# PETERSON'S®
## GRADUATE PROGRAMS IN THE HUMANITIES, ARTS & SOCIAL SCIENCES

# 2018

## About Peterson's®

Peterson's®, a Nelnet company, as been your trusted educational publisher for over 50 years. It's a milestone we're quite proud of, as we continue to offer the most accurate, dependable, high-quality education content in the field, providing you with everything you need to succeed. No matter where you are on your academic or professional path, you can rely on Peterson's publications and its online information at **www.petersons.com** for the most up-to-date education exploration data, expert test-prep tools, and the highest quality career success resources—everything you need to achieve your educational goals. For our complete line of products visit www.petersons.com.

For more information, contact Peterson's, 3 Columbia Circle, Suite 205, Albany, NY 12203-5158; 800-338-3282 Ext. 54229; or find us online at **www.petersons.com.**

# CONTENTS

## ACADEMIC AND PROFESSIONAL PROGRAMS IN INTERDISCIPLINARY STUDIES

## ACADEMIC AND PROFESSIONAL PROGRAMS IN THE SOCIAL SCIENCES

# A Note from the Peterson's Editors

The six volumes of Peterson's *Graduate and Professional Programs*, the only annually updated reference work of its kind, provide wide-ranging information on the graduate and professional programs offered by accredited colleges and universities in the United States, U.S. territories, and Canada and by those institutions outside the United States that are accredited by U.S. accrediting bodies. More than 44,000 individual academic and professional programs at more than 2,300 institutions are listed. Peterson's *Graduate and Professional Programs* have been used for more than fifty years by prospective graduate and professional students, placement counselors, faculty advisers, and all others interested in postbaccalaureate education.

*Graduate & Professional Programs: An Overview* contains information on institutions as a whole, while the other books in the series are devoted to specific academic and professional fields:

- *Graduate Programs in the Biological/Biomedical Sciences & Health-Related Medical Professions*

- *Graduate Programs in Business, Education, Information Studies, Law & Social Work*

- *Graduate Programs in Engineering & Applied Sciences*

- *Graduate Programs in the Humanities, Arts & Social Sciences*

- *Graduate Programs in the Physical Sciences, Mathematics, Agricultural Sciences, the Environment & Natural Resources*

The books may be used individually or as a set. For example, if you have chosen a field of study but do not know what institution you want to attend or if you have a college or university in mind but have not chosen an academic field of study, it is best to begin with the Overview guide.

*Graduate & Professional Programs: An Overview* presents several directories to help you identify programs of study that might interest you; you can then research those programs further in the other books in the series by using the Directory of Graduate and Professional Programs by Field, which lists 500 fields and gives the names of those institutions that offer graduate degree programs in each.

For geographical or financial reasons, you may be interested in attending a particular institution and will want to know what it has to offer. You should turn to the Directory of Institutions and Their Offerings, which lists the degree programs available at each institution. As in the Directory of Graduate and Professional Programs by Field, the level of degrees offered is also indicated.

All books in the series include advice on graduate education, including topics such as admissions tests, financial aid, and accreditation. **The Graduate Adviser** includes two essays and information about accreditation. The first essay, "The Admissions Process," discusses general admission requirements, admission tests, factors to consider when selecting a graduate school or program, when and how to apply, and how admission decisions are made. Special information for international students and tips for minority students are also included. The second essay, "Financial Support," is an overview of the broad range of support available at the graduate level. Fellowships, scholarships, and grants; assistantships and internships; federal and private loan programs, as well as Federal Work-Study; and the GI bill are detailed. This essay concludes with advice on applying for need-based financial aid. "Accreditation and Accrediting Agencies" gives information on accreditation and its purpose and lists institutional accrediting agencies first and then specialized accrediting agencies relevant to each volume's specific fields of study.

With information on more than 40,000 graduate programs in more than 500 disciplines, Peterson's *Graduate and Professional Programs* give you all the information you need about the programs that are of interest to you in three formats: **Profiles** (capsule summaries of basic information), **Displays** (information that an institution or program wants to emphasize), and **Close-Ups** (written by administrators, with more expansive information than the **Profiles**, emphasizing different aspects of the programs). By using these various formats of program information, coupled with **Appendixes** and **Indexes** covering directories and subject areas for all six books, you will find that these guides provide the most comprehensive, accurate, and up-to-date graduate study information available.

Peterson's publishes a full line of resources with information you need to guide you through the graduate admissions process. Peterson's publications can be found at college libraries and career centers and your local bookstore or library—or visit us on the Web at www.petersons.com.

Colleges and universities will be pleased to know that Peterson's helped you in your selection. Admissions staff members are more than happy to answer questions, address specific problems, and help in any way they can. The editors at Peterson's wish you great success in your graduate program search!

# THE GRADUATE ADVISER

# The Admissions Process

Generalizations about graduate admissions practices are not always helpful because each institution has its own set of guidelines and procedures. Nevertheless, some broad statements can be made about the admissions process that may help you plan your strategy.

## Factors Involved in Selecting a Graduate School or Program

Selecting a graduate school and a specific program of study is a complex matter. Quality of the faculty; program and course offerings; the nature, size, and location of the institution; admission requirements; cost; and the availability of financial assistance are among the many factors that affect one's choice of institution. Other considerations are job placement and achievements of the program's graduates and the institution's resources, such as libraries, laboratories, and computer facilities. If you are to make the best possible choice, you need to learn as much as you can about the schools and programs you are considering before you apply.

The following steps may help you narrow your choices.

- Talk to alumni of the programs or institutions you are considering to get their impressions of how well they were prepared for work in their fields of study.
- Remember that graduate school requirements change, so be sure to get the most up-to-date information possible.
- Talk to department faculty members and the graduate adviser at your undergraduate institution. They often have information about programs of study at other institutions.
- Visit the websites of the graduate schools in which you are interested to request a graduate catalog. Contact the department chair in your chosen field of study for additional information about the department and the field.
- Visit as many campuses as possible. Call ahead for an appointment with the graduate adviser in your field of interest and be sure to check out the facilities and talk to students.

## General Requirements

Graduate schools and departments have requirements that applicants for admission must meet. Typically, these requirements include undergraduate transcripts (which provide information about undergraduate grade point average and course work applied toward a major), admission test scores, and letters of recommendation. Most graduate programs also ask for an essay or personal statement that describes your personal reasons for seeking graduate study. In some fields, such as art and music, portfolios or auditions may be required in addition to other evidence of talent. Some institutions require that the applicant have an undergraduate degree in the same subject as the intended graduate major.

Most institutions evaluate each applicant on the basis of the applicant's total record, and the weight accorded any given factor varies widely from institution to institution and from program to program.

## The Application Process

You should begin the application process at least one year before you expect to begin your graduate study. Find out the application deadline for each institution (many are provided in the **Profile** section of this guide). Go to the institution's website and find out if you can apply online. If not, request a paper application form. Fill out this form thoroughly and neatly. Assume that the school needs all the information it is requesting and that the admissions officer will be sensitive to the neatness and overall quality of what you submit. Do not supply more information than the school requires.

The institution may ask at least one question that will require a three- or four-paragraph answer. Compose your response on the assumption that the admissions officer is interested in both what you think and how you express yourself. Keep your statement brief and to the point, but, at the same time, include all pertinent information about your past experiences and your educational goals. Individual statements vary greatly in style and content, which helps admissions officers differentiate among applicants. Many graduate departments give considerable weight to the statement in making their admissions decisions, so be sure to take the time to prepare a thoughtful and concise statement.

If recommendations are a part of the admissions requirements, carefully choose the individuals you ask to write them. It is generally best to ask current or former professors to write the recommendations, provided they are able to attest to your intellectual ability and motivation for doing the work required of a graduate student. It is advisable to provide stamped, preaddressed envelopes to people being asked to submit recommendations on your behalf.

Completed applications, including references, transcripts, and admission test scores, should be received at the institution by the specified date.

Be advised that institutions do not usually make admissions decisions until all materials have been received. Enclose a self-addressed postcard with your application, requesting confirmation of receipt. Allow at least ten days for the return of the postcard before making further inquiries.

If you plan to apply for financial support, it is imperative that you file your application early.

### ADMISSION TESTS

The major testing program used in graduate admissions is the Graduate Record Examinations (GRE®) testing program, sponsored by the GRE Board and administered by Educational Testing Service, Princeton, New Jersey.

The Graduate Record Examinations testing program consists of a General Test and eight Subject Tests. The General Test measures critical thinking, verbal reasoning, quantitative reasoning, and analytical writing skills. It is offered as an Internet-based test (iBT) in the United States, Canada, and many other countries.

The GRE® General Test's questions were designed to reflect the kind of thinking that students need to do in graduate or business school and demonstrate that students are indeed ready for graduate-level work.

- **Verbal Reasoning**—Measures ability to analyze and evaluate written material and synthesize information obtained from it, analyze relationships among component parts of sentences, and recognize relationships among words and concepts.
- **Quantitative Reasoning**—Measures problem-solving ability, focusing on basic concepts of arithmetic, algebra, geometry, and data analysis.
- **Analytical Writing**—Measures critical thinking and analytical writing skills, specifically the ability to articulate and support complex ideas clearly and effectively.

The computer-based GRE® General Test is offered year-round at Prometric™ test centers and on specific dates at testing locations outside of the Prometric test center network. Appointments are scheduled on a first-come, first-served basis. The GRE® General Test is also offered as a paper-based test three times a year in areas where computer-based testing is not available.

You can take the computer-delivered GRE® General Test once every twenty-one days, up to five times within any continuous rolling twelve-month period (365 days)—even if you canceled your scores on a previously taken test. You may take the paper-based GRE® General Test as often as it is offered.

Three scores are reported on the General Test:

1. A **Verbal Reasoning score** is reported on a 130–170 score scale, in 1-point increments.

2. A **Quantitative Reasoning score** is reported on a 130–170 score scale, in 1-point increments.

3. An **Analytical Writing score** is reported on a 0–6 score level, in half-point increments.

The GRE® Subject Tests measure achievement and assume undergraduate majors or extensive background in the following eight disciplines:

- Biochemistry, Cell and Molecular Biology
- Biology
- Chemistry
- Computer Science
- Literature in English
- Mathematics
- Physics
- Psychology

The Subject Tests are available three times per year as paper-based administrations around the world. Testing time is approximately 2 hours and 50 minutes. You can obtain more information about the GRE® by visiting the ETS website at www.ets.org or consulting the *GRE® Information and Registration Bulletin*. The *Bulletin* can be obtained at many undergraduate colleges. You can also download it from the ETS website or obtain it by contacting Graduate Record Examinations, Educational Testing Service, P.O. Box 6000, Princeton, NJ 08541-6000; phone: 609-771-7670.

If you expect to apply for admission to a program that requires any of the GRE® tests, you should select a test date well in advance of the application deadline. Scores on the computer-based General Test are reported within ten to fifteen days; scores on the paper-based Subject Tests are reported within six weeks.

Another testing program, the Miller Analogies Test® (MAT®), is administered at more than 500 Controlled Testing Centers, licensed by Pearson, in the United States, Canada, and other countries. The MAT® computer-based test is now available. Testing time is 60 minutes. The test consists of 120 partial analogies. You can obtain the *Candidate Information Booklet,* which contains a list of test centers and instructions for taking the test, from http://www.milleranalogies.com or by calling 800-328-5999 (toll-free).

Check the specific requirements of the programs to which you are applying.

# How Admission Decisions Are Made

The program you apply to is directly involved in the admissions process. Although the final decision is usually made by the graduate dean (or an associate) or the faculty admissions committee, recommendations from faculty members in your intended field are important. At some institutions, an interview is incorporated into the decision process.

# A Special Note for International Students

In addition to the steps already described, there are some special considerations for international students who intend to apply for graduate study in the United States. All graduate schools require an indication of competence in English. The purpose of the Test of English as a Foreign Language (TOEFL®) is to evaluate the English proficiency of people who are nonnative speakers of English and want to study at colleges and universities where English is the language of instruction. The TOEFL® is administered by Educational Testing Service (ETS) under the general direction of a policy board established by the College Board and the Graduate Record Examinations Board.

The TOEFL® iBT assesses the four basic language skills: listening, reading, writing, and speaking. It was administered for the first time in September 2005, and ETS continues to introduce the TOEFL® iBT in selected cities. The Internet-based test is administered at secure, official test centers. The testing time is approximately 4 hours. Because the TOEFL® iBT includes a speaking section, the Test of Spoken English (TSE) is no longer needed.

The TOEFL® is also offered in the paper-based format in areas of the world where Internet-based testing is not available. The paper-based TOEFL® consists of three sections—listening comprehension, structure and written expression, and reading comprehension. The testing time is approximately 3 hours. The Test of Written English (TWE®) is also given. The TWE® is a 30-minute essay that measures the examinee's ability to compose in English. Examinees receive a TWE® score separate from their TOEFL® score. The *Information Bulletin* contains information on local fees and registration procedures.

The TOEFL® paper-based test (TOEFL® PBT) began being phased out in mid-2012. For those who may have taken the TOEFL® PBT, scores remain valid for two years after the test date. The Test of Written English (TWE®) is also given. The TWE® is a 30-minute essay that measures the examinee's ability to compose in English. Examinees receive a TWE® score separate from their TOEFL® score. The Information Bulletin contains information on local fees and registration procedures.

Additional information and registration materials are available from TOEFL® Services, Educational Testing Service, P.O. Box 6151, Princeton, New Jersey 08541-6151. Phone: 609-771-7100. Website: www.toefl.org.

International students should apply especially early because of the number of steps required to complete the admissions process. Furthermore, many United States graduate schools have a limited number of spaces for international students, and many more students apply than the schools can accommodate.

International students may find financial assistance from institutions very limited. The U.S. government requires international applicants to submit a certification of support, which is a statement attesting to the applicant's financial resources. In addition, international students *must* have health insurance coverage.

# Tips for Minority Students

Indicators of a university's values in terms of diversity are found both in its recruitment programs and its resources directed to student success. Important questions: Does the institution vigorously recruit minorities for its graduate programs? Is there funding available to help with the costs associated with visiting the school? Are minorities represented in the institution's brochures or website or on their faculty rolls? What campus-based resources or services (including assistance in locating housing or career counseling and placement) are available? Is funding available to members of underrepresented groups?

At the program level, it is particularly important for minority students to investigate the "climate" of a program under consideration. How many minority students are enrolled and how many have graduated? What opportunities are there to work with diverse faculty and mentors whose research interests match yours? How are conflicts resolved or concerns addressed? How interested are faculty in building strong and supportive relations with students? "Climate" concerns should be addressed by posing questions to various individuals, including faculty members, current students, and alumni.

Information is also available through various organizations, such as the Hispanic Association of Colleges & Universities (HACU), and publications such as *Diverse Issues in Higher Education* and *Hispanic Outlook* magazine. There are also books devoted to this topic, such as *The Multicultural Student's Guide to Colleges* by Robert Mitchell.

# Financial Support

The range of financial support at the graduate level is very broad. The following descriptions will give you a general idea of what you might expect and what will be expected of you as a financial support recipient.

## Fellowships, Scholarships, and Grants

These are usually outright awards of a few hundred to many thousands of dollars with no service to the institution required in return. Fellowships and scholarships are usually awarded on the basis of merit and are highly competitive. Grants are made on the basis of financial need or special talent in a field of study. Many fellowships, scholarships, and grants not only cover tuition, fees, and supplies but also include stipends for living expenses with allowances for dependents. However, the terms of each should be examined because some do not permit recipients to supplement their income with outside work. Fellowships, scholarships, and grants may vary in the number of years for which they are awarded.

In addition to the availability of these funds at the university or program level, many excellent fellowship programs are available at the national level and may be applied for before and during enrollment in a graduate program. A listing of many of these programs can be found at the Council of Graduate Schools' website: http://www.cgsnet.org. There is a wealth of information in the "Programs" and "Awards" sections.

## Assistantships and Internships

Many graduate students receive financial support through assistantships, particularly involving teaching or research duties. It is important to recognize that such appointments should not be viewed simply as employment relationships but rather should constitute an integral and important part of a student's graduate education. As such, the appointments should be accompanied by strong faculty mentoring and increasingly responsible apprenticeship experiences. The specific nature of these appointments in a given program should be considered in selecting that graduate program.

### TEACHING ASSISTANTSHIPS

These usually provide a salary and full or partial tuition remission and may also provide health benefits. Unlike fellowships, scholarships, and grants, which require no service to the institution, teaching assistantships require recipients to provide the institution with a specific amount of undergraduate teaching, ideally related to the student's field of study. Some teaching assistants are limited to grading papers, compiling bibliographies, taking notes, or monitoring laboratories. At some graduate schools, teaching assistants must carry lighter course loads than regular full-time students.

### RESEARCH ASSISTANTSHIPS

These are very similar to teaching assistantships in the manner in which financial assistance is provided. The difference is that recipients are given basic research assignments in their disciplines rather than teaching responsibilities. The work required is normally related to the student's field of study; in most instances, the assistantship supports the student's thesis or dissertation research.

### ADMINISTRATIVE INTERNSHIPS

These are similar to assistantships in application of financial assistance funds, but the student is given an assignment on a part-time basis, usually as a special assistant with one of the university's administrative offices. The assignment may not necessarily be directly related to the recipient's discipline.

### RESIDENCE HALL AND COUNSELING ASSISTANTSHIPS

These assistantships are frequently assigned to graduate students in psychology, counseling, and social work, but they may be offered to students in other disciplines, especially if the student has worked in this capacity during his or her undergraduate years. Duties can vary from being available in a dean's office for a specific number of hours for consultation with undergraduates to living in campus residences and being responsible for both counseling and administrative tasks or advising student activity groups. Residence hall assistantships often include a room and board allowance and, in some cases, tuition assistance and stipends. Contact the Housing and Student Life Office for more information.

## Health Insurance

The availability and affordability of health insurance is an important issue and one that should be considered in an applicant's choice of institution and program. While often included with assistantships and fellowships, this is not always the case and, even if provided, the benefits may be limited. It is important to note that the U.S. government requires international students to have health insurance.

## The GI Bill

This provides financial assistance for students who are veterans of the United States armed forces. If you are a veteran, contact your local Veterans Administration office to determine your eligibility and to get full details about benefits. There are a number of programs that offer educational benefits to current military enlistees. Some states have tuition assistance programs for members of the National Guard. Contact the VA office at the college for more information.

## Federal Work-Study Program (FWS)

Employment is another way some students finance their graduate studies. The federally funded Federal Work-Study Program provides eligible students with employment opportunities, usually in public and private nonprofit organizations. Federal funds pay up to 75 percent of the wages, with the remainder paid by the employing agency. FWS is available to graduate students who demonstrate financial need. Not all schools have these funds, and some only award them to undergraduates. Each school sets its application deadline and workstudy earnings limits. Wages vary and are related to the type of work done. You must file the Free Application for Federal Student Aid (FAFSA) to be eligible for this program.

## Loans

Many graduate students borrow to finance their graduate programs when other sources of assistance (which do not have to be repaid) prove insufficient. You should always read and understand the terms of any loan program before submitting your application.

### FEDERAL DIRECT LOANS

**Federal Direct Loans.** The Federal Direct Loan Program offers a variable-fixed interest rate loan to graduate students with the Department of Education acting as the lender. Students receive a new rate with each new loan, but that rate is fixed for the life of the loan. Beginning with loans made on or after July 1, 2013, the interest rate for loans made each July 1st to June 30th period are determined based on the last 10-year Treasury note auction prior to June 1st of that year, plus an added percentage. The interest rate can be no higher than 9.5%.

Beginning July 1, 2012, the Federal Direct Loan for graduate students is an unsubsidized loan. Under the *unsubsidized* program, the grad borrower pays the interest on the loan from the day proceeds are issued and is responsible for paying interest during all periods. If the borrower chooses not to pay the interest while in school, or during the grace periods, deferment, or forbearance, the interest accrues and will be capitalized.

Graduate students may borrow up to $20,500 per year through the Direct Loan Program, up to a cumulative maximum of $138,500, including undergraduate borrowing. No more than $65,500 of the $138,500 can be from subsidized loans, including loans the grad borrower may have received for periods of enrollment that began before July 1, 2012, or for prior undergraduate borrowing. You may borrow up to the cost of attendance at the school in which you are enrolled or will attend, minus estimated financial assistance from other federal, state, and private sources, up to a maximum of $20,500. Grad borrowers who reach the aggregate loan limit over the course of their education cannot receive additional loans; however, if they repay some of their loans to bring the outstanding balance below the aggregate limit, they could be eligible to borrow again, up to that limit.

For Unsubsidized loans first disbursed on or after July 1, 2015, and before July 1, 2017, the interest rate was 5.31%. For those first disbursed on or after July 1, 2017, and before July 1, 2018, the interest rate is 6%.

A fee is deducted from the loan proceeds upon disbursement. Loans with a first disbursement on or after July 1, 2010 but before July 1, 2012, have a borrower origination fee of 1 percent. For loans disbursed after July 1, 2012, these fee deductions no longer apply. The Budget Control Act of 2011, signed into law on August 2, 2011, eliminated Direct Subsidized Loan eligibility for graduate and professional students for periods of enrollment beginning on or after July 1, 2012, and terminated the authority of the Department of Education to offer most repayment incentives to Direct Loan borrowers for loans disbursed on or after July 1, 2012.

Under the *subsidized* Federal Direct Loan Program, repayment begins six months after your last date of enrollment on at least a half-time basis. Under the *unsubsidized* program, repayment of interest begins within thirty days from disbursement of the loan proceeds, and repayment of the principal begins six months after your last enrollment on at least a half-time basis. Some borrowers may choose to defer interest payments while they are in school. The accrued interest is added to the loan balance when the borrower begins repayment. There are several repayment options.

**Federal Perkins Loans.** The Federal Perkins Loan is available to students demonstrating financial need and is administered directly by the school. Not all schools have these funds, and some may award them to undergraduates only. Eligibility is determined from the information you provide on the FAFSA. The school will notify you of your eligibility.

Eligible graduate students may borrow up to $8,000 per year, up to a maximum of $60,000, including undergraduate borrowing (even if your previous Perkins Loans have been repaid). The interest rate for Federal Perkins Loans is 5 percent, and no interest accrues while you remain in school at least half-time. Students who are attending less than half-time need to check with their school to determine the length of their grace period. There are no guarantee, loan, or disbursement fees. Repayment begins nine months after your last date of enrollment on at least a half-time basis and may extend over a maximum of ten years with no prepayment penalty.

**Federal Direct Graduate PLUS Loans.** Effective July 1, 2006, graduate and professional students are eligible for Graduate PLUS loans. This program allows students to borrow up to the cost of attendance, less any other aid received. These loans have a fixed interest rate (7.0% for the 2017–2018 academic year), and interest begins to accrue at the time of disbursement. Beginning with loans made on or after July 1, 2013, the interest rate for loans made each July 1st to June 30th period are deter-

mined based on the last 10-year Treasury note auction prior to June 1st of that year. The interest rate can be no higher than 10.5%. The PLUS loans do involve a credit check; a PLUS borrower may obtain a loan with a cosigner if his or her credit is not good enough. Grad PLUS loans may be deferred while a student is in school and for the six months following a drop below half-time enrollment. For more information, you should contact a representative in your college's financial aid office.

**Deferring Your Federal Loan Repayments.** If you borrowed under the Federal Direct Loan Program, Federal Direct PLUS Loan Program, or the Federal Perkins Loan Program for previous undergraduate or graduate study, your payments may be deferred when you return to graduate school, depending on when you borrowed and under which program.

There are other deferment options available if you are temporarily unable to repay your loan. Information about these deferments is provided at your entrance and exit interviews. If you believe you are eligible for a deferment of your loan payments, you must contact your lender or loan servicer to request a deferment. The deferment must be filed prior to the time your payment is due, and it must be re-filed when it expires if you remain eligible for deferment at that time.

## SUPPLEMENTAL (PRIVATE) LOANS

Many lending institutions offer supplemental loan programs and other financing plans, such as the ones described here, to students seeking additional assistance in meeting their education expenses. Some loan programs target all types of graduate students; others are designed specifically for business, law, or medical students. In addition, you can use private loans not specifically designed for education to help finance your graduate degree.

If you are considering borrowing through a supplemental or private loan program, you should carefully consider the terms and be sure to read the fine print. Check with the program sponsor for the most current terms that will be applicable to the amounts you intend to borrow for graduate study. Most supplemental loan programs for graduate study offer unsubsidized, credit-based loans. In general, a credit-ready borrower is one who has a satisfactory credit history or no credit history at all. A creditworthy borrower generally must pass a credit test to be eligible to borrow or act as a cosigner for the loan funds.

Many supplemental loan programs have minimum and maximum annual loan limits. Some offer amounts equal to the cost of attendance minus any other aid you will receive for graduate study. If you are planning to borrow for several years of graduate study, consider whether there is a cumulative or aggregate limit on the amount you may borrow. Often this cumulative or aggregate limit will include any amounts you borrowed and have not repaid for undergraduate or previous graduate study.

The combination of the annual interest rate, loan fees, and the repayment terms you choose will determine how much you will repay over time. Compare these features in combination before you decide which loan program to use. Some loans offer interest rates that are adjusted monthly, quarterly, or annually. Some offer interest rates that are lower during the in-school, grace, and deferment periods and then increase when you begin repayment. Some programs include a loan origination fee, which is usually deducted from the principal amount you receive when the loan is disbursed and must be repaid along with the interest and other principal when you graduate, withdraw from school, or drop below half-time study. Sometimes the loan fees are reduced if you borrow with a qualified cosigner. Some programs allow you to defer interest and/or principal payments while you are enrolled in graduate school. Many programs allow you to capitalize your interest payments; the interest due on your loan is added to the outstanding balance of your loan, so you don't have to repay immediately, but this increases the amount you owe. Other programs allow you to pay the interest as you go, which reduces the amount you later have to repay. The private loan market is very competitive, and your financial aid office can help you evaluate these programs.

# Applying for Need-Based Financial Aid

Schools that award federal and institutional financial assistance based on need will require you to complete the FAFSA and, in some cases, an institutional financial aid application.

If you are applying for federal student assistance, you **must** complete the FAFSA. A service of the U.S. Department of Education, the FAFSA is free to all applicants. Most applicants apply online at www.fafsa.ed.gov. Paper applications are available at the financial aid office of your local college.

After your FAFSA information has been processed, you will receive a Student Aid Report (SAR). If you provided an e-mail address on the FAFSA, this will be sent to you electronically; otherwise, it will be mailed to your home address.

Follow the instructions on the SAR if you need to correct information reported on your original application. If your situation changes after you file your FAFSA, contact your financial aid officer to discuss amending your information. You can also appeal your financial aid award if you have extenuating circumstances.

If you would like more information on federal student financial aid, visit the FAFSA website or download the most recent version of *Funding Education Beyond High School: The Guide to Federal Student Aid* at http://studentaid.ed.gov/students/publications/student_guide/index.html. This guide is also available in Spanish.

The U.S. Department of Education also has a toll-free number for questions concerning federal student aid programs. The number is 1-800-4-FED AID (1-800-433-3243). If you are hearing impaired, call toll-free, 1-800-730-8913.

# Summary

Remember that these are generalized statements about financial assistance at the graduate level. Because each institution allots its aid differently, you should communicate directly with the school and the specific department of interest to you. It is not unusual, for example, to find that an endowment vested within a specific department supports one or more fellowships. You may fit its requirements and specifications precisely.

# Accreditation and Accrediting Agencies

Colleges and universities in the United States, and their individual academic and professional programs, are accredited by nongovernmental agencies concerned with monitoring the quality of education in this country. Agencies with both regional and national jurisdictions grant accreditation to institutions as a whole, while specialized bodies acting on a nationwide basis—often national professional associations—grant accreditation to departments and programs in specific fields.

Institutional and specialized accrediting agencies share the same basic concerns: the purpose an academic unit—whether university or program—has set for itself and how well it fulfills that purpose, the adequacy of its financial and other resources, the quality of its academic offerings, and the level of services it provides. Agencies that grant institutional accreditation take a broader view, of course, and examine university-wide or college-wide services with which a specialized agency may not concern itself.

Both types of agencies follow the same general procedures when considering an application for accreditation. The academic unit prepares a self-evaluation, focusing on the concerns mentioned above and usually including an assessment of both its strengths and weaknesses; a team of representatives of the accrediting body reviews this evaluation, visits the campus, and makes its own report; and finally, the accrediting body makes a decision on the application. Often, even when accreditation is granted, the agency makes a recommendation regarding how the institution or program can improve. All institutions and programs are also reviewed every few years to determine whether they continue to meet established standards; if they do not, they may lose their accreditation.

Accrediting agencies themselves are reviewed and evaluated periodically by the U.S. Department of Education and the Council for Higher Education Accreditation (CHEA). Recognized agencies adhere to certain standards and practices, and their authority in matters of accreditation is widely accepted in the educational community.

This does not mean, however, that accreditation is a simple matter, either for schools wishing to become accredited or for students deciding where to apply. Indeed, in certain fields the very meaning and methods of accreditation are the subject of a good deal of debate. For their part, those applying to graduate school should be aware of the safeguards provided by regional accreditation, especially in terms of degree acceptance and institutional longevity. Beyond this, applicants should understand the role that specialized accreditation plays in their field, as this varies considerably from one discipline to another. In certain professional fields, it is necessary to have graduated from a program that is accredited in order to be eligible for a license to practice, and in some fields the federal government also makes this a hiring requirement. In other disciplines, however, accreditation is not as essential, and there can be excellent programs that are not accredited. In fact, some programs choose not to seek accreditation, although most do.

Institutions and programs that present themselves for accreditation are sometimes granted the status of candidate for accreditation, or what is known as "preaccreditation." This may happen, for example, when an academic unit is too new to have met all the requirements for accreditation. Such status signifies initial recognition and indicates that the school or program in question is working to fulfill all requirements; it does not, however, guarantee that accreditation will be granted.

## Institutional Accrediting Agencies—Regional

### MIDDLE STATES ASSOCIATION OF COLLEGES AND SCHOOLS

Accredits institutions in Delaware, District of Columbia, Maryland, New Jersey, New York, Pennsylvania, Puerto Rico, and the Virgin Islands.

Dr. Elizabeth Sibolski, President
Middle States Commission on Higher Education
3624 Market Street, Second Floor West
Philadelphia, Pennsylvania 19104
Phone: 267-284-5000
Fax: 215-662-5501
E-mail: info@msche.org
Website: www.msche.org

### NEW ENGLAND ASSOCIATION OF SCHOOLS AND COLLEGES

Accredits institutions in Connecticut, Maine, Massachusetts, New Hampshire, Rhode Island, and Vermont.

Dr. Barbara E. Brittingham, President/Director
Commission on Institutions of Higher Education
3 Burlington Woods Drive, Suite 100
Burlington, Massachusetts 01803-4531
Phone: 855-886-3272 or 781-425-7714
Fax: 781-425-1001
E-mail: cihe@neasc.org
Website: http://cihe.neasc.org

### THE HIGHER LEARNING COMMISSION

Accredits institutions in Arizona, Arkansas, Colorado, Illinois, Indiana, Iowa, Kansas, Michigan, Minnesota, Missouri, Nebraska, New Mexico, North Dakota, Ohio, Oklahoma, South Dakota, West Virginia, Wisconsin, and Wyoming.

Dr. Barbara Gellman-Danley, President
The Higher Learning Commission
230 South LaSalle Street, Suite 7-500
Chicago, Illinois 60604-1413
Phone: 800-621-7440 or 312-263-0456
Fax: 312-263-7462
E-mail: info@hlcommission.org
Website: www.hlcommission.org

### NORTHWEST COMMISSION ON COLLEGES AND UNIVERSITIES

Accredits institutions in Alaska, Idaho, Montana, Nevada, Oregon, Utah, and Washington.

Dr. Sandra E. Elman, President
8060 165th Avenue, NE, Suite 100
Redmond, Washington 98052
Phone: 425-558-4224
Fax: 425-376-0596
E-mail: selman@nwccu.org
Website: www.nwccu.org

### SOUTHERN ASSOCIATION OF COLLEGES AND SCHOOLS

Accredits institutions in Alabama, Florida, Georgia, Kentucky, Louisiana, Mississippi, North Carolina, South Carolina, Tennessee, Texas, and Virginia.

Dr. Belle S. Wheelan, President
Commission on Colleges
1866 Southern Lane
Decatur, Georgia 30033-4097
Phone: 404-679-4500 Ext. 4504
Fax: 404-679-4558
E-mail: questions@sacscoc.org
Website: www.sacscoc.org

### WESTERN ASSOCIATION OF SCHOOLS AND COLLEGES

Accredits institutions in California, Guam, and Hawaii.

Dr. Mary Ellen Petrisko, President
Accrediting Commission for Senior Colleges and Universities
985 Atlantic Avenue, Suite 100
Alameda, California 94501
Phone: 510-748-9001
Fax: 510-748-9797
E-mail: wasc@wascsenior.org
Website: http://www.wascsenior.org/

## Institutional Accrediting Agencies—Other

*ACCREDITING COUNCIL FOR INDEPENDENT COLLEGES AND SCHOOLS*
Anthony S. Bieda, Executive in Charge
750 First Street, NE, Suite 980
Washington, DC 20002-4241
Phone: 202-336-6780
Fax: 202-842-2593
E-mail: info@acics.org
Website: www.acics.org

*DISTANCE EDUCATION AND ACCREDITING COMMISSION (DEAC)*
Accrediting Commission
Leah Matthews, Executive Director
1101 17th Street, NW, Suite 808
Washington, DC 20036-4704
Phone: 202-234-5100
Fax: 202-332-1386
E-mail: info@deac.org
Website: www.deac.org

## Specialized Accrediting Agencies

*ACUPUNCTURE AND ORIENTAL MEDICINE*
Mark S. McKenzie, LAc MsOM DiplOM, Executive Director
Accreditation Commission for Acupuncture and Oriental Medicine
8941 Aztec Drive
Eden Prairie, Minnesota 55347
Phone: 952-212-2434
Fax: 301-313-0912
E-mail: coordinator@acaom.org
Website: www.acaom.org

*ALLIED HEALTH*
Kathleen Megivern, Executive Director
Commission on Accreditation of Allied Health Education Programs (CAAHEP)
25400 US Hwy 19 North, Suite 158
Clearwater, Florida 33763
Phone: 727-210-2350
Fax: 727-210-2354
E-mail: mail@caahep.org
Website: www.caahep.org

*ART AND DESIGN*
Karen P. Moynahan, Executive Director
National Association of Schools of Art and Design (NASAD)
Commission on Accreditation
11250 Roger Bacon Drive, Suite 21
Reston, Virginia 20190-5248
Phone: 703-437-0700
Fax: 703-437-6312
E-mail: info@arts-accredit.org
Website: http://nasad.arts-accredit.org

*ATHLETIC TRAINING EDUCATION*
Micki Cuppett, Executive Director
Commission on Accreditation of Athletic Training Education (CAATE)
6850 Austin Center Blvd., Suite 100
Austin, Texas 78731-3184
Phone: 512-733-9700
E-mail: micki@caate.net
Website: www.caate.net

*AUDIOLOGY EDUCATION*
Doris Gordon, Executive Director
Accreditation Commission for Audiology Education (ACAE)
11480 Commerce Park Drive, Suite 220
Reston, Virginia 20191
Phone: 202-986-9550
Fax: 202-986-9500
E-mail: info@acaeaccred.org
Website: www.acaeaccred.org

*AVIATION*
Dr. Gary J. Northam, Executive Director
Aviation Accreditation Board International (AABI)
3410 Skyway Drive
Auburn, Alabama 36830
Phone: 334-844-2431
Fax: 334-844-2432
E-mail: bayenva@auburn.edu
Website: www.aabi.aero

*BUSINESS*
Robert D. Reid, Executive Vice President and Chief Accreditation Officer
AACSB International—The Association to Advance Collegiate Schools of Business
777 South Harbour Island Boulevard, Suite 750
Tampa, Florida 33602
Phone: 813-769-6500
Fax: 813-769-6559
E-mail: bob@aacsb.edu
Website: www.aacsb.edu

*BUSINESS EDUCATION*
Dennis N. Gash, President and Chief Executive Officer
International Assembly for Collegiate Business Education (IACBE)
11257 Strang Line Road
Lenexa, Kansas 66215
Phone: 913-631-3009
Fax: 913-631-9154
E-mail:iacbe@iacbe.org
Website: www.iacbe.org

*CHIROPRACTIC*
Craig S. Little, President
Council on Chiropractic Education (CCE)
Commission on Accreditation
8049 North 85th Way
Scottsdale, Arizona 85258-4321
Phone: 480-443-8877 or 888-443-3506
Fax: 480-483-7333
E-mail: cce@cce-usa.org
Website: www.cce-usa.org

*CLINICAL LABORATORY SCIENCES*
Dianne M. Cearlock, Ph.D., Chief Executive Officer
National Accrediting Agency for Clinical Laboratory Sciences
5600 North River Road, Suite 720
Rosemont, Illinois 60018-5119
Phone: 773-714-8880 or 847-939-3597
Fax: 773-714-8886
E-mail: info@naacls.org
Website: www.naacls.org

*CLINICAL PASTORAL EDUCATION*
Trace Haythorn, Executive Director
Association for Clinical Pastoral Education, Inc.
1549 Clairmont Road, Suite 103
Decatur, Georgia 30033-4611
Phone: 404-320-1472
Fax: 404-320-0849
E-mail: acpe@acpe.edu
Website: www.acpe.edu

*DANCE*
Karen P. Moynahan, Executive Director
National Association of Schools of Dance (NASD)
Commission on Accreditation
11250 Roger Bacon Drive, Suite 21
Reston, Virginia 20190-5248
Phone: 703-437-0700
Fax: 703-437-6312
E-mail: info@arts-accredit.org
Website: http://nasd.arts-accredit.org

*DENTISTRY*
Dr. Sherin Tooks, Director
Commission on Dental Accreditation
American Dental Association
211 East Chicago Avenue, Suite 1900
Chicago, Illinois 60611
Phone: 312-440-4643 or 800-621-8099
E-mail: accreditation@ada.org
Website: www.ada.org

*DIETETICS AND NUTRITION*
Mary B. Gregoire, Ph.D., Executive Director; RD, FADA, FAND
Academy of Nutrition and Dietetics
Accreditation Council for Education in Nutrition and Dietetics (ACEND)
120 South Riverside Plaza, Suite 2000
Chicago, Illinois 60606-6995
Phone: 800-877-1600 Ext. 5400 or 312-899-0040
Fax: 312-899-4817
E-mail: acend@eatright.org
Website: www.eatright.org/ACEND

*EDUCATION PREPARATION*
Christopher Koch, President
Council for the Accreditation of Education Preparation (CAEP)
1140 19th Street NW, Suite 400
Washington, DC 20036
Phone: 202-223-0077
Fax: 202-296-6620
E-mail: caep@caepnet.org
Website: www.caepnet.org

*ENGINEERING*
Michael Milligan, Ph.D., PE, Executive Director
Accreditation Board for Engineering and Technology, Inc. (ABET)
415 North Charles Street
Baltimore, Maryland 21201
Phone: 410-347-7700
E-mail: accreditation@abet.org
Website: www.abet.org

*FORENSIC SCIENCES*
Nancy J. Jackson, Director of Development and Accreditation
American Academy of Forensic Sciences (AAFS)
Forensic Science Education Program Accreditation Commission
(FEPAC)
410 North 21st Street
Colorado Springs, Colorado 80904
Phone: 719-636-1100
Fax: 719-636-1993
E-mail: njackson@aafs.org
Website: www.fepac-edu.org

*FORESTRY*
Carol L. Redelsheimer
Director of Science and Education
Society of American Foresters
5400 Grosvenor Lane
Bethesda, Maryland 20814-2198
Phone: 301-897-8720 or 866-897-8720

Fax: 301-897-3690
E-mail: redelsheimerc@safnet.org
Website: www.safnet.org

*HEALTHCARE MANAGEMENT*
Commission on Accreditation of Healthcare Management Education
(CAHME)
Anthony Stanowski, President and CEO
1700 Rockville Pike
Suite 400
Rockville, Maryland 20852
Phone: 301-998-6101
E-mail: info@cahme.org
Website: www.cahme.org

*HEALTH INFORMATICS AND HEALTH MANAGEMENT*
Claire Dixon-Lee, Executive Director
Commission on Accreditation for Health Informatics and Information
Management Education (CAHIIM)
233 North Michigan Avenue, 21st Floor
Chicago, Illinois 60601-5800
Phone: 312-233-1100
Fax: 312-233-1948
E-mail:E-mail: claire.dixon-lee@cahiim.org
Website: www.cahiim.org

*HUMAN SERVICE EDUCATION*
Dr. Elaine Green, President
Council for Standards in Human Service Education (CSHSE)
3337 Duke Street
Alexandria, Virginia 22314
Phone: 571-257-3959
E-mail: info@cshse.org
Web: http://www.cshse.org

*INTERIOR DESIGN*
Holly Mattson, Executive Director
Council for Interior Design Accreditation
206 Grandview Avenue, Suite 350
Grand Rapids, Michigan 49503-4014
Phone: 616-458-0400
Fax: 616-458-0460
E-mail: info@accredit-id.org
Website: www.accredit-id.org

*JOURNALISM AND MASS COMMUNICATIONS*
Susanne Shaw, Executive Director
Accrediting Council on Education in Journalism and Mass
Communications (ACEJMC)
School of Journalism
Stauffer-Flint Hall
University of Kansas
1435 Jayhawk Boulevard
Lawrence, Kansas 66045-7575
Phone: 785-864-3973
Fax: 785-864-5225
E-mail: sshaw@ku.edu
Website: http://www2.ku.edu/~acejmc/

*LANDSCAPE ARCHITECTURE*
Kristopher D. Pritchard, Executive Director
Landscape Architectural Accreditation Board (LAAB)
American Society of Landscape Architects (ASLA)
636 Eye Street, NW
Washington, DC 20001-3736
Phone: 202-216-2359
Fax: 202-898-1185
E-mail: info@asla.org
Website: www.asla.org

*LAW*
Barry Currier, Managing Director of Accreditation & Legal Education
American Bar Association
321 North Clark Street, 21st Floor
Chicago, Illinois 60654
Phone: 312-988-6738
Fax: 312-988-5681
E-mail: legaled@americanbar.org
Website: http://www.americanbar.org/groups/legal_education/
    resources/accreditation.html

*LIBRARY*
Karen O'Brien, Director
Office for Accreditation
American Library Association
50 East Huron Street
Chicago, Illinois 60611-2795
Phone: 312-280-2432
Fax: 312-280-2433
E-mail: accred@ala.org
Website: www.ala.org/accreditation/

*MARRIAGE AND FAMILY THERAPY*
Tanya A. Tamarkin, Director of Educational Affairs
Commission on Accreditation for Marriage and Family Therapy
    Education (COAMFTE)
American Association for Marriage and Family Therapy
112 South Alfred Street
Alexandria, Virginia 22314-3061
Phone: 703-838-9808
Fax: 703-838-9805
E-mail: coa@aamft.org
Website: www.aamft.org

*MEDICAL ILLUSTRATION*
Kathleen Megivern, Executive Director
Commission on Accreditation of Allied Health Education Programs
    (CAAHEP)
1361 Park Street
Clearwater, Florida 33756
Phone: 727-210-2350
Fax: 727-210-2354
E-mail: mail@caahep.org
Website: www.caahep.org

*MEDICINE*
Liaison Committee on Medical Education (LCME)
Robert B. Hash, M.D., LCME Secretary
American Medical Association
Council on Medical Education
330 North Wabash Avenue, Suite 39300
Chicago, Illinois 60611-5885
Phone: 312-464-4933
E-mail: lcme@aamc.org
Website: www.ama-assn.org

Liaison Committee on Medical Education (LCME)
Heather Lent, M.A., Director
Accreditation Services
Association of American Medical Colleges
655 K Street, NW
Washington, DC 20001-2399
Phone: 202-828-0596
E-mail: lcme@aamc.org
Website: www.lcme.org

*MUSIC*
Karen P. Moynahan, Executive Director
National Association of Schools of Music (NASM)
Commission on Accreditation
11250 Roger Bacon Drive, Suite 21
Reston, Virginia 20190-5248
Phone: 703-437-0700
Fax: 703-437-6312
E-mail: info@arts-accredit.org
Website: http://nasm.arts-accredit.org/

*NATUROPATHIC MEDICINE*
Daniel Seitz, J.D., Ed.D., Executive Director
Council on Naturopathic Medical Education
P.O. Box 178
Great Barrington, Massachusetts 01230
Phone: 413-528-8877
E-mail: www.cnme.org/contact.html
Website: www.cnme.org

*NURSE ANESTHESIA*
Francis R.Gerbasi, Ph.D., CRNA, COA Executive Director
Council on Accreditation of Nurse Anesthesia Educational Programs
    (CoA-NAEP)
American Association of Nurse Anesthetists
222 South Prospect Avenue, Suite 304
Park Ridge, Illinois 60068-4010
Phone: 847-655-1160
Fax: 847-692-7137
E-mail: accreditation@coa.us.com
Website: http://home.coa.us.com

*NURSE EDUCATION*
Jennifer L. Butlin, Executive Director
Commission on Collegiate Nursing Education (CCNE)
One Dupont Circle, NW, Suite 530
Washington, DC 20036-1120
Phone: 202-887-6791
Fax: 202-887-8476
E-mail: jbutlin@aacn.nche.edu
Website: www.aacn.nche.edu/accreditation

Marsal P. Stoll, Chief Executive Officer
Accreditation Commission for Education in Nursing (ACEN)
3343 Peachtree Road, NE, Suite 850
Atlanta, Georgia 30326
Phone: 404-975-5000
Fax: 404-975-5020
E-mail: mstoll@acenursing.org
Website: www.acenursing.org

*NURSE MIDWIFERY*
Heather L. Maurer, M.A., Executive Director
Accreditation Commission for Midwifery Education (ACME)
American College of Nurse-Midwives
8403 Colesville Road, Suite 1550
Silver Spring, Maryland 20910
Phone: 240-485-1800
Fax: 240-485-1818
E-mail: info@acnm.org
Website: www.midwife.org/Program-Accreditation

*NURSE PRACTITIONER*
Gay Johnson, CEO
National Association of Nurse Practitioners in Women's Health
Council on Accreditation
505 C Street, NE
Washington, DC 20002
Phone: 202-543-9693 Ext. 1
Fax: 202-543-9858
E-mail: info@npwh.org
Website: www.npwh.org

*NURSING*
Marsal P. Stoll, Chief Executive Director
Accreditation Commission for Education in Nursing (ACEN)
3343 Peachtree Road, NE, Suite 850
Atlanta, Georgia 30326
Phone: 404-975-5000
Fax: 404-975-5020
E-mail: info@acenursing.org
Website: www.acenursing.org

*OCCUPATIONAL THERAPY*
Heather Stagliano, DHSc, OTR/L, Executive Director
The American Occupational Therapy Association, Inc.
4720 Montgomery Lane, Suite 200
Bethesda, Maryland 20814-3449
Phone: 301-652-6611 Ext. 2682
TDD: 800-377-8555
Fax: 240-762-5150
E-mail: accred@aota.org
Website: www.aoteonline.org

*OPTOMETRY*
Joyce L. Urbeck, Administrative Director
Accreditation Council on Optometric Education (ACOE)
American Optometric Association
243 North Lindbergh Boulevard
St. Louis, Missouri 63141-7881
Phone: 314-991-4100, Ext. 4246
Fax: 314-991-4101
E-mail: accredit@aoa.org
Website: www.theacoe.org

*OSTEOPATHIC MEDICINE*
Director, Department of Accreditation
Commission on Osteopathic College Accreditation (COCA)
American Osteopathic Association
142 East Ontario Street
Chicago, Illinois 60611
Phone: 312-202-8048
Fax: 312-202-8202
E-mail: predoc@osteopathic.org
Website: www.aoacoca.org

*PHARMACY*
Peter H. Vlasses, PharmD, Executive Director
Accreditation Council for Pharmacy Education
135 South LaSalle Street, Suite 4100
Chicago, Illinois 60603-4810
Phone: 312-664-3575
Fax: 312-664-4652
E-mail: csinfo@acpe-accredit.org
Website: www.acpe-accredit.org

*PHYSICAL THERAPY*
Sandra Wise, Senior Director
Commission on Accreditation in Physical Therapy Education (CAPTE)
American Physical Therapy Association (APTA)
1111 North Fairfax Street
Alexandria, Virginia 22314-1488
Phone: 703-706-3245
Fax: 703-706-3387
E-mail: accreditation@apta.org
Website: www.capteonline.org

*PHYSICIAN ASSISTANT STUDIES*
Sharon L. Luke, Executive Director
Accredittion Review Commission on Education for the Physician
    Assistant, Inc. (ARC-PA)
12000 Findley Road, Suite 150
Johns Creek, Georgia 30097
Phone: 770-476-1224
Fax: 770-476-1738
E-mail: arc-pa@arc-pa.org
Website: www.arc-pa.org

*PLANNING*
Ms. Shonagh Merits, Executive Director
American Institute of Certified Planners/Association of Collegiate
    Schools of Planning/American Planning Association
Planning Accreditation Board (PAB)
2334 West Lawrence Avenue, Suite 209
Chicago, Illinois 60625
Phone: 773-334-7200
E-mail: smerits@planningaccreditationboard.org
Website: www.planningaccreditationboard.org

*PODIATRIC MEDICINE*
Alan R. Tinkleman, M.P.A., Executive Director
Council on Podiatric Medical Education (CPME)
American Podiatric Medical Association (APMA)
9312 Old Georgetown Road
Bethesda, Maryland 20814-1621
Phone: 301-581-9200
Fax: 301-571-4903
Website: www.cpme.org

*PSYCHOLOGY AND COUNSELING*
Jacqueline Remondet Wall, CEO of the Accrediting Unit,
Office of Program Consultation and Accreditation
American Psychological Association
750 First Street, NE
Washington, DC 20002-4202
Phone: 202-336-5979 or 800-374-2721
TDD/TTY: 202-336-6123
Fax: 202-336-5978
E-mail: apaaccred@apa.org
Website: www.apa.org/ed/accreditation

Carol L. Bobby, Ph.D., Executive Director
Council for Accreditation of Counseling and Related Educational
    Programs (CACREP)
1001 North Fairfax Street, Suite 510
Alexandria, Virginia 22314
Phone: 703-535-5990
Fax: 703-739-6209
E-mail: cacrep@cacrep.org
Website: www.cacrep.org

Richard M. McFall, Executive Director
Psychological Clinical Science Accreditation System (PCSAS)
1101 East Tenth Street
IU Psychology Building
Bloomington, Indiana 47405-7007
Phone: 812-856-2570
Fax: 812-322-5545
E-mail: rmmcfall@pcsas.org
Website: www.pcsas.org

*PUBLIC HEALTH*
Laura Rasar King, M.P.H., MCHES, Executive Director
Council on Education for Public Health
1010 Wayne Avenue, Suite 220
Silver Spring, Maryland 20910
Phone: 202-789-1050
Fax: 202-789-1895
E-mail: Lking@ceph.org
Website: www.ceph.org

*PUBLIC POLICY, AFFAIRS AND ADMINISTRATION*
Crystal Calarusse, Chief Accreditation Officer
Commission on Peer Review and Accreditation
Network of Schools of Public Policy, Affairs, and Administration
(NASPAA-COPRA)
1029 Vermont Avenue, NW, Suite 1100
Washington, DC 20005
Phone: 202-628-8965
Fax: 202-626-4978
E-mail: copra@naspaa.org
Website: www.naspaa.org

*RADIOLOGIC TECHNOLOGY*
Leslie Winter, Chief Executive Officer Joint Review Committee on
Education in Radiologic Technology (JRCERT)
20 North Wacker Drive, Suite 2850
Chicago, Illinois 60606-3182
Phone: 312-704-5300
Fax: 312-704-5304
E-mail: mail@jrcert.org
Web: www.jrcert.org

*REHABILITATION EDUCATION*
Frank Lane, Ph.D., Executive Director
Council on Rehabilitation Education (CORE)
Commission on Standards and Accreditation
1699 Woodfield Road, Suite 300
Schaumburg, Illinois 60173
Phone: 847-944-1345
Fax: 847-944-1346
E-mail: flane@core-rehab.org
Website: www.core-rehab.org

*RESPIRATORY CARE*
Thomas Smalling, Executive Director
Commission on Accreditation for Respiratory Care (CoARC)
1248 Harwood Road
Bedford, Texas 76021-4244
Phone: 817-283-2835
Fax: 817-354-8519
E-mail: tom@coarc.com
Website: www.coarc.com

*SOCIAL WORK*
Dr. Stacey Borasky, Director of Accreditation
Office of Social Work Accreditation
Council on Social Work Education
1701 Duke Street, Suite 200
Alexandria, Virginia 22314
Phone: 703-683-8080
Fax: 703-519-2078
E-mail: info@cswe.org
Website: www.cswe.org

*SPEECH-LANGUAGE PATHOLOGY AND AUDIOLOGY*
Patrima L. Tice, Accreditation Executive Director
American Speech-Language-Hearing Association
Council on Academic Accreditation in Audiology and Speech-Language
    Pathology
2200 Research Boulevard #310
Rockville, Maryland 20850-3289
Phone: 301-296-5700
Fax: 301-296-8750
E-mail: accreditation@asha.org
Website: http://caa.asha.org

*TEACHER EDUCATION*
Christopher A. Koch, President
National Council for Accreditation of Teacher Education (NCATE)
Teacher Education Accreditation Council (TEAC)
1140 19th Street, Suite 400
Washington, DC 20036
Phone: 202-223-0077
Fax: 202-296-6620
E-mail: caep@caepnet.org
Website: www.ncate.org

*TECHNOLOGY*
Michale S. McComis, Ed.D., Executive Director
Accrediting Commission of Career Schools and Colleges
2101 Wilson Boulevard, Suite 302
Arlington, Virginia 22201
Phone: 703-247-4212
Fax: 703-247-4533
E-mail: mccomis@accsc.org
Website: www.accsc.org

*TECHNOLOGY, MANAGEMENT, AND APPLIED ENGINEERING*
Kelly Schild, Director of Accreditation
The Association of Technology, Management, and Applied Engineering
(ATMAE)
275 N. York Street, Suite 401
Elmhurst, Illinois 60126
Phone: 630-433-4514
Fax: 630-563-9181
E-mail: Kelly@atmae.org
Website: www.atmae.org

*THEATER*
Karen P. Moynahan, Executive Director
National Association of Schools of Theatre Commission on
    Accreditation
11250 Roger Bacon Drive, Suite 21
Reston, Virginia 20190
Phone: 703-437-0700
Fax: 703-437-6312
E-mail: info@arts-accredit.org
Website: http://nast.arts-accredit.org/

*THEOLOGY*
Dr. Bernard Fryshman, Executive VP
Emeritus and Interim Executive Director
Association of Advanced Rabbinical and Talmudic Schools (AARTS)
Accreditation Commission
11 Broadway, Suite 405
New York, New York 10004
Phone: 212-363-1991
Fax: 212-533-5335
E-mail: office@aarts-schools.org

Daniel O. Aleshire, Executive Director
Association of Theological Schools in the United States and Canada
    (ATS)
Commission on Accrediting
10 Summit Park Drive
Pittsburgh, Pennsylvania 15275
Phone: 412-788-6505
Fax: 412-788-6510
E-mail: ats@ats.edu
Website: www.ats.edu

Dr. Timothy Eaton, Interim President
Transnational Association of Christian Colleges and Schools (TRACS)
Accreditation Commission
15935 Forest Road
Forest, Virginia 24551
Phone: 434-525-9539
Fax: 434-525-9538
E-mail: info@tracs.org
Website: www.tracs.org

*VETERINARY MEDICINE*
Dr. Karen Brandt, Director of Education and Research
American Veterinary Medical Association (AVMA)
Council on Education
1931 North Meacham Road, Suite 100
Schaumburg, Illinois 60173-4360
Phone: 847-925-8070 Ext. 6674
Fax: 847-285-5732
E-mail: info@avma.org
Website: www.avma.org

# How to Use These Guides

As you identify the particular programs and institutions that interest you, you can use both the *Graduate & Professional Programs: An Overview* volume and the specialized volumes in the series to obtain detailed information.

- *Graduate Programs in the Biological/Biomedical Sciences & Health-Related Professions*
- *Graduate Programs in Business, Education, Information Studies, Law & Social Work*
- *Graduate Programs in Engineering & Applied Sciences*
- *Graduate Programs the Humanities, Arts & Social Sciences*
- *Graduate Programs in the Physical Sciences, Mathematics, Agricultural Sciences, the Environment & Natural Resources*

Each of the specialized volumes in the series is divided into sections that contain one or more directories devoted to programs in a particular field. If you do not find a directory devoted to your field of interest in a specific volume, consult "Directories and Subject Areas" (located at the end of each volume). After you have identified the correct volume, consult the "Directories and Subject Areas in This Book" index, which shows (as does the more general directory) what directories cover subjects not specifically named in a directory or section title.

Each of the specialized volumes in the series has a number of general directories. These directories have entries for the largest unit at an institution granting graduate degrees in that field. For example, the general Engineering and Applied Sciences directory in the *Graduate Programs in Engineering & Applied Sciences* volume consists of **Profiles** for colleges, schools, and departments of engineering and applied sciences.

General directories are followed by other directories, or sections, that give more detailed information about programs in particular areas of the general field that has been covered. The general Engineering and Applied Sciences directory, in the previous example, is followed by nineteen sections with directories in specific areas of engineering, such as Chemical Engineering, Industrial/Management Engineering, and Mechanical Engineering.

Because of the broad nature of many fields, any system of organization is bound to involve a certain amount of overlap. Environmental studies, for example, is a field whose various aspects are studied in several types of departments and schools. Readers interested in such studies will find information on relevant programs in the *Graduate Programs in the Biological/Biomedical Sciences & Health-Related Professions* volume under Ecology and Environmental Biology and Environmental and Occupational Health; in the *Graduate Programs in the Physical Sciences, Mathematics, Agricultural Sciences, the Environment & Natural Resources* volume under Environmental Management and Policy and Natural Resources; and in the *Graduate Programs in Engineering & Applied Sciences* volume under Energy Management and Policy and Environmental Engineering. To help you find all of the programs of interest to you, the introduction to each section within the specialized volumes includes, if applicable, a paragraph suggesting other sections and directories with information on related areas of study.

## Directory of Institutions with Programs in the Humanities, Arts, and Social Sciences

This directory lists institutions in alphabetical order and includes beneath each name the academic fields in which each institution offers graduate programs. The degree level in each field is also indicated, provided that the institution has supplied that information in response to Peterson's Annual Survey of Graduate and Professional Institutions.

An M indicates that a master's degree program is offered; a D indicates that a doctoral degree program is offered; an O signifies that other advanced degrees (e.g., certificates or specialist degrees) are offered; and an * (asterisk) indicates that a **Close-Up** and/or **Display** is located in this volume. See the index, "Close-Ups and Displays," for the specific page number.

## Profiles of Academic and Professional Programs in the Specialized Volumes

Each section of **Profiles** has a table of contents that lists the Program Directories, **Displays**, and **Close-Ups**. Program Directories consist of the **Profiles** of programs in the relevant fields, with **Displays** following if programs have chosen to include them. **Close-Ups**, which are more individualized statements, are also listed for those graduate schools or programs that have chosen to submit them.

The **Profiles** found in the 500 directories in the specialized volumes provide basic data about the graduate units in capsule form for quick reference. To make these directories as useful as possible, **Profiles** are generally listed for an institution's smallest academic unit within a subject area. In other words, if an institution has a College of Liberal Arts that administers many related programs, the **Profile** for the individual program (e.g., Program in History), not the entire College, appears in the directory.

There are some programs that do not fit into any current directory and are not given individual **Profiles**. The directory structure is reviewed annually in order to keep this number to a minimum and to accommodate major trends in graduate education.

The following outline describes the **Profile** information found in the guides and explains how best to use that information. Any item that does not apply to or was not provided by a graduate unit is omitted from its listing. The format of the **Profiles** is constant, making it easy to compare one institution with another and one program with another.

A ★ graphic next to the school's name indicates the institution has additional detailed information in a "Premium Profile" on Petersons.com. After reading their information here, you can learn more about the school by visiting www.petersons.com and searching for that particular college or university's graduate program.

**Identifying Information.** The institution's name, in boldface type, is followed by a complete listing of the administrative structure for that field of study. (For example, University of Akron, Buchtel College of Arts and Sciences, Department of Theoretical and Applied Mathematics, Program in Mathematics.) The last unit listed is the one to which all information in the **Profile** pertains. The institution's city, state, and zip code follow.

**Offerings.** Each field of study offered by the unit is listed with all postbaccalaureate degrees awarded. Degrees that are not preceded by a specific concentration are awarded in the general field listed in the unit name. Frequently, fields of study are broken down into subspecializations, and those appear following the degrees awarded; for example, "Offerings in secondary education (M.Ed.), including English education, mathematics education, science education." Students enrolled in the M.Ed. program would be able to specialize in any of the three fields mentioned.

**Professional Accreditation.** Some **Profiles** indicate whether a program is professionally accredited. Because it is possible for a program to receive or lose professional accreditation at any time, students entering fields in which accreditation is important to a career should verify the status of programs by contacting either the chairperson or the appropriate accrediting association.

**Jointly Offered Degrees.** Explanatory statements concerning programs that are offered in cooperation with other institutions are included in the list of degrees offered. This occurs most commonly on a regional basis (for example, two state universities offering a cooperative Ph.D. in special education) or where the specialized nature of the institutions encourages joint efforts (a J.D./M.B.A. offered by a law school at an institution with no formal business programs and an institution with a business school but lacking a law school). Only programs that are truly cooperative are listed; those involving only limited course work at another institution are not. Interested students should contact the heads of such units for further information.

**Program Availability.** This may include the following: part-time, evening/weekend, online only, 100% online, blended/hybrid learning, and/or minimal on-campus study. When information regarding the availability of part-time or evening/weekend study appears in the **Profile**, it means that students are able to earn a degree exclusively through such study. Blended/hybrid learning describe those courses in which some traditional in-class time has been replaced by online learning activities. Hybrid courses take advantage of the best features of both face-to-face and online learning.

**Postbaccalaureate Distance Learning Degrees.** A postbaccalaureate distance learning degree program signifies that course requirements can be fulfilled with minimal or no on-campus study.

**Faculty.** Figures on the number of faculty members actively involved with graduate students through teaching or research are separated into full- and part-time as well as men and women whenever the information has been supplied.

**Students.** Figures for the number of students enrolled in graduate and professional programs pertain to the semester of highest enrollment from the 2016–17 academic year. These figures are broken down into full- and part-time and men and women whenever the data have been supplied. Information on the number of matriculated students enrolled in the unit who are members of a minority group or are international students appears here. The average age of the matriculated students is followed by the number of applicants, the percentage accepted, and the number enrolled for fall 2016.

**Degrees Awarded.** The number of degrees awarded in the calendar year is listed. Many doctoral programs offer a terminal master's degree if students leave the program after completing only part of the requirements for a doctoral degree; that is indicated here. All degrees are classified into one of four types: master's, doctoral, first professional, and other advanced degrees. A unit may award one or several degrees at a given level; however, the data are only collected by type and may therefore represent several different degree programs.

**Degree Requirements.** The information in this section is also broken down by type of degree, and all information for a degree level pertains to all degrees of that type unless otherwise specified. Degree requirements are collected in a simplified form to provide some very basic information on the nature of the program and on foreign language, thesis or dissertation, comprehensive exam, and registration requirements. Many units also provide a short list of additional requirements, such as fieldwork or an internship. For complete information on graduation requirements, contact the graduate school or program directly.

**Entrance Requirements.** Entrance requirements are broken down into the four degree levels of master's, doctoral, first professional, and other advanced degrees. Within each level, information may be provided in two basic categories: entrance exams and other requirements. The entrance exams are identified by the standard acronyms used by the testing agencies, unless they are not well known. Other entrance requirements are quite varied, but they often contain an undergraduate or graduate grade point average (GPA). Unless otherwise stated, the GPA is calculated on a 4.0 scale and is listed as a minimum required for admission. Additional exam requirements/recommendations for international students may be listed here. Application deadlines for domestic and international students, the application fee, and whether electronic applications are accepted may be listed here. Note that the deadline should be used for reference only; these dates are subject to change, and students interested in applying should always contact the graduate unit directly about application procedures and deadlines.

**Expenses.** The typical cost of study for the 2017–2018 academic year (2016–17 if 2017–18 figures were not available) is given in two basic categories: tuition and fees. Cost of study may be quite complex at a graduate institution. There are often sliding scales for part-time study, a different cost for first-year students, and other variables that make it impossible to completely cover the cost of study for each graduate program. To provide the most usable information, figures are given for full-time study for a full year where available and for part-time study in terms of a per-unit rate (per credit, per semester hour, etc.). Occasionally, variances may be noted in tuition and fees for reasons such

as the type of program, whether courses are taken during the day or evening, whether courses are at the master's or doctoral level, or other institution-specific reasons. Respondents were also given the opportunity to provide more specific and detailed tuition and fees information at the unit level. When provided, this information will appear in place of any typical costs entered elsewhere on the university-level survey. Expenses are usually subject to change; for exact costs at any given time, contact your chosen schools and programs directly. Keep in mind that the tuition of Canadian institutions is usually given in Canadian dollars.

**Financial Support.** This section contains data on the number of awards administered by the institution and given to graduate students during the 2016–17 academic year. The first figure given represents the total number of students receiving financial support enrolled in that unit. If the unit has provided information on graduate appointments, these are broken down into three major categories: fellowships give money to graduate students to cover the cost of study and living expenses and are not based on a work obligation or research commitment, research assistantships provide stipends to graduate students for assistance in a formal research project with a faculty member, and teaching assistantships provide stipends to graduate students for teaching or for assisting faculty members in teaching undergraduate classes. Within each category, figures are given for the total number of awards, the average yearly amount per award, and whether full or partial tuition reimbursements are awarded. In addition to graduate appointments, the availability of several other financial aid sources is covered in this section. Tuition waivers are routinely part of a graduate appointment, but units sometimes waive part or all of a student's tuition even if a graduate appointment is not available. Federal WorkStudy is made available to students who demonstrate need and meet the federal guidelines; this form of aid normally includes 10 or more hours of work per week in an office of the institution. Institutionally sponsored loans are low-interest loans available to graduate students to cover both educational and living expenses. Career-related internships or fieldwork offer money to students who are participating in a formal off-campus research project or practicum. Grants, scholarships, traineeships, unspecified assistantships, and other awards may also be noted. The availability of financial support to part-time students is also indicated here.

Some programs list the financial aid application deadline and the forms that need to be completed for students to be eligible for financial awards. There are two forms: FAFSA, the Free Application for Federal Student Aid, which is required for federal aid, and the CSS PROFILE®.

**Faculty Research.** Each unit has the opportunity to list several keyword phrases describing the current research involving faculty members and graduate students. Space limitations prevent the unit from listing complete information on all research programs. The total expenditure for funded research from the previous academic year may also be included.

**Unit Head and Application Contact.** The head of the graduate program for each unit may be listed with academic title, phone and fax numbers, and e-mail address. In addition to the unit head's contact information, many graduate programs also list a separate contact for application and admission information, followed by the graduate school, program, or department's website. If no unit head or application contact is given, you should contact the overall institution for information on graduate admissions.

# Displays and Close-Ups

The **Displays** and **Close-Ups** are supplementary insertions submitted by deans, chairs, and other administrators who wish to offer an additional, more individualized statement to readers. A number of graduate school and program administrators have attached a **Display** ad near the **Profile** listing. Here you will find information that an institution or program wants to emphasize. The **Close-Ups** are by their very nature more expansive and flexible than the **Profiles**, and the administrators who have written them may emphasize different aspects of their programs. All of the **Close-Ups** are organized in the same way (with the exception of a few that describe research and training opportunities instead of degree programs), and in each one you will find information on the same basic topics, such as programs of study, research facilities, tuition and fees, financial aid, and application procedures. If an institution or program has submitted a **Close-Up**, a boldface cross-reference appears below its **Profile**. As with the **Displays**, all of the **Close-Ups** in the guides have been submitted by choice; the absence of a **Display** or **Close-Up** does not reflect any type of editorial judgment on the part of Peterson's, and their presence in the guides should not be taken as an indication of status, quality, or approval. Statements regarding a university's objectives and accomplishments are a reflection of its own beliefs and are not the opinions of the Peterson's editors.

## Appendixes

This section contains two appendixes. The first, "Institutional Changes Since the 2017 Edition," lists institutions that have closed, merged, or changed their name or status since the last edition of the guides. The second, "Abbreviations Used in the Guides," gives abbreviations of degree names, along with what those abbreviations stand for. These appendixes are identical in all six volumes of *Peterson's Graduate and Professional Programs*.

## Indexes

There are three indexes presented here. The first index, "Close-Ups and Displays," gives page references for all programs that have chosen to place **Close-Ups** and **Displays** in this volume. It is arranged alphabetically by institution; within institutions, the arrangement is alphabetical by subject area. It is not an index to all programs in the book's directories of **Profiles**; readers must refer to the directories themselves for **Profile** information on programs that have not submitted the additional, more individualized statements. The second index, "Directories and Subject Areas in Other Books in This Series", gives book references for the directories in the specialized volumes and also includes cross-references for subject area names not used in the directory structure, for example, "Computing Technology (see Computer Science)." The third index, "Directories and Subject Areas in This Book," gives page references for the directories in this volume and cross-references for subject area names not used in this volume's directory structure.

## Data Collection Procedures

The information published in the directories and Profiles of all the books is collected through Peterson's Annual Survey of Graduate and Professional Institutions. The survey is sent each spring to nearly 2,300 institutions offering postbaccalaureate degree programs, including accredited institutions in the United States, U.S. territories, and Canada and those institutions outside the United States that are accredited by U.S. accrediting bodies. Deans and other administrators complete these surveys, providing information on programs in the 500 academic and professional fields covered in the guides as well as overall institutional information. While every effort has been made to ensure the accuracy and completeness of the data, information is sometimes unavailable or changes occur after publication deadlines. All usable information received in time for publication has been included. The omission of any particular item from a directory or Profile signifies either that the item is not applicable to the institution or program or that information was not available. Profiles of programs scheduled to begin during the 2017–18 academic year cannot, obviously, include statistics on enrollment or, in many cases, the number of faculty members. If no usable data were submitted by an institution, its name, address, and program name appear in order to indicate the availability of graduate work.

## Criteria for Inclusion in This Guide

To be included in this guide, an institution must have full accreditation or be a candidate for accreditation (preaccreditation) status by an institutional or specialized accrediting body recognized by the U.S. Department of Education or the Council for Higher Education Accreditation (CHEA). Institutional accrediting bodies, which review each institution as a whole, include the six regional associations of schools and colleges (Middle States, New England, North Central, Northwest, Southern, and Western), each of which is responsible for a specified portion of the United States and its territories. Other institutional accrediting bodies are national in scope and accredit specific kinds of institutions (e.g., Bible colleges, independent colleges, and rabbinical and Talmudic schools). Program registration by the New York State Board of Regents is considered to be the equivalent of institutional accreditation, since the board requires that all programs offered by an institution meet its standards before recognition is granted. A Canadian institution must be chartered and authorized to grant degrees by the provincial government, affiliated with a chartered institution, or accredited by a recognized U.S. accrediting body. This guide also includes institutions outside the United States that are accredited by these U.S. accrediting bodies. There are recognized specialized or professional accrediting bodies in more than fifty different fields, each of which is authorized to accredit institutions or specific programs in its particular field. For specialized institutions that offer programs in one field only, we designate this to be the equivalent of institutional accreditation. A full explanation of the accrediting process and complete information on recognized institutional (regional and national) and specialized accrediting bodies can be found online at www.chea.org or at www.ed.gov/admins/finaid/accred/index.html.

# DIRECTORY OF INSTITUTIONS WITH PROGRAMS IN THE HUMANITIES, ARTS & SOCIAL SCIENCES

**ABILENE CHRISTIAN UNIVERSITY**
| | |
|---|---|
| Clinical Psychology | M |
| Communication—General | M |
| Conflict Resolution and Mediation/Peace Studies | M,O |
| Counseling Psychology | M |
| English | M |
| Liberal Studies | M |
| Marriage and Family Therapy | M |
| Missions and Missiology | M |
| Pastoral Ministry and Counseling | M,D |
| Psychology—General | M |
| Religion | M |
| Rhetoric | M |
| School Psychology | O |
| Theology | M |
| Writing | M |

**ACADEMY OF ART UNIVERSITY**
| | |
|---|---|
| Applied Arts and Design—General | M |
| Architecture | M |
| Art History | M |
| Art/Fine Arts | M |
| Arts Journalism | M |
| Computer Art and Design | M |
| Film, Television, and Video Production | M |
| Graphic Design | M |
| Illustration | M |
| Industrial Design | M |
| Interior Design | M |
| Internet and Interactive Multimedia | M |
| Landscape Architecture | M |
| Music | M |
| Photography | M |
| Textile Design | M |
| Theater | M |
| Writing | M |

**ACADIA UNIVERSITY**
| | |
|---|---|
| Clinical Psychology | M |
| English | M |
| Geographic Information Systems | M |
| Philosophy | M |
| Political Science | M |
| Psychology—General | M |
| Sociology | M |
| Sustainable Development | M |
| Theology | M,D |

**ADAMS STATE UNIVERSITY**
| | |
|---|---|
| Art/Fine Arts | M |
| History | M |

**ADELPHI UNIVERSITY**
| | |
|---|---|
| Art/Fine Arts | M |
| Clinical Psychology | D |
| Counseling Psychology | M |
| Emergency Management | O |
| Gerontology | M,O |
| Psychology—General | M |
| Public Administration | O |
| School Psychology | M |
| Writing | M |

**ADLER GRADUATE SCHOOL**
| | |
|---|---|
| Addictions/Substance Abuse Counseling | M |
| Art Therapy | M |
| Clinical Psychology | M |
| Counseling Psychology | M |
| Marriage and Family Therapy | M |
| Psychoanalysis and Psychotherapy | M |

**ADLER UNIVERSITY**
| | |
|---|---|
| Addictions/Substance Abuse Counseling | M,D,O |
| Art Therapy | M,D,O |
| Clinical Psychology | M,D,O |
| Counseling Psychology | M,D,O |
| Criminal Justice and Criminology | M,D,O |
| Emergency Management | M,D,O |
| Forensic Psychology | M,D,O |
| Health Psychology | M,D,O |
| Industrial and Organizational Psychology | M,D,O |
| Marriage and Family Therapy | M,D,O |
| Psychoanalysis and Psychotherapy | M,D,O |
| Psychology—General | M,D,O* |
| Public Administration | M,D,O |
| Public Policy | M,D,O |
| Rehabilitation Counseling | M,D,O |
| Social Psychology | M,D,O |
| Sport Psychology | M,D,O |

**ADRIAN COLLEGE**
| | |
|---|---|
| Criminal Justice and Criminology | M |

**ALABAMA AGRICULTURAL AND MECHANICAL UNIVERSITY**
| | |
|---|---|
| Child and Family Studies | M |
| Clinical Psychology | M,O |
| Clothing and Textiles | M |
| Counseling Psychology | M,O |
| Family and Consumer Sciences-General | M |
| Human Development | M |
| Psychology—General | M,O |
| Rehabilitation Counseling | M,O |
| School Psychology | M |
| Urban and Regional Planning | M |

**ALABAMA STATE UNIVERSITY**
| | |
|---|---|
| Forensic Sciences | M |
| History | M |
| Rehabilitation Counseling | M |

**ALASKA PACIFIC UNIVERSITY**
| | |
|---|---|
| Counseling Psychology | M |
| Interdisciplinary Studies | M |
| Liberal Studies | M |

**ALBANY STATE UNIVERSITY**
| | |
|---|---|
| Criminal Justice and Criminology | M |
| Economic Development | M |
| Economics | M |

| | |
|---|---|
| Public Administration | M |
| Public Policy | M |

**ALBERTUS MAGNUS COLLEGE**
| | |
|---|---|
| Art Therapy | M |
| Criminal Justice and Criminology | M |
| Liberal Studies | M |
| Writing | M |

**ALCORN STATE UNIVERSITY**
| | |
|---|---|
| Agricultural Economics and Agribusiness | M |

**ALFRED UNIVERSITY**
| | |
|---|---|
| Applied Arts and Design—General | M |
| Art/Fine Arts | M,D |
| Computer Art and Design | M |
| Counseling Psychology | M,D,O |
| Internet and Interactive Multimedia | M |
| Public Administration | M |
| School Psychology | M,D,O |

**ALLIANT INTERNATIONAL UNIVERSITY–FRESNO**
| | |
|---|---|
| Clinical Psychology | D |
| Forensic Psychology | D |
| Industrial and Organizational Psychology | M,D |
| Psychology—General | M,D |

**ALLIANT INTERNATIONAL UNIVERSITY–IRVINE**
| | |
|---|---|
| Forensic Psychology | D |
| Forensic Sciences | D |
| Marriage and Family Therapy | M,D |
| School Psychology | M,D,O |

**ALLIANT INTERNATIONAL UNIVERSITY–LOS ANGELES**
| | |
|---|---|
| Addictions/Substance Abuse Counseling | M |
| Clinical Psychology | D |
| Forensic Psychology | D |
| Gerontology | M |
| Health Psychology | D |
| Industrial and Organizational Psychology | M,D |
| Marriage and Family Therapy | M,D |
| Psychology—General | M,D |
| School Psychology | M,D,O |
| Social Psychology | D |

**ALLIANT INTERNATIONAL UNIVERSITY–SACRAMENTO**
| | |
|---|---|
| Clinical Psychology | D |
| Forensic Psychology | D |
| Marriage and Family Therapy | M,D |
| Psychology—General | M,D |

**ALLIANT INTERNATIONAL UNIVERSITY–SAN DIEGO**
| | |
|---|---|
| Clinical Psychology | M,D |
| Forensic Psychology | D |
| Industrial and Organizational Psychology | M,D |
| Marriage and Family Therapy | M,D |
| Psychology—General | M,D |
| School Psychology | M,D,O |

**ALLIANT INTERNATIONAL UNIVERSITY–SAN FRANCISCO**
| | |
|---|---|
| Clinical Psychology | M,D,O |
| Criminal Justice and Criminology | M |
| Forensic Psychology | M,D |
| Industrial and Organizational Psychology | M,D |
| Psychology—General | M,D,O |
| School Psychology | M,D,O |

**ALVERNIA UNIVERSITY**
| | |
|---|---|
| Liberal Studies | M |
| Social Psychology | M |

**ALVERNO COLLEGE**
| | |
|---|---|
| Social Psychology | M |

**AMBERTON UNIVERSITY**
| | |
|---|---|
| Child and Family Studies | M |
| Counseling Psychology | M |
| Interdisciplinary Studies | M |

**AMBROSE UNIVERSITY**
| | |
|---|---|
| Pastoral Ministry and Counseling | M,O |
| Religion | M,O |
| Theology | M,O |

**AMERICAN BAPTIST SEMINARY OF THE WEST**
| | |
|---|---|
| Pastoral Ministry and Counseling | M |
| Theology | M |

**AMERICAN CONSERVATORY THEATER**
| | |
|---|---|
| Theater | M,O |

**AMERICAN FILM INSTITUTE CONSERVATORY**
| | |
|---|---|
| Film, Television, and Video Production | M |

**AMERICAN GRADUATE SCHOOL IN PARIS**
| | |
|---|---|
| International Affairs | M,D |

**AMERICAN INTERCONTINENTAL UNIVERSITY ONLINE**
| | |
|---|---|
| Industrial and Organizational Psychology | M |

**AMERICAN INTERNATIONAL COLLEGE**
| | |
|---|---|
| Clinical Psychology | M,D,O |
| Counseling Psychology | M,D |
| Forensic Psychology | M,D,O |
| Psychology—General | M,D,O |

**AMERICAN JEWISH UNIVERSITY**
| | |
|---|---|
| Jewish Studies | M |
| Theology | M |

**AMERICAN MUSEUM OF NATURAL HISTORY–RICHARD GILDER GRADUATE SCHOOL**
| | |
|---|---|
| Museum Studies | D |

**AMERICAN PUBLIC UNIVERSITY SYSTEM**
| | |
|---|---|
| American Studies | M |
| Classics | M |
| Conflict Resolution and Mediation/Peace Studies | M |
| Criminal Justice and Criminology | M |
| Emergency Management | M |
| Forensic Sciences | M |
| History | M |
| Homeland Security | M |
| Humanities | M |
| International Affairs | M |
| Military and Defense Studies | M |
| National Security | M |
| Political Science | M |
| Psychology—General | M |
| Public Administration | M |
| Public History | M |
| Public Policy | M |
| Western European Studies | M |

**AMERICAN UNIVERSITY**
| | |
|---|---|
| American Studies | M,D,O |
| Anthropology | M,D,O |
| Applied Social Research | M,O |
| Art History | M |
| Arts Administration | M,O |
| Asian Studies | O |
| Clinical Psychology | M,D,O |
| Cognitive Sciences | M,D,O |
| Communication—General | M,D |
| Comparative Literature | M |
| Conflict Resolution and Mediation/Peace Studies | M,D,O |
| Criminal Justice and Criminology | M,D |
| Cultural Studies | M,D,O |
| Economics | M,D,O |
| Ethics | M,D,O |
| Film, Television, and Video Production | M |
| French | M,O |
| Gender Studies | M,D,O |
| History | M,D |
| International Affairs | M,D,O |
| International Development | M,D,O |
| International Economics | M,D,O |
| Journalism | M |
| Latin American Studies | M,O |
| Mass Communication | M,D,O |
| Media Studies | M,D |
| Music | M,O |
| Philosophy | M |
| Political Science | M,D,O |
| Psychology—General | M,D,O |
| Public Administration | M,D,O |
| Public Affairs | M |
| Public Policy | M,D |
| Russian | M,O |
| Sociology | M,O |
| Spanish | M,O |
| Sustainable Development | M,D,O |
| Western European Studies | M,D,O |
| Women's Studies | O |
| Writing | M |

**THE AMERICAN UNIVERSITY IN CAIRO**
| | |
|---|---|
| Broadcast Journalism | M,O |
| Communication—General | M,D,O |
| Comparative Literature | M,O |
| Economic Development | M,O |
| Economics | M,O |
| English | M,O |
| Gender Studies | M,O |
| Journalism | M,O |
| Mass Communication | M,O |
| Near and Middle Eastern Languages | M,O |
| Near and Middle Eastern Studies | M,O |
| Philosophy | M,O |
| Psychology—General | M,O |
| Public Administration | M,O |
| Sustainable Development | M,D,O |
| Women's Studies | M,O |

**AMERICAN UNIVERSITY OF ARMENIA**
| | |
|---|---|
| Economics | M |
| International Affairs | M |
| Political Science | M |

**AMERICAN UNIVERSITY OF BEIRUT**
| | |
|---|---|
| Agricultural Economics and Agribusiness | M |
| American Studies | M,D |
| Anthropology | M,D |
| Archaeology | M,D |
| Art History | M,D |
| Clinical Psychology | M,D |
| Economics | M,D |
| English | M,D |
| History | M,D |
| International Affairs | M,D |
| Media Studies | M,D |
| Near and Middle Eastern Languages | M,D |
| Near and Middle Eastern Studies | M,D |
| Political Science | M,D |
| Psychology—General | M,D |
| Public Administration | M,D |
| Public Policy | M,D |
| Sociology | M,D |
| Urban and Regional Planning | M,D |
| Urban Design | M,D |

**THE AMERICAN UNIVERSITY OF PARIS**
| | |
|---|---|
| Communication—General | M |
| Conflict Resolution and Mediation/Peace Studies | M |
| Cultural Studies | M |
| International Affairs | M |
| Near and Middle Eastern Studies | M |
| Public Policy | M |

**AMERICAN UNIVERSITY OF PUERTO RICO**
| | |
|---|---|
| Criminal Justice and Criminology | M |

**THE AMERICAN UNIVERSITY OF ROME**
| | |
|---|---|
| Historic Preservation | M |
| Religion | M |

**AMERICAN UNIVERSITY OF SHARJAH**
| | |
|---|---|
| Translation and Interpretation | M |
| Urban and Regional Planning | M |

**AMRIDGE UNIVERSITY**
| | |
|---|---|
| Counseling Psychology | M,D |
| Marriage and Family Therapy | M,D |
| Pastoral Ministry and Counseling | M,D |
| Religion | M,D |
| Theology | M,D |

**ANABAPTIST MENNONITE BIBLICAL SEMINARY**
| | |
|---|---|
| Conflict Resolution and Mediation/Peace Studies | M,O |
| Ethics | M,O |
| International Affairs | M,O |
| Pastoral Ministry and Counseling | M,O |
| Public Administration | M,O |
| Theology | M,O |

**ANDERSON UNIVERSITY (IN)**
| | |
|---|---|
| Missions and Missiology | M,D |
| Theology | M,D |

**ANDERSON UNIVERSITY (SC)**
| | |
|---|---|
| Criminal Justice and Criminology | M |
| Pastoral Ministry and Counseling | M,D |

**ANDREWS UNIVERSITY**
| | |
|---|---|
| Architecture | M |
| Clinical Psychology | M |
| Communication—General | M |
| Counseling Psychology | M,D |
| Developmental Psychology | M,D |
| Economics | M |
| English | M |
| International Development | M |
| Music | M |
| Pastoral Ministry and Counseling | M,D,O |
| Psychology—General | M,D,O |
| School Psychology | M,O |
| Social Psychology | M |
| Theology | M,D,O |
| Urban and Regional Planning | M |

**ANGELO STATE UNIVERSITY**
| | |
|---|---|
| Applied Psychology | M |
| Communication—General | M |
| Counseling Psychology | M |
| Criminal Justice and Criminology | M |
| English | M |
| Homeland Security | M |
| Industrial and Organizational Psychology | M |
| Media Studies | M |
| National Security | M |
| Psychology—General | M |

**ANNA MARIA COLLEGE**
| | |
|---|---|
| Art/Fine Arts | M,O |
| Counseling Psychology | M |
| Criminal Justice and Criminology | M |
| Emergency Management | M,O |
| Industrial and Organizational Psychology | M |
| Public Administration | M |

**ANTIOCH UNIVERSITY LOS ANGELES**
| | |
|---|---|
| Clinical Psychology | M |
| Psychology—General | M |
| Sustainable Development | M |
| Writing | M,O |

**ANTIOCH UNIVERSITY MIDWEST**
| | |
|---|---|
| Applied Psychology | M |
| Conflict Resolution and Mediation/Peace Studies | M |
| Interdisciplinary Studies | M |
| Social Sciences | M |

**ANTIOCH UNIVERSITY NEW ENGLAND**
| | |
|---|---|
| Addictions/Substance Abuse Counseling | M |
| Applied Behavior Analysis | M,O |
| Applied Psychology | M,D,O |
| Clinical Psychology | M,D |
| Counseling Psychology | M |
| Humanities | M |
| Interdisciplinary Studies | M |
| Marriage and Family Therapy | M,D,O |
| Sustainable Development | M,O |
| Therapies—Dance, Drama, and Music | M,O |

**ANTIOCH UNIVERSITY SANTA BARBARA**
| | |
|---|---|
| Clinical Psychology | M,D |
| Writing | M |

**ANTIOCH UNIVERSITY SEATTLE**
| | |
|---|---|
| Psychology—General | M,D |

**APEX SCHOOL OF THEOLOGY**
| | |
|---|---|
| Theology | M,D |

**APPALACHIAN BIBLE COLLEGE**
| | |
|---|---|
| Pastoral Ministry and Counseling | M |

**APPALACHIAN STATE UNIVERSITY**
| | |
|---|---|
| American Studies | M |
| Clinical Psychology | M |
| Counseling Psychology | M |
| Cultural Studies | M |
| English | M |
| Geographic Information Systems | M |
| Geography | M |
| Health Psychology | M |
| History | M |
| Marriage and Family Therapy | M |
| Music | M |
| Political Science | M |

Psychology—General M
Public Administration M
School Psychology M
Therapies—Dance, Drama, and
Music M

## AQUINAS INSTITUTE OF THEOLOGY
Music M,D,O
Pastoral Ministry and Counseling M
Theology M,D,O

## ARCADIA UNIVERSITY
Applied Behavior Analysis M
Conflict Resolution and
Mediation/Peace Studies M
Counseling Psychology M
English M
Forensic Sciences M
Genetic Counseling M
Humanities M
International Affairs M
Marriage and Family Therapy M
Psychology—General M,D,O
Theater M
Writing M

## ARGOSY UNIVERSITY, ATLANTA
Clinical Psychology M,D,O
Forensic Psychology M,D,O
Health Psychology M,D,O
Industrial and Organizational
Psychology M,D,O
Marriage and Family Therapy M,D,O
Psychology—General M,D,O
Social Psychology M,D,O
Sport Psychology M,D,O

## ARGOSY UNIVERSITY, CHICAGO
Clinical Psychology M,D
Counseling Psychology D
Forensic Psychology D
Health Psychology D
Human Development D
Industrial and Organizational
Psychology M,D
Marriage and Family Therapy M
Psychoanalysis and Psychotherapy D
Psychology—General M,D
Public Administration M,D
Social Psychology M,D

## ARGOSY UNIVERSITY, DALLAS
Clinical Psychology M,D
Forensic Psychology M
Industrial and Organizational
Psychology M
Psychology—General M,D
Public Administration M,D
School Psychology M,D
Social Psychology M

## ARGOSY UNIVERSITY, DENVER
Clinical Psychology M,D
Counseling Psychology M,D
Forensic Psychology M,D
Industrial and Organizational
Psychology M,D
Marriage and Family Therapy M,D
Psychology—General M,D
Public Administration M,D

## ARGOSY UNIVERSITY, HAWAI'I
Addictions/Substance Abuse
Counseling O
Clinical Psychology M,D,O
Counseling Psychology D
Forensic Psychology M
Marriage and Family Therapy M
Psychology—General M,D,O
School Psychology M

## ARGOSY UNIVERSITY, INLAND EMPIRE
Clinical Psychology M,D
Counseling Psychology M,D
Forensic Psychology M,D
Industrial and Organizational
Psychology M,D
Marriage and Family Therapy M,D
Psychology—General M,D
Public Administration M,D
Sport Psychology M,D

## ARGOSY UNIVERSITY, LOS ANGELES
Clinical Psychology M,D
Counseling Psychology M,D
Forensic Psychology M,D
Marriage and Family Therapy M,D
Psychology—General M,D
Public Administration M,D

## ARGOSY UNIVERSITY, NASHVILLE
Counseling Psychology M,D
Psychology—General M,D

## ARGOSY UNIVERSITY, NORTHERN VIRGINIA
Clinical Psychology M,D
Counseling Psychology M,D
Forensic Psychology M,D
Health Psychology M,D
Marriage and Family Therapy M,D
Psychology—General M,D
Public Administration M,D
Social Psychology M,D

## ARGOSY UNIVERSITY, ORANGE COUNTY
Clinical Psychology M,D
Counseling Psychology M,D
Forensic Psychology M
Marriage and Family Therapy M,D
Psychology—General M,D
Public Administration M,D,O
Sport Psychology M

## ARGOSY UNIVERSITY, PHOENIX
Clinical Psychology M,D
Counseling Psychology M
Forensic Psychology M
Industrial and Organizational
Psychology M
Psychology—General M,D
Public Administration M,D
School Psychology M,D
Sport Psychology M,D

## ARGOSY UNIVERSITY, SALT LAKE CITY
Counseling Psychology M,D
Forensic Psychology M,D
Marriage and Family Therapy M,D
Psychology—General M,D
Public Administration M,D

## ARGOSY UNIVERSITY, SAN DIEGO
Clinical Psychology M,D
Counseling Psychology M,D
Forensic Psychology M,D
Marriage and Family Therapy M,D
Psychology—General M,D
Public Administration M,D

## ARGOSY UNIVERSITY, SAN FRANCISCO BAY AREA
Clinical Psychology M,D
Counseling Psychology M,D
Forensic Psychology M
Psychology—General M,D
Public Administration M,D
Sport Psychology M,D

## ARGOSY UNIVERSITY, SARASOTA
Counseling Psychology M,D
Forensic Psychology M,D
Marriage and Family Therapy M,D
Pastoral Ministry and Counseling M,D
Psychology—General M,D
Public Administration M,D,O
School Psychology M,D,O
Social Psychology M,D

## ARGOSY UNIVERSITY, SCHAUMBURG
Clinical Psychology M,D
Corporate and Organizational
Communication M,D,O
Counseling Psychology M,O
Forensic Psychology M,O
Industrial and Organizational
Psychology M,O
Psychology—General M,O
Public Administration M,D,O
Sport Psychology M,O

## ARGOSY UNIVERSITY, SEATTLE
Clinical Psychology M,D,O
Counseling Psychology M,D
Psychology—General M,D,O
Public Administration M,D

## ARGOSY UNIVERSITY, TAMPA
Clinical Psychology M,D
Counseling Psychology M,D
Industrial and Organizational
Psychology M,D
Marriage and Family Therapy M,D
Psychology—General M,D
Public Administration M,D

## ARGOSY UNIVERSITY, TWIN CITIES
Clinical Psychology M,D,O
Forensic Psychology M,D,O
Health Psychology M,D,O
Industrial and Organizational
Psychology M,D,O
Marriage and Family Therapy M,D,O
Psychology—General M,D
Public Administration M,D

## ARIZONA STATE UNIVERSITY AT THE TEMPE CAMPUS
African Studies M,D,O
Agricultural Economics and
Agribusiness D
Anthropology M,D,O
Applied Arts and Design—
General M,D
Applied Behavior Analysis M,D
Applied Psychology M
Archaeology M,D,O
Architectural History D
Architecture M,D
Art History M,D
Art/Fine Arts M,D
Arts Administration M,D
Building Science M,D
Child and Family Studies M,D
Chinese M,D
Clinical Psychology M,D
Cognitive Sciences M,D
Communication—General M,D
Comparative Literature M,D,O
Counseling Psychology D
Criminal Justice and Criminology M,D,O
Cultural Studies M,D
Dance M
Developmental Psychology M,D
Economics D
Emergency Management M,D
English M,D,O
Environmental Design D
Ethics M,D
Film, Television, and Video
Production M
French M
Gender Studies M,D,O
Geographic Information Systems M,D,O
Geography M,D,O
German M
Gerontology M,D,O

History of Science and Technology M,D
History M,D,O
Homeland Security M,D
Human Development M,D
Interdisciplinary Studies M
Japanese M
Journalism M,D
Landscape Architecture M,D
Liberal Studies M
Linguistics M,D,O
Marriage and Family Therapy M,D,O
Mass Communication M,D
Media Studies M,D
Medieval and Renaissance Studies M,D,O
Museum Studies M,D,O
Music M,D,O
Philosophy M,D,O
Political Science M,D
Psychology—General M,D
Public Administration M,D
Public Affairs M,D
Public History M,D,O
Public Policy M,D,O
Publishing M,D,O
Religion M,D,O
Rhetoric M,D,O
Social Psychology M,D
Sociology M,D
Spanish M,D,O
Sustainable Development M,D,O
Textile Design M,D
Theater M,D
Therapies—Dance, Drama, and
Music M,D
Translation and Interpretation M,D,O
Urban and Regional Planning M,D,O
Urban Design M,D
Urban Studies M,D,O
Writing M

## ARKANSAS STATE UNIVERSITY
Addictions/Substance Abuse
Counseling M,O
Clinical Psychology M,O
Communication—General M,O
Criminal Justice and Criminology M,O
Emergency Management M,O
English M,O
Gerontology M,D,O
Health Communication M,O
Historic Preservation M,O
History M,O
Journalism M
Mass Communication M
Media Studies M
Music M,O
Political Science M,O
Public Administration M,O
Rehabilitation Counseling M,O
School Psychology M,O
Sociology M,O

## ARKANSAS TECH UNIVERSITY
Emergency Management M
English M
History M
Journalism M
Liberal Studies M
Psychology—General M
Sociology M

## ARLINGTON BAPTIST COLLEGE
Theology M

## ARMSTRONG STATE UNIVERSITY
American Studies M
Corporate and Organizational
Communication M,O
Criminal Justice and Criminology M,O
History M
Public History M
Western European Studies M
Writing M,O

## ARTCENTER COLLEGE OF DESIGN
Art/Fine Arts M
Computer Art and Design M
Environmental Design M
Film, Television, and Video
Production M
Graphic Design M
Industrial Design M

## THE ART INSTITUTE OF CALIFORNIA–SAN FRANCISCO, A CAMPUS OF ARGOSY UNIVERSITY
Computer Art and Design M
Film, Television, and Video
Production M

## THE ART INSTITUTE OF DALLAS, A BRANCH OF MIAMI INTERNATIONAL UNIVERSITY OF ART & DESIGN
Applied Arts and Design—
General M

## ASBURY THEOLOGICAL SEMINARY
Missions and Missiology M,D,O
Pastoral Ministry and Counseling M,D,O
Theology M,D,O

## ASBURY UNIVERSITY
Child and Family Studies M
Classics M
English M
French M
Spanish M
Writing M

## ASHLAND THEOLOGICAL SEMINARY
Clinical Psychology M,D
Pastoral Ministry and Counseling M,D
Theology M,D

## ASHLAND UNIVERSITY
Corporate and Organizational
Communication M
History M
Political Science M
Writing M

## ASHWORTH COLLEGE
Criminal Justice and Criminology M

## ASSEMBLIES OF GOD THEOLOGICAL SEMINARY
Cultural Studies M,D
Missions and Missiology M,D
Pastoral Ministry and Counseling M,D
Theology M,D

## ASSUMPTION COLLEGE
Addictions/Substance Abuse
Counseling O
Applied Behavior Analysis M,O
Child and Family Studies M,O
Counseling Psychology M,O
Economics M,O
Rehabilitation Counseling M,O
School Psychology M,O
Social Sciences O

## ATHABASCA UNIVERSITY
Applied Psychology M,O
Architecture M,O
Art Therapy M,O
Counseling Psychology M,O
Cultural Studies M,O
Interdisciplinary Studies M,O
International Development M,O

## THE ATHENAEUM OF OHIO
Theology M,O

## ATLANTIC SCHOOL OF THEOLOGY
Pastoral Ministry and Counseling M,O
Theology M,O

## ATLANTIC UNIVERSITY
Pastoral Ministry and Counseling O
Psychoanalysis and Psychotherapy O
Transpersonal and Humanistic
Psychology M

## ATLANTIC UNIVERSITY COLLEGE
Graphic Design M

## A.T. STILL UNIVERSITY
Sport Psychology M,D,O

## AUBURN UNIVERSITY
Agricultural Economics and
Agribusiness M
Applied Economics D
Architecture M
Building Science M
Child and Family Studies M,D
Clothing and Textiles M,D
Communication—General M,O
Economics M
English M,D,O
Geography M
History M,D,O
Human Development M,D
Industrial Design M
Landscape Architecture M
Political Science M,D,O
Psychology—General M,D
Public Administration M,D,O
Sociology M
Spanish M
Technical Communication M,D,O
Urban and Regional Planning M

## AUBURN UNIVERSITY AT MONTGOMERY
Clinical Psychology M
Criminal Justice and Criminology M,O
Emergency Management M
Geographic Information Systems M
Homeland Security M,O
International Affairs M,D,O
Liberal Studies M,D,O
Political Science M,D,O
Psychology—General M
Public Administration M,D,O
Public Policy M,D,O
Writing M

## AUGUSTA UNIVERSITY
Medical Illustration M
Psychology—General M
Social Sciences M

## AURORA UNIVERSITY
Applied Behavior Analysis M
Homeland Security M
Public Policy M

## AUSTIN GRADUATE SCHOOL OF THEOLOGY
Theology M

## AUSTIN PEAY STATE UNIVERSITY
Clinical Psychology M
Communication—General M
Counseling Psychology M
English M
Industrial and Organizational
Psychology M
Military and Defense Studies M
Music M
Psychology—General M

## AUSTIN PRESBYTERIAN THEOLOGICAL SEMINARY
Pastoral Ministry and Counseling M,D
Theology M,D

---

*M—masters degree; D—doctorate; O—other advanced degree; \*—Close-Up and/or Display*

## AVE MARIA UNIVERSITY
| | |
|---|---|
| Pastoral Ministry and Counseling | M,D |
| Theology | M,D |

## AVILA UNIVERSITY
| | |
|---|---|
| Counseling Psychology | M |
| Psychology—General | M |

## AZUSA PACIFIC UNIVERSITY
| | |
|---|---|
| Art/Fine Arts | M |
| Clinical Psychology | M,D |
| Ethics | M |
| International Affairs | M |
| Marriage and Family Therapy | M |
| Music | M |
| Pastoral Ministry and Counseling | M |
| Psychology—General | M,D |
| Public Administration | M |
| School Psychology | M |
| Theology | M,D |
| Urban Studies | M |

## BABEL UNIVERSITY PROFESSIONAL SCHOOL OF TRANSLATION
| | |
|---|---|
| Translation and Interpretation | M |

## BAKER UNIVERSITY
| | |
|---|---|
| Liberal Studies | M |

## BAKKE GRADUATE UNIVERSITY
| | |
|---|---|
| Pastoral Ministry and Counseling | M,D |
| Theology | M,D |

## BALL STATE UNIVERSITY
| | |
|---|---|
| Anthropology | M,O |
| Applied Behavior Analysis | M |
| Architecture | M |
| Art/Fine Arts | M |
| Clinical Psychology | M,D |
| Cognitive Sciences | M |
| Communication—General | M,O |
| Counseling Psychology | M,D |
| Criminal Justice and Criminology | M,O |
| Economic Development | M,O |
| Emergency Management | M,O |
| English | M,D |
| Family and Consumer Sciences-General | M |
| Geographic Information Systems | M,O |
| Geography | M,O |
| Historic Preservation | M |
| History | M |
| Homeland Security | M,O |
| Human Development | M,D,O |
| Interior Design | M |
| Internet and Interactive Multimedia | M |
| Journalism | M |
| Landscape Architecture | M |
| Linguistics | M |
| Music | M,D,O |
| Photography | M |
| Political Science | M |
| Psychology—General | M |
| Public Administration | M,O |
| Rehabilitation Counseling | M,D |
| Rhetoric | M,D |
| School Psychology | M,D,O |
| Social Psychology | M |
| Sociology | M |
| Speech and Interpersonal Communication | M |
| Sport Psychology | M |
| Urban and Regional Planning | M,O |
| Urban Design | M |
| Writing | M,D |

## BANK STREET COLLEGE OF EDUCATION
| | |
|---|---|
| Child and Family Studies | M |

## BAPTIST BIBLE COLLEGE
| | |
|---|---|
| Cultural Studies | M |
| Pastoral Ministry and Counseling | M |
| Theology | M |

## THE BAPTIST COLLEGE OF FLORIDA
| | |
|---|---|
| Music | M |
| Pastoral Ministry and Counseling | M |
| Religion | M |
| Theology | M |

## BAPTIST MISSIONARY ASSOCIATION THEOLOGICAL SEMINARY
| | |
|---|---|
| Theology | M |

## BAPTIST THEOLOGICAL SEMINARY AT RICHMOND
| | |
|---|---|
| Pastoral Ministry and Counseling | M,D,O |
| Religion | M,D,O |
| Theology | M,D,O |

## BARCLAY COLLEGE
| | |
|---|---|
| Theology | M |

## BARD COLLEGE
| | |
|---|---|
| Art/Fine Arts | M |
| Economics | M |
| Museum Studies | M |
| Music | M,O |
| Photography | M |

## BARD GRADUATE CENTER
| | |
|---|---|
| Art History | M,D* |
| Decorative Arts | M,D |

## BARRY UNIVERSITY
| | |
|---|---|
| Art/Fine Arts | M |
| Clinical Psychology | M,O |
| Communication—General | M,O |
| Corporate and Organizational Communication | M,O |
| Liberal Studies | M |
| Marriage and Family Therapy | M,O |
| Pastoral Ministry and Counseling | M,D |
| Photography | M |
| Psychology—General | M,O |
| Public Administration | M |
| Rehabilitation Counseling | M,O |

## BARUCH COLLEGE OF THE CITY UNIVERSITY OF NEW YORK
| | |
|---|---|
| Arts Administration | M |
| Corporate and Organizational Communication | M |
| Counseling Psychology | M |
| Economics | M |
| Industrial and Labor Relations | M |
| Industrial and Organizational Psychology | M,D |
| International Affairs | M* |
| International Economics | M |
| International Trade Policy | M |
| Public Administration | M |
| Public Policy | M |
| Sustainable Development | M |

## BASTYR UNIVERSITY
| | |
|---|---|
| Counseling Psychology | M,O |
| Environmental Design | M,O |
| Health Psychology | M,O |
| Landscape Architecture | M,O |

## BAYAMÓN CENTRAL UNIVERSITY
| | |
|---|---|
| Industrial and Organizational Psychology | M |
| Marriage and Family Therapy | M,O |
| Rehabilitation Counseling | M,O |

## BAYLOR UNIVERSITY
| | |
|---|---|
| American Studies | M |
| Applied Behavior Analysis | M,D,O |
| Clinical Psychology | D |
| Communication—General | M |
| Economics | M |
| English | M,D |
| History | M,D |
| Interdisciplinary Studies | D |
| International Affairs | M,D |
| Journalism | M |
| Museum Studies | M |
| Music | M,D |
| Philosophy | M,D |
| Political Science | M,D |
| Psychology—General | M,D |
| Public Administration | M,D |
| Public Policy | M,D |
| Religion | M,D |
| School Psychology | M,D,O |
| Sociology | M,D |
| Spanish | M |
| Theater | M |
| Theology | M,D |

## BAY PATH UNIVERSITY
| | |
|---|---|
| Addictions/Substance Abuse Counseling | M |
| Applied Behavior Analysis | M |
| Clinical Psychology | M |
| Developmental Psychology | M |
| Writing | M |

## BECKER COLLEGE
| | |
|---|---|
| Counseling Psychology | M |
| Social Psychology | M |

## BELHAVEN UNIVERSITY (MS)
| | |
|---|---|
| Public Administration | M |

## BELLARMINE UNIVERSITY
| | |
|---|---|
| Communication—General | M |

## BELLEVUE UNIVERSITY
| | |
|---|---|
| Corporate and Organizational Communication | M |
| Criminal Justice and Criminology | M |
| Military and Defense Studies | M |
| National Security | M |
| Public Administration | M |

## BEMIDJI STATE UNIVERSITY
| | |
|---|---|
| English | M |

## BENEDICTINE UNIVERSITY
| | |
|---|---|
| Clinical Psychology | M |
| Emergency Management | M |
| Women's Studies | M |

## BENNINGTON COLLEGE
| | |
|---|---|
| Dance | M |
| Music | M |
| Writing | M |

## BERKLEE COLLEGE OF MUSIC
| | |
|---|---|
| Music | M,O |
| Theater | M,O |
| Therapies—Dance, Drama, and Music | M,O |

## BETHANY GLOBAL UNIVERSITY
| | |
|---|---|
| Pastoral Ministry and Counseling | M |

## BETHANY THEOLOGICAL SEMINARY
| | |
|---|---|
| Conflict Resolution and Mediation/Peace Studies | M,O |
| Pastoral Ministry and Counseling | M,O |
| Religion | M,O |
| Theology | M,O |

## BETHEL COLLEGE
| | |
|---|---|
| Pastoral Ministry and Counseling | M |
| Theology | M |

## BETHEL SEMINARY
| | |
|---|---|
| Classics | M,D,O |
| Clinical Psychology | M,D,O |
| Marriage and Family Therapy | M,D,O |
| Missions and Missiology | M,D,O |
| Near and Middle Eastern Languages | M,D,O |
| Pastoral Ministry and Counseling | M,D,O |
| Religion | M,D,O |
| Theology | M,D,O |

## BETHEL UNIVERSITY (MN)
| | |
|---|---|
| Counseling Psychology | M,D,O |

## BETHEL UNIVERSITY (TN)
| | |
|---|---|
| Conflict Resolution and Mediation/Peace Studies | M |

## BETHESDA UNIVERSITY
| | |
|---|---|
| Music | M |
| Religion | M |
| Theology | M |

## BETH HAMEDRASH SHAAREI YOSHER INSTITUTE
| | |
|---|---|
| Theology | M |

## BETH HATALMUD RABBINICAL COLLEGE
| | |
|---|---|
| Theology | M |

## BETH MEDRASH GOVOHA
| | |
|---|---|
| Theology | M |

## BETHUNE-COOKMAN UNIVERSITY
| | |
|---|---|
| Theology | M |

## BEULAH HEIGHTS UNIVERSITY
| | |
|---|---|
| Religion | M |

## BEXLEY SEABURY SEMINARY
| | |
|---|---|
| Theology | M,D,O |

## BIBLICAL THEOLOGICAL SEMINARY
| | |
|---|---|
| Missions and Missiology | M,D,O |
| Pastoral Ministry and Counseling | M,D,O |
| Theology | M,D,O |

## BINGHAMTON UNIVERSITY, STATE UNIVERSITY OF NEW YORK
| | |
|---|---|
| Anthropology | M,D |
| Art History | M,D |
| Asian Studies | M,O |
| Asian-American Studies | M,O |
| Clinical Psychology | D |
| Cognitive Sciences | D |
| Comparative Literature | M,D |
| Cultural Studies | M,D |
| Economics | M,D |
| English | M,D |
| French | M |
| Geography | M |
| History | M,D |
| Italian | M |
| Music | M |
| Philosophy | M,D |
| Political Science | M,D |
| Psychology—General | D |
| Public Administration | M |
| Sociology | M,D |
| Spanish | M |
| Sustainable Development | M |
| Theater | M |
| Translation and Interpretation | D,O |
| Writing | M,D |

## BIOLA UNIVERSITY
| | |
|---|---|
| Anthropology | M,D,O |
| Clinical Psychology | D |
| Cultural Studies | M,D,O |
| Jewish Studies | M,D,O |
| Linguistics | M,D,O |
| Missions and Missiology | M,D,O |
| Pastoral Ministry and Counseling | M,D,O |
| Psychology—General | D |
| Religion | M,D,O |
| Theology | M,D,O |

## BLOOMSBURG UNIVERSITY OF PENNSYLVANIA
| | |
|---|---|
| School Psychology | M |

## BOB JONES UNIVERSITY
| | |
|---|---|
| Art/Fine Arts | M,D,O |
| English | M,D,O |
| Film, Television, and Video Production | M,D,O |
| Graphic Design | M,D,O |
| History | M,D,O |
| Illustration | M,D,O |
| Journalism | M,D,O |
| Media Studies | M,D,O |
| Music | M,D,O |
| Pastoral Ministry and Counseling | M,D,O |
| Religion | M,D,O |
| Rhetoric | M,D,O |
| Speech and Interpersonal Communication | M,D,O |
| Theater | M,D,O |
| Theology | M,D,O |

## BOISE STATE UNIVERSITY
| | |
|---|---|
| Anthropology | M |
| Art/Fine Arts | M |
| Communication—General | M |
| Criminal Justice and Criminology | M |
| History | M |
| Interdisciplinary Studies | M |
| Music | M |
| Political Science | M |
| Public Administration | M,D,O |
| Public Policy | M,D,O |
| Rhetoric | M |
| Technical Communication | M |
| Writing | M |

## BORICUA COLLEGE
| | |
|---|---|
| Latin American Studies | M |

## BOSTON ARCHITECTURAL COLLEGE
| | |
|---|---|
| Architecture | M |
| Historic Preservation | M |
| Interior Design | M |
| Landscape Architecture | M |
| Sustainable Development | M |

## BOSTON COLLEGE
| | |
|---|---|
| Applied Psychology | M,D |
| Classics | M |
| Counseling Psychology | M,D |
| Developmental Psychology | M,D |
| East European and Russian Studies | M |
| Economics | D |

## BOSTON COLLEGE (continued)
| | |
|---|---|
| English | M,D |
| French | M,D |
| History | M |
| Italian | M |
| Linguistics | M |
| Pastoral Ministry and Counseling | M,D,O |
| Philosophy | M,D |
| Political Science | M,D |
| Psychology—General | D |
| Russian | M |
| Sociology | M,D |
| Spanish | M |
| Theology | M,D |
| Western European Studies | M,D |

## BOSTON GRADUATE SCHOOL OF PSYCHOANALYSIS
| | |
|---|---|
| Counseling Psychology | M |
| Developmental Psychology | O |
| Psychoanalysis and Psychotherapy | M,D,O |
| Psychology—General | M |

## BOSTON UNIVERSITY
| | |
|---|---|
| African-American Studies | M |
| American Studies | D |
| Anthropology | M,D |
| Archaeology | M,D |
| Art History | M,D,O |
| Art/Fine Arts | M |
| Arts Administration | M,O |
| Classics | M,D |
| Communication—General | M,D |
| Corporate and Organizational Communication | M |
| Counseling Psychology | M |
| Criminal Justice and Criminology | M |
| Cultural Studies | M |
| Economic Development | M |
| Economics | M,D |
| Emergency Management | M |
| English | M,D |
| Ethics | M,D |
| Film, Television, and Video Production | M |
| Forensic Sciences | M |
| French | M,D |
| Genetic Counseling | M |
| Geographic Information Systems | M,D |
| Geography | M,D |
| Graphic Design | M |
| Health Communication | M |
| Hispanic and Latin American Languages | M,D |
| Historic Preservation | M |
| History | M,D |
| International Affairs | M* |
| Internet and Interactive Multimedia | M,O |
| Journalism | M |
| Linguistics | M,D |
| Mass Communication | M |
| Media Studies | M,D |
| Missions and Missiology | M,D |
| Museum Studies | M,D,O |
| Music | M,D,O |
| Pastoral Ministry and Counseling | M,D |
| Philosophy | M,D |
| Political Science | D |
| Psychology—General | M,D |
| Religion | M,D |
| Romance Languages | M,D |
| Sociology | M,D |
| Theater | M,O |
| Theology | M,D |
| Urban and Regional Planning | M |
| Urban Studies | M |
| Writing | M |

## BOWIE STATE UNIVERSITY
| | |
|---|---|
| Corporate and Organizational Communication | M,O |
| Counseling Psychology | M |
| English | M |
| Public Administration | M |

## BOWLING GREEN STATE UNIVERSITY
| | |
|---|---|
| American Studies | M,D |
| Applied Arts and Design—General | M |
| Art History | M |
| Art/Fine Arts | M |
| Clinical Psychology | M |
| Communication—General | M,D |
| Computer Art and Design | M |
| Criminal Justice and Criminology | M |
| Demography and Population Studies | M,D |
| Developmental Psychology | M,D |
| English | M,D |
| Experimental Psychology | M,D |
| Film, Television, and Video Production | M,D |
| French | M |
| German | M |
| Graphic Design | M |
| History | M,D |
| Industrial and Organizational Psychology | M,D |
| Interdisciplinary Studies | M,D |
| Media Studies | M,D |
| Music | M,D |
| Philosophy | M,D |
| Psychology—General | M,D |
| Public Administration | M,D |
| Rhetoric | M,D |
| Social Psychology | M,D |
| Sociology | M,D |
| Spanish | M |
| Technical Communication | M,D |
| Theater | M,D |
| Writing | M,D |

## BRADLEY UNIVERSITY
| | |
|---|---|
| Art/Fine Arts | M |
| Clinical Psychology | M |
| Counseling Psychology | M |
| English | M |

| | | | |
|---|---|---|---|
| Graphic Design | M | | |
| Human Development | M | | |
| Photography | M | | |

## BRANDEIS UNIVERSITY

| | |
|---|---|
| Anthropology | M,D |
| Art/Fine Arts | O |
| Child and Family Studies | M,D |
| Classics | M |
| Cognitive Sciences | M,D |
| Conflict Resolution and Mediation/Peace Studies | M |
| Developmental Psychology | M,D |
| Disability Studies | D |
| Economics | M,D |
| English | M,D |
| Gender Studies | M,D |
| Genetic Counseling | M |
| History | M,D |
| Humanities | M |
| International Affairs | M |
| Internet and Interactive Multimedia | M |
| Jewish Studies | M,D |
| Linguistics | M |
| Music | M,D |
| Near and Middle Eastern Languages | M,D |
| Near and Middle Eastern Studies | M,D |
| Philosophy | M |
| Political Science | M,D |
| Psychology—General | M,D |
| Public Policy | M |
| Social Psychology | M,D |
| Sociology | M,D |
| Sustainable Development | M |
| Theater | M |
| Women's Studies | M,D |

## BRANDMAN UNIVERSITY

| | |
|---|---|
| Counseling Psychology | M |
| Marriage and Family Therapy | M |
| Psychology—General | M |
| Public Administration | M |

## BRANDON UNIVERSITY

| | |
|---|---|
| Music | M |
| Rural Planning and Studies | M,O |

## BRENAU UNIVERSITY

| | |
|---|---|
| Interior Design | M |
| Psychology—General | M |

## BRIDGEWATER STATE UNIVERSITY

| | |
|---|---|
| Criminal Justice and Criminology | M |
| English | M |
| Psychology—General | M |
| Public Administration | M |

## BRIERCREST SEMINARY

| | |
|---|---|
| Marriage and Family Therapy | M |
| Missions and Missiology | M |
| Pastoral Ministry and Counseling | M |
| Religion | M |
| Theology | M |

## BRIGHAM YOUNG UNIVERSITY

| | |
|---|---|
| Anthropology | M |
| Applied Psychology | D |
| Art/Fine Arts | M |
| Child and Family Studies | M,D |
| Classics | M |
| Clinical Psychology | D |
| Cognitive Sciences | D |
| Communication—General | M |
| Comparative and Interdisciplinary Arts | M |
| Comparative Literature | M |
| Counseling Psychology | M,D,O |
| Developmental Psychology | D |
| English | M |
| Film, Television, and Video Production | M |
| French | M |
| Hispanic and Latin American Languages | M |
| Human Development | M,D |
| Humanities | M |
| International Affairs | M |
| Linguistics | M,D |
| Marriage and Family Therapy | M,D |
| Mass Communication | M |
| Music | M |
| Political Science | M |
| Portuguese | M |
| Psychology—General | D |
| Public Administration | M |
| Rhetoric | M |
| School Psychology | M,D,O |
| Sociology | M |
| Spanish | M |
| Theater | M |
| Writing | M |

## BRITE DIVINITY SCHOOL

| | |
|---|---|
| Pastoral Ministry and Counseling | M,D,O |
| Theology | M,D,O |

## BROCK UNIVERSITY

| | |
|---|---|
| Child and Family Studies | M |
| Classics | M |
| Comparative Literature | M |
| Cultural Studies | M |
| Disability Studies | M,O |
| Economics | M |
| English | M |
| Geography | M |
| History | M |
| Human Development | M,D |
| International Affairs | M |
| Philosophy | M |
| Political Science | M |
| Psychology—General | M,D |
| Public Policy | M |

| | |
|---|---|
| Social Psychology | M,D |
| Sociology | M |

## BROOKLYN COLLEGE OF THE CITY UNIVERSITY OF NEW YORK

| | |
|---|---|
| Art History | M |
| Art/Fine Arts | M |
| Arts Administration | M,D,O |
| Counseling Psychology | M,D,O |
| Economics | M |
| English | M |
| Experimental Psychology | M,D |
| Film, Television, and Video Production | M |
| Film, Television, and Video Theory and Criticism | M |
| French | M |
| History | M |
| Industrial and Organizational Psychology | M,D |
| International Affairs | M |
| Internet and Interactive Multimedia | M |
| Jewish Studies | M |
| Liberal Studies | M |
| Media Studies | M |
| Music | M |
| Photography | M |
| Political Science | M |
| Psychology—General | M,D |
| Public Policy | M |
| School Psychology | M,O |
| Social Psychology | M,D |
| Sociology | M,D |
| Spanish | M |
| Speech and Interpersonal Communication | M,D |
| Thanatology | M |
| Theater | M |
| Urban Studies | M |
| Writing | M |

## BROWN UNIVERSITY

| | |
|---|---|
| American Studies | M,D |
| Anthropology | M,D |
| Archaeology | D |
| Art History | D |
| Asian Studies | D |
| Classics | M,D |
| Cognitive Sciences | M,D |
| Comparative Literature | D |
| East European and Russian Studies | M,D |
| Economics | D |
| English | M,D |
| French | D |
| German | D |
| Hispanic Studies | D |
| History of Science and Technology | D |
| History | M,D |
| Italian | D |
| Latin American Studies | M,D |
| Linguistics | M,D |
| Music | D |
| Near and Middle Eastern Studies | D |
| Philosophy | D |
| Political Science | D |
| Psychology—General | M,D |
| Public Policy | M |
| Publishing | M,D |
| Religion | D |
| Russian | M,D |
| Slavic Languages | M,D |
| Sociology | M,D |
| Theater | M,D |
| Western European Studies | M,D |
| Writing | M,D |

## BRYANT UNIVERSITY

| | |
|---|---|
| Communication—General | M,O |
| Corporate and Organizational Communication | M,O |
| International Economics | M,O |
| Mass Communication | M,O |

## BRYN ATHYN COLLEGE OF THE NEW CHURCH

| | |
|---|---|
| Religion | M |
| Theology | M |

## BRYN MAWR COLLEGE

| | |
|---|---|
| Archaeology | M,D |
| Art History | M,D |
| Classics | M,D |

## BUCKNELL UNIVERSITY

| | |
|---|---|
| English | M |
| Psychology—General | M |

## BUFFALO STATE COLLEGE, STATE UNIVERSITY OF NEW YORK

| | |
|---|---|
| Applied Economics | M |
| Criminal Justice and Criminology | M |
| Economics | M |
| English | M |
| Historic Preservation | M,O |
| History | M |
| Interdisciplinary Studies | M |

## BUTLER UNIVERSITY

| | |
|---|---|
| Art/Fine Arts | M |
| Clinical Psychology | M,O |
| English | M |
| History | M |
| Music | M |
| Writing | M |

## BYZANTINE CATHOLIC SEMINARY OF SAINTS CYRIL AND METHODIUS

| | |
|---|---|
| Theology | M |

## CAIRN UNIVERSITY

| | |
|---|---|
| Applied Behavior Analysis | M,O |
| Pastoral Ministry and Counseling | M |

## CALDWELL UNIVERSITY

| | |
|---|---|
| Applied Behavior Analysis | M,D,O |
| Art Therapy | M,O |
| Counseling Psychology | M,O |
| School Psychology | M,O |

## CALIFORNIA BAPTIST UNIVERSITY

| | |
|---|---|
| Architecture | M |
| Communication—General | M |
| Counseling Psychology | M |
| Disability Studies | M |
| English | M |
| Forensic Psychology | M |
| Music | M |
| Pastoral Ministry and Counseling | M |
| Public Administration | M |
| School Psychology | M |

## CALIFORNIA COAST UNIVERSITY

| | |
|---|---|
| Criminal Justice and Criminology | M |
| Psychology—General | M |

## CALIFORNIA COLLEGE OF THE ARTS

| | |
|---|---|
| Applied Arts and Design— General | M |
| Architecture | M |
| Art/Fine Arts | M |
| Computer Art and Design | M |
| Film, Television, and Video Production | M |
| Film, Television, and Video Theory and Criticism | M |
| Graphic Design | M |
| Industrial Design | M |
| Interdisciplinary Studies | M |
| Media Studies | M |
| Museum Studies | M |
| Photography | M |
| Textile Design | M |
| Writing | M |

## CALIFORNIA INSTITUTE OF INTEGRAL STUDIES

| | |
|---|---|
| Art Therapy | M,D |
| Asian Studies | M,D |
| Clinical Psychology | M,D |
| Counseling Psychology | M,D |
| Cultural Anthropology | M,D |
| Health Psychology | M,D |
| Humanities | M,D |
| Interdisciplinary Studies | M,D |
| Music | M,D |
| Philosophy | M,D |
| Psychology—General | M,D |
| Religion | M,D |
| Social Psychology | M,D |
| Theater | M,D |
| Theology | M,D |
| Therapies—Dance, Drama, and Music | M,D |
| Transpersonal and Humanistic Psychology | M,D |
| Women's Studies | M,D |
| Writing | M,D |

## CALIFORNIA INSTITUTE OF TECHNOLOGY

| | |
|---|---|
| Social Sciences | M,D |

## CALIFORNIA INSTITUTE OF THE ARTS

| | |
|---|---|
| Applied Arts and Design— General | M,O |
| Art/Fine Arts | M,O |
| Dance | M,O |
| Film, Television, and Video Production | M,O |
| Graphic Design | M,O |
| Music | M,O |
| Photography | M,O |
| Theater | M,O |
| Writing | M,O |

## CALIFORNIA LUTHERAN UNIVERSITY

| | |
|---|---|
| Clinical Psychology | M,D |
| Economics | M,O |
| Marriage and Family Therapy | M,D |
| Psychology—General | M,D |
| Public Policy | M,O |
| Theology | M,D,O |

## CALIFORNIA POLYTECHNIC STATE UNIVERSITY, SAN LUIS OBISPO

| | |
|---|---|
| Agricultural Economics and Agribusiness | M |
| Architecture | M |
| Economics | M |
| English | M |
| History | M |
| Political Science | M |
| Psychology—General | M |
| Urban and Regional Planning | M |

## CALIFORNIA STATE POLYTECHNIC UNIVERSITY, POMONA

| | |
|---|---|
| Architecture | M |
| Economics | M |
| English | M |
| History | M |
| Interior Design | M |
| Landscape Architecture | M |
| Psychology—General | M |
| Public Administration | M |
| Urban and Regional Planning | M |

## CALIFORNIA STATE UNIVERSITY, BAKERSFIELD

| | |
|---|---|
| Anthropology | M |
| Counseling Psychology | M |
| English | M |
| History | M |

| | |
|---|---|
| Interdisciplinary Studies | M |
| Public Administration | M |
| Sociology | M |
| Spanish | M |

## CALIFORNIA STATE UNIVERSITY, CHICO

| | |
|---|---|
| Anthropology | M |
| Applied Psychology | M |
| Art History | M |
| Art/Fine Arts | M |
| Communication—General | M |
| Criminal Justice and Criminology | M |
| English | M |
| History | M |
| Marriage and Family Therapy | M |
| Museum Studies | M |
| Political Science | M |
| Psychology—General | M |
| Public Administration | M |
| School Psychology | M |
| Social Sciences | M |

## CALIFORNIA STATE UNIVERSITY, DOMINGUEZ HILLS

| | |
|---|---|
| Applied Social Research | M,O |
| Clinical Psychology | M |
| Conflict Resolution and Mediation/Peace Studies | M |
| English | M,O |
| Health Psychology | M |
| Humanities | M |
| Marriage and Family Therapy | M |
| Psychology—General | M |
| Public Administration | M |
| Rhetoric | M,O |
| School Psychology | M |
| Sociology | M,O |

## CALIFORNIA STATE UNIVERSITY, EAST BAY

| | |
|---|---|
| Anthropology | M |
| Child and Family Studies | M |
| Communication—General | M |
| Economics | M |
| English | M |
| Geography | M |
| History | M |
| Interdisciplinary Studies | M |
| Internet and Interactive Multimedia | M |
| Marriage and Family Therapy | M |
| Music | M |
| Public Administration | M |
| Public History | M |
| Public Policy | M |
| School Psychology | M |
| Social Psychology | M |
| Writing | M |

## CALIFORNIA STATE UNIVERSITY, FRESNO

| | |
|---|---|
| Applied Arts and Design— General | M |
| Applied Behavior Analysis | M,O |
| Art/Fine Arts | M |
| Communication—General | M |
| Counseling Psychology | M |
| Criminal Justice and Criminology | M |
| English | M |
| Experimental Psychology | M,O |
| History | M |
| Human Development | M,D |
| Linguistics | M |
| Marriage and Family Therapy | M |
| Music | M |
| Psychology—General | M,O |
| Public Administration | M |
| Rehabilitation Counseling | M |
| Rhetoric | M |
| School Psychology | M,O |
| Spanish | M |
| Sport Psychology | M |
| Writing | M |

## CALIFORNIA STATE UNIVERSITY, FULLERTON

| | |
|---|---|
| American Studies | M |
| Anthropology | M |
| Clinical Psychology | M |
| Communication—General | M |
| Economics | M |
| English | M |
| Film, Television, and Video Production | M |
| Geography | M |
| Gerontology | M |
| History | M |
| Linguistics | M |
| Mass Communication | M |
| Music | M |
| Political Science | M |
| Psychology—General | M |
| Public Administration | M |
| Social Psychology | M |
| Sociology | M |
| Spanish | M |
| Speech and Interpersonal Communication | M |
| Theater | M |

## CALIFORNIA STATE UNIVERSITY, LONG BEACH

| | |
|---|---|
| African Studies | M |
| Anthropology | M |
| Art/Fine Arts | M |
| Asian Studies | M |
| Asian-American Studies | M |
| Communication—General | M |
| Criminal Justice and Criminology | M |
| Dance | M |
| Economics | M |

Emergency Management — M
English — M
French — M
Geography — M
German — M
Gerontology — M
History — M
Industrial and Organizational
   Psychology — M
Linguistics — M,O
Marriage and Family Therapy — M,D
Music — M
Near and Middle Eastern Studies — M
Philosophy — M
Political Science — M
Psychology—General — M
Public Administration — M,O
Public Policy — M,O
Religion — M
Spanish — M
Sport Psychology — M
Theater — M
Writing — M

## CALIFORNIA STATE UNIVERSITY, LOS ANGELES
Anthropology — M
Applied Arts and Design—
   General — M
Art History — M
Art Therapy — M
Art/Fine Arts — M
Child and Family Studies — M
Child Development — M
Communication—General — M
Criminal Justice and Criminology — M
Economics — M
English — M,O
French — M
Geography — M
Graphic Design — M
Hispanic Studies — M
History — M
Latin American Studies — M
Music — M,O
Philosophy — M
Photography — M
Political Science — M
Psychology—General — M
Public Administration — M
Rehabilitation Counseling — M,D
School Psychology — M,D
Sociology — M
Spanish — M
Textile Design — M
Theater — M

## CALIFORNIA STATE UNIVERSITY MARITIME ACADEMY
Emergency Management — M

## CALIFORNIA STATE UNIVERSITY, NORTHRIDGE
Anthropology — M
Archaeology — M
Art History — M
Art/Fine Arts — M
Clinical Psychology — M
Communication—General — M
Comparative Literature — M
English — M
Experimental Psychology — M
Family and Consumer
   Sciences-General — M
Film, Television, and Video
   Production — M
Geography — M
Hispanic Studies — M
History — M
Journalism — M
Linguistics — M
Marriage and Family Therapy — M
Mass Communication — M
Music — M
Political Science — M
Psychology—General — M
Public Administration — M,O*
Rhetoric — M
School Psychology — M
Sociology — M
Spanish — M
Speech and Interpersonal
   Communication — M
Theater — M
Writing — M

## CALIFORNIA STATE UNIVERSITY, SACRAMENTO
Anthropology — M
Applied Behavior Analysis — M
Art/Fine Arts — M
Child Development — M,D
Communication—General — M
Counseling Psychology — M
Criminal Justice and Criminology — M
English — M
Industrial and Organizational
   Psychology — M
Music — M
Political Science — M
Psychology—General — M
Public Administration — M
Public History — M,D
Public Policy — M
School Psychology — M,D
Sociology — M
Writing — M

## CALIFORNIA STATE UNIVERSITY, SAN BERNARDINO
Archaeology — M
Art/Fine Arts — M
Child Development — M
Clinical Psychology — M
Communication—General — M

Corporate and Organizational
   Communication — M
Counseling Psychology — M
Criminal Justice and Criminology — M
English — M
Experimental Psychology — M
Industrial and Organizational
   Psychology — M
Interdisciplinary Studies — M
Music — M
National Security — M
Psychology—General — M
Public Administration — M
Rehabilitation Counseling — M
Social Sciences — M
Spanish — M
Writing — M

## CALIFORNIA STATE UNIVERSITY, SAN MARCOS
Child and Family Studies — M
English — M
Hispanic and Latin American
   Languages — M
Hispanic Studies — M
History — M
Psychology—General — M
Sociology — M
Spanish — M
Writing — M

## CALIFORNIA STATE UNIVERSITY, STANISLAUS
Applied Behavior Analysis — M
Counseling Psychology — M
Criminal Justice and Criminology — M
English — M,O
Genetic Counseling — M
History — M
Interdisciplinary Studies — M
International Affairs — M
Psychology—General — M
Public Administration — M
Rhetoric — M,O
Sustainable Development — M
Writing — M,O

## CALIFORNIA UNIVERSITY OF MANAGEMENT AND SCIENCES
Economics — M,D

## CALIFORNIA UNIVERSITY OF PENNSYLVANIA
Clinical Psychology — M
Counseling Psychology — M
Criminal Justice and Criminology — M
School Psychology — M
Sport Psychology — M

## CALUMET COLLEGE OF SAINT JOSEPH
Criminal Justice and Criminology — M

## CALVARY UNIVERSITY
Pastoral Ministry and Counseling — M
Theology — M

## CALVIN THEOLOGICAL SEMINARY
Missions and Missiology — M,D
Pastoral Ministry and Counseling — M
Religion — M
Theology — M,D

## CAMBRIDGE COLLEGE
Addictions/Substance Abuse
   Counseling — M,O
Conflict Resolution and
   Mediation/Peace Studies — M
Counseling Psychology — M,O
Forensic Psychology — M,O
Interdisciplinary Studies — M,D,O
Marriage and Family Therapy — M,O
Psychology—General — M,O
School Psychology — M,D,O

## CAMERON UNIVERSITY
Psychology—General — M

## CAMPBELLSVILLE UNIVERSITY
Marriage and Family Therapy — M
Music — M
Social Sciences — M
Theology — M

## CAMPBELL UNIVERSITY
Interdisciplinary Studies — M
Pastoral Ministry and Counseling — M,D
Theology — M,D

## CANADIAN SOUTHERN BAPTIST SEMINARY
Pastoral Ministry and Counseling — M
Religion — M
Theology — M

## CANISIUS COLLEGE
Anthropology — M
Corporate and Organizational
   Communication — M
School Psychology — M
Social Psychology — M

## CAPELLA UNIVERSITY
Addictions/Substance Abuse
   Counseling — M,D
Applied Behavior Analysis — M
Child and Family Studies — M
Clinical Psychology — M
Counseling Psychology — M
Criminal Justice and Criminology — M
Developmental Psychology — M
Emergency Management — M
Gerontology — M
Homeland Security — M
Industrial and Organizational
   Psychology — M,D
Marriage and Family Therapy — M
Psychology—General — M,D
Public Administration — M
School Psychology — M,D

Sport Psychology — M

## CAPITAL UNIVERSITY
Music — M

## CARDINAL STRITCH UNIVERSITY
Clinical Psychology — M
Liberal Studies — M
Pastoral Ministry and Counseling — M
Psychology—General — M
Religion — M

## CAREY THEOLOGICAL COLLEGE
Theology — M,D

## CARIBBEAN UNIVERSITY
Art History — M,D
Criminal Justice and Criminology — M,D
Museum Studies — M,D

## CARLETON UNIVERSITY
Anthropology — M
Architecture — M
Art History — M
Canadian Studies — M,D
Cognitive Sciences — D
Communication—General — M,D
Comparative Literature — D
Conflict Resolution and
   Mediation/Peace Studies — M,O
East European and Russian Studies — M,O
Economics — M,D
English — M,D
Film, Television, and Video
   Production — M
French — M
Geography — M,D
History — M,D
Industrial Design — M
International Affairs — M,D
Journalism — M,D
Linguistics — M
Music — M
Philosophy — M
Political Science — M,D
Psychology—General — M,D
Public Administration — M,D
Public Policy — M,D
Sociology — M,D
Western European Studies — M,O

## CARLOS ALBIZU UNIVERSITY
Clinical Psychology — M,D
Industrial and Organizational
   Psychology — M,D
Psychology—General — M,D

## CARLOS ALBIZU UNIVERSITY, MIAMI CAMPUS
Clinical Psychology — M,D
Counseling Psychology — M,D
Industrial and Organizational
   Psychology — M,D
Marriage and Family Therapy — M,D
Psychology—General — M,D
School Psychology — M,D

## CARLOW UNIVERSITY
Addictions/Substance Abuse
   Counseling — M,O
Counseling Psychology — M,D,O
Forensic Sciences — M
Writing — M

## CARNEGIE MELLON UNIVERSITY
African Studies — D
African-American Studies — D
Applied Arts and Design—
   General — M,D
Architecture — M,D
Art/Fine Arts — M
Arts Administration — M
Building Science — M,D
Cognitive Sciences — D
Communication—General — M,D
Comparative Literature — M,D
Computer Art and Design — M
Corporate and Organizational
   Communication — M
Criminal Justice and Criminology — M
Cultural Studies — D
Developmental Psychology — D
Economics — D
English — M,D
Film, Television, and Video
   Production — D
Gender Studies — D
History of Science and Technology — D
History — D
Industrial and Labor Relations — D
Linguistics — M,D
Media Studies — M
Music — M
Philosophy — M,D
Psychology—General — D
Public Administration — M
Public Policy — M,D
Publishing — M
Rhetoric — M,D
Social Psychology — D
Social Sciences — D
Sustainable Development — M,D
Technical Writing — M
Theater — M
Urban Design — M,D
Women's Studies — D
Writing — M

## CAROLINA CHRISTIAN COLLEGE
Pastoral Ministry and Counseling — M

## CARSON-NEWMAN UNIVERSITY
Theology — M

## CASE WESTERN RESERVE UNIVERSITY
Anthropology — M,D
Art History — M,D
Clinical Psychology — D

Cognitive Sciences — M
Comparative Literature — M
Dance — M,D
English — M,D
Experimental Psychology — D
French — M
Genetic Counseling — M
History — M,D
Linguistics — M
Museum Studies — M
Music — M,D
Political Science — M,D
Psychology—General — M,D
Sociology — M,D
Theater — M

## CASTLETON UNIVERSITY
Forensic Psychology — M
Psychology—General — M

## CATHOLIC DISTANCE UNIVERSITY
Theology — M

## CATHOLIC THEOLOGICAL UNION
Missions and Missiology — M,D,O
Pastoral Ministry and Counseling — M,D,O
Theology — M,D,O

## THE CATHOLIC UNIVERSITY OF AMERICA
American Studies — M,D
Anthropology — M
Applied Psychology — M
Architecture — M,O
Classics — M,D,O
Clinical Psychology — M,D
Criminal Justice and Criminology — M,D
Economic Development — M
English — M,D,O
Experimental Psychology — M,D
Hispanic Studies — M,D
History — M,D
International Affairs — M,D
Latin American Studies — M,D
Medieval and Renaissance Studies — M,D,O
Music — M,D
Near and Middle Eastern Languages — M,D
Near and Middle Eastern Studies — M,D,O
Pastoral Ministry and Counseling — M,D,O
Philosophy — M,D,O
Political Science — M,D
Psychology—General — M,D
Public Policy — M
Religion — M,D,O
Rhetoric — M,D,O
Sociology — M
Spanish — M,D
Sustainable Development — M,O
Theater — M,O.
Theology — M,D,O
Urban and Regional Planning — M,O
Western European Studies — M,D

## CEDAR CREST COLLEGE
Art Therapy — M
Forensic Sciences — M
Writing — M

## CEDARVILLE UNIVERSITY
Pastoral Ministry and Counseling — M,D

## CENTENARY UNIVERSITY
Counseling Psychology — M

## CENTRAL BAPTIST THEOLOGICAL SEMINARY
Missions and Missiology — M,O
Theology — M,O

## CENTRAL CONNECTICUT STATE UNIVERSITY
Communication—General — M,O
Criminal Justice and Criminology — M
French — M,O
Geography — M
German — M,O
Graphic Design — M
History — M
International Affairs — M
Italian — M,O
Marriage and Family Therapy — M,O
Psychology—General — M
Rehabilitation Counseling — M,O
School Psychology — M,O
Spanish — M,O

## CENTRAL EUROPEAN UNIVERSITY
Anthropology — M,D
Cognitive Sciences — D
Economics — M,D
Gender Studies — M,D
History — M,D
International Affairs — M,D
Medieval and Renaissance Studies — M,D
Philosophy — M,D
Political Science — M,D
Public Administration — M,D
Public Policy — M,D
Sociology — M,D

## CENTRAL MICHIGAN UNIVERSITY
American Indian/Native American
   Studies — M
American Studies — M,O
Applied Psychology — M
Child and Family Studies — M
Clinical Psychology — D
Clothing and Textiles — M,O
Communication—General — M
Counseling Psychology — M,D,O
Cultural Studies — M
Economics — M
English — M
Experimental Psychology — M,D
Family and Consumer
   Sciences-General — M,O
Film, Television, and Video
   Production — M

Film, Television, and Video
  Theory and Criticism — M
Gender Studies — M
Geographic Information Systems — M
Gerontology — M,O
Health Psychology — M,D
History — M,O
Human Development — M,O
Humanities — M
Industrial and Organizational
  Psychology — M,D
International Affairs — M,O
Media Studies — M
Music — M
Political Science — M,O
Psychology—General — M,D,O
Public Administration — M,O
School Psychology — D,O
Spanish — M
Western European Studies — M,O
Writing — M

## CENTRAL WASHINGTON UNIVERSITY
Art/Fine Arts — M
Child and Family Studies — M
Counseling Psychology — M
English — M
Experimental Psychology — M
Family and Consumer
  Sciences-General — M
History — M
Interdisciplinary Studies — M
Music — M
Psychology—General — M
School Psychology — M
Theater — M

## CENTRAL YESHIVA TOMCHEI TMIMIM-LUBAVITCH
Jewish Studies — M
Theology — M

## CENTRO DE ESTUDIOS AVANZADOS DE PUERTO RICO Y EL CARIBE
History — M,D
Latin American Studies — M,D

## CHAMINADE UNIVERSITY OF HONOLULU
Child Development — M
Counseling Psychology — M
Criminal Justice and Criminology — M
Marriage and Family Therapy — M
Pastoral Ministry and Counseling — M
School Psychology — M
Theology — M

## CHAMPLAIN COLLEGE
Conflict Resolution and
  Mediation/Peace Studies — M
Forensic Sciences — M
Internet and Interactive
  Multimedia — M
Media Studies — M

## CHAPMAN UNIVERSITY
Cultural Studies — M,D,O
Disability Studies — M,D,O
English — M
Film, Television, and Video
  Production — M
Health Communication — M
Holocaust and Genocide Studies — M
International Affairs — M
Marriage and Family Therapy — M
School Psychology — M,D,O
Writing — M

## CHARLESTON SOUTHERN UNIVERSITY
Criminal Justice and Criminology — M

## CHARLOTTE CHRISTIAN COLLEGE AND THEOLOGICAL SEMINARY
Cultural Studies — M
Missions and Missiology — M
Music — M
Pastoral Ministry and Counseling — M
Religion — M
Theology — M

## CHATHAM UNIVERSITY
Communication—General — M
Computer Art and Design — M
Counseling Psychology — M,D
Developmental Psychology — M,D
Film, Television, and Video
  Production — M
Health Communication — M
Health Psychology — M,D
Industrial and Organizational
  Psychology — M,D
Interior Design — M
Landscape Architecture — M
Marriage and Family Therapy — M,D
Sport Psychology — M,D
Women's Studies — M
Writing — M

## CHESTNUT HILL COLLEGE
Clinical Psychology — M,D,O
Counseling Psychology — M,O
Marriage and Family Therapy — M,D,O
Psychology—General — M,D,O

## CHEYNEY UNIVERSITY OF PENNSYLVANIA
Public Administration — M

## THE CHICAGO SCHOOL OF PROFESSIONAL PSYCHOLOGY
Applied Behavior Analysis — M,D
Clinical Psychology — M
Forensic Psychology — M,D

Industrial and Organizational
  Psychology — M,D
Psychology—General — M,D
School Psychology — D,O

## THE CHICAGO SCHOOL OF PROFESSIONAL PSYCHOLOGY AT DOWNTOWN LOS ANGELES
Applied Behavior Analysis — M,D
Clinical Psychology — M,D
Forensic Psychology — D
Industrial and Organizational
  Psychology — M
Marriage and Family Therapy — M,D

## THE CHICAGO SCHOOL OF PROFESSIONAL PSYCHOLOGY AT IRVINE
Clinical Psychology — D
Forensic Psychology — D
Marriage and Family Therapy — M,D
Psychology—General — D

## THE CHICAGO SCHOOL OF PROFESSIONAL PSYCHOLOGY: ONLINE
Applied Psychology — M,O
Forensic Psychology — M,O
Industrial and Organizational
  Psychology — M,D,O
Psychology—General — M,D

## CHICAGO STATE UNIVERSITY
Criminal Justice and Criminology — M
English — M
Geographic Information Systems — M
Geography — M
History — M
Writing — M

## CHICAGO THEOLOGICAL SEMINARY
Ethics — M,D
Pastoral Ministry and Counseling — M,D
Religion — M,D
Theology — M,D

## CHRISTENDOM COLLEGE
Theology — M

## CHRISTIAN BROTHERS UNIVERSITY
Religion — M

## CHRISTIAN THEOLOGICAL SEMINARY
Marriage and Family Therapy — M,D
Pastoral Ministry and Counseling — M,D
Religion — M,D
Theology — M,D

## CHRISTIE'S EDUCATION
Art History — M
Art/Fine Arts — O
Arts Administration — M,O
Museum Studies — M

## CHRIST THE KING SEMINARY
Pastoral Ministry and Counseling — M
Theology — M

## CHURCH DIVINITY SCHOOL OF THE PACIFIC
Theology — M,D,O

## CINCINNATI CHRISTIAN UNIVERSITY
Pastoral Ministry and Counseling — M
Religion — M
Theology — M

## THE CITADEL, THE MILITARY COLLEGE OF SOUTH CAROLINA
English — M
Hispanic Studies — O
History — M,O
Homeland Security — M,O
Interdisciplinary Studies — M,O
Military and Defense Studies — M,O
National Security — M,O
Political Science — M
Psychology—General — M,O
School Psychology — M,O
Social Sciences — M

## CITY COLLEGE OF THE CITY UNIVERSITY OF NEW YORK
Architecture — M
Art History — M
Art/Fine Arts — M
Classics — M
Clinical Psychology — M,D
Computer Art and Design — M
Corporate and Organizational
  Communication — M
Economics — M
English — M
Graphic Design — M
History — M
International Affairs — M
Landscape Architecture — M
Media Studies — M
Museum Studies — M
Psychology—General — M,D
Public Administration — M,D
Sociology — M
Spanish — M
Sustainable Development — M
Urban Design — M
Writing — M

## CITY UNIVERSITY OF SEATTLE
Counseling Psychology — M

## CITY VISION UNIVERSITY
Pastoral Ministry and Counseling — M

## CLAREMONT GRADUATE UNIVERSITY
African Studies — M,D,O
American Studies — M,D,O

Art/Fine Arts — M
Arts Administration — M
Cognitive Sciences — M,D,O
Comparative Literature — M,D
Computer Art and Design — M
Cultural Studies — M,D,O
Developmental Psychology — M,D,O
Economic Development — M,D,O
Economics — M,D,O
English — M,D
Ethics — M,D
Film, Television, and Video
  Theory and Criticism — M,D
Geographic Information Systems — M,D,O
Health Psychology — M,D,O
History — M,D,O
Human Development — M,D,O
Humanities — M,D,O
Industrial and Organizational
  Psychology — M,D,O
International Affairs — M,D
International Economics — M,D,O
Media Studies — M,D,O
Museum Studies — M,D
Music — M,D
Philosophy — M,D
Photography — M
Political Science — M,D
Psychology—General — M,D,O
Public Policy — M,D,O
Religion — M,D
Social Psychology — M,D,O
Theology — M,D
Western European Studies — M,D,O
Women's Studies — M,D
Writing — M

## CLAREMONT LINCOLN UNIVERSITY
Ethics — M
Pastoral Ministry and Counseling — M
Religion — M

## CLAREMONT SCHOOL OF THEOLOGY
Ethics — M,D
Pastoral Ministry and Counseling — M,D
Religion — M,D
Theology — M,D

## CLARION UNIVERSITY OF PENNSYLVANIA
Clinical Psychology — M
Communication—General — M

## CLARK ATLANTA UNIVERSITY
African-American Studies — M,D
Criminal Justice and Criminology — M
Economics — M
English — M,D
History — M,D
Political Science — M,D
Public Administration — M
Romance Languages — M
Sociology — M
Women's Studies — M,D

## CLARKSON UNIVERSITY
Interdisciplinary Studies — M,D
Sustainable Development — M,D

## CLARKS SUMMIT UNIVERSITY
Communication—General — M,D
Cultural Studies — M
English — M
Missions and Missiology — M
Pastoral Ministry and Counseling — M,D
Philosophy — M
Religion — M,D
Theology — M,D

## CLARK UNIVERSITY
American Studies — D
Clinical Psychology — D
Communication—General — M
Developmental Psychology — D
Economics — D
English — M
Geographic Information Systems — M
Geography — D
History — D
Holocaust and Genocide Studies — M
International Development — M
Public Administration — M,O
Social Psychology — D
Sustainable Development — M
Urban and Regional Planning — M

## CLAYTON STATE UNIVERSITY
Applied Psychology — M
Clinical Psychology — M
Criminal Justice and Criminology — M
Developmental Psychology — M
History — M
Liberal Studies — M
Psychology—General — M

## CLEMSON UNIVERSITY
Applied Economics — M,D
Applied Psychology — M
Architecture — M,O
Communication—General — M,D
Computer Art and Design — M
Counseling Psychology — M,O
Economics — M,D
Emergency Management — M,O
English — M
Environmental Design — D
Family and Consumer
  Sciences-General — D,O
Historic Preservation — M,O
History — M
Homeland Security — M,O
Human Development — M,O
Industrial and Organizational
  Psychology — D

Landscape Architecture — M
Political Science — M,O
Psychology—General — D
Public Administration — M,D,O
Public Policy — D,O
Rhetoric — D
School Psychology — M,O
Sociology — M
Sustainable Development — M,O
Urban and Regional Planning — M
Writing — M

## CLEVELAND INSTITUTE OF MUSIC
Music — M,D,O

## CLEVELAND STATE UNIVERSITY
Art History — M
Communication—General — M,D,O
Counseling Psychology — M,D,O
Economic Development — M,O
Economics — M,O
English — M
History — M
Industrial and Labor Relations — M
International Affairs — M
International Economics — M
Museum Studies — M
Music — M
Philosophy — M,O
Psychology—General — M,D,O
Public Administration — M,D,O
Public Affairs — D
Spanish — M
Sustainable Development — M,O
Urban and Regional Planning — M,O
Urban Studies — M,D,O
Writing — M

## COASTAL CAROLINA UNIVERSITY
Liberal Studies — M
Writing — M

## THE COLBURN SCHOOL CONSERVATORY OF MUSIC
Music — M,O

## COLGATE ROCHESTER CROZER DIVINITY SCHOOL
Conflict Resolution and
  Mediation/Peace Studies — M,D,O
Theology — M,D,O

## THE COLLEGE AT BROCKPORT, STATE UNIVERSITY OF NEW YORK
American Studies — M
Art/Fine Arts — M
Arts Administration — M,O
Communication—General — M
Counseling Psychology — M,O
Dance — M
English — M,O
Forensic Sciences — M,O
Gerontology — M,O
History of Medicine — M,O
History — M
Liberal Studies — M
Psychology—General — M
Public Administration — M,O
Public History — M
Writing — M,O

## COLLÈGE DOMINICAIN DE PHILOSOPHIE ET DE THÉOLOGIE
Philosophy — M,D
Theology — M,D,O

## COLLEGE FOR CREATIVE STUDIES
Applied Arts and Design—
  General — M
Art/Fine Arts — M

## COLLEGE OF CHARLESTON
Arts Administration — O
English — M
Historic Preservation — M
History — M
Public Administration — M
Urban and Regional Planning — O
Writing — M

## COLLEGE OF EMMANUEL AND ST. CHAD
Theology — M,D,O

## THE COLLEGE OF NEW JERSEY
Addictions/Substance Abuse
  Counseling — M,O
English — M
Gender Studies — O
Marriage and Family Therapy — O

## THE COLLEGE OF NEW ROCHELLE
Art Therapy — M
Communication—General — M,O
Counseling Psychology — M,O
Marriage and Family Therapy — M
Public Administration — M
School Psychology — M
Thanatology — M,O

## COLLEGE OF SAINT ELIZABETH
Counseling Psychology — M,D,O
Criminal Justice and Criminology — M
Forensic Psychology — M,D,O
Psychology—General — M,D,O
Public Administration — M
Theology — M

## COLLEGE OF ST. JOSEPH
Addictions/Substance Abuse
  Counseling — M
Clinical Psychology — M
Counseling Psychology — M
Psychology—General — M

*M—masters degree; D—doctorate; O—other advanced degree; *—Close-Up and/or Display*

School Psychology — M
Social Psychology — M

**THE COLLEGE OF SAINT ROSE**
Counseling Psychology — M,O
School Psychology — M,O

**COLLEGE OF STATEN ISLAND OF THE CITY UNIVERSITY OF NEW YORK**
African Studies — M
American Studies — M
Clinical Psychology — M
Counseling Psychology — M
English — M,O
Film, Television, and Video Theory and Criticism — M
History — M,O
Latin American Studies — M
Liberal Studies — M
Media Studies — M
Near and Middle Eastern Studies — M
Western European Studies — M

**THE COLLEGE OF WILLIAM AND MARY**
Addictions/Substance Abuse Counseling — M,D
American Studies — M,D
Anthropology — M,D
English — M,D
Geographic Information Systems — M,D
History — M,D
Marriage and Family Therapy — M,D
Psychology—General — M
Public Policy — M
School Psychology — M,O

**COLORADO CHRISTIAN UNIVERSITY**
Counseling Psychology — M

**THE COLORADO COLLEGE**
American Studies — M
Humanities — M
Liberal Studies — M

**COLORADO SCHOOL OF MINES**
International Affairs — O
Mineral Economics — M,D

**COLORADO STATE UNIVERSITY**
Agricultural Economics and Agribusiness — M,D
Anthropology — M
Art History — M
Art/Fine Arts — M
Arts Administration — M
Child and Family Studies — M,D
Consumer Economics — M
Economics — M,D
English — M
Ethnic Studies — M
French — M
German — M
Historic Preservation — M
History — M
Human Development — M,D
Interior Design — M
International Development — M
Landscape Architecture — M,D
Liberal Studies — M
Marriage and Family Therapy — M,D
Media Studies — M,D
Museum Studies — M
Music — M,D
Philosophy — M
Political Science — M,D
Psychology—General — M,D
Public History — M
Rhetoric — M
Sociology — M,D
Spanish — M
Speech and Interpersonal Communication — M,D
Sustainable Development — M
Therapies—Dance, Drama, and Music — M
Writing — M

**COLORADO STATE UNIVERSITY–GLOBAL CAMPUS**
Criminal Justice and Criminology — M

**COLORADO TECHNICAL UNIVERSITY AURORA**
Conflict Resolution and Mediation/Peace Studies — M
Criminal Justice and Criminology — M

**COLORADO TECHNICAL UNIVERSITY COLORADO SPRINGS**
Conflict Resolution and Mediation/Peace Studies — M,D
Criminal Justice and Criminology — M

**COLUMBIA COLLEGE (MO)**
Criminal Justice and Criminology — M

**COLUMBIA COLLEGE (SC)**
Conflict Resolution and Mediation/Peace Studies — M

**COLUMBIA COLLEGE CHICAGO**
Arts Administration — M
Comparative and Interdisciplinary Arts — M
Film, Television, and Video Production — M
Journalism — M
Music — M
Photography — M
Therapies—Dance, Drama, and Music — M,O
Writing — M

**COLUMBIA INTERNATIONAL UNIVERSITY**
Cultural Studies — M,D,O
Missions and Missiology — M,D,O
Pastoral Ministry and Counseling — M,D,O
Theology — M,D,O

**COLUMBIA SOUTHERN UNIVERSITY**
Criminal Justice and Criminology — M
Emergency Management — M

**COLUMBIA THEOLOGICAL SEMINARY**
Theology — M,D

**COLUMBIA UNIVERSITY**
African Studies — M,D
African-American Studies — M,D
American Studies — M,D
Anthropology — M,D
Archaeology — M,D
Architecture — M,D
Art History — M,D
Art/Fine Arts — M,D*
Asian Studies — M,D,O
Classics — M,D
Communication—General — M,D
Comparative Literature — M,D
Conflict Resolution and Mediation/Peace Studies — M
Corporate and Organizational Communication — M
East European and Russian Studies — M,D
Economics — M,D
English — M,D
Environmental Design — M
Ethics — M,D
Film, Television, and Video Production — M
French — M,D
German — M,D
Hispanic Studies — M,D
Historic Preservation — M,O
History — M,D
International Affairs — M,D
Italian — M,D
Japanese — M,D
Jewish Studies — M,D
Journalism — M,D
Landscape Architecture — M
Latin American Studies — M,D
Medieval and Renaissance Studies — M,D
Museum Studies — M,D
Music — M,D
Near and Middle Eastern Studies — M,D
Philosophy — M,D
Photography — M
Political Science — M,D
Psychology—General — M,D
Public Administration — M
Public Policy — M
Religion — M,D
Romance Languages — M,D
Russian — M,D
Slavic Languages — M,D
Social Sciences — M,D
Sociology — M,D
Spanish — M,D
Sustainable Development — M,D
Theater — M,D
Translation and Interpretation — M,D
Urban and Regional Planning — M,D
Western European Studies — M,D
Writing — M

**COLUMBUS STATE UNIVERSITY**
Clinical Psychology — M,D,O
Criminal Justice and Criminology — M,O
History — M,O
Homeland Security — M
Music — M,O
Political Science — M
Public Administration — M
Theater — M
Urban Studies — M

**CONCORDIA LUTHERAN SEMINARY**
Theology — M,O

**CONCORDIA SEMINARY**
Theology — M,D,O

**CONCORDIA THEOLOGICAL SEMINARY**
Theology — M,D

**CONCORDIA UNIVERSITY (CANADA)**
Anthropology — M,D
Applied Arts and Design—General — M,O
Art History — M,D
Art Therapy — M
Art/Fine Arts — M
Child and Family Studies — M
Clinical Psychology — D,O
Communication—General — M,D,O
Computer Art and Design — M,O
Cultural Anthropology — O
Economic Development — O
Economics — M,D,O
English — M,D
Film, Television, and Video Production — M,D
Film, Television, and Video Theory and Criticism — M,D
French — M,O
Geography — M,D,O
History — M,D
Humanities — D
Interdisciplinary Studies — M,D
Internet and Interactive Multimedia — M,D,O
Jewish Studies — M
Journalism — M,O
Linguistics — M,O
Media Studies — M,D,O
Music — O
Philosophy — M
Political Science — M,D
Psychology—General — M
Public Administration — O
Public Affairs — M
Public Policy — M,D
Religion — M,D
Sociology — M,D

Textile Design — M
Theology — M
Therapies—Dance, Drama, and Music — M,O
Translation and Interpretation — M,O
Urban and Regional Planning — O
Urban Studies — M,D,O
Writing — M

**CONCORDIA UNIVERSITY CHICAGO**
Counseling Psychology — M
Gerontology — M
Liberal Studies — M
Music — M
Psychology—General — M
Religion — M

**CONCORDIA UNIVERSITY IRVINE**
Applied Social Research — M
Cultural Studies — M
International Affairs — M*
Religion — M
Theology — M

**CONCORDIA UNIVERSITY, NEBRASKA**
Pastoral Ministry and Counseling — M

**CONCORDIA UNIVERSITY OF EDMONTON**
Religion — M
Theology — M

**CONCORDIA UNIVERSITY, ST. PAUL**
Child and Family Studies — M,D
Corporate and Organizational Communication — M
Criminal Justice and Criminology — M,D

**CONCORDIA UNIVERSITY WISCONSIN**
Child and Family Studies — M
Corporate and Organizational Communication — M
Music — M
Public Administration — M

**CONSERVATORIO DE MUSICA DE PUERTO RICO**
Music — O

**CONVERSE COLLEGE**
English — M
History — M
Liberal Studies — M
Marriage and Family Therapy — M
Music — M
Political Science — M

**COOPER UNION FOR THE ADVANCEMENT OF SCIENCE AND ART**
Architecture — M

**COPENHAGEN BUSINESS SCHOOL**
Economics — M,D
Public Administration — M,D

**COPPIN STATE UNIVERSITY**
Addictions/Substance Abuse Counseling — M
Criminal Justice and Criminology — M
Rehabilitation Counseling — M

**CORBAN UNIVERSITY**
Pastoral Ministry and Counseling — M,D,O
Theology — M,D,O

**CORNELL UNIVERSITY**
African Studies — M,D
African-American Studies — M,D
Agricultural Economics and Agribusiness — M,D
American Studies — M,D
Anthropology — D
Applied Economics — M,D
Archaeology — M,D
Architectural History — M,D
Architecture — M,D
Art History — D
Art/Fine Arts — M
Asian Languages — M,D
Asian Studies — M,D
Child and Family Studies — M,D
Classics — D
Clothing and Textiles — M,D
Cognitive Sciences — D
Communication—General — M,D
Comparative Literature — D
Computer Art and Design — M,D
Conflict Resolution and Mediation/Peace Studies — M,D
Consumer Economics — M,D
Corporate and Organizational Communication — M,D
Cultural Anthropology — D
Cultural Studies — M,D
Demography and Population Studies — M,D
Developmental Psychology — M,D
East European and Russian Studies — M,D
Economic Development — M,D
Economics — M,D
English — M
Environmental Design — M,D
Ethnic Studies — M,D
Experimental Psychology — D
French — D
Gender Studies — M,D
German — M,D
Health Communication — M,D
Hispanic and Latin American Languages — D
Historic Preservation — M
History — M,D
History of Science and Technology — M,D
Human Development — M,D
Industrial and Labor Relations — M,D
Interior Design — M
International Affairs — D
Italian — D
Jewish Studies — M,D

Landscape Architecture — M
Latin American Studies — M,D
Linguistics — M,D
Media Studies — M,D
Medieval and Renaissance Studies — M,D
Music — M,D
Near and Middle Eastern Studies — M,D
Philosophy — D
Photography — M,D
Political Science — D
Psychology—General — M
Public Affairs — M
Public Policy — M,D
Religion — M,D
Romance Languages — M,D
Rural Sociology — M,D
Scandinavian Languages — M,D
Slavic Languages — M,D
Social Psychology — M,D
Sociology — M,D
Spanish — D
Sustainable Development — M,D
Textile Design — M,D
Theater — D
Urban and Regional Planning — M,D
Urban Design — M,D
Western European Studies — M,D
Women's Studies — M,D
Writing — M,D

**COVENANT THEOLOGICAL SEMINARY**
Pastoral Ministry and Counseling — M,D,O
Theology — M,D,O

**CRANBROOK ACADEMY OF ART**
Architecture — M
Art/Fine Arts — M
Photography — M
Textile Design — M

**CREIGHTON UNIVERSITY**
Anthropology — M
Asian Studies — M
Conflict Resolution and Mediation/Peace Studies — M,O
English — M
International Affairs — M
School Psychology — M
Theology — M
Western European Studies — M
Writing — M

**CRISWELL COLLEGE**
Jewish Studies — M
Pastoral Ministry and Counseling — M
Theology — M

**CROWN COLLEGE**
Theology — M

**CUMBERLAND UNIVERSITY**
Public Administration — M

**CUNY GRADUATE SCHOOL OF JOURNALISM**
Journalism — M

**CURRY COLLEGE**
Criminal Justice and Criminology — M

**CURTIS INSTITUTE OF MUSIC**
Music — M

**DAEMEN COLLEGE**
Arts Administration — M

**DALHOUSIE UNIVERSITY**
Anthropology — M,D
Architecture — M
Classics — M,D
Clinical Psychology — M,D
Economics — M,D
English — M,D
French — M
German — M
History — M,D
Interdisciplinary Studies — D
International Development — M
Music — M
Philosophy — M,D
Political Science — M,D
Psychology—General — M,D
Public Administration — M,O
Rural Planning and Studies — M
Sociology — M,D
Urban and Regional Planning — M

**DALLAS BAPTIST UNIVERSITY**
Asian Studies — M
Communication—General — M
Conflict Resolution and Mediation/Peace Studies — M
Corporate and Organizational Communication — M
Counseling Psychology — M
Criminal Justice and Criminology — M
Interdisciplinary Studies — M
International Affairs — M
Liberal Studies — M
Missions and Missiology — M
Pastoral Ministry and Counseling — M,D
Religion — M
Theology — M
Western European Studies — M

**DALLAS THEOLOGICAL SEMINARY**
Child and Family Studies — M,D,O
Jewish Studies — M,D,O
Media Studies — M,D,O
Missions and Missiology — M,D,O
Pastoral Ministry and Counseling — M,D,O
Philosophy — M,D,O
Religion — M,D,O
Theology — M,D,O

**DARTMOUTH COLLEGE**
Cognitive Sciences — D
Comparative Literature — M
Liberal Studies — M*

Music M
Psychology—General D

**DELAWARE STATE UNIVERSITY**
Historic Preservation M

**DELAWARE VALLEY UNIVERSITY**
Agricultural Economics and
  Agribusiness M
Counseling Psychology M
Developmental Psychology M
Social Psychology M

**DELL'ARTE INTERNATIONAL SCHOOL OF PHYSICAL THEATRE**
Theater M

**DELTA STATE UNIVERSITY**
Criminal Justice and Criminology M
Gender Studies M
Liberal Studies M
Philosophy M
Religion M
Urban and Regional Planning M

**DENVER SEMINARY**
Marriage and Family Therapy M,D,O
Pastoral Ministry and Counseling M,D,O
Religion M,D,O
Theology M,D,O

**DEPAUL UNIVERSITY**
Applied Economics M
Chinese M
Clinical Psychology M,D
Communication—General M
Computer Art and Design M,D
Corporate and Organizational
  Communication M
Counseling Psychology M,D
Economics M
English M
Film, Television, and Video
  Production M,D
Film, Television, and Video
  Theory and Criticism M
French M
German M
Health Communication M
History M
Interdisciplinary Studies M
International Affairs M
Internet and Interactive
  Multimedia M,D
Italian M
Japanese M
Journalism M
Liberal Studies M
Media Studies M
Music M,O
Near and Middle Eastern Languages M
Psychology—General M,D
Public Administration M
Public Policy M
Publishing M
Rhetoric M
School Psychology M,D
Sociology M
Spanish M
Sustainable Development M
Theater M
Urban Design M
Women's Studies M
Writing M

**DEREE - THE AMERICAN COLLEGE OF GREECE**
Applied Psychology M
Communication—General M

**DESALES UNIVERSITY**
Criminal Justice and Criminology M,O
Forensic Sciences M,O
Gerontology M,D,O

**DEVRY UNIVERSITY–FOLSOM CAMPUS**
Public Administration M

**DIGIPEN INSTITUTE OF TECHNOLOGY**
Computer Art and Design M

**DIGITAL MEDIA ARTS COLLEGE**
Computer Art and Design M
Graphic Design M
Media Studies M

**DOMINICAN HOUSE OF STUDIES, PONTIFICAL FACULTY OF THE IMMACULATE CONCEPTION**
Theology M,D,O

**DOMINICAN SCHOOL OF PHILOSOPHY AND THEOLOGY**
Philosophy M,O
Theology M,O

**DOMINICAN UNIVERSITY**
Conflict Resolution and
  Mediation/Peace Studies M

**DOMINICAN UNIVERSITY OF CALIFORNIA**
Art History M
Counseling Psychology M
English M
Gender Studies M
History M
Humanities M
Marriage and Family Therapy M
Music M
Philosophy M
Political Science M
Religion M
Writing M

**DRAKE UNIVERSITY**
Communication—General M
Public Administration M

**DREW UNIVERSITY**
American Studies M,D,O
Art/Fine Arts M,D,O
Conflict Resolution and
  Mediation/Peace Studies M,D,O
Cultural Studies M,D,O
English M,D,O
French M,D,O
History M,D,O
Italian M,D,O
Liberal Studies M,D,O
Public History M,D,O
Religion M,D,O
Theology M,D,O
Western European Studies M,D,O
Writing M,D,O

**DREXEL UNIVERSITY**
Applied Arts and Design—
  General M*
Applied Behavior Analysis M,D
Art Therapy M,O
Arts Administration M
Clinical Psychology D
Communication—General M
Computer Art and Design M
Corporate and Organizational
  Communication M
Economics M,D,O
Emergency Management M
Film, Television, and Video
  Production M
Forensic Psychology D
Health Psychology D
History of Science and Technology M
Homeland Security M
Interior Design M
Marriage and Family Therapy M,D
Mass Communication M
Media Studies M
Psychology—General M,D
Technical Communication M
Technical Writing M
Textile Design M
Therapies—Dance, Drama, and
  Music M,O

**DRURY UNIVERSITY**
Communication—General M

**DUKE UNIVERSITY**
Art History M,D
Art/Fine Arts M,D
Asian Studies M,O
Biological Anthropology D
Classics D
Clinical Psychology D
Cognitive Sciences D
Comparative Literature D
Cultural Anthropology D
Developmental Psychology D
Economics M,D
English D
Ethics M,O
Experimental Psychology D
French D
German D
Gerontology M,D,O
Health Psychology D
History M,D
Human Development D
Humanities M
International Development M
Italian D
Latin American Studies M,D
Liberal Studies M
Media Studies M
Music D
Philosophy D
Political Science M,D
Psychology—General D
Public Policy M,D
Religion M,D
Slavic Languages M,O
Sociology M,D
Spanish D
Theology M,D

**DUQUESNE UNIVERSITY**
Classics M
Clinical Psychology M,D,O
Communication—General M,D
Counseling Psychology M,D,O
English M,D
Forensic Sciences M
History M
Marriage and Family Therapy M,D,O
Music M,O
Philosophy M,D
Psychology—General D
Public History M
Rhetoric M,D
School Psychology M,D
Theology M,D

**EARLHAM SCHOOL OF RELIGION**
Religion M
Theology M

**EAST CAROLINA UNIVERSITY**
Addictions/Substance Abuse
  Counseling M,D,O
American Studies M
Anthropology M
Applied Economics M
Art/Fine Arts M
Child and Family Studies M,D
Child Development M,D
Clinical Psychology M,D

Comparative Literature M,D,O
Criminal Justice and Criminology M,O
Economic Development M,O
English M,D,O
Family and Consumer
  Sciences-General M
Geographic Information Systems M,O
Geography M,O
Gerontology M,O
Graphic Design M
Health Communication M
Health Psychology M,D
History M
Illustration M
Industrial and Organizational
  Psychology M,D
International Affairs M
Linguistics M,D,O
Marriage and Family Therapy M,D
Military and Defense Studies M
Music M,D,O
Photography M
Political Science M,O
Public Administration M,O
Public History M,O
Rehabilitation Counseling M,D,O
Rhetoric M,D,O
Rural Planning and Studies M,O
Sociology M
Technical Communication M,O
Textile Design M
Therapies—Dance, Drama, and
  Music M,O
Urban and Regional Planning M,O
Western European Studies M
Writing M,D,O

**EAST CENTRAL UNIVERSITY**
Criminal Justice and Criminology M
Psychology—General M
Rehabilitation Counseling M

**EASTERN ILLINOIS UNIVERSITY**
Art/Fine Arts M
Clinical Psychology M,O
Economics M
English M
Family and Consumer
  Sciences-General M
Geographic Information Systems M
Gerontology M
History M
Music M
Political Science M
Psychology—General M
Public History M
School Psychology M,O
Speech and Interpersonal
  Communication M
Sustainable Development M

**EASTERN KENTUCKY UNIVERSITY**
Clinical Psychology M,O
Criminal Justice and Criminology M
English M
History M
Industrial and Organizational
  Psychology M,O
Music M
Political Science M
Psychology—General M,O
Public Administration M
School Psychology M,O
Urban and Regional Planning M
Writing M

**EASTERN MENNONITE UNIVERSITY**
Conflict Resolution and
  Mediation/Peace Studies M,O
Pastoral Ministry and Counseling M,O
Religion M,O
Theology M,O

**EASTERN MICHIGAN UNIVERSITY**
African-American Studies O
Art/Fine Arts M
Arts Administration M
Clinical Psychology M,D
Clothing and Textiles M
Communication—General M
Corporate and Organizational
  Communication M,O
Criminal Justice and Criminology M
Cultural Studies O
Dance M
Economics M,O
English M
Gender Studies M
Geographic Information Systems M,O
Gerontology O
Historic Preservation M,O
History M
Interior Design M
Linguistics M
Museum Studies M,O
Music M
Philosophy M
Psychology—General M,D
Public Administration M,O
Public Policy M,O
Social Sciences M
Sociology M
Sustainable Development M,O
Technical Communication M,O
Theater M
Urban and Regional Planning M,O
Women's Studies M,O
Writing M,O

**EASTERN NAZARENE COLLEGE**
Counseling Psychology M
Marriage and Family Therapy M

**EASTERN NEW MEXICO UNIVERSITY**
Anthropology M
Communication—General M
English M

**EASTERN OREGON UNIVERSITY**
Writing M

**EASTERN UNIVERSITY**
Applied Behavior Analysis M,O
Child and Family Studies D
Communication—General M,D,O
Counseling Psychology M,O
Cultural Anthropology M
Economic Development M
French M,D,O
International Development M
Marriage and Family Therapy D
Pastoral Ministry and Counseling M,D
Public Policy M,D
School Psychology M,O
Spanish M,D,O
Theology M,D
Urban and Regional Planning M
Urban Studies M

**EASTERN VIRGINIA MEDICAL SCHOOL**
Art Therapy M
Clinical Psychology D

**EASTERN WASHINGTON UNIVERSITY**
Applied Psychology M
Clinical Psychology M
Communication—General M
Counseling Psychology M
English M
Experimental Psychology M
History M
Interdisciplinary Studies M
Music M
Psychology—General M,O
Public Administration M
Rhetoric M
School Psychology O
Technical Communication M
Urban and Regional Planning M
Writing M

**EAST STROUDSBURG UNIVERSITY OF PENNSYLVANIA**
Geography M
History M
Political Science M
Public Administration M

**EAST TENNESSEE STATE UNIVERSITY**
Art/Fine Arts M
Communication—General M
Computer Art and Design M,O
Corporate and Organizational
  Communication M
Criminal Justice and Criminology M,O
Economic Development M,O
English M,O
History M,O
Human Development M
Liberal Studies M,O
Political Science M
Psychology—General D
Public Administration M,O
Sociology M
Urban and Regional Planning M,O

**EAST TEXAS BAPTIST UNIVERSITY**
Counseling Psychology M
Pastoral Ministry and Counseling M
Religion M

**ECUMENICAL THEOLOGICAL SEMINARY**
Pastoral Ministry and Counseling D
Theology M

**EDEN THEOLOGICAL SEMINARY**
Theology M,D

**EDGEWOOD COLLEGE**
Marriage and Family Therapy M

**EDINBORO UNIVERSITY OF PENNSYLVANIA**
Anthropology M
Art Therapy M,O
Art/Fine Arts M
Clinical Psychology M,O
Communication—General M
Counseling Psychology M,O
History M
Political Science M
Rehabilitation Counseling M,O
School Psychology M,O

**ELIZABETH CITY STATE UNIVERSITY**
Geographic Information Systems M

**ELMHURST COLLEGE**
Geographic Information Systems M
Industrial and Organizational
  Psychology M

**ELMS COLLEGE**
Religion M

**ELON UNIVERSITY**
Internet and Interactive
  Multimedia M

**EMBRY-RIDDLE AERONAUTICAL UNIVERSITY–PRESCOTT**
Military and Defense Studies M

**EMBRY-RIDDLE AERONAUTICAL UNIVERSITY–WORLDWIDE**
International Affairs M

**EMERSON COLLEGE**
Broadcast Journalism M

---

*M—masters degree; D—doctorate; O—other advanced degree; *—Close-Up and/or Display*

| | |
|---|---|
| Communication—General | M |
| Corporate and Organizational Communication | M |
| Film, Television, and Video Production | M |
| Journalism | M |
| Media Studies | M |
| Publishing | M |
| Theater | M |
| Writing | M |

**EMILY CARR UNIVERSITY OF ART + DESIGN**

| | |
|---|---|
| Applied Arts and Design—General | M |
| Art/Fine Arts | M |
| Computer Art and Design | M |

**EMORY & HENRY COLLEGE**

| | |
|---|---|
| American Studies | M |
| History | M |

**EMORY UNIVERSITY**

| | |
|---|---|
| Anthropology | D |
| Art History | D |
| Clinical Psychology | D |
| Cognitive Sciences | D |
| Comparative Literature | D,O |
| Developmental Psychology | D |
| Economics | D |
| English | D,O |
| Ethics | M,D |
| Film, Television, and Video Theory and Criticism | M,D,O |
| French | D |
| Genetic Counseling | M |
| History | D |
| Interdisciplinary Studies | D |
| Music | M |
| Pastoral Ministry and Counseling | M,D |
| Philosophy | D,O |
| Political Science | D |
| Portuguese | D,O |
| Psychology—General | D |
| Religion | D |
| Sociology | D |
| Spanish | D,O |
| Sustainable Development | M |
| Theology | M,D |
| Women's Studies | D,O |

**EMPORIA STATE UNIVERSITY**

| | |
|---|---|
| Art Therapy | M |
| Clinical Psychology | M |
| Counseling Psychology | M |
| English | M |
| Forensic Sciences | M,O |
| History | M |
| Industrial and Organizational Psychology | M |
| Music | M |
| Psychology—General | M |
| Rehabilitation Counseling | M |
| School Psychology | M,O |

**ENDICOTT COLLEGE**

| | |
|---|---|
| Applied Behavior Analysis | M,D |
| Homeland Security | M |
| Interior Design | M |

**EPISCOPAL DIVINITY SCHOOL**

| | |
|---|---|
| Theology | M,D,O |

**ERIKSON INSTITUTE**

| | |
|---|---|
| Child Development | M |
| Developmental Psychology | M,O |
| Human Development | M,O |

**ERSKINE THEOLOGICAL SEMINARY**

| | |
|---|---|
| Theology | M,D |

**EVANGELICAL SEMINARY**

| | |
|---|---|
| Marriage and Family Therapy | M |
| Missions and Missiology | M |
| Pastoral Ministry and Counseling | M |
| Theology | M |

**EVANGELICAL SEMINARY OF PUERTO RICO**

| | |
|---|---|
| Theology | M,D |

**EVANGEL UNIVERSITY**

| | |
|---|---|
| Clinical Psychology | M |
| Counseling Psychology | M |
| Psychology—General | M |
| School Psychology | M |

**THE EVERGREEN STATE COLLEGE**

| | |
|---|---|
| Public Administration | M |

**EXCELSIOR COLLEGE**

| | |
|---|---|
| Conflict Resolution and Mediation/Peace Studies | M,O |
| Criminal Justice and Criminology | M,O |
| Emergency Management | M |
| Homeland Security | M |
| Internet and Interactive Multimedia | M,O |
| Liberal Studies | M |
| Public Administration | M |

**FAIRFIELD UNIVERSITY**

| | |
|---|---|
| Addictions/Substance Abuse Counseling | M,O |
| American Studies | M |
| Applied Behavior Analysis | M,O |
| Applied Psychology | M,O |
| Child and Family Studies | M,O |
| Clinical Psychology | M,O |
| Communication—General | M |
| Counseling Psychology | M,O |
| Internet and Interactive Multimedia | M,O |
| Marriage and Family Therapy | M,O |
| Pastoral Ministry and Counseling | M,O |
| Public Administration | M |
| School Psychology | M,O |
| Writing | M |

**FAIRLEIGH DICKINSON UNIVERSITY, COLLEGE AT FLORHAM**

| | |
|---|---|
| Clinical Psychology | M |
| Corporate and Organizational Communication | M |
| Counseling Psychology | M |
| Industrial and Organizational Psychology | M |
| Psychology—General | M,O |
| Public Administration | M |
| Writing | M |

**FAIRLEIGH DICKINSON UNIVERSITY, METROPOLITAN CAMPUS**

| | |
|---|---|
| Art/Fine Arts | M |
| Clinical Psychology | M,D |
| Communication—General | M |
| Comparative Literature | M |
| Criminal Justice and Criminology | M |
| English | M |
| Experimental Psychology | M,O |
| Forensic Psychology | M |
| History | M |
| Homeland Security | M |
| International Affairs | M |
| Media Studies | M |
| Political Science | M |
| Psychology—General | M,D,O |
| Public Administration | M,O |
| School Psychology | M,D |

**FAIRMONT STATE UNIVERSITY**

| | |
|---|---|
| Criminal Justice and Criminology | M |

**FAITH BAPTIST BIBLE COLLEGE AND THEOLOGICAL SEMINARY**

| | |
|---|---|
| Pastoral Ministry and Counseling | M |
| Religion | M |
| Theology | M |

**FAITH EVANGELICAL COLLEGE & SEMINARY**

| | |
|---|---|
| Theology | M,D |

**FAITH THEOLOGICAL SEMINARY**

| | |
|---|---|
| Theology | M,D |

**FASHION INSTITUTE OF TECHNOLOGY**

| | |
|---|---|
| Applied Arts and Design—General | M* |
| Art History | M* |
| Arts Administration | M* |
| Clothing and Textiles | M* |
| Illustration | M* |
| Museum Studies | M* |

**FAULKNER UNIVERSITY**

| | |
|---|---|
| Criminal Justice and Criminology | M |
| History | M |
| Liberal Studies | M |
| Missions and Missiology | M |
| Pastoral Ministry and Counseling | M |
| Theology | M |

**FAYETTEVILLE STATE UNIVERSITY**

| | |
|---|---|
| Criminal Justice and Criminology | M |
| Psychology—General | M |
| Sociology | M |

**FELICIAN UNIVERSITY**

| | |
|---|---|
| Counseling Psychology | M |

**FERRIS STATE UNIVERSITY**

| | |
|---|---|
| Applied Arts and Design—General | M |
| Architecture | M |
| Art/Fine Arts | M |
| Criminal Justice and Criminology | M |
| Photography | M |

**FIELDING GRADUATE UNIVERSITY**

| | |
|---|---|
| Child Development | D,O |
| Clinical Psychology | D,O |
| Forensic Psychology | D,O |
| Health Psychology | D,O |
| Human Development | M,D,O |
| Media Studies | M,D,O |
| Psychology—General | M,D,O |

**FISK UNIVERSITY**

| | |
|---|---|
| Clinical Psychology | M |
| Psychology—General | M |

**FITCHBURG STATE UNIVERSITY**

| | |
|---|---|
| Communication—General | M,O |
| Counseling Psychology | M |
| English | M,O |
| History | M,O |
| Interdisciplinary Studies | O |
| Psychology—General | O |

**FIVE TOWNS COLLEGE**

| | |
|---|---|
| Music | M,D |

**FLORIDA AGRICULTURAL AND MECHANICAL UNIVERSITY**

| | |
|---|---|
| Architecture | M |
| Criminal Justice and Criminology | M |
| History | M |
| Journalism | M |
| Landscape Architecture | M |
| Political Science | M |
| Psychology—General | M |
| Public Administration | M |
| Social Psychology | M |
| Social Sciences | M |

**FLORIDA ATLANTIC UNIVERSITY**

| | |
|---|---|
| Anthropology | M |
| Applied Arts and Design—General | M |
| Art/Fine Arts | M |
| Communication—General | M,O |
| Comparative and Interdisciplinary Arts | M,D |
| Comparative Literature | M |
| Criminal Justice and Criminology | M |
| Economics | M |
| English | M |

| | |
|---|---|
| Film, Television, and Video Production | M,O |
| French | M |
| German | M |
| Graphic Design | M |
| History | M |
| Linguistics | M |
| Media Studies | M,O |
| Music | M |
| Political Science | M |
| Psychology—General | M |
| Public Administration | M,D |
| Sociology | M |
| Spanish | M |
| Theater | M |
| Urban and Regional Planning | M |
| Women's Studies | M |

**FLORIDA GULF COAST UNIVERSITY**

| | |
|---|---|
| Criminal Justice and Criminology | M |
| English | M |
| Forensic Sciences | M |
| History | M |
| Interdisciplinary Studies | M |
| Public Administration | M |

**FLORIDA INSTITUTE OF TECHNOLOGY**

| | |
|---|---|
| Applied Behavior Analysis | M,D |
| Clinical Psychology | D |
| Communication—General | M |
| Emergency Management | M,D |
| Industrial and Organizational Psychology | M,D |
| Interdisciplinary Studies | M |
| Psychology—General | M,D |
| Public Administration | M,D |

**FLORIDA INTERNATIONAL UNIVERSITY**

| | |
|---|---|
| African Studies | M |
| Applied Behavior Analysis | M,D |
| Architecture | M |
| Art/Fine Arts | M,O |
| Asian Studies | M |
| Clinical Psychology | M,D,O |
| Cognitive Sciences | M,D |
| Communication—General | M |
| Counseling Psychology | M,D,O |
| Criminal Justice and Criminology | M,D |
| Developmental Psychology | M,D |
| Economics | M,D |
| Emergency Management | M |
| English | M |
| Forensic Sciences | M,D |
| History | M,D |
| Industrial and Organizational Psychology | M,D |
| Interior Design | M,O |
| International Affairs | M,D |
| Journalism | M |
| Landscape Architecture | M |
| Latin American Studies | M |
| Liberal Studies | M |
| Linguistics | M |
| Mass Communication | M |
| Museum Studies | M,O |
| Music | M |
| Political Science | M,D |
| Psychology—General | M,D |
| Public Administration | M,D |
| Public Affairs | M,D |
| Rehabilitation Counseling | M,D,O |
| Religion | M |
| School Psychology | M,D,O |
| Sociology | M,D |
| Spanish | M,D |
| Writing | M |

**FLORIDA NATIONAL UNIVERSITY**

| | |
|---|---|
| Public Administration | M |

**FLORIDA STATE UNIVERSITY**

| | |
|---|---|
| American Studies | M,D |
| Applied Behavior Analysis | M |
| Applied Economics | M,D |
| Applied Social Research | M,D |
| Archaeology | M,D |
| Architecture | M |
| Art History | M,D |
| Art/Fine Arts | M |
| Arts Administration | M,D |
| Asian Studies | M |
| Child and Family Studies | M,D |
| Classics | M,D |
| Clinical Psychology | D |
| Cognitive Sciences | D |
| Communication—General | M,D |
| Corporate and Organizational Communication | M,D |
| Counseling Psychology | D |
| Criminal Justice and Criminology | M,D |
| Cultural Studies | M,D |
| Dance | M |
| Demography and Population Studies | M,D |
| Developmental Psychology | D |
| East European and Russian Studies | M |
| Economics | M,D |
| English | M,D |
| Family and Consumer Sciences-General | M,D |
| Film, Television, and Video Production | M* |
| French | M,D |
| Geographic Information Systems | M,D |
| Geography | M,D |
| German | M |
| History | M,D |
| Industrial Design | M |
| Interior Design | M |
| International Affairs | M |
| Italian | M |
| Marriage and Family Therapy | M,D |
| Media Studies | M,D |
| Museum Studies | M,D |
| Music | M,D |
| Philosophy | M,D |
| Political Science | M,D |

| | |
|---|---|
| Psychology—General | M,D |
| Public Administration | M,D,O |
| Public History | M,D,O |
| Public Policy | M,D,O |
| Religion | M,D |
| Rhetoric | M,D |
| School Psychology | D |
| Slavic Languages | M |
| Social Psychology | D |
| Sociology | M,D |
| Spanish | M,D |
| Sport Psychology | M,D |
| Theater | M |
| Therapies—Dance, Drama, and Music | M,D |
| Urban and Regional Planning | M,D |
| Writing | M,D |

**FONTBONNE UNIVERSITY**

| | |
|---|---|
| Art/Fine Arts | M |
| Family and Consumer Sciences-General | M |
| Health Communication | M |
| Theater | M |

**FORDHAM UNIVERSITY**

| | |
|---|---|
| Applied Psychology | M,D |
| Classics | M,D |
| Clinical Psychology | D |
| Communication—General | M |
| Counseling Psychology | M,D |
| Developmental Psychology | D |
| Economic Development | M,O |
| Economics | M,D,O |
| Emergency Management | M |
| English | M,D |
| Ethics | M,D |
| History | M,D |
| International Affairs | M,O |
| International Development | M,O |
| International Economics | M,O |
| Media Studies | M |
| Medieval and Renaissance Studies | M,O |
| Pastoral Ministry and Counseling | M,D,O |
| Philosophy | M,D |
| Political Science | M |
| Psychology—General | M,D |
| Religion | M,D,O |
| School Psychology | M,D |
| Theater | M |
| Theology | M,D |
| Urban Studies | M |

**FORT HAYS STATE UNIVERSITY**

| | |
|---|---|
| Art/Fine Arts | M |
| Communication—General | M |
| English | M |
| Geography | M |
| History | M |
| Liberal Studies | M |
| Psychology—General | M,O |
| School Psychology | O |

**FORT VALLEY STATE UNIVERSITY**

| | |
|---|---|
| Counseling Psychology | M |
| Rehabilitation Counseling | M |

**FRAMINGHAM STATE UNIVERSITY**

| | |
|---|---|
| Art/Fine Arts | M |
| Psychology—General | M |
| Public Administration | M |
| Spanish | M |

**FRANCISCAN SCHOOL OF THEOLOGY**

| | |
|---|---|
| Theology | M |

**FRANCISCAN UNIVERSITY OF STEUBENVILLE**

| | |
|---|---|
| Clinical Psychology | M |
| Counseling Psychology | M |
| Philosophy | M |
| Theology | M |

**FRANCIS MARION UNIVERSITY**

| | |
|---|---|
| Applied Psychology | M,O |
| Clinical Psychology | M,O |
| Counseling Psychology | M,O |
| Psychology—General | M,O |
| School Psychology | M,O |

**FRANKLIN UNIVERSITY**

| | |
|---|---|
| Corporate and Organizational Communication | M |

**FREDERICK S. PARDEE RAND GRADUATE SCHOOL**

| | |
|---|---|
| Public Policy | D |

**FREED-HARDEMAN UNIVERSITY**

| | |
|---|---|
| Ethics | M |
| Pastoral Ministry and Counseling | M |
| Theology | M |

**FRESNO PACIFIC UNIVERSITY**

| | |
|---|---|
| Conflict Resolution and Mediation/Peace Studies | M,O |
| Interdisciplinary Studies | M |
| Marriage and Family Therapy | M |
| Missions and Missiology | M |
| Pastoral Ministry and Counseling | M |
| School Psychology | M |
| Theology | M |
| Urban Studies | M |

**FRIENDS UNIVERSITY**

| | |
|---|---|
| Marriage and Family Therapy | M |

**FROSTBURG STATE UNIVERSITY**

| | |
|---|---|
| Counseling Psychology | M |
| Interdisciplinary Studies | M |
| Psychology—General | M |

**FULLER THEOLOGICAL SEMINARY**

| | |
|---|---|
| Clinical Psychology | M,D,O |
| Marriage and Family Therapy | M,D,O |
| Missions and Missiology | M,D,O |
| Music | M,D,O |
| Pastoral Ministry and Counseling | M,D,O |
| Theology | M,D,O |

## FULL SAIL UNIVERSITY
| | |
|---|---|
| Art/Fine Arts | M |
| Computer Art and Design | M |
| Graphic Design | M |
| Internet and Interactive Multimedia | M |
| Journalism | M |
| Media Studies | M |
| Writing | M |

## FUTURE GENERATIONS GRADUATE SCHOOL
| | |
|---|---|
| Social Psychology | M |
| Sustainable Development | M |
| Urban and Regional Planning | M |

## GALLAUDET UNIVERSITY
| | |
|---|---|
| Clinical Psychology | M,D,O |
| Counseling Psychology | M,D,O |
| Linguistics | M,D,O |
| Public Administration | M,D,O |
| School Psychology | M,D,O |
| Translation and Interpretation | M,D,O |

## GANNON UNIVERSITY
| | |
|---|---|
| Clinical Psychology | M |
| Counseling Psychology | M |
| Criminal Justice and Criminology | M |
| English | M |
| Health Communication | M |
| Pastoral Ministry and Counseling | M,O |
| Public Administration | M |
| Theology | M,O |

## GARDNER-WEBB UNIVERSITY
| | |
|---|---|
| Counseling Psychology | M |
| Cultural Studies | M,D |
| English | M |
| Missions and Missiology | M,D |
| Pastoral Ministry and Counseling | M,D |
| Psychology—General | M |
| School Psychology | M |
| Theology | M,D |

## GARRETT-EVANGELICAL THEOLOGICAL SEMINARY
| | |
|---|---|
| Music | M,D |
| Pastoral Ministry and Counseling | M,D |
| Theology | M,D |

## GATEWAY SEMINARY
| | |
|---|---|
| Pastoral Ministry and Counseling | M,D,O |
| Theology | M,D,O |

## GENERAL THEOLOGICAL SEMINARY
| | |
|---|---|
| Pastoral Ministry and Counseling | M |
| Religion | M,D,O |
| Theology | M,D,O |

## GENEVA COLLEGE
| | |
|---|---|
| Clinical Psychology | M |
| Counseling Psychology | M |
| Marriage and Family Therapy | M |
| Pastoral Ministry and Counseling | M |
| Psychology—General | M |

## GEORGE FOX UNIVERSITY
| | |
|---|---|
| Clinical Psychology | M,D,O |
| Counseling Psychology | M,O |
| Cultural Studies | M,D,O |
| Marriage and Family Therapy | M,O |
| Pastoral Ministry and Counseling | M,D,O |
| School Psychology | M,O |
| Theology | M,D,O |

## GEORGE MASON UNIVERSITY
| | |
|---|---|
| Anthropology | M,D |
| Applied Psychology | M,D,O |
| Art History | M |
| Art/Fine Arts | M |
| Arts Administration | M,O |
| Cognitive Sciences | M,D,O |
| Communication—General | M,D,O |
| Conflict Resolution and Mediation/Peace Studies | M,D,O |
| Criminal Justice and Criminology | M,D |
| Cultural Studies | D |
| Developmental Psychology | M,D,O |
| Economics | M,D |
| English | M,D,O |
| Ethics | M |
| Forensic Sciences | M |
| French | M |
| Gender Studies | M |
| Geographic Information Systems | M,D,O |
| Geography | M,D,O |
| Graphic Design | M |
| History | M,D |
| Industrial and Organizational Psychology | M,D,O |
| Interdisciplinary Studies | M |
| International Affairs | M |
| Linguistics | M,D,O |
| Music | M,D |
| National Security | M,D,O |
| Near and Middle Eastern Studies | M,O |
| Philosophy | M |
| Photography | M |
| Political Science | M,D |
| Psychology—General | M,D,O |
| Public Administration | M |
| Public Affairs | M |
| Public Policy | M,D |
| Religion | M |
| Sociology | M,D |
| Women's Studies | M |
| Writing | M |

## GEORGETOWN UNIVERSITY
| | |
|---|---|
| American Studies | M,D |
| Asian Studies | M |
| Communication—General | M |
| Comparative Literature | M,D |
| Conflict Resolution and Mediation/Peace Studies | M |
| East European and Russian Studies | M |
| Economic Development | D |
| Economics | D |
| Emergency Management | M,D |
| English | M |
| Ethics | M,D |
| German | M,D |
| History | M,D |
| Human Development | M,D |
| Humanities | D |
| Industrial and Labor Relations | M,D |
| Interdisciplinary Studies | M,D |
| International Affairs | M,D |
| International Development | M |
| Internet and Interactive Multimedia | M |
| Journalism | M,D |
| Latin American Studies | M |
| Liberal Studies | M,D |
| Linguistics | M,D |
| Media Studies | M,D |
| Medieval and Renaissance Studies | M,D |
| Near and Middle Eastern Languages | M,O |
| Near and Middle Eastern Studies | M,D |
| Philosophy | M,D |
| Political Science | M,D |
| Psychology—General | D |
| Public Policy | M,D |
| Religion | M,D |
| Spanish | M,D |
| Theology | D |
| Urban and Regional Planning | M,D |
| Western European Studies | M |

## THE GEORGE WASHINGTON UNIVERSITY
| | |
|---|---|
| Addictions/Substance Abuse Counseling | M |
| American Studies | M,D |
| Anthropology | M,D |
| Applied Psychology | D |
| Art History | M |
| Art Therapy | M,O |
| Art/Fine Arts | M,O |
| Asian Studies | M |
| Clinical Psychology | M,D |
| Cognitive Sciences | D |
| Communication—General | M |
| Criminal Justice and Criminology | M,O |
| Dance | M,O |
| East European and Russian Studies | M |
| Economics | M,D |
| Emergency Management | M,D,O |
| English | M,D |
| Folklore | M,D |
| Forensic Psychology | O |
| Forensic Sciences | M,O |
| Gender Studies | O |
| Geography | M,O |
| Health Communication | M,D |
| Historic Preservation | M,D |
| History | M,D |
| Human Development | M |
| Interior Design | M |
| International Affairs | M,D |
| International Development | M,D |
| International Trade Policy | M |
| Latin American Studies | M |
| Mass Communication | M,O |
| Military and Defense Studies | M |
| Museum Studies | M,D,O |
| National Security | M,D |
| Near and Middle Eastern Studies | M |
| Philosophy | M |
| Photography | M,O |
| Political Science | M,D |
| Psychology—General | M,D,O |
| Public Administration | M,D |
| Public Affairs | M,O |
| Public Policy | M,D |
| Publishing | M |
| Rehabilitation Counseling | M |
| Religion | M |
| Social Psychology | D |
| Sociology | M |
| Theater | M,O |
| Western European Studies | M |
| Women's Studies | M,O |

## GEORGIA CHRISTIAN UNIVERSITY
| | |
|---|---|
| Missions and Missiology | M,D |
| Music | M |
| Pastoral Ministry and Counseling | M,D |
| Theology | M,D |

## GEORGIA COLLEGE & STATE UNIVERSITY
| | |
|---|---|
| Art Therapy | M |
| Criminal Justice and Criminology | M |
| English | M |
| History | M |
| Public Administration | M |
| Therapies—Dance, Drama, and Music | M |
| Writing | M |

## GEORGIA INSTITUTE OF TECHNOLOGY
| | |
|---|---|
| Architecture | M,D |
| Building Science | M,D |
| Computer Art and Design | M,D |
| Economic Development | M,D |
| Economics | M,D |
| Geographic Information Systems | M,D |
| History of Science and Technology | M,D |
| Industrial Design | M |
| International Affairs | M |
| Internet and Interactive Multimedia | M,D |
| Music | M,D |
| Psychology—General | M,D |

## GEORGIAN COURT UNIVERSITY
| | |
|---|---|
| Applied Behavior Analysis | M,O |
| Clinical Psychology | M,O |
| Computer Art and Design | M,O |
| Counseling Psychology | M,O |
| Health Psychology | M,O |
| Homeland Security | M,O |
| School Psychology | M,O |
| Theology | M,O |

## GEORGIA SOUTHERN UNIVERSITY
| | |
|---|---|
| Applied Economics | M,O |
| Art/Fine Arts | M |
| Clinical Psychology | M |
| English | M |
| Graphic Design | M |
| History | M |
| Music | M |
| Psychology—General | M |
| Public Administration | M |
| Public History | M,O |
| School Psychology | M,O |
| Sociology | M |
| Spanish | M |

## GEORGIA STATE UNIVERSITY
| | |
|---|---|
| African-American Studies | M |
| Anthropology | M |
| Art History | M |
| Art/Fine Arts | M |
| Clinical Psychology | D |
| Clothing and Textiles | M |
| Cognitive Sciences | D |
| Communication—General | M,D |
| Counseling Psychology | M,O |
| Criminal Justice and Criminology | M,D,O |
| Cultural Studies | M,O |
| Developmental Psychology | D |
| Economic Development | M,D,O |
| Economics | M,D |
| Emergency Management | M,D,O |
| English | M,D |
| Film, Television, and Video Production | M,D |
| Forensic Sciences | M |
| French | M,O |
| Geographic Information Systems | O |
| Geography | M,D |
| German | O |
| Gerontology | M,O |
| Graphic Design | M |
| Historic Preservation | M,D |
| History | M,D |
| Human Development | M,D,O |
| Industrial and Labor Relations | M,D |
| Interior Design | M |
| Latin American Studies | M,O |
| Linguistics | M,D |
| Mass Communication | M,D |
| Media Studies | M,D |
| Music | M,D,O |
| Philosophy | M |
| Photography | M,D |
| Political Science | M |
| Psychology—General | D |
| Public Administration | M,D |
| Public History | M,D |
| Public Policy | M,D,O |
| Rehabilitation Counseling | M |
| Religion | M |
| Rhetoric | M,D |
| School Psychology | M,D,O |
| Social Psychology | D |
| Sociology | M,D |
| Spanish | M,D |
| Speech and Interpersonal Communication | M,D |
| Translation and Interpretation | O |
| Urban and Regional Planning | M,D,O |
| Women's Studies | M,O |
| Writing | M,D |

## GLOBAL UNIVERSITY
| | |
|---|---|
| Missions and Missiology | M,D |
| Pastoral Ministry and Counseling | M,D |
| Theology | M,D |

## GODDARD COLLEGE
| | |
|---|---|
| Art Therapy | M |
| Clinical Psychology | M |
| Comparative and Interdisciplinary Arts | M |
| Interdisciplinary Studies | M |
| Psychology—General | M |
| Writing | M |

## GOLDEN GATE UNIVERSITY
| | |
|---|---|
| Corporate and Organizational Communication | M,D,O |
| Forensic Sciences | M,O |
| Psychology—General | M,O |
| Public Administration | M,D,O |

## GONZAGA UNIVERSITY
| | |
|---|---|
| Marriage and Family Therapy | M |
| Philosophy | M |
| Theology | M |

## GORDON-CONWELL THEOLOGICAL SEMINARY
| | |
|---|---|
| Archaeology | M,D |
| Missions and Missiology | M,D |
| Pastoral Ministry and Counseling | M,D |
| Religion | M,D |
| Theology | M,D |

## GOUCHER COLLEGE
| | |
|---|---|
| Arts Administration | M |
| Computer Art and Design | M |
| Cultural Studies | M |

## Public Policy / Georgian Court heading area
| | |
|---|---|
| Public Policy | M,D |
| Urban and Regional Planning | M,D |
| Urban Design | M,D |

## GOVERNORS STATE UNIVERSITY
| | |
|---|---|
| Addictions/Substance Abuse Counseling | M |
| Art/Fine Arts | M |
| Communication—General | M |
| Counseling Psychology | M |
| Criminal Justice and Criminology | M |
| English | M |
| Film, Television, and Video Production | M |
| Media Studies | M |
| Photography | M |
| Political Science | M |
| Psychology—General | M |
| Public Administration | M |

## GRACE COLLEGE
| | |
|---|---|
| Clinical Psychology | M |

## GRACE COLLEGE OF DIVINITY
| | |
|---|---|
| Religion | M |

## GRACELAND UNIVERSITY (IA)
| | |
|---|---|
| Religion | M |
| Theology | M |

## GRACE MISSION UNIVERSITY
| | |
|---|---|
| Missions and Missiology | M,D |

## GRACE SCHOOL OF THEOLOGY
| | |
|---|---|
| Theology | M |

## GRACE THEOLOGICAL SEMINARY
| | |
|---|---|
| Cultural Studies | M,D,O |
| Missions and Missiology | M,D,O |
| Pastoral Ministry and Counseling | M,D,O |
| Theology | M,D,O |
| Women's Studies | M,D,O |

## GRACE UNIVERSITY
| | |
|---|---|
| Counseling Psychology | M |
| Pastoral Ministry and Counseling | M |
| Theology | M |

## THE GRADUATE CENTER, CITY UNIVERSITY OF NEW YORK
| | |
|---|---|
| Anthropology | D |
| Archaeology | D |
| Architectural History | D |
| Art History | D |
| Classics | M,D |
| Clinical Psychology | D |
| Cognitive Sciences | D |
| Comparative Literature | M,D |
| Criminal Justice and Criminology | D |
| Cultural Anthropology | D |
| Developmental Psychology | D |
| Economics | D |
| English | D |
| Experimental Psychology | D |
| French | D |
| German | M,D |
| Hispanic and Latin American Languages | D |
| History | D |
| Industrial and Organizational Psychology | D |
| Interdisciplinary Studies | M,D |
| Italian | M,D |
| Liberal Studies | M |
| Linguistics | M,D |
| Medieval and Renaissance Studies | M,D |
| Music | D |
| Philosophy | M,D |
| Political Science | M,D |
| Psychology—General | M,D |
| Public Policy | M,D |
| Social Psychology | D |
| Sociology | D |
| Theater | D |
| Urban Studies | M,D |
| Women's Studies | M,D |

## GRADUATE INSTITUTE OF APPLIED LINGUISTICS
| | |
|---|---|
| Linguistics | M,O |

## GRADUATE THEOLOGICAL UNION
| | |
|---|---|
| Art History | M,D,O |
| Cultural Studies | M,D,O |
| Ethics | M,D,O |
| Jewish Studies | M,D,O |
| Religion | M,D,O |
| Social Sciences | M,D,O |
| Theology | M,D,O |

## GRAMBLING STATE UNIVERSITY
| | |
|---|---|
| Criminal Justice and Criminology | M |
| English | M,D,O |
| Mass Communication | M |
| Political Science | M |
| Public Administration | M |

## GRAND CANYON UNIVERSITY
| | |
|---|---|
| Cognitive Sciences | D |
| Emergency Management | M |
| Industrial and Organizational Psychology | D |
| Pastoral Ministry and Counseling | D |
| Psychology—General | D |

## GRAND RAPIDS THEOLOGICAL SEMINARY OF CORNERSTONE UNIVERSITY
| | |
|---|---|
| Missions and Missiology | M |
| Pastoral Ministry and Counseling | M |
| Religion | M |
| Theology | M |

## GRAND VALLEY STATE UNIVERSITY
| | |
|---|---|
| Communication—General | M |
| Criminal Justice and Criminology | M |
| English | M |

Historic Preservation — M
Writing — M

*M—masters degree; D—doctorate; O—other advanced degree; *—Close-Up and/or Display*

Linguistics M
Public Administration M
School Psychology M,O

**GRATZ COLLEGE**
Holocaust and Genocide Studies M,D
Jewish Studies M,O

**GREENVILLE COLLEGE**
Pastoral Ministry and Counseling M

**HAMLINE UNIVERSITY**
Public Administration M,D
Writing M

**HAMPTON UNIVERSITY**
Architecture M
Pastoral Ministry and Counseling M,D,O

**HARDING SCHOOL OF THEOLOGY**
Pastoral Ministry and Counseling M,D
Religion M,D
Theology M,D

**HARDING UNIVERSITY**
Counseling Psychology M
Marriage and Family Therapy M
Pastoral Ministry and Counseling M

**HARDIN-SIMMONS UNIVERSITY**
Counseling Psychology M
English M
History M
Marriage and Family Therapy M
Music M
Pastoral Ministry and Counseling M,D
Psychology—General M
Religion M
Theology M,D

**HARRISON MIDDLETON UNIVERSITY**
Comparative Literature M,D
Humanities M,D
Interdisciplinary Studies M,D
Philosophy M,D
Religion M,D
Social Sciences M,D

**HARTFORD SEMINARY**
Pastoral Ministry and Counseling M,D,O
Religion M,D,O
Theology M,D,O

**HARVARD UNIVERSITY**
African Studies D
African-American Studies D
American Studies D
Anthropology M,D
Archaeology M,D
Architectural History D
Architecture M,D
Art History D
Asian Languages M,D
Asian Studies M,D
Celtic Languages D
Chinese D
Classics D
Cognitive Sciences M,D
Communication—General M,O
Comparative Literature D
Demography and Population Studies M,D
Developmental Psychology D
East European and Russian Studies D
Economics D
English M,D,O
Experimental Psychology D
French M,D
German D
History of Science and Technology M,D
History D
Human Development M
International Affairs D
International Development M
Italian M,D
Japanese D
Jewish Studies M,D
Journalism M,O
Landscape Architecture M,D
Liberal Studies M,O
Linguistics D
Medieval and Renaissance Studies D
Museum Studies M,O
Music M,D
Near and Middle Eastern Languages M,D
Near and Middle Eastern Studies M,D
Philosophy M,D
Political Science M,D
Portuguese M
Psychology—General D
Public Administration M
Public Policy M,D
Religion D
Russian D
Scandinavian Languages D
Slavic Languages D
Social Psychology D
Sociology D
Spanish M,D
Technical Communication M
Theology M
Urban and Regional Planning M,D
Urban Design M

**HAWAI'I PACIFIC UNIVERSITY**
Clinical Psychology M
Communication—General M
Economics M
Liberal Studies M
Military and Defense Studies M
Sustainable Development M

**HAZELDEN GRADUATE SCHOOL OF ADDICTION STUDIES**
Addictions/Substance Abuse
  Counseling M,O

**HEBREW COLLEGE**
Jewish Studies M,O

Music M,O
Theology M

**HEBREW UNION COLLEGE–JEWISH INSTITUTE OF RELIGION (NY)**
Jewish Studies M
Music M
Near and Middle Eastern Languages D
Theology M,D

**HEC MONTREAL**
Applied Economics M
Arts Administration O
Corporate and Organizational
  Communication O
Sustainable Development O

**HEIDELBERG UNIVERSITY**
Clinical Psychology M
Counseling Psychology M
School Psychology M

**HENDERSON STATE UNIVERSITY**
Counseling Psychology M,O
Liberal Studies M

**HENLEY-PUTNAM UNIVERSITY**
Conflict Resolution and
  Mediation/Peace Studies M
Homeland Security M
Military and Defense Studies M
National Security D

**HERITAGE CHRISTIAN UNIVERSITY**
Classics M
Pastoral Ministry and Counseling M
Religion M

**HERITAGE COLLEGE AND SEMINARY**
Theology M,O

**HERITAGE UNIVERSITY**
English M

**HIGH POINT UNIVERSITY**
Corporate and Organizational
  Communication M
History M

**HILBERT COLLEGE**
Criminal Justice and Criminology M
Public Administration M

**HILLSDALE COLLEGE**
Political Science M,D

**HIRAM COLLEGE**
Interdisciplinary Studies M

**HODGES UNIVERSITY**
Clinical Psychology M
Counseling Psychology M

**HOFSTRA UNIVERSITY**
Addictions/Substance Abuse
  Counseling M,O
Applied Behavior Analysis M,D,O
Art Therapy M,O
Art/Fine Arts M,D,O
Clinical Psychology M,D
Counseling Psychology M
English M
Family and Consumer
  Sciences-General M,D,O
Human Development M
Humanities M,D,O
Industrial and Organizational
  Psychology M,D
Journalism M
Linguistics M,D,O
Marriage and Family Therapy M,O
Psychology—General M
Rehabilitation Counseling M,O
School Psychology M,O
Social Psychology M,D
Sustainable Development M
Urban Design M
Writing M

**HOLLINS UNIVERSITY**
Art/Fine Arts M
Dance M
English M
Film, Television, and Video
  Production M
Film, Television, and Video
  Theory and Criticism M
Humanities M
Illustration M
Interdisciplinary Studies M
Liberal Studies M
Music M
Social Sciences M
Theater M,O
Writing M,O

**HOLMES INSTITUTE**
Pastoral Ministry and Counseling M

**HOLY APOSTLES COLLEGE AND SEMINARY**
Theology M

**HOLY CROSS GREEK ORTHODOX SCHOOL OF THEOLOGY**
Theology M

**HOLY FAMILY UNIVERSITY**
Counseling Psychology M,D
Criminal Justice and Criminology M,D

**HOLY NAMES UNIVERSITY**
Counseling Psychology M
Forensic Psychology M
Music M,O
Pastoral Ministry and Counseling M
Writing M

**HOOD COLLEGE**
Art/Fine Arts M,O
Clinical Psychology M

Human Development M
Humanities M
Psychology—General M
Public Administration M
School Psychology M

**HOOD THEOLOGICAL SEMINARY**
Theology M,D

**HOPE INTERNATIONAL UNIVERSITY**
International Development M
Marriage and Family Therapy M
Missions and Missiology M
Music M
Religion M

**HOUGHTON COLLEGE**
Music M

**HOUSTON BAPTIST UNIVERSITY**
Art/Fine Arts M
Counseling Psychology M
Liberal Studies M
Near and Middle Eastern Languages M
Pastoral Ministry and Counseling M
Philosophy M
Psychology—General M
School Psychology M
Theology M

**HOUSTON GRADUATE SCHOOL OF THEOLOGY**
Pastoral Ministry and Counseling M,D
Theology M,D

**HOWARD PAYNE UNIVERSITY**
Criminal Justice and Criminology M
Pastoral Ministry and Counseling M
Theology M

**HOWARD UNIVERSITY**
African Studies M,D
Applied Arts and Design—
  General M
Art History M
Art/Fine Arts M
Clinical Psychology M,D
Communication—General M,D
Corporate and Organizational
  Communication M,D
Counseling Psychology D
Developmental Psychology M,D
Economics M,D
English M,D
Experimental Psychology M,D
Film, Television, and Video
  Production M
French M
History M,D
Mass Communication M,D
Media Studies M,D
Music M
Philosophy M
Photography M
Political Science M,D
Psychology—General M,D
Public Administration M
School Psychology M,D
Social Psychology M,D
Sociology M,D
Spanish M
Theology M,D

**HUMBOLDT STATE UNIVERSITY**
Anthropology M
Counseling Psychology M
Developmental Psychology M
English M
Psychology—General M
School Psychology M
Social Psychology M
Social Sciences M
Sociology M

**HUNTER COLLEGE OF THE CITY UNIVERSITY OF NEW YORK**
Anthropology M
Applied Social Research M
Art History M
Art/Fine Arts M
Chinese M
Classics M
Comparative Literature M
Economics M
French M
Geographic Information Systems M,O
Geography M,O
History M
Italian M
Media Studies M
Music M
Psychology—General M,O
Rehabilitation Counseling M
Romance Languages M
Sociology M
Spanish M
Sustainable Development M,O
Theater M
Urban and Regional Planning M
Urban Studies M
Writing M

**HUNTINGTON UNIVERSITY**
Missions and Missiology M,D
Pastoral Ministry and Counseling M,D

**HUSSON UNIVERSITY**
Clinical Psychology M
Counseling Psychology M
Criminal Justice and Criminology M
School Psychology M
Social Psychology M

**ICAHN SCHOOL OF MEDICINE AT MOUNT SINAI**
Genetic Counseling M,D

**IDAHO STATE UNIVERSITY**
Anthropology M
Art/Fine Arts M
Clinical Psychology D
Counseling Psychology M,D,O
English M,D,O
Experimental Psychology D
Geographic Information Systems M,O
History M
Interdisciplinary Studies M
Marriage and Family Therapy M,D,O
Political Science M,D
Psychology—General D
Public Administration M
Rhetoric M
School Psychology M,D,O
Sociology M
Speech and Interpersonal
  Communication M
Theater M

**IGLOBAL UNIVERSITY**
Public Administration M

**ILIFF SCHOOL OF THEOLOGY**
Pastoral Ministry and Counseling M,D
Religion M,D
Theology M,D

**ILLINOIS INSTITUTE OF TECHNOLOGY**
Applied Arts and Design—
  General M,D
Architecture M,D
Clinical Psychology M,D
Communication—General M,D
Corporate and Organizational
  Communication M
Humanities M,D
Industrial and Organizational
  Psychology M,D
Landscape Architecture M,D
Psychology—General M,D
Public Administration M
Rehabilitation Counseling M,D
Technical Writing M,D

**ILLINOIS STATE UNIVERSITY**
Agricultural Economics and
  Agribusiness M
Archaeology M
Art History M
Art/Fine Arts M
Clinical Psychology M,D,O
Cognitive Sciences M,D,O
Communication—General M
Counseling Psychology M
Criminal Justice and Criminology M
Developmental Psychology M,D,O
Economics M
English M,D,O
Family and Consumer
  Sciences-General M
French M
German M
Graphic Design M
History M
Industrial and Organizational
  Psychology M,D,O
Music M
Photography M
Political Science M
Psychology—General M,D,O
School Psychology D,O
Sociology M
Spanish M
Textile Design M
Theater M
Writing O

**IMMACULATA UNIVERSITY**
Clinical Psychology M,D,O
Counseling Psychology M,D,O
Forensic Psychology M,D,O
Psychoanalysis and Psychotherapy M,D,O
Psychology—General M,D,O
School Psychology M,D,O
Therapies—Dance, Drama, and
  Music M

**INDIANA STATE UNIVERSITY**
Art/Fine Arts M
Clinical Psychology M,D,O
Communication—General M
Criminal Justice and Criminology M
English M
Graphic Design M
History M
Linguistics M,D,O
Media Studies M
Music M
Photography M
Psychology—General M,D
Public Administration M
School Psychology M,D,O
Spanish M,D,O
Writing M

**INDIANA TECH**
Psychology—General M

**INDIANA UNIVERSITY BLOOMINGTON**
African Studies M
African-American Studies M,D
Anthropology M,D
Applied Arts and Design—
  General M
Archaeology M
Art/Fine Arts M
Arts Administration M
Asian Languages M,D
Asian Studies M,D
Chinese M,D
Classics M,D
Cognitive Sciences D
Comparative Literature M,D
Criminal Justice and Criminology M,D
Developmental Psychology D

East European and Russian Studies M,O
Economic Development M,D,O
Economics M,D
English M,D
Folklore M,D
French M,D
Gender Studies D
Geography D
German M,D
Hispanic and Latin American
 Languages M,D
History of Science and Technology M,D
History M,D,O
International Development M,D,O
Italian M,D
Japanese M,D
Jewish Studies M
Latin American Studies M
Linguistics M,D
Media Studies M,D
Medieval and Renaissance Studies M,D
Music M,D,O
Near and Middle Eastern Languages M,D
Philosophy M,D,O
Political Science M,D
Portuguese M,D
Psychology—General D
Public Administration M,D,O
Public Affairs M,D,O
Public Policy M,O
Religion M,D
Rhetoric M,D
School Psychology M,D,O
Slavic Languages M,D
Social Psychology D
Social Sciences M,D,O
Sociology M,D
Spanish M,D
Theater M,D
Western European Studies M
Writing M,D

**INDIANA UNIVERSITY KOKOMO**
Public Administration M,O
Public Policy M,O

**INDIANA UNIVERSITY NORTHWEST**
Addictions/Substance Abuse
 Counseling M,O
Counseling Psychology M,O
Criminal Justice and Criminology M,O
Gender Studies M,O
Liberal Studies M,O
Public Administration M,O
Public Affairs M,O
Urban Studies M,O

**INDIANA UNIVERSITY OF PENNSYLVANIA**
Archaeology M
Art/Fine Arts M
Clinical Psychology M,D
Communication—General D
Criminal Justice and Criminology M,D
English M
Geographic Information Systems M,O
Geography M
Hispanic and Latin American
 Languages M
History M
Industrial and Labor Relations M
Media Studies D
Music M
Psychology—General M,D
Public Affairs M
Public History M
School Psychology D,O
Social Psychology M
Sociology M
Urban and Regional Planning M

**INDIANA UNIVERSITY–PURDUE UNIVERSITY FORT WAYNE**
Communication—General M
English M,O
Marriage and Family Therapy M,O
Public Policy M,O

**INDIANA UNIVERSITY–PURDUE UNIVERSITY INDIANAPOLIS**
Addictions/Substance Abuse
 Counseling M,D
Art Therapy M
Art/Fine Arts M
Child and Family Studies M
Clinical Psychology M,D
Communication—General M,D
Computer Art and Design M
Criminal Justice and Criminology M,O
Economics M
Emergency Management M,O
English M
Forensic Sciences M
Gender Studies M
Geographic Information Systems M,O
Graphic Design M
Health Communication M,D
History M
Homeland Security M,O
Industrial and Organizational
 Psychology M,D
Internet and Interactive
 Multimedia M,D
Liberal Studies M,D,O
Museum Studies M,O
Music M,D
Philanthropic Studies M,D
Philosophy M,O
Photography M
Political Science M,O
Psychology—General M,D
Public Administration M,O

Public Affairs M,O
Public History M,O
Social Sciences M,D
Sociology M
Technical Communication M
Therapies—Dance, Drama, and
 Music M,D
Writing M,O

**INDIANA UNIVERSITY SOUTH BEND**
Addictions/Substance Abuse
 Counseling M,O
Clinical Psychology M,O
Communication—General M,D
Counseling Psychology M,O
English M,O
International Affairs M,O
Liberal Studies M,O
Marriage and Family Therapy M,O
Music M,D
Public Administration M,O
Public Affairs M,O
School Psychology M,O
Writing M,O

**INDIANA UNIVERSITY SOUTHEAST**
Interdisciplinary Studies M,O

**INDIANA WESLEYAN UNIVERSITY**
Addictions/Substance Abuse
 Counseling M
Counseling Psychology M
Marriage and Family Therapy M
Pastoral Ministry and Counseling M
Social Psychology M
Theology M

**INSTITUTE FOR CHRISTIAN STUDIES**
Philosophy M,D
Political Science M,D
Theology M,D

**INSTITUTE FOR DOCTORAL STUDIES IN THE VISUAL ARTS**
Art/Fine Arts D
Philosophy D

**THE INSTITUTE FOR THE PSYCHOLOGICAL SCIENCES**
Clinical Psychology M,D

**INSTITUTE OF AMERICAN INDIAN ARTS**
Writing M

**INSTITUTE OF PUBLIC ADMINISTRATION**
Public Administration M,O

**THE INSTITUTE OF WORLD POLITICS**
Military and Defense Studies M,O
National Security M,O
Political Science M,O
Public Affairs M,O
Public Policy M,O

**INSTITUTO CENTROAMERICANO DE ADMINISTRACIÓN DE EMPRESAS**
Agricultural Economics and
 Agribusiness M
Sustainable Development M

**INSTITUTO TECNOLOGICO DE SANTO DOMINGO**
Communication—General M,O
Counseling Psychology M,O
Economics M,O
Gender Studies M,O
Humanities M,O
International Affairs M,O
Linguistics M,O
Marriage and Family Therapy M,O
Sustainable Development M,O

**INSTITUTO TECNOLÓGICO Y DE ESTUDIOS SUPERIORES DE MONTERREY, CAMPUS CENTRAL DE VERACRUZ**
Humanities M

**INSTITUTO TECNOLÓGICO Y DE ESTUDIOS SUPERIORES DE MONTERREY, CAMPUS CIUDAD DE MÉXICO**
Economics M,D
Humanities M,D

**INSTITUTO TECNOLÓGICO Y DE ESTUDIOS SUPERIORES DE MONTERREY, CAMPUS CIUDAD JUÁREZ**
Humanities M
Public Administration M

**INSTITUTO TECNOLÓGICO Y DE ESTUDIOS SUPERIORES DE MONTERREY, CAMPUS CIUDAD OBREGÓN**
Communication—General M
International Affairs M

**INSTITUTO TECNOLÓGICO Y DE ESTUDIOS SUPERIORES DE MONTERREY, CAMPUS ESTADO DE MÉXICO**
Architecture M,D
Humanities M,D

**INSTITUTO TECNOLÓGICO Y DE ESTUDIOS SUPERIORES DE MONTERREY, CAMPUS IRAPUATO**
Architecture M,D
Humanities M,D

**INSTITUTO TECNOLÓGICO Y DE ESTUDIOS SUPERIORES DE MONTERREY, CAMPUS MONTERREY**
Communication—General M,D

**INTER AMERICAN UNIVERSITY OF PUERTO RICO, AGUADILLA CAMPUS**
Counseling Psychology M
Criminal Justice and Criminology M

**INTER AMERICAN UNIVERSITY OF PUERTO RICO, METROPOLITAN CAMPUS**
American Studies M,D
Counseling Psychology M,D
Criminal Justice and Criminology M
English M
History M,D
Industrial and Labor Relations M,D
Industrial and Organizational
 Psychology M,D
Pastoral Ministry and Counseling D
Psychology—General M,D
School Psychology M,D
Spanish M
Theology D
Women's Studies M

**INTER AMERICAN UNIVERSITY OF PUERTO RICO, PONCE CAMPUS**
Criminal Justice and Criminology M
Spanish M

**INTER AMERICAN UNIVERSITY OF PUERTO RICO, SAN GERMÁN CAMPUS**
Art/Fine Arts M
Counseling Psychology M,D
Graphic Design M
Music M
Photography M
Psychology—General M,D
School Psychology M

**INTERDENOMINATIONAL THEOLOGICAL CENTER**
Pastoral Ministry and Counseling M,D
Theology M,D

**INTERIOR DESIGNERS INSTITUTE**
Interior Design M

**INTERNATIONAL BAPTIST COLLEGE AND SEMINARY**
Pastoral Ministry and Counseling M,D
Theology M

**INTERNATIONAL TECHNOLOGICAL UNIVERSITY**
Computer Art and Design M

**INTERNATIONAL UNIVERSITY IN GENEVA**
Communication—General M,D
International Affairs M,D
Media Studies M,D
Public Administration M,D

**IONA COLLEGE**
Counseling Psychology M,O
Criminal Justice and Criminology M,O
English M
Experimental Psychology M,O
Forensic Sciences M,O
History M
Industrial and Organizational
 Psychology M,O
Marriage and Family Therapy M
Mass Communication M
Psychology—General M,O
School Psychology M,O
Spanish M

**IOWA STATE UNIVERSITY OF SCIENCE AND TECHNOLOGY**
Agricultural Economics and
 Agribusiness M,D
Anthropology M
Applied Arts and Design—
 General M,D
Architecture M
Art/Fine Arts M
Child and Family Studies M,D
Clothing and Textiles M,D
Cognitive Sciences M,D
Corporate and Organizational
 Communication M,D
Counseling Psychology M,D
Economics M,D
English M,D
Family and Consumer
 Sciences-General M
Graphic Design M
History M,D
Human Development M,D
Industrial Design M
Interdisciplinary Studies M
Interior Design M
Journalism M
Landscape Architecture M
Linguistics M,D
Mass Communication M
Political Science M
Psychology—General M,D
Public Administration M
Rhetoric M,D
Rural Planning and Studies D
Rural Sociology M,D
Social Psychology M,D
Sociology M,D
Sustainable Development M,D
Urban and Regional Planning M
Writing M,D

**ITHACA COLLEGE**
Art/Fine Arts M
Internet and Interactive
 Multimedia M
Music M
Photography M
Spanish M
Writing M

**JACKSON STATE UNIVERSITY**
Clinical Psychology M,D
Criminal Justice and Criminology M
English M
History M
Political Science M
Psychology—General D
Public Administration M,D
Public Affairs M,D
Public Policy M,D
School Psychology M
Sociology M
Urban and Regional Planning M,D

**JACKSONVILLE STATE UNIVERSITY**
Criminal Justice and Criminology M
Emergency Management M,D
English M
History M
Liberal Studies M
Music M
Political Science M
Psychology—General M

**JACKSONVILLE UNIVERSITY**
Art/Fine Arts M
Counseling Psychology M
Dance M
Public Policy M

**JAMES MADISON UNIVERSITY**
American Studies M
Applied Behavior Analysis M
Art History M
Art/Fine Arts M
Clinical Psychology D
Communication—General M
Counseling Psychology D
English M
Experimental Psychology M
Forensic Sciences M
History M
Music M,D
Photography M
Political Science M
Psychology—General M
Public Administration M
Public History M
Rhetoric M
School Psychology M,D,O
Technical Writing M
Writing M

**THE JEWISH THEOLOGICAL SEMINARY**
Jewish Studies M,D
Music M
Religion M
Theology M,D,O
Women's Studies M,D

**JOHN BROWN UNIVERSITY**
Clinical Psychology M,O
Counseling Psychology M,O
Ethics M
Marriage and Family Therapy M,O

**JOHN CARROLL UNIVERSITY**
Counseling Psychology M,O
English M
Humanities M
Religion M
Theology M

**JOHN F. KENNEDY UNIVERSITY**
Art/Fine Arts M
Comparative and Interdisciplinary
 Arts M
Counseling Psychology M
Health Psychology M
Industrial and Organizational
 Psychology M,O
Museum Studies M,O
Psychology—General M,D,O
Sport Psychology M
Transpersonal and Humanistic
 Psychology M

**JOHN JAY COLLEGE OF CRIMINAL JUSTICE OF THE CITY UNIVERSITY OF NEW YORK**
Criminal Justice and Criminology M,D
Forensic Psychology M,D
Forensic Sciences M,D
Public Administration M
Public Policy M,D

**JOHN PAUL THE GREAT CATHOLIC UNIVERSITY**
Theology M

**JOHNS HOPKINS UNIVERSITY**
Addictions/Substance Abuse
 Counseling M,D
Anthropology D
Applied Behavior Analysis O
Applied Economics M
Archaeology D
Art History M,D
Asian Studies M,D,O
Classics D
Clinical Psychology M,D
Cognitive Sciences D
Communication—General M,O
Comparative Literature D
Counseling Psychology M,O

---

*M—masters degree; D—doctorate; O—other advanced degree; *—Close-Up and/or Display*

Demography and Population Studies — M,D
Economics — D
English — M,D
Film, Television, and Video Production — M
French — D
Genetic Counseling — M,D
Geographic Information Systems — M,O
German — D
Health Communication — M,D
History of Science and Technology — M,D
History — D
Homeland Security — M,O
International Affairs — M,D,O
International Development — M,D,O
International Economics — M,D,O
Italian — D
Liberal Studies — M,O
Media Studies — M
Medical Illustration — M
Military and Defense Studies — M
Museum Studies — M,O
Music — M,D,O
Near and Middle Eastern Languages — D
Near and Middle Eastern Studies — D
Philosophy — M,D
Political Science — M,D,O
Psychology—General — D
Public Administration — M,O
Public Policy — M,D
Romance Languages — D
Social Sciences — M,D
Sociology — M,D
Spanish — D
Technical Writing — M,O
Writing — M,O

**JOHNSON & WALES UNIVERSITY**
Addictions/Substance Abuse Counseling — M
Clinical Psychology — M
Criminal Justice and Criminology — M

**JOHNSON STATE COLLEGE**
Addictions/Substance Abuse Counseling — M
Applied Behavior Analysis — M
Art/Fine Arts — M
Computer Art and Design — M
Photography — M
School Psychology — M

**JOHNSON UNIVERSITY**
Clinical Psychology — M,D,O
Cultural Studies — M,D,O
Pastoral Ministry and Counseling — M,D,O
Theology — M,D,O

**JOHN WESLEY UNIVERSITY**
Pastoral Ministry and Counseling — M,D
Theology — M,D

**THE JUDGE ADVOCATE GENERAL'S SCHOOL, U.S. ARMY**
Military and Defense Studies — M

**JUDSON UNIVERSITY**
Architecture — M
Clinical Psychology — M
Pastoral Ministry and Counseling — M
Sustainable Development — M
Urban Design — M

**THE JUILLIARD SCHOOL**
Music — M,D,O
Theater — M,D,O

**KANSAS STATE UNIVERSITY**
Agricultural Economics and Agribusiness — M,D
Architecture — M
Art/Fine Arts — M
Child and Family Studies — M,D,O
Child Development — M,D,O
Clothing and Textiles — M,D
Communication—General — M,D,O
Conflict Resolution and Mediation/Peace Studies — M,D,O
Consumer Economics — M,D,O
Economics — M,D
English — M,O
Environmental Design — D
Family and Consumer Sciences-General — M,D,O
Gender Studies — O
Geographic Information Systems — M,D,O
Geography — M,O
Gerontology — M,O
Health Communication — M
History — M,D
Human Development — M,D,O
Interdisciplinary Studies — M,O
Journalism — M
Landscape Architecture — M
Marriage and Family Therapy — M,D,O
Mass Communication — M
Music — M
National Security — M,D
Political Science — M
Psychology—General — M,D
Public Administration — M
Sociology — M,D
Theater — M
Urban and Regional Planning — M
Women's Studies — O

**KAPLAN UNIVERSITY, DAVENPORT CAMPUS**
Criminal Justice and Criminology — M
Political Science — M,O

**KEAN UNIVERSITY**
Addictions/Substance Abuse Counseling — M
Child and Family Studies — M
Clinical Psychology — M,D
Communication—General — M

Counseling Psychology — M
Criminal Justice and Criminology — M
Forensic Psychology — M
Holocaust and Genocide Studies — M
Industrial and Organizational Psychology — M
Liberal Studies — M,O
Marriage and Family Therapy — M,O
Psychology—General — M
Public Administration — M
School Psychology — D,O
Writing — M

**KEENE STATE COLLEGE**
School Psychology — M,O

**KEHILATH YAKOV RABBINICAL SEMINARY**
Theology — M

**KEISER UNIVERSITY**
Criminal Justice and Criminology — M
Homeland Security — M
Industrial and Organizational Psychology — M,D
Psychology—General — M,D

**KENNESAW STATE UNIVERSITY**
American Studies — M
Architecture — M
Communication—General — M
Conflict Resolution and Mediation/Peace Studies — M,D
Criminal Justice and Criminology — M
Ethics — O
International Affairs — M
Public Administration — M
Writing — M

**KENRICK-GLENNON SEMINARY**
Theology — M

**KENT STATE UNIVERSITY**
Anthropology — M
Architecture — M
Art History — M
Art/Fine Arts — M
Biological Anthropology — M,D
Child and Family Studies — M
Clinical Psychology — M,D
Communication—General — M
Conflict Resolution and Mediation/Peace Studies — M,D
Counseling Psychology — M
Criminal Justice and Criminology — M,D
Economics — M
English — M,D
Environmental Design — M
Experimental Psychology — M,D
French — M,D
Geographic Information Systems — M,D
Geography — M,D
German — M,D
Gerontology — M,D
Graphic Design — M
History — M,D
Human Development — M
Illustration — M
Japanese — M,D
Journalism — M
Landscape Architecture — M
Liberal Studies — M
Linguistics — M,D
Mass Communication — M
Media Studies — M
Music — M,D
Near and Middle Eastern Languages — M,D
Philosophy — M
Political Science — M,D
Psychology—General — M,D
Public Administration — M,D
Rehabilitation Counseling — M
Rhetoric — M,D
Russian — M,D
School Psychology — M,D,O
Sociology — M,D
Spanish — M,D
Theater — M
Translation and Interpretation — M,D
Urban Design — M
Writing — M,D

**KENTUCKY CHRISTIAN UNIVERSITY**
Religion — M
Theology — M

**KENTUCKY STATE UNIVERSITY**
Psychology—General — M
Public Administration — M,D

**KEUKA COLLEGE**
Criminal Justice and Criminology — M

**THE KING'S UNIVERSITY**
Pastoral Ministry and Counseling — M,D,O
Theology — M,D,O

**KINGSWOOD UNIVERSITY**
Pastoral Ministry and Counseling — M
Theology — M

**KNOX COLLEGE**
Theology — M,D

**KNOX THEOLOGICAL SEMINARY**
Classics — M
Pastoral Ministry and Counseling — D
Religion — M
Theology — M

**KUTZTOWN UNIVERSITY OF PENNSYLVANIA**
Clinical Psychology — M
Counseling Psychology — M
English — M
Internet and Interactive Multimedia — M
Marriage and Family Therapy — M
Public Administration — M

**LAGRANGE COLLEGE**
Clinical Psychology — M

**LAGUNA COLLEGE OF ART & DESIGN**
Art/Fine Arts — M

**LAKE FOREST COLLEGE**
American Studies — M
Art/Fine Arts — M
French — M
History — M
Liberal Studies — M
Philosophy — M
Spanish — M
Writing — M

**LAKEHEAD UNIVERSITY**
Clinical Psychology — M,D
Economics — M
English — M
Experimental Psychology — M,D
Gerontology — M,D
History — M
Psychology—General — M,D
Sociology — M
Women's Studies — M,D

**LAKELAND UNIVERSITY**
Theology — M

**LAMAR UNIVERSITY**
Clinical Psychology — M
Counseling Psychology — M
Criminal Justice and Criminology — M
English — M
Family and Consumer Sciences-General — M
History — M
Industrial and Organizational Psychology — M
Music — M
Political Science — M
Psychology—General — M
Public Administration — M
Spanish — M

**LANCASTER BIBLE COLLEGE**
Counseling Psychology — M,D
Marriage and Family Therapy — M,D
Pastoral Ministry and Counseling — M,D,O
Theology — M,D,O

**LANCASTER THEOLOGICAL SEMINARY**
Art History — M,D,O
Ethics — M,D,O
Religion — M,D,O
Theology — M,D,O

**LANDER UNIVERSITY**
Emergency Management — M

**LANGSTON UNIVERSITY**
Rehabilitation Counseling — M

**LA SALLE UNIVERSITY**
American Studies — M,O
Clinical Psychology — M,D
Communication—General — M,O
Corporate and Organizational Communication — M,O
Counseling Psychology — M
Developmental Psychology — M,D
English — M,O
Forensic Sciences — M,O
Gerontology — M,D,O
Health Psychology — M,D
Hispanic Studies — M,O
History — M,O
Latin American Studies — M,O
Marriage and Family Therapy — M
Media Studies — M,O
Pastoral Ministry and Counseling — M
Psychology—General — M,D
Public History — M,O
Translation and Interpretation — M,O
Western European Studies — M,O

**LASELL COLLEGE**
Communication—General — M,O
Corporate and Organizational Communication — M,O
Criminal Justice and Criminology — M,O
Emergency Management — M,O
Health Communication — M,O
Homeland Security — M,O

**LA SIERRA UNIVERSITY**
Communication—General — M
English — M
Pastoral Ministry and Counseling — M
Religion — M
School Psychology — M
Writing — M

**LAURENTIAN UNIVERSITY**
Applied Psychology — M
Applied Social Research — M
Experimental Psychology — M
History — M
Human Development — M
Humanities — M
Psychology—General — M
Sociology — M
Technical Writing — O

**LAWRENCE TECHNOLOGICAL UNIVERSITY**
Architecture — M,O
Communication—General — M,O
Interior Design — M,O
Technical Communication — M,O
Urban Design — M,O

**LEBANESE AMERICAN UNIVERSITY**
International Affairs — M

**LEBANON VALLEY COLLEGE**
Ethics — M

**LEE UNIVERSITY**
Art/Fine Arts — M,O
Child Development — M
Counseling Psychology — M
Economics — M,O
English — M,O
Ethics — M
History — M,O
Marriage and Family Therapy — M
Music — M
Pastoral Ministry and Counseling — M
Religion — M
Spanish — M,O
Theology — M

**LEHIGH UNIVERSITY**
American Studies — M,D,O
Counseling Psychology — M,D,O
Economics — M,D
English — M,D
History — M,D
Interdisciplinary Studies — M,D
International Development — M,D,O
Political Science — M
Psychology—General — M,D
Public History — M,D
School Psychology — D,O
Sociology — M
Sustainable Development — M,O

**LEHMAN COLLEGE OF THE CITY UNIVERSITY OF NEW YORK**
Art/Fine Arts — M
English — M
History — M
Spanish — M

**LE MOYNE COLLEGE**
Arts Administration — M
Urban Studies — M,O

**LENOIR-RHYNE UNIVERSITY**
Addictions/Substance Abuse Counseling — M
Clinical Psychology — M
Counseling Psychology — M
Sustainable Development — M
Theology — M
Writing — M

**LESLEY UNIVERSITY**
Art Therapy — M,D,O
Art/Fine Arts — M,D,O
Clinical Psychology — M,D,O
Conflict Resolution and Mediation/Peace Studies — M,D,O
Counseling Psychology — M,D,O
Health Psychology — M,D,O
Interdisciplinary Studies — M,D,O
International Affairs — M,D,O
Photography — M
Psychology—General — M,D,O
School Psychology — M,D,O
Social Psychology — M,D,O
Sustainable Development — M,D,O
Therapies—Dance, Drama, and Music — M,D,O
Urban and Regional Planning — M,D,O
Women's Studies — M,D,O
Writing — M,D,O

**LETOURNEAU UNIVERSITY**
Counseling Psychology — M
Marriage and Family Therapy — M
Psychology—General — M
School Psychology — M

**LEWIS & CLARK COLLEGE**
Addictions/Substance Abuse Counseling — M
Counseling Psychology — M
Marriage and Family Therapy — M
School Psychology — M,O

**LEWIS UNIVERSITY**
Clinical Psychology — M
Counseling Psychology — M
Criminal Justice and Criminology — M

**LEXINGTON THEOLOGICAL SEMINARY**
Theology — M,D

**LIBERTY UNIVERSITY**
Addictions/Substance Abuse Counseling — M,D,O
Art/Fine Arts — M
Child and Family Studies — M,D,O
Clinical Psychology — M,D,O
Communication—General — M
Counseling Psychology — M,D,O
Criminal Justice and Criminology — M,D,O
Emergency Management — M,D,O
English — M
History — M
International Affairs — M,D,O
Marriage and Family Therapy — M,D,O
Military and Defense Studies — M,D,O
Missions and Missiology — M,D
Music — M,D
Pastoral Ministry and Counseling — M,D,O
Public Administration — M,D,O
Public Policy — M
Religion — M,D,O
Theology — M,D,O

**LIM COLLEGE**
Clothing and Textiles — M
Textile Design — M

**LINCOLN CHRISTIAN SEMINARY**
Pastoral Ministry and Counseling — M,D
Theology — M,D

**LINCOLN CHRISTIAN UNIVERSITY**
Cultural Studies — M
Pastoral Ministry and Counseling — M
Philosophy — M

Religion — M
Theology — M

**LINCOLN UNIVERSITY (MO)**
Criminal Justice and Criminology — M
History — M
Public Administration — M
Public Policy — M
Sociology — M

**LINDENWOOD UNIVERSITY**
Communication—General — M,O
Counseling Psychology — M,D,O
Criminal Justice and Criminology — M,O
Film, Television, and Video
    Production — M
Media Studies — M,O
Public Administration — M
School Psychology — M,D,O
Writing — M

**LINDENWOOD UNIVERSITY–BELLEVILLE**
Communication—General — M
Computer Art and Design — M
Criminal Justice and Criminology — M
Internet and Interactive
    Multimedia — M
Media Studies — M

**LINDSEY WILSON COLLEGE**
Counseling Psychology — M,D
Human Development — M,D
Internet and Interactive
    Multimedia — M

**LIPSCOMB UNIVERSITY**
Applied Behavior Analysis — M,D,O
Clinical Psychology — M,O
Conflict Resolution and
    Mediation/Peace Studies — M,O
Counseling Psychology — M,O
English — M,D,O
Film, Television, and Video
    Production — M
Marriage and Family Therapy — M,O
Pastoral Ministry and Counseling — M,D,O
Psychology—General — M,O
Public Administration — M
Public Policy — M
Sustainable Development — M,O
Theology — M,D,O
Writing — M

**LOCK HAVEN UNIVERSITY OF PENNSYLVANIA**
Clinical Psychology — M
Counseling Psychology — M
Sport Psychology — M

**LOGOS EVANGELICAL SEMINARY**
Theology — M,D,O

**LOMA LINDA UNIVERSITY**
Addictions/Substance Abuse
    Counseling — M,D,O
Applied Social Research — M,D
Child and Family Studies — M,D,O
Clinical Psychology — D
Criminal Justice and Criminology — M,D
Gerontology — M,D
Marriage and Family Therapy — M,D,O
Psychology—General — D
Religion — M

**LONDON METROPOLITAN UNIVERSITY**
Applied Psychology — M,D
Architecture — M,D
Arts Administration — M,D
Child and Family Studies — M,D
Clinical Psychology — M,D
Conflict Resolution and
    Mediation/Peace Studies — M,D
Counseling Psychology — M,D
Criminal Justice and Criminology — M,D
Emergency Management — M,D
Forensic Psychology — M,D
Homeland Security — M,D
Industrial and Organizational
    Psychology — M,D
International Affairs — M,D
Internet and Interactive
    Multimedia — M,D
Military and Defense Studies — M,D
Near and Middle Eastern Languages — M,D
Public Administration — M,D
Public Policy — M,D
Translation and Interpretation — M,D
Urban Design — M,D
Women's Studies — M,D
Writing — M,D

**LONG ISLAND UNIVERSITY–BRENTWOOD CAMPUS**
Clinical Psychology — M,O
Counseling Psychology — M,O

**LONG ISLAND UNIVERSITY–HUDSON**
Addictions/Substance Abuse
    Counseling — M,O
Counseling Psychology — M,O
Marriage and Family Therapy — M,O
Public Administration — M,O
School Psychology — M,O

**LONG ISLAND UNIVERSITY–LIU BROOKLYN**
Applied Behavior Analysis — M
Clinical Psychology — M,D,O
Counseling Psychology — M,O
English — M,D,O
Forensic Sciences — M,D,O
Gerontology — M,O
Marriage and Family Therapy — M
Media Studies — M,D,O

Political Science — M,D,O
Psychology—General — M,D,O
Public Administration — M,O
Sociology — M,D,O
Urban Studies — M,D,O
Writing — M,D,O

**LONG ISLAND UNIVERSITY–LIU POST**
Applied Behavior Analysis — M
Art Therapy — M
Art/Fine Arts — M
Clinical Psychology — M,D,O
Counseling Psychology — M,D,O
Criminal Justice and Criminology — M,O
English — M,O
Genetic Counseling — M,O
Geographic Information Systems — M,O
Gerontology — M,O
History — M,D,O
Interdisciplinary Studies — M,O
Internet and Interactive
    Multimedia — M
Music — M
Political Science — M,O
Psychology—General — M,O
Public Administration — M,O
School Psychology — M,D,O
Sustainable Development — M,O
Theater — M

**LORAS COLLEGE**
Applied Psychology — M
Pastoral Ministry and Counseling — M
Theology — M

**LOUISIANA COLLEGE**
Pastoral Ministry and Counseling — M
Theology — M

**LOUISIANA STATE UNIVERSITY AND AGRICULTURAL & MECHANICAL COLLEGE**
Agricultural Economics and
    Agribusiness — M,D
Anthropology — M,D
Applied Arts and Design—
    General — M
Architecture — M
Art History — M
Art/Fine Arts — M
Clinical Psychology — M,D
Cognitive Sciences — M,D
Communication—General — M,D
Comparative Literature — M,D
Developmental Psychology — M,D
Economics — M,D
English — M,D
Family and Consumer
    Sciences-General — M,D
French — M,D
Geography — M,D
Graphic Design — M
Hispanic Studies — M
History — M,D
Internet and Interactive
    Multimedia — M
Landscape Architecture — M
Liberal Studies — M
Mass Communication — M,D
Media Studies — M,D
Music — M,D
Philosophy — M
Photography — M
Political Science — M,D
Psychology—General — M,D
Public Administration — M,D
School Psychology — M,D
Sociology — M,D
Theater — M,D
Writing — M,D

**LOUISIANA STATE UNIVERSITY HEALTH SCIENCES CENTER**
Rehabilitation Counseling — M

**LOUISIANA STATE UNIVERSITY IN SHREVEPORT**
Liberal Studies — M
School Psychology — O

**LOUISIANA TECH UNIVERSITY**
Applied Arts and Design—
    General — M
Architecture — M
Art/Fine Arts — M
Counseling Psychology — M,D
Economics — M,D
English — M,O
Family and Consumer
    Sciences-General — M
Graphic Design — M
History — M
Industrial and Organizational
    Psychology — M,D
Photography — M
Psychology—General — M,D
Technical Writing — M,O
Theater — M

**LOUISVILLE PRESBYTERIAN THEOLOGICAL SEMINARY**
Religion — M,D
Theology — M,D

**LOURDES UNIVERSITY**
Theology — M

**LOYOLA MARYMOUNT UNIVERSITY**
Counseling Psychology — M
English — M
Film, Television, and Video
    Production — M
Marriage and Family Therapy — M
Pastoral Ministry and Counseling — M

Philosophy — M
School Psychology — M
Theology — M
Writing — M

**LOYOLA UNIVERSITY CHICAGO**
Clinical Psychology — M,D
Communication—General — M
Corporate and Organizational
    Communication — M
Counseling Psychology — D
Criminal Justice and Criminology — M,D
Developmental Psychology — M,D
Economics — M
English — M,D
Ethics — M
History — M,D
Humanities — M
Pastoral Ministry and Counseling — M,O
Philosophy — M,D
Political Science — M,D
Psychology—General — M,D
Public History — M,D
Public Policy — M
School Psychology — D,O
Social Psychology — M,D
Sociology — M,D
Spanish — M
Theology — M,D,O
Urban Studies — M

**LOYOLA UNIVERSITY MARYLAND**
Clinical Psychology — M,D,O
Counseling Psychology — M,O
Liberal Studies — M
Media Studies — M
Psychology—General — M,D,O
Theology — M

**LOYOLA UNIVERSITY NEW ORLEANS**
Clinical Psychology — M
Criminal Justice and Criminology — M
Music — M
Theology — M,O
Therapies—Dance, Drama, and
    Music — M

**LUBBOCK CHRISTIAN UNIVERSITY**
Theology — M

**LUTHERAN SCHOOL OF THEOLOGY AT CHICAGO**
Pastoral Ministry and Counseling — M,D
Theology — M,D

**LUTHERAN THEOLOGICAL SEMINARY AT GETTYSBURG**
Pastoral Ministry and Counseling — M,D
Religion — M,D
Theology — M,D

**THE LUTHERAN THEOLOGICAL SEMINARY AT PHILADELPHIA**
Pastoral Ministry and Counseling — M,D,O
Religion — M,D,O
Theology — M,D,O

**LUTHERAN THEOLOGICAL SEMINARY SASKATOON**
Ethics — M,D
Pastoral Ministry and Counseling — M,D
Religion — M,D
Theology — M,D

**LUTHER RICE COLLEGE & SEMINARY**
Pastoral Ministry and Counseling — M,D
Religion — M,D
Theology — M,D

**LUTHER SEMINARY**
Missions and Missiology — M,D
Pastoral Ministry and Counseling — M,D
Theology — M,D

**LYNCHBURG COLLEGE**
Clinical Psychology — M
Counseling Psychology — M
Music — M
School Psychology — M

**LYNN UNIVERSITY**
Applied Psychology — M
Communication—General — M,O
Computer Art and Design — M,O
Counseling Psychology — M
Criminal Justice and Criminology — M
Internet and Interactive
    Multimedia — M,O
Mass Communication — M,O
Media Studies — M,O
Music — M,O

**MACHZIKEI HADATH RABBINICAL COLLEGE**
Theology — O

**MADONNA UNIVERSITY**
Clinical Psychology — M
Criminal Justice and Criminology — M
Liberal Studies — M
Pastoral Ministry and Counseling — M
Psychology—General — M
Theology — M

**MAHARISHI UNIVERSITY OF MANAGEMENT**
Asian Studies — M,D
Writing — M

**MAINE COLLEGE OF ART**
Art/Fine Arts — M

**MALONE UNIVERSITY**
Theology — M

**MANHATTAN COLLEGE**
English — M,O

**MANHATTAN SCHOOL OF MUSIC**
Music — M,D,O

**MANHATTANVILLE COLLEGE**
Corporate and Organizational
    Communication — M
Writing — M

**MANSFIELD UNIVERSITY OF PENNSYLVANIA**
Music — M
Psychology—General — M

**MAPLE SPRINGS BAPTIST BIBLE COLLEGE AND SEMINARY**
Pastoral Ministry and Counseling — M,D,O
Theology — M,D,O

**MARANATHA BAPTIST UNIVERSITY**
Cultural Studies — M
Pastoral Ministry and Counseling — M
Religion — M
Theology — M

**MARIAN UNIVERSITY (WI)**
Thanatology — M

**MARIETTA COLLEGE**
Psychology—General — M

**MARIST COLLEGE**
Communication—General — M
Corporate and Organizational
    Communication — M
Counseling Psychology — M,O
Museum Studies — M
Psychology—General — M,O
Public Administration — M
School Psychology — M,O

**MARLBORO COLLEGE**
Internet and Interactive
    Multimedia — M,O

**MARQUETTE UNIVERSITY**
Clinical Psychology — M,D
Communication—General — M,O
Counseling Psychology — M,D
Economics — M,O
English — M,D
Ethics — M,D
Health Communication — M,O
History — M,D
Interdisciplinary Studies — D
International Affairs — M,D
Journalism — M,O
Mass Communication — M,O
Philosophy — M,D
Political Science — M
Psychology—General — D
Social Psychology — M
Spanish — M
Speech and Interpersonal
    Communication — M,O
Theology — M,D

**MARSHALL UNIVERSITY**
Classics — M,O
Clinical Psychology — M,D,O
Communication—General — M
Criminal Justice and Criminology — M
English — M,O
Forensic Sciences — M,O
Geography — M,O
History — M,O
Humanities — M,O
Journalism — M
Music — M
Political Science — M
Psychology—General — M,D,O
Public Administration — M
School Psychology — O
Sociology — M

**MARTIN UNIVERSITY**
Pastoral Ministry and Counseling — M
Psychology—General — M
Social Psychology — M

**MARY BALDWIN UNIVERSITY**
English — M
Theater — M

**MARYGROVE COLLEGE**
English — M
Translation and Interpretation — O

**MARYLAND INSTITUTE COLLEGE OF ART**
Applied Arts and Design—
    General — M
Art/Fine Arts — M,O
Film, Television, and Video
    Production — M
Graphic Design — M
Illustration — M
Museum Studies — M
Photography — M

**MARYLHURST UNIVERSITY**
Art Therapy — M,O
Interdisciplinary Studies — M
Theology — M

**MARYMOUNT CALIFORNIA UNIVERSITY**
International Development — M
Social Psychology — M

**MARYMOUNT UNIVERSITY**
Clinical Psychology — M
Counseling Psychology — M
English — M,O
Forensic Psychology — M
Interior Design — M
Pastoral Ministry and Counseling — M

*M—masters degree; D—doctorate; O—other advanced degree; *—Close-Up and/or Display*

## MARYVILLE UNIVERSITY OF SAINT LOUIS
| | |
|---|---|
| Addictions/Substance Abuse Counseling | M |
| Marriage and Family Therapy | M |
| Rehabilitation Counseling | M |
| Therapies—Dance, Drama, and Music | M |

## MARYWOOD UNIVERSITY
| | |
|---|---|
| Architecture | M |
| Art Therapy | M,O |
| Art/Fine Arts | M |
| Clinical Psychology | M,D |
| Communication—General | M |
| Counseling Psychology | M |
| Criminal Justice and Criminology | M |
| Gerontology | M |
| Graphic Design | M |
| Human Development | D |
| Illustration | M |
| Interdisciplinary Studies | D |
| Interior Design | M |
| Photography | M |
| Psychology—General | M |
| Public Administration | M |

## MASSACHUSETTS COLLEGE OF ART AND DESIGN
| | |
|---|---|
| Applied Arts and Design— General | M,O |
| Architecture | M |
| Art/Fine Arts | M,O |
| Film, Television, and Video Production | M,O |
| Interdisciplinary Studies | M,O |
| Media Studies | M,O |
| Photography | M,O |
| Textile Design | M,O |

## MASSACHUSETTS INSTITUTE OF TECHNOLOGY
| | |
|---|---|
| Archaeology | M,D,O |
| Architectural History | M,D |
| Architecture | M,D |
| Art History | M,D |
| Cognitive Sciences | D |
| Economics | M,D |
| History of Science and Technology | D |
| Linguistics | D |
| Media Studies | M,D |
| Philosophy | D |
| Political Science | M,D |
| Social Sciences | D |
| Technical Writing | M |
| Urban and Regional Planning | M,D |
| Urban Studies | M,D |
| Writing | M |

## MASSACHUSETTS MARITIME ACADEMY
| | |
|---|---|
| Emergency Management | M |

## THE MASTER'S UNIVERSITY
| | |
|---|---|
| Pastoral Ministry and Counseling | M,D |
| Theology | M,D |

## MCCORMICK THEOLOGICAL SEMINARY
| | |
|---|---|
| Pastoral Ministry and Counseling | M,D,O |
| Theology | M,D,O |

## MCDANIEL COLLEGE
| | |
|---|---|
| Gerontology | M,O |
| Liberal Studies | M,O |
| Writing | M,O |

## MCGILL UNIVERSITY
| | |
|---|---|
| Agricultural Economics and Agribusiness | M |
| Anthropology | M,D |
| Architecture | M,D,O |
| Art History | M,D |
| Asian Studies | M,D |
| Clinical Psychology | M,D |
| Communication—General | M |
| Counseling Psychology | M,D,O |
| Developmental Psychology | M,D,O |
| Economics | M,D |
| English | M,D |
| Experimental Psychology | M,D |
| Forensic Sciences | M,D,O |
| French | M,D |
| Genetic Counseling | M |
| Geography | M,D |
| German | M,D |
| Hispanic Studies | M,D |
| History of Medicine | M |
| History | M,D |
| International Development | M,D,O |
| Italian | M,D |
| Jewish Studies | M |
| Linguistics | M,D |
| Music | M,D |
| Near and Middle Eastern Studies | M,D,O |
| Philosophy | M,D |
| Political Science | M,D |
| Psychology—General | M,D |
| Religion | M,D |
| Russian | M |
| School Psychology | M,D,O |
| Sociology | M,D |
| Theology | M,D |
| Urban and Regional Planning | M,D |

## MCKENDREE UNIVERSITY
| | |
|---|---|
| Clinical Psychology | M |
| Counseling Psychology | M |

## MCMASTER UNIVERSITY
| | |
|---|---|
| Anthropology | M,D |
| Classics | M,D |
| Cultural Studies | M,D |
| Economics | M,D |
| English | M,D |
| French | M |
| Geography | M,D |
| History | M,D |
| Industrial and Labor Relations | M |

| | |
|---|---|
| International Affairs | M,D |
| Pastoral Ministry and Counseling | M,D,O |
| Philosophy | M,D |
| Political Science | M,D |
| Psychology—General | M,D |
| Public Administration | M,D |
| Public Affairs | M,D |
| Public Policy | M,D |
| Religion | M,D |
| Sociology | M,D |
| Theology | M,D |

## MCNALLY SMITH COLLEGE OF MUSIC
| | |
|---|---|
| Music | M |

## MCNEESE STATE UNIVERSITY
| | |
|---|---|
| Addictions/Substance Abuse Counseling | M |
| Applied Behavior Analysis | M |
| Counseling Psychology | M |
| Criminal Justice and Criminology | M |
| English | M |
| Experimental Psychology | M |
| Psychology—General | M |
| School Psychology | M |
| Writing | M |

## MEADVILLE LOMBARD THEOLOGICAL SCHOOL
| | |
|---|---|
| Pastoral Ministry and Counseling | M,D |
| Theology | M,D |

## MEDAILLE COLLEGE
| | |
|---|---|
| Clinical Psychology | M,D |
| Counseling Psychology | M,D |
| Marriage and Family Therapy | M,D |
| Psychology—General | M,D |

## MEMORIAL UNIVERSITY OF NEWFOUNDLAND
| | |
|---|---|
| Anthropology | M,D |
| Archaeology | M,D |
| Classics | M |
| Clinical Psychology | M,D |
| Cultural Anthropology | M,D |
| Economics | M |
| English | M,D |
| Experimental Psychology | M,D |
| Folklore | M,D |
| French | M |
| Gender Studies | M,D |
| Geography | M,D |
| German | M |
| History | M |
| Humanities | M |
| Industrial and Labor Relations | M |
| Linguistics | M,D |
| Music | M,D |
| Philosophy | M,D |
| Political Science | M |
| Psychology—General | M,D |
| Religion | M |
| Sociology | M,D |

## MEMPHIS COLLEGE OF ART
| | |
|---|---|
| Applied Arts and Design— General | M |
| Art/Fine Arts | M |
| Illustration | M |
| Photography | M |

## MEMPHIS THEOLOGICAL SEMINARY
| | |
|---|---|
| Theology | M,D |

## MERCER UNIVERSITY
| | |
|---|---|
| Clinical Psychology | M,D |
| Criminal Justice and Criminology | M,D |
| Gerontology | M,D |
| Music | M |
| Pastoral Ministry and Counseling | M,D |
| Rehabilitation Counseling | M,D |
| School Psychology | M,D |
| Theology | M,D |

## MERCY COLLEGE
| | |
|---|---|
| Counseling Psychology | M,O |
| English | M |
| Marriage and Family Therapy | M,O |
| Psychology—General | M |
| School Psychology | M |

## MERCYHURST UNIVERSITY
| | |
|---|---|
| Anthropology | M |
| Applied Behavior Analysis | M |
| Archaeology | M |
| Biological Anthropology | M |
| Criminal Justice and Criminology | M,O |
| Forensic Sciences | M |

## MERRIMACK COLLEGE
| | |
|---|---|
| Clinical Psychology | M |
| Criminal Justice and Criminology | M,O |
| Public Affairs | M |
| School Psychology | M,O |

## MESIVTA OF EASTERN PARKWAY–YESHIVA ZICHRON MEILECH
| | |
|---|---|
| Theology | |

## MESIVTA TORAH VODAATH RABBINICAL SEMINARY
| | |
|---|---|
| Theology | |

## MESIVTHA TIFERETH JERUSALEM OF AMERICA
| | |
|---|---|
| Theology | |

## MESSIAH COLLEGE
| | |
|---|---|
| Clinical Psychology | M,O |
| Counseling Psychology | M,O |
| Marriage and Family Therapy | M,O |
| Music | M |

## METHODIST THEOLOGICAL SCHOOL IN OHIO
| | |
|---|---|
| Theology | M,D |

## METHODIST UNIVERSITY
| | |
|---|---|
| Criminal Justice and Criminology | M |

## METROPOLITAN COLLEGE OF NEW YORK
| | |
|---|---|
| Emergency Management | M |
| Media Studies | M |
| Public Administration | M |
| Public Affairs | M |

## METROPOLITAN STATE UNIVERSITY
| | |
|---|---|
| Criminal Justice and Criminology | M |
| Liberal Studies | M |
| Psychology—General | M,D |
| Public Administration | M,D,O |
| Technical Writing | M |

## MIAMI INTERNATIONAL UNIVERSITY OF ART & DESIGN
| | |
|---|---|
| Applied Arts and Design— General | M |
| Film, Television, and Video Production | M |

## MIAMI UNIVERSITY
| | |
|---|---|
| Architecture | M |
| Art/Fine Arts | M |
| Child and Family Studies | M |
| Demography and Population Studies | M,D |
| Economics | M |
| English | M,D |
| French | M |
| Geography | M |
| Gerontology | M |
| History | M |
| Interior Design | M |
| Music | M |
| Philosophy | M |
| Political Science | M |
| Psychology—General | M,D |
| Theater | M |

## MICHIGAN SCHOOL OF PROFESSIONAL PSYCHOLOGY
| | |
|---|---|
| Clinical Psychology | M,D |
| Psychology—General | M,D |
| Transpersonal and Humanistic Psychology | M,D |

## MICHIGAN STATE UNIVERSITY
| | |
|---|---|
| African Studies | M,D |
| African-American Studies | M,D |
| Agricultural Economics and Agribusiness | M,D |
| American Studies | M,D |
| Anthropology | M,D |
| Art/Fine Arts | M |
| Child and Family Studies | M,D |
| Child Development | M,D |
| Communication—General | M |
| Computer Art and Design | M |
| Criminal Justice and Criminology | M,D |
| Economics | M,D |
| English | M,D |
| Environmental Design | M,D |
| Forensic Sciences | M,D |
| French | M,D |
| Geography | M,D |
| German | M,D |
| Health Communication | M |
| Hispanic and Latin American Languages | M,D |
| Hispanic Studies | M,D |
| History | M,D |
| Industrial and Labor Relations | M,D |
| Interior Design | M,D |
| Journalism | M |
| Latin American Studies | D |
| Linguistics | M,D |
| Marriage and Family Therapy | M,D |
| Media Studies | M,D |
| Music | M,D |
| Philosophy | M,D |
| Political Science | M,D |
| Portuguese | M,D |
| Psychology—General | M,D |
| Rehabilitation Counseling | M,D,O |
| Rhetoric | M,D |
| Romance Languages | M,D |
| School Psychology | M,D,O |
| Sociology | M,D |
| Spanish | M,D |
| Theater | M |
| Therapies—Dance, Drama, and Music | M,D |
| Urban and Regional Planning | M,D |
| Writing | M,D |

## MICHIGAN TECHNOLOGICAL UNIVERSITY
| | |
|---|---|
| Archaeology | M,D |
| Cognitive Sciences | M,D,O |
| Cultural Studies | M,D |
| Geographic Information Systems | M |
| Interdisciplinary Studies | M,D,O |
| Mineral Economics | M |
| Rhetoric | M,D |

## MID-AMERICA BAPTIST THEOLOGICAL SEMINARY
| | |
|---|---|
| Theology | M,D |

## MID-AMERICA BAPTIST THEOLOGICAL SEMINARY NORTHEAST BRANCH
| | |
|---|---|
| Theology | M |

## MID-AMERICA CHRISTIAN UNIVERSITY
| | |
|---|---|
| Counseling Psychology | M |
| Marriage and Family Therapy | M |
| Pastoral Ministry and Counseling | M |
| Public Administration | M |

## MIDAMERICA NAZARENE UNIVERSITY
| | |
|---|---|
| Clinical Psychology | M |
| Marriage and Family Therapy | M |
| School Psychology | M |

## MID-AMERICA REFORMED SEMINARY
| | |
|---|---|
| Theology | M |

## MIDDLEBURY COLLEGE
| | |
|---|---|
| Chinese | M |
| English | M,D |
| French | M,D |
| German | M,D |
| Italian | M,D |
| Near and Middle Eastern Languages | M |
| Russian | M,D |
| Spanish | M,D |

## MIDDLEBURY INSTITUTE OF INTERNATIONAL STUDIES AT MONTEREY
| | |
|---|---|
| Conflict Resolution and Mediation/Peace Studies | M |
| International Affairs | M |
| International Development | M |
| International Trade Policy | M |
| Public Administration | M |
| Translation and Interpretation | M |

## MIDDLE GEORGIA STATE UNIVERSITY
| | |
|---|---|
| Forensic Sciences | M |

## MIDDLE TENNESSEE STATE UNIVERSITY
| | |
|---|---|
| Clinical Psychology | M,O |
| Counseling Psychology | M |
| Criminal Justice and Criminology | M |
| Economics | M,D |
| English | M,D |
| Experimental Psychology | M |
| French | M |
| Gender Studies | O |
| German | M |
| Gerontology | O |
| History | M |
| Industrial and Organizational Psychology | M,O |
| International Affairs | M |
| Mass Communication | M |
| Music | M |
| Political Science | M |
| Psychology—General | M,O |
| Public History | D |
| School Psychology | M,O |
| Sociology | M |
| Spanish | M |
| Women's Studies | O |

## MIDWESTERN BAPTIST THEOLOGICAL SEMINARY
| | |
|---|---|
| Music | M,D,O |
| Pastoral Ministry and Counseling | M,D,O |
| Theology | M,D,O |

## MIDWESTERN STATE UNIVERSITY
| | |
|---|---|
| Clinical Psychology | M |
| Counseling Psychology | M |
| Criminal Justice and Criminology | M,O |
| English | M,D |
| History | M |
| Philosophy | M,D |
| Political Science | M |

## MIDWESTERN UNIVERSITY, DOWNERS GROVE CAMPUS
| | |
|---|---|
| Clinical Psychology | M,D |

## MIDWESTERN UNIVERSITY, GLENDALE CAMPUS
| | |
|---|---|
| Clinical Psychology | D |

## MILLERSVILLE UNIVERSITY OF PENNSYLVANIA
| | |
|---|---|
| Applied Arts and Design— General | M |
| Art/Fine Arts | M |
| Clinical Psychology | M |
| Emergency Management | M |
| English | M,O |
| French | M |
| Geographic Information Systems | M |
| German | M |
| History | M |
| Psychology—General | M |
| School Psychology | M |
| Spanish | M |
| Writing | M,O |

## MILLIGAN COLLEGE
| | |
|---|---|
| Clinical Psychology | M,O |
| Missions and Missiology | M,D,O |
| Pastoral Ministry and Counseling | M,D,O |
| Religion | M,D,O |
| Theology | M,D,O |

## MILLS COLLEGE
| | |
|---|---|
| Applied Economics | M |
| Art/Fine Arts | M |
| Dance | M |
| English | M,O |
| Illustration | M,O |
| Interdisciplinary Studies | M,O |
| Music | M |
| Photography | M |
| Public Policy | M |
| Translation and Interpretation | M,O |
| Writing | M,O |

## MINNEAPOLIS COLLEGE OF ART AND DESIGN
| | |
|---|---|
| Applied Arts and Design— General | M |
| Art/Fine Arts | M,O |
| Computer Art and Design | O |
| Film, Television, and Video Production | |
| Graphic Design | M,O |
| Illustration | M |
| Photography | M |
| Sustainable Development | O |

## MINNESOTA STATE UNIVERSITY MANKATO
| | |
|---|---|
| Anthropology | M |
| Art/Fine Arts | M |

| | |
|---|---|
| Clinical Psychology | M,D |
| Communication—General | M,O |
| Corporate and Organizational Communication | M,O |
| Counseling Psychology | M,D |
| Criminal Justice and Criminology | M |
| English | M,O |
| Ethnic Studies | M |
| French | M |
| Gender Studies | M |
| Geography | M |
| Gerontology | M |
| History | M |
| Industrial and Organizational Psychology | M,D |
| Interdisciplinary Studies | M |
| Music | M,O |
| Psychology—General | M,D |
| Public Administration | M |
| Rehabilitation Counseling | M |
| School Psychology | M,D |
| Sociology | M |
| Spanish | M |
| Technical Communication | M |
| Theater | M |
| Urban and Regional Planning | M,O |
| Urban Studies | M,O |
| Women's Studies | M |
| Writing | M,O |

**MINNESOTA STATE UNIVERSITY MOORHEAD**

| | |
|---|---|
| School Psychology | M,O |

**MINOT STATE UNIVERSITY**

| | |
|---|---|
| School Psychology | O |

**MIRRER YESHIVA**

| | |
|---|---|
| Theology | M |

**MISSISSIPPI COLLEGE**

| | |
|---|---|
| Art/Fine Arts | M |
| Communication—General | M |
| Corporate and Organizational Communication | M |
| Counseling Psychology | M |
| Criminal Justice and Criminology | M,O |
| English | M |
| History | M,O |
| Liberal Studies | M |
| Marriage and Family Therapy | M,O |
| Music | M |
| Political Science | M,O |
| Social Sciences | M,O |

**MISSISSIPPI STATE UNIVERSITY**

| | |
|---|---|
| Agricultural Economics and Agribusiness | M |
| American Studies | M,D |
| Anthropology | M |
| Child and Family Studies | M,D |
| Clinical Psychology | M,D,O |
| Cognitive Sciences | M,D |
| Economics | M,D |
| English | M |
| Geography | M |
| History | M,D |
| Human Development | M,D |
| Internet and Interactive Multimedia | M,D,O |
| Landscape Architecture | M |
| Political Science | M,D |
| Psychology—General | M,D |
| Public Administration | M,D |
| Public Policy | M,D |
| Rehabilitation Counseling | M,D,O |
| School Psychology | M,D,O |
| Sociology | M,D |
| Sustainable Development | M,D |
| Western European Studies | M,D |

**MISSISSIPPI VALLEY STATE UNIVERSITY**

| | |
|---|---|
| Criminal Justice and Criminology | M |

**MISSOURI BAPTIST UNIVERSITY**

| | |
|---|---|
| Pastoral Ministry and Counseling | M,O |

**MISSOURI SOUTHERN STATE UNIVERSITY**

| | |
|---|---|
| Criminal Justice and Criminology | M |

**MISSOURI STATE UNIVERSITY**

| | |
|---|---|
| Applied Behavior Analysis | M,O |
| Art/Fine Arts | M |
| Child and Family Studies | M |
| Clinical Psychology | M,O |
| Communication—General | M,O |
| Counseling Psychology | M |
| Criminal Justice and Criminology | M,O |
| English | M,O |
| Experimental Psychology | M,O |
| Film, Television, and Video Production | M,O |
| Geography | M |
| History | M,O |
| Homeland Security | M,O |
| Industrial and Organizational Psychology | M,O |
| International Affairs | M |
| Military and Defense Studies | M |
| Music | M |
| Political Science | M,O |
| Psychology—General | M,O |
| Public Administration | M,O |
| Religion | M,O |
| Theater | M |
| Urban and Regional Planning | M |
| Writing | M |

**MISSOURI VALLEY COLLEGE**

| | |
|---|---|
| Social Psychology | M |

**MISSOURI WESTERN STATE UNIVERSITY**

| | |
|---|---|
| Forensic Sciences | M,O |
| Media Studies | M |
| Rhetoric | M,O |
| Technical Communication | M,O |
| Writing | M,O |

**MOLLOY COLLEGE**

| | |
|---|---|
| Clinical Psychology | M |
| Criminal Justice and Criminology | M,O |
| English | M,O |
| Spanish | M,O |
| Therapies—Dance, Drama, and Music | M |

**MONMOUTH UNIVERSITY**

| | |
|---|---|
| Addictions/Substance Abuse Counseling | M,O |
| American Studies | M |
| Anthropology | M |
| Applied Behavior Analysis | M,O |
| Communication—General | M,O |
| Corporate and Organizational Communication | M,O |
| Counseling Psychology | M,O |
| Criminal Justice and Criminology | M,O |
| English | M |
| History | M |
| Homeland Security | M,O |
| Media Studies | M,O |
| Psychology—General | M,O |
| Public Policy | M |
| Rhetoric | M |
| School Psychology | M,O |
| Western European Studies | M |
| Writing | M |

**MONROE COLLEGE**

| | |
|---|---|
| Criminal Justice and Criminology | M |

**MONTANA STATE UNIVERSITY**

| | |
|---|---|
| American Indian/Native American Studies | M |
| Architecture | M |
| Art History | M |
| Art/Fine Arts | M |
| English | M |
| Film, Television, and Video Production | M |
| History | M,D |
| Human Development | M |
| Psychology—General | M |
| Public Administration | M |
| School Psychology | M,D,O |

**MONTANA STATE UNIVERSITY BILLINGS**

| | |
|---|---|
| Applied Behavior Analysis | M |
| Communication—General | M |
| Counseling Psychology | M |
| Interdisciplinary Studies | M |
| Psychology—General | M |
| Rehabilitation Counseling | M |

**MONTANA TECH OF THE UNIVERSITY OF MONTANA**

| | |
|---|---|
| Interdisciplinary Studies | M |
| Technical Communication | M |

**MONTCLAIR STATE UNIVERSITY**

| | |
|---|---|
| Addictions/Substance Abuse Counseling | O |
| Art/Fine Arts | M |
| Arts Administration | M |
| Child and Family Studies | M,D,O |
| Child Development | M,O |
| Clinical Psychology | M |
| Conflict Resolution and Mediation/Peace Studies | M,O |
| Corporate and Organizational Communication | M |
| Disability Studies | M,O |
| English | M |
| Forensic Psychology | O |
| French | M |
| Geographic Information Systems | O |
| Industrial and Organizational Psychology | M |
| Linguistics | M,O |
| Music | M,O |
| Political Science | M,O |
| Psychology—General | M |
| Social Sciences | M |
| Spanish | M |
| Sustainable Development | M |
| Theater | M |
| Therapies—Dance, Drama, and Music | M,O |
| Translation and Interpretation | O |
| Writing | O |

**MOODY BIBLE INSTITUTE**

| | |
|---|---|
| Pastoral Ministry and Counseling | M,O |
| Theology | M,O |
| Urban Studies | M,O |

**MOODY THEOLOGICAL SEMINARY–MICHIGAN**

| | |
|---|---|
| Counseling Psychology | M,O |
| Religion | M,O |
| Theology | M,O |

**MOORE COLLEGE OF ART & DESIGN**

| | |
|---|---|
| Art/Fine Arts | M |
| Arts Administration | M |
| Communication—General | M |
| Interior Design | M |

**MORAVIAN THEOLOGICAL SEMINARY**

| | |
|---|---|
| Pastoral Ministry and Counseling | M |
| Theology | M,O |

**MOREHEAD STATE UNIVERSITY**

| | |
|---|---|
| Art/Fine Arts | M |

| | |
|---|---|
| Clinical Psychology | M |
| Communication—General | M |
| Counseling Psychology | M |
| Criminal Justice and Criminology | M |
| English | M |
| Experimental Psychology | M |
| Gerontology | M |
| Graphic Design | M |
| Music | M |
| Psychology—General | M |
| Public Administration | M |
| Public Policy | M |
| Sociology | M |

**MORGAN STATE UNIVERSITY**

| | |
|---|---|
| African-American Studies | M,D |
| Architecture | M |
| Economics | M |
| English | M,D |
| Historic Preservation | M,D |
| History | M |
| International Affairs | M |
| Landscape Architecture | M |
| Museum Studies | M,D |
| Music | M |
| Psychology—General | M,D |
| Sociology | M |
| Urban and Regional Planning | M |

**MOUNT ALOYSIUS COLLEGE**

| | |
|---|---|
| Psychology—General | M |
| Social Psychology | M |

**MOUNT ANGEL SEMINARY**

| | |
|---|---|
| Theology | M |

**MOUNT MARTY COLLEGE**

| | |
|---|---|
| Pastoral Ministry and Counseling | M |

**MOUNT MARY UNIVERSITY**

| | |
|---|---|
| Art Therapy | M,D |
| Clinical Psychology | M,O |
| Counseling Psychology | M,O |
| English | M |
| Internet and Interactive Multimedia | M |
| Rehabilitation Counseling | M |
| Writing | M |

**MOUNT MERCY UNIVERSITY**

| | |
|---|---|
| Criminal Justice and Criminology | M |
| Marriage and Family Therapy | M |

**MOUNT ST. JOSEPH UNIVERSITY**

| | |
|---|---|
| Pastoral Ministry and Counseling | M,O |
| Religion | M,O |
| Theology | M,O |

**MOUNT SAINT MARY COLLEGE**

| | |
|---|---|
| Child Development | M,O |

**MOUNT SAINT MARY'S UNIVERSITY (CA)**

| | |
|---|---|
| Counseling Psychology | M,D,O |
| English | M,D,O |
| Film, Television, and Video Production | M,D,O |
| Humanities | M,D,O |
| Religion | M,D,O |
| Writing | M,D,O |

**MOUNT ST. MARY'S UNIVERSITY (MD)**

| | |
|---|---|
| Philosophy | M |
| Theology | M |

**MOUNT SAINT VINCENT UNIVERSITY**

| | |
|---|---|
| Child and Family Studies | M |
| Gerontology | M |
| School Psychology | M |
| Women's Studies | M |

**MOUNT VERNON NAZARENE UNIVERSITY**

| | |
|---|---|
| Theology | M |

**MULTNOMAH UNIVERSITY**

| | |
|---|---|
| Theology | M,D |

**MURRAY STATE UNIVERSITY**

| | |
|---|---|
| Clinical Psychology | M |
| Corporate and Organizational Communication | M |
| Economics | M |
| English | M |
| History | M |
| Mass Communication | M |
| Music | M |
| Psychology—General | M |
| Public Affairs | M |
| Writing | M |

**NAROPA UNIVERSITY**

| | |
|---|---|
| Art Therapy | M |
| Counseling Psychology | M |
| Psychoanalysis and Psychotherapy | M |
| Religion | M |
| Theater | M |
| Theology | M |
| Therapies—Dance, Drama, and Music | M |
| Writing | M |

**NASHOTAH HOUSE THEOLOGICAL SEMINARY**

| | |
|---|---|
| Pastoral Ministry and Counseling | M,D,O |
| Religion | M,D,O |
| Theology | M,D,O |

**NATIONAL DEFENSE UNIVERSITY**

| | |
|---|---|
| Homeland Security | M |
| Military and Defense Studies | M |
| National Security | M |

**THE NATIONAL GRADUATE SCHOOL OF QUALITY MANAGEMENT**

| | |
|---|---|
| Homeland Security | M,D |

**NATIONAL INTELLIGENCE UNIVERSITY**

| | |
|---|---|
| Military and Defense Studies | M |

**NATIONAL LOUIS UNIVERSITY**

| | |
|---|---|
| Human Development | M,D,O |
| Psychology—General | M,D,O |
| Public Policy | M,D,O |
| School Psychology | M,D,O |
| Writing | M,D,O |

**NATIONAL UNIVERSITY**

| | |
|---|---|
| Clinical Psychology | M,O |
| Counseling Psychology | M,O |
| Criminal Justice and Criminology | M |
| Film, Television, and Video Production | M |
| Internet and Interactive Multimedia | M |
| Journalism | M |
| Public Administration | M |
| Writing | M,O |

**NAVAJO TECHNICAL UNIVERSITY**

| | |
|---|---|
| American Indian/Native American Studies | M |

**NAVAL POSTGRADUATE SCHOOL**

| | |
|---|---|
| Conflict Resolution and Mediation/Peace Studies | M,D |
| Geographic Information Systems | M,D,O |
| Homeland Security | M,D |
| Military and Defense Studies | M,D |
| National Security | M,D,O |

**NAVAL WAR COLLEGE**

| | |
|---|---|
| National Security | M |

**NAZARENE THEOLOGICAL SEMINARY**

| | |
|---|---|
| Cultural Studies | M,D |
| Theology | M,D |

**NAZARETH COLLEGE OF ROCHESTER**

| | |
|---|---|
| Art Therapy | M |
| Music | M |
| Therapies—Dance, Drama, and Music | M |

**NEBRASKA WESLEYAN UNIVERSITY**

| | |
|---|---|
| Forensic Sciences | M |
| History | M |

**NER ISRAEL RABBINICAL COLLEGE**

| | |
|---|---|
| Theology | M,D,O |

**NER ISRAEL YESHIVA COLLEGE OF TORONTO**

| | |
|---|---|
| Theology | M |

**NEUMANN UNIVERSITY**

| | |
|---|---|
| Clinical Psychology | M,D,O |
| Pastoral Ministry and Counseling | M,D,O |

**NEW BRUNSWICK THEOLOGICAL SEMINARY**

| | |
|---|---|
| Pastoral Ministry and Counseling | M,D |
| Theology | M,D |

**NEW CHARTER UNIVERSITY**

| | |
|---|---|
| Criminal Justice and Criminology | M |
| Public Administration | M |

**NEW ENGLAND COLLEGE**

| | |
|---|---|
| Counseling Psychology | M |
| International Affairs | M |
| Public Policy | M |
| Writing | M |

**NEW ENGLAND COLLEGE OF BUSINESS AND FINANCE**

| | |
|---|---|
| Ethics | M |

**NEW ENGLAND CONSERVATORY OF MUSIC**

| | |
|---|---|
| Music | M,D,O |

**NEW HAMPSHIRE INSTITUTE OF ART**

| | |
|---|---|
| Art/Fine Arts | M |
| Photography | M |
| Writing | M |

**NEW JERSEY CITY UNIVERSITY**

| | |
|---|---|
| Art/Fine Arts | M |
| Criminal Justice and Criminology | M,D,O |
| Music | M |
| National Security | M,D,O |
| Urban Studies | M |

**NEW JERSEY INSTITUTE OF TECHNOLOGY**

| | |
|---|---|
| Architecture | M,D |
| Emergency Management | M,D,O |
| History | M,D,O |
| Sustainable Development | M,D,O |
| Technical Communication | M,D,O |
| Urban Studies | M,D |

**NEWMAN THEOLOGICAL COLLEGE**

| | |
|---|---|
| Theology | M |

**NEWMAN UNIVERSITY**

| | |
|---|---|
| Theology | M |

**NEW MEXICO HIGHLANDS UNIVERSITY**

| | |
|---|---|
| American Studies | M |
| Anthropology | M |
| Clinical Psychology | M |
| Computer Art and Design | M |
| Counseling Psychology | M |
| English | M |
| History | M |
| Internet and Interactive Multimedia | M |
| Media Studies | M |
| Political Science | M |
| Psychology—General | M |
| Public Affairs | M |
| Rhetoric | M |

---

*M—masters degree; D—doctorate; O—other advanced degree; \*—Close-Up and/or Display*

Sociology — M
Writing — M

**NEW MEXICO STATE UNIVERSITY**
Agricultural Economics and
  Agribusiness — M,D
Anthropology — M,O
Art History — M
Art/Fine Arts — M
Clothing and Textiles — M
Communication—General — M
Corporate and Organizational
  Communication — M,D
Counseling Psychology — M,D,O
Criminal Justice and Criminology — M
Cultural Studies — M,D,O
Economic Development — M,D,O
Economics — M,D,O
English — M,D
Family and Consumer
  Sciences-General — M
Geography — M
History — M
Interdisciplinary Studies — M,D
Museum Studies — M,O
Music — M
Political Science — M
Psychology—General — M,D
Public Administration — M
Rhetoric — M,D
School Psychology — M,D,O
Sociology — M
Spanish — M,D,O
Writing — M,D

**NEW ORLEANS BAPTIST THEOLOGICAL SEMINARY**
Music — M,D
Pastoral Ministry and Counseling — M,D
Theology — M,D

**NEW SAINT ANDREWS COLLEGE**
Religion — M,O
Theology — M,O

**THE NEW SCHOOL**
Anthropology — M,D
Applied Arts and Design—
  General — M
Applied Social Research — M,D
Architecture — M
Art/Fine Arts — M
Clinical Psychology — M,D
Clothing and Textiles — M
Cognitive Sciences — M,D
Computer Art and Design — M
Economics — M,D
History — M,D
Industrial Design — M
Interior Design — M
International Affairs — M
International Economics — M,D
Liberal Studies — M
Lighting Design — M
Media Studies — M,O
Museum Studies — M
Music — M,O
Philosophy — M,D
Photography — M
Political Science — M,D
Psychoanalysis and Psychotherapy — M,D
Psychology—General — M,D
Public Policy — D
Social Psychology — M,D
Social Sciences — M,D
Sociology — M,D
Textile Design — M
Theater — M
Urban Design — M
Urban Studies — M
Writing — M

**NEWSCHOOL OF ARCHITECTURE AND DESIGN**
Architecture — M

**NEW YORK ACADEMY OF ART**
Art/Fine Arts — M

**NEW YORK FILM ACADEMY**
Film, Television, and Video
  Production — M
Photography — M

**NEW YORK INSTITUTE OF TECHNOLOGY**
Applied Arts and Design—
  General — M
Architecture — M
Art/Fine Arts — M
Arts Administration — M,O
Communication—General — M
Computer Art and Design — M
Graphic Design — M
Industrial and Labor Relations — M,O
Interdisciplinary Studies — M
Urban Design — M

**NEW YORK MEDICAL COLLEGE**
Emergency Management — M,D,O
Psychology—General — M,D,O

**NEW YORK SCHOOL OF INTERIOR DESIGN**
Interior Design — M
Lighting Design — M
Sustainable Development — M

**NEW YORK STUDIO SCHOOL OF DRAWING, PAINTING AND SCULPTURE**
Art/Fine Arts — M,O*

**NEW YORK THEOLOGICAL SEMINARY**
Theology — M,D

**NEW YORK UNIVERSITY**
African Studies — M,D,O
American Studies — M,D

Anthropology — M,D
Applied Arts and Design—
  General — M
Applied Economics — M,D,O
Applied Psychology — M,D,O
Applied Social Research — M
Archaeology — M,D
Architectural History — M
Art History — M,D
Art Therapy — M
Art/Fine Arts — M,D,O
Arts Administration — M
Asian Studies — M,D
Chinese — M,D,O
Classics — M,D,O
Cognitive Sciences — M,D,O
Communication—General — M,D
Comparative Literature — M,D
Computer Art and Design — M
Conflict Resolution and
  Mediation/Peace Studies — M,O
Corporate and Organizational
  Communication — M
Counseling Psychology — M,D,O
Cultural Studies — M,D,O
Dance — M,D
Demography and Population Studies — M,D
Developmental Psychology — M,D
Economics — M,D,O
English — M,D
Film, Television, and Video
  Production — M
French — M,D,O
German — M,D
Graphic Design — M
Historic Preservation — M
History — M,D,O
Human Development — M,D,O
Humanities — M,O
Industrial and Organizational
  Psychology — M,D,O
Interdisciplinary Studies — M
International Affairs — M,D
International Development — M,O
Internet and Interactive
  Multimedia — M,O
Italian — M,D,O
Japanese — M,D,O
Jewish Studies — M,D,O
Journalism — M,O
Latin American Studies — M,O
Linguistics — M,D
Media Studies — M,D,O
Museum Studies — M,D,O
Music — M,D,O
National Security — M,O
Near and Middle Eastern Studies — M,D,O
Philosophy — M,D
Political Science — M,D
Portuguese — M,D
Psychoanalysis and Psychotherapy — M,D,O
Psychology—General — M,D,O
Public Administration — M,D,O
Public History — M
Public Policy — M
Publishing — M
Religion — M,O
Romance Languages — M,D
Russian — M
Slavic Languages — M
Social Psychology — M,D,O
Social Sciences — M,D
Sociology — M,D
Spanish — M,D,O
Speech and Interpersonal
  Communication — M,D
Sustainable Development — M
Theater — M,D,O
Therapies—Dance, Drama, and
  Music — M
Translation and Interpretation — M
Urban and Regional Planning — M
Urban Studies — M
Western European Studies — M
Writing — M

**NIAGARA UNIVERSITY**
Counseling Psychology — M,O
Criminal Justice and Criminology — M
Interdisciplinary Studies — M
School Psychology — M

**NICHOLLS STATE UNIVERSITY**
Clinical Psychology — M,O
School Psychology — M,O

**NORFOLK STATE UNIVERSITY**
Art/Fine Arts — M
Clinical Psychology — M
Communication—General — M
Criminal Justice and Criminology — M
Media Studies — M
Music — M
Psychology—General — M,D
Social Psychology — M
Urban Studies — M

**NORTH CAROLINA AGRICULTURAL AND TECHNICAL STATE UNIVERSITY**
African-American Studies — M
Agricultural Economics and
  Agribusiness — M
Applied Economics — M
Child and Family Studies — M
Child Development — M
Computer Art and Design — M
Consumer Economics — M
English — M
Graphic Design — M

**NORTH CAROLINA CENTRAL UNIVERSITY**
Criminal Justice and Criminology — M
English — M
History — M
Music — M

Psychology—General — M
Public Administration — M

**NORTH CAROLINA STATE UNIVERSITY**
Agricultural Economics and
  Agribusiness — M
Anthropology — M
Applied Arts and Design—
  General — M,D
Architecture — M
Clothing and Textiles — D
Communication—General — M
Computer Art and Design — D
Cultural Anthropology — M
Developmental Psychology — D
Economics — M,D
English — M
Experimental Psychology — D
French — M
Geographic Information Systems — M,D
Graphic Design — M
History — M
Industrial and Organizational
  Psychology — D
Industrial Design — M
International Affairs — M
Landscape Architecture — M
Liberal Studies — M
Psychology—General — D
Public Administration — M,D
Public History — M
Rhetoric — D
School Psychology — D
Social Psychology — M
Sociology — M,D
Spanish — M
Technical Communication — M
Writing — M

**NORTH CENTRAL COLLEGE**
Cultural Studies — M
Liberal Studies — M

**NORTHCENTRAL UNIVERSITY**
Marriage and Family Therapy — M,D,O
Psychology—General — M

**NORTH DAKOTA STATE UNIVERSITY**
Agricultural Economics and
  Agribusiness — M
Anthropology — M
Architecture — M
Child and Family Studies — M,D,O*
Child Development — M
Clinical Psychology — M,D
Clothing and Textiles — M,O
Cognitive Sciences — M,D
Communication—General — M,D
Consumer Economics — M,O
Counseling Psychology — M,D
Criminal Justice and Criminology — M,D
Developmental Psychology — D
English — M,D
Family and Consumer
  Sciences-General — M
Gerontology — M,O
Health Psychology — M,D
History — M,D
Marriage and Family Therapy — D
Mass Communication — M,D
Music — M,D
Psychology—General — M,D
Rhetoric — M,D*
School Psychology — M,D
Social Psychology — M,D
Social Sciences — M
Sociology — M
Speech and Interpersonal
  Communication — M,D
Urban and Regional Planning — M
Urban Studies — M,D
Writing — M,D

**NORTHEASTERN ILLINOIS UNIVERSITY**
English — M
Geography — M
Gerontology — M
History — M
Latin American Studies — M
Linguistics — M
Marriage and Family Therapy — M
Music — M
Political Science — M
Rehabilitation Counseling — M
Social Psychology — M
Speech and Interpersonal
  Communication — M
Writing — M

**NORTHEASTERN SEMINARY AT ROBERTS WESLEYAN COLLEGE**
Theology — M,D

**NORTHEASTERN STATE UNIVERSITY**
Addictions/Substance Abuse
  Counseling — M
American Indian/Native American
  Studies — M
Communication—General — M
Counseling Psychology — M
Criminal Justice and Criminology — M
English — M
Psychology—General — M

**NORTHEASTERN UNIVERSITY**
Applied Arts and Design—
  General — M
Applied Behavior Analysis — M,D,O
Architecture — M
Art/Fine Arts — M
Corporate and Organizational
  Communication — M
Counseling Psychology — M,D,O
Criminal Justice and Criminology — M,D
Economic Development — M
Economics — M,D
English — M,D

Geographic Information Systems — M
History — M,D
Homeland Security — M,D
Interdisciplinary Studies — M,D,O
International Affairs — M,D
Internet and Interactive
  Multimedia — M
Journalism — M
Political Science — M
Psychology—General — M,D
Public Administration — M,D
Public History — M,D
Public Policy — M,D,O
School Psychology — M,D,O
Sociology — M,D
Technical Communication — M
Urban Studies — M,D

**NORTHERN ARIZONA UNIVERSITY**
Anthropology — M
Archaeology — M
Clinical Psychology — M
Communication—General — M
Counseling Psychology — M,D,O
Criminal Justice and Criminology — M
Cultural Anthropology — M
English — M,D,O
Ethnic Studies — O
Gender Studies — O
Geographic Information Systems — M,O
Geography — M,O
History — M
Human Development — O
Liberal Studies — M
Linguistics — M,D,O
Music — M,O
Political Science — M,D,O
Psychology—General — M
Public Administration — M,D,O
Rhetoric — M,D,O
School Psychology — M,D,O
Sociology — M
Spanish — M
Sustainable Development — M
Urban and Regional Planning — M,O
Women's Studies — O
Writing — M,D,O

**NORTHERN ILLINOIS UNIVERSITY**
Anthropology — M
Art/Fine Arts — M
Child and Family Studies — M
Communication—General — M
Dance — M
Economics — M
English — M,D
French — M
Geography — M,D
History — M,D
Music — M,O
Philosophy — M
Political Science — M,D
Psychology—General — M,D
Public Administration — M
Romance Languages — M
Sociology — M
Spanish — M
Theater — M

**NORTHERN KENTUCKY UNIVERSITY**
Clinical Psychology — M
Communication—General — M,O
Counseling Psychology — M
Cultural Studies — M,O
English — M,O
Geographic Information Systems — M,O
Health Psychology — M,O
Industrial and Organizational
  Psychology — M,O
Liberal Studies — M
Marriage and Family Therapy — M,O
Media Studies — M,O
Music — M
Public Administration — M,O
Public History — M
Rhetoric — M,O
Writing — M,O

**NORTHERN MICHIGAN UNIVERSITY**
Applied Behavior Analysis — M,O
Criminal Justice and Criminology — M,O
English — M,O
Psychology—General — M,O
Public Administration — M,O
Theater — M,O
Writing — M,O

**NORTHERN SEMINARY**
Pastoral Ministry and Counseling — M,D
Religion — M,D
Theology — M,D

**NORTHERN STATE UNIVERSITY**
Clinical Psychology — M
Counseling Psychology — M

**NORTH GREENVILLE UNIVERSITY**
Pastoral Ministry and Counseling — M,D

**NORTH PARK THEOLOGICAL SEMINARY**
Pastoral Ministry and Counseling — M,O
Theology — M,D

**NORTH PARK UNIVERSITY**
Music — M

**NORTHWEST CHRISTIAN UNIVERSITY**
Counseling Psychology — M

**NORTHWESTERN OKLAHOMA STATE UNIVERSITY**
American Studies — M
Counseling Psychology — M

**NORTHWESTERN STATE UNIVERSITY OF LOUISIANA**
Art/Fine Arts — M

Clinical Psychology — M
English — M
Homeland Security — M
Music — M
Psychology—General — M

**NORTHWESTERN UNIVERSITY**
African Studies — O
African-American Studies — D
American Studies — M
Anthropology — D
Art History — D
Art/Fine Arts — M
Arts Administration — M
Broadcast Journalism — M
Clinical Psychology — D
Cognitive Sciences — D
Communication—General — M,D
Comparative Literature — M,D
Corporate and Organizational
   Communication — M,D
Economics — D
English — M,D
Ethics — M
Film, Television, and Video
   Production — M,D
French — D,O
Gender Studies — O
Genetic Counseling — M
German — D
History — M,D
Human Development — D
International Affairs — M,D,O
Internet and Interactive
   Multimedia — M
Italian — D,O
Journalism — M
Liberal Studies — M
Linguistics — D
Marriage and Family Therapy — M
Media Studies — M,D
Music — M,D
Philosophy — D
Political Science — D
Portuguese — D
Psychology—General — D
Public Administration — M
Public Policy — M,D
Publishing — M
Religion — M,D
Rhetoric — M,D
Slavic Languages — D
Social Psychology — D
Sociology — M,D
Spanish — D
Speech and Interpersonal
   Communication — M,D
Theater — M,D
Writing — M

**NORTHWEST MISSOURI STATE UNIVERSITY**
Agricultural Economics and
   Agribusiness — M
English — M,O
Geographic Information Systems — M,O

**NORTHWEST NAZARENE UNIVERSITY**
Addictions/Substance Abuse
   Counseling — M
Clinical Psychology — M
Marriage and Family Therapy — M
Missions and Missiology — M
Pastoral Ministry and Counseling — M
Religion — M
School Psychology — M
Theology — M

**NORTHWEST UNIVERSITY**
Counseling Psychology — M,D
Cultural Studies — M
Missions and Missiology — M
Pastoral Ministry and Counseling — M
Psychology—General — M,D
Theology — M
Urban and Regional Planning — M,D

**NORWICH UNIVERSITY**
Conflict Resolution and
   Mediation/Peace Studies — M
Criminal Justice and Criminology — M
Emergency Management — M
History — M
International Affairs — M
International Development — M
Military and Defense Studies — M
Public Administration — M
Public Policy — M

**NOTRE DAME COLLEGE (OH)**
Homeland Security — M,O

**NOTRE DAME DE NAMUR UNIVERSITY**
Art Therapy — M
Clinical Psychology — M
English — M
Marriage and Family Therapy — M
Music — M,O
Psychology—General — M
Public Administration — M
Public Affairs — M

**NOTRE DAME OF MARYLAND UNIVERSITY**
Communication—General — M
Liberal Studies — M

**NOTRE DAME SEMINARY**
Theology — M

**NOVA SOUTHEASTERN UNIVERSITY**
Art/Fine Arts — M,D,O
Clinical Psychology — M,D,O

Conflict Resolution and
   Mediation/Peace Studies — M,D,O
Counseling Psychology — M,D,O
Emergency Management — M,D,O
Experimental Psychology — M,D,O
Forensic Psychology — M,D,O
Humanities — M,D,O
Interdisciplinary Studies — M,D,O
Marriage and Family Therapy — M,D,O
Psychology—General — M,D,O
Public Administration — M
School Psychology — M,D,O
Social Sciences — M,D,O

**NSCAD UNIVERSITY**
Applied Arts and Design—
   General — M
Art/Fine Arts — M

**NYACK COLLEGE**
Counseling Psychology — M
Marriage and Family Therapy — M
Missions and Missiology — M,D
Pastoral Ministry and Counseling — M
Religion — M
Theology — M,D

**OAKLAND CITY UNIVERSITY**
Theology — M,D

**OAKLAND UNIVERSITY**
Applied Behavior Analysis — M,O
Counseling Psychology — M,D,O
Economics — M,O
English — M
History — M
Liberal Studies — M
Linguistics — M,O
Music — M,D
Public Administration — M,O

**OAKWOOD UNIVERSITY**
Pastoral Ministry and Counseling — M

**OBERLIN COLLEGE**
Music — M,O

**OBLATE SCHOOL OF THEOLOGY**
African-American Studies — M,D,O
Pastoral Ministry and Counseling — M,D,O
Religion — M,D,O
Theology — M,D,O

**OHIO CHRISTIAN UNIVERSITY**
Pastoral Ministry and Counseling — M
Theology — M

**OHIO DOMINICAN UNIVERSITY**
English — M
Theology — M

**THE OHIO STATE UNIVERSITY**
African Studies — M,D
African-American Studies — M,D
Agricultural Economics and
   Agribusiness — M,D
Anthropology — M,D
Architecture — M,D
Art History — M,D
Art/Fine Arts — M
Arts Administration — M
Asian Languages — M
Asian Studies — M
Child and Family Studies — M,D
Chinese — M,D
Classics — M,D
Clinical Psychology — D
Cognitive Sciences — D
Communication—General — M,D
Computer Art and Design — M
Dance — M,D
Developmental Psychology — D
East European and Russian Studies — M,D
Economics — M,D
English — M,D
Family and Consumer
   Sciences-General — M,D
French — M,D
Gender Studies — M,D
Geography — M,D
German — M,D
History — M,D
Human Development — M,D
Industrial and Labor Relations — M,D
Industrial Design — M
Interdisciplinary Studies — M,D
Interior Design — M
Internet and Interactive
   Multimedia — M
Italian — M,D
Japanese — M,D
Landscape Architecture — M
Latin American Studies — M
Linguistics — M,D
Music — M,D
Near and Middle Eastern Languages — M,D
Philosophy — M,D
Political Science — D
Portuguese — M,D
Psychology—General — D
Public Administration — M,D
Public Affairs — M,D
Public Policy — M,D
Rural Sociology — M,D
Slavic Languages — M,D
Social Psychology — D
Social Sciences — M,D
Sociology — D
Spanish — M,D
Theater — M,D
Urban and Regional Planning — M,D
Women's Studies — M,D

**OHIO UNIVERSITY**
African Studies — M
Applied Economics — M
Art History — M
Art/Fine Arts — M
Asian Studies — M
Child and Family Studies — M
Child Development — M
Clinical Psychology — D
Communication—General — M,D
Comparative and Interdisciplinary
   Arts — D
Consumer Economics — M
Corporate and Organizational
   Communication — M,D
Economics — M
English — M,D
Experimental Psychology — D
Film, Television, and Video
   Production — M
Film, Television, and Video
   Theory and Criticism — M
French — M
Geography — M
Graphic Design — M
Health Communication — M,D
History — M,D
Industrial and Organizational
   Psychology — D
International Affairs — M
International Development — M
Journalism — M,D
Latin American Studies — M
Linguistics — M,D
Media Studies — M,D
Music — M,O
Philosophy — M
Photography — M
Political Science — M
Psychology—General — D
Public Administration — M,O
Rehabilitation Counseling — M,D
Rhetoric — M,D
Social Sciences — M
Sociology — M
Spanish — M
Speech and Interpersonal
   Communication — M,D
Theater — M
Therapies—Dance, Drama, and
   Music — M,O

**OHR HAMEIR THEOLOGICAL SEMINARY**
Theology — M

**OKLAHOMA BAPTIST UNIVERSITY**
Marriage and Family Therapy — M

**OKLAHOMA CHRISTIAN UNIVERSITY**
Theology — M

**OKLAHOMA CITY UNIVERSITY**
Applied Behavior Analysis — M
Criminal Justice and Criminology — M
Music — M
Photography — M
Sociology — M
Writing — M

**OKLAHOMA STATE UNIVERSITY**
Agricultural Economics and
   Agribusiness — M,D
Applied Arts and Design—
   General — M,D
Applied Behavior Analysis — M,D,O
Applied Psychology — M,D,O
Art History — M
Child and Family Studies — M,D
Clinical Psychology — M,D
Clothing and Textiles — M,D
Consumer Economics — M,D
Economics — M,D
Emergency Management — M,D
English — M,D
Family and Consumer
   Sciences-General — M,D
Geography — M,D
Graphic Design — M
Health Psychology — M,D,O
History — M,D
Human Development — M,D
International Affairs — M,D,O
Landscape Architecture — M
Marriage and Family Therapy — M,D
Mass Communication — M
Music — M
Philosophy — M
Political Science — M,D
Psychology—General — M,D
Sociology — M,D
Theater — M
Writing — M,D

**OKLAHOMA STATE UNIVERSITY CENTER FOR HEALTH SCIENCES**
Forensic Sciences — M

**OKLAHOMA WESLEYAN UNIVERSITY**
Theology — M

**OLD DOMINION UNIVERSITY**
Applied Psychology — D
Clinical Psychology — D
Computer Art and Design — M
Conflict Resolution and
   Mediation/Peace Studies — M,D
Counseling Psychology — M,D,O
Criminal Justice and Criminology — M,D
Cultural Studies — M,D
Economics — M
English — M,D
History — M
Humanities — M

Industrial and Organizational
   Psychology — D
International Affairs — M,D
International Development — M,D
Linguistics — M
Psychology—General — M
Public Administration — M,D
School Psychology — M,D,O
Sociology — M
Speech and Interpersonal
   Communication — M
Urban Studies — D
Women's Studies — M
Writing — M

**OLIVET NAZARENE UNIVERSITY**
Religion — M
Theology — M

**OPEN UNIVERSITY**
History — M
Music — M
Philosophy — M

**ORAL ROBERTS UNIVERSITY**
Marriage and Family Therapy — M,D
Missions and Missiology — M,D
Near and Middle Eastern Languages — M,D
Pastoral Ministry and Counseling — M,D
Theology — M,D

**OREGON COLLEGE OF ART AND CRAFT**
Art/Fine Arts — M

**OREGON HEALTH & SCIENCE UNIVERSITY**
Gerontology — M,O

**OREGON STATE UNIVERSITY**
Anthropology — M,D
Child and Family Studies — M,D
Clinical Psychology — M,D
Clothing and Textiles — M,D
Cognitive Sciences — M,D
Economic Development — M,D
Economics — M
English — M
Ethics — M
Gender Studies — M,D
Geographic Information Systems — M
Geography — M,D
Health Psychology — M
Hispanic Studies — M
History of Medicine — M,D
History of Science and Technology — M,D
Human Development — M,D
Interdisciplinary Studies — M
Psychology—General — M,D
Public Policy — M
Religion — M
School Psychology — M,D
Social Sciences — M,D
Women's Studies — M
Writing — M

**OREGON STATE UNIVERSITY–CASCADES**
School Psychology — M
Social Psychology — M

**OTIS COLLEGE OF ART AND DESIGN**
Art/Fine Arts — M
Graphic Design — M
Photography — M
Writing — M

**OTTAWA UNIVERSITY**
Art Therapy — M
Counseling Psychology — M
Marriage and Family Therapy — M
Pastoral Ministry and Counseling — M
School Psychology — M

**OUR LADY OF THE LAKE UNIVERSITY**
Counseling Psychology — D
English — M
Psychology—General — M
School Psychology — M
Sociology — M
Writing — M

**OXFORD GRADUATE SCHOOL**
Child and Family Studies — M,D
Religion — M,D
Sociology — M,D

**PACE UNIVERSITY**
Addictions/Substance Abuse
   Counseling — M,D
Art/Fine Arts — M,O
Clinical Psychology — M,D
Counseling Psychology — M,D
Developmental Psychology — M,D
Economics — O
Emergency Management — M
English — M,O
Forensic Sciences — M
Homeland Security — M
International Economics — O
Internet and Interactive
   Multimedia — M,D,O
Media Studies — M
Psychology—General — M
Public Administration — M
Publishing — M,O
School Psychology — M,D
Sustainable Development — M,D
Theater — M

**PACIFICA GRADUATE INSTITUTE**
Clinical Psychology — M,D
Counseling Psychology — M,D
Psychology—General — M,D

*M—masters degree; D—doctorate; O—other advanced degree; *—Close-Up and/or Display*

## PACIFIC LUTHERAN UNIVERSITY
| | |
|---|---|
| Marriage and Family Therapy | M |
| Writing | M |

## PACIFIC NORTHWEST COLLEGE OF ART
| | |
|---|---|
| Applied Arts and Design— General | M |
| Art/Fine Arts | M |
| Cultural Studies | M |

## PACIFIC OAKS COLLEGE
| | |
|---|---|
| Human Development | M |
| Marriage and Family Therapy | M |

## PACIFIC RIM CHRISTIAN UNIVERSITY
| | |
|---|---|
| Pastoral Ministry and Counseling | M |

## PACIFIC SCHOOL OF RELIGION
| | |
|---|---|
| Religion | M,D,O |
| Theology | M,D,O |

## PACIFIC UNIVERSITY
| | |
|---|---|
| Clinical Psychology | M,D |
| Psychology—General | M,D |
| Writing | M |

## PALM BEACH ATLANTIC UNIVERSITY
| | |
|---|---|
| Addictions/Substance Abuse Counseling | M |
| Counseling Psychology | M |
| Marriage and Family Therapy | M |
| Theology | M |

## PALO ALTO UNIVERSITY
| | |
|---|---|
| Clinical Psychology | M,D |
| Counseling Psychology | M |
| Marriage and Family Therapy | M |
| Psychology—General | M,D |

## PARIS COLLEGE OF ART
| | |
|---|---|
| Art/Fine Arts | M |
| Interior Design | M |
| Media Studies | M |
| Photography | M |
| Textile Design | M |

## PARK UNIVERSITY
| | |
|---|---|
| Emergency Management | M,O |
| Music | M,O |
| Public Administration | M,O |
| Public Affairs | M,O |
| Writing | M,O |

## PAYNE THEOLOGICAL SEMINARY
| | |
|---|---|
| Theology | M |

## PENN STATE HARRISBURG
| | |
|---|---|
| American Studies | M,D,O |
| Applied Behavior Analysis | M,D,O |
| Applied Psychology | M,D,O |
| Clinical Psychology | M,D,O |
| Communication—General | M,D,O |
| Criminal Justice and Criminology | M,D,O |
| Folklore | M,D,O |
| Health Psychology | M,D,O |
| Historic Preservation | M,D,O |
| Homeland Security | M,D,O |
| Humanities | M,D,O |
| Museum Studies | M,D,O |
| Psychology—General | M,D,O |
| Public Administration | M,D,O |
| Public Affairs | M,D,O |
| Social Psychology | M,D,O |
| Writing | M,D,O |

## PENN STATE UNIVERSITY PARK
| | |
|---|---|
| Agricultural Economics and Agribusiness | M,D,O |
| Anthropology | M,D |
| Architecture | M,D |
| Art History | M,D |
| Art/Fine Arts | M,D,O |
| Child and Family Studies | M,D |
| Communication—General | M,D |
| Comparative Literature | M,D |
| Criminal Justice and Criminology | M,D |
| Economic Development | M,D,O |
| Economics | M,D |
| English | M,D |
| Forensic Sciences | M |
| French | M,D |
| Geographic Information Systems | M,D |
| Geography | M,D |
| German | M,D |
| History | M,D |
| Human Development | M,D |
| Industrial and Labor Relations | M |
| International Affairs | M |
| Landscape Architecture | M,D |
| Linguistics | M |
| Mass Communication | M,D |
| Media Studies | M,D |
| Music | M,D,O |
| Philosophy | M,D |
| Political Science | M,D |
| Psychology—General | M,D,O |
| Rural Sociology | M,D |
| Russian | M,D |
| School Psychology | M,D,O |
| Sociology | M,D |
| Spanish | M,D |
| Sustainable Development | M |
| Theater | M |
| Urban and Regional Planning | M,D,O |

## PENNSYLVANIA ACADEMY OF THE FINE ARTS
| | |
|---|---|
| Art/Fine Arts | M,O |

## PENSACOLA CHRISTIAN COLLEGE
| | |
|---|---|
| Art/Fine Arts | M,D,O |
| Graphic Design | M,D,O |
| Music | M,D,O |
| Theater | M,D,O |

## PENTECOSTAL THEOLOGICAL SEMINARY
| | |
|---|---|
| Pastoral Ministry and Counseling | M,D |
| Theology | M,D |

## PEPPERDINE UNIVERSITY
| | |
|---|---|
| American Studies | M |
| Clinical Psychology | M,D |
| Communication—General | M |
| Conflict Resolution and Mediation/Peace Studies | M |
| Economics | M |
| Humanities | M |
| International Affairs | M,D |
| Marriage and Family Therapy | M,D |
| Media Studies | M |
| Pastoral Ministry and Counseling | M |
| Political Science | M |
| Psychology—General | M,D |
| Public Policy | M |
| Religion | M |
| Writing | M |

## PERU STATE COLLEGE
| | |
|---|---|
| Economics | M |

## PFEIFFER UNIVERSITY
| | |
|---|---|
| Theology | M |

## PHILADELPHIA COLLEGE OF OSTEOPATHIC MEDICINE
| | |
|---|---|
| Applied Behavior Analysis | M,D,O |
| Clinical Psychology | M,D,O |
| Counseling Psychology | M,D,O |
| Forensic Sciences | M |
| Industrial and Organizational Psychology | M,D,O |
| Psychology—General | M,D,O* |
| School Psychology | M,D,O |

## PHILADELPHIA UNIVERSITY
| | |
|---|---|
| Architecture | M |
| Art/Fine Arts | M |
| Clothing and Textiles | M |
| Emergency Management | M |
| Geography | M |
| Industrial Design | M |
| Interior Design | M |
| Internet and Interactive Multimedia | M |
| Social Psychology | M |
| Sustainable Development | M |
| Textile Design | M |
| Urban and Regional Planning | M |

## PHILLIPS GRADUATE UNIVERSITY
| | |
|---|---|
| Art Therapy | M |
| Marriage and Family Therapy | M |

## PHILLIPS THEOLOGICAL SEMINARY
| | |
|---|---|
| Ethics | M,D |
| Missions and Missiology | M,D |
| Music | M,D |
| Pastoral Ministry and Counseling | D |
| Theology | M,D |

## PHOENIX SEMINARY
| | |
|---|---|
| Counseling Psychology | M,D,O |
| Pastoral Ministry and Counseling | M,D,O |
| Theology | M,D,O |

## PIEDMONT INTERNATIONAL UNIVERSITY
| | |
|---|---|
| Pastoral Ministry and Counseling | M,D |
| Theology | M,D |

## PITTSBURGH THEOLOGICAL SEMINARY
| | |
|---|---|
| Pastoral Ministry and Counseling | M,D |
| Theology | M,D |

## PITTSBURG STATE UNIVERSITY
| | |
|---|---|
| Clinical Psychology | M |
| Communication—General | M |
| English | M |
| Graphic Design | M,O |
| History | M |
| Music | M |
| Psychology—General | M |
| School Psychology | O |
| Writing | M |

## PLYMOUTH STATE UNIVERSITY
| | |
|---|---|
| Clinical Psychology | M,O |
| Cultural Studies | M |
| Historic Preservation | M |
| School Psychology | M,O |

## POINT LOMA NAZARENE UNIVERSITY
| | |
|---|---|
| Clinical Psychology | M |
| Pastoral Ministry and Counseling | M |
| Theology | M |

## POINT PARK UNIVERSITY
| | |
|---|---|
| Clinical Psychology | M |
| Communication—General | M |
| Criminal Justice and Criminology | M |
| Journalism | M |
| Mass Communication | M |
| Music | M |
| Theater | M |

## POLYTECHNIC UNIVERSITY OF PUERTO RICO
| | |
|---|---|
| Landscape Architecture | M |

## PONCE HEALTH SCIENCES UNIVERSITY
| | |
|---|---|
| Clinical Psychology | D |

## PONTIFICAL CATHOLIC UNIVERSITY OF PUERTO RICO
| | |
|---|---|
| Art/Fine Arts | M |
| Clinical Psychology | D |
| Criminal Justice and Criminology | M |
| Hispanic Studies | M,O |
| History | M |
| Industrial and Organizational Psychology | D |
| Psychology—General | M,D |

## Public Administration, etc.
| | |
|---|---|
| Public Administration | M |
| Rehabilitation Counseling | M |
| Spanish | M,O |
| Theology | M |

## PONTIFICAL COLLEGE JOSEPHINUM
| | |
|---|---|
| Theology | M |

## PONTIFICAL JOHN PAUL II INSTITUTE FOR STUDIES ON MARRIAGE AND FAMILY
| | |
|---|---|
| Ethics | M,D,O |
| Marriage and Family Therapy | M,D,O |
| Theology | M,D,O |

## PONTIFICIA UNIVERSIDAD CATOLICA MADRE Y MAESTRA
| | |
|---|---|
| Architecture | M |
| Building Science | M |
| Clinical Psychology | M |
| Criminal Justice and Criminology | M |
| Developmental Psychology | M |
| Forensic Psychology | M |
| Interior Design | M |
| International Affairs | M |
| Landscape Architecture | M |
| Psychology—General | M |

## POPE ST. JOHN XXIII NATIONAL SEMINARY
| | |
|---|---|
| Theology | M |

## PORTLAND STATE UNIVERSITY
| | |
|---|---|
| Anthropology | M,D,O |
| Applied Economics | M,D |
| Applied Social Research | M,D |
| Architecture | M |
| Art/Fine Arts | M |
| Conflict Resolution and Mediation/Peace Studies | M |
| Criminal Justice and Criminology | M,D |
| Economics | M,D,O |
| English | M |
| French | M |
| Geography | M,D |
| German | M |
| Gerontology | M,D,O |
| History | M |
| Japanese | M |
| Music | M |
| Political Science | M,D |
| Psychology—General | M,D,O |
| Public Administration | M,D |
| Public Affairs | M,D |
| Public Policy | M,D |
| Sociology | M,D,O |
| Spanish | M |
| Speech and Interpersonal Communication | M,O |
| Theater | M |
| Urban and Regional Planning | M |
| Urban Studies | M,D |

## POST UNIVERSITY
| | |
|---|---|
| Addictions/Substance Abuse Counseling | M |
| Public Administration | M |

## PRAIRIE VIEW A&M UNIVERSITY
| | |
|---|---|
| Architecture | M |
| Clinical Psychology | M,D |
| Forensic Psychology | M,D |
| Sociology | M |

## PRATT INSTITUTE
| | |
|---|---|
| Applied Arts and Design— General | M,O* |
| Architecture | M* |
| Art History | M |
| Art Therapy | M |
| Art/Fine Arts | M* |
| Arts Administration | M |
| Graphic Design | M |
| Historic Preservation | M |
| Industrial Design | M |
| Interior Design | M |
| Internet and Interactive Multimedia | M |
| Media Studies | M* |
| Music | M |
| Sustainable Development | M |
| Therapies—Dance, Drama, and Music | M |
| Urban and Regional Planning | M |
| Urban Design | M |
| Writing | M |

## PRESCOTT COLLEGE
| | |
|---|---|
| Art Therapy | M |
| Art/Fine Arts | M |
| Counseling Psychology | M |
| Health Psychology | M |
| Humanities | M |
| Psychoanalysis and Psychotherapy | M |

## PRESIDIO GRADUATE SCHOOL (CA)
| | |
|---|---|
| Agricultural Economics and Agribusiness | M,O |

## PRINCETON THEOLOGICAL SEMINARY
| | |
|---|---|
| Religion | M,D |
| Theology | M,D |

## PRINCETON UNIVERSITY
| | |
|---|---|
| Anthropology | D |
| Archaeology | D |
| Architecture | M,D |
| Asian Studies | D |
| Classics | D |
| Comparative Literature | D |
| Demography and Population Studies | D,O |
| Economics | D,O |
| English | D |
| French | D |
| German | D |
| History of Science and Technology | D |
| History | D |
| International Affairs | M,D |

## Princeton University (cont.)
| | |
|---|---|
| Music | D |
| Near and Middle Eastern Studies | M,D |
| Philosophy | D |
| Political Science | D |
| Portuguese | D |
| Psychology—General | D |
| Public Affairs | M,D,O |
| Public Policy | M,D |
| Religion | D |
| Russian | D |
| Slavic Languages | D |
| Sociology | D,O |
| Spanish | D |

## PROVIDENCE COLLEGE
| | |
|---|---|
| American Studies | M |
| History | M |
| Theology | M |

## PROVIDENCE UNIVERSITY COLLEGE & THEOLOGICAL SEMINARY
| | |
|---|---|
| Counseling Psychology | M,D,O |
| Missions and Missiology | M,D,O |
| Pastoral Ministry and Counseling | M,D,O |
| Theology | M,D,O |

## PURCHASE COLLEGE, STATE UNIVERSITY OF NEW YORK
| | |
|---|---|
| Art History | M |
| Art/Fine Arts | M |
| Music | M |

## PURDUE UNIVERSITY
| | |
|---|---|
| Agricultural Economics and Agribusiness | M,D |
| American Studies | M,D |
| Anthropology | M,D |
| Applied Arts and Design— General | M,D |
| Art/Fine Arts | M,D |
| Child and Family Studies | M,D |
| Child Development | M,D |
| Clinical Psychology | D |
| Cognitive Sciences | D |
| Communication—General | M,D |
| Comparative Literature | M,D |
| Computer Art and Design | M,D |
| Consumer Economics | M,D |
| Economics | D |
| English | M,D |
| Family and Consumer Sciences-General | M,D |
| French | M,D |
| German | M,D |
| History | M,D |
| Human Development | M,D |
| Industrial and Organizational Psychology | D |
| Industrial Design | M,D |
| Interior Design | M,D |
| Japanese | M,D |
| Linguistics | M,D |
| Marriage and Family Therapy | M,D |
| Philosophy | M,D |
| Photography | M,D |
| Political Science | M,D |
| Psychology—General | D |
| Sociology | M,D |
| Spanish | M,D |
| Sport Psychology | M,D |
| Theater | M |
| Writing | M,D |

## PURDUE UNIVERSITY NORTHWEST
| | |
|---|---|
| Child and Family Studies | M |
| Child Development | M |
| Communication—General | M |
| Counseling Psychology | M |
| English | M |
| History | M |
| Marriage and Family Therapy | M |
| School Psychology | M |

## QUEENS COLLEGE OF THE CITY UNIVERSITY OF NEW YORK
| | |
|---|---|
| Applied Behavior Analysis | M,O |
| Applied Social Research | M |
| Art History | M |
| Art/Fine Arts | M |
| Child and Family Studies | M,O |
| Counseling Psychology | M,O |
| Developmental Psychology | M,O |
| Economics | M |
| English | M,O |
| Family and Consumer Sciences-General | M,O |
| French | M |
| Hispanic and Latin American Languages | M |
| History | M,O |
| Italian | M |
| Liberal Studies | M |
| Linguistics | M,O |
| Media Studies | M |
| Music | M |
| Psychology—General | M,O |
| Romance Languages | M |
| School Psychology | M,O |
| Sociology | M |
| Spanish | M |
| Urban Studies | M |
| Writing | M,O |

## QUEEN'S UNIVERSITY AT KINGSTON
| | |
|---|---|
| Canadian Studies | M |
| Classics | M |
| Clinical Psychology | M,D |
| Cognitive Sciences | M,D |
| Communication—General | M,D |
| Developmental Psychology | M,D |
| English | M,D |
| French | M,D |
| Gender Studies | M,D |
| Geography | M,D |
| German | M |
| Hispanic Studies | M |

Industrial and Labor Relations — M
International Affairs — M,D
Philosophy — M,D
Political Science — M,D
Psychology—General — M,D
Public Policy — M
Religion — M
Social Psychology — M
Sociology — M,D
Spanish — M
Sport Psychology — M,D
Theology — M,O
Urban and Regional Planning — M
Women's Studies — M,D

**QUEENS UNIVERSITY OF CHARLOTTE**
Communication—General — M
Interior Design — M
Writing — M

**QUINCY UNIVERSITY**
Communication—General — M
School Psychology — M

**QUINNIPIAC UNIVERSITY**
Broadcast Journalism — M
Communication—General — M
Film, Television, and Video
  Production — M
Internet and Interactive
  Multimedia — M
Journalism — M

**RABBINICAL ACADEMY MESIVTA RABBI CHAIM BERLIN**
Theology — O

**RABBINICAL COLLEGE BETH SHRAGA**
Theology

**RABBINICAL COLLEGE BOBOVER YESHIVA B'NEI ZION**
Theology

**RABBINICAL COLLEGE OF LONG ISLAND**
Theology

**RABBINICAL SEMINARY OF AMERICA**
Theology

**RADFORD UNIVERSITY**
Art/Fine Arts — M
Corporate and Organizational
  Communication — M
Counseling Psychology — D
Criminal Justice and Criminology — M,O
English — M
Music — M
School Psychology — O

**RANDALL UNIVERSITY**
Pastoral Ministry and Counseling — M

**RECONSTRUCTIONIST RABBINICAL COLLEGE**
Jewish Studies — M,D,O
Theology — M,D,O
Women's Studies — M,D,O

**REED COLLEGE**
Liberal Studies — M

**REFORMED EPISCOPAL SEMINARY**
Theology — M

**REFORMED PRESBYTERIAN THEOLOGICAL SEMINARY**
Theology — M,D

**REFORMED THEOLOGICAL SEMINARY–ATLANTA CAMPUS**
Theology — M,D,O

**REFORMED THEOLOGICAL SEMINARY–CHARLOTTE CAMPUS**
Pastoral Ministry and Counseling — M,D
Religion — M,D
Theology — M,D

**REFORMED THEOLOGICAL SEMINARY–HOUSTON CAMPUS**
Religion — M

**REFORMED THEOLOGICAL SEMINARY–JACKSON CAMPUS**
Marriage and Family Therapy — M,D,O
Missions and Missiology — M,D,O
Pastoral Ministry and Counseling — M,D,O
Religion — M,D,O
Theology — M,D,O

**REFORMED THEOLOGICAL SEMINARY–ORLANDO CAMPUS**
Pastoral Ministry and Counseling — M,D,O
Theology — M,D,O

**REFORMED THEOLOGICAL SEMINARY–WASHINGTON D.C.**
Religion — M
Theology — M

**REGENT COLLEGE**
Theology — M,O

**REGENT'S UNIVERSITY LONDON**
International Affairs — M

**REGENT UNIVERSITY**
American Studies — M
Clinical Psychology — M,D,O
Communication—General — M,D
Conflict Resolution and
  Mediation/Peace Studies — M,D
Corporate and Organizational
  Communication — M,D,O
Counseling Psychology — M,D,O
Criminal Justice and Criminology — M,D

Cultural Studies — M,D
Emergency Management — M
Film, Television, and Video
  Production — M,D
History — M,D
Homeland Security — M
Interdisciplinary Studies — M,D,O
International Affairs — M
Journalism — M
Marriage and Family Therapy — M,D,O
Missions and Missiology — M
National Security — M,D
Pastoral Ministry and Counseling — M,D,O
Political Science — M
Psychoanalysis and Psychotherapy — M,D
Public Administration — M
Public Policy — M
Religion — M,D
Theater — M,D
Theology — M,D
Writing — M,D

**REGIS COLLEGE (CANADA)**
Pastoral Ministry and Counseling — M
Philosophy — M,D,O
Theology — M,D,O

**REGIS COLLEGE (MA)**
Applied Behavior Analysis — M
Corporate and Organizational
  Communication — M
Counseling Psychology — M,D,O
Cultural Studies — M
Public Affairs — M

**REGIS UNIVERSITY**
Criminal Justice and Criminology — M,O
Developmental Psychology — M,D,O
Economics — M,O
Marriage and Family Therapy — M,D,O
Writing — M,O

**RENSSELAER POLYTECHNIC INSTITUTE**
Architecture — M,D
Art/Fine Arts — D
Building Science — M,D
Cognitive Sciences — D
Computer Art and Design — D
History of Science and Technology — M,D
Interdisciplinary Studies — M,D
Lighting Design — M,D
Rhetoric — M,D
Speech and Interpersonal
  Communication — M,D

**RHODE ISLAND COLLEGE**
Art/Fine Arts — M
Arts Administration — M
Counseling Psychology — M,O
English — M,O
Health Psychology — M,O
History — M
Psychology—General — M,O
Public Administration — M
School Psychology — M,O
Writing — M,O

**RHODE ISLAND SCHOOL OF DESIGN**
Applied Arts and Design—
  General — M
Architecture — M
Art/Fine Arts — M
Computer Art and Design — M
Graphic Design — M
Industrial Design — M
Interior Design — M
Landscape Architecture — M
Media Studies — M
Photography — M
Textile Design — M

**RICE UNIVERSITY**
African Studies — D
American Studies — D
Anthropology — M,D
Archaeology — M,D
Architecture — M,D
Art History — D
Cognitive Sciences — M,D
Cultural Anthropology — M,D
Economics — M,D
English — M,D
History — M,D
Industrial and Organizational
  Psychology — M,D
Jewish Studies — D
Liberal Studies — M
Linguistics — M,D
Music — M,D
Near and Middle Eastern Studies — D
Philosophy — M,D
Political Science — D
Psychology—General — M,D
Religion — D
Sociology — D
Urban Design — M,D

**RICHMOND, THE AMERICAN INTERNATIONAL UNIVERSITY IN LONDON**
Art History — M
International Affairs — M

**RICHMONT GRADUATE UNIVERSITY**
Clinical Psychology — M
Marriage and Family Therapy — M
Pastoral Ministry and Counseling — M,O

**RIDER UNIVERSITY**
Applied Psychology — M
Corporate and Organizational
  Communication — M
French — O

German — O
Music — M
School Psychology — O
Spanish — O

**RIVIER UNIVERSITY**
Clinical Psychology — M
Counseling Psychology — M,D,O
English — M
Experimental Psychology — M
Psychology—General — M
Writing — M

**THE ROBERT E. WEBBER INSTITUTE FOR WORSHIP STUDIES**
Religion — M,D

**ROBERT MORRIS UNIVERSITY**
Counseling Psychology — M,D,O
Internet and Interactive
  Multimedia — M,D

**ROBERT MORRIS UNIVERSITY ILLINOIS**
Arts Administration — M
Criminal Justice and Criminology — M
Media Studies — M

**ROBERTS WESLEYAN COLLEGE**
Child and Family Studies — M
Clinical Psychology — M,D
Psychology—General — M,D
School Psychology — M,D

**ROCHESTER COLLEGE**
Missions and Missiology — M

**ROCHESTER INSTITUTE OF TECHNOLOGY**
Architecture — M
Art/Fine Arts — M
Communication—General — M
Computer Art and Design — M
Criminal Justice and Criminology — M
Experimental Psychology — M
Film, Television, and Video
  Production — M
Graphic Design — M
Industrial Design — M
Interdisciplinary Studies — M
Internet and Interactive
  Multimedia — O
Media Studies — M
Medical Illustration — M
Photography — M
Psychology—General — M,O
Public Policy — M
School Psychology — M,O
Sustainable Development — M,D
Translation and Interpretation — M

**ROCKY MOUNTAIN COLLEGE OF ART + DESIGN**
Arts Administration — M
Internet and Interactive
  Multimedia — M

**ROGER WILLIAMS UNIVERSITY**
Architectural History — M
Architecture — M
Art History — M
Clinical Psychology — M
Criminal Justice and Criminology — M
Forensic Psychology — M
Historic Preservation — M
Public Administration — M

**ROLLINS COLLEGE**
Applied Behavior Analysis — M
Liberal Studies — M

**ROOSEVELT UNIVERSITY**
Anthropology — M
Applied Economics — M
Clinical Psychology — M
Communication—General — M
Corporate and Organizational
  Communication — M
Economics — M
English — M
Gender Studies — M,O
History — M
Industrial and Organizational
  Psychology — M,D
Journalism — M
Music — M,O
Political Science — M
Psychology—General — M,D
Public Administration — M
Sociology — M
Spanish — M
Theater — M
Women's Studies — M,O
Writing — M

**ROSALIND FRANKLIN UNIVERSITY OF MEDICINE AND SCIENCE**
Clinical Psychology — M,D
Interdisciplinary Studies — D
Psychology—General — M,D

**ROSEMONT COLLEGE**
Counseling Psychology — M
Publishing — M
Writing — M

**ROWAN UNIVERSITY**
Applied Behavior Analysis — M,O
Arts Administration — M
Clinical Psychology — M,O
Corporate and Organizational
  Communication — O
Criminal Justice and Criminology — M
History — M,O
Media Studies — O
Music — M

Psychology—General — M,O
Publishing — O
Rhetoric — O
School Psychology — M,O
Theater — M
Writing — M,O

**ROYAL MILITARY COLLEGE OF CANADA**
Military and Defense Studies — M,D

**ROYAL ROADS UNIVERSITY**
Conflict Resolution and
  Mediation/Peace Studies — M
Emergency Management — M,O

**RUTGERS UNIVERSITY–CAMDEN**
Child Development — M,D
Criminal Justice and Criminology — M
English — M
History — M
International Affairs — M
International Development — M
Liberal Studies — M
Psychology—General — M
Public Administration — M
Public History — M
Public Policy — M
Writing — M

**RUTGERS UNIVERSITY–NEWARK**
American Studies — M,D
Clothing and Textiles — M
Cognitive Sciences — D
Criminal Justice and Criminology — M,D
Economics — M,D
English — M
History — M
International Affairs — M,D
Music — M
Political Science — M
Psychology—General — D
Public Administration — M
Public Policy — M,D,O
Rehabilitation Counseling — M,D
Social Psychology — D
Urban Studies — M,D
Writing — M

**RUTGERS UNIVERSITY–NEW BRUNSWICK**
African Studies — D
African-American Studies — D
Agricultural Economics and
  Agribusiness — M
Anthropology — M,D
Applied Arts and Design—
  General — M
Applied Psychology — M,D
Art History — M,D,O
Art/Fine Arts — M
Asian Studies — M,D
Classics — M,D
Clinical Psychology — D
Cognitive Sciences — D
Communication—General — M,D
Comparative Literature — M,D
Counseling Psychology — M
Economics — M,D
Emergency Management — M,D,O
English — D
French — M,D
Gender Studies — M,D
Geography — M,D
German — M,D
Health Psychology — D
Historic Preservation — M,D,O
History of Medicine — D
History of Science and Technology — D
History — D
Industrial and Labor Relations — M,D
Interdisciplinary Studies — D
International Affairs — M,D
Italian — M,D
Jewish Studies — M,O
Linguistics — M
Medieval and Renaissance Studies — D
Music — M,D,O
Philosophy — D
Political Science — D
Psychology—General — D
Public Policy — M,D
Religion — M,O
School Psychology — M,D
Social Psychology — D
Sociology — M,D
Spanish — M,D
Theater — M
Translation and Interpretation — M,D
Urban and Regional Planning — M,D
Women's Studies — M,D
Writing — M

**RYERSON UNIVERSITY**
Arts Administration — M

**SACRED HEART MAJOR SEMINARY**
Pastoral Ministry and Counseling — M
Theology — M

**SACRED HEART SCHOOL OF THEOLOGY**
Theology — M,O

**SACRED HEART UNIVERSITY**
Applied Psychology — M
Communication—General — M
Criminal Justice and Criminology — M
Film, Television, and Video
  Production — M
Industrial and Organizational
  Psychology — M
Journalism — M

---

*M—masters degree; D—doctorate; O—other advanced degree; *—Close-Up and/or Display*

Media Studies — M
Social Psychology — M

**SAGE GRADUATE SCHOOL**
Applied Behavior Analysis — M,O
Counseling Psychology — M
Forensic Psychology — M,O
Gerontology — M
Psychology—General — M,O
Social Psychology — M

**SAGINAW VALLEY STATE UNIVERSITY**
Chinese — M
Communication—General — M
Media Studies — M
Public Administration — M

**ST. AMBROSE UNIVERSITY**
Criminal Justice and Criminology — M
Pastoral Ministry and Counseling — M

**ST. ANDREW'S COLLEGE**
Theology — M,D,O

**ST. ANDREW'S COLLEGE IN WINNIPEG**
Theology — M

**ST. AUGUSTINE'S SEMINARY OF TORONTO**
Pastoral Ministry and Counseling — M,O
Theology — M,O

**ST. BERNARD'S SCHOOL OF THEOLOGY AND MINISTRY**
Pastoral Ministry and Counseling — M,O
Theology — M,O

**ST. BONAVENTURE UNIVERSITY**
Corporate and Organizational
  Communication — M
Counseling Psychology — M,O
Rehabilitation Counseling — M,O
Religion — M,O
Social Psychology — M,O

**ST. CATHERINE UNIVERSITY**
Pastoral Ministry and Counseling — M,O
Theology — M,O

**SAINT CHARLES BORROMEO SEMINARY, OVERBROOK**
Religion — M
Theology — M

**ST. CLOUD STATE UNIVERSITY**
Applied Behavior Analysis — M
Applied Economics — M
Archaeology — M
Child and Family Studies — M
Criminal Justice and Criminology — M
Economics — M
English — M
Geography — M
Gerontology — M
Historic Preservation — M
History — M
Industrial and Organizational
  Psychology — M
Marriage and Family Therapy — M
Mass Communication — M
Music — M
Psychology—General — M,D
Rehabilitation Counseling — M
Social Psychology — M

**ST. EDWARD'S UNIVERSITY**
Counseling Psychology — M
Humanities — M,O
Liberal Studies — M,O
Sustainable Development — M

**ST. FRANCIS XAVIER UNIVERSITY**
Cultural Studies — M
Urban and Regional Planning — M

**ST. JOHN FISHER COLLEGE**
Counseling Psychology — M
French — M

**ST. JOHN'S COLLEGE (MD)**
Liberal Studies — M

**ST. JOHN'S COLLEGE (NM)**
Asian Languages — M
Asian Studies — M
Liberal Studies — M

**ST. JOHN'S SEMINARY (CA)**
Pastoral Ministry and Counseling — M
Theology — M

**SAINT JOHN'S SEMINARY (MA)**
Religion — M
Theology — M

**SAINT JOHN'S UNIVERSITY (MN)**
Music — M
Pastoral Ministry and Counseling — M
Theology — M

**ST. JOHN'S UNIVERSITY (NY)**
Asian Studies — M,O
Clinical Psychology — M,D,O
Counseling Psychology — M,D,O
Criminal Justice and Criminology — M
English — M,D
Experimental Psychology — M
History — M,D
International Affairs — M,O
Liberal Studies — M
Museum Studies — M
Political Science — M,O
Psychology—General — M,D
Public Administration — M,D
Public History — M,D
School Psychology — M,D
Sociology — M
Spanish — M
Theology — M

**ST. JOSEPH'S COLLEGE, NEW YORK**
Forensic Sciences — M
Writing — M

**SAINT JOSEPH'S COLLEGE OF MAINE**
Pastoral Ministry and Counseling — M

**ST. JOSEPH'S SEMINARY**
Pastoral Ministry and Counseling — M
Religion — M
Theology — M

**SAINT JOSEPH'S UNIVERSITY**
Criminal Justice and Criminology — M,O
Psychology—General — M,O
Writing — M

**ST. LAWRENCE UNIVERSITY**
Human Development — M,O

**SAINT LEO UNIVERSITY**
Criminal Justice and Criminology — M
Emergency Management — M
Forensic Sciences — M
Theology — M,O
Writing — M

**SAINT LOUIS UNIVERSITY**
American Studies — M,D
Clinical Psychology — M,D
Communication—General — M
English — M,D
Experimental Psychology — M,D
French — M
Geographic Information Systems — M,D,O
History — M,D
Human Development — M,D,O
Industrial and Organizational
  Psychology — M,D
Marriage and Family Therapy — M,D,O
Philosophy — M,D
Political Science — M,D
Psychology—General — M,D
Public Administration — M,D,O
Public Policy — M,D,O
Spanish — M
Theology — M,D
Urban Studies — M,D,O

**SAINT LOUIS UNIVERSITY–MADRID CAMPUS**
English — M
Spanish — M

**SAINT MARTIN'S UNIVERSITY**
Counseling Psychology — M
Social Psychology — M

**SAINT MARY-OF-THE-WOODS COLLEGE**
Art Therapy — M,O
Therapies—Dance, Drama, and
  Music — M

**SAINT MARY'S COLLEGE OF CALIFORNIA**
Conflict Resolution and
  Mediation/Peace Studies — M
Dance — M
Marriage and Family Therapy — M,O
School Psychology — M,O
Writing — M

**SAINT MARY SEMINARY AND GRADUATE SCHOOL OF THEOLOGY**
Theology — M,D

**ST. MARY'S SEMINARY AND UNIVERSITY**
Theology — M,D,O

**SAINT MARY'S UNIVERSITY (CANADA)**
Applied Psychology — M,D
Canadian Studies — M,O
Criminal Justice and Criminology — M
Gender Studies — M
History — M
Industrial and Organizational
  Psychology — M,D
International Development — M,O
Philosophy — M
Psychology—General — M,D
Religion — M
Theology — M
Women's Studies — M

**ST. MARY'S UNIVERSITY (UNITED STATES)**
Communication—General — M,O
Conflict Resolution and
  Mediation/Peace Studies — M,O
Counseling Psychology — M
English — M
Homeland Security — M,O
Industrial and Organizational
  Psychology — M
International Affairs — M,O
International Development — M,O
Marriage and Family Therapy — M,D
Public Administration — M,O
Public Policy — M,O
Theology — M

**SAINT MARY'S UNIVERSITY OF MINNESOTA**
Addictions/Substance Abuse
  Counseling — M,O
Arts Administration — M
Counseling Psychology — M,D,O
Geographic Information Systems — M,O
Human Development — M
International Development — M
Marriage and Family Therapy — M
Philanthropic Studies — M

**SAINT MEINRAD SCHOOL OF THEOLOGY**
Theology — M

**SAINT MICHAEL'S COLLEGE**
Clinical Psychology — M

**ST. NORBERT COLLEGE**
Liberal Studies — M
Theology — M

**ST. PATRICK'S SEMINARY & UNIVERSITY**
Theology — M,O

**SAINT PAUL SCHOOL OF THEOLOGY**
Theology — M,D

**SAINT PAUL UNIVERSITY**
Conflict Resolution and
  Mediation/Peace Studies — M
Counseling Psychology — M
Marriage and Family Therapy — M
Missions and Missiology — M
Pastoral Ministry and Counseling — M,D,O
Theology — M,D,O

**ST. PETER'S SEMINARY**
Theology — M

**SAINT PETER'S UNIVERSITY**
Applied Behavior Analysis — M
Criminal Justice and Criminology — M
Public Administration — M

**SAINTS CYRIL AND METHODIUS SEMINARY**
Pastoral Ministry and Counseling — M
Theology — M

**ST. STEPHEN'S COLLEGE**
Pastoral Ministry and Counseling — M,D
Theology — M,D

**ST. THOMAS UNIVERSITY**
Arts Administration — M
Communication—General — M,D,O
Counseling Psychology — M
Criminal Justice and Criminology — M,O
Film, Television, and Video
  Production — M
Hispanic Studies — M,O
Marriage and Family Therapy — M,O
Pastoral Ministry and Counseling — M,D,O
Public Administration — M,O
Theology — M,D,O

**ST. TIKHON'S ORTHODOX THEOLOGICAL SEMINARY**
Theology — M

**ST. VINCENT DE PAUL REGIONAL SEMINARY**
Theology — M

**SAINT VINCENT SEMINARY**
Pastoral Ministry and Counseling — M
Theology — M

**ST. VLADIMIR'S ORTHODOX THEOLOGICAL SEMINARY**
Theology — M,D

**SAINT XAVIER UNIVERSITY**
Spanish — M

**SALEM STATE UNIVERSITY**
Counseling Psychology — M,O
Criminal Justice and Criminology — M
English — M
Geography — M
History — M
Psychology—General — M,O
Spanish — M

**SALISBURY UNIVERSITY**
American Studies — M
Conflict Resolution and
  Mediation/Peace Studies — M
English — M
Film, Television, and Video
  Theory and Criticism — M
Geographic Information Systems — M
History — M
Rhetoric — M
Writing — M

**SALVE REGINA UNIVERSITY**
Addictions/Substance Abuse
  Counseling — M,O
Conflict Resolution and
  Mediation/Peace Studies — M,D
Counseling Psychology — M,O
Criminal Justice and Criminology — M,O
Forensic Sciences — M,O
Homeland Security — M,O
Humanities — M,D
International Affairs — M,O
Rehabilitation Counseling — M,O
Religion — M,D

**SAMFORD UNIVERSITY**
Applied Arts and Design—
  General — M
Music — M
Theology — M,D

**SAM HOUSTON STATE UNIVERSITY**
Clinical Psychology — M,D,O
Communication—General — M
Criminal Justice and Criminology — M,D
Dance — M
English — M
Family and Consumer
  Sciences-General — M
Forensic Sciences — M,D
Geographic Information Systems — M,O
History — M
Homeland Security — M
Humanities — M,D,O
Internet and Interactive
  Multimedia — M
Music — M
Political Science — M

Psychology—General — M,D,O
Public Administration — M
Publishing — M
School Psychology — M,D,O
Sociology — M
Spanish — M
Writing — M

**SAN DIEGO STATE UNIVERSITY**
Anthropology — M
Applied Arts and Design—
  General — M
Art History — M
Art/Fine Arts — M
Asian Studies — M
Child and Family Studies — M
Child Development — M
Clinical Psychology — M,D
Communication—General — M
Criminal Justice and Criminology — M
Economics — M
Emergency Management — M,D
English — M
Environmental Design — M
Film, Television, and Video
  Production — M
Gender Studies — O
Geography — M,D
Gerontology — M
Graphic Design — M
Health Psychology — M,D
History — M
Industrial and Organizational
  Psychology — M,D
Interdisciplinary Studies — M
Interior Design — M
Internet and Interactive
  Multimedia — M
Latin American Studies — M
Liberal Studies — M
Linguistics — M,O
Media Studies — M
Music — M
Philosophy — M
Political Science — M
Psychology—General — M,D
Public Administration — M
Rehabilitation Counseling — M
Rhetoric — M
Romance Languages — M
School Psychology — M
Sociology — M
Spanish — M
Theater — M
Urban and Regional Planning — M
Western European Studies — M
Women's Studies — M
Writing — M

**SAN FRANCISCO ART INSTITUTE**
Art History — M
Art/Fine Arts — M,O
Museum Studies — M

**SAN FRANCISCO CONSERVATORY OF MUSIC**
Music — M,O

**SAN FRANCISCO STATE UNIVERSITY**
Anthropology — M
Applied Arts and Design—
  General — M
Archaeology — M
Art History — M
Art/Fine Arts — M
Asian-American Studies — M
Chinese — M
Classics — M
Clinical Psychology — M,O
Comparative Literature — M
Counseling Psychology — M,O
Criminal Justice and Criminology — M
Cultural Anthropology — M
Cultural Studies — M
Developmental Psychology — M,O
Economics — M
English — M,O
Ethnic Studies — M
Family and Consumer
  Sciences-General — M
Film, Television, and Video
  Production — M
Film, Television, and Video
  Theory and Criticism — M
French — M
Geographic Information Systems — M
Geography — M
German — M
Gerontology — M
History — M
Humanities — M
Industrial and Organizational
  Psychology — M,O
International Affairs — M
Italian — M
Japanese — M
Liberal Studies — M
Linguistics — M
Marriage and Family Therapy — M,O
Media Studies — M
Museum Studies — M
Music — M
Philosophy — M
Political Science — M
Psychology—General — M,O
Public Administration — M
Public Policy — M
Rehabilitation Counseling — M,O
School Psychology — M,O
Social Psychology — M,O
Spanish — M
Speech and Interpersonal
  Communication — M
Theater — M

Women's Studies M
Writing M

**SAN FRANCISCO THEOLOGICAL SEMINARY**
Theology M,D

**SAN JOSE STATE UNIVERSITY**
Anthropology M,O
Art History M,O
Child Development M,D,O
Clinical Psychology M,O
Communication—General M,O
Economics M,O
English M,O
Experimental Psychology M,O
French M,O
Geography M,O
Hispanic Studies M,O
History M,O
Industrial and Organizational
　Psychology M,O
Linguistics M,O
Mass Communication M,O
Media Studies M,O
Music M,O
Philosophy M,O
Photography M,O
Psychology—General M,O
Public Administration M,O
School Psychology M,D,O
Sociology M,O
Spanish M,O
Sustainable Development M,O
Theater M,O
Writing M,O

**SANTA CLARA UNIVERSITY**
Counseling Psychology M
Ethics M,D,O
Pastoral Ministry and Counseling M,D,O
Religion M,D,O
Theology M,D,O

**SARAH LAWRENCE COLLEGE**
Child Development M
Dance M
Genetic Counseling M
History M
Theater M
Women's Studies M
Writing M

**SAVANNAH COLLEGE OF ART AND DESIGN**
Applied Arts and Design—
　General M
Architectural History M
Architecture M
Art History M
Art/Fine Arts M
Arts Administration M
Clothing and Textiles M
Computer Art and Design M
Film, Television, and Video
　Production M
Film, Television, and Video
　Theory and Criticism M
Graphic Design M
Historic Preservation M
Illustration M
Industrial Design M
Interior Design M
Internet and Interactive
　Multimedia M
Media Studies M
Music M
Photography M
Sustainable Development M
Textile Design M
Theater M
Urban Design M
Writing M

**SAVANNAH STATE UNIVERSITY**
Public Administration M
Urban and Regional Planning M
Urban Studies M

**SAYBROOK UNIVERSITY**
Clinical Psychology M
Counseling Psychology M
Health Psychology M,D
Marriage and Family Therapy M,D
Psychology—General M,D
Sustainable Development M,D
Transpersonal and Humanistic
　Psychology M,D

**SCHILLER INTERNATIONAL UNIVERSITY**
International Affairs M

**SCHOOL OF ADVANCED AIR AND SPACE STUDIES**
Military and Defense Studies M

**SCHOOL OF ARCHITECTURE AT TALIESIN**
Architecture M*

**SCHOOL OF THE ART INSTITUTE OF CHICAGO**
Applied Arts and Design—
　General M
Architecture M
Art History M
Art Therapy M
Art/Fine Arts M
Arts Administration M
Arts Journalism M
Film, Television, and Video
　Production M
Graphic Design M

Historic Preservation M
Interior Design M
Journalism M
Music M
Photography M
Textile Design M,O
Writing M,O

**SCHOOL OF VISUAL ARTS (NY)**
Applied Arts and Design—
　General M
Art History M
Art Therapy M
Art/Fine Arts M
Computer Art and Design M
Cultural Studies M
Film, Television, and Video
　Production M
Graphic Design M
Illustration M
Internet and Interactive
　Multimedia M
Photography M
Writing M

**SCHREINER UNIVERSITY**
Ethics M

**SEATTLE PACIFIC UNIVERSITY**
Clinical Psychology D
Industrial and Organizational
　Psychology M,D
Marriage and Family Therapy M,O
Religion M,O
Theology M,O
Writing M

**THE SEATTLE SCHOOL OF THEOLOGY AND PSYCHOLOGY**
Counseling Psychology M
Psychology—General M
Religion M
Theology M

**SEATTLE UNIVERSITY**
Arts Administration M
Criminal Justice and Criminology M,O
Forensic Sciences M,O
Marriage and Family Therapy M
Pastoral Ministry and Counseling M
Psychology—General M
Public Administration M
School Psychology M,O
Theology M,D,O
Transpersonal and Humanistic
　Psychology M

**SELMA UNIVERSITY**
Pastoral Ministry and Counseling M
Religion M

**SEMINARY OF THE SOUTHWEST**
Theology M

**SETON HALL UNIVERSITY**
Asian Studies M
Communication—General M
Corporate and Organizational
　Communication M
Counseling Psychology M,D
English M
Experimental Psychology M
History M
International Affairs M,O
Jewish Studies M,O
Marriage and Family Therapy M
Museum Studies M
Pastoral Ministry and Counseling M,O
Psychology—General M,D
Public Administration M,O
Public Policy M,O
Religion M,O
School Psychology M
Speech and Interpersonal
　Communication M
Sport Psychology M
Theology M,O

**SETON HILL UNIVERSITY**
Art Therapy M
Holocaust and Genocide Studies O
Marriage and Family Therapy M
Writing M,O

**SEWANEE: THE UNIVERSITY OF THE SOUTH**
English M
Theology M,D
Writing M

**SHASTA BIBLE COLLEGE**
Pastoral Ministry and Counseling M

**SHAW UNIVERSITY**
Theology M

**SHENANDOAH UNIVERSITY**
Applied Behavior Analysis M
Music M,D,O
Therapies—Dance, Drama, and
　Music M,D,O

**SHEPHERDS THEOLOGICAL SEMINARY**
Pastoral Ministry and Counseling M
Theology M

**SHEPHERD UNIVERSITY (CA)**
Computer Art and Design M
Music M
Theology M,D

**SHILOH UNIVERSITY**
Pastoral Ministry and Counseling M,D
Theology M,D

**SHIPPENSBURG UNIVERSITY OF PENNSYLVANIA**
Clinical Psychology M,D,O
Communication—General M
Criminal Justice and Criminology M
Geography M,O
History M,O
Marriage and Family Therapy M,D,O
Psychology—General M
Public Administration M
Public History M
Sociology M

**SH'OR YOSHUV RABBINICAL COLLEGE**
Theology M

**SIENA HEIGHTS UNIVERSITY**
Clinical Psychology M,O
Counseling Psychology M,O

**SILVER LAKE COLLEGE OF THE HOLY FAMILY**
Music M

**SIMMONS COLLEGE**
Applied Behavior Analysis M,D,O
Communication—General M
Cultural Studies M
English M
Gender Studies M
History M
Public Policy M
Writing M,D,O

**SIMON FRASER UNIVERSITY**
Anthropology M,D
Archaeology M,D
Communication—General M,D
Comparative and Interdisciplinary
　Arts M,D
Criminal Justice and Criminology M,D
Cultural Studies D
Economics M,D
English M,D
French M
Gender Studies M,D
Geography M,D
Gerontology M,D
History M,D
Humanities M
International Affairs M
Latin American Studies M,O
Liberal Studies M
Linguistics M,D
Philosophy M,D
Political Science M,D
Psychology—General M
Public Policy M
Publishing M
Sociology M,D
Urban Studies M,O
Women's Studies M,D

**SIMPSON COLLEGE**
Criminal Justice and Criminology M

**SIMPSON UNIVERSITY**
Counseling Psychology M
Missions and Missiology M
Pastoral Ministry and Counseling M

**SIOUX FALLS SEMINARY**
Marriage and Family Therapy M
Pastoral Ministry and Counseling M
Religion M
Theology M,D,O

**SIT GRADUATE INSTITUTE**
Conflict Resolution and
　Mediation/Peace Studies M
International Affairs M
Sustainable Development M

**SLIPPERY ROCK UNIVERSITY OF PENNSYLVANIA**
Clinical Psychology M
Counseling Psychology M
Criminal Justice and Criminology M
English M
History M
School Psychology M
Therapies—Dance, Drama, and
　Music M

**SMITH COLLEGE**
Dance M
French M
History M
Spanish M
Theater M
Women's Studies O

**SOFIA UNIVERSITY**
Clinical Psychology M,D
Counseling Psychology M,D
Psychology—General M,D
Transpersonal and Humanistic
　Psychology M,D

**SONOMA STATE UNIVERSITY**
Anthropology M
Clinical Psychology M
Counseling Psychology M
English M
History M
Interdisciplinary Studies M
Political Science M,O
Public Administration M,O
Public History M
School Psychology M
Writing M

**SOTHEBY'S INSTITUTE OF ART–LONDON**
Art/Fine Arts M

Arts Administration M
Decorative Arts M

**SOTHEBY'S INSTITUTE OF ART–NEW YORK**
Art/Fine Arts M
Arts Administration M
Decorative Arts M

**SOUTH CAROLINA STATE UNIVERSITY**
Agricultural Economics and
　Agribusiness M
Child and Family Studies M
English M
Family and Consumer
　Sciences-General M
Rehabilitation Counseling M

**SOUTH DAKOTA STATE UNIVERSITY**
Communication—General M
Consumer Economics M
Economics M
English M
Family and Consumer
　Sciences-General M
Geography M
Industrial and Organizational
　Psychology M
Journalism M
Sociology M,D

**SOUTHEASTERN BAPTIST THEOLOGICAL SEMINARY**
Ethics M,D
Missions and Missiology M,D
Music M,D
Philosophy M,D
Psychology—General M,D
Theology M,D
Women's Studies M,D

**SOUTHEASTERN LOUISIANA UNIVERSITY**
Communication—General M
English M
History M
Industrial and Organizational
　Psychology M
Music M
Psychology—General M
Sociology M
Writing M

**SOUTHEASTERN OKLAHOMA STATE UNIVERSITY**
Clinical Psychology M
Counseling Psychology M

**SOUTHEASTERN UNIVERSITY (FL)**
Counseling Psychology M
Marriage and Family Therapy M
Pastoral Ministry and Counseling M,D
Theology M,D
Urban and Regional Planning M

**SOUTHEAST MISSOURI STATE UNIVERSITY**
Counseling Psychology M,O
Criminal Justice and Criminology M
English M
Historic Preservation M,O
History M,O
Public Administration M
Public History M

**SOUTHERN ADVENTIST UNIVERSITY**
Counseling Psychology M
Missions and Missiology M
Psychology—General M
Religion M
Theology M

**SOUTHERN ARKANSAS UNIVERSITY–MAGNOLIA**
Public Administration M

**THE SOUTHERN BAPTIST THEOLOGICAL SEMINARY**
Missions and Missiology M,D
Pastoral Ministry and Counseling M,D
Philosophy M,D
Religion M,D
Theology M,D

**SOUTHERN CALIFORNIA INSTITUTE OF ARCHITECTURE**
Architecture M*

**SOUTHERN CALIFORNIA SEMINARY**
Counseling Psychology M,D
Marriage and Family Therapy M,D
Psychology—General M,D
Religion M,D
Theology M,D

**SOUTHERN CONNECTICUT STATE UNIVERSITY**
English M
History M
Political Science M
Psychology—General M
School Psychology M,O
Sociology M
Women's Studies M

**SOUTHERN EVANGELICAL SEMINARY**
Jewish Studies M,D,O
Missions and Missiology M,D,O
Near and Middle Eastern Studies M,D,O
Pastoral Ministry and Counseling M,D,O
Philosophy M,D,O
Religion M,D,O
Theology M,D,O

*M—masters degree; D—doctorate; O—other advanced degree; *—Close-Up and/or Display*

## SOUTHERN ILLINOIS UNIVERSITY CARBONDALE

| | |
|---|---|
| Agricultural Economics and Agribusiness | M |
| Anthropology | M,D |
| Applied Arts and Design—General | M |
| Architecture | M |
| Art/Fine Arts | M |
| Clinical Psychology | M,D |
| Communication—General | M,D |
| Counseling Psychology | M,D |
| Criminal Justice and Criminology | M,D |
| Cultural Studies | M |
| Economics | M,D |
| English | M,D |
| Experimental Psychology | M,D |
| Geography | M,D |
| History | M,D |
| Homeland Security | M |
| Linguistics | M |
| Mass Communication | M,D |
| Media Studies | M,D |
| Music | M |
| Philosophy | M,D |
| Political Science | M,D |
| Psychology—General | M,D |
| Public Administration | M |
| Rhetoric | M,D |
| Sociology | M,D |
| Speech and Interpersonal Communication | M,D |
| Theater | M,D |
| Writing | M |

## SOUTHERN ILLINOIS UNIVERSITY EDWARDSVILLE

| | |
|---|---|
| Art Therapy | M |
| Art/Fine Arts | M |
| Clinical Psychology | M |
| Corporate and Organizational Communication | M |
| Cultural Anthropology | M |
| Economics | M |
| English | M,O |
| Geography | M |
| Health Communication | M |
| History | M |
| Industrial and Organizational Psychology | M |
| Interdisciplinary Studies | M |
| Mass Communication | M |
| Media Studies | O |
| Museum Studies | O |
| Music | M |
| Psychology—General | M,O |
| Public Administration | M |
| School Psychology | O |
| Sociology | M |
| Speech and Interpersonal Communication | M |
| Sport Psychology | M |
| Sustainable Development | M |
| Writing | M |

## SOUTHERN METHODIST UNIVERSITY

| | |
|---|---|
| Anthropology | M,D |
| Applied Economics | M,D |
| Art History | M,D |
| Art/Fine Arts | M |
| Arts Administration | M |
| Clinical Psychology | D |
| Conflict Resolution and Mediation/Peace Studies | M |
| Economics | M,D |
| English | M,D |
| Ethics | M,D |
| Experimental Psychology | M,D |
| History | M,D |
| Liberal Studies | M |
| Medieval and Renaissance Studies | M |
| Music | M |
| Photography | M |
| Psychology—General | D |
| Religion | M,D |
| Sustainable Development | M,D |
| Theater | M |
| Theology | M |

## SOUTHERN NAZARENE UNIVERSITY

| | |
|---|---|
| Counseling Psychology | M |
| Marriage and Family Therapy | M |
| Psychology—General | M |

## SOUTHERN NEW HAMPSHIRE UNIVERSITY

| | |
|---|---|
| Child Development | M,D,O |
| Conflict Resolution and Mediation/Peace Studies | M,O |
| Ethics | M,O |
| Industrial and Labor Relations | M,O |
| Internet and Interactive Multimedia | M,O |
| Psychology—General | M,O |
| Writing | M,O |

## SOUTHERN OREGON UNIVERSITY

| | |
|---|---|
| Counseling Psychology | M |
| French | M |
| Interdisciplinary Studies | M |
| Music | M |
| Psychology—General | M |
| Spanish | M |
| Theater | M |

## SOUTHERN UNIVERSITY AND AGRICULTURAL AND MECHANICAL COLLEGE

| | |
|---|---|
| Criminal Justice and Criminology | M |
| History | M |
| Mass Communication | M |
| Political Science | M |
| Psychology—General | M |
| Public Administration | M |
| Public Policy | D |

| | |
|---|---|
| Rehabilitation Counseling | M |
| Social Sciences | M |

## SOUTHERN UNIVERSITY AT NEW ORLEANS

| | |
|---|---|
| Criminal Justice and Criminology | M |
| Museum Studies | M |

## SOUTHERN UTAH UNIVERSITY

| | |
|---|---|
| Arts Administration | M |
| Communication—General | M |
| Music | M |
| Public Administration | M |

## SOUTHERN WESLEYAN UNIVERSITY

| | |
|---|---|
| Pastoral Ministry and Counseling | M |

## SOUTH FLORIDA BIBLE COLLEGE AND THEOLOGICAL SEMINARY

| | |
|---|---|
| Theology | M |

## SOUTH UNIVERSITY (AL)

| | |
|---|---|
| Counseling Psychology | M |
| Criminal Justice and Criminology | M |
| Public Administration | M |

## SOUTH UNIVERSITY

| | |
|---|---|
| Counseling Psychology | M |
| Criminal Justice and Criminology | M |
| Public Administration | M |

## SOUTH UNIVERSITY

| | |
|---|---|
| Criminal Justice and Criminology | M |

## SOUTH UNIVERSITY (GA)

| | |
|---|---|
| Counseling Psychology | M |
| Criminal Justice and Criminology | M |
| Pastoral Ministry and Counseling | D |
| Public Administration | M |

## SOUTH UNIVERSITY (MI)

| | |
|---|---|
| Counseling Psychology | M |
| Pastoral Ministry and Counseling | D |

## SOUTH UNIVERSITY (NC)

| | |
|---|---|
| Counseling Psychology | M |

## SOUTH UNIVERSITY (OH)

| | |
|---|---|
| Clinical Psychology | M |
| Counseling Psychology | M |

## SOUTH UNIVERSITY (SC)

| | |
|---|---|
| Counseling Psychology | M |
| Criminal Justice and Criminology | M |

## SOUTH UNIVERSITY (TX)

| | |
|---|---|
| Counseling Psychology | M |

## SOUTH UNIVERSITY

| | |
|---|---|
| Counseling Psychology | M |

## SOUTH UNIVERSITY

| | |
|---|---|
| Counseling Psychology | M |

## SOUTHWESTERN ASSEMBLIES OF GOD UNIVERSITY

| | |
|---|---|
| Counseling Psychology | M |
| History | M |
| Missions and Missiology | M |
| Pastoral Ministry and Counseling | M |
| Religion | M |
| Theology | M |

## SOUTHWESTERN BAPTIST THEOLOGICAL SEMINARY

| | |
|---|---|
| Missions and Missiology | M,D |
| Music | M,D |
| Near and Middle Eastern Studies | M,D |
| Pastoral Ministry and Counseling | M,D,O |
| Theology | M,D |

## SOUTHWESTERN CHRISTIAN UNIVERSITY

| | |
|---|---|
| Missions and Missiology | M |
| Pastoral Ministry and Counseling | M |

## SOUTHWESTERN COLLEGE (KS)

| | |
|---|---|
| Criminal Justice and Criminology | M |

## SOUTHWESTERN COLLEGE (NM)

| | |
|---|---|
| Art Therapy | M |
| Counseling Psychology | M,O |
| Health Psychology | O |
| Psychology—General | O |
| Social Psychology | O |
| Thanatology | M,O |

## SOUTHWESTERN OKLAHOMA STATE UNIVERSITY

| | |
|---|---|
| Music | M |
| School Psychology | M |

## SOUTHWEST UNIVERSITY

| | |
|---|---|
| Criminal Justice and Criminology | M |

## SOUTHWEST UNIVERSITY OF VISUAL ARTS

| | |
|---|---|
| Art/Fine Arts | M |
| Photography | M |

## SPALDING UNIVERSITY

| | |
|---|---|
| Clinical Psychology | M,D |
| Corporate and Organizational Communication | M |
| Psychology—General | M,D |
| Writing | M |

## SPERTUS INSTITUTE FOR JEWISH LEARNING AND LEADERSHIP

| | |
|---|---|
| Jewish Studies | M,D |

## SPRING ARBOR UNIVERSITY

| | |
|---|---|
| Child and Family Studies | M |
| Communication—General | M |
| Counseling Psychology | M |
| Pastoral Ministry and Counseling | M |
| Theology | M |

## SPRINGFIELD COLLEGE

| | |
|---|---|
| Addictions/Substance Abuse Counseling | M |
| Art Therapy | M,O |
| Clinical Psychology | M,D,O |

| | |
|---|---|
| Counseling Psychology | M,D,O |
| Industrial and Organizational Psychology | M,D,O |
| Rehabilitation Counseling | M |
| Sport Psychology | M,D,O |

## SPRING HILL COLLEGE

| | |
|---|---|
| Art/Fine Arts | M,O |
| English | M,O |
| Ethics | M,O |
| History | M,O |
| Liberal Studies | M,O |
| Pastoral Ministry and Counseling | M,O |
| Theology | M,O |

## STANFORD UNIVERSITY

| | |
|---|---|
| Anthropology | M,D |
| Applied Arts and Design—General | M,D,O |
| Archaeology | M,D |
| Art/Fine Arts | M,D |
| Asian Languages | M,D |
| Asian Studies | M |
| Chinese | M,D |
| Classics | M,D |
| Communication—General | M,D |
| Comparative Literature | D |
| Cultural Studies | M,D |
| East European and Russian Studies | M |
| Economics | D |
| English | M,D |
| Film, Television, and Video Production | M,D |
| French | M,D |
| German | M,D |
| History | M,D |
| Italian | M,D |
| Japanese | M,D |
| Linguistics | M,D |
| Music | M,D |
| Philosophy | M,D |
| Political Science | M,D |
| Psychology—General | D |
| Religion | D |
| Slavic Languages | D |
| Sociology | D |
| Spanish | M,D |
| Sustainable Development | M,D,O |
| Theater | M,D |

## STARR KING SCHOOL FOR THE MINISTRY

| | |
|---|---|
| Theology | M |

## STATE UNIVERSITY OF NEW YORK AT FREDONIA

| | |
|---|---|
| Interdisciplinary Studies | M |
| Music | M |

## STATE UNIVERSITY OF NEW YORK AT NEW PALTZ

| | |
|---|---|
| Art/Fine Arts | M |
| Counseling Psychology | M,O |
| English | M |
| French | M,O |
| Music | M |
| Psychology—General | M,O |
| Spanish | M,O |
| Therapies—Dance, Drama, and Music | M |

## STATE UNIVERSITY OF NEW YORK AT OSWEGO

| | |
|---|---|
| Art/Fine Arts | M |
| Child and Family Studies | M |
| Communication—General | M |
| Consumer Economics | M |
| Corporate and Organizational Communication | M |
| Counseling Psychology | M |
| English | M |
| Graphic Design | M |
| Health Communication | M |
| History | M |
| Internet and Interactive Multimedia | M |

## STATE UNIVERSITY OF NEW YORK AT PLATTSBURGH

| | |
|---|---|
| Clinical Psychology | M,O |
| Counseling Psychology | M,O |
| Psychology—General | M,O |
| School Psychology | M,O |

## STATE UNIVERSITY OF NEW YORK COLLEGE AT CORTLAND

| | |
|---|---|
| English | M |
| History | M |

## STATE UNIVERSITY OF NEW YORK COLLEGE AT OLD WESTBURY

| | |
|---|---|
| Counseling Psychology | M |
| Liberal Studies | M |

## STATE UNIVERSITY OF NEW YORK COLLEGE AT ONEONTA

| | |
|---|---|
| Museum Studies | M |

## STATE UNIVERSITY OF NEW YORK COLLEGE AT POTSDAM

| | |
|---|---|
| Communication—General | M |
| English | M |
| Music | M |

## STATE UNIVERSITY OF NEW YORK COLLEGE OF ENVIRONMENTAL SCIENCE AND FORESTRY

| | |
|---|---|
| Economics | M,D |
| Geographic Information Systems | M,D |
| Landscape Architecture | M |
| Sustainable Development | M,D,O |
| Urban and Regional Planning | M,D |
| Urban Design | M |

## STATE UNIVERSITY OF NEW YORK EMPIRE STATE COLLEGE

| | |
|---|---|
| Economic Development | M |

| | |
|---|---|
| Industrial and Labor Relations | M |
| Liberal Studies | M |
| Public Policy | M |

## STEPHEN F. AUSTIN STATE UNIVERSITY

| | |
|---|---|
| Applied Arts and Design—General | M |
| Art/Fine Arts | M |
| Communication—General | M |
| English | M |
| Family and Consumer Sciences-General | M |
| History | M |
| Interdisciplinary Studies | M |
| Mass Communication | M |
| Music | M |
| Psychology—General | M |
| Public Administration | M |
| School Psychology | M |

## STEPHENS COLLEGE

| | |
|---|---|
| Addictions/Substance Abuse Counseling | M,O |
| Clinical Psychology | M,O |
| Writing | M,O |

## STETSON UNIVERSITY

| | |
|---|---|
| Counseling Psychology | M |
| Marriage and Family Therapy | M |
| Writing | M |

## STEVENS INSTITUTE OF TECHNOLOGY

| | |
|---|---|
| Communication—General | M,D,O |
| Computer Art and Design | M,D,O |
| Corporate and Organizational Communication | O |
| Ethics | M,O |
| Film, Television, and Video Production | M |
| Internet and Interactive Multimedia | M,D,O |
| Media Studies | M |

## STEVENSON UNIVERSITY

| | |
|---|---|
| Communication—General | M |
| Forensic Sciences | M |

## STOCKTON UNIVERSITY

| | |
|---|---|
| American Studies | M,O |
| Criminal Justice and Criminology | M |
| Holocaust and Genocide Studies | M |

## STONY BROOK UNIVERSITY, STATE UNIVERSITY OF NEW YORK

| | |
|---|---|
| Addictions/Substance Abuse Counseling | M,O |
| African Studies | M,O |
| Anthropology | M,D |
| Art History | M,D |
| Art/Fine Arts | M |
| Asian Studies | M |
| Asian-American Studies | M |
| Clinical Psychology | D |
| Cognitive Sciences | D |
| Comparative Literature | M,D,O |
| Cultural Studies | M,D,O |
| Economics | M,D |
| English | M,D,O |
| Film, Television, and Video Production | M |
| French | M |
| Gender Studies | O |
| Geographic Information Systems | O |
| Health Communication | M,O |
| Health Psychology | D |
| Hispanic and Latin American Languages | M,D |
| History | M,D |
| Italian | M |
| Journalism | M,O |
| Liberal Studies | M,O |
| Linguistics | M,D |
| Music | M,D |
| Philosophy | M,D,O |
| Political Science | M,D |
| Psychology—General | M,D |
| Public Policy | M |
| Romance Languages | M |
| Social Psychology | D |
| Sociology | M,D |
| Theater | M |
| Women's Studies | O |
| Writing | M,O |

## STRATFORD UNIVERSITY (VA)

| | |
|---|---|
| Forensic Sciences | M |

## STRAYER UNIVERSITY

| | |
|---|---|
| Public Administration | M |

## SUFFOLK UNIVERSITY

| | |
|---|---|
| Applied Arts and Design—General | M |
| Clinical Psychology | M,D,O |
| Corporate and Organizational Communication | M |
| Counseling Psychology | M,D,O |
| Criminal Justice and Criminology | M |
| Ethics | M,O |
| Graphic Design | M |
| Interior Design | M |
| Political Science | M,O |
| Psychology—General | M,D,O |
| Public Administration | M |
| Public Policy | M |
| School Psychology | M,D,O |

## SUL ROSS STATE UNIVERSITY

| | |
|---|---|
| Art History | M |
| Art/Fine Arts | M |
| Criminal Justice and Criminology | M |
| Emergency Management | M |
| English | M |
| History | M |
| Political Science | M |
| Psychology—General | M |

## SUM BIBLE COLLEGE & THEOLOGICAL SEMINARY
Pastoral Ministry and Counseling — M
Religion — M
Theology — M

## SYRACUSE UNIVERSITY
Addictions/Substance Abuse Counseling — M,O
African Studies — M
African-American Studies — M
Anthropology — M,D
Applied Arts and Design—General — M
Architecture — M
Art History — M
Art/Fine Arts — M
Arts Journalism — M
Broadcast Journalism — M
Child and Family Studies — M,D
Clinical Psychology — M,D
Cognitive Sciences — D
Communication—General — M,D
Computer Art and Design — M
Conflict Resolution and Mediation/Peace Studies — O
Disability Studies — O
Economics — M,D
Emergency Management — O
English — M,D
Film, Television, and Video Production — M
Film, Television, and Video Theory and Criticism — M
Forensic Sciences — M,O
French — M
Geography — M,D
History — M,D
Illustration — M
International Affairs — M
Journalism — M
Linguistics — M
Marriage and Family Therapy — M,D
Mass Communication — M,D
Media Studies — M
Museum Studies — M
Music — M
Philosophy — M,D
Photography — M
Political Science — M,D,O
Public Administration — M,D
Public Affairs — M
Religion — M,D
Rhetoric — M,D
School Psychology — M,D,O
Social Psychology — D
Social Sciences — M,D
Sociology — M,D
Spanish — M
Urban and Regional Planning — O
Writing — M,D

## TALMUDIC UNIVERSITY
Theology — M

## TARLETON STATE UNIVERSITY
Applied Psychology — M
Communication—General — M
Counseling Psychology — M
Criminal Justice and Criminology — M
Economics — M
English — M
History — M
Political Science — M
Public Administration — M

## TAYLOR COLLEGE AND SEMINARY
Cultural Studies — M,O
Missions and Missiology — M,O
Theology — M

## TEACHERS COLLEGE, COLUMBIA UNIVERSITY
Anthropology — M,D
Applied Behavior Analysis — M,D,O
Applied Psychology — M,D
Arts Administration — M,D,O
Clinical Psychology — M,D
Communication—General — M,D
Counseling Psychology — M,D
Developmental Psychology — M,D
Economics — M,D
Industrial and Organizational Psychology — M,D
Interdisciplinary Studies — M,D
International Affairs — M,D,O
Linguistics — M,D,O
Philosophy — M,D,O
Political Science — M,D
Psychology—General — M,D
School Psychology — M,D,O
Social Psychology — M,D
Sociology — M,D

## TELSHE YESHIVA–CHICAGO
Jewish Studies — O

## TEMPLE UNIVERSITY
African-American Studies — M,D
Anthropology — D
Architecture — M
Art History — M,D
Art/Fine Arts — M
Arts Administration — M,D
Communication—General — M,D
Corporate and Organizational Communication — M
Counseling Psychology — M,D,O
Criminal Justice and Criminology — M,D
Dance — M,D
Economics — M,D
English — M,D

Film, Television, and Video Production — M
Geographic Information Systems — M,D,O
Geography — M,D,O
Gerontology — D
Graphic Design — M
History — M,D
Industrial and Organizational Psychology — M,D,O
Journalism — M
Landscape Architecture — M
Media Studies — M
Music — M,D
Philosophy — M,D
Photography — M
Political Science — M,D
Psychology—General — M,D
Religion — M,D
School Psychology — M,D,O
Social Psychology — M,D,O
Sociology — M,D
Spanish — M,D
Sustainable Development — M,O
Textile Design — M
Theater — M
Therapies—Dance, Drama, and Music — M,D
Urban and Regional Planning — M,O
Urban Studies — M,D,O
Writing — M,D

## TENNESSEE STATE UNIVERSITY
Counseling Psychology — M
Criminal Justice and Criminology — M
Family and Consumer Sciences-General — M,D
Psychology—General — M
Public Administration — M,D

## TENNESSEE TECHNOLOGICAL UNIVERSITY
Applied Behavior Analysis — D
English — M
Internet and Interactive Multimedia — M

## TEXAS A&M INTERNATIONAL UNIVERSITY
Counseling Psychology — M
Criminal Justice and Criminology — M
English — M,D
Hispanic Studies — M,D
History — M,D
Political Science — M,D
Psychology—General — M
Public Administration — M
Social Sciences — M
Translation and Interpretation — M,D

## TEXAS A&M UNIVERSITY
Agricultural Economics and Agribusiness — M,D
Anthropology — M,D
Architecture — M,D
Art/Fine Arts — M
Clinical Psychology — M,D
Communication—General — M,D
Counseling Psychology — M,D
Cultural Studies — M
Economics — M,D
English — M,D
Geography — M,D
History — M,D
Homeland Security — M,O
Industrial and Organizational Psychology — M,D
International Affairs — M,O
Landscape Architecture — M,D
Music — M
National Security — M,O
Philosophy — M,D
Political Science — M,D
Psychology—General — M,D
Public Administration — M,O
Public Affairs — M,O
School Psychology — M,D
Sociology — M,D
Spanish — M,D
Urban and Regional Planning — M,D

## TEXAS A&M UNIVERSITY–CENTRAL TEXAS
Clinical Psychology — M,O
Criminal Justice and Criminology — M,O
Experimental Psychology — M,O
History — M,O
Liberal Studies — M,O
Marriage and Family Therapy — M,O
Political Science — M,O
School Psychology — M,O

## TEXAS A&M UNIVERSITY–COMMERCE
Art/Fine Arts — M,D,O
Criminal Justice and Criminology — M,D,O
English — M,D,O
Film, Television, and Video Theory and Criticism — M,D,O
History — M,D,O
Linguistics — M,D,O
Music — M,D,O
Political Science — M,D,O
Psychology—General — M,D,O
Public History — M,D,O
School Psychology — M,D,O
Sociology — M,D,O
Spanish — M,D,O
Theater — M,D,O
Writing — M,D,O

## TEXAS A&M UNIVERSITY–CORPUS CHRISTI
Art/Fine Arts — M
Clinical Psychology — M

Communication—General — M
English — M
History — M
Psychology—General — M
Public Administration — M

## TEXAS A&M UNIVERSITY–KINGSVILLE
Agricultural Economics and Agribusiness — M,D
Criminal Justice and Criminology — M,D
Cultural Studies — M
English — M
Family and Consumer Sciences-General — M
Hispanic Studies — D
Music — M
Psychology—General — M
Sociology — M
Spanish — M
Sustainable Development — D

## TEXAS A&M UNIVERSITY–SAN ANTONIO
English — M

## TEXAS A&M UNIVERSITY–TEXARKANA
Counseling Psychology — M
English — M
Interdisciplinary Studies — M
Psychology—General — M

## TEXAS CHRISTIAN UNIVERSITY
American Studies — M,D
Art History — M
Art/Fine Arts — M
Cognitive Sciences — M,D
Communication—General — M
Corporate and Organizational Communication — M
Criminal Justice and Criminology — M,D
Developmental Psychology — M,D
English — M,D
Experimental Psychology — M,D
Gerontology — D
History — M,D
Latin American Studies — M,D
Liberal Studies — M
Mass Communication — M,D
Music — M,D
Psychology—General — M,D
Rhetoric — M,D
Social Psychology — M,D
Speech and Interpersonal Communication — M

## TEXAS SOUTHERN UNIVERSITY
Art/Fine Arts — M
Communication—General — M
Criminal Justice and Criminology — M,D
English — M
Family and Consumer Sciences-General — M
History — M
Music — M
Psychology—General — M
Public Administration — M
Sociology — M
Urban and Regional Planning — M,D

## TEXAS STATE UNIVERSITY
Anthropology — M
Applied Arts and Design—General — M
Child and Family Studies — M
Communication—General — M
Computer Art and Design — M
Criminal Justice and Criminology — M,D
English — M
Ethics — M
Family and Consumer Sciences-General — M
Geographic Information Systems — D
Geography — M
Gerontology — M
Graphic Design — M
History — M
Interdisciplinary Studies — M
International Affairs — M
Marriage and Family Therapy — M
Mass Communication — M
Music — M
Philosophy — M
Political Science — M
Psychology—General — M
Public Administration — M
Rhetoric — M
School Psychology — O
Social Psychology — M
Sociology — M
Spanish — M
Sustainable Development — M
Technical Communication — M
Theater — M
Writing — M

## TEXAS TECH UNIVERSITY
Agricultural Economics and Agribusiness — M,D
Anthropology — M
Applied Economics — M,D
Architecture — M,D
Art History — M
Art/Fine Arts — M,D
Child and Family Studies — M,D
Classics — M,D
Clinical Psychology — M,D
Communication—General — M,D
Consumer Economics — M,D
Counseling Psychology — M,D
Cultural Studies — M,D
Economics — M,D
English — M,D
Environmental Design — M,D

Experimental Psychology — M,D
Family and Consumer Sciences-General — M,D
Forensic Sciences — M
Geography — M,D
German — M,D
Gerontology — M,D
History — M,D
Human Development — M,D
Interdisciplinary Studies — M,D
Interior Design — M,D
Landscape Architecture — M
Linguistics — M,D
Marriage and Family Therapy — M,D
Mass Communication — M,D
Media Studies — M,D
Museum Studies — M,D
Music — M,D
Philosophy — M
Political Science — M
Psychology—General — M,D
Public Administration — M,D
Rhetoric — M,D
Romance Languages — M,D
Sociology — M,D
Spanish — M,D
Sustainable Development — M,D
Technical Writing — M,D
Theater — M

## TEXAS TECH UNIVERSITY HEALTH SCIENCES CENTER
Rehabilitation Counseling — M

## TEXAS WESLEYAN UNIVERSITY
Counseling Psychology — M,D
Marriage and Family Therapy — M,D

## TEXAS WOMAN'S UNIVERSITY
Art/Fine Arts — M
Child and Family Studies — M,D
Child Development — M,D
Counseling Psychology — M,D,O
Dance — M,D
English — M,D
Gender Studies — M,D
History — M
Marriage and Family Therapy — M,D
Music — M
Political Science — M
Psychology—General — M,D,O
Rhetoric — M,D
School Psychology — M,D,O
Sociology — M,D
Theater — M
Women's Studies — M

## THEOLOGICAL UNIVERSITY OF THE CARIBBEAN
Missions and Missiology — M,D
Pastoral Ministry and Counseling — M,D

## THOMAS EDISON STATE UNIVERSITY
Homeland Security — O
Liberal Studies — M
Public Administration — M

## THOMAS JEFFERSON UNIVERSITY
Applied Economics — M,D,O
Genetic Counseling — M
Marriage and Family Therapy — M

## THOMAS UNIVERSITY
Rehabilitation Counseling — M
Social Psychology — M

## TIFFIN UNIVERSITY
Art/Fine Arts — M
Communication—General — M
Criminal Justice and Criminology — M
English — M
Film, Television, and Video Theory and Criticism — M
Forensic Psychology — M
Homeland Security — M
Humanities — M
Psychology—General — M
Writing — M

## TORONTO SCHOOL OF THEOLOGY
Theology — M,D

## TOURO COLLEGE
Counseling Psychology — M,D
Industrial and Organizational Psychology — M,D
Internet and Interactive Multimedia — M
Jewish Studies — M

## TOWSON UNIVERSITY
Art History — M
Art/Fine Arts — M
Child and Family Studies — M,O
Communication—General — M
Corporate and Organizational Communication — M
Counseling Psychology — M
Experimental Psychology — M
Forensic Sciences — M
Geography — M
Homeland Security — M,O
Internet and Interactive Multimedia — M,D,O
Jewish Studies — M,O
Liberal Studies — M
Music — M
Psychology—General — M
School Psychology — M
Social Sciences — M
Theater — M
Women's Studies — M,O
Writing — M

---

*M—masters degree; D—doctorate; O—other advanced degree; *—Close-Up and/or Display*

## TRENT UNIVERSITY

| | |
|---|---|
| American Indian/Native American Studies | M,D |
| Anthropology | M |
| Canadian Studies | M,D |
| Cultural Studies | D |
| Geography | M,D |

## TREVECCA NAZARENE UNIVERSITY

| | |
|---|---|
| Marriage and Family Therapy | M,D |
| Pastoral Ministry and Counseling | M |
| Religion | M |

## TRIDENT UNIVERSITY INTERNATIONAL

| | |
|---|---|
| Conflict Resolution and Mediation/Peace Studies | M,D |
| Criminal Justice and Criminology | M,D |
| Emergency Management | M,D,O |
| Public Administration | M,D |

## TRINE UNIVERSITY

| | |
|---|---|
| Criminal Justice and Criminology | M |
| Emergency Management | M |
| Forensic Psychology | M |
| Public Administration | M |

## TRINITY BIBLE COLLEGE AND GRADUATE SCHOOL

| | |
|---|---|
| Missions and Missiology | M |
| Theology | M |

## TRINITY CHRISTIAN COLLEGE

| | |
|---|---|
| Counseling Psychology | M |

## TRINITY COLLEGE (CANADA)

| | |
|---|---|
| Music | M,D,O |
| Pastoral Ministry and Counseling | M,D,O |
| Theology | M,D,O |

## TRINITY COLLEGE (UNITED STATES)

| | |
|---|---|
| American Studies | M |
| Cultural Studies | M |
| English | M |
| Media Studies | M |
| Museum Studies | M |
| Public Policy | M |
| Writing | M |

## TRINITY INTERNATIONAL UNIVERSITY

| | |
|---|---|
| Archaeology | M,D,O |
| Counseling Psychology | M,D,O |
| Missions and Missiology | M,D,O |
| Pastoral Ministry and Counseling | M,D,O |
| Theology | M,D,O |

## TRINITY INTERNATIONAL UNIVERSITY FLORIDA

| | |
|---|---|
| Counseling Psychology | M |
| Religion | M,O |

## TRINITY LUTHERAN SEMINARY

| | |
|---|---|
| African-American Studies | M |
| Missions and Missiology | M |
| Music | M |
| Pastoral Ministry and Counseling | M |
| Theology | M |

## TRINITY SCHOOL FOR MINISTRY

| | |
|---|---|
| Missions and Missiology | M,D,O |
| Pastoral Ministry and Counseling | M,D,O |
| Religion | M,D,O |
| Theology | M,D,O |

## TRINITY UNIVERSITY

| | |
|---|---|
| School Psychology | M |

## TRINITY WASHINGTON UNIVERSITY

| | |
|---|---|
| Clinical Psychology | M |
| Communication—General | M |
| Counseling Psychology | M |
| National Security | M |

## TRINITY WESTERN UNIVERSITY

| | |
|---|---|
| Counseling Psychology | M |
| English | M |
| History | M |
| Humanities | M |
| Interdisciplinary Studies | M |
| Linguistics | M |
| Pastoral Ministry and Counseling | M,D |
| Philosophy | M |
| Theology | M,D |

## TRI-STATE BIBLE COLLEGE

| | |
|---|---|
| Theology | M |

## TROPICAL AGRICULTURE RESEARCH AND HIGHER EDUCATION CENTER

| | |
|---|---|
| Agricultural Economics and Agribusiness | M,D |

## TROY UNIVERSITY

| | |
|---|---|
| Communication—General | M |
| Corporate and Organizational Communication | M |
| Criminal Justice and Criminology | M |
| Economic Development | M |
| Economics | M |
| History | M |
| International Affairs | M |
| Public Administration | M |
| Social Sciences | M |

## TRUETT MCCONNELL UNIVERSITY

| | |
|---|---|
| Theology | M |

## TRUMAN STATE UNIVERSITY

| | |
|---|---|
| English | M |
| Music | M |

## TUFTS UNIVERSITY

| | |
|---|---|
| Archaeology | M |
| Art History | M |
| Art/Fine Arts | M,O |
| Child and Family Studies | M,D |
| Child Development | M,D |
| Classics | M |
| Cognitive Sciences | M,D |
| Conflict Resolution and Mediation/Peace Studies | M,D |
| Economics | M |

| | |
|---|---|
| English | M,D |
| Family and Consumer Sciences-General | M |
| French | M |
| German | M |
| Health Communication | M,D,O |
| History | M,D |
| Human Development | M,D |
| Interdisciplinary Studies | D |
| International Affairs | M |
| International Development | M,D |
| Museum Studies | M |
| Music | M |
| Philosophy | M |
| Psychology—General | M,D |
| Public Administration | O |
| Public Policy | M |
| School Psychology | M,O |
| Theater | M,D |
| Urban and Regional Planning | M |
| Urban Studies | M |

## TULANE UNIVERSITY

| | |
|---|---|
| Anthropology | D |
| Architecture | M |
| Art History | M |
| Art/Fine Arts | M |
| Classics | M |
| Dance | M |
| Economics | M,D |
| Emergency Management | M,D |
| English | M |
| French | M,D |
| History | M,D |
| Interdisciplinary Studies | D |
| International Development | M,D |
| Latin American Studies | M,D |
| Liberal Studies | M |
| Music | M |
| Philosophy | M,D |
| Political Science | D |
| Portuguese | M,D |
| Psychology—General | M,D |
| Sociology | M |
| Spanish | M,D |
| Theater | M |

## TUSKEGEE UNIVERSITY

| | |
|---|---|
| Agricultural Economics and Agribusiness | M |

## TYNDALE UNIVERSITY COLLEGE & SEMINARY

| | |
|---|---|
| Missions and Missiology | M,O |
| Pastoral Ministry and Counseling | M,O |
| Theology | M,O |

## UNIFICATION THEOLOGICAL SEMINARY

| | |
|---|---|
| Pastoral Ministry and Counseling | M,D |
| Religion | M,D |
| Theology | M,D |

## UNIFORMED SERVICES UNIVERSITY OF THE HEALTH SCIENCES

| | |
|---|---|
| Clinical Psychology | D |
| Psychology—General | D |

## UNION COLLEGE (KY)

| | |
|---|---|
| Clinical Psychology | M |
| Counseling Psychology | M |
| Psychology—General | M |
| School Psychology | M |

## UNION INSTITUTE & UNIVERSITY

| | |
|---|---|
| Clinical Psychology | M |
| Cultural Studies | M |
| History | M,D |
| Interdisciplinary Studies | M |
| Public Policy | M |
| Writing | M |

## UNION THEOLOGICAL SEMINARY IN THE CITY OF NEW YORK

| | |
|---|---|
| Theology | M,D |

## UNION UNIVERSITY

| | |
|---|---|
| Cultural Studies | M |
| Pastoral Ministry and Counseling | M,D |
| Religion | M |

## UNITED STATES ARMY COMMAND AND GENERAL STAFF COLLEGE

| | |
|---|---|
| Military and Defense Studies | M |

## UNITED STATES INTERNATIONAL UNIVERSITY–AFRICA

| | |
|---|---|
| Addictions/Substance Abuse Counseling | M |
| Conflict Resolution and Mediation/Peace Studies | M |
| Counseling Psychology | M |
| Health Psychology | M |
| International Affairs | M |

## UNITED TALMUDICAL SEMINARY

| | |
|---|---|
| Theology | M |

## UNITED THEOLOGICAL SEMINARY

| | |
|---|---|
| Pastoral Ministry and Counseling | M,D |
| Theology | M,D |

## UNITED THEOLOGICAL SEMINARY OF THE TWIN CITIES

| | |
|---|---|
| Art/Fine Arts | M,D,O |
| Asian Studies | M,D,O |
| Conflict Resolution and Mediation/Peace Studies | M,D,O |
| Ethnic Studies | M,D,O |
| Humanities | M,D,O |
| Pastoral Ministry and Counseling | M,D,O |
| Religion | M,D,O |
| Theology | M,D,O |
| Women's Studies | M,D,O |

## UNITY COLLEGE

| | |
|---|---|
| Sustainable Development | M |

## UNIVERSIDAD AUTONOMA DE GUADALAJARA

| | |
|---|---|
| Architecture | M,D |
| Computer Art and Design | M,D |
| Corporate and Organizational Communication | M,D |
| Film, Television, and Video Production | M,D |
| Internet and Interactive Multimedia | M,D |
| Philosophy | M,D |
| Public Policy | M,D |
| Spanish | M,D |
| Translation and Interpretation | M,D |

## UNIVERSIDAD CENTRAL DEL CARIBE

| | |
|---|---|
| Addictions/Substance Abuse Counseling | M |

## UNIVERSIDAD DE IBEROAMERICA

| | |
|---|---|
| Clinical Psychology | M,D |
| Forensic Psychology | M,D |

## UNIVERSIDAD DE LAS AMERICAS, A.C.

| | |
|---|---|
| International Affairs | M |
| Marriage and Family Therapy | M |
| Psychology—General | M |

## UNIVERSIDAD DE LAS AMÉRICAS PUEBLA

| | |
|---|---|
| American Studies | M |
| Anthropology | M |
| Archaeology | M |
| Computer Art and Design | M |
| Economics | M |
| English | M |
| Linguistics | M |
| Psychology—General | M |

## UNIVERSIDAD DEL ESTE

| | |
|---|---|
| Agricultural Economics and Agribusiness | M |
| Criminal Justice and Criminology | M |
| Public Policy | M |

## UNIVERSIDAD DEL TURABO

| | |
|---|---|
| Art/Fine Arts | M |
| Arts Administration | M |
| Conflict Resolution and Mediation/Peace Studies | M |
| Counseling Psychology | M,D,O |
| Criminal Justice and Criminology | M |
| Forensic Psychology | M,D,O |
| Forensic Sciences | M |

## UNIVERSIDAD IBEROAMERICANA

| | |
|---|---|
| Corporate and Organizational Communication | M,D |

## UNIVERSIDAD METROPOLITANA

| | |
|---|---|
| Counseling Psychology | M |

## UNIVERSIDAD NACIONAL PEDRO HENRIQUEZ URENA

| | |
|---|---|
| Architecture | M |
| Historic Preservation | M |
| International Affairs | M |
| Political Science | M |

## UNIVERSITÉ DE MONCTON

| | |
|---|---|
| Economics | M |
| French | M,D |
| History | M,D |
| Public Administration | M |

## UNIVERSITÉ DE MONTRÉAL

| | |
|---|---|
| Anthropology | M,D |
| Art History | M,D |
| Classics | M |
| Communication—General | M,D |
| Comparative Literature | M,D |
| Criminal Justice and Criminology | M,D |
| Demography and Population Studies | M,D |
| Developmental Psychology | M,D |
| Economics | M,D,O |
| Emergency Management | O |
| English | M,D |
| Environmental Design | M,D,O |
| Film, Television, and Video Theory and Criticism | M,D |
| French | M,D |
| Genetic Counseling | M |
| Geography | M,D,O |
| German | M |
| Hispanic and Latin American Languages | M,D |
| History | M,D |
| Industrial and Labor Relations | M,D,O |
| International Affairs | M,O |
| Linguistics | M,D,O |
| Museum Studies | M |
| Music | M,D,O |
| Philosophy | M,D |
| Political Science | M,D |
| Psychology—General | O |
| Public Policy | M |
| Religion | M,D,O |
| Sociology | M,D |
| Spanish | M |
| Theology | M,D,O |
| Translation and Interpretation | M,D,O |
| Urban and Regional Planning | M,D,O |

## UNIVERSITÉ DE SAINT-BONIFACE

| | |
|---|---|
| Canadian Studies | M |

## UNIVERSITÉ DE SHERBROOKE

| | |
|---|---|
| Canadian Studies | M,D |
| Comparative Literature | M,D |
| Conflict Resolution and Mediation/Peace Studies | M,D,O |
| Corporate and Organizational Communication | M |
| Economic Development | D |
| Economics | M,D,O |
| Ethics | M,D,O |
| French | M,D |
| Geography | M,D |

| | |
|---|---|
| Gerontology | M |
| History | M |
| Linguistics | M,D,O |
| Philosophy | M,D |
| Psychology—General | M |
| Public Administration | M |
| Religion | M,D |
| Theater | M |
| Theology | M,D,O |

## UNIVERSITÉ DU QUÉBEC À CHICOUTIMI

| | |
|---|---|
| Art/Fine Arts | M |
| Canadian Studies | M |
| Comparative Literature | M |
| Ethics | O |
| French | O |
| Linguistics | M |
| Theology | M,D |

## UNIVERSITÉ DU QUÉBEC À MONTRÉAL

| | |
|---|---|
| Art History | M,D |
| Art/Fine Arts | M |
| Communication—General | M,D |
| Comparative Literature | M,D |
| Dance | M |
| Economics | M,D |
| Geographic Information Systems | O |
| Geography | M |
| History | M,D |
| Linguistics | M,D |
| Museum Studies | M |
| Philosophy | M,D |
| Political Science | M,D |
| Psychology—General | D |
| Public Administration | M |
| Religion | M,D |
| Sociology | M,D |
| Urban Studies | M,D |

## UNIVERSITÉ DU QUÉBEC À RIMOUSKI

| | |
|---|---|
| Comparative Literature | M,D |
| Ethics | M,O |
| Social Psychology | M |
| Urban and Regional Planning | M,D,O |

## UNIVERSITÉ DU QUÉBEC À TROIS-RIVIÈRES

| | |
|---|---|
| Communication—General | M,O |
| Comparative Literature | M |
| Industrial and Labor Relations | O |
| Philosophy | M,D |
| Psychology—General | D,O |

## UNIVERSITÉ DU QUÉBEC, ÉCOLE NATIONALE D'ADMINISTRATION PUBLIQUE

| | |
|---|---|
| Public Administration | D,O |
| Urban Studies | M |

## UNIVERSITÉ DU QUÉBEC EN OUTAOUAIS

| | |
|---|---|
| Industrial and Labor Relations | M,D,O |
| Urban and Regional Planning | M |

## UNIVERSITÉ DU QUÉBEC, INSTITUT NATIONAL DE LA RECHERCHE SCIENTIFIQUE

| | |
|---|---|
| Demography and Population Studies | M,D,O |
| Urban Studies | M,D,O |

## UNIVERSITÉ LAVAL

| | |
|---|---|
| Agricultural Economics and Agribusiness | M |
| Anthropology | M,D |
| Archaeology | M,D |
| Architecture | M |
| Art History | M,D |
| Art/Fine Arts | M |
| Clinical Psychology | D |
| Comparative Literature | M,D |
| Consumer Economics | O |
| Economics | M,D |
| English | M,D |
| Ethics | O |
| Ethnic Studies | M,D |
| Film, Television, and Video Theory and Criticism | M,D |
| Geographic Information Systems | M,O |
| Geography | M,D |
| Gerontology | O |
| Graphic Design | M |
| History | M,D |
| Industrial and Labor Relations | M,D |
| International Affairs | M,D |
| Journalism | O |
| Linguistics | M,D |
| Mass Communication | M,D |
| Museum Studies | O |
| Music | M,D |
| Philosophy | M,D |
| Political Science | M,D |
| Psychology—General | D |
| Religion | M,D |
| Rural Planning and Studies | O |
| Social Psychology | D |
| Sociology | M,D |
| Spanish | M,D |
| Theater | M,D |
| Theology | M,D |
| Translation and Interpretation | M,O |
| Urban and Regional Planning | M,D |
| Women's Studies | O |

## UNIVERSITY AT ALBANY, STATE UNIVERSITY OF NEW YORK

| | |
|---|---|
| African Studies | M |
| African-American Studies | M |
| Anthropology | M,D |
| Art/Fine Arts | M |
| Clinical Psychology | M,D |
| Cognitive Sciences | M,D |
| Communication—General | M,D |
| Counseling Psychology | M,D |
| Criminal Justice and Criminology | M,D |
| Demography and Population Studies | M,D,O |
| Economics | M,D,O |
| Emergency Management | O |

English M,D
Forensic Sciences M
Geographic Information Systems M,O
Geography M
History M,D,O
Homeland Security M,D,O
Industrial and Organizational
  Psychology M,D
Latin American Studies M,D,O
Liberal Studies M
Philosophy M,D
Political Science M,D
Psychology—General M,D
Public Administration M,D,O
Public History M,D,O
Public Policy M,D,O
Social Psychology M,D
Sociology M,D,O
Spanish M,D
Urban and Regional Planning M
Urban Studies M,D,O
Women's Studies M

**UNIVERSITY AT BUFFALO, THE STATE UNIVERSITY OF NEW YORK**
American Studies M,D,O
Anthropology M,D
Architecture M
Art History M,D
Art/Fine Arts M,D
Arts Administration M
Canadian Studies M,D,O
Classics M,D,O
Communication—General M,D
Comparative Literature M,D
Counseling Psychology M,D,O
Economics M,D,O
English M,D,O
Film, Television, and Video
  Theory and Criticism M,D,O
French M,D,O
Gender Studies M,D,O
Geographic Information Systems M,D
Geography M
German M,D,O
Historic Preservation M,D,O
History M,D,O
Humanities M
Interdisciplinary Studies M
Linguistics M,D
Media Studies M,D,O
Museum Studies M,D
Music M,D,O
Philosophy M,D
Political Science M,D
Psychology—General M,D
Public History M,D,O
Rehabilitation Counseling M,D,O
Romance Languages M,D
Social Sciences M
Sociology M,D
Spanish M,D,O
Theater M,D
Urban and Regional Planning M,D,O
Urban Design M,D,O

**UNIVERSITY OF ADVANCING TECHNOLOGY**
Internet and Interactive
  Multimedia M

**THE UNIVERSITY OF AKRON**
Arts Administration M
Child and Family Studies M
Child Development M
Clinical Psychology M
Clothing and Textiles M
Communication—General M
Counseling Psychology M,D
Economics M
English M
Gerontology D
History M,D
Industrial and Organizational
  Psychology M,D
Marriage and Family Therapy M
Music M
Political Science M
Psychology—General M,D
Public Administration M
School Psychology M,D
Sociology M,D
Spanish M
Theater M
Writing M

**THE UNIVERSITY OF ALABAMA**
American Studies M
Anthropology M,D
Art History M
Art/Fine Arts M
Child and Family Studies M
Clinical Psychology D
Clothing and Textiles M
Communication—General M
Consumer Economics M
Criminal Justice and Criminology M
Economics M,D
English M,D
Experimental Psychology D
Family and Consumer
  Sciences-General M,D
French M,D
Geographic Information Systems M,D
Geography M,D
German M,D
History M,D
Human Development M
Interdisciplinary Studies D
Journalism M
Marriage and Family Therapy M
Mass Communication D

Music M,D
Photography M
Political Science M,D
Psychology—General D
Public Administration M,D
Rhetoric M,D
Romance Languages M,D
Spanish M,D
Speech and Interpersonal
  Communication M
Theater M
Women's Studies M
Writing M,D

**THE UNIVERSITY OF ALABAMA AT BIRMINGHAM**
Anthropology M
Art History M
Clinical Psychology M
Communication—General M
Criminal Justice and Criminology M
Developmental Psychology M,D
English M
Forensic Sciences M
Genetic Counseling M
Health Psychology M,D
History M
Interdisciplinary Studies D
Music M
Psychology—General M
Public Administration M
Rhetoric M
Sociology D
Writing M

**THE UNIVERSITY OF ALABAMA IN HUNTSVILLE**
English M,O
History M
Industrial and Organizational
  Psychology M
Psychology—General M
Public Affairs M
Technical Writing M,O

**UNIVERSITY OF ALASKA ANCHORAGE**
Anthropology M
Clinical Psychology M,D
English M
Interdisciplinary Studies M
Psychology—General M,D
Public Administration M
Social Psychology M,D
Writing M

**UNIVERSITY OF ALASKA FAIRBANKS**
Anthropology M
Art/Fine Arts M
Clinical Psychology D
Communication—General M
Computer Art and Design M
Corporate and Organizational
  Communication M
Criminal Justice and Criminology M
Cultural Studies M
Economics M
Emergency Management M
English M
Geographic Information Systems M
History M
Homeland Security M
Interdisciplinary Studies M,D
Linguistics M
Music M
Northern Studies M
Photography M
Psychology—General D
Rural Planning and Studies M
Social Psychology M,D,O
Sustainable Development M,D
Writing M

**UNIVERSITY OF ALASKA SOUTHEAST**
Public Administration M

**UNIVERSITY OF ALBERTA**
Agricultural Economics and
  Agribusiness M,D
Anthropology M,D
Applied Arts and Design—
  General M
Archaeology M,D
Art History M
Art/Fine Arts M
Asian Studies M
Chinese M
Classics M,D
Clothing and Textiles M
Communication—General M
Counseling Psychology M,D
Criminal Justice and Criminology M,D
Demography and Population Studies M,D
East European and Russian Studies M,D
Economics M,D
English M,D
Family and Consumer
  Sciences-General M,D
Folklore M,D
French M,D
German M,D
Hispanic Studies M,D
History M,D
Industrial and Labor Relations D
Italian M,D
Japanese M
Linguistics M,D
Music M,D
Philosophy M,D
Political Science M,D
Psychology—General M,D
Rural Sociology M,D
School Psychology M,D
Slavic Languages M,D

Sociology M,D
Theater M

**UNIVERSITY OF ANTELOPE VALLEY**
Criminal Justice and Criminology M

**THE UNIVERSITY OF ARIZONA**
African Studies M,D,O
Agricultural Economics and
  Agribusiness M
American Indian/Native American
  Studies M,D
Anthropology M,D,O
Architecture M
Art History M,D
Art/Fine Arts M
Asian Studies M,D
Child and Family Studies M,D,O
Classics M
Communication—General M,D
Counseling Psychology M
Dance M
Economics M,D
English M,D
Family and Consumer
  Sciences-General D
Film, Television, and Video
  Theory and Criticism M
French M
Gender Studies M,D,O
Geographic Information Systems M,D,O
Geography M,D,O
German M,D
History M,D,O
Human Development M,D,O
Interdisciplinary Studies M
Journalism M
Landscape Architecture M
Latin American Studies M
Linguistics M,D
Music M,D
Near and Middle Eastern Studies M,D,O
Philosophy M,D
Political Science M,D
Psychology—General M,D
Public Administration M,D,O
Public Policy M,D,O
Rehabilitation Counseling M,D
Rhetoric M,D
Russian M
School Psychology D,O
Sociology M,D
Spanish M,D
Theater M
Urban and Regional Planning M
Women's Studies M,D,O
Writing M

**UNIVERSITY OF ARKANSAS**
Agricultural Economics and
  Agribusiness M
Anthropology M,D
Art/Fine Arts M
Communication—General M
Comparative Literature M,D
Economics M,D
English M,D
Family and Consumer
  Sciences-General M
French M
Geography M
German M
History M,D
Interdisciplinary Studies M,D
Journalism M
Music M
Philosophy M,D
Political Science M
Psychology—General M,D
Public Administration M
Public Policy D
Rehabilitation Counseling M,D
Sociology M
Spanish M
Theater M
Writing M

**UNIVERSITY OF ARKANSAS AT LITTLE ROCK**
Applied Psychology M
Art History M
Art/Fine Arts M
Conflict Resolution and
  Mediation/Peace Studies O
Criminal Justice and Criminology M,D
Gerontology O
Interdisciplinary Studies M
Mass Communication M
Psychology—General M
Public Administration M
Public Affairs M,O
Public History M
Rehabilitation Counseling M,O
Rhetoric M
Speech and Interpersonal
  Communication M
Technical Writing M
Writing M

**UNIVERSITY OF ARKANSAS FOR MEDICAL SCIENCES**
Genetic Counseling M,D

**UNIVERSITY OF BALTIMORE**
Applied Arts and Design—
  General M
Applied Psychology M
Conflict Resolution and
  Mediation/Peace Studies M
Counseling Psychology M
Criminal Justice and Criminology M
Ethics M
Graphic Design M,D

Public Administration M,D
Public Affairs M,D
Publishing M
Writing M

**UNIVERSITY OF BRIDGEPORT**
Applied Arts and Design—
  General M
Asian Studies M
Clinical Psychology M
Communication—General M
Conflict Resolution and
  Mediation/Peace Studies M
Counseling Psychology M
International Affairs M
Media Studies M
Social Psychology M

**THE UNIVERSITY OF BRITISH COLUMBIA**
Anthropology M,D
Archaeology M,D
Architecture M
Art History M,D
Art/Fine Arts M,D
Asian Studies M,D
Classics M,D
Clinical Psychology M,D
Cognitive Sciences M,D
Counseling Psychology M,D,O
Developmental Psychology M,D
East European and Russian Studies M,D
Economics M,D
English M,D
Ethnic Studies M,D
Film, Television, and Video
  Production M
Film, Television, and Video
  Theory and Criticism M
French M,D
Gender Studies M,D
Genetic Counseling M
Geography M,D
German M,D
Health Psychology M,D
Hispanic Studies M,D
History M,D
Human Development M,D,O
International Affairs M
Journalism M
Landscape Architecture M
Linguistics M,D
Museum Studies M,D
Music M,D
Pacific Area/Pacific Rim Studies M
Philosophy M,D
Political Science M,D
Psychology—General M,D
Public Policy M
Religion M,D
School Psychology M,D,O
Social Psychology M,D
Sociology M,D
Theater M,D
Urban and Regional Planning M,D
Urban Design M
Writing M,D

**UNIVERSITY OF CALGARY**
Anthropology M,D
Applied Psychology M,D
Archaeology M
Architecture M,D
Art/Fine Arts M
Classics M,D
Clinical Psychology M,D
Communication—General M,D
Counseling Psychology M,D
Economics M,D
English M,D
Environmental Design M,D
French M,D
Geography M,D
German M,D
History M,D
Linguistics M,D
Military and Defense Studies M,D
Music M,D
Philosophy M,D
Political Science M,D
Psychology—General M,D
Religion M,D
School Psychology M,D
Sociology M,D
Spanish M,D
Sustainable Development M,D
Theater M

**UNIVERSITY OF CALIFORNIA, BERKELEY**
Addictions/Substance Abuse
  Counseling O
African-American Studies D
Agricultural Economics and
  Agribusiness D
Anthropology D
Applied Arts and Design—
  General O
Archaeology M,D
Architectural History M,D
Architecture M,D
Art History D
Art/Fine Arts M,O
Asian Languages M,D
Asian Studies M,D
Building Science D
Chinese D
Classics M,D
Comparative Literature D
Counseling Psychology O
Demography and Population Studies M,D
Economics D

| | |
|---|---|
| English | D |
| Environmental Design | M,D |
| Ethnic Studies | D |
| Film, Television, and Video Theory and Criticism | D |
| Folklore | M |
| French | D |
| Geography | D |
| German | D |
| Hispanic and Latin American Languages | D |
| History of Science and Technology | D |
| History | M,D |
| Human Development | M,D |
| Industrial and Labor Relations | D |
| Interior Design | O |
| International Affairs | M |
| Italian | D |
| Japanese | D |
| Journalism | M |
| Landscape Architecture | M,D,O |
| Linguistics | D |
| Music | D |
| Near and Middle Eastern Studies | M,D |
| Philosophy | D |
| Political Science | D |
| Psychology—General | D |
| Public Affairs | M |
| Public Policy | M,D |
| Religion | D |
| Rhetoric | D |
| Romance Languages | D |
| Russian | D |
| Scandinavian Languages | D |
| Slavic Languages | D |
| Sociology | D |
| Spanish | D |
| Sustainable Development | M,O |
| Theater | D |
| Urban and Regional Planning | M,D |
| Urban Design | M,D |
| Writing | O |

### UNIVERSITY OF CALIFORNIA, DAVIS

| | |
|---|---|
| Agricultural Economics and Agribusiness | M,D |
| American Indian/Native American Studies | M,D |
| Anthropology | M,D |
| Art History | M |
| Art/Fine Arts | M |
| Child Development | M |
| Clothing and Textiles | M |
| Communication—General | M |
| Comparative Literature | D |
| Cultural Studies | M,D |
| Economics | M,D |
| English | M,D |
| Forensic Sciences | M |
| French | D |
| Geography | M,D |
| German | M,D |
| History | M,D |
| Human Development | D |
| Linguistics | M,D |
| Music | M,D |
| Philosophy | M,D |
| Political Science | M,D |
| Psychology—General | D |
| Sociology | M,D |
| Spanish | M,D |
| Textile Design | M |
| Theater | M,D |
| Urban and Regional Planning | M |
| Writing | M,D |

### UNIVERSITY OF CALIFORNIA, IRVINE

| | |
|---|---|
| Anthropology | M,D |
| Art/Fine Arts | M,D |
| Asian Languages | M,D |
| Chinese | M,D |
| Classics | M,D |
| Comparative Literature | M,D |
| Criminal Justice and Criminology | M,D |
| Cultural Studies | D |
| Dance | M |
| Demography and Population Studies | M |
| Economics | M,D |
| English | M,D |
| Environmental Design | D |
| French | M,D |
| Genetic Counseling | M |
| German | M,D |
| History | M,D |
| Japanese | M,D |
| Music | M |
| Philosophy | M,D |
| Political Science | D |
| Psychology—General | D |
| Sociology | D |
| Spanish | M,D |
| Theater | M,D |
| Urban and Regional Planning | M,D |
| Urban Studies | M,D |
| Writing | M |

### UNIVERSITY OF CALIFORNIA, LOS ANGELES

| | |
|---|---|
| African Studies | M |
| African-American Studies | M |
| American Indian/Native American Studies | M |
| Anthropology | M,D |
| Applied Arts and Design—General | M |
| Applied Social Research | M,D |
| Archaeology | M,D |
| Architecture | M,D |
| Art History | M,D |
| Art/Fine Arts | M |
| Asian Languages | M,D |
| Asian Studies | M,D |
| Asian-American Studies | M |
| Classics | M,D |
| Comparative Literature | M,D |
| Dance | M,D |
| Economics | M,D |
| English | M,D |
| Film, Television, and Video Production | M,D |
| French | M,D |
| Gender Studies | M,D |
| Geography | M,D |
| German | M,D |
| Hispanic and Latin American Languages | D |
| Historic Preservation | M |
| History | M,D |
| Italian | M,D |
| Latin American Studies | M |
| Linguistics | M,D |
| Media Studies | M,D |
| Music | M,D |
| Near and Middle Eastern Languages | M,D |
| Near and Middle Eastern Studies | M,D |
| Philosophy | M,D |
| Political Science | M,D |
| Portuguese | M |
| Psychology—General | M,D |
| Public Policy | M |
| Scandinavian Languages | M,D |
| Slavic Languages | M,D |
| Sociology | M,D |
| Spanish | M,D |
| Theater | M,D |
| Urban and Regional Planning | M,D |
| Urban Design | M,D |

### UNIVERSITY OF CALIFORNIA, MERCED

| | |
|---|---|
| Cognitive Sciences | M,D |
| Psychology—General | M,D |
| Social Sciences | M,D |
| Sociology | M,D |

### UNIVERSITY OF CALIFORNIA, RIVERSIDE

| | |
|---|---|
| Anthropology | M,D |
| Art History | M,D |
| Art/Fine Arts | M |
| Asian Studies | M |
| Classics | D |
| Comparative Literature | M,D |
| Cultural Studies | D |
| Dance | M |
| Economics | M,D |
| English | M,D |
| Ethnic Studies | D |
| Hispanic Studies | M,D |
| History | M,D |
| Music | M,D |
| Philosophy | M,D |
| Political Science | M,D |
| Psychology—General | D |
| Public Policy | M,D |
| Religion | M,D |
| School Psychology | M,D,O |
| Sociology | M,D |
| Spanish | M,D |
| Writing | M |

### UNIVERSITY OF CALIFORNIA, SAN DIEGO

| | |
|---|---|
| Anthropology | D |
| Art History | M,D |
| Art/Fine Arts | M,D |
| Clinical Psychology | D |
| Cognitive Sciences | D |
| Communication—General | D |
| Dance | M,D |
| Economics | D |
| English | M,D |
| Ethnic Studies | D |
| History of Science and Technology | D |
| History | M,D |
| International Affairs | M,D |
| International Development | M |
| International Economics | M |
| Jewish Studies | M,D |
| Latin American Studies | M |
| Linguistics | D |
| Music | M,D |
| Philosophy | M,D |
| Political Science | M,D |
| Psychology—General | D |
| Public Policy | M |
| Sociology | D |
| Theater | M,D |
| Writing | M,D |

### UNIVERSITY OF CALIFORNIA, SAN FRANCISCO

| | |
|---|---|
| Anthropology | D |
| History of Science and Technology | M,D |
| Sociology | D |

### UNIVERSITY OF CALIFORNIA, SANTA BARBARA

| | |
|---|---|
| African-American Studies | D |
| Agricultural Economics and Agribusiness | M,D |
| Anthropology | M,D |
| Art History | D |
| Art/Fine Arts | M |
| Asian Languages | M,D |
| Asian Studies | M,D |
| Classics | M,D |
| Clinical Psychology | M,D,O |
| Cognitive Sciences | M,D |
| Communication—General | D |
| Comparative Literature | M,D |
| Counseling Psychology | M,D,O |
| Cultural Anthropology | M,D |
| Cultural Studies | M,D |
| Economics | M,D |
| English | D |
| Film, Television, and Video Production | D |
| French | M,D |
| Geography | M,D |

| | |
|---|---|
| Hispanic and Latin American Languages | M,D |
| Hispanic Studies | D |
| History | D |
| Interdisciplinary Studies | D |
| International Affairs | M,D |
| Latin American Studies | M |
| Linguistics | M,D |
| Media Studies | M,D |
| Medieval and Renaissance Studies | M,D |
| Music | M,D |
| Philosophy | D |
| Political Science | M,D |
| Portuguese | M,D |
| Psychology—General | D |
| Public History | D |
| Religion | M,D |
| School Psychology | M,D,O |
| Social Sciences | D |
| Sociology | D |
| Spanish | M,D |
| Speech and Interpersonal Communication | D |
| Sustainable Development | M,D |
| Theater | M,D |
| Translation and Interpretation | M,D |
| Women's Studies | M,D |
| Writing | M |

### UNIVERSITY OF CALIFORNIA, SANTA CRUZ

| | |
|---|---|
| Anthropology | D |
| Applied Economics | M |
| Art/Fine Arts | M,D |
| Communication—General | O |
| Comparative Literature | M,D |
| Computer Art and Design | M,D |
| Cultural Anthropology | D |
| Economics | D |
| English | M,D |
| Film, Television, and Video Theory and Criticism | D |
| History | D |
| Humanities | D |
| Interdisciplinary Studies | M,D |
| International Affairs | M |
| Linguistics | M,D |
| Music | M,D |
| Philosophy | M,D |
| Political Science | D |
| Psychology—General | D |
| Social Sciences | D |
| Sociology | D |
| Theater | O |
| Writing | M |

### UNIVERSITY OF CENTRAL ARKANSAS

| | |
|---|---|
| Computer Art and Design | M |
| Counseling Psychology | M,O |
| Economic Development | M,O |
| Economics | M |
| English | M |
| Family and Consumer Sciences-General | M |
| Film, Television, and Video Production | M |
| Geographic Information Systems | M,O |
| Geography | M,O |
| History | M |
| Music | M,O |
| Psychology—General | M,D,O |
| School Psychology | M,D,O |
| Social Psychology | M |
| Urban and Regional Planning | M,O |
| Writing | M |

### UNIVERSITY OF CENTRAL FLORIDA

| | |
|---|---|
| Anthropology | M,O |
| Applied Psychology | M,D |
| Art/Fine Arts | M |
| Child Development | M,O |
| Clinical Psychology | M,D |
| Communication—General | M,O |
| Computer Art and Design | M |
| Corporate and Organizational Communication | M,O |
| Criminal Justice and Criminology | M,D,O |
| Emergency Management | M |
| English | M,D,O |
| Experimental Psychology | M,D |
| Film, Television, and Video Production | M |
| Forensic Sciences | M,D |
| Geographic Information Systems | M |
| History | M |
| Homeland Security | M,O |
| Industrial and Organizational Psychology | M,D |
| Interdisciplinary Studies | M,O |
| Marriage and Family Therapy | M,O |
| Music | M |
| National Security | M,D,O |
| Political Science | M,D,O |
| Psychology—General | M,D |
| Public Administration | M,O |
| Public Affairs | O |
| School Psychology | O |
| Sociology | M,D |
| Spanish | M |
| Theater | M |
| Urban and Regional Planning | M,O |
| Writing | M,D,O |

### UNIVERSITY OF CENTRAL MISSOURI

| | |
|---|---|
| Communication—General | M,D |
| Counseling Psychology | M,D,O |
| Criminal Justice and Criminology | M,D,O |
| English | M,D,O |
| Gerontology | M,D,O |
| History | M,D,O |
| Music | M,D,O |
| Psychology—General | M,D,O |
| Sociology | M,D,O |
| Theater | M,D,O |

### UNIVERSITY OF CENTRAL OKLAHOMA

| | |
|---|---|
| Addictions/Substance Abuse Counseling | M |
| Applied Arts and Design—General | M |
| Child and Family Studies | M |
| Counseling Psychology | M |
| Criminal Justice and Criminology | M |
| English | M |
| Experimental Psychology | M |
| Family and Consumer Sciences-General | M |
| Forensic Psychology | M |
| Forensic Sciences | M |
| Gerontology | M |
| History | M |
| Human Development | M |
| Interdisciplinary Studies | M |
| International Affairs | M |
| Marriage and Family Therapy | M |
| Museum Studies | M |
| Music | M |
| Political Science | M |
| Psychology—General | M |
| Public Administration | M |
| School Psychology | M |
| Sociology | M |
| Writing | M |

### UNIVERSITY OF CHARLESTON

| | |
|---|---|
| Forensic Sciences | M |

### UNIVERSITY OF CHICAGO

| | |
|---|---|
| Anthropology | D |
| Archaeology | D |
| Art History | M,D |
| Art/Fine Arts | M |
| Asian Languages | D |
| Asian Studies | M,D |
| Classics | M,D |
| Comparative Literature | M,D |
| Economics | M,D,O |
| Emergency Management | M |
| English | M,D |
| Ethics | D |
| Film, Television, and Video Theory and Criticism | D |
| French | D |
| Gender Studies | M |
| German | M,D |
| History | M |
| Human Development | D |
| Humanities | M |
| International Affairs | M |
| Italian | D |
| Latin American Studies | M |
| Liberal Studies | M |
| Linguistics | M,D |
| Media Studies | M,D |
| Medieval and Renaissance Studies | D |
| Music | M,D |
| Near and Middle Eastern Languages | D |
| Near and Middle Eastern Studies | M,D |
| Pastoral Ministry and Counseling | M |
| Philosophy | M,D |
| Political Science | D |
| Psychology—General | D |
| Public Policy | M,D |
| Religion | M,D |
| Romance Languages | M,D |
| Slavic Languages | M |
| Social Sciences | M,D |
| Sociology | D |
| Spanish | D |
| Theater | M |
| Theology | D |
| Writing | M |

### UNIVERSITY OF CINCINNATI

| | |
|---|---|
| Addictions/Substance Abuse Counseling | M,D,O |
| Anthropology | M |
| Applied Arts and Design—General | M |
| Applied Economics | M |
| Architecture | M |
| Art History | M |
| Art/Fine Arts | M |
| Arts Administration | M,D |
| Classics | M,D |
| Clinical Psychology | D |
| Communication—General | M |
| Criminal Justice and Criminology | M,D |
| Economics | D |
| English | M,D |
| Experimental Psychology | D |
| French | M,D |
| Genetic Counseling | M |
| Geography | M,D |
| German | M,D |
| Graphic Design | M |
| History | M,D |
| Industrial and Labor Relations | M |
| Industrial Design | M |
| Interdisciplinary Studies | D |
| Interior Design | M |
| Music | M,D,O |
| Philosophy | M,D |
| Political Science | M,D |
| Psychology—General | D |
| Romance Languages | M,D |
| School Psychology | D,O |
| Sociology | M,D |
| Spanish | M,D |
| Textile Design | M |
| Theater | M |
| Urban and Regional Planning | M |
| Women's Studies | M |

### UNIVERSITY OF COLORADO BOULDER

| | |
|---|---|
| Anthropology | M,D |
| Art History | M |
| Art/Fine Arts | M |
| Asian Studies | M,D |
| Chinese | M,D |

| | |
|---|---|
| Classics | M,D |
| Communication—General | M,D |
| Comparative Literature | M,D |
| Dance | M,D |
| Economics | M,D |
| English | M,D |
| Ethnic Studies | D |
| Film, Television, and Video Production | M |
| French | M,D |
| Geography | M,D |
| German | M |
| Hispanic and Latin American Languages | M,D |
| History | M,D |
| Internet and Interactive Multimedia | D |
| Japanese | M,D |
| Journalism | M |
| Linguistics | M,D |
| Mass Communication | M,D |
| Media Studies | M,D |
| Museum Studies | M |
| Music | M,D |
| Philosophy | M,D |
| Photography | M |
| Political Science | M,D |
| Psychology—General | M,D |
| Religion | M |
| Sociology | D |
| Spanish | M,D |
| Theater | M |
| Writing | M,D |

### UNIVERSITY OF COLORADO COLORADO SPRINGS
| | |
|---|---|
| Communication—General | M |
| Criminal Justice and Criminology | M |
| Geography | M |
| History | M |
| Interdisciplinary Studies | M |
| Psychology—General | M,D |
| Public Administration | M |
| Public Affairs | M |
| Sociology | M |

### UNIVERSITY OF COLORADO DENVER
| | |
|---|---|
| American Studies | M |
| Anthropology | M |
| Archaeology | M |
| Architectural History | D |
| Architecture | M |
| Art/Fine Arts | M |
| Clinical Psychology | M,D |
| Communication—General | M |
| Corporate and Organizational Communication | M |
| Counseling Psychology | M |
| Criminal Justice and Criminology | M,D |
| Economic Development | M |
| Economics | M |
| Emergency Management | M,D |
| English | M |
| Forensic Sciences | M |
| Gender Studies | M |
| Genetic Counseling | M,D |
| Geographic Information Systems | M,D |
| Health Psychology | M,D |
| Historic Preservation | M |
| History | M,D |
| Homeland Security | M |
| Human Development | M,D,O |
| Humanities | M |
| International Affairs | M |
| Landscape Architecture | M |
| Linguistics | M |
| Marriage and Family Therapy | M |
| Military and Defense Studies | M,D |
| Music | M |
| Political Science | M,D |
| Public Administration | M,D |
| Public Affairs | M,D |
| Public History | M |
| Rhetoric | M |
| School Psychology | M,D,O |
| Sociology | M |
| Spanish | M |
| Sustainable Development | M,D |
| Urban and Regional Planning | M,D |
| Urban Design | M,D |
| Western European Studies | M |
| Women's Studies | M |
| Writing | M |

### UNIVERSITY OF CONNECTICUT
| | |
|---|---|
| Agricultural Economics and Agribusiness | M,D |
| Anthropology | M,D |
| Applied Arts and Design— General | M |
| Child and Family Studies | M,D |
| Clinical Psychology | M,D |
| Cognitive Sciences | M,D |
| Communication—General | M |
| Counseling Psychology | M,D |
| Developmental Psychology | M,D |
| Economics | M,D |
| English | M,D |
| Experimental Psychology | M,D |
| Geography | M,D |
| History | M,D |
| Human Development | M,D |
| Industrial and Organizational Psychology | M,D |
| International Affairs | M |
| Jewish Studies | M |
| Latin American Studies | M |
| Linguistics | M,D |
| Medieval and Renaissance Studies | M,D |
| Music | M,D |
| Philosophy | M,D |
| Political Science | M,D |

| | |
|---|---|
| Psychology—General | M,D |
| Public Administration | M |
| Social Psychology | M,D |
| Sociology | M,D |
| Theater | M |
| Western European Studies | M |

### UNIVERSITY OF DALLAS
| | |
|---|---|
| American Studies | M |
| Art/Fine Arts | M |
| Classics | M |
| Comparative Literature | D |
| English | M |
| Humanities | M |
| Pastoral Ministry and Counseling | M |
| Philosophy | M,D |
| Political Science | M,D |
| Psychology—General | M |
| Theology | M |

### UNIVERSITY OF DAYTON
| | |
|---|---|
| Clinical Psychology | M,O |
| Communication—General | M |
| Counseling Psychology | M,O |
| Cultural Studies | M |
| English | M |
| Human Development | M,O |
| Pastoral Ministry and Counseling | M,D |
| Psychology—General | M |
| Public Administration | M |
| Rhetoric | M |
| School Psychology | M,O |
| Theology | M,D |
| Writing | M |

### UNIVERSITY OF DELAWARE
| | |
|---|---|
| Agricultural Economics and Agribusiness | M |
| American Studies | M |
| Applied Arts and Design— General | M |
| Art History | M,D |
| Art/Fine Arts | M |
| Child and Family Studies | M,D |
| Chinese | M |
| Clinical Psychology | D |
| Clothing and Textiles | M |
| Cognitive Sciences | M,D |
| Communication—General | M |
| Criminal Justice and Criminology | M,D |
| Economics | M,D |
| Emergency Management | M,D |
| English | M,D |
| French | M |
| Geography | M,D |
| German | M |
| Historic Preservation | M |
| History of Science and Technology | M,D |
| History | M,D |
| Human Development | M,D |
| International Affairs | M |
| Liberal Studies | M |
| Linguistics | M,D |
| Music | M |
| Political Science | M,D |
| Psychology—General | D |
| Public Administration | M* |
| Public Policy | M,D |
| School Psychology | M,D,O |
| Social Psychology | D |
| Sociology | M,D |
| Spanish | M |
| Theater | M |
| Translation and Interpretation | M |
| Urban Studies | M,D |

### UNIVERSITY OF DENVER
| | |
|---|---|
| Anthropology | M |
| Archaeology | M |
| Art History | M |
| Art/Fine Arts | M |
| Child and Family Studies | M,D,O |
| Clinical Psychology | M,D |
| Cognitive Sciences | D |
| Communication—General | M,D,O |
| Computer Art and Design | M |
| Conflict Resolution and Mediation/Peace Studies | M |
| Counseling Psychology | M,D,O |
| Criminal Justice and Criminology | M,O |
| Cultural Anthropology | M |
| Cultural Studies | M,O |
| Developmental Psychology | D |
| Economics | M |
| Emergency Management | M,O |
| English | M,D |
| Forensic Psychology | M,D |
| Geographic Information Systems | M,O |
| History | M,O |
| Homeland Security | M,D,O |
| International Affairs | M,D,O |
| International Development | M,D,O |
| Marriage and Family Therapy | M,D,O |
| Mass Communication | M |
| Media Studies | M |
| Museum Studies | M |
| Music | M,O |
| Psychology—General | M,D |
| Public Policy | M |
| Religion | M,D,O |
| Rhetoric | M,D |
| School Psychology | M,D,O |
| Social Psychology | D |
| Speech and Interpersonal Communication | M,D |
| Sport Psychology | M,D |
| Translation and Interpretation | M,O |
| Writing | M,D,O |

### UNIVERSITY OF DETROIT MERCY
| | |
|---|---|
| Addictions/Substance Abuse Counseling | M,D,O |

| | |
|---|---|
| Clinical Psychology | M,D,O |
| Criminal Justice and Criminology | M,D,O |
| Economics | M,D,O |
| Ethics | M,O |
| Forensic Sciences | M,O |
| Industrial and Organizational Psychology | M,D,O |
| Industrial Design | M,D |
| Liberal Studies | M,D,O |
| School Psychology | M,D,O |
| Urban and Regional Planning | M |

### UNIVERSITY OF DUBUQUE
| | |
|---|---|
| Communication—General | M |
| Theology | M,D |

### UNIVERSITY OF EVANSVILLE
| | |
|---|---|
| Public Administration | M |

### THE UNIVERSITY OF FINDLAY
| | |
|---|---|
| Public Administration | M |
| Rhetoric | M,D |
| Writing | M,D |

### UNIVERSITY OF FLORIDA
| | |
|---|---|
| Agricultural Economics and Agribusiness | M,D |
| Anthropology | M,D |
| Architecture | M,D |
| Art History | M,D |
| Art/Fine Arts | M,D |
| Child Development | M |
| Classics | M,D |
| Clinical Psychology | M,D |
| Communication—General | M,D |
| Computer Art and Design | M,D |
| Counseling Psychology | M,D |
| Criminal Justice and Criminology | M,D |
| Economics | M,D |
| Emergency Management | M |
| English | M,D |
| Family and Consumer Sciences-General | M |
| Forensic Sciences | M,O |
| French | M,D |
| Gender Studies | M |
| Geographic Information Systems | M,D |
| Geography | M,D |
| German | M,D |
| Health Communication | M,D,O |
| Health Psychology | M,D |
| Historic Preservation | M,D |
| History | M,D |
| Interdisciplinary Studies | M,D |
| Interior Design | M,D |
| International Affairs | M |
| International Development | M,D,O |
| Jewish Studies | M |
| Journalism | M,D |
| Landscape Architecture | M,D |
| Latin American Studies | M,O |
| Linguistics | M,D,O |
| Marriage and Family Therapy | M,D,O |
| Mass Communication | M,D |
| Museum Studies | M |
| Music | M,D |
| Philosophy | M,D |
| Political Science | M,D,O |
| Psychology—General | M,D |
| Public Affairs | M,D,O |
| Religion | M,D |
| School Psychology | M,D,O |
| Social Sciences | M,O |
| Sociology | M,D |
| Spanish | M,D |
| Sustainable Development | M,O |
| Theater | M |
| Urban and Regional Planning | M,D |
| Women's Studies | M,O |
| Writing | M,D |

### UNIVERSITY OF FORT LAUDERDALE
| | |
|---|---|
| Pastoral Ministry and Counseling | M |

### UNIVERSITY OF GEORGIA
| | |
|---|---|
| Agricultural Economics and Agribusiness | M,D |
| Anthropology | M,D |
| Applied Economics | M,D |
| Art History | M,D |
| Art/Fine Arts | M,D |
| Child and Family Studies | M |
| Classics | M |
| Clothing and Textiles | M,D |
| Communication—General | M,D |
| Comparative Literature | M,D |
| Economics | M,D |
| English | M,D |
| Environmental Design | M |
| Family and Consumer Sciences-General | M,D |
| French | M,D |
| Geography | M,D |
| German | M,D |
| Gerontology | O |
| Historic Preservation | M |
| History | M,D |
| Interior Design | M,D |
| International Affairs | M,D |
| Italian | M,D |
| Journalism | M,D |
| Landscape Architecture | M |
| Linguistics | M,D |
| Mass Communication | M,D |
| Music | M,D |
| Philosophy | M,D |
| Political Science | M,D |
| Portuguese | M,D |
| Psychology—General | D |
| Public Administration | M,D |
| Public Policy | M,D |
| Religion | M |
| Sociology | M,D |

| | |
|---|---|
| Spanish | M,D |
| Sustainable Development | M,D |
| Theater | M,D |
| Women's Studies | O |

### UNIVERSITY OF GREAT FALLS
| | |
|---|---|
| Counseling Psychology | M |
| Criminal Justice and Criminology | M |

### UNIVERSITY OF GUAM
| | |
|---|---|
| Art/Fine Arts | M |
| English | M |
| Graphic Design | M |
| Pacific Area/Pacific Rim Studies | M |
| Public Administration | M |

### UNIVERSITY OF GUELPH
| | |
|---|---|
| Agricultural Economics and Agribusiness | M,D |
| Anthropology | M,D |
| Applied Psychology | M,D |
| Art/Fine Arts | M |
| Child and Family Studies | M,D |
| Clinical Psychology | M,D |
| Cognitive Sciences | M,D |
| Comparative Literature | D |
| Consumer Economics | M |
| Criminal Justice and Criminology | M,D |
| Demography and Population Studies | M,D |
| Economics | M,D |
| English | M |
| French | M |
| Geography | M,D |
| History | M,D |
| Human Development | M,D |
| Industrial and Organizational Psychology | M,D |
| International Development | M,D |
| Landscape Architecture | M |
| Marriage and Family Therapy | M |
| Medieval and Renaissance Studies | D |
| Philosophy | M,D |
| Political Science | M |
| Psychology—General | M,D |
| Public Administration | M |
| Public Policy | M |
| Rural Planning and Studies | M,D |
| Social Psychology | M,D |
| Sociology | M |
| Theater | M |
| Western European Studies | M |

### UNIVERSITY OF HARTFORD
| | |
|---|---|
| Architecture | M |
| Art/Fine Arts | M |
| Clinical Psychology | M,D |
| Communication—General | M |
| Experimental Psychology | M |
| Music | M,D,O |
| Psychology—General | M,D |
| School Psychology | M |

### UNIVERSITY OF HAWAII AT HILO
| | |
|---|---|
| Counseling Psychology | M |
| Cultural Studies | M,D |

### UNIVERSITY OF HAWAII AT MANOA
| | |
|---|---|
| American Studies | M,D,O |
| Anthropology | M,D |
| Architecture | D |
| Art History | M |
| Art/Fine Arts | M |
| Asian Languages | M,D |
| Asian Studies | O |
| Chinese | M,D,O |
| Clinical Psychology | M,D,O |
| Communication—General | M,O |
| Conflict Resolution and Mediation/Peace Studies | M,O |
| Cultural Studies | O |
| Dance | M,D |
| Demography and Population Studies | O |
| Disability Studies | O |
| Economics | M,D |
| Emergency Management | O |
| English | M |
| French | M |
| Geography | M,D,O |
| Historic Preservation | O |
| History | M,D |
| International Affairs | O |
| International Development | M,D,O |
| Japanese | M,D,O |
| Linguistics | M,D |
| Museum Studies | O |
| Music | M,D |
| Pacific Area/Pacific Rim Studies | M,O |
| Philosophy | M,D |
| Political Science | M,D |
| Psychology—General | M,D,O |
| Public Administration | M,O |
| Public Policy | M |
| Religion | M |
| Social Psychology | M,D,O |
| Sociology | M,D |
| Spanish | M |
| Speech and Interpersonal Communication | M |
| Sustainable Development | M,D,O |
| Theater | M,D |
| Urban and Regional Planning | M,D,O |
| Women's Studies | O |

### UNIVERSITY OF HOLY CROSS
| | |
|---|---|
| Marriage and Family Therapy | M |

### UNIVERSITY OF HOUSTON
| | |
|---|---|
| Anthropology | M |
| Applied Economics | M,D |
| Architecture | M |
| Art History | M |
| Art/Fine Arts | M |
| Clinical Psychology | M,D |
| Communication—General | M |

---

*M—masters degree; D—doctorate; O—other advanced degree; *—Close-Up and/or Display*

Comparative Literature — M
Counseling Psychology — M,D
Cultural Studies — M
Developmental Psychology — M,D
Economics — M,D
Family and Consumer
    Sciences-General — M
Health Communication — M
Hispanic Studies — M,D
History — M,D
Industrial and Organizational
    Psychology — M,D
Linguistics — M,D
Mass Communication — M
Music — M,D
Philosophy — M
Political Science — M,D
Psychology—General — M,D
Public Administration — M,D
Public Policy — M
Social Psychology — M,D
Sociology — M
Spanish — M,D
Speech and Interpersonal
    Communication — M
Theater — M
Writing — M,D

**UNIVERSITY OF HOUSTON–CLEAR LAKE**
Clinical Psychology — M
Criminal Justice and Criminology — M
Cultural Studies — M
English — M
History — M
Humanities — M
Marriage and Family Therapy — M
Psychology—General — M
School Psychology — M
Sociology — M

**UNIVERSITY OF HOUSTON–DOWNTOWN**
Criminal Justice and Criminology — M
English — M
Rhetoric — M
Technical Communication — M

**UNIVERSITY OF HOUSTON–VICTORIA**
Counseling Psychology — M
Economic Development — M
Forensic Psychology — M
Forensic Sciences — M
Interdisciplinary Studies — M
Psychology—General — M
Publishing — M
School Psychology — M
Writing — M

**UNIVERSITY OF IDAHO**
Agricultural Economics and
    Agribusiness — M
American Indian/Native American
    Studies — D
Anthropology — M
Applied Economics — M
Architecture — M
Art/Fine Arts — M
Conflict Resolution and
    Mediation/Peace Studies — D
Consumer Economics — M
English — M
Experimental Psychology — M,D
Geography — M,D
History — M,D
Interdisciplinary Studies — M
Landscape Architecture — M
Music — M
Philosophy — M,D
Political Science — M,D
Psychology—General — M,D
Public Administration — M,D
Rehabilitation Counseling — M,O
Theater — M
Urban and Regional Planning — M
Writing — M

**UNIVERSITY OF ILLINOIS AT CHICAGO**
Anthropology — M,D
Applied Arts and Design—
    General — M
Architecture — M
Art History — M,D
Art/Fine Arts — M,D
Communication—General — M,D
Criminal Justice and Criminology — M,D
Developmental Psychology — M,D
Disability Studies — M,D
East European and Russian Studies — M,D
Economics — M,D
English — M,D
Forensic Sciences — M
French — M
Geography — M
German — M,D
Graphic Design — M
Hispanic and Latin American
    Languages — M,D
Hispanic Studies — M,D
History — M,D
Human Development — M
Interdisciplinary Studies — D
Latin American Studies — M
Linguistics — M
Medical Illustration — M
Museum Studies — M,D
Philosophy — M,D
Political Science — M,D
Psychology—General — M,D
Public Administration — M,D
Slavic Languages — M,D
Sociology — M,D
Spanish — M,D
Urban and Regional Planning — M,D

**UNIVERSITY OF ILLINOIS AT SPRINGFIELD**
Addictions/Substance Abuse
    Counseling — M,O
Child and Family Studies — M,O
Communication—General — M
Emergency Management — M,O
English — M,O
Gerontology — M,O
History — M
Homeland Security — M,O
Human Development — M
Interdisciplinary Studies — M
Journalism — M
Political Science — M
Public Administration — M,D,O
Public History — M
Social Studies — M,O

**UNIVERSITY OF ILLINOIS AT URBANA–CHAMPAIGN**
African Studies — M
Agricultural Economics and
    Agribusiness — M,D
Anthropology — M,D
Applied Arts and Design—
    General — M,D
Applied Economics — M,D
Architecture — M,D
Art History — M,D
Art/Fine Arts — M
Asian Languages — M,D
Asian Studies — M,D
Classics — M,D
Communication—General — M,D
Comparative Literature — M,D
Consumer Economics — M,D
Dance — M
East European and Russian Studies — M,D
Economics — M,D
English — M,D
French — M,D
Geography — M,D
German — M,D
Graphic Design — M
History — M,D
Human Development — M,D
Industrial and Labor Relations — M,D
Industrial Design — M
Interdisciplinary Studies — D
Italian — M,D
Journalism — M
Landscape Architecture — M
Latin American Studies — M
Linguistics — M,D
Media Studies — M,D
Music — M,D
Near and Middle Eastern Studies — M
Philosophy — M,D
Photography — M
Political Science — M,D
Portuguese — M,D
Psychology—General — M,D
Religion — M
Romance Languages — D
Slavic Languages — M,D
Sociology — M,D
Spanish — M,D
Theater — M,D
Translation and Interpretation — M
Urban and Regional Planning — M,D
Western European Studies — M
Writing — M,D

**UNIVERSITY OF INDIANAPOLIS**
Anthropology — M
Art/Fine Arts — M
Clinical Psychology — M,D
Counseling Psychology — M,D
English — M
Gerontology — M,D,O
History — M
International Affairs — M
Psychology—General — M,D
Sociology — M

**THE UNIVERSITY OF IOWA**
American Studies — M,D
Anthropology — M,D
Art History — M,D
Art/Fine Arts — M
Asian Languages — M
Asian Studies — M
Chinese — M
Classics — M,D
Communication—General — M,D
Counseling Psychology — M,D,O
Dance — M
Economics — D
English — M,D
Film, Television, and Video
    Production — M
Film, Television, and Video
    Theory and Criticism — M,D
French — M,D
Geographic Information Systems — M,D,O
Geography — M,D,O
History — M,D
Journalism — M,D
Linguistics — M,D
Marriage and Family Therapy — M,D
Mass Communication — M,D
Media Studies — M,D
Music — M,D
Philosophy — D
Political Science — D
Psychology—General — M,D,O
Rehabilitation Counseling — M,D
Religion — M,D
Rhetoric — M
School Psychology — M,D,O
Sociology — M,D
Spanish — M,D
Speech and Interpersonal
    Communication — M,D

Theater — M
Urban and Regional Planning — M
Women's Studies — O
Writing — M,D

**THE UNIVERSITY OF KANSAS**
African Studies — M,O
African-American Studies — M,O
American Indian/Native American
    Studies — M,O
American Studies — M,D
Anthropology — M,D
Applied Arts and Design—
    General — M
Applied Behavior Analysis — M,D,O
Architecture — M,D
Art History — M,D
Art/Fine Arts — M,O
Asian Languages — M,O
Asian Studies — M,O
Classics — M
Clinical Psychology — M,D
Cognitive Sciences — M,D
Communication—General — M,D,O
Counseling Psychology — M,D
Cultural Studies — M,D
Developmental Psychology — M,D
East European and Russian Studies — M,O
Economics — M,D
English — M,D
Film, Television, and Video
    Theory and Criticism — M,D
French — M,D
Geographic Information Systems — M,D,O
Geography — M,D,O
German — M,D
Gerontology — D
Historic Preservation — M,D,O
History — M,D
Interdisciplinary Studies — D
International Affairs — M
Journalism — M,D
Latin American Studies — M,O
Linguistics — M,D
Media Studies — M,O
Museum Studies — M
Music — M,D
Near and Middle Eastern Studies — M,O
Philosophy — M,D
Political Science — M,D
Psychology—General — M,D
Public Administration — M,D,O
Religion — M,D
School Psychology — D,O
Slavic Languages — M,D
Social Psychology — M,D
Sociology — D
Spanish — M,D
Textile Design — M
Theater — M,D
Therapies—Dance, Drama, and
    Music — M,D
Urban and Regional Planning — M
Urban Design — M,D,O
Writing — M,D

**UNIVERSITY OF KENTUCKY**
Agricultural Economics and
    Agribusiness — M,D
Anthropology — M,D
Applied Arts and Design—
    General — M
Architecture — M
Art History — M
Art/Fine Arts — M
Arts Administration — M
Child and Family Studies — M,D
Classics — M
Communication—General — M,D
Counseling Psychology — M,D,O
Economics — M,D
English — M,D
Geography — M,D
German — M
Gerontology — D,O
Hispanic Studies — M
Historic Preservation — M
History — M,D
Interior Design — M
International Affairs — M
Music — M,D
Philosophy — M,D
Political Science — M,D
Psychology—General — M,D
Public Administration — M,D
Public Policy — M,D,O
Rehabilitation Counseling — M,D
School Psychology — M,D,O
Sociology — M,D
Therapies—Dance, Drama, and
    Music — M,D

**UNIVERSITY OF KING'S COLLEGE**
Journalism — M
Writing — M

**UNIVERSITY OF LA VERNE**
Child and Family Studies — M
Child Development — M
Clinical Psychology — D
English — M,D
Gerontology — M,O
Marriage and Family Therapy — M,D
Psychology—General — M,D
Public Administration — M,D
School Psychology — M,O

**UNIVERSITY OF LETHBRIDGE**
Addictions/Substance Abuse
    Counseling — M,D
American Indian/Native American
    Studies — M,D
Anthropology — M,D
Archaeology — M,D
Art/Fine Arts — M,D
Canadian Studies — M,D

Counseling Psychology — M,D
Economics — M,D
English — M,D
French — M,D
Gender Studies — M,D
Geographic Information Systems — M,D
Geography — M,D
German — M,D
Media Studies — M,D
Music — M,D
Philosophy — M,D
Political Science — M,D
Psychology—General — M,D
Religion — M,D
Sociology — M,D
Spanish — M,D
Theater — M,D
Urban Studies — M,D
Women's Studies — M,D

**UNIVERSITY OF LOUISIANA AT LAFAYETTE**
American Studies — D
Cognitive Sciences — D
Communication—General — M
English — M,D
Folklore — M,D
French — M,D
History — M
Mass Communication — M
Music — M
Psychology—General — M
Rehabilitation Counseling — M
Rhetoric — M,D
Writing — M,D

**UNIVERSITY OF LOUISIANA AT MONROE**
Clinical Psychology — M
Communication—General — M
Counseling Psychology — M
Criminal Justice and Criminology — M
English — M
Family and Consumer
    Sciences-General — M,D
Forensic Psychology — M
Gerontology — M,O
History — M
Marriage and Family Therapy — M,D
Psychology—General — M
Public Administration — M
Speech and Interpersonal
    Communication — M,D

**UNIVERSITY OF LOUISVILLE**
Addictions/Substance Abuse
    Counseling — M,D,O
African Studies — M
African-American Studies — M
Anthropology — M
Applied Arts and Design—
    General — M,D
Applied Behavior Analysis — M,D
Art History — M,D
Art Therapy — M,D
Clinical Psychology — D
Cognitive Sciences — D
Communication—General — M
Counseling Psychology — M,D
Criminal Justice and Criminology — M,D
Cultural Studies — M,D
Developmental Psychology — D
English — M,D
Experimental Psychology — D
French — M,O
Geography — M
Gerontology — M,D,O
History — M,O
Humanities — M,D
Interdisciplinary Studies — M,D
Linguistics — M,D
Marriage and Family Therapy — M,D,O
Museum Studies — M,D
Music — M
Philosophy — M,D
Political Science — M
Psychology—General — D
Public Administration — M,D
Public Affairs — M,D
Public History — M,O
Public Policy — M,D
Rhetoric — M,D
School Psychology — M,D
Sociology — M,D
Spanish — M,O
Theater — M
Urban and Regional Planning — M,D
Urban Studies — M,D
Women's Studies — M,O
Writing — M,D

**UNIVERSITY OF MAINE**
Agricultural Economics and
    Agribusiness — M
Anthropology — D
Art/Fine Arts — M
Communication—General — M,D
Economics — M
English — M
French — M
History — M,D
Human Development — M,D,O
Interdisciplinary Studies — M,D
International Affairs — M
Music — M
Psychology—General — M,D

**UNIVERSITY OF MANAGEMENT AND TECHNOLOGY**
Criminal Justice and Criminology — M,O
Homeland Security — M
Public Administration — M,O

**THE UNIVERSITY OF MANCHESTER**
Anthropology — M,D
Archaeology — M,D

Architecture M,D
Art History D
Art/Fine Arts M,D
Arts Administration D
Asian Studies M,D
Chinese M,D
Classics D
Clinical Psychology M,D
Clothing and Textiles M,D
Conflict Resolution and
    Mediation/Peace Studies D
Counseling Psychology M,D
Criminal Justice and Criminology M,D
Cultural Studies M,D
Developmental Psychology M,D
Economics D
English D
Environmental Design M,D
French M,D
Geography M,D
German M,D
Hispanic Studies M,D
History of Medicine M,D
History of Science and Technology M,D
History D
Industrial and Labor Relations M
Industrial and Organizational
    Psychology D
International Affairs D
International Development M,D
Italian M,D
Japanese M,D
Landscape Architecture M,D
Latin American Studies M,D
Linguistics M,D
Museum Studies D
Music D
Near and Middle Eastern Languages M,D
Near and Middle Eastern Studies M,D
Philosophy M,D
Political Science M,D
Psychology—General M,D
Religion D
Russian M,D
Slavic Languages M,D
Social Sciences M,D
Sociology M,D
Spanish M,D
Textile Design M,D
Theater D
Theology D
Translation and Interpretation M,D
Writing D

**UNIVERSITY OF MANITOBA**
Agricultural Economics and
    Agribusiness M,D
American Indian/Native American
    Studies M
Anthropology M,D
Architecture M
Canadian Studies M
Child and Family Studies M
Classics M
Clinical Psychology M,D
Clothing and Textiles M
Disability Studies M
Economics M,D
English M,D
Family and Consumer
    Sciences-General M
French M,D
Geography M,D
German M
History M,D
Interdisciplinary Studies M,D
Interior Design M
Landscape Architecture M
Linguistics M,D
Music M
Northern Studies M
Philosophy M
Political Science M
Psychology—General M,D
Public Administration M
Religion M,D
School Psychology M,D
Slavic Languages M
Sociology M,D
Urban and Regional Planning M

**UNIVERSITY OF MARY HARDIN-BAYLOR**
Clinical Psychology M
Counseling Psychology M
Marriage and Family Therapy M

**UNIVERSITY OF MARYLAND, BALTIMORE**
Ethics O
Genetic Counseling M
Gerontology M,D
Thanatology O

**UNIVERSITY OF MARYLAND, BALTIMORE COUNTY**
Applied Psychology D
Clinical Psychology M,D
Cognitive Sciences D
Communication—General M
Computer Art and Design M
Dance M
Developmental Psychology D
Economics M,D
Emergency Management M,D,O
English M
Geographic Information Systems M,O
Geography M,D
Gerontology M,D
History M
Industrial and Organizational
    Psychology M
Linguistics M

Music O
Psychology—General M,D
Public History M,D
Public Policy M,D,O
Social Psychology M,D
Social Sciences D
Sociology M
Theater M
Urban Studies M,D

**UNIVERSITY OF MARYLAND, COLLEGE PARK**
Agricultural Economics and
    Agribusiness M,D
American Studies M,D
Anthropology M
Architecture M
Art History M,D
Art Therapy M,D,O
Art/Fine Arts M,D
Broadcast Journalism M,D
Child and Family Studies M,D
Classics M
Clinical Psychology M,D
Cognitive Sciences D
Communication—General M,D
Comparative Literature M,D
Counseling Psychology M,D,O
Criminal Justice and Criminology M,D
Dance M
Developmental Psychology M,D
Economics M,D
English M,D
Experimental Psychology M,D
Family and Consumer
    Sciences-General M,D
French M,D
Geography M,D
German M,D
Historic Preservation M,O
History M,D
Human Development M,D
Industrial and Organizational
    Psychology M,D
Jewish Studies M
Journalism M,D
Landscape Architecture M
Linguistics M,D
Marriage and Family Therapy M,D
Media Studies M,D
Music M,D
Philosophy M,D
Political Science D
Portuguese M,D
Psychology—General M,D
Public Administration M
Public Policy M,D
Rehabilitation Counseling M,D,O
School Psychology M,D
Social Psychology M,D
Sociology M,D
Spanish M,D
Speech and Interpersonal
    Communication M,D
Survey Methodology M,D
Sustainable Development M
Theater M,D
Urban and Regional Planning M,D
Women's Studies M,D
Writing M,D

**UNIVERSITY OF MARYLAND EASTERN SHORE**
Criminal Justice and Criminology M
Rehabilitation Counseling M

**UNIVERSITY OF MASSACHUSETTS AMHERST**
African-American Studies M,D
Agricultural Economics and
    Agribusiness M,D
American Studies M,D
Anthropology M,D
Architecture M
Art History M
Art/Fine Arts M
Child and Family Studies M,D,O
Chinese M
Classics M
Clinical Psychology M,D
Cognitive Sciences M,D
Communication—General M,D
Comparative Literature M,D
Conflict Resolution and
    Mediation/Peace Studies M,D
Developmental Psychology M,D
Economics M,D
English M,D
French M
Geography M
German M,D
Hispanic and Latin American
    Languages M,D
Historic Preservation M
History M,D
Industrial and Labor Relations M
Interior Design M
Italian M
Japanese M
Landscape Architecture M
Linguistics M,D
Music M,D
Philosophy M,D
Political Science M,D
Portuguese M,D
Psychology—General M,D
Public Administration M
Public Policy M
Rhetoric M,D
Scandinavian Languages M
School Psychology M,D,O

Social Psychology M,D
Sociology M,D
Spanish M,D
Sustainable Development M
Theater M
Urban and Regional Planning M,D
Writing M,D

**UNIVERSITY OF MASSACHUSETTS BOSTON**
American Studies M
Applied Economics M
Archaeology M
Classics M
Clinical Psychology D
Cognitive Sciences M
Conflict Resolution and
    Mediation/Peace Studies M,O
Counseling Psychology M,D
Cultural Studies M
English M
Gerontology M,D,O
History M
International Affairs M
International Development M,D
Linguistics M,D
Marriage and Family Therapy M
Public Administration M
Public Policy M,D
Rehabilitation Counseling M
School Psychology M,D
Sociology M,D
Urban and Regional Planning M
Writing M

**UNIVERSITY OF MASSACHUSETTS DARTMOUTH**
Applied Arts and Design—
    General M
Applied Behavior Analysis M,O
Art/Fine Arts M,O
Clinical Psychology M,O
Computer Art and Design M
Experimental Psychology M,O
Illustration M
Internet and Interactive
    Multimedia M
Latin American Studies M,D
Photography M
Portuguese M,D
Psychology—General M,O
Public Administration M
Public Policy M,O
Writing M,O

**UNIVERSITY OF MASSACHUSETTS LOWELL**
Conflict Resolution and
    Mediation/Peace Studies M
Criminal Justice and Criminology M
Economic Development M,O
Economics M,O
Music M
Psychology—General M
Social Psychology M
Sociology M,O
Urban and Regional Planning M,O

**UNIVERSITY OF MASSACHUSETTS MEDICAL SCHOOL**
Interdisciplinary Studies M,D

**UNIVERSITY OF MEMPHIS**
African-American Studies M,D,O
Anthropology M
Applied Behavior Analysis M,D,O
Archaeology M,D,O
Architecture M
Art History M,O
Art/Fine Arts M,O
Clinical Psychology M,D,O
Communication—General M,D
Comparative Literature M,D,O
Counseling Psychology M,D
Criminal Justice and Criminology M,D
Economics M,D
English M,D,O
Experimental Psychology M,D,O
Film, Television, and Video
    Production M,D
French M
Gender Studies O
Geographic Information Systems M,D,O
Geography M,D,O
Graphic Design M,O
History M,D
Interdisciplinary Studies M,D,O
Journalism M,O
Liberal Studies M,O
Linguistics M,D,O
Museum Studies M,O
Music M,D
Near and Middle Eastern Studies M,D
Philosophy M,D
Photography M,O
Political Science M
Psychology—General M,D,O
Public Administration M,O
Public Policy M,O
Rehabilitation Counseling M
School Psychology M,D,O
Social Sciences M,D
Sociology M
Spanish M
Theater M
Urban and Regional Planning M
Writing M,D,O

**UNIVERSITY OF MIAMI**
Architecture M
Art History M
Art/Fine Arts M

Broadcast Journalism M,D
Clinical Psychology M,D
Communication—General M,D
Counseling Psychology D
Developmental Psychology M,D
English M,D
Film, Television, and Video
    Production M,D
Film, Television, and Video
    Theory and Criticism M,D
French D
Geography M
Graphic Design M
History M,D
International Affairs M,D
Internet and Interactive
    Multimedia M
Journalism M,D
Latin American Studies M
Liberal Studies M
Marriage and Family Therapy M,O
Music M,D,O
Philosophy M,D
Photography M
Political Science M
Psychology—General M,D
Romance Languages D
Sociology M,D
Spanish M,D
Therapies—Dance, Drama, and
    Music M,D,O
Urban Design M

**UNIVERSITY OF MICHIGAN**
American Studies M,D
Anthropology D
Applied Arts and Design—
    General M,D
Applied Economics M
Archaeology M
Architecture M
Art History M,D
Art/Fine Arts M
Asian Languages D
Asian Studies M,D,O
Classics M,D,O
Clinical Psychology D
Cognitive Sciences D
Communication—General D
Comparative Literature D
Cultural Anthropology D
Dance M
Developmental Psychology D
East European and Russian Studies M,O
Economics M,D
English M,D,O
Film, Television, and Video
    Theory and Criticism D,O
French D
Genetic Counseling M,D
German M,D,O
History D,O
Italian D
Jewish Studies M,D,O
Landscape Architecture M
Linguistics D
Mass Communication D
Media Studies M
Music M,D,O
Near and Middle Eastern Languages M,D
Near and Middle Eastern Studies M,D
Philosophy M,D
Political Science D
Psychology—General D,O
Public Policy M,D
Religion M,D
Slavic Languages M,D
Social Psychology D
Social Sciences D
Sociology D
Spanish D
Survey Methodology M,D,O
Sustainable Development M,D
Urban and Regional Planning D,O
Urban Design M
Women's Studies D,O
Writing M

**UNIVERSITY OF MICHIGAN–DEARBORN**
Clinical Psychology M
Criminal Justice and Criminology M
Health Psychology M
Public Administration M

**UNIVERSITY OF MICHIGAN–FLINT**
American Studies M
Art/Fine Arts M
Arts Administration M
Communication—General M
Criminal Justice and Criminology M
English M
Gender Studies M
Gerontology M,D,O
International Affairs M
Museum Studies M
Music M
Political Science M
Public Administration M
Rhetoric M
Social Sciences M
Writing M

**UNIVERSITY OF MINNESOTA, DULUTH**
Anthropology M
Art/Fine Arts M
Criminal Justice and Criminology M
English M
Graphic Design M
Liberal Studies M
Music M
Sociology M

*M—masters degree; D—doctorate; O—other advanced degree; *—Close-Up and/or Display*

**UNIVERSITY OF MINNESOTA, TWIN CITIES CAMPUS**
American Studies — D
Anthropology — M,D
Applied Arts and Design—General — M,D,O
Applied Economics — M,D
Archaeology — M,D
Architecture — M
Art History — M,D
Art/Fine Arts — M
Asian Languages — D
Asian Studies — D
Child and Family Studies — M,D
Child Development — M,D
Classics — M,D
Clinical Psychology — D
Clothing and Textiles — M,D,O
Cognitive Sciences — D
Communication—General — M,D,O
Comparative Literature — D
Counseling Psychology — D
Cultural Studies — D
Economics — M,D
English — M,D
French — M,D
Genetic Counseling — M,D
Geographic Information Systems — M,D
Geography — M,D
German — M,D
Hispanic and Latin American Languages — M,D
History of Medicine — M,D
History of Science and Technology — M,D
History — M,D
Industrial and Labor Relations — M
Industrial and Organizational Psychology — D
Interdisciplinary Studies — D
Interior Design — M,D,O
International Development — M
Landscape Architecture — M
Linguistics — M,D
Marriage and Family Therapy — M,D
Mass Communication — M,D
Medieval and Renaissance Studies — M,D
Music — M,D
Philosophy — M,D
Political Science — D
Portuguese — M,D
Psychology—General — D
Public Affairs — M,D
Public Policy — M,D
Religion — M,D
Scandinavian Languages — M,D
School Psychology — M,D,O
Social Psychology — D
Sociology — M,D
Spanish — M,D
Textile Design — M,D,O
Theater — M,D
Urban and Regional Planning — M,D
Women's Studies — D

**UNIVERSITY OF MISSISSIPPI**
Anthropology — M,D
Art/Fine Arts — M,D
Economics — M,D
English — M,D
Experimental Psychology — M,D
History — M,D
Journalism — M
Music — M,D
Philosophy — M,D
Political Science — M,D

**UNIVERSITY OF MISSOURI**
Agricultural Economics and Agribusiness — M,D,O
Anthropology — M,D
Archaeology — M,D
Architecture — M,D
Art History — M
Art/Fine Arts — M,D
Child and Family Studies — M,D
Classics — M,D
Clothing and Textiles — M,D
Communication—General — M,D
Comparative Literature — M,D
Conflict Resolution and Mediation/Peace Studies — M,D,O
Consumer Economics — M,D,O
Counseling Psychology — M,D,O
Economics — M,D
English — M,D
Family and Consumer Sciences-General — M,D,O
French — M,D
Geographic Information Systems — M,D,O
Geography — M,O
German — M
Gerontology — M,D,O
Health Communication — M,D
History — M,D
Human Development — M,D
Journalism — M,D
Music — M
Philosophy — D
Political Science — M,D
Psychology—General — M,D
Public Administration — M,D,O
Public Affairs — M,D,O
Public Policy — M,D,O
Religion — M
Romance Languages — M,D
Rural Sociology — M,D
Russian — M
School Psychology — M,D,O
Sociology — D
Spanish — M,D
Theater — M,D

**UNIVERSITY OF MISSOURI–KANSAS CITY**
Art/Fine Arts — M,D

Counseling Psychology — M,D,O
Criminal Justice and Criminology — M
Economics — M,D
English — M,D
French — M
History — M,D
Interdisciplinary Studies — D
Music — M,D
Political Science — M
Psychology—General — M,D
Public Administration — M,D
Public Affairs — M
Romance Languages — M
Social Psychology — M,D
Sociology — M
Spanish — M
Theater — M
Therapies—Dance, Drama, and Music — M,D

**UNIVERSITY OF MISSOURI–ST. LOUIS**
American Studies — M,D
Clinical Psychology — M,D,O
Communication—General — M
Counseling Psychology — M,D
Criminal Justice and Criminology — M,D
Economics — M
English — M
Gerontology — M,O
Industrial and Organizational Psychology — M,D,O
Marriage and Family Therapy — M,D
Media Studies — M
Museum Studies — M,O
Philosophy — M
Political Science — M,D
Psychology—General — M,D,O
Public Administration — M,D
Public History — M,O
Public Policy — M,D,O
School Psychology — M,D,O
Writing — M

**UNIVERSITY OF MOBILE**
Marriage and Family Therapy — M

**UNIVERSITY OF MONTANA**
Anthropology — M,D
Art History — M
Art/Fine Arts — M
Child and Family Studies — M,D,O
Clinical Psychology — M,D,O
Communication—General — M
Computer Art and Design — M
Counseling Psychology — M,D,O
Criminal Justice and Criminology — M
Cultural Studies — M,D,O
Developmental Psychology — M,D,O
Economics — M
English — M
Experimental Psychology — M,D
Film, Television, and Video Production — M
French — M
Geography — M
German — M
History — M,D
Interdisciplinary Studies — M,D
Internet and Interactive Multimedia — M
Journalism — M
Linguistics — M,D
Music — M
Philosophy — M
Photography — M
Political Science — M
Psychology—General — M,D,O
Public Administration — M
Rural Planning and Studies — M
Rural Sociology — M
School Psychology — M,D,O
Sociology — M
Spanish — M
Theater — M
Writing — M

**UNIVERSITY OF MONTEVALLO**
English — M

**UNIVERSITY OF NEBRASKA AT KEARNEY**
Counseling Psychology — M,O
English — M
History — M
School Psychology — M,O
Writing — M

**UNIVERSITY OF NEBRASKA AT OMAHA**
Applied Behavior Analysis — M,D,O
Art/Fine Arts — M,O
Communication—General — M,O
Criminal Justice and Criminology — M,D,O
Economics — M
English — M,O
Geographic Information Systems — M,O
Geography — M
Gerontology — M,D,O
History — M
Industrial and Organizational Psychology — M,D,O
Music — M
National Security — M,O
Political Science — M,O
Psychology—General — M,D,O
Public Administration — M,D,O
School Psychology — M,D,O
Sociology — M
Technical Communication — M,O
Writing — M

**UNIVERSITY OF NEBRASKA–LINCOLN**
Agricultural Economics and Agribusiness — M,D
Anthropology — M
Archaeology — M,D
Architecture — M,D

Art History — M
Art/Fine Arts — M
Child and Family Studies — M,D
Child Development — M,D
Classics — M
Clinical Psychology — M,D
Clothing and Textiles — M,D
Cognitive Sciences — M,D,O
Communication—General — M
Comparative Literature — M,D
Consumer Economics — M,D
Corporate and Organizational Communication — M,D
Counseling Psychology — M,D,O
Developmental Psychology — M,D,O
Economics — M,D
English — M,D
Family and Consumer Sciences-General — M,D
French — M,D
Geography — M,D
German — M,D
Gerontology — M,D
History — M,D
Human Development — M,D,O
Interior Design — M,D
Journalism — M
Marriage and Family Therapy — M
Mass Communication — M
Music — M,D
Philosophy — M,D
Political Science — M,D,O
Psychology—General — M,D,O
Public Policy — M,D
Rhetoric — M,D
School Psychology — M,D,O
Social Psychology — M,D
Sociology — M,D
Spanish — M,D
Speech and Interpersonal Communication — M,D
Survey Methodology — M,D
Theater — M
Urban and Regional Planning — M,D
Writing — M,D

**UNIVERSITY OF NEBRASKA MEDICAL CENTER**
Applied Behavior Analysis — M,D
Emergency Management — M

**UNIVERSITY OF NEVADA, LAS VEGAS**
Addictions/Substance Abuse Counseling — M,D,O
Anthropology — M,D
Applied Economics — M,O
Architecture — M,O
Art/Fine Arts — M
Clinical Psychology — M,D,O
Communication—General — M
Counseling Psychology — M,D,O
Criminal Justice and Criminology — M,D
Economics — M
Emergency Management — M,D,O
English — M,D
Film, Television, and Video Production — M,O
Hispanic Studies — M
History — M,D
Journalism — M
Marriage and Family Therapy — M
Media Studies — M
Music — M,D,O
Political Science — M,D
Psychology—General — M,D,O
Public Administration — M,D,O
Public Affairs — M,D,O
Public Policy — M,D,O
Sociology — M,D
Theater — M
Writing — M,D,O

**UNIVERSITY OF NEVADA, RENO**
Agricultural Economics and Agribusiness — M,D
Anthropology — M,D
Applied Economics — M,D
Art/Fine Arts — M
Child and Family Studies — M
Clinical Psychology — D
Cognitive Sciences — M,D
Criminal Justice and Criminology — M
Economics — M,D
English — M,D
French — M
Geography — M,D
German — M
History — M,D
Human Development — M
Journalism — M
Music — M
Philosophy — M
Political Science — M,D
Psychology—General — M,D
Public Administration — M
Social Psychology — D
Sociology — M
Spanish — M
Speech and Interpersonal Communication — M
Western European Studies — D

**UNIVERSITY OF NEW BRUNSWICK FREDERICTON**
Anthropology — M
Applied Economics — M
Classics — M
Conflict Resolution and Mediation/Peace Studies — M
Economics — M
English — M,D
History — M,D
Interdisciplinary Studies — M
International Development — M
Political Science — M

Psychology—General — M,D
Public Administration — M
Public Policy — M
Sociology — M,D
Sustainable Development — M
Urban and Regional Planning — M

**UNIVERSITY OF NEW BRUNSWICK SAINT JOHN**
Clinical Psychology — M,D
Experimental Psychology — M,D
Psychology—General — M,D

**UNIVERSITY OF NEW HAMPSHIRE**
Addictions/Substance Abuse Counseling — M,O
Art/Fine Arts — M
Child and Family Studies — M,O
Comparative Literature — M,D
Economics — M,D
English — M,D
Geographic Information Systems — O
History — M,D
Liberal Studies — M
Linguistics — M,D
Marriage and Family Therapy — M,O
Museum Studies — M,D
Music — M
Political Science — M,O
Psychology—General — D
Public Administration — M,O
Public Policy — M
Sociology — M,D
Spanish — M
Writing — M,D

**UNIVERSITY OF NEW HAVEN**
Conflict Resolution and Mediation/Peace Studies — M,O
Criminal Justice and Criminology — M,D,O
Emergency Management — M,O
Forensic Psychology — M,D,O
Forensic Sciences — M,D,O
Geographic Information Systems — M,O
Industrial and Labor Relations — M,O
Industrial and Organizational Psychology — M,O
National Security — M,O
Public Administration — M,O
Social Psychology — M,O
Urban and Regional Planning — M,O

**UNIVERSITY OF NEW MEXICO**
American Indian/Native American Studies — M,D
American Studies — M,D
Anthropology — M,D
Archaeology — M,D
Architecture — M,D
Art History — M,D
Art/Fine Arts — M
Child and Family Studies — M,D
Clinical Psychology — D
Cognitive Sciences — D
Communication—General — M,D
Comparative Literature — M,D
Cultural Studies — M,D
Dance — M
Developmental Psychology — D
Economics — M,D
English — M,D
Ethnic Studies — M,D
French — M
Geography — M
German — M,D
Health Psychology — D
Historic Preservation — O
History — M,D
Human Development — M,D
International Development — M,D
International Economics — M,D
Landscape Architecture — M
Latin American Studies — M,D
Linguistics — M,D
Music — M
Philosophy — M,D
Photography — M,D
Political Science — M,D
Portuguese — M,D
Psychology—General — D
Public Administration — M
Sociology — M,D
Spanish — M,D
Theater — M
Urban and Regional Planning — M
Writing — M

**UNIVERSITY OF NEW ORLEANS**
Art/Fine Arts — M
Arts Administration — M
Economics — D
English — M
Film, Television, and Video Production — M
Geography — M
History — M
Music — M
Political Science — M,D
Psychology—General — M,D
Public Administration — M
Romance Languages — M
Sociology — M
Theater — M
Urban and Regional Planning — M
Urban Studies — M,D

**UNIVERSITY OF NORTH ALABAMA**
Child and Family Studies — M
Clinical Psychology — M
Criminal Justice and Criminology — M
Economic Development — M
English — M
Geographic Information Systems — M
History — M
Interdisciplinary Studies — M

Political Science M
Public History M

## UNIVERSITY OF NORTH CAROLINA AT ASHEVILLE
Cultural Studies M,O
Liberal Studies M,O
Sustainable Development M,O

## THE UNIVERSITY OF NORTH CAROLINA AT CHAPEL HILL
Anthropology M,D
Archaeology M,D
Art History M,D
Art/Fine Arts M
Classics M,D
Clinical Psychology D
Cognitive Sciences D
Communication—General D
Developmental Psychology D
East European and Russian Studies M
Economics M,D
English M,D
Folklore M
French M,D
Geography M,D
German M,D
Health Psychology M,D
History M,D
Italian M,D
Latin American Studies M,D,O
Linguistics M,D
Mass Communication M,D,O
Music M,D
Philosophy M,D
Political Science M,D,O
Portuguese M,D
Psychology—General D
Public Administration M
Public Policy D
Rehabilitation Counseling M,D
Religion M,D
Romance Languages M,D
School Psychology M,D
Social Psychology D
Sociology M,D
Spanish M,D
Theater M
Urban and Regional Planning M,D

## THE UNIVERSITY OF NORTH CAROLINA AT CHARLOTTE
Addictions/Substance Abuse
  Counseling M,D,O
African Studies O
Anthropology M
Applied Economics M,O
Architecture M
Arts Administration M,O
Child and Family Studies M,D,O
Child Development M,D,O
Cognitive Sciences M,D,O
Communication—General M
Criminal Justice and Criminology M
Cultural Studies M,O
Economics M,O
Emergency Management M,O
English M,O
Ethics M,O
Gender Studies M,D,O
Geographic Information Systems M,D
Geography M,D
Gerontology M,D,O
Health Psychology M,D,O
History M
Industrial and Organizational
  Psychology M,D,O
Interdisciplinary Studies M,D,O
Latin American Studies M,D,O
Liberal Studies M,D,O
Linguistics M,O
Music O
Philosophy M,O
Psychology—General M,D,O
Public Administration M,O
Public Policy M,D,O
Religion M
Sociology M
Spanish M,O
Technical Writing M,O
Theater M,D,O
Translation and Interpretation M,O
Urban and Regional Planning M,O
Urban Design M
Women's Studies M,D,O
Writing M,O

## THE UNIVERSITY OF NORTH CAROLINA AT GREENSBORO
Applied Economics M
Architecture M,O
Art/Fine Arts M
Child and Family Studies M,D
Classics M
Clinical Psychology M,D
Cognitive Sciences M,D
Communication—General M
Conflict Resolution and
  Mediation/Peace Studies M,O
Counseling Psychology M,D,O
Criminal Justice and Criminology M
Dance M
Developmental Psychology M,D
Economic Development M,D,O
Economics D
English M,D
Film, Television, and Video
  Production M
French M
Gender Studies M
Genetic Counseling M
Geographic Information Systems M,D,O

Geography M,D,O
Gerontology M,O
Hispanic and Latin American
  Languages M,O
Hispanic Studies M,O
Historic Preservation M,O
History M,D,O
Human Development M,O
Interior Design M,O
Liberal Studies M
Marriage and Family Therapy M,D,O
Media Studies M
Museum Studies M,D
Music M,D
Political Science M,O
Psychology—General M
Public Affairs M,O
Rhetoric M
School Psychology M,D,O
Social Psychology M,O
Sociology M
Spanish M,O
Technical Writing M,D,O
Textile Design M,D
Theater M
Women's Studies M,D,O
Writing M

## THE UNIVERSITY OF NORTH CAROLINA AT PEMBROKE
Counseling Psychology M
Public Administration M

## UNIVERSITY OF NORTH CAROLINA SCHOOL OF THE ARTS
Film, Television, and Video
  Production M
Music M,O
Theater M

## THE UNIVERSITY OF NORTH CAROLINA WILMINGTON
Applied Behavior Analysis M
Conflict Resolution and
  Mediation/Peace Studies M
Criminal Justice and Criminology M
English M
Gerontology M,O
History M
Liberal Studies M
Psychology—General M
Public Administration M
Sociology M
Spanish M
Writing M

## UNIVERSITY OF NORTH DAKOTA
Applied Economics M
Art/Fine Arts M
Clinical Psychology M,D
Communication—General D
Counseling Psychology M,D
Criminal Justice and Criminology D
English M,D
Forensic Psychology M
Geographic Information Systems M
Geography M
History M,D
Linguistics M
Music M,D
Psychology—General M,D
Public Administration M
Sociology M

## UNIVERSITY OF NORTHERN BRITISH COLUMBIA
Disability Studies M,D,O
Gender Studies M,D,O
History M,D,O
Interdisciplinary Studies M,D,O
International Affairs M,D,O
Political Science M,D,O
Psychology—General M,D,O

## UNIVERSITY OF NORTHERN COLORADO
Communication—General M
Criminal Justice and Criminology M
English M
Gerontology M,D
History M
Music M,D
Psychology—General M,D
Rehabilitation Counseling M,D
School Psychology O
Social Psychology M,D
Sociology M
Sport Psychology M

## UNIVERSITY OF NORTHERN IOWA
Art/Fine Arts M
Communication—General M
Counseling Psychology M
English M
Gender Studies M
Geography M
History M
Music M
Psychology—General M
Public History M
Public Policy M
School Psychology M,O
Social Sciences M
Spanish M
Women's Studies M
Writing M

## UNIVERSITY OF NORTH FLORIDA
Applied Behavior Analysis M
Counseling Psychology M
Criminal Justice and Criminology M
Economics M
English M

Ethics M,O
History M
Philosophy M,O
Psychology—General M
Public Administration M,O
Translation and Interpretation M
Writing M

## UNIVERSITY OF NORTH GEORGIA
Anthropology M
Clinical Psychology M
Criminal Justice and Criminology M
History M
International Affairs M
Philosophy M
Public Administration M

## UNIVERSITY OF NORTH TEXAS
Anthropology M,D,O
Applied Arts and Design—
  General M,D,O
Applied Behavior Analysis M,D,O
Art History M,D,O
Art/Fine Arts M,D,O
Child and Family Studies M,D,O
Clinical Psychology M,D,O
Communication—General M,D,O
Counseling Psychology M,D,O
Criminal Justice and Criminology M,D,O
Economics M,D,O
Emergency Management M,D,O
English M,D,O
Film, Television, and Video
  Production M,D,O
French M,D,O
Geography M,D,O
Gerontology M,D,O
History M,D,O
Human Development M,D,O
Interdisciplinary Studies M,D,O
Interior Design M,D,O
International Affairs M,D,O
Internet and Interactive
  Multimedia M,D,O
Journalism M,D,O
Linguistics M,D,O
Museum Studies M,D,O
Music M,D,O
Philosophy M,D,O
Political Science M,D,O
Psychology—General M,D,O
Public Administration M,D,O
Rehabilitation Counseling M,D,O
Sociology M,D,O
Spanish M,D,O
Textile Design M,D,O
Writing M,D,O

## UNIVERSITY OF NORTH TEXAS AT DALLAS
Clinical Psychology M
Criminal Justice and Criminology M
Public Administration M

## UNIVERSITY OF NORTH TEXAS HEALTH SCIENCE CENTER AT FORT WORTH
Forensic Sciences M,D

## UNIVERSITY OF NORTHWESTERN–ST. PAUL
Pastoral Ministry and Counseling M
Theology M

## UNIVERSITY OF NOTRE DAME
Applied Arts and Design—
  General M
Architecture M
Art History M
Art/Fine Arts M
Cognitive Sciences D
Comparative Literature D
Conflict Resolution and
  Mediation/Peace Studies M,D
Counseling Psychology D
Developmental Psychology D
Economics M,D
English M,D
French M
Graphic Design M
History of Science and Technology M,D
History M,D
Industrial Design M
International Affairs M
Italian M
Latin American Studies M
Medieval and Renaissance Studies M,D
Philosophy D
Photography M
Political Science D
Psychology—General D
Religion M
Romance Languages M
Sociology D
Spanish M
Sustainable Development M
Theology M,D
Writing M

## UNIVERSITY OF OKLAHOMA
Addictions/Substance Abuse
  Counseling M
American Indian/Native American
  Studies M
Anthropology M,D
Applied Behavior Analysis M,D
Applied Economics M,D
Archaeology M,D
Architecture M,D
Art History M,D
Art/Fine Arts M
Clinical Psychology M,O
Communication—General M,D

Corporate and Organizational
  Communication M,D
Counseling Psychology M,D
Criminal Justice and Criminology M,O
Cultural Studies M,D
Dance M
Economic Development M,D
Economics M,D
English M,D
French M,D
Gender Studies O
Geography M,D
German M,D
Health Communication M
History of Science and Technology M,D
History M,D
Industrial and Organizational
  Psychology M,D
Interdisciplinary Studies M,D
Interior Design M,D,O
International Affairs M
Journalism M,D
Landscape Architecture M
Liberal Studies M,O
Mass Communication M,D
Music M,D,O
Philosophy M,D
Political Science M,D
Psychology—General M,D,O
Public Administration M
Rhetoric M,D
School Psychology M
Sociology M,D
Spanish M,D
Sustainable Development M,D
Theater M
Urban and Regional Planning M
Women's Studies O
Writing M

## UNIVERSITY OF OKLAHOMA HEALTH SCIENCES CENTER
Genetic Counseling M
Homeland Security M

## UNIVERSITY OF OREGON
Anthropology M,D
Architecture M
Art History M,D
Art/Fine Arts M
Arts Administration M
Asian Languages M,D
Asian Studies M
Chinese M,D
Classics M
Clinical Psychology D
Cognitive Sciences M,D
Communication—General M,D
Comparative Literature M,D
Dance M
Developmental Psychology M,D
Economics M,D
English M,D
Folklore M
French M
Geography M,D
German M,D
Historic Preservation M
History M,D
Interdisciplinary Studies M
Interior Design M
International Affairs M
Italian M
Japanese M,D
Journalism M,D
Landscape Architecture M
Linguistics M,D
Media Studies M,D
Music M,D
Philosophy M,D
Political Science M,D
Psychology—General M,D
Public Policy M
Romance Languages M,D
Russian M
Social Psychology M,D
Sociology M,D
Spanish M
Theater M,D
Urban and Regional Planning M
Writing M

## UNIVERSITY OF OTTAWA
Anthropology M
Canadian Studies D
Classics M,D
Communication—General M
Criminal Justice and Criminology M,D
Economics M,D
English M,D
French M,D
Geography M,D
History D,O
Interdisciplinary Studies D,O
International Development M
Linguistics M,D
Music M,O
Philosophy M,D
Political Science M,D
Psychology—General D,O
Public Administration D
Religion M,D
Sociology M
Spanish M,D
Theater M
Translation and Interpretation M,D
Women's Studies M

## UNIVERSITY OF PENNSYLVANIA
African Studies M,D
Anthropology M,D
Applied Economics D

---

*M—masters degree; D—doctorate; O—other advanced degree; \*—Close-Up and/or Display*

Applied Psychology — M
Archaeology — M,D
Architecture — M,D,O
Art History — M,O
Art/Fine Arts — M,O
Asian Studies — M,D
Classics — M,D
Communication—General — D
Comparative Literature — M,D
Computer Art and Design — M,D
Counseling Psychology — M
Criminal Justice and Criminology — M,D
Demography and Population Studies — M,D
Economic Development — M,O
Economics — M,D
English — M,D
Ethics — M,D
French — M,D
Geographic Information Systems — M,D,O
German — M,D
Graphic Design — M,O
Historic Preservation — M,O
History of Science and Technology — M,D
History — M,D
Human Development — M
International Affairs — M
Internet and Interactive Multimedia — M,O
Italian — M,D
Landscape Architecture — M,O
Liberal Studies — M
Linguistics — M,D
Music — M,D
Near and Middle Eastern Studies — M,D
Philosophy — M,D
Political Science — M,D,O
Psychology—General — D
Public Administration — M,O
Public Policy — M,D
Religion — D
Romance Languages — M,D
Sociology — M,D
Spanish — M,D
Urban and Regional Planning — M,D,O
Urban Design — M,D,O

**UNIVERSITY OF PHILOSOPHICAL RESEARCH**
Psychology—General — M
Theology — M

**UNIVERSITY OF PHOENIX–ATLANTA CAMPUS**
Public Administration — M

**UNIVERSITY OF PHOENIX–AUGUSTA CAMPUS**
Criminal Justice and Criminology — M
Public Administration — M

**UNIVERSITY OF PHOENIX–BAY AREA CAMPUS**
Criminal Justice and Criminology — M
Marriage and Family Therapy — M
Public Administration — M,D

**UNIVERSITY OF PHOENIX–CENTRAL VALLEY CAMPUS**
Gerontology — M
Marriage and Family Therapy — M
Public Administration — M

**UNIVERSITY OF PHOENIX–CHARLOTTE CAMPUS**
Gerontology — M

**UNIVERSITY OF PHOENIX–COLORADO CAMPUS**
Public Administration — M
School Psychology — M

**UNIVERSITY OF PHOENIX–COLORADO SPRINGS DOWNTOWN CAMPUS**
Gerontology — M
Public Administration — M
School Psychology — M,O

**UNIVERSITY OF PHOENIX–COLUMBUS GEORGIA CAMPUS**
Public Administration — M

**UNIVERSITY OF PHOENIX–DALLAS CAMPUS**
Criminal Justice and Criminology — M
Public Administration — M

**UNIVERSITY OF PHOENIX–HAWAII CAMPUS**
Gerontology — M
Public Administration — M

**UNIVERSITY OF PHOENIX–HOUSTON CAMPUS**
Public Administration — M

**UNIVERSITY OF PHOENIX–JERSEY CITY CAMPUS**
Criminal Justice and Criminology — M
Psychology—General — M
Public Administration — M

**UNIVERSITY OF PHOENIX–LAS VEGAS CAMPUS**
Counseling Psychology — M
Marriage and Family Therapy — M
Public Administration — M
School Psychology — M

**UNIVERSITY OF PHOENIX–NORTH FLORIDA CAMPUS**
Public Administration — M

**UNIVERSITY OF PHOENIX–ONLINE CAMPUS**
Conflict Resolution and Mediation/Peace Studies — M,O
Criminal Justice and Criminology — M
Homeland Security — M

Industrial and Organizational Psychology — M,D,O
Psychology—General — M,O
Public Administration — M,O

**UNIVERSITY OF PHOENIX–PHOENIX CAMPUS**
Clinical Psychology — M
Counseling Psychology — M
Criminal Justice and Criminology — M
Homeland Security — M
Marriage and Family Therapy — M
Psychology—General — M
Public Administration — M
Social Psychology — M

**UNIVERSITY OF PHOENIX–SACRAMENTO VALLEY CAMPUS**
Public Administration — M

**UNIVERSITY OF PHOENIX–SAN ANTONIO CAMPUS**
Criminal Justice and Criminology — M
Public Administration — M

**UNIVERSITY OF PHOENIX–SAN DIEGO CAMPUS**
Public Administration — M

**UNIVERSITY OF PHOENIX–SOUTHERN ARIZONA CAMPUS**
Psychology—General — M

**UNIVERSITY OF PHOENIX–SOUTHERN CALIFORNIA CAMPUS**
Criminal Justice and Criminology — M
Homeland Security — M
Marriage and Family Therapy — M
Psychology—General — M
Public Administration — M

**UNIVERSITY OF PHOENIX–SOUTH FLORIDA CAMPUS**
Public Administration — M

**UNIVERSITY OF PHOENIX–UTAH CAMPUS**
School Psychology — M

**UNIVERSITY OF PHOENIX–WASHINGTON D.C. CAMPUS**
Criminal Justice and Criminology — M
Gerontology — M,D
Industrial and Organizational Psychology — M,D
Psychology—General — M,D
Public Administration — M,D

**UNIVERSITY OF PHOENIX–WESTERN WASHINGTON CAMPUS**
Criminal Justice and Criminology — M

**UNIVERSITY OF PITTSBURGH**
African Studies — O
Anthropology — M,D
Applied Behavior Analysis — M,D
Applied Psychology — M,D
Architectural History — M,D
Art History — M,O
Asian Studies — M
Chinese — D
Clinical Psychology — D
Communication—General — M,D
Criminal Justice and Criminology — M
Cultural Studies — O
Developmental Psychology — M,D
Disability Studies — O
East European and Russian Studies — O
Economics — M,D
English — M,D
Film, Television, and Video Theory and Criticism — M,D,O
French — M,D
Genetic Counseling — M,D,O
Geographic Information Systems — M,D
Hispanic and Latin American Languages — M,D
History of Science and Technology — D
History — M,D
Interdisciplinary Studies — D
International Affairs — M,D,O
International Development — M,D
Italian — M,D
Japanese — M
Latin American Studies — O
Medieval and Renaissance Studies — O
Military and Defense Studies — M
Music — M,D
Philosophy — D
Political Science — M,D
Psychology—General — D
Public Administration — M,D
Public Policy — M,D
Slavic Languages — M,D
Sociology — M,D
Spanish — M,D
Theater — M,D
Urban and Regional Planning — M
Western European Studies — O
Women's Studies — O
Writing — M,D

**UNIVERSITY OF PORTLAND**
Communication—General — M
Corporate and Organizational Communication — M
Pastoral Ministry and Counseling — M
Theater — M

**UNIVERSITY OF PRINCE EDWARD ISLAND**
Geography — M

**UNIVERSITY OF PUERTO RICO, MAYAGÜEZ CAMPUS**
Agricultural Economics and Agribusiness — M

English — M
Hispanic Studies — M
Rural Sociology — M

**UNIVERSITY OF PUERTO RICO, MEDICAL SCIENCES CAMPUS**
Demography and Population Studies — M
Gerontology — M,O

**UNIVERSITY OF PUERTO RICO, RÍO PIEDRAS CAMPUS**
Architecture — M
Clinical Psychology — M,D
Communication—General — M
Comparative Literature — M
Economic Development — M
Economics — M
English — M,D
Family and Consumer Sciences-General — M
Hispanic Studies — M,D
History — M,D
Industrial and Organizational Psychology — M,D
Journalism — M
Linguistics — M,D
Mass Communication — M
Philosophy — M
Psychology—General — M,D
Public Administration — M
Public Policy — M
Rehabilitation Counseling — M
Social Psychology — M,D
Sociology — M
Translation and Interpretation — M,O
Urban and Regional Planning — M

**UNIVERSITY OF PUGET SOUND**
Counseling Psychology — M

**UNIVERSITY OF REDLANDS**
Geographic Information Systems — M
Music — M

**UNIVERSITY OF REGINA**
Anthropology — M
Applied Economics — M
Applied Psychology — M,D
Art/Fine Arts — M
Canadian Studies — M,D
Clinical Psychology — M,D
Criminal Justice and Criminology — M
Economics — M,D,O
English — M,D
Experimental Psychology — M,D
Film, Television, and Video Production — M
French — M
Geography — M,D
Gerontology — M
History — M
Interdisciplinary Studies — M
Journalism — M
Linguistics — M
Music — M
Philosophy — M
Political Science — M
Psychology—General — M,D
Public Administration — M,D,O
Public Policy — M,D,O
Religion — M
Social Sciences — M
Sociology — M
Women's Studies — M
Writing — M,D

**UNIVERSITY OF RHODE ISLAND**
Anthropology — M
Archaeology — M
Child and Family Studies — M
Clinical Psychology — M,D
Communication—General — M
Computer Art and Design — M
Counseling Psychology — M
Economics — M,D
English — M,D
Forensic Sciences — M,D,O
Gender Studies — M,D,O
History — M
Human Development — M
Industrial and Labor Relations — M,O
International Affairs — M
Marriage and Family Therapy — M
Music — M
Political Science — M
Psychology—General — M,D
Public Administration — M
Public Policy — M
School Psychology — M,D
Spanish — M
Sport Psychology — M
Women's Studies — O

**UNIVERSITY OF ROCHESTER**
American Studies — M,D
Art History — D
Art/Fine Arts — D
Clinical Psychology — D
Cognitive Sciences — D
Developmental Psychology — D
Economics — M,D
English — M,D
Historic Preservation — M
History — M,D
Human Development — M,D
International Affairs — M,D
Linguistics — M,D
Marriage and Family Therapy — M
Music — D
Philosophy — D
Photography — M
Political Science — D
Psychology—General — D
Social Psychology — M,D
Translation and Interpretation — M,O
Western European Studies — M,D

**UNIVERSITY OF ST. FRANCIS (IL)**
Forensic Sciences — M,O

**UNIVERSITY OF SAINT FRANCIS (IN)**
Art/Fine Arts — M
Clinical Psychology — M,O
Counseling Psychology — M,O

**UNIVERSITY OF SAINT JOSEPH**
Applied Behavior Analysis — M,O
Clinical Psychology — M,O
Counseling Psychology — M,O
Gerontology — O
Marriage and Family Therapy — M

**UNIVERSITY OF SAINT MARY**
Counseling Psychology — M
Psychology—General — M

**UNIVERSITY OF SAINT MARY OF THE LAKE–MUNDELEIN SEMINARY**
Pastoral Ministry and Counseling — M,D
Theology — M,D

**UNIVERSITY OF ST. MICHAEL'S COLLEGE**
Jewish Studies — M,D,O
Pastoral Ministry and Counseling — M,D,O
Theology — M,D

**UNIVERSITY OF ST. THOMAS (MN)**
Art History — M
Criminal Justice and Criminology — M,D
English — M
Ethics — M,D
Human Development — M
Music — M,D
Pastoral Ministry and Counseling — M
Psychology—General — M,D
Religion — M
Theology — M

**UNIVERSITY OF ST. THOMAS (TX)**
Liberal Studies — M
Music — M
Pastoral Ministry and Counseling — M
Philosophy — M,D
Public Administration — M
Public Policy — M
Religion — M
Theology — M

**UNIVERSITY OF SAN DIEGO**
Conflict Resolution and Mediation/Peace Studies — M
Counseling Psychology — M
Criminal Justice and Criminology — M
International Affairs — M
Marriage and Family Therapy — M
Theater — M

**UNIVERSITY OF SAN FRANCISCO**
Applied Behavior Analysis — M
Asian Studies — M
Clinical Psychology — D
Communication—General — M
Counseling Psychology — M
Economics — M
International Affairs — M
International Development — M
Marriage and Family Therapy — M
Museum Studies — M
Pacific Area/Pacific Rim Studies — M
Public Administration — M
Public Affairs — M
Urban Studies — M
Writing — M

**UNIVERSITY OF SASKATCHEWAN**
Agricultural Economics and Agribusiness — M,D,O
Anthropology — M,D
Archaeology — M,D
Art/Fine Arts — M
Canadian Studies — M,D
East European and Russian Studies — M
Economics — M,O
English — M,D
French — M
Gender Studies — M,D
Geography — M,D
German — M
History — M,D
Music — M
Philosophy — M
Political Science — M
Psychology—General — M,D
Public Affairs — M,D
Public Policy — M,D
Religion — M
Sociology — M,D
Theater — M
Women's Studies — M

**THE UNIVERSITY OF SCRANTON**
Art/Fine Arts — M
Clinical Psychology — M
Counseling Psychology — M
Rehabilitation Counseling — M
Theology — M

**UNIVERSITY OF SOUTH AFRICA**
Anthropology — M,D
Archaeology — M,D
Art History — M,D
Classics — M,D
Clinical Psychology — M,D
Communication—General — M,D
Counseling Psychology — M,D
Criminal Justice and Criminology — M,D
Economics — M,D
English — M,D
Ethics — M,D
Family and Consumer Sciences-General — M,D
French — M,D
Geography — M,D
German — M,D

History M,D
Human Development M,D
Industrial and Organizational
Psychology M,D
Italian M,D
Linguistics M,D
Missions and Missiology M,D
Music M,D
Near and Middle Eastern Languages M,D
Near and Middle Eastern Studies M,D
Pastoral Ministry and Counseling M,D
Philosophy M,D
Political Science M,D
Portuguese M,D
Psychology—General M,D
Public Administration M,D
Religion M,D
Romance Languages M,D
Russian M,D
Sociology M,D
Spanish M,D
Theology M,D

### UNIVERSITY OF SOUTH ALABAMA
Art/Fine Arts M
Clinical Psychology M,D
Communication—General M
Counseling Psychology M
English M
History M
Interdisciplinary Studies M,D
Music M
Psychology—General M
Public Administration M
Sociology M
Writing M

### UNIVERSITY OF SOUTH CAROLINA
Anthropology M,D
Art History M
Art/Fine Arts M
Clinical Psychology M,D
Comparative Literature M,D
Consumer Economics M
Criminal Justice and Criminology M,D
Economics M,D
English M,D
Experimental Psychology M,D
French M,D
Genetic Counseling M
Geography M,D
German M,D
Gerontology O
Historic Preservation M,O
History M,D,O
International Affairs M,D
Journalism M,D
Linguistics M,D,O
Media Studies M
Museum Studies M,O
Music M,D,O
Philosophy M,D
Political Science M,D
Psychology—General M,D
Public Administration M
Public History M,O
Rehabilitation Counseling M,O
Religion M
School Psychology D
Social Psychology M,D
Sociology M,D
Spanish M,D
Speech and Interpersonal
Communication M,D
Theater M,D
Women's Studies O
Writing M,D

### UNIVERSITY OF SOUTH CAROLINA AIKEN
Applied Psychology M
Clinical Psychology M

### THE UNIVERSITY OF SOUTH DAKOTA
Addictions/Substance Abuse
Counseling M
Art/Fine Arts M
Clinical Psychology M,D
Communication—General M
Criminal Justice and Criminology M
English M,D
Graphic Design M
History M
Human Development M,D,O
Interdisciplinary Studies M
Music M
Photography M
Political Science M,D
Psychology—General M,D
Public Administration M,D
Public Policy M,D
School Psychology M,D,O
Theater M

### UNIVERSITY OF SOUTHERN CALIFORNIA
American Studies D
Architecture M,D
Art History M,D,O
Art/Fine Arts M,D,O
Arts Administration M
Asian Languages M,D
Asian Studies M,D
Child and Family Studies M,D
Classics M,D
Clinical Psychology M,D
Cognitive Sciences M,D
Communication—General M,D
Comparative Literature D
Computer Art and Design M
Corporate and Organizational
Communication M

Cultural Studies D
Developmental Psychology M,D
Economic Development M,D
Economics M,D
English M,D
Film, Television, and Video
Production M
Film, Television, and Video
Theory and Criticism M,D
Geographic Information Systems M,O
Geography M,O
Gerontology M,D,O
Health Communication M,D
History D
Homeland Security M,O
International Affairs M,D
Internet and Interactive
Multimedia M,D,O
Journalism M
Latin American Studies D
Linguistics M,D
Marriage and Family Therapy M
Media Studies M,D
Music M,D,O
Philosophy M,D
Photography M
Political Science M,D
Psychology—General M,D
Public Administration M,O
Public Policy M,D,O
Rhetoric D
Slavic Languages M,D
Social Psychology M,D
Sociology D
Spanish D
Sustainable Development M,D,O
Theater M,D
Urban and Regional Planning M,D,O
Writing M,D

### UNIVERSITY OF SOUTHERN INDIANA
Communication—General M
Cultural Studies M
English M
Gerontology M,D,O
Liberal Studies M
Public Administration M

### UNIVERSITY OF SOUTHERN MAINE
Addictions/Substance Abuse
Counseling M,O
American Studies M,O
Applied Behavior Analysis M,O
Counseling Psychology M,O
Cultural Studies M,O
Music M
Public Policy M
Rehabilitation Counseling M,O
School Psychology M,O
Urban and Regional Planning M,O
Writing M

### UNIVERSITY OF SOUTHERN MISSISSIPPI
Anthropology M
Applied Behavior Analysis M,D
Child and Family Studies M
Clinical Psychology M,D
Counseling Psychology M,D
Criminal Justice and Criminology M,D
Economic Development M
Economics M
English M,D
Forensic Sciences M,D
Geography M,D
History M,D
International Development M,D
Marriage and Family Therapy M
Mass Communication M,D
Music M,D
Political Science M,D
Psychology—General M,D
School Psychology M,D
Speech and Interpersonal
Communication M,D
Theater M
Writing M,D

### UNIVERSITY OF SOUTH FLORIDA
Addictions/Substance Abuse
Counseling M,O
African Studies M,O
American Studies M,D
Anthropology M,D,O
Applied Behavior Analysis M,O
Archaeology M,D,O
Architecture M
Art History M
Art/Fine Arts M
Child and Family Studies M,D,O
Clinical Psychology D
Cognitive Sciences D
Communication—General M,D
Comparative Literature O
Corporate and Organizational
Communication M,O
Counseling Psychology M,O
Criminal Justice and Criminology M,D
Economics M,D
Emergency Management O
English M,D,O
Film, Television, and Video
Theory and Criticism M
Forensic Sciences M,D,O
French M
Gender Studies M
Geographic Information Systems M,D,O
Geography O
Gerontology M,D,O
History M,D
Humanities M

Industrial and Organizational
Psychology D
Interdisciplinary Studies M,D
International Affairs M,D,O
Internet and Interactive
Multimedia M,O
Journalism M,O
Latin American Studies M,D,O
Liberal Studies M
Linguistics M,D
Marriage and Family Therapy M,D,O
Mass Communication M,O
Media Studies M
Museum Studies O
Music M,D
Philosophy M,D
Political Science M,D,O
Psychology—General M,D,O
Public Administration M,D,O
Public Affairs O
Rehabilitation Counseling M,D,O
Religion M,D
Rhetoric M,D
School Psychology M,D,O
Sociology M,D
Spanish M,D
Sustainable Development M,O
Technical Communication O
Urban and Regional Planning M,D,O
Urban Design M
Western European Studies M,D
Women's Studies M
Writing M,D,O

### UNIVERSITY OF SOUTH FLORIDA, ST. PETERSBURG
Computer Art and Design M
Journalism M
Liberal Studies M
Media Studies M
Psychology—General M

### UNIVERSITY OF SOUTH FLORIDA SARASOTA-MANATEE
Criminal Justice and Criminology M
Liberal Studies M
Social Sciences M

### THE UNIVERSITY OF TAMPA
Writing M

### THE UNIVERSITY OF TENNESSEE
Anthropology M,D
Applied Psychology M,D
Archaeology M,D
Architecture M
Art/Fine Arts M
Child and Family Studies M,D
Clinical Psychology M,D
Clothing and Textiles M,D
Communication—General M,D
Consumer Economics M,D
Counseling Psychology M,D
Criminal Justice and Criminology M,D
Cultural Anthropology M,D
Economics M,D
English M,D
Experimental Psychology M,D
Family and Consumer
Sciences-General D
French M,D
Geography M,D
German M,D
Gerontology M
Graphic Design M
History M,D
Industrial and Organizational
Psychology D
Italian D
Journalism M,D
Landscape Architecture M
Linguistics D
Media Studies M,D
Music M
Philosophy M,D
Photography M
Political Science M,D
Portuguese D
Psychology—General M,D
Public Administration M
Rehabilitation Counseling M,D
Religion M,D
Russian D
School Psychology M,D,O
Sociology M,D
Spanish M,D
Speech and Interpersonal
Communication M,D
Theater M

### THE UNIVERSITY OF TENNESSEE AT CHATTANOOGA
Criminal Justice and Criminology M
English M
Ethics M,O
Experimental Psychology M
Industrial and Organizational
Psychology M
Music M
Political Science M,O
Psychology—General M
Public Administration M,O
Rhetoric M
School Psychology M,D,O
Social Psychology M,D,O
Writing M

### THE UNIVERSITY OF TENNESSEE AT MARTIN
Addictions/Substance Abuse
Counseling M

Agricultural Economics and
Agribusiness M
Child and Family Studies M
Child Development M
Communication—General M
Family and Consumer
Sciences-General M
Interdisciplinary Studies M
Social Psychology M

### THE UNIVERSITY OF TEXAS AT ARLINGTON
Anthropology M
Architecture M
Art/Fine Arts M
Communication—General M
Criminal Justice and Criminology M
Economics M
English M,D
Experimental Psychology M,D
Film, Television, and Video
Production M
French M
Health Psychology M,D
History M,D
Industrial and Organizational
Psychology M,D
Landscape Architecture M
Linguistics M,D
Music M
Political Science M
Psychology—General M,D
Public Administration M
Public Policy M,D
Sociology M
Spanish M
Urban and Regional Planning D

### THE UNIVERSITY OF TEXAS AT AUSTIN
African Studies M,D
American Studies M,D
Anthropology M,D
Applied Arts and Design—
General M
Archaeology M,D
Architectural History M,D
Architecture M
Art History M,D
Art/Fine Arts M
Asian Languages M,D
Asian Studies M,D
Child and Family Studies M,D
Child Development M,D
Classics M,D
Clinical Psychology D
Communication—General M,D
Comparative Literature M,D
Counseling Psychology M,D
Cultural Studies M,D
Dance M,D
Developmental Psychology D
East European and Russian Studies M,D
Economics M,D
English M,D
Family and Consumer
Sciences-General M,D
Film, Television, and Video
Production M,D
Folklore M,D
French M,D
Geography M,D
German M,D
Hispanic and Latin American
Languages M,D
Hispanic Studies M
Historic Preservation M
History M,D
Human Development M,D
Interior Design M
Italian M,D
Journalism M,D
Landscape Architecture M
Latin American Studies M
Linguistics M,D
Media Studies M,D
Mineral Economics M
Music M,D
Near and Middle Eastern Languages M,D
Near and Middle Eastern Studies M,D
Philosophy D
Political Science M,D
Portuguese M,D
Psychology—General D
Public Administration M,D
Public Affairs M,D
Public History M,D
Public Policy M,D
Rehabilitation Counseling M,D
Romance Languages M,D
School Psychology M,D
Slavic Languages M,D
Sociology M,D
Spanish M,D
Sport Psychology M,D
Sustainable Development M
Theater M,D
Urban and Regional Planning M,D
Urban Design M
Writing M,D

### THE UNIVERSITY OF TEXAS AT DALLAS
Child and Family Studies M,D
Cognitive Sciences M,D
Communication—General M,D
Comparative Literature M,D
Criminal Justice and Criminology M,D
Economics M,D
Geographic Information Systems M,D
Geography M,D
History M,D
Humanities M,D
Interdisciplinary Studies M

M—masters degree; D—doctorate; O—other advanced degree; *—Close-Up and/or Display

Internet and Interactive
   Multimedia — M,D
Latin American Studies — M,D
Political Science — M,D
Psychology—General — M,D
Public Administration — M,D
Public Policy — M,D

### THE UNIVERSITY OF TEXAS AT EL PASO
Anthropology — M,O
Applied Psychology — M,O
Art/Fine Arts — M
Clinical Psychology — M,D
Communication—General — M
Economics — M
English — M,D,O
Experimental Psychology — M,D
History — M,D
Interdisciplinary Studies — M
Liberal Studies — M
Linguistics — M,O
Music — M
Philosophy — M
Political Science — M
Psychology—General — M,D
Rehabilitation Counseling — M
Rhetoric — M,D,O
Sociology — M,O
Spanish — M,O
Writing — M,D,O

### THE UNIVERSITY OF TEXAS AT SAN ANTONIO
Anthropology — M,D
Applied Behavior Analysis — M,O
Architecture — M
Art History — M
Art/Fine Arts — M
Communication—General — M
Criminal Justice and Criminology — M
Cultural Studies — M,D
Demography and Population Studies — D
Economics — M
English — M,D
History — M
Interdisciplinary Studies — M,D
Music — M
Philosophy — M
Political Science — M
Psychology—General — M,D
Public Administration — M
School Psychology — M,O
Sociology — M
Spanish — M
Urban and Regional Planning — M

### THE UNIVERSITY OF TEXAS AT TYLER
Art History — M
Art/Fine Arts — M
Clinical Psychology — M
Communication—General — M
Counseling Psychology — M
Criminal Justice and Criminology — M
English — M
History — M
Interdisciplinary Studies — M
Marriage and Family Therapy — M
Political Science — M
Psychology—General — M
Public Administration — M
School Psychology — M
Social Sciences — M
Sociology — M

### THE UNIVERSITY OF TEXAS HEALTH SCIENCE CENTER AT HOUSTON
Genetic Counseling — M,D

### THE UNIVERSITY OF TEXAS HEALTH SCIENCE CENTER AT SAN ANTONIO
Interdisciplinary Studies — D

### THE UNIVERSITY OF TEXAS MEDICAL BRANCH
Demography and Population Studies — D
Humanities — M,D

### THE UNIVERSITY OF TEXAS OF THE PERMIAN BASIN
Applied Psychology — M
Clinical Psychology — M
Criminal Justice and Criminology — M
English — M
Experimental Psychology — M
History — M
Political Science — M
Psychology—General — M
Spanish — M

### THE UNIVERSITY OF TEXAS RIO GRANDE VALLEY
Anthropology — M
Art/Fine Arts — M
Clinical Psychology — M
Communication—General — M,O
Criminal Justice and Criminology — M
English — M
Experimental Psychology — M
History — M
Interdisciplinary Studies — M
Music — M
Psychology—General — M
Public Administration — M
Public Affairs — M
Public Policy — M
Rehabilitation Counseling — M,D
Rhetoric — M
School Psychology — M
Sociology — M
Spanish — M
Theater — M,O
Writing — M

### THE UNIVERSITY OF TEXAS SOUTHWESTERN MEDICAL CENTER
Clinical Psychology — D
Rehabilitation Counseling — M

### THE UNIVERSITY OF THE ARTS
Art/Fine Arts — M
Industrial Design — M
Museum Studies — M
Music — M

### UNIVERSITY OF THE CUMBERLANDS
Clinical Psychology — D
Counseling Psychology — M
Religion — M
Theater — M,D,O

### UNIVERSITY OF THE DISTRICT OF COLUMBIA
Architecture — M
Counseling Psychology — M
Homeland Security — M
Public Administration — M
Rehabilitation Counseling — M

### UNIVERSITY OF THE FRASER VALLEY
Criminal Justice and Criminology — M

### UNIVERSITY OF THE INCARNATE WORD
Clothing and Textiles — M
Communication—General — M
Pastoral Ministry and Counseling — M

### UNIVERSITY OF THE PACIFIC
Communication—General — M
International Affairs — M,D
Music — M
Psychology—General — M
Public Policy — M,D
School Psychology — M,D,O
Therapies—Dance, Drama, and
   Music — M

### UNIVERSITY OF THE ROCKIES
Psychology—General — M,D

### UNIVERSITY OF THE SACRED HEART
Broadcast Journalism — M,O
Communication—General — M,O
Conflict Resolution and
   Mediation/Peace Studies — M
Cultural Studies — M
Film, Television, and Video
   Production — M,O
Internet and Interactive
   Multimedia — M,O
Writing — M

### UNIVERSITY OF THE SCIENCES
Health Psychology — M
Technical Writing — M,O

### UNIVERSITY OF THE SOUTHWEST
Counseling Psychology — M

### UNIVERSITY OF THE VIRGIN ISLANDS
Liberal Studies — M
School Psychology — M,D,O
Social Sciences — M

### UNIVERSITY OF THE WEST
Psychology—General — M
Religion — M,D
Theology — M

### THE UNIVERSITY OF TOLEDO
Clinical Psychology — M,D
Communication—General — O
Criminal Justice and Criminology — M,O
Economics — M,D,O
Emergency Management — M,O
English — M,D
Experimental Psychology — M,D
French — M
Gender Studies — O
Geographic Information Systems — M,D,O
Geography — M,D,O
German — M
Gerontology — M,O
History — M,D
Liberal Studies — M
Music — M,O
Philosophy — M
Political Science — M,O
Psychology—General — M,D
Public Administration — M,O
School Psychology — M,D,O
Sociology — M
Spanish — M
Urban and Regional Planning — M,D,O
Women's Studies — O
Writing — M,O

### UNIVERSITY OF TORONTO
Anthropology — M,D
Architecture — M
Art History — M,D
Asian Studies — M,D
Classics — M,D
Comparative Literature — M,D
Criminal Justice and Criminology — M,D
East European and Russian Studies — M
Economics — M,D
English — M,D
Film, Television, and Video
   Theory and Criticism — M,D
French — M,D
Gender Studies — M,D
Genetic Counseling — M
Geography — M,D
German — M,D
History of Science and Technology — M,D
History — M,D
Industrial and Labor Relations — M
International Affairs — M
Italian — M,D
Landscape Architecture — M
Linguistics — M,D
Medieval and Renaissance Studies — M,D

Museum Studies — M
Music — M,D
Near and Middle Eastern Studies — M,D
Philosophy — M,D
Political Science — M,D
Portuguese — M,D
Psychology—General — M,D
Religion — M,D
Slavic Languages — M,D
Social Sciences — M,D
Sociology — M,D
Spanish — M,D
Theater — M,D
Urban and Regional Planning — M,D
Urban Design — M,D
Women's Studies — M,D
Writing — M,D

### THE UNIVERSITY OF TULSA
American Indian/Native American
   Studies — M,D,O
Anthropology — M,D
Art/Fine Arts — M
Clinical Psychology — M,D
English — M,D
History — M
Industrial and Organizational
   Psychology — M,D
Museum Studies — M
Psychology—General — M,D

### UNIVERSITY OF UTAH
American Studies — M,D
Anthropology — M,D
Architecture — M
Art History — M
Art/Fine Arts — M
Asian Studies — M
Child and Family Studies — M
Clinical Psychology — M,D,O
Communication—General — M,D
Comparative Literature — M,D
Consumer Economics — M
Counseling Psychology — M,D,O
Dance — M,O
Economics — M,D
English — M,D
Film, Television, and Video
   Production — M
French — M,D
Geographic Information Systems — M,D
Geography — M,D
Gerontology — M,O
Graphic Design — M
History — M
Human Development — M
Humanities — M
International Affairs — M,D
Internet and Interactive
   Multimedia — M
Latin American Studies — M
Linguistics — M,D
Music — M,D
Near and Middle Eastern Languages — M,D
Near and Middle Eastern Studies — M,D
Philosophy — M,D
Photography — M
Political Science — D
Psychology—General — M,D
Public Administration — M,D
Public Policy — M,D
Rhetoric — M,D
School Psychology — M,D,O
Sociology — M,D
Spanish — M,D
Urban and Regional Planning — M,D
Urban Design — M,D
Writing — M,D

### UNIVERSITY OF VALLEY FORGE
Music — M
Religion — M
Theology — M

### UNIVERSITY OF VERMONT
Agricultural Economics and
   Agribusiness — M
Applied Economics — M
Clinical Psychology — D
Communication—General — M
Counseling Psychology — M
English — M
German — M
Historic Preservation — M
History — M
Interdisciplinary Studies — M
Psychology—General — D
Public Administration — M

### UNIVERSITY OF VICTORIA
Anthropology — M
Art History — M,D
Art/Fine Arts — M,D
Asian Studies — M
Child and Family Studies — M,D
Classics — M,D
Clinical Psychology — M,D
Computer Art and Design — M
Conflict Resolution and
   Mediation/Peace Studies — M,D
Counseling Psychology — M,D
Developmental Psychology — M,D
Economics — M,D
English — M,D
Experimental Psychology — M,D
Film, Television, and Video
   Production — M
French — M
Geography — M,D
German — M
Hispanic Studies — M
History — M,D
Human Development — M
Italian — M
Linguistics — M,D
Music — M,D

Pacific Area/Pacific Rim Studies — M
Philosophy — M
Photography — M
Political Science — M,D
Psychology—General — M,D
Public Administration — M
Social Psychology — M,D
Sociology — M,D
Theater — M
Writing — M

### UNIVERSITY OF VIRGINIA
Anthropology — M,D
Architectural History — M,D
Art History — M,D
Asian Studies — M
Classics — M,D
Clinical Psychology — D
Economics — M,D
English — M,D
French — M,D
German — M
History — M,D
Interdisciplinary Studies — M,D
International Affairs — M,D
Landscape Architecture — M
Linguistics — M
Music — M,D
Near and Middle Eastern Studies — M,D
Philosophy — M,D
Political Science — M,D
Psychology—General — M,D
Public Policy — M,D
Religion — M,D
School Psychology — M,D
Slavic Languages — M,D
Sociology — M,D
Spanish — M,D
Theater — M
Urban and Regional Planning — M
Writing — M

### UNIVERSITY OF WASHINGTON
Anthropology — M,D
Applied Arts and Design—
   General — M
Architecture — M,D,O
Art History — M,D
Art/Fine Arts — M
Asian Languages — M,D
Asian Studies — M,D
Chinese — M,D
Classics — M,D
Clinical Psychology — D
Cognitive Sciences — D
Communication—General — M,D
Comparative Literature — M,D
Dance — M
Developmental Psychology — D
East European and Russian Studies — M
Economics — M,D
English — M,D
French — M,D
Geography — M,D
German — M,D
Hispanic and Latin American
   Languages — M
Historic Preservation — O
History — M,D
Human Development — M,D
Industrial Design — M
International Affairs — D
Italian — M,D
Japanese — M,D
Landscape Architecture — M
Lighting Design — M,D,O
Linguistics — M,D
Museum Studies — M
Music — M,D
Near and Middle Eastern Studies — M,D
Philosophy — M,D
Photography — M
Political Science — M,D
Portuguese — M
Psychology—General — D
Public Administration — M,D
Public Affairs — M,D
Public Policy — M,D
Religion — M,D
Russian — M,D
Scandinavian Languages — M,D
School Psychology — M,D
Slavic Languages — M,D
Social Psychology — D
Social Sciences — M,D
Sociology — M,D
Spanish — M
Sustainable Development — M,D
Technical Communication — M,D,O
Theater — M,D
Urban and Regional Planning — M,D
Urban Design — M,D,O
Women's Studies — D
Writing — M

### UNIVERSITY OF WASHINGTON, BOTHELL
Cultural Studies — M
Public Policy — M
Writing — M

### UNIVERSITY OF WASHINGTON, TACOMA
Interdisciplinary Studies — M

### UNIVERSITY OF WATERLOO
Anthropology — M
Architecture — M
Art/Fine Arts — M
Economic Development — M
Economics — M,D
English — M,D
French — M,D
Geography — M,D
German — M,D
History — M,D

International Affairs — M,D
Near and Middle Eastern Studies — M
Philosophy — M,D
Political Science — M,D
Psychology—General — M,D
Public Affairs — M
Religion — D
Russian — M,D
Sociology — M,D
Technical Writing — M,D
Urban and Regional Planning — M

**THE UNIVERSITY OF WEST ALABAMA**
Child Development — M,O
Experimental Psychology — M
History — M
Marriage and Family Therapy — M
School Psychology — M,O

**THE UNIVERSITY OF WESTERN ONTARIO**
Anthropology — M,D
Classics — M
Comparative Literature — M,D
Counseling Psychology — M
Economics — M,D
English — M,D
French — M,D
Geography — M,D
History — M,D
Interdisciplinary Studies — M,D
Journalism — M
Media Studies — M,D
Music — M,D
Philosophy — M,D
Political Science — M,D
Psychology—General — M,D
Sociology — M,D
Spanish — M,D
Sustainable Development — M

**UNIVERSITY OF WEST FLORIDA**
American Studies — M
Anthropology — M
Applied Behavior Analysis — M
Applied Psychology — M
Archaeology — M
Communication—General — M
Counseling Psychology — M
Criminal Justice and Criminology — M
English — M
Experimental Psychology — M
History — M
Industrial and Organizational Psychology — M
Political Science — M
Psychology—General — M
Public History — M
Writing — M

**UNIVERSITY OF WEST GEORGIA**
Criminal Justice and Criminology — M,D,O
English — M,O
Geographic Information Systems — M,O
History — M,O
Museum Studies — M,O
Music — M,O
Psychology—General — M,D,O
Public Administration — M,D,O
Public History — M,O
Sociology — M,D,O
Urban and Regional Planning — M,D,O

**UNIVERSITY OF WINDSOR**
Applied Psychology — M,D
Art/Fine Arts — M
Clinical Psychology — M,D
Communication—General — M
Criminal Justice and Criminology — M,D
Economics — M
English — M
History — M
Philosophy — M
Political Science — M
Psychology—General — M,D
Social Psychology — M,D
Sociology — M,D
Writing — M

**THE UNIVERSITY OF WINNIPEG**
History — M
Marriage and Family Therapy — M,O
Public Administration — M
Religion — M
Theology — M

**UNIVERSITY OF WISCONSIN–EAU CLAIRE**
English — M
History — M
Psychology—General — M,O
School Psychology — M,O
Writing — M

**UNIVERSITY OF WISCONSIN–LA CROSSE**
Psychology—General — M,O
School Psychology — M,O

**UNIVERSITY OF WISCONSIN–MADISON**
African Studies — M,D
African-American Studies — M
Agricultural Economics and Agribusiness — M,D
American Studies — M,D
Anthropology — D
Applied Arts and Design—General — M,D
Applied Economics — M,D
Archaeology — D
Art History — M,D
Art/Fine Arts — M
Arts Administration — M
Asian Languages — M,D

Asian Studies — M,D
Child and Family Studies — M,D
Chinese — M,D
Classics — M,D
Clinical Psychology — D
Cognitive Sciences — D
Communication—General — M,D
Comparative Literature — M,D
Consumer Economics — M,D
Counseling Psychology — D
Cultural Anthropology — D
Demography and Population Studies — M,D
Developmental Psychology — D
Economics — M
English — M,D
Family and Consumer Sciences-General — M,D
Film, Television, and Video Theory and Criticism — M,D
Folklore — M,D
French — M,D,O
Genetic Counseling — M,D
Geographic Information Systems — M,D,O
Geography — M,D,O
German — M,D
History of Science and Technology — M,D
History — M,D
Human Development — M,D
Italian — M,D
Japanese — M,D
Jewish Studies — M,D
Journalism — M,D
Landscape Architecture — M
Latin American Studies — M,D
Linguistics — M,D
Mass Communication — M,D
Media Studies — M,D
Music — M,D
Near and Middle Eastern Languages — M,D
Near and Middle Eastern Studies — M,D
Philosophy — M,D
Political Science — D
Portuguese — M,D
Psychology—General — D
Public Affairs — M
Rehabilitation Counseling — M,D
Rhetoric — M,D
Rural Sociology — M,D
Scandinavian Languages — M,D
Slavic Languages — M,D
Social Psychology — D
Sociology — M,D
Spanish — M,D
Speech and Interpersonal Communication — M,D
Sustainable Development — M
Theater — M,D
Urban and Regional Planning — M,D
Women's Studies — M,D
Writing — M,D

**UNIVERSITY OF WISCONSIN–MILWAUKEE**
African Studies — D
Anthropology — M,D,O
Applied Arts and Design—General — M
Applied Behavior Analysis — M,D
Archaeology — M,D,O
Architecture — M,D,O
Art History — M
Biological Anthropology — M,D,O
Classics — M,O
Clinical Psychology — M,D
Communication—General — M,D,O
Comparative Literature — M,O
Conflict Resolution and Mediation/Peace Studies — M,D,O
Corporate and Organizational Communication — M,D,O
Counseling Psychology — M,D,O
Criminal Justice and Criminology — M,O
Cultural Anthropology — M,D,O
Developmental Psychology — M,D,O
Economics — M,D
English — M,D
Experimental Psychology — M,D
Film, Television, and Video Theory and Criticism — M,D
French — M,O
Gender Studies — M,O
Geographic Information Systems — M,D,O
Geography — M,D
German — M,D
Gerontology — M,D,O
Health Psychology — M,D
History — M,D
Industrial and Labor Relations — M,D
International Economics — M,D
Liberal Studies — M
Linguistics — M,D,O
Marriage and Family Therapy — M,D,O
Mass Communication — M,D,O
Media Studies — M,D
Museum Studies — M,D,O
Philosophy — M
Political Science — M
Portuguese — M
Psychology—General — M,D
Public Administration — M
Public History — M,D
Rhetoric — M,D,O
School Psychology — M,D,O
Social Psychology — M,D,O
Sociology — M,D
Spanish — M,O
Translation and Interpretation — M,O
Urban and Regional Planning — M
Women's Studies — M,O
Writing — M,D

**UNIVERSITY OF WISCONSIN–OSHKOSH**
English — M
Experimental Psychology — M
Industrial and Organizational Psychology — M
Psychology—General — M
Public Administration — M

**UNIVERSITY OF WISCONSIN–PLATTEVILLE**
Criminal Justice and Criminology — M

**UNIVERSITY OF WISCONSIN–RIVER FALLS**
Art/Fine Arts — M
School Psychology — M,O

**UNIVERSITY OF WISCONSIN–STEVENS POINT**
Communication—General — M
Corporate and Organizational Communication — M
English — M
Family and Consumer Sciences-General — M
History — M
Human Development — M
Media Studies — M
Speech and Interpersonal Communication — M

**UNIVERSITY OF WISCONSIN–STOUT**
Applied Psychology — M
Art/Fine Arts — M
Clinical Psychology — M
Counseling Psychology — M
Marriage and Family Therapy — M
Rehabilitation Counseling — M
School Psychology — M,O
Technical Communication — M

**UNIVERSITY OF WISCONSIN–SUPERIOR**
Art History — M
Art Therapy — M
Art/Fine Arts — M
Communication—General — M
Mass Communication — M
School Psychology — M
Social Psychology — M
Speech and Interpersonal Communication — M
Theater — M

**UNIVERSITY OF WISCONSIN–WHITEWATER**
Communication—General — M
Corporate and Organizational Communication — M
Mass Communication — M
Psychology—General — M,O
School Psychology — M,O

**UNIVERSITY OF WYOMING**
Agricultural Economics and Agribusiness — M
American Studies — M
Anthropology — M,D
Applied Economics — M
Child Development — M
Communication—General — M
Consumer Economics — M
Economics — M,D
English — M
French — M
Geography — M
German — M
History — M
International Affairs — M
Music — M
Philosophy — M
Political Science — M
Psychology—General — M,D
Public Administration — M
Rural Planning and Studies — M
Sociology — M
Spanish — M
Writing — M

**UPPER IOWA UNIVERSITY**
Emergency Management — M
Homeland Security — M
Public Administration — M

**URBANA UNIVERSITY**
Criminal Justice and Criminology — M

**URSHAN GRADUATE SCHOOL OF THEOLOGY**
Theology — M

**URSULINE COLLEGE**
Art Therapy — M
Historic Preservation — M
Liberal Studies — M
Pastoral Ministry and Counseling — M
Theology — M

**UTAH STATE UNIVERSITY**
American Studies — M
Applied Economics — M
Art/Fine Arts — M
Child and Family Studies — M,D
Clinical Psychology — M,D
Communication—General — M
Consumer Economics — M
Counseling Psychology — M,D
Disability Studies — M,D,O
Economics — M
English — M
Family and Consumer Sciences-General — M,D
Folklore — M
Geography — M,D
History — M

Human Development — M,D
Interior Design — M
Landscape Architecture — M
Marriage and Family Therapy — M,D
Political Science — M
Psychology—General — M,D
Rehabilitation Counseling — M
School Psychology — M,D
Sociology — M,D
Theater — M
Urban and Regional Planning — M,D
Writing — M

**UTICA COLLEGE**
Criminal Justice and Criminology — M
Forensic Sciences — M
Liberal Studies — M

**VALDOSTA STATE UNIVERSITY**
English — M
Marriage and Family Therapy — M,O
Music — M
Psychology—General — M,O
Rhetoric — M

**VALPARAISO UNIVERSITY**
Arts Administration — M
Chinese — M
Clinical Psychology — M
Communication—General — M,O
English — M,O
Ethics — M,O
History — M,O
International Economics — M
International Trade Policy — M
Liberal Studies — M,O
Media Studies — M,O
Psychology—General — M
School Psychology — M,O
Theology — M

**VANCOUVER SCHOOL OF THEOLOGY**
Religion — M,O
Theology — M,O

**VANDERBILT UNIVERSITY**
Anthropology — M,D
Child and Family Studies — M
Classics — M
Economic Development — M,D
Economics — M,D
English — M,D
French — M,D
German — M,D
History — M,D
Human Development — M
Latin American Studies — M
Liberal Studies — M
Philosophy — M,D
Political Science — M,D
Portuguese — M,D
Psychology—General — D
Public Policy — D
Religion — M,D
Sociology — M,D
Spanish — M,D
Theology — M
Urban and Regional Planning — M
Writing — M

**VANGUARD UNIVERSITY OF SOUTHERN CALIFORNIA**
Clinical Psychology — M
Religion — M
Theology — M

**VERMONT COLLEGE OF FINE ARTS**
Art/Fine Arts — M
Film, Television, and Video Production — M
Graphic Design — M
Music — M
Publishing — M
Writing — M

**VICTORIA UNIVERSITY**
Theology — M,D,O

**VILLANOVA UNIVERSITY**
Classics — M
Communication—General — M
English — M
Hispanic Studies — M
History — M
Liberal Studies — M
Missions and Missiology — M
Philosophy — D
Political Science — M
Psychology—General — M
Public Administration — M,O
Theater — M
Theology — M,D

**VIRGINIA BAPTIST COLLEGE**
Theology — M

**VIRGINIA BEACH THEOLOGICAL SEMINARY**
Pastoral Ministry and Counseling — M
Theology — M

**VIRGINIA COLLEGE IN BIRMINGHAM**
Criminal Justice and Criminology — M

**VIRGINIA COMMONWEALTH UNIVERSITY**
Art History — M,D
Art/Fine Arts — M,D
Clinical Psychology — D
Communication—General — D
Counseling Psychology — M,D
Criminal Justice and Criminology — M,O
Economics — M
Emergency Management — M,O
English — M

---

*M—masters degree; D—doctorate; O—other advanced degree; \*—Close-Up and/or Display*

Film, Television, and Video Production M,D
Forensic Sciences M
Geographic Information Systems O
Gerontology M,D
Health Psychology D
History M
Homeland Security M,O
Interdisciplinary Studies M,D
Interior Design M
Journalism M
Mass Communication M,D
Media Studies M,D
Museum Studies M
Music M
Photography M,D
Political Science M,D,O
Public Administration M
Public Affairs M,D,O
Public Policy D
Rehabilitation Counseling M
Sociology M
Theater M
Urban and Regional Planning M
Writing M

**VIRGINIA INTERNATIONAL UNIVERSITY**
Computer Art and Design M,O
International Affairs M
Linguistics M
Public Administration M

**VIRGINIA POLYTECHNIC INSTITUTE AND STATE UNIVERSITY**
Agricultural Economics and Agribusiness M,D
Applied Economics M,D
Architecture M,D,O
Building Science M,D,O
Communication—General M,D,O
Economics M,D
English M,D,O
Environmental Design M,D
Geographic Information Systems M,D
Geography M,D
History of Science and Technology M,D,O
History M,D,O
Human Development M,D
Humanities M,D,O
Interdisciplinary Studies M,D
International Affairs M,D,O
Internet and Interactive Multimedia M,D,O
Landscape Architecture M,D,O
Liberal Studies M,O
National Security M
Philosophy M,D,O
Political Science M,D,O
Psychology—General M,D
Public Administration M,D,O
Public Affairs M,D,O
Public Policy M,D
Rhetoric M,D,O
Sociology M,D,O
Theater M
Urban and Regional Planning M,D,O
Urban Studies M,D,O
Writing M,D,O

**VIRGINIA STATE UNIVERSITY**
Clinical Psychology M,D
Criminal Justice and Criminology M
Economics M
Health Psychology M,D
Interdisciplinary Studies M
Media Studies M
Psychology—General M,D

**VIRGINIA THEOLOGICAL SEMINARY**
Theology M,D

**VIRGINIA UNION UNIVERSITY**
Theology M,D

**VIRGINIA UNIVERSITY OF LYNCHBURG**
Pastoral Ministry and Counseling M,D
Religion M,D

**VITERBO UNIVERSITY**
Addictions/Substance Abuse Counseling M
Counseling Psychology M
Developmental Psychology M
Ethics M,O
Health Psychology M
Pastoral Ministry and Counseling M,O

**WAKE FOREST UNIVERSITY**
Communication—General M
English M
Liberal Studies M
Psychology—General M
Religion M
Speech and Interpersonal Communication M

**WALDEN UNIVERSITY**
Addictions/Substance Abuse Counseling M,D
Applied Psychology M,D,O
Child and Family Studies M,D
Clinical Psychology M,D,O
Communication—General M,D,O
Conflict Resolution and Mediation/Peace Studies M,D,O
Counseling Psychology M,D,O
Criminal Justice and Criminology M,D,O
Emergency Management M,D,O
Forensic Psychology M,D,O
Gerontology M,D
Health Psychology M,D,O
Homeland Security M,D,O
Industrial and Organizational Psychology M,D,O
Interdisciplinary Studies M,D,O
International Affairs M,D,O
International Development M,D,O
Marriage and Family Therapy M,D

Political Science M,D,O
Psychology—General M,D,O
Public Administration M,D,O
Public Policy M,D,O
Social Psychology M,D,O
Sustainable Development M,D,O

**WALDORF UNIVERSITY**
Criminal Justice and Criminology M
Emergency Management M
Public Administration M

**WALSH UNIVERSITY**
Counseling Psychology M
Pastoral Ministry and Counseling M
Theology M

**WARREN WILSON COLLEGE**
Writing M

**WARTBURG THEOLOGICAL SEMINARY**
Theology M

**WASHBURN UNIVERSITY**
Addictions/Substance Abuse Counseling M
Clinical Psychology M
Criminal Justice and Criminology M
Liberal Studies M
Psychology—General M

**WASHINGTON ADVENTIST UNIVERSITY**
Counseling Psychology M
Public Administration M
Religion M

**WASHINGTON & JEFFERSON COLLEGE**
Applied Economics M,O
Thanatology M,O
Writing M,O

**WASHINGTON STATE UNIVERSITY**
Agricultural Economics and Agribusiness M,D,O
American Studies M,D
Anthropology M,D
Archaeology M,D
Architecture M
Art/Fine Arts M
Clinical Psychology M,D
Clothing and Textiles M
Communication—General M,D
Corporate and Organizational Communication M,D
Counseling Psychology M,D
Criminal Justice and Criminology M,D
Cultural Anthropology M,D
Cultural Studies M,D,O
Economics M,D
English M,D
Experimental Psychology M,D
History M,D
Human Development D
Interdisciplinary Studies D
Interior Design M
Landscape Architecture M
Music M
Political Science M,D,O
Psychology—General M,D
Public Affairs M,D,O
Sociology M,D

**WASHINGTON UNIVERSITY IN ST. LOUIS**
Anthropology D
Archaeology M,D
Architecture M
Art History M,D
Art/Fine Arts M
Asian Languages M,D
Asian Studies M,D
Child and Family Studies M,D
Chinese M,D
Classics M,D
Comparative Literature M,D
Dance M
Developmental Psychology D
Economics D
English M,D
French D
German D
Gerontology M,D
History D
Japanese M,D
Jewish Studies M
Music M
Near and Middle Eastern Studies M
Philosophy D
Political Science D
Psychology—General D
Religion M
Romance Languages D
Spanish D
Speech and Interpersonal Communication M,D
Theater M
Urban Design M
Writing M

**WAYLAND BAPTIST UNIVERSITY**
Counseling Psychology M
Criminal Justice and Criminology M
History M
Homeland Security M
Humanities M
Interdisciplinary Studies M
Pastoral Ministry and Counseling M
Religion M
Theology M

**WAYNESBURG UNIVERSITY**
Addictions/Substance Abuse Counseling M,D
Clinical Psychology M,D
Counseling Psychology M,D
Criminal Justice and Criminology M,D

**WAYNE STATE COLLEGE**
Communication—General M

**WAYNE STATE UNIVERSITY**
African Studies M,D,O
American Studies M,D,O
Anthropology M,D,O
Applied Behavior Analysis M,D,O
Art History M
Art/Fine Arts M,D,O
Asian Studies M,D
Clinical Psychology M,D
Cognitive Sciences M,D
Communication—General M,D,O
Conflict Resolution and Mediation/Peace Studies M,D,O
Counseling Psychology M,D,O
Criminal Justice and Criminology M
Dance M,D,O
Developmental Psychology M,D
Economic Development M,D,O
Economics M,D
English M,D
Film, Television, and Video Theory and Criticism M,D
French M,D
Gender Studies M,D,O
Genetic Counseling M,D
German M,D,O
Gerontology M
Graphic Design M
Health Communication M,D,O
History of Science and Technology M,D,O
History M,D,O
Industrial and Labor Relations M,D
Industrial and Organizational Psychology M,D
Industrial Design M
Interior Design M
International Economics M,D
Italian M,D
Journalism M,D,O
Linguistics M
Media Studies M,D,O
Music M,D,O
Near and Middle Eastern Languages M,D
Near and Middle Eastern Studies M,D
Philosophy M
Photography M
Political Science M,D
Psychology—General M,D
Public Administration M,D
Public History M,D,O
Public Policy M,D
Rehabilitation Counseling M,D
Rhetoric M,D
Romance Languages M,D
School Psychology M,D,O
Social Psychology M,D
Sociology M,D
Spanish M
Textile Design M
Theater M
Urban and Regional Planning M,D
Urban Studies M
Western European Studies M,D,O
Writing M,D

**WEBBER INTERNATIONAL UNIVERSITY**
Criminal Justice and Criminology M

**WEBER STATE UNIVERSITY**
Communication—General M
English M

**WEBSTER UNIVERSITY**
Art History M
Art/Fine Arts M
Communication—General M,O
Corporate and Organizational Communication M
Counseling Psychology M
Criminal Justice and Criminology M,D,O
Forensic Sciences M
Gerontology M
International Affairs M
Internet and Interactive Multimedia M
Media Studies M
Music M
Psychology—General M
Public Administration M,D,O

**WENTWORTH INSTITUTE OF TECHNOLOGY**
Architecture M

**WESLEYAN UNIVERSITY**
Liberal Studies M,O
Music M,D
Writing M

**WESLEY BIBLICAL SEMINARY**
Linguistics M
Missions and Missiology M
Pastoral Ministry and Counseling M
Religion M
Theology M
Translation and Interpretation M

**WESLEY THEOLOGICAL SEMINARY**
Theology M,D

**WEST CHESTER UNIVERSITY OF PENNSYLVANIA**
Clinical Psychology M,D,O
Communication—General M
Criminal Justice and Criminology M
Cultural Studies M
Emergency Management M,O
English M,O
Ethics M,O
French M,O
Geographic Information Systems M,O
Geography M,O
German M,O
Gerontology M,O

History M
Holocaust and Genocide Studies M,O
Humanities M,O
Industrial and Organizational Psychology M,D,O
Music M,O
Philosophy M,O
Psychology—General M,D,O
Public Administration M,O
Public Affairs M,O
Spanish M,O
Sustainable Development M,O
Urban and Regional Planning M,O
Writing M,O

**WESTERN CAROLINA UNIVERSITY**
Applied Arts and Design—General M
Art/Fine Arts M
English M
History M
Psychology—General M
Public Affairs M

**WESTERN CONNECTICUT STATE UNIVERSITY**
Art/Fine Arts M
Clinical Psychology M
Criminal Justice and Criminology M
English M
History M
Illustration M
Writing M

**WESTERN ILLINOIS UNIVERSITY**
Clinical Psychology M,O
Communication—General M
Criminal Justice and Criminology M
Economic Development M
Economics M
English M,O
Experimental Psychology M,O
Geographic Information Systems M,O
Geography M,O
History M,O
Liberal Studies M
Museum Studies M,O
Music M
Political Science M
Psychology—General M,O
School Psychology M,O
Social Psychology M,O
Sociology M
Sustainable Development M,O
Theater M
Writing M,O

**WESTERN KENTUCKY UNIVERSITY**
Anthropology M
Applied Economics M
Clinical Psychology M,O
Communication—General M,O
Comparative Literature M
Corporate and Organizational Communication M,O
Counseling Psychology M
Criminal Justice and Criminology M
English M
Experimental Psychology M,O
French M
German M
History M
Homeland Security M
Industrial and Organizational Psychology M,O
Interdisciplinary Studies M,O
Marriage and Family Therapy M
Political Science M
Psychology—General M,O
Public Administration M
School Psychology M,O
Sociology M
Spanish M
Writing M

**WESTERN MICHIGAN UNIVERSITY**
Anthropology M
Applied Arts and Design—General M
Applied Economics M,D
Clinical Psychology M,D
Communication—General M
Counseling Psychology M,D
Economics M,D
English M,D
Family and Consumer Sciences-General M
Geographic Information Systems M,O
Geography M,D,O
History M,D
Industrial and Organizational Psychology M,D
International Affairs M,O
Music M,O
Philosophy M
Political Science M,D
Psychology—General M,D
Public Administration M,D,O
Public Affairs M,D,O
Rehabilitation Counseling M
Religion M
Sociology M,D
Spanish M,D
Therapies—Dance, Drama, and Music M,O
Writing M,D

**WESTERN MICHIGAN UNIVERSITY THOMAS M. COOLEY LAW SCHOOL**
Homeland Security M
National Security M,D

**WESTERN NEW ENGLAND UNIVERSITY**
Applied Behavior Analysis M,D
Communication—General M
Writing M

**WESTERN NEW MEXICO UNIVERSITY**
Interdisciplinary Studies M

**WESTERN OREGON UNIVERSITY**
Criminal Justice and Criminology — M
Music — M
Rehabilitation Counseling — M

**WESTERN SEMINARY**
Pastoral Ministry and Counseling — M,D,O
Religion — M,O
Theology — M,O
Women's Studies — M

**WESTERN SEMINARY–SACRAMENTO CAMPUS**
Marriage and Family Therapy — M
Pastoral Ministry and Counseling — M,O
Theology — M,O
Women's Studies — O

**WESTERN SEMINARY–SAN JOSE CAMPUS**
Marriage and Family Therapy — M,O
Pastoral Ministry and Counseling — M,O
Theology — M,O
Women's Studies — M,O

**WESTERN STATE COLORADO UNIVERSITY**
Film, Television, and Video Production — M
Writing — M

**WESTERN THEOLOGICAL SEMINARY**
Pastoral Ministry and Counseling — M,D,O
Theology — M,D,O

**WESTERN WASHINGTON UNIVERSITY**
Anthropology — M
Counseling Psychology — M
English — M
Experimental Psychology — M
Geography — M
History — M
Music — M
Political Science — M
Psychology—General — M
Rehabilitation Counseling — M

**WESTFIELD STATE UNIVERSITY**
Applied Behavior Analysis — M
Counseling Psychology — M
Criminal Justice and Criminology — M
English — M
Forensic Psychology — M
History — M
Psychology—General — M
Public Administration — M
Speech and Interpersonal Communication — M

**WEST LIBERTY UNIVERSITY**
Criminal Justice and Criminology — M

**WESTMINSTER COLLEGE (UT)**
Communication—General — M
Counseling Psychology — M
Writing — M

**WESTMINSTER SEMINARY CALIFORNIA**
Religion — M
Theology — M

**WESTMINSTER THEOLOGICAL SEMINARY**
Missions and Missiology — M,D,O
Pastoral Ministry and Counseling — M,D,O
Religion — M,D,O
Theology — M,D,O

**WEST TEXAS A&M UNIVERSITY**
Agricultural Economics and Agribusiness — M
Art/Fine Arts — M
Communication—General — M
Criminal Justice and Criminology — M
Economics — M
English — M
History — M
Interdisciplinary Studies — M
Music — M
Psychology—General — M

**WEST VIRGINIA STATE UNIVERSITY**
Criminal Justice and Criminology — M
Media Studies — M

**WEST VIRGINIA UNIVERSITY**
African Studies — M,D
African-American Studies — M,D
Agricultural Economics and Agribusiness — M
American Studies — M,D
Art History — M
Art/Fine Arts — M
Asian Studies — M,D
Child and Family Studies — M
Clinical Psychology — M,D
Communication—General — M,D
Corporate and Organizational Communication — M,D,O
Counseling Psychology — D
Developmental Psychology — M,D
Economic Development — M,D
Economics — M,D
English — M,D
Forensic Sciences — M,D
French — M
Geographic Information Systems — M,D
Geography — M,D
Graphic Design — M
History of Science and Technology — M,D
History — M,D
Human Development — M
Industrial and Labor Relations — M
International Affairs — M,D
International Economics — M,D
Journalism — M,O

Latin American Studies — M
Liberal Studies — M
Linguistics — M
Music — M,D
Political Science — M,D
Psychology—General — M,D
Public Administration — M
Public Policy — M,D
Rehabilitation Counseling — M
Sociology — M,D
Spanish — M
Sport Psychology — M,D
Sustainable Development — D
Theater — M
Urban and Regional Planning — M,D
Writing — M

**WEST VIRGINIA WESLEYAN COLLEGE**
Writing — M

**WHEATON COLLEGE**
Archaeology — M,D
Clinical Psychology — M,D
Counseling Psychology — M,D
Cultural Studies — M,O
Marriage and Family Therapy — M,D
Missions and Missiology — M,O
Pastoral Ministry and Counseling — M,D
Psychology—General — M,D
Theology — M,D

**WHEELOCK COLLEGE**
Child and Family Studies — M
Human Development — M

**WHITTIER COLLEGE**
Child Development — M

**WHITWORTH UNIVERSITY**
Theology — M

**WICHITA STATE UNIVERSITY**
Anthropology — M
Art/Fine Arts — M
Clinical Psychology — D
Communication—General — M
Criminal Justice and Criminology — M
Economics — M
English — M
Gerontology — M
History — M
International Economics — M
Liberal Studies — M
Music — M
Photography — M
Psychology—General — D
Public Administration — M
School Psychology — M,D,O
Social Psychology — D
Sociology — M
Spanish — M
Writing — M

**WIDENER UNIVERSITY**
Clinical Psychology — D
Criminal Justice and Criminology — M
Liberal Studies — M
Psychology—General — M
Public Administration — M

**WILBERFORCE UNIVERSITY**
Rehabilitation Counseling — M

**WILFRID LAURIER UNIVERSITY**
American Studies — M,D
Canadian Studies — M,D
Cognitive Sciences — M,D
Communication—General — M
Conflict Resolution and Mediation/Peace Studies — D
Criminal Justice and Criminology — M
Cultural Studies — M
Developmental Psychology — M,D
Economics — M,D
English — M,D
Film, Television, and Video Theory and Criticism — M,D
Gender Studies — M
Geography — M,D
History — M,D
International Affairs — M,D
International Economics — M
Media Studies — M
Pastoral Ministry and Counseling — M,D,O
Philosophy — M
Political Science — M,D
Psychology—General — M,D
Public Policy — M
Religion — M,D
Social Psychology — M,D
Social Sciences — M
Sociology — M
Theology — M,D,O
Therapies—Dance, Drama, and Music — M

**WILKES UNIVERSITY**
Writing — M

**WILLAMETTE UNIVERSITY**
Conflict Resolution and Mediation/Peace Studies — M,D

**WILLIAM CAREY UNIVERSITY**
Counseling Psychology — M
Psychology—General — M

**WILLIAM JAMES COLLEGE**
Applied Psychology — M,D
Clinical Psychology — M,D,O
Counseling Psychology — M,D
Forensic Psychology — M,D,O
Industrial and Organizational Psychology — M,D,O
Psychology—General — M,D,O
School Psychology — M,D,O

**WILLIAM PATERSON UNIVERSITY OF NEW JERSEY**
Clinical Psychology — M,D
Counseling Psychology — M,D
English — M,D
History — M
Music — M
Public Policy — M,D
Sociology — M,D
Writing — M,D

**WILLIAMS COLLEGE**
Art History — M
Economic Development — M

**WILMINGTON UNIVERSITY**
Clinical Psychology — M
Counseling Psychology — M
Criminal Justice and Criminology — M
Geographic Information Systems — M
Homeland Security — M,D
Internet and Interactive Multimedia — M
Public Administration — M,D

**WILSON COLLEGE**
Art/Fine Arts — M
Cultural Studies — M
Dance — M
English — M
Humanities — M
Women's Studies — M

**WINEBRENNER THEOLOGICAL SEMINARY**
Counseling Psychology — M,D
Theology — M,D

**WINONA STATE UNIVERSITY**
English — M

**WINSTON-SALEM STATE UNIVERSITY**
Rehabilitation Counseling — M

**WINTHROP UNIVERSITY**
Art/Fine Arts — M
Arts Administration — M
English — M
History — M
Liberal Studies — M
Music — M
Psychology—General — M,O

**WISCONSIN SCHOOL OF PROFESSIONAL PSYCHOLOGY**
Clinical Psychology — M,D
Psychology—General — M,D

**WON INSTITUTE OF GRADUATE STUDIES**
Religion — M

**WOODBURY UNIVERSITY**
Architecture — M

**WORCESTER POLYTECHNIC INSTITUTE**
Interdisciplinary Studies — M,D,O
Internet and Interactive Multimedia — M
Social Sciences — M,D,O

**WORCESTER STATE UNIVERSITY**
History — M
School Psychology — O
Spanish — M

**WRIGHT INSTITUTE**
Clinical Psychology — D
Counseling Psychology — M
Psychology—General — D

**WRIGHT STATE UNIVERSITY**
Applied Behavior Analysis — M
Applied Economics — M
Clinical Psychology — D
Criminal Justice and Criminology — M
Economics — M
English — M
History — M
Humanities — M
Industrial and Organizational Psychology — M,D
Psychology—General — M,D
Public Administration — M
Rehabilitation Counseling — M
Urban Studies — M

**WYCLIFFE COLLEGE**
Religion — M,D,O
Theology — M,D,O

**XAVIER UNIVERSITY**
Clinical Psychology — M,D
Counseling Psychology — M
Criminal Justice and Criminology — M
English — M
Ethics — M
Industrial and Organizational Psychology — M,D
Pastoral Ministry and Counseling — M
Psychology—General — M,D
Sustainable Development — M
Theology — M

**XAVIER UNIVERSITY OF LOUISIANA**
Pastoral Ministry and Counseling — M
Theology — M

**YALE UNIVERSITY**
African Studies — M
African-American Studies — D
American Studies — D
Anthropology — M,D
Applied Arts and Design—General — M
Archaeology — M,D
Architecture — M,D

Art History — D
Art/Fine Arts — M
Asian Languages — D
Asian Studies — M
Classics — M,D
Clinical Psychology — D
Cognitive Sciences — D
Comparative Literature — D
Developmental Psychology — D
East European and Russian Studies — M,D
Economic Development — M
Economics — M,D
English — M,D
Environmental Design — M,D
Film, Television, and Video Theory and Criticism — D
French — M,D
German — D
Graphic Design — M
History of Medicine — M,D
History of Science and Technology — M,D
History — M
International Affairs — M
International Economics — M
Italian — D
Latin American Studies — D
Linguistics — D
Medieval and Renaissance Studies — M,D
Music — M,D,O
Near and Middle Eastern Languages — M,D
Near and Middle Eastern Studies — M
Philosophy — D
Photography — M
Political Science — D
Portuguese — D
Psychology—General — D
Religion — D
Russian — D
Slavic Languages — D
Social Psychology — D
Social Sciences — M,D
Sociology — D
Spanish — D
Theater — M,D,O
Theology — M
Writing — M,D,O

**YESHIVA BETH MOSHE**
Theology — O

**YESHIVA DERECH CHAIM**
Religion — D

**YESHIVA KARLIN STOLIN RABBINICAL INSTITUTE**
Theology — O

**YESHIVA OF NITRA RABBINICAL COLLEGE**
Theology

**YESHIVA SHAAR HATORAH TALMUDIC RESEARCH INSTITUTE**
Theology

**YESHIVATH ZICHRON MOSHE**
Theology — O

**YESHIVA UNIVERSITY**
Clinical Psychology — D
Conflict Resolution and Mediation/Peace Studies — M,D
Counseling Psychology — M
Economics — M,D
Health Psychology — D
Jewish Studies — M,D
Psychology—General — M,D
School Psychology — D

**YORK UNIVERSITY**
Anthropology — M,D
Applied Arts and Design—General — M
Art History — M,D
Art/Fine Arts — M,D
Communication—General — M,D
Dance — M,D
Disability Studies — M,D
Economics — M,D
Emergency Management — M
English — M,D
Film, Television, and Video Production — M,D
French — M,D
Gender Studies — M,D
Geography — M,D
History — M,D
Humanities — M,D
Interdisciplinary Studies — M
International Affairs — M
Linguistics — M,D
Music — M,D
Philosophy — M,D
Political Science — M,D
Psychology—General — M,D
Public Administration — M
Public Affairs — M
Public Policy — M
Sociology — M,D
Theater — M,D
Translation and Interpretation — M
Women's Studies — M,D

**YOUNGSTOWN STATE UNIVERSITY**
Applied Behavior Analysis — M
Counseling Psychology — M
Criminal Justice and Criminology — M
Economics — M
English — M
Gerontology — M
History — M
Music — M
Psychology—General — M
School Psychology — M

---

*M—masters degree; D—doctorate; O—other advanced degree; \*—Close-Up and/or Display*

# ACADEMIC AND PROFESSIONAL PROGRAMS IN THE ARTS AND ARCHITECTURE

# Section 1
# Applied Arts and Design

This section contains a directory of institutions offering graduate work in applied arts and design, followed by in-depth entries submitted by institutions that chose to prepare detailed program descriptions. Additional information about programs listed in the directory but not augmented by an in-depth entry may be obtained by writing directly to the dean of a graduate school or chair of a department at the address given in the directory.

For programs offering related work, see also in this book *Architecture* and *Art and Art History*. In another guide in this series: **Graduate Programs in Business, Education, Information Studies, Law & Social Work**
See *Advertising and Public Relations*

## CONTENTS

# Applied Arts and Design—General

**Academy of Art University,** Graduate Programs, School of Advertising, San Francisco, CA 94105-3410. Offers advertising (MFA); advertising and branded media technology (MA). *Program availability:* Part-time, 100% online. *Faculty:* 6 full-time (2 women), 20 part-time/adjunct (6 women). *Students:* 85 full-time (56 women), 24 part-time (16 women); includes 16 minority (2 Black or African American, non-Hispanic/Latino; 1 American Indian or Alaska Native, non-Hispanic/Latino; 7 Asian, non-Hispanic/Latino; 6 Hispanic/Latino), 72 international. Average age 28. 32 applicants, 100% accepted, 16 enrolled. In 2016, 47 master's awarded. *Degree requirements:* For master's, final review. *Entrance requirements:* For master's, statement of intent; resume; portfolio/reel; official college transcripts. *Application deadline:* Applications are processed on a rolling basis. Application fee: $50. Electronic applications accepted. *Expenses:* Tuition: Part-time $982 per unit. *Financial support:* Career-related internships or fieldwork, Federal Work-Study, and scholarships/grants available. Financial award application deadline: 8/10; financial award applicants required to submit FAFSA. *Unit head:* 800-544-ARTS, Call: info@academyart.edu. *Application contact:* 800-544-ARTS, E-mail: info@academyart.edu.
Website: http://www.academyart.edu/advertising-school/index.html

**Alfred University,** Graduate School, College of Ceramics, School of Art and Design, Alfred, NY 14802. Offers ceramic art (MFA); electronic integrated arts (MFA); painting (MFA); sculpture/dimensional studies (MFA). *Accreditation:* NASAD. *Faculty:* 19 full-time (11 women), 14 part-time/adjunct (9 women). *Students:* 34 full-time (18 women); includes 2 minority (1 Asian, non-Hispanic/Latino; 1 Hispanic/Latino), 10 international. Average age 28. 32 applicants, 66% accepted, 19 enrolled. In 2016, 15 master's awarded. *Degree requirements:* For master's, thesis, exhibit. *Entrance requirements:* For master's, portfolio. Additional exam requirements/recommendations for international students: Required—TOEFL (minimum score 550 paper-based; 80 iBT), IELTS (minimum score 6). *Application deadline:* For fall admission, 1/15 for domestic and international students. Application fee: $60. Electronic applications accepted. *Expenses:* Contact institution. *Financial support:* In 2016–17, 34 students received support. Teaching assistantships with full tuition reimbursements available and tuition waivers (full) available. Financial award application deadline: 8/1; financial award applicants required to submit FAFSA. *Faculty research:* Ceramic art, sculpture, glass art, new media, time-based media. *Unit head:* Gerar Edizel, Interim Dean, 607-871-2412, E-mail: fedizel@alfred.edu. *Application contact:* Sara Love, Coordinator of Graduate Admissions, 607-871-2115, Fax: 607-871-2198, E-mail: gradinquiry@alfred.edu.
Website: http://art.alfred.edu/graduate/

**Arizona State University at the Tempe campus,** Herberger Institute for Design and the Arts, The Design School, Tempe, AZ 85287-1605. Offers architecture (M Arch); building design/built environment (MS); design (MSD), including arts, media, and engineering, healthcare and healing environments (MSD, PhD), industrial design, interaction design, interior design, new product innovation, visual communication design; design, environment and the arts (PhD), including design, digital culture, healthcare and healing environments (MSD, PhD), history, theory, and criticism; landscape architecture (MLA); urban design (MUD); MA/MBA. *Accreditation:* NASAD. Terminal master's awarded for partial completion of doctoral program. *Degree requirements:* For master's, thesis optional, interactive Program of Study (iPOS) submitted before completing 50 percent of required credit hours; for doctorate, comprehensive exam, thesis/dissertation, interactive Program of Study (iPOS) submitted before completing 50 percent of required credit hours. *Entrance requirements:* For master's, GRE General Test, minimum GPA of 3.0 or equivalent in last 2 years of work leading to bachelor's degree, design/creative works portfolio, 3 references, statement of intent; for doctorate, GRE, master's degree in architecture, graphic design, industrial design, interior design, landscape architecture, or art history or equivalent standing; statement of purpose; 3 letters of recommendation; indication of potential faculty mentor; sample of written work. Additional exam requirements/recommendations for international students: Required—TOEFL (minimum score 600 paper-based; 100 iBT). Electronic applications accepted.

**The Art Institute of Dallas, a branch of Miami International University of Art & Design,** Program in Design and Media Management, Dallas, TX 75231-5993. Offers MA.

**Bowling Green State University,** Graduate College, College of Arts and Sciences, School of Art, Bowling Green, OH 43403. Offers 2-D studio art (MA, MFA); 3-D studio art (MA, MFA); art education (MA); art history (MA); computer art (MA); design (MFA); digital arts (MFA); graphics (MFA). *Accreditation:* NASAD. *Program availability:* Part-time. *Degree requirements:* For master's, thesis or alternative, final exhibit (MFA). *Entrance requirements:* For master's, GRE General Test (MA), slide portfolio (15-20 slides). Additional exam requirements/recommendations for international students: Required—TOEFL. *Application deadline:* For fall admission, 2/15 for domestic students. Application fee: $30. Electronic applications accepted. *Financial support:* Research assistantships with full and partial tuition reimbursements, teaching assistantships with full and partial tuition reimbursements, career-related internships or fieldwork, institutionally sponsored loans, and unspecified assistantships available. Support available to part-time students. Financial award applicants required to submit FAFSA. *Faculty research:* Computer animation and virtual reality, Spanish still-life painting from 1600 to 1800, art and psychotherapy, Japanese wood-firing techniques in ceramics, non-toxic printmaking technologies. *Unit head:* Dr. Katerina Ruedi Ray, Director, 419-372-8575. *Application contact:* Marisa Cline, Graduate Coordinator, 419-372-2786, E-mail: mlcline@bgsu.edu.

**California College of the Arts,** Graduate Programs, Design Program, San Francisco, CA 94107. Offers graphic design (MFA); industrial design (MFA); interaction design (MFA). *Accreditation:* NASAD. *Faculty:* 6 full-time (2 women), 26 part-time/adjunct (10 women). *Students:* 105 full-time (67 women); includes 14 minority (1 Black or African American, non-Hispanic/Latino; 8 Asian, non-Hispanic/Latino; 5 Hispanic/Latino), 67 international. Average age 26. 384 applicants, 36% accepted, 45 enrolled. In 2016, 9 master's awarded. *Degree requirements:* For master's, exhibit. *Entrance requirements:* For master's, appropriate bachelor's degree, portfolio, resume, letters of recommendation, transcripts. Additional exam requirements/recommendations for international students: Required—TOEFL, IELTS, or PTE. *Application deadline:* For fall admission, 1/10 for domestic and international students. Applications are processed on a rolling basis. Application fee: $70. Electronic applications accepted. *Expenses:* $1,641 per unit, $49,230 per year tuition; $490 fees. *Financial support:* In 2016–17, fellowships (averaging $22,000 per year), teaching assistantships (averaging $2,000 per year) were awarded; career-related internships or fieldwork, Federal Work-Study, scholarships/grants, health care benefits, and unspecified assistantships also available. Financial award application deadline: 7/31; financial award applicants required to submit FAFSA. *Unit head:* Jon Sueda, Graduate Chair, 415-551-9283, Fax: 415-703-9539, E-mail:

jsueda@cca.edu. *Application contact:* Wes Fanelli, Assistant Director of Graduate Admissions, 415-703-9533, Fax: 415-703-9539, E-mail: wfanelli@cca.edu.

**California College of the Arts,** Graduate Programs, MBA in Design Strategy Program, San Francisco, CA 94107. Offers MBA. *Accreditation:* NASAD. *Faculty:* 2 full-time (1 woman), 14 part-time/adjunct (3 women). *Students:* 86 full-time (57 women); includes 23 minority (4 Black or African American, non-Hispanic/Latino; 11 Asian, non-Hispanic/Latino; 7 Hispanic/Latino; 1 Native Hawaiian or other Pacific Islander, non-Hispanic/Latino), 35 international. Average age 30. 141 applicants, 94% accepted, 39 enrolled. In 2016, 54 master's awarded. *Degree requirements:* For master's, thesis. *Entrance requirements:* Additional exam requirements/recommendations for international students: Required—TOEFL, IELTS, or PTE. *Application deadline:* For fall admission, 1/10 for domestic and international students. Applications are processed on a rolling basis. Application fee: $70. Electronic applications accepted. *Expenses:* $1,641 per unit, $49,230 per year tuition; $490 fees. *Financial support:* Federal Work-Study and scholarships/grants available. Financial award application deadline: 7/31; financial award applicants required to submit FAFSA. *Unit head:* Nathan Shedroff, Program Chair, 800-447-1ART, E-mail: nshedroff@cca.edu. *Application contact:* Wes Fanelli, Assistant Director of Graduate Admissions, 415-703-9533, Fax: 415-703-9539, E-mail: wfanelli@cca.edu.

**California Institute of the Arts,** School of Art, Valencia, CA 91355-2340. Offers art (MFA, Adv C); graphic design (MFA, Adv C); photography (MFA, Adv C). *Accreditation:* NASAD (one or more programs are accredited). *Degree requirements:* For master's, final project. *Entrance requirements:* For master's, portfolio. Additional exam requirements/recommendations for international students: Required—TOEFL. Electronic applications accepted.

**California State University, Fresno,** Division of Research and Graduate Studies, College of Arts and Humanities, Department of Art and Design, Fresno, CA 93740-8027. Offers art (MA). *Program availability:* Part-time, evening/weekend. *Degree requirements:* For master's, thesis or alternative. *Entrance requirements:* For master's, GRE General Test, minimum GPA of 3.0, portfolio. Additional exam requirements/recommendations for international students: Required—TOEFL. *Application deadline:* For fall admission, 5/1 for domestic and international students; for spring admission, 10/1 for domestic and international students. Applications are processed on a rolling basis. Application fee: $55. Electronic applications accepted. *Financial support:* Career-related internships or fieldwork, Federal Work-Study, and scholarships/grants available. Support available to part-time students. Financial award application deadline: 3/1; financial award applicants required to submit FAFSA. *Faculty research:* Art history, graphic design, studio art. *Unit head:* Martin R. Valencia, Chair, 559-278-2612, Fax: 559-278-4706, E-mail: mvalencia@csufresno.edu. *Application contact:* Prof. Paula Durette, Graduate Program Coordinator, 559-278-2249, Fax: 559-278-4706, E-mail: pdurrette@csufresno.edu.
Website: http://www.fresnostate.edu/artshum/artanddesign/

**California State University, Los Angeles,** Graduate Studies, College of Arts and Letters, Department of Art, Los Angeles, CA 90032-8530. Offers art (MA), including art education, art history, art therapy, ceramics, metals, and textiles, design (MA, MFA), painting, sculpture, and graphic arts, photography; fine arts (MFA), including crafts, design (MA, MFA), studio arts. *Accreditation:* NASAD (one or more programs are accredited). *Program availability:* Part-time, evening/weekend. *Degree requirements:* For master's, comprehensive exam, project or thesis. *Entrance requirements:* For master's, portfolio. Additional exam requirements/recommendations for international students: Required—TOEFL (minimum score 500 paper-based). Electronic applications accepted. *Faculty research:* The artist and the book, conceptual art, ceramic processes, computer graphics, architectural graphics.

**Carnegie Mellon University,** College of Fine Arts, School of Design, Program in Design, Pittsburgh, PA 15213-3891. Offers MA, D Des, PhD. *Degree requirements:* For doctorate, one foreign language, comprehensive exam, thesis/dissertation. *Entrance requirements:* For doctorate, GRE, portfolio of relevant work. Additional exam requirements/recommendations for international students: Required—TOEFL (minimum score 600 paper-based). *Faculty research:* Design theory, typography and information design, new product development, organizational behavior, interaction design.

**College for Creative Studies,** Graduate Programs, Detroit, MI 48202-4034. Offers color and materials design (MFA); integrated design (MFA); interaction design (MFA); transportation design (MFA). *Accreditation:* NASAD.

**Concordia University,** School of Graduate Studies, Faculty of Fine Arts, Department of Design and Computation Arts, Montréal, QC H3G 1M8, Canada. Offers design (M Des); digital technologies in design art practice (Certificate).

★ **Drexel University,** Westphal College of Media Arts and Design, Philadelphia, PA 19104-2875. Offers arts administration (MS); design research (MS); digital media (MS); fashion design (MS); interior architecture and design (MS); museum leadership (MS); television management (MS); MS/MBA. *Accreditation:* NASAD. *Program availability:* Part-time, evening/weekend. *Faculty:* 127 full-time (51 women), 184 part-time/adjunct (87 women). *Students:* 126 full-time (98 women), 115 part-time (82 women); includes 61 minority (37 Black or African American, non-Hispanic/Latino; 5 Asian, non-Hispanic/Latino; 15 Hispanic/Latino; 4 Two or more races, non-Hispanic/Latino), 56 international. Average age 29. In 2016, 84 master's awarded. *Entrance requirements:* For master's, interview. Additional exam requirements/recommendations for international students: Required—TOEFL. *Application deadline:* For fall admission, 8/21 for domestic students; for spring admission, 3/5 for domestic students. Applications are processed on a rolling basis. Application fee: $50. Electronic applications accepted. *Expenses:* Contact institution. *Financial support:* Research assistantships, teaching assistantships, career-related internships or fieldwork, and unspecified assistantships available. Support available to part-time students. Financial award application deadline: 2/1. *Unit head:* College Recruitment Office, 215-895-1675, Fax: 215-895-5838. *Application contact:* Graduate Admissions Office, 215-895-6700, E-mail: enroll@drexel.edu.
Website: http://www.drexel.edu/westphal/

See Display on next page and Close-Up on page 99.

**Emily Carr University of Art + Design,** Program in Applied Arts, Vancouver, BC V6H 3R9, Canada. Offers design (M Des); media arts (MAA); visual arts (MAA). *Degree requirements:* For master's, internship, thesis project. *Entrance requirements:* For master's, minimum overall GPA of 3.0, visual portfolio, 3 letters of recommendation, resume/curriculum vitae. Additional exam requirements/recommendations for international students: Required—TOEFL (minimum score 570 paper-based; 84 iBT), IELTS (minimum score 6.5), Michigan English Language Assessment Battery (minimum score 81). Electronic applications accepted.

**Fashion Institute of Technology,** School of Graduate Studies, New York, NY 10001-5992. Offers MA, MFA, MPS. *Accreditation:* NASAD. *Program availability:* Part-time, evening/weekend. *Degree requirements:* For master's, thesis. *Entrance requirements:* For master's, portfolio, letters of recommendation, resume, interview. Additional exam requirements/recommendations for international students: Required— TOEFL (minimum score 550 paper-based; 80 iBT). *Application deadline:* For fall admission, 2/15 priority date for domestic and international students. Applications are processed on a rolling basis. Application fee: $50. Electronic applications accepted. *Expenses:* Tuition, state resident: full-time $10,870; part-time $453 per credit. Tuition, nonresident: full-time $22,210; part-time $925 per credit. *Required fees:* $745. *Financial support:* Federal Work-Study and scholarships/grants available. Financial award applicants required to submit FAFSA. *Faculty research:* Fashion history, material conservation, international marketing and global sourcing, sustainable economic development, luxury braiding in China. *Unit head:* Dr. Mary Davis, Dean, 212-217-4300. *Application contact:* Carole deSantis, Administrative Secretary, Graduate Admissions, 212-217-4314, Fax: 212-217-5156, E-mail: carole_desantis@fitnyc.edu.
Website: http://www.fitnyc.edu/graduate-studies/

**See Display on next page and Close-Up on page 103.**

**Ferris State University,** Kendall College of Art and Design, Grand Rapids, MI 49503. Offers architecture (M Arch); art education (MAE); design (MA); drawing (MFA); painting (MFA); photography (MFA); printmaking (MFA); visual and critical studies (MA). *Program availability:* Part-time. *Faculty:* 15 full-time (10 women), 9 part-time/adjunct (2 women). *Students:* 40 full-time (33 women), 5 part-time (3 women); includes 9 minority (3 Black or African American, non-Hispanic/Latino; 3 Asian, non-Hispanic/Latino; 3 Hispanic/Latino), 6 international. Average age 30. 43 applicants, 53% accepted, 16 enrolled. In 2016, 16 master's awarded. *Degree requirements:* For master's, thesis, seminars. *Entrance requirements:* For master's, portfolio, 3 letters of recommendation, curriculum vitae, artist statement, letter of intent. Additional exam requirements/ recommendations for international students: Required—TOEFL (minimum score 70 iBT). *Application deadline:* For fall admission, 2/1 priority date for domestic and international students; for spring admission, 11/1 priority date for domestic and international students. Applications are processed on a rolling basis. Application fee: $0. Electronic applications accepted. *Expenses:* $1,017 per credit hour plus $390 fees per year. *Financial support:* In 2016–17, 32 students received support, including 8 fellowships (averaging $16,781 per year); scholarships/grants and unspecified assistantships also available. Financial award application deadline: 2/1; financial award applicants required to submit FAFSA. *Unit head:* Leslie Bellavance, President, 616-451-2787. *Application contact:* Thomas Post, Graduate Recruitment Specialist, 616-451-2787, Fax: 616-831-9689, E-mail: thomaspost@ferris.edu.
Website: http://www.kcad.edu/

**Florida Atlantic University,** Dorothy F. Schmidt College of Arts and Letters, Department of Visual Arts and Art History, Boca Raton, FL 33431-0991. Offers visual art (MFA), including ceramics, graphic design, visual art. *Faculty:* 14 full-time (10 women). *Students:* 15 full-time (12 women), 1 (woman) part-time; includes 6 minority (1 Black or African American, non-Hispanic/Latino; 1 Asian, non-Hispanic/Latino; 3 Hispanic/Latino; 1 Two or more races, non-Hispanic/Latino). Average age 37. 23 applicants, 26% accepted, 4 enrolled. In 2016, 3 master's awarded. *Degree requirements:* For master's, one foreign language, project. *Entrance requirements:* For master's, GRE General Test, minimum GPA of 3.0 during last 60 hours of course work, slide portfolio. *Application deadline:* For fall admission, 2/21 for domestic and international students; for spring admission, 10/1 for domestic and international students. Application fee: $30. Electronic applications accepted. *Expenses:* Tuition, state resident: full-time $7392; part-time $369.82 per credit hour. Tuition, nonresident: full-time $19,432; part-time $1024.81 per

credit hour. *Financial support:* Research assistantships with full tuition reimbursements, teaching assistantships with full tuition reimbursements, career-related internships or fieldwork, Federal Work-Study, and institutionally sponsored loans available. Financial award applicants required to submit FAFSA. *Faculty research:* Painting, ceramics (traditional and non-traditional), installation, video and interactive sculpture. *Unit head:* Dr. Eric Landes, Interim Chair, 954-236-1106, E-mail: elandes1@fau.edu. *Application contact:* James A. Novak, Associate Professor/Graduate Coordinator/Advisor, 561-297-2430, Fax: 561-297-3078, E-mail: jnovak@fau.edu.
Website: http://www.fau.edu/VAAH/

**Howard University,** Graduate School, Division of Fine Arts, Department of Art, Program in Fine Arts, Washington, DC 20059-0002. Offers 3D reality (sculpture and ceramics) (MFA); design (MFA); electronic studio (MFA); painting (MFA); photography (MFA). *Accreditation:* NASAD. *Degree requirements:* For master's, comprehensive exam, thesis, exhibit. *Entrance requirements:* For master's, minimum GPA of 3.0, portfolio.

**Illinois Institute of Technology,** Graduate College, Institute of Design, Chicago, IL 60654. Offers M Des, MDM, PhD, M Des/MBA. *Program availability:* Part-time. Terminal master's awarded for partial completion of doctoral program. *Degree requirements:* For master's, comprehensive exam (for some programs), thesis (for some programs); for doctorate, one foreign language, comprehensive exam, thesis/ dissertation. *Entrance requirements:* For master's, GRE (minimum score 310); GMAT (minimum score 600), bachelor's degree, minimum GPA of 3.0, official transcripts, portfolio (for applicants with design degrees), minimum of two years of professional experience; for doctorate, GRE General Test (minimum score 1000 Quantitative and Verbal, 3.5 Analytical Writing), master's degree in design from accredited institution, official transcripts, portfolio. Additional exam requirements/recommendations for international students: Required—TOEFL (minimum score 100 iBT); Recommended— IELTS (minimum score 7). Electronic applications accepted. *Expenses:* Contact institution. *Faculty research:* Data visualization, urbanism, big data, digital tools, future of work.

**Indiana University Bloomington,** University Graduate School, College of Arts and Sciences, School of Art and Design, Bloomington, IN 47405-7000. Offers apparel merchandising (MS); studio art (MFA). *Accreditation:* NASAD (one or more programs are accredited). *Students:* 64 full-time (39 women), 12 part-time (5 women); includes 12 minority (1 Black or African American, non-Hispanic/Latino; 3 Asian, non-Hispanic/ Latino; 6 Hispanic/Latino; 2 Two or more races, non-Hispanic/Latino), 8 international. Average age 31. 104 applicants, 22% accepted, 23 enrolled. In 2016, 13 master's awarded. *Entrance requirements:* For master's, portfolio (MFA). Additional exam requirements/recommendations for international students: Required—TOEFL. *Application deadline:* For fall admission, 1/15 for domestic students, 12/1 for international students. Application fee: $55 ($65 for international students). Electronic applications accepted. *Financial support:* Fellowships with tuition reimbursements, research assistantships with tuition reimbursements, teaching assistantships with tuition reimbursements, career-related internships or fieldwork, Federal Work-Study, scholarships/grants, tuition waivers (full and partial), and stipends available. *Unit head:* Peg Faimon, Founding Dean, 812-855-2561, E-mail: pfaimon@indiana.edu. *Application contact:* Toni Arcuri, Graduate Services Coordinator, 812-855-0188, E-mail: sofagrad@indiana.edu.
Website: https://soad.indiana.edu/

**Iowa State University of Science and Technology,** Department of Apparel, Events, and Hospitality Management, Ames, IA 50011-1078. Offers apparel, merchandising, and design (MS, PhD); hospitality management (MS, PhD). *Program availability:* Online learning. *Degree requirements:* For doctorate, thesis/dissertation.

*Applied Arts and Design—General*

*Entrance requirements:* For master's and doctorate, GRE General Test. Additional exam requirements/recommendations for international students: Required—TOEFL (minimum score 550 paper-based; 79 iBT), IELTS (minimum score 6.5). *Application deadline:* For fall admission, 2/1 priority date for domestic and international students. Application fee: $40 ($90 for international students). Electronic applications accepted. *Application contact:* Ann Marie Fiore, Director of Graduate Education, 515-294-9303, E-mail: amfiore@iastate.edu.
Website: http://www.aeshm.hs.iastate.edu/graduate-programs/amd/

**Louisiana State University and Agricultural & Mechanical College,** Graduate School, College of Art and Design, Baton Rouge, LA 70803. Offers M Arch, M Sc, MA, MFA, MLA. *Accreditation:* ASLA (one or more programs are accredited); NASAD (one or more programs are accredited).

**Louisiana Tech University,** Graduate School, College of Liberal Arts, MFA Program, Ruston, LA 71272. Offers graphic design (MFA); photography (MFA); studio (MFA). *Accreditation:* NASAD. *Program availability:* Part-time. *Degree requirements:* For master's, exhibit. *Entrance requirements:* For master's, GRE General Test, portfolio. *Application deadline:* For fall admission, 5/12 for domestic students. Applications are processed on a rolling basis. Application fee: $40 ($50 for international students). Electronic applications accepted. *Financial support:* Fellowships, career-related internships or fieldwork, Federal Work-Study, institutionally sponsored loans, and unspecified assistantships available. Financial award application deadline: 2/15. *Unit head:* Frank Hamrick, Graduate Coordinator, 318-257-4154, Fax: 318-257-4890, E-mail: fhamrick@latech.edu. *Application contact:* Marilyn J. Robinson, Assistant to the Dean of the Graduate School, 318-257-2924, Fax: 318-257-4487.
Website: http://design.latech.edu/master-of-fine-arts/

**Maryland Institute College of Art,** Graduate Studies, Design Leadership MBA/MA Program, Baltimore, MD 21201. Offers MBA/MA. Program offered in collaboration with The Johns Hopkins University. *Students:* 20 full-time (10 women); includes 7 minority (2 Black or African American, non-Hispanic/Latino; 2 Asian, non-Hispanic/Latino; 1 Hispanic/Latino; 2 Two or more races, non-Hispanic/Latino), 3 international. *Entrance requirements:* Additional exam requirements/recommendations for international students: Required—TOEFL (minimum score 100 iBT) or IELTS (minimum score 7). *Application deadline:* For fall admission, 1/15 priority date for domestic and international students; for spring admission, 4/1 for domestic and international students. Applications are processed on a rolling basis. Application fee: $100. Electronic applications accepted. *Expenses:* Contact institution. *Financial support:* Scholarships/grants available. Financial award applicants required to submit FAFSA. *Unit head:* David Gracyalny, Vice Provost for Research/Dean, 410-225-5273, E-mail: dgracyalny@mica.edu. *Application contact:* Chris D. Harring, Director of Graduate Admission, 410-225-2256, Fax: 410-225-5275, E-mail: graduate@mica.edu.
Website: http://www.designleadershipmba.com/

**Maryland Institute College of Art,** Graduate Studies, MPS Program in Business of Art and Design, Baltimore, MD 21201. Offers MPS. *Program availability:* Part-time. *Faculty:* 15 part-time/adjunct (6 women). *Students:* 20 part-time (10 women); includes 5 minority (2 Black or African American, non-Hispanic/Latino; 1 Asian, non-Hispanic/Latino; 2 Hispanic/Latino). Average age 27. 53 applicants, 47% accepted, 20 enrolled. In 2016, 20 master's awarded. *Degree requirements:* For master's, business plan presentation. *Entrance requirements:* For master's, essay, resume. Additional exam requirements/recommendations for international students: Required—TOEFL (minimum score 550 paper-based; 80 iBT), IELTS (minimum score 6.5). *Application deadline:* For fall admission, 1/15 for domestic and international students; for spring admission, 4/1 for domestic and international students. Application fee: $70. Electronic applications accepted. *Expenses:* Contact institution. *Financial support:* In 2016–17, 20 students received support, including 20 fellowships (averaging $3,400 per year); scholarships/grants also available. Financial award application deadline: 1/15; financial award applicants required to submit FAFSA. *Unit head:* Heather Bradbury, Manager, 410-225-2220, Fax: 410-225-2229, E-mail: hbradbury@mica.edu. *Application contact:* Chris D. Harring, Director of Graduate Admission, 410-225-2256, Fax: 410-225-5275, E-mail: graduate@mica.edu.
Website: http://www.mica.edu/Programs_of_Study/Graduate_Programs/The_Business_of_Art_and_Design_(Online_MPS).html

**Maryland Institute College of Art,** Graduate Studies, MPS Program in Information Visualization, Baltimore, MD 21201. Offers MPS. *Program availability:* Part-time, online learning. *Faculty:* 13 part-time/adjunct (8 women). *Students:* 20 full-time (11 women); includes 2 minority (1 Black or African American, non-Hispanic/Latino; 1 Hispanic/Latino). Average age 31. 35 applicants, 71% accepted, 20 enrolled. In 2016, 20 master's awarded. *Entrance requirements:* For master's, curriculum vitae/resume, visualization portfolio, bachelor's degree in any field. Additional exam requirements/recommendations for international students: Required—TOEFL (minimum score 550 paper-based; 80 iBT). *Application deadline:* For fall admission, 1/15 priority date for domestic students, 1/15 for international students. Application fee: $75. Electronic applications accepted. *Expenses:* Contact institution. *Financial support:* In 2016–17, 20 fellowships (averaging $3,500 per year) were awarded; scholarships/grants also available. Financial award application deadline: 1/15; financial award applicants required to submit FAFSA. *Unit head:* Heather Bradbury, Manager of Business of Art and Design Master's Program, 410-225-2220, Fax: 410-225-2229, E-mail: hbradbury@mica.edu. *Application contact:* Chris D. Harring, Director of Graduate Admission, 410-225-2256, Fax: 410-225-5275, E-mail: graduate@mica.edu.
Website: http://www.mica.edu/Programs_of_Study/Graduate_Programs/Information_Visualization_(Online_MPS).html

**Maryland Institute College of Art,** Graduate Studies, Program in Social Design, Baltimore, MD 21201. Offers MPS. *Program availability:* Part-time/adjunct. *Students:* 14 full-time (9 women); includes 5 minority (1 Black or African American, non-Hispanic/Latino; 1 Asian, non-Hispanic/Latino; 2 Hispanic/Latino; 1 Two or more races, non-Hispanic/Latino). Average age 27. 60 applicants, 30% accepted, 14 enrolled. In 2016, 14 master's awarded. *Degree requirements:* For master's, thesis, thesis project, exhibition, project presentation. *Entrance requirements:* For master's, portfolio, bachelor's degree in any field. Additional exam requirements/recommendations for international students: Required—TOEFL (minimum score 550 paper-based; 80 iBT), IELTS (minimum score 6.5). *Application deadline:* For fall admission, 1/15 priority date for domestic students, 1/15 for international students. Applications are processed on a rolling basis. Application fee: $75. Electronic applications accepted. *Expenses:* Contact institution. *Financial support:* In 2016–17, 8 students received support, including 14 fellowships (averaging $13,000 per year), 14 teaching assistantships (averaging $3,200 per year); scholarships/grants also available. Financial award application deadline: 1/15. *Unit head:* Michael S. Weikert, Director, 410-276-2015, E-mail: graduate@mica.edu. *Application contact:* Chris D. Harring, Director of Graduate Admission, 410-225-2256, Fax: 410-225-5275, E-mail: graduate@mica.edu.
Website: http://www.mica.edu/Programs_of_Study/Graduate_Programs/Social_Design_(MA).html

**Massachusetts College of Art and Design,** Graduate Programs, MFA Program, Boston, MA 02115-5882. Offers 2D fine arts (MFA), including painting, printmaking; 3D fine arts (MFA), including ceramics, fibers, glass, jewelry and metalsmithing, sculpture; design (MFA, Postbaccalaureate Certificate), including dynamic media; fine arts (MFA), including interdisciplinary; media arts (MFA, Postbaccalaureate Certificate), including film/video (MFA), photography. *Accreditation:* NASAD. *Faculty:* 40 full-time (19 women), 55 part-time/adjunct (23 women). *Students:*

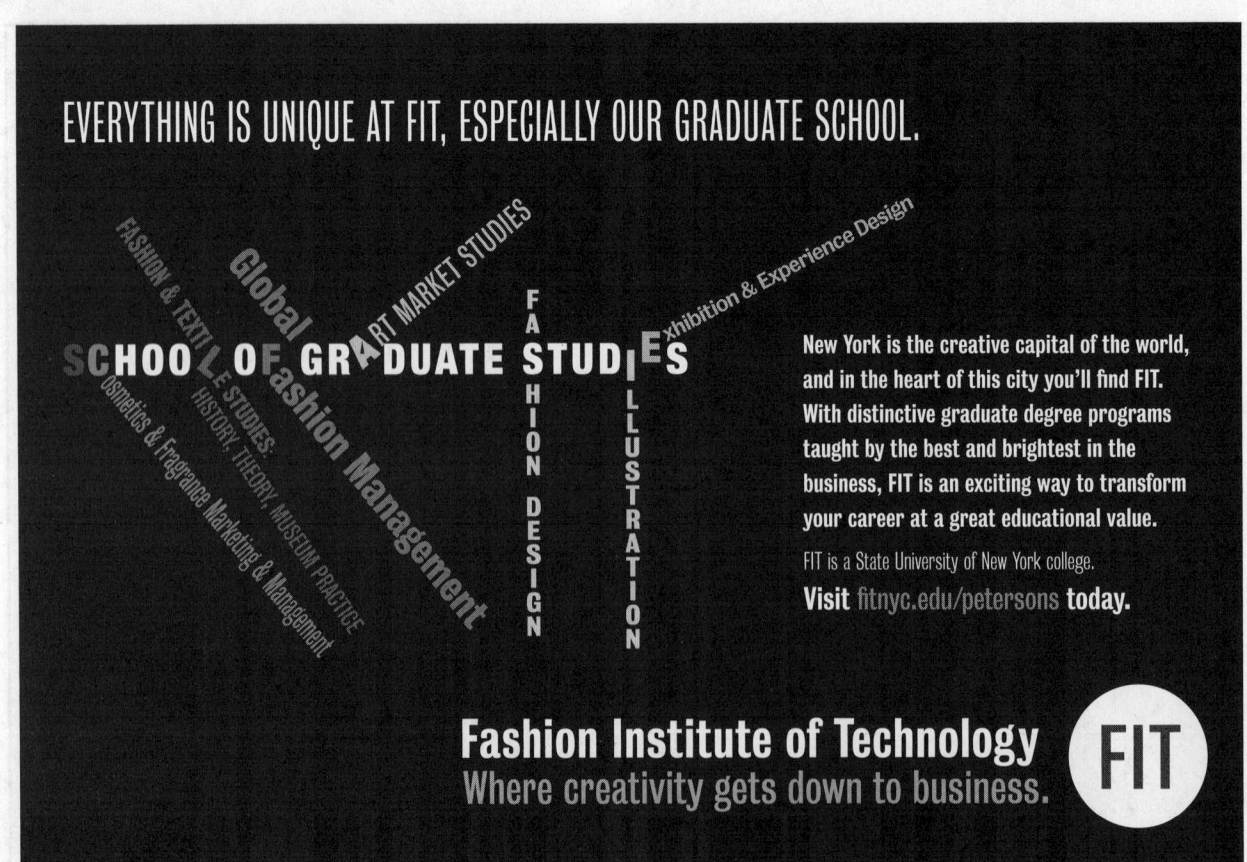

58 full-time (39 women), 16 part-time (12 women); includes 10 minority (1 Black or African American, non-Hispanic/Latino; 4 Asian, non-Hispanic/Latino; 4 Hispanic/Latino; 1 Native Hawaiian or other Pacific Islander, non-Hispanic/Latino), 28 international. 247 applicants, 52% accepted, 47 enrolled. In 2016, 34 master's, 3 other advanced degrees awarded. *Degree requirements:* For master's, thesis, thesis exhibition (for fine arts programs); thesis project and document (for design/dynamic media program). *Entrance requirements:* For master's, portfolio, college transcripts, resume, statement of purpose, letters of reference, interview, 6 credits of art history taken prior to or during MFA program; for Postbaccalaureate Certificate, portfolio, college transcripts, resume, statement of purpose, letters of reference, interview. Additional exam requirements/ recommendations for international students: Required—TOEFL (minimum score 550 paper-based; 85 iBT); Recommended—IELTS (minimum score 6.5). *Application deadline:* For fall admission, 1/4 priority date for domestic and international students; for summer admission, 1/4 priority date for domestic and international students. Application fee: $90. Electronic applications accepted. *Expenses:* $780 per credit tuition. *Financial support:* In 2016–17, 57 students received support, including 33 teaching assistantships (averaging $2,160 per year); fellowships, research assistantships, career-related internships or fieldwork, scholarships/grants, tuition waivers (partial), unspecified assistantships, and 6-8 one-term adjunct co-teaching positions; 27 full-year general assistantships also available. Support available to part-time students. Financial award application deadline: 1/4; financial award applicants required to submit FAFSA. *Faculty research:* Painting and printmaking, sculpture, photography, film and video, dynamic media design. *Unit head:* Paul Paturzo, Dean of Graduate Studies, 617-879-7166, E-mail: pjpaturzo@massart.edu. *Application contact:* Lauren O'Neill, Assistant Director of Graduate Admissions, 617-879-7222, E-mail: gradadmissions@massart.edu. Website: http://www.massart.edu/Admissions/Graduate_Programs.html

**Massachusetts College of Art and Design,** Graduate Programs, Program in Design Innovation, Boston, MA 02115-5882. Offers M Des. *Faculty:* 4 full-time (0 women), 9 part-time/adjunct (4 women). *Students:* 9 full-time (3 women), 3 international. 42 applicants, 48% accepted, 9 enrolled. *Degree requirements:* For master's, thesis, thesis project. *Entrance requirements:* For master's, portfolio, college transcripts, resume, statement of purpose, letters of reference, interview. Additional exam requirements/recommendations for international students: Required—TOEFL (minimum score 550 paper-based; 85 iBT); Recommended—IELTS (minimum score 6.5). *Application deadline:* For fall admission, 1/4 priority date for domestic and international students. Application fee: $90. Electronic applications accepted. *Expenses:* $780 per credit. *Financial support:* In 2016–17, 9 students received support, including 1 research assistantship (averaging $2,160 per year), 4 teaching assistantships (averaging $2,160 per year); career-related internships or fieldwork, Federal Work-Study, scholarships/ grants, tuition waivers (partial), and unspecified assistantships also available. Support available to part-time students. Financial award application deadline: 1/4; financial award applicants required to submit FAFSA. *Unit head:* Paul Paturzo, Dean of Graduate Studies, 617-879-7166, E-mail: pjpaturzo@massart.edu. *Application contact:* Lauren O'Neill, Assistant Director of Graduate Admissions, 617-879-7222, E-mail: gradadmissions@massart.edu. Website: http://www.massart.edu/Admissions/Graduate_Programs.html

**Memphis College of Art,** Graduate Programs, Memphis, TN 38104-2764. Offers MA, MAT, MFA. *Accreditation:* NASAD. *Program availability:* Part-time, evening/ weekend. *Faculty:* 27 full-time (16 women), 25 part-time/adjunct (13 women). *Students:* 17 full-time (13 women), 23 part-time (14 women); includes 14 minority (10 Black or African American, non-Hispanic/Latino; 2 Hispanic/Latino; 2 Two or more races, non-Hispanic/Latino), 2 international. Average age 32. 39 applicants, 51% accepted, 13 enrolled. In 2016, 17 master's awarded. *Degree requirements:* For master's, thesis. *Entrance requirements:* For master's, portfolio, interview, resume, artist statement. Additional exam requirements/recommendations for international students: Required— TOEFL (minimum score 525 paper-based). *Application deadline:* For fall admission, 2/1 for domestic students, 3/1 for international students; for spring admission, 11/1 for domestic and international students. Application fee: $50. Electronic applications accepted. *Expenses:* Tuition: Full-time $32,400; part-time $3875 per course. *Required fees:* $700; $250 per course. Tuition and fees vary according to program. *Financial support:* In 2016–17, 40 students received support, including 8 teaching assistantships (averaging $3,000 per year); career-related internships or fieldwork, Federal Work-Study, scholarships/grants, unspecified assistantships, and teaching professional tuition discounts also available. Financial award application deadline: 8/1; financial award applicants required to submit FAFSA. *Unit head:* Haley Cafiero, Interim Vice President for Academic Affairs, 901-272-5100, Fax: 901-272-5104, E-mail: hcafiero@mca.edu. *Application contact:* Katey Henriksen, Director of Admissions, 901-272-5151, Fax: 901-272-5158, E-mail: khenriksen@mca.edu.

**Miami International University of Art & Design,** Program in Design and Media Management, Miami, FL 33132-1418. Offers MA.

**Millersville University of Pennsylvania,** College of Graduate Studies and Adult Learning, College of Arts, Humanities and Social Sciences, Department of Art and Design, Millersville, PA 17551-0302. Offers art education (M Ed). *Accreditation:* NASAD; NCATE. *Program availability:* Part-time. *Faculty:* 12 full-time (8 women). *Students:* 2 full-time (1 woman), 13 part-time (9 women); includes 2 minority (1 Asian, non-Hispanic/ Latino; 1 Hispanic/Latino). Average age 31. 5 applicants, 100% accepted, 3 enrolled. In 2016, 4 master's awarded. *Degree requirements:* For master's, comprehensive exam, thesis optional. *Entrance requirements:* For master's, teaching certificate (unless enrolled in post baccalaureate certificate at same time); portfolio (if not MU graduate). Additional exam requirements/recommendations for international students: Required— TOEFL (minimum score 600 paper-based), IELTS (minimum score 6). *Application deadline:* Applications are processed on a rolling basis. Application fee: $40. Electronic applications accepted. *Expenses:* $483 per credit resident tuition; $725 per credit non-resident tuition. *Financial support:* Unspecified assistantships available. Financial award application deadline: 3/15; financial award applicants required to submit FAFSA. *Faculty research:* Ceramics; representational painting; material investigations involving bronze casting, steel forming and fabrication, mold-making, wood working; art educator's professional learning, assessment in the arts, and postmodern; interactive design fundamentals, interdisciplinary design, interaction, visual storytelling and digital narrative forms and choice-based approaches to teaching art. *Unit head:* Deborah S. Sigel, Chair, 717-871-7249, Fax: 717-871-2004, E-mail: deborah.sigel@millersville.edu. *Application contact:* Dr. Victor S. DeSantis, Dean of College of Graduate Studies and Adult Learning/Associate Provost for Civic and Community Engagement, 717-871-7619, Fax: 717-871-7954, E-mail: victor.desantis@millersville.edu. Website: http://www.millersville.edu/art/

**Minneapolis College of Art and Design,** Program in Visual Studies, Minneapolis, MN 55404-4347. Offers animation (MFA); comic art (MFA); drawing (MFA); filmmaking (MFA); fine arts (MFA); furniture design (MFA); graphic design (MFA); illustration (MFA); interactive media (MFA); painting (MFA); photography (MFA); printmaking (MFA); sculpture (MFA). *Accreditation:* NASAD. *Program availability:* Part-time. *Degree requirements:* For master's, thesis, thesis exhibit. *Entrance requirements:* For master's, portfolio of visual artwork, resume, 3 letters of recommendation. Additional exam requirements/recommendations for international students: Required—TOEFL

(minimum score 550 paper-based; 79 iBT). Electronic applications accepted. *Faculty research:* Visual arts: animation, comic art, drawing, filmmaking, furniture design, graphic design, illustration, interactive media, painting, photography, printmaking, sculpture.

**The New School,** Parsons Paris, Paris, NY 10011, France. Offers MA. *Program availability:* Part-time. *Faculty:* 5 full-time (2 women), 43 part-time/adjunct (26 women). *Students:* 27 full-time (22 women), 1 (woman) part-time; includes 6 minority (1 Black or African American, non-Hispanic/Latino; 2 Asian, non-Hispanic/Latino; 1 Hispanic/Latino; 2 Two or more races, non-Hispanic/Latino), 16 international. Average age 27. 46 applicants, 96% accepted, 16 enrolled. In 2016, 5 master's awarded. *Entrance requirements:* For master's, transcripts, resume, statement of purpose. *Application deadline:* Applications are processed on a rolling basis. Application fee: $50. Electronic applications accepted. *Expenses:* Contact institution. *Financial support:* Scholarships/ grants available. Financial award applicants required to submit FAFSA. *Unit head:* Prof. Susan Taylor-Leduc, Dean, 33-176217661, E-mail: leducs@newschool.edu. *Application contact:* Mike Fakih, Director of Admissions, Parsons Paris, 33 176 21 76 67, E-mail: thinkparsonsparis@newschool.edu.

**The New School,** Parsons School of Design, Program in Design Studies, New York, NY 10011. Offers MFA. *Program availability:* Part-time. *Faculty:* 23 full-time (16 women), 18 part-time/adjunct (13 women). *Students:* 16 full-time (14 women), 1 (woman) part-time; includes 4 minority (3 Hispanic/Latino; 1 Two or more races, non-Hispanic/Latino), 10 international. Average age 26. 21 applicants, 81% accepted, 7 enrolled. In 2016, 19 master's awarded. *Degree requirements:* For master's, thesis. *Entrance requirements:* For master's, transcripts, resume, statement of purpose, recommendation letters, interview. Additional exam requirements/recommendations for international students: Required—TOEFL (minimum score 92 iBT), IELTS (minimum score 7), PTE (minimum score 63). *Application deadline:* For fall admission, 1/1 priority date for domestic and international students. Applications are processed on a rolling basis. Application fee: $50. Electronic applications accepted. *Expenses:* Contact institution. *Financial support:* Research assistantships, teaching assistantships, career-related internships or fieldwork, scholarships/grants, and unspecified assistantships available. Support available to part-time students. Financial award application deadline: 2/1; financial award applicants required to submit FAFSA. *Faculty research:* Social action and innovation, social media, social sciences, urban realm, history, theory, criticism, and curation of design. *Total annual research expenditures:* $106,000. *Unit head:* Susan Yelavich, Director, 212-229-8916 Ext. 3767, E-mail: yelavics@newschool.edu. *Application contact:* Courtney Malenius, Director of Graduate Admission, 212-229-5150 Ext. 4011, E-mail: thinkparsonsgrad@newschool.edu. Website: http://www.newschool.edu/parsons/

**The New School,** Parsons School of Design, Program in Transdisciplinary Design (TransDesign), New York, NY 10011. Offers MFA. *Program availability:* Part-time. *Faculty:* 41 full-time (18 women), 6 part-time/adjunct (5 women). *Students:* 37 full-time (28 women); includes 8 minority (1 American Indian or Alaska Native, non-Hispanic/ Latino; 3 Asian, non-Hispanic/Latino; 4 Hispanic/Latino), 21 international. Average age 28. 79 applicants, 71% accepted, 19 enrolled. In 2016, 16 master's awarded. *Degree requirements:* For master's, thesis. *Entrance requirements:* For master's, transcripts, resume, statement of purpose, recommendation letters, portfolio, interview. Additional exam requirements/recommendations for international students: Required—TOEFL (minimum score 91 iBT), IELTS (minimum score 7), PTE (minimum score 63). *Application deadline:* For fall admission, 1/1 priority date for domestic and international students. Applications are processed on a rolling basis. Application fee: $50. Electronic applications accepted. *Expenses:* Contact institution. *Financial support:* Research assistantships, teaching assistantships, career-related internships or fieldwork, scholarships/grants, and unspecified assistantships available. Support available to part-time students. Financial award application deadline: 2/1; financial award applicants required to submit FAFSA. *Faculty research:* Service design; social practice and innovation; sustainable design; systems; urban design/urban studies. *Unit head:* Lara Penin, Director, 212-229-8908 Ext. 4329, E-mail: peninl@newschool.edu. *Application contact:* Courtney Malenius, Director of Graduate Admissions, 212-229-5150 Ext. 4011, E-mail: maleniuc@newschool.edu. Website: http://www.newschool.edu/parsons

**New York Institute of Technology,** College of Arts and Sciences, Department of Digital Art and Design, Old Westbury, NY 11568-8000. Offers computer graphics (MFA), including animation, fine arts and technology, graphic design. *Program availability:* Part-time, evening/weekend. *Faculty:* 7 full-time (4 women), 6 part-time/adjunct (2 women). *Students:* 42 full-time (30 women), 12 part-time (6 women); includes 6 minority (3 Black or African American, non-Hispanic/Latino; 1 Asian, non-Hispanic/Latino; 2 Hispanic/ Latino), 42 international. Average age 27. 41 applicants, 68% accepted, 14 enrolled. In 2016, 31 master's awarded. *Degree requirements:* For master's, thesis. *Entrance requirements:* For master's, BFA or equivalent; minimum undergraduate GPA of 3.0; digital portfolio. Additional exam requirements/recommendations for international students: Required—TOEFL (minimum score 79 iBT), IELTS (minimum score 6). *Application deadline:* For fall admission, 6/1 for domestic and international students. Applications are processed on a rolling basis. Application fee: $50. Electronic applications accepted. *Expenses:* $1,215 per credit. *Financial support:* Career-related internships or fieldwork, Federal Work-Study, scholarships/grants, tuition waivers (full and partial), and unspecified assistantships available. Support available to part-time students. Financial award application deadline: 3/1; financial award applicants required to submit FAFSA. *Faculty research:* Graphic design, animation, art and technology, virtual reality, sculpture. *Unit head:* Terry Nauheim, Department Chair, 516-686-7881, Fax: 212-261-1742, E-mail: tnauheim@nyit.edu. *Application contact:* Alice Dolitsky, Director, Graduate Admissions, 516-686-7520, Fax: 516-686-1116, E-mail: nyitgrad@nyit.edu. Website: http://www.nyit.edu/arts_and_sciences/department_of_digital_art_design

**New York University,** Tisch School of the Arts, Department of Design for Stage and Film, New York, NY 10012-1019. Offers MFA. *Degree requirements:* For master's, thesis. *Entrance requirements:* For master's, interview, portfolio. Additional exam requirements/recommendations for international students: Required—TOEFL (minimum score 620 paper-based; 105 iBT), IELTS. Electronic applications accepted.

**North Carolina State University,** Graduate School, College of Design, Program in Art and Design, Raleigh, NC 27695. Offers MAD. *Degree requirements:* For master's, thesis optional. Electronic applications accepted.

**North Carolina State University,** Graduate School, College of Design, Program in Design, Raleigh, NC 27695. Offers PhD. *Degree requirements:* For doctorate, thesis/ dissertation. *Entrance requirements:* For doctorate, GRE. Electronic applications accepted. *Faculty research:* Design and cognition, children's environments, community design, ecological design, sustainable communities and urban spatial development.

**Northeastern University,** College of Arts, Media and Design, Boston, MA 02115-5096. Offers architecture (M Arch); game science and design (MS); information design and visualization (MFA); interdisciplinary arts (MFA); journalism (MA); music industry leadership (MS); studio art (MFA); sustainable building systems (MS); sustainable urban environments (M Des). *Faculty:* 142 full-time (55 women), 80 part-time/adjunct (34

*Applied Arts and Design—General*

women). *Students:* 239 full-time (147 women), 16 part-time (12 women). In 2016, 83 master's awarded. Application fee: $75. Electronic applications accepted. *Expenses:* $1,365 per credit. *Financial support:* Applicants required to submit FAFSA. *Unit head:* Dr. Elizabeth Hudson, Dean. *Application contact:* Jane Amidon, Associate Dean for Graduate Programs and Research, 617-373-4614, E-mail: gscamd@northeastern.edu. Website: http://www.northeastern.edu/camd/

**NSCAD University,** Program in Fine Arts, Halifax, NS B3J 3J6, Canada. Offers craft (MFA); design (M Des); fine and media arts (MFA). *Degree requirements:* For master's, thesis, exhibit. *Entrance requirements:* For master's, portfolio, at least 5 art history classes. Additional exam requirements/recommendations for international students: Required—Michigan English Language Assessment Battery (minimum score: 80), CanTEST (minimum score: 4.5), CAEL (minimum score: 70); Recommended—TOEFL (minimum score 575 paper-based; 90 iBT), IELTS (minimum score 6.5).

**Oklahoma State University,** College of Human Sciences, Department of Design, Housing and Merchandising, Stillwater, OK 74078. Offers MS, PhD. *Faculty:* 16 full-time (12 women). *Students:* 5 full-time (3 women), 7 part-time (all women); includes 1 minority (Black or African American, non-Hispanic/Latino), 6 international. Average age 27. 18 applicants, 39% accepted, 7 enrolled. In 2016, 1 master's awarded. *Degree requirements:* For master's, thesis (for some programs); for doctorate, comprehensive exam, thesis/dissertation. *Entrance requirements:* For master's and doctorate, GRE or GMAT. Additional exam requirements/recommendations for international students: Required—TOEFL (minimum score 550 paper-based; 79 iBT). *Application deadline:* For fall admission, 3/1 priority date for international students; for spring admission, 8/1 priority date for international students. Applications are processed on a rolling basis. Application fee: $40 ($75 for international students). Electronic applications accepted. *Expenses:* Tuition, state resident: full-time $3775; part-time $209.70 per credit hour. Tuition, nonresident: full-time $14,851; part-time $825.05 per credit hour. *Required fees:* $2027; $112.60 per credit hour. Tuition and fees vary according to campus/location. *Financial support:* In 2016–17, 6 research assistantships (averaging $5,203 per year), 6 teaching assistantships (averaging $9,894 per year) were awarded; career-related internships or fieldwork, Federal Work-Study, scholarships/grants, health care benefits, tuition waivers (partial), and unspecified assistantships also available. Support available to part-time students. Financial award application deadline: 3/1; financial award applicants required to submit FAFSA. *Faculty research:* Environmental sciences design, housing and merchandising; creativity and physical environment; product development, production and evaluation; experimental learning and critical thinking; technology strategies and assessment; customer expectation and satisfaction. *Unit head:* Dr. Jane Swinney, Interim Department Head, 405-744-6552, Fax: 405-744-6910, E-mail: jane.swinney@okstate.edu. *Application contact:* Dr. Christine Johnson, Associate Dean for Research and Graduate Studies, 405-744-1744, E-mail: christine.johnson@okstate.edu. Website: http://humansciences.okstate.edu/dhm/

**Pacific Northwest College of Art,** Program in Applied Craft and Design, Portland, OR 97209. Offers MFA. Program offered in collaboration with Oregon College of Art & Craft. *Accreditation:* NASAD. *Entrance requirements:* For master's, resume, 2 letters of recommendation, portfolio.

**Pacific Northwest College of Art,** Program in Collaborative Design, Portland, OR 97209. Offers MFA.

**Pratt Institute,** School of Art, Brooklyn, NY 11205-3899. Offers MFA, MPS, MS, Adv C, MA/MFA, MS/MFA, MS/MS. *Accreditation:* NASAD (one or more programs are accredited). *Program availability:* Part-time. *Faculty:* 22 full-time (13 women), 141 part-time/adjunct (68 women). *Students:* 346 full-time (289 women), 8 part-time (6 women); includes 81 minority (26 Black or African American, non-Hispanic/Latino; 1 American Indian or Alaska Native, non-Hispanic/Latino; 16 Asian, non-Hispanic/Latino; 30 Hispanic/Latino; 8 Two or more races, non-Hispanic/Latino), 146 international. Average age 27. 858 applicants, 47% accepted, 144 enrolled. In 2016, 170 master's awarded. *Degree requirements:* For master's, thesis. *Entrance requirements:* For master's, portfolio. Additional exam requirements/recommendations for international students: Required—TOEFL (minimum score 550 paper-based; 79 iBT). *Application deadline:* For fall admission, 1/5 for domestic and international students; for spring admission, 10/1 for domestic and international students. Application fee: $50 ($90 for international students). Electronic applications accepted. *Expenses:* $29,646 full-time tuition, $1,938 fees. *Financial support:* Career-related internships or fieldwork, Federal Work-Study, institutionally sponsored loans, scholarships/grants, health care benefits, and unspecified assistantships available. Support available to part-time students. Financial award application deadline: 2/1; financial award applicants required to submit FAFSA. *Faculty research:* Painting, drawing, photography, sculpture, integrated practices and printmaking; art therapy; four-dimensional design; digital arts; art and design education. *Unit head:* Gerry Snyder, Dean, 718-636-3619, E-mail: gsnyder@pratt.edu. *Application contact:* Natalie Capannelli, Director of Graduate Admissions, 718-636-3551, Fax: 718-399-4242, E-mail: ncapanne@pratt.edu.
Website: https://www.pratt.edu/academics/school-of-art/graduate-school-of-art/
See Display on page 156 and Close-Up on page 209.

**Pratt Institute,** School of Design, Brooklyn, NY 11205-3899. Offers MFA, MID, MS. *Program availability:* Part-time. *Faculty:* 12 full-time (5 women), 136 part-time/adjunct (56 women). *Students:* 367 full-time (278 women), 7 part-time (6 women); includes 55 minority (8 Black or African American, non-Hispanic/Latino; 27 Asian, non-Hispanic/Latino; 17 Hispanic/Latino; 1 Native Hawaiian or other Pacific Islander, non-Hispanic/Latino; 2 Two or more races, non-Hispanic/Latino), 233 international. Average age 26. 947 applicants, 45% accepted, 133 enrolled. In 2016, 151 master's awarded. *Degree requirements:* For master's, thesis. *Entrance requirements:* For master's, letters of recommendation, portfolio. Additional exam requirements/recommendations for international students: Required—TOEFL (minimum score 575 paper-based; 90 iBT). *Application deadline:* For fall admission, 1/5 for domestic and international students; for spring admission, 10/1 for domestic and international students. Application fee: $50 ($90 for international students). Electronic applications accepted. *Expenses:* $29,646 full-time tuition, $1,938 fees. *Financial support:* Career-related internships or fieldwork, Federal Work-Study, institutionally sponsored loans, scholarships/grants, health care benefits, and unspecified assistantships available. Support available to part-time students. Financial award application deadline: 2/1; financial award applicants required to submit FAFSA. *Unit head:* Anita Cooney, Dean, School of Design, 718-687-5744, Fax: 718-636-3410, E-mail: acooney@pratt.edu. *Application contact:* Natalie Capannelli, Director of Graduate Admissions, 718-636-3551, Fax: 718-636-3670, E-mail: ncapanne@pratt.edu.
Website: https://www.pratt.edu/academics/school-of-design/graduate-school-of-design/
See Display on this page and Close-Up on page 105.

**Pratt Institute,** School of Liberal Arts and Sciences, History of Art and Design Program, Brooklyn, NY 11205-3899. Offers MS, MS/MFA, MS/MS. *Accreditation:* NASAD. *Program availability:* Part-time. *Faculty:* 7 full-time (6 women), 35 part-time/adjunct (22 women). *Students:* 34 full-time (31 women), 1 (woman) part-time; includes 7 minority (1 American Indian or Alaska Native, non-Hispanic/Latino; 1 Asian, non-

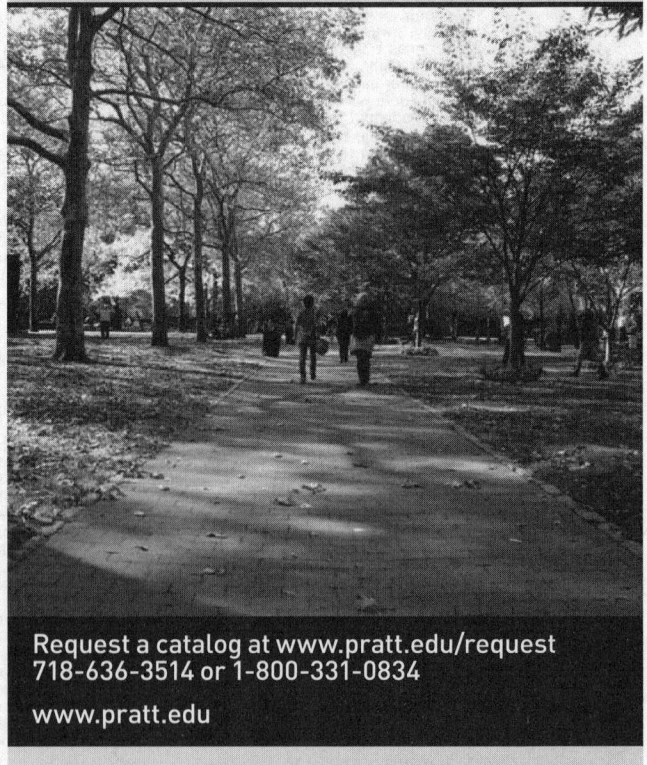

Hispanic/Latino; 3 Hispanic/Latino; 2 Two or more races, non-Hispanic/Latino), 4 international. Average age 27. 30 applicants, 83% accepted, 6 enrolled. In 2016, 17 master's awarded. *Degree requirements:* For master's, one foreign language, thesis. *Entrance requirements:* For master's, GRE General Test, letters of recommendation, writing sample, portfolio. Additional exam requirements/recommendations for international students: Required—TOEFL (minimum score 600 paper-based; 100 iBT). *Application deadline:* For fall admission, 1/5 for domestic and international students; for spring admission, 10/1 for domestic and international students. Application fee: $50 ($90 for international students). Electronic applications accepted. *Expenses:* $29,646 full-time tuition, $1,938 fees. *Financial support:* Career-related internships or fieldwork, Federal Work-Study, institutionally sponsored loans, scholarships/grants, health care benefits, and unspecified assistantships available. Support available to part-time students. Financial award application deadline: 2/1; financial award applicants required to submit CSS PROFILE or FAFSA. *Faculty research:* Conservation techniques, women artists from previous centuries, art of sixteenth-century Veneto, design history, nineteenth-century Germany. *Unit head:* Gayle Rodda Kurtz, Chairperson, 718-636-3532, Fax: 718-687-5925, E-mail: gkurtz@pratt.edu. *Application contact:* Natalie Capannelli, Director of Graduate Admissions, 718-636-3551, Fax: 718-399-4242, E-mail: ncapanne@pratt.edu. Website: https://www.pratt.edu/academics/liberal-arts-and-sciences/history-of-art-design-grad/

**See Display on page 746 and Close-Up on page 769.**

**Purdue University,** Graduate School, College of Liberal Arts, Department of Art and Design, West Lafayette, IN 47907. Offers art education (MA, PhD); industrial design (MFA); integrated studio arts (MFA); interior design (MFA); photography (MFA); visual communications design (MFA). *Accreditation:* NASAD; NAST. *Program availability:* Part-time. *Students:* 20 full-time (14 women), 1 part-time (0 women); includes 1 minority (Two or more races, non-Hispanic/Latino), 16 international. Average age 26. 97 applicants, 26% accepted, 10 enrolled. In 2016, 6 master's awarded. *Degree requirements:* For master's, terminal exhibit, project, or thesis. *Entrance requirements:* For master's, GRE General Test (for art education), minimum undergraduate GPA of 3.0 or equivalent; 9 undergraduate hours in an art or design history; BA in art (for MA in art education); for doctorate, GRE General Test (minimum scores 600 in verbal and 1000 total), master's degree in art education or art with teaching certification; 3 years of teaching experience at the K-12 level. Additional exam requirements/recommendations for international students: Required—TOEFL (minimum score 550 paper-based; 77 iBT). *Application deadline:* For fall admission, 2/1 for domestic students; 2/1 priority date for international students. Applications are processed on a rolling basis. Application fee: $60 ($75 for international students). Electronic applications accepted. *Financial support:* Teaching assistantships with tuition reimbursements and career-related internships or fieldwork available. Support available to part-time students. Financial award applicants required to submit FAFSA. *Faculty research:* Design, fine arts, photography, acting, directing, theatre technology. *Unit head:* Harry T. Bulow, Head of the Graduate Program, 765-494-3056, E-mail: hbulow@purdue.edu. *Application contact:* Sara J. Unser, Graduate Contact, 765-494-8662, E-mail: sunser@purdue.edu. Website: https://www.cla.purdue.edu/vpa/ad/

**Rhode Island School of Design,** Division of Architecture and Design, Department of Furniture Design, Providence, RI 02903-2784. Offers MFA. *Faculty:* 9 full-time (3 women), 17 part-time/adjunct (6 women). *Students:* 22 full-time (12 women); includes 6 minority (5 Asian, non-Hispanic/Latino; 1 Hispanic/Latino), 8 international. Average age 28. 28 applicants, 54% accepted, 9 enrolled. In 2016, 8 master's awarded. *Degree requirements:* For master's, thesis, exhibition. *Entrance requirements:* For master's, portfolio, statement of purpose, 3 letters of recommendation. Additional exam requirements/recommendations for international students: Required—TOEFL (minimum score 580 paper-based; 93 iBT). *Application deadline:* For fall admission, 2/1 for domestic and international students. Application fee: $60. Electronic applications accepted. *Expenses:* Tuition: Full-time $46,800. *Required fees:* $310. *Financial support:* Fellowships, research assistantships, teaching assistantships, Federal Work-Study, scholarships/grants, and unspecified assistantships available. Financial award application deadline: 2/15; financial award applicants required to submit FAFSA. *Unit head:* John Dunnigan, Department Head, 401-454-6384, Fax: 401-454-6566, E-mail: jdunniga@risd.edu. *Application contact:* Molly Pettengil, Assistant Director for Graduate Recruitment, 401-454-6312, Fax: 401-454-6309, E-mail: mpetteng@risd.edu. Website: http://www.risd.edu/academics/furniture-design/

**Rhode Island School of Design,** Graduate Studies, Providence, RI 02903-2784. Offers MA, MAT, MFA. *Accreditation:* NASAD (one or more programs are accredited). *Faculty:* 14 full-time (5 women), 23 part-time/adjunct (9 women). *Students:* 49 full-time (40 women); includes 7 minority (5 Asian, non-Hispanic/Latino; 1 Hispanic/Latino; 1 Two or more races, non-Hispanic/Latino), 18 international. Average age 27. 182 applicants, 32% accepted, 32 enrolled. In 2016, 31 master's awarded. *Degree requirements:* For master's, thesis, exhibition. *Entrance requirements:* For master's, portfolio, statement of purpose, three letters of recommendation. Additional exam requirements/recommendations for international students: Required—TOEFL (minimum score 580 paper-based; 93 iBT). *Application deadline:* For fall admission, 2/1 for domestic and international students. Application fee: $60. Electronic applications accepted. *Expenses:* Tuition: Full-time $46,800. *Required fees:* $310. *Financial support:* Fellowships, research assistantships, teaching assistantships, Federal Work-Study, scholarships/grants, and unspecified assistantships available. Financial award application deadline: 2/15; financial award applicants required to submit FAFSA. Website: http://www.risd.edu/academics/graduate-studies/

**Rutgers University–New Brunswick,** Mason Gross School of the Arts, Theater Department, New Brunswick, NJ 08901. Offers acting (MFA); design (MFA); playwriting (MFA); stage management (MFA); technical direction (MFA). *Degree requirements:* For master's, thesis (for some programs), performance project. *Entrance requirements:* For master's, audition, interview, portfolio. Additional exam requirements/recommendations for international students: Required—TOEFL (minimum score 550 paper-based), IELTS (minimum score 7). Electronic applications accepted. *Faculty research:* Faculty of working professional.

**Samford University,** School of the Arts, Birmingham, AL 35229. Offers design studies (MS); music (MM); music education (MME). MME program offered in traditional, fifth year non-traditional, and national board cohort formats. *Accreditation:* NASM. *Program availability:* Part-time, evening/weekend, online learning. *Faculty:* 9 full-time (4 women), 3 part-time/adjunct (1 woman). *Students:* 11 full-time (5 women); includes 4 minority (all Black or African American, non-Hispanic/Latino), 1 international. Average age 30. 9 applicants, 100% accepted, 5 enrolled. In 2016, 7 master's awarded. Terminal master's awarded for partial completion of doctoral program. *Degree requirements:* For master's, comprehensive exam, recital. *Entrance requirements:* For master's, audition. Additional exam requirements/recommendations for international students: Required—TOEFL (minimum score 90 iBT). *Application deadline:* For fall admission, 11/15 for domestic and international students; for spring admission, 4/15 for domestic and international students; for summer admission, 8/1 for domestic and international students. Applications are processed on a rolling basis. Application fee: $35. Electronic applications accepted. *Expenses:* Tuition: Full-time $18,530; part-time $789 per credit hour. *Required fees:* $610. Tuition and fees vary according to course load, degree level,

program and student level. *Financial support:* In 2016–17, 10 students received support. Federal Work-Study, scholarships/grants, and unspecified assistantships available. Financial award application deadline: 3/1; financial award applicants required to submit FAFSA. *Unit head:* Dr. Joseph Hopkin, Dean of the School of the Arts/Professor, 205-726-2778, Fax: 205-726-2615, E-mail: jhopkins@samford.edu. *Application contact:* Dr. Demondrae L. Thurman, Director of Graduate Studies/Professor of Music, 205-726-2389, Fax: 205-726-2615, E-mail: dthurman@samford.edu. Website: http://www.samford.edu/arts

**San Diego State University,** Graduate and Research Affairs, College of Professional Studies and Fine Arts, School of Art, Design and Art History, San Diego, CA 92182. Offers art history (MA); studio arts (MA, MFA), including applied design, environmental design, graphic design, interior design, painting and printmaking, sculpture. *Accreditation:* NASAD (one or more programs are accredited). *Degree requirements:* For master's, variable foreign language requirement, thesis. *Entrance requirements:* For master's, GRE General Test, bachelor's degree in related field, slide portfolio, typed slide information sheet, 2 letters of recommendation. Additional exam requirements/recommendations for international students: Required—TOEFL. Electronic applications accepted.

**San Francisco State University,** Division of Graduate Studies, College of Liberal and Creative Arts, School of Design, San Francisco, CA 94132-1722. Offers industrial arts (MA). *Expenses:* Tuition, state resident: full-time $6738. Tuition, nonresident: full-time $15,666. *Required fees:* $1012. Tuition and fees vary according to degree level and program. *Unit head:* Dr. Christina Sabee, Acting Director, 415-338-2211, Fax: 415-338-7770, E-mail: design@sfsu.edu. *Application contact:* Prof. Hsiao-Yun Chu, Graduate Coordinator, 415-338-2430, Fax: 415-338-7770, E-mail: hychu@sfsu.edu. Website: http://design.sfsu.edu/

**Savannah College of Art and Design,** Graduate School, Program in Service Design, Savannah, GA 31402-3146. Offers MFA. *Program availability:* Part-time. *Faculty:* 2 full-time (1 woman). *Students:* 11 full-time (7 women), 4 part-time (3 women); includes 2 minority (1 Black or African American, non-Hispanic/Latino; 1 Asian, non-Hispanic/Latino), 9 international. Average age 28. 31 applicants, 65% accepted, 3 enrolled. In 2016, 4 master's awarded. *Degree requirements:* For master's, thesis. *Entrance requirements:* For master's, GRE (recommended), portfolio (submitted in digital format), audition or writing submission, resume, statement of purpose, two letters of recommendation. Additional exam requirements/recommendations for international students: Required—TOEFL (minimum score 550 paper-based, 85 iBT) or IELTS (minimum score 6.5). *Application deadline:* For fall admission, 4/1 for domestic and international students. Applications are processed on a rolling basis. Application fee: $40. Electronic applications accepted. *Expenses:* Tuition: Full-time $36,045. Tuition and fees vary according to course load. *Financial support:* Career-related internships or fieldwork, Federal Work-Study, and scholarships/grants available. Financial award application deadline: 4/1; financial award applicants required to submit FAFSA. *Unit head:* Xenia Viladas, Academic Program Coordinator. *Application contact:* Jenny Jaquillard, Executive Director of Admissions, Recruitment and Events, 912-525-5100, Fax: 912-525-5985, E-mail: admission@scad.edu. Website: http://www.scad.edu/academics/programs/service-design

**School of the Art Institute of Chicago,** Graduate Division, Department of Architecture, Interior Architecture, and Designed Objects, Program in Designed Objects, Chicago, IL 60603-3103. Offers M Des. *Entrance requirements:* Additional exam requirements/recommendations for international students: Required—TOEFL, IELTS.

**School of the Art Institute of Chicago,** Graduate Division, Department of Architecture, Interior Architecture, and Designed Objects, Program in Design for Emerging Technologies, Chicago, IL 60603-3103. Offers MFA. *Entrance requirements:* Additional exam requirements/recommendations for international students: Required—TOEFL, IELTS.

**School of the Art Institute of Chicago,** Graduate Division, Department of Architecture, Interior Architecture, and Designed Objects, Program in Interior Architecture, Chicago, IL 60603-3103. Offers M Arc. *Entrance requirements:* Additional exam requirements/recommendations for international students: Required—TOEFL, IELTS.

**School of Visual Arts,** Graduate Programs, Design Department, New York, NY 10010-3994. Offers MFA. *Accreditation:* NASAD. *Degree requirements:* For master's, thesis, 60 credits, including all required courses; minimum cumulative GPA of 3.0; residency of two academic years. *Entrance requirements:* For master's, portfolio that reflects wide range of design work and fluency in type and typography. Additional exam requirements/recommendations for international students: Required—TOEFL (minimum score 550 paper-based; 79 iBT). *Expenses:* Contact institution. *Faculty research:* Design, graphic design, multimedia.

**School of Visual Arts,** Graduate Programs, Design for Social Innovation Department, New York, NY 10010-3994. Offers MFA. *Degree requirements:* For master's, thesis, 60 credits, including all required courses, with minimum cumulative GPA of 3.0; residency of two academic years. *Entrance requirements:* For master's, resume/curriculum vitae; statement of purpose; portfolio; personal interview. Additional exam requirements/recommendations for international students: Required—TOEFL (minimum score 550 paper-based; 79 iBT). Electronic applications accepted. *Expenses:* Contact institution.

**School of Visual Arts,** Graduate Programs, Products of Design Department, New York, NY 10010-3994. Offers MFA. *Degree requirements:* For master's, thesis, 60 credits, including all required courses; minimum cumulative GPA 3.0; residency of two academic years. *Entrance requirements:* For master's, portfolio. Additional exam requirements/recommendations for international students: Required—TOEFL (minimum score 550 paper-based; 79 iBT). Electronic applications accepted.

**School of Visual Arts,** Graduate Programs, Program in Branding, New York, NY 10010-3994. Offers MPS. *Degree requirements:* For master's, thesis, 36 credits, including all required courses; minimum cumulative GPA of 3.0; residency of one academic year. *Entrance requirements:* For master's, writing sample, statement of purpose. Additional exam requirements/recommendations for international students: Required—TOEFL (minimum score 550 paper-based; 79 iBT). *Expenses:* Contact institution.

**School of Visual Arts,** Graduate Programs, Program in Design Research, Writing and Criticism, New York, NY 10010-3994. Offers MA. *Degree requirements:* For master's, thesis, 64 credits, including all required courses, with minimum cumulative GPA of 3.0; residency of two academic years. *Entrance requirements:* For master's, short essay critiquing design object, event or concept; writing sample of published or unpublished writing between 1,000 and 2,000 words; personal interview. Additional exam requirements/recommendations for international students: Required—TOEFL (minimum score 550 paper-based; 79 iBT). Electronic applications accepted.

**Southern Illinois University Carbondale,** Graduate School, College of Liberal Arts, School of Art and Design, Carbondale, IL 62901-4701. Offers drawing (MFA); fiber/weaving (MFA); glass (MFA); metalsmithing/blacksmithing (MFA); painting (MFA). *Accreditation:* NASAD. *Degree requirements:* For master's, thesis or alternative.

## Applied Arts and Design—General

*Entrance requirements:* For master's, minimum GPA of 2.7, portfolio, slides. Additional exam requirements/recommendations for international students: Required—TOEFL. *Faculty research:* Prints/woodcuts, foundry, watercolor.

**Stanford University,** School of Engineering, Department of Civil and Environmental Engineering, Stanford, CA 94305-2004. Offers atmosphere and energy (MS, PhD); construction (MS), including construction engineering and management, design-construction integration, sustainable design and construction; environmental engineering and science (MS, PhD, Eng); environmental fluid mechanics and hydrology (PhD); geomechanics (MS); structural engineering (MS). Terminal master's awarded for partial completion of doctoral program. *Degree requirements:* For doctorate; thesis/dissertation, qualifying exam; for Eng, thesis. *Entrance requirements:* For master's, doctorate, and Eng, GRE General Test. Additional exam requirements/recommendations for international students: Required—TOEFL. Electronic applications accepted. *Expenses: Tuition:* Full-time $47,331. *Required fees:* $609.

**Stanford University,** School of Humanities and Sciences, Department of Art and Art History, Stanford, CA 94305-2004. Offers art history (PhD); art practice (MFA); design (MFA); documentary film and video (MFA); MS/MFA. *Degree requirements:* For master's, thesis (for some programs), faculty reviews; for doctorate, 2 foreign languages, thesis/dissertation. *Entrance requirements:* For master's and doctorate, GRE General Test. Additional exam requirements/recommendations for international students: Required—TOEFL. Electronic applications accepted. *Expenses: Tuition:* Full-time $47,331. *Required fees:* $609.

**Stephen F. Austin State University,** Graduate School, College of Fine Arts, School of Art, Nacogdoches, TX 75962. Offers art (MA); design (MFA); drawing (MFA); painting (MFA); sculpture (MFA). *Accreditation:* NASAD. *Program availability:* Part-time. *Degree requirements:* For master's, comprehensive exam, thesis, exhibit. *Entrance requirements:* For master's, GRE General Test, portfolio. Additional exam requirements/recommendations for international students: Required—TOEFL. *Faculty research:* Printmaking, jewelry, photography, ceramics, art history.

**Suffolk University,** New England School of Art and Design, Boston, MA 02108-2770. Offers graphic design (MA); interior architecture (MA). *Program availability:* Part-time, evening/weekend. *Faculty:* 12 full-time (8 women), 20 part-time/adjunct (12 women). *Students:* 37 full-time (30 women), 25 part-time (23 women); includes 11 minority (1 Black or African American, non-Hispanic/Latino; 7 Asian, non-Hispanic/Latino; 3 Hispanic/Latino), 19 international. Average age 29. 63 applicants, 73% accepted, 20 enrolled. In 2016, 29 master's awarded. *Entrance requirements:* For master's, GRE (for MFA), art portfolio, interview, 2 letters of recommendation, resume; letter of intent (for MFA). Additional exam requirements/recommendations for international students: Required—TOEFL (minimum score 550 paper-based; 80 iBT). *Application deadline:* For fall admission, 3/15 priority date for domestic and international students; for spring admission, 10/15 priority date for domestic and international students. Applications are processed on a rolling basis. Application fee: $50. Electronic applications accepted. *Expenses:* $24,436 per year full-time tuition, $1,144 per credit hour part-time tuition, $52 per year student activity fee, $180 per course studio fee. *Financial support:* In 2016–17, 44 students received support, including 40 fellowships (averaging $6,900 per year); career-related internships or fieldwork, Federal Work-Study, institutionally sponsored loans, scholarships/grants, and unspecified assistantships also available. Financial award application deadline: 4/1; financial award applicants required to submit FAFSA. *Faculty research:* Sustainable design, lighting and technology, design education, environmental graphic design, designing for the non-profit sector. *Unit head:* Audrey Goldstein, Department Chair, 617-997-4290, E-mail: agoldstein@suffolk.edu. *Application contact:* Mara Marzocchi, Associate Director of Graduate Admissions, 617-573-8302, Fax: 617-305-1733, E-mail: grad.admission@suffolk.edu. Website: http://www.suffolk.edu/nesad/

**Syracuse University,** College of Visual and Performing Arts, MFA Program in Art Video, Syracuse, NY 13244. Offers MFA. *Accreditation:* NASAD. *Program availability:* Part-time, online learning. *Degree requirements:* For master's, thesis or alternative. *Entrance requirements:* For master's, portfolio, artist statement, three letters of recommendation, transcripts, personal statement/essay, resume. Additional exam requirements/recommendations for international students: Required—TOEFL (minimum score 100 iBT), IELTS. *Application deadline:* For fall admission, 2/1 priority date for domestic and international students. Application fee: $75. Electronic applications accepted. *Expenses: Tuition:* Full-time $25,974; part-time $1443 per credit hour. *Required fees:* $802; $50 per course. Tuition and fees vary according to course load and program. *Financial support:* Fellowships with full tuition reimbursements, teaching assistantships with tuition reimbursements, and tuition waivers available. Financial award application deadline: 1/1; financial award applicants required to submit FAFSA. *Faculty research:* Aesthetic possibilities of subject, genre, and media technologies from personal points of view. *Unit head:* Prof. Tom Sherman, Department of Transmedia, 315-443-1202, E-mail: twsherma@syr.edu. *Application contact:* Therese West, Information Contact, 315-443-0137, E-mail: admissg@syr.edu.

**Texas State University,** The Graduate College, College of Fine Arts and Communication, Program in Theatre Arts, San Marcos, TX 78666. Offers design (MFA); directing (MFA); dramatic writing (MFA); theatre history, dramatic criticism and dramaturgy (MA). *Program availability:* Part-time, evening/weekend. *Faculty:* 17 full-time (9 women), 2 part-time/adjunct. *Students:* 18 full-time (8 women), 1 (woman) part-time; includes 3 minority (2 Black or African American, non-Hispanic/Latino; 1 Two or more races, non-Hispanic/Latino). Average age 33. 25 applicants, 44% accepted, 8 enrolled. In 2016, 11 master's awarded. *Degree requirements:* For master's, comprehensive exam, thesis (for some programs). *Entrance requirements:* For master's, GRE General Test (minimum preferred score of 300), baccalaureate degree from regionally-accredited institution with minimum GPA of 2.75 in last 60 hours of undergraduate course work, 2 letters of recommendation, statement of purpose, curriculum vitae/resume; writing sample (for playwriting applicants only); interview (for directing applicants only). Additional exam requirements/recommendations for international students: Required—TOEFL (minimum score 550 paper-based; 78 iBT), IELTS (minimum score 6.5). *Application deadline:* For fall admission, 3/15 for domestic and international students. Applications are processed on a rolling basis. Application fee: $40 ($90 for international students). Electronic applications accepted. *Expenses:* $4,851 per semester. *Financial support:* In 2016–17, 18 teaching assistantships (averaging $13,246 per year) were awarded; research assistantships, Federal Work-Study, institutionally sponsored loans, scholarships/grants, and unspecified assistantships also available. Support available to part-time students. Financial award application deadline: 3/1; financial award applicants required to submit FAFSA. *Unit head:* Dr. Sandra Mayo, Graduate Advisor, 512-245-7889, Fax: 512-245-8440, E-mail: th_gradadvisor@txstate.edu. *Application contact:* Dr. Andrea Golato, Dean of Graduate School, 512-245-2581, Fax: 512-245-8365, E-mail: gradcollege@txstate.edu.
Website: http://www.theatreanddance.txstate.edu/

**University of Alberta,** Faculty of Graduate Studies and Research, Department of Art and Design, Edmonton, AB T6G 2E1, Canada. Offers drawing (MFA); history of art, design, and visual culture (MA); industrial design (M Des); painting (MFA); printmaking (MFA); sculpture (MFA); visual communication design (M Des). *Degree requirements:*

For master's, thesis. *Entrance requirements:* For master's, portfolio (MFA and MDES). Additional exam requirements/recommendations for international students: Required—TOEFL (minimum score 550 paper-based).

**University of Baltimore,** Yale Gordon College of Arts and Sciences, Program in Integrated Design, Baltimore, MD 21201-5779. Offers MFA. *Program availability:* Part-time, evening/weekend. *Entrance requirements:* Additional exam requirements/recommendations for international students: Required—TOEFL (minimum score 550 paper-based). Electronic applications accepted. *Expenses:* Contact institution. *Faculty research:* Information and graphics design, economics, hypermedia communications.

**University of Bridgeport,** Shintaro Akatsu School of Design, Bridgeport, CT 06604. Offers design management (MPS). *Program availability:* Part-time, evening/weekend. *Entrance requirements:* Additional exam requirements/recommendations for international students: Recommended—TOEFL (minimum score 550 paper-based; 80 iBT), IELTS (minimum score 6.5). Electronic applications accepted.

**University of California, Berkeley,** UC Berkeley Extension, Certificate Programs in Art and Design, Berkeley, CA 94720-1500. Offers interior design and interior architecture (Certificate); landscape architecture (Certificate); visual arts (Postbaccalaureate Certificate).

**University of California, Los Angeles,** Graduate Division, School of the Arts and Architecture, Department of Design Media Arts, Los Angeles, CA 90095. Offers MFA. *Degree requirements:* For master's, comprehensive exam. *Entrance requirements:* For master's, bachelor's degree; minimum undergraduate GPA of 3.0 (or its equivalent if letter grade system not used); portfolio. Additional exam requirements/recommendations for international students: Required—TOEFL. Electronic applications accepted. *Expenses:* Contact institution.

**University of Central Oklahoma,** The Jackson College of Graduate Studies, College of Fine Arts and Design, Department of Design and Interior Design, Edmond, OK 73034-5209. Offers design (MFA). *Accreditation:* NASAD. *Program availability:* Part-time, online learning. *Degree requirements:* For master's, thesis. *Entrance requirements:* For master's, essay, portfolio. Additional exam requirements/recommendations for international students: Required—TOEFL (minimum score 550 paper-based; 79 iBT), IELTS (minimum score 6.5). Electronic applications accepted. *Faculty research:* Design pedagogy in foundations curriculum, social media in design education, typography and its evolution in digital media, cross-cultural design, historical preservation for adaptive reuse.

**University of Cincinnati,** Graduate School, College of Design, Architecture, Art, and Planning, School of Design, Cincinnati, OH 45221. Offers fashion design (M Des); graphic design (M Des); industrial design (M Des); interaction design (M Des); product development (M Des). *Accreditation:* NASAD. *Degree requirements:* For master's, thesis. *Entrance requirements:* For master's, undergraduate degree in design or related field, 2 years of work experience in design or related field. Additional exam requirements/recommendations for international students: Required—TOEFL. Electronic applications accepted. *Expenses: Tuition, area resident:* Full-time $12,790; part-time $389 per credit hour. Tuition, state resident: full-time $13,290; part-time $419 per credit hour. Tuition, nonresident: full-time $24,532; part-time $976 per credit hour. *International tuition:* $24,832 full-time. *Required fees:* $3958; $140 per credit hour. Tuition and fees vary according to course load, degree level, program and reciprocity agreements. *Faculty research:* Design theory, interdisciplinary design topics.

**University of Connecticut,** Graduate School, School of Fine Arts, Department of Dramatic Arts, Storrs, CT 06269. Offers acting (MA, MFA); design (MA, MFA); puppetry (MA, MFA); technical direction (MA, MFA). *Degree requirements:* For master's, comprehensive exam. *Entrance requirements:* Additional exam requirements/recommendations for international students: Required—TOEFL (minimum score 550 paper-based). Electronic applications accepted.

**University of Delaware,** College of Arts and Sciences, Department of Art, Newark, DE 19716. Offers MA, MFA. *Degree requirements:* For master's, exposition paper final exhibition. *Entrance requirements:* For master's, portfolio of creative work. Electronic applications accepted. *Faculty research:* Painting, printmaking, ceramics, photography, sculpture.

**University of Illinois at Chicago,** College of Architecture, Design and the Arts, School of Design, Chicago, IL 60607-7128. Offers graphic design (M Des); industrial design (M Des). *Accreditation:* NASAD (one or more programs are accredited). *Degree requirements:* For master's, thesis, exhibit. *Entrance requirements:* For master's, MAT, portfolio. Additional exam requirements/recommendations for international students: Required—TOEFL. Electronic applications accepted. *Expenses:* Contact institution.

**University of Illinois at Urbana–Champaign,** Graduate College, College of Fine and Applied Arts, School of Art and Design, Champaign, IL 61820. Offers Ed M, MA, MFA, PhD. *Accreditation:* NASAD. *Entrance requirements:* For master's, minimum GPA of 3.0.

**The University of Kansas,** Graduate Studies, School of Architecture, Design, and Planning, Department of Design, Lawrence, KS 66045. Offers design management (MA); interaction design (MA). *Accreditation:* NASAD. *Program availability:* Part-time. *Students:* 4 full-time (1 woman), 20 part-time (13 women); includes 4 minority (1 Black or African American, non-Hispanic/Latino; 1 Asian, non-Hispanic/Latino; 2 Two or more races, non-Hispanic/Latino), 5 international. Average age 33. 14 applicants, 86% accepted, 6 enrolled. In 2016, 10 master's awarded. *Entrance requirements:* For master's, GRE (preferred), curriculum vitae or resume; statement of design philosophy and approach; official transcripts; three recommendations; portfolio of design work or, if previous degree was not in design-related discipline, samples of written work or other creative artifacts produced. Additional exam requirements/recommendations for international students: Required—TOEFL, IELTS. *Application deadline:* For fall admission, 4/15 priority date for domestic and international students; for spring admission, 11/15 priority date for domestic and international students. Application fee: $65 ($85 for international students). Electronic applications accepted. *Financial support:* Fellowships, teaching assistantships, Federal Work-Study, scholarships/grants, and unspecified assistantships available. Financial award application deadline: 2/1; financial award applicants required to submit FAFSA. *Faculty research:* Interaction design, design management, photography, graphic design, industrial design. *Unit head:* Andrea Herstowski, Chair, 785-864-2956, E-mail: hestow@ku.edu. *Application contact:* Gera Elliott, Graduate Admission Coordinator, 785-864-3167, E-mail: archku@ku.edu. Website: http://design.ku.edu/

**University of Kentucky,** Graduate School, College of Design, Lexington, KY 40506-0032. Offers M Arch, MAIDM, MHP, MSIDM. *Accreditation:* NASAD. *Entrance requirements:* For master's, GRE, minimum GPA of 2.75. Additional exam requirements/recommendations for international students: Required—TOEFL (minimum score 550 paper-based). Electronic applications accepted.

**University of Louisville,** Graduate School, College of Arts and Sciences, Department of Fine Arts, Louisville, KY 40292. Offers art history (MA, PhD); curatorial studies (MA); studio art (MFA), including design. *Faculty:* 23 full-time (9 women), 6 part-time/adjunct (4 women). *Students:* 20 full-time (14 women), 6 part-time (4 women);

includes 5 minority (2 Asian, non-Hispanic/Latino; 1 Hispanic/Latino; 2 Two or more races, non-Hispanic/Latino). Average age 34. 34 applicants, 56% accepted, 11 enrolled. In 2016, 1 master's, 1 doctorate awarded. *Degree requirements:* For master's, one foreign language, thesis. *Entrance requirements:* For doctorate, MA. Additional exam requirements/recommendations for international students: Required—TOEFL (minimum score 550 paper-based; 80 iBT), IELTS (minimum score 6.5). *Application deadline:* For fall admission, 1/15 priority date for domestic and international students. Application fee: $60. *Expenses:* $12,000. *Financial support:* In 2016–17, 7 teaching assistantships with full tuition reimbursements (averaging $12,000 per year) were awarded; research assistantships, scholarships/grants, health care benefits, and unspecified assistantships also available. Financial award application deadline: 1/15. *Faculty research:* Sustainability and environmental design, media theory, cross cultural and critical theories, Installation, urban and public art. *Total annual research expenditures:* $81,639. *Unit head:* Dr. Scott L. Massey, Associate Professor and Chair, 502-852-6794, Fax: 502-852-6791, E-mail: s.massey@louisville.edu. *Application contact:* Theresa Berbet, Senior Advisor, 502-852-6147, Fax: 502-852-6791, E-mail: tberbet@louisville.edu. Website: http://art.louisville.edu

**University of Louisville,** Graduate School, College of Arts and Sciences, Department of Theatre Arts, Louisville, KY 40292-0001. Offers design (MFA); performance (MFA). *Accreditation:* NAST. *Program availability:* Part-time. *Faculty:* 11 full-time (5 women), 4 part-time/adjunct (3 women). *Students:* 11 full-time (7 women); includes 6 minority (5 Black or African American, non-Hispanic/Latino; 1 Hispanic/Latino). Average age 28. 6 applicants, 67% accepted, 3 enrolled. In 2016, 2 master's awarded. *Degree requirements:* For master's, variable foreign language requirement, performance project and monograph. *Entrance requirements:* For master's, audition. Additional exam requirements/recommendations for international students: Required—TOEFL. *Application deadline:* For spring admission, 4/15 for domestic and international students. Application fee: $60. Electronic applications accepted. *Expenses:* Contact institution. *Financial support:* In 2016–17, 3 teaching assistantships (averaging $12,000 per year) were awarded; health care benefits also available. Financial award application deadline: 2/15; financial award applicants required to submit FAFSA. *Faculty research:* Social justice, African American theatre, African diaspora theatre, costume history and design, lighting design, scenic design. *Unit head:* Dr. Nefertiti Burton, Chair, 502-852-8444, Fax: 502-852-7235, E-mail: ncburt01@louisville.edu. *Application contact:* Libby Leggett, Director, Graduate Admissions, 502-852-3101, Fax: 502-852-6536, E-mail: gradadm@louisville.edu. Website: http://louisville.edu/theatrearts/

**University of Massachusetts Dartmouth,** Graduate School, College of Visual and Performing Arts, Department of Design, North Dartmouth, MA 02747-2300. Offers digital media (MFA); digital multi-media (MFA); graphic design (MFA); illustration (MFA); photography (MFA); typography (MFA). *Accreditation:* NASAD. *Program availability:* Part-time. *Faculty:* 16 full-time (7 women), 3 part-time/adjunct (1 woman). *Students:* 1 (woman) full-time, 10 part-time (7 women), 6 international. Average age 28. 30 applicants, 43% accepted, 4 enrolled. In 2016, 1 degree awarded. *Degree requirements:* For master's, visual thesis, written thesis. *Entrance requirements:* For master's, statement of purpose (minimum of 300 words), resume, 2 letters of recommendation, official transcripts, portfolio (20 images representing applicant's art work, process of thinking, implementation of concepts and studio production). Additional exam requirements/recommendations for international students: Required—TOEFL (minimum score 533 paper-based; 72 iBT). *Application deadline:* For fall admission, 1/11 priority date for domestic students, 12/9 priority date for international students; for spring admission, 10/15 priority date for domestic students, 9/15 priority date for international students. Applications are processed on a rolling basis. Application fee: $60. Electronic applications accepted. *Expenses:* Tuition, state resident: full-time $14,994; part-time $624.75 per credit. Tuition, nonresident: full-time $27,068; part-time $1127.83 per credit. *Required fees:* $405; $25.88 per credit. Tuition and fees vary according to course load and reciprocity agreements. *Financial support:* In 2016–17, 2 fellowships (averaging $2,600 per year) were awarded; teaching assistantships, scholarships/grants, unspecified assistantships, and studio assistantships also available. Support available to part-time students. Financial award application deadline: 3/1; financial award applicants required to submit FAFSA. *Faculty research:* Web design, multimedia design, broadcast design, product design, typography, illustration, photography and design for arts. *Total annual research expenditures:* $113,333. *Unit head:* Ziddi Msagni, Graduate Program Director, Visual Design, 508-999-9291, E-mail: zmsagni@umassd.edu. *Application contact:* Steven Briggs, Director of Marketing and Recruitment for Graduate Studies, 508-999-8604, Fax: 508-999-8183, E-mail: graduate@umassd.edu. Website: http://www.umassd.edu/cvpa/graduate/visualdesign/

**University of Michigan,** College of Engineering, Department of Integrative Systems and Design, Ann Arbor, MI 48109. Offers automotive engineering (M Eng); design science (MS, PhD); energy systems engineering (M Eng, MS); global automotive and manufacturing engineering (M Eng); manufacturing engineering (M Eng, D Eng); pharmaceutical engineering (M Eng); robotics and autonomous vehicles (M Eng); systems engineering and design (M Eng); MBA/M Eng; MSE/MS. *Program availability:* Part-time, online learning. *Students:* 147 full-time (33 women), 234 part-time (39 women). 315 applicants, 8% accepted, 13 enrolled. In 2016, 158 master's, 2 doctorates awarded. Terminal master's awarded for partial completion of doctoral program. *Degree requirements:* For master's, capstone project; for doctorate, thesis/dissertation. *Entrance requirements:* For master's, GRE; for doctorate, GRE, 2 years of work experience. Additional exam requirements/recommendations for international students: Required—TOEFL (minimum score 560 paper-based). *Application deadline:* Applications are processed on a rolling basis. Electronic applications accepted. *Expenses:* Tuition, state resident: full-time $21,466; part-time $1152 per credit hour. Tuition, nonresident: full-time $43,346; part-time $2367 per credit hour. Part-time tuition and fees vary according to course load, degree level and program. *Financial support:* Fellowships, research assistantships with full tuition reimbursements, teaching assistantships with full tuition reimbursements, career-related internships or fieldwork, scholarships/grants, and unspecified assistantships available. Financial award applicants required to submit FAFSA. *Faculty research:* Automotive engineering, design science, energy systems engineering, engineering sustainable systems, financial engineering, global automotive and manufacturing engineering, integrated microsystems, manufacturing engineering, pharmaceutical engineering, robotics and autonomous vehicles. *Total annual research expenditures:* $292,225. *Unit head:* Prof. Panos Papalambros, Department Chair, 734-647-8401, E-mail: pyp@umich.edu. *Application contact:* Kathy Bishar, Senior Graduate Coordinator, 734-764-3312, E-mail: kbishar@umich.edu. Website: http://www.isd.engin.umich.edu

**University of Michigan,** Rackham Graduate School, Penny W. Stamps School of Art and Design, Ann Arbor, MI 48109. Offers art and design (MFA); integrative design (M Des). *Accreditation:* NASAD. *Faculty:* 37. *Students:* 19 (13 women); includes 2 minority (1 Black or African American, non-Hispanic/Latino; 1 Asian, non-Hispanic/Latino). 146 applicants, 8% accepted, 10 enrolled. In 2016, 6 master's awarded. *Degree requirements:* For master's, thesis, exhibit (MFA), slide lecture. *Entrance requirements:* For master's, portfolio. Additional exam requirements/recommendations for international students: Required—TOEFL (minimum score 560 paper-based; 84 iBT), IELTS

(minimum score 6.5). *Application deadline:* For fall admission, 1/1 for domestic and international students. Application fee: $75 ($90 for international students). Electronic applications accepted. *Expenses:* Tuition, state resident: full-time $21,466; part-time $1152 per credit hour. Tuition, nonresident: full-time $43,346; part-time $2367 per credit hour. Part-time tuition and fees vary according to course load, degree level and program. *Financial support:* In 2016–17, 19 students received support. Fellowships with tuition reimbursements available, research assistantships with tuition reimbursements available, teaching assistantships with tuition reimbursements available, Federal Work-Study, scholarships/grants, health care benefits, tuition waivers (full and partial), and unspecified assistantships available. Support available to part-time students. Financial award application deadline: 1/1. *Faculty research:* Creative expression, social engagement, commercial design, collaborative research, preparation for teaching. *Unit head:* Gunalan Nadarajan, Dean, 734-763-4093, E-mail: artdes-dean@umich.edu. *Application contact:* Meghan Jellema, Graduate Programs Coordinator, 734-763-5247, E-mail: stamps-graduate-info@umich.edu. Website: http://stamps.umich.edu/

**University of Minnesota, Twin Cities Campus,** Graduate School, College of Design, Department of Design, Housing, and Apparel, Minneapolis, MN 55455-0213. Offers apparel (MA, MS, PhD); design communication (MA, MS, PhD); housing studies (MA, MS, PhD, Postbaccalaureate Certificate); interactive design (MFA); interior design (MA, MS, PhD). *Program availability:* Part-time. *Degree requirements:* For master's and Postbaccalaureate Certificate, comprehensive exam, thesis (for some programs); for doctorate, comprehensive exam, thesis/dissertation. *Entrance requirements:* For master's, GRE General Test, minimum GPA of 3.0 (preferred), portfolio, 3 letters of recommendation; for doctorate, GRE General Test, minimum GPA of 3.0 (preferred), portfolio, 3 letters of recommendation, writing sample; for Postbaccalaureate Certificate, GRE General Test, minimum GPA of 3.0 (preferred). Additional exam requirements/recommendations for international students: Required—TOEFL (minimum score 550 paper-based; 79 iBT). Electronic applications accepted. *Faculty research:* Housing policy and community development; consumer behavior; interactive design; design history; social, cultural, and behavioral issues related to designed environments.

**University of North Texas,** Robert B. Toulouse School of Graduate Studies, Denton, TX 76203-5459. Offers accounting (MS); applied anthropology (MA, MS); applied behavior analysis (Certificate); applied geography (MA); applied technology and performance improvement (M Ed, MS); art education (MA); art history (MA); art museum education (Certificate); arts leadership (Certificate); audiology (Au D); behavior analysis (MS); behavioral science (PhD); biochemistry and molecular biology (MS); biology (MA, MS); biomedical engineering (MS); business analysis (MS); chemistry (MS); clinical health psychology (PhD); communication studies (MA, MS); computer engineering (MS); computer science (MS); counseling (M Ed, MS), including clinical mental health counseling (MS), college and university counseling, elementary school counseling, secondary school counseling; creative writing (MA); criminal justice (MS); curriculum and instruction (M Ed); decision sciences (MBA); design (MA, MFA), including fashion design (MFA), innovation studies, interior design (MFA); early childhood studies (MS); economics (MS); educational leadership (M Ed, Ed D); educational psychology (MS, PhD), including family studies (MS), gifted and talented (MS), human development (MS), learning and cognition (MS), research, measurement and evaluation (MS); electrical engineering (MS); emergency management (MPA); engineering technology (MS); English (MA); English as a second language (MA); environmental science (MS); finance (MBA, MS); financial management (MPA); French (MA); health services management (MBA); higher education (M Ed, Ed D); history (MA, MS); hospitality management (MS); human resources management (MPA); information science (MS); information systems (PhD); information technologies (MBA); interdisciplinary studies (MA, MS); international studies (MA); international sustainable tourism (MS); jazz studies (MM); journalism (MA, MJ, Graduate Certificate), including interactive and virtual digital communication (Graduate Certificate), narrative journalism (Graduate Certificate), public relations (Graduate Certificate); kinesiology (MS); linguistics (MA); local government management (MPA); logistics (PhD); logistics and supply chain management (MBA); long-term care, senior housing, and aging services (MA); management (PhD); marketing (MBA); mathematics (MS); mechanical and energy engineering (MS, PhD); music (MA), including ethnomusicology, music theory, musicology, performance; music composition (PhD); music education (MM Ed, PhD); nonprofit management (MPA); operations and supply chain management (MBA); performance (MM, DMA); philosophy (MA); political science (MA); professional and technical communication (MA); radio, television and film (MA, MFA); rehabilitation counseling (Certificate); sociology (MA); Spanish (MA); special education (M Ed); speech-language pathology (MS); strategic management (MBA); studio art (MFA); teaching (M Ed); MBA/MS. *Program availability:* Part-time, evening/weekend, online learning. Terminal master's awarded for partial completion of doctoral program. *Degree requirements:* For master's, variable foreign language requirement, comprehensive exam (for some programs), thesis (for some programs); for doctorate, variable foreign language requirement, comprehensive exam (for some programs), thesis/dissertation; for other advanced degree, variable foreign language requirement, comprehensive exam (for some programs). *Entrance requirements:* For master's and doctorate, GRE, GMAT. Additional exam requirements/recommendations for international students: Required—TOEFL (minimum score 550 paper-based; 79 iBT). Electronic applications accepted.

**University of Notre Dame,** Graduate School, College of Arts and Letters, Division of Humanities, Department of Art, Art History, and Design, Notre Dame, IN 46556. Offers art history (MA); design (MFA), including graphic design, industrial design; studio art (MFA), including ceramics, painting, photography, printmaking, sculpture. *Accreditation:* NASAD. *Degree requirements:* For master's, comprehensive exam (for some programs), thesis. *Entrance requirements:* For master's, GRE General Test, minimum GPA of 3.0. Additional exam requirements/recommendations for international students: Required—TOEFL (minimum score 600 paper-based; 80 iBT). Electronic applications accepted. *Faculty research:* Studio art practice in ceramics, printing, photography, printmaking and sculpture, graphic design and industrial design, digital imaging in design and photography, Renaissance and American art history, contemporary art theory and criticism.

**The University of Texas at Austin,** Graduate School, College of Fine Arts, Department of Art and Art History, Program in Design, Austin, TX 78712-1111. Offers MFA. *Accreditation:* NASAD. *Degree requirements:* For master's, thesis, oral exam, exhibition. *Entrance requirements:* For master's, minimum GPA of 3.0, portfolio. Electronic applications accepted.

**University of Washington,** Graduate School, College of Arts and Sciences, School of Art, Division of Design, Seattle, WA 98195. Offers industrial design (MFA); visual communication design (MFA).

**University of Wisconsin–Madison,** Graduate School, School of Human Ecology, Program in Design Studies, Madison, WI 53706. Offers MFA, MS, PhD. *Degree requirements:* For master's, thesis (for some programs); for doctorate, comprehensive exam, thesis/dissertation. *Entrance requirements:* For master's, portfolio, scholarly paper, 3 letters of recommendation from faculty; for doctorate, letters of recommendation, scholarly paper. Additional exam requirements/recommendations for international students: Required—TOEFL (minimum score 580 paper-based; 92 iBT).

*Applied Arts and Design—General*

*Faculty research:* Feng shui, material culture, behavior and environment, use of pattern to enhance environment, design visualization.

**University of Wisconsin–Milwaukee,** Graduate School, College of Health Sciences, Department of Occupational Science and Technology, Milwaukee, WI 53201-0413. Offers assistive technology and design (MS); ergonomics (MS). *Accreditation:* AOTA. *Students:* 92 full-time (84 women), 4 part-time (3 women); includes 7 minority (3 Asian, non-Hispanic/Latino; 1 Hispanic/Latino; 3 Two or more races, non-Hispanic/Latino). Average age 26. 90 applicants, 40% accepted, 32 enrolled. In 2016, 34 master's awarded. *Degree requirements:* For master's, thesis or alternative. *Entrance requirements:* Additional exam requirements/recommendations for international students: Required—TOEFL (minimum score 550 paper-based; 79 iBT), IELTS (minimum score 6.5). *Application deadline:* For fall admission, 1/1 priority date for domestic students; for spring admission, 9/1 for domestic students. Applications are processed on a rolling basis. Application fee: $56 ($75 for international students). *Financial support:* Fellowships, research assistantships, teaching assistantships, and unspecified assistantships available. Support available to part-time students. Financial award application deadline: 4/15. *Unit head:* Jay Kapellusch, PhD, Department Chair, 414-229-5292, Fax: 414-229-2619, E-mail: kap@uwm.edu. *Application contact:* Bhagwant S. Sindhu, PhD, Graduate Program Coordinator, 414-229-1180, Fax: 414-229-5100, E-mail: sindhu@uwm.edu.
Website: http://uwm.edu/healthsciences/academics/occupational-science-technology/

**Western Carolina University,** Graduate School, College of Fine and Performing Arts, School of Art and Design, Cullowhee, NC 28723. Offers MFA. *Accreditation:* NASAD. *Program availability:* Part-time. *Degree requirements:* For master's, thesis. *Entrance requirements:* For master's, GRE, appropriate undergraduate degree, portfolio, letters of recommendation. Additional exam requirements/recommendations for international students: Required—TOEFL (minimum score 550 paper-based; 79 iBT). *Expenses:* Tuition, state resident: full-time $2174. Tuition, nonresident: full-time $7377.

*Required fees:* $1442. Part-time tuition and fees vary according to course load. *Faculty research:* Art and society, visual literacy, vernacular cultural studies and oral history, environments for aging, health and leisure.

**Western Michigan University,** Graduate College, College of Fine Arts, Gwen Frostic School of Art, Kalamazoo, MI 49008. Offers art education (MA). *Accreditation:* NASAD. *Degree requirements:* For master's, thesis or alternative.

**Yale University,** School of Art, New Haven, CT 06520-8339. Offers graphic design (MFA); painting/printmaking (MFA); photography (MFA); sculpture (MFA). *Faculty:* 10 full-time (5 women), 35 part-time/adjunct (12 women). *Students:* 127 full-time (65 women); includes 17 minority (8 Black or African American, non-Hispanic/Latino; 5 Asian, non-Hispanic/Latino; 4 Hispanic/Latino), 35 international. Average age 28. 1,003 applicants, 6% accepted, 61 enrolled. In 2016, 61 master's awarded. *Degree requirements:* For master's, thesis (for some programs). *Entrance requirements:* Additional exam requirements/recommendations for international students: Required—TOEFL (minimum score 550 paper-based; 100 iBT). *Application deadline:* For fall admission, 1/4 for domestic and international students. Application fee: $100. Electronic applications accepted. *Expenses:* Contact institution. *Financial support:* In 2016–17, 110 students received support, including 61 teaching assistantships (averaging $2,000 per year); Federal Work-Study, scholarships/grants, and unspecified assistantships also available. Financial award application deadline: 3/1; financial award applicants required to submit FAFSA. *Unit head:* Marta Kuzma, Dean, 203-432-2606. *Application contact:* Patricia Ann DeChiara, Director of Academic Affairs, 203-432-2600, E-mail: artschool.info@yale.edu.
Website: http://www.yale.edu/art/

**York University,** Faculty of Graduate Studies, Faculty of Fine Arts, Program in Design, Toronto, ON M3J 1P3, Canada. Offers M Des. Electronic applications accepted.

# Computer Art and Design

**Academy of Art University,** Graduate Programs, School of Graphic Design, San Francisco, CA 94105-3410. Offers graphic design (MFA); graphic design and digital media (MA). *Accreditation:* NASAD. *Program availability:* Part-time, 100% online. *Faculty:* 7 full-time (1 woman), 33 part-time/adjunct (15 women). *Students:* 220 full-time (162 women), 145 part-time (103 women); includes 49 minority (14 Black or African American, non-Hispanic/Latino; 1 American Indian or Alaska Native, non-Hispanic/Latino; 16 Asian, non-Hispanic/Latino; 14 Hispanic/Latino; 2 Native Hawaiian or other Pacific Islander, non-Hispanic/Latino; 2 Two or more races, non-Hispanic/Latino), 242 international. Average age 29. 130 applicants, 100% accepted, 80 enrolled. In 2016, 38 master's awarded. *Degree requirements:* For master's, final review. *Entrance requirements:* For master's, statement of intent; resume; portfolio/reel; official college transcripts. *Application deadline:* Applications are processed on a rolling basis. Application fee: $50. Electronic applications accepted. *Expenses: Tuition:* Part-time $982 per unit. *Financial support:* Career-related internships or fieldwork, Federal Work-Study, and scholarships/grants available. Financial award application deadline: 8/10; financial award applicants required to submit FAFSA. *Unit head:* 800-544-ARTS, E-mail: info@academyart.edu. *Application contact:* 800-544-ARTS, E-mail: info@academyart.edu.
Website: http://www.academyart.edu/graphic-design-school/index.html

**Academy of Art University,** Graduate Programs, School of Visual Development, San Francisco, CA 94105-3410. Offers MA, MFA. *Program availability:* Part-time, 100% online. *Faculty:* 5 full-time (0 women), 17 part-time/adjunct (2 women). *Students:* 152 full-time (85 women), 80 part-time (44 women); includes 44 minority (8 Black or African American, non-Hispanic/Latino; 1 American Indian or Alaska Native, non-Hispanic/Latino; 16 Asian, non-Hispanic/Latino; 15 Hispanic/Latino; 4 Two or more races, non-Hispanic/Latino), 124 international. Average age 28. 45 applicants, 100% accepted, 36 enrolled. In 2016, 33 master's awarded. *Degree requirements:* For master's, final review. *Entrance requirements:* For master's, statement of intent; resume; portfolio/reel; official college transcripts. *Application deadline:* Applications are processed on a rolling basis. Application fee: $50. Electronic applications accepted. *Expenses: Tuition:* Part-time $982 per unit. *Financial support:* Career-related internships or fieldwork, Federal Work-Study, and scholarships/grants available. Financial award application deadline: 8/10; financial award applicants required to submit FAFSA. *Unit head:* 800-544-ARTS, E-mail: info@academyart.edu. *Application contact:* 800-544-ARTS, E-mail: info@academyart.edu.
Website: https://www.academyart.edu/academics/visual-development

**Academy of Art University,** Graduate Programs, School of Web Design and New Media, San Francisco, CA 94105-3410. Offers MA, MFA. *Program availability:* Part-time, 100% online. *Faculty:* 9 full-time (3 women), 49 part-time/adjunct (16 women). *Students:* 273 full-time (176 women), 136 part-time (87 women); includes 53 minority (10 Black or African American, non-Hispanic/Latino; 32 Asian, non-Hispanic/Latino; 1 Hispanic/Latino; 1 Native Hawaiian or other Pacific Islander, non-Hispanic/Latino; 3 Two or more races, non-Hispanic/Latino), 287 international. Average age 29. 98 applicants, 100% accepted, 78 enrolled. In 2016, 104 master's awarded. *Degree requirements:* For master's, final review. *Entrance requirements:* For master's, statement of intent; resume; portfolio/reel; official college transcripts. *Application deadline:* Applications are processed on a rolling basis. Application fee: $50. Electronic applications accepted. *Expenses: Tuition:* Part-time $982 per unit. *Financial support:* Career-related internships or fieldwork, Federal Work-Study, and scholarships/grants available. Financial award application deadline: 8/10; financial award applicants required to submit FAFSA. *Unit head:* 800-544-ARTS, E-mail: info@academyart.edu. *Application contact:* 800-544-ARTS, E-mail: info@academyart.edu.
Website: http://www.academyart.edu/computer-arts-school/index.html

**Alfred University,** Graduate School, College of Ceramics, School of Art and Design, Alfred, NY 14802. Offers ceramic art (MFA); electronic integrated arts (MFA); painting (MFA); sculpture/dimensional studies (MFA). *Accreditation:* NASAD. *Faculty:* 19 full-time (11 women), 14 part-time/adjunct (9 women). *Students:* 34 full-time (18 women); includes 2 minority (1 Asian, non-Hispanic/Latino; 1 Hispanic/Latino), 10 international. Average age 28. 32 applicants, 66% accepted, 19 enrolled. In 2016, 15 master's awarded. *Degree requirements:* For master's, thesis, exhibit. *Entrance requirements:* For master's, portfolio. Additional exam requirements/recommendations for international students: Required—TOEFL (minimum score 550 paper-based; 80 iBT), IELTS (minimum score 6). *Application deadline:* For fall admission, 1/15 for domestic and international students. Application fee: $60. Electronic applications accepted. *Expenses:* Contact institution. *Financial support:* In 2016–17, 34 students received support.

Teaching assistantships with full tuition reimbursements available and tuition waivers (full) available. Financial award application deadline: 8/1; financial award applicants required to submit FAFSA. *Faculty research:* Ceramic art, sculpture, glass art, new media, time-based media. *Unit head:* Gerar Edizel, Interim Dean, 607-871-2412, E-mail: fedizel@alfred.edu. *Application contact:* Sara Love, Coordinator of Graduate Admissions, 607-871-2115, Fax: 607-871-2198, E-mail: gradinquiry@alfred.edu.
Website: http://art.alfred.edu/graduate/

**ArtCenter College of Design,** Graduate Media Design Practices Program, Pasadena, CA 91103. Offers MFA. *Accreditation:* NASAD. *Degree requirements:* For master's, thesis, studio project. *Entrance requirements:* For master's, portfolio. Additional exam requirements/recommendations for international students: Required—TOEFL (minimum score 100 iBT), IELTS (minimum score 7). Electronic applications accepted.

**The Art Institute of California–San Francisco, a campus of Argosy University,** Program in Computer Animation, San Francisco, CA 94102-4928. Offers MFA.

**Bowling Green State University,** Graduate College, College of Arts and Sciences, School of Art, Bowling Green, OH 43403. Offers 2-D studio art (MA, MFA); 3-D studio art (MA, MFA); art education (MA); art history (MA); computer art (MA); design (MFA); digital arts (MFA); graphics (MFA). *Accreditation:* NASAD. *Program availability:* Part-time. *Degree requirements:* For master's, thesis or alternative, final exhibit (MFA). *Entrance requirements:* For master's, GRE General Test (MA), slide portfolio (15-20 slides). Additional exam requirements/recommendations for international students: Required—TOEFL. *Application deadline:* For fall admission, 2/15 for domestic students. Application fee: $30. Electronic applications accepted. *Financial support:* Research assistantships with full and partial tuition reimbursements, teaching assistantships with full and partial tuition reimbursements, career-related internships or fieldwork, institutionally sponsored loans, and unspecified assistantships available. Support available to part-time students. Financial award applicants required to submit FAFSA. *Faculty research:* Computer animation and virtual reality, Spanish still-life painting from 1600 to 1800, art and psychotherapy, Japanese wood-firing techniques in ceramics, non-toxic printmaking technologies. *Unit head:* Dr. Katerina Ruedi Ray, Director, 419-372-8575. *Application contact:* Marisa Cline, Graduate Coordinator, 419-372-2786, E-mail: mlcline@bgsu.edu.

**California College of the Arts,** Graduate Programs, Design Program, San Francisco, CA 94107. Offers graphic design (MFA); industrial design (MFA); interaction design (MFA). *Accreditation:* NASAD. *Faculty:* 6 full-time (2 women), 26 part-time/adjunct (10 women). *Students:* 105 full-time (67 women); includes 14 minority (1 Black or African American, non-Hispanic/Latino; 8 Asian, non-Hispanic/Latino; 5 Hispanic/Latino), 67 international. Average age 26. 384 applicants, 36% accepted, 45 enrolled. In 2016, 9 master's awarded. *Degree requirements:* For master's, thesis, exhibit. *Entrance requirements:* For master's, appropriate bachelor's degree, portfolio, resume, letters of recommendation, transcripts. Additional exam requirements/recommendations for international students: Required—TOEFL, IELTS, or PTE. *Application deadline:* For fall admission, 1/10 for domestic and international students. Applications are processed on a rolling basis. Application fee: $70. Electronic applications accepted. *Expenses:* $1,641 per unit, $49,230 per year tuition; $490 fees. *Financial support:* In 2016–17, fellowships (averaging $22,000 per year), teaching assistantships (averaging $2,000 per year) were awarded; career-related internships or fieldwork, Federal Work-Study, scholarships/grants, health care benefits, and unspecified assistantships also available. Financial award application deadline: 7/31; financial award applicants required to submit FAFSA. *Unit head:* Jon Sueda, Graduate Chair, 415-551-9283, Fax: 415-703-9539, E-mail: jsueda@cca.edu. *Application contact:* Wes Fanelli, Assistant Director of Graduate Admissions, 415-703-9533, Fax: 415-703-9539, E-mail: wfanelli@cca.edu.

**Carnegie Mellon University,** College of Fine Arts, School of Design, Program in Design for Interactions, Pittsburgh, PA 15213-3891. Offers M Des. *Program availability:* Part-time. *Degree requirements:* For master's, thesis. *Entrance requirements:* For master's, GRE, portfolio of relevant work. Additional exam requirements/recommendations for international students: Required—TOEFL (minimum score 600 paper-based). *Faculty research:* Interaction and emotion, visual interface design, robotics, visualization and diagramming, design theory.

**Chatham University,** Program in Film and Digital Technology, Pittsburgh, PA 15232-2826. Offers MFA. *Program availability:* Part-time, evening/weekend. *Degree requirements:* For master's, thesis, capstone project. *Entrance requirements:* Additional exam requirements/recommendations for international students: Required—TOEFL (minimum score 600 paper-based; 100 iBT), IELTS (minimum score 7), TWE. Electronic applications accepted. Application fee is waived when completed online. *Expenses: Tuition:* Full-time $16,254; part-time $903 per credit hour. *Required fees:* $468; $26 per credit hour.

**City College of the City University of New York,** Graduate School, Division of Humanities and the Arts, Department of Art, Program in Fine Arts, New York, NY 10031-9198. Offers advertising design (MFA); ceramic design (MFA); digital and interdisciplinary art practice (MFA); painting (MFA); printmaking (MFA); sculpture (MFA); wood and metal design (MFA). *Degree requirements:* For master's, thesis exhibit. *Entrance requirements:* For master's, 20-slide portfolio. Additional exam requirements/recommendations for international students: Required—TOEFL (minimum score 577 paper-based; 90 iBT). Electronic applications accepted. Tuition and fees vary according to course load, degree level and program.

**Claremont Graduate University,** Graduate Programs, School of Arts and Humanities, Department of Art, Claremont, CA 91711. Offers digital media (MFA); drawing (MFA); installation (MFA); painting (MFA); performance (MFA); photography (MFA); sculpture (MFA); studio (MFA). *Program availability:* Part-time. *Faculty:* 3 full-time (1 woman). *Students:* 38 full-time (25 women), 1 part-time (0 women); includes 12 minority (1 Black or African American, non-Hispanic/Latino; 4 Asian, non-Hispanic/Latino; 6 Hispanic/Latino; 1 Two or more races, non-Hispanic/Latino), 8 international. Average age 35. In 2016, 18 master's awarded. *Degree requirements:* For master's, final project show. *Entrance requirements:* For master's, BA in art or BFA, slide review. Additional exam requirements/recommendations for international students: Required—TOEFL (minimum score 75 iBT). *Application deadline:* For fall admission, 2/1 priority date for domestic and international students. Applications are processed on a rolling basis. Application fee: $80. Electronic applications accepted. *Expenses:* Contact institution. *Financial support:* Fellowships, research assistantships, teaching assistantships, Federal Work-Study, institutionally sponsored loans, and scholarships/grants available. Support available to part-time students. Financial award application deadline: 2/15; financial award applicants required to submit FAFSA. *Faculty research:* Acoustic sculpture, feminization of abstraction, installation sculpture. *Unit head:* David Amico, Chair, 909-607-8216, E-mail: david.amico@cgu.edu. *Application contact:* Amy Sandefur, Assistant Director of Admissions, 909-607-9101, E-mail: jennifer.gracia@cgu.edu.
Website: https://www.cgu.edu/academics/program/mfa/

**Clemson University,** Graduate School, College of Engineering, Computing and Applied Sciences, School of Computing, MFA Program in Digital Production Arts, Clemson, SC 29634. Offers MFA. *Accreditation:* NASAD. *Program availability:* Part-time. *Faculty:* 12 full-time (1 woman). *Students:* 33 full-time (11 women); includes 5 minority (both Hispanic/Latino), 2 international. Average age 25. 32 applicants, 72% accepted, 17 enrolled. In 2016, 12 master's awarded. *Degree requirements:* For master's, thesis. *Entrance requirements:* For master's, GRE General Test, portfolio of artistic work (computer programming samples, art samples, writing sample), letters of recommendation, unofficial transcripts. Additional exam requirements/recommendations for international students: Required—TOEFL (minimum score 550 paper-based; 80 iBT), IELTS (minimum score 6.5). *Application deadline:* For fall admission, 5/15 priority date for domestic students, 4/15 priority date for international students. Applications are processed on a rolling basis. Application fee: $80 ($90 for international students). Electronic applications accepted. *Expenses:* $18,028 per semester full-time, $1,986 per credit hour part-time. *Financial support:* In 2016–17, 10 students received support, including 2 research assistantships with partial tuition reimbursements available (averaging $10,596 per year), 3 teaching assistantships with partial tuition reimbursements available (averaging $16,650 per year); career-related internships or fieldwork, traineeships, and unspecified assistantships also available. Financial award application deadline: 1/1. *Faculty research:* Distributed rendering, fluids and simulation, computer animation and graphics, game design, motion. *Unit head:* Dr. Donald House, Visual Computing Division Chair, 864-656-2844, E-mail: dhouse@clemson.edu. *Application contact:* Dr. Victor Zordan, Director of Digital Production Arts, 864-656-4144, E-mail: vbz@clemson.edu.
Website: https://www.cs.clemson.edu/dpa/

**Concordia University,** School of Graduate Studies, Faculty of Fine Arts, Department of Design and Computation Arts, Montréal, QC H3G 1M8, Canada. Offers design (M Des); digital technologies in design art practice (Certificate).

**Cornell University,** Graduate School, Graduate Fields of Architecture, Art and Planning, Field of Architecture, Ithaca, NY 14853. Offers architectural design (M Arch); architectural science (MS); computer graphics (MS); history of architecture (MA, PhD); history of urban development (MA, PhD); theory and criticism of architecture (M Arch); urban design (M Arch). *Degree requirements:* For master's, one foreign language, thesis (MA, MS); for doctorate, 2 foreign languages, comprehensive exam, thesis/dissertation. *Entrance requirements:* For master's, GRE General Test, 5-year bachelor's degree in architecture, portfolio (M Arch), 3 letters of recommendation; for doctorate, GRE General Test, 3 letters of recommendation. Additional exam requirements/recommendations for international students: Required—TOEFL (minimum score 600 paper-based; 77 iBT). Electronic applications accepted. *Faculty research:* Architectural design and urban design, theory and criticism of architecture, computer graphics, building technology and environmental science, history of architecture and history of urban-development.

**DePaul University,** College of Computing and Digital Media, Chicago, IL 60604. Offers animation (MA, MFA); business information technology (MS); cinema (MFA); cinema production (MS); computational finance (MS); computer and information sciences (PhD); computer game development (MS); computer information and network security (MS); computer science (MS); e-commerce technology (MS); health informatics (MS); human-computer interaction (MS); information systems (MS); information technology project management (MS); network engineering and management (MS); predictive analytics (MS); screenwriting (MFA); software engineering (MS); JD/MS. *Program availability:* Part-time, evening/weekend, online learning. *Degree requirements:* For master's, thesis (for some programs); for doctorate, comprehensive exam, thesis/dissertation. *Entrance requirements:* For master's, GRE or GMAT (for MS in computational finance only), bachelor's degree, resume (MS in predictive analytics only), IT experience (MS in information technology project management only), portfolio review (all MFA programs and MA in animation); for doctorate, GRE, master's degree in computer science. Additional exam requirements/recommendations for international students: Required—TOEFL (minimum score 590 paper-based; 80 iBT), IELTS (minimum score 6.5), PTE (minimum score 53). Electronic applications accepted. *Expenses:* Contact institution. *Faculty research:* Data mining, computer science, human-computer interaction, security, animation and film.

**DigiPen Institute of Technology,** Graduate Programs, Redmond, WA 98052. Offers computer science (MS); digital art and animation (MFA). *Program availability:* Part-time. *Faculty:* 28 full-time (7 women), 14 part-time/adjunct (1 woman). *Students:* 51 full-time (8 women), 27 part-time (5 women); includes 8 minority (3 Asian, non-Hispanic/Latino; 4 Hispanic/Latino; 1 Two or more races, non-Hispanic/Latino), 41 international. Average age 28. 107 applicants, 47% accepted, 21 enrolled. In 2016, 23 master's awarded. *Degree requirements:* For master's, comprehensive exam (for some

programs), thesis (for some programs). *Entrance requirements:* For master's, GRE General Test (for MS), art portfolio (for MFA); official transcripts from all post-secondary education including final transcript indicating degree earned, statement of purpose, and 2 letters of recommendation. Additional exam requirements/recommendations for international students: Required—TOEFL (minimum score 550 paper-based; 80 iBT). *Application deadline:* For fall admission, 2/1 priority date for domestic and international students; for spring admission, 7/1 for domestic and international students. Applications are processed on a rolling basis. Application fee: $35. Electronic applications accepted. *Expenses:* Contact institution. *Financial support:* In 2016–17, 4 students received support, including 1 fellowship (averaging $9,500 per year); career-related internships or fieldwork and scholarships/grants also available. Financial award application deadline: 5/1; financial award applicants required to submit FAFSA. *Faculty research:* Procedural modeling, computer graphics and visualization, human-computer interaction, fuzzy numbers and fuzzy analysis, modeling under spistemic uncertainty, nonlinear image processing, mathematical representation of surfaces, advanced computer graphic rendering techniques, mathematical physics, computer music and sound synthesis. *Unit head:* Angela Kugler, Senior Vice President, 425-895-4438, Fax: 425-558-0378, E-mail: akugler@digipen.edu. *Application contact:* Danial Powers, Director of Admissions, 425-629-5071, Fax: 425-558-0378, E-mail: dpowers@digipen.edu.

**Digital Media Arts College,** Graduate Programs, Boca Raton, FL 33487. Offers graphic design (MFA); special FX animation (MFA).

★ **Drexel University,** Westphal College of Media Arts and Design, Program in Digital Media, Philadelphia, PA 19104-2875. Offers MS. *Faculty:* 12 full-time (1 woman), 17 part-time/adjunct (1 woman). *Students:* 32 full-time (15 women), 5 part-time (2 women); includes 9 minority (3 Black or African American, non-Hispanic/Latino; 2 Asian, non-Hispanic/Latino; 2 Hispanic/Latino; 2 Two or more races, non-Hispanic/Latino), 12 international. Average age 26. In 2016, 15 master's awarded. *Degree requirements:* For master's, thesis (including oral presentation, written statement, and copy of completed media work). *Entrance requirements:* For master's, interview. Additional exam requirements/recommendations for international students: Required—TOEFL (minimum score 550 paper-based; 80 iBT). *Application deadline:* For fall admission, 8/21 for domestic students; for spring admission, 3/5 for domestic students. Applications are processed on a rolling basis. Application fee: $50. Electronic applications accepted. *Expenses: Tuition:* Full-time $32,184; part-time $1192 per credit hour. *Required fees:* $280. Tuition and fees vary according to campus/location and program. *Financial support:* Research assistantships, teaching assistantships, career-related internships or fieldwork, and unspecified assistantships available. Financial award application deadline: 2/1. *Unit head:* Dr. Karin S. Kuenstler, Head, 215-895-2383. *Application contact:* Director of Graduate Admissions, 215-895-6700, Fax: 215-895-5939, E-mail: enroll@drexel.edu.

**See Display on page 63 and Close-Up on page 99.**

**East Tennessee State University,** School of Graduate Studies, College of Business and Technology, Department of Engineering Technology, Surveying and Digital Media, Johnson City, TN 37614. Offers MS, Postbaccalaureate Certificate. *Program availability:* Part-time. *Degree requirements:* For master's, comprehensive exam, thesis optional, capstone. *Entrance requirements:* For master's, bachelor's degree in technical or related area, minimum GPA of 3.0; for Postbaccalaureate Certificate, minimum GPA of 2.5, three letters of recommendation. Additional exam requirements/recommendations for international students: Required—TOEFL (minimum score 550 paper-based; 79 iBT). Electronic applications accepted. *Faculty research:* Computer-integrated manufacturing, alternative energy, sustainability, CAD/CAM, organizational change.

**Emily Carr University of Art + Design,** Program in Digital Media, Vancouver, BC V5T 0C6, Canada. Offers MDM. *Degree requirements:* For master's, internship. *Entrance requirements:* For master's, portfolio, minimum undergraduate B+ average, 3 reference letters. Additional exam requirements/recommendations for international students: Required—TOEFL (minimum score 93 iBT), IELTS (minimum score 6.5), PTE (minimum score 62). Electronic applications accepted.

**Full Sail University,** Game Design Master of Science Program - Campus, Winter Park, FL 32792-7437. Offers MS.

**Georgia Institute of Technology,** Graduate Studies, Ivan Allen College of Liberal Arts, School of Literature, Media, and Communication, Atlanta, GA 30332-0001. Offers digital media (MS, PhD). *Program availability:* Part-time. Terminal master's awarded for partial completion of doctoral program. *Degree requirements:* For master's, thesis optional, project studio, paid internship, responsible conduct of research training; for doctorate, comprehensive exam, thesis/dissertation, portfolio review, responsible conduct of research training. *Entrance requirements:* For master's and doctorate, GRE, three letters of recommendation, transcripts from each college/university attended, design portfolio, statement of purpose. Additional exam requirements/recommendations for international students: Required—TOEFL (minimum score 650 paper-based; 114 iBT). Electronic applications accepted. *Faculty research:* New media studies.

**Georgian Court University,** School of Business and Digital Media, Lakewood, NJ 08701-2697. Offers business (MBA); business essentials (Certificate); nonprofit management (Certificate). *Program availability:* Part-time, evening/weekend. *Faculty:* 7 full-time (3 women), 11 part-time/adjunct (4 women). *Students:* 29 full-time (22 women), 40 part-time (26 women); includes 22 minority (7 Black or African American, non-Hispanic/Latino; 2 Asian, non-Hispanic/Latino; 9 Hispanic/Latino; 4 Two or more races, non-Hispanic/Latino). Average age 31. 55 applicants, 49% accepted, 13 enrolled. In 2016, 34 master's, 3 other advanced degrees awarded. *Entrance requirements:* For master's, GMAT or CPA exam, 3 letters of recommendation. Additional exam requirements/recommendations for international students: Required—TOEFL (minimum score 550 paper-based). *Application deadline:* For fall admission, 8/15 priority date for domestic students, 5/1 for international students; for spring admission, 1/15 priority date for domestic students, 10/1 for international students. Applications are processed on a rolling basis. Application fee: $40. Electronic applications accepted. *Expenses: Tuition:* Full-time $15,079; part-time $839 per credit. *Required fees:* $968; $496 per credit. Tuition and fees vary according to campus/location and program. *Financial support:* Scholarships/grants, health care benefits, and unspecified assistantships available. Financial award application deadline: 4/15; financial award applicants required to submit FAFSA. *Unit head:* Dr. Janice Warner, Dean, 732-987-2662, Fax: 732-987-2024, E-mail: jwarner@georgian.edu. *Application contact:* Patrick Givens, Director of Graduate and Professional Studies Admissions, 732-987-2736, Fax: 732-987-2000, E-mail: gps@georgian.edu.
Website: http://georgian.edu/academics/school-of-business/

**Goucher College,** MA and MFA Programs, Baltimore, MD 21204-2794. Offers arts administration (MA); creative nonfiction (MFA); cultural sustainability (MA); digital arts (MA, MFA); environmental studies (MA); historic preservation (MA); management (MA). *Program availability:* Part-time, evening/weekend, blended/hybrid learning. *Faculty:* 6 full-time (4 women), 100 part-time/adjunct (56 women). *Students:* 70 full-time (50 women), 69 part-time (52 women); includes 15 minority (7 Black or African American, non-Hispanic/Latino; 1 American Indian or Alaska Native, non-Hispanic/Latino; 1 Asian, non-Hispanic/Latino; 4 Hispanic/Latino; 2 Two or more races, non-Hispanic/Latino), 2

## Computer Art and Design

international. 74 applicants, 88% accepted, 42 enrolled. In 2016, 83 master's awarded. *Degree requirements:* For master's, thesis, e-portfolio. *Entrance requirements:* For master's, digital portfolio (for MA, MFA in digital arts); writing sample (for MFA in creative nonfiction). Additional exam requirements/recommendations for international students: Required—TOEFL (minimum score 550 paper-based; 80 iBT). *Application deadline:* Applications are processed on a rolling basis. Application fee: $75. Electronic applications accepted. *Expenses:* Contact institution. *Financial support:* Scholarships/grants and unspecified assistantships available. Financial award application deadline: 4/15; financial award applicants required to submit FAFSA. *Unit head:* Leslie Rubinkowski, Assistant Provost, 410-337-6200, E-mail: leslie.rubinkowski@goucher.edu. *Application contact:* Shelby Hillers, Admissions Coordinator, 410-337-6200, Fax: 410-337-6200, E-mail: shelby.hillers@goucher.edu.
Website: http://www.goucher.edu/grad

**Indiana University–Purdue University Indianapolis,** Herron School of Art and Design, Indianapolis, IN 46202. Offers art therapy (MA); visual art (MFA), including ceramics, furniture design, painting and drawing, photography and intermedia, printmaking, sculpture; visual communication design (MFA). *Faculty:* 26 full-time (13 women), 16 part-time/adjunct (11 women). *Students:* 56 full-time (40 women), 1 (woman) part-time; includes 8 minority (4 Black or African American, non-Hispanic/Latino; 2 Asian, non-Hispanic/Latino; 2 Hispanic/Latino), 7 international. Average age 31. 72 applicants, 53% accepted, 25 enrolled. In 2016, 22 master's awarded. *Degree requirements:* For master's, thesis. *Entrance requirements:* For master's, personal statement, resume, recommendations, portfolio, transcripts (18 credit hours of studio art and 12 credit hours of psychology, including 3 credit hours of developmental psychology and 3 credit hours of abnormal psychology for MA). Additional exam requirements/recommendations for international students: Recommended—TOEFL (minimum score 550 paper-based; 79 iBT), IELTS (minimum score 6.5). *Application deadline:* For fall admission, 1/15 for domestic and international students; for spring admission, 11/1 for domestic students, 10/15 for international students. Application fee: $60 ($65 for international students). Electronic applications accepted. *Expenses:* Contact institution. *Financial support:* In 2016–17, 55 students received support, including 36 fellowships (averaging $2,830 per year), 11 teaching assistantships (averaging $3,609 per year); research assistantships, Federal Work-Study, scholarships/grants, health care benefits, tuition waivers, and unspecified assistantships also available. Financial award application deadline: 2/1. *Faculty research:* Contemporary digital narratives for the homoerotic trope; sound articulated 3D print; neuroscience, art and related therapeutics; automotive and aeronautical design and fabrication; technological detritus. *Total annual research expenditures:* $22,990. *Unit head:* Prof. Valerie Eickmeier, Dean, 317-278-9470, Fax: 317-278-9471, E-mail: herron@iupui.edu. *Application contact:* Abbey Chambers, Herron Office of Admissions and Student Services, 317-378-9400, E-mail: herron4u@iupui.edu.
Website: http://herron.iupui.edu/

**International Technological University,** Program in Digital Arts, San Jose, CA 95134. Offers MA. *Program availability:* Part-time. *Degree requirements:* For master's, capstone project. *Entrance requirements:* Additional exam requirements/recommendations for international students: Required—TOEFL, IELTS. Electronic applications accepted.

**Johnson State College,** Program in Studio Arts, Johnson, VT 05656. Offers ceramics (MFA); digital media (MFA); drawing (MFA); painting (MFA); photography (MFA); printmaking (MFA); sculpture (MFA). *Program availability:* Part-time, online learning. *Degree requirements:* For master's, thesis. *Entrance requirements:* For master's, portfolio. Additional exam requirements/recommendations for international students: Required—TOEFL. *Application deadline:* For fall admission, 3/1 for domestic students, 2/1 for international students. Applications are processed on a rolling basis. Electronic applications accepted. Application fee is waived when completed online. *Expenses:* Contact institution. *Financial support:* Teaching assistantships and unspecified assistantships available. Support available to part-time students. Financial award application deadline: 3/1; financial award applicants required to submit FAFSA. *Application contact:* Catherine H. Higley, Administrative Assistant, 800-635-2356 Ext. 1244, Fax: 802-635-1248, E-mail: catherine.higley@jsc.edu.
Website: http://www.jsc.edu/academics/fine-arts-department/majors-and-minors/mfa-in-studio-arts/

**Lindenwood University–Belleville,** Graduate Programs, Belleville, IL 62226. Offers business administration (MBA); communications (MA), including digital and multimedia, media management, promotions, training and development; counseling (MA); criminal justice administration (MS); education (MA); healthcare administration (MS); human resource management (MS); school administration (MA); teaching (MAT).

**Lynn University,** Eugene M. and Christine E. Lynn College of International Communication, Boca Raton, FL 33431-5598. Offers communication and media (MS), including digital media, media studies and practice; digital media (Certificate). *Program availability:* Part-time, evening/weekend. *Faculty:* 15 full-time (8 women), 6 part-time/adjunct (3 women). *Students:* 24 full-time (20 women), 15 part-time (14 women); includes 11 minority (7 Black or African American, non-Hispanic/Latino; 2 Asian, non-Hispanic/Latino; 2 Hispanic/Latino), 14 international. Average age 27. 38 applicants, 87% accepted, 17 enrolled. In 2016, 18 master's, 1 other advanced degree awarded. *Degree requirements:* For master's, project or thesis. *Entrance requirements:* For master's, resume, letter of recommendation, official transcripts, bachelor's degree from accredited institution, personal statement. Additional exam requirements/recommendations for international students: Required—TOEFL (minimum score 550 paper-based; 80 iBT), IELTS (minimum score 6.5). *Application deadline:* For fall admission, 8/18 for domestic students, 8/4 for international students; for spring admission, 12/15 for domestic students, 12/1 for international students; for summer admission, 4/17 for domestic students, 4/3 for international students. Applications are processed on a rolling basis. Application fee: $45. Electronic applications accepted. *Expenses:* $725 per credit hour. *Financial support:* In 2016–17, 7 students received support. Career-related internships or fieldwork, Federal Work-Study, institutionally sponsored loans, scholarships/grants, tuition waivers (partial), and unspecified assistantships available. Support available to part-time students. Financial award application deadline: 8/1; financial award applicants required to submit FAFSA. *Unit head:* Dr. David L. Jaffe, Dean, 561-237-7099, Fax: 561-237-7097, E-mail: djaffe@lynn.edu. *Application contact:* Steven Pruitt, Director of Graduate Admission, 561-237-7834, Fax: 561-237-7100, E-mail: admission@lynn.edu.
Website: http://www.lynn.edu/academics/colleges/international-communication

**Michigan State University,** The Graduate School, College of Communication Arts and Sciences, Department of Telecommunication, Information Studies, and Media, East Lansing, MI 48824. Offers digital media arts and technology (MA); information and telecommunication management (MA); information, policy and society (MA); serious game design (MA). *Entrance requirements:* Additional exam requirements/recommendations for international students: Required—TOEFL. Electronic applications accepted.

**Minneapolis College of Art and Design,** Certificate Programs, Minneapolis, MN 55404-4347. Offers design (Certificate); fine arts (Certificate); graphic design (Certificate); media (Certificate); sustainable design (Certificate). *Program availability:* Part-time, online learning. *Degree requirements:* For Certificate, final project. *Entrance requirements:* For degree, resume, portfolio, letter of recommendation. Additional exam requirements/recommendations for international students: Required—TOEFL (minimum score 550 paper-based; 79 iBT). Electronic applications accepted. *Faculty research:* Visual arts.

**New Mexico Highlands University,** Graduate Studies, School of Business, Media and Technology, Department of Media Arts and Technology, Las Vegas, NM 87701. Offers media arts and computer science (MA), including media arts.

**The New School,** Parsons School of Design, Program in Design and Technology, New York, NY 10011. Offers MFA. Program also offered at Paris, France campus. *Faculty:* 49 full-time (27 women), 28 part-time/adjunct (11 women). *Students:* 155 full-time (115 women), 1 (woman) part-time; includes 25 minority (7 Black or African American, non-Hispanic/Latino; 1 American Indian or Alaska Native, non-Hispanic/Latino; 8 Asian, non-Hispanic/Latino; 7 Hispanic/Latino; 2 Two or more races, non-Hispanic/Latino), 105 international. Average age 26. 313 applicants, 72% accepted, 82 enrolled. In 2016, 96 master's awarded. *Degree requirements:* For master's, thesis, exam, written essay. *Entrance requirements:* For master's, transcripts, resume, statement of purpose, recommendation letters, portfolio, interview. Additional exam requirements/recommendations for international students: Required—TOEFL (minimum score 92 iBT), IELTS (minimum score 7), PTE (minimum score 63). *Application deadline:* For fall admission, 1/1 for domestic and international students. Applications are processed on a rolling basis. Application fee: $50. Electronic applications accepted. *Expenses:* Contact institution. *Financial support:* Research assistantships, teaching assistantships, career-related internships or fieldwork, Federal Work-Study, scholarships/grants, unspecified assistantships, and travel funding; tuition waivers for students who are also New School employees available. Support available to part-time students. Financial award application deadline: 2/1; financial award applicants required to submit FAFSA. *Faculty research:* Mobile and application design, web/UI/UX design, new media art, game design, motion graphics and digital filmmaking. *Unit head:* Sven Travis, Program Director, 212-229-8908 Ext. 4342, E-mail: traviss@newschool.edu. *Application contact:* Courtney Malenius, Director of Graduate Admission, 212-229-5150 Ext. 4011, E-mail: thinkparsonsgrad@newschool.edu.
Website: http://www.newschool.edu/

**New York Institute of Technology,** College of Arts and Sciences, Department of Digital Art and Design, Old Westbury, NY 11568-8000. Offers computer graphics (MFA), including animation, fine arts and technology, graphic design. *Program availability:* Part-time, evening/weekend. *Faculty:* 7 full-time (4 women), 6 part-time/adjunct (2 women). *Students:* 42 full-time (30 women), 12 part-time (6 women); includes 6 minority (3 Black or African American, non-Hispanic/Latino; 1 Asian, non-Hispanic/Latino; 2 Hispanic/Latino), 42 international. Average age 27. 41 applicants, 68% accepted, 14 enrolled. In 2016, 31 master's awarded. *Degree requirements:* For master's, thesis. *Entrance requirements:* For master's, BFA or equivalent; minimum undergraduate GPA of 3.0; digital portfolio. Additional exam requirements/recommendations for international students: Required—TOEFL (minimum score 79 iBT), IELTS (minimum score 6). *Application deadline:* For fall admission, 6/1 for domestic and international students. Applications are processed on a rolling basis. Application fee: $50. Electronic applications accepted. *Expenses:* $1,215 per credit. *Financial support:* Career-related internships or fieldwork, Federal Work-Study, scholarships/grants, tuition waivers (full and partial), and unspecified assistantships available. Support available to part-time students. Financial award application deadline: 3/1; financial award applicants required to submit FAFSA. *Faculty research:* Graphic design, animation, art and technology, virtual reality, sculpture. *Unit head:* Terry Nauheim, Department Chair, 516-686-7881, Fax: 212-261-1742, E-mail: tnauheim@nyit.edu. *Application contact:* Alice Dolitsky, Director, Graduate Admissions, 516-686-7520, Fax: 516-686-1116, E-mail: nyitgrad@nyit.edu.
Website: http://www.nyit.edu/arts_and_sciences/department_of_digital_art_design

**New York University,** School of Continuing and Professional Studies, Division of Programs in Business, Program in Graphic Communications Management and Technology, New York, NY 10012-1019. Offers MA. *Program availability:* Part-time, evening/weekend. *Degree requirements:* For master's, thesis, capstone, research course. *Entrance requirements:* For master's, GRE or GMAT (only upon request), relevant professional work, internship or volunteer experience. Additional exam requirements/recommendations for international students: Required—TOEFL (minimum score 600 paper-based; 100 iBT), IELTS (minimum score 7). Electronic applications accepted.

**New York University,** School of Continuing and Professional Studies, Division of Programs in Business, Program in Interactive Motion Graphics and Visual Effects, New York, NY 10012-1019. Offers MS. *Program availability:* Part-time. *Degree requirements:* For master's, thesis, project. *Entrance requirements:* For master's, bachelor's degree, resume with relevant professional work, internship or volunteer experience, two letters of recommendation, statement of purpose. Additional exam requirements/recommendations for international students: Required—TOEFL (minimum score 600 paper-based; 100 iBT), IELTS (minimum score 7). Electronic applications accepted.

**North Carolina Agricultural and Technical State University,** School of Graduate Studies, School of Technology, Department of Graphic Communication Systems and Technological Studies, Greensboro, NC 27411. Offers graphic communication systems (MSTM); technology education (MAT). *Accreditation:* NCATE (one or more programs are accredited). *Program availability:* Part-time, evening/weekend. *Degree requirements:* For master's, comprehensive exam, thesis or alternative, qualifying exam. *Entrance requirements:* For master's, GRE General Test, minimum GPA of 3.0.

**North Carolina State University,** Graduate School, College of Humanities and Social Sciences, Program in Communication, Rhetoric, and Digital Media, Raleigh, NC 27695. Offers PhD.

**The Ohio State University,** Graduate School, College of Arts and Sciences, Division of Arts and Humanities, Department of Design, Columbus, OH 43210. Offers design (MA); design research and development (MFA); digital animation and interactive media (MFA). *Accreditation:* NASAD. *Program availability:* Part-time. *Faculty:* 15. *Students:* 23 full-time (12 women), 7 international. Average age 29. In 2016, 8 master's awarded. *Degree requirements:* For master's, project or thesis. *Entrance requirements:* For master's, GRE General Test (for all applicants with cumulative GPA below 3.0), portfolio. Additional exam requirements/recommendations for international students: Recommended—TOEFL (minimum score 550 paper-based; 79 iBT). *Application deadline:* For fall admission, 12/13 priority date for domestic students, 11/30 priority date for international students; for spring admission, 3/1 for domestic students, 2/1 for international students. Applications are processed on a rolling basis. Application fee: $60 ($70 for international students). Electronic applications accepted. *Financial support:* Fellowships with tuition reimbursements, research assistantships with tuition reimbursements, teaching assistantships with tuition reimbursements, career-related internships or fieldwork, Federal Work-Study, institutionally sponsored loans, and unspecified assistantships available. Support available to part-time students. Financial award application deadline: 5/1. *Unit head:* Dr. Mary Anne Beecher, Chair, 614-688-

6746, E-mail: beecher.17@osu.edu. *Application contact:* Graduate and Professional Admissions, 614-292-9444, Fax: 614-292-3895, E-mail: gpadmissions@osu.edu. Website: http://design.osu.edu/

**Old Dominion University,** College of Arts and Letters, Program in Lifespan and Digital Communication, Norfolk, VA 23529. Offers MA. *Accreditation:* NASAD. *Program availability:* Part-time, evening/weekend. *Faculty:* 15 full-time (5 women). *Students:* 9 full-time (6 women), 17 part-time (13 women); includes 14 minority (7 Black or African American, non-Hispanic/Latino; 2 Asian, non-Hispanic/Latino; 3 Hispanic/Latino; 2 Two or more races, non-Hispanic/Latino), 1 international. Average age 33. 14 applicants, 86% accepted, 12 enrolled. In 2016, 6 master's awarded. *Degree requirements:* For master's, comprehensive exam or thesis. *Entrance requirements:* For master's, GRE. Additional exam requirements/recommendations for international students: Recommended—TOEFL (minimum score 550 paper-based; 79 iBT). *Application deadline:* For fall admission, 6/15 for domestic students, 4/15 for international students. Applications are processed on a rolling basis. Application fee: $50. Electronic applications accepted. *Expenses:* $8,604 tuition; $346 fees. *Financial support:* In 2016–17, 10 students received support, including 1 research assistantship (averaging $10,000 per year), 7 teaching assistantships (averaging $10,000 per year); 3 assistantships (averaging $5000) also available. Financial award application deadline: 6/15. *Faculty research:* Family communication, digital media studies, lifespan communication, social media, screenwriting. *Unit head:* Dr. Thomas J. Socha, Graduate Program Director, 757-683-3833, E-mail: tsocha@odu.edu. *Application contact:* Dr. David C. Earnest, Associate Dean, 757-683-6077, Fax: 757-683-5746, E-mail: dearnest@odu.edu. Website: http://www.odu.edu/commtheatre/graduate#.VzDZI032bGg

**Purdue University,** Graduate School, College of Technology, Department of Computer Graphics Technology, West Lafayette, IN 47907. Offers MS, PhD. *Faculty:* 20 full-time (5 women). *Students:* 33 full-time (13 women), 17 part-time (8 women); includes 6 minority (1 Black or African American, non-Hispanic/Latino; 2 American Indian or Alaska Native, non-Hispanic/Latino; 2 Asian, non-Hispanic/Latino; 1 Hispanic/Latino), 25 international. Average age 25. 40 applicants, 75% accepted, 20 enrolled. In 2016, 10 master's awarded. *Degree requirements:* For master's, thesis; for doctorate, thesis/dissertation. *Entrance requirements:* For master's, GRE (minimum scores: 50th percentile, 150 on verbal, 150 on quantitative, 4.0 analytical). Additional exam requirements/recommendations for international students: Required—TOEFL (minimum score 550 paper-based; 77 iBT); Recommended—TWE. *Application deadline:* For fall admission, 4/1 for domestic and international students; for spring admission, 10/1 for domestic students, 9/1 for international students; for summer admission, 4/1 for domestic students, 2/15 for international students. Applications are processed on a rolling basis. Application fee: $60 ($75 for international students). Electronic applications accepted. *Financial support:* Research assistantships and teaching assistantships available. *Unit head:* Patrick Connolly, Head, 765-496-3943, E-mail: connollp@purdue.edu. *Application contact:* Cathy Noerenberg, Graduate Contact, 765-496-6368, E-mail: cnoerenb@purdue.edu. Website: http://www.tech.purdue.edu/cgt/

**Rensselaer Polytechnic Institute,** Graduate School, School of Humanities, Arts, and Social Sciences, Program in Electronic Arts, Troy, NY 12180-3590. Offers PhD. *Faculty:* 23 full-time (10 women), 1 (woman) part-time/adjunct. *Students:* 19 full-time (11 women), 1 part-time (0 women). 29 applicants, 48% accepted, 6 enrolled. In 2016, 1 doctorate awarded. *Degree requirements:* For doctorate, comprehensive exam. *Entrance requirements:* Additional exam requirements/recommendations for international students: Required—TOEFL (minimum score 570 paper-based; 88 iBT), IELTS (minimum score 6.5), PTE (minimum score 60). *Application deadline:* For fall admission, 1/1 priority date for domestic and international students. Applications are processed on a rolling basis. Application fee: $75. Electronic applications accepted. *Expenses:* Tuition: Full-time $49,520; part-time $2060 per credit hour. *Required fees:* $2617. *Financial support:* In 2016–17, research assistantships (averaging $22,000 per year), teaching assistantships with full tuition reimbursements (averaging $22,000 per year) were awarded; scholarships/grants also available. Financial award application deadline: 1/1. *Unit head:* Dr. Shawn Lawson, Graduate Program Director, 518-276-2206, E-mail: lawsos2@rpi.edu. *Application contact:* Office of Graduate Admissions, 518-276-6216, E-mail: gradadmissions@rpi.edu. Website: http://www.arts.rpi.edu/pl/graduate-programs

**Rhode Island School of Design,** Graduate Studies, Department of Digital and Media, Providence, RI 02903-2784. Offers MFA. *Faculty:* 4 full-time (2 women), 13 part-time/adjunct (3 women). *Students:* 27 full-time (19 women); includes 6 minority (4 Asian, non-Hispanic/Latino; 1 Hispanic/Latino; 1 Two or more races, non-Hispanic/Latino), 12 international. Average age 28. 140 applicants, 19% accepted, 13 enrolled. In 2016, 14 master's awarded. *Degree requirements:* For master's, thesis, exhibition. *Entrance requirements:* For master's, portfolio, statement of purpose, 3 letters of recommendation. Additional exam requirements/recommendations for international students: Required—TOEFL (minimum score 580 paper-based; 93 iBT). *Application deadline:* For fall admission, 2/1 for domestic and international students. Application fee: $60. Electronic applications accepted. *Expenses:* Tuition: Full-time $46,800. *Required fees:* $310. *Financial support:* Fellowships, research assistantships, teaching assistantships, Federal Work-Study, scholarships/grants, and unspecified assistantships available. Financial award application deadline: 2/15; financial award applicants required to submit FAFSA. *Unit head:* Shona Kitchen, Head, 401-454-6139, Fax: 401-277-4966, E-mail: skitchen@risd.edu. *Application contact:* Molly Pettengil, Assistant Director for Graduate Recruitment, 401-454-6312, Fax: 401-454-6309, E-mail: mpetteng@risd.edu. Website: http://www.risd.edu/academics/digital-media/

**Rochester Institute of Technology,** Graduate Enrollment Services, College of Imaging Arts and Sciences, School of Design, MFA Program in Visual Communication Design, Rochester, NY 14623-5603. Offers MFA. *Accreditation:* NASAD. *Program availability:* Part-time. *Students:* 59 full-time (47 women), 29 part-time (16 women); includes 7 minority (2 Asian, non-Hispanic/Latino; 3 Hispanic/Latino; 2 Two or more races, non-Hispanic/Latino), 70 international. Average age 29. 201 applicants, 43% accepted, 27 enrolled. In 2016, 20 master's awarded. *Degree requirements:* For master's, thesis, thesis exhibition. *Entrance requirements:* For master's, GRE, portfolio, minimum GPA of 3.0 (recommended). Additional exam requirements/recommendations for international students: Required—TOEFL (minimum score 550 paper-based; 90 iBT), IELTS (minimum score 7), PTE (minimum score 58). *Application deadline:* For fall admission, 2/15 priority date for domestic and international students. Applications are processed on a rolling basis. Application fee: $60. Electronic applications accepted. *Expenses:* $1,742 per credit hour. *Financial support:* In 2016–17, 46 students received support. Teaching assistantships with partial tuition reimbursements available, career-related internships or fieldwork, scholarships/grants, and unspecified assistantships available. Support available to part-time students. Financial award applicants required to submit FAFSA. *Faculty research:* Motion graphics for design and interaction; experiential design for physical and virtual environments; augmented and virtual reality applications within education, advertising and consumer products; visual design for user experience and interactive solutions. *Unit head:* Adam Smith, Graduate Program Director, 585-475-4552, Fax: 585-475-7533, E-mail: aesfaa@rit.edu. *Application*

*contact:* Diane Ellison, Associate Vice President, Graduate Enrollment Services, 585-475-2229, Fax: 585-475-7164, E-mail: gradinfo@rit.edu. Website: http://cias.rit.edu/schools/design/graduate-visual-communication-design

**Rochester Institute of Technology,** Graduate Enrollment Services, College of Imaging Arts and Sciences, School of Film and Animation, MFA Program in Film and Animation, Rochester, NY 14623. Offers MFA. *Program availability:* Part-time. *Students:* 44 full-time (21 women), 7 part-time (2 women); includes 5 minority (1 Black or African American, non-Hispanic/Latino; 2 Asian, non-Hispanic/Latino; 2 Hispanic/Latino), 33 international. Average age 26. 119 applicants, 50% accepted, 20 enrolled. In 2016, 17 master's awarded. *Degree requirements:* For master's, thesis. *Entrance requirements:* For master's, GRE, portfolio, minimum GPA of 3.0 (recommended). Additional exam requirements/recommendations for international students: Required—TOEFL (minimum score 550 paper-based; 82 iBT), IELTS (minimum score 6.5), PTE (minimum score 58). *Application deadline:* For fall admission, 2/15 priority date for domestic and international students. Applications are processed on a rolling basis. Application fee: $60. Electronic applications accepted. *Expenses:* $1,742 per credit hour. *Financial support:* In 2016–17, 32 students received support. Teaching assistantships with partial tuition reimbursements available, career-related internships or fieldwork, scholarships/grants, and unspecified assistantships available. Support available to part-time students. Financial award applicants required to submit FAFSA. *Faculty research:* 3-D printing, super 8 cameras, color and projection, gaming and storytelling, special effects including virtual reality. *Unit head:* Thomas Gasek, Graduate Program Director, 585-475-7403, E-mail: tdgpph@rit.edu. *Application contact:* Diane Ellison, Associate Vice President, Graduate Enrollment Services, 585-475-2229, Fax: 585-475-7164, E-mail: gradinfo@rit.edu. Website: http://cias.rit.edu/schools/film-animation/graduate-film-and-animation

**Savannah College of Art and Design,** Graduate School, Program in Animation, Savannah, GA 31402-3146. Offers MA, MFA. *Program availability:* Part-time, 100% online. *Faculty:* 27 full-time (4 women), 6 part-time/adjunct (2 women). *Students:* 178 full-time (105 women), 70 part-time (30 women); includes 43 minority (29 Black or African American, non-Hispanic/Latino; 1 American Indian or Alaska Native, non-Hispanic/Latino; 6 Asian, non-Hispanic/Latino; 7 Hispanic/Latino), 119 international. Average age 26. 218 applicants, 58% accepted, 75 enrolled. In 2016, 41 master's awarded. *Degree requirements:* For master's, final project (for MA); thesis (for MFA). *Entrance requirements:* For master's, GRE (recommended), portfolio (submitted in digital format), audition or writing submission, resume, statement of purpose, two letters of recommendation. Additional exam requirements/recommendations for international students: Required—TOEFL (minimum score 550 paper-based, 85 iBT), IELTS (minimum score 6.5), or ACTFL. *Application deadline:* For fall admission, 4/1 for domestic and international students. Applications are processed on a rolling basis. Application fee: $40. Electronic applications accepted. *Expenses:* Tuition: Full-time $36,045. Tuition and fees vary according to course load. *Financial support:* Career-related internships or fieldwork, Federal Work-Study, and scholarships/grants available. Financial award application deadline: 4/1; financial award applicants required to submit FAFSA. *Unit head:* Greg Araya, Chair, Animation. *Application contact:* Jenny Jaquillard, Executive Director of Admissions, Recruitment and Events, 912-525-5100, Fax: 912-525-5985, E-mail: admission@scad.edu. Website: http://www.scad.edu/academics/programs/animation

**Savannah College of Art and Design,** Graduate School, Program in Interactive Design and Game Development, Savannah, GA 31402-3146. Offers MA, MFA. *Program availability:* Part-time, 100% online. *Faculty:* 14 full-time (4 women), 5 part-time/adjunct (0 women). *Students:* 66 full-time (29 women), 34 part-time (8 women); includes 10 minority (2 Black or African American, non-Hispanic/Latino; 6 Asian, non-Hispanic/Latino; 2 Hispanic/Latino), 56 international. Average age 28. 124 applicants, 40% accepted, 22 enrolled. In 2016, 27 master's awarded. *Degree requirements:* For master's, final project (for MA); thesis (for MFA). *Entrance requirements:* For master's, GRE (recommended), portfolio (submitted in digital format), audition or writing submission, resume, statement of purpose, two letters of recommendation. Additional exam requirements/recommendations for international students: Required—TOEFL (minimum score 550 paper-based, 85 iBT), IELTS (minimum score 6.5), or ACTFL. *Application deadline:* For fall admission, 4/1 for domestic and international students. Applications are processed on a rolling basis. Application fee: $40. Electronic applications accepted. *Expenses:* Tuition: Full-time $36,045. Tuition and fees vary according to course load. *Financial support:* Career-related internships or fieldwork, Federal Work-Study, and scholarships/grants available. Financial award application deadline: 4/1; financial award applicants required to submit FAFSA. *Unit head:* SuAnne Fu, Chair, Interactive Design and Game Development. *Application contact:* Jenny Jaquillard, Executive Director of Admissions, Recruitment and Events, 912-525-5100, Fax: 912-525-5985, E-mail: admission@scad.edu. Website: http://www.scad.edu/academics/programs/interactive-design-and-game-development

**Savannah College of Art and Design,** Graduate School, Program in Motion Media Design, Savannah, GA 31402-3146. Offers MA, MFA. *Program availability:* Part-time, 100% online. *Faculty:* 14 full-time (5 women), 7 part-time/adjunct (5 women). *Students:* 56 full-time (35 women), 20 part-time (8 women); includes 12 minority (9 Black or African American, non-Hispanic/Latino; 1 Asian, non-Hispanic/Latino; 2 Hispanic/Latino), 40 international. Average age 30. 51 applicants, 61% accepted, 20 enrolled. In 2016, 22 master's awarded. *Degree requirements:* For master's, final project (for MA); thesis (for MFA). *Entrance requirements:* For master's, GRE (recommended), portfolio (submitted in digital format), audition or writing submission, resume, statement of purpose, two letters of recommendation. Additional exam requirements/recommendations for international students: Required—TOEFL (minimum score 550 paper-based, 85 iBT), IELTS (minimum score 6.5), or ACTFL. *Application deadline:* For fall admission, 4/1 for domestic and international students. Applications are processed on a rolling basis. Application fee: $40. Electronic applications accepted. *Expenses:* Tuition: Full-time $36,045. Tuition and fees vary according to course load. *Financial support:* Career-related internships or fieldwork, Federal Work-Study, and scholarships/grants available. Financial award application deadline: 4/1; financial award applicants required to submit FAFSA. *Unit head:* Kelly Carlton, Chair, Motion Media Design. *Application contact:* Jenny Jaquillard, Executive Director of Admissions, Recruitment and Events, 912-525-5100, Fax: 912-525-5985, E-mail: admission@scad.edu. Website: http://www.scad.edu/academics/programs/motion-media-design

**School of Visual Arts,** Graduate Programs, Computer Art Department, New York, NY 10010-3994. Offers MFA. *Accreditation:* NASAD. *Degree requirements:* For master's, thesis, 60 credits, including all required courses; minimum GPA of 3.0; matriculation of two academic years. *Entrance requirements:* For master's, portfolio; 3-5 minute sample reel showing best work; statement of purpose; official transcript; 3 letters of recommendation; resume/curriculum vitae. Additional exam requirements/recommendations for international students: Required—TOEFL (minimum score 550 paper-based; 79 iBT). Electronic applications accepted. *Expenses:* Contact institution.

**Shepherd University,** Hollywood CG School of Digital Arts, Los Angeles, CA 90065. Offers game art and design (MSIT); visual effects and animation (MSIT). *Degree requirements:* For master's, exam, thesis, or portfolio.

## Computer Art and Design

**Stevens Institute of Technology,** Graduate School, Charles V. Schaefer Jr. School of Engineering and Science, Department of Computer Science, Hoboken, NJ 07030. Offers computer graphics (Certificate), including computer graphics; computer science (MS, PhD); computer systems (Certificate), including computer systems; cybersecurity (MS); database management systems (Certificate), including databases; distributed systems (Certificate), including distributed systems; elements of computer science (Certificate), including cybersecurity; enterprise and cloud computing (MS); enterprise computing (Certificate), including enterprise and cloud computing; enterprise security and information assurance (Certificate), including enterprise security and information assurance; health informatics (Certificate), including health informatics; multimedia experience and management (Certificate), including multimedia experience and management; networks and systems administration (Certificate), including cloud computing; service oriented computing (Certificate), including service oriented computing. *Program availability:* Part-time, evening/weekend. *Faculty:* 21 full-time (4 women), 13 part-time/adjunct (2 women). *Students:* 436 full-time (124 women), 72 part-time (12 women); includes 27 minority (4 Black or African American, non-Hispanic/Latino; 21 Asian, non-Hispanic/Latino; 1 Hispanic/Latino; 1 Two or more races, non-Hispanic/Latino), 423 international. Average age 25. 1,183 applicants, 54% accepted, 184 enrolled. In 2016, 225 master's, 4 doctorates, 18 other advanced degrees awarded. Terminal master's awarded for partial completion of doctoral program. *Degree requirements:* For master's, thesis optional, minimum B average in major field and overall; for doctorate, comprehensive exam (for some programs), thesis/dissertation; for Certificate, minimum B average. *Entrance requirements:* Additional exam requirements/recommendations for international students: Required—TOEFL (minimum score 74 iBT), IELTS (minimum score 6). *Application deadline:* For fall admission, 6/1 for domestic students, 4/15 for international students; for spring admission, 11/30 for domestic students, 11/1 for international students. Applications are processed on a rolling basis. Application fee: $65. Electronic applications accepted. *Expenses:* Contact institution. *Financial support:* Fellowships, research assistantships, teaching assistantships, career-related internships or fieldwork, Federal Work-Study, scholarships/grants, and unspecified assistantships available. Financial award application deadline: 2/15; financial award applicants required to submit FAFSA. *Faculty research:* Computer security, computer vision, dynamic scene analysis, privacy-preserving data mining, visualization. *Unit head:* Giuseppe Ateniese, Director, 201-216-3741, E-mail: gatenies@stevens.edu. *Application contact:* Graduate Admissions, 888-783-8367, Fax: 888-511-1306, E-mail: graduate@stevens.edu. Website: https://www.stevens.edu/schaefer-school-engineering-science/departments/computer-science

**Syracuse University,** College of Visual and Performing Arts, MFA Program in Computer Art, Syracuse, NY 13244. Offers art video (MFA). *Degree requirements:* For master's, thesis or alternative. *Entrance requirements:* For master's, portfolio, artist statement, three letters of recommendation, transcripts, personal statement/essay, resume. Additional exam requirements/recommendations for international students: Required—TOEFL (minimum score 100 iBT), IELTS. *Application deadline:* For fall admission, 2/1 priority date for domestic and international students. Application fee: $75. Electronic applications accepted. *Expenses: Tuition:* Full-time $25,974; part-time $1443 per credit hour. *Required fees:* $802; $50 per course. Tuition and fees vary according to course load and program. *Financial support:* Fellowships with full tuition reimbursements and teaching assistantships with tuition reimbursements available. Financial award application deadline: 1/1; financial award applicants required to submit FAFSA. *Faculty research:* Aesthetic possibilities of subject, genre, media technologies from personal points of view, strategies for making art in the video medium, including performance, narrative, documentary, site-specific, and multi-channel installation. *Unit head:* Prof. Annina Rust, Associate Professor/Program Coordinator, Computer Art and Animation, 315-443-1202, E-mail: arust@syr.edu. *Application contact:* Therese West, Information Contact, 315-443-0137, E-mail: admissg@syr.edu.

**Texas State University,** The Graduate College, College of Fine Arts and Communication, Program in Communication Design, San Marcos, TX 78666. Offers MFA. *Program availability:* Part-time. *Faculty:* 8 full-time (4 women), 2 part-time/adjunct (0 women). *Students:* 18 full-time (13 women), 28 part-time (19 women); includes 15 minority (1 Black or African American, non-Hispanic/Latino; 1 Asian, non-Hispanic/Latino; 11 Hispanic/Latino; 2 Two or more races, non-Hispanic/Latino), 4 international. Average age 36. 35 applicants, 54% accepted, 14 enrolled. In 2016, 6 master's awarded. *Degree requirements:* For master's, comprehensive exam, thesis. *Entrance requirements:* For master's, related baccalaureate degree from regionally-accredited institution with minimum GPA of 2.75 in last 60 hours of undergraduate course work, portfolio, 3 letters of recommendation, academic and professional statement of purpose. Additional exam requirements/recommendations for international students: Required—TOEFL (minimum score 550 paper-based; 78 iBT), IELTS (minimum score 6.5). *Application deadline:* For fall admission, 3/31 for domestic and international students; for spring admission, 10/31 for domestic students, 10/1 for international students. Applications are processed on a rolling basis. Application fee: $40 ($90 for international students). Electronic applications accepted. *Expenses:* $4,851 per semester. *Financial support:* In 2016–17, 28 students received support, including 7 teaching assistantships (averaging $14,621 per year); research assistantships, Federal Work-Study, institutionally sponsored loans, scholarships/grants, and unspecified assistantships also available. Support available to part-time students. Financial award application deadline: 3/1; financial award applicants required to submit FAFSA. *Unit head:* Dr. Claudia Roeschmann, Graduate Advisor, 512-245-7450, E-mail: cr29@txstate.edu. *Application contact:* Dr. Andrea Golato, Dean of Graduate School, 512-245-2581, Fax: 512-245-8365, E-mail: gradcollege@txstate.edu. Website: http://www.finearts.txstate.edu/Art/mfacomdes/

**Universidad Autonoma de Guadalajara,** Graduate Programs, Guadalajara, Mexico. Offers administrative law and justice (LL M); advertising and corporate communications (MA); architecture (M Arch); business (MBA); computational science (MCC); education (Ed M, Ed D); English-Spanish translation (MA); entrepreneurship and management (MBA); integrated management of digital animation (MA); international business (MIB); international corporate law (LL M); internet technologies (MS); manufacturing systems (MMS); occupational health (MS); philosophy (MA, PhD); power electronics (MS); quality systems (MQS); renewable energy (MS); social evaluation of projects (MBA); strategic market research (MBA); tax law (MA); teaching mathematics (MA).

**Universidad de las Américas Puebla,** Division of Graduate Studies, School of Humanities, Program in Information Design, Puebla, Mexico. Offers MA. *Program availability:* Part-time, evening/weekend. *Degree requirements:* For master's, one foreign language, thesis. *Entrance requirements:* Additional exam requirements/recommendations for international students: Required—TOEFL. *Faculty research:* Typography, project development, organizational image.

**University of Alaska Fairbanks,** College of Liberal Arts, Department of Art, Fairbanks, AK 99775-5640. Offers art (MFA); ceramics (MFA); computer art (MFA); drawing (MFA); painting (MFA); photography (MFA); printmaking (MFA); sculpture (MFA). *Program availability:* Part-time. *Faculty:* 7 full-time (4 women). *Students:* 4 full-time (3 women), 1 (woman) part-time; includes 2 minority (1 Hispanic/Latino; 1 Native

Hawaiian or other Pacific Islander, non-Hispanic/Latino). Average age 38. 4 applicants, 50% accepted, 1 enrolled. In 2016, 2 master's awarded. *Degree requirements:* For master's, comprehensive exam, oral defense of project or thesis. *Entrance requirements:* For master's, portfolio of work about 20 slides or appropriate equivalent depending on field of study. Additional exam requirements/recommendations for international students: Required—TOEFL (minimum score 550 paper-based; 79 iBT), IELTS (minimum score 6.5). *Application deadline:* For fall admission, 6/1 for domestic students, 3/1 for international students; for spring admission, 10/15 for domestic students, 9/1 for international students. Applications are processed on a rolling basis. Application fee: $60. Electronic applications accepted. *Expenses:* Tuition, state resident: full-time $7992; part-time $444 per credit. Tuition, nonresident: full-time $16,326; part-time $907 per credit. *Required fees:* $39 per credit. $322 per semester. Tuition and fees vary according to course level, course load, campus/location, program and reciprocity agreements. *Financial support:* In 2016–17, 3 teaching assistantships with full tuition reimbursements (averaging $5,717 per year) were awarded; fellowships with full tuition reimbursements, research assistantships with full tuition reimbursements, Federal Work-Study, scholarships/grants, health care benefits, and unspecified assistantships also available. Support available to part-time students. Financial award application deadline: 7/1; financial award applicants required to submit FAFSA. *Faculty research:* Computer art, survey of arts in Alaska, found object art, visualization and animation, painting from the wilderness. *Unit head:* David Mollett, Chair, 907-474-7530, Fax: 907-474-5853, E-mail: uaf-art@alaska.edu. *Application contact:* Mary Kreta, Director of Admissions, 907-474-7500, Fax: 907-474-7097, E-mail: admissions@uaf.edu. Website: http://www.uaf.edu/art/

**University of California, Santa Cruz,** Division of Graduate Studies, Division of the Arts, Department of Film and Digital Media, Santa Cruz, CA 95064. Offers PhD. *Degree requirements:* For doctorate, one foreign language, thesis/dissertation, qualifying exams. *Entrance requirements:* For doctorate, GRE. Additional exam requirements/recommendations for international students: Required—TOEFL (minimum score 550 paper-based; 83 iBT); Recommended—IELTS (minimum score 8). Electronic applications accepted. *Faculty research:* Integrating critical and creative practice, working across media, pursuing new modes of social and political engagement, fostering global cultural citizenship.

**University of California, Santa Cruz,** Division of Graduate Studies, Division of the Arts, Program in Digital Arts and New Media, Santa Cruz, CA 95064. Offers MFA. *Degree requirements:* For master's, thesis, written paper. *Entrance requirements:* Additional exam requirements/recommendations for international students: Required—TOEFL (minimum score 550 paper-based; 83 iBT); Recommended—IELTS (minimum score 8). Electronic applications accepted. *Faculty research:* Mechatronics, participatory culture, performative technologies, playable media.

**University of Central Arkansas,** Graduate School, College of Fine Arts and Communication, Program in Digital Filmmaking, Conway, AR 72035-0001. Offers MFA. *Accreditation:* NASAD. *Degree requirements:* For master's, thesis. *Entrance requirements:* For master's, GRE General Test, minimum GPA of 2.7. Additional exam requirements/recommendations for international students: Required—TOEFL (minimum score 550 paper-based). Electronic applications accepted.

**University of Central Florida,** College of Arts and Humanities, School of Visual Arts and Design, Orlando, FL 32816. Offers digital media (MA); emerging media (MFA), including digital media, entrepreneurial digital cinema, studio art and the computer. *Program availability:* Part-time. *Faculty:* 57 full-time (23 women), 15 part-time/adjunct (4 women). *Students:* 26 full-time (12 women), 13 part-time (3 women); includes 7 minority (3 Black or African American, non-Hispanic/Latino; 1 Asian, non-Hispanic/Latino; 3 Hispanic/Latino), 2 international. Average age 31. 49 applicants, 57% accepted, 19 enrolled. In 2016, 7 master's awarded. *Degree requirements:* For master's, comprehensive exam, thesis or alternative. *Entrance requirements:* Additional exam requirements/recommendations for international students: Required—TOEFL. *Application deadline:* For fall admission, 7/1 for domestic students. Application fee: $30. Electronic applications accepted. *Expenses:* Tuition, state resident: part-time $288.16 per credit hour. Tuition, nonresident: part-time $1071.31 per credit hour. *Financial support:* In 2016–17, 15 students received support, including 4 fellowships with partial tuition reimbursements available (averaging $10,000 per year), 2 research assistantships with partial tuition reimbursements available (averaging $3,214 per year), 13 teaching assistantships with partial tuition reimbursements available (averaging $7,570 per year); scholarships/grants and unspecified assistantships also available. Financial award application deadline: 1/1; financial award applicants required to submit FAFSA. *Unit head:* Dr. Rudy McDaniel, Interim Director, 407-823-3145, E-mail: rudy@ucf.edu. *Application contact:* Assistant Director, Graduate Admissions, 407-823-2766, Fax: 407-823-6442, E-mail: gradadmissions@ucf.edu. Website: http://svad.cah.ucf.edu/

**University of Denver,** Division of Arts, Humanities and Social Sciences, Program in Emergent Digital Practices, Denver, CO 80208. Offers MA, MFA. *Program availability:* Part-time. *Faculty:* 17 full-time (5 women). *Students:* 7 full-time (1 woman), 255 part-time (150 women); includes 55 minority (16 Black or African American, non-Hispanic/Latino; 4 American Indian or Alaska Native, non-Hispanic/Latino; 4 Asian, non-Hispanic/Latino; 21 Hispanic/Latino; 3 Native Hawaiian or other Pacific Islander, non-Hispanic/Latino; 7 Two or more races, non-Hispanic/Latino), 9 international. Average age 33. 121 applicants, 86% accepted, 70 enrolled. In 2016, 87 master's awarded. *Degree requirements:* For master's, thesis (for some programs), project or thesis. *Entrance requirements:* For master's, GRE General Test, bachelor's degree, transcripts, personal statement, resume or curriculum vitae, three letters of recommendation. Additional exam requirements/recommendations for international students: Required—TOEFL (minimum score 620 paper-based; 105 iBT). *Application deadline:* For fall admission, 1/20 priority date for domestic and international students. Applications are processed on a rolling basis. Application fee: $65. Electronic applications accepted. *Expenses:* $29,022 per year full-time. *Financial support:* In 2016–17, 10 students received support, including 4 teaching assistantships with tuition reimbursements available (averaging $7,500 per year); Federal Work-Study, scholarships/grants, and unspecified assistantships also available. Financial award application deadline: 2/15; financial award applicants required to submit FAFSA. *Faculty research:* Bio-art, humane games, creative coding, audio/video art and animation, online activism. *Unit head:* Dr. Rafael Fajardo, Associate Professor and Director, 303-871-7716, E-mail: rfajardo@du.edu. *Application contact:* Dr. Laleh Mehran, Assistant Professor and Graduate Director, 303-871-3264, E-mail: laleh.mehran@du.edu. Website: http://www.du.edu/ahss/edp

**University of Florida,** Graduate School, College of The Arts, School of Art and Art History, Gainesville, FL 32611. Offers art (MA), including digital arts and sciences; art education (MA); art history (MA, PhD); museology (MA), including historic preservation. *Accreditation:* NASAD. *Program availability:* Online learning. *Degree requirements:* For master's, project or thesis (MFA); 1 foreign language (MA in art history); for doctorate, 2 foreign languages, comprehensive exam, thesis/dissertation. *Entrance requirements:* For master's, GRE General Test, portfolio (MFA), writing sample (MA), minimum GPA 3.0; for doctorate, GRE General Test, minimum GPA of 3.0. Additional exam requirements/recommendations for international students: Required—TOEFL (minimum score 550 paper-based; 80 iBT), IELTS (minimum score 6). Electronic applications accepted. *Faculty research:* Studio production, art historical studies of style context.

**University of Florida,** Graduate School, Herbert Wertheim College of Engineering and College of Liberal Arts and Sciences, Department of Computer and Information Science and Engineering, Gainesville, FL 32611. Offers computer engineering (ME, MS, PhD); computer science (MS); digital arts and sciences (MS). *Program availability:* Part-time, online learning. Terminal master's awarded for partial completion of doctoral program. *Degree requirements:* For master's, comprehensive exam, thesis optional; for doctorate, comprehensive exam, thesis/dissertation. *Entrance requirements:* For master's and doctorate, minimum GPA of 3.0. Additional exam requirements/recommendations for international students: Required—TOEFL (minimum score 550 paper-based; 80 iBT), IELTS (minimum score 6). Electronic applications accepted. *Faculty research:* Computer systems and computer networking; high-performance computing and algorithm; database and machine learning; computer graphics, vision, and intelligent systems; human center computing and digital art.

**University of Maryland, Baltimore County,** The Graduate School, College of Arts, Humanities and Social Sciences, Department of Visual Arts, MFA in Intermedia and Digital Arts Program, Baltimore, MD 21250. Offers MFA. *Faculty:* 24 full-time (13 women), 15 part-time/adjunct (7 women). *Students:* 15 full-time (8 women); includes 4 minority (1 Black or African American, non-Hispanic/Latino; 1 Asian, non-Hispanic/Latino; 2 Two or more races, non-Hispanic/Latino), 4 international. Average age 30. 22 applicants, 27% accepted, 4 enrolled. In 2016, 3 master's awarded. *Degree requirements:* For master's, oral defense, exhibition, written thesis. *Entrance requirements:* For master's, minimum GPA of 3.0, portfolio. Additional exam requirements/recommendations for international students: Required—TOEFL. *Application deadline:* For fall admission, 2/1 for domestic and international students. Applications are processed on a rolling basis. Application fee: $50. Electronic applications accepted. *Expenses:* Contact institution. *Financial support:* In 2016–17, 16 students received support, including 16 research assistantships with partial tuition reimbursements available (averaging $22,325 per year); institutionally sponsored loans, scholarships/grants, health care benefits, and unspecified assistantships also available. Financial award application deadline: 2/1. *Faculty research:* Interactive art, video, electronic media, photography, animation, print media, sound, performance, installation, cinematic arts. *Unit head:* Prof. Lisa Moren, Graduate Program Director, 410-455-2490, Fax: 410-455-1053, E-mail: lmoren@umbc.edu.
Website: http://imda.umbc.edu

**University of Massachusetts Dartmouth,** Graduate School, College of Visual and Performing Arts, Department of Design, North Dartmouth, MA 02747-2300. Offers digital media (MFA); digital multi-media (MFA); graphic design (MFA); illustration (MFA); photography (MFA); typography (MFA). *Accreditation:* NASAD. *Program availability:* Part-time. *Faculty:* 16 full-time (7 women), 3 part-time/adjunct (1 woman). *Students:* 1 (woman) full-time, 10 part-time (7 women), 6 international. Average age 28. 30 applicants, 43% accepted, 4 enrolled. In 2016, 1 degree awarded. *Degree requirements:* For master's, visual thesis, written thesis. *Entrance requirements:* For master's, statement of purpose (minimum of 300 words), resume, 2 letters of recommendation, official transcripts, portfolio (20 images representing applicant's art work, process of thinking, implementation of concepts and studio production). Additional exam requirements/recommendations for international students: Required—TOEFL (minimum score 533 paper-based; 72 iBT). *Application deadline:* For fall admission, 1/11 priority date for domestic students, 12/9 priority date for international students; for spring admission, 10/15 priority date for domestic students, 9/15 priority date for international students. Applications are processed on a rolling basis. Application fee: $60. Electronic applications accepted. *Expenses:* Tuition, state resident: full-time $14,994; part-time $624.75 per credit. Tuition, nonresident: full-time $27,068; part-time $1127.83 per credit. *Required fees:* $405; $25.88 per credit. Tuition and fees vary according to course load and reciprocity agreements. *Financial support:* In 2016–17, 2 fellowships (averaging $2,600 per year) were awarded; teaching assistantships, scholarships/grants, unspecified assistantships, and studio assistantships also available. Support available to part-time students. Financial award application deadline: 3/1; financial award applicants required to submit FAFSA. *Faculty research:* Web design, multimedia design, broadcast design, product design, typography, illustration, photography and design for arts. *Total annual research expenditures:* $113,333. *Unit head:* Ziddi Msagni, Graduate Program Director, Visual Design, 508-999-9291, E-mail: zmsagni@umassd.edu. *Application contact:* Steven Briggs, Director of Marketing and Recruitment for Graduate Studies, 508-999-8604, Fax: 508-999-8183, E-mail: graduate@umassd.edu.
Website: http://www.umassd.edu/cvpa/graduate/visualdesign/

**University of Montana,** Graduate School, College of Visual and Performing Arts, School of Media Arts, Missoula, MT 59812-0002. Offers digital filmmaking (MFA); integrated digital media (MFA).

**University of Pennsylvania,** School of Engineering and Applied Science, Department of Computer and Information Science, Philadelphia, PA 19104. Offers computer and information science (MSE, PhD); computer and information technology (MCIT); computer graphics and game technology (MSE). *Program availability:* Part-time. *Faculty:* 53 full-time (6 women), 8 part-time/adjunct (2 women). *Students:* 304 full-time (84 women), 96 part-time (36 women); includes 38 minority (4 Black or African American, non-Hispanic/Latino; 26 Asian, non-Hispanic/Latino; 6 Hispanic/Latino; 2 Two

or more races, non-Hispanic/Latino), 233 international. Average age 26. 2,114 applicants, 17% accepted, 209 enrolled. In 2016, 142 master's, 14 doctorates awarded. *Degree requirements:* For master's, comprehensive exam, thesis optional; for doctorate, comprehensive exam, thesis/dissertation. *Entrance requirements:* For master's and doctorate, GRE. Additional exam requirements/recommendations for international students: Required—TOEFL (minimum score 100 iBT), IELTS (minimum score 7). *Application deadline:* For fall admission, 3/15 priority date for domestic and international students. Application fee: $80. Electronic applications accepted. *Expenses:* Tuition: Full-time $31,068; part-time $5762 per course. *Required fees:* $3200; $336 per course. Full-time tuition and fees vary according to degree level, program and student level. Part-time tuition and fees vary according to course load, degree level and program. *Faculty research:* Artificial intelligence, robotics, software engineering, computational linguistics, machine learning. *Application contact:* William Fenton, Assistant Director of Graduate Admissions, 215-898-4542, Fax: 215-573-5577, E-mail: gradstudies@seas.upenn.edu. Website: http://www.cis.upenn.edu/prospective-students/graduate/

**University of Rhode Island,** Graduate School, College of Arts and Sciences, Graduate School of Library and Information Studies, Kingston, RI 02881. Offers libraries, leadership and transforming communities (MLIS); organization of digital media (MLIS); school library media (MLIS); MLIS/MA; MLIS/MPA. *Accreditation:* ALA (one or more programs are accredited). *Program availability:* Part-time. *Faculty:* 4 full-time (all women). *Students:* 31 full-time (23 women), 71 part-time (61 women); includes 3 minority (1 Black or African American, non-Hispanic/Latino; 2 Asian, non-Hispanic/Latino). In 2016, 31 master's awarded. *Degree requirements:* For master's, comprehensive exam. *Entrance requirements:* For master's, GRE or MAT if undergraduate GPA below 3.3, 2 letters of recommendation. Additional exam requirements/recommendations for international students: Required—TOEFL. *Application deadline:* For fall admission, 6/15 for domestic students, 2/1 for international students; for spring admission, 10/15 for domestic students, 7/15 for international students; for summer admission, 3/15 for domestic students. Application fee: $65. Electronic applications accepted. *Expenses:* Tuition, state resident: full-time $11,796; part-time $655 per credit. Tuition, nonresident: full-time $24,206; part-time $1345 per credit. *Required fees:* $1546; $44 per credit. One-time fee: $155 full-time; $35 part-time. *Financial support:* In 2016–17, 1 teaching assistantship (averaging $17,184 per year) was awarded; research assistantships also available. Financial award application deadline: 1/15; financial award applicants required to submit FAFSA. *Unit head:* Dr. Valerie Karno, Director, Graduate School of Library and Information Studies, 401-874-4682, Fax: 401-874-4127, E-mail: karno@uri.edu. *Application contact:* GSLIS Student Services Office, 401-874-2872, Fax: 401-874-5787, E-mail: stefaniemetko@mail.uri.edu.
Website: http://www.uri.edu/artsci/lsc/

**University of Southern California,** Graduate School, School of Cinematic Arts, Division of Animation and Digital Arts, Los Angeles, CA 90089. Offers MFA. *Degree requirements:* For master's, thesis, digital media and research documentation. *Entrance requirements:* Additional exam requirements/recommendations for international students: Recommended—TOEFL. Electronic applications accepted. *Expenses:* Contact institution. *Faculty research:* Character animation, visual effects, motion graphics, documentary animation, experimental animation.

**University of South Florida, St. Petersburg,** College of Arts and Sciences, St. Petersburg, FL 33701. Offers digital journalism and design (MA); environmental science and policy (MA, MS); Florida studies (MLA); journalism and media studies (MA); liberal studies (MLA); psychology (MA). *Program availability:* Part-time, online learning. *Degree requirements:* For master's, comprehensive exam, thesis or project. *Entrance requirements:* For master's, GRE, LSAT, MCAT (varies by program), letter of intent, 3 letters of recommendation, writing samples, bachelor's degree from regionally-accredited institution with minimum GPA of 3.0 overall or in upper two years. Additional exam requirements/recommendations for international students: Required—TOEFL (minimum score 550 paper-based; 79 iBT); Recommended—IELTS. Electronic applications accepted.

**University of Victoria,** Faculty of Graduate Studies, Faculty of Fine Arts, Department of Visual Arts, Victoria, BC V8W 2Y2, Canada. Offers digital multimedia (MFA); drawing (MFA); painting (MFA); photography (MFA); sculpture (MFA); video (MFA). *Degree requirements:* For master's, exhibit, oral exam. *Entrance requirements:* For master's, portfolio, BFA. Additional exam requirements/recommendations for international students: Required—TOEFL (minimum score 575 paper-based), IELTS (minimum score 7). Electronic applications accepted.

**Virginia International University,** School of Computer Information Systems, Fairfax, VA 22030. Offers business intelligence (Graduate Certificate); business intelligence and data analytics (MIS); computer science (MS), including computer animation and gaming, cybersecurity, data management networking, intelligent systems, software applications development, software engineering; cybersecurity (MIS); data management (MIS); enterprise project management (MIS); health informatics (MIS); information assurance (MIS); information systems (Graduate Certificate); information systems management (MS, Graduate Certificate); information technology (MS); information technology audit and compliance (Graduate Certificate); knowledge management (MIS); software engineering (MS). *Program availability:* Part-time, online learning. *Entrance requirements:* For master's, bachelor's degree. Additional exam requirements/recommendations for international students: Required—TOEFL (minimum score 550 paper-based; 80 iBT), IELTS. Electronic applications accepted.

# Graphic Design

**Academy of Art University,** Graduate Programs, School of Graphic Design, San Francisco, CA 94105-3410. Offers graphic design (MFA); graphic design and digital media (MA). *Accreditation:* NASAD. *Program availability:* Part-time, 100% online. *Faculty:* 7 full-time (1 woman), 33 part-time/adjunct (15 women). *Students:* 220 full-time (162 women), 145 part-time (103 women); includes 49 minority (14 Black or African American, non-Hispanic/Latino; 1 American Indian or Alaska Native, non-Hispanic/Latino; 16 Asian, non-Hispanic/Latino; 14 Hispanic/Latino; 2 Native Hawaiian or other Pacific Islander, non-Hispanic/Latino; 2 Two or more races, non-Hispanic/Latino), 242 international. Average age 29. 130 applicants, 100% accepted, 80 enrolled. In 2016, 38 master's awarded. *Degree requirements:* For master's, final review. *Entrance requirements:* For master's, statement of intent; resume; portfolio/reel; official college transcripts. *Application deadline:* Applications are processed on a rolling basis. Application fee: $50. Electronic applications accepted. *Expenses:* Tuition: Part-time $982 per unit. *Financial support:* Career-related internships or fieldwork, Federal Work-Study, and scholarships/grants available. Financial award application deadline: 8/10;

financial award applicants required to submit FAFSA. *Unit head:* 800-544-ARTS, E-mail: info@academyart.edu. *Application contact:* 800-544-ARTS, E-mail: info@academyart.edu.
Website: http://www.academyart.edu/graphic-design-school/index.html

**ArtCenter College of Design,** Graduate Graphic Design Program, Pasadena, CA 91103. Offers MFA. *Entrance requirements:* Additional exam requirements/recommendations for international students: Required—TOEFL (minimum score 100 iBT) or IELTS (minimum score 7).

**Atlantic University College,** Program in Graphic Arts, Guaynabo, PR 00970. Offers digital graphic design (MGD). *Program availability:* Part-time. *Degree requirements:* For master's, thesis. *Entrance requirements:* For master's, minimum GPA of 3.0, 2 letters of recommendation, portfolio, interview. *Faculty research:* Digital design, technology.

## Graphic Design

**Bob Jones University,** Graduate Programs, Greenville, SC 29614. Offers accountancy (MS); Bible (MA); Bible translation (MA); Biblical studies (Certificate); broadcast management (MS); business administration (MBA); church history (MA, PhD); church ministries (MA); church music (MM); cinema and video production (MA); counseling (MS); curriculum and instruction (Ed D); divinity (M Div); dramatic production (MA); educational leadership (MS, Ed D, Ed S); elementary education (M Ed, MAT); English (M Ed, MA, MAT); fine arts (MA); graphic design (MA); history (M Ed, MA); illustration (MA); interpretative speech (MA); mathematics (M Ed, MAT); medical missions (Certificate); ministry (MM, D Min); multi-categorical special education (M Ed, MAT); music (M Ed); New Testament interpretation (PhD); Old Testament interpretation (PhD); orchestral instrument performance (MM); organ performance (MM); pastoral studies (MA); personnel services (MS, Ed S); piano pedagogy (MM); piano performance (MM); platform arts (MA); radio and television broadcasting (MS); rhetoric and public address (MA); secondary education (M Ed); studio art (MA); teaching Bible (MA); theology (MA, PhD); voice performance (MM); youth ministries (MA); M Div/MM.

**Boston University,** College of Fine Arts, School of Visual Arts, Boston, MA 02226. Offers art education (MA); graphic design (MFA); painting (MFA); sculpture (MFA); studio teaching (MA). *Faculty:* 17 full-time, 4 part-time/adjunct. *Students:* 197 full-time (166 women), 3 part-time (all women); includes 24 minority (2 Black or African American, non-Hispanic/Latino; 9 Asian, non-Hispanic/Latino; 8 Hispanic/Latino; 5 Two or more races, non-Hispanic/Latino), 58 international. Average age 31. 257 applicants, 27% accepted, 21 enrolled. In 2016, 122 master's awarded. *Entrance requirements:* For master's, portfolio. Additional exam requirements/recommendations for international students: Required—TOEFL (minimum score 90 iBT), IELTS (minimum score 7). *Application deadline:* For fall admission, 2/1 for domestic and international students. Applications are processed on a rolling basis. Application fee: $80. *Expenses:* Contact institution. *Financial support:* In 2016–17, 36 students received support. Fellowships, teaching assistantships, scholarships/grants, and unspecified assistantships available. Financial award application deadline: 2/1. *Unit head:* Jeannette Guillemin, Interim Director, 617-353-3371. *Application contact:* Jessica Caccamo, Assistant Director, 617-353-3371. E-mail: visuarts@bu.edu.

**Bowling Green State University,** Graduate College, College of Arts and Sciences, School of Art, Bowling Green, OH 43403. Offers 2-D studio art (MA, MFA); 3-D studio art (MA, MFA); art education (MA); art history (MA); computer art (MA); design (MFA); digital arts (MFA); graphics (MFA). *Accreditation:* NASAD. *Program availability:* Part-time. *Degree requirements:* For master's, thesis or alternative, final exhibit (MFA). *Entrance requirements:* For master's, GRE General Test (MA), slide portfolio (15-20 slides). Additional exam requirements/recommendations for international students: Required—TOEFL. *Application deadline:* For fall admission, 2/15 for domestic students. Application fee: $30. Electronic applications accepted. *Financial support:* Research assistantships with full and partial tuition reimbursements, teaching assistantships with full and partial tuition reimbursements, career-related internships or fieldwork, institutionally sponsored loans, and unspecified assistantships available. Support available to part-time students. Financial award applicants required to submit FAFSA. *Faculty research:* Computer animation and virtual reality, Spanish still-life painting from 1600 to 1800, art and psychotherapy, Japanese wood-firing techniques in ceramics, non-toxic printmaking technologies. *Unit head:* Dr. Katerina Ruedi Ray, Director, 419-372-8575. *Application contact:* Marisa Cline, Graduate Coordinator, 419-372-2786, E-mail: mlcline@bgsu.edu.

**Bradley University,** The Graduate School, Slane College of Communications and Fine Arts, Department of Art, Peoria, IL 61625-0002. Offers ceramics (MA, MFA); drawing (MA, MFA); graphic design (MA, MFA); painting (MA, MFA); photography (MA, MFA); printmaking (MA, MFA); sculpture (MA, MFA). *Accreditation:* NASAD. *Program availability:* Part-time. *Degree requirements:* For master's, comprehensive exam, thesis, final exhibit. *Entrance requirements:* For master's, portfolio, 2 letters of recommendation. Additional exam requirements/recommendations for international students: Required—TOEFL (minimum score 550 paper-based; 79 iBT). *Application deadline:* For fall admission, 4/1 priority date for domestic and international students; for spring admission, 11/1 priority date for domestic and international students. Applications are processed on a rolling basis. Application fee: $40 ($50 for international students). Electronic applications accepted. *Expenses: Tuition:* Full-time $7650; part-time $850 per credit. *Required fees:* $50 per credit. One-time fee: $100 full-time. *Financial support:* Teaching assistantships with full and partial tuition reimbursements, scholarships/grants, tuition waivers (partial), and unspecified assistantships available. Support available to part-time students. Financial award application deadline: 4/1. *Unit head:* Gary Will, Chairperson, 309-677-2967, E-mail: pkrainak@bradley.edu. *Application contact:* Kayla Carroll, Director of International Admission and Student Services, 309-677-2375, E-mail: klcarroll@fsmail.bradley.edu.
Website: http://www.bradley.edu/academic/departments/art/

**California College of the Arts,** Graduate Programs, Design Program, San Francisco, CA 94107. Offers graphic design (MFA); industrial design (MFA); interaction design (MFA). *Accreditation:* NASAD. *Faculty:* 6 full-time (2 women), 26 part-time/adjunct (10 women). *Students:* 105 full-time (67 women); includes 14 minority (1 Black or African American, non-Hispanic/Latino; 8 Asian, non-Hispanic/Latino; 5 Hispanic/Latino), 67 international. Average age 26. 384 applicants, 36% accepted, 45 enrolled. In 2016, 9 master's awarded. *Degree requirements:* For master's, thesis, exhibit. *Entrance requirements:* For master's, appropriate bachelor's degree, portfolio, resume, letters of recommendation, transcripts. Additional exam requirements/recommendations for international students: Required—TOEFL, IELTS, or PTE. *Application deadline:* For fall admission, 1/10 for domestic and international students. Applications are processed on a rolling basis. Application fee: $70. Electronic applications accepted. *Expenses:* $1,641 per unit, $49,230 per year tuition; $490 fees. *Financial support:* In 2016–17, fellowships (averaging $22,000 per year), teaching assistantships (averaging $2,000 per year) were awarded; career-related internships or fieldwork, Federal Work-Study, scholarships/grants, health care benefits, and unspecified assistantships also available. Financial award application deadline: 7/31; financial award applicants required to submit FAFSA. *Unit head:* Jon Sueda, Graduate Chair, 415-551-9283, Fax: 415-703-9539, E-mail: jsueda@cca.edu. *Application contact:* Wes Fanelli, Assistant Director of Graduate Admissions, 415-703-9533, Fax: 415-703-9539, E-mail: wfanelli@cca.edu.

**California Institute of the Arts,** School of Art, Valencia, CA 91355-2340. Offers art (MFA, Adv C); graphic design (MFA, Adv C); photography (MFA, Adv C). *Accreditation:* NASAD (one or more programs are accredited). *Degree requirements:* For master's, final project. *Entrance requirements:* For master's, portfolio. Additional exam requirements/recommendations for international students: Required—TOEFL. Electronic applications accepted.

**California State University, Los Angeles,** Graduate Studies, College of Arts and Letters, Department of Art, Los Angeles, CA 90032-8530. Offers art (MA), including art education, art history, art therapy, ceramics, metals, and textiles, design (MA, MFA); painting, sculpture, and graphic arts, photography; fine arts (MFA), including crafts, design (MA, MFA), studio arts. *Accreditation:* NASAD (one or more programs are accredited). *Program availability:* Part-time, evening/weekend. *Degree requirements:* For master's, comprehensive exam, project or thesis. *Entrance requirements:* For master's, portfolio. Additional exam requirements/recommendations for international

students: Required—TOEFL (minimum score 500 paper-based). Electronic applications accepted. *Faculty research:* The artist and the book, conceptual art, ceramic processes, computer graphics, architectural graphics.

**Central Connecticut State University,** School of Graduate Studies, College of Liberal Arts and Social Sciences, Department of Design, New Britain, CT 06050-4010. Offers information design (MA). *Program availability:* Part-time, evening/weekend. *Faculty:* 2 full-time (1 woman), 1 (woman) part-time/adjunct. *Students:* 8 full-time (4 women), 4 part-time (all women); includes 2 minority (1 Black or African American, non-Hispanic/Latino; 1 Asian, non-Hispanic/Latino). Average age 31. 11 applicants, 82% accepted, 5 enrolled. In 2016, 4 master's awarded. *Degree requirements:* For master's, thesis or alternative, research project. *Entrance requirements:* For master's, portfolio, minimum undergraduate GPA of 3.0, essay. Additional exam requirements/recommendations for international students: Required—TOEFL (minimum score 550 paper-based; 79 iBT). *Application deadline:* For fall admission, 6/1 for domestic students, 5/1 for international students; for spring admission, 11/1 for domestic and international students. Applications are processed on a rolling basis. Application fee: $50. Electronic applications accepted. *Expenses: Tuition, area resident:* Full-time $6497; part-time $606 per credit. Tuition, state resident: full-time $9748; part-time $622 per credit. Tuition, nonresident: full-time $18,102; part-time $622 per credit. *Required fees:* $4459; $246 per credit. *Financial support:* In 2016–17, 2 students received support. Career-related internships or fieldwork, Federal Work-Study, scholarships/grants, and unspecified assistantships available. Support available to part-time students. Financial award application deadline: 3/1; financial award applicants required to submit FAFSA. *Unit head:* Dr. Eleanor Thornton, Chair, 860-832-2564, E-mail: thorntone@ccsu.edu. *Application contact:* Patricia Gardner, Associate Director of Graduate Studies, 860-832-2350, Fax: 860-832-2362.
Website: http://www.design.ccsu.edu/

**City College of the City University of New York,** Graduate School, Division of Humanities and the Arts, Department of Art, Program in Fine Arts, New York, NY 10031-9198. Offers advertising design (MFA); ceramic design (MFA); digital and interdisciplinary art practice (MFA); painting (MFA); printmaking (MFA); sculpture (MFA); wood and metal design (MFA). *Degree requirements:* For master's, thesis exhibit. *Entrance requirements:* For master's, 20-slide portfolio. Additional exam requirements/recommendations for international students: Required—TOEFL (minimum score 577 paper-based; 90 iBT). Electronic applications accepted. Tuition and fees vary according to course load, degree level and program.

**Digital Media Arts College,** Graduate Programs, Boca Raton, FL 33487. Offers graphic design (MFA); special FX animation (MFA).

**East Carolina University,** Graduate School, College of Fine Arts and Communication, School of Art and Design, Greenville, NC 27858-4353. Offers art education (MA Ed); ceramics (MFA); graphic design (MFA); illustration (MFA); metal design (MFA); painting and drawing (MFA); photography (MFA); printmaking (MFA); sculpture (MFA); textile design (MFA); wood design (MFA). *Accreditation:* NASAD (one or more programs are accredited). *Program availability:* Part-time, evening/weekend. *Students:* 25 full-time (15 women), 17 part-time (12 women); includes 5 minority (2 Asian, non-Hispanic/Latino; 2 Hispanic/Latino; 1 Two or more races, non-Hispanic/Latino). Average age 33. 37 applicants, 62% accepted, 16 enrolled. In 2016, 17 master's awarded. *Degree requirements:* For master's, comprehensive exam, thesis (for some programs). *Entrance requirements:* For master's, GRE General Test or MAT, portfolio. Additional exam requirements/recommendations for international students: Required—TOEFL. *Application deadline:* For fall admission, 2/1 for domestic students; for spring admission, 10/1 for domestic students. Applications are processed on a rolling basis. Application fee: $50. *Financial support:* Research assistantships with partial tuition reimbursements, teaching assistantships with partial tuition reimbursements, and Federal Work-Study available. Support available to part-time students. Financial award application deadline: 6/1. *Unit head:* Michael H. Drought, Director, 252-328-6665, E-mail: droughtm@ecu.edu. *Application contact:* Dr. Linda H. Nelson, Information Contact, 252-328-1286, E-mail: nelsonlh@ecu.edu.
Website: http://www.ecu.edu/cs-cfac/soad/gradschool.cfm

**Florida Atlantic University,** Dorothy F. Schmidt College of Arts and Letters, Department of Visual Arts and Art History, Boca Raton, FL 33431-0991. Offers visual art (MFA), including ceramics, graphic design, visual art. *Faculty:* 14 full-time (10 women). *Students:* 15 full-time (12 women), 1 (woman) part-time; includes 6 minority (1 Black or African American, non-Hispanic/Latino; 1 Asian, non-Hispanic/Latino; 3 Hispanic/Latino; 1 Two or more races, non-Hispanic/Latino). Average age 37. 23 applicants, 26% accepted, 4 enrolled. In 2016, 3 master's awarded. *Degree requirements:* For master's, one foreign language, project. *Entrance requirements:* For master's, GRE General Test, minimum GPA of 3.0 during last 60 hours of course work, slide portfolio. *Application deadline:* For fall admission, 2/21 for domestic and international students; for spring admission, 10/1 for domestic and international students. Application fee: $30. Electronic applications accepted. *Expenses:* Tuition, state resident: full-time $7392; part-time $369.82 per credit hour. Tuition, nonresident: full-time $19,432; part-time $1024.81 per credit hour. *Financial support:* Research assistantships with full tuition reimbursements, teaching assistantships with full tuition reimbursements, career-related internships or fieldwork, Federal Work-Study, and institutionally sponsored loans available. Financial award applicants required to submit FAFSA. *Faculty research:* Painting, ceramics (traditional and non-traditional), installation, video and interactive sculpture. *Unit head:* Dr. Eric Landes, Interim Chair, 954-236-1106, E-mail: elandes1@fau.edu. *Application contact:* James A. Novak, Associate Professor/Graduate Coordinator/Advisor, 561-297-2430, Fax: 561-297-3078, E-mail: jnovak@fau.edu.
Website: http://www.fau.edu/VAAH/

**Full Sail University,** Game Design Master of Science Program - Campus, Winter Park, FL 32792-7437. Offers MS.

**George Mason University,** College of Visual and Performing Arts, Program in Graphic Design, Fairfax, VA 22030. Offers MA. *Faculty:* 19 full-time (9 women), 31 part-time/adjunct (13 women). *Students:* 3 full-time (all women), 8 part-time (5 women); includes 4 minority (3 Black or African American, non-Hispanic/Latino; 1 Hispanic/Latino), 4 international. Average age 27. 9 applicants, 33% accepted, 2 enrolled. In 2016, 5 master's awarded. *Degree requirements:* For master's, final project. *Entrance requirements:* For master's, 2 official transcripts; goals statement; 3 letters of recommendation; writing sample; portfolio CD/DVD with 20 examples of design work. Additional exam requirements/recommendations for international students: Required—TOEFL (minimum score 575 paper-based; 88 iBT), IELTS (minimum score 6.5), PTE (minimum score 59). *Application deadline:* For fall admission, 2/1 for domestic students. Application fee: $75 ($80 for international students). Electronic applications accepted. *Expenses:* Tuition, state resident: full-time $10,628; part-time $443 per credit. Tuition, nonresident: full-time $29,306; part-time $1221 per credit. *Required fees:* $3096; $129 per credit. Tuition and fees vary according to program. *Financial support:* Career-related internships or fieldwork, Federal Work-Study, and scholarships/grants available. Support available to part-time students. Financial award application deadline: 3/1; financial award applicants required to submit FAFSA. *Unit head:* Don Starr, Director, 703-993-8642, Fax: 703-993-8798, E-mail: dstarr@gmu.edu. *Application contact:* Nikki Brugnoli-Whipkey, Administrative Assistant for Graduate Study, 703-993-5792, Fax:

703-993-8798, E-mail: nbrugnol@gmu.edu.
Website: http://soa.gmu.edu/areasofconcentration/graphicdesign/

**George Mason University,** College of Visual and Performing Arts, Program in Visual and Performing Arts, Fairfax, VA 22030. Offers drawing (MFA); new media (MFA); painting (MFA); photography (MFA); printmaking (MFA); sculpture (MFA). *Accreditation:* NASAD. *Faculty:* 18 full-time (9 women), 38 part-time/adjunct (19 women). *Students:* 3 full-time (2 women), 2 part-time (1 woman). Average age 34. 15 applicants, 27% accepted, 3 enrolled. In 2016, 6 master's awarded. *Degree requirements:* For master's, comprehensive experience, studio project or thesis. *Entrance requirements:* For master's, official transcripts; 3 letters of recommendation; letter of intent; resume; professional goals statement. Additional exam requirements/recommendations for international students: Required—TOEFL (minimum score 575 paper-based; 88 iBT), IELTS (minimum score 6.5), PTE (minimum score 59). Application fee: $75 ($80 for international students). Electronic applications accepted. *Expenses:* Tuition, state resident: full-time $10,628; part-time $443 per credit. Tuition, nonresident: full-time $29,306; part-time $1221 per credit. *Required fees:* $3096; $129 per credit. Tuition and fees vary according to program. *Financial support:* Career-related internships or fieldwork, Federal Work-Study, scholarships/grants, unspecified assistantships, and health care benefits (for full-time research or teaching assistantship recipients) available. Support available to part-time students. Financial award application deadline: 3/1; financial award applicants required to submit FAFSA. *Faculty research:* Digital arts, painting, photography, print-making, sculpture; combined art forms in in-disciplinary projects including installation, performance, publishing, time or writing-based; combined creative and critical approaches. *Unit head:* Lisa Kahn, Associate Dean, 703-993-4541, E-mail: lkahn2@gmu.edu. *Application contact:* Nikki Brugnoli-Whipkey, Graduate Studies Administrative Assistant, 703-993-5792, Fax: 703-993-8798, E-mail: rbrugnol@gmu.edu.
Website: http://soa.gmu.edu

**Georgia Southern University,** Jack N. Averitt College of Graduate Studies, College of Liberal Arts and Social Sciences, Program in Art, Statesboro, GA 30460. Offers fine arts (MFA), including 2D graphic design, 2D studio art, 3D studio art. *Accreditation:* NASAD. *Program availability:* Part-time. *Students:* 11 full-time (7 women), 3 part-time (2 women); includes 1 minority (Black or African American, non-Hispanic/Latino), 3 international. Average age 34. 9 applicants, 89% accepted, 4 enrolled. In 2016, 4 master's awarded. *Degree requirements:* For master's, thesis, exhibition. *Entrance requirements:* For master's, minimum GPA of 3.0; 18 semester hours of course work in studio art, 9 in art history; portfolio; letters of reference. Additional exam requirements/recommendations for international students: Required—TOEFL (minimum score 550 paper-based; 80 iBT), IELTS (minimum score 6). *Application deadline:* For fall admission, 3/1 priority date for domestic and international students; for spring admission, 10/1 priority date for domestic students, 10/1 for international students. Applications are processed on a rolling basis. Application fee: $50. Electronic applications accepted. *Expenses:* Tuition, state resident: full-time $7236; part-time $277 per semester hour. Tuition, nonresident: full-time $27,118; part-time $1105 per semester hour. *Required fees:* $2092. *Financial support:* In 2016–17, 1 student received support, including 4 fellowships with full tuition reimbursements available (averaging $7,750 per year); career-related internships or fieldwork, Federal Work-Study, scholarships/grants, tuition waivers (full), and unspecified assistantships also available. Support available to part-time students. Financial award application deadline: 4/15; financial award applicants required to submit FAFSA. *Faculty research:* International design trends; graphic design social awareness campaigns; functional design; public sculpture; fine art painting, drawing, printmaking, paper and book arts; folk art; Georgia artists archive, technology, design, contemporary, traditional studio. *Unit head:* Dr. Robert Farber, Department Chair, 912-478-5358, Fax: 912-478-5104, E-mail: rfarber@georgiasouthern.edu.
Website: http://class.georgiasouthern.edu/art

**Georgia State University,** College of Arts and Sciences, Ernest G. Welch School of Art and Design, Program in Studio Art, Atlanta, GA 30302-3083. Offers ceramics (MFA); drawing and painting (MFA); graphic design (MFA); interior design (MFA); photography (MFA); printmaking (MFA); sculpture (MFA); textiles (MFA). *Accreditation:* NASAD. *Degree requirements:* For master's, thesis. *Application deadline:* For fall admission, 1/6 for domestic and international students; for spring admission, 1/15 priority date for domestic and international students. Application fee: $50. Electronic applications accepted. *Expenses:* Tuition, state resident: full-time $6876; part-time $382 per credit hour. Tuition, nonresident: full-time $22,374; part-time $1243 per credit hour. *Required fees:* $2128; $1064 per term. Part-time tuition and fees vary according to course load and program. *Financial support:* In 2016–17, fellowships with full tuition reimbursements (averaging $11,000 per year), teaching assistantships with full tuition reimbursements (averaging $7,000 per year) were awarded; research assistantships, scholarships/grants, and unspecified assistantships also available. Financial award application deadline: 4/15; financial award applicants required to submit FAFSA. *Faculty research:* Advertising and typography, new media, traditional media, three-dimensional art, architectural and environmental design. *Unit head:* Michael White, Director, Welch School of Art and Design, 404-413-5221, Fax: 404-413-5261, E-mail: mwhite@gsu.edu. *Application contact:* Hubert Stanley Anderson, Director of Graduate Studies, 404-413-5229, Fax: 404-413-5261, E-mail: artgrad@gsu.edu.
Website: http://artdesign.gsu.edu/graduate/admissions/masters-of-fine-arts-in-studio/

**Illinois State University,** Graduate School, College of Fine Arts, School of Art, Normal, IL 61790-2200. Offers art history (MA, MS); ceramics (MFA, MS); drawing (MFA, MS); fibers (MFA, MS); glass (MFA, MS); graphic design (MFA, MS); metals (MFA, MS); painting (MFA, MS); photography (MFA, MS); printmaking (MFA, MS); sculpture (MFA, MS). *Accreditation:* NASAD (one or more programs are accredited). *Degree requirements:* For master's, thesis or alternative, internship. *Entrance requirements:* For master's, portfolio, sample of scholarly writing.

**Indiana State University,** College of Graduate and Professional Studies, College of Arts and Sciences, Department of Art and Design, Terre Haute, IN 47809. Offers ceramics (MA, MFA); drawing (MA, MFA); graphic design (MA, MFA); painting (MA, MFA); photography (MA, MFA); printmaking (MA, MFA); sculpture (MA, MFA). *Accreditation:* NASAD (one or more programs are accredited). *Program availability:* Part-time. *Degree requirements:* For master's, thesis or alternative, departmental qualifying exam. *Entrance requirements:* For master's, portfolio. Additional exam requirements/recommendations for international students: Required—TOEFL (minimum score 500 paper-based).

**Indiana University–Purdue University Indianapolis,** Herron School of Art and Design, Indianapolis, IN 46202. Offers art therapy (MA); visual art (MFA), including ceramics, furniture design, painting and drawing, photography and intermedia, printmaking, sculpture; visual communication design (MFA). *Faculty:* 26 full-time (13 women), 16 part-time/adjunct (11 women). *Students:* 56 full-time (40 women), 1 (woman) part-time; includes 8 minority (4 Black or African American, non-Hispanic/Latino; 2 Asian, non-Hispanic/Latino; 2 Hispanic/Latino), 7 international. Average age 31. 72 applicants, 53% accepted, 25 enrolled. In 2016, 22 master's awarded. *Degree requirements:* For master's, thesis. *Entrance requirements:* For master's, personal statement, resume, recommendations, portfolio, transcripts (18 credit hours of studio art

and 12 credit hours of psychology, including 3 credit hours of developmental psychology and 3 credit hours of abnormal psychology for MA. Additional exam requirements/recommendations for international students: Recommended—TOEFL (minimum score 550 paper-based; 79 iBT), IELTS (minimum score 6.5). *Application deadline:* For fall admission, 1/15 for domestic and international students; for spring admission, 11/1 for domestic students, 10/15 for international students. Application fee: $60 ($65 for international students). Electronic applications accepted. *Expenses:* Contact institution. *Financial support:* In 2016–17, 55 students received support, including 36 fellowships (averaging $2,830 per year), 11 teaching assistantships (averaging $3,609 per year); research assistantships, Federal Work-Study, scholarships/grants, health care benefits, tuition waivers, and unspecified assistantships also available. Financial award application deadline: 2/1. *Faculty research:* Contemporary digital narratives for the homoerotic trope; sound articulated 3D print; neuroscience, art and related therapeutics; automotive and aeronautical design and fabrication; technological detritus. *Total annual research expenditures:* $22,990. *Unit head:* Prof. Valerie Eickmeier, Dean, 317-278-9470, Fax: 317-278-9471, E-mail: herron@iupui.edu. *Application contact:* Abbey Chambers, Herron Office of Admissions and Student Services, 317-378-9400, E-mail: herron4u@iupui.edu.
Website: http://herron.iupui.edu/

**Inter American University of Puerto Rico, San Germán Campus,** Graduate Studies Center, Program in Fine Arts, San Germán, PR 00683-5008. Offers drawing (MFA); graphic design (MFA); painting (MFA); photography (MFA); printmaking (MFA); sculpture (MFA). *Program availability:* Part-time, evening/weekend. *Degree requirements:* For master's, comprehensive exam, thesis. *Entrance requirements:* For master's, GRE General Test or EXADEP, minimum GPA of 3.0.

**Iowa State University of Science and Technology,** Program in Graphic Design, Ames, IA 50011. Offers MA, MFA. *Accreditation:* NASAD. *Entrance requirements:* Additional exam requirements/recommendations for international students: Required—TOEFL (minimum score 550 paper-based; 79 iBT), IELTS (minimum score 6). *Application deadline:* For fall admission, 2/1 for domestic students; for spring admission, 4/15 for domestic students. Application fee: $60 ($90 for international students). Electronic applications accepted. *Application contact:* Meredith Foley, Application Contact, 515-294-0816, Fax: 515-294-2725, E-mail: merfoley@iastate.edu.
Website: http://www.design.iastate.edu/graphicdesign/graduateprograms.php?

**Kent State University,** College of Communication and Information, School of Visual Communication Design, Kent, OH 44242-0001. Offers MA, MFA. *Accreditation:* NASAD. *Program availability:* Part-time. *Faculty:* 16 full-time (7 women). *Students:* 27 full-time (15 women), 8 part-time (5 women); includes 6 minority (4 Black or African American, non-Hispanic/Latino; 1 Asian, non-Hispanic/Latino; 1 Two or more races, non-Hispanic/Latino), 11 international. Average age 28. 25 applicants, 88% accepted, 12 enrolled. In 2016, 7 master's awarded. *Degree requirements:* For master's, thesis optional. *Entrance requirements:* For master's, goal statement, autobiographical statement, 3 letters of recommendation, transcripts, link to personal online portfolio. Additional exam requirements/recommendations for international students: Required—TOEFL (minimum score: paper-based 525, iBT 71), Michigan English Language Assessment Battery (minimum score of 75), IELTS (minimum score of 6.0), PTE Academic (minimum score of 48), or completion of ELS level 112 Intensive Program. *Application deadline:* For fall admission, 3/1 for domestic and international students; for spring admission, 10/1 for domestic and international students. Applications are processed on a rolling basis. Application fee: $45 ($70 for international students). Electronic applications accepted. *Expenses:* Tuition, state resident: full-time $10,864; part-time $495 per credit hour. Tuition, nonresident: full-time $18,380; part-time $837 per credit hour. *Financial support:* Scholarships/grants and unspecified assistantships available. Financial award application deadline: 3/1. *Unit head:* Dr. David Robins, Interim Director, 330-672-2782, E-mail: drobins@kent.edu. *Application contact:* Ken Visocky O'Grady, Graduate Coordinator and Associate Professor, 330-672-1353, E-mail: kogrady@kent.edu.
Website: http://www.kent.edu/vcd/

**Louisiana State University and Agricultural & Mechanical College,** Graduate School, College of Art and Design, School of Art, Program in Studio Art, Baton Rouge, LA 70803. Offers ceramics (MFA); graphic design (MFA); painting and drawing (MFA); photography (MFA); printmaking (MFA); sculpture (MFA). *Accreditation:* NASAD.

**Louisiana Tech University,** Graduate School, College of Liberal Arts, MFA Program, Ruston, LA 71272. Offers graphic design (MFA); photography (MFA); studio (MFA). *Accreditation:* NASAD. *Program availability:* Part-time. *Degree requirements:* For master's, exhibit. *Entrance requirements:* For master's, GRE General Test, portfolio. *Application deadline:* For fall admission, 5/12 for domestic students. Applications are processed on a rolling basis. Application fee: $40 ($50 for international students). Electronic applications accepted. *Financial support:* Fellowships, career-related internships or fieldwork, Federal Work-Study, institutionally sponsored loans, and unspecified assistantships available. Financial award application deadline: 2/15. *Unit head:* Frank Hamrick, Graduate Coordinator, 318-257-4154, Fax: 318-257-4890, E-mail: fhamrick@latech.edu. *Application contact:* Marilyn J. Robinson, Assistant to the Dean of the Graduate School, 318-257-2924, Fax: 318-257-4487.
Website: http://design.latech.edu/master-of-fine-arts/

**Maryland Institute College of Art,** Graduate Studies, MA Program in Graphic Design, Baltimore, MD 21201. Offers MA. *Faculty:* 1 (woman) full-time. *Students:* 17 full-time (11 women); includes 4 minority (2 Black or African American, non-Hispanic/Latino; 1 Asian, non-Hispanic/Latino; 1 Two or more races, non-Hispanic/Latino), 4 international. Average age 26. *Entrance requirements:* Additional exam requirements/recommendations for international students: Required—TOEFL (minimum score 550 paper-based; 80 iBT), IELTS (minimum score 6.5). *Application deadline:* For fall admission, 1/15 priority date for domestic and international students; for spring admission, 4/1 for domestic and international students. Application fee: $75. Electronic applications accepted. *Expenses:* Tuition: Full-time $45,290; part-time $1510 per credit. *Required fees:* $1700. One-time fee: $335 full-time. Full-time tuition and fees vary according to course load. *Financial support:* In 2016–17, 17 students received support, including 17 fellowships (averaging $5,500 per year); scholarships/grants also available. Financial award application deadline: 1/15; financial award applicants required to submit FAFSA. *Unit head:* Sandra Maxa, Director, 410-669-2382, Fax: 410-225-2408, E-mail: graduate@mica.edu. *Application contact:* Chris D. Harring, Director of Graduate Admission, 410-225-2256, Fax: 410-225-5275, E-mail: graduate@mica.edu.
Website: http://www.mica.edu/Programs_of_Study/Post-Baccalaureate_Certificate_in_Graphic_Design.html

**Maryland Institute College of Art,** Graduate Studies, MFA Program in Graphic Design, Baltimore, MD 21201. Offers MFA. *Faculty:* 2 full-time (both women), 7 part-time/adjunct (2 women). *Students:* 28 full-time (17 women); includes 4 minority (1 Asian, non-Hispanic/Latino; 1 Hispanic/Latino; 2 Two or more races, non-Hispanic/Latino), 8 international. Average age 27. 250 applicants, 10% accepted, 15 enrolled. In 2016, 15 master's awarded. *Degree requirements:* For master's, thesis, exhibit and thesis documentation. *Entrance requirements:* For master's, portfolio, bachelor's degree in any field. Additional exam requirements/recommendations for international students: Required—TOEFL (minimum score 550 paper-based; 80 iBT), IELTS (minimum score

*Graphic Design*

6.5). *Application deadline:* For fall admission, 1/15 for domestic and international students. Application fee: $75. Electronic applications accepted. *Expenses:* Contact institution. *Financial support:* In 2016–17, 28 students received support, including 28 fellowships (averaging $13,000 per year), 28 teaching assistantships (averaging $3,200 per year); career-related internships or fieldwork and scholarships/grants also available. Financial award application deadline: 1/15. *Unit head:* Ellen Lupton, Director, 410-225-5274, Fax: 410-225-5275. *Application contact:* Chris D. Harring, Director, Graduate Admission, 410-225-2256, Fax: 410-225-5275, E-mail: graduate@mica.edu.

**Marywood University,** Academic Affairs, Insalaco College of Creative and Performing Arts, Art Department, Program in Visual Arts, Scranton, PA 18509-1598. Offers clay (MFA); graphic design (MFA); illustration (MFA); painting (MFA); photography (MFA); printmaking (MFA); sculpture (MFA). *Accreditation:* NASAD. *Program availability:* Part-time. Electronic applications accepted. *Expenses:* Contact institution.

**Minneapolis College of Art and Design,** Certificate Programs, Minneapolis, MN 55404-4347. Offers design (Certificate); fine arts (Certificate); graphic design (Certificate); media (Certificate); sustainable design (Certificate). *Program availability:* Part-time, online learning. *Degree requirements:* For Certificate, final project. *Entrance requirements:* For degree, resume, portfolio, letter of recommendation. Additional exam requirements/recommendations for international students: Required—TOEFL (minimum score 550 paper-based; 79 iBT). Electronic applications accepted. *Faculty research:* Visual arts.

**Minneapolis College of Art and Design,** Program in Visual Studies, Minneapolis, MN 55404-4347. Offers animation (MFA); comic art (MFA); drawing (MFA); filmmaking (MFA); fine arts (MFA); furniture design (MFA); graphic design (MFA); illustration (MFA); interactive media (MFA); painting (MFA); photography (MFA); printmaking (MFA); sculpture (MFA). *Accreditation:* NASAD. *Program availability:* Part-time. *Degree requirements:* For master's, thesis, thesis exhibit. *Entrance requirements:* For master's, portfolio of visual artwork, resume, 3 letters of recommendation. Additional exam requirements/recommendations for international students: Required—TOEFL (minimum score 550 paper-based; 79 iBT). Electronic applications accepted. *Faculty research:* Visual arts: animation, comic art, drawing, filmmaking, furniture design, graphic design, illustration, interactive media, painting, photography, printmaking, sculpture.

**Morehead State University,** Graduate Programs, Caudill College of Arts, Humanities and Social Sciences, Department of Art and Design, Morehead, KY 40351. Offers art education (MA); graphic design (MA); studio art (MA). *Accreditation:* NASAD. *Program availability:* Part-time, evening/weekend. *Degree requirements:* For master's, comprehensive exam, thesis (for some programs), oral exam during exhibition. *Entrance requirements:* For master's, GRE General Test, minimum undergraduate GPA of 3.0 in major, 2.5 overall; portfolio; bachelor's degree in art. Additional exam requirements/recommendations for international students: Required—TOEFL (minimum score 500 paper-based). Electronic applications accepted. *Faculty research:* Computer art, painting, drawing, ceramics, photography.

**New York Institute of Technology,** College of Arts and Sciences, Department of Digital Art and Design, Old Westbury, NY 11568-8000. Offers computer graphics (MFA), including animation, fine arts and technology, graphic design. *Program availability:* Part-time, evening/weekend. *Faculty:* 7 full-time (4 women), 6 part-time/adjunct (2 women). *Students:* 42 full-time (30 women), 12 part-time (6 women); includes 6 minority (3 Black or African American, non-Hispanic/Latino; 1 Asian, non-Hispanic/Latino; 2 Hispanic/Latino), 42 international. Average age 27. 41 applicants, 68% accepted, 14 enrolled. In 2016, 31 master's awarded. *Degree requirements:* For master's, thesis. *Entrance requirements:* For master's, BFA or equivalent; minimum undergraduate GPA of 3.0; digital portfolio. Additional exam requirements/recommendations for international students: Required—TOEFL (minimum score 79 iBT), IELTS (minimum score 6). *Application deadline:* For fall admission, 6/1 for domestic and international students. Applications are processed on a rolling basis. Application fee: $50. Electronic applications accepted. *Expenses:* $1,215 per credit. *Financial support:* Career-related internships or fieldwork, Federal Work-Study, scholarships/grants, tuition waivers (full and partial), and unspecified assistantships available. Support available to part-time students. Financial award application deadline: 3/1; financial award applicants required to submit FAFSA. *Faculty research:* Graphic design, animation, art and technology, virtual reality, sculpture. *Unit head:* Terry Nauheim, Department Chair, 516-686-7881, Fax: 212-261-1742, E-mail: tnauheim@nyit.edu. *Application contact:* Alice Dolitsky, Director, Graduate Admissions, 516-686-7520, Fax: 516-686-1116, E-mail: nyitgrad@nyit.edu.
Website: http://www.nyit.edu/arts_and_sciences/department_of_digital_art_design

**New York University,** School of Continuing and Professional Studies, Division of Programs in Business, Program in Graphic Communications Management and Technology, New York, NY 10012-1019. Offers MA. *Program availability:* Part-time, evening/weekend. *Degree requirements:* For master's, thesis, capstone, research course. *Entrance requirements:* For master's, GRE or GMAT (only upon request), relevant professional work, internship or volunteer experience. Additional exam requirements/recommendations for international students: Required—TOEFL (minimum score 600 paper-based; 100 iBT), IELTS (minimum score 7). Electronic applications accepted.

**North Carolina Agricultural and Technical State University,** School of Graduate Studies, School of Technology, Department of Graphic Communication Systems and Technological Studies, Greensboro, NC 27411. Offers graphic communication systems (MSTM); technology education (MAT). *Accreditation:* NCATE (one or more programs are accredited). *Program availability:* Part-time, evening/weekend. *Degree requirements:* For master's, comprehensive exam, thesis or alternative, qualifying exam. *Entrance requirements:* For master's, GRE General Test, minimum GPA of 3.0.

**North Carolina State University,** Graduate School, College of Design, Department of Graphic Design, Raleigh, NC 27695. Offers MGD. *Accreditation:* NASAD. *Degree requirements:* For master's, thesis optional, oral exam. *Entrance requirements:* For master's, GRE General Test, portfolio. Electronic applications accepted. *Faculty research:* Typography, graphic design, interaction design, design and cognition, design and culture.

**Ohio University,** Graduate College, College of Fine Arts, School of Art, Athens, OH 45701-2979. Offers art history (MA); ceramics (MFA); graphic design (MFA); painting (MFA); photography (MFA); printmaking (MFA); sculpture (MFA). *Program availability:* Part-time. *Degree requirements:* For master's, thesis. *Entrance requirements:* For master's, portfolio. Additional exam requirements/recommendations for international students: Required—TOEFL (minimum score 550 paper-based; 80 iBT) or IELTS (minimum score 6.5). *Application deadline:* For fall admission, 2/1 for domestic and international students. Application fee: $50 ($55 for international students). Electronic applications accepted. *Financial support:* Teaching assistantships with full and partial tuition reimbursements, career-related internships or fieldwork, Federal Work-Study, institutionally sponsored loans, scholarships/grants, tuition waivers (partial), and unspecified assistantships available. Financial award application deadline: 2/1. *Faculty*

*research:* Vapor-fired ceramics, video installation, art theory, digital photography, mixed and interdisciplinary media work. *Unit head:* David LaPalombara, Director, 740-593-4290, Fax: 740-593-0457, E-mail: lapalomb@ohio.edu. *Application contact:* Alexandra Hibbitt, Chair, Graduate Programs, 740-593-4293, Fax: 740-593-0457, E-mail: hibbitt@ohio.edu.
Website: http://www.finearts.ohio.edu/art/

**Oklahoma State University,** College of Arts and Sciences, Department of Art, Graphic Design and Art History, Stillwater, OK 74078. Offers art history (MA); graphic design (MA). *Faculty:* 22 full-time (13 women), 4 part-time/adjunct (0 women). *Students:* 9 full-time (6 women), 2 part-time (1 woman); includes 3 minority (1 American Indian or Alaska Native, non-Hispanic/Latino; 2 Hispanic/Latino), 1 international. Average age 28. 20 applicants, 50% accepted, 6 enrolled. *Entrance requirements:* Additional exam requirements/recommendations for international students: Required—TOEFL. *Application deadline:* For fall admission, 3/1 for domestic students; for spring admission, 8/1 for domestic students. Application fee: $40 ($75 for international students). Electronic applications accepted. *Expenses:* Tuition, state resident: full-time $3775; part-time $209.70 per credit hour. Tuition, nonresident: full-time $14,851; part-time $825.05 per credit hour. *Required fees:* $2027; $112.60 per credit hour. Tuition and fees vary according to campus/location. *Financial support:* In 2016–17, 9 research assistantships (averaging $12,768 per year), 2 teaching assistantships (averaging $5,741 per year) were awarded. Financial award applicants required to submit FAFSA. *Unit head:* Dr. Rebecca Brienen, Head, E-mail: rebecca.brienen@okstate.edu.
Website: http://art.okstate.edu/

**Otis College of Art and Design,** Program in Graphic Design, Los Angeles, CA 90045-9785. Offers MFA. *Entrance requirements:* Additional exam requirements/recommendations for international students: Required—TOEFL (minimum score 600 paper-based). Electronic applications accepted.

**Pensacola Christian College,** Graduate Studies, Pensacola, FL 32503-2267. Offers business administration (MBA); curriculum and instruction (MS, Ed D, Ed S); dramatics (MFA); educational leadership (MS, Ed D, Ed S); graphic design (MA, MFA); music (MA); nursing (MSN); performance studies (MA); studio art (MA, MFA).

**Pittsburg State University,** Graduate School, College of Technology, Department of Technology and Workforce Learning, Pittsburg, KS 66762. Offers career and technical education (MS); human resource development (MS); technology (MS), including automotive technology, construction management, graphic design, graphics management, innovation in technology, personnel development, technology management, workforce learning; workforce development and education (Ed S). *Program availability:* Part-time, evening/weekend, 100% online, blended/hybrid learning. *Students:* 171 (79 women); includes 20 minority (4 Black or African American, non-Hispanic/Latino; 5 American Indian or Alaska Native, non-Hispanic/Latino; 2 Asian, non-Hispanic/Latino; 4 Hispanic/Latino; 5 Two or more races, non-Hispanic/Latino), 61 international. In 2016, 62 master's, 2 other advanced degrees awarded. *Degree requirements:* For master's, thesis or alternative; for Ed S, thesis optional. *Entrance requirements:* Additional exam requirements/recommendations for international students: Required—TOEFL (minimum score 520 paper-based; 68 iBT), IELTS (minimum score 6), PTE (minimum score 47). *Application deadline:* For fall admission, 7/15 for domestic students, 6/1 for international students; for spring admission, 12/15 for domestic students, 10/15 for international students; for summer admission, 5/15 for domestic students, 4/1 for international students. Applications are processed on a rolling basis. Application fee: $35 ($60 for international students). Electronic applications accepted. *Expenses:* Contact institution. *Financial support:* In 2016–17, 8 teaching assistantships with full tuition reimbursements (averaging $5,500 per year) were awarded; career-related internships or fieldwork also available. Financial award application deadline: 2/1; financial award applicants required to submit FAFSA. *Unit head:* Dr. John Iley, Chairperson, 620-235-4373, E-mail: jiley@pittstate.edu. *Application contact:* Lisa Allen, Assistant Director of Graduate and Continuing Studies, 620-235-4218, Fax: 620-235-4219, E-mail: lallen@pittstate.edu.

**Pratt Institute,** School of Art, Program in Digital Arts, Brooklyn, NY 11205-3899. Offers MFA, MS/MFA. *Accreditation:* NASAD. *Faculty:* 5 full-time (1 woman), 27 part-time/adjunct (8 women). *Students:* 64 full-time (50 women), 4 part-time (3 women); includes 8 minority (1 Black or African American, non-Hispanic/Latino; 4 Asian, non-Hispanic/Latino; 3 Hispanic/Latino), 51 international. Average age 26. 210 applicants, 33% accepted, 25 enrolled. In 2016, 29 master's awarded. *Degree requirements:* For master's, thesis, exhibit. *Entrance requirements:* For master's, portfolio or video, letters of recommendation. Additional exam requirements/recommendations for international students: Required—TOEFL (minimum score 550 paper-based; 79 iBT). *Application deadline:* For fall admission, 1/5 for domestic and international students; for spring admission, 10/1 for domestic and international students. Application fee: $50 ($90 for international students). Electronic applications accepted. *Expenses:* $29,646 full-time tuition, $1,938 fees. *Financial support:* Career-related internships or fieldwork, Federal Work-Study, institutionally sponsored loans, scholarships/grants, health care benefits, and unspecified assistantships available. Support available to part-time students. Financial award application deadline: 2/1; financial award applicants required to submit FAFSA. *Unit head:* Peter Patchen, Chair, 718-636-3693, Fax: 718-399-4494, E-mail: ppatchen@pratt.edu. *Application contact:* Natalie Capannelli, Director of Graduate Admissions, 718-636-3551, Fax: 718-399-4242, E-mail: ncapanne@pratt.edu.
Website: https://www.pratt.edu/academics/school-of-art/graduate-school-of-art/digital-arts-grad/

**See Display on page 156 and Close-Up on page 209.**

**Pratt Institute,** School of Design, Program in Communications Design, Brooklyn, NY 11205-3899. Offers MFA. *Accreditation:* NASAD. *Program availability:* Part-time. *Faculty:* 5 full-time (2 women), 35 part-time/adjunct (14 women). *Students:* 134 full-time (103 women), 4 part-time (3 women); includes 15 minority (3 Black or African American, non-Hispanic/Latino; 8 Asian, non-Hispanic/Latino; 4 Hispanic/Latino), 103 international. Average age 25. 365 applicants, 50% accepted, 50 enrolled. In 2016, 57 master's awarded. *Degree requirements:* For master's, thesis. *Entrance requirements:* For master's, portfolio, letters of recommendation. Additional exam requirements/recommendations for international students: Required—TOEFL (minimum score 575 paper-based; 90 iBT). *Application deadline:* For fall admission, 1/5 for domestic and international students; for spring admission, 10/1 for domestic and international students. Application fee: $50 ($90 for international students). Electronic applications accepted. *Expenses:* $29,646 full-time tuition, $1,938 fees. *Financial support:* Career-related internships or fieldwork, Federal Work-Study, institutionally sponsored loans, scholarships/grants, health care benefits, and unspecified assistantships available. Support available to part-time students. Financial award application deadline: 2/1; financial award applicants required to submit FAFSA. *Faculty research:* Graphics, film, photography, media presentations, computer graphics for community service organizations. *Unit head:* Santiago Piedrafita Iglesias, Chairperson, 212-647-7640, Fax: 212-367-2481, E-mail: spiedraf@pratt.edu. *Application contact:* Natalie Capannelli, Director of Graduate Admissions, 718-636-3551, Fax: 718-399-4242, E-mail: ncapanne@pratt.edu.

Website: https://www.pratt.edu/academics/school-of-design/graduate-school-of-design/grad-communications-design/

**See Display on page 66 and Close-Up on page 105.**

**Rhode Island School of Design,** Division of Architecture and Design, Department of Graphic Design, Providence, RI 02903-2784. Offers MFA. *Accreditation:* NASAD. *Faculty:* 10 full-time (5 women), 13 part-time/adjunct (5 women). *Students:* 34 full-time (23 women); includes 9 minority (6 Asian, non-Hispanic/Latino; 2 Hispanic/Latino; 1 Two or more races, non-Hispanic/Latino), 11 international. Average age 28. 299 applicants, 10% accepted, 15 enrolled. In 2016, 14 master's awarded. *Degree requirements:* For master's, thesis, exhibition. *Entrance requirements:* For master's, portfolio, statement of purpose, 3 letters of recommendation. Additional exam requirements/recommendations for international students: Required—TOEFL (minimum score 580 paper-based; 93 iBT). *Application deadline:* For fall admission, 2/1 for domestic and international students. Application fee: $60. Electronic applications accepted. *Expenses: Tuition:* Full-time $46,800. *Required fees:* $310. *Financial support:* Fellowships, research assistantships, teaching assistantships, Federal Work-Study, scholarships/grants, and unspecified assistantships available. Financial award application deadline: 2/15; financial award applicants required to submit FAFSA. *Unit head:* John Caserta, Department Head, 401-454-6131, Fax: 401-454-6117, E-mail: jcaserta@risd.edu. *Application contact:* Molly Pettengil, Assistant Director for Graduate Recruitment, 401-454-6312, Fax: 401-454-6309, E-mail: mpetteng@risd.edu.
Website: http://www.risd.edu/academics/graphic-design/

**Rochester Institute of Technology,** Graduate Enrollment Services, College of Imaging Arts and Sciences, School of Design, MFA Program in Visual Communication Design, Rochester, NY 14623-5603. Offers MFA. *Accreditation:* NASAD. *Program availability:* Part-time. *Students:* 59 full-time (47 women), 29 part-time (16 women); includes 7 minority (2 Asian, non-Hispanic/Latino; 3 Hispanic/Latino; 2 Two or more races, non-Hispanic/Latino), 70 international. Average age 29. 201 applicants, 43% accepted, 27 enrolled. In 2016, 20 master's awarded. *Degree requirements:* For master's, thesis, thesis exhibition. *Entrance requirements:* For master's, GRE, portfolio, minimum GPA of 3.0 (recommended). Additional exam requirements/recommendations for international students: Required—TOEFL (minimum score 550 paper-based; 90 iBT), IELTS (minimum score 7), PTE (minimum score 58). *Application deadline:* For fall admission, 2/15 priority date for domestic and international students. Applications are processed on a rolling basis. Application fee: $60. Electronic applications accepted. *Expenses:* $1,742 per credit hour. *Financial support:* In 2016–17, 46 students received support. Teaching assistantships with partial tuition reimbursements available, career-related internships or fieldwork, scholarships/grants, and unspecified assistantships available. Support available to part-time students. Financial award applicants required to submit FAFSA. *Faculty research:* Motion graphics for design and interaction; experiential design for physical and digital environments; augmented and virtual reality applications within education, advertising and consumer products; visual design for user experience and interactive solutions. *Unit head:* Adam Smith, Graduate Program Director, 585-475-4552, Fax: 585-475-7533, E-mail: aesfaa@rit.edu. *Application contact:* Diane Ellison, Associate Vice President, Graduate Enrollment Services, 585-475-2229, Fax: 585-475-7164, E-mail: gradinfo@rit.edu.
Website: http://cias.rit.edu/schools/design/graduate-visual-communication-design

**Rochester Institute of Technology,** Graduate Enrollment Services, College of Imaging Arts and Sciences, School of Media Sciences, MS Program in Print Media, Rochester, NY 14623-5603. Offers MS. *Program availability:* Part-time. *Students:* 14 full-time (7 women), 5 part-time (4 women), 16 international. Average age 25. 11 applicants, 73% accepted, 3 enrolled. In 2016, 1 master's awarded. *Degree requirements:* For master's, thesis. *Entrance requirements:* For master's, GRE, minimum GPA of 3.0 (recommended). Additional exam requirements/recommendations for international students: Required—TOEFL (minimum score 550 paper-based; 80 iBT), IELTS (minimum score 6.5), PTE (minimum score 58). *Application deadline:* For fall admission, 2/15 priority date for domestic and international students. Applications are processed on a rolling basis. Application fee: $60. Electronic applications accepted. *Expenses:* $1,742 per credit hour. *Financial support:* In 2016–17, 12 students received support. Research assistantships with partial tuition reimbursements available, teaching assistantships with partial tuition reimbursements available, career-related internships or fieldwork, scholarships/grants, and unspecified assistantships available. Support available to part-time students. Financial award applicants required to submit FAFSA. *Faculty research:* 3D, functional, and packaging print processes; color management; cross-media publishing; operations management; digital printing. *Unit head:* Christine Heusner, Graduate Program Director, 585-475-4627, E-mail: cxhppr@rit.edu. *Application contact:* Diane Ellison, Associate Vice President, Graduate Enrollment Services, 585-475-2229, Fax: 585-475-7164, E-mail: gradinfo@rit.edu.
Website: http://cias.rit.edu/schools/media-sciences/graduate-graduate-print-media

**San Diego State University,** Graduate and Research Affairs, College of Professional Studies and Fine Arts, School of Art, Design and Art History, San Diego, CA 92182. Offers art history (MA); studio arts (MA, MFA), including applied arts, environmental design, graphic design, interior design, painting and printmaking, sculpture. *Accreditation:* NASAD (one or more programs are accredited). *Degree requirements:* For master's, variable foreign language requirement, thesis. *Entrance requirements:* For master's, GRE General Test, bachelor's degree in related field, slide portfolio, typed slide information sheet, 2 letters of recommendation. Additional exam requirements/recommendations for international students: Required—TOEFL. Electronic applications accepted.

**Savannah College of Art and Design,** Graduate School, Program in Advertising, Savannah, GA 31402-3146. Offers MA, MFA. *Program availability:* Part-time. *Faculty:* 9 full-time (3 women), 6 part-time/adjunct (2 women). *Students:* 33 full-time (21 women), 8 part-time (4 women); includes 19 minority (13 Black or African American, non-Hispanic/Latino; 1 American Indian or Alaska Native, non-Hispanic/Latino; 2 Asian, non-Hispanic/Latino; 3 Hispanic/Latino), 12 international. Average age 27. 53 applicants, 26% accepted, 6 enrolled. In 2016, 18 master's awarded. *Degree requirements:* For master's, final project (for MA); thesis (for MFA). *Entrance requirements:* For master's, GRE (recommended), portfolio (submitted in digital format), audition or writing submission, resume, statement of purpose, two letters of recommendation. Additional exam requirements/recommendations for international students: Required—TOEFL (minimum score 550 paper-based, 85 iBT), IELTS (minimum score 6.5), or ACTFL. *Application deadline:* For fall admission, 4/1 for domestic and international students. Applications are processed on a rolling basis. Application fee: $40. Electronic applications accepted. *Expenses: Tuition:* Full-time $36,045. Tuition and fees vary according to course load. *Financial support:* Fellowships, career-related internships or fieldwork, Federal Work-Study, and scholarships/grants available. Financial award application deadline: 4/1; financial award applicants required to submit FAFSA. *Unit head:* Emily Sander, Chair of Advertising Design. *Application contact:* Jenny Jaquillard, Executive Director of Admissions, Recruitment and Events, 912-525-5100, Fax: 912-525-5985, E-mail: admission@scad.edu.
Website: http://www.scad.edu/academics/programs/advertising

**Savannah College of Art and Design,** Graduate School, Program in Graphic Design and Visual Experience, Savannah, GA 31402-3146. Offers MA, MFA. *Program availability:* Part-time, 100% online. *Faculty:* 21 full-time (10 women), 14 part-time/adjunct (6 women). *Students:* 85 full-time (58 women), 53 part-time (39 women); includes 19 minority (10 Black or African American, non-Hispanic/Latino; 3 Asian, non-Hispanic/Latino; 6 Hispanic/Latino), 59 international. Average age 29. 325 applicants, 34% accepted, 54 enrolled. In 2016, 61 master's awarded. *Degree requirements:* For master's, capstone course (for MA); thesis (for MFA). *Entrance requirements:* For master's, GRE (recommended), portfolio (submitted in digital format), audition or writing submission, resume, statement of purpose, two letters of recommendation. Additional exam requirements/recommendations for international students: Required—TOEFL (minimum score 550 paper-based, 85 iBT), IELTS (minimum score 6.5), or ACTFL. *Application deadline:* For fall admission, 4/1 for domestic and international students. Applications are processed on a rolling basis. Application fee: $40. Electronic applications accepted. *Expenses: Tuition:* Full-time $36,045. Tuition and fees vary according to course load. *Financial support:* Career-related internships or fieldwork, Federal Work-Study, and scholarships/grants available. Financial award application deadline: 4/1; financial award applicants required to submit FAFSA. *Unit head:* Jason Fox, Chair, Graphic Design and Visual Experience. *Application contact:* Jenny Jaquillard, Executive Director of Admissions, Recruitment and Events, 912-525-5100, Fax: 912-525-5985, E-mail: admission@scad.edu.
Website: http://www.scad.edu/academics/programs/graphic-design

**School of the Art Institute of Chicago,** Graduate Division, Department of Visual Communication, Chicago, IL 60603-3103. Offers MFA. *Entrance requirements:* Additional exam requirements/recommendations for international students: Required—TOEFL, IELTS.

**School of Visual Arts,** Graduate Programs, Program in Visual Narrative, New York, NY 10010-3994. Offers MFA. Summer admission only. *Degree requirements:* For master's, thesis, 60 credits, including all required courses. *Entrance requirements:* For master's, portfolio, statement of purpose; unique and complete short story/visual narrative (minimum 2-5 pages/images, or 2-5 minutes for video or animation submissions). Additional exam requirements/recommendations for international students: Required—TOEFL (minimum score 550 paper-based; 79 iBT). Electronic applications accepted. *Faculty research:* Storytelling, animation, design, illustration, art history, painting, printmaking, writing, graphic novels.

**State University of New York at Oswego,** Graduate Studies, Department of Art, Oswego, NY 13126. Offers art (MA); graphic design and digital media (MA). *Accreditation:* NASAD. *Program availability:* Part-time. *Degree requirements:* For master's, exhibit, final presentation. *Entrance requirements:* For master's, slides of previous work. Additional exam requirements/recommendations for international students: Required—TOEFL (minimum score 560 paper-based). *Faculty research:* Ancient and primitive art, nineteenth century art, medieval art, Renaissance art.

**Suffolk University,** New England School of Art and Design, Boston, MA 02108-2770. Offers graphic design (MA); interior architecture (MA). *Program availability:* Part-time, evening/weekend. *Faculty:* 12 full-time (8 women), 20 part-time/adjunct (12 women). *Students:* 37 full-time (30 women), 25 part-time (23 women); includes 11 minority (1 Black or African American, non-Hispanic/Latino; 7 Asian, non-Hispanic/Latino; 3 Hispanic/Latino), 19 international. Average age 29. 63 applicants, 73% accepted, 20 enrolled. In 2016, 29 master's awarded. *Entrance requirements:* For master's, GRE (for MFA), art portfolio, interview, 2 letters of recommendation, resume; letter of intent (for MFA). Additional exam requirements/recommendations for international students: Required—TOEFL (minimum score 550 paper-based; 80 iBT). *Application deadline:* For fall admission, 3/15 priority date for domestic and international students; for spring admission, 10/15 priority date for domestic and international students. Applications are processed on a rolling basis. Application fee: $50. Electronic applications accepted. *Expenses:* $24,436 per year full-time tuition, $1,144 per credit hour part-time tuition, $52 per year student activity fee, $180 per course studio fee. *Financial support:* In 2016–17, 44 students received support, including 40 fellowships (averaging $6,900 per year); career-related internships or fieldwork, Federal Work-Study, institutionally sponsored loans, scholarships/grants, and unspecified assistantships also available. Financial award application deadline: 4/1; financial award applicants required to submit FAFSA. *Faculty research:* Sustainable design, lighting and technology, design education, environmental graphic design, designing for the non-profit sector. *Unit head:* Audrey Goldstein, Department Chair, 617-997-4290, E-mail: agoldstein@suffolk.edu. *Application contact:* Mara Marzocchi, Associate Director of Graduate Admissions, 617-573-8302, Fax: 617-305-1733, E-mail: grad.admission@suffolk.edu.
Website: http://www.suffolk.edu/nesad/

**Temple University,** Tyler School of Art, Department of Graphic Arts and Design, Philadelphia, PA 19122-6096. Offers graphic and interactive design (MFA); photography (MFA); printmaking (MFA). *Degree requirements:* For master's, essay, exhibit. *Entrance requirements:* For master's, minimum GPA of 3.0, slide portfolio, 40 credits in studio art, 12 credits in art history, letters of recommendation, resume/curriculum vitae. Additional exam requirements/recommendations for international students: Required—TOEFL (minimum score 550 paper-based; 79 iBT), IELTS (minimum score 6.5). Electronic applications accepted. *Expenses:* Contact institution.

**Texas State University,** The Graduate College, College of Fine Arts and Communication, Program in Communication Design, San Marcos, TX 78666. Offers MFA. *Program availability:* Part-time. *Faculty:* 8 full-time (4 women), 2 part-time/adjunct (0 women). *Students:* 18 full-time (13 women), 28 part-time (19 women); includes 15 minority (1 Black or African American, non-Hispanic/Latino; 1 Asian, non-Hispanic/Latino; 11 Hispanic/Latino; 2 Two or more races, non-Hispanic/Latino), 4 international. Average age 36. 35 applicants, 54% accepted, 14 enrolled. In 2016, 6 master's awarded. *Degree requirements:* For master's, comprehensive exam, thesis. *Entrance requirements:* For master's, related baccalaureate degree from regionally-accredited institution with minimum GPA of 2.75 in last 60 hours of undergraduate course work, portfolio, 3 letters of recommendation, academic and professional statement of purpose. Additional exam requirements/recommendations for international students: Required—TOEFL (minimum score 550 paper-based; 78 iBT), IELTS (minimum score 6.5). *Application deadline:* For fall admission, 3/31 for domestic and international students; for spring admission, 10/31 for domestic students, 10/1 for international students. Applications are processed on a rolling basis. Application fee: $40 ($90 for international students). Electronic applications accepted. *Expenses:* $4,851 per semester. *Financial support:* In 2016–17, 28 students received support, including 7 teaching assistantships (averaging $14,621 per year); research assistantships, Federal Work-Study, institutionally sponsored loans, scholarships/grants, and unspecified assistantships also available. Support available to part-time students. Financial award application deadline: 3/1; financial award applicants required to submit FAFSA. *Unit head:* Claudia Roeschmann, Graduate Advisor, 512-245-7450, E-mail: cr29@txstate.edu. *Application contact:* Dr. Andrea Golato, Dean of Graduate School, 512-245-2581, Fax: 512-245-8365, E-mail: gradcollege@txstate.edu.
Website: http://www.finearts.txstate.edu/Art/mfacomdes/

*Graphic Design*

**Université Laval,** Faculty of Architecture, Planning and Visual Arts, School of Visual Arts, Programs in Visual Arts, Québec, QC G1K 7P4, Canada. Offers graphic design and multimedia (MA); visual arts (MA). *Degree requirements:* For master's, thesis (for some programs). *Entrance requirements:* For master's, technical exam, interview, mastery of pertinent software, knowledge of French. Electronic applications accepted.

**University of Baltimore,** Graduate School, Yale Gordon College of Arts and Sciences, Doctoral Program in Information and Interaction Design, Baltimore, MD 21201-5779. Offers DS. *Program availability:* Part-time, evening/weekend. *Entrance requirements:* For doctorate, minimum GPA of 3.2, previous graduate study in related discipline, portfolio, resume. Electronic applications accepted.

**University of Baltimore,** Graduate School, Yale Gordon College of Arts and Sciences, Program in Publications Design, Baltimore, MD 21201-5779. Offers MA. *Program availability:* Part-time, evening/weekend. *Degree requirements:* For master's, seminar project. *Entrance requirements:* For master's, minimum GPA of 3.0, portfolio, interview. Additional exam requirements/recommendations for international students: Required—TOEFL (minimum score 550 paper-based). Electronic applications accepted. *Faculty research:* Communication theory, graphic design, media technology.

**University of Cincinnati,** Graduate School, College of Design, Architecture, Art, and Planning, School of Design, Cincinnati, OH 45221. Offers fashion design (M Des); graphic design (M Des); industrial design (M Des); interaction design (M Des); product development (M Des). *Accreditation:* NASAD. *Degree requirements:* For master's, thesis. *Entrance requirements:* For master's, undergraduate degree in design or related field, 2 years of work experience in design or related field. Additional exam requirements/recommendations for international students: Required—TOEFL. Electronic applications accepted. *Expenses: Tuition, area resident:* Full-time $12,790; part-time $389 per credit hour. Tuition, state resident: full-time $13,290; part-time $419 per credit hour. Tuition, nonresident: full-time $24,532; part-time $976 per credit hour. International tuition: $24,832 full-time. *Required fees:* $3958; $140 per credit hour. Tuition and fees vary according to course load, degree level, program and reciprocity agreements. *Faculty research:* Design theory, interdisciplinary design topics.

**University of Guam,** Office of Graduate Studies, College of Liberal Arts and Social Sciences, Division of Fine Arts, Mangilao, GU 96923. Offers ceramics (MA); graphics (MA); painting (MA). *Degree requirements:* For master's, thesis or alternative, exhibit, final oral exam. *Entrance requirements:* For master's, GRE General Test, portfolio. Additional exam requirements/recommendations for international students: Required—TOEFL.

**University of Illinois at Chicago,** College of Architecture, Design and the Arts, School of Design, Chicago, IL 60607-7128. Offers graphic design (M Des); industrial design (M Des). *Accreditation:* NASAD (one or more programs are accredited). *Degree requirements:* For master's, thesis, exhibit. *Entrance requirements:* For master's, MAT, portfolio. Additional exam requirements/recommendations for international students: Required—TOEFL. Electronic applications accepted. *Expenses:* Contact institution.

**University of Illinois at Urbana–Champaign,** Graduate College, College of Fine and Applied Arts, School of Art and Design, Program in Design and Media, Champaign, IL 61820. Offers art and design (MFA), including new media; graphic design (MFA); industrial design (MFA). *Accreditation:* NASAD.

**University of Memphis,** Graduate School, College of Communication and Fine Arts, Department of Art, Memphis, TN 38152. Offers art history (MA), including Egyptian art and archaeology, general art history; ceramics (MFA); graphic design (MFA); museum studies (Graduate Certificate); painting (MFA); printmaking/photography (MFA); sculpture (MFA). *Accreditation:* NASAD (one or more programs are accredited). *Program availability:* Part-time. *Faculty:* 20 full-time (7 women), 1 part-time/adjunct (0 women). *Students:* 22 full-time (16 women), 10 part-time (9 women); includes 9 minority (2 Black or African American, non-Hispanic/Latino; 1 Asian, non-Hispanic/Latino; 3 Hispanic/Latino; 3 Two or more races, non-Hispanic/Latino). Average age 29. 18 applicants, 78% accepted, 11 enrolled. In 2016, 17 master's, 16 other advanced degrees awarded. *Degree requirements:* For master's, 2 foreign languages, comprehensive exam, thesis, image identification exam, qualifying exam; for Graduate Certificate, internship. *Entrance requirements:* For master's, GRE General Test or MAT, portfolio (MFA), letter of intent, sample of undergraduate writing, two letters of recommendation; for Graduate Certificate, three letters of recommendation, letter of intent. *Application deadline:* For fall admission, 2/15 for domestic students; for spring admission, 11/1 for domestic students. Applications are processed on a rolling basis. Application fee: $35 ($60 for international students). *Expenses:* $5,231.50 per semester full-time in-state, $9,623.50 full-time out-of-state. *Financial support:* In 2016–17, 36 students received support, including 20 research assistantships with full tuition reimbursements available (averaging $9,800 per year); teaching assistantships with full tuition reimbursements available, Federal Work-Study, scholarships/grants, and unspecified assistantships also available. Financial award application deadline: 2/1; financial award applicants required to submit FAFSA. *Faculty research:* Online collaborative learning, advanced art history studies, electronic publishing/design, studio arts, architectural studies. *Unit head:* Prof. Richard Lou, Chair, 901-678-2217, Fax: 901-678-2735, E-mail: ralou@memphis.edu. *Application contact:* Niles Wallice, Coordinator of Graduate Studies, 901-678-4899.
Website: http://memphis.edu/art/

**University of Miami,** Graduate School, College of Arts and Sciences, Department of Art and Art History, Coral Gables, FL 33124. Offers art history (MA); ceramics/glass (MFA); graphic design/multimedia (MFA); painting (MFA); photography/digital imaging (MFA); printmaking (MFA); sculpture (MFA). *Program availability:* Part-time. *Degree requirements:* For master's, variable foreign language requirement, thesis, exhibit (MFA), comprehensive exam (MA). *Entrance requirements:* For master's, GRE General Test (MA), research paper (MA), slide portfolio (MFA). Additional exam requirements/recommendations for international students: Required—TOEFL. Electronic applications accepted. *Faculty research:* Installation art, public art.

**University of Minnesota, Duluth,** Graduate School, School of Fine Arts, Department of Art and Design, Duluth, MN 55812-2496. Offers graphic design (MFA). *Accreditation:* NASAD. *Program availability:* Part-time. *Degree requirements:* For master's, final exhibit, project, supporting paper. *Entrance requirements:* For master's, minimum GPA of 3.0, writing sample, slide portfolio. Additional exam requirements/recommendations for international students: Required—TOEFL (minimum score 550 paper-based). *Faculty research:* Motion graphics, graphic design history, interactive design, typography, education.

**University of Notre Dame,** Graduate School, College of Arts and Letters, Division of Humanities, Department of Art, Art History, and Design, Notre Dame, IN 46556. Offers art history (MA); design (MFA), including graphic design, industrial design; studio art (MFA), including ceramics, painting, photography, printmaking, sculpture. *Accreditation:* NASAD. *Degree requirements:* For master's, comprehensive exam (for some programs), thesis. *Entrance requirements:* For master's, GRE General Test, minimum GPA of 3.0. Additional exam requirements/recommendations for international students: Required—TOEFL (minimum score 600 paper-based; 80 iBT). Electronic applications accepted. *Faculty research:* Studio art practice in ceramics, printing, photography, printmaking and sculpture, graphic design and industrial design, digital imaging in design and photography, Renaissance and American art history, contemporary art theory and criticism.

**University of Pennsylvania,** School of Design, Department of Fine Arts, Philadelphia, PA 19104. Offers emerging design and research (Certificate); fine arts (MFA); time-based and interactive media (Certificate). *Faculty:* 7 full-time (3 women), 1 part-time/adjunct (0 women). *Students:* 34 full-time (23 women), 1 part-time (0 women); includes 10 minority (1 Black or African American, non-Hispanic/Latino; 2 Asian, non-Hispanic/Latino; 5 Hispanic/Latino; 2 Two or more races, non-Hispanic/Latino), 4 international. Average age 28. 131 applicants, 39% accepted, 18 enrolled. In 2016, 20 master's awarded. *Degree requirements:* For master's, thesis. *Application deadline:* Applications are processed on a rolling basis. Electronic applications accepted. *Expenses: Tuition:* Full-time $31,068; part-time $5762 per course. *Required fees:* $3200; $336 per course. Full-time tuition and fees vary according to degree level, program and student level. Part-time tuition and fees vary according to course load, degree level and program. *Financial support:* In 2016–17, 30 students received support, including teaching assistantships (averaging $6,000 per year); fellowships with full tuition reimbursements available, research assistantships, Federal Work-Study, scholarships/grants, health care benefits, and unspecified assistantships also available. Financial award applicants required to submit FAFSA. *Faculty research:* Performance art, photography and video, drawing and painting, sculpture, animation and creative research. *Unit head:* Joshua Mosley, Professor/Chair/Director of Graduate Program, 215-898-8374, E-mail: jmosley@design.upenn.edu. *Application contact:* Leighann Bogner, Administrative Assistant, 215-898-8374, Fax: 215-573-2459, E-mail: mfa@pobox.upenn.edu.
Website: http://www.design.upenn.edu/mfa

**The University of South Dakota,** Graduate School, College of Fine Arts, Department of Art, Vermillion, SD 57069. Offers art education (MFA); ceramics (MFA); graphic design (MFA); painting (MFA); photography (MFA); printmaking (MFA); sculpture (MFA). *Accreditation:* NASAD. *Degree requirements:* For master's, thesis or alternative. *Entrance requirements:* For master's, portfolio, minimum GPA of 2.7. Additional exam requirements/recommendations for international students: Required—TOEFL (minimum score 550 paper-based; 79 iBT). Electronic applications accepted.

**The University of Tennessee,** Graduate School, College of Arts and Sciences, School of Art, Knoxville, TN 37996. Offers ceramics (MFA); drawing (MFA); graphic design (MFA); inter-area studies (MFA); media arts (MFA); painting (MFA); printmaking (MFA); sculpture (MFA); watercolor (MFA). *Accreditation:* NASAD. *Degree requirements:* For master's, thesis or alternative, exhibit. *Entrance requirements:* For master's, portfolio, minimum GPA of 2.7. Additional exam requirements/recommendations for international students: Required—TOEFL. Electronic applications accepted.

**University of Utah,** Graduate School, College of Fine Arts, Department of Art and Art History, Salt Lake City, UT 84112-0380. Offers art history (MA); ceramics (MFA); community-based art education (MFA); drawing (MFA); graphic design (MFA); painting (MFA); photography/digital imaging (MFA); printmaking (MFA); sculpture/intermedia (MFA). *Faculty:* 18 full-time (10 women), 22 part-time/adjunct (11 women). *Students:* 6 full-time (2 women); includes 2 minority (both Hispanic/Latino). 48 applicants, 31% accepted, 10 enrolled. In 2016, 7 master's awarded. *Degree requirements:* For master's, variable foreign language requirement, comprehensive exam (for some programs), thesis or alternative, exhibit and final project paper (for MFA). *Entrance requirements:* For master's, CD portfolio (MFA), writing sample (MA), curriculum vitae, letters of recommendation, letter of intent. Additional exam requirements/recommendations for international students: Required—TOEFL (minimum score 575 paper-based; 75 iBT). *Application deadline:* For fall admission, 1/15 priority date for domestic and international students. Application fee: $55 ($65 for international students). Electronic applications accepted. *Expenses:* Contact institution. *Financial support:* In 2016–17, 6 students received support, including 2 fellowships, 6 research assistantships with partial tuition reimbursements available, 34 teaching assistantships with partial tuition reimbursements available, Federal Work-Study, institutionally sponsored loans, scholarships/grants, tuition waivers (partial), unspecified assistantships, and stipends also available. Financial award application deadline: 1/15; financial award applicants required to submit FAFSA. *Faculty research:* Studio art, European art history, Asian art history, Latin American art history, twentieth-century/contemporary art history. *Total annual research expenditures:* $54,906. *Unit head:* Prof. Brian Snapp, Chair, 801-581-8677, Fax: 801-585-6171, E-mail: b.snapp@utah.edu. *Application contact:* Prof. Kim Martinez, Director of Graduate Studies, 801-581-8677, Fax: 801-585-6171, E-mail: kim.martinez@art.utah.edu.
Website: http://www.art.utah.edu/

**Vermont College of Fine Arts,** MFA in Graphic Design Program, Montpelier, VT 05602. Offers MFA. *Faculty:* 10 part-time/adjunct (5 women). *Students:* 41 full-time (21 women); includes 10 minority (3 Black or African American, non-Hispanic/Latino; 1 Asian, non-Hispanic/Latino; 6 Hispanic/Latino). Average age 37. 31 applicants, 74% accepted, 14 enrolled. In 2016, 15 master's awarded. *Degree requirements:* For master's, thesis. *Application deadline:* For fall admission, 7/13 priority date for domestic and international students; for spring admission, 1/15 priority date for domestic and international students. Applications are processed on a rolling basis. Application fee: $75. Electronic applications accepted. *Expenses:* Contact institution. *Financial support:* Scholarships/grants available. Financial award applicants required to submit FAFSA. *Unit head:* Jennifer Renko, Program Director, 866-934-8232 Ext. 8896, E-mail: jennifer.renko@vcfa.edu. *Application contact:* Jennifer Renko, Program Director, 866-934-8232 Ext. 8896, E-mail: jennifer.renko@vcfa.edu.
Website: http://www.vcfa.edu/graphic-design

**Wayne State University,** College of Fine, Performing and Communication Arts, James Pearson Duffy Department of Art and Art History, Detroit, MI 48202. Offers art (MA, MFA), including ceramics, drawing, fibers, graphic design, industrial design (MA), interior design (MA), metalsmithing, painting, photography, printmaking, sculpture; art history (MA). *Students:* 15 full-time (10 women), 9 part-time (7 women); includes 6 minority (2 Black or African American, non-Hispanic/Latino; 1 Asian, non-Hispanic/Latino; 1 Hispanic/Latino; 2 Two or more races, non-Hispanic/Latino), 2 international. Average age 34. 49 applicants, 12% accepted, 3 enrolled. In 2016, 7 master's awarded. *Degree requirements:* For master's, thesis (for some programs), essay or thesis. *Entrance requirements:* For master's, BFA or another degree and equivalent course work, portfolio, personal interview, reference letters, statement of intent (except for art history program). Additional exam requirements/recommendations for international students: Required—TOEFL (minimum score 550 paper-based; 79 iBT), TWE (minimum score 5.5), Michigan English Language Assessment Battery (minimum score 85); Recommended—IELTS (minimum score 6.5). *Application deadline:* For fall admission, 2/1 for domestic and international students; for winter admission, 10/1 for domestic and international students. Application fee: $50. Electronic applications accepted. *Expenses:* $17,240 per year resident tuition and fees, $34,434 per year non-resident tuition and fees. *Financial support:* In 2016–17, 21 students received support, including 1 fellowship with tuition reimbursement available (averaging $16,000 per year), 6 teaching assistantships with tuition reimbursements available (averaging $17,994 per year); research assistantships, scholarships/grants, and unspecified assistantships also

available. Support available to part-time students. Financial award applicants required to submit FAFSA. *Faculty research:* Integration of the human figure into urban and rural landscape in painting; performance art utilizing digital media and video; exploration of race, gender, and culture through creative practice (including art, design, and art history); ongoing investigation and elaboration of visual art traditions in diverse media; continued scholarship in the history of art. *Unit head:* Dr. John Richardson, Chair, 313-577-2980, Fax: 313-577-3491, E-mail: af5343@wayne.edu. *Application contact:* 313-577-2980, E-mail: art@wayne.edu.
Website: http://art.wayne.edu/

**West Virginia University,** College of Creative Arts, School of Art and Design, Morgantown, WV 26506. Offers art education (MA); art history (MA); ceramics (MFA); graphic design (MFA); painting (MFA); printmaking (MFA); sculpture (MFA); studio art (MA). *Accreditation:* NASAD. *Degree requirements:* For master's, thesis, exhibit. *Entrance requirements:* For master's, minimum GPA of 2.75, portfolio. Additional exam requirements/recommendations for international students: Required—TOEFL. *Expenses:* Contact institution. *Faculty research:* Medieval art history.

**Yale University,** School of Art, New Haven, CT 06520-8339. Offers graphic design (MFA); painting/printmaking (MFA); photography (MFA); sculpture (MFA). *Faculty:* 10 full-time (5 women), 35 part-time/adjunct (12 women). *Students:* 127 full-time (65 women); includes 17 minority (8 Black or African American, non-Hispanic/Latino; 5 Asian, non-Hispanic/Latino; 4 Hispanic/Latino), 35 international. Average age 28. 1,003 applicants, 6% accepted, 61 enrolled. In 2016, 61 master's awarded. *Degree requirements:* For master's, thesis (for some programs). *Entrance requirements:* Additional exam requirements/recommendations for international students: Required—TOEFL (minimum score 550 paper-based; 100 iBT). *Application deadline:* For fall admission, 1/4 for domestic and international students. Application fee: $100. Electronic applications accepted. *Expenses:* Contact institution. *Financial support:* In 2016–17, 110 students received support, including 61 teaching assistantships (averaging $2,000 per year); Federal Work-Study, scholarships/grants, and unspecified assistantships also available. Financial award application deadline: 3/1; financial award applicants required to submit FAFSA. *Unit head:* Marta Kuzma, Dean, 203-432-2606. *Application contact:* Patricia Ann DeChiara, Director of Academic Affairs, 203-432-2600,
E-mail: artschool.info@yale.edu.
Website: http://www.yale.edu/art/

# Illustration

**Academy of Art University,** Graduate Programs, School of Illustration, San Francisco, CA 94105-3410. Offers MA, MFA. *Accreditation:* NASAD. *Program availability:* Part-time, 100% online. *Faculty:* 9 full-time (2 women), 39 part-time/adjunct (17 women). *Students:* 142 full-time (94 women), 98 part-time (67 women); includes 32 minority (9 Black or African American, non-Hispanic/Latino; 5 Asian, non-Hispanic/Latino; 14 Hispanic/Latino; 4 Two or more races, non-Hispanic/Latino), 120 international. Average age 30. 71 applicants, 100% accepted, 46 enrolled. In 2016, 78 master's awarded. *Degree requirements:* For master's, final review. *Entrance requirements:* For master's, statement of intent; resume; portfolio/reel; official college transcripts. *Application deadline:* Applications are processed on a rolling basis. Application fee: $50. Electronic applications accepted. *Expenses:* Tuition: Part-time $982 per unit. *Financial support:* Career-related internships or fieldwork, Federal Work-Study, and scholarships/grants available. Financial award application deadline: 8/10; financial award applicants required to submit FAFSA. *Unit head:* 800-544-ARTS, E-mail: info@academyart.edu. *Application contact:* 800-544-ARTS, E-mail: info@academyart.edu.
Website: http://www.academyart.edu/illustration-school/index.html

**Bob Jones University,** Graduate Programs, Greenville, SC 29614. Offers accountancy (MS); Bible (MA); Bible translation (MA); Biblical studies (Certificate); broadcast management (MS); business administration (MBA); church history (MA, PhD); church ministries (MA); church music (MM); cinema and video production (MA); counseling (MS); curriculum and instruction (Ed D); divinity (M Div); dramatic production (MA); educational leadership (MS, Ed D, Ed S); elementary education (M Ed, MAT); English (M Ed, MA, MAT); fine arts (MA); graphic design (MA); history (M Ed, MA); illustration (MA); interpretative speech (MA); mathematics (M Ed, MAT); medical missions (Certificate); ministry (MM, D Min); multi-categorical special education (M Ed, MAT); music (M Ed); New Testament interpretation (PhD); Old Testament interpretation (PhD); orchestral instrument performance (MM); organ performance (MM); pastoral studies (MA); personnel services (MS, Ed S); piano pedagogy (MM); piano performance (MM); platform arts (MA); radio and television broadcasting (MS); rhetoric and public address (MA); secondary education (M Ed); studio art (MA); teaching Bible (MA); theology (MA, PhD); voice performance (MM); youth ministries (MA); M Div/MM.

**East Carolina University,** Graduate School, College of Fine Arts and Communication, School of Art and Design, Greenville, NC 27858-4353. Offers art education (MA Ed); ceramics (MFA); graphic design (MFA); illustration (MFA); metal design (MFA); painting and drawing (MFA); photography (MFA); printmaking (MFA); sculpture (MFA); textile design (MFA); wood design (MFA). *Accreditation:* NASAD (one or more programs are accredited). *Program availability:* Part-time, evening/weekend. *Students:* 25 full-time (15 women), 17 part-time (12 women); includes 5 minority (2 Asian, non-Hispanic/Latino; 2 Hispanic/Latino; 1 Two or more races, non-Hispanic/Latino). Average age 33. 37 applicants, 62% accepted, 16 enrolled. In 2016, 17 master's awarded. *Degree requirements:* For master's, comprehensive exam, thesis (for some programs). *Entrance requirements:* For master's, GRE General Test or MAT, portfolio. Additional exam requirements/recommendations for international students: Required—TOEFL. *Application deadline:* For fall admission, 2/1 for domestic students; for spring admission, 10/1 for domestic students. Applications are processed on a rolling basis. Application fee: $50. *Financial support:* Research assistantships with partial tuition reimbursements, teaching assistantships with partial tuition reimbursements, and Federal Work-Study available. Support available to part-time students. Financial award application deadline: 6/1. *Unit head:* Michael H. Drought, Director, 252-328-6665, E-mail: droughtm@ecu.edu. *Application contact:* Dr. Linda H. Nelson, Information Contact, 252-328-1286, E-mail: nelsonlh@ecu.edu.
Website: http://www.ecu.edu/cs-cfac/soad/gradschool.cfm

**Fashion Institute of Technology,** School of Graduate Studies, Program in Illustration, New York, NY 10001-5992. Offers MFA. *Students:* 28. 88 applicants, 20% accepted, 16 enrolled. In 2016, 10 master's awarded. *Degree requirements:* For master's, thesis. *Entrance requirements:* Additional exam requirements/recommendations for international students: Required—TOEFL (minimum score 550 paper-based). *Application deadline:* For fall admission, 2/15 priority date for domestic and international students. Applications are processed on a rolling basis. Application fee: $50. Electronic applications accepted. *Expenses:* Tuition, state resident: full-time $10,870; part-time $453 per credit. Tuition, nonresident: full-time $22,210; part-time $925 per credit. *Required fees:* $745. *Unit head:* Melanie Reim, Associate Chairperson, 212-217-4317. *Application contact:* Administrative Secretary, Graduate Admissions, 212-217-4300, Fax: 212-217-5156, E-mail: gradinfo@fitnyc.edu.
Website: http://www.fitnyc.edu/illustration-mfa

**See Display on next page and Close-Up on page 103.**

**Hollins University,** Graduate Programs, Program in Children's Literature, Roanoke, VA 24020. Offers children's book writing and illustrating (MFA); children's literature (MA, MFA). Program offered during summer only. *Program availability:* Part-time. *Faculty:* 2 full-time (both women), 8 part-time/adjunct (7 women). *Students:* 40 full-time (38 women), 6 part-time (5 women); includes 6 minority (1 Black or African American, non-Hispanic/Latino; 1 Asian, non-Hispanic/Latino; 3 Hispanic/Latino; 1 Two or more races, non-Hispanic/Latino). Average age 35. 24 applicants, 96% accepted, 10 enrolled. In 2016, 11 master's awarded. *Degree requirements:* For master's, one foreign language, comprehensive exam, thesis. *Entrance requirements:* For master's, transcripts, letters of recommendation, portfolio, personal statement of educational objectives. Additional exam requirements/recommendations for international students: Required—TOEFL (minimum score 550 paper-based; 79 iBT), IELTS (minimum score 6.5). *Application deadline:* For summer admission, 2/15 for domestic and international students. Application fee: $40. Electronic applications accepted. *Expenses:* Contact institution. *Financial support:* Fellowships, Federal Work-Study, and scholarships/grants available. Support available to part-time students. Financial award application deadline: 2/15; financial award applicants required to submit FAFSA. *Faculty research:* Fantasy, children's film, young adult fiction, gender studies, mythology and folk tales, children's poetry, picture books. *Unit head:* Amanda Cockrell, Director, 540-362-6024, Fax: 540-362-6642, E-mail: acockrell@hollins.edu. *Application contact:* Cathy S. Koon, Manager of Graduate Services, 540-362-6326, Fax: 540-362-6288, E-mail: ckoon@hollins.edu.

**Kent State University,** College of Communication and Information, School of Visual Communication Design, Kent, OH 44242-0001. Offers MA, MFA. *Accreditation:* NASAD. *Program availability:* Part-time. *Faculty:* 16 full-time (7 women). *Students:* 27 full-time (15 women), 8 part-time (5 women); includes 6 minority (4 Black or African American, non-Hispanic/Latino; 1 Asian, non-Hispanic/Latino; 1 Two or more races, non-Hispanic/Latino), 11 international. Average age 28. 25 applicants, 88% accepted, 12 enrolled. In 2016, 7 master's awarded. *Degree requirements:* For master's, thesis optional. *Entrance requirements:* For master's, goal statement, autobiographical statement, 3 letters of recommendation, transcripts, link to personal online portfolio. Additional exam requirements/recommendations for international students: Required—TOEFL (minimum score: paper-based 525, iBT 71), Michigan English Language Assessment Battery (minimum score of 75), IELTS (minimum score of 6.0), PTE Academic (minimum score of 48), or completion of ELS level 112 Intensive Program. *Application deadline:* For fall admission, 3/1 for domestic and international students; for spring admission, 10/1 for domestic and international students. Applications are processed on a rolling basis. Application fee: $45 ($70 for international students). Electronic applications accepted. *Expenses:* Tuition, state resident: full-time $10,864; part-time $495 per credit hour. Tuition, nonresident: full-time $18,380; part-time $837 per credit hour. *Financial support:* Scholarships/grants and unspecified assistantships available. Financial award application deadline: 3/1. *Unit head:* Dr. David Robins, Interim Director, 330-672-2782, E-mail: drobins@kent.edu. *Application contact:* Ken Visocky O'Grady, Graduate Coordinator and Associate Professor, 330-672-1353, E-mail: kogrady@kent.edu.
Website: http://www.kent.edu/vcd

**Maryland Institute College of Art,** Graduate Studies, Program in Illustration Practice, Baltimore, MD 21201. Offers MFA. *Faculty:* 4 full-time (all women). *Students:* 29 full-time (17 women); includes 9 minority (8 Asian, non-Hispanic/Latino; 1 Two or more races, non-Hispanic/Latino), 8 international. Average age 24. 100 applicants, 20% accepted, 14 enrolled. In 2016, 14 master's awarded. *Degree requirements:* For master's, thesis, exhibition. *Entrance requirements:* For master's, portfolio, writing sample, bachelor's degree in any field. Additional exam requirements/recommendations for international students: Required—TOEFL (minimum score 550 paper-based; 80 iBT), IELTS (minimum score 6.5). *Application deadline:* For fall admission, 1/15 for domestic and international students. Application fee: $75. Electronic applications accepted. *Expenses:* Contact institution. *Financial support:* In 2016–17, 10 students received support, including 14 fellowships (averaging $13,000 per year), 14 teaching assistantships (averaging $3,200 per year); career-related internships or fieldwork and scholarships/grants also available. Financial award application deadline: 1/15. *Unit head:* Whitney Sherman, Director, 410-225-3177, Fax: 410-225-2408, E-mail: graduate@mica.edu. *Application contact:* Chris D. Harring, Director of Graduate Admission, 410-225-2256, Fax: 410-225-5275, E-mail: graduate@mica.edu.
Website: http://www.mica.edu/Programs_of_Study/Graduate_Programs/Illustration_Practice_(MFA).html

**Marywood University,** Academic Affairs, Insalaco College of Creative and Performing Arts, Art Department, Program in Visual Arts, Scranton, PA 18509-1598. Offers clay (MFA); graphic design (MFA); illustration (MFA); painting (MFA); photography (MFA); printmaking (MFA); sculpture (MFA). *Accreditation:* NASAD. *Program availability:* Part-time. Electronic applications accepted. *Expenses:* Contact institution.

**Memphis College of Art,** Graduate Programs, MFA Program, Memphis, TN 38104-2764. Offers illustration (MFA); metals (MFA); painting/drawing (MFA); photography (MFA); studio art (MFA). *Accreditation:* NASAD. *Program availability:* Part-time. *Faculty:* 27 full-time (16 women), 25 part-time/adjunct (13 women). *Students:* 17 full-time (13 women), 3 part-time (2 women); includes 4 minority (2 Black or African American, non-Hispanic/Latino; 2 Hispanic/Latino), 2 international. Average age 30. 24 applicants, 50% accepted, 4 enrolled. In 2016, 14 master's awarded. *Degree requirements:* For master's, thesis, thesis exhibit. *Entrance requirements:* For master's, portfolio, interview, resume, artist statement. Additional exam requirements/recommendations for international students: Required—TOEFL (minimum score 525 paper-based). *Application deadline:* For fall admission, 2/1 priority date for domestic and international students; for spring admission, 11/1 priority date for domestic and international students. Application fee: $50. Electronic applications accepted. *Expenses:* $33,100. *Financial support:* In 2016–17, 20 students received support, including 8 fellowships (averaging $4,000 per year), 5

## Illustration

teaching assistantships (averaging $3,000 per year); career-related internships or fieldwork, Federal Work-Study, scholarships/grants, and unspecified assistantships also available. Financial award application deadline: 8/1; financial award applicants required to submit FAFSA. *Unit head:* O. Gustavo Plascenicia, Director, 901-272-5100, E-mail: ogplascencia@mca.edu. *Application contact:* Katey Henriksen, Director of Admissions, 901-272-5151, Fax: 901-272-5158, E-mail: khenriksen@mca.edu.

**Mills College,** Graduate Studies, Department of English, Oakland, CA 94613-1000. Offers book and creative writing (MFA); literature (MA); poetry (MFA); prose (MFA); Spanish creative writing (Certificate); translation (MFA). *Program availability:* Part-time. *Faculty:* 4 full-time (3 women), 4 part-time/adjunct (3 women). *Students:* 47 full-time (38 women), 2 part-time (both women); includes 28 minority (8 Black or African American, non-Hispanic/Latino; 3 Asian, non-Hispanic/Latino; 9 Hispanic/Latino; 8 Two or more races, non-Hispanic/Latino). Average age 32. 78 applicants, 95% accepted, 27 enrolled. In 2016, 29 master's awarded. *Degree requirements:* For master's, comprehensive exam, thesis. *Entrance requirements:* For master's, 15-20 page writing sample. Additional exam requirements/recommendations for international students: Required—TOEFL (minimum score 600 paper-based; 100 iBT), IELTS (minimum score 7). *Application deadline:* For fall admission, 12/15 priority date for domestic students, 12/15 for international students. Applications are processed on a rolling basis. Application fee: $50. Electronic applications accepted. *Expenses: Tuition:* Full-time $31,620. *Required fees:* $1118. Tuition and fees vary according to course load, degree level and program. *Financial support:* In 2016–17, 40 students received support, including 22 fellowships with partial tuition reimbursements available (averaging $9,099 per year), 18 teaching assistantships with tuition reimbursements available (averaging $4,798 per year); research assistantships and scholarships/grants also available. Support available to part-time students. Financial award application deadline: 2/1; financial award applicants required to submit FAFSA. *Faculty research:* Creative writing, African-American literature, Victorian women writers, theories of sexuality, Shakespeare. *Unit head:* Dr. Ajuan Mance, Chair of the English Department, 510-430-2218, E-mail: dcady@mills.edu. *Application contact:* Robynne Lofton, Director of Admissions, 510-430-3295, Fax: 510-430-2159, E-mail: grad-admission@mills.edu. Website: http://www.mills.edu/english/

**Mills College,** Graduate Studies, Program in Book Art and Creative Writing, Oakland, CA 94613-1000. Offers MFA. *Program availability:* Part-time. *Faculty:* 5 full-time (4 women), 8 part-time/adjunct (7 women). *Students:* 4 full-time (all women), 3 part-time (2 women); includes 1 minority (Hispanic/Latino). Average age 28. 12 applicants, 100% accepted, 2 enrolled. In 2016, 3 master's awarded. *Degree requirements:* For master's, thesis project. *Entrance requirements:* For master's, visual portfolio of 15-25 images, written portfolio sample (for creative writing program). Additional exam requirements/recommendations for international students: Required—TOEFL (minimum score 600 paper-based; 100 iBT), IELTS (minimum score 7). *Application deadline:* For fall admission, 12/15 priority date for domestic students, 12/15 for international students. Application fee: $50. Electronic applications accepted. *Expenses: Tuition:* Full-time $31,620. *Required fees:* $1118. Tuition and fees vary according to course load, degree level and program. *Financial support:* In 2016–17, 15 students received support, including 9 fellowships with tuition reimbursements available (averaging $9,719 per year), 6 teaching assistantships with tuition reimbursements available (averaging $6,302 per year). Financial award application deadline: 2/1; financial award applicants required to submit FAFSA. *Unit head:* Kathleen Walkup, Professor of Book Arts, 510-430-2001, Fax: 510-430-2159, E-mail: kwalk@mills.edu. *Application contact:* Robynne Lofton, Director of Admissions, 510-430-3295, Fax: 510-430-2159, E-mail: grad-admission@mills.edu. Website: http://www.mills.edu/academics/graduate/eng/programs/MFA_in_bookart.php

**Minneapolis College of Art and Design,** Program in Visual Studies, Minneapolis, MN 55404-4347. Offers animation (MFA); comic art (MFA); drawing (MFA); filmmaking (MFA); fine arts (MFA); furniture design (MFA); graphic design (MFA); illustration (MFA); interactive media (MFA); painting (MFA); photography (MFA); printmaking (MFA); sculpture (MFA). *Accreditation:* NASAD. *Program availability:* Part-time. *Degree requirements:* For master's, thesis, thesis exhibit. *Entrance requirements:* For master's, portfolio of visual artwork, resume, 3 letters of recommendation. Additional exam requirements/recommendations for international students: Required—TOEFL (minimum score 550 paper-based; 79 iBT). Electronic applications accepted. *Faculty research:* Visual arts: animation, comic art, drawing, filmmaking, furniture design, graphic design, illustration, interactive media, painting, photography, printmaking, sculpture.

**Savannah College of Art and Design,** Graduate School, Program in Illustration, Savannah, GA 31402-3146. Offers MA, MFA. *Program availability:* Part-time, 100% online. *Faculty:* 15 full-time (3 women), 3 part-time/adjunct (1 woman). *Students:* 114 full-time (84 women), 48 part-time (33 women); includes 19 minority (4 Black or African American, non-Hispanic/Latino; 1 American Indian or Alaska Native, non-Hispanic/Latino; 5 Asian, non-Hispanic/Latino; 9 Hispanic/Latino), 73 international. Average age 29. 159 applicants, 53% accepted, 44 enrolled. In 2016, 20 master's awarded. *Degree requirements:* For master's, final project (for MA); thesis (for MFA). *Entrance requirements:* For master's, GRE (recommended), portfolio (submitted in digital format), audition or writing submission, resume, statement of purpose, two letters of recommendation. Additional exam requirements/recommendations for international students: Required—TOEFL (minimum score 550 paper-based, 85 iBT), IELTS (minimum score 6.5), or ACTFL. *Application deadline:* For fall admission, 4/1 for domestic and international students. Applications are processed on a rolling basis. Application fee: $40. Electronic applications accepted. *Expenses: Tuition:* Full-time $36,045. Tuition and fees vary according to course load. *Financial support:* Career-related internships or fieldwork, Federal Work-Study, and scholarships/grants available. Financial award application deadline: 4/1; financial award applicants required to submit FAFSA. *Unit head:* George Spears, Chair, Illustration and Sequential Art. *Application contact:* Jenny Jaquillard, Executive Director of Admissions, Recruitment and Events, 912-525-5100, Fax: 912-525-5985, E-mail: admission@scad.edu. Website: http://www.scad.edu/academics/programs/illustration

**Savannah College of Art and Design,** Graduate School, Program in Sequential Art, Savannah, GA 31402-3146. Offers MA, MFA. *Program availability:* Part-time. *Faculty:* 13 full-time (1 woman), 5 part-time/adjunct (3 women). *Students:* 36 full-time (26 women), 4 part-time (2 women); includes 10 minority (3 Black or African American, non-Hispanic/Latino; 2 Asian, non-Hispanic/Latino; 5 Hispanic/Latino), 11 international. Average age 27. 36 applicants, 47% accepted, 13 enrolled. In 2016, 18 master's awarded. *Degree requirements:* For master's, final project (for MA); thesis (for MFA). *Entrance requirements:* For master's, GRE (recommended), portfolio (submitted in digital format), audition or writing submission, resume, statement of purpose, two letters of recommendation. Additional exam requirements/recommendations for international students: Required—TOEFL (minimum score 550 paper-based, 85 iBT), IELTS (minimum score 6.5), or ACTFL. *Application deadline:* For fall admission, 4/1 for domestic and international students. Applications are processed on a rolling basis. Application fee: $40. Electronic applications accepted. *Expenses: Tuition:* Full-time $36,045. Tuition and fees vary according to course load. *Financial support:* Career-related internships or fieldwork, Federal Work-Study, and scholarships/grants available. Financial award application deadline: 4/1; financial award applicants required to submit FAFSA. *Unit head:* George Spears, Chair, Illustration and Sequential Art. *Application contact:* Jenny Jaquillard, Executive Director of Admissions, Recruitment and Events,

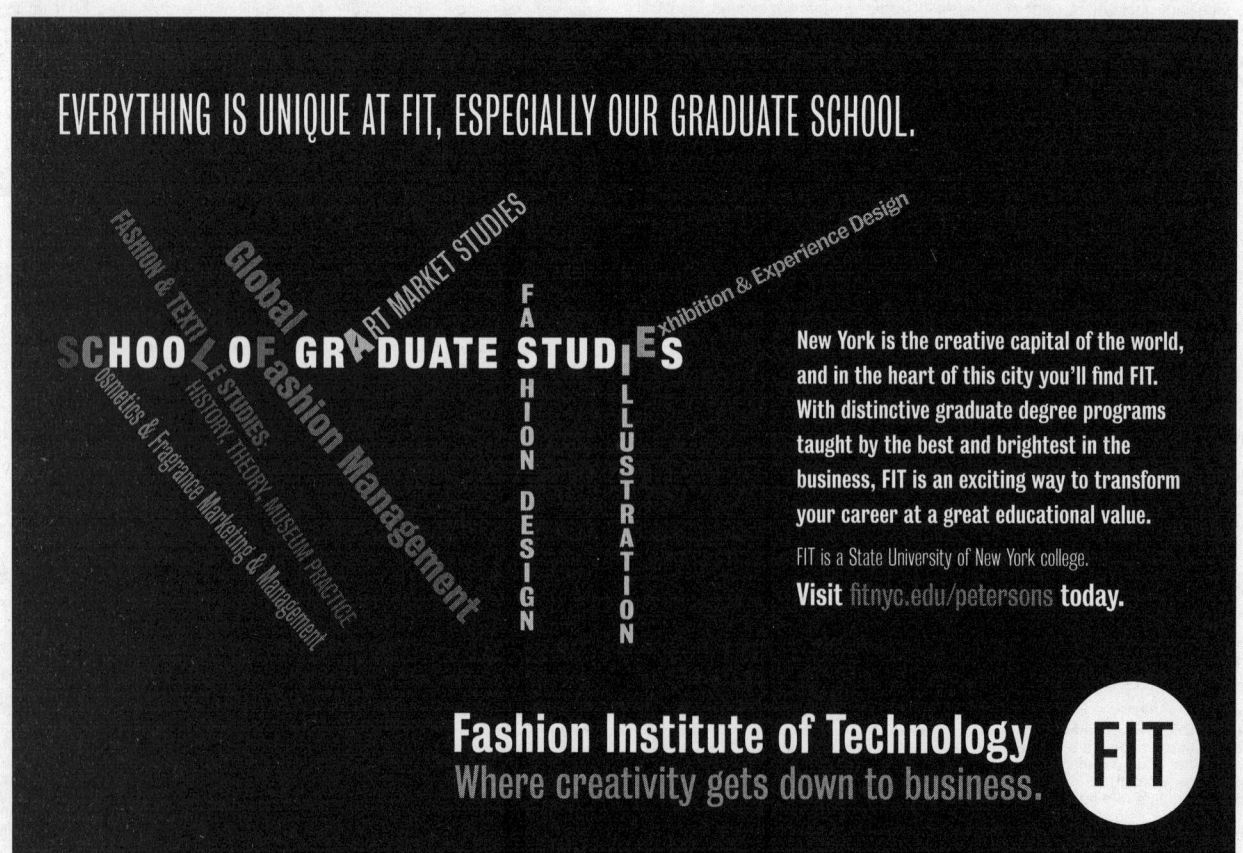

912-525-5100, Fax: 912-525-5985, E-mail: admission@scad.edu. Website: http://www.scad.edu/academics/programs/sequential-art

**School of Visual Arts,** Graduate Programs, Illustration as Visual Essay Department, New York, NY 10010-3994. Offers MFA. *Accreditation:* NASAD. *Degree requirements:* For master's, thesis, 60 credits, including all required courses; residency of two academic years. *Entrance requirements:* For master's, portfolio of work (still images) submitted through SlideRoom. Additional exam requirements/recommendations for international students: Required—TOEFL (minimum score 100 iBT). Electronic applications accepted. *Faculty research:* Illustration, fine arts, computer art, writing, art history, art direction.

**Syracuse University,** College of Visual and Performing Arts, MFA Program in Illustration, Syracuse, NY 13244. Offers MFA. In 2016, 1 master's awarded. *Degree requirements:* For master's, thesis or alternative. *Entrance requirements:* For master's, portfolio, artist statement, three letters of recommendation, academic transcripts, personal statement/essay, resume. Additional exam requirements/recommendations for international students: Required—TOEFL (minimum score 100 iBT), IELTS. *Application deadline:* For fall admission, 2/1 priority date for domestic and international students. Application fee: $75. Electronic applications accepted. *Expenses: Tuition:* Full-time $25,974; part-time $1443 per credit hour. *Required fees:* $802; $50 per course. Tuition and fees vary according to course load and program. *Financial support:* Fellowships with full tuition reimbursements and teaching assistantships with tuition reimbursements available. Financial award application deadline: 1/1. *Faculty research:* Illustration skills and concepts. *Unit head:* Prof. James Ransome, Associate Professor/Graduate Program Coordinator, 315-443-1138, E-mail: jransome@syr.edu. *Application contact:* Therese West, Information Contact, 315-443-0137, E-mail: admissg@syr.edu. Website: http://vpa.syr.edu/academics/art/graduate/illustration/

**University of Massachusetts Dartmouth,** Graduate School, College of Visual and Performing Arts, Department of Design, North Dartmouth, MA 02747-2300. Offers digital media (MFA); digital multi-media (MFA); graphic design (MFA); illustration (MFA); photography (MFA); typography (MFA). *Accreditation:* NASAD. *Program availability:* Part-time. *Faculty:* 16 full-time (7 women), 3 part-time/adjunct (1 woman). *Students:* 1 (woman) full-time, 10 part-time (7 women), 6 international. Average age 28. 30 applicants, 43% accepted, 4 enrolled. In 2016, 1 degree awarded. *Degree requirements:*

For master's, visual thesis, written thesis. *Entrance requirements:* For master's, statement of purpose (minimum of 300 words), resume, 2 letters of recommendation, official transcripts, portfolio (20 images representing applicant's art work, process of thinking, implementation of concepts and studio production). Additional exam requirements/recommendations for international students: Required—TOEFL (minimum score 533 paper-based; 72 iBT). *Application deadline:* For fall admission, 1/11 priority date for domestic students, 12/9 priority date for international students; for spring admission, 10/15 priority date for domestic students, 9/15 priority date for international students. Applications are processed on a rolling basis. Application fee: $60. Electronic applications accepted. *Expenses:* Tuition, state resident: full-time $14,994; part-time $624.75 per credit. Tuition, nonresident: full-time $27,068; part-time $1127.83 per credit. *Required fees:* $405; $25.88 per credit. Tuition and fees vary according to course load and reciprocity agreements. *Financial support:* In 2016–17, 2 fellowships (averaging $2,600 per year) were awarded; teaching assistantships, scholarships/grants, unspecified assistantships, and studio assistantships also available. Support available to part-time students. Financial award application deadline: 3/1; financial award applicants required to submit FAFSA. *Faculty research:* Web design, multimedia design, broadcast design, product design, typography, illustration, photography and design for arts. *Total annual research expenditures:* $113,333. *Unit head:* Ziddi Msagni, Graduate Program Director, Visual Design, 508-999-9291, E-mail: zmsagni@umassd.edu. *Application contact:* Steven Briggs, Director of Marketing and Recruitment for Graduate Studies, 508-999-8604, Fax: 508-999-8183, E-mail: graduate@umassd.edu. Website: http://www.umassd.edu/cvpa/graduate/visualdesign/

**Western Connecticut State University,** Division of Graduate Studies, School of Visual and Performing Arts, Department of Art, Danbury, CT 06810-6885. Offers illustration (MFA); painting (MFA). *Program availability:* Part-time. *Degree requirements:* For master's, individual exhibition of artwork, review of student's progress prior to admission to final semester, completion of program in 6 years. *Entrance requirements:* For master's, portfolio review, minimum GPA of 2.5. Additional exam requirements/recommendations for international students: Recommended—TOEFL (minimum score 550 paper-based; 79 iBT), IELTS (minimum score 6). *Expenses:* Contact institution. *Faculty research:* Proficiency in both traditional and digital processes.

# Industrial Design

**Academy of Art University,** Graduate Programs, School of Industrial Design, San Francisco, CA 94105-3410. Offers MA, MFA. *Program availability:* Part-time, 100% online. *Faculty:* 4 full-time (0 women), 29 part-time/adjunct (3 women). *Students:* 90 full-time (26 women), 56 part-time (23 women); includes 17 minority (3 Black or African American, non-Hispanic/Latino; 7 Asian, non-Hispanic/Latino; 6 Hispanic/Latino; 1 Native Hawaiian or other Pacific Islander, non-Hispanic/Latino), 105 international. Average age 29. 64 applicants, 100% accepted, 27 enrolled. In 2016, 25 master's awarded. *Degree requirements:* For master's, final review. *Entrance requirements:* For master's, statement of intent; resume; portfolio/reel; official college transcripts. *Application deadline:* Applications are processed on a rolling basis. Application fee: $50. Electronic applications accepted. *Expenses: Tuition:* Part-time $982 per unit. *Financial support:* Career-related internships or fieldwork, Federal Work-Study, and scholarships/grants available. Financial award application deadline: 8/10; financial award applicants required to submit FAFSA. *Unit head:* 800-544-ARTS, E-mail: info@academyart.edu. *Application contact:* 800-544-ARTS, E-mail: info@academyart.edu. Website: http://www.academyart.edu/industrial-design-school/index.html

**ArtCenter College of Design,** Graduate Industrial Design Program, Pasadena, CA 91103. Offers MS. *Accreditation:* NASAD. *Degree requirements:* For master's, thesis, studio project. *Entrance requirements:* For master's, portfolio. Additional exam requirements/recommendations for international students: Required—TOEFL (minimum score 100 iBT), IELTS (minimum score 7). Electronic applications accepted.

**Auburn University,** Graduate School, College of Architecture, Design, and Construction, Department of Industrial Design, Auburn University, AL 36849. Offers MID. *Accreditation:* NASAD. *Program availability:* Part-time. *Faculty:* 19 full-time (4 women). *Students:* 27 full-time (13 women), 6 part-time (1 woman); includes 2 minority (both Black or African American, non-Hispanic/Latino), 24 international. Average age 25. 50 applicants, 44% accepted, 14 enrolled. In 2016, 9 master's awarded. *Entrance requirements:* For master's, GRE General Test. *Application deadline:* Applications are processed on a rolling basis. Application fee: $50 ($60 for international students). Electronic applications accepted. *Expenses:* Tuition, state resident: full-time $9072; part-time $504 per credit hour. Tuition, nonresident: full-time $27,216; part-time $1512 per credit hour. *Required fees:* $812 per semester. Tuition and fees vary according to degree level and program. *Financial support:* Federal Work-Study available. Support available to part-time students. Financial award application deadline: 3/15; financial award applicants required to submit FAFSA. *Faculty research:* Design of space living facilities, color use in business communications. *Unit head:* Clark E. Lundell, Head, 334-844-2364. *Application contact:* Dr. George Flowers, Dean of the Graduate School, 334-844-2125. Website: http://www.auburn.edu/academic/architecture/ind/menu.html

**California College of the Arts,** Graduate Programs, Design Program, San Francisco, CA 94107. Offers graphic design (MFA); industrial design (MFA); interaction design (MFA). *Accreditation:* NASAD. *Faculty:* 6 full-time (2 women), 26 part-time/adjunct (10 women). *Students:* 105 full-time (67 women); includes 14 minority (1 Black or African American, non-Hispanic/Latino; 8 Asian, non-Hispanic/Latino; 5 Hispanic/Latino), 67 international. Average age 26. 384 applicants, 36% accepted, 45 enrolled. In 2016, 9 master's awarded. *Degree requirements:* For master's, thesis, exhibit. *Entrance requirements:* For master's, appropriate bachelor's degree, portfolio, resume, letters of recommendation, transcripts. Additional exam requirements/recommendations for international students: Required—TOEFL, IELTS, or PTE. *Application deadline:* For fall admission, 1/10 for domestic and international students. Applications are processed on a rolling basis. Application fee: $70. Electronic applications accepted. *Expenses:* $1,641 per unit, $49,230 per year tuition; $490 fees. *Financial support:* In 2016–17, fellowships (averaging $22,000 per year), teaching assistantships (averaging $2,000 per year) were awarded; career-related internships or fieldwork, Federal Work-Study, scholarships/grants, health care benefits, and unspecified assistantships also available. Financial award application deadline: 7/31; financial award applicants required to submit FAFSA. *Unit head:* Jon Sueda, Graduate Chair, 415-551-9283, Fax: 415-703-9539, E-mail: jsueda@cca.edu. *Application contact:* Wes Fanelli, Assistant Director of Graduate Admissions, 415-703-9533, Fax: 415-703-9539, E-mail: wfanelli@cca.edu.

**Carleton University,** Faculty of Graduate Studies, Faculty of Engineering and Design, School of Industrial Design, Ottawa, ON K1S 5B6, Canada. Offers M Des. *Degree requirements:* For master's, thesis optional. *Entrance requirements:* For master's, honors degree. Additional exam requirements/recommendations for international students: Required—TOEFL.

**Florida State University,** The Graduate School, College of Human Sciences, Department of Retail, Merchandising and Product Development, Tallahassee, FL 32306. Offers MS. *Program availability:* Part-time. *Faculty:* 6 full-time (5 women). *Students:* 5 full-time (all women), 1 (woman) part-time; includes 4 minority (2 Black or African American, non-Hispanic/Latino; 2 Hispanic/Latino). 8 applicants, 63% accepted, 3 enrolled. In 2016, 2 master's awarded. *Degree requirements:* For master's, thesis optional. *Entrance requirements:* For master's, GRE General Test, minimum upper-division GPA of 3.0. Additional exam requirements/recommendations for international students: Required—TOEFL (minimum score 550 paper-based; 80 iBT). *Application deadline:* For fall admission, 4/1 for domestic and international students; for spring admission, 10/1 for domestic and international students. Applications are processed on a rolling basis. Application fee: $30. Electronic applications accepted. *Expenses:* Tuition, state resident: full-time $7263; part-time $403.51 per credit hour. Tuition, nonresident: full-time $18,087; part-time $1004.85 per credit hour. *Required fees:* $1365; $75.81 per credit hour. $20 per semester. Tuition and fees vary according to campus/location. *Financial support:* In 2016–17, 7 students received support, including 4 research assistantships (averaging $4,329 per year), 8 teaching assistantships with full tuition reimbursements available (averaging $4,615 per year); career-related internships or fieldwork, institutionally sponsored loans, scholarships/grants, and unspecified assistantships also available. Financial award application deadline: 1/15; financial award applicants required to submit FAFSA. *Faculty research:* Global merchandising and product development. *Total annual research expenditures:* $35,875. *Unit head:* Dr. Robert C. Hickner, Interim Department Chair, 850-644-2498, Fax: 850-645-4673, E-mail: rhickner@fsu.edu. Website: http://humansciences.fsu.edu/departments/retail-merchandising-and-product-development

**Georgia Institute of Technology,** Graduate Studies, College of Architecture, School of Industrial Design, Atlanta, GA 30332-0001. Offers MID. *Accreditation:* NASAD. *Degree requirements:* For master's, thesis optional.

**Iowa State University of Science and Technology,** Program in Industrial Design, Ames, IA 50011. Offers MID. *Accreditation:* NASAD. *Entrance requirements:* For master's, GRE, curriculum vitae, portfolio, letters of recommendation, interview. Additional exam requirements/recommendations for international students: Required—TOEFL (minimum score 587 paper-based; 95 iBT), IELTS (minimum score 7). *Application deadline:* For fall admission, 3/15 for domestic students; for spring admission, 10/1 for domestic students. Application fee: $60 ($90 for international students). Electronic applications accepted. *Application contact:* Meredith Foley, Application Contact, 515-294-0816, Fax: 515-294-2348, E-mail: merfoley@iastate.edu. Website: http://www.design.iastate.edu/industrialdesign/graduateprogram.php

**The New School,** Parsons School of Design, Program in Industrial Design, New York, NY 10011. Offers MFA. *Program availability:* Part-time. *Faculty:* 26 full-time (7 women), 5 part-time/adjunct (3 women). *Students:* 31 full-time (23 women); includes 7 minority (1 Black or African American, non-Hispanic/Latino; 1 Asian, non-Hispanic/Latino; 4 Hispanic/Latino; 1 Two or more races, non-Hispanic/Latino), 14 international. Average age 27. 130 applicants, 27% accepted, 17 enrolled. *Degree requirements:* For master's, thesis. *Entrance requirements:* For master's, transcripts, resume, statement of purpose, recommendation letters, portfolio, interview. Additional exam requirements/recommendations for international students: Required—TOEFL (minimum score 92 iBT), IELTS (minimum score 7), PTE (minimum score 63). *Application deadline:* For fall admission, 1/1 priority date for domestic and international students. Applications are processed on a rolling basis. Application fee: $50. Electronic applications accepted. *Expenses:* Contact institution. *Financial support:* Research assistantships, teaching assistantships, career-related internships or fieldwork, scholarships/grants, unspecified assistantships, and travel funding; tuition waivers for students who are also New School

## Industrial Design

employees available. Support available to part-time students. Financial award application deadline: 2/1; financial award applicants required to submit FAFSA. *Faculty research:* Materials and manufacturing; physical computing/wearable technology; social practice and Innovation; sustainable product development. *Unit head:* Rama Chorpash, Director, 212-229-5600, E-mail: chorpasr@newschool.edu. *Application contact:* Courtney Malenius, Director of Graduate Admissions, 212-229-5150 Ext. 4011, E-mail: maleniuc@newschool.edu.
Website: https://www.newschool.edu/parsons

**North Carolina State University,** Graduate School, College of Design, Department of Industrial Design, Raleigh, NC 27695. Offers MID. *Accreditation:* NASAD. *Program availability:* Part-time. *Degree requirements:* For master's, thesis optional, oral exam, project. *Entrance requirements:* For master's, GRE General Test (recommended), portfolio. Electronic applications accepted. *Faculty research:* Computer graphics, ergonomics, product design.

**The Ohio State University,** Graduate School, College of Arts and Sciences, Division of Arts and Humanities, Department of Design, Columbus, OH 43210. Offers design (MA); design research and development (MFA); digital animation and interactive media (MFA). *Accreditation:* NASAD. *Program availability:* Part-time. *Faculty:* 15. *Students:* 23 full-time (12 women), 7 international. Average age 29. In 2016, 8 master's awarded. *Degree requirements:* For master's, project or thesis. *Entrance requirements:* For master's, GRE General Test (for all applicants with cumulative GPA below 3.0), portfolio. Additional exam requirements/recommendations for international students: Recommended—TOEFL (minimum score 550 paper-based; 79 iBT). *Application deadline:* For fall admission, 12/13 priority date for domestic students, 11/30 priority date for international students; for spring admission, 3/1 for domestic students, 2/1 for international students. Applications are processed on a rolling basis. Application fee: $60 ($70 for international students). Electronic applications accepted. *Financial support:* Fellowships with tuition reimbursements, research assistantships with tuition reimbursements, teaching assistantships with tuition reimbursements, career-related internships or fieldwork, Federal Work-Study, institutionally sponsored loans, and unspecified assistantships available. Support available to part-time students. Financial award application deadline: 5/1. *Unit head:* Dr. Mary Anne Beecher, Chair, 614-688-6746, E-mail: beecher.17@osu.edu. *Application contact:* Graduate and Professional Admissions, 614-292-9444, Fax: 614-292-3895, E-mail: gpadmissions@osu.edu.
Website: http://design.osu.edu/

**Philadelphia University,** School of Design and Engineering, Program in Industrial Design, Philadelphia, PA 19144. Offers MS. *Accreditation:* NASAD. *Program availability:* Part-time, evening/weekend. *Degree requirements:* For master's, project. *Entrance requirements:* For master's, essay; portfolio (recommended). Additional exam requirements/recommendations for international students: Required—TOEFL (minimum score 79 iBT), IELTS (minimum score 6.5).

**Pratt Institute,** School of Design, Program in Industrial Design, Brooklyn, NY 11205-3899. Offers MID. *Accreditation:* NASAD. *Program availability:* Part-time. *Faculty:* 4 full-time (1 woman), 39 part-time/adjunct (13 women). *Students:* 37 full-time (17 women); includes 12 minority (5 Asian, non-Hispanic/Latino; 4 Hispanic/Latino; 1 Native Hawaiian or other Pacific Islander, non-Hispanic/Latino; 2 Two or more races, non-Hispanic/Latino), 38 international. Average age 27. 270 applicants, 21% accepted, 27 enrolled. In 2016, 22 master's awarded. *Degree requirements:* For master's, thesis. *Entrance requirements:* For master's, portfolio, letters of recommendation. Additional exam requirements/recommendations for international students: Required—TOEFL (minimum score 575 paper-based; 90 iBT). *Application deadline:* For fall admission, 1/5 for domestic and international students; for spring admission, 10/1 for domestic and international students. Application fee: $50 ($90 for international students). Electronic applications accepted. *Expenses:* $29,646 full-time tuition, $1,938 fees. *Financial support:* Career-related internships or fieldwork, Federal Work-Study, institutionally sponsored loans, scholarships/grants, health care benefits, and unspecified assistantships available. Support available to part-time students. Financial award application deadline: 2/1; financial award applicants required to submit FAFSA. *Faculty research:* Universal design, design ethics, sustainability in design. *Unit head:* Constantin Boym, Chairperson, 718-636-3520, E-mail: cboym@pratt.edu. *Application contact:* Natalie Capannelli, Director of Graduate Admissions, 718-636-3551, Fax: 718-399-4242, E-mail: ncapanne@pratt.edu.
Website: https://www.pratt.edu/academics/school-of-design/graduate-school-of-design/industrial-design-grad/

See Display on page 66 and Close-Up on page 105.

**Pratt Institute,** School of Design, Program in Package Design, Brooklyn, NY 11205-3899. Offers MS. *Accreditation:* NASAD. *Program availability:* Part-time. *Faculty:* 5 full-time (2 women), 35 part-time/adjunct (14 women). *Students:* 40 full-time (34 women), 1 (woman) part-time; includes 8 minority (1 Black or African American, non-Hispanic/Latino; 4 Asian, non-Hispanic/Latino; 3 Hispanic/Latino), 29 international. Average age 25. 40 applicants, 93% accepted, 19 enrolled. In 2016, 12 master's awarded. *Degree requirements:* For master's, thesis. *Entrance requirements:* For master's, portfolio, letters of recommendation. Additional exam requirements/recommendations for international students: Required—TOEFL (minimum score 575 paper-based; 90 iBT). *Application deadline:* For fall admission, 1/5 for domestic and international students; for spring admission, 10/1 for domestic and international students. Application fee: $50 ($90 for international students). Electronic applications accepted. *Expenses:* $29,646 full-time tuition, $1,938 fees. *Financial support:* Career-related internships or fieldwork, Federal Work-Study, institutionally sponsored loans, scholarships/grants, health care benefits, and unspecified assistantships available. Support available to part-time students. Financial award application deadline: 2/1; financial award applicants required to submit FAFSA. *Unit head:* Santiago Piedrafita Iglesias, Chairperson, 212-647-7640, Fax: 212-367-2481, E-mail: spiedraf@pratt.edu. *Application contact:* Natalie Capannelli, Director of Graduate Admissions, 718-636-3551, Fax: 718-399-4242, E-mail: ncapanne@pratt.edu.
Website: https://www.pratt.edu/academics/school-of-design/graduate-school-of-design/grad-communications-design/package-design-ms/

See Display on page 66 and Close-Up on page 105.

**Purdue University,** Graduate School, College of Liberal Arts, Department of Art and Design, West Lafayette, IN 47907. Offers art education (MA, PhD); industrial design (MFA); integrated studio arts (MFA); interior design (MFA); photography (MFA); visual communications design (MFA). *Accreditation:* NASAD; NAST. *Program availability:* Part-time. *Students:* 20 full-time (14 women), 1 part-time (0 women); includes 1 minority (Two or more races, non-Hispanic/Latino), 16 international. Average age 26. 97 applicants, 26% accepted, 10 enrolled. In 2016, 6 master's awarded. *Degree requirements:* For master's, terminal exhibit, project, or thesis. *Entrance requirements:* For master's, GRE General Test (for art education), minimum undergraduate GPA of 3.0 or equivalent; 9 undergraduate hours in an art or design history; BA in art (for MA in art education); for doctorate, GRE General Test (minimum scores 600 in verbal and 1000 total), master's degree in art education or art with teaching certification; 3 years of teaching experience at the K-12 level. Additional exam requirements/recommendations for international students: Required—TOEFL (minimum score 550 paper-based; 77 iBT).

*Application deadline:* For fall admission, 2/1 for domestic students, 2/1 priority date for international students. Applications are processed on a rolling basis. Application fee: $60 ($75 for international students). Electronic applications accepted. *Financial support:* Teaching assistantships with tuition reimbursements and career-related internships or fieldwork available. Support available to part-time students. Financial award applicants required to submit FAFSA. *Faculty research:* Design, fine arts, photography, acting, directing, theatre technology. *Unit head:* Harry T. Bulow, Head of the Graduate Program, 765-494-3056, E-mail: hbulow@purdue.edu. *Application contact:* Sara J. Unser, Graduate Contact, 765-494-8662, E-mail: sunser@purdue.edu.
Website: https://www.cla.purdue.edu/vpa/ad/

**Rhode Island School of Design,** Division of Architecture and Design, Department of Industrial Design, Providence, RI 02903-2784. Offers MID. *Accreditation:* NASAD. *Faculty:* 10 full-time (3 women), 34 part-time/adjunct (11 women). *Students:* 43 full-time (24 women); includes 6 minority (4 Asian, non-Hispanic/Latino; 2 Hispanic/Latino), 16 international. Average age 27. 233 applicants, 15% accepted, 14 enrolled. In 2016, 19 master's awarded. *Degree requirements:* For master's, thesis, exhibition. *Entrance requirements:* For master's, portfolio, statement of purpose, 3 letters of recommendation. Additional exam requirements/recommendations for international students: Required—TOEFL (minimum score 580 paper-based; 93 iBT). *Application deadline:* For fall admission, 2/1 for domestic and international students. Application fee: $60. Electronic applications accepted. *Expenses: Tuition:* Full-time $46,800. *Required fees:* $310. *Financial support:* Fellowships, research assistantships, teaching assistantships, Federal Work-Study, scholarships/grants, and unspecified assistantships available. Financial award application deadline: 2/15; financial award applicants required to submit FAFSA. *Unit head:* Charlie Cannon, Department Head, 401-454-6160, Fax: 401-454-6157, E-mail: idgradprogram@risd.edu. *Application contact:* Molly Pettengil, Assistant Director for Graduate Recruitment, 401-454-6312, Fax: 401-454-6309, E-mail: mpetteng@risd.edu.
Website: http://www.risd.edu/academics/industrial-design/

**Rochester Institute of Technology,** Graduate Enrollment Services, College of Imaging Arts and Sciences, School of Design, MFA Program in Industrial Design, Rochester, NY 14623-5603. Offers MFA. *Accreditation:* NASAD. *Program availability:* Part-time. *Students:* 38 full-time (23 women), 14 part-time (7 women); includes 3 minority (2 Asian, non-Hispanic/Latino; 1 Hispanic/Latino), 38 international. Average age 26. 189 applicants, 32% accepted, 20 enrolled. In 2016, 10 master's awarded. *Degree requirements:* For master's, thesis, thesis exhibition. *Entrance requirements:* For master's, GRE, portfolio, minimum GPA of 3.0 (recommended). Additional exam requirements/recommendations for international students: Required—TOEFL (minimum score 550 paper-based; 90 iBT), IELTS (minimum score 7), PTE (minimum score 58). *Application deadline:* For fall admission, 2/15 priority date for domestic and international students. Applications are processed on a rolling basis. Application fee: $60. Electronic applications accepted. *Expenses:* $1,742 per credit hour. *Financial support:* In 2016–17, 31 students received support. Teaching assistantships with partial tuition reimbursements available, career-related internships or fieldwork, scholarships/grants, and unspecified assistantships available. Support available to part-time students. Financial award applicants required to submit FAFSA. *Faculty research:* User-centered design, accessible technology, interdisciplinary collaboration, digital fabrication, sustainability. *Unit head:* Alex Lobos, Graduate Program Director, 585-475-7417, E-mail: alex.lobos@rit.edu. *Application contact:* Diane Ellison, Associate Vice President, Graduate Enrollment Services, 585-475-2229, Fax: 585-475-7164, E-mail: gradinfo@rit.edu.
Website: http://cias.rit.edu/schools/design/graduate-industrial-design

**Savannah College of Art and Design,** Graduate School, Program in Industrial Design, Savannah, GA 31402-3146. Offers MA, MFA. *Program availability:* Part-time. *Faculty:* 14 full-time (1 woman), 4 part-time/adjunct (0 women). *Students:* 132 full-time (63 women), 22 part-time (10 women); includes 9 minority (2 Black or African American, non-Hispanic/Latino; 4 Asian, non-Hispanic/Latino; 2 Hispanic/Latino; 1 Native Hawaiian or other Pacific Islander, non-Hispanic/Latino), 125 international. Average age 25. 150 applicants, 75% accepted, 50 enrolled. In 2016, 32 master's awarded. *Degree requirements:* For master's, final project (for MA); thesis (for MFA). *Entrance requirements:* For master's, GRE (recommended), portfolio (submitted in digital format), audition or writing submission, resume, statement of purpose, two letters of recommendation. Additional exam requirements/recommendations for international students: Required—TOEFL (minimum score 550 paper-based, 85 iBT), IELTS (minimum score 6.5), or ACTFL. *Application deadline:* For fall admission, 4/1 for domestic and international students. Applications are processed on a rolling basis. Application fee: $40. Electronic applications accepted. *Expenses:* Tuition: Full-time $36,045. Tuition and fees vary according to course load. *Financial support:* Career-related internships or fieldwork, Federal Work-Study, and scholarships/grants available. Financial award application deadline: 4/1; financial award applicants required to submit FAFSA. *Unit head:* Victor Ermoli, Dean, School of Design. *Application contact:* Jenny Jaquillard, Executive Director of Admissions, Recruitment and Events, 912-525-5100, Fax: 912-525-5985, E-mail: admission@scad.edu.
Website: http://www.scad.edu/academics/programs/industrial-design

**University of Cincinnati,** Graduate School, College of Design, Architecture, Art, and Planning, School of Design, Cincinnati, OH 45221. Offers fashion design (M Des); graphic design (M Des); industrial design (M Des); interaction design (M Des); product development (M Des). *Accreditation:* NASAD. *Degree requirements:* For master's, thesis. *Entrance requirements:* For master's, undergraduate degree in design or related field, 2 years of work experience in design or related field. Additional exam requirements/recommendations for international students: Required—TOEFL. Electronic applications accepted. *Expenses: Tuition, area resident:* Full-time $12,790; part-time $389 per credit hour. Tuition, state resident: full-time $13,290; part-time $419 per credit hour. Tuition, nonresident: full-time $24,532; part-time $976 per credit hour. International tuition: $24,832 full-time. *Required fees:* $3958; $140 per credit hour. Tuition and fees vary according to course load, degree level, program and reciprocity agreements. *Faculty research:* Design theory, interdisciplinary design topics.

**University of Detroit Mercy,** College of Engineering and Science, Detroit, MI 48221. Offers chemistry (MS); civil and environmental engineering (DE); electrical and computer engineering (ME); electrical engineering (DE); engineering management (M Eng Mgt); environmental engineering (MEE); mechanical engineering (MME, DE); product development (MS); software engineering (MSSE); teaching of mathematics (MATM). *Program availability:* Part-time, evening/weekend. *Degree requirements:* For doctorate, thesis/dissertation. Electronic applications accepted. Application fee is waived when completed online. *Expenses:* Contact institution.

**University of Illinois at Urbana–Champaign,** Graduate College, College of Fine and Applied Arts, School of Art and Design, Program in Design and Media, Champaign, IL 61820. Offers art and design (MFA), including new media; graphic design (MFA); industrial design (MFA). *Accreditation:* NASAD.

**University of Notre Dame,** Graduate School, College of Arts and Letters, Division of Humanities, Department of Art, Art History, and Design, Notre Dame, IN 46556. Offers art history (MA); design (MFA), including graphic design, industrial design; studio art (MFA), including ceramics, painting, photography, printmaking, sculpture.

*Accreditation:* NASAD. *Degree requirements:* For master's, comprehensive exam (for some programs), thesis. *Entrance requirements:* For master's, GRE General Test, minimum GPA of 3.0. Additional exam requirements/recommendations for international students: Required—TOEFL (minimum score 600 paper-based; 80 iBT). Electronic applications accepted. *Faculty research:* Studio art practice in ceramics, printing, photography, printmaking and sculpture, graphic design and industrial design, digital imaging in design and photography, Renaissance and American art history, contemporary art theory and criticism.

**The University of the Arts,** College of Art, Media and Design, Department of Industrial Design, Philadelphia, PA 19102-4944. Offers MID. *Accreditation:* NASAD. *Degree requirements:* For master's, thesis. *Entrance requirements:* For master's, portfolio of 20 pieces that showcases self-generated projects, professional assignments or projects developed in a previous program; official transcripts; three letters of recommendation; one- to two-page statement of professional plans and goals; personal interview; resume or curriculum vitae; statement of intent. Additional exam requirements/recommendations for international students: Required—TOEFL (minimum score 580 paper-based, 92 iBT) or IELTS (minimum score 6.5).

**University of Washington,** Graduate School, College of Arts and Sciences, School of Art, Division of Design, Seattle, WA 98195. Offers industrial design (MFA); visual communication design (MFA).

**Wayne State University,** College of Fine, Performing and Communication Arts, James Pearson Duffy Department of Art and Art History, Detroit, MI 48202. Offers art (MA, MFA), including ceramics, drawing, fibers, graphic design, industrial design (MA), interior design (MA), metalsmithing, painting, photography, printmaking, sculpture; art history (MA). *Students:* 15 full-time (10 women), 9 part-time (7 women); includes 6 minority (2 Black or African American, non-Hispanic/Latino; 1 Asian, non-Hispanic/ Latino; 1 Hispanic/Latino; 2 Two or more races, non-Hispanic/Latino), 2 international. Average age 34. 49 applicants, 12% accepted, 3 enrolled. In 2016, 7 master's awarded. *Degree requirements:* For master's, thesis (for some programs), essay or thesis. *Entrance requirements:* For master's, BFA or another degree and equivalent course work, portfolio, personal interview, reference letters, statement of intent (except for art history program). Additional exam requirements/recommendations for international students: Required—TOEFL (minimum score 550 paper-based; 79 iBT), TWE (minimum score 5.5), Michigan English Language Assessment Battery (minimum score 85); Recommended—IELTS (minimum score 6.5). *Application deadline:* For fall admission, 2/1 for domestic and international students; for winter admission, 10/1 for domestic and international students. Application fee: $50. Electronic applications accepted. *Expenses:* $17,240 per year resident tuition and fees, $34,434 per year non-resident tuition and fees. *Financial support:* In 2016–17, 21 students received support, including 1 fellowship with tuition reimbursement available (averaging $16,000 per year), 6 teaching assistantships with tuition reimbursement available (averaging $17,994 per year); research assistantships, scholarships/grants, and unspecified assistantships also available. Support available to part-time students. Financial award applicants required to submit FAFSA. *Faculty research:* Integration of the human figure into urban and rural landscape in painting; performance art utilizing digital media and video; exploration of race, gender, and culture through creative practice (including art, design, and art history); ongoing investigation and elaboration of visual art traditions in diverse media; continued scholarship in the history of art. *Unit head:* Dr. John Richardson, Chair, 313-577-2980, Fax: 313-577-3491, E-mail: af5343@wayne.edu. *Application contact:* 313-577-2980, E-mail: art@wayne.edu.
Website: http://art.wayne.edu/

# Interior Design

**Academy of Art University,** Graduate Programs, School of Interior Architecture and Design, San Francisco, CA 94105-3410. Offers MA, MFA. *Accreditation:* CIDA. *Program availability:* Part-time, 100% online. *Faculty:* 4 full-time (1 woman), 23 part-time/adjunct (10 women). *Students:* 137 full-time (100 women), 100 part-time (91 women); includes 39 minority (16 Black or African American, non-Hispanic/Latino; 13 Asian, non-Hispanic/Latino; 7 Hispanic/Latino; 3 Two or more races, non-Hispanic/Latino), 120 international. Average age 32. 96 applicants, 100% accepted, 56 enrolled. In 2016, 60 master's awarded. *Degree requirements:* For master's, final review. *Entrance requirements:* For master's, statement of intent; resume; portfolio/reel; official college transcripts. *Application deadline:* Applications are processed on a rolling basis. Application fee: $50. Electronic applications accepted. *Expenses: Tuition:* Part-time $982 per unit. *Financial support:* Career-related internships or fieldwork, Federal Work-Study, and scholarships/grants available. Financial award application deadline: 8/10; financial award applicants required to submit FAFSA. *Unit head:* 800-544-ARTS, E-mail: info@academyart.edu. *Application contact:* 800-544-ARTS, E-mail: info@academyart.edu.
Website: http://www.academyart.edu/interior-design-school/index.html

**Ball State University,** Graduate School, College of Applied Sciences and Technology, Department of Family and Consumer Sciences, Muncie, IN 47306. Offers family and consumer science (MS), including apparel design (MA, MS), fashion merchandising (MA, MS), interior design (MA, MS), residential property management (MA, MS); family and consumer sciences (MA), including apparel design (MA, MS), fashion merchandising (MA, MS), interior design (MA, MS), residential property management (MA, MS); nutrition and dietetics (MA, MS). *Program availability:* Part-time, evening/weekend, 100% online. *Degree requirements:* For master's, thesis or alternative. *Entrance requirements:* For master's, letter of intent, resume, two letters of recommendation, portfolio (for interior design option). Additional exam requirements/recommendations for international students: Required—TOEFL (minimum score 550 paper-based; 79 iBT), IELTS (minimum score 6.5). Electronic applications accepted. *Faculty research:* Maternal and infant nutrition, nutrition education.

**Boston Architectural College,** Graduate Programs, Boston, MA 02115-2795. Offers architecture (M Arch); historic preservation (MDS); interior design (MID); landscape architecture (MLA); sustainable design (MDS). *Accreditation:* CIDA. *Degree requirements:* For master's, thesis. *Entrance requirements:* For master's, portfolio (recommended). Electronic applications accepted.

**Brenau University,** Sydney O. Smith Graduate School, College of Fine Arts and Humanities, Gainesville, GA 30501. Offers interior design (MID). *Accreditation:* CIDA. *Program availability:* Part-time. *Degree requirements:* For master's, internship; portfolio. *Entrance requirements:* For master's, portfolio review, minimum GPA of 3.0, resume. Additional exam requirements/recommendations for international students: Required—TOEFL (minimum score 500 paper-based; 61 iBT); Recommended—IELTS (minimum score 5). Electronic applications accepted.

**California State Polytechnic University, Pomona,** Program in Interior Architecture, Pomona, CA 91768-2557. Offers MIA. Program offered in partnership with UCLA Extension. *Accreditation:* CIDA. *Program availability:* Part-time, evening/weekend. *Students:* 19 full-time (all women), 39 part-time (35 women); includes 12 minority (3 Black or African American, non-Hispanic/Latino; 8 Asian, non-Hispanic/Latino; 1 Hispanic/Latino), 20 international. Average age 30. 31 applicants, 100% accepted, 27 enrolled. In 2016, 49 master's awarded. *Entrance requirements:* Additional exam requirements/recommendations for international students: Required—TOEFL. *Application deadline:* Applications are processed on a rolling basis. Application fee: $55. Electronic applications accepted. *Expenses:* Contact institution. *Financial support:* Application deadline: 3/2; applicants required to submit FAFSA. *Unit head:* George R. Proctor, Program Coordinator, 909-869-4728, Fax: 909-869-4331, E-mail: grproctor@cpp.edu. *Application contact:* Andrew M. Wright, Director of Admissions, 909-869-3130, Fax: 909-869-4529, E-mail: awright@cpp.edu.
Website: http://www.cpp.edu/~ceu/degree-programs/interior-architecture/index.shtml

**Chatham University,** Program in Interior Architecture, Pittsburgh, PA 15232-2826. Offers MIA. *Accreditation:* CIDA. *Program availability:* Part-time, evening/weekend, online learning. *Entrance requirements:* Additional exam requirements/recommendations for international students: Required—TOEFL (minimum score 600 paper-based; 100 iBT), IELTS (minimum score 7), TWE. Electronic applications accepted. Application fee is waived when completed online. *Expenses: Tuition:* Full-time $16,254; part-time $903 per credit hour. *Required fees:* $468; $26 per credit hour. *Faculty research:* Sustainability.

**Colorado State University,** College of Health and Human Sciences, Department of Design and Merchandising, Fort Collins, CO 80523-1574. Offers apparel and merchandising (MS); interior design (MS). *Program availability:* Part-time. *Faculty:* 7 full-time (all women). *Students:* 10 full-time (7 women), 9 part-time (all women), 4 international. Average age 31. 12 applicants, 100% accepted, 5 enrolled. In 2016, 11 master's awarded. *Degree requirements:* For master's, thesis or alternative. *Entrance requirements:* For master's, minimum cumulative undergraduate GPA of 3.0; bachelor's degree from four-year, accredited institution. Additional exam requirements/recommendations for international students: Required—TOEFL (minimum score 550 paper-based; 80 iBT). *Application deadline:* For fall admission, 3/1 priority date for domestic and international students; for spring admission, 10/15 priority date for domestic and international students. Applications are processed on a rolling basis. Application fee: $60 ($70 for international students). Electronic applications accepted. *Expenses:* Tuition, state resident: full-time $9628. Tuition, nonresident: full-time $23,603. *Required fees:* $2253; $528.14 per credit hour. $264.07 per semester. Tuition and fees vary according to course load and program. *Financial support:* In 2016–17, 9 students received support, including 5 research assistantships with full and partial tuition reimbursements available (averaging $6,966 per year), 2 teaching assistantships with full and partial tuition reimbursements available (averaging $8,708 per year); fellowships with full and partial tuition reimbursements available, Federal Work-Study, scholarships/grants, health care benefits, and unspecified assistantships also available. Financial award application deadline: 3/1. *Faculty research:* Consumer behavior, creativity and innovation, design/product development, social responsibility, social/cultural/historical aspects of the near environment. *Total annual research expenditures:* $41,861. *Unit head:* Dr. Nancy Miller, Professor and Department Head, 970-491-5811, Fax: 970-491-4855, E-mail: nancy.miller@colostate.edu. *Application contact:* Dr. Jennifer Ogle, Professor and Graduate Coordinator, 970-491-3794, Fax: 970-491-4855, E-mail: jennifer.ogle@colostate.edu.
Website: http://www.dm.chhs.colostate.edu/

**Cornell University,** Graduate School, Graduate Fields of Human Ecology, Field of Design and Environmental Analysis, Ithaca, NY 14853. Offers applied research in human-environment relations (MS); facilities planning and management (MS); housing and design (MS); human factors and ergonomics (MS); human-environment relations (MS); interior design (MA, MPS). *Degree requirements:* For master's, thesis. *Entrance requirements:* For master's, GRE General Test, portfolio or slides of recent work; bachelor's degree in interior design, architecture or related design discipline; 2 letters of recommendation. Additional exam requirements/recommendations for international students: Required—TOEFL (minimum score 600 paper-based; 105 iBT). Electronic applications accepted. *Faculty research:* Facility planning and management, environmental psychology, housing, interior design, ergonomics and human factors.

★ **Drexel University,** Westphal College of Media Arts and Design, Program in Interior Architecture and Design, Philadelphia, PA 19104-2875. Offers MS. *Accreditation:* CIDA; NASAD. *Faculty:* 14 full-time (9 women), 2 part-time/adjunct (0 women). *Students:* 34 full-time (33 women), 1 part-time; includes 5 minority (2 Black or African American, non-Hispanic/Latino; 3 Hispanic/Latino), 9 international. Average age 28. In 2016, 18 master's awarded. *Degree requirements:* For master's, comprehensive exam, thesis. *Entrance requirements:* For master's, interview. Additional exam requirements/recommendations for international students: Required—TOEFL. *Application deadline:* For fall admission, 8/21 for domestic students; for spring admission, 3/5 for domestic students. Applications are processed on a rolling basis. Application fee: $50. Electronic applications accepted. *Expenses: Tuition:* Full-time $32,184; part-time $1192 per credit hour. *Required fees:* $280. Tuition and fees vary according to campus/location and program. *Financial support:* Teaching assistantships and unspecified assistantships available. Financial award application deadline: 2/1. *Faculty research:* History of commercial interiors, hospice spaces, environmental sculpture, painting. *Unit head:* Rena Cumby, Director, 215-895-4943. *Application contact:* Director of Graduate Admissions, 215-895-6700, Fax: 215-895-5939, E-mail: enroll@drexel.edu.

**See Display on page 63 and Close-Up on page 99.**

**Eastern Michigan University,** Graduate School, College of Technology, School of Visual and Built Environments, Program in Interior Design, Ypsilanti, MI 48197. Offers MS. *Program availability:* Part-time, evening/weekend, online learning. *Students:* 14 full-time (all women), 8 part-time (6 women); includes 3 minority (1 Black or African American, non-Hispanic/Latino; 2 Asian, non-Hispanic/Latino), 12 international. Average age 30. 11 applicants, 82% accepted, 4 enrolled. In 2016, 5 master's awarded. *Entrance requirements:* Additional exam requirements/recommendations for international

*Interior Design*

students: Required—TOEFL. *Application deadline:* Applications are processed on a rolling basis. Application fee: $45. *Financial support:* Fellowships, research assistantships with full tuition reimbursements, teaching assistantships with full tuition reimbursements, career-related internships or fieldwork, Federal Work-Study, institutionally sponsored loans, scholarships/grants, tuition waivers (partial), and unspecified assistantships available. Support available to part-time students. Financial award applicants required to submit FAFSA. *Application contact:* Dr. Shinming Shyu, Graduate Program Coordinator, 734-487-6419, Fax: 734-487-8755, E-mail: sshyu@emich.edu.

**Endicott College,** Van Loan School of Graduate and Professional Studies, Program in Interior Architecture, Beverly, MA 01915-2096. Offers MA, MFA. *Accreditation:* NASAD. *Faculty:* 1 (woman) full-time, 9 part-time/adjunct (5 women). *Students:* 14 full-time (11 women), 5 part-time (all women); includes 2 minority (1 Asian, non-Hispanic/Latino; 1 Hispanic/Latino), 3 international. Average age 28. 11 applicants, 100% accepted, 7 enrolled. In 2016, 9 master's awarded. *Degree requirements:* For master's, thesis. *Entrance requirements:* For master's, statement of professional goals, two letters of recommendation, interview, undergraduate transcript. Additional exam requirements/recommendations for international students: Required—TOEFL (minimum score 550 paper-based; 79 iBT). *Application deadline:* Applications are processed on a rolling basis. Application fee: $50. Electronic applications accepted. *Expenses:* Contact institution. *Financial support:* Applicants required to submit FAFSA. *Faculty research:* Community outreach design studio, interior design practice. *Unit head:* Myoung Joo Chun, Director of Graduate Interior Design Programs, 978-232-2545, Fax: 978-232-3000, E-mail: mchun@endicott.edu. *Application contact:* Ian Menchini, Director, Graduate Enrollment and Advising, 978-232-5292, Fax: 978-232-3000, E-mail: imenchin@endicott.edu.
Website: http://www.endicott.edu/VanLoan/Graduate-Studies/Interior-Architecture.aspx

**Florida International University,** College of Communication, Architecture and The Arts, Department of Interior Architecture, Miami, FL 33199. Offers MA, MIA, Certificate. *Accreditation:* CIDA. *Faculty:* 3 full-time (1 woman), 6 part-time/adjunct (all women). *Students:* 33 full-time (27 women); includes 22 minority (1 Asian, non-Hispanic/Latino; 21 Hispanic/Latino), 5 international. Average age 29. 18 applicants, 44% accepted, 4 enrolled. In 2016, 25 master's awarded. *Entrance requirements:* For master's, GRE or minimum GPA of 3.0 in upper-level undergraduate work, portfolio. Additional exam requirements/recommendations for international students: Required—TOEFL (minimum score 550 paper-based; 80 iBT). *Application deadline:* For fall admission, 2/1 for domestic and international students. Application fee: $30. Electronic applications accepted. *Expenses:* Tuition, state resident: full-time $8912; part-time $446 per credit hour. Tuition, nonresident: full-time $21,393; part-time $992 per credit hour. *Required fees:* $2185; $195 per semester. Tuition and fees vary according to program. *Financial support:* Institutionally sponsored loans and scholarships/grants available. Financial award application deadline: 3/1; financial award applicants required to submit FAFSA. *Unit head:* Janine King, Chair, 305-348-6630, Fax: 305-348-2650, E-mail: janine.king@fiu.edu. *Application contact:* Nanett Rojas, Assistant Director, Graduate Admissions, 305-348-7464, Fax: 305-348-7441, E-mail: gradadm@fiu.edu.
Website: http://carta.fiu.edu

**Florida State University,** The Graduate School, College of Fine Arts, Department of Interior Architecture and Design, Tallahassee, FL 32306. Offers MFA, MS. *Accreditation:* NASAD (one or more programs are accredited). *Program availability:* Part-time. *Faculty:* 9 full-time (7 women), 9 part-time/adjunct (3 women). *Students:* 20 full-time (17 women); includes 5 minority (1 Black or African American, non-Hispanic/Latino; 4 American Indian or Alaska Native, non-Hispanic/Latino), 3 international. Average age 27. 47 applicants, 53% accepted, 25 enrolled. In 2016, 22 master's awarded. *Degree requirements:* For master's, thesis or alternative. *Entrance requirements:* For master's, GRE General Test, minimum GPA of 3.0 during previous 2 years. Additional exam requirements/recommendations for international students: Required—TOEFL (minimum score 550 paper-based; 80 iBT). *Application deadline:* For fall admission, 7/1 for domestic students, 5/1 for international students; for summer admission, 3/1 for domestic and international students. Applications are processed on a rolling basis. Application fee: $30. Electronic applications accepted. *Expenses:* Tuition, state resident: full-time $7263; part-time $403.51 per credit hour. Tuition, nonresident: full-time $18,087; part-time $1004.85 per credit hour. *Required fees:* $1365; $75.81 per credit hour. $20 per semester. Tuition and fees vary according to campus/location. *Financial support:* In 2016–17, 13 teaching assistantships with tuition reimbursements (averaging $5,000 per year) were awarded; career-related internships or fieldwork and unspecified assistantships also available. Financial award applicants required to submit FAFSA. *Faculty research:* Social responsibility issues, graphics techniques, history of interiors, computer-aided design and drafting, pedagogy. *Unit head:* Dr. Lisa K. Waxman, Chairman, 850-644-8326, Fax: 850-644-3112, E-mail: lwaxman@fsu.edu. *Application contact:* Dr. Marlo Ransdell, Director of Graduate Studies, 850-645-6831, Fax: 850-644-3112, E-mail: mransdell@fsu.edu.
Website: http://interiordesign.fsu.edu/

**The George Washington University,** Columbian College of Arts and Sciences, Corcoran School of the Arts and Design, Washington, DC 20007. Offers art and the book (MA); art education (MA, MAT); exhibition design (MA); interior design (MA); new media photojournalism (MA). *Accreditation:* NASAD. *Program availability:* Part-time. *Entrance requirements:* Additional exam requirements/recommendations for international students: Required—TOEFL (minimum score 95 iBT).

**The George Washington University,** Columbian College of Arts and Sciences, Department of Fine Arts and Art History, Program in Interior Design, Washington, DC 20052. Offers MA, MFA. *Faculty:* 2 full-time (both women). *Students:* 32 full-time (30 women), 11 part-time (all women); includes 17 minority (12 Black or African American, non-Hispanic/Latino; 1 Asian, non-Hispanic/Latino; 2 Hispanic/Latino; 2 Two or more races, non-Hispanic/Latino), 2 international. Average age 30. 61 applicants, 62% accepted, 21 enrolled. In 2016, 45 master's awarded. *Entrance requirements:* Additional exam requirements/recommendations for international students: Required—TOEFL (minimum score 550 paper-based; 80 iBT). *Application deadline:* For fall admission, 3/1 for domestic students, 1/15 for international students; for spring admission, 10/1 for domestic students, 9/1 for international students. *Financial support:* Application deadline: 1/15. *Unit head:* Stephanie Travis, Chair, E-mail: stravis@gwu.edu. *Application contact:* Information Contact, 202-994-6085, Fax: 202-994-8657, E-mail: art@gwu.edu.

**Georgia State University,** College of Arts and Sciences, Ernest G. Welch School of Art and Design, Program in Studio Art, Atlanta, GA 30302-3083. Offers ceramics (MFA); drawing and painting (MFA); graphic design (MFA); interior design (MFA); photography (MFA); printmaking (MFA); sculpture (MFA); textiles (MFA). *Accreditation:* NASAD. *Degree requirements:* For master's, thesis. *Application deadline:* For fall admission, 1/6 for domestic and international students; for spring admission, 1/15 priority date for domestic and international students. Application fee: $50. Electronic applications accepted. *Expenses:* Tuition, state resident: full-time $6876; part-time $382 per credit hour. Tuition, nonresident: full-time $22,374; part-time $1243 per credit hour. *Required fees:* $2128; $1064 per term. Part-time tuition and fees vary according to course load and program. *Financial support:* In 2016–17, fellowships with full tuition reimbursements (averaging $11,000 per year), teaching assistantships with full tuition reimbursements (averaging $7,000 per year) were awarded; research assistantships, scholarships/grants, and unspecified assistantships also available. Financial award application deadline: 4/15; financial award applicants required to submit FAFSA. *Faculty research:* Advertising and typography, new media, traditional media, three-dimensional art, architectural and environmental design. *Unit head:* Michael White, Director, Welch School of Art and Design, 404-413-5221, Fax: 404-413-5261, E-mail: mwhite@gsu.edu. *Application contact:* Hubert Stanley Anderson, Director of Graduate Studies, 404-413-5229, Fax: 404-413-5261, E-mail: artgrad@gsu.edu.
Website: http://artdesign.gsu.edu/graduate/admissions/masters-of-fine-arts-in-studio/

**Interior Designers Institute,** Graduate Program, Newport Beach, CA 92660. Offers MA.

**Iowa State University of Science and Technology,** Program in Interior Design, Ames, IA 50011. Offers MA, MFA. *Accreditation:* NASAD. *Entrance requirements:* For master's, GRE. Additional exam requirements/recommendations for international students: Required—TOEFL (minimum score 550 paper-based; 79 iBT), IELTS (minimum score 6.5). *Application deadline:* For fall admission, 2/1 for domestic students. Application fee: $60 ($90 for international students). Electronic applications accepted. *Application contact:* Meredith Foley, Application Contact, 515-294-0816, Fax: 515-294-2348, E-mail: merfoley@iastate.edu.
Website: http://www.design.iastate.edu/interiordesign/graduateprograms.php

**Lawrence Technological University,** College of Architecture and Design, Southfield, MI 48075-1058. Offers architecture (M Arch); build information modeling (Graduate Certificate); interior design (MID); transportation design (Graduate Certificate); urban design (MUD). *Accreditation:* NASAD. *Program availability:* Part-time, evening/weekend. *Faculty:* 14 full-time (2 women), 13 part-time/adjunct (3 women). *Students:* 8 full-time (3 women), 159 part-time (69 women); includes 15 minority (2 Black or African American, non-Hispanic/Latino; 4 Asian, non-Hispanic/Latino; 7 Hispanic/Latino; 2 Two or more races, non-Hispanic/Latino), 50 international. Average age 30. 119 applicants, 58% accepted, 43 enrolled. In 2016, 78 master's awarded. *Degree requirements:* For master's, thesis optional. *Entrance requirements:* Additional exam requirements/recommendations for international students: Required—TOEFL (minimum score 550 paper-based; 79 iBT). *Application deadline:* For fall admission, 5/22 for international students; for spring admission, 10/11 for international students; for summer admission, 2/16 for international students. Applications are processed on a rolling basis. Application fee: $50. Electronic applications accepted. *Expenses: Tuition:* Full-time $14,868; part-time $1062 per credit. *Required fees:* $75 per semester. Tuition and fees vary according to campus/location. *Financial support:* In 2016–17, 43 students received support, including 8 research assistantships with partial tuition reimbursements available (averaging $6,000 per year), 24 teaching assistantships (averaging $5,000 per year); career-related internships or fieldwork, scholarships/grants, and unspecified assistantships also available. Financial award application deadline: 4/1; financial award applicants required to submit FAFSA. *Faculty research:* Public interest design/social practice; digital fabrication and practice; design education; sustainable urbanism; Detroit architecture, Minoru Yamasaki and mid-twentieth century architecture. *Total annual research expenditures:* $260,728. *Unit head:* Prof. Karl Daubmann, Dean/Professor, 248-204-2805, E-mail: archdean@ltu.edu. *Application contact:* Jane Rohrback, Director of Admissions, 248-204-3160, Fax: 248-204-2228, E-mail: admissions@ltu.edu.
Website: http://www.ltu.edu/architecture_and_design/index.asp

**Marymount University,** School of Arts and Sciences, Program in Interior Design, Arlington, VA 22207-4299. Offers MA. *Accreditation:* CIDA. *Program availability:* Part-time, evening/weekend. *Faculty:* 11 full-time (9 women), 7 part-time/adjunct (6 women). *Students:* 36 full-time (34 women), 26 part-time (24 women); includes 15 minority (7 Black or African American, non-Hispanic/Latino; 1 Asian, non-Hispanic/Latino; 6 Hispanic/Latino; 1 Native Hawaiian or other Pacific Islander, non-Hispanic/Latino), 13 international. Average age 32. 38 applicants, 100% accepted, 26 enrolled. In 2016, 8 master's awarded. *Degree requirements:* For master's, thesis, 3-6 semesters applied design studio work. *Entrance requirements:* For master's, two letters of recommendation, resume, personal statement, portfolio, transcript showing minimum of 30 credits in liberal arts and sciences coursework. Additional exam requirements/recommendations for international students: Required—TOEFL (minimum score 600 paper-based; 96 iBT), IELTS (minimum score 6.5). *Application deadline:* For fall admission, 7/15 priority date for domestic and international students; for spring admission, 11/1 priority date for domestic and international students; for summer admission, 4/15 priority date for domestic and international students. Applications are processed on a rolling basis. Application fee: $40. Electronic applications accepted. *Expenses: Tuition:* Full-time $8460; part-time $940 per credit hour. *Required fees:* $10 per credit hour. One-time fee: $240 part-time. Tuition and fees vary according to program. *Financial support:* In 2016–17, 10 students received support, including 1 research assistantship with tuition reimbursement available, 5 teaching assistantships with tuition reimbursements available; career-related internships or fieldwork, Federal Work-Study, scholarships/grants, and unspecified assistantships also available. Support available to part-time students. Financial award applicants required to submit FAFSA. *Unit head:* Douglas R. Seidler, Chair, Interior Design, 703-284-1671, Fax: 703-284-3859, E-mail: douglas.seidler@marymount.edu. *Application contact:* Francesca Reed, Director, Graduate Admissions, 703-284-5901, Fax: 703-527-3815, E-mail: grad.admissions@marymount.edu.
Website: http://www.marymount.edu/Academics/School-of-Arts-Sciences/Graduate-Programs/Interior-Design-MA

**Marywood University,** Academic Affairs, School of Architecture, Program in Interior Architecture/Design, Scranton, PA 18509-1598. Offers MA. *Degree requirements:* For master's, thesis. *Entrance requirements:* For master's, resume, personal essay, portfolio.

**Miami University,** College of Creative Arts, Department of Architecture and Interior Design, Oxford, OH 45056. Offers M Arch. *Accreditation:* NASAD. *Students:* 24 full-time (12 women); includes 1 minority (Two or more races, non-Hispanic/Latino), 9 international. Average age 26. In 2016, 15 master's awarded. *Expenses:* Tuition, state resident: full-time $12,890; part-time $564 per credit hour. Tuition, nonresident: full-time $29,604; part-time $1260 per credit hour. *Required fees:* $638. Part-time tuition and fees vary according to course load and program. *Unit head:* Mary Rogero, Interim Chair, 513-529-4903, E-mail: rogeromr@miamioh.edu. *Application contact:* Craig Hinrichs, Professor/Director of Graduate Studies, 513-529-7036, E-mail: hinriccl@miamioh.edu.
Website: http://www.MiamiOH.edu/architecture

**Michigan State University,** The Graduate School, College of Agriculture and Natural Resources and College of Social Science, School of Planning, Design and Construction, East Lansing, MI 48824. Offers construction management (MS, PhD); environmental design (MA); interior design and facilities management (MA); international planning studies (MIPS); urban and regional planning (MURP). *Degree requirements:* For master's, thesis or alternative. *Entrance requirements:* Additional exam requirements/recommendations for international students: Required—TOEFL. Electronic applications accepted.

**Moore College of Art & Design,** Program in Interior Design, Philadelphia, PA 19103. Offers MFA. *Accreditation:* NASAD. *Program availability:* Evening/weekend. *Degree requirements:* For master's, thesis, internship, thesis exhibition. *Entrance requirements:* For master's, minimum GPA of 3.0, on-site interview, portfolio, 3 letters of recommendation, resume.

**The New School,** Parsons School of Design, Program in Interior Design, New York, NY 10011. Offers interior design (MFA); lighting design (MFA). *Program availability:* Part-time. *Faculty:* 26 full-time (7 women), 18 part-time/adjunct (10 women). *Students:* 55 full-time (43 women), 1 (woman) part-time; includes 5 minority (1 Asian, non-Hispanic/Latino; 2 Hispanic/Latino; 1 Native Hawaiian or other Pacific Islander, non-Hispanic/Latino; 1 Two or more races, non-Hispanic/Latino), 34 international. Average age 27. 184 applicants, 40% accepted, 21 enrolled. In 2016, 19 master's awarded. *Degree requirements:* For master's, thesis. *Entrance requirements:* For master's, transcripts, resume, statement of purpose, recommendation letters, portfolio, interviews. Additional exam requirements/recommendations for international students: Required—TOEFL (minimum score 92 iBT), IELTS (minimum score 7), PTE (minimum score 63). *Application deadline:* For fall admission, 1/1 priority date for domestic and international students. Applications are processed on a rolling basis. Application fee: $50. Electronic applications accepted. *Expenses:* Contact institution. *Financial support:* Research assistantships, teaching assistantships, career-related internships or fieldwork, scholarships/grants, and unspecified assistantships available. Support available to part-time students. Financial award application deadline: 2/1; financial award applicants required to submit FAFSA. *Faculty research:* Design research; integrated design; interior design; landscape architecture and design; materials and fabrication; sustainable design; textiles. *Unit head:* Alfred Zollinger, Director, 212-229-8955 Ext. 2779, E-mail: zollinga@newschool.edu. *Application contact:* Courtney Malenius, Director of Graduate Admissions, 212-229-5150 Ext. 4011, E-mail: maleniuc@newschool.edu.
Website: http://www.newschool.edu/parsons

**The New School,** Parsons School of Design, Program in Lighting Design, New York, NY 10011. Offers MFA, M Arch/MFA. *Accreditation:* NASAD. *Program availability:* Part-time. *Faculty:* 26 full-time (7 women), 11 part-time/adjunct (9 women). *Students:* 29 full-time (25 women); includes 2 minority (1 Asian, non-Hispanic/Latino; 1 Hispanic/Latino), 24 international. Average age 27. 42 applicants, 64% accepted, 17 enrolled. In 2016, 21 master's awarded. *Degree requirements:* For master's, thesis. *Entrance requirements:* For master's, transcripts, resume, statement of purpose, recommendation letters, portfolio, interviews. Additional exam requirements/recommendations for international students: Required—TOEFL (minimum score 92 iBT), IELTS (minimum score 7), PTE (minimum score 63). *Application deadline:* For fall admission, 1/1 priority date for domestic and international students. Applications are processed on a rolling basis. Application fee: $50. Electronic applications accepted. *Expenses:* Contact institution. *Financial support:* Research assistantships, teaching assistantships, career-related internships or fieldwork, scholarships/grants, and unspecified assistantships available. Support available to part-time students. Financial award application deadline: 2/1; financial award applicants required to submit FAFSA. *Faculty research:* Integrated environments; energy conservation, urban planning, light and perception. *Unit head:* Glenn Shrum, Director, 212-229-8900 Ext. 4853, E-mail: shrumg@newschool.edu. *Application contact:* Courtney Malenius, Director of Graduate Admissions, 212-229-5150 Ext. 4011, E-mail: maleniuc@newschool.edu.
Website: http://www.newschool.edu/parsons

**New York School of Interior Design,** Program in Healthcare Interior Design, New York, NY 10021-5110. Offers MPS. *Entrance requirements:* For master's, portfolio, resume, undergraduate degree in interior design or closely-related field. Additional exam requirements/recommendations for international students: Required—TOEFL (minimum score 550 paper-based; 79 iBT). Electronic applications accepted.

**New York School of Interior Design,** Program in Interior Design (Post-Professional Level), New York, NY 10021-5110. Offers MFA. *Degree requirements:* For master's, thesis. *Entrance requirements:* For master's, portfolio, resume, undergraduate degree in interior design or closely-related field. Additional exam requirements/recommendations for international students: Required—TOEFL (minimum score 550 paper-based; 79 iBT). Electronic applications accepted.

**New York School of Interior Design,** Program in Interior Design (Professional-Level), New York, NY 10021-5110. Offers MFA. *Accreditation:* CIDA; NASAD. *Degree requirements:* For master's, thesis. *Entrance requirements:* For master's, portfolio, resume, undergraduate degree in interior design or closely-related field. Additional exam requirements/recommendations for international students: Required—TOEFL (minimum score 550 paper-based; 79 iBT). Electronic applications accepted. *Faculty research:* History, theory, aesthetics, sociology, and green design; landscape, lighting, furniture, product, and set design.

**The Ohio State University,** Graduate School, College of Arts and Sciences, Division of Arts and Humanities, Department of Design, Columbus, OH 43210. Offers design (MA); design research and development (MFA); digital animation and interactive media (MFA). *Accreditation:* NASAD. *Program availability:* Part-time. *Faculty:* 15. *Students:* 23 full-time (12 women), 7 international. Average age 29. In 2016, 8 master's awarded. *Degree requirements:* For master's, project or thesis. *Entrance requirements:* For master's, GRE General Test (for all applicants with cumulative GPA below 3.0), portfolio. Additional exam requirements/recommendations for international students: Recommended—TOEFL (minimum score 550 paper-based; 79 iBT). *Application deadline:* For fall admission, 12/13 priority date for domestic students, 11/30 priority date for international students; for spring admission, 3/1 for domestic students, 2/1 for international students. Applications are processed on a rolling basis. Application fee: $60 ($70 for international students). Electronic applications accepted. *Financial support:* Fellowships with tuition reimbursements, research assistantships with tuition reimbursements, teaching assistantships with tuition reimbursements, career-related internships or fieldwork, Federal Work-Study, institutionally sponsored loans, and unspecified assistantships available. Support available to part-time students. Financial award application deadline: 5/1. *Unit head:* Dr. Mary Anne Beecher, Chair, 614-688-6746, E-mail: beecher.17@osu.edu. *Application contact:* Graduate and Professional Admissions, 614-292-9444, Fax: 614-292-3895, E-mail: gpadmissions@osu.edu.
Website: http://design.osu.edu/

**Paris College of Art,** Graduate Programs, Paris, France. Offers accessories design (MA); fashion design: new materials and technologies (MA); fashion film and photography (MA); interior design (MA); transdisciplinary new media (MA, MFA). *Entrance requirements:* Additional exam requirements/recommendations for international students: Required—TOEFL or IELTS.

**Philadelphia University,** College of Architecture and the Built Environment, Program in Interior Architecture, Philadelphia, PA 19144. Offers MS.

**Pontificia Universidad Catolica Madre y Maestra,** Graduate School, Faculty of Sciences and Humanities, Santiago, Dominican Republic. Offers architecture (M Arch), including architecture of interiors, architecture of tourist lodgings, landscaping; early childhood education (M Ed).

**Pratt Institute,** School of Design, Program in Interior Design, Brooklyn, NY 11205-3899. Offers MFA. *Accreditation:* NASAD. *Program availability:* Part-time. *Faculty:* 3 full-time (2 women), 62 part-time/adjunct (29 women). *Students:* 118 full-time (101 women), 2 part-time (both women); includes 20 minority (4 Black or African American, non-Hispanic/Latino; 10 Asian, non-Hispanic/Latino; 6 Hispanic/Latino), 63 international. Average age 26. 272 applicants, 54% accepted, 37 enrolled. In 2016, 60 master's awarded. *Degree requirements:* For master's, thesis. *Entrance requirements:* For master's, portfolio, letters of recommendation. Additional exam requirements/recommendations for international students: Required—TOEFL (minimum score 575 paper-based; 90 iBT). *Application deadline:* For fall admission, 1/5 for domestic and international students; for spring admission, 10/1 for domestic and international students. Application fee: $50 ($90 for international students). Electronic applications accepted. *Expenses:* $29,646 full-time tuition, $1,938 fees. *Financial support:* Career-related internships or fieldwork, Federal Work-Study, institutionally sponsored loans, scholarships/grants, health care benefits, and unspecified assistantships available. Support available to part-time students. Financial award application deadline: 2/1; financial award applicants required to submit FAFSA. *Unit head:* Anita Cooney, Dean, School of Design, 718-687-5744, Fax: 718-636-3410, E-mail: acooney@pratt.edu. *Application contact:* Natalie Capannelli, Director of Graduate Admissions, 718-636-3551, Fax: 718-636-3670, E-mail: ncapanne@pratt.edu.
Website: https://www.pratt.edu/academics/school-of-design/graduate-school-of-design/interior-design-grad/

**See Display on page 66 and Close-Up on page 105.**

**Purdue University,** Graduate School, College of Liberal Arts, Department of Art and Design, West Lafayette, IN 47907. Offers art education (MA, PhD); industrial design (MFA); integrated studio arts (MFA); interior design (MFA); photography (MFA); visual communications design (MFA). *Accreditation:* NASAD; NAST. *Program availability:* Part-time. *Students:* 20 full-time (14 women), 1 part-time (0 women); includes 1 minority (Two or more races, non-Hispanic/Latino), 16 international. Average age 26. 97 applicants, 26% accepted, 10 enrolled. In 2016, 6 master's awarded. *Degree requirements:* For master's, terminal exhibit, project, or thesis. *Entrance requirements:* For master's, GRE General Test (for art education), minimum undergraduate GPA of 3.0 or equivalent; 9 undergraduate hours in an art or design history; BA in art (for MA in art education); for doctorate, GRE General Test (minimum scores 600 in verbal and 1000 total), master's degree in art education or art with teaching certification; 3 years of teaching experience at the K-12 level. Additional exam requirements/recommendations for international students: Required—TOEFL (minimum score 550 paper-based; 77 iBT). *Application deadline:* For fall admission, 2/1 for domestic students, 2/1 priority date for international students. Applications are processed on a rolling basis. Application fee: $60 ($75 for international students). Electronic applications accepted. *Financial support:* Teaching assistantships with tuition reimbursements and career-related internships or fieldwork available. Support available to part-time students. Financial award applicants required to submit FAFSA. *Faculty research:* Design, fine arts, photography, acting, directing, theatre technology. *Unit head:* Harry T. Bulow, Head of the Graduate Program, 765-494-3056, E-mail: hbulow@purdue.edu. *Application contact:* Sara J. Unser, Graduate Contact, 765-494-8662, E-mail: sunser@purdue.edu.
Website: https://www.cla.purdue.edu/vpa/ad/

**Queens University of Charlotte,** College of Arts and Sciences, Charlotte, NC 28274-0002. Offers creative writing (MFA); interior design (MA). *Program availability:* Part-time, online learning. Electronic applications accepted.

**Rhode Island School of Design,** Division of Architecture and Design, Department of Interior Architecture, Providence, RI 02903-2784. Offers adaptive reuse (MA); interior studies/adaptive reuse (M Des); interior studies/exhibition and narrative environments (M Des). *Faculty:* 9 full-time (3 women), 25 part-time/adjunct (8 women). *Students:* 74 full-time (59 women); includes 6 minority (2 Black or African American, non-Hispanic/Latino; 2 Asian, non-Hispanic/Latino; 1 Hispanic/Latino; 1 Two or more races, non-Hispanic/Latino), 60 international. Average age 25. 153 applicants, 48% accepted, 43 enrolled. In 2016, 36 master's awarded. *Degree requirements:* For master's, thesis, exhibition. *Entrance requirements:* For master's, portfolio, statement of purpose, 3 letters of recommendation. Additional exam requirements/recommendations for international students: Required—TOEFL (minimum score 580 paper-based; 93 iBT). *Application deadline:* For fall admission, 2/1 for domestic and international students. Application fee: $60. Electronic applications accepted. *Expenses:* Contact institution. *Financial support:* Fellowships, research assistantships, teaching assistantships, Federal Work-Study, scholarships/grants, and unspecified assistantships available. Financial award application deadline: 2/15; financial award applicants required to submit FAFSA. *Unit head:* Liliane Wong, Department Head, 401-454-6272, Fax: 401-277-4962, E-mail: lwong@risd.edu. *Application contact:* Molly Pettengil, Assistant Director for Graduate Recruitment, 401-454-6312, Fax: 401-454-6309, E-mail: mpetteng@risd.edu.
Website: http://www.risd.edu/academics/interior-architecture/

**San Diego State University,** Graduate and Research Affairs, College of Professional Studies and Fine Arts, School of Art, Design and Art History, San Diego, CA 92182. Offers art history (MA); studio arts (MA, MFA), including applied design, environmental design, graphic design, interior design, painting and printmaking, sculpture. *Accreditation:* NASAD (one or more programs are accredited). *Degree requirements:* For master's, variable foreign language requirement, thesis. *Entrance requirements:* For master's, GRE General Test, bachelor's degree in related field, slide portfolio, typed slide information sheet, 2 letters of recommendation. Additional exam requirements/recommendations for international students: Required—TOEFL. Electronic applications accepted.

**Savannah College of Art and Design,** Graduate School, Program in Interior Design, Savannah, GA 31402-3146. Offers MA, MFA. *Program availability:* Part-time, 100% online. *Faculty:* 17 full-time (10 women), 5 part-time/adjunct (2 women). *Students:* 84 full-time (67 women), 17 part-time (12 women); includes 9 minority (1 Black or African American, non-Hispanic/Latino; 2 Asian, non-Hispanic/Latino; 6 Hispanic/Latino), 74 international. Average age 27. 247 applicants, 34% accepted, 35 enrolled. In 2016, 40 master's awarded. *Degree requirements:* For master's, final project (for MA); thesis (for MFA). *Entrance requirements:* For master's, GRE (recommended), portfolio (submitted in digital format), audition or writing submission, resume, statement of purpose, two letters of recommendation. Additional exam requirements/recommendations for international students: Required—TOEFL (minimum score 550 paper-based, 85 iBT), IELTS (minimum score 6.5), or ACTFL. *Application deadline:* For fall admission, 4/1 for domestic and international students. Applications are processed on a rolling basis. Application fee: $40. Electronic applications accepted. *Expenses: Tuition:* Full-time $36,045. Tuition and fees vary according to course load. *Financial support:* Career-related internships or fieldwork, Federal Work-Study, and scholarships/grants available. Financial award application deadline: 4/1; financial award applicants required to submit FAFSA. *Unit head:* Khoi Vo, Chair, Interior Design. *Application contact:* Jenny Jaquillard, Executive Director of Admissions, Recruitment and Events, 912-525-5100, Fax: 912-525-5985, E-mail: admission@scad.edu.
Website: http://www.scad.edu/academics/programs/interior-design

*Interior Design*

**School of the Art Institute of Chicago,** Graduate Division, Department of Architecture, Interior Architecture, and Designed Objects, Chicago, IL 60603-3103. Offers architecture (M Arc); design for emerging technologies (MFA); designed objects (M Des); interior architecture (M Arc). *Entrance requirements:* Additional exam requirements/recommendations for international students: Required—TOEFL, IELTS.

**Suffolk University,** New England School of Art and Design, Boston, MA 02108-2770. Offers graphic design (MA); interior architecture (MA). *Program availability:* Part-time, evening/weekend. *Faculty:* 12 full-time (8 women), 20 part-time/adjunct (12 women). *Students:* 37 full-time (30 women), 25 part-time (23 women); includes 11 minority (1 Black or African American, non-Hispanic/Latino; 7 Asian, non-Hispanic/Latino; 3 Hispanic/Latino), 19 international. Average age 29. 63 applicants, 73% accepted, 20 enrolled. In 2016, 29 master's awarded. *Entrance requirements:* For master's, GRE (for MFA), art portfolio, interview, 2 letters of recommendation, resume; letter of intent (for MFA). Additional exam requirements/recommendations for international students: Required—TOEFL (minimum score 550 paper-based; 80 iBT). *Application deadline:* For fall admission, 3/15 priority date for domestic and international students; for spring admission, 10/15 priority date for domestic and international students. Applications are processed on a rolling basis. Application fee: $50. Electronic applications accepted. *Expenses:* $24,436 per year full-time tuition, $1,144 per credit hour part-time tuition, $52 per year student activity fee, $180 per course studio fee. *Financial support:* In 2016–17, 44 students received support, including 40 fellowships (averaging $6,900 per year); career-related internships or fieldwork, Federal Work-Study, institutionally sponsored loans, scholarships/grants, and unspecified assistantships also available. Financial award application deadline: 4/1; financial award applicants required to submit FAFSA. *Faculty research:* Sustainable design, lighting and technology, design education, environmental graphic design, designing for the non-profit sector. *Unit head:* Audrey Goldstein, Department Chair, 617-997-4290, E-mail: agoldstein@suffolk.edu. *Application contact:* Mara Marzocchi, Associate Director of Graduate Admissions, 617-573-8302, Fax: 617-305-1733, E-mail: grad.admission@suffolk.edu.
Website: http://www.suffolk.edu/nesad/

**Texas Tech University,** Graduate School, College of Human Sciences, Department of Design, Lubbock, TX 79409-1220. Offers environmental design (MS); interior and environmental design (PhD). *Program availability:* Part-time. *Faculty:* 10 full-time (8 women), 1 (woman) part-time/adjunct. *Students:* 15 full-time (9 women), 5 part-time (4 women); includes 1 minority (Hispanic/Latino), 13 international. Average age 34. 19 applicants, 53% accepted, 5 enrolled. In 2016, 9 master's, 5 doctorates awarded. *Degree requirements:* For master's, comprehensive exam, thesis or alternative; for doctorate, comprehensive exam, thesis/dissertation. *Entrance requirements:* For master's, 3 recommendation letters, design portfolio, 500-word written statement (reason for pursuing degree), resume; for doctorate, GRE, 3 recommendation letters, design portfolio, 500-word written statement (reason for pursuing degree), resume. Additional exam requirements/recommendations for international students: Required—TOEFL (minimum score 550 paper-based, 79 iBT) or IELTS (6.5). *Application deadline:* For fall admission, 6/1 priority date for domestic students, 1/15 priority date for international students; for spring admission, 9/1 priority date for domestic students, 6/15 priority date for international students. Applications are processed on a rolling basis. Application fee: $75. Electronic applications accepted. *Expenses:* $315 per credit hour full-time resident tuition, $723 per credit hour full-time non-resident tuition; $50.50 per credit hour fee plus $608 per term fee. *Financial support:* In 2016–17, 17 students received support, including 16 fellowships (averaging $7,220 per year), 10 research assistantships (averaging $8,312 per year); teaching assistantships, scholarships/grants, and unspecified assistantships also available. Financial award application deadline: 4/15; financial award applicants required to submit FAFSA. *Faculty research:* Healthcare and the built environment, sustainability, vulnerable populations, historic preservation, evidence-based design. *Total annual research expenditures:* $34,363. *Unit head:* Dr. Sharran F. Parkinson, Chair, 806-742-3031, Fax: 806-742-1639, E-mail: sharran.parkinson@ttu.edu. *Application contact:* Dr. Kristi Gaines, Graduate Programs Director, 806-742-3050, Fax: 806-742-1639, E-mail: kristi.gaines@ttu.edu.
Website: http://www.depts.ttu.edu/hs/dod/

**University of California, Berkeley,** UC Berkeley Extension, Certificate Programs in Art and Design, Berkeley, CA 94720-1500. Offers interior design and interior architecture (Certificate); landscape architecture (Certificate); visual arts (Postbaccalaureate Certificate).

**University of Cincinnati,** Graduate School, College of Design, Architecture, Art, and Planning, School of Architecture and Interior Design, Cincinnati, OH 45221. Offers architecture (M Arch). *Accreditation:* NASAD. *Degree requirements:* For master's, one foreign language, thesis. *Entrance requirements:* Additional exam requirements/recommendations for international students: Required—TOEFL. *Expenses:* Tuition, area resident: Full-time $12,790; part-time $389 per credit hour. Tuition, state resident: full-time $13,290; part-time $419 per credit hour. Tuition, nonresident: full-time $24,532; part-time $976 per credit hour. *International tuition:* $24,832 full-time. *Required fees:* $3958; $140 per credit hour. Tuition and fees vary according to course load, degree level, program and reciprocity agreements. *Faculty research:* Theory and history of architecture.

**University of Florida,** Graduate School, College of Design, Construction and Planning, Department of Interior Design, Gainesville, FL 32611. Offers historic preservation (MID); interior design (MID); sustainable design (MID). *Degree requirements:* For master's, thesis. *Entrance requirements:* For master's, GRE General Test, minimum GPA of 3.0. Additional exam requirements/recommendations for international students: Required—TOEFL (minimum score 550 paper-based; 80 iBT), IELTS (minimum score 6). *Faculty research:* Sustainable design and environmentally significant behaviors; design innovation, creativity, methods and pedagogy; lighting and color design and perception; historic preservation; design for special populations.

**University of Florida,** Graduate School, College of Design, Construction and Planning, Doctoral Program in Design, Construction and Planning, Gainesville, FL 32611. Offers construction management (PhD); design, construction and planning (PhD); geographic information systems (PhD); historic preservation (PhD); interior design (PhD); landscape architecture (PhD); urban and regional planning (PhD). *Degree requirements:* For doctorate, thesis/dissertation. *Entrance requirements:* For doctorate, GRE General Test, minimum GPA of 3.0. Additional exam requirements/recommendations for international students: Required—TOEFL (minimum score 550 paper-based; 80 iBT), IELTS (minimum score 6). Electronic applications accepted. *Faculty research:* Architecture, building construction, urban and regional planning.

**University of Georgia,** College of Family and Consumer Sciences, Department of Textiles, Merchandising, and Interiors, Athens, GA 30602. Offers historical and cultural aspects of dress and textiles (MS); interior environments (MS); international merchandising (MS); merchandising and international trade (MS); polymer, fiber and textile science (MS); polymer, fiber, and textile sciences (PhD). *Degree requirements:* For master's, thesis; for doctorate, thesis/dissertation. *Entrance requirements:* For master's and doctorate, GRE General Test. *Application deadline:* For fall admission, 7/1 priority date for domestic students; for spring admission, 11/15 for domestic students. Application fee: $50. Electronic applications accepted. *Financial support:* Fellowships, research assistantships, teaching assistantships, and unspecified assistantships available. *Unit head:* Dr. Patricia K. Hunt-Hurst, Department Head, 706-542-4891, Fax: 706-542-4862, E-mail: phunt@fcs.uga.edu. *Application contact:* Suraj Sharma, Graduate Coordinator, 706-542-7353, E-mail: ssharma@uga.edu.
Website: http://www.fcs.uga.edu/tmi/

**University of Kentucky,** Graduate School, College of Design, Program in Interior Design, Merchandising, and Textiles, Lexington, KY 40506-0032. Offers interior design (MA). *Degree requirements:* For master's, comprehensive exam, thesis optional. *Entrance requirements:* For master's, GRE General Test, minimum undergraduate GPA of 2.75. Additional exam requirements/recommendations for international students: Required—TOEFL (minimum score 550 paper-based). Electronic applications accepted. *Faculty research:* Interior design, apparel merchandising, textile evaluation, creativity in design, social-psychological aspects of dress and interiors.

**University of Manitoba,** Faculty of Graduate Studies, Faculty of Architecture, Department of Interior Design, Winnipeg, MB R3T 2N2, Canada. Offers MID. *Accreditation:* CIDA.

**University of Massachusetts Amherst,** Graduate School, College of Humanities and Fine Arts, Department of Architecture, Amherst, MA 01003. Offers architecture (M Arch); design (MS); design in historic preservation (MS). *Program availability:* Part-time. *Degree requirements:* For master's, thesis or alternative, project. *Entrance requirements:* For master's, GRE General Test (for M Arch only), 3 letters of recommendation (M Arch only); portfolio. Additional exam requirements/recommendations for international students: Required—TOEFL (minimum score 550 paper-based; 80 iBT), IELTS (minimum score 6.5). Electronic applications accepted.

**University of Minnesota, Twin Cities Campus,** Graduate School, College of Design, Department of Design, Housing, and Apparel, Minneapolis, MN 55455-0213. Offers apparel (MA, MS, PhD); design communication (MA, MS, PhD); housing studies (MA, MS, PhD, Postbaccalaureate Certificate); interactive design (MFA); interior design (MA, MS, PhD). *Program availability:* Part-time. *Degree requirements:* For master's and Postbaccalaureate Certificate, comprehensive exam, thesis (for some programs); for doctorate, comprehensive exam, thesis/dissertation. *Entrance requirements:* For master's, GRE General Test, minimum GPA of 3.0 (preferred), portfolio, 3 letters of recommendation; for doctorate, GRE General Test, minimum GPA of 3.0 (preferred), portfolio, 3 letters of recommendation, writing sample; for Postbaccalaureate Certificate, GRE General Test, minimum GPA of 3.0 (preferred). Additional exam requirements/recommendations for international students: Required—TOEFL (minimum score 550 paper-based; 79 iBT). Electronic applications accepted. *Faculty research:* Housing policy and community development; consumer behavior; interactive design; design history; social, cultural, and behavioral issues related to designed environments.

**University of Nebraska–Lincoln,** Graduate College, College of Architecture, Department of Architecture, Lincoln, NE 68588. Offers architecture (M Arch, MS, PhD); interior design (MS); M Arch/MBA; M Arch/MCRP. *Entrance requirements:* Additional exam requirements/recommendations for international students: Required—TOEFL. Electronic applications accepted.

**The University of North Carolina at Greensboro,** Graduate School, College of Arts and Sciences, Department of Interior Architecture, Greensboro, NC 27412-5001. Offers historic preservation (Certificate); interior architecture (MS); museum studies (Certificate). *Degree requirements:* For master's, thesis. *Entrance requirements:* For master's, GRE General Test or MAT, bachelor's degree in interior design, interview, portfolio. Additional exam requirements/recommendations for international students: Required—TOEFL. Electronic applications accepted.

**University of North Texas,** Robert B. Toulouse School of Graduate Studies, Denton, TX 76203-5459. Offers accounting (MS); applied anthropology (MA, MS); applied behavior analysis (Certificate); applied geography (MA); applied technology and performance improvement (M Ed, MS); art education (MA); art history (MA); art museum education (Certificate); arts leadership (Certificate); audiology (Au D); behavior analysis (MS); behavioral science (PhD); biochemistry and molecular biology (MS); biology (MA, MS); biomedical engineering (MS); business analysis (MS); chemistry (MS); clinical health psychology (PhD); communication studies (MA, MS); computer engineering (MS); computer science (MS); counseling (M Ed, MS), including clinical mental health counseling (MS), college and university counseling, elementary school counseling, secondary school counseling; creative writing (MA); criminal justice (MS); curriculum and instruction (M Ed); decision sciences (MBA); design (MA, MFA), including fashion design (MFA), innovation studies, interior design (MFA); early childhood studies (MS); economics (MS); educational leadership (M Ed, Ed D); educational psychology (MS, PhD), including family studies (MS), gifted and talented (MS), human development (MS), learning and cognition (MS), research, measurement and evaluation (MS); electrical engineering (MS); emergency management (MPA); engineering technology (MS); English (MA); English as a second language (MA); environmental science (MS); finance (MBA, MS); financial management (MPA); French (MA); health services management (MBA); higher education (M Ed, Ed D); history (MA, MS); hospitality management (MS); human resources management (MPA); information science (MS); information systems (PhD); information technologies (MBA); interdisciplinary studies (MA, MS); international studies (MA); international sustainable tourism (MS); jazz studies (MM); journalism (MA, MJ, Graduate Certificate), including interactive and virtual digital communication (Graduate Certificate), narrative journalism (Graduate Certificate), public relations (Graduate Certificate); kinesiology (MS); linguistics (MA); local government management (MPA); logistics (PhD); logistics and supply chain management (MBA); long-term care, senior housing, and aging services (MA); management (PhD); marketing (MBA); mathematics (MA, MS); mechanical and energy engineering (MS, PhD); music (MA), including ethnomusicology, music theory, musicology, performance; music composition (PhD); music education (MM Ed, PhD); nonprofit management (MPA); operations and supply chain management (MBA); performance (MM, DMA); philosophy (MA); political science (MA); professional and technical communication (MA); radio, television and film (MA, MFA); rehabilitation counseling (Certificate); sociology (MA); Spanish (MA); special education (M Ed); speech-language pathology (MA); strategic management (MBA); studio art (MFA); teaching (M Ed); MBA/MS. *Program availability:* Part-time, evening/weekend, online learning. Terminal master's awarded for partial completion of doctoral program. *Degree requirements:* For master's, variable foreign language requirement, comprehensive exam (for some programs), thesis (for some programs); for doctorate, variable foreign language requirement, comprehensive exam (for some programs), thesis/dissertation; for other advanced degree, variable foreign language requirement, comprehensive exam (for some programs). *Entrance requirements:* For master's and doctorate, GRE, GMAT. Additional exam requirements/recommendations for international students: Required—TOEFL (minimum score 550 paper-based; 79 iBT). Electronic applications accepted.

**University of Oklahoma,** College of Architecture, Division of Interior Design, Norman, OK 73019. Offers interior design (MS); planning, design and construction (PhD); professional applications of interior design (Graduate Certificate). *Program availability:* Part-time. *Students:* 6 full-time (5 women); includes 2 minority (both American Indian or Alaska Native, non-Hispanic/Latino), 2 international. Average age 34. 11 applicants, 55% accepted, 4 enrolled. In 2016, 1 master's awarded. *Degree*

requirements: For master's, comprehensive exam, project or thesis; for doctorate, comprehensive exam, thesis/dissertation. *Entrance requirements:* For master's, letter of intent, 3 letters of recommendation; for doctorate, graduate degree in interior design or related field, portfolio of design work, letter of intent, three letters of recommendation; for Graduate Certificate, undergraduate degree in interior design or related field, portfolio of design work, letter of intent, three letters of recommendation. Additional exam requirements/recommendations for international students: Required—TOEFL (minimum score 79 iBT) or IELTS (minimum score 6.5). *Application deadline:* Applications are processed on a rolling basis. Application fee: $50 ($100 for international students). Electronic applications accepted. *Expenses:* Tuition, state resident: full-time $4886; part-time $203.60 per credit hour. Tuition, nonresident: full-time $18,989; part-time $791.20 per credit hour. *Required fees:* $3283; $126.25 per credit hour. $126.50 per semester. *Financial support:* In 2016–17, 3 students received support, including 3 research assistantships with partial tuition reimbursements available (averaging $10,372 per year); teaching assistantships with full and partial tuition reimbursements available, career-related internships or fieldwork, scholarships/grants, tuition waivers, and unspecified assistantships also available. Financial award application deadline: 6/1; financial award applicants required to submit FAFSA. *Faculty research:* Environment and human behavior; indoor environmental quality; pedagogical exploration; building information modeling (BIM) for cognitive spatial problem solving; community health and environmental design. *Unit head:* Mia Kile, Academic Director and Associate Professor, 405-325-1051, Fax: 405-325-7558, E-mail: mkile@ou.edu. *Application contact:* Dr. Suchismita Bhattacharjee, Assistant Professor and Graduate Liaison, 405-325-2548, Fax: 405-325-7558, E-mail: suchi@ou.edu.
Website: http://www.ou.edu/architecture/interior_design.html

**University of Oregon,** Graduate School, School of Architecture and Allied Arts, Department of Architecture, Eugene, OR 97403. Offers architecture (M Arch); interior architecture (MI Arch). *Accreditation:* CIDA. *Degree requirements:* For master's, thesis (for some programs). *Entrance requirements:* For master's, GRE General Test. Additional exam requirements/recommendations for international students: Required—TOEFL. *Faculty research:* Innovation in housing design and design production, climate responsive design, passive heating and cooling, computer software development for design applications, vernacular architecture.

**The University of Texas at Austin,** Graduate School, School of Architecture, Program in Interior Design, Austin, TX 78712-1111. Offers MID.

**Utah State University,** School of Graduate Studies, College of Humanities, Arts and Social Sciences, Program in Interior Design, Logan, UT 84322. Offers MS. *Program availability:* Part-time, online learning. *Entrance requirements:* For master's, GRE General Test, MAT, minimum GPA of 3.0. Additional exam requirements/ recommendations for international students: Required—TOEFL.

**Virginia Commonwealth University,** Graduate School, School of the Arts, Richmond, VA 23284-9005. Offers art education (MAE, PhD); art history (MA, PhD), including curatorial (PhD), historical studies, museum studies (MA); ceramics (MFA); design (MFA), including interior environments, visual communications; fibers (MFA); furniture design (MFA); glassworking (MFA); jewelry/metalworking (MFA); kinetic imaging (MFA); music (MM), including music education; painting (MFA); photography and film (MFA); printmaking (MFA); sculpture (MFA); theatre (MFA), including costume design, pedagogy/literature, pedagogy/performance, scene design/technical theatre. *Program availability:* Part-time. *Entrance requirements:* For doctorate, GRE General Test, writing sample. Additional exam requirements/recommendations for international students: Required—TOEFL (minimum score 600 paper-based; 100 iBT). *Application deadline:* For fall admission, 1/15 priority date for domestic students. Application fee: $50. Electronic applications accepted. *Financial support:* Fellowships, teaching assistantships, career-related internships or fieldwork, Federal Work-Study, institutionally sponsored loans, and tuition waivers (full and partial) available. Support available to part-time students. Financial award applicants required to submit FAFSA. *Unit head:* Joseph H. Seipel, Dean, 804-828-2787, Fax: 804-828-6469, E-mail: arts@vcu.edu. *Application contact:* Jack H. Risley, Associate Dean for Academic Affairs, 804-828-2787, Fax: 804-828-6469, E-mail: jhrisley@vcu.edu.
Website: http://www.vcu.edu/arts/

**Washington State University,** College of Agricultural, Human, and Natural Resource Sciences, Program in Interior Design and Landscape Architecture, Pullman, WA 99164-2220. Offers MA, MS. Programs offered at the Pullman campus. *Program availability:* Part-time. *Degree requirements:* For master's, comprehensive exam, thesis (for some programs), oral exam. *Entrance requirements:* For master's, portfolio. Additional exam requirements/recommendations for international students: Required—TOEFL or IELTS. Electronic applications accepted. *Faculty research:* Digital fabrication, design pedagogy, proportional systems, American architecture and urbanism, design leadership.

**Wayne State University,** College of Fine, Performing and Communication Arts, James Pearson Duffy Department of Art and Art History, Detroit, MI 48202. Offers art (MA, MFA), including ceramics, drawing, fibers, graphic design, industrial design (MA), interior design (MA), metalsmithing, painting, photography, printmaking, sculpture; art history (MA). *Students:* 15 full-time (10 women), 9 part-time (7 women); includes 6 minority (2 Black or African American, non-Hispanic/Latino; 1 Asian, non-Hispanic/ Latino; 1 Hispanic/Latino; 2 Two or more races, non-Hispanic/Latino), 2 international. Average age 34. 49 applicants, 12% accepted, 3 enrolled. In 2016, 7 master's awarded. *Degree requirements:* For master's, thesis (for some programs), essay or thesis. *Entrance requirements:* For master's, BFA or another degree and equivalent course work, portfolio, personal interview, reference letters, statement of intent (except for art history program). Additional exam requirements/recommendations for international students: Required—TOEFL (minimum score 550 paper-based; 79 iBT), TWE (minimum score 5.5), Michigan English Language Assessment Battery (minimum score 85); Recommended—IELTS (minimum score 6.5). *Application deadline:* For fall admission, 2/1 for domestic and international students; for winter admission, 10/1 for domestic and international students. Application fee: $50. Electronic applications accepted. *Expenses:* $17,240 per year resident tuition and fees, $34,434 per year non-resident tuition and fees. *Financial support:* In 2016–17, 21 students received support, including 1 fellowship with tuition reimbursement available (averaging $16,000 per year), 6 teaching assistantships with tuition reimbursements available (averaging $17,994 per year); research assistantships, scholarships/grants, and unspecified assistantships also available. Support available to part-time students. Financial award applicants required to submit FAFSA. *Faculty research:* Integration of the human figure into urban and rural landscape in painting; performance art utilizing digital media and video; exploration of race, gender, and culture through creative practice (including art, design, and art history); ongoing investigation and elaboration of visual art traditions in diverse media; continued scholarship in the history of art. *Unit head:* Dr. John Richardson, Chair, 313-577-2980, Fax: 313-577-3491, E-mail: af5343@wayne.edu. *Application contact:* 313-577-2980, E-mail: art@wayne.edu.
Website: http://art.wayne.edu/

# Medical Illustration

**Augusta University,** College of Allied Health Sciences, Program in Medical Illustration, Augusta, GA 30912. Offers MS. *Accreditation:* ARCMI. *Degree requirements:* For master's, thesis or alternative, project. *Entrance requirements:* For master's, GRE General Test, portfolio. Additional exam requirements/recommendations for international students: Required—TOEFL (minimum score 550 paper-based; 79 iBT). Electronic applications accepted. *Faculty research:* Digital visual communication modalities, information science education, Southwestern Native American art pedagogy, medical illustration pedagogy, public health/visual education.

**Johns Hopkins University,** School of Medicine, Graduate Programs in Medicine, Department of Art as Applied to Medicine, Baltimore, MD 21205. Offers medical and biological illustration (MA). *Accreditation:* ARCMI. *Faculty:* 10 full-time (4 women), 12 part-time/adjunct (3 women). *Students:* 14 full-time (12 women); includes 2 minority (1 Black or African American, non-Hispanic/Latino; 1 Asian, non-Hispanic/Latino), 3 international. Average age 26. 61 applicants, 11% accepted, 7 enrolled. In 2016, 8 master's awarded. *Degree requirements:* For master's, thesis. *Entrance requirements:* Additional exam requirements/recommendations for international students: Recommended—TOEFL. *Application deadline:* For fall admission, 1/15 for domestic and international students. Application fee: $110. Electronic applications accepted. *Expenses:* $50,160 tuition, $475 university health service fee, $740 matriculation fee. *Financial support:* In 2016–17, 14 students received support. Scholarships/grants available. Financial award application deadline: 5/31; financial award applicants required to submit FAFSA. *Faculty research:* Visualization, digital media, animation and 3D modeling, instructional design, anaplastology and 3D printing. *Unit head:* Corinne Sandone, Director, 410-955-3213, Fax: 410-955-1085, E-mail: medart-info@jhmi.edu. *Application contact:* Dacia M. Balch, Administrative Coordinator, 410-955-3213, Fax: 410-955-1085, E-mail: medart-info@jhmi.edu.
Website: http://medicalart.johnshopkins.edu/

**Rochester Institute of Technology,** Graduate Enrollment Services, College of Health Sciences and Technology, Health Sciences Department, MFA Program in Medical Illustration, Rochester, NY 14623-5603. Offers MFA. *Program availability:* Part-time. *Students:* 9 full-time (5 women), 2 part-time (1 woman); includes 2 minority (1 Black or African American, non-Hispanic/Latino; 1 Hispanic/Latino), 3 international. Average age 29. 15 applicants, 40% accepted, 4 enrolled. In 2016, 2 master's awarded. *Degree requirements:* For master's, thesis. *Entrance requirements:* For master's, portfolio, minimum GPA of 3.0 (recommended). Additional exam requirements/ recommendations for international students: Required—TOEFL (minimum score 550 paper-based; 79 iBT), IELTS (minimum score 6.5), PTE (minimum score 58). *Application deadline:* Applications are processed on a rolling basis. Application fee: $60. Electronic applications accepted. *Expenses:* $1,742 per credit hour. *Financial support:* In 2016–17, 9 students received support. Teaching assistantships with partial tuition reimbursements available, career-related internships or fieldwork, scholarships/grants, and unspecified assistantships available. Support available to part-time students. Financial award applicants required to submit FAFSA. *Faculty research:* Medical and scientific visualization, medical game design and interactive media, three-dimensional modeling and animation, medical information design and graphics, molecular graphics. *Unit head:* James Perkins, Graduate Program Director, 585-475-5697, Fax: 585-475-6447, E-mail: japfaa@rit.edu. *Application contact:* Diane Ellison, Associate Vice President, Graduate Enrollment Services, 585-475-2229, Fax: 585-475-7164, E-mail: gradinfo@rit.edu.
Website: http://www.rit.edu/healthsciences/graduate-programs/medical-illustration

**University of Illinois at Chicago,** College of Applied Health Sciences, Program in Biomedical Visualization, Chicago, IL 60607-7128. Offers MS. *Accreditation:* ARCMI. *Degree requirements:* For master's, thesis. *Entrance requirements:* For master's, GRE General Test, minimum GPA of 2.75. Additional exam requirements/recommendations for international students: Required—TOEFL. Electronic applications accepted. *Expenses:* Contact institution. *Faculty research:* Medical illustration, graphics, reconstruction, anatomical modeling.

# Photography

**Academy of Art University,** Graduate Programs, School of Photography, San Francisco, CA 94105-3410. Offers MA, MFA. *Accreditation:* NASAD. *Program availability:* Part-time, 100% online. *Faculty:* 10 full-time (5 women), 35 part-time/adjunct (14 women). *Students:* 117 full-time (59 women), 145 part-time (90 women); includes 48 minority (13 Black or African American, non-Hispanic/Latino; 3 American Indian or Alaska Native, non-Hispanic/Latino; 10 Asian, non-Hispanic/Latino; 16 Hispanic/Latino;

3 Native Hawaiian or other Pacific Islander, non-Hispanic/Latino; 3 Two or more races, non-Hispanic/Latino), 87 international. Average age 36. 75 applicants, 100% accepted, 57 enrolled. In 2016, 54 master's awarded. *Degree requirements:* For master's, final review. *Entrance requirements:* For master's, statement of intent; resume; portfolio/reel; official college transcripts. *Application deadline:* Applications are processed on a rolling basis. Application fee: $50. Electronic applications accepted. *Expenses: Tuition:* Part-time $982 per unit. *Financial support:* Career-related internships or fieldwork, Federal Work-Study, and scholarships/grants available. Financial award application deadline: 8/10; financial award applicants required to submit FAFSA. *Unit head:* 800-544-ARTS, E-mail: info@academyart.edu. *Application contact:* 800-544-ARTS, E-mail: info@academyart.edu.
Website: http://www.academyart.edu/photography-school/index.html

**Ball State University,** Graduate School, College of Fine Arts, School of Art, Muncie, IN 47306. Offers fine arts (MFA), including animation, glass; visual arts studio (MA), including ceramics, drawing, metals, painting, photography and intermedia arts, printmaking, sculpture. *Accreditation:* NASAD. *Program availability:* Part-time. *Entrance requirements:* For master's, minimum baccalaureate GPA of 2.75 or 3.0 in latter half of baccalauareate, goals statement, digital portfolio of artwork, resume, transcripts of all college-level course work, three letters of recommendation. Additional exam requirements/recommendations for international students: Required—TOEFL (minimum score 550 paper-based; 79 iBT), IELTS (minimum score 6.5). Electronic applications accepted. *Expenses:* Contact institution.

**Bard College,** International Center of Photography, Annandale-on-Hudson, NY 12504. Offers advanced photographic studies (MFA).

**Barry University,** College of Arts and Sciences, Department of Fine Arts, Miami Shores, FL 33161-6695. Offers photography (MA, MFA). *Degree requirements:* For master's, thesis (for some programs). *Entrance requirements:* For master's, GRE General Test, minimum GPA of 3.0. Electronic applications accepted. *Faculty research:* Inclusion education, exceptional education, art-based assessments.

**Bradley University,** The Graduate School, Slane College of Communications and Fine Arts, Department of Art, Peoria, IL 61625-0002. Offers ceramics (MA, MFA); drawing (MA, MFA); graphic design (MA, MFA); painting (MA, MFA); photography (MA, MFA); printmaking (MA, MFA); sculpture (MA, MFA). *Accreditation:* NASAD. *Program availability:* Part-time. *Degree requirements:* For master's, comprehensive exam, thesis, final exhibit. *Entrance requirements:* For master's, portfolio, 2 letters of recommendation. Additional exam requirements/recommendations for international students: Required—TOEFL (minimum score 550 paper-based; 79 iBT). *Application deadline:* For fall admission, 4/1 priority date for domestic and international students; for spring admission, 11/1 priority date for domestic and international students. Applications are processed on a rolling basis. Application fee: $40 ($50 for international students). Electronic applications accepted. *Expenses: Tuition:* Full-time $7650; part-time $850 per credit. *Required fees:* $50 per credit. One-time fee: $100 full-time. *Financial support:* Teaching assistantships with full and partial tuition reimbursements, scholarships/grants, tuition waivers (partial), and unspecified assistantships available. Support available to part-time students. Financial award application deadline: 4/1. *Unit head:* Gary Will, Chairperson, 309-677-2967, E-mail: pkrainak@bradley.edu. *Application contact:* Kayla Carroll, Director of International Admission and Student Services, 309-677-2375, E-mail: klcarroll@fsmail.bradley.edu.
Website: http://www.bradley.edu/academic/departments/art/

**Brooklyn College of the City University of New York,** School of Visual, Media and Performing Arts, Department of Art, Brooklyn, NY 11210-2889. Offers art history (MA); digital art (MFA); drawing and painting (MFA); photography (MFA); printmaking (MFA); sculpture (MFA). *Program availability:* Part-time. *Degree requirements:* For master's, thesis. *Entrance requirements:* For master's, bachelor's degree in art, portfolio, 2 letters of recommendation. Additional exam requirements/recommendations for international students: Required—TOEFL (minimum score 500 paper-based; 61 iBT). Electronic applications accepted.

**California College of the Arts,** Graduate Programs, Fine Arts Programs, San Francisco, CA 94107. Offers ceramics (MFA); film/video/performance (MFA); glass (MFA); interdisciplinary studies (MFA); jewelry/metal arts (MFA); media studies (MFA); painting/drawing (MFA); photography (MFA); printmaking (MFA); sculpture (MFA); textiles (MFA); wood/furniture (MFA). *Accreditation:* NASAD. *Faculty:* 23 full-time (14 women), 17 part-time/adjunct (12 women). *Students:* 75 full-time (55 women); includes 20 minority (7 Black or African American, non-Hispanic/Latino; 2 American Indian or Alaska Native, non-Hispanic/Latino; 6 Asian, non-Hispanic/Latino; 5 Hispanic/Latino), 15 international. Average age 29. 224 applicants, 54% accepted, 43 enrolled. In 2016, 27 master's awarded. *Degree requirements:* For master's, thesis, exhibit. *Entrance requirements:* For master's, appropriate bachelor's degree, portfolio, resume, 2 letters of recommendation, transcript. Additional exam requirements/recommendations for international students: Required—TOEFL, IELTS, or PTE. *Application deadline:* For fall admission, 1/10 for domestic and international students. Applications are processed on a rolling basis. Application fee: $70. Electronic applications accepted. *Expenses:* $1,641 per unit, $49,230 per year tuition; $490 fees. *Financial support:* In 2016–17, fellowships (averaging $42,000 per year), teaching assistantships (averaging $2,000 per year) were awarded; career-related internships or fieldwork, Federal Work-Study, scholarships/grants, health care benefits, and unspecified assistantships also available. Financial award application deadline: 7/31; financial award applicants required to submit FAFSA. *Unit head:* James Gobel, Chair, 415-551-9214, Fax: 415-703-9539, E-mail: jgobel@cca.edu. *Application contact:* Wes Fanelli, Assistant Director of Graduate Admissions, 415-703-9533, Fax: 415-703-9539, E-mail: wfanelli@cca.edu.

**California Institute of the Arts,** School of Art, Valencia, CA 91355-2340. Offers art (MFA, Adv C); graphic design (MFA, Adv C); photography (MFA, Adv C). *Accreditation:* NASAD (one or more programs are accredited). *Degree requirements:* For master's, final project. *Entrance requirements:* For master's, portfolio. Additional exam requirements/recommendations for international students: Required—TOEFL. Electronic applications accepted.

**California State University, Los Angeles,** Graduate Studies, College of Arts and Letters, Department of Art, Los Angeles, CA 90032-8530. Offers art (MA), including art education, art history, art therapy, ceramics, metals, and textiles, design (MA, MFA), painting, sculpture, and graphic arts, photography; fine arts (MFA), including crafts, design (MA, MFA), studio arts. *Accreditation:* NASAD (one or more programs are accredited). *Program availability:* Part-time, evening/weekend. *Degree requirements:* For master's, comprehensive exam, project or thesis. *Entrance requirements:* For master's, portfolio. Additional exam requirements/recommendations for international students: Required—TOEFL (minimum score 500 paper-based). Electronic applications accepted. *Faculty research:* The artist and the book, conceptual art, ceramic processes, computer graphics, architectural graphics.

**Claremont Graduate University,** Graduate Programs, School of Arts and Humanities, Department of Art, Claremont, CA 91711. Offers digital media (MFA); drawing (MFA); installation (MFA); painting (MFA); performance (MFA); photography (MFA); sculpture (MFA); studio (MFA). *Program availability:* Part-time. *Faculty:* 3 full-time (1 woman). *Students:* 38 full-time (25 women), 1 part-time (0 women); includes 12

minority (1 Black or African American, non-Hispanic/Latino; 4 Asian, non-Hispanic/Latino; 6 Hispanic/Latino; 1 Two or more races, non-Hispanic/Latino), 8 international. Average age 35. In 2016, 18 master's awarded. *Degree requirements:* For master's, final project show. *Entrance requirements:* For master's, BA in art or BFA, slide review. Additional exam requirements/recommendations for international students: Required—TOEFL (minimum score 75 iBT). *Application deadline:* For fall admission, 2/1 priority date for domestic and international students. Applications are processed on a rolling basis. Application fee: $80. Electronic applications accepted. *Expenses:* Contact institution. *Financial support:* Fellowships, research assistantships, teaching assistantships, Federal Work-Study, institutionally sponsored loans, and scholarships/grants available. Support available to part-time students. Financial award application deadline: 2/15; financial award applicants required to submit FAFSA. *Faculty research:* Acoustic sculpture, feminization of abstraction, installation sculpture. *Unit head:* David Amico, Chair, 909-607-8216, E-mail: david.amico@cgu.edu. *Application contact:* Amy Sandefur, Assistant Director of Admissions, 909-607-9101, E-mail: jennifer.gracia@cgu.edu.
Website: https://www.cgu.edu/academics/program/mfa

**Columbia College Chicago,** Graduate School, Department of Photography, Chicago, IL 60605-1996. Offers MFA. *Degree requirements:* For master's, thesis. *Entrance requirements:* For master's, self-assessment essay, portfolio, resume, letters of recommendation. Additional exam requirements/recommendations for international students: Required—TOEFL (minimum score 600 paper-based; 100 iBT). Electronic applications accepted. *Expenses:* Contact institution.

**Columbia University,** School of the Arts, Visual Arts Program, New York, NY 10027. Offers new genres (MFA); painting (MFA); photography (MFA); printmaking (MFA); sculpture (MFA). *Degree requirements:* For master's, thesis. *Entrance requirements:* For master's, 3 letters of recommendation, portfolio, resume. Additional exam requirements/recommendations for international students: Required—TOEFL (minimum score 600 paper-based; 100 iBT). Electronic applications accepted.

**See Display on page 147 and Close-Up on page 201.**

**Cornell University,** Graduate School, Graduate Fields of Architecture, Art and Planning, Field of Art, Ithaca, NY 14853. Offers creative visual arts (MFA), including painting, photography, printmaking, sculpture. *Degree requirements:* For master's, thesis, exhibit. *Entrance requirements:* For master's, slide portfolio of 10-20 slides, 3 letters of recommendation, resume. Additional exam requirements/recommendations for international students: Required—TOEFL (minimum score 550 paper-based; 77 iBT). Electronic applications accepted. *Faculty research:* Painting, sculpture, photography, printmaking.

**Cornell University,** Graduate School, Graduate Fields of Arts and Sciences, Field of History of Art, Archaeology and Visual Studies, Ithaca, NY 14853. Offers 19th century art (PhD); African, African American and African diaspora (PhD); American art (PhD); ancient art and archaeology (PhD); Asian American art (PhD); Baroque art (PhD); comparative modernities (PhD); digital art (PhD); East Asian art (PhD); history of photography (PhD); Islamic art (PhD); Latin American art (PhD); medieval art (PhD); modern art (PhD); Renaissance art (PhD); Southeast Asian art (PhD); theory and criticism (PhD); visual studies (PhD). *Degree requirements:* For doctorate, one foreign language, comprehensive exam, thesis/dissertation, general exams in 3 areas. *Entrance requirements:* For doctorate, GRE General Test, sample of written work, 3 letters of recommendation. Additional exam requirements/recommendations for international students: Required—TOEFL (minimum score 550 paper-based; 77 iBT). Electronic applications accepted.

**Cranbrook Academy of Art,** Graduate School, Program in Fine Arts, Bloomfield Hills, MI 48303-0801. Offers 2d design (MFA); 3d design (MFA); ceramics (MFA); fiber (MFA); metalsmithing (MFA); painting (MFA); photography (MFA); print media (MFA); sculpture (MFA). *Accreditation:* NASAD. *Degree requirements:* For master's, thesis, exhibit. *Entrance requirements:* Additional exam requirements/recommendations for international students: Required—TOEFL (minimum score 85 iBT). *Application deadline:* For fall admission, 2/1 priority date for domestic and international students. Application fee: $85. Electronic applications accepted. *Expenses: Tuition, area resident:* Full-time $37,375. *Required fees:* $1460. *Financial support:* Federal Work-Study and scholarships/grants available. Financial award application deadline: 2/15; financial award applicants required to submit FAFSA. *Unit head:* Christopher Scoates, Director, 248-645-3301, Fax: 248-645-3591. *Application contact:* Leslie Tobakos, Registrar/Financial Aid and Admissions Manager, 248-645-3360, Fax: 248-645-3591, E-mail: ltobakos@cranbrook.edu.

**East Carolina University,** Graduate School, College of Fine Arts and Communication, School of Art and Design, Greenville, NC 27858-4353. Offers art education (MA Ed); ceramics (MFA); graphic design (MFA); illustration (MFA); metal design (MFA); painting and drawing (MFA); photography (MFA); printmaking (MFA); sculpture (MFA); textile design (MFA); wood design (MFA). *Accreditation:* NASAD (one or more programs are accredited). *Program availability:* Part-time, evening/weekend. *Students:* 25 full-time (15 women), 17 part-time (12 women); includes 5 minority (2 Asian, non-Hispanic/Latino; 2 Hispanic/Latino; 1 Two or more races, non-Hispanic/Latino). Average age 33. 37 applicants, 62% accepted, 16 enrolled. In 2016, 17 master's awarded. *Degree requirements:* For master's, comprehensive exam, thesis (for some programs). *Entrance requirements:* For master's, GRE General Test or MAT, portfolio. Additional exam requirements/recommendations for international students: Required—TOEFL. *Application deadline:* For fall admission, 2/1 for domestic students; for spring admission, 10/1 for domestic students. Applications are processed on a rolling basis. Application fee: $50. *Financial support:* Research assistantships with partial tuition reimbursements, teaching assistantships with partial tuition reimbursements, and Federal Work-Study available. Support available to part-time students. Financial award application deadline: 6/1. *Unit head:* Michael H. Drought, Director, 252-328-6665, E-mail: droughtm@ecu.edu. *Application contact:* Dr. Linda H. Nelson, Information Contact, 252-328-1286, E-mail: nelsonlh@ecu.edu.
Website: http://www.ecu.edu/cs-cfac/soad/gradschool.cfm

**Ferris State University,** Kendall College of Art and Design, Grand Rapids, MI 49503. Offers architecture (M Arch); art education (MAE); drawing (MFA); painting (MFA); photography (MFA); printmaking (MFA); visual and critical studies (MA). *Program availability:* Part-time. *Faculty:* 15 full-time (10 women), 9 part-time/adjunct (2 women). *Students:* 40 full-time (33 women), 5 part-time (3 women); includes 9 minority (3 Black or African American, non-Hispanic/Latino; 3 Asian, non-Hispanic/Latino; 3 Hispanic/Latino), 6 international. Average age 30. 43 applicants, 53% accepted, 16 enrolled. In 2016, 16 master's awarded. *Degree requirements:* For master's, thesis, seminars. *Entrance requirements:* For master's, portfolio, 3 letters of recommendation, curriculum vitae, artist statement, letter of intent. Additional exam requirements/recommendations for international students: Required—TOEFL (minimum score 70 iBT). *Application deadline:* For fall admission, 2/1 priority date for domestic and international students; for spring admission, 11/1 priority date for domestic and international students. Applications are processed on a rolling basis. Application fee: $0. Electronic applications accepted. *Expenses:* $1,017 per credit hour plus $390 fees per year. *Financial support:* In 2016–17, 32 students received support, including 8 fellowships (averaging $16,781 per year); scholarships/grants and unspecified assistantships also available. Financial award application deadline: 2/1; financial award applicants required to submit FAFSA. *Unit head:* Leslie Bellavance, President, 616-451-2787. *Application contact:* Thomas Post, Graduate Recruitment Specialist, 616-451-2787, Fax: 616-831-9689, E-mail: thomaspost@ferris.edu. Website: http://www.kcad.edu/

**George Mason University,** College of Visual and Performing Arts, Program in Visual and Performing Arts, Fairfax, VA 22030. Offers drawing (MFA); new media (MFA); painting (MFA); photography (MFA); printmaking (MFA); sculpture (MFA). *Accreditation:* NASAD. *Faculty:* 18 full-time (9 women), 38 part-time/adjunct (19 women). *Students:* 3 full-time (2 women), 2 part-time (1 woman). Average age 34. 15 applicants, 27% accepted, 3 enrolled. In 2016, 6 master's awarded. *Degree requirements:* For master's, comprehensive experience, studio project or thesis. *Entrance requirements:* For master's, official transcripts; 3 letters of recommendation; letter of intent; resume; professional goals statement. Additional exam requirements/recommendations for international students: Required—TOEFL (minimum score 575 paper-based; 88 iBT), IELTS (minimum score 6.5), PTE (minimum score 59). Application fee: $75 ($80 for international students). Electronic applications accepted. *Expenses:* Tuition, state resident: full-time $10,628; part-time $443 per credit. Tuition, nonresident: full-time $29,306; part-time $1221 per credit. *Required fees:* $3096; $129 per credit. Tuition and fees vary according to program. *Financial support:* Career-related internships or fieldwork, Federal Work-Study, scholarships/grants, unspecified assistantships, and health care benefits (for full-time research or teaching assistantship recipients) available. Support available to part-time students. Financial award application deadline: 3/1; financial award applicants required to submit FAFSA. *Faculty research:* Digital arts, painting, photography, print-making, sculpture; combined art forms in in-disciplinary projects including installation, performance, publishing, time or writing-based; combined creative and critical approaches. *Unit head:* Lisa Kahn, Associate Dean, 703-993-4541, E-mail: lkahn2@gmu.edu. *Application contact:* Nikki Brugnoli-Whipkey, Graduate Studies Administrative Assistant, 703-993-5792, Fax: 703-993-8798, E-mail: rbrugnol@gmu.edu. Website: http://soa.gmu.edu

**The George Washington University,** Columbian College of Arts and Sciences, Corcoran School of the Arts and Design, Washington, DC 20007. Offers art and the book (MA); art education (MA, MAT); exhibition design (MA); interior design (MA); new media photojournalism (MA). *Accreditation:* NASAD. *Program availability:* Part-time. *Entrance requirements:* Additional exam requirements/recommendations for international students: Required—TOEFL (minimum score 95 iBT).

**The George Washington University,** Columbian College of Arts and Sciences, Department of Fine Arts and Art History, Washington, DC 20052. Offers art history (MA), including art history, museum training; ceramics (MFA); drawing/painting (MFA); interior design (MFA), including interior architecture and design; new media (MFA); photography (MFA); sculpture (MFA). *Accreditation:* CIDA. *Program availability:* Part-time, evening/weekend. *Faculty:* 16 full-time (10 women). *Students:* 75 full-time (56 women), 15 part-time (13 women); includes 20 minority (6 Black or African American, non-Hispanic/Latino; 7 Asian, non-Hispanic/Latino; 6 Hispanic/Latino; 1 Two or more races, non-Hispanic/Latino), 22 international. Average age 29. 103 applicants, 83% accepted, 35 enrolled. In 2016, 43 master's awarded. *Entrance requirements:* For master's, GRE General Test, bachelor's degree in field, minimum GPA of 3.0. Additional exam requirements/recommendations for international students: Required—TOEFL (minimum score 550 paper-based; 80 iBT). *Application deadline:* For fall admission, 3/1 priority date for domestic students, 1/15 priority date for international students; for spring admission, 10/1 priority date for domestic students, 9/1 priority date for international students. Applications are processed on a rolling basis. Application fee: $75. Electronic applications accepted. *Financial support:* In 2016–17, 12 students received support. Fellowships, teaching assistantships, career-related internships or fieldwork, Federal Work-Study, and tuition waivers available. Financial award application deadline: 1/15. *Unit head:* Phil Jacks, Chair, 202-994-6085, E-mail: pjacks@gwu.edu. *Application contact:* Information Contact, 202-994-6085, Fax: 202-994-8657, E-mail: art@gwu.edu. Website: http://art.columbian.gwu.edu/

**Georgia State University,** College of Arts and Sciences, Department of Communication, Atlanta, GA 30302-3083. Offers film, video, and digital imaging (MA), including critical studies, production, screenwriting; human communication and social influence (MA); mass communication (MA); media and society (PhD); moving image studies (PhD); public communication (PhD); rhetoric and politics (PhD). *Program availability:* Part-time. *Faculty:* 57 full-time (34 women). *Students:* 113 full-time (69 women), 56 part-time (33 women); includes 59 minority (37 Black or African American, non-Hispanic/Latino; 1 American Indian or Alaska Native, non-Hispanic/Latino; 2 Asian, non-Hispanic/Latino; 9 Hispanic/Latino; 10 Two or more races, non-Hispanic/Latino), 18 international. Average age 32. 134 applicants, 58% accepted, 47 enrolled. In 2016, 22 master's, 11 doctorates awarded. *Degree requirements:* For master's, variable foreign language requirement, thesis (for some programs); for doctorate, comprehensive exam, thesis/dissertation. *Entrance requirements:* For master's and doctorate, GRE. Additional exam requirements/recommendations for international students: Required—TOEFL (minimum score 550 paper-based; 80 iBT), IELTS (minimum score 6.5). *Application deadline:* For fall admission, 2/10 for domestic and international students; for spring admission, 10/15 for domestic and international students. Application fee: $50. Electronic applications accepted. *Expenses:* Tuition, state resident: full-time $6876; part-time $382 per credit hour. Tuition, nonresident: full-time $22,374; part-time $1243 per credit hour. *Required fees:* $2128; $1064 per term. Part-time tuition and fees vary according to course load and program. *Financial support:* In 2016–17, fellowships with tuition reimbursements (averaging $15,000 per year), teaching assistantships with tuition reimbursements (averaging $15,000 per year) were awarded; career-related internships or fieldwork and unspecified assistantships also available. Financial award applicants required to submit FAFSA. *Faculty research:* New media, mass media and journalism, rhetoric, film and media studies, film production. *Unit head:* Dr. Greg Lisby, Chair, 404-413-5639, Fax: 404-413-5634, E-mail: glisby@gsu.edu. Website: http://communication.gsu.edu

**Georgia State University,** College of Arts and Sciences, Ernest G. Welch School of Art and Design, Program in Studio Art, Atlanta, GA 30302-3083. Offers ceramics (MFA); drawing and painting (MFA); graphic design (MFA); interior design (MFA); photography (MFA); printmaking (MFA); sculpture (MFA); textiles (MFA). *Accreditation:* NASAD. *Degree requirements:* For master's, thesis. *Application deadline:* For fall admission, 1/6 for domestic and international students; for spring admission, 1/15 priority date for domestic and international students. Application fee: $50. Electronic applications accepted. *Expenses:* Tuition, state resident: full-time $6876; part-time $382 per credit hour. Tuition, nonresident: full-time $22,374; part-time $1243 per credit hour. *Required fees:* $2128; $1064 per term. Part-time tuition and fees vary according to course load and program. *Financial support:* In 2016–17, fellowships with full tuition reimbursements (averaging $11,000 per year), teaching assistantships with full tuition reimbursements (averaging $7,000 per year) were awarded; research assistantships, scholarships/grants, and unspecified assistantships also available. Financial award application deadline: 4/15; financial award applicants required to submit FAFSA. *Faculty research:*

Advertising and typography, new media, traditional media, three-dimensional art, architectural and environmental design. *Unit head:* Michael White, Director, Welch School of Art and Design, 404-413-5221, Fax: 404-413-5261, E-mail: mwhite@gsu.edu. *Application contact:* Hubert Stanley Anderson, Director of Graduate Studies, 404-413-5229, Fax: 404-413-5261, E-mail: artgrad@gsu.edu. Website: http://artdesign.gsu.edu/graduate/admissions/masters-of-fine-arts-in-studio/

**Governors State University,** College of Arts and Sciences, Program in Independent Film and Digital Imaging, University Park, IL 60484. Offers MFA. *Program availability:* Part-time. *Faculty:* 91 full-time (43 women), 125 part-time/adjunct (64 women). *Students:* 11 full-time (6 women), 10 part-time (6 women); includes 11 minority (9 Black or African American, non-Hispanic/Latino; 1 Hispanic/Latino; 1 Two or more races, non-Hispanic/Latino), 2 international. Average age 39. 10 applicants, 70% accepted, 4 enrolled. In 2016, 8 master's awarded. *Entrance requirements:* Additional exam requirements/recommendations for international students: Required—TOEFL (minimum score 550 paper-based; 80 iBT), IELTS. *Application deadline:* For fall admission, 4/1 for domestic students. Application fee: $50. Electronic applications accepted. *Expenses:* $307 per credit hour; $38 per term or $76 per credit hour fees. *Financial support:* Application deadline: 5/1; applicants required to submit FAFSA. *Unit head:* Lori Montalbano, Chair of Division of Communication, Visual and Performing Arts, 708-235-2802, E-mail: lmontalbano@govst.edu. *Application contact:* Yakeea Daniels, Assistant Vice President for Enrollment Services/Director of Admission, 708-534-4510, E-mail: ydaniels@govst.edu.

**Howard University,** Graduate School, Division of Fine Arts, Department of Art, Program in Fine Arts, Washington, DC 20059-0002. Offers 3D reality (sculpture and ceramics) (MFA); design (MFA); electronic studio (MFA); painting (MFA); photography (MFA). *Accreditation:* NASAD. *Degree requirements:* For master's, comprehensive exam, thesis, exhibit. *Entrance requirements:* For master's, minimum GPA of 3.0, portfolio.

**Illinois State University,** Graduate School, College of Fine Arts, School of Art, Normal, IL 61790-2200. Offers art history (MA, MS); ceramics (MFA, MS); drawing (MFA, MS); fibers (MFA, MS); glass (MFA, MS); graphic design (MFA, MS); metals (MFA, MS); painting (MFA, MS); photography (MFA, MS); printmaking (MFA, MS); sculpture (MFA, MS). *Accreditation:* NASAD (one or more programs are accredited). *Degree requirements:* For master's, thesis or alternative, internship. *Entrance requirements:* For master's, portfolio, sample of scholarly writing.

**Indiana State University,** College of Graduate and Professional Studies, College of Arts and Sciences, Department of Art and Design, Terre Haute, IN 47809. Offers ceramics (MA, MFA); drawing (MA, MFA); graphic design (MA, MFA); painting (MA, MFA); photography (MA, MFA); printmaking (MA, MFA); sculpture (MA, MFA). *Accreditation:* NASAD (one or more programs are accredited). *Program availability:* Part-time. *Degree requirements:* For master's, thesis or alternative, departmental qualifying exam. *Entrance requirements:* For master's, portfolio. Additional exam requirements/recommendations for international students: Required—TOEFL (minimum score 550 paper-based).

**Indiana University–Purdue University Indianapolis,** Herron School of Art and Design, Indianapolis, IN 46202. Offers art therapy (MA); visual art (MFA), including ceramics, furniture design, painting and drawing, photography and intermedia, printmaking, sculpture; visual communication design (MFA). *Faculty:* 26 full-time (13 women), 16 part-time/adjunct (11 women). *Students:* 56 full-time (40 women), 1 (woman) part-time; includes 8 minority (4 Black or African American, non-Hispanic/Latino; 2 Asian, non-Hispanic/Latino; 2 Hispanic/Latino), 7 international. Average age 31. 72 applicants, 53% accepted, 25 enrolled. In 2016, 22 master's awarded. *Degree requirements:* For master's, thesis. *Entrance requirements:* For master's, personal statement, resume, recommendations, portfolio, transcripts (18 credit hours of studio art and 12 credit hours of psychology, including 3 credit hours of developmental psychology and 3 credit hours of abnormal psychology for MA). Additional exam requirements/recommendations for international students: Recommended—TOEFL (minimum score 550 paper-based; 79 iBT), IELTS (minimum score 6.5). *Application deadline:* For fall admission, 1/15 for domestic and international students; for spring admission, 11/1 for domestic students, 10/15 for international students). Electronic applications accepted. *Expenses:* Contact institution. *Financial support:* In 2016–17, 55 students received support, including 36 fellowships (averaging $2,830 per year), 11 teaching assistantships (averaging $3,609 per year); research assistantships, Federal Work-Study, scholarships/grants, health care benefits, tuition waivers, and unspecified assistantships also available. Financial award application deadline: 2/1. *Faculty research:* Contemporary digital narratives for the homoerotic trope; sound articulated 3D print; neuroscience, art and related therapeutics; automotive and aeronautical design and fabrication; technological detritus. *Total annual research expenditures:* $22,990. *Unit head:* Prof. Valerie Eickmeier, Dean, 317-278-9470, Fax: 317-278-9471, E-mail: herron@iupui.edu. *Application contact:* Abbey Chambers, Herron Office of Admissions and Student Services, 317-378-9400, E-mail: herron4u@iupui.edu. Website: http://herron.iupui.edu/

**Inter American University of Puerto Rico, San Germán Campus,** Graduate Studies Center, Program in Fine Arts, San Germán, PR 00683-5008. Offers drawing (MFA); graphic design (MFA); painting (MFA); photography (MFA); printmaking (MFA); sculpture (MFA). *Program availability:* Part-time, evening/weekend. *Degree requirements:* For master's, comprehensive exam, thesis. *Entrance requirements:* For master's, GRE General Test or EXADEP, minimum GPA of 3.0.

**Ithaca College,** Roy H. Park School of Communications, Program in Image Text, Ithaca, NY 14850. Offers MFA. *Program availability:* Part-time-only. *Faculty:* 3 full-time (1 woman). *Students:* 8 part-time (3 women); includes 1 minority (Hispanic/Latino). Average age 28. 15 applicants, 87% accepted, 8 enrolled. *Degree requirements:* For master's, thesis optional. *Entrance requirements:* Additional exam requirements/recommendations for international students: Required—TOEFL (minimum score 550 paper-based; 80 iBT). *Application deadline:* For fall admission, 3/15 for domestic and international students; for spring admission, 12/1 for domestic and international students. Applications are processed on a rolling basis. Application fee: $40. Electronic applications accepted. *Expenses:* Contact institution. *Financial support:* In 2016–17, 7 students received support, including 7 fellowships (averaging $5,089 per year); career-related internships or fieldwork, Federal Work-Study, and scholarships/grants also available. Support available to part-time students. Financial award application deadline: 3/1; financial award applicants required to submit CSS PROFILE or FAFSA. *Unit head:* Nicholas Muellner, Co-Director, 607- 274-1984, E-mail: nmuellner@ithaca.edu. *Application contact:* Nicole Eversley Bradwell, Director, Office of Admission, 607-274-3124, Fax: 607-274-1263, E-mail: admission@ithaca.edu. Website: http://www.ithaca.edu/gradprograms/image-text

**James Madison University,** The Graduate School, College of Visual and Performing Arts, School of Art, Design and Art History, Harrisonburg, VA 22802. Offers art education (MA); studio art (MA, MFA), including ceramics (MFA), drawing/painting (MFA), intermedia (MFA), metal/jewelry (MFA), photography (MFA), sculpture (MFA). *Accreditation:* NASAD. *Program availability:* Part-time. *Faculty:* 25 full-time (15 women).

## Photography

*Students:* 10 full-time (6 women), 1 (woman) part-time, 1 international. Average age 30. 18 applicants, 39% accepted, 6 enrolled. In 2016, 6 master's awarded. Application fee: $55. Electronic applications accepted. *Financial support:* In 2016–17, 10 students received support, including 3 teaching assistantships with full tuition reimbursements available (averaging $9,284 per year); Federal Work-Study and 7 assistantships (averaging $7911) also available. Financial award application deadline: 3/1; financial award applicants required to submit FAFSA. *Unit head:* Dr. Kathy A. Schwartz, Director of School of Art, Design and Art History, 540-568-6216, E-mail: schwarka@jmu.edu. *Application contact:* Lynette D. Michael, Director of Graduate Student Admissions, 540-568-6131 Ext. 6395, Fax: 540-568-7860, E-mail: michaeld@jmu.edu. Website: http://www.jmu.edu/artandarthistory/

**Johnson State College,** Program in Studio Arts, Johnson, VT 05656. Offers ceramics (MFA); digital media (MFA); drawing (MFA); painting (MFA); photography (MFA); printmaking (MFA); sculpture (MFA). *Program availability:* Part-time, online learning. *Degree requirements:* For master's, thesis. *Entrance requirements:* For master's, portfolio. Additional exam requirements/recommendations for international students: Required—TOEFL. *Application deadline:* For fall admission, 3/1 for domestic students, 2/1 for international students. Applications are processed on a rolling basis. Electronic applications accepted. Application fee is waived when completed online. *Expenses:* Contact institution. *Financial support:* Teaching assistantships and unspecified assistantships available. Support available to part-time students. Financial award application deadline: 3/1; financial award applicants required to submit FAFSA. *Application contact:* Catherine H. Higley, Administrative Assistant, 800-635-2356 Ext. 1244, Fax: 802-635-1248, E-mail: catherine.higley@jsc.edu. Website: http://www.jsc.edu/academics/fine-arts-department/majors-and-minors/mfa-in-studio-arts/

**Lesley University,** College of Art and Design, Cambridge, MA 02138-2790. Offers photography (MFA); visual arts (MFA). *Program availability:* Part-time. *Degree requirements:* For master's, thesis, final exhibition of thesis work. *Entrance requirements:* For master's, portfolio, resume, personal statement. Additional exam requirements/recommendations for international students: Required—TOEFL (minimum score 550 paper-based; 80 iBT). Electronic applications accepted. *Faculty research:* Graphic design; Web and multimedia design; book, advertising and editorial illustration; animation; documentary photography; photojournalism; fine arts photography; fine arts; art education.

**Louisiana State University and Agricultural & Mechanical College,** Graduate School, College of Art and Design, School of Art, Program in Studio Art, Baton Rouge, LA 70803. Offers ceramics (MFA); graphic design (MFA); painting and drawing (MFA); photography (MFA); printmaking (MFA); sculpture (MFA). *Accreditation:* NASAD.

**Louisiana Tech University,** Graduate School, College of Liberal Arts, MFA Program, Ruston, LA 71272. Offers graphic design (MFA); photography (MFA); studio (MFA). *Accreditation:* NASAD. *Program availability:* Part-time. *Degree requirements:* For master's, exhibit. *Entrance requirements:* For master's, GRE General Test, portfolio. *Application deadline:* For fall admission, 5/12 for domestic students. Applications are processed on a rolling basis. Application fee: $40 ($50 for international students). Electronic applications accepted. *Financial support:* Fellowships, career-related internships or fieldwork, Federal Work-Study, institutionally sponsored loans, and unspecified assistantships available. Financial award application deadline: 2/15. *Unit head:* Frank Hamrick, Graduate Coordinator, 318-257-4154, Fax: 318-257-4890, E-mail: fhamrick@latech.edu. *Application contact:* Marilyn J. Robinson, Assistant to the Dean of the Graduate School, 318-257-2924, Fax: 318-257-4487. Website: http://design.latech.edu/master-of-fine-arts/

**Maryland Institute College of Art,** Graduate Studies, MFA Program in Photographic and Electronic Media, Baltimore, MD 21201. Offers MFA. *Accreditation:* NASAD. *Faculty:* 1 (woman) full-time, 5 part-time/adjunct (1 woman). *Students:* 28 full-time (18 women); includes 6 minority (1 Black or African American, non-Hispanic/Latino; 1 Asian, non-Hispanic/Latino; 1 Hispanic/Latino; 3 Two or more races, non-Hispanic/Latino), 5 international. Average age 27. 100 applicants, 30% accepted, 14 enrolled. In 2016, 14 master's awarded. *Degree requirements:* For master's, thesis, exhibit and thesis documentation. *Entrance requirements:* For master's, portfolio, bachelor's degree in any field. Additional exam requirements/recommendations for international students: Required—TOEFL (minimum score 550 paper-based; 80 iBT), IELTS (minimum score 6.5). *Application deadline:* For fall admission, 1/15 for domestic and international students. Application fee: $75. Electronic applications accepted. *Expenses:* Contact institution. *Financial support:* In 2016–17, 28 students received support, including 28 fellowships (averaging $13,000 per year), 28 teaching assistantships (averaging $3,200 per year); career-related internships or fieldwork and scholarships/grants also available. Financial award application deadline: 1/15. *Unit head:* Timothy Druckrey, Director, 410-225-5274, Fax: 410-225-5275, E-mail: graduate@mica.edu. *Application contact:* Chris D. Harring, Director, Graduate Admission, 410-225-2256, Fax: 410-225-5275, E-mail: graduate@mica.edu. Website: http://www.mica.edu/Programs_of_Study/Graduate_Programs/Photographic_and_Electronic_Media_(MFA).html

**Marywood University,** Academic Affairs, Insalaco College of Creative and Performing Arts, Art Department, Program in Studio Art, Scranton, PA 18509-1598. Offers clay (MA); painting (MA); photography (MA); printmaking (MA); sculpture (MA). *Accreditation:* NASAD. Electronic applications accepted. *Faculty research:* Texture and line in clay, cast bronze sculpture, color theories, book art and illustration, sculptural form.

**Marywood University,** Academic Affairs, Insalaco College of Creative and Performing Arts, Art Department, Program in Visual Arts, Scranton, PA 18509-1598. Offers clay (MFA); graphic design (MFA); illustration (MFA); painting (MFA); photography (MFA); printmaking (MFA); sculpture (MFA). *Accreditation:* NASAD. *Program availability:* Part-time. Electronic applications accepted. *Expenses:* Contact institution.

**Massachusetts College of Art and Design,** Graduate Programs, MFA Program, Boston, MA 02115-5882. Offers 2D fine arts (MFA), including painting, printmaking; 3D fine arts (MFA), including ceramics, fibers, glass, jewelry and metalsmithing, sculpture; design (MFA, Postbaccalaureate Certificate), including dynamic media; fine arts (MFA), including interdisciplinary; media arts (MFA, Postbaccalaureate Certificate), including film/video (MFA), photography. *Accreditation:* NASAD. *Faculty:* 40 full-time (19 women), 55 part-time/adjunct (23 women). *Students:* 58 full-time (39 women), 16 part-time (12 women); includes 10 minority (1 Black or African American, non-Hispanic/Latino; 4 Asian, non-Hispanic/Latino; 4 Hispanic/Latino; 1 Native Hawaiian or other Pacific Islander, non-Hispanic/Latino), 28 international. 247 applicants, 52% accepted, 47 enrolled. In 2016, 34 master's, 3 other advanced degrees awarded. *Degree requirements:* For master's, thesis, thesis exhibition (for fine arts programs); thesis project and document (for design/dynamic media program). *Entrance requirements:* For master's, portfolio, college transcripts, resume, statement of purpose, letters of reference, interview, 6 credits of art history taken prior to or during MFA program; for Postbaccalaureate Certificate, portfolio, college transcripts, resume, statement of purpose, letters of reference, interview. Additional exam requirements/

recommendations for international students: Required—TOEFL (minimum score 550 paper-based; 85 iBT); Recommended—IELTS (minimum score 6.5). *Application deadline:* For fall admission, 1/4 priority date for domestic and international students; for summer admission, 1/4 priority date for domestic and international students. Application fee: $90. Electronic applications accepted. *Expenses:* $780 per credit tuition. *Financial support:* In 2016–17, 57 students received support, including 33 teaching assistantships (averaging $2,160 per year); fellowships, research assistantships, career-related internships or fieldwork, scholarships/grants, tuition waivers (partial), unspecified assistantships, and 6-8 one-term adjunct co-teaching positions; 27 full-year general assistantships also available. Support available to part-time students. Financial award application deadline: 1/4; financial award applicants required to submit FAFSA. *Faculty research:* Painting and printmaking, sculpture, photography, film and video, dynamic media design. *Unit head:* Paul Paturzo, Dean of Graduate Studies, 617-879-7166, E-mail: pjpaturzo@massart.edu. *Application contact:* Lauren O'Neill, Assistant Director of Graduate Admissions, 617-879-7222, E-mail: gradadmissions@massart.edu. Website: http://www.massart.edu/Admissions/Graduate_Programs.html

**Memphis College of Art,** Graduate Programs, MFA Program, Memphis, TN 38104-2764. Offers illustration (MFA); metals (MFA); painting/drawing (MFA); photography (MFA); studio art (MFA). *Accreditation:* NASAD. *Program availability:* Part-time. *Faculty:* 27 full-time (16 women), 25 part-time/adjunct (13 women). *Students:* 17 full-time (13 women), 3 part-time (2 women); includes 4 minority (2 Black or African American, non-Hispanic/Latino; 2 Hispanic/Latino), 2 international. Average age 30. 24 applicants, 50% accepted, 4 enrolled. In 2016, 14 master's awarded. *Degree requirements:* For master's, thesis, thesis exhibit. *Entrance requirements:* For master's, portfolio, interview, resume, artist statement. Additional exam requirements/recommendations for international students: Required—TOEFL (minimum score 525 paper-based). *Application deadline:* For fall admission, 2/1 priority date for domestic and international students; for spring admission, 11/1 priority date for domestic and international students. Application fee: $50. Electronic applications accepted. *Expenses:* $33,100. *Financial support:* In 2016–17, 20 students received support, including 8 fellowships (averaging $4,000 per year), 5 teaching assistantships (averaging $3,000 per year); career-related internships or fieldwork, Federal Work-Study, scholarships/grants, and unspecified assistantships also available. Financial award application deadline: 8/1; financial award applicants required to submit FAFSA. *Unit head:* O. Gustavo Plascencia, Director, 901-272-5100, E-mail: ogplascencia@mca.edu. *Application contact:* Katey Henriksen, Director of Admissions, 901-272-5151, Fax: 901-272-5158, E-mail: khenriksen@mca.edu.

**Mills College,** Graduate Studies, Department of Art, Oakland, CA 94613-1000. Offers art (MFA); ceramics (MFA); intermedia (MFA); painting (MFA); photography (MFA); sculpture (MFA). *Faculty:* 3 full-time (2 women), 5 part-time/adjunct (2 women). *Students:* 20 full-time (11 women); includes 5 minority (1 Black or African American, non-Hispanic/Latino; 4 Hispanic/Latino). Average age 31. 31 applicants, 74% accepted, 9 enrolled. In 2016, 9 master's awarded. *Degree requirements:* For master's, thesis or alternative, exhibit. *Entrance requirements:* For master's, portfolio, artist statement. Additional exam requirements/recommendations for international students: Required—TOEFL (minimum score 550 paper-based; 80 iBT) or IELTS (minimum score 6). *Application deadline:* For fall admission, 2/1 for domestic students, 12/15 for international students. Application fee: $50. Electronic applications accepted. *Expenses:* Contact institution. *Financial support:* In 2016–17, 34 students received support, including 21 fellowships with partial tuition reimbursements available (averaging $11,360 per year), 13 teaching assistantships with partial tuition reimbursements available (averaging $12,200 per year); scholarships/grants and unspecified assistantships also available. Financial award application deadline: 2/1; financial award applicants required to submit FAFSA. *Faculty research:* Experimental film and video, public art projects, ecological design, contemporary art philosophy, sound installations. *Unit head:* Dr. Mary-Ann Milford, Professor of Art History, 510-430-2117. *Application contact:* Robynne Lofton, Director of Admissions, 510-430-3295, Fax: 510-430-2159, E-mail: grad-admission@mills.edu. Website: http://www.mills.edu/art

**Minneapolis College of Art and Design,** Program in Visual Studies, Minneapolis, MN 55404-4347. Offers animation (MFA); comic art (MFA); drawing (MFA); filmmaking (MFA); fine arts (MFA); furniture design (MFA); graphic design (MFA); illustration (MFA); interactive media (MFA); painting (MFA); photography (MFA); printmaking (MFA); sculpture (MFA). *Accreditation:* NASAD. *Program availability:* Part-time. *Degree requirements:* For master's, thesis, thesis exhibit. *Entrance requirements:* For master's, portfolio of visual artwork, resume, 3 letters of recommendation. Additional exam requirements/recommendations for international students: Required—TOEFL (minimum score 550 paper-based; 79 iBT). Electronic applications accepted. *Faculty research:* Visual arts: animation, comic art, drawing, filmmaking, furniture design, graphic design, illustration, interactive media, painting, photography, printmaking, sculpture.

**New Hampshire Institute of Art,** Graduate Studies, Manchester, NH 03104. Offers art education (MA); creative writing (MFA); photography (MFA); teaching visual arts (MAT); visual arts (MFA); writing for stage and screen (MFA). *Accreditation:* NASAD. *Faculty:* 31 part-time/adjunct (14 women). *Students:* 59 full-time (42 women), 6 part-time (3 women); includes 2 minority (1 Asian, non-Hispanic/Latino; 1 Hispanic/Latino). Average age 43. 36 applicants, 58% accepted, 12 enrolled. In 2016, 2 master's awarded. *Degree requirements:* For master's, thesis, corresponding exhibition and artist talk. *Entrance requirements:* For master's, writing sample or visual art portfolio; curriculum vitae; transcripts; letters of recommendation. Additional exam requirements/recommendations for international students: Required—TOEFL (minimum score 530 paper-based; 71 iBT). *Application deadline:* For fall admission, 5/1 priority date for domestic students; for spring admission, 11/1 priority date for domestic students. Applications are processed on a rolling basis. Application fee: $75. Electronic applications accepted. *Expenses:* $9,745 tuition per semester/residency plus $745 residency fee. *Financial support:* In 2016–17, 2 teaching assistantships (averaging $1,200 per year) were awarded; scholarships/grants and unspecified assistantships also available. Support available to part-time students. Financial award application deadline: 6/1; financial award applicants required to submit FAFSA. *Faculty research:* Fine arts - visual arts, photography, creative writing, writing for stage and screen; art education. *Unit head:* Lucinda Bliss, Dean of Graduate Studies, 603-836 2522, E-mail: lucindabliss@nhia.edu. *Application contact:* Moriah Billups, Graduate Admissions Coordinator, 603-836 2588, E-mail: gradadmissions@nhia.edu. Website: http://www.nhia.edu/graduate-studies

**The New School,** Parsons School of Design, Program in Photography, New York, NY 10011. Offers MFA. *Program availability:* Part-time. *Faculty:* 49 full-time (27 women), 5 part-time/adjunct (2 women). *Students:* 13 full-time (7 women), 18 part-time (14 women); includes 6 minority (4 Asian, non-Hispanic/Latino; 1 Hispanic/Latino; 1 Two or more races, non-Hispanic/Latino), 16 international. Average age 27. 84 applicants, 40% accepted, 18 enrolled. In 2016, 8 master's awarded. *Degree requirements:* For master's, thesis. *Entrance requirements:* For master's, transcripts, resume, statement of purpose, recommendation letters, portfolio, interview. Additional exam requirements/recommendations for international students: Required—TOEFL (minimum score 92 iBT), IELTS (minimum score 7), PTE (minimum score 63). *Application deadline:* For fall

admission, 1/1 priority date for domestic and international students. Applications are processed on a rolling basis. Application fee: $50. Electronic applications accepted. *Expenses:* Contact institution. *Financial support:* Research assistantships, teaching assistantships, career-related internships or fieldwork, scholarships/grants, unspecified assistantships, and travel funding; tuition waivers for students who are also New School employees available. Support available to part-time students. Financial award application deadline: 2/1; financial award applicants required to submit FAFSA. *Faculty research:* Photography and video; performance; visual culture studies; new imaging technologies. *Unit head:* Arthur Ou, Director, 212-229-8923 Ext. 2893, E-mail: oua@newschool.edu. *Application contact:* Courtney Malenius, Director of Graduate Admissions, 212-229-5150 Ext. 4011, E-mail: maleniuc@newschool.edu.
Website: http://www.newschool.edu/parsons

**New York Film Academy,** Program in Filmmaking–Los Angeles, Burbank, CA 91505. Offers acting for film (MFA); cinematography (MFA); documentary film (MFA); film and media production (MA); filmmaking (MFA); game design (MFA); photography (MFA); producing (MA, MFA); screenwriting (MA, MFA). *Accreditation:* NASAD.

**New York Film Academy,** Program in Filmmaking–South Beach, Florida, Miami Beach, FL 33139. Offers acting for film (MFA); cinematography (MFA); documentary film (MFA); film and media production (MA); filmmaking (MFA); game design (MFA); photography (MFA); producing (MA, MFA); screenwriting (MA, MFA).

**Ohio University,** Graduate College, College of Fine Arts, School of Art, Athens, OH 45701-2979. Offers art history (MA); ceramics (MFA); graphic design (MFA); painting (MFA); photography (MFA); printmaking (MFA); sculpture (MFA). *Program availability:* Part-time. *Degree requirements:* For master's, thesis. *Entrance requirements:* For master's, portfolio. Additional exam requirements/recommendations for international students: Required—TOEFL (minimum score 550 paper-based; 80 iBT) or IELTS (minimum score 6.5). *Application deadline:* For fall admission, 2/1 for domestic and international students. Application fee: $50 ($55 for international students). Electronic applications accepted. *Financial support:* Teaching assistantships with full and partial tuition reimbursements, career-related internships or fieldwork, Federal Work-Study, institutionally sponsored loans, scholarships/grants, tuition waivers (partial), and unspecified assistantships available. Financial award application deadline: 2/1. *Faculty research:* Vapor-fired ceramics, video installation, art theory, digital photography, mixed and interdisciplinary media work. *Unit head:* David LaPalombara, Director, 740-593-4290, Fax: 740-593-0457, E-mail: lapalomb@ohio.edu. *Application contact:* Alexandra Hibbitt, Chair, Graduate Programs, 740-593-4293, Fax: 740-593-0457, E-mail: hibbitt@ohio.edu.
Website: http://www.finearts.ohio.edu/art/

**Ohio University,** Graduate College, Scripps College of Communication, School of Visual Communication, Athens, OH 45701-2979. Offers MA. *Entrance requirements:* For master's, minimum GPA of 2.5, portfolio. Additional exam requirements/recommendations for international students: Required—TOEFL (minimum score 600 paper-based; 100 iBT) or IELTS (minimum score 7). *Application deadline:* For fall admission, 2/1 for domestic students, 12/14 for international students. Application fee: $50 ($55 for international students). Electronic applications accepted. *Financial support:* Federal Work-Study, institutionally sponsored loans, and tuition waivers (partial) available. Financial award applicants required to submit FAFSA. *Faculty research:* Photojournalism (including documentary photography), commercial photography (including illustrative photography), picture editing, informational graphics/publication design, interactive multimedia, visual media management. *Unit head:* Terry Eiler, Director, 740-595-4895, Fax: 740-593-0190, E-mail: eiler@ohio.edu. *Application contact:* Stan Alost, Assistant Director, 740-597-1756, Fax: 740-593-0190, E-mail: alost@ohio.edu.
Website: http://www.viscom.ohiou.edu/

**Oklahoma City University,** Petree College of Arts and Sciences, Oklahoma City, OK 73106-1402. Offers applied behavioral studies (M Ed); applied sociology: nonprofit leadership (MA); creative writing (MFA); criminology (MS); early childhood education (M Ed); elementary education (M Ed); general studies (MLA); leadership/management (MLA); moving image arts (MFA); professional counseling (M Ed); teaching (MA); teaching English to speakers of other languages (MA). *Program availability:* Part-time, evening/weekend. *Faculty:* 11 full-time (5 women), 15 part-time/adjunct (6 women). *Students:* 77 full-time (55 women), 46 part-time (30 women); includes 32 minority (13 Black or African American, non-Hispanic/Latino; 1 American Indian or Alaska Native, non-Hispanic/Latino; 2 Asian, non-Hispanic/Latino; 12 Hispanic/Latino; 4 Two or more races, non-Hispanic/Latino), 37 international. Average age 34. 92 applicants, 74% accepted, 46 enrolled. In 2016, 72 master's awarded. *Degree requirements:* For master's, capstone/practicum. *Entrance requirements:* For master's, bachelor's degree from accredited institution with minimum GPA of 3.0, essay, recommendation letters. Additional exam requirements/recommendations for international students: Required—TOEFL (minimum score 550 paper-based; 80 iBT). *Application deadline:* Applications are processed on a rolling basis. Application fee: $50. Electronic applications accepted. *Expenses:* Contact institution. *Financial support:* In 2016–17, 16 students received support. Federal Work-Study, institutionally sponsored loans, scholarships/grants, and tuition waivers (full and partial) available. Support available to part-time students. Financial award application deadline: 6/1; financial award applicants required to submit FAFSA. *Unit head:* Dr. Amy Cataldi, Dean, 405-208-5446, Fax: 405-208-5447, E-mail: acataldi@okcu.edu. *Application contact:* Michael Harrington, Director of Graduate Admissions, 800-633-7242, Fax: 405-208-5356, E-mail: gadmissions@okcu.edu.
Website: http://www.okcu.edu/petree/

**Otis College of Art and Design,** Program in Fine Arts, Los Angeles, CA 90045-9785. Offers new genres (MFA); painting (MFA); photography (MFA); sculpture (MFA). *Accreditation:* NASAD. *Degree requirements:* For master's, thesis. *Entrance requirements:* For master's, portfolio. Additional exam requirements/recommendations for international students: Required—TOEFL (minimum score 600 paper-based). Electronic applications accepted.

**Paris College of Art,** Graduate Programs, Paris, France. Offers accessories design (MA); fashion design: new materials and technologies (MA); fashion film and photography (MA); interior design (MA); transdisciplinary new media (MA, MFA). *Entrance requirements:* Additional exam requirements/recommendations for international students: Required—TOEFL or IELTS.

**Purdue University,** Graduate School, College of Liberal Arts, Department of Art and Design, West Lafayette, IN 47907. Offers art education (MA, PhD); industrial design (MFA); integrated studio arts (MFA); interior design (MFA); photography (MFA); visual communications design (MFA). *Accreditation:* NASAD; NAST. *Program availability:* Part-time. *Students:* 20 full-time (14 women), 1 part-time (0 women); includes 1 minority (Two or more races, non-Hispanic/Latino), 16 international. Average age 26. 97 applicants, 26% accepted, 10 enrolled. In 2016, 6 master's awarded. *Degree requirements:* For master's, terminal exhibit, project, or thesis. *Entrance requirements:* For master's, GRE General Test (for art education), minimum undergraduate GPA of 3.0 or equivalent; 9 undergraduate hours in an art or design history; BA in art (for MA in art education); for doctorate, GRE General Test (minimum scores 600 in verbal and 1000 total), master's degree in art education or art with teaching certification; 3 years of

teaching experience at the K-12 level. Additional exam requirements/recommendations for international students: Required—TOEFL (minimum score 550 paper-based; 77 iBT). *Application deadline:* For fall admission, 2/1 for domestic students, 2/1 priority date for international students. Applications are processed on a rolling basis. Application fee: $60 ($75 for international students). Electronic applications accepted. *Financial support:* Teaching assistantships with tuition reimbursements and career-related internships or fieldwork available. Support available to part-time students. Financial award applicants required to submit FAFSA. *Faculty research:* Design, fine arts, photography, acting, directing, theatre technology. *Unit head:* Harry T. Bulow, Head of the Graduate Program, 765-494-3056, E-mail: hbulow@purdue.edu. *Application contact:* Sara J. Unser, Graduate Contact, 765-494-8662, E-mail: sunser@purdue.edu.
Website: https://www.cla.purdue.edu/vpa/ad/

**Rhode Island School of Design,** Division of Fine Arts, Department of Photography, Providence, RI 02903-2784. Offers MFA. *Accreditation:* NASAD. *Faculty:* 7 full-time (5 women), 7 part-time/adjunct (2 women). *Students:* 14 full-time (5 women); includes 3 minority (2 Black or African American, non-Hispanic/Latino; 1 Hispanic/Latino), 4 international. Average age 26. 110 applicants, 15% accepted, 7 enrolled. In 2016, 7 master's awarded. *Degree requirements:* For master's, thesis, exhibition. *Entrance requirements:* For master's, portfolio, statement of purpose, 3 letters of recommendation. Additional exam requirements/recommendations for international students: Required—TOEFL (minimum score 580 paper-based; 93 iBT). *Application deadline:* For fall admission, 2/1 for domestic and international students. Application fee: $60. Electronic applications accepted. *Expenses: Tuition:* Full-time $46,800. *Required fees:* $310. *Financial support:* Fellowships, research assistantships, teaching assistantships, Federal Work-Study, scholarships/grants, and unspecified assistantships available. Financial award application deadline: 2/15; financial award applicants required to submit FAFSA. *Unit head:* Steve Smith, Department Head, 401-454-6122, Fax: 401-454-6385, E-mail: photo@risd.edu. *Application contact:* Molly Pettengil, Assistant Director for Graduate Recruitment, 401-454-6312, Fax: 401-454-6309, E-mail: mpetteng@risd.edu.
Website: http://www.risd.edu/academics/photography

**Rochester Institute of Technology,** Graduate Enrollment Services, College of Imaging Arts and Sciences, School of Photographic Arts and Sciences, MFA Program in Imaging Arts, Photography and Related Media, Rochester, NY 14623-5603. Offers MFA. *Accreditation:* NASAD. *Program availability:* Part-time. *Students:* 11 full-time (7 women), 3 part-time (2 women); includes 1 minority (Asian, non-Hispanic/Latino), 6 international. Average age 30. 65 applicants, 32% accepted, 6 enrolled. In 2016, 2 master's awarded. *Degree requirements:* For master's, thesis, exhibit. *Entrance requirements:* For master's, GRE, portfolio, minimum GPA of 3.0 (recommended). Additional exam requirements/recommendations for international students: Required—TOEFL (minimum score 550 paper-based; 90 iBT), IELTS (minimum score 6.5), PTE (minimum score 58). *Application deadline:* For fall admission, 2/15 priority date for domestic and international students. Applications are processed on a rolling basis. Application fee: $60. Electronic applications accepted. *Expenses:* $1,742 per credit hour. *Financial support:* In 2016–17, 11 students received support. Teaching assistantships with partial tuition reimbursements available, career-related internships or fieldwork, scholarships/grants, and unspecified assistantships available. Support available to part-time students. Financial award applicants required to submit FAFSA. *Faculty research:* Histories and theories of photography, contemporary art, American art and visual culture, and critical theory; photo books, visual narrative and expanded/experimental forms of documentary; contemporary fine art photography practice as personal document; public space, social practice, sensory observation, walking and mapping; relationship between the constructed image, photography as object, and fiction in contemporary practice. *Unit head:* Christine Shank, Graduate Program Director, 585-475-2616, Fax: 585-475-5804, E-mail: crspph@rit.edu. *Application contact:* Diane Ellison, Associate Vice President, Graduate Enrollment Services, 585-475-2229, Fax: 585-475-7164, E-mail: gradinfo@rit.edu.
Website: http://cias.rit.edu/schools/photographic-arts-sciences/graduate-imaging-arts

**San Jose State University,** Graduate Studies and Research, College of Humanities and the Arts, San Jose, CA 95192-0001. Offers art (MA, MFA), including art history and visual culture (MA), digital media art (MFA), photography (MFA), pictorial art (MFA), spatial art (MFA); computational linguistics (Certificate); English (MA, MFA), including creative writing (MFA); French (MA); humanities and arts (Certificate); linguistics (MA); music (MA); philosophy (MA); professional and technical communication (Certificate); Spanish (MA); teaching English to speakers of other languages (MA); TESOL (Certificate); theatre arts (MA). Electronic applications accepted.

**Savannah College of Art and Design,** Graduate School, Program in Photography, Savannah, GA 31402-3146. Offers MA, MFA. *Program availability:* Part-time, 100% online. *Faculty:* 19 full-time (8 women), 9 part-time/adjunct (2 women). *Students:* 64 full-time (29 women), 34 part-time (19 women); includes 18 minority (11 Black or African American, non-Hispanic/Latino; 1 American Indian or Alaska Native, non-Hispanic/Latino; 6 Hispanic/Latino), 32 international. Average age 32. 125 applicants, 32% accepted, 17 enrolled. In 2016, 26 master's awarded. *Degree requirements:* For master's, final portfolio (for MA); thesis (for MFA). *Entrance requirements:* For master's, GRE (recommended), portfolio (submitted in digital format), audition or writing submission, resume, statement of purpose, two letters of recommendation. Additional exam requirements/recommendations for international students: Required—TOEFL (minimum score 550 paper-based, 85 iBT), IELTS (minimum score 6.5), or ACTFL. *Application deadline:* For fall admission, 4/1 for domestic and international students. Applications are processed on a rolling basis. Application fee: $40. Electronic applications accepted. *Expenses: Tuition:* Full-time $36,045. Tuition and fees vary according to course load. *Financial support:* Career-related internships or fieldwork, Federal Work-Study, and scholarships/grants available. Financial award application deadline: 4/1; financial award applicants required to submit FAFSA. *Unit head:* Rick English, Chair, Photography. *Application contact:* Jenny Jaquillard, Executive Director of Admissions, Recruitment and Events, 912-525-5100, Fax: 912-525-5985, E-mail: admission@scad.edu.
Website: http://www.scad.edu/academics/photography

**School of the Art Institute of Chicago,** Graduate Division, Department of Photography, Chicago, IL 60603-3103. Offers MFA. *Accreditation:* NASAD. *Entrance requirements:* Additional exam requirements/recommendations for international students: Required—TOEFL.

**School of Visual Arts,** Graduate Programs, Digital Photography Department, New York, NY 10010-3994. Offers MPS. *Program availability:* Part-time, online learning. *Degree requirements:* For master's, thesis, 33 credits, including all required courses; minimum GPA of 3.0; thesis project culminating in online project, printed book and exhibition. *Entrance requirements:* For master's, image portfolio which represents 1-3 photographically cohesive bodies of work based on style, concept and execution. Additional exam requirements/recommendations for international students: Required—TOEFL (minimum score 550 paper-based; 79 iBT). Electronic applications accepted. *Faculty research:* Professional photography, digital-imaging technologies.

*Photography*

**School of Visual Arts,** Graduate Programs, Fashion Photography Department, New York, NY 10010-3994. Offers MPS. *Degree requirements:* For master's, 30 credits, including all required courses; minimum cumulative GPA of 3.0; original, challenging and provocative portfolio of images. *Entrance requirements:* For master's, portfolio, writing sample. Additional exam requirements/recommendations for international students: Required—TOEFL (minimum score 550 paper-based; 79 iBT). Electronic applications accepted. *Expenses:* Contact institution.

**School of Visual Arts,** Graduate Programs, Program in Photography, Video and Related Media, New York, NY 10010-3994. Offers MFA. *Accreditation:* NASAD. *Degree requirements:* For master's, 60 credits and all course requirements; minimum GPA of 3.3; thesis project. *Entrance requirements:* For master's, portfolio (still images and/or videos) through SlideRoom. Additional exam requirements/recommendations for international students: Required—TOEFL (minimum score 550 paper-based; 79 iBT). Electronic applications accepted. *Faculty research:* Contemporary and responsible creative initiatives, including experimental, narrative or documentary video, installation and conceptual art, tableau and real-world-witness photography.

**Southern Methodist University,** Meadows School of the Arts, Division of Art, Dallas, TX 75275. Offers studio art (MFA), including ceramics, drawing, painting, photography, printmaking, sculpture. *Accreditation:* NASAD. *Degree requirements:* For master's, thesis or alternative, exhibit. *Entrance requirements:* For master's, BFA or equivalent, letters of recommendation, portfolio. Additional exam requirements/recommendations for international students: Required—TOEFL (minimum score 550 paper-based; 80 iBT). *Faculty research:* American stoneware, Southwestern furniture traditions, photographic apparatus and techniques, American ceramists, architecture.

**Southwest University of Visual Arts,** MFA Programs, Tucson, AZ 85716-2505. Offers motion arts (MFA); painting and drawing (MFA); photography (MFA).

**Syracuse University,** College of Visual and Performing Arts, MFA Program in Art Photography, Syracuse, NY 13244. Offers MFA. *Accreditation:* NASAD. *Degree requirements:* For master's, thesis or alternative. *Entrance requirements:* For master's, personal statement, portfolio, three letters of recommendation, transcripts. Additional exam requirements/recommendations for international students: Required—TOEFL (minimum score 100 iBT). *Application deadline:* For fall admission, 2/1 priority date for domestic and international students. Application fee: $75. Electronic applications accepted. *Expenses: Tuition:* Full-time $25,974; part-time $1443 per credit hour. *Required fees:* $802; $50 per course. Tuition and fees vary according to course load and program. *Financial support:* Fellowships with full tuition reimbursements, teaching assistantships with tuition reimbursements, and tuition waivers available. Financial award application deadline: 1/1. *Faculty research:* Light work, art photography, art theory, art criticism. *Unit head:* Prof. Laura Heyman, Associate Professor/Program Coordinator, 315-443-1198, E-mail: lheyman@syr.edu. *Application contact:* Therese West, Administrative Assistant, 315-443-0137, E-mail: thwest@syr.edu. Website: http://vpa.syr.edu/academics/transmedia/graduate/art-photography/

**Syracuse University,** S. I. Newhouse School of Public Communications, MS in Photography Program, Syracuse, NY 13244. Offers MS. *Students:* Average age 29. *Degree requirements:* For master's, thesis optional, special project. *Entrance requirements:* For master's, portfolio, resume, official transcripts, personal statement, three letters of recommendation. Additional exam requirements/recommendations for international students: Required—TOEFL (minimum score 600 paper-based; 100 iBT). *Application deadline:* For summer admission, 1/15 priority date for domestic and international students. Application fee: $45. Electronic applications accepted. *Expenses: Tuition:* Full-time $25,974; part-time $1443 per credit hour. *Required fees:* $802; $50 per course. Tuition and fees vary according to course load and program. *Financial support:* Fellowships with full tuition reimbursements, research assistantships with partial tuition reimbursements, teaching assistantships with partial tuition reimbursements, and Federal Work-Study available. Financial award application deadline: 2/1. *Faculty research:* Visual communications theory and practice, advertising and illustration photography, picture and multimedia editing, media law. *Unit head:* Prof. Bruce Strong, Chair, Multimedia Photography and Design, 315-443-2304, Fax: 315-443-3946, E-mail: pcgrad@syr.edu. *Application contact:* Martha Coria, Graduate Records, 315-443-4039, Fax: 315-443-1834, E-mail: pcgrad@syr.edu. Website: http://newhouse.syr.edu/

**Temple University,** Tyler School of Art, Department of Graphic Arts and Design, Philadelphia, PA 19122-6096. Offers graphic and interactive design (MFA); photography (MFA); printmaking (MFA). *Degree requirements:* For master's, essay, exhibit. *Entrance requirements:* For master's, minimum GPA of 3.0, slide portfolio, 40 credits in studio art, 12 credits in art history, letters of recommendation, resume/curriculum vitae. Additional exam requirements/recommendations for international students: Required—TOEFL (minimum score 550 paper-based; 79 iBT), IELTS (minimum score 6.5). Electronic applications accepted. *Expenses:* Contact institution.

**The University of Alabama,** Graduate School, College of Arts and Sciences, Department of Art and Art History, Tuscaloosa, AL 35487. Offers art history (MA); studio art (MA, MFA), including ceramics, painting, photography, printmaking, sculpture. *Accreditation:* NASAD. *Program availability:* Part-time. *Faculty:* 19 full-time (12 women), 1 part-time/adjunct (0 women). *Students:* 18 full-time (13 women), 4 part-time (3 women); includes 3 minority (1 Black or African American, non-Hispanic/Latino; 1 Asian, non-Hispanic/Latino; 1 Hispanic/Latino), 1 international. Average age 30. 17 applicants, 41% accepted, 5 enrolled. In 2016, 7 master's awarded. *Degree requirements:* For master's, one foreign language, comprehensive exam (for some programs), oral exam, thesis statement, exhibit (studio art), thesis (art history). *Entrance requirements:* For master's, GRE General Test or MAT (art history), minimum GPA of 3.0, BFA or equivalent (studio art). Additional exam requirements/recommendations for international students: Required—TOEFL (minimum score 550 paper-based). *Application deadline:* For fall admission, 3/15 for domestic and international students; for spring admission, 10/15 for domestic and international students. Applications are processed on a rolling basis. Application fee: $50 ($60 for international students). Electronic applications accepted. *Expenses:* Tuition, state resident: full-time $10,470. Tuition, nonresident: full-time $26,950. *Financial support:* In 2016–17, 8 students received support, including 2 fellowships with full tuition reimbursements available, 14 teaching assistantships with tuition reimbursements available (averaging $15,427 per year); career-related internships or fieldwork, institutionally sponsored loans, scholarships/grants, and unspecified assistantships also available. Financial award application deadline: 7/14. *Faculty research:* Nineteenth-century American, Medieval Europe, Baroque, twentieth-century, and African American Art History. *Unit head:* Jason Guynes, Chair, 205-348-9944, Fax: 205-348-0287, E-mail: jguynes@ua.edu. *Application contact:* Sarah Marshall, Graduate Coordinator, 205-348-1890, Fax: 205-348-5967, E-mail: smarsh@ua.edu. Website: http://www.art.ua.edu/

**University of Alaska Fairbanks,** College of Liberal Arts, Department of Art, Fairbanks, AK 99775-5640. Offers art (MFA); ceramics (MFA); computer art (MFA); drawing (MFA); painting (MFA); photography (MFA); printmaking (MFA); sculpture (MFA). *Program availability:* Part-time. *Faculty:* 7 full-time (4 women). *Students:* 4 full-time (3 women), 1 (woman) part-time; includes 2 minority (1 Hispanic/Latino; 1 Native Hawaiian or other Pacific Islander, non-Hispanic/Latino). Average age 38. 4 applicants, 50% accepted, 1 enrolled. In 2016, 2 master's awarded. *Degree requirements:* For master's, comprehensive exam, oral defense of project or thesis. *Entrance requirements:* For master's, portfolio of work including about 20 slides or appropriate equivalent depending on field of study. Additional exam requirements/recommendations for international students: Required—TOEFL (minimum score 550 paper-based; 79 iBT), IELTS (minimum score 6.5). *Application deadline:* For fall admission, 6/1 for domestic students, 3/1 for international students; for spring admission, 10/15 for domestic students, 9/1 for international students. Applications are processed on a rolling basis. Application fee: $60. Electronic applications accepted. *Expenses:* Tuition, state resident: full-time $7992; part-time $444 per credit. Tuition, nonresident: full-time $16,326; part-time $907 per credit. *Required fees:* $39 per credit. $322 per semester. Tuition and fees vary according to course level, course load, campus/location, program and reciprocity agreements. *Financial support:* In 2016–17, 3 teaching assistantships with full tuition reimbursements (averaging $5,717 per year) were awarded; fellowships with full tuition reimbursements, research assistantships with full tuition reimbursements, Federal Work-Study, scholarships/grants, health care benefits, and unspecified assistantships also available. Support available to part-time students. Financial award application deadline: 7/1; financial award applicants required to submit FAFSA. *Faculty research:* Computer art, survey of arts in Alaska, found object art, visualization and animation, painting from the wilderness. *Unit head:* David Mollett, Chair, 907-474-7530, Fax: 907-474-5853, E-mail: uaf-art@alaska.edu. *Application contact:* Mary Kreta, Director of Admissions, 907-474-7500, Fax: 907-474-7097, E-mail: admissions@uaf.edu. Website: http://www.uaf.edu/art/

**University of Colorado Boulder,** Graduate School, College of Arts and Sciences, Department of Art and Art History, Boulder, CO 80309. Offers art history (MA), including contemporary art criticism, early twentieth-century art, nineteenth-century art, Russian and Soviet art; ceramics (MFA); photography and media arts (MFA); printmaking (MFA); sculpture (MFA). *Faculty:* 25 full-time (12 women). *Students:* 47 full-time (33 women); includes 8 minority (1 Black or African American, non-Hispanic/Latino; 6 Hispanic/Latino; 1 Two or more races, non-Hispanic/Latino), 1 international. Average age 29. 173 applicants, 8% accepted, 13 enrolled. In 2016, 20 master's awarded. Terminal master's awarded for partial completion of doctoral program. *Degree requirements:* For master's, variable foreign language requirement, comprehensive exam, thesis (for some programs). *Entrance requirements:* For master's, GRE General Test, minimum undergraduate GPA of 3.0, portfolio. *Application deadline:* For fall admission, 1/15 for domestic students, 12/1 for international students). Electronic applications accepted. Application fee is waived when completed online. *Financial support:* In 2016–17, 179 students received support, including 73 fellowships (averaging $1,882 per year), 42 teaching assistantships with full and partial tuition reimbursements available (averaging $30,614 per year); institutionally sponsored loans, scholarships/grants, health care benefits, and unspecified assistantships also available. Financial award application deadline: 1/15; financial award applicants required to submit FAFSA. *Faculty research:* Visual arts, fine arts, sculpture, installation art, inter-arts: interdisciplinary art forms. *Application contact:* E-mail: finearts@colorado.edu. Website: http://www.colorado.edu/arts

**University of Illinois at Urbana–Champaign,** Graduate College, College of Fine and Applied Arts, School of Art and Design, Program in Studio Arts, Champaign, IL 61820. Offers art and design (MFA); crafts (MFA); metals (MFA); painting (MFA); photography (MFA); sculpture (MFA). *Accreditation:* NASAD. *Entrance requirements:* For master's, minimum GPA of 3.0.

**University of Massachusetts Dartmouth,** Graduate School, College of Visual and Performing Arts, Department of Design, North Dartmouth, MA 02747-2300. Offers digital media (MFA); digital multi-media (MFA); graphic design (MFA); illustration (MFA); photography (MFA); typography (MFA). *Accreditation:* NASAD. *Program availability:* Part-time. *Faculty:* 16 full-time (7 women), 3 part-time/adjunct (1 woman). *Students:* 1 (woman) full-time, 10 part-time (7 women), 6 international. Average age 28. 30 applicants, 43% accepted, 4 enrolled. In 2016, 1 degree awarded. *Degree requirements:* For master's, visual thesis, written thesis. *Entrance requirements:* For master's, statement of purpose (minimum of 300 words), resume, 2 letters of recommendation, official transcripts, portfolio (20 images representing applicant's art work, process of thinking, implementation of concepts and studio production). Additional exam requirements/recommendations for international students: Required—TOEFL (minimum score 533 paper-based; 72 iBT). *Application deadline:* For fall admission, 1/11 priority date for domestic students, 12/9 priority date for international students; for spring admission, 10/15 priority date for domestic students, 9/15 priority date for international students. Applications are processed on a rolling basis. Application fee: $60. Electronic applications accepted. *Expenses:* Tuition, state resident: full-time $14,994; part-time $624.75 per credit. Tuition, nonresident: full-time $27,068; part-time $1127.83 per credit. *Required fees:* $405; $25.88 per credit. Tuition and fees vary according to course load and reciprocity agreements. *Financial support:* In 2016–17, 2 fellowships (averaging $2,600 per year) were awarded; teaching assistantships, scholarships/grants, unspecified assistantships, and studio assistantships also available. Support available to part-time students. Financial award application deadline: 3/1; financial award applicants required to submit FAFSA. *Faculty research:* Web design, multimedia design, broadcast design, product design, typography, illustration, photography and design for arts. *Total annual research expenditures:* $113,333. *Unit head:* Ziddi Msagni, Graduate Program Director, Visual Design, 508-999-9291, E-mail: zmsagni@umassd.edu. *Application contact:* Steven Briggs, Director of Marketing and Recruitment for Graduate Studies, 508-999-8604, Fax: 508-999-8183, E-mail: graduate@umassd.edu. Website: http://www.umassd.edu/cvpa/graduate/visualdesign/

**University of Memphis,** Graduate School, College of Communication and Fine Arts, Department of Art, Memphis, TN 38152. Offers art history (MA), including Egyptian art and archaeology, general art history; ceramics (MFA); graphic design (MFA); museum studies (Graduate Certificate); painting (MFA); printmaking/photography (MFA); sculpture (MFA). *Accreditation:* NASAD (one or more programs are accredited). *Program availability:* Part-time. *Faculty:* 20 full-time (7 women), 1 part-time/adjunct (0 women). *Students:* 22 full-time (16 women), 10 part-time (9 women); includes 9 minority (2 Black or African American, non-Hispanic/Latino; 1 Asian, non-Hispanic/Latino; 3 Hispanic/Latino; 3 Two or more races, non-Hispanic/Latino). Average age 29. 18 applicants, 78% accepted, 11 enrolled. In 2016, 17 master's, 16 other advanced degrees awarded. *Degree requirements:* For master's, 2 foreign languages, comprehensive exam, thesis, image identification exam, qualifying exam; for Graduate Certificate, internship. *Entrance requirements:* For master's, GRE General Test or MAT, portfolio (MFA), letter of intent, sample of undergraduate writing, two letters of recommendation; for Graduate Certificate, three letters of recommendation, letter of intent. *Application deadline:* For fall admission, 2/15 for domestic students; for spring admission, 11/1 for domestic students. Applications are processed on a rolling basis. Application fee: $35 ($60 for international students). *Expenses:* $5,231.50 per semester full-time in-state, $9,623.50 full-time out-of-state. *Financial support:* In 2016–17, 36 students received support, including 20 research assistantships with full tuition

reimbursements available (averaging $9,800 per year); teaching assistantships with full tuition reimbursements available, Federal Work-Study, scholarships/grants, and unspecified assistantships also available. Financial award application deadline: 2/1; financial award applicants required to submit FAFSA. *Faculty research:* Online collaborative learning, advanced art history studies, electronic publishing/design, studio arts, architectural studies. *Unit head:* Prof. Richard Lou, Chair, 901-678-2217, Fax: 901-678-2735, E-mail: ralou@memphis.edu. *Application contact:* Niles Wallice, Coordinator of Graduate Studies, 901-678-4899.
Website: http://memphis.edu/art/

**University of Miami,** Graduate School, College of Arts and Sciences, Department of Art and Art History, Coral Gables, FL 33124. Offers art history (MA); ceramics/glass (MFA); graphic design/multimedia (MFA); painting (MFA); photography/digital imaging (MFA); printmaking (MFA); sculpture (MFA). *Program availability:* Part-time. *Degree requirements:* For master's, variable foreign language requirement, thesis, exhibit (MFA), comprehensive exam (MFA). *Entrance requirements:* For master's, GRE General Test (MA), research paper (MA), slide portfolio (MFA). Additional exam requirements/recommendations for international students: Required—TOEFL. Electronic applications accepted. *Faculty research:* Installation art, public art.

**University of Montana,** Graduate School, College of Visual and Performing Arts, School of Art, Missoula, MT 59812-0002. Offers fine arts (MA), including art, art history; photography (MFA). *Accreditation:* NASAD (one or more programs are accredited). *Degree requirements:* For master's, thesis exhibit. *Entrance requirements:* For master's, GRE General Test, portfolio.

**University of New Mexico,** Graduate Studies, College of Fine Arts, Program in Art History, Albuquerque, NM 87131. Offers art history (MA); art of the Americas (MA); history of architecture (PhD); history of graphic arts (PhD); history of photography (PhD); modern Latin American art (PhD); Native American art (PhD); Pre-Columbian art and architecture (PhD); Spanish colonial art (PhD). *Program availability:* Part-time. *Faculty:* 4 full-time (2 women). *Students:* 8 full-time (all women), 22 part-time (19 women); includes 9 minority (3 American Indian or Alaska Native, non-Hispanic/Latino; 5 Hispanic/Latino; 1 Two or more races, non-Hispanic/Latino), 3 international. Average age 40. 19 applicants, 42% accepted, 4 enrolled. In 2016, 5 master's, 1 doctorate awarded. *Degree requirements:* For master's, one foreign language, comprehensive exam (for some programs), thesis, symposium; for doctorate, 2 foreign languages, comprehensive exam, thesis/dissertation, symposium. *Entrance requirements:* Additional exam requirements/recommendations for international students: Required—TOEFL (minimum score 550 paper-based), IELTS (minimum score 6). *Application deadline:* For fall admission, 1/15 for domestic students; for spring admission, 1/15 for domestic students. Application fee: $50. Electronic applications accepted. *Financial support:* Fellowships, research assistantships with tuition reimbursements, teaching assistantships with partial tuition reimbursements, Federal Work-Study, institutionally sponsored loans, scholarships/grants, health care benefits, and unspecified assistantships available. Support available to part-time students. Financial award application deadline: 3/1; financial award applicants required to submit FAFSA. *Faculty research:* Native American, modern Latin American, pre-Columbian, architectural, American, medieval, Spanish Colonial, and Latin American art; history of photography. *Unit head:* Prof. Mary Tsiongas, Chair, 505-277-5861, Fax: 505-277-5955, E-mail: tsiongas@unm.edu. *Application contact:* Kat Heatherington, Graduate Advisor, 505-277-6672, Fax: 505-277-5955, E-mail: art255@unm.edu.
Website: http://art.unm.edu/

**University of Notre Dame,** Graduate School, College of Arts and Letters, Division of Humanities, Department of Art, Art History, and Design, Notre Dame, IN 46556. Offers art history (MA); design (MFA), including graphic design, industrial design; studio art (MFA), including ceramics, painting, photography, printmaking, sculpture. *Accreditation:* NASAD. *Degree requirements:* For master's, comprehensive exam (for some programs), thesis. *Entrance requirements:* For master's, GRE General Test, minimum GPA of 3.0. Additional exam requirements/recommendations for international students: Required—TOEFL (minimum score 600 paper-based; 80 iBT). Electronic applications accepted. *Faculty research:* Studio art practice in ceramics, printing, photography, printmaking and sculpture, graphic design and industrial design, digital imaging in design and photography, Renaissance and American art history, contemporary art theory and criticism.

**University of Rochester,** School of Arts and Sciences, Program in Photographic Preservation and Collections Management, Rochester, NY 14627. Offers MA. Program offered jointly with George Eastman House. *Program availability:* Part-time. *Students:* 15 full-time (10 women). Average age 29. 18 applicants, 78% accepted, 5 enrolled. In 2016, 2 master's awarded. *Degree requirements:* For master's, thesis (for some programs). *Entrance requirements:* Additional exam requirements/recommendations for international students: Required—TOEFL (minimum score 600 paper-based; 100 iBT). *Application deadline:* For fall admission, 3/3 for domestic students. Application fee: $60. Electronic applications accepted. *Expenses:* $1,583 per credit. *Faculty research:* Photographic preservation, collections management, photography. *Unit head:* Joan Saab, Co-Director, 585-275-4287, E-mail: joan.saab@rochester.edu. *Application contact:* Lorna Maier, Administrative Assistant, 585-275-9249, E-mail: lmaier@ur.rochester.edu.
Website: http://www.rochester.edu/college/ppcm

**The University of South Dakota,** Graduate School, College of Fine Arts, Department of Art, Vermillion, SD 57069. Offers art education (MFA); ceramics (MFA); graphic design (MFA); painting (MFA); photography (MFA); printmaking (MFA); sculpture (MFA). *Accreditation:* NASAD. *Degree requirements:* For master's, thesis or alternative. *Entrance requirements:* For master's, portfolio, minimum GPA of 2.7. Additional exam requirements/recommendations for international students: Required—TOEFL (minimum score 550 paper-based; 79 iBT). Electronic applications accepted.

**University of Southern California,** Graduate School, Roski School of Fine Arts, Graduate Programs in Fine Arts, Los Angeles, CA 90089. Offers new genres (MFA); painting/drawing (MFA); photography (MFA); sculpture (MFA). *Degree requirements:* For master's, thesis. *Entrance requirements:* For master's, portfolio, artist statement, 3 letters of recommendation. Additional exam requirements/recommendations for international students: Required—TOEFL (minimum score 600 paper-based; 100 iBT). Electronic applications accepted. *Faculty research:* Fine art production in the areas of photography, video, sculpture, drawing, and performance.

**The University of Tennessee,** Graduate School, College of Arts and Sciences, School of Art, Knoxville, TN 37996. Offers ceramics (MFA); drawing (MFA); graphic design (MFA); inter-area studies (MFA); media arts (MFA); painting (MFA); printmaking (MFA); sculpture (MFA); watercolor (MFA). *Accreditation:* NASAD. *Degree requirements:* For master's, thesis or alternative, exhibit. *Entrance requirements:* For master's, portfolio, minimum GPA of 2.7. Additional exam requirements/recommendations for international students: Required—TOEFL. Electronic applications accepted.

**University of Utah,** Graduate School, College of Fine Arts, Department of Art and Art History, Salt Lake City, UT 84112-0380. Offers art history (MA); ceramics (MFA); community-based art education (MFA); drawing (MFA); graphic design (MFA); painting

(MFA); photography/digital imaging (MFA); printmaking (MFA); sculpture/intermedia (MFA). *Faculty:* 18 full-time (10 women), 22 part-time/adjunct (11 women). *Students:* 6 full-time (2 women); includes 2 minority (both Hispanic/Latino). 48 applicants, 31% accepted, 10 enrolled. In 2016, 7 master's awarded. *Degree requirements:* For master's, variable foreign language requirement, comprehensive exam (for some programs), thesis or alternative, exhibit and final project paper (for MFA). *Entrance requirements:* For master's, CD portfolio (MFA), writing sample (MA), curriculum vitae, letters of recommendation, letter of intent. Additional exam requirements/recommendations for international students: Required—TOEFL (minimum score 575 paper-based; 75 iBT). *Application deadline:* For fall admission, 1/15 priority date for domestic and international students. Application fee: $55 ($65 for international students). Electronic applications accepted. *Expenses:* Contact institution. *Financial support:* In 2016–17, 6 students received support, including 2 fellowships, 6 research assistantships with partial tuition reimbursements available, 34 teaching assistantships with partial tuition reimbursements available; Federal Work-Study, institutionally sponsored loans, scholarships/grants, tuition waivers (partial), unspecified assistantships, and stipends also available. Financial award application deadline: 1/15; financial award applicants required to submit FAFSA. *Faculty research:* Studio art, European art history, Asian art history, Latin American art history, twentieth-century/contemporary art history. *Total annual research expenditures:* $54,906. *Unit head:* Prof. Brian Snapp, Chair, 801-581-8677, Fax: 801-585-6171, E-mail: b.snapp@utah.edu. *Application contact:* Prof. Kim Martinez, Director of Graduate Studies, 801-581-8677, Fax: 801-585-6171, E-mail: kim.martinez@art.utah.edu.
Website: http://www.art.utah.edu/

**University of Victoria,** Faculty of Graduate Studies, Faculty of Fine Arts, Department of Visual Arts, Victoria, BC V8W 2Y2, Canada. Offers digital multimedia (MFA); drawing (MFA); painting (MFA); photography (MFA); sculpture (MFA); video (MFA). *Degree requirements:* For master's, exhibit, oral exam. *Entrance requirements:* For master's, portfolio, BFA. Additional exam requirements/recommendations for international students: Required—TOEFL (minimum score 575 paper-based), IELTS (minimum score 7). Electronic applications accepted.

**University of Washington,** Graduate School, College of Arts and Sciences, School of Art, Division of Art, Seattle, WA 98195. Offers painting and drawing (MFA); photography (MFA). *Degree requirements:* For master's, thesis, exhibit. *Entrance requirements:* For master's, BFA or equivalent academic work in art, 20 slide portfolio. Additional exam requirements/recommendations for international students: Required—TOEFL. Electronic applications accepted.

**Virginia Commonwealth University,** Graduate School, School of the Arts, Richmond, VA 23284-9005. Offers art education (MAE, PhD); art history (MA, PhD), including curatorial (PhD), historical studies, museum studies (MA); ceramics (MFA); design (MFA), including interior environments, visual communications; fibers (MFA); furniture design (MFA); glassworking (MFA); jewelry/metalworking (MFA); kinetic imaging (MFA); music (MM), including music education; painting (MFA); photography and film (MFA); printmaking (MFA); sculpture (MFA); theatre (MFA), including costume design, pedagogy/literature, pedagogy/performance, scene design/technical theatre. *Program availability:* Part-time. *Entrance requirements:* For doctorate, GRE General Test, writing sample. Additional exam requirements/recommendations for international students: Required—TOEFL (minimum score 600 paper-based; 100 iBT). *Application deadline:* For fall admission, 1/15 priority date for domestic students. Application fee: $50. Electronic applications accepted. *Financial support:* Fellowships, teaching assistantships, career-related internships or fieldwork, Federal Work-Study, institutionally sponsored loans, and tuition waivers (full and partial) available. Support available to part-time students. Financial award applicants required to submit FAFSA. *Unit head:* Joseph H. Seipel, Dean, 804-828-2787, Fax: 804-828-6469, E-mail: arts@vcu.edu. *Application contact:* Jack H. Risley, Associate Dean for Academic Affairs, 804-828-2787, Fax: 804-828-6469, E-mail: jhrisley@vcu.edu.
Website: http://www.vcu.edu/arts/

**Wayne State University,** College of Fine, Performing and Communication Arts, James Pearson Duffy Department of Art and Art History, Detroit, MI 48202. Offers art (MA, MFA), including ceramics, drawing, fibers, graphic design, industrial design (MA), interior design (MA), metalsmithing, painting, photography, printmaking, sculpture; art history (MA). *Students:* 15 full-time (10 women), 9 part-time (7 women); includes 6 minority (2 Black or African American, non-Hispanic/Latino; 1 Asian, non-Hispanic/Latino; 1 Hispanic/Latino; 2 Two or more races, non-Hispanic/Latino), 2 international. Average age 34. 49 applicants, 12% accepted, 3 enrolled. In 2016, 7 master's awarded. *Degree requirements:* For master's, thesis (for some programs), essay or thesis. *Entrance requirements:* For master's, BFA or another degree and equivalent course work, portfolio, personal interview, reference letters, statement of intent (except for art history program). Additional exam requirements/recommendations for international students: Required—TOEFL (minimum score 550 paper-based; 79 iBT), TWE (minimum score 5.5), Michigan English Language Assessment Battery (minimum score 85); Recommended—IELTS (minimum score 6.5). *Application deadline:* For fall admission, 2/1 for domestic and international students; for winter admission, 10/1 for domestic and international students. Application fee: $50. Electronic applications accepted. *Expenses:* $17,240 per year resident tuition and fees, $34,434 per year non-resident tuition and fees. *Financial support:* In 2016–17, 21 students received support, including 1 fellowship with tuition reimbursement available (averaging $16,000 per year), 6 teaching assistantships with tuition reimbursements available (averaging $17,994 per year); research assistantships, scholarships/grants, and unspecified assistantships also available. Support available to part-time students. Financial award applicants required to submit FAFSA. *Faculty research:* Integration of the human figure into urban and rural landscape in painting; performance art utilizing digital media and video; exploration of race, gender, and culture through creative practice (including art, design, and art history); ongoing investigation and elaboration of visual art traditions in diverse media; continued scholarship in the history of art. *Unit head:* Dr. John Richardson, Chair, 313-577-2980, Fax: 313-577-3491, E-mail: af5343@wayne.edu. *Application contact:* 313-577-2980, Fax: 313-577-2980, E-mail: art@wayne.edu.
Website: http://art.wayne.edu/

**Wichita State University,** Graduate School, College of Fine Arts, School of Art, Design and Creative Industries, Wichita, KS 67260. Offers studio arts (MFA), including ceramics, painting, photo media, printmaking, sculpture. *Accreditation:* NASAD. *Unit head:* Prof. Jeff Pulaski, Director, 316-978-3555, Fax: 316-978-5418, E-mail: jeff.pulaski1@wichita.edu. *Application contact:* Jordan Oleson, Admissions Coordinator, 316-978-3095, Fax: 316-978-3253, E-mail: jordan.oleson@wichita.edu.
Website: http://www.wichita.edu/artdesign

**Yale University,** School of Art, New Haven, CT 06520-8339. Offers graphic design (MFA); painting/printmaking (MFA); photography (MFA); sculpture (MFA). *Faculty:* 10 full-time (5 women), 35 part-time/adjunct (12 women). *Students:* 127 full-time (65 women); includes 17 minority (8 Black or African American, non-Hispanic/Latino; 5 Asian, non-Hispanic/Latino; 4 Hispanic/Latino), 35 international. Average age 28. 1,003 applicants, 6% accepted, 61 enrolled. In 2016, 61 master's awarded. *Degree requirements:* For master's, thesis (for some programs). *Entrance requirements:* Additional exam requirements/recommendations for international students: Required—

TOEFL (minimum score 550 paper-based; 100 iBT). *Application deadline:* For fall admission, 1/4 for domestic and international students. Application fee: $100. Electronic applications accepted. *Expenses:* Contact institution. *Financial support:* In 2016–17, 110 students received support, including 61 teaching assistantships (averaging $2,000 per year); Federal Work-Study, scholarships/grants, and unspecified assistantships also available. Financial award application deadline: 3/1; financial award applicants required to submit FAFSA. *Unit head:* Marta Kuzma, Dean, 203-432-2606. *Application contact:* Patricia Ann DeChiara, Director of Academic Affairs, 203-432-2600, E-mail: artschool.info@yale.edu.
Website: http://www.yale.edu/art/

# Textile Design

**Academy of Art University,** Graduate Programs, Program in Costume Design, San Francisco, CA 94105-3410. Offers MFA. *Program availability:* Part-time, evening/weekend, 100% online. *Faculty:* 23 full-time (14 women), 70 part-time/adjunct (54 women). *Students:* 3 full-time (2 women); includes 1 minority (Asian, non-Hispanic/Latino), 1 international. Average age 34. 4 applicants, 100% accepted, 3 enrolled. *Degree requirements:* For master's, final review. *Entrance requirements:* For master's, statement of intent; resume; portfolio/reel; official college transcripts. *Application deadline:* Applications are processed on a rolling basis. Application fee: $100. Electronic applications accepted. *Expenses: Tuition:* Part-time $982 per unit. *Financial support:* Career-related internships or fieldwork, Federal Work-Study, and scholarships/grants available. Financial award application deadline: 8/10; financial award applicants required to submit FAFSA. *Application contact:* 800-544-ARTS, E-mail: info@academyart.edu.
Website: http://www.academyart.edu/academics/fashion/graduate-degrees

**Academy of Art University,** Graduate Programs, School of Fashion, San Francisco, CA 94105-3410. Offers costume design (MA, MFA); fashion (MA, MFA); fashion journalism (MA); fashion marketing and brand management (MFA); fashion merchandising (MA); fashion merchandising and management (MFA); fashion product development (MFA); textile design (MFA). *Program availability:* Part-time, 100% online. *Faculty:* 27 full-time (17 women), 62 part-time/adjunct (47 women). *Students:* 376 full-time (335 women), 196 part-time (184 women); includes 154 minority (81 Black or African American, non-Hispanic/Latino; 2 American Indian or Alaska Native, non-Hispanic/Latino; 36 Asian, non-Hispanic/Latino; 25 Hispanic/Latino; 1 Native Hawaiian or other Pacific Islander, non-Hispanic/Latino; 9 Two or more races, non-Hispanic/Latino), 306 international. Average age 29. 190 applicants, 100% accepted, 114 enrolled. In 2016, 137 master's awarded. *Degree requirements:* For master's, final review. *Entrance requirements:* For master's, statement of intent; resume; portfolio/reel; official college transcripts. *Application deadline:* Applications are processed on a rolling basis. Application fee: $50. Electronic applications accepted. *Expenses: Tuition:* Part-time $982 per unit. *Financial support:* Career-related internships or fieldwork, Federal Work-Study, and scholarships/grants available. Financial award application deadline: 8/10; financial award applicants required to submit FAFSA. *Unit head:* 800-544-ARTS, E-mail: info@academyart.edu. *Application contact:* 800-544-ARTS, E-mail: info@academyart.edu.
Website: http://www.academyart.edu/fashion-school/index.html

**Arizona State University at the Tempe campus,** Herberger Institute for Design and the Arts, School of Art, Tempe, AZ 85287-1505. Offers art education (MA); art history (MA); ceramics (MFA); design, environment and the arts (PhD), including history, theory and criticism; drawing (MFA); fibers (MFA); intermedia (MFA); metals (MFA); museum studies (MFA); painting (MFA); printmaking (MFA); sculpture (MFA); wood (MFA); MFA/MA. Terminal master's awarded for partial completion of doctoral program. *Degree requirements:* For master's, thesis/exhibition (MFA, MA in art education); interactive Program of Study (iPOS) submitted before completing 50 percent of required credit hours; for doctorate, comprehensive exam, thesis/dissertation, interactive Program of Study (iPOS) submitted before completing 50 percent of required credit hours. *Entrance requirements:* For master's, GRE or MAT, minimum GPA of 3.0 or equivalent in last 2 years of work leading to bachelor's degree; for doctorate, GRE, master's degree in architecture, graphic design, industrial design, interior design, landscape architecture, or art history or equivalent standing; statement of purpose; 3 letters of recommendation; indication of potential faculty mentor; sample of written work. Additional exam requirements/recommendations for international students: Required—TOEFL, IELTS, or PTE. Electronic applications accepted.

**California College of the Arts,** Graduate Programs, Fine Arts Programs, San Francisco, CA 94107. Offers ceramics (MFA); film/video/performance (MFA); glass (MFA); interdisciplinary studies (MFA); jewelry/metal arts (MFA); media studies (MFA); painting/drawing (MFA); photography (MFA); printmaking (MFA); sculpture (MFA); textiles (MFA); wood/furniture (MFA). *Accreditation:* NASAD. *Faculty:* 23 full-time (14 women), 17 part-time/adjunct (12 women). *Students:* 75 full-time (55 women); includes 20 minority (7 Black or African American, non-Hispanic/Latino; 2 American Indian or Alaska Native, non-Hispanic/Latino; 6 Asian, non-Hispanic/Latino; 5 Hispanic/Latino), 15 international. Average age 29. 224 applicants, 54% accepted, 43 enrolled. In 2016, 27 master's awarded. *Degree requirements:* For master's, thesis, exhibit. *Entrance requirements:* For master's, appropriate bachelor's degree, portfolio, resume, 2 letters of recommendation, transcript. Additional exam requirements/recommendations for international students: Required—TOEFL, IELTS, or PTE. *Application deadline:* For fall admission, 1/10 for domestic and international students. Applications are processed on a rolling basis. Application fee: $70. Electronic applications accepted. *Expenses:* $1,641 per unit, $49,230 per year tuition; $490 fees. *Financial support:* In 2016–17, fellowships (averaging $42,000 per year), teaching assistantships (averaging $2,000 per year) were awarded; career-related internships or fieldwork, Federal Work-Study, scholarships/grants, health care benefits, and unspecified assistantships also available. Financial award application deadline: 7/31; financial award applicants required to submit FAFSA. *Unit head:* James Gobel, Chair, 415-551-9214, Fax: 415-703-9539, E-mail: jgobel@cca.edu. *Application contact:* Wes Fanelli, Assistant Director of Graduate Admissions, 415-703-9533, Fax: 415-703-9539, E-mail: wfanelli@cca.edu.

**California State University, Los Angeles,** Graduate Studies, College of Arts and Letters, Department of Art, Los Angeles, CA 90032-8530. Offers art (MA), including art education, art history, art therapy, ceramics, metals, and textiles, design (MA, MFA), painting, sculpture, and graphic arts, photography; fine arts (MFA), including crafts, design (MA, MFA), studio arts. *Accreditation:* NASAD (one or more programs are accredited). *Program availability:* Part-time, evening/weekend. *Degree requirements:* For master's, comprehensive exam, project or thesis. *Entrance requirements:* For master's, portfolio. Additional exam requirements/recommendations for international students: Required—TOEFL (minimum score 500 paper-based). Electronic applications accepted. *Faculty research:* The artist and the book, conceptual art, ceramic processes, computer graphics, architectural graphics.

**Concordia University,** School of Graduate Studies, Faculty of Fine Arts, Department of Studio Arts, Montréal, QC H3G 1M8, Canada. Offers studio arts (MFA), including fibers and material practices, film production, intermedia, painting and drawing,

photography, print media, sculpture. *Degree requirements:* For master's, thesis or alternative. *Entrance requirements:* For master's, portfolio.

**Cornell University,** Graduate School, Graduate Fields of Human Ecology, Field of Fiber Science and Apparel Design, Ithaca, NY 14853. Offers apparel design (MA, MPS); fiber science (MS, PhD); polymer science (MS, PhD); textile science (MS, PhD). *Degree requirements:* For master's, thesis (MA, MS), project paper (MPS); for doctorate, comprehensive exam, thesis/dissertation. *Entrance requirements:* For master's, GRE General Test, 2 letters of recommendation, portfolio (for functional apparel design); for doctorate, GRE General Test, 2 letters of recommendation. Additional exam requirements/recommendations for international students: Required—TOEFL (minimum score 600 paper-based; 77 iBT). Electronic applications accepted. *Faculty research:* Apparel design, consumption, mass customization, 3-D body scanning.

**Cranbrook Academy of Art,** Graduate School, Program in Fine Arts, Bloomfield Hills, MI 48303-0801. Offers 2d design (MFA); 3d design (MFA); ceramics (MFA); fiber (MFA); metalsmithing (MFA); painting (MFA); photography (MFA); print media (MFA); sculpture (MFA). *Accreditation:* NASAD. *Degree requirements:* For master's, thesis, exhibit. *Entrance requirements:* Additional exam requirements/recommendations for international students: Required—TOEFL (minimum score 85 iBT). *Application deadline:* For fall admission, 2/1 priority date for domestic and international students. Application fee: $85. Electronic applications accepted. *Expenses: Tuition, area resident:* Full-time $37,375. *Required fees:* $1460. *Financial support:* Federal Work-Study and scholarships/grants available. Financial award application deadline: 2/15; financial award applicants required to submit FAFSA. *Unit head:* Christopher Scoates, Director, 248-645-3301, Fax: 248-645-3591. *Application contact:* Leslie Tobakos, Registrar/Financial Aid and Admissions Manager, 248-645-3360, Fax: 248-645-3591, E-mail: ltobakos@cranbrook.edu.

★ **Drexel University,** Westphal College of Media Arts and Design, Program in Fashion Design, Philadelphia, PA 19104-2875. Offers MS. *Accreditation:* NASAD. *Faculty:* 1 (woman) full-time. *Students:* 21 full-time (all women), 5 part-time (all women); includes 9 minority (6 Black or African American, non-Hispanic/Latino; 1 Asian, non-Hispanic/Latino; 1 Hispanic/Latino; 1 Two or more races, non-Hispanic/Latino), 11 international. Average age 28. In 2016, 4 master's awarded. *Degree requirements:* For master's, thesis, portfolio review. *Entrance requirements:* For master's, interview. Additional exam requirements/recommendations for international students: Required—TOEFL. *Application deadline:* For fall admission, 8/21 for domestic students; for spring admission, 3/5 for domestic students. Applications are processed on a rolling basis. Application fee: $50. Electronic applications accepted. *Expenses: Tuition:* Full-time $32,184; part-time $1192 per credit hour. *Required fees:* $280. Tuition and fees vary according to campus/location and program. *Financial support:* Research assistantships, teaching assistantships, career-related internships or fieldwork, and unspecified assistantships available. Financial award application deadline: 2/1. *Unit head:* Renee Weiss Chase, Director, 215-895-2412. *Application contact:* Director of Graduate Admissions, 215-895-6700, Fax: 215-895-5939, E-mail: enroll@drexel.edu.
**See Display on page 63 and Close-Up on page 99.**

**East Carolina University,** Graduate School, College of Fine Arts and Communication, School of Art and Design, Greenville, NC 27858-4353. Offers art education (MA Ed); ceramics (MFA); graphic design (MFA); illustration (MFA); metal design (MFA); painting and drawing (MFA); photography (MFA); printmaking (MFA); sculpture (MFA); textile design (MFA); wood design (MFA). *Accreditation:* NASAD (one or more programs are accredited). *Program availability:* Part-time, evening/weekend. *Students:* 25 full-time (15 women), 17 part-time (12 women); includes 5 minority (2 Asian, non-Hispanic/Latino; 2 Hispanic/Latino; 1 Two or more races, non-Hispanic/Latino). Average age 33. 37 applicants, 62% accepted, 16 enrolled. In 2016, 17 master's awarded. *Degree requirements:* For master's, comprehensive exam, thesis (for some programs). *Entrance requirements:* For master's, GRE General Test or MAT, portfolio. Additional exam requirements/recommendations for international students: Required—TOEFL. *Application deadline:* For fall admission, 2/1 for domestic students; for spring admission, 10/1 for domestic students. Applications are processed on a rolling basis. Application fee: $50. *Financial support:* Research assistantships with partial tuition reimbursements, teaching assistantships with partial tuition reimbursements, and Federal Work-Study available. Support available to part-time students. Financial award application deadline: 6/1. *Unit head:* Michael H. Drought, Director, 252-328-6665, E-mail: droughtm@ecu.edu. *Application contact:* Dr. Linda H. Nelson, Information Contact, 252-328-1286, E-mail: nelsonlh@ecu.edu.
Website: http://www.ecu.edu/cs-cfac/soad/gradschool.cfm

**Illinois State University,** Graduate School, College of Fine Arts, School of Art, Normal, IL 61790-2200. Offers art history (MA, MS); ceramics (MFA, MS); drawing (MFA, MS); fibers (MFA, MS); glass (MFA, MS); graphic design (MFA, MS); metals (MFA, MS); painting (MFA, MS); photography (MFA, MS); printmaking (MFA, MS); sculpture (MFA, MS). *Accreditation:* NASAD (one or more programs are accredited). *Degree requirements:* For master's, thesis or alternative, internship. *Entrance requirements:* For master's, portfolio, sample of scholarly writing.

**LIM College,** MBA Program, New York, NY 10022-5268. Offers entrepreneurship (MBA); fashion management (MBA). *Accreditation:* ACBSP. *Entrance requirements:* For master's, interview. Additional exam requirements/recommendations for international students: Required—TOEFL (minimum score 550 paper-based; 80 iBT), IELTS (minimum score 6.5).

**Massachusetts College of Art and Design,** Graduate Programs, MFA Program, Boston, MA 02115-5882. Offers 2D fine arts (MFA), including painting, printmaking; 3D fine arts (MFA), including ceramics, fibers, glass, jewelry and metalsmithing, sculpture; design (MFA, Postbaccalaureate Certificate), including dynamic media; fine arts (MFA), including interdisciplinary; media arts (MFA, Postbaccalaureate Certificate), including film/video (MFA), photography. *Accreditation:* NASAD. *Faculty:* 40 full-time (19 women), 55 part-time/adjunct (23 women). *Students:* 58 full-time (39 women), 16 part-time (12 women); includes 10 minority (1 Black or African American, non-Hispanic/Latino; 4 Asian, non-Hispanic/Latino; 4 Hispanic/Latino; 1 Native Hawaiian or other Pacific Islander, non-Hispanic/Latino), 28 international. 247

applicants, 52% accepted, 47 enrolled. In 2016, 34 master's, 3 other advanced degrees awarded. *Degree requirements:* For master's, thesis, thesis exhibition (for fine arts programs); thesis project and document (for design/dynamic media program). *Entrance requirements:* For master's, portfolio, college transcripts, resume, statement of purpose, letters of reference, interview, 6 credits of art history taken prior to or during MFA program; for Postbaccalaureate Certificate, portfolio, college transcripts, resume, statement of purpose, letters of reference, interview. Additional exam requirements/recommendations for international students: Required—TOEFL (minimum score 550 paper-based; 85 iBT); Recommended—IELTS (minimum score 6.5). *Application deadline:* For fall admission, 1/4 priority date for domestic and international students; for summer admission, 1/4 priority date for domestic and international students. Application fee: $90. Electronic applications accepted. *Expenses:* $780 per credit tuition. *Financial support:* In 2016–17, 57 students received support, including 33 teaching assistantships (averaging $2,160 per year); fellowships, research assistantships, career-related internships or fieldwork, scholarships/grants, tuition waivers (partial), unspecified assistantships, and 6-8 one-term adjunct co-teaching positions; 27 full-year general assistantships also available. Support available to part-time students. Financial award application deadline: 1/4; financial award applicants required to submit FAFSA. *Faculty research:* Painting and printmaking, sculpture, photography, film and video, dynamic media design. *Unit head:* Paul Paturzo, Dean of Graduate Studies, 617-879-7166, E-mail: pjpaturzo@massart.edu. *Application contact:* Lauren O'Neill, Assistant Director of Graduate Admissions, 617-879-7222, E-mail: gradadmissions@massart.edu.
Website: http://www.massart.edu/Admissions/Graduate_Programs.html

**The New School,** Parsons School of Design, Program in Fashion Design and Society, New York, NY 10011. Offers MFA. *Program availability:* Part-time. *Faculty:* 22 full-time (15 women), 4 part-time/adjunct (2 women). *Students:* 30 full-time (25 women); includes 2 minority (1 Black or African American, non-Hispanic/Latino; 1 Asian, non-Hispanic/Latino), 26 international. Average age 25. 180 applicants, 14% accepted, 17 enrolled. In 2016, 13 master's awarded. *Degree requirements:* For master's, thesis. *Entrance requirements:* For master's, transcripts, resume, statement of purpose, recommendation letters, portfolio. Additional exam requirements/recommendations for international students: Required—TOEFL (minimum score 92 iBT), IELTS (minimum score 7), PTE (minimum score 63). *Application deadline:* For fall admission, 1/1 priority date for domestic and international students. Applications are processed on a rolling basis. Application fee: $50. Electronic applications accepted. *Expenses:* Contact institution. *Financial support:* Research assistantships, teaching assistantships, career-related internships or fieldwork, scholarships/grants, and unspecified assistantships available. Support available to part-time students. Financial award application deadline: 2/1; financial award applicants required to submit FAFSA. *Faculty research:* Fashion systems, textiles materials and fabrication, physical computing/wearable technology; sustainable design. *Unit head:* Shelley Fox, Director, 212-229-8966 Ext. 2746, E-mail: foxs@newschool.edu. *Application contact:* Courtney Malenius, Director of Graduate Admissions, 212-229-5150 Ext. 4011, E-mail: maleniuc@newschool.edu.
Website: http://www.newschool.edu/parsons

**The New School,** Parsons School of Design, Program in Fashion Studies, New York, NY 10011. Offers MA. Program also offered at Paris, France campus. *Program availability:* Part-time. *Faculty:* 23 full-time (16 women), 1 (woman) part-time/adjunct. *Students:* 53 full-time (46 women), 6 part-time (all women); includes 16 minority (5 Black or African American, non-Hispanic/Latino; 4 Asian, non-Hispanic/Latino; 6 Hispanic/Latino; 1 Two or more races, non-Hispanic/Latino), 30 international. Average age 25. 87 applicants, 59% accepted, 29 enrolled. In 2016, 30 master's awarded. *Degree requirements:* For master's, thesis. *Entrance requirements:* For master's, transcripts, resume, statement of purpose, recommendation letters, interview. Additional exam requirements/recommendations for international students: Required—TOEFL (minimum score 92 iBT), IELTS (minimum score 7), PTE (minimum score 63). *Application deadline:* For fall admission, 1/1 priority date for domestic and international students. Applications are processed on a rolling basis. Application fee: $50. Electronic applications accepted. *Expenses:* Contact institution. *Financial support:* Research assistantships, teaching assistantships, career-related internships or fieldwork, scholarships/grants, unspecified assistantships, and travel funding; tuition waivers for students who are also New School employees available. Support available to part-time students. Financial award application deadline: 2/1; financial award applicants required to submit FAFSA. *Faculty research:* Branding, cultural studies, fashion history, theory and criticism, materials and fabrication, visual culture studies. *Unit head:* Francesca Granata, Director, 212-229-8916 Ext. 3876, E-mail: granataf@newschool.edu. *Application contact:* Courtney Malenius, Director of Graduate Admissions, 212-229-5150 Ext. 4011, E-mail: maleniuc@newschool.edu.
Website: http://www.newschool.edu/parsons

**Paris College of Art,** Graduate Programs, Paris, France. Offers accessories design (MA); fashion design: new materials and technologies (MA); fashion film and photography (MA); interior design (MA); transdisciplinary new media (MA, MFA). *Entrance requirements:* Additional exam requirements/recommendations for international students: Required—TOEFL or IELTS.

**Philadelphia University,** School of Design and Engineering, Program in Textile Design, Philadelphia, PA 19144. Offers MS. *Program availability:* Part-time. *Entrance requirements:* For master's, GRE or MAT, minimum GPA of 2.8. Additional exam requirements/recommendations for international students: Required—TOEFL (minimum score 550 paper-based; 79 iBT). Electronic applications accepted.

**Rhode Island School of Design,** Division of Fine Arts, Department of Textiles, Providence, RI 02903-2784. Offers MFA. *Accreditation:* NASAD. *Faculty:* 9 full-time (4 women), 10 part-time/adjunct (6 women). *Students:* 11 full-time (10 women); includes 2 minority (1 Asian, non-Hispanic/Latino; 1 Hispanic/Latino), 4 international. Average age 28. 55 applicants, 16% accepted, 6 enrolled. In 2016, 5 master's awarded. *Degree requirements:* For master's, thesis, exhibition. *Entrance requirements:* For master's, portfolio, statement of purpose, 3 letters of recommendation. Additional exam requirements/recommendations for international students: Required—TOEFL (minimum score 580 paper-based; 93 iBT). *Application deadline:* For fall admission, 2/1 for domestic and international students. Application fee: $60. Electronic applications accepted. *Expenses:* Tuition: Full-time $46,800. *Required fees:* $310. *Financial support:* Fellowships, research assistantships, teaching assistantships, Federal Work-Study, scholarships/grants, and unspecified assistantships available. Financial award application deadline: 2/15; financial award applicants required to submit FAFSA. *Unit head:* Anais Missakian, Department Head, 401-427-6967, Fax: 401-277-4883, E-mail: amissaki@risd.edu. *Application contact:* Molly Pettengil, Assistant Director for Graduate Recruitment, 401-454-6312, Fax: 401-454-6309, E-mail: mpetteng@risd.edu.
Website: http://www.risd.edu/academics/textiles

**Savannah College of Art and Design,** Graduate School, Program in Fashion, Savannah, GA 31402-3146. Offers MA, MFA. *Program availability:* Part-time, 100% online. *Faculty:* 23 full-time (15 women), 6 part-time/adjunct (all women). *Students:* 55 full-time (46 women), 19 part-time (16 women); includes 17 minority (12 Black or African American, non-Hispanic/Latino; 2 Asian, non-Hispanic/Latino; 3 Hispanic/Latino), 49 international. Average age 27. 125 applicants, 40% accepted, 27 enrolled. In 2016, 16 master's awarded. *Degree requirements:* For master's, final project (for MA); thesis (for

MFA). *Entrance requirements:* For master's, GRE (recommended), portfolio (submitted in digital format), audition or writing submission, resume, statement of purpose, two letters of recommendation. Additional exam requirements/recommendations for international students: Required—TOEFL (minimum score 550 paper-based, 85 iBT), IELTS (minimum score 6.5), or ACTFL. *Application deadline:* For fall admission, 4/1 for domestic and international students. Applications are processed on a rolling basis. Application fee: $40. Electronic applications accepted. *Expenses:* Tuition: Full-time $36,045. Tuition and fees vary according to course load. *Financial support:* Career-related internships or fieldwork, Federal Work-Study, and scholarships/grants available. Financial award application deadline: 4/1; financial award applicants required to submit FAFSA. *Application contact:* Jenny Jaquillard, Executive Director of Admissions, Recruitment and Events, 912-525-5100, Fax: 912-525-5985, E-mail: admission@scad.edu.
Website: http://www.scad.edu/academics/programs/fashion

**Savannah College of Art and Design,** Graduate School, Program in Fibers, Savannah, GA 31402-3146. Offers MA, MFA. *Program availability:* Part-time. *Faculty:* 8 full-time (7 women), 3 part-time/adjunct (all women). *Students:* 19 full-time (17 women), 4 part-time (all women); includes 2 minority (1 Black or African American, non-Hispanic/Latino; 1 Asian, non-Hispanic/Latino), 12 international. Average age 26. 28 applicants, 39% accepted, 8 enrolled. In 2016, 10 master's awarded. *Degree requirements:* For master's, final project (for MA); thesis (for MFA). *Entrance requirements:* For master's, GRE (recommended), portfolio (submitted in digital format), audition or writing submission, resume, statement of purpose, two letters of recommendation. Additional exam requirements/recommendations for international students: Required—TOEFL (minimum score 550 paper-based, 85 iBT), IELTS (minimum score 6.5), or ACTFL. *Application deadline:* For fall admission, 4/1 for domestic and international students. Applications are processed on a rolling basis. Application fee: $40. Electronic applications accepted. *Expenses:* Tuition: Full-time $36,045. Tuition and fees vary according to course load. *Financial support:* Career-related internships or fieldwork, Federal Work-Study, and scholarships/grants available. Financial award application deadline: 4/1; financial award applicants required to submit FAFSA. *Unit head:* Cayewah Easley, Chair, Fibers. *Application contact:* Jenny Jaquillard, Executive Director of Admissions, Recruitment and Events, 912-525-5100, Fax: 912-525-5985, E-mail: admission@scad.edu.
Website: http://www.scad.edu/academics/programs/fibers

**Savannah College of Art and Design,** Graduate School, Program in Luxury and Fashion Management, Savannah, GA 31402-3146. Offers MA, MFA. *Program availability:* Part-time, 100% online. *Faculty:* 12 full-time (4 women), 1 (woman) part-time/adjunct. *Students:* 99 full-time (89 women), 49 part-time (40 women); includes 44 minority (35 Black or African American, non-Hispanic/Latino; 6 Asian, non-Hispanic/Latino; 3 Hispanic/Latino), 66 international. Average age 27. 200 applicants, 39% accepted, 45 enrolled. In 2016, 54 master's awarded. *Degree requirements:* For master's, final project (for MA); thesis (for MFA). *Entrance requirements:* For master's, GRE (recommended), portfolio (submitted in digital format), audition or writing submission, resume, statement of purpose, two letters of recommendation. Additional exam requirements/recommendations for international students: Required—TOEFL (minimum score 550 paper-based, 85 iBT), IELTS (minimum score 6.5), or ACTFL. *Application deadline:* For fall admission, 4/1 for domestic and international students. Applications are processed on a rolling basis. Application fee: $40. Electronic applications accepted. *Expenses:* Tuition: Full-time $36,045. Tuition and fees vary according to course load. *Financial support:* Career-related internships or fieldwork, Federal Work-Study, and scholarships/grants available. Financial award application deadline: 4/1; financial award applicants required to submit FAFSA. *Unit head:* Alessandro Cannata, Academic Program Coordinator. *Application contact:* Jenny Jaquillard, Executive Director of Admissions, Recruitment and Events, 912-525-5100, Fax: 912-525-5985, E-mail: admission@scad.edu.
Website: http://www.scad.edu/academics/programs/luxury-and-fashion-management

**School of the Art Institute of Chicago,** Graduate Division, Program in Fashion, Body, and Garment, Chicago, IL 60603-3103. Offers M Des, Certificate.

**Temple University,** Tyler School of Art, Department of Crafts, Philadelphia, PA 19122-6096. Offers ceramics/glass (MFA); fibers and material studies (MFA); metals/jewelry/CAD-CAM (MFA). *Degree requirements:* For master's, essay, exhibit. *Entrance requirements:* For master's, minimum GPA of 3.0, slide portfolio, 40 credits in studio art, 12 credits in art history, letters of recommendation, resume/curriculum vitae. Additional exam requirements/recommendations for international students: Required—TOEFL (minimum score 550 paper-based; 79 iBT), IELTS (minimum score 6.5). Electronic applications accepted. *Expenses:* Contact institution.

**University of California, Davis,** Graduate Studies, Program in Textile Arts and Costume Design, Davis, CA 95616. Offers MFA. *Degree requirements:* For master's, presentation of an individual project/body of work. *Entrance requirements:* For master's, minimum GPA of 3.0, portfolio. Additional exam requirements/recommendations for international students: Required—TOEFL (minimum score 550 paper-based). Electronic applications accepted. *Faculty research:* Historic ethnographic and contemporary costume and textile design, computer-aided design.

**University of Cincinnati,** Graduate School, College of Design, Architecture, Art, and Planning, School of Design, Cincinnati, OH 45221. Offers fashion design (M Des); graphic design (M Des); industrial design (M Des); interaction design (M Des); product development (M Des). *Accreditation:* NASAD. *Degree requirements:* For master's, thesis. *Entrance requirements:* For master's, undergraduate degree in design or related field, 2 years of work experience in design or related field. Additional exam requirements/recommendations for international students: Required—TOEFL. Electronic applications accepted. *Expenses: Tuition, area resident:* Full-time $12,790; part-time $389 per credit hour. Tuition, state resident: full-time $13,290; part-time $419 per credit hour. Tuition, nonresident: full-time $24,532; part-time $976 per credit hour. *International tuition:* $24,832 full-time. *Required fees:* $3958; $140 per credit hour. Tuition and fees vary according to course load, degree level, program and reciprocity agreements. *Faculty research:* Design theory, interdisciplinary design topics.

**The University of Kansas,** Graduate Studies, College of Liberal Arts and Sciences, Department of Visual Art, Lawrence, KS 66045. Offers ceramics (MFA); drawing and painting (MFA); expanded media (MFA); metalsmithing/jewelry (MFA); printmaking (MFA); sculpture (MFA); textiles/fibers (MFA); visual art education (MA). *Accreditation:* NASAD. *Program availability:* Part-time. *Students:* 27 full-time (13 women), 3 part-time (all women); includes 3 minority (1 American Indian or Alaska Native, non-Hispanic/Latino; 2 Two or more races, non-Hispanic/Latino), 6 international. Average age 31. 40 applicants, 28% accepted, 10 enrolled. In 2016, 12 master's awarded. *Entrance requirements:* For master's, portfolio, official transcript, minimum GPA of 3.0, 3 letters of recommendation. Additional exam requirements/recommendations for international students: Required—TOEFL. *Application deadline:* For fall admission, 5/1 for domestic and international students; for spring admission, 12/1 for domestic and international students. Application fee: $65 ($85 for international students). Electronic applications accepted. *Financial support:* Fellowships, teaching assistantships, Federal Work-Study, scholarships/grants, and unspecified assistantships available. Financial award application deadline: 1/15; financial award

## Textile Design

applicants required to submit FAFSA. *Faculty research:* Metal and glass casting; mapping, indigenous lands and history; wood fire kilns; Japanese block printing techniques. *Unit head:* Mary Anne Jordan, Chair, 785-864-2952, E-mail: majordan@ku.edu. *Application contact:* Lauren Chaney, Graduate Admissions Contact, 785-864-2306, E-mail: lkchaney@ku.edu.
Website: http://art.ku.edu/

**The University of Manchester,** School of Materials, Manchester, United Kingdom. Offers advanced aerospace materials engineering (M Sc); advanced metallic systems (PhD); biomedical materials (M Phil, M Sc, PhD); ceramics and glass (M Phil, M Sc, PhD); composite materials (M Sc, PhD); corrosion and protection (M Phil, M Sc, PhD); materials (M Phil, PhD); metallic materials (M Phil, M Sc, PhD); nanostructural materials (M Phil, M Sc, PhD); paper science (M Phil, M Sc, PhD); polymer science and engineering (M Phil, M Sc, PhD); technical textiles (M Sc); textile design, fashion and management (M Phil, M Sc, PhD); textile science and technology (M Phil, M Sc, PhD); textiles (M Phil, PhD); textiles and fashion (M Ent).

**University of Minnesota, Twin Cities Campus,** Graduate School, College of Design, Department of Design, Housing, and Apparel, Minneapolis, MN 55455-0213. Offers apparel (MA, MS, PhD); design communication (MA, MS, PhD); housing studies (MA, MS, PhD, Postbaccalaureate Certificate); interactive design (MFA); interior design (MA, MS, PhD). *Program availability:* Part-time. *Degree requirements:* For master's and Postbaccalaureate Certificate, comprehensive exam, thesis (for some programs); for doctorate, comprehensive exam, thesis/dissertation. *Entrance requirements:* For master's, GRE General Test, minimum GPA of 3.0 (preferred), portfolio, 3 letters of recommendation; for doctorate, GRE General Test, minimum GPA of 3.0 (preferred), portfolio, 3 letters of recommendation, writing sample; for Postbaccalaureate Certificate, GRE General Test, minimum GPA of 3.0 (preferred). Additional exam requirements/recommendations for international students: Required—TOEFL (minimum score 550 paper-based; 79 iBT). Electronic applications accepted. *Faculty research:* Housing policy and community development; consumer behavior; interactive design; design history; social, cultural, and behavioral issues related to designed environments.

**The University of North Carolina at Greensboro,** Graduate School, Bryan School of Business and Economics, Department of Consumer, Apparel, and Retail Studies, Greensboro, NC 27412-5001. Offers MS, PhD. *Degree requirements:* For master's, one foreign language; for doctorate, one foreign language, thesis/dissertation. *Entrance requirements:* For master's and doctorate, GRE General Test. Additional exam requirements/recommendations for international students: Required—TOEFL. Electronic applications accepted. *Faculty research:* Impact of phosphate removal, protective clothing for pesticide workers, fabric hand: subjective and objective measurements.

**University of North Texas,** Robert B. Toulouse School of Graduate Studies, Denton, TX 76203-5459. Offers accounting (MS); applied anthropology (MA, MS); applied behavior analysis (Certificate); applied geography (MA); applied technology and performance improvement (M Ed, MS); art education (MA); art history (MA); art museum education (Certificate); arts leadership (Certificate); audiology (Au D); behavior analysis (MS); behavioral science (PhD); biochemistry and molecular biology (MS); biology (MA, MS); biomedical engineering (MS); business analysis (MS); chemistry (MS); clinical health psychology (PhD); communication studies (MA, MS); computer engineering (MS); computer science (MS); counseling (M Ed, MS), including clinical mental health counseling (MS), college and university counseling, elementary school counseling, secondary school counseling; creative writing (MA); criminal justice (MS); curriculum and instruction (M Ed); decision sciences (MBA); design (MA, MFA), including fashion design (MFA), innovation studies, interior design (MFA); early childhood studies (MS); economics (MS); educational leadership (M Ed, Ed D); educational psychology (MS, PhD), including family studies (MS), gifted and talented (MS), human development (MS), learning and cognition (MS), research, measurement and evaluation (MS); electrical engineering (MS); emergency management (MPA); engineering technology (MS); English (MA); English as a second language (MA); environmental science (MS); finance (MBA, MS); financial management (MPA); French (MA); health services management

(MBA); higher education (M Ed, Ed D); history (MA, MS); hospitality management (MS); human resources management (MPA); information science (MS); information systems (PhD); information technologies (MBA); interdisciplinary studies (MA, MS); international studies (MA); international sustainable tourism (MS); jazz studies (MM); journalism (MA, MJ, Graduate Certificate), including interactive and virtual digital communication (Graduate Certificate), narrative journalism (Graduate Certificate), public relations (Graduate Certificate); kinesiology (MS); linguistics (MA); local government management (MPA); logistics (PhD); logistics and supply chain management (MBA); long-term care, senior housing, and aging services (MA); management (PhD); marketing (MBA); mathematics (MA, MS); mechanical and energy engineering (MS, PhD); music (MA), including ethnomusicology, music theory, musicology, performance; music composition (PhD); music education (MM Ed, PhD); nonprofit management (MPA); operations and supply chain management (MBA); performance (MM, DMA); philosophy (MA); political science (MA); professional and technical communication (MA); radio, television and film (MA, MFA); rehabilitation counseling (Certificate); sociology (MA); Spanish (MA); special education (M Ed); speech-language pathology (MA); strategic management (MBA); studio art (MFA); teaching (M Ed); MBA/MS. *Program availability:* Part-time, evening/weekend, online learning. Terminal master's awarded for partial completion of doctoral program. *Degree requirements:* For master's, variable foreign language requirement, comprehensive exam (for some programs), thesis (for some programs); for doctorate, variable foreign language requirement, comprehensive exam (for some programs), thesis/dissertation; for other advanced degree, variable foreign language requirement, comprehensive exam (for some programs). *Entrance requirements:* For master's and doctorate, GRE, GMAT. Additional exam requirements/recommendations for international students: Required—TOEFL (minimum score 550 paper-based; 79 iBT). Electronic applications accepted.

**Wayne State University,** College of Fine, Performing and Communication Arts, James Pearson Duffy Department of Art and Art History, Detroit, MI 48202. Offers art (MA, MFA), including ceramics, drawing, fibers, graphic design, industrial design (MA), interior design (MA), metalsmithing, painting, photography, printmaking, sculpture; art history (MA). *Students:* 15 full-time (10 women), 9 part-time (7 women); includes 6 minority (2 Black or African American, non-Hispanic/Latino; 1 Asian, non-Hispanic/Latino; 1 Hispanic/Latino; 2 Two or more races, non-Hispanic/Latino), 2 international. Average age 34. 49 applicants, 12% accepted, 3 enrolled. In 2016, 7 master's awarded. *Degree requirements:* For master's, thesis (for some programs), essay or thesis. *Entrance requirements:* For master's, BFA or another degree and equivalent course work, portfolio, personal interview, reference letters, statement of intent (except for art history program). Additional exam requirements/recommendations for international students: Required—TOEFL (minimum score 550 paper-based; 79 iBT), TWE (minimum score 5.5), Michigan English Language Assessment Battery (minimum score 85); Recommended—IELTS (minimum score 6.5). *Application deadline:* For fall admission, 2/1 for domestic and international students; for winter admission, 10/1 for domestic and international students. Application fee: $50. Electronic applications accepted. *Expenses:* $17,240 per year resident tuition and fees, $34,434 per year non-resident tuition and fees. *Financial support:* In 2016–17, 21 students received support, including 1 fellowship with tuition reimbursement available (averaging $16,000 per year), 6 teaching assistantships with tuition reimbursements available (averaging $17,994 per year); research assistantships, scholarships/grants, and unspecified assistantships also available. Support available to part-time students. Financial award applicants required to submit FAFSA. *Faculty research:* Integration of the human figure into urban and rural landscape in painting; performance art utilizing digital media and video; exploration of race, gender, and culture through creative practice (including art, design, and art history); ongoing investigation and elaboration of visual art traditions in diverse media; continued scholarship in the history of art. *Unit head:* Dr. John Richardson, Chair, 313-577-2980, Fax: 313-577-3491, E-mail: af5343@wayne.edu. *Application contact:* 313-577-2980, E-mail: art@wayne.edu.
Website: http://art.wayne.edu/

# DREXEL UNIVERSITY
## Westphal College of Media Arts & Design

 For more information, visit http://petersons.to/drexelu_media-arts-design

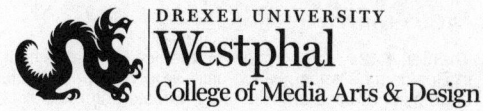

## Programs of Study

The Antoinette Westphal College of Media Arts & Design at Drexel University offers nine Master of Science (M.S.) degree programs that combine classroom study, studio work, and professional experience under the supervision of faculty with outstanding industry backgrounds. Master's degrees are offered in arts administration, design research, digital media, fashion design, interior architecture and design, retail and merchandising, museum leadership, television management, and urban strategy.

The College's professionally oriented programs prepare students to begin or enhance careers in the design, media, and nonprofit arts sectors. Class sizes are kept small, and students are exposed to their professions through exchanges with a full-time faculty of talented industry practitioners and part-time instructors drawn from their fields. Two qualities define Westphal's graduate programs: an emphasis on experiential learning through studio instruction and a focus on the real-world challenges of professional practice.

Drexel is ranked among the Top 100 National Universities as chosen by *U.S. News & World Report*. The website The Business of Fashion has ranked Westphal College's fashion design program among the top 10 fashion schools worldwide; DesignIntelligence has ranked the graduate interior design program at Drexel University among the top 10 in the nation, and The Princeton Review has ranked Westphal's graduate game design program eighth in the country. Drexel has also been recognized nationally for its campus security, use of technology, and outreach to military members and veterans.

**Arts Administration (M.S.):** Westphal offers two pathways to the Master of Science in Arts Administration degree program: on campus and online. The campus-based course of study provides experience and networking opportunities through Philadelphia arts organizations, and the online course puts students in contact with national leaders in the field.

Philadelphia consistently ranks among Travel and Leisure readers' favorite cities for cultural attractions, including theater, dance, and museums. As members of Westphal's Arts Administration Graduate Association, students can further develop professional connections and build experience by planning and participating in local and regional events, including an annual art auction and National Arts Advocacy Day lobbying activities in Washington, D.C.

**Fashion Design (M.S.):** Drexel's graduate fashion design program prepares students for work in fashion and costume design, merchandising, and curating historical textiles and designs. The internationally recognized Robert and Penny Fox Historic Costume Collection at Drexel's UBRN Center is one of the oldest research collections in the United States, with more than 14,000 objects dating back to the sixteenth century and more recent pieces, such as clothing worn by Greta Garbo.

The M.S. in Fashion Design degree program strongly emphasizes studio work, and the Student Fashion Club puts members in touch with major players in the industry through showroom visits, trunk shows, and designer events. High-profile club guests have included designers Vera Wang, Anna Sui, Josie Natori, and David Yurman, along with designers for Ralph Lauren, Coach, Lilly Pulitzer, and Anthropologie.

**Digital Media (M.S./Ph.D.):** Westphal's Master of Science in Digital Media degree program gives students an interdisciplinary, project-oriented experience with 3-D modeling and animation, game design, and projects sponsored by industry or funded by government grants. Both The Princeton Review and GamePro Media rank Drexel's graduate video game design program in their top 10.

Digital media students have access to RePlay, Drexel's interdisciplinary lab at the UBRN Center, run by Westphal and Drexel's College of Computing and Informatics. RePlay provides more than 100 high-powered workstations, an assortment of consoles and controllers across a number of brands, motion-capture systems, 3-D scanners, and eye-trackers, as well as multiple recording studios and an 80-seat 3-D theater.

The program reflects the fast-paced, constantly evolving field in which art, technology, and science intersect. Westphal digital media graduates have gone on to work with Disney, Pixar, Microsoft, and other industry leaders.

**Design Research (M.S.):** The Master of Science in Design Research considers complex multidisciplinary problems beyond the scope of traditional boundaries within individual design disciplines. This ethical, human-centered, and international perspective on twenty-first century design enables students to explore and develop a critical understanding of design as theory, concept, and practice in service to current and future challenges.

This 46-credit program offers two concentrated paths of study: Design and Technology or Environmental Design and Health. Students can tailor a unique educational pathway engaging with Drexel's multiple colleges to suit their academic needs. Working alongside Drexel's world-class faculty students practice design research and apply solutions that are in demand prepare for long-term career growth and success.

**Interior Architecture and Design (M.S.):** The M.S. in Interior Architecture and Design degree program at Drexel University is one of only 14 such programs certified by the Council for Interior Design Accreditation in the U.S. and Canada. As such, its graduates are qualified to sit for the National Council for Interior Design Qualification's Interior Design Fundamentals Exam. Westphal's program is also certified by the National Association of Schools of Art and Design.

Graduate students in Westphal's interior architecture and design program are trained in design, technology, ethics, and sustainability to prepare for work on public, private, and institutional projects. Most of the program's students graduate with job offers from top-tier firms.

**Museum Leadership (M.S.):** Westphal's M.S. in Museum Leadership degree program sets itself apart with its emphasis on technology, audience and resource development, education, and financial management in addition to traditional topics such as conserving and curating collections. The program is designed to prepare graduates to lead and grow traditional museums as well as arboreta, zoos, children's museums, historic homes, and other kinds of museums.

**Retail & Merchandising (Online M.S.):** Westphal's online master's program in retail and merchandising provides a broad overview of the industry, focusing on topics such as branding, fashion, visual communication, omnichannel marketing, product development, and supply chain management. Considering both theoretical and practical approaches, the curriculum will develop students' ability to think critically, research and solve problems, and implement innovative solutions in a dynamic global marketplace.

The forecasted job growth shows a strong need for managers possessing a nimbleness in retail operations, merchandise management, customer relations, strategic planning, product analysis, advanced problem solving, and human resource development. Students who graduate from the M.S. in Retail & Merchandising program will be able to pursue positions such as retail corporate manager, retail sales manager, manufacturer sales representative, educator, and more.

**Television Management (M.S./M.B.A.):** Students in the Paul F. Harron Graduate Program in Television Management have the option of pursuing a Master of Science on campus or online, or a dual Master of Science and Master of Business Administration (M.B.A.) path.

Both programs offer evening classes and flexible options to accommodate working adults, and both degree plans give students lots of hands-on learning opportunities through Drexel University Television (DUTV), the new Television in Service to Society civic-engagement program, and internships in Philadelphia, the fourth-largest television market in the U.S., as well as with national broadcast and cable networks.

**Urban Strategy (M.S):** The next generation of 21st century urbanists will face complex social, environmental and economic problems in an increasingly dynamic and interconnected world. Westphal's Urban Strategy program prepares students to meet those challenges through a two-year, 48-credit interdisciplinary master's degree program that brings together Drexel's expertise in design, engineering, business, policy, and public health. Students will hone their skills in real-time through practical engagement and experiential learning. The program combines rigorous training in critical thinking and analytical methods, while grounding students in historical, political, and economic context.

The Urban Strategy program is housed in Philadelphia, a city increasingly known for its vitality, livability, and continuous transformation. Students will learn firsthand what makes Philadelphia work, and the struggles the city and region continue to face. Urban Strategy students will have a front row seat as Drexel embarks on an ambitious plan to transform the district around 30th Street Station into Schuylkill Yards: a 14-acre hub for living, learning, and innovation. The program's reach is global as well; students will have opportunities to travel and learn about best practices in contemporary urbanism from a network of partners around the world.

Through a partnership with the Lindy Institute for Urban Innovation, students will have access to respected scholars and practitioners from around the world, who will serve as their teachers, advisers, and mentors, in addition to seasoned Drexel faculty. Graduates of the Urban Strategy program will gain public and private sector employment, including positions in government agencies, design firms, think tanks, community development corporations, and beyond.

## Facilities

The Westphal College of Media Arts & Design is located in the state-of-the-art URBN Center. Students enjoy specialized facilities, including design studios, recording studios, computer laboratories, television studios and a television station, an art gallery, the Historic Costume Collection, and the Mandell

Theater, a 424-seat proscenium theater. Mandell is host to the Professionals in Residence Project, which pairs working theater professionals with Drexel students. Facilities are designed to foster interdisciplinary collaboration and hands-on learning.

## THE FACULTY

Westphal faculty members are leaders in their industries. For example, Westphal Dean *Allen Sabinson* is the former president of production at Miramax Films and has held senior positions at A&E, TNT, ABC, ICM, NBC, and Showtime.

*Neville K. Vakharia*, director of the on-campus Arts Administration program, was the director of the Cultural Data Project (now DataArts) at The Pew Charitable Trusts, overseeing its strategic direction, operations, and national expansion. His research centers on the role that technology, innovation, and knowledge play in building sustainable, resilient, and relevant organizations and communities. He serves on the board of directors of CultureWorks Greater Philadelphia, the Philadelphia Cultural Fund, and the editorial board of *Artivate*.

*Jean Brody*, Head of the online Arts Administration program, has more than 25 years' experience in education and the arts, and has worked in a variety of roles with Philadelphia arts organizations including the Philadelphia Theatre Caravan, Hedgerow Theatre, Point Breeze Performing Arts Center, the Theatre Alliance of Greater Philadelphia, Relâche, Inc., and more.

*Dr. Danielle Rice*, Director of the Museum Leadership program, served as the Executive Director of the Delaware Art Museum since June 2005. Prior to that, Dr. Rice worked at the Philadelphia Museum of Art for 19 years where she served as senior curator of education and associate director for programs.

*Michael G. Wagner*, Associate Professor and the Director of the Digital Media Program, is the scientific director of Ludwig, a curriculum-based physics learning game for middle schools that has been awarded the German Game Developer Award for Best Serious Game, 2011.

*Diana Nicholas*, Associate Director of the Interior Architecture & Design program and Director of Design Research program, ran a solo practice in Philadelphia executing residential interiors, storefront revitalization, space planning, and adaptive interior nonprofit reuse for over 10 years. She has exhibited widely and taught architecture and interior design for 16 years at various schools and universities. She has presented research works at both national and international conferences. Her work has been published and exhibited in a variety of academic journals including ARCH IN-Form, ARCC, and ACSA.

*Kathi Martin*, Head of the Fashion graduate program, has her work in the Permanent Collection of the Philadelphia Museum of Art and has been in editorials in *British Vogue, Women's Wear Daily, The New York Times Magazine, Harpers & Queen*, and other fashion magazines.

*Albert Tedesco*, director of the Paul F. Harron Graduate Program in Television Management is also the president of Medianex, Incorporated, a marketing communications and management-consulting firm, and directs the documentary laboratory there. Tedesco created and directed the foundation-supported and award-winning video documentary laboratory at Drexel and was the founding vice-president and general manager of WWSG-TV57, Philadelphia's first hybrid television station.

*Andrew Zitcer*, Director of the Urban Strategy program, teaches courses in research and methods, creative placemaking, and cultural policy. Andrew's research focuses on cooperative social and economic practices, as well as the role of arts in community and economic development. His work has been published in *Urban Geography, Antipode, Planning Theory & Practice*, and the *Journal of Planning Education and Research*.

*Dr. Joseph Hancock*, Director of the Retail & Merchandising program, is an international authority in the area of fashion branding as a form of storytelling. He started in academia after 20 years in the retailing industry having worked for such legendary brands as The Gap Incorporated, The Limited Corporation, and Target Corporation. He is a published author of several prominent retail industry books, and the executive director for Events for the Popular Culture/American Culture Associations (PCA/ACA).

## Financial Aid

Drexel's graduate scholarship options include merit-based dean's fellowships and awards, Drexel Grad Grants for undergraduate alumni who are returning for master's degrees, and the Yellow Ribbon matching-funds program for eligible veterans.

Work-study opportunities for full-time students include teaching, research, and graduate assistant positions. Part-time graduate students who work during the day may be able to earn academic credit for up to six months of paid work in their chosen fields through Drexel's Graduate Co-op Program.

## Costs

Tuition for programs in the Westphal College of Media Arts and Design for the 2016–17 academic year was $966 per credit hour, with fees of $280 for full-time students and $140 for part-time students.

## Location

Philadelphia is the nation's fifth-largest city, with a metropolitan population of nearly 6 million. It is renowned for its historical sites and the diversity of its neighborhoods, and as a hub of the pharmaceutical, electronics, cable, design, and finance industries. The city offers countless arts, entertainment, and recreational attractions including museums, galleries, theaters, major league sports franchises, and one of the nation's largest urban park systems, as well as first-class shopping, dining, and nightlife.

The Westphal College of Media Arts & Design is located on Drexel's University City Campus in Philadelphia's University City neighborhood, which is also home to the University of Pennsylvania, the University of the Sciences, and the Restaurant School at Walnut Hill College.

## The University

Drexel University is a private, nonsectarian coeducational university, founded in 1891 by financier and philanthropist Anthony J. Drexel. Today it is a top-tier, comprehensive research university, enrolling nearly 16,000 undergraduates and more than 9,000 graduate, professional, and certificate students on four separate campuses. The University's colleges and schools offer over 80 undergraduate majors, and more than 70 master's and 30 doctoral programs. Drexel is fully accredited by the Middle States Association of Colleges and Schools, with additional programs accredited by their respective top professional accreditation bodies. Students come from all 50 U.S. states and 133 other countries.

## Applying

Applicants may only apply to one program at a time. More information is available online at www.drexel.edu/grad/apply.

## Correspondence and Information

Tia James, Assistant Director of Recruitment
Antoinette Westphal College of Media Arts & Design
Drexel University
3501 Market Street
The URBN Center, 1A 10 C
Philadelphia, Pennsylvania 19104
Phone: 215-895-1834
Website: http://drexel.edu/westphal

URBN Center, Drexel University, Philadelphia, Pennsylvania.

URBN Center, Drexel University, Philadelphia, PA.

# FASHION INSTITUTE OF TECHNOLOGY

*State University of New York*

*M.A. in Exhibition and Experience Design*

 For more information, visit http://petersons.to/fitexhibitiondesign

## Programs of Study

The Fashion Institute of Technology (FIT), a State University of New York (SUNY) college of art and design, business, and technology, is home to a mix of innovative achievers, creative thinkers, and industry pioneers. FIT fosters interdisciplinary initiatives, advances research, and provides access to an international network of professionals. With a reputation for excellence, FIT offers its diverse student body access to world-class faculty, dynamic and relevant curricula, and a superior education at an affordable cost. It offers seven programs of graduate study. The programs in Art Market Studies; Exhibition and Experience Design; and Fashion and Textile Studies: History, Theory, Museum Practice lead to the Master of Arts (M.A.) degree. The Illustration and Fashion Design programs lead to the Master of Fine Arts (M.F.A.) degree. The Master of Professional Studies (M.P.S.) degree programs are Cosmetics and Fragrance Marketing and Management, and Global Fashion Management.

The 39-credit, full-time Exhibition and Experience Design M.A. program prepares students for careers in the exhibition design profession, teaching them how to convey intellectual content, incite emotion, and engage audiences within the designed environment. The studio-driven, 16-month course of study centers on the designer's role within the exhibition team, with emphasis on the development of both design and conceptual development skills. Students may also choose to attend on a part time basis. Students explore exhibitions in museums, historic sites, expositions, retail venues, and public arenas, while working with narrative, audience research, architecture, environmental graphics, lighting, rendering, model-making, and production. All graduating students complete an independent qualifying paper and applied exhibition design project. An internship elective is available to interested students upon completion of their degree requirements.

## Research Facilities

The School of Graduate Studies is primarily located in the campus's Shirley Goodman Resource Center, which also houses the Gladys Marcus Library and The Museum at FIT. School of Graduate Studies facilities include conference rooms; a fully equipped conservation laboratory; a multipurpose laboratory for conservation projects and the dressing of mannequins; storage facilities for costume and textile materials; a graduate student lounge with computer and printer access; a graduate student library reading room with computers, reference materials, and copies of past classes' qualifying and thesis papers; specialized wireless classrooms; traditional and digital illustration studios; and classrooms equipped with model stands, easels, and drafting tables.

The Gladys Marcus Library houses more than 300,000 volumes of print, nonprint, and digital resources. Specialized holdings include industry reference materials, manufacturers' catalogs, original fashion sketches and scrapbooks, photographs, portfolios of plates, and sample books. The FIT Digital Library provides access to over 90 searchable online databases.

The Museum at FIT houses one of the world's most important collections of clothing and textiles and is the only museum in New York City dedicated to the art of fashion. The permanent collection encompasses more than 50,000 garments and accessories dating from the eighteenth century, with particular strength in twentieth-century fashion, as well as 30,000 textiles and 100,000 textile swatches. Each year, nearly 100,000 visitors are drawn to the museum's award-winning exhibitions and public programs.

## Financial Aid

FIT directly administers its institutional grants, scholarships, and loans. Federal funding administered by the college may include Federal Perkins Loans, federally subsidized and unsubsidized Direct Loans for students, Grad PLUS loans, and the Federal Work-Study Program. Priority for institutionally administered funds is given to students enrolled and designated as full-time.

## Cost of Study

Tuition for New York State residents is $5,603 per semester, or $467 per credit. Out-of-state residents' tuition is $11,449 per semester, or $954 per credit. Tuition and fees are subject to change at the discretion of FIT's Board of Trustees. Additional expenses—for class materials, textbooks, and travel—may apply and vary per program.

## Living and Housing Costs

On-campus housing is available to graduate students. Traditional residence hall accommodations (including meal plan) cost from $5,887 to $7,074 per semester. Apartment-style housing options (not including meal plan) cost from $6,299 to $10,495 per semester.

## Student Group

Enrollment in the School of Graduate Studies is approximately 200 students per academic year, allowing considerable individual advisement. Students come to FIT from throughout the country and around the world.

## Student Outcomes

Graduates of the Exhibition and Experience Design program find employment with architectural and exhibition design firms, museums, historic trusts, and special-events companies.

## Location

FIT is located in Manhattan's Chelsea neighborhood, at the heart of the advertising, visual arts, marketing, fashion, business, design, and communications industries. Students are connected to New York City and gain unparalleled exposure to their field through guest lectures, field trips, internships, and sponsored competitions. The location provides access to major museums, galleries, and auction houses as well as dining, entertainment, and shopping options. The campus is near subway, bus, and commuter rail lines.

*Fashion Institute of Technology*

### Applying

Applicants to all School of Graduate Studies programs must hold a baccalaureate degree in an appropriate major from a college or university, with a cumulative GPA of 3.0 or higher. International students from non-English-speaking countries are required to submit minimum TOEFL scores of 550 on the written test, 213 on the computer test, or 80 on the Internet test. Each major has additional, specialized prerequisites for admission; for detailed information, students should visit the School of Graduate Studies on FIT's website.

Domestic and international students use the same application when seeking admission. The deadline for completed applications with transcripts and supplemental materials is March 15 for the Exhibition and Experience Design program. After the deadline date, applicants are considered on a rolling admissions basis. Candidates may apply online at fitnyc.edu/gradstudies.

### Correspondence and Information

School of Graduate Studies
Shirley Goodman Resource Center, Room E315
Fashion Institute of Technology
227 West 27 Street
New York, New York 10001-5992
Phone: 212-217-4300
Fax: 212-217-4301
E-mail: gradinfo@fitnyc.edu
Websites: fitnyc.edu/gradstudies
　　　　　fitnyc.edu/exhibitiondesign

### THE FACULTY

A partial list of faculty members is below. Guest lecturers are not included.

Christina Lyons, Chair, M.S., Pratt.
Isabella Bruno, M.A., Fashion Institute of Technology.
Rob Cohen, Ph.D., Suffolk.
Brenda Cowan, M.S.Ed., Bank Street College of Education.
Robin Drake, B.S., Pratt.
Joseph Karadin, B.Arch., Cornell.
Jorge Martinez, B.F.A., Michigan.
John Newman, M.A., Parsons.
Hannah Rawe, B.F.A., Cooper Union.
Michael Stiller, B.A., Bard.
Kate Schein Waisman, M.S.Ed., Bank Street College of Education.
Michele Y. Washington, M.S., Pratt.
Jackson Young, B.F.A., Parsons.

# FASHION INSTITUTE OF TECHNOLOGY

*State University of New York*

*M.F.A. in Illustration*

 For more information, visit http://petersons.to/fitillustration

## Programs of Study

The Fashion Institute of Technology (FIT), a State University of New York (SUNY) college of art and design, business, and technology, is home to a mix of innovative achievers, creative thinkers, and industry pioneers. FIT fosters interdisciplinary initiatives, advances research, and provides access to an international network of professionals. With a reputation for excellence, FIT offers its diverse student body access to world-class faculty, dynamic and relevant curricula, and a superior education at an affordable cost. It offers seven programs of graduate study. The programs in Art Market Studies; Exhibition and Experience Design; and Fashion and Textile Studies: History, Theory, Museum Practice lead to the Master of Arts (M.A.) degree. The Illustration and Fashion Design programs lead to the Master of Fine Arts (M.F.A.) degree. The Master of Professional Studies (M.P.S.) programs are Cosmetics and Fragrance Marketing and Management, and Global Fashion Management.

The 60-credit evening and weekend Illustration M.F.A. program is designed for working professionals seeking advanced study to further develop their skills as master illustrators. The program focuses on high-level techniques, new media applications, and illustration business practices. The curriculum encompasses digital and traditional studio methods, entrepreneurial research and writing, and opportunities in new and emerging markets. The program features assignments that mirror marketplace demands and specifications, regular guest lecturers, an intensive trip to the West Coast that provides opportunities for interactions with artists at film and entertainment studios, and regular off-campus engagement with New York City's art and design world. Students complete a visual thesis project and an independently researched and written master's thesis.

## Research Facilities

The School of Graduate Studies is primarily located in the campus's Shirley Goodman Resource Center, which also houses the Gladys Marcus Library and The Museum at FIT. School of Graduate Studies facilities include conference rooms; a fully equipped conservation laboratory; a multipurpose laboratory for conservation projects and the dressing of mannequins; storage facilities for costume and textile materials; a graduate student lounge with computer and printer access; a graduate student library reading room with computers, reference materials, and copies of past classes' qualifying and thesis papers; specialized wireless classrooms; traditional and digital illustration studios; and classrooms equipped with model stands, easels, and drafting tables.

The Gladys Marcus Library houses more than 300,000 volumes of print, nonprint, and digital resources. Specialized holdings include industry reference materials, manufacturers' catalogs, original fashion sketches and scrapbooks, photographs, portfolios of plates, and sample books. The FIT Digital Library provides access to over 90 searchable online databases.

The Museum at FIT houses one of the world's most important collections of clothing and textiles and is the only museum in New York City dedicated to the art of fashion. The permanent collection encompasses more than 50,000 garments and accessories dating from the eighteenth century to the present, with particular strength in twentieth-century fashion, as well as 30,000 textiles and 100,000 textile swatches. Each year, nearly 100,000 visitors are drawn to the museum's award-winning exhibitions and public programs.

## Financial Aid

FIT directly administers its institutional grants, scholarships, and loans. Federal funding administered by the college may include Federal Perkins Loans, federally subsidized and unsubsidized Direct Loans for students, Grad PLUS loans, and the Federal Work-Study Program. Priority for institutionally administered funds is given to students enrolled and designated as full-time.

## Cost of Study

Tuition for New York State residents is $5,603 per semester, or $467 per credit. Out-of-state residents' tuition is $11,449 per semester, or $954 per credit. Tuition and fees are subject to change at the discretion of FIT's Board of Trustees. Additional expenses—for class materials, textbooks, and travel—may apply and vary per program.

## Living and Housing Costs

On-campus housing is available to graduate students. Traditional residence hall accommodations (including meal plan) cost from $5,887 to $7,074 per semester. Apartment-style housing options (not including meal plan) cost from $6,299 to $10,495 per semester.

## Student Group

Enrollment in the School of Graduate Studies is approximately 200 students per academic year, allowing considerable individualized advisement. Students come to FIT from throughout the country and around the world.

## Student Outcomes

Students in the Illustration program graduate with a personal vision, an entrepreneurial spirit, and the skills needed to succeed as freelance illustrators.

## Location

FIT is located in Manhattan's Chelsea neighborhood, at the heart of the advertising, visual arts, marketing, fashion, business, design, and communications industries. Students are connected to New York City and gain unparalleled exposure to their field through guest lectures, field trips, internships, and sponsored competitions. The location provides access to major museums, galleries, and auction houses as well as dining, entertainment, and shopping options. The campus is near subway, bus, and commuter rail lines.

## Applying

Applicants to all School of Graduate Studies programs must hold a baccalaureate degree in an appropriate major from a college or university, with a cumulative GPA of 3.0 or higher. International students from non-English-speaking countries are required to submit minimum TOEFL scores of 550 on the written test, 213 on the computer test, or 80 on the Internet test. Each major has additional, specialized prerequisites for admission; for detailed information, students should visit the School of Graduate Studies on FIT's website.

Domestic and international students use the same application when seeking admission. The deadline for completed applications with transcripts and supplemental materials is March 15 for the Illustration program. After the deadline date, applicants are considered on a rolling admissions basis. Candidates may apply online at fitnyc.edu/gradstudies.

*Fashion Institute of Technology*

**Correspondence and Information**

School of Graduate Studies
Shirley Goodman Resource Center, Room E315
Fashion Institute of Technology
227 West 27 Street
New York, New York 10001-5992
Phone: 212-217-4300
Fax: 212-217-4301
E-mail: gradinfo@fitnyc.edu
Websites: fitnyc.edu/gradstudies
　　　　　 fitnyc.edu/illustration-mfa

## THE FACULTY

A partial list of faculty members is below. Guest lecturers are not included.

Daniel Abraham, J.D., Miami (Florida).
Jonathan Bartlett, MFA, School of Visual Arts.
Richard Borge, MFA, University of Arizona
Steve Brodner, B.F.A., Cooper Union.
Celia Bullwinkel, M.F.A., School of Visual Arts.

Denise Carvalho, Ph.D., University of California, Davis.
Dennis Dittrich, M.F.A., Syracuse.
Rudy Gutierrez, B.F.A., Pratt.
Michael Hyde, Ph.D., NYU.
Aya Kakeda, M.F.A., School of Visual Arts.
Monika Maniecki, M.F.A., Fashion Institute of Technology.
Anelle Miller, B.F.A., Parsons.

John Nickle, M.F.A., South Florida.
Cheryl Phelps, B.F.A., Memphis College of Art.
Melanie Reim, M.F.A., Syracuse.
Martha Rich, M.F.A., Pennsylvania.

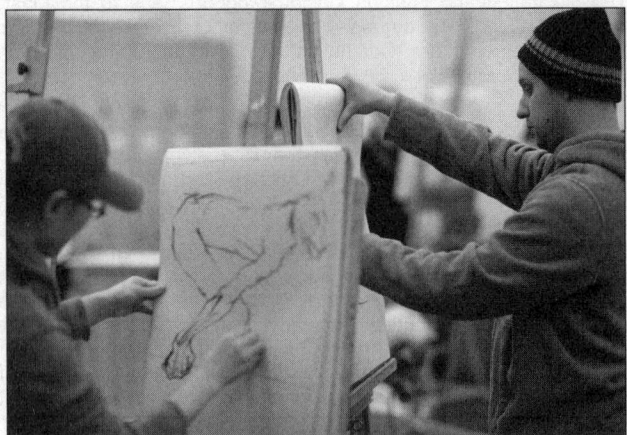

# PRATT INSTITUTE
## *School of Design*

## Programs of Study

Pratt has been educating professionals for productive careers in the field of design since its founding in 1887. Pratt's School of Design, one of the largest of its kind, offers an outstanding professional art and design education taught by a faculty of working professionals who bring high standards and current practices to the classroom. Faculty members have received more than eighteen Tiffany, Fulbright, and Guggenheim awards as well as other prestigious professional awards. Pratt's graduate interior design program was ranked first nationally by *DesignIntelligence* (2017). *U.S. News & World Report* ranked Pratt's interior design program among the best in the country, communications design was ranked twelfth, and industrial design was ranked fifth.

Pratt offers master's degrees in a variety of programs, including Master of Fine Arts in Communications Design and Interior Design, Master of Science in Package Design, and Master of Industrial Design. All are located on the main Brooklyn campus.

Graduates of Pratt's design programs have the competitive edge needed to obtain top administrative and creative positions in design studios, businesses, various industries, and arts organizations.

All graduate design curricula include supportive course work in the humanities. Students can choose from a wide array of course offerings, including art and design history, comparative literature, philosophy, foreign languages, and social sciences. The graduate programs require the completion of 30 to 68 credits and last from 1½ to 3 years, depending on the curriculum and the number of prerequisites that have not been met at the time of admission. For the granting of degrees, all of the graduate programs require the submission of a thesis or a comparable effort. For the M.F.A., an exhibition and supporting corollary statement are required. Candidates for the M.S. and the M.I.D. degrees must present a thesis project that demonstrates a meaningful contribution to design and documents the supportive research that informs all phases of design and construction.

## Research Facilities

The Pratt Library contains 186,589 bound volumes, serial backfiles, and other material (including government documents); 251,603 audiovisual materials; and 3,996 microforms and subscribes to 925 periodicals.

Pratt maintains numerous studios, shops, and technical facilities for work in all media as well as state-of-the-art computer facilities. Digital arts labs include state-of-the-art Macintosh, PC/NT, and UNIX operating systems as well as digital video and audio systems. Pratt also has extensive gallery space for exhibitions.

## Financial Aid

Financial aid awards are offered through a variety of institutional, state, and federally funded programs. These include Graduate Scholarships awarded by departments to incoming students on the basis of merit, endowed and restricted scholarships for continuing students, and student employment. Assistantships are awarded on a competitive basis to continuing students in all departments. Special alumni-sponsored fellowships are also available.

## Cost of Study

Graduate tuition for 2017–18 is $30,834 per year (full-time 18 credits, $1,713 per credit) and student fees are $1,974 per year. The cost of books and supplies varies widely, depending on the program in which the student is enrolled.

## Living and Housing Costs

Limited campus housing is available on a first-come, first-served basis. Housing costs average $18,880 per academic year. There is a plentiful supply of moderately priced rentals in the immediate area and in adjacent neighborhoods for married students seeking housing and for those students choosing to reside off campus.

## Student Group

In educating more than four generations of students to be creative, technically skilled, and adaptable professionals, Pratt has gained an international reputation that attracts more than 4,600 undergraduate and graduate students annually from forty-eight states and eighty-one countries.

## Location

Pratt Institute's 25-acre, parklike main campus is situated among the turn-of-the-century mansions, Victorian brownstones, and wide, tree-lined boulevards of Clinton Hill, one of Brooklyn's historic neighborhoods. Midtown Manhattan, the heart of New York City, is only 25 minutes away by subway and offers students a vast array of professional, cultural, and recreational opportunities. Pratt's Manhattan campus is located in the Chelsea district.

## The Institute

A private, nonsectarian institute of higher education, Pratt Institute was founded by the industrialist and philanthropist Charles Pratt. Changing with the needs and requirements of the professional world for which it prepares its graduates, Pratt today educates 3,310 undergraduate and 1,349 graduate students for careers in art and design, architecture, and library and information science.

## Applying

The deadline for applications and all supporting materials, including portfolio, is January 5. Applicants should complete the application process online. Early submission of applications with all necessary credentials is highly desirable. Applications received after these dates are considered if openings exist in a particular program. For applicants who intend to file for financial aid, the FAFSA should be filed by March 1 for fall entrance and by October 1 for spring entrance.

## Correspondence and Information

Graduate Admissions Office
Pratt Institute
200 Willoughby Avenue
Brooklyn, New York 11205
United States
Phone: 718-636-3514
     800-331-0834 (toll-free)
Fax: 718-399-4242
E-mail: admissions@pratt.edu
Website: http://www.pratt.edu
     http://www.pratt.edu/admissions/request-information (to request information)

# THE FACULTY

**Anita Cooney, Dean**

## Communications/Package Design

Santiago Piedrafita, Chair, Associate Professor; M.S. Pratt.
David Burke, Acting Assistant Chair.
Barry Berger, Associate Professor; B.I.D., Pratt.
Jean Brennan, Adjunct Professor; M.S., Pratt.
Thomas Delaney, Visiting Instructor; A.A.S., F.I.T.
Antonio DiSpigna, Full-Time Tenure Professor; B.F.A., Pratt.
David Frisco, Adjunct Professor; M.F.A., Yale.
Kevin Gatta, Distinguished Professor with Tenure; M.S., Pratt.
J. Roger Guilfoyle, Adjunct Professor; B.A., Creighton; CCE.
Richard Hall, Visiting Assistant Professor, M.F.A. Pratt.
William Hilson, Adjunct Professor; M.S., NYIT; CCE.
Michelle Hinebrook, Adjunct Assistant Instructor; M.F.A., Cranbrook.
Allen Hori, Visiting Associate Professor; M.F.A., Cranbrook Academy of Art.
Thomas Klinkowstein, Adjunct Professor; M.S., Syracuse; CCE.
Gusty Lange, Adjunct Professor; M.P.S., Pratt, CCE.
Christina Latina, Visiting Assistant Professor; M.F.A. Pratt.
EunSun Lee, Adjunct Associate Professor; M.S., Pratt.
Alex Liebergesell, Associate Professor; M.F.A., Yale.
Katya Moorman, Associate Professor; M.F.A., Cranbrook.
Ann Morris, Adjunct Assistant Professor; M.A., CUNY, Hunter.
Eric O'Toole, Adjunct Associate Professor; M.F.A., Pratt; CCE.
Marc Rosen, Visiting Associate Professor; M.S., Pratt.
Gaia Scagnetti, Assistant Professor; Ph.D., Politecnico di Milano.
Natalie Sims, Visiting Assistant Professor; M.F.A., Pratt.
Ryan Waller, Adjunct Assistant Professor; M.F.A., Yale.
Pirco Wolfframm, Adjunct Associate Professor; M.F.A., California Institute of the Arts; CCE.
Alisa Zamir, Professor; M.S., Pratt.

## Industrial Design

Constantin Boym, Chair, Professor; M.Design, Domus Academy (Milan).
Audrey Lapiner, Acting Assistant Chair.
Lawrence Au, Visiting Instructor; B.I.D., Pratt.
Peter Barna, Associate Professor; M.I.D., Pratt.
Harvey Bernstein, Adjunct Professor; M.S., Pratt; CCE.
Meri Bourgard-Rohrs, Visiting Professor; M.F.A., Pratt; CCE.
Gina Caspi, Visiting Professor; M.I.D. Pratt.
Esther Beke Cohen, Visiting Instructor; M.I.D. Pratt.
Justin Crocker, Visiting Instructor, M.I.D. Pratt.
Lucia DeRespinis, Adjunct Professor; B.I.D., Pratt; CCE.
Kate Hixon, Adjunct Associate Professor; CCE.
Michael Hobbs, Visiting Instructor; B.F.A. RISD.
Matthew Hoey, Visiting Assistant Professor; B.Arch, Temple University.
Jeffrey Kapec, Visiting Associate Professor; B.I.D., Pratt.

## Pratt Institute

Robert Langhorn, Adjunct Associate Professor; Royal College of Art, London.
Jay Levy, Visiting Assistant Professor; M.Arch., Columbia University.
Kate Lewis, Visiting Assistant Professor; M.A., Central Saint Martins.
Jong. S. (Mark) Lim, Adjunct Professor; M.F.A., Pratt, CCE.
Scott Lundberg, Adjunct Associate Professor; M.I.D., Pratt; CCE.
Frederick McSwain, Visiting Assistant Professor; B.A., University of North Carolina at Wilmington.
Frank Millero, Visiting Assistant Professor; M.I.D., Pratt.
Katrin Mueller-Russo, Professor; Dipl Des., Hochschule fur Dildende Kunste (Germany).
Karol Murlak, Associate Professor; Ph.D., Academy of Fine Arts in Warsaw, Poland.
William Niemeier, Visiting Assistant Professor; A.A.S., F.I.T.
Judith Nylen, Visiting Assistant Professor; M.F.A., Pratt.
Rebeccah Pailes-Friedman, Adjunct Associate Professor; M.I.D., Pratt.
Peter Ragonetti, Visiting Instructor; B.I.D., Pratt.
Michael Schafler, Visiting Assistant Professor; M.I.D. Pratt.
Alex Schweder, Visiting Associate Professor; Ph.D., University of Cambridge.
Irvin Tepper, Adjunct Professor; M.F.A., Washington (Seattle), CCE.
Jonathan Thayer, Associate Professor; B.I.D., Pratt.
William Jeffrey Tolbert, Adjunct Associate Professor; M.F.A., Yale.
Ignacio Urbina Polo, Associate Professor; M.S., Universidad Federal de Santa Catarina (Brazil).
Rebecca Welz, Adjunct Professor; B.A., SUNY Empire State College; CCE.
Allen Wilpon, Visiting Associate Professor; M.I.D., Pratt; M.D., Domus Academy, Milan.
Laura Wing, Visiting Assistant Professor; M.F.A. Parsons.
Henry Yoo, Adjunct Professor; M.I.D., Pratt, CCE.

### Interior Design

Alison B. Snyder, Chair, Professor; M.Arch., GSAPP, Columbia University.
Tania Sofia Branquinho, Acting Assistant Chair, Visiting Assistant Professor; M.Arch., Pratt.
Virna Abraham, Visiting Assistant Professor; M.F.A., Parsons.
Severino Alfonso, Visiting Assistant Professor; M.S., Columbia.
Eric Ansel, Visiting Assistant Professor; M.Arch., Pratt.
Tarek Ashkar, Visiting Assistant Professor; M.Arch., Harvard.
Peter Lind Barna, Professor; M.I.D., Pratt.
Francesca Bastianini, Visiting Instructor; M.F.A., Parsons.
Jacob Bek, Visiting Assistant Professor; M.Sc., Architectural Association School of Architecture.
David Black, Visiting Assistant Professor; M.Arch, Illinois at Chicago.
Mary Burke, Adjunct Associate Professor; M.S., Columbia.
Tania Chau, Visiting Assistant Professor; M.S., Pratt.
Der Sean Chou, Visiting Assistant Professor; M.S., NYU.
Annie Coggan, Visiting Assistant Professor; M.Arch., Southern California Institute of Architecture.
James Conti, Adjunct Associate Professor; M.F.A., Ohio State.
James Counts Jr., Visting Assistant Professor; M.S., Columbia.
Wendy Cronk, Visiting Assistant Professor; M.Arch., Harvard.
Asli Erdem, Visiting Assistant Professor; M.Arch, Rensselaer.
Kim Farrah, Visiting Assistant Professor; M.S. Pratt.
Philip Farrell, Adjunct Professor; M.S., Pratt.
David C. Foley, Visiting Professor; M.Arch., Notre Dame.
Thom Forsythe, Visiting Assistant Professor; M.S., Pratt.
Andrew Freeman, Visiting Instructor; B.F.A., B.G.D. Rhode Island School of Design.
Pavlina Gantcheva, Visiting Assistant Professor; M.S., Columbia.
Randi Halpern, Visiting Assistant Professor; B.F.A. NYIT.
Dalia Hamati, Visiting Assistant Professor; M.S., Columbia.
Adam Hayes, Visiting Instructor; B.Arch., Rice.
John Heida, Visiting Assistant Professor; B.Arch., Rice.
Claudia Hernandez, Visiting Assistant Professor; M.S., Columbia.
Sarah Hill, Visiting Assistant Professor; M.S., Pratt.
Lindsay Homer, Visiting Associate Professor; M.S., Pratt.
Benjamin Howes, Visiting Assistant Professor; M.S., Stevens.
Sheryl Kasak, Adjunct Associate Professor; M.S., Columbia.
Ted Kilcommons, Visiting Instructor; B.A., Texas.
Eugene Kwak, Visiting Assistant Professor; M.S., Columbia.
Chelsea Limbird, Visiting Assistant Professor; M.Arch., Rhode Island School of Design.
Jason Livingston, Visiting Assistant Professor; M.F.A., NYU.
Cam Lorendo, Adjunct Associate Professor; B.A., Parsons.
Addy Madorsky, Visiting Assistant Professor; M.S., Pratt.
Michael Maggio, Visiting Assistant Professor; M.A., Buffalo, SUNY.
William Mangold, Adjunct Assistant Professor; Ph.D., CUNY Graduate Center.
William McLoughlin, Visiting Instructor; B.Arch, Rhode Island School of Design/Brown.
Anthony Mekel, Visiting Associate Professor; B.Arch., Pratt.
Francine Monaco, Adjunct Associate Professor; B.Arch., Cincinnati.
Marius Myking, Visiting Assistant Professor; M.S., Pratt.
John Nafziger, Visiting Assistant Professor; M.Arch. II, Yale.
Robert Nassar, Visiting Associate Professor; B.F.A., Syracuse.
Latoya Nelson, Visiting Assistant Professor; M.Arch., Pennsylvania.
Joseph E. Nocella, Visiting Assistant Professor; M.Arch., Kansas.
Tetsu Ohara, Visiting Assistant Professor; certificate of architecture, Harvard.

Jon Otis, Professor; M.S., Massachusetts.
Danny Pang, Visiting Assistant Professor; M.S., Pratt.
Regis Pean, Visiting Assistant Professor; M.Arch, Technical University (Austria).
Sal Raffone, Visiting Assistant Professor; M.Arch., Harvard; M.B.A., Columbia.
J. Woodson Rainey Jr., Visiting Assistant Professor; B.Arch., Utah.
Christian Rietzke, Visiting Assistant Professor; M.Arch., Pratt.
Ben Rosenblum, Visiting Assistant Professor; M.Arch, Yale.
Rachely Rotem, Visiting Assistant Professor; M.S., Columbia.
Mary-Jo Schlachter, Visiting Assistant Professor; M.Arch., Pennsylvania.
Irina Schneid, Visiting Assistant Professor; M.Arch., Cornell.
Deborah Schneiderman, Associate Professor; M.Arch., Southern California Institute of Architecture, RA, LEED AP.
Alex Schweder, Visiting Associate Professor; Ph.D., University of Cambridge, U.K.
Coren Sharples, Visiting Assistant Professor; M.Arch., Columbia.
Hazel Siegel, Visiting Assistant Professor; M.F.A., CUNY, Hunter.
Andrew Simons, Visiting Assistant Professor; B.F.A., Carnegie Mellon.
Darius Somers, Visiting Assistant Professor; M.S., Columbia.
Suzanne Song, Visiting Assistant Professor; M.S.A.A.D., GSAPP, Columbia.
Sarah Strauss, Visiting Associate Professor; M.Arch., Yale.
Keena Suh, Associate Professor; M.Arch., Columbia.
Karin Tehve, Associate Professor; M.Arch., Harvard.
Jack Travis, Adjunct Professor; M.Arch., Illinois at Urbana–Champaign.
Loukia Tsafoulia, Visiting Assistant Professor; M.S.A.A.D., Columbia.
Kathryn van Voorhees, Visiting Assistant Professor; architectural designer and educator.
Kevin Walz, Visiting Associate Professor; Pratt.
William Watson, Visiting Assistant Professor; M.Arch., Texas at Austin.
Henry Weintraub, Visiting Assistant Professor; M.A., Bard.
Alexandra Winton, Visiting Associate Professor; M.A., Bard.
Piotr Woronkowicz, Visiting Instructor; B.S., Art Center College of Design.
Edwin Zawadzki, Visiting Assistant Professor; M.Arch., Yale.
Michael Zuckerman, Adjunct Professor; B.Arch., CUNY, City College; RA, LEED, AP.

© 2017 Bob Handelman

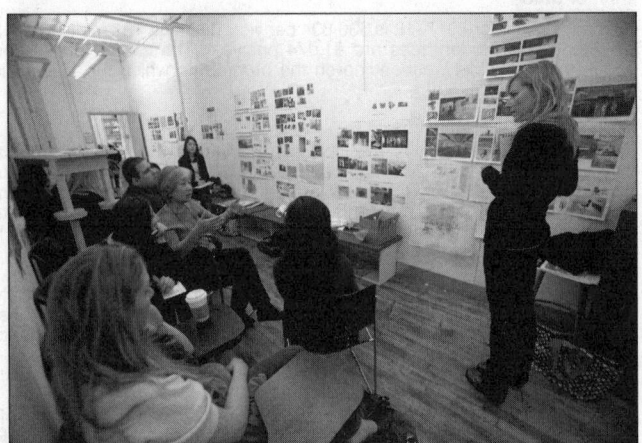

© 2017 Bob Handelman

# Section 2
# Architecture

This section contains a directory of institutions offering graduate work in architecture, followed by in-depth entries submitted by institutions that chose to prepare detailed program descriptions. Additional information about programs listed in the directory but not augmented by an in-depth entry may be obtained by writing directly to the dean of a graduate school or chair of a department at the address given in the directory.

For programs offering related work, see also in this book *Applied Arts and Design, Art and Art History,* and *Public, Regional, and Industrial Affairs.* In another guide in this series:

**Graduate Programs in Engineering & Applied Sciences**
See *Civil and Environmental Engineering*

## CONTENTS

# Architectural History

**Arizona State University at the Tempe campus,** Herberger Institute for Design and the Arts, The Design School, PhD Program in Design, Environment and the Arts, Tempe, AZ 85287-2105. Offers design (PhD); digital culture (PhD); healthcare and healing environments (PhD); history, theory, and criticism (PhD). *Degree requirements:* For doctorate, comprehensive exam, thesis/dissertation, interactive Program of Study (iPOS) submitted before completing 50 percent of required credit hours. *Entrance requirements:* For doctorate, GRE, master's degree in architecture, graphic design, industrial design, interior design, landscape architecture, or art history or equivalent standing; statement of purpose; 3 letters of recommendation; indication of potential faculty mentor; sample of written work. Additional exam requirements/recommendations for international students: Required—TOEFL, IELTS, or PTE. Electronic applications accepted. *Expenses:* Contact institution.

**Cornell University,** Graduate School, Graduate Fields of Architecture, Art and Planning, Field of Architecture, Ithaca, NY 14853. Offers architectural design (M Arch); architectural science (MS); computer graphics (MS); history of architecture (MA, PhD); history of urban development (MA, PhD); theory and criticism of architecture (M Arch); urban design (M Arch). *Degree requirements:* For master's, one foreign language, thesis (MA, MS); for doctorate, 2 foreign languages, comprehensive exam, thesis/dissertation. *Entrance requirements:* For master's, GRE General Test, 5-year bachelor's degree in architecture, portfolio (M Arch), 3 letters of recommendation; for doctorate, GRE General Test, 3 letters of recommendation. Additional exam requirements/recommendations for international students: Required—TOEFL (minimum score 600 paper-based, 77 iBT). Electronic applications accepted. *Faculty research:* Architectural design and urban design, theory and criticism of architecture, computer graphics, building technology and environmental science, history of architecture and history of urban-development.

**The Graduate Center, City University of New York,** Graduate Studies, Program in Art History, New York, NY 10016-4039. Offers architecture (PhD); graphic arts (PhD); painting (PhD); photography (PhD); sculpture (PhD). *Degree requirements:* For doctorate, 2 foreign languages, thesis/dissertation. *Entrance requirements:* For doctorate, GRE General Test. Additional exam requirements/recommendations for international students: Required—TOEFL. Electronic applications accepted.

**Harvard University,** Graduate School of Arts and Sciences, Department of History of Art and Architecture, Cambridge, MA 02138. Offers ancient art (PhD); ancient Near Eastern art (PhD); Baroque art (PhD); Byzantine art (PhD); classical art (PhD); Indian art (PhD); Islamic art (PhD); Japanese and Chinese art (PhD); medieval art (PhD); modern art (PhD); Renaissance and modern architecture (PhD); Renaissance art (PhD). *Degree requirements:* For doctorate, variable foreign language requirement, thesis/dissertation, general exams; reading exams in French, German, and Italian. *Entrance requirements:* For doctorate, GRE General Test. Additional exam requirements/recommendations for international students: Required—TOEFL.

**Massachusetts Institute of Technology,** School of Architecture and Planning, Department of Architecture, Cambridge, MA 02139. Offers architecture (M Arch, PhD), including building technology (PhD); design and computation (PhD); history and theory of architecture (PhD); history and theory of art (PhD); architecture studies (SM Arch S); art, culture and technology (SMACT); building technology (SMBT). *Faculty:* 36 full-time (13 women). *Students:* 224 full-time (106 women); includes 46 minority (5 Black or African American, non-Hispanic/Latino; 11 Asian, non-Hispanic/Latino; 22 Hispanic/Latino; 8 Two or more races, non-Hispanic/Latino), 113 international. Average age 28. 1,165 applicants, 12% accepted, 82 enrolled. In 2016, 58 master's, 10 doctorates awarded. *Degree requirements:* For master's, thesis; for doctorate, comprehensive exam, thesis/dissertation. *Entrance requirements:* For master's and doctorate, GRE General Test. Additional exam requirements/recommendations for international students: Required—TOEFL, IELTS. *Application deadline:* For fall admission, 12/31 for domestic and international students. Application fee: $75. Electronic applications accepted. *Expenses: Tuition:* Full-time $46,400; part-time $725 per credit. One-time fee: $312 full-time. Full-time tuition and fees vary according to course load and program. *Financial support:* In 2016–17, 189 students received support, including 128 fellowships (averaging $23,600 per year), 31 research assistantships (averaging $33,200 per year), 34 teaching assistantships (averaging $34,700 per year); Federal Work-Study, institutionally sponsored loans, scholarships/grants, traineeships, health care benefits, unspecified assistantships, and resident tutors also available. Support available to part-time students. Financial award application deadline: 5/1; financial award applicants required to submit FAFSA. *Faculty research:* Architecture; urbanism; building technology and sustainability; computation and design; history, theory, and criticism; art, culture, and technology. *Total annual research expenditures:* $3.5 million. *Unit head:* Prof. J. Meejin Yoon, Department Head, 617-253-7791, E-mail: arch@mit.edu. *Application contact:* 617-715-4490. Website: http://architecture.mit.edu/

**New York University,** Graduate School of Arts and Science, Program in Historical and Sustainable Architecture, New York, NY 10012-1019. Offers MA. *Entrance requirements:* For master's, GRE, writing sample.

**Roger Williams University,** School of Architecture, Art and Historic Preservation, Bristol, RI 02809. Offers architecture (M Arch); art and architectural history (MA); historical preservation (MS). *Faculty:* 15 full-time (4 women), 4 part-time/adjunct (2 women). *Students:* 100 full-time (43 women), 1 part-time (0 women); includes 14 minority (3 Black or African American, non-Hispanic/Latino; 1 Asian, non-Hispanic/Latino; 6 Hispanic/Latino; 4 Two or more races, non-Hispanic/Latino), 4 international. Average age 25. 77 applicants, 95% accepted, 48 enrolled. In 2016, 43 master's awarded. *Degree requirements:* For master's, thesis. *Entrance requirements:* For master's, portfolio, 2 letters of recommendation, college transcript, letter of intent. Additional exam requirements/recommendations for international students: Required—TOEFL (minimum score 85 iBT), IELTS (minimum score 6.5). *Application deadline:* For fall admission, 4/1 for domestic students; for spring admission, 1/1 for domestic students. Application fee: $50. Electronic applications accepted. Application fee is waived when completed online. *Expenses:* $1,408 per credit hour (for M Arch); $843 per credit hour (for MS and MA). *Financial support:* In 2016–17, 95 students received support, including 91 research assistantships (averaging $2,753 per year); scholarships/grants and unspecified assistantships also available. Financial award application deadline: 4/1; financial award applicants required to submit FAFSA. *Unit head:* Stephen White, Dean, 401-254-3607, E-mail: swhite@rwu.edu. *Application contact:* Marcus Hanscom, Director of Graduate Admissions, 401-254-6200, Fax: 401-254-3345, E-mail: gradadmit@rwu.edu.
Website: http://www.rwu.edu/academics/departments/architecture.htm#dual

**Savannah College of Art and Design,** Graduate School, Program in Architectural History, Savannah, GA 31402-3146. Offers MFA. *Program availability:* Part-time. *Faculty:* 8 full-time (1 woman). *Students:* 1 (woman) full-time, 2 part-time (both women). Average age 26. 3 applicants, 33% accepted, 1 enrolled. In 2016, 3 master's awarded. *Degree requirements:* For master's, thesis. *Entrance requirements:* For master's, GRE (recommended), portfolio (submitted in digital format), audition or writing submission, resume, statement of purpose, two letters of recommendation. Additional exam requirements/recommendations for international students: Required—TOEFL (minimum score 550 paper-based, 85 iBT), IELTS (minimum score 6.5), or ACTFL. *Application deadline:* For fall admission, 4/1 for domestic and international students. Applications are processed on a rolling basis. Application fee: $40. Electronic applications accepted. *Expenses: Tuition:* Full-time $36,045. Tuition and fees vary according to course load. *Financial support:* Career-related internships or fieldwork, Federal Work-Study, and scholarships/grants available. Financial award application deadline: 4/1; financial award applicants required to submit FAFSA. *Unit head:* Dr. Robin Williams, Chair, Architectural History. *Application contact:* Jenny Jaquillard, Executive Director of Admissions, Recruitment and Events, 912-525-5100, Fax: 912-525-5985, E-mail: admission@scad.edu.
Website: http://www.scad.edu/academics/programs/architectural-history

**University of California, Berkeley,** Graduate Division, College of Environmental Design, Department of Architecture, Berkeley, CA 94720-1500. Offers architecture (M Arch); building science (MS, PhD); building structures, construction and materials (MS, PhD); design theories, methods, and practices (MS, PhD); environmental design in developing countries (MS, PhD); history of architecture and urbanism (MS, PhD); social and cultural processes in architecture and urbanism (MS, PhD); M Arch/MCP; M Arch/MS; MLA/M Arch. *Students:* 178 full-time (84 women); includes 34 minority (4 Black or African American, non-Hispanic/Latino; 1 American Indian or Alaska Native, non-Hispanic/Latino; 13 Asian, non-Hispanic/Latino; 16 Hispanic/Latino), 85 international. Average age 30. 1,047 applicants, 68 enrolled. In 2016, 42 master's, 7 doctorates awarded. *Degree requirements:* For master's, thesis; for doctorate, thesis/dissertation, qualifying exam. *Entrance requirements:* For master's and doctorate, GRE General Test, minimum GPA of 3.0, 3 letters of recommendation. Additional exam requirements/recommendations for international students: Required—TOEFL (minimum score 570 paper-based; 90 iBT). *Application deadline:* For fall admission, 12/7 for domestic students. Application fee: $105 ($125 for international students). Electronic applications accepted. Application fee is waived when completed online. *Financial support:* Fellowships, research assistantships, teaching assistantships, career-related internships or fieldwork, institutionally sponsored loans, health care benefits, and unspecified assistantships available. *Unit head:* Prof. Tom Buresh, Chair, 510-642-4942. *Application contact:* Lois H. Ito Koch, Student Affairs Officer, 510-642-5577, Fax: 510-643-5607, E-mail: archgrad@berkeley.edu. Website: http://arch.ced.berkeley.edu/

**University of Colorado Denver,** College of Architecture and Planning, Program in Design and Planning, Denver, CO 80217. Offers history of architecture, landscape and urbanism (PhD); sustainable and healthy environments (PhD). *Program availability:* Part-time. *Faculty:* 8 full-time (3 women), 9 part-time/adjunct (1 woman). *Students:* 6 full-time (2 women), 9 part-time (6 women); includes 1 minority (Hispanic/Latino), 5 international. Average age 35. 21 applicants, 14% accepted, 3 enrolled. In 2016, 3 doctorates awarded. *Degree requirements:* For doctorate, comprehensive exam, thesis/dissertation. *Entrance requirements:* For doctorate, GRE (minimum score of 158 for both verbal and quantitative; writing 4.0), minimum undergraduate GPA of 3.0, graduate 3.5; writing sample; three letters of recommendation; statement of personal and professional goals. Additional exam requirements/recommendations for international students: Required—TOEFL (minimum score 80 iBT); Recommended—IELTS (minimum score 6.8). *Application deadline:* For fall admission, 2/2 for domestic students, 1/2 for international students; for spring admission, 10/1 for domestic students. Application fee: $50 ($75 for international students). Electronic applications accepted. *Expenses:* Contact institution. *Financial support:* In 2016–17, 6 students received support. Fellowships, research assistantships, teaching assistantships, Federal Work-Study, institutionally sponsored loans, scholarships/grants, traineeships, and unspecified assistantships available. Financial award application deadline: 4/1; financial award applicants required to submit FAFSA. *Faculty research:* Land use and environmental planning and design; design and planning processes and practices; history, theory, and criticism of the built environment. *Unit head:* Dr. Osman Attmann, Director, 303-315-0032, E-mail: o.attmann@ucdenver.edu. *Application contact:* Rachael Kuroiwa, Manager of Admissions and Outreach, 303-315-2325, E-mail: rachael.kuroiwa@ucdenver.edu. Website: http://www.ucdenver.edu/academics/colleges/ArchitecturePlanning/Academics/DegreePrograms/PhD/Pages/PhD.aspx

**University of Pittsburgh,** Dietrich School of Arts and Sciences, Department of History of Art and Architecture, Pittsburgh, PA 15260. Offers MA, PhD. *Faculty:* 13 full-time (6 women). *Students:* 31 full-time (27 women); includes 6 minority (3 Hispanic/Latino; 1 Native Hawaiian or other Pacific Islander, non-Hispanic/Latino; 3 Two or more races, non-Hispanic/Latino), 6 international. Average age 32. 50 applicants, 20% accepted, 4 enrolled. In 2016, 2 master's, 5 doctorates awarded. *Degree requirements:* For master's, one foreign language, thesis or alternative, paper; for doctorate, 2 foreign languages, comprehensive exam, thesis/dissertation, teaching portfolio. *Entrance requirements:* For master's and doctorate, GRE General Test, 3 letters of recommendation, writing sample, personal statement, transcripts, foreign language questionnaire. Additional exam requirements/recommendations for international students: Required—TOEFL (minimum score 550 paper-based; 90 iBT). *Application deadline:* For fall admission, 12/15 for domestic and international students. Application fee: $50. Electronic applications accepted. *Expenses:* $21,748 per year, in-state, full-time; $35,904 per year, out-of-state, full-time. *Financial support:* In 2016–17, 28 students received support, including 9 fellowships with full tuition reimbursements available (averaging $21,692 per year), 7 research assistantships with full tuition reimbursements available (averaging $17,905 per year), 6 teaching assistantships with full tuition reimbursements available (averaging $17,905 per year); career-related internships or fieldwork, Federal Work-Study, scholarships/grants, health care benefits, tuition waivers (partial), and unspecified assistantships also available. Financial award application deadline: 12/15. *Faculty research:* Medieval European art and architecture, modern architecture, modern and contemporary art, history of photography, Japanese art history, 20th century German art, contemporary Chinese art, art of the United States, ancient Roman art. *Unit head:* Dr. Barbara McCloskey, Chair, 412-648-2417, Fax: 412-648-2792, E-mail: barbara.mccloskey@pitt.edu. *Application contact:* Corrin Trombley, Graduate Administrator, 412-648-2400, Fax: 412-648-2792, E-mail: cot12@pitt.edu. Website: http://www.haa.pitt.edu

**The University of Texas at Austin,** Graduate School, School of Architecture, Program in Architectural History, Austin, TX 78712-1111. Offers MA, PhD. *Degree requirements:* For doctorate, thesis/dissertation.

**University of Virginia,** School of Architecture, Department of Architectural History, Charlottesville, VA 22903. Offers M Arch H, PhD. *Faculty:* 6 full-time (2 women). *Students:* 14 full-time (7 women), 1 (woman) part-time, 1 international. Average age 27.

19 applicants, 89% accepted, 7 enrolled. In 2016, 11 master's awarded. *Degree requirements:* For master's, one foreign language, thesis. *Entrance requirements:* For master's, GRE General Test, 3 letters of recommendation. Additional exam requirements/recommendations for international students: Required—TOEFL (minimum score 600 paper-based; 90 iBT). *Application deadline:* For fall admission, 1/5 for domestic and international students. Applications are processed on a rolling basis. Application fee: $60. Electronic applications accepted. *Expenses:* Tuition, state resident: full-time $15,026; part-time $834 per credit hour. Tuition, nonresident: full-time $25,168; part-time $1378 per credit hour. *Required fees:* $2654. *Financial support:* Career-related internships or fieldwork, Federal Work-Study, and institutionally sponsored loans available. Financial award applicants required to submit FAFSA. *Faculty research:* Urban form, nineteenth- and twentieth-century American architecture. *Unit head:* Lisa Reilly, Chair, 434-924-1316, Fax: 434-982-2678, E-mail: lar2f@virginia.edu. *Application contact:* Kristine Nelson, Director of Admissions and Financial Aid, 434-924-6442, Fax: 434-982-2678, E-mail: arch-admissions@virginia.edu. Website: http://www.arch.virginia.edu/academics/disciplines/history

# Architecture

**Academy of Art University,** Graduate Programs, School of Architecture, San Francisco, CA 94105-3410. Offers advanced architectural design (MA); architecture (M Arch). *Program availability:* Part-time, 100% online. *Faculty:* 8 full-time (3 women), 32 part-time/adjunct (6 women). *Students:* 115 full-time (45 women), 81 part-time (32 women); includes 40 minority (9 Black or African American, non-Hispanic/Latino; 9 Asian, non-Hispanic/Latino; 22 Hispanic/Latino), 65 international. Average age 34. 109 applicants, 100% accepted, 44 enrolled. In 2016, 41 master's awarded. *Degree requirements:* For master's, final review. *Entrance requirements:* For master's, statement of intent; resume; portfolio/reel; official college transcripts. *Application deadline:* Applications are processed on a rolling basis. Application fee: $50. Electronic applications accepted. *Expenses:* Tuition: Part-time $982 per unit. *Financial support:* Career-related internships or fieldwork, Federal Work-Study, and scholarships/grants available. Financial award application deadline: 8/10; financial award applicants required to submit FAFSA. *Unit head:* 800-544-ARTS, E-mail: info@academyart.edu. *Application contact:* 800-544-ARTS, E-mail: info@academyart.edu. Website: http://www.academyart.edu/architecture-school/index.html

**Andrews University,** School of Graduate Studies, School of Architecture, Art and Design, Berrien Springs, MI 49104. Offers M Arch. *Faculty:* 9 full-time (3 women), 1 (woman) part-time/adjunct. *Students:* 11 full-time (5 women), 2 part-time (both women); includes 8 minority (1 Black or African American, non-Hispanic/Latino; 1 Asian, non-Hispanic/Latino; 5 Hispanic/Latino; 1 Native Hawaiian or other Pacific Islander, non-Hispanic/Latino), 2 international. Average age 30. In 2016, 12 master's awarded. *Entrance requirements:* For master's, GRE. Additional exam requirements/recommendations for international students: Required—TOEFL (minimum score 550 paper-based). *Application deadline:* Applications are processed on a rolling basis. Application fee: $40. Electronic applications accepted. *Faculty research:* Irish archaeology, place making, town planning, Waldensian architecture, international community development. *Unit head:* Carey Carscallen, Dean, 269-471-6003. *Application contact:* Justina Clayburn, Supervisor of Graduate Admission, 800-253-2874, Fax: 269-471-6321, E-mail: graduate@andrews.edu.

**Arizona State University at the Tempe campus,** Herberger Institute for Design and the Arts, The Design School, Tempe, AZ 85287-1605. Offers architecture (M Arch); building design/built environment (MS); design (MSD), including arts, media, and engineering, healthcare and healing environments (MSD, PhD), industrial design, interaction design, interior design, new product innovation, visual communication design; design, environment and the arts (PhD), including design, digital culture, healthcare and healing environments (MSD, PhD), history, theory, and criticism; landscape architecture (MLA); urban design (MUD); MA/MBA. *Accreditation:* NASAD. Terminal master's awarded for partial completion of doctoral program. *Degree requirements:* For master's, thesis optional, interactive Program of Study (iPOS) submitted before completing 50 percent of required credit hours; for doctorate, comprehensive exam, thesis/dissertation, interactive Program of Study (iPOS) submitted before completing 50 percent of required credit hours. *Entrance requirements:* For master's, GRE General Test, minimum GPA of 3.0 or equivalent in last 2 years of work leading to bachelor's degree, design/creative works portfolio, 3 references, statement of intent; for doctorate, GRE, master's degree in architecture, graphic design, industrial design, interior design, landscape architecture, or art history or equivalent standing; statement of purpose; 3 letters of recommendation; indication of potential faculty mentor; sample of written work. Additional exam requirements/recommendations for international students: Required—TOEFL (minimum score 600 paper-based; 100 iBT). Electronic applications accepted.

**Athabasca University,** Faculty of Science and Technology, Athabasca, AB T9S 3A3, Canada. Offers architecture (Postgraduate Diploma); information systems (M Sc). *Program availability:* Part-time, online learning. *Degree requirements:* For master's, thesis optional. *Entrance requirements:* For master's, B Sc in computing or other bachelor's degree and IT experience. Electronic applications accepted. *Expenses:* Contact institution. *Faculty research:* Distributed systems multimedia, computer science education, e-services.

**Auburn University,** Graduate School, College of Architecture, Design, and Construction, Auburn University, AL 36849. Offers MBC, MCP, MID, MIDC, ML Arch, MPA/MCP. *Program availability:* Part-time. *Faculty:* 62 full-time (14 women), 7 part-time/adjunct (1 woman). *Students:* 79 full-time (36 women), 68 part-time (21 women); includes 27 minority (12 Black or African American, non-Hispanic/Latino; 4 Asian, non-Hispanic/Latino; 8 Hispanic/Latino; 1 Native Hawaiian or other Pacific Islander, non-Hispanic/Latino; 2 Two or more races, non-Hispanic/Latino), 41 international. Average age 31. 223 applicants, 71% accepted, 66 enrolled. In 2016, 73 master's awarded. *Entrance requirements:* For master's, GRE General Test. *Application deadline:* Applications are processed on a rolling basis. Application fee: $50 ($60 for international students). Electronic applications accepted. *Expenses:* Contact institution. *Financial support:* Fellowships and Federal Work-Study available. Support available to part-time students. Financial award application deadline: 3/15; financial award applicants required to submit FAFSA. *Unit head:* Dr. Vini Nathan, Dean/Chair, 334-844-4285. *Application contact:* Dr. George Flowers, Dean of the Graduate School, 334-844-2125. Website: http://www.cadc.auburn.edu/

**Ball State University,** Graduate School, College of Architecture and Planning, Department of Architecture, Program in Architecture, Muncie, IN 47306. Offers architecture (M Arch, M Arch II). *Program availability:* Part-time. *Degree requirements:* For master's, thesis. *Entrance requirements:* For master's, GRE (if cumulative baccalaureate GPA is below 3.0), minimum baccalaureate GPA of 2.75 or 3.0 in latter half of baccalaureate, resume, statement of purpose, portfolio, three letters of reference. Additional exam requirements/recommendations for international students: Required—TOEFL (minimum score 550 paper-based; 79 iBT), IELTS (minimum score 6.5). Electronic applications accepted. *Expenses:* Contact institution.

**Boston Architectural College,** Graduate Programs, Boston, MA 02115-2795. Offers architecture (M Arch); historic preservation (MDS); interior design (MID); landscape architecture (MLA); sustainable design (MDS). *Accreditation:* CIDA. *Degree requirements:* For master's, thesis. *Entrance requirements:* For master's, portfolio (recommended). Electronic applications accepted.

**California Baptist University,** Program in Architecture, Riverside, CA 92504-3206. Offers M Arch. *Faculty:* 8 full-time (3 women), 5 part-time/adjunct (2 women). *Students:* 73 full-time (28 women), 2 part-time (1 woman); includes 46 minority (8 Black or African American, non-Hispanic/Latino; 1 American Indian or Alaska Native, non-Hispanic/Latino; 4 Asian, non-Hispanic/Latino; 31 Hispanic/Latino; 1 Native Hawaiian or other Pacific Islander, non-Hispanic/Latino; 1 Two or more races, non-Hispanic/Latino), 3 international. Average age 21. *Degree requirements:* For master's, thesis, internship, professional practice, minimum cumulative GPA of 2.75 by the end of the first semester of the third year, progress review after the fifth full-time semester in the program. *Entrance requirements:* Additional exam requirements/recommendations for international students: Required—TOEFL (minimum score 80 iBT). *Application deadline:* For fall admission, 8/1 priority date for domestic students, 7/1 for international students; for spring admission, 12/1 priority date for domestic students, 11/1 for international students. Applications are processed on a rolling basis. Application fee: $45. Electronic applications accepted. *Expenses:* Contact institution. *Financial support:* Federal Work-Study and scholarships/grants available. Financial award applicants required to submit CSS PROFILE or FAFSA. *Faculty research:* Architectural design, urbanism, interdisciplinary design thought, psychology of human interaction to the built environment, aesthetic perception. *Unit head:* Mark Roberson, Dean, College of Architecture, Visual Arts and Design, 951-552-8652, E-mail: maroberson@calbaptist.edu. Website: http://cbucavad.com/architecture/

**California College of the Arts,** Graduate Programs, Master of Architecture Program, San Francisco, CA 94107. Offers advanced architecture design (MAAD); architecture (M Arch). *Faculty:* 5 full-time (2 women), 11 part-time/adjunct (5 women). *Students:* 59 full-time (29 women); includes 19 minority (2 Black or African American, non-Hispanic/Latino; 1 American Indian or Alaska Native, non-Hispanic/Latino; 8 Asian, non-Hispanic/Latino; 8 Hispanic/Latino), 20 international. Average age 28. In 2016, 21 master's awarded. *Degree requirements:* For master's, thesis. *Entrance requirements:* For master's, appropriate bachelor's degree, portfolio, resume, minimum 2 letters of recommendation, essay, transcripts. Additional exam requirements/recommendations for international students: Required—TOEFL, IELTS, or PTE. *Application deadline:* For fall admission, 1/10 for domestic and international students. Applications are processed on a rolling basis. Application fee: $70. Electronic applications accepted. *Expenses:* $1,641 per unit, $49,230 per year tuition; $490 fees. *Financial support:* In 2016–17, fellowships (averaging $22,000 per year), teaching assistantships (averaging $2,000 per year) were awarded; career-related internships or fieldwork, Federal Work-Study, scholarships/grants, and health care benefits also available. Financial award application deadline: 7/31; financial award applicants required to submit FAFSA. *Unit head:* Nataly Gattegno, Chair, 415-703-9516, E-mail: ngattegno@cca.edu. *Application contact:* Wes Fanelli, Assistant Director of Graduate Admissions, 415-703-9533, Fax: 415-703-9539, E-mail: wfanelli@cca.edu.

**California Polytechnic State University, San Luis Obispo,** College of Architecture and Environmental Design, Department of Architecture, San Luis Obispo, CA 93407. Offers MS. *Program availability:* Part-time. *Faculty:* 6 full-time (2 women), 1 part-time/adjunct (0 women). *Students:* 11 full-time (4 women), 5 part-time (4 women); includes 2 minority (both Hispanic/Latino), 3 international. Average age 24. 22 applicants, 23% accepted, 2 enrolled. In 2016, 10 master's awarded. *Degree requirements:* For master's, thesis. *Application deadline:* For fall admission, 4/1 for domestic and international students; for winter admission, 11/1 for domestic students, 6/30 for international students. Applications are processed on a rolling basis. Application fee: $55. Electronic applications accepted. *Expenses:* Tuition, state resident: full-time $6738; part-time $3906 per year. Tuition, nonresident: full-time $15,666; part-time $8370 per year. *Required fees:* $3603; $3141 per unit. $1047 per term. *Financial support:* Fellowships, research assistantships, teaching assistantships, and institutionally sponsored loans available. Financial award application deadline: 3/2; financial award applicants required to submit FAFSA. *Faculty research:* Computer-assisted design, decision support systems, building science, facilities management. *Unit head:* Thomas Fowler, Graduate Coordinator, 805-756-2981, E-mail: tfowler@calpoly.edu. Website: http://www.architecture.calpoly.edu/

**California State Polytechnic University, Pomona,** Program in Architecture, Pomona, CA 91768-2557. Offers M Arch. *Program availability:* Part-time, evening/weekend. *Students:* 43 full-time (21 women), 2 part-time (1 woman); includes 23 minority (7 Asian, non-Hispanic/Latino; 16 Hispanic/Latino), 8 international. Average age 28. 19 applicants, 100% accepted, 18 enrolled. In 2016, 24 master's awarded. *Entrance requirements:* Additional exam requirements/recommendations for international students: Required—TOEFL. *Application deadline:* Applications are processed on a rolling basis. Application fee: $55. Electronic applications accepted. *Expenses:* Contact institution. *Financial support:* Application deadline: 3/2; applicants required to submit FAFSA. *Unit head:* Dr. Weimin Li, Graduate Coordinator, 909-869-2715, Fax: 909-869-2580, E-mail: wli@cpp.edu. *Application contact:* Andrew M. Wright, Director of Admissions, 909-869-3130, Fax: 909-869-4529, E-mail: awright@cpp.edu. Website: https://env.cpp.edu/la/degree/master-landscape-architecture

**Carleton University,** Faculty of Graduate Studies, Faculty of Engineering and Design, School of Architecture, Ottawa, ON K1S 5B6, Canada. Offers design studies (M Arch). *Degree requirements:* For master's, thesis. *Entrance requirements:* For master's, honors degree. Additional exam requirements/recommendations for international students: Required—TOEFL. *Faculty research:* Theoretical issues in architecture and culture, cultural diversity, architecture and technoscientific culture.

## Architecture

**Carnegie Mellon University,** College of Fine Arts, School of Architecture, Pittsburgh, PA 15213-3891. Offers architecture (MSA); architecture, engineering, and construction management (PhD); building performance and diagnostics (MS, PhD); computational design (MS, PhD); engineering construction management (MSA); tangible interaction design (MTID); urban design (MUD). Terminal master's awarded for partial completion of doctoral program. *Degree requirements:* For doctorate, thesis/dissertation. *Entrance requirements:* For master's and doctorate, GRE General Test. Additional exam requirements/recommendations for international students: Required—TOEFL.

**The Catholic University of America,** School of Architecture and Planning, Washington, DC 20064. Offers architecture and planning (M Arch, MS Arch St); city and regional planning (M Arch); facilities management (MS Arch); regional development (Certificate); sustainable design (M Arch, Certificate). *Program availability:* Part-time. *Faculty:* 20 full-time (7 women), 15 part-time/adjunct (1 woman). *Students:* 69 full-time (28 women), 21 part-time (13 women); includes 35 minority (11 Black or African American, non-Hispanic/Latino; 5 Asian, non-Hispanic/Latino; 11 Hispanic/Latino; 8 Two or more races, non-Hispanic/Latino), 13 international. Average age 28. 73 applicants, 84% accepted, 24 enrolled. In 2016, 42 master's awarded. *Degree requirements:* For master's, thesis. *Entrance requirements:* For master's, GRE (minimum score: 1000), minimum GPA of 2.8, portfolio, statement of purpose, official copies of academic transcripts, three letters of recommendation. Additional exam requirements/recommendations for international students: Required—TOEFL (minimum score 550 paper-based; 80 iBT). *Application deadline:* For fall admission, 1/15 priority date for domestic students, 7/1 for international students; for spring admission, 10/15 priority date for domestic students, 11/1 for international students. Applications are processed on a rolling basis. Application fee: $55. Electronic applications accepted. *Expenses:* $43,380 per year; $1,170 per credit; $200 per semester part-time fees. *Financial support:* Fellowships, research assistantships, teaching assistantships, Federal Work-Study, scholarships/grants, tuition waivers (full and partial), and unspecified assistantships available. Financial award application deadline: 2/1; financial award applicants required to submit FAFSA. *Faculty research:* Architectural history, cultural studies/sacred space, design technologies, digital media, real estate development, urban design. *Total annual research expenditures:* $93,903. *Unit head:* Randall Ott, Dean, 202-319-5784, Fax: 202-319-2023, E-mail: ott@cua.edu. *Application contact:* Director of Graduate Admissions, 202-319-5057, Fax: 202-319-6533, E-mail: cua-admissions@cua.edu.
Website: http://architecture.cua.edu/

**City College of the City University of New York,** Graduate School, The Bernard and Anne Spitzer School of Architecture, Program in Architecture, New York, NY 10031-9198. Offers M Arch. *Entrance requirements:* For master's, GRE. Additional exam requirements/recommendations for international students: Required—TOEFL (minimum score 550 paper-based). Tuition and fees vary according to course load, degree level and program.

**Clemson University,** Graduate School, College of Architecture, Arts, and Humanities, School of Architecture, Clemson, SC 29634. Offers architecture (M Arch, MS, Certificate, including animated architecture (MS); architectural and urban history, theory and criticism (MS); community build (Certificate), community research and design (MS), health (M Arch, MS). *Faculty:* 28 full-time (7 women), 8 part-time/adjunct (4 women). *Students:* 102 full-time (54 women), 2 part-time (1 woman); includes 9 minority (2 Black or African American, non-Hispanic/Latino; 3 Asian, non-Hispanic/Latino; 3 Hispanic/Latino; 1 Two or more races, non-Hispanic/Latino), 30 international. Average age 25. 269 applicants, 35% accepted, 43 enrolled. In 2016, 38 master's, 11 other advanced degrees awarded. *Degree requirements:* For master's, thesis (for some programs). *Entrance requirements:* For master's, GRE General Test, design portfolio, unofficial transcripts, letters of recommendation, personal statement. Additional exam requirements/recommendations for international students: Required—TOEFL (minimum score 80 iBT); Recommended—IELTS (minimum score 6.5). *Application deadline:* For fall admission, 1/15 for domestic and international students. Applications are processed on a rolling basis. Application fee: $80 ($90 for international students). Electronic applications accepted. *Expenses:* $5,617 per semester full-time resident, $11,194 per semester full-time non-resident, $697 per credit hour part-time resident, $1,392 per credit hour part-time non-resident. *Financial support:* In 2016–17, 104 students received support, including 59 fellowships with partial tuition reimbursements available (averaging $1,256 per year), 20 research assistantships with partial tuition reimbursements available (averaging $4,200 per year); career-related internships or fieldwork and unspecified assistantships also available. Financial award application deadline: 1/15. *Faculty research:* Architecture and health, sustainable design, community design-build, architectural robotics, digital fabrication. *Total annual research expenditures:* $89,088. *Unit head:* Kate Schwennsen, Director, 864-656-3895, E-mail: kschwen@clemson.edu. *Application contact:* Dr. Peter Laurence, Graduate Director, 864-656-1499, E-mail: plauren@clemson.edu.
Website: https://www.clemson.edu/caah/departments/architecture/index.html

**Columbia University,** Graduate School of Architecture, Planning, and Preservation, Program in Advanced Architectural Design, New York, NY 10027. Offers MS. *Entrance requirements:* For master's, GRE General Test.

**Columbia University,** Graduate School of Architecture, Planning, and Preservation, Program in Architecture, New York, NY 10027. Offers M Arch, PhD, M Arch/MS. PhD offered through the Graduate School of Arts and Science. *Degree requirements:* For master's, thesis optional. *Entrance requirements:* For master's, GRE General Test.

**Cooper Union for the Advancement of Science and Art,** Irwin S. Chanin School of Architecture, New York, NY 10003. Offers M Arch II. *Faculty:* 14 full-time (4 women), 19 part-time/adjunct (6 women). *Students:* 13 full-time (9 women), 10 international. Average age 26. 66 applicants, 29% accepted, 14 enrolled. In 2016, 6 master's awarded. *Degree requirements:* For master's, thesis. *Entrance requirements:* For master's, GRE, official transcripts from all colleges and universities from which applicant received credit; three recommendation letters; resumé/curriculum vitae; written essay. Additional exam requirements/recommendations for international students: Required—TOEFL (minimum score 600 paper-based; 100 iBT). *Application deadline:* For fall admission, 1/31 for domestic and international students. Application fee: $75. Electronic applications accepted. *Expenses:* Contact institution. *Financial support:* In 2016–17, 14 students received support. Tuition waivers (partial) and tuition scholarships offered to exceptional students available. Financial award application deadline: 5/1; financial award applicants required to submit FAFSA. *Unit head:* Nader Tehrani, Dean, 212-353-4220, E-mail: ntehrani@cooper.edu. *Application contact:* Chabeli Lajara, Administrative Assistant, 212-353-4120, E-mail: admissions@cooper.edu.
Website: http://cooper.edu/architecture

**Cornell University,** Graduate School, Graduate Fields of Architecture, Art and Planning, Field of Architecture, Ithaca, NY 14853. Offers architectural design (M Arch); architectural science (MS); computer graphics (MS); history of architecture (MA, PhD); history of urban development (MA, PhD); theory and criticism of architecture (M Arch); urban design (M Arch). *Degree requirements:* For master's, one foreign language, thesis (MA, MS); for doctorate, 2 foreign languages, comprehensive exam, thesis/dissertation. *Entrance requirements:* For master's, GRE General Test, 5-year bachelor's degree in

architecture, portfolio (M Arch), 3 letters of recommendation; for doctorate, GRE General Test, 3 letters of recommendation. Additional exam requirements/recommendations for international students: Required—TOEFL (minimum score 600 paper-based; 77 iBT). Electronic applications accepted. *Faculty research:* Architectural design and urban design, theory and criticism of architecture, computer graphics, building technology and environmental science, history of architecture and history of urban-development.

**Cranbrook Academy of Art,** Graduate School, Program in Architecture, Bloomfield Hills, MI 48303-0801. Offers M Arch. *Degree requirements:* For master's, thesis, exhibit. *Entrance requirements:* Additional exam requirements/recommendations for international students: Required—TOEFL (minimum score 85 iBT). *Application deadline:* For fall admission, 2/1 priority date for domestic and international students. Application fee: $85. Electronic applications accepted. *Expenses: Tuition, area resident:* Full-time $37,375. *Required fees:* $1460. *Financial support:* Federal Work-Study and scholarships/grants available. Financial award application deadline: 2/15; financial award applicants required to submit FAFSA. *Unit head:* Ceren Bingol, Interim Head, 248-645-3462, Fax: 248-645-3591, E-mail: cbingol@cranbrook.edu. *Application contact:* Leslie Tobakos, Registrar/Financial Aid and Admissions Manager, 248-645-3360, Fax: 248-645-3591, E-mail: ltobakos@cranbrook.edu.

**Dalhousie University,** Faculty of Architecture and Planning, Halifax, NS B3J 2X4, Canada. Offers M Arch, M Eng, M Plan, MEDS, MPS. *Degree requirements:* For master's, thesis. *Entrance requirements:* Additional exam requirements/recommendations for international students: Required—1 of 5 approved tests: TOEFL, IELTS, CANTEST, CAEL, Michigan English Language Assessment Battery. Electronic applications accepted.

**Ferris State University,** Kendall College of Art and Design, Grand Rapids, MI 49503. Offers architecture (M Arch); art education (MAE); design (MA); drawing (MFA); painting (MFA); photography (MFA); printmaking (MFA); visual and critical studies (MA). *Program availability:* Part-time. *Faculty:* 15 full-time (10 women), 9 part-time/adjunct (2 women). *Students:* 40 full-time (33 women), 5 part-time (3 women); includes 9 minority (3 Black or African American, non-Hispanic/Latino; 3 Asian, non-Hispanic/Latino; 3 Hispanic/Latino), 6 international. Average age 30. 43 applicants, 53% accepted, 16 enrolled. In 2016, 16 master's awarded. *Degree requirements:* For master's, thesis, seminars. *Entrance requirements:* For master's, portfolio, 3 letters of recommendation, curriculum vitae, artist statement, letter of intent. Additional exam requirements/recommendations for international students: Required—TOEFL (minimum score 70 iBT). *Application deadline:* For fall admission, 2/1 priority date for domestic and international students; for spring admission, 11/1 priority date for domestic and international students. Applications are processed on a rolling basis. Application fee: $0. Electronic applications accepted. *Expenses:* $1,017 per credit hour plus $390 fees per year. *Financial support:* In 2016–17, 32 students received support, including 8 fellowships (averaging $16,781 per year); scholarships/grants and unspecified assistantships also available. Financial award application deadline: 2/1; financial award applicants required to submit FAFSA. *Unit head:* Leslie Bellavance, President, 616-451-2787. *Application contact:* Thomas Post, Graduate Recruitment Specialist, 616-451-2787, Fax: 616-831-9689, E-mail: thomaspost@ferris.edu.
Website: http://www.kcad.edu/

**Florida Agricultural and Mechanical University,** Division of Graduate Studies, Research, and Continuing Education, School of Architecture, Tallahassee, FL 32307-3200. Offers architectural studies (MS Arch); architecture (professional) (M Arch); landscape architecture (MLA). *Program availability:* Part-time. *Degree requirements:* For master's, thesis. *Entrance requirements:* For master's, GRE General Test, minimum GPA of 3.0, portfolio. Additional exam requirements/recommendations for international students: Required—TOEFL (minimum score 550 paper-based). *Faculty research:* Environmental technology, post-occupancy evaluation, building economics, design methods, computer-aided design.

**Florida International University,** College of Communication, Architecture and The Arts, Department of Architecture, Miami, FL 33199. Offers M Arch, MA. *Program availability:* Part-time, evening/weekend. *Faculty:* 12 full-time (1 woman), 18 part-time/adjunct (7 women). *Students:* 135 full-time (78 women), 4 part-time (1 woman); includes 96 minority (6 Black or African American, non-Hispanic/Latino; 3 Asian, non-Hispanic/Latino; 86 Hispanic/Latino; 1 Two or more races, non-Hispanic/Latino), 20 international. Average age 26. 113 applicants, 43% accepted, 19 enrolled. In 2016, 104 master's awarded. *Entrance requirements:* For master's, GRE or minimum GPA of 3.0 in upper-level undergraduate work, portfolio. Additional exam requirements/recommendations for international students: Required—TOEFL (minimum score 550 paper-based; 80 iBT). *Application deadline:* For fall admission, 2/1 for domestic and international students. Application fee: $30. Electronic applications accepted. *Expenses:* Tuition, state resident: full-time $8912; part-time $446 per credit hour. Tuition, nonresident: full-time $21,393; part-time $992 per credit hour. *Required fees:* $2185; $195 per semester. Tuition and fees vary according to program. *Financial support:* Institutionally sponsored loans and scholarships/grants available. Financial award application deadline: 3/1; financial award applicants required to submit FAFSA. *Unit head:* Jason Chandler, Chair, 305-348-6913, E-mail: jason.chandler@fiu.edu. *Application contact:* Nanett Rojas, Assistant Director, Graduate Admissions, 305-348-7464, Fax: 305-348-7441, E-mail: gradadm@fiu.edu. Website: http://carta.fiu.edu/

**Florida State University,** The Graduate School, College of Fine Arts, Department of Interior Architecture and Design, Tallahassee, FL 32306. Offers MFA, MS. *Accreditation:* NASAD (one or more programs are accredited). *Program availability:* Part-time. *Faculty:* 9 full-time (7 women), 9 part-time/adjunct (3 women). *Students:* 20 full-time (17 women); includes 5 minority (1 Black or African American, non-Hispanic/Latino; 4 American Indian or Alaska Native, non-Hispanic/Latino), 3 international. Average age 27. 47 applicants, 53% accepted, 25 enrolled. In 2016, 22 master's awarded. *Degree requirements:* For master's, thesis or alternative. *Entrance requirements:* For master's, GRE General Test, minimum GPA of 3.0 during previous 2 years. Additional exam requirements/recommendations for international students: Required—TOEFL (minimum score 550 paper-based; 80 iBT). *Application deadline:* For fall admission, 7/1 for domestic students, 5/1 for international students; for summer admission, 3/1 for domestic and international students. Applications are processed on a rolling basis. Application fee: $30. Electronic applications accepted. *Expenses:* Tuition, state resident: full-time $7263; part-time $403.51 per credit hour. Tuition, nonresident: full-time $18,087; part-time $1004.85 per credit hour. *Required fees:* $1365; $75.81 per credit hour. $20 per semester. Tuition and fees vary according to campus/location. *Financial support:* In 2016–17, 13 teaching assistantships with tuition reimbursements (averaging $5,000 per year) were awarded; career-related internships or fieldwork and unspecified assistantships also available. Financial award applicants required to submit FAFSA. *Faculty research:* Social responsibility issues, graphics techniques, history of interiors, computer-aided design and drafting, pedagogy. *Unit head:* Dr. Lisa K. Waxman, Chairman, 850-644-8326, Fax: 850-644-3112, E-mail: lwaxman@fsu.edu. *Application contact:* Dr. Marlo Ransdell, Director of Graduate Studies, 850-645-6831, Fax: 850-644-3112, E-mail: mransdell@fsu.edu.
Website: http://interiordesign.fsu.edu/

**Georgia Institute of Technology,** Graduate Studies, College of Architecture, Doctoral Program in Architecture, Atlanta, GA 30332-0001. Offers PhD. *Program availability:*

Part-time, online learning. *Degree requirements:* For doctorate, comprehensive exam, thesis/dissertation. *Entrance requirements:* For doctorate, GRE General Test. Additional exam requirements/recommendations for international students: Required—TOEFL (minimum score 600 paper-based). Electronic applications accepted.

**Georgia Institute of Technology,** Graduate Studies, College of Architecture, Master's Program in Architecture, Atlanta, GA 30332-0001. Offers M Arch, MS, M Arch/MCRP. *Program availability:* Part-time. *Degree requirements:* For master's, thesis or alternative. *Entrance requirements:* For master's, GRE General Test. Additional exam requirements/recommendations for international students: Required—TOEFL (minimum score 600 paper-based). Electronic applications accepted.

**Georgia Institute of Technology,** Graduate Studies, College of Architecture, School of City and Regional Planning, Atlanta, GA 30332-0001. Offers city and regional planning (PhD); economic development (MCRP); environmental planning and management (MCRP); geographic information systems (MCRP); land and community development (MCRP); land use planning (MCRP); transportation (MCRP); urban design (MCRP); MCP/MSCE. *Accreditation:* ACSP. *Degree requirements:* For master's, thesis, internship. *Entrance requirements:* For master's, GRE General Test, minimum GPA of 2.7. Additional exam requirements/recommendations for international students: Required—TOEFL. Electronic applications accepted.

**Hampton University,** School of Engineering and Technology, Hampton, VA 23668. Offers architecture (M Arch). *Faculty:* 8 full-time (5 women), 2 part-time/adjunct (0 women). *Students:* 12 full-time (7 women), 7 part-time (2 women); includes 16 minority (14 Black or African American, non-Hispanic/Latino; 2 Asian, non-Hispanic/Latino), 2 international. Average age 27. In 2016, 15 master's awarded. Electronic applications accepted. *Expenses: Tuition:* Full-time $10,776; part-time $548 per credit hour. *Required fees:* $35; $35 per credit hour. Tuition and fees vary according to course load and program. *Financial support:* Applicants required to submit FAFSA. *Faculty research:* Design at the water's edge, impact of climate change on coastal regions, innovation in design, historic preservation and documentation, sustainability and energy efficiency. *Total annual research expenditures:* $10,000. *Unit head:* Dr. Joyce Shirazi, Dean, 757-728-6970, Fax: 757-728-6972, E-mail: joyce.shirazi@hamptonu.edu. *Application contact:* Robert Easter, Chair, Architecture Department, 757-727-5441, Fax: 757-728-6680. Website: http://set.hamptonu.edu/

**Harvard University,** Graduate School of Arts and Sciences, Committee on Architecture, Landscape Architecture, and Urban Planning, Cambridge, MA 02138. Offers architecture (PhD); landscape architecture (PhD); urban planning (PhD). *Accreditation:* ACSP. *Degree requirements:* For doctorate, one foreign language, thesis/dissertation, oral exam. *Entrance requirements:* For doctorate, GRE General Test. Additional exam requirements/recommendations for international students: Required—TOEFL.

**Harvard University,** Graduate School of Design, Department of Architecture, Cambridge, MA 02138. Offers M Arch. *Degree requirements:* For master's, thesis (for some programs). *Entrance requirements:* For master's, GRE General Test. Additional exam requirements/recommendations for international students: Required—TOEFL (minimum score 600 paper-based; 104 iBT). Electronic applications accepted.

**Harvard University,** Graduate School of Design, Program in Design, Cambridge, MA 02138. Offers Dr DES. *Entrance requirements:* For doctorate, GRE General Test. Additional exam requirements/recommendations for international students: Required—TOEFL (minimum score 600 paper-based; 104 iBT). Electronic applications accepted.

**Harvard University,** Graduate School of Design, Program in Design Studies, Cambridge, MA 02138. Offers M Des S. *Entrance requirements:* For master's, GRE General Test. Additional exam requirements/recommendations for international students: Required—TOEFL (minimum score 600 paper-based; 104 iBT). Electronic applications accepted.

**Illinois Institute of Technology,** Graduate College, College of Architecture, Chicago, IL 60616. Offers M Arch, MLA, MS Arch, PhD, MLA/M Arch. *Accreditation:* ASLA. *Program availability:* Part-time. Terminal master's awarded for partial completion of doctoral program. *Degree requirements:* For master's, comprehensive exam (for some programs), thesis (for some programs); for doctorate, comprehensive exam, thesis/dissertation. *Entrance requirements:* For master's, GRE General Test (minimum score 292 Quantitative and Verbal, 2.5 Analytical Writing), minimum college GPA of 3.0, official transcripts, portfolio, 3 letters of recommendation, professional statement; for doctorate, GRE General Test (minimum score 900 Quantitative and Verbal, 2.5 Analytical Writing), minimum GPA of 3.5, official transcripts, portfolio, 3 letters of recommendation, professional statement. Additional exam requirements/recommendations for international students: Required—TOEFL (minimum score 550 paper-based; 80 iBT). Electronic applications accepted. *Faculty research:* Sustainable design and efficiency; the influence of climate and environment on building form; emerging urbanisms; computer applications (such as 3-D modeling); the design, planning and structure of high-rise buildings.

**Instituto Tecnológico y de Estudios Superiores de Monterrey, Campus Estado de México,** Professional and Graduate Division, Estado de Mexico, Mexico. Offers administration of information technologies (MITA); architecture (M Arch); business administration (GMBA, MBA); computer sciences (MCS, PhD); education (M Ed); educational institution administration (MAD); educational technology and innovation (PhD); electronic commerce (MEC); environmental systems (MS); finance (MAF); humanistic studies (MHS); information sciences and knowledge management (MISKM); information systems (MS); manufacturing systems (MS); marketing (MEM); quality systems and productivity (MS); science and materials engineering (PhD); telecommunications management (MTM). *Program availability:* Part-time, online learning. *Degree requirements:* For master's, one foreign language, thesis (for some programs); for doctorate, one foreign language, thesis/dissertation. *Entrance requirements:* For master's, E-PAEP 500, interview; for doctorate, E-PAEP 500, research proposal. Additional exam requirements/recommendations for international students: Required—TOEFL (minimum score 550 paper-based). *Faculty research:* Surface treatments by plasmas, mechanical properties, robotics, graphical computing, mechatronics security protocols.

**Instituto Tecnológico y de Estudios Superiores de Monterrey, Campus Irapuato,** Graduate Programs, Irapuato, Mexico. Offers administration (MBA); administration of information technology (MAIT); administration of telecommunications (MAT); architecture (M Arch); computer science (MCS); education (M Ed); educational administration (MEA); educational innovation and technology (DEIT); educational technology (MET); electronic commerce (MBA); environmental administration and planning (MEAP); environmental systems (MS); finances (MBA); humanistic studies (MHS); international management for Latin American executives (MIMLAE); library and information science (MLIS); manufacturing quality management (MMQM); marketing research (MBA).

**Iowa State University of Science and Technology,** Department of Architecture, Ames, IA 50011. Offers architectural studies (MSAS); architecture (M Arch, MS); M Arch/MBA; M Arch/MCRP; M Arch/MS. *Degree requirements:* For master's, thesis (for some programs). *Entrance requirements:* For master's, GRE General Test,

portfolio, letters of reference. Additional exam requirements/recommendations for international students: Required—TOEFL (minimum score 600 paper-based; 79 iBT), IELTS (minimum score 7). *Application deadline:* For fall admission, 1/4 priority date for domestic and international students; for spring admission, 10/4 for domestic and international students. Application fee: $60 ($90 for international students). Electronic applications accepted. *Financial support:* In 2016–17, 30 students received support. Tuition waivers (partial) available. Financial award applicants required to submit FAFSA. *Faculty research:* Computer-aided architectural design, social dimensions of urban architecture, designing for the elderly, energy utilization in buildings, architectural theory. *Application contact:* Meredith Foley, Application Contact, 515-294-0816, Fax: 515-294-2348, E-mail: merfoley@iastate.edu.
Website: http://www.design.iastate.edu/architecture/graduateprograms.php

**Judson University,** Master of Architecture Program, Elgin, IL 60123-1498. Offers architecture (M Arch); sustainable design (M Arch); traditional architecture and urbanism (M Arch). *Program availability:* Part-time. *Faculty:* 9 full-time (3 women), 1 part-time/adjunct (1 woman). *Students:* 19 full-time (5 women); includes 5 minority (1 Black or African American, non-Hispanic/Latino; 3 Hispanic/Latino; 1 Two or more races, non-Hispanic/Latino). Average age 22. 24 applicants, 83% accepted, 19 enrolled. In 2016, 16 master's awarded. *Degree requirements:* For master's, thesis optional, 1600-hour practicum/preceptorship completed prior to enrollment. *Entrance requirements:* For master's, GRE, Judson BA in architecture or equivalent; minimum cumulative undergraduate GPA of 2.75, 3.0 in architecture; comprehensive portfolio; letter of intent. Additional exam requirements/recommendations for international students: Required—TOEFL (minimum score 550 paper-based), IELTS (minimum score 6.5). *Application deadline:* For fall admission, 2/15 priority date for domestic and international students; for winter admission, 11/15 for domestic students; for spring admission, 11/15 for domestic and international students. Applications are processed on a rolling basis. Application fee: $100. Electronic applications accepted. *Expenses:* Contact institution. *Financial support:* In 2016–17, 19 students received support, including 1 fellowship with partial tuition reimbursement available (averaging $5,000 per year), 1 research assistantship with partial tuition reimbursement available (averaging $5,000 per year), 12 teaching assistantships with partial tuition reimbursements available (averaging $2,500 per year); unspecified assistantships also available. Financial award application deadline: 7/1; financial award applicants required to submit FAFSA. *Faculty research:* Sustainable design, urbanism, daylighting, acoustics, digital media and fabrication. *Unit head:* Ian Hoffman, Chair, 847-628-1014, E-mail: ihoffman@judsonu.edu. *Application contact:* Molly Smith, Director of Admissions, 847-628-2521, E-mail: molly.smith@judsonu.edu. Website: http://www.judsonu.edu/ArchMaster/

**Kansas State University,** Graduate School, College of Architecture, Planning and Design, Department of Architecture, Manhattan, KS 66506. Offers M Arch, MS Arch. *Program availability:* Part-time. *Faculty:* 18 full-time (3 women), 6 part-time/adjunct (2 women). *Students:* 156 full-time (64 women), 7 part-time (3 women); includes 35 minority (6 Black or African American, non-Hispanic/Latino; 7 Asian, non-Hispanic/Latino; 13 Hispanic/Latino; 9 Two or more races, non-Hispanic/Latino), 27 international. Average age 23. 129 applicants, 75% accepted, 79 enrolled. In 2016, 73 master's awarded. *Degree requirements:* For master's, thesis optional, residency. *Entrance requirements:* For master's, portfolio, minimum GPA of 3.0. Additional exam requirements/recommendations for international students: Required—TOEFL (minimum score 95 iBT), IELTS (minimum score 7). *Application deadline:* For fall admission, 2/1 priority date for domestic students, 1/1 priority date for international students; for spring admission, 8/1 priority date for domestic and international students. Applications are processed on a rolling basis. Application fee: $90 ($100 for international students). Electronic applications accepted. *Expenses:* Tuition, state resident: full-time $9670. Tuition, nonresident: full-time $21,828. *Required fees:* $862. *Financial support:* In 2016–17, 18 teaching assistantships with full tuition reimbursements (averaging $7,500 per year) were awarded; research assistantships, institutionally sponsored loans, and scholarships/grants also available. Support available to part-time students. Financial award application deadline: 3/1; financial award applicants required to submit FAFSA. *Faculty research:* Design theory, environment behavior and place studies, ecological and sustainable design, computer-assisted design and fabrication. *Unit head:* Matthew Knox, Professor and Head, 785-532-5953, Fax: 785-532-6722, E-mail: mknox@ksu.edu. *Application contact:* R. Todd Gabbard, Associate Head and Director of Graduate Programs, 785-532-1129, Fax: 785-532-6722, E-mail: rtodd@ksu.edu. Website: http://apdesign.k-state.edu/arch/

**Kennesaw State University,** College of Architecture and Construction Management, Department of Architecture, Kennesaw, GA 30144. Offers MS Arch.

**Kent State University,** College of Architecture and Environmental Design, Kent, OH 44240. Offers architecture (M Arc); architecture and environmental design (MS); health care design (MHCD); landscape architecture (MLA); urban design (MUD); M Arch/MBA; M Arch/MUD. *Program availability:* Part-time. *Faculty:* 20 full-time (3 women). *Students:* 75 full-time (31 women), 7 part-time (2 women); includes 6 minority (3 Black or African American, non-Hispanic/Latino; 1 American Indian or Alaska Native, non-Hispanic/Latino; 2 Hispanic/Latino), 10 international. Average age 25. 125 applicants, 56% accepted, 58 enrolled. In 2016, 55 master's awarded. *Degree requirements:* For master's, thesis (for some programs), project (for some programs). *Entrance requirements:* For master's, GRE, statement of purpose, curriculum vitae, transcripts, 3 letters of recommendation, portfolio. Additional exam requirements/recommendations for international students: Required—TOEFL (minimum scores of 550 paper-based, 80 iBT), Michigan English Language Assessment Battery (77), IELTS (6.5), or PTE (54). *Application deadline:* For fall admission, 1/15 for domestic and international students. Applications are processed on a rolling basis. Application fee: $45 ($70 for international students). Electronic applications accepted. *Expenses:* Tuition, state resident: full-time $10,864; part-time $495 per credit hour. Tuition, nonresident: full-time $18,380; part-time $837 per credit hour. *Financial support:* Research assistantships with full tuition reimbursements, teaching assistantships with full tuition reimbursements, Federal Work-Study, scholarships/grants, and unspecified assistantships available. Financial award application deadline: 2/1. *Unit head:* Mark Mistur, Dean, E-mail: mmistur1@kent.edu. *Application contact:* Johnathan Fleming, Assistant Professor and Director, Master of Architecture, 330-672-0934, E-mail: jpflemi1@kent.edu. Website: http://www.kent.edu/caed

**Lawrence Technological University,** College of Architecture and Design, Southfield, MI 48075-1058. Offers architecture (M Arch); build information modeling (Graduate Certificate); interior design (MID); transportation design (Graduate Certificate); urban design (MUD). *Accreditation:* NASAD. *Program availability:* Part-time, evening/weekend. *Faculty:* 14 full-time (2 women), 13 part-time/adjunct (3 women). *Students:* 8 full-time (3 women), 159 part-time (69 women); includes 15 minority (2 Black or African American, non-Hispanic/Latino; 4 Asian, non-Hispanic/Latino; 7 Hispanic/Latino; 2 Two or more races, non-Hispanic/Latino), 50 international. Average age 30. 119 applicants, 58% accepted, 43 enrolled. In 2016, 78 master's awarded. *Degree requirements:* For master's, thesis optional. *Entrance requirements:* Additional exam requirements/recommendations for international students: Required—TOEFL (minimum score 550 paper-based; 79 iBT). *Application deadline:* For fall admission, 5/22 for international students; for spring admission, 10/11 for international students; for summer admission, 2/16 for international students. Applications are processed on a rolling basis.

## Architecture

Application fee: $50. Electronic applications accepted. *Expenses: Tuition:* Full-time $14,868; part-time $1062 per credit. *Required fees:* $75 per semester. Tuition and fees vary according to campus/location. *Financial support:* In 2016–17, 43 students received support, including 8 research assistantships with partial tuition reimbursements available (averaging $6,000 per year), 24 teaching assistantships (averaging $5,000 per year); career-related internships or fieldwork, scholarships/grants, and unspecified assistantships also available. Financial award application deadline: 4/1; financial award applicants required to submit FAFSA. *Faculty research:* Public interest design/social practice; digital fabrication and practice; design education; sustainable urbanism; Detroit architecture, Minoru Yamasaki and mid-twentieth century architecture. *Total annual research expenditures:* $260,728. *Unit head:* Prof. Karl Daubmann, Dean/Professor, 248-204-2805, Fax: 248-204-2228, E-mail: archdean@ltu.edu. *Application contact:* Jane Rohrback, Director of Admissions, 248-204-3160, Fax: 248-204-2228, E-mail: admissions@ltu.edu. Website: http://www.ltu.edu/architecture_and_design/index.asp

**London Metropolitan University,** Graduate Programs, London, United Kingdom. Offers applied psychology (M Sc); architecture (MA); biomedical science (M Sc); blood science (M Sc); cancer pharmacology (M Sc); computer networking and cyber security (M Sc); computing and information systems (M Sc); conference interpreting (MA); counter-terrorism studies (M Sc); creative, digital and professional writing (MA); crime, violence and prevention (M Sc); criminology (M Sc); curating contemporary art (MA); data analytics (M Sc); digital media (MA); early childhood studies (MA); education (MA, Ed D); financial services law, regulation and compliance (LL M); food science (M Sc); forensic psychology (M Sc); health and social care management and policy (M Sc); human nutrition (M Sc); human resource management (MA); human rights and international conflict (MA); information technology (M Sc); intelligence and security studies (M Sc); international oil, gas and energy law (LL M); international relations (MA); interpreting (MA); learning and teaching in higher education (MA); legal practice (LL M); media and entertainment law (LL M); organizational and consumer psychology (M Sc); psychological therapy (M Sc); psychology of mental health (M Sc); public health (M Sc); public policy and management (MPA); security studies (M Sc); social work (M Sc); spatial planning and urban design (MA); sports therapy (M Sc); supporting older children and young people with dyslexia (MA); teaching languages (MA), including Arabic, English; translation (MA); woman and child abuse (MA).

**Louisiana State University and Agricultural & Mechanical College,** Graduate School, College of Art and Design, School of Architecture, Baton Rouge, LA 70803. Offers M Arch.

**Louisiana Tech University,** Graduate School, College of Liberal Arts, Architecture Program, Ruston, LA 71272. Offers M Arch. *Entrance requirements:* For master's, GRE General Test. *Application deadline:* For fall admission, 7/29 for domestic students; for spring admission, 2/3 for domestic students. Applications are processed on a rolling basis. Application fee: $40 ($50 for international students). *Financial support:* Application deadline: 2/1. *Unit head:* Damon Caldwell, Graduate Coordinator, 318-257-5259, Fax: 318-257-4687, E-mail: caldwell@latech.edu. *Application contact:* Marilyn J. Robinson, Assistant to the Dean of the Graduate School, 318-257-2924, Fax: 318-257-4487. Website: http://design.latech.edu/architecture/

**Marywood University,** Academic Affairs, School of Architecture, Program in Architecture, Scranton, PA 18509-1598. Offers M Arch. *Program availability:* Part-time. *Degree requirements:* For master's, thesis project.

**Massachusetts College of Art and Design,** Graduate Programs, Program in Architecture, Boston, MA 02115-5882. Offers M Arch. *Faculty:* 6 full-time (3 women), 19 part-time/adjunct (5 women). *Students:* 27 full-time (14 women), 1 (woman) part-time; includes 7 minority (3 Black or African American, non-Hispanic/Latino; 3 Asian, non-Hispanic/Latino; 1 Hispanic/Latino), 8 international. 43 applicants, 79% accepted, 12 enrolled. In 2016, 9 master's awarded. *Degree requirements:* For master's, thesis, thesis project. *Entrance requirements:* For master's, portfolio, college transcripts, resume, statement of purpose, letters of reference, interview. Additional exam requirements/recommendations for international students: Required—TOEFL (minimum score 550 paper-based; 85 iBT); Recommended—IELTS (minimum score 6). *Application deadline:* For summer admission, 1/4 priority date for domestic and international students. Application fee: $90. Electronic applications accepted. *Expenses:* $780 per credit. *Financial support:* In 2016–17, 20 students received support, including 1 research assistantship (averaging $2,160 per year), 4 teaching assistantships (averaging $2,160 per year); career-related internships or fieldwork, scholarships/grants, tuition waivers (partial), and 8 general assistantships also available. Support available to part-time students. Financial award application deadline: 1/4; financial award applicants required to submit FAFSA. *Faculty research:* Sustainability, civic engagement, community development, digital teaching tools. *Unit head:* Paul Paturzo, Dean of Graduate Studies, 617-879-7166, E-mail: pjpaturzo@massart.edu. *Application contact:* Lauren O'Neill, Assistant Director of Graduate Admissions, 617-879-7222, E-mail: gradadmissions@massart.edu. Website: http://www.massart.edu/Admissions/Graduate_Programs.html

**Massachusetts Institute of Technology,** School of Architecture and Planning, Department of Architecture, Cambridge, MA 02139. Offers architecture (M Arch, PhD), including building technology (PhD), design and computation (PhD), history and theory of architecture (PhD), history and theory of art (PhD); architecture studies (SM Arch S); art, culture and technology (SMACT); building technology (SMBT). *Faculty:* 36 full-time (13 women). *Students:* 224 full-time (106 women); includes 46 minority (5 Black or African American, non-Hispanic/Latino; 11 Asian, non-Hispanic/Latino; 22 Hispanic/Latino; 8 Two or more races, non-Hispanic/Latino), 113 international. Average age 28. 1,165 applicants, 12% accepted, 82 enrolled. In 2016, 58 master's, 10 doctorates awarded. *Degree requirements:* For master's, thesis; for doctorate, comprehensive exam, thesis/dissertation. *Entrance requirements:* For master's and doctorate, GRE General Test. Additional exam requirements/recommendations for international students: Required—TOEFL, IELTS. *Application deadline:* For fall admission, 12/31 for domestic and international students. Application fee: $75. Electronic applications accepted. *Expenses: Tuition:* Full-time $46,400; part-time $725 per credit. One-time fee: $312 full-time. Full-time tuition and fees vary according to course load and program. *Financial support:* In 2016–17, 189 students received support, including 128 fellowships (averaging $23,600 per year), 31 research assistantships (averaging $33,200 per year), 34 teaching assistantships (averaging $34,700 per year); Federal Work-Study, institutionally sponsored loans, scholarships/grants, traineeships, health care benefits, unspecified assistantships, and resident tutors also available. Support available to part-time students. Financial award application deadline: 5/1; financial award applicants required to submit FAFSA. *Faculty research:* Architecture; urbanism; building technology and sustainability; computation and design; history, theory, and criticism; art, culture, and technology. *Total annual research expenditures:* $3.5 million. *Unit head:* Prof. J. Meejin Yoon, Department Head, 617-253-7791, E-mail: arch@mit.edu. *Application contact:* 617-715-4400. Website: http://architecture.mit.edu/

**McGill University,** Faculty of Graduate and Postdoctoral Studies, Faculty of Engineering, School of Architecture, Montréal, QC H3A 2T5, Canada. Offers affordable homes (M Arch II, Diploma); architectural history and theory (M Arch II); architecture (PhD); domestic environment (M Arch II); domestic environments (Diploma); minimum cost housing in developing countries (M Arch II, Diploma); professional architecture (M Arch I).

**Miami University,** College of Creative Arts, Department of Architecture and Interior Design, Oxford, OH 45056. Offers M Arch. *Accreditation:* NASAD. *Students:* 24 full-time (12 women); includes 1 minority (Two or more races, non-Hispanic/Latino), 9 international. Average age 26. In 2016, 15 master's awarded. *Expenses:* Tuition, state resident: full-time $12,890; part-time $564 per credit hour. Tuition, nonresident: full-time $29,604; part-time $1260 per credit hour. *Required fees:* $638. Part-time tuition and fees vary according to course load and program. *Unit head:* Mary Rogero, Interim Chair, 513-529-4903, E-mail: rogeromr@miamioh.edu. *Application contact:* Craig Hinrichs, Professor/Director of Graduate Studies, 513-529-7036, E-mail: hinriccl@miamioh.edu. Website: http://www.MiamiOH.edu/architecture

**Montana State University,** The Graduate School, College of Arts and Architecture, School of Architecture, Bozeman, MT 59717. Offers M Arch. *Program availability:* Part-time. *Degree requirements:* For master's, comprehensive exam. *Entrance requirements:* For master's, GRE General Test, minimum cumulative GPA of 3.0, portfolio, 3 letters of recommendation. Additional exam requirements/recommendations for international students: Required—TOEFL (minimum score 550 paper-based). Electronic applications accepted. *Faculty research:* Sustainability, architecture as craft, visualization, stewardship, community design, design build.

**Morgan State University,** School of Graduate Studies, Institute of Architecture and Planning, Program in Architecture, Baltimore, MD 21251. Offers M Arch. *Degree requirements:* For master's, thesis. *Entrance requirements:* Additional exam requirements/recommendations for international students: Required—TOEFL (minimum score 550 paper-based).

**New Jersey Institute of Technology,** College of Architecture and Design, Newark, NJ 07102. Offers architecture (M Arch, MS Arch); infrastructure planning (MIP); urban systems (PhD). *Program availability:* Part-time, evening/weekend. *Faculty:* 31 full-time (8 women), 37 part-time/adjunct (14 women). *Students:* 40 full-time (23 women), 6 part-time (0 women); includes 10 minority (1 Black or African American, non-Hispanic/Latino; 3 Asian, non-Hispanic/Latino; 5 Hispanic/Latino; 1 Two or more races, non-Hispanic/Latino), 19 international. Average age 30. 129 applicants, 37% accepted, 10 enrolled. In 2016, 16 master's, 4 doctorates awarded. Terminal master's awarded for partial completion of doctoral program. *Degree requirements:* For master's, thesis (for some programs). *Entrance requirements:* For master's, GRE General Test, minimum GPA of 3.0. Additional exam requirements/recommendations for international students: Required—TOEFL (minimum score 550 paper-based; 79 iBT). *Application deadline:* For fall admission, 6/1 priority date for domestic students, 5/1 priority date for international students; for spring admission, 11/15 priority date for domestic and international students. Applications are processed on a rolling basis. Application fee: $75. Electronic applications accepted. *Expenses:* Contact institution. *Financial support:* In 2016–17, 31 students received support, including 6 teaching assistantships (averaging $22,500 per year); fellowships, career-related internships or fieldwork, Federal Work-Study, institutionally sponsored loans, scholarships/grants, traineeships, unspecified assistantships, and studio assistantships (1 averaging $10,000) also available. Financial award application deadline: 1/15. *Faculty research:* Building sciences, community and urban design history and theory, computer-aided architecture, material dynamics. *Unit head:* Anthony W. Schuman, Interim Dean, 973-596-6370, E-mail: anthony.w.schuman@njit.edu. *Application contact:* Stephen Eck, Director of Admissions, 973-596-3300, Fax: 973-596-3461, E-mail: admissions@njit.edu. Website: http://architecture.njit.edu/

**The New School,** Parsons School of Design, Program in Architecture, New York, NY 10011. Offers M Arch, M Arch/MFA. *Faculty:* 26 full-time (7 women), 26 part-time/adjunct (16 women). *Students:* 75 full-time (39 women), 1 (woman) part-time; includes 20 minority (5 Black or African American, non-Hispanic/Latino; 4 Asian, non-Hispanic/Latino; 11 Hispanic/Latino), 23 international. Average age 26. 191 applicants, 67% accepted, 20 enrolled. In 2016, 43 master's awarded. *Degree requirements:* For master's, thesis. *Entrance requirements:* For master's, GRE, transcripts, resume, statement of purpose, recommendation letters, portfolio, interview. Additional exam requirements/recommendations for international students: Required—TOEFL (minimum score 92 iBT), IELTS (minimum score 7), PTE (minimum score 63). *Application deadline:* For fall admission, 1/1 for domestic and international students. Applications are processed on a rolling basis. Application fee: $50. Electronic applications accepted. *Expenses:* Contact institution. *Financial support:* Research assistantships, teaching assistantships, career-related internships or fieldwork, Federal Work-Study, scholarships/grants, unspecified assistantships, and travel funding; tuition waivers for students who are also New School employees available. Support available to part-time students. Financial award application deadline: 2/1; financial award applicants required to submit FAFSA. *Faculty research:* Engineering, urban planning, landscape design, interior design; architectural history, theory, and criticism. *Unit head:* Joel Towers, Executive Dean, Parsons School of Design, 212-229-8950 Ext. 4393, E-mail: towersj@newschool.edu. *Application contact:* Courtney Malenius, Director of Graduate Admission, 212-229-5150 Ext. 4011, E-mail: thinkparsonsgrad@newschool.edu. Website: http://www.newschool.edu/

**NewSchool of Architecture and Design,** Program in Architecture, San Diego, CA 92101-6634. Offers M Arch, MS. *Program availability:* Part-time, online learning. *Degree requirements:* For master's, thesis. *Entrance requirements:* For master's, portfolio, interview. Additional exam requirements/recommendations for international students: Required—TOEFL, IELTS. *Faculty research:* Urban studies, regional studies, environmental design, structures, cross-cultural studies.

**New York Institute of Technology,** School of Architecture and Design, Old Westbury, NY 11568-8000. Offers architecture, urban and regional design (MS). *Program availability:* Part-time. *Faculty:* 3 full-time (1 woman), 3 part-time/adjunct (0 women). *Students:* 20 full-time (14 women), all international. Average age 26. 55 applicants, 25% accepted, 9 enrolled. In 2016, 7 master's awarded. *Entrance requirements:* For master's, professional architecture or landscape architecture degree from accredited college or university approved by the NAAB or equivalent; minimum undergraduate GPA of 3.0; digital portfolio; curriculum vitae; personal essay; two letters of recommendation. Additional exam requirements/recommendations for international students: Required—TOEFL (minimum score 79 iBT), IELTS (minimum score 6). *Application deadline:* For fall admission, 3/1 for domestic and international students. Applications are processed on a rolling basis. Application fee: $50. Electronic applications accepted. *Expenses:* $1,215 per credit. *Financial support:* Career-related internships or fieldwork, Federal Work-Study, institutionally sponsored loans, scholarships/grants, tuition waivers (full and partial), and unspecified assistantships available. Support available to part-time students. Financial award application deadline: 3/1; financial award applicants required to submit FAFSA. *Faculty research:* Resilient cities, compact morphology, new town development, pedestrian-friendly public realm. *Unit head:* Jeffrey Raven, Graduate Director, 212-261-1547, E-mail: jraven@nyit.edu. *Application contact:* Alice Dolitsky, Director, Graduate Admissions, 516-686-7520, Fax: 516-686-1116, E-mail: nyitgrad@nyit.edu. Website: http://www.nyit.edu/architecture

**North Carolina State University,** Graduate School, College of Design, School of Architecture, Raleigh, NC 27695. Offers M Arch. *Degree requirements:* For master's, thesis optional, oral exam, project. *Entrance requirements:* For master's, GRE General Test, portfolio. Electronic applications accepted. *Faculty research:* Architectural design, architectural history and theory, construction materials, sustainable design.

**North Dakota State University,** College of Graduate and Interdisciplinary Studies, College of Arts, Humanities and Social Sciences, Department of Architecture and Landscape Architecture, Fargo, ND 58102. Offers architecture (M Arch). Electronic applications accepted.

**Northeastern University,** College of Arts, Media and Design, Boston, MA 02115-5096. Offers architecture (M Arch); game science and design (MS); information design and visualization (MFA); interdisciplinary arts (MFA); journalism (MA); music industry leadership (MS); studio art (MFA); sustainable building systems (MS); sustainable urban environments (M Des). *Faculty:* 142 full-time (55 women), 80 part-time/adjunct (34 women). *Students:* 239 full-time (147 women), 16 part-time (12 women). In 2016, 83 master's awarded. *Application fee:* $75. Electronic applications accepted. *Expenses:* $1,365 per credit. *Financial support:* Applicants required to submit FAFSA. *Unit head:* Dr. Elizabeth Hudson, Dean. *Application contact:* Jane Amidon, Associate Dean for Graduate Programs and Research, 617-373-4614, E-mail: gscamd@northeastern.edu. Website: http://www.northeastern.edu/camd/

**The Ohio State University,** Graduate School, College of Engineering, Austin E. Knowlton School of Architecture, Columbus, OH 43210. Offers architecture (M Arch); city and regional planning (MCRP, PhD); landscape architecture (M Land Arch). *Accreditation:* ACSP; ASLA. *Faculty:* 41. *Students:* 191 full-time (83 women), 4 part-time. Average age 26. In 2016, 60 master's, 2 doctorates awarded. *Degree requirements:* For doctorate, thesis/dissertation. *Entrance requirements:* For master's, GRE or GMAT (city and regional planning), portfolio (for architecture and landscape architecture); for doctorate, GRE or GMAT (city and regional planning), example of research or written work. Additional exam requirements/recommendations for international students: Required—TOEFL (minimum score 600 paper-based; 100 iBT), Michigan English Language Assessment Battery (minimum score 86); Recommended—IELTS (minimum score 8). *Application deadline:* For fall admission, 1/1 priority date for domestic students, 11/30 priority date for international students. Applications are processed on a rolling basis. Application fee: $60 ($70 for international students). Electronic applications accepted. *Financial support:* Fellowships with tuition reimbursements, research assistantships with tuition reimbursements, Federal Work-Study, institutionally sponsored loans, and unspecified assistantships available. Support available to part-time students. *Unit head:* Michael B. Cadwell, Professor/Director, 614-292-3174, E-mail: cadwell.1@osu.edu. *Application contact:* Graduate and Professional Admissions, 614-292-9444, Fax: 614-292-3895, E-mail: gpadmissions@osu.edu. Website: http://knowlton.osu.edu/

**Penn State University Park,** Graduate School, College of Arts and Architecture, Stuckeman School of Architecture and Landscape Architecture, University Park, PA 16802. Offers architecture (M Arch, MS, PhD); geodesign (MPS); landscape architecture (MLA, MS). *Accreditation:* ASLA. *Unit head:* Dr. Barbara O. Korner, Dean, 814-865-2592, Fax: 814-865-2018. *Application contact:* Lori Hawn, Director, Graduate Student Services, 814-865-1795, Fax: 814-863-4627, E-mail: l-gswww@lists.psu.edu. Website: https://stuckeman.psu.edu/

**Philadelphia University,** College of Architecture and the Built Environment, Program in Architecture, Philadelphia, PA 19144. Offers architecture (M Arch); high performance building (MS). *Entrance requirements:* For master's, bachelor's degree, official undergraduate transcripts, current resume, two letters of recommendation, portfolio of relevant work, personal essay describing intended research.

**Pontificia Universidad Catolica Madre y Maestra,** Graduate School, Faculty of Sciences and Humanities, Santiago, Dominican Republic. Offers architecture (M Arch), including architecture of interiors, architecture of tourist lodgings, landscaping; early childhood education (M Ed).

**Portland State University,** Graduate Studies, College of the Arts, School of Architecture, Portland, OR 97207-0751. Offers M Arch. *Faculty:* 14 full-time (5 women), 16 part-time/adjunct (6 women). *Students:* 54 full-time (30 women), 8 part-time (5 women); includes 9 minority (2 Black or African American, non-Hispanic/Latino; 6 Hispanic/Latino; 1 Two or more races, non-Hispanic/Latino), 5 international. Average age 31. 60 applicants, 58% accepted, 22 enrolled. In 2016, 26 master's awarded. *Degree requirements:* For master's, thesis optional. *Entrance requirements:* Additional exam requirements/recommendations for international students: Required—TOEFL (minimum score 550 paper-based; 80 iBT), IELTS (minimum score 6.5). *Application deadline:* For fall admission, 6/22 for domestic students; for summer admission, 5/23 for domestic students. Applications are processed on a rolling basis. Application fee: $65. Electronic applications accepted. *Expenses:* Contact institution. *Financial support:* In 2016–17, 6 research assistantships with tuition reimbursements (averaging $5,882 per year), 9 teaching assistantships with tuition reimbursements (averaging $5,325 per year) were awarded; Federal Work-Study, institutionally sponsored loans, scholarships/grants, and unspecified assistantships also available. Support available to part-time students. *Total annual research expenditures:* $77,837. *Unit head:* Prof. Clive Knights, Director, 503-725-3349, E-mail: knightsc@pdx.edu. *Application contact:* 503-725-8405, Fax: 503-725-8318. Website: https://www.pdx.edu/architecture/

**Prairie View A&M University,** School of Architecture, Prairie View, TX 77446. Offers M Arch, MCD. *Program availability:* Part-time, evening/weekend. *Faculty:* 3 full-time (0 women), 3 part-time/adjunct (1 woman). *Students:* 45 full-time (23 women), 18 part-time (12 women); includes 54 minority (46 Black or African American, non-Hispanic/Latino; 1 American Indian or Alaska Native, non-Hispanic/Latino; 7 Hispanic/Latino), 8 international. Average age 30. 46 applicants, 91% accepted, 36 enrolled. In 2016, 24 master's awarded. *Degree requirements:* For master's, comprehensive exam, thesis. *Entrance requirements:* For master's, GRE General Test, portfolio (M Arch), minimum GPA of 2.75. Additional exam requirements/recommendations for international students: Required—TOEFL (minimum score 550 paper-based; 79 iBT). *Application deadline:* For fall admission, 5/1 priority date for domestic and international students; for spring admission, 10/1 priority date for domestic students, 9/1 priority date for international students; for summer admission, 3/1 priority date for domestic students, 2/1 priority date for international students. Applications are processed on a rolling basis. Application fee: $50. Electronic applications accepted. *Expenses:* Tuition, state resident: full-time $4362; part-time $273.48 per credit hour. Tuition, nonresident: full-time $12,390; part-time $534.10 per credit hour. *Required fees:* $2782; $178.26 per credit hour. *Financial support:* Career-related internships or fieldwork, Federal Work-Study, institutionally sponsored loans, scholarships/grants, tuition waivers (full and partial), and unspecified assistantships available. Support available to part-time students. Financial award application deadline: 4/1; financial award applicants required to submit FAFSA. *Faculty research:* Community management, sustainable design. *Unit head:* Dr. Ikhlas Sabouni, Dean, 936-261-9800, Fax: 936-261-2350, E-mail: isabouni@pvamu.edu. *Application contact:* Pauline Walker, Administrative Assistant II, Research and Graduate Studies, 936-261-3521, Fax: 936-261-3529, E-mail: pmwalker@pvamu.edu.

**Pratt Institute,** School of Architecture, Program in Architecture, Brooklyn, NY 11205-3899. Offers architecture (first-professional) (M Arch); architecture (post-professional) (MS Arch). *Faculty:* 4 full-time (1 woman), 40 part-time/adjunct (11 women). *Students:* 172 full-time (93 women), 2 part-time (1 woman); includes 33 minority (1 Black or African American, non-Hispanic/Latino; 12 Asian, non-Hispanic/Latino; 18 Hispanic/Latino; 2 Two or more races, non-Hispanic/Latino), 90 international. Average age 26. 418 applicants, 72% accepted, 60 enrolled. In 2016, 71 master's awarded. *Degree requirements:* For master's, thesis. *Entrance requirements:* For master's, GRE (for M Arch only), B Arch (for MS Arch only), portfolio, letters of recommendation. Additional exam requirements/recommendations for international students: Required—TOEFL (minimum score 550 paper-based; 79 iBT). *Application deadline:* For fall admission, 1/5 for domestic and international students; for spring admission, 10/1 for domestic and international students. Application fee: $50 ($90 for international students). Electronic applications accepted. *Expenses:* $29,646 full-time tuition, $1,938 fees. *Financial support:* Career-related internships or fieldwork, Federal Work-Study, institutionally sponsored loans, scholarships/grants, health care benefits, and unspecified assistantships available. Support available to part-time students. Financial award application deadline: 2/1; financial award applicants required to submit FAFSA. *Faculty research:* Design theory, advanced structural systems, urban investigations. *Unit head:* William J. Mac Donald, Chairperson, 718-636-4308, E-mail: wmacdona@pratt.edu. *Application contact:* Natalie Capannelli, Director of Graduate Admissions, 718-636-3551, Fax: 718-399-4242, E-mail: ncapanne@pratt.edu. Website: https://www.pratt.edu/academics/architecture/grad-arch-urban-design/grad-dept-architecture/

**See Display on next page and Close-Up on page 137.**

**Princeton University,** Graduate School, School of Architecture, Princeton, NJ 08544-1019. Offers M Arch, PhD. Terminal master's awarded for partial completion of doctoral program. *Degree requirements:* For master's, thesis; for doctorate, 2 foreign languages, comprehensive exam, thesis/dissertation. *Entrance requirements:* For master's, GRE General Test, design portfolio, math, 2 semesters of physics, and art/architecture survey; for doctorate, GRE General Test, samples of written work. Additional exam requirements/recommendations for international students: Required—TOEFL (minimum score 600 paper-based). Electronic applications accepted. *Faculty research:* Design, urban studies, landscape architecture, media and information technologies in architecture.

**Rensselaer Polytechnic Institute,** Graduate School, School of Architecture, Program in Architectural Acoustics, Troy, NY 12180-3590. Offers architectural sciences (MS, PhD). Terminal master's awarded for partial completion of doctoral program. *Degree requirements:* For master's, thesis; for doctorate, comprehensive exam, thesis/dissertation. *Entrance requirements:* For master's and doctorate, GRE General Test. Additional exam requirements/recommendations for international students: Required—TOEFL (minimum score 570 paper-based; 88 iBT), IELTS (minimum score 6.5), PTE (minimum score 60). Electronic applications accepted. *Expenses: Tuition:* Full-time $49,520; part-time $2060 per credit hour. *Required fees:* $2617.

**Rensselaer Polytechnic Institute,** Graduate School, School of Architecture, Program in Built Ecologies, Troy, NY 12180-3590. Offers MS, PhD. *Degree requirements:* For master's, thesis; for doctorate, comprehensive exam, thesis/dissertation. *Entrance requirements:* For master's and doctorate, GRE General Test. Additional exam requirements/recommendations for international students: Required—TOEFL (minimum score 570 paper-based; 88 iBT), IELTS (minimum score 6.5), PTE (minimum score 60). Electronic applications accepted. *Expenses: Tuition:* Full-time $49,520; part-time $2060 per credit hour. *Required fees:* $2617.

**Rensselaer Polytechnic Institute,** Graduate School, School of Architecture, Program in Lighting, Troy, NY 12180-3590. Offers architectural sciences (MS, PhD); lighting (MS). *Degree requirements:* For master's, comprehensive exam, thesis; for doctorate, comprehensive exam, thesis/dissertation. *Entrance requirements:* For master's and doctorate, GRE. Additional exam requirements/recommendations for international students: Required—TOEFL (minimum score 570 paper-based; 88 iBT), IELTS (minimum score 6.5), PTE (minimum score 60). Electronic applications accepted. *Expenses: Tuition:* Full-time $49,520; part-time $2060 per credit hour. *Required fees:* $2617. *Faculty research:* Applications and design, automotive and street lighting, aviation lighting, controls, daylighting, energy and environment, health and vision, LEDs, outdoor lighting, residential lighting, security lighting.

**Rhode Island School of Design,** Division of Architecture and Design, Department of Architecture, Providence, RI 02903-2784. Offers M Arch. *Faculty:* 21 full-time (7 women), 23 part-time/adjunct (6 women). *Students:* 82 full-time (53 women); includes 16 minority (3 Black or African American, non-Hispanic/Latino; 8 Asian, non-Hispanic/Latino; 5 Hispanic/Latino), 47 international. Average age 26. 315 applicants, 42% accepted, 30 enrolled. In 2016, 32 master's awarded. *Degree requirements:* For master's, thesis, exhibition. *Entrance requirements:* For master's, portfolio, statement of purpose, 3 letters of recommendation. Additional exam requirements/recommendations for international students: Required—TOEFL (minimum score 580 paper-based; 93 iBT). *Application deadline:* For fall admission, 2/1 for domestic and international students. Application fee: $60. Electronic applications accepted. *Expenses: Tuition:* Full-time $46,800. *Required fees:* $310. *Financial support:* Fellowships, research assistantships, teaching assistantships, Federal Work-Study, scholarships/grants, and unspecified assistantships available. Financial award application deadline: 2/15; financial award applicants required to submit FAFSA. *Unit head:* Laura Briggs, Department Head, 401-454-6281, Fax: 401-454-6299, E-mail: lbriggs@risd.edu. *Application contact:* Molly Pettengil, Assistant Director for Graduate Recruitment, 401-454-6312, Fax: 401-454-6309, E-mail: mpetteng@risd.edu. Website: http://www.risd.edu/academics/architecture/

**Rice University,** Graduate Programs, School of Architecture, Houston, TX 77251-1892. Offers architecture (M Arch, D Arch); urban design (M Arch). *Degree requirements:* For master's, thesis optional; for doctorate, thesis/dissertation. *Entrance requirements:* For master's and doctorate, GRE. Additional exam requirements/recommendations for international students: Required—TOEFL (minimum score 600 paper-based; 100 iBT). Electronic applications accepted.

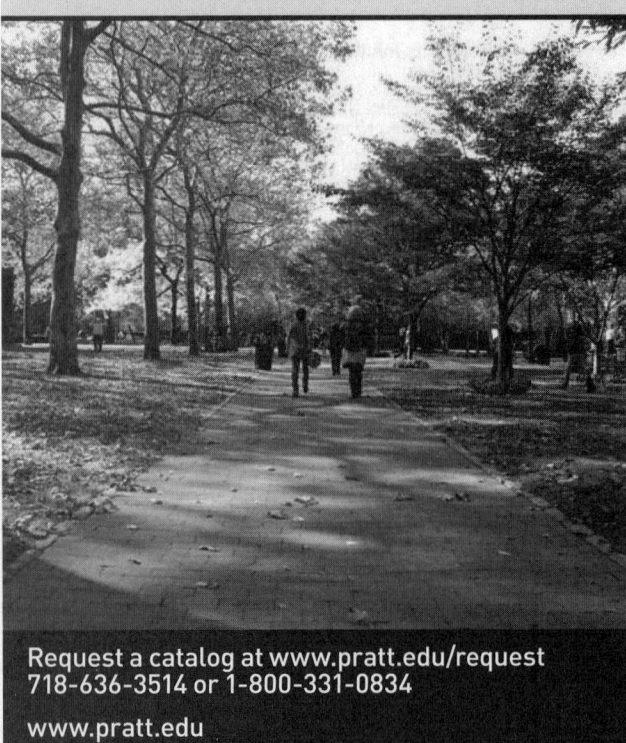
**Rochester Institute of Technology,** Graduate Enrollment Services, Golisano Institute for Sustainability, Architecture and Sustainability Department, M Arch Program in Architecture, Rochester, NY 14623. Offers M Arch. *Students:* 39 full-time (20 women), 8 part-time (4 women); includes 1 minority (Hispanic/Latino), 24 international. Average age 29. 63 applicants, 86% accepted, 9 enrolled. In 2016, 3 master's awarded. *Degree requirements:* For master's, thesis. *Entrance requirements:* For master's, GRE, minimum GPA of 3.0 (recommended), portfolio. Additional exam requirements/recommendations for international students: Required—TOEFL (minimum score 550 paper-based; 79 iBT), IELTS (minimum score 6.5), PTE (minimum score 58). *Application deadline:* For fall admission, 2/15 priority date for domestic and international students. Applications are processed on a rolling basis. Application fee: $60. Electronic applications accepted. *Expenses:* $1,742 per credit hour. *Financial support:* In 2016–17, 39 students received support. Teaching assistantships with partial tuition reimbursements available, career-related internships or fieldwork, scholarships/grants, and unspecified assistantships available. Financial award applicants required to submit FAFSA. *Faculty research:* Architecture and sustainability, design resiliency, and net zero energy/high performance buildings; renewable energy, environmentally responsive architecture and passive/natural building design and systems; sustainable urban design; socially responsible design and livable communities; traditional and classical architecture; theory and history of architecture and urban form. *Unit head:* Dennis Andrejko, Program Chairman, 585-475-7363, E-mail: info@sustainability.rit.edu. *Application contact:* Diane Ellison, Associate Vice President, Graduate Enrollment Services, 585-475-2229, Fax: 585-475-7164, E-mail: gradinfo@rit.edu. Website: http://www.rit.edu/gis/academics/master-architecture/overview

**Roger Williams University,** School of Architecture, Art and Historic Preservation, Bristol, RI 02809. Offers architecture (M Arch); art and architectural history (MA); historical preservation (MS). *Faculty:* 15 full-time (4 women), 4 part-time/adjunct (2 women). *Students:* 100 full-time (43 women), 1 part-time (0 women); includes 14 minority (3 Black or African American, non-Hispanic/Latino; 1 Asian, non-Hispanic/Latino; 6 Hispanic/Latino; 4 Two or more races, non-Hispanic/Latino), 4 international. Average age 25. 77 applicants, 95% accepted, 48 enrolled. In 2016, 43 master's awarded. *Degree requirements:* For master's, thesis. *Entrance requirements:* For master's, portfolio, 2 letters of recommendation, college transcript, letter of intent. Additional exam requirements/recommendations for international students: Required—TOEFL (minimum score 85 iBT), IELTS (minimum score 6.5). *Application deadline:* For fall admission, 4/1 for domestic students; for spring admission, 1/1 for domestic students. Application fee: $50. Electronic applications accepted. Application fee is waived when completed online. *Expenses:* $1,408 per credit hour (for M Arch); $843 per credit hour (for MS and MA). *Financial support:* In 2016–17, 95 students received support, including 91 research assistantships (averaging $2,753 per year); scholarships/grants and unspecified assistantships also available. Financial award application deadline: 4/1; financial award applicants required to submit FAFSA. *Unit head:* Stephen White, Dean, 401-254-3607, E-mail: swhite@rwu.edu. *Application contact:* Marcus Hanscom, Director of Graduate Admissions, 401-254-6200, Fax: 401-254-3345, E-mail: gradadmit@rwu.edu. Website: http://www.rwu.edu/academics/departments/architecture.htm#dual

**Savannah College of Art and Design,** Graduate School, Program in Architecture, Savannah, GA 31402-3146. Offers M Arch. *Program availability:* Part-time. *Faculty:* 20 full-time (8 women), 4 part-time/adjunct (0 women). *Students:* 86 full-time (36 women), 24 part-time (9 women); includes 18 minority (8 Black or African American, non-Hispanic/Latino; 2 Asian, non-Hispanic/Latino; 8 Hispanic/Latino), 56 international. Average age 26. 133 applicants, 61% accepted, 30 enrolled. In 2016, 30 master's awarded. *Degree requirements:* For master's, thesis. *Entrance requirements:* For master's, GRE (recommended), portfolio (submitted in digital format), audition or writing submission, resume, statement of purpose, two letters of recommendation. Additional exam requirements/recommendations for international students: Required—TOEFL (minimum score 550 paper-based, 85 iBT), IELTS (minimum score 6.5), or ACTFL. *Application deadline:* For fall admission, 4/1 for domestic and international students. Applications are processed on a rolling basis. Application fee: $40. Electronic applications accepted. *Expenses: Tuition:* Full-time $36,045. Tuition and fees vary according to course load. *Financial support:* Career-related internships or fieldwork, Federal Work-Study, and scholarships/grants available. Financial award application deadline: 4/1; financial award applicants required to submit FAFSA. *Faculty research:* Computer-aided design, photovoltaic-powered environmental control. *Unit head:* Ivan Chow, Dean, School of Building Arts. *Application contact:* Jenny Jaquillard, Executive Director of Admissions, Recruitment and Events, 912-525-5100, Fax: 912-525-5985, E-mail: admission@scad.edu. Website: http://www.scad.edu/academics/programs/architecture

**School of Architecture at Taliesin,** Graduate Program, Scottsdale, AZ 85259. Offers M Arch. Summer session held in Spring Green, WI. *Faculty:* 3 full-time (1 woman), 17 part-time/adjunct (4 women). *Students:* 16 full-time (4 women); includes 1 minority (Hispanic/Latino), 5 international. Average age 29. 27 applicants, 44% accepted, 8 enrolled. In 2016, 12 master's awarded. *Degree requirements:* For master's, thesis or alternative. *Entrance requirements:* For master's, interviews, portfolio, statement of purpose, resume, 3 letters of recommendation, transcripts. Additional exam requirements/recommendations for international students: Required—TOEFL, IELTS. *Application deadline:* For fall admission, 3/1 for domestic and international students. Applications are processed on a rolling basis. Application fee: $50. Electronic applications accepted. Application fee is waived when completed online. *Expenses:* Contact institution. *Financial support:* In 2016–17, 1 student received support. Career-related internships or fieldwork, scholarships/grants, and traineeships available. Financial award application deadline: 7/1; financial award applicants required to submit FAFSA. *Faculty research:* Architecture, landscape architecture, materials design, design. *Unit head:* Aaron A. Betsky, Dean, 480-860-2700, Fax: 480-391-4009, E-mail: abetsky@taliesin.edu. *Application contact:* Jerry Kavalieratos, Director of Admissions and Student Services, 480-627-5345, E-mail: jkavalieratos@taliesin.edu. Website: https://www.taliesin.edu

**See Display on next page and Close-Up on page 139.**

**TALIESIN**

FRANK LLOYD WRIGHT SCHOOL OF ARCHITECTURE

challenge
architectural
conventions

Master of Architecture
& Immersion Experience

www.taliesin.edu

**School of the Art Institute of Chicago,** Graduate Division, Department of Architecture, Interior Architecture, and Designed Objects, Chicago, IL 60603-3103. Offers architecture (M Arc); design for emerging technologies (MFA); designed objects (M Des); interior architecture (M Arc). *Entrance requirements:* Additional exam requirements/recommendations for international students: Required—TOEFL, IELTS.

★ **Southern California Institute of Architecture,** Graduate Program in Architecture, Los Angeles, CA 90013. Offers M Arch. *Degree requirements:* For master's, thesis, final thesis project. *Entrance requirements:* For master's, GRE General Test, portfolio, 3 letters of recommendation, transcripts, statement of purpose, resume. Additional exam requirements/recommendations for international students: Required—TOEFL (minimum score 583 paper-based, 90 iBT) or IELTS (minimum score 6.5). Electronic applications accepted.
**See Display on next page and Close-Up on page 141.**

**Southern Illinois University Carbondale,** Graduate School, College of Applied Science, School of Architecture, Carbondale, IL 62901-4701. Offers M Arch. *Entrance requirements:* Additional exam requirements/recommendations for international students: Required—TOEFL (minimum score 550 paper-based; 80 iBT). Electronic applications accepted.

**Syracuse University,** School of Architecture, Master of Architecture Program, Syracuse, NY 13244. Offers M Arch. *Entrance requirements:* For master's, GRE, online portfolio of creative and/or professional work in architecture, the visual arts, design, and/or affiliated fields; personal statement of purpose; official transcripts; three letters of recommendation. Additional exam requirements/recommendations for international students: Required—TOEFL, IELTS. *Application deadline:* For fall admission, 1/15 priority date for domestic students, 1/1 priority date for international students. *Expenses:* Tuition: Full-time $25,974; part-time $1443 per credit hour. *Required fees:* $802; $50 per course. Tuition and fees vary according to course load and program. *Financial support:* Fellowships, research assistantships, teaching assistantships, and scholarships/grants available. *Unit head:* Brian Lonsway, Chair, 315-443-2316, E-mail: blonsway@syr.edu. *Application contact:* Vittoria Buccina, Director, Graduate and Undergraduate Recruitment, 315-443-5074, E-mail: vabuccin@syr.edu.
Website: http://soa.syr.edu/programs/graduate/march/

**Syracuse University,** School of Architecture, MS in Architecture Program, Syracuse, NY 13244. Offers MS. *Entrance requirements:* For master's, GRE (recommended), online portfolio of creative and/or professional work in architecture, the visual arts, design, and/or affiliated fields; personal statement of purpose; research proposal; official transcripts; three letters of recommendation. Additional exam requirements/recommendations for international students: Required—TOEFL, IELTS. *Application deadline:* For fall admission, 1/15 for domestic and international students. *Expenses:* Tuition: Full-time $25,974; part-time $1443 per credit hour. *Required fees:* $802; $50 per course. Tuition and fees vary according to course load and program. *Financial support:* Fellowships, research assistantships, teaching assistantships, and scholarships/grants available. *Unit head:* Brian Lonsway, Associate Professor/Graduate Chair, 315-443-2316, E-mail: blonsway@syr.edu. *Application contact:* Vittoria Buccina, Director, Graduate and Undergraduate Recruitment, 315-443-5074, E-mail: vabuccin@syr.edu.
Website: http://soa.syr.edu/programs/graduate/ms-in-architecture/

**Temple University,** Tyler School of Art, Department of Architecture, Philadelphia, PA 19122-6096. Offers M Arch. *Program availability:* Part-time. *Degree requirements:* For master's, thesis optional. *Entrance requirements:* For master's, GRE, portfolio, letters of recommendation, resume/curriculum vitae, minimum GPA of 3.0. Additional exam requirements/recommendations for international students: Required—TOEFL (minimum score 550 paper-based; 79 iBT), IELTS (minimum score 6.5). Electronic applications accepted. *Expenses:* Contact institution.

**Texas A&M University,** College of Architecture, Department of Architecture, College Station, TX 77843. Offers architecture (M Arch, MS, PhD). *Faculty:* 33. *Students:* 152 full-time (77 women), 11 part-time (2 women); includes 22 minority (3 Black or African American, non-Hispanic/Latino; 6 Asian, non-Hispanic/Latino; 13 Hispanic/Latino), 87 international. Average age 29. 263 applicants, 52% accepted, 56 enrolled. In 2016, 45 master's, 5 doctorates awarded. *Degree requirements:* For master's, comprehensive exam, thesis; for doctorate, comprehensive exam, thesis/dissertation. *Entrance requirements:* For master's, GRE General Test, portfolio, letters of recommendation; for doctorate, GRE General Test. Additional exam requirements/recommendations for international students: Required—TOEFL (minimum score 550 paper-based; 80 iBT), IELTS (minimum score 6), PTE (minimum score 53). *Application deadline:* For fall admission, 12/15 priority date for domestic and international students. Applications are processed on a rolling basis. Application fee: $50 ($90 for international students). Electronic applications accepted. *Expenses:* Contact institution. *Financial support:* In 2016–17, 111 students received support, including 2 fellowships with tuition reimbursements available (averaging $13,697 per year), 24 research assistantships with tuition reimbursements available (averaging $3,447 per year), 53 teaching assistantships with tuition reimbursements available (averaging $6,017 per year); career-related internships or fieldwork, institutionally sponsored loans, scholarships/grants, traineeships, health care benefits, tuition waivers (full and partial), and unspecified assistantships also available. Support available to part-time students. Financial award application deadline: 3/15; financial award applicants required to submit FAFSA. *Faculty research:* Energy optimization, architecture pedagogy, environment and behavior. *Unit head:* Dr. Ward Wells, Head, 979-845-1015, Fax: 979-862-1571, E-mail: ward-wells@tamu.edu. *Application contact:* Graduate Admissions, 979-845-1060, E-mail: graduate-admissions@tamu.edu.
Website: http://dept.arch.tamu.edu/

**Texas Tech University,** Graduate School, College of Architecture, Lubbock, TX 79409-2091. Offers architecture (M Arch, MS); land-use planning, management, and design (PhD); MBA/M Arch. *Program availability:* Part-time. *Faculty:* 33 full-time (8 women), 16 part-time/adjunct (5 women). *Students:* 84 full-time (26 women), 20 part-time (5 women); includes 45 minority (3 Black or African American, non-Hispanic/Latino; 38 Hispanic/Latino; 4 Two or more races, non-Hispanic/Latino), 22 international. Average age 26. 71 applicants, 58% accepted, 19 enrolled. In 2016, 38 master's, 2 doctorates awarded. *Degree requirements:* For master's, comprehensive exam (for some programs), thesis (for some programs); for doctorate, comprehensive exam, thesis/dissertation. *Entrance requirements:* For master's, GRE General Test, portfolio; for doctorate, GRE General Test. Additional exam requirements/recommendations for international students: Required—TOEFL (minimum score 550 paper-based; 79 iBT). *Application deadline:* For fall admission, 6/1 priority date for domestic students, 1/15 priority date for international students; for spring admission, 9/1 priority date for domestic students, 6/15 priority date for international students. Applications are processed on a rolling basis. Application fee: $75. Electronic applications accepted. *Expenses:* $325 per credit hour full-time resident tuition, $733 per credit hour full-time non-resident tuition; $53.75 per credit hour fee plus $608 per term fee. *Financial support:* In 2016–17, 83 students received support, including 83 fellowships (averaging $4,422 per year); research assistantships, teaching assistantships, career-related internships or fieldwork,

SCIᴛ⅃ᴛC

Los Angeles

Master of Architecture — M.Arch

MS in Architectural Technologies

MS in Design Theory and Pedagogy

MS in Design of Cities

MA in Fiction and Entertainment

sciarc.edu

Federal Work-Study, institutionally sponsored loans, scholarships/grants, traineeships, health care benefits, and unspecified assistantships also available. Support available to part-time students. Financial award application deadline: 2/1; financial award applicants required to submit FAFSA. *Faculty research:* Digital design construction and fabrication, community development and design, health care design, historic preservation, visualization, sustainable architecture. *Total annual research expenditures:* $42,138. *Unit head:* Prof. James Williamson, Dean, 806-742-3136, Fax: 806-742-1400, E-mail: james.p.williamson@ttu.edu. *Application contact:* Jeff Rammage, Graduate Advisor, 806-742-3169, Fax: 806-742-1400, E-mail: jeffrey.rammage@ttu.edu. Website: http://www.arch.ttu.edu/architecture/

**Tulane University,** School of Architecture, New Orleans, LA 70118-5669. Offers M Arch, M Arch II, MPS, MSRED. *Program availability:* Part-time. *Degree requirements:* For master's, thesis. *Entrance requirements:* For master's, GRE, portfolio. Additional exam requirements/recommendations for international students: Required—TOEFL. *Expenses:* Contact institution. *Faculty research:* Design topics, preservation and environmental conservation, architecture and human health, computing.

**Universidad Autonoma de Guadalajara,** Graduate Programs, Guadalajara, Mexico. Offers administrative law and justice (LL M); advertising and corporate communications (MA); architecture (M Arch); business (MBA); computational science (MCC); education (Ed M, Ed D); English-Spanish translation (MA); entrepreneurship and management (MBA); integrated management of digital animation (MA); international business (MIB); international corporate law (LL M); internet technologies (MS); manufacturing systems (MMS); occupational health (MS); philosophy (MA, PhD); power electronics (MS); quality systems (MQS); renewable energy (MS); social evaluation of projects (MBA); strategic market research (MBA); tax law (MA); teaching mathematics (MA).

**Universidad Nacional Pedro Henriquez Urena,** Graduate School, Santo Domingo, Dominican Republic. Offers agricultural diversity (MS), including horticultural/fruit production, tropical animal production; conservation of monuments and cultural assets (M Arch); ecology and environment (MS); environmental engineering (MEE); international relations (MA); natural resource management (MS); political science (MA); project optimization (MPM); project feasibility (MPM); project management (MPM); sanitation engineering (ME); science for teachers (MS); tropical Caribbean architecture (M Arch).

**Université Laval,** Faculty of Architecture, Planning and Visual Arts, School of Architecture, Program in Architecture, Québec, QC G1K 7P4, Canada. Offers M Arch, M Sc. *Program availability:* Part-time. *Degree requirements:* For master's, thesis (for some programs). *Entrance requirements:* For master's, mastery of software (CAO), knowledge of French and English. Electronic applications accepted.

**University at Buffalo, the State University of New York,** Graduate School, School of Architecture and Planning, Department of Architecture, Buffalo, NY 14214. Offers architecture (M Arch); ecological practices (MS Arch); historic preservation and urban design (MS Arch); inclusive design (MS Arch); real estate development (MS Arch); situated technology (MS Arch); M Arch/MBA; M Arch/MFA; M Arch/MUP. *Faculty:* 32 full-time (11 women), 9 part-time/adjunct (3 women). *Students:* 134 full-time (56 women), 15 part-time (5 women); includes 29 minority (12 Black or African American, non-Hispanic/Latino; 5 Asian, non-Hispanic/Latino; 8 Hispanic/Latino; 4 Two or more races, non-Hispanic/Latino), 27 international. Average age 25. 267 applicants, 34% accepted, 63 enrolled. In 2016, 44 master's awarded. *Degree requirements:* For master's, thesis or alternative, project. *Entrance requirements:* For master's, GRE, portfolio, 3 letters of recommendation, transcripts, 500-word personal statement. Additional exam requirements/recommendations for international students: Required—TOEFL (minimum score 79 iBT), IELTS (minimum score 6.5). *Application deadline:* For fall admission, 1/1 priority date for domestic and international students. Application fee: $75. Electronic applications accepted. *Expenses:* Contact institution. *Financial support:* In 2016–17, 5 students received support, including 5 fellowships with full tuition reimbursements available (averaging $11,040 per year), 2 research assistantships with partial tuition reimbursements available (averaging $13,200 per year), 43 teaching assistantships with partial tuition reimbursements available (averaging $4,337 per year); career-related internships or fieldwork, Federal Work-Study, scholarships/grants, health care benefits, and unspecified assistantships also available. Financial award application deadline: 3/1; financial award applicants required to submit FAFSA. *Faculty research:* Ecological practices, inclusive design, material culture, situated technologies, urban design. *Total annual research expenditures:* $3.8 million. *Unit head:* Prof. Omar Khan, Chair, 716-829-3483 Ext. 105, Fax: 716-829-3256, E-mail: omar.khan@buffalo.edu. *Application contact:* Debra Eggebrecht, Assistant to the Chair, 716-829-3486 Ext. 105, Fax: 716-829-3256, E-mail: dle2@buffalo.edu. Website: http://www.ap.buffalo.edu/architecture/

**The University of Arizona,** College of Architecture, Planning, and Landscape Architecture, School of Architecture, Tucson, AZ 85721. Offers M Arch, MS. *Entrance requirements:* For master's, GRE, 3 letters of recommendation, statement of purpose, portfolio, resume. Additional exam requirements/recommendations for international students: Required—TOEFL (minimum score 550 paper-based; 79 iBT). Electronic applications accepted.

**The University of British Columbia,** Faculty of Applied Science, School of Architecture and Landscape Architecture, Vancouver, BC V6T 1Z2, Canada. Offers architecture (M Arch, MASA); landscape architecture (MASLA, MLA, MUD), including advanced studies in landscape architecture (MASLA), landscape architecture (MLA), urban design (MUD); M Arch/MLA. *Degree requirements:* For master's, thesis. *Entrance requirements:* For master's, portfolio, resume, statement of interest, 3 reference letters. Additional exam requirements/recommendations for international students: Required—TOEFL, IELTS. Application fee: $100 Canadian dollars ($162 Canadian dollars for international students). Electronic applications accepted. *Expenses:* Contact institution. *Financial support:* Fellowships, research assistantships, teaching assistantships, Federal Work-Study, institutionally sponsored loans, scholarships/grants, and tuition waivers (partial) available. *Faculty research:* Energy and resource use of buildings, advanced design research, urban design and community activism, advanced research in computer applications, cultural studies. *Application contact:* Jaynus O'Donnell, Graduate Program Staff, 604-822-2779, E-mail: jodonnell@sala.ubc.ca. Website: http://www.sala.ubc.ca

**University of Calgary,** Faculty of Graduate Studies, Faculty of Environmental Design, Calgary, AB T2N 1N4, Canada. Offers architecture (M Arch); environmental design (M Env Des, PhD); planning (M Plan). *Degree requirements:* For master's, thesis; for doctorate, thesis/dissertation. *Entrance requirements:* For master's, minimum GPA 3.0; for doctorate, minimum GPA 3.5. Additional exam requirements/recommendations for international students: Required—TOEFL (minimum score 550 paper-based). *Faculty research:* Sustainable development in architecture, planning and product design, energy and environment, impact assessment, ecotourism.

**University of California, Berkeley,** Graduate Division, College of Environmental Design, Department of Architecture, Berkeley, CA 94720-1500. Offers architecture (M Arch); building science (MS, PhD); building structures, construction and materials (MS, PhD); design theories, methods, and practices (MS, PhD); environmental design in developing countries (MS, PhD); history of architecture and urbanism (MS, PhD); social and cultural processes in architecture and urbanism (MS, PhD); M Arch/MCP; M Arch/MS; MLA/M Arch. *Students:* 178 full-time (84 women); includes 34 minority (4 Black or African American, non-Hispanic/Latino; 1 American Indian or Alaska Native, non-Hispanic/Latino; 13 Asian, non-Hispanic/Latino; 16 Hispanic/Latino), 85 international. Average age 30. 1,047 applicants, 68 enrolled. In 2016, 42 master's, 7 doctorates awarded. *Degree requirements:* For master's, thesis; for doctorate, thesis/dissertation, qualifying exam. *Entrance requirements:* For master's and doctorate, GRE General Test, minimum GPA 3.0, 3 letters of recommendation. *Additional exam requirements/recommendations for international students:* Required—TOEFL (minimum score 570 paper-based; 90 iBT). *Application deadline:* For fall admission, 12/7 for domestic students. Application fee: $105 ($125 for international students). Electronic applications accepted. Application fee is waived when completed online. *Financial support:* Fellowships, research assistantships, teaching assistantships, career-related internships or fieldwork, institutionally sponsored loans, health care benefits, and unspecified assistantships available. *Unit head:* Prof. Tom Buresh, Chair, 510-642-4942. *Application contact:* Lois H. Ito Koch, Student Affairs Officer, 510-642-5577, Fax: 510-643-5607, E-mail: archgrad@berkeley.edu. Website: http://arch.ced.berkeley.edu/

**University of California, Los Angeles,** Graduate Division, School of the Arts and Architecture, Department of Architecture and Urban Design, Los Angeles, CA 90095. Offers M Arch, MA, PhD. *Degree requirements:* For master's, comprehensive exam (M Arch I, II); thesis (MA); for doctorate, 2 foreign languages, thesis/dissertation, oral and written qualifying exams. *Entrance requirements:* For master's, GRE General Test, bachelor's degree; minimum undergraduate GPA of 3.0 (or its equivalent if letter grade system not used); writing sample (MA only); portfolio (M Arch only); for doctorate, GRE General Test, bachelor's degree; minimum undergraduate GPA of 3.5 (or its equivalent if letter grade system not used); writing sample. *Additional exam requirements/recommendations for international students:* Required—TOEFL. Electronic applications accepted. *Expenses:* Contact institution.

**University of Cincinnati,** Graduate School, College of Design, Architecture, Art, and Planning, School of Architecture and Interior Design, Cincinnati, OH 45221. Offers architecture (M Arch). *Accreditation:* NASAD. *Degree requirements:* For master's, one foreign language, thesis. *Entrance requirements:* *Additional exam requirements/recommendations for international students:* Required—TOEFL. *Expenses: Tuition, area resident:* Full-time $12,790; part-time $389 per credit hour. Tuition, state resident: full-time $13,290; part-time $419 per credit hour. Tuition, nonresident: full-time $24,532; part-time $976 per credit hour. *International tuition:* $24,832 full-time. *Required fees:* $3958; $140 per credit hour. Tuition and fees vary according to course load, degree level, program and reciprocity agreements. *Faculty research:* Theory and history of architecture.

**University of Colorado Denver,** College of Architecture and Planning, Program in Architecture, Denver, CO 80217. Offers M Arch. *Program availability:* Part-time. *Faculty:* 16 full-time (4 women), 16 part-time/adjunct (6 women). *Students:* 179 full-time (83 women), 3 part-time (0 women); includes 30 minority (2 Black or African American, non-Hispanic/Latino; 2 Asian, non-Hispanic/Latino; 20 Hispanic/Latino; 6 Two or more races, non-Hispanic/Latino), 7 international. Average age 28. 214 applicants, 44% accepted, 59 enrolled. In 2016, 69 master's awarded. *Degree requirements:* For master's, thesis optional. *Entrance requirements:* For master's, GRE, portfolio; sample of writing or work project; three letters of recommendation; statement of purpose. *Additional exam requirements/recommendations for international students:* Required—TOEFL (minimum score 75 iBT). *Application deadline:* For fall admission, 1/15 for domestic students, 12/15 for international students; for spring admission, 10/1 for domestic and international students. Application fee: $50 ($75 for international students). Electronic applications accepted. *Expenses:* Contact institution. *Financial support:* In 2016–17, 37 students received support. Fellowships, research assistantships, teaching assistantships, Federal Work-Study, institutionally sponsored loans, scholarships/grants, and traineeships available. Financial award application deadline: 4/1; financial award applicants required to submit FAFSA. *Faculty research:* Architectural design; history, theory, and criticism of architecture; regional and environmental issues; sustainability; intervention and transformation in the urban and rural landscape. *Unit head:* Ekaterini Vlahos, Chair/Director of the Center of Preservation Research, 303-315-0573, E-mail: kat.vlahos@ucdenver.edu. *Application contact:* Rachael Kuroiwa, Manager of Admissions and Outreach, 303-315-2325, E-mail: rachael.kuroiwa@ucdenver.edu. Website: http://www.ucdenver.edu/academics/colleges/ArchitecturePlanning/Academics/DegreePrograms/MArch/Pages/MArch.aspx

**University of Florida,** Graduate School, College of Design, Construction and Planning, Doctoral Program in Design, Construction and Planning, Gainesville, FL 32611. Offers construction management (PhD); design, construction and planning (PhD); geographic information systems (PhD); historic preservation (PhD); interior design (PhD); landscape architecture (PhD); urban and regional planning (PhD). *Degree requirements:* For doctorate, thesis/dissertation. *Entrance requirements:* For doctorate, GRE General Test, minimum GPA of 3.0. *Additional exam requirements/recommendations for international students:* Required—TOEFL (minimum score 550 paper-based; 80 iBT), IELTS (minimum score 6). Electronic applications accepted. *Faculty research:* Architecture, building construction, urban and regional planning.

**University of Florida,** Graduate School, College of Design, Construction and Planning, School of Architecture, Gainesville, FL 32611. Offers architecture (M Arch, MSAS); historic preservation (M Arch, MSAS); sustainable architecture (M Arch, MSAS); sustainable design (M Arch, MSAS). *Program availability:* Online learning. *Entrance requirements:* For master's, GRE General Test, minimum GPA of 3.0. *Additional exam requirements/recommendations for international students:* Required—TOEFL (minimum score 550 paper-based; 80 iBT), IELTS (minimum score 6).

**University of Hartford,** College of Engineering, Technology and Architecture, Program in Architecture, West Hartford, CT 06117-1599. Offers M Arch. *Entrance requirements:* For master's, 3 letters of recommendation, portfolio. *Additional exam requirements/recommendations for international students:* Required—TOEFL (minimum score 550 paper-based).

**University of Hawaii at Manoa,** School of Architecture, Honolulu, HI 96822. Offers D Arch. *Program availability:* Part-time. *Entrance requirements:* *Additional exam requirements/recommendations for international students:* Required—TOEFL, IELTS. *Faculty research:* Housing, future cities, environmental studies, preservation, professional practice.

**University of Houston,** College of Architecture, Houston, TX 77204. Offers architecture (MS); architecture studies (MA); space architecture (MS). *Entrance requirements:* For master's, GRE General Test. *Additional exam requirements/recommendations for international students:* Required—TOEFL (minimum score 550 paper-based; 79 iBT), IELTS (minimum score 6.5). Electronic applications accepted. *Faculty research:* Community-based design; twentieth century architecture, urbanism, and design; extreme environments; design build; green building components and digital technology.

**University of Idaho,** College of Graduate Studies, College of Art and Architecture, Moscow, ID 83844. Offers architecture (M Arch); art (MFA); bioregional planning and community design (MS); integrated architecture and design (MS); landscape architecture (MLA). *Faculty:* 14 full-time, 2 part-time/adjunct (0 women). *Students:* 67 full-time, 9 part-time. Average age 28. In 2016, 42 master's awarded. *Entrance requirements:* For master's, minimum GPA of 3.0. *Additional exam requirements/recommendations for international students:* Required—TOEFL. *Application deadline:* For fall admission, 8/1 for domestic students; for spring admission, 12/15 for domestic students. Applications are processed on a rolling basis. Application fee: $60. Electronic applications accepted. *Expenses:* Tuition, state resident: full-time $6460; part-time $414 per credit hour. Tuition, nonresident: full-time $21,268; part-time $1237 per credit hour. *Required fees:* $2070; $60 per credit hour. Full-time tuition and fees vary according to course load and reciprocity agreements. *Financial support:* Applicants required to submit FAFSA. *Faculty research:* Sustainability in communities, urban research, virtual technology, bioregional planning, environment and behavior interaction. *Unit head:* Dr. Shauna Corry, Interim Dean, 208-885-4409, E-mail: caa@uidaho.edu. *Application contact:* Sean Scoggin, Graduate Recruitment Coordinator, 208-885-4001, Fax: 208-885-4406, E-mail: graduateadmissions@uidaho.edu. Website: http://www.uidaho.edu/caa

**University of Illinois at Chicago,** College of Architecture, Design and the Arts, School of Architecture, Chicago, IL 60607-7128. Offers M Arch, MA, MS, MS Arch. *Entrance requirements:* For master's, GRE General Test, portfolio, minimum GPA of 3.0 in the last 60 hours of coursework, 3 letters of recommendation, statement of intent. *Additional exam requirements/recommendations for international students:* Required—TOEFL or IELTS. Electronic applications accepted. *Expenses:* Contact institution. *Faculty research:* Contemporary design, history and theory, technology, urbanism.

**University of Illinois at Urbana–Champaign,** Graduate College, College of Fine and Applied Arts, School of Architecture, Champaign, IL 61820. Offers architectural studies (MS); architecture (M Arch, PhD); M Arch/MBA; M Arch/MS; M Arch/MUP; MCS/M Arch.

**The University of Kansas,** Graduate Studies, School of Architecture, Design, and Planning, Department of Architecture, Lawrence, KS 66045. Offers architectural acoustics (Certificate); architecture (M Arch, PhD); health and wellness (Certificate); historic preservation (Certificate); urban design (Certificate). *Students:* 107 full-time (52 women), 15 part-time (7 women); includes 17 minority (5 Black or African American, non-Hispanic/Latino; 6 Asian, non-Hispanic/Latino; 4 Hispanic/Latino; 2 Two or more races, non-Hispanic/Latino), 35 international. Average age 26. 115 applicants, 71% accepted, 20 enrolled. In 2016, 85 master's, 2 doctorates awarded. Terminal master's awarded for partial completion of doctoral program. *Entrance requirements:* For master's, GRE, transcript; resume; minimum GPA of 3.0; statement of purpose; letters of recommendation; portfolio of design work, or samples of written work or other creative artifacts produced if previous degree was not in a design-related discipline; for doctorate, GRE, transcript, resume, minimum GPA of 3.0, statement of purpose, letters of recommendation, research-informed writing sample, exhibit of work illustrating applicant's interests and abilities in areas related to the design disciplines. *Additional exam requirements/recommendations for international students:* Required—TOEFL, IELTS. *Application deadline:* For fall admission, 1/15 priority date for domestic and international students; for summer admission, 1/15 priority date for domestic and international students. Application fee: $65 ($85 for international students). Electronic applications accepted. *Financial support:* Fellowships, research assistantships, teaching assistantships, scholarships/grants, health care benefits, and unspecified assistantships available. Financial award application deadline: 1/15; financial award applicants required to submit FAFSA. *Faculty research:* Design build, sustainability, emergent technology, healthy places, urban design. *Unit head:* Prof. Jae Chang, Chair, 785-864-1446, E-mail: jdchang@ku.edu. *Application contact:* Gera Elliott, Admissions Coordinator, 785-864-3167, Fax: 785-864-5185, E-mail: archku@ku.edu. Website: http://architecture.ku.edu/

**University of Kentucky,** Graduate School, College of Design, School of Architecture, Lexington, KY 40506-0032. Offers M Arch. *Degree requirements:* For master's, comprehensive exam. *Entrance requirements:* For master's, GRE General Test, minimum undergraduate GPA of 2.75. *Additional exam requirements/recommendations for international students:* Required—TOEFL (minimum score 550 paper-based). Electronic applications accepted.

**The University of Manchester,** School of Environment and Development, Manchester, United Kingdom. Offers architecture (M Phil, PhD); development policy and management (M Phil, PhD); human geography (M Phil, PhD); physical geography (M Phil, PhD); planning and landscape (M Phil, PhD).

**University of Manitoba,** Faculty of Graduate Studies, Faculty of Architecture, Department of Architecture, Winnipeg, MB R3T 2N2, Canada. Offers M Arch. *Degree requirements:* For master's, thesis or alternative.

**University of Maryland, College Park,** Academic Affairs, School of Architecture, Planning and Preservation, Program in Architecture, College Park, MD 20742. Offers M Arch, M Arch/MCP. *Program availability:* Part-time, evening/weekend. *Entrance requirements:* For master's, GRE General Test, portfolio, minimum GPA of 3.0, letters of recommendation. *Additional exam requirements/recommendations for international students:* Required—TOEFL. Electronic applications accepted. *Faculty research:* Design, history, theory.

**University of Massachusetts Amherst,** Graduate School, College of Humanities and Fine Arts, Department of Architecture, Amherst, MA 01003. Offers architecture (M Arch); design (MS); design in historic preservation (MS). *Program availability:* Part-time. *Degree requirements:* For master's, thesis or alternative. *Entrance requirements:* For master's, GRE General Test (for M Arch only), 3 letters of recommendation (M Arch only); portfolio. *Additional exam requirements/recommendations for international students:* Required—TOEFL (minimum score 550 paper-based; 80 iBT), IELTS (minimum score 6.5). Electronic applications accepted.

**University of Memphis,** Graduate School, College of Communication and Fine Arts, Department of Architecture, Memphis, TN 38152. Offers M Arch. *Program availability:* Part-time. *Faculty:* 5 full-time (2 women), 2 part-time/adjunct (1 woman). *Students:* 10 full-time (6 women), 3 part-time (0 women); includes 6 minority (1 Black or African American, non-Hispanic/Latino; 1 Asian, non-Hispanic/Latino; 4 Hispanic/Latino), 3 international. Average age 32. 4 applicants, 100% accepted, 2 enrolled. In 2016, 10 master's awarded. *Degree requirements:* For master's, thesis or alternative. *Entrance requirements:* For master's, portfolio; letters of recommendation; statement of intent; pre-professional undergraduate degree in architecture, environmental design, or equivalent. *Additional exam requirements/recommendations for international students:* Required—TOEFL (minimum score 550 paper-based; 79 iBT). *Application deadline:* For fall admission, 3/15 for domestic students. Application fee: $35 ($60 for international students). Electronic applications accepted. *Expenses:* $5,231.50 per semester full-time in-state, $9,623.50 full-time out-of-state. *Financial support:* In 2016–17, 7 students received support, including 7 research assistantships with full tuition reimbursements available (averaging $10,142 per year); teaching assistantships with full tuition

*Architecture*

reimbursements available, Federal Work-Study, scholarships/grants, and unspecified assistantships also available. Financial award application deadline: 2/1; financial award applicants required to submit FAFSA. *Unit head:* Michael D. Hagge, Chair, 901-678-2724, Fax: 901-678-1755, E-mail: mdhagge@memphis.edu. *Application contact:* Sherry Brian, Director of Graduate Studies, 901-678-3302, Fax: 901-678-1755. Website: http://architecture.memphis.edu

**University of Miami,** Graduate School, School of Architecture, Coral Gables, FL 33124. Offers architecture (M Arch); suburb and town design (M Arch). *Entrance requirements:* For master's, GRE General Test, minimum GPA of 3.0, portfolio. Additional exam requirements/recommendations for international students: Required—TOEFL. Electronic applications accepted. *Faculty research:* Housing, town planning, retrofit.

**University of Michigan,** Taubman College of Architecture and Urban Planning, Master of Architecture Program, Ann Arbor, MI 48109. Offers M Arch, M Arch/M Eng, M Arch/MSE, M Arch/MUD, MBA/M Arch. *Faculty:* 53 full-time (18 women), 24 part-time/adjunct (9 women). *Students:* 326 full-time (156 women); includes 62 minority (11 Black or African American, non-Hispanic/Latino; 28 Asian, non-Hispanic/Latino; 13 Hispanic/Latino; 10 Two or more races, non-Hispanic/Latino), 138 international. 728 applicants, 67% accepted, 184 enrolled. In 2016, 129 master's awarded. *Degree requirements:* For master's, thesis or alternative, thesis studio. *Entrance requirements:* Additional exam requirements/recommendations for international students: Required—TOEFL (minimum score 100 iBT), GRE. *Application deadline:* For fall admission, 1/15 for domestic and international students. Application fee: $75 ($90 for international students). Electronic applications accepted. *Expenses:* Contact institution. *Financial support:* In 2016–17, 169 students received support, including 32 teaching assistantships with full tuition reimbursements available (averaging $25,000 per year); scholarships/grants also available. Financial award application deadline: 1/15; financial award applicants required to submit FAFSA. *Unit head:* Sharon Haar, Architecture Program Chair, 734-764-1300, E-mail: haar@umich.edu. *Application contact:* Gerry Kreiner, Admissions Officer, 734-615-0431, E-mail: taubmancollegestudentservices@umich.edu. Website: http://taubmancollege.umich.edu/architecture/degrees/master-architecture

**University of Michigan,** Taubman College of Architecture and Urban Planning, Master of Science in Architecture Design and Research Program, Ann Arbor, MI 48109. Offers design and health (MS); digital technologies (MS); material systems (MS). *Faculty:* 10 full-time (5 women). *Students:* 22 full-time (10 women), 18 international. 62 applicants, 79% accepted, 18 enrolled. In 2016, 12 master's awarded. *Degree requirements:* For master's, thesis or alternative, capstone studio. *Entrance requirements:* Additional exam requirements/recommendations for international students: Required—TOEFL (minimum score 83 iBT), GRE. *Application deadline:* For fall admission, 1/15 for domestic students. Application fee: $75 ($90 for international students). Electronic applications accepted. *Expenses:* Contact institution. *Financial support:* In 2016–17, 22 students received support. Scholarships/grants available. Financial award application deadline: 1/15; financial award applicants required to submit FAFSA. *Unit head:* Sharon Haar, Architecture Program Chair, 734-764-1300, E-mail: haar@umich.edu. *Application contact:* Mike Smith, Admissions Officer, 734-647-2187, E-mail: taubmancollegestudentservices@umich.edu. Website: http://taubmancollege.umich.edu/architecture/degrees/master-science-architecture

**University of Minnesota, Twin Cities Campus,** Graduate School, College of Design, School of Architecture, Minneapolis, MN 55455-0213. Offers architecture (M Arch); sustainable design (MS). First professional and post-professional tracks available in M Arch program. *Degree requirements:* For master's, thesis (for some programs). *Entrance requirements:* For master's, GRE General Test, suggested GPA of 3.0, portfolio. Additional exam requirements/recommendations for international students: Required—TOEFL (minimum score 550 paper-based; 79 iBT). *Expenses:* Contact institution. *Faculty research:* History, daylighting, computer-aided design, sustainable design, structures.

**University of Missouri,** Office of Research and Graduate Studies, College of Human Environmental Sciences, Department of Architectural Studies, Columbia, MO 65211. Offers M Arch, PhD. *Entrance requirements:* For master's, GRE General Test, minimum GPA of 3.0. Additional exam requirements/recommendations for international students: Required—TOEFL (minimum score 500 paper-based; 61 iBT). Electronic applications accepted. *Expenses:* Tuition, state resident: full-time $6347; part-time $352.60 per credit hour. Tuition, nonresident: full-time $17,379; part-time $965.50 per credit hour. *Required fees:* $1035. Tuition and fees vary according to course load, campus/location and program.

**University of Nebraska–Lincoln,** Graduate College, College of Architecture, Department of Architecture, Graduate Program in Architecture, Lincoln, NE 68588. Offers MS, PhD. *Degree requirements:* For master's, comprehensive exam, thesis. *Entrance requirements:* For master's, GRE General Test. Additional exam requirements/recommendations for international students: Required—TOEFL (minimum score 550 paper-based). Electronic applications accepted. *Faculty research:* Housing, environmental design, architectural history, sustainable design, rural architecture.

**University of Nebraska–Lincoln,** Graduate College, College of Architecture, Department of Architecture, Professional Program in Architecture, Lincoln, NE 68588. Offers M Arch, M Arch/MBA, M Arch/MCRP. *Entrance requirements:* For master's, GRE General Test. Additional exam requirements/recommendations for international students: Required—TOEFL. *Faculty research:* Housing, environmental design, architectural history, sustainable design, rural architecture.

**University of Nevada, Las Vegas,** Graduate College, College of Fine Arts, School of Architecture, Las Vegas, NV 89154. Offers architecture (M Arch); healthcare interior design (MHID); hospitality design (Certificate). *Program availability:* Part-time. *Faculty:* 9 full-time (3 women), 5 part-time/adjunct (0 women). *Students:* 41 full-time (19 women), 6 part-time (4 women); includes 24 minority (6 Asian, non-Hispanic/Latino; 15 Hispanic/Latino; 1 Native Hawaiian or other Pacific Islander, non-Hispanic/Latino; 2 Two or more races, non-Hispanic/Latino), 6 international. Average age 28. 30 applicants, 80% accepted, 13 enrolled. In 2016, 21 master's awarded. *Degree requirements:* For master's, thesis (for some programs), professional project; for Certificate, defense of design/research presentation. *Entrance requirements:* For master's, GRE General Test, design portfolio; writing sample; bachelor's degree with minimum GPA of 3.0; for Certificate, portfolio of original work. Additional exam requirements/recommendations for international students: Required—TOEFL (minimum score 550 paper-based; 80 iBT), IELTS (minimum score 7). *Application deadline:* For fall admission, 1/15 for domestic students. Application fee: $60 ($95 for international students). Electronic applications accepted. *Expenses:* $269.25 per credit, $792 per 3-credit course; $9,634 per year resident; $23,274 per year non-resident; $7,094 fees non-resident (7 credits or more); $1,307 annual health insurance fee. *Financial support:* In 2016–17, 4 research assistantships (averaging $10,000 per year), 10 teaching assistantships with partial tuition reimbursements (averaging $10,000 per year) were awarded; institutionally sponsored loans, scholarships/grants, health care benefits, and unspecified assistantships also available. Financial award application deadline: 3/15. *Faculty research:* Hospitality design, urban studies/design, building science and sustainability,

healthcare design, design for aging populations, educational design. *Total annual research expenditures:* $195,894. *Unit head:* Dr. Alfredo Fernandez-Gonzalez, Director/Professor, 702-895-1141, Fax: 702-895-1119, E-mail: alfredo.fernandez@unlv.edu. *Application contact:* Dr. Glenn Nowak, Graduate Coordinator, 702-895-1076, Fax: 702-895-1119, E-mail: glenn.nowak@unlv.edu. Website: http://architecture.unlv.edu/

**University of New Mexico,** Graduate Studies, College of Fine Arts, Program in Art History, Albuquerque, NM 87131. Offers art history (MA); art of the Americas (MA); history of architecture (PhD); history of graphic arts (PhD); history of photography (PhD); modern Latin American art (PhD); Native American art (PhD); Pre-Columbian art and architecture (PhD); Spanish colonial art (PhD). *Program availability:* Part-time. *Faculty:* 4 full-time (all women). *Students:* 8 full-time (all women), 22 part-time (19 women); includes 9 minority (3 American Indian or Alaska Native, non-Hispanic/Latino; 5 Hispanic/Latino; 1 Two or more races, non-Hispanic/Latino), 3 international. Average age 40. 19 applicants, 42% accepted, 4 enrolled. In 2016, 5 master's, 1 doctorate awarded. *Degree requirements:* For master's, one foreign language, comprehensive exam (for some programs), thesis, symposium; for doctorate, 2 foreign languages, comprehensive exam, thesis/dissertation, symposium. *Entrance requirements:* Additional exam requirements/recommendations for international students: Required—TOEFL (minimum score 550 paper-based), IELTS (minimum score 6). *Application deadline:* For fall admission, 1/15 for domestic students; for spring admission, 1/15 for domestic students. Application fee: $50. Electronic applications accepted. *Financial support:* Fellowships, research assistantships with tuition reimbursements, teaching assistantships with partial tuition reimbursements, Federal Work-Study, institutionally sponsored loans, scholarships/grants, health care benefits, and unspecified assistantships available. Support available to part-time students. Financial award application deadline: 3/1; financial award applicants required to submit FAFSA. *Faculty research:* Native American, modern Latin American, pre-Columbian, architectural, American, medieval, Spanish Colonial, and Latin American art; history of photography. *Unit head:* Prof. Mary Tsiongas, Chair, 505-277-5861, Fax: 505-277-5955, E-mail: tsiongas@unm.edu. *Application contact:* Kat Heatherington, Graduate Advisor, 505-277-6672, Fax: 505-277-5955, E-mail: art255@unm.edu. Website: http://art.unm.edu/

**University of New Mexico,** Graduate Studies, School of Architecture and Planning, Program in Architecture, Albuquerque, NM 87131-2039. Offers M Arch. *Faculty:* 15 full-time (5 women), 5 part-time/adjunct (1 woman). *Students:* 72 full-time (25 women), 4 part-time (2 women); includes 31 minority (1 Black or African American, non-Hispanic/Latino; 6 American Indian or Alaska Native, non-Hispanic/Latino; 1 Asian, non-Hispanic/Latino; 23 Hispanic/Latino), 20 international. Average age 30. 88 applicants, 45% accepted, 30 enrolled. In 2016, 30 master's awarded. *Degree requirements:* For master's, thesis (for some programs). *Entrance requirements:* For master's, experience in field. Additional exam requirements/recommendations for international students: Required—TOEFL (minimum score 550 paper-based; 79 iBT). *Application deadline:* For fall admission, 2/1 priority date for domestic students. Application fee: $50. Electronic applications accepted. *Financial support:* Fellowships, research assistantships with partial tuition reimbursements, scholarships/grants, health care benefits, and unspecified assistantships available. Financial award application deadline: 3/1; financial award applicants required to submit FAFSA. *Faculty research:* Professional practice, design theory, sustainable environments, architecture and children, environment and behavior. *Unit head:* Geraldine Forbes Isais, Director, 505-277-3303, Fax: 505-277-0076, E-mail: gforbes@unm.edu. *Application contact:* Elizabeth M. Rowe, Senior Academic Advisor, 505-277-1303, Fax: 505-277-0076, E-mail: mitziv@unm.edu. Website: http://saap.unm.edu/

**The University of North Carolina at Charlotte,** College of Arts and Architecture, School of Architecture, Charlotte, NC 28223-0001. Offers architecture (M Arch I, M Arch II); urban design (MUD). *Faculty:* 21 full-time (7 women). *Students:* 100 full-time (57 women), 2 part-time (1 woman); includes 21 minority (9 Black or African American, non-Hispanic/Latino; 1 Asian, non-Hispanic/Latino; 8 Hispanic/Latino; 3 Two or more races, non-Hispanic/Latino), 23 international. Average age 25. 164 applicants, 74% accepted, 47 enrolled. In 2016, 31 master's awarded. *Degree requirements:* For master's, design studio or thesis. *Entrance requirements:* For master's, GRE, official transcripts from all previous college-level institution(s); statement of purpose explaining reasons for wanting to study in the School of Architecture; three recommendations from persons familiar with the applicant's personal and professional qualifications; resume or curriculum vitae; portfolio. Additional exam requirements/recommendations for international students: Required—TOEFL (minimum score 523 paper-based, 70 iBT) or IELTS (6.5). *Application deadline:* For fall admission, 1/15 priority date for domestic and international students. Applications are processed on a rolling basis. Application fee: $75. Electronic applications accepted. *Expenses:* Contact institution. *Financial support:* In 2016–17, 33 students received support, including 25 research assistantships (averaging $7,500 per year), 8 teaching assistantships (averaging $3,112 per year); institutionally sponsored loans, scholarships/grants, and unspecified assistantships also available. Financial award application deadline: 3/1; financial award applicants required to submit FAFSA. *Faculty research:* Urban design studies for local and regional municipalities and community groups, high performance building and optimization protocols, daylighting and energy analysis, digital design and fabrication components, and interactive visualization; refinement of regionally specific computer-aided analysis tools used to evaluate total building energy performance, and the economic valuation of architectural systems and their design attributes. *Total annual research expenditures:* $35,367. *Unit head:* Kenneth A. Lambla, Dean, 704-687-0090, E-mail: kalambla@uncc.edu. *Application contact:* Kathy B. Giddings, Director of Graduate Admissions, 704-687-5503, Fax: 704-687-1668, E-mail: gradadm@uncc.edu. Website: http://coaa.uncc.edu/academics/school-of-architecture

**The University of North Carolina at Greensboro,** Graduate School, College of Arts and Sciences, Department of Interior Architecture, Greensboro, NC 27412-5001. Offers historic preservation (Certificate); interior architecture (MS); museum studies (Certificate). *Degree requirements:* For master's, thesis. *Entrance requirements:* For master's, GRE General Test or MAT, bachelor's degree in interior design, interview, portfolio. Additional exam requirements/recommendations for international students: Required—TOEFL. Electronic applications accepted.

**University of Notre Dame,** Graduate School, School of Architecture, Notre Dame, IN 46556. Offers architectural design and urbanism (M ADU); architecture (M Arch). *Degree requirements:* For master's, thesis or alternative. *Entrance requirements:* For master's, GRE General Test, portfolio. Additional exam requirements/recommendations for international students: Required—TOEFL (minimum score 600 paper-based; 80 iBT). Electronic applications accepted. *Faculty research:* Architectural theory, urban design, classical and traditional architecture and urbanism.

**University of Oklahoma,** College of Architecture, Division of Architecture, Norman, OK 73019-6141. Offers architecture (MS, PhD); data and digital representation (M Arch); design entrepreneurship and real estate (M Arch); resilient planning, design, and construction (M Arch). *Program availability:* Part-time. *Faculty:* 38 full-time (16 women), 1 part-time/adjunct (0 women). *Students:* 35 full-time (19 women), 9 part-time (4 women); includes 6 minority (1 Black or African American, non-Hispanic/Latino; 1

American Indian or Alaska Native, non-Hispanic/Latino; 1 Asian, non-Hispanic/Latino; 3 Two or more races, non-Hispanic/Latino), 17 international. Average age 31. 47 applicants, 47% accepted, 16 enrolled. In 2016, 14 master's awarded. Terminal master's awarded for partial completion of doctoral program. *Degree requirements:* For master's, variable foreign language requirement; for doctorate, variable foreign language requirement, comprehensive exam, thesis/dissertation. *Entrance requirements:* Additional exam requirements/recommendations for international students: Required—TOEFL (minimum score 79 iBT) or IELTS (minimum score 6.5). *Application deadline:* For spring admission, 5/1 for domestic students, 3/1 for international students. Applications are processed on a rolling basis. Application fee: $50 ($100 for international students). Electronic applications accepted. *Expenses:* Tuition, state resident: full-time $4886; part-time $203.60 per credit hour. Tuition, nonresident: full-time $18,989; part-time $791.20 per credit hour. *Required fees:* $3283; $126.25 per credit hour. $126.50 per semester. *Financial support:* In 2016–17, 25 students received support, including 10 research assistantships with partial tuition reimbursements available (averaging $10,372 per year), 2 teaching assistantships with partial tuition reimbursements available (averaging $12,686 per year); career-related internships or fieldwork, scholarships/grants, health care benefits, tuition waivers, and unspecified assistantships also available. Financial award application deadline: 6/1; financial award applicants required to submit FAFSA. *Faculty research:* Resiliency and sustainability; data and digital representation; design entrepreneurship and real estate. *Unit head:* Dr. Stephanie Pilat, Director, 405-325-9352, Fax: 405-325-7588, E-mail: architecture.director@ou.edu. *Application contact:* Marjorie Callahan, Graduate Liaison, Fax: 405-325-7588, E-mail: mcallahan@ou.edu.
Website: http://arch.coa.ou.edu

**University of Oregon,** Graduate School, School of Architecture and Allied Arts, Department of Architecture, Eugene, OR 97403. Offers architecture (M Arch); interior architecture (MI Arch). *Accreditation:* CIDA. *Degree requirements:* For master's, thesis (for some programs). *Entrance requirements:* For master's, GRE General Test. Additional exam requirements/recommendations for international students: Required—TOEFL. *Faculty research:* Innovation in housing design and design production, climate responsive design, passive heating and cooling, computer software development for design applications, vernacular architecture.

**University of Pennsylvania,** School of Design, Department of Architecture, Philadelphia, PA 19104. Offers architecture (M Arch, PhD); ecological architecture (Certificate); environmental building design (MEBD). *Program availability:* Part-time. *Faculty:* 13 full-time (4 women), 14 part-time/adjunct (3 women). *Students:* 373 full-time (206 women), 3 part-time (2 women); includes 51 minority (4 Black or African American, non-Hispanic/Latino; 30 Asian, non-Hispanic/Latino; 11 Hispanic/Latino; 6 Two or more races, non-Hispanic/Latino), 242 international. Average age 26. 838 applicants, 45% accepted, 142 enrolled. In 2016, 103 master's, 1 doctorate, 22 other advanced degrees awarded. *Expenses: Tuition:* Full-time $31,068; part-time $5762 per course. *Required fees:* $3200; $336 per course. Full-time tuition and fees vary according to degree level, program and student level. Part-time tuition and fees vary according to course load, degree level and program.

**University of Puerto Rico, Río Piedras Campus,** School of Architecture, San Juan, PR 00931-3300. Offers M Arch. *Program availability:* Part-time. *Entrance requirements:* For master's, comprehensive exam, thesis, design project. *Entrance requirements:* For master's, PAEG or GRE, bachelor's degree in architecture, interview, minimum GPA of 3.0, portfolio, 2 letters of recommendation.

**University of Southern California,** Graduate School, School of Architecture, Los Angeles, CA 90089. Offers M Arch, MBS, MHP, MLA, PhD, M Arch/M Pl, MLA/M Pl. Terminal master's awarded for partial completion of doctoral program. *Degree requirements:* For master's, thesis (for some programs); for doctorate, thesis/dissertation. *Entrance requirements:* For master's and doctorate, GRE. Additional exam requirements/recommendations for international students: Required—TOEFL (minimum score 100 iBT). Electronic applications accepted. *Faculty research:* Urban housing; advanced digital simulation, computation, and representation; building skins; parametric design; advanced seismic research.

**University of South Florida,** College of The Arts, School of Architecture and Community Design, Tampa, FL 33620-9951. Offers architecture (M Arch); urban and community design (MUCD). *Faculty:* 10 full-time (1 woman). *Students:* 103 full-time (40 women), 13 part-time (8 women); includes 41 minority (6 Black or African American, non-Hispanic/Latino; 6 Asian, non-Hispanic/Latino; 26 Hispanic/Latino; 3 Two or more races, non-Hispanic/Latino), 17 international. Average age 25. 83 applicants, 43% accepted, 25 enrolled. In 2016, 51 master's awarded. *Degree requirements:* For master's, comprehensive exam, thesis. *Entrance requirements:* For master's, GRE General Test, minimum undergraduate GPA of 3.0 in last 60 hours of coursework; three letters of recommendation; portfolio or creative work; written statement of intent; prerequisite courses in physics, calculus, and AutoCAD. Additional exam requirements/recommendations for international students: Required—TOEFL (minimum score 550 paper-based; 79 iBT) or IELTS (minimum score 6.5). *Application deadline:* For fall admission, 2/1 priority date for domestic students, 2/1 for international students. Applications are processed on a rolling basis. Application fee: $30. Electronic applications accepted. *Expenses:* Tuition, state resident: full-time $7766; part-time $431.43 per credit hour. Tuition, nonresident: full-time $15,789; part-time $877.17 per credit hour. *Required fees:* $37 per term. *Financial support:* In 2016–17, 48 students received support, including 3 teaching assistantships with tuition reimbursements available (averaging $9,360 per year); Federal Work-Study, scholarships/grants, and unspecified assistantships also available. *Faculty research:* Urban community design and planning; public space infrastructure; conditions of suburban sprawl; redevelopment strategies for abandoned commercial centers and edges; sustainability; influences of technology, cultural identity and interpretation and social values on architectural design; epistemology of design thinking; tropical architecture; high-density urbanism; design benevolence; economic development/community revitalization; housing/residential development; development regulations. *Total annual research expenditures:* $403,084. *Unit head:* Dr. Robert MacLeod, Director and Professor, School of Architecture and Community Design, 813-974-6015, Fax: 813-974-2557, E-mail: rmacleod@arch.usf.edu. *Application contact:* Mildred Abreu, Academic Advisor, 813-974-1216, Fax: 813-974-2557, E-mail: abreu@arch.usf.edu.
Website: http://www.arch.usf.edu

**The University of Tennessee,** Graduate School, College of Architecture and Design, Program in Architecture, Knoxville, TN 37996. Offers architecture (professional) (M Arch); architecture (research) (M Arch). *Degree requirements:* For master's, thesis. *Entrance requirements:* For master's, GRE General Test, minimum GPA of 3.0, 3 letters of recommendation, samples of portfolio work (highly recommended for professional track). Additional exam requirements/recommendations for international students: Required—TOEFL (minimum score 550 paper-based).

**The University of Texas at Arlington,** Graduate School, College of Architecture, Planning and Public Affairs, Program in Architecture, Arlington, TX 76019. Offers M Arch. *Degree requirements:* For master's, thesis. *Entrance requirements:* For master's, GRE General Test, minimum GPA of 3.0, portfolio (for those with previous design degrees). Additional exam requirements/recommendations for international

students: Required—TOEFL (minimum score 575 paper-based; 91 iBT). *Application deadline:* For fall admission, 6/1 for domestic students, 4/1 for international students; for spring admission, 10/15 for domestic students, 9/15 for international students. Applications are processed on a rolling basis. Application fee: $50 ($60 for international students). *Financial support:* Research assistantships with partial tuition reimbursements, teaching assistantships with full tuition reimbursements, career-related internships or fieldwork, scholarships/grants, and unspecified assistantships available. Financial award application deadline: 6/1; financial award applicants required to submit FAFSA. *Faculty research:* Regional landscapes/native materials, urban densification, urban design, sustainable design principles. *Unit head:* David Jones, Associate Dean, 817-272-2801, Fax: 817-272-5098, E-mail: djonesarch@uta.edu. *Application contact:* Ana Maria Peredo-Manor, Administrative Assistant, 817-272-2801, Fax: 817-272-5098, E-mail: ampmanor@uta.edu.
Website: http://www.uta.edu/architecture/

**The University of Texas at Austin,** Graduate School, School of Architecture, Program in Architecture, Austin, TX 78712-1111. Offers M Arch, MSAS. *Entrance requirements:* For master's, GRE, transcripts, portfolio, statement of interest, references.

**The University of Texas at San Antonio,** College of Architecture, Department of Architecture, San Antonio, TX 78249-0617. Offers M Arch, MS Arch. *Program availability:* Part-time. *Faculty:* 19 full-time (5 women), 2 part-time/adjunct (0 women). *Students:* 63 full-time (35 women), 25 part-time (11 women); includes 57 minority (2 Black or African American, non-Hispanic/Latino; 6 Asian, non-Hispanic/Latino; 49 Hispanic/Latino), 12 international. Average age 28. 74 applicants, 70% accepted, 29 enrolled. In 2016, 30 master's awarded. *Degree requirements:* For master's, comprehensive exam (for some programs), thesis optional. *Entrance requirements:* For master's, GRE General Test, bachelor's degree with 18 credit hours in field of study or in another appropriate field of study, 2 letters of recommendation, statement of purpose. Additional exam requirements/recommendations for international students: Required—TOEFL (minimum score 550 paper-based; 79 iBT), IELTS (minimum score 6.5). Application fee: $45 ($80 for international students). Electronic applications accepted. *Financial support:* In 2016–17, research assistantships (averaging $3,500 per year) were awarded; teaching assistantships and tuition waivers (partial) also available. Financial award applicants required to submit FAFSA. *Faculty research:* Building energy performance and sustainability, architectural and heritage tourism, regionalism and architectural theory, Mexican and Latin American architecture, medieval and Renaissance architecture, historic preservation and conservation, urban and regional planning, materials. *Total annual research expenditures:* $147,433. *Unit head:* Dr. Vincent Canizaro, Chair, 210-458-3039, E-mail: vincent.canizaro@utsa.edu. *Application contact:* Dr. Sedef Doganer, Graduate Advisor of Record, 210-458-3037, Fax: 210-458-3016, E-mail: sedef.doganer@utsa.edu.
Website: http://architecture.utsa.edu/academic-programs/department-of-architecture/

**University of the District of Columbia,** College of Agriculture, Urban Sustainability and Environmental Sciences, Program in Architecture, Washington, DC 20008-1175. Offers M Arch, M Arch II.

**University of Toronto,** School of Graduate Studies, John H. Daniels Faculty of Architecture, Landscape, and Design, Toronto, ON M5S 1A1, Canada. Offers M Arch, MLA, MUD, MVS. *Entrance requirements:* For master's, minimum B average; 3 letters of reference; resume; 3 writing samples; 5 samples of design work, drawing, or work in a related field, statement of interest. Additional exam requirements/recommendations for international students: Required—TOEFL (minimum score 580 paper-based; 93 iBT), IELTS (minimum score 7), TWE (minimum score 5), Michigan English Language Assessment Battery (minimum score 85), COPE (minimum score 76). Electronic applications accepted. *Expenses:* Contact institution.

**University of Utah,** Graduate School, College of Architecture and Planning, School of Architecture, Salt Lake City, UT 84112. Offers architectural studies (MS); architecture (M Arch). *Program availability:* Part-time. *Faculty:* 18 full-time (9 women), 20 part-time/adjunct (5 women). *Students:* 59 full-time (15 women), 3 part-time (0 women); includes 10 minority (1 Black or African American, non-Hispanic/Latino; 2 Asian, non-Hispanic/Latino; 5 Hispanic/Latino; 2 Two or more races, non-Hispanic/Latino), 6 international. Average age 28. 67 applicants, 87% accepted, 34 enrolled. In 2016, 33 master's awarded. *Degree requirements:* For master's, thesis (for some programs), comprehensive project. *Entrance requirements:* For master's, minimum undergraduate GPA of 3.0; portfolio; statement of purpose; letters of recommendation. Additional exam requirements/recommendations for international students: Required—TOEFL (minimum score 575 paper-based). *Application deadline:* For fall admission, 1/1 for domestic students, 12/1 for international students. Application fee: $55 ($65 for international students). Electronic applications accepted. *Expenses:* Contact institution. *Financial support:* In 2016–17, 36 students received support, including 15 fellowships (averaging $3,375 per year), 29 teaching assistantships (averaging $3,375 per year); research assistantships, career-related internships or fieldwork, scholarships/grants, and unspecified assistantships also available. Financial award application deadline: 3/1; financial award applicants required to submit FAFSA. *Faculty research:* History, design, acoustics, photography, structures, architecture of the American West, architectural communication and representation, impact of technology, design-build. *Total annual research expenditures:* $62,017. *Unit head:* Mira Locher, Chair, 801-585-8946, E-mail: locher@arch.utah.edu. *Application contact:* Mayra Godin Focht, Administrative Officer/Advisor, 801-585-5354, Fax: 801-585-1565, E-mail: mayra@arch.utah.edu.
Website: http://www.arch.utah.edu/?school_of_architecture

**University of Washington,** Graduate School, College of Built Environments, Department of Architecture, Seattle, WA 98195. Offers architecture (M Arch, MS); built environment (PhD); design computing (Certificate); design firm leadership and management (Certificate); historic preservation (Certificate); lighting (Certificate); urban design (Certificate). *Degree requirements:* For master's, thesis. *Entrance requirements:* For master's, GRE General Test, minimum GPA of 3.0, portfolio, 3 letters of recommendation. Additional exam requirements/recommendations for international students: Required—TOEFL. *Faculty research:* Lighting, materials, computing theory, media, culture, environment.

**University of Waterloo,** Graduate Studies, Faculty of Engineering, School of Architecture, Waterloo, ON N2L 3G1, Canada. Offers M Arch. *Program availability:* Part-time. *Degree requirements:* For master's, thesis. *Entrance requirements:* For master's, bachelor's degree in pre-professional architecture. Additional exam requirements/recommendations for international students: Required—TOEFL, IELTS, PTE. Electronic applications accepted.

**University of Wisconsin–Milwaukee,** Graduate School, School of Architecture and Urban Planning, Department of Architecture, Milwaukee, WI 53201-0413. Offers architecture (M Arch, MS Arch, PhD); geographic information systems (Graduate Certificate). *Students:* 114 full-time (51 women), 15 part-time (4 women); includes 18 minority (3 Black or African American, non-Hispanic/Latino; 1 American Indian or Alaska Native, non-Hispanic/Latino; 6 Asian, non-Hispanic/Latino; 2 Hispanic/Latino; 6 Two or more races, non-Hispanic/Latino), 21 international. Average age 30. 131 applicants, 59% accepted, 42 enrolled. In 2016, 65 master's, 1 doctorate, 11 other advanced

## Architecture

degrees awarded. *Degree requirements:* For master's, comprehensive exam, thesis; for doctorate, comprehensive exam, thesis/dissertation. *Entrance requirements:* For master's, GRE General Test, portfolio. Additional exam requirements/recommendations for international students: Required—TOEFL (minimum score 600 paper-based; 100 iBT), IELTS (minimum score 7). *Application deadline:* For fall admission, 1/1 priority date for domestic students; for spring admission, 9/1 for domestic students. Applications are processed on a rolling basis. Application fee: $56 ($96 for international students). Electronic applications accepted. *Financial support:* In 2016–17, 3 fellowships, 20 teaching assistantships were awarded; career-related internships or fieldwork, health care benefits, unspecified assistantships, and project assistantships also available. Support available to part-time students. Financial award application deadline: 4/15; financial award applicants required to submit FAFSA. *Unit head:* Robert Greenstreet, Dean. *Application contact:* Student Advising Office, 414-229-4015, E-mail: sarup-grad@uwm.edu.
Website: https://uwm.edu/sarup/architecture/

**Virginia Polytechnic Institute and State University,** Graduate School, College of Architecture and Urban Studies, Blacksburg, VA 24061. Offers architecture (MS Arch); architecture and design research (PhD); building/construction science and management (MS); creative technologies (MFA); environmental design and planning (PhD); landscape architecture (MLA); planning, governance, and globalization (PhD); public administration (MPA); public administration/public affairs (PhD, Certificate); public and international affairs (MPIA); urban and regional planning (MURP). *Accreditation:* ASLA (one or more programs are accredited). *Faculty:* 136 full-time (53 women). *Students:* 371 full-time (185 women), 210 part-time (104 women); includes 118 minority (49 Black or African American, non-Hispanic/Latino; 1 American Indian or Alaska Native, non-Hispanic/Latino; 30 Asian, non-Hispanic/Latino; 32 Hispanic/Latino; 6 Two or more races, non-Hispanic/Latino), 137 international. Average age 31. 566 applicants, 55% accepted, 160 enrolled. In 2016, 137 master's, 24 doctorates awarded. *Degree requirements:* For master's, comprehensive exam (for some programs), thesis (for some programs); for doctorate, comprehensive exam (for some programs), thesis/dissertation (for some programs). *Entrance requirements:* For master's and doctorate, GRE/GMAT. Additional exam requirements/recommendations for international students: Required—TOEFL (minimum score 80 iBT). *Application deadline:* For fall admission, 8/1 for domestic students, 4/1 for international students; for spring admission, 1/1 for domestic students, 9/1 for international students. Applications are processed on a rolling basis. Application fee: $75. Electronic applications accepted. *Expenses:* Tuition, state resident: full-time $12,467; part-time $692.50 per credit hour. Tuition, nonresident: full-time $25,095; part-time $1394.25 per credit hour. *Required fees:* $2669; $491.50 per semester. Tuition and fees vary according to course load, campus/location and program. *Financial support:* In 2016–17, 11 research assistantships with full tuition reimbursements (averaging $19,474 per year), 45 teaching assistantships with full tuition reimbursements (averaging $16,014 per year) were awarded. Financial award application deadline: 3/1; financial award applicants required to submit FAFSA. *Total annual research expenditures:* $3.6 million. *Unit head:* Dr. A. J. Davis, Dean, 540-231-6416, Fax: 540-231-6332, E-mail: davisa@vt.edu. *Application contact:* Christine Mattsson-Coon, Executive Assistant, 540-231-6416, Fax: 540-231-6332, E-mail: cmattsso@vt.edu.
Website: http://www.caus.vt.edu/

**Washington State University,** Voiland College of Engineering and Architecture, Program in Architecture, Pullman, WA 99164-2220. Offers architecture (M Arch). *Degree requirements:* For master's, comprehensive exam, thesis, oral exam. *Entrance requirements:* For master's, minimum GPA of 3.0, 3 letters of recommendation, personal statement, portfolio. Additional exam requirements/recommendations for international students: Required—TOEFL (minimum score 80 iBT), IELTS. *Faculty research:* Cultural, technological, and environmental design; integrated project delivery; American architecture and urbanism; land use and planning; design for rural communities and aging populations.

**Washington University in St. Louis,** Sam Fox School of Design and Visual Arts, Program in Architecture, St. Louis, MO 63130-4899. Offers M Arch, MLA, M Arch/MBA, M Arch/MCM, M Arch/MSW, M Arch/MUD, MLA/M Arch. *Degree requirements:* For master's, final project. *Entrance requirements:* For master's, GRE General Test, portfolio. Additional exam requirements/recommendations for international students: Required—TOEFL (minimum score 550 paper-based; 80 iBT), TWE. Electronic applications accepted. *Faculty research:* Urban design development issues.

**Wentworth Institute of Technology,** Department of Architecture, Boston, MA 02115-5998. Offers M Arch. *Faculty:* 14 full-time (7 women), 13 part-time/adjunct (5 women). *Students:* 75 full-time (34 women), 3 part-time (2 women); includes 14 minority (5 Black or African American, non-Hispanic/Latino; 3 Asian, non-Hispanic/Latino; 2 Hispanic/Latino; 4 Two or more races, non-Hispanic/Latino), 7 international. Average age 24. 121 applicants, 83% accepted, 69 enrolled. In 2016, 78 master's awarded. *Degree requirements:* For master's, thesis project. *Entrance requirements:* For master's, GRE, statement of objectives, resume or curriculum vitae, recommendation letters, official transcripts, portfolio. Additional exam requirements/recommendations for international students: Required—TOEFL (minimum score 525 paper-based). *Application deadline:* For fall admission, 1/15 priority date for domestic and international students. Applications are processed on a rolling basis. Application fee: $50. Electronic applications accepted. *Expenses:* Contact institution. *Financial support:* In 2016–17, 88 students received support, including 87 fellowships (averaging $6,100 per year), 37 teaching assistantships (averaging $2,700 per year). Financial award application deadline: 5/1; financial award applicants required to submit FAFSA. *Unit head:* Michael Macphail, Architecture Department Chair, 617-989-4455, E-mail: macphailm@wit.edu. *Application contact:* Kelly Hutzell, Director of Graduate Programs, 617-989-4494, E-mail: hutzelk@wit.edu.
Website: http://www.wit.edu/arch/

**Woodbury University,** School of Architecture, Burbank, CA 91504-1099. Offers M Arch, MIA, MS Arch. *Degree requirements:* For master's, thesis. *Entrance requirements:* For master's, GRE (if undergraduate GPA is below 3.0), 3 letters of recommendation, portfolio, essay, interview, resume, academic transcripts. Additional exam requirements/recommendations for international students: Required—TOEFL (minimum score 550 paper-based; 83 iBT), IELTS (minimum score 6.5). *Expenses:* Contact institution.

**Yale University,** School of Architecture, New Haven, CT 06520. Offers M Arch, M Env Des, MEM, PhD, M Arch/M Env Des, M Arch/MBA. *Entrance requirements:* For master's, GRE General Test, design portfolio. Additional exam requirements/recommendations for international students: Required—TOEFL. Electronic applications accepted. *Expenses:* Contact institution.

# Building Science

**Arizona State University at the Tempe campus,** Herberger Institute for Design and the Arts, The Design School, Tempe, AZ 85287-1605. Offers architecture (M Arch); building design/built environment (MS); design (MSD), including arts, media, and engineering, healthcare and healing environments (MSD, PhD), industrial design, interaction design, interior design, new product innovation, visual communication design; design, environment and the arts (PhD), including design, digital culture, healthcare and healing environments (MSD, PhD), history, theory, and criticism; landscape architecture (MLA); urban design (MUD); MA/MBA. *Accreditation:* NASAD. Terminal master's awarded for partial completion of doctoral program. *Degree requirements:* For master's, thesis optional, interactive Program of Study (iPOS) submitted before completing 50 percent of required credit hours; for doctorate, comprehensive exam, thesis/dissertation, interactive Program of Study (iPOS) submitted before completing 50 percent of required credit hours. *Entrance requirements:* For master's, GRE General Test, minimum GPA of 3.0 or equivalent in last 2 years of work leading to bachelor's degree, design/creative works portfolio, 3 references, statement of intent; for doctorate, GRE, master's degree in architecture, graphic design, industrial design, interior design, landscape architecture, or art history or equivalent standing; statement of purpose; 3 letters of recommendation; indication of potential faculty mentor; sample of written work. Additional exam requirements/recommendations for international students: Required—TOEFL (minimum score 600 paper-based; 100 iBT). Electronic applications accepted.

**Auburn University,** Graduate School, College of Architecture, Design, and Construction, McWhorter School of Building Science, Program in Integrated Design and Construction, Auburn University, AL 36849. Offers MIDC. *Expenses:* Tuition, state resident: full-time $9072; part-time $504 per credit hour. Tuition, nonresident: full-time $27,216; part-time $1512 per credit hour. *Required fees:* $812 per semester. Tuition and fees vary according to degree level and program. *Unit head:* Dr. Vini Nathan, Dean, 334-844-4524. *Application contact:* Dr. George Flowers, Dean of the Graduate School, 334-844-2125.
Website: http://cadc.auburn.edu/construction/construction-masters-degrees-programs/integrated-design-and-const

**Carnegie Mellon University,** College of Fine Arts, School of Architecture, Pittsburgh, PA 15213-3891. Offers architecture (MSA); architecture, engineering, and construction management (PhD); building performance and diagnostics (MS, PhD); computational design (MS, PhD); engineering construction management (MSA); tangible interaction design (MTID); urban design (MUD). Terminal master's awarded for partial completion of doctoral program. *Degree requirements:* For doctorate, thesis/dissertation. *Entrance requirements:* For master's and doctorate, GRE General Test. Additional exam requirements/recommendations for international students: Required—TOEFL.

**Georgia Institute of Technology,** Graduate Studies, College of Architecture, School of Building Construction, Atlanta, GA 30332-0001. Offers building construction (PhD); integrated facility and property management (MS); integrated project delivery systems (MS); program management (MS); residential construction development (MS).

*Program availability:* Part-time, evening/weekend. *Entrance requirements:* For master's and doctorate, GRE or GMAT. Additional exam requirements/recommendations for international students: Required—TOEFL (minimum score 550 paper-based). Electronic applications accepted. *Faculty research:* Design-build, mold, indoor air quality, real estate.

**Pontificia Universidad Catolica Madre y Maestra,** Graduate School, Faculty of Engineering Sciences, Santiago, Dominican Republic. Offers earthquake engineering (ME); logistics management (ME).

**Rensselaer Polytechnic Institute,** Graduate School, School of Architecture, Program in Built Ecologies, Troy, NY 12180-3590. Offers MS, PhD. *Degree requirements:* For master's, thesis; for doctorate, comprehensive exam, thesis/dissertation. *Entrance requirements:* For master's and doctorate, GRE General Test. Additional exam requirements/recommendations for international students: Required—TOEFL (minimum score 570 paper-based; 88 iBT), IELTS (minimum score 6.5), PTE (minimum score 60). Electronic applications accepted. *Expenses:* Tuition: Full-time $49,520; part-time $2060 per credit hour. *Required fees:* $2617.

**University of California, Berkeley,** Graduate Division, College of Environmental Design, Department of Architecture, Berkeley, CA 94720-1500. Offers architecture (M Arch); building science (MS, PhD); building structures, construction and materials (MS, PhD); design theories, methods, and practices (MS, PhD); environmental design in developing countries (MS, PhD); history of architecture and urbanism (MS, PhD); social and cultural processes in architecture and urbanism (MS, PhD); M Arch/MCP; M Arch/MS; MLA/M Arch. *Students:* 178 full-time (84 women); includes 34 minority (4 Black or African American, non-Hispanic/Latino; 1 American Indian or Alaska Native, non-Hispanic/Latino; 13 Asian, non-Hispanic/Latino; 16 Hispanic/Latino), 85 international. Average age 30. 1,047 applicants, 68 enrolled. In 2016, 42 master's, 7 doctorates awarded. *Degree requirements:* For master's, thesis; for doctorate, thesis/dissertation, qualifying exam. *Entrance requirements:* For master's and doctorate, GRE General Test, minimum GPA of 3.0, 3 letters of recommendation. Additional exam requirements/recommendations for international students: Required—TOEFL (minimum score 570 paper-based; 90 iBT). *Application deadline:* For fall admission, 12/7 for domestic students. Application fee: $105 ($125 for international students). Electronic applications accepted. Application fee is waived when completed online. *Financial support:* Fellowships, research assistantships, teaching assistantships, career-related internships or fieldwork, institutionally sponsored loans, health care benefits, and unspecified assistantships available. *Unit head:* Prof. Tom Buresh, Chair, 510-642-4942. *Application contact:* Lois H. Ito Koch, Student Affairs Officer, 510-642-5577, Fax: 510-643-5607, E-mail: archgrad@berkeley.edu.
Website: http://arch.ced.berkeley.edu/

**Virginia Polytechnic Institute and State University,** Graduate School, College of Architecture and Urban Studies, Blacksburg, VA 24061. Offers architecture (MS Arch); architecture and design research (PhD); building/construction science and management (MS); creative technologies (MFA); environmental design and planning (PhD); landscape architecture (MLA); planning, governance, and globalization (PhD);

public administration (MPA); public administration/public affairs (PhD, Certificate); public and international affairs (MPIA); urban and regional planning (MURP). *Accreditation:* ASLA (one or more programs are accredited). *Faculty:* 136 full-time (53 women). *Students:* 371 full-time (185 women), 210 part-time (104 women); includes 118 minority (49 Black or African American, non-Hispanic/Latino; 1 American Indian or Alaska Native, non-Hispanic/Latino; 30 Asian, non-Hispanic/Latino; 32 Hispanic/Latino; 6 Two or more races, non-Hispanic/Latino), 137 international. Average age 31. 566 applicants, 55% accepted, 160 enrolled. In 2016, 137 master's, 24 doctorates awarded. *Degree requirements:* For master's, comprehensive exam (for some programs), thesis (for some programs); for doctorate, comprehensive exam (for some programs), thesis/dissertation (for some programs). *Entrance requirements:* For master's and doctorate, GRE/GMAT. Additional exam requirements/recommendations for international students: Required— TOEFL (minimum score 80 iBT). *Application deadline:* For fall admission, 8/1 for domestic students, 4/1 for international students; for spring admission, 1/1 for domestic

students, 9/1 for international students. Applications are processed on a rolling basis. Application fee: $75. Electronic applications accepted. *Expenses:* Tuition, state resident: full-time $12,467; part-time $692.50 per credit hour. Tuition, nonresident: full-time $25,095; part-time $1394.25 per credit hour. *Required fees:* $2669; $491.50 per semester. Tuition and fees vary according to course load, campus/location and program. *Financial support:* In 2016–17, 11 research assistantships with full tuition reimbursements (averaging $19,474 per year), 45 teaching assistantships with full tuition reimbursements (averaging $16,014 per year) were awarded. Financial award application deadline: 3/1; financial award applicants required to submit FAFSA. *Total annual research expenditures:* $3.6 million. *Unit head:* Dr. A. J. Davis, Dean, 540-231-6416, Fax: 540-231-6332, E-mail: davisa@vt.edu. *Application contact:* Christine Mattsson-Coon, Executive Assistant, 540-231-6416, Fax: 540-231-6332, E-mail: cmattsso@vt.edu.
Website: http://www.caus.vt.edu/

# Environmental Design

**Arizona State University at the Tempe campus,** Herberger Institute for Design and the Arts, The Design School, PhD Program in Design, Environment and the Arts, Tempe, AZ 85287-2105. Offers design (PhD); digital culture (PhD); healthcare and healing environments (PhD); history, theory, and criticism (PhD). *Degree requirements:* For doctorate, comprehensive exam, thesis/dissertation, interactive Program of Study (iPOS) submitted before completing 50 percent of required credit hours. *Entrance requirements:* For doctorate, GRE, master's degree in architecture, graphic design, industrial design, interior design, landscape architecture, or art history or equivalent standing; statement of purpose; 3 letters of recommendation; indication of potential faculty mentor; sample of written work. Additional exam requirements/recommendations for international students: Required—TOEFL, IELTS, or PTE. Electronic applications accepted. *Expenses:* Contact institution.

**ArtCenter College of Design,** Graduate Environmental Design Program, Pasadena, CA 91103. Offers furniture and fixtures (MS); spatial experience (MS). *Degree requirements:* For master's, thesis. *Entrance requirements:* For master's, portfolio. Additional exam requirements/recommendations for international students: Required—TOEFL (minimum score 100 iBT), IELTS (minimum score 7). Electronic applications accepted.

**Bastyr University,** School of Natural Health Arts and Sciences, Kenmore, WA 98028-4966. Offers counseling psychology (MA); holistic landscape design (Certificate); midwifery (MS); nutrition (MS); nutrition and clinical health psychology (MS). *Accreditation:* AND. *Program availability:* Part-time. *Degree requirements:* For master's, thesis optional. *Entrance requirements:* For master's, 1-2 years' basic sciences course work (depending on program). Additional exam requirements/recommendations for international students: Required—TOEFL (minimum score 550 paper-based; 79 iBT). *Faculty research:* Whole-food nutrition for type 2 diabetes; meditation in end-of-life care; stress management; Qi Gong, Tai Chi and yoga for older adults; Echinacea and immunology.

**Clemson University,** Graduate School, College of Architecture, Arts, and Humanities, Program in Planning, Design and the Built Environment, Clemson, SC 29634. Offers planning, design and the built environment (PhD), including architectural design, technology and construction processes, built environment and health, regional/community development and design, restoration, sustainability and land ecology. *Faculty:* 31 full-time (10 women). *Students:* 21 full-time (14 women); includes 1 minority (Black or African American, non-Hispanic/Latino), 12 international. Average age 32. 27 applicants, 22% accepted, 6 enrolled. In 2016, 1 doctorate awarded. *Degree requirements:* For doctorate, comprehensive exam, thesis/dissertation. *Entrance requirements:* For doctorate, GRE General Test, official transcripts, letters of recommendation, statement of purpose, portfolio. Additional exam requirements/recommendations for international students: Required—TOEFL (minimum score 80 iBT), IELTS (minimum score 7). *Application deadline:* For fall admission, 2/1 priority date for domestic and international students. Applications are processed on a rolling basis. Application fee: $80 ($90 for international students). Electronic applications accepted. *Expenses:* $4,841 per semester full-time resident, $9,640 per semester full-time non-resident, $612 per credit hour part-time resident, $1,223 per credit hour part-time non-resident. *Financial support:* In 2016–17, 20 students received support, including 5 research assistantships with partial tuition reimbursements available (averaging $19,440 per year), 15 teaching assistantships with partial tuition reimbursements available (averaging $14,875 per year); career-related internships or fieldwork and unspecified assistantships also available. Financial award application deadline: 2/1. *Faculty research:* Built environment and health; restoration, sustainability and land ecology; regional/community design and development; technology, materials and construction processes; real estate development. *Unit head:* Dr. Mickey Lauria, Program Director, 864-656-0520, E-mail: mlauria@clemson.edu.
Website: http://www.clemson.edu/caah/departments/pdbe/index.html

**Columbia University,** School of Continuing Education, Program in Landscape Design, New York, NY 10027. Offers MS. *Program availability:* Part-time. *Entrance requirements:* For master's, minimum undergraduate GPA of 3.0. Additional exam requirements/recommendations for international students: Required—American Language Program placement test.

**Cornell University,** Graduate School, Graduate Fields of Human Ecology, Field of Design and Environmental Analysis, Ithaca, NY 14853. Offers applied research in human-environment relations (MS); facilities planning and management (MS); housing and design (MS); human factors and ergonomics (MS); human-environment relations (MS); interior design (MA, MPS). *Degree requirements:* For master's, thesis. *Entrance requirements:* For master's, GRE General Test, portfolio or slides of recent work; bachelor's degree in interior design, architecture or related design discipline; 2 letters of recommendation. Additional exam requirements/recommendations for international students: Required—TOEFL (minimum score 600 paper-based; 105 iBT). Electronic applications accepted. *Faculty research:* Facility planning and management, environmental psychology, housing, interior design, ergonomics and human factors.

**Kansas State University,** Graduate School, College of Architecture, Planning and Design, Interdisciplinary Doctoral Program in Environmental Design and Planning, Manhattan, KS 66506. Offers PhD. *Faculty:* 3 full-time (2 women). *Students:* 5 full-time (4 women), 3 part-time (2 women); includes 2 minority (both Black or African American, non-Hispanic/Latino), 4 international. Average age 33. 10 applicants, 40% accepted, 4 enrolled. In 2016, 4 doctorates awarded. *Degree requirements:* For doctorate, comprehensive exam, thesis/dissertation, preliminary exam, oral exam. *Entrance requirements:* For doctorate, GRE, transcript(s), statement of intent, three letters of

recommendation, portfolio. Additional exam requirements/recommendations for international students: Required—TOEFL (minimum score 600 paper-based; 100 iBT), IELTS (minimum score 7), PTE (minimum score 70). *Application deadline:* For fall admission, 1/1 priority date for domestic and international students. Applications are processed on a rolling basis. Application fee: $90 ($100 for international students). Electronic applications accepted. *Expenses:* Tuition, state resident: full-time $9670. Tuition, nonresident: full-time $21,828. *Required fees:* $862. *Financial support:* In 2016–17, 5 students received support. Research assistantships, teaching assistantships, scholarships/grants, and unspecified assistantships available. Financial award applicants required to submit FAFSA. *Faculty research:* Sustainability, place-making, design, planning. *Unit head:* Dr. David H. Sachs, Director of PhD Program, 785-532-1183, E-mail: sachs@ksu.edu. *Application contact:* Ann Cook, Administrative Assistant, 785-532-5950, E-mail: amcook@ksu.edu.
Website: http://apdesign.k-state.edu/academics/phd/

**Kent State University,** College of Architecture and Environmental Design, Kent, OH 44240. Offers architecture (M Arc); architecture and environmental design (MS); health care design (MHCD); landscape architecture (MLA); urban design (MUD); M Arch/MBA; M Arch/MUD. *Program availability:* Part-time. *Faculty:* 20 full-time (3 women). *Students:* 75 full-time (31 women), 7 part-time (2 women); includes 6 minority (3 Black or African American, non-Hispanic/Latino; 1 American Indian or Alaska Native, non-Hispanic/Latino; 2 Hispanic/Latino), 10 international. Average age 25. 125 applicants, 56% accepted, 58 enrolled. In 2016, 55 master's awarded. *Degree requirements:* For master's, thesis (for some programs), project (for some programs). *Entrance requirements:* For master's, GRE, statement of purpose, curriculum vitae, transcripts, 3 letters of recommendation, portfolio. Additional exam requirements/recommendations for international students: Required—TOEFL (minimum scores of 550 paper-based, 80 iBT), Michigan English Language Assessment Battery (77), IELTS (6.5), or PTE (54). *Application deadline:* For fall admission, 1/15 for domestic and international students. Applications are processed on a rolling basis. Application fee: $45 ($70 for international students). Electronic applications accepted. *Expenses:* Tuition, state resident: full-time $10,864; part-time $495 per credit hour. Tuition, nonresident: full-time $18,380; part-time $837 per credit hour. *Financial support:* Research assistantships with full tuition reimbursements, teaching assistantships with full tuition reimbursements, Federal Work-Study, scholarships/grants, and unspecified assistantships available. Financial award application deadline: 2/1. *Unit head:* Mark Mistur, Dean, E-mail: mmistur1@kent.edu. *Application contact:* Johnathan Fleming, Assistant Professor and Director, Master of Architecture, 330-672-0934, E-mail: jpflemi1@kent.edu.
Website: http://www.kent.edu/caed

**Michigan State University,** The Graduate School, College of Agriculture and Natural Resources and College of Social Science, School of Planning, Design and Construction, East Lansing, MI 48824. Offers construction management (MS, PhD); environmental design (MA); interior design and facilities management (MA); international planning studies (MIPS); urban and regional planning (MURP). *Degree requirements:* For master's, thesis or alternative. *Entrance requirements:* Additional exam requirements/recommendations for international students: Required—TOEFL. Electronic applications accepted.

**San Diego State University,** Graduate and Research Affairs, College of Professional Studies and Fine Arts, School of Art, Design and Art History, San Diego, CA 92182. Offers art history (MA); studio arts (MA, MFA), including applied design, environmental design, graphic design, interior design, painting and printmaking, sculpture. *Accreditation:* NASAD (one or more programs are accredited). *Degree requirements:* For master's, variable foreign language requirement, thesis. *Entrance requirements:* For master's, GRE General Test, bachelor's degree in related field, slide portfolio, typed slide information sheet, 2 letters of recommendation. Additional exam requirements/recommendations for international students: Required—TOEFL. Electronic applications accepted.

**Texas Tech University,** Graduate School, College of Human Sciences, Department of Design, Lubbock, TX 79409-1220. Offers environmental design (MS); interior and environmental design (PhD). *Program availability:* Part-time. *Faculty:* 10 full-time (8 women), 1 (woman) part-time/adjunct. *Students:* 15 full-time (9 women), 5 part-time (4 women); includes 1 minority (Hispanic/Latino), 13 international. Average age 34. 19 applicants, 53% accepted, 5 enrolled. In 2016, 9 master's, 5 doctorates awarded. *Degree requirements:* For master's, comprehensive exam, thesis or alternative; for doctorate, comprehensive exam, thesis/dissertation. *Entrance requirements:* For master's, 3 recommendation letters, design portfolio, 500-word written statement (reason for pursuing degree), resume; for doctorate, GRE, 3 recommendation letters, design portfolio, 500-word written statement (reason for pursuing degree), resume. Additional exam requirements/recommendations for international students: Required— TOEFL (minimum score 550 paper-based, 79 iBT) or IELTS (6.5). *Application deadline:* For fall admission, 6/1 priority date for domestic students, 1/15 priority date for international students; for spring admission, 9/1 priority date for domestic students, 6/15 priority date for international students. Applications are processed on a rolling basis. Application fee: $75. Electronic applications accepted. *Expenses:* $315 per credit hour full-time resident tuition, $723 per credit hour full-time non-resident tuition; $50.50 per credit hour fee plus $608 per term fee. *Financial support:* In 2016–17, 17 students received support, including 16 fellowships (averaging $7,220 per year), 10 research assistantships (averaging $8,312 per year); teaching assistantships, scholarships/grants, and unspecified assistantships also available. Financial award application deadline: 4/15; financial award applicants required to submit FAFSA. *Faculty research:*

## Environmental Design

Healthcare and the built environment, sustainability, vulnerable populations, historic preservation, evidence-based design. *Total annual research expenditures:* $34,363. *Unit head:* Dr. Sharran F. Parkinson, Chair, 806-742-3031, Fax: 806-742-1639, E-mail: sharran.parkinson@ttu.edu. *Application contact:* Dr. Kristi Gaines, Graduate Programs Director, 806-742-3050, Fax: 806-742-1639, E-mail: kristi.gaines@ttu.edu. Website: http://www.depts.ttu.edu/hs/dod/

**Université de Montréal,** Faculty of Environmental Design and Planning, Montréal, QC H3C 3J7, Canada. Offers environmental design and planning (M Sc A, PhD); environmental planning and design projects (DESS); game design (DESS); urban management for developing countries (DESS); urban planning (M Urb). DESS programs offered jointly with HEC Montreal and Ecole Polytechnique de Montréal. *Accreditation:* ACSP. *Degree requirements:* For doctorate, thesis/dissertation, general exam. Electronic applications accepted. *Expenses:* Contact institution. *Faculty research:* Wayfinding, environmental evaluation, housing studies, urban design, urban and regional planning.

**University of Calgary,** Faculty of Graduate Studies, Faculty of Environmental Design, Calgary, AB T2N 1N4, Canada. Offers architecture (M Arch); environmental design (M Env Des, PhD); planning (M Plan). *Degree requirements:* For master's, thesis; for doctorate, thesis/dissertation. *Entrance requirements:* For master's, minimum GPA of 3.0; for doctorate, minimum GPA of 3.5. Additional exam requirements/ recommendations for international students: Required—TOEFL (minimum score 550 paper-based). *Faculty research:* Sustainable development in architecture, planning and product design, energy and environment, impact assessment, ecotourism.

**University of California, Berkeley,** Graduate Division, College of Environmental Design, Department of Landscape Architecture and Environmental Planning, Berkeley, CA 94720-1500. Offers landscape architecture (MLA), including environmental planning, landscape design and site planning, urban and community design; landscape architecture and environmental planning (PhD); MLA/M Arch; MLA/MCP. *Accreditation:* ASLA (one or more programs are accredited). *Faculty:* 13 full-time, 6 part-time/adjunct. *Students:* 84 full-time (52 women); includes 19 minority (1 Black or African American, non-Hispanic/Latino; 5 Asian, non-Hispanic/Latino; 13 Hispanic/Latino), 26 international. Average age 30. 263 applicants, 30 enrolled. In 2016, 27 master's, 3 doctorates awarded. *Degree requirements:* For master's, comprehensive exam (for some programs), thesis (for some programs), professional project or thesis; for doctorate, one foreign language, thesis/dissertation, qualifying exam. *Entrance requirements:* For master's, GRE General Test, minimum GPA of 3.0, portfolio; for doctorate, GRE General Test, master's degree (strongly recommended), minimum GPA of 3.0, sample of written work, 3 letters of recommendation. Additional exam requirements/ recommendations for international students: Required—TOEFL (minimum score 570 paper-based; 90 iBT). *Application deadline:* For fall admission, 12/7 for domestic students. Application fee: $105 ($125 for international students). Electronic applications accepted. *Financial support:* Fellowships, research assistantships, teaching assistantships, career-related internships or fieldwork, Federal Work-Study, institutionally sponsored loans, and unspecified assistantships available. *Unit head:* Prof. Louise Mozingo, Chair, 510-643-6165, Fax: 510-643-6166. *Application contact:* 510-642-2965, Fax: 510-643-6166, E-mail: laepgrad@berkeley.edu. Website: http://laep.ced.berkeley.edu/

**University of California, Irvine,** School of Social Ecology, Programs in Social Ecology, Irvine, CA 92697. Offers environmental analysis and design (PhD); epidemiology and public health (PhD); social ecology (PhD). *Students:* 8 full-time (6 women), 2 part-time (both women), 1 international. Average age 32. 9 applicants, 22% accepted, 1 enrolled. In 2016, 2 doctorates awarded. Application fee: $105 ($125 for international students). *Unit head:* Tim-Allen Bruckner, Professor, 949-824-5797, Fax: 949-824-1845, E-mail: tim.bruckner@uci.edu. *Application contact:* Jennifer Craig,

Director of Graduate Student Services, 949-824-5918, Fax: 949-824-1845, E-mail: craigj@uci.edu. Website: http://socialecology.uci.edu/core/graduate-se-core-programs

**University of Georgia,** College of Environment and Design, Athens, GA 30602. Offers environmental planning and design (MEPD); historic preservation (MHP); landscape architecture (MLA). *Application deadline:* For fall admission, 7/1 priority date for domestic students; for spring admission, 11/15 for domestic students. Application fee: $50. *Unit head:* Daniels J. Nadenicek, Acting Dean, 706-542-1100, Fax: 706-542-4485, E-mail: dnadeni@uga.edu. *Application contact:* Umit Yilmaz, Graduate Coordinator, 706-542-4720, E-mail: yilmaz@uga.edu. Website: http://www.ced.uga.edu

**The University of Manchester,** School of Environment and Development, Manchester, United Kingdom. Offers architecture (M Phil, PhD); development policy and management (M Phil, PhD); human geography (M Phil, PhD); physical geography (M Phil, PhD); planning and landscape (M Phil, PhD).

**Virginia Polytechnic Institute and State University,** Graduate School, College of Architecture and Urban Studies, Blacksburg, VA 24061. Offers architecture (MS Arch); architecture and design research (PhD); building/construction science and management (MS); creative technologies (MFA); environmental design and planning (PhD); landscape architecture (MLA); planning, governance, and globalization (PhD); public administration (MPA); public administration/public affairs (PhD, Certificate); public and international affairs (MPIA); urban and regional planning (MURP). *Accreditation:* ASLA (one or more programs are accredited). *Faculty:* 136 full-time (53 women). *Students:* 371 full-time (185 women), 210 part-time (104 women); includes 118 minority (49 Black or African American, non-Hispanic/Latino; 1 American Indian or Alaska Native, non-Hispanic/Latino; 30 Asian, non-Hispanic/Latino; 32 Hispanic/Latino; 6 Two or more races, non-Hispanic/Latino), 137 international. Average age 31. 566 applicants, 55% accepted, 160 enrolled. In 2016, 137 master's, 24 doctorates awarded. *Degree requirements:* For master's, comprehensive exam (for some programs), thesis (for some programs); for doctorate, comprehensive exam (for some programs), thesis/dissertation (for some programs). *Entrance requirements:* For master's and doctorate, GRE/GMAT. Additional exam requirements/recommendations for international students: Required— TOEFL (minimum score 80 iBT). *Application deadline:* For fall admission, 8/1 for domestic students, 4/1 for international students; for spring admission, 1/1 for domestic students, 9/1 for international students. Applications are processed on a rolling basis. Application fee: $75. Electronic applications accepted. *Expenses:* Tuition, state resident: full-time $12,467; part-time $692.50 per credit hour. Tuition, nonresident: full-time $25,095; part-time $1394.25 per credit hour. *Required fees:* $2669; $491.50 per semester. Tuition and fees vary according to course load, campus/location and program. *Financial support:* In 2016–17, 11 research assistantships with full tuition reimbursements (averaging $19,474 per year), 45 teaching assistantships with full tuition reimbursements (averaging $16,014 per year) were awarded. Financial award application deadline: 3/1; financial award applicants required to submit FAFSA. *Total annual research expenditures:* $3.6 million. *Unit head:* Dr. A. J. Davis, Dean, 540-231-6416, Fax: 540-231-6332, E-mail: davisa@vt.edu. *Application contact:* Christine Mattsson-Coon, Executive Assistant, 540-231-6416, Fax: 540-231-6332, E-mail: cmattsso@vt.edu. Website: http://www.caus.vt.edu

**Yale University,** School of Architecture, New Haven, CT 06520. Offers M Arch, M Env Des, MEM, PhD, M Arch/M Env Des, M Arch/MBA. *Entrance requirements:* For master's, GRE General Test, design portfolio. Additional exam requirements/ recommendations for international students: Required—TOEFL. Electronic applications accepted. *Expenses:* Contact institution.

# Historic Preservation

**The American University of Rome,** Graduate School, Rome, Italy. Offers religious studies (MA); sustainable cultural heritage (MA). *Degree requirements:* For master's, thesis, internship. *Entrance requirements:* For master's, bachelor's degree in the liberal arts, humanities or social sciences; minimum GPA of 2.75. Additional exam requirements/recommendations for international students: Required—TOEFL (minimum score 550 paper-based; 80 iBT), IELTS (minimum score 6.5). Electronic applications accepted. *Faculty research:* Sustainable cultural heritage, archaeology in Europe and Italy.

**Arkansas State University,** Graduate School, College of Humanities and Social Sciences, Heritage Studies Program, State University, AR 72467. Offers heritage studies (MA, PhD). *Program availability:* Part-time. *Degree requirements:* For master's, comprehensive exam, thesis or alternative, portfolio; for doctorate, comprehensive exam, thesis/dissertation, portfolio. *Entrance requirements:* For master's, GRE, MAT or GMAT, appropriate bachelor's degree, letters of reference, official transcript, interview, letter of interest, writing sample, immunization records; for doctorate, GRE, MAT, or GMAT, appropriate bachelor's or master's degree, interview, letters of reference, official transcript, letter of interest, writing sample, immunization records. Additional exam requirements/recommendations for international students: Required—TOEFL (minimum score 550 paper-based; 79 iBT), IELTS (minimum score 6), PTE (minimum score 56). Electronic applications accepted.

**Ball State University,** Graduate School, College of Architecture and Planning, Department of Architecture, Program in Historic Preservation, Muncie, IN 47306. Offers MS. *Program availability:* Part-time. *Degree requirements:* For master's, thesis. *Entrance requirements:* For master's, minimum baccalaureate GPA of 2.75 or 3.0 in latter half of baccalaureate, resume, statement of purpose, academic writing sample, three letters of recommendation. Additional exam requirements/recommendations for international students: Required—TOEFL (minimum score 550 paper-based; 79 iBT), IELTS (minimum score 6.5). Electronic applications accepted. *Expenses:* Contact institution.

**Boston Architectural College,** Graduate Programs, Boston, MA 02115-2795. Offers architecture (M Arch); historic preservation (MDS); interior design (MID); landscape architecture (MLA); sustainable design (MDS). *Accreditation:* CIDA. *Degree requirements:* For master's, thesis. *Entrance requirements:* For master's, portfolio (recommended). Electronic applications accepted.

**Boston University,** Graduate School of Arts and Sciences, Program in Preservation Studies, Boston, MA 02215. Offers MA, JD/MA. *Students:* 8 full-time (6 women), 2 part-time (1 woman); includes 1 minority (Hispanic/Latino), 3 international. Average age 25. 17 applicants, 94% accepted, 3 enrolled. In 2016, 1 master's awarded. *Degree*

*requirements:* For master's, thesis or alternative, internship, major project. *Entrance requirements:* For master's, GRE General Test, scholarly writing sample, 3 letters of recommendation, transcripts, curriculum vitae, personal statement. Additional exam requirements/recommendations for international students: Required—TOEFL (minimum score 550 paper-based; 84 iBT). *Application deadline:* For fall admission, 4/1 for domestic and international students; for spring admission, 11/15 for domestic and international students. Application fee: $95. Electronic applications accepted. *Financial support:* In 2016–17, 2 students received support. Career-related internships or fieldwork, Federal Work-Study, scholarships/grants, and unspecified assistantships available. Support available to part-time students. Financial award application deadline: 1/15. *Unit head:* Daniel Bluestone, Director, 617-358-7332, Fax: 617-353-2556, E-mail: dblues@bu.edu. *Application contact:* Julia Kline, Senior Program Coordinator, 617-353-2948, Fax: 617-353-2556, E-mail: jgawle@bu.edu. Website: http://www.bu.edu/amnesp/ma/

**Buffalo State College, State University of New York,** The Graduate School, Faculty of Arts and Humanities, Department of Art Conservation, Buffalo, NY 14222-1095. Offers art conservation (CAS); conservation of historic works and art works (MA). *Degree requirements:* For master's, final oral exam; for CAS, internship. *Entrance requirements:* For master's, GRE General Test, minimum GPA of 2.8. Additional exam requirements/recommendations for international students: Required—TOEFL (minimum score 550 paper-based). *Faculty research:* Mechanics of deterioration of art, conservation of materials.

**Clemson University,** Graduate School, College of Architecture, Arts, and Humanities, Program in Historic Preservation, Charleston, SC 29403. Offers MS, Certificate. *Faculty:* 2 full-time (1 woman), 14 part-time/adjunct (6 women). *Students:* 15 full-time (11 women); includes 2 minority (1 Hispanic/Latino; 1 Two or more races, non-Hispanic/Latino). Average age 25. 40 applicants, 55% accepted, 14 enrolled. In 2016, 12 master's awarded. *Degree requirements:* For master's, thesis. *Entrance requirements:* For master's, GRE General Test, official transcripts, letters of recommendation. Additional exam requirements/recommendations for international students: Required—TOEFL (minimum score 80 iBT), IELTS (minimum score 6.5). *Application deadline:* For fall admission, 2/15 for domestic and international students. Application fee: $80 ($90 for international students). Electronic applications accepted. *Expenses:* $14,700 per semester tuition, $428 per semester full-time fees. *Financial support:* In 2016–17, 12 students received support, including 12 fellowships with partial tuition reimbursements available (averaging $5,583 per year). Financial award application deadline: 2/15. *Faculty research:* Historic preservation, architectural history, architectural forensics, materials science. *Unit head:* Kate Schwennsen, Director, School of Architecture, 864-656-3895, E-mail: kschwen@clemson.edu. *Application* *contact:* Dr. Carter Hudgins, Director of the Graduate Program in Historic Preservation, 843-937-9596, E-mail: chudgin@clemson.edu. Website: http://www.clemson.edu/caah/departments/historic-preservation/

**College of Charleston,** Graduate School, School of the Arts, Program in Historic Preservation, Charleston, SC 29424-0001. Offers MS. Program offered in collaboration with Clemson University. *Degree requirements:* For master's, thesis optional. *Entrance requirements:* For master's, GRE. Additional exam requirements/recommendations for international students: Required—TOEFL (minimum score 81 iBT). Application fee: $45. Electronic applications accepted. *Financial support:* Career-related internships or fieldwork, Federal Work-Study, scholarships/grants, and unspecified assistantships available. Support available to part-time students. Financial award application deadline: 4/1; financial award applicants required to submit FAFSA. *Unit head:* Karen Chandler, Director, 843-953-5474. *Application contact:* Karen Chandler, Director, 843-953-5474. Website: http://arthistory.cofc.edu/grad-progs/

**Colorado State University,** College of Liberal Arts, Department of History, Fort Collins, CO 80523-1776. Offers liberal arts (MA); public history (MA), including cultural resource management, historic preservation, museum studies. *Program availability:* Part-time. *Faculty:* 6 full-time (2 women), 1 part-time/adjunct (0 women). *Students:* 25 full-time (14 women), 4 part-time (1 woman); includes 2 minority (1 American Indian or Alaska Native, non-Hispanic/Latino; 1 Hispanic/Latino). Average age 28. 23 applicants, 61% accepted, 13 enrolled. In 2016, 6 master's awarded. *Degree requirements:* For master's, one foreign language, comprehensive exam, thesis (for some programs), minimum final grade of B- in history courses counted toward degree. *Entrance requirements:* For master's, GRE General Test, 21 credits in history, statement of purpose, 3 letters of reference. Additional exam requirements/recommendations for international students: Required—TOEFL, IELTS. *Application deadline:* For fall admission, 2/1 priority date for domestic and international students. Application fee: $60 ($70 for international students). Electronic applications accepted. *Expenses:* Tuition, state resident: full-time $9628. Tuition, nonresident: full-time $23,603. *Required fees:* $2253; $528.14 per credit hour. $264.07 per semester. Tuition and fees vary according to course load and program. *Financial support:* In 2016–17, 22 students received support, including 1 research assistantship with full tuition reimbursement available (averaging $13,932 per year), 23 teaching assistantships with full tuition reimbursements available (averaging $13,932 per year); fellowships with full tuition reimbursements available and health care benefits also available. Financial award application deadline: 3/1; financial award applicants required to submit FAFSA. *Faculty research:* United states and north America; public and environmental history; modern world; religion; women, gender and sexuality. *Total annual research expenditures:* $281,014. *Unit head:* Dr. Doug Yarrington, Department Chair, 970-491-6801, Fax: 970-491-2941, E-mail: doug.yarrington@colostate.edu. *Application contact:* Diane Margolf, Graduate Studies Committee Chair, 970-491-5671, Fax: 970-491-2941, E-mail: diane.margolf@colostate.edu. Website: http://history.colostate.edu/

**Columbia University,** Graduate School of Architecture, Planning, and Preservation, Program in Historic Preservation, New York, NY 10027. Offers MS, Certificate, M Arch/MS, MS/MS. *Degree requirements:* For master's, thesis. *Entrance requirements:* For master's, GRE General Test.

**Cornell University,** Graduate School, Graduate Fields of Architecture, Art and Planning, Field of City and Regional Planning, Ithaca, NY 14853. Offers city and regional planning (MRP, PhD); environmental planning and design (MRP, PhD); historic preservation planning (MA); international development planning (MRP, PhD); planning theory and systems analysis (MRP, PhD); regional economics and development planning (MRP, PhD); regional science (MRP, PhD); social and health systems planning (MRP, PhD); urban and regional theory (MRP, PhD); urban planning history (MRP, PhD). *Accreditation:* ACSP (one or more programs are accredited). *Degree requirements:* For master's, thesis (MA); for doctorate, comprehensive exam, thesis/dissertation. *Entrance requirements:* For master's and doctorate, GRE General Test, 2 letters of recommendation. Additional exam requirements/recommendations for international students: Required—TOEFL (minimum score 600 paper-based; 77 iBT). Electronic applications accepted. *Faculty research:* Land use planning, economic development, international development, historic preservation, community development.

**Delaware State University,** Graduate Programs, Department of History, Philosophy and Political Sciences, Dover, DE 19901-2277. Offers historic preservation (MA). *Entrance requirements:* Additional exam requirements/recommendations for international students: Required—TOEFL (minimum score 550 paper-based). Electronic applications accepted.

**Eastern Michigan University,** Graduate School, College of Arts and Sciences, Department of Geography and Geology, Programs in Historic Preservation, Ypsilanti, MI 48197. Offers heritage interpretation and museum practice (MS); historic preservation (Graduate Certificate); preservation planning and administration (MS); recording, documentation and digital cultural heritage (MS). *Program availability:* Part-time, evening/weekend, online learning. *Students:* 17 full-time (16 women), 42 part-time (28 women); includes 9 minority (2 Black or African American, non-Hispanic/Latino; 5 Hispanic/Latino; 2 Two or more races, non-Hispanic/Latino). Average age 36. 25 applicants, 76% accepted, 12 enrolled. In 2016, 22 master's, 5 other advanced degrees awarded. *Entrance requirements:* Additional exam requirements/recommendations for international students: Required—TOEFL. *Application deadline:* Applications are processed on a rolling basis. Application fee: $45. *Financial support:* Fellowships, research assistantships with full tuition reimbursements, teaching assistantships with full tuition reimbursements, career-related internships or fieldwork, Federal Work-Study, institutionally sponsored loans, scholarships/grants, tuition waivers (partial), and unspecified assistantships available. Support available to part-time students. Financial award applicants required to submit FAFSA. *Application contact:* Dr. Ted Ligibel, Program Director, 734-487-0232, Fax: 734-487-6979, E-mail: tligibel@emich.edu.

**The George Washington University,** Columbian College of Arts and Sciences, Department of American Studies, Washington, DC 20052. Offers American studies (PhD); folk life (MA); historic preservation (MA); material culture (MA). *Program availability:* Part-time, evening/weekend. *Faculty:* 18 full-time (14 women), 15 part-time/adjunct (10 women). *Students:* 18 full-time (14 women), 15 part-time (10 women); includes 9 minority (5 Black or African American, non-Hispanic/Latino; 3 Asian, non-Hispanic/Latino; 1 Hispanic/Latino). Average age 29. 87 applicants, 29% accepted, 10 enrolled. In 2016, 7 master's, 13 doctorates awarded. Terminal master's awarded for partial completion of doctoral program. *Degree requirements:* For master's, comprehensive exam; for doctorate, one foreign language, thesis/dissertation, general exam. *Entrance requirements:* For master's and doctorate, GRE General Test, minimum GPA of 3.0. Additional exam requirements/recommendations for international students: Required—TOEFL (minimum score 550 paper-based; 80 iBT). *Application deadline:* For fall admission, 1/15 priority date for domestic and international students; for spring admission, 10/1 for domestic students. Application fee: $75. *Financial support:* In 2016–17, 22 students received support. Fellowships, research assistantships, teaching assistantships, career-related internships or fieldwork, Federal Work-Study, institutionally sponsored loans, and tuition waivers available. Financial award application deadline: 1/15. *Unit head:* Melanie McAlister, Chair, 202-994-7244, E-mail:

jam@gwu.edu. *Application contact:* Information Contact, 202-994-6070, Fax: 202-994-8651, E-mail: amst@gwu.edu. Website: http://departments.columbian.gwu.edu/americanstudies/

**Georgia State University,** College of Arts and Sciences, Department of History, Program in Heritage Preservation, Atlanta, GA 30302-3083. Offers MHP. *Program availability:* Part-time. *Degree requirements:* For master's, comprehensive exam, thesis optional, 42 hours of credit. *Entrance requirements:* For master's, GRE General Test, statement of purpose, three letters of recommendation, official transcripts. Additional exam requirements/recommendations for international students: Required—TOEFL (minimum score 550 paper-based; 80 iBT). *Application deadline:* For fall admission, 3/15 priority date for domestic and international students; for spring admission, 10/15 priority date for domestic and international students. Applications are processed on a rolling basis. Application fee: $50. Electronic applications accepted. *Expenses:* Tuition, state resident: full-time $6876; part-time $382 per credit hour. Tuition, nonresident: full-time $22,374; part-time $1243 per credit hour. *Required fees:* $2128; $1064 per term. Part-time tuition and fees vary according to course load and program. *Financial support:* In 2016–17, fellowships with full tuition reimbursements (averaging $5,100 per year), research assistantships with full tuition reimbursements (averaging $5,100 per year) were awarded; career-related internships or fieldwork, Federal Work-Study, scholarships/grants, and unspecified assistantships also available. Support available to part-time students. Financial award application deadline: 7/15. *Faculty research:* Materials conservation, preservation planning, cultural preservation, public history, oral history, twentieth-century American history. *Unit head:* Dr. Michelle Brattain, Chair, 404-413-6352, E-mail: mbrattain@gsu.edu. *Application contact:* Richard Laub, Director of Heritage Preservation Program, 404-413-6365, E-mail: rlaub@gsu.edu. Website: http://www.gsu.edu/~wwwhis

**Georgia State University,** College of Arts and Sciences, Department of History, Program in History, Atlanta, GA 30302-3083. Offers historic preservation (MA); history (PhD); public history (MA); world history (MA). *Program availability:* Part-time, evening/weekend. Terminal master's awarded for partial completion of doctoral program. *Degree requirements:* For master's, one foreign language, comprehensive exam, thesis optional, continuous enrollment; 6 hours of thesis credits; for doctorate, 2 foreign languages, comprehensive exam, thesis/dissertation, dissertation prospectus and prospectus defense; dissertation defense; residency; continuous enrollment; 6 hours of thesis credits. *Entrance requirements:* For master's, GRE, BA in history; statement of purpose; writing sample; three letters of recommendation; official transcripts; for doctorate, GRE, MA in history; master's thesis; statement of purpose; writing sample; three letters of recommendation; official transcripts; appropriate language skills. Additional exam requirements/recommendations for international students: Required—TOEFL (minimum score 550 paper-based; 80 iBT). *Application deadline:* For fall admission, 3/15 for domestic and international students; for spring admission, 10/15 for domestic and international students. Applications are processed on a rolling basis. Application fee: $50. Electronic applications accepted. *Expenses:* Tuition, state resident: full-time $6876; part-time $382 per credit hour. Tuition, nonresident: full-time $22,374; part-time $1243 per credit hour. *Required fees:* $2128; $1064 per term. Part-time tuition and fees vary according to course load and program. *Financial support:* Research assistantships with tuition reimbursements, teaching assistantships with tuition reimbursements, and scholarships/grants available. Financial award application deadline: 2/15; financial award applicants required to submit FAFSA. *Faculty research:* Nineteenth- and twentieth-century U.S. history, early modern European history, modern European history, world history, public history. *Unit head:* Dr. Michelle Brattain, Chair, 404-413-6352, Fax: 404-413-6384, E-mail: mbrattain@gsu.edu. *Application contact:* Dr. Joe Perry, Director of Graduate Studies, 404-413-6374, Fax: 404-413-6384, E-mail: jbperry@gsu.edu. Website: http://www.gsu.edu/~wwwhis

**Goucher College,** MA and MFA Programs, Baltimore, MD 21204-2794. Offers arts administration (MA); creative nonfiction (MFA); cultural sustainability (MA); digital arts (MA, MFA); environmental studies (MA); historic preservation (MA); management (MA). *Program availability:* Part-time, evening/weekend, blended/hybrid learning. *Faculty:* 6 full-time (4 women), 100 part-time/adjunct (56 women). *Students:* 70 full-time (50 women), 69 part-time (52 women); includes 15 minority (7 Black or African American, non-Hispanic/Latino; 1 American Indian or Alaska Native, non-Hispanic/Latino; 1 Asian, non-Hispanic/Latino; 4 Hispanic/Latino; 2 Two or more races, non-Hispanic/Latino), 2 international. 74 applicants, 88% accepted, 42 enrolled. In 2016, 83 master's awarded. *Degree requirements:* For master's, thesis, e-portfolio. *Entrance requirements:* For master's, digital portfolio (for MA, MFA in digital arts); writing sample (for MFA in creative nonfiction). Additional exam requirements/recommendations for international students: Required—TOEFL (minimum score 550 paper-based; 80 iBT). *Application deadline:* Applications are processed on a rolling basis. Application fee: $75. Electronic applications accepted. *Expenses:* Contact institution. *Financial support:* Scholarships/grants and unspecified assistantships available. Financial award application deadline: 4/15; financial award applicants required to submit FAFSA. *Unit head:* Leslie Rubinkowski, Assistant Provost, 410-337-6200, E-mail: leslie.rubinkowski@goucher.edu. *Application contact:* Shelby Hillers, Admissions Coordinator, 410-337-6200, Fax: 410-337-6200, E-mail: shelby.hillers@goucher.edu. Website: http://www.goucher.edu/grad

**Morgan State University,** School of Graduate Studies, College of Liberal Arts, Department of History and Geography, Baltimore, MD 21251. Offers African-American studies (MA); history (MA, PhD); museum studies and historic preservation (MA). *Program availability:* Part-time, evening/weekend. *Degree requirements:* For master's, comprehensive exam, thesis; for doctorate, comprehensive exam, thesis/dissertation. *Entrance requirements:* For master's, minimum GPA of 2.5; for doctorate, GRE or MAT. Additional exam requirements/recommendations for international students: Required—TOEFL (minimum score 550 paper-based). *Faculty research:* Women's history, African diaspora history, urban history.

**New York University,** Graduate School of Arts and Science, Institute of Fine Arts, Program in Conservation Training, New York, NY 10012-1019. Offers MA/Diploma.

**Penn State Harrisburg,** Graduate School, School of Humanities, Middletown, PA 17057. Offers American studies (MA, PhD); communications (MA); heritage and museum practice (Certificate); humanities (MA); writing instruction specialist (Certificate). *Program availability:* Evening/weekend. *Unit head:* Dr. Mukund S. Kulkarni, Chancellor, 717-948-6105, Fax: 717-948-6452. *Application contact:* Robert W. Coffman, Jr., Director of Enrollment Management, Admissions, 717-948-6250, Fax: 717-948-6325, E-mail: hbgadmit@psu.edu. Website: https://harrisburg.psu.edu/humanities

**Plymouth State University,** Program in Historic Preservation, Plymouth, NH 03264-1595. Offers MA. *Degree requirements:* For master's, thesis or practicum.

**Pratt Institute,** School of Architecture, Program in Historic Preservation, New York, NY 10011. Offers MS. *Program availability:* Part-time. *Faculty:* 5 full-time (2 women), 8 part-time/adjunct (4 women). *Students:* 27 full-time (16 women); includes 6 minority (1 Black or African American, non-Hispanic/Latino; 4 Hispanic/Latino; 1 Two or more races, non-Hispanic/Latino), 8 international. Average age 31. 37 applicants, 97% accepted, 14

## Historic Preservation

enrolled. In 2016, 11 master's awarded. *Degree requirements:* For master's, thesis. *Entrance requirements:* For master's, writing sample, bachelor's degree, transcripts, letters of recommendation, portfolio. Additional exam requirements/recommendations for international students: Required—TOEFL (minimum score 575 paper-based; 90 iBT). *Application deadline:* For fall admission, 1/5 for domestic and international students; for spring admission, 10/1 for domestic and international students. Application fee: $50 ($90 for international students). Electronic applications accepted. *Expenses:* $29,646 full-time tuition, $1,938 fees. *Financial support:* Career-related internships or fieldwork, Federal Work-Study, institutionally sponsored loans, scholarships/grants, health care benefits, and unspecified assistantships available. Support available to part-time students. Financial award application deadline: 2/1; financial award applicants required to submit FAFSA. *Unit head:* Thomas Hanrahan, Dean of Architecture, 718-399-4308, E-mail: hanrahan@pratt.edu. *Application contact:* Natalie Capannelli, Director of Graduate Admissions, 718-636-3551, Fax: 718-399-4242, E-mail: ncapanne@pratt.edu. Website: https://www.pratt.edu/academics/architecture/historic-preservation/

**See Display on page 114 and Close-Up on page 137.**

**Roger Williams University,** School of Architecture, Art and Historic Preservation, Bristol, RI 02809. Offers architecture (M Arch); art and architectural history (MA); historical preservation (MS). *Faculty:* 15 full-time (4 women), 4 part-time/adjunct (2 women). *Students:* 100 full-time (43 women), 1 part-time (0 women); includes 14 minority (3 Black or African American, non-Hispanic/Latino; 1 Asian, non-Hispanic/Latino; 6 Hispanic/Latino; 4 Two or more races, non-Hispanic/Latino), 4 international. Average age 25. 77 applicants, 95% accepted, 48 enrolled. In 2016, 43 master's awarded. *Degree requirements:* For master's, thesis. *Entrance requirements:* For master's, portfolio, 2 letters of recommendation, college transcript, letter of intent. Additional exam requirements/recommendations for international students: Required—TOEFL (minimum score 85 iBT), IELTS (minimum score 6.5). *Application deadline:* For fall admission, 4/1 for domestic students; for spring admission, 1/1 for domestic students. Application fee: $50. Electronic applications accepted. Application fee is waived when completed online. *Expenses:* $1,408 per credit hour (for M Arch); $843 per credit hour (for MS and MA). *Financial support:* In 2016–17, 95 students received support, including 91 research assistantships (averaging $2,753 per year); scholarships/grants and unspecified assistantships also available. Financial award application deadline: 4/1; financial award applicants required to submit FAFSA. *Unit head:* Stephen White, Dean, 401-254-3607, E-mail: swhite@rwu.edu. *Application contact:* Marcus Hanscom, Director of Graduate Admissions, 401-254-6200, Fax: 401-254-3345, E-mail: gradadmit@rwu.edu.
Website: http://www.rwu.edu/academics/departments/architecture.htm#dual

**Rutgers University–New Brunswick,** Graduate School-New Brunswick, Program in Art History, Piscataway, NJ 08854-8097. Offers art history (MA, PhD); curatorial studies (Certificate); historic preservation (Certificate). *Program availability:* Part-time. Terminal master's awarded for partial completion of doctoral program. *Degree requirements:* For master's, one foreign language, comprehensive exam; for doctorate, 2 foreign languages, comprehensive exam, thesis/dissertation. *Entrance requirements:* For master's and doctorate, GRE General Test, writing sample. Additional exam requirements/recommendations for international students: Required—TOEFL (minimum score 550 paper-based). Electronic applications accepted. *Faculty research:* Ancient and medieval art and architecture; Renaissance and Baroque art and architecture; modern and contemporary art and architecture; Italian studies; the arts of Asia, Africa, and the Americas.

**Rutgers University–New Brunswick,** Graduate School-New Brunswick, Program in Cultural Heritage and Preservation Studies, Piscataway, NJ 08854-8097. Offers cultural heritage and preservation studies (MA); historic preservation (Certificate).

**St. Cloud State University,** School of Graduate Studies, College of Social Sciences, Program in Cultural Resource Management Archeology, St. Cloud, MN 56301-4498. Offers MS. *Entrance requirements:* For master's, GRE General Test, minimum GPA of 2.75. Additional exam requirements/recommendations for international students: Required—Michigan English Language Assessment Battery; Recommended—TOEFL (minimum score 550 paper-based).

**Savannah College of Art and Design,** Graduate School, Program in Preservation Design, Savannah, GA 31402-3146. Offers MA, MFA. *Program availability:* Part-time. *Faculty:* 5 full-time (0 women). *Students:* 28 full-time (26 women), 16 part-time (13 women); includes 2 minority (1 Black or African American, non-Hispanic/Latino; 1 Hispanic/Latino). Average age 34. 59 applicants, 39% accepted, 16 enrolled. In 2016, 21 master's awarded. *Degree requirements:* For master's, thesis (for some programs), preservation practicum (for MA); thesis (for MFA). *Entrance requirements:* For master's, GRE (recommended), portfolio (submitted in digital format), audition or writing submission, resume, statement of purpose, two letters of recommendation. Additional exam requirements/recommendations for international students: Required—TOEFL (minimum score 550 paper-based, 85 iBT), IELTS (minimum score 6.5), or ACTFL. *Application deadline:* For fall admission, 4/1 for domestic and international students. Applications are processed on a rolling basis. Application fee: $40. Electronic applications accepted. *Expenses: Tuition:* Full-time $36,045. Tuition and fees vary according to course load. *Financial support:* Career-related internships or fieldwork, Federal Work-Study, and scholarships/grants available. Financial award application deadline: 4/1; financial award applicants required to submit FAFSA. *Unit head:* Ivan Chow, Dean, School of Building Arts. *Application contact:* Jenny Jaquillard, Executive Director of Admissions, Recruitment and Events, 912-525-5100, Fax: 912-525-5985, E-mail: admission@scad.edu.
Website: http://www.scad.edu/academics/programs/preservation-design

**School of the Art Institute of Chicago,** Graduate Division, Program in Historic Preservation, Chicago, IL 60603-3103. Offers MSHP. *Entrance requirements:* Additional exam requirements/recommendations for international students: Required—TOEFL, IELTS.

**Southeast Missouri State University,** School of Graduate Studies, Department of History, Cape Girardeau, MO 63701-4799. Offers heritage interpretation (Certificate); historic preservation (Certificate); history (MA); public history (MA), including heritage education, historic preservation. *Program availability:* Part-time, evening/weekend. *Faculty:* 11 full-time (3 women). *Students:* 8 full-time (2 women), 19 part-time (7 women); includes 2 minority (both Hispanic/Latino). Average age 31. 13 applicants, 92% accepted, 7 enrolled. In 2016, 8 master's awarded. *Degree requirements:* For master's, comprehensive exam (for some programs), thesis or comprehensive exams plus a capstone project/paper (for history); thesis or internship plus advanced project in applied history and comprehensive exams (for public history). *Entrance requirements:* For master's, minimum GPA of 2.75; 24 semester hours of undergraduate credit in history; letter of intent indicating how past experiences have prepared the candidate for graduate study and what the candidate expects to achieve through graduate study; two letters of recommendation; academic or professional writing sample; for Certificate, minimum GPA of 2.75; letter of intent indicating how past experiences have prepared the candidate for graduate study and what the candidate expects to achieve through graduate study; two letters of recommendation; academic or professional writing sample. Additional exam requirements/recommendations for international students:

Required—TOEFL (minimum score 550 paper-based; 79 iBT), IELTS (minimum score 6), PTE (minimum score 53). *Application deadline:* For fall admission, 8/1 for domestic students, 6/1 for international students; for spring admission, 11/21 for domestic students, 10/1 for international students; for summer admission, 5/15 for domestic students. Applications are processed on a rolling basis. Application fee: $30 ($40 for international students). Electronic applications accepted. *Expenses:* Tuition, state resident: full-time $3130; part-time $260.80 per credit hour. Tuition, nonresident: full-time $5842; part-time $486.80 per credit hour. *Required fees:* $33.70 per credit hour. *Financial support:* In 2016–17, 5 students received support, including 4 teaching assistantships with full tuition reimbursements available; career-related internships or fieldwork, Federal Work-Study, scholarships/grants, traineeships, tuition waivers (full), and unspecified assistantships also available. Financial award application deadline: 6/30; financial award applicants required to submit FAFSA. *Faculty research:* Medieval Europe; modern Europe including Britain, Germany, France, Russia, and Spain; colonial and nineteenth-century America; twentieth-century America and American West; public history and historic preservation; Latin America. *Unit head:* Dr. Wayne Bowen, Chairperson/Professor of History, 573-651-2179, Fax: 573-651-5114, E-mail: wbowen@semo.edu. *Application contact:* Dr. Vicky McAlister, Graduate Coordinator/Assistant Professor of History, 573-651-2763, Fax: 573-651-5114, E-mail: vmcalister@semo.edu.

**Universidad Nacional Pedro Henriquez Urena,** Graduate School, Santo Domingo, Dominican Republic. Offers agricultural diversity (MS), including horticultural/fruit production, tropical animal production; conservation of monuments and cultural assets (M Arch); ecology and environment (MS); environmental engineering (MEE); international relations (MA); natural resource management (MS); political science (MA); project optimization (MPM); project feasibility (MPM); project management (MPM); sanitation engineering (ME); science for teachers (MS); tropical Caribbean architecture (M Arch).

**University at Buffalo, the State University of New York,** Graduate School, School of Architecture and Planning, Department of Architecture, Buffalo, NY 14214. Offers architecture (M Arch); ecological practices (MS Arch); historic preservation and urban design (MS Arch); inclusive design (MS Arch); real estate development (MS Arch); situated technology (MS Arch); M Arch/MBA; M Arch/MFA; M Arch/MUP. *Faculty:* 32 full-time (11 women), 9 part-time/adjunct (3 women). *Students:* 134 full-time (56 women), 15 part-time (5 women); includes 29 minority (12 Black or African American, non-Hispanic/Latino; 5 Asian, non-Hispanic/Latino; 8 Hispanic/Latino; 4 Two or more races, non-Hispanic/Latino), 27 international. Average age 25. 267 applicants, 34% accepted, 63 enrolled. In 2016, 44 master's awarded. *Degree requirements:* For master's, thesis or alternative, project. *Entrance requirements:* For master's, GRE, portfolio, 3 letters of recommendation, transcripts, 500-word personal statement. Additional exam requirements/recommendations for international students: Required—TOEFL (minimum score 79 iBT), IELTS (minimum score 6.5). *Application deadline:* For fall admission, 1/1 priority date for domestic and international students. Application fee: $75. Electronic applications accepted. *Expenses:* Contact institution. *Financial support:* In 2016–17, 5 students received support, including 5 fellowships with full tuition reimbursements available (averaging $11,040 per year), 2 research assistantships with partial tuition reimbursements available (averaging $13,200 per year), 43 teaching assistantships with partial tuition reimbursements available (averaging $4,337 per year); career-related internships or fieldwork, Federal Work-Study, scholarships/grants, health care benefits, and unspecified assistantships also available. Financial award application deadline: 3/1; financial award applicants required to submit FAFSA. *Faculty research:* Ecological practices, inclusive design, material culture, situated technologies, urban design. *Total annual research expenditures:* $3.8 million. *Unit head:* Prof. Omar Khan, Chair, 716-829-3483 Ext. 105, Fax: 716-829-3256, E-mail: omar.khan@buffalo.edu. *Application contact:* Debra Eggebrecht, Assistant to the Chair, 716-829-3486 Ext. 105, Fax: 716-829-3256, E-mail: dle2@buffalo.edu.
Website: http://www.ap.buffalo.edu/architecture/

**University at Buffalo, the State University of New York,** Graduate School, School of Architecture and Planning, Department of Urban and Regional Planning, Buffalo, NY 14214. Offers historic preservation (Certificate); urban and regional planning (PhD); JD/MUP; M Arch/MUP. *Accreditation:* ACSP. *Program availability:* Part-time. *Faculty:* 14 full-time (6 women), 12 part-time/adjunct (3 women). *Students:* 78 full-time (29 women), 12 part-time (7 women); includes 19 minority (11 Black or African American, non-Hispanic/Latino; 1 Asian, non-Hispanic/Latino; 5 Hispanic/Latino; 2 Two or more races, non-Hispanic/Latino), 24 international. Average age 27. 216 applicants, 23% accepted, 36 enrolled. In 2016, 34 master's awarded. *Degree requirements:* For master's, thesis or alternative, project; for doctorate, thesis/dissertation. *Entrance requirements:* For master's, minimum GPA of 3.0, resume, 3 letters of recommendation, 500-word personal statement, transcripts; for doctorate, GRE, transcripts, 3 letters of recommendation, minimum GPA of 3.0, resume, research statement, writing sample. Additional exam requirements/recommendations for international students: Required—TOEFL (minimum score 79 iBT), IELTS (minimum score 6.5). *Application deadline:* For fall admission, 3/1 priority date for domestic and international students; for spring admission, 10/31 priority date for domestic students, 10/1 priority date for international students. Applications are processed on a rolling basis. Application fee: $75. Electronic applications accepted. *Expenses:* Contact institution. *Financial support:* In 2016–17, 3 students received support, including 3 fellowships with full tuition reimbursements available (averaging $10,400 per year), 5 research assistantships with tuition reimbursements available (averaging $8,751 per year), 15 teaching assistantships with partial tuition reimbursements available (averaging $3,684 per year); career-related internships or fieldwork, Federal Work-Study, institutionally sponsored loans, scholarships/grants, health care benefits, and unspecified assistantships also available. Financial award application deadline: 3/1; financial award applicants required to submit FAFSA. *Faculty research:* Economic and international development, environmental and land use planning, GIS and spatial analysis, urban design and physical planning, neighborhood planning and community development, historic preservation. *Total annual research expenditures:* $3.8 million. *Unit head:* Dr. Ernest Sternberg, Professor, 716-829-3671 Ext. 109, Fax: 716-829-3256, E-mail: ezs@buffalo.edu. *Application contact:* Norma Everett, Assistant to the Chair, 716-829-3283, Fax: 716-829-3256, E-mail: norma.everett@buffalo.edu.
Website: http://www.ap.buffalo.edu/planning/

**University of California, Los Angeles,** Graduate Division, College of Letters and Science, Interdepartmental Program in Conservation of Archaeological and Ethnographic Materials, Los Angeles, CA 90095. Offers MA. *Degree requirements:* For master's, one foreign language, thesis, eleven-month internship. *Entrance requirements:* For master's, GRE General Test, bachelor's degree; minimum undergraduate GPA of 3.0 (or its equivalent if letter grade system not used); proficiency in one foreign language; portfolio; writing sample; documented practical experience; interview. Additional exam requirements/recommendations for international students: Required—TOEFL.

**University of Colorado Denver,** College of Architecture and Planning, Program in Historic Preservation, Denver, CO 80217. Offers MS. *Students:* 10 full-time (6 women), 3 part-time (1 woman); includes 1 minority (Hispanic/Latino). Average age 31. 13

applicants, 31% accepted, 4 enrolled. In 2016, 7 master's awarded. *Degree requirements:* For master's, thesis, 45 credit hours. *Entrance requirements:* For master's, GRE (recommended, especially for students with an undergraduate GPA of less than 3.0), portfolio of creative work; sample of writing or work project. Additional exam requirements/recommendations for international students: Required—TOEFL (minimum score 75 iBT). *Application deadline:* For fall admission, 3/15 priority date for domestic students, 2/15 priority date for international students. Applications are processed on a rolling basis. Application fee: $50 ($75 for international students). Electronic applications accepted. *Expenses:* Contact institution. *Financial support:* In 2016–17, 2 students received support. Fellowships, research assistantships, teaching assistantships, Federal Work-Study, institutionally sponsored loans, scholarships/ grants, and traineeships available. Financial award application deadline: 4/1; financial award applicants required to submit FAFSA. *Faculty research:* Rural cultural landscapes; vernacular architecture; cultural preservation; architectural conservation, heritage, and policy. *Unit head:* Dr. Christopher Koziol, Director, 303-556-6516, E-mail: christopher.koziol@ucdenver.edu. *Application contact:* Rachael Kuroiwa, Manager of Admissions and Outreach, 303-315-2325, E-mail: rachael.kuroiwa@ucdenver.edu. Website: http://www.ucdenver.edu/academics/colleges/ArchitecturePlanning/ Academics/DegreePrograms/MSHP/Pages/MSHP.aspx

**University of Delaware,** College of Arts and Sciences, Department of Art Conservation, Newark, DE 19716. Offers art conservation (MS); preservation studies (PhD). *Degree requirements:* For master's, internship, portfolio, oral exam, oral presentation. *Entrance requirements:* For master's, GRE General Test, course work in chemistry, art history/anthropology and studio art; minimum of 400 hours of conservation experience. Additional exam requirements/recommendations for international students: Recommended—TOEFL. Electronic applications accepted. *Faculty research:* Emergency response cleaning techniques, degradation process, art history, artists, materials, techniques of preservation and treatment.

**University of Delaware,** College of Arts and Sciences, School of Public Policy and Administration, Program in Urban Affairs and Public Policy, Newark, DE 19716. Offers governance planning and management (PhD); historic preservation (MA); social and urban policy (PhD); technology, environment and society (PhD); urban affairs and public policy (MA). *Program availability:* Part-time. Terminal master's awarded for partial completion of doctoral program. *Degree requirements:* For master's, analytical paper or thesis; for doctorate, thesis/dissertation. *Entrance requirements:* For master's, GRE General Test, minimum GPA of 3.0; for doctorate, GRE General Test, minimum GPA of 3.5. Additional exam requirements/recommendations for international students: Required—TOEFL. Electronic applications accepted. *Faculty research:* Political economy; social policy analysis; technology and society; historic preservation; urban policy.

**University of Florida,** Graduate School, College of Liberal Arts and Sciences, Department of History, Gainesville, FL 32611. Offers historic preservation (MA, PhD); history (MA, PhD); Jewish studies (MA); women's and gender studies (PhD); JD/MA; JD/PhD. *Program availability:* Part-time. Terminal master's awarded for partial completion of doctoral program. *Degree requirements:* For master's, variable foreign language requirement, thesis optional, 30 credit hours; for doctorate, variable foreign language requirement, comprehensive exam, thesis/dissertation, 90 credit hours. *Entrance requirements:* For master's and doctorate, GRE General Test, minimum GPA of 3.0. Additional exam requirements/recommendations for international students: Required—TOEFL (minimum score 550 paper-based; 80 iBT), IELTS (minimum score 6). Electronic applications accepted. *Faculty research:* Latin American and Caribbean history, nineteenth century U.S. history, medieval European history, African history and Atlantic world history.

**University of Georgia,** College of Environment and Design, Athens, GA 30602. Offers environmental planning and design (MEPD); historic preservation (MHP); landscape architecture (MLA). *Application deadline:* For fall admission, 7/1 priority date for domestic students; for spring admission, 11/15 for domestic students. Application fee: $50. *Unit head:* Daniels J. Nadenicek, Acting Dean, 706-542-1100, Fax: 706-542-4485, E-mail: dnadeni@uga.edu. *Application contact:* Umit Yilmaz, Graduate Coordinator, 706-542-4720, E-mail: yilmaz@uga.edu. Website: http://www.ced.uga.edu

**University of Hawaii at Manoa,** Graduate Division, College of Arts and Humanities, Department of American Studies, Program in Historic Preservation, Honolulu, HI 96822. Offers Graduate Certificate. *Program availability:* Part-time. *Entrance requirements:* Additional exam requirements/recommendations for international students: Required—TOEFL (minimum score 600 paper-based; 100 iBT), IELTS (minimum score 7).

**The University of Kansas,** Graduate Studies, School of Architecture, Design, and Planning, Department of Architecture, Lawrence, KS 66045. Offers architectural acoustics (Certificate); architecture (M Arch, PhD); health and wellness (Certificate); historic preservation (Certificate); urban design (Certificate). *Students:* 107 full-time (52 women), 15 part-time (7 women); includes 17 minority (5 Black or African American, non-Hispanic/Latino; 6 Asian, non-Hispanic/Latino; 4 Hispanic/Latino; 2 Two or more races, non-Hispanic/Latino), 35 international. Average age 26. 115 applicants, 71% accepted, 20 enrolled. In 2016, 85 master's, 2 doctorates awarded. Terminal master's awarded for partial completion of doctoral program. *Entrance requirements:* For master's, GRE, transcript; resume; minimum GPA of 3.0; statement of purpose; letters of recommendation; portfolio of design work, or samples of written work or other creative artifacts produced if previous degree was not in a design-related discipline; for doctorate, GRE, transcript, resume, minimum GPA of 3.0, statement of purpose, letters of recommendation, research-informed writing sample, exhibit of work illustrating applicant's interests and abilities in areas related to the design disciplines. Additional exam requirements/recommendations for international students: Required—TOEFL, IELTS. *Application deadline:* For fall admission, 1/15 priority date for domestic and international students; for summer admission, 1/15 priority date for domestic and international students. Application fee: $65 ($85 for international students). Electronic applications accepted. *Financial support:* Fellowships, research assistantships, teaching assistantships, scholarships/grants, health care benefits, and unspecified assistantships available. Financial award application deadline: 1/15; financial award applicants required to submit FAFSA. *Faculty research:* Design build, sustainability, emergent technology, healthy places, urban design. *Unit head:* Prof. Jae Chang, Chair, 785-864-1446, E-mail: jdchang@ku.edu. *Application contact:* Gera Elliott, Admissions Coordinator, 785-864-3167, Fax: 785-864-5185, E-mail: archku@ku.edu. Website: http://architecture.ku.edu/

**University of Kentucky,** Graduate School, College of Design, Department of Historic Preservation, Lexington, KY 40506-0032. Offers MHP. *Degree requirements:* For master's, comprehensive exam. *Entrance requirements:* For master's, GRE General Test, minimum undergraduate GPA of 2.75. Additional exam requirements/ recommendations for international students: Required—TOEFL (minimum score 550 paper-based). Electronic applications accepted.

**University of Maryland, College Park,** Academic Affairs, School of Architecture, Planning and Preservation, Program in Historic Preservation, College Park, MD 20742.

Offers MHP, Certificate. *Degree requirements:* For Certificate, thesis. *Entrance requirements:* For master's, GRE, minimum GPA of 3.0, 3 letters of recommendation, writing sample. Additional exam requirements/recommendations for international students: Required—TOEFL. Electronic applications accepted.

**University of Massachusetts Amherst,** Graduate School, College of Humanities and Fine Arts, Department of Architecture, Amherst, MA 01003. Offers architecture (M Arch); design (MS); design in historic preservation (MS). *Program availability:* Part-time. *Degree requirements:* For master's, thesis or alternative, project. *Entrance requirements:* For master's, GRE General Test (for M Arch only), 3 letters of recommendation (M Arch only); portfolio. Additional exam requirements/ recommendations for international students: Required—TOEFL (minimum score 550 paper-based; 80 iBT), IELTS (minimum score 6.5). Electronic applications accepted.

**University of New Mexico,** Graduate Studies, School of Architecture and Planning, Program in Historic Preservation and Regionalism, Albuquerque, NM 87131-2039. Offers Graduate Certificate. *Program availability:* Part-time, evening/weekend. *Faculty:* 1 (woman) full-time, 2 part-time/adjunct (0 women). *Students:* 2 full-time (both women), 6 part-time (3 women); includes 2 minority (1 American Indian or Alaska Native, non-Hispanic/Latino; 1 Hispanic/Latino), 2 international. Average age 41. 6 applicants, 83% accepted, 4 enrolled. In 2016, 9 Graduate Certificates awarded. *Application deadline:* For fall admission, 11/1 priority date for domestic students; for spring admission, 3/1 priority date for domestic students. Application fee: $50. Electronic applications accepted. *Financial support:* Research assistantships, career-related internships or fieldwork, and scholarships/grants available. Support available to part-time students. *Unit head:* Chris Wilson, Director, 505-277-3303, Fax: 505-277-0897, E-mail: chwilson@unm.edu. *Application contact:* Elizabeth M. Rowe, Senior Academic Adviser, 505-277-1303, Fax: 505-277-0076, E-mail: erowe@unm.edu. Website: http://saap.unm.edu/

**The University of North Carolina at Greensboro,** Graduate School, College of Arts and Sciences, Department of Interior Architecture, Greensboro, NC 27412-5001. Offers historic preservation (Certificate); interior architecture (MS); museum studies (Certificate). *Degree requirements:* For master's, thesis. *Entrance requirements:* For master's, GRE General Test or MAT, bachelor's degree in interior design, interview, portfolio. Additional exam requirements/recommendations for international students: Required—TOEFL. Electronic applications accepted.

**University of Oregon,** Graduate School, School of Architecture and Allied Arts, Program in Historic Preservation, Eugene, OR 97403. Offers MS. *Degree requirements:* For master's, thesis, internship. *Entrance requirements:* For master's, participation in Pacific Northwest Field School. Additional exam requirements/recommendations for international students: Required—TOEFL. *Faculty research:* Vernacular architecture, Native American architecture, masonry structure and details, wood construction systems, cultural landscapes.

**University of Pennsylvania,** School of Design, Program in Historic Preservation, Philadelphia, PA 19104. Offers MS, Certificate. *Faculty:* 3 full-time (0 women), 1 part-time/adjunct (0 women). *Students:* 47 full-time (34 women), 3 part-time (all women); includes 6 minority (4 Black or African American, non-Hispanic/Latino; 2 Asian, non-Hispanic/Latino), 8 international. Average age 27. 47 applicants, 100% accepted, 25 enrolled. In 2016, 20 master's, 6 other advanced degrees awarded. *Degree requirements:* For master's, thesis. *Entrance requirements:* For master's, GRE, official academic transcripts, 3 letters of recommendation, course in computer-aided drafting (preferably AutoCad). Additional exam requirements/recommendations for international students: Required—TOEFL (minimum score 600 paper-based; 100 iBT). *Application deadline:* For fall admission, 1/12 for domestic students. Application fee: $80. *Expenses:* Tuition: Full-time $31,068; part-time $5762 per course. *Required fees:* $3200; $336 per course. Full-time tuition and fees vary according to degree level, program and student level. Part-time tuition and fees vary according to course load, degree level and program. *Financial support:* Research assistantships, teaching assistantships, career-related internships or fieldwork, Federal Work-Study, institutionally sponsored loans, scholarships/grants, and unspecified assistantships available. Financial award application deadline: 4/15; financial award applicants required to submit FAFSA. *Faculty research:* Theories and methods of preservation planning, historic building technology and conservation of building materials, ways in which visual culture inform planning and design, cultural policy and the economics of preservation. *Unit head:* Dr. Randall F. Mason, Chair/Associate Professor, 215-898-3169, Fax: 215-573-6326, E-mail: rfmason@upenn.edu. *Application contact:* Nadine Beauharnois, Administrative Assistant, 215-898-3169, Fax: 215-573-6326, E-mail: pennhsvp@upenn.edu. Website: http://www.design.upenn.edu/historic-preservation

**University of Rochester,** School of Arts and Sciences, Program in Photographic Preservation and Collections Management, Rochester, NY 14627. Offers MA. Program offered jointly with George Eastman House. *Program availability:* Part-time. *Students:* 15 full-time (10 women). Average age 29. 18 applicants, 78% accepted, 5 enrolled. In 2016, 2 master's awarded. *Degree requirements:* For master's, thesis (for some programs). *Entrance requirements:* Additional exam requirements/recommendations for international students: Required—TOEFL (minimum score 600 paper-based; 100 iBT). *Application deadline:* For fall admission, 3/3 for domestic students. Application fee: $60. Electronic applications accepted. *Expenses:* $1,583 per credit. *Faculty research:* Photographic preservation, collections management, photography. *Unit head:* Joan Saab, Co-Director, 585-275-4287, E-mail: joan.saab@rochester.edu. *Application contact:* Lorna Maier, Administrative Assistant, 585-275-9249, E-mail: lmaier@ur.rochester.edu. Website: http://www.rochester.edu/college/ppcm

**University of South Carolina,** The Graduate School, College of Arts and Sciences, Department of History, Program in Public History, Columbia, SC 29208. Offers archive management (MA); historic preservation (MA); museum administration (MA); museum management (Certificate); MLIS/MA. *Degree requirements:* For master's, one foreign language, thesis, internship. *Entrance requirements:* For master's, GRE General Test, writing sample. Additional exam requirements/recommendations for international students: Required—TOEFL. Electronic applications accepted. *Faculty research:* Museum studies, historic preservation, archives administration.

**The University of Texas at Austin,** Graduate School, School of Architecture, Program in Historic Preservation, Austin, TX 78712-1111. Offers M Arch, MS, MSCRP.

**University of Vermont,** Graduate College, College of Arts and Sciences, Program in Historic Preservation, Burlington, VT 05405. Offers MS. *Entrance requirements:* For master's, GRE General Test, sample project or equivalent. Additional exam requirements/recommendations for international students: Required—TOEFL (minimum score 550 paper-based; 80 iBT). Electronic applications accepted. *Expenses:* Tuition, state resident: full-time $5814. Tuition, nonresident: full-time $14,670. *Faculty research:* Architectural environment.

**University of Washington,** Graduate School, College of Built Environments, Interdisciplinary Program in Historic Preservation, Seattle, WA 98195. Offers Certificate. Offered in cooperation with the Departments of Architecture, Landscape Architecture, and Urban Design and Planning. *Program availability:* Part-time. Electronic applications accepted. *Faculty research:* History of the built environment, historic preservation planning, vernacular architecture, ethnic and gender issues in preservation, restoration.

**Ursuline College,** School of Graduate Studies, Program in Historic Preservation, Pepper Pike, OH 44124-4398. Offers MA. *Program availability:* Part-time. *Faculty:* 1 (woman) full-time, 1 part-time/adjunct (0 women). *Students:* 2 full-time (both women), 5 part-time (3 women); includes 1 minority (Black or African American, non-Hispanic/Latino), 34 international. Average age 41. 2 applicants, 100% accepted, 1 enrolled. *Degree requirements:* For master's, thesis. *Entrance requirements:* For master's, minimum undergraduate GPA of 3.0. Additional exam requirements/recommendations for international students: Required—TOEFL (minimum score 500 paper-based; 80 iBT). *Application deadline:* For fall admission, 8/1 priority date for domestic students. Applications are processed on a rolling basis. Application fee: $25. Electronic applications accepted. *Expenses:* $1,052 per semester credit hour. *Financial support:* In 2016–17, 2 students received support. Scholarships/grants available. Financial award application deadline: 3/1; financial award applicants required to submit FAFSA. *Unit head:* Dr. Bari Stith, Director, 440-646-8135, Fax: 440-684-6088, E-mail: bstith@ursuline.edu. *Application contact:* Melanie Steele, Director, Graduate Admission, 440-646-8146, Fax: 440-684-6138, E-mail: graduateadmissions@ursuline.edu.

# Landscape Architecture

**Academy of Art University,** Graduate Programs, School of Landscape Architecture, San Francisco, CA 94105-3410. Offers MA, MFA. *Program availability:* Part-time, 100% online. *Faculty:* 1 (woman) full-time, 14 part-time/adjunct (7 women). *Students:* 31 full-time (18 women), 8 part-time (6 women); includes 1 minority (Asian, non-Hispanic/Latino), 34 international. Average age 27. 15 applicants, 100% accepted, 10 enrolled. In 2016, 10 master's awarded. *Degree requirements:* For master's, final review. *Entrance requirements:* For master's, statement of intent; resume; portfolio/reel; official college transcripts. *Application deadline:* Applications are processed on a rolling basis. Application fee: $50. Electronic applications accepted. *Expenses: Tuition:* Part-time $982 per unit. *Financial support:* Career-related internships or fieldwork, Federal Work-Study, and scholarships/grants available. Financial award application deadline: 8/10; financial award applicants required to submit FAFSA. *Unit head:* 800-544-ARTS, E-mail: info@academyart.edu. *Application contact:* 800-544-ARTS, E-mail: info@academyart.edu.
Website: http://www.academyart.edu/landscape-architecture-school/index.html

**Arizona State University at the Tempe campus,** Herberger Institute for Design and the Arts, The Design School, Tempe, AZ 85287-1605. Offers architecture (M Arch); building design/built environment (MS); design (MSD), including arts, media, and engineering, healthcare and healing environments (MSD, PhD), industrial design, interaction design, interior design, new product innovation, visual communication design; design, environment and the arts (PhD), including design, digital culture, healthcare and healing environments (MSD, PhD), history, theory, and criticism; landscape architecture (MLA); urban design (MUD); MA/MBA. *Accreditation:* NASAD. Terminal master's awarded for partial completion of doctoral program. *Degree requirements:* For master's, thesis optional, interactive Program of Study (iPOS) submitted before completing 50 percent of required credit hours; for doctorate, comprehensive exam, thesis/dissertation, interactive Program of Study (iPOS) submitted before completing 50 percent of required credit hours. *Entrance requirements:* For master's, GRE General Test, minimum GPA of 3.0 or equivalent in last 2 years of work leading to bachelor's degree, design/creative works portfolio, 3 references, statement of intent; for doctorate, GRE, master's degree in architecture, graphic design, industrial design, interior design, landscape architecture, or art history or equivalent standing; statement of purpose; 3 letters of recommendation; indication of potential faculty mentor; sample of written work. Additional exam requirements/recommendations for international students: Required—TOEFL (minimum score 600 paper-based; 100 iBT). Electronic applications accepted.

**Auburn University,** Graduate School, College of Architecture, Design, and Construction, Program in Landscape Architecture, Auburn University, AL 36849. Offers ML Arch. *Accreditation:* ASLA. *Faculty:* 24 full-time (7 women), 5 part-time/adjunct (0 women). *Students:* 23 full-time (14 women), 1 part-time (0 women); includes 4 minority (2 Black or African American, non-Hispanic/Latino; 1 Asian, non-Hispanic/Latino; 1 Hispanic/Latino), 13 international. Average age 25. 42 applicants, 69% accepted, 13 enrolled. In 2016, 14 master's awarded. *Entrance requirements:* For master's, 3 letters of recommendation. Application fee: $50 ($60 for international students). *Expenses:* Tuition, state resident: full-time $9072; part-time $504 per credit hour. Tuition, nonresident: full-time $27,216; part-time $1512 per credit hour. *Required fees:* $812 per semester. Tuition and fees vary according to degree level and program. *Financial support:* Applicants required to submit FAFSA. *Unit head:* David Hill, Chair, 334-844-5449. *Application contact:* Dr. George Flowers, Dean of the Graduate School, 334-844-2125.

**Ball State University,** Graduate School, College of Architecture and Planning, Department of Landscape Architecture, Muncie, IN 47306. Offers MLA. *Accreditation:* ASLA. *Program availability:* Part-time. *Degree requirements:* For master's, thesis. *Entrance requirements:* For master's, minimum baccalaureate GPA of 2.75 or 3.0 in latter half of baccalaureate, resume, three letters of reference, copies of all transcripts, portfolio, writing sample. Additional exam requirements/recommendations for international students: Required—TOEFL (minimum score 550 paper-based; 79 iBT), IELTS (minimum score 6.5). Electronic applications accepted. *Expenses:* Contact institution.

**Bastyr University,** School of Natural Health Arts and Sciences, Kenmore, WA 98028-4966. Offers counseling psychology (MA); holistic landscape design (Certificate); midwifery (MS); nutrition (MS); nutrition and clinical health psychology (MS). *Accreditation:* AND. *Program availability:* Part-time. *Degree requirements:* For master's, thesis optional. *Entrance requirements:* For master's, 1-2 years' basic sciences course work (depending on program). Additional exam requirements/recommendations for international students: Required—TOEFL (minimum score 550 paper-based; 79 iBT). *Faculty research:* Whole-food nutrition for type 2 diabetes; meditation in end-of-life care; stress management; Qi Gong, Tai Chi and yoga for older adults; Echinacea and immunology.

**Boston Architectural College,** Graduate Programs, Boston, MA 02115-2795. Offers architecture (M Arch); historic preservation (MDS); interior design (MID); landscape architecture (MLA); sustainable design (MDS). *Accreditation:* CIDA. *Degree requirements:* For master's, thesis. *Entrance requirements:* For master's, portfolio (recommended). Electronic applications accepted.

**California State Polytechnic University, Pomona,** Program in Landscape Architecture, Pomona, CA 91768-2557. Offers M Land Arch. *Accreditation:* ASLA. *Program availability:* Part-time, evening/weekend. *Students:* 17 full-time (7 women), 8 part-time (7 women); includes 7 minority (2 Asian, non-Hispanic/Latino; 4 Hispanic/Latino; 1 Two or more races, non-Hispanic/Latino), 7 international. Average age 31. 8 applicants, 100% accepted, 8 enrolled. In 2016, 25 master's awarded. *Entrance requirements:* Additional exam requirements/recommendations for international students: Required—TOEFL. *Application deadline:* Applications are processed on a rolling basis. Application fee: $55. Electronic applications accepted. *Expenses:* Contact institution. *Financial support:* Application deadline: 3/2; applicants required to submit FAFSA. *Unit head:* Dr. Weimin Li, Graduate Coordinator, 909-869-2715, Fax: 909-869-2580, E-mail: wli@cpp.edu. *Application contact:* Andrew M. Wright, Director of Admissions, 909-869-3130, Fax: 909-869-4529, E-mail: awright@cpp.edu.
Website: https://env.cpp.edu/la/degree/master-landscape-architecture

**Chatham University,** Program in Landscape Architecture, Pittsburgh, PA 15232-2826. Offers landscape architecture (ML Arch); landscape design and development (MA). *Accreditation:* ASLA. *Program availability:* Part-time, evening/weekend. *Degree requirements:* For master's, thesis, capstone project. *Entrance requirements:* For master's, portfolio. Additional exam requirements/recommendations for international students: Required—TOEFL (minimum score 600 paper-based; 100 iBT), IELTS (minimum score 7), TWE. Electronic applications accepted. Application fee is waived when completed online. *Expenses: Tuition:* Full-time $16,254; part-time $903 per credit hour. *Required fees:* $468; $26 per credit hour. *Faculty research:* Sustainability.

**City College of the City University of New York,** Graduate School, The Bernard and Anne Spitzer School of Architecture, Program in Landscape Architecture, New York, NY 10031-9198. Offers MLA. Tuition and fees vary according to course load, degree level and program.

**Clemson University,** Graduate School, College of Architecture, Arts, and Humanities, Department of Landscape Architecture, Clemson, SC 29634. Offers MLA. *Accreditation:* ASLA. *Faculty:* 8 full-time (3 women). *Students:* 23 full-time (16 women), 17 international. Average age 25. 44 applicants, 50% accepted, 4 enrolled. In 2016, 7 master's awarded. *Degree requirements:* For master's, thesis or alternative. *Entrance requirements:* For master's, GRE General Test, unofficial transcripts, letters of recommendation, portfolio of creative and design work. Additional exam requirements/recommendations for international students: Required—TOEFL (minimum score 80 iBT), IELTS (minimum score 6.5). *Application deadline:* For fall admission, 2/15 priority date for domestic and international students. Applications are processed on a rolling basis. Application fee: $80 ($90 for international students). Electronic applications accepted. *Expenses:* $4,841 per semester full-time resident, $9,640 per semester full-time non-resident; $612 per credit hour part-time resident, $1,223 per credit hour part-time non-resident. *Financial support:* In 2016–17, 14 students received support, including 7 research assistantships with partial tuition reimbursements available (averaging $4,509 per year); career-related internships or fieldwork and unspecified assistantships also available. Financial award application deadline: 2/15. *Total annual research expenditures:* $21,259. *Unit head:* Dr. Mary Padua, Founding Chair, 864-656-3925, E-mail: mgpadua@clemson.edu. *Application contact:* Dr. Hala Nassar, Program Coordinator, Master of Landscape Architecture, 864-656-2499, E-mail: hnassar@clemson.edu.
Website: https://www.clemson.edu/caah/departments/la/

**Colorado State University,** College of Agricultural Sciences, Department of Horticulture and Landscape Architecture, Fort Collins, CO 80523-1173. Offers MLA, MS, PhD. *Program availability:* Part-time. *Faculty:* 15 full-time (3 women), 1 (woman) part-time/adjunct. *Students:* 19 full-time (7 women), 27 part-time (11 women); includes 3 minority (2 Hispanic/Latino; 1 Two or more races, non-Hispanic/Latino), 13 international. Average age 34. 33 applicants, 67% accepted, 4 enrolled. In 2016, 9 master's, 1 doctorate awarded. *Degree requirements:* For master's, thesis (for some programs); for doctorate, comprehensive exam, thesis/dissertation. *Entrance requirements:* For master's, GRE General Test (minimum score of 300 combined Verbal and Quantitative sections), minimum GPA of 3.0, letters of reference, related bachelor's degree or experience, transcripts, resume/curriculum vitae, statement of purpose; for doctorate, GRE General Test (minimum score of 300 combined Verbal and Quantitative sections), minimum GPA of 3.0, letters of reference, statement of purpose, related bachelor's degree or experience, resume/curriculum vitae, transcripts. Additional exam requirements/recommendations for international students: Required—TOEFL (minimum score 550 paper-based; 80 iBT), IELTS (minimum score 6.5). *Application deadline:* For fall admission, 4/1 for domestic and international students; for spring admission, 9/1 for domestic and international students; for summer admission, 1/1 for domestic and international students. Applications are processed on a rolling basis. Application fee: $60 ($70 for international students). Electronic applications accepted. *Expenses:* Tuition, state resident: full-time $9628. Tuition, nonresident: full-time $23,603. *Required fees:* $2253; $528.14 per credit hour. $264.07 per semester. Tuition and fees vary according to course load and program. *Financial support:* In 2016–17, 2 fellowships with full and partial tuition reimbursements (averaging $31,806 per year), 8 research assistantships with partial tuition reimbursements (averaging $16,020 per year), 7 teaching assistantships with partial tuition reimbursements (averaging $12,954 per year) were awarded; scholarships/grants and unspecified assistantships also available. Financial award application deadline: 2/15; financial award applicants required to submit FAFSA. *Faculty research:* Specialty crops, environmental physiology, water conservation, perennial research, cancer prevention through dietary intervention. *Total annual research expenditures:* $1.3 million. *Unit head:* Dr. Jessica G. Davis, Department Head/Professor, 970-491-7018, Fax: 970-491-7745, E-mail: jessica.davis@colostate.edu. *Application contact:* Kathi Nietfeld, Graduate Coordinator, 970-491-7018, Fax: 970-491-7745, E-mail: kathi.nietfeld@colostate.edu.
Website: http://hortla.agsci.colostate.edu

**Columbia University,** School of Continuing Education, Program in Landscape Design, New York, NY 10027. Offers MS. *Program availability:* Part-time. *Entrance requirements:* For master's, minimum undergraduate GPA of 3.0. Additional exam requirements/recommendations for international students: Required—American Language Program placement test.

**Cornell University,** Graduate School, Graduate Fields of Agriculture and Life Sciences and Graduate Fields of Architecture, Art and Planning, Field of Landscape Architecture, Ithaca, NY 14853. Offers MLA, MPS. *Accreditation:* ASLA. *Degree* *requirements:* For master's, project or thesis. *Entrance requirements:* For master's, GRE General Test (recommended), portfolio, 2 letters of recommendation. Additional exam requirements/recommendations for international students: Required—TOEFL (minimum score 550 paper-based; 77 iBT). Electronic applications accepted. *Faculty research:* Urban horticulture and landscape design, urban design research, cultural landscape history, women in landscape architecture, landscape design language, Japanese landscape architecture.

**Florida Agricultural and Mechanical University,** Division of Graduate Studies, Research, and Continuing Education, School of Architecture, Tallahassee, FL 32307-3200. Offers architectural studies (MS Arch); architecture (professional) (M Arch); landscape architecture (MLA). *Program availability:* Part-time. *Degree requirements:* For master's, thesis. *Entrance requirements:* For master's, GRE General Test, minimum GPA of 3.0, portfolio. Additional exam requirements/recommendations for international students: Required—TOEFL (minimum score 550 paper-based). *Faculty research:* Environmental technology, post-occupancy evaluation, building economics, design methods, computer-aided design.

**Florida International University,** College of Communication, Architecture and The Arts, Department of Landscape Architecture, Miami, FL 33199. Offers MLA. *Accreditation:* ASLA. *Program availability:* Part-time. *Faculty:* 4 full-time (2 women), 3 part-time/adjunct (2 women). *Students:* 32 full-time (15 women); includes 14 minority (2 Black or African American, non-Hispanic/Latino; 1 Asian, non-Hispanic/Latino; 10 Hispanic/Latino; 1 Two or more races, non-Hispanic/Latino), 5 international. Average age 28. 32 applicants, 34% accepted, 6 enrolled. In 2016, 10 master's awarded. *Entrance requirements:* For master's, GRE or minimum GPA of 3.0 in upper-level undergraduate work, portfolio. Additional exam requirements/recommendations for international students: Required—TOEFL (minimum score 550 paper-based; 80 iBT). *Application deadline:* For fall admission, 2/1 for domestic and international students. Application fee: $30. Electronic applications accepted. *Expenses:* Tuition, state resident: full-time $8912; part-time $446 per credit hour. Tuition, nonresident: full-time $21,393; part-time $992 per credit hour. *Required fees:* $2185; $195 per semester. Tuition and fees vary according to program. *Financial support:* Institutionally sponsored loans and scholarships/grants available. Financial award application deadline: 3/1; financial award applicants required to submit FAFSA. *Unit head:* Jason Chandler, Chair, 305-348-6913, E-mail: jason.chandler@fiu.edu. *Application contact:* Nanett Rojas, Assistant Director, Graduate Admissions, 305-348-7464, Fax: 305-348-7441, E-mail: gradadm@fiu.edu.
Website: http://carta.fiu.edu/landscape/

**Harvard University,** Graduate School of Arts and Sciences, Committee on Architecture, Landscape Architecture, and Urban Planning, Cambridge, MA 02138. Offers architecture (PhD); landscape architecture (PhD); urban planning (PhD). *Accreditation:* ACSP. *Degree requirements:* For doctorate, one foreign language, thesis/dissertation, oral exam. *Entrance requirements:* For doctorate, GRE General Test. Additional exam requirements/recommendations for international students: Required—TOEFL.

**Harvard University,** Graduate School of Design, Department of Landscape Architecture, Cambridge, MA 02138. Offers MLA. *Accreditation:* ASLA. *Entrance requirements:* For master's, GRE General Test. Additional exam requirements/recommendations for international students: Required—TOEFL (minimum score 600 paper-based; 104 iBT). Electronic applications accepted.

**Illinois Institute of Technology,** Graduate College, College of Architecture, Chicago, IL 60616. Offers M Arch, MLA, MS Arch, PhD, MLA/M Arch. *Accreditation:* ASLA. *Program availability:* Part-time. Terminal master's awarded for partial completion of doctoral program. *Degree requirements:* For master's, comprehensive exam (for some programs), thesis (for some programs); for doctorate, comprehensive exam, thesis/dissertation. *Entrance requirements:* For master's, GRE General Test (minimum score 292 Quantitative and Verbal, 2.5 Analytical Writing), minimum college GPA of 3.0, official transcripts, portfolio, 3 letters of recommendation, professional statement; for doctorate, GRE General Test (minimum score 900 Quantitative and Verbal, 2.5 Analytical Writing), minimum GPA of 3.5, official transcripts, portfolio, 3 letters of recommendation, professional statement. Additional exam requirements/recommendations for international students: Required—TOEFL (minimum score 550 paper-based; 80 iBT). Electronic applications accepted. *Faculty research:* Sustainable design and efficiency; the influence of climate and environment on building form; emerging urbanisms; computer applications (such as 3-D modeling); the design, planning and structure of high-rise buildings.

**Iowa State University of Science and Technology,** Department of Landscape Architecture, Ames, IA 50011. Offers MLA, MS, MCRP/MLA. *Accreditation:* ASLA. *Program availability:* Part-time. *Degree requirements:* For master's, thesis. *Entrance requirements:* For master's, GRE (highly recommended), portfolio. Additional exam requirements/recommendations for international students: Required—TOEFL (minimum score 600 paper-based; 79 iBT), IELTS (minimum score 7). *Application deadline:* For fall admission, 2/1 priority date for domestic and international students. Application fee: $60 ($90 for international students). Electronic applications accepted. *Financial support:* Institutionally sponsored loans available. Financial award application deadline: 2/15; financial award applicants required to submit FAFSA. *Faculty research:* Landscape ecology, geographic information systems, landscape perception, historic preservation, resource management, design. *Total annual research expenditures:* $1.2 million. *Application contact:* Meredith Foley, Application Contact, 515-294-0816, Fax: 515-294-2348, E-mail: landarch@iastate.edu.
Website: http://www.design.iastate.edu/landscapearchitecture/graduateprograms.php

**Kansas State University,** Graduate School, College of Architecture, Planning and Design, Department of Landscape Architecture and Regional and Community Planning, Manhattan, KS 66506. Offers community planning (MS); landscape architecture (MLA); regional and community planning (MRCP). MS offered online through the Great Plains Interactive Distance Education Alliance: Iowa State University, University of Nebraska, North Dakota State University, South Dakota State University. *Accreditation:* ACSP; ASLA. *Program availability:* Part-time, 100% online. *Faculty:* 17 full-time (6 women), 1 (woman) part-time/adjunct. *Students:* 41 full-time (25 women), 18 part-time (11 women); includes 9 minority (2 Black or African American, non-Hispanic/Latino; 1 Asian, non-Hispanic/Latino; 3 Hispanic/Latino; 3 Two or more races, non-Hispanic/Latino), 4 international. Average age 26. 47 applicants, 62% accepted, 20 enrolled. In 2016, 27 master's awarded. Terminal master's awarded for partial completion of doctoral program. *Degree requirements:* For master's, thesis, oral exam. *Entrance requirements:* Additional exam requirements/recommendations for international students: Required—TOEFL (minimum score 600 paper-based), IELTS (minimum score 6.5). *Application deadline:* For fall admission, 2/1 priority date for domestic and international students; for spring admission, 8/1 priority date for domestic and international students. Applications are processed on a rolling basis. Application fee: $80. Electronic applications accepted. *Expenses:* Tuition, state resident: full-time $9670. Tuition, nonresident: full-time $21,828. *Required fees:* $862. *Financial support:* In 2016–17, 2 research assistantships (averaging $9,500 per year), 10 teaching assistantships with full tuition reimbursements (averaging $7,366 per year) were awarded; fellowships, career-related internships or fieldwork, Federal Work-Study,

institutionally sponsored loans, and scholarships/grants also available. Support available to part-time students. Financial award application deadline: 3/15; financial award applicants required to submit FAFSA. *Faculty research:* Community planning and design, design and implementation, geospatial modeling, fluvial and green systems, transportation systems. *Total annual research expenditures:* $110,033. *Unit head:* Prof. Stephanie Rolley, Head, 785-532-5961, Fax: 785-532-6722, E-mail: srolley@ksu.edu. *Application contact:* Jody Hodges, Application Contact, 785-532-5961, Fax: 785-532-6722, E-mail: jodyhodges@ksu.edu.
Website: http://apdesign.k-state.edu/larcp/

**Kent State University,** College of Architecture and Environmental Design, Kent, OH 44240. Offers architecture (M Arc); architecture and environmental design (MS); health care design (MHCD); landscape architecture (MLA); urban design (MUD); M Arch/MBA; M Arch/MUD. *Program availability:* Part-time. *Faculty:* 20 full-time (3 women). *Students:* 75 full-time (31 women), 7 part-time (2 women); includes 6 minority (3 Black or African American, non-Hispanic/Latino; 1 American Indian or Alaska Native, non-Hispanic/Latino; 2 Hispanic/Latino), 10 international. Average age 25. 125 applicants, 56% accepted, 58 enrolled. In 2016, 55 master's awarded. *Degree requirements:* For master's, thesis (for some programs), project (for some programs). *Entrance requirements:* For master's, GRE, statement of purpose, curriculum vitae, transcripts, 3 letters of recommendation, portfolio. Additional exam requirements/recommendations for international students: Required—TOEFL (minimum scores of 550 paper-based, 80 iBT), Michigan English Language Assessment Battery (77), IELTS (6.5), or PTE (54). *Application deadline:* For fall admission, 1/15 for domestic and international students. Applications are processed on a rolling basis. Application fee: $45 ($70 for international students). Electronic applications accepted. *Expenses:* Tuition, state resident: full-time $10,864; part-time $495 per credit hour. Tuition, nonresident: full-time $18,380; part-time $837 per credit hour. *Financial support:* Research assistantships with full tuition reimbursements, teaching assistantships with full tuition reimbursements, Federal Work-Study, scholarships/grants, and unspecified assistantships available. Financial award application deadline: 2/1. *Unit head:* Mark Mistur, Dean, E-mail: mmistur1@kent.edu. *Application contact:* Johnathan Fleming, Assistant Professor and Director, Master of Architecture, 330-672-0934, E-mail: jpflemi1@kent.edu.
Website: http://www.kent.edu/caed

**Louisiana State University and Agricultural & Mechanical College,** Graduate School, College of Art and Design, Robert Reich School of Landscape Architecture, Baton Rouge, LA 70803. Offers MLA. *Accreditation:* ASLA.

**Mississippi State University,** College of Agriculture and Life Sciences, Department of Landscape Architecture, Mississippi State, MS 39762. Offers MLA. *Accreditation:* ASLA. *Program availability:* Part-time. *Faculty:* 10 full-time (2 women). *Students:* 8 full-time (6 women), 1 part-time (0 women); includes 2 minority (1 Black or African American, non-Hispanic/Latino; 1 Hispanic/Latino), 2 international. Average age 37. 10 applicants, 80% accepted, 2 enrolled. In 2016, 9 master's awarded. *Degree requirements:* For master's, thesis. *Entrance requirements:* For master's, GRE or minimum GPA of 3.0 in upper-division major emphasis courses from accredited university, minimum GPA of 2.8 on bachelor's degree. Additional exam requirements/recommendations for international students: Required—TOEFL (minimum score 600 paper-based; 100 iBT); Recommended—IELTS (minimum score 7.5). *Application deadline:* For fall admission, 7/1 for domestic students, 5/1 for international students; for spring admission, 10/1 for domestic students, 9/1 for international students. Applications are processed on a rolling basis. Application fee: $60. Electronic applications accepted. *Expenses:* Tuition, state resident: full-time $7670; part-time $852.50 per credit hour. Tuition, nonresident: full-time $20,790; part-time $2310.50 per credit hour. Part-time tuition and fees vary according to course load. *Financial support:* In 2016–17, 2 research assistantships with full tuition reimbursements (averaging $16,360 per year), 4 teaching assistantships with partial tuition reimbursements (averaging $7,120 per year) were awarded; Federal Work-Study, institutionally sponsored loans, tuition waivers (partial), and unspecified assistantships also available. Financial award application deadline: 4/1; financial award applicants required to submit FAFSA. *Faculty research:* Design pedagogy, low impact development, conservation planning, wildlife/urban interfacing planning, sustainable communities, watershed planning, historical landscapes, decision support system development, Center for Sustainable Design. *Unit head:* Dr. Sadik C. Artunc, Professor and Department Head, 662-325-7894, Fax: 662-325-7893, E-mail: sa303@msstate.edu. *Application contact:* Marina Hunt, Admissions and Enrollment Assistant, 662-325-5188, Fax: 662-325-7893, E-mail: mhunt@grad.msstate.edu.
Website: http://www.lalc.msstate.edu

**Morgan State University,** School of Graduate Studies, Institute of Architecture and Planning, Program in Landscape Architecture, Baltimore, MD 21251. Offers MLA. *Accreditation:* ASLA. *Degree requirements:* For master's, thesis. *Entrance requirements:* Additional exam requirements/recommendations for international students: Required—TOEFL (minimum score 550 paper-based). *Faculty research:* Philosophy and design, urban design, design history and theory, computer-aided design and community design.

**North Carolina State University,** Graduate School, College of Design, Department of Landscape Architecture, Raleigh, NC 27695. Offers MLA. *Accreditation:* ASLA. *Degree requirements:* For master's, thesis optional, oral exam, project. *Entrance requirements:* For master's, GRE General Test (recommended), portfolio. Electronic applications accepted. *Faculty research:* Community development and co-operative engagement, landscape planning and design.

**The Ohio State University,** Graduate School, College of Engineering, Austin E. Knowlton School of Architecture, Columbus, OH 43210. Offers architecture (M Arch); city and regional planning (MCRP, PhD); landscape architecture (M Land Arch). *Accreditation:* ACSP; ASLA. *Faculty:* 41. *Students:* 191 full-time (83 women), 4 part-time. Average age 26. In 2016, 60 master's, 2 doctorates awarded. *Degree requirements:* For doctorate, thesis/dissertation. *Entrance requirements:* For master's, GRE or GMAT (city and regional planning), portfolio (for architecture and landscape architecture); for doctorate, GRE or GMAT (city and regional planning), example of research or written work. Additional exam requirements/recommendations for international students: Required—TOEFL (minimum score 600 paper-based; 100 iBT), Michigan English Language Assessment Battery (minimum score 86); Recommended—IELTS (minimum score 8). *Application deadline:* For fall admission, 1/1 priority date for domestic students, 11/30 priority date for international students. Applications are processed on a rolling basis. Application fee: $60 ($70 for international students). Electronic applications accepted. *Financial support:* Fellowships with tuition reimbursements, research assistantships with tuition reimbursements, Federal Work-Study, institutionally sponsored loans, and unspecified assistantships available. Support available to part-time students. *Unit head:* Michael B. Cadwell, Professor/Director, 614-292-3174, E-mail: cadwell.1@osu.edu. *Application contact:* Graduate and Professional Admissions, 614-292-9444, Fax: 614-292-3895, E-mail: gpadmissions@osu.edu.
Website: http://knowlton.osu.edu/

**Oklahoma State University,** College of Agricultural Science and Natural Resources, Department of Horticulture and Landscape Architecture, Stillwater, OK 74078. Offers crop science (PhD); environmental science (PhD); horticulture (M Ag,

## Landscape Architecture

MS); plant science (PhD). *Faculty:* 18 full-time (5 women), 1 part-time/adjunct (0 women). *Students:* 1 full-time (0 women), 13 part-time (3 women); includes 1 minority (Black or African American, non-Hispanic/Latino), 8 international. Average age 28. 6 applicants, 50% accepted, 2 enrolled. In 2016, 4 master's awarded. *Degree requirements:* For master's, thesis (for some programs); for doctorate, comprehensive exam, thesis/dissertation. *Entrance requirements:* For master's and doctorate, GRE or GMAT. Additional exam requirements/recommendations for international students: Required—TOEFL (minimum score 550 paper-based; 79 iBT). *Application deadline:* For fall admission, 3/1 priority date for international students; for spring admission, 8/1 priority date for international students. Applications are processed on a rolling basis. Application fee: $40 ($75 for international students). Electronic applications accepted. *Expenses:* Tuition, state resident: full-time $3775; part-time $209.70 per credit hour. Tuition, nonresident: full-time $14,851; part-time $825.05 per credit hour. *Required fees:* $2027; $112.60 per credit hour. Tuition and fees vary according to campus/location. *Financial support:* In 2016–17, 16 research assistantships (averaging $13,535 per year) were awarded; teaching assistantships, career-related internships or fieldwork, Federal Work-Study, scholarships/grants, health care benefits, tuition waivers (partial), and unspecified assistantships also available. Support available to part-time students. Financial award application deadline: 3/1; financial award applicants required to submit FAFSA. *Faculty research:* Stress and postharvest physiology; water utilization and runoff; integrated pest management (IPM) systems and nursery, turf, floriculture, vegetable, net and fruit produces and natural resources, food extraction, and processing; public garden management. *Unit head:* Dr. Janet Cole, Department Head, 405-744-5414, Fax: 405-744-9709. *Application contact:* Dr. Sheryl Tucker, Dean, 405-744-7099, Fax: 405-744-0355, E-mail: gradi@okstate.edu.
Website: http://www.hortla.okstate.edu/

**Penn State University Park,** Graduate School, College of Arts and Architecture, Stuckeman School of Architecture and Landscape Architecture, University Park, PA 16802. Offers architecture (M Arch, MS, PhD); geodesign (MPS); landscape architecture (MLA, MS). *Accreditation:* ASLA. *Unit head:* Dr. Barbara O. Korner, Dean, 814-865-2592, Fax: 814-865-2018. *Application contact:* Lori Hawn, Director, Graduate Student Services, 814-865-1795, Fax: 814-863-4627, E-mail: l-gswww@lists.psu.edu.
Website: https://stuckeman.psu.edu/

**Polytechnic University of Puerto Rico,** Graduate School, Hato Rey, PR 00918. Offers business administration (MBA), including computer information systems, general management, management of information systems, management of international enterprises; civil engineering (ME, MS); computer engineering (ME, MS); computer science (MCS, MS); electrical engineering (ME, MS); engineering management (MEM); environmental management (MEM); landscape architecture (M Land Arch); manufacturing competitiveness (MMC, MS); manufacturing engineering (ME, MS); mechanical engineering (M Mech E). *Program availability:* Part-time, evening/weekend. *Entrance requirements:* For master's, 3 letters of recommendation.

**Pontificia Universidad Catolica Madre y Maestra,** Graduate School, Faculty of Sciences and Humanities, Santiago, Dominican Republic. Offers architecture (M Arch), including architecture of interiors, architecture of tourist lodgings, landscaping; early childhood education (M Ed).

**Rhode Island School of Design,** Division of Architecture and Design, Department of Landscape Architecture, Providence, RI 02903-2784. Offers MLA. *Accreditation:* ASLA. *Faculty:* 15 full-time (8 women), 37 part-time/adjunct (15 women). *Students:* 84 full-time (59 women); includes 4 minority (2 Asian, non-Hispanic/Latino; 2 Hispanic/Latino), 68 international. Average age 25. 138 applicants, 75% accepted, 33 enrolled. In 2016, 23 master's awarded. *Degree requirements:* For master's, thesis, exhibition. *Entrance requirements:* For master's, portfolio, statement of purpose, 3 letters of recommendation. Additional exam requirements/recommendations for international students: Required—TOEFL (minimum score 580 paper-based; 93 iBT). *Application deadline:* For fall admission, 2/1 for domestic and international students. Application fee: $60. Electronic applications accepted. *Expenses: Tuition:* Full-time $46,800. *Required fees:* $310. *Financial support:* Fellowships, research assistantships, teaching assistantships, Federal Work-Study, scholarships/grants, and unspecified assistantships available. Financial award application deadline: 2/15; financial award applicants required to submit FAFSA. *Unit head:* Scheri Fultineer, Department Head and Graduate Program Director, 401-454-6282, Fax: 401-454-6299, E-mail: sfultine@risd.edu. *Application contact:* Molly Pettengil, Assistant Director for Graduate Recruitment, 401-454-6312, Fax: 401-454-6309, E-mail: mpetteng@risd.edu.
Website: http://www.risd.edu/academics/landscape-architecture/

**State University of New York College of Environmental Science and Forestry,** Department of Landscape Architecture, Syracuse, NY 13210-2779. Offers community design and planning (MLA, MS); cultural landscape studies and conservation (MLA, MS); landscape and urban ecology (MLA, MS). *Accreditation:* ASLA (one or more programs are accredited). *Faculty:* 11 full-time (4 women), 9 part-time/adjunct (3 women). *Students:* 31 full-time (17 women), 3 part-time (2 women); includes 4 minority (2 Black or African American, non-Hispanic/Latino; 1 Asian, non-Hispanic/Latino; 1 Hispanic/Latino), 6 international. Average age 26. 53 applicants, 72% accepted, 12 enrolled. In 2016, 9 master's awarded. *Degree requirements:* For master's, comprehensive exam (for some programs), thesis (for some programs). *Entrance requirements:* For master's, GRE General Test, minimum GPA of 3.0. Additional exam requirements/recommendations for international students: Required—TOEFL (minimum score 550 paper-based; 80 iBT), IELTS (minimum score 6), or STEP Eiken (grade 1). *Application deadline:* For fall admission, 2/1 priority date for domestic and international students; for spring admission, 11/1 priority date for domestic and international students. Applications are processed on a rolling basis. Application fee: $60. *Expenses:* Tuition, state resident: full-time $10,870; part-time $453 per credit. Tuition, nonresident: full-time $22,210; part-time $925 per credit. *Required fees:* $1075; $89.22 per credit. *Financial support:* In 2016–17, 16 students received support. Application deadline: 6/30; applicants required to submit FAFSA. *Faculty research:* Site analysis and design, city and regional planning, community environments. *Total annual research expenditures:* $437,597. *Unit head:* Dr. Douglas Johnston, Chair, 315-470-6544, Fax: 315-470-6540, E-mail: dmjohnst@esf.edu. *Application contact:* Scott Shannon, Associate Provost for Instruction/Dean of the Graduate School, 315-470-6599, Fax: 315-470-6978, E-mail: esfgrad@esf.edu.
Website: http://www.esf.edu/la/

**Temple University,** Tyler School of Art, Department of Landscape Architecture and Horticulture, Ambler, PA 19122. Offers landscape architecture (ML Arch), including ecological restoration. *Accreditation:* ASLA. *Program availability:* Part-time. *Entrance requirements:* For master's, GRE or GMAT, 2 letters of recommendation, minimum undergraduate GPA of 3.0, statement of goals. Additional exam requirements/recommendations for international students: Required—TOEFL (minimum score 550 paper-based; 79 iBT). *Faculty research:* Seasonal landscape performance, landscape performance, green urban schoolyards, intersection of landscape arch practice and research, community engagement and service.

**Texas A&M University,** College of Architecture, Department of Landscape Architecture and Urban Planning, College Station, TX 77843. Offers land and property development (MLPD); landscape architecture (MLA); urban and regional planning (MUP); urban and regional science (PhD). *Accreditation:* ACSP (one or more programs are accredited); ASLA (one or more programs are accredited). *Faculty:* 28. *Students:* 161 full-time (88 women), 14 part-time (7 women); includes 21 minority (2 Black or African American, non-Hispanic/Latino; 5 Asian, non-Hispanic/Latino; 13 Hispanic/Latino; 1 Native Hawaiian or other Pacific Islander, non-Hispanic/Latino), 102 international. Average age 28. 186 applicants, 66% accepted, 56 enrolled. In 2016, 69 master's, 10 doctorates awarded. Terminal master's awarded for partial completion of doctoral program. *Degree requirements:* For master's, thesis optional, professional internship; for doctorate, comprehensive exam, thesis/dissertation, seminar. *Entrance requirements:* For master's, GMAT or GRE General Test, portfolio (MLA), minimum GPA of 3.0; for doctorate, GMAT or GRE General Test. Additional exam requirements/recommendations for international students: Required—TOEFL (minimum score 550 paper-based; 80 iBT), IELTS (minimum score 6), PTE (minimum score 53). *Application deadline:* For fall admission, 12/1 priority date for domestic and international students; for spring admission, 8/1 for domestic students. Applications are processed on a rolling basis. Application fee: $50 ($90 for international students). Electronic applications accepted. *Expenses:* Contact institution. *Financial support:* In 2016–17, 123 students received support, including 3 fellowships with tuition reimbursements available (averaging $6,298 per year), 43 research assistantships with tuition reimbursements available (averaging $4,626 per year), 12 teaching assistantships with tuition reimbursements available (averaging $7,956 per year); career-related internships or fieldwork, institutionally sponsored loans, scholarships/grants, traineeships, health care benefits, tuition waivers (full and partial), and unspecified assistantships also available. Support available to part-time students. Financial award application deadline: 3/15; financial award applicants required to submit FAFSA. *Faculty research:* Erosion control/water quality, geographic information systems/spatial information technology, transport hazards, international sustainable development. *Unit head:* Dr. Forster Ndubisi, Head, 979-845-1019, Fax: 979-862-1784. *Application contact:* Thena Morris, Administrative Assistant, 979-458-4306, E-mail: t-morris@tamu.edu.
Website: http://laup.arch.tamu.edu/

**Texas Tech University,** Graduate School, College of Agricultural Sciences and Natural Resources, Department of Landscape Architecture, Lubbock, TX 79409-2121. Offers MLA. *Accreditation:* ASLA. *Program availability:* Part-time. *Faculty:* 8 full-time (4 women). *Students:* 11 full-time (6 women), 2 part-time (1 woman); includes 1 minority (Hispanic/Latino), 3 international. Average age 29. 16 applicants, 56% accepted, 3 enrolled. In 2016, 3 master's awarded. Terminal master's awarded for partial completion of doctoral program. *Degree requirements:* For master's, thesis or alternative. *Entrance requirements:* For master's, formal approval from departmental committee. Additional exam requirements/recommendations for international students: Required—TOEFL (minimum score 550 paper-based; 79 iBT). *Application deadline:* For fall admission, 6/1 priority date for domestic students, 1/15 priority date for international students; for spring admission, 9/1 priority date for domestic students, 6/15 priority date for international students. Applications are processed on a rolling basis. Application fee: $75. Electronic applications accepted. *Expenses:* $325 per credit hour full-time resident tuition, $733 per credit hour full-time non-resident tuition; $53.75 per credit hour fee plus $608 per term fee. *Financial support:* In 2016–17, 11 students received support, including 10 fellowships (averaging $3,619 per year), 4 research assistantships (averaging $10,275 per year); teaching assistantships, career-related internships or fieldwork, scholarships/grants, and unspecified assistantships also available. Financial award application deadline: 4/15; financial award applicants required to submit FAFSA. *Faculty research:* Landscape performance, landscape modeling, environmental planning and design, therapeutic landscapes, GIS and CAD fused workflows in landscape architecture. *Total annual research expenditures:* $42,232. *Unit head:* Prof. Eric A. Bernard, Professor and Chairperson, 806-742-2858, Fax: 806-742-0770, E-mail: eric.bernard@ttu.edu.
Website: http://www.larc.ttu.edu/

**The University of Arizona,** College of Architecture, Planning, and Landscape Architecture, Landscape Architecture Program, Tucson, AZ 85721. Offers ML Arch. *Accreditation:* ASLA. *Degree requirements:* For master's, thesis. *Entrance requirements:* For master's, minimum GPA of 3.2, 3 letters of reference, statement of intent, portfolio, transcripts. Additional exam requirements/recommendations for international students: Required—TOEFL (minimum score 600 paper-based). Electronic applications accepted. *Faculty research:* Children's environments, cultural landscapes, arid lands plant communities, geographic information systems and science, computer-aided drafting and design (CAD).

**The University of British Columbia,** Faculty of Applied Science, School of Architecture and Landscape Architecture, Program in Landscape Architecture, Vancouver, BC V6T 1Z2, Canada. Offers advanced studies in landscape architecture (MASLA); landscape architecture (MLA); urban design (MUD); M Arch/MLA. *Degree requirements:* For master's, comprehensive exam or thesis. *Entrance requirements:* For master's, portfolio. Additional exam requirements/recommendations for international students: Required—TOEFL. Application fee: $100 Canadian dollars ($162 Canadian dollars for international students). Electronic applications accepted. *Expenses:* Contact institution. *Financial support:* Fellowships, institutionally sponsored loans, scholarships/grants, and tuition waivers (partial) available. *Faculty research:* Landscape design, urban-rural interface, urban ecology, sustainable development, collaborative planning and community forestry. *Application contact:* Tara Deans, Program Assistant, 604-822-3445, E-mail: tdeans@sala.ubc.ca.
Website: http://www.larc.ubc.ca

**University of California, Berkeley,** Graduate Division, College of Environmental Design, Department of Landscape Architecture and Environmental Planning, Berkeley, CA 94720-1500. Offers landscape architecture (MLA), including environmental planning, landscape design and site planning, urban and community design; landscape architecture and environmental planning (PhD); MLA/M Arch; MLA/MCP. *Accreditation:* ASLA (one or more programs are accredited). *Faculty:* 13 full-time, 6 part-time/adjunct. *Students:* 84 full-time (52 women); includes 19 minority (1 Black or African American, non-Hispanic/Latino; 5 Asian, non-Hispanic/Latino; 13 Hispanic/Latino), 26 international. Average age 30. 263 applicants, 30 enrolled. In 2016, 27 master's, 3 doctorates awarded. *Degree requirements:* For master's, comprehensive exam (for some programs), thesis (for some programs), professional project or thesis; for doctorate, one foreign language, thesis/dissertation, qualifying exam. *Entrance requirements:* For master's, GRE General Test, minimum GPA of 3.0, portfolio; for doctorate, GRE General Test, master's degree (strongly recommended), minimum GPA of 3.0, sample of written work, 3 letters of recommendation. Additional exam requirements/recommendations for international students: Required—TOEFL (minimum score 570 paper-based; 90 iBT). *Application deadline:* For fall admission, 12/7 for domestic students. Application fee: $105 ($125 for international students). Electronic applications accepted. *Financial support:* Fellowships, research assistantships, teaching assistantships, career-related internships or fieldwork, Federal Work-Study, institutionally sponsored loans, and unspecified assistantships available. *Unit head:* Prof. Louise Mozingo, Chair, 510-643-6165, Fax: 510-643-6166. *Application contact:* 510-642-2965, Fax: 510-643-6166, E-mail: laepgrad@berkeley.edu.
Website: http://laep.ced.berkeley.edu/

**University of California, Berkeley,** UC Berkeley Extension, Certificate Programs in Art and Design, Berkeley, CA 94720-1500. Offers interior design and interior architecture (Certificate); landscape architecture (Certificate); visual arts (Postbaccalaureate Certificate).

**University of Colorado Denver,** College of Architecture and Planning, Program in Landscape Architecture, Denver, CO 80217. Offers MLA. *Accreditation:* ASLA. *Program availability:* Part-time. *Faculty:* 8 full-time (4 women), 2 part-time/adjunct (1 woman). *Students:* 52 full-time (27 women), 1 (woman) part-time; includes 4 minority (1 Hispanic/Latino; 3 Two or more races, non-Hispanic/Latino), 12 international. Average age 28. 75 applicants, 49% accepted, 19 enrolled. In 2016, 27 master's awarded. *Degree requirements:* For master's, thesis optional, six-semester sequence of course work totaling 90 semester hours. *Entrance requirements:* For master's, GRE (recommended for students with an undergraduate GPA of 3.0 or lower), portfolio of creative work; statement of purpose; three letters of recommendation. Additional exam requirements/recommendations for international students: Required—TOEFL (minimum score 75 iBT). *Application deadline:* For fall admission, 2/1 for domestic students, 1/1 priority date for international students. Application fee: $50 ($75 for international students). Electronic applications accepted. *Expenses:* Contact institution. *Financial support:* In 2016–17, 21 students received support. Fellowships, research assistantships, teaching assistantships, Federal Work-Study, institutionally sponsored loans, scholarships/grants, traineeships, and unspecified assistantships available. Financial award application deadline: 4/1; financial award applicants required to submit FAFSA. *Faculty research:* Landscape architectural design theory and process, urban design, advanced landscape technologies, landscape planning. *Unit head:* Ann Komara, Associate Professor and Chair, 303-315-2428, E-mail: ann.komara@ucdenver.edu. *Application contact:* Rachael Kuroiwa, Manager of Admissions and Outreach, 303-315-2325, E-mail: rachael.kuroiwa@ucdenver.edu.
Website: http://www.ucdenver.edu/academics/colleges/ArchitecturePlanning/Academics/DegreePrograms/MLA/Pages/MLA.aspx

**University of Florida,** Graduate School, College of Design, Construction and Planning, Department of Landscape Architecture, Gainesville, FL 32611. Offers geographic information systems (MLA); historic preservation (MLA); landscape architecture (MLA); sustainable design (MLA); wetland sciences (MLA). *Accreditation:* ASLA. *Program availability:* Part-time. *Degree requirements:* For master's, thesis, internship. *Entrance requirements:* For master's, GRE General Test, minimum GPA of 3.0. Additional exam requirements/recommendations for international students: Required—TOEFL (minimum score 550 paper-based; 80 iBT), IELTS (minimum score 6). Electronic applications accepted. *Faculty research:* Landscape reclamation, community development, landscape ethics, land-use planning, international conservation.

**University of Florida,** Graduate School, College of Design, Construction and Planning, Doctoral Program in Design, Construction and Planning, Gainesville, FL 32611. Offers construction management (PhD); design, construction and planning (PhD); geographic information systems (PhD); historic preservation (PhD); interior design (PhD); landscape architecture (PhD); urban and regional planning (PhD). *Degree requirements:* For doctorate, thesis/dissertation. *Entrance requirements:* For doctorate, GRE General Test, minimum GPA of 3.0. Additional exam requirements/recommendations for international students: Required—TOEFL (minimum score 550 paper-based; 80 iBT), IELTS (minimum score 6). Electronic applications accepted. *Faculty research:* Architecture, building construction, urban and regional planning.

**University of Georgia,** College of Environment and Design, Athens, GA 30602. Offers environmental planning and design (MEPD); historic preservation (MHP); landscape architecture (MLA). *Application deadline:* For fall admission, 7/1 priority date for domestic students; for spring admission, 11/15 for domestic students. Application fee: $50. *Unit head:* Daniels J. Nadenicek, Acting Dean, 706-542-1100, Fax: 706-542-4485, E-mail: dnadeni@uga.edu. *Application contact:* Umit Yilmaz, Graduate Coordinator, 706-542-4720, E-mail: yilmaz@uga.edu.
Website: http://www.ced.uga.edu

**University of Guelph,** Graduate Studies, Ontario Agricultural College, School of Environmental Design and Rural Development, Landscape Architecture Program, Guelph, ON N1G 2W1, Canada. Offers MLA. *Degree requirements:* For master's, thesis. *Entrance requirements:* For master's, minimum B- average during previous 2 years of honors degree, portfolio and questionnaire. Additional exam requirements/recommendations for international students: Required—TOEFL (minimum score 600 paper-based; 89 iBT), IELTS (minimum score 7), Canadian Academic Language Assessment, Michigan English Language Assessment Battery. Electronic applications accepted. *Faculty research:* Land planning, human factors in design, landscape assessment (biophysical and cultural), landscape ecology and restoration, community design.

**University of Idaho,** College of Graduate Studies, College of Art and Architecture, Moscow, ID 83844. Offers architecture (M Arch); art (MFA); bioregional planning and community design (MS); integrated architecture and design (MS); landscape architecture (MLA). *Accreditation:* NASAD. *Faculty:* 14 full-time, 2 part-time/adjunct (0 women). *Students:* 67 full-time, 9 part-time. Average age 28. In 2016, 42 master's awarded. *Entrance requirements:* For master's, minimum GPA of 3.0. Additional exam requirements/recommendations for international students: Required—TOEFL. *Application deadline:* For fall admission, 8/1 for domestic students; for spring admission, 12/15 for domestic students. Applications are processed on a rolling basis. Application fee: $60. Electronic applications accepted. *Expenses:* Tuition, state resident: full-time $6460; part-time $414 per credit hour. Tuition, nonresident: full-time $21,268; part-time $1237 per credit hour. *Required fees:* $2070; $60 per credit hour. Full-time tuition and fees vary according to course load and reciprocity agreements. *Financial support:* Applicants required to submit FAFSA. *Faculty research:* Sustainability in communities, urban research, virtual technology, bioregional planning, environment and behavior interaction. *Unit head:* Dr. Shauna Corry, Interim Dean, 208-885-4409, E-mail: caa@uidaho.edu. *Application contact:* Sean Scoggin, Graduate Recruitment Coordinator, 208-885-4001, Fax: 208-885-4406, E-mail: graduateadmissions@uidaho.edu.
Website: http://www.uidaho.edu/caa

**University of Illinois at Urbana–Champaign,** Graduate College, College of Fine and Applied Arts, Department of Landscape Architecture, Champaign, IL 61820. Offers MLA, PhD, MLA/MUP. *Accreditation:* ASLA.

**The University of Manchester,** School of Environment and Development, Manchester, United Kingdom. Offers architecture (M Phil, PhD); development policy and management (M Phil, PhD); human geography (M Phil, PhD); physical geography (M Phil, PhD); planning and landscape (M Phil, PhD).

**University of Manitoba,** Faculty of Graduate Studies, Faculty of Architecture, Department of Landscape Architecture, Winnipeg, MB R3T 2N2, Canada. Offers M Land Arch. *Accreditation:* ASLA. *Degree requirements:* For master's, thesis or alternative.

**University of Maryland, College Park,** Academic Affairs, College of Agriculture and Natural Resources, Department of Plant Science and Landscape Architecture, Landscape Architecture Program, College Park, MD 20742. Offers MLA. *Accreditation:* ASLA. *Entrance requirements:* Additional exam requirements/recommendations for international students: Required—TOEFL. Electronic applications accepted. *Faculty research:* Cereal crop production, soil and water conservation, turf management, x-ray diffraction.

**University of Massachusetts Amherst,** Graduate School, College of Social and Behavioral Sciences, Department of Landscape Architecture and Regional Planning, Dual Degree Program in Landscape Architecture and Regional Planning, Amherst, MA 01003. Offers MLA/MRP. *Accreditation:* ACSP; ASLA. *Program availability:* Part-time. *Entrance requirements:* Additional exam requirements/recommendations for international students: Required—TOEFL (minimum score 550 paper-based; 80 iBT), IELTS (minimum score 6.5). Electronic applications accepted.

**University of Massachusetts Amherst,** Graduate School, College of Social and Behavioral Sciences, Department of Landscape Architecture and Regional Planning, Program in Landscape Architecture, Amherst, MA 01003. Offers MLA, MLA/M Arch. *Accreditation:* ASLA. *Program availability:* Part-time. *Degree requirements:* For master's, thesis or alternative. *Entrance requirements:* For master's, GRE General Test, portfolio. Additional exam requirements/recommendations for international students: Required—TOEFL (minimum score 550 paper-based; 80 iBT), IELTS (minimum score 6.5). Electronic applications accepted.

**University of Michigan,** School for Environment and Sustainability, Program in Landscape Architecture, Ann Arbor, MI 48109. Offers MLA, MLA/M Arch, MLA/MBA, MURP/MLA. Offered through the Rackham Graduate School. *Accreditation:* ASLA (one or more programs are accredited). *Faculty:* 5 full-time (2 women), 4 part-time/adjunct (2 women). *Students:* 44 full-time (35 women); includes 5 minority (1 Black or African American, non-Hispanic/Latino; 2 Hispanic/Latino; 2 Two or more races, non-Hispanic/Latino), 25 international. Average age 27. 115 applicants. In 2016, 12 master's awarded. *Degree requirements:* For master's, thesis, practicum or group project. *Entrance requirements:* For master's, GRE General Test. Additional exam requirements/recommendations for international students: Required—TOEFL (minimum score 560 paper-based; 84 iBT) or IELTS (minimum score 6.5). *Application deadline:* For fall admission, 4/30 for domestic and international students. Application fee: $75 ($90 for international students). Electronic applications accepted. *Expenses:* Tuition, state resident: full-time $21,466; part-time $1152 per credit hour. Tuition, nonresident: full-time $43,346; part-time $2367 per credit hour. Part-time tuition and fees vary according to course load, degree level and program. *Financial support:* Fellowships, research assistantships, teaching assistantships, career-related internships or fieldwork, Federal Work-Study, scholarships/grants, and health care benefits available. Financial award application deadline: 1/6; financial award applicants required to submit FAFSA. *Faculty research:* Environmentally responsible design, ecological processes, human behavior, and ecological function. *Unit head:* Prof. Stan Jones, Professor, 734-764-6453, Fax: 734-734-2195, E-mail: stanj@umich.edu. *Application contact:* Sara O'Brien, Director of Academic Programs, 734-764-6453, Fax: 734-936-2195, E-mail: seas-admissions@umich.edu.
Website: http://seas.umich.edu/academics/la

**University of Minnesota, Twin Cities Campus,** Graduate School, College of Design, Department of Landscape Architecture, Minneapolis, MN 55455-0213. Offers MLA, MS. *Accreditation:* ASLA (one or more programs are accredited). *Degree requirements:* For master's, thesis (MS). *Entrance requirements:* For master's, GRE General Test (MS), suggested GPA of 3.0. Additional exam requirements/recommendations for international students: Required—TOEFL (minimum score 550 paper-based; 79 iBT). Electronic applications accepted. *Expenses:* Contact institution. *Faculty research:* Landscape history, landscape ecology, urban design, sustainable design, public art/space.

**University of New Mexico,** Graduate Studies, School of Architecture and Planning, Program in Landscape Architecture, Albuquerque, NM 87131-2039. Offers MLA. *Accreditation:* ASLA. *Program availability:* Part-time. *Faculty:* 2 full-time (1 woman), 4 part-time/adjunct (2 women). *Students:* 24 full-time (10 women), 2 part-time (1 woman); includes 3 minority (2 Black or African American, non-Hispanic/Latino; 1 Hispanic/Latino), 7 international. Average age 30. 21 applicants, 43% accepted, 5 enrolled. In 2016, 22 master's awarded. *Degree requirements:* For master's, comprehensive exam, thesis optional, portfolio review, thesis studio. *Entrance requirements:* For master's, minimum GPA of 3.0. Additional exam requirements/recommendations for international students: Required—TOEFL. *Application deadline:* For fall admission, 2/15 priority date for domestic students, 2/15 for international students; for spring admission, 11/1 for domestic and international students. Applications are processed on a rolling basis. Application fee: $50. Electronic applications accepted. *Expenses:* Contact institution. *Financial support:* Research assistantships with partial tuition reimbursements, teaching assistantships with partial tuition reimbursements, scholarships/grants, health care benefits, tuition waivers (partial), and unspecified assistantships available. Financial award application deadline: 3/1; financial award applicants required to submit FAFSA. *Faculty research:* Cultural landscape studies, urban design and sustainability, landscape and infrastructure. *Unit head:* Dr. Alfred Simon, Director, 505-277-4120, Fax: 505-277-0897, E-mail: asimon@unm.edu. *Application contact:* Elizabeth M. Rowe, Senior Academic Advisor, 505-277-1303, Fax: 505-277-0076, E-mail: erowe@unm.edu.
Website: http://saap.unm.edu/

**University of Oklahoma,** College of Architecture, Division of Landscape Architecture, Norman, OK 73019. Offers landscape architectural studies (MLA); landscape architecture (MLA); MRCP/MLA. *Accreditation:* ASLA. *Students:* 19 full-time (13 women), 1 part-time (0 women); includes 4 minority (2 Asian, non-Hispanic/Latino; 2 Two or more races, non-Hispanic/Latino), 8 international. Average age 28. 22 applicants, 45% accepted, 8 enrolled. In 2016, 2 master's awarded. Terminal master's awarded for partial completion of doctoral program. *Degree requirements:* For master's, comprehensive exam. *Entrance requirements:* Additional exam requirements/recommendations for international students: Required—TOEFL (minimum score 79 iBT) or IELTS (minimum score 6.5). *Application deadline:* For fall admission, 2/15 priority date for domestic and international students. Applications are processed on a rolling basis. Application fee: $50 ($100 for international students). Electronic applications accepted. *Expenses:* Tuition, state resident: full-time $4886; part-time $203.60 per credit hour. Tuition, nonresident: full-time $18,989; part-time $791.20 per credit hour. *Required fees:* $3283; $126.25 per credit hour. $126.50 per semester. *Financial support:* In 2016–17, 19 students received support, including 11 research assistantships with full and partial tuition reimbursements available (averaging $13,671 per year); scholarships/grants and unspecified assistantships also available. Financial award application deadline: 6/1; financial award applicants required to submit FAFSA. *Faculty research:* Human behavior in environment, green roofs, geodesign. *Unit head:* Leehu Loon, Associate Dean and Director, 405-325-1519, Fax: 405-325-7558, E-mail: lloon@ou.edu.
Website: http://la.ou.edu

**University of Oregon,** Graduate School, School of Architecture and Allied Arts, Department of Landscape Architecture, Eugene, OR 97403. Offers MLA. *Accreditation:* ASLA. *Degree requirements:* For master's, thesis or alternative, project. *Entrance requirements:* For master's, portfolio. Additional exam requirements/recommendations

*Landscape Architecture*

for international students: Required—TOEFL. *Faculty research:* Design, landscape planning analysis, history and theory, computer applications.

**University of Pennsylvania,** School of Design, Department of Landscape Architecture, Philadelphia, PA 19104. Offers landscape architecture (MLA); landscape studies (Certificate). *Accreditation:* ASLA (one or more programs are accredited). *Program availability:* Part-time. *Faculty:* 7 full-time (3 women), 6 part-time/adjunct (2 women). *Students:* 102 full-time (62 women), 3 part-time (all women); includes 11 minority (2 Black or African American, non-Hispanic/Latino; 1 American Indian or Alaska Native, non-Hispanic/Latino; 2 Asian, non-Hispanic/Latino; 5 Hispanic/Latino; 1 Two or more races, non-Hispanic/Latino), 70 international. Average age 26. 297 applicants, 44% accepted, 65 enrolled. In 2016, 40 master's, 4 Certificates awarded. *Expenses:* Tuition: Full-time $31,068; part-time $5762 per course. *Required fees:* $3200; $336 per course. Full-time tuition and fees vary according to degree level, program and student level. Part-time tuition and fees vary according to course load, degree level and program. *Financial support:* Teaching assistantships available. Financial award application deadline: 2/1.

**The University of Tennessee,** Graduate School, College of Architecture and Design, Program in Landscape Architecture, Knoxville, TN 37996. Offers landscape architecture (MLA); landscape architecture (research) (MA, MS). *Accreditation:* ASLA. *Degree requirements:* For master's, oral exam, project and thesis optional (MLA), oral exam and thesis (MA, MS). *Entrance requirements:* For master's, GRE General Test, minimum GPA of 3.0, 3 letters of recommendation, samples of portfolio work. Additional exam requirements/recommendations for international students: Required—TOEFL (minimum score 550 paper-based).

**The University of Texas at Arlington,** Graduate School, College of Architecture, Planning and Public Affairs, Program in Landscape Architecture, Arlington, TX 76019. Offers MLA. *Program availability:* Part-time, evening/weekend. *Degree requirements:* For master's, thesis. *Entrance requirements:* For master's, GRE General Test, minimum GPA of 3.0, portfolio. Additional exam requirements/recommendations for international students: Required—TOEFL (minimum score 575 paper-based; 80 iBT). *Application deadline:* For fall admission, 1/15 for domestic and international students. Applications are processed on a rolling basis. Application fee: $50. *Financial support:* Fellowships, research assistantships with partial tuition reimbursements, teaching assistantships with partial tuition reimbursements, career-related internships or fieldwork, and tuition waivers (partial) available. Financial award application deadline: 6/1; financial award applicants required to submit FAFSA. *Unit head:* Dr. Pat D. Taylor, Program Director, 817-272-2801, Fax: 817-272-5098, E-mail: pdt@uta.edu. *Application contact:* David Jones, Associate Dean, 817-272-2801, Fax: 817-272-5098, E-mail: djonesarch@uta.edu.

**The University of Texas at Austin,** Graduate School, School of Architecture, Program in Landscape Architecture, Austin, TX 78712-1111. Offers MLA. *Accreditation:* ASLA.

**University of Toronto,** School of Graduate Studies, John H. Daniels Faculty of Architecture, Landscape, and Design, Toronto, ON M5S 1A1, Canada. Offers M Arch, MLA, MUD, MVS. *Entrance requirements:* For master's, minimum B average; 3 letters of reference; resume; 3 writing samples; 5 samples of design work, drawing, or work in a related field, statement of interest. Additional exam requirements/recommendations for international students: Required—TOEFL (minimum score 580 paper-based; 93 iBT), IELTS (minimum score 7), TWE (minimum score 5), Michigan English Language Assessment Battery (minimum score 85), COPE (minimum score 76). Electronic applications accepted. *Expenses:* Contact institution.

**University of Virginia,** School of Architecture, Department of Landscape Architecture, Charlottesville, VA 22903. Offers M Land Arch. *Accreditation:* ASLA. *Faculty:* 2 full-time (1 woman), 1 (woman) part-time/adjunct. *Students:* 56 full-time (38 women), 1 part-time (0 women); includes 5 minority (2 Asian, non-Hispanic/Latino; 2 Hispanic/Latino; 1 Two or more races, non-Hispanic/Latino), 21 international. Average age 26. 180 applicants, 40% accepted, 27 enrolled. In 2016, 12 master's awarded. *Entrance requirements:* For master's, GRE General Test, 3 letters of recommendation; portfolio. Additional exam requirements/recommendations for international students: Required—TOEFL (minimum score 600 paper-based; 90 iBT). *Application deadline:* For fall admission, 1/15 for domestic students, 1/16 for international students. Applications are processed on a rolling basis. Application fee: $60. Electronic applications accepted. *Expenses:* Tuition, state resident: full-time $15,026; part-time $834 per credit hour. Tuition, nonresident: full-time $25,168; part-time $1378 per credit hour. *Required fees:* $2654. *Financial support:* Applicants required to submit FAFSA. *Faculty research:* History of landscape architecture. *Unit head:* Teresa Gali-Izard, Chair, 434-924-6465, Fax: 434-982-2678, E-mail: teg2q@virginia.edu. *Application contact:* Kristine Nelson, Director of Graduate Admissions and Financial Aid, 434-924-6442, Fax: 434-982-2678,

E-mail: arch-admissions@virginia.edu.
Website: http://www.arch.virginia.edu/academics/disciplines/landscape

**University of Washington,** Graduate School, College of Built Environments, Department of Landscape Architecture, Seattle, WA 98195. Offers MLA. *Accreditation:* ASLA. *Degree requirements:* For master's, thesis. *Entrance requirements:* For master's, GRE, minimum GPA of 3.0. Additional exam requirements/recommendations for international students: Required—TOEFL. *Faculty research:* Cultural landscape, history of gardens, urban stream restoration, campus master planning, urban ecology.

**University of Wisconsin–Madison,** Graduate School, College of Agricultural and Life Sciences, Department of Landscape Architecture, Madison, WI 53076. Offers MA, MS. *Program availability:* Part-time. *Degree requirements:* For master's, thesis. *Entrance requirements:* For master's, GRE (recommended), samples of creative work. Additional exam requirements/recommendations for international students: Required—TOEFL (minimum score 580 paper-based). Electronic applications accepted. *Faculty research:* Urban/landscape ecology, land restoration, cultural resource preservation, community design, conservation studies.

**Utah State University,** School of Graduate Studies, College of Humanities, Arts and Social Sciences, Department of Landscape Architecture and Environmental Planning, Logan, UT 84322. Offers bioregional planning (MS); landscape architecture (MLA). *Accreditation:* ASLA (one or more programs are accredited). *Degree requirements:* For master's, thesis. *Entrance requirements:* For master's, GRE General Test, minimum GPA of 3.0. Additional exam requirements/recommendations for international students: Required—TOEFL. *Faculty research:* Visual resource management, planning for wildlife, agricultural land preservation, watershed planning, community planning and design.

**Virginia Polytechnic Institute and State University,** Graduate School, College of Architecture and Urban Studies, Blacksburg, VA 24061. Offers architecture (MS Arch); architecture and design research (PhD); building/construction science and management (MS); creative technologies (MFA); environmental design and planning (PhD); landscape architecture (MLA); planning, governance, and globalization (PhD); public administration (MPA); public administration/public affairs (PhD, Certificate); public and international affairs (MPIA); urban and regional planning (MURP). *Accreditation:* ASLA (one or more programs are accredited). *Faculty:* 136 full-time (53 women). *Students:* 371 full-time (185 women), 210 part-time (104 women); includes 118 minority (49 Black or African American, non-Hispanic/Latino; 1 American Indian or Alaska Native, non-Hispanic/Latino; 30 Asian, non-Hispanic/Latino; 32 Hispanic/Latino; 6 Two or more races, non-Hispanic/Latino), 137 international. Average age 31. 566 applicants, 55% accepted, 160 enrolled. In 2016, 137 master's, 24 doctorates awarded. *Degree requirements:* For master's, comprehensive exam (for some programs), thesis (for some programs); for doctorate, comprehensive exam (for some programs), thesis/dissertation (for some programs). *Entrance requirements:* For master's and doctorate, GRE/GMAT. Additional exam requirements/recommendations for international students: Required—TOEFL (minimum score 80 iBT). *Application deadline:* For fall admission, 8/1 for domestic students, 4/1 for international students; for spring admission, 1/1 for domestic students, 9/1 for international students. Applications are processed on a rolling basis. Application fee: $75. Electronic applications accepted. *Expenses:* Tuition, state resident: full-time $12,467; part-time $692.50 per credit hour. Tuition, nonresident: full-time $25,095; part-time $1394.25 per credit hour. *Required fees:* $2669; $491.50 per semester. Tuition and fees vary according to course load, campus/location and program. *Financial support:* In 2016–17, 11 research assistantships with full tuition reimbursements (averaging $19,474 per year), 45 teaching assistantships with full tuition reimbursements (averaging $16,014 per year) were awarded. Financial award application deadline: 3/1; financial award applicants required to submit FAFSA. *Total annual research expenditures:* $3.6 million. *Unit head:* Dr. A. J. Davis, Dean, 540-231-6416, Fax: 540-231-6332, E-mail: davisa@vt.edu. *Application contact:* Christine Mattsson-Coon, Executive Assistant, 540-231-6416, Fax: 540-231-6332, E-mail: cmattsso@vt.edu.
Website: http://www.caus.vt.edu/

**Washington State University,** College of Agricultural, Human, and Natural Resource Sciences, Program in Interior Design and Landscape Architecture, Pullman, WA 99164-2220. Offers MA, MS. Programs offered at the Pullman campus. *Program availability:* Part-time. *Degree requirements:* For master's, comprehensive exam, thesis (for some programs), oral exam. *Entrance requirements:* For master's, portfolio. Additional exam requirements/recommendations for international students: Required—TOEFL or IELTS. Electronic applications accepted. *Faculty research:* Digital fabrication, design pedagogy, proportional systems, American architecture and urbanism, design leadership.

# Lighting Design

**The New School,** Parsons School of Design, Program in Lighting Design, New York, NY 10011. Offers MFA, M Arch/MFA. *Accreditation:* NASAD. *Program availability:* Part-time. *Faculty:* 26 full-time (7 women), 11 part-time/adjunct (9 women). *Students:* 29 full-time (25 women); includes 2 minority (1 Asian, non-Hispanic/Latino; 1 Hispanic/Latino), 24 international. Average age 27. 42 applicants, 64% accepted, 17 enrolled. In 2016, 21 master's awarded. *Degree requirements:* For master's, thesis. *Entrance requirements:* For master's, transcripts, resume, statement of purpose, recommendation letters, portfolio, interviews. Additional exam requirements/recommendations for international students: Required—TOEFL (minimum score 92 iBT), IELTS (minimum score 7), PTE (minimum score 63). *Application deadline:* For fall admission, 1/1 priority date for domestic and international students. Applications are processed on a rolling basis. Application fee: $50. Electronic applications accepted. *Expenses:* Contact institution. *Financial support:* Research assistantships, teaching assistantships, career-related internships or fieldwork, scholarships/grants, and unspecified assistantships available. Support available to part-time students. Financial award application deadline: 2/1; financial award applicants required to submit FAFSA. *Faculty research:* Integrated environments; energy conservation, urban planning, light and perception. *Unit head:* Glenn Shrum, Director, 212-229-8900 Ext. 4853, E-mail: shrumg@newschool.edu. *Application contact:* Courtney Malenius, Director of Graduate Admissions, 212-229-5150 Ext. 4011, E-mail: maleniuc@newschool.edu.
Website: http://www.newschool.edu/parsons

**New York School of Interior Design,** Program in Interior Lighting Design, New York, NY 10021-5110. Offers MPS. *Entrance requirements:* For master's, portfolio, resume, undergraduate degree in interior design or closely-related field. Additional exam requirements/recommendations for international students: Required—TOEFL (minimum score 79 iBT). Electronic applications accepted.

**Rensselaer Polytechnic Institute,** Graduate School, School of Architecture, PhD Program in Architectural Sciences, Troy, NY 12180-3590. Offers architectural acoustics (PhD); built ecologies (PhD); lighting (PhD). *Degree requirements:* For doctorate, comprehensive exam (for some programs), thesis/dissertation. *Entrance requirements:* For doctorate, GRE. Additional exam requirements/recommendations for international students: Required—TOEFL (minimum score 570 paper-based; 88 iBT), IELTS (minimum score 6.5), PTE (minimum score 60). Electronic applications accepted. *Expenses: Tuition:* Full-time $49,520; part-time $2060 per credit hour. *Required fees:* $2617. *Faculty research:* Architectural acoustics, built ecologies, lighting.

**Rensselaer Polytechnic Institute,** Graduate School, School of Architecture, Program in Lighting, Troy, NY 12180-3590. Offers architectural sciences (MS, PhD); lighting (MS). *Degree requirements:* For master's, comprehensive exam, thesis; for doctorate, comprehensive exam, thesis/dissertation. *Entrance requirements:* For master's and doctorate, GRE. Additional exam requirements/recommendations for international students: Required—TOEFL (minimum score 570 paper-based; 88 iBT), IELTS (minimum score 6.5), PTE (minimum score 60). Electronic applications accepted. *Expenses: Tuition:* Full-time $49,520; part-time $2060 per credit hour. *Required fees:* $2617. *Faculty research:* Applications and design, automotive and street lighting, aviation lighting, controls, daylighting, energy and environment, health and vision, LEDs, outdoor lighting, residential lighting, security lighting.

**University of Washington,** Graduate School, College of Built Environments, Department of Architecture, Seattle, WA 98195. Offers architecture (M Arch, MS); built environment (PhD); design computing (Certificate); design firm leadership and management (Certificate); historic preservation (Certificate); lighting (Certificate); urban design (Certificate). *Degree requirements:* For master's, thesis. *Entrance requirements:* For master's, GRE General Test, minimum GPA of 3.0, portfolio, 3 letters of recommendation. Additional exam requirements/recommendations for international students: Required—TOEFL. *Faculty research:* Lighting, materials, computing theory, media, culture, environment.

# Urban Design

**American University of Beirut,** Graduate Programs, Faculty of Engineering and Architecture, 11-0236, Lebanon. Offers applied energy (ME); civil engineering (PhD); electrical and computer engineering (PhD); energy studies (MS); engineering management (MEM); environmental and water resources (ME); environmental technology (MSES); mechanical engineering (ME, PhD); urban design (MUD); urban planning and policy (MUPP). *Program availability:* Part-time, evening/weekend, 100% online. *Faculty:* 99 full-time (22 women), 1 part-time/adjunct (0 women). *Students:* 308 full-time (143 women), 86 part-time (39 women). Average age 26. 430 applicants, 69% accepted, 125 enrolled. In 2016, 103 master's, 7 doctorates awarded. Terminal master's awarded for partial completion of doctoral program. *Degree requirements:* For master's, comprehensive exam, thesis optional; for doctorate, comprehensive exam, thesis/dissertation. *Entrance requirements:* For doctorate, GRE. Additional exam requirements/recommendations for international students: Required—TOEFL (minimum score 573 paper-based; 88 iBT); Recommended—IELTS (minimum score 7). *Application deadline:* For fall admission, 2/10 priority date for domestic and international students; for spring admission, 11/2 priority date for domestic students, 11/2 for international students. Application fee: $50. Electronic applications accepted. *Expenses:* Contact institution. *Financial support:* In 2016–17, 22 students received support, including 94 fellowships with full tuition reimbursements available (averaging $18,200 per year), 44 research assistantships with full tuition reimbursements available (averaging $7,596 per year), 124 teaching assistantships with full tuition reimbursements available (averaging $1,056 per year); career-related internships or fieldwork, Federal Work-Study, institutionally sponsored loans, scholarships/grants, traineeships, health care benefits, tuition waivers, and unspecified assistantships also available. Support available to part-time students. Financial award application deadline: 12/20. *Total annual research expenditures:* $1.5 million. *Unit head:* Prof. Alan Shihadeh, Interim Dean, 961-1350000 Ext. 3400, Fax: 961-1744462, E-mail: as20@aub.edu.lb. *Application contact:* Dr. Salim Kanaan, Director, Admissions Office, 961-1350000 Ext. 2594, Fax: 961-1750775, E-mail: sk00@aub.edu.lb.
Website: http://www.aub.edu.lb/fea/fea_home/Pages/index.aspx

**Arizona State University at the Tempe campus,** Herberger Institute for Design and the Arts, The Design School, Tempe, AZ 85287-1605. Offers architecture (M Arch); building design/built environment (MS); design (MSD), including arts, media, and engineering, healthcare and healing environments (MSD, PhD), industrial design, interaction design, interior design, new product innovation, visual communication design; design, environment and the arts (PhD), including design, digital culture, healthcare and healing environments (MSD, PhD), history, theory, and criticism; landscape architecture (MLA); urban design (MUD); MA/MBA. *Accreditation:* NASAD. Terminal master's awarded for partial completion of doctoral program. *Degree requirements:* For master's, thesis optional, interactive Program of Study (iPOS) submitted before completing 50 percent of required credit hours; for doctorate, comprehensive exam, thesis/dissertation, interactive Program of Study (iPOS) submitted before completing 50 percent of required credit hours. *Entrance requirements:* For master's, GRE General Test, minimum GPA of 3.0 or equivalent in last 2 years of work leading to bachelor's degree, design/creative works portfolio, 3 references, statement of intent; for doctorate, GRE, master's degree in architecture, graphic design, industrial design, interior design, landscape architecture, or art history or equivalent standing; statement of purpose; 3 letters of recommendation; indication of potential faculty mentor; sample of written work. Additional exam requirements/recommendations for international students: Required—TOEFL (minimum score 600 paper-based; 100 iBT). Electronic applications accepted.

**Ball State University,** Graduate School, College of Architecture and Planning, Interdepartmental Program in Urban Design, Muncie, IN 47306. Offers MUD. *Entrance requirements:* For master's, minimum cumulative baccalaureate GPA of 2.75 or 3.0 for latter half of baccalaureate, curriculum vitae or resume, statement of professional intent, portfolio of professional/academic work, writing sample. Additional exam requirements/recommendations for international students: Required—TOEFL (minimum score 550 paper-based; 79 iBT), IELTS (minimum score 6.5). Electronic applications accepted. *Expenses:* Contact institution.

**Carnegie Mellon University,** College of Fine Arts, School of Architecture, Pittsburgh, PA 15213-3891. Offers architecture (MSA); architecture, engineering, and construction management (PhD); building performance and diagnostics (MS, PhD); computational design (MS, PhD); engineering construction management (MSA); tangible interaction design (MTID); urban design (MUD). Terminal master's awarded for partial completion of doctoral program. *Degree requirements:* For doctorate, thesis/dissertation. *Entrance requirements:* For master's and doctorate, GRE General Test. Additional exam requirements/recommendations for international students: Required—TOEFL.

**City College of the City University of New York,** Graduate School, The Bernard and Anne Spitzer School of Architecture, Program in Urban Design, New York, NY 10031-9198. Offers MUP. *Program availability:* Part-time. *Degree requirements:* For master's, thesis. *Entrance requirements:* For master's, portfolio, professional degree in architecture or equivalent. Additional exam requirements/recommendations for international students: Required—TOEFL (minimum score 550 paper-based). Tuition and fees vary according to course load, degree level and program. *Faculty research:* Real estate, planning, law.

**Cornell University,** Graduate School, Graduate Fields of Architecture, Art and Planning, Field of Architecture, Ithaca, NY 14853. Offers architectural design (M Arch); architectural science (MS); computer graphics (MS); history of architecture (MA, PhD); history of urban development (MA, PhD); theory and criticism of architecture (M Arch); urban design (M Arch). *Degree requirements:* For master's, one foreign language, thesis (MA, MS); for doctorate, 2 foreign languages, comprehensive exam, thesis/dissertation. *Entrance requirements:* For master's, GRE General Test, 5-year bachelor's degree in architecture, portfolio (M Arch), 3 letters of recommendation; for doctorate, GRE General Test, 3 letters of recommendation. Additional exam requirements/recommendations for international students: Required—TOEFL (minimum score 600 paper-based; 77 iBT). Electronic applications accepted. *Faculty research:* Architectural design and urban design, theory and criticism of architecture, computer graphics, building technology and environmental science, history of architecture and history of urban-development.

**DePaul University,** College of Liberal Arts and Social Sciences, Chicago, IL 60614. Offers Arabic (MA); Chinese (MA); English (MA); French (MA); German (MA); history (MA); interdisciplinary studies (MA, MS); international public service (MS); international studies (MA); Italian (MA); Japanese (MA); leadership and policy studies (MS); liberal studies (MA); new media studies (MA); nonprofit management (MNM); public administration (MPA); public health (MPH); public service management (MS); social work (MSW); sociology (MA); Spanish (MA); sustainable urban development (MA); women and gender studies (MA); writing and publishing (MA); writing, rhetoric, and discourse (MA); MA/PhD. *Program availability:* Part-time, evening/weekend, online learning. Terminal master's awarded for partial completion of doctoral program. *Degree requirements:* For master's, variable foreign language requirement, comprehensive exam (for some programs), thesis (for some programs). Electronic applications accepted.

**Georgia Institute of Technology,** Graduate Studies, College of Architecture, School of City and Regional Planning, Atlanta, GA 30332-0001. Offers city and regional planning (PhD); economic development (MCRP); environmental planning and management (MCRP); geographic information systems (MCRP); land and community development (MCRP); land use planning (MCRP); transportation (MCRP); urban design (MCRP); MCP/MSCE. *Accreditation:* ACSP. *Degree requirements:* For master's, thesis, internship. *Entrance requirements:* For master's, GRE General Test, minimum GPA of 2.7. Additional exam requirements/recommendations for international students: Required—TOEFL. Electronic applications accepted.

**Harvard University,** Graduate School of Design, Department of Urban Planning and Design, Cambridge, MA 02138. Offers urban planning (MUP); urban planning and design (MAUD, MLAUD). *Accreditation:* ACSP (one or more programs are accredited). *Entrance requirements:* For master's, GRE General Test. Additional exam requirements/recommendations for international students: Required—TOEFL (minimum score 600 paper-based; 104 iBT). Electronic applications accepted.

**Hofstra University,** College of Liberal Arts and Sciences, Programs in Biology, Hempstead, NY 11549. Offers biology (MA, MS); urban ecology (MA, MS). *Program availability:* Part-time, evening/weekend. *Students:* 16 full-time (9 women), 10 part-time (3 women); includes 14 minority (5 Black or African American, non-Hispanic/Latino; 1 American Indian or Alaska Native, non-Hispanic/Latino; 1 Asian, non-Hispanic/Latino; 6 Hispanic/Latino; 1 Two or more races, non-Hispanic/Latino), 1 international. Average age 25. 23 applicants, 57% accepted, 7 enrolled. In 2016, 8 master's awarded. *Degree requirements:* For master's, thesis, minimum GPA of 3.0. *Entrance requirements:* For master's, GRE, bachelor's degree in biology or equivalent, 2 letters of recommendation, essay. Additional exam requirements/recommendations for international students: Required—TOEFL (minimum score 550 paper-based; 80 iBT). *Application deadline:* Applications are processed on a rolling basis. Application fee: $75. Electronic applications accepted. *Expenses: Tuition:* Full-time $1240. *Required fees:* $970. Tuition and fees vary according to program. *Financial support:* In 2016–17, 21 students received support, including 17 fellowships with full and partial tuition reimbursements available (averaging $4,315 per year); research assistantships with full and partial tuition reimbursements available, career-related internships or fieldwork, Federal Work-Study, institutionally sponsored loans, scholarships/grants, tuition waivers (full and partial), and unspecified assistantships also available. Support available to part-time students. Financial award applicants required to submit FAFSA. *Faculty research:* G protein-coupled receptor signaling in human vascular cells, endocytic adaptor and scaffold proteins regulators of cell-to-cell communication, extracellular vesicles as critical biomarkers for vascular inflammation and cancer; molecular and biochemical adaptations of marine invertebrates to hypoxia and immune challenge, characterization of genetic variation via molecular markers. *Unit head:* Dr. Nicholas Santangelo, Program Director, 516-463-7394, Fax: 516-463-5112, E-mail: nicholas.santangelo@hofstra.edu. *Application contact:* Sunil Samuel, Assistant Vice President of Admissions, 516-463-4723, Fax: 516-463-4664, E-mail: graduateadmission@hofstra.edu.
Website: http://www.hofstra.edu/hclas

**Judson University,** Master of Architecture Program, Elgin, IL 60123-1498. Offers architecture (M Arch); sustainable design (M Arch); traditional architecture and urbanism (M Arch). *Program availability:* Part-time. *Faculty:* 9 full-time (3 women), 3 part-time/adjunct (1 woman). *Students:* 19 full-time (5 women); includes 5 minority (1 Black or African American, non-Hispanic/Latino; 3 Hispanic/Latino; 1 Two or more races, non-Hispanic/Latino). Average age 22. 24 applicants, 83% accepted, 19 enrolled. In 2016, 16 master's awarded. *Degree requirements:* For master's, thesis optional, 1600-hour practicum/preceptorship completed prior to enrollment. *Entrance requirements:* For master's, GRE, Judson BA in architecture or equivalent; minimum cumulative undergraduate GPA of 2.75, 3.0 in architecture; comprehensive portfolio; letter of intent. Additional exam requirements/recommendations for international students: Required—TOEFL (minimum score 550 paper-based), IELTS (minimum score 6.5). *Application deadline:* For fall admission, 2/15 priority date for domestic and international students; for winter admission, 11/15 for domestic students; for spring admission, 11/15 for domestic and international students. Applications are processed on a rolling basis. Application fee: $100. Electronic applications accepted. *Expenses:* Contact institution. *Financial support:* In 2016–17, 19 students received support, including 1 fellowship with partial tuition reimbursement available (averaging $5,000 per year), 1 research assistantship with partial tuition reimbursement available (averaging $5,000 per year), 12 teaching assistantships with partial tuition reimbursements available (averaging $2,500 per year); unspecified assistantships also available. Financial award application deadline: 7/1; financial award applicants required to submit FAFSA. *Faculty research:* Sustainable design, urbanism, daylighting, acoustics, digital media and fabrication. *Unit head:* Ian Hoffman, Chair, 847-628-1014, E-mail: ihoffman@judsonu.edu. *Application contact:* Molly Smith, Director of Admissions, 847-628-2521, E-mail: molly.smith@judsonu.edu.
Website: http://www.judsonu.edu/ArchMaster/

**Kent State University,** College of Architecture and Environmental Design, Kent, OH 44240. Offers architecture (M Arc); architecture and environmental design (MS); health care design (MHCD); landscape architecture (MLA); urban design (MUD); M Arch/MBA; M Arch/MUD. *Program availability:* Part-time. *Faculty:* 20 full-time (3 women). *Students:* 75 full-time (31 women), 7 part-time (2 women); includes 6 minority (3 Black or African

## Urban Design

American, non-Hispanic/Latino; 1 American Indian or Alaska Native, non-Hispanic/Latino; 2 Hispanic/Latino), 10 international. Average age 25. 125 applicants, 56% accepted, 58 enrolled. In 2016, 55 master's awarded. *Degree requirements:* For master's, thesis (for some programs), project (for some programs). *Entrance requirements:* For master's, GRE, statement of purpose, curriculum vitae, transcripts, 3 letters of recommendation. Additional exam requirements/recommendations for international students: Required—TOEFL (minimum scores of 550 paper-based, 80 iBT), Michigan English Language Assessment Battery (77), IELTS (6.5), or PTE (54). *Application deadline:* For fall admission, 1/15 for domestic and international students. Applications are processed on a rolling basis. Application fee: $45 ($70 for international students). Electronic applications accepted. *Expenses:* Tuition, state resident: full-time $10,864; part-time $495 per credit hour. Tuition, nonresident: full-time $18,380; part-time $837 per credit hour. *Financial support:* Research assistantships with full tuition reimbursements, teaching assistantships with full tuition reimbursements, Federal Work-Study, scholarships/grants, and unspecified assistantships available. Financial award application deadline: 2/1. *Unit head:* Mark Mistur, Dean, E-mail: mmistur1@kent.edu. *Application contact:* Johnathan Fleming, Assistant Professor and Director, Master of Architecture, 330-672-0934, E-mail: jpflemi1@kent.edu.
Website: http://www.kent.edu/caed

**Lawrence Technological University,** College of Architecture and Design, Southfield, MI 48075-1058. Offers architecture (M Arch); build information modeling (Graduate Certificate); interior design (MID); transportation design (Graduate Certificate); urban design (MUD). *Accreditation:* NASAD. *Program availability:* Part-time, evening/weekend. *Faculty:* 14 full-time (2 women), 13 part-time/adjunct (3 women). *Students:* 8 full-time (3 women), 159 part-time (69 women); includes 15 minority (2 Black or African American, non-Hispanic/Latino; 4 Asian, non-Hispanic/Latino; 7 Hispanic/Latino; 2 Two or more races, non-Hispanic/Latino), 50 international. Average age 30. 119 applicants, 58% accepted, 43 enrolled. In 2016, 78 master's awarded. *Degree requirements:* For master's, thesis optional. *Entrance requirements:* Additional exam requirements/recommendations for international students: Required—TOEFL (minimum score 550 paper-based; 79 iBT). *Application deadline:* For fall admission, 5/22 for international students; for spring admission, 10/11 for international students; for summer admission, 2/16 for international students. Applications are processed on a rolling basis. Application fee: $50. Electronic applications accepted. *Expenses: Tuition:* Full-time $14,868; part-time $1062 per credit. *Required fees:* $75 per semester. Tuition and fees vary according to campus/location. *Financial support:* In 2016–17, 43 students received support, including 6 research assistantships with partial tuition reimbursements available (averaging $6,000 per year), 24 teaching assistantships (averaging $5,000 per year); career-related internships or fieldwork, scholarships/grants, and unspecified assistantships also available. Financial award application deadline: 4/1; financial award applicants required to submit FAFSA. *Faculty research:* Public interest design/social practice; digital fabrication and practice; design education; sustainable urbanism; Detroit architecture, Minoru Yamasaki and mid-twentieth century architecture. *Total annual research expenditures:* $260,728. *Unit head:* Prof. Karl Daubmann, Dean/Professor, 248-204-2805, E-mail: archdean@ltu.edu. *Application contact:* Jane Rohrback, Director of Admissions, 248-204-3160, Fax: 248-204-2228, E-mail: admissions@ltu.edu.
Website: http://www.ltu.edu/architecture_and_design/index.asp

**London Metropolitan University,** Graduate Programs, London, United Kingdom. Offers applied psychology (M Sc); architecture (MA); biomedical science (M Sc); blood science (M Sc); cancer pharmacology (M Sc); computer networking and cyber security (M Sc); computing and information systems (M Sc); conference interpreting (MA); counter-terrorism studies (M Sc); creative, digital and professional writing (MA); crime, violence and prevention (M Sc); criminology (M Sc); curating contemporary art (MA); data analytics (M Sc); digital media (MA); early childhood studies (MA); education (MA, Ed D); financial services law, regulation and compliance (LL M); food science (M Sc); forensic psychology (M Sc); health and social care management and policy (M Sc); human nutrition (M Sc); human resource management (MA); human rights and international conflict (MA); information technology (M Sc); intelligence and security studies (M Sc); international oil, gas and energy law (LL M); international relations (MA); interpreting (MA); learning and teaching in higher education (MA); legal practice (LL M); media and entertainment law (LL M); organizational and consumer psychology (MA); psychological therapy (M Sc); psychology of mental health (M Sc); public health (M Sc); public policy and management (MPA); security studies (M Sc); social work (M Sc); spatial planning and urban design (MA); sports therapy (M Sc); supporting older children and young people with dyslexia (MA); teaching languages (MA), including Arabic, English; translation (MA); woman and child abuse (MA).

**The New School,** Parsons School of Design, Program in Design and Urban Ecologies, New York, NY 10011. Offers MS. *Program availability:* Part-time. *Faculty:* 41 full-time (18 women), 4 part-time/adjunct (1 woman). *Students:* 20 full-time (14 women), 1 (woman) part-time; includes 3 minority (2 Black or African American, non-Hispanic/Latino; 1 Two or more races, non-Hispanic/Latino), 12 international. Average age 26. 48 applicants, 88% accepted, 13 enrolled. In 2016, 20 master's awarded. *Degree requirements:* For master's, thesis. *Entrance requirements:* For master's, transcripts, resume, statement of purpose, recommendation letters, portfolio, interview. Additional exam requirements/recommendations for international students: Required—TOEFL (minimum score 92 iBT), IELTS (minimum score 7), PTE (minimum score 63). *Application deadline:* For fall admission, 1/1 priority date for domestic and international students. Applications are processed on a rolling basis. Application fee: $50. Electronic applications accepted. *Expenses:* Contact institution. *Financial support:* Research assistantships, teaching assistantships, career-related internships or fieldwork, Federal Work-Study, scholarships/grants, unspecified assistantships, and travel funding; tuition waivers for students who are also New School employees available. Support available to part-time students. Financial award application deadline: 2/1; financial award applicants required to submit FAFSA. *Faculty research:* Urban planning, environmental enterprises, community organizing, public policy, non-profit management. *Unit head:* Miodrag Mitrasinovic, Chair, Urban Council, 212-229-8970 Ext. 4722, E-mail: mitrasim@newschool.edu. *Application contact:* Courtney Malenius, Director of Graduate Admission, 212-229-5150 Ext. 4011, E-mail: thinkparsonsgrad@newschool.edu.
Website: http://www.newschool.edu/parsons

**The New School,** Parsons School of Design, Program in Theories of Urban Practice, New York, NY 10011. Offers MA. *Program availability:* Part-time. *Faculty:* 41 full-time (18 women), 4 part-time/adjunct (1 woman). *Students:* 18 full-time (8 women), 3 part-time (2 women); includes 7 minority (1 Black or African American, non-Hispanic/Latino; 3 Asian, non-Hispanic/Latino; 2 Hispanic/Latino; 1 Two or more races, non-Hispanic/Latino), 6 international. Average age 28. 25 applicants, 92% accepted, 10 enrolled. In 2016, 7 master's awarded. *Degree requirements:* For master's, thesis. *Entrance requirements:* For master's, transcripts, resume, statement of purpose, recommendation letters, portfolio or writing sample, interview. Additional exam requirements/recommendations for international students: Required—TOEFL (minimum score 92 iBT), IELTS (minimum score 7), PTE (minimum score 63). *Application deadline:* For fall admission, 1/1 priority date for domestic and international students. Applications are processed on a rolling basis. Application fee: $50. Electronic applications accepted. *Expenses:* Contact institution. *Financial support:* Research assistantships, teaching assistantships, career-related internships or fieldwork, scholarships/grants, and

unspecified assistantships available. Support available to part-time students. Financial award application deadline: 2/1; financial award applicants required to submit FAFSA. *Faculty research:* Architecture; ecosystems/environmental systems; landscape design; service design; social practice and innovation. *Unit head:* Gabriela Perez Rendon, Co-Chair, Urban Council, 212-229-8970 Ext. 1335, E-mail: perezreg@newschool.edu. *Application contact:* Courtney Malenius, Director of Graduate Admissions, 212-229-5150 Ext. 4011, E-mail: maleniuc@newschool.edu.
Website: http://www.newschool.edu/parsons

**New York Institute of Technology,** School of Architecture and Design, Old Westbury, NY 11568-8000. Offers architecture, urban and regional design (MS). *Program availability:* Part-time. *Faculty:* 3 full-time (1 woman), 3 part-time/adjunct (0 women). *Students:* 20 full-time (14 women), all international. Average age 26. 55 applicants, 25% accepted, 9 enrolled. In 2016, 7 master's awarded. *Entrance requirements:* For master's, professional architecture or landscape architecture degree from accredited college or university approved by the NAAB or equivalent; minimum undergraduate GPA of 3.0; digital portfolio; curriculum vitae; personal essay; two letters of recommendation. Additional exam requirements/recommendations for international students: Required—TOEFL (minimum score 79 iBT), IELTS (minimum score 6). *Application deadline:* For fall admission, 3/1 for domestic and international students. Applications are processed on a rolling basis. Application fee: $50. Electronic applications accepted. *Expenses:* $1,215 per credit. *Financial support:* Career-related internships or fieldwork, Federal Work-Study, institutionally sponsored loans, scholarships/grants, tuition waivers (full and partial), and unspecified assistantships available. Support available to part-time students. Financial award application deadline: 3/1; financial award applicants required to submit FAFSA. *Faculty research:* Resilient cities, compact morphology, new town development, pedestrian-friendly public realm. *Unit head:* Jeffrey Raven, Graduate Director, 212-261-1547, E-mail: jraven@nyit.edu. *Application contact:* Alice Dolitsky, Director, Graduate Admissions, 516-686-7520, Fax: 516-686-1116, E-mail: nyitgrad@nyit.edu.
Website: http://www.nyit.edu/architecture

**Pratt Institute,** School of Architecture, Program in Architecture and Urban Design, Brooklyn, NY 11205-3899. Offers MS. *Faculty:* 4 part-time/adjunct (2 women). *Students:* 9 full-time (2 women); includes 2 minority (1 Asian, non-Hispanic/Latino; 1 Hispanic/Latino), 7 international. Average age 28. 72 applicants, 65% accepted, 8 enrolled. In 2016, 8 master's awarded. *Degree requirements:* For master's, thesis. *Entrance requirements:* For master's, portfolio, letters of recommendation. Additional exam requirements/recommendations for international students: Required—TOEFL (minimum score 550 paper-based; 79 iBT). *Application deadline:* For fall admission, 1/5 for domestic and international students; for spring admission, 10/1 for domestic and international students. Application fee: $50 ($90 for international students). Electronic applications accepted. *Expenses:* $29,646 full-time tuition, $1,938 fees. *Financial support:* Career-related internships or fieldwork, Federal Work-Study, institutionally sponsored loans, scholarships/grants, health care benefits, and unspecified assistantships available. Support available to part-time students. Financial award application deadline: 2/1; financial award applicants required to submit FAFSA. *Faculty research:* Urban development process; historical, social, and economic implications of planning. *Unit head:* William J. Mac Donald, Chairperson, 718-399-4357, E-mail: wmacdona@pratt.edu. *Application contact:* Natalie Capannelli, Director of Graduate Admissions, 718-636-3551, Fax: 718-399-4242, E-mail: ncapanne@pratt.edu.
Website: https://www.pratt.edu/academics/architecture/grad-arch-urban-design/

**See Display on page 114 and Close-Up on page 137.**

**Rice University,** Graduate Programs, School of Architecture, Houston, TX 77251-1892. Offers architecture (M Arch, D Arch); urban design (M Arch). *Degree requirements:* For master's, thesis optional; for doctorate, thesis/dissertation. *Entrance requirements:* For master's and doctorate, GRE. Additional exam requirements/recommendations for international students: Required—TOEFL (minimum score 600 paper-based; 100 iBT). Electronic applications accepted.

**Savannah College of Art and Design,** Graduate School, Program in Urban Design, Savannah, GA 31402-3146. Offers MUD. *Program availability:* Part-time. *Faculty:* 1 full-time (0 women), 1 part-time/adjunct (0 women). *Students:* 8 full-time (6 women), 1 (woman) part-time, 8 international. Average age 29. 31 applicants, 42% accepted, 3 enrolled. In 2016, 5 master's awarded. *Degree requirements:* For master's, thesis. *Entrance requirements:* For master's, GRE (recommended), portfolio (submitted in digital format), audition or writing submission, resume, statement of purpose, two letters of recommendation. Additional exam requirements/recommendations for international students: Required—TOEFL (minimum score 550 paper-based, 85 iBT), IELTS (minimum score 6.5), or ACTFL. *Application deadline:* For fall admission, 4/1 for domestic and international students. Applications are processed on a rolling basis. Application fee: $40. Electronic applications accepted. *Expenses: Tuition:* Full-time $36,045. Tuition and fees vary according to course load. *Financial support:* Career-related internships or fieldwork, Federal Work-Study, and scholarships/grants available. Financial award application deadline: 4/1; financial award applicants required to submit FAFSA. *Unit head:* Ivan Chow, Dean, School of Building Arts. *Application contact:* Jenny Jaquillard, Executive Director of Admissions, Recruitment and Events, 912-525-5100, Fax: 912-525-5985, E-mail: admission@scad.edu.
Website: http://www.scad.edu/academics/programs/urban-design

**State University of New York College of Environmental Science and Forestry,** Department of Landscape Architecture, Syracuse, NY 13210-2779. Offers community design and planning (MLA, MS); cultural landscape studies and conservation (MLA, MS); landscape and urban ecology (MLA, MS). *Accreditation:* ASLA (one or more programs are accredited). *Faculty:* 11 full-time (4 women), 9 part-time/adjunct (3 women). *Students:* 31 full-time (17 women), 3 part-time (2 women); includes 4 minority (2 Black or African American, non-Hispanic/Latino; 1 Asian, non-Hispanic/Latino; 1 Hispanic/Latino), 6 international. Average age 26. 53 applicants, 72% accepted, 12 enrolled. In 2016, 9 master's awarded. *Degree requirements:* For master's, comprehensive exam (for some programs), thesis (for some programs). *Entrance requirements:* For master's, GRE General Test, minimum GPA of 3.0. Additional exam requirements/recommendations for international students: Required—TOEFL (minimum score 550 paper-based; 80 iBT), IELTS (minimum score 6), or STEP Eiken (grade 1). *Application deadline:* For fall admission, 2/1 priority date for domestic and international students; for spring admission, 11/1 priority date for domestic and international students. Applications are processed on a rolling basis. Application fee: $60. *Expenses:* Tuition, state resident: full-time $10,870; part-time $453 per credit. Tuition, nonresident: full-time $22,210; part-time $925 per credit. *Required fees:* $1075; $89.22 per credit. *Financial support:* In 2016–17, 16 students received support. Application deadline: 6/30; applicants required to submit FAFSA. *Faculty research:* Site analysis and design, city and regional planning, community environments. *Total annual research expenditures:* $437,597. *Unit head:* Dr. Douglas Johnston, Chair, 315-470-6544, Fax: 315-470-6540, E-mail: dmjohnst@esf.edu. *Application contact:* Scott Shannon, Associate Provost for Instruction/Dean of the Graduate School, 315-470-6599, Fax: 315-470-6978, E-mail: esfgrad@esf.edu.
Website: http://www.esf.edu/la/

**University at Buffalo, the State University of New York,** Graduate School, School of Architecture and Planning, Department of Architecture, Buffalo, NY 14214. Offers architecture (M Arch); ecological practices (MS Arch); historic preservation and urban design (MS Arch); inclusive design (MS Arch); real estate development (MS Arch); situated technology (MS Arch); M Arch/MBA; M Arch/MFA; M Arch/MUP. *Faculty:* 32 full-time (11 women), 9 part-time/adjunct (3 women). *Students:* 134 full-time (56 women), 15 part-time (5 women); includes 29 minority (12 Black or African American, non-Hispanic/Latino; 5 Asian, non-Hispanic/Latino; 8 Hispanic/Latino; 4 Two or more races, non-Hispanic/Latino), 27 international. Average age 25. 267 applicants, 34% accepted, 63 enrolled. In 2016, 44 master's awarded. *Degree requirements:* For master's, thesis or alternative, project. *Entrance requirements:* For master's, GRE, portfolio, 3 letters of recommendation, transcripts, 500-word personal statement. Additional exam requirements/recommendations for international students: Required—TOEFL (minimum score 79 iBT), IELTS (minimum score 6.5). *Application deadline:* For fall admission, 1/1 priority date for domestic and international students. Application fee: $75. Electronic applications accepted. *Expenses:* Contact institution. *Financial support:* In 2016–17, 5 students received support, including 5 fellowships with full tuition reimbursements available (averaging $11,040 per year), 2 research assistantships with partial tuition reimbursements available (averaging $13,200 per year), 43 teaching assistantships with partial tuition reimbursements available (averaging $4,337 per year); career-related internships or fieldwork, Federal Work-Study, scholarships/grants, health care benefits, and unspecified assistantships also available. Financial award application deadline: 3/1; financial award applicants required to submit FAFSA. *Faculty research:* Ecological practices, inclusive design, material culture, situated technologies, urban design. *Total annual research expenditures:* $3.8 million. *Unit head:* Prof. Omar Khan, Chair, 716-829-3483 Ext. 105, Fax: 716-829-3256, E-mail: omar.khan@buffalo.edu. *Application contact:* Debra Eggebrecht, Assistant to the Chair, 716-829-3486 Ext. 105, Fax: 716-829-3256, E-mail: dle2@buffalo.edu. Website: http://www.ap.buffalo.edu/architecture/

**University at Buffalo, the State University of New York,** Graduate School, School of Architecture and Planning, Department of Urban and Regional Planning, Buffalo, NY 14214. Offers historic preservation (Certificate); urban and regional planning (PhD); JD/MUP; M Arch/MUP. *Accreditation:* ACSP. *Program availability:* Part-time. *Faculty:* 14 full-time (6 women), 12 part-time/adjunct (3 women). *Students:* 78 full-time (29 women), 12 part-time (7 women); includes 19 minority (11 Black or African American, non-Hispanic/Latino; 1 Asian, non-Hispanic/Latino; 5 Hispanic/Latino; 2 Two or more races, non-Hispanic/Latino), 24 international. Average age 27. 216 applicants, 23% accepted, 36 enrolled. In 2016, 34 master's awarded. *Degree requirements:* For master's, thesis or alternative, project; for doctorate, thesis/dissertation. *Entrance requirements:* For master's, minimum GPA of 3.0, resume, 3 letters of recommendation, 500-word personal statement, transcripts; for doctorate, GRE, transcripts, 3 letters of recommendation, minimum GPA of 3.0, resume, research statement, writing sample. Additional exam requirements/recommendations for international students: Required—TOEFL (minimum score 79 iBT), IELTS (minimum score 6.5). *Application deadline:* For fall admission, 3/1 priority date for domestic and international students; for spring admission, 10/31 priority date for domestic students, 10/1 priority date for international students. Applications are processed on a rolling basis. Application fee: $75. Electronic applications accepted. *Expenses:* Contact institution. *Financial support:* In 2016–17, 3 students received support, including 3 fellowships with full tuition reimbursements available (averaging $10,400 per year), 5 research assistantships with tuition reimbursements available (averaging $8,751 per year), 15 teaching assistantships with partial tuition reimbursements available (averaging $3,684 per year); career-related internships or fieldwork, Federal Work-Study, institutionally sponsored loans, scholarships/grants, health care benefits, and unspecified assistantships also available. Financial award application deadline: 3/1; financial award applicants required to submit FAFSA. *Faculty research:* Economic and international development, environmental and land use planning, GIS and spatial analysis, urban design and physical planning, neighborhood planning and community development, historic preservation. *Total annual research expenditures:* $3.8 million. *Unit head:* Dr. Ernest Sternberg, Professor, 716-829-3671 Ext. 109, Fax: 716-829-3256, E-mail: ezs@buffalo.edu. *Application contact:* Norma Everett, Assistant to the Chair, 716-829-3283, Fax: 716-829-3256, E-mail: norma.everett@buffalo.edu. Website: http://www.ap.buffalo.edu/planning/

**The University of British Columbia,** Faculty of Applied Science, School of Architecture and Landscape Architecture, Program in Landscape Architecture, Vancouver, BC V6T 1Z2, Canada. Offers advanced studies in landscape architecture (MASLA); landscape architecture (MLA); urban design (MUD); M Arch/MLA. *Degree requirements:* For master's, comprehensive exam or thesis. *Entrance requirements:* For master's, portfolio. Additional exam requirements/recommendations for international students: Required—TOEFL. Application fee: $100 Canadian dollars ($162 Canadian dollars for international students). Electronic applications accepted. *Expenses:* Contact institution. *Financial support:* Fellowships, institutionally sponsored loans, scholarships/grants, and tuition waivers (partial) available. *Faculty research:* Landscape design, urban-rural interface, urban ecology, sustainable development, collaborative planning and community forestry. *Application contact:* Tara Deans, Program Assistant, 604-822-3445, E-mail: tdeans@sala.ubc.ca. Website: http://www.larc.ubc.ca

**University of California, Berkeley,** Graduate Division, College of Environmental Design, Department of Architecture, Berkeley, CA 94720-1500. Offers architecture (M Arch); building science (MS, PhD); building structures, construction and materials (MS, PhD); design theories, methods, and practices (MS, PhD); environmental design in developing countries (MS, PhD); history of architecture and urbanism (MS, PhD); social and cultural processes in architecture and urbanism (MS, PhD); M Arch/MCP; M Arch/MS; MLA/M Arch. *Students:* 178 full-time (84 women); includes 34 minority (4 Black or African American, non-Hispanic/Latino; 1 American Indian or Alaska Native, non-Hispanic/Latino; 13 Asian, non-Hispanic/Latino; 16 Hispanic/Latino), 85 international. Average age 30. 1,047 applicants, 68 enrolled. In 2016, 42 master's, 7 doctorates awarded. *Degree requirements:* For master's, thesis; for doctorate, thesis/dissertation, qualifying exam. *Entrance requirements:* For master's and doctorate, GRE General Test, minimum GPA of 3.0, 3 letters of recommendation. Additional exam requirements/recommendations for international students: Required—TOEFL (minimum score 570 paper-based; 90 iBT). *Application deadline:* For fall admission, 12/7 for domestic students. Application fee: $105 ($125 for international students). Electronic applications accepted. Application fee is waived when completed online. *Financial support:* Fellowships, research assistantships, teaching assistantships, career-related internships or fieldwork, institutionally sponsored loans, health care benefits, and unspecified assistantships available. *Unit head:* Prof. Tom Buresh, Chair, 510-642-4942. *Application contact:* Lois H. Ito Koch, Student Affairs Officer, 510-642-5577, Fax: 510-643-5607, E-mail: archgrad@berkeley.edu. Website: http://arch.ced.berkeley.edu/

**University of California, Berkeley,** Graduate Division, College of Environmental Design, Department of Landscape Architecture and Environmental Planning, Berkeley, CA 94720-1500. Offers landscape architecture (MLA), including environmental planning, landscape design and site planning, urban and community design; landscape architecture and environmental planning (PhD); MLA/M Arch; MLA/MCP. *Accreditation:* ASLA (one or more programs are accredited). *Faculty:* 13 full-time, 6 part-time/adjunct. *Students:* 84 full-time (52 women); includes 19 minority (1 Black or African American, non-Hispanic/Latino; 5 Asian, non-Hispanic/Latino; 13 Hispanic/Latino), 26 international. Average age 30. 263 applicants, 30 enrolled. In 2016, 27 master's, 3 doctorates awarded. *Degree requirements:* For master's, comprehensive exam (for some programs), thesis (for some programs), professional project or thesis; for doctorate, one foreign language, thesis/dissertation, qualifying exam. *Entrance requirements:* For master's, GRE General Test, minimum GPA of 3.0, portfolio; for doctorate, GRE General Test, master's degree (strongly recommended), minimum GPA of 3.0, sample of written work, 3 letters of recommendation. Additional exam requirements/recommendations for international students: Required—TOEFL (minimum score 570 paper-based; 90 iBT). *Application deadline:* For fall admission, 12/7 for domestic students. Application fee: $105 ($125 for international students). Electronic applications accepted. *Financial support:* Fellowships, research assistantships, teaching assistantships, career-related internships or fieldwork, Federal Work-Study, institutionally sponsored loans, and unspecified assistantships available. *Unit head:* Prof. Louise Mozingo, Chair, 510-643-6165, Fax: 510-643-6166. *Application contact:* 510-642-2965, Fax: 510-643-6166, E-mail: laepgrad@berkeley.edu. Website: http://laep.ced.berkeley.edu/

**University of California, Berkeley,** Graduate Division, College of Environmental Design, Group in Urban Design, Berkeley, CA 94720-1500. Offers MUD. *Faculty:* 13 full-time, 6 part-time/adjunct. *Students:* 9 full-time (6 women); includes 1 minority (Hispanic/Latino), 8 international. Average age 29. 98 applicants, 9 enrolled. In 2016, 6 master's awarded. *Degree requirements:* For master's, thesis (for some programs), professional project or thesis. *Entrance requirements:* For master's, GRE General Test, minimum GPA of 3.0, portfolio, 3 letters of recommendation. Additional exam requirements/recommendations for international students: Required—TOEFL (minimum score 570 paper-based; 90 iBT). *Application deadline:* For fall admission, 12/14 for domestic students. Application fee: $105 ($125 for international students). Electronic applications accepted. *Financial support:* Unspecified assistantships available. *Unit head:* Prof. Harrison Fraker, Co-Chair, 510-642-4022. *Application contact:* Tony Tieu, Student Affairs Officer, 510-642-2965, Fax: 510-643-6166, E-mail: laepgrad@berkeley.edu. Website: http://mud.ced.berkeley.edu/

**University of California, Los Angeles,** Graduate Division, School of the Arts and Architecture, Department of Architecture and Urban Design, Los Angeles, CA 90095. Offers M Arch, MA, PhD. *Degree requirements:* For master's, comprehensive exam (M Arch I, II); thesis (MA); for doctorate, 2 foreign languages, thesis/dissertation, oral and written qualifying exams. *Entrance requirements:* For master's, GRE General Test, bachelor's degree; minimum undergraduate GPA of 3.0 (or its equivalent if letter grade system not used); writing sample (MA only); portfolio (M Arch only); for doctorate, GRE General Test, bachelor's degree; minimum undergraduate GPA of 3.5 (or its equivalent if letter grade system not used); writing sample. Additional exam requirements/recommendations for international students: Required—TOEFL. Electronic applications accepted. *Expenses:* Contact institution.

**University of Colorado Denver,** College of Architecture and Planning, Program in Design and Planning, Denver, CO 80217. Offers history of architecture, landscape and urbanism (PhD); sustainable and healthy environments (PhD). *Program availability:* Part-time. *Faculty:* 8 full-time (3 women), 9 part-time/adjunct (1 woman). *Students:* 6 full-time (2 women), 9 part-time (6 women); includes 1 minority (Hispanic/Latino), 5 international. Average age 35. 21 applicants, 14% accepted, 3 enrolled. In 2016, 3 doctorates awarded. *Degree requirements:* For doctorate, comprehensive exam, thesis/dissertation. *Entrance requirements:* For doctorate, GRE (minimum score of 158 for both verbal and quantitative; writing 4.0), minimum undergraduate GPA of 3.0, graduate 3.5; writing sample; three letters of recommendation; statement of personal and professional goals. Additional exam requirements/recommendations for international students: Required—TOEFL (minimum score 80 iBT); Recommended—IELTS (minimum score 6.8). *Application deadline:* For fall admission, 2/2 for domestic students, 1/2 for international students; for spring admission, 10/1 for domestic students. Application fee: $50 ($75 for international students). Electronic applications accepted. *Expenses:* Contact institution. *Financial support:* In 2016–17, 6 students received support. Fellowships, research assistantships, teaching assistantships, Federal Work-Study, institutionally sponsored loans, scholarships/grants, traineeships, and unspecified assistantships available. Financial award application deadline: 4/1; financial award applicants required to submit FAFSA. *Faculty research:* Land use and environmental planning and design; design and planning processes and practices; history, theory, and criticism of the built environment. *Unit head:* Dr. Osman Attmann, Director, 303-315-0032, E-mail: o.attmann@ucdenver.edu. *Application contact:* Rachael Kuroiwa, Manager of Admissions and Outreach, 303-315-2325, E-mail: rachael.kuroiwa@ucdenver.edu. Website: http://www.ucdenver.edu/academics/colleges/ArchitecturePlanning/Academics/DegreePrograms/PhD/Pages/PhD.aspx

**University of Colorado Denver,** College of Architecture and Planning, Program in Urban Design, Denver, CO 80217. Offers MUD. *Program availability:* Part-time. *Students:* 17 full-time (8 women), 1 (woman) part-time, 14 international. Average age 29. 28 applicants, 61% accepted, 8 enrolled. In 2016, 7 master's awarded. *Degree requirements:* For master's, thesis optional, 36 credits, including an independent study, internship, or additional elective. *Entrance requirements:* For master's, GRE (for students with an undergraduate GPA below 3.0), BA in related field; prior professional degree; portfolio of creative work; statement of purpose; resume. Additional exam requirements/recommendations for international students: Required—TOEFL (minimum score 75 iBT). *Application deadline:* For fall admission, 2/15 priority date for domestic students, 1/15 priority date for international students; for spring admission, 10/1 for domestic students. Applications are processed on a rolling basis. Application fee: $50 ($75 for international students). Electronic applications accepted. *Expenses:* Contact institution. *Financial support:* In 2016–17, 17 students received support. Fellowships, research assistantships, teaching assistantships, Federal Work-Study, institutionally sponsored loans, scholarships/grants, and traineeships available. Financial award application deadline: 4/1; financial award applicants required to submit FAFSA. *Faculty research:* Architecture of the city, architectural experimentation and exploration, composition and decomposition, intervention and transformation in the urban and rural landscape. *Unit head:* Ann Komara, Associate Professor/Director, 303-315-2428, E-mail: ann.komara@ucdenver.edu. *Application contact:* Rachael Kuroiwa, Manager of Admissions and Outreach, 303-315-2325, E-mail: rachael.kuroiwa@ucdenver.edu. Website: http://www.ucdenver.edu/academics/colleges/ArchitecturePlanning/Academics/DegreePrograms/MUD/Pages/MUD.aspx

**University of Colorado Denver,** School of Education and Human Development, Program in Educational Leadership and Innovation, Denver, CO 80217. Offers educational studies and research (PhD), including administrative leadership and policy, early childhood special education, math education, research, assessment and evaluation, science education, urban ecologies. *Program availability:* Part-time, evening/weekend. *Students:* 30 full-time (25 women), 14 part-time (11 women); includes 16 minority (7 Black or African American, non-Hispanic/Latino; 1 American Indian or Alaska

*Urban Design*

Native, non-Hispanic/Latino; 1 Asian, non-Hispanic/Latino; 6 Hispanic/Latino; 1 Two or more races, non-Hispanic/Latino, 5 international. Average age 40. 21 applicants, 67% accepted, 8 enrolled. In 2016, 3 doctorates awarded. *Degree requirements:* For doctorate, comprehensive exam, thesis/dissertation, 75 credit hours (for PhD). *Entrance requirements:* For doctorate, GRE or equivalent, resume or curriculum vitae, letters of recommendation, master's degree or equivalent, completion of basic or advanced statistics course with minimum B grade. Additional exam requirements/recommendations for international students: Required—TOEFL (minimum score 537 paper-based; 75 iBT); Recommended—IELTS (minimum score 6.5). *Application deadline:* For fall admission, 12/1 priority date for domestic students, 11/1 priority date for international students. Applications are processed on a rolling basis. Application fee: $50 ($75 for international students). Electronic applications accepted. *Expenses:* Contact institution. *Financial support:* In 2016–17, 45 students received support. Fellowships, research assistantships, teaching assistantships, Federal Work-Study, institutionally sponsored loans, scholarships/grants, and traineeships available. Financial award application deadline: 4/1; financial award applicants required to submit FAFSA. *Faculty research:* Administrative leadership and policy studies, early childhood education, research in diversity, paraprofessionals in education, urban schools lab. *Unit head:* 303-315-6300, E-mail: education@ucdenver.edu. *Application contact:* 303-315-6300, E-mail: education@ucdenver.edu.
Website: http://www.ucdenver.edu/academics/colleges/SchoolOfEducation/Academics/Doctorate/Pages/PhD%20in%20Education%20and%20Human%20Development.aspx

**The University of Kansas,** Graduate Studies, School of Architecture, Design, and Planning, Department of Architecture, Lawrence, KS 66045. Offers architectural acoustics (Certificate); architecture (M Arch, PhD); health and wellness (Certificate); historic preservation (Certificate); urban design (Certificate). *Students:* 107 full-time (52 women), 15 part-time (7 women); includes 17 minority (5 Black or African American, non-Hispanic/Latino; 6 Asian, non-Hispanic/Latino; 4 Hispanic/Latino; 2 Two or more races, non-Hispanic/Latino), 35 international. Average age 26. 115 applicants, 71% accepted, 20 enrolled. In 2016, 85 master's, 2 doctorates awarded. Terminal master's awarded for partial completion of doctoral program. *Entrance requirements:* For master's, GRE, transcript; resume; minimum GPA of 3.0; statement of purpose; letters of recommendation, portfolio of design work, or samples of written work or other creative artifacts produced if previous degree was not in a design-related discipline; for doctorate, GRE, transcript, resume, minimum GPA of 3.0, statement of purpose, letters of recommendation, research-informed writing sample, exhibit of work illustrating applicant's interests and abilities in areas related to the design disciplines. Additional exam requirements/recommendations for international students: Required—TOEFL, IELTS. *Application deadline:* For fall admission, 1/15 priority date for domestic and international students; for summer admission, 1/15 priority date for domestic and international students. Application fee: $65 ($85 for international students). Electronic applications accepted. *Financial support:* Fellowships, research assistantships, teaching assistantships, scholarships/grants, health care benefits, and unspecified assistantships available. Financial award application deadline: 1/15; financial award applicants required to submit FAFSA. *Faculty research:* Design build, sustainability, emergent technology, healthy places, urban design. *Unit head:* Jae Chang, Chair, 785-864-1446, E-mail: jdchang@ku.edu. *Application contact:* Gera Elliott, Admissions Coordinator, 785-864-3167, Fax: 785-864-5185, E-mail: archku@ku.edu.
Website: http://architecture.ku.edu/

**University of Miami,** Graduate School, School of Architecture, Program in Suburb and Town Design, Coral Gables, FL 33124. Offers M Arch. *Entrance requirements:* For master's, GRE General Test, minimum GPA of 3.0, portfolio. Additional exam requirements/recommendations for international students: Required—TOEFL. Electronic applications accepted.

**University of Michigan,** Taubman College of Architecture and Urban Planning, Master of Urban Design Program, Ann Arbor, MI 48109. Offers MUD, MUD/M Arch. *Faculty:* 5 full-time (2 women), 1 (woman) part-time/adjunct. *Students:* 14 full-time (10 women), 11 international. 72 applicants, 86% accepted, 9 enrolled. In 2016, 9 master's awarded. *Degree requirements:* For master's, thesis or alternative. *Entrance requirements:* Additional exam requirements/recommendations for international students: Required—TOEFL (minimum score 100 iBT), GRE. *Application deadline:* For fall admission, 1/15 for domestic and international students. Application fee: $75 ($90 for international students). Electronic applications accepted. *Expenses:* Contact institution. *Financial support:* In 2016–17, 13 students received support. Scholarships/grants available. Financial award application deadline: 1/15; financial award applicants required to submit FAFSA. *Unit head:* Sharon Haar, Architecture Program Chair, 734-764-1300, E-mail: haar@umich.edu. *Application contact:* Mike Smith, Admission Officer, 734-647-2187, E-mail: taubmancollegestudentservices@umich.edu.
Website: http://taubmancollege.umich.edu/architecture/degrees/master-urban-design

**The University of North Carolina at Charlotte,** College of Arts and Architecture, School of Architecture, Charlotte, NC 28223-0001. Offers architecture (M Arch I, M Arch II); urban design (MUD). *Faculty:* 21 full-time (7 women). *Students:* 100 full-time (57 women), 2 part-time (1 woman); includes 21 minority (9 Black or African American, non-Hispanic/Latino; 1 Asian, non-Hispanic/Latino; 8 Hispanic/Latino; 3 Two or more races, non-Hispanic/Latino), 23 international. Average age 25. 164 applicants, 74% accepted, 47 enrolled. In 2016, 31 master's awarded. *Degree requirements:* For master's, design studio or thesis. *Entrance requirements:* For master's, GRE, official transcripts from all previous college-level institution(s); statement of purpose explaining reasons for wanting to study in the School of Architecture; three recommendations from persons familiar with the applicant's personal and professional qualifications; resume or curriculum vitae; portfolio. Additional exam requirements/recommendations for international students: Required—TOEFL (minimum score 523 paper-based, 70 iBT) or IELTS (6.5). *Application deadline:* For fall admission, 1/15 priority date for domestic and international students. Applications are processed on a rolling basis. Application fee: $75. Electronic applications accepted. *Expenses:* Contact institution. *Financial support:* In 2016–17, 33 students received support, including 25 research assistantships (averaging $7,500 per year), 8 teaching assistantships (averaging $3,112 per year); institutionally sponsored loans, scholarships/grants, and unspecified assistantships also available. Financial award application deadline: 3/1; financial award applicants required to submit FAFSA. *Faculty research:* Urban design studies for local and regional municipalities and community groups, high performance building and optimization protocols, daylighting and energy analysis, digital design and fabrication components, and interactive visualization; refinement of regionally specific computer-aided analysis tools used to evaluate total building energy performance, and the economic valuation of architectural systems and their design attributes. *Total annual research expenditures:* $35,367. *Unit head:* Kenneth A. Lambla, Dean, 704-687-0090, E-mail: kalambla@uncc.edu. *Application contact:* Kathy B. Giddings, Director of Graduate Admissions, 704-687-5503, Fax: 704-687-1668, E-mail: gradadm@uncc.edu.
Website: http://coaa.uncc.edu/academics/school-of-architecture

**University of Pennsylvania,** School of Design, Department of City and Regional Planning, Philadelphia, PA 19104. Offers city and regional planning (PhD); city planning (MCP); GIS and spatial analysis (Certificate); land preservation (Certificate); urban design (Certificate); urban redevelopment (Certificate); urban spatial analytics (MUSA).

*Accreditation:* ACSP (one or more programs are accredited). *Program availability:* Part-time. *Faculty:* 13 full-time (5 women), 4 part-time/adjunct (0 women). *Students:* 136 full-time (77 women), 15 part-time (11 women); includes 22 minority (5 Black or African American, non-Hispanic/Latino; 8 Asian, non-Hispanic/Latino; 6 Hispanic/Latino; 1 Native Hawaiian or other Pacific Islander, non-Hispanic/Latino; 2 Two or more races, non-Hispanic/Latino), 56 international. Average age 27. 419 applicants, 58% accepted, 90 enrolled. In 2016, 76 master's, 8 doctorates awarded. *Degree requirements:* For doctorate, thesis/dissertation. *Entrance requirements:* Additional exam requirements/recommendations for international students: Required—TOEFL (minimum score 100 iBT); Recommended—IELTS (minimum score 7), TSE (minimum score 68). *Application deadline:* For spring admission, 1/12 for domestic students. Application fee: $80. Electronic applications accepted. *Expenses: Tuition:* Full-time $31,068; part-time $5762 per course. *Required fees:* $3200; $336 per course. Full-time tuition and fees vary according to degree level, program and student level. Part-time tuition and fees vary according to course load, degree level and program. *Financial support:* In 2016–17, 39 teaching assistantships (averaging $2,000 per year) were awarded; fellowships, research assistantships, and Federal Work-Study also available. Financial award application deadline: 2/15; financial award applicants required to submit FAFSA. *Faculty research:* Transportation planning, community and economic development, public private development, land use and environmental planning, urban design. *Unit head:* Dr. John Landis, Department Chair, 215-746-2340, E-mail: jlan@design.upenn.edu. *Application contact:* Roslynne Carter, Administrative Assistant, 215-898-8330, Fax: 215-898-5730, E-mail: admissions@design.upenn.edu.
Website: https://www.design.upenn.edu/city-regional-planning

**University of South Florida,** College of The Arts, School of Architecture and Community Design, Tampa, FL 33620-9951. Offers architecture (M Arch); urban and community design (MUCD). *Faculty:* 10 full-time (1 woman). *Students:* 103 full-time (40 women), 13 part-time (8 women); includes 41 minority (6 Black or African American, non-Hispanic/Latino; 6 Asian, non-Hispanic/Latino; 26 Hispanic/Latino; 3 Two or more races, non-Hispanic/Latino), 17 international. Average age 25. 83 applicants, 43% accepted, 25 enrolled. In 2016, 51 master's awarded. *Degree requirements:* For master's, comprehensive exam, thesis. *Entrance requirements:* For master's, GRE General Test, minimum undergraduate GPA of 3.0 in last 60 hours of coursework; three letters of recommendation; portfolio or creative work; written statement of intent; prerequisite courses in physics, calculus, and AutoCAD. Additional exam requirements/recommendations for international students: Required—TOEFL (minimum score 550 paper-based; 79 iBT) or IELTS (minimum score 6.5). *Application deadline:* For fall admission, 2/1 priority date for domestic students, 2/1 for international students. Applications are processed on a rolling basis. Application fee: $30. Electronic applications accepted. *Expenses:* Tuition, state resident: full-time $7766; part-time $431.43 per credit hour. Tuition, nonresident: full-time $15,789; part-time $877.17 per credit hour. *Required fees:* $37 per term. *Financial support:* In 2016–17, 48 students received support, including 3 teaching assistantships with tuition reimbursements available (averaging $9,360 per year); Federal Work-Study, scholarships/grants, and unspecified assistantships also available. *Faculty research:* Urban community design and planning; public space infrastructure; conditions of suburban sprawl; redevelopment strategies for abandoned commercial centers and edges; sustainability; influences of technology, cultural identity and interpretation and social values on architectural design; epistemology of design thinking; tropical architecture; high-density urbanism; design benevolence; economic development/community revitalization; housing/residential development; development regulations. *Total annual research expenditures:* $403,084. *Unit head:* Dr. Robert MacLeod, Director and Professor, School of Architecture and Community Design, 813-974-6015, Fax: 813-974-2557, E-mail: rmacleod@arch.usf.edu. *Application contact:* Mildred Abreu, Academic Advisor, 813-974-1216, Fax: 813-974-2557, E-mail: abreu@arch.usf.edu.
Website: http://www.arch.usf.edu/

**The University of Texas at Austin,** Graduate School, School of Architecture, Program in Urban Design, Austin, TX 78712-1111. Offers M Arch, MSUD.

**University of Toronto,** School of Graduate Studies, Faculty of Arts and Science, Department of Geography, Program in Planning, Toronto, ON M5S 1A1, Canada. Offers M Sc Pl, MUDS, PhD. *Program availability:* Part-time. *Degree requirements:* For master's, summer internship. *Entrance requirements:* For master's, bachelor's degree in planning, geography, social science or a closely related professional field, minimum B+ average in final year, 3 letters of reference; for doctorate, minimum A- or equivalent standing in previous master's program. Additional exam requirements/recommendations for international students: Required—TOEFL (minimum score 580 paper-based; 93 iBT), TWE (minimum score 5). Electronic applications accepted. *Expenses:* Contact institution.

**University of Toronto,** School of Graduate Studies, John H. Daniels Faculty of Architecture, Landscape, and Design, Toronto, ON M5S 1A1, Canada. Offers M Arch, MLA, MUD, MVS. *Entrance requirements:* For master's, minimum B average; 3 letters of reference; resume; 3 writing samples; 5 samples of design work, drawing, or work in a related field, statement of interest. Additional exam requirements/recommendations for international students: Required—TOEFL (minimum score 580 paper-based; 93 iBT), IELTS (minimum score 7), TWE (minimum score 5), Michigan English Language Assessment Battery (minimum score 85), COPE (minimum score 76). Electronic applications accepted. *Expenses:* Contact institution.

**University of Utah,** Graduate School, College of Architecture and Planning, Department of City and Metropolitan Planning, Salt Lake City, UT 84112. Offers city and metropolitan planning (MCMP), including ecological planning, small town and resort planning, smart growth and transportation, urban design; metropolitan planning, policy and design (PhD). *Program availability:* Part-time. *Faculty:* 7 full-time (3 women), 25 part-time/adjunct (9 women). *Students:* 42 full-time (21 women), 14 part-time (4 women); includes 6 minority (6 Asian, non-Hispanic/Latino; 1 Hispanic/Latino; 2 Two or more races, non-Hispanic/Latino), 11 international. Average age 30. 33 applicants, 100% accepted, 16 enrolled. In 2016, 15 master's, 3 doctorates awarded. *Degree requirements:* For master's, thesis or alternative, comprehensive project; for doctorate, thesis/dissertation. *Entrance requirements:* For master's, GRE, minimum undergraduate GPA of 3.0; for doctorate, GRE, minimum GPA of 3.5. Additional exam requirements/recommendations for international students: Required—TOEFL (minimum score 500 paper-based; 61 iBT); Recommended—IELTS (minimum score 6). *Application deadline:* For fall admission, 1/15 priority date for domestic and international students; for spring admission, 11/1 for domestic and international students. Applications are processed on a rolling basis. Application fee: $55 ($65 for international students). Electronic applications accepted. *Expenses:* Contact institution. *Financial support:* In 2016–17, 25 students received support, including 1 fellowship with full tuition reimbursement available (averaging $25,000 per year), 3 research assistantships with tuition reimbursements available (averaging $16,000 per year), 21 teaching assistantships with tuition reimbursements available (averaging $10,000 per year); career-related internships or fieldwork, Federal Work-Study, scholarships/grants, health care benefits, and unspecified assistantships also available. Financial award application deadline: 1/15; financial award applicants required to submit FAFSA. *Faculty research:* Transportation, land-use, smart growth, public health, climate change, urban design,

sustainable communities, community-based decision-making process, urban morphology, theory and practice in scenario-planning techniques, community-engaged teaching methodologies, interactions between federal environmental policies and state/local community development patterns, values in architecture and planning practices. *Total annual research expenditures:* $689,627. *Unit head:* Reid Ewing, Chair, 801-585-3745, Fax: 801-581-8217, E-mail: ewing@arch.utah.edu. *Application contact:* Saolo Utu, Recruitment and Admissions Advisor, 801-581-2361, Fax: 801-581-8217, E-mail: recruitment@arch.utah.edu.
Website: http://www.plan.utah.edu/

**University of Washington,** Graduate School, College of Built Environments, Department of Urban Design and Planning, Seattle, WA 98195. Offers urban design and planning (PhD); urban planning (MUP). *Accreditation:* ACSP (one or more programs are accredited). *Degree requirements:* For master's, thesis or alternative; for doctorate, thesis/dissertation. *Entrance requirements:* For master's and doctorate, GRE General Test, minimum GPA of 3.0. Additional exam requirements/recommendations for international students: Required—TOEFL. *Faculty research:* Land-use and growth management, urban form and travel behavior, geographic information systems/remote sensing, historic preservation, urban ecology and environmental planning.

**University of Washington,** Graduate School, College of Built Environments, Interdisciplinary Program in Urban Design, Seattle, WA 98195. Offers Certificate. Electronic applications accepted. *Faculty research:* Urban design process; urban form; place theory; place analysis; race, class, and gender in community design.

**Washington University in St. Louis,** Sam Fox School of Design and Visual Arts, Program in Urban Design, St. Louis, MO 63130-4899. Offers MUD, M Arch/MUD, MUD/MSW. *Entrance requirements:* For master's, GRE General Test, portfolio. Additional exam requirements/recommendations for international students: Required—TOEFL (minimum score 600 paper-based; 100 iBT), TWE. *Faculty research:* Urban design development issues: city revitalization, sustainability and suburbanization; urban history and visualization of urban form.

# PRATT INSTITUTE
## School of Architecture

 For more information, visit http://petersons.to/prattarchitecture

## Programs of Study

The School of Architecture is dedicated to maintaining the connection between design theory and practice and to extending the range of knowledge necessary to an understanding of the built environment. The diversity of programs within the School and the accessibility of other programs within the Institute enable students to pursue a wide range of interests. Students can take electives in fine arts, film, digital arts, industrial design, furniture design, interior design, and photography as well as electives in advanced architectural theory, design, technology, and management. The School has many internationally recognized faculty members who bring to the graduate programs a strong theoretical base and the high standards of their professional work. The programs are distinguished by strong studio cultures and creative approaches to architectural design. Many special courses are offered in contemporary theoretical and critical issues, advanced computing and media, building technology, architectural history, and experimental structures. Students are exposed to the professional world through optional internship programs that place them in outstanding New York architectural offices, public agencies, and nonprofit design institutions, giving them firsthand work experience and credit towards their degree.

The School of Architecture offers a total of nine graduate programs. There are two graduate architecture programs: the first-professional accredited Master of Architecture (M.Arch.) and the post-professional Master of Architecture (M.S.Arch.). There are also seven Master of Science programs: Architecture and Urban Design, City and Regional Planning, Sustainable Environmental Systems, Facilities Management, Historic Preservation, Urban Placemaking and Management, and Real Estate Practice.

The three-year M.Arch. first-professional program is designed for students holding a four-year undergraduate program in any field, including architecture. Graduate courses and seminars are designed to familiarize students with all aspects of the discipline and practice of architecture. Design studios at Pratt find many of their coordinates within the rich territory of New York City. However, the program also reaches into areas worldwide and into other frames, such as global marketplaces, digital worlds, and historical, theoretical, and political networks. This program is fully accredited by NAAB. Students with a B.S. in Architecture or other non-professional degree should apply for this M.Arch. program. Applicants with four-year, B.Sc. in Architecture or B.Sc.Eng. in Architecture may qualify for advanced standing (shortening the time to two years). The post-professional M.S.Arch., a summer/fall/spring program, is for those who hold an accredited architecture degree or the equivalent. The program takes three semesters to complete. Students with significant professional experience can also apply for work credit, which reduces total credit-hour requirements. The post-professional M.S.Arch. allows intensive theoretical and technical engagement of architecture and the city and stresses research and experimentation concentrating on the relations between architecture and other urban forms, scales, and forces. Research is conducted primarily within the analytic and synthetic content of the design studio and culminates in a required thesis.

The Master of Science in Architecture and Urban Design program is intended for students who are interested in careers that enhance the growth and development of the built urban environments, the context for an urban laboratory. The 33-credit program requires 17 hours of design studio and research, with the balance of the credits in required courses in urban history, theory, infrastructure, and implementation and electives in law, transportation, housing, and preservation. The program is open to those with professional undergraduate degrees in architecture and is a summer/fall/spring program.

The six programs offered by Pratt's Programs for Sustainable Planning and Development (PSPD)—the M.S. in City and Regional Planning (CRP), the M.S. in Sustainable Environmental Systems (SES), the M.S. in Historic Preservation, the M.S. in Urban Placemaking and Management, the M.S. in Facilities Management (FM), and the M.S. in Real Estate Practice (REP)—emphasize planning and preservation practice rooted in the principles of sustainability, equity, and public participation.

The curricula are designed to build the professional skills and knowledge of students who desire to affect the built, natural, and social environments of the nation's cities and communities in positive ways. CRP and SES courses are offered in the evenings, enabling students to work full-time. The City and Regional planning program offers specializations in community development, environmental planning, physical planning, and preservation planning. The CRP program requires the completion of 60 credits, including the thesis or the Demonstration of Professional Competence course. The Urban Placemaking and Management program requires the completion of 40 credits. The curriculum of study includes Design and Infrastructure, Economics, Planning and Policy and Management. The SES program requires 40 credits of course work and includes a focus on sustainability. The REP program is 36 credits designed to be completed in three full-time terms of study in the afternoon and evenings.

Students with undergraduate degrees in architecture and engineering may have up to 9 credits waived in either the CRP or SES program.

PSPD's Historic Preservation program is a two-year graduate program leading to the M.S. in Historic Preservation. The program, designed primarily for full-time students and based at the Brooklyn campus, is a 44-credit sequence of courses that provides studies in community planning, history, interpretation, design, policy, and regulatory practice.

Recognizing that today's field of preservation requires more than curatorial management, the program fosters the knowledge preservationists must have in order to participate in policy-making to revitalize urban areas, suburban communities, and rural landscapes. With its urban focus, the program emphasizes hands-on work and makes extensive use of New York City's rich resources.

All five graduate programs in the PSPD maintain strong ties with Pratt's architecture and design programs and with the Pratt Center for Community Development, an innovative center for the practice of planning, design, and policy work that focuses on increasing quality of life and affecting social change in New York City's diverse communities.

The M.S. in Facilities Management program prepares individuals to assume leadership roles in corporations, institutions, and government. The degree requires the completion of 45 credits of course work and the 5-credit Demonstration of Professional Competence course, for a total of 50 credits. Students entering the program with prior professional experience or graduate work in related fields may be eligible for advanced standing; up to 12 credits may be waived. The facilities management program, accredited by IFMA, is offered at the Pratt Manhattan Center on an evening schedule, allowing maximum flexibility to combine full-time work with study and research. Students may take courses in any of the programs in PSPD.

## Research Facilities

The Pratt Library has grown with the Institute to house one of the finest collections of reference material on art, design, and architecture.

Pratt maintains numerous studios, shops, and technical facilities for work in all media, as well as state-of-the-art computer facilities. Pratt also has extensive gallery space for the exhibition of works by the student body, alumni, faculty members, and well-known architects and designers.

## Financial Aid

Financial aid awards are offered through a variety of institutional, state, and federally funded programs. These include Graduate Scholarships awarded by departments to incoming students on the basis of merit, as well as endowed and restricted scholarships for continuing students, and student employment. Assistantships are awarded on a competitive basis to continuing students in all departments. Special alumni-sponsored fellowships are also available.

## Cost of Study

Graduate tuition for 2017–18 is $ $30,834 per year (full-time 18 credits, $1,713 per credit). Student fees are $1,974 per semester. The cost of books and supplies varies widely, depending on the program in which the student is enrolled.

## Living and Housing Costs

Campus housing continues to be expanded to meet student needs and is available for single students on a first-come, first-served basis. Housing costs average $18,880 per academic year. There is a plentiful supply of moderately priced rentals in the immediate area and in adjacent neighborhoods for married students seeking housing as well as for those students choosing to reside off campus.

## Student Group

There are 366 students enrolled in Pratt's School of Architecture graduate programs; 57 percent are women. They come from all parts of the United States and the world. The graduate programs are noted for an exceptional placement ratio, with more than 85 percent of the graduating students finding employment before graduation.

## Location

Pratt Institute is located in the Clinton Hill section of Brooklyn, on a 25-acre park-like campus. Pratt's Manhattan campus houses the Institute's graduate arts and cultural management, communications design, design management, facilities management, and library and information science programs as well as offering courses in architecture, city and regional planning, creative arts therapy, and urban design.

## The Institute

A private, nonsectarian institute of higher education, Pratt Institute was founded in 1887 by the industrialist and philanthropist Charles Pratt. Today, Pratt educates 3,310 undergraduates and 1,349 graduate students for careers in art and design, architecture, and library and information science.

## Applying

The deadline for applications and all supporting materials, including portfolio, is January 5. Applicants should complete the application process online. Early submission of applications with all necessary credentials is highly desirable. Applications received after these dates are considered if openings exist in a particular program. For applicants who intend to file for financial aid, the FAFSA should be filed by March 1 for fall entrance and by October 1 for spring entrance.

## Correspondence and Information

Graduate Admissions Office
Pratt Institute
200 Willoughby Avenue
Brooklyn, New York 11205
Phone: 718-636-3514
      800-331-0834 (toll-free outside New York State)
Fax: 718-399-4242
E-mail: admissions@pratt.edu
Website: http://www.pratt.edu

## THE FACULTY

Thomas Hanrahan, Dean; M.Arch., Harvard; AIA, NCARB.

### Architecture

David Erdman, Chair.
Philip Parker, Assistant Chair, Adjunct Associate Professor; M.Arch., Yale.

Nick Agneta, Adjunct Associate Professor; B.Arch., Cooper Union; AIA.
Carlos Arnaiz, Adjunct Assistant Professor; M.Arch., Harvard.
Kutan Ayata, Adjunct Assistant Professor; M.Arch., Princeton.
Alexandra Barker, Adjunct Assistant Professor; M.Arch., Harvard.
Stephanie Bayard, Adjunct Assistant Professor; M.S., Columbia.
Meta Brunzema, Adjunct Associate Professor; M.Arch., Columbia.
Robert Cervellione, Visiting Instructor; M.Arch., Pratt.
Steven J. Chang, Adjunct Assistant Professor; B.Arch., Berkeley; AIA.
Cristobal Correa, Assistant Professor; M.S.C.E., MIT.
Theo David, Professor; M.Arch., Yale.
Manuel DeLanda, Adjunct Professor; B.F.A., School of Visual Arts.
Deborah Gans, Professor; M.Arch., Princeton.
James Garrison, Adjunct Associate Professor; B.Arch., Syracuse.
Erik Ghenoiu, Adjunct Associate Professor; Ph.D., Harvard.
Jose Gonzalez, Visiting Assistant Professor; M.S., Columbia.
Catherine Ingraham, Professor; Ph.D., Johns Hopkins.

## SECTION 2: ARCHITECTURE

### Pratt Institute

Hina Jamelle, Visiting Assistant Professor; M.Arch., Michigan.
Robert Kearns, Visiting Assistant Professor; M.A.E., Penn State.
Karel Klein, Adjunct Associate Professor; M.Arch., Columbia.
Carisima Koenig, Visiting Instructor; M.Arch., Iowa State.
Mehmet Ferda Kolatan, Visiting Assistant Professor; M.S.A.A.D., Columbia.
Sulan Kolatan, Adjunct Professor; M.S.Arch., Columbia.
Craig Konyk, Adjunct Associate Professor; M.Arch., Virginia.
Christopher Kroner, Adjunct Assistant Professor; M.Arch., Columbia.
Sameer Kumar, Adjunct Professor; M.Arch., Pennsylvania.
Sanford Kwinter, Professor, Ph.D., Columbia.
Thomas Leeser, Associate Professor.
Carla Leitao, Adjunct Assistant Professor; M.S.AAD., Columbia.
John Lobell, Professor; M.Arch., Pennsylvania.
Ariane Lourie-Harrison, Adjunct Associate Professor, Ph.D., NYU.
Peter Macapia, Adjunct Assistant Professor; Ph.D., Columbia.
William MacDonald, Professor; M.S.Arch, Columbia.
Radhi Majmuder, Adjunct Assistant Professor; M.S., Columbia.
Rosalinda Malibiran, Visiting Assistant Professor; M.Arch., Columbia.
Elliott Maltby, Adjunct Associate Professor; M.L.A., Berkeley.
Deborah McGuinness, Visiting Associate Professor, B.S., Villanova.
Benjamin Martinson, Visiting Instructor; M.Arch., Pratt.
Bruce Nichol, Visiting Professor, Graduate Diploma, Architecture,
     Oxford Brookes University; ARB, RIBA.
Signe Nielsen, Adjunct Professor; B.S., Pratt.
Brian Ringley, Visiting Assistant Professor; M.Arch., Cincinnati.
David Ruy, Associate Professor; M.Arch., Columbia.
Richard Scherr, Director, Facilities Planning; M.S.Arch., Columbia.
Erich Schoenenberger, Adjunct Associate Professor; M.S.AAD., Columbia.
Paul Segal, Adjunct Professor; M.F.A., Princeton; FAIA.
Benjamin Shepherd, Adjunct Associate Professor; M.A., Yale.
Maria Sieira, Adjunct Assistant Instructor; M.Arch., Pennsylvania.
Henry Smith-Miller, Adjunct Professor; M.Arch., Pennsylvania.
Roland Snooks, Adjunct Assistant Professor; M.S.AAD., Columbia.
Michael Szivos, Visiting Assistant Professor; M.S.AAD., Columbia.
Jeffrey Taras, Visiting Instructor; M.Arch., Columbia.
Maria Ludovica Tramontin, Adjunct Assistant Professor; Ph.D., Cagliari (Italy).
Nanako Umemoto-Reiser, Adjunct Professor; B.Arch., Cooper Union.
Jason Vigneri-Beane, Adjunct Associate Professor; M.Arch., Iowa State.
John Christopher Whitelaw, Visiting Instructor; M.Arch., Columbia.

### Urban Design
David Erdman, Chair.
Philip Parker, Assistant Chair; M.Arch., Yale.

Carlos Arnaiz, Adjunct Assistant Professor; M.Arch., Harvard.
Stephanie Bayard, Adjunct Assistant Professor; M.S.AAD, Columbia.
Meta Brunzema, Adjunct Associate Professor; M.Arch., Columbia.
Jose Gonzales, Visiting Assistant Professor; M.S.AAD., Columbia.
Mehmet Ferda Kolatan, Visiting Assistant Professor; M.S.AAD., Columbia.
Sulan Kolatan, Adjunct Professor; M.S.Arch., Columbia.
Carla Leitao, Adjunct Associate Professor; M.S.AAD., Columbia.
William MacDonald, Professor, M.S. Arch, Columbia.
Elliot Maltby, Adjunct Associate Professor; M.L.A., Berkeley.
Benjamin Martinson, Visiting Instructor; M.Arch., Pratt.
Signe Nielsen, Adjunct Professor; B.S., Pratt.
David Ruy, Associate Professor; M.Arch., Columbia.
Erich Schoenenberger, Visiting Instructor; M.S.AAD., Columbia.
Nanako Umemoto-Reiser, Adjunct Professor; B.Arch., Cooper Union.

### Planning and the Environment (City and Regional Planning, Sustainable Environmental Systems, Urban Placemaking and Management)
Eve Baron, Chair, Ph.D. Rutgers.
David Burney, Academic Coordinator of Urban Placemaking and Management,
     Associate Professor; M.S., London.
Jaime Stein, Academic Coordinator, Sustainable Environmental Systems; M.S., Pratt.

Bridget Anderson, Visiting Assistant Professor; M.P.A., Columbia.
Alec Appelbaum, Visiting Assistant Professor; M.B.A., Yale.
Caron Atlas, Visiting Assistant Professor; M.A., Chicago.
Eddie Bautista, Visiting Assistant Professor; M.S.C.R.P., Pratt.
Jenifer Becker, Visiting Assistant Professor; M.S., Pratt.
Bethany Bingham, Visiting Assistant Professor, M.S., Pratt.
Michael Bobker, Visiting Assistant Professor; M.S., NYIT.
Carlton Brown, Visiting Assistant Professor; B.Arch., Princeton.
Joan Byron, Visiting Assistant Professor; B.Arch., Pratt.
Damon Chaky, Assistant Professor; Ph.D., Rensselaer Polytechnic Institute.
Carter Craft, Visiting Assistant Professor; M.U.P., NYU.
Steve Davies, Professor, M.Arch, California–Berkeley.
Mike Flynn, Visiting Assistant Professor; M.S.C.R.P., Pratt.
Michael Freedman-Schnapp, Visiting Assistant Professor; M.S.U.P., NYU.
Adam Friedman, Visiting Assistant Professor; J.D., Yeshiva.
Mindy Fullilove, Visiting Assistant Professor; M.D., Columbia.
Christine Gaspar, Adjunct Associate Professor; M.Arch, M.C.P., MIT.
Moses Gates, Visiting Assistant Professor; M.U.P., Hunter College.
Ben Gibberd, Visiting Assistant Professor; M.A., Edinburgh.
Ingrid Haftel, Visiting Assistant Professor; M.A., Chicago.
Eva Hanhardt, Visiting Assistant Professor; M.U.P., NYU.
Will Hart, Visiting Assistant Professor; M.L.A., Georgia.
Daniel Hernandez, Visiting Assistant Professor; M.Arch., UCLA.
George Jacquemart, Visiting Assistant Professor; M.S.U.P., Stanford; PE.
Tom Jost, Visiting Assistant Professor; M.U.D., Pratt.
David Kallick, Visiting Assistant Professor; B.A., Yale.
Gillian Kaye, Visiting Assistant Professor; B.A., Columbia.
Gavin Kearney, Visiting Assistant Professor; J.D., Minnesota.
Sarah Kogel-Smucker, Visiting Assistant Professor; J.D., Boston College.
Raj Kottamasu, Visiting Assistant Professor; M.C.P. with Urban Design Certificate, MIT.
Tanu Kumar, Visiting Assistant Professor; M.S., Cornell.
Frank Lang, Visiting Assistant Professor; M.Arch., Pennsylvania; RA.
Matthew Lister, Visiting Assistant Professor.
Setha Low, Visiting Assistant Professor; Ph.D., Berkeley.
Alan Mallach, Visiting Assistant Professor; B.A., Yale.
Elliott Maltby, Adjunct Associate Professor; M.L.A., Berkeley.
Paul Mankiewicz, Visiting Associate Professor; Ph.D., CUNY.
Michael Marella, Visiting Assistant Professor; M.C.P. with Urban Design Certificate, MIT.
Jonathan Martin, Associate Professor; Ph.D., Cornell.
Jonathan Marvel, Visiting Assistant Professor; M.Arch., Harvard, FAIA.
William Menking, Professor; M.S.C.R.P., Pratt.
Jon Meyers, Visiting Assistnat Professor; M.B.A., Columbia.

Norman Mintz, Visiting Associate Professor; M.S., Columbia.
Mariana Mogilevich, Visiting Assistant Professor; Ph.D., Harvard.
Eliza Montgomery, Visiting Assistant Professor; AIA.
Gita Nandan, Visiting Assistant Professor; M.Arch., Berkeley.
Mercedes Narciso, Adjunct Associate Professor; M.S.C.R.P., Pratt.
Signe Nielsen, Adjunct Professor; B.L.Arch., CUNY, City College.
Cynthia Kikitin, Visiting Assistant Professor; M.A., NYU.
Larisa Ortiz Pu-Folkes, Visiting Assistant Professor; M.S., Massachusetts.
Juan Camilo Osorio, Visiting Assistant Professor; M.S., Massachusetts.
Steven Romalewski, Visiting Assistant Professor; M.S., Columbia.
Carolyn Schaeberle, Visiting Assistant Professor; M.S.I.D., Pratt.
David Seiter, Visiting Assistant Professor; M.L.A., Pennsylvania.
John Shapiro, Associate Professor; M.S.C.R.P., Pratt; AICP.
Ronald Shiffman, Professor; M.S.C.R.P., Pratt; FAICP, FAIA.
Mitchell Siver, Professor, M.S. Hunter College.
Toby Snyder, Visiting Assistant Professor; M.Arch., Rhode Island School of Design.
Ira Stern, Visiting Assistant Professor; M.S.C.R.P., Pratt.
Gelvin Stevenson, Visiting Associate Professor; Ph.D., Washington (St. Louis).
Samara Swanston, Visiting Assistant Professor; J.D., St. John's (New York).
Lacey Tauber, Visiting Assistant Professor; M.S., Pratt.
Adia Ware, Visiting Assistant Professor, M.S., Pratt.
Meg Walker, Visiting Assistant Professor; M.Arch., Columbia.
Ben Wellington, Visiting Assistant Professor; Ph.D., NYU.
Barika Williams, Visiting Assistant Professor; M.C.P., MIT.
Don Weinreich, Visiting Assistant Professor; FAIA, LEED AP.
Ayse Yonder, Professor; Ph.D., Berkeley.

### Historic Preservation
Nadya Nenadich, Adjunct Associate Professor, Academic Coordinator, Graduate Center for
     Planning; Ph.D., Polytechnic University of Cataluna.

Lisa Ackerman, Visiting Assistant Professor; M.B.A., NYU.
Beth Bingham, Visiting Assistant Professor; M.S., Pratt.
Patrick Ciccone, Visiting Assistant Professor; M.S., Columbia.
Carol Clark, Visiting Associate Professor; M.S., Columbia.
Pat Fisher-Olsen, Visiting Assistant Professor; M.S., Pratt.
Norman Mintz, Visiting Associate Professor, M.S. Columbia.
Christopher Neville, Visiting Assistant Professor; M.S., Columbia.
Laura Klar Phillips, Visiting Assistant Professor.
Theodore Prudon, Adjunct Professor; Ph.D., Columbia; FAIA.
Lacey Tauber, Visiting Assistant Professor; M.S., Pratt.
Andrew Wasserman, Adjunct Associate Professor.
Vicki Weiner, Adjunct Associate Professor; M.S., Columbia.
Kevin Wolfe, Visiting Assistant Professor; M.Arch., Columbia.

### Facilities Management and Real Estate Practice
Regina Ford Cahill, Chair, Associate Professor; M.S., Pratt.

Lennart Andersson, Visiting Assistant Professor; M.Arch., Savannah College of Art and Design.
Matthias Ebinger, Visiting Assistant Professor; M.S., NYU.
William Henry, Visiting Assistant Professor; B.Arch., NYU.
Stephen LoGrasso, Visiting Assistant Professor; B.S., NYIT.
Harriet Markis, Adjunct Associate Professor; M.Eng., Cornell.
Mary J. Matthews, Professor Emerita; M.S., Boston College.
Gerald F. McGowan, Visiting Associate Professor; M.B.A., NYU.
Martin McManus, Visiting Assistant Professor; B.B.A., Pace.
Russell Olson, Visiting Assistant Professor; M.S., Pratt.
John Osborn, Visiting Associate Professor; J.D., South Carolina.
Edward Re, Adjunct Associate Professor; M.S., Pratt.
Norman Rosenfeld, Adjunct Associate Professor; B.Arch., Pratt.
Audrey L. Schultz, Associate Professor; Ph.D., Salford; FMP, ASC, CIB.
Marjorie St. Ellin, Visiting Assistant Professor; B.S., Pratt.
Mira Tsymuk, Visiting Assistant Professor; M.A., CUNY, Hunter.

© 2017 Bob Handelman

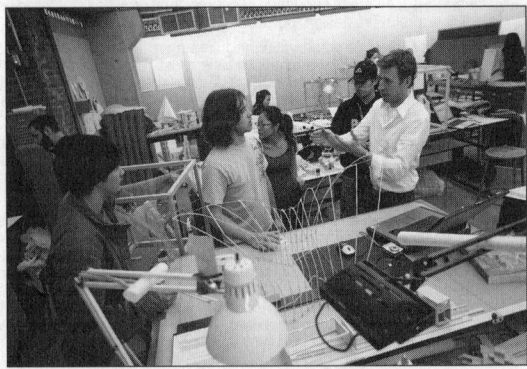

© 2017 Bob Handelman

# THE SCHOOL OF ARCHITECTURE AT TALIESIN
## *Master of Architecture Program*

 For more information, visit http://petersons.to/franklloydwrightarchitecture

## Programs of Study

Founded by Frank Lloyd Wright in 1932 as an alternative to traditional architectural education, the School of Architecture at Taliesin today provides a professional Master of Architecture (M.Arch.) degree in an intensive, in-residence academic environment. The program is designed for self-motivated students who thrive in a multifaceted environment focusing on rigorous design, critical thinking, exploration, and hands-on learning.

The Master of Architecture (M.Arch.) program prepares students in advanced design, professional practice, and hands-on application while immersing them in the communities Wright designed at Taliesin in Spring Green, Wisconsin, and Taliesin West in Scottsdale, Arizona.

The School's small scale facilitates an individualized educational experience and fosters a close and dynamic relationship between students, faculty, and staff. Students explore the discipline through work in the design studio, through architectural practice, in seminars with noted scholars, and on design-build projects.

The Taliesin community empowers students to be leaders within the framework of residence life and provides a rich set of experiences outside the architectural discipline. Students host key events, create design identities for campus initiatives, help prepare meals, garden in on-campus gardens, perform music, and exhibit design projects to invited audiences. More information is available at http://www.taliesin.edu/program.html.

## Philosophy

Before new apprentices would arrive, Frank Lloyd Wright would famously tell them to bring four things: a drafting pencil, a hammer, a sleeping bag, and a tuxedo. The logic behind these requirements remains the same today: to learn by drawing, by making, by being there, and by being part of a civilized conversation about the past, present, and future of our culture. Students learn how to embrace and celebrate diverse cultures and customs while also developing the art and methods they need to explain their designs and converse with others. Once a month, students participate in Taliesin Evenings, which fill the campus with music, dance, and dialogue with members of the community. Students thus have the opportunity to meet with faculty and visitors both for formal education

and for cultural and social events, participating in everything from making music to doing the dishes.

The education at Taliesin is immersive and offers the opportunity to work side by side with professors, participating in hands-on projects all day and into the evening. The School of Architecture at Taliesin also embodies Wright's concepts of organic architecture; to build with the land rather than just upon it. The design process unfolds out of existing cultural and physical condition, materials, and landscapes into well-crafted frameworks for human activities.

## Curriculum

The mission of the School of Architecture at Taliesin is to be a place where students learn how to make a human-made environment that is more sustainable, open, and beautiful. The School's curriculum is based on the notion of learning by doing and experience through experimentation. The School trains the next generation of architects to be designers, thinkers, and visionaries, but also fully formed citizens and human beings. All of the core faculty members are practicing architects, and thus bring to the studio not only the principles and methodology of architecture, but also real-world experience.

The Core Curriculum comprises three phases: foundation, exploration, and synthesis. Studios, workshops, and classes designated as Core are required activities, and occur at intervals throughout the student's course of study. The Core Curriculum includes design studios, classes, architectural practice activities, research, and shelter construction and preservation projects. Students are required to attend all Core offerings, which may be complimented with independent study as approved by faculty. Core requirements may be adjusted based on evaluation of prior work.

## Living and Self-Discovery

Continuing a tradition begun in 1937, the School operates seasonally at two locations. From mid-October through mid-May, the School is in session at Taliesin West in Scottsdale, Arizona. Mid-May through mid-October is spent at Taliesin in Spring Green, Wisconsin. The Taliesin educational experience is closely linked to its two architecturally stunning campuses and is fueled by the year-round educational community. This intense and rewarding residential experience is shaped by two forces that bear essential relevance on the experience of architecture: the force of the landscape as captured in the genius loci (spirit of place) of the two campuses, and the force of self-discovery in the context of a living culture of architecture. The migration travels provide opportunities to visit places of interest, architectural sites, and experience the vast landscapes between Arizona and Wisconsin.

Taliesin students live on-campus and participate in the life of the academic community. Housing is available in rooms within the historic campus and in the experimental dwellings designed by previous students built in the landscape surrounding the campus core. In keeping with Taliesin tradition, students are provided the opportunity to design, build, and live in their own experimental structures as a component of their learning program and personal portfolio.

The community component of the program is based on Wright's strongly-held belief that, "a great architect is not made by way of a brain nearly so much as he is made by way of a cultivated, enriched heart." Community involvement at Taliesin provides opportunities for students to explore the social and cultural contexts of architecture and to integrate and apply the content, philosophies, and disciplines of all learning through the experience and social interaction of daily living and community maintenance.

Through participation in community, students learn to apply critical thinking and creative problem solving in challenging situations that arise as part of projects of any size; and they learn to resolve the human problems that occur whenever people attempt to work together cooperatively. Students come from a wide variety of cultural and socioeconomic backgrounds, yet are expected to leave Taliesin prepared to function as professionals. Community participation, by providing students with opportunities to develop social skills, conversational skills, leadership and collaborative skills, and cultural awareness, prepares them to enter the architectural profession with the poise and confidence needed to interact with clients of all kinds.

With nearly 90 percent of all graduates actively working in the architectural field, the School of Architecture at Taliesin's practice of discovery and invention builds architects who can thrive within the context of the rapidly changing world.

## Cost of Study

The cost of attendance is $42,525 annually and covers tuition, room/board, food, accident insurance, and facility fee. There are scholarships and financial aid available for those who qualify.

## Correspondence and Information

Director of Admissions
The School of Architecture at Taliesin
Taliesin West
P.O. Box 4430
Scottsdale, Arizona 85261-4430
United States
Phone: 480-627-5345
E-mail: admissions@taliesin.edu
Website: http://www.taliesin.edu

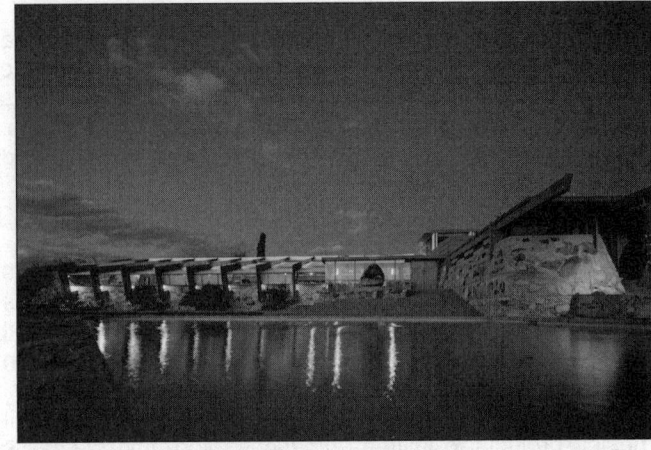

The historic studio at Taliesin West.

# SOUTHERN CALIFORNIA INSTITUTE OF ARCHITECTURE
*Master of Architecture Programs*

SCI-Arc

## Programs of Study

The Master of Architecture (M.Arch.) programs at Southern California Institute of Architecture (SCI-Arc) seek to advance the next generation of the architectural discipline. They emphasize formal exploration, innovation in architectural practice, contemporary experimentation, speculation, and creative freedom. The programs also give students the opportunity to work closely with expert faculty mentors and top consultants in the field.

The Southern California Institute of Architecture has received national recognition for excellence in architectural education. The M.Arch. programs have accreditation from the National Architectural Accrediting Board (NAAB). DesignIntelligence ranked the Institute in more categories on its list of America's Top Architectural Schools 2017 than any other school in the nation: #3 for Computer Applications, #3 for Top Regional Graduate Program in the West, #4 for Design Skills, and #4 for Graduate Programs Most Admired by Deans and Chairs.

**M.Arch. 1 Program:** This three-year (seven terms) program of rigorous course work is designed for individuals with bachelor's degrees in any field. Its curriculum consists of a core sequence, advanced studios, seminars, and a thesis.

The four semesters of core courses provide a framework for the field as well as a strong foundation for experimentation and critical inquiry. Each semester includes a design studio that links with courses in applied studies, visual studies, and history and theory. This provides students with an in-depth understanding of the relationship between architecture, representation, social change, and technology. With each semester, students strengthen their ability to address multifaceted architectural issues while testing their design and intellectual principles.

After completing the core sequence, students choose from an assortment of advanced studios and seminars. They explore the latest technological innovations, develop new approaches to design analysis, and use applied research to create new ideas and methods. Their studies culminate with an extensively researched architectural thesis that's presented at a public exhibition.

**M.Arch. 2 Program:** This two-year (five-terms) program was created for individuals with four-year degrees in architecture (or the equivalent). Emphasizing the most current developments in design fabrication, the M.Arch 2 program. It enables students to review and build upon knowledge acquired during their undergraduate studies and introduces them to advanced critical viewpoints about contemporary architectural issues. It also allows students to examine the complex and changing relationships between architecture and cultural, economic, political, and social change.

The program consists of a two-term core sequence with a studio emphasis on computational design and continues with one year of vertical studios and elective seminars before culminating with a thoroughly researched thesis that's presented at a public exhibition.

## Facilities

Within its quarter-mile-long campus, SCI-Arc offers students an integrated suite of resources that support academic progress and experimentation.

The Magic Box, SCI-Arc's technologically transformative digital fabrication lab, expands the school's experimental approach to design. The SCI-Arc Robot House is a platform for experimentation and speculation on the future of architecture, situated conceptually and physically between studio and shop, academy and industry.

SCI-Arc's 6,000-square-foot fabrication shop is equipped with a wide array of metal and woodworking machinery and tools, supporting hands-on experimentation with materials and construction. The SCI-Arc Art and Architecture Supply Store serves both the student body and the downtown community, offering competitive prices for architecture and art supplies. The Print Center at SCI-Arc provides students and faculty with access to a variety of regular and large-format high-resolution color plotters and printers at a fraction of typical service center prices.

SCI-Arc also has several galleries, making it the only cultural institution in Los Angeles committed to exhibiting experimental projects by contemporary architects. The Kappe Library is the largest academic library in Southern California focused on architecture, and welcomes both students and outside architectural researchers.

## Financial Aid

SCI-Arc works with students to find the right means to fund their education. Available financial aid options include Federal Pell Grants, Federal Supplemental Educational Opportunity Grants (FSEOG), and Federal Education Loans. State aid is available for California students. A limited number of merit- and need-based scholarships are also available for both U.S. and international students.

It is recommended that all eligible students file the Free Application for Federal Student Aid (FAFSA) regardless of income.

## Cost of Study

For the 2017–18 academic year, tuition and fees for Master of Architecture programs total $21,900 per semester. The cost of course supplies and books is estimated at $3,050 per semester.

## Living and Housing Costs

SCI-Arc does not provide on-campus housing. Most students live in apartments or lofts close to the campus in the Arts District of downtown Los Angeles, or in surrounding communities, many accessible by bike or public transportation. Students live in the Arts District itself or the nearby communities of Little Tokyo, Echo Park, Chinatown, Silver Lake, and Koreatown. Each community has a distinctive flavor that can best be understood by visiting. Some have easily accessible public transportation, others may require a vehicle. While finding housing in any new city can be challenging, most SCI-Arc students are able to find suitable accommodations within a week or two. Room and board for an academic year is estimated at $5,500 per semester.

## Student Outcomes

M.Arch. students graduate prepared to create structures and spaces that improve quality of life and change how humans interact with one other and their environments. Upon graduation, they enter a promising job market. According to the US Bureau of Labor Statistics, employment of architects is expected to grow 7 percent from 2014 to 2024. This is as fast as the average for all occupations.

## Location

The Institute is located in the historic Santa Fe Freight Depot in the Arts District of Los Angeles (LA), California in the western region of the United States. Its vibrant campus includes design studios and galleries as well as a fabrication lab, fabrication shop, store, library, and print center. Located in downtown LA, the Arts District offers a variety of galleries, shops, restaurants, coffee shops, and nightlife venues. Attractions include

## SECTION 2: ARCHITECTURE

### Southern California Institute of Architecture

A+D Museum, Alchemy Works, Blacktop Coffee, Hauser Wirth & Schimmel, and Hennessey + Ingalls.

### The Institute

Founded in 1972, Southern California Institute of Architecture is one the few independent architecture schools in the nation. It offers undergraduate, graduate, and post-graduate programs in architecture, architectural technologies, design theory and pedagogy, fiction and entertainment, and urban design.

SCI-Arc's mission is to reimagine the very edges of architecture, educating architects to engage, speculate, and innovate; to examine everything about the built environment, from design and materials to culture and experience; to ask provocative questions that provoke new thinking and prompt new theoretical constructs; to be international leaders in creating the future of architecture; and to create designs that change how people interact with each other and their environment.

The purpose of SCI-Arc is to assist students, faculty, staff, and the public in the exploration of architectural ideas and issues. Its organization is centered on the idea of the practicing architect as educator, inflecting top-down direction with vigorous open participation and strong individual autonomy. For more than forty years, SCI-Arc has maintained a reputation of risk and excellence.

### Faculty

SCI-Arc faculty members are scholars and practitioners from around the world. They're actively involved with modern architectural production and discourse.

Argentine-born Architect Maxi Spina is the principal of the international design firm, Maxi Spina Architecture, which is based in Los Angeles. His firm's work has been extensively exhibited and published. Furthermore, it has received honors from *Architect Magazine*, the Association of Collegiate Schools of Architecture (ACSA), Chicago Athenaeum, and the Los Angeles Chapter of the American Institute of Architects (AIA-LA).

Architect David Ross is the principal of DRA, a Los Angeles-based architecture studio. For the past 15 years, he has worked with several top architects like Diller + Scofidio and Steven Holl Architects.

Information about other faculty members can be found at https://sciarc. edu/institution/people/faculty.

SCI-Arc also provides lectures and symposia that enhance classroom and hands-on learning. Guest lecturers include prominent architects, artists, curators, historians, professors, writers, and other experts. Recent and upcoming symposia include Drawing Conclusions Symposium, Architecture in the Age of Digital Media, and SCI-Arc Tokyo Symposium.

### Applying

SCI-Arc receives applications from students all over the United States and around the world. SCI-Arc is committed to shaping student experiences as they pursue undergraduate, graduate, and postgraduate degrees. Applications for all graduate and postgraduate programs are accepted for the fall semester only. Successful applicants generally demonstrate a strong academic record, compelling letters of recommendation, and a portfolio of distinct work.

Applicants need to complete the online application form and submit all additional required application materials through SlideRoom. Required application materials include: online application form, $85 nonrefundable application fee, portfolio of creative work, personal statement, resume, academic transcripts, three letters of recommendation, GRE test scores, and TOEFL/IELTS test scores (for international applicants only).

Graduate applicants will be notified of their admission status between the months of March and April. Students who accept SCI-Arc's offer of admission are required to submit a nonrefundable deposit, which reserves their place in the entering class.

Applicants placed on the waiting list will be notified on a rolling basis as positions become available in the entering class.

Students accepted to SCI-Arc may defer their acceptance for up to one academic year.

### Correspondence and Information

Southern California Institute of Architecture
960 East 3rd Street
Los Angeles, California 90013
United States
Phone: 213-613-2200
E-mail: admissions@sciarc.edu
Website: https://sciarc.edu

# Section 3
# Art and Art History

This section contains a directory of institutions offering graduate work in art and art history, followed by in-depth entries submitted by institutions that chose to prepare detailed program descriptions. Additional information about programs listed in the directory but not augmented by an in-depth entry may be obtained by writing directly to the dean of a graduate school or chair of a department at the address given in the directory.

For programs offering related work, see also in this book *Applied Arts and Design; Architecture; Area and Cultural Studies; Film, Television, and Video; Performing Arts;* and *Sociology, Anthropology, and Archaeology.* In another guide in this series:

**Graduate Programs in Business, Education, Information Studies, Law & Social Work**
See *Subject Areas (Art Education)*

## CONTENTS

### Program Directories

### Displays and Close-Ups

### See also:

# Art/Fine Arts

**Academy of Art University,** Graduate Programs, School of Fine Art, San Francisco, CA 94105-3410. Offers figurative painting (MFA). *Accreditation:* NASAD. *Program availability:* Part-time, 100% online. *Faculty:* 18 full-time (8 women), 38 part-time/adjunct (17 women). *Students:* 72 full-time (49 women), 162 part-time (123 women); includes 43 minority (9 Black or African American, non-Hispanic/Latino; 2 American Indian or Alaska Native, non-Hispanic/Latino; 11 Asian, non-Hispanic/Latino; 15 Hispanic/Latino; 2 Native Hawaiian or other Pacific Islander, non-Hispanic/Latino; 4 Two or more races, non-Hispanic/Latino), 53 international. Average age 42. 64 applicants, 100% accepted, 34 enrolled. In 2016, 60 master's awarded. *Degree requirements:* For master's, final review. *Entrance requirements:* For master's, statement of intent; resume; portfolio/reel; official college transcripts. *Application deadline:* Applications are processed on a rolling basis. Application fee: $50. Electronic applications accepted. *Expenses: Tuition:* Part-time $982 per unit. *Financial support:* Career-related internships or fieldwork, Federal Work-Study, and scholarships/grants available. Financial award application deadline: 8/10; financial award applicants required to submit FAFSA. *Unit head:* 800-544-ARTS, E-mail: info@academyart.edu. *Application contact:* 800-544-ARTS, E-mail: info@academyart.edu.
Website: http://www.academyart.edu/fine-art-school/index.html

**Academy of Art University,** Graduate Programs, School of Jewelry and Metal Arts, San Francisco, CA 94105-3410. Offers MA, MFA. *Program availability:* Part-time, 100% online. *Faculty:* 2 full-time (both women), 9 part-time/adjunct (5 women). *Students:* 36 full-time (30 women), 8 part-time (all women); includes 5 minority (1 Black or African American, non-Hispanic/Latino; 3 Asian, non-Hispanic/Latino; 1 Hispanic/Latino), 31 international. Average age 30. 14 applicants, 100% accepted, 12 enrolled. In 2016, 8 master's awarded. *Degree requirements:* For master's, final review. *Entrance requirements:* For master's, statement of intent; resume; portfolio/reel; official college transcripts. *Application deadline:* Applications are processed on a rolling basis. Application fee: $50. Electronic applications accepted. *Expenses: Tuition:* Part-time $982 per unit. *Financial support:* Career-related internships or fieldwork, Federal Work-Study, and scholarships/grants available. Financial award application deadline: 8/10; financial award applicants required to submit FAFSA. *Unit head:* 800-544-ARTS, E-mail: info@academyart.edu. *Application contact:* 800-544-ARTS, E-mail: info@academyart.edu.
Website: http://www.academyart.edu/jewelry-and-metal-arts-school/

**Adams State University,** The Graduate School, Department of Art, Alamosa, CO 81101. Offers MA. *Program availability:* Part-time. *Degree requirements:* For master's, thesis, departmental qualifying exam. *Entrance requirements:* For master's, GRE General Test or MAT, minimum undergraduate GPA of 2.75.

**Adelphi University,** College of Arts and Sciences, Department of Art and Art History, Garden City, NY 11530-0701. Offers studio art (MA). *Program availability:* Part-time. *Entrance requirements:* For master's, essay, portfolio, 2 letters of recommendation. Additional exam requirements/recommendations for international students: Required—TOEFL (minimum score 550 paper-based; 80 iBT), IELTS (minimum score 6.5). *Application deadline:* For fall admission, 5/1 for international students; for spring admission, 12/1 for international students. Applications are processed on a rolling basis. Application fee: $50. Electronic applications accepted. *Expenses:* Contact institution. *Financial support:* Research assistantships with full and partial tuition reimbursements, teaching assistantships, career-related internships or fieldwork, institutionally sponsored loans, scholarships/grants, traineeships, and unspecified assistantships available. Support available to part-time students. Financial award application deadline: 2/15; financial award applicants required to submit FAFSA. *Unit head:* David Hornung, Chairperson, 516-877-4458, E-mail: hornung@adelphi.edu. *Application contact:* Christine Murphy, Director of Admissions, 516-877-3050, Fax: 516-877-3039, E-mail: graduateadmissions@adelphi.edu.
Website: http://academics.adelphi.edu/artsci/art/

**Alfred University,** Graduate School, College of Ceramics, Inamori School of Engineering, Alfred, NY 14802. Offers biomaterials engineering (MS); ceramic engineering (MS, PhD); electrical engineering (MS); glass science (MS, PhD); materials science and engineering (MS, PhD); mechanical engineering (MS). *Program availability:* Part-time. *Faculty:* 18 full-time (1 woman). *Students:* 26 full-time (6 women), 16 part-time (4 women); includes 1 minority (Hispanic/Latino), 12 international. Average age 27. 14 applicants, 79% accepted, 10 enrolled. In 2016, 13 master's, 5 doctorates awarded. *Degree requirements:* For master's, thesis; for doctorate, thesis/dissertation. *Entrance requirements:* Additional exam requirements/recommendations for international students: Required—TOEFL (minimum score 590 paper-based; 90 iBT), IELTS (minimum score 6.5). *Application deadline:* For fall admission, 3/1 priority date for domestic students, 3/15 for international students; for spring admission, 10/1 priority date for domestic students, 10/1 for international students. Applications are processed on a rolling basis. Application fee: $60. Electronic applications accepted. *Expenses:* Contact institution. *Financial support:* Fellowships with full tuition reimbursements, research assistantships with full tuition reimbursements, teaching assistantships with full tuition reimbursements, tuition waivers (full and partial), and unspecified assistantships available. Financial award application deadline: 8/1; financial award applicants required to submit FAFSA. *Faculty research:* X-ray diffraction, biomaterials and polymers, thin-film processing, electronic and optical ceramics, solid-state chemistry. *Unit head:* Dr. Alistair N. Cormack, Dean, 607-871-2422, E-mail: cormack@alfred.edu. *Application contact:* Sara Love, Coordinator of Graduate Admissions, 607-871-2115, Fax: 607-871-2198, E-mail: gradinquiry@alfred.edu.
Website: http://engineering.alfred.edu/grad/

**Alfred University,** Graduate School, College of Ceramics, School of Art and Design, Alfred, NY 14802. Offers ceramic art (MFA); electronic integrated arts (MFA); painting (MFA); sculpture/dimensional studies (MFA). *Accreditation:* NASAD. *Faculty:* 19 full-time (11 women), 14 part-time/adjunct (9 women). *Students:* 34 full-time (18 women); includes 2 minority (1 Asian, non-Hispanic/Latino; 1 Hispanic/Latino), 10 international. Average age 28. 32 applicants, 66% accepted, 19 enrolled. In 2016, 15 master's awarded. *Degree requirements:* For master's, thesis, exhibit. *Entrance requirements:* For master's, portfolio. Additional exam requirements/recommendations for international students: Required—TOEFL (minimum score 550 paper-based), IELTS (minimum score 6). *Application deadline:* For fall admission, 1/15 for domestic and international students. Application fee: $60. Electronic applications accepted. *Expenses:* Contact institution. *Financial support:* In 2016–17, 34 students received support. Teaching assistantships with full tuition reimbursements available and tuition waivers (full) available. Financial award application deadline: 8/1; financial award applicants required to submit FAFSA. *Faculty research:* Ceramic art, sculpture, glass art, new media, time-based media. *Unit head:* Gerar Edizel, Interim Dean, 607-871-2412, E-mail: fedizel@alfred.edu. *Application contact:* Sara Love, Coordinator of Graduate

Admissions, 607-871-2115, Fax: 607-871-2198, E-mail: gradinquiry@alfred.edu.
Website: http://art.alfred.edu/graduate/

**Anna Maria College,** Graduate Division, Program in Education, Paxton, MA 01612. Offers early childhood education (M Ed); education (CAGS); elementary education (M Ed); English language arts (M Ed); visual arts (M Ed). *Program availability:* Part-time, evening/weekend. *Entrance requirements:* For master's, bachelor's degree in liberal arts or sciences, minimum GPA of 3.0. Additional exam requirements/recommendations for international students: Required—TOEFL (minimum score 500 paper-based). Electronic applications accepted.

**Arizona State University at the Tempe campus,** Herberger Institute for Design and the Arts, School of Art, Tempe, AZ 85287-1505. Offers art education (MA); art history (MA); ceramics (MFA); design, environment and the arts (PhD), including history, theory and criticism; drawing (MFA); fibers (MFA); intermedia (MFA); metals (MFA); museum studies (MFA); painting (MFA); printmaking (MFA); sculpture (MFA); wood (MFA); MFA/MA. Terminal master's awarded for partial completion of doctoral program. *Degree requirements:* For master's, thesis/exhibition (MFA, MA in art education); interactive Program of Study (iPOS) submitted before completing 50 percent of required credit hours; for doctorate, comprehensive exam, thesis/dissertation, interactive Program of Study (iPOS) submitted before completing 50 percent of required credit hours. *Entrance requirements:* For master's, GRE or MAT, minimum GPA of 3.0 or equivalent in last 2 years of work leading to bachelor's degree; for doctorate, GRE, master's degree in architecture, graphic design, industrial design, interior design, landscape architecture, or art history or equivalent standing; statement of purpose; 3 letters of recommendation; indication of potential faculty mentor; sample of written work. Additional exam requirements/recommendations for international students: Required—TOEFL, IELTS, or PTE. Electronic applications accepted.

**ArtCenter College of Design,** Graduate Art Program, Pasadena, CA 91103. Offers MFA. *Accreditation:* NASAD. *Degree requirements:* For master's, thesis. *Entrance requirements:* For master's, portfolio. Additional exam requirements/recommendations for international students: Required—TOEFL (minimum score 100 iBT), IELTS (minimum score 7). Electronic applications accepted.

**Azusa Pacific University,** College of Liberal Arts and Sciences, Program in Fine Arts in Visual Art, Azusa, CA 91702-7000. Offers MFA. *Accreditation:* NASAD.

**Ball State University,** Graduate School, College of Fine Arts, School of Art, Muncie, IN 47306. Offers fine arts (MFA), including animation, glass; visual arts studio (MA), including ceramics, drawing, metals, painting, photography and intermedia arts, printmaking, sculpture. *Accreditation:* NASAD. *Program availability:* Part-time. *Entrance requirements:* For master's, minimum baccalaureate GPA of 2.75 or 3.0 in latter half of baccalaureate, goals statement, digital portfolio of artwork, resume, transcripts of all college-level course work, three letters of recommendation. Additional exam requirements/recommendations for international students: Required—TOEFL (minimum score 550 paper-based; 79 iBT), IELTS (minimum score 6.5). Electronic applications accepted. *Expenses:* Contact institution.

**Bard College,** Milton Avery Graduate School of the Arts, Annandale-on-Hudson, NY 12504. Offers MFA. *Degree requirements:* For master's, thesis, project, 8-week summer residency, independent study. *Entrance requirements:* For master's, interview, portfolio, 2 letters of recommendation, history of work in the arts. Additional exam requirements/recommendations for international students: Required—TOEFL (minimum score 550 paper-based). Electronic applications accepted. *Faculty research:* Original work in painting, writing, sculpture, photography, video/film, sound/music.

**Barry University,** College of Arts and Sciences, Department of Fine Arts, Miami Shores, FL 33161-6695. Offers photography (MA, MFA). *Degree requirements:* For master's, thesis (for some programs). *Entrance requirements:* For master's, GRE General Test, minimum GPA of 3.0. Electronic applications accepted. *Faculty research:* Inclusion education, exceptional education, art-based assessments.

**Bob Jones University,** Graduate Programs, Greenville, SC 29614. Offers accountancy (MS); Bible (MA); Bible translation (MA); Biblical studies (Certificate); broadcast management (MS); business administration (MBA); church history (MA, PhD); church ministries (MA); church music (MM); cinema and video production (MA); counseling (MS); curriculum and instruction (Ed D); divinity (M Div); dramatic production (MA); educational leadership (MS, Ed D, Ed S); elementary education (M Ed, MAT); English (M Ed, MA, MAT); fine arts (MA); graphic design (MA); history (M Ed, MA); illustration (MA); interpretative speech (MA); mathematics (M Ed, MAT); medical missions (Certificate); ministry (MM, D Min); multi-categorical special education (M Ed, MAT); music (M Ed); New Testament interpretation (PhD); Old Testament interpretation (PhD); orchestral instrument performance (MM); organ performance (MM); pastoral studies (MA); personnel services (MS, Ed S); piano pedagogy (MM); piano performance (MM); platform arts (MA); radio and television broadcasting (MS); rhetoric and public address (MA); secondary education (M Ed); studio art (MA); teaching Bible (MA); theology (MA, PhD); voice performance (MM); youth ministries (MA); M Div/MM.

**Boise State University,** College of Arts and Sciences, Department of Art, Boise, ID 83725. Offers art education (MA); visual arts (MFA). *Program availability:* Part-time. *Faculty:* 8. *Students:* 8 full-time (5 women), 4 part-time (2 women); includes 1 minority (Hispanic/Latino). Average age 38. 22 applicants, 23% accepted, 4 enrolled. In 2016, 5 master's awarded. *Degree requirements:* For master's, thesis optional. *Entrance requirements:* For master's, minimum GPA of 3.0, portfolio. Additional exam requirements/recommendations for international students: Required—TOEFL (minimum score 550 paper-based; 80 iBT), IELTS (minimum score 6). *Application deadline:* For fall admission, 1/15 priority date for domestic and international students. Application fee: $80 ($110 for international students). Electronic applications accepted. *Expenses:* Tuition, state resident: full-time $6058; part-time $358 per credit hour. Tuition, nonresident: full-time $20,108; part-time $608 per credit hour. *Required fees:* $2108. Tuition and fees vary according to program. *Financial support:* In 2016–17, 1 student received support, including 2 teaching assistantships (averaging $5,541 per year); scholarships/grants and unspecified assistantships also available. Financial award application deadline: 1/15; financial award applicants required to submit FAFSA. *Unit head:* Dr. Kathleen Keys, Department Chair, 208-426-1230, E-mail: kathleenkeys@boisestate.edu. *Application contact:* Chad Erpelding, Graduate Program Coordinator, 208-426-4081, E-mail: chaderpelding@boisestate.edu.
Website: http://art.boisestate.edu/gradprogram/

**Boston University,** College of Fine Arts, School of Visual Arts, Boston, MA 02226. Offers art education (MA); graphic design (MFA); painting (MFA); sculpture (MFA); studio teaching (MA). *Faculty:* 17 full-time, 4 part-time/adjunct. *Students:* 197 full-time (166 women), 3 part-time (all women); includes 24 minority (2 Black or African American, non-Hispanic/Latino; 9 Asian, non-Hispanic/Latino; 8 Hispanic/Latino; 5 Two or more races, non-Hispanic/Latino), 58 international. Average age 31. 257 applicants, 27% accepted, 21 enrolled. In 2016, 122 master's awarded. *Entrance requirements:* For master's, portfolio. Additional exam requirements/recommendations for international students: Required—TOEFL (minimum score 90 iBT), IELTS (minimum score 7). *Application deadline:* For fall admission, 2/1 for domestic and international students. Applications are processed on a rolling basis. Application fee: $80. *Expenses:* Contact institution. *Financial support:* In 2016–17, 36 students received support. Fellowships, teaching assistantships, scholarships/grants, and unspecified assistantships available. Financial award application deadline: 2/1. *Unit head:* Jeannette Guillemin, Interim Director, 617-353-3371. *Application contact:* Jessica Caccamo, Assistant Director, 617-353-3371, E-mail: visuarts@bu.edu.

**Bowling Green State University,** Graduate College, College of Arts and Sciences, School of Art, Bowling Green, OH 43403. Offers 2-D studio art (MA, MFA); 3-D studio art (MA, MFA); art education (MA); art history (MA); computer art (MA); design (MFA); digital arts (MFA); graphics (MFA). *Accreditation:* NASAD. *Program availability:* Part-time. *Degree requirements:* For master's, thesis or alternative, final exhibit (MFA). *Entrance requirements:* For master's, GRE General Test (MA), slide portfolio (15-20 slides). Additional exam requirements/recommendations for international students: Required—TOEFL. *Application deadline:* For fall admission, 2/15 for domestic students. Application fee: $30. Electronic applications accepted. *Financial support:* Research assistantships with full and partial tuition reimbursements, teaching assistantships with full and partial tuition reimbursements, career-related internships or fieldwork, institutionally sponsored loans, and unspecified assistantships available. Support available to part-time students. Financial award applicants required to submit FAFSA. *Faculty research:* Computer animation and virtual reality, Spanish still-life painting from 1600 to 1800, art and psychotherapy, Japanese wood-firing techniques in ceramics, non-toxic printmaking technologies. *Unit head:* Dr. Katerina Ruedi Ray, Director, 419-372-8575. *Application contact:* Marisa Cline, Graduate Coordinator, 419-372-2786, E-mail: mlcline@bgsu.edu.

**Bradley University,** The Graduate School, Slane College of Communications and Fine Arts, Department of Art, Peoria, IL 61625-0002. Offers ceramics (MA, MFA); drawing (MA, MFA); graphic design (MA, MFA); painting (MA, MFA); photography (MA, MFA); printmaking (MA, MFA); sculpture (MA, MFA). *Accreditation:* NASAD. *Program availability:* Part-time. *Degree requirements:* For master's, comprehensive exam, thesis, final exhibit. *Entrance requirements:* For master's, portfolio, 2 letters of recommendation. Additional exam requirements/recommendations for international students: Required—TOEFL (minimum score 550 paper-based; 79 iBT). *Application deadline:* For fall admission, 4/1 priority date for domestic and international students; for spring admission, 11/1 priority date for domestic and international students. Applications are processed on a rolling basis. Application fee: $40 ($50 for international students). Electronic applications accepted. *Expenses:* Tuition: Full-time $7650; part-time $850 per credit. *Required fees:* $50 per credit. One-time fee: $100 full-time. *Financial support:* Teaching assistantships with full and partial tuition reimbursements, scholarships/grants, tuition waivers (partial), and unspecified assistantships available. Support available to part-time students. Financial award application deadline: 4/1. *Unit head:* Gary Will, Chairperson, 309-677-2967, E-mail: pkrainak@bradley.edu. *Application contact:* Kayla Carroll, Director of International Admission and Student Services, 309-677-2375, E-mail: klcarroll@fsmail.bradley.edu.
Website: http://www.bradley.edu/academic/departments/art/

**Brandeis University,** Graduate School of Arts and Sciences, Program in Studio Art, Waltham, MA 02454-9110. Offers Postbaccalaureate Certificate. *Faculty:* 15 full-time (8 women), 2 part-time/adjunct (0 women). *Students:* 18 full-time (15 women); includes 4 minority (3 Asian, non-Hispanic/Latino; 1 Hispanic/Latino), 1 international. 5 applicants, 100% accepted, 2 enrolled. *Degree requirements:* For Postbaccalaureate Certificate, exhibit of work. *Entrance requirements:* For degree, resume, sample of work, slide list, letters of recommendation, transcript(s). Additional exam requirements/recommendations for international students: Required—TOEFL (minimum score 600 paper-based; 100 iBT); Recommended—IELTS (minimum score 7), TSE (minimum score 68). *Application deadline:* For fall admission, 6/15 for domestic students. Applications are processed on a rolling basis. Application fee: $75. Electronic applications accepted. *Expenses:* Contact institution. *Financial support:* In 2016–17, 21 teaching assistantships with partial tuition reimbursements (averaging $2,000 per year) were awarded; unspecified assistantships also available. Financial award application deadline: 6/15; financial award applicants required to submit FAFSA. *Faculty research:* Painting, sculpture. *Unit head:* Prof. Sean Downey, Faculty Coordinator, 781-736-2660, Fax: 781-736-2672, E-mail: sdowney@brandeis.edu. *Application contact:* Christine Dunant, Department Administrator, 781-736-2655, Fax: 781-736-2672, E-mail: cdunant@brandeis.edu.
Website: http://www.brandeis.edu/departments/finearts/postbac/index.html

**Brigham Young University,** Graduate Studies, College of Fine Arts and Communications, Department of Art, Provo, UT 84602-6414. Offers art education (MA); studio arts (MFA). Art education applications accepted biennially. *Accreditation:* NASAD. *Faculty:* 13 full-time (2 women). *Students:* 24 full-time (14 women); includes 4 minority (2 Asian, non-Hispanic/Latino; 1 Hispanic/Latino; 1 Native Hawaiian or other Pacific Islander, non-Hispanic/Latino). Average age 26. 16 applicants, 13% accepted, 2 enrolled. In 2016, 7 master's awarded. *Degree requirements:* For master's, one foreign language, comprehensive exam, thesis, selected project (for MFA); curriculum project (for art education). *Entrance requirements:* For master's, minimum GPA of 3.0 (for MFA, MA in art education), portfolio submitted on a flash drive (for MFA); writing samples (for MA). Additional exam requirements/recommendations for international students: Required—TOEFL (minimum score 580 paper-based; 85 iBT). *Application deadline:* For fall admission, 2/1 for domestic and international students. Application fee: $50. Electronic applications accepted. *Expenses:* Tuition: Full-time $6680; part-time $393 per credit. Tuition and fees vary according to course load, program and student's religious affiliation. *Financial support:* In 2016–17, 16 students received support. Teaching assistantships with partial tuition reimbursements available, scholarships/grants, and tuition waivers (partial) available. Financial award application deadline: 2/1. *Faculty research:* Methodology-standards-assessment, exploration of art making processes, new genre, installation, photography, theory and critical studies, art history. *Unit head:* Prof. Gary C. Barton, Chair, 801-422-4429, Fax: 801-422-0695, E-mail: garold_barton@byu.edu. *Application contact:* Sharon Lyn Heelis, Secretary, 801-422-4429, Fax: 801-422-0695, E-mail: sharon_heelis@byu.edu.
Website: http://art.byu.edu/

**Brooklyn College of the City University of New York,** School of Visual, Media and Performing Arts, Department of Art, Brooklyn, NY 11210-2889. Offers art history (MA); digital art (MFA); drawing and painting (MFA); photography (MFA); printmaking (MFA); sculpture (MFA). *Program availability:* Part-time. *Degree requirements:* For master's, thesis. *Entrance requirements:* For master's, bachelor's degree in art, portfolio, 2 letters of recommendation. Additional exam requirements/recommendations for international students: Required—TOEFL (minimum score 500 paper-based; 61 iBT). Electronic applications accepted.

**Butler University,** Jordan College of the Arts, Indianapolis, IN 46208-3485. Offers composition (MM); conducting (MM); music education (MM); music history (MM).

*Accreditation:* NASM. *Program availability:* Part-time. *Faculty:* 29 full-time (10 women), 36 part-time/adjunct (18 women). *Students:* 16 full-time (5 women), 21 part-time (4 women); includes 7 minority (3 Black or African American, non-Hispanic/Latino; 1 Asian, non-Hispanic/Latino; 1 Hispanic/Latino; 2 Two or more races, non-Hispanic/Latino), 1 international. Average age 26. 41 applicants, 66% accepted, 13 enrolled. In 2016, 16 master's awarded. *Degree requirements:* For master's, variable foreign language requirement, comprehensive exam, thesis (for some programs). *Entrance requirements:* For master's, GRE General Test (for MA in musicology), audition, interview, three letters of recommendation, transcripts, sample works. Additional exam requirements/recommendations for international students: Required—TOEFL (minimum score 550 paper-based; 79 iBT), IELTS (minimum score 6). *Application deadline:* For fall admission, 2/1 for domestic and international students; for spring admission, 12/15 for domestic and international students; for summer admission, 4/15 for domestic and international students. Applications are processed on a rolling basis. Application fee: $0. Electronic applications accepted. *Expenses:* Contact institution. *Financial support:* Scholarships/grants, tuition waivers (full and partial), and unspecified assistantships available. Financial award application deadline: 7/15; financial award applicants required to submit FAFSA. *Faculty research:* Music neuroscience; woodwind pedagogy and repertoire; music of the Renaissance; Johannes Kepler and Johannes Ockeghem; music criticism in early 20th-century Germany and Austria; Arabic choral music; pedagogy of music theory. *Unit head:* Michele Jarvis, Interim Dean, 317-940-9231, E-mail: mjarvis@butler.edu. *Application contact:* Diane Dubord, Graduate Student Services Specialist, 317-940-8107, E-mail: ddubord@butler.edu.
Website: http://www.butler.edu/jca/

**California College of the Arts,** Graduate Programs, Fine Arts Programs, San Francisco, CA 94107. Offers ceramics (MFA); film/video/performance (MFA); glass (MFA); interdisciplinary studies (MFA); jewelry/metal arts (MFA); media studies (MFA); painting/drawing (MFA); photography (MFA); printmaking (MFA); sculpture (MFA); textiles (MFA); wood/furniture (MFA). *Accreditation:* NASAD. *Faculty:* 23 full-time (14 women), 17 part-time/adjunct (12 women). *Students:* 75 full-time (55 women); includes 20 minority (7 Black or African American, non-Hispanic/Latino; 2 American Indian or Alaska Native, non-Hispanic/Latino; 6 Asian, non-Hispanic/Latino; 5 Hispanic/Latino), 15 international. Average age 29. 224 applicants, 54% accepted, 43 enrolled. In 2016, 27 master's awarded. *Degree requirements:* For master's, thesis, exhibit. *Entrance requirements:* For master's, appropriate bachelor's degree, portfolio, resume, 2 letters of recommendation, transcript. Additional exam requirements/recommendations for international students: Required—TOEFL, IELTS, or PTE. *Application deadline:* For fall admission, 1/10 for domestic and international students. Applications are processed on a rolling basis. Application fee: $70. Electronic applications accepted. *Expenses:* $1,641 per unit, $49,230 per year tuition; $490 fees. *Financial support:* In 2016–17, fellowships (averaging $42,000 per year), teaching assistantships (averaging $2,000 per year) were awarded; career-related internships or fieldwork, Federal Work-Study, scholarships/grants, health care benefits, and unspecified assistantships also available. Financial award application deadline: 7/31; financial award applicants required to submit FAFSA. *Unit head:* James Gobel, Chair, 415-551-9214, Fax: 415-703-9539, E-mail: jgobel@cca.edu. *Application contact:* Wes Fanelli, Assistant Director of Graduate Admissions, 415-703-9533, Fax: 415-703-9539, E-mail: wfanelli@cca.edu.

**California College of the Arts,** Graduate Programs, Visual and Critical Studies Program, San Francisco, CA 94107. Offers MA. *Faculty:* 1 (woman) full-time, 4 part-time/adjunct (3 women). *Students:* 15 full-time (14 women); includes 7 minority (1 Black or African American, non-Hispanic/Latino; 6 Hispanic/Latino), 2 international. Average age 32. 6 applicants, 83% accepted, 2 enrolled. In 2016, 10 master's awarded. *Degree requirements:* For master's, thesis. *Entrance requirements:* For master's, portfolio, resume, 2 letters of recommendation, transcripts, essay, interview. Additional exam requirements/recommendations for international students: Required—TOEFL, IELTS, or PTE. *Application deadline:* For fall admission, 1/10 for domestic and international students. Applications are processed on a rolling basis. Application fee: $70. Electronic applications accepted. *Expenses:* $1,641 per unit, $39,384 per year tuition; $490 fees. *Financial support:* Fellowships, teaching assistantships, career-related internships or fieldwork, Federal Work-Study, scholarships/grants, and health care benefits available. Financial award application deadline: 7/31; financial award applicants required to submit FAFSA. *Unit head:* Tirza Latimer, Chair, 415-551-9250, E-mail: tlatimer@cca.edu. *Application contact:* Wes Fanelli, Assistant Director of Graduate Admissions, 415-703-9533, Fax: 415-703-9539, E-mail: wfanelli@cca.edu.
Website: https://www.cca.edu/academics/graduate/visual-critical-studies

**California Institute of the Arts,** School of Art, Valencia, CA 91355-2340. Offers art (MFA, Adv C); graphic design (MFA, Adv C); photography (MFA, Adv C). *Accreditation:* NASAD (one or more programs are accredited). *Degree requirements:* For master's, final project. *Entrance requirements:* For master's, portfolio. Additional exam requirements/recommendations for international students: Required—TOEFL. Electronic applications accepted.

**California State University, Chico,** Office of Graduate Studies, College of Humanities and Fine Arts, Department of Art and Art History, Program in Fine Arts, Chico, CA 95929-0722. Offers art studio (MFA). *Accreditation:* NASAD. *Students:* 3 full-time (2 women), 1 (woman) part-time; includes 2 minority (1 Asian, non-Hispanic/Latino; 1 Two or more races, non-Hispanic/Latino). 11 applicants, 45% accepted, 4 enrolled. In 2016, 2 master's awarded. *Degree requirements:* For master's, thesis or alternative, exhibition with written evaluation of work. *Entrance requirements:* For master's, three letters of recommendation, statement of purpose, media portfolio. Additional exam requirements/recommendations for international students: Required—TOEFL (minimum score 550 paper-based; 80 iBT), IELTS (minimum score 6.5), PTE (minimum score 59). *Application deadline:* For fall admission, 3/1 for domestic and international students; for spring admission, 9/15 for domestic and international students. Application fee: $55. Electronic applications accepted. *Financial support:* Scholarships/grants available. Financial award application deadline: 3/1; financial award applicants required to submit FAFSA. *Unit head:* Cameron Crawford, Graduate Advisor, 530-898-5331, Fax: 530-898-4171, E-mail: art@csuchico.edu. *Application contact:* Judy L. Morris, Graduate Admissions Coordinator, 530-898-5416, Fax: 530-898-3342, E-mail: jlmorris@csuchico.edu.

**California State University, Fresno,** Division of Research and Graduate Studies, College of Arts and Humanities, Department of Art and Design, Fresno, CA 93740-8027. Offers art (MA). *Program availability:* Part-time, evening/weekend. *Degree requirements:* For master's, thesis or alternative. *Entrance requirements:* For master's, GRE General Test, minimum GPA of 3.0, portfolio. Additional exam requirements/recommendations for international students: Required—TOEFL. *Application deadline:* For fall admission, 5/1 for domestic and international students; for spring admission, 10/1 for domestic and international students. Applications are processed on a rolling basis. Application fee: $55. Electronic applications accepted. *Financial support:* Career-related internships or fieldwork, Federal Work-Study, and scholarships/grants available. Support available to part-time students. Financial award application deadline: 3/1; financial award applicants required to submit FAFSA. *Faculty research:* Art history, graphic design, studio art. *Unit head:* Martin R. Valencia, Chair, 559-278-2612, Fax: 559-278-4706, E-mail: mvalencia@csufresno.edu. *Application contact:* Prof. Paula

## Art/Fine Arts

Durette, Graduate Program Coordinator, 559-278-2249, Fax: 559-278-4706, E-mail: pdurrette@csufresno.edu. Website: http://www.fresnostate.edu/artshum/artanddesign/

**California State University, Long Beach,** Graduate Studies, College of the Arts, Department of Art, Long Beach, CA 90840. Offers art education (MA); studio art (MFA). *Accreditation:* NASAD. *Program availability:* Part-time. *Degree requirements:* For master's, thesis (for some programs). *Entrance requirements:* For master's, minimum GPA of 3.0 in last 60 hours. *Application deadline:* For fall admission, 7/1 for domestic students; for spring admission, 12/1 for domestic students. Applications are processed on a rolling basis. Application fee: $55. Electronic applications accepted. *Financial support:* Federal Work-Study, institutionally sponsored loans, and scholarships/grants available. Financial award application deadline: 3/2. *Unit head:* Prof. David Hadlock, Chair, 562-985-7908, Fax: 562-985-1650, E-mail: dhadlock@csulb.edu. *Application contact:* Margaret Black, Graduate Advisor, 562-985-7910, Fax: 562-985-1650.

**California State University, Los Angeles,** Graduate Studies, College of Arts and Letters, Department of Art, Los Angeles, CA 90032-8530. Offers art (MA), including art education, art history, art therapy, ceramics, metals, and textiles, design (MA, MFA), painting, sculpture, and graphic arts, photography; fine arts (MFA), including crafts, design (MA, MFA), studio arts. *Accreditation:* NASAD (one or more programs are accredited). *Program availability:* Part-time, evening/weekend. *Degree requirements:* For master's, comprehensive exam, project or thesis. *Entrance requirements:* For master's, portfolio. Additional exam requirements/recommendations for international students: Required—TOEFL (minimum score 500 paper-based). Electronic applications accepted. *Faculty research:* The artist and the book, conceptual art, ceramic processes, computer graphics, architectural graphics.

**California State University, Northridge,** Graduate Studies, College of Arts, Media, and Communication, Department of Art, Northridge, CA 91330. Offers art education (MA); art history (MA); studio art (MA, MFA); visual communications (MA, MFA). *Accreditation:* NASAD. *Faculty:* 23 full-time (10 women), 75 part-time/adjunct (38 women). *Students:* 22 full-time (15 women), 5 part-time (2 women); includes 12 minority (1 Asian, non-Hispanic/Latino; 8 Hispanic/Latino; 3 Two or more races, non-Hispanic/Latino), 3 international. Average age 30. 51 applicants, 27% accepted, 12 enrolled. *Application deadline:* For fall admission, 11/30 for domestic students. Application fee: $55. *Expenses:* Tuition, state resident: full-time $4152. *Financial support:* Application deadline: 3/1. *Unit head:* Prof. Edward Alfano, Chair, 818-677-2242, E-mail: art.dept@csun.edu. Website: http://www.csun.edu/art/

**California State University, Sacramento,** Office of Graduate Studies, College of Arts and Letters, Department of Art, Sacramento, CA 95819. Offers studio art (MA). *Accreditation:* NASAD. *Program availability:* Part-time. *Students:* 8 full-time (3 women), 2 part-time (both women); includes 5 minority (3 Asian, non-Hispanic/Latino; 2 Hispanic/Latino). Average age 31. 11 applicants, 64% accepted, 5 enrolled. In 2016, 2 master's awarded. *Degree requirements:* For master's, culminating exhibition of student's work; passage of Writing Proficiency Examination or approved waiver. *Entrance requirements:* For master's, BA in art or its equivalent, including 12 units in art history; minimum GPA of 2.5 in last 60 units attempted; approval by studio faculty review of other submitted materials. Additional exam requirements/recommendations for international students: Required—TOEFL (minimum score 550 paper-based; 80 iBT). *Application deadline:* For fall admission, 2/15 for domestic students, 1/15 for international students; for spring admission, 9/15 for domestic students, 8/15 for international students. Applications are processed on a rolling basis. Application fee: $55. Electronic applications accepted. *Expenses:* $4,302 full-time tuition and fees per semester, $2,796 part-time. *Financial support:* Career-related internships or fieldwork and Federal Work-Study available. Support available to part-time students. Financial award application deadline: 3/1; financial award applicants required to submit FAFSA. *Unit head:* Carolyn Gibbs, Chair, 916-278-7515, Fax: 916-278-7287, E-mail: carolyng@csus.edu. *Application contact:* Jose Martinez, Graduate Admissions Supervisor, 916-278-7871, E-mail: martinj@skymail.csus.edu. Website: http://www.al.csus.edu/art

**California State University, San Bernardino,** Graduate Studies, College of Arts and Letters, Program in Studio Art, San Bernardino, CA 92407. Offers MA. *Accreditation:* NCATE. *Faculty:* 3 full-time (2 women). *Students:* 11 full-time (5 women), 1 (woman) part-time; includes 5 minority (1 Black or African American, non-Hispanic/Latino; 2 Hispanic/Latino; 2 Two or more races, non-Hispanic/Latino). 10 applicants, 50% accepted, 4 enrolled. In 2016, 4 master's awarded. *Entrance requirements:* Additional exam requirements/recommendations for international students: Required—TOEFL. Application fee: $55. *Expenses:* Tuition, state resident: full-time $7843; part-time $5011.20 per year. Tuition and fees vary according to course load, degree level, program and reciprocity agreements. *Unit head:* Dr. Matthew Poole, Dean, 909-537-5808, E-mail: matthew.poole@csusb.edu. *Application contact:* Dr. Francisca Beer, Dean of Graduate Studies, 909-537-5058, E-mail: fbeer@csusb.edu.

**Carnegie Mellon University,** College of Fine Arts, School of Art, Pittsburgh, PA 15213-3891. Offers MFA. *Degree requirements:* For master's, thesis, exhibit. *Entrance requirements:* For master's, portfolio. Additional exam requirements/recommendations for international students: Required—TOEFL.

**Central Washington University,** Graduate Studies and Research, College of Arts and Humanities, Department of Art, Ellensburg, WA 98926. Offers MA, MFA. *Degree requirements:* For master's, thesis or alternative. *Entrance requirements:* For master's, minimum GPA of 3.0, portfolio. Additional exam requirements/recommendations for international students: Required—TOEFL (minimum score 550 paper-based; 79 iBT) or IELTS (minimum score 6.5). Electronic applications accepted.

**Christie's Education,** Certificate Program in Modern and Contemporary Art in New York, New York, NY 10020. Offers Certificate. *Program availability:* Part-time. *Faculty:* 5 full-time (4 women). *Students:* 6 (4 women). *Application deadline:* Applications are processed on a rolling basis. Application fee: $95. *Expenses:* Contact institution. *Unit head:* Dr. Julie Reiss, Program Director, 212-355-1501 Ext. 3307, E-mail: jreiss@christies.edu. *Application contact:* Hilary Smith, Recruitment and Admissions Officer, 212-355-1501 Ext. 3309, Fax: 212-355-7370, E-mail: hsmith@christies.edu. Website: https://www.christies.edu/new-york/courses/certificate-modern-contemporary-art.aspx

**City College of the City University of New York,** Graduate School, Division of Humanities and the Arts, Department of Art, Program in Fine Arts, New York, NY 10031-9198. Offers advertising design (MFA); ceramic design (MFA); digital and interdisciplinary art practice (MFA); painting (MFA); printmaking (MFA); sculpture (MFA); wood and metal design (MFA). *Degree requirements:* For master's, thesis exhibit. *Entrance requirements:* For master's, 20-slide portfolio. Additional exam requirements/recommendations for international students: Required—TOEFL (minimum score 577 paper-based; 90 iBT). Electronic applications accepted. Tuition and fees vary according to course load, degree level and program.

**Claremont Graduate University,** Graduate Programs, School of Arts and Humanities, Department of Art, Claremont, CA 91711. Offers digital media (MFA); drawing (MFA); installation (MFA); painting (MFA); performance (MFA); photography (MFA); sculpture (MFA); studio (MFA). *Program availability:* Part-time. *Faculty:* 3 full-time (1 woman). *Students:* 38 full-time (25 women), 1 part-time (0 women); includes 12 minority (1 Black or African American, non-Hispanic/Latino; 4 Asian, non-Hispanic/Latino; 6 Hispanic/Latino; 1 Two or more races, non-Hispanic/Latino), 8 international. Average age 35. In 2016, 18 master's awarded. *Degree requirements:* For master's, final project show. *Entrance requirements:* For master's, BA in art or BFA, slide review. Additional exam requirements/recommendations for international students: Required—TOEFL (minimum score 75 iBT). *Application deadline:* For fall admission, 2/1 priority date for domestic and international students. Applications are processed on a rolling basis. Application fee: $80. Electronic applications accepted. *Expenses:* Contact institution. *Financial support:* Fellowships, research assistantships, teaching assistantships, Federal Work-Study, institutionally sponsored loans, and scholarships/grants available. Support available to part-time students. Financial award application deadline: 2/15; financial award applicants required to submit FAFSA. *Faculty research:* Acoustic sculpture, feminization of abstraction, installation sculpture. *Unit head:* David Amico, Chair, 909-607-8216, E-mail: david.amico@cgu.edu. *Application contact:* Amy Sandefur, Assistant Director of Admissions, 909-607-9101, E-mail: jennifer.gracia@cgu.edu. Website: https://www.cgu.edu/academics/program/mfa/

**The College at Brockport, State University of New York,** School of Arts and Sciences, Visual Studies Workshop, Brockport, NY 14420-2997. Offers MFA. *Faculty:* 2 full-time (1 woman). *Students:* 11 full-time (7 women), 3 part-time (1 woman); includes 2 minority (1 Asian, non-Hispanic/Latino; 1 Two or more races, non-Hispanic/Latino), 1 international. 16 applicants, 56% accepted, 7 enrolled. In 2016, 4 master's awarded. *Degree requirements:* For master's, thesis or alternative, internship, final project. *Entrance requirements:* For master's, slides, portfolio, video or CD/DVD, including work description; letters of recommendation; minimum GPA of 3.0; statement of objectives. Additional exam requirements/recommendations for international students: Required—TOEFL (minimum score 550 paper-based; 79 iBT), IELTS (minimum score 6.5). *Application deadline:* For fall admission, 2/15 priority date for domestic and international students. Application fee: $50. Electronic applications accepted. *Expenses:* Contact institution. *Financial support:* Federal Work-Study and scholarships/grants available. Support available to part-time students. Financial award application deadline: 3/15; financial award applicants required to submit FAFSA. *Faculty research:* Photography, film, video, digital media, artists' books. *Unit head:* Tate Shaw, Executive Director, 585-442-8676, Fax: 585-442-1992, E-mail: tshaw@brockport.edu. *Application contact:* Danielle A. Welch, Graduate Admissions Counselor, 585-395-5465, Fax: 585-395-2515. Website: http://www.vsw.org

**College for Creative Studies,** Graduate Programs, Detroit, MI 48202-4034. Offers color and materials design (MFA); integrated design (MFA); interaction design (MFA); transportation design (MFA). *Accreditation:* NASAD.

**Colorado State University,** College of Liberal Arts, Department of Art and Art History, Fort Collins, CO 80523-1779. Offers studio art (MFA). *Faculty:* 15 full-time (9 women), 3 part-time/adjunct (1 woman). *Students:* 14 full-time (9 women), 2 part-time (1 woman); includes 2 minority (1 American Indian or Alaska Native, non-Hispanic/Latino; 1 Two or more races, non-Hispanic/Latino). Average age 32. 40 applicants, 18% accepted, 3 enrolled. In 2016, 4 master's awarded. *Degree requirements:* For master's, comprehensive exam (for some programs), thesis (for some programs), exhibition. *Entrance requirements:* For master's, portfolio, three letters of recommendation, transcripts, statement of purpose, resume, artist statement. Additional exam requirements/recommendations for international students: Required—TOEFL (minimum score 550 paper-based; 80 iBT). *Application deadline:* For fall admission, 2/1 priority date for domestic and international students. Applications are processed on a rolling basis. Application fee: $60 ($70 for international students). Electronic applications accepted. *Expenses:* Tuition, state resident: full-time $9628. Tuition, nonresident: full-time $23,603. *Required fees:* $2253; $528.14 per credit hour. $264.07 per semester. Tuition and fees vary according to course load and program. *Financial support:* In 2016–17, 8 teaching assistantships with partial tuition reimbursements (averaging $12,191 per year) were awarded; Federal Work-Study, scholarships/grants, and unspecified assistantships also available. Financial award application deadline: 3/1; financial award applicants required to submit FAFSA. *Faculty research:* African art history, bronze castings, etching/lithography, pre-Columbian art history, contemporary crafts. *Total annual research expenditures:* $27,924. *Unit head:* Suzanne Faris, Department Chair/Associate Professor, 970-491-6774, Fax: 970-491-0505, E-mail: suzanne.faris@colostate.edu. *Application contact:* Kathleen Chynoweth, Graduate Contact, 970-491-6775, E-mail: kathleen.chynoweth@colostate.edu. Website: http://art.colostate.edu/

**Columbia University,** Graduate School of Arts and Sciences, New York, NY 10027. Offers African-American studies (MA); American studies (MA); anthropology (MA, PhD); art history and archaeology (MA, PhD); astronomy (PhD); biological sciences (PhD); biotechnology (MA); chemical physics (PhD); chemistry (PhD); classical studies (MA, PhD); classics (MA, PhD); climate and society (MA); conservation biology (MA); earth and environmental sciences (PhD); East Asia: regional studies (MA); East Asian languages and cultures (MA, PhD); ecology, evolution and environmental biology (MA), including conservation biology; ecology, evolution, and environmental biology (PhD), including ecology and evolutionary biology, evolutionary primatology; economics (MA, PhD); English and comparative literature (MA, PhD); French and Romance philology (MA, PhD); Germanic languages (MA, PhD); global French studies (MA); global thought (MA); Hispanic cultural studies (MA); history (PhD); history and literature (MA); human rights studies (MA); Islamic studies (MA); Italian (MA, PhD); Japanese pedagogy (MA); Jewish studies (MA); Latin America and the Caribbean: regional studies (MA); Latin American and Iberian cultures (PhD); mathematics (MA, PhD), including finance (MA); medieval and Renaissance studies (MA); Middle Eastern, South Asian, and African studies (MA, PhD); modern art: critical and curatorial studies (MA); modern European studies (MA); museum anthropology (MA); music (DMA, PhD); oral history (MA); philosophical foundations of physics (MA); philosophy (MA, PhD); physics (PhD); political science (MA, PhD); psychology (PhD); quantitative methods in the social sciences (MA); religion (MA, PhD); Russia, Eurasia and East Europe: regional studies (MA); Russian translation (MA); Slavic cultures (MA); Slavic languages (MA, PhD); sociology (MA, PhD); South Asian studies (MA); statistics (MA, PhD); theatre (PhD). Dual-degree programs require admission to both Graduate School of Arts and Sciences and another Columbia school. *Program availability:* Part-time. Terminal master's awarded for partial completion of doctoral program. *Degree requirements:* For master's, variable foreign language requirement, comprehensive exam (for some programs), thesis (for some programs); for doctorate, variable foreign language requirement, comprehensive exam (for some programs), thesis/dissertation. *Entrance requirements:* For master's and doctorate, GRE General Test, GRE Subject Test (for some programs). Additional exam requirements/recommendations for international students: Required—TOEFL, IELTS. Electronic applications accepted.

**Columbia University,** School of the Arts, Visual Arts Program, New York, NY 10027. Offers new genres (MFA); painting (MFA); photography (MFA); printmaking (MFA); sculpture (MFA). *Degree requirements:* For master's, thesis. *Entrance requirements:* For master's, 3 letters of recommendation, portfolio, resume. Additional exam requirements/

recommendations for international students: Required—TOEFL (minimum score 600 paper-based; 100 iBT). Electronic applications accepted.

See Display below and Close-Up on page 201.

**Concordia University,** School of Graduate Studies, Faculty of Fine Arts, Department of Studio Arts, Montréal, QC H3G 1M8, Canada. Offers studio arts (MFA), including fibers and material practices, film production, intermedia, painting and drawing, photography, print media, sculpture. *Degree requirements:* For master's, thesis or alternative. *Entrance requirements:* For master's, portfolio.

**Cornell University,** Graduate School, Graduate Fields of Architecture, Art and Planning, Field of Art, Ithaca, NY 14853. Offers creative visual arts (MFA), including painting, photography, printmaking, sculpture. *Degree requirements:* For master's, thesis, exhibit. *Entrance requirements:* For master's, slide portfolio of 10-20 slides, 3 letters of recommendation, resume. Additional exam requirements/recommendations for international students: Required—TOEFL (minimum score 550 paper-based; 77 iBT). Electronic applications accepted. *Faculty research:* Painting, sculpture, photography, printmaking.

**Cranbrook Academy of Art,** Graduate School, Program in Fine Arts, Bloomfield Hills, MI 48303-0801. Offers 2d design (MFA); 3d design (MFA); ceramics (MFA); fiber (MFA); metalsmithing (MFA); painting (MFA); photography (MFA); print media (MFA); sculpture (MFA). *Accreditation:* NASAD. *Degree requirements:* For master's, thesis, exhibit. *Entrance requirements:* Additional exam requirements/recommendations for international students: Required—TOEFL (minimum score 85 iBT). *Application deadline:* For fall admission, 2/1 priority date for domestic and international students. Application fee: $85. Electronic applications accepted. *Expenses: Tuition, area resident:* Full-time $37,375. *Required fees:* $1460. *Financial support:* Federal Work-Study and scholarships/grants available. Financial award application deadline: 2/15; financial award applicants required to submit FAFSA. *Unit head:* Christopher Scoates, Director, 248-645-3301, Fax: 248-645-3591. *Application contact:* Leslie Tobakos, Registrar/Financial Aid and Admissions Manager, 248-645-3360, Fax: 248-645-3591, E-mail: ltobakos@cranbrook.edu.

**Drew University,** Caspersen School of Graduate Studies, Madison, NJ 07940-1493. Offers conflict resolution and leadership (Certificate), including community leadership, moderation, peace building; history and culture (MA, PhD), including American history, book history, British history, European history, Holocaust and genocide (M Litt, MA, D Litt, PhD), intellectual history, Irish history, print culture, public history; K-12 education (MAT), including art, biology, chemistry, elementary education, English, French, Italian, math, secondary education, special education, teacher of students with disabilities; liberal studies (M Litt, D Litt), including history, Holocaust and genocide (M Litt, MA, D Litt, PhD), Irish/Irish-American studies, literature (M Litt, MMH, D Litt, DMH, CMH), religion, spirituality, teaching in the two-year college, writing; medical humanities (MMH, DMH, CMH), including arts, health, healthcare, literature (M Litt, MMH, D Litt, DMH, CMH), scientific research; poetry (MFA). *Program availability:* Part-time, evening/weekend. *Faculty:* 4 full-time (2 women), 31 part-time/adjunct (16 women). *Students:* 62 full-time (41 women), 199 part-time (130 women); includes 38 minority (17 Black or African American, non-Hispanic/Latino; 3 Asian, non-Hispanic/Latino; 17 Hispanic/Latino; 1 Two or more races, non-Hispanic/Latino), 3 international. Average age 27. 93 applicants, 81% accepted, 46 enrolled. In 2016, 39 master's, 27 doctorates, 26 other advanced degrees awarded. Terminal master's awarded for partial completion of doctoral program. *Degree requirements:* For master's and other advanced degree, thesis (for some programs); for doctorate, one foreign language, comprehensive exam (for some programs), thesis/dissertation. *Entrance requirements:* For master's, PRAXIS Core and Subject Area tests (for MAT), resume, transcripts, writing sample, personal statement, letters of recommendation; for doctorate, GRE (PhD in history and culture),

resume, transcripts, writing sample, personal statement, letters of recommendation. Additional exam requirements/recommendations for international students: Required—TOEFL (minimum score 587 paper-based; 94 iBT), IELTS (minimum score 7), TWE (minimum score 4). *Application deadline:* For fall admission, 8/1 for domestic students, 6/1 for international students; for spring admission, 12/1 for domestic students, 10/1 for international students. Applications are processed on a rolling basis. Application fee: $35. Electronic applications accepted. Tuition and fees vary according to program. *Financial support:* Fellowships, research assistantships, teaching assistantships, career-related internships or fieldwork, Federal Work-Study, scholarships/grants, and unspecified assistantships available. Support available to part-time students. Financial award applicants required to submit FAFSA. *Application contact:* Leanne Horinko, Director of Caspersen Admissions, 973-408-3280, E-mail: gradm@drew.edu. Website: http://www.drew.edu/caspersen

**Duke University,** Graduate School, Department of Art, Art History and Visual Studies, Durham, NC 27708-0764. Offers historical and cultural visualization (MA); history of art (PhD). *Degree requirements:* For doctorate, thesis/dissertation. *Entrance requirements:* For doctorate, GRE General Test. Additional exam requirements/recommendations for international students: Required—TOEFL (minimum score 577 paper-based; 90 iBT) or IELTS (minimum score 7). Electronic applications accepted.

**East Carolina University,** Graduate School, College of Fine Arts and Communication, School of Art and Design, Greenville, NC 27858-4353. Offers art education (MA Ed); ceramics (MFA); graphic design (MFA); illustration (MFA); metal design (MFA); painting and drawing (MFA); photography (MFA); printmaking (MFA); sculpture (MFA); textile design (MFA); wood design (MFA). *Accreditation:* NASAD (one or more programs are accredited). *Program availability:* Part-time, evening/weekend. *Students:* 25 full-time (15 women), 17 part-time (12 women); includes 5 minority (2 Asian, non-Hispanic/Latino; 2 Hispanic/Latino; 1 Two or more races, non-Hispanic/Latino). Average age 33. 37 applicants, 62% accepted, 16 enrolled. In 2016, 17 master's awarded. *Degree requirements:* For master's, comprehensive exam, thesis (for some programs). *Entrance requirements:* For master's, GRE General Test or MAT, portfolio. Additional exam requirements/recommendations for international students: Required—TOEFL. *Application deadline:* For fall admission, 2/1 for domestic students; for spring admission, 10/1 for domestic students. Applications are processed on a rolling basis. Application fee: $50. *Financial support:* Research assistantships with partial tuition reimbursements, teaching assistantships with partial tuition reimbursements, and Federal Work-Study available. Support available to part-time students. Financial award application deadline: 6/1. *Unit head:* Michael H. Drought, Director, 252-328-6665, E-mail: droughtm@ecu.edu. *Application contact:* Dr. Linda H. Nelson, Information Contact, 252-328-1286, E-mail: nelsonlh@ecu.edu. Website: http://www.ecu.edu/cs-cfac/soad/gradschool.cfm

**Eastern Illinois University,** Graduate School, College of Arts and Humanities, Department of Art, Charleston, IL 61920. Offers art (MA); art education (MA); community arts (MA). *Accreditation:* NASAD. *Program availability:* Part-time, evening/weekend, online learning. *Degree requirements:* For master's, comprehensive exam (for some programs), thesis (for some programs). *Entrance requirements:* For master's, GMAT or GRE. Additional exam requirements/recommendations for international students: Required—TOEFL (minimum score 500 paper-based; 61 iBT), IELTS (minimum score 6). Electronic applications accepted.

**Eastern Michigan University,** Graduate School, College of Arts and Sciences, School of Art and Design, Program in Studio Art, Ypsilanti, MI 48197. Offers MA, MFA. *Program availability:* Part-time, evening/weekend, online learning. *Students:* 14 full-time (13 women), 9 part-time (6 women); includes 6 minority (1 American Indian or Alaska Native, non-Hispanic/Latino; 3 Asian, non-Hispanic/Latino; 1 Hispanic/Latino; 1 Two or more races, non-Hispanic/Latino). Average age 35. 11 applicants, 55% accepted, 3 enrolled. In 2016, 6 master's awarded. *Application deadline:* Applications are processed on a rolling basis. Application fee: $45. *Financial support:* Fellowships, research assistantships with full tuition reimbursements, teaching assistantships with full tuition reimbursements, career-related internships or fieldwork, Federal Work-Study, institutionally sponsored loans, scholarships/grants, and unspecified assistantships available. Support available to part-time students. *Application contact:* Michael Reedy, Graduate Coordinator, 734-487-1268, Fax: 734-487-2324, E-mail: mreedy@emich.edu.

**East Tennessee State University,** School of Graduate Studies, College of Arts and Sciences, Department of Art and Design, Johnson City, TN 37614. Offers studio art (MFA). *Accreditation:* NASAD. *Degree requirements:* For master's, thesis, exhibit, oral exam. *Entrance requirements:* For master's, GRE General Test, portfolio, bachelor's degree in art, minimum GPA of 3.0, three letters of recommendation. Additional exam requirements/recommendations for international students: Required—TOEFL (minimum score 550 paper-based; 79 iBT). Electronic applications accepted. *Faculty research:* Art history, ceramics, drawing, fibers, graphic design, installation, jewelry/metalsmithing, mixed media, new media, painting, photography, printmaking, sculpture, video.

**Edinboro University of Pennsylvania,** Department of Art, Edinboro, PA 16444. Offers art education (MA); fine arts (MFA), including ceramics (MA, MFA), metals/jewelry, painting (MA, MFA), printmaking (MA, MFA), sculpture (MA, MFA); studio art (MA), including ceramics (MA, MFA), jewelry/metals, painting (MA, MFA), printmaking (MA, MFA), sculpture (MA, MFA). *Accreditation:* NASAD. *Program availability:* Evening/weekend. *Degree requirements:* For master's, comprehensive exam, thesis or alternative, competency exam, exhibit, portfolio. *Entrance requirements:* For master's, GRE or MAT, interview, minimum QPA of 2.5, portfolio. Electronic applications accepted.

**Emily Carr University of Art + Design,** Program in Applied Arts, Vancouver, BC V6H 3R9, Canada. Offers design (M Des); media arts (MAA); visual arts (MAA). *Degree requirements:* For master's, internship, thesis project. *Entrance requirements:* For master's, minimum overall GPA of 3.0, visual portfolio, 3 letters of recommendation, resume/curriculum vitae. Additional exam requirements/recommendations for international students: Required—TOEFL (minimum score 570 paper-based; 84 iBT), IELTS (minimum score 6.5), Michigan English Language Assessment Battery (minimum score 81). Electronic applications accepted.

**Fairleigh Dickinson University, Metropolitan Campus,** University College: Arts, Sciences, and Professional Studies, School of Art and Media Studies, Teaneck, NJ 07666-1914. Offers MA.

**Ferris State University,** Kendall College of Art and Design, Grand Rapids, MI 49503. Offers architecture (M Arch); art education (MAE); design (MA); drawing (MFA); painting (MFA); photography (MFA); printmaking (MFA); visual and critical studies (MA). *Program availability:* Part-time. *Faculty:* 15 full-time (10 women), 9 part-time/adjunct (2 women). *Students:* 40 full-time (33 women), 5 part-time (3 women); includes 9 minority (3 Black or African American, non-Hispanic/Latino; 3 Asian, non-Hispanic/Latino; 3 Hispanic/Latino), 6 international. Average age 30. 43 applicants, 53% accepted, 16 enrolled. In 2016, 16 master's awarded. *Degree requirements:* For master's, thesis, seminars. *Entrance requirements:* For master's, portfolio, 3 letters of recommendation, curriculum vitae, artist statement, letter of intent. Additional exam requirements/recommendations for international students: Required—TOEFL (minimum score 70 iBT). *Application deadline:* For fall admission, 2/1 priority date for domestic and international students; for spring admission, 11/1 priority date for domestic and international students. Applications are processed on a rolling basis. Application fee: $0. Electronic applications accepted. *Expenses:* $1,017 per credit hour plus $390 fees per year. *Financial support:* In 2016–17, 32 students received support, including 8 fellowships (averaging $16,781 per year); scholarships/grants and unspecified assistantships also available. Financial award application deadline: 2/1; financial award applicants required to submit FAFSA. *Unit head:* Leslie Bellavance, President, 616-451-2787. *Application contact:* Thomas Post, Graduate Recruitment Specialist, 616-451-2787, Fax: 616-831-9689, E-mail: thomaspost@ferris.edu.
Website: http://www.kcad.edu/

**Florida Atlantic University,** Dorothy F. Schmidt College of Arts and Letters, Department of Visual Arts and Art History, Boca Raton, FL 33431-0991. Offers visual art (MFA), including ceramics, graphic design, visual art. *Faculty:* 14 full-time (10 women). *Students:* 15 full-time (12 women), 1 (woman) part-time; includes 6 minority (1 Black or African American, non-Hispanic/Latino; 1 Asian, non-Hispanic/Latino; 3 Hispanic/Latino; 1 Two or more races, non-Hispanic/Latino). Average age 37. 23 applicants, 26% accepted, 4 enrolled. In 2016, 3 master's awarded. *Degree requirements:* For master's, one foreign language, project. *Entrance requirements:* For master's, GRE General Test, minimum GPA of 3.0 during last 60 hours of course work, slide portfolio. *Application deadline:* For fall admission, 2/21 for domestic and international students; for spring admission, 10/1 for domestic and international students. Application fee: $30. Electronic applications accepted. *Expenses:* Tuition, state resident: full-time $7392; part-time $369.82 per credit hour. Tuition, nonresident: full-time $19,432; part-time $1024.81 per credit hour. *Financial support:* Research assistantships with full tuition reimbursements, teaching assistantships with full tuition reimbursements, career-related internships or fieldwork, Federal Work-Study, and institutionally sponsored loans available. Financial award applicants required to submit FAFSA. *Faculty research:* Painting, ceramics (traditional and non-traditional), installation, video and interactive sculpture. *Unit head:* Dr. Eric Landes, Interim Chair, 954-236-1106, E-mail: elandes1@fau.edu. *Application contact:* James A. Novak, Associate Professor/Graduate Coordinator/Advisor, 561-297-2430, Fax: 561-297-3078, E-mail: jnovak@fau.edu.
Website: http://www.fau.edu/VAAH/

**Florida International University,** College of Communication, Architecture and The Arts, Department of Art and Art History, Miami, FL 33199. Offers museum studies (Graduate Certificate); studio art (MFA). *Accreditation:* NASAD. *Program availability:* Part-time, evening/weekend. *Faculty:* 13 full-time (6 women), 17 part-time/adjunct (10 women). *Students:* 24 full-time (16 women), 9 part-time (6 women); includes 23 minority (4 Black or African American, non-Hispanic/Latino; 19 Hispanic/Latino). Average age 39. 22 applicants, 68% accepted, 11 enrolled. In 2016, 5 master's awarded. *Entrance requirements:* For master's, minimum GPA of 3.0 in upper-level coursework, 3 letters of recommendation, 20 slides of creative work. Additional exam requirements/recommendations for international students: Required—TOEFL (minimum score 550 paper-based; 80 iBT). *Application deadline:* For fall admission, 2/1 for domestic and international students. Application fee: $30. Electronic applications accepted. *Expenses:* Tuition, state resident: full-time $8912; part-time $446 per credit hour. Tuition, nonresident: full-time $21,393; part-time $992 per credit hour. *Required fees:* $2185; $195 per semester. Tuition and fees vary according to program. *Financial support:* Institutionally sponsored loans and scholarships/grants available. Financial award application deadline: 3/1; financial award applicants required to submit FAFSA. *Unit head:* Dr. Jacek Kolasinski, Chair, 305-348-3362, Fax: 305-348-0513, E-mail: jacek.kolasinski@fiu.edu. *Application contact:* Nanett Rojas, Assistant Director, Graduate Admissions, 305-348-7464, Fax: 305-348-7441, E-mail: gradadm@fiu.edu.
Website: http://carta.fiu.edu/arts/

**Florida State University,** The Graduate School, College of Fine Arts, Department of Art, Tallahassee, FL 32306. Offers MFA. *Accreditation:* NASAD. *Faculty:* 20 full-time (12 women), 33 part-time/adjunct (22 women). *Students:* 31 full-time (23 women); includes 8 minority (3 Black or African American, non-Hispanic/Latino; 1 Asian, non-Hispanic/Latino; 4 Hispanic/Latino). Average age 26. 63 applicants, 24% accepted, 10 enrolled. In 2016, 12 master's awarded. *Degree requirements:* For master's, thesis, creative thesis project, short thesis paper. *Entrance requirements:* Additional exam requirements/recommendations for international students: Required—TOEFL (minimum score 550 paper-based). *Application deadline:* For fall admission, 2/1 priority date for domestic and international students. Application fee: $40. Electronic applications accepted. *Expenses:* Tuition, state resident: full-time $7263; part-time $403.51 per credit hour. Tuition, nonresident: full-time $18,087; part-time $1004.85 per credit hour. *Required fees:* $1365; $75.81 per credit hour. $20 per semester. Tuition and fees vary according to campus/location. *Financial support:* In 2016–17, 31 students received support, including 31 teaching assistantships (averaging $5,000 per year); fellowships, Federal Work-Study, scholarships/grants, tuition waivers (full), and unspecified assistantships also available. *Faculty research:* Photography, painting, sculpture, printmaking, ceramics. *Unit head:* Carolyn Henne, Department Chair, 850-644-7254, E-mail: chenne@fsu.edu. *Application contact:* Elizabeth DiDonna, Graduate Admissions Officer, 850-644-8252, E-mail: edidonna@fsu.edu.
Website: http://art.fsu.edu/

**Fontbonne University,** Graduate Programs, St. Louis, MO 63105-3098. Offers accounting (MBA, MS); art (MA); art (K-12) (MAT); business (MBA); computer science (MS); deaf education (MA); early intervention in deaf education (MA); education (MA), including autism spectrum disorders, curriculum and instruction, diverse learners, early childhood education, reading, special education; elementary education (MAT); family and consumer sciences (MA), including multidisciplinary health communication studies; fine arts (MFA); instructional design and technology (MS); management and leadership (MM); middle school education (MAT); secondary education (MAT); special education (MAT); speech-language pathology (MS); supply chain management (MS); theatre (MA). *Program availability:* Part-time, evening/weekend, online learning. *Faculty:* 32 full-time (24 women), 43 part-time/adjunct (26 women). *Students:* 456 full-time (313 women), 102 part-time (77 women); includes 138 minority (118 Black or African American, non-Hispanic/Latino; 1 American Indian or Alaska Native, non-Hispanic/Latino; 7 Asian, non-Hispanic/Latino; 9 Hispanic/Latino; 3 Two or more races, non-Hispanic/Latino), 37 international. *Degree requirements:* For master's, comprehensive exam (for some programs), thesis (for some programs). *Entrance requirements:* Additional exam requirements/recommendations for international students: Required—TOEFL (minimum score 500 paper-based; 65 iBT). *Application deadline:* For fall admission, 8/1 for international students; for spring admission, 12/1 for international students. Applications are processed on a rolling basis. Application fee: $25 ($30 for international students). Electronic applications accepted. *Expenses: Tuition:* Full-time $8436; part-time $703 per credit hour. *Required fees:* $18 per credit hour. Tuition and fees vary according to course load. *Financial support:* Teaching assistantships with partial tuition reimbursements and scholarships/grants available. Support available to part-time students. Financial award application deadline: 4/1; financial award applicants required to submit FAFSA. *Unit head:* Dr. Carey Adams, Vice President for Academic Affairs, 314-719-3609, E-mail: cadams@fontbonne.edu. *Application contact:* Lauryn Filip, Coordinator, Graduate Admission and Professional Studies, 314-889-4650, E-mail: admissions@fontbonne.edu.
Website: https://www.fontbonne.edu/academics/graduate-programs/

**Fort Hays State University,** Graduate School, College of Arts and Sciences, Department of Art and Design, Hays, KS 67601-4099. Offers studio art (MFA). *Program availability:* Part-time. *Degree requirements:* For master's, comprehensive exam, thesis. *Entrance requirements:* For master's, slides. Additional exam requirements/recommendations for international students: Required—TOEFL (minimum score 550 paper-based; 79 iBT). Electronic applications accepted. *Faculty research:* Migration art of Germanic tribes, iconographic and stylistic development, graphic design, photography, lithography.

**Framingham State University,** Continuing Education, Program in Art, Framingham, MA 01701-9101. Offers M Ed. *Accreditation:* NASAD.

**Full Sail University,** Education Media Design and Technology Master of Science Program - Online, Winter Park, FL 32792-7437. Offers MS. *Program availability:* Online learning. *Entrance requirements:* Additional exam requirements/recommendations for international students: Required—TOEFL (minimum score 550 paper-based; 79 iBT).

**Full Sail University,** Media Design Master of Fine Arts Program - Online, Winter Park, FL 32792-7437. Offers MFA. *Program availability:* Online learning.

**George Mason University,** College of Visual and Performing Arts, Program in Visual and Performing Arts, Fairfax, VA 22030. Offers drawing (MFA); new media (MFA); painting (MFA); photography (MFA); printmaking (MFA); sculpture (MFA). *Accreditation:* NASAD. *Faculty:* 18 full-time (9 women), 38 part-time/adjunct (19 women). *Students:* 3 full-time (2 women), 2 part-time (1 woman). Average age 34. 15 applicants, 27% accepted, 3 enrolled. In 2016, 6 master's awarded. *Degree requirements:* For master's, comprehensive experience, studio project or thesis. *Entrance requirements:* For master's, official transcripts; 3 letters of recommendation; letter of intent; resume; professional goals statement. Additional exam requirements/recommendations for international students: Required—TOEFL (minimum score 575 paper-based; 88 iBT), IELTS (minimum score 6.5), PTE (minimum score 59). Application fee: $75 ($80 for international students). Electronic applications accepted. *Expenses:* Tuition, state resident: full-time $10,628; part-time $443 per credit. Tuition, nonresident: full-time $29,306; part-time $1221 per credit. *Required fees:* $3096; $129 per credit. Tuition and fees vary according to program. *Financial support:* Career-related internships or fieldwork, Federal Work-Study, scholarships/grants, unspecified assistantships, and health care benefits (for full-time research or teaching assistantship recipients) available. Support available to part-time students. Financial award application deadline: 3/1; financial award applicants required to submit FAFSA. *Faculty research:* Digital arts, painting, photography, print-making, sculpture; combined art forms in in-disciplinary projects including installation, performance, publishing, time or writing-based; combined creative and critical approaches. *Unit head:* Lisa Kahn, Associate Dean, 703-993-4541, E-mail: lkahn2@gmu.edu. *Application contact:* Nikki Brugnoli-Whipkey, Graduate Studies Administrative Assistant, 703-993-5792, Fax: 703-993-8798, E-mail: rbrugnol@gmu.edu.
Website: http://soa.gmu.edu

**The George Washington University,** Columbian College of Arts and Sciences, Department of Fine Arts and Art History, Washington, DC 20052. Offers art history (MA), including art history, museum training; ceramics (MFA); drawing/painting (MFA); interior design (MFA), including interior architecture and design; new media (MFA); photography (MFA); sculpture (MFA). *Accreditation:* CIDA. *Program availability:* Part-time, evening/weekend. *Faculty:* 16 full-time (10 women). *Students:* 75 full-time (56 women), 15 part-time (13 women); includes 20 minority (6 Black or African American, non-Hispanic/Latino; 7 Asian, non-Hispanic/Latino; 6 Hispanic/Latino; 1 Two or more races, non-Hispanic/Latino), 22 international. Average age 29. 103 applicants, 83% accepted, 35 enrolled. In 2016, 43 master's awarded. *Entrance requirements:* For master's, GRE

General Test, bachelor's degree in field, minimum GPA of 3.0. Additional exam requirements/recommendations for international students: Required—TOEFL (minimum score 550 paper-based; 80 iBT). *Application deadline:* For fall admission, 3/1 priority date for domestic students, 1/15 priority date for international students; for spring admission, 10/1 priority date for domestic students, 9/1 priority date for international students. Applications are processed on a rolling basis. Application fee: $75. Electronic applications accepted. *Financial support:* In 2016–17, 12 students received support. Fellowships, teaching assistantships, career-related internships or fieldwork, Federal Work-Study, and tuition waivers available. Financial award application deadline: 1/15. *Unit head:* Phil Jacks, Chair, 202-994-6085, E-mail: pjacks@gwu.edu. *Application contact:* Information Contact, 202-994-6085, Fax: 202-994-8657, E-mail: art@gwu.edu. Website: http://art.columbian.gwu.edu/

**Georgia Southern University,** Jack N. Averitt College of Graduate Studies, College of Liberal Arts and Social Sciences, Program in Art, Statesboro, GA 30460. Offers fine arts (MFA), including 2D graphic design, 2D studio art, 3D studio art. *Accreditation:* NASAD. *Program availability:* Part-time. *Students:* 11 full-time (7 women), 3 part-time (2 women); includes 1 minority (Black or African American, non-Hispanic/Latino), 3 international. Average age 34. 9 applicants, 89% accepted, 4 enrolled. In 2016, 4 master's awarded. *Degree requirements:* For master's, thesis, exhibition. *Entrance requirements:* For master's, minimum GPA of 3.0; 18 semester hours of course work in studio art, 9 in art history; portfolio; letters of reference. Additional exam requirements/recommendations for international students: Required—TOEFL (minimum score 550 paper-based; 80 iBT), IELTS (minimum score 6). *Application deadline:* For fall admission, 3/1 priority date for domestic and international students; for spring admission, 10/1 priority date for domestic students, 10/1 for international students. Applications are processed on a rolling basis. Application fee: $50. Electronic applications accepted. *Expenses:* Tuition, state resident: full-time $7236; part-time $277 per semester hour. Tuition, nonresident: full-time $27,118; part-time $1105 per semester hour. *Required fees:* $2092. *Financial support:* In 2016–17, 1 student received support, including 4 fellowships with full tuition reimbursements available (averaging $7,750 per year); career-related internships or fieldwork, Federal Work-Study, scholarships/grants, tuition waivers (full), and unspecified assistantships also available. Support available to part-time students. Financial award application deadline: 4/15; financial award applicants required to submit FAFSA. *Faculty research:* International design trends; graphic design social awareness campaigns; functional design; public sculpture; fine art painting, drawing, printmaking, paper and book arts; folk art; Georgia artists archive, technology, design, contemporary, traditional studio. *Unit head:* Dr. Robert Farber, Department Chair, 912-478-5358, Fax: 912-478-5104, E-mail: rfarber@georgiasouthern.edu. Website: http://class.georgiasouthern.edu/art

**Georgia State University,** College of Arts and Sciences, Ernest G. Welch School of Art and Design, Program in Studio Art, Atlanta, GA 30302-3083. Offers ceramics (MFA); drawing and painting (MFA); graphic design (MFA); interior design (MFA); photography (MFA); printmaking (MFA); sculpture (MFA); textiles (MFA). *Accreditation:* NASAD. *Degree requirements:* For master's, thesis. *Application deadline:* For fall admission, 1/6 for domestic and international students; for spring admission, 1/15 priority date for domestic and international students. Application fee: $50. Electronic applications accepted. *Expenses:* Tuition, state resident: full-time $6876; part-time $382 per credit hour. Tuition, nonresident: full-time $22,374; part-time $1243 per credit hour. *Required fees:* $2128; $1064 per term. Part-time tuition and fees vary according to course load and program. *Financial support:* In 2016–17, fellowships with full tuition reimbursements (averaging $11,000 per year), teaching assistantships with full tuition reimbursements (averaging $7,000 per year) were awarded; research assistantships, scholarships/grants, and unspecified assistantships also available. Financial award application deadline: 4/15; financial award applicants required to submit FAFSA. *Faculty research:* Advertising and typography, new media, traditional media, three-dimensional art, architectural and environmental design. *Unit head:* Michael White, Director, Welch School of Art and Design, 404-413-5221, Fax: 404-413-5261, E-mail: mwhite@gsu.edu. *Application contact:* Hubert Stanley Anderson, Director of Graduate Studies, 404-413-5229, Fax: 404-413-5261, E-mail: artgrad@gsu.edu. Website: http://artdesign.gsu.edu/graduate/admissions/masters-of-fine-arts-in-studio/

**Governors State University,** College of Arts and Sciences, Program in Art, University Park, IL 60484. Offers MA. *Program availability:* Part-time. *Faculty:* 91 full-time (43 women), 125 part-time/adjunct (64 women). *Students:* 1 (woman) full-time, 10 part-time (5 women); includes 6 minority (5 Black or African American, non-Hispanic/Latino; 1 Hispanic/Latino). Average age 36. 11 applicants, 45% accepted, 5 enrolled. In 2016, 3 master's awarded. *Entrance requirements:* Additional exam requirements/recommendations for international students: Required—TOEFL (minimum score 550 paper-based; 80 iBT), IELTS. *Application deadline:* For fall admission, 4/1 for domestic students. Application fee: $50. Electronic applications accepted. *Expenses:* $307 per credit hour; $38 per term or $76 per credit hour fees. *Financial support:* Application deadline: 5/1; applicants required to submit FAFSA. *Unit head:* Lori Montalbano, Chair of Division of Communication, Visual and Performing Arts, 708-235-2802, E-mail: lmontalbano@govst.edu. *Application contact:* Yakeea Daniels, Assistant Vice President for Enrollment Services/Director of Admission, 708-534-4510, E-mail: ydaniels@govst.edu.

**Hofstra University,** School of Education, Programs in Teacher Education, Hempstead, NY 11549. Offers bilingual education (MA, Advanced Certificate); bilingual extension (Advanced Certificate), including education/speech language pathology; business education (MS Ed); early childhood and childhood education (MS Ed); early childhood education (MA, MS Ed); education technology (Advanced Certificate); elementary education (MA, MS Ed), including science, technology, engineering, and mathematics (STEM) (MA); English education (MS Ed); family and consumer science (MS Ed); fine arts and music education (Advanced Certificate); fine arts education (MS Ed); foreign language and TESOL (MS Ed); foreign language education (MS Ed), including French, German, Russian, Spanish; learning and teaching (Ed D), including applied linguistics, art education, arts and humanities, early childhood education, English education, human development, math education, math, science, and technology, multicultural education, physical education, science education, social studies education, special education; mathematics education (MA, MS Ed); middle school extension (Advanced Certificate), including grades 5-6, grades 7-9; music education (MA, MS Ed); science education (MA, MS Ed), including biology, chemistry, earth science, geology, physics; secondary education (Advanced Certificate); social studies education (MA, MS Ed); teaching languages other than English and TESOL (MS Ed); TESOL (MS Ed, Advanced Certificate). *Program availability:* Part-time, evening/weekend, blended/hybrid learning. *Students:* 139 full-time (97 women), 145 part-time (106 women); includes 60 minority (15 Black or African American, non-Hispanic/Latino; 1 American Indian or Alaska Native, non-Hispanic/Latino; 12 Asian, non-Hispanic/Latino; 31 Hispanic/Latino; 1 Two or more races, non-Hispanic/Latino), 21 international. Average age 29. 255 applicants, 86% accepted, 122 enrolled. In 2016, 101 master's, 4 doctorates, 43 other advanced degrees awarded. *Degree requirements:* For master's, comprehensive exam, thesis (for some programs), exit project, student teaching, fieldwork, electronic portfolio, curriculum project, minimum GPA of 3.0; for doctorate, thesis/dissertation; for Advanced Certificate, 3 foreign languages, comprehensive exam (for some programs), thesis project. *Entrance requirements:* For master's, GRE, MAT, 2 letters of recommendation, portfolio,

teacher certification (MA), interview, essay; for doctorate, GMAT, GRE, LSAT, or MAT; for Advanced Certificate, 2 letters of recommendation, essay, interview and/or portfolio, teaching certificate. Additional exam requirements/recommendations for international students: Required—TOEFL (minimum score 550 paper-based; 80 iBT). *Application deadline:* Applications are processed on a rolling basis. Application fee: $75. Electronic applications accepted. *Expenses: Tuition:* Full-time $1240. *Required fees:* $970. Tuition and fees vary according to program. *Financial support:* In 2016–17, 149 students received support, including 58 fellowships with full and partial tuition reimbursements available (averaging $5,309 per year), 5 research assistantships with full and partial tuition reimbursements available (averaging $7,073 per year); career-related internships or fieldwork, Federal Work-Study, institutionally sponsored loans, scholarships/grants, traineeships, tuition waivers (full and partial), and unspecified assistantships also available. Support available to part-time students. Financial award applicants required to submit FAFSA. *Faculty research:* Educational interventions that foster critical-thinking skills; teachers' attitudes about professional development; threats to teacher quality. *Unit head:* Dr. Eustace Thompson, Chairperson, 516-463-5749, Fax: 516-463-6275, E-mail: eustace.g.thompson@hofstra.edu. *Application contact:* Sunil Samuel, Assistant Vice President of Admissions, 516-463-4723, Fax: 516-463-4664, E-mail: graduateadmission@hofstra.edu. Website: http://www.hofstra.edu/education/

**Hollins University,** Graduate Programs, Program in Liberal Studies, Roanoke, VA 24020. Offers humanities (MALS); interdisciplinary studies (MALS); leadership (MALS); social sciences (MALS); visual and performing arts (MALS). *Program availability:* Part-time, evening/weekend. *Degree requirements:* For master's, thesis. *Entrance requirements:* For master's, three letters of recommendation, interview, bachelor's degree, undergraduate transcripts, statement of educational objectives. Additional exam requirements/recommendations for international students: Required—TOEFL (minimum score 550 paper-based; 80 iBT), IELTS (minimum score 6.5). *Application deadline:* Applications are processed on a rolling basis. Application fee: $40. Electronic applications accepted. *Expenses:* $395 per credit hour. *Financial support:* Fellowships and scholarships/grants available. Support available to part-time students. Financial award application deadline: 7/15; financial award applicants required to submit FAFSA. *Faculty research:* Diversity, gender and women's studies, political science, leadership. *Unit head:* Director, 540-362-6576, Fax: 540-362-6288, E-mail: hugrad@hollins.edu. *Application contact:* Cathy S. Koon, Manager of Graduate Programs, 540-362-6326, Fax: 540-362-6288, E-mail: ckoon@hollins.edu. Website: http://www.hollins.edu/academics/graduate-degrees/liberal-studies/

**Hood College,** Graduate School, Program in Ceramic Arts, Frederick, MD 21701-8575. Offers ceramic arts (Certificate); ceramics (MA, MFA). *Program availability:* Part-time, evening/weekend. *Faculty:* 1 full-time, 6 part-time/adjunct. *Students:* 3 full-time (2 women), 21 part-time (10 women); includes 1 minority (Hispanic/Latino). Average age 36. 4 applicants, 100% accepted, 4 enrolled. In 2016, 7 master's, 3 other advanced degrees awarded. *Degree requirements:* For master's, comprehensive exam (for some programs), thesis (for some programs), capstone project. *Entrance requirements:* For master's, minimum GPA of 2.75, artist statement, resume (MFA), 2 letters of recommendation, portfolio of 20 images; for Certificate, portfolio of 12 images. Additional exam requirements/recommendations for international students: Required—TOEFL (minimum score 575 paper-based; 89 iBT), IELTS (minimum score 6.5). *Application deadline:* For fall admission, 8/15 priority date for domestic students, 8/5 for international students; for spring admission, 12/1 priority date for domestic students, 12/1 for international students; for summer admission, 5/1 priority date for domestic students, 4/15 for international students. Applications are processed on a rolling basis. Application fee: $35. Electronic applications accepted. *Expenses: Tuition:* Part-time $450 per credit hour. *Required fees:* $105 per term. Part-time tuition and fees vary according to degree level, campus/location and program. *Financial support:* Tuition waivers (partial) and unspecified assistantships available. Financial award applicants required to submit FAFSA. *Unit head:* April Boulton, Interim Dean of the Graduate School, 301-696-3600, E-mail: gofurther@hood.edu. *Application contact:* Jan Marcus, Assistant Director of Graduate Admissions, 301-696-3600, E-mail: gofurther@hood.edu. Website: http://www.hood.edu/graduate

**Houston Baptist University,** School of Fine Arts, Houston, TX 77074-3298. Offers studio art (MFA). *Program availability:* Part-time, evening/weekend. *Faculty:* 8 full-time (2 women), 2 part-time/adjunct (1 woman). *Students:* 21 full-time (14 women); includes 7 minority (1 Black or African American, non-Hispanic/Latino; 1 Asian, non-Hispanic/Latino; 3 Hispanic/Latino; 2 Two or more races, non-Hispanic/Latino), 3 international. Average age 33. 44 applicants, 34% accepted, 9 enrolled. In 2016, 11 master's awarded. *Degree requirements:* For master's, comprehensive exam. *Entrance requirements:* For master's, minimum GPA of 2.5, essay/personal statement, resume, bachelor's degree transcript, digital portfolio. Additional exam requirements/recommendations for international students: Required—TOEFL (minimum score 80 iBT), IELTS (minimum score 6.5). *Application deadline:* For fall admission, 4/1 for domestic students, 2/1 for international students. Applications are processed on a rolling basis. Application fee: $0 ($100 for international students). Electronic applications accepted. Application fee is waived when completed online. *Expenses:* $2,000 per 3-hour course; $1,275 annual general fee; $1,060 annual technology fee. *Financial support:* In 2016–17, 5 students received support. Federal Work-Study and scholarships/grants available. Support available to part-time students. Financial award application deadline: 4/1; financial award applicants required to submit FAFSA. *Unit head:* Dr. Jason Lester, Dean, 281-649-3339, E-mail: jlester@hbu.edu. *Application contact:* Dr. Michael Collins, Program Director, 281-649-3624, E-mail: mcollins@hbu.edu. Website: http://www.hbu.edu/mfa

**Howard University,** Graduate School, Division of Fine Arts, Department of Art, Program in Fine Arts, Washington, DC 20059-0002. Offers 3D reality (sculpture and ceramics) (MFA); design (MFA); electronic studio (MFA); painting (MFA); photography (MFA). *Accreditation:* NASAD. *Degree requirements:* For master's, comprehensive exam, thesis, exhibit. *Entrance requirements:* For master's, minimum GPA of 3.0, portfolio.

**Hunter College of the City University of New York,** Graduate School, School of Arts and Sciences, Department of Art and Art History, Program in Studio Art, New York, NY 10013. Offers MFA. *Program availability:* Part-time, evening/weekend. *Students:* 8 full-time (6 women), 107 part-time (57 women); includes 25 minority (10 Black or African American, non-Hispanic/Latino; 7 Asian, non-Hispanic/Latino; 8 Hispanic/Latino), 21 international. Average age 31. 380 applicants, 11% accepted, 24 enrolled. In 2016, 20 master's awarded. *Degree requirements:* For master's, exhibit, project. *Entrance requirements:* For master's, minimum of 24 credits of course work in studio art, 9 in art history; portfolio; minimum GPA of 3.0 overall and in art courses; statement of purpose; two letters of recommendation. Additional exam requirements/recommendations for international students: Required—TOEFL (minimum score 550 paper-based; 60 iBT). *Application deadline:* For fall admission, 1/15 for domestic students. Application fee: $125. *Financial support:* Career-related internships or fieldwork, Federal Work-Study, scholarships/grants, and tuition waivers (partial) available. Support available to part-time students. Financial award application deadline: 4/15. *Faculty research:* Color theory, public printmaking and environmental commissions in painting and sculpture, graphics,

*Art/Fine Arts*

ceramics, contemporary film and video. *Unit head:* Joel Carreiro, Director, 212-650-3398. *Application contact:* William Zlata, Director for Graduate Admissions, 212-772-4482, Fax: 212-650-3336, E-mail: admissions@hunter.cuny.edu. Website: http://www.mfa205hudson.org/

**Idaho State University,** Office of Graduate Studies, College of Arts and Letters, Department of Art and Pre-Architecture, Pocatello, ID 83209-8004. Offers art (MFA). *Program availability:* Part-time. *Degree requirements:* For master's, comprehensive exam, thesis, exhibit, 2 year minimum participation in program, oral exam. *Entrance requirements:* For master's, GRE General Test, GMAT or MAT, minimum GPA of 3.0 in all upper-division classes, portfolio of work, 3 letters of recommendation. Additional exam requirements/recommendations for international students: Required—TOEFL (minimum score 550 paper-based; 80 iBT). Electronic applications accepted. *Faculty research:* Computerized weaving, anodizing refractory metals, viscosity printing, neon, ceramic shell casting.

**Illinois State University,** Graduate School, College of Fine Arts, Program in Arts Technology, Normal, IL 61790-2200. Offers MS. *Accreditation:* NASAD. *Degree requirements:* For master's, thesis or alternative.

**Illinois State University,** Graduate School, College of Fine Arts, School of Art, Normal, IL 61790-2200. Offers art history (MA, MS); ceramics (MFA, MS); drawing (MFA, MS); fibers (MFA, MS); glass (MFA, MS); graphic design (MFA, MS); metals (MFA, MS); painting (MFA, MS); photography (MFA, MS); printmaking (MFA, MS); sculpture (MFA, MS). *Accreditation:* NASAD (one or more programs are accredited). *Degree requirements:* For master's, thesis or alternative, internship. *Entrance requirements:* For master's, portfolio, sample of scholarly writing.

**Indiana State University,** College of Graduate and Professional Studies, College of Arts and Sciences, Department of Art and Design, Terre Haute, IN 47809. Offers ceramics (MA, MFA); drawing (MA, MFA); graphic design (MA, MFA); painting (MA, MFA); photography (MA, MFA); printmaking (MA, MFA); sculpture (MA, MFA). *Accreditation:* NASAD (one or more programs are accredited). *Program availability:* Part-time. *Degree requirements:* For master's, thesis or alternative, departmental qualifying exam. *Entrance requirements:* For master's, portfolio. Additional exam requirements/recommendations for international students: Required—TOEFL (minimum score 550 paper-based).

**Indiana University Bloomington,** University Graduate School, College of Arts and Sciences, School of Art and Design, Bloomington, IN 47405-7000. Offers apparel merchandising (MS); studio art (MFA). *Accreditation:* NASAD (one or more programs are accredited). *Students:* 64 full-time (39 women), 12 part-time (5 women); includes 12 minority (1 Black or African American, non-Hispanic/Latino; 3 Asian, non-Hispanic/Latino; 6 Hispanic/Latino; 2 Two or more races, non-Hispanic/Latino), 8 international. Average age 31. 104 applicants, 22% accepted, 23 enrolled. In 2016, 13 master's awarded. *Entrance requirements:* For master's, portfolio (MFA). Additional exam requirements/recommendations for international students: Required—TOEFL. *Application deadline:* For fall admission, 1/15 for domestic students, 12/1 for international students. Application fee: $55 ($65 for international students). Electronic applications accepted. *Financial support:* Fellowships with tuition reimbursements, research assistantships with tuition reimbursements, teaching assistantships with tuition reimbursements, career-related internships or fieldwork, Federal Work-Study, scholarships/grants, tuition waivers (full and partial), and stipends available. *Unit head:* Peg Faimon, Founding Dean, 812-855-2561, E-mail: pfaimon@indiana.edu. *Application contact:* Toni Arcuri, Graduate Services Coordinator, 812-855-0188, E-mail: sofagrad@indiana.edu. Website: https://soad.indiana.edu/

**Indiana University of Pennsylvania,** School of Graduate Studies and Research, College of Fine Arts, Department of Art, MA Program in Art, Indiana, PA 15705. Offers MA. *Accreditation:* NASAD. *Program availability:* Part-time. *Faculty:* 7 full-time (3 women). *Students:* 2 full-time (1 woman), 2 part-time (both women). Average age 27. 7 applicants, 86% accepted, 4 enrolled. In 2016, 1 master's awarded. *Degree requirements:* For master's, thesis optional. *Entrance requirements:* For master's, 3 letters of recommendation, portfolio. Additional exam requirements/recommendations for international students: Required—TOEFL (minimum score 540 paper-based). *Application deadline:* For fall admission, 4/15 priority date for domestic students. Applications are processed on a rolling basis. Application fee: $50. Electronic applications accepted. *Expenses:* Tuition, state resident: full-time $8694; part-time $483 per credit. Tuition, nonresident: full-time $13,050; part-time $725 per credit. *Required fees:* $157 per credit. $50 per term. Tuition and fees vary according to course load and program. *Financial support:* In 2016–17, 2 research assistantships with tuition reimbursements (averaging $1,000 per year) were awarded; fellowships, career-related internships or fieldwork, Federal Work-Study, scholarships/grants, and unspecified assistantships also available. Support available to part-time students. Financial award application deadline: 4/15; financial award applicants required to submit FAFSA. *Unit head:* Dr. Susan Palmisano, Graduate Coordinator, 724-357-2530, E-mail: palmisan@iup.edu. Website: http://www.iup.edu/art/grad/default.aspx

**Indiana University of Pennsylvania,** School of Graduate Studies and Research, College of Fine Arts, Department of Art, Master of Fine Arts Program, Indiana, PA 15705. Offers MFA. *Program availability:* Part-time. *Faculty:* 7 full-time (3 women). *Students:* 19 full-time (12 women), 4 part-time (3 women); includes 3 minority (1 Black or African American, non-Hispanic/Latino; 2 Two or more races, non-Hispanic/Latino), 1 international. Average age 28. 16 applicants, 81% accepted, 10 enrolled. In 2016, 8 master's awarded. *Degree requirements:* For master's, thesis, thesis/exhibition. *Entrance requirements:* For master's, 2 letters of recommendation, art slides. Additional exam requirements/recommendations for international students: Required—TOEFL (minimum score 540 paper-based). *Application deadline:* For fall admission, 2/15 priority date for domestic students. Application fee: $50. Electronic applications accepted. *Expenses:* Tuition, state resident: full-time $8694; part-time $483 per credit. Tuition, nonresident: full-time $13,050; part-time $725 per credit. *Required fees:* $157 per credit. $50 per term. Tuition and fees vary according to course load and program. *Financial support:* In 2016–17, 14 research assistantships with tuition reimbursements (averaging $2,520 per year) were awarded; fellowships with full tuition reimbursements, career-related internships or fieldwork, Federal Work-Study, scholarships/grants, and unspecified assistantships also available. Support available to part-time students. Financial award application deadline: 4/15; financial award applicants required to submit FAFSA. *Unit head:* Dr. Susan Palmisano, Graduate Coordinator, 724-357-2536, E-mail: palmisan@iup.edu. Website: http://www.iup.edu/art/grad/default.aspx

**Indiana University–Purdue University Indianapolis,** Herron School of Art and Design, Indianapolis, IN 46202. Offers art therapy (MA); visual art (MFA), including ceramics, furniture design, painting and drawing, photography and intermedia, printmaking, sculpture; visual communication design (MFA). *Faculty:* 26 full-time (13 women), 16 part-time/adjunct (11 women). *Students:* 56 full-time (40 women), 1 (woman) part-time; includes 8 minority (4 Black or African American, non-Hispanic/Latino; 2 Asian, non-Hispanic/Latino; 2 Hispanic/Latino), 7 international. Average age 31. 72 applicants, 53%

accepted, 25 enrolled. In 2016, 22 master's awarded. *Degree requirements:* For master's, thesis. *Entrance requirements:* For master's, personal statement, resume, recommendations, portfolio, transcripts (18 credit hours of studio art and 12 credit hours of psychology, including 3 credit hours of developmental psychology and 3 credit hours of abnormal psychology for MA). Additional exam requirements/recommendations for international students: Recommended—TOEFL (minimum score 550 paper-based; 79 iBT), IELTS (minimum score 6.5). *Application deadline:* For fall admission, 1/15 for domestic and international students; for spring admission, 11/1 for domestic students, 10/15 for international students. Application fee: $60 ($65 for international students). Electronic applications accepted. *Expenses:* Contact institution. *Financial support:* In 2016–17, 55 students received support, including 36 fellowships (averaging $2,830 per year), 11 teaching assistantships (averaging $3,609 per year); research assistantships, Federal Work-Study, scholarships/grants, health care benefits, tuition waivers, and unspecified assistantships also available. Financial award application deadline: 2/1. *Faculty research:* Contemporary digital narratives for the homoerotic trope; sound articulated 3D print; neuroscience, art and related therapeutics; automotive and aeronautical design and fabrication; technological detritus. *Total annual research expenditures:* $22,990. *Unit head:* Prof. Valerie Eickmeier, Dean, 317-278-9470, Fax: 317-278-9471, E-mail: herron@iupui.edu. *Application contact:* Abbey Chambers, Herron Office of Admissions and Student Services, 317-378-9400, E-mail: herron4u@iupui.edu. Website: http://herron.iupui.edu/

**Institute for Doctoral Studies in the Visual Arts,** PhD Program in Visual Art: Philosophy, Aesthetics, and Art Theory, Portland, ME 04102. Offers aesthetics (PhD); art theory (PhD); philosophy (PhD). *Program availability:* Online learning. *Faculty:* 3 full-time, 7 part-time/adjunct. *Students:* 56 full-time. *Degree requirements:* For doctorate, comprehensive exam, thesis/dissertation, dissertation defense. *Entrance requirements:* For doctorate, curriculum vitae, writing sample, portfolio, interview. *Application deadline:* Applications are processed on a rolling basis. Application fee: $56. Electronic applications accepted. Application fee is waived when completed online. *Financial support:* Fellowships, teaching assistantships, and scholarships/grants available. Financial award applicants required to submit FAFSA. *Faculty research:* Visual culture, cultural studies, feminism, contemporary art. *Application contact:* Molly M. Davis, Director of Administration/Co-Director of Admissions, 207-771-8887, E-mail: info@idsva.edu. Website: https://www.idsva.edu

**Inter American University of Puerto Rico, San Germán Campus,** Graduate Studies Center, Program in Fine Arts, San Germán, PR 00683-5008. Offers drawing (MFA); graphic design (MFA); painting (MFA); photography (MFA); printmaking (MFA); sculpture (MFA). *Program availability:* Part-time, evening/weekend. *Degree requirements:* For master's, comprehensive exam, thesis. *Entrance requirements:* For master's, GRE General Test or EXADEP, minimum GPA of 3.0.

**Iowa State University of Science and Technology,** Program in Integrated Visual Arts, Ames, IA 50011. Offers MFA. *Accreditation:* NASAD. *Entrance requirements:* Additional exam requirements/recommendations for international students: Required—TOEFL (minimum score 550 paper-based; 79 iBT), IELTS (minimum score 6.5). *Application deadline:* For fall admission, 2/1 priority date for domestic students. *Application contact:* Meredith Foley, Application Contact, 515-294-0816, Fax: 515-294-2348, E-mail: merfoley@iastate.edu. Website: http://www.design.iastate.edu/integratedstudioarts/graduateprogram.php

**Ithaca College,** Roy H. Park School of Communications, Program in Image Text, Ithaca, NY 14850. Offers MFA. *Program availability:* Part-time-only. *Faculty:* 3 full-time (1 woman). *Students:* 8 part-time (3 women); includes 1 minority (Hispanic/Latino). Average age 28. 15 applicants, 87% accepted, 8 enrolled. *Degree requirements:* For master's, thesis optional. *Entrance requirements:* Additional exam requirements/recommendations for international students: Required—TOEFL (minimum score 550 paper-based; 80 iBT). *Application deadline:* For fall admission, 3/15 for domestic and international students; for spring admission, 12/1 for domestic and international students. Applications are processed on a rolling basis. Application fee: $40. Electronic applications accepted. *Expenses:* Contact institution. *Financial support:* In 2016–17, 7 students received support, including 7 fellowships (averaging $5,089 per year); career-related internships or fieldwork, Federal Work-Study, and scholarships/grants also available. Support available to part-time students. Financial award application deadline: 3/1; financial award applicants required to submit CSS PROFILE or FAFSA. *Unit head:* Nicholas Muellner, Co-Director, 607-274-1984, E-mail: nmuellner@ithaca.edu. *Application contact:* Nicole Eversley Bradwell, Director, Office of Admission, 607-274-3124, Fax: 607-274-1263, E-mail: admission@ithaca.edu. Website: http://www.ithaca.edu/gradprograms/image-text

**Jacksonville University,** College of Fine Arts, MFA in Visual Arts Program, Jacksonville, FL 32211. Offers MFA. *Degree requirements:* For master's, thesis, portfolio. *Expenses:* Tuition: Full-time $13,320. One-time fee: $50 part-time. Tuition and fees vary according to course load, degree level, campus/location and program.

**James Madison University,** The Graduate School, College of Visual and Performing Arts, School of Art, Design and Art History, Harrisonburg, VA 22802. Offers art education (MA); studio art (MA, MFA), including ceramics (MFA), drawing/painting (MFA), intermedia (MFA), metal/jewelry (MFA), photography (MFA), sculpture (MFA). *Accreditation:* NASAD. *Program availability:* Part-time. *Faculty:* 25 full-time (15 women). *Students:* 10 full-time (6 women), 1 (woman) part-time, 1 international. Average age 30. 18 applicants, 39% accepted, 6 enrolled. In 2016, 6 master's awarded. Application fee: $55. Electronic applications accepted. *Financial support:* In 2016–17, 10 students received support, including 3 teaching assistantships with full tuition reimbursements available (averaging $9,284 per year); Federal Work-Study and 7 assistantships (averaging $7911) also available. Financial award application deadline: 3/1; financial award applicants required to submit FAFSA. *Unit head:* Dr. Kathy A. Schwartz, Director of School of Art, Design and Art History, 540-568-6216, E-mail: schwarka@jmu.edu. *Application contact:* Lynette D. Michael, Director of Graduate Student Admissions, 540-568-6131 Ext. 6395, Fax: 540-568-7860, E-mail: michaeld@jmu.edu. Website: http://www.jmu.edu/artandarthistory/

**John F. Kennedy University,** Graduate School of Holistic Studies, Department of Arts and Consciousness, Program in Studio Arts, Pleasant Hill, CA 94523-4817. Offers MFA. *Program availability:* Part-time, evening/weekend. *Degree requirements:* For master's, thesis or alternative. *Entrance requirements:* For master's, interview, portfolio. Additional exam requirements/recommendations for international students: Required—TOEFL. *Expenses:* Contact institution.

**Johnson State College,** Program in Studio Arts, Johnson, VT 05656. Offers ceramics (MFA); digital media (MFA); drawing (MFA); painting (MFA); photography (MFA); printmaking (MFA); sculpture (MFA). *Program availability:* Part-time, online learning. *Degree requirements:* For master's, thesis. *Entrance requirements:* For master's, portfolio. Additional exam requirements/recommendations for international students: Required—TOEFL. *Application deadline:* For fall admission, 3/1 for domestic students, 2/1 for international students. Applications are processed on a rolling basis. Electronic applications accepted. Application fee is waived when completed online. *Expenses:* Contact institution. *Financial support:* Teaching assistantships and unspecified assistantships available. Support available to part-time students. Financial award application deadline: 3/1; financial award applicants required to submit FAFSA. *Application contact:* Catherine H. Higley, Administrative Assistant, 800-635-2356 Ext. 1244, Fax: 802-635-1248, E-mail: catherine.higley@jsc.edu. Website: http://www.jsc.edu/academics/fine-arts-department/majors-and-minors/mfa-in-studio-arts/

**Kansas State University,** Graduate School, College of Arts and Sciences, Department of Art, Manhattan, KS 66506. Offers MFA. *Accreditation:* NASAD. *Faculty:* 18 full-time (7 women), 7 part-time/adjunct (5 women). *Students:* 12 full-time (9 women); includes 2 minority (both Hispanic/Latino). Average age 26. 20 applicants, 25% accepted, 3 enrolled. In 2016, 7 master's awarded. *Degree requirements:* For master's, thesis, gallery exhibit. *Entrance requirements:* For master's, slides of artistic work, portfolio, official transcripts, recommendation form/letters, statement of purpose. Additional exam requirements/recommendations for international students: Required—TOEFL (minimum score 550 paper-based; 79 iBT). *Application deadline:* For fall admission, 1/15 for domestic students, 1/1 for international students; for spring admission, 10/1 for domestic students, 8/1 for international students. Application fee: $50 ($75 for international students). Electronic applications accepted. *Expenses:* Tuition, state resident: full-time $9670. Tuition, nonresident: full-time $21,828. *Required fees:* $862. *Financial support:* In 2016–17, 16 students received support, including 16 teaching assistantships with full tuition reimbursements available (averaging $8,323 per year); career-related internships or fieldwork, institutionally sponsored loans, scholarships/grants, and unspecified assistantships also available. Support available to part-time students. Financial award application deadline: 3/1; financial award applicants required to submit FAFSA. *Faculty research:* Drawing, painting, sculpture, metalsmithing, graphic design, digital/experimental media, ceramics, printmaking. *Unit head:* Prof. Matthew S. Gaynor, Interim Head, 785-532-6605, Fax: 785-532-0334, E-mail: matthewgaynor@ksu.edu. *Application contact:* Prof. Nancy Murrow, Director of Graduate Studies, 785-532-6605, Fax: 785-532-0334, E-mail: nmurrow@ksu.edu. Website: http://art.ksu.edu

**Kent State University,** College of the Arts, School of Art, Kent, OH 44242-0001. Offers art education (MA); art history (MA); crafts (MA, MFA), including glass; fine arts (MA, MFA), including fashion (MA). *Accreditation:* NASAD (one or more programs are accredited). *Program availability:* Part-time, online learning. *Faculty:* 23 full-time (15 women). *Students:* 51 full-time (23 women), 167 part-time (120 women); includes 18 minority (8 Black or African American, non-Hispanic/Latino; 1 American Indian or Alaska Native, non-Hispanic/Latino; 1 Asian, non-Hispanic/Latino; 4 Hispanic/Latino; 1 Native Hawaiian or other Pacific Islander, non-Hispanic/Latino; 3 Two or more races, non-Hispanic/Latino), 25 international. Average age 31. 57 applicants, 53% accepted, 21 enrolled. In 2016, 30 master's awarded. *Degree requirements:* For master's, comprehensive exam, thesis (for some programs), 1 foreign language (for art history); final project (for crafts and fine arts). *Entrance requirements:* For master's, transcripts, goal statement, 3 letters of recommendation, curriculum vitae, portfolio. Additional exam requirements/recommendations for international students: Required—TOEFL (minimum score of 575 paper-based, 90 iBT), IELTS (minimum score of 7.0), Michigan English Language Assessment Battery (minimum score of 85), or PTE (minimum score of 68). *Application deadline:* For fall admission, 2/2 for domestic and international students; for spring admission, 10/15 for domestic and international students. Applications are processed on a rolling basis. Application fee: $45 ($70 for international students). Electronic applications accepted. *Expenses:* Tuition, state resident: full-time $10,864; part-time $495 per credit hour. Tuition, nonresident: full-time $18,380; part-time $837 per credit hour. *Financial support:* Career-related internships or fieldwork, scholarships/grants, and unspecified assistantships available. Financial award application deadline: 2/2. *Unit head:* Michael J. Loderstedt, Interim Director/Professor, Print Media and Photography, 330-672-2192, E-mail: mloderst@kent.edu. *Application contact:* Linda Hoeptner Poling, Graduate Coordinator and Associate Professor of Art Education, 330-672-7895, E-mail: lhoeptne@kent.edu. Website: http://www.kent.edu/art

**Laguna College of Art & Design,** Graduate Program, Laguna Beach, CA 92651-1136. Offers painting (MFA). *Accreditation:* NASAD. *Entrance requirements:* For master's, BA with a studio concentration or BFA, minimum GPA of 3.0 in studio subjects, portfolio, resume. Additional exam requirements/recommendations for international students: Required—TOEFL (minimum score 550 paper-based). Electronic applications accepted.

**Lake Forest College,** Graduate Program in Liberal Studies, Lake Forest, IL 60045. Offers American studies (MLS); environmental studies (MLS); history (MLS); Medieval and Renaissance art (MLS); philosophy (MLS); Spanish (MLS); writing (MLS). *Program availability:* Part-time, evening/weekend. *Faculty:* 9 full-time (3 women), 1 part-time/adjunct (0 women). *Students:* 1 full-time (0 women), 38 part-time (20 women); includes 5 minority (1 Black or African American, non-Hispanic/Latino; 2 Asian, non-Hispanic/Latino; 2 Hispanic/Latino). Average age 38. 19 applicants, 53% accepted, 7 enrolled. In 2016, 4 master's awarded. *Degree requirements:* For master's, thesis optional, 8 courses, including at least 3 interdisciplinary seminars. *Entrance requirements:* For master's, transcript, essay, interview. Additional exam requirements/recommendations for international students: Required—TOEFL (minimum score 550 paper-based; 83 iBT); Recommended—IELTS (minimum score 6.5). *Application deadline:* For fall admission, 7/15 priority date for domestic students, 6/1 priority date for international students; for spring admission, 12/1 priority date for domestic students, 10/1 priority date for international students. Applications are processed on a rolling basis. Application fee: $30. *Expenses:* $2,600 per course. *Financial support:* In 2016–17, 2 students received support. Partial tuition grants for full-time teachers available. *Faculty research:* Realigning of the international order; Renaissance women artists; literature of Latin Americans in the U.S.; modern Chinese history; environmental biology. *Unit head:* Prof. D. L. LeMahieu, Director, 847-735-5133, Fax: 847-735-6291, E-mail: lemahieu@lakeforest.edu. *Application contact:* Prof. Carol Gayle, Associate Director, 847-735-5083, Fax: 847-735-6291, E-mail: gayle@lakeforest.edu. Website: http://www.lakeforest.edu/academics/programs/mls

**Lake Forest College,** Master of Arts in Teaching Program, Lake Forest, IL 60045. Offers elementary education (MAT); K-12 French (MAT); K-12 music (MAT); K-12 Spanish (MAT); K-12 visual art (MAT); secondary biology (MAT); secondary chemistry (MAT); secondary English (MAT); secondary history (MAT); secondary mathematics (MAT). *Degree requirements:* For master's, comprehensive exam, portfolio. *Entrance requirements:* For master's, GRE.

**Lee University,** Program in Education, Cleveland, TN 37320-3450. Offers art (MAT); curriculum and instruction (M Ed, Ed S); early childhood (M Ed, Ed S); educational leadership (M Ed, Ed S); elementary education (MAT); English and math (MAT); English and science (MAT); English and social studies (MAT); higher education administration (MS); history (MAT); history and economics (MAT); math and science (MAT); math and social studies (MAT); middle grades (MAT); science and social studies (MASW); secondary education (MAT); Spanish (MAT); special education (M Ed, MAT); TESOL (MAT). *Accreditation:* NCATE. *Program availability:* Part-time. *Faculty:* 13 full-time (6 women), 9 part-time/adjunct (4 women). *Students:* 35 full-time (27 women), 50 part-time (32 women); includes 12 minority (5 Black or African American, non-Hispanic/Latino; 5 Hispanic/Latino; 2 Two or more races, non-Hispanic/Latino), 4 international. Average age 30. 43 applicants, 79% accepted, 28 enrolled. In 2016, 42 master's, 6 other advanced degrees awarded. *Degree requirements:* For master's, variable foreign language requirement, thesis optional, internship. *Entrance requirements:* For master's, MAT or GRE General Test, minimum undergraduate GPA of 2.75, 3 letters of recommendation, interview, writing sample, official transcripts, background check; for Ed S, minimum undergraduate and master's GPA of 2.75, official transcripts for undergraduate and master's degrees. Additional exam requirements/recommendations for international students: Required—TOEFL (minimum score 61 iBT). *Application deadline:* For fall admission, 6/1 priority date for domestic and international students; for spring admission, 11/1 priority date for domestic and international students; for summer admission, 4/1 priority date for domestic and international students. Applications are processed on a rolling basis. Application fee: $25. Electronic applications accepted. *Expenses: Tuition:* Full-time $11,367; part-time $632 per credit hour. *Required fees:* $35 per term. One-time fee: $25. Tuition and fees vary according to program. *Financial support:* In 2016–17, 42 students received support. Career-related internships or fieldwork, Federal Work-Study, institutionally sponsored loans, scholarships/grants, and unspecified assistantships available. Financial award application deadline: 3/1; financial award applicants required to submit FAFSA. *Unit head:* Dr. William Kamm, Director, 423-614-8544, E-mail: wkamm@leeuniversity.edu. *Application contact:* Crystal Keeter, Graduate Education Secretary, 423-614-8544, E-mail: ckeeter@leeuniversity.edu. Website: http://www.leeuniversity.edu/academics/graduate/education

**Lehman College of the City University of New York,** School of Arts and Humanities, Department of Art, Bronx, NY 10468-1589. Offers MA. *Program availability:* Part-time, evening/weekend. *Entrance requirements:* For master's, 33 undergraduate credits in art, interview, portfolio. *Faculty research:* Graphic art, modern and contemporary art, sculpture, primitive and pre-Columbian art, medieval art.

**Lesley University,** College of Art and Design, Cambridge, MA 02138-2790. Offers photography (MFA); visual arts (MFA). *Program availability:* Part-time. *Degree requirements:* For master's, thesis, final exhibition of thesis work. *Entrance requirements:* For master's, portfolio, resume, personal statement. Additional exam requirements/recommendations for international students: Required—TOEFL (minimum score 550 paper-based; 80 iBT). Electronic applications accepted. *Faculty research:* Graphic design; Web and multimedia design; book, advertising and editorial illustration; animation; documentary photography; photojournalism; fine arts photography; fine arts; art education.

**Lesley University,** Graduate School of Education, Cambridge, MA 02138-2790. Offers arts, community, and education (M Ed); autism studies (Certificate); curriculum and instruction (M Ed, CAGS); early childhood education (M Ed); ecological teaching and learning (MS); educational studies (PhD), including adult learning, educational leadership, individually designed; elementary education (M Ed); emergent technologies for educators (Certificate); ESLArts: language learning through the arts (M Ed); high school education (M Ed); individually designed (M Ed); integrated teaching through the arts (M Ed); literacy for K-8 classroom teachers (M Ed); mathematics education (M Ed); middle school education (M Ed); moderate disabilities (M Ed); online learning (Certificate); reading (CAGS); science in education (M Ed); severe disabilities (M Ed); special needs (CAGS); specialist teacher of reading (M Ed); teacher of visual art (M Ed); technology in education (M Ed, CAGS). *Accreditation:* TEAC. *Program availability:* Part-time, evening/weekend, online learning. *Degree requirements:* For master's, practicum; for doctorate, thesis/dissertation. *Entrance requirements:* For master's, Massachusetts Tests for Educator Licensure (MTEL), transcripts, statement of purpose, recommendations; interview (for special education); for doctorate, GRE General Test, transcripts, statement of purpose, recommendations, interview, master's degree, resume; for other advanced degree, interview, master's degree. Additional exam requirements/recommendations for international students: Required—TOEFL (minimum score 550 paper-based; 80 iBT). Electronic applications accepted. *Faculty research:* Assessment in literacy, mathematics and science; autism spectrum disorders; instructional technology and online learning; multicultural education and English language learners.

**Liberty University,** School of Communication and Creative Arts, Lynchburg, VA 24515. Offers strategic communication (MA); studio and digital arts (MFA). *Program availability:* Part-time. *Students:* 120 full-time (82 women), 142 part-time (90 women); includes 56 minority (45 Black or African American, non-Hispanic/Latino; 1 Asian, non-Hispanic/Latino; 1 Hispanic/Latino; 9 Two or more races, non-Hispanic/Latino), 12 international. Average age 32. 384 applicants, 33% accepted, 66 enrolled. In 2016, 58 master's awarded. *Degree requirements:* For master's, thesis (for some programs). *Entrance requirements:* For master's, minimum undergraduate GPA of 3.0, faculty recommendation, written statement of purpose, writing sample. Additional exam requirements/recommendations for international students: Required—TOEFL (minimum score 600 paper-based; 100 iBT). *Application deadline:* For fall admission, 6/1 for domestic students; for spring admission, 11/1 for domestic students. Applications are processed on a rolling basis. Application fee: $50. Electronic applications accepted. *Financial support:* Federal Work-Study and unspecified assistantships available. Financial award applicants required to submit FAFSA. *Unit head:* Dr. Norman Mintle, Dean, 434-582-2077, E-mail: cvkramer@liberty.edu. *Application contact:* Dr. Terry Elam, Director of Graduate Admissions, 434-582-2111, Fax: 434-582-7836, E-mail: gradadmissions@liberty.edu.

**Long Island University–LIU Post,** College of Arts, Communications and Design, Brookville, NY 11548-1300. Offers art (MA); clinical art therapy (MA); clinical art therapy and counseling (MA); digital game design and development (MFA); fine arts and design (MFA); interactive multimedia arts (MA); music (MA); theater (MA); theatre (MFA). *Faculty:* 36 full-time (19 women), 144 part-time/adjunct (74 women). *Students:* 123 full-time (91 women), 21 part-time (18 women); includes 25 minority (6 Black or African American, non-Hispanic/Latino; 1 American Indian or Alaska Native, non-Hispanic/Latino; 6 Asian, non-Hispanic/Latino; 11 Hispanic/Latino; 1 Two or more races, non-Hispanic/Latino), 32 international. 175 applicants, 73% accepted, 46 enrolled. In 2016, 68 master's awarded. *Degree requirements:* For master's, variable foreign language requirement, comprehensive exam (for some programs), thesis (for some programs). *Entrance requirements:* For master's, performance audition or portfolio. Additional exam requirements/recommendations for international students: Required—TOEFL (minimum score 550 paper-based; 79 iBT). *Application deadline:* Applications are processed on a rolling basis. Application fee: $50. Electronic applications accepted. *Expenses: Tuition:* Full-time $28,272; part-time $1178 per credit. *Required fees:* $451 per term. Tuition and fees vary according to degree level and program. *Financial support:* In 2016–17, 6 research assistantships with partial tuition reimbursements (averaging $1,020 per year), 14 teaching assistantships with partial tuition reimbursements (averaging $670 per year) were awarded; career-related internships or fieldwork, Federal Work-Study, institutionally sponsored loans, scholarships/grants, tuition waivers (full and partial), and unspecified assistantships also available. Support available to part-time students. Financial award application deadline: 2/15; financial award applicants required to submit FAFSA. *Faculty research:* Game design, new plays, musical theatre, compositions for wind symphony, jazz ensemble, jazz combo and vocal jazz. *Unit head:* Dr. Christine Kerr, Acting Dean, 516-299-2309, E-mail: christine.kerr@liu.edu. *Application contact:* Carol Zerah, Director of Graduate Admissions, 516-299-2900, Fax: 516-299-2137,

## Art/Fine Arts

E-mail: post-enroll@liu.edu.
Website: http://www.liu.edu/CWPost/Academics/School-of-Visual-Arts-Communications-and-Digital-Technologies

**Louisiana State University and Agricultural & Mechanical College,** Graduate School, College of Art and Design, School of Art, Program in Studio Art, Baton Rouge, LA 70803. Offers ceramics (MFA); graphic design (MFA); painting and drawing (MFA); photography (MFA); printmaking (MFA); sculpture (MFA). *Accreditation:* NASAD.

**Louisiana Tech University,** Graduate School, College of Liberal Arts, MFA Program, Ruston, LA 71272. Offers graphic design (MFA); photography (MFA); studio (MFA). *Accreditation:* NASAD. *Program availability:* Part-time. *Degree requirements:* For master's, exhibit. *Entrance requirements:* For master's, GRE General Test, portfolio. *Application deadline:* For fall admission, 5/12 for domestic students. Applications are processed on a rolling basis. Application fee: $40 ($50 for international students). Electronic applications accepted. *Financial support:* Fellowships, career-related internships or fieldwork, Federal Work-Study, institutionally sponsored loans, and unspecified assistantships available. Financial award application deadline: 2/15. *Unit head:* Frank Hamrick, Graduate Coordinator, 318-257-4154, Fax: 318-257-4890, E-mail: fhamrick@latech.edu. *Application contact:* Marilyn J. Robinson, Assistant to the Dean of the Graduate School, 318-257-2924, Fax: 318-257-4487.
Website: http://design.latech.edu/master-of-fine-arts/

**Maine College of Art,** Program in Studio Art, Portland, ME 04101. Offers MA, MFA. *Accreditation:* NASAD. *Degree requirements:* For master's, thesis, studio thesis exhibition. *Entrance requirements:* Additional exam requirements/recommendations for international students: Required—TOEFL (minimum score 550 paper-based). Electronic applications accepted.

**Maryland Institute College of Art,** Graduate Studies, LeRoy E. Hoffberger School of Painting, Baltimore, MD 21201. Offers MFA. *Accreditation:* NASAD. *Faculty:* 1 (woman) full-time, 2 part-time/adjunct (0 women). *Students:* 20 full-time (12 women); includes 4 minority (1 Black or African American, non-Hispanic/Latino; 1 Asian, non-Hispanic/Latino; 1 Hispanic/Latino; 1 Two or more races, non-Hispanic/Latino), 4 international. Average age 27. 200 applicants, 10% accepted, 10 enrolled. In 2016, 10 master's awarded. *Degree requirements:* For master's, thesis, exhibit and thesis documentation. *Entrance requirements:* For master's, portfolio, bachelor's degree in any field. Additional exam requirements/recommendations for international students: Required—TOEFL (minimum score 550 paper-based; 80 iBT), IELTS (minimum score 6.5). *Application deadline:* For fall admission, 1/15 for domestic and international students. Application fee: $75. Electronic applications accepted. *Expenses:* Contact institution. *Financial support:* In 2016–17, 20 students received support, including 20 fellowships (averaging $13,000 per year), 20 teaching assistantships (averaging $3,200 per year); career-related internships or fieldwork and scholarships/grants also available. Financial award application deadline: 1/15; financial award applicants required to submit FAFSA. *Unit head:* Joan Waltemath, Director, 410-225-5274, Fax: 410-225-5275, E-mail: graduate@mica.edu. *Application contact:* Chris D. Harring, Director of Graduate Admission, 410-225-2256, Fax: 410-225-5275, E-mail: graduate@mica.edu.
Website: http://www.mica.edu/Programs_of_Study/Graduate_Programs/Hoffberger_School_of_Painting.html

**Maryland Institute College of Art,** Graduate Studies, Mount Royal School of Art, Baltimore, MD 21217. Offers painting (MFA). *Faculty:* 1 full-time (0 women), 6 part-time/adjunct (3 women). *Students:* 28 full-time (17 women); includes 3 minority (1 Asian, non-Hispanic/Latino; 2 Two or more races, non-Hispanic/Latino), 5 international. Average age 27. 175 applicants, 11% accepted, 15 enrolled. In 2016, 15 master's awarded. *Degree requirements:* For master's, thesis, exhibit and thesis documentation. *Entrance requirements:* For master's, 40 credits in studio art, bachelor's degree in any field. Additional exam requirements/recommendations for international students: Required—TOEFL (minimum score 550 paper-based; 80 iBT), IELTS (minimum score 6.5). *Application deadline:* For fall admission, 1/15 for domestic and international students. Application fee: $75. Electronic applications accepted. *Expenses:* Contact institution. *Financial support:* In 2016–17, 28 students received support, including 28 fellowships (averaging $13,000 per year), 28 teaching assistantships (averaging $3,200 per year); career-related internships or fieldwork and scholarships/grants also available. Financial award application deadline: 1/15. *Unit head:* Luca Buvoli, Director, 410-225-5274, Fax: 410-225-5275, E-mail: graduate@mica.edu. *Application contact:* Chris D. Harring, Director, Graduate Admission, 410-225-2256, Fax: 410-225-5275, E-mail: graduate@mica.edu.
Website: http://www.mica.edu/Programs_of_Study/Graduate_Programs/Mount_Royal_School_of_Art_(Multidisciplinary_MFA).html

**Maryland Institute College of Art,** Graduate Studies, MPS Program in Business of Art and Design, Baltimore, MD 21201. Offers MPS. *Program availability:* Part-time. *Faculty:* 15 part-time/adjunct (6 women). *Students:* 20 part-time (10 women); includes 5 minority (2 Black or African American, non-Hispanic/Latino; 1 Asian, non-Hispanic/Latino; 2 Hispanic/Latino). Average age 27. 53 applicants, 47% accepted, 20 enrolled. In 2016, 20 master's awarded. *Degree requirements:* For master's, business plan presentation. *Entrance requirements:* For master's, essay, resume. Additional exam requirements/recommendations for international students: Required—TOEFL (minimum score 550 paper-based; 80 iBT), IELTS (minimum score 6.5). *Application deadline:* For fall admission, 1/15 for domestic and international students; for spring admission, 4/1 for domestic and international students. Application fee: $70. Electronic applications accepted. *Expenses:* Contact institution. *Financial support:* In 2016–17, 20 students received support, including 20 fellowships (averaging $3,400 per year); scholarships/grants also available. Financial award application deadline: 1/15; financial award applicants required to submit FAFSA. *Unit head:* Heather Bradbury, Manager, 410-225-2220, Fax: 410-225-2229, E-mail: hbradbury@mica.edu. *Application contact:* Chris D. Harring, Director of Graduate Admission, 410-225-2256, Fax: 410-225-5275, E-mail: graduate@mica.edu.
Website: http://www.mica.edu/Programs_of_Study/Graduate_Programs/The_Business_of_Art_and_Design_(Online_MPS).html

**Maryland Institute College of Art,** Graduate Studies, Post Baccalaureate Certificate Program in Fine Arts, Baltimore, MD 21201. Offers Postbaccalaureate Certificate. *Faculty:* 1 full-time (0 women), 1 (woman) part-time/adjunct. *Students:* 23 full-time (13 women); includes 4 minority (3 Asian, non-Hispanic/Latino; 1 Hispanic/Latino), 3 international. Average age 27. In 2016, 23 Postbaccalaureate Certificates awarded. *Degree requirements:* For Postbaccalaureate Certificate, thesis, exhibition and documentation. *Entrance requirements:* For degree, portfolio, 40 studio credits, 6 credits in art history. Additional exam requirements/recommendations for international students: Required—TOEFL (minimum score 550 paper-based; 80 iBT), IELTS (minimum score 6.5). *Application deadline:* For fall admission, 1/15 priority date for domestic and international students; for spring admission, 11/15 for domestic and international students. Application fee: $75. Electronic applications accepted. *Expenses:* Contact institution. *Financial support:* In 2016–17, 22 students received support, including 22 fellowships with partial tuition reimbursements available (averaging $7,000 per year); scholarships/grants also available. Financial award application deadline: 1/15; financial award applicants required to submit FAFSA. *Unit head:* William Schmidt, Director, 410-230-0568. *Application contact:* Chris D. Harring, Director of Graduate Admission, 410-

225-2256, Fax: 410-225-5275, E-mail: graduate@mica.edu.
Website: http://www.mica.edu/Programs_of_Study/Post-Baccalaureate_Certificate_in_Fine_Art.html

**Maryland Institute College of Art,** Graduate Studies, Program in Community Arts, Baltimore, MD 21201. Offers MFA. *Program availability:* Part-time. *Faculty:* 3 full-time (2 women), 2 part-time/adjunct (both women). *Students:* 20 full-time (18 women); includes 4 minority (2 Black or African American, non-Hispanic/Latino; 1 Hispanic/Latino; 1 Two or more races, non-Hispanic/Latino), 1 international. Average age 27. 35 applicants, 43% accepted, 10 enrolled. In 2016, 10 master's awarded. *Degree requirements:* For master's, thesis, exhibition and thesis documentation. *Entrance requirements:* For master's, portfolio, bachelor's degree in any field. Additional exam requirements/recommendations for international students: Required—TOEFL (minimum score 550 paper-based; 80 iBT), IELTS (minimum score 6.5). *Application deadline:* For fall admission, 1/15 for domestic and international students. Applications are processed on a rolling basis. Application fee: $75. Electronic applications accepted. *Expenses:* Contact institution. *Financial support:* In 2016–17, 20 students received support, including 20 fellowships (averaging $13,000 per year), 20 teaching assistantships (averaging $3,200 per year); career-related internships or fieldwork and scholarships/grants also available. Financial award application deadline: 1/15. *Unit head:* Ken Krafchek, Director, 410-225-5274, Fax: 410-225-5275, E-mail: graduate@mica.edu. *Application contact:* Chris D. Harring, Director, Graduate Admission, 410-225-2256, Fax: 410-225-5275, E-mail: graduate@mica.edu.

**Maryland Institute College of Art,** Graduate Studies, Program in Studio Art, Baltimore, MD 21201. Offers MFA. Offered during summer only. *Faculty:* 3 full-time (1 woman), 1 (woman) part-time/adjunct. *Students:* 37 full-time (26 women); includes 8 minority (2 Black or African American, non-Hispanic/Latino; 2 Asian, non-Hispanic/Latino; 2 Hispanic/Latino; 2 Two or more races, non-Hispanic/Latino), 1 international. Average age 38. 85 applicants, 18% accepted, 10 enrolled. In 2016, 10 master's awarded. *Degree requirements:* For master's, thesis, exhibition, final paper. *Entrance requirements:* For master's, portfolio, 40 studio credits, 6 credits in art history, bachelor's degree in any field. Additional exam requirements/recommendations for international students: Required—TOEFL (minimum score 550 paper-based; 80 iBT), IELTS (minimum score 6.5). *Application deadline:* For fall admission, 1/15 priority date for domestic students, 1/15 for international students. Application fee: $75. Electronic applications accepted. *Expenses:* Contact institution. *Financial support:* In 2016–17, 37 fellowships (averaging $6,500 per year) were awarded; career-related internships or fieldwork and scholarships/grants also available. Financial award application deadline: 1/15. *Unit head:* Zlata Baum, Director, 410-225-2297, Fax: 410-225-2257. *Application contact:* Chris D. Harring, Director of Graduate Admission, 410-225-2256, Fax: 410-225-5275, E-mail: graduate@mica.edu.
Website: http://www.mica.edu/Programs_of_Study/Graduate_Programs/Studio_Art_(Online_and_Low-Residency_MFA).html

**Maryland Institute College of Art,** Graduate Studies, Rinehart School of Sculpture, Baltimore, MD 21201. Offers MFA. *Accreditation:* NASAD. *Faculty:* 3 full-time (2 women), 2 part-time/adjunct (both women). *Students:* 15 full-time (9 women); includes 4 minority (3 Asian, non-Hispanic/Latino; 1 Native Hawaiian or other Pacific Islander, non-Hispanic/Latino). Average age 27. 80 applicants, 25% accepted, 8 enrolled. In 2016, 5 master's awarded. *Degree requirements:* For master's, thesis, exhibition. *Entrance requirements:* For master's, portfolio, bachelor's degree in any field. Additional exam requirements/recommendations for international students: Required—TOEFL (minimum score 550 paper-based; 80 iBT), IELTS (minimum score 6.5). *Application deadline:* For fall admission, 1/15 for domestic and international students. Application fee: $75. Electronic applications accepted. *Expenses:* Contact institution. *Financial support:* In 2016–17, 11 students received support, including 15 fellowships with partial tuition reimbursements available (averaging $13,000 per year), 11 teaching assistantships (averaging $3,200 per year); career-related internships or fieldwork and scholarships/grants also available. Financial award application deadline: 1/15; financial award applicants required to submit FAFSA. *Unit head:* Maren Hassinger, Director, 410-225-2271, Fax: 410-225-2408. *Application contact:* Chris D. Harring, Director of Graduate Admission, 410-225-2256, Fax: 410-225-2408, E-mail: graduate@mica.edu.
Website: http://www.mica.edu/Programs_of_Study/Graduate_Programs/Rinehart_School_of_Sculpture_(MFA).html

**Marywood University,** Academic Affairs, Insalaco College of Creative and Performing Arts, Art Department, Program in Studio Art, Scranton, PA 18509-1598. Offers clay (MA); painting (MA); photography (MA); printmaking (MA); sculpture (MA). *Accreditation:* NASAD. Electronic applications accepted. *Faculty research:* Texture and line in clay, cast bronze sculpture, color theories, book art and illustration, sculptural form.

**Marywood University,** Academic Affairs, Insalaco College of Creative and Performing Arts, Art Department, Program in Visual Arts, Scranton, PA 18509-1598. Offers clay (MFA); graphic design (MFA); illustration (MFA); painting (MFA); photography (MFA); printmaking (MFA); sculpture (MFA). *Accreditation:* NASAD. *Program availability:* Part-time. Electronic applications accepted. *Expenses:* Contact institution.

**Massachusetts College of Art and Design,** Graduate Programs, MFA Program, Boston, MA 02115-5882. Offers 2D fine arts (MFA), including painting, printmaking; 3D fine arts (MFA), including ceramics, fibers, glass, jewelry and metalsmithing, sculpture; design (MFA, Postbaccalaureate Certificate), including dynamic media; fine arts (MFA), including interdisciplinary; media arts (MFA, Postbaccalaureate Certificate), including film/video (MFA), photography. *Accreditation:* NASAD. *Faculty:* 40 full-time (19 women), 55 part-time/adjunct (23 women). *Students:* 58 full-time (39 women), 16 part-time (12 women); includes 10 minority (1 Black or African American, non-Hispanic/Latino; 4 Asian, non-Hispanic/Latino; 4 Hispanic/Latino; 1 Native Hawaiian or other Pacific Islander, non-Hispanic/Latino), 28 international. 247 applicants, 52% accepted, 47 enrolled. In 2016, 34 master's, 3 other advanced degrees awarded. *Degree requirements:* For master's, thesis, thesis exhibition (for fine arts programs); thesis project and document (for design/dynamic media program). *Entrance requirements:* For master's, portfolio, college transcripts, resume, statement of purpose, letters of reference, interview, 6 credits of art history taken prior to or during MFA program; for Postbaccalaureate Certificate, portfolio, college transcripts, resume, statement of purpose, letters of reference, interview. Additional exam requirements/recommendations for international students: Required—TOEFL (minimum score 550 paper-based; 85 iBT); Recommended—IELTS (minimum score 6.5). *Application deadline:* For fall admission, 1/4 priority date for domestic and international students; for summer admission, 1/4 priority date for domestic and international students. Application fee: $90. Electronic applications accepted. *Expenses:* $780 per credit tuition. *Financial support:* In 2016–17, 57 students received support, including 33 teaching assistantships (averaging $2,160 per year); fellowships, research assistantships, career-related internships or fieldwork, scholarships/grants, tuition waivers (partial), unspecified assistantships, and 6-8 one-term adjunct co-teaching positions; 27 full-year general assistantships also available. Support available to part-time students. Financial award application deadline: 1/4; financial award applicants required to submit FAFSA. *Faculty research:* Painting and printmaking, sculpture, photography, film and video, dynamic media design. *Unit head:* Paul Paturzo, Dean of Graduate Studies, 617-879-7166, E-mail: pjpaturzo@massart.edu. *Application contact:* Lauren O'Neill, Assistant Director of

Graduate Admissions, 617-879-7222, E-mail: gradadmissions@massart.edu. Website: http://www.massart.edu/Admissions/Graduate_Programs.html

**Memphis College of Art,** Graduate Programs, MFA Program, Memphis, TN 38104-2764. Offers illustration (MFA); metals (MFA); painting/drawing (MFA); photography (MFA); studio art (MFA). *Accreditation:* NASAD. *Program availability:* Part-time. *Faculty:* 27 full-time (16 women), 25 part-time/adjunct (13 women). *Students:* 17 full-time (13 women), 3 part-time (2 women); includes 4 minority (2 Black or African American, non-Hispanic/Latino; 2 Hispanic/Latino), 2 international. Average age 30. 24 applicants, 50% accepted, 4 enrolled. In 2016, 14 master's awarded. *Degree requirements:* For master's, thesis, thesis exhibit. *Entrance requirements:* For master's, portfolio, interview, resume, artist statement. Additional exam requirements/recommendations for international students: Required—TOEFL (minimum score 525 paper-based). *Application deadline:* For fall admission, 2/1 priority date for domestic and international students; for spring admission, 11/1 priority date for domestic and international students. Application fee: $50. Electronic applications accepted. *Expenses:* $33,100. *Financial support:* In 2016–17, 20 students received support, including 8 fellowships (averaging $4,000 per year), 5 teaching assistantships (averaging $3,000 per year); career-related internships or fieldwork, Federal Work-Study, scholarships/grants, and unspecified assistantships also available. Financial award application deadline: 8/1; financial award applicants required to submit FAFSA. *Unit head:* O. Gustavo Plascenicia, Director, 901-272-5100, E-mail: ogplascencia@mca.edu. *Application contact:* Katey Henriksen, Director of Admissions, 901-272-5151, Fax: 901-272-5158, E-mail: khenriksen@mca.edu.

**Miami University,** College of Creative Arts, Department of Art, Oxford, OH 45056. Offers art education (MA); studio art (MFA). *Accreditation:* NASAD (one or more programs are accredited). *Students:* 22 full-time (11 women), 2 part-time (1 woman); includes 6 minority (2 Black or African American, non-Hispanic/Latino; 2 Asian, non-Hispanic/Latino; 1 Hispanic/Latino; 1 Two or more races, non-Hispanic/Latino), 4 international. Average age 33. In 2016, 4 master's awarded. *Expenses:* Tuition, state resident: full-time $12,890; part-time $564 per credit hour. Tuition, nonresident: full-time $29,604; part-time $1260 per credit hour. *Required fees:* $638. Part-time tuition and fees vary according to course load and program. *Unit head:* Thomas Effler, Interim Chair, 513-529-2900, E-mail: art@miamioh.edu. Website: http://www.MiamiOH.edu/art

**Michigan State University,** The Graduate School, College of Arts and Letters, Department of Art and Art History, East Lansing, MI 48824. Offers studio art (MFA). *Entrance requirements:* For master's, minimum GPA of 3.0, portfolio, resume. Additional exam requirements/recommendations for international students: Required—TOEFL, Michigan State University ELT ( minimum score 85), Michigan English Language Assessment Battery (minimum score 83). Electronic applications accepted.

**Millersville University of Pennsylvania,** College of Graduate Studies and Adult Learning, College of Arts, Humanities and Social Sciences, Department of Art and Design, Millersville, PA 17551-0302. Offers art education (M Ed). *Accreditation:* NASAD; NCATE. *Program availability:* Part-time. *Faculty:* 12 full-time (8 women). *Students:* 2 full-time (1 woman), 13 part-time (9 women); includes 2 minority (1 Asian, non-Hispanic/Latino; 1 Hispanic/Latino). Average age 31. 5 applicants, 100% accepted, 3 enrolled. In 2016, 4 master's awarded. *Degree requirements:* For master's, comprehensive exam, thesis optional. *Entrance requirements:* For master's, teaching certificate (unless enrolled in post baccalaureate certificate at same time); portfolio (if not MU graduate). Additional exam requirements/recommendations for international students: Required—TOEFL (minimum score 600 paper-based), IELTS (minimum score 6). *Application deadline:* Applications are processed on a rolling basis. Application fee: $40. Electronic applications accepted. *Expenses:* $483 per credit resident tuition; $725 per credit non-resident tuition. *Financial support:* Unspecified assistantships available. Financial award application deadline: 3/15; financial award applicants required to submit FAFSA. *Faculty research:* Ceramics; representational painting; material investigations involving bronze casting, steel forming and fabrication, mold-making, wood working; art educator's professional learning, assessment in the arts, and postmodern; interactive design fundamentals, interdisciplinary design, interaction, visual storytelling and digital narrative forms and choice-based approaches to teaching art. *Unit head:* Deborah S. Sigel, Chair, 717-871-7249, Fax: 717-871-2004, E-mail: deborah.sigel@millersville.edu. *Application contact:* Dr. Victor S. DeSantis, Dean of College of Graduate Studies and Adult Learning/Associate Provost for Civic and Community Engagement, 717-871-7619, Fax: 717-871-7954, E-mail: victor.desantis@millersville.edu. Website: http://www.millersville.edu/art/

**Mills College,** Graduate Studies, Department of Art, Oakland, CA 94613-1000. Offers art (MFA); ceramics (MFA); intermedia (MFA); painting (MFA); photography (MFA); sculpture (MFA). *Faculty:* 3 full-time (2 women), 5 part-time/adjunct (2 women). *Students:* 20 full-time (11 women); includes 5 minority (1 Black or African American, non-Hispanic/Latino; 4 Hispanic/Latino). Average age 31. 31 applicants, 74% accepted, 9 enrolled. In 2016, 9 master's awarded. *Degree requirements:* For master's, thesis or alternative, exhibit. *Entrance requirements:* For master's, portfolio, artist statement. Additional exam requirements/recommendations for international students: Required—TOEFL (minimum score 550 paper-based; 80 iBT) or IELTS (minimum score 6). *Application deadline:* For fall admission, 2/1 for domestic students, 12/15 for international students. Application fee: $50. Electronic applications accepted. *Expenses:* Contact institution. *Financial support:* In 2016–17, 34 students received support, including 21 fellowships with partial tuition reimbursements available (averaging $11,360 per year), 13 teaching assistantships with partial tuition reimbursements available (averaging $12,200 per year); scholarships/grants and unspecified assistantships also available. Financial award application deadline: 2/1; financial award applicants required to submit FAFSA. *Faculty research:* Experimental film and video, public art projects, ecological design, contemporary art philosophy, sound installations. *Unit head:* Dr. Mary-Ann Milford, Professor of Art History, 510-430-2117. *Application contact:* Robynne Lofton, Director of Admissions, 510-430-3295, Fax: 510-430-2159, E-mail: grad-admission@mills.edu. Website: http://www.mills.edu/art

**Minneapolis College of Art and Design,** Certificate Programs, Minneapolis, MN 55404-4347. Offers design (Certificate); fine arts (Certificate); graphic design (Certificate); media (Certificate); sustainable design (Certificate). *Program availability:* Part-time, online learning. *Degree requirements:* For Certificate, final project. *Entrance requirements:* For degree, resume, portfolio, letter of recommendation. Additional exam requirements/recommendations for international students: Required—TOEFL (minimum score 550 paper-based; 79 iBT). Electronic applications accepted. *Faculty research:* Visual arts.

**Minneapolis College of Art and Design,** Program in Visual Studies, Minneapolis, MN 55404-4347. Offers animation (MFA); comic art (MFA); drawing (MFA); filmmaking (MFA); fine arts (MFA); furniture design (MFA); graphic design (MFA); illustration (MFA); interactive media (MFA); painting (MFA); photography (MFA); printmaking (MFA); sculpture (MFA). *Accreditation:* NASAD. *Program availability:* Part-time. *Degree requirements:* For master's, thesis, thesis exhibit. *Entrance requirements:* For master's, portfolio of visual artwork, resume, 3 letters of recommendation. Additional exam requirements/recommendations for international students: Required—TOEFL (minimum score 550 paper-based; 79 iBT). Electronic applications accepted. *Faculty research:*

Visual arts: animation, comic art, drawing, filmmaking, furniture design, graphic design, illustration, interactive media, painting, photography, printmaking, sculpture.

**Minnesota State University Mankato,** College of Graduate Studies and Research, College of Arts and Humanities, Department of Art, Mankato, MN 56001. Offers art (MA); art education (MAT). *Accreditation:* NASAD (one or more programs are accredited). *Program availability:* Part-time. *Students:* 5 full-time (3 women), 7 part-time (3 women). *Degree requirements:* For master's, one foreign language, comprehensive exam, thesis or alternative. *Entrance requirements:* For master's, portfolio, three letters of reference. Additional exam requirements/recommendations for international students: Required—TOEFL. *Application deadline:* For fall admission, 3/15 priority date for domestic students. Applications are processed on a rolling basis. Application fee: $40. Electronic applications accepted. *Financial support:* Research assistantships, teaching assistantships with full tuition reimbursements, and unspecified assistantships available. Financial award application deadline: 3/15; financial award applicants required to submit FAFSA. *Unit head:* Brian Frink, Chairperson, 507-389-5213, E-mail: brian.frink@mnsu.edu. Website: http://www.mnsu.edu/artdept/

**Mississippi College,** Graduate School, College of Arts and Sciences, School of Christian Studies and the Arts, Department of Art, Clinton, MS 39058. Offers M Ed, MA, MFA. *Program availability:* Part-time, evening/weekend. *Degree requirements:* For master's, one foreign language, comprehensive exam, thesis (for some programs). *Entrance requirements:* For master's, GRE or NTE, minimum GPA of 2.5. Additional exam requirements/recommendations for international students: Recommended—TOEFL, IELTS. Electronic applications accepted.

**Missouri State University,** Graduate College, College of Arts and Letters, Department of Art and Design, Springfield, MO 65897. Offers visual studies (MFA). *Program availability:* Part-time. *Faculty:* 14 full-time (7 women). *Students:* 9 full-time (6 women), 3 part-time (2 women); includes 1 minority (Two or more races, non-Hispanic/Latino), 4 international. Average age 32. 11 applicants, 27% accepted, 2 enrolled. In 2016, 4 master's awarded. *Degree requirements:* For master's, comprehensive exam, thesis, exhibition. *Entrance requirements:* For master's, digital portfolio; 300- to 800-word statement describing reasons and goals behind applicant's interest in graduate study and direction of intended research; at least three letters of recommendation from individuals able to speak of applicant's academic achievements and potential. Additional exam requirements/recommendations for international students: Required—TOEFL (minimum score 550 paper-based; 79 iBT), IELTS (minimum score 6). *Application deadline:* For fall admission, 7/20 priority date for domestic students, 5/1 for international students; for spring admission, 12/20 priority date for domestic students, 9/1 for international students. Applications are processed on a rolling basis. Application fee: $35 ($50 for international students). Electronic applications accepted. *Expenses:* Tuition, state resident: full-time $5830. Tuition, nonresident: full-time $10,708. *Required fees:* $1130. Tuition and fees vary according to class time, course level, course load and program. *Financial support:* In 2016–17, 5 teaching assistantships with full tuition reimbursements (averaging $8,772 per year) were awarded; Federal Work-Study and unspecified assistantships also available. Financial award application deadline: 3/31; financial award applicants required to submit FAFSA. *Unit head:* Vonda Yarberry, Interim Department Head, 417-837-2330, E-mail: artanddesign@missouristate.edu. *Application contact:* Michael Edwards, Coordinator of Graduate Admissions, 417-836-5330, Fax: 417-836-6200, E-mail: michaeledwards@missouristate.edu. Website: http://art.missouristate.edu/

**Montana State University,** The Graduate School, College of Arts and Architecture, School of Art, Bozeman, MT 59717. Offers art (MFA); art history (MA). *Accreditation:* NASAD (one or more programs are accredited). *Program availability:* Part-time. *Degree requirements:* For master's, comprehensive exam, thesis. *Entrance requirements:* For master's, GRE General Test, undergraduate degree in art. Additional exam requirements/recommendations for international students: Required—TOEFL (minimum score 550 paper-based). Electronic applications accepted. *Faculty research:* Encaustic painting, wild clay research, environmentally friendly kiln fuel, Roman wall paintings, French revolutionary portraiture.

**Montclair State University,** The Graduate School, College of the Arts, Program in Fine Art, Montclair, NJ 07043-1624. Offers museum management (MA); studio (MA). *Accreditation:* NASAD. *Program availability:* Part-time, evening/weekend. *Degree requirements:* For master's, project. *Entrance requirements:* For master's, GRE or MAT, 2 letters of recommendation, essay. Electronic applications accepted. *Expenses:* Tuition, state resident: part-time $553 per credit. Tuition, nonresident: part-time $854 per credit. *Required fees:* $91 per credit. Tuition and fees vary according to program.

**Montclair State University,** The Graduate School, College of the Arts, Program in Studio Art, Montclair, NJ 07043-1624. Offers MFA. *Accreditation:* NASAD. *Program availability:* Part-time, evening/weekend. *Degree requirements:* For master's, project. *Entrance requirements:* For master's, 2 letters of recommendation, essay. Additional exam requirements/recommendations for international students: Required—TOEFL (minimum score 83 iBT), IELTS (minimum score 6.5). Electronic applications accepted. *Expenses:* Tuition, state resident: part-time $553 per credit. Tuition, nonresident: part-time $854 per credit. *Required fees:* $91 per credit. Tuition and fees vary according to program.

**Moore College of Art & Design,** Program in Studio Art, Philadelphia, PA 19103. Offers MFA. *Accreditation:* NASAD. *Degree requirements:* For master's, thesis. *Entrance requirements:* For master's, bachelor's degree in visual arts or another field with completion of 15 art history credits; minimum GPA of 3.0; on-site interview; portfolio; 3 letters of recommendation; resume.

**Morehead State University,** Graduate Programs, Caudill College of Arts, Humanities and Social Sciences, Department of Art and Design, Morehead, KY 40351. Offers art education (MA); graphic design (MA); studio art (MA). *Accreditation:* NASAD. *Program availability:* Part-time, evening/weekend. *Degree requirements:* For master's, comprehensive exam, thesis (for some programs), oral exam during exhibition. *Entrance requirements:* For master's, GRE General Test, minimum undergraduate GPA of 3.0 in major, 2.5 overall; portfolio; bachelor's degree in art. Additional exam requirements/recommendations for international students: Required—TOEFL (minimum score 500 paper-based). Electronic applications accepted. *Faculty research:* Computer art, painting, drawing, ceramics, photography.

**New Hampshire Institute of Art,** Graduate Studies, Manchester, NH 03104. Offers art education (MA); creative writing (MFA); photography (MFA); teaching visual arts (MAT); visual arts (MFA); writing for stage and screen (MFA). *Accreditation:* NASAD. *Faculty:* 31 part-time/adjunct (14 women). *Students:* 59 full-time (42 women), 6 part-time (3 women); includes 2 minority (1 Asian, non-Hispanic/Latino; 1 Hispanic/Latino). Average age 43. 36 applicants, 58% accepted, 12 enrolled. In 2016, 2 master's awarded. *Degree requirements:* For master's, thesis, corresponding exhibition and artist talk. *Entrance requirements:* For master's, writing sample or visual art portfolio; curriculum vitae; transcripts; letters of recommendation. Additional exam requirements/recommendations for international students: Required—TOEFL (minimum score 530 paper-based; 71 iBT). *Application deadline:* For fall admission, 5/1 priority date for domestic students; for spring admission, 11/1 priority date for domestic students. Applications are processed

on a rolling basis. Application fee: $75. Electronic applications accepted. *Expenses:* $9,745 tuition per semester/residency plus $745 residency fee. *Financial support:* In 2016–17, 2 teaching assistantships (averaging $1,200 per year) were awarded; scholarships/grants and unspecified assistantships also available. Support available to part-time students. Financial award application deadline: 6/1; financial award applicants required to submit FAFSA. *Faculty research:* Fine arts - visual arts, photography, creative writing, writing for stage and screen; art education. *Unit head:* Lucinda Bliss, Dean of Graduate Studies, 603-836 2522, E-mail: lucindabliss@nhia.edu. *Application contact:* Moriah Billups, Graduate Admissions Coordinator, 603-836 2588, E-mail: gradadmissions@nhia.edu.
Website: http://www.nhia.edu/graduate-studies

**New Jersey City University,** William J. Maxwell College of Arts and Sciences, Department of Art, Jersey City, NJ 07305-1597. Offers art (MFA); art education (MA); studio art (MFA). *Accreditation:* NASAD. *Program availability:* Part-time, evening/weekend. *Degree requirements:* For master's, thesis or alternative, exhibit. *Entrance requirements:* For master's, portfolio. Additional exam requirements/recommendations for international students: Required—TOEFL (minimum score 79 iBT).

**New Mexico State University,** College of Arts and Sciences, Department of Art, Las Cruces, NM 88003. Offers art history (MA); studio art (MFA). *Program availability:* Part-time. *Faculty:* 10 full-time (7 women). *Students:* 14 full-time (8 women), 2 part-time (both women); includes 7 minority (1 Black or African American, non-Hispanic/Latino; 6 Hispanic/Latino), 1 international. Average age 33. 14 applicants, 57% accepted, 3 enrolled. In 2016, 4 master's awarded. *Degree requirements:* For master's, one foreign language, comprehensive exam (for some programs), thesis, thesis exhibit. *Entrance requirements:* For master's, portfolio (for MFA); 10-20 page paper (for MA). Additional exam requirements/recommendations for international students: Required—TOEFL (minimum score 550 paper-based; 79 iBT), IELTS (minimum score 6.5). *Application deadline:* For fall admission, 1/20 for domestic students; for spring admission, 11/15 for domestic students. Application fee: $40 ($50 for international students). Electronic applications accepted. *Expenses:* Tuition, state resident: full-time $4086. Tuition, nonresident: full-time $14,254. *Required fees:* $853. Tuition and fees vary according to course load. *Financial support:* In 2016–17, 14 students received support, including 2 fellowships (averaging $4,088 per year), 13 teaching assistantships (averaging $15,105 per year); career-related internships or fieldwork, Federal Work-Study, scholarships/grants, traineeships, health care benefits, and unspecified assistantships also available. Support available to part-time students. Financial award application deadline: 3/1. *Faculty research:* Art history, painting, graphic design, sculpture, ceramics, photography. Total annual research expenditures: $3,118. *Unit head:* Dr. Julia Barello, Department Head, 575-646-1705, Fax: 575-646-8036, E-mail: jbarello@nmsu.edu. *Application contact:* 575-646-1705, Fax: 575-646-8036, E-mail: artdept@nmsu.edu.
Website: http://artdepartment.nmsu.edu/

**The New School,** Parsons School of Design, Program in Fine Arts, New York, NY 10011. Offers MFA. *Program availability:* Part-time. *Faculty:* 49 full-time (27 women), 21 part-time/adjunct (13 women). *Students:* 47 full-time (30 women); includes 10 minority (3 Black or African American, non-Hispanic/Latino; 2 Asian, non-Hispanic/Latino; 5 Hispanic/Latino), 22 international. Average age 27. 113 applicants, 43% accepted, 25 enrolled. In 2016, 15 master's awarded. *Degree requirements:* For master's, thesis. *Entrance requirements:* For master's, transcripts, resume, statement of purpose, recommendation letters, portfolio, interview. Additional exam requirements/recommendations for international students: Required—TOEFL (minimum score 92 iBT), IELTS (minimum score 7), PTE (minimum score 63). *Application deadline:* For fall admission, 1/1 priority date for domestic and international students. Applications are processed on a rolling basis. Application fee: $50. Electronic applications accepted. *Expenses:* Contact institution. *Financial support:* Research assistantships, teaching assistantships, career-related internships or fieldwork, scholarships/grants, and unspecified assistantships available. Support available to part-time students. Financial award application deadline: 2/1; financial award applicants required to submit FAFSA. *Faculty research:* New genres; performance; photography and video; visual culture studies; art history, theory, and criticism; cultural studies. *Unit head:* Simone Douglas, Director, 212-229-8950, E-mail: douglass@newschool.edu. *Application contact:* Courtney Malenius, Director of Graduate Admissions, 212-229-5150 Ext. 4011, E-mail: maleniuc@newschool.edu. Website: http://www.newschool.edu/parsons

**New York Academy of Art,** Master of Fine Arts Program, New York, NY 10013-2911. Offers drawing (MFA), including anatomy, printmaking; painting (MFA), including anatomy, printmaking; sculpture (MFA), including anatomy, printmaking. *Accreditation:* NASAD. *Faculty:* 5 full-time (1 woman), 31 part-time/adjunct (13 women). *Students:* 119 full-time (76 women); includes 22 minority (4 Black or African American, non-Hispanic/Latino; 1 American Indian or Alaska Native, non-Hispanic/Latino; 4 Asian, non-Hispanic/Latino; 8 Hispanic/Latino; 2 Native Hawaiian or other Pacific Islander, non-Hispanic/Latino; 3 Two or more races, non-Hispanic/Latino), 33 international. Average age 30. 115 applicants, 77% accepted, 55 enrolled. In 2016, 49 master's awarded. *Degree requirements:* For master's, thesis. *Entrance requirements:* For master's, portfolio, essay, two letters of recommendation, curriculum vitae or resume, official undergraduate transcripts. Additional exam requirements/recommendations for international students: Required—TOEFL (minimum score 550 paper-based; 80 iBT), IELTS (minimum score 6.5). *Application deadline:* For fall admission, 1/17 priority date for domestic and international students. Application fee: $80. Electronic applications accepted. Application fee is waived when completed online. *Expenses:* Contact institution. *Financial support:* In 2016–17, 92 students received support, including 3 fellowships (averaging $10,000 per year); career-related internships or fieldwork, Federal Work-Study, and scholarships/grants also available. Financial award application deadline: 9/1; financial award applicants required to submit FAFSA. *Faculty research:* Drawing, painting, sculpture, anatomy, printmaking. Total annual research expenditures: $27,000. *Unit head:* David Kratz, President, 212-966-0300. *Application contact:* Katie Hemmer, Director of Admissions/Registrar, 212-842-5961, E-mail: khemmer@nyaa.edu.
Website: http://www.nyaa.edu/

**New York Institute of Technology,** College of Arts and Sciences, Department of Digital Art and Design, Old Westbury, NY 11568-8000. Offers computer graphics (MFA), including animation, fine arts and technology, graphic design. *Program availability:* Part-time, evening/weekend. *Faculty:* 7 full-time (4 women), 6 part-time/adjunct (2 women). *Students:* 42 full-time (30 women), 12 part-time (6 women); includes 6 minority (3 Black or African American, non-Hispanic/Latino; 1 Asian, non-Hispanic/Latino; 2 Hispanic/Latino), 42 international. Average age 27. 41 applicants, 68% accepted, 14 enrolled. In 2016, 31 master's awarded. *Degree requirements:* For master's, thesis. *Entrance requirements:* For master's, BFA or equivalent; minimum undergraduate GPA of 3.0; digital portfolio. Additional exam requirements/recommendations for international students: Required—TOEFL (minimum score 79 iBT), IELTS (minimum score 6). *Application deadline:* For fall admission, 6/1 for domestic and international students. Applications are processed on a rolling basis. Application fee: $50. Electronic applications accepted. *Expenses:* $1,215 per credit. *Financial support:* Career-related internships or fieldwork, Federal Work-Study, scholarships/grants, tuition waivers (full and partial), and unspecified assistantships available. Support available to part-time students. Financial award application deadline: 3/1; financial award applicants required

to submit FAFSA. *Faculty research:* Graphic design, animation, art and technology, virtual reality, sculpture. *Unit head:* Terry Nauheim, Department Chair, 516-686-7881, Fax: 212-261-1742, E-mail: tnauheim@nyit.edu. *Application contact:* Alice Dolitsky, Director, Graduate Admissions, 516-686-7520, Fax: 516-686-1116, E-mail: nyitgrad@nyit.edu.
Website: http://www.nyit.edu/arts_and_sciences/department_of_digital_art_design

**New York Studio School of Drawing, Painting and Sculpture,** Certificate Program, New York, NY 10011. Offers studio art (Certificate).

**New York Studio School of Drawing, Painting and Sculpture,** MFA Program, New York, NY 10011. Offers painting (MFA); sculpture (MFA).
**See Display on next page and Close-Up on page 207.**

**New York University,** Graduate School of Arts and Science, Institute of Fine Arts, New York, NY 10012-1019. Offers art history and archaeology (MA, PhD), including architectural studies (PhD), art history and archaeology, classical art and archaeology (PhD), curatorial studies (PhD), East and South Asian art (PhD), Near Eastern art and archaeology (PhD); MA/Diploma; PhD/Certificate. *Program availability:* Part-time. Terminal master's awarded for partial completion of doctoral program. *Degree requirements:* For master's, 2 foreign languages, thesis or alternative, 2 qualifying papers; for doctorate, 2 foreign languages, thesis/dissertation. *Entrance requirements:* For master's, GRE General Test; for doctorate, GRE General Test, MA. Additional exam requirements/recommendations for international students: Required—TOEFL.

**New York University,** Steinhardt School of Culture, Education, and Human Development, Department of Art and Art Professions, Program in Studio Art, New York, NY 10003. Offers MA, MFA, Advanced Certificate. *Program availability:* Part-time. *Degree requirements:* For master's, thesis (for some programs). *Entrance requirements:* For master's, portfolio, interview, presentation. Additional exam requirements/recommendations for international students: Required—TOEFL (minimum score 100 iBT). Electronic applications accepted. *Faculty research:* Media and culture, video art and digital media, multimedia works, critical theory, memory and history, performance and text.

**New York University,** Steinhardt School of Culture, Education, and Human Development, Department of Art and Art Professions, Program in Visual Culture, New York, NY 10003. Offers costume studies (MA); MA/MS. *Program availability:* Part-time. *Degree requirements:* For master's, thesis (for some programs). *Entrance requirements:* Additional exam requirements/recommendations for international students: Required—TOEFL (minimum score 100 iBT). Electronic applications accepted. *Faculty research:* Textiles as material culture, contemporary visual culture and globalization, cultural theory.

**New York University,** Tisch School of the Arts, Program in Arts Politics, New York, NY 10012-1019. Offers MA. *Degree requirements:* For master's, thesis. *Entrance requirements:* For master's, professional resume, writing sample, statement of purpose. Additional exam requirements/recommendations for international students: Required—TOEFL or IELTS.

**Norfolk State University,** School of Graduate Studies, School of Liberal Arts, Department of Fine Arts, Norfolk, VA 23504. Offers visual studies (MA, MFA). *Program availability:* Part-time. *Degree requirements:* For master's, thesis or alternative. *Entrance requirements:* For master's, portfolio, interview, letters of recommendation. Additional exam requirements/recommendations for international students: Required—TOEFL (minimum score 500 paper-based).

**Northeastern University,** College of Arts, Media and Design, Boston, MA 02115-5096. Offers architecture (M Arch); game science and design (MS); information design and visualization (MFA); interdisciplinary arts (MFA); journalism (MA); music industry leadership (MS); studio art (MFA); sustainable building systems (MS); sustainable urban environments (M Des). *Faculty:* 142 full-time (55 women), 80 part-time/adjunct (34 women). *Students:* 239 full-time (147 women), 16 part-time (12 women). In 2016, 83 master's awarded. Application fee: $75. Electronic applications accepted. *Expenses:* $1,365 per credit. *Financial support:* Applicants required to submit FAFSA. *Unit head:* Dr. Elizabeth Hudson, Dean. *Application contact:* Jane Amidon, Associate Dean for Graduate Programs and Research, 617-373-4614, E-mail: gscamd@northeastern.edu.
Website: http://www.northeastern.edu/camd/

**Northern Illinois University,** Graduate School, College of Visual and Performing Arts, School of Art, De Kalb, IL 60115-2854. Offers MA, MFA, MS. *Accreditation:* NASAD (one or more programs are accredited). *Program availability:* Part-time, evening/weekend. *Faculty:* 36 full-time (15 women), 1 (woman) part-time/adjunct. *Students:* 50 full-time (36 women), 22 part-time (13 women); includes 13 minority (1 Black or African American, non-Hispanic/Latino; 3 Asian, non-Hispanic/Latino; 8 Hispanic/Latino; 1 Two or more races, non-Hispanic/Latino), 4 international. Average age 32. 64 applicants, 50% accepted, 16 enrolled. In 2016, 21 master's awarded. *Degree requirements:* For master's, variable foreign language requirement, comprehensive exam, thesis (for some programs), show or project. *Entrance requirements:* For master's, GRE General Test, minimum GPA of 2.75, portfolio. Additional exam requirements/recommendations for international students: Required—TOEFL (minimum score 550 paper-based). *Application deadline:* For fall and spring admission, 3/1 for domestic and international students. Applications are processed on a rolling basis. Application fee: $40. Electronic applications accepted. *Financial support:* In 2016–17, 28 research assistantships with full tuition reimbursements, 24 teaching assistantships with full tuition reimbursements were awarded; fellowships with full tuition reimbursements, career-related internships or fieldwork, Federal Work-Study, scholarships/grants, tuition waivers (full), and staff assistantships also available. Support available to part-time students. Financial award applicants required to submit FAFSA. *Faculty research:* Art education, portfolio assessment, central European design history, relationship between modern art and industrialism. *Unit head:* John Siblik, Director, 815-753-7850, Fax: 815-753-7701, E-mail: jsiblik@niu.edu. *Application contact:* Kurt Schultz, Graduate Coordinator, 815-753-1473, E-mail: artgradcoordinator@niu.edu.
Website: http://www.niu.edu/art/

**Northwestern State University of Louisiana,** Graduate Studies and Research, School of Creative and Performing Arts, Program in Art, Natchitoches, LA 71497. Offers fine and graphic arts (MA). *Accreditation:* NASAD. *Degree requirements:* For master's, comprehensive exam, thesis or alternative. *Entrance requirements:* For master's, GRE General Test, minimum undergraduate GPA of 2.5. Additional exam requirements/recommendations for international students: Required—TOEFL. Electronic applications accepted.

**Northwestern University,** The Graduate School, Judd A. and Marjorie Weinberg College of Arts and Sciences, Department of Art Theory and Practice, Evanston, IL 60208. Offers visual arts (MFA). Admissions and degrees offered through The Graduate School. *Degree requirements:* For master's, essay, exhibit. *Entrance requirements:* For master's, 20 slides of recent work. Additional exam requirements/recommendations for international students: Required—TOEFL. Electronic applications accepted.

**Nova Southeastern University,** College of Arts, Humanities, and Social Sciences, Fort Lauderdale, FL 33314-7796. Offers advanced conflict resolution practice (Graduate Certificate); college student affairs (MS); conflict analysis and resolution (MS, PhD);

cross-disciplinary studies (MA); family studies (Graduate Certificate); family systems health care (Graduate Certificate); family therapy (MS, PhD); marriage and family therapy (DMFT); peace studies (Graduate Certificate); qualitative research (Graduate Certificate); solution focused coaching (Graduate Certificate). *Accreditation:* AAMFT/COAMFTE (one or more programs are accredited). *Program availability:* Part-time, evening/weekend, 100% online, blended/hybrid learning. *Faculty:* 29 full-time (18 women), 27 part-time/adjunct (21 women). *Students:* 306 full-time (242 women), 889 part-time (683 women); includes 677 minority (403 Black or African American, non-Hispanic/Latino; 2 American Indian or Alaska Native, non-Hispanic/Latino; 20 Asian, non-Hispanic/Latino; 224 Hispanic/Latino; 1 Native Hawaiian or other Pacific Islander, non-Hispanic/Latino; 27 Two or more races, non-Hispanic/Latino), 53 international. Average age 37. 624 applicants, 61% accepted, 285 enrolled. In 2016, 303 master's, 71 doctorates, 34 other advanced degrees awarded. *Degree requirements:* For master's, thesis optional, comprehensive exams, portfolios (for some programs), table-top exams (for some programs); for doctorate, comprehensive exam, thesis/dissertation, qualifying exams, portfolios (for some programs). *Entrance requirements:* For master's, interview, minimum GPA of 3.0, writing sample; for doctorate, interview, minimum GPA of 3.5, master's degree in related field, writing sample; for Graduate Certificate, minimum GPA of 3.0. Additional exam requirements/recommendations for international students: Required—TOEFL. *Application deadline:* For fall admission, 5/17 priority date for domestic and international students; for winter admission, 12/1 priority date for domestic and international students; for spring admission, 4/1 priority date for domestic and international students. Applications are processed on a rolling basis. Application fee: $50. Electronic applications accepted. *Expenses:* $1,005. *Financial support:* In 2016–17, 170 students received support. Career-related internships or fieldwork, Federal Work-Study, scholarships/grants, and unspecified assistantships available. Financial award application deadline: 4/1; financial award applicants required to submit CSS PROFILE. *Faculty research:* Conflict resolution, family therapy, peace research, international conflict, multi-disciplinary studies, college student affairs, national security affairs, health care conflict resolution, family systems health care, advanced family systems, qualitative research, solution-focused coaching. *Unit head:* Dr. Honggang Yang, Dean, 954-262-3016, Fax: 954-262-3968, E-mail: yangh@nova.edu. *Application contact:* Marcia Arango, Student Recruitment Coordinator, 954-262-3006, Fax: 954-262-3968, E-mail: marango@nsu.nova.edu.
Website: http://cahss.nova.edu/

**NSCAD University,** Program in Fine Arts, Halifax, NS B3J 3J6, Canada. Offers craft (MFA); design (M Des); fine and media arts (MFA). *Degree requirements:* For master's, thesis, exhibit. *Entrance requirements:* For master's, portfolio, at least 5 art history classes. Additional exam requirements/recommendations for international students: Required—Michigan English Language Assessment Battery (minimum score: 80), CanTEST (minimum score: 4.5), CAEL (minimum score: 70); Recommended—TOEFL (minimum score 575 paper-based; 90 iBT), IELTS (minimum score 6.5).

**The Ohio State University,** Graduate School, College of Arts and Sciences, Division of Arts and Humanities, Department of Art, Columbus, OH 43210. Offers MFA. *Accreditation:* NASAD. *Faculty:* 19. *Students:* 40 full-time (24 women), 9 international. Average age 29. In 2016, 24 master's awarded. *Degree requirements:* For master's, thesis, exhibit, oral exams. *Entrance requirements:* For master's, GRE General Test (if GPA cumulative average is less than 3.0), electronic portfolio. Additional exam requirements/recommendations for international students: Required—Michigan English Language Assessment Battery (minimum score 82); Recommended—TOEFL (minimum score 550 paper-based; 79 iBT), IELTS (minimum score 7). *Application deadline:* For fall admission, 12/31 priority date for domestic students, 11/30 priority date for international students; for spring admission, 3/1 for domestic students, 2/1 for international students. Applications are processed on a rolling basis. Application fee: $60 ($70 for international

students). Electronic applications accepted. *Financial support:* Fellowships with tuition reimbursements, teaching assistantships with tuition reimbursements, Federal Work-Study, institutionally sponsored loans, and unspecified assistantships available. Support available to part-time students. *Unit head:* Rebecca Harvey, Chair, 614-292-5072, E-mail: harvey.113@osu.edu. *Application contact:* Graduate and Professional Admissions, 614-292-9444, Fax: 614-292-3895, E-mail: gpadmissions@osu.edu. Website: http://art.osu.edu/

**Ohio University,** Graduate College, College of Fine Arts, School of Art, Athens, OH 45701-2979. Offers art history (MA); ceramics (MFA); graphic design (MFA); painting (MFA); photography (MFA); printmaking (MFA); sculpture (MFA). *Program availability:* Part-time. *Degree requirements:* For master's, thesis. *Entrance requirements:* For master's, portfolio. Additional exam requirements/recommendations for international students: Required—TOEFL (minimum score 550 paper-based; 80 iBT) or IELTS (minimum score 6.5). *Application deadline:* For fall admission, 2/1 for domestic and international students. Application fee: $50 ($55 for international students). Electronic applications accepted. *Financial support:* Teaching assistantships with full and partial tuition reimbursements, career-related internships or fieldwork, Federal Work-Study, institutionally sponsored loans, scholarships/grants, tuition waivers (partial), and unspecified assistantships available. Financial award application deadline: 2/1. *Faculty research:* Vapor-fired ceramics, video installation, art theory, digital photography, mixed and interdisciplinary media work. *Unit head:* David LaPalombara, Director, 740-593-4290, Fax: 740-593-0457, E-mail: lapalomb@ohio.edu. *Application contact:* Alexandra Hibbitt, Chair, Graduate Programs, 740-593-4293, Fax: 740-593-0457, E-mail: hibbitt@ohio.edu. Website: http://www.finearts.ohio.edu/art/

**Oregon College of Art and Craft,** MFA Program, Portland, OR 97225. Offers craft (MFA). *Accreditation:* NASAD.

**Otis College of Art and Design,** Program in Fine Arts, Los Angeles, CA 90045-9785. Offers new genres (MFA); painting (MFA); photography (MFA); sculpture (MFA). *Accreditation:* NASAD. *Degree requirements:* For master's, thesis. *Entrance requirements:* For master's, portfolio. Additional exam requirements/recommendations for international students: Required—TOEFL (minimum score 600 paper-based). Electronic applications accepted.

**Otis College of Art and Design,** Program in Public Practice, Los Angeles, CA 90045-9785. Offers MFA. *Entrance requirements:* Additional exam requirements/recommendations for international students: Required—TOEFL (minimum score 600 paper-based). Electronic applications accepted.

**Pace University,** School of Education, New York, NY 10038. Offers adolescent education (MST), including biology, business education, chemistry, earth science, English, foreign languages, mathematics, physics, social studies, visual arts; childhood education (MST); early childhood development, learning and intervention (MST); educational technology studies (MS); inclusive adolescent education (MST), including biology, business education, chemistry, earth science, English, foreign languages, mathematics, physics, social studies, visual arts; integrated instruction for educational technology (Certificate); integrated instruction for literacy and technology (Certificate); literacy (MS Ed); special education (MS Ed). *Accreditation:* NCATE. *Program availability:* Part-time, evening/weekend, blended/hybrid learning. *Faculty:* 19 full-time (13 women), 86 part-time/adjunct (49 women). *Students:* 115 full-time (97 women), 543 part-time (381 women); includes 280 minority (137 Black or African American, non-Hispanic/Latino; 1 American Indian or Alaska Native, non-Hispanic/Latino; 40 Asian, non-Hispanic/Latino; 87 Hispanic/Latino; 15 Two or more races, non-Hispanic/Latino), 13 international. Average age 30. 181 applicants, 78% accepted, 72 enrolled. In 2016, 193 master's, 9 other advanced degrees awarded. *Degree requirements:* For master's, certification exams. *Entrance requirements:* For master's, GRE, interview, teaching

*Art/Fine Arts*

certificate (except for MST). Additional exam requirements/recommendations for international students: Required—TOEFL (minimum score 88 iBT), IELTS or PTE. *Application deadline:* For fall admission, 8/1 priority date for domestic students, 6/1 for international students; for spring admission, 12/1 priority date for domestic students, 10/1 for international students. Applications are processed on a rolling basis. Application fee: $70. Electronic applications accepted. *Expenses:* Contact institution. *Financial support:* In 2016–17, 17 students received support, including 17 research assistantships with partial tuition reimbursements available (averaging $6,020 per year); career-related internships or fieldwork and Federal Work-Study also available. Financial award application deadline: 9/1; financial award applicants required to submit FAFSA. *Faculty research:* STEM education, TESOL, teacher education, special education, language and literary development. *Total annual research expenditures:* $290,153. *Unit head:* Dr. Xiao-Lei Wang, Dean, School of Education, 914-773-3876, E-mail: xwang@pace.edu. *Application contact:* Susan Ford-Goldschein, Director of Graduate Admissions, 212-346-1531, Fax: 212-346-1585, E-mail: graduateadmission@pace.edu. Website: http://www.pace.edu/school-of-education

**Pacific Northwest College of Art,** Program in Visual Studies, Portland, OR 97209. Offers MFA. *Accreditation:* NASAD.

**Paris College of Art,** Graduate Programs, Paris, France. Offers accessories design (MA); fashion design: new materials and technologies (MA); fashion film and photography (MA); interior design (MA); transdisciplinary new media (MA, MFA). *Entrance requirements:* Additional exam requirements/recommendations for international students: Required—TOEFL or IELTS.

**Penn State University Park,** Graduate School, College of Arts and Architecture, School of Visual Arts, University Park, PA 16802. Offers art (MFA); art education (MPS, MS, PhD, Certificate). *Unit head:* Dr. Barbara O. Korner, Dean, 814-865-2592, Fax: 814-865-2018. *Application contact:* Lori Hawn, Director, Graduate Student Services, 814-865-1795, Fax: 814-863-4627, E-mail: l-gswww@lists.psu.edu. Website: http://sova.psu.edu/

**Pennsylvania Academy of the Fine Arts,** Division of Graduate Studies, Philadelphia, PA 19102. Offers drawing (MFA, Postbaccalaureate Certificate); painting (MFA, Postbaccalaureate Certificate); printmaking (MFA, Postbaccalaureate Certificate); sculpture (MFA, Postbaccalaureate Certificate). MFA program also available in a low-residency format. *Accreditation:* NASAD (one or more programs are accredited). *Degree requirements:* For master's, thesis exhibit. *Entrance requirements:* For master's, 10-20 slides of work and slide list or SlideRoom submission, 3 letters of recommendation, bachelor's degree, statement of purpose. Additional exam requirements/recommendations for international students: Required—TOEFL (minimum score 600 paper-based; 100 iBT), IELTS (minimum score 6). Electronic applications accepted.

**Pensacola Christian College,** Graduate Studies, Pensacola, FL 32503-2267. Offers business administration (MBA); curriculum and instruction (MS, Ed D, Ed S); dramatics (MFA); educational leadership (MS, Ed D, Ed S); graphic design (MA, MFA); music (MA); nursing (MSN); performance studies (MA); studio art (MA, MFA).

**Philadelphia University,** School of Design and Engineering, Program in Surface Imaging, Philadelphia, PA 19144. Offers MS.

**Pontifical Catholic University of Puerto Rico,** College of Arts and Humanities, Department of Fine Arts, Ponce, PR 00717-0777. Offers painting and drawing (MA).

**Portland State University,** Graduate Studies, College of the Arts, School of Art and Design, Portland, OR 97207-0751. Offers drawing (MFA); mixed media (MFA); painting (MFA); printmaking (MFA); sculpture (MFA). *Faculty:* 22 full-time (16 women), 54 part-time/adjunct (29 women). *Students:* 19 full-time (12 women), 3 part-time (2 women), 5 international. Average age 32. 57 applicants, 25% accepted, 7 enrolled. In 2016, 7 master's awarded. *Degree requirements:* For master's, variable foreign language requirement, thesis, exhibit. *Entrance requirements:* For master's, minimum GPA of 3.0 in upper-division course work or 2.75 overall, portfolio, 3 letters of recommendation. Additional exam requirements/recommendations for international students: Required—TOEFL (minimum score 550 paper-based; 80 iBT), IELTS (minimum score 6.5). *Application deadline:* For fall admission, 3/1 for domestic and international students. Application fee: $65. *Expenses:* Contact institution. *Financial support:* In 2016–17, 6 research assistantships with tuition reimbursements (averaging $1,775 per year), 10 teaching assistantships with partial tuition reimbursements (averaging $1,775 per year) were awarded; Federal Work-Study, scholarships/grants, and unspecified assistantships also available. Support available to part-time students. Financial award application deadline: 3/1; financial award applicants required to submit FAFSA. *Total annual research expenditures:* $77,837. *Unit head:* Patricia Boas, Director, 503-725-3300, Fax: 503-725-4541, E-mail: boasp@pdx.edu. *Application contact:* 503-725-3515, Fax: 503-725-4541, E-mail: askmfa@pdx.edu. Website: https://www.pdx.edu/art-design/

**Pratt Institute,** School of Art, Program in Fine Arts, Brooklyn, NY 11205-3899. Offers MFA. *Accreditation:* NASAD. *Program availability:* Part-time. *Faculty:* 10 full-time (5 women), 78 part-time/adjunct (33 women). *Students:* 83 full-time (52 women), 4 part-time (3 women); includes 16 minority (1 Black or African American, non-Hispanic/Latino; 1 American Indian or Alaska Native, non-Hispanic/Latino; 6 Asian, non-Hispanic/Latino; 4 Hispanic/Latino; 4 Two or more races, non-Hispanic/Latino), 42 international. Average age 27. 277 applicants, 44% accepted, 23 enrolled. In 2016, 47 master's awarded. *Degree requirements:* For master's, thesis, exhibit. *Entrance requirements:* For master's, portfolio, letters of recommendation. Additional exam requirements/recommendations for international students: Required—TOEFL (minimum score 550 paper-based; 79 iBT). *Application deadline:* For fall admission, 1/5 for domestic and international students; for spring admission, 10/1 for domestic and international students. Application fee: $50 ($90 for international students). Electronic applications accepted. *Expenses:* $29,646 full-time tuition, $1,938 fees. *Financial support:* Career-related internships or fieldwork, Federal Work-Study, institutionally sponsored loans, scholarships/grants, health care benefits, and unspecified assistantships available. Support available to part-time students. Financial award application deadline: 2/1; financial award applicants required to submit FAFSA. *Unit head:* Jane South, Chairperson, 718-636-3634, E-mail: jsouth@pratt.edu. *Application contact:* Natalie Capannelli, Director of Graduate Admissions, 718-636-3551, Fax: 718-399-4242, E-mail: ncapanne@pratt.edu. Website: https://www.pratt.edu/academics/school-of-art/graduate-school-of-art/graduate-fine-arts/

See Display on this page and Close-Up on page 209.

**Prescott College,** Graduate Programs, Program in Arts and Humanities, Prescott, AZ 86301. Offers humanities (MA); social justice and human rights (MA); student-directed independent study (MA). *Program availability:* Part-time, online learning. *Faculty:* 3 full-time (0 women). *Students:* 3 full-time (1 woman), 13 part-time (10 women); includes 1 minority (Hispanic/Latino). Average age 42. 28 applicants, 79% accepted, 17 enrolled. In 2016, 20 master's awarded. *Degree requirements:* For master's, thesis, fieldwork or internship, practicum. *Entrance requirements:* For master's, 2 letters of recommendation, resume, essay. Additional exam requirements/recommendations for international students: Required—TOEFL (minimum score 500 paper-based). *Application deadline:* For fall admission, 4/15 priority date for domestic and international students; for spring admission, 9/15 priority date for domestic and international students. Applications are processed on a rolling basis. Application fee: $40. Electronic applications accepted. *Expenses: Tuition:* Full-time $19,680. One-time fee: $260 part-time. *Financial support:* Fellowships, research assistantships, teaching assistantships, career-related internships or fieldwork, Federal Work-Study, institutionally sponsored loans, scholarships/grants, traineeships, health care benefits, tuition waivers, and unspecified assistantships available. Support available to part-time students. Financial award applicants required to submit FAFSA. *Unit head:* Ellen Greenblum, 928-350-3209, E-mail: egreenblum@prescott.edu. *Application contact:* Amber Harris, Assistant Director, Graduate Admissions, 928-615-8446, Fax: 928-776-5242, E-mail: amber.harris@prescott.edu.

**Purchase College, State University of New York,** School of Art and Design, Purchase, NY 10577-1400. Offers visual arts (MFA). *Accreditation:* NASAD. *Degree requirements:* For master's, thesis, exhibit. *Entrance requirements:* For master's, portfolio. *Application deadline:* For fall admission, 2/15 for domestic students. Applications are processed on a rolling basis. Application fee: $85. Electronic applications accepted. *Expenses:* Tuition, state resident: full-time $10,870; part-time $453 per credit. Tuition, nonresident: full-time $22,210; part-time $925 per credit. *Required fees:* $1737. *Financial support:* Fellowships, teaching assistantships, Federal Work-Study, scholarships/grants, and tuition waivers (partial) available. Support available to part-time students. Financial award application deadline: 3/15; financial award applicants required to submit FAFSA. *Unit head:* Steven Lam, Director, 914-251-6750, Fax: 914-251-6793, E-mail: steven.lam@purchase.edu. *Application contact:* Sabrina Johnston, Admission Counselor, 914-251-6479, Fax: 914-251-6314, E-mail: admissn@purchase.edu.
Website: https://www.purchase.edu/academics/art-and-design/

**Purdue University,** Graduate School, College of Liberal Arts, Department of Art and Design, West Lafayette, IN 47907. Offers art education (MA, PhD); industrial design (MFA); integrated studio arts (MFA); interior design (MFA); photography (MFA); visual communications design (MFA). *Accreditation:* NASAD; NAST. *Program availability:* Part-time. *Students:* 20 full-time (14 women), 1 part-time (0 women); includes 1 minority (Two or more races, non-Hispanic/Latino), 16 international. Average age 26. 97 applicants, 26% accepted, 10 enrolled. In 2016, 6 master's awarded. *Degree requirements:* For master's, terminal exhibit, project, or thesis. *Entrance requirements:* For master's, GRE General Test (for art education), minimum undergraduate GPA of 3.0 or equivalent; 9 undergraduate hours in an art or design history; BA in art (for MA in art education); for doctorate, GRE General Test (minimum scores 600 in verbal and 1000 total), master's degree in art education or art with teaching certification; 3 years of teaching experience at the K-12 level. Additional exam requirements/recommendations for international students: Required—TOEFL (minimum score 550 paper-based; 77 iBT). *Application deadline:* For fall admission, 2/1 for domestic students, 2/1 priority date for international students. Applications are processed on a rolling basis. Application fee: $60 ($75 for international students). Electronic applications accepted. *Financial support:* Teaching assistantships with tuition reimbursements and career-related internships or fieldwork available. Support available to part-time students. Financial award applicants required to submit FAFSA. *Faculty research:* Design, fine arts, photography, acting, directing, theatre technology. *Unit head:* Harry T. Bulow, Head of the Graduate Program, 765-494-3056, E-mail: hbulow@purdue.edu. *Application contact:* Sara J. Unser, Graduate Contact, 765-494-8662, E-mail: sunser@purdue.edu.
Website: https://www.cla.purdue.edu/vpa/ad/

**Queens College of the City University of New York,** Arts and Humanities Division, Department of Art, Queens, NY 11367-1597. Offers art history (MA); studio art (MFA). *Program availability:* Part-time. *Faculty:* 18 full-time (6 women), 56 part-time/adjunct (32 women). *Students:* 15 full-time (8 women), 25 part-time (21 women); includes 11 minority (5 Black or African American, non-Hispanic/Latino; 2 Asian, non-Hispanic/Latino; 4 Hispanic/Latino), 5 international. Average age 36. 25 applicants, 44% accepted, 8 enrolled. In 2016, 11 master's awarded. *Degree requirements:* For master's, thesis, comprehensive exam (for art history program). *Entrance requirements:* For master's, minimum GPA of 3.0. Additional exam requirements/recommendations for international students: Required—TOEFL, IELTS. *Application deadline:* For fall admission, 4/1 for domestic students; for spring admission, 11/1 for domestic students. Applications are processed on a rolling basis. Application fee: $125. Electronic applications accepted. *Expenses:* Tuition, state resident: full-time $5065; part-time $425 per credit. Tuition, nonresident: part-time $780 per credit. *Required fees:* $522; $397 per credit. Part-time tuition and fees vary according to course load and program. *Financial support:* Career-related internships or fieldwork available. Financial award application deadline: 4/1; financial award applicants required to submit FAFSA. *Unit head:* Dr. Antonio Gonzalez, Chairperson, 718-997-4800, E-mail: antonio.gonzalez@qc.cuny.edu.

**Radford University,** College of Graduate Studies and Research, Program in Art, Radford, VA 24142. Offers MFA. *Accreditation:* NASAD. *Program availability:* Part-time. *Faculty:* 12 full-time (6 women), 2 part-time/adjunct (both women). *Students:* 19 full-time (12 women), 9 part-time (5 women); includes 6 minority (2 Black or African American, non-Hispanic/Latino; 1 American Indian or Alaska Native, non-Hispanic/Latino; 2 Asian, non-Hispanic/Latino; 1 Hispanic/Latino), 2 international. Average age 35. 17 applicants, 82% accepted, 9 enrolled. In 2016, 6 master's awarded. *Degree requirements:* For master's, comprehensive exam. *Entrance requirements:* For master's, statement of philosophy; minimum GPA of 2.75, 2 letters of reference, BFA or commensurate collegiate course work, 20 slides or CD of recent work, resume and official transcripts (for studio art); minimum GPA of 3.0 (preferred) and three letters of reference (for design thinking). Additional exam requirements/recommendations for international students: Required—TOEFL (minimum score 550 paper-based; 79 iBT), IELTS (minimum score 6.5). *Application deadline:* For fall admission, 2/15 priority date for domestic students, 12/1 for international students; for spring admission, 7/1 for international students. Applications are processed on a rolling basis. Application fee: $50. Electronic applications accepted. *Expenses:* $685 per credit hour in-state tuition and fees, $704 per credit hour out-of-state tuition and fees. *Financial support:* In 2016–17, 13 students received support, including 1 research assistantship (averaging $11,000 per year), 5 teaching assistantships (averaging $9,500 per year); scholarships/grants and unspecified assistantships also available. Support available to part-time students. Financial award application deadline: 3/1; financial award applicants required to submit FAFSA. *Unit head:* Dr. Roann Barris, Chair, 540-831-5778, E-mail: rbarris@radford.edu. Website: http://www.radford.edu/content/cvpa/home/art.html

**Rensselaer Polytechnic Institute,** Graduate School, School of Humanities, Arts, and Social Sciences, Program in Electronic Arts, Troy, NY 12180-3590. Offers PhD. *Faculty:* 23 full-time (10 women), 1 (woman) part-time/adjunct. *Students:* 19 full-time (11 women), 1 part-time (0 women). 29 applicants, 48% accepted, 6 enrolled. In 2016, 1 doctorate awarded. *Degree requirements:* For doctorate, comprehensive exam. *Entrance requirements:* Additional exam requirements/recommendations for international students: Required—TOEFL (minimum score 570 paper-based; 88 iBT), IELTS (minimum score 6.5), PTE (minimum score 60). *Application deadline:* For fall

admission, 1/1 priority date for domestic and international students. Applications are processed on a rolling basis. Application fee: $75. Electronic applications accepted. *Expenses: Tuition:* Full-time $49,520; part-time $2060 per credit hour. *Required fees:* $2617. *Financial support:* In 2016–17, research assistantships (averaging $22,000 per year), teaching assistantships with full tuition reimbursements (averaging $22,000 per year) were awarded; scholarships/grants also available. Financial award application deadline: 1/1. *Unit head:* Dr. Shawn Lawson, Graduate Program Director, 518-276-2206, E-mail: lawsos2@rpi.edu. *Application contact:* Office of Graduate Admissions, 518-276-6216, E-mail: gradadmissions@rpi.edu.
Website: http://www.arts.rpi.edu/pl/graduate-programs

**Rhode Island College,** School of Graduate Studies, Faculty of Arts and Sciences, Department of Art, Providence, RI 02908-1991. Offers art education (MA, MAT); media studies (MA). *Accreditation:* NASAD (one or more programs are accredited). *Program availability:* Part-time, evening/weekend. *Faculty:* 6 full-time (3 women), 2 part-time/adjunct (1 woman). *Students:* 7 full-time (5 women), 5 part-time (4 women); includes 1 minority (Hispanic/Latino). Average age 33. In 2016, 4 master's awarded. *Degree requirements:* For master's, thesis. *Entrance requirements:* For master's, GRE General Test, portfolio (MA), 3 letters of recommendation, interview. Additional exam requirements/recommendations for international students: Recommended—TOEFL (minimum score 550 paper-based; 79 iBT). *Application deadline:* For fall admission, 3/1 for domestic students. Applications are processed on a rolling basis. Application fee: $50. Electronic applications accepted. *Expenses:* Tuition, state resident: full-time $8928; part-time $372 per credit. Tuition, nonresident: full-time $17,376; part-time $724 per credit. *Required fees:* $604; $22 per credit. One-time fee: $74. *Financial support:* In 2016–17, 2 teaching assistantships with full tuition reimbursements (averaging $1,500 per year) were awarded; career-related internships or fieldwork, Federal Work-Study, scholarships/grants, health care benefits, and unspecified assistantships also available. Support available to part-time students. Financial award application deadline: 5/15; financial award applicants required to submit FAFSA. *Unit head:* Prof. Richard Whitten, Chair, 401-456-9635. *Application contact:* Graduate Studies, 401-456-8700.
Website: http://www.ric.edu/art/index.php

**Rhode Island School of Design,** Division of Fine Arts, Department of Ceramics, Providence, RI 02903-2784. Offers MFA. *Accreditation:* NASAD. *Faculty:* 7 full-time (4 women), 7 part-time/adjunct (3 women). *Students:* 10 full-time (5 women); includes 2 minority (1 Black or African American, non-Hispanic/Latino; 1 Asian, non-Hispanic/Latino), 5 international. Average age 27. 17 applicants, 47% accepted, 4 enrolled. In 2016, 6 master's awarded. *Degree requirements:* For master's, thesis, exhibition. *Entrance requirements:* For master's, portfolio, statement of purpose, 3 letters of recommendation. Additional exam requirements/recommendations for international students: Required—TOEFL (minimum score 580 paper-based; 93 iBT). *Application deadline:* For fall admission, 2/1 for domestic and international students. Application fee: $60. Electronic applications accepted. *Expenses: Tuition:* Full-time $46,800. *Required fees:* $310. *Financial support:* Fellowships, research assistantships, teaching assistantships, Federal Work-Study, scholarships/grants, and unspecified assistantships available. Financial award applicants required to submit FAFSA. *Unit head:* Katy Schimert, Department Head and Graduate Program Director, 401-454-6190, Fax: 401-454-6191, E-mail: kchimer@risd.edu. *Application contact:* Molly Pettengil, Assistant Director for Graduate Recruitment, 401-454-6312, Fax: 401-454-6309, E-mail: mpetteng@risd.edu.
Website: http://www.risd.edu/academics/ceramics/

**Rhode Island School of Design,** Division of Fine Arts, Department of Glass, Providence, RI 02903-2784. Offers MFA. *Accreditation:* NASAD. *Faculty:* 3 full-time (2 women), 2 part-time/adjunct (1 woman). *Students:* 5 full-time (3 women); includes 1 minority (Two or more races, non-Hispanic/Latino), 2 international. Average age 26. 8 applicants, 38% accepted, 2 enrolled. In 2016, 2 master's awarded. *Degree requirements:* For master's, thesis, exhibition. *Entrance requirements:* For master's, portfolio, statement of purpose, 3 letters of recommendation. Additional exam requirements/recommendations for international students: Required—TOEFL (minimum score 580 paper-based; 93 iBT). *Application deadline:* For fall admission, 2/1 for domestic and international students. Application fee: $60. Electronic applications accepted. *Expenses: Tuition:* Full-time $46,800. *Required fees:* $310. *Financial support:* Fellowships, research assistantships, teaching assistantships, Federal Work-Study, scholarships/grants, and unspecified assistantships available. Financial award application deadline: 2/15; financial award applicants required to submit FAFSA. *Unit head:* Rachel Berwick, Department Head and Graduate Program Director, 401-454-6190, Fax: 401-454-6680, E-mail: rberwick@risd.edu. *Application contact:* Molly Pettengil, Assistant Director for Graduate Recruitment, 401-454-6312, Fax: 401-454-6309, E-mail: mpetteng@risd.edu.
Website: http://www.risd.edu/academics/glass/

**Rhode Island School of Design,** Division of Fine Arts, Department of Jewelry and Metalsmithing, Providence, RI 02903-2784. Offers MFA. *Accreditation:* NASAD. *Faculty:* 5 full-time (3 women), 8 part-time/adjunct (3 women). *Students:* 8 full-time (all women); includes 1 minority (Asian, non-Hispanic/Latino), 5 international. Average age 26. 37 applicants, 22% accepted, 5 enrolled. In 2016, 5 master's awarded. *Degree requirements:* For master's, thesis, exhibition. *Entrance requirements:* For master's, portfolio, statement of purpose, 3 letters of recommendation. Additional exam requirements/recommendations for international students: Required—TOEFL (minimum score 580 paper-based; 93 iBT). *Application deadline:* For fall admission, 2/1 for domestic and international students. Application fee: $60. Electronic applications accepted. *Expenses: Tuition:* Full-time $46,800. *Required fees:* $310. *Financial support:* Fellowships, research assistantships, teaching assistantships, Federal Work-Study, scholarships/grants, and unspecified assistantships available. Financial award application deadline: 2/15; financial award applicants required to submit FAFSA. *Unit head:* Tracy Steepy, Department Head, 401-454-6190, Fax: 401-454-6191, E-mail: jewelry@risd.edu. *Application contact:* Molly Pettengil, Assistant Director for Graduate Recruitment, 401-454-6312, Fax: 401-454-6309, E-mail: empetteng@risd.edu.
Website: http://www.risd.edu/academic/jewelry-metalsmithing/

**Rhode Island School of Design,** Division of Fine Arts, Department of Painting, Providence, RI 02903-2784. Offers MFA. *Accreditation:* NASAD. *Faculty:* 7 full-time (2 women), 8 part-time/adjunct (4 women). *Students:* 20 full-time (13 women); includes 6 minority (2 Asian, non-Hispanic/Latino; 4 Hispanic/Latino), 4 international. Average age 29. 254 applicants, 6% accepted, 10 enrolled. In 2016, 10 master's awarded. *Degree requirements:* For master's, thesis, exhibition. *Entrance requirements:* For master's, portfolio, statement of purpose, 3 letters of recommendation. Additional exam requirements/recommendations for international students: Required—TOEFL (minimum score 580 paper-based; 93 iBT). *Application deadline:* For fall admission, 2/1 for domestic and international students. Application fee: $60. Electronic applications accepted. *Expenses: Tuition:* Full-time $46,800. *Required fees:* $310. *Financial support:* Fellowships, teaching assistantships, Federal Work-Study, institutionally sponsored loans, scholarships/grants, and unspecified assistantships available. Financial award application deadline: 2/15; financial award applicants required to submit FAFSA. *Unit head:* David Frazer, Department Head, 401-454-6158, Fax: 401-454-6681, E-mail: dfrazer@risd.edu. *Application contact:* Molly Pettengil, Assistant Director for Graduate

Recruitment, 401-454-6312, Fax: 401-454-6309, E-mail: mpetteng@risd.edu. Website: http://www.risd.edu/academics/painting/

**Rhode Island School of Design,** Division of Fine Arts, Department of Printmaking, Providence, RI 02903-2784. Offers MFA. *Faculty:* 8 full-time (5 women), 11 part-time/adjunct (5 women). *Students:* 12 full-time (all women); includes 2 minority (1 Black or African American, non-Hispanic/Latino; 1 Hispanic/Latino), 5 international. Average age 27. 41 applicants, 34% accepted, 6 enrolled. In 2016, 8 master's awarded. *Degree requirements:* For master's, thesis, exhibition. *Entrance requirements:* For master's, portfolio, statement of purpose, 3 letters of recommendation. Additional exam requirements/recommendations for international students: Required—TOEFL (minimum score 580 paper-based; 93 iBT). *Application deadline:* For fall admission, 2/1 for domestic and international students. Application fee: $60. Electronic applications accepted. *Expenses: Tuition:* Full-time $46,800. *Required fees:* $310. *Financial support:* Fellowships, research assistantships, teaching assistantships, Federal Work-Study, scholarships/grants, and unspecified assistantships available. Financial award application deadline: 2/15; financial award applicants required to submit FAFSA. *Unit head:* Henry Ferreira, Department Head, 401-454-6224, Fax: 401-454-6707, E-mail: hferreir@risd.edu. *Application contact:* Molly Pettengil, Assistant Director for Graduate Recruitment, 401-454-6312, Fax: 401-454-6309, E-mail: mpetteng@risd.edu. Website: http://www.risd.edu/academics/printmaking/

**Rhode Island School of Design,** Division of Fine Arts, Department of Sculpture, Providence, RI 02903-2784. Offers MFA. *Accreditation:* NASAD. *Faculty:* 8 full-time (2 women), 6 part-time/adjunct (2 women). *Students:* 10 full-time (6 women); includes 1 minority (Asian, non-Hispanic/Latino), 4 international. Average age 29. 69 applicants, 28% accepted, 5 enrolled. In 2016, 6 master's awarded. *Degree requirements:* For master's, thesis, exhibition. *Entrance requirements:* For master's, portfolio, statement of purpose, 3 letters of recommendation. Additional exam requirements/recommendations for international students: Required—TOEFL (minimum score 580 paper-based; 93 iBT). *Application deadline:* For fall admission, 2/1 for domestic and international students. Application fee: $60. Electronic applications accepted. *Expenses: Tuition:* Full-time $46,800. *Required fees:* $310. *Financial support:* Fellowships, research assistantships, teaching assistantships, Federal Work-Study, scholarships/grants, and unspecified assistantships available. Financial award application deadline: 2/15; financial award applicants required to submit FAFSA. *Unit head:* Lisi Raskin, Department Head, 401-454-6190, Fax: 401-454-6191, E-mail: sculpture@risd.edu. *Application contact:* Molly Pettengil, Assistant Director for Graduate Recruitment, 401-454-6312, Fax: 401-454-6309, E-mail: mpetteng@risd.edu. Website: http://www.risd.edu/academics/sculpture/

**Rochester Institute of Technology,** Graduate Enrollment Services, College of Imaging Arts and Sciences, School for American Crafts, MFA Program in Ceramics, Rochester, NY 14623. Offers MFA. *Accreditation:* NASAD. *Program availability:* Part-time. *Students:* 7 full-time (4 women); includes 1 minority (Asian, non-Hispanic/Latino), 3 international. Average age 31. 8 applicants, 63% accepted, 2 enrolled. In 2016, 2 master's awarded. *Degree requirements:* For master's, thesis. *Entrance requirements:* For master's, GRE, portfolio, minimum GPA of 3.0 (recommended). Additional exam requirements/recommendations for international students: Required—TOEFL (minimum score 550 paper-based; 79 iBT), IELTS (minimum score 6.5), PTE (minimum score 58). *Application deadline:* Applications are processed on a rolling basis. Application fee: $60. Electronic applications accepted. *Expenses:* $1,742 per credit hour. *Financial support:* In 2016–17, 6 students received support. Teaching assistantships with partial tuition reimbursements available, career-related internships or fieldwork, scholarships/grants, and unspecified assistantships available. Support available to part-time students. Financial award applicants required to submit FAFSA. *Faculty research:* Aesthetics, techniques, and theory. *Unit head:* Jane Shellenbarger, Graduate Program Director, 585-475-7562, Fax: 585-475-6447, E-mail: sac@rit.edu. *Application contact:* Diane Ellison, Associate Vice President, Graduate Enrollment Services, 585-475-2229, Fax: 585-475-7164, E-mail: gradinfo@rit.edu. Website: http://cias.rit.edu/schools/american-crafts/graduate-ceramics-graduate

**Rochester Institute of Technology,** Graduate Enrollment Services, College of Imaging Arts and Sciences, School for American Crafts, MFA Program in Furniture Design, Rochester, NY 14623-5603. Offers MFA. *Program availability:* Part-time. *Students:* 3 full-time (2 women), 6 part-time (3 women), 6 international. Average age 29. 17 applicants, 41% accepted, 1 enrolled. In 2016, 1 master's awarded. *Degree requirements:* For master's, thesis, thesis project/exhibition. *Entrance requirements:* For master's, GRE, portfolio, minimum GPA of 3.0 (recommended). Additional exam requirements/recommendations for international students: Required—TOEFL (minimum score 570 paper-based; 80 iBT), IELTS (minimum score 6.5), PTE (minimum score 58). *Application deadline:* Applications are processed on a rolling basis. Application fee: $60. Electronic applications accepted. *Expenses:* $1,742 per credit hour. *Financial support:* In 2016–17, 1 student received support. Teaching assistantships with partial tuition reimbursements available, career-related internships or fieldwork, scholarships/grants, and unspecified assistantships available. Support available to part-time students. Financial award applicants required to submit FAFSA. *Faculty research:* Technology, contemporary art, science, craft; sculptural form in furniture. *Unit head:* Andy Buck, Graduate Program Director, 585-475-2636, Fax: 585-475-6447, E-mail: sac@rit.edu. *Application contact:* Diane Ellison, Associate Vice President, Graduate Enrollment Services, 585-475-2229, Fax: 585-475-7164, E-mail: gradinfo@rit.edu. Website: http://cias.rit.edu/schools/american-crafts/graduate-woodworking-graduate

**Rochester Institute of Technology,** Graduate Enrollment Services, College of Imaging Arts and Sciences, School for American Crafts, MFA Program in Glass, Rochester, NY 14623-5603. Offers MFA. *Accreditation:* NASAD. *Program availability:* Part-time. *Students:* 5 full-time (3 women), 1 (woman) part-time, 4 international. Average age 29. 6 applicants. *Degree requirements:* For master's, thesis. *Entrance requirements:* For master's, GRE, portfolio, minimum GPA of 3.0 (recommended). Additional exam requirements/recommendations for international students: Required—TOEFL (minimum score 540 paper-based; 80 iBT), IELTS (minimum score 6), PTE (minimum score 58). *Application deadline:* For fall admission, 2/15 priority date for domestic and international students. Applications are processed on a rolling basis. Application fee: $60. Electronic applications accepted. *Expenses:* $1,742 per credit hour. *Financial support:* In 2016–17, 4 students received support. Teaching assistantships with partial tuition reimbursements available, career-related internships or fieldwork, scholarships/grants, and unspecified assistantships available. Support available to part-time students. Financial award applicants required to submit FAFSA. *Faculty research:* Technology, multi-media sculpture, contemporary art, science, craft. *Unit head:* Michael Rogers, Graduate Program Director, 585-475-7562, Fax: 585-475-6447, E-mail: sac@rit.edu. *Application contact:* Diane Ellison, Associate Vice President, Graduate Enrollment Services, 585-475-2229, Fax: 585-475-7164, E-mail: gradinfo@rit.edu. Website: http://cias.rit.edu/schools/american-crafts/graduate-glass

**Rochester Institute of Technology,** Graduate Enrollment Services, College of Imaging Arts and Sciences, School for American Crafts, MFA Program in Metals and Jewelry Design, Rochester, NY 14623-5603. Offers MFA. *Accreditation:* NASAD. *Program availability:* Part-time. *Students:* 14 full-time (12 women), 7 part-time (5 women); includes 2 minority (both Asian, non-Hispanic/Latino), 16 international. Average age 26.

36 applicants, 28% accepted, 6 enrolled. In 2016, 4 master's awarded. *Degree requirements:* For master's, thesis. *Entrance requirements:* For master's, GRE, portfolio, minimum GPA of 3.0 (recommended). Additional exam requirements/recommendations for international students: Required—TOEFL (minimum score 550 paper-based; 79 iBT), IELTS (minimum score 6.5), PTE (minimum score 58). *Application deadline:* For fall admission, 2/15 priority date for domestic and international students. Applications are processed on a rolling basis. Application fee: $60. Electronic applications accepted. *Expenses:* $1,742 per credit hour. *Financial support:* In 2016–17, 13 students received support. Teaching assistantships with partial tuition reimbursements available, career-related internships or fieldwork, scholarships/grants, and unspecified assistantships available. Support available to part-time students. Financial award applicants required to submit FAFSA. *Faculty research:* Computer aided design, computer aided manufacturing, material process research, creation of a body of work. *Unit head:* Juan Carlos Caballero-Perez, Graduate Program Director, 585-475-2654, Fax: 585-475-7562, E-mail: sac@rit.edu. *Application contact:* Diane Ellison, Associate Vice President, Graduate Enrollment Services, 585-475-2229, Fax: 585-475-7164, E-mail: gradinfo@rit.edu. Website: http://cias.rit.edu/schools/american-crafts/graduate-metalcrafts-graduate

**Rochester Institute of Technology,** Graduate Enrollment Services, College of Imaging Arts and Sciences, School of Art, MFA Program in Fine Arts Studio, Rochester, NY 14623. Offers fine arts studio (MFA). *Accreditation:* NASAD. *Program availability:* Part-time. *Students:* 10 full-time (5 women), 3 part-time (all women); includes 1 minority (Black or African American, non-Hispanic/Latino), 4 international. Average age 31. 31 applicants, 61% accepted, 7 enrolled. In 2016, 9 master's awarded. *Degree requirements:* For master's, thesis (for some programs). *Entrance requirements:* For master's, GRE, portfolio, minimum GPA of 3.0 (recommended). Additional exam requirements/recommendations for international students: Required—TOEFL (minimum score 550 paper-based; 79 iBT), IELTS (minimum score 6.5), PTE (minimum score 58). *Application deadline:* For fall admission, 2/15 priority date for domestic and international students. Applications are processed on a rolling basis. Application fee: $60. Electronic applications accepted. *Expenses:* $1,742 per credit hour. *Financial support:* In 2016–17, 6 students received support. Teaching assistantships with partial tuition reimbursements available, career-related internships or fieldwork, scholarships/grants, and unspecified assistantships available. Support available to part-time students. Financial award applicants required to submit FAFSA. *Faculty research:* Art therapy, art criticism, art restoration, gallery and museum management, set and display design, master printmaking, and sculptural casting and foundry fabrication; contemporary and historical art; art education. *Unit head:* Denton Crawford, Graduate Program Director, 585-475-7562, E-mail: denton@rit.edu. *Application contact:* Diane Ellison, Associate Vice President, Graduate Enrollment Services, 585-475-2229, Fax: 585-475-7164, E-mail: gradinfo@rit.edu. Website: http://cias.rit.edu/schools/art/graduate-fine-arts-studio

**Rutgers University–New Brunswick,** Mason Gross School of the Arts, Visual Arts Department, New Brunswick, NJ 08901. Offers drawing (MFA); painting (MFA); sculpture (MFA); visual arts (MFA). *Degree requirements:* For master's, thesis, exhibit. *Entrance requirements:* For master's, portfolio. Additional exam requirements/recommendations for international students: Required—TOEFL (minimum score 550 paper-based), IELTS (minimum score 7). Electronic applications accepted. *Faculty research:* Media, painting, sculpture, photography, film.

**San Diego State University,** Graduate and Research Affairs, College of Professional Studies and Fine Arts, School of Art, Design and Art History, San Diego, CA 92182. Offers art history (MA); studio arts (MA, MFA), including applied design, environmental design, graphic design, interior design, painting and printmaking, sculpture. *Accreditation:* NASAD (one or more programs are accredited). *Degree requirements:* For master's, variable foreign language requirement, thesis. *Entrance requirements:* For master's, GRE General Test, bachelor's degree in related field, slide portfolio, typed slide information sheet, 2 letters of recommendation. Additional exam requirements/recommendations for international students: Required—TOEFL. Electronic applications accepted.

**San Francisco Art Institute,** Master of Fine Arts Programs, San Francisco, CA 94133. Offers studio art (MFA, Certificate), including art and technology (MFA); film (MFA); new genres (MFA); painting (MFA); photography (MFA); printmaking (MFA); sculpture (MFA); MFA/MA. *Accreditation:* NASAD. *Faculty:* 18 full-time (9 women), 41 part-time/adjunct (20 women). *Students:* 135 full-time (84 women), 24 part-time (16 women); includes 36 minority (2 Black or African American, non-Hispanic/Latino; 6 Asian, non-Hispanic/Latino; 21 Hispanic/Latino; 1 Native Hawaiian or other Pacific Islander, non-Hispanic/Latino; 6 Two or more races, non-Hispanic/Latino), 61 international. Average age 30. 295 applicants, 66% accepted, 64 enrolled. In 2016, 78 master's, 8 other advanced degrees awarded. *Degree requirements:* For master's, thesis. *Entrance requirements:* For master's and Certificate, portfolio. Additional exam requirements/recommendations for international students: Required—TOEFL (minimum score 580 paper-based; 92 iBT), IELTS (minimum score 7). *Application deadline:* For spring admission, 11/1 priority date for domestic and international students. Applications are processed on a rolling basis. Application fee: $85. Electronic applications accepted. *Expenses: Tuition:* Full-time $46,010; part-time $2020 per credit. *Required fees:* $870; $870 per credit. *Financial support:* Fellowships, teaching assistantships, career-related internships or fieldwork, Federal Work-Study, scholarships/grants, and unspecified assistantships available. Support available to part-time students. Financial award application deadline: 3/1; financial award applicants required to submit FAFSA. *Faculty research:* Studio art, international art exhibitions, neurohumanities, experimental music, virtual reality 360 degree film. *Unit head:* Tony Labat, Chair, Master of Fine Arts Department, 415-351-3574, Fax: 415-641-1205, E-mail: tlabat@sfai.edu. *Application contact:* Jana Rumberger, Director of Graduate Admissions, 415-351-3507, Fax: 415-749-4592, E-mail: jrumberger@sfai.edu. Website: http://www.sfai.edu/degree-programs/graduate

**San Francisco State University,** Division of Graduate Studies, College of Liberal and Creative Arts, School of Art, San Francisco, CA 94132-1722. Offers art (MFA); art history (MA). *Accreditation:* NASAD (one or more programs are accredited). *Expenses:* Tuition, state resident: full-time $6738. Tuition, nonresident: full-time $15,666. *Required fees:* $1012. Tuition and fees vary according to degree level and program. *Unit head:* Gail Dawson, Director, 415-338-2176, Fax: 415-338-6537, E-mail: gdawson@sfsu.edu. *Application contact:* Prof. Susan Belau, Associate Professor and Graduate Coordinator, 415-338-1591, Fax: 415-338-6537, E-mail: sbelau@sfsu.edu. Website: http://www.art.sfsu.edu

**Savannah College of Art and Design,** Graduate School, Program in Accessory Design, Savannah, GA 31402-3146. Offers MA, MFA. *Program availability:* Part-time. *Faculty:* 5 full-time (3 women). *Students:* 14 full-time (12 women), 2 part-time (both women); includes 4 minority (1 Asian, non-Hispanic/Latino; 3 Hispanic/Latino), 7 international. Average age 27. 15 applicants, 40% accepted, 4 enrolled. In 2016, 4 master's awarded. *Degree requirements:* For master's, final project (for MA); thesis (for MFA). *Entrance requirements:* For master's, GRE (recommended), portfolio (submitted in digital format), audition or writing submission, resume, statement of purpose, two letters of recommendation. Additional exam requirements/recommendations for

international students: Required—TOEFL (minimum score 550 paper-based, 85 iBT), IELTS (minimum score 6.5), or ACTFL. *Application deadline:* For fall admission, 4/1 for domestic and international students. Applications are processed on a rolling basis. Application fee: $40. Electronic applications accepted. *Expenses: Tuition:* Full-time $36,045. Tuition and fees vary according to course load. *Financial support:* Career-related internships or fieldwork and Federal Work-Study available. Financial award application deadline: 4/1; financial award applicants required to submit FAFSA. *Unit head:* Michael Fink, Dean, School of Fashion. *Application contact:* Jenny Jaquillard, Executive Director of Admissions, Recruitment and Events, 912-525-5100, Fax: 912-525-5985, E-mail: admission@scad.edu.
Website: http://www.scad.edu/academics/programs/accessory-design

**Savannah College of Art and Design,** Graduate School, Program in Furniture Design, Savannah, GA 31402-3146. Offers MA, MFA. *Program availability:* Part-time. *Faculty:* 5 full-time (1 woman). *Students:* 16 full-time (7 women), 3 part-time (all women); includes 1 minority (Hispanic/Latino), 15 international. Average age 26. 18 applicants, 56% accepted, 5 enrolled. In 2016, 9 master's awarded. *Degree requirements:* For master's, final project (for MA); thesis (for MFA). *Entrance requirements:* For master's, GRE (recommended), portfolio (submitted in digital format), audition or writing submission, resume, statement of purpose, two letters of recommendation. Additional exam requirements/recommendations for international students: Required—TOEFL (minimum score 550 paper-based, 85 iBT), IELTS (minimum score 6.5), or ACTFL. *Application deadline:* For fall admission, 4/1 for domestic and international students. Applications are processed on a rolling basis. Application fee: $40. Electronic applications accepted. *Expenses: Tuition:* Full-time $36,045. Tuition and fees vary according to course load. *Financial support:* Career-related internships or fieldwork, Federal Work-Study, and scholarships/grants available. Financial award application deadline: 4/1; financial award applicants required to submit FAFSA. *Unit head:* Fred Spector, Academic Program Coordinator. *Application contact:* Jenny Jaquillard, Executive Director of Admissions, Recruitment and Events, 912-525-5100, Fax: 912-525-5985, E-mail: admission@scad.edu.
Website: http://www.scad.edu/academics/programs/furniture-design

**Savannah College of Art and Design,** Graduate School, Program in Jewelry, Savannah, GA 31402-3146. Offers MA, MFA. *Program availability:* Part-time. *Faculty:* 4 full-time (3 women). *Students:* 23 full-time (22 women), 4 part-time (3 women); includes 1 minority (Black or African American, non-Hispanic/Latino), 24 international. Average age 28. 29 applicants, 66% accepted, 7 enrolled. In 2016, 4 master's awarded. *Degree requirements:* For master's, final project (for MA); thesis (for MFA). *Entrance requirements:* For master's, GRE (recommended), portfolio (submitted in digital format), audition or writing submission, resume, statement of purpose, two letters of recommendation. Additional exam requirements/recommendations for international students: Required—TOEFL (minimum score 550 paper-based, 85 iBT), IELTS (minimum score 6.5), or ACTFL. *Application deadline:* For fall admission, 4/1 for domestic and international students. Applications are processed on a rolling basis. Application fee: $40. Electronic applications accepted. *Expenses: Tuition:* Full-time $36,045. Tuition and fees vary according to course load. *Financial support:* Career-related internships or fieldwork, Federal Work-Study, and scholarships/grants available. Financial award application deadline: 4/1; financial award applicants required to submit FAFSA. *Unit head:* Jay Song, Chair, Jewelry. *Application contact:* Jenny Jaquillard, Executive Director of Admissions, Recruitment and Events, 912-525-5100, Fax: 912-525-5985, E-mail: admission@scad.edu.
Website: http://www.scad.edu/academics/programs/jewelry

**Savannah College of Art and Design,** Graduate School, Program in Painting, Savannah, GA 31402-3146. Offers MA, MFA. *Program availability:* Part-time, 100% online. *Faculty:* 10 full-time (2 women), 2 part-time/adjunct (1 woman). *Students:* 57 full-time (39 women), 21 part-time (11 women); includes 12 minority (5 Black or African American, non-Hispanic/Latino; 1 American Indian or Alaska Native, non-Hispanic/Latino; 2 Asian, non-Hispanic/Latino; 4 Hispanic/Latino), 22 international. Average age 34. 112 applicants, 31% accepted, 18 enrolled. In 2016, 23 master's awarded. *Degree requirements:* For master's, final project (for MA); thesis (for MFA). *Entrance requirements:* For master's, GRE (recommended), portfolio (submitted in digital format), audition or writing submission, resume, statement of purpose, two letters of recommendation. Additional exam requirements/recommendations for international students: Required—TOEFL (minimum score 550 paper-based, 85 iBT), IELTS (minimum score 6.5), or ACTFL. *Application deadline:* For fall admission, 4/1 for domestic and international students. Applications are processed on a rolling basis. Application fee: $40. Electronic applications accepted. *Expenses: Tuition:* Full-time $36,045. Tuition and fees vary according to course load. *Financial support:* Career-related internships or fieldwork, Federal Work-Study, and scholarships/grants available. Financial award application deadline: 4/1; financial award applicants required to submit FAFSA. *Unit head:* Thomas Francis, Academic Program Coordinator. *Application contact:* Jenny Jaquillard, Executive Director of Admissions, Recruitment and Events, 912-525-5100, Fax: 912-525-5985, E-mail: admission@scad.edu.
Website: http://www.scad.edu/academics/programs/painting

**Savannah College of Art and Design,** Graduate School, Program in Printmaking, Savannah, GA 31402-3146. Offers MFA. *Program availability:* Part-time. *Faculty:* 4 full-time (3 women), 2 part-time/adjunct (0 women). *Students:* 1 (woman) full-time, 1 (woman) part-time, 1 international. Average age 26. 9 applicants, 56% accepted, 1 enrolled. In 2016, 7 master's awarded. *Degree requirements:* For master's, thesis. *Entrance requirements:* For master's, GRE (recommended), portfolio (submitted in digital format), audition or writing submission, resume, statement of purpose, two letters of recommendation. Additional exam requirements/recommendations for international students: Required—TOEFL (minimum score 550 paper-based, 85 iBT), IELTS (minimum score 6.5), or ACTFL. *Application deadline:* For fall admission, 4/1 for domestic and international students. Applications are processed on a rolling basis. Application fee: $40. Electronic applications accepted. *Expenses: Tuition:* Full-time $36,045. Tuition and fees vary according to course load. *Financial support:* Career-related internships or fieldwork, Federal Work-Study, and scholarships/grants available. Financial award application deadline: 4/1; financial award applicants required to submit FAFSA. *Unit head:* Robert Brown, Chair, Printmaking. *Application contact:* Jenny Jaquillard, Executive Director of Admissions, Recruitment and Events, 912-525-5100, Fax: 912-525-5985, E-mail: admission@scad.edu.
Website: http://www.scad.edu/academics/programs/printmaking

**Savannah College of Art and Design,** Graduate School, Program in Sculpture, Savannah, GA 31402-3146. Offers MA, MFA. *Program availability:* Part-time. *Faculty:* 2 full-time (1 woman), 1 part-time/adjunct (0 women). *Students:* 7 full-time (4 women), 2 part-time (0 women), 5 international. Average age 36. 11 applicants, 55% accepted, 1 enrolled. In 2016, 6 master's awarded. *Degree requirements:* For master's, final project (for MA); thesis (for MFA). *Entrance requirements:* For master's, GRE (recommended), portfolio (submitted in digital format), audition or writing submission, resume, statement of purpose, two letters of recommendation. Additional exam requirements/recommendations for international students: Required—TOEFL (minimum score 550 paper-based, 85 iBT), IELTS (minimum score 6.5), or ACTFL. *Application deadline:* For fall admission, 4/1 for domestic and international students. Applications are processed

on a rolling basis. Application fee: $40. Electronic applications accepted. *Expenses: Tuition:* Full-time $36,045. Tuition and fees vary according to course load. *Financial support:* Career-related internships or fieldwork, Federal Work-Study, and scholarships/grants available. Financial award application deadline: 4/1; financial award applicants required to submit FAFSA. *Unit head:* Susan Krause, Chair, Sculpture. *Application contact:* Jenny Jaquillard, Executive Director of Admissions, Recruitment and Events, 912-525-5100, Fax: 912-525-5985, E-mail: admission@scad.edu.
Website: http://www.scad.edu/academics/programs/sculpture

**Savannah College of Art and Design,** Graduate School, Program in Visual Effects, Savannah, GA 31402-3146. Offers MA, MFA. *Program availability:* Part-time. *Faculty:* 14 full-time (4 women), 1 part-time/adjunct (0 women). *Students:* 44 full-time (17 women), 11 part-time (6 women); includes 12 minority (3 Black or African American, non-Hispanic/Latino; 3 Asian, non-Hispanic/Latino; 6 Hispanic/Latino), 34 international. Average age 27. 36 applicants, 36% accepted, 9 enrolled. In 2016, 24 master's awarded. *Degree requirements:* For master's, final project (for MA); thesis (for MFA). *Entrance requirements:* For master's, GRE (recommended), portfolio (submitted in digital format), audition or writing submission, resume, statement of purpose, two letters of recommendation. Additional exam requirements/recommendations for international students: Required—TOEFL (minimum score 550 paper-based, 85 iBT), IELTS (minimum score 6.5), or ACTFL. *Application deadline:* For fall admission, 4/1 for domestic and international students. Applications are processed on a rolling basis. Application fee: $40. Electronic applications accepted. *Expenses: Tuition:* Full-time $36,045. Tuition and fees vary according to course load. *Financial support:* Application deadline: 4/1; applicants required to submit FAFSA. *Unit head:* Max Almy, Dean, School of Digital Media. *Application contact:* Jenny Jaquillard, Executive Director of Admissions, Recruitment and Events, 912-525-5100, Fax: 912-525-5985, E-mail: admission@scad.edu.
Website: http://www.scad.edu/academics/programs/visual-effects

**School of the Art Institute of Chicago,** Graduate Division, Department of Art and Technology Studies, Chicago, IL 60603-3103. Offers MFA. *Entrance requirements:* Additional exam requirements/recommendations for international students: Required—TOEFL, IELTS. Electronic applications accepted.

**School of the Art Institute of Chicago,** Graduate Division, Department of Ceramics, Chicago, IL 60603-3103. Offers MFA. *Accreditation:* NASAD. *Entrance requirements:* Additional exam requirements/recommendations for international students: Required—TOEFL, IELTS. Electronic applications accepted.

**School of the Art Institute of Chicago,** Graduate Division, Department of Fiber and Material Studies, Chicago, IL 60603-3103. Offers MFA. *Accreditation:* NASAD. *Entrance requirements:* Additional exam requirements/recommendations for international students: Required—TOEFL, IELTS.

**School of the Art Institute of Chicago,** Graduate Division, Department of Painting and Drawing, Chicago, IL 60603-3103. Offers MFA. *Accreditation:* NASAD. *Entrance requirements:* Additional exam requirements/recommendations for international students: Required—TOEFL, IELTS.

**School of the Art Institute of Chicago,** Graduate Division, Department of Printmaking, Chicago, IL 60603-3103. Offers MFA. *Accreditation:* NASAD. *Entrance requirements:* Additional exam requirements/recommendations for international students: Required—TOEFL (minimum score 550 paper-based; 80 iBT), IELTS (minimum score 6.5).

**School of the Art Institute of Chicago,** Graduate Division, Department of Sculpture, Chicago, IL 60603-3103. Offers MFA. *Accreditation:* NASAD. *Entrance requirements:* Additional exam requirements/recommendations for international students: Required—TOEFL, IELTS.

**School of the Art Institute of Chicago,** Graduate Division, Program in Visual and Critical Studies, Chicago, IL 60603-3103. Offers MA.

**School of Visual Arts,** Graduate Programs, Art Practice Department, New York, NY 10010-3994. Offers MFA. *Degree requirements:* For master's, thesis. *Entrance requirements:* For master's, portfolio submitted through SlideRoom; 500- to 750-word writing sample. Additional exam requirements/recommendations for international students: Required—TOEFL (minimum score 550 paper-based; 100 iBT), IELTS (minimum score 8). Electronic applications accepted.

**School of Visual Arts,** Graduate Programs, Computer Art Department, New York, NY 10010-3994. Offers MFA. *Accreditation:* NASAD. *Degree requirements:* For master's, thesis, 60 credits, including all required courses; minimum GPA of 3.0; matriculation of two academic years. *Entrance requirements:* For master's, portfolio; 3-5 minute sample reel showing best work; statement of purpose; official transcript; 3 letters of recommendation; resume/curriculum vitae. Additional exam requirements/recommendations for international students: Required—TOEFL (minimum score 550 paper-based; 79 iBT). Electronic applications accepted. *Expenses:* Contact institution.

**School of Visual Arts,** Graduate Programs, Design Department, New York, NY 10010-3994. Offers MFA. *Accreditation:* NASAD. *Degree requirements:* For master's, thesis, 60 credits, including all required courses; minimum cumulative GPA of 3.0; residency of two academic years. *Entrance requirements:* For master's, portfolio that reflects wide range of design work and fluency in type and typography. Additional exam requirements/recommendations for international students: Required—TOEFL (minimum score 550 paper-based; 79 iBT). *Expenses:* Contact institution. *Faculty research:* Design, graphic design, multimedia.

**School of Visual Arts,** Graduate Programs, Illustration as Visual Essay Department, New York, NY 10010-3994. Offers MFA. *Accreditation:* NASAD. *Degree requirements:* For master's, thesis, 60 credits, including all required courses; residency of two academic years. *Entrance requirements:* For master's, portfolio of work (still images) submitted through SlideRoom. Additional exam requirements/recommendations for international students: Required—TOEFL (minimum score 100 iBT). Electronic applications accepted. *Faculty research:* Illustration, fine arts, computer art, writing, art history, art direction.

**School of Visual Arts,** Graduate Programs, Program in Fine Arts, New York, NY 10010-3994. Offers MFA. *Accreditation:* NASAD. *Degree requirements:* For master's, thesis, 60 credits, including all required courses; residency of two academic years. *Entrance requirements:* For master's, CD portfolio of work with exactly 12 images. Additional exam requirements/recommendations for international students: Required—TOEFL (minimum score 550 paper-based; 79 iBT). Electronic applications accepted.

**School of Visual Arts,** Graduate Programs, Program in Photography, Video and Related Media, New York, NY 10010-3994. Offers MFA. *Accreditation:* NASAD. *Degree requirements:* For master's, thesis, 60 credits and all course requirements; minimum GPA of 3.3; thesis project. *Entrance requirements:* For master's, portfolio (still images and/or videos) through SlideRoom. Additional exam requirements/recommendations for international students: Required—TOEFL (minimum score 550 paper-based; 79 iBT). Electronic applications accepted. *Faculty research:* Contemporary and responsible creative initiatives, including experimental, narrative or documentary video, installation and conceptual art, tableau and real-world-witness photography.

### Art/Fine Arts

**Sotheby's Institute of Art–London,** Graduate Programs, London, United Kingdom. Offers art business (MA); contemporary art (MA); fine and decorative art and design (MA); modern and contemporary Asian art (MA). *Faculty:* 41 full-time (25 women). *Students:* 181 full-time (159 women). *Degree requirements:* For master's, thesis. *Entrance requirements:* Additional exam requirements/recommendations for international students: Required—IELTS (minimum score 7). *Application deadline:* Applications are processed on a rolling basis. Electronic applications accepted. *Expenses: Tuition:* Full-time 24,900 British pounds. Tuition and fees vary according to class time, program and student level. *Application contact:* Jessica Bearne, Admissions Manager, 44 20 7462 3250, E-mail: j.bearne@sothebysinstitute.com.

**Sotheby's Institute of Art–New York,** Graduate Programs, New York, NY 10021. Offers art business (MA); contemporary art (MA); fine and decorative art and design (MA). *Accreditation:* NASAD. *Entrance requirements:* For master's, academic transcripts, two letters of academic reference, personal statement, writing sample, curriculum vitae/resume, interview. Additional exam requirements/recommendations for international students: Required—TOEFL (minimum score 100 iBT), IELTS (minimum score 7). Electronic applications accepted.

**Southern Illinois University Carbondale,** Graduate School, College of Liberal Arts, School of Art and Design, Carbondale, IL 62901-4701. Offers drawing (MFA); fiber/weaving (MFA); glass (MFA); metalsmithing/blacksmithing (MFA); painting (MFA). *Accreditation:* NASAD. *Degree requirements:* For master's, thesis or alternative. *Entrance requirements:* For master's, minimum GPA of 2.7, portfolio, slides. Additional exam requirements/recommendations for international students: Required—TOEFL. *Faculty research:* Prints/woodcuts, foundry, watercolor.

**Southern Illinois University Edwardsville,** Graduate School, College of Arts and Sciences, Department of Art and Design, Program in Art Studio, Edwardsville, IL 62026-0001. Offers MFA. *Accreditation:* NASAD. *Program availability:* Part-time. *Degree requirements:* For master's, thesis, exhibition. *Entrance requirements:* For master's, portfolio. Additional exam requirements/recommendations for international students: Required—TOEFL (minimum score 550 paper-based; 79 iBT), IELTS (minimum score 6.5). Electronic applications accepted.

**Southern Methodist University,** Meadows School of the Arts, Division of Art, Dallas, TX 75275. Offers studio art (MFA), including ceramics, drawing, painting, photography, printmaking, sculpture. *Accreditation:* NASAD. *Degree requirements:* For master's, thesis or alternative, exhibit. *Entrance requirements:* For master's, BFA or equivalent, letters of recommendation, portfolio. Additional exam requirements/recommendations for international students: Required—TOEFL (minimum score 550 paper-based; 80 iBT). *Faculty research:* American stoneware, Southwestern furniture traditions, photographic apparatus and techniques, American ceramists, architecture.

**Southwest University of Visual Arts,** MFA Programs, Tucson, AZ 85716-2505. Offers motion arts (MFA); painting and drawing (MFA); photography (MFA).

**Spring Hill College,** Graduate Programs, Program in Liberal Arts, Mobile, AL 36608-1791. Offers fine arts (MLA); history and social science (MLA); leadership and ethics (MLA, Postbaccalaureate Certificate); literature (MLA); studio art (Postbaccalaureate Certificate). *Program availability:* Part-time, evening/weekend. *Faculty:* 5 full-time (0 women), 2 part-time/adjunct (1 woman). *Students:* 2 full-time (1 woman), 31 part-time (10 women); includes 4 minority (3 Black or African American, non-Hispanic/Latino; 1 Hispanic/Latino), 3 international. Average age 35. In 2016, 7 master's, 1 other advanced degree awarded. *Degree requirements:* For master's, capstone course, completion of program within 6 years of initial admittance. *Entrance requirements:* For master's, bachelor's degree with minimum undergraduate GPA of 3.0 or graduate/professional degree. Additional exam requirements/recommendations for international students: Required—TOEFL (minimum score 550 paper-based; 80 iBT), IELTS (minimum score 6.5), CPE or CAE (minimum score C), Michigan English Language Assessment Battery (minimum score 90). *Application deadline:* For fall admission, 8/1 priority date for domestic and international students; for spring admission, 12/1 priority date for domestic and international students. Applications are processed on a rolling basis. Application fee: $25 ($35 for international students). Electronic applications accepted. *Expenses:* Contact institution. *Financial support:* Applicants required to submit FAFSA. *Unit head:* Dr. Thomas J. Hoffman, Director, 251-380-4184, Fax: 251-460-2115, E-mail: thoffman@shc.edu. *Application contact:* Robert Stewart, Vice President of Enrollment, 251-380-3030, Fax: 251-460-2186, E-mail: rstewart@shc.edu. Website: http://ug.shc.edu/graduate-degrees/master-liberal-arts/

**Stanford University,** School of Humanities and Sciences, Department of Art and Art History, Stanford, CA 94305-2004. Offers art history (PhD); art practice (MFA); design (MFA); documentary film and video (MFA); MS/MFA. *Degree requirements:* For master's, thesis (for some programs), faculty reviews; for doctorate, 2 foreign languages, thesis/dissertation. *Entrance requirements:* For master's and doctorate, GRE General Test. Additional exam requirements/recommendations for international students: Required—TOEFL. Electronic applications accepted. *Expenses: Tuition:* Full-time $47,331. *Required fees:* $609.

**State University of New York at New Paltz,** Graduate School, School of Fine and Performing Arts, Department of Fine Arts, New Paltz, NY 12561. Offers ceramics (MFA); metal (MFA); painting/drawing (MFA); printmaking (MFA); sculpture (MFA). *Accreditation:* NASAD. *Program availability:* Part-time, evening/weekend. *Students:* 31 full-time (26 women), 1 (woman) part-time; includes 2 minority (1 Asian, non-Hispanic/Latino; 1 Two or more races, non-Hispanic/Latino), 6 international. 69 applicants, 42% accepted, 11 enrolled. In 2016, 16 master's awarded. *Degree requirements:* For master's, thesis, portfolio, exhibit (MFA). *Entrance requirements:* For master's, minimum GPA of 3.0, portfolio. Additional exam requirements/recommendations for international students: Required—TOEFL (minimum score 550 paper-based; 80 iBT), IELTS (minimum score 6.5). *Application deadline:* For fall admission, 2/15 priority date for domestic and international students. Applications are processed on a rolling basis. Application fee: $50. Electronic applications accepted. *Financial support:* In 2016–17, 7 teaching assistantships with partial tuition reimbursements (averaging $5,000 per year) were awarded; unspecified assistantships also available. Financial award application deadline: 8/1. *Unit head:* Prof. Anne Galperin, Chair, 845-257-3833, E-mail: galperia@newpaltz.edu. *Application contact:* Prof. Matthew Friday, Graduate Coordinator, 845-257-2609, E-mail: fridaym@newpaltz.edu. Website: http://www.newpaltz.edu/

**State University of New York at Oswego,** Graduate Studies, Department of Art, Oswego, NY 13126. Offers art (MA); graphic design and digital media (MA). *Accreditation:* NASAD. *Program availability:* Part-time. *Degree requirements:* For master's, exhibit, final presentation. *Entrance requirements:* For master's, slides of previous work. Additional exam requirements/recommendations for international students: Required—TOEFL (minimum score 560 paper-based). *Faculty research:* Ancient and primitive art, nineteenth century art, medieval art, Renaissance art.

**Stephen F. Austin State University,** Graduate School, College of Fine Arts, School of Art, Nacogdoches, TX 75962. Offers art (MA); design (MFA); drawing (MFA); painting (MFA); sculpture (MFA). *Accreditation:* NASAD. *Program availability:* Part-time. *Degree requirements:* For master's, comprehensive exam, thesis, exhibit. *Entrance requirements:* For master's, GRE General Test, portfolio. Additional exam requirements/

recommendations for international students: Required—TOEFL. *Faculty research:* Printmaking, jewelry, photography, ceramics, art history.

**Stony Brook University, State University of New York,** Graduate School, College of Arts and Sciences, Department of Art, Program in Studio Art, Stony Brook, NY 11794. Offers MFA. *Students:* 11 full-time (9 women); includes 4 minority (1 Black or African American, non-Hispanic/Latino; 3 Hispanic/Latino), 2 international. Average age 32. 10 applicants, 50% accepted, 3 enrolled. In 2016, 4 master's awarded. *Degree requirements:* For master's, comprehensive exam, thesis, reading knowledge of German, French, or Italian; exhibition. *Entrance requirements:* For master's, GRE General Test, minimum undergraduate GPA of 3.0. Additional exam requirements/recommendations for international students: Required—TOEFL. *Application deadline:* For fall admission, 1/15 priority date for domestic students; for spring admission, 10/1 for domestic students. Application fee: $100. *Expenses:* Contact institution. *Unit head:* Dr. Barbara Frank, Chair, 631-632-7250, E-mail: barbara.frank@stonybrook.edu. *Application contact:* Lisa Perez, Coordinator, 631-632-7270, Fax: 631-632-7261, E-mail: lisa.perez@stonybrook.edu. Website: http://art.stonybrook.edu/graduate-programs/mfa-program/

**Sul Ross State University,** College of Arts and Sciences, Department of Fine Arts and Communication, Alpine, TX 79832. Offers art history (MA); studio art (MA), including art education. *Program availability:* Part-time. *Degree requirements:* For master's, oral or written exam. *Entrance requirements:* For master's, GRE General Test, minimum GPA of 2.5 in last 60 hours of undergraduate work. *Faculty research:* Ceramic sculpture, watercolor, wood sculpture, rock art.

**Syracuse University,** College of Visual and Performing Arts, MFA Program in Studio Arts, Syracuse, NY 13244. Offers MFA. *Accreditation:* NASAD. *Program availability:* Part-time. *Degree requirements:* For master's, thesis or alternative. *Entrance requirements:* For master's, portfolio, three letters of recommendation, resume, personal statement. Additional exam requirements/recommendations for international students: Required—TOEFL (minimum score 100 iBT). *Application deadline:* For fall admission, 2/1 priority date for domestic and international students. Application fee: $75. Electronic applications accepted. *Expenses: Tuition:* Full-time $25,974; part-time $1443 per credit hour. *Required fees:* $802; $50 per course. Tuition and fees vary according to course load and program. *Financial support:* Fellowships with full tuition reimbursements, teaching assistantships with tuition reimbursements, and tuition waivers available. Financial award application deadline: 1/1; financial award applicants required to submit FAFSA. *Faculty research:* Ceramics, drawing, jewelry and metalsmithing, painting, print media and graphic art, and sculpture. *Unit head:* Prof. Joanna Spitzner, Associate Professor/Studio Arts Graduate Program Coordinator, 315-443-5698, E-mail: jspitzne@syr.edu. *Application contact:* Therese West, Information Contact, 315-443-0137, E-mail: admissg@syr.edu. Website: http://vpa.syr.edu/academics/art/graduate/studio-arts/

**Temple University,** Tyler School of Art, Department of Crafts, Philadelphia, PA 19122-6096. Offers ceramics/glass (MFA); fibers and material studies (MFA); metals/jewelry/CAD-CAM (MFA). *Degree requirements:* For master's, essay, exhibit. *Entrance requirements:* For master's, minimum GPA of 3.0, slide portfolio, 40 credits in studio art, 12 credits in art history, letters of recommendation, resume/curriculum vitae. Additional exam requirements/recommendations for international students: Required—TOEFL (minimum score 550 paper-based; 79 iBT), IELTS (minimum score 6.5). Electronic applications accepted. *Expenses:* Contact institution.

**Temple University,** Tyler School of Art, Department of Graphic Arts and Design, Philadelphia, PA 19122-6096. Offers graphic and interactive design (MFA); photography (MFA); printmaking (MFA). *Degree requirements:* For master's, essay, exhibit. *Entrance requirements:* For master's, minimum GPA of 3.0, slide portfolio, 40 credits in studio art, 12 credits in art history, letters of recommendation, resume/curriculum vitae. Additional exam requirements/recommendations for international students: Required—TOEFL (minimum score 550 paper-based; 79 iBT), IELTS (minimum score 6.5). Electronic applications accepted. *Expenses:* Contact institution.

**Temple University,** Tyler School of Art, Department of Painting, Drawing, and Sculpture, Philadelphia, PA 19122-6096. Offers painting (MFA); sculpture (MFA). *Degree requirements:* For master's, essay, exhibit. *Entrance requirements:* For master's, minimum GPA of 3.0, slide portfolio, 40 credits in studio art, 12 credits in art history, letters of recommendation, resume/curriculum vitae. Additional exam requirements/recommendations for international students: Required—TOEFL (minimum score 550 paper-based; 79 iBT), IELTS (minimum score 6.5). Electronic applications accepted. *Expenses:* Contact institution.

**Texas A&M University,** College of Architecture, Department of Visualization, College Station, TX 77843. Offers MFA, MS. *Faculty:* 17. *Students:* 68 full-time (34 women), 27 part-time (8 women); includes 21 minority (1 Black or African American, non-Hispanic/Latino; 7 Asian, non-Hispanic/Latino; 1 Two or more races, non-Hispanic/Latino), 19 international. Average age 27. 43 applicants, 86% accepted, 23 enrolled. In 2016, 13 master's awarded. *Entrance requirements:* Additional exam requirements/recommendations for international students: Required—TOEFL (minimum score 550 paper-based; 80 iBT), TWE, PTE (minimum score 53). *Application deadline:* For fall admission, 1/5 for domestic students. Application fee: $50 ($90 for international students). *Expenses:* Contact institution. *Financial support:* In 2016–17, 73 students received support, including 20 research assistantships with tuition reimbursements available (averaging $2,912 per year), 45 teaching assistantships with tuition reimbursements available (averaging $4,133 per year); career-related internships or fieldwork, institutionally sponsored loans, scholarships/grants, traineeships, health care benefits, tuition waivers (full and partial), and unspecified assistantships also available. Support available to part-time students. Financial award application deadline: 12/15; financial award applicants required to submit FAFSA. *Unit head:* Dr. Tim McLaughlin, Department Head, 979-845-3465, E-mail: timm@viz.tamu.edu. *Application contact:* Dr. Frederic Parke, Associate Head of Department/Graduate Program Coordinator, 979-845-6596, E-mail: parke@viz.tamu.edu. Website: http://viz.arch.tamu.edu/

**Texas A&M University–Commerce,** College of Humanities, Social Sciences and Arts, Commerce, TX 75429-3011. Offers applied criminology (MS); applied linguistics (MA, MS); art (MA, MFA); Christianity in history (Graduate Certificate); computational linguistics (Graduate Certificate); creative writing (Graduate Certificate); English (MA, MS, PhD); film studies (Graduate Certificate); history (MA, MS); music (MM); political science (MA, MS); public history (Graduate Certificate); sociology (MS); Spanish (MA); studies in children's and adolescent literature and culture (Graduate Certificate); teaching English to speakers of other languages (Graduate Certificate); theater (MA, MS). *Program availability:* Part-time. *Faculty:* 53 full-time (26 women), 7 part-time/adjunct (7 women). *Students:* 87 full-time (55 women), 528 part-time (362 women); includes 198 minority (86 Black or African American, non-Hispanic/Latino; 2 American Indian or Alaska Native, non-Hispanic/Latino; 8 Asian, non-Hispanic/Latino; 84 Hispanic/Latino; 18 Two or more races, non-Hispanic/Latino), 27 international. Average age 37. 333 applicants, 56% accepted, 149 enrolled. In 2016, 66 master's, 8 doctorates awarded. *Degree requirements:* For master's, one foreign language, comprehensive exam, thesis (for some programs); for doctorate, one foreign language, comprehensive

exam, thesis/dissertation, departmental qualifying exam. *Entrance requirements:* For master's and doctorate, GRE General Test. Additional exam requirements/recommendations for international students: Required—TOEFL (minimum score 550 paper-based; 79 iBT), IELTS (minimum score 6). *Application deadline:* Applications are processed on a rolling basis. Application fee: $50. Electronic applications accepted. *Expenses:* Contact institution. *Financial support:* In 2016–17, 255 students received support, including 9 research assistantships with partial tuition reimbursements available (averaging $9,000 per year), 68 teaching assistantships with partial tuition reimbursements available (averaging $9,000 per year); Federal Work-Study, institutionally sponsored loans, scholarships/grants, health care benefits, and unspecified assistantships also available. Financial award application deadline: 5/1; financial award applicants required to submit FAFSA. *Unit head:* Dr. Salvatore Attardo, Dean, 903-886-5166, Fax: 903-886-5774, E-mail: salvatore.attardo@tamuc.edu. *Application contact:* Shelby Miller, Graduate Recruiter, 903-468-8123, Fax: 903-886-5774, E-mail: shelby.miller@tamuc.edu.
Website: http://www.tamuc.edu/academics/graduateSchool/programs/humanitiesSocialScienceArts/default.aspx

**Texas A&M University–Corpus Christi,** College of Graduate Studies, College of Liberal Arts, Program in Studio Art, Corpus Christi, TX 78412-5503. Offers MFA. *Program availability:* Part-time, evening/weekend. *Students:* 16 full-time (7 women), 3 part-time (1 woman); includes 5 minority (1 Asian, non-Hispanic/Latino; 4 Hispanic/Latino), 1 international. Average age 31. 11 applicants, 55% accepted, 4 enrolled. In 2016, 4 master's awarded. *Degree requirements:* For master's, comprehensive exam, thesis. *Entrance requirements:* For master's, essay (300-500 words); 3 letters of recommendation; CD of .jpg image files of applicant's art work. Additional exam requirements/recommendations for international students: Required—TOEFL (minimum score 550 paper-based; 79 iBT), IELTS (minimum score 6.5). *Application deadline:* For fall admission, 3/1 priority date for domestic and international students; for spring admission, 10/1 priority date for domestic and international students. Applications are processed on a rolling basis. Application fee: $50 ($70 for international students). Electronic applications accepted. *Financial support:* Research assistantships, teaching assistantships, career-related internships or fieldwork, Federal Work-Study, institutionally sponsored loans, scholarships/grants, health care benefits, and unspecified assistantships available. Support available to part-time students. Financial award application deadline: 3/15; financial award applicants required to submit FAFSA. *Unit head:* Jack Gron, Head, 361-825-3473, E-mail: jack.gron@tamucc.edu. *Application contact:* Graduate Admissions Coordinator, 361-825-2177, Fax: 361-825-2755, E-mail: gradweb@tamucc.edu.
Website: http://cla.tamucc.edu/art/graduate/art_grad.html

**Texas Christian University,** College of Fine Arts, School of Art, Fort Worth, TX 76129. Offers art history (MA); studio art (MFA), including painting, printmaking, sculpture. *Accreditation:* NASAD. *Faculty:* 12 full-time (5 women), 3 part-time/adjunct (2 women). *Students:* 17 full-time (16 women), 1 (woman) part-time; includes 2 minority (both Hispanic/Latino), 2 international. Average age 30. 24 applicants, 46% accepted, 9 enrolled. In 2016, 7 master's awarded. *Degree requirements:* For master's, variable foreign language requirement, comprehensive exam, thesis. *Entrance requirements:* For master's, GRE General Test (for MA). Additional exam requirements/recommendations for international students: Required—TOEFL (minimum score 550 paper-based; 80 iBT). *Application deadline:* For fall admission, 2/1 for domestic and international students. Application fee: $60. Electronic applications accepted. *Expenses:* Contact institution. *Financial support:* In 2016–17, 18 students received support, including 17 teaching assistantships (averaging $10,000 per year); institutionally sponsored loans, scholarships/grants, health care benefits, tuition waivers (full and partial), and unspecified assistantships also available. Financial award application deadline: 4/15. *Unit head:* Dr. Sally Packard, Director, 817-257-7643, E-mail: s.packard@tcu.edu. *Application contact:* Donna Smolik, TCU College of Fine Arts Graduate Office, 817-257-7603, Fax: 817-257-5672, E-mail: cfagradinfo@tcu.edu.
Website: http://www.art.tcu.edu/

**Texas Southern University,** College of Liberal Arts and Behavioral Sciences, Department of Fine Arts, Houston, TX 77004-4584. Offers fine arts (MA); music (MA). *Program availability:* Part-time. *Degree requirements:* For master's, one foreign language, comprehensive exam, recital. *Entrance requirements:* For master's, GRE General Test, minimum GPA of 2.5. Additional exam requirements/recommendations for international students: Required—TOEFL. Electronic applications accepted. *Faculty research:* Music theory, choral music, composition, percussion composition, ethnic musicology.

**Texas Tech University,** Graduate School, J.T. and Margaret Talkington College of Visual and Performing Arts, Fine Arts Doctoral Program, Lubbock, TX 79409. Offers PhD. *Accreditation:* NAST. *Students:* 52 full-time (33 women), 44 part-time (28 women); includes 12 minority (3 Black or African American, non-Hispanic/Latino; 1 Asian, non-Hispanic/Latino; 4 Hispanic/Latino; 4 Two or more races, non-Hispanic/Latino), 17 international. Average age 37. 27 applicants, 48% accepted, 11 enrolled. In 2016, 3 doctorates awarded. *Degree requirements:* For doctorate, variable foreign language requirement, comprehensive exam, thesis/dissertation. *Entrance requirements:* For doctorate, GRE General Test (for some specializations). Additional exam requirements/recommendations for international students: Required—TOEFL (minimum score 550 paper-based; 79 iBT). *Application deadline:* For fall admission, 6/1 priority date for domestic students, 1/15 priority date for international students; for spring admission, 9/1 priority date for domestic students, 6/15 priority date for international students. Applications are processed on a rolling basis. Application fee: $75. Electronic applications accepted. *Expenses:* $325 per credit hour full-time resident tuition, $733 per credit hour full-time non-resident tuition; $53.75 per credit hour fee plus $608 per term fee. *Financial support:* In 2016–17, 66 students received support, including 66 fellowships (averaging $4,485 per year); research assistantships, teaching assistantships, Federal Work-Study, institutionally sponsored loans, scholarships/grants, health care benefits, tuition waivers (partial), and unspecified assistantships also available. Financial award applicants required to submit FAFSA. *Faculty research:* Art criticism and theory, music, theatre arts, arts education, history of arts, interdisciplinary arts. *Unit head:* Dr. Brian D. Steele, Director/Associate Dean, College of Visual and Performing Arts, 806-742-0700, Fax: 806-742-0695, E-mail: brian.steele@ttu.edu.
Website: http://www.fadp.vpa.ttu.edu

**Texas Tech University,** Graduate School, J.T. and Margaret Talkington College of Visual and Performing Arts, School of Art, Lubbock, TX 79409. Offers art (MFA); art education (MAE); art history (MA). *Accreditation:* NASAD (one or more programs are accredited). *Program availability:* Part-time, online learning. *Faculty:* 32 full-time (14 women), 8 part-time/adjunct (5 women). *Students:* 36 full-time (23 women), 26 part-time (19 women); includes 15 minority (1 Black or African American, non-Hispanic/Latino; 1 Asian, non-Hispanic/Latino; 11 Hispanic/Latino; 2 Two or more races, non-Hispanic/Latino), 4 international. Average age 35. 39 applicants, 62% accepted, 19 enrolled. In 2016, 19 master's awarded. *Degree requirements:* For master's, variable foreign language requirement, comprehensive exam, thesis (for some programs), exhibition (for MFA). *Entrance requirements:* For master's, GRE (for MA). Additional exam requirements/recommendations for international students: Required—TOEFL (minimum

score 550 paper-based; 79 iBT), IELTS (minimum score 6.5). *Application deadline:* For fall admission, 6/1 priority date for domestic students, 1/15 priority date for international students; for spring admission, 9/1 priority date for domestic students, 6/15 priority date for international students. Applications are processed on a rolling basis. Application fee: $75. Electronic applications accepted. *Expenses:* $325 per credit hour full-time resident tuition, $733 per credit hour full-time non-resident tuition; $53.75 per credit hour fee plus $608 per term fee. *Financial support:* In 2016–17, 60 students received support, including 57 fellowships (averaging $2,318 per year), 56 teaching assistantships (averaging $9,357 per year); research assistantships, Federal Work-Study, institutionally sponsored loans, scholarships/grants, health care benefits, tuition waivers (partial), and unspecified assistantships also available. Financial award application deadline: 2/15; financial award applicants required to submit FAFSA. *Faculty research:* Modern and contemporary art; contemporary Chicano/a art; transformation of multidisciplinary approach to printmaking; figurative painting and an intense interest in space as metaphor for community; working-class, sexuality and race issues; letter press posters; conceptual three dimensional concepts. *Total annual research expenditures:* $11,986. *Unit head:* Prof. Lydia Thompson, Director and Professor, 806-742-3825 Ext. 255, E-mail: lydia.thompson@ttu.edu. *Application contact:* Linda Rumbelow, Academic Advisor, 806-742-3825 Ext. 222, E-mail: linda.rumbelow@ttu.edu.
Website: http://www.art.ttu.edu

**Texas Woman's University,** Graduate School, College of Arts and Sciences, School of the Arts, Department of Visual Arts, Denton, TX 76201. Offers art (MA, MFA). *Faculty:* 18 full-time (17 women), 11 part-time/adjunct (9 women). *Students:* Average age 35. In 2016, 9 master's awarded. *Degree requirements:* For master's, comprehensive exam, thesis (for some programs), exhibit (MFA), oral exam, thesis or professional paper (MA). *Entrance requirements:* For master's, portfolio, interview, current curriculum vitae, letter of intent, 3 letters of recommendation (for MFA only). Additional exam requirements/recommendations for international students: Required—TOEFL (minimum score 550 paper-based; 79 iBT). *Application deadline:* For fall admission, 2/15 priority date for domestic students, 2/15 for international students; for spring admission, 10/15 priority date for domestic students, 7/1 for international students. Applications are processed on a rolling basis. Application fee: $50 ($75 for international students). Electronic applications accepted. *Expenses:* Tuition, state resident: full-time $9046; part-time $251 per credit hour. Tuition, nonresident: full-time $22,922; part-time $614 per credit hour. International tuition: $23,046 full-time. *Required fees:* $2690; $1285 per credit hour. One-time fee: $50. Tuition and fees vary according to course level, course load, program and reciprocity agreements. *Financial support:* Research assistantships, teaching assistantships, career-related internships or fieldwork, Federal Work-Study, institutionally sponsored loans, scholarships/grants, traineeships, health care benefits, and unspecified assistantships available. Support available to part-time students. Financial award application deadline: 3/1; financial award applicants required to submit FAFSA. *Faculty research:* Art education and electronic technology, film noir, handmade paper, one-of-a kind art books, new media. *Unit head:* Prof. Gary Washmon, Interim Chair, 940-898-2530, Fax: 940-898-2496, E-mail: gwashmon@twu.edu. *Application contact:* Dr. Samuel Wheeler, Assistant Director of Admissions, 940-898-3188, Fax: 940-898-3081, E-mail: wheelersr@twu.edu.
Website: http://www.twu.edu/visual-arts/

**Tiffin University,** Program in Humanities, Tiffin, OH 44883-2161. Offers art and visual media (MH); communication (MH); creative writing (MH); English (MH); film studies (MH); humanities (MH); individualized studies (MH). *Program availability:* Part-time, evening/weekend, online only, 100% online, blended/hybrid learning. *Students:* 17 full-time (15 women), 116 part-time (75 women); includes 25 minority (15 Black or African American, non-Hispanic/Latino; 2 Asian, non-Hispanic/Latino; 6 Hispanic/Latino; 2 Two or more races, non-Hispanic/Latino). Average age 36. 84 applicants, 80% accepted, 43 enrolled. In 2016, 42 master's awarded. *Entrance requirements:* For master's, work experience. Additional exam requirements/recommendations for international students: Required—TOEFL (minimum score 550 paper-based; 79 iBT). *Application deadline:* For fall admission, 9/1 for domestic students; for spring admission, 1/9 for domestic students. Applications are processed on a rolling basis. Application fee: $50. Electronic applications accepted. Application fee is waived when completed online. *Expenses:* Contact institution. *Financial support:* Unspecified assistantships available. Financial award applicants required to submit FAFSA. *Unit head:* Dr. Jason Slone, Program Chair, 419-448-5851, Fax: 419-443-5002, E-mail: slonedj@tiffin.edu. *Application contact:* Nikki Hintze, Director of Graduate and Distance Education Academic Advising, 800-968-6446 Ext. 3596, Fax: 419-443-5002, E-mail: hintzenm@tiffin.edu.

**Towson University,** Program in Studio Arts, Towson, MD 21252-0001. Offers MFA. *Students:* 12 full-time (5 women), 7 part-time (4 women); includes 6 minority (2 Black or African American, non-Hispanic/Latino; 1 Asian, non-Hispanic/Latino; 1 Hispanic/Latino; 2 Two or more races, non-Hispanic/Latino), 1 international. *Entrance requirements:* For master's, bachelor's degree, preferably in art; portfolio; minimum GPA of 3.0; letter of intent; current resume; 2 letters of recommendation. *Application deadline:* For fall admission, 2/1 for domestic students; for spring admission, 11/1 for domestic students. Application fee: $45. Electronic applications accepted. *Expenses:* Tuition, state resident: full-time $7580; part-time $379 per unit. Tuition, nonresident: full-time $15,700; part-time $785 per unit. *Required fees:* $2480. *Financial support:* Application deadline: 4/1. *Unit head:* Prof. Tonia Matthews, Graduate Program Director, 410-704-2803, E-mail: tmatthews@towson.edu. *Application contact:* Coverley Beidleman, Assistant Director of Graduate Admissions, 410-704-2113, Fax: 410-704-3030, E-mail: grads@towson.edu.
Website: http://www.towson.edu/cofac/departments/art/grad/studio/index.html

**Tufts University,** School of the Museum of Fine Arts, Medford, MA 02155. Offers art education (MAT); studio art (MFA, Postbaccalaureate Certificate). *Accreditation:* NASAD (one or more programs are accredited). Terminal master's awarded for partial completion of doctoral program. *Degree requirements:* For master's, thesis (for some programs), exhibition thesis. *Entrance requirements:* For master's, BFA (preferred) or bachelor's degree or equivalent in related area; portfolio; for Postbaccalaureate Certificate, portfolio, BFA or equivalent. Additional exam requirements/recommendations for international students: Required—TOEFL (minimum score 550 paper-based). Electronic applications accepted. *Expenses:* Tuition: Full-time $49,892; part-time $1248 per credit hour. *Required fees:* $844. Full-time tuition and fees vary according to degree level, program and student level. Part-time tuition and fees vary according to course load. *Faculty research:* Public art commissions, National Endowment for the Arts grant recipients, international exhibitions.

**Tulane University,** School of Liberal Arts, Department of Art, New Orleans, LA 70118-5669. Offers history of art (MA); studio art (MFA). PhD held jointly with Roger Thayer Stone Center for Latin American Studies. *Degree requirements:* For master's, one foreign language, thesis. *Entrance requirements:* For master's, GRE General Test, minimum B average in undergraduate course work. Additional exam requirements/recommendations for international students: Required—TOEFL. Electronic applications accepted. *Expenses:* Tuition: Full-time $50,920; part-time $2829 per credit hour. *Required fees:* $2040; $44.50 per credit hour. $580 per term. Tuition and fees vary according to course load, degree level and program.

*Art/Fine Arts*

**United Theological Seminary of the Twin Cities,** Graduate Programs, New Brighton, MN 55112-2598. Offers advanced theological studies (Diploma); justice and peace studies (M Div, MA); leadership toward racial justice (M Div, MA, Certificate); Methodist studies (M Div, MA, Certificate); ministry (D Min); ministry renewal and professional development (Certificate); pastoral care and counseling (M Div, MA, MARL); religion and theology (MA); theological and religious studies (Certificate); theology and the arts (M Div, MA); urban ministry (M Div, MA, MARL); women's studies: religion, theology and ministry (M Div, MA). *Accreditation:* ACIPE; ATS. *Program availability:* Part-time, evening/weekend. *Degree requirements:* For master's, thesis; for doctorate, comprehensive exam, thesis/dissertation. *Entrance requirements:* For master's, minimum GPA of 2.75; strong analytical, reflective thinking and writing skills; vocational and academic goals compatible with those of Seminary; for doctorate, M Div or equivalent, minimum GPA of 3.0, 3 years experience in professional ministry; for other advanced degree, BA or equivalent life experience; strong analytical, reflective thinking and writing skills (Certificate); proficiency in English language, previous study of theology at a theological school, recommendation of student's denomination (Diploma). Additional exam requirements/recommendations for international students: Required—TOEFL (minimum score 550 paper-based).

**Universidad del Turabo,** Graduate Programs, Programs in Education, Program in Teaching of Fine Arts, Gurabo, PR 00778-3030. Offers M Ed. *Students:* 11 full-time (10 women), 18 part-time (15 women); all minorities (all Hispanic/Latino). Average age 33. 31 applicants, 68% accepted, 18 enrolled. In 2016, 22 master's awarded. *Entrance requirements:* For master's, GRE, EXADEP, GMAT, interview, official transcript, essay, recommendation letters. *Application deadline:* Applications are processed on a rolling basis. Application fee: $25. Electronic applications accepted. *Financial support:* Institutionally sponsored loans available. Financial award applicants required to submit FAFSA. *Unit head:* Israel Rodríguez, Dean, 787-743-7979. *Application contact:* Diriee Rodríguez, Admissions Director, 787-743-7979 Ext. 4453, E-mail: admisiones-ut@suagm.edu.
Website: http://ut.suagm.edu/es/educacion

**Université du Québec à Chicoutimi,** Graduate Programs, Program in Fine Arts, Chicoutimi, QC G7H 2B1, Canada. Offers MA. Program offered jointly with Université du Québec à Montréal. *Program availability:* Part-time. *Degree requirements:* For master's, thesis optional. *Entrance requirements:* For master's, appropriate bachelor's degree, proficiency in French.

**Université du Québec à Montréal,** Graduate Programs, Program in Fine Arts, Montréal, QC H3C 3P8, Canada. Offers MA. Program offered jointly with Université du Québec à Chicoutimi. *Program availability:* Part-time. *Degree requirements:* For master's, thesis optional. *Entrance requirements:* For master's, appropriate bachelor's degree or equivalent, proficiency in French.

**Université Laval,** Faculty of Architecture, Planning and Visual Arts, School of Visual Arts, Programs in Visual Arts, Québec, QC G1K 7P4, Canada. Offers graphic design and multimedia (MA); visual arts (MA). *Degree requirements:* For master's, thesis (for some programs). *Entrance requirements:* For master's, technical exam, interview, mastery of pertinent software, knowledge of French. Electronic applications accepted.

**University at Albany, State University of New York,** College of Arts and Sciences, Department of Art and Art History, Albany, NY 12222-0001. Offers art (MA, MFA). *Faculty:* 7 full-time (5 women), 3 part-time/adjunct (0 women). *Students:* 27 full-time (18 women); includes 3 minority (2 Black or African American, non-Hispanic/Latino; 1 Hispanic/Latino), 1 international. Average age 26. 38 applicants, 63% accepted, 18 enrolled. In 2016, 18 master's awarded. *Degree requirements:* For master's, exhibit. *Entrance requirements:* For master's, portfolio. Additional exam requirements/recommendations for international students: Required—TOEFL (minimum score 550 paper-based). *Application deadline:* For fall admission, 4/15 for domestic and international students; for spring admission, 11/1 for domestic and international students. Application fee: $75. *Expenses:* Tuition, state resident: full-time $10,870; part-time $453 per credit hour. Tuition, nonresident: full-time $22,210; part-time $925 per credit hour. *International tuition:* $21,550 full-time. *Required fees:* $1864; $96 per credit hour. *Financial support:* Federal Work-Study available. Financial award application deadline: 4/1. *Faculty research:* Art history, sculpture, painting and drawing, photography, digital media. *Unit head:* Rachel Dressler, Chair, 518-442-4020, Fax: 518-442-4807. *Application contact:* Michael DeRensis, Director, Graduate Admissions, 518-442-3980, Fax: 518-442-3922, E-mail: graduate@albany.edu.
Website: http://www.albany.edu/finearts

**University at Buffalo, the State University of New York,** Graduate School, College of Arts and Sciences, Department of Art, Buffalo, NY 14260. Offers studio art (MFA); visual studies (MA, PhD), including critical museum studies (MA), visual studies. *Faculty:* 13 full-time (5 women). *Students:* 37 full-time (24 women); includes 6 minority (2 Black or African American, non-Hispanic/Latino; 2 Asian, non-Hispanic/Latino; 2 Hispanic/Latino), 5 international. Average age 30. 87 applicants, 36% accepted, 17 enrolled. *Degree requirements:* For master's, thesis, exhibition, written research paper; for doctorate, comprehensive exam, thesis/dissertation. *Entrance requirements:* For master's, bachelor's degree with minimum GPA of 3.0, work samples, three letters of reference, statement of purpose; for doctorate, GRE. Additional exam requirements/recommendations for international students: Required—TOEFL (minimum score 550 paper-based; 79 iBT). *Application deadline:* For fall admission, 1/10 for domestic and international students. Application fee: $75. Electronic applications accepted. *Financial support:* In 2016–17, 24 students received support, including 24 teaching assistantships with full tuition reimbursements available (averaging $13,424 per year); fellowships with full tuition reimbursements available, career-related internships or fieldwork, Federal Work-Study, institutionally sponsored loans, health care benefits, and unspecified assistantships also available. Support available to part-time students. Financial award application deadline: 2/7; financial award applicants required to submit FAFSA. *Faculty research:* Studio practice, visual studies, design, new media. *Unit head:* Joan Linder, Chair, 716-645-0539, Fax: 716-645-6970, E-mail: joannder@buffalo.edu. *Application contact:* Prof. Stephanie Rothenberg, Director of Graduate Studies, 716-645-6878, Fax: 716-645-6970, E-mail: sjr6@buffalo.edu.
Website: http://art.buffalo.edu

**The University of Alabama,** Graduate School, College of Arts and Sciences, Department of Art and Art History, Tuscaloosa, AL 35487. Offers art history (MA); studio art (MA, MFA), including ceramics, painting, photography, printmaking, sculpture. *Accreditation:* NASAD. *Program availability:* Part-time. *Faculty:* 19 full-time (12 women), 1 part-time/adjunct (0 women). *Students:* 18 full-time (13 women), 4 part-time (3 women); includes 3 minority (1 Black or African American, non-Hispanic/Latino; 1 Asian, non-Hispanic/Latino; 1 Hispanic/Latino), 1 international. Average age 30. 17 applicants, 41% accepted, 5 enrolled. In 2016, 7 master's awarded. *Degree requirements:* For master's, one foreign language, comprehensive exam (for some programs), oral exam, thesis statement, exhibit (studio art), thesis (art history). *Entrance requirements:* For master's, GRE General Test or MAT (art history), minimum GPA of 3.0, BFA or equivalent (studio art). Additional exam requirements/recommendations for international students: Required—TOEFL (minimum score 550 paper-based). *Application deadline:* For fall admission, 3/15 for domestic and international students; for spring admission, 10/15 for domestic and international students. Applications are processed on a rolling

basis. Application fee: $50 ($60 for international students). Electronic applications accepted. *Expenses:* Tuition, state resident: full-time $10,470. Tuition, nonresident: full-time $26,950. *Financial support:* In 2016–17, 8 students received support, including 2 fellowships with full tuition reimbursements available, 14 teaching assistantships with tuition reimbursements available (averaging $15,427 per year); career-related internships or fieldwork, institutionally sponsored loans, scholarships/grants, and unspecified assistantships also available. Financial award application deadline: 7/14. *Faculty research:* Nineteenth-century American, Medieval European, Baroque, twentieth-century, and African American Art History. *Unit head:* Jason Guynes, Chair, 205-348-9944, Fax: 205-348-0287, E-mail: jguynes@ua.edu. *Application contact:* Sarah Marshall, Graduate Coordinator, 205-348-1890, Fax: 205-348-5967, E-mail: smarsh@ua.edu.
Website: http://www.art.ua.edu/

**University of Alaska Fairbanks,** College of Liberal Arts, Department of Art, Fairbanks, AK 99775-5640. Offers art (MFA); ceramics (MFA); computer art (MFA); drawing (MFA); painting (MFA); photography (MFA); printmaking (MFA); sculpture (MFA). *Program availability:* Part-time. *Faculty:* 7 full-time (3 women), 1 (woman) part-time; includes 2 minority (1 Hispanic/Latino; 1 Native Hawaiian or other Pacific Islander, non-Hispanic/Latino). Average age 38. 4 applicants, 50% accepted, 1 enrolled. In 2016, 2 master's awarded. *Degree requirements:* For master's, comprehensive exam, oral defense of project or thesis. *Entrance requirements:* For master's, portfolio of work including about 20 slides or appropriate equivalent depending on field of study. Additional exam requirements/recommendations for international students: Required—TOEFL (minimum score 550 paper-based; 79 iBT), IELTS (minimum score 6.5). *Application deadline:* For fall admission, 6/1 for domestic students, 3/1 for international students; for spring admission, 10/15 for domestic students, 9/1 for international students. Applications are processed on a rolling basis. Application fee: $60. Electronic applications accepted. *Expenses:* Tuition, state resident: full-time $7992; part-time $444 per credit. Tuition, nonresident: full-time $16,326; part-time $907 per credit. *Required fees:* $39 per credit. $322 per semester. Tuition and fees vary according to course level, course load, campus/location, program and reciprocity agreements. *Financial support:* In 2016–17, 3 teaching assistantships with full tuition reimbursements (averaging $5,717 per year) were awarded; fellowships with full tuition reimbursements, research assistantships with full tuition reimbursements, Federal Work-Study, scholarships/grants, health care benefits, and unspecified assistantships also available. Support available to part-time students. Financial award application deadline: 7/1; financial award applicants required to submit FAFSA. *Faculty research:* Computer art, survey of arts in Alaska, found object art, visualization and animation, painting from the wilderness. *Unit head:* David Mollett, Chair, 907-474-7530, Fax: 907-474-5853, E-mail: uaf-art@alaska.edu. *Application contact:* Mary Kreta, Director of Admissions, 907-474-7500, Fax: 907-474-7097, E-mail: admissions@uaf.edu.
Website: http://www.uaf.edu/art/

**University of Alberta,** Faculty of Graduate Studies and Research, Department of Art and Design, Edmonton, AB T6G 2E1, Canada. Offers drawing (MFA); history of art, design, and visual culture (MA); industrial design (M Des); painting (MFA); printmaking (MFA); sculpture (MFA); visual communication design (M Des). *Degree requirements:* For master's, thesis. *Entrance requirements:* For master's, portfolio (MFA and MDES). Additional exam requirements/recommendations for international students: Required—TOEFL (minimum score 550 paper-based).

**The University of Arizona,** College of Fine Arts, School of Art, Program in Art, Tucson, AZ 85721. Offers MFA. *Entrance requirements:* Additional exam requirements/recommendations for international students: Required—TOEFL (minimum score 550 paper-based; 79 iBT). Electronic applications accepted.

**University of Arkansas,** Graduate School, J. William Fulbright College of Arts and Sciences, Department of Art, Fayetteville, AR 72701. Offers MFA. In 2016, 6 master's awarded. *Degree requirements:* For master's, exhibit or thesis. *Application deadline:* For fall admission, 4/1 for international students; for spring admission, 10/1 for international students. Applications are processed on a rolling basis. Application fee: $40 ($50 for international students). Electronic applications accepted. *Financial support:* In 2016–17, 11 research assistantships were awarded; fellowships, teaching assistantships, career-related internships or fieldwork, and Federal Work-Study also available. Support available to part-time students. Financial award application deadline: 4/1; financial award applicants required to submit FAFSA. *Unit head:* Jeannie Hulen, Department Chairperson, 479-575-5202, Fax: 479-575-2062, E-mail: jhulen@uark.edu. *Application contact:* Marc Mitchell, Graduate Coordinator, 479-575-2062, Fax: 479-575-2062, E-mail: mmitch@uark.edu.
Website: http://art.uark.edu

**University of Arkansas at Little Rock,** Graduate School, College of Arts, Letters, and Sciences, Department of Art, Little Rock, AR 72204-1099. Offers art education (MA); art history (MA); studio art (MA). *Accreditation:* NASAD. *Program availability:* Part-time. *Degree requirements:* For master's, 4 foreign languages, oral exam, oral defense of thesis or exhibit. *Entrance requirements:* For master's, portfolio review or term paper evaluation, minimum GPA of 2.7.

**The University of British Columbia,** Faculty of Arts and Faculty of Graduate Studies, Department of Art History, Visual Art, and Theory, Vancouver, BC V6T 1Z2, Canada. Offers art history (MA, PhD); critical and curatorial studies (MA); visual art (MFA). *Degree requirements:* For master's, one foreign language, thesis, final exhibition (MFA, MA in critical and curatorial studies); for doctorate, 2 foreign languages, comprehensive exam, thesis/dissertation. *Entrance requirements:* For master's, bachelor's degree with minimum B+ average (MFA, MA in critical and curatorial studies), A- (MA in art history); for doctorate, master's degree with minimum A- average. Additional exam requirements/recommendations for international students: Required—TOEFL. Application fee: $100 Canadian dollars ($162 Canadian dollars for international students). Electronic applications accepted. *Expenses:* $4,802 per year tuition and fees, $8,436 per year international. *Financial support:* Fellowships, research assistantships, teaching assistantships, Federal Work-Study, scholarships/grants, health care benefits, tuition waivers (full), and unspecified assistantships available. *Faculty research:* Conceptual art, Asian art, indigenous North American art, post-second war art, eighteenth- and nineteenth-century art, curatorial, digital art. *Application contact:* Bryn Dharmaratne, Graduate Program Staff, 604-822-4340, Fax: 604-822-9003, E-mail: ahva.grad@ubc.ca.
Website: http://www.ahva.ubc.ca

**University of Calgary,** Faculty of Graduate Studies, Faculty of Arts, Department of Art, Calgary, AB T2N 1N4, Canada. Offers MA, MFA. *Degree requirements:* For master's, thesis. *Entrance requirements:* Additional exam requirements/recommendations for international students: Required—TOEFL. *Faculty research:* Painting, sculpture, drawing, photography, printmaking, new media.

**University of California, Berkeley,** Graduate Division, College of Letters and Science, Department of Art Practice, Berkeley, CA 94720-1500. Offers MFA. *Faculty:* 7 full-time, 12 part-time/adjunct. *Students:* 12 full-time (9 women); includes 5 minority (1 Black or African American, non-Hispanic/Latino; 3 Asian, non-Hispanic/Latino; 1 Hispanic/Latino), 1 international. Average age 31. 139 applicants, 6 enrolled. In 2016, 6 master's awarded. *Entrance requirements:* For master's, GRE General Test, minimum GPA of

3.0, sample of work, 3 letters of recommendation. Additional exam requirements/recommendations for international students: Required—TOEFL (minimum score 570 paper-based; 90 iBT). *Application deadline:* For fall admission, 12/16 for domestic students. Application fee: $105 ($125 for international students). Electronic applications accepted. *Financial support:* Fellowships, teaching assistantships, institutionally sponsored loans, health care benefits, and unspecified assistantships available. Financial award applicants required to submit FAFSA. *Unit head:* Prof. Allan Desouza, Chair, 501-642-2582. *Application contact:* Dee Levister, Graduate Assistant, 510-643-2582, Fax: 510-643-0884, E-mail: artgrad@berkeley.edu.
Website: http://art.berkeley.edu

**University of California, Berkeley,** UC Berkeley Extension, Certificate Programs in Art and Design, Berkeley, CA 94720-1500. Offers interior design and interior architecture (Certificate); landscape architecture (Certificate); visual arts (Postbaccalaureate Certificate).

**University of California, Davis,** Graduate Studies, Program in Art, Davis, CA 95616. Offers MFA. *Degree requirements:* For master's, final exhibit. *Entrance requirements:* For master's, minimum GPA of 3.0, portfolio. Additional exam requirements/recommendations for international students: Required—TOEFL (minimum score 550 paper-based). Electronic applications accepted. *Faculty research:* Drawing, painting, photography, video, interactive art.

**University of California, Irvine,** Claire Trevor School of the Arts, Department of Art, Irvine, CA 92697. Offers MFA. *Students:* 37 full-time (21 women); includes 15 minority (2 Black or African American, non-Hispanic/Latino; 3 Asian, non-Hispanic/Latino; 6 Hispanic/Latino; 4 Two or more races, non-Hispanic/Latino), 2 international. Average age 30. 141 applicants, 14% accepted, 15 enrolled. In 2016, 12 master's awarded. *Degree requirements:* For master's, thesis. *Entrance requirements:* For master's, minimum GPA of 3.0. *Application deadline:* For fall admission, 1/15 for domestic and international students. Applications are processed on a rolling basis. Application fee: $105 ($125 for international students). Electronic applications accepted. *Financial support:* Fellowships with tuition reimbursements, research assistantships with tuition reimbursements, teaching assistantships with tuition reimbursements, institutionally sponsored loans, traineeships, health care benefits, and unspecified assistantships available. Financial award application deadline: 3/1; financial award applicants required to submit FAFSA. *Faculty research:* Experimental concepts, processes relevant to contemporary issues. *Unit head:* John Medina, Department Manager, 949-824-4917, Fax: 949-824-4106, E-mail: jcmedina@uci.edu. *Application contact:* Kevin Appel, Graduate Advisor, Fax: 949-824-5297, E-mail: kappel@uci.edu.
Website: http://www.arts.uci.edu/ctsa-academic-departments-art-department

**University of California, Irvine,** School of Humanities, Department of Art History, Irvine, CA 92697. Offers visual studies (MA, PhD). Program offered jointly with Department of Film and Media Studies. *Students:* 29 full-time (17 women); includes 10 minority (3 Asian, non-Hispanic/Latino; 5 Hispanic/Latino; 2 Two or more races, non-Hispanic/Latino), 2 international. Average age 30. 86 applicants, 22% accepted, 8 enrolled. In 2016, 1 master's, 5 doctorates awarded. *Degree requirements:* For doctorate, thesis/dissertation. *Entrance requirements:* For master's, GRE, minimum GPA of 3.0; for doctorate, GRE General Test, writing sample. Additional exam requirements/recommendations for international students: Required—TOEFL (minimum score 550 paper-based). *Application deadline:* For fall admission, 12/15 for domestic and international students. Application fee: $105 ($125 for international students). Electronic applications accepted. *Financial support:* Fellowships, teaching assistantships, institutionally sponsored loans, traineeships, health care benefits, and unspecified assistantships available. Financial award application deadline: 3/1; financial award applicants required to submit FAFSA. *Faculty research:* Interdisciplinary study and research in art history, critical theory, women's studies, cultural studies, film studies. *Unit head:* Prof. Cecile Whiting, Chair, 949-824-2464, E-mail: cwhiting@uci.edu. *Application contact:* Lucas Hilderbrand, Director of Graduate Studies for Visual Studies, 949-824-1124, Fax: 949-824-2865, E-mail: lucas.h@uci.edu.
Website: http://www.hnet.uci.edu/arthistory/

**University of California, Los Angeles,** Graduate Division, School of the Arts and Architecture, Department of Art, Los Angeles, CA 90095. Offers MFA. *Degree requirements:* For master's, comprehensive exam. *Entrance requirements:* For master's, bachelor's degree; minimum undergraduate GPA of 3.0 (or its equivalent if letter grade system not used); portfolio. Additional exam requirements/recommendations for international students: Required—TOEFL. Electronic applications accepted. *Expenses:* Contact institution.

**University of California, Riverside,** Graduate Division, Program in Visual Arts, Riverside, CA 92521-0102. Offers MFA. *Degree requirements:* For master's, thesis. *Entrance requirements:* For master's, portfolio, minimum GPA of 3.2. Additional exam requirements/recommendations for international students: Required—TOEFL (minimum score 550 paper-based; 80 iBT). Electronic applications accepted. *Expenses:* Tuition, state resident: full-time $16,666. Tuition, nonresident: full-time $31,768. *Required fees:* $11,055.54 per quarter. $3685.18 per quarter. Tuition and fees vary according to campus/location and program. *Faculty research:* Painting, photography, sculpture, digital art, video.

**University of California, San Diego,** Graduate Division, Department of Visual Arts, La Jolla, CA 92093. Offers art history, theory and criticism (PhD), including anthropogony, visual arts; visual arts (MFA). *Students:* 67 full-time (36 women). 159 applicants, 26% accepted, 20 enrolled. In 2016, 16 master's, 9 doctorates awarded. *Degree requirements:* For master's, comprehensive exam, thesis; for doctorate, 2 foreign languages, comprehensive exam, thesis/dissertation, reading knowledge of at least two of the foreign languages commonly used by scholars engaged in the advanced study in art history, theory, and criticism. *Entrance requirements:* For master's, electronic portfolio; for doctorate, GRE General Test, electronic portfolio. Additional exam requirements/recommendations for international students: Required—TOEFL (minimum score 550 paper-based; 80 iBT), IELTS (minimum score 7). *Application deadline:* For fall admission, 12/4 for domestic students. Application fee: $105 ($125 for international students). Electronic applications accepted. *Expenses:* Tuition, state resident: full-time $11,220. Tuition, nonresident: full-time $26,322. *Required fees:* $1864. *Financial support:* Fellowships, research assistantships, teaching assistantships, career-related internships or fieldwork, scholarships/grants, and readerships available. Financial award applicants required to submit FAFSA. *Faculty research:* Contemporary art, ancient art, critical design, new media/software/hardware. *Unit head:* Jack Greenstein, Chair, 858-534-0418, E-mail: jgreenstein@ucsd.edu. *Application contact:* Katherine Edwards, Graduate Program Coordinator, 858-822-3882, E-mail: vis-grad@ucsd.edu.
Website: http://visarts.ucsd.edu/

**University of California, Santa Barbara,** Graduate Division, College of Letters and Sciences, Division of Humanities and Fine Arts, Department of Art, Santa Barbara, CA 93106-7120. Offers MFA. *Degree requirements:* For master's, thesis, exhibition. *Entrance requirements:* Additional exam requirements/recommendations for international students: Required—TOEFL (minimum score 550 paper-based; 80 iBT), IELTS (minimum score 7). Electronic applications accepted. *Faculty research:* Digital media, interactive media, spatial studies, public space art, book arts.

**University of California, Santa Cruz,** Division of Graduate Studies, Division of the Arts, Program in Digital Arts and New Media, Santa Cruz, CA 95064. Offers MFA. *Degree requirements:* For master's, thesis, written paper. *Entrance requirements:* Additional exam requirements/recommendations for international students: Required—TOEFL (minimum score 550 paper-based; 83 iBT); Recommended—IELTS (minimum score 8). Electronic applications accepted. *Faculty research:* Mechatronics, participatory culture, performative technologies, playable media.

**University of California, Santa Cruz,** Division of Graduate Studies, Division of the Arts, Program in Visual Studies, Santa Cruz, CA 95064. Offers PhD. *Degree requirements:* For doctorate, one foreign language, thesis/dissertation, qualifying exams. *Entrance requirements:* For doctorate, GRE, writing sample under 20 pages, 3 letters of recommendation. Additional exam requirements/recommendations for international students: Required—TOEFL (minimum score 550 paper-based; 83 iBT); Recommended—IELTS (minimum score 8). Electronic applications accepted. *Faculty research:* Opportunity to consider the role of social and cultural forces in guiding how and what their members see, concentration on cultures in Africa, the Americas, Asia, Europe, and the Pacific Islands.

**University of Central Florida,** College of Arts and Humanities, School of Visual Arts and Design, Orlando, FL 32816. Offers digital media (MA); emerging media (MFA), including digital media, entrepreneurial digital cinema, studio art and the computer. *Program availability:* Part-time. *Faculty:* 57 full-time (23 women), 15 part-time/adjunct (4 women). *Students:* 26 full-time (12 women), 13 part-time (3 women); includes 7 minority (3 Black or African American, non-Hispanic/Latino; 1 Asian, non-Hispanic/Latino; 3 Hispanic/Latino), 2 international. Average age 31. 49 applicants, 57% accepted, 19 enrolled. In 2016, 7 master's awarded. *Degree requirements:* For master's, comprehensive exam, thesis or alternative. *Entrance requirements:* Additional exam requirements/recommendations for international students: Required—TOEFL. *Application deadline:* For fall admission, 7/1 for domestic students. Application fee: $30. Electronic applications accepted. *Expenses:* Tuition, state resident: part-time $288.16 per credit hour. Tuition, nonresident: part-time $1071.31 per credit hour. *Financial support:* In 2016–17, 15 students received support, including 4 fellowships with partial tuition reimbursements available (averaging $10,000 per year), 2 research assistantships with partial tuition reimbursements available (averaging $3,214 per year), 13 teaching assistantships with partial tuition reimbursements available (averaging $7,570 per year); scholarships/grants and unspecified assistantships also available. Financial award application deadline: 3/1; financial award applicants required to submit FAFSA. *Unit head:* Dr. Rudy McDaniel, Interim Director, 407-823-3145, E-mail: rudy@ucf.edu. *Application contact:* Assistant Director, Graduate Admissions, 407-823-2766, Fax: 407-823-6442, E-mail: gradadmissions@ucf.edu.
Website: http://svad.cah.ucf.edu/

**University of Chicago,** Division of the Humanities, Department of Visual Arts, Chicago, IL 60637. Offers MFA. *Students:* 16 full-time (7 women); includes 3 minority (1 Black or African American, non-Hispanic/Latino; 2 Hispanic/Latino), 1 international. 85 applicants, 14% accepted, 8 enrolled. In 2016, 8 master's awarded. *Degree requirements:* For master's, thesis presentation and exhibition. *Entrance requirements:* Additional exam requirements/recommendations for international students: Required—TOEFL (minimum score 104 iBT), IELTS (minimum score 7). *Application deadline:* For fall admission, 12/15 for domestic and international students. Application fee: $90. Electronic applications accepted. *Financial support:* Fellowships, Federal Work-Study, institutionally sponsored loans, scholarships/grants, and tuition waivers (full and partial) available. Financial award application deadline: 12/15; financial award applicants required to submit FAFSA. *Unit head:* Dr. Jessica Stockholder, Chair, 773-753-4821. *Application contact:* Michael Beetley, Assistant Dean of Students, Admissions and Fellowships, 773-702-1552, Fax: 773-834-9148, E-mail: humanitiesadmissions@uchicago.edu.
Website: http://dova.uchicago.edu/

**University of Cincinnati,** Graduate School, College of Design, Architecture, Art, and Planning, School of Art, Program in Fine Arts, Cincinnati, OH 45221. Offers MFA. *Accreditation:* NASAD. *Program availability:* Part-time. *Degree requirements:* For master's, thesis, oral exam. *Entrance requirements:* Additional exam requirements/recommendations for international students: Required—TOEFL. Electronic applications accepted. *Expenses:* Tuition, area resident: Full-time $12,790; part-time $389 per credit hour. Tuition, state resident: full-time $13,290; part-time $419 per credit hour. Tuition, nonresident: full-time $24,532; part-time $976 per credit hour. *International tuition:* $24,832 full-time. *Required fees:* $3958; $140 per credit hour. Tuition and fees vary according to course load, degree level, program and reciprocity agreements. *Faculty research:* Painting, drawing, ceramics, printmaking, sculpture.

**University of Colorado Boulder,** Graduate School, College of Arts and Sciences, Department of Art and Art History, Boulder, CO 80309. Offers art history (MA), including contemporary art criticism, early twentieth-century art, nineteenth-century art, Russian and Soviet art; ceramics (MFA); photography and media arts (MFA); printmaking (MFA); sculpture (MFA). *Faculty:* 25 full-time (12 women). *Students:* 47 full-time (33 women); includes 8 minority (1 Black or African American, non-Hispanic/Latino; 6 Hispanic/Latino; 1 Two or more races, non-Hispanic/Latino), 1 international. Average age 29. 173 applicants, 8% accepted, 13 enrolled. In 2016, 20 master's awarded. Terminal master's awarded for partial completion of doctoral program. *Degree requirements:* For master's, variable foreign language requirement, comprehensive exam, thesis (for some programs). *Entrance requirements:* For master's, GRE General Test, minimum undergraduate GPA of 3.0, portfolio. *Application deadline:* For fall admission, 1/15 for domestic students, 12/1 for international students. Electronic applications accepted. Application fee is waived when completed online. *Financial support:* In 2016–17, 179 students received support, including 73 fellowships (averaging $1,882 per year), 42 teaching assistantships with full and partial tuition reimbursements available (averaging $30,614 per year); institutionally sponsored loans, scholarships/grants, health care benefits, and unspecified assistantships also available. Financial award application deadline: 1/15; financial award applicants required to submit FAFSA. *Faculty research:* Visual arts, fine arts, sculpture, installation art, inter-arts: interdisciplinary art forms. *Application contact:* E-mail: finearts@colorado.edu.
Website: http://www.colorado.edu/arts

**University of Colorado Denver,** College of Liberal Arts and Sciences, Program in Humanities, Denver, CO 80217. Offers community health science (MSS); humanities (MH); international studies (MSS); philosophy and theory (MH); social justice (MSS); society and the environment (MSS); visual studies (MH); women's and gender studies (MSS). *Program availability:* Part-time, evening/weekend. *Faculty:* 3 full-time (1 woman). *Students:* 12 full-time (6 women), 15 part-time (7 women); includes 6 minority (1 American Indian or Alaska Native, non-Hispanic/Latino; 3 Hispanic/Latino; 2 Two or more races, non-Hispanic/Latino). Average age 41. 4 applicants, 100% accepted, 4 enrolled. In 2016, 5 master's awarded. *Degree requirements:* For master's, 36 credit hours, project or thesis. *Entrance requirements:* For master's, writing sample, statement of purpose/letter of intent, three letters of recommendation. Additional exam requirements/recommendations for international students: Required—TOEFL (minimum score 537 paper-based; 75 iBT); Recommended—IELTS (minimum score 6.5).

*Art/Fine Arts*

*Application deadline:* For fall admission, 5/15 for domestic students, 5/15 priority date for international students; for spring admission, 10/15 for domestic students, 10/15 priority date for international students; for summer admission, 3/15 for domestic and international students. Application fee: $50 ($75 for international students). Electronic applications accepted. *Expenses:* Tuition, state resident: full-time $11,006; part-time $474 per credit. Tuition, nonresident: full-time $28,212; part-time $1264 per credit hour. *Required fees:* $256 per semester. One-time fee: $94.32. Tuition and fees vary according to campus/location and program. *Financial support:* In 2016–17, 2 students received support. Fellowships, research assistantships, teaching assistantships, Federal Work-Study, institutionally sponsored loans, scholarships/grants, and traineeships available. Financial award application deadline: 4/1; financial award applicants required to submit FAFSA. *Faculty research:* Women and gender in the classical Mediterranean, communication theory and democracy, relationship between psychology and philosophy. *Unit head:* Margaret Woodhull, Director of Humanities, 303-315-3568, E-mail: margaret.woodhull@ucdenver.edu. *Application contact:* Angela Beale, Program Assistant, 303-315-3565, E-mail: mastershs@ucdenver.edu.
Website: http://www.ucdenver.edu/academics/colleges/CLAS/Programs/HumanitiesSocialSciences/Programs/Pages/MasterofHumanities.aspx

**University of Dallas,** Braniff Graduate School of Liberal Arts, Program in Art, Irving, TX 75062-4736. Offers MA, MFA. *Program availability:* Part-time. *Degree requirements:* For master's, exhibit, oral exam. *Entrance requirements:* For master's, GRE General Test, portfolio. Additional exam requirements/recommendations for international students: Required—TOEFL (minimum score 550 paper-based). *Faculty research:* Ceramics, printmaking, sculpture, art history, religious imagery and architecture.

**University of Delaware,** College of Arts and Sciences, Department of Art, Newark, DE 19716. Offers MA, MFA. *Degree requirements:* For master's, exposition paper final exhibition. *Entrance requirements:* For master's, portfolio of creative work. Electronic applications accepted. *Faculty research:* Painting, printmaking, ceramics, photography, sculpture.

**University of Denver,** Division of Arts, Humanities and Social Sciences, School of Art and Art History, Denver, CO 80208. Offers art history (MA); museum studies (MA). *Accreditation:* NASAD. *Program availability:* Part-time. *Faculty:* 16 full-time (10 women), 8 part-time/adjunct (7 women). *Students:* 3 full-time (all women), 12 part-time (all women). Average age 25. 29 applicants, 83% accepted, 6 enrolled. In 2016, 5 master's awarded. *Degree requirements:* For master's, one foreign language, comprehensive exam, research paper or thesis project. *Entrance requirements:* For master's, GRE General Test, transcripts, personal statement, writing sample, three letters of recommendation. Additional exam requirements/recommendations for international students: Required—TOEFL (minimum score 550 paper-based; 80 iBT). *Application deadline:* For fall admission, 1/31 priority date for domestic and international students. Applications are processed on a rolling basis. Application fee: $65. Electronic applications accepted. *Expenses:* $29,022 per year full-time. *Financial support:* In 2016–17, 14 students received support, including 4 teaching assistantships with tuition reimbursements available (averaging $7,500 per year); research assistantships with tuition reimbursements available, career-related internships or fieldwork, Federal Work-Study, institutionally sponsored loans, scholarships/grants, and unspecified assistantships also available. Support available to part-time students. Financial award application deadline: 2/15; financial award applicants required to submit FAFSA. *Faculty research:* Abstract expressionist women painters, Chichen Itza, the cult of St. Ursula, rock poster art of the psychedelic era. *Unit head:* Dr. Catherine Chauvin, Associate Professor and Director, 303-871-2367, Fax: 303-871-4112, E-mail: catherine.chauvin@du.edu. *Application contact:* Dr. Annette Stott, Acting Graduate Art History Advisor, 303-871-3278, Fax: 303-871-4112, E-mail: astott@du.edu.
Website: http://www.du.edu/ahss/art/index.html

**University of Florida,** Graduate School, College of The Arts, School of Art and Art History, Gainesville, FL 32611. Offers art (MA), including digital arts and sciences; art education (MA); art history (MA, PhD); museology (MA), including historic preservation. *Accreditation:* NASAD. *Program availability:* Online learning. *Degree requirements:* For master's, project or thesis (MFA); 1 foreign language (MA in art history); for doctorate, 2 foreign languages, comprehensive exam, thesis/dissertation. *Entrance requirements:* For master's, GRE General Test, portfolio (MFA), writing sample (MA), minimum GPA 3.0; for doctorate, GRE General Test, minimum GPA of 3.0. Additional exam requirements/recommendations for international students: Required—TOEFL (minimum score 550 paper-based; 80 iBT), IELTS (minimum score 6). Electronic applications accepted. *Faculty research:* Studio production, art historical studies of style context.

**University of Georgia,** Franklin College of Arts and Sciences, Lamar Dodd School of Art, Athens, GA 30602. Offers art (MFA, PhD); art history (MA). *Accreditation:* NASAD (one or more programs are accredited). *Degree requirements:* For doctorate, one foreign language, thesis/dissertation. *Entrance requirements:* For master's and doctorate, GRE General Test. *Application deadline:* For fall admission, 7/1 priority date for domestic students; for spring admission, 11/15 for domestic students. Application fee: $50. Electronic applications accepted. *Financial support:* Fellowships, research assistantships, teaching assistantships, and unspecified assistantships available. *Unit head:* Prof. Georgia Strange, Director, 706-542-1600, Fax: 706-542-0226, E-mail: strange@uga.edu. *Application contact:* Isabelle Wallace, Graduate Coordinator, 706-542-1624, E-mail: iwallace@uga.edu.
Website: http://art.uga.edu/

**University of Guam,** Office of Graduate Studies, College of Liberal Arts and Social Sciences, Division of Fine Arts, Mangilao, GU 96923. Offers ceramics (MA); graphics (MA); painting (MA). *Degree requirements:* For master's, thesis or alternative, exhibit, final oral exam. *Entrance requirements:* For master's, GRE General Test, portfolio. Additional exam requirements/recommendations for international students: Required—TOEFL.

**University of Guelph,** Graduate Studies, College of Arts, School of Fine Art and Music, Guelph, ON N1G 2W1, Canada. Offers studio art (MFA). *Degree requirements:* For master's, exhibition, support paper, oral defense. *Entrance requirements:* For master's, minimum B- average during previous 2 years of course work. Additional exam requirements/recommendations for international students: Required—TOEFL. Electronic applications accepted. *Faculty research:* Studio practice in painting, sculpture, print, photo, drawing, video.

**University of Hartford,** Hartford Art School, West Hartford, CT 06117-1599. Offers MFA. *Program availability:* Part-time. *Degree requirements:* For master's, thesis. *Entrance requirements:* For master's, portfolio, 3 letters of recommendation. Additional exam requirements/recommendations for international students: Required—TOEFL (minimum score 550 paper-based). Electronic applications accepted. *Expenses:* Contact institution.

**University of Hawaii at Manoa,** Graduate Division, College of Arts and Humanities, Department of Art and Art History, Honolulu, HI 96822. Offers art history (MA); visual arts (MFA). *Program availability:* Part-time. *Degree requirements:* For master's, thesis optional. *Entrance requirements:* For master's, GRE General Test, BFA, 18 hours of course work in art history. Additional exam requirements/recommendations for international students: Required—TOEFL (minimum score 550 paper-based; 79 iBT),

IELTS (minimum score 7). *Faculty research:* Painting, sculpture, glass, design, printmaking.

**University of Houston,** College of Liberal Arts and Social Sciences, School of Art, Houston, TX 77204. Offers art history (MA); interdisciplinary practice and emerging forms (MFA); painting (MFA); studio art (MFA). *Entrance requirements:* For master's, baccalaureate degree, portfolio. Electronic applications accepted. *Faculty research:* Painting, sculpture, photography/installation/video, graphic design and typography, art history (Pre-Columbian to Surrealism).

**University of Idaho,** College of Graduate Studies, College of Art and Architecture, Moscow, ID 83844. Offers architecture (M Arch); art (MFA); bioregional planning and community design (MS); integrated architecture and design (MS); landscape architecture (MLA). *Accreditation:* NASAD. *Faculty:* 14 full-time, 2 part-time/adjunct (0 women). *Students:* 67 full-time, 9 part-time. Average age 28. In 2016, 42 master's awarded. *Entrance requirements:* For master's, minimum GPA of 3.0. Additional exam requirements/recommendations for international students: Required—TOEFL. *Application deadline:* For fall admission, 8/1 for domestic students; for spring admission, 12/15 for domestic students. Applications are processed on a rolling basis. Application fee: $60. Electronic applications accepted. *Expenses:* Tuition, state resident: full-time $6460; part-time $414 per credit hour. Tuition, nonresident: full-time $21,268; part-time $1237 per credit hour. *Required fees:* $2070; $60 per credit hour. Full-time tuition and fees vary according to course load and reciprocity agreements. *Financial support:* Applicants required to submit FAFSA. *Faculty research:* Sustainability in communities, urban research, virtual technology, bioregional planning, environment and behavior interaction. *Unit head:* Dr. Shauna Corry, Interim Dean, 208-885-4409, E-mail: caa@uidaho.edu. *Application contact:* Sean Scoggin, Graduate Recruitment Coordinator, 208-885-4001, Fax: 208-885-4406, E-mail: graduateadmissions@uidaho.edu.
Website: http://www.uidaho.edu/caa

**University of Illinois at Chicago,** College of Architecture, Design and the Arts, School of Art and Art History, Chicago, IL 60607-7128. Offers art history (MA); electronic visualization (MFA); museum and exhibition studies (MA); new media arts (MFA). *Program availability:* Part-time, evening/weekend. Terminal master's awarded for partial completion of doctoral program. *Degree requirements:* For master's, one foreign language, thesis or alternative; for doctorate, thesis/dissertation. *Entrance requirements:* For master's, GRE General Test, minimum GPA 2.75, 3 letters of recommendation; for doctorate, GRE General Test, MA in art history or equivalent, minimum GPA of 3.0. Additional exam requirements/recommendations for international students: Required—TOEFL. Electronic applications accepted. *Expenses:* Contact institution. *Faculty research:* Modern painting and sculpture, history of architecture, city planning and design, history of photography.

**University of Illinois at Urbana–Champaign,** Graduate College, College of Fine and Applied Arts, School of Art and Design, Program in Design and Media, Champaign, IL 61820. Offers art and design (MFA), including new media; graphic design (MFA); industrial design (MFA). *Accreditation:* NASAD.

**University of Illinois at Urbana–Champaign,** Graduate College, College of Fine and Applied Arts, School of Art and Design, Program in Studio Arts, Champaign, IL 61820. Offers art and design (MFA); crafts (MFA); metals (MFA); painting (MFA); photography (MFA); sculpture (MFA). *Accreditation:* NASAD. *Entrance requirements:* For master's, minimum GPA of 3.0.

**University of Indianapolis,** Graduate Programs, College of Arts and Sciences, Department of Art, Indianapolis, IN 46227-3697. Offers MA. *Accreditation:* NASAD. *Program availability:* Part-time, evening/weekend. *Entrance requirements:* For master's, GRE Subject Test, 3 letters of recommendation, portfolio. Additional exam requirements/recommendations for international students: Required—TOEFL.

**The University of Iowa,** Graduate College, College of Liberal Arts and Sciences, School of Art and Art History, Programs in Studio Art, Iowa City, IA 52242-1316. Offers MA, MFA. *Faculty:* 25 full-time (15 women), 2 part-time/adjunct (both women). *Students:* 55 full-time (38 women), 2 part-time; includes 7 minority (2 Black or African American, non-Hispanic/Latino; 2 Asian, non-Hispanic/Latino; 1 Hispanic/Latino; 2 Two or more races, non-Hispanic/Latino), 7 international. 160 applicants, 28% accepted, 35 enrolled. In 2016, 41 master's awarded. *Degree requirements:* For master's, thesis, final exam. *Entrance requirements:* For master's, portfolio. Additional exam requirements/recommendations for international students: Required—TOEFL (minimum score 550 paper-based; 81 iBT). *Application deadline:* For fall admission, 2/1 for domestic and international students. Application fee: $50 ($75 for international students). Electronic applications accepted. *Financial support:* In 2016–17, 58 students received support, including 2 research assistantships with full and partial tuition reimbursements available (averaging $9,132 per year), 64 teaching assistantships with full and partial tuition reimbursements available (averaging $9,132 per year); fellowships, career-related internships or fieldwork, Federal Work-Study, institutionally sponsored loans, scholarships/grants, health care benefits, and unspecified assistantships also available. Support available to part-time students. Financial award application deadline: 2/1. *Faculty research:* Ceramics, painting, design, printmaking, photography, sculpture. *Unit head:* Prof. Isabel Barbuzza, Director of Graduate Studies, 319-335-1789, Fax: 319-384-2715. *Application contact:* Laura Jorgensen, Graduate Program Coordinator, 319-335-1758, Fax: 319-335-1774, E-mail: art@uiowa.edu.

**The University of Kansas,** Graduate Studies, College of Liberal Arts and Sciences, Department of English, Lawrence, KS 66045. Offers creative writing (MFA), including fine arts/creative writing; English (MA, PhD). *Program availability:* Part-time. *Students:* 93 full-time (57 women), 3 part-time (1 woman); includes 14 minority (7 Black or African American, non-Hispanic/Latino; 1 Asian, non-Hispanic/Latino; 3 Two or more races, non-Hispanic/Latino), 8 international. Average age 30. 143 applicants, 29% accepted, 28 enrolled. In 2016, 9 master's, 3 doctorates awarded. *Entrance requirements:* For master's and doctorate, GRE General Test, two examples of academic writing; resume; statement of approximately 500 words describing interests, training, experience (including teaching experience), academic ability, and goals; three letters of recommendation; official transcripts. Additional exam requirements/recommendations for international students: Required—TOEFL or IELTS. *Application deadline:* For fall admission, 12/31 for domestic and international students. Application fee: $65 ($85 for international students). Electronic applications accepted. *Financial support:* Fellowships, research assistantships, teaching assistantships, and unspecified assistantships available. *Faculty research:* Ecocriticism and science/science fiction writing; gender and sexuality studies; U.S. ethnic literatures, race, and diaspora studies; composition, rhetoric, and language studies; creative writing. *Unit head:* Anna Neill, Chair, 785-864-2521, E-mail: aneill@ku.edu. *Application contact:* Lydia Ash, Graduate Secretary, 785-864-2518, E-mail: lash@ku.edu.
Website: http://www.english.ku.edu

**The University of Kansas,** Graduate Studies, College of Liberal Arts and Sciences, Department of Visual Art, Program in Visual Art Education, Lawrence, KS 66045. Offers MA. *Program availability:* Part-time. *Students:* 3 full-time (all women), 2 part-time (both women). Average age 34. 2 applicants, 100% accepted, 2 enrolled. In 2016, 4 master's awarded. *Entrance requirements:* For master's, portfolio, 3 letters of recommendation, minimum GPA of 3.0. Additional exam requirements/recommendations for international students: Required—TOEFL (minimum score 570 paper-based) or IELTS (minimum score 6.5). *Application deadline:* For fall admission, 5/1 for domestic and international students; for spring admission, 12/1 for domestic and international students. Application fee: $65 ($85 for international students). Electronic applications accepted. *Financial support:* Teaching assistantships, Federal Work-Study, scholarships/grants, and unspecified assistantships available. *Faculty research:* Emphasizing a balance of studio, art history, and education courses. *Unit head:* Mary Anne Jordan, Chairperson, 785-864-2952, E-mail: majordan@ku.edu. *Application contact:* Lauren Chaney, Graduate Admissions Contact, 785-864-2306, E-mail: lkchaney@ku.edu. Website: http://art.ku.edu/programs/visual_art_education/

**University of Kentucky,** Graduate School, College of Fine Arts, Program in Art Studio, Lexington, KY 40506-0032. Offers MFA. *Accreditation:* NASAD. *Degree requirements:* For master's, comprehensive exam. *Entrance requirements:* For master's, GRE General Test, minimum undergraduate GPA of 2.75. Additional exam requirements/recommendations for international students: Required—TOEFL (minimum score 550 paper-based). Electronic applications accepted.

**University of Lethbridge,** School of Graduate Studies, Lethbridge, AB T1K 3M4, Canada. Offers addictions counseling (M Sc); agricultural biotechnology (M Sc); agricultural studies (M Sc, MA); anthropology (MA); archaeology (M Sc, MA); art (MA, MFA); biochemistry (M Sc); biological sciences (M Sc); biomolecular science (PhD); biosystems and biodiversity (PhD); Canadian studies (MA); chemistry (M Sc); computer science (M Sc); computer science and geographical information science (M Sc); counseling (MC); counseling psychology (M Ed); dramatic arts (MA); earth, space, and physical science (PhD); economics (MA); education (MA, PhD); educational leadership (M Ed); English (MA); environmental science (M Sc); evolution and behavior (PhD); exercise science (M Sc); French (MA); French/German (MA); French/Spanish (MA); general education (M Ed); geography (M Sc, MA); German (MA); health sciences (M Sc); individualized multidisciplinary (M Sc, MA); kinesiology (M Sc, MA); management (M Sc), including accounting, finance, human resource management and labor relations, information systems, international management, marketing, policy and strategy; mathematics (M Sc); music (M Mus, MA); Native American studies (MA); neuroscience (M Sc, PhD); new media (MA, MFA); nursing (M Sc, MN); philosophy (MA); physics (M Sc); political science (MA); psychology (M Sc, MA); religious studies (MA); sociology (MA); theatre and dramatic arts (MFA); theoretical and computational science (PhD); urban and regional studies (MA); women and gender studies (MA). *Program availability:* Part-time, evening/weekend. *Degree requirements:* For master's, thesis (for some programs); for doctorate, comprehensive exam, thesis/dissertation. *Entrance requirements:* For master's, GMAT (for M Sc in management), bachelor's degree in related field, minimum GPA of 3.0 during previous 20 graded semester courses, 2 years' teaching or related experience (M Ed); for doctorate, master's degree, minimum graduate GPA of 3.5. Additional exam requirements/recommendations for international students: Required—TOEFL (minimum score 580 paper-based; 93 iBT). Electronic applications accepted. *Faculty research:* Movement and brain plasticity, gibberellin physiology, photosynthesis, carbon cycling, molecular properties of main-group ring components.

**University of Maine,** Graduate School, Intermedia Program, Orono, ME 04469. Offers MFA. *Accreditation:* NASAD. *Faculty:* 9 full-time (4 women), 4 part-time/adjunct (3 women). *Students:* 18 full-time (7 women), 13 part-time (4 women); includes 6 minority (4 American Indian or Alaska Native, non-Hispanic/Latino; 1 Hispanic/Latino; 1 Two or more races, non-Hispanic/Latino), 1 international. Average age 43. 20 applicants, 100% accepted, 9 enrolled. In 2016, 7 master's awarded. Terminal master's awarded for partial completion of doctoral program. *Degree requirements:* For master's, comprehensive exam, thesis. *Entrance requirements:* For master's, portfolio. Additional exam requirements/recommendations for international students: Required—TOEFL. Application fee: $65. *Expenses:* Tuition, state resident: full-time $7524; part-time $2508 per credit. Tuition, nonresident: full-time $24,498; part-time $8166 per credit. *Required fees:* $1148; $571 per credit. *Financial support:* In 2016–17, 12 students received support, including 5 teaching assistantships (averaging $14,600 per year); Federal Work-Study, scholarships/grants, health care benefits, and unspecified assistantships also available. Financial award application deadline: 3/1; financial award applicants required to submit FAFSA. *Faculty research:* Intermedia, bio-art, art and science, Fluxus, activist art. *Total annual research expenditures:* $4,000. *Unit head:* Dr. Owen Smith, Director, 207-581-4389, E-mail: owen.smith@umit.maine.edu. *Application contact:* Scott G. Delcourt, Assistant Vice President for Graduate Studies and Senior Associate Dean, 207-581-3291, Fax: 207-581-3232, E-mail: graduate@maine.edu. Website: http://intermediamfa.org

**The University of Manchester,** School of Arts, Histories and Cultures, Manchester, United Kingdom. Offers anthropology, media and performance (PhD); applied theatre professional (PhD); archaeology (PhD); art history and visual studies (PhD); arts management and cultural policy (PhD); classics and ancient history (PhD); composition (PhD); creative writing (PhD); drama (PhD); economic and social history (PhD); electroacoustic composition (PhD); English and American studies (PhD); history (PhD); humanitarianism and conflict response (PhD); museology (PhD); music (PhD); musicology (PhD); religions and theology (PhD).

**The University of Manchester,** School of Materials, Manchester, United Kingdom. Offers advanced aerospace materials engineering (M Sc); advanced metallic systems (PhD); biomedical materials (M Phil, M Sc, PhD); ceramics and glass (M Phil, M Sc, PhD); composite materials (M Sc, PhD); corrosion and protection (M Phil, M Sc, PhD); materials (M Phil, M Sc, PhD); metallic materials (M Phil, M Sc, PhD); nanostructural materials (M Phil, M Sc, PhD); paper science (M Phil, M Sc, PhD); polymer science and engineering (M Phil, M Sc, PhD); technical textiles (M Sc); textile design, fashion and management (M Phil, M Sc, PhD); textile science and technology (M Phil, M Sc, PhD); textiles (M Phil, PhD); textiles and fashion (M Ent).

**University of Maryland, College Park,** Academic Affairs, College of Arts and Humanities, Department of Art, College Park, MD 20742. Offers MFA. *Degree requirements:* For master's, thesis, oral defense. *Entrance requirements:* For master's, minimum GPA of 3.0, portfolio, 20 digital images, 3 letters of recommendation. Electronic applications accepted. *Faculty research:* Studio art.

**University of Massachusetts Amherst,** Graduate School, College of Humanities and Fine Arts, Department of Art, Amherst, MA 01003. Offers art (MA, MFA), including art education (MA), studio art (MFA). *Program availability:* Part-time. *Degree requirements:* For master's, comprehensive exam (for some programs), thesis (for some programs). *Entrance requirements:* For master's, portfolio. Additional exam requirements/recommendations for international students: Required—TOEFL (minimum score 550 paper-based; 80 iBT), IELTS (minimum score 6.5). Electronic applications accepted.

**University of Massachusetts Dartmouth,** Graduate School, College of Visual and Performing Arts, Department of Artisanry, North Dartmouth, MA 02747-2300. Offers ceramics (MFA, Postbaccalaureate Certificate); fibers (MFA, Postbaccalaureate Certificate); jewelry/metals (MFA, Postbaccalaureate Certificate); wood/furniture design (MFA, Postbaccalaureate Certificate). *Accreditation:* NASAD. *Program availability:* Part-time. *Faculty:* 5 full-time (3 women), 2 part-time/adjunct (1 woman). *Students:* 9 full-time

(8 women), 7 part-time (6 women); includes 2 minority (1 Black or African American, non-Hispanic/Latino; 1 Two or more races, non-Hispanic/Latino), 2 international. Average age 35. 22 applicants, 73% accepted, 5 enrolled. In 2016, 6 master's, 2 other advanced degrees awarded. *Degree requirements:* For master's, visual thesis, written thesis. *Entrance requirements:* For master's, statement of purpose (minimum of 300 words), resume, 2 letters of recommendation, official transcripts, portfolio (20 images representing applicant's art work, process of thinking, implementation of concepts, and studio production); for Postbaccalaureate Certificate, statement of purpose (minimum of 300 words), resume, 3 letters of recommendation, official transcripts, portfolio (10 images representing applicant's art work, process of thinking, implementation of concepts and studio production). Additional exam requirements/recommendations for international students: Required—TOEFL (minimum score 533 paper-based; 72 iBT). *Application deadline:* For fall admission, 1/11 priority date for domestic students, 12/9 priority date for international students; for spring admission, 10/15 priority date for domestic students, 9/15 priority date for international students. Applications are processed on a rolling basis. Application fee: $60. Electronic applications accepted. *Expenses:* Tuition, state resident: full-time $14,994; part-time $624.75 per credit. Tuition, nonresident: full-time $27,068; part-time $1127.83 per credit. *Required fees:* $405; $25.88 per credit. Tuition and fees vary according to course load and reciprocity agreements. *Financial support:* In 2016–17, 5 fellowships (averaging $2,783 per year) were awarded; institutionally sponsored loans, scholarships/grants, unspecified assistantships, and studio assistantships, distinguished art fellowships also available. Financial award application deadline: 3/1; financial award applicants required to submit FAFSA. *Faculty research:* Hand-building, wheeling-throwing, fabrication of jewelry, sculptural objects, slip casting. *Total annual research expenditures:* $113,333. *Unit head:* James Lawton, Graduate Program Director, Artisanry, 508-999-8906, E-mail: jlawton@umassd.edu. *Application contact:* Steven Briggs, Director of Marketing and Recruitment for Graduate Studies, 508-999-8604, Fax: 508-999-8183, E-mail: graduate@umassd.edu.
Website: http://www.umassd.edu/cvpa/graduate/artisanry

**University of Massachusetts Dartmouth,** Graduate School, College of Visual and Performing Arts, Department of Fine Arts, North Dartmouth, MA 02747-2300. Offers drawing (MFA, Postbaccalaureate Certificate); painting (MFA, Postbaccalaureate Certificate); printmaking (MFA, Postbaccalaureate Certificate); sculpture (MFA, Postbaccalaureate Certificate). *Program availability:* Part-time. *Faculty:* 9 full-time (3 women), 3 part-time/adjunct (1 woman). *Students:* 9 full-time (4 women), 6 part-time (2 women); includes 2 minority (both Hispanic/Latino). Average age 43. 23 applicants, 48% accepted, 6 enrolled. In 2016, 10 master's awarded. *Degree requirements:* For master's, visual thesis, written thesis. *Entrance requirements:* For master's, statement of purpose (minimum of 300 words), resume, 2 letters of recommendation, official transcripts, portfolio (20 images representing applicant's art work, process of thinking, implementation of concepts and studio production); for Postbaccalaureate Certificate, statement of purpose (minimum of 300 words), resume, 3 letters of recommendation, official transcripts, portfolio (10 images representing applicant's art work, process of thinking, implementation of concepts and studio production). Additional exam requirements/recommendations for international students: Required—TOEFL (minimum score 533 paper-based; 72 iBT). *Application deadline:* For fall admission, 1/11 priority date for domestic students, 12/9 priority date for international students; for spring admission, 10/15 priority date for domestic students, 9/15 priority date for international students. Applications are processed on a rolling basis. Application fee: $60. Electronic applications accepted. *Expenses:* Tuition, state resident: full-time $14,994; part-time $624.75 per credit. Tuition, nonresident: full-time $27,068; part-time $1127.83 per credit. *Required fees:* $405; $25.88 per credit. Tuition and fees vary according to course load and reciprocity agreements. *Financial support:* In 2016–17, 6 fellowships (averaging $2,600 per year) were awarded; institutionally sponsored loans, scholarships/grants, and studio assistantships also available. Support available to part-time students. Financial award application deadline: 3/1; financial award applicants required to submit FAFSA. *Faculty research:* Painting, printmaking, drawing, figurative sculpture plaster media, prehistoric rock art, petroglyphs and pictographs. *Total annual research expenditures:* $113,334. *Unit head:* Suzanne Schiresan, Graduate Program Director, Fine Arts, 508-999-8908, E-mail: sschiresan@umassd.edu. *Application contact:* Steven Briggs, Director of Marketing and Recruitment for Graduate Studies, 508-999-8604, Fax: 508-999-8183, E-mail: graduate@umassd.edu.
Website: http://www.umassd.edu/cvpa/graduate/finearts

**University of Memphis,** Graduate School, College of Communication and Fine Arts, Department of Art, Memphis, TN 38152. Offers art history (MA), including Egyptian art and archaeology, general art history; ceramics (MFA); graphic design (MFA); museum studies (Graduate Certificate); painting (MFA); printmaking/photography (MFA); sculpture (MFA). *Accreditation:* NASAD (one or more programs are accredited). *Program availability:* Part-time. *Faculty:* 20 full-time (7 women), 1 part-time/adjunct (0 women). *Students:* 22 full-time (16 women), 10 part-time (9 women); includes 9 minority (2 Black or African American, non-Hispanic/Latino; 1 Asian, non-Hispanic/Latino; 3 Hispanic/Latino; 3 Two or more races, non-Hispanic/Latino). Average age 29. 18 applicants, 78% accepted, 11 enrolled. In 2016, 17 master's, 16 other advanced degrees awarded. *Degree requirements:* For master's, 2 foreign languages, comprehensive exam, thesis, image identification exam, qualifying exam; for Graduate Certificate, internship. *Entrance requirements:* For master's, GRE General Test or MAT, portfolio (MFA), letter of intent, sample of undergraduate writing, two letters of recommendation; for Graduate Certificate, three letters of recommendation, letter of intent. *Application deadline:* For fall admission, 2/15 for domestic students; for spring admission, 11/1 for domestic students. Applications are processed on a rolling basis. Application fee: $35 ($60 for international students). *Expenses:* $5,231.50 per semester full-time in-state, $9,623.50 full-time out-of-state. *Financial support:* In 2016–17, 36 students received support, including 20 research assistantships with full tuition reimbursements available (averaging $9,800 per year); teaching assistantships with full tuition reimbursements available, Federal Work-Study, scholarships/grants, and unspecified assistantships also available. Financial award application deadline: 2/1; financial award applicants required to submit FAFSA. *Faculty research:* Online collaborative learning, advanced art history studies, electronic publishing/design, studio arts, architectural studies. *Unit head:* Prof. Richard Lou, Chair, 901-678-2217, Fax: 901-678-2735, E-mail: ralou@memphis.edu. *Application contact:* Niles Wallice, Coordinator of Graduate Studies, 901-678-4899.
Website: http://memphis.edu/art/

**University of Miami,** Graduate School, College of Arts and Sciences, Department of Art and Art History, Coral Gables, FL 33124. Offers art history (MA); ceramics/glass (MFA); graphic design/multimedia (MFA); painting (MFA); photography/digital imaging (MFA); printmaking (MFA); sculpture (MFA). *Program availability:* Part-time. *Degree requirements:* For master's, variable foreign language requirement, thesis, exhibit (MFA), comprehensive exam (MA). *Entrance requirements:* For master's, GRE General Test (MA), research paper (MA), slide portfolio (MFA). Additional exam requirements/recommendations for international students: Required—TOEFL. Electronic applications accepted. *Faculty research:* Installation art, public art.

**University of Michigan,** Rackham Graduate School, Penny W. Stamps School of Art and Design, Ann Arbor, MI 48109. Offers art and design (MFA); integrative design

*Art/Fine Arts*

(M Des). *Accreditation:* NASAD. *Faculty:* 37. *Students:* 19 (13 women); includes 2 minority (1 Black or African American, non-Hispanic/Latino; 1 Asian, non-Hispanic/Latino). 146 applicants, 8% accepted, 10 enrolled. In 2016, 6 master's awarded. *Degree requirements:* For master's, thesis, exhibit (MFA), slide lecture. *Entrance requirements:* For master's, portfolio. Additional exam requirements/recommendations for international students: Required—TOEFL (minimum score 560 paper-based; 84 iBT), IELTS (minimum score 6.5). *Application deadline:* For fall admission, 1/1 for domestic and international students. Application fee: $75 ($90 for international students). Electronic applications accepted. *Expenses:* Tuition, state resident: full-time $21,466; part-time $1152 per credit hour. Tuition, nonresident: full-time $43,346; part-time $2367 per credit hour. Part-time tuition and fees vary according to course load, degree level and program. *Financial support:* In 2016–17, 19 students received support. Fellowships with tuition reimbursements available, research assistantships with tuition reimbursements available, teaching assistantships with tuition reimbursements available, Federal Work-Study, scholarships/grants, health care benefits, tuition waivers (full and partial), and unspecified assistantships available. Support available to part-time students. Financial award application deadline: 1/1. *Faculty research:* Creative expression, social engagement, commercial design, collaborative research, preparation for teaching. *Unit head:* Gunalan Nadarajan, Dean, 734-763-4093, E-mail: artdes-dean@umich.edu. *Application contact:* Meghan Jellema, Graduate Programs Coordinator, 734-763-5247, E-mail: stamps-graduate-info@umich.edu. Website: http://stamps.umich.edu/

**University of Michigan–Flint,** Graduate Programs, Program in Arts Administration, Flint, MI 48502. Offers museum and visual arts (MA), including museum and visual arts, performance. *Program availability:* Part-time. *Faculty:* 5 full-time (4 women), 3 part-time/adjunct (all women). *Students:* 7 full-time (6 women), 5 part-time (3 women); includes 2 minority (both Black or African American, non-Hispanic/Latino). Average age 39. 11 applicants, 55% accepted, 3 enrolled. In 2016, 3 master's awarded. *Degree requirements:* For master's, thesis, internship. *Entrance requirements:* For master's, bachelor's degree in the arts (visual art, theatre, dance, music, etc.) from regionally-accredited institution; minimum cumulative undergraduate GPA of 3.0. Additional exam requirements/recommendations for international students: Required—TOEFL (minimum score 84 iBT), IELTS (minimum score 6.5). *Application deadline:* For fall admission, 8/1 for domestic students, 5/1 for international students; for winter admission, 11/15 for domestic students, 9/1 for international students. Applications are processed on a rolling basis. Application fee: $55. Electronic applications accepted. *Expenses:* Contact institution. *Financial support:* Federal Work-Study, scholarships/grants, and unspecified assistantships available. Support available to part-time students. Financial award application deadline: 3/1; financial award applicants required to submit FAFSA. *Unit head:* Nicole Broughton, Director, 810-237-6522, E-mail: broughn@umflint.edu. *Application contact:* Bradley T. Maki, Director of Graduate Admissions, 810-762-3171, Fax: 810-766-6789, E-mail: bmaki@umflint.edu. Website: http://www.umflint.edu/graduateprograms/arts-administration-ma

**University of Minnesota, Duluth,** Graduate School, School of Fine Arts, Department of Art and Design, Duluth, MN 55812-2496. Offers graphic design (MFA). *Accreditation:* NASAD. *Program availability:* Part-time. *Degree requirements:* For master's, final exhibit, project, supporting paper. *Entrance requirements:* For master's, minimum GPA of 3.0, writing sample, slide portfolio. Additional exam requirements/recommendations for international students: Required—TOEFL (minimum score 550 paper-based). *Faculty research:* Motion graphics, graphic design history, interactive design, typography, education.

**University of Minnesota, Twin Cities Campus,** Graduate School, College of Liberal Arts, Department of Art, Minneapolis, MN 55455. Offers MFA. *Degree requirements:* For master's, oral exam, supporting paper, thesis exhibit. *Entrance requirements:* For master's, portfolio, letters of recommendation, minimum GPA 3.0. Additional exam requirements/recommendations for international students: Required—TOEFL (minimum score 550 paper-based; 79 iBT); Recommended—IELTS (minimum score 6.5). Electronic applications accepted. *Faculty research:* Performed photography, image as code and symbol, cast metal sculpture, performance and installations, high-fired salt glazed and utilitarian ceramic earthenware, contemporary theory, multimedia, video and electronic technology.

**University of Mississippi,** Graduate School, College of Liberal Arts, University, MS 38677. Offers anthropology (MA); biology (MS, PhD); chemistry (MS, PhD); economics (MA, PhD); English (MA, PhD); experimental psychology (PhD); history (MA, PhD); mathematics (MS, PhD); modern languages (MA); music (MM); philosophy (MA); physics (MA, MS, PhD); political science (MA, PhD); studio art (MFA). *Program availability:* Part-time. *Faculty:* 472 full-time (263 women), 75 part-time/adjunct (35 women). *Students:* 415 full-time (210 women), 57 part-time (20 women); includes 70 minority (35 Black or African American, non-Hispanic/Latino; 13 Asian, non-Hispanic/Latino; 14 Hispanic/Latino; 8 Two or more races, non-Hispanic/Latino), 102 international. Average age 27. *Degree requirements:* For doctorate, thesis/dissertation. *Entrance requirements:* For master's, GRE General Test, minimum GPA of 3.0; for doctorate, GRE General Test. Additional exam requirements/recommendations for international students: Required—TOEFL. *Application deadline:* For fall admission, 4/1 for domestic students; for spring admission, 10/1 for domestic students. Applications are processed on a rolling basis. Application fee: $40. Electronic applications accepted. *Financial support:* Fellowships, research assistantships, teaching assistantships, career-related internships or fieldwork, Federal Work-Study, institutionally sponsored loans, scholarships/grants, and unspecified assistantships available. Financial award application deadline: 3/1; financial award applicants required to submit FAFSA. *Unit head:* Dr. Lee Michael Cohen, Dean, 662-915-7177, Fax: 662-915-5792, E-mail: libarts@olemiss.edu. *Application contact:* Dr. Christy M. Wyandt, Associate Dean of Graduate School, 662-915-7474, Fax: 662-915-7577, E-mail: cwyandt@olemiss.edu. Website: https://www.olemiss.edu

**University of Missouri,** Office of Research and Graduate Studies, College of Arts and Science, Department of Art, Columbia, MO 65211. Offers MFA. *Faculty:* 18 full-time (7 women), 9 part-time/adjunct (7 women). *Students:* 22 full-time (7 women); includes 1 minority (Hispanic/Latino), 1 international. Average age 32. *Degree requirements:* For master's, thesis. *Entrance requirements:* For master's, GRE General Test, minimum GPA of 3.0. Additional exam requirements/recommendations for international students: Required—TOEFL (minimum score 550 paper-based; 80 iBT), IELTS (minimum score 6.5). *Application deadline:* For fall admission, 1/1 priority date for domestic students, 1/1 for international students; for winter admission, 9/1 for domestic and international students; for spring admission, 2/1 for domestic students. Applications are processed on a rolling basis. Application fee: $75 ($90 for international students). Electronic applications accepted. *Expenses:* Tuition, state resident: full-time $6347; part-time $352.60 per credit hour. Tuition, nonresident: full-time $17,379; part-time $965.50 per credit hour. *Required fees:* $1035. Tuition and fees vary according to course load, campus/location and program. *Financial support:* Research assistantships with full tuition reimbursements, teaching assistantships with full tuition reimbursements, institutionally sponsored loans, health care benefits, and unspecified assistantships available. Support available to part-time students. *Faculty research:* Painting, digital art,

new media, photography, ceramics. Website: http://art.missouri.edu/mfa-program.html

**University of Missouri–Kansas City,** College of Arts and Sciences, Department of Art and Art History, Kansas City, MO 64110-2499. Offers MA, PhD. PhD (interdisciplinary) offered through the School of Graduate Studies. *Program availability:* Part-time. *Faculty:* 10 full-time (5 women), 9 part-time/adjunct (4 women). *Students:* 1 (woman) full-time, 24 part-time (17 women); includes 4 minority (1 Black or African American, non-Hispanic/Latino; 3 Hispanic/Latino), 1 international. Average age 39. 12 applicants, 58% accepted, 7 enrolled. In 2016, 13 master's awarded. Terminal master's awarded for partial completion of doctoral program. *Degree requirements:* For master's, thesis, qualifying exam; for doctorate, thesis/dissertation, exams. *Entrance requirements:* For master's, good general education in the humanities. Additional exam requirements/recommendations for international students: Required—TOEFL (minimum score 550 paper-based; 80 iBT). *Application deadline:* For fall admission, 3/1 priority date for domestic and international students; for spring admission, 10/15 for domestic and international students. Applications are processed on a rolling basis. Application fee: $45 ($50 for international students). Electronic applications accepted. *Financial support:* In 2016–17, 1 teaching assistantship with partial tuition reimbursement (averaging $10,800 per year) was awarded; career-related internships or fieldwork, Federal Work-Study, institutionally sponsored loans, and tuition waivers (full and partial) also available. Support available to part-time students. Financial award application deadline: 3/1; financial award applicants required to submit FAFSA. *Faculty research:* Painting, electronic media, Western and non-Western art history, photography. *Unit head:* Barry Anderson, Department Chair, 816-235-2988, Fax: 816-235-5507, E-mail: andersonbs@umkc.edu. *Application contact:* Tamara Byland, Director of Admissions, 816-235-1111, Fax: 816-235-5544, E-mail: admit@umkc.edu. Website: http://cas.umkc.edu/art

**University of Montana,** Graduate School, College of Visual and Performing Arts, School of Art, Missoula, MT 59812-0002. Offers fine arts (MA), including art, art history; photography (MFA). *Accreditation:* NASAD (one or more programs are accredited). *Degree requirements:* For master's, thesis exhibit. *Entrance requirements:* For master's, GRE General Test, portfolio.

**University of Nebraska at Omaha,** Graduate Studies, College of Communication, Fine Arts and Media, School of the Arts, Omaha, NE 68182. Offers MA. *Accreditation:* NASAD. *Program availability:* Part-time. *Faculty:* 12 full-time (5 women). *Students:* 4 full-time (2 women), 2 part-time (1 woman); includes 1 minority (Hispanic/Latino). Average age 27. 7 applicants, 43% accepted, 3 enrolled. *Degree requirements:* For master's, comprehensive exam, thesis (for some programs). *Entrance requirements:* For master's, minimum GPA of 3.0, statement of purpose, writing sample, 2 letters of recommendation, transcripts. Additional exam requirements/recommendations for international students: Required—TOEFL, IELTS, PTE. *Application deadline:* For fall admission, 2/22 for domestic students; for spring admission, 10/1 for domestic students. Applications are processed on a rolling basis. Application fee: $45. Electronic applications accepted. *Financial support:* In 2016–17, 3 students received support, including 1 research assistantship with tuition reimbursement available, 2 teaching assistantships with tuition reimbursements available; fellowships, Federal Work-Study, scholarships/grants, health care benefits, tuition waivers (full), and unspecified assistantships also available. Support available to part-time students. Financial award application deadline: 3/1; financial award applicants required to submit FAFSA. *Unit head:* Dr. Jack Zerbe, Director, 402-554-2341, E-mail: graduate@unomaha.edu. *Application contact:* Dr. Cynthia Phaneuf, Graduate Program Chair, 402-554-2341, E-mail: graduate@unomaha.edu.

**University of Nebraska–Lincoln,** Graduate College, College of Fine and Performing Arts, Department of Art and Art History, Lincoln, NE 68588. Offers art history (MA); studio art (MFA). *Accreditation:* NASAD. *Degree requirements:* For master's, thesis. *Entrance requirements:* For master's, slide portfolio. Additional exam requirements/recommendations for international students: Required—TOEFL (minimum score 550 paper-based). Electronic applications accepted. *Faculty research:* Classical archaeology, contemporary art, printmaking, photography.

**University of Nevada, Las Vegas,** Graduate College, College of Fine Arts, Department of Art, Las Vegas, NV 89154-5013. Offers MFA. *Accreditation:* NASAD. *Program availability:* Part-time. *Faculty:* 7 full-time (1 woman), 1 (woman) part-time/adjunct. *Students:* 10 full-time (4 women); includes 2 minority (both Hispanic/Latino). Average age 34. 20 applicants, 30% accepted, 5 enrolled. In 2016, 4 master's awarded. *Degree requirements:* For master's, comprehensive exam, thesis. *Entrance requirements:* For master's, bachelor's degree, 20 slides of work. Additional exam requirements/recommendations for international students: Required—TOEFL (minimum score 550 paper-based; 80 iBT), IELTS (minimum score 7). *Application deadline:* For fall admission, 3/1 for domestic students. Application fee: $60 ($95 for international students). Electronic applications accepted. *Expenses:* $269.25 per credit, $792 per 3-credit course; $9,634 per year resident; $23,274 per year non-resident; $7,094 fees non-resident (7 credits or more); $1,307 annual health insurance fee. *Financial support:* In 2016–17, 10 teaching assistantships with partial tuition reimbursements (averaging $15,000 per year) were awarded; institutionally sponsored loans, scholarships/grants, health care benefits, and unspecified assistantships also available. Financial award application deadline: 3/15. *Faculty research:* Studio arts: printmaking, sculpture, mixed media, photography, film and digital; graphic design; art history, theory and criticism. *Unit head:* Dr. Louisa McDonald, Chair/Professor, 702-895-2717, Fax: 702-895-4346, E-mail: louisa.mcdonald@unlv.edu. *Application contact:* Dr. Pasha Rafat, Graduate Coordinator, 702-895-3110, Fax: 702-895-4346, E-mail: pasha.rafat@unlv.edu. Website: http://art.unlv.edu/

**University of Nevada, Reno,** Graduate School, College of Liberal Arts, Department of Fine Arts, Reno, NV 89557. Offers MFA. *Degree requirements:* For master's, thesis optional. *Entrance requirements:* For master's, minimum GPA of 2.75. Additional exam requirements/recommendations for international students: Required—TOEFL (minimum score 500 paper-based; 61 iBT), IELTS (minimum score 6). Electronic applications accepted. *Faculty research:* Ceramics; digital-media; drawing; painting; performance; photography; printmaking; sculpture; video; studio program supported by a strong emphasis in the areas of contemporary art, theory and criticism.

**University of New Hampshire,** Graduate School, College of Liberal Arts, Program in Painting, Durham, NH 03824. Offers MFA. Program offered in fall only. *Program availability:* Part-time. *Degree requirements:* For master's, thesis or alternative. *Entrance requirements:* For master's, slide portfolio. Additional exam requirements/recommendations for international students: Required—TOEFL (minimum score 550 paper-based; 80 iBT). Electronic applications accepted.

**University of New Mexico,** Graduate Studies, College of Fine Arts, Program in Studio Art, Albuquerque, NM 87131. Offers MFA. *Faculty:* 24 full-time (18 women), 2 part-time/adjunct (1 woman). *Students:* 36 full-time (22 women), 7 part-time (5 women); includes 5 minority (1 American Indian or Alaska Native, non-Hispanic/Latino; 3 Hispanic/Latino; 1 Two or more races, non-Hispanic/Latino), 4 international. Average age 32. 90 applicants, 29% accepted, 12 enrolled. In 2016, 14 master's awarded. *Degree requirements:* For master's, comprehensive exam, thesis or alternative, studio reviews,

qualifying exams. *Entrance requirements:* Additional exam requirements/recommendations for international students: Required—TOEFL (minimum score 550 paper-based), IELTS (minimum score 6). *Application deadline:* For fall admission, 1/15 for domestic and international students. Application fee: $50. Electronic applications accepted. *Financial support:* Fellowships, research assistantships with tuition reimbursements, teaching assistantships with partial tuition reimbursements, Federal Work-Study, institutionally sponsored loans, scholarships/grants, health care benefits, and unspecified assistantships available. Support available to part-time students. Financial award application deadline: 3/1; financial award applicants required to submit FAFSA. *Faculty research:* Photography, painting, drawing, print making, sculpture, ceramics, electronic arts, art and ecology. *Unit head:* Prof. Mary Tsiongas, Chair, 505-277-5861, Fax: 505-277-5955, E-mail: tsiongas@unm.edu. *Application contact:* Kat Heatherington, Graduate Advisor, 505-277-6672, Fax: 505-277-5955, E-mail: art255@unm.edu.
Website: http://art.unm.edu/graduate-programs/

**University of New Orleans,** Graduate School, College of Liberal Arts, Department of Fine Arts, New Orleans, LA 70148. Offers MFA. *Accreditation:* NASAD. *Degree requirements:* For master's, thesis. *Entrance requirements:* For master's, GRE General Test, slide review. Additional exam requirements/recommendations for international students: Required—TOEFL (minimum score 550 paper-based; 79 iBT), IELTS (minimum score 6.5). Electronic applications accepted. *Faculty research:* Large-scale painting and sculpture, black-and-white and color photography, computer graphics.

**The University of North Carolina at Chapel Hill,** Graduate School, College of Arts and Sciences, Department of Art, Studio Art Program, Chapel Hill, NC 27599. Offers MFA. *Degree requirements:* For master's, variable foreign language requirement. *Entrance requirements:* For master's, minimum GPA of 3.0, portfolio. Electronic applications accepted. *Faculty research:* Environmental installation, painting, photography, mixed media, printmaking.

**The University of North Carolina at Greensboro,** Graduate School, College of Arts and Sciences, Department of Art, Greensboro, NC 27412-5001. Offers studio arts (MFA). *Degree requirements:* For master's, thesis (for some programs). *Entrance requirements:* For master's, GRE General Test, 39 hours of course work in studio art, 15 hours of course work in art history, portfolio. Additional exam requirements/recommendations for international students: Required—TOEFL. Electronic applications accepted.

**University of North Dakota,** Graduate School, College of Arts and Sciences, Department of Visual Arts, Grand Forks, ND 58202. Offers MFA. *Accreditation:* NASAD. *Degree requirements:* For master's, thesis and alternative, comprehensive evaluation, professional exhibition. *Entrance requirements:* For master's, minimum GPA of 3.0. Additional exam requirements/recommendations for international students: Required—TOEFL (minimum score 550 paper-based; 79 iBT), IELTS (minimum score 6.5). *Application deadline:* For fall admission, 8/1 priority date for domestic students, 5/1 priority date for international students; for spring admission, 12/1 priority date for domestic students, 9/1 priority date for international students. Applications are processed on a rolling basis. Application fee: $35. Electronic applications accepted. *Financial support:* Fellowships with full and partial tuition reimbursements, research assistantships, teaching assistantships with full tuition reimbursements, Federal Work-Study, institutionally sponsored loans, scholarships/grants, health care benefits, tuition waivers (full and partial), and unspecified assistantships available. Support available to part-time students. Financial award application deadline: 3/15; financial award applicants required to submit FAFSA. *Faculty research:* Ceramics, drawing, metalsmithing, printmaking, painting. *Unit head:* Dr. Anita Monsebroten, Graduate Director, 701-777-2257, Fax: 701-777-2903, E-mail: anita_monsebroten@und.nodak.edu. *Application contact:* Matt Anderson, Admissions Specialist, 701-777-2947, Fax: 701-777-3619, E-mail: matthew.anderson@gradschool.und.edu.
Website: http://arts-sciences.und.edu/art-design/index.cfm

**University of Northern Iowa,** Graduate College, College of Humanities, Arts and Sciences, Department of Art, Cedar Falls, IA 50614. Offers art education (MA). *Program availability:* Part-time, evening/weekend. *Degree requirements:* For master's, comprehensive exam (for some programs), thesis or alternative. *Entrance requirements:* For master's, minimum GPA of 3.0, portfolio. Additional exam requirements/recommendations for international students: Required—TOEFL (minimum score 500 paper-based; 61 iBT). Electronic applications accepted.

**University of North Texas,** Robert B. Toulouse School of Graduate Studies, Denton, TX 76203-5459. Offers accounting (MS); applied anthropology (MA, MS); applied behavior analysis (Certificate); applied geography (MA); applied technology and performance improvement (M Ed, MS); art education (MA); art history (MA); art museum education (Certificate); arts leadership (Certificate); audiology (Au D); behavior analysis (MS); behavioral science (PhD); biochemistry and molecular biology (MS); biology (MA, MS); biomedical engineering (MS); business analysis (MS); chemistry (MS); clinical health psychology (PhD); communication studies (MA, MS); computer engineering (MS); computer science (MS); counseling (M Ed, MS), including clinical mental health counseling (MS), college and university counseling, elementary school counseling, secondary school counseling; creative writing (MA); criminal justice (MS); curriculum and instruction (M Ed); decision sciences (MBA); design (MA, MFA), including fashion design (MFA), innovation studies, interior design (MFA); early childhood studies (MS); economics (MS); educational leadership (M Ed, Ed D); educational psychology (MS, PhD), including family studies (MS), gifted and talented (MS), human development (MS), learning and cognition (MS), research, measurement and evaluation (MS); electrical engineering (MS); emergency management (MPA); engineering technology (MS); English (MA); English as a second language (MA); environmental science (MS); finance (MBA, MS); financial management (MPA); French (MA); health services management (MBA); higher education (M Ed, Ed D); history (MA, MS); hospitality management (MS); human resources management (MPA); information science (MS); information systems (PhD); information technologies (MBA); interdisciplinary studies (MA, MS); international studies (MA); international sustainable tourism (MS); jazz studies (MM); journalism (MA, MJ, Graduate Certificate), including interactive and virtual digital communication (Graduate Certificate), narrative journalism (Graduate Certificate), public relations (Graduate Certificate); kinesiology (MS); linguistics (MA); local government management (MPA); logistics (PhD); logistics and supply chain management (MBA); long-term care, senior housing, and aging services (MA); management (PhD); marketing (MBA); mathematics (MA, MS); mechanical and energy engineering (MS, PhD); music (MA), including ethnomusicology, music theory, musicology, performance; music composition (PhD); music education (MM Ed, PhD); nonprofit management (MPA); operations and supply chain management (MBA); performance (MM, DMA); philosophy (MA); political science (MA); professional and technical communication (MA); radio, television and film (MA, MFA); rehabilitation counseling (Certificate); sociology (MA); Spanish (MA); special education (M Ed); speech-language pathology (MA); strategic management (MBA); studio art (MFA); teaching (M Ed); MBA/MS. *Program availability:* Part-time, evening/weekend, online learning. Terminal master's awarded for partial completion of doctoral program. *Degree requirements:* For master's, variable foreign language requirement, comprehensive exam (for some programs), thesis (for some

programs); for doctorate, variable foreign language requirement, comprehensive exam (for some programs), thesis/dissertation; for other advanced degree, variable foreign language requirement, comprehensive exam (for some programs). *Entrance requirements:* For master's and doctorate, GRE, GMAT. Additional exam requirements/recommendations for international students: Required—TOEFL (minimum score 550 paper-based; 79 iBT). Electronic applications accepted.

**University of Notre Dame,** Graduate School, College of Arts and Letters, Division of Humanities, Department of Art, Art History, and Design, Notre Dame, IN 46556. Offers art history (MA); design (MFA), including graphic design, industrial design; studio art (MFA), including ceramics, painting, photography, printmaking, sculpture. *Accreditation:* NASAD. *Degree requirements:* For master's, comprehensive exam (for some programs), thesis. *Entrance requirements:* For master's, GRE General Test, minimum GPA of 3.0. Additional exam requirements/recommendations for international students: Required—TOEFL (minimum score 600 paper-based; 80 iBT). Electronic applications accepted. *Faculty research:* Studio art practice in ceramics, printing, photography, printmaking and sculpture, graphic design and industrial design, digital imaging in design and photography, Renaissance and American art history, contemporary art theory and criticism.

**University of Oklahoma,** Weitzenhoffer Family College of Fine Arts, School of Visual Arts, Program in Art, Norman, OK 73019. Offers art, technology and culture (MFA); ceramics (MFA); painting (MFA); printmaking (MFA); sculpture (MFA); visual communication (MFA). Applicants admitted in fall only. *Students:* 26 full-time (16 women); includes 8 minority (2 Asian, non-Hispanic/Latino; 2 Hispanic/Latino; 4 Two or more races, non-Hispanic/Latino), 2 international. Average age 30. 20 applicants, 35% accepted, 7 enrolled. In 2016, 7 master's awarded. Terminal master's awarded for partial completion of doctoral program. *Entrance requirements:* Additional exam requirements/recommendations for international students: Required—TOEFL (minimum score 79 iBT) or IELTS (minimum score 6.5). *Application deadline:* For fall admission, 2/1 for domestic and international students. Electronic applications accepted. Application fee: $50 ($100 for international students). Electronic applications accepted. *Expenses:* Tuition, state resident: full-time $4886; part-time $203.60 per credit hour. Tuition, nonresident: full-time $18,989; part-time $791.20 per credit hour. *Required fees:* $3283; $126.25 per credit hour. $126.50 per semester. *Financial support:* In 2016–17, 13 students received support. Fellowships with full and partial tuition reimbursements available, research assistantships with full tuition reimbursements available, teaching assistantships with full tuition reimbursements available, Federal Work-Study, institutionally sponsored loans, scholarships/grants, health care benefits, tuition waivers (partial), and unspecified assistantships available. Financial award application deadline: 6/1; financial award applicants required to submit FAFSA. *Faculty research:* 3D printing and sculpture, photography, painting, and installation art. *Unit head:* Dr. Bette Talvacchia, Director, 405-325-6210, Fax: 405-325-1668, E-mail: bette.talvacchia-1@ou.edu. *Application contact:* Jason Cytacki, Graduate Coordinator, E-mail: jason.cytacki@ou.edu.
Website: http://art.ou.edu

**University of Oregon,** Graduate School, School of Architecture and Allied Arts, Department of Art, Eugene, OR 97403. Offers MFA. *Accreditation:* NASAD. *Degree requirements:* For master's, thesis or alternative. *Entrance requirements:* For master's, BFA or equivalent. Additional exam requirements/recommendations for international students: Required—TOEFL.

**University of Pennsylvania,** School of Design, Department of Fine Arts, Philadelphia, PA 19104. Offers emerging design and research (Certificate); fine arts (MFA); time-based and interactive media (Certificate). *Faculty:* 7 full-time (3 women), 1 part-time/adjunct (0 women). *Students:* 34 full-time (23 women), 1 part-time (0 women); includes 10 minority (1 Black or African American, non-Hispanic/Latino; 2 Asian, non-Hispanic/Latino; 5 Hispanic/Latino; 2 Two or more races, non-Hispanic/Latino), 4 international. Average age 28. 131 applicants, 39% accepted, 18 enrolled. In 2016, 20 master's awarded. *Degree requirements:* For master's, thesis. *Application deadline:* Applications are processed on a rolling basis. Electronic applications accepted. *Expenses:* Tuition: Full-time $31,068; part-time $5762 per course. *Required fees:* $3200; $336 per course. Full-time tuition and fees vary according to degree level, program and student level. Part-time tuition and fees vary according to course load, degree level and program. *Financial support:* In 2016–17, 30 students received support, including teaching assistantships (averaging $6,000 per year); fellowships with full tuition reimbursements available, research assistantships, Federal Work-Study, scholarships/grants, health care benefits, and unspecified assistantships also available. Financial award applicants required to submit FAFSA. *Faculty research:* Performance art, photography and video, drawing and painting, sculpture, animation and creative research. *Unit head:* Joshua Mosley, Professor/Chair/Director of Graduate Program, 215-898-8374, E-mail: jmosley@design.upenn.edu. *Application contact:* Leighann Bogner, Administrative Assistant, 215-898-8374, Fax: 215-573-2459, E-mail: mfa@pobox.upenn.edu.
Website: http://www.design.upenn.edu/mfa

**University of Regina,** Faculty of Graduate Studies and Research, Faculty of Media, Art, and Performance, Department of Visual Arts, Regina, SK S4S 0A2, Canada. Offers ceramics (MFA); drawing (MFA); interdisciplinary studies (MA, MFA); intermedia (MFA); painting (MFA); sculpture (MFA). *Faculty:* 9 full-time (5 women), 3 part-time/adjunct (1 woman). *Students:* 7 full-time (5 women). 6 applicants, 50% accepted. In 2016, 3 master's awarded. *Degree requirements:* For master's, exhibition, support paper, oral defense. *Entrance requirements:* For master's, documentation of recent work. Additional exam requirements/recommendations for international students: Required—TOEFL (minimum score 580 paper-based; 80 iBT), IELTS (minimum score 6.5), PTE (minimum score 59). *Application deadline:* For fall admission, 1/15 for domestic and international students. Application fee: $100. Electronic applications accepted. *Financial support:* In 2016–17, 5 fellowships (averaging $6,000 per year), 3 teaching assistantships (averaging $2,501 per year) were awarded; scholarships/grants also available. Financial award application deadline: 6/15. *Faculty research:* Contemporary visual art theory and practice; art history; curatorial practice; print media; drawing/painting, sculpture, and ceramics. *Unit head:* Leesa Streifler, Department Head, 306-585-5574, Fax: 306-585-5526, E-mail: leesa.steifler@uregina.ca. *Application contact:* Dr. Robert Truszkowski, Graduate Coordinator, Visual Arts, 306-585-5574, Fax: 306-585-5526, E-mail: robert.truszkowski@uregina.ca.

**University of Rochester,** School of Arts and Sciences, Department of Art and Art History, Rochester, NY 14627. Offers visual and cultural studies (PhD). *Faculty:* 11 full-time (6 women). *Students:* 31 full-time (21 women); includes 7 minority (1 Black or African American, non-Hispanic/Latino; 2 Asian, non-Hispanic/Latino; 3 Hispanic/Latino; 1 Two or more races, non-Hispanic/Latino), 10 international. Average age 30. 57 applicants, 14% accepted, 5 enrolled. In 2016, 4 doctorates awarded. Terminal master's awarded for partial completion of doctoral program. *Degree requirements:* For doctorate, one foreign language, thesis/dissertation, qualifying exam. *Entrance requirements:* For doctorate, GRE General Test, personal statement, three letters of recommendation, official undergraduate and graduate transcripts, writing sample. Additional exam requirements/recommendations for international students: Required—TOEFL (minimum score 600 paper-based; 100 iBT). *Application deadline:* For fall admission, 1/15 for domestic and international students. Application fee: $60. Electronic applications accepted. *Expenses:* $1,538 per credit hour. *Financial support:* Fellowships and tuition

*Art/Fine Arts*

waivers (full and partial) available. *Faculty research:* Visual culture from a social-historical perspective. *Unit head:* Rachel Haidu, Director of Graduate Program in Visual and Cultural Studies, 585-275-4112, E-mail: rachel.haidu@rochester.edu. *Application contact:* Martin Collier, Administrator, 585-275-7451. Website: http://www.rochester.edu/College/aah/

**University of Saint Francis,** Graduate School, Department of Visual Art and Communication, Fort Wayne, IN 46808-3994. Offers studio art (MA). *Accreditation:* NASAD. *Program availability:* Part-time, evening/weekend, blended/hybrid learning. *Faculty:* 4 full-time (1 woman). *Students:* 4 part-time (all women); includes 1 minority (Asian, non-Hispanic/Latino). Average age 35. In 2016, 2 master's awarded. *Degree requirements:* For master's, thesis, exhibit. *Entrance requirements:* For master's, undergraduate degree in art; minimum undergraduate GPA of 3.0; portfolio; essay; resume; three professional recommendations. Additional exam requirements/recommendations for international students: Required—TOEFL (minimum score 550 paper-based) or IELTS (minimum score 6.5). *Application deadline:* Applications are processed on a rolling basis. Application fee: $0. Electronic applications accepted. *Expenses:* Tuition: Full-time $16,290; part-time $905 per credit hour. *Required fees:* $25 per credit hour. $140 per semester. Tuition and fees vary according to campus/location and program. *Financial support:* In 2016–17, 2 students received support. Federal Work-Study, scholarships/grants, and unspecified assistantships available. Support available to part-time students. Financial award application deadline: 3/10; financial award applicants required to submit FAFSA. *Unit head:* Cara Wade, School of Creative Arts Graduate Studies Program Director, 260-399-7700 Ext. 8016, Fax: 260-399-8171, E-mail: cwade@sf.edu. *Application contact:* Kyle Richardson, Enrollment Services Specialist, 260-399-7700 Ext. 6310, Fax: 260-399-8152, E-mail: krichardson@sf.edu. Website: http://www.sf.edu/graduate/

**University of Saskatchewan,** College of Graduate Studies and Research, College of Arts and Science, Department of Art and Art History, Saskatoon, SK S7N 5A2, Canada. Offers MFA. *Program availability:* Part-time. *Degree requirements:* For master's, thesis. *Entrance requirements:* Additional exam requirements/recommendations for international students: Required—TOEFL (minimum score 80 iBT); Recommended—IELTS (minimum score 6.5).

**The University of Scranton,** College of Arts and Sciences, Scranton, PA 18510. Offers MA, MS. *Program availability:* Part-time, evening/weekend, 100% online. *Degree requirements:* For master's, comprehensive exam (for some programs), thesis (for some programs), capstone experience. *Entrance requirements:* For master's, GMAT (for MBA), minimum GPA of 3.0, three letters of reference. Additional exam requirements/recommendations for international students: Required—TOEFL (minimum score 500 paper-based; 80 iBT), IELTS (minimum score 6.5). Electronic applications accepted.

**University of South Alabama,** College of Arts and Sciences, Department of Visual Arts, Mobile, AL 36688. Offers creative technologies and practice (MFA). *Faculty:* 7 full-time (3 women). *Students:* 4 full-time (1 woman); includes 1 minority (Hispanic/Latino). Average age 30. 8 applicants, 75% accepted, 4 enrolled. *Degree requirements:* For master's, thesis, 4 semesters of residency. *Entrance requirements:* For master's, minimum undergraduate GPA of 3.0, letter of intent, resume, three letters of recommendation, portfolio. Additional exam requirements/recommendations for international students: Required—TOEFL (minimum score 525 paper-based; 71 iBT), IELTS (minimum score 6). *Application deadline:* For fall admission, 2/15 priority date for domestic students. Applications are processed on a rolling basis. Application fee: $35. Electronic applications accepted. *Expenses:* Tuition, state resident: full-time $9768; part-time $407 per credit hour. Tuition, nonresident: full-time $19,536; part-time $814 per credit hour. *Financial support:* Fellowships, teaching assistantships, career-related internships or fieldwork, and unspecified assistantships available. Financial award application deadline: 2/15; financial award applicants required to submit FAFSA. *Faculty research:* Glass vessel and color formation, eighteenth-century art, material culture, and identity through sculptural applications. *Unit head:* Diane Gibbs, Interim Chairperson, 251-461-1696, E-mail: dgibbs@southalabama.edu. *Application contact:* Dr. Eric Loomis, Associate Dean, College of Arts and Sciences, 251-460-7811, Fax: 251-461-1744, E-mail: ejloomis@southalabama.edu. Website: http://www.southalabama.edu/colleges/artsandsci/art/

**University of South Carolina,** The Graduate School, College of Arts and Sciences, Department of Art, Columbia, SC 29208. Offers art education (IMA, MA, MAT); art history (MA); art studio (MA); media arts (MMA); studio art (MFA). *Accreditation:* NASAD. *Degree requirements:* For master's, comprehensive exam (for some programs), thesis (for some programs). *Entrance requirements:* For master's, GRE General Test or MAT, portfolio. Additional exam requirements/recommendations for international students: Required—TOEFL. Electronic applications accepted. *Faculty research:* Script writing, teaching art at the elementary and secondary levels of education, history of art and architecture.

**The University of South Dakota,** Graduate School, College of Fine Arts, Department of Art, Vermillion, SD 57069. Offers art education (MFA); ceramics (MFA); graphic design (MFA); painting (MFA); photography (MFA); printmaking (MFA); sculpture (MFA). *Accreditation:* NASAD. *Degree requirements:* For master's, thesis or alternative. *Entrance requirements:* For master's, portfolio, minimum GPA of 2.7. Additional exam requirements/recommendations for international students: Required—TOEFL (minimum score 550 paper-based; 79 iBT). Electronic applications accepted.

**University of Southern California,** Graduate School, Dana and David Dornsife College of Letters, Arts and Sciences, Department of Art History, Los Angeles, CA 90089. Offers art history (MA, PhD); visual studies (Graduate Certificate). *Degree requirements:* For doctorate, 2 foreign languages, comprehensive exam, thesis/dissertation, 60 units. *Entrance requirements:* For doctorate, GRE. Additional exam requirements/recommendations for international students: Required—TOEFL. *Faculty research:* Ancient, medieval, Renaissance, eighteenth-nineteenth century, contemporary.

**University of Southern California,** Graduate School, Roski School of Fine Arts, Graduate Programs in Fine Arts, Los Angeles, CA 90089. Offers new genres (MFA); painting/drawing (MFA); photography (MFA); sculpture (MFA). *Degree requirements:* For master's, thesis. *Entrance requirements:* For master's, portfolio, artist statement, 3 letters of recommendation. Additional exam requirements/recommendations for international students: Required—TOEFL (minimum score 600 paper-based; 100 iBT). Electronic applications accepted. *Faculty research:* Fine art production in the areas of photography, video, sculpture, drawing, and performance.

**University of South Florida,** College of The Arts, School of Art and Art History, Tampa, FL 33620-9951. Offers art (MFA); art history (MA). *Accreditation:* NASAD. *Program availability:* Part-time. *Faculty:* 20 full-time (10 women). *Students:* 35 full-time (17 women), 2 part-time (both women); includes 10 minority (7 Hispanic/Latino; 3 Two or more races, non-Hispanic/Latino), 3 international. Average age 29. 60 applicants, 27% accepted, 16 enrolled. In 2016, 16 master's awarded. *Degree requirements:* For master's, comprehensive exam, thesis, exhibition (for MFA). *Entrance requirements:* For master's, GRE General Test, bachelor's degree from regionally-accredited institution with minimum GPA of 3.0 in upper-division coursework or graduate degree from regionally-accredited institution; portfolio; goals statement (for MA in art history). Additional exam requirements/recommendations for international students: Required—

TOEFL (minimum score 550 paper-based; 79 iBT) or IELTS (minimum score 6.5). *Application deadline:* For fall admission, 1/15 for domestic students, 2/1 for international students; for spring admission, 10/15 for domestic students, 9/15 for international students; for summer admission, 2/15 for domestic students, 1/15 for international students. Application fee: $30. Electronic applications accepted. *Expenses:* Tuition, state resident: full-time $7766; part-time $431.43 per credit hour. Tuition, nonresident: full-time $15,789; part-time $877.17 per credit hour. *Required fees:* $37 per term. *Financial support:* In 2016–17, 33 students received support, including 37 teaching assistantships with partial tuition reimbursements available (averaging $9,440 per year); scholarships/grants, health care benefits, and unspecified assistantships also available. Support available to part-time students. Financial award application deadline: 2/15; financial award applicants required to submit FAFSA. *Faculty research:* Contemporary art and role of the artist, identity strategies, political iconography, art practice and technology, the construction of race in art. *Total annual research expenditures:* $113,801. *Unit head:* Prof. Wallace Wilson, Director, 813-974-2360, Fax: 813-974-9226, E-mail: wwilson2@usf.edu. *Application contact:* Prof. Neil Bender, Associate Professor and Graduate Program Director, 813-974-2360, Fax: 813-974-9226, E-mail: nb2@usf.edu. Website: http://www.art.usf.edu

**The University of Tennessee,** Graduate School, College of Arts and Sciences, School of Art, Knoxville, TN 37996. Offers ceramics (MFA); drawing (MFA); graphic design (MFA); inter-area studies (MFA); media arts (MFA); painting (MFA); printmaking (MFA); sculpture (MFA); watercolor (MFA). *Accreditation:* NASAD. *Degree requirements:* For master's, thesis or alternative, exhibit. *Entrance requirements:* For master's, portfolio, minimum GPA of 2.7. Additional exam requirements/recommendations for international students: Required—TOEFL. Electronic applications accepted.

**The University of Texas at Arlington,** Graduate School, College of Liberal Arts, Department of Art and Art History, Arlington, TX 76019. Offers film and video (MFA); glass (MFA); intermedia (MFA); visual communication (MFA). *Accreditation:* NASAD. *Degree requirements:* For master's, thesis or alternative, mid- and final program reviews; exhibition. *Entrance requirements:* For master's, GRE, minimum GPA of 3.0, 3 letters of recommendation, portfolio, resume. Additional exam requirements/recommendations for international students: Required—TOEFL (minimum score 550 paper-based). *Application deadline:* For fall admission, 1/15 priority date for domestic and international students; for spring admission, 10/15 priority date for domestic and international students. Applications are processed on a rolling basis. Electronic applications accepted. *Financial support:* Fellowships with full tuition reimbursements, research assistantships, teaching assistantships, scholarships/grants, and unspecified assistantships available. Financial award applicants required to submit FAFSA. *Unit head:* Prof. Robert Hower, Chair/Professor, 817-272-2891, Fax: 817-272-2805, E-mail: hower@uta.edu. *Application contact:* Prof. Nancy Palmeri, Graduate Advisor/Associate Professor, 817-272-2891, Fax: 817-272-2805, E-mail: palmeri@uta.edu. Website: http://www.uta.edu/art

**The University of Texas at Austin,** Graduate School, College of Fine Arts, Department of Art and Art History, Program in Studio Art, Austin, TX 78712-1111. Offers MFA. *Accreditation:* NASAD. *Degree requirements:* For master's, thesis, oral exam. *Entrance requirements:* For master's, minimum GPA of 3.0, portfolio of 15 slides. Electronic applications accepted. *Faculty research:* Painting, sculpture, transmedia, photography, printmaking.

**The University of Texas at El Paso,** Graduate School, College of Liberal Arts, Department of Art, El Paso, TX 79968-0001. Offers art education (MA); studio art (MA). *Program availability:* Part-time, evening/weekend. *Degree requirements:* For master's, thesis optional. *Entrance requirements:* For master's, minimum GPA of 3.0, digital portfolio, letters of recommendation. Additional exam requirements/recommendations for international students: Required—TOEFL; Recommended—IELTS. Electronic applications accepted.

**The University of Texas at San Antonio,** College of Liberal and Fine Arts, Department of Art and Art History, San Antonio, TX 78249-0617. Offers art (MFA); art history (MA). *Accreditation:* NASAD (one or more programs are accredited). *Faculty:* 11 full-time (5 women), 2 part-time/adjunct (0 women). *Students:* 18 full-time (13 women), 4 part-time (2 women); includes 10 minority (9 Hispanic/Latino; 1 Two or more races, non-Hispanic/Latino), 1 international. Average age 30. 19 applicants, 37% accepted, 4 enrolled. In 2016, 10 master's awarded. *Entrance requirements:* For master's, GRE General Test, portfolio, minimum GPA of 3.0 in last 60 hours, 3 letters of recommendation, statement of purpose. Additional exam requirements/recommendations for international students: Required—TOEFL (minimum score 550 paper-based; 79 iBT), IELTS (minimum score 6.5). *Application deadline:* For fall admission, 7/1 for domestic students, 4/1 for international students; for spring admission, 11/1 for domestic students, 9/1 for international students. Application fee: $45 ($80 for international students). *Unit head:* Dr. Gregory Elliott, Department Chair, 210-458-4352, Fax: 210-458-4356, E-mail: greg.elliott@utsa.edu. *Application contact:* Monica Rodriguez, Director of Graduate Admissions, 210-458-4331, Fax: 210-458-4332, E-mail: graduatestudies@utsa.edu. Website: http://art.utsa.edu/

**The University of Texas at Tyler,** College of Arts and Sciences, Department of Art and Art History, Tyler, TX 75799-0001. Offers art history (MA); interdisciplinary (MAIS); studio art (MFA). *Degree requirements:* For master's, thesis, graduate committee review. *Entrance requirements:* For master's, minimum GPA of 3.0. Additional exam requirements/recommendations for international students: Required—TOEFL. *Faculty research:* Classical myths in contemporary art, social issues in contemporary art, casting methods, Renaissance art.

**The University of Texas Rio Grande Valley,** College of Fine Arts, School of Art, Edinburg, TX 78539. Offers MFA. *Program availability:* Part-time, evening/weekend, online learning. Terminal master's awarded for partial completion of doctoral program. *Degree requirements:* For master's, thesis, thesis show of artwork. *Entrance requirements:* For master's, bachelor's degree in fine arts, portfolio, minimum GPA of 2.5. Tuition and fees vary according to course load and program. *Faculty research:* Painting, photography, graphic design, sculpture, bronze casting, performance.

**The University of the Arts,** College of Art, Media and Design, Department of Book Arts/Printmaking, Philadelphia, PA 19102-4944. Offers MFA. *Accreditation:* NASAD. *Degree requirements:* For master's, thesis. *Entrance requirements:* For master's, portfolio of 20-30 digital images showing work that represents applicant's full range of studio experience, preferably including printmaking and book arts; official transcripts from each undergraduate or graduate school attended; three letters of recommendation; one- to two-page statement of professional plans and goals; personal interview. Additional exam requirements/recommendations for international students: Required—TOEFL (minimum score 580 paper-based, 92 iBT) or IELTS (minimum score 6.5).

**The University of the Arts,** College of Art, Media and Design, Program in Studio Art, Philadelphia, PA 19102-4944. Offers MFA. *Degree requirements:* For master's, thesis, summer residency. *Entrance requirements:* For master's, official transcripts from each undergraduate or graduate school attended, three letters of recommendation, one- to two-page statement of professional plans and goals, personal interview, portfolio.

Additional exam requirements/recommendations for international students: Required—TOEFL (minimum score 580 paper-based, 92 iBT) or IELTS (minimum score 6.5).

**The University of Tulsa,** Graduate School, Kendall College of Arts and Sciences, School of Art, Tulsa, OK 74104-3189. Offers MA, MFA, MTA. *Program availability:* Part-time. *Faculty:* 9 full-time (5 women), 2 part-time/adjunct (0 women). *Students:* 6 full-time (4 women), 1 part-time (0 women); includes 1 minority (Asian, non-Hispanic/Latino). Average age 38. 9 applicants, 33% accepted, 3 enrolled. In 2016, 5 master's awarded. *Degree requirements:* For master's, comprehensive exam (for some programs), thesis (for some programs). *Entrance requirements:* For master's, portfolio. Additional exam requirements/recommendations for international students: Required—TOEFL (minimum score 577 paper-based; 91 iBT), IELTS (minimum score 6.5). *Application deadline:* For fall admission, 2/1 for domestic and international students. Application fee: $55. Electronic applications accepted. *Expenses: Tuition:* Full-time $22,230; part-time $1235 per credit hour. *Required fees:* $990 per semester. Tuition and fees vary according to course load. *Financial support:* In 2016–17, 6 students received support, including 3 fellowships with full tuition reimbursements available (averaging $2,666 per year), 5 teaching assistantships with full tuition reimbursements available (averaging $13,410 per year); career-related internships or fieldwork, Federal Work-Study, scholarships/grants, traineeships, health care benefits, tuition waivers (full and partial), and unspecified assistantships also available. Support available to part-time students. Financial award application deadline: 2/1; financial award applicants required to submit FAFSA. *Faculty research:* Drawing, painting, printmaking, ceramics, graphic design, photography. *Unit head:* Prof. Teresa Valero, Director, 918-631-3513, Fax: 918-631-3423, E-mail: maria-valero@utulsa.edu. *Application contact:* Prof. Michelle Martin, Program Advisor, 918-631-2736, Fax: 918-631-3423, E-mail: michelle-martin@utulsa.edu.
Website: http://artsandsciences.utulsa.edu/academics/departments-schools/art/

**The University of Tulsa,** Graduate School, Kendall College of Arts and Sciences, School of Urban Education, Program in Teaching Arts, Tulsa, OK 74104-3189. Offers art (MTA); biology (MTA); English (MTA); history (MTA); mathematics (MTA). *Program availability:* Part-time. *Students:* 1 (woman) full-time. Average age 26. 4 applicants, 50% accepted, 1 enrolled. In 2016, 1 master's awarded. *Entrance requirements:* For master's, GRE General Test. Additional exam requirements/recommendations for international students: Required—TOEFL (minimum score 577 paper-based), IELTS (minimum score 6.5). *Application deadline:* Applications are processed on a rolling basis. Application fee: $55. Electronic applications accepted. *Expenses: Tuition:* Full-time $22,230; part-time $1235 per credit hour. *Required fees:* $990 per semester. Tuition and fees vary according to course load. *Financial support:* In 2016–17, 1 student received support, including 1 teaching assistantship with full tuition reimbursement available (averaging $13,410 per year); fellowships with tuition reimbursements available, research assistantships with tuition reimbursements available, career-related internships or fieldwork, Federal Work-Study, scholarships/grants, health care benefits, tuition waivers (full and partial), and unspecified assistantships also available. Support available to part-time students. Financial award application deadline: 2/1; financial award applicants required to submit FAFSA. *Unit head:* Dr. Sharon Baker, Chair, 918-631-2238, Fax: 918-631-3721, E-mail: sharon-baker@utulsa.edu. *Application contact:* Dr. David Brown, Advisor, 918-631-2719, Fax: 918-631-2133, E-mail: david-brown@utulsa.edu.

**University of Utah,** Graduate School, College of Fine Arts, Department of Art and Art History, Salt Lake City, UT 84112-0380. Offers art history (MA); ceramics (MFA); community-based art education (MFA); drawing (MFA); graphic design (MFA); painting (MFA); photography/digital imaging (MFA); printmaking (MFA); sculpture/intermedia (MFA). *Faculty:* 18 full-time (10 women), 22 part-time/adjunct (11 women). *Students:* 6 full-time (2 women); includes 2 minority (both Hispanic/Latino). 48 applicants, 31% accepted, 10 enrolled. In 2016, 7 master's awarded. *Degree requirements:* For master's, variable foreign language requirement, comprehensive exam (for some programs), thesis or alternative, exhibit and final project paper (for MFA). *Entrance requirements:* For master's, CD portfolio (MFA), writing sample (MA), curriculum vitae, letters of recommendation, letter of intent. Additional exam requirements/recommendations for international students: Required—TOEFL (minimum score 575 paper-based; 75 iBT). *Application deadline:* For fall admission, 1/15 priority date for domestic and international students. Application fee: $55 ($65 for international students). Electronic applications accepted. *Expenses:* Contact institution. *Financial support:* In 2016–17, 6 students received support, including 2 fellowships, 6 research assistantships with partial tuition reimbursements available, 34 teaching assistantships with partial tuition reimbursements available; Federal Work-Study, institutionally sponsored loans, scholarships/grants, tuition waivers (partial), unspecified assistantships, and stipends also available. Financial award application deadline: 1/15; financial award applicants required to submit FAFSA. *Faculty research:* Studio art, European art history, Asian art history, Latin American art history, twentieth-century/contemporary art history. *Total annual research expenditures:* $54,906. *Unit head:* Prof. Brian Snapp, Chair, 801-581-8677, Fax: 801-585-6171, E-mail: b.snapp@utah.edu. *Application contact:* Prof. Kim Martinez, Director of Graduate Studies, 801-581-8677, Fax: 801-585-6171, E-mail: kim.martinez@art.utah.edu.
Website: http://www.art.utah.edu/

**University of Victoria,** Faculty of Graduate Studies, Faculty of Fine Arts, Department of Visual Arts, Victoria, BC V8W 2Y2, Canada. Offers digital multimedia (MFA); drawing (MFA); painting (MFA); photography (MFA); sculpture (MFA); video (MFA). *Degree requirements:* For master's, exhibit, oral exam. *Entrance requirements:* For master's, portfolio, BFA. Additional exam requirements/recommendations for international students: Required—TOEFL (minimum score 575 paper-based), IELTS (minimum score 7). Electronic applications accepted.

**University of Washington,** Graduate School, College of Arts and Sciences, School of Art, Division of Art, Seattle, WA 98195. Offers painting and drawing (MFA); photography (MFA). *Degree requirements:* For master's, thesis, exhibit. *Entrance requirements:* For master's, BFA or equivalent academic work in art, 20 slide portfolio. Additional exam requirements/recommendations for international students: Required—TOEFL. Electronic applications accepted.

**University of Waterloo,** Graduate Studies, Faculty of Arts, Department of Fine Arts, Waterloo, ON N2L 3G1, Canada. Offers studio art (MFA). *Degree requirements:* For master's, thesis exhibit. *Entrance requirements:* For master's, honors degree, minimum A- average, sample of work. Additional exam requirements/recommendations for international students: Required—TOEFL, IELTS, PTE. Electronic applications accepted. *Faculty research:* Ceramic sculpture, computer imaging, painting, drawing, contemporary art theory.

**University of Windsor,** Faculty of Graduate Studies, Faculty of Arts and Social Sciences, School of Visual Arts, Windsor, ON N9B 3P4, Canada. Offers MFA. *Degree requirements:* For master's, thesis. *Entrance requirements:* For master's, minimum B average, portfolio. Additional exam requirements/recommendations for international students: Required—TOEFL (minimum score 560 paper-based). Electronic applications accepted.

**University of Wisconsin–Madison,** Graduate School, School of Education, Department of Art, Madison, WI 53706-1380. Offers art (MA, MFA); art education (MA). *Accreditation:* NASAD. Electronic applications accepted.

**University of Wisconsin–River Falls,** Outreach and Graduate Studies, College of Arts and Science, Program in Fine Arts, River Falls, WI 54022. Offers MSE.

**University of Wisconsin–Stout,** Graduate School, College of Arts, Humanities and Social Sciences, Menomonie, WI 54751. Offers design (MFA); technical and professional communication (MS). *Accreditation:* NASAD.

**University of Wisconsin–Superior,** Graduate Division, Department of Visual Arts, Superior, WI 54880. Offers art education (MA); art history (MA); art therapy (MA); studio arts (MA). *Program availability:* Part-time. *Degree requirements:* For master's, comprehensive exam, exhibit. *Entrance requirements:* For master's, minimum GPA of 2.75, portfolio. Electronic applications accepted.

**Utah State University,** School of Graduate Studies, College of Humanities, Arts and Social Sciences, Department of Art, Logan, UT 84322. Offers MA, MFA. *Accreditation:* NASAD. *Degree requirements:* For master's, thesis, exhibit. *Entrance requirements:* For master's, GRE General Test or MAT, minimum GPA of 3.0, slide portfolio of art. Additional exam requirements/recommendations for international students: Required—TOEFL. *Faculty research:* Painting, drawing, sculpture, ceramics, photography.

**Vermont College of Fine Arts,** MFA in Visual Art Program, Montpelier, VT 05602. Offers MFA. *Faculty:* 12 part-time/adjunct (6 women). *Students:* 41 full-time (30 women); includes 6 minority (1 Black or African American, non-Hispanic/Latino; 3 Hispanic/Latino; 1 Native Hawaiian or other Pacific Islander, non-Hispanic/Latino; 1 Two or more races, non-Hispanic/Latino), 3 international. Average age 44. 45 applicants, 58% accepted, 16 enrolled. In 2016, 24 master's awarded. *Degree requirements:* For master's, thesis. *Entrance requirements:* For master's, BFA, BA, or BS from accredited college or university, or Diploma from recognized professional art school, substantial experience in making art; thirty semester hours in undergraduate study (preferred). *Application deadline:* For fall admission, 2/15 priority date for domestic students, 2/15 for international students; for spring admission, 9/15 priority date for domestic students, 9/15 for international students. Applications are processed on a rolling basis. Application fee: $75. Electronic applications accepted. *Expenses:* Contact institution. *Financial support:* Scholarships/grants available. Financial award applicants required to submit FAFSA. *Unit head:* Danielle Dahline, Program Director, 802-828-8703, E-mail: danielle.dahline@vcfa.edu. *Application contact:* Thatiana Oliveria, Assistant Director of Admissions, 802-828-8636, E-mail: thatiana.oliveria@vcfa.edu.
Website: http://www.vcfa.edu/visual-art

**Virginia Commonwealth University,** Graduate School, College of Humanities and Sciences, School of Mass Communications, Program in Media, Art, and Text, Richmond, VA 23284-9005. Offers PhD. *Entrance requirements:* For doctorate, GRE. Additional exam requirements/recommendations for international students: Required—TOEFL (minimum score 600 paper-based; 100 iBT); Recommended—IELTS (minimum score 6.5). *Application deadline:* For fall admission, 1/15 for domestic students. Application fee: $50. Electronic applications accepted. *Unit head:* Dr. Eric G. Garberson, Graduate Program Director, 804-828-7295, E-mail: eggarberson@vcu.edu. *Application contact:* Thom Didato, Graduate Programs Adviser, 804-828-1329, E-mail: tndidato@vcu.edu.

**Virginia Commonwealth University,** Graduate School, School of the Arts, Richmond, VA 23284-9005. Offers art education (MAE, PhD); art history (MA, PhD), including curatorial (PhD), historical studies, museum studies (MA); ceramics (MFA); design (MFA), including interior environments, visual communications; fibers (MFA); furniture design (MFA); glassworking (MFA); jewelry/metalworking (MFA); kinetic imaging (MFA); music (MM), including music education; painting (MFA); photography and film (MFA); printmaking (MFA); sculpture (MFA); theatre (MFA), including costume design, pedagogy/literature, pedagogy/performance, scene design/technical theatre. *Program availability:* Part-time. *Entrance requirements:* For doctorate, GRE General Test, writing sample. Additional exam requirements/recommendations for international students: Required—TOEFL (minimum score 600 paper-based; 100 iBT). *Application deadline:* For fall admission, 1/15 priority date for domestic students. Application fee: $50. Electronic applications accepted. *Financial support:* Fellowships, teaching assistantships, career-related internships or fieldwork, Federal Work-Study, institutionally sponsored loans, and tuition waivers (full and partial) available. Support available to part-time students. Financial award applicants required to submit FAFSA. *Unit head:* Joseph H. Seipel, Dean, 804-828-2787, Fax: 804-828-6469, E-mail: arts@vcu.edu. *Application contact:* Jack H. Risley, Associate Dean for Academic Affairs, 804-828-2787, Fax: 804-828-6469, E-mail: jhrisley@vcu.edu.
Website: http://www.vcu.edu/arts/

**Washington State University,** College of Arts and Sciences, Department of Fine Arts, Pullman, WA 99164. Offers MFA. Programs offered at the Pullman campus. *Degree requirements:* For master's, comprehensive exam (for some programs), thesis, exhibit, oral exam. *Entrance requirements:* For master's, statement of intent, portfolio of no more than 15 images on CD/DVD. Additional exam requirements/recommendations for international students: Required—TOEFL (minimum score 550 paper-based), IELTS. Electronic applications accepted. *Faculty research:* Polynesian art, museum representation, number theory.

**Washington University in St. Louis,** Sam Fox School of Design and Visual Arts, Graduate School of Art, St. Louis, MO 63130-4899. Offers visual art (MFA). *Accreditation:* NASAD. *Faculty:* 16 full-time (7 women), 5 part-time/adjunct (3 women). *Students:* 44 full-time (25 women); includes 6 minority (1 Black or African American, non-Hispanic/Latino; 1 American Indian or Alaska Native, non-Hispanic/Latino; 2 Asian, non-Hispanic/Latino; 1 Hispanic/Latino; 1 Two or more races, non-Hispanic/Latino), 9 international. Average age 28. 47 applicants, 91% accepted, 20 enrolled. In 2016, 22 master's awarded. *Degree requirements:* For master's, thesis, exhibition. *Entrance requirements:* For master's, portfolio, resume, transcripts, 3 letters of recommendation. Additional exam requirements/recommendations for international students: Required—TOEFL (minimum score 577 paper-based; 90 iBT), IELTS (minimum score 7.5). *Application deadline:* For fall admission, 1/15 for domestic and international students. Application fee: $40. Electronic applications accepted. *Expenses:* Contact institution. *Financial support:* In 2016–17, 44 students received support. Fellowships with partial tuition reimbursements available, Federal Work-Study, institutionally sponsored loans, scholarships/grants, and unspecified assistantships available. Financial award application deadline: 2/15; financial award applicants required to submit FAFSA. *Faculty research:* New media, design, fine arts. *Unit head:* Prof. Heather Corcoran, Director of the College and Graduate School of Art, 314-935-6500, Fax: 314-935-4862, E-mail: hcorcoran@wustl.edu. *Application contact:* Prof. Patricia Olynyk, Director of the Graduate School of Art, 314-935-5884, Fax: 314-935-8413, E-mail: olynyk@wustl.edu.
Website: http://samfoxschool.wustl.edu/

**Wayne State University,** College of Fine, Performing and Communication Arts, James Pearson Duffy Department of Art and Art History, Detroit, MI 48202. Offers art (MA, MFA), including ceramics, drawing, fibers, graphic design, industrial design (MA), interior design (MA), metalsmithing, painting, photography, printmaking, sculpture; art history (MA). *Students:* 15 full-time (10 women), 9 part-time (7 women); includes 6

*Art/Fine Arts*

minority (2 Black or African American, non-Hispanic/Latino; 1 Asian, non-Hispanic/Latino; 1 Hispanic/Latino; 2 Two or more races, non-Hispanic/Latino), 2 international. Average age 34. 49 applicants, 12% accepted, 3 enrolled. In 2016, 7 master's awarded. *Degree requirements:* For master's, thesis (for some programs), essay or thesis. *Entrance requirements:* For master's, BFA or another degree and equivalent course work, portfolio, personal interview, reference letters, statement of intent (except for art history program). Additional exam requirements/recommendations for international students: Required—TOEFL (minimum score 550 paper-based; 79 iBT), TWE (minimum score 5.5), Michigan English Language Assessment Battery (minimum score 85); Recommended—IELTS (minimum score 6.5). *Application deadline:* For fall admission, 2/1 for domestic and international students; for winter admission, 10/1 for domestic and international students. Application fee: $50. Electronic applications accepted. *Expenses:* $17,240 per year resident tuition and fees, $34,434 per year non-resident tuition and fees. *Financial support:* In 2016–17, 21 students received support, including 1 fellowship with tuition reimbursement available (averaging $16,000 per year), 6 teaching assistantships with tuition reimbursements available (averaging $17,994 per year); research assistantships, scholarships/grants, and unspecified assistantships also available. Support available to part-time students. Financial award application required to submit FAFSA. *Faculty research:* Integration of the human figure into urban and rural landscape in painting; performance art utilizing digital media and video; exploration of race, gender, and culture through creative practice (including art, design, and art history); ongoing investigation and elaboration of visual art traditions in diverse media; continued scholarship in the history of art. *Unit head:* Dr. John Richardson, Chair, 313-577-2980, Fax: 313-577-3491, E-mail: af5343@wayne.edu. *Application contact:* 313-577-2980, E-mail: art@wayne.edu.
Website: http://art.wayne.edu/

**Webster University,** Leigh Gerdine College of Fine Arts, Department of Art, Design, and Art History, St. Louis, MO 63119-3194. Offers art history and criticism (MA). *Program availability:* Part-time. *Degree requirements:* For master's, thesis. *Entrance requirements:* For master's, BA or BFA in related field, interview, portfolio. Additional exam requirements/recommendations for international students: Required—TOEFL. *Application deadline:* Applications are processed on a rolling basis. Application fee: $35 ($50 for international students). *Expenses:* Tuition: Full-time $21,900; part-time $730 per credit hour. Tuition and fees vary according to campus/location and program. *Financial support:* Federal Work-Study available. Support available to part-time students. Financial award application deadline: 4/1; financial award applicants required to submit FAFSA. *Unit head:* Tom K. Lang, Chair, 314-968-7171, E-mail: langtk@webster.edu. *Application contact:* Jeffrey Hughes, Director, Graduate Program, 314-968-7159, E-mail: hughesja@webster.edu.
Website: http://www.webster.edu/depts/finearts/art/

**Western Carolina University,** Graduate School, College of Fine and Performing Arts, Cullowhee, NC 28723. Offers MFA. *Accreditation:* NASAD. *Program availability:* Part-time. *Degree requirements:* For master's, comprehensive exam, thesis optional. *Entrance requirements:* For master's, GRE, appropriate undergraduate degree, portfolio, letters of recommendation, letter of intent, live audition and/or interview. Additional exam requirements/recommendations for international students: Required—TOEFL (minimum score 550 paper-based; 79 iBT). *Expenses:* Tuition: state resident: full-time $2174. Tuition, nonresident: full-time $7377. *Required fees:* $1442. Part-time tuition and fees vary according to course load. *Faculty research:* Vernacular cultural studies and oral history, sound mixing for television, music technology.

**Western Connecticut State University,** Division of Graduate Studies, School of Visual and Performing Arts, Department of Art, Danbury, CT 06810-6885. Offers illustration (MFA); painting (MFA). *Program availability:* Part-time. *Degree requirements:* For master's, individual exhibition of artwork, review of student's progress prior to admission to final semester, completion of program in 6 years. *Entrance requirements:* For master's, portfolio review, minimum GPA of 2.5. Additional exam requirements/recommendations for international students: Recommended—TOEFL (minimum score 550 paper-based; 79 iBT), IELTS (minimum score 6). *Expenses:* Contact institution. *Faculty research:* Proficiency in both traditional and digital processes.

**West Texas A&M University,** College of Fine Arts and Humanities, Department of Art, Theatre and Dance, Canyon, TX 79016-0001. Offers studio art (MFA). *Program availability:* Part-time. *Degree requirements:* For master's, comprehensive exam, thesis optional. *Entrance requirements:* For master's, GRE General Test. Additional exam requirements/recommendations for international students: Required—TOEFL (minimum score 550 paper-based). *Application deadline:* For fall admission, 4/10 for domestic students. Applications are processed on a rolling basis. Application fee: $40 ($75 for international students). Electronic applications accepted. *Financial support:* In 2016–17,

research assistantships (averaging $6,500 per year) were awarded; fellowships, teaching assistantships with partial tuition reimbursements, career-related internships or fieldwork, Federal Work-Study, institutionally sponsored loans, and tuition waivers (partial) also available. Support available to part-time students. Financial award applicants required to submit CSS PROFILE or FAFSA. *Faculty research:* Ceramics, graphic design, woodblock prints, art education, aesthetics. *Unit head:* Stephen Crandall, Head, 806-651-2799, Fax: 806-651-2818, E-mail: scrandall@wtamu.edu. *Application contact:* Administrative Assistant, 806-651-2777.
Website: http://www.wtamu.edu/academics/art-theatre-dance.aspx

**West Virginia University,** College of Creative Arts, School of Art and Design, Morgantown, WV 26506. Offers art education (MA); art history (MA); ceramics (MFA); graphic design (MFA); painting (MFA); printmaking (MFA); sculpture (MFA); studio art (MA). *Accreditation:* NASAD. *Degree requirements:* For master's, thesis, exhibit. *Entrance requirements:* For master's, minimum GPA of 2.75, portfolio. Additional exam requirements/recommendations for international students: Required—TOEFL. *Expenses:* Contact institution. *Faculty research:* Medieval art history.

**Wichita State University,** Graduate School, College of Fine Arts, School of Art, Design and Creative Industries, Wichita, KS 67260. Offers studio arts (MFA), including ceramics, painting, photo media, printmaking, sculpture. *Accreditation:* NASAD. *Unit head:* Prof. Jeff Pulaski, Director, 316-978-3555, Fax: 316-978-5418, E-mail: jeff.pulaski1@wichita.edu. *Application contact:* Jordan Oleson, Admissions Coordinator, 316-978-3095, Fax: 316-978-3253, E-mail: jordan.oleson@wichita.edu.
Website: http://www.wichita.edu/artdesign

**Wilson College,** Graduate Programs, Chambersburg, PA 17201-1285. Offers accounting (M Acc); choreography and visual art (MFA); education (M Ed); healthcare management for sustainability (MHM); humanities (MA), including art and culture, critical/cultural theory, English language and literature, women's studies; management (MSM); nursing (MSN), including nursing education, nursing leadership and management. *Program availability:* Evening/weekend. *Degree requirements:* For master's, project. *Entrance requirements:* For master's, PRAXIS, minimum undergraduate cumulative GPA of 3.0, 2 letters of recommendation, current certification for eligibility to teach in grades K-12, resume, personal interview. Electronic applications accepted.

**Winthrop University,** College of Visual and Performing Arts, Department of Art, Rock Hill, SC 29733. Offers art (MFA); art administration (MA); art education (MA). *Accreditation:* NASAD. *Program availability:* Part-time. *Degree requirements:* For master's, comprehensive exam (for some programs), thesis (for some programs), documented exhibit, oral exam. *Entrance requirements:* For master's, GRE General Test or MAT, PRAXIS (for MA), minimum GPA of 3.0, resume, slide portfolio, teaching certificate (MA). Additional exam requirements/recommendations for international students: Required—TOEFL (minimum score 550 paper-based; 79 iBT), IELTS (minimum score 6). Electronic applications accepted. *Expenses:* Tuition, state resident: full-time $14,312; part-time $599 per credit hour. Tuition, nonresident: full-time $27,570; part-time $1153 per credit hour.

**Yale University,** School of Art, New Haven, CT 06520-8339. Offers graphic design (MFA); painting/printmaking (MFA); photography (MFA); sculpture (MFA). *Faculty:* 10 full-time (5 women), 35 part-time/adjunct (12 women). *Students:* 127 full-time (65 women); includes 17 minority (8 Black or African American, non-Hispanic/Latino; 5 Asian, non-Hispanic/Latino; 4 Hispanic/Latino), 35 international. Average age 28. 1,003 applicants, 6% accepted, 61 enrolled. In 2016, 61 master's awarded. *Degree requirements:* For master's, thesis (for some programs). *Entrance requirements:* Additional exam requirements/recommendations for international students: Required—TOEFL (minimum score 550 paper-based; 100 iBT). *Application deadline:* For fall admission, 1/4 for domestic and international students. Application fee: $100. Electronic applications accepted. *Expenses:* Contact institution. *Financial support:* In 2016–17, 110 students received support, including 61 teaching assistantships (averaging $2,000 per year); Federal Work-Study, scholarships/grants, and unspecified assistantships also available. Financial award application deadline: 3/1; financial award applicants required to submit FAFSA. *Unit head:* Marta Kuzma, Dean, 203-432-2606. *Application contact:* Patricia Ann DeChiara, Director of Academic Affairs, 203-432-2600, E-mail: artschool.info@yale.edu.
Website: http://www.yale.edu/art/

**York University,** Faculty of Graduate Studies, Faculty of Fine Arts, Program in Visual Arts, Toronto, ON M3J 1P3, Canada. Offers MFA, PhD. *Degree requirements:* For master's, thesis. *Entrance requirements:* For master's, portfolio. Electronic applications accepted.

# Art History

**Academy of Art University,** Graduate Programs, School of Art History, San Francisco, CA 94105-3410. Offers MA. *Program availability:* Part-time, 100% online. *Faculty:* 1 (woman) full-time, 2 part-time/adjunct (1 woman). *Students:* 14 full-time (all women), 44 part-time (40 women); includes 9 minority (1 Black or African American, non-Hispanic/Latino; 1 Asian, non-Hispanic/Latino; 7 Hispanic/Latino), 4 international. Average age 34. 24 applicants, 100% accepted, 10 enrolled. In 2016, 10 master's awarded. *Degree requirements:* For master's, final review. *Entrance requirements:* For master's, statement of intent; resume; portfolio/reel; official college transcripts. *Application deadline:* Applications are processed on a rolling basis. Application fee: $50. Electronic applications accepted. *Expenses:* Tuition: Part-time $982 per unit. *Financial support:* Career-related internships or fieldwork, Federal Work-Study, and scholarships/grants available. Financial award application deadline: 8/10; financial award applicants required to submit FAFSA. *Unit head:* 800-544-ARTS, E-mail: info@academyart.edu. *Application contact:* 800-544-ARTS, E-mail: info@academyart.edu.
Website: http://www.academyart.edu/art-history/

**American University,** College of Arts and Sciences, Department of Art, Washington, DC 20016-8004. Offers art history (MA); studio art (MFA). *Program availability:* Part-time. *Faculty:* 18 full-time (11 women), 23 part-time/adjunct (14 women). *Students:* 26 full-time (23 women), 8 part-time (7 women); includes 2 minority (both Asian, non-Hispanic/Latino), 2 international. Average age 29. 47 applicants, 72% accepted, 15 enrolled. In 2016, 18 master's awarded. *Degree requirements:* For master's, comprehensive exam. *Entrance requirements:* For master's, GRE, portfolio or writing sample, statement of purpose, transcripts, 2 letters of recommendation. Additional exam requirements/recommendations for international students: Required—TOEFL (minimum score 100 iBT), IELTS (minimum score 7), PTE (minimum score 68). *Application deadline:* For fall admission, 2/1 priority date for domestic students. Application fee: $55.

*Expenses:* $1,579 per credit tuition; $690 mandatory fees. *Financial support:* Unspecified assistantships available. Financial award application deadline: 1/15; financial award applicants required to submit FAFSA. *Unit head:* Zoe Charlton, Department Chair, 202-885-3851, Fax: 202-885-1132, E-mail: charlton@american.edu. *Application contact:* Kathleen Clowery, Associate Director, Graduate Admissions, 202-885-3620, Fax: 202-885-1344, E-mail: clowery@american.edu.
Website: http://www.american.edu/cas/art/

**American University of Beirut,** Graduate Programs, Faculty of Arts and Sciences, Beirut, Lebanon. Offers anthropology (MA); Arab and Middle Eastern history (PhD); Arabic language and literature (MA, PhD); archaeology (MA); art history and curating (MA); biology (MS); cell and molecular biology (PhD); chemistry (MS); clinical psychology (MA); computational sciences (MS); computer science (MS); economics (MA); education (MA); English language (MA); English literature (MA); environmental policy planning (MS); financial economics (MAFE); geology (MS); history (MA); Islamic studies (MA); mathematics (MS); media studies (MA); Middle Eastern studies (MA); physics (MS); political studies (MA); psychology (MA); public administration (MA); public policy and international affairs (MA); sociology (MA); statistics (MA, MS); theoretical physics (PhD); transnational American studies (MA). *Program availability:* Part-time. *Faculty:* 133 full-time (42 women), 6 part-time/adjunct (2 women). *Students:* 240 full-time (172 women), 227 part-time (166 women). Average age 27. 286 applicants, 67% accepted, 108 enrolled. In 2016, 60 master's, 3 doctorates awarded. Terminal master's awarded for partial completion of doctoral program. *Degree requirements:* For master's, one foreign language, comprehensive exam, thesis (for some programs); for doctorate, one foreign language, comprehensive exam, thesis/dissertation. *Entrance requirements:* For master's, GRE (for some MA, MS programs), letters of recommendation; for doctorate, GRE, letters of recommendation. Additional exam requirements/

recommendations for international students: Required—TOEFL (minimum score 600 paper-based; 97 iBT), IELTS (minimum score 7). *Application deadline:* For fall admission, 4/3 for domestic students; for winter admission, 11/3 for domestic students. Application fee: $50. Electronic applications accepted. *Expenses:* Contact institution. *Financial support:* In 2016–17, 4 fellowships (averaging $11,200 per year), 18 research assistantships (averaging $5,400 per year) were awarded; teaching assistantships, career-related internships or fieldwork, Federal Work-Study, institutionally sponsored loans, scholarships/grants, traineeships, health care benefits, tuition waivers (full), and unspecified assistantships also available. Support available to part-time students. *Faculty research:* Development economics, spatial econometrics, health economics, labor economics, energy economics, hydrogeology, geophysics, petrophysics, structural geology, mineralogy, petrology, geochemistry, multilingualism, comparative/world literature, translation studies, book histories/ cultures, biocatalysis, molecular recognition, photocatalysis, photophysical and biophysical chemistry, probe chemistry, machine learning, data science. *Unit head:* Dr. Nadia Maria El Cheikh, Dean, Faculty of Arts and Sciences, 961-1374374 Ext. 3800, Fax: 961-1744461, E-mail: nmcheikh@aub.edu.lb. *Application contact:* Dr. Salim Kanaan, Director, Admissions Office, 961-1350000 Ext. 2590, Fax: 961-1750775, E-mail: sk00@aub.edu.lb. Website: http://www.aub.edu.lb/fas/

**Arizona State University at the Tempe campus,** Herberger Institute for Design and the Arts, School of Art, Tempe, AZ 85287-1505. Offers art education (MA); art history (MA); ceramics (MFA); design, environment and the arts (PhD), including history, theory and criticism; drawing (MFA); fibers (MFA); intermedia (MFA); metals (MFA); museum studies (MFA); painting (MFA); printmaking (MFA); sculpture (MFA); wood (MFA); MFA/MA. Terminal master's awarded for partial completion of doctoral program. *Degree requirements:* For master's, thesis/exhibition (MFA, MA in art education); interactive Program of Study (iPOS) submitted before completing 50 percent of required credit hours; for doctorate, comprehensive exam, thesis/dissertation, interactive Program of Study (iPOS) submitted before completing 50 percent of required credit hours. *Entrance requirements:* For master's, GRE or MAT, minimum GPA of 3.0 or equivalent in last 2 years of work leading to bachelor's degree; for doctorate, GRE, master's degree in architecture, graphic design, industrial design, interior design, landscape architecture, or art history or equivalent standing; statement of purpose; 3 letters of recommendation; indication of potential faculty mentor; sample of written work. Additional exam requirements/recommendations for international students: Required—TOEFL, IELTS, or PTE. Electronic applications accepted.

**Bard Graduate Center,** Graduate Studies, New York, NY 10024-3602. Offers M Phil, MA, PhD. *Program availability:* Part-time. *Faculty:* 15 full-time (7 women), 5 part-time/adjunct (4 women). *Students:* 67 full-time (55 women), 11 part-time (all women). In 2016, 23 master's, 5 doctorates awarded. *Degree requirements:* For master's, one foreign language, thesis, internship; for doctorate, 2 foreign languages, thesis/dissertation, 3 field exams. *Entrance requirements:* For master's, GRE General Test, writing sample, 3 letters of recommendation; for doctorate, GRE General Test, MA, master's thesis or equivalent, 3 letters of recommendation. Additional exam requirements/recommendations for international students: Required—TOEFL. *Application deadline:* For fall admission, 1/6 for domestic and international students. Application fee: $70. *Financial support:* Fellowships with tuition reimbursements, research assistantships, teaching assistantships, career-related internships or fieldwork, institutionally sponsored loans, scholarships/grants, traineeships, health care benefits, and unspecified assistantships available. Financial award application deadline: 1/6; financial award applicants required to submit FAFSA. *Faculty research:* New York and American material culture; modern design history; history and theory of museums; early Modern Europe; global Middle Ages; archaeology, anthropology, and material culture; cultures of conservation. *Unit head:* Susan Weber, Founder and Director, 212-501-3000,

Fax: 212-501-3079. *Application contact:* Elena Pinto Simon, Dean for Academic Administration, Student and Alumni Affairs, 212-501-3057, Fax: 212-501-3065, E-mail: simon@bgc.bard.edu. Website: http://www.bgc.bard.edu

**See Display below and Close-Up on page 199.**

**Binghamton University, State University of New York,** Graduate School, Harpur College of Arts and Sciences, Department of Art History, Binghamton, NY 13902-6000. Offers MA, PhD. *Program availability:* Part-time. *Faculty:* 8 full-time (4 women), 1 (woman) part-time/adjunct. *Students:* 13 full-time (8 women), 20 part-time (18 women); includes 4 minority (3 Asian, non-Hispanic/Latino; 1 Hispanic/Latino), 14 international. Average age 33. 20 applicants, 85% accepted, 5 enrolled. In 2016, 3 master's, 4 doctorates awarded. Terminal master's awarded for partial completion of doctoral program. *Degree requirements:* For master's, one foreign language, comprehensive exam, thesis; for doctorate, 2 foreign languages, comprehensive exam, thesis/dissertation. *Entrance requirements:* For master's and doctorate, GRE General Test, writing sample. Additional exam requirements/recommendations for international students: Required—TOEFL (minimum score 80 iBT). *Application deadline:* Applications are processed on a rolling basis. Application fee: $75. Electronic applications accepted. *Financial support:* In 2016–17, 13 students received support, including 9 teaching assistantships with full tuition reimbursements available (averaging $15,000 per year); career-related internships or fieldwork, Federal Work-Study, institutionally sponsored loans, scholarships/grants, health care benefits, and unspecified assistantships also available. Financial award application deadline: 2/15; financial award applicants required to submit FAFSA. *Faculty research:* History of art and architecture. *Unit head:* Dr. Tom McDonough, Chair, 607-777-2847, E-mail: tmcdonou@binghamton.edu. *Application contact:* Ben Balkaya, Assistant Dean and Director, 607-777-2151, Fax: 607-777-2501, E-mail: balkaya@binghamton.edu. Website: http://www.binghamton.edu/art-history/

**Boston University,** Graduate School of Arts and Sciences, Department of History of Art and Architecture, Boston, MA 02215. Offers art history (MA, PhD); museum studies (Certificate). *Accreditation:* NASAD. *Students:* 61 full-time (52 women), 6 part-time (4 women); includes 8 minority (2 Black or African American, non-Hispanic/Latino; 2 Asian, non-Hispanic/Latino; 4 Hispanic/Latino), 6 international. Average age 31. 139 applicants, 35% accepted, 15 enrolled. In 2016, 9 master's, 7 doctorates awarded. Terminal master's awarded for partial completion of doctoral program. *Degree requirements:* For master's, one foreign language, comprehensive exam, thesis or alternative, scholarly paper; for doctorate, 2 foreign languages, comprehensive exam, thesis/dissertation. *Entrance requirements:* For master's and doctorate, GRE General Test, 3 letters of recommendation, transcripts, personal statement, curriculum vitae, writing sample, foreign language proficiency; for Certificate, GRE General Test. Additional exam requirements/recommendations for international students: Required—TOEFL (minimum score 550 paper-based; 84 iBT). *Application deadline:* For fall admission, 1/5 for domestic and international students; for spring admission, 10/15 for domestic and international students. Application fee: $95. Electronic applications accepted. *Financial support:* In 2016–17, 43 students received support, including 17 fellowships with full tuition reimbursements available (averaging $21,500 per year), 10 teaching assistantships with full tuition reimbursements available (averaging $21,500 per year); career-related internships or fieldwork, Federal Work-Study, scholarships/grants, health care benefits, and unspecified assistantships also available. Financial award application deadline: 1/5. *Unit head:* Dr. Alice Tseng, Chair, 617-353-1458, Fax: 617-353-3243, E-mail: aytseng@bu.edu. *Application contact:* Cheryl Crombie, Administrative Assistant, 617-353-2522, Fax: 617-353-3243, E-mail: ccrombie@bu.edu. Website: http://www.bu.edu/AH/

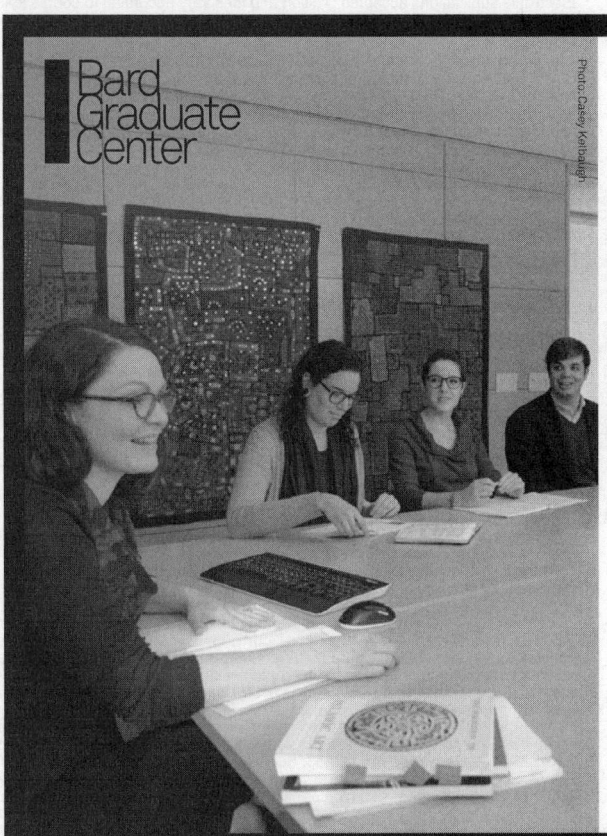

*Art History*

**Bowling Green State University,** Graduate College, College of Arts and Sciences, School of Art, Bowling Green, OH 43403. Offers 2-D studio art (MA, MFA); 3-D studio art (MA, MFA); art education (MA); art history (MA); computer art (MA); design (MFA); digital arts (MFA); graphics (MFA). *Accreditation:* NASAD. *Program availability:* Part-time. *Degree requirements:* For master's, thesis or alternative, final exhibit (MFA). *Entrance requirements:* For master's, GRE General Test (MA), slide portfolio (15-20 slides). Additional exam requirements/recommendations for international students: Required—TOEFL. *Application deadline:* For fall admission, 2/15 for domestic students. Application fee: $30. Electronic applications accepted. *Financial support:* Research assistantships with full and partial tuition reimbursements, teaching assistantships with full and partial tuition reimbursements, career-related internships or fieldwork, institutionally sponsored loans, and unspecified assistantships available. Support available to part-time students. Financial award applicants required to submit FAFSA. *Faculty research:* Computer animation and virtual reality, Spanish still-life painting from 1600 to 1800, art and psychotherapy, Japanese wood-firing techniques in ceramics, non-toxic printmaking technologies. *Unit head:* Dr. Katerina Ruedi Ray, Director, 419-372-8575. *Application contact:* Marisa Cline, Graduate Coordinator, 419-372-2786, E-mail: mlcline@bgsu.edu.

**Brooklyn College of the City University of New York,** School of Visual, Media and Performing Arts, Department of Art, Brooklyn, NY 11210-2889. Offers art history (MA); digital art (MFA); drawing and painting (MFA); photography (MFA); printmaking (MFA); sculpture (MFA). *Program availability:* Part-time. *Degree requirements:* For master's, thesis. *Entrance requirements:* For master's, bachelor's degree in art, portfolio, 2 letters of recommendation. Additional exam requirements/recommendations for international students: Required—TOEFL (minimum score 500 paper-based; 61 iBT). Electronic applications accepted.

**Brown University,** Graduate School, Department of History of Art and Architecture, Providence, RI 02912. Offers PhD. *Degree requirements:* For doctorate, 2 foreign languages, thesis/dissertation, oral exam. *Entrance requirements:* For doctorate, GRE General Test, MA with distinction.

**Brown University,** Graduate School, Joukowsky Institute for Archaeology and the Ancient World, Providence, RI 02912. Offers PhD. *Degree requirements:* For doctorate, thesis/dissertation.

**Bryn Mawr College,** Graduate School of Arts and Sciences, Department of History of Art, Bryn Mawr, PA 19010-2899. Offers MA, PhD. *Program availability:* Part-time. *Faculty:* 6 full-time (4 women), 1 part-time/adjunct (0 women). *Students:* 19 full-time (14 women), 3 part-time (all women); includes 4 minority (3 Hispanic/Latino; 1 Native Hawaiian or other Pacific Islander, non-Hispanic/Latino), 1 international. Average age 29. 24 applicants, 25% accepted, 5 enrolled. In 2016, 3 master's, 2 doctorates awarded. Terminal master's awarded for partial completion of doctoral program. *Degree requirements:* For master's, 2 foreign languages, thesis; for doctorate, 2 foreign languages, comprehensive exam, thesis/dissertation. *Entrance requirements:* For master's and doctorate, GRE General Test, transcripts, three letters of recommendation, statement of interest, resume or curriculum vitae. Additional exam requirements/recommendations for international students: Required—TOEFL (minimum score 600 paper-based; 100 iBT), IELTS (minimum score 7). *Application deadline:* For fall admission, 12/15 for domestic and international students. Application fee: $50. Electronic applications accepted. *Expenses: Tuition:* Full-time $40,620; part-time $6770 per unit. Tuition and fees vary according to program. *Financial support:* In 2016–17, 22 students received support, including 14 fellowships with tuition reimbursements available (averaging $18,642 per year), 4 teaching assistantships with tuition reimbursements available (averaging $16,625 per year); Federal Work-Study, scholarships/grants, health care benefits, tuition waivers, and unspecified assistantships also available. Support available to part-time students. Financial award application deadline: 12/15. *Unit head:* Maria Dantis, Graduate Program Administrator, 610-526-5074, E-mail: gsas@brynmawr.edu.

**California State University, Chico,** Office of Graduate Studies, College of Humanities and Fine Arts, Department of Art and Art History, Program in Art History, Chico, CA 95929-0722. Offers MA. *Accreditation:* NASAD. *Students:* 2 applicants, 100% accepted, 2 enrolled. In 2016, 1 master's awarded. *Degree requirements:* For master's, thesis, examination. *Entrance requirements:* For master's, 2 letters of recommendation; statement of purpose; two upper-division art history papers. Additional exam requirements/recommendations for international students: Required—TOEFL (minimum score 550 paper-based; 80 iBT), IELTS (minimum score 6.5), PTE (minimum score 59). *Application deadline:* For fall admission, 3/1 for domestic and international students; for spring admission, 9/15 for domestic and international students. Application fee: $55. Electronic applications accepted. *Financial support:* Scholarships/grants available. Financial award application deadline: 3/1; financial award applicants required to submit FAFSA. *Unit head:* Dr. Robert Herhusky, Chair, 530-898-4560, Fax: 530-898-4171, E-mail: art@csuchico.edu. *Application contact:* Judy L. Morris, Graduate Admissions Coordinator, 530-898-5416, Fax: 530-898-3342, E-mail: jlmorris@csuchico.edu. Website: http://www.csuchico.edu/art/programs/ma.shtml

**California State University, Los Angeles,** Graduate Studies, College of Arts and Letters, Department of Art, Los Angeles, CA 90032-8530. Offers art (MA), including art education, art history, art therapy, ceramics, metals and textiles, design (MA, MFA), painting, sculpture, and graphic arts, photography; fine arts (MFA), including crafts, design (MA, MFA), studio arts. *Accreditation:* NASAD (one or more programs are accredited). *Program availability:* Part-time, evening/weekend. *Degree requirements:* For master's, comprehensive exam, project or thesis. *Entrance requirements:* For master's, portfolio. Additional exam requirements/recommendations for international students: Required—TOEFL (minimum score 500 paper-based). Electronic applications accepted. *Faculty research:* The artist and the book, conceptual art, ceramic processes, computer graphics, architectural graphics.

**California State University, Northridge,** Graduate Studies, College of Arts, Media, and Communication, Department of Art, Northridge, CA 91330. Offers art education (MA); art history (MA); studio art (MA, MFA); visual communications (MA, MFA). *Accreditation:* NASAD. *Faculty:* 23 full-time (10 women), 75 part-time/adjunct (38 women). *Students:* 22 full-time (15 women), 5 part-time (2 women); includes 12 minority (1 Asian, non-Hispanic/Latino; 8 Hispanic/Latino; 3 Two or more races, non-Hispanic/Latino), 3 international. Average age 30. 51 applicants, 27% accepted, 12 enrolled. *Application deadline:* For fall admission, 11/30 for domestic students. Application fee: $55. *Expenses:* Tuition, state resident: full-time $4152. *Financial support:* Application deadline: 3/1. *Unit head:* Prof. Edward Alfano, Chair, 818-677-2242, E-mail: art.dept@csun.edu. Website: http://www.csun.edu/art/

**Caribbean University,** Graduate School, Bayamón, PR 00960-0493. Offers administration and supervision (MA Ed); criminal justice (MA); curriculum and instruction (MA Ed, PhD), including elementary education (MA Ed), English education (MA Ed), history education (MA Ed), mathematics education (MA Ed), primary education (MA Ed), science education (MA Ed), Spanish education (MA Ed); educational technology in instructional systems (MA Ed); gerontology (MSN); human resources (MBA); museology, archiving and art history (MA Ed); neonatal pediatrics (MSN); physical education (MA Ed); special education (MA Ed). *Entrance requirements:* For master's, interview, minimum GPA of 2.5.

**Carleton University,** Faculty of Graduate Studies, Faculty of Arts and Social Sciences, School for Studies in Art and Culture, Program in Art History: Art and its Institutions, Ottawa, ON K1S 5B6, Canada. Offers MA. *Degree requirements:* For master's, thesis. *Entrance requirements:* For master's, honors degree.

**Case Western Reserve University,** School of Graduate Studies, Department of Art History and Art, Program in Art History, Cleveland, OH 44106. Offers MA, PhD. Programs offered jointly with The Cleveland Museum of Art. *Program availability:* Part-time. *Faculty:* 9 full-time (8 women), 2 part-time/adjunct (1 woman). *Students:* 9 full-time (8 women), 2 part-time (both women); includes 2 minority (both Two or more races, non-Hispanic/Latino), 1 international. Average age 28. 18 applicants, 33% accepted, 3 enrolled. In 2016, 7 master's awarded. *Degree requirements:* For master's, one foreign language, comprehensive exam; for doctorate, 2 foreign languages, comprehensive exam, thesis/dissertation. *Entrance requirements:* For master's, GRE General Test, 2 samples of written work; for doctorate, GRE General Test, 2 samples of written work, MA thesis. Additional exam requirements/recommendations for international students: Required—TOEFL (minimum score 600 paper-based; 100 iBT). *Application deadline:* For fall admission, 1/1 priority date for domestic students. Applications are processed on a rolling basis. Application fee: $50. Electronic applications accepted. *Expenses: Tuition:* Full-time $42,576; part-time $1774 per credit hour. *Required fees:* $34. Tuition and fees vary according to course load and program. *Financial support:* Fellowships, research assistantships, teaching assistantships, career-related internships or fieldwork, and tuition waivers available. Financial award application deadline: 1/1; financial award applicants required to submit FAFSA. *Faculty research:* Greek art and architecture, Northern Baroque art, Italian Baroque sculpture, abstract expressionism, Indian art, nineteenth-century French art, American and contemporary art. *Unit head:* Catherine Scallen, Associate Professor/Chair, 216-368-2383, Fax: 216-368-4681, E-mail: catherine.scallen@case.edu. *Application contact:* Deborah Tenenbaum, Department Assistant, 216-368-4118, Fax: 216-368-4681, E-mail: deborah.tenenbaum@case.edu. Website: http://arthistory.case.edu/graduate/art-history/

**Christie's Education,** MA Program in Modern and Contemporary Art and the Market, New York, NY 10020. Offers MA. *Program availability:* Part-time. *Faculty:* 5 full-time (4 women). *Students:* 47 full-time (43 women), 4 part-time (all women). In 2016, 21 master's awarded. *Degree requirements:* For master's, one foreign language, thesis, internship. *Entrance requirements:* For master's, writing sample, 3 letters of recommendation. *Application deadline:* For fall admission, 1/15 priority date for domestic and international students. Applications are processed on a rolling basis. Application fee: $95. *Expenses:* Contact institution. *Financial support:* In 2016–17, 3 students received support. Scholarships/grants and unspecified assistantships available. Financial award applicants required to submit FAFSA. *Unit head:* Dr. Julie Reiss, Program Director, 212-355-1501 Ext. 3307, Fax: 212-355-7370, E-mail: jreiss@christies.edu. *Application contact:* Hilary Smith, Recruitment and Admissions Officer, 212-355-1501 Ext. 3309, Fax: 212-355-7370, E-mail: hsmith@christies.edu. Website: https://www.christies.com/new-york/courses/masters-modern-contemporary-art-markets.aspx

**City College of the City University of New York,** Graduate School, Division of Humanities and the Arts, Department of Art, Programs in Art History and Museum Studies, New York, NY 10031-9198. Offers art history (MA); art museum education (MA); museum studies (MA). *Program availability:* Part-time. *Degree requirements:* For master's, one foreign language, thesis. *Entrance requirements:* For master's, minimum GPA of 3.0, portfolio, art history paper. Additional exam requirements/recommendations for international students: Required—TOEFL (minimum score 577 paper-based; 90 iBT). Electronic applications accepted. Tuition and fees vary according to course load, degree level and program. *Faculty research:* Egyptian, Greek, medieval, Romanesque, and Ottoman art.

**Cleveland State University,** College of Graduate Studies, College of Liberal Arts and Social Sciences, Department of History, Cleveland, OH 44115. Offers art history (MA); museum studies (MA). *Program availability:* Part-time, evening/weekend. *Faculty:* 13 full-time (4 women). *Students:* 10 full-time (6 women), 7 part-time (4 women); includes 3 minority (1 Hispanic/Latino; 2 Two or more races, non-Hispanic/Latino). Average age 30. 21 applicants, 90% accepted, 6 enrolled. In 2016, 14 master's awarded. *Degree requirements:* For master's, thesis optional. *Entrance requirements:* For master's, minimum GPA of 3.0, bachelor's degree in history (or related field for art history). Additional exam requirements/recommendations for international students: Required—TOEFL (minimum score 550 paper-based; 78 iBT). *Application deadline:* For fall admission, 7/1 priority date for domestic students, 5/15 for international students; for spring admission, 11/15 for domestic students, 11/1 for international students; for summer admission, 4/1 for domestic students, 3/15 for international students. Applications are processed on a rolling basis. Application fee: $40. Electronic applications accepted. *Expenses:* Tuition, state resident: full-time $9565. Tuition, nonresident: full-time $17,980. Tuition and fees vary according to program. *Financial support:* In 2016–17, 7 students received support, including research assistantships with full tuition reimbursements available (averaging $8,600 per year); career-related internships or fieldwork, tuition waivers (full and partial), and unspecified assistantships also available. Financial award application deadline: 4/15. *Faculty research:* Africa and African diaspora, European history, Middle Eastern history, Latin American/Caribbean history, American history, gender and sexuality. *Unit head:* Dr. Elizabeth A. Lehfeldt, Chairperson, 216-687-3920, Fax: 216-687-5592, E-mail: e.lehfeldt@csuohio.edu. *Application contact:* Dr. Karen Sotiropoulos, Graduate Director, 216-687-3940, E-mail: r.s.shelton@csuohio.edu. Website: http://www.csuohio.edu/history/

**Colorado State University,** College of Liberal Arts, Department of Art and Art History, Fort Collins, CO 80523-1779. Offers studio art (MFA). *Faculty:* 15 full-time (9 women), 3 part-time/adjunct (1 woman). *Students:* 14 full-time (9 women), 2 part-time (1 woman); includes 2 minority (1 American Indian or Alaska Native, non-Hispanic/Latino; 1 Two or more races, non-Hispanic/Latino). Average age 32. 40 applicants, 18% accepted, 3 enrolled. In 2016, 4 master's awarded. *Degree requirements:* For master's, comprehensive exam (for some programs), thesis (for some programs), exhibition. *Entrance requirements:* For master's, portfolio, three letters of recommendation, transcripts, statement of purpose, resume, artist statement. Additional exam requirements/recommendations for international students: Required—TOEFL (minimum score 550 paper-based; 80 iBT). *Application deadline:* For fall admission, 2/1 priority date for domestic and international students. Applications are processed on a rolling basis. Application fee: $60 ($70 for international students). Electronic applications accepted. *Expenses:* Tuition, state resident: full-time $9628. Tuition, nonresident: full-time $23,603. *Required fees:* $2253; $528.14 per credit hour. $264.07 per semester. Tuition and fees vary according to course load and program. *Financial support:* In 2016–17, 8 teaching assistantships with partial tuition reimbursements (averaging $12,191 per year) were awarded; Federal Work-Study, scholarships/grants, and unspecified assistantships also available. Financial award application deadline: 3/1; financial award applicants required to submit FAFSA. *Faculty research:* African art history, bronze castings, etching/lithography, pre-Columbian art history, contemporary crafts. *Total annual research expenditures:* $27,924. *Unit head:* Suzanne Faris, Department Chair/Associate Professor, 970-491-6774, Fax: 970-491-0505, E-mail: suzanne.faris@colostate.edu. *Application contact:* Kathleen Chynoweth, Graduate Contact, 970-491-6775, E-mail: kathleen.chynoweth@colostate.edu. Website: http://art.colostate.edu/

**Columbia University,** Graduate School of Arts and Sciences, New York, NY 10027. Offers African-American studies (MA); American studies (MA); anthropology (MA, PhD); art history and archaeology (MA, PhD); astronomy (PhD); biological sciences (PhD); biotechnology (MA); chemical physics (PhD); chemistry (PhD); classical studies (MA, PhD); classics (MA, PhD); climate and society (MA); conservation biology (MA); earth and environmental sciences (PhD); East Asia: regional studies (MA); East Asian languages and cultures (MA, PhD); ecology, evolution and environmental biology (MA), including conservation biology; ecology, evolution, and environmental biology (PhD), including ecology and evolutionary biology, evolutionary primatology; economics (MA, PhD); English and comparative literature (MA, PhD); French and Romance philology (MA, PhD); Germanic languages (MA, PhD); global French studies (MA); global thought (MA); Hispanic cultural studies (MA); history (PhD); history and literature (MA); human rights studies (MA); Islamic studies (MA); Italian (MA, PhD); Japanese pedagogy (MA); Jewish studies (MA); Latin America and the Caribbean: regional studies (MA); Latin American and Iberian cultures (PhD); mathematics (MA, PhD), including finance (MA); medieval and Renaissance studies (MA); Middle Eastern, South Asian, and African studies (MA, PhD); modern art: critical and curatorial studies (MA); modern European studies (MA); museum anthropology (MA); music (DMA, PhD); oral history (MA); philosophical foundations of physics (MA); philosophy (MA, PhD); physics (PhD); political science (MA, PhD); psychology (PhD); quantitative methods in the social sciences (MA); religion (MA, PhD); Russia, Eurasia and East Europe: regional studies (MA); Russian translation (MA); Slavic cultures (MA); Slavic languages (MA, PhD); sociology (MA, PhD); South Asian studies (MA); statistics (MA, PhD); theatre (PhD). Dual-degree programs require admission to both Graduate School of Arts and Sciences and another Columbia school. *Program availability:* Part-time. Terminal master's awarded for partial completion of doctoral program. *Degree requirements:* For master's, variable foreign language requirement, comprehensive exam (for some programs), thesis (for some programs); for doctorate, variable foreign language requirement, comprehensive exam (for some programs), thesis/dissertation. *Entrance requirements:* For master's and doctorate, GRE General Test, GRE Subject Test (for some programs). Additional exam requirements/recommendations for international students: Required—TOEFL, IELTS. Electronic applications accepted.

**Concordia University,** School of Graduate Studies, Faculty of Fine Arts, Department of Art History, Montréal, QC H3G 1M8, Canada. Offers MA, PhD. PhD program offered jointly with Universityé Laval, Universityé de Montréal, and Universityé du Québec à Montréal. *Degree requirements:* For master's, one foreign language, thesis. *Entrance requirements:* For master's, BFA or equivalent, minimum B average in major. *Faculty research:* Ancient and modern Canadian art and architecture, Canadian decorative arts, museum studies.

**Cornell University,** Graduate School, Graduate Fields of Arts and Sciences, Field of History of Art, Archaeology and Visual Studies, Ithaca, NY 14853. Offers 19th century art (PhD); African, African American and African diaspora (PhD); American art (PhD); ancient art and archaeology (PhD); Asian American art (PhD); Baroque art (PhD); comparative modernities (PhD); digital art (PhD); East Asian art (PhD); history of photography (PhD); Islamic art (PhD); Latin American art (PhD); medieval art (PhD); modern art (PhD); Renaissance art (PhD); Southeast Asian art (PhD); theory and criticism (PhD); visual studies (PhD). *Degree requirements:* For doctorate, one foreign language, comprehensive exam, thesis/dissertation, general exams in 3 areas. *Entrance requirements:* For doctorate, GRE General Test, sample of written work, 3 letters of recommendation. Additional exam requirements/recommendations for international students: Required—TOEFL (minimum score 550 paper-based; 77 iBT). Electronic applications accepted.

**Dominican University of California,** School of Arts, Humanities and Social Sciences, Humanities Program, San Rafael, CA 94901-2298. Offers applied music (MA); art history (MA); creative writing (MA); gender studies (MA); history (MA); literature (MA); philosophy (MA); political theory (MA); religion (MA). *Program availability:* Part-time. *Degree requirements:* For master's, thesis or alternative. *Entrance requirements:* For master's, minimum GPA of 3.0, interview. Additional exam requirements/recommendations for international students: Required—TOEFL (minimum score 550 paper-based; 80 iBT), IELTS (minimum score 6.5). Electronic applications accepted. Application fee is waived when completed online. *Expenses:* Contact institution.

**Duke University,** Graduate School, Department of Art, Art History and Visual Studies, Durham, NC 27708-0764. Offers historical and cultural visualization (MA); history of art (PhD). *Degree requirements:* For doctorate, thesis/dissertation. *Entrance requirements:* For doctorate, GRE General Test. Additional exam requirements/recommendations for international students: Required—TOEFL (minimum score 577 paper-based; 90 iBT), or IELTS (minimum score 7). Electronic applications accepted.

**Emory University,** Laney Graduate School, Department of Art History, Atlanta, GA 30322-1100. Offers PhD. *Degree requirements:* For doctorate, 2 foreign languages, comprehensive exam, thesis/dissertation, oral exam. *Entrance requirements:* For doctorate, GRE General Test. Additional exam requirements/recommendations for international students: Required—TOEFL. Electronic applications accepted.

**Fashion Institute of Technology,** School of Graduate Studies, Program in Art Market Studies, New York, NY 10001-5992. Offers MA. *Accreditation:* NASAD. *Students:* 13. 23 applicants, 43% accepted, 5 enrolled. *Degree requirements:* For master's, thesis or alternative, internship. *Entrance requirements:* For master's, GRE General Test, previous course work in art history, 4 semesters of a foreign language. Additional exam requirements/recommendations for international students: Required—TOEFL (minimum score 550 paper-based). *Application deadline:* For fall admission, 2/15 priority date for domestic and international students. Applications are processed on a rolling basis. Application fee: $50. Electronic applications accepted. *Expenses:* Tuition, state resident: full-time $10,870; part-time $453 per credit. Tuition, nonresident: full-time $22,210; part-time $925 per credit. *Required fees:* $745. *Financial support:* Federal Work-Study and scholarships/grants available. Financial award applicants required to submit FAFSA. *Unit head:* Natasha Degen, Associate Chairperson, 212-217-4300. *Application contact:* Administrative Coordinator, 212-217-4300. Website: http://www.fitnyc.edu/art-market/

See Display on page 193 and Close-Up on page 203.

**Florida State University,** The Graduate School, College of Fine Arts, Department of Art History, Tallahassee, FL 32306. Offers art history (MA, PhD); museum and cultural heritage studies (MA). *Accreditation:* NASAD. *Program availability:* Part-time. *Faculty:* 11 full-time (4 women), 9 part-time/adjunct (5 women). *Students:* 48 full-time (43 women), 6 part-time (5 women); includes 10 minority (1 Black or African American, non-Hispanic/Latino; 2 Asian, non-Hispanic/Latino; 6 Hispanic/Latino; 1 Two or more races, non-Hispanic/Latino). Average age 32. 35 applicants, 91% accepted, 21 enrolled. In 2016, 14 master's, 1 doctorate awarded. Terminal master's awarded for partial

completion of doctoral program. *Degree requirements:* For master's, one foreign language, thesis (for some programs), capstone project (for some programs); for doctorate, 2 foreign languages, comprehensive exam, thesis/dissertation. *Entrance requirements:* For master's, GRE General Test, minimum GPA of 3.0; for doctorate, GRE General Test, minimum GPA of 3.5. Additional exam requirements/recommendations for international students: Required—TOEFL (minimum score 550 paper-based; 80 iBT), IELTS (minimum score 6.5). *Application deadline:* For fall admission, 4/1 for domestic and international students. Applications are processed on a rolling basis. Application fee: $35. Electronic applications accepted. *Expenses:* $479.32 per credit hour in-state, $1,110.72 per credit hour out-of-state. *Financial support:* In 2016–17, 34 students received support, including 7 fellowships with full tuition reimbursements available (averaging $10,900 per year), 19 research assistantships with full tuition reimbursements available (averaging $5,395 per year), 8 teaching assistantships with full tuition reimbursements available (averaging $6,609 per year); career-related internships or fieldwork, Federal Work-Study, institutionally sponsored loans, and unspecified assistantships also available. Financial award application deadline: 1/1; financial award applicants required to submit FAFSA. *Faculty research:* Modern art and critical theory, medieval, Renaissance and Baroque, Pre-Columbian and Spanish Colonial, visual arts of the Americas. *Unit head:* Dr. Adam Jolles, Associate Professor of Art History/Department Chair, 850-644-7066, E-mail: ajolles@fsu.edu. *Application contact:* Juan Barcelo-Gonzalez, Academic Program Specialist/Graduate Student Advisor, 850-644-8207, E-mail: juan.barcelo@fsu.edu. Website: http://arthistory.fsu.edu/

**George Mason University,** College of Humanities and Social Sciences, Department of History and Art History, Program in Art History, Fairfax, VA 22030. Offers MA. *Accreditation:* NASAD. *Faculty:* 8 full-time (6 women), 7 part-time/adjunct (6 women). *Students:* 3 full-time (all women), 3 part-time (all women); includes 2 minority (1 Asian, non-Hispanic/Latino; 1 Hispanic/Latino). Average age 25. 8 applicants, 75% accepted, 1 enrolled. In 2016, 11 master's awarded. *Degree requirements:* For master's, variable foreign language requirement, comprehensive exam, thesis optional. *Entrance requirements:* For master's, GRE (waived for those who hold another graduate degree or received their undergraduate degree 10 or more years ago), expanded goals statement; 2 letters of recommendation; resume; official transcript. Additional exam requirements/recommendations for international students: Required—TOEFL (minimum score 575 paper-based; 88 iBT), IELTS (minimum score 6.5), PTE (minimum score 59). *Application deadline:* For fall admission, 3/15 for domestic students. Application fee: $75 ($80 for international students). Electronic applications accepted. *Expenses:* Tuition, state resident: full-time $10,628; part-time $443 per credit. Tuition, nonresident: full-time $29,306; part-time $1221 per credit. *Required fees:* $3096; $129 per credit. Tuition and fees vary according to program. *Financial support:* Career-related internships or fieldwork, Federal Work-Study, scholarships/grants, unspecified assistantships, and health care benefits (for full-time research or teaching assistantship recipients) available. Support available to part-time students. Financial award application deadline: 3/1; financial award applicants required to submit FAFSA. *Faculty research:* Exhibit on Pompeii: ancient art, southeast Asia; history on Buddhist art, twentieth century Latin America interchange, Silk Road Project, American art on visual imagery. *Unit head:* Michele Greet, Director, 703-993-3479, Fax: 703-993-1251, E-mail: mgreet@gmu.edu. *Application contact:* Emily Gibson, Graduate Coordinator, 703-993-1248, Fax: 703-993-1251, E-mail: egibson5@gmu.edu. Website: http://historyarthistory.gmu.edu/programs/la-ma-ah

**The George Washington University,** Columbian College of Arts and Sciences, Department of Fine Arts and Art History, Program in Art History, Washington, DC 20052. Offers art history (MA); museum training (MA). *Program availability:* Part-time, evening/ weekend. *Students:* 11 full-time (10 women), 2 part-time (both women); includes 1 minority (Hispanic/Latino), 1 international. Average age 27. 33 applicants, 88% accepted, 8 enrolled. In 2016, 7 master's awarded. *Degree requirements:* For master's, one foreign language, comprehensive exam, thesis or alternative. *Entrance requirements:* For master's, GRE General Test, bachelor's degree in field, minimum GPA of 3.0. Additional exam requirements/recommendations for international students: Required—TOEFL (minimum score 550 paper-based; 80 iBT). *Application deadline:* For fall admission, 3/1 priority date for domestic students, 1/15 priority date for international students; for spring admission, 10/1 priority date for domestic students, 9/1 priority date for international students. Applications are processed on a rolling basis. Application fee: $75. Electronic applications accepted. *Financial support:* In 2016–17, 3 students received support. Fellowships, teaching assistantships, career-related internships or fieldwork, and Federal Work-Study available. Financial award application deadline: 1/15. *Unit head:* Thomas K. Brown, Chair, 202-994-9067, E-mail: thbrown@gwu.edu. *Application contact:* Information Contact, 202-994-6085, Fax: 202-994-8657, E-mail: art@gwu.edu.

**Georgia State University,** College of Arts and Sciences, Ernest G. Welch School of Art and Design, Program in Art History, Atlanta, GA 30302-3083. Offers MA. *Accreditation:* NASAD. *Degree requirements:* For master's, one foreign language, comprehensive exam, thesis. *Application deadline:* For fall admission, 1/6 for domestic and international students; for spring admission, 1/15 priority date for domestic and international students. Application fee: $50. Electronic applications accepted. *Expenses:* Tuition, state resident: full-time $6876; part-time $382 per credit hour. Tuition, nonresident: full-time $22,374; part-time $1243 per credit hour. *Required fees:* $2128; $1064 per term. Part-time tuition and fees vary according to course load and program. *Financial support:* In 2016–17, research assistantships with full tuition reimbursements (averaging $6,000 per year) were awarded; fellowships, scholarships/grants, and unspecified assistantships also available. Financial award application deadline: 4/15; financial award applicants required to submit FAFSA. *Faculty research:* Ancient Egyptian tomb painting, nineteenth- and early twentieth-century French representations of primitive mankind, contemporary women artists, early modern images of devotion and death, images of the wet nurse in Afro-Brazilian art. *Unit head:* Michael White, Director, Welch School of Art and Design, 404-413-5221, Fax: 404-413-5261, E-mail: mwhite@gsu.edu. *Application contact:* Hubert Stanley Anderson, Director of Graduate Studies, 404-413-5229, Fax: 404-413-5261, E-mail: artgrad@gsu.edu. Website: http://artdesign.gsu.edu/graduate/admissions/master-of-arts-in-art-history/

**The Graduate Center, City University of New York,** Graduate Studies, Program in Art History, New York, NY 10016-4039. Offers architecture (PhD); graphic arts (PhD); painting (PhD); photography (PhD); sculpture (PhD). *Degree requirements:* For doctorate, 2 foreign languages, thesis/dissertation. *Entrance requirements:* For doctorate, GRE General Test. Additional exam requirements/recommendations for international students: Required—TOEFL. Electronic applications accepted.

**Graduate Theological Union,** Graduate Programs, Berkeley, CA 94709-1212. Offers art and religion (MA, PhD, Th D); biblical languages (MA); biblical studies (MA); Biblical studies (PhD, Th D); Buddhist studies (MA); Christian spirituality (MA, PhD, Th D); cultural and historical studies of religions (MA, PhD, Th D); ethics and social theory (PhD, Th D); history (MA, PhD, Th D); homiletics (MA, PhD, Th D); interdisciplinary studies (PhD, Th D); Jewish studies (MA, PhD, Th D, Certificate); liturgical studies (MA, PhD, Th D); Near Eastern religions (PhD, Th D); Orthodox Christian studies (MA); religion and psychology (MA, PhD, Th D); religion and society/ethics and social theory

## Art History

(MA); systematic and philosophical theology (MA, PhD, Th D). PhD programs in Jewish studies and Near Eastern religions offered jointly with University of California, Berkeley. *Accreditation:* ATS. Terminal master's awarded for partial completion of doctoral program. *Degree requirements:* For master's, one foreign language, thesis; for doctorate, one foreign language, comprehensive exam, thesis/dissertation. *Entrance requirements:* For master's, GRE General Test; for doctorate, GRE General Test, MA or M Div. Additional exam requirements/recommendations for international students: Required—TOEFL. Electronic applications accepted.

**Harvard University,** Graduate School of Arts and Sciences, Department of History of Art and Architecture, Cambridge, MA 02138. Offers ancient art (PhD); ancient Near Eastern art (PhD); Baroque art (PhD); Byzantine art (PhD); classical art (PhD); Indian art (PhD); Islamic art (PhD); Japanese and Chinese art (PhD); medieval art (PhD); modern art (PhD); Renaissance and modern architecture (PhD); Renaissance art (PhD). *Degree requirements:* For doctorate, variable foreign language requirement, thesis/dissertation, general exams; reading exams in French, German, and Italian. *Entrance requirements:* For doctorate, GRE General Test. Additional exam requirements/recommendations for international students: Required—TOEFL.

**Howard University,** Graduate School, Division of Fine Arts, Department of Art, Program in Art History, Washington, DC 20059-0002. Offers art history (MA); history of art and visual culture (MA). *Accreditation:* NASAD. *Program availability:* Part-time. *Degree requirements:* For master's, comprehensive exam, thesis. *Entrance requirements:* For master's, GRE General Test, minimum GPA of 3.0, BA in art history or related field, portfolio.

**Hunter College of the City University of New York,** Graduate School, School of Arts and Sciences, Department of Art and Art History, Program in Art History, New York, NY 10065-5085. Offers MA. *Program availability:* Part-time, evening/weekend. *Students:* 85 part-time (77 women); includes 12 minority (4 Black or African American, non-Hispanic/Latino; 5 Asian, non-Hispanic/Latino; 3 Hispanic/Latino), 4 international. Average age 32. 67 applicants, 85% accepted, 26 enrolled. In 2016, 14 master's awarded. *Degree requirements:* For master's, one foreign language, comprehensive exam, thesis. *Entrance requirements:* For master's, GRE General Test, minimum 12 credits of course work in art history, reading knowledge of a foreign language (Italian, French, German, or Spanish), 2 letters of recommendation, statement of purpose, writing sample. Additional exam requirements/recommendations for international students: Required—TOEFL (minimum score 550 paper-based; 60 iBT). *Application deadline:* For fall admission, 2/1 for domestic students; for spring admission, 10/1 for domestic students. *Financial support:* Teaching assistantships, career-related internships or fieldwork, Federal Work-Study, scholarships/grants, and tuition waivers (partial) available. Support available to part-time students. Financial award application deadline: 4/15. *Faculty research:* Islamic art, Renaissance and Baroque, Impressionism, critical theory, Modernism. *Application contact:* William Zlata, Director for Graduate Admissions, 212-772-4482, Fax: 212-650-3336, E-mail: admissions@hunter.cuny.edu.
Website: http://www.hunter.cuny.edu/art/art-history/ma-program

**Illinois State University,** Graduate School, College of Fine Arts, School of Art, Normal, IL 61790-2200. Offers art history (MA, MS); ceramics (MFA, MS); drawing (MFA, MS); fibers (MFA, MS); glass (MFA, MS); graphic design (MFA, MS); metals (MFA, MS); painting (MFA, MS); photography (MFA, MS); printmaking (MFA, MS); sculpture (MFA, MS). *Accreditation:* NASAD (one or more programs are accredited). *Degree requirements:* For master's, thesis or alternative, internship. *Entrance requirements:* For master's, portfolio, sample of scholarly writing.

**James Madison University,** The Graduate School, College of Visual and Performing Arts, School of Art, Design and Art History, Harrisonburg, VA 22802. Offers art education (MA); studio art (MA, MFA), including ceramics (MFA), drawing/painting (MFA), intermedia (MFA), metal/jewelry (MFA), photography (MFA), sculpture (MFA). *Accreditation:* NASAD. *Program availability:* Part-time. *Faculty:* 25 full-time (15 women). *Students:* 10 full-time (6 women), 1 (woman) part-time, 1 international. Average age 30. 18 applicants, 39% accepted, 6 enrolled. In 2016, 6 master's awarded. Application fee: $55. Electronic applications accepted. *Financial support:* In 2016–17, 10 students received support, including 3 teaching assistantships with full tuition reimbursements available (averaging $9,284 per year); Federal Work-Study and 7 assistantships (averaging $7911) also available. Financial award application deadline: 3/1; financial award applicants required to submit FAFSA. *Unit head:* Dr. Kathy A. Schwartz, Director of School of Art, Design and Art History, 540-568-6216, E-mail: schwarka@jmu.edu. *Application contact:* Lynette D. Michael, Director of Graduate Student Admissions, 540-568-6131 Ext. 6395, Fax: 540-568-7860, E-mail: michaeld@jmu.edu.
Website: http://www.jmu.edu/artandarthistory/

**Johns Hopkins University,** Zanvyl Krieger School of Arts and Sciences, Department of History of Art, Baltimore, MD 21218. Offers MA, PhD. Terminal master's awarded for partial completion of doctoral program. *Degree requirements:* For master's, 2 foreign languages; for doctorate, 2 foreign languages, thesis/dissertation. *Entrance requirements:* For master's and doctorate, GRE General Test. Additional exam requirements/recommendations for international students: Required—TOEFL (minimum score 600 paper-based; 100 iBT), IELTS. Electronic applications accepted. *Faculty research:* Modern art, Renaissance art, medieval art, Roman art.

**Kent State University,** College of the Arts, School of Art, Kent, OH 44242-0001. Offers art education (MA); art history (MA); crafts (MA, MFA), including glass; fine arts (MA, MFA), including fashion (MA). *Accreditation:* NASAD (one or more programs are accredited). *Program availability:* Part-time, online learning. *Faculty:* 23 full-time (15 women). *Students:* 51 full-time (23 women), 167 part-time (120 women); includes 18 minority (8 Black or African American, non-Hispanic/Latino; 1 American Indian or Alaska Native, non-Hispanic/Latino; 1 Asian, non-Hispanic/Latino; 4 Hispanic/Latino; 1 Native Hawaiian or other Pacific Islander, non-Hispanic/Latino; 3 Two or more races, non-Hispanic/Latino), 25 international. Average age 31. 57 applicants, 53% accepted, 21 enrolled. In 2016, 30 master's awarded. *Degree requirements:* For master's, comprehensive exam, thesis (for some programs), 1 foreign language (for art history); final project (for crafts and fine arts). *Entrance requirements:* For master's, transcripts, goal statement, 3 letters of recommendation, curriculum vitae, portfolio. Additional exam requirements/recommendations for international students: Required—TOEFL (minimum score of 575 paper-based, 90 iBT), IELTS (minimum score of 7.0), Michigan English Language Assessment Battery (minimum score of 85), or PTE (minimum score of 68). *Application deadline:* For fall admission, 2/2 for domestic and international students; for spring admission, 10/15 for domestic and international students. Applications are processed on a rolling basis. Application fee: $45 ($70 for international students). Electronic applications accepted. *Expenses:* Tuition, state resident: full-time $10,864; part-time $495 per credit hour. Tuition, nonresident: full-time $18,380; part-time $837 per credit hour. *Financial support:* Career-related internships or fieldwork, scholarships/grants, and unspecified assistantships available. Financial award application deadline: 2/2. *Unit head:* Michael J. Loderstedt, Interim Director/Professor, Print Media and Photography, 330-672-2192, E-mail: mloderst@kent.edu. *Application contact:* Linda Hoeptner Poling, Graduate Coordinator and Associate Professor of Art Education, 330-672-7895, E-mail: lhoeptne@kent.edu.
Website: http://www.kent.edu/art

**Lancaster Theological Seminary,** Graduate and Professional Programs, Lancaster, PA 17603-2812. Offers biblical studies (MAR); Christian education (MAR); Christianity and the arts (MAR); church history (MAR); congregational life (MAR); lay leadership (Certificate); theological studies (M Div); theology (D Min); theology and ethics (MAR). *Accreditation:* ACIPE; ATS. *Degree requirements:* For doctorate, thesis/dissertation.

**Louisiana State University and Agricultural & Mechanical College,** Graduate School, College of Art and Design, School of Art, Program in Art History, Baton Rouge, LA 70803. Offers MA. *Accreditation:* NASAD.

**Massachusetts Institute of Technology,** School of Architecture and Planning, Department of Architecture, Cambridge, MA 02139. Offers architecture (M Arch, PhD), including building technology (PhD), design and computation (PhD), history and theory of architecture (PhD), history and theory of art (PhD); architecture studies (SM Arch S); art, culture and technology (SMACT); building technology (SMBT). *Faculty:* 36 full-time (13 women). *Students:* 224 full-time (106 women); includes 46 minority (5 Black or African American, non-Hispanic/Latino; 11 Asian, non-Hispanic/Latino; 22 Hispanic/Latino; 8 Two or more races, non-Hispanic/Latino), 113 international. Average age 28. 1,165 applicants, 12% accepted, 82 enrolled. In 2016, 58 master's, 10 doctorates awarded. *Degree requirements:* For master's, thesis; for doctorate, comprehensive exam, thesis/dissertation. *Entrance requirements:* For master's and doctorate, GRE General Test. Additional exam requirements/recommendations for international students: Required—TOEFL, IELTS. *Application deadline:* For fall admission, 12/31 for domestic and international students. Application fee: $75. Electronic applications accepted. *Expenses:* Tuition: Full-time $46,400; part-time $725 per credit. One-time fee: $312 full-time. Full-time tuition and fees vary according to course load and program. *Financial support:* In 2016–17, 189 students received support, including 128 fellowships (averaging $23,600 per year), 31 research assistantships (averaging $33,200 per year), 34 teaching assistantships (averaging $34,700 per year); Federal Work-Study, institutionally sponsored loans, scholarships/grants, traineeships, health care benefits, unspecified assistantships, and resident tutors also available. Support available to part-time students. Financial award application deadline: 5/1; financial award applicants required to submit FAFSA. *Faculty research:* Architecture; urbanism; building technology and sustainability; computation and design; history, theory, and criticism; art, culture, and technology. *Total annual research expenditures:* $3.5 million. *Unit head:* Prof. J. Meejin Yoon, Department Head, 617-253-7791, E-mail: arch@mit.edu. *Application contact:* 617-715-4490.
Website: http://architecture.mit.edu/

**McGill University,** Faculty of Graduate and Postdoctoral Studies, Faculty of Arts, Department of Art History and Communication Studies, Montréal, QC H3A 2T5, Canada. Offers MA, PhD.

**Montana State University,** The Graduate School, College of Arts and Architecture, School of Art, Bozeman, MT 59717. Offers art (MFA); art history (MA). *Accreditation:* NASAD (one or more programs are accredited). *Program availability:* Part-time. *Degree requirements:* For master's, comprehensive exam, thesis. *Entrance requirements:* For master's, GRE General Test, undergraduate degree in art. Additional exam requirements/recommendations for international students: Required—TOEFL (minimum score 550 paper-based). Electronic applications accepted. *Faculty research:* Encaustic painting, wild clay research, environmentally friendly kiln fuel, Roman wall paintings, French revolutionary portraiture.

**New Mexico State University,** College of Arts and Sciences, Department of Art, Las Cruces, NM 88003. Offers art history (MA); studio art (MFA). *Program availability:* Part-time. *Faculty:* 10 full-time (7 women). *Students:* 14 full-time (8 women), 2 part-time (both women); includes 7 minority (1 Black or African American, non-Hispanic/Latino; 6 Hispanic/Latino), 1 international. Average age 33. 14 applicants, 57% accepted, 3 enrolled. In 2016, 4 master's awarded. *Degree requirements:* For master's, one foreign language, comprehensive exam (for some programs), thesis, thesis exhibit. *Entrance requirements:* For master's, portfolio (for MFA); 10-20 page paper (for MA). Additional exam requirements/recommendations for international students: Required—TOEFL (minimum score 550 paper-based; 79 iBT), IELTS (minimum score 6.5). *Application deadline:* For fall admission, 1/20 for domestic students; for spring admission, 11/15 for domestic students. Application fee: $40 ($50 for international students). Electronic applications accepted. *Expenses:* Tuition, state resident: full-time $4086. Tuition, nonresident: full-time $14,254. *Required fees:* $853. Tuition and fees vary according to course load. *Financial support:* In 2016–17, 14 students received support, including 2 fellowships (averaging $4,088 per year), 13 teaching assistantships (averaging $15,105 per year); career-related internships or fieldwork, Federal Work-Study, scholarships/grants, traineeships, health care benefits, and unspecified assistantships also available. Support available to part-time students. Financial award application deadline: 3/1. *Faculty research:* Art history, painting, graphic design, sculpture, ceramics, photography. *Total annual research expenditures:* $3,118. *Unit head:* Dr. Julia Barello, Department Head, 575-646-1705, Fax: 575-646-8036, E-mail: jbarello@nmsu.edu. *Application contact:* 575-646-1705, Fax: 575-646-8036, E-mail: artdept@nmsu.edu.
Website: http://artdepartment.nmsu.edu/

**New York University,** Graduate School of Arts and Science, Institute of Fine Arts, Program in Art History and Archaeology, New York, NY 10012-1019. Offers architectural studies (PhD); art history and archaeology (MA, PhD); classical art and archaeology (PhD); curatorial studies (PhD); East and South Asian art (PhD); Near Eastern art and archaeology (PhD); MA/Diploma; PhD/Certificate. *Program availability:* Part-time. Terminal master's awarded for partial completion of doctoral program. *Degree requirements:* For master's, 2 foreign languages, thesis or alternative, 2 qualifying papers; for doctorate, 2 foreign languages, thesis/dissertation. *Entrance requirements:* For master's, GRE General Test; for doctorate, GRE General Test, MA. Additional exam requirements/recommendations for international students: Required—TOEFL.

**Northwestern University,** The Graduate School, Judd A. and Marjorie Weinberg College of Arts and Sciences, Department of Art History, Evanston, IL 60208. Offers PhD. Admissions and degrees offered through The Graduate School. *Degree requirements:* For doctorate, 2 foreign languages, comprehensive exam, thesis/dissertation, major and minor field exercises. *Entrance requirements:* For doctorate, GRE General Test. Additional exam requirements/recommendations for international students: Required—TOEFL. Electronic applications accepted. *Faculty research:* Modern American and European art and architecture, prehistoric and ancient art, central Asian art, medieval manuscripts and early printed books, history of museums, art of Western Africa, theory of culture.

**The Ohio State University,** Graduate School, College of Arts and Sciences, Division of Arts and Humanities, Department of History of Art, Columbus, OH 43210. Offers MA, PhD. *Accreditation:* NASAD. *Faculty:* 13. *Students:* 29 full-time (25 women), 3 part-time (all women), 8 international. Average age 33. In 2016, 4 master's, 5 doctorates awarded. Terminal master's awarded for partial completion of doctoral program. *Degree requirements:* For master's, one foreign language, thesis optional; for doctorate, 2 foreign languages, thesis/dissertation. *Entrance requirements:* For master's and doctorate, GRE General Test. Additional exam requirements/recommendations for international students: Required—TOEFL (minimum score 550 paper-based; 79 iBT), Michigan English Language Assessment Battery (minimum score 82); Recommended—

IELTS (minimum score 7). *Application deadline:* For fall admission, 12/1 priority date for domestic and international students; for winter admission, 12/1 for domestic students, 11/1 for international students; for spring admission, 3/1 for domestic students, 2/1 for international students. Applications are processed on a rolling basis. Application fee: $60 ($70 for international students). Electronic applications accepted. *Financial support:* Fellowships with tuition reimbursements, teaching assistantships with tuition reimbursements, Federal Work-Study, and institutionally sponsored loans available. Support available to part-time students. *Faculty research:* Western and Oriental art, African art and archaeology. *Unit head:* Dr. Lisa Florman, Chair and Professor, 614-292-7481, E-mail: florman.4@osu.edu. *Application contact:* Graduate and Professional Admissions, 614-292-9444, Fax: 614-292-3895, E-mail: gpadmissions@osu.edu. Website: http://history-of-art.osu.edu/

**Ohio University,** Graduate College, College of Fine Arts, School of Art, Athens, OH 45701-2979. Offers art history (MA); ceramics (MFA); graphic design (MFA); painting (MFA); photography (MFA); printmaking (MFA); sculpture (MFA). *Program availability:* Part-time. *Degree requirements:* For master's, thesis. *Entrance requirements:* For master's, portfolio. Additional exam requirements/recommendations for international students: Required—TOEFL (minimum score 550 paper-based; 80 iBT) or IELTS (minimum score 6.5). *Application deadline:* For fall admission, 2/1 for domestic and international students. Application fee: $50 ($55 for international students). Electronic applications accepted. *Financial support:* Teaching assistantships with full and partial tuition reimbursements, career-related internships or fieldwork, Federal Work-Study, institutionally sponsored loans, scholarships/grants, tuition waivers (partial), and unspecified assistantships available. Financial award application deadline: 2/1. *Faculty research:* Vapor-fired ceramics, video installation, art theory, digital photography, mixed and interdisciplinary media work. *Unit head:* David LaPalombara, Director, 740-593-4290, Fax: 740-593-0457, E-mail: lapalomb@ohio.edu. *Application contact:* Alexandra Hibbitt, Chair, Graduate Programs, 740-593-4293, Fax: 740-593-0457, E-mail: hibbitt@ohio.edu. Website: http://www.finearts.ohio.edu/art/

**Oklahoma State University,** College of Arts and Sciences, Department of Art, Graphic Design and Art History, Stillwater, OK 74078. Offers art history (MA); graphic design (MA). *Faculty:* 22 full-time (13 women), 4 part-time/adjunct (0 women). *Students:* 9 full-time (6 women), 2 part-time (1 woman); includes 3 minority (1 American Indian or Alaska Native, non-Hispanic/Latino; 2 Hispanic/Latino), 1 international. Average age 28. 20 applicants, 50% accepted, 6 enrolled. *Entrance requirements:* Additional exam requirements/recommendations for international students: Required—TOEFL. *Application deadline:* For fall admission, 3/1 for domestic students; for spring admission, 8/1 for domestic students. Application fee: $40 ($75 for international students). Electronic applications accepted. *Expenses:* Tuition, state resident: full-time $3775; part-time $209.70 per credit hour. Tuition, nonresident: full-time $14,851; part-time $825.05 per credit hour. *Required fees:* $2027; $112.60 per credit hour. Tuition and fees vary according to campus/location. *Financial support:* In 2016–17, 9 research assistantships (averaging $12,768 per year), 2 teaching assistantships (averaging $5,741 per year) were awarded. Financial award applicants required to submit FAFSA. *Unit head:* Dr. Rebecca Brienen, Head, E-mail: rebecca.brienen@okstate.edu. Website: http://art.okstate.edu/

**Penn State University Park,** Graduate School, College of Arts and Architecture, Department of Art History, University Park, PA 16802. Offers MA, PhD. *Unit head:* Dr. Barbara O. Korner, Dean, 814-865-2592, Fax: 814-865-2018. *Application contact:* Lori Hawn, Director, Graduate Student Services, 814-865-1795, Fax: 814-863-4627, E-mail: l-gswww@lists.psu.edu. Website: http://arthistory.psu.edu/

**Pratt Institute,** School of Liberal Arts and Sciences, History of Art and Design Program, Brooklyn, NY 11205-3899. Offers MS, MS/MFA, MS/MS. *Accreditation:* NASAD. *Program availability:* Part-time. *Faculty:* 7 full-time (6 women), 35 part-time/adjunct (22 women). *Students:* 34 full-time (31 women), 1 (woman) part-time; includes 7 minority (1 American Indian or Alaska Native, non-Hispanic/Latino; 1 Asian, non-Hispanic/Latino; 3 Hispanic/Latino; 2 Two or more races, non-Hispanic/Latino), 4 international. Average age 27. 30 applicants, 83% accepted, 6 enrolled. In 2016, 17 master's awarded. *Degree requirements:* For master's, one foreign language, thesis. *Entrance requirements:* For master's, GRE General Test, letters of recommendation, writing sample, portfolio. Additional exam requirements/recommendations for international students: Required—TOEFL (minimum score 600 paper-based; 100 iBT). *Application deadline:* For fall admission, 1/5 for domestic and international students; for spring admission, 10/1 for domestic and international students. Application fee: $50 ($90 for international students). Electronic applications accepted. *Expenses:* $29,646 full-time tuition, $1,938 fees. *Financial support:* Career-related internships or fieldwork, Federal Work-Study, institutionally sponsored loans, scholarships/grants, health care benefits, and unspecified assistantships available. Support available to part-time students. Financial award application deadline: 2/1; financial award applicants required to submit CSS PROFILE or FAFSA. *Faculty research:* Conservation techniques, women artists from previous centuries, art of sixteenth-century Veneto, design history, nineteenth-century Germany. *Unit head:* Gayle Rodda Kurtz, Chairperson, 718-636-3532, Fax: 718-687-5925, E-mail: gkurtz@pratt.edu. *Application contact:* Natalie Capannelli, Director of Graduate Admissions, 718-636-3551, Fax: 718-399-4242, E-mail: ncapanne@pratt.edu. Website: https://www.pratt.edu/academics/liberal-arts-and-sciences/history-of-art-design-grad/

**See Display on page 156 and Close-Up on page 209.**

**Purchase College, State University of New York,** School of Humanities, Purchase, NY 10577-1400. Offers art history (MA). *Accreditation:* NASAD. *Degree requirements:* For master's, one foreign language, thesis. *Entrance requirements:* For master's, BA or BFA, previous course work in art history, three letters of recommendation, personal statement, 1-2 writing samples, official transcripts. Additional exam requirements/ recommendations for international students: Required—TOEFL or IELTS. *Application deadline:* For fall admission, 3/1 for domestic students. Application fee: $80. Electronic applications accepted. *Expenses:* Tuition, state resident: full-time $10,870; part-time $453 per credit. Tuition, nonresident: full-time $22,210; part-time $925 per credit. *Required fees:* $1737. *Financial support:* Fellowships, Federal Work-Study, scholarships/grants, and tuition waivers (partial) available. Support available to part-time students. Financial award application deadline: 3/15; financial award applicants required to submit FAFSA. *Unit head:* Ross Daly, Chair, 914-251-6550. *Application contact:* Sabrina Johnston, Admissions Counselor, 914-251-6479, Fax: 914-251-6314, E-mail: admissn@purchase.edu. Website: https://www.purchase.edu/academics/school-of-humanities/

**Queens College of the City University of New York,** Arts and Humanities Division, Department of Art, Queens, NY 11367-1597. Offers art history (MA); studio art (MFA). *Program availability:* Part-time. *Faculty:* 18 full-time (6 women), 56 part-time/adjunct (32 women). *Students:* 15 full-time (8 women), 25 part-time (21 women); includes 11 minority (5 Black or African American, non-Hispanic/Latino; 2 Asian, non-Hispanic/Latino; 4 Hispanic/Latino), 5 international. Average age 36. 25 applicants, 44% accepted, 8 enrolled. In 2016, 11 master's awarded. *Degree requirements:* For master's,

thesis, comprehensive exam (for art history program). *Entrance requirements:* For master's, minimum GPA of 3.0. Additional exam requirements/recommendations for international students: Required—TOEFL, IELTS. *Application deadline:* For fall admission, 4/1 for domestic students; for spring admission, 11/1 for domestic students. Applications are processed on a rolling basis. Application fee: $125. Electronic applications accepted. *Expenses:* Tuition, state resident: full-time $5065; part-time $425 per credit. Tuition, nonresident: part-time $780 per credit. *Required fees:* $522; $397 per credit. Part-time tuition and fees vary according to course load and program. *Financial support:* Career-related internships or fieldwork available. Financial award application deadline: 4/1; financial award applicants required to submit FAFSA. *Unit head:* Dr. Antonio Gonzalez, Chairperson, 718-997-4800, E-mail: antonio.gonzalez@qc.cuny.edu.

**Rice University,** Graduate Programs, School of Humanities, Department of Art History, Houston, TX 77251-1892. Offers PhD.

**Richmond, The American International University in London,** MA in Art History Program, Richmond, United Kingdom. Offers MA. *Program availability:* Part-time. *Degree requirements:* For master's, thesis. *Entrance requirements:* For master's, minimum GPA of 3.0. Additional exam requirements/recommendations for international students: Required—TOEFL, IELTS. Electronic applications accepted. *Expenses:* Contact institution. *Faculty research:* Archaeology of art and representation, contemporary paganisms, nineteenth century modernisms, American twentieth century art, sound media.

**Roger Williams University,** School of Architecture, Art and Historic Preservation, Bristol, RI 02809. Offers architecture (M Arch); art and architectural history (MA); historical preservation (MS). *Faculty:* 15 full-time (4 women), 4 part-time/adjunct (2 women). *Students:* 100 full-time (43 women), 1 part-time (0 women); includes 14 minority (3 Black or African American, non-Hispanic/Latino; 1 Asian, non-Hispanic/Latino; 6 Hispanic/Latino; 4 Two or more races, non-Hispanic/Latino), 4 international. Average age 25. 77 applicants, 95% accepted, 48 enrolled. In 2016, 43 master's awarded. *Degree requirements:* For master's, thesis. *Entrance requirements:* For master's, portfolio, 2 letters of recommendation, college transcript, letter of intent. Additional exam requirements/recommendations for international students: Required—TOEFL (minimum score 85 iBT), IELTS (minimum score 6.5). *Application deadline:* For fall admission, 4/1 for domestic students; for spring admission, 1/1 for domestic students. Application fee: $50. Electronic applications accepted. Application fee is waived when completed online. *Expenses:* $1,408 per credit hour (for M Arch); $843 per credit hour (for MS and MA). *Financial support:* In 2016–17, 95 students received support, including 91 research assistantships (averaging $2,753 per year); scholarships/grants and unspecified assistantships also available. Financial award application deadline: 4/1; financial award applicants required to submit FAFSA. *Unit head:* Stephen White, Dean, 401-254-3607, E-mail: swhite@rwu.edu. *Application contact:* Marcus Hanscom, Director of Graduate Admissions, 401-254-6200, Fax: 401-254-3345, E-mail: gradadmit@rwu.edu. Website: http://www.rwu.edu/academics/departments/architecture.htm#dual

**Rutgers University–New Brunswick,** Graduate School-New Brunswick, Program in Art History, Piscataway, NJ 08854-8097. Offers art history (MA, PhD); curatorial studies (Certificate); historic preservation (Certificate). *Program availability:* Part-time. Terminal master's awarded for partial completion of doctoral program. *Degree requirements:* For master's, one foreign language, comprehensive exam; for doctorate, 2 foreign languages, comprehensive exam, thesis/dissertation. *Entrance requirements:* For master's and doctorate, GRE General Test, writing sample. Additional exam requirements/recommendations for international students: Required—TOEFL (minimum score 550 paper-based). Electronic applications accepted. *Faculty research:* Ancient and medieval art and architecture; Renaissance and Baroque art and architecture; modern and contemporary art and architecture; Italian studies; the arts of Asia, Africa, and the Americas.

**San Diego State University,** Graduate and Research Affairs, College of Professional Studies and Fine Arts, School of Art, Design and Art History, San Diego, CA 92182. Offers art history (MA); studio arts (MA, MFA), including applied design, environmental design, graphic design, interior design, painting and printmaking, sculpture. *Accreditation:* NASAD (one or more programs are accredited). *Degree requirements:* For master's, variable foreign language requirement, thesis. *Entrance requirements:* For master's, GRE General Test, bachelor's degree in related field, slide portfolio, typed slide information sheet, 2 letters of recommendation. Additional exam requirements/recommendations for international students: Required—TOEFL. Electronic applications accepted.

**San Francisco Art Institute,** Master of Arts Programs, San Francisco, CA 94133. Offers exhibition and museum studies (MA); history and theory of contemporary art (MA). *Faculty:* 3 full-time (all women), 12 part-time/adjunct (7 women). *Students:* 6 full-time (all women), 3 part-time (all women); includes 1 minority (Asian, non-Hispanic/Latino), 3 international. Average age 27. 20 applicants, 60% accepted, 5 enrolled. In 2016, 9 master's awarded. *Degree requirements:* For master's, thesis. *Entrance requirements:* For master's, statement of purpose, writing samples. Additional exam requirements/recommendations for international students: Required—TOEFL (minimum score 600 paper-based; 100 iBT), IELTS (minimum score 7.5). *Application deadline:* Applications are processed on a rolling basis. Application fee: $85. Electronic applications accepted. *Expenses:* Full-time $46,010; part-time $2020 per credit. *Required fees:* $870; $870 per credit. *Financial support:* Fellowships, teaching assistantships, career-related internships or fieldwork, Federal Work-Study, scholarships/grants, and unspecified assistantships available. Support available to part-time students. Financial award application deadline: 3/1; financial award applicants required to submit FAFSA. *Unit head:* Claire Daigle, Chair, Master of Arts Department, 415-351-3573, Fax: 415-641-1205, E-mail: cdaigle@sfai.edu. *Application contact:* Jana Rumberger, Director of Graduate Admissions, 415-351-3507, Fax: 415-749-4592, E-mail: jrumberger@sfai.edu. Website: http://www.sfai.edu/degree-programs/graduate/ma

**San Francisco State University,** Division of Graduate Studies, College of Liberal and Creative Arts, School of Art, San Francisco, CA 94132-1722. Offers art (MFA); art history (MA). *Accreditation:* NASAD (one or more programs are accredited). *Expenses:* Tuition, state resident: full-time $6738. Tuition, nonresident: full-time $15,666. *Required fees:* $1012. Tuition and fees vary according to degree level and program. *Unit head:* Gail Dawson, Director, 415-338-2176, Fax: 415-338-6537, E-mail: gdawson@sfsu.edu. *Application contact:* Prof. Susan Belau, Associate Professor and Graduate Coordinator, 415-338-1591, Fax: 415-338-6537, E-mail: sbelau@sfsu.edu. Website: http://www.art.sfsu.edu

**San Jose State University,** Graduate Studies and Research, College of Humanities and the Arts, San Jose, CA 95192-0001. Offers art (MA, MFA), including art history and visual culture (MA), digital media art (MFA), photography (MFA), pictorial art (MFA), spatial art (MFA); computational linguistics (Certificate); English (MA, MFA), including creative writing (MFA); French (MA); humanities and arts (Certificate); linguistics (MA); music (MA); philosophy (MA); professional and technical communication (Certificate);

## Art History

Spanish (MA); teaching English to speakers of other languages (MA); TESOL (Certificate); theatre arts (MA). Electronic applications accepted.

**Savannah College of Art and Design,** Graduate School, Program in Art History, Savannah, GA 31402-3146. Offers MA. *Program availability:* Part-time. *Faculty:* 39 full-time (24 women), 7 part-time/adjunct (5 women). *Students:* 5 full-time (4 women), 5 part-time (all women); includes 1 minority (Black or African American, non-Hispanic/Latino). Average age 31. 22 applicants, 32% accepted, 3 enrolled. In 2016, 6 master's awarded. *Degree requirements:* For master's, one foreign language, comprehensive exam, thesis. *Entrance requirements:* For master's, GRE (recommended), portfolio (submitted in digital format), audition or writing submission, resume, statement of purpose, two letters of recommendation. Additional exam requirements/recommendations for international students: Required—TOEFL (minimum score 550 paper-based, 85 iBT), IELTS (minimum score 6.5), or ACTFL. *Application deadline:* For fall admission, 4/1 for domestic and international students. Applications are processed on a rolling basis. Application fee: $40. Electronic applications accepted. *Expenses: Tuition:* Full-time $36,045. Tuition and fees vary according to course load. *Financial support:* Career-related internships or fieldwork, Federal Work-Study, and scholarships/grants available. Financial award application deadline: 4/1; financial award applicants required to submit FAFSA. *Faculty research:* Contemporary art. *Unit head:* Dr. Geoffrey Taylor, Chair, Art History. *Application contact:* Jenny Jaquillard, Executive Director of Admissions, Recruitment and Events, 912-525-5100, Fax: 912-525-5985, E-mail: admission@scad.edu.
Website: http://www.scad.edu/academics/programs/art-history

**School of the Art Institute of Chicago,** Graduate Division, Program in Modern Art History, Theory, and Criticism, Chicago, IL 60603-3103. Offers MA. *Accreditation:* NASAD. *Entrance requirements:* For master's, GRE. Additional exam requirements/recommendations for international students: Required—TOEFL, IELTS.

**School of Visual Arts,** Graduate Programs, Program in Curatorial Practice, New York, NY 10010-3994. Offers MA.

**Southern Methodist University,** Meadows School of the Arts, Division of Art History, Dallas, TX 75275. Offers art history (MA); rhetorics of art, space and culture (PhD). *Program availability:* Part-time, evening/weekend. *Degree requirements:* For master's, one foreign language, thesis, translation exam. *Entrance requirements:* For master's, GRE, 12 upper-level hours in art history, sample research paper. Additional exam requirements/recommendations for international students: Required—TOEFL (minimum score 550 paper-based; 80 iBT). *Faculty research:* American art, nineteenth- and twentieth-century art, classical and Byzantine art, Hispanic art, Mesoamerican art, Renaissance-Baroque.

**Stony Brook University, State University of New York,** Graduate School, College of Arts and Sciences, Department of Art, Program in Art History and Criticism, Stony Brook, NY 11794. Offers MA, PhD. *Program availability:* Part-time. *Students:* 40 full-time (28 women); includes 7 minority (1 American Indian or Alaska Native, non-Hispanic/Latino; 3 Asian, non-Hispanic/Latino; 2 Hispanic/Latino; 1 Two or more races, non-Hispanic/Latino), 5 international. Average age 30. 39 applicants, 67% accepted, 10 enrolled. In 2016, 4 master's, 1 doctorate awarded. *Degree requirements:* For master's, comprehensive exam, thesis, reading knowledge of German or French; for doctorate, comprehensive exam, thesis/dissertation, qualifying paper, reading knowledge of German and French, qualifying examination. *Entrance requirements:* For master's, GRE General Test, minimum undergraduate GPA of 3.0; for doctorate, GRE General Test, minimum graduate GPA of 3.0. Additional exam requirements/recommendations for international students: Required—TOEFL (minimum score 550 paper-based), IELTS (minimum score 6.5). *Application deadline:* For fall admission, 1/15 for domestic students; for spring admission, 10/1 for domestic students. Application fee: $100. *Expenses:* Contact institution. *Financial support:* Fellowships, research assistantships, and teaching assistantships available. Financial award applicants required to submit FAFSA. *Unit head:* Dr. Barbara Frank, Director, 631-632-4250, E-mail: barbara.frank@stonybrook.edu. *Application contact:* Lisa Perez, Coordinator, 631-632-7270, E-mail: lisa.a.perez@stonybrook.edu.
Website: http://art.stonybrook.edu/graduate-programs/maph-d-programs/

**Sul Ross State University,** College of Arts and Sciences, Department of Fine Arts and Communication, Alpine, TX 79832. Offers art history (MA); studio art (MA), including art education. *Program availability:* Part-time. *Degree requirements:* For master's, oral or written exam. *Entrance requirements:* For master's, GRE General Test, minimum GPA of 2.5 in last 60 hours of undergraduate work. *Faculty research:* Ceramic sculpture, watercolor, wood sculpture, rock art.

**Syracuse University,** College of Arts and Sciences, MA Program in Art History, Syracuse, NY 13244. Offers MA. *Students:* Average age 27. *Degree requirements:* For master's, one foreign language, symposium presentation. *Entrance requirements:* For master's, GRE, competency exam in the history of art, bachelor's degree, normally as art history major, at accredited institution; academic transcripts of all undergraduate studies. Additional exam requirements/recommendations for international students: Required—TOEFL (minimum score 100 iBT). *Application deadline:* For fall admission, 1/1 for domestic and international students. Application fee: $75. Electronic applications accepted. *Expenses: Tuition:* Full-time $25,974; part-time $1443 per credit hour. *Required fees:* $802; $50 per course. Tuition and fees vary according to course load and program. *Financial support:* Fellowships with full tuition reimbursements, teaching assistantships with tuition reimbursements, career-related internships or fieldwork, and scholarships/grants available. Financial award application deadline: 1/1; financial award applicants required to submit FAFSA. *Faculty research:* Literature of art criticism, historical methodology, art and culture of various world traditions, cultural management, galleries and the art market. *Unit head:* Sascha Scott, Assistant Professor and Director of Graduate Studies for Art and Music Histories, 315-443-5033, E-mail: sscott04@syr.edu. *Application contact:* Maureen Verone, Administrative Assistant to the Chair, 315-443-4185, E-mail: mverone@syr.edu.
Website: http://amh.syr.edu/

**Temple University,** Tyler School of Art, Department of Art History, Philadelphia, PA 19122-6096. Offers MA, PhD. *Program availability:* Part-time. Terminal master's awarded for partial completion of doctoral program. *Degree requirements:* For master's, 2 foreign languages, thesis, comprehensive slide exam; for doctorate, 2 foreign languages, thesis/dissertation, qualifying exam. *Entrance requirements:* For master's, GRE General Test, minimum GPA of 3.0, letters of recommendation, resume/curriculum vitae, writing sample; for doctorate, GRE, MA in art history, minimum GPA of 3.0, letters of recommendation, resume/curriculum vitae, writing sample. Additional exam requirements/recommendations for international students: Required—TOEFL (minimum score 550 paper-based; 79 iBT), IELTS (minimum score 6.5). Electronic applications accepted. *Expenses:* Contact institution. *Faculty research:* Aegean, Greek, and Roman art; early Christian art; medieval art and architecture; Renaissance and Baroque painting, sculpture, and architecture; nineteenth- and twentieth-century painting and sculpture.

**Texas Christian University,** College of Fine Arts, School of Art, Fort Worth, TX 76129. Offers art history (MA); studio art (MFA), including painting, printmaking, sculpture. *Accreditation:* NASAD. *Faculty:* 12 full-time (5 women), 3 part-time/adjunct (2 women).

*Students:* 17 full-time (16 women), 1 (woman) part-time; includes 2 minority (both Hispanic/Latino), 2 international. Average age 30. 24 applicants, 46% accepted, 9 enrolled. In 2016, 7 master's awarded. *Degree requirements:* For master's, variable foreign language requirement, comprehensive exam, thesis. *Entrance requirements:* For master's, GRE General Test (for MA). Additional exam requirements/recommendations for international students: Required—TOEFL (minimum score 550 paper-based; 80 iBT). *Application deadline:* For fall admission, 2/1 for domestic and international students. Application fee: $60. Electronic applications accepted. *Expenses:* Contact institution. *Financial support:* In 2016–17, 18 students received support, including 17 teaching assistantships (averaging $10,000 per year); institutionally sponsored loans, scholarships/grants, health care benefits, tuition waivers (full and partial), and unspecified assistantships also available. Financial award application deadline: 4/15. *Unit head:* Dr. Sally Packard, Director, 817-257-7643, E-mail: s.packard@tcu.edu. *Application contact:* Donna Smolik, TCU College of Fine Arts Graduate Office, 817-257-7603, Fax: 817-257-5672, E-mail: cfagradinfo@tcu.edu.
Website: http://www.art.tcu.edu/

**Texas Tech University,** Graduate School, J.T. and Margaret Talkington College of Visual and Performing Arts, School of Art, Lubbock, TX 79409. Offers (MFA); art education (MAE); art history (MA). *Accreditation:* NASAD (one or more programs are accredited). *Program availability:* Part-time, online learning. *Faculty:* 32 full-time (14 women), 8 part-time/adjunct (5 women). *Students:* 36 full-time (23 women), 26 part-time (19 women); includes 15 minority (1 Black or African American, non-Hispanic/Latino; 6 Asian, non-Hispanic/Latino; 11 Hispanic/Latino; 2 Two or more races, non-Hispanic/Latino), 4 international. Average age 35. 39 applicants, 62% accepted, 19 enrolled. In 2016, 19 master's awarded. *Degree requirements:* For master's, variable foreign language requirement, comprehensive exam, thesis (for some programs), exhibition (for MFA). *Entrance requirements:* For master's, GRE (for MA). Additional exam requirements/recommendations for international students: Required—TOEFL (minimum score 550 paper-based; 79 iBT), IELTS (minimum score 6.5). *Application deadline:* For fall admission, 6/1 priority date for domestic students, 1/15 priority date for international students; for spring admission, 9/1 priority date for domestic students, 6/15 priority date for international students. Applications are processed on a rolling basis. Application fee: $75. Electronic applications accepted. *Expenses:* $325 per credit hour full-time resident tuition, $733 per credit hour full-time non-resident tuition; $53.75 per credit hour fee plus $608 per term fee. *Financial support:* In 2016–17, 60 students received support, including 57 fellowships (averaging $2,318 per year), 56 teaching assistantships (averaging $9,357 per year); research assistantships, Federal Work-Study, institutionally sponsored loans, scholarships/grants, health care benefits, tuition waivers (partial), and unspecified assistantships also available. Financial award application deadline: 2/15; financial award applicants required to submit FAFSA. *Faculty research:* Modern and contemporary art; contemporary Chicano/a art; transformation of multidisciplinary approach to printmaking; figurative painting and an intense interest in space as metaphor for community; working-class, sexuality and race issues; letter press posters; conceptual three dimensional concepts. *Total annual research expenditures:* $11,986. *Unit head:* Prof. Lydia Thompson, Director and Professor, 806-742-3825 Ext. 255, E-mail: lydia.thompson@ttu.edu. *Application contact:* Linda Rumbelow, Academic Advisor, 806-742-3825 Ext. 222, E-mail: linda.rumbelow@ttu.edu.
Website: http://www.art.ttu.edu

**Towson University,** Program in Professional Studies, Towson, MD 21252-0001. Offers art history (MA); individualized plan (MA). *Program availability:* Part-time, evening/weekend. *Students:* 10 full-time (6 women), 13 part-time (11 women); includes 5 minority (4 Black or African American, non-Hispanic/Latino; 1 Two or more races, non-Hispanic/Latino). *Degree requirements:* For master's, thesis optional. *Entrance requirements:* For master's, minimum GPA of 3.0, essay. *Application deadline:* Applications are processed on a rolling basis. Application fee: $45. Electronic applications accepted. *Expenses:* Tuition, state resident: full-time $7580; part-time $379 per unit. Tuition, nonresident: full-time $15,700; part-time $785 per unit. *Required fees:* $2480. *Financial support:* Application deadline: 4/1. *Unit head:* Dr. James Smith, Graduate Program Director, 410-704-4620, E-mail: jmsmith@towson.edu. *Application contact:* Coverley Beidleman, Assistant Director of Graduate Admissions, 410-704-2113, Fax: 410-704-3030, E-mail: grads@towson.edu.
Website: http://www.towson.edu/cla/departments/interdisciplinary/grad/professional/

**Tufts University,** Graduate School of Arts and Sciences, Department of Art and Art History, Medford, MA 02155. Offers art history (MA); art history and museum studies (MA). *Students:* 15 full-time (12 women); includes 3 minority (1 Black or African American, non-Hispanic/Latino; 1 Asian, non-Hispanic/Latino; 1 Hispanic/Latino). Average age 26. 66 applicants, 42% accepted, 7 enrolled. In 2016, 11 master's awarded. *Degree requirements:* For master's, one foreign language, thesis (for some programs). *Entrance requirements:* For master's, GRE General Test. Additional exam requirements/recommendations for international students: Required—TOEFL (minimum score 550 paper-based; 80 iBT), IELTS (minimum score 6.5). *Application deadline:* For fall admission, 1/15 for domestic and international students. Application fee: $85. Electronic applications accepted. *Expenses:* $49,982 full-time tuition (for MA). *Financial support:* In 2016–17, 14 students received support. Teaching assistantships, Federal Work-Study, scholarships/grants, tuition waivers (full and partial), and unspecified assistantships available. Financial award application deadline: 1/15. *Unit head:* Karen Overbey, Graduate Program Director, 617-627-3395. *Application contact:* Office of Graduate Admissions, 617-627-3395, E-mail: gradadmissions@tufts.edu.
Website: http://ase.tufts.edu/art/

**Tulane University,** School of Liberal Arts, Department of Art, New Orleans, LA 70118-5669. Offers history of art (MA); studio art (MFA). PhD held jointly with Roger Thayer Stone Center for Latin American Studies. *Degree requirements:* For master's, one foreign language, thesis. *Entrance requirements:* For master's, GRE General Test, minimum B average in undergraduate course work. Additional exam requirements/recommendations for international students: Required—TOEFL. Electronic applications accepted. *Expenses: Tuition:* Full-time $50,920; part-time $2829 per credit hour. *Required fees:* $2040; $44.50 per credit hour. $580 per term. Tuition and fees vary according to course load, degree level and program.

**Université de Montréal,** Faculty of Arts and Sciences, Department of Art History and Film Studies, Montréal, QC H3C 3J7, Canada. Offers art history (MA, PhD); film studies (MA, PhD). Programs offered jointly with Concordia University, Université Laval, and Université du Québec à Montréal. *Degree requirements:* For master's, thesis. Electronic applications accepted. *Faculty research:* Western art from the Middle Ages, classic and modern theory, modern and contemporary art, Canadian art.

**Université du Québec à Montréal,** Graduate Programs, Program in Art Studies, Montréal, QC H3C 3P8, Canada. Offers art history (PhD); art studies (MA); study and practices of the arts (PhD). *Program availability:* Part-time. *Degree requirements:* For master's, thesis; for doctorate, thesis/dissertation. *Entrance requirements:* For master's, appropriate bachelor's degree or equivalent, proficiency in French; for doctorate, appropriate master's degree or equivalent, proficiency in French.

**Université Laval,** Faculty of Letters, Department of History, Programs in Art History, Québec, QC G1K 7P4, Canada. Offers MA, PhD. PhD offered jointly with Concordia University, Université de Montréal, and Université du Québec à Montréal. Terminal

master's awarded for partial completion of doctoral program. *Degree requirements:* For master's, thesis; for doctorate, comprehensive exam, thesis/dissertation. *Entrance requirements:* For master's, English test (comprehension of written English), knowledge of French; for doctorate, English test (comprehension of written English), knowledge of French and English, knowledge of a third language. Electronic applications accepted.

**University at Buffalo, the State University of New York,** Graduate School, College of Arts and Sciences, Department of Art, Program in Visual Studies, Buffalo, NY 14260. Offers critical museum studies (MA); visual studies (MA, PhD). *Program availability:* Part-time. *Faculty:* 6 full-time (2 women). *Students:* 13 full-time (9 women), 3 international. Average age 27. 35 applicants, 31% accepted, 5 enrolled. *Degree requirements:* For master's, thesis, field exam; for doctorate, one foreign language, thesis/dissertation. *Entrance requirements:* Additional exam requirements/recommendations for international students: Required—TOEFL (minimum score 79 iBT). *Application deadline:* For fall admission, 2/1 priority date for domestic students; for spring admission, 10/15 priority date for domestic students. Applications are processed on a rolling basis. Application fee: $50. Electronic applications accepted. *Financial support:* In 2016–17, 6 teaching assistantships with full tuition reimbursements (averaging $8,400 per year) were awarded; career-related internships or fieldwork, Federal Work-Study, institutionally sponsored loans, tuition waivers (partial), and unspecified assistantships also available. Support available to part-time students. Financial award application deadline: 2/28; financial award applicants required to submit FAFSA. *Unit head:* Joan Linder, Chair, 716-645-0539, Fax: 716-645-6970, E-mail: joannder@buffalo.edu. *Application contact:* Dr. Jonathan Katz, 716-645-6878, Fax: 716-645-5978.
Website: http://art.buffalo.edu

**The University of Alabama,** Graduate School, College of Arts and Sciences, Department of Art and Art History, Tuscaloosa, AL 35487. Offers art history (MA); studio art (MA, MFA), including ceramics, painting, photography, printmaking, sculpture. *Accreditation:* NASAD. *Program availability:* Part-time. *Faculty:* 19 full-time (12 women), 1 part-time/adjunct (0 women). *Students:* 18 full-time (13 women), 4 part-time (3 women); includes 3 minority (1 Black or African American, non-Hispanic/Latino; 1 Asian, non-Hispanic/Latino; 1 Hispanic/Latino), 1 international. Average age 30. 17 applicants, 41% accepted, 5 enrolled. In 2016, 7 master's awarded. *Degree requirements:* For master's, one foreign language, comprehensive exam (for some programs), oral exam, thesis statement, exhibit (studio art), thesis (art history). *Entrance requirements:* For master's, GRE General Test or MAT (art history), minimum GPA of 3.0, BFA or equivalent (studio art). Additional exam requirements/recommendations for international students: Required—TOEFL (minimum score 550 paper-based). *Application deadline:* For fall admission, 3/15 for domestic and international students; for spring admission, 10/15 for domestic and international students. Applications are processed on a rolling basis. Application fee: $50 ($60 for international students). Electronic applications accepted. *Expenses:* Tuition, state resident: full-time $10,470. Tuition, nonresident: full-time $26,950. *Financial support:* In 2016–17, 8 students received support, including 2 fellowships with full tuition reimbursements available, 14 teaching assistantships with tuition reimbursements available (averaging $15,427 per year); career-related internships or fieldwork, institutionally sponsored loans, scholarships/grants, and unspecified assistantships also available. Financial award application deadline: 7/14. *Faculty research:* Nineteenth-century American, Medieval Europe, Baroque, twentieth-century, and African American Art History. *Unit head:* Jason Guynes, Chair, 205-348-9944, Fax: 205-348-0287, E-mail: jguynes@ua.edu. *Application contact:* Sarah Marshall, Graduate Coordinator, 205-348-1890, Fax: 205-348-5967, E-mail: smarsh@ua.edu.
Website: http://www.art.ua.edu/

**The University of Alabama at Birmingham,** College of Arts and Sciences, Program in Art History, Birmingham, AL 35294. Offers MA. Program offered jointly with The University of Alabama (Tuscaloosa). *Accreditation:* NASAD. *Program availability:* Part-time-only, evening/weekend. *Faculty:* 4 full-time (all women). *Students:* 4 full-time (3 women), 4 part-time (3 women); includes 1 minority (Two or more races, non-Hispanic/Latino), 2 international. Average age 29. 4 applicants, 50% accepted, 1 enrolled. In 2016, 4 master's awarded. Terminal master's awarded for partial completion of doctoral program. *Degree requirements:* For master's, one foreign language, comprehensive exam, thesis optional. *Entrance requirements:* For master's, GRE General Test, minimum GPA of 3.0. *Application deadline:* For fall admission, 4/1 for domestic students; for spring admission, 10/1 for domestic students. Applications are processed on a rolling basis. Electronic applications accepted. Full-time tuition and fees vary according to course load and program. *Financial support:* Research assistantships, Federal Work-Study, and tuition waivers (partial) available. Financial award application deadline: 5/1. *Faculty research:* Race and representation in American art; Hindu temple architecture; the evolving image of the artist in nineteenth-century France through the lens of the artist's studio; animation and realism in early Netherlandish painting; animals in art. *Unit head:* Dr. Cathleen Cummings, Graduate Advisor, 205-934-4941, E-mail: cathleen@uab.edu. *Application contact:* Susan Noblitt Banks, Director of Graduate School Operations, 205-934-8227, Fax: 205-934-8413, E-mail: gradschool@uab.edu.
Website: http://www.uab.edu/cas/art/areas-of-study/ma-art-history

**University of Alberta,** Faculty of Graduate Studies and Research, Department of Art and Design, Edmonton, AB T6G 2E1, Canada. Offers drawing (MFA); history of art, design, and visual culture (MA); industrial design (M Des); painting (MFA); printmaking (MFA); sculpture (MFA); visual communication design (M Des). *Degree requirements:* For master's, thesis. *Entrance requirements:* For master's, portfolio (MFA and MDES). Additional exam requirements/recommendations for international students: Required—TOEFL (minimum score 550 paper-based).

**The University of Arizona,** College of Fine Arts, School of Art, Program in Art History, Tucson, AZ 85721. Offers MA. *Accreditation:* NASAD. *Program availability:* Part-time. Terminal master's awarded for partial completion of doctoral program. *Degree requirements:* For master's, one foreign language, thesis. *Entrance requirements:* For master's, GRE, 3 letters of recommendation, resume or curriculum vitae, writing sample. Additional exam requirements/recommendations for international students: Required—TOEFL (minimum score 550 paper-based; 79 iBT). Electronic applications accepted. *Faculty research:* American art, history of photography, Mexican art, contemporary African art.

**The University of Arizona,** College of Fine Arts, School of Art, Program in Art History and Education, Tucson, AZ 85721. Offers PhD. *Degree requirements:* For doctorate, thesis/dissertation. *Entrance requirements:* Additional exam requirements/recommendations for international students: Required—TOEFL (minimum score 550 paper-based; 79 iBT). Electronic applications accepted.

**The University of Arizona,** College of Fine Arts, School of Art, Program in History and Theory of Art, Tucson, AZ 85721. Offers PhD. *Entrance requirements:* Additional exam requirements/recommendations for international students: Required—TOEFL (minimum score 550 paper-based; 79 iBT).

**University of Arkansas at Little Rock,** Graduate School, College of Arts, Letters, and Sciences, Department of Art, Little Rock, AR 72204-1099. Offers art education (MA); art history (MA); studio art (MA). *Accreditation:* NASAD. *Program availability:* Part-time.

*Degree requirements:* For master's, 4 foreign languages, oral exam, oral defense of thesis or exhibit. *Entrance requirements:* For master's, portfolio review or term paper evaluation, minimum GPA of 2.7.

**The University of British Columbia,** Faculty of Arts and Faculty of Graduate Studies, Department of Art History, Visual Art, and Theory, Vancouver, BC V6T 1Z2, Canada. Offers art history (MA, PhD); critical and curatorial studies (MA); visual art (MFA). *Degree requirements:* For master's, one foreign language, thesis, final exhibition (MFA, MA in critical and curatorial studies); for doctorate, 2 foreign languages, comprehensive exam, thesis/dissertation. *Entrance requirements:* For master's, bachelor's degree with minimum B+ average (MFA, MA in critical and curatorial studies), A- (MA in art history); for doctorate, master's degree with minimum A- average. Additional exam requirements/recommendations for international students: Required—TOEFL. Application fee: $100 Canadian dollars ($162 Canadian dollars for international students). Electronic applications accepted. *Expenses:* $4,802 per year tuition and fees, $8,436 per year international. *Financial support:* Fellowships, research assistantships, teaching assistantships, Federal Work-Study, scholarships/grants, health care benefits, tuition waivers (full), and unspecified assistantships available. *Faculty research:* Conceptual art, Asian art, indigenous North American art, post-second war art, eighteenth- and nineteenth-century art, curatorial, digital art. *Application contact:* Bryn Dharmaratne, Graduate Program Staff, 604-822-4340, Fax: 604-822-9003, E-mail: ahva.grad@ubc.ca.
Website: http://www.ahva.ubc.ca

**University of California, Berkeley,** Graduate Division, College of Letters and Science, Department of History of Art, Berkeley, CA 94720-1500. Offers PhD. *Students:* 39 full-time (28 women); includes 10 minority (1 Black or African American, non-Hispanic/Latino; 6 Asian, non-Hispanic/Latino; 3 Hispanic/Latino), 2 international. Average age 32. 156 applicants, 6 enrolled. In 2016, 7 doctorates awarded. *Degree requirements:* For doctorate, 2 foreign languages, thesis/dissertation, qualifying exam. *Entrance requirements:* For doctorate, GRE General Test, minimum GPA of 3.0, 3 letters of recommendation. Additional exam requirements/recommendations for international students: Required—TOEFL (minimum score 570 paper-based; 90 iBT). *Application deadline:* For fall admission, 12/1 for domestic students. Application fee: $105 ($125 for international students). Electronic applications accepted. *Financial support:* Fellowships, research assistantships, teaching assistantships, career-related internships or fieldwork, Federal Work-Study, institutionally sponsored loans, health care benefits, tuition waivers (full and partial), and unspecified assistantships available. Financial award applicants required to submit FAFSA. *Faculty research:* Modernism, Italian Renaissance art and architecture, Gothic art and architecture, women artists' representations of the body, the body in ancient Greece. *Unit head:* Prof. Bonnie Wade, Chair, 510-643-7290, Fax: 510-643-2185, E-mail: art_history@berkeley.edu. *Application contact:* Marcus Norman, 510-642-5510, Fax: 540-643-2185, E-mail: mdn@berkeley.edu.
Website: http://arthistory.berkeley.edu

**University of California, Davis,** Graduate Studies, Program in Art History, Davis, CA 95616. Offers MA. *Degree requirements:* For master's, thesis. *Entrance requirements:* For master's, GRE, minimum GPA of 3.0, writing sample. Additional exam requirements/recommendations for international students: Required—TOEFL (minimum score 550 paper-based). Electronic applications accepted.

**University of California, Los Angeles,** Graduate Division, College of Letters and Science, Department of Art History, Los Angeles, CA 90095. Offers MA, PhD. Terminal master's awarded for partial completion of doctoral program. *Degree requirements:* For master's, one foreign language, thesis; for doctorate, one foreign language, thesis/dissertation, oral and written qualifying exams. *Entrance requirements:* For doctorate, GRE General Test, master's degree; minimum undergraduate GPA of 3.0 (or its equivalent if letter grade system not used); thesis or research paper, language survey. Additional exam requirements/recommendations for international students: Required—TOEFL. Electronic applications accepted.

**University of California, Riverside,** Graduate Division, Department of Art History, Riverside, CA 92521-0102. Offers MA, PhD. *Program availability:* Part-time. *Degree requirements:* For master's, one foreign language, thesis. *Entrance requirements:* For master's, GRE General Test, sample of written work, minimum GPA of 3.2. Additional exam requirements/recommendations for international students: Required—TOEFL (minimum score 550 paper-based; 80 iBT). Electronic applications accepted. *Expenses:* Tuition, state resident: full-time $16,666. Tuition, nonresident: full-time $31,768. *Required fees:* $11,055.54 per quarter. $3685.18 per quarter. Tuition and fees vary according to campus/location and program. *Faculty research:* Ancient, medieval, Renaissance, seventeenth and eighteenth century art; modern European art; contemporary art and theory; modern architecture and urbanism; history of photography.

**University of California, San Diego,** Graduate Division, Department of Visual Arts, La Jolla, CA 92093. Offers art history, theory and criticism (PhD), including anthropogony, visual arts; visual arts (MFA). *Students:* 67 full-time (36 women). 159 applicants, 26% accepted, 20 enrolled. In 2016, 16 master's, 9 doctorates awarded. *Degree requirements:* For master's, comprehensive exam, thesis; for doctorate, 2 foreign languages, comprehensive exam, thesis/dissertation, reading knowledge of at least two of the foreign languages commonly used by scholars engaged in the advanced study in art history, theory, and criticism. *Entrance requirements:* For master's, electronic portfolio; for doctorate, GRE General Test, electronic portfolio. Additional exam requirements/recommendations for international students: Required—TOEFL (minimum score 550 paper-based; 80 iBT), IELTS (minimum score 7). *Application deadline:* For fall admission, 12/4 for domestic students. Application fee: $105 ($125 for international students). Electronic applications accepted. *Expenses:* Tuition, state resident: full-time $11,220. Tuition, nonresident: full-time $26,322. *Required fees:* $1864. *Financial support:* Fellowships, research assistantships, teaching assistantships, career-related internships or fieldwork, scholarships/grants, and readerships available. Financial award applicants required to submit FAFSA. *Faculty research:* Contemporary art, ancient art, critical design, new media/software/hardware. *Unit head:* Jack Greenstein, Chair, 858-534-0418, E-mail: jgreenstein@ucsd.edu. *Application contact:* Katherine Edwards, Graduate Program Coordinator, 858-822-3882, E-mail: vis-grad@ucsd.edu.
Website: http://visarts.ucsd.edu/

**University of California, Santa Barbara,** Graduate Division, College of Letters and Sciences, Division of Humanities and Fine Arts, Department of History of Art and Architecture, Santa Barbara, CA 93106-2014. Offers art history (PhD), including art history, European medieval studies, feminist studies; MA/PhD. Terminal master's awarded for partial completion of doctoral program. *Degree requirements:* For doctorate, 2 foreign languages, comprehensive exam, thesis/dissertation. *Entrance requirements:* For doctorate, GRE. Additional exam requirements/recommendations for international students: Required—TOEFL (minimum score 550 paper-based; 80 iBT), IELTS (minimum score 7). Electronic applications accepted. *Faculty research:* History of architecture, Renaissance-Italian, Baroque, American, Chinese, Japanese, contemporary, Northern Renaissance.

**University of Chicago,** Division of the Humanities, Department of Art History, Chicago, IL 60637. Offers PhD. *Students:* 54 full-time (41 women); includes 9 minority (2 Black or African American, non-Hispanic/Latino; 5 Asian, non-Hispanic/Latino; 2 Hispanic/

## Art History

Latino), 13 international. 128 applicants, 8% accepted, 7 enrolled. In 2016, 3 doctorates awarded. Terminal master's awarded for partial completion of doctoral program. *Degree requirements:* For doctorate, variable foreign language requirement, comprehensive exam, thesis/dissertation. *Entrance requirements:* For doctorate, GRE General Test. Additional exam requirements/recommendations for international students: Required—TOEFL (minimum score 104 iBT), IELTS (minimum score 7). *Application deadline:* For fall admission, 12/15 for domestic and international students. Application fee: $90. Electronic applications accepted. *Financial support:* Fellowships with full tuition reimbursements, teaching assistantships with full tuition reimbursements, Federal Work-Study, institutionally sponsored loans, scholarships/grants, and health care benefits available. Financial award application deadline: 12/15; financial award applicants required to submit FAFSA. *Faculty research:* Global ancient art history, Asian art history, modern and contemporary art history, Latin American art history, built environment. *Unit head:* Christine Mehring, Chair, 773-702-0278, E-mail: mehring@uchicago.edu. *Application contact:* Michael Beetley, Assistant Dean of Students, Admissions, 773-702-1552, Fax: 773-834-9148, E-mail: humanitiesadmissions@uchicago.edu.
Website: http://arthistory.uchicago.edu

**University of Chicago,** Division of the Humanities, Master of Arts Program in the Humanities, Chicago, IL 60637. Offers art history (MA); cinema and media studies (MA); classic languages (MA); comparative literature (MA); creative writing (MA); cultural policy studies (MA); digital humanities (MA); East Asian languages and civilizations (MA); English language and literature (MA); gender and sexuality studies (MA); Germanic studies (MA); linguistics (MA); music (MA); near Eastern languages and civilizations (MA); philosophy (MA); poetics (MA); race, politics and culture (MA); Romance languages and literatures (MA); Slavic languages and literatures (MA); South Asian languages and civilizations (MA); theater and performance studies (MA). *Students:* 80 full-time (43 women), 7 part-time (3 women); includes 20 minority (5 Black or African American, non-Hispanic/Latino; 1 American Indian or Alaska Native, non-Hispanic/Latino; 6 Asian, non-Hispanic/Latino; 5 Hispanic/Latino; 3 Two or more races, non-Hispanic/Latino), 11 international. Average age 26. 706 applicants, 15% accepted, 42 enrolled. In 2016, 92 master's awarded. *Degree requirements:* For master's, thesis. *Entrance requirements:* For master's, GRE General Test. Additional exam requirements/recommendations for international students: Required—TOEFL (minimum score 104 iBT), IELTS (minimum score 7). *Application deadline:* For fall admission, 1/3 for domestic and international students. Application fee: $90. Electronic applications accepted. *Financial support:* In 2016–17, 8 fellowships with partial tuition reimbursements (averaging $12,000 per year) were awarded; Federal Work-Study, institutionally sponsored loans, scholarships/grants, and tuition waivers (partial) also available. Financial award application deadline: 12/15; financial award applicants required to submit FAFSA. *Unit head:* Malynne Sternstein, Co-Director, 773-834-1201, Fax: 773-834-7526. *Application contact:* Program Coordinator, 773-834-1201, Fax: 773-834-7526, E-mail: ma-humanities@uchicago.edu.
Website: http://maph.uchicago.edu/

**University of Cincinnati,** Graduate School, College of Design, Architecture, Art, and Planning, School of Art, Program in Art History, Cincinnati, OH 45221. Offers MA. *Accreditation:* NASAD. *Program availability:* Part-time. *Degree requirements:* For master's, one foreign language, comprehensive exam, thesis. Electronic applications accepted. *Expenses: Tuition, area resident:* Full-time $12,790; part-time $389 per credit hour. Tuition, state resident: full-time $13,290; part-time $419 per credit hour. Tuition, nonresident: full-time $24,532; part-time $976 per credit hour. *International tuition:* $24,832 full-time. *Required fees:* $3958; $140 per credit hour. Tuition and fees vary according to course load, degree level, program and reciprocity agreements.

**University of Colorado Boulder,** Graduate School, College of Arts and Sciences, Department of Art and Art History, Boulder, CO 80309. Offers art history (MA), including contemporary art criticism, early twentieth-century art, nineteenth-century art, Russian and Soviet art; ceramics (MFA); photography and media arts (MFA); printmaking (MFA); sculpture (MFA). *Faculty:* 25 full-time (12 women). *Students:* 47 full-time (33 women); includes 8 minority (1 Black or African American, non-Hispanic/Latino; 6 Hispanic/Latino; 1 Two or more races, non-Hispanic/Latino), 1 international. Average age 29. 173 applicants, 8% accepted, 13 enrolled. In 2016, 20 master's awarded. Terminal master's awarded for partial completion of doctoral program. *Degree requirements:* For master's, variable foreign language requirement, comprehensive exam, thesis (for some programs). *Entrance requirements:* For master's, GRE General Test, minimum undergraduate GPA of 3.0, portfolio. *Application deadline:* For fall admission, 1/15 for domestic students, 12/1 for international students. Application fee: $60 ($80 for international students). Electronic applications accepted. Application fee is waived when completed online. *Financial support:* In 2016–17, 179 students received support, including 73 fellowships (averaging $1,882 per year), 42 teaching assistantships with full and partial tuition reimbursements available (averaging $30,614 per year); institutionally sponsored loans, scholarships/grants, health care benefits, and unspecified assistantships also available. Financial award application deadline: 1/15; financial award applicants required to submit FAFSA. *Faculty research:* Visual arts, fine arts, sculpture, installation art, inter-arts: interdisciplinary art forms. *Application contact:* E-mail: finearts@colorado.edu.
Website: http://www.colorado.edu/arts

**University of Delaware,** College of Arts and Sciences, Department of Art History, Newark, DE 19716. Offers MA, PhD. *Program availability:* Part-time. *Degree requirements:* For master's, one foreign language, thesis; for doctorate, 2 foreign languages, comprehensive exam, thesis/dissertation. *Entrance requirements:* For master's and doctorate, GRE General Test, writing sample. Additional exam requirements/recommendations for international students: Required—TOEFL. Electronic applications accepted. *Faculty research:* Art of Europe and the United States, art theory, vernacular architecture, medieval manuscripts, African art and architecture.

**University of Denver,** Division of Arts, Humanities and Social Sciences, School of Art and Art History, Denver, CO 80208. Offers art history (MA); museum studies (MA). *Accreditation:* NASAD. *Program availability:* Part-time. *Faculty:* 16 full-time (10 women), 8 part-time/adjunct (7 women). *Students:* 3 full-time (all women), 12 part-time (all women). Average age 25. 29 applicants, 83% accepted, 6 enrolled. In 2016, 5 master's awarded. *Degree requirements:* For master's, one foreign language, comprehensive exam, research paper or thesis project. *Entrance requirements:* For master's, GRE General Test, transcripts, personal statement, writing sample, three letters of recommendation. Additional exam requirements/recommendations for international students: Required—TOEFL (minimum score 550 paper-based; 80 iBT). *Application deadline:* For fall admission, 1/31 priority date for domestic and international students. Applications are processed on a rolling basis. Application fee: $65. Electronic applications accepted. *Expenses:* $29,022 per year full-time. *Financial support:* In 2016–17, 14 students received support, including 4 teaching assistantships with tuition reimbursements available (averaging $7,500 per year); research assistantships with tuition reimbursements available, career-related internships or fieldwork, Federal Work-Study, institutionally sponsored loans, scholarships/grants, and unspecified assistantships also available. Support available to part-time students. Financial award application deadline: 2/15; financial award applicants required to submit FAFSA. *Faculty research:* Abstract expressionist women painters, Chichen Itza, the cult of St. Ursula,

rock poster art of the psychedelic era. *Unit head:* Dr. Catherine Chauvin, Associate Professor and Director, 303-871-2367, Fax: 303-871-4112, E-mail: catherine.chauvin@du.edu. *Application contact:* Dr. Annette Stott, Acting Graduate Art History Advisor, 303-871-3278, Fax: 303-871-4112, E-mail: astott@du.edu.
Website: http://www.du.edu/ahss/art/index.html

**University of Florida,** Graduate School, College of The Arts, School of Art and Art History, Gainesville, FL 32611. Offers art (MA), including digital arts and sciences; art education (MA); art history (MA, PhD); museology (MA), including historic preservation. *Accreditation:* NASAD. *Program availability:* Online learning. *Degree requirements:* For master's, project or thesis (MFA); 1 foreign language (MA in art history); for doctorate, 2 foreign languages, comprehensive exam, thesis/dissertation. *Entrance requirements:* For master's, GRE General Test, portfolio (MFA); writing sample (MA), minimum GPA 3.0; for doctorate, GRE General Test, minimum GPA of 3.0. Additional exam requirements/recommendations for international students: Required—TOEFL (minimum score 550 paper-based; 80 iBT), IELTS (minimum score 6). Electronic applications accepted. *Faculty research:* Studio production, art historical studies of style context.

**University of Georgia,** Franklin College of Arts and Sciences, Lamar Dodd School of Art, Athens, GA 30602. Offers art (MFA, PhD); art history (MA). *Accreditation:* NASAD (one or more programs are accredited). *Degree requirements:* For doctorate, one foreign language, thesis/dissertation. *Entrance requirements:* For master's and doctorate, GRE General Test. *Application deadline:* For fall admission, 7/1 priority date for domestic students; for spring admission, 11/15 for domestic students. Application fee: $50. Electronic applications accepted. *Financial support:* Fellowships, research assistantships, teaching assistantships, and unspecified assistantships available. *Unit head:* Prof. Georgia Strange, Director, 706-542-1600, Fax: 706-542-0226, E-mail: strange@uga.edu. *Application contact:* Isabelle Wallace, Graduate Coordinator, 706-542-1624, E-mail: iwallace@uga.edu.
Website: http://art.uga.edu/

**University of Hawaii at Manoa,** Graduate Division, College of Arts and Humanities, Department of Art and Art History, Program in Art History, Honolulu, HI 96822. Offers MA. *Program availability:* Part-time. *Entrance requirements:* Additional exam requirements/recommendations for international students: Required—TOEFL (minimum score 600 paper-based; 100 iBT); Recommended—IELTS.

**University of Houston,** College of Liberal Arts and Social Sciences, School of Art, Houston, TX 77204. Offers art history (MA); interdisciplinary practice and emerging forms (MFA); painting (MFA); studio art (MFA). *Entrance requirements:* For master's, baccalaureate degree, portfolio. Electronic applications accepted. *Faculty research:* Painting, sculpture, photography/installation/video, graphic design and typography, art history (Pre-Columbian to Surrealism).

**University of Illinois at Chicago,** College of Architecture, Design and the Arts, School of Art and Art History, Chicago, IL 60607-7128. Offers art history (MA); electronic visualization (MFA); museum and exhibition studies (MA); new media arts (MFA). *Program availability:* Part-time, evening/weekend. Terminal master's awarded for partial completion of doctoral program. *Degree requirements:* For master's, one foreign language, thesis or alternative; for doctorate, thesis/dissertation. *Entrance requirements:* For master's, GRE General Test, minimum GPA of 2.75, 3 letters of recommendation; for doctorate, GRE General Test, MA in art history or equivalent, minimum GPA of 3.0. Additional exam requirements/recommendations for international students: Required—TOEFL. Electronic applications accepted. *Expenses:* Contact institution. *Faculty research:* Modern painting and sculpture, history of architecture, city planning and design, history of photography.

**University of Illinois at Urbana–Champaign,** Graduate College, College of Fine and Applied Arts, School of Art and Design, Program in Art History, Champaign, IL 61820. Offers MA, PhD. *Accreditation:* NASAD.

**The University of Iowa,** Graduate College, College of Liberal Arts and Sciences, School of Art and Art History, Program in Art History, Iowa City, IA 52242-1316. Offers MA, PhD. *Faculty:* 10 full-time (5 women), 1 (woman) part-time/adjunct. *Students:* 25 full-time (21 women), 1 (woman) part-time; includes 2 minority (both Hispanic/Latino), 2 international. 20 applicants, 65% accepted, 9 enrolled. In 2016, 5 doctorates awarded. *Degree requirements:* For master's, one foreign language, thesis, exam; for doctorate, 2 foreign languages, comprehensive exam, thesis/dissertation, final exams. *Entrance requirements:* For master's, GRE General Test; for doctorate, GRE General Test, MA in art history. Additional exam requirements/recommendations for international students: Required—TOEFL (minimum score 550 paper-based; 81 iBT). *Application deadline:* For fall admission, 12/15 for domestic and international students. Application fee: $50 ($75 for international students). Electronic applications accepted. *Financial support:* In 2016–17, 16 students received support, including 1 research assistantship with full and partial tuition reimbursement available (averaging $9,132 per year), 15 teaching assistantships with full and partial tuition reimbursements available (averaging $9,132 per year); fellowships, career-related internships or fieldwork, Federal Work-Study, institutionally sponsored loans, scholarships/grants, health care benefits, and unspecified assistantships also available. Support available to part-time students. Financial award application deadline: 12/15. *Faculty research:* African (Oceanic), Asian, ancient (3000 B.C.-300 A.D.), medieval, Renaissance, Baroque, eighteenth- and nineteenth-century European, American (includes Pre-Columbian, Native American, and African American), and Modern/Contemporary. *Unit head:* Dorothy Johnson, Area Head for Art History, 319-335-1784, E-mail: dorothy-johnson@uiowa.edu. *Application contact:* Laura Jorgensen, Graduate Program Coordinator, 319-335-1758, Fax: 319-335-1774, E-mail: art@uiowa.edu.

**The University of Kansas,** Graduate Studies, College of Liberal Arts and Sciences, The Kress Foundation Department of Art History, Lawrence, KS 66045. Offers MA, PhD/MA. *Program availability:* Part-time. *Students:* 41 full-time (35 women), 6 part-time (5 women); includes 2 minority (1 Asian, non-Hispanic/Latino; 1 Two or more races, non-Hispanic/Latino), 16 international. Average age 30. 36 applicants, 83% accepted, 10 enrolled. In 2016, 3 master's, 4 doctorates awarded. Terminal master's awarded for partial completion of doctoral program. *Entrance requirements:* For master's and doctorate, GRE, resume or curriculum vitae, one-page statement of educational and career objectives, writing sample (preferably an art history paper), copy or scan of official transcripts. Additional exam requirements/recommendations for international students: Required—TOEFL. *Application deadline:* For fall admission, 1/1 for domestic and international students. Application fee: $65 ($85 for international students). Electronic applications accepted. *Financial support:* Fellowships, research assistantships, teaching assistantships, career-related internships or fieldwork, scholarships/grants, health care benefits, and unspecified assistantships available. Financial award application deadline: 1/1. *Faculty research:* American, Asian, European, and modern art; Medieval/Renaissance. *Unit head:* David Cateforis, Chair, 785-864-1491, E-mail: dcat@ku.edu. *Application contact:* Lisa Cloar, Graduate Admissions Contact, 785-864-4713, Fax: 785-864-5091, E-mail: arthist@ku.edu.
Website: http://arthistory.ku.edu/

**University of Kentucky,** Graduate School, College of Fine Arts, Program in Art History, Lexington, KY 40506-0032. Offers MA. *Accreditation:* NASAD. *Degree requirements:* For master's, 2 foreign languages, comprehensive exam, thesis. *Entrance requirements:*

For master's, GRE General Test, minimum undergraduate GPA of 2.75. Additional exam requirements/recommendations for international students: Required—TOEFL (minimum score 550 paper-based). Electronic applications accepted. *Faculty research:* Northern European prints and drawings, nineteenth century French painting and drawing, Roman sarcophagus sculpture, manuscript illumination, history and theory of photography.

**University of Louisville,** Graduate School, College of Arts and Sciences, Department of Fine Arts, Louisville, KY 40292. Offers art history (MA, PhD); curatorial studies (MA); studio art (MFA), including design. *Faculty:* 23 full-time (9 women), 6 part-time/adjunct (4 women). *Students:* 20 full-time (14 women), 6 part-time (4 women); includes 5 minority (2 Asian, non-Hispanic/Latino; 1 Hispanic/Latino; 2 Two or more races, non-Hispanic/Latino). Average age 34. 34 applicants, 56% accepted, 11 enrolled. In 2016, 1 master's, 1 doctorate awarded. *Degree requirements:* For master's, one foreign language, thesis. *Entrance requirements:* For doctorate, MA. Additional exam requirements/recommendations for international students: Required—TOEFL (minimum score 550 paper-based; 80 iBT), IELTS (minimum score 6.5). *Application deadline:* For fall admission, 1/15 priority date for domestic and international students. Application fee: $60. *Expenses:* $12,000. *Financial support:* In 2016–17, 7 teaching assistantships with full tuition reimbursements (averaging $12,000 per year) were awarded; research assistantships, scholarships/grants, health care benefits, and unspecified assistantships also available. Financial award application deadline: 1/15. *Faculty research:* Sustainability and environmental design, media theory, cross cultural and critical theories, Installation, urban and public art. *Total annual research expenditures:* $81,639. *Unit head:* Dr. Scott L. Massey, Associate Professor and Chair, 502-852-6794, Fax: 502-852-6791, E-mail: s.massey@louisville.edu. *Application contact:* Theresa Berbet, Senior Advisor, 502-852-6147, Fax: 502-852-6791, E-mail: tberbet@louisville.edu. Website: http://art.louisville.edu

**The University of Manchester,** School of Arts, Histories and Cultures, Manchester, United Kingdom. Offers anthropology, media and performance (PhD); applied theatre professional (PhD); archaeology (PhD); art history and visual studies (PhD); arts management and cultural policy (PhD); classics and ancient history (PhD); composition (PhD); creative writing (PhD); drama (PhD); economic and social history (PhD); electroacoustic composition (PhD); English and American studies (PhD); history (PhD); humanitarianism and conflict response (PhD); museology (PhD); music (PhD); musicology (PhD); religions and theology (PhD).

**University of Maryland, College Park,** Academic Affairs, College of Arts and Humanities, Department of Art History and Archaeology, College Park, MD 20742. Offers art history (MA, PhD). *Degree requirements:* For master's, one foreign language, thesis, oral exam; for doctorate, 2 foreign languages, thesis/dissertation, oral exam. *Entrance requirements:* For master's, GRE General Test, minimum GPA of 3.0, writing sample, 3 letters of recommendation. Additional exam requirements/recommendations for international students: Required—TOEFL. Electronic applications accepted. *Faculty research:* Western, African, pre-Columbian, American, and East Asian art.

**University of Massachusetts Amherst,** Graduate School, College of Humanities and Fine Arts, Department of the History of Art and Architecture, Amherst, MA 01003. Offers MA. *Accreditation:* NASAD. *Program availability:* Part-time. *Degree requirements:* For master's, comprehensive exam, journal-level knowledge of French, German, or Italian. *Entrance requirements:* For master's, GRE General Test, 7-20 page writing sample. Additional exam requirements/recommendations for international students: Required—TOEFL (minimum score 550 paper-based; 80 iBT), IELTS (minimum score 6.5). Electronic applications accepted.

**University of Memphis,** Graduate School, College of Communication and Fine Arts, Department of Art, Memphis, TN 38152. Offers art history (MA), including Egyptian art and archaeology, general art history; ceramics (MFA); graphic design (MFA); museum studies (Graduate Certificate); painting (MFA); printmaking/photography (MFA); sculpture (MFA). *Accreditation:* NASAD (one or more programs are accredited). *Program availability:* Part-time. *Faculty:* 20 full-time (7 women), 1 part-time/adjunct (0 women). *Students:* 22 full-time (16 women), 10 part-time (9 women); includes 9 minority (2 Black or African American, non-Hispanic/Latino; 1 Asian, non-Hispanic/Latino; 3 Hispanic/Latino; 3 Two or more races, non-Hispanic/Latino). Average age 29. 18 applicants, 78% accepted, 11 enrolled. In 2016, 17 master's, 16 other advanced degrees awarded. *Degree requirements:* For master's, 2 foreign languages, comprehensive exam, thesis, image identification exam, qualifying exam; for Graduate Certificate, internship. *Entrance requirements:* For master's, GRE General Test or MAT, portfolio (MFA), letter of intent, sample of undergraduate writing, two letters of recommendation; for Graduate Certificate, three letters of recommendation, letter of intent. *Application deadline:* For fall admission, 2/15 for domestic students; for spring admission, 11/1 for domestic students. Applications are processed on a rolling basis. Application fee: $35 ($60 for international students). *Expenses:* $5,231.50 per semester full-time in-state, $9,623.50 full-time out-of-state. *Financial support:* In 2016–17, 36 students received support, including 20 research assistantships with full tuition reimbursements available (averaging $9,800 per year); teaching assistantships with full tuition reimbursements available, Federal Work-Study, scholarships/grants, and unspecified assistantships also available. Financial award application deadline: 2/1; financial award applicants required to submit FAFSA. *Faculty research:* Online collaborative learning, advanced art history studies, electronic publishing/design, studio arts, architectural studies. *Unit head:* Prof. Richard Lou, Chair, 901-678-2217, Fax: 901-678-2735, E-mail: ralou@memphis.edu. *Application contact:* Niles Wallice, Coordinator of Graduate Studies, 901-678-4899. Website: http://memphis.edu/art/

**University of Miami,** Graduate School, College of Arts and Sciences, Department of Art and Art History, Coral Gables, FL 33124. Offers art history (MA); ceramics/glass (MFA); graphic design/multimedia (MFA); painting (MFA); photography/digital imaging (MFA); printmaking (MFA); sculpture (MFA). *Program availability:* Part-time. *Degree requirements:* For master's, variable foreign language requirement, thesis, exhibit (MFA), comprehensive exam (MA). *Entrance requirements:* For master's, GRE General Test (MA), research paper (MA), slide portfolio (MFA). Additional exam requirements/recommendations for international students: Required—TOEFL. Electronic applications accepted. *Faculty research:* Installation art, public art.

**University of Michigan,** Rackham Graduate School, College of Literature, Science, and the Arts, Department of History of Art, Ann Arbor, MI 48109-1357. Offers PhD. *Degree requirements:* For doctorate, 2 foreign languages, thesis/dissertation, preliminary examinations, oral defense of dissertation. *Entrance requirements:* For doctorate, GRE General Test. Additional exam requirements/recommendations for international students: Recommended—TOEFL. Electronic applications accepted. *Expenses:* Tuition, state resident: full-time $21,466; part-time $1152 per credit hour. Tuition, nonresident: full-time $43,346; part-time $2367 per credit hour. Part-time tuition and fees vary according to course load, degree level and program. *Faculty research:* Asian, African and African-American, ancient, medieval and Byzantine, early modern, and modern art.

**University of Michigan,** Rackham Graduate School, College of Literature, Science, and the Arts, Interdepartmental Program in Classical Art and Archaeology, Ann Arbor, MI 48109-1390. Offers MA, PhD. *Faculty:* 17 full-time (8 women), 4 part-time/adjunct (2 women). *Students:* 28 full-time (19 women); includes 4 minority (1 Black or African American, non-Hispanic/Latino; 1 Asian, non-Hispanic/Latino; 2 Hispanic/Latino), 7 international. 59 applicants, 15% accepted, 4 enrolled. In 2016, 3 doctorates awarded. *Degree requirements:* For doctorate, 4 foreign languages, comprehensive exam, thesis/dissertation, ancient history exam, qualifying exam, preliminary exam. *Entrance requirements:* For doctorate, GRE General Test. Additional exam requirements/recommendations for international students: Required—TOEFL (minimum score 560 paper-based; 84 iBT). *Application deadline:* For fall admission, 12/1 for domestic and international students. Application fee: $75 ($90 for international students). Electronic applications accepted. *Expenses:* Tuition, state resident: full-time $21,466; part-time $1152 per credit hour. Tuition, nonresident: full-time $43,346; part-time $2367 per credit hour. Part-time tuition and fees vary according to course load, degree level and program. *Financial support:* In 2016–17, 22 students received support, including 9 fellowships with full tuition reimbursements available (averaging $19,737 per year), 1 research assistantship with full tuition reimbursement available (averaging $19,304 per year), 9 teaching assistantships with full tuition reimbursements available (averaging $19,737 per year); career-related internships or fieldwork, health care benefits, and summer research funding, ad hoc conference travel funding also available. Financial award application deadline: 4/15. *Faculty research:* Prehistoric art and archaeology, Greek art and archaeology, Roman art and archaeology, Near Eastern art and archaeology, archaeological theory and methodology. *Total annual research expenditures:* $13,500. *Unit head:* Prof. Lisa Nevett, Graduate Program Director, 734-764-8581, Fax: 734-763-8976, E-mail: lcnevett@umich.edu. *Application contact:* Alexander Zwinak, Graduate Program Coordinator, 734-764-6323, Fax: 734-763-8976, E-mail: ipcaa.office@umich.edu. Website: http://lsa.umich.edu/ipcaa/

**University of Minnesota, Twin Cities Campus,** Graduate School, College of Liberal Arts, Department of Art History, Minneapolis, MN 55455. Offers MA, PhD. *Faculty:* 14 full-time (8 women). *Students:* 22 full-time (18 women); includes 4 minority (2 Black or African American, non-Hispanic/Latino; 1 Hispanic/Latino; 1 Two or more races, non-Hispanic/Latino), 3 international. Average age 27. 45 applicants, 11% accepted, 5 enrolled. In 2016, 4 master's, 3 doctorates awarded. Terminal master's awarded for partial completion of doctoral program. *Degree requirements:* For master's, one foreign language, comprehensive exam, thesis or alternative; for doctorate, 2 foreign languages, comprehensive exam, thesis/dissertation. *Entrance requirements:* For master's, GRE, 3 letters of recommendation, writing sample, statement of purpose; for doctorate, transcripts, 3 letters of recommendation, writing sample. Additional exam requirements/recommendations for international students: Required—TOEFL (minimum score 550 paper-based; 79 iBT). *Application deadline:* For fall admission, 1/1 for domestic and international students. Application fee: $75 ($95 for international students). Electronic applications accepted. *Financial support:* In 2016–17, 19 students received support, including 4 fellowships with full tuition reimbursements available (averaging $25,000 per year), 2 research assistantships with full tuition reimbursements available (averaging $19,500 per year), 13 teaching assistantships with full tuition reimbursements available (averaging $19,500 per year); career-related internships or fieldwork, institutionally sponsored loans, scholarships/grants, health care benefits, and unspecified assistantships also available. Financial award application deadline: 1/1. *Faculty research:* Art and archaeology of Persia and the ancient Iranian world, Islamic art, South Asian art, early modern Europe and the Atlantic world, modern and contemporary North America. *Unit head:* Prof. Jane Blocker, Chair, 612-624-4500, Fax: 612-626-8679, E-mail: block023@umn.edu. *Application contact:* Sara Enfield, DGS Assistant, 612-624-4500, Fax: 612-626-8679, E-mail: arthist@umn.edu. Website: https://cla.umn.edu/art-history

**University of Minnesota, Twin Cities Campus,** Graduate School, College of Liberal Arts, Department of Classical and Near Eastern Studies, Minneapolis, MN 55455-0213. Offers ancient and medieval art and archaeology (MA, PhD); classics (MA, PhD); Greek (MA, PhD); Latin (MA, PhD); religions in antiquity (MA). *Program availability:* Part-time. Terminal master's awarded for partial completion of doctoral program. *Degree requirements:* For master's, 2 foreign languages, comprehensive exam, thesis or alternative; for doctorate, variable foreign language requirement, comprehensive exam, thesis/dissertation. *Entrance requirements:* For master's and doctorate, GRE, 3 letters of recommendation, writing sample, copies of transcripts, personal statement. Additional exam requirements/recommendations for international students: Required—TOEFL. Electronic applications accepted. *Faculty research:* Greek and Latin literature, religions in antiquity, ancient Near East.

**University of Missouri,** Office of Research and Graduate Studies, College of Arts and Science, Department of Art History and Archaeology, Columbia, MO 65211. Offers MA, PhD. *Students:* 26 full-time (23 women), 1 (woman) part-time; includes 2 minority (both Hispanic/Latino), 1 international. Average age 32. Terminal master's awarded for partial completion of doctoral program. *Degree requirements:* For master's, 2 foreign languages, thesis; for doctorate, 2 foreign languages, thesis/dissertation. *Entrance requirements:* For master's, GRE General Test (minimum score 1000 verbal and quantitative, 4.5 analytical), minimum GPA of 3.0, 3.3 in major field; at least 3 semesters in appropriate foreign language; for doctorate, GRE General Test, minimum GPA of 3.0; MA or equivalent in art history or classical archaeology; master's thesis. Additional exam requirements/recommendations for international students: Required—TOEFL (minimum score 500 paper-based; 61 iBT), IELTS (minimum score 5.5). *Application deadline:* For fall admission, 1/18 priority date for domestic students. Applications are processed on a rolling basis. Application fee: $75 ($90 for international students). Electronic applications accepted. *Expenses:* Tuition, state resident: full-time $6347; part-time $352.60 per credit hour. Tuition, nonresident: full-time $17,379; part-time $965.50 per credit hour. *Required fees:* $1035. Tuition and fees vary according to course load, campus/location and program. *Financial support:* Fellowships with full tuition reimbursements, research assistantships with full tuition reimbursements, teaching assistantships with full tuition reimbursements, institutionally sponsored loans, health care benefits, and unspecified assistantships available. *Faculty research:* Classical Mediterranean archaeology, medieval and Renaissance art, art and architecture of modern Europe and the Americas. Website: http://aha.missouri.edu/

**University of Montana,** Graduate School, College of Visual and Performing Arts, School of Art, Missoula, MT 59812-0002. Offers fine arts (MA), including art, art history; photography (MFA). *Accreditation:* NASAD (one or more programs are accredited). *Degree requirements:* For master's, thesis exhibit. *Entrance requirements:* For master's, GRE General Test, portfolio.

**University of Nebraska–Lincoln,** Graduate College, College of Fine and Performing Arts, Department of Art and Art History, Lincoln, NE 68588. Offers art history (MA); studio art (MFA). *Accreditation:* NASAD. *Degree requirements:* For master's, thesis. *Entrance requirements:* For master's, slide portfolio. Additional exam requirements/recommendations for international students: Required—TOEFL (minimum score 550 paper-based). Electronic applications accepted. *Faculty research:* Classical archaeology, contemporary art, printmaking, photography.

**University of New Mexico,** Graduate Studies, College of Fine Arts, Program in Art History, Albuquerque, NM 87131. Offers art history (MA); art of the Americas (MA);

*Art History*

history of architecture (PhD); history of graphic arts (PhD); history of photography (PhD); modern Latin American art (PhD); Native American art (PhD); Pre-Columbian art and architecture (PhD); Spanish colonial art (PhD). *Program availability:* Part-time. *Faculty:* 4 full-time (2 women). *Students:* 8 full-time (all women), 22 part-time (19 women); includes 9 minority (3 American Indian or Alaska Native, non-Hispanic/Latino; 5 Hispanic/Latino; 1 Two or more races, non-Hispanic/Latino), 3 international. Average age 40. 19 applicants, 42% accepted, 4 enrolled. In 2016, 5 master's, 1 doctorate awarded. *Degree requirements:* For master's, one foreign language, comprehensive exam (for some programs), thesis, symposium; for doctorate, 2 foreign languages, comprehensive exam, thesis/dissertation, symposium. *Entrance requirements:* Additional exam requirements/recommendations for international students: Required—TOEFL (minimum score 550 paper-based), IELTS (minimum score 6). *Application deadline:* For fall admission, 1/15 for domestic students; for spring admission, 1/15 for domestic students. Application fee: $50. Electronic applications accepted. *Financial support:* Fellowships, research assistantships with tuition reimbursements, teaching assistantships with partial tuition reimbursements, Federal Work-Study, institutionally sponsored loans, scholarships/grants, health care benefits, and unspecified assistantships available. Support available to part-time students. Financial award application deadline: 3/1; financial award applicants required to submit FAFSA. *Faculty research:* Native American, modern Latin American, pre-Columbian, architectural, American, medieval, Spanish Colonial, and Latin American art; history of photography. *Unit head:* Prof. Mary Tsiongas, Chair, Fax: 505-277-5861, Fax: 505-277-5955, E-mail: tsiongas@unm.edu. *Application contact:* Kat Heatherington, Graduate Advisor, 505-277-6672, Fax: 505-277-5955, E-mail: art255@unm.edu.
Website: http://art.unm.edu.

**The University of North Carolina at Chapel Hill,** Graduate School, College of Arts and Sciences, Department of Art, Program in Art History, Chapel Hill, NC 27599. Offers MA, PhD. *Degree requirements:* For master's, one foreign language, comprehensive exam, thesis; for doctorate, one foreign language, comprehensive exam, thesis/dissertation. *Entrance requirements:* For master's and doctorate, GRE General Test, minimum GPA of 3.0.

**University of North Texas,** Robert B. Toulouse School of Graduate Studies, Denton, TX 76203-5459. Offers accounting (MS); applied anthropology (MA, MS); applied behavior analysis (Certificate); applied geography (MA); applied technology and performance improvement (M Ed, MS); art education (MA); art history (MA); art museum education (Certificate); arts leadership (Certificate); audiology (Au D); behavior analysis (MS); behavioral science (PhD); biochemistry and molecular biology (MS); biology (MA, MS); biomedical engineering (MS); business analysis (MS); chemistry (MS); clinical health psychology (PhD); communication studies (MA, MS); computer engineering (MS); computer science (MS); counseling (M Ed), including clinical mental health counseling (MS), college and university counseling, elementary school counseling, secondary school counseling; creative writing (MA); criminal justice (MS); curriculum and instruction (M Ed); decision sciences (MBA); design (MA, MFA), including fashion design (MFA), innovation studies, interior design (MFA); early childhood studies (MS); economics (MS); educational leadership (M Ed, Ed D); educational psychology (MS, PhD), including family studies (MS), gifted and talented (MS), human development (MS), learning and cognition (MS), research, measurement and evaluation (MS); electrical engineering (MS); emergency management (MPA); engineering technology (MS); English (MA); English as a second language (MA); environmental science (MS); finance (MBA, MS); financial management (MPA); French (MA); health services management (MBA); higher education (M Ed, Ed D); history (MA, MS); hospitality management (MS); human resources management (MPA); information science (MS); information systems (PhD); information technologies (MBA); interdisciplinary studies (MA, MS); international studies (MA); international sustainable tourism (MS); jazz studies (MM); journalism (MA, MJ, Graduate Certificate), including interactive and virtual digital communication (Graduate Certificate), narrative journalism (Graduate Certificate), public relations (Graduate Certificate); kinesiology (MS); linguistics (MA); local government management (MPA); logistics (PhD); logistics and supply chain management (MBA); long-term care, senior housing, and aging services (MA); management (PhD); marketing (MBA); mathematics (MA, MS); mechanical and energy engineering (MS, PhD); music (MA), including ethnomusicology, music theory, musicology, performance; music composition (PhD); music education (MM Ed, PhD); nonprofit management (MPA); operations and supply chain management (MBA); performance (MM, DMA); philosophy (MA); political science (MA); professional and technical communication (MA); radio, television and film (MA, MFA); rehabilitation counseling (Certificate); sociology (MA); Spanish (MA); special education (M Ed); speech-language pathology (MA); strategic management (MBA); studio art (MFA); teaching (M Ed); MBA/MS. *Program availability:* Part-time, evening/weekend, online learning. Terminal master's awarded for partial completion of doctoral program. *Degree requirements:* For master's, variable foreign language requirement, comprehensive exam (for some programs), thesis (for some programs); for doctorate, variable foreign language requirement, comprehensive exam (for some programs), thesis/dissertation; for other advanced degree, variable foreign language requirement, comprehensive exam (for some programs). *Entrance requirements:* For master's and doctorate, GRE, GMAT. Additional exam requirements/recommendations for international students: Required—TOEFL (minimum score 550 paper-based; 79 iBT). Electronic applications accepted.

**University of Notre Dame,** Graduate School, College of Arts and Letters, Division of Humanities, Department of Art, Art History, and Design, Notre Dame, IN 46556. Offers art history (MA); design (MFA), including graphic design, industrial design; studio art (MFA), including ceramics, painting, photography, printmaking, sculpture. *Accreditation:* NASAD. *Degree requirements:* For master's, comprehensive exam (for some programs), thesis. *Entrance requirements:* For master's, GRE General Test, minimum GPA of 3.0. Additional exam requirements/recommendations for international students: Required—TOEFL (minimum score 600 paper-based; 80 iBT). Electronic applications accepted. *Faculty research:* Studio art practice in ceramics, printing, photography, printmaking and sculpture, graphic design and industrial design, digital imaging in design and photography, Renaissance and American art history, contemporary art theory and criticism.

**University of Oklahoma,** Weitzenhoffer Family College of Fine Arts, School of Visual Arts, Program in Art History, Norman, OK 73019. Offers art history (MA); art of the American West (PhD); Native American art history (PhD). *Students:* 16 full-time (14 women), 26 part-time (24 women); includes 10 minority (2 American Indian or Alaska Native, non-Hispanic/Latino; 2 Hispanic/Latino; 6 Two or more races, non-Hispanic/Latino). Average age 34. 10 applicants, 70% accepted, 6 enrolled. *Degree requirements:* For master's, 2 foreign languages, comprehensive exam, thesis; for doctorate, 2 foreign languages, comprehensive exam, thesis/dissertation. *Entrance requirements:* For master's and doctorate, GRE. Additional exam requirements/recommendations for international students: Required—TOEFL (minimum score 79 iBT) or IELTS (minimum score 6.5). *Application deadline:* For fall admission, 2/1 for domestic and international students; for spring admission, 10/1 for domestic and international students. Application fee: $50 ($100 for international students). Electronic applications accepted. *Expenses:* Tuition, state resident: full-time $4886; part-time $203.60 per credit hour. Tuition, nonresident: full-time $18,989; part-time $791.20 per credit hour. Required fees: $3283; $126.25 per credit hour. $126.50 per semester. *Financial*

*support:* In 2016–17, 17 students received support. Fellowships with full and partial tuition reimbursements available, research assistantships with full tuition reimbursements available, teaching assistantships with full tuition reimbursements available, career-related internships or fieldwork, institutionally sponsored loans, scholarships/grants, health care benefits, tuition waivers (partial), and unspecified assistantships available. Support available to part-time students. Financial award application deadline: 6/1; financial award applicants required to submit FAFSA. *Faculty research:* Medieval, Renaissance, contemporary, 19th century, Native American. *Unit head:* Dr. Bette Talvacchia, Director, 405-325-6210, Fax: 405-325-1668, E-mail: bette.talvacchia-1@ou.edu. *Application contact:* Dr. Jackson Rushing, Graduate Coordinator, 405-325-6919, E-mail: jackson_rushing@ou.edu.
Website: http://art.ou.edu

**University of Oregon,** Graduate School, School of Architecture and Allied Arts, Department of Art History, Eugene, OR 97403. Offers MA, PhD. *Degree requirements:* For master's, one foreign language, thesis or alternative; for doctorate, 2 foreign languages, thesis/dissertation. *Entrance requirements:* For master's, GRE General Test, minimum GPA of 3.0; for doctorate, minimum GPA of 3.0. Additional exam requirements/recommendations for international students: Required—TOEFL. *Faculty research:* Scytho-Siberian art, modern Chinese painting, European landscape painting, American architecture, German expressionist graphics.

**University of Pennsylvania,** School of Arts and Sciences, Graduate Group in the History of Art, Philadelphia, PA 19104. Offers AM, PhD. *Faculty:* 28 full-time (12 women), 9 part-time/adjunct (5 women). *Students:* 50 full-time (40 women), 2 part-time (1 woman); includes 10 minority (1 Black or African American, non-Hispanic/Latino; 3 Asian, non-Hispanic/Latino; 4 Hispanic/Latino; 2 Two or more races, non-Hispanic/Latino), 6 international. Average age 29. 164 applicants, 12% accepted, 8 enrolled. In 2016, 2 master's, 4 doctorates awarded. Terminal master's awarded for partial completion of doctoral program. *Expenses:* Tuition: Full-time $31,068; part-time $5762 per course. *Required fees:* $3200; $336 per course. Full-time tuition and fees vary according to degree level, program and student level. Part-time tuition and fees vary according to course load, degree level and program.
Website: http://www.sas.upenn.edu/arthistory/graduate/about-the-program

**University of Pittsburgh,** Dietrich School of Arts and Sciences, Department of History of Art and Architecture, Pittsburgh, PA 15260. Offers MA, PhD. *Faculty:* 13 full-time (6 women). *Students:* 31 full-time (27 women); includes 6 minority (2 Hispanic/Latino; 1 Native Hawaiian or other Pacific Islander, non-Hispanic/Latino; 3 Two or more races, non-Hispanic/Latino), 6 international. Average age 32. 50 applicants, 20% accepted, 4 enrolled. In 2016, 2 master's, 5 doctorates awarded. *Degree requirements:* For master's, one foreign language, thesis or alternative, paper; for doctorate, 2 foreign languages, comprehensive exam, thesis/dissertation, teaching portfolio. *Entrance requirements:* For master's and doctorate, GRE General Test, 3 letters of recommendation, writing sample, personal statement, transcripts, foreign language questionnaire. Additional exam requirements/recommendations for international students: Required—TOEFL (minimum score 550 paper-based; 90 iBT). *Application deadline:* For fall admission, 12/15 for domestic and international students. Application fee: $50. Electronic applications accepted. *Expenses:* $21,748 per year, in-state, full-time; $35,904 per year, out-of-state, full-time. *Financial support:* In 2016–17, 28 students received support, including 9 fellowships with full tuition reimbursements available (averaging $21,692 per year), 7 research assistantships with full tuition reimbursements available (averaging $17,905 per year), 6 teaching assistantships with full tuition reimbursements available (averaging $17,905 per year); career-related internships or fieldwork, Federal Work-Study, scholarships/grants, health care benefits, tuition waivers (partial), and unspecified assistantships also available. Financial award application deadline: 12/15. *Faculty research:* Medieval European art and architecture, modern architecture, modern and contemporary art, history of photography, Japanese art history, 20th century German art, contemporary Chinese art, art of the United States, ancient Roman art. *Unit head:* Dr. Barbara McCloskey, Chair, 412-648-2417, Fax: 412-648-2792, E-mail: barbara.mccloskey@pitt.edu. *Application contact:* Corrin Trombley, Graduate Administrator, 412-648-2400, Fax: 412-648-2792, E-mail: cot12@pitt.edu.
Website: http://www.haa.pitt.edu

**University of Rochester,** School of Arts and Sciences, Department of Art and Art History, Rochester, NY 14627. Offers visual and cultural studies (PhD). *Faculty:* 11 full-time (6 women). *Students:* 31 full-time (21 women); includes 7 minority (1 Black or African American, non-Hispanic/Latino; 2 Asian, non-Hispanic/Latino; 3 Hispanic/Latino; 1 Two or more races, non-Hispanic/Latino), 10 international. Average age 30. 57 applicants, 14% accepted, 5 enrolled. In 2016, 4 doctorates awarded. Terminal master's awarded for partial completion of doctoral program. *Degree requirements:* For doctorate, one foreign language, thesis/dissertation, qualifying exam. *Entrance requirements:* For doctorate, GRE General Test, personal statement, three letters of recommendation, official undergraduate and graduate transcripts, writing sample. Additional exam requirements/recommendations for international students: Required—TOEFL (minimum score 600 paper-based; 100 iBT). *Application deadline:* For fall admission, 1/15 for domestic and international students. Application fee: $60. Electronic applications accepted. *Expenses:* $1,538 per credit hour. *Financial support:* Fellowships and tuition waivers (full and partial) available. *Faculty research:* Visual culture from a social-historical perspective. *Unit head:* Rachel Haidu, Director of Graduate Program in Visual and Cultural Studies, 585-275-4112, E-mail: rachel.haidu@rochester.edu. *Application contact:* Martin Collier, Administrator, 585-275-7451.
Website: http://www.rochester.edu/College/aah/

**University of St. Thomas,** Graduate Studies, College of Arts and Sciences, Department of Art History, St. Paul, MN 55105. Offers MA. *Program availability:* Part-time, evening/weekend. *Degree requirements:* For master's, oral exam, reading proficiency in 1 foreign language. *Entrance requirements:* For master's, bachelor's degree in art history or related field; 3 letters of recommendation; writing sample; personal statement. Additional exam requirements/recommendations for international students: Required—TOEFL (minimum score 80 iBT). *Application deadline:* For fall admission, 3/1 for domestic and international students; for spring admission, 11/1 for domestic and international students; for summer admission, 3/1 for domestic and international students. Electronic applications accepted. *Expenses:* Contact institution. *Financial support:* Fellowships with partial tuition reimbursements, research assistantships, career-related internships or fieldwork, institutionally sponsored loans, scholarships/grants, and unspecified assistantships available. Support available to part-time students. Financial award application deadline: 4/1; financial award applicants required to submit FAFSA. *Faculty research:* Pictorial narrative and theory, Mesoamerican art, Chinese manuscript painting, Africa and African diaspora, architectural history, Modernism. *Unit head:* Victoria Young, Chair, 651-962-5855, Fax: 651-962-5861, E-mail: vmyoung@stthomas.edu. *Application contact:* Dr. Heather Shirey, Director of Graduate Studies, 651-962-5572, Fax: 651-962-5861, E-mail: hmshirey@stthomas.edu.
Website: http://www.stthomas.edu/arthistory/

**University of South Africa,** College of Human Sciences, Pretoria, South Africa. Offers adult education (M Ed); African languages (MA, PhD); African politics (MA, PhD); Afrikaans (MA, PhD); ancient history (MA, PhD); ancient Near Eastern studies (MA,

PhD); anthropology (MA, PhD); applied linguistics (MA); Arabic (MA, PhD); archaeology (MA); art history (MA); Biblical archaeology (MA); Biblical studies (M Th, D Th, PhD); Christian spirituality (M Th, D Th); church history (M Th, D Th); classical studies (MA, PhD); clinical psychology (MA); communication (MA, PhD); comparative education (M Ed, Ed D); consulting psychology (D Admin, D Com, PhD); curriculum studies (M Ed, Ed D); development studies (M Admin, MA, D Admin, PhD); didactics (M Ed, Ed D); education (M Tech); education management (M Ed, Ed D); educational psychology (M Ed); English (MA); environmental education (M Ed); French (MA, PhD); German (MA, PhD); Greek (MA); guidance and counseling (M Ed); health studies (MA, PhD), including health sciences education (MA), health services management (MA), medical and surgical nursing science (critical care general) (MA), midwifery and neonatal nursing science (MA), trauma and emergency care (MA); history (MA, PhD); history of education (Ed D); inclusive education (M Ed, Ed D); information and communications technology policy and regulation (MA); information science (MA, MIS, PhD); international politics (MA, PhD); Islamic studies (MA, PhD); Italian (MA, PhD); Judaica (MA, PhD); linguistics (MA, PhD); mathematical education (M Ed); mathematics education (MA); missiology (M Th, D Th); modern Hebrew (MA); musicology (MA, MMus, D Mus, PhD); natural science education (M Ed); New Testament (M Th, D Th); Old Testament (D Th); pastoral therapy (M Th, D Th); philosophy (MA); philosophy of education (M Ed, Ed D); politics (MA, PhD); Portuguese (MA, PhD); practical theology (M Th, D Th); psychology (MA, MS, PhD); psychology of education (M Ed, Ed D); public health (MA); religious studies (MA, D Th, PhD); Romance languages (MA); Russian (MA, PhD); Semitic languages (MA, PhD); social behavior studies in HIV/AIDS (MA); social science (mental health) (MA); social science in development studies (MA); social science in psychology (MA); social science in social work (MA); social science in sociology (MA); social work (MSW, DSW, PhD); socio-education (M Ed, Ed D); sociolinguistics (MA); sociology (MA, PhD); Spanish (MA, PhD); systematic theology (M Th, D Th); TESOL (teaching English to speakers of other languages) (MA); theological ethics (M Th, D Th); theory of literature (MA, PhD); urban ministries (D Th); urban ministry (M Th).

**University of South Carolina,** The Graduate School, College of Arts and Sciences, Department of Art, Program in Art History, Columbia, SC 29208. Offers MA. *Accreditation:* NASAD. *Program availability:* Part-time. *Degree requirements:* For master's, one foreign language, comprehensive exam, thesis. *Entrance requirements:* For master's, GRE General Test or MAT, writing sample. Additional exam requirements/recommendations for international students: Required—TOEFL. Electronic applications accepted. *Faculty research:* History of art and architecture.

**University of Southern California,** Graduate School, Dana and David Dornsife College of Letters, Arts and Sciences, Department of Art History, Los Angeles, CA 90089. Offers art history (MA, PhD); visual studies (Graduate Certificate). *Degree requirements:* For doctorate, 2 foreign languages, comprehensive exam, thesis/dissertation, 60 units. *Entrance requirements:* For doctorate, GRE. Additional exam requirements/recommendations for international students: Required—TOEFL. *Faculty research:* Ancient, medieval, Renaissance, eighteenth-nineteenth century, contemporary.

**University of South Florida,** College of The Arts, School of Art and Art History, Tampa, FL 33620-9951. Offers art (MFA); art history (MA). *Accreditation:* NASAD. *Program availability:* Part-time. *Faculty:* 20 full-time (10 women). *Students:* 35 full-time (17 women), 2 part-time (both women); includes 10 minority (7 Hispanic/Latino; 3 Two or more races, non-Hispanic/Latino), 3 international. Average age 29. 60 applicants, 27% accepted, 16 enrolled. In 2016, 16 master's awarded. *Degree requirements:* For master's, comprehensive exam, thesis, exhibition (for MFA). *Entrance requirements:* For master's, GRE General Test, bachelor's degree from regionally-accredited institution with minimum GPA of 3.0 in upper-division coursework or graduate degree from regionally-accredited institution; portfolio; goals statement (for MA in art history). Additional exam requirements/recommendations for international students: Required—TOEFL (minimum score 550 paper-based; 79 iBT) or IELTS (minimum score 6.5). *Application deadline:* For fall admission, 1/15 for domestic students, 2/1 for international students; for spring admission, 10/15 for domestic students, 9/15 for international students; for summer admission, 2/15 for domestic students, 1/15 for international students. Application fee: $30. Electronic applications accepted. *Expenses:* Tuition, state resident: full-time $7766; part-time $431.43 per credit hour. Tuition, nonresident: full-time $15,789; part-time $877.17 per credit hour. *Required fees:* $37 per term. *Financial support:* In 2016–17, 33 students received support, including 37 teaching assistantships with partial tuition reimbursements available (averaging $9,440 per year); scholarships/grants, health care benefits, and unspecified assistantships also available. Support available to part-time students. Financial award application deadline: 2/15; financial award applicants required to submit FAFSA. *Faculty research:* Contemporary art and role of the artist, identity strategies, political iconography, art practice and technology, the construction of race in art. *Total annual research expenditures:* $113,801. *Unit head:* Prof. Wallace Wilson, Director, 813-974-2360, Fax: 813-974-9226, E-mail: wwilson2@usf.edu. *Application contact:* Prof. Neil Bender, Associate Professor and Graduate Program Director, 813-974-2360, Fax: 813-974-9226, E-mail: nb2@usf.edu.
Website: http://www.art.usf.edu

**The University of Texas at Austin,** Graduate School, College of Fine Arts, Department of Art and Art History, Program in Art History, Austin, TX 78712-1111. Offers MA, PhD. *Accreditation:* NASAD. *Program availability:* Part-time. *Degree requirements:* For master's, one foreign language, thesis; for doctorate, 2 foreign languages, thesis/dissertation, oral and written qualifying exam. *Entrance requirements:* For master's, GRE General Test, 2 samples of written work; for doctorate, GRE General Test, minimum GPA of 3.0, 2 samples of written work. Electronic applications accepted.

**The University of Texas at San Antonio,** College of Liberal and Fine Arts, Department of Art and Art History, San Antonio, TX 78249-0617. Offers art (MFA); art history (MA). *Accreditation:* NASAD (one or more programs are accredited). *Faculty:* 11 full-time (5 women), 2 part-time/adjunct (0 women). *Students:* 18 full-time (13 women), 4 part-time (2 women); includes 10 minority (9 Hispanic/Latino; 1 Two or more races, non-Hispanic/Latino), 1 international. Average age 30. 19 applicants, 37% accepted, 4 enrolled. In 2016, 10 master's awarded. *Entrance requirements:* For master's, GRE General Test, portfolio, minimum GPA of 3.0 in last 60 hours, 3 letters of recommendation, statement of purpose. Additional exam requirements/recommendations for international students: Required—TOEFL (minimum score 550 paper-based; 79 iBT), IELTS (minimum score 6.5). *Application deadline:* For fall admission, 7/1 for domestic students, 4/1 for international students; for spring admission, 11/1 for domestic students, 9/1 for international students. Application fee: $45 ($80 for international students). *Unit head:* Dr. Gregory Elliott, Department Chair, 210-458-4352, Fax: 210-458-4356, E-mail: greg.elliott@utsa.edu. *Application contact:* Monica Rodriguez, Director of Graduate Admissions, 210-458-4331, Fax: 210-458-4332, E-mail: graduatestudies@utsa.edu.
Website: http://art.utsa.edu

**The University of Texas at Tyler,** College of Arts and Sciences, Department of Art and Art History, Tyler, TX 75799-0001. Offers art history (MA); interdisciplinary (MAIS); studio art (MFA). *Degree requirements:* For master's, thesis, graduate committee review. *Entrance requirements:* For master's, minimum GPA of 3.0. Additional exam requirements/recommendations for international students: Required—TOEFL. *Faculty*

*research:* Classical myths in contemporary art, social issues in contemporary art, casting methods, Renaissance art.

**University of Toronto,** School of Graduate Studies, Faculty of Arts and Science, Department of Art, Toronto, ON M5S 1A1, Canada. Offers art history (MA, PhD). *Program availability:* Part-time. *Degree requirements:* For master's, 2 foreign languages, language proficiency exams; for doctorate, 2 foreign languages, comprehensive exam, thesis/dissertation. *Entrance requirements:* For master's, coursework in a foreign language, 3 letters of reference, sample research paper, minimum B+ average in senior art history and/or humanities courses; for doctorate, minimum A- average in senior art history and/or humanities courses, 2 letters of reference, sample research paper. Electronic applications accepted.

**University of Utah,** Graduate School, College of Fine Arts, Department of Art and Art History, Program in Art History, Salt Lake City, UT 84112-0380. Offers MA. *Faculty:* 6 full-time (4 women), 1 (woman) part-time/adjunct. *Students:* 7 full-time (6 women), 1 (woman) part-time; includes 2 minority (1 Asian, non-Hispanic/Latino; 1 Hispanic/Latino). 13 applicants, 31% accepted, 1 enrolled. In 2016, 3 master's awarded. Terminal master's awarded for partial completion of doctoral program. *Degree requirements:* For master's, one foreign language, comprehensive exam, thesis, qualifying paper, thesis defense. *Entrance requirements:* For master's, curriculum vitae, academic writing sample, letters of recommendation. Additional exam requirements/recommendations for international students: Required—TOEFL (minimum score 80 iBT). *Application deadline:* For fall admission, 2/1 for domestic and international students. Application fee: $55 ($65 for international students). Electronic applications accepted. *Expenses:* $7,010 (first-year). *Financial support:* In 2016–17, 7 students received support, including 5 teaching assistantships with partial tuition reimbursements available (averaging $7,500 per year); scholarships/grants and tuition reduction also available. Financial award application deadline: 2/1; financial award applicants required to submit FAFSA. *Faculty research:* Asian, Latin American, Renaissance/Baroque, European/American, twentieth century/contemporary, and medieval art. *Unit head:* Prof. Elizabeth A. Peterson, Director, 801-581-8677, Fax: 801-585-6171. *Application contact:* Dr. Jessen Kelly, Director of Graduate Studies, 801-581-8677, Fax: 801-585-6171, E-mail: jessen.kelly@utah.edu.
Website: http://www.arthistory.utah.edu/

**University of Victoria,** Faculty of Graduate Studies, Faculty of Fine Arts, Department of History in Art, Victoria, BC V8W 2Y2, Canada. Offers MA, PhD. *Degree requirements:* For master's, one foreign language, thesis (for some programs), oral defense; for doctorate, 2 foreign languages, comprehensive exam, thesis/dissertation, oral defense. *Entrance requirements:* For master's, minimum B+ average in undergraduate course work; for doctorate, minimum B+ average in graduate course work. Additional exam requirements/recommendations for international students: Required—TOEFL (minimum score 575 paper-based), IELTS (minimum score 7). Electronic applications accepted. *Faculty research:* Europe, Southeast Asia, China and Islamic world, architecture of North America and the Islamic World, film.

**University of Virginia,** College and Graduate School of Arts and Sciences, Program in Art and Architectural History, Charlottesville, VA 22903. Offers MA, PhD. *Faculty:* 24 full-time (13 women), 2 part-time/adjunct (1 woman). *Students:* 30 full-time (18 women); includes 5 minority (1 Black or African American, non-Hispanic/Latino; 2 Asian, non-Hispanic/Latino; 1 Hispanic/Latino; 1 Two or more races, non-Hispanic/Latino), 2 international. Average age 31. 64 applicants, 14% accepted, 5 enrolled. In 2016, 9 doctorates awarded. *Degree requirements:* For master's, one foreign language, comprehensive exam, thesis; for doctorate, 2 foreign languages, thesis/dissertation, oral exam. *Entrance requirements:* For master's and doctorate, GRE, 2 letters of recommendation. *Application deadline:* For fall admission, 12/7 for domestic and international students. Applications are processed on a rolling basis. Application fee: $60. Electronic applications accepted. *Expenses:* Tuition, state resident: full-time $15,026; part-time $834 per credit hour. Tuition, nonresident: full-time $25,168; part-time $1378 per credit hour. *Required fees:* $2654. *Financial support:* Application deadline: 12/7. *Unit head:* Larry Goedde, Chair, 434-924-3541, Fax: 434-924-3647, E-mail: artdept@virginia.edu. *Application contact:* Sheila Crane, Director of Graduate Studies, 434-243-2342, Fax: 434-924-3647, E-mail: artdept@virginia.edu.
Website: http://www.virginia.edu/art/phd-program/

**University of Washington,** Graduate School, College of Arts and Sciences, School of Art, Division of Art History, Seattle, WA 98195. Offers MA, PhD. Terminal master's awarded for partial completion of doctoral program. *Degree requirements:* For master's, 2 foreign languages, practicum or thesis; for doctorate, 2 foreign languages, thesis/dissertation. *Entrance requirements:* For master's, GRE General Test, minimum undergraduate GPA of 3.0, undergraduate major in art history or equivalent; for doctorate, GRE General Test, MA in art history, minimum graduate GPA of 3.0. Additional exam requirements/recommendations for international students: Required—TOEFL (minimum score 580 paper-based). Electronic applications accepted. *Faculty research:* European-American (all periods), Japanese, Chinese, African, and Native American art.

**University of Wisconsin–Madison,** Graduate School, College of Letters and Science, Department of Art History, Madison, WI 53706-1380. Offers MA, PhD. *Program availability:* Part-time. Terminal master's awarded for partial completion of doctoral program. *Degree requirements:* For master's, one foreign language; for doctorate, 2 foreign languages, thesis/dissertation. *Entrance requirements:* For master's and doctorate, GRE. Additional exam requirements/recommendations for international students: Required—TOEFL. Electronic applications accepted. *Faculty research:* Twentieth-century, African art, Italian Renaissance, Dutch, material culture.

**University of Wisconsin–Milwaukee,** Graduate School, College of Letters and Science, Department of Art History, Milwaukee, WI 53201-0413. Offers MA. *Program availability:* Part-time. *Students:* 5 full-time (all women), 11 part-time (9 women), 1 international. Average age 28. 7 applicants, 86% accepted, 3 enrolled. In 2016, 8 master's awarded. *Degree requirements:* For master's, one foreign language, comprehensive exam, thesis or alternative. *Entrance requirements:* For master's, GRE. Additional exam requirements/recommendations for international students: Required—TOEFL (minimum score 550 paper-based; 79 iBT), IELTS (minimum score 6.5). *Application deadline:* For fall admission, 1/1 priority date for domestic students; for spring admission, 9/1 for domestic students. Applications are processed on a rolling basis. Application fee: $56 ($96 for international students). *Financial support:* In 2016–17, 7 teaching assistantships were awarded; fellowships, research assistantships, career-related internships or fieldwork, and unspecified assistantships also available. Support available to part-time students. Financial award application deadline: 4/15; financial award applicants required to submit FAFSA. *Faculty research:* Ancient Mediterranean art through contemporary Western art, Chinese art, Pre-Columbian art, film, theory. *Unit head:* Tanya Tiffany, Chair, 414-229-3466, E-mail: tanyatif@uwm.edu. *Application contact:* Derek Counts, General Information Contact, 414-229-3466, E-mail: dbc@uwm.edu.
Website: https://uwm.edu/arthistory/

**University of Wisconsin–Superior,** Graduate Division, Department of Visual Arts, Superior, WI 54880-4500. Offers art education (MA); art history (MA); art therapy (MA); studio arts (MA). *Program availability:* Part-time. *Degree requirements:* For master's,

comprehensive exam, exhibit. *Entrance requirements:* For master's, minimum GPA of 2.75, portfolio. Electronic applications accepted.

**Virginia Commonwealth University,** Graduate School, School of the Arts, Department of Art History, Richmond, VA 23284-9005. Offers curatorial (PhD); historical studies (MA, PhD); museum studies (MA). *Accreditation:* NASAD. *Degree requirements:* For master's, thesis; for doctorate, comprehensive exam, thesis/dissertation. *Entrance requirements:* For master's and doctorate, GRE General Test. *Application deadline:* For fall admission, 1/15 for domestic students. Application fee: $50. Electronic applications accepted. *Financial support:* Fellowships, teaching assistantships, career-related internships or fieldwork, Federal Work-Study, and institutionally sponsored loans available. Support available to part-time students. Financial award application deadline: 3/15; financial award applicants required to submit FAFSA. *Faculty research:* Modern, nineteenth-century, Renaissance, American, and medieval art. *Unit head:* Dr. Dina Bangdel, Director of Graduate Studies, 804-628-7027, Fax: 804-828-7468, E-mail: dbangdel@vcu.edu. *Application contact:* Dr. Margaret A. Lindauer, Graduate Program Director, 804-828-2784, E-mail: malindauer@vcu.edu.
Website: http://www.vcu.edu/artweb/History/

**Washington University in St. Louis,** The Graduate School, Department of Art History and Archaeology, St. Louis, MO 63130-4899. Offers AM, PhD. *Degree requirements:* For doctorate, 2 foreign languages, comprehensive exam, thesis/dissertation. *Entrance requirements:* For master's and doctorate, GRE General Test, sample of written work. Electronic applications accepted. *Faculty research:* Ancient, medieval, Renaissance, early modern European, modern and contemporary European and American, and Asian art history; classical archaeology.

**Wayne State University,** College of Fine, Performing and Communication Arts, James Pearson Duffy Department of Art and Art History, Detroit, MI 48202. Offers art (MA, MFA), including ceramics, drawing, fibers, graphic design, industrial design (MA), interior design (MA), metalsmithing, painting, photography, printmaking, sculpture; art history (MA). *Students:* 15 full-time (10 women), 9 part-time (7 women); includes 6 minority (2 Black or African American, non-Hispanic/Latino; 1 Asian, non-Hispanic/Latino; 1 Hispanic/Latino; 2 Two or more races, non-Hispanic/Latino), 2 international. Average age 34. 49 applicants, 12% accepted, 3 enrolled. In 2016, 7 master's awarded. *Degree requirements:* For master's, thesis (for some programs), essay or thesis. *Entrance requirements:* For master's, BFA or another degree and equivalent course work, portfolio, personal interview, reference letters, statement of intent (except for art history program). Additional exam requirements/recommendations for international students: Required—TOEFL (minimum score 550 paper-based; 79 iBT), TWE (minimum score 5.5), Michigan English Language Assessment Battery (minimum score 85); Recommended—IELTS (minimum score 6.5). *Application deadline:* For fall admission, 2/1 for domestic and international students; for winter admission, 10/1 for domestic and international students. Application fee: $50. Electronic applications accepted. *Expenses:* $17,240 per year resident tuition and fees, $34,434 per year non-resident tuition and fees. *Financial support:* In 2016–17, 21 students received support, including 1 fellowship with tuition reimbursement available (averaging $16,000 per year), 6 teaching assistantships with tuition reimbursements available (averaging $17,994 per year); research assistantships, scholarships/grants, and unspecified assistantships also

available. Support available to part-time students. Financial award applicants required to submit FAFSA. *Faculty research:* Integration of the human figure into urban and rural landscape in painting; performance art utilizing digital media and video; exploration of race, gender, and culture through creative practice (including art, design, and art history); ongoing investigation and elaboration of visual art traditions in diverse media; continued scholarship in the history of art. *Unit head:* Dr. John Richardson, Chair, 313-577-2980, Fax: 313-577-3491, E-mail: af5343@wayne.edu. *Application contact:* 313-577-2980, E-mail: art@wayne.edu.
Website: http://art.wayne.edu/

**Webster University,** Leigh Gerdine College of Fine Arts, Department of Art, Design, and Art History, St. Louis, MO 63119-3194. Offers art history and criticism (MA). *Program availability:* Part-time. *Degree requirements:* For master's, thesis. *Entrance requirements:* For master's, BA or BFA in related field, interview, portfolio. Additional exam requirements/recommendations for international students: Required—TOEFL. *Application deadline:* Applications are processed on a rolling basis. Application fee: $35 ($50 for international students). *Expenses: Tuition:* Full-time $21,900; part-time $730 per credit hour. Tuition and fees vary according to campus/location and program. *Financial support:* Federal Work-Study available. Support available to part-time students. Financial award application deadline: 4/1; financial award applicants required to submit FAFSA. *Unit head:* Tom K. Lang, Chair, 314-968-7171, E-mail: langtk@webster.edu. *Application contact:* Jeffrey Hughes, Director, Graduate Program, 314-968-7159, E-mail: hughesja@webster.edu.
Website: http://www.webster.edu/depts/finearts/art/

**West Virginia University,** College of Creative Arts, School of Art and Design, Morgantown, WV 26506. Offers art education (MA); art history (MA); ceramics (MFA); graphic design (MFA); painting (MFA); printmaking (MFA); sculpture (MFA); studio art (MA). *Accreditation:* NASAD. *Degree requirements:* For master's, thesis, exhibit. *Entrance requirements:* For master's, minimum GPA of 2.75, portfolio. Additional exam requirements/recommendations for international students: Required—TOEFL. *Expenses:* Contact institution. *Faculty research:* Medieval art history.

**Williams College,** Graduate Program in the History of Art, Williamstown, MA 01267. Offers development economics (MA); history of art (MA). MA in history of art offered jointly with Sterling and Francine Clark Art Institute. *Degree requirements:* For master's, 2 foreign languages, symposium paper and lecture. *Entrance requirements:* For master's, GRE General Test. Additional exam requirements/recommendations for international students: Required—TOEFL. Electronic applications accepted.

**Yale University,** Graduate School of Arts and Sciences, Department of History of Art, New Haven, CT 06520. Offers PhD. *Degree requirements:* For doctorate, 2 foreign languages, thesis/dissertation. *Entrance requirements:* For doctorate, GRE General Test.

**York University,** Faculty of Graduate Studies, Faculty of Fine Arts, Program in Art History, Toronto, ON M3J 1P3, Canada. Offers MA, PhD. *Program availability:* Part-time. *Degree requirements:* For master's, one foreign language, thesis or alternative. Electronic applications accepted.

# Arts Administration

**American University,** College of Arts and Sciences, Department of Performing Arts, Washington, DC 20016-8053. Offers art management (MA); audio production (Certificate); audio technology (MA); international arts management (Certificate); technology in arts management (Certificate). *Program availability:* Part-time, evening/weekend. *Faculty:* 28 full-time (14 women), 41 part-time/adjunct (15 women). *Students:* 46 full-time (28 women), 21 part-time (9 women); includes 25 minority (18 Black or African American, non-Hispanic/Latino; 3 Hispanic/Latino; 1 Native Hawaiian or other Pacific Islander, non-Hispanic/Latino; 3 Two or more races, non-Hispanic/Latino), 11 international. Average age 29. 115 applicants, 77% accepted, 30 enrolled. In 2016, 44 master's, 7 other advanced degrees awarded. *Degree requirements:* For master's, comprehensive exam, thesis or alternative. *Entrance requirements:* For master's, GRE, minimum GPA of 3.0, statement of purpose, transcripts, 2 letters of recommendation, resume, art portfolio; for Certificate, bachelor's degree, statement of purpose, transcripts, resume, art portfolio. Additional exam requirements/recommendations for international students: Required—TOEFL (minimum score 100 iBT), IELTS, PTE (minimum score 68). *Application deadline:* For fall admission, 2/1 priority date for domestic students; for spring admission, 11/1 priority date for domestic students. Application fee: $55. *Expenses:* $1,579 per credit tuition; $690 mandatory fees. *Financial support:* Unspecified assistantships available. Financial award application deadline: 2/1; financial award applicants required to submit FAFSA. *Unit head:* Dr. Daniel Abraham, Department Chair, 202-885-3427, Fax: 202-885-1092, E-mail: dabraham@american.edu. *Application contact:* Kathleen Clowery, Director, Graduate Admissions, 202-885-3620, Fax: 202-885-1344, E-mail: clowery@american.edu.
Website: http://www.american.edu/cas/performing-arts/

**Arizona State University at the Tempe campus,** Herberger Institute for Design and the Arts, School of Film, Dance and Theatre, Tempe, AZ 85287-2002. Offers dance (MFA), including dance, interdisciplinary digital media and performance; theatre (MA, MFA, PhD), including arts entrepreneurship and management (MFA), directing (MFA), dramatic writing (MFA), interdisciplinary digital media and performance (MFA), performance (MFA), performance design (MFA), theatre (MFA), theatre and performance of the Americas (PhD), theatre for youth (MFA, PhD). Terminal master's awarded for partial completion of doctoral program. *Degree requirements:* For master's, comprehensive exam (for some programs), thesis (for some programs), applied project (for some programs); interactive Program of Study (iPOS) submitted before completing 50 percent of required credit hours; for doctorate, comprehensive exam, thesis/dissertation, interactive Program of Study (iPOS) submitted before completing 50 percent of required credit hours. *Entrance requirements:* For master's, GRE or MAT, minimum GPA of 3.0 in last 2 years of work leading to bachelor's degree (depending on program); for doctorate, GRE, minimum GPA of 3.0 or equivalent in last 2 years of work leading to bachelor's degree, 3 letters of recommendation, resume, scholarly writing sample, statement of purpose. Additional exam requirements/recommendations for international students: Required—TOEFL, IELTS, or PTE. Electronic applications accepted.

**Baruch College of the City University of New York,** Weissman School of Arts and Sciences, Program in Arts Administration, New York, NY 10010-5585. Offers MA. *Program availability:* Part-time, evening/weekend. *Faculty:* 4 full-time (2 women), 4 part-time/adjunct (2 women). *Students:* 78. 31 applicants, 97% accepted, 24 enrolled.

*Degree requirements:* For master's, thesis or alternative, arts consultancy project. *Entrance requirements:* For master's, GRE/GMAT. Additional exam requirements/recommendations for international students: Required—TOEFL or IELTS. *Application deadline:* For fall admission, 4/1 priority date for domestic and international students; for spring admission, 11/1 priority date for domestic and international students. Application fee: $125. Electronic applications accepted. *Financial support:* Research assistantships, teaching assistantships, career-related internships or fieldwork, Federal Work-Study, scholarships/grants, and unspecified assistantships available. Financial award applicants required to submit FAFSA. *Faculty research:* Art policy; art administration; leadership, governance and strategic planning; government-nongovernment relations; immigration policy; policing; twentieth-century and contemporary art; ethics and policymaking; race, politics and social justice; visual culture of the Great War; intersections of dance, theatre, visual art, and technology; spectacle entertainments and strategies of visual display in performance culture. *Application contact:* Cathy Levkulic, Assistant Director, Graduate Studies, 646-312-4493, Fax: 646-312-3871, E-mail: wsas.graduate.studies@baruch.cuny.edu.
Website: http://www.baruch.cuny.edu/wsas/academics/ma-arts-administration/index.html

**Boston University,** Metropolitan College, Program in Arts Administration, Boston, MA 02215. Offers arts administration (MS, Graduate Certificate); fundraising management (Graduate Certificate). *Program availability:* Part-time, evening/weekend. *Faculty:* 2 full-time (0 women), 16 part-time/adjunct (5 women). *Students:* 26 full-time (24 women), 86 part-time (76 women); includes 8 minority (4 Black or African American, non-Hispanic/Latino; 3 Asian, non-Hispanic/Latino; 1 Hispanic/Latino), 33 international. Average age 29. 136 applicants, 55% accepted, 30 enrolled. In 2016, 43 master's awarded. *Degree requirements:* For master's, internship. *Entrance requirements:* Additional exam requirements/recommendations for international students: Required—TOEFL (minimum score 95 iBT). *Application deadline:* For fall admission, 4/1 priority date for domestic students, 2/1 priority date for international students; for spring admission, 11/15 priority date for domestic and international students. Applications are processed on a rolling basis. Application fee: $85. Electronic applications accepted. *Expenses:* Contact institution. *Financial support:* In 2016–17, 6 research assistantships (averaging $8,400 per year) were awarded; career-related internships or fieldwork, unspecified assistantships, and 6 office assistantships (averaging $4200) also available. Support available to part-time students. Financial award applicants required to submit FAFSA. *Faculty research:* Cultural policy, artists' rights, museum practices, audience development. *Unit head:* Dr. Lanfranco Aceti, Associate Professor of the Practice/Director, 617-353-4064, Fax: 617-353-1230, E-mail: artsad@bu.edu. *Application contact:* Raquel Peula, Program Administrator, 617-353-4064, Fax: 617-358-1230, E-mail: rpeula@bu.edu.
Website: http://www.bu.edu/artsadmin/programs/

**Brooklyn College of the City University of New York,** School of Visual, Media and Performing Arts, Department of Theater, Brooklyn, NY 11210-2889. Offers acting (MFA); design and technical theater (MFA); directing (MFA); performing arts management (MFA); theater history and criticism (MA). *Program availability:* Part-time. *Degree requirements:* For master's, thesis, professional residency. *Entrance requirements:* For master's, audition or interview, 18 credits in theater, 2 letters of

recommendation, essay. Additional exam requirements/recommendations for international students: Required—TOEFL. Electronic applications accepted. *Faculty research:* Multiculturalism and the arts, art education, arts collaboration.

**Carnegie Mellon University,** Heinz College, School of Public Policy and Management, Master of Arts Management Program, Pittsburgh, PA 15213-3891. Offers MAM. *Degree requirements:* For master's, internship. *Entrance requirements:* For master's, GRE or GMAT, college-level course in advanced algebra/pre-calculus; college-level courses in economics and statistics (recommended). Additional exam requirements/ recommendations for international students: Required—TOEFL or IELTS. Electronic applications accepted.

**Christie's Education,** Certificate Program in Art Business, New York, NY 10020. Offers Certificate. *Application deadline:* Applications are processed on a rolling basis. Electronic applications accepted. *Expenses:* $3,000 per module. *Unit head:* Dr. Marisa Kayyem, Director of Continuing Education, 212-355-1501, Fax: 212-355-7370, E-mail: mkayyem@christies.edu. *Application contact:* Catherine Warden, Academic Coordinator, 212-355-1501, Fax: 212-355-7370, E-mail: shortcoursesus@christies.edu. Website: https://www.christies.edu/new-york/courses/certificate-art-business.aspx

**Christie's Education,** MA Program in Art, Law and Business, New York, NY 10020. Offers MA. *Program availability:* Part-time. *Faculty:* 3 full-time (2 women). *Students:* 13 full-time (12 women). *Degree requirements:* For master's, capstone project, internship. *Entrance requirements:* For master's, bachelor's degree or equivalent international degree, official transcripts from all post-secondary institutions attended. *Application deadline:* For fall admission, 1/15 priority date for domestic and international students. Applications are processed on a rolling basis. Application fee: $95. *Financial support:* In 2016–17, 1 student received support. Scholarships/grants and unspecified assistantships available. Financial award applicants required to submit FAFSA. *Unit head:* Noah Kupferman, Program Director, 212-355-1501 Ext. 7101, E-mail: nkupferman@christies.edu. *Application contact:* Hilary Smith, Recruitment and Admissions Officer, 212-355-1501 Ext. 3309, Fax: 212-355-7370, E-mail: hsmith@christies.edu.

**Claremont Graduate University,** Graduate Programs, Peter F. Drucker and Masatoshi Ito Graduate School of Management, Program in Art Business, Claremont, CA 91711-6160. Offers MA. Program offered in conjunction with Sotheby's Institute of Art–Los Angeles. *Faculty:* 3 full-time (1 woman). *Students:* 57 full-time (49 women), 4 part-time (2 women); includes 6 minority (1 Black or African American, non-Hispanic/Latino; 3 Asian, non-Hispanic/Latino; 1 Hispanic/Latino; 1 Native Hawaiian or other Pacific Islander, non-Hispanic/Latino), 18 international. Average age 29. In 2016, 29 master's awarded. *Degree requirements:* For master's, project seminar. *Entrance requirements:* Additional exam requirements/recommendations for international students: Required—TOEFL (minimum score 75 iBT). *Application deadline:* For fall admission, 2/1 priority date for domestic and international students. Applications are processed on a rolling basis. Application fee: $80. Electronic applications accepted. *Expenses: Tuition:* Full-time $44,328; part-time $1847 per unit. *Required fees:* $600; $300 per semester. Tuition and fees vary according to course load and program. *Financial support:* Federal Work-Study, institutionally sponsored loans, and scholarships/grants available. Support available to part-time students. *Unit head:* Jonathan Neil, Director, 909-607-0619, E-mail: jonathan.neil@cgu.edu. *Application contact:* Matt O'Connor, Assistant Director of Admissions, 909-607-1185, E-mail: matthew.o'connor2@cgu.edu. Website: https://www.cgu.edu/academics/program/art-business/

**Claremont Graduate University,** Graduate Programs, Program in Arts Management, Claremont, CA 91711. Offers MA. Program offered in conjunction with Sotheby's Institute of Art–Los Angeles. *Faculty:* 2 full-time (0 women). *Students:* 23 full-time (all women), 21 part-time (17 women); includes 16 minority (3 Black or African American, non-Hispanic/Latino; 3 Asian, non-Hispanic/Latino; 9 Hispanic/Latino; 1 Two or more races, non-Hispanic/Latino), 15 international. Average age 32. In 2016, 13 master's awarded. *Entrance requirements:* For master's, GRE General Test. Additional exam requirements/recommendations for international students: Required—TOEFL (minimum score 75 iBT). *Application deadline:* For fall admission, 2/1 priority date for domestic and international students. Applications are processed on a rolling basis. Application fee: $80. Electronic applications accepted. *Expenses: Tuition:* Full-time $44,328; part-time $1847 per unit. *Required fees:* $600; $300 per semester. Tuition and fees vary according to course load and program. *Financial support:* Fellowships, research assistantships, teaching assistantships, Federal Work-Study, institutionally sponsored loans, and scholarships/grants available. Support available to part-time students. Financial award application deadline: 2/15; financial award applicants required to submit FAFSA. *Unit head:* Jonathan Neil, Director, Center for Management in the Creative Industries, 909-607-9109, Fax: 909-621-8330, E-mail: jonathan.neil@cgu.edu. *Application contact:* Matt O'Connor, Assistant Director of Admissions, 909-607-1185, E-mail: matthew.o'connor2@cgu.edu. Website: https://www.cgu.edu/academics/program/arts-management/

**The College at Brockport, State University of New York,** School of Business and Management, Department of Public Administration, Brockport, NY 14420-2997. Offers arts administration (AGC); nonprofit management (AGC); public administration (MPA), including health care management, nonprofit management, public management. *Accreditation:* NASPAA. *Program availability:* Part-time, evening/weekend. *Faculty:* 5 full-time (3 women), 5 part-time/adjunct (1 woman). *Students:* 59 full-time (41 women), 100 part-time (60 women); includes 32 minority (16 Black or African American, non-Hispanic/Latino; 5 Asian, non-Hispanic/Latino; 8 Hispanic/Latino; 3 Two or more races, non-Hispanic/Latino), 3 international. 82 applicants, 89% accepted, 53 enrolled. In 2016, 42 master's, 10 other advanced degrees awarded. *Degree requirements:* For master's, thesis or alternative. *Entrance requirements:* For master's, GRE or minimum GPA of 3.0, letters of recommendation, statement of objectives, current resume. Additional exam requirements/recommendations for international students: Required—TOEFL (minimum score 550 paper-based; 79 iBT), IELTS (minimum score 6.5). *Application deadline:* For fall admission, 8/15 priority date for domestic and international students; for spring admission, 1/15 priority date for domestic and international students; for summer admission, 4/15 priority date for domestic and international students. Application fee: $50. Electronic applications accepted. *Expenses:* Contact institution. *Financial support:* In 2016–17, 1 fellowship with full tuition reimbursement (averaging $7,500 per year), 1 teaching assistantship with full tuition reimbursement (averaging $6,000 per year) were awarded; Federal Work-Study, scholarships/grants, and unspecified assistantships also available. Support available to part-time students. Financial award application deadline: 3/15; financial award applicants required to submit FAFSA. *Faculty research:* E-government, performance management, nonprofits and policy implementation, Medicaid and disabilities. *Unit head:* Dr. Celia Watt, Graduate Director, 585-395-5538, Fax: 585-395-2172, E-mail: cwatt@brockport.edu. *Application contact:* Danielle A. Welch, Graduate Admissions Counselor, 585-395-2525, Fax: 585-395-2515. Website: http://www.brockport.edu/pubadmin

**College of Charleston,** Graduate School, School of the Arts, Program in Arts Management, Charleston, SC 29424-0001. Offers Certificate. *Program availability:* Part-time, evening/weekend. *Entrance requirements:* For degree, minimum GPA of 3.0, writing sample. Additional exam requirements/recommendations for international students: Required—TOEFL (minimum score 81 iBT). *Application deadline:* For fall admission, 4/1 for domestic students; for spring admission, 11/1 for domestic students. Application fee: $45. *Unit head:* Karen Chandler, Director, 843-953-5474. *Application contact:* Karen Chandler, Director, 843-953-5474. Website: http://artsmgmt.cofc.edu/

**Colorado State University,** College of Liberal Arts, LEAP Institute for the Arts, Fort Collins, CO 80523. Offers MALCM. *Program availability:* Part-time, evening/weekend, 100% online. *Students:* 7 part-time (6 women); includes 1 minority (Black or African American, non-Hispanic/Latino). Average age 31. 4 applicants, 100% accepted, 3 enrolled. *Degree requirements:* For master's, comprehensive exam, internship. *Entrance requirements:* For master's, minimum GPA of 3.0, official transcripts, 3 letters of recommendation, personal statement, resume. Additional exam requirements/ recommendations for international students: Required—TOEFL (minimum score 550 paper-based; 80 iBT). *Application deadline:* For fall admission, 4/15 for domestic and international students; for spring admission, 9/15 for domestic and international students; for summer admission, 2/15 for domestic and international students. Applications are processed on a rolling basis. Application fee: $60 ($70 for international students). Electronic applications accepted. *Expenses:* Contact institution. *Financial support:* In 2016–17, 3 students received support. Fellowships, research assistantships, teaching assistantships, career-related internships or fieldwork, scholarships/grants, and tuition award waivers available. Financial award application deadline: 3/1; financial award applicants required to submit FAFSA. *Faculty research:* Arts and cultural management, discourse of practice, arts and cultural policy, culturally sustainable entrepreneurship, cultural citizenship, everyday aesthetics. *Unit head:* Dr. Constance DeVereaux, Director, 970-491-3902, E-mail: constance.devereaux@colostate.edu. *Application contact:* Dulcie Willis, Coordinator, 970-491-3746, E-mail: dulcie.willis@colostate.edu. Website: http://leap.colostate.edu/

**Columbia College Chicago,** Graduate School, Department of Business and Entrepreneurship, Chicago, IL 60605-1996. Offers arts, entertainment and media management (MA), including visual arts management. *Program availability:* Part-time. *Degree requirements:* For master's, thesis, internship. *Entrance requirements:* For master's, GRE (recommended), self-assessment essay, resume, letters of recommendation. Additional exam requirements/recommendations for international students: Required—TOEFL (minimum score 600 paper-based; 100 iBT). Electronic applications accepted. *Expenses:* Contact institution.

**Daemen College,** Department of Visual and Performing Arts, Amherst, NY 14226-3592. Offers arts administration (MS). *Entrance requirements:* For master's, bachelor's degree from an accredited institution; at least two letters of recommendation; minimum undergraduate GPA of 2.75 or GRE/GMAT.

**Drexel University,** Westphal College of Media Arts and Design, Program in Arts Administration, Philadelphia, PA 19104-2875. Offers MS. *Accreditation:* NASAD. *Program availability:* Part-time, evening/weekend. *Faculty:* 2 full-time (both women), 6 part-time/adjunct (5 women). *Students:* 15 full-time (14 women), 60 part-time (46 women); includes 15 minority (11 Black or African American, non-Hispanic/Latino; 1 Asian, non-Hispanic/Latino; 3 Hispanic/Latino), 7 international. Average age 29. In 2016, 28 master's awarded. *Degree requirements:* For master's, thesis, internship. *Entrance requirements:* For master's, GRE, interview, minimum GPA of 3.0, previous course work in arts and business. Additional exam requirements/recommendations for international students: Required—TOEFL. *Application deadline:* For fall admission, 8/21 for domestic students; for spring admission, 3/5 for domestic students. Applications are processed on a rolling basis. Application fee: $50. Electronic applications accepted. *Expenses: Tuition:* Full-time $32,184; part-time $1192 per credit hour. *Required fees:* $280. Tuition and fees vary according to campus/location and program. *Financial support:* Teaching assistantships, career-related internships or fieldwork, and unspecified assistantships available. Support available to part-time students. Financial award application deadline: 2/1. *Faculty research:* Evaluation of art administration structures, funding for the arts, impact of politics in the arts, computer applications. *Unit head:* Cecelia Fitzgibbon, Program Coordinator, 215-895-2451, Fax: 215-895-2452. *Application contact:* Director of Graduate Admissions, 215-895-6700, Fax: 215-895-5939.

See Display on page 63 and Close-Up on page 99.

**Eastern Michigan University,** Graduate School, College of Arts and Sciences, School of Communication, Media and Theatre Arts, Program in Arts Administration, Ypsilanti, MI 48197. Offers MA. *Program availability:* Part-time, evening/weekend, online learning. *Students:* 3 full-time (all women), 2 part-time (both women); includes 2 minority (1 Black or African American, non-Hispanic/Latino; 1 Hispanic/Latino), 1 international. Average age 29. 14 applicants, 57% accepted. In 2016, 1 master's awarded. *Entrance requirements:* Additional exam requirements/recommendations for international students: Required—TOEFL. *Application deadline:* Applications are processed on a rolling basis. Application fee: $45. *Financial support:* Fellowships, research assistantships with full tuition reimbursements, teaching assistantships with full tuition reimbursements, career-related internships or fieldwork, Federal Work-Study, institutionally sponsored loans, scholarships/grants, tuition waivers (partial), and unspecified assistantships available. Support available to part-time students. Financial award applicants required to submit FAFSA. *Unit head:* Dr. Susan Booth, Coordinator, 734-487-1220, Fax: 734-487-3443, E-mail: sbooth1@emich.edu.

**Fashion Institute of Technology,** School of Graduate Studies, Program in Art Market Studies, New York, NY 10001-5992. Offers MA. *Accreditation:* NASAD. *Students:* 13. 23 applicants, 43% accepted, 5 enrolled. *Degree requirements:* For master's, thesis or alternative, internship. *Entrance requirements:* For master's, GRE General Test, previous course work in art history, 4 semesters of a foreign language. Additional exam requirements/recommendations for international students: Required—TOEFL (minimum score 550 paper-based). *Application deadline:* For fall admission, 2/15 priority date for domestic and international students. Applications are processed on a rolling basis. Application fee: $50. Electronic applications accepted. *Expenses:* Tuition, state resident: full-time $10,870; part-time $453 per credit. Tuition, nonresident: full-time $22,210; part-time $925 per credit. *Required fees:* $745. *Financial support:* Federal Work-Study and scholarships/grants available. Financial award applicants required to submit FAFSA. *Unit head:* Natasha Degen, Associate Chairperson, 212-217-4300. *Application contact:* Administrative Coordinator, 212-217-4300. Website: http://www.fitnyc.edu/art-market/

See Display on page 193 and Close-Up on page 203.

**Florida State University,** The Graduate School, College of Music, Tallahassee, FL 32306. Offers accompanying (MM); arts administration (MA); choral conducting (MM); composition (MM, DM); ethnomusicology (MM); general music (MA); instrumental accompanying (MM); instrumental conducting (MM); jazz studies (MM); music theory (MM, PhD); music therapy (MM); musicology (MM, PhD), including ethnomusicology (PhD), historical musicology (PhD); opera (MM, DM); performance (MM, DM); piano pedagogy (MM); piano technology (MA); vocal accompanying (MM). *Accreditation:* NASM. *Program availability:* Part-time. *Faculty:* 79 full-time, 2 part-time/adjunct. *Students:* 324 full-time (156 women); includes 87 minority (26 Black or African American, non-Hispanic/Latino; 1 American Indian or Alaska Native, non-Hispanic/Latino; 32 Asian, non-Hispanic/Latino; 26 Hispanic/Latino; 2 Native Hawaiian or other Pacific Islander, non-Hispanic/Latino). Average age 26. 737 applicants, 42% accepted, 138 enrolled. In

## Arts Administration

2016, 120 master's, 36 doctorates awarded. *Degree requirements:* For master's, variable foreign language requirement, comprehensive exam (for some programs), thesis (for some programs), departmental qualifying exam; for doctorate, variable foreign language requirement, comprehensive exam (for some programs), thesis/dissertation, departmental qualifying exam. *Entrance requirements:* For master's, GRE General Test (for some programs), audition, minimum GPA of 3.0; for doctorate, GRE General Test (for some programs), audition, master's degree, minimum GPA of 3.0. Additional exam requirements/recommendations for international students: Required—TOEFL (minimum score 590 paper-based; 97 iBT), IELTS (minimum score 7.5). *Application deadline:* For fall admission, 7/1 for domestic and international students; for spring admission, 11/1 for domestic and international students; for summer admission, 3/1 for domestic students. Applications are processed on a rolling basis. Application fee: $30. Electronic applications accepted. *Expenses:* Tuition, state resident: full-time $7263; part-time $403.51 per credit hour. Tuition, nonresident: full-time $18,087; part-time $1004.85 per credit hour. *Required fees:* $1365; $75.81 per credit hour. $20 per semester. Tuition and fees vary according to campus/location. *Financial support:* In 2016–17, 222 students received support, including 2 fellowships with full tuition reimbursements available (averaging $15,000 per year), 14 research assistantships with full and partial tuition reimbursements available (averaging $5,900 per year), 201 teaching assistantships with full and partial tuition reimbursements available (averaging $5,900 per year); career-related internships or fieldwork, scholarships/grants, tuition waivers (full and partial), and unspecified assistantships also available. Support available to part-time students. Financial award application deadline: 2/28; financial award applicants required to submit FAFSA. *Faculty research:* Music therapy in NICU units, music of the Americas, music theory pedagogy, music performance. *Unit head:* Dr. Patricia Flowers, Dean, 850-644-4361, Fax: 850-644-2033, E-mail: pjflowers@fsu.edu. *Application contact:* Kris Watson, Director of Admissions, 850-645-2126, Fax: 850-644-2033, E-mail: krwatson@fsu.edu. Website: http://www.music.fsu.edu/

**George Mason University,** College of Visual and Performing Arts, Program in Arts Management, Fairfax, VA 22030. Offers MA, Certificate. *Accreditation:* NASAD. *Faculty:* 4 full-time (3 women), 5 part-time/adjunct (4 women). *Students:* 43 full-time (36 women), 43 part-time (39 women); includes 18 minority (6 Black or African American, non-Hispanic/Latino; 2 Asian, non-Hispanic/Latino; 6 Hispanic/Latino; 1 Native Hawaiian or other Pacific Islander, non-Hispanic/Latino; 3 Two or more races, non-Hispanic/Latino), 23 international. Average age 27. 62 applicants, 60% accepted, 19 enrolled. In 2016, 35 master's, 2 other advanced degrees awarded. *Degree requirements:* For master's, internship. *Entrance requirements:* For master's and Certificate, GRE (recommended), undergraduate degree with minimum GPA of 3.0, official transcripts, 2 letters of recommendation, statement of purpose, resume. Additional exam requirements/recommendations for international students: Required—TOEFL (minimum score 575 paper-based; 88 iBT), IELTS (minimum score 6.5), PTE (minimum score 59). *Application deadline:* For fall admission, 2/15 for domestic and international students. Application fee: $75 ($80 for international students). Electronic applications accepted. *Expenses:* Tuition, state resident: full-time $10,628; part-time $443 per credit. Tuition, nonresident: full-time $29,306; part-time $1221 per credit. *Required fees:* $3096; $129 per credit. Tuition and fees vary according to program. *Financial support:* Career-related internships or fieldwork, Federal Work-Study, and scholarships/grants available. Support available to part-time students. Financial award application deadline: 3/1; financial award applicants required to submit FAFSA. *Faculty research:* Information technology for arts managers, special topics in arts management, directions in gallery management, arts in society, public relations/marketing strategies for art organizations. *Unit head:* Claire Huschle, Program Director, 703-993-8719, Fax: 703-993-9829, E-mail: chuschle@gmu.edu. *Application contact:* Elizabeth Ricks, Program Coordinator, 703-993-8926, Fax: 703-993-9829, E-mail: ericks@gmu.edu. Website: http://artsmanagement.gmu.edu/arts-management-ma/

**Goucher College,** MA and MFA Programs, Baltimore, MD 21204-2794. Offers arts administration (MA); creative nonfiction (MFA); cultural sustainability (MA); digital arts (MA, MFA); environmental studies (MA); historic preservation (MA); management (MA). *Program availability:* Part-time, evening/weekend, blended/hybrid learning. *Faculty:* 6 full-time (4 women), 100 part-time/adjunct (56 women). *Students:* 70 full-time (50 women), 69 part-time (52 women); includes 15 minority (7 Black or African American, non-Hispanic/Latino; 1 American Indian or Alaska Native, non-Hispanic/Latino; 1 Asian, non-Hispanic/Latino; 4 Hispanic/Latino; 2 Two or more races, non-Hispanic/Latino), 2 international. 74 applicants, 88% accepted, 42 enrolled. In 2016, 83 master's awarded. *Degree requirements:* For master's, thesis, e-portfolio. *Entrance requirements:* For master's, digital portfolio (for MA, MFA in digital arts); writing sample (for MFA in creative nonfiction). Additional exam requirements/recommendations for international students: Required—TOEFL (minimum score 550 paper-based; 80 iBT). *Application deadline:* Applications are processed on a rolling basis. Application fee: $75. Electronic applications accepted. *Expenses:* Contact institution. *Financial support:* Scholarships/grants and unspecified assistantships available. Financial award application deadline: 4/15; financial award applicants required to submit FAFSA. *Unit head:* Leslie Rubinkowski, Assistant Provost, 410-337-6200, E-mail: leslie.rubinkowski@goucher.edu. *Application contact:* Shelby Hillers, Admissions Coordinator, 410-337-6200, Fax: 410-337-6200, E-mail: shelby.hillers@goucher.edu. Website: http://www.goucher.edu/grad

**HEC Montreal,** School of Business Administration, Graduate Diploma Programs in Administration, Program in Management of Cultural Organizations, Montréal, QC H3T 2A7, Canada. Offers Graduate Diploma. All courses are given in French. *Students:* 34 full-time (30 women), 101 part-time (86 women). 80 applicants, 80% accepted, 57 enrolled. In 2016, 40 Graduate Diplomas awarded. *Degree requirements:* For Graduate Diploma, one foreign language. *Entrance requirements:* For degree, bachelor's degree (not in administration, preferably cultural field), one year of work experience. *Application deadline:* For fall admission, 4/15 for domestic and international students; for winter admission, 9/15 for domestic and international students. Application fee: $86 Canadian dollars. Electronic applications accepted. *Expenses:* Tuition, area resident: Part-time $77.80 Canadian dollars per credit. Tuition, state resident: full-time $2797 Canadian dollars; part-time $240.92 Canadian dollars per credit. Tuition, nonresident: full-time $8673 Canadian dollars; part-time $531.43 Canadian dollars per credit. International tuition: $19,131 Canadian dollars full-time. *Required fees:* $1699 Canadian dollars; $40.58 Canadian dollars per credit. $67.32 Canadian dollars per term. Tuition and fees vary according to degree level and program. *Financial support:* In 2016–17, 814 students received support. Research assistantships, teaching assistantships, and scholarships/grants available. Financial award application deadline: 9/2. *Unit head:* Renaud Lachance, Director, 514-340-7165, E-mail: renaud.lachance@hec.ca. *Application contact:* Anny Caron, Administrative Director, 514-340-3598, Fax: 514-340-6411, E-mail: anny.caron@hec.ca. Website: http://www.hec.ca/programmes/dess/dess-gestion-organismes-culturels/index.html

**Indiana University Bloomington,** School of Public and Environmental Affairs, Program in Arts Administration, Bloomington, IN 47405-7000. Offers MAAA. *Program availability:* Part-time. *Degree requirements:* For master's, final internship. *Entrance requirements:* For master's, GRE or GMAT. Additional exam requirements/recommendations for international students: Required—TOEFL or IELTS. Electronic applications accepted. *Faculty research:* Cultural policy, nonprofit management, and pricing for the arts.

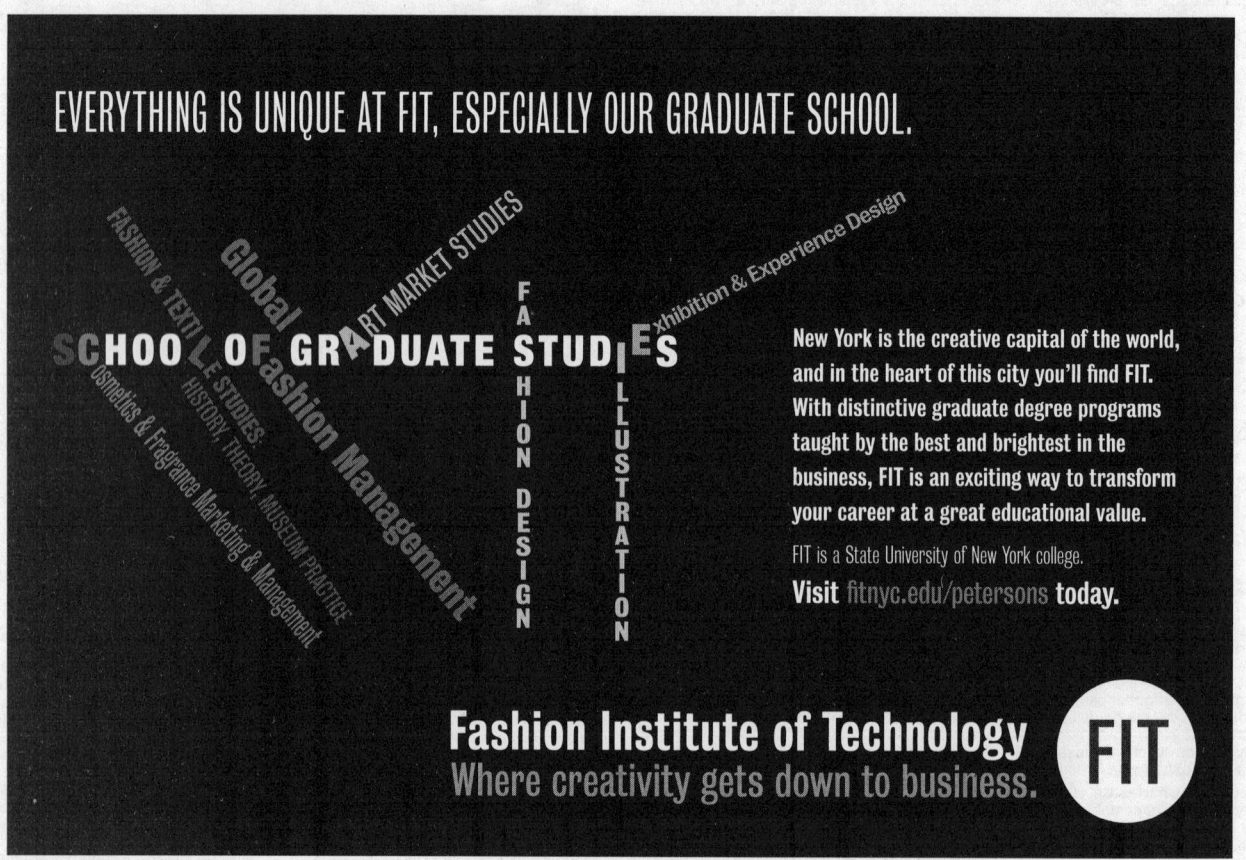

**Le Moyne College,** Program in Arts Administration, Syracuse, NY 13214. Offers MS. *Program availability:* Part-time, evening/weekend. *Faculty:* 1 full-time (0 women), 2 part-time/adjunct (both women). *Students:* 10 full-time (6 women), 6 part-time (5 women); includes 3 minority (1 Black or African American, non-Hispanic/Latino; 1 American Indian or Alaska Native, non-Hispanic/Latino; 1 Hispanic/Latino). Average age 29. 16 applicants, 94% accepted, 14 enrolled. *Degree requirements:* For master's, capstone consulting project. *Entrance requirements:* For master's, bachelor's degree with minimum GPA of 2.8, two letters of recommendation, resumé, interview. Additional exam requirements/recommendations for international students: Required—TOEFL (minimum score 550 paper-based; 79 iBT); Recommended—IELTS (minimum score 6.5). *Application deadline:* For fall admission, 7/1 priority date for domestic and international students; for spring admission, 11/1 priority date for domestic and international students; for summer admission, 4/1 priority date for domestic and international students. Applications are processed on a rolling basis. Application fee: $50. Electronic applications accepted. *Expenses:* $700 per credit hour. *Financial support:* In 2016–17, 3 students received support. Career-related internships or fieldwork, scholarships/grants, and health care benefits available. Financial award applicants required to submit FAFSA. *Unit head:* Travis Newton, Assistant Professor and Director of Arts Administration, 315-445-4201, E-mail: newtontm@lemoyne.edu. *Application contact:* Kristen P. Richards, Senior Director of Enrollment Management, 315-445-5444, Fax: 315-445-6092, E-mail: trapaskp@lemoyne.edu.
Website: http://www.lemoyne.edu/Learn/Colleges-Schools-Centers/College-of-Arts-Sciences/Majors-Minors/Arts-Administration

**London Metropolitan University,** Graduate Programs, London, United Kingdom. Offers applied psychology (M Sc); architecture (MA); biomedical science (M Sc); blood science (M Sc); cancer pharmacology (M Sc); computer networking and cyber security (M Sc); computing and information systems (M Sc); conference interpreting (MA); counter-terrorism studies (M Sc); creative, digital and professional writing (MA); crime, violence and prevention (M Sc); criminology (M Sc); curating contemporary art (MA); data analytics (M Sc); digital media (MA); early childhood studies (MA); education (MA, Ed D); financial services law, regulation and compliance (LL M); food science (M Sc); forensic psychology (M Sc); health and social care management and policy (MA); human nutrition (M Sc); human resource management (MA); human rights and international conflict (MA); information technology (M Sc); intelligence and security studies (M Sc); international oil, gas and energy law (LL M); international relations (MA); interpreting (MA); learning and teaching in higher education (MA); legal practice (LL M); media and entertainment law (LL M); organizational and consumer psychology (M Sc); psychological therapy (M Sc); psychology of mental health (M Sc); public health (M Sc); public policy and management (MPA); security studies (M Sc); social work (M Sc); spatial planning and urban design (MA); sports therapy (M Sc); supporting older children and young people with dyslexia (MA); teaching languages (MA), including Arabic, English; translation (MA); woman and child abuse (MA).

**Montclair State University,** The Graduate School, College of the Arts, MA Program in Theatre, Montclair, NJ 07043-1624. Offers arts management (MA); production/stage management (MA); theatre studies (MA). *Accreditation:* NAST. *Program availability:* Part-time, evening/weekend. *Degree requirements:* For master's, comprehensive exam, thesis or alternative. *Entrance requirements:* For master's, GRE General Test, 2 letters of recommendation. Additional exam requirements/recommendations for international students: Required—TOEFL (minimum score 83 iBT) or IELTS (minimum score 6.5). Electronic applications accepted. *Expenses:* Tuition, state resident: part-time $553 per credit. Tuition, nonresident: part-time $854 per credit. *Required fees:* $91 per credit. Tuition and fees vary according to program. *Faculty research:* Dancetury, Arab and Muslim images in American drama, Neil LaBute and playwriting, directing, Robert Edmond Jones.

**Moore College of Art & Design,** Program in Community Practice, Philadelphia, PA 19103. Offers MFA. *Degree requirements:* For master's, thesis.

**New York Institute of Technology,** School of Interdisciplinary Studies and Education, Program in Leadership in the Arts and Entertainment Industries, Old Westbury, NY 11568-8000. Offers arts and entertainment leadership (Advanced Certificate); leadership in the arts and entertainment industries (MA). *Program availability:* Part-time, evening/weekend. *Faculty:* 3 full-time (2 women), 1 part-time/adjunct (0 women). *Students:* 3 full-time (all women), 1 (woman) part-time; includes 1 minority (Two or more races, non-Hispanic/Latino), 3 international. Average age 27. 3 applicants, 100% accepted, 2 enrolled. *Degree requirements:* For master's, practicum, capstone seminar. *Entrance requirements:* For master's, bachelor's degree in the arts and/or in-depth knowledge of at least one performing art discipline; demonstration of at least three years of progressively responsible positions in management or an organization in a performing arts industry sector; interview via Skype or phone; resume; personal statement; two letters of recommendation; for Advanced Certificate, bachelor's degree in the arts and/or in-depth knowledge of at least one performing art discipline; some experience in management; interview via Skype or phone; resume; two letters of recommendation. Additional exam requirements/recommendations for international students: Required—TOEFL (minimum score 79 iBT), IELTS (minimum score 6). *Application deadline:* Applications are processed on a rolling basis. Application fee: $50. Electronic applications accepted. *Expenses:* $1,215 per credit. *Financial support:* Career-related internships or fieldwork, Federal Work-Study, scholarships/grants, tuition waivers (full and partial), and unspecified assistantships available. Support available to part-time students. Financial award application deadline: 3/1; financial award applicants required to submit FAFSA. *Unit head:* David Milch, Program Director, 212-261-1639, E-mail: dmilch@nyit.edu. *Application contact:* Alice Dolitsky, Director, Graduate Admissions, 516-686-7520, Fax: 516-686-1116, E-mail: nyitgrad@nyit.edu.
Website: http://www.nyit.edu/degrees/arts_entertainment_leadership_ma

**New York University,** Steinhardt School of Culture, Education, and Human Development, Department of Art and Art Professions, Program in Visual Arts Administration, New York, NY 10003. Offers MA. *Program availability:* Part-time. *Degree requirements:* For master's, thesis (for some programs). *Entrance requirements:* For master's, interview. Additional exam requirements/recommendations for international students: Required—TOEFL (minimum score 100 iBT). Electronic applications accepted. *Faculty research:* Corporate philanthropy, contemporary art and culture, public art and urban development, cultural policy, arts advocacy.

**New York University,** Steinhardt School of Culture, Education, and Human Development, Department of Music and Performing Arts Professions, Program in Performing Arts Administration, New York, NY 10012. Offers MA. *Program availability:* Part-time. *Degree requirements:* For master's, thesis (for some programs). *Entrance requirements:* For master's, interview. Additional exam requirements/recommendations for international students: Required—TOEFL (minimum score 100 iBT). Electronic applications accepted. *Faculty research:* Legal dimensions of arts management, global arts management, cultural policy.

**New York University,** Tisch School of the Arts, Program in Arts Politics, New York, NY 10012-1019. Offers MA. *Degree requirements:* For master's, thesis. *Entrance requirements:* For master's, professional resume, writing sample, statement of purpose. Additional exam requirements/recommendations for international students: Required—TOEFL or IELTS.

**Northwestern University,** The Graduate School, School of Communication, Program in Leadership for Creative Enterprises, Evanston, IL 60208. Offers MS.

**The Ohio State University,** Graduate School, College of Arts and Sciences, Division of Arts and Humanities, Department of Arts Administration, Education and Policy, Program in Arts Policy and Administration, Columbus, OH 43210. Offers MA. *Faculty:* 11. *Students:* 7 full-time (3 women). Average age 25. In 2016, 4 master's awarded. *Degree requirements:* For master's, thesis. *Entrance requirements:* For master's, GRE General Test. Additional exam requirements/recommendations for international students: Required—TOEFL (minimum score 600 paper-based; 100 iBT); Recommended—IELTS (minimum score 8). *Application deadline:* For fall and spring admission, 11/30 priority date for domestic and international students. Applications are processed on a rolling basis. Application fee: $60 ($70 for international students). Electronic applications accepted. *Financial support:* Fellowships with tuition reimbursements, teaching assistantships with tuition reimbursements, career-related internships or fieldwork, and unspecified assistantships available. Support available to part-time students. Financial award application deadline: 4/5. *Faculty research:* Public policy and advocacy. *Unit head:* Dr. Karen Hutzel, Chair and Associate Professor, 614-292-9852, E-mail: hutzel.4@osu.edu. *Application contact:* Graduate and Professional Admissions, 614-292-6031, Fax: 614-292-3656, E-mail: gpadmissions@osu.edu.
Website: http://aaep.osu.edu/arts-policy-administration-ma-program

**Pratt Institute,** School of Art, Program in Arts and Cultural Management, New York, NY 10011. Offers MPS. *Program availability:* Part-time, evening/weekend. *Faculty:* 4 part-time/adjunct (2 women). *Students:* 36 full-time (35 women); includes 6 minority (3 Black or African American, non-Hispanic/Latino; 1 Asian, non-Hispanic/Latino; 3 Hispanic/Latino; 1 Two or more races, non-Hispanic/Latino), 19 international. Average age 25. 121 applicants, 51% accepted, 21 enrolled. In 2016, 23 master's awarded. *Degree requirements:* For master's, thesis. *Entrance requirements:* For master's, letters of recommendation, portfolio. Additional exam requirements/recommendations for international students: Required—TOEFL (minimum score 600 paper-based; 100 iBT). *Application deadline:* For fall admission, 1/5 for domestic and international students; for spring admission, 10/1 for domestic and international students. Application fee: $50 ($90 for international students). Electronic applications accepted. *Expenses:* $29,646 full-time tuition, $1,938 fees. *Financial support:* Career-related internships or fieldwork, Federal Work-Study, institutionally sponsored loans, scholarships/grants, health care benefits, and unspecified assistantships available. Support available to part-time students. Financial award application deadline: 2/1; financial award applicants required to submit FAFSA. *Unit head:* Dr. Mary McBride, Director, 212-647-7538, E-mail: mmcb1033@pratt.edu. *Application contact:* Natalie Capannelli, Director of Graduate Admissions, 718-636-3551, Fax: 718-399-4242, E-mail: ncapanne@pratt.edu.
Website: https://www.pratt.edu/academics/school-of-art/graduate-school-of-art/arts-cultural-management/

**Pratt Institute,** School of Art, Program in Design Management, New York, NY 10011. Offers MPS. *Program availability:* Part-time. *Faculty:* 7 part-time/adjunct (3 women). *Students:* 43 full-time (36 women); includes 8 minority (3 Black or African American, non-Hispanic/Latino; 1 Asian, non-Hispanic/Latino; 4 Hispanic/Latino), 31 international. Average age 27. 81 applicants, 62% accepted, 21 enrolled. In 2016, 20 master's awarded. *Degree requirements:* For master's, thesis. *Entrance requirements:* For master's, letters of recommendation, portfolio. Additional exam requirements/recommendations for international students: Required—TOEFL (minimum score 600 paper-based; 100 iBT). *Application deadline:* For fall admission, 1/5 for domestic and international students; for spring admission, 10/1 for domestic and international students. Application fee: $50 ($90 for international students). Electronic applications accepted. *Expenses:* $29,646 full-time tuition, $1,938 fees. *Financial support:* Career-related internships or fieldwork, Federal Work-Study, institutionally sponsored loans, scholarships/grants, health care benefits, and unspecified assistantships available. Support available to part-time students. Financial award application deadline: 2/1; financial award applicants required to submit FAFSA. *Unit head:* Dr. Mary McBride, Chairperson, 212-647-7538, E-mail: mmcb1033@pratt.edu. *Application contact:* Natalie Capannelli, Director of Graduate Admissions, 718-636-3551, Fax: 718-399-4242, E-mail: ncapanne@pratt.edu.
Website: https://www.pratt.edu/academics/school-of-art/graduate-school-of-art/design-management/

See Display on page 156 and Close-Up on page 209.

**Rhode Island College,** School of Graduate Studies, Faculty of Arts and Sciences, Department of Art, Providence, RI 02908-1991. Offers art education (MA, MAT); media studies (MA). *Accreditation:* NASAD (one or more programs are accredited). *Program availability:* Part-time, evening/weekend. *Faculty:* 6 full-time (3 women), 2 part-time/adjunct (1 woman). *Students:* 7 full-time (5 women), 5 part-time (4 women); includes 1 minority (Hispanic/Latino). Average age 33. In 2016, 4 master's awarded. *Degree requirements:* For master's, thesis. *Entrance requirements:* For master's, GRE General Test, portfolio (MA), 3 letters of recommendation, interview. Additional exam requirements/recommendations for international students: Recommended—TOEFL (minimum score 550 paper-based; 79 iBT). *Application deadline:* For fall admission, 3/1 for domestic students. Applications are processed on a rolling basis. Application fee: $50. Electronic applications accepted. *Expenses:* Tuition, state resident: full-time $8928; part-time $372 per credit. Tuition, nonresident: full-time $17,376; part-time $724 per credit. *Required fees:* $604; $22 per credit. One-time fee: $74. *Financial support:* In 2016–17, 2 teaching assistantships with full tuition reimbursements (averaging $1,500 per year) were awarded; career-related internships or fieldwork, Federal Work-Study, scholarships/grants, health care benefits, and unspecified assistantships also available. Support available to part-time students. Financial award application deadline: 5/15; financial award applicants required to submit FAFSA. *Unit head:* Prof. Richard Whitten, Chair, 401-456-9635. *Application contact:* Graduate Studies, 401-456-8700.
Website: http://www.ric.edu/art/index.php

**Robert Morris University Illinois,** Morris Graduate School of Management, Chicago, IL 60605. Offers accounting (MBA); accounting/finance (MBA); business analytics (MIS); design and media (MM); design management (MM); educational technology (MM); health care administration (MM); higher education administration (MM); human resource management (MBA); information security (MIS); information systems (MBA, MIS); law enforcement administration (MM); management (MBA); management/finance (MBA); management/human resource management (MBA); mobile computing (MIS); sports administration (MM). *Program availability:* Part-time, evening/weekend. *Faculty:* 4 full-time (1 woman), 25 part-time/adjunct (5 women). *Students:* 196 full-time (98 women), 151 part-time (85 women); includes 200 minority (114 Black or African American, non-Hispanic/Latino; 17 Asian, non-Hispanic/Latino; 67 Hispanic/Latino; 2 Two or more races, non-Hispanic/Latino), 23 international. Average age 33. 174 applicants, 61% accepted, 97 enrolled. In 2016, 190 master's awarded. *Entrance requirements:* For master's, official transcripts and letters of recommendation (for some programs); written personal statement. Additional exam requirements/recommendations for international students: Required—TOEFL (minimum score 550 paper-based). *Application deadline:* Applications are processed on a rolling basis. Application fee: $20 ($100 for international students). Electronic applications accepted. *Expenses:* Tuition: Full-time $16,500; part-time $2750 per course. *Financial support:* In 2016–17, 444 students received support.

## *Arts Administration*

Federal Work-Study, scholarships/grants, and unspecified assistantships available. Support available to part-time students. Financial award applicants required to submit FAFSA. *Unit head:* Kayed Akkawi, Dean, 312-935-6050, Fax: 312-935-6020, E-mail: kakkawi@robertmorris.edu. *Application contact:* Danielle Naffziger, Vice President of Marketing and Enrollment, 312-935-4812, Fax: 312-935-6020, E-mail: dnaffziger@robertmorris.edu.

**Rocky Mountain College of Art + Design,** Program in Education, Leadership + Emerging Technologies, Lakewood, CO 80214. Offers MA. *Accreditation:* NASAD. *Program availability:* Online learning.

**Rowan University,** Graduate School, College of Performing Arts, Department of Theatre and Dance, Glassboro, NJ 08028-1701. Offers theatre arts administration (MA). *Accreditation:* NASAD. Electronic applications accepted.

**Ryerson University,** School of Graduate Studies, Program in Photographic Preservation and Collections Management, Toronto, ON M5B 2K3, Canada. Offers MA.

**Saint Mary's University of Minnesota,** Schools of Graduate and Professional Programs, Graduate School of Business and Technology, Arts and Cultural Management Program, Winona, MN 55987-1399. Offers MA. Tuition and fees vary according to degree level and program. *Unit head:* Paula Justich, Director, 612-728-5165, Fax: 612-728-5121, E-mail: pjustich@smumn.edu. *Application contact:* James Callinan, Director of Admissions for Graduate and Professional Programs, 612-728-5185, Fax: 612-728-5121, E-mail: jcallina@smumn.edu. *Website:* http://www.smumn.edu/ACM

**St. Thomas University,** School of Leadership Studies, Program in Art Management, Miami Gardens, FL 33054-6459. Offers MA.

**Savannah College of Art and Design,** Graduate School, Program in Business Design and Arts Leadership, Savannah, GA 31402-3146. Offers MA. *Program availability:* Part-time, 100% online. *Faculty:* 5 full-time (1 woman), 3 part-time/adjunct (1 woman). *Students:* 35 full-time (31 women), 51 part-time (44 women); includes 27 minority (18 Black or African American, non-Hispanic/Latino; 1 Asian, non-Hispanic/Latino; 6 Hispanic/Latino; 1 Native Hawaiian or other Pacific Islander, non-Hispanic/Latino; 1 Two or more races, non-Hispanic/Latino), 26 international. Average age 29. 115 applicants, 40% accepted, 28 enrolled. In 2016, 56 master's awarded. *Degree requirements:* For master's, final project. *Entrance requirements:* For master's, GRE (recommended), portfolio (submitted in digital format), audition or writing submission, resume, statement of purpose, two letters of recommendation. Additional exam requirements/recommendations for international students: Required—TOEFL (minimum score 550 paper-based, 85 iBT), IELTS (minimum score 6.5), or ACTFL. *Application deadline:* For fall admission, 4/1 for domestic and international students. Applications are processed on a rolling basis. Application fee: $40. Electronic applications accepted. *Expenses: Tuition:* Full-time $36,045. Tuition and fees vary according to course load. *Financial support:* Career-related internships or fieldwork, Federal Work-Study, and scholarships/grants available. Financial award application deadline: 4/1; financial award applicants required to submit FAFSA. *Unit head:* Anita Akella, Academic Program Coordinator. *Application contact:* Jenny Jaquillard, Executive Director of Admissions, Recruitment and Events, 912-525-5100, Fax: 912-525-5985, E-mail: admission@scad.edu. *Website:* http://www.scad.edu/academics/programs/business-design-and-arts-leadership

**Savannah College of Art and Design,** Graduate School, Program in Design Management, Savannah, GA 31402-3146. Offers MA, MFA. *Program availability:* Part-time, 100% online. *Faculty:* 17 full-time (2 women), 8 part-time/adjunct (4 women). *Students:* 49 full-time (36 women), 65 part-time (48 women); includes 17 minority (6 Black or African American, non-Hispanic/Latino; 4 Asian, non-Hispanic/Latino; 7 Hispanic/Latino), 42 international. Average age 30. 91 applicants, 42% accepted, 24 enrolled. In 2016, 44 master's awarded. *Degree requirements:* For master's, final project (for MA); thesis (for MFA). *Entrance requirements:* For master's, GRE (recommended), portfolio (submitted in digital format), audition or writing submission, resume, statement of purpose, two letters of recommendation. Additional exam requirements/recommendations for international students: Required—TOEFL (minimum score 550 paper-based, 85 iBT), IELTS (minimum score 6.5), or ACTFL. *Application deadline:* For fall admission, 4/1 for domestic and international students. Applications are processed on a rolling basis. Application fee: $40. Electronic applications accepted. *Expenses: Tuition:* Full-time $36,045. Tuition and fees vary according to course load. *Financial support:* Career-related internships or fieldwork, Federal Work-Study, and scholarships/grants available. Financial award application deadline: 4/1; financial award applicants required to submit FAFSA. *Unit head:* Bill Lee, Chair, Design Management. *Application contact:* Jenny Jaquillard, Executive Director of Admissions, Recruitment and Events, 912-525-5100, Fax: 912-525-5985, E-mail: admission@scad.edu. *Website:* http://www.scad.edu/academics/programs/design-management

**School of the Art Institute of Chicago,** Graduate Division, Program in Arts Administration and Policy, Chicago, IL 60603-3103. Offers MAAAP. *Accreditation:* NASAD. *Degree requirements:* For master's, thesis, telephone interview. *Entrance requirements:* Additional exam requirements/recommendations for international students: Required—TOEFL, IELTS. *Faculty research:* Latin American artists, activist art, community-based art.

**Seattle University,** College of Arts and Sciences, Program in Arts Leadership, Seattle, WA 98122-1090. Offers MFA. *Program availability:* Part-time, evening/weekend. *Faculty:* 6 full-time (4 women), 9 part-time/adjunct (4 women). *Students:* 1 (woman) full-time, 62 part-time (49 women); includes 18 minority (9 Black or African American, non-Hispanic/Latino; 3 Asian, non-Hispanic/Latino; 3 Hispanic/Latino; 3 Two or more races, non-Hispanic/Latino), 10 international. Average age 30. 73 applicants, 84% accepted, 33 enrolled. In 2016, 35 master's awarded. *Degree requirements:* For master's, summary capstone project presentation and paper. *Entrance requirements:* For master's, minimum GPA of 3.0; 2 years of management in nonprofit, comparable work, or volunteer experience. Additional exam requirements/recommendations for international students: Required—TOEFL, IELTS. *Application deadline:* For fall admission, 3/15 for domestic students, 4/1 for international students. Applications are processed on a rolling basis. Application fee: $55. Electronic applications accepted. *Financial support:* In 2016–17, 23 students received support. Application deadline: 3/15; applicants required to submit FAFSA. *Faculty research:* Leadership succession planning, social media in arts marketing, audience development. *Unit head:* Kevin Maifeld, Director, 206-296-5370, E-mail: maifeldk@seattleu.edu. *Application contact:* Janet Shandley, Associate Dean of Graduate Admissions, 206-296-5900, Fax: 206-298-5656, E-mail: grad_admissions@seattleu.edu. *Website:* https://www.seattleu.edu/artsci/mfa/

**Sotheby's Institute of Art–London,** Graduate Programs, London, United Kingdom. Offers art business (MA); contemporary art (MA); fine and decorative art and design (MA); modern and contemporary Asian art (MA). *Faculty:* 41 full-time (25 women). *Students:* 181 full-time (159 women). *Degree requirements:* For master's, thesis. *Entrance requirements:* Additional exam requirements/recommendations for international students: Required—IELTS (minimum score 7). *Application deadline:* Applications are processed on a rolling basis. Electronic applications accepted. *Expenses: Tuition:* Full-time 24,900 British pounds. Tuition and fees vary according to

class time, program and student level. *Application contact:* Jessica Bearne, Admissions Manager, 44 20 7462 3250, E-mail: j.bearne@sothebysinstitute.com.

**Sotheby's Institute of Art–New York,** Graduate Programs, New York, NY 10021. Offers art business (MA); contemporary art (MA); fine and decorative art and design (MA). *Accreditation:* NASAD. *Entrance requirements:* For master's, academic transcripts, two letters of academic reference, personal statement, writing sample, curriculum vitae/resume, interview. Additional exam requirements/recommendations for international students: Required—TOEFL (minimum score 100 iBT), IELTS (minimum score 7). Electronic applications accepted.

**Southern Methodist University,** Meadows School of the Arts, Division of Arts Management and Arts Entrepreneurship, Dallas, TX 75275. Offers international arts management (MM); MA/MBA. MM offered jointly with Bocconi University Graduate School of Management in Milan and HEC Montreal. *Entrance requirements:* For master's, GMAT. Additional exam requirements/recommendations for international students: Required—TOEFL (minimum score 600 paper-based; 100 iBT). Electronic applications accepted.

**Southern Utah University,** Program in Arts Administration, Cedar City, UT 84720-2498. Offers MA, MFA. *Program availability:* Part-time, online learning. *Faculty:* 1 (woman) full-time, 4 part-time/adjunct (1 woman). *Students:* 10 full-time (6 women), 27 part-time (22 women); includes 8 minority (2 Asian, non-Hispanic/Latino; 5 Hispanic/Latino; 1 Native Hawaiian or other Pacific Islander, non-Hispanic/Latino), 1 international. Average age 31. 47 applicants, 77% accepted, 32 enrolled. In 2016, 10 master's awarded. *Entrance requirements:* For master's, bachelor's degree, interview, 3 letters of recommendation, resume, minimum undergraduate GPA of 3.0, written statement of purpose, transcripts. Additional exam requirements/recommendations for international students: Required—TOEFL (minimum score 550 paper-based, 79 iBT) or IELTS (minimum score 6). *Application deadline:* For fall admission, 2/15 for domestic and international students. Applications are processed on a rolling basis. Application fee: $60 ($65 for international students). Electronic applications accepted. *Expenses:* $7,692 per year resident or online full-time; $23,384 per year on-campus non-resident full-time. *Financial support:* Tuition waivers and unspecified assistantships available. *Unit head:* Rachel Bishop, Program Director/Assistant Professor, 435-586-7873, Fax: 435-865-8657, E-mail: bishopr@suu.edu. *Website:* https://www.suu.edu/pva/aa/academic.html

**Teachers College, Columbia University,** Department of Arts and Humanities, New York, NY 10027. Offers applied linguistics (MA, Ed D); art and art education (Ed M, MA, Ed D, Ed DCT); arts administration (MA); bilingual and bicultural education (MA); global competence (Certificate); history and education (Ed D, PhD); music and music education (Ed DCT); philosophy and education (MA, Ed D, PhD); social studies education (Ed M, PhD); teaching English to speakers of other languages (Ed M); teaching of English and English education (Ed M, MA, Ed D, PhD), including English education (Ed M, Ed D, PhD), teaching of English (MA); teaching of social studies (MA); TESOL (MA, Ed D). *Program availability:* Part-time, evening/weekend. *Students:* 429 full-time (329 women), 467 part-time (332 women); includes 268 minority (62 Black or African American, non-Hispanic/Latino; 1 American Indian or Alaska Native, non-Hispanic/Latino; 108 Asian, non-Hispanic/Latino; 76 Hispanic/Latino; 21 Two or more races, non-Hispanic/Latino), 212 international. 1,068 applicants, 53% accepted, 272 enrolled. Terminal master's awarded for partial completion of doctoral program. *Expenses: Tuition:* Full-time $36,288; part-time $1512 per credit. *Required fees:* $438 per semester. One-time fee: $510 full-time. Full-time tuition and fees vary according to course load. *Financial support:* Fellowships, research assistantships, teaching assistantships, career-related internships or fieldwork, Federal Work-Study, institutionally sponsored loans, tuition waivers (full and partial), and unspecified assistantships available. Support available to part-time students. *Unit head:* Prof. William Gaudelli, Department Chair, 212-678-3150, E-mail: wg74@columbia.edu. *Application contact:* David Estrella, Director of Admissions, 212-678-3305, Fax: 212-678-4171, E-mail: estrella@tc.columbia.edu. *Website:* http://www.tc.edu/a%26h/

**Temple University,** Tyler School of Art, Department of Art History, Philadelphia, PA 19122-6096. Offers MA, PhD. *Program availability:* Part-time. Terminal master's awarded for partial completion of doctoral program. *Degree requirements:* For master's, 2 foreign languages, thesis, comprehensive slide exam; for doctorate, 2 foreign languages, thesis/dissertation, qualifying exam. *Entrance requirements:* For master's, GRE General Test, minimum GPA of 3.0, letters of recommendation, resume/curriculum vitae, writing sample; for doctorate, GRE, MA in art history, minimum GPA of 3.0, letters of recommendation, resume/curriculum vitae, writing sample. Additional exam requirements/recommendations for international students: Required—TOEFL (minimum score 550 paper-based; 79 iBT), IELTS (minimum score 6.5). Electronic applications accepted. *Expenses:* Contact institution. *Faculty research:* Aegean, Greek, and Roman art; early Christian art; medieval art and architecture; Renaissance and Baroque painting, sculpture, and architecture; nineteenth- and twentieth-century painting and sculpture.

**Universidad del Turabo,** Graduate Programs, School of Social Sciences and Humanities, Programs in Public Affairs, Program in Arts Administration, Gurabo, PR 00778-3030. Offers MPA. *Students:* 4 full-time (2 women), 4 part-time (3 women); all minorities (all Hispanic/Latino). Average age 31. 12 applicants, 50% accepted, 5 enrolled. In 2016, 4 master's awarded. *Entrance requirements:* For master's, GRE, EXADEP or GMAT, interview, essay, official transcript, recommendation letters. *Application deadline:* Applications are processed on a rolling basis. Application fee: $25. Electronic applications accepted. *Financial support:* Institutionally sponsored loans available. Financial award applicants required to submit FAFSA. *Unit head:* María del Carmen Santos, Dean, 787-743-7979 Ext. 4232. *Application contact:* Diriee Rodríguez, Admissions Director, 787-743-7979 Ext. 4453, E-mail: admisiones-ut@suagm.edu. *Website:* http://ut.suagm.edu/es/sociales

**University at Buffalo, the State University of New York,** Graduate School, College of Arts and Sciences, Arts Management Program, Buffalo, NY 14260. Offers MA. *Program availability:* Part-time. *Faculty:* 3 full-time (2 women), 1 (woman) part-time/adjunct. *Students:* 17 full-time (16 women), 1 part-time (0 women), 9 international. Average age 24. 52 applicants, 62% accepted, 8 enrolled. In 2016, 1 master's awarded. *Degree requirements:* For master's, thesis. *Entrance requirements:* For master's, curriculum vitae, academic essay, personal statement, 2 letters of recommendation, official transcripts; bank statements, supporting documentation, and passport (for international students). Additional exam requirements/recommendations for international students: Required—TOEFL or IELTS. *Application deadline:* For fall admission, 2/1 priority date for domestic and international students. Applications are processed on a rolling basis. Application fee: $45. Electronic applications accepted. *Expenses:* $13,347 per year resident, $24,687 per year non-resident, $26,395 per year international. *Financial support:* In 2016–17, 1 student received support, including 1 fellowship with full tuition reimbursement available. Financial award application deadline: 8/15; financial award applicants required to submit FAFSA. *Faculty research:* Cultural policy, arts management, museums and the public space, performing arts and digital media, cultural frameworks. *Unit head:* Prof. Franck Bauchard, Director, 716-645-2437, Fax: 716-645-6737, E-mail: artsmgmt@buffalo.edu. *Application contact:* Anne Gullotti, Assistant to the

Director, 716-645-0766, Fax: 716-645-6737, E-mail: artsmgmt@buffalo.edu. Website: http://www.buffalo.edu/cas/arts_management.html

**The University of Akron,** Graduate School, Buchtel College of Arts and Sciences, School of Dance, Theatre, and Arts Administration, Program in Arts Administration, Akron, OH 44325. Offers MA. *Accreditation:* NASAD. *Students:* 16 full-time (13 women), 7 part-time (6 women); includes 4 minority (3 Black or African American, non-Hispanic/Latino; 1 Two or more races, non-Hispanic/Latino), 2 international. Average age 29. 17 applicants, 76% accepted, 11 enrolled. In 2016, 8 master's awarded. *Degree requirements:* For master's, thesis. *Entrance requirements:* For master's, minimum GPA of 2.75, 300-word statement of intent summarizing student background and outlining career goals. Additional exam requirements/recommendations for international students: Required—TOEFL (minimum score 550 paper-based; 79 iBT), IELTS (minimum score 6.5). *Application deadline:* For fall admission, 3/15 for domestic and international students. Application fee: $45 ($70 for international students). Electronic applications accepted. *Expenses:* Tuition, state resident: full-time $8618; part-time $359 per credit hour. Tuition, nonresident: full-time $17,149; part-time $715 per credit hour. *Required fees:* $1652. *Unit head:* Dr. J. Thomas Dukes, 330-972-7948, E-mail: jtdukes@uakron.edu. *Application contact:* Elisa Gargarella, Coordinator, Arts Administration, 330-972-8325, E-mail: gelisa@uakron.edu. Website: http://www.uakron.edu/dtaa/artsadmin/

**University of Cincinnati,** Graduate School, College-Conservatory of Music, Division of Theatre Arts, Production and Arts Administration, Cincinnati, OH 45221. Offers arts administration (MA); directing (MFA); theater design and production (MFA); voice and opera (MM, DMA); MBA/MA. *Accreditation:* NAST (one or more programs are accredited). *Degree requirements:* For master's, final project. *Entrance requirements:* For master's, GMAT (MA), audition/interview. Additional exam requirements/recommendations for international students: Required—TOEFL (minimum score 520 paper-based). Electronic applications accepted. *Expenses: Tuition, area resident:* Full-time $12,790; part-time $389 per credit hour. Tuition, state resident: full-time $13,290; part-time $419 per credit hour. Tuition, nonresident: full-time $24,532; part-time $976 per credit hour. *International tuition:* $24,832 full-time. *Required fees:* $3958; $140 per credit hour. Tuition and fees vary according to course load, degree level, program and reciprocity agreements.

**University of Kentucky,** Graduate School, College of Fine Arts, Program in Arts Administration, Lexington, KY 40506-0032. Offers MA.

**The University of Manchester,** School of Arts, Histories and Cultures, Manchester, United Kingdom. Offers anthropology, media and performance (PhD); applied theatre professional (PhD); archaeology (PhD); art history and visual studies (PhD); arts management and cultural policy (PhD); classics and ancient history (PhD); composition (PhD); creative writing (PhD); drama (PhD); economic and social history (PhD); electroacoustic composition (PhD); English and American studies (PhD); history (PhD); humanitarianism and conflict response (PhD); museology (PhD); music (PhD); musicology (PhD); religions and theology (PhD).

**University of Michigan–Flint,** Graduate Programs, Program in Arts Administration, Flint, MI 48502. Offers museum and visual arts (MA), including museum and visual arts, performance. *Program availability:* Part-time. *Faculty:* 5 full-time (4 women), 3 part-time/adjunct (all women). *Students:* 7 full-time (6 women), 5 part-time (3 women); includes 2 minority (both Black or African American, non-Hispanic/Latino). Average age 39. 11 applicants, 55% accepted, 3 enrolled. In 2016, 3 master's awarded. *Degree requirements:* For master's, thesis, internship. *Entrance requirements:* For master's, bachelor's degree in the arts (visual art, theatre, dance, music, etc.) from regionally-accredited institution; minimum cumulative undergraduate GPA of 3.0. Additional exam requirements/recommendations for international students: Required—TOEFL (minimum score 84 iBT), IELTS (minimum score 6.5). *Application deadline:* For fall admission, 8/1 for domestic students, 5/1 for international students; for winter admission, 11/15 for domestic students, 9/1 for international students. Applications are processed on a rolling basis. Application fee: $55. Electronic applications accepted. *Expenses:* Contact institution. *Financial support:* Federal Work-Study, scholarships/grants, and unspecified assistantships available. Support available to part-time students. Financial award application deadline: 3/1; financial award applicants required to submit FAFSA. *Unit head:* Nicole Broughton, Director, 810-237-6522, E-mail: broughn@umflint.edu. *Application contact:* Bradley T. Maki, Director of Graduate Admissions, 810-762-3171, Fax: 810-766-6789, E-mail: bmaki@umflint.edu. Website: http://www.umflint.edu/graduateprograms/arts-administration-ma

**University of New Orleans,** Graduate School, College of Liberal Arts, Program in Arts Administration, New Orleans, LA 70148. Offers MA. *Program availability:* Part-time. *Degree requirements:* For master's, internship. *Entrance requirements:* For master's, GRE General Test. Additional exam requirements/recommendations for international students: Required—TOEFL (minimum score 550 paper-based; 79 iBT), IELTS (minimum score 6.5). Electronic applications accepted.

**The University of North Carolina at Charlotte,** College of Liberal Arts and Sciences, Department of Political Science and Public Administration, Charlotte, NC 28223-0001. Offers emergency management (Graduate Certificate); non-profit management (Graduate Certificate); public administration (MPA), including arts administration, emergency management, non-profit management, public budgeting and finance, urban management and policy; public budgeting and finance (Graduate Certificate); urban management and policy (Graduate Certificate). *Accreditation:* NASPAA. *Program availability:* Part-time, evening/weekend. *Faculty:* 19 full-time (10 women), 3 part-time/adjunct (0 women). *Students:* 25 full-time (17 women), 57 part-time (39 women); includes 23 minority (14 Black or African American, non-Hispanic/Latino; 1 American Indian or Alaska Native, non-Hispanic/Latino; 2 Asian, non-Hispanic/Latino; 4 Hispanic/Latino; 2 Two or more races, non-Hispanic/Latino). Average age 30. 55 applicants, 73% accepted, 30 enrolled. In 2016, 31 master's, 12 other advanced degrees awarded. *Degree requirements:* For master's, research project or thesis. *Entrance requirements:* For master's, GRE General Test, bachelor's degree, or its equivalent, from accredited college or university; minimum undergraduate GPA of 3.0; 3 letters of recommendation; statement of purpose; for Graduate Certificate, statement of purpose (1-2 pages in length) explaining applicant's career goals, how the Certificate fits into achieving those goals, and any relevant work experience; official transcripts; letters of recommendation.

Additional exam requirements/recommendations for international students: Required—TOEFL (minimum score 523 paper-based, 70 iBT) or IELTS (6.5). *Application deadline:* For fall admission, 8/1 for domestic and international students; for spring admission, 12/1 for domestic and international students. Applications are processed on a rolling basis. Application fee: $75. Electronic applications accepted. *Expenses:* Tuition, state resident: full-time $4252. Tuition, nonresident: full-time $17,423. *Required fees:* $3026. Tuition and fees vary according to course load and program. *Financial support:* In 2016–17, 9 students received support, including 9 research assistantships (averaging $7,117 per year); career-related internships or fieldwork, Federal Work-Study, institutionally sponsored loans, scholarships/grants, and unspecified assistantships also available. Support available to part-time students. Financial award application deadline: 3/1; financial award applicants required to submit FAFSA. *Total annual research expenditures:* $477,651. *Unit head:* Dr. Greg Weeks, Chair, 704-687-7574, E-mail: gbweeks@uncc.edu. *Application contact:* Kathy B. Giddings, Director of Graduate Admissions, 704-687-5503, Fax: 704-687-1668, E-mail: gradadm@uncc.edu. Website: http://politicalscience.uncc.edu/

**University of Oregon,** Graduate School, School of Architecture and Allied Arts, Program in Arts and Administration, Eugene, OR 97403. Offers arts management (MA, MS); media management (MA, MS). *Degree requirements:* For master's, summer internship, thesis/project. *Entrance requirements:* For master's, minimum GPA of 3.0; bachelor's degree in history, practice of visual, performing arts or other related degree. Additional exam requirements/recommendations for international students: Required—TOEFL. *Faculty research:* Museum education, arts program evaluation, community arts, information management, arts marketing.

**University of Southern California,** Graduate School, Roski School of Fine Arts, Art and Curatorial Practices in the Public Sphere Program, Los Angeles, CA 90089. Offers MA. *Degree requirements:* For master's, thesis, practicum exhibition. *Entrance requirements:* For master's, GRE, personal statement, writing sample, three letters of recommendation. Additional exam requirements/recommendations for international students: Required—TOEFL (minimum score 600 paper-based; 100 iBT). Electronic applications accepted. *Faculty research:* Curatorial studies, exhibition histories, modern and contemporary art, public art.

**University of Wisconsin–Madison,** Graduate School, Wisconsin School of Business, Wisconsin Full-Time MBA Program, Madison, WI 53706. Offers applied security analysis (MBA); arts administration (MBA); brand and product management (MBA); corporate finance and investment banking (MBA); marketing research (MBA); operations and technology management (MBA); real estate (MBA); risk management and insurance (MBA); strategic human resource management (MBA); supply chain management (MBA). *Faculty:* 125 full-time (32 women), 48 part-time/adjunct (11 women). *Students:* 197 full-time (73 women); includes 30 minority (11 Black or African American, non-Hispanic/Latino; 9 Asian, non-Hispanic/Latino; 10 Hispanic/Latino), 42 international. Average age 29. 728 applicants, 26% accepted, 99 enrolled. In 2016, 100 master's awarded. *Entrance requirements:* For master's, GMAT or GRE, bachelor's or equivalent degree, 2 years of work experience, essay, letter of recommendation, resume. Additional exam requirements/recommendations for international students: Required—TOEFL (minimum score 100 iBT), IELTS (minimum score 7.5). *Application deadline:* For fall admission, 9/28 for domestic students, 11/1 for international students; for winter admission, 11/2 for domestic students, 12/16 for international students; for spring admission, 1/11 for domestic students, 2/24 for international students; for summer admission, 3/1 for domestic students, 4/14 for international students. Applications are processed on a rolling basis. Application fee: $75 ($81 for international students). Electronic applications accepted. *Expenses:* $7,947 per semester resident tuition, $2,430 fees; $16,082 per semester resident tuition, $2,830 fees. *Financial support:* In 2016–17, 178 students received support, including 8 fellowships with full tuition reimbursements available (averaging $56,413 per year), 23 research assistantships with full tuition reimbursements available (averaging $42,151 per year), 51 teaching assistantships with full tuition reimbursements available (averaging $39,963 per year); scholarships/grants, health care benefits, and unspecified assistantships also available. Financial award application deadline: 4/11. *Faculty research:* Forms of competition and outcomes in dual distribution systems; explaining the accuracy of revised forecasts; supply chain planning for random demand surges; advanced demand information in a multi-product system; the effects of presentation salience and measurement subjectivity on nonprofessional investors' fair value judgments. *Unit head:* Prof. Ella Mae Matsumura, Associate Dean, Full-time MBA Program, 608-262-9731, E-mail: ematsumura@bus.wisc.edu. *Application contact:* Mary Lewitzke, Assistant Director of Admissions and Recruiting, Full-time MBA Program, 608-262-4000, E-mail: mlewitzke@bus.wisc.edu. Website: http://www.bus.wisc.edu/mba

**Valparaiso University,** Graduate School and Continuing Education, Program in Arts and Entertainment Administration, Valparaiso, IN 46383. Offers MA. *Program availability:* Part-time, evening/weekend. *Degree requirements:* For master's, internship or research project. *Entrance requirements:* Additional exam requirements/recommendations for international students: Required—TOEFL (minimum score 550 paper-based; 80 iBT), IELTS (minimum score 6). Electronic applications accepted. *Expenses: Tuition:* Full-time $11,070; part-time $615 per credit hour. *Required fees:* $116 per semester. Tuition and fees vary according to course load, degree level and program.

**Winthrop University,** College of Visual and Performing Arts, Department of Art, Rock Hill, SC 29733. Offers art (MFA); art administration (MA); art education (MA). *Accreditation:* NASAD. *Program availability:* Part-time. *Degree requirements:* For master's, comprehensive exam (for some programs), thesis (for some programs), documented exhibit, oral exam. *Entrance requirements:* For master's, GRE General Test or MAT, PRAXIS (for MA), minimum GPA of 3.0, resume, slide portfolio, teaching certificate (MA). Additional exam requirements/recommendations for international students: Required—TOEFL (minimum score 550 paper-based; 79 iBT), IELTS (minimum score 6). Electronic applications accepted. *Expenses:* Tuition, state resident: full-time $14,312; part-time $599 per credit hour. Tuition, nonresident: full-time $27,570; part-time $1153 per credit hour.

# Art Therapy

---

**Adler Graduate School,** Program in Adlerian Counseling and Psychotherapy, Richfield, MN 55423. Offers Adlerian studies (MA); art therapy (MA); clinical mental health counseling (MA); co-occurring mental health and substance abuse disorders (MA);

marriage and family therapy (MA); school counseling (MA). *Program availability:* Part-time, evening/weekend. *Faculty:* 71 part-time/adjunct (55 women). *Students:* 298 part-time (225 women); includes 51 minority (40 Black or African American, non-Hispanic/

## Art Therapy

Latino; 6 American Indian or Alaska Native, non-Hispanic/Latino; 5 Hispanic/Latino). *Degree requirements:* For master's, thesis or alternative, 500-700 hour internship (depending on license choice). *Entrance requirements:* For master's, interview, official transcripts, minimum cumulative GPA of 3.0. *Application deadline:* Applications are processed on a rolling basis. Application fee: $50. Electronic applications accepted. *Financial support:* Career-related internships or fieldwork and tuition waivers available. Support available to part-time students. Financial award applicants required to submit FAFSA. *Unit head:* Dr. Dan Haugen, President, 612-767-7048, Fax: 612-861-7559, E-mail: haugen@alfredadler.edu. *Application contact:* Evelyn B. Haas, Director of Admissions, 612-767-7044, Fax: 612-861-7559, E-mail: ev@alfredadler.edu.

**Adler University,** Programs in Psychology, Chicago, IL 60602. Offers advanced Adlerian psychotherapy (Certificate); art therapy (MA); clinical mental health counseling (MA); clinical neuropsychology (Certificate); clinical psychology (Psy D); community psychology (MA); counseling and organizational psychology (MA); counseling psychology (MA); counselor education and supervision (PhD); couple and family therapy (DCFT); criminology (MA); emergency management leadership (MA); forensic psychology (MA); marriage and family counseling (MA); marriage and family therapy (Certificate); military psychology (MA); nonprofit management (MA); organizational psychology (MA); police psychology (MA); public policy and administration (MA); rehabilitation counseling (MA); sport and health psychology (MA); substance abuse counseling (Certificate); Psy D/Certificate; Psy D/MACAT; Psy D/MACP; Psy D/MAMFC; Psy D/MASAC. *Accreditation:* APA. *Program availability:* Part-time, evening/weekend, online learning. Terminal master's awarded for partial completion of doctoral program. *Degree requirements:* For master's, thesis or alternative, oral exam, practicum; for doctorate, thesis/dissertation, clinical exam, internship, oral exam, practicum, written qualifying exam. *Entrance requirements:* For master's, 12 semester hours in psychology, minimum GPA of 3.0; for doctorate, 18 semester hours in psychology, minimum GPA of 3.25; for Certificate, appropriate master's or doctoral degree. Additional exam requirements/recommendations for international students: Required—TOEFL (minimum score 550 paper-based; 79 iBT). Electronic applications accepted.

**See Display on page 982 and Close-Up on page 1225.**

**Albertus Magnus College,** Master of Arts in Art Therapy Program, New Haven, CT 06511-1189. Offers MAAT. *Program availability:* Part-time. *Faculty:* 3 full-time (all women), 13 part-time/adjunct (10 women). *Students:* 20 full-time (19 women), 18 part-time (17 women); includes 2 minority (1 Asian, non-Hispanic/Latino; 1 Hispanic/Latino). Average age 28. In 2016, 15 master's awarded. *Degree requirements:* For master's, thesis, 725-hour internship; 60 credits. *Entrance requirements:* For master's, interview, writing sample, portfolio (original art), 15 credits in psychology, 18 credits in studio art. Additional exam requirements/recommendations for international students: Required—TOEFL (minimum score 120 iBT). *Application deadline:* For fall admission, 5/1 for domestic students; for spring admission, 11/1 for domestic students. Applications are processed on a rolling basis. Application fee: $50. Electronic applications accepted. *Expenses:* Contact institution. *Financial support:* Federal Work-Study and unspecified assistantships available. Support available to part-time students. Financial award application deadline: 8/15; financial award applicants required to submit FAFSA. *Unit head:* Abbe Miller, Director, 203-773-8543, Fax: 203-773-3117, E-mail: amiller@albertus.edu. *Application contact:* Dr. Sean O'Connell, Vice President for Academic Affairs, 203-777-8539, Fax: 203-777-3701, E-mail: soconnell@albertus.edu. Website: http://www.albertus.edu/art-therapy/ms/

**Athabasca University,** Program in Counseling, Athabasca, AB T9S 3A3, Canada. Offers applied psychology (Post Master's Certificate); art therapy (MC); career counseling (MC); counseling (Advanced Certificate); counseling psychology (MC); school counseling (MC).

**Caldwell University,** Graduate Studies, Department of Psychology, Caldwell, NJ 07006-6195. Offers art therapy (MA); counseling (MA), including art therapy, mental health, school counseling; director of school counseling (Post-Master's Certificate); professional counselor (Post-Master's Certificate); school counselor (Post-Master's Certificate). *Accreditation:* ACA. *Program availability:* Part-time, evening/weekend. *Degree requirements:* For master's, comprehensive exam. *Entrance requirements:* For master's, GRE or MAT, interview. Electronic applications accepted. *Faculty research:* Counseling, school counseling, art therapy.

**California Institute of Integral Studies,** School of Professional Psychology and Health, San Francisco, CA 94103. Offers clinical psychology (Psy D); community mental health (MA); drama therapy (MA); expressive arts therapy (MA); human sexuality (PhD); integral counseling psychology (MA); integrative health studies (MA); psychological studies (MA); somatic psychology (MA). *Program availability:* Part-time, evening/weekend, 100% online, blended/hybrid learning. *Students:* 526 full-time (408 women), 113 part-time (96 women); includes 173 minority (34 Black or African American, non-Hispanic/Latino; 5 American Indian or Alaska Native, non-Hispanic/Latino; 31 Asian, non-Hispanic/Latino; 58 Hispanic/Latino; 1 Native Hawaiian or other Pacific Islander, non-Hispanic/Latino; 44 Two or more races, non-Hispanic/Latino; 52 international. Average age 38. 319 applicants, 85% accepted, 164 enrolled. In 2016, 157 master's, 21 doctorates awarded. *Degree requirements:* For doctorate, comprehensive exam, thesis/dissertation. *Entrance requirements:* For master's, minimum GPA of 3.0, letters of recommendation, writing sample; for doctorate, GRE, MA in psychology or social work with appropriate practical experience for advanced standing, or BA with a minimum GPA of 3.1; letters of recommendation; writing sample. Additional exam requirements/recommendations for international students: Required—TOEFL. *Application deadline:* For fall admission, 2/1 priority date for domestic and international students; for spring admission, 10/15 priority date for domestic and international students. Applications are processed on a rolling basis. Application fee: $65. Electronic applications accepted. *Expenses:* Tuition: Full-time $19,728; part-time $1098 per semester hour. *Required fees:* $320; $320 per semester hour. *Financial support:* Research assistantships with tuition reimbursements, teaching assistantships with tuition reimbursements, career-related internships or fieldwork, Federal Work-Study, and scholarships/grants available. Support available to part-time students. Financial award application deadline: 4/15; financial award applicants required to submit FAFSA. *Faculty research:* Transpersonal psychology, somatic psychology, expressive arts therapy, drama therapy, community mental health, ecopsychology, integrative health, human sexuality. *Application contact:* Ellen Durst, Director of Admissions, 415-575-6100, Fax: 415-575-1268, E-mail: admissions@ciis.edu.

**California State University, Los Angeles,** Graduate Studies, College of Arts and Letters, Department of Art, Los Angeles, CA 90032-8530. Offers art (MA), including art education, art history, art therapy, ceramics, metals, and textiles, design (MA, MFA), painting, sculpture, and graphic arts, photography; fine arts (MFA), including crafts, design (MA, MFA), studio arts. *Accreditation:* NASAD (one or more programs are accredited). *Program availability:* Part-time, evening/weekend. *Degree requirements:* For master's, comprehensive exam, project or thesis. *Entrance requirements:* For master's, portfolio. Additional exam requirements/recommendations for international students: Required—TOEFL (minimum score 500 paper-based). Electronic applications

accepted. *Faculty research:* The artist and the book, conceptual art, ceramic processes, computer graphics, architectural graphics.

**Cedar Crest College,** Program in Art Therapy, Allentown, PA 18104-6196. Offers MA. *Program availability:* Part-time, evening/weekend, blended/hybrid learning. *Faculty:* 2 full-time (both women), 4 part-time/adjunct (all women). *Students:* 16 full-time (all women), 7 part-time (all women); includes 2 minority (1 Asian, non-Hispanic/Latino; 1 Hispanic/Latino). Average age 31. In 2016, 7 master's awarded. *Application deadline:* Applications are processed on a rolling basis. Electronic applications accepted. *Expenses:* $821 per credit. *Unit head:* Rebecca Arnold, Director, 610-437-4471 Ext. 3594, E-mail: rarnold@cedarcrest.edu. *Application contact:* Mary Ellen Hickes, Director of School of Adult and Graduate Education, 610-437-4471, E-mail: sage@cedarcrest.edu.
Website: http://sage.cedarcrest.edu/graduate/master-of-arts-in-art-therapy/

**The College of New Rochelle,** Graduate School, Division of Art and Communication Studies, Program in Art Therapy, New Rochelle, NY 10805-2308. Offers art therapy (MS); art therapy/counseling (MS). *Program availability:* Part-time, evening/weekend. *Degree requirements:* For master's, thesis, practicum, fieldwork, internship. *Entrance requirements:* For master's, 12 credits in psychology, portfolio. *Faculty research:* Phototherapy, assessment and evaluation, developmental stages in art, creativity and mental illness.

**Concordia University,** School of Graduate Studies, Faculty of Fine Arts, Department of Creative Arts Therapies, Montréal, QC H3G 1M8, Canada. Offers art therapy (MA); drama therapy (MA); music therapy (MA).

**Drexel University,** College of Nursing and Health Professions, Department of Creative Arts Therapies, Specialization in Art Therapy, Philadelphia, PA 19104-2875. Offers MA, PMC. *Accreditation:* NASAD. *Students:* 31 full-time (30 women), 1 (woman) part-time; includes 8 minority (4 Black or African American, non-Hispanic/Latino; 1 Asian, non-Hispanic/Latino; 1 Hispanic/Latino; 2 Two or more races, non-Hispanic/Latino), 1 international. Average age 26. In 2016, 26 master's awarded. *Degree requirements:* For master's, comprehensive exam, thesis. *Entrance requirements:* For master's, GRE General Test or MAT, interview, minimum GPA of 2.75, portfolio. *Application deadline:* For fall admission, 3/1 for domestic students. Applications are processed on a rolling basis. Application fee: $50. Electronic applications accepted. *Expenses:* Tuition: Full-time $32,184; part-time $1192 per credit hour. *Required fees:* $280. Tuition and fees vary according to campus/location and program. *Financial support:* Career-related internships or fieldwork, Federal Work-Study, and institutionally sponsored loans available. Support available to part-time students. Financial award application deadline: 5/1; financial award applicants required to submit FAFSA. *Unit head:* Nancy Gerber, Director, 215-762-6928, E-mail: nancy.gerber@drexel.edu. *Application contact:* Director of Graduate Admissions, 215-895-6700, Fax: 215-895-5939, E-mail: enroll@drexel.edu.

**Eastern Virginia Medical School,** Graduate Art Therapy and Counseling Program, Norfolk, VA 23501-1980. Offers MS. *Degree requirements:* For master's, thesis, internship. *Entrance requirements:* For master's, 12 credit hours in psychology, including abnormal and developmental; 18 credit hours in studio art; face-to-face interview; portfolio (diverse media preferred). Electronic applications accepted. *Expenses:* Contact institution.

**Edinboro University of Pennsylvania,** Department of Counseling, School Psychology and Special Education, Edinboro, PA 16444. Offers counseling (MA), including art therapy, clinical mental health counseling, college counseling, rehabilitation counseling, school counseling; educational psychology (M Ed); school psychology (Ed S); special education (M Ed), including autism, behavior management. *Accreditation:* ACA. *Program availability:* Part-time, evening/weekend. *Degree requirements:* For master's, thesis or alternative, competency exam; for Ed S, thesis or alternative. *Entrance requirements:* For master's and Ed S, GRE or MAT, minimum QPA of 2.5. Electronic applications accepted.

**Emporia State University,** Program in Art Therapy, Emporia, KS 66801-5415. Offers MS. *Accreditation:* NASAD. *Program availability:* Part-time. *Faculty:* 11 full-time (7 women), 1 (woman) part-time/adjunct. *Students:* 30 full-time (27 women), 4 part-time (all women); includes 4 minority (1 American Indian or Alaska Native, non-Hispanic/Latino; 2 Hispanic/Latino; 1 Two or more races, non-Hispanic/Latino). 36 applicants, 83% accepted, 13 enrolled. In 2016, 12 master's awarded. *Degree requirements:* For master's, comprehensive exam or thesis, internship. *Entrance requirements:* For master's, GRE General Test or MAT, essay sample, appropriate bachelor's degree. Additional exam requirements/recommendations for international students: Required—TOEFL (minimum score 520 paper-based; 68 iBT). *Application deadline:* For fall admission, 6/1 for domestic students; for spring admission, 10/1 for domestic students. Applications are processed on a rolling basis. Application fee: $30 ($75 for international students). Electronic applications accepted. *Expenses:* Tuition, state resident: full-time $5922; part-time $246.75 per credit hour. Tuition, nonresident: full-time $18,414; part-time $767.25 per credit hour. *Required fees:* $1884; $78.50 per credit hour. *Financial support:* In 2016–17, 7 research assistantships with full tuition reimbursements (averaging $7,353 per year), 4 teaching assistantships with full tuition reimbursements (averaging $7,335 per year) were awarded; career-related internships or fieldwork, Federal Work-Study, institutionally sponsored loans, health care benefits, and unspecified assistantships also available. Financial award application deadline: 3/15; financial award applicants required to submit FAFSA. *Unit head:* Dr. Katrina Miller, Interim Chair, 620-341-5231, E-mail: kmille12@emporia.edu. *Application contact:* Mary Sewell, Admissions Coordinator, 800-950-GRAD, Fax: 620-341-5909, E-mail: msewell@emporia.edu.

**The George Washington University,** Columbian College of Arts and Sciences, Program in Art Therapy, Washington, DC 20052. Offers MA, Graduate Certificate. *Faculty:* 5 full-time (4 women). *Students:* 49 full-time (46 women), 12 part-time (11 women); includes 17 minority (5 Black or African American, non-Hispanic/Latino; 2 Asian, non-Hispanic/Latino; 7 Hispanic/Latino; 3 Two or more races, non-Hispanic/Latino), 9 international. Average age 30. 75 applicants, 59% accepted, 29 enrolled. In 2016, 24 master's awarded. *Degree requirements:* For master's, internship, practicum paper. *Entrance requirements:* For master's, GRE General Test, interview, minimum GPA of 3.0; for Graduate Certificate, interview, minimum GPA of 3.0. Additional exam requirements/recommendations for international students: Required—TOEFL (minimum score 550 paper-based; 80 iBT). *Application deadline:* For fall admission, 1/1 priority date for domestic students. Application fee: $75. *Financial support:* In 2016–17, 11 students received support. Fellowships with partial tuition reimbursements available, career-related internships or fieldwork, Federal Work-Study, institutionally sponsored loans, and tuition waivers available. *Unit head:* Heidi Bardot, Director, 202-994-4148, E-mail: hbardot@gwu.edu. *Application contact:* Information Contact, 202-994-6285, Fax: 202-994-1404, E-mail: artx@gwu.edu.
Website: http://arttherapy.columbian.gwu.edu/program-options

**Georgia College & State University,** Graduate School, College of Health Sciences, Program in Art Therapy, Milledgeville, GA 31061. Offers MA. *Program availability:* Part-time. *Students:* 9 full-time (7 women), 2 part-time (both women); includes 4 minority (3 Black or African American, non-Hispanic/Latino; 1 Hispanic/Latino). Average age 33. 3 applicants, 100% accepted, 2 enrolled. In 2016, 6 master's awarded. *Degree* *requirements:* For master's, comprehensive exam, minimum GPA of 3.0, thesis or clinical project. *Entrance requirements:* For master's, GRE or MAT, 2 letters of reference; minimum undergraduate GPA of 2.75; official transcript; 12 credit hours in psychology, 18 in studio art; 12 pieces of recent artwork; essay; interview (in-person or via Skype). *Application deadline:* For fall admission, 7/1 priority date for domestic students; for spring admission, 11/1 priority date for domestic students; for summer admission, 3/1 priority date for domestic students. Applications are processed on a rolling basis. Application fee: $40. Electronic applications accepted. *Expenses:* $288 per credit hour in-state tuition; $1,027 per credit hour out-of-state; fees vary by hours enrolled. *Financial support:* In 2016–17, 2 students received support. Unspecified assistantships available. Financial award application deadline: 3/1; financial award applicants required to submit FAFSA. *Unit head:* Dr. Chesley Mercado, Program Coordinator, Art Therapy, 478-445-2645, Fax: 478-445-4532, E-mail: chesley.mercado@gcsu.edu. *Application contact:* Kate Marshall, Graduate Admissions Coordinator, 478-445-1184, Fax: 478-445-1336, E-mail: grad-admit@gcsu.edu. Website: http://catalog.gcsu.edu/en/2015-2016/Graduate-Catalog/College-of-Health-Sciences/Master-of-Arts-with-a-Major-in-Art-Therapy

**Goddard College,** Graduate Division, Master of Arts in Psychology Program, Plainfield, VT 05667-9432. Offers expressive arts therapy (MA); psychology (MA); sexual orientation (MA). *Program availability:* Part-time, online learning. *Degree requirements:* For master's, thesis or alternative, clinical internship. *Entrance requirements:* For master's, eight specific undergraduate prerequisite courses taken within previous five years (or preparatory semester at Goddard), statement of purpose, 3 letters of recommendation, interview. Electronic applications accepted.

**Hofstra University,** School of Health Professions and Human Services, Programs in Counseling, Hempstead, NY 11549. Offers counseling (MS Ed, PD); creative arts therapy (MA); interdisciplinary transition specialist (Advanced Certificate); marriage and family therapy (MA); mental health counseling (MA, Advanced Certificate), including alcohol and substance abuse (Advanced Certificate); rehabilitation administration (PD); rehabilitation counseling (MS Ed, Advanced Certificate); rehabilitation counseling in mental health (MS Ed, Advanced Certificate); school counselor bilingual extension (Advanced Certificate). *Accreditation:* ACA. *Program availability:* Part-time, evening/weekend. *Students:* 116 full-time (100 women), 66 part-time (59 women); includes 48 minority (18 Black or African American, non-Hispanic/Latino; 11 Asian, non-Hispanic/Latino; 17 Hispanic/Latino; 2 Two or more races, non-Hispanic/Latino), 5 international. Average age 29. 166 applicants, 81% accepted, 66 enrolled. In 2016, 71 master's, 7 other advanced degrees awarded. *Degree requirements:* For master's, comprehensive exam (for some programs), thesis (for some programs), internship, practicum, student teaching, seminars, minimum GPA of 3.0. *Entrance requirements:* For master's, GRE, interview, letters of recommendation, portfolio, essay, professional experience, certification; for other advanced degree, GRE, interview, letters of recommendation, essay, professional experience, resume, master's degree. Additional exam requirements/recommendations for international students: Required—TOEFL (minimum score 550 paper-based; 80 iBT). *Application deadline:* Applications are processed on a rolling basis. Application fee: $75. Electronic applications accepted. *Expenses: Tuition:* Full-time $1240. *Required fees:* $970. Tuition and fees vary according to program. *Financial support:* In 2016–17, 76 students received support, including 40 fellowships with full and partial tuition reimbursements available (averaging $3,465 per year), 5 research assistantships with full and partial tuition reimbursements available (averaging $6,939 per year); career-related internships or fieldwork, Federal Work-Study, institutionally sponsored loans, scholarships/grants, traineeships, tuition waivers (full and partial), and unspecified assistantships also available. Support available to part-time students. Financial award applicants required to submit FAFSA. *Faculty research:* The constructs of hope and grit; the efficacy of support groups in treating eating disorders; attitudes of primary care physicians related to providing integrated care with mental health counselors; expanding the counselor identity through disability cultural competence; vocational evaluation and assessment collaboration; disability cultural competence. *Unit head:* Dr. Jamie Mitus, Chairperson, 516-463-5759, E-mail: jamie.s.mitus@hofstra.edu. *Application contact:* Sunil Samuel, Assistant Vice President of Admissions, 516-463-4723, Fax: 516-463-4664, E-mail: graduateadmission@hofstra.edu. Website: http://www.hofstra.edu/academics/colleges/healthscienceshumanservices/

**Indiana University–Purdue University Indianapolis,** Herron School of Art and Design, Indianapolis, IN 46202. Offers art therapy (MA); visual art (MFA), including ceramics, furniture design, painting and drawing, photography and intermedia, printmaking, sculpture; visual communication design (MFA). *Faculty:* 26 full-time (13 women), 16 part-time/adjunct (11 women). *Students:* 56 full-time (40 women), 1 (woman) part-time; includes 8 minority (4 Black or African American, non-Hispanic/Latino; 2 Asian, non-Hispanic/Latino; 2 Hispanic/Latino), 7 international. Average age 31. 72 applicants, 53% accepted, 25 enrolled. In 2016, 22 master's awarded. *Degree requirements:* For master's, thesis. *Entrance requirements:* For master's, personal statement, resume, recommendations, portfolio, transcripts (18 credit hours of studio art and 12 credit hours of psychology, including 3 credit hours of developmental psychology and 3 credit hours of abnormal psychology for MA). Additional exam requirements/recommendations for international students: Recommended—TOEFL (minimum score 550 paper-based; 79 iBT), IELTS (minimum score 6.5). *Application deadline:* For fall admission, 1/15 for domestic and international students; for spring admission, 11/1 for domestic students, 10/15 for international students. Application fee: $60 ($65 for international students). Electronic applications accepted. *Expenses:* Contact institution. *Financial support:* In 2016–17, 55 students received support, including 36 fellowships (averaging $2,830 per year), 11 teaching assistantships (averaging $3,609 per year); research assistantships, Federal Work-Study, scholarships/grants, health care benefits, tuition waivers, and unspecified assistantships also available. Financial award application deadline: 2/1. *Faculty research:* Contemporary digital narratives for the homoerotic trope; sound articulated 3D print; neuroscience, art and related therapeutics; automotive and aeronautical design and fabrication; technological detritus. *Total annual research expenditures:* $22,990. *Unit head:* Prof. Valerie Eickmeier, Dean, 317-278-9470, Fax: 317-278-9471, E-mail: herron@iupui.edu. *Application contact:* Abbey Chambers, Herron Office of Admissions and Student Services, 317-378-9400, E-mail: herron4u@iupui.edu. Website: http://herron.iupui.edu/

**Lesley University,** Graduate School of Arts and Social Sciences, Cambridge, MA 02138-2790. Offers clinical mental health counseling (MA), including holistic counseling, school and community counseling, trauma studies; counseling psychology (MA, CAGS), including professional counseling (MA), school counseling (MA); creative writing (MFA); expressive therapies (MA, PhD, CAGS), including art (MA), clinical mental health counseling (MA), dance (MA), expressive therapies (MA), music (MA); independent studies (CAGS); independent study (MA); intercultural relations (MA, CAGS); interdisciplinary studies (MA), including individualized studies, integrative holistic health, mindfulness studies, peace and conflict transformation, trauma sensitive assessment, intervention, and consultation, women's studies; urban environmental leadership (MA). *Program availability:* Part-time, online learning. *Degree requirements:* For master's, internship, practicum, thesis (for expressive therapies); for doctorate, thesis/dissertation, arts apprenticeship, field placement; for CAGS, thesis, internship (for counseling psychology, expressive therapies). *Entrance requirements:* For master's, MAT

(counseling psychology), interview, writing samples, art portfolio; for doctorate, GRE or MAT, interview, master's degree; for CAGS, interview, master's degree. Additional exam requirements/recommendations for international students: Required—TOEFL (minimum score 550 paper-based; 80 iBT). Electronic applications accepted. *Faculty research:* Psychotherapy and culture; psychotherapy and psychological trauma; women's issues in art, teaching and psychotherapy; community-based art, psycho-spiritual inquiry.

**Long Island University–LIU Post,** College of Arts, Communications and Design, Brookville, NY 11548-1300. Offers art (MA); clinical art therapy (MA); clinical art therapy and counseling (MA); digital game design and development (MA); fine arts and design (MFA); interactive multimedia arts (MA); music (MA); theater (MA); theatre (MFA). *Faculty:* 36 full-time (19 women), 144 part-time/adjunct (74 women). *Students:* 123 full-time (91 women), 21 part-time (18 women); includes 25 minority (6 Black or African American, non-Hispanic/Latino; 1 American Indian or Alaska Native, non-Hispanic/Latino; 6 Asian, non-Hispanic/Latino; 11 Hispanic/Latino; 1 Two or more races, non-Hispanic/Latino), 32 international. 175 applicants, 73% accepted, 46 enrolled. In 2016, 68 master's awarded. *Degree requirements:* For master's, variable foreign language requirement, comprehensive exam (for some programs), thesis (for some programs). *Entrance requirements:* For master's, performance audition or portfolio. Additional exam requirements/recommendations for international students: Required—TOEFL (minimum score 550 paper-based; 79 iBT). *Application deadline:* Applications are processed on a rolling basis. Application fee: $50. Electronic applications accepted. *Expenses: Tuition:* Full-time $28,272; part-time $1178 per credit. *Required fees:* $451 per term. Tuition and fees vary according to degree level and program. *Financial support:* In 2016–17, 6 research assistantships with partial tuition reimbursements (averaging $1,020 per year), 14 teaching assistantships with partial tuition reimbursements (averaging $670 per year) were awarded; career-related internships or fieldwork, Federal Work-Study, institutionally sponsored loans, scholarships/grants, tuition waivers (full and partial), and unspecified assistantships also available. Support available to part-time students. Financial award application deadline: 2/15; financial award applicants required to submit FAFSA. *Faculty research:* Game design, new plays, musical theatre, compositions for wind symphony, jazz ensemble, jazz combo and vocal jazz. *Unit head:* Dr. Christine Kerr, Acting Dean, 516-299-2309, E-mail: christine.kerr@liu.edu. *Application contact:* Carol Zerah, Director of Graduate Admissions, 516-299-2900, Fax: 516-299-2137, E-mail: post-enroll@liu.edu. Website: http://www.liu.edu/CWPost/Academics/School-of-Visual-Arts-Communications-and-Digital-Technologies

**Marylhurst University,** Department of Art Therapy Counseling, Marylhurst, OR 97036-0261. Offers MA, PGC. *Program availability:* Part-time. *Students:* 36 (34 women); includes 10 minority (2 Hispanic/Latino; 8 Two or more races, non-Hispanic/Latino). Average age 32. In 2016, 15 master's awarded. *Degree requirements:* For master's, comprehensive exam, clinical portfolio, three art projects and papers. *Entrance requirements:* For master's, official transcripts from regionally-accredited institution, resume including experience working with people (minimum 300 hours of volunteered or paid experience), recommendations, statement of intent, art portfolio, minimum GPA of 3.0, interview with department faculty, background check. Additional exam requirements/recommendations for international students: Required—PTE, TOEFL (minimum score 79 iBT) or IELTS (minimum score 6.5). *Application deadline:* For fall admission, 1/31 priority date for domestic and international students. Applications are processed on a rolling basis. Application fee: $0. Electronic applications accepted. *Expenses:* Contact institution. *Financial support:* Career-related internships or fieldwork and scholarships/grants available. Support available to part-time students. Financial award application deadline: 2/1; financial award applicants required to submit FAFSA. *Faculty research:* Scientific approaches to art therapy research, child and adolescent psychotherapy, multicultural counseling. *Unit head:* Mary Andrus, Director of Art Therapy Counseling, 503-534-7046, E-mail: mandrus@marylhurst.edu. *Application contact:* Maruska Lynch, Graduate Admissions Counselor, 503-699-6322, E-mail: admissions@marylhurst.edu.

**Marywood University,** Academic Affairs, Insalaco College of Creative and Performing Arts, Art Department, Program in Art Therapy, Scranton, PA 18509-1598. Offers MA, Graduate Certificate. *Accreditation:* NASAD. *Program availability:* Part-time. Electronic applications accepted.

**Mount Mary University,** Graduate Programs, Program in Art Therapy, Milwaukee, WI 53222-4597. Offers MS, DAT. *Program availability:* Part-time, evening/weekend. *Faculty:* 4 full-time (2 women), 11 part-time/adjunct (8 women). *Students:* 48 full-time (46 women), 20 part-time (all women); includes 9 minority (2 Black or African American, non-Hispanic/Latino; 4 Asian, non-Hispanic/Latino; 1 Hispanic/Latino; 2 Two or more races, non-Hispanic/Latino), 4 international. Average age 32. 68 applicants, 63% accepted, 22 enrolled. In 2016, 21 master's, 1 doctorate awarded. *Degree requirements:* For master's, thesis or alternative, internship; for doctorate, culminating project and pre-graduation defense. *Entrance requirements:* For master's, minimum GPA of 3.0; for doctorate, minimum GPA of 3.5. Additional exam requirements/recommendations for international students: Required—TOEFL (minimum score 550 paper-based; 80 iBT); Recommended—IELTS (minimum score 6.5). *Application deadline:* For fall admission, 10/31 priority date for domestic and international students; for summer admission, 3/15 for domestic and international students. Application fee: $45. Electronic applications accepted. *Expenses:* Contact institution. *Financial support:* Career-related internships or fieldwork, Federal Work-Study, and unspecified assistantships available. Support available to part-time students. Financial award application deadline: 5/1; financial award applicants required to submit FAFSA. *Faculty research:* Art-based research in art therapy, consensus-group supervision, art therapy in public school programs. *Unit head:* Dr. Chris Belkofer, Graduate Program Director, 414-930-3120, E-mail: belkofec@mtmary.edu. *Application contact:* Kirk Heller de Messer, Director, Graduate Admissions, 414-930-3221, E-mail: hellerk@mtmary.edu. Website: http://www.mtmary.edu/majors-programs/graduate/art-therapy/

**Naropa University,** Graduate Programs, Program in Clinical Mental Health Counseling, Concentration in Transpersonal Art Therapy, Boulder, CO 80302-6697. Offers MA. *Faculty:* 10 full-time (7 women), 23 part-time/adjunct (17 women). *Students:* 52 full-time (51 women), 1 (woman) part-time; includes 8 minority (1 American Indian or Alaska Native, non-Hispanic/Latino; 1 Asian, non-Hispanic/Latino; 4 Hispanic/Latino; 2 Two or more races, non-Hispanic/Latino), 1 international. Average age 29. 52 applicants, 60% accepted, 19 enrolled. In 2016, 16 master's awarded. *Degree requirements:* For master's, internship, 190 direct art contact hours of studio-based work, counseling practicum. *Entrance requirements:* For master's, interview, visual art portfolio, statement of interest, 2 letters of recommendation, transcripts. Additional exam requirements/recommendations for international students: Required—TOEFL (minimum score 550 paper-based; 80 iBT). *Application deadline:* For fall admission, 1/15 priority date for domestic and international students. Applications are processed on a rolling basis. Application fee: $60. Electronic applications accepted. *Expenses:* $22,560 for first year. *Financial support:* In 2016–17, 15 students received support, including 2 research assistantships with partial tuition reimbursements available (averaging $1,875 per year); career-related internships or fieldwork, scholarships/grants, tuition waivers (partial), and unspecified assistantships also available. Support available to part-time students. Financial award application deadline: 3/1; financial award applicants required to submit

## Art Therapy

**FAFSA.** *Unit head:* Dr. Deborah Bowman, Dean, Graduate School of Counseling and Psychology, 303-546-3559, E-mail: bowman@naropa.edu. *Application contact:* Office of Admissions, 303-546-3572, Fax: 303-546-3583, E-mail: admissions@naropa.edu. Website: http://www.naropa.edu/academics/masters/clinical-mental-health-counseling/art-therapy/index.php

**Nazareth College of Rochester,** Graduate Studies, Department of Creative Arts Therapy, Rochester, NY 14618. Offers art therapy (MS); music therapy (MS). *Program availability:* Part-time. *Students:* 36 full-time (32 women), 10 part-time (9 women); includes 3 minority (1 Black or African American, non-Hispanic/Latino; 2 Asian, non-Hispanic/Latino). Average age 25. 64 applicants, 55% accepted, 20 enrolled. *Entrance requirements:* For master's, minimum GPA of 3.0; portfolio review (art therapy); audition (music therapy). Additional exam requirements/recommendations for international students: Required—TOEFL (minimum score 550 paper-based, 79 iBT) or IELTS (6.5). *Application deadline:* For fall admission, 1/15 for domestic students. Electronic applications accepted. *Expenses: Tuition:* Part-time $880 per credit hour. Part-time tuition and fees vary according to course load, degree level and program. *Financial support:* Unspecified assistantships available. Financial award application deadline: 3/1; financial award applicants required to submit FAFSA. *Unit head:* Dr. Bryan Hunter, Chair, Creative Arts Therapy, 585-389-2702, E-mail: bhunter7@naz.edu. *Application contact:* Judith Baker, Director, Transfer and Graduate Admissions, 585-531-1154, Fax: 585-389-2826, E-mail: gradadmissions@naz.edu.

**New York University,** Steinhardt School of Culture, Education, and Human Development, Department of Art and Art Professions, Program in Art Therapy, New York, NY 10003. Offers MA. *Program availability:* Part-time. *Degree requirements:* For master's, thesis (for some programs). *Entrance requirements:* For master's, interview, portfolio. Additional exam requirements/recommendations for international students: Required—TOEFL (minimum score 100 iBT). Electronic applications accepted. *Faculty research:* Art therapy in non-clinical settings, international art therapy.

**Notre Dame de Namur University,** Division of Academic Affairs, College of Arts and Sciences, Program in Art Therapy Psychology, Belmont, CA 94002-1908. Offers art therapy (MA). *Program availability:* Part-time. *Degree requirements:* For master's, thesis, oral presentation, portfolio. *Entrance requirements:* For master's, interview, minimum GPA of 2.5. Additional exam requirements/recommendations for international students: Required—TOEFL (minimum score 550 paper-based; 79 iBT). Electronic applications accepted.

**Ottawa University,** Graduate Studies-Arizona, Program in Professional Counseling, Ottawa, KS 66067-3399. Offers Christian counseling (MA); expressive arts therapy (MA); marriage and family therapy (MA); treatment of trauma, abuse and deprivation (MA). Programs offered in Mesa, Phoenix, Tempe and West Valley, AZ. *Program availability:* Part-time, evening/weekend, online learning. *Degree requirements:* For master's, comprehensive exam, thesis or alternative, field experience, practicum. *Entrance requirements:* For master's, minimum undergraduate GPA of 3.0; course work in theories of personality, abnormal psychology, and human growth and development. Additional exam requirements/recommendations for international students: Required—TOEFL (minimum score 550 paper-based).

**Phillips Graduate University,** Programs in Marriage and Family Therapy and School Counseling, Chatsworth, CA 91311. Offers art therapy (MA); marriage and family therapy (MA); school counseling (MA). *Program availability:* Evening/weekend. *Degree requirements:* For master's, comprehensive exam, thesis. *Entrance requirements:* For master's, minimum GPA of 2.5. Electronic applications accepted. *Faculty research:* Integration of interpersonal psychological theory, systems approach, firsthand experiential learning.

**Pratt Institute,** School of Art, Programs in Creative Arts Therapy, Brooklyn, NY 11205-3899. Offers art therapy and creativity development (MPS); dance/movement therapy (MS). *Accreditation:* NASAD (one or more programs are accredited). *Program availability:* Part-time. *Faculty:* 3 full-time (all women), 22 part-time/adjunct (19 women). *Students:* 109 full-time (108 women); includes 38 minority (17 Black or African American, non-Hispanic/Latino; 4 Asian, non-Hispanic/Latino; 14 Hispanic/Latino; 3 Two or more races, non-Hispanic/Latino), 3 international. Average age 29. 149 applicants, 58% accepted, 44 enrolled. In 2016, 47 master's awarded. *Degree requirements:* For master's, thesis. *Entrance requirements:* For master's, letters of recommendation, portfolio. Additional exam requirements/recommendations for international students: Required—TOEFL (minimum score 600 paper-based; 100 iBT). *Application deadline:* For fall admission, 1/5 for domestic and international students; for spring admission, 10/1 for domestic and international students. Applications are processed on a rolling basis. Application fee: $50 ($90 for international students). Electronic applications accepted. *Expenses:* $29,646 full-time tuition, $1,938 fees. *Financial support:* Career-related internships or fieldwork, Federal Work-Study, institutionally sponsored loans, scholarships/grants, health care benefits, and unspecified assistantships available. Support available to part-time students. Financial award application deadline: 2/1; financial award applicants required to submit FAFSA. *Faculty research:* Psychology and aesthetic interaction, art therapy and AIDS, art therapy and autism, art diagnosis. *Unit head:* Dina Schapiro, Assistant Chairperson, 718-399-4267, Fax: 718-636-3597, E-mail: dschapir@pratt.edu. *Application contact:* Natalie Capannelli, Director of Graduate Admissions, 718-636-3551, Fax: 718-399-4242, E-mail: ncapanne@pratt.edu. Website: https://www.pratt.edu/academics/school-of-art/graduate-school-of-art/creative-arts-therapy/

**See Display on page 156 and Close-Up on page 209.**

**Prescott College,** Graduate Programs, Program in Counseling and Psychology, Prescott, AZ 86301. Offers adventure-based psychotherapy (MA); counseling psychology (MA); ecopsychology (MA); ecotherapy (MA); equine-assisted mental health (MA); expressive arts therapy (MA); somatic psychology (MA); student-directed independent study (MA). *Program availability:* Part-time, online learning. *Faculty:* 4 full-time (2 women), 9 part-time/adjunct (6 women). *Students:* 45 full-time (41 women), 139 part-time (113 women); includes 26 minority (1 Black or African American, non-Hispanic/Latino; 4 American Indian or Alaska Native, non-Hispanic/Latino; 2 Asian, non-Hispanic/Latino; 7 Hispanic/Latino; 1 Native Hawaiian or other Pacific Islander, non-Hispanic/Latino; 11 Two or more races, non-Hispanic/Latino), 7 international. Average age 38. 129 applicants, 84% accepted, 69 enrolled. In 2016, 24 master's awarded. Terminal master's awarded for partial completion of doctoral program. *Degree requirements:* For master's, thesis, fieldwork or internship, practicum. *Entrance requirements:* For master's, 2 letters of recommendation, resume. Additional exam requirements/recommendations for international students: Required—TOEFL (minimum score 500 paper-based). *Application deadline:* For fall admission, 4/15 priority date for domestic and international students; for spring admission, 9/15 priority date for domestic and international students. Applications are processed on a rolling basis. Application fee: $40. Electronic applications accepted. *Expenses: Tuition:* Full-time $19,680. One-time fee: $260 part-time. *Financial support:* Fellowships, research assistantships, teaching assistantships, career-related internships or fieldwork, Federal Work-Study, institutionally sponsored loans, scholarships/grants, traineeships, health care benefits, tuition waivers, and unspecified assistantships available. Support available to part-time students. Financial award applicants required to submit FAFSA. *Unit head:* Dr. Stacey

Carillo, Department Chair for Counseling, E-mail: stacey.carillo@prescott.edu. *Application contact:* Robert Monk, Graduate Admissions Counselor, 928-350-2109, E-mail: robert.monk@prescott.edu.

**Saint Mary-of-the-Woods College,** Master of Arts in Art Therapy Program, Saint Mary of the Woods, IN 47876. Offers MA, Post-Master's Certificate. *Program availability:* Evening/weekend, online learning. *Faculty:* 2 full-time (both women). *Students:* 144 full-time (139 women); includes 20 minority (all Two or more races, non-Hispanic/Latino). Average age 37. *Entrance requirements:* For degree, 12 credit hours each in general psychology, abnormal psychology, theories of personality, and developmental psychology; 18 credit hours in studio art skills. Application fee: $0. Electronic applications accepted. *Expenses:* Contact institution. *Financial support:* Scholarships/grants available. Financial award applicants required to submit FAFSA. *Unit head:* Dr. Jill McNutt, Director, 812-535-5160, E-mail: jmcnutt@smwc.edu. Website: http://www.smwc.edu/graduate/maat/

**School of the Art Institute of Chicago,** Graduate Division, Program in Art Therapy, Chicago, IL 60603-3103. Offers MAAT. Program offered jointly with Rush University. *Accreditation:* NASAD. *Degree requirements:* For master's, thesis, personal interview. *Entrance requirements:* Additional exam requirements/recommendations for international students: Required—TOEFL, IELTS. *Faculty research:* Migrane, ousider art, community-based practice.

**School of Visual Arts,** Graduate Programs, Art Therapy Department, New York, NY 10010-3994. Offers MPS. *Degree requirements:* For master's, thesis, 60 credits, including all required courses; minimum cumulative GPA of 3.0; residency of two academic years; internship. *Entrance requirements:* For master's, interview; 18 credits (or equivalent) in studio art and 12 credits in psychology (developmental and abnormal required; courses in introduction to psychology and theories of personality recommended); 15 to 20 digital images on CD. Additional exam requirements/recommendations for international students: Required—TOEFL (minimum score 550 paper-based; 79 iBT). Electronic applications accepted.

**Seton Hill University,** Program in Art Therapy, Greensburg, PA 15601. Offers MA. *Program availability:* Part-time. *Entrance requirements:* For master's, portfolio; 3 letters of recommendation; letter of intent; transcripts; writing sample (APA style); resume. Additional exam requirements/recommendations for international students: Required—TOEFL (minimum score 650 paper-based; 114 iBT), IELTS (minimum score 7). Electronic applications accepted.

**Southern Illinois University Edwardsville,** Graduate School, College of Arts and Sciences, Department of Art and Design, Program in Art Therapy Counseling, Edwardsville, IL 62026-0001. Offers MA. *Program availability:* Part-time. *Degree requirements:* For master's, thesis or alternative, project. *Entrance requirements:* For master's, MAT, portfolio. Additional exam requirements/recommendations for international students: Required—TOEFL (minimum score 550 paper-based; 79 iBT), IELTS (minimum score 6.5). Electronic applications accepted.

**Southwestern College,** Program in Art Therapy/Counseling, Santa Fe, NM 87502-4788. Offers MA. *Program availability:* Part-time, evening/weekend. *Degree requirements:* For master's, internship. *Entrance requirements:* For master's, resume, slide portfolio, interview, 3 letters of reference. Additional exam requirements/recommendations for international students: Required—TOEFL.

**Springfield College,** Graduate Programs, Program in Art Therapy, Springfield, MA 01109-3797. Offers M Ed, MS, CAGS. *Program availability:* Part-time. *Degree requirements:* For master's, research project, final art exhibition. *Entrance requirements:* For master's, portfolio. Additional exam requirements/recommendations for international students: Required—TOEFL (minimum score 550 paper-based). Electronic applications accepted. *Expenses: Tuition:* Full-time $29,640; part-time $988 per credit. *Required fees:* $195. *Faculty research:* Stage development in art, psychopathology of expression, art history and art therapy.

**University of Louisville,** Graduate School, College of Education and Human Development, Department of Counseling and Human Development, Louisville, KY 40292-0001. Offers counseling and personnel services (M Ed, PhD), including art therapy (M Ed), clinical mental health counseling (M Ed), college student personnel, counseling psychology, counselor education and supervision (PhD), educational psychology, measurement, and evaluation (PhD), school counseling (M Ed). *Accreditation:* APA; NCATE. *Program availability:* Part-time, evening/weekend. *Students:* 148 full-time (115 women), 58 part-time (42 women); includes 52 minority (36 Black or African American, non-Hispanic/Latino; 1 American Indian or Alaska Native, non-Hispanic/Latino; 4 Asian, non-Hispanic/Latino; 7 Hispanic/Latino; 4 Two or more races, non-Hispanic/Latino), 2 international. Average age 28. 206 applicants, 56% accepted, 73 enrolled. In 2016, 38 master's, 1 doctorate awarded. *Degree requirements:* For doctorate, comprehensive exam, thesis/dissertation. *Entrance requirements:* For master's and doctorate, GRE General Test. Application fee: $60. *Expenses:* Tuition, state resident: full-time $12,246; part-time $681 per credit hour. Tuition, nonresident: full-time $25,486; part-time $1417 per credit hour. *Required fees:* $196. Tuition and fees vary according to program and reciprocity agreements. *Financial support:* Fellowships, research assistantships, teaching assistantships, career-related internships or fieldwork, Federal Work-Study, scholarships/grants, health care benefits, and unspecified assistantships available. Financial award application deadline: 6/1; financial award applicants required to submit FAFSA. *Faculty research:* Mental health services and under-served populations; health disparities and outcomes; well-being identity development; measurement and evaluation. *Total annual research expenditures:* $295,684. *Unit head:* Dr. Mark M. Leach, Interim Chair/Professor, 502-852-0588, Fax: 502-852-0629, E-mail: m.leach@louisville.edu. *Application contact:* Betty Hampton, Director of Graduate Student Services, 502-852-5597, Fax: 502-852-1465, E-mail: edadvise@louisville.edu. Website: http://www.louisville.edu/education/departments/ecpy

**University of Maryland, College Park,** Academic Affairs, College of Education, Department of Counseling, Higher Education and Special Education, College Park, MD 20742. Offers college student personnel (M Ed, MA); college student personnel administration (PhD); community counseling (CAGS); community/career counseling (M Ed, MA); counseling and personnel services (M Ed, MA, PhD), including art therapy (M Ed), college student personnel (M Ed), counseling and personnel services (PhD), counseling psychology (M Ed), mental health counseling (M Ed), school counseling (M Ed); counseling psychology (PhD); counselor education (PhD); rehabilitation counseling (M Ed, MA, AGSC); school counseling (M Ed, MA); school psychology (M Ed, MA, PhD). *Accreditation:* ACA (one or more programs are accredited); APA (one or more programs are accredited); NCATE. *Program availability:* Part-time, evening/weekend, online learning. *Degree requirements:* For master's, thesis (for some programs); for doctorate, thesis/dissertation. *Entrance requirements:* For master's, GRE General Test or MAT, minimum GPA of 3.0, 3 letters of recommendation; for doctorate, GRE General Test or MAT, minimum GPA of 3.5, 3 letters of recommendation. Additional exam requirements/recommendations for international students: Required—TOEFL. Electronic applications accepted. *Faculty research:* Educational psychology, counseling, health.

**University of Wisconsin–Superior,** Graduate Division, Department of Visual Arts, Superior, WI 54880-4500. Offers art education (MA); art history (MA); art therapy (MA); studio arts (MA). *Program availability:* Part-time. *Degree requirements:* For master's, comprehensive exam, exhibit. *Entrance requirements:* For master's, minimum GPA of 2.75, portfolio. Electronic applications accepted.

**Ursuline College,** School of Graduate Studies, Program in Counseling and Art Therapy, Pepper Pike, OH 44124-4398. Offers MA. *Program availability:* Part-time. *Faculty:* 4 full-time (3 women), 1 (woman) part-time/adjunct. *Students:* 37 applicants, 97% accepted, 22 enrolled. In 2016, 22 master's awarded. *Degree requirements:* For master's, thesis, 700-hour internship. *Entrance requirements:* For master's, BA in psychology, social sciences, or related field; minimum undergraduate GPA of 3.0; portfolio; work experience with human service agency. Additional exam requirements/recommendations for international students: Required—TOEFL (minimum score 500 paper-based; 80 iBT). *Application deadline:* For fall admission, 8/1 priority date for domestic students. Applications are processed on a rolling basis. Application fee: $25. Electronic applications accepted. *Expenses:* $1,094 per credit hour. *Financial support:* In 2016–17, 21 students received support. Scholarships/grants available. Financial award application deadline: 3/1; financial award applicants required to submit FAFSA. *Faculty research:* LGBTQ issues, affirmative counseling, wellness, holistic care, creativity and mental health, creativity and clinical supervision, expressive therapies and counselor education, mindfulness and family therapy. *Unit head:* Gail Rule-Hoffman, Director, 440-646-8138, Fax: 440-684-6135. *Application contact:* Stephanie Pratt, Graduate Admission Coordinator, 440-646-8119, Fax: 440-684-6138, E-mail: graduateadmissions@ursuline.edu.

# Decorative Arts

**Bard Graduate Center,** Graduate Studies, New York, NY 10024-3602. Offers M Phil, MA, PhD. *Program availability:* Part-time. *Faculty:* 15 full-time (7 women), 5 part-time/adjunct (4 women). *Students:* 67 full-time (55 women), 11 part-time (all women). In 2016, 23 master's, 5 doctorates awarded. *Degree requirements:* For master's, one foreign language, thesis, internship; for doctorate, 2 foreign languages, thesis/dissertation, 3 field exams. *Entrance requirements:* For master's, GRE General Test, writing sample, 3 letters of recommendation; for doctorate, GRE General Test, MA, master's thesis or equivalent, 3 letters of recommendation. Additional exam requirements/recommendations for international students: Required—TOEFL. *Application deadline:* For fall admission, 1/6 for domestic and international students. Application fee: $70. *Financial support:* Fellowships with tuition reimbursements, research assistantships, teaching assistantships, career-related internships or fieldwork, institutionally sponsored loans, scholarships/grants, traineeships, health care benefits, and unspecified assistantships available. Financial award application deadline: 1/6; financial award applicants required to submit FAFSA. *Faculty research:* New York and American material culture; modern design history; history and theory of museums; early Modern Europe; global Middle Ages; archaeology, anthropology, and material culture; cultures of conservation. *Unit head:* Susan Weber, Founder and Director, 212-501-3000, Fax: 212-501-3079. *Application contact:* Elena Pinto Simon, Dean for Academic Administration, Student and Alumni Affairs, 212-501-3057, Fax: 212-501-3065, E-mail: simon@bgc.bard.edu.
Website: http://www.bgc.bard.edu

See Display on page 171 and Close-Up on page 199.

**Sotheby's Institute of Art–London,** Graduate Programs, London, United Kingdom. Offers art business (MA); contemporary art (MA); fine and decorative art and design (MA); modern and contemporary Asian art (MA). *Faculty:* 41 full-time (25 women). *Students:* 181 full-time (159 women). *Degree requirements:* For master's, thesis. *Entrance requirements:* Additional exam requirements/recommendations for international students: Required—IELTS (minimum score 7). *Application deadline:* Applications are processed on a rolling basis. Electronic applications accepted. *Expenses: Tuition:* Full-time 24,900 British pounds. Tuition and fees vary according to class time, program and student level. *Application contact:* Jessica Bearne, Admissions Manager, 44 20 7462 3250, E-mail: j.bearne@sothebysinstitute.com.

**Sotheby's Institute of Art–New York,** Graduate Programs, New York, NY 10021. Offers art business (MA); contemporary art (MA); fine and decorative art and design (MA). *Accreditation:* NASAD. *Entrance requirements:* For master's, academic transcripts, two letters of academic reference, personal statement, writing sample, curriculum vitae/resume, interview. Additional exam requirements/recommendations for international students: Required—TOEFL (minimum score 100 iBT), IELTS (minimum score 7). Electronic applications accepted.

# Museum Studies

**American Museum of Natural History–Richard Gilder Graduate School,** Program in Comparative Biology, New York, NY 10024. Offers PhD. *Degree requirements:* For doctorate, thesis/dissertation, qualifying examination. *Entrance requirements:* For doctorate, GRE General Test (taken within the past five years); GRE Subject Test (recommended), BA, BS, or equivalent degree from accredited institution; official transcripts; essay;. Additional exam requirements/recommendations for international students: Required—TOEFL (minimum score 600 paper-based; 100 iBT), IELTS (minimum score 7).

**Arizona State University at the Tempe campus,** College of Liberal Arts and Sciences, School of Human Evolution and Social Change, Tempe, AZ 85287-2402. Offers anthropology (MA, PhD), including anthropology (PhD), archaeology (PhD), bioarchaeology (PhD), evolutionary (PhD), museum studies (MA), sociocultural (PhD); applied mathematics for the life and social sciences (PhD); environmental social science (PhD), including environmental social science, urbanism; global health (MA, PhD), including complex adaptive systems science (PhD), evolutionary global health sciences (PhD), health and culture (PhD), urbanism (PhD); immigration studies (Graduate Certificate). Terminal master's awarded for partial completion of doctoral program. *Degree requirements:* For master's, thesis or alternative, interactive Program of Study (iPOS) submitted before completing 50 percent of required credit hours; for doctorate, comprehensive exam, thesis/dissertation, interactive Program of Study (iPOS) submitted before completing 50 percent of required credit hours. *Entrance requirements:* For master's and doctorate, GRE, minimum GPA of 3.0 or equivalent in last 2 years of work leading to bachelor's degree. Additional exam requirements/recommendations for international students: Required—TOEFL, IELTS, or PTE. Electronic applications accepted.

**Arizona State University at the Tempe campus,** Herberger Institute for Design and the Arts, School of Art, Tempe, AZ 85287-1505. Offers art education (MA); art history (MA); ceramics (MFA); design, environment and the arts (PhD), including history, theory and criticism; drawing (MFA); fibers (MFA); intermedia (MFA); metals (MFA); museum studies (MFA); painting (MFA); printmaking (MFA); sculpture (MFA); wood (MFA); MFA/MA. Terminal master's awarded for partial completion of doctoral program. *Degree requirements:* For master's, thesis/exhibition (MFA, MA in art education); interactive Program of Study (iPOS) submitted before completing 50 percent of required credit hours; for doctorate, comprehensive exam, thesis/dissertation, interactive Program of Study (iPOS) submitted before completing 50 percent of required credit hours. *Entrance requirements:* For master's, GRE or MAT, minimum GPA of 3.0 or equivalent in last 2 years of work leading to bachelor's degree; for doctorate, GRE, master's degree in architecture, graphic design, industrial design, interior design, landscape architecture, or art history or equivalent standing; statement of purpose; 3 letters of recommendation; indication of potential faculty mentor; sample of written work. Additional exam requirements/recommendations for international students: Required—TOEFL, IELTS, or PTE. Electronic applications accepted.

**Bard College,** Center for Curatorial Studies, Annandale-on-Hudson, NY 12504. Offers MA. *Degree requirements:* For master's, thesis, exhibition. *Entrance requirements:* For master's, exhibition review, 3 letters of recommendation. Additional exam requirements/recommendations for international students: Required—TOEFL (minimum score 550 paper-based). Electronic applications accepted. *Expenses:* Contact institution. *Faculty research:* Contemporary art, history of exhibition, curatorial practice.

**Baylor University,** Graduate School, College of Arts and Sciences, Department of Museum Studies, Waco, TX 76798. Offers MA. *Program availability:* Part-time. *Faculty:* 3 full-time (2 women), 4 part-time/adjunct (1 woman). *Students:* 6 full-time (5 women), 9 part-time (all women); includes 2 minority (1 Black or African American, non-Hispanic/Latino; 1 Hispanic/Latino). Average age 25. 32 applicants, 81% accepted, 4 enrolled. In 2016, 9 master's awarded. *Degree requirements:* For master's, comprehensive exam, thesis or alternative. *Entrance requirements:* For master's, GRE General Test. Additional exam requirements/recommendations for international students: Required—TOEFL (minimum score 550 paper-based; 80 iBT). *Application deadline:* For fall admission, 2/15 priority date for domestic and international students. Applications are processed on a rolling basis. Application fee: $50. Electronic applications accepted. *Expenses: Tuition:* Full-time $28,494; part-time $1583 per credit hour. *Required fees:* $167 per credit hour. Tuition and fees vary according to course load and program. *Financial support:* In 2016–17, 13 students received support, including 13 research assistantships with partial tuition reimbursements available (averaging $9,000 per year); career-related internships or fieldwork, Federal Work-Study, scholarships/grants, tuition waivers (full and partial), and unspecified assistantships also available. Support available to part-time students. Financial award application deadline: 2/15; financial award applicants required to submit FAFSA. *Faculty research:* Material culture, archival collections, 19th-century U.S. history, digitization, American decorative arts. *Unit head:* Dr. Julie Holcomb, Graduate Program Director, 254-710-1233, Fax: 254-710-1173, E-mail: julie_holcomb@baylor.edu. *Application contact:* Lisa Rieger, Administrative Assistant, 254-710-1233, Fax: 254-710-1173, E-mail: lisa_rieger@baylor.edu. Website: http://www.baylor.edu/Museum_Studies/

**Boston University,** Graduate School of Arts and Sciences, Department of History of Art and Architecture, Boston, MA 02215. Offers art history (MA, PhD); museum studies (Certificate). *Accreditation:* NASAD. *Students:* 61 full-time (52 women), 6 part-time (4 women); includes 8 minority (2 Black or African American, non-Hispanic/Latino; 2 Asian, non-Hispanic/Latino; 4 Hispanic/Latino), 6 international. Average age 31. 139 applicants, 35% accepted, 15 enrolled. In 2016, 9 master's, 7 doctorates awarded. Terminal master's awarded for partial completion of doctoral program. *Degree requirements:* For master's, one foreign language, comprehensive exam, thesis or alternative, scholarly paper; for doctorate, 2 foreign languages, comprehensive exam, thesis/dissertation. *Entrance requirements:* For master's and doctorate, GRE General Test, 3 letters of recommendation, transcripts, personal statement, curriculum vitae, writing sample, foreign language proficiency; for Certificate, GRE General Test. Additional exam requirements/recommendations for international students: Required—TOEFL (minimum score 550 paper-based; 84 iBT). *Application deadline:* For fall admission, 1/5 for domestic and international students; for spring admission, 10/15 for domestic and international students. Application fee: $95. Electronic applications accepted. *Financial support:* In 2016–17, 43 students received support, including 17 fellowships with full tuition reimbursements available (averaging $21,500 per year), 10 teaching assistantships with full tuition reimbursements available (averaging $21,500 per year); career-related internships or fieldwork, Federal Work-Study, scholarships/grants, health care benefits, and unspecified assistantships also available. Financial award application deadline: 1/5. *Unit head:* Alice Tseng, Chair, 617-353-1458, Fax: 617-353-3243, E-mail: aytseng@bu.edu. *Application contact:* Cheryl Crombie, Administrative Assistant, 617-353-2522, Fax: 617-353-3243, E-mail: ccrombie@bu.edu. Website: http://www.bu.edu/AH/

*Museum Studies*

**California College of the Arts,** Graduate Programs, Curatorial Practice Program, San Francisco, CA 94107. Offers MA. *Faculty:* 2 full-time (both women), 2 part-time/adjunct (both women). *Students:* 13 full-time (11 women); includes 1 minority (Hispanic/Latino), 6 international. Average age 29. 24 applicants, 83% accepted, 8 enrolled. In 2016, 7 master's awarded. *Degree requirements:* For master's, thesis, exhibit. *Entrance requirements:* For master's, appropriate bachelor's degree, portfolio, resume, letters of recommendation, transcript. Additional exam requirements/recommendations for international students: Required—TOEFL, IELTS, or PTE. *Application deadline:* For fall admission, 1/10 priority date for domestic and international students. Applications are processed on a rolling basis. Application fee: $70. Electronic applications accepted. *Expenses:* $39,384 tuition per year, $490 fees per year. *Financial support:* In 2016–17, teaching assistantships (averaging $2,000 per year) were awarded; career-related internships or fieldwork, Federal Work-Study, scholarships/grants, health care benefits, and unspecified assistantships also available. Financial award application deadline: 7/31; financial award applicants required to submit FAFSA. *Unit head:* James Voorhies, Dean of Fine Arts, 415-551-9249, E-mail: jvoorhies@cca.edu. *Application contact:* Wes Fanelli, Assistant Director of Graduate Admissions, 415-703-9533, Fax: 415-703-9539, E-mail: wfanelli@cca.edu.

**California State University, Chico,** Office of Graduate Studies, College of Behavioral and Social Sciences, Department of Anthropology, Chico, CA 95929-0722. Offers anthropology (MA); museum studies (MA). *Faculty:* 11 full-time (4 women), 6 part-time/adjunct (5 women). *Students:* 12 full-time (8 women), 12 part-time (10 women); includes 5 minority (3 Hispanic/Latino; 2 Two or more races, non-Hispanic/Latino). 58 applicants, 16% accepted, 5 enrolled. In 2016, 9 master's awarded. *Degree requirements:* For master's, comprehensive exam, thesis, oral examination. *Entrance requirements:* For master's, GRE General Test, two letters of recommendation, statement of purpose, curriculum vitae, writing sample. Additional exam requirements/recommendations for international students: Required—TOEFL (minimum score 550 paper-based; 80 iBT), IELTS (minimum score 6.5), PTE (minimum score 59). *Application deadline:* For fall admission, 1/15 for domestic and international students. Application fee: $55. Electronic applications accepted. *Financial support:* Fellowships, career-related internships or fieldwork, institutionally sponsored loans, scholarships/grants, and unspecified assistantships available. Financial award application deadline: 3/1; financial award applicants required to submit FAFSA. *Unit head:* Jesse Dizard, Chair, 530-898-6193, Fax: 530-898-6143, E-mail: anth@csuchico.edu. *Application contact:* Judy L. Morris, Graduate Admissions Coordinator, 530-898-6880, Fax: 530-898-6889, E-mail: jlmorris@csuchico.edu.
Website: http://www.csuchico.edu/anth/

**Caribbean University,** Graduate School, Bayamón, PR 00960-0493. Offers administration and supervision (MA Ed); criminal justice (MA); curriculum and instruction (MA Ed, PhD), including elementary education (MA Ed), English education (MA Ed), history education (MA Ed), mathematics education (MA Ed), primary education (MA Ed), science education (MA Ed), Spanish education (MA Ed); educational technology in instructional systems (MA Ed); gerontology (MSN); human resources (MBA); museology, archiving and art history (MA Ed); neonatal pediatrics (MSN); physical education (MA Ed); special education (MA Ed). *Entrance requirements:* For master's, interview, minimum GPA of 2.5.

**Case Western Reserve University,** School of Graduate Studies, Department of Art History and Art, Program in Art History and Museum Studies, Cleveland, OH 44106. Offers MA. *Program availability:* Part-time. *Faculty:* 9 full-time (8 women), 2 part-time/adjunct (1 woman). *Students:* 2 full-time (both women), 3 part-time (2 women). Average age 24. 11 applicants, 55% accepted, 2 enrolled. In 2016, 1 master's awarded. *Degree requirements:* For master's, one foreign language, comprehensive exam. *Entrance requirements:* For master's, GRE General Test, 2 samples of written work; 3 letters of recommendation. Additional exam requirements/recommendations for international students: Required—TOEFL (minimum score 600 paper-based; 100 iBT). *Application deadline:* For fall admission, 1/1 priority date for domestic students. Applications are processed on a rolling basis. Application fee: $50. Electronic applications accepted. *Expenses: Tuition:* Full-time $42,576; part-time $1774 per credit hour. *Required fees:* $34. Tuition and fees vary according to course load and program. *Financial support:* Fellowships, research assistantships, teaching assistantships, career-related internships or fieldwork, and tuition waivers available. Financial award application deadline: 1/1. *Faculty research:* Greek art and architecture, Northern Baroque art, Italian Renaissance and Baroque, abstract expressionism, East Asian art, nineteenth-century French art, American and contemporary art. *Unit head:* Catherine Scallen, Associate Professor/Chair, 216-368-2383, Fax: 216-368-4681, E-mail: catherine.scallen@case.edu. *Application contact:* Deborah Tenenbaum, Department Assistant, 216-368-4118, Fax: 216-368-4681, E-mail: deborah.tenenbaum@case.edu.
Website: http://arthistory.case.edu/graduate/art-history/

**Christie's Education,** MA Program in Modern and Contemporary Art and the Market, New York, NY 10020. Offers MA. *Program availability:* Part-time. *Faculty:* 5 full-time (4 women). *Students:* 47 full-time (43 women), 4 part-time (all women). In 2016, 21 master's awarded. *Degree requirements:* For master's, one foreign language, thesis, internship. *Entrance requirements:* For master's, writing sample, 3 letters of recommendation. *Application deadline:* For fall admission, 1/15 priority date for domestic and international students. Applications are processed on a rolling basis. Application fee: $95. *Expenses:* Contact institution. *Financial support:* In 2016–17, 3 students received support. Scholarships/grants and unspecified assistantships available. Financial award applicants required to submit FAFSA. *Unit head:* Dr. Julie Reiss, Program Director, 212-355-1501 Ext. 3307, Fax: 212-355-7370, E-mail: jreiss@christies.edu. *Application contact:* Hilary Smith, Recruitment and Admissions Officer, 212-355-1501 Ext. 3309, Fax: 212-355-7370, E-mail: hsmith@christies.edu.
Website: https://www.christies.edu/new-york/courses/masters-modern-contemporary-art-markets.aspx

**City College of the City University of New York,** Graduate School, Division of Humanities and the Arts, Department of Art, Programs in Art History and Museum Studies, New York, NY 10031-9198. Offers art history (MA); art museum education (MA); museum studies (MA). *Program availability:* Part-time. *Degree requirements:* For master's, one foreign language, thesis. *Entrance requirements:* For master's, minimum GPA of 3.0, portfolio, art history paper. Additional exam requirements/recommendations for international students: Required—TOEFL (minimum score 577 paper-based; 90 iBT). Electronic applications accepted. Tuition and fees vary according to course load, degree level and program. *Faculty research:* Egyptian, Greek, medieval, Romanesque, and Ottoman art.

**Claremont Graduate University,** Graduate Programs, School of Arts and Humanities, Department of Cultural Studies, Claremont, CA 91711-6160. Offers Africana studies (Certificate); cultural studies (MA, PhD); media studies (MA, PhD); museum studies (MA). *Program availability:* Part-time. *Faculty:* 5 full-time (1 woman). *Students:* 47 full-time (35 women), 84 part-time (8 women); includes 28 minority (5 Black or African American, non-Hispanic/Latino; 1 American Indian or Alaska Native, non-Hispanic/Latino; 7 Asian, non-Hispanic/Latino; 12 Hispanic/Latino; 3 Two or more races, non-Hispanic/Latino), 5 international. Average age 35. In 2016, 4 master's, 2 doctorates, 1 other advanced degree awarded. *Entrance requirements:* For master's and doctorate,

GRE General Test. Additional exam requirements/recommendations for international students: Required—TOEFL (minimum score 75 iBT). *Application deadline:* For fall admission, 2/1 priority date for domestic and international students. Applications are processed on a rolling basis. Application fee: $80. Electronic applications accepted. *Expenses: Tuition:* Full-time $44,328; part-time $1847 per unit. *Required fees:* $600; $300 per semester. Tuition and fees vary according to course load and program. *Financial support:* Fellowships, research assistantships, Federal Work-Study, institutionally sponsored loans, and scholarships/grants available. Support available to part-time students. Financial award application deadline: 2/15; financial award applicants required to submit FAFSA. *Unit head:* David Luis-Brown, Chair, 909-607-3337, E-mail: david.luis-brown@cgu.edu. *Application contact:* Amy Sandefur, Assistant Director of Admissions, 909-607-9101, E-mail: amy.sandefur@cgu.edu.
Website: https://www.cgu.edu/departments/cultural-studies/

**Cleveland State University,** College of Graduate Studies, College of Liberal Arts and Social Sciences, Department of History, Cleveland, OH 44115. Offers art history (MA); museum studies (MA). *Program availability:* Part-time, evening/weekend. *Faculty:* 13 full-time (4 women), 7 part-time (4 women); includes 3 minority (1 Hispanic/Latino; 2 Two or more races, non-Hispanic/Latino). Average age 30. 21 applicants, 90% accepted, 6 enrolled. In 2016, 14 master's awarded. *Degree requirements:* For master's, thesis optional. *Entrance requirements:* For master's, minimum GPA of 3.0, bachelor's degree in history (or related field for art history). Additional exam requirements/recommendations for international students: Required—TOEFL (minimum score 550 paper-based; 78 iBT). *Application deadline:* For fall admission, 7/1 priority date for domestic students, 5/15 for international students; for spring admission, 11/15 for domestic students, 11/1 for international students; for summer admission, 4/1 for domestic students, 3/15 for international students. Applications are processed on a rolling basis. Application fee: $40. Electronic applications accepted. *Expenses:* Tuition, state resident: full-time $9565. Tuition, nonresident: full-time $17,980. Tuition and fees vary according to program. *Financial support:* In 2016–17, 7 students received support, including research assistantships with full tuition reimbursements available (averaging $8,600 per year); career-related internships or fieldwork, tuition waivers (full and partial), and unspecified assistantships also available. Financial award application deadline: 4/15. *Faculty research:* Africa and African diaspora, European history, Middle Eastern history, Latin American/Caribbean history, American history, gender and sexuality. *Unit head:* Dr. Elizabeth A. Lehfeldt, Chairperson, 216-687-3920, Fax: 216-687-5592, E-mail: e.lehfeldt@csuohio.edu. *Application contact:* Dr. Karen Sotiropoulos, Graduate Director, 216-687-3940, E-mail: r.s.shelton@csuohio.edu.
Website: http://www.csuohio.edu/history/

**Colorado State University,** College of Liberal Arts, Department of History, Fort Collins, CO 80523-1776. Offers liberal arts (MA); public history (MA), including cultural resource management, historic preservation, museum studies. *Program availability:* Part-time. *Faculty:* 6 full-time (2 women), 1 part-time/adjunct (0 women). *Students:* 25 full-time (14 women), 4 part-time (1 woman); includes 2 minority (1 American Indian or Alaska Native, non-Hispanic/Latino; 1 Hispanic/Latino). Average age 28. 23 applicants, 61% accepted, 13 enrolled. In 2016, 6 master's awarded. *Degree requirements:* For master's, one foreign language, comprehensive exam, thesis (for some programs), minimum final grade of B- in history courses counted toward degree. *Entrance requirements:* For master's, GRE General Test, 21 credits in history, statement of purpose, 3 letters of reference. Additional exam requirements/recommendations for international students: Required—TOEFL, IELTS. *Application deadline:* For fall admission, 2/1 priority date for domestic and international students. Application fee: $60 ($70 for international students). Electronic applications accepted. *Expenses:* Tuition, state resident: full-time $9628. Tuition, nonresident: full-time $23,603. *Required fees:* $2253; $528.14 per credit hour. $264.07 per semester. Tuition and fees vary according to course load and program. *Financial support:* In 2016–17, 22 students received support, including 1 research assistantship with full tuition reimbursement available (averaging $13,932 per year), 23 teaching assistantships with full tuition reimbursements available (averaging $13,932 per year); fellowships with full tuition reimbursements available and health care benefits also available. Financial award application deadline: 3/1; financial award applicants required to submit FAFSA. *Faculty research:* United states and north America; public and environmental history; modern world; religion; women, gender and sexuality. *Total annual research expenditures:* $281,014. *Unit head:* Dr. Doug Yarrington, Department Chair, 970-491-6801, Fax: 970-491-2941, E-mail: doug.yarrington@colostate.edu. *Application contact:* Diane Margolf, Graduate Studies Committee Chair, 970-491-5671, Fax: 970-491-2941, E-mail: diane.margolf@colostate.edu.
Website: http://history.colostate.edu/

**Columbia University,** Graduate School of Arts and Sciences, New York, NY 10027. Offers African-American studies (MA); American studies (MA); anthropology (MA, PhD); art history and archaeology (MA, PhD); astronomy (PhD); biological sciences (PhD); biotechnology (MA); chemical physics (PhD); chemistry (PhD); classical studies (MA, PhD); classics (MA, PhD); climate and society (MA); conservation biology (MA); earth and environmental sciences (PhD); East Asia: regional studies (MA); East Asian languages and cultures (MA, PhD); ecology, evolution and environmental biology (MA), including conservation biology; ecology, evolution, and environmental biology (PhD), including ecology and evolutionary biology, evolutionary primatology; economics (MA, PhD); English and comparative literature (MA, PhD); French and Romance philology (MA, PhD); Germanic languages (MA, PhD); global French studies (MA); global thought (MA); Hispanic cultural studies (MA); history (PhD); history and literature (MA); human rights studies (MA); Islamic studies (MA); Italian (MA, PhD); Japanese pedagogy (MA); Jewish studies (MA); Latin America and the Caribbean: regional studies (MA); Latin American and Iberian cultures (PhD); mathematics (MA, PhD), including finance (MA); medieval and Renaissance studies (MA); Middle Eastern, South Asian, and African studies (MA, PhD); modern art: critical and curatorial studies (MA); modern European studies (MA); museum anthropology (MA); music (DMA, PhD); oral history (MA); philosophical foundations of physics (MA); philosophy (MA, PhD); physics (PhD); political science (MA, PhD); psychology (PhD); quantitative methods in the social sciences (MA); religion (MA, PhD); Russia, Eurasia and East Europe: regional studies (MA); Russian translation (MA); Slavic cultures (MA); Slavic languages (MA, PhD); sociology (MA, PhD); South Asian studies (MA); statistics (MA, PhD); theatre (PhD). Dual-degree programs require admission to both Graduate School of Arts and Sciences and another Columbia school. *Program availability:* Part-time. Terminal master's awarded for partial completion of doctoral program. *Degree requirements:* For master's, variable foreign language requirement, comprehensive exam (for some programs); thesis (for some programs); for doctorate, variable foreign language requirement, comprehensive exam (for some programs), thesis/dissertation. *Entrance requirements:* For master's and doctorate, GRE General Test, GRE Subject Test (for some programs). Additional exam requirements/recommendations for international students: Required—TOEFL, IELTS. Electronic applications accepted.

**Eastern Michigan University,** Graduate School, College of Arts and Sciences, Department of Geography and Geology, Programs in Historic Preservation, Ypsilanti, MI 48197. Offers heritage interpretation and museum practice (MS); historic preservation (Graduate Certificate); preservation planning and administration (MS); recording, documentation and digital cultural heritage (MS). *Program availability:* Part-time, evening/weekend, online learning. *Students:* 17 full-time (16 women), 42 part-time (28 women); includes 9 minority (2 Black or African American, non-Hispanic/Latino; 5 Hispanic/Latino; 2 Two or more races, non-Hispanic/Latino). Average age 36. 25 applicants, 76% accepted, 12 enrolled. In 2016, 22 master's, 5 other advanced degrees awarded. *Entrance requirements:* Additional exam requirements/recommendations for international students: Required—TOEFL. *Application deadline:* Applications are processed on a rolling basis. Application fee: $45. *Financial support:* Fellowships, research assistantships with full tuition reimbursements, teaching assistantships with full tuition reimbursements, career-related internships or fieldwork, Federal Work-Study, institutionally sponsored loans, scholarships/grants, tuition waivers (partial), and unspecified assistantships available. Support available to part-time students. Financial award applicants required to submit FAFSA. *Application contact:* Dr. Ted Ligibel, Program Director, 734-487-0232, Fax: 734-487-6979, E-mail: tligibel@emich.edu.

**Fashion Institute of Technology,** School of Graduate Studies, Exhibition and Experience Design Program, New York, NY 10001-5992. Offers MA. *Students:* 20. 32 applicants, 34% accepted, 11 enrolled. In 2016, 13 master's awarded. *Degree requirements:* For master's, qualifying project. *Entrance requirements:* Additional exam requirements/recommendations for international students: Required—TOEFL (minimum score 550 paper-based). *Application deadline:* For fall admission, 2/15 priority date for domestic and international students. Applications are processed on a rolling basis. Application fee: $50. Electronic applications accepted. *Expenses:* Tuition, state resident: full-time $10,870; part-time $453 per credit. Tuition, nonresident: full-time $22,210; part-time $925 per credit. *Required fees:* $745. *Unit head:* Christina Lyons, Chair, 212-217-4302, E-mail: christina_lyons@fitnyc.edu. *Application contact:* Administrative Secretary, Graduate Admissions, 212-217-4300, Fax: 212-217-5156, E-mail: gradinfo@fitnyc.edu.
Website: http://www.fitnyc.edu/exhibition-design/

See Display on page 63 and Close-Up on page 101.

**Fashion Institute of Technology,** School of Graduate Studies, Program in Fashion and Textile Studies: History, Theory, Museum Practice, New York, NY 10001-5992. Offers MA. *Accreditation:* NASAD. *Students:* 36. 49 applicants, 31% accepted, 14 enrolled. *Degree requirements:* For master's, one foreign language, thesis, internship. *Entrance requirements:* For master's, GRE General Test or GRE Subject Test, previous course work in art history and chemistry, 4 semesters of a foreign language. Additional exam requirements/recommendations for international students: Required—TOEFL (minimum score 550 paper-based). *Application deadline:* For fall admission, 2/15 priority date for domestic and international students. Applications are processed on a rolling basis. Application fee: $50. Electronic applications accepted. *Expenses:* Tuition, state resident: full-time $10,870; part-time $453 per credit. Tuition, nonresident: full-time $22,210; part-time $925 per credit. *Required fees:* $745. *Financial support:* Federal Work-Study and scholarships/grants available. Financial award applicants required to submit FAFSA. *Unit head:* Denyse Montegut, Associate Chair, 212-217-4308. *Application contact:* Administrative Coordinator, 212-217-4300, E-mail: gradinfo@fitnyc.edu.
Website: http://www.fitnyc.edu/fashion-textile-history/

See Display on page 184 and Close-Up on page 205.

**Florida International University,** College of Communication, Architecture and The Arts, Department of Art and Art History, Miami, FL 33199. Offers museum studies (Graduate Certificate); studio art (MFA). *Accreditation:* NASAD. *Program availability:* Part-time, evening/weekend. *Faculty:* 13 full-time (6 women), 17 part-time/adjunct (10 women). *Students:* 24 full-time (16 women), 9 part-time (6 women); includes 23 minority (4 Black or African American, non-Hispanic/Latino; 19 Hispanic/Latino). Average age 39.

22 applicants, 68% accepted, 11 enrolled. In 2016, 5 master's awarded. *Entrance requirements:* For master's, minimum GPA of 3.0 in upper-level coursework, 3 letters of recommendation, 20 slides of creative work. Additional exam requirements/recommendations for international students: Required—TOEFL (minimum score 550 paper-based; 80 iBT). *Application deadline:* For fall admission, 2/1 for domestic and international students. Application fee: $30. Electronic applications accepted. *Expenses:* Tuition, state resident: full-time $8912; part-time $446 per credit hour. Tuition, nonresident: full-time $21,393; part-time $992 per credit hour. *Required fees:* $2185; $195 per semester. Tuition and fees vary according to program. *Financial support:* Institutionally sponsored loans and scholarships/grants available. Financial award application deadline: 3/1; financial award applicants required to submit FAFSA. *Unit head:* Dr. Jacek Kolasinski, Chair, 305-348-3362, Fax: 305-348-0513, E-mail: jacek.kolasinski@fiu.edu. *Application contact:* Nanett Rojas, Assistant Director, Graduate Admissions, 305-348-7464, Fax: 305-348-7441, E-mail: gradadm@fiu.edu.
Website: http://carta.fiu.edu/arts/

**Florida State University,** The Graduate School, College of Fine Arts, Department of Art History, Tallahassee, FL 32306. Offers art history (MA, PhD); museum and cultural heritage studies (MA). *Accreditation:* NASAD. *Program availability:* Part-time. *Faculty:* 11 full-time (4 women), 9 part-time/adjunct (5 women). *Students:* 48 full-time (43 women), 6 part-time (5 women); includes 10 minority (1 Black or African American, non-Hispanic/Latino; 2 Asian, non-Hispanic/Latino; 6 Hispanic/Latino; 1 Two or more races, non-Hispanic/Latino). Average age 32. 35 applicants, 91% accepted, 21 enrolled. In 2016, 14 master's, 1 doctorate awarded. Terminal master's awarded for partial completion of doctoral program. *Degree requirements:* For master's, one foreign language, thesis (for some programs), capstone project (for some programs); for doctorate, 2 foreign languages, comprehensive exam, thesis/dissertation. *Entrance requirements:* For master's, GRE General Test, minimum GPA of 3.0; for doctorate, GRE General Test, minimum GPA of 3.5. Additional exam requirements/recommendations for international students: Required—TOEFL (minimum score 550 paper-based; 80 iBT), IELTS (minimum score 6.5). *Application deadline:* For fall admission, 4/1 for domestic and international students. Applications are processed on a rolling basis. Application fee: $35. Electronic applications accepted. *Expenses:* $479.32 per credit hour in-state, $1,110.72 per credit hour out-of-state. *Financial support:* In 2016–17, 34 students received support, including 7 fellowships with full tuition reimbursements available (averaging $10,900 per year), 19 research assistantships with full tuition reimbursements available (averaging $5,395 per year), 8 teaching assistantships with full tuition reimbursements available (averaging $6,609 per year); career-related internships or fieldwork, Federal Work-Study, institutionally sponsored loans, and unspecified assistantships also available. Financial award application deadline: 1/1; financial award applicants required to submit FAFSA. *Faculty research:* Modern art and critical theory, medieval, Renaissance and Baroque, Pre-Columbian and Spanish Colonial, visual arts of the Americas. *Unit head:* Dr. Adam Jolles, Associate Professor of Art History/Department Chair, 850-644-7066, E-mail: ajolles@fsu.edu. *Application contact:* Juan Barcelo-Gonzalez, Academic Program Specialist/Graduate Student Advisor, 850-644-8207, E-mail: juan.barcelo@fsu.edu.
Website: http://arthistory.fsu.edu/

**The George Washington University,** Columbian College of Arts and Sciences, Department of Anthropology, Washington, DC 20052. Offers anthropology (MA, PhD); international development (MA); medical anthropology (MA); museum training (MA). *Program availability:* Part-time, evening/weekend. *Faculty:* 15 full-time (6 women). *Students:* 27 full-time (20 women), 11 part-time (8 women); includes 12 minority (1 Black or African American, non-Hispanic/Latino; 2 Asian, non-Hispanic/Latino; 5 Hispanic/Latino; 4 Two or more races, non-Hispanic/Latino), 6 international. Average age 28. 86 applicants, 33% accepted, 9 enrolled. In 2016, 10 master's awarded. *Degree*

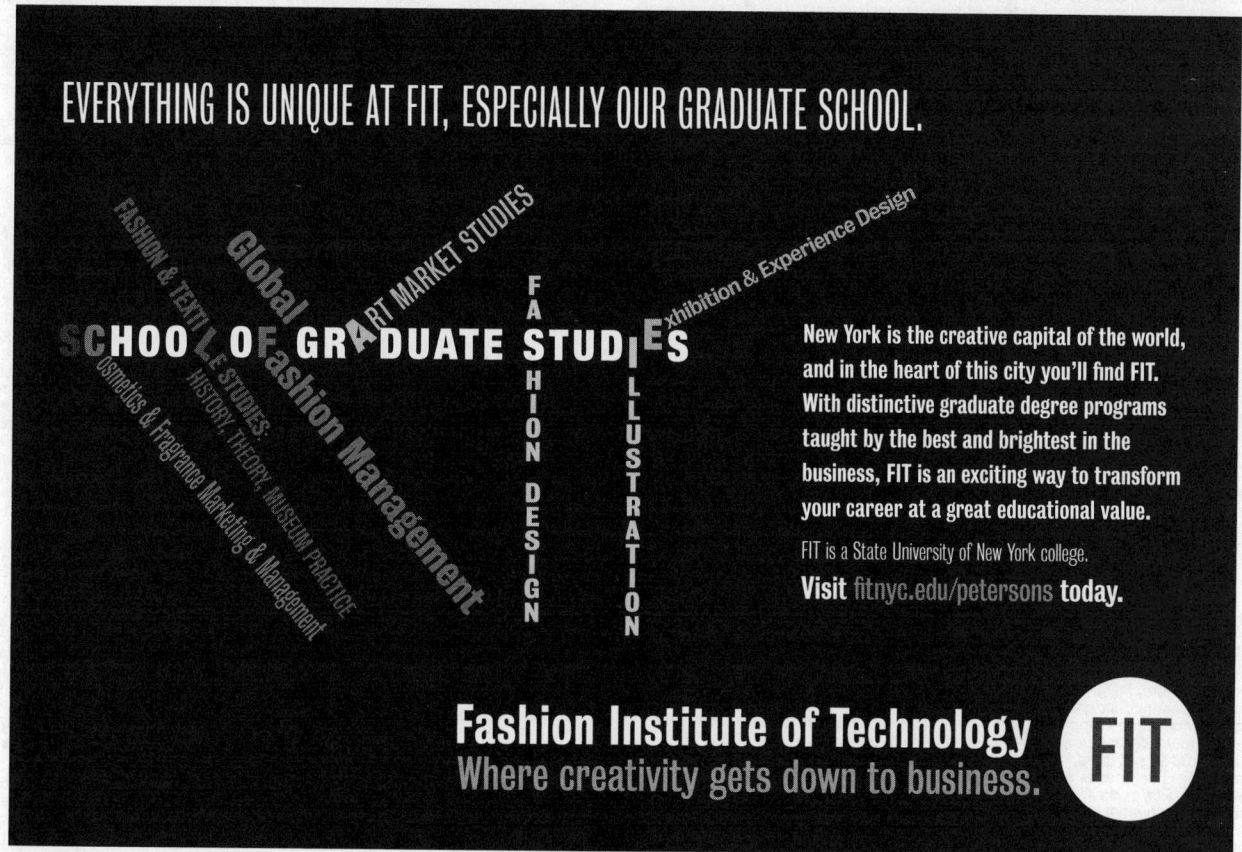

*requirements:* For master's, one foreign language, comprehensive exam, thesis or alternative. *Entrance requirements:* For master's, GRE General Test, minimum GPA of 3.0. Additional exam requirements/recommendations for international students: Required—TOEFL (minimum score 550 paper-based; 80 iBT). *Application deadline:* For fall admission, 1/15 priority date for international students; for spring admission, 9/15 priority date for domestic students, 9/1 priority date for international students. Applications are processed on a rolling basis. Application fee: $75. Electronic applications accepted. *Financial support:* In 2016–17, 8 students received support. Fellowships, teaching assistantships, career-related internships or fieldwork, and Federal Work-Study available. Financial award application deadline: 1/15. *Unit head:* Richard Grinker, Chair, 202-994-6984, E-mail: rgrink@email.gwu.edu. *Application contact:* Information Contact, 202-994-6075, E-mail: anth@gwu.edu. Website: http://anthropology.columbian.gwu.edu/

**The George Washington University,** Columbian College of Arts and Sciences, Department of Fine Arts and Art History, Program in Art History, Washington, DC 20052. Offers art history (MA); museum training (MA). *Program availability:* Part-time, evening/weekend. *Students:* 11 full-time (10 women), 2 part-time (both women); includes 1 minority (Hispanic/Latino), 1 international. Average age 27. 33 applicants, 88% accepted, 8 enrolled. In 2016, 7 master's awarded. *Degree requirements:* For master's, one foreign language, comprehensive exam, thesis or alternative. *Entrance requirements:* For master's, GRE General Test, bachelor's degree in field, minimum GPA of 3.0. Additional exam requirements/recommendations for international students: Required—TOEFL (minimum score 550 paper-based; 80 iBT). *Application deadline:* For fall admission, 3/1 priority date for domestic students, 1/15 priority date for international students; for spring admission, 10/1 priority date for domestic students, 9/1 priority date for international students. Applications are processed on a rolling basis. Application fee: $75. Electronic applications accepted. *Financial support:* In 2016–17, 3 students received support. Fellowships, teaching assistantships, career-related internships or fieldwork, and Federal Work-Study available. Financial award application deadline: 1/15. *Unit head:* Thomas K. Brown, Chair, 202-994-9067, E-mail: thbrown@gwu.edu. *Application contact:* Information Contact, 202-994-6085, Fax: 202-994-8657, E-mail: art@gwu.edu.

**The George Washington University,** Columbian College of Arts and Sciences, Program in Museum Studies, Washington, DC 20052. Offers museum collections management and care (Graduate Certificate); museum studies (MA). *Program availability:* Part-time, evening/weekend. *Faculty:* 5 full-time (all women). *Students:* 98 full-time (91 women), 38 part-time (33 women); includes 17 minority (1 Black or African American, non-Hispanic/Latino; 8 Asian, non-Hispanic/Latino; 6 Hispanic/Latino; 2 Two or more races, non-Hispanic/Latino), 7 international. Average age 26. 196 applicants, 73% accepted, 59 enrolled. In 2016, 46 master's, 8 other advanced degrees awarded. *Degree requirements:* For master's, comprehensive exam, internship. *Entrance requirements:* For master's, GRE General Test, minimum GPA of 3.0. Additional exam requirements/recommendations for international students: Required—TOEFL (minimum score 550 paper-based; 80 iBT). *Application deadline:* For fall admission, 2/1 priority date for domestic students, 1/15 priority date for international students; for spring admission, 10/15 priority date for domestic students, 9/1 priority date for international students. Applications are processed on a rolling basis. Application fee: $75. Electronic applications accepted. *Financial support:* In 2016–17, 15 students received support. Fellowships with tuition reimbursements available, career-related internships or fieldwork, Federal Work-Study, institutionally sponsored loans, and tuition waivers available. Financial award application deadline: 1/15. *Unit head:* Kym S. Rice, Director, 202-994-0165, Fax: 202-994-7034, E-mail: kym@gwu.edu. *Application contact:* Information Contact, 202-994-7030, Fax: 202-994-7034, E-mail: mstd@gwu.edu. Website: http://museumstudies.columbian.gwu.edu/

**Harvard University,** Extension School, Cambridge, MA 02138-3722. Offers applied sciences (CAS); biotechnology (ALM); educational technologies (ALM); educational technology (CET); English for graduate and professional studies (DGP); environmental management (ALM, CEM); information technology (ALM); journalism (ALM); liberal arts (ALM); management (ALM, CM); mathematics for teaching (ALM); museum studies (ALM); premedical studies (Diploma); publication and communication (CPC). *Program availability:* Part-time, evening/weekend. *Degree requirements:* For master's, thesis. *Entrance requirements:* For master's, 3 completed graduate courses with grade of B or higher. Additional exam requirements/recommendations for international students: Required—TOEFL (minimum score 600 paper-based), TWE (minimum score 5). *Expenses:* Contact institution.

**Indiana University–Purdue University Indianapolis,** School of Liberal Arts, Department of Museum Studies, Indianapolis, IN 46202. Offers MS, Certificate. *Entrance requirements:* For master's, GRE.

**John F. Kennedy University,** School of Education and Liberal Arts, Department of Museum Studies, Berkeley, CA 94702. Offers museum studies (MA, Certificate), including administration, collections management, public programming. *Program availability:* Part-time. *Degree requirements:* For master's, project. *Entrance requirements:* For master's, interview. Additional exam requirements/recommendations for international students: Required—TOEFL, TWE. *Faculty research:* Emerging museum philosophies, multicultural diversity issues in museums, trends in collections management and preventive conservation, effective programming techniques and application for diverse audiences.

**Johns Hopkins University,** Zanvyl Krieger School of Arts and Sciences, Advanced Academic Programs, Program in Museum Studies, Washington, DC 20036. Offers digital curation (Certificate); museum studies (MA). *Program availability:* Part-time, evening/weekend, online learning. *Entrance requirements:* For master's, minimum GPA of 3.0. Additional exam requirements/recommendations for international students: Required—TOEFL (minimum score 100 iBT). Electronic applications accepted.

**Marist College,** Graduate Programs, School of Communication and the Arts, Poughkeepsie, NY 12601-1387. Offers communication (MA); integrated marketing communication (MA); museum studies (MA). *Program availability:* Part-time, online learning. *Degree requirements:* For master's, thesis or comprehensive exam. *Entrance requirements:* For master's, GRE, minimum undergraduate GPA of 3.0, resume, 3 letters of recommendation. Additional exam requirements/recommendations for international students: Required—TOEFL (minimum score 550 paper-based; 80 iBT); Recommended—IELTS (minimum score 6.5). Electronic applications accepted.

**Maryland Institute College of Art,** Graduate Studies, MFA Program in Curatorial Practice, Baltimore, MD 21201. Offers MFA. *Faculty:* 2 full-time (0 women), 4 part-time/adjunct (1 woman). *Students:* 20 full-time (18 women); includes 9 minority (3 Black or African American, non-Hispanic/Latino; 1 Asian, non-Hispanic/Latino; 2 Hispanic/Latino; 3 Two or more races, non-Hispanic/Latino), 3 international. Average age 27. 40 applicants, 38% accepted, 10 enrolled. In 2016, 10 master's awarded. *Degree requirements:* For master's, thesis, exhibit and thesis documentation. *Entrance requirements:* For master's, portfolio, bachelor's degree in any field. Additional exam requirements/recommendations for international students: Required—TOEFL (minimum score 550 paper-based; 80 iBT), IELTS (minimum score 6.5). *Application deadline:* For fall admission, 1/15 for domestic and international students. Application fee: $75.

Electronic applications accepted. *Expenses:* Contact institution. *Financial support:* In 2016–17, 10 students received support, including 20 fellowships (averaging $13,000 per year), 10 teaching assistantships (averaging $3,200 per year); career-related internships or fieldwork and scholarships/grants also available. Financial award application deadline: 1/15. *Unit head:* Jose Ruiz, Director, 410-225-5274, Fax: 410-225-5275, E-mail: graduate@mica.edu. *Application contact:* Chris D. Harring, Director, Graduate Admission, 410-225-2256, Fax: 410-225-5275, E-mail: graduate@mica.edu. Website: http://www.mica.edu/Programs_of_Study/Graduate_Programs/Curatorial_Practice_(MFA).html

**Morgan State University,** School of Graduate Studies, College of Liberal Arts, Department of History and Geography, Baltimore, MD 21251. Offers African-American studies (MA); history (MA, PhD); museum studies and historic preservation (MA). *Program availability:* Part-time, evening/weekend. *Degree requirements:* For master's, comprehensive exam, thesis; for doctorate, comprehensive exam, thesis/dissertation. *Entrance requirements:* For master's, minimum GPA of 2.5; for doctorate, GRE or MAT. Additional exam requirements/recommendations for international students: Required—TOEFL (minimum score 550 paper-based). *Faculty research:* Women's history, African diaspora history, urban history.

**New Mexico State University,** College of Arts and Sciences, Department of Anthropology, Las Cruces, NM 88003. Offers anthropology (MA); cultural resource management (Graduate Certificate); museum studies (Graduate Certificate). *Program availability:* Part-time. *Faculty:* 9 full-time (5 women), 1 part-time/adjunct (0 women). *Students:* 35 full-time (23 women), 22 part-time (16 women); includes 20 minority (2 Black or African American, non-Hispanic/Latino; 1 American Indian or Alaska Native, non-Hispanic/Latino; 15 Hispanic/Latino; 2 Two or more races, non-Hispanic/Latino), 2 international. Average age 32. 27 applicants, 67% accepted, 12 enrolled. In 2016, 16 master's, 7 other advanced degrees awarded. *Degree requirements:* For master's, comprehensive exam (for some programs), thesis or internship. *Entrance requirements:* For master's, minimum undergraduate GPA of 3.0. Additional exam requirements/recommendations for international students: Required—TOEFL (minimum score 550 paper-based; 79 iBT), IELTS (minimum score 6.5). *Application deadline:* For fall admission, 2/1 priority date for domestic and international students; for spring admission, 10/1 priority date for domestic and international students. Applications are processed on a rolling basis. Application fee: $40 ($50 for international students). Electronic applications accepted. *Expenses:* Tuition, state resident: full-time $4086. Tuition, nonresident: full-time $14,254. *Required fees:* $853. Tuition and fees vary according to course load. *Financial support:* In 2016–17, 27 students received support, including 5 fellowships (averaging $4,088 per year), 2 research assistantships (averaging $8,482 per year), 11 teaching assistantships (averaging $10,097 per year); career-related internships or fieldwork, Federal Work-Study, scholarships/grants, traineeships, health care benefits, and unspecified assistantships also available. Support available to part-time students. Financial award application deadline: 3/1. *Faculty research:* Native American culture and society, Latin America and border studies, prehistoric and historic archaeology, medical anthropology, applied anthropology, museum studies. *Total annual research expenditures:* $31,819. *Unit head:* Dr. Rani Alexander, Department Head, 575-646-2725, E-mail: raalexan@nmsu.edu. *Application contact:* Dr. Lois Stanford, Graduate Advisor, 575-646-6092, E-mail: lstanfor@nmsu.edu. Website: http://anthropology.nmsu.edu

**The New School,** Parsons Paris, Program in History of Design and Curatorial Studies, New York, NY 10011. Offers MA. Program offered in cooperation with the Musee des Arts Decoratifs. *Program availability:* Part-time. *Faculty:* 5 full-time (2 women). *Students:* 11 full-time (10 women), 1 (woman) part-time; includes 2 minority (1 Asian, non-Hispanic/Latino; 1 Hispanic/Latino), 7 international. Average age 29. 14 applicants, 86% accepted, 4 enrolled. In 2016, 3 master's awarded. *Degree requirements:* For master's, one foreign language, thesis optional. *Entrance requirements:* For master's, transcripts, resume, statement of purpose. Additional exam requirements/recommendations for international students: Required—TOEFL (minimum score 92 iBT), IELTS (minimum score 7), PTE (minimum score 63). *Application deadline:* Applications are processed on a rolling basis. Application fee: $50. Electronic applications accepted. *Expenses:* Contact institution. *Financial support:* Research assistantships, teaching assistantships, career-related internships or fieldwork, and scholarships/grants available. *Faculty research:* Curation, art history, 20th century art and design. *Unit head:* Emmanuel Guy, Director, 33-176217661, E-mail: guye@newschool.edu. *Application contact:* Mike Fakih, Director of Admissions, Parsons Paris, 33 176 21 76 67, E-mail: thinkparsonsparis@newschool.edu.

**The New School,** Parsons School of Design, Program in the History of Design and Curatorial Studies, New York, NY 10011. Offers MA. Program offered jointly with the Cooper-Hewitt Museum and the Smithsonian Institution. *Accreditation:* NASAD. *Program availability:* Part-time. *Faculty:* 23 full-time (16 women), 18 part-time/adjunct (13 women). *Students:* 42 full-time (34 women), 22 part-time (20 women); includes 12 minority (5 Black or African American, non-Hispanic/Latino; 2 Asian, non-Hispanic/Latino; 4 Hispanic/Latino; 1 Two or more races, non-Hispanic/Latino), 14 international. Average age 31. 76 applicants, 78% accepted, 25 enrolled. In 2016, 8 master's awarded. *Degree requirements:* For master's, one foreign language, thesis. *Entrance requirements:* For master's, transcripts, resume, statement of purpose, recommendation letters. Additional exam requirements/recommendations for international students: Required—TOEFL (minimum score 92 iBT), IELTS (minimum score 7), PTE (minimum score 63). *Application deadline:* For fall admission, 1/1 priority date for domestic and international students. Applications are processed on a rolling basis. Application fee: $50. Electronic applications accepted. *Expenses:* Contact institution. *Financial support:* Fellowships, research assistantships, teaching assistantships, career-related internships or fieldwork, scholarships/grants, and unspecified assistantships available. Support available to part-time students. Financial award application deadline: 2/1; financial award applicants required to submit FAFSA. *Faculty research:* Design history, theory, and criticism; cultural studies; curatorial practice; decorative arts; design research. *Unit head:* Sarah Lichtman, Director, E-mail: lichtmas@newschool.edu. *Application contact:* Courtney Malenius, Director of Graduate Admissions, 212-229-5150 Ext. 4011, E-mail: maleniuc@newschool.edu. Website: http://www.newschool.edu/parsons

**New York University,** Graduate School of Arts and Science, Program in Museum Studies, New York, NY 10012-1019. Offers museum studies (MA, Advanced Certificate), including Africana studies (MA), Hebrew and Judaic studies (MA), Latin American and Caribbean studies (MA), Near Eastern studies (MA). *Program availability:* Part-time, evening/weekend. *Entrance requirements:* For master's, GRE General Test; for Advanced Certificate, master's degree or PhD. Additional exam requirements/recommendations for international students: Required—TOEFL. *Faculty research:* Modern and contemporary art, history of museums and exhibitions, conservation of cultural materials, museum anthropology, ethnography.

**Penn State Harrisburg,** Graduate School, School of Humanities, Middletown, PA 17057. Offers American studies (MA, PhD); communications (MA); heritage and museum practice (Certificate); humanities (MA); writing instruction specialist (Certificate). *Program availability:* Evening/weekend. *Unit head:* Dr. Mukund S. Kulkarni,

Chancellor, 717-948-6105, Fax: 717-948-6452. *Application contact:* Robert W. Coffman, Jr., Director of Enrollment Management, Admissions, 717-948-6250, Fax: 717-948-6325, E-mail: hbgadmit@psu.edu.
Website: https://harrisburg.psu.edu/humanities

**St. John's University,** St. John's College of Liberal Arts and Sciences, Department of Art and Design, Queens, NY 11439. Offers MA. *Degree requirements:* For master's, internship. *Entrance requirements:* For master's, BA with at least 24 credits in art history or a major in a related area in the humanities and coursework in art history; minimum cumulative undergraduate GPA of 3.0 overall and in major.

**San Francisco Art Institute,** Master of Arts Programs, San Francisco, CA 94133. Offers exhibition and museum studies (MA); history and theory of contemporary art (MA). *Faculty:* 3 full-time (all women), 12 part-time/adjunct (7 women). *Students:* 6 full-time (all women), 3 part-time (all women); includes 1 minority (Asian, non-Hispanic/Latino), 3 international. Average age 27. 20 applicants, 60% accepted, 5 enrolled. In 2016, 9 master's awarded. *Degree requirements:* For master's, thesis. *Entrance requirements:* For master's, statement of purpose, writing samples. Additional exam requirements/recommendations for international students: Required—TOEFL (minimum score 600 paper-based; 100 iBT), IELTS (minimum score 7.5). *Application deadline:* Applications are processed on a rolling basis. Application fee: $85. Electronic applications accepted. *Expenses:* Tuition: Full-time $46,010; part-time $2020 per credit. *Required fees:* $870; $870 per credit. *Financial support:* Fellowships, teaching assistantships, career-related internships or fieldwork, Federal Work-Study, scholarships/grants, and unspecified assistantships available. Support available to part-time students. Financial award application deadline: 3/1; financial award applicants required to submit FAFSA. *Unit head:* Claire Daigle, Chair, Master of Arts Department, 415-351-3573, Fax: 415-641-1205, E-mail: cdaigle@sfai.edu. *Application contact:* Jana Rumberger, Director of Graduate Admissions, 415-351-3507, Fax: 415-749-4592, E-mail: jrumberger@sfai.edu.
Website: http://www.sfai.edu/degree-programs/graduate/ma

**San Francisco State University,** Division of Graduate Studies, College of Liberal and Creative Arts, Museum Studies Program, San Francisco, CA 94132-1722. Offers MA. *Program availability:* Part-time. *Expenses:* Tuition, state resident: full-time $6738. Tuition, nonresident: full-time $15,666. *Required fees:* $1012. Tuition and fees vary according to degree level and program. *Financial support:* Career-related internships or fieldwork and Federal Work-Study available. *Unit head:* Dr. Edward Luby, Program Director, 415-338-3163, Fax: 415-338-6537, E-mail: emluby@sfsu.edu.
Website: http://museum.sfsu.edu/

**Seton Hall University,** College of Communication and the Arts, South Orange, NJ 07079-2697. Offers museum professions (MA), including exhibition development, museum education, museum management, museum registration; public relations (MA); strategic communication (MA). *Program availability:* Part-time, evening/weekend, online learning. *Degree requirements:* For master's, thesis. *Entrance requirements:* Additional exam requirements/recommendations for international students: Required—TOEFL. Electronic applications accepted. *Faculty research:* Managerial communication, communication consulting, communication and development.

**Southern Illinois University Edwardsville,** Graduate School, College of Arts and Sciences, Department of Historical Studies, Program in Museum Studies, Edwardsville, IL 62026-0001. Offers Postbaccalaureate Certificate. *Program availability:* Part-time, evening/weekend. *Entrance requirements:* Additional exam requirements/recommendations for international students: Required—TOEFL (minimum score 550 paper-based; 79 iBT), IELTS (minimum score 6.5). Electronic applications accepted.

**Southern University at New Orleans,** School of Graduate Studies, New Orleans, LA 70126-1009. Offers criminal justice (MA); management information systems (MS); museum studies (MA); social work (MSW). *Accreditation:* CSWE. *Program availability:* Part-time, evening/weekend. *Degree requirements:* For master's, thesis. *Entrance requirements:* For master's, GRE/GMAT. Additional exam requirements/recommendations for international students: Required—TOEFL.

**State University of New York College at Oneonta,** Graduate Programs, Cooperstown Graduate Program in Museum Studies, Cooperstown, NY 13326. Offers history museum studies (MA); science museum studies (MA). *Students:* 29 full-time (23 women), 2 part-time (1 woman). Average age 25. 93 applicants, 34% accepted, 31 enrolled. *Degree requirements:* For master's, research paper or thesis. *Entrance requirements:* For master's, GRE General Test. *Application deadline:* For fall admission, 1/10 for domestic students. Application fee: $50. *Expenses:* Contact institution. *Unit head:* Dr. Gretchen Sorin, Director, 607-547-2586, Fax: 607-547-8926, E-mail: gretchen.sorin@oneonta.edu. *Application contact:* Patrick J. Mente, Director of Graduate Studies, 607-436-2523, Fax: 607-436-3084, E-mail: gradstudies@oneonta.edu.
Website: http://cgpmuseumstudies.org/

**Syracuse University,** College of Visual and Performing Arts, MA Program in Museum Studies, Syracuse, NY 13244. Offers MA. *Accreditation:* NASAD. In 2016, 15 master's awarded. *Degree requirements:* For master's, thesis or alternative. *Entrance requirements:* For master's, three letters of recommendation, academic transcripts, personal statement/essay, academic writing sample, resume. Additional exam requirements/recommendations for international students: Required—TOEFL (minimum score 100 iBT), IELTS. *Application deadline:* For fall admission, 2/1 priority date for domestic and international students. Application fee: $75. Electronic applications accepted. *Expenses:* Tuition: Full-time $25,974; part-time $1443 per credit hour. *Required fees:* $802; $50 per course. Tuition and fees vary according to course load and program. *Financial support:* Fellowships with full tuition reimbursements and teaching assistantships with tuition reimbursements available. Financial award application deadline: 1/1; financial award applicants required to submit FAFSA. *Faculty research:* Museum preparation and installation, museum graphics and communications, museum development, print history and processes. *Unit head:* Emily Stokes-Rees, Professor/Program Coordinator, Museum Studies, 315-443-2455, Fax: 315-443-1303, E-mail: ewstokes@syr.edu. *Application contact:* Therese West, Information Contact, 315-443-0137, E-mail: admissg@syr.edu.
Website: http://vpa.syr.edu/

**Texas Tech University,** Graduate School, Interdisciplinary Programs, Lubbock, TX 79409. Offers arid land studies (MS); biotechnology (MS); interdisciplinary studies (MA, MS); museum science (MA); wind science and engineering (PhD); JD/MS. *Program availability:* Part-time. *Faculty:* 10 full-time (4 women). *Students:* 122 full-time (56 women), 83 part-time (46 women); includes 78 minority (25 Black or African American, non-Hispanic/Latino; 1 American Indian or Alaska Native, non-Hispanic/Latino; 2 Asian, non-Hispanic/Latino; 41 Hispanic/Latino; 1 Native Hawaiian or other Pacific Islander, non-Hispanic/Latino; 8 Two or more races, non-Hispanic/Latino), 32 international. Average age 29. 114 applicants, 71% accepted, 60 enrolled. In 2016, 55 master's, 1 doctorate awarded. Terminal master's awarded for partial completion of doctoral program. *Degree requirements:* For master's, comprehensive exam (for some programs), thesis (for some programs); for doctorate, comprehensive exam, thesis/dissertation (for some programs). *Entrance requirements:* Additional exam requirements/recommendations for international students: Required—TOEFL (minimum

score 550 paper-based; 79 iBT), IELTS (minimum score 6.5), PTE (minimum score 60), Cambridge Advanced (B), Cambridge Proficiency (C), ELS English for Academic Purposes (Level 112). *Application deadline:* For fall admission, 6/1 priority date for domestic students, 1/15 priority date for international students; for spring admission, 9/1 priority date for domestic students, 6/15 priority date for international students. Applications are processed on a rolling basis. Application fee: $75. Electronic applications accepted. *Expenses:* Tuition, state resident: full-time $7200; part-time $300 per credit hour. Tuition, nonresident: full-time $16,992; part-time $708 per credit hour. *Required fees:* $2428; $50.50 per credit hour. $608 per semester. Tuition and fees vary according to program. *Financial support:* In 2016–17, 116 students received support, including 107 fellowships (averaging $4,360 per year), 10 research assistantships (averaging $10,619 per year), 7 teaching assistantships (averaging $9,152 per year); scholarships/grants and unspecified assistantships also available. Financial award application deadline: 4/15; financial award applicants required to submit FAFSA. *Total annual research expenditures:* $2 million. *Unit head:* Dr. Mark Sheridan, Vice Provost for Graduate and Postdoctoral Affairs/Dean of the Graduate School, 806-742-2787, Fax: 806-742-1746, E-mail: mark.sheridan@ttu.edu. *Application contact:* Amanda Wysinger, Academic Advisor, 806-834-0822, Fax: 806-742-4038, E-mail: amanda.wysinger@ttu.edu.
Website: http://www.depts.ttu.edu/gradschool/about/INDS/index.php

**Trinity College,** Graduate Programs, Program in American Studies, Hartford, CT 06106-3100. Offers American culture studies (MA); museums and communities (MA). *Program availability:* Part-time, evening/weekend. *Degree requirements:* For master's, thesis or alternative. *Entrance requirements:* For master's, minimum GPA of 3.0.

**Tufts University,** Graduate School of Arts and Sciences, Department of Art and Art History, Medford, MA 02155. Offers art history (MA); art history and museum studies (MA). *Students:* 15 full-time (12 women); includes 3 minority (1 Black or African American, non-Hispanic/Latino; 1 Asian, non-Hispanic/Latino; 1 Hispanic/Latino). Average age 26. 46 applicants, 42% accepted, 7 enrolled. In 2016, 11 master's awarded. *Degree requirements:* For master's, one foreign language, thesis (for some programs). *Entrance requirements:* For master's, GRE General Test. Additional exam requirements/recommendations for international students: Required—TOEFL (minimum score 550 paper-based; 80 iBT), IELTS (minimum score 6.5). *Application deadline:* For fall admission, 1/15 for domestic and international students. Application fee: $85. Electronic applications accepted. *Expenses:* $49,982 full-time tuition (for MA). *Financial support:* In 2016–17, 14 students received support. Teaching assistantships, Federal Work-Study, scholarships/grants, tuition waivers (full and partial), and unspecified assistantships available. Financial award application deadline: 1/15. *Unit head:* Karen Overbey, Graduate Program Director, 617-627-3395. *Application contact:* Office of Graduate Admissions, 617-627-3395, E-mail: gradadmissions@tufts.edu.
Website: http://ase.tufts.edu/art/

**Tufts University,** Graduate School of Arts and Sciences, Department of History, Medford, MA 02155. Offers history (MA, PhD), including global history (PhD); history and museum studies (MA). *Students:* 23 full-time (16 women); includes 4 minority (1 Black or African American, non-Hispanic/Latino; 2 Asian, non-Hispanic/Latino; 1 Two or more races, non-Hispanic/Latino), 5 international. Average age 26. 57 applicants, 42% accepted, 7 enrolled. In 2016, 4 master's awarded. Terminal master's awarded for partial completion of doctoral program. *Degree requirements:* For master's, one foreign language, thesis optional; for doctorate, 2 foreign languages, comprehensive exam, thesis/dissertation. *Entrance requirements:* For master's and doctorate, GRE General Test, writing sample. Additional exam requirements/recommendations for international students: Required—TOEFL (minimum score 550 paper-based; 80 iBT), IELTS (minimum score 6.5). *Application deadline:* For fall admission, 1/15 for domestic and international students. Applications are processed on a rolling basis. Application fee: $85. Electronic applications accepted. *Expenses:* $49,982 full-time tuition (for MA); $29,936 full-time tuition (for PhD). *Financial support:* In 2016–17, 20 students received support. Teaching assistantships, Federal Work-Study, scholarships/grants, tuition waivers (full and partial), and unspecified assistantships available. Financial award application deadline: 1/15. *Unit head:* Dr. Steven Marrone, Graduate Program Director. *Application contact:* Office of Graduate Admissions, 617-627-3395, E-mail: gradadmissions@tufts.edu.
Website: http://www.ase.tufts.edu/history/

**Tufts University,** Graduate School of Arts and Sciences, Graduate Certificate Programs, Museum Studies Program, Medford, MA 02155. Offers Certificate. *Program availability:* Part-time, evening/weekend. *Expenses:* Contact institution.

**Université de Montréal,** Faculty of Arts and Sciences, Program in Museology, Montréal, QC H3C 3J7, Canada. Offers MA. Program offered jointly with Université du Québec à Montréal. Electronic applications accepted. *Faculty research:* Museum exhibits, museum education, natural science and museums, new technologies and museums.

**Université du Québec à Montréal,** Graduate Programs, Program in Museology, Montréal, QC H3C 3P8, Canada. Offers MA. *Program availability:* Part-time. *Entrance requirements:* For master's, appropriate bachelor's degree or equivalent and proficiency in French.

**Université Laval,** Faculty of Letters, Department of History, Program in Museology, Québec, QC G1K 7P4, Canada. Offers Diploma. *Program availability:* Part-time. *Entrance requirements:* For degree, English exam (comprehension of English), knowledge of French. Electronic applications accepted.

**University at Buffalo, the State University of New York,** Graduate School, College of Arts and Sciences, Department of Art, Program in Visual Studies, Buffalo, NY 14260. Offers critical museum studies (MA); visual studies (MA, PhD). *Program availability:* Part-time. *Faculty:* 6 full-time (2 women). *Students:* 13 full-time (9 women), 3 international. Average age 27. 35 applicants, 31% accepted, 5 enrolled. *Degree requirements:* For master's, thesis, field exam; for doctorate, one foreign language, thesis/dissertation. *Entrance requirements:* Additional exam requirements/recommendations for international students: Required—TOEFL (minimum score 79 iBT). *Application deadline:* For fall admission, 2/1 priority date for domestic students; for spring admission, 10/15 priority date for domestic students. Applications are processed on a rolling basis. Application fee: $50. Electronic applications accepted. *Financial support:* In 2016–17, 6 teaching assistantships with full tuition reimbursements (averaging $8,400 per year) were awarded; career-related internships or fieldwork, Federal Work-Study, institutionally sponsored loans, tuition waivers (partial), and unspecified assistantships also available. Support available to part-time students. Financial award application deadline: 2/28; financial award applicants required to submit FAFSA. *Unit head:* Joan Linder, Chair, 716-645-0539, Fax: 716-645-6970, E-mail: joannder@buffalo.edu. *Application contact:* Dr. Jonathan Katz, 716-645-6878, Fax: 716-645-5978.
Website: http://art.buffalo.edu

**The University of British Columbia,** Faculty of Arts and Faculty of Graduate Studies, Department of Art History, Visual Art, and Theory, Vancouver, BC V6T 1Z2, Canada. Offers art history (MA, PhD); critical and curatorial studies (MA); visual art (MFA). *Degree requirements:* For master's, one foreign language, thesis, final exhibition (MFA,

## Museum Studies

MA in critical and curatorial studies); for doctorate, 2 foreign languages, comprehensive exam, thesis/dissertation. *Entrance requirements:* For master's, bachelor's degree with minimum B+ average (MFA, MA in critical and curatorial studies), A- (MA in art history); for doctorate, master's degree with minimum A- average. Additional exam requirements/recommendations for international students: Required—TOEFL. Application fee: $100 Canadian dollars ($162 Canadian dollars for international students). Electronic applications accepted. *Expenses:* $4,802 per year tuition and fees, $8,436 per year international. *Financial support:* Fellowships, research assistantships, teaching assistantships, Federal Work-Study, scholarships/grants, health care benefits, tuition waivers (full), and unspecified assistantships available. *Faculty research:* Conceptual art, Asian art, indigenous North American art, post-second war art, eighteenth- and nineteenth-century art, curatorial, digital art. *Application contact:* Bryn Dharmaratne, Graduate Program Staff, 604-822-4340, Fax: 604-822-9003, E-mail: ahva.grad@ubc.ca. Website: http://www.ahva.ubc.ca

**University of Central Oklahoma,** The Jackson College of Graduate Studies, College of Liberal Arts, Department of History, Edmond, OK 73034-5209. Offers history (MA); museum studies (MA). *Program availability:* Part-time. *Degree requirements:* For master's, one foreign language, comprehensive exam (for some programs), thesis (for some programs). *Entrance requirements:* For master's, GRE, writing sample, essay. Additional exam requirements/recommendations for international students: Required—TOEFL (minimum score 550 paper-based; 79 iBT), IELTS (minimum score 6.5). Electronic applications accepted. *Faculty research:* China, Russia, civil war, American naval logistics.

**University of Colorado Boulder,** Graduate School, Museum and Field Studies Program, Boulder, CO 80309. Offers MS. *Students:* 15 full-time (14 women); includes 2 minority (1 American Indian or Alaska Native, non-Hispanic/Latino; 1 Two or more races, non-Hispanic/Latino), 1 international. Average age 27. 45 applicants, 20% accepted, 8 enrolled. In 2016, 8 master's awarded. Terminal master's awarded for partial completion of doctoral program. *Degree requirements:* For master's, comprehensive exam, thesis or alternative. *Entrance requirements:* For master's, GRE General Test, GRE Subject Test, minimum undergraduate GPA of 3.0. *Application deadline:* For fall admission, 1/15 for domestic students, 12/1 for international students. Application fee: $60 ($80 for international students). Electronic applications accepted. Application fee is waived when completed online. *Financial support:* In 2016–17, 58 students received support, including 19 fellowships (averaging $4,602 per year), 3 research assistantships with full and partial tuition reimbursements available (averaging $24,240 per year), 13 teaching assistantships with full and partial tuition reimbursements available (averaging $23,152 per year); institutionally sponsored loans, scholarships/grants, health care benefits, and unspecified assistantships also available. Financial award application deadline: 2/1; financial award applicants required to submit FAFSA. *Total annual research expenditures:* $458,595. *Application contact:* E-mail: mfsinfo@colorado.edu. Website: http://cumuseum.colorado.edu/

**University of Denver,** Division of Arts, Humanities and Social Sciences, Department of Anthropology, Denver, CO 80208. Offers archaeology (MA); cultural anthropology (MA); museum and heritage studies (MA). *Program availability:* Part-time. *Faculty:* 8 full-time (2 women). *Students:* 3 full-time (all women), 17 part-time (16 women); includes 2 minority (1 American Indian or Alaska Native, non-Hispanic/Latino; 1 Hispanic/Latino). Average age 25. 47 applicants, 43% accepted, 11 enrolled. In 2016, 11 master's awarded. *Degree requirements:* For master's, one foreign language, comprehensive exam, thesis (for some programs), tool, foreign language literacy, or course work. *Entrance requirements:* For master's, GRE General Test, bachelor's degree, transcripts, personal statement, two letters of recommendation. Additional exam requirements/recommendations for international students: Required—TOEFL (minimum score 550 paper-based; 80 iBT). *Application deadline:* For fall admission, 2/4 priority date for domestic and international students. Applications are processed on a rolling basis. Application fee: $65. Electronic applications accepted. *Expenses:* $29,022 per year full-time. *Financial support:* In 2016–17, 19 students received support, including 6 teaching assistantships with tuition reimbursements available (averaging $6,667 per year); career-related internships or fieldwork, Federal Work-Study, institutionally sponsored loans, scholarships/grants, and unspecified assistantships also available. Support available to part-time students. Financial award application deadline: 2/15; financial award applicants required to submit FAFSA. *Faculty research:* Human diversity, human rights, historic archaeology, museums and heritage, high-tech field methods. *Unit head:* Dr. Larry Conyers, Professor and Chair, 303-871-2684, Fax: 303-871-2437, E-mail: lconyers@du.edu. *Application contact:* Dr. Larry Conyers, Professor and Director of Graduate Program, 303-871-2684, Fax: 303-871-2437, E-mail: lconyers@du.edu. Website: http://www.du.edu/ahss/anthropology

**University of Denver,** Division of Arts, Humanities and Social Sciences, School of Art and Art History, Denver, CO 80208. Offers art history (MA); museum studies (MA). *Accreditation:* NASAD. *Program availability:* Part-time. *Faculty:* 16 full-time (10 women), 8 part-time/adjunct (7 women). *Students:* 3 full-time (all women), 12 part-time (all women). Average age 25. 29 applicants, 83% accepted, 6 enrolled. In 2016, 5 master's awarded. *Degree requirements:* For master's, one foreign language, comprehensive exam, research paper or thesis project. *Entrance requirements:* For master's, GRE General Test, transcripts, personal statement, writing sample, three letters of recommendation. Additional exam requirements/recommendations for international students: Required—TOEFL (minimum score 550 paper-based; 80 iBT). *Application deadline:* For fall admission, 1/31 priority date for domestic and international students. Applications are processed on a rolling basis. Application fee: $65. Electronic applications accepted. *Expenses:* $29,022 per year full-time. *Financial support:* In 2016–17, 14 students received support, including 4 teaching assistantships with tuition reimbursements available (averaging $7,500 per year); research assistantships with tuition reimbursements available, career-related internships or fieldwork, Federal Work-Study, institutionally sponsored loans, scholarships/grants, and unspecified assistantships also available. Support available to part-time students. Financial award application deadline: 2/15; financial award applicants required to submit FAFSA. *Faculty research:* Abstract expressionist women painters, Chichen Itza, the cult of St. Ursula, rock poster art of the psychedelic era. *Unit head:* Dr. Catherine Chauvin, Associate Professor and Chair, 303-871-2367, Fax: 303-871-4112, E-mail: catherine.chauvin@du.edu. *Application contact:* Dr. Annette Stott, Acting Graduate Art History Advisor, 303-871-3278, Fax: 303-871-4112, E-mail: astott@du.edu. Website: http://www.du.edu/ahss/art/index.html

**University of Florida,** Graduate School, College of The Arts, School of Art and Art History, Gainesville, FL 32611. Offers art (MA), including digital arts and sciences; art education (MA); art history (MA, PhD); museology (MA), including historic preservation. *Accreditation:* NASAD. *Program availability:* Online learning. *Degree requirements:* For master's, project or thesis (MFA); 1 foreign language (MA in art history); for doctorate, 2 foreign languages, comprehensive exam, thesis/dissertation. *Entrance requirements:* For master's, GRE General Test, portfolio (MFA), writing sample (MA), minimum GPA 3.0; for doctorate, GRE General Test, minimum GPA of 3.0. Additional exam requirements/recommendations for international students: Required—TOEFL (minimum score 550 paper-based; 80 iBT), IELTS (minimum score 6). Electronic applications accepted. *Faculty research:* Studio production, art historical studies of style context.

**University of Hawaii at Manoa,** Graduate Division, College of Arts and Humanities, Department of American Studies, Program in Museum Studies, Honolulu, HI 96822. Offers Graduate Certificate. *Program availability:* Part-time. *Entrance requirements:* Additional exam requirements/recommendations for international students: Required—TOEFL (minimum score 600 paper-based; 100 iBT), IELTS (minimum score 7).

**University of Illinois at Chicago,** College of Architecture, Design and the Arts, School of Art and Art History, Chicago, IL 60607-7128. Offers art history (MA); electronic visualization (MFA); museum and exhibition studies (MA); new media arts (MFA). *Program availability:* Part-time, evening/weekend. Terminal master's awarded for partial completion of doctoral program. *Degree requirements:* For master's, one foreign language, thesis or alternative; for doctorate, thesis/dissertation. *Entrance requirements:* For master's, GRE General Test, minimum GPA of 2.75, 3 letters of recommendation; for doctorate, GRE General Test, MA in art history or equivalent, minimum GPA of 3.0. Additional exam requirements/recommendations for international students: Required—TOEFL. Electronic applications accepted. *Expenses:* Contact institution. *Faculty research:* Modern painting and sculpture, history of architecture, city planning and design, history of photography.

**The University of Kansas,** Graduate Studies, College of Liberal Arts and Sciences, Museum Studies Program, Lawrence, KS 66045-7545. Offers MA, Graduate Certificate. *Program availability:* Part-time. *Students:* 16 full-time (14 women), 2 part-time (both women). Average age 28. 34 applicants, 56% accepted, 8 enrolled. In 2016, 9 master's, 1 other advanced degree awarded. *Entrance requirements:* For master's, GRE, 3 letters of recommendation, resume, writing sample, statement of purpose, official transcripts. Additional exam requirements/recommendations for international students: Required—TOEFL. *Application deadline:* For fall admission, 1/1 priority date for domestic and international students. Application fee: $65 ($85 for international students). Electronic applications accepted. *Financial support:* Research assistantships, career-related internships or fieldwork, and unspecified assistantships available. Financial award application deadline: 1/1. *Faculty research:* Museum studies, audience evaluation, community engagement, material culture, anthropology, historical and legal backgrounds by which museums have come to control culturally-sensitive objects. *Unit head:* Dr. Peter H. Welsh, Director, 785-864-5702, E-mail: phwelsh@ku.edu. *Application contact:* Kay Isbell, Graduate Academic Advisor, 785-864-2306, E-mail: kisbell@ku.edu. Website: http://museumstudies.ku.edu/

**University of Louisville,** Graduate School, College of Arts and Sciences, Department of Fine Arts, Louisville, KY 40292. Offers art history (MA, PhD); curatorial studies (MA); studio art (MFA), including design. *Faculty:* 23 full-time (9 women), 6 part-time/adjunct (4 women). *Students:* 20 full-time (14 women), 6 part-time (4 women); includes 5 minority (2 Asian, non-Hispanic/Latino; 1 Hispanic/Latino; 2 Two or more races, non-Hispanic/Latino). Average age 34. 34 applicants, 56% accepted, 11 enrolled. In 2016, 1 master's, 1 doctorate awarded. *Degree requirements:* For master's, one foreign language, thesis. *Entrance requirements:* For doctorate, MA. Additional exam requirements/recommendations for international students: Required—TOEFL (minimum score 550 paper-based; 80 iBT), IELTS (minimum score 6.5). *Application deadline:* For fall admission, 1/15 priority date for domestic and international students. Application fee: $60. *Expenses:* $12,000. *Financial support:* In 2016–17, 7 teaching assistantships with full tuition reimbursements (averaging $12,000 per year) were awarded; research assistantships, scholarships/grants, health care benefits, and unspecified assistantships also available. Financial award application deadline: 1/15. *Faculty research:* Sustainability and environmental design, media theory, cross cultural and critical theories, Installation, urban and public art. *Total annual research expenditures:* $81,639. *Unit head:* Dr. Scott L. Massey, Associate Professor and Chair, 502-852-6794, Fax: 502-852-6791, E-mail: s.massey@louisville.edu. *Application contact:* Theresa Berbet, Senior Advisor, 502-852-6147, Fax: 502-852-6791, E-mail: tberbet@louisville.edu. Website: http://art.louisville.edu

**The University of Manchester,** School of Arts, Histories and Cultures, Manchester, United Kingdom. Offers anthropology, media and performance (PhD); applied theatre professional (PhD); archaeology (PhD); art history and visual studies (PhD); arts management and cultural policy (PhD); classics and ancient history (PhD); composition (PhD); creative writing (PhD); drama (PhD); economic and social history (PhD); electroacoustic composition (PhD); English and American studies (PhD); history (PhD); humanitarianism and conflict response (PhD); museology (PhD); music (PhD); musicology (PhD); religions and theology (PhD).

**University of Memphis,** Graduate School, College of Arts and Sciences, Program in Interdisciplinary Studies, Memphis, TN 38152. Offers museum studies (Graduate Certificate); women's and gender studies (Graduate Certificate). *Faculty:* 2 full-time (1 woman), 7 part-time (3 women); includes 3 minority (1 Black or African American, non-Hispanic/Latino; 1 Hispanic/Latino; 1 Two or more races, non-Hispanic/Latino), 6 international. Average age 30. 19 applicants, 79% accepted, 6 enrolled. In 2016, 6 Graduate Certificates awarded. *Degree requirements:* For Graduate Certificate, minimum GPA of 3.0. *Entrance requirements:* For degree, GRE, letter of interest, undergraduate transcript. Additional exam requirements/recommendations for international students: Required—TOEFL (minimum score 550 paper-based). *Application deadline:* For fall admission, 4/3 for domestic students. Application fee: $35 ($60 for international students). *Expenses:* Contact institution. *Financial support:* In 2016–17, 11 students received support, including 8 research assistantships with full tuition reimbursements available (averaging $11,736 per year); teaching assistantships with full tuition reimbursements available, Federal Work-Study, scholarships/grants, and unspecified assistantships also available. Financial award application deadline: 2/1; financial award applicants required to submit FAFSA. *Unit head:* Dr. Henry A. Kurtz, Dean, 901-678-2251, Fax: 901-678-4831, E-mail: hkurtz@memphis.edu. *Application contact:* Dr. Kathy Schultz, Director of Women's and Gender Studies, 901-678-2651, E-mail: klschltz@memphis.edu. Website: http://www.memphis.edu/isc/

**University of Memphis,** Graduate School, College of Communication and Fine Arts, Department of Art, Memphis, TN 38152. Offers art history (MA), including Egyptian art and archaeology, general art history; ceramics (MFA); graphic design (MFA); museum studies (Graduate Certificate); painting (MFA); printmaking/photography (MFA); sculpture (MFA). *Accreditation:* NASAD (one or more programs are accredited). *Program availability:* Part-time. *Faculty:* 20 full-time (7 women), 1 part-time/adjunct (0 women). *Students:* 22 full-time (16 women), 10 part-time (9 women); includes 9 minority (2 Black or African American, non-Hispanic/Latino; 1 Asian, non-Hispanic/Latino; 3 Hispanic/Latino; 3 Two or more races, non-Hispanic/Latino). Average age 29. 18 applicants, 78% accepted, 11 enrolled. In 2016, 17 master's, 16 other advanced degrees awarded. *Degree requirements:* For master's, 2 foreign languages, comprehensive exam, thesis, image identification exam, qualifying exam; for Graduate Certificate, internship. *Entrance requirements:* For master's, GRE General Test or MAT, portfolio (MFA), letter of intent, sample of undergraduate writing, two letters of recommendation; for Graduate Certificate, three letters of recommendation, letter of intent. *Application deadline:* For fall admission, 2/15 for domestic students; for spring admission, 11/1 for domestic students. Applications are processed on a rolling basis. Application fee: $35 ($60 for international students). *Expenses:* $5,231.50 per semester full-time in-state, $9,623.50 full-time out-of-state. *Financial support:* In 2016–17, 36

students received support, including 20 research assistantships with full tuition reimbursements available (averaging $9,800 per year); teaching assistantships with full tuition reimbursements available, Federal Work-Study, scholarships/grants, and unspecified assistantships also available. Financial award application deadline: 2/1; financial award applicants required to submit FAFSA. *Faculty research:* Online collaborative learning, advanced art history studies, electronic publishing/design, studio arts, architectural studies. *Unit head:* Prof. Richard Lou, Chair, 901-678-2217, Fax: 901-678-2735, E-mail: ralou@memphis.edu. *Application contact:* Niles Wallice, Coordinator of Graduate Studies, 901-678-4899.
Website: http://memphis.edu/art/

**University of Michigan–Flint,** Graduate Programs, Program in Arts Administration, Flint, MI 48502. Offers museum and visual arts (MA), including museum and visual arts, performance. *Program availability:* Part-time. *Faculty:* 5 full-time (4 women), 3 part-time/adjunct (all women). *Students:* 7 full-time (6 women), 5 part-time (3 women); includes 2 minority (both Black or African American, non-Hispanic/Latino). Average age 39. 11 applicants, 55% accepted, 3 enrolled. In 2016, 3 master's awarded. *Degree requirements:* For master's, thesis, internship. *Entrance requirements:* For master's, bachelor's degree in the arts (visual art, theatre, dance, music, etc.) from regionally-accredited institution; minimum cumulative undergraduate GPA of 3.0. Additional exam requirements/recommendations for international students: Required—TOEFL (minimum score 84 iBT), IELTS (minimum score 6.5). *Application deadline:* For fall admission, 8/1 for domestic students, 5/1 for international students; for winter admission, 11/15 for domestic students, 9/1 for international students. Applications are processed on a rolling basis. Application fee: $55. Electronic applications accepted. *Expenses:* Contact institution. *Financial support:* Federal Work-Study, scholarships/grants, and unspecified assistantships available. Support available to part-time students. Financial award application deadline: 3/1; financial award applicants required to submit FAFSA. *Unit head:* Nicole Broughton, Director, 810-237-6522, E-mail: broughn@umflint.edu. *Application contact:* Bradley T. Maki, Director of Graduate Admissions, 810-762-3171, Fax: 810-766-6789, E-mail: bmaki@umflint.edu.
Website: http://www.umflint.edu/graduateprograms/arts-administration-ma

**University of Missouri–St. Louis,** College of Arts and Sciences, Department of History, St. Louis, MO 63121. Offers history (MA); museum studies (MA, Certificate); public history and cultural heritage (Certificate). *Program availability:* Part-time, evening/weekend. *Faculty:* 11 full-time (3 women), 8 part-time/adjunct (0 women). *Students:* 21 full-time (19 women), 35 part-time (11 women); includes 8 minority (5 Black or African American, non-Hispanic/Latino; 2 Asian, non-Hispanic/Latino; 1 Hispanic/Latino), 1 international. Average age 35. 36 applicants, 86% accepted, 20 enrolled. *Degree requirements:* For master's, thesis (for some programs). *Entrance requirements:* For master's, writing sample; minimum GPA of 2.75 (for history), 3.2 (for museum studies). Additional exam requirements/recommendations for international students: Required—TOEFL (minimum score 550 paper-based; 79 iBT), IELTS (minimum score 6.5). *Application deadline:* For fall admission, 3/15 for domestic and international students; for spring admission, 10/15 for domestic and international students. Applications are processed on a rolling basis. Application fee: $50 ($40 for international students). Electronic applications accepted. *Financial support:* Research assistantships with tuition reimbursements, teaching assistantships with tuition reimbursements, and career-related internships or fieldwork available. Financial award applicants required to submit FAFSA. *Faculty research:* United States, European, East Asian, Latin American, and African history. *Unit head:* Dr. Andrew Hurley, Director of Graduate Studies, 314-516-4805, Fax: 314-516-5781, E-mail: ahurley@umsl.edu. *Application contact:* 314-516-5458, Fax: 314-516-6996, E-mail: gradadm@umsl.edu.
Website: http://www.umsl.edu/~umslhistory/

**University of New Hampshire,** Graduate School, College of Liberal Arts, Department of History, Durham, NH 03824. Offers history (MA, PhD); museum studies (MA). *Program availability:* Part-time. *Degree requirements:* For master's, thesis or alternative; for doctorate, 2 foreign languages, thesis/dissertation. *Entrance requirements:* For master's and doctorate, GRE General Test. Additional exam requirements/recommendations for international students: Required—TOEFL (minimum score 550 paper-based; 80 iBT). Electronic applications accepted.

**The University of North Carolina at Greensboro,** Graduate School, College of Arts and Sciences, Department of History, Greensboro, NC 27412-5001. Offers historic preservation (Certificate); history (MA); museum studies (Certificate); U.S. history (PhD). *Program availability:* Part-time. *Entrance requirements:* For master's, GRE General Test. Additional exam requirements/recommendations for international students: Required—TOEFL. Electronic applications accepted. *Faculty research:* Simultaneous discovery in science, progressive social reform, Robert Mayer.

**The University of North Carolina at Greensboro,** Graduate School, College of Arts and Sciences, Department of Interior Architecture, Greensboro, NC 27412-5001. Offers historic preservation (Certificate); interior architecture (MS); museum studies (Certificate). *Degree requirements:* For master's, thesis. *Entrance requirements:* For master's, GRE General Test or MAT, bachelor's degree in interior design, interview, portfolio. Additional exam requirements/recommendations for international students: Required—TOEFL. Electronic applications accepted.

**University of North Texas,** Robert B. Toulouse School of Graduate Studies, Denton, TX 76203-5459. Offers accounting (MS); applied anthropology (MA, MS); applied behavior analysis (Certificate); applied geography (MA); applied technology and performance improvement (M Ed, MS); art education (MA); art history (MA); art museum education (Certificate); arts leadership (Certificate); audiology (Au D); behavior analysis (MS); behavioral science (PhD); biochemistry and molecular biology (MS); biology (MA, MS); biomedical engineering (MS); business analysis (MS); chemistry (MS); clinical health psychology (PhD); communication studies (MA, MS); computer engineering (MS); computer science (MS); counseling (M Ed, MS), including clinical mental health counseling (MS), college and university counseling, elementary school counseling, secondary school counseling; creative writing (MA); criminal justice (MS); curriculum and instruction (M Ed); decision sciences (MBA); design (MA, MFA), including fashion design (MFA), innovation studies, interior design (MFA); early childhood studies (MS); economics (MS); educational leadership (M Ed, Ed D); educational psychology (MS, PhD), including family studies (MS), gifted and talented (MS), human development (MS), learning and cognition (MS), research, measurement and evaluation (MS); electrical engineering (MS); emergency management (MPA); engineering technology (MS); English (MA); English as a second language (MA); environmental science (MS); finance (MBA, MS); financial management (MBA); French (MA); health services management (MBA); higher education (M Ed, Ed D); history (MA, MS); hospitality management (MS); human resources management (MPA); information science (MS); information systems (PhD); information technologies (MBA); interdisciplinary studies (MA, MS); international studies (MA); international sustainable tourism (MS); jazz studies (MM); journalism (MA, MJ, Graduate Certificate), including interactive and virtual digital communication (Graduate Certificate), narrative journalism (Graduate Certificate), public relations (Graduate Certificate); kinesiology (MS); linguistics (MA); local government management (MPA); logistics (PhD); logistics and supply chain management (MBA); long-term care, senior housing, and aging services (MA); management (PhD); marketing (MBA); mathematics (MA, MS); mechanical and energy engineering (MS, PhD); music

(MA), including ethnomusicology, music theory, musicology, performance; music composition (PhD); music education (MM Ed, PhD); nonprofit management (MPA); operations and supply chain management (MBA); performance (MM, DMA); philosophy (MA); political science (MA); professional and technical communication (MA); radio, television and film (MA, MFA); rehabilitation counseling (Certificate); sociology (MA); Spanish (MA); special education (M Ed); speech-language pathology (MA); strategic management (MBA); studio art (MFA); teaching (M Ed); MBA/MS. *Program availability:* Part-time, evening/weekend, online learning. Terminal master's awarded for partial completion of doctoral program. *Degree requirements:* For master's, variable foreign language requirement, comprehensive exam (for some programs), thesis (for some programs); for doctorate, variable foreign language requirement, comprehensive exam (for some programs), thesis/dissertation; for other advanced degree, variable foreign language requirement, comprehensive exam (for some programs). *Entrance requirements:* For master's and doctorate, GRE, GMAT. Additional exam requirements/recommendations for international students: Required—TOEFL (minimum score 550 paper-based; 79 iBT). Electronic applications accepted.

**University of San Francisco,** College of Arts and Sciences, Museum Studies Program, San Francisco, CA 94117-1080. Offers MA. *Program availability:* Part-time. *Faculty:* 2 full-time (both women), 3 part-time/adjunct (all women). *Students:* 25 full-time (23 women), 22 part-time (18 women); includes 10 minority (1 Black or African American, non-Hispanic/Latino; 3 Asian, non-Hispanic/Latino; 5 Hispanic/Latino; 1 Two or more races, non-Hispanic/Latino), 10 international. Average age 28. 92 applicants, 58% accepted, 21 enrolled. In 2016, 17 master's awarded. *Entrance requirements:* Additional exam requirements/recommendations for international students: Required—TOEFL, IELTS, PTE. *Application deadline:* For fall admission, 2/1 for domestic and international students. Electronic applications accepted. *Expenses: Tuition:* Full-time $23,310; part-time $1295 per credit. Tuition and fees vary according to course load, degree level, campus/location and program. *Financial support:* In 2016–17, 25 students received support. Teaching assistantships available. Financial award applicants required to submit FAFSA. *Unit head:* Dr. Marjorie Schwarzer, Dean, 415-422-5685. *Application contact:* Mark Landerghini, Information Contact, 415-422-5101, Fax: 415-422-2217, E-mail: asgraduate@usfca.edu.
Website: https://www.usfca.edu/arts-sciences/graduate-programs/museum-studies

**University of South Carolina,** The Graduate School, College of Arts and Sciences, Department of History, Program in Public History, Columbia, SC 29208. Offers archive management (MA); historic preservation (MA); museum administration (MA); museum management (Certificate); MLIS/MA. *Degree requirements:* For master's, one foreign language, thesis, internship. *Entrance requirements:* For master's, GRE General Test, writing sample. Additional exam requirements/recommendations for international students: Required—TOEFL. Electronic applications accepted. *Faculty research:* Museum studies, historic preservation, archives administration.

**University of South Florida,** Innovative Education, Tampa, FL 33620-9951. Offers adult, career and higher education (Graduate Certificate), including college teaching, leadership in developing human resources, leadership in higher education; Africana studies (Graduate Certificate), including diasporas and health disparities, genocide and human rights; aging studies (Graduate Certificate), including gerontology; art research (Graduate Certificate), including museum studies; business foundations (Graduate Certificate); chemical and biomedical engineering (Graduate Certificate), including materials science and engineering, water, health and sustainability; child and family studies (Graduate Certificate), including positive behavior support; civil and industrial engineering (Graduate Certificate), including transportation systems analysis; community and family health (Graduate Certificate), including maternal and child health, social marketing and public health, violence and injury: prevention and intervention, women's health; criminology (Graduate Certificate), including criminal justice administration; educational measurement and research (Graduate Certificate), including evaluation; English (Graduate Certificate), including comparative literary studies, creative writing, professional and technical communication; entrepreneurship (Graduate Certificate); environmental health (Graduate Certificate), including safety management; epidemiology and biostatistics (Graduate Certificate), including applied biostatistics, biostatistics, concepts and tools of epidemiology, epidemiology, epidemiology of infectious diseases; geography, environment and planning (Graduate Certificate), including community development, environmental policy and management, geographical information systems; geology (Graduate Certificate), including hydrogeology; global health (Graduate Certificate), including disaster management, global health and Latin American and Caribbean studies, global health practice, humanitarian assistance, infection control; government and international affairs (Graduate Certificate), including Cuban studies, globalization studies; health policy and management (Graduate Certificate), including health management and leadership, public health policy and programs; hearing specialist: early intervention (Graduate Certificate); industrial and management systems engineering (Graduate Certificate), including systems engineering, technology management; information studies (Graduate Certificate), including school library media specialist; information systems/decision sciences (Graduate Certificate), including analytics and business intelligence; instructional technology (Graduate Certificate), including distance education, Florida digital/virtual educator, instructional design, multimedia design, Web design; internal medicine, bioethics and medical humanities (Graduate Certificate), including biomedical ethics; Latin American and Caribbean studies (Graduate Certificate); mass communications (Graduate Certificate), including multimedia journalism; mathematics and statistics (Graduate Certificate), including mathematics; medicine (Graduate Certificate), including aging and neuroscience, bioinformatics, biotechnology, brain fitness and memory management, clinical investigation, health informatics, health sciences, integrative weight management, intellectual property, medicine and gender, metabolic and nutritional medicine, metabolic cardiology, pharmacy sciences; national and competitive intelligence (Graduate Certificate); psychological and social foundations (Graduate Certificate), including career counseling, college teaching, diversity in education, mental health counseling, school counseling; public affairs (Graduate Certificate), including nonprofit management, public management, research administration; public health (Graduate Certificate), including environmental health, health equity, public health generalist, translational research in adolescent behavioral health; public health practices (Graduate Certificate), including planning for healthy communities; rehabilitation and mental health counseling (Graduate Certificate), including integrative mental health care, marriage and family therapy, rehabilitation technology; secondary education (Graduate Certificate), including ESOL, foreign language education: culture and content, foreign language education: professional; social work (Graduate Certificate), including geriatric social work/clinical gerontology; special education (Graduate Certificate), including autism spectrum disorder, disabilities education: severe/profound; world languages (Graduate Certificate), including teaching English as a second language (TESL) or foreign language. *Expenses:* Tuition, state resident: full-time $7766; part-time $431.43 per credit hour. Tuition, nonresident: full-time $15,789; part-time $877.17 per credit hour. *Required fees:* $37 per term. *Unit head:* Kathy Barnes, Interdisciplinary Programs Coordinator, 813-974-8031, Fax: 813-974-7061, E-mail: barnesk@usf.edu. *Application contact:* Karen Tylinski, Metro Initiatives, 813-974-9943, Fax: 813-974-7061, E-mail: ktylinsk@usf.edu.
Website: http://www.usf.edu/innovative-education/

*Museum Studies*

**The University of the Arts,** College of Art, Media and Design, Department of Museum Studies, Philadelphia, PA 19102-4944. Offers museum communication (MA); museum education (MA); museum exhibition planning and design (MFA). *Accreditation:* NASAD. *Degree requirements:* For master's, thesis, internship. *Entrance requirements:* For master's, official transcripts, three letters of recommendation, one- to two-page statement, personal interview; academic writing sample and examples of work (for museum communication); two examples of academic and professional writing (for museum education); portfolio and/or writing samples (for museum exhibition planning and design). Additional exam requirements/recommendations for international students: Required—TOEFL (minimum score 580 paper-based, 92 iBT) or IELTS (minimum score 6.5).

**University of Toronto,** School of Graduate Studies, Faculty of Information, Program in Museum Studies, Toronto, ON M5S 1A1, Canada. Offers MM St. *Entrance requirements:* Additional exam requirements/recommendations for international students: Required—TOEFL (minimum score 580 paper-based; 93 iBT), TWE (minimum score 5). Electronic applications accepted. *Expenses:* Contact institution.

**The University of Tulsa,** Graduate School, Program in Museum Science and Management, Tulsa, OK 74104-3189. Offers MA. *Program availability:* Part-time. *Faculty:* 9 full-time (1 woman). *Students:* 7 full-time (4 women), 1 (woman) part-time; includes 2 minority (both American Indian or Alaska Native, non-Hispanic/Latino). Average age 28. 9 applicants, 44% accepted, 3 enrolled. In 2016, 2 master's awarded. *Degree requirements:* For master's, final semester internship or independent research project. *Entrance requirements:* For master's, GRE General Test. Additional exam requirements/recommendations for international students: Required—TOEFL (minimum score 575 paper-based; 91 iBT), IELTS (minimum score 6.5). *Application deadline:* Applications are processed on a rolling basis. Application fee: $55. Electronic applications accepted. *Expenses: Tuition:* Full-time $22,230; part-time $1235 per credit hour. *Required fees:* $990 per semester. Tuition and fees vary according to course load. *Financial support:* In 2016–17, 6 students received support, including 2 research assistantships with full tuition reimbursements available (averaging $5,571 per year), 5 teaching assistantships with full tuition reimbursements available (averaging $12,069 per year); fellowships with full tuition reimbursements available, career-related internships or fieldwork, Federal Work-Study, scholarships/grants, health care benefits, tuition waivers (full and partial), and unspecified assistantships also available. Support available to part-time students. Financial award application deadline: 2/1; financial award applicants required to submit FAFSA. *Unit head:* Dr. Bob Pickering, Director, 918-596-2706, Fax: 918-596-2770, E-mail: bob-pickering@utulsa.edu. *Application contact:* Graduate School, 918-631-2336, Fax: 918-631-2156, E-mail: grad@utulsa.edu. Website: http://graduate.utulsa.edu/academics/museum-science-management-program/

**University of Washington,** Graduate School, Museology Graduate Program, Seattle, WA 98195. Offers MA. *Faculty:* 4 full-time (3 women), 14 part-time/adjunct (10 women). *Students:* 71 full-time (61 women); includes 12 minority (1 Black or African American, non-Hispanic/Latino; 4 American Indian or Alaska Native, non-Hispanic/Latino; 4 Asian, non-Hispanic/Latino; 3 Hispanic/Latino), 4 international. Average age 26. 111 applicants, 63% accepted, 34 enrolled. In 2016, 33 master's awarded. *Degree requirements:* For master's, thesis. *Entrance requirements:* For master's, GRE General Test, baccalaureate degree; minimum GPA of 3.0 during last 2 years (60 semester credits and 90 quarter credits) of courses. Additional exam requirements/recommendations for international students: Required—TOEFL (minimum score 580 paper-based; 92 iBT). *Application deadline:* For fall admission, 1/15 for domestic and international students. Application fee: $85. Electronic applications accepted. *Expenses:* $5,894 per quarter tuition (up to 18 credits), non-refundable $45 registration fee, $41 quarterly technology fee, $236 quarterly services and activities fee, $80 quarterly U-PASS fee. *Financial support:* In 2016–17, 3 research assistantships were awarded; career-related internships or fieldwork, Federal Work-Study, institutionally sponsored loans, and scholarships/grants also available. Financial award application deadline: 1/15; financial award applicants required to submit FAFSA. *Faculty research:* Collection management, audience research and evaluation, informal learning, museums and social change, museum administration. *Unit head:* Dr. Jessica Luke, Director, 206-685-3496, E-mail: uwmuse@uw.edu. *Application contact:* Dylan High, Student Experience Coordinator, 206-221-0713, E-mail: uwmuse@uw.edu. Website: http://uw.edu/museology

**University of West Georgia,** College of Arts and Humanities, Carrollton, GA 30118. Offers English (MA); history (MA); museum studies (Postbaccalaureate Certificate); music performance (M Mus); music teacher education (M Mus); public history (Postbaccalaureate Certificate). *Program availability:* Part-time, evening/weekend, 100% online, blended/hybrid learning. *Faculty:* 70 full-time (39 women). *Students:* 23 full-time (16 women), 55 part-time (33 women); includes 18 minority (10 Black or African American, non-Hispanic/Latino; 1 American Indian or Alaska Native, non-Hispanic/Latino; 5 Hispanic/Latino; 2 Two or more races, non-Hispanic/Latino), 1 international. Average age 31. 24 applicants, 100% accepted, 23 enrolled. In 2016, 34 master's, 6 other advanced degrees awarded. *Entrance requirements:* Additional exam

requirements/recommendations for international students: Required—TOEFL (minimum score 523 paper-based; 69 iBT); Recommended—IELTS (minimum score 6.5). *Application deadline:* For fall admission, 8/1 for domestic students, 6/1 for international students; for spring admission, 11/15 for domestic students, 10/15 for international students; for summer admission, 5/15 for domestic students, 3/30 for international students. Applications are processed on a rolling basis. Application fee: $40. Electronic applications accepted. *Expenses:* Tuition, state resident: full-time $5316; part-time $222 per semester hour. Tuition, nonresident: full-time $20,658; part-time $861 per semester hour. *Required fees:* $1962. Tuition and fees vary according to course load, degree level and program. *Financial support:* Fellowships, research assistantships, teaching assistantships, career-related internships or fieldwork, Federal Work-Study, institutionally sponsored loans, scholarships/grants, and unspecified assistantships available. Support available to part-time students. Financial award application deadline: 4/1; financial award applicants required to submit FAFSA. *Unit head:* Dr. Pauline D. Gagnon, Dean of Arts and Humanities, 678-839-5450, Fax: 678-839-5451, E-mail: pgagnon@westga.edu. *Application contact:* Dr. Toby Ziglar, Assistant Dean of the Graduate School, 678-839-1394, Fax: 678-839-1395, E-mail: graduate@westga.edu. Website: http://www.westga.edu/coah

**University of Wisconsin–Milwaukee,** Graduate School, College of Letters and Science, Department of Anthropology, Milwaukee, WI 53201-0413. Offers anthropology (MS, PhD), including archaeology (MS), biological anthropology (MS), cultural anthropology (MS); museum studies (Graduate Certificate). *Students:* 58 full-time (43 women), 36 part-time (29 women); includes 8 minority (1 American Indian or Alaska Native, non-Hispanic/Latino; 2 Hispanic/Latino; 5 Two or more races, non-Hispanic/Latino), 1 international. Average age 32. 46 applicants, 100% accepted, 20 enrolled. In 2016, 17 master's, 2 doctorates, 14 other advanced degrees awarded. *Degree requirements:* For master's, thesis or alternative; for doctorate, one foreign language, thesis/dissertation, departmental qualifying exam. *Entrance requirements:* For master's, GRE; for doctorate, GRE, minimum GPA of 3.0, master's degree. Additional exam requirements/recommendations for international students: Required—TOEFL (minimum score 550 paper-based; 79 iBT), IELTS (minimum score 6.5). *Application deadline:* For fall admission, 1/1 priority date for domestic students; for spring admission, 9/1 for domestic students. Applications are processed on a rolling basis. Application fee: $56 ($96 for international students). *Financial support:* In 2016–17, 4 fellowships, 2 research assistantships, 26 teaching assistantships were awarded; career-related internships or fieldwork, unspecified assistantships, and project assistantships also available. Support available to part-time students. Financial award application deadline: 4/15; financial award applicants required to submit FAFSA. *Unit head:* Thomas Malaby, Department Chair, 414-229-5247, E-mail: malaby@uwm.edu. *Application contact:* General Information Contact, 414-229-4982, Fax: 414-229-6967, E-mail: gradschool@uwm.edu. Website: https://uwm.edu/letters-science/programs/?discipline-Anthropology

**Virginia Commonwealth University,** Graduate School, School of the Arts, Department of Art History, Richmond, VA 23284-9005. Offers curatorial (PhD); historical studies (MA, PhD); museum studies (MA). *Accreditation:* NASAD. *Degree requirements:* For master's, thesis; for doctorate, comprehensive exam, thesis/dissertation. *Entrance requirements:* For master's and doctorate, GRE General Test. *Application deadline:* For fall admission, 1/15 for domestic students. Application fee: $50. Electronic applications accepted. *Financial support:* Fellowships, teaching assistantships, career-related internships or fieldwork, Federal Work-Study, and institutionally sponsored loans available. Support available to part-time students. Financial award application deadline: 3/15; financial award applicants required to submit FAFSA. *Faculty research:* Modern, nineteenth-century, Renaissance, American, and medieval art. *Unit head:* Dr. Dina Bangdel, Director of Graduate Studies, 804-628-7027, Fax: 804-828-7468, E-mail: dbangdel@vcu.edu. *Application contact:* Dr. Margaret A. Lindauer, Graduate Program Director, 804-828-2784, E-mail: malindauer@vcu.edu. Website: http://www.vcu.edu/artweb/History/

**Western Illinois University,** School of Graduate Studies, College of Fine Arts and Communication, Program in Museum Studies, Macomb, IL 61455-1390. Offers MA, Certificate. *Accreditation:* NASAD. *Program availability:* Part-time. *Students:* 18 full-time (14 women), 14 part-time (9 women); includes 2 minority (1 Black or African American, non-Hispanic/Latino; 1 Two or more races, non-Hispanic/Latino). Average age 29. 28 applicants, 96% accepted, 18 enrolled. In 2016, 9 master's, 2 other advanced degrees awarded. *Entrance requirements:* For master's, minimum GPA of 3.0. Additional exam requirements/recommendations for international students: Required—TOEFL (minimum score 600 paper-based; 100 iBT). *Application deadline:* Applications are processed on a rolling basis. Application fee: $30. Electronic applications accepted. *Financial support:* In 2016–17, 9 students received support. Unspecified assistantships available. Financial award applicants required to submit FAFSA. *Unit head:* Dr. Pam White, Director, 309-762-9481, E-mail: pj-white@wiu.edu. *Application contact:* Dr. Nancy Parsons, Associate Provost and Director of Graduate Studies, 309-298-1806, Fax: 309-298-2345, E-mail: grad-office@wiu.edu. Website: http://wiu.edu/museumstudies/

# BARD GRADUATE CENTER: DECORATIVE ARTS, DESIGN HISTORY, MATERIAL CULTURE

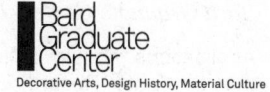

## Programs of Study

Bard Graduate Center is a graduate institute affiliated with Bard College that studies the cultural history of the material world. Founded in 1993, it offers M.A. and Ph.D. degrees in Decorative Arts, Design History, Material Culture. Its teaching, research, and exhibitions draw on methodologies and approaches from art and design history, decorative arts, economic history, history of technology, philosophy, anthropology, and archaeology. Areas of particular strength include New York and American material culture, modern design history, history and theory of museums, early modern Europe, global Middle Ages, archaeology, anthropology, and material culture, and cultures of conservation. Hands-on examination of materials and objects is a key part of the curriculum and there is an extensive connection to special programs and exhibition projects with the Metropolitan Museum of Art, the New-York Historical Society, the Brooklyn Museum of Art, the American Museum of Natural History, the Frick Collection, and the Museum of Arts and Design, among other major cultural institutions. As part of their studies, all M.A. students undertake an internship at one of more than 250 institutions around the world and participate in an international study trip. Bard Graduate Center's programs prepare students for careers or career advancement in museums and galleries; auction houses; government agencies; art-related education, research, publishing, and communications; and landscape and historic preservation.

## Research and Facilities

Bard Graduate Center occupies two six-story town houses at 18 and 38 West 86th Street in Manhattan. The buildings' elegantly appointed rooms provide an aesthetically appropriate setting for the study of the decorative arts. Its facilities include a 50,000-volume research library, a digital media research lab, exhibition galleries, classrooms, faculty offices, student lounges, outdoor terraces, symposium spaces, and administrative offices.

A semiannual interdisciplinary journal, *West 86th: A Journal of Decorative Arts, Design History, and Material Culture,* which features scholarly articles that focus on the wider crossroads where the decorative arts meet design history and material culture, is published in collaboration with the University of Chicago Press as is *Source: Notes on the History of Art.* Bard Graduate Center also publishes *Cultural Histories of the Material World*, a book series that is dedicated to showing how attention to materiality can contribute to a more precise historical understanding of specific times, places, ways, and means.

## Financial Aid

Bard Graduate Center offers fellowships, scholarships, and a student campus employment program. Aid is awarded on the basis of need and merit. Financial aid applications are due by January 5. About 85 percent of students receive some financial aid.

## Cost of Study

The average annual tuition for incoming full-time students in the 2017–18 academic year was $37,665 for M.A. students, based on a cost of $1,395 per credit. Tuition for Ph.D. students averaged $33,480 for incoming full-time students in the 2017–18 academic year; they vary for subsequent years of doctoral work. Students may contact the Office of Admissions for more detailed and updated fee schedules.

## Living and Housing Costs

Bard Hall, located at 410 West 58th Street, provides housing for students, faculty members, and visiting scholars. Nine residential floors offer a variety of furnished studios and one- and two-bedroom suites with kitchens and baths. Apartments are offered year-round. For the 2017–18 academic year, the cost of a studio unit was approximately $17,899, a one-bedroom unit was $21,458, and a two-bedroom unit was $17,723 per student.

## Student Group

Bard Graduate Center enrolls approximately 20–25 M.A. students and approximately 3 Ph.D. students into the program annually. Applications are received from many countries and from across the United States. Bard Graduate Center welcomes students of all ages and backgrounds as well as working professionals.

## Location

Bard Graduate Center is located on the Upper West Side of Manhattan, near Central Park. It is situated in a landmark neighborhood conveniently served by public transportation, with easy access to the innumerable museums, libraries, auction houses, and galleries of metropolitan New York.

## Applying

Students are admitted to the graduate programs annually for fall admission. The application deadline for admission and financial aid is January 5. Applicants to the M.A. program must have a bachelor's degree or the equivalent; applicants to the Ph.D. program are expected to have completed a master's degree in either the decorative arts or a related field. Because of the interdisciplinary nature of the program, there are no limitations on the M.A. applicant's prior field of study. Successful applicants, however, will have had some previous study, training, or work experience in the history of art, architecture, anthropology, archeology, history, the decorative arts, cultural history, or material culture studies.

## Bard Graduate Center: Decorative Arts, Design History, Material Culture

Applications should include scores on the General Test of the Graduate Record Examinations (GRE), three letters of recommendation, a short resume, a sample of scholarly writing, and a statement of intent describing academic and professional objectives. International candidates must submit TOEFL scores and a Certification of Finances. An interview is required. The application fee for 2017–18 is $70.

### Correspondence and Information

Office of Admissions
Bard Graduate Center
38 West 86th Street
New York, New York 10024
Phone: 212-501-3056
Fax: 212-501-3065
E-mail: admissions@bgc.bard.edu
Website: http://www.bgc.bard.edu/admissions

### THE FACULTY AND THEIR RESEARCH

Bard Graduate Center maintains a distinguished core of full-time faculty members, supplemented by eminent decorative arts scholars visiting from a broad range of national and international museums and institutions of higher learning.

### Bard Graduate Center Faculty

Susan Weber, Iris Horowitz Professor in the History of the Decorative Arts and Director; Ph.D., Royal College of Art. Eighteenth- and nineteenth-century decorative arts topics.

Peter N. Miller, Professor and Dean; Ph.D., University of Cambridge. History of historical research.

Abigail Krasner Balbale, Assistant Professor; Ph.D., Harvard University. Islamic art and material culture studies.

Jeffrey Collins, Professor; Ph.D., Yale University. Seventeenth- and eighteenth-century art and culture.

Ivan Gaskell, Professor; Ph.D., University of Cambridge. Material culture of North America and Europe, sixteenth through twentieth centuries.

Aaron Glass, Associate Professor; Ph.D., New York University. Native peoples of the Northwest Coast, museums and anthropology.

Freyja Hartzell, Assistant Professor; Ph.D., Yale University. Nineteenth- and twentieth-century European decorative arts and material culture.

Deborah L. Krohn, Associate Professor and Director of Masters Studies; Ph.D., Harvard University. Italian renaissance decorative arts and material culture.

Meredith B. Linn, Assistant Professor; Ph.D., Columbia University. Historical archeology.

François Louis, Associate Professor; Ph.D., University of Zurich. History of Chinese design and visual culture, material culture of Medieval China.

Michele Majer, Assistant Professor; M.A., New York University. European and American clothing and textiles, costume historian.

Andrew Morrall, Professor and Chair of Academic Programs; Ph.D., Courtauld Institute of Art, London University. Early modern Northern European fine and applied arts.

Elizabeth Simpson, Professor and Director of Doctoral Studies; Ph.D., University of Pennsylvania. Greek, Roman, Ancient Near Eastern, and Egyptian art and archaeology.

Paul Stirton, Associate Professor; Ph.D. University of Glasgow. Nineteenth- and twentieth-century European design and architecture.

Ittai Weinryb, Associate Professor; Ph.D., Johns Hopkins University. Medieval European artistic and material culture.

Catherine Whalen, Associate Professor; Ph.D., Yale University. American material culture studies, craft and design history.

Elissa Auther, Windgate Research Curator, Museum of Arts and Design and Visiting Associate Professor; Ph.D., University of Maryland, College Park.

Alicia Boswell, Andrew W. Mellon Postdoctoral Fellow, Cultures of Conservation; Ph.D. candidate, University of California, San Diego.

Jennifer L. Mass, Andrew W. Mellon Professor of Cultural Heritage Science; Ph.D., Cornell University.

Urmila Mohan, Bard Graduate Center-AMNH Postdoctoral Fellow in Museum Anthropology; Ph.D., University College, London.

Charlotte Vignon, Curator of Decorative Arts, The Frick Collection and Visiting Assistant Professor; Ph.D., Paris-Sorbonne University.

Kenneth Ames, Professor Emeritus; Ph.D., University of Pennsylvania. American and European decorative arts and material culture.

Pat Kirkham, Professor Emerita; Ph.D., University of London. Histories of design, architecture, and objects; material culture; film; gender.

Professor Michele Majer and her students admire Bard Graduate Center's Focus Gallery's Staging Fashion exhibition, the culmination of a multipart seminar course.

Bard Graduate Center students working on digital projects in the Digital Media Lab.

# COLUMBIA UNIVERSITY

*School of the Arts*
*Programs in Film, Theatre, Visual Arts, Writing, and Sound Art*

## Programs of Study

Columbia University School of the Arts offers M.F.A. degree programs in Film (areas of study include screenwriting/directing, creative producing, and TV writing); Theatre (concentrations in acting, directing, dramaturgy, playwriting, stage management, and theatre management & producing); Visual Arts (areas of study include painting, photography, printmaking, sculpture, new genres, and a program in Sound Art in association with the Department of Music); Writing (concentrations in fiction, nonfiction, and poetry, with the option of pursuing a joint course of study in writing and literary translation); and an M.A. degree program in Film and Media Studies. In addition, a Ph.D. in Drama and Theatre is available through the Graduate School of Arts and Sciences, and a joint J.D./M.F.A. in Theatre Management & Producing is available in conjunction with Columbia Law School. The School also offers summer programs, including master classes, workshops, and credit and noncredit courses in film, theatre, visual arts, and writing, and an array of international programs in partnership with Columbia University's Global Centers.

The School of the Arts typically enrolls full-time students only, except for the M.A. in Film and Media Studies program, which students can attend part-time. The M.F.A. degree programs require 60 points of completed course work. Once the 60 points of course work are completed, each student completes a thesis and/or internships, often under "research arts" student status.

For all specific program requirements and information, prospective students should visit http://arts.columbia.edu/petersons.

## Resources and Facilities

The School of the Arts is located on Columbia's Morningside Campus in the vibrant Upper West Side of Manhattan, with New York City's world-renowned museums, Broadway and Off-Broadway theaters, film centers, galleries, cultural foundations, and literary hubs all nearby. The School is also home to Miller Theatre, the LeRoy Neiman Center for Print Studies, the Columbia University Arts Initiative, and the Office of Public Programs and Engagement. In 2017, the School opened the Lenfest Center for the Arts, a multi-arts venue designed as a hub for the presentation and creation of art across disciplines on the University's new Manhattanville campus. The Lenfest hosts exhibitions, performances, screenings, symposia, readings, and lectures that present new, global voices and perspectives, as well as an exciting, publicly accessible home for Columbia's Miriam and Ira D. Wallach Art Gallery. The University's 22 libraries and countless research centers and institutes are all also available to students.

## Financial Aid

The School of the Arts and Columbia University Office of Student Financial Planning work carefully with students to arrange the financing of their degrees. Scholarships, fellowships, federal work-study, on-campus employment, loan packages, and other options are available for eligible students. Students are encouraged to actively explore all options, even before acceptance into the School, to develop a plan to support the costs of graduate study. Each year, the School awards more than $10 million in student financial support.

More information is available at http://arts.columbia.edu/financing-your-degree/petersons.

## Cost of Study

M.F.A. tuition and fees for 2017–18 are approximately $60,000 for each of the first two years, based on full-time matriculation of 12 to 18 credits per semester. M.F.A. students who have completed the two-year coursework requirement pay a reduced tuition (in 2017–18) of $2,450 per semester while progressing toward completion of the required thesis. A thesis fee may also be assessed by the student's program (details available at http://arts.columbia.edu/expenses/petersons). The time to completion of the thesis requirement varies by program and by the nature and scope of the student's chosen project. M.A. students pay approximately $54,000 in 2017–18 tuition and fees for the first year, then pay a reduced tuition during their third and final semester.

## Living and Housing Costs

The University estimates that students need about $30,000 per year to cover living expenses and housing in New York City. Students can find housing around campus in the Morningside Heights neighborhood, in surrounding Manhattan neighborhoods and boroughs, and in the greater New York area. Columbia University apartment housing consists of a limited number of apartment shares; dormitory-style rooms; and one-bedroom, studio, and family units for which priority is given to couples and families. This housing is primarily located within walking distance of campus.

For additional details, visit http://facilities.columbia.edu/housing.

## Student Group

In fall 2016, the School enrolled over 850 students from 53 countries: 323 in film programs, 162 in theatre programs, 316 in writing programs, 56 in visual arts programs, and 6 in sound art programs.

## Location

Columbia University (including Barnard College and Teachers College) occupies approximately 18 square blocks in the Morningside Heights area of Manhattan. The School of the Arts is on the Morningside Campus, at 116th Street and Broadway on the Upper West Side of Manhattan. The School also operates the Lenfest Center for the Arts on Columbia's new Manhattanville Campus, at 129th and Broadway.

## The University and the School

Columbia, founded in 1754, is comprised of three undergraduate schools, 14 graduate and professional schools, and affiliates Barnard College and Teachers College.

Additional information is available at http://www.columbia.edu/.

## The Faculty

The faculty comprises acclaimed and internationally renowned artists, film and theatre directors, playwrights, producers, poets, writers of fiction and nonfiction, critics, and scholars. Additional information about full-time and adjunct faculty members is available at http://arts.columbia.edu/faculty/petersons.

## Columbia University

### Applying

Applications are accepted for the fall semester only. The cost for the fall 2017 online application is $110. The GRE is not required for application. TOEFL scores for international students are good for two years from the test date. Applicants whose scores were received over two years ago must retake the test and resubmit their current scores with the admissions application. Applicants should request that TOEFL direct results to school code 2171, department code 15.

Students whose transcripts reflect advanced study at an institution where English is the primary language of instruction may request to have the TOEFL requirement waived by e-mailing admissions-arts@columbia.edu. An original certified transcript from the institution, in English, will be required to verify the waiver request. If no transcript has been received, the offer of admission will be provisional until the School receives and approves the official transcript.

Deadlines and more information are available at http://arts.columbia.edu/apply/petersons.

### Correspondence and Information

Office of Admissions
School of the Arts
Columbia University
305 Dodge Hall, MC 1808
2960 Broadway
New York, New York 10027
United States
Phone: 212-854-2134
E-mail: admissions-arts@columbia.edu
Website: http://arts.columbia.edu/petersons

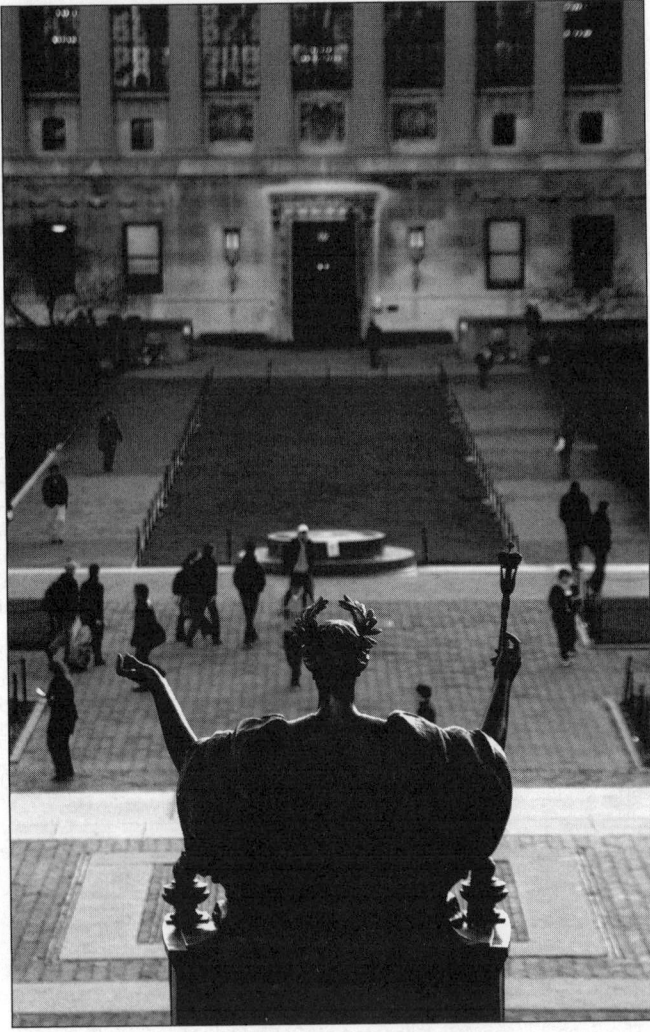

# FASHION INSTITUTE OF TECHNOLOGY
*State University of New York*
*M.A. in Art Market Studies*

 For more information, visit http://petersons.to/fitartmarket

## Programs of Study

The Fashion Institute of Technology (FIT), a State University of New York (SUNY) college of art and design, business, and technology, is home to a mix of innovative achievers, creative thinkers, and industry pioneers. FIT fosters interdisciplinary initiatives, advances research, and provides access to an international network of professionals. With a reputation for excellence, FIT offers its diverse student body access to world-class faculty, dynamic and relevant curricula, and a superior education at an affordable cost. It offers seven programs of graduate study. The programs in Art Market Studies; Exhibition and Experience Design; and Fashion and Textile Studies: History, Theory, Museum Practice lead to the Master of Arts (M.A.) degree. The Illustration and Fashion Design programs lead to the Master of Fine Arts (M.F.A.) degree. The Master of Professional Studies (M.P.S.) degree programs are Cosmetics and Fragrance Marketing and Management and Global Fashion Management.

Art Market Studies is a 39-credit, full-time program that provides students with the tools to forge careers in the business of art. Its interdisciplinary nature reflects the diversity of professional opportunities available to graduates—whether in galleries, auction houses, online platforms, museums, or nonprofit organizations. The curriculum aims to balance practical skills with academic rigor, as well as core business and legal concepts with industry-specific knowledge. In addition to course work in valuation and appraisal, art law, marketing, gallery operations, the auction business, and the history of contemporary art, students in the program are required to pursue an internship with an art-related business or organization. Students also gain hands-on experience through a practicum in which they assemble an exhibition from concept to execution.

## Research Facilities

The School of Graduate Studies is primarily located in the campus's Shirley Goodman Resource Center, which also houses the Gladys Marcus Library and The Museum at FIT. School of Graduate Studies facilities include conference rooms; a fully equipped conservation laboratory; a multipurpose laboratory for conservation projects and the dressing of mannequins; storage facilities for costume and textile materials; a graduate student lounge with computer and printer access; a graduate student library reading room with computers, reference materials, and copies of past classes' qualifying and thesis papers; specialized wireless classrooms; traditional and digital illustration studios; and classrooms equipped with model stands, easels, and drafting tables.

The Gladys Marcus Library houses more than 300,000 volumes of print, nonprint, and digital resources. Specialized holdings include industry reference materials, manufacturers' catalogs, original fashion sketches and scrapbooks, photographs, portfolios of plates, and sample books. The FIT Digital Library provides access to over 90 searchable online databases.

The Museum at FIT houses one of the world's most important collections of clothing and textiles and is the only museum in New York City dedicated to the art of fashion. The permanent collection encompasses more than 50,000 garments and accessories dating from the eighteenth century to the present, with particular strength in twentieth-century fashion, as well as 30,000 textiles and 100,000 textile swatches. Each year, nearly 100,000 visitors are drawn to the museum's award-winning exhibitions and public programs.

## Financial Aid

FIT directly administers its institutional grants, scholarships, and loans. Federal funding administered by the college may include Federal Perkins Loans, federally subsidized and unsubsidized Direct Loans for students, Grad PLUS loans, and the Federal Work-Study Program. Priority for institutionally administered funds is given to students enrolled and designated as full-time.

## Cost of Study

Tuition for New York State residents is $5,603 per semester, or $467 per credit. Out-of-state residents' tuition is $11,449 per semester, or $954 per credit. Tuition and fees are subject to change at the discretion of FIT's Board of Trustees. Additional expenses—for class materials, textbooks, and travel—may apply and vary per program.

## Living and Housing Costs

On-campus housing is available to graduate students. Traditional residence hall accommodations (including meal plan) cost from $5,887 to $7,074 per semester. Apartment-style housing options (not including meal plan) cost from $6,299 to $10,495 per semester.

## Student Group

Enrollment in the School of Graduate Studies is approximately 200 students per academic year, allowing considerable individual advisement. Students come to FIT from throughout the country and around the world.

## Student Outcomes

Art Market Studies graduates forge careers in a broad range of for-profit and nonprofit art organizations—among them,

*Fashion Institute of Technology*

commercial art galleries, auction houses, art fairs, museums, foundations, online platforms, and art appraisal firms.

## Location

FIT is located in Manhattan's Chelsea neighborhood, at the heart of the advertising, visual arts, marketing, fashion, business, design, and communications industries. Students are connected to New York City and gain unparalleled exposure to their field through guest lectures, field trips, internships, and sponsored competitions. The location provides access to major museums, galleries, and auction houses as well as dining, entertainment, and shopping options. The campus is near subway, bus, and commuter rail lines.

## Applying

Applicants to all School of Graduate Studies programs must hold a baccalaureate degree in an appropriate major from a college or university, with a cumulative GPA of 3.0 or higher. International students from non-English-speaking countries are required to submit minimum TOEFL scores of 550 on the written test, 213 on the computer test, or 80 on the Internet test. Each major has additional, specialized prerequisites for admission; for detailed information, students should visit the School of Graduate Studies on FIT's website. Students applying to the Art Market Studies program must submit GRE scores.

Domestic and international students use the same application when seeking admission. The deadline for completed applications with transcripts and supplemental materials is February 15 for the Art Market Studies program. After the deadline date, applicants are considered on a rolling admissions basis. Candidates may apply online at fitnyc.edu/gradstudies.

## Correspondence and Information

School of Graduate Studies
Shirley Goodman Resource Center, Room E315
Fashion Institute of Technology
227 West 27 Street
New York, New York 10001-5992
Phone: 212-217-4300
Fax: 212-217-4301
E-mail: gradinfo@fitnyc.edu
Websites: fitnyc.edu/gradstudies
        fitnyc.edu/artmarket

## THE FACULTY

A partial list of faculty members is below. Guest lecturers are not included.

Natasha Degen, Chair; Ph.D. and M.Phil., Trinity College (England).
Catherine Hannah Behrend, M.B.A., NYU; Certificate in Executive Education, INSEAD (France).
Mari Dumett, Ph.D., Boston University.
Chad Laird, M.A., Stony Brook, SUNY.
Florence Lynch, M.A., Fashion Institute of Technology.
Donald McMichael, M.B.A., Duke.
John Reed, M.F.A., Columbia.
Holly Shen, M.A., NYU.
Gayle M. Skluzacek, B.A., Barat.

# FASHION INSTITUTE OF TECHNOLOGY
*State University of New York*

*M.A. in Fashion and Textile Studies: History, Theory, Museum Practice*

 For more information, visit http://petersons.to/fitfashiontextile

## Programs of Study

The Fashion Institute of Technology (FIT), a State University of New York (SUNY) college of art and design, business, and technology, is home to a mix of innovative achievers, creative thinkers, and industry pioneers. FIT fosters interdisciplinary initiatives, advances research, and provides access to an international network of professionals. With a reputation for excellence, FIT offers its diverse student body access to world-class faculty, dynamic and relevant curricula, and a superior education at an affordable cost. It offers seven programs of graduate study. The programs in Art Market Studies; Exhibition and Experience Design; and Fashion and Textile Studies: History, Theory, Museum Practice lead to the Master of Arts (M.A.) degree. The Illustration and Fashion Design programs lead to the Master of Fine Arts (M.F.A.) degree. The Master of Professional Studies (M.P.S.) degree programs are Cosmetics and Fragrance Marketing and Management, and Global Fashion Management.

The 48-credit, full- or part-time Fashion and Textile Studies: History, Theory, Museum Practice M.A. program prepares students for professional curatorial, conservation, education, and other scholarly careers that focus on historical clothing, accessories, textiles, and related materials. The curriculum incorporates conservation skills, current collections management methods, exhibition techniques, art historical methodologies, material culture studies, and gender studies. The program draws on the resources of The Museum at FIT, one of the world's largest collections of clothing, textiles, and accessories. Students may elect either a conservation or curatorial emphasis; they may also select up to two independent study courses with an appropriate focus on their chosen specialization. All students are required to complete an internship in the field, write a qualifying paper based on original research, and take an active role in a yearlong course culminating in a professional exhibition.

## Research Facilities

The School of Graduate Studies is primarily located in the campus's Shirley Goodman Resource Center, which also houses the Gladys Marcus Library and The Museum at FIT. School of Graduate Studies facilities include conference rooms; a fully equipped conservation laboratory; a multipurpose laboratory for conservation projects and the dressing of mannequins; storage facilities for costume and textile materials; a graduate student lounge with computer and printer access; a graduate student library reading room with computers, reference materials, and copies of past classes' qualifying and thesis papers; specialized wireless classrooms; traditional and digital illustration studios; and classrooms equipped with model stands, easels, and drafting tables.

The Gladys Marcus Library houses more than 300,000 volumes of print, nonprint, and digital resources. Specialized holdings include industry reference materials, manufacturers' catalogs, original fashion sketches and scrapbooks, photographs, portfolios of plates, and sample books. The FIT Digital Library provides access to over 90 searchable online databases.

The Museum at FIT houses one of the world's most important collections of clothing and textiles and is the only museum in New York City dedicated to the art of fashion. The permanent collection encompasses more than 50,000 garments and accessories dating from the eighteenth century, with particular strength in twentieth-century fashion, as well as 30,000 textiles and 100,000 textile swatches. Each year, nearly 100,000 visitors are drawn to the museum's award-winning exhibitions and public programs.

## Financial Aid

FIT directly administers its institutional grants, scholarships, and loans. Federal funding administered by the college may include Federal Perkins Loans, federally subsidized and unsubsidized Direct Loans for students, Grad PLUS loans, and the Federal Work-Study Program. Priority for institutionally administered funds is given to students enrolled and designated as full-time.

## Cost of Study

Tuition for New York State residents is $5,603 per semester, or $467 per credit. Out-of-state residents' tuition is $11,449 per semester, or $954 per credit. Tuition and fees are subject to change at the discretion of FIT's Board of Trustees. Additional expenses—for class materials, textbooks, and travel—may apply and vary per program.

## Living and Housing Costs

On-campus housing is available to graduate students. Traditional residence hall accommodations (including meal plan) cost from $5,887 to $7,074 per semester. Apartment-style housing options (not including meal plan) cost from $6,299 to $10,495 per semester.

## Student Group

Enrollment in the School of Graduate Studies is approximately 200 students per academic year, allowing considerable individualized advisement. Students come to FIT from throughout the country and around the world.

## Student Outcomes

Graduates of the Fashion and Textile Studies: History, Theory, Museum Practice program find positions as museum curators, research specialists, collections managers and registrars, historic house directors, museum educators, independent exhibition curators, corporate curators, fashion and textile historians, costume and textile conservators, auction house department specialists and researchers, vintage clothing and textile dealers, and consultants.

## Location

FIT is located in Manhattan's Chelsea neighborhood, at the heart of the advertising, visual arts, marketing, fashion, business, design, and communications industries. Students are connected to New York City and gain unparalleled exposure to their field through guest lectures, field trips, internships, and sponsored competitions. The location provides access to major museums, galleries, and auction houses as well as dining, entertainment, and shopping options. The campus is near subway, bus, and commuter rail lines.

## Applying

Applicants to all School of Graduate Studies programs must hold a baccalaureate degree in an appropriate major from a college or university, with a cumulative GPA of 3.0 or higher. International students from non-English-speaking countries are required to submit minimum TOEFL scores of 550 on the written test, 213 on the computer test, or 80 on the Internet test. Students applying to the Fashion and Textile Studies: History, Theory, Museum Practice program must submit GRE scores. Each major has additional, specialized prerequisites for admission; for detailed information, students should visit the School of Graduate Studies on FIT's website.

*Fashion Institute of Technology*

Domestic and international students use the same application when seeking admission. The deadline for completed applications with transcripts and supplemental materials is February 15 for the Fashion and Textile Studies: History, Theory, Museum Practice program. After the deadline date, applicants are considered on a rolling admissions basis. Candidates may apply online at fitnyc.edu/gradstudies.

### Correspondence and Information

School of Graduate Studies
Shirley Goodman Resource Center, Room E315
Fashion Institute of Technology
227 West 27 Street
New York, New York 10001-5992
Phone: 212-217-4300
Fax: 212-217-4301
E-mail: gradinfo@fitnyc.edu
Websites: fitnyc.edu/gradstudies
　　　　　 fitnyc.edu/fashiontextilehistory

### THE FACULTY

A partial list of faculty members is below. Guest lecturers are not included.

Denyse Montegut, Chair; Ph.D. candidate, Delaware.
June Burns Bové, M.A., NYU.
Sarah Byrd, M.A., Fashion Institute of Technology.
Joyce Denney, M.A., University of Missouri-Columbia; M.A., Columbia.
Lourdes Font, Ph.D., NYU.
Rebecca Kelly, M.S., University of Rhode Island.
Desire Koslin, Ph.D., NYU.
Bernice Morris, Ph.D. candidate, Delaware.
Sarah Reiter, M.S., Delaware.
Sarah Scaturro, B.A., Colorado.
Valerie Soll, B.A., Oregon.
Deborah Trupin, M.A., NYU.

# NEW YORK STUDIO SCHOOL OF DRAWING, PAINTING & SCULPTURE

*Master of Fine Arts Program*

 http://petersons.to/nystudioschoolmfa

## Programs of Study

The New York Studio School is committed to providing aspiring artists with a significant education that will last a lifetime. Students are encouraged to question and think about the practice of drawing, painting, and sculpture at all times. Master of Fine Arts (MFA) students graduate from the program with an ambitious studio practice, a developed understanding of the language of art, and an enlarged imagination stirred by an established work ethic.

During the first year of study, students choose a core faculty member with whom they work alongside in an Atelier model. Faculty members are present in the classrooms two days each week, and students are expected to work on the objectives set by the instructors throughout the week. Students work more independently, with Faculty studio visits in their second year. MFA candidates work in private and semi-private studios toward the completion of their individual thesis projects.

The MFA programs are offered with concentrations in painting or in sculpture and are based on maintaining a full-time, rigorous studio practice. Students are engaged to work a minimum of 40 hours per week for the duration of their two years at the School. Studio practice is balanced with Critical Studies courses and instructed critiques. Lectures and seminars are held throughout the semester, as well as small group discussion with current and visiting faculty. Students must complete 60 credits to successfully achieve the Master of Fine Arts degree and credits must include all required courses. A residency of at least two academic years is necessary to complete the degree. Students have access to their studios on a full-time basis. New York City's museums, arts organizations, and culture serve as a resource to all students.

The School's internationally recognized Marathon Programs were developed in 1988 by Dean Graham Nickson, to establish the momentum and dedication for the rest of the semester at the start of the program year. The program has since expanded to become a core component of the School's curriculum. The interest in the Marathon Programs has led to a wider audience of participants outside the full-time student body. Renowned artists, art historians, dealers, collectors, art educators, writers, journalists, and students of all levels and affiliations have since experienced the intensity of the program. The Marathon Sessions are offered three times during the academic year: fall, spring, and summer.

## Research Facilities

The John McEnroe Library's mission is to support the New York Studio School's programs and courses by providing materials and information for students, faculty, staff, and visiting lecturers. Holdings include monographs on artists, art historical texts, art periodicals, and exhibition catalogs, as well as an extensive lecture archive, comprising audio and video recordings of lectures from the past thirty years, featuring artists, historians, critics, and philosophers.

The library provides an online catalog to check the holdings of the collection, as well as access to research databases and indexes that aid in scholarly research.

## Financial Aid

The financial aid programs are part of the School's desire to attract qualified students from diverse backgrounds. Any student who would like to be considered for financial assistance from the School must complete a financial aid application and submit it to Student Services by the deadline date each year. Financial aid scholarships are contingent on the continuation of satisfactory progress in all enrolled courses and are available to all full-time enrolled students. Scholarships are available for part-time students during the summer session.

## Cost of Study

For the 2017–18 academic year, the cost for the MFA program is $11,937.50 per semester. The cost for the Certificate program is $7,925 per semester. For additional, up-to-date cost information, prospective students should visit www.nyss.org/admissions-services/tuition-fees-financial-aid/.

## Living and Housing Costs

The School does not have facilities to house students. Upon acceptance, students receive information on housing opportunities in New York, including listings of temporary accommodations and help on searching for suitable living situations. The School is easily accessible by public transport from the outer boroughs and New Jersey. Rents in the outer boroughs tend to be lower than in Manhattan. Less expensive situations can be found through sublets or by living with roommates. Students should plan to find proper accommodations prior to the start of classes.

## Student Group

The Studio School welcomes a diverse demographic of students varying in ages and geographical origins; one third of the full-time student body is composed of international students. At the Studio School, the incentive to work comes from the students themselves without the distraction of too many diversionary projects or assignments. The students here are excited to remain in the studio and to concentrate on their independent work.

The measure of each student's development is particular to that individual, and progresses without the pressure of producing accomplished works. The amount learned in the process is the criterion of success. At the School, the pursuit of authenticity tends to reject the distractions of style or the rush for novelty. Response to the contemporary does not lessen the excitement of discovery within the art of the past. No dichotomy between realism and abstraction is assumed at the School. On the contrary, perceptual experience is encouraged to lead the student to the discovery of abstract equivalents, to a deepening grasp of the plastic means.

## Location

The School is located on West 8th Street, between Sixth Avenue/Avenue of the Americas and Fifth Avenue. It is accessible by subway or the PATH train. The School occupies eight historic buildings with an extraordinary cultural and artistic history. Occupied by various artists, and the original site of the Whitney Museum of American Art from 1931 to 1954, the School's physical home has been a place where art has been created, discussed, and displayed for over a century. In the 50 years that the School has been on West 8th Street, artists and students alike have found both inspiration and comfort in continuing the tradition of drawing, painting, and sculpting in the historic spaces that have played such an important role in the history of art in America.

*New York Studio School of Drawing, Painting & Sculpture*

## Applying

The application deadline for MFA applicants is February 15. Late applications are reviewed on a case-by-case basis; however late applicants may not be eligible for financial aid. MFA candidates are accepted exclusively for enrollment in the fall semester. Applicants must have a bachelor's degree or equivalent to be considered for admission. Forms must be completed online at https://nyss.slideroom.com/#/Login.

Completed applications include the application form, two required essays, a $90 nonrefundable application fee, two letters of recommendation, 20 jpeg images of student work, and official transcripts from all previous institutions that resulted in the applicant's undergraduate degree. Detailed instructions are available as part of the application form. Partial applications will not be considered. Prospective candidates will be invited for an interview with the Admissions Committee.

For additional information, prospective students should visit http://www.nyss.org/admissions-services/application-requirements/.

## Correspondence and Information

New York Studio School
8 West 8th Street
New York, New York 10011
United States
Phone: 212-673-6466
Fax: 212-777-0996
E-mail: info@nyss.org
Website: http://www.nyss.org/programs-courses/mfa-painting-sculpture/

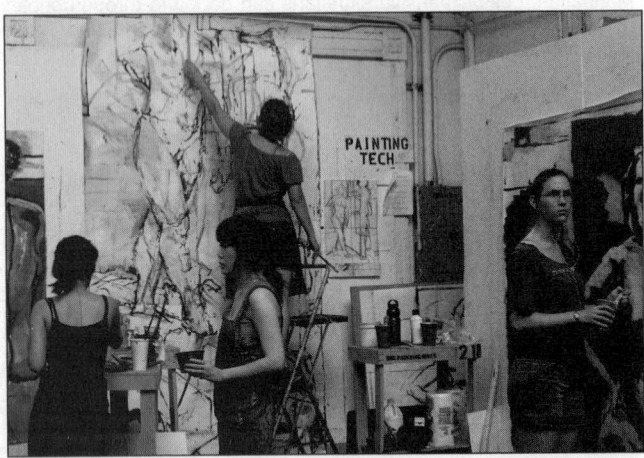

The School's internationally recognized Marathon programs were developed by Dean Graham Nickson, initially as a measure for the rest of the semester at the start of the program year. All MFA and Certificate candidates begin in the fall and spring semesters with either a Drawing or Sculpture Marathon.

## THE FACULTY

David Cohen, art critic and curator; publisher of *artcritical.com.*

Garth Evans, sculptor; studied at Manchester Junior and Regional Colleges of Art and the Slade School of Fine Art (London).

Bruce Gagnier, sculptor; M.F.A., Columbia. National Academician represented by Lori Bookstein Fine Art.

Judy Glantzman, painter; B.F.A., Rhode Island School of Design. Represented by the Betty Cuningham Gallery, New York City.

Bill Jensen, painter; B.F.A. and M.F.A., University of Minnesota. Represented by Cheim & Read Gallery, New York.

Elisa Jensen, painter; M.A., Smith College and the New York Studio School.

Jilaine Jones , sculptor; studied at the College of Ceramics, Alfred University; School of the Museum of Fine Arts; and New York Studio School.

John Lees, painter; B.F.A. and M.F.A., Otis Art Institute. Represented by Betty Cuningham Gallery.

Leonid Lerman, sculptor; studied drawing and sculpture at the Odessa (Russia) School of Art and the Professional School of Mosaics and Woodcarving.

Margrit Lewczuk, painter; studied at Queens College and the Brooklyn Museum Art School.

John Newman, sculptor; B.A., Oberlin College; M.F.A., Yale School of Art.

Graham Nickson, painting and drawing; B.A., Camberwell School of Arts & Crafts; M.A., Royal College of Art (London).

Ophrah Shemesh, painter; educated at Bezalel Academy of Art and Design (Jerusalem) and the New York Studio School.

Kyle Staver, painter; M.F.A., Yale School of Art. Guggenheim Memorial Foundation Fellowship 2015; represented by Kent Fine Art.

Lee Tribe, sculptor; educated at Saint Martin's School of Art and Birmingham School of Art (England) and the New York Studio School.

Karen Wilkin, art historian and critic; educated at Barnard College and Columbia University. Fulbright and Woodrow Wilson Fellow.

Second-year MFA candidates are provided with semi-private to private studios, allowing for growth and development of their creative practice.

# PRATT INSTITUTE
*School of Art*

## Programs of Study

Pratt has been educating professionals for productive careers in the fields of art and design since its founding in 1887. Pratt's School of Art offers an outstanding professional art education taught by a faculty of working professionals that brings high standards and current practices to the classroom. Faculty members have received more than eighteen Tiffany, Fulbright, and Guggenheim awards as well as other prestigious professional awards.

Pratt offers master's degrees in a variety of programs, including Master of Fine Arts in Digital Arts (including animation) or Fine Art (painting and drawing, photography, printmaking, sculpture, and integrated practices); Master of Art in Art and Design Education (teacher certification) and Master of Science in Dance/Movement Therapy; and Master of Professional Studies in Art Therapy and Creativity Development, Arts and Cultural Management, or Design Management. A post-baccalaureate New York State certification program for the teaching of art in grades pre-K–12 is available for fine arts graduate students. Pratt also offers a dual degree in Fine Arts and History of Art and Design, Fine Arts and Library and Information Science and a dual degree in Digital Arts and Library Science as well as various certificates for holders of the M.S. in Library Science including Museum Studies, Archives, and Library and Information Studies.

Art and Design Education graduates are prepared to pursue teaching careers in pre-K–12 schools, museums and cultural institutions, or colleges. Graduates of the Creative Arts Therapy program work in psychiatric, medical rehabilitation, geriatric and family therapy, school, substance abuse, and child-life settings. They also learn to work with a variety of patient populations, including patients with eating disorders and the homeless.

All graduate art curricula include supportive course work in the humanities. Students can choose from a wide array of course offerings, including art and design history, comparative literature, philosophy, foreign languages, and social sciences. The graduate programs require the completion of 30 to 68 credits (75 credits for the M.S./M.F.A. dual-degree program) and last from 1½ to 3 years, depending on the curriculum and the number of prerequisites that have not been met at the time of admission. For the granting of degrees, all of the graduate programs require the submission of a thesis or a comparable effort. For the M.F.A., an exhibition and supporting corollary statement are required. For the M.P.S. in Art Therapy and the M.S. in Dance/Movement Therapy, the thesis project may involve research, an extended case study, the development of a project implementing innovative techniques in therapy, or the opportunity to publish an article. For the M.P.S. in Design Management, the thesis project is the preparation of a business case study.

## Research Facilities

The Pratt Library contains 186,589 bound volumes, serial backfiles, and other material (including government documents); 251,603 audiovisual materials; and 3,996 microforms and subscribes to 925 periodicals.

Pratt maintains numerous studios, shops, and technical facilities for work in all media as well as state-of-the-art computer facilities. Digital arts labs include state-of-the-art Macintosh, PC/NT, and UNIX operating systems as well as digital video and audio systems. Pratt also has extensive gallery space for exhibitions.

## Financial Aid

Financial aid awards are offered through a variety of institutional, state, and federally funded programs. These include Graduate Scholarships awarded by departments to incoming students on the basis of merit, endowed and restricted scholarships for continuing students, and student employment. Assistantships are awarded on a competitive basis to continuing students in all departments. Special alumni-sponsored fellowships are also available.

## Cost of Study

Graduate tuition for 2017–18 is $30,834 per year (full-time 18 credits, $1,713 per credit) and student fees are $1,974 per year. The cost of books and supplies varies widely, depending on the program in which the student is enrolled.

## Living and Housing Costs

Campus housing continues to be expanded to meet students' needs and is available for single students on a first-come, first-served basis. Housing costs average $18,800 per academic year. Pratt offers limited graduate student housing two blocks away from the campus. There is a plentiful supply of moderately priced rentals in the immediate area and in adjacent neighborhoods for married students seeking housing and for those students choosing to reside off campus.

## Student Group

In educating more than five generations of students to be creative, technically skilled, and adaptable professionals, Pratt has gained an international reputation that attracts over 4,600 undergraduate and graduate students annually from 48 states and 81 countries.

## Location

Pratt Institute's 25-acre, parklike main campus is situated among the turn-of-the-century mansions, Victorian brownstones, and wide, tree-lined boulevards of Clinton Hill, one of Brooklyn's historic neighborhoods. Midtown Manhattan, the heart of New York City, is only 25 minutes away by subway and offers students a vast array of professional, cultural, and recreational opportunities. Pratt also maintains a campus in Manhattan's Chelsea district. Pratt Manhattan houses the Institute's graduate arts and cultural management and design management programs.

## The Institute

A private, nonsectarian institute of higher education, Pratt Institute was founded by the industrialist and philanthropist Charles Pratt. Changing with the needs and requirements of the professional world for which it prepares its graduates, Pratt today educates 3,310 undergraduate and 1,349 graduate students for careers in art and design, architecture, and library and information science.

## Applying

The deadline for applications and all supporting materials, including portfolio, is January 5. Applicants should complete the application process online. Early submission of applications with all necessary credentials is highly desirable. Applications received after these dates are considered if openings exist in a particular program. For applicants who intend to file for financial aid, the FAFSA should be filed by March 1 for fall entrance and by October 1 for spring entrance.

## Correspondence and Information

Graduate Admissions Office
Pratt Institute
200 Willoughby Avenue
Brooklyn, New York 11205
United States
Phone: 718-636-3514
     800-331-0834 (toll-free)
Fax: 718-399-4242
E-mail: admissions@pratt.edu
Website: http://www.pratt.edu
     http://www.pratt.edu/admissions/request-information (to request information)

## THE FACULTY

**Gerry Snyder, Dean**
Camille Martin, Assistant Dean, School of Design; M.Arch., Washington University St. Louis.

### Art and Design Education
Heather Lewis, Chair, Professor; Ph.D., NYU.
Mirland Terlonge, Assistant to the Chair.
Caitlin Cahill, Visiting Instructor; M.A., TESOL, City College.
Phillip DeSantis, Visiting Instructor; M.A., Brooklyn College.
Mary Elmer-Dewitt, Adjunct Assistant Professor; M.S., Pratt.
Borinquen Gallo, Assistant Professor; M.F.A., CUNY, Hunter.
Sarah Holcomb, Visiting Instructor; M.S., Pratt.
Ann Holt, Visiting Instructor; Ph.D., Penn State.
Tara Kopp, Visiting Assistant Professor; M.F.A. and Adv. Cert., Pratt.
Rebecca Krucoff, Visiting Assistant Professor; M.S.Ed., Bank Street College.
Monica Marino, Visiting Instructor; M.S., Hunter.
Joshua Millis, Visiting Instructor; M.F.A., Art Institute of Chicago.
Ryan Minezzi, Visiting Instructor; M.S., Pratt.
Kelly Normand, Visiting Instructor; M.S., Pratt.
Rachel Ropiek, Visiting Instructor; M.A, Courtauld Institute of Art, London.
Patrick Rowe, Visiting Instructor; M.F.A., M.S. Pratt.
Theodora Skipitares, Associate Professor; M.F.A., NYU.
Jaret Vadera, Visiting Instructor; M.F.A., Yale .
Aileen Wilson, Professor, Ed.D., Columbia.

### Arts and Cultural Management
Mary McBride, Chair; Professor, Ph.D., NYU.
Christopher Shrum, Associate Professor; Ph.D., Fielding Graduate University.
Catherine Ashcraft, Visiting Assistant Professor; Ph.D., MIT.
Catherine Cacho-Leary, Visiting Assistant Professor; M.B.A., Keller Graduate School of Management.
Laurence DeGaetano, Adjunct Assistant Professor; M.B.A., NYU.
Dyanis De Jesus, Visiting Assistant Professor; M.P.S., Pratt.
Tyra Nicole Dumars, Visiting Assistant Professor; M.P.S., Pratt.
Kristen Earls, Visiting Assistant Professor; M.A., NYU.
Scott Fiaschetti, Visiting Associate Professor; V.P. of Insights and Strategy, Questus, Inc.
Larry Gibbs, Visiting Assistant Professor; Product and Technology Officer of March Warden Consulting.
Richard Green, Professor; Consultant specializing in developing organizational change strategies and the improvement of internal team processes.
Jeffrey Klein, Visiting Assistant Professor; J.D., Fordham.
Antonio Ponton-Nunez, Visiting Assistant Professor; M.P.S., Pratt.
Christina Rosan, Visiting Assistant Professor; Ph.D., MIT.
JoJo Spiker, Visiting Assistant Professor; M.P.S., Pratt.
Denise Tahara, Visiting Associate Professor; Ph.D., NYU.
Tiffany Townsend, Visiting Assistant Professor; M.S., Columbia.
Kelly Kocinski Trager, Visiting Associate Professor; J.D., Brooklyn Law.
Alicia Whiteman, Visiting Assistant Professor; M.P.S., Pratt.

### Creative Arts Therapy
Julie Miller, Chair; M.A./M.S., Hunter; LCSW, LCAT, BC-DMT.
Dina Schapiro, Assistant Chair, Director Graduate Art Therapy Program; M.P.S., Pratt; LCAT, ATR-BC.
Linda Siegel, Director of Graduate Art Therapy Program, Assistant Professor; LCAT, ATR-BC.
Joan Wittig, Director of Graduate Dance/Movement Therapy Program, Associate Professor; M.S., CUNY, Hunter; LCAT, BC-DMT.
Claudia Bader, Visiting Instructor; M.P.S., Pratt; LCAT, LP, NCPsychA, ATR-BC.
Joachim Boenig, Adjunct Assistant Professor; LCAT, ATR.
Shannon Bradley, Visiting Instructor; M.S., Pratt; LCAT, ATR-BC.
Corinna Brown, Visiting Instructor; M.S., CUNY, Hunter; LCAT, BC-DMT.
Kimberly Bush, Adjunct Assistant Professor; M.F.A., Parsons; LCAT, ATR-BC.
Jean Davis, Adjunct Associate Professor; M.P.S., Pratt; CCE, LCAT, ATR-BC.
Christina Devereaux, Visiting Assistant Professor; Ph.D., Santa Barbara Graduate Institute; LCAT, LMHC, BC-DMT.
Ted Ehrhardt, Adjunct Assistant Professor; M.S., CUNY, Hunter; CCE, LCAT, BC-DMT, CMA.
Cara Gallo, Visiting Instructor; M.S., CUNY, Hunter; LCAT, BC-DMT.
Alison Gigl-George, Adjunct Assistant Professor; LCAT, ATR-BC.
Valerie Hubbs, Visiting Instructor; M.S., CUNY, Hunter; LCAT, BC-DMT.
Melissa Klay, Adjunct Instructor; Ph.D., Pacifica Graduate; LCAT, ATR-BC.
Judith Luongo, Adjunct Associate Professor; M.P.S., Pratt; CCE, LCAT, LP, ATR.
Briana MacWilliam, Visiting Instructor; M.S., Pratt; LCAT, ATR-BC.
Deniz Oktay, Visiting Instructor; M.S., Pratt.
Sean Plunkett, Visiting Instructor; M.P.S., Pratt.
Deborah Rice, Visiting Professor; M.P.S., Pratt; LCAT, LMHC, ATR.

## Pratt Institute

Maria Rivera, Visiting Instructor; M.S., Pratt; LCAT, BC-DMT.
Sara Rothstein, Visiting Instructor; M.P.S., Pratt; LCAT, ATR.
Jean Seibel, Visiting Instructor; M.S., Hunter College; LCAT, BC-DMT.
Lauren Smith, Visiting Instructor; M.P.S., Pratt.
Elissa White, Visiting Assistant Professor; LCAT, BC-DMT.
Eva Teirstein Young, Visiting Instructor; M.P.S., Pratt; LCAT, ATR-BC.

### Design Management

Mary McBride, Chair, Professor; Ph.D., NYU.
Catherine Ashcraft, Visiting Assistant Professor; Ph.D., MIT.
Laurence DeGaetano, Adjunct Assistant Professor; M.B.A., NYU.
Dyanis DeJesus, Visiting Assistant Professor; M.P.S., Pratt.
Tyra Nicole Dumars, Visiting Assistant Professor, M.P.S., Pratt.
Roger Dunbar, Visiting Professor; Ph.D., Cornell.
Scott Fiaschetti, Visiting Associate Professor; V.P., Insights and Strategy, Questus, Inc.
Larry Gibbs, Visiting Assistant Professor; Product and Technology Officer, March Warden Consulting.
Richard Green, Professor; Consultant specializing in developing organizational change strategies and the improvement of internal team processes.
Mung Ki Woo, Visiting Assistant Professor; Ecole Polytechnique and Telecom Paris Tech.
Jacqueline McCormack, Adjunct Associate Professor; M.P.S., Pratt.
James Murray, Visiting Assistant Professor; M.P.S., Pratt.
Christina Rosan, Visiting Assistant Professor; Ph.D., MIT.
Rachel Starobinsky, Visiting Assistant Professor; M.P.S., Pratt.
Jo Ann Stonier, Visiting Assistant Professor; J.D., St. John's (New York).
Denise Tahara, Visiting Associate Professor; Ph.D., NYU.
Yutaka Takiura, Visiting Assistant Professor; M.Arch Urban Design, Pennsylvania; M.Arch., IIT.
Kelly Kocinski Trager, Visiting Associate Professor; J.D., Brooklyn Law.
Marvin Waldman, Visiting Assistant Professor; M.B.A., CUNY, Baruch.

### Digital Arts

Peter Patchen, Chair; M.F.A., Oregon.
Carla Gannis, Assistant Chair; M.F.A., Boston University.
Dan Augsburger, Visiting Instructor; M.F.A. Savannah College of Art and Design.
Justin Berry, Visiting Assistant Professor; M.F.A., Art Institute of Chicago.
Liubomir Borissov, Associate Professor; Ph.D., Columbia.
Michael Bourbeau, Visiting Instructor; M.F.A., School of Visual Arts.
Svjetlana Bukvich-Nichols, Visiting Associate Professor; M.F.A., Rensselaer.
Blake Carrington, Assistant Professor; M.F.A., Syracuse.
Elliot Cowan, Visiting Instructor; B.A., Independent College of Art and Design.
Edward Darino, Adjunct Assistant Professor; M.F.A., NYU; Ph.D., UEU on New Technologies.
Marianna Ellenberg, Visiting Instructor; M.A., Slade School of Art.
Mike Enright, Adjunct Assistant Professor; M.F.A., California Institute of the Arts.
Kay Hines, Adjunct Assistant Professor; B.A., Barnard.
Faith Holland, Visiting Instructor; M.F.A., School of Visual Arts.
Kenneth Hughes, Visiting Instructor.
Everett Kane, Assistant Professor; M.F.A., Art Center College of Design.
Hyunsuk Kim, Visiting Instructor.
Jacques Khouri, Visiting Instructor; M.F.A., Savannah College of Art and Design.
Linda Lauro-Lazin, Adjunct Associate Professor, M.A., NYIT.
David Mattingly, Visiting Instructor; M.F.A., Art Center.
Genevieve Okupniak, Visiting Instructor, M.F.A., California Institute of the Arts.
Michael J. O'Rourke, Professor; Ed.M., Harvard.
Mira Scharf, Visiting Instructor; M.F.A., UCLA.
Claudia Tait, Associate Professor; M.F.A., Maryland.
Michael Tanzillo, Visiting Instructor; M.F.A., Savannah College of Art and Design.
Katherine Torn, Visiting Instructor; M.F.A., Art Institute of Chicago.
Lukas Wadya, Visiting Instructor; M.F.A., School of Visual Arts.
Gregory Webb, Adjunct Instructor.
Daniel Weisbard, Visiting Instructor; M.F.A., RIT.
Elizabeth White, Visiting Instructor; M.F.A., School of Visual Arts.
Bryan Zanisnik, Visiting Instructor; M.F.A., Hunter.

### Fine Arts

Jane South, Chair of Fine Arts; M.F.A., UNC Greensboro.
Stephen Hilger, Chair of Photography; M.F.A., Columbia.
Nat Meade, Assistant Chair of Fine Arts, Visiting Instructor; M.F.A., Pratt.
Dina Weiss, Assistant Chair, Visiting Instructor; M.F.A., Parsons.
Ann Agee, Visiting Associate Professor; M.F.A. ,Yale.
David Alban, Visiting Assistant Professor; M.F.A., Cranbrook Academy of Art.
Ruby Omyinyechi Amanze, Visiting Assistant Professor; M.F.A., Cranbrook.
Adam Apostolos, Visiting Instructor; Sculpture technician.
Karen Bachmann, Visiting Assistant Professor; B.F.A., Pratt.
Lisha Bai, Adjunct Assistant Professor; M.F.A., Yale.
Lisa Bateman, Adjunct Associate Professor; M.F.A., Virginia Commonwealth.
Michael Brennan, Adjunct Assistant Professor; M.F.A., Pratt.
Deborah Bright; M.F.A., University of Chicago.
Mona Brody, Adjunct Associate Professor; M.F.A., Vermont College.
Howard Buchwald, Professor; M.A., CUNY, Hunter.
David Butler, Adjunct Associate Professor; M.F.A., Washington (Seattle).
Kathy Butterly, Visiting Associate Professor; M.F.A., UC Davis.
William Carroll, Visiting Associate Professor; M.F.A., CUNY, Queens.
Nanette Carter, Adjunct Associate Professor, Coordinator for Drawing; M.F.A., Pratt.
Deborah Chaney, Visiting Associate Professor; B.F.A. , Tamarind Master Printer.
David Cohen, Visiting Associate Professor; M.A., Courtauld Institute of Art (London).
Angela Conant, Visiting Assistant Professor; M.F.A., SVA.
James Costanzo, Adjunct Associate Professor; M.F.A., Iowa.
Grayson Cox, Visiting Assistant Professor; M.F.A., Columbia.
Peggy Cyphers, Adjunct Professor; M.F.A., Pratt.
Pradeep Dalal, Visiting Assistant Director; M.F.A., Bard.
Gregory Drasler, Adjunct Associate Professor; M.F.A., University of Illinois.
Kelly Driscoll, Assistant Professor; M.F.A., CUNY, City College.
Samuel Evensen, Visiting Assistant Professor; M.F.A., New York Academy of Art.
Brad Ewing, Visiting Instructor; M.F.A., Rhode Island School of Design.
Patrick Fenton, Visiting Assistant Professor; M.F.A., Stanford.
Allen Frame, Adjunct Associate Professor; B.A., Harvard.
Linda Francis, Adjunct Professor; M.A., CUNY, Hunter.
Michael Fujita, Visiting Instructor; M.F.A., Alfred.
Joseph Fyfe, Adjunct Associate Professor; B.F.A., University of the Arts.
Brice Garrett, Visiting Assistant Professor; M.F.A., Konstfack University, Stockholm, Sweden.
Anne Gilman, Adjunct Associate Professor; M.F.A., CUNY, Brooklyn.

Jonathan Goodman, Visiting Assistant Professor; M.A., Pennsylvania.
David Gothard, Visiting Assistant Professor; B.F.A., Pratt.
Toni Greenbaum, Visiting Associate Professor; M.A., Hunter.
Nancy Grimes, Adjunct Associate Professor; M.F.A., Art Institute of Chicago.
Raphael Griswold, Visiting Assistant Professor; M.F.A., Brooklyn College.
Aubrey Hillman; M.F.A., University of Oregon.
Vera Iliatova, Visiting Assistant Professor; M.F.A., Yale.
Yasu Izaki, Visiting Instructor; M.F.A., Pratt.
Russell Jones, Visiting Assistant Professor; M.A., Metropolitan University of Manchester.
Shirley Kaneda, Professor; B.F.A., Parsons.
Michael Kirk, Adjunct Professor; M.F.A., Pratt.
Ross Knight, Visiting Assistant Professor; B.F.A., Minnesota, Twin Cities.
Vivien Knussi, Assistant Professor; Ph.D., Columbia.
Peter Kruty, Visiting Assistant Professor; M.A., Alabama.
Julia Kunin, Visiting Associate Professor; M.F.A., Rutgers.
Alexander Kvares, Visiting Assistant Professor, M.F.A., University of Texas.
Benjamin LaRocco, Visiting Assistant Professor; M.F.A., Pratt.
David Lantow, Visiting Associate Professor; M.F.A., CUNY, Brooklyn.
Catherine Lecleire, Adjunct Associate Professor; M.F.A., USC.
Jenny Lee, Adjunct Professor, B.F.A., Cooper Union.
Frank Lind, Professor; M.F.A., Pratt.
Patricia Madeja, Associate Professor; B.F.A., Pratt.
Ann Mandelbaum, Adjunct Professor; M.F.A., Pratt.
Dennis Masback, Adjunct Professor; M.F.A., Washington (St. Louis).
Mary Mattingly, Visiting Assistant Professor; B.F.A., Pacific Northwest College of Art.
Jen Mazza, Visiting Assistant Professor; M.F.A., Rutgers.
J. Martin Mazzora, Visiting Assistant Professor; M.F.A., American.
Jennifer Melby, Adjunct Associate Professor; M.F.A., Pratt.
Anne Messner, Professor; B.F.A., Pratt.
Curtis Mitchell, Adjunct Professor; M.F.A., Yale.
John Monti, Professor; M.F.A., Pratt.
Donna Moran, Professor; M.F.A., Pratt.
Robert Morgan, Adjunct Professor; Ph.D., NYU.
Dominique Nahas, Adjunct Associate Professor; M.A., NYU.
Mario Naves, Adjunct Assistant Professor; M.F.A., Pratt.
Sarah Nicholls, Visiting Assistant Professor; B.A., Sarah Lawrence.
Thirwell Nolen, Adjunct Associate Professor; M.Arch., Georgia Tech.
John O'Connor, Visiting Assistant Professor; M.F.A., Pratt.
Catherine Redmond, Adjunct Associate Professor; B.A., SUNY at Binghamton.
William Richards, Adjunct Associate Professor; M.F.A., New Mexico.
Caitlin Riordan, Visiting Instructor; B.F.A., Maine College of Art.
Mary Beth Rozkewicz, Adjunct Associate Professor; B.F.A., SUNY.
Alan Ruiz, Visiting Assistant Professor; M.F.A., Yale.
Stuart Sachs, Visiting Assistant Professor; Sculptor.
Analia Segal, Visiting Associate Professor; M.A., NYU.
Jason Segall, Visiting Instructor; M.F.A., Alfred University.
Beverly Semmes, Visiting Assistant Professor; M.F.A., Yale.
Steven Sergiovanni, Visiting Assistant Professor; M.A., NYU.
Carla Shapiro, Adjunct Assistant Professor; B.F.A., Syracuse.
Jean Shin, Adjunct Professor; M.S., Pratt.
Gerald Siciliano, Adjunct Professor; M.S., Pratt.
Robbin Silverberg, Adjunct Associate Professor; B.A., Princeton.
Joseph Smith, Professor; M.F.A., NYU.
Judith Solodkin, Visiting Associate Professor; M.F.A., Columbia.
Laurel Sparks, Visiting Associate Professor; M.F.A., Bard.
Joseph Stauber, Adjunct Assistant Professor; M.F.A., SUNY Purchase.
Jason Stopa, Visiting Assistant Professor; M.F.A., Pratt.
Irvin Tepper, Adjunct Professor; M.F.A., Washington (Seattle).
Christopher Verstegen, Visiting Instructor, Studio and Gallery Supervisor; M.F.A., Pratt.
Timothy Veske-McMahon, Visiting Assistant Professor; M.F.A., Cranbrook.
Emily Weiner, Visiting Assistant Professor; M.F.A., School of Visual Arts.
Christopher White, Adjunct Assistant Professor; B.A., Harvard.
Rachel Wiecking, Visiting Assistant Professor; M.F.A., Purchase, SUNY.
Chris Wright, Adjunct Associate Professor; M.F.A., Pratt.
SeoKyeong Yoon, Studio and Gallery Manager; M.F.A., Pratt.
Robert Zakarian, Professor; M.F.A., Pratt.
Katrin Zimmerman, Visiting Assistant Professor; M.A., School of Oriental and African Studies (London).

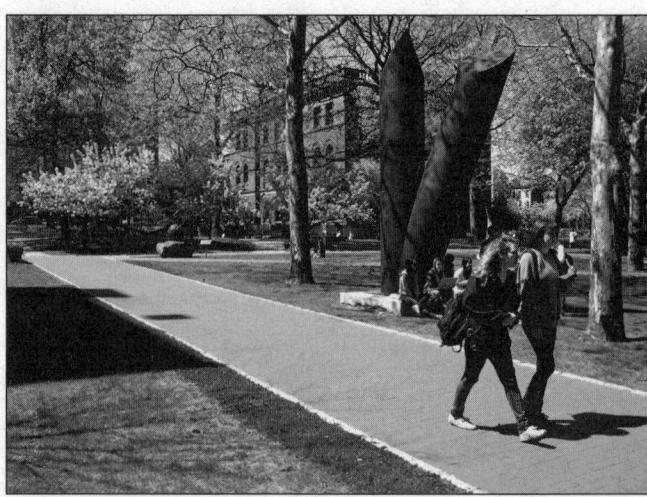

©2017 Bob Handelman

# Section 4
# Comparative and Interdisciplinary Arts

This section contains a directory of institutions offering graduate work in comparative and interdisciplinary arts. Additional information about programs listed in the directory may be obtained by writing directly to the dean of a graduate school or chair of a department at the address given in the directory.

For programs offering related work, see also in this book *Applied Arts and Design, Architecture, Art and Art History,* and *Performing Arts.* In another guide in this series:

**Graduate Programs in Business, Education, Information Studies, Law & Social Work**

See *Subject Areas (Art Education)*

## CONTENTS

**Program Directory**

# Comparative and Interdisciplinary Arts

**Brigham Young University,** Graduate Studies, College of Humanities, Department of Comparative Arts and Letters, Provo, UT 84602. Offers comparative studies (MA). *Faculty:* 29 full-time (8 women). *Students:* 19 full-time (12 women), 1 part-time (0 women); includes 1 minority (Hispanic/Latino). Average age 29. 12 applicants, 67% accepted, 6 enrolled. In 2016, 5 master's awarded. *Degree requirements:* For master's, 2 foreign languages, comprehensive exam, thesis. *Entrance requirements:* For master's, GRE, minimum GPA of 3.0 in last 60 hours, writing sample, foreign language experience. Additional exam requirements/recommendations for international students: Required—TOEFL (minimum score 580 paper-based; 85 iBT), IELTS (minimum score 7). *Application deadline:* For fall admission, 3/1 for domestic and international students. Application fee: $50. Electronic applications accepted. *Expenses: Tuition:* Full-time $6680; part-time $393 per credit. Tuition and fees vary according to course load, program and student's religious affiliation. *Financial support:* In 2016–17, 19 students received support, including 33 fellowships with partial tuition reimbursements available (averaging $2,566 per year), 4 research assistantships (averaging $1,500 per year), 29 teaching assistantships (averaging $2,658 per year); scholarships/grants, tuition waivers (full and partial), unspecified assistantships, and student instructorships also available. Support available to part-time students. *Faculty research:* Latin American literature and translation, Mormon women artists, documentary photography, Lucan studies, African Mormon women's oral histories. *Unit head:* Dr. Roger Macfarlane, Graduate Coordinator/Professor of Classical Studies, 801-422-9078, Fax: 801-422-0305, E-mail: macfarlane@byu.edu. *Application contact:* Andrea Kristensen, Graduate Program Manager, 801-422-2996, Fax: 801-422-0305, E-mail: andrea_kristensen@byu.edu. Website: http://cal.byu.edu/

**Columbia College Chicago,** Graduate School, Department of Interdisciplinary Arts, Chicago, IL 60605-1996. Offers interdisciplinary arts (MA); interdisciplinary arts and media (MFA); interdisciplinary book and paper arts (MFA). *Program availability:* Part-time, evening/weekend, online learning. *Degree requirements:* For master's, thesis. *Entrance requirements:* For master's, self-assessment essay, work sample, interview, letters of recommendation. Additional exam requirements/recommendations for international students: Required—TOEFL (minimum score 600 paper-based; 100 iBT). Electronic applications accepted. *Expenses:* Contact institution.

**Florida Atlantic University,** Dorothy F. Schmidt College of Arts and Letters, Department of Comparative Studies, Boca Raton, FL 33431-0991. Offers MA, PhD. *Program availability:* Part-time. *Students:* 26 full-time (17 women), 21 part-time (16 women); includes 14 minority (4 Black or African American, non-Hispanic/Latino; 9 Hispanic/Latino; 1 Two or more races, non-Hispanic/Latino), 6 international. Average age 40. 18 applicants, 67% accepted, 10 enrolled. In 2016, 7 doctorates awarded. *Degree requirements:* For doctorate, one foreign language, comprehensive exam, thesis/dissertation. *Entrance requirements:* For doctorate, GRE, minimum GPA of 3.5, 3 references. Additional exam requirements/recommendations for international students: Required—TOEFL (minimum score 500 paper-based; 61 iBT), IELTS (minimum score 6). *Application deadline:* For fall admission, 2/1 priority date for domestic and international students. Applications are processed on a rolling basis. Application fee: $30. *Expenses:* Tuition, state resident: full-time $7392; part-time $369.82 per credit hour. Tuition, nonresident: full-time $19,432; part-time $1024.81 per credit hour. *Financial support:* Teaching assistantships with tuition reimbursements available.

*Faculty research:* Arts, humanities, social sciences. *Unit head:* Dr. Nancy Poulson, 561-297-3845, E-mail: npoulson@fau.edu.
Website: http://www.fau.edu/comparativestudies/

**Goddard College,** Graduate Division, Master of Fine Arts in Interdisciplinary Arts Program, Plainfield, VT 05667-9432. Offers MFA. *Program availability:* Online learning. *Degree requirements:* For master's, thesis. *Entrance requirements:* For master's, relevant undergraduate degree, 3 letters of recommendation, interview, portfolio, artistic resume. Electronic applications accepted.

**John F. Kennedy University,** Graduate School of Holistic Studies, Department of Arts and Consciousness, Program in Transformative Arts, Pleasant Hill, CA 94523-4817. Offers MA. *Program availability:* Part-time, evening/weekend. *Degree requirements:* For master's, thesis or alternative. *Entrance requirements:* For master's, interview. Additional exam requirements/recommendations for international students: Required—TOEFL. *Expenses:* Contact institution.

**Ohio University,** Graduate College, College of Fine Arts, School of Interdisciplinary Arts, Athens, OH 45701-2979. Offers PhD. *Degree requirements:* For doctorate, 2 foreign languages, comprehensive exam, thesis/dissertation. *Entrance requirements:* For doctorate, GRE or MAT, master's degree. Additional exam requirements/recommendations for international students: Required—TOEFL (minimum score 575 paper-based; 91 iBT) or IELTS (minimum score 7). *Application deadline:* For fall admission, 1/31 priority date for domestic and international students. Application fee: $50 ($55 for international students). Electronic applications accepted. *Financial support:* Teaching assistantships with tuition reimbursements, Federal Work-Study, and institutionally sponsored loans available. Financial award application deadline: 1/31. *Faculty research:* Comparative studies of theater, music, and the visual arts. *Unit head:* Charles S. Buchanan, Director, 740-593-9413, E-mail: buchanac@ohio.edu.
Website: http://www.ohiou.edu/interarts/index.htm

**Simon Fraser University,** Office of Graduate Studies and Postdoctoral Fellows, Faculty of Communication, Art and Technology, School for the Contemporary Arts, Vancouver, BC V6B 5K3, Canada. Offers MA, MFA. *Faculty:* 30 full-time (13 women). *Students:* 39 full-time (23 women), 3 part-time (2 women). 59 applicants, 44% accepted, 18 enrolled. In 2016, 20 master's awarded. *Degree requirements:* For master's, thesis or alternative. *Entrance requirements:* For master's, portfolio; minimum GPA of 3.0 (on scale of 4.33) or 3.33 based on last 60 credits of undergraduate courses. Additional exam requirements/recommendations for international students: Recommended—TOEFL (minimum score 580 paper-based; 93 iBT), IELTS (minimum score 7), TWE (minimum score 5). *Application deadline:* For fall admission, 1/23 for domestic and international students. Application fee: $90 ($125 for international students). Electronic applications accepted. *Financial support:* In 2016–17, 31 students received support, including 5 fellowships (averaging $5,200 per year), teaching assistantships (averaging $5,608 per year); research assistantships and scholarships/grants also available. *Faculty research:* Dance theory, screenplays, drawing and painting, acting, electroacoustic music. *Unit head:* Arne Eigenfeldt, Graduate Chair, Fax: 778-782-5907, E-mail: ca-grad-chair@sfu.ca. *Application contact:* Barbara Adler, Graduate Secretary, 778-782-9593, Fax: 778-782-5907, E-mail: mfagrad@sfu.ca.
Website: http://www.sfu.ca/sca

# Section 5
# Film, Television, and Video

This section contains a directory of institutions offering graduate work in film, television, and video. Additional information about programs listed in the directory but not augmented by an in-depth entry may be obtained by writing directly to the dean of a graduate school or chair of a department at the address given in the directory.

For programs offering related work, see also in this book *Art and Art History* and *Communication and Media*. In the other guides in this series:

**Graduate Programs in Engineering & Applied Sciences**
See *Telecommunications*
**Graduate Programs in Business, Education, Information Studies, Law & Social Work**
See *Advertising and Public Relations*

## CONTENTS

# Film, Television, and Video Production

**Academy of Art University,** Graduate Programs, School of Animation and Visual Effects, San Francisco, CA 94105-3410. Offers 3D animation (MFA). *Program availability:* Part-time, 100% online. *Faculty:* 20 full-time (6 women), 64 part-time/adjunct (9 women). *Students:* 297 full-time (138 women), 156 part-time (65 women); includes 73 minority (22 Black or African American, non-Hispanic/Latino; 2 American Indian or Alaska Native, non-Hispanic/Latino; 19 Asian, non-Hispanic/Latino; 24 Hispanic/Latino; 1 Native Hawaiian or other Pacific Islander, non-Hispanic/Latino; 5 Two or more races, non-Hispanic/Latino), 276 international. Average age 29. 109 applicants, 100% accepted, 74 enrolled. In 2016, 120 master's awarded. *Degree requirements:* For master's, final review. *Entrance requirements:* For master's, statement of intent; resume; portfolio/reel; official college transcripts. *Application deadline:* Applications are processed on a rolling basis. Application fee: $50. Electronic applications accepted. *Expenses: Tuition:* Part-time $982 per unit. *Financial support:* Career-related internships or fieldwork, Federal Work-Study, and scholarships/grants available. Financial award application deadline: 8/10; financial award applicants required to submit FAFSA. *Unit head:* 800-544-ARTS, E-mail: info@academyart.edu. *Application contact:* 800-544-ARTS, E-mail: info@academyart.edu. Website: http://www.academyart.edu/animation-school/index.html

**Academy of Art University,** Graduate Programs, School of Motion Pictures and Television, San Francisco, CA 94105-3410. Offers MFA. *Program availability:* Part-time, 100% online. *Faculty:* 9 full-time (1 woman), 48 part-time/adjunct (14 women). *Students:* 185 full-time (87 women), 79 part-time (35 women); includes 41 minority (18 Black or African American, non-Hispanic/Latino; 3 American Indian or Alaska Native, non-Hispanic/Latino; 4 Asian, non-Hispanic/Latino; 11 Hispanic/Latino; 5 Two or more races, non-Hispanic/Latino), 166 international. Average age 30. 58 applicants, 100% accepted, 40 enrolled. In 2016, 83 master's awarded. *Degree requirements:* For master's, final review. *Entrance requirements:* For master's, statement of intent; resume; portfolio/reel; official college transcripts. *Application deadline:* Applications are processed on a rolling basis. Application fee: $50. Electronic applications accepted. *Expenses: Tuition:* Part-time $982 per unit. *Financial support:* Career-related internships or fieldwork, Federal Work-Study, and scholarships/grants available. Financial award application deadline: 8/10; financial award applicants required to submit FAFSA. *Unit head:* 800-544-ARTS, E-mail: info@academyart.edu. *Application contact:* 800-544-ARTS, E-mail: info@academyart.edu. Website: http://www.academyart.edu/film-school/index.html

**Academy of Art University,** Graduate Programs, School of Music Production and Sound Design for Visual Media, San Francisco, CA 94105-3410. Offers music scoring and composition (MA, MFA); sound design (MA, MFA). *Program availability:* Part-time, 100% online. *Faculty:* 4 full-time (0 women), 22 part-time/adjunct (3 women). *Students:* 97 full-time (46 women), 32 part-time (10 women); includes 21 minority (10 Black or African American, non-Hispanic/Latino; 1 American Indian or Alaska Native, non-Hispanic/Latino; 2 Asian, non-Hispanic/Latino; 6 Hispanic/Latino; 1 Native Hawaiian or other Pacific Islander, non-Hispanic/Latino; 1 Two or more races, non-Hispanic/Latino), 86 international. Average age 29. 31 applicants, 100% accepted, 27 enrolled. In 2016, 38 master's awarded. *Degree requirements:* For master's, final review. *Entrance requirements:* For master's, statement of intent; resume; portfolio/reel; official college transcripts. *Application deadline:* Applications are processed on a rolling basis. Application fee: $50. Electronic applications accepted. *Expenses: Tuition:* Part-time $982 per unit. *Financial support:* Career-related internships or fieldwork, Federal Work-Study, and scholarships/grants available. Financial award application deadline: 8/10; financial award applicants required to submit FAFSA. *Unit head:* 800-544-ARTS, E-mail: info@academyart.edu. *Application contact:* 800-544-ARTS, E-mail: info@academyart.edu. Website: http://www.academyart.edu/music-for-visual-media/index.html

**Academy of Art University,** Graduate Programs, School of Writing for Film, Television and Digital Media, San Francisco, CA 94105-3410. Offers MFA. *Program availability:* Part-time, 100% online. *Faculty:* 2 full-time (1 woman), 9 part-time/adjunct (2 women). *Students:* 11 full-time (7 women), 17 part-time (8 women); includes 10 minority (5 Black or African American, non-Hispanic/Latino; 1 American Indian or Alaska Native, non-Hispanic/Latino; 2 Hispanic/Latino; 2 Two or more races, non-Hispanic/Latino), 4 international. Average age 35. 4 applicants, 100% accepted, 3 enrolled. *Degree requirements:* For master's, final review. *Entrance requirements:* For master's, statement of intent; resume; portfolio/reel; official college transcripts. *Application deadline:* Applications are processed on a rolling basis. Application fee: $50. Electronic applications accepted. *Expenses: Tuition:* Part-time $982 per unit. *Financial support:* Career-related internships or fieldwork, Federal Work-Study, and scholarships/grants available. Financial award application deadline: 8/10; financial award applicants required to submit FAFSA. *Unit head:* 800-544-ARTS, E-mail: info@academyart.edu. *Application contact:* 800-544-ARTS, E-mail: info@academyart.edu. Website: http://www.academyart.edu/academics/writing-film-television-digital-media

**American Film Institute Conservatory,** Graduate Program, Los Angeles, CA 90027-1657. Offers cinematography (MFA); directing (MFA); editing (MFA); producing (MFA); production design (MFA); screenwriting (MFA). *Degree requirements:* For master's, thesis. *Entrance requirements:* Additional exam requirements/recommendations for international students: Required—TOEFL (minimum score 600 paper-based; 100 iBT), IELTS (minimum score 7). Electronic applications accepted. *Faculty research:* Film production, TV production.

**American University,** School of Communication, Film and Electronic Media Program, Washington, DC 20016-8001. Offers MFA. *Students:* 13 full-time (9 women), 4 part-time (0 women); includes 8 minority (4 Black or African American, non-Hispanic/Latino; 3 Hispanic/Latino; 1 Two or more races, non-Hispanic/Latino), 1 international. *Degree requirements:* For master's, comprehensive exam, thesis or alternative. *Entrance requirements:* For master's, GRE General Test. Additional exam requirements/recommendations for international students: Required—TOEFL (minimum score 600 paper-based; 100 iBT), IELTS. *Application deadline:* For fall admission, 2/1 priority date for domestic and international students. Applications are processed on a rolling basis. Application fee: $50. Electronic applications accepted. *Expenses: Tuition:* Full-time $28,422; part-time $1579 per credit hour. *Required fees:* $690; $200 per term. Tuition and fees vary according to course load, degree level and program. *Financial support:* Fellowships with partial tuition reimbursements, research assistantships with partial tuition reimbursements, teaching assistantships with partial tuition reimbursements, career-related internships or fieldwork, Federal Work-Study, institutionally sponsored loans, scholarships/grants, tuition waivers (partial), and unspecified assistantships available. Financial award application deadline: 2/1; financial award applicants required to submit FAFSA. *Faculty research:* Documentary film production, social media, media and public policy, visual literacy, new technology. *Unit head:* Prof. Brigid Maher, Director, Film and Media Arts Division, 202-885-2664, Fax: 202-885-2019, E-mail:

bmaher@american.edu. *Application contact:* Leila Hernandez, Program Coordinator, Student Services, 202-885-2040, Fax: 202-885-2019, E-mail: leila@american.edu. Website: http://www.american.edu/soc/film/degrees/MFA-FLEM.cfm

**American University,** School of Communication, Film and Video Program, Washington, DC 20016-8001. Offers film and media arts (MA). *Program availability:* Part-time. *Degree requirements:* For master's, comprehensive exam, thesis or alternative. *Entrance requirements:* Additional exam requirements/recommendations for international students: Required—TOEFL (minimum score 660 paper-based; 100 iBT), IELTS (minimum score 7). *Application deadline:* For fall admission, 2/1 priority date for domestic and international students. Applications are processed on a rolling basis. Application fee: $55. Electronic applications accepted. *Expenses: Tuition:* Full-time $28,422; part-time $1579 per credit hour. *Required fees:* $690; $200 per term. Tuition and fees vary according to course load, degree level and program. *Financial support:* Research assistantships with partial tuition reimbursements, teaching assistantships with partial tuition reimbursements, career-related internships or fieldwork, Federal Work-Study, institutionally sponsored loans, scholarships/grants, tuition waivers (partial), and unspecified assistantships available. Financial award application deadline: 2/1; financial award applicants required to submit FAFSA. *Faculty research:* Documentary film and video production, visual literacy, Eastern European cinema, media and public policy, social media. *Unit head:* Prof. Brigid Maher, Director, Film and Media Arts Division, 202-885-2664, Fax: 202-885-2019, E-mail: bmaher@american.edu. *Application contact:* Leila Hernandez, Program Coordinator, Student Services, 202-885-2040, Fax: 202-885-2019, E-mail: leila@american.edu.

**American University,** School of Communication, Weekend Programs in Communication, Washington, DC 20016-8001. Offers journalism and digital storytelling (MA); producing film, TV and video (MA). *Accreditation:* ACEJMC. *Program availability:* Part-time, evening/weekend. *Students:* 66 part-time (41 women); includes 45 minority (31 Black or African American, non-Hispanic/Latino; 4 Asian, non-Hispanic/Latino; 7 Hispanic/Latino; 3 Two or more races, non-Hispanic/Latino), 1 international. 111 applicants, 31% accepted, 19 enrolled. *Degree requirements:* For master's, comprehensive exam, thesis or alternative. *Entrance requirements:* Additional exam requirements/recommendations for international students: Required—TOEFL (minimum score 600 paper-based; 100 iBT). *Application deadline:* For fall admission, 8/1 for domestic students. Applications are processed on a rolling basis. Application fee: $55. Electronic applications accepted. *Expenses: Tuition:* Full-time $28,422; part-time $1579 per credit hour. *Required fees:* $690; $200 per term. Tuition and fees vary according to course load, degree level and program. *Financial support:* Institutionally sponsored loans and tuition waivers available. Financial award applicants required to submit FAFSA. *Unit head:* Christine Rials, Assistant Director for Graduate Admissions, 202-885-2040, E-mail: crials@american.edu. *Application contact:* Christine Rials, Assistant Director for Graduate Admissions, 202-885-2040, E-mail: crials@american.edu. Website: http://american.edu/soc/admissions/weekend.cfm

**Arizona State University at the Tempe campus,** College of Liberal Arts and Sciences, Department of English, Program in Film and Media Studies, Tempe, AZ 85287-0402. Offers American media and popular culture (MAS). *Program availability:* Part-time, evening/weekend, online learning. *Degree requirements:* For master's, integrated project. *Entrance requirements:* For master's, minimum GPA of 3.0 or equivalent in last 2 years of work leading to bachelor's degree. Additional exam requirements/recommendations for international students: Required—TOEFL, IELTS, or PTE. Electronic applications accepted. *Expenses:* Contact institution.

**ArtCenter College of Design,** Graduate Film Program, Pasadena, CA 91103. Offers MFA. *Accreditation:* NASAD. *Degree requirements:* For master's, thesis. *Entrance requirements:* For master's, portfolio. Additional exam requirements/recommendations for international students: Required—TOEFL (minimum score 100 iBT), IELTS (minimum score 7). Electronic applications accepted.

**The Art Institute of California–San Francisco, a campus of Argosy University,** Program in Computer Animation, San Francisco, CA 94102-4928. Offers MFA.

**Bob Jones University,** Graduate Programs, Greenville, SC 29614. Offers accountancy (MS); Bible (MA); Bible translation (MA); Biblical studies (Certificate); broadcast management (MS); business administration (MBA); church history (MA, PhD); church ministries (MA); church music (MM); cinema and video production (MA); counseling (MS); curriculum and instruction (Ed D); divinity (M Div); dramatic production (MA); educational leadership (MS, Ed D, Ed S); elementary education (M Ed, MAT); English (M Ed, MA, MAT); fine arts (MA); graphic design (MA); history (M Ed, MA); illustration (MA); interpretative speech (MA); mathematics (M Ed, MAT); medical missions (Certificate); ministry (MM, D Min); multi-categorical special education (M Ed, MAT); music (M Ed); New Testament interpretation (PhD); Old Testament interpretation (PhD); orchestral instrument performance (MM); organ performance (MM); pastoral studies (MA); personnel services (MS, Ed S); piano pedagogy (MM); piano performance (MM); platform arts (MA); radio and television broadcasting (MS); rhetoric and public address (MA); secondary education (M Ed); studio art (MA); teaching Bible (MA); theology (MA, PhD); voice performance (MM); youth ministries (MA); M Div/MM.

**Boston University,** College of Communication, Department of Film and Television, Boston, MA 02215. Offers MFA, MS. *Program availability:* Part-time. *Faculty:* 17 full-time, 25 part-time/adjunct. *Students:* 86 full-time (47 women), 13 part-time (9 women); includes 27 minority (7 Black or African American, non-Hispanic/Latino; 2 American Indian or Alaska Native, non-Hispanic/Latino; 5 Asian, non-Hispanic/Latino; 9 Hispanic/Latino; 4 Two or more races, non-Hispanic/Latino), 16 international. Average age 26. 352 applicants, 41% accepted, 67 enrolled. In 2016, 31 master's awarded. *Degree requirements:* For master's, thesis. *Entrance requirements:* For master's, GRE General Test, resume, writing and creative samples, letters of recommendation. Additional exam requirements/recommendations for international students: Required—TOEFL (minimum score 600 paper-based; 100 iBT), IELTS (minimum score 7). *Application deadline:* For fall admission, 5/1 for domestic and international students. Applications are processed on a rolling basis. Application fee: $95. Electronic applications accepted. *Financial support:* Research assistantships, teaching assistantships with partial tuition reimbursements, career-related internships or fieldwork, Federal Work-Study, institutionally sponsored loans, scholarships/grants, and unspecified assistantships available. Support available to part-time students. Financial award application deadline: 5/1; financial award applicants required to submit FAFSA. *Unit head:* Paul Schneider, Chairman, 617-353-3483, Fax: 617-353-1084, E-mail: ftvchair@bu.edu. *Application contact:* Haley Nielsen, Administrator of Admission and Financial Aid, 617-353-3481, E-mail: comgrad@bu.edu. Website: http://www.bu.edu/com/academics/film-tv/

**Bowling Green State University,** Graduate College, College of Arts and Sciences, Department of Theatre and Film, Bowling Green, OH 43403. Offers MA, PhD.

*Film, Television, and Video Production*

*Accreditation:* NAST. *Program availability:* Part-time. Terminal master's awarded for partial completion of doctoral program. *Degree requirements:* For master's, thesis or alternative; for doctorate, comprehensive exam, thesis/dissertation, 9 hour research tool. *Entrance requirements:* For master's and doctorate, GRE General Test. Additional exam requirements/recommendations for international students: Required—TOEFL. *Application deadline:* For fall admission, 1/15 for domestic students. Application fee: $30. Electronic applications accepted. *Financial support:* Fellowships with full tuition reimbursements, research assistantships with full tuition reimbursements, teaching assistantships with full tuition reimbursements, Federal Work-Study, and unspecified assistantships available. Financial award applicants required to submit FAFSA. *Faculty research:* Theatre history, dramatic theory, cultural studies, performance studies, American theatre history. *Unit head:* Dr. Lesa Lockford, Chair, 419-372-2222, Fax: 419-372-7186, E-mail: theatrefilm@bgsu.edu. *Application contact:* Dr. Jonathan Chambers, Graduate Coordinator, 419-372-9618.

**Brigham Young University,** Graduate Studies, College of Fine Arts and Communications, Department of Theatre and Media Arts, Provo, UT 84602-6404. Offers MA. *Accreditation:* NAST. *Program availability:* Evening/weekend. *Faculty:* 18 full-time (6 women). *Students:* 5 full-time (2 women); includes 1 minority (Asian, non-Hispanic/Latino). Average age 31. In 2016, 6 master's awarded. *Degree requirements:* For master's, comprehensive exam, thesis, 32 hours, oral defense. *Entrance requirements:* For master's, GRE, two samples of scholarly writing, letter of intent, three letters of recommendation. Additional exam requirements/recommendations for international students: Required—TOEFL (minimum score 580 paper-based; 85 iBT). *Application deadline:* For fall admission, 4/1 priority date for domestic and international students. Application fee: $50. Electronic applications accepted. *Expenses: Tuition:* Full-time $6680; part-time $393 per credit. Tuition and fees vary according to course load, program and student's religious affiliation. *Financial support:* In 2016–17, 6 students received support, including 6 teaching assistantships with full and partial tuition reimbursements available; research assistantships, career-related internships or fieldwork, scholarships/grants, and unspecified assistantships also available. Support available to part-time students. *Faculty research:* History, literary and screen theory, curatorial studies, critical race theory, popular culture, performance philosophy, women's studies, and media literacy. *Unit head:* Dr. Megan Sanborn Jones, Graduate Coordinator, 801-422-1321, E-mail: msjones@byu.edu. *Application contact:* Lindsi Michelle Neilson, Graduate Secretary, 801-422-3750, E-mail: lindsi_neilson@byu.edu. Website: http://cfac.byu.edu/departments/tma

**Brooklyn College of the City University of New York,** School of Visual, Media and Performing Arts, Department of Television and Radio, Brooklyn, NY 11210-2889. Offers media studies (MS); television production (MFA). *Program availability:* Part-time, evening/weekend. *Degree requirements:* For master's, comprehensive exam. *Entrance requirements:* For master's, GRE General Test or MAT, 12 credits in television/radio with a minimum B average, 2 letters of recommendation. Additional exam requirements/recommendations for international students: Required—TOEFL (minimum score 580 paper-based; 92 iBT). Electronic applications accepted. *Faculty research:* Criticism, research methods, audience behavior, policy and regulation, program history, international television and radio.

**Brooklyn College of the City University of New York,** School of Visual, Media and Performing Arts, Feirstein Graduate School of Cinema, Brooklyn, NY 11210-2889. Offers cinema arts (MFA); cinema studies (MA).

**California College of the Arts,** Graduate Programs, Fine Arts Programs, San Francisco, CA 94107. Offers ceramics (MFA); film/video/performance (MFA); glass (MFA); interdisciplinary studies (MFA); jewelry/metal arts (MFA); media studies (MFA); painting/drawing (MFA); photography (MFA); printmaking (MFA); sculpture (MFA); textiles (MFA); wood/furniture (MFA). *Accreditation:* NASAD. *Faculty:* 23 full-time (14 women), 17 part-time/adjunct (12 women). *Students:* 75 full-time (55 women); includes 20 minority (7 Black or African American, non-Hispanic/Latino; 2 American Indian or Alaska Native, non-Hispanic/Latino; 6 Asian, non-Hispanic/Latino; 5 Hispanic/Latino), 15 international. Average age 29. 224 applicants, 54% accepted, 43 enrolled. In 2016, 27 master's awarded. *Degree requirements:* For master's, thesis, exhibit. *Entrance requirements:* For master's, appropriate bachelor's degree, portfolio, resume, 2 letters of recommendation, transcript. Additional exam requirements/recommendations for international students: Required—TOEFL, IELTS, or PTE. *Application deadline:* For fall admission, 1/10 for domestic and international students. Applications are processed on a rolling basis. Application fee: $70. Electronic applications accepted. *Expenses:* $1,641 per unit, $49,230 per year tuition; $490 fees. *Financial support:* In 2016–17, fellowships (averaging $42,000 per year), teaching assistantships (averaging $2,000 per year) were awarded; career-related internships or fieldwork, Federal Work-Study, scholarships/ grants, health care benefits, and unspecified assistantships also available. Financial award application deadline: 7/31; financial award applicants required to submit FAFSA. *Unit head:* James Gobel, Chair, 415-551-9214, Fax: 415-703-9539, E-mail: jgobel@cca.edu. *Application contact:* Wes Fanelli, Assistant Director of Graduate Admissions, 415-703-9533, Fax: 415-703-9539, E-mail: wfanelli@cca.edu.

**California Institute of the Arts,** School of Film/Video, Valencia, CA 91355-2340. Offers experimental animation (MFA); film directing (MFA, Adv C); film/video (Adv C). *Entrance requirements:* For master's, portfolio. Additional exam requirements/recommendations for international students: Required—TOEFL. Electronic applications accepted. *Faculty research:* Experimental and character animation, experimental film/video, video graphics.

**California State University, Fullerton,** Graduate Studies, College of Communications, Department of Cinema and Television Arts, Fullerton, CA 92834-9480. Offers screenwriting (MFA). *Degree requirements:* For master's, final project. *Entrance requirements:* For master's, bachelor's degree from accredited university; samples of competent and creative writing, such as original screenplays, teleplays, theatrical plays, or other narrative work; essay; three letters of recommendation. Application fee: $55. Electronic applications accepted. *Expenses:* Tuition, state resident: full-time $3369; part-time $1953 per unit. Tuition, nonresident: full-time $3915; part-time $2499 per unit. Tuition and fees vary according to course load, degree level and program. *Unit head:* Garrett Hart, Chair, 657-278-4635, E-mail: gshart@fullerton.edu. *Application contact:* Admissions/Applications, 657-278-2371. Website: http://communications.fullerton.edu/ctva/

**California State University, Northridge,** Graduate Studies, College of Arts, Media, and Communication, Department of Cinema and Television Arts, Northridge, CA 91330. Offers screenwriting (MA). *Faculty:* 14 full-time (6 women), 48 part-time/adjunct (18 women). *Students:* 27 full-time (11 women), 5 part-time; includes 8 minority (1 Asian, non-Hispanic/Latino; 4 Hispanic/Latino; 3 Two or more races, non-Hispanic/Latino), 1 international. Average age 39. 47 applicants, 32% accepted, 13 enrolled. *Entrance requirements:* For master's, GRE (if cumulative undergraduate GPA less than 3.0). Application fee: $55. *Expenses:* Tuition, state resident: full-time $4152. *Unit head:* Jon Stahl, Chair, 818-677-3192. Website: http://www.ctva.csun.edu/

**Carleton University,** Faculty of Graduate Studies, Faculty of Arts and Social Sciences, School for Studies in Art and Culture, Program in Film Studies, Ottawa, ON K1S 5B6,

Canada. Offers MA. *Degree requirements:* For master's, thesis. *Entrance requirements:* For master's, honors degree. Additional exam requirements/recommendations for international students: Required—TOEFL.

**Carnegie Mellon University,** College of Fine Arts, School of Drama, Pittsburgh, PA 15213-3891. Offers design (MFA); directing (MFA); dramatic writing (MFA); production technology and management (MFA); video and media design (MFA). *Degree requirements:* For master's, thesis (for some programs). *Entrance requirements:* For master's, audition, portfolio review, interview. Additional exam requirements/ recommendations for international students: Required—TOEFL. *Faculty research:* Developing voice and speech compact disc.

**Carnegie Mellon University,** School of Computer Science and College of Fine Arts, Program in Entertainment Technology, Pittsburgh, PA 15213-3891. Offers MET.

**Central Michigan University,** College of Graduate Studies, College of Communication and Fine Arts, School of Broadcasting and Cinematic Arts, Mount Pleasant, MI 48859. Offers electronic media management (MA); electronic media production (MA); electronic media studies (MA); film theory and criticism (MA). *Program availability:* Part-time. *Degree requirements:* For master's, thesis or alternative. *Entrance requirements:* For master's, undergraduate degree in broadcasting, film studies, or an associated discipline with minimum GPA of 2.7. Electronic applications accepted. *Faculty research:* Multimedia production, film history and criticism, writing and promotions, international broadcasting and media systems, history of American broadcasting.

**Chapman University,** Dodge College of Film and Media Arts, Orange, CA 92866. Offers documentary filmmaking (MFA); film and television producing (MFA); film production (MFA); film studies (MA); production design (MFA); screenwriting (MFA); JD/ MFA; MBA/MFA. *Faculty:* 44 full-time (11 women), 69 part-time/adjunct (26 women). *Students:* 241 full-time (115 women), 6 part-time (1 woman); includes 45 minority (13 Black or African American, non-Hispanic/Latino; 8 Asian, non-Hispanic/Latino; 19 Hispanic/Latino; 5 Two or more races, non-Hispanic/Latino), 99 international. Average age 26. 467 applicants, 50% accepted, 113 enrolled. In 2016, 79 master's awarded. *Degree requirements:* For master's, thesis. *Entrance requirements:* For master's, GRE (if undergraduate GPA less than 3.0), minimum undergraduate GPA of 2.5, creative portfolio. Additional exam requirements/recommendations for international students: Required—TOEFL (minimum score 550 paper-based, 80 iBT), IELTS (6.5), PTE Academic (53), or CAE. *Application deadline:* For fall admission, 12/1 for domestic students. Application fee: $60. Electronic applications accepted. *Expenses:* Contact institution. *Financial support:* Fellowships, Federal Work-Study, and scholarships/grants available. Financial award applicants required to submit FAFSA. *Unit head:* Robert Bassett, Dean, 714-997-6715, E-mail: bassett@chapman.edu. *Application contact:* Lauren Kacura, Assistant Director of Admissions, 714-744-7856, E-mail: kacura@chapman.edu.

**Chatham University,** Program in Film and Digital Technology, Pittsburgh, PA 15232-2826. Offers MFA. *Program availability:* Part-time, evening/weekend. *Degree requirements:* For master's, thesis, capstone project. *Entrance requirements:* Additional exam requirements/recommendations for international students: Required—TOEFL (minimum score 600 paper-based; 100 iBT), IELTS (minimum score 7), TWE. Electronic applications accepted. Application fee is waived when completed online. *Expenses: Tuition:* Full-time $16,254; part-time $903 per credit hour. *Required fees:* $468; $26 per credit hour.

**Columbia College Chicago,** Graduate School, Department of Cinema Art and Science, Chicago, IL 60605-1996. Offers cinema directing (MFA); creative producing (MFA). *Program availability:* Part-time. *Degree requirements:* For master's, thesis, film project. *Entrance requirements:* For master's, self-assessment essay, work samples, interview, case study. Additional exam requirements/recommendations for international students: Required—TOEFL (minimum score 550 paper-based). Electronic applications accepted.

**Columbia University,** School of the Arts, Film Program, New York, NY 10027. Offers creative producing (MFA); directing (MFA); film studies (MA); screenwriting (MFA). *Degree requirements:* For master's, thesis. *Entrance requirements:* For master's, 3 letters of recommendation, writing sample, complete a scene, feature film treatment (optional visual submission). Additional exam requirements/recommendations for international students: Required—TOEFL (minimum score 600 paper-based; 100 iBT). Electronic applications accepted.

See Display on page 147 and Close-Up on page 201.

**Concordia University,** School of Graduate Studies, Faculty of Fine Arts, Department of Studio Arts, Montréal, QC H3G 1M8, Canada. Offers studio arts (MFA), including fibers and material practices, film production, intermedia, painting and drawing, photography, print media, sculpture. *Degree requirements:* For master's, thesis or alternative. *Entrance requirements:* For master's, portfolio.

**Concordia University,** School of Graduate Studies, Faculty of Fine Arts, Mel Hoppenheim School of Cinema, Montréal, QC H3G 1M8, Canada. Offers film and moving image studies (PhD); film production (MFA); film studies (MA).

**DePaul University,** College of Computing and Digital Media, Chicago, IL 60604. Offers animation (MA, MFA); business information technology (MS); cinema (MFA); cinema production (MS); computational finance (MS); computer and information sciences (PhD); computer game development (MS); computer information and network security (MS); computer science (MS); e-commerce technology (MS); health informatics (MS); human-computer interaction (MS); information systems (MS); information technology project management (MS); network engineering and management (MS); predictive analytics (MS); screenwriting (MFA); software engineering (MS); JD/MS. *Program availability:* Part-time, evening/weekend, online learning. *Degree requirements:* For master's, thesis (for some programs); for doctorate, comprehensive exam, thesis/dissertation. *Entrance requirements:* For master's, GRE or GMAT (for MS in computational finance only), bachelor's degree, resume (MS in predictive analytics only), IT experience (MS in information technology project management only), portfolio review (all MFA programs and MA in animation); for doctorate, GRE, master's degree in computer science. Additional exam requirements/recommendations for international students: Required— TOEFL (minimum score 590 paper-based; 80 iBT), IELTS (minimum score 6.5), PTE (minimum score 53). Electronic applications accepted. *Expenses:* Contact institution. *Faculty research:* Data mining, computer science, human-computer interaction, security, animation and film.

**Drexel University,** Westphal College of Media Arts and Design, Program in Television Management, Philadelphia, PA 19104-2875. Offers MS, MS/MBA. *Faculty:* 3 part-time/ adjunct (2 women). *Students:* 11 full-time (4 women), 40 part-time (25 women); includes 18 minority (13 Black or African American, non-Hispanic/Latino; 5 Hispanic/Latino), 15 international. Average age 30. In 2016, 13 master's awarded. *Expenses: Tuition:* Full-time $32,184; part-time $1192 per credit hour. *Required fees:* $280. Tuition and fees vary according to campus/location and program. *Unit head:* College Recruitment Office, 215-895-1675, Fax: 215-895-5838. *Application contact:* Graduate Admissions Office, 215-895-6700, E-mail: enroll@drexel.edu.

See Display on page 63 and Close-Up on page 99.

*Film, Television, and Video Production*

**Emerson College,** Graduate Studies, School of the Arts, Department of Visual and Media Arts, Program in Writing for Film and Television, Boston, MA 02116-4624. Offers MFA. *Faculty:* 85 full-time (48 women), 6 part-time/adjunct (3 women). *Students:* 13 full-time (7 women). Average age 34. 37 applicants, 65% accepted, 12 enrolled. *Entrance requirements:* Additional exam requirements/recommendations for international students: Required—TOEFL (minimum score 577 paper-based), IELTS (minimum score 7). *Application deadline:* Applications are processed on a rolling basis. Application fee: $60 ($75 for international students). Electronic applications accepted. *Financial support:* In 2016–17, 11 students received support, including 11 fellowships (averaging $5,700 per year). *Application contact:* Leanda Ferland, Director of Graduate Admission, 617-824-8610, Fax: 617-824-8614, E-mail: gradapp@emerson.edu.
Website: http://www.emerson.edu/visual-and-media-arts/low-residency-mfa

**Florida Atlantic University,** Dorothy F. Schmidt College of Arts and Letters, School of Communication and Multimedia Studies, Boca Raton, FL 33431-0991. Offers communication studies (MA); film and video (Certificate); media, technology and entertainment (MFA). *Program availability:* Part-time. *Faculty:* 25 full-time (8 women). *Students:* 21 full-time (15 women), 17 part-time (9 women); includes 16 minority (6 Black or African American, non-Hispanic/Latino; 1 Asian, non-Hispanic/Latino; 9 Hispanic/Latino), 3 international. Average age 33. 39 applicants, 72% accepted, 14 enrolled. In 2016, 8 master's awarded. *Degree requirements:* For master's, one foreign language, comprehensive exam (for some programs), thesis (for some programs). *Entrance requirements:* For master's, GRE General Test, minimum GPA of 3.0, essay, letters of recommendation. *Application deadline:* For fall admission, 7/1 priority date for domestic students, 4/1 for international students; for spring admission, 11/1 for domestic students, 10/1 for international students. Applications are processed on a rolling basis. Application fee: $30. Electronic applications accepted. *Expenses:* Tuition, state resident: full-time $7392; part-time $369.82 per credit hour. Tuition, nonresident: full-time $19,432; part-time $1024.81 per credit hour. *Financial support:* Teaching assistantships with partial tuition reimbursements, Federal Work-Study, institutionally sponsored loans, scholarships/grants, and unspecified assistantships available. Support available to part-time students. Financial award application deadline: 3/1; financial award applicants required to submit FAFSA. *Faculty research:* Cultural studies, gender studies, film, communication theory, journalism, new media. *Unit head:* Dr. David Williams, Director, 561-297-0045, Fax: 561-297-2615, E-mail: dcwill@fau.edu. *Application contact:* Dr. Eric M. Freedman, Graduate Coordinator, 561-297-2534, Fax: 561-297-2615, E-mail: efreedma@fau.edu.
Website: http://www.fau.edu/scms/

⭐ **Florida State University,** The Graduate School, College of Motion Picture Arts, Tallahassee, FL 32306-2350. Offers film production (MFA); screenwriting (MFA). *Faculty:* 24 full-time (7 women), 3 part-time/adjunct (1 woman). *Students:* 59 full-time (25 women); includes 29 minority (9 Black or African American, non-Hispanic/Latino; 13 Asian, non-Hispanic/Latino; 4 Hispanic/Latino; 3 Two or more races, non-Hispanic/Latino). Average age 25. 187 applicants, 16% accepted, 30 enrolled. In 2016, 30 master's awarded. *Degree requirements:* For master's, thesis, thesis film project. *Entrance requirements:* For master's, GRE (for MFA in writing), minimum GPA of 3.0, resume, statement of purpose, writing sample, 3 letters of recommendation, creative portfolio. Additional exam requirements/recommendations for international students: Required—TOEFL (minimum score 550 paper-based; 80 iBT). *Application deadline:* For fall admission, 12/1 for domestic and international students. Application fee: $30. Electronic applications accepted. *Expenses:* $44,639 in-state (for production degree); $30,739 in-state (for writing degree). *Financial support:* In 2016–17, 20 students received support, including 20 teaching assistantships with partial tuition reimbursements available (averaging $5,500 per year); institutionally sponsored loans and unspecified assistantships also available. Financial award application deadline: 12/

1; financial award applicants required to submit FAFSA. *Faculty research:* Producing, screenwriting, directing, cinematography, editing. *Unit head:* Reb Braddock, Interim Dean, 850-644-0453, Fax: 850-644-2626. *Application contact:* Gloria McElroy, Staff Director of Admissions and Recruitment, 850-644-8524, Fax: 850-644-2626, E-mail: gmcelroy@fsu.edu.
Website: http://film.fsu.edu/

**See Display below and Close-Up on page 225.**

**Georgia State University,** College of Arts and Sciences, Department of Communication, Atlanta, GA 30302-3083. Offers film, video, and digital imaging (MA), including critical studies, production, screenwriting; human communication and social influence (MA); mass communication (MA); media and society (PhD); moving image studies (PhD); public communication (PhD); rhetoric and politics (PhD). *Program availability:* Part-time. *Faculty:* 57 full-time (34 women). *Students:* 113 full-time (69 women), 56 part-time (33 women); includes 59 minority (37 Black or African American, non-Hispanic/Latino; 1 American Indian or Alaska Native, non-Hispanic/Latino; 2 Asian, non-Hispanic/Latino; 9 Hispanic/Latino; 10 Two or more races, non-Hispanic/Latino), 18 international. Average age 32. 134 applicants, 58% accepted, 47 enrolled. In 2016, 22 master's, 11 doctorates awarded. *Degree requirements:* For master's, variable foreign language requirement, thesis (for some programs); for doctorate, comprehensive exam, thesis/dissertation. *Entrance requirements:* For master's and doctorate, GRE. Additional exam requirements/recommendations for international students: Required—TOEFL (minimum score 550 paper-based; 80 iBT), IELTS (minimum score 6.5). *Application deadline:* For fall admission, 2/10 for domestic and international students; for spring admission, 10/15 for domestic and international students. Application fee: $50. Electronic applications accepted. *Expenses:* Tuition, state resident: full-time $6876; part-time $382 per credit hour. Tuition, nonresident: full-time $22,374; part-time $1243 per credit hour. *Required fees:* $2128; $1064 per term. Part-time tuition and fees vary according to course load and program. *Financial support:* In 2016–17, fellowships with tuition reimbursements (averaging $15,000 per year), teaching assistantships with tuition reimbursements (averaging $15,000 per year) were awarded; career-related internships or fieldwork and unspecified assistantships also available. Financial award applicants required to submit FAFSA. *Faculty research:* New media, mass media and journalism, rhetoric, film and media studies, film production. *Unit head:* Dr. Greg Lisby, Chair, 404-413-5636, Fax: 404-413-5634, E-mail: glisby@gsu.edu.
Website: http://communication.gsu.edu

**Governors State University,** College of Arts and Sciences, Program in Independent Film and Digital Imaging, University Park, IL 60484. Offers MFA. *Program availability:* Part-time. *Faculty:* 91 full-time (43 women), 125 part-time/adjunct (64 women). *Students:* 11 full-time (6 women), 10 part-time (6 women); includes 11 minority (9 Black or African American, non-Hispanic/Latino; 1 Hispanic/Latino; 1 Two or more races, non-Hispanic/Latino), 2 international. Average age 39. 10 applicants, 70% accepted, 4 enrolled. In 2016, 8 master's awarded. *Entrance requirements:* Additional exam requirements/recommendations for international students: Required—TOEFL (minimum score 550 paper-based; 80 iBT), IELTS. *Application deadline:* For fall admission, 4/1 for domestic students. Application fee: $50. Electronic applications accepted. *Expenses:* $307 per credit hour; $38 per term or $76 per credit hour fees. *Financial support:* Application deadline: 5/1; applicants required to submit FAFSA. *Unit head:* Lori Montalbano, Chair of Division of Communication, Visual and Performing Arts, 708-235-2802, E-mail: lmontalbano@govst.edu. *Application contact:* Yakeea Daniels, Assistant Vice President for Enrollment Services/Director of Admission, 708-534-4510, E-mail: ydaniels@govst.edu.

**Hollins University,** Graduate Programs, Program in Screenwriting and Film Studies, Roanoke, VA 24020. Offers screenwriting (MFA); screenwriting and film studies (MA).

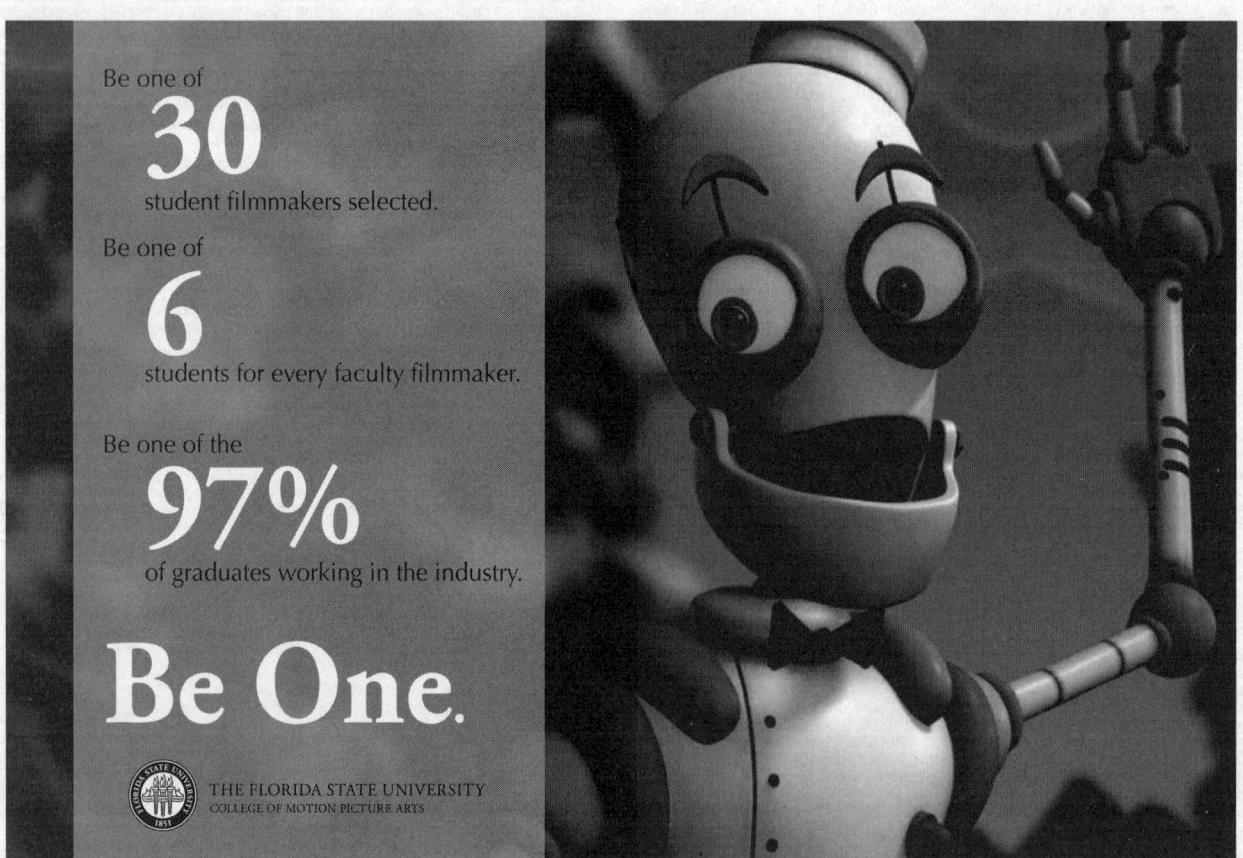

Be one of
**30**
student filmmakers selected.

Be one of
**6**
students for every faculty filmmaker.

Be one of the
**97%**
of graduates working in the industry.

**Be One.**

THE FLORIDA STATE UNIVERSITY
COLLEGE OF MOTION PICTURE ARTS

Program offered during summer only. *Program availability:* Part-time. *Degree requirements:* For master's, one foreign language, comprehensive exam, thesis. *Entrance requirements:* For master's, letters of recommendation, portfolio. Additional exam requirements/recommendations for international students: Required—TOEFL (minimum score 550 paper-based; 80 iBT), IELTS (minimum score 6.5). *Application deadline:* For summer admission, 2/15 for domestic and international students. Application fee: $40. Electronic applications accepted. *Expenses:* $830 per credit hour. *Financial support:* Fellowships, Federal Work-Study, institutionally sponsored loans, and scholarships/grants available. Support available to part-time students. Financial award application deadline: 2/15; financial award applicants required to submit FAFSA. *Faculty research:* Censorship, minorities in film, writing for television, new media. *Unit head:* Dr. Tim Albaugh, Director, 540-362-6575, E-mail: hugrad@hollins.edu. *Application contact:* Cathy S. Koon, Manager of Graduate Programs, 540-362-6326, Fax: 540-362-6288, E-mail: ckoon@hollins.edu.
Website: https://www.hollins.edu/academics/graduate-degrees/mfa-screenwriting-film-studies/

**Howard University,** School of Communications, Department of Radio, Television and Film, Washington, DC 20059-0002. Offers film (MFA). *Program availability:* Part-time. *Degree requirements:* For master's, thesis optional. *Entrance requirements:* For master's, GRE General Test, minimum GPA of 3.0.

**Johns Hopkins University,** Zanvyl Krieger School of Arts and Sciences, Advanced Academic Programs, Program in Film and Media, Baltimore, MD 21218. Offers MA. Students choose two concentrations from business, sound, and writing. *Program availability:* Part-time.

**Lindenwood University,** Graduate Programs, School of Arts, Media, and Communications, St. Charles, MO 63301-1695. Offers cinema and media arts (MFA). *Program availability:* Part-time. *Faculty:* 17 full-time (6 women), 6 part-time/adjunct (5 women). *Students:* 15 full-time (8 women), 5 part-time (3 women); includes 4 minority (2 Black or African American, non-Hispanic/Latino; 1 Hispanic/Latino; 1 Two or more races, non-Hispanic/Latino), 3 international. Average age 30. 16 applicants, 56% accepted, 6 enrolled. In 2016, 8 master's awarded. *Degree requirements:* For master's, thesis (for some programs), minimum cumulative GPA of 3.0. *Entrance requirements:* For master's, audition or interview, minimum GPA of 3.0, portfolio, letter of recommendation. Additional exam requirements/recommendations for international students: Required—TOEFL (minimum score 550 paper-based; 80 iBT); Recommended—IELTS (minimum score 6.5). *Application deadline:* For fall admission, 8/28 priority date for domestic and international students; for spring admission, 1/8 for domestic students, 1/8 priority date for international students; for summer admission, 6/5 priority date for domestic and international students. Applications are processed on a rolling basis. Application fee: $30 ($100 for international students). Electronic applications accepted. *Expenses:* Tuition: Full-time $15,672; part-time $453 per credit hour. *Required fees:* $205 per semester. Tuition and fees vary according to course level, course load and degree level. *Financial support:* In 2016–17, 12 students received support. Career-related internships or fieldwork, institutionally sponsored loans, scholarships/grants, tuition waivers (partial), and unspecified assistantships available. Financial award application deadline: 6/30; financial award applicants required to submit FAFSA. *Unit head:* Dr. Joseph Alsobrook, Dean, School of Arts, Media, and Communications, 636-949-4164, Fax: 636-949-4910, E-mail: jalsobrook@lindenwood.edu. *Application contact:* Tyler Kostich, Director, Evening and Graduate Admissions, 636-949-4138, Fax: 636-949-4109, E-mail: adultadmissions@lindenwood.edu.
Website: http://www.lindenwood.edu/academics/academic-schools/school-of-arts-media-and-communications/

**Lipscomb University,** Program in Film and Creative Media, Nashville, TN 37204-3951. Offers writer/director (MFA); MFA/MBA. *Program availability:* Part-time, evening/weekend. *Faculty:* 5 full-time (1 woman), 4 part-time/adjunct (1 woman). *Students:* 21 full-time (14 women), 6 part-time (5 women); includes 12 minority (10 Black or African American, non-Hispanic/Latino; 1 Hispanic/Latino; 1 Two or more races, non-Hispanic/Latino), 1 international. Average age 30. 21 applicants, 48% accepted, 8 enrolled. In 2016, 7 master's awarded. *Degree requirements:* For master's, professional practicum, portfolio. *Entrance requirements:* For master's, GRE or MAT, 2 references, resume, video portfolio. Additional exam requirements/recommendations for international students: Required—TOEFL (minimum score 570 paper-based; 80 iBT). *Application deadline:* Applications are processed on a rolling basis. Application fee: $50 ($75 for international students). Electronic applications accepted. *Expenses:* $966 per hour. *Financial support:* Unspecified assistantships available. Financial award applicants required to submit FAFSA. *Unit head:* David DeBorde, Director, 615-966-7111, E-mail: david.deborde@lipscomb.edu. *Application contact:* Josh Link, Recruiting and Marketing Coordinator, 615-966-6005, E-mail: josh.link@lipscomb.edu.
Website: http://www.lipscomb.edu/cinematicarts/graduate-programs

**Loyola Marymount University,** School of Film and Television, Department of Production, Program in Film and Television Production, Los Angeles, CA 90045-8347. Offers MFA. *Students:* 77 full-time (29 women), 1 part-time (0 women); includes 22 minority (8 Black or African American, non-Hispanic/Latino; 3 Asian, non-Hispanic/Latino; 8 Hispanic/Latino; 3 Two or more races, non-Hispanic/Latino), 37 international. Average age 26. 150 applicants, 42% accepted, 29 enrolled. In 2016, 24 master's awarded. *Degree requirements:* For master's, thesis, film. *Entrance requirements:* For master's, GRE, creative work, 2 letters of recommendation, personal statement. Additional exam requirements/recommendations for international students: Required—TOEFL (minimum score 600 paper-based; 100 iBT). *Application deadline:* For fall admission, 1/10 for domestic students. Application fee: $50. Electronic applications accepted. *Financial support:* In 2016–17, 58 students received support, including 9 research assistantships, 11 teaching assistantships; career-related internships or fieldwork and scholarships/grants also available. Support available to part-time students. Financial award application deadline: 6/30; financial award applicants required to submit FAFSA. *Unit head:* Kennedy Wheatley, Program Director, 310-338-3765, E-mail: kwheatle@lmu.edu. *Application contact:* Chake H. Kouyoumjian, Associate Dean of Graduate Studies, 310-338-2721, E-mail: ckouyoum@lmu.edu.
Website: http://sftv.lmu.edu/academics/graduateprograms/filmandtvproduction/

**Loyola Marymount University,** School of Film and Television, Department of Screenwriting, Program in Writing and Producing for Television, Los Angeles, CA 90045-2659. Offers MFA. *Students:* 45 full-time (30 women); includes 19 minority (8 Black or African American, non-Hispanic/Latino; 1 American Indian or Alaska Native, non-Hispanic/Latino; 7 Hispanic/Latino; 3 Two or more races, non-Hispanic/Latino), 2 international. Average age 26. 44 applicants, 55% accepted, 13 enrolled. In 2016, 11 master's awarded. *Entrance requirements:* For master's, GRE, personal statement, letters of recommendation, creative work or writing sample. Additional exam requirements/recommendations for international students: Required—TOEFL (minimum score 600 paper-based; 100 iBT). *Application deadline:* For fall admission, 1/10 for domestic students. Application fee: $50. Electronic applications accepted. *Financial support:* In 2016–17, 30 students received support, including 1 research assistantship, 3 teaching assistantships. Financial award application deadline: 6/30; financial award applicants required to submit FAFSA. *Unit head:* Karol Hoeffner, Graduate Director, 310-338-3033, E-mail: khoeffne@lmu.edu. *Application contact:* Chake H. Kouyoumjian,

Associate Dean of Graduate Studies, 310-338-2721, E-mail: ckouyoum@lmu.edu.
Website: http://sftv.lmu.edu/academics/graduateprograms/writingandproducingfortv/

**Maryland Institute College of Art,** Graduate Studies, Program in Filmmaking, Baltimore, MD 21201. Offers MFA. *Faculty:* 5 full-time (2 women). *Degree requirements:* For master's, thesis film and screening, written thesis. *Entrance requirements:* For master's, portfolio, writing samples, bachelor's degree in any field. Additional exam requirements/recommendations for international students: Required—TOEFL (minimum score 550 paper-based; 80 iBT), IELTS (minimum score 6.5). *Application deadline:* For fall admission, 1/15 priority date for domestic students. Application fee: $75. Electronic applications accepted. *Expenses:* Contact institution. *Financial support:* In 2016–17, 12 students received support, including 12 fellowships (averaging $13,000 per year); career-related internships or fieldwork and scholarships/grants also available. Financial award application deadline: 1/15. *Unit head:* Patrick Wright, Director. *Application contact:* Chris D. Harring, Director of Graduate Admission, 410-225-2256, Fax: 410-225-5275, E-mail: graduate@mica.edu.
Website: http://www.mica.edu/Programs_of_Study/Graduate_Programs/Filmmaking_(MFA).html

**Massachusetts College of Art and Design,** Graduate Programs, MFA Program, Boston, MA 02115-5882. Offers 2D fine arts (MFA), including painting, printmaking; 3D fine arts (MFA), including ceramics, fibers, glass, jewelry and metalsmithing, sculpture; design (MFA, Postbaccalaureate Certificate), including dynamic media; fine arts (MFA), including interdisciplinary; media arts (MFA, Postbaccalaureate Certificate), including film/video (MFA), photography. *Accreditation:* NASAD. *Faculty:* 40 full-time (19 women), 55 part-time/adjunct (23 women). *Students:* 58 full-time (39 women), 16 part-time (12 women); includes 10 minority (1 Black or African American, non-Hispanic/Latino; 4 Asian, non-Hispanic/Latino; 4 Hispanic/Latino; 1 Native Hawaiian or other Pacific Islander, non-Hispanic/Latino), 28 international. 247 applicants, 52% accepted, 47 enrolled. In 2016, 34 master's, 3 other advanced degrees awarded. *Degree requirements:* For master's, thesis, thesis exhibition (for fine arts programs); thesis project and document (for design/dynamic media program). *Entrance requirements:* For master's, portfolio, college transcripts, resume, statement of purpose, letters of reference, interview, 6 credits of art history taken prior to or during MFA program; for Postbaccalaureate Certificate, portfolio, college transcripts, resume, statement of purpose, letters of reference, interview. Additional exam requirements/recommendations for international students: Required—TOEFL (minimum score 550 paper-based; 85 iBT); Recommended—IELTS (minimum score 6.5). *Application deadline:* For fall admission, 1/4 priority date for domestic and international students; for summer admission, 1/4 priority date for domestic and international students. Application fee: $90. Electronic applications accepted. *Expenses:* $780 per credit tuition. *Financial support:* In 2016–17, 57 students received support, including 33 teaching assistantships (averaging $2,160 per year); fellowships, research assistantships, career-related internships or fieldwork, scholarships/grants, tuition waivers (partial), unspecified assistantships, and 6-8 one-term adjunct co-teaching positions; 27 full-year general assistantships also available. Support available to part-time students. Financial award application deadline: 1/4; financial award applicants required to submit FAFSA. *Faculty research:* Painting and printmaking, sculpture, photography, film and video, dynamic media design. *Unit head:* Paul Paturzo, Dean of Graduate Studies, 617-879-7166, E-mail: pjpaturzo@massart.edu. *Application contact:* Lauren O'Neill, Assistant Director of Graduate Admissions, 617-879-7222, E-mail: gradadmissions@massart.edu.
Website: http://www.massart.edu/Admissions/Graduate_Programs.html

**Miami International University of Art & Design,** Program in Film, Miami, FL 33132-1418. Offers MFA. *Program availability:* Online learning.

**Minneapolis College of Art and Design,** Program in Visual Studies, Minneapolis, MN 55404-4347. Offers animation (MFA); comic art (MFA); drawing (MFA); filmmaking (MFA); fine arts (MFA); furniture design (MFA); graphic design (MFA); illustration (MFA); interactive media (MFA); painting (MFA); photography (MFA); printmaking (MFA); sculpture (MFA). *Accreditation:* NASAD. *Program availability:* Part-time. *Degree requirements:* For master's, thesis, thesis exhibition. *Entrance requirements:* For master's, portfolio of visual artwork, resume, 3 letters of recommendation. Additional exam requirements/recommendations for international students: Required—TOEFL (minimum score 550 paper-based; 79 iBT). Electronic applications accepted. *Faculty research:* Visual arts: animation, comic art, drawing, filmmaking, furniture design, graphic design, illustration, interactive media, painting, photography, printmaking, sculpture.

**Missouri State University,** Graduate College, Interdisciplinary Program in Professional Studies, Springfield, MO 65897. Offers administrative studies (Certificate); applied communication (MS); criminal justice (MS); environmental management (MS); homeland security (MS); individualized (MS); screenwriting and producing (MS); sports management (MS). *Program availability:* Part-time, evening/weekend, 100% online, blended/hybrid learning. *Students:* 60 full-time (34 women), 66 part-time (29 women); includes 17 minority (7 Black or African American, non-Hispanic/Latino; 1 Asian, non-Hispanic/Latino; 5 Hispanic/Latino; 4 Two or more races, non-Hispanic/Latino), 43 international. Average age 33. 76 applicants, 58% accepted, 38 enrolled. In 2016, 48 master's awarded. *Degree requirements:* For master's, comprehensive exam, thesis or alternative. *Entrance requirements:* For master's, GRE, GMAT (if GPA less than 3.0). Additional exam requirements/recommendations for international students: Required—TOEFL (minimum score 550 paper-based; 79 iBT), IELTS (minimum score 6). *Application deadline:* For fall admission, 7/15 priority date for domestic students; for spring admission, 12/1 priority date for domestic students; for summer admission, 5/1 for domestic students. Applications are processed on a rolling basis. Application fee: $35 ($50 for international students). Electronic applications accepted. *Expenses:* Tuition, state resident: full-time $5830. Tuition, nonresident: full-time $10,708. *Required fees:* $1130. Tuition and fees vary according to class time, course level, course load and program. *Financial support:* Career-related internships or fieldwork, Federal Work-Study, institutionally sponsored loans, scholarships/grants, and unspecified assistantships available. Support available to part-time students. Financial award application deadline: 3/31; financial award applicants required to submit FAFSA. *Unit head:* Dr. Gerald Masterson, Program Director, 417-836-5251, Fax: 417-836-6888, E-mail: mps@missouristate.edu. *Application contact:* Michael Edwards, Coordinator of Graduate Admissions, 417-836-5330, Fax: 417-836-6200, E-mail: michaeledwards@missouristate.edu.
Website: http://mps.missouristate.edu

**Montana State University,** The Graduate School, College of Arts and Architecture, School of Film and Photography, Bozeman, MT 59717. Offers science and natural history filmmaking (MFA). *Program availability:* Part-time. *Degree requirements:* For master's, comprehensive exam. *Entrance requirements:* For master's, GRE General Test, minimum GPA of 3.0, resume, 3 letters of recommendation. Additional exam requirements/recommendations for international students: Required—TOEFL (minimum score 550 paper-based). Electronic applications accepted. *Faculty research:* Science and natural history filmmaking, science communication, public outreach, new media production, environmental communication.

**Mount Saint Mary's University,** Graduate Division, Los Angeles, CA 90049. Offers business administration (MBA); counseling psychology (MS); creative writing (MFA); education (MS, Certificate); film and television (MFA); health policy and management

### Film, Television, and Video Production

(MS); humanities (MA); nursing (MSN, Certificate); physical therapy (DPT); religious studies (MA). *Program availability:* Part-time, evening/weekend. *Faculty:* 50 full-time (35 women), 116 part-time/adjunct (81 women). *Students:* 670 full-time (518 women), 147 part-time (116 women); includes 414 minority (73 Black or African American, non-Hispanic/Latino; 4 American Indian or Alaska Native, non-Hispanic/Latino; 60 Asian, non-Hispanic/Latino; 259 Hispanic/Latino; 7 Native Hawaiian or other Pacific Islander, non-Hispanic/Latino; 11 Two or more races, non-Hispanic/Latino), 4 international. Average age 32. 1,398 applicants, 21% accepted, 242 enrolled. In 2016, 170 master's, 28 doctorates, 35 other advanced degrees awarded. *Entrance requirements:* Additional exam requirements/recommendations for international students: Required—TOEFL. *Application deadline:* For fall admission, 6/30 priority date for domestic and international students; for spring admission, 10/30 priority date for domestic and international students; for summer admission, 3/30 priority date for domestic and international students. Applications are processed on a rolling basis. Application fee: $50. Electronic applications accepted. *Expenses: Tuition:* Full-time $9983; part-time $829 per unit. One-time fee: $135. Tuition and fees vary according to degree level and program. *Financial support:* Career-related internships or fieldwork, Federal Work-Study, institutionally sponsored loans, and tuition waivers (full and partial) available. Support available to part-time students. Financial award application deadline: 3/15; financial award applicants required to submit FAFSA. *Unit head:* Albert Ramos, Director of Graduate Admissions, 213-477-2800, E-mail: gradprograms@msmu.edu. *Application contact:* Shawn Peters, Graduate Admission Counselor, 213-477-2676, E-mail: gradprograms@msmu.edu.
Website: http://www.msmu.edu/graduate-programs/

**National University,** Academic Affairs, School of Professional Studies, La Jolla, CA 92037-1011. Offers criminal justice (MCJ); digital cinema (MFA); digital journalism (MA); juvenile justice (MS); public administration (MPA), including human resource management. *Program availability:* Part-time, evening/weekend, 100% online, blended/hybrid learning. *Faculty:* 21 full-time (8 women), 35 part-time/adjunct (9 women). *Students:* 280 full-time (155 women), 100 part-time (54 women); includes 226 minority (76 Black or African American, non-Hispanic/Latino; 1 American Indian or Alaska Native, non-Hispanic/Latino; 27 Asian, non-Hispanic/Latino; 102 Hispanic/Latino; 3 Native Hawaiian or other Pacific Islander, non-Hispanic/Latino; 17 Two or more races, non-Hispanic/Latino), 3 international. Average age 37. In 2016, 21 master's awarded. *Degree requirements:* For master's, thesis (for some programs). *Entrance requirements:* For master's, interview, minimum GPA of 2.5. Additional exam requirements/recommendations for international students: Required—TOEFL (minimum score 550 paper-based; 79 iBT), IELTS (minimum score 6). *Application deadline:* Applications are processed on a rolling basis. Application fee: $60 ($65 for international students). Electronic applications accepted. *Financial support:* Career-related internships or fieldwork, institutionally sponsored loans, scholarships/grants, and tuition waivers (partial) available. Support available to part-time students. Financial award application deadline: 6/30; financial award applicants required to submit FAFSA. *Unit head:* School of Professional Studies, 800-628-8648, E-mail: sops@nu.edu. *Application contact:* Brandon Jouganatos, Vice President for Enrollment Services, 800-628-8648, E-mail: advisor@nu.edu.
Website: http://www.nu.edu/OurPrograms/School-of-Professional-Studies.html

**New York Film Academy,** Program in Filmmaking–Los Angeles, Burbank, CA 91505. Offers acting for film (MFA); cinematography (MFA); documentary film (MFA); film and media production (MA); filmmaking (MFA); game design (MFA); photography (MFA); producing (MA, MFA); screenwriting (MA, MFA). *Accreditation:* NASAD.

**New York Film Academy,** Program in Filmmaking–South Beach, Florida, Miami Beach, FL 33139. Offers acting for film (MFA); cinematography (MFA); documentary film (MFA); film and media production (MA); filmmaking (MFA); game design (MFA); photography (MFA); producing (MA, MFA); screenwriting (MA, MFA).

**New York University,** Tisch School of the Arts, Kanbar Institute of Film and Television, New York, NY 10012-1019. Offers MFA. *Degree requirements:* For master's, 4 films. *Entrance requirements:* For master's, portfolio. Additional exam requirements/recommendations for international students: Required—TOEFL or IELTS. Electronic applications accepted.

**New York University,** Tisch School of the Arts, Program in Moving Image Archiving and Preservation, New York, NY 10012-1019. Offers MA. *Degree requirements:* For master's, internship. *Entrance requirements:* For master's, GRE. Additional exam requirements/recommendations for international students: Required—TOEFL or IELTS. Electronic applications accepted.

**Northwestern University,** The Graduate School, School of Communication, Department of Radio, Television and Film, Evanston, IL 60208. Offers documentary media (MFA); screen cultures (MA, PhD); writing for the screen and stage (MFA). Admissions and degrees offered through The Graduate School. *Program availability:* Part-time. Terminal master's awarded for partial completion of doctoral program. *Degree requirements:* For master's, comprehensive exam or thesis; for doctorate, thesis/dissertation, qualifying exam. *Entrance requirements:* For master's and doctorate, GRE General Test. Additional exam requirements/recommendations for international students: Required—TOEFL. Electronic applications accepted. *Faculty research:* Art and new media, media theory and criticism, gender, media history, documentary.

**Ohio University,** Graduate College, College of Fine Arts, School of Film, Athens, OH 45701-2979. Offers film (MFA); film studies (MA). *Degree requirements:* For master's, one foreign language, thesis. *Entrance requirements:* Additional exam requirements/recommendations for international students: Required—TOEFL (minimum score 550 paper-based; 80 iBT) or IELTS (minimum score 6.5). *Application deadline:* For fall admission, 2/1 for domestic and international students. Application fee: $50 ($55 for international students). Electronic applications accepted. *Financial support:* Research assistantships with full tuition reimbursements, teaching assistantships with full tuition reimbursements, institutionally sponsored loans, scholarships/grants, tuition waivers (full and partial), and unspecified assistantships available. Financial award application deadline: 2/1. *Faculty research:* Scriptwriting, sound, editing, cinematography, film theory, digital post production. *Unit head:* Steven Ross, Director, 740-593-9969, Fax: 740-593-1328, E-mail: rosss2@ohio.edu. *Application contact:* Dr. Jody Lamb, Associate Dean, 740-593-1811, E-mail: lambj@ohio.edu.
Website: http://www.finearts.ohio.edu/film/

**Quinnipiac University,** School of Communications, Program in Interactive Media, Hamden, CT 06518-1940. Offers interactive media (MS); media design (MS); social media (MS); UX design (MS). *Program availability:* Part-time, evening/weekend, online only, 100% online. *Faculty:* 2 full-time (1 woman), 10 part-time/adjunct (5 women). *Students:* 5 full-time (3 women), 74 part-time (51 women); includes 23 minority (13 Black or African American, non-Hispanic/Latino; 2 Asian, non-Hispanic/Latino; 6 Hispanic/Latino; 2 Two or more races, non-Hispanic/Latino). 50 applicants, 86% accepted, 38 enrolled. In 2016, 48 master's awarded. *Entrance requirements:* For master's, minimum GPA of 3.0, portfolio or writing sample. Additional exam requirements/recommendations for international students: Required—TOEFL (minimum score 575 paper-based; 90 iBT), IELTS (minimum score 6.5). *Application deadline:* For fall admission, 7/30 priority date for domestic students, 4/30 priority date for international students; for spring admission,

12/30 priority date for domestic students, 9/30 priority date for international students. Applications are processed on a rolling basis. Application fee: $45. Electronic applications accepted. *Expenses:* Contact institution. *Financial support:* Federal Work-Study and unspecified assistantships available. Financial award application deadline: 6/1; financial award applicants required to submit FAFSA. *Faculty research:* User experience, social media, semiotics and communication, online distribution of news, Web-based interventions for research. *Unit head:* Phillip Simon, Director, 203-582-8274, E-mail: phillip.simon@qu.edu. *Application contact:* Quinnipiac University Online Admissions Office, 800-462-1944, E-mail: quonlineadmissions@qu.edu.
Website: https://quonline.quinnipiac.edu/online-programs/online-graduate-programs/ms-in-interactive-media/

**Regent University,** Graduate School, School of Communication and the Arts, Virginia Beach, VA 23464-9800. Offers communication (MA, PhD), including media and arts management and promotion (MA), political communication (MA), strategic communication (MA); directing for cinema/television (MFA); film and TV (MA), including producing, production, script writing; journalism (MA); producing for cinema/television (MFA); script and screenwriting (MFA); theatre (MA). *Program availability:* Part-time, 100% online, blended/hybrid learning. *Faculty:* 19 full-time (3 women), 51 part-time/adjunct (17 women). *Students:* 92 full-time (52 women), 344 part-time (225 women); includes 163 minority (116 Black or African American, non-Hispanic/Latino; 6 American Indian or Alaska Native, non-Hispanic/Latino; 7 Asian, non-Hispanic/Latino; 25 Hispanic/Latino; 1 Native Hawaiian or other Pacific Islander, non-Hispanic/Latino; 8 Two or more races, non-Hispanic/Latino), 8 international. Average age 37. 368 applicants, 52% accepted, 124 enrolled. In 2016, 91 master's, 7 doctorates awarded. *Degree requirements:* For master's, thesis or alternative; for doctorate, thesis/dissertation. *Entrance requirements:* For master's, transcripts, writing sample, resume, audition (for MFA programs); for doctorate, GRE General Test, resume, writing sample, recommendations, interview, transcripts, personal goals statement. Additional exam requirements/recommendations for international students: Required—TOEFL (minimum score 577 paper-based). *Application deadline:* For fall admission, 3/1 priority date for domestic students; for spring admission, 10/1 priority date for domestic students. Applications are processed on a rolling basis. Application fee: $50. Electronic applications accepted. *Expenses:* $685 per credit (for MA); $895 per credit (for MFA in acting); $885 per credit (for PhD); $250 per semester technology fee. *Financial support:* In 2016–17, 178 students received support, including 2 fellowships (averaging $10,000 per year); career-related internships or fieldwork, scholarships/grants, and unspecified assistantships also available. Support available to part-time students. *Faculty research:* Screenwriting, digital media production, communication, acting, directing. *Unit head:* Dr. Mitch Land, Dean, 757-352-4916, Fax: 757-352-4291, E-mail: mland@regent.edu. *Application contact:* Heidi Cece, Assistant Vice President of Enrollment Management, 800-373-5504, Fax: 757-352-4381, E-mail: admissions@regent.edu.
Website: http://www.regent.edu/sca/

**Rochester Institute of Technology,** Graduate Enrollment Services, College of Imaging Arts and Sciences, School of Film and Animation, MFA Program in Film and Animation, Rochester, NY 14623. Offers MFA. *Program availability:* Part-time. *Students:* 44 full-time (21 women), 7 part-time (2 women); includes 5 minority (1 Black or African American, non-Hispanic/Latino; 2 Asian, non-Hispanic/Latino; 2 Hispanic/Latino), 33 international. Average age 26. 119 applicants, 50% accepted, 20 enrolled. In 2016, 17 master's awarded. *Degree requirements:* For master's, thesis. *Entrance requirements:* For master's, GRE, portfolio, minimum GPA of 3.0 (recommended). Additional exam requirements/recommendations for international students: Required—TOEFL (minimum score 550 paper-based; 82 iBT), IELTS (minimum score 6.5), PTE (minimum score 58). *Application deadline:* For fall admission, 2/15 priority date for domestic and international students. Applications are processed on a rolling basis. Application fee: $60. Electronic applications accepted. *Expenses:* $1,742 per credit hour. *Financial support:* In 2016–17, 32 students received support. Teaching assistantships with partial tuition reimbursements available, career-related internships or fieldwork, scholarships/grants, and unspecified assistantships available. Support available to part-time students. Financial award applicants required to submit FAFSA. *Faculty research:* 3-D printing, super 8 cameras, color and projection, gaming and storytelling, special effects including virtual reality. *Unit head:* Thomas Gasek, Graduate Program Director, 585-475-7403, E-mail: tdgpph@rit.edu. *Application contact:* Diane Ellison, Associate Vice President, Graduate Enrollment Services, 585-475-2229, Fax: 585-475-7164, E-mail: gradinfo@rit.edu.
Website: http://cias.rit.edu/schools/film-animation/graduate-film-and-animation

**Rochester Institute of Technology,** Graduate Enrollment Services, College of Imaging Arts and Sciences, School of Photographic Arts and Sciences, MFA Program in Imaging Arts, Photography and Related Media, Rochester, NY 14623-5603. Offers MFA. *Accreditation:* NASAD. *Program availability:* Part-time. *Students:* 11 full-time (7 women), 3 part-time (2 women); includes 1 minority (Asian, non-Hispanic/Latino), 6 international. Average age 30. 65 applicants, 32% accepted, 6 enrolled. In 2016, 2 master's awarded. *Degree requirements:* For master's, thesis, exhibit. *Entrance requirements:* For master's, GRE, portfolio, minimum GPA of 3.0 (recommended). Additional exam requirements/recommendations for international students: Required—TOEFL (minimum score 550 paper-based; 90 iBT), IELTS (minimum score 6.5), PTE (minimum score 58). *Application deadline:* For fall admission, 2/15 priority date for domestic and international students. Applications are processed on a rolling basis. Application fee: $60. Electronic applications accepted. *Expenses:* $1,742 per credit hour. *Financial support:* In 2016–17, 11 students received support. Teaching assistantships with partial tuition reimbursements available, career-related internships or fieldwork, scholarships/grants, and unspecified assistantships available. Support available to part-time students. Financial award applicants required to submit FAFSA. *Faculty research:* Histories and theories of photography, contemporary art, American art and visual culture, and critical theory; photo books, visual narrative and expanded/experimental forms of documentary; contemporary fine art photography practice as personal document; public space, social practice, sensory observation, walking and mapping; relationship between the constructed image, photography as object, and fiction in contemporary practice. *Unit head:* Christine Shank, Graduate Program Director, 585-475-2616, Fax: 585-475-5804, E-mail: crspph@rit.edu. *Application contact:* Diane Ellison, Associate Vice President, Graduate Enrollment Services, 585-475-2229, Fax: 585-475-7164, E-mail: gradinfo@rit.edu.
Website: http://cias.rit.edu/schools/photographic-arts-sciences/graduate-imaging-arts

**Sacred Heart University,** Graduate Programs, College of Arts and Sciences, School of Communication and Media Arts, Fairfield, CT 06825. Offers corporate communications and public relations (MA Comm); digital multimedia journalism (MA Comm); digital multimedia production (MA Comm); film and television production (MA); media literacy and digital culture (MA), including children, health and media, media and social justice, political action and media production; sports communication and media (MA), including athletic communications and promotions, sports broadcasting. *Program availability:* Part-time, evening/weekend. *Faculty:* 9 full-time (1 woman), 3 part-time/adjunct (2 women). *Students:* 60 full-time (34 women), 44 part-time (23 women); includes 23 minority (14 Black or African American, non-Hispanic/Latino; 7 Hispanic/Latino; 2 Two or more races, non-Hispanic/Latino), 18 international. Average age 26. 135 applicants, 93% accepted, 72 enrolled. In 2016, 69 master's awarded. *Degree requirements:* For

*Film, Television, and Video Production*

master's, thesis or alternative. *Entrance requirements:* For master's, bachelor's degree. Additional exam requirements/recommendations for international students: Required—TOEFL (minimum score 570 paper-based, 80 iBT), TWE, or IELTS (6.5); Recommended—TSE. *Application deadline:* Applications are processed on a rolling basis. Application fee: $75. Electronic applications accepted. *Expenses:* $935 per credit. *Financial support:* Unspecified assistantships available. Financial award applicants required to submit FAFSA. *Unit head:* Dr. Andrew Miller, Chair, 203-396-8087, E-mail: millera@sacredheart.edu. *Application contact:* William Sweeney, Director of Graduate Admissions Operations, 203-365-7619, Fax: 203-365-4732, E-mail: graduatestudies@sacredheart.edu. Website: http://www.sacredheart.edu/academics/collegeofartssciences/academicdepartments/communicationmediastudies/

**St. Thomas University,** School of Leadership Studies, Program in Electronic Media, Miami Gardens, FL 33054-6459. Offers MA.

**San Diego State University,** Graduate and Research Affairs, College of Professional Studies and Fine Arts, School of Theater, Television and Film, Program in Television, Film, and New Media Production, San Diego, CA 92182. Offers MA. *Entrance requirements:* For master's, GRE General Test, 3 letters of recommendation, resume, sample reel, influential book list, influential films list, hobby list. Additional exam requirements/recommendations for international students: Required—TOEFL. Electronic applications accepted. *Faculty research:* Experimental film and television programs, documentary film, television research and production.

**San Francisco State University,** Division of Graduate Studies, College of Liberal and Creative Arts, School of Cinema, San Francisco, CA 94132-1722. Offers MA, MFA. *Expenses:* Tuition, state resident: full-time $6738. Tuition, nonresident: full-time $15,666. *Required fees:* $1012. Tuition and fees vary according to degree level and program. *Unit head:* Dr. Britta Sjogren, Director, 415-338-1629, E-mail: cinedept@sfsu.edu. *Application contact:* Dr. R. L. Rutsky, MA Coordinator, 415-405-3400, Fax: 415-338-0906, E-mail: rlrutsky@sfsu.edu. Website: http://www.cinema.sfsu.edu/

**Savannah College of Art and Design,** Graduate School, Program in Animation, Savannah, GA 31402-3146. Offers MA, MFA. *Program availability:* Part-time, 100% online. *Faculty:* 27 full-time (4 women), 6 part-time/adjunct (2 women). *Students:* 178 full-time (105 women), 70 part-time (30 women); includes 43 minority (29 Black or African American, non-Hispanic/Latino; 1 American Indian or Alaska Native, non-Hispanic/Latino; 6 Asian, non-Hispanic/Latino; 7 Hispanic/Latino), 119 international. Average age 26. 218 applicants, 58% accepted, 75 enrolled. In 2016, 41 master's awarded. *Degree requirements:* For master's, final project (for MA); thesis (for MFA). *Entrance requirements:* For master's, GRE (recommended), portfolio (submitted in digital format), audition or writing submission, resume, statement of purpose, two letters of recommendation. Additional exam requirements/recommendations for international students: Required—TOEFL (minimum score 550 paper-based, 85 iBT), IELTS (minimum score 6.5), or ACTFL. *Application deadline:* For fall admission, 4/1 for domestic and international students. Applications are processed on a rolling basis. Application fee: $40. Electronic applications accepted. *Expenses:* Tuition: Full-time $36,045. Tuition and fees vary according to course load. *Financial support:* Career-related internships or fieldwork, Federal Work-Study, and scholarships/grants available. Financial award application deadline: 4/1; financial award applicants required to submit FAFSA. *Unit head:* Greg Araya, Chair, Animation. *Application contact:* Jenny Jaquillard, Executive Director of Admissions, Recruitment and Events, 912-525-5100, Fax: 912-525-5985, E-mail: admission@scad.edu. Website: http://www.scad.edu/academics/programs/animation

**Savannah College of Art and Design,** Graduate School, Program in Film and Television, Savannah, GA 31402-3146. Offers MA, MFA. *Program availability:* Part-time. *Faculty:* 13 full-time (2 women), 3 part-time/adjunct (2 women). *Students:* 137 full-time (64 women), 25 part-time (17 women); includes 43 minority (33 Black or African American, non-Hispanic/Latino; 2 American Indian or Alaska Native, non-Hispanic/Latino; 1 Asian, non-Hispanic/Latino; 7 Hispanic/Latino), 73 international. Average age 27. 265 applicants, 55% accepted, 60 enrolled. In 2016, 23 master's awarded. *Degree requirements:* For master's, final project (for MA); thesis (for MFA). *Entrance requirements:* For master's, GRE (recommended), portfolio (submitted in digital format), audition or writing submission, resume, statement of purpose, two letters of recommendation. Additional exam requirements/recommendations for international students: Required—TOEFL (minimum score 550 paper-based, 85 iBT), IELTS (minimum score 6.5), or ACTFL. *Application deadline:* For fall admission, 4/1 for domestic and international students. Applications are processed on a rolling basis. Application fee: $40. Electronic applications accepted. *Expenses:* Tuition: Full-time $36,045. Tuition and fees vary according to course load. *Financial support:* Career-related internships or fieldwork, Federal Work-Study, and scholarships/grants available. Financial award application deadline: 4/1; financial award applicants required to submit FAFSA. *Unit head:* Donald Moffett, Chair, Film and Television. *Application contact:* Jenny Jaquillard, Executive Director of Admissions, Recruitment and Events, 912-525-5100, Fax: 912-525-5985, E-mail: admission@scad.edu. Website: http://www.scad.edu/academics/programs/film-and-television

**Savannah College of Art and Design,** Graduate School, Program in Sound Design, Savannah, GA 31402-3146. Offers MA, MFA. *Program availability:* Part-time. *Faculty:* 8 full-time (0 women), 1 (woman) part-time/adjunct. *Students:* 23 full-time (6 women), 4 part-time (3 women); includes 7 minority (4 Black or African American, non-Hispanic/Latino; 1 Asian, non-Hispanic/Latino; 2 Hispanic/Latino), 6 international. Average age 25. 30 applicants, 50% accepted, 9 enrolled. In 2016, 17 master's awarded. *Degree requirements:* For master's, final project (for MA); thesis (for MFA). *Entrance requirements:* For master's, GRE (recommended), portfolio (submitted in digital format), audition or writing submission, resume, statement of purpose, two letters of recommendation. Additional exam requirements/recommendations for international students: Required—TOEFL (minimum score 550 paper-based, 85 iBT), IELTS (minimum score 6.5), or ACTFL. *Application deadline:* For fall admission, 4/1 for domestic and international students. Applications are processed on a rolling basis. Application fee: $40. Electronic applications accepted. *Expenses:* Tuition: Full-time $36,045. Tuition and fees vary according to course load. *Financial support:* Career-related internships or fieldwork, Federal Work-Study, and scholarships/grants available. Financial award application deadline: 4/1; financial award applicants required to submit FAFSA. *Unit head:* Robin Beauchamp, Chair, Sound Design. *Application contact:* Jenny Jaquillard, Executive Director of Admissions, Recruitment and Events, 912-525-5100, Fax: 912-525-5985, E-mail: admission@scad.edu. Website: http://www.scad.edu/academics/programs/sound-design

**School of the Art Institute of Chicago,** Graduate Division, Department of Film, Video, and New Media, Chicago, IL 60603-3103. Offers MFA. *Accreditation:* NASAD. *Degree requirements:* For master's, thesis exhibit. *Entrance requirements:* Additional exam requirements/recommendations for international students: Required—TOEFL (minimum score 550 paper-based; 80 iBT), IELTS (minimum score 6.5). Electronic applications accepted.

**School of the Art Institute of Chicago,** Graduate Division, Department of Sound, Chicago, IL 60603-3103. Offers MFA. *Entrance requirements:* Additional exam requirements/recommendations for international students: Required—TOEFL, IELTS.

**School of Visual Arts,** Graduate Programs, Directing Department, New York, NY 10010-3994. Offers MPS. *Degree requirements:* For master's, thesis, 36 credits, including all required courses; minimum GPA of 3.0; completion and marketing of his or her thesis film. *Entrance requirements:* For master's, portfolio. Additional exam requirements/recommendations for international students: Required—TOEFL (minimum score 550 paper-based; 79 iBT).

**School of Visual Arts,** Graduate Programs, Program in Photography, Video and Related Media, New York, NY 10010-3994. Offers MFA. *Accreditation:* NASAD. *Degree requirements:* For master's, thesis, 60 credits and all course requirements; minimum GPA of 3.3; thesis project. *Entrance requirements:* For master's, portfolio (still images and/or videos) through SlideRoom. Additional exam requirements/recommendations for international students: Required—TOEFL (minimum score 550 paper-based; 79 iBT). Electronic applications accepted. *Faculty research:* Contemporary and responsible creative initiatives, including experimental, narrative or documentary video, installation and conceptual art, tableau and real-world-witness photography.

**School of Visual Arts,** Graduate Programs, Social Documentary Film Department, New York, NY 10010-3994. Offers MFA. *Degree requirements:* For master's, thesis, 60 credits, including all required courses; minimum cumulative GPA of 3.0; residency of two academic years. *Entrance requirements:* For master's, concise treatment for documentary film production; video work or still imagery; visual documentation of a subject (for applicants without prior filmmaking experience). Additional exam requirements/recommendations for international students: Required—TOEFL (minimum score 550 paper-based; 79 iBT). Electronic applications accepted. *Expenses:* Contact institution.

**Stanford University,** School of Humanities and Sciences, Department of Art and Art History, Stanford, CA 94305-2004. Offers art history (PhD); art practice (MFA); design (MFA); documentary film and video (MFA); MS/MFA. *Degree requirements:* For master's, thesis (for some programs), faculty reviews; for doctorate, 2 foreign languages, thesis/dissertation. *Entrance requirements:* For master's and doctorate, GRE General Test. Additional exam requirements/recommendations for international students: Required—TOEFL. Electronic applications accepted. *Expenses:* Tuition: Full-time $47,331. *Required fees:* $609.

**Stevens Institute of Technology,** Graduate School, Charles V. Schaefer Jr. School of Engineering and Science, Interdisciplinary Program in Media and Broadcast Engineering, Hoboken, NJ 07030. Offers MS. *Students:* 3 applicants, 33% accepted. *Degree requirements:* For master's, thesis optional, minimum B average in major field and overall. *Entrance requirements:* Additional exam requirements/recommendations for international students: Required—TOEFL (minimum score 74 iBT), IELTS (minimum score 6). *Application deadline:* For fall admission, 6/1 for domestic students, 4/15 for international students; for spring admission, 11/30 for domestic students, 11/1 for international students. *Expenses:* Tuition: Full-time $33,328; part-time $1501 per credit. *Required fees:* $1186; $566 per credit. $283 per semester. *Unit head:* Dr. Keith G. Sheppard, Interim Dean, 201-216-5263. *Application contact:* Graduate Admissions, 888-783-8367, Fax: 888-555-1306, E-mail: graduate@stevens.edu.

**Stony Brook University, State University of New York,** Stony Brook Southampton, Program in Film, Stony Brook, NY 11794. Offers MFA. *Students:* 19 full-time (8 women), 12 part-time (9 women); includes 4 minority (1 Asian, non-Hispanic/Latino; 3 Hispanic/Latino), 2 international. 15 applicants, 80% accepted, 6 enrolled. In 2016, 2 master's awarded. *Degree requirements:* For master's, thesis. *Entrance requirements:* Additional exam requirements/recommendations for international students: Required—TOEFL. *Application deadline:* For fall admission, 1/15 for domestic students; for spring admission, 10/1 for domestic students. Application fee: $100. *Expenses:* Contact institution. *Unit head:* Christine Vachon, Director, 631-632-5030, E-mail: christine.vachon@stonybrook.edu. *Application contact:* Margaret S. Grigonis, Coordinator, 631-632-5028, Fax: 631-632-2576, E-mail: margaret.grigonis@stonybrook.edu. Website: http://www.stonybrook.edu/southampton/mfa/film/index.html

**Syracuse University,** College of Visual and Performing Arts, MFA Program in Film, Syracuse, NY 13244. Offers MFA. *Degree requirements:* For master's, thesis or alternative. *Entrance requirements:* For master's, portfolio, artist statement, three letters of recommendation, academic transcripts, personal statement/essay, resume. Additional exam requirements/recommendations for international students: Required—TOEFL (minimum score 100 iBT). *Application deadline:* For fall admission, 2/1 priority date for domestic and international students. Application fee: $75. Electronic applications accepted. *Expenses:* Tuition: Full-time $25,974; part-time $1443 per credit hour. *Required fees:* $802; $50 per course. Tuition and fees vary according to course load and program. *Financial support:* Fellowships with full tuition reimbursements and teaching assistantships with tuition reimbursements available. Financial award application deadline: 1/1; financial award applicants required to submit FAFSA. *Faculty research:* Film production, global cinema, historical, artistic, and international film contexts. *Unit head:* Owen Shapiro, Professor/Film Program Coordinator, 315-443-2214, E-mail: ojshapir@syr.edu. *Application contact:* Therese West, Information Contact, 315-443-0137, E-mail: admissg@syr.edu. Website: http://vpa.syr.edu/academics/transmedia/graduate/film/

**Syracuse University,** S. I. Newhouse School of Public Communications, MA Program in Documentary Film and History, Syracuse, NY 13244. Offers MA. *Students:* Average age 31. *Degree requirements:* For master's, thesis or alternative. *Entrance requirements:* For master's, GRE General Test, resume, official transcripts, personal statement, three letters of recommendation. Additional exam requirements/recommendations for international students: Required—TOEFL (minimum score 100 iBT). *Application deadline:* For fall admission, 2/1 for international students; for summer admission, 1/15 priority date for domestic and international students. Application fee: $45. Electronic applications accepted. *Expenses:* Tuition: Full-time $25,974; part-time $1443 per credit hour. *Required fees:* $802; $50 per course. Tuition and fees vary according to course load and program. *Financial support:* Fellowships with full tuition reimbursements, research assistantships with partial tuition reimbursements, and teaching assistantships with partial tuition reimbursements available. Financial award application deadline: 2/1. *Faculty research:* View production, distribution, new media, applications to education. *Unit head:* Richard Breyer, Co-Director, Documentary Film and History/Professor, 315-443-9249, E-mail: rlbreyer@syr.edu. *Application contact:* Martha Coria, Graduate Records Office, 315-443-4039, Fax: 315-443-1834, E-mail: pcgrad@syr.edu. Website: http://newhouse.syr.edu/

**Temple University,** Center for the Performing and Cinematic Arts, Division of Theater, Film and Media Arts, Department of Film and Media Arts, Philadelphia, PA 19122. Offers MA, MFA. *Program availability:* Part-time. *Degree requirements:* For master's, comprehensive exam, project. *Entrance requirements:* For master's, minimum GPA of 3.0; exhibit. Additional exam requirements/recommendations for international students: Required—TOEFL (minimum score 600 paper-based; 100 iBT). Electronic applications

## Film, Television, and Video Production

accepted. *Expenses:* Contact institution. *Faculty research:* Documentary/experimental film, narrative film, digital media arts, film and media studies, screenwriting.

**Universidad Autonoma de Guadalajara,** Graduate Programs, Guadalajara, Mexico. Offers administrative law and justice (LL M); advertising and corporate communications (MA); architecture (M Arch); business (MBA); computational science (MCC); education (Ed M, Ed D); English-Spanish translation (MA); entrepreneurship and management (MBA); integrated management of digital animation (MA); international business (MIB); international corporate law (LL M); internet technologies (MS); manufacturing systems (MMS); occupational health (MS); philosophy (MA, PhD); power electronics (MS); quality systems (MQS); renewable energy (MS); social evaluation of projects (MBA); strategic market research (MBA); tax law (MA); teaching mathematics (MA).

**The University of British Columbia,** Faculty of Arts, Creative Writing Program, Vancouver, BC V6T 1Z1, Canada. Offers creative writing (MFA); creative writing and theatre (MFA); film production and creative writing (MFA). *Program availability:* Part-time, online learning. *Degree requirements:* For master's, thesis. *Entrance requirements:* For master's, sample of written work. Additional exam requirements/recommendations for international students: Required—TOEFL. Application fee: $100 Canadian dollars ($162 Canadian dollars for international students). Electronic applications accepted. *Expenses:* $4,802 per year tuition and fees, $8,436 per year international; $592 per credit, $996 per credit international (online). *Financial support:* Fellowships, teaching assistantships, Federal Work-Study, institutionally sponsored loans, and unspecified assistantships available. *Faculty research:* Writing of fiction; poetry, creative nonfiction, plays for stage, screen, television, radio, writing for children and translation, song lyrics and libretto, new media and graphic novel. *Application contact:* Heather Miller, Graduate Program Staff, 604-822-0699, E-mail: crwr.grad@ubc.ca.
Website: http://creativewriting.ubc.ca/

**The University of British Columbia,** Faculty of Arts and Faculty of Graduate Studies, Department of Theatre and Film, Film Program, Vancouver, BC V6T 1Z2, Canada. Offers film production (MFA); film studies (MA). *Degree requirements:* For master's, variable foreign language requirement, comprehensive exam, thesis (MA); thesis or project (MFA). *Entrance requirements:* For master's, portfolio (MFA). Additional exam requirements/recommendations for international students: Required—TOEFL. Application fee: $100 Canadian dollars ($162 Canadian dollars for international students). *Expenses:* $4,802 per year tuition and fees, $8,436 per year international. *Financial support:* Fellowships, research assistantships, and teaching assistantships available. *Faculty research:* Film theory and violence; American and European cinema; cult cinema; Irish cinema. *Application contact:* Zanna Downes, Graduate Program Staff, 604-822-6037, Fax: 604-822-0508, E-mail: fipr.sec@ubc.ca.
Website: http://theatrefilm.ubc.ca/

**University of California, Los Angeles,** Graduate Division, School of Theater, Film and Television, Department of Film, Television, and Digital Media, Los Angeles, CA 90034. Offers animation (MFA); cinema and media studies (MA, PhD); cinematography (MFA); production (MFA); screenwriting (MFA). *Degree requirements:* For master's, comprehensive exam; for doctorate, one foreign language, thesis/dissertation, oral and written qualifying exams. *Entrance requirements:* For master's, GRE General Test (for MA applicants), bachelor's degree; minimum undergraduate GPA of 3.0 (or its equivalent if letter grade system not used); writing sample (for MA); for doctorate, GRE General Test, master's degree; minimum undergraduate GPA of 3.0 (or its equivalent if letter grade system not used); writing sample. Additional exam requirements/recommendations for international students: Required—TOEFL. Electronic applications accepted. *Expenses:* Contact institution.

**University of California, Los Angeles,** Graduate Division, School of Theater, Film and Television, Interdepartmental Program in Moving Image Archive Studies, Los Angeles, CA 90095. Offers MA. *Degree requirements:* For master's, comprehensive exam, thesis. *Entrance requirements:* For master's, bachelor's degree; minimum undergraduate GPA of 3.0 (or its equivalent if letter grade system not used); writing sample. Additional exam requirements/recommendations for international students: Required—TOEFL. Electronic applications accepted.

**University of California, Santa Barbara,** Graduate Division, College of Letters and Sciences, Division of Humanities and Fine Arts, Department of Film and Media Studies, Santa Barbara, CA 93106-4010. Offers PhD, MA/PhD. Terminal master's awarded for partial completion of doctoral program. *Degree requirements:* For doctorate, one foreign language, comprehensive exam, thesis/dissertation. *Entrance requirements:* For doctorate, GRE, MA in film/media studies or equivalent. Additional exam requirements/recommendations for international students: Required—TOEFL (minimum score 600 paper-based; 100 iBT), IELTS (minimum score 7). Electronic applications accepted. *Faculty research:* Classical film theory, film and television history, historiography, cultural studies, global media, media industries, regulation and policy.

**University of Central Arkansas,** Graduate School, College of Fine Arts and Communication, Program in Digital Filmmaking, Conway, AR 72035-0001. Offers MFA. *Accreditation:* NASAD. *Degree requirements:* For master's, thesis. *Entrance requirements:* For master's, GRE General Test, minimum GPA of 2.7. Additional exam requirements/recommendations for international students: Required—TOEFL (minimum score 550 paper-based). Electronic applications accepted.

**University of Central Florida,** College of Arts and Humanities, School of Visual Arts and Design, Orlando, FL 32816. Offers digital media (MA); emerging media (MFA), including digital media, entrepreneurial digital cinema, studio art and the computer. *Program availability:* Part-time. *Faculty:* 57 full-time (23 women), 15 part-time/adjunct (4 women). *Students:* 26 full-time (12 women), 13 part-time (3 women); includes 7 minority (3 Black or African American, non-Hispanic/Latino; 1 Asian, non-Hispanic/Latino; 2 Hispanic/Latino), 2 international. Average age 31. 49 applicants, 57% accepted, 19 enrolled. In 2016, 7 master's awarded. *Degree requirements:* For master's, comprehensive exam, thesis or alternative. *Entrance requirements:* Additional exam requirements/recommendations for international students: Required—TOEFL. *Application deadline:* For fall admission, 7/1 for domestic students. Application fee: $30. Electronic applications accepted. *Expenses:* Tuition, state resident: part-time $288.16 per credit hour. Tuition, nonresident: part-time $1071.31 per credit hour. *Financial support:* In 2016–17, 15 students received support, including 4 fellowships with partial tuition reimbursements available (averaging $10,000 per year), 2 research assistantships with partial tuition reimbursements available (averaging $3,214 per year), 13 teaching assistantships with partial tuition reimbursements available (averaging $7,570 per year); scholarships/grants and unspecified assistantships also available. Financial award application deadline: 3/1; financial award applicants required to submit FAFSA. *Unit head:* Dr. Rudy McDaniel, Interim Director, 407-823-3145, E-mail: rudy@ucf.edu. *Application contact:* Assistant Director, Graduate Admissions, 407-823-2766, Fax: 407-823-6442, E-mail: gradadmissions@ucf.edu.
Website: http://svad.cah.ucf.edu/

**University of Colorado Boulder,** Graduate School, College of Media, Communication and Information, Program in Critical Media Practices, Boulder, CO 80309. Offers interdisciplinary documentary media practices (MFA). *Faculty:* 4 full-time (2 women). *Students:* 7 full-time (5 women). Average age 32. 13 applicants, 23% accepted, 3

enrolled. *Application deadline:* For fall admission, 1/15 for domestic students, 12/1 for international students. Application fee: $60 ($80 for international students). Electronic applications accepted. Application fee is waived when completed online. *Financial support:* In 2016–17, 24 students received support, including 4 fellowships (averaging $1,750 per year), 7 research assistantships with full and partial tuition reimbursements available (averaging $32,610 per year), 4 teaching assistantships with full and partial tuition reimbursements available (averaging $15,103 per year); institutionally sponsored loans, scholarships/grants, health care benefits, and unspecified assistantships also available. Financial award application deadline: 2/1; financial award applicants required to submit FAFSA. *Faculty research:* Arts/humanities/cultural activities, cinema/video, inter-arts: interdisciplinary art forms, media arts, visual arts. *Application contact:* E-mail: cmci.dcmp@colorado.edu.
Website: http://www.colorado.edu/cmci/academics/critical-media-practices

**The University of Iowa,** Graduate College, College of Liberal Arts and Sciences, Department of Cinema and Comparative Literature, Program in Film and Video Production, Iowa City, IA 52242-1316. Offers MFA. *Degree requirements:* For master's, thesis (for some programs), exam. *Entrance requirements:* For master's, GRE General Test, minimum GPA of 3.0. Additional exam requirements/recommendations for international students: Required—TOEFL (minimum score 550 paper-based; 81 iBT). Electronic applications accepted.

**University of Memphis,** Graduate School, College of Communication and Fine Arts, Department of Communication, Memphis, TN 38152. Offers communication (MA); communication arts (PhD); film and video production (MA). *Program availability:* Part-time. *Faculty:* 13 full-time (6 women). *Students:* 20 full-time (8 women), 23 part-time (12 women); includes 14 minority (7 Black or African American, non-Hispanic/Latino; 2 Asian, non-Hispanic/Latino; 2 Hispanic/Latino; 3 Two or more races, non-Hispanic/Latino), 2 international. Average age 35. 38 applicants, 68% accepted, 17 enrolled. In 2016, 13 master's, 1 doctorate awarded. *Degree requirements:* For master's, comprehensive exam, thesis or alternative, culminating project; for doctorate, comprehensive exam, thesis/dissertation. *Entrance requirements:* For master's and doctorate, GRE General Test, personal goal statement, letters of recommendation, writing sample. Additional exam requirements/recommendations for international students: Required—TOEFL (minimum score 600 paper-based). *Application deadline:* For fall admission, 1/13 priority date for domestic students. Applications are processed on a rolling basis. Application fee: $35 ($60 for international students). *Expenses:* $5,231.50 per semester full-time in-state, $9,623.50 full-time out-of-state. *Financial support:* In 2016–17, 27 students received support, including 6 research assistantships with full tuition reimbursements available (averaging $12,000 per year), 12 teaching assistantships with full tuition reimbursements available (averaging $22,042 per year); Federal Work-Study, scholarships/grants, and unspecified assistantships also available. Financial award application deadline: 2/1; financial award applicants required to submit FAFSA. *Faculty research:* Rhetoric, media studies, applied communication (health communication). *Unit head:* Dr. Sandra Sarkela, Interim Department Chair, 901-678-2565, Fax: 901-678-4331, E-mail: ssarkela@memphis.edu. *Application contact:* Dr. Antonio de Velasco, Coordinator of Graduate Studies, 901-678-3185, Fax: 901-678-4331, E-mail: adevelsc@memphis.edu.
Website: http://www.memphis.edu/ccfa/index.php

**University of Miami,** Graduate School, School of Communication, Coral Gables, FL 33124. Offers communication (PhD); communication studies (MA); film studies (MA, PhD); motion pictures (MFA), including production, producing, and screenwriting; print journalism (MA); public relations (MA); Spanish language journalism (MA); television broadcast journalism (MA). *Program availability:* Part-time. *Degree requirements:* For master's, comprehensive exam (for some programs), thesis (for some programs); for doctorate, comprehensive exam, thesis/dissertation. *Entrance requirements:* For master's, GRE General Test; for doctorate, GRE General Test, master's thesis or scholarly research. Additional exam requirements/recommendations for international students: Required—TOEFL (minimum score 600 paper-based; 100 iBT). Electronic applications accepted. *Faculty research:* Communication studies, mass communication, international/interpersonal communication, film studies, journalism.

**University of Montana,** Graduate School, College of Visual and Performing Arts, School of Media Arts, Missoula, MT 59812-0002. Offers digital filmmaking (MFA); integrated digital media (MFA).

**University of Nevada, Las Vegas,** Graduate College, College of Fine Arts, Department of Film, Las Vegas, NV 89154-5015. Offers film/writing for dramatic media (MFA); writing for dramatic media (Certificate). *Program availability:* Part-time. *Faculty:* 2 full-time (0 women). *Students:* 8 full-time (6 women); includes 1 minority (Black or African American, non-Hispanic/Latino), 3 international. Average age 33. 17 applicants, 18% accepted, 2 enrolled. In 2016, 2 master's awarded. *Degree requirements:* For master's, thesis, creative project and defense; for Certificate, creative project and defense. *Entrance requirements:* For master's, writing sample. Additional exam requirements/recommendations for international students: Required—TOEFL (minimum score 550 paper-based; 80 iBT), IELTS (minimum score 7). *Application deadline:* For fall admission, 1/15 for domestic students. Application fee: $60 ($95 for international students). Electronic applications accepted. *Expenses:* $269.25 per credit, $792 per 3-credit course; $9,634 per year resident; $23,274 per year non-resident; $7,094 fees non-resident (7 credits or more); $1,307 annual health insurance fee. *Financial support:* In 2016–17, 8 teaching assistantships with partial tuition reimbursements (averaging $15,250 per year) were awarded; institutionally sponsored loans, scholarships/grants, health care benefits, and unspecified assistantships also available. Financial award application deadline: 3/15. *Faculty research:* Screenplay, stage play, television series, Web entertainment content, production. *Unit head:* Dr. Heather Addison, Chair/Professor, 702-895-3547, Fax: 702-895-4395, E-mail: heather.addison@unlv.edu. *Application contact:* Dr. Sean Clark, Graduate Coordinator, 702-895-2442, Fax: 702-895-4395, E-mail: sean.clark@unlv.edu.
Website: http://film.unlv.edu/

**University of New Orleans,** Graduate School, College of Liberal Arts, Department of Film and Theatre, New Orleans, LA 70148. Offers design (MFA); film production (MFA); theatre performance (MFA), including acting, directing. *Accreditation:* NAST. *Degree requirements:* For master's, comprehensive exam, thesis. *Entrance requirements:* Additional exam requirements/recommendations for international students: Required—TOEFL (minimum score 550 paper-based; 79 iBT), IELTS (minimum score 6.5). Electronic applications accepted. *Faculty research:* Mass communication theory, nineteenth and twentieth century theater history, film criticism and history.

**The University of North Carolina at Greensboro,** Graduate School, College of Arts and Sciences, Department of Media Studies, Greensboro, NC 27412-5001. Offers film and video production (MFA).

**University of North Carolina School of the Arts,** School of Filmmaking, Winston-Salem, NC 27127-2738. Offers creative producing (MFA); film music composition (MFA); screenwriting (MFA). *Entrance requirements:* For master's, audition, performance, portfolio, interview. Additional exam requirements/recommendations for international students: Required—TOEFL. *Application deadline:* For fall admission, 4/1 priority date for domestic students. Applications are processed on a rolling basis.

Application fee: $95 ($100 for international students). Electronic applications accepted. *Expenses:* Tuition, state resident: full-time $7996; part-time $444 per credit hour. Tuition, nonresident: full-time $21,403; part-time $1189 per credit hour. *Required fees:* $2769; $153.83 per credit hour. *Financial support:* Fellowships, research assistantships, career-related internships or fieldwork, and Federal Work-Study available. Support available to part-time students. Financial award application deadline: 3/15; financial award applicants required to submit FAFSA. *Unit head:* Susan Ruskin, Dean, 336-770-1334, Fax: 336-770-1339, E-mail: ruskins@uncsa.edu. *Application contact:* Sheeler Lawson, Director of Admissions, 336-770-3290, Fax: 336-770-3370, E-mail: admissions@uncsa.edu.
Website: http://www.uncsa.edu/filmmaking/

**University of North Texas,** Robert B. Toulouse School of Graduate Studies, Denton, TX 76203-5459. Offers accounting (MS); applied anthropology (MA, MS); applied behavior analysis (Certificate); applied geography (MA); applied technology and performance improvement (M Ed, MS); art education (MA); art history (MA); art museum education (Certificate); arts leadership (Certificate); audiology (Au D); behavior analysis (MS); behavioral science (PhD); biochemistry and molecular biology (MS); biology (MA, MS); biomedical engineering (MS); business analysis (MS); chemistry (MS); clinical health psychology (PhD); communication studies (MA, MS); computer engineering (MS); computer science (MS); counseling (M Ed, MS), including clinical mental health counseling (MS), college and university counseling, elementary school counseling, secondary school counseling; creative writing (MA); criminal justice (MS); curriculum and instruction (M Ed); decision sciences (MBA); design (MA, MFA), including fashion design (MFA), innovation studies, interior design (MFA); early childhood studies (MS); economics (MS); educational leadership (M Ed, Ed D); educational psychology (MS, PhD), including family studies (MS), gifted and talented (MS), human development (MS), learning and cognition (MS), research, measurement and evaluation (MS); electrical engineering (MS); emergency management (MPA); engineering technology (MS); English (MA); English as a second language (MA); environmental science (MS); finance (MBA, MS); financial management (MBA); French (MA); health services management (MBA); higher education (M Ed, Ed D); history (MA, MS); hospitality management (MS); human resources management (MPA); information science (MS); information systems (PhD); information technologies (MBA); interdisciplinary studies (MA, MS); international studies (MA); international sustainable tourism (MS); jazz studies (MM); journalism (MA, MJ, Graduate Certificate), including interactive and virtual digital communication (Graduate Certificate), narrative journalism (Graduate Certificate), public relations (Graduate Certificate); kinesiology (MS); linguistics (MA); local government management (MPA); logistics (PhD); logistics and supply chain management (MBA); long-term care, senior housing, and aging services (MS); management (PhD); marketing (MBA); mathematics (MA, MS); mechanical and energy engineering (MS, PhD); music (MA), including ethnomusicology, music theory, musicology, performance; music composition (PhD); music education (MM Ed, PhD); nonprofit management (MPA); operations and supply chain management (MBA); performance (MM, DMA); philosophy (MA); political science (MA); professional and technical communication (MA); radio, television and film (MA, MFA); rehabilitation counseling (Certificate); sociology (MA); Spanish (MA); special education (M Ed); speech-language pathology (MA); strategic management (MBA); studio art (MFA); teaching (M Ed); MBA/MS. *Program availability:* Part-time, evening/weekend, online learning. Terminal master's awarded for partial completion of doctoral program. *Degree requirements:* For master's, variable foreign language requirement, comprehensive exam (for some programs), thesis (for some programs); for doctorate, variable foreign language requirement, comprehensive exam (for some programs), thesis/dissertation; for other advanced degree, variable foreign language requirement, comprehensive exam (for some programs). *Entrance requirements:* For master's and doctorate, GRE, GMAT. Additional exam requirements/recommendations for international students: Required—TOEFL (minimum score 550 paper-based; 79 iBT). Electronic applications accepted.

**University of Regina,** Faculty of Graduate Studies and Research, Faculty of Media, Art, and Performance, Department of Film, Regina, SK S4S 0A2, Canada. Offers media production (MFA); media studies (MA). *Program availability:* Part-time. *Faculty:* 13 full-time (7 women). *Students:* 5 full-time (4 women), 1 (woman) part-time. 4 applicants. In 2016, 2 master's awarded. *Degree requirements:* For master's, thesis (for some programs). *Entrance requirements:* For master's, two writing samples (for MA); media-based support material (for MFA). Additional exam requirements/recommendations for international students: Required—TOEFL (minimum score 600 paper-based; 93 iBT), IELTS (minimum score 7), PTE (minimum score 59). *Application deadline:* For fall admission, 1/15 for domestic and international students. Application fee: $100. Electronic applications accepted. *Financial support:* In 2016–17, 1 fellowship (averaging $6,000 per year), 2 teaching assistantships (averaging $2,501 per year) were awarded; scholarships/grants also available. Financial award application deadline: 6/15. *Faculty research:* Dramatic, documentary, and experimental film and video; new and interactive media; animation through a range of artistic, aesthetic, technical, and theoretical skills and knowledge; general and specialized study in media arts production; media arts theory. *Unit head:* Dr. Kathryn Bracht, Department Head, 306-585-5590, E-mail: kathryn.bracht@uregina.ca. *Application contact:* Dr. Rebecca Caines, Graduate Coordinator, 306-585-5520, E-mail: rebecca.caines@uregina.ca.

**University of Southern California,** Graduate School, School of Cinematic Arts, Division of Animation and Digital Arts, Los Angeles, CA 90089. Offers MFA. *Degree requirements:* For master's, thesis, digital media and research documentation. *Entrance requirements:* Additional exam requirements/recommendations for international students: Recommended—TOEFL. Electronic applications accepted. *Expenses:* Contact institution. *Faculty research:* Character animation, visual effects, motion graphics, documentary animation, experimental animation.

**University of Southern California,** Graduate School, School of Cinematic Arts, Division of Film and Television Production, Los Angeles, CA 90089. Offers MFA. Terminal master's awarded for partial completion of doctoral program. *Degree requirements:* For master's, advanced project. *Entrance requirements:* Additional exam requirements/recommendations for international students: Required—TOEFL (minimum score 600 paper-based). Electronic applications accepted. *Faculty research:* Documentary filmmaking, narrative filmmaking, initiatives related to health issues, science foundation project, global workshops in China.

**University of Southern California,** Graduate School, School of Cinematic Arts, The Peter Stark Producing Program, Los Angeles, CA 90089. Offers motion picture producing (MFA). *Degree requirements:* For master's, thesis, set curriculum, oral examination. *Entrance requirements:* For master's, GRE. Additional exam requirements/recommendations for international students: Required—TOEFL (minimum score 600 paper-based; 100 iBT), IELTS (minimum score 7). Electronic applications accepted.

**University of Southern California,** Graduate School, School of Cinematic Arts, Writing for Screen and Television Division, Los Angeles, CA 90089. Offers MFA. *Degree requirements:* For master's, thesis or alternative. *Entrance requirements:* For master's, GRE. Additional exam requirements/recommendations for international students: Required—TOEFL. Electronic applications accepted. *Faculty research:* Dramatic storytelling, new media content and distribution, television and film character development, theory of storytelling, interactive writing.

**The University of Texas at Arlington,** Graduate School, College of Liberal Arts, Department of Art and Art History, Arlington, TX 76019. Offers film and video (MFA); glass (MFA); intermedia (MFA); visual communication (MFA). *Accreditation:* NASAD. *Degree requirements:* For master's, thesis or alternative, mid- and final program reviews; exhibition. *Entrance requirements:* For master's, GRE, minimum GPA of 3.0, 3 letters of recommendation, portfolio, resume. Additional exam requirements/recommendations for international students: Required—TOEFL (minimum score 550 paper-based). *Application deadline:* For fall admission, 1/15 priority date for domestic and international students; for spring admission, 10/15 priority date for domestic and international students. Applications are processed on a rolling basis. Electronic applications accepted. *Financial support:* Fellowships with full tuition reimbursements, research assistantships, teaching assistantships, scholarships/grants, and unspecified assistantships available. Financial award applicants required to submit FAFSA. *Unit head:* Prof. Robert Hower, Chair/Professor, 817-272-2891, Fax: 817-272-2805, E-mail: hower@uta.edu. *Application contact:* Prof. Nancy Palmeri, Graduate Advisor/Associate Professor, 817-272-2891, Fax: 817-272-2805, E-mail: palmeri@uta.edu.
Website: http://www.uta.edu/art

**The University of Texas at Austin,** Graduate School, College of Communication, Department of Radio-Television-Film, Austin, TX 78712-1111. Offers film and media production (MFA); media studies (MA, PhD); screenwriting (MFA). *Degree requirements:* For master's, thesis (for some programs); for doctorate, thesis/dissertation. *Entrance requirements:* For master's and doctorate, GRE General Test. Electronic applications accepted. *Faculty research:* International communication, film studies, media and culture, telecommunication and new media, gender and sexuality.

**The University of Texas at Austin,** Graduate School, Michener Center for Writers, Austin, TX 78712-1111. Offers fiction (MFA); playwriting (MFA); poetry (MFA); screenwriting (MFA). Electronic applications accepted.

**University of the Sacred Heart,** Graduate Programs, Department of Communication, San Juan, PR 00914-0383. Offers contemporary culture and media (MA); digital journalism (MA, Certificate); editing for media (MA, Certificate); public relations (MA, Certificate); publicity (MA, Certificate); scriptwriting (MA, Certificate). *Program availability:* Part-time, evening/weekend. *Degree requirements:* For master's, thesis.

**University of Utah,** Graduate School, College of Fine Arts, Film and Media Arts Department, Salt Lake City, UT 84112-0380. Offers MFA. *Program availability:* Part-time. *Faculty:* 8 full-time (4 women), 17 part-time/adjunct (5 women). *Students:* 13 full-time (9 women); includes 2 minority (1 Asian, non-Hispanic/Latino; 1 Hispanic/Latino), 3 international. Average age 29. 27 applicants, 15% accepted, 4 enrolled. In 2016, 10 master's awarded. *Degree requirements:* For master's, comprehensive exam, film or video portfolio. *Entrance requirements:* For master's, minimum GPA of 3.0. Additional exam requirements/recommendations for international students: Required—TOEFL (minimum score 500 paper-based). *Application deadline:* For fall admission, 11/30 for domestic and international students. Application fee: $55 ($65 for international students). *Expenses:* Tuition, state resident: full-time $9011; part-time $3918.24 per credit hour. Tuition, nonresident: full-time $22,154; part-time $11,665.42 per credit hour. *Financial support:* In 2016–17, 13 students received support, including 13 teaching assistantships with full and partial tuition reimbursements available (averaging $10,523 per year); career-related internships or fieldwork, Federal Work-Study, institutionally sponsored loans, scholarships/grants, health care benefits, and unspecified assistantships also available. Financial award application deadline: 12/31; financial award applicants required to submit FAFSA. *Faculty research:* Film history, criticism, cultural studies, production of narrative and documentary films. *Unit head:* Prof. Kevin D. Hanson, Chair, 801-581-7428, Fax: 801-585-3192, E-mail: kevin.hanson@utah.edu. *Application contact:* Prof. Chris Lippard, Director of Graduate Studies, 801-585-9358, Fax: 801-585-3192, E-mail: chris.lippard@utah.edu. Website: http://www.film.utah.edu

**University of Victoria,** Faculty of Graduate Studies, Faculty of Fine Arts, Department of Visual Arts, Victoria, BC V8W 2Y2, Canada. Offers digital multimedia (MFA); drawing (MFA); painting (MFA); photography (MFA); sculpture (MFA); video (MFA). *Degree requirements:* For master's, exhibit, oral exam. *Entrance requirements:* For master's, portfolio, BFA. Additional exam requirements/recommendations for international students: Required—TOEFL (minimum score 575 paper-based), IELTS (minimum score 7). Electronic applications accepted.

**Vermont College of Fine Arts,** MFA in Film Program, Montpelier, VT 05602. Offers MFA. *Faculty:* 7 part-time/adjunct (3 women). *Students:* 31 full-time (13 women); includes 5 minority (1 Black or African American, non-Hispanic/Latino; 1 American Indian or Alaska Native, non-Hispanic/Latino; 1 Hispanic/Latino; 1 Native Hawaiian or other Pacific Islander, non-Hispanic/Latino; 1 Two or more races, non-Hispanic/Latino), 1 international. Average age 39. In 2016, 18 master's awarded. *Degree requirements:* For master's, thesis. *Application deadline:* For fall admission, 8/15 for domestic students; for spring admission, 2/15 for domestic students. Applications are processed on a rolling basis. Application fee: $75. Electronic applications accepted. *Expenses:* Contact institution. *Financial support:* Application deadline: 6/15; applicants required to submit FAFSA. *Unit head:* Stephen Pite, Director, 802-828-8529, E-mail: stephen.pite@vcfa.edu. *Application contact:* Jennifer Skinder, Assistant Director of Admissions, 802-828-8829, E-mail: jennifer.skinder@vcfa.edu.
Website: http://www.vcfa.edu/film

**Virginia Commonwealth University,** Graduate School, School of the Arts, Richmond, VA 23284-9005. Offers art education (MAE, PhD); art history (MA, PhD), including curatorial (PhD), historical studies, museum studies (MA); ceramics (MFA); design (MFA), including interior environments, visual communications; fibers (MFA); furniture design (MFA); glassworking (MFA); jewelry/metalworking (MFA); kinetic imaging (MFA); music (MM), including music education; painting (MFA); photography and film (MFA); printmaking (MFA); sculpture (MFA); theatre (MFA), including costume design, pedagogy/literature, pedagogy/performance, scene design/technical theatre. *Program availability:* Part-time. *Entrance requirements:* For doctorate, GRE General Test, writing sample. Additional exam requirements/recommendations for international students: Required—TOEFL (minimum score 600 paper-based; 100 iBT). *Application deadline:* For fall admission, 1/15 priority date for domestic students. Application fee: $50. Electronic applications accepted. *Financial support:* Fellowships, teaching assistantships, career-related internships or fieldwork, Federal Work-Study, institutionally sponsored loans, and tuition waivers (full and partial) available. Support available to part-time students. Financial award applicants required to submit FAFSA. *Unit head:* Joseph H. Seipel, Dean, 804-828-2787, Fax: 804-828-6469, E-mail: arts@vcu.edu. *Application contact:* Jack H. Risley, Associate Dean for Academic Affairs, 804-828-2787, Fax: 804-828-6469, E-mail: jhrisley@vcu.edu.
Website: http://www.vcu.edu/arts/

**Western State Colorado University,** Program in Creative Writing, Gunnison, CO 81231. Offers mainstream genre fiction (MFA); poetry (MFA); screenwriting (MFA). *Program availability:* Online learning. *Degree requirements:* For master's, thesis.

**York University,** Faculty of Graduate Studies, Faculty of Fine Arts, Program in Film, Toronto, ON M3J 1P3, Canada. Offers MA, MFA, PhD. *Degree requirements:* For master's, thesis. *Entrance requirements:* For master's, portfolio. Electronic applications accepted.

# Film, Television, and Video Theory and Criticism

**Brooklyn College of the City University of New York,** School of Visual, Media and Performing Arts, Feirstein Graduate School of Cinema, Brooklyn, NY 11210-2889. Offers cinema arts (MFA); cinema studies (MA).

**California College of the Arts,** Graduate Programs, Visual and Critical Studies Program, San Francisco, CA 94107. Offers MA. *Faculty:* 1 (woman) full-time, 4 part-time/adjunct (3 women). *Students:* 15 full-time (14 women); includes 7 minority (1 Black or African American, non-Hispanic/Latino; 6 Hispanic/Latino), 2 international. Average age 32. 6 applicants, 83% accepted, 2 enrolled. In 2016, 10 master's awarded. *Degree requirements:* For master's, thesis. *Entrance requirements:* For master's, portfolio, resume, 2 letters of recommendation, transcripts, essay, interview. Additional exam requirements/recommendations for international students: Required—TOEFL, IELTS, or PTE. *Application deadline:* For fall admission, 1/10 for domestic and international students. Applications are processed on a rolling basis. Application fee: $70. Electronic applications accepted. *Expenses:* $1,641 per unit, $39,384 per year tuition; $490 fees. *Financial support:* Fellowships, teaching assistantships, career-related internships or fieldwork, Federal Work-Study, scholarships/grants, and health care benefits available. Financial award application deadline: 7/31; financial award applicants required to submit FAFSA. *Unit head:* Tirza Latimer, Chair, 415-551-9250, E-mail: tlatimer@cca.edu. *Application contact:* Wes Fanelli, Assistant Director of Graduate Admissions, 415-703-9533, Fax: 415-703-9539, E-mail: wfanelli@cca.edu.
Website: https://www.cca.edu/academics/graduate/visual-critical-studies

**Central Michigan University,** College of Graduate Studies, College of Communication and Fine Arts, School of Broadcasting and Cinematic Arts, Mount Pleasant, MI 48859. Offers electronic media management (MA); electronic media production (MA); electronic media studies (MA); film theory and criticism (MA). *Program availability:* Part-time. *Degree requirements:* For master's, thesis or alternative. *Entrance requirements:* For master's, undergraduate degree in broadcasting, film studies, or an associated discipline with minimum GPA of 2.7. Electronic applications accepted. *Faculty research:* Multimedia production, film history and criticism, writing and promotions, international broadcasting and media systems, history of American broadcasting.

**Claremont Graduate University,** Graduate Programs, School of Arts and Humanities, Department of English, Claremont, CA 91711-6160. Offers American studies (MA, PhD); critical theory (MA, PhD); early modern studies (MA, PhD); English (M Phil, MA, PhD); literary theory (PhD); literature (MA, PhD); literature and creative writing (MA); literature and film (MA); MBA/MA; MBA/PhD. *Program availability:* Part-time. *Faculty:* 3 full-time (1 woman), 1 part-time/adjunct (0 women). *Students:* 61 full-time (46 women), 20 part-time (14 women); includes 23 minority (4 Black or African American, non-Hispanic/Latino; 1 American Indian or Alaska Native, non-Hispanic/Latino; 9 Asian, non-Hispanic/Latino; 4 Hispanic/Latino; 5 Two or more races, non-Hispanic/Latino), 6 international. Average age 37. In 2016, 10 master's, 8 doctorates awarded. *Entrance requirements:* For master's and doctorate, GRE General Test. Additional exam requirements/recommendations for international students: Required—TOEFL (minimum score 75 iBT). *Application deadline:* For fall admission, 2/1 priority date for domestic and international students. Applications are processed on a rolling basis. Application fee: $80. Electronic applications accepted. *Expenses: Tuition:* Full-time $44,328; part-time $1847 per unit. *Required fees:* $600; $300 per semester. Tuition and fees vary according to course load and program. *Financial support:* Fellowships, Federal Work-Study, institutionally sponsored loans, and scholarships/grants available. Support available to part-time students. Financial award application deadline: 2/15; financial award applicants required to submit FAFSA. *Faculty research:* American, comparative, and English Renaissance literature; modernism; feminist literature and theory. *Unit head:* Lori Anne Ferrell, Chair, 909-607-2652, E-mail: lorianne.ferrell@cgu.edu. *Application contact:* Amy Sandefur, Assistant Director of Admissions, 909-607-9101, E-mail: amy.sandefur@cgu.edu.
Website: https://www.cgu.edu/departments/english/

**College of Staten Island of the City University of New York,** Graduate Programs, Division of Humanities and Social Sciences, Program in Cinema and Media Studies, Staten Island, NY 10314-6600. Offers MA. *Program availability:* Part-time, evening/weekend. *Faculty:* 4 full-time, 1 part-time/adjunct. *Students:* 10 part-time. Average age 31. 12 applicants, 58% accepted, 4 enrolled. In 2016, 1 master's awarded. *Degree requirements:* For master's, comprehensive exam (for some programs), 36 credits in cinema and media studies courses; written thesis, production thesis, or examination. *Entrance requirements:* For master's, bachelor's degree with minimum B average in undergraduate cinema studies or communications courses; 10-12 page writing sample; three letters of recommendation; 1-2 page statement of intent detailing interest in field, background in film and media studies, and/or research interests. Additional exam requirements/recommendations for international students: Required—TOEFL (minimum score 550 paper-based; 79 iBT), IELTS (minimum score 6.5). *Application deadline:* For fall admission, 6/15 priority date for domestic and international students; for spring admission, 11/25 priority date for domestic and international students. Applications are processed on a rolling basis. Application fee: $125. Electronic applications accepted. *Expenses:* Tuition, state resident: full-time $10,130; part-time $425 per credit. Tuition, nonresident: full-time $18,720; part-time $780 per credit. *Required fees:* $181.10 per semester. Tuition and fees vary according to program. *Faculty research:* Political communication, Latino/a media and audience, gender and sexuality, representation of race and ethnicity, video surveillance. *Unit head:* Jillian Baez, Graduate Program Coordinator, 718-982-2143, E-mail: cinemamasters@csi.cuny.edu. *Application contact:* Sasha Spence, Associate Director for Graduate Admissions, 718-982-2019, Fax: 718-982-2500, E-mail: sasha.spence@csi.cuny.edu.
Website: http://csivc.csi.cuny.edu/mediaculture/files

**Concordia University,** School of Graduate Studies, Faculty of Fine Arts, Mel Hoppenheim School of Cinema, Montréal, QC H3G 1M8, Canada. Offers film and moving image studies (PhD); film production (MFA); film studies (MA).

**DePaul University,** College of Communication, Chicago, IL 60614. Offers digital communication and media arts (MA); health communication (MA); journalism (MA); media and cinema studies (MA); organizational and multicultural communication (MA); public relations and advertising (MA); relational communication (MA). *Program availability:* Part-time, evening/weekend. *Entrance requirements:* Additional exam requirements/recommendations for international students: Required—TOEFL (minimum score 590 paper-based; 96 iBT), IELTS (minimum score 7.5) or PTE. Electronic applications accepted.

**Emory University,** Laney Graduate School, Department of Film Studies, Atlanta, GA 30322-1100. Offers MA, PhD/Certificate. *Degree requirements:* For master's, comprehensive exam, thesis or alternative. *Entrance requirements:* For master's, GRE General Test, 3 letters of reference, 2 writing samples. Additional exam requirements/recommendations for international students: Required—TOEFL. Electronic applications

accepted. *Faculty research:* International film history, film theory, film style, feminism and film, reception.

**Emory University,** Laney Graduate School, Department of Spanish and Portuguese, Atlanta, GA 30322-1100. Offers comparative literature (Certificate); film studies (Certificate); Spanish (PhD); women's studies (Certificate). *Degree requirements:* For doctorate, 2 foreign languages, comprehensive exam, thesis/dissertation. *Entrance requirements:* For doctorate, GRE General Test. Additional exam requirements/recommendations for international students: Required—TOEFL. Electronic applications accepted. *Faculty research:* Spanish literature, Spanish American literature, literary theory, criticism, cultural studies.

**Hollins University,** Graduate Programs, Program in Screenwriting and Film Studies, Roanoke, VA 24020. Offers screenwriting (MFA); screenwriting and film studies (MA). Program offered during summer only. *Program availability:* Part-time. *Degree requirements:* For master's, one foreign language, comprehensive exam, thesis. *Entrance requirements:* For master's, letters of recommendation, portfolio. Additional exam requirements/recommendations for international students: Required—TOEFL (minimum score 550 paper-based; 80 iBT), IELTS (minimum score 6.5). *Application deadline:* For summer admission, 2/15 for domestic and international students. Application fee: $40. Electronic applications accepted. *Expenses:* $830 per credit hour. *Financial support:* Fellowships, Federal Work-Study, institutionally sponsored loans, and scholarships/grants available. Support available to part-time students. Financial award application deadline: 2/15; financial award applicants required to submit FAFSA. *Faculty research:* Censorship, minorities in film, writing for television, new media. *Unit head:* Dr. Tim Albaugh, Director, 540-362-6575, E-mail: hugrad@hollins.edu. *Application contact:* Cathy S. Koon, Manager of Graduate Programs, 540-362-6326, Fax: 540-362-6288, E-mail: ckoon@hollins.edu.
Website: https://www.hollins.edu/academics/graduate-degrees/mfa-screenwriting-film-studies/

**Ohio University,** Graduate College, College of Fine Arts, School of Film, Athens, OH 45701-2979. Offers film (MFA); film studies (MA). *Degree requirements:* For master's, one foreign language, thesis. *Entrance requirements:* Additional exam requirements/recommendations for international students: Required—TOEFL (minimum score 550 paper-based; 80 iBT) or IELTS (minimum score 6.5). *Application deadline:* For fall admission, 2/1 for domestic and international students. Application fee: $50 ($55 for international students). Electronic applications accepted. *Financial support:* Research assistantships with full tuition reimbursements, teaching assistantships with full tuition reimbursements, institutionally sponsored loans, scholarships/grants, tuition waivers (full and partial), and unspecified assistantships available. Financial award application deadline: 2/1. *Faculty research:* Scriptwriting, sound, editing, cinematography, film theory, digital post production. *Unit head:* Steven Ross, Director, 740-593-9969, Fax: 740-593-1328, E-mail: rosss2@ohio.edu. *Application contact:* Dr. Jody Lamb, Associate Dean, 740-593-1811, E-mail: lambj@ohio.edu.
Website: http://www.finearts.ohio.edu/film/

**Salisbury University,** Department of English, Salisbury, MD 21801-6837. Offers English (MA), including creative writing, film, literature, secondary education, TESOL, writing and rhetoric. *Program availability:* Part-time. *Faculty:* 11 full-time (5 women), 1 (woman) part-time/adjunct. *Students:* 11 full-time (9 women), 24 part-time (19 women); includes 1 minority (Black or African American, non-Hispanic/Latino), 4 international. Average age 33. 18 applicants, 67% accepted, 9 enrolled. In 2016, 17 master's awarded. *Degree requirements:* For master's, comprehensive exam, thesis optional. *Entrance requirements:* Additional exam requirements/recommendations for international students: Required—TOEFL (minimum score 550 paper-based, 79 iBT) or IELTS (6.5). *Application deadline:* For fall admission, 8/1 for domestic and international students; for spring admission, 1/1 for domestic and international students. Application fee: $65. Electronic applications accepted. *Expenses:* $381 per credit hour resident tuition, $670 per credit hour non-resident tuition; $84 per credit hour fees. *Financial support:* In 2016–17, 2 students received support, including 11 teaching assistantships with full tuition reimbursements available (averaging $9,395 per year); career-related internships or fieldwork and scholarships/grants also available. Support available to part-time students. Financial award application deadline: 3/1; financial award applicants required to submit FAFSA. *Faculty research:* Literature; linguistics; film studies; rhetoric and composition; TESOL. *Unit head:* Dr. Christopher Vilmar, Graduate Program Director, English, 410-677-6511, E-mail: csvilmar@salisbury.edu.
Website: http://www.salisbury.edu/gsr/gradstudies/ENGpage.html

**San Francisco State University,** Division of Graduate Studies, College of Liberal and Creative Arts, School of Cinema, San Francisco, CA 94132-1722. Offers MA, MFA. *Expenses:* Tuition, state resident: full-time $6738. Tuition, nonresident: full-time $15,666. *Required fees:* $1012. Tuition and fees vary according to degree level and program. *Unit head:* Dr. Britta Sjogren, Director, 415-338-1629, Fax: 415-338-0906, E-mail: cinedept@sfsu.edu. *Application contact:* Dr. R. L. Rutsky, MA Coordinator, 415-405-3400, Fax: 415-338-0906, E-mail: rlrutsky@sfsu.edu.
Website: http://www.cinema.sfsu.edu/

**Savannah College of Art and Design,** Graduate School, Program in Cinema Studies, Savannah, GA 31402-3146. Offers MA. *Program availability:* Part-time. *Faculty:* 2 full-time (1 woman). *Students:* 3 full-time (2 women), 5 part-time (4 women); includes 2 minority (1 Black or African American, non-Hispanic/Latino; 1 Hispanic/Latino). Average age 27. 6 applicants, 50% accepted, 2 enrolled. In 2016, 3 master's awarded. *Degree requirements:* For master's, thesis. *Entrance requirements:* For master's, GRE (recommended), portfolio (submitted in digital format), audition or writing submission, resume, statement of purpose, two letters of recommendation. Additional exam requirements/recommendations for international students: Required—TOEFL (minimum score 550 paper-based, 85 iBT), IELTS (minimum score 6.5), or ACTFL. *Application deadline:* For fall admission, 4/1 for domestic and international students. Applications are processed on a rolling basis. Application fee: $40. Electronic applications accepted. *Expenses: Tuition:* Full-time $36,045. Tuition and fees vary according to course load. *Financial support:* Career-related internships or fieldwork, Federal Work-Study, and scholarships/grants available. Financial award application deadline: 4/1; financial award applicants required to submit FAFSA. *Unit head:* Dr. Geoffrey Taylor, Chair, Art History. *Application contact:* Jenny Jaquillard, Executive Director of Admissions, Recruitment and Events, 912-525-5100, Fax: 912-525-5985, E-mail: admission@scad.edu.
Website: http://www.scad.edu/academics/programs/cinema-studies

**Syracuse University,** S. I. Newhouse School of Public Communications, MA Program in Documentary Film and History, Syracuse, NY 13244. Offers MA. *Students:* Average age 31. *Degree requirements:* For master's, thesis or alternative. *Entrance requirements:* For master's, GRE General Test, resume, official transcripts, personal statement, three letters of recommendation. Additional exam requirements/

recommendations for international students: Required—TOEFL (minimum score 100 iBT). *Application deadline:* For fall admission, 2/1 for international students; for summer admission, 1/15 priority date for domestic and international students. Application fee: $45. Electronic applications accepted. *Expenses:* Tuition: Full-time $25,974; part-time $1443 per credit hour. *Required fees:* $802; $50 per course. Tuition and fees vary according to course load and program. *Financial support:* Fellowships with full tuition reimbursements, research assistantships with partial tuition reimbursements, and teaching assistantships with partial tuition reimbursements available. Financial award application deadline: 2/1. *Faculty research:* View production, distribution, new media, applications to education. *Unit head:* Richard Breyer, Co-Director, Documentary Film and History/Professor, 315-443-9249, E-mail: rlbreyer@syr.edu. *Application contact:* Martha Coria, Graduate Records Office, 315-443-4039, Fax: 315-443-1834, E-mail: pcgrad@syr.edu.
Website: http://newhouse.syr.edu/

**Texas A&M University–Commerce,** College of Humanities, Social Sciences and Arts, Commerce, TX 75429-3011. Offers applied criminology (MS); applied linguistics (MA, MS); art (MA, MFA); Christianity in history (Graduate Certificate); computational linguistics (Graduate Certificate); creative writing (Graduate Certificate); English (MA, MS, PhD); film studies (Graduate Certificate); history (MA, MS); music (MM); political science (MA, MS); public history (Graduate Certificate); sociology (MS); Spanish (MA); studies in children's and adolescent literature and culture (Graduate Certificate); teaching English to speakers of other languages (Graduate Certificate); theater (MA, MS). *Program availability:* Part-time. *Faculty:* 53 full-time (26 women), 7 part-time/adjunct (2 women). *Students:* 87 full-time (55 women), 528 part-time (362 women); includes 198 minority (86 Black or African American, non-Hispanic/Latino; 2 American Indian or Alaska Native, non-Hispanic/Latino; 8 Asian, non-Hispanic/Latino; 84 Hispanic/Latino; 18 Two or more races, non-Hispanic/Latino), 27 international. Average age 37. 333 applicants, 56% accepted, 149 enrolled. In 2016, 66 master's, 8 doctorates awarded. *Degree requirements:* For master's, one foreign language, comprehensive exam, thesis (for some programs); for doctorate, one foreign language, comprehensive exam, thesis/dissertation, departmental qualifying exam. *Entrance requirements:* For master's and doctorate, GRE General Test. Additional exam requirements/recommendations for international students: Required—TOEFL (minimum score 550 paper-based; 79 iBT), IELTS (minimum score 6). *Application deadline:* Applications are processed on a rolling basis. Application fee: $50. Electronic applications accepted. *Expenses:* Contact institution. *Financial support:* In 2016–17, 255 students received support, including 9 research assistantships with partial tuition reimbursements available (averaging $9,000 per year), 68 teaching assistantships with partial tuition reimbursements available (averaging $9,000 per year); Federal Work-Study, institutionally sponsored loans, scholarships/grants, health care benefits, and unspecified assistantships also available. Financial award application deadline: 5/1; financial award applicants required to submit FAFSA. *Unit head:* Dr. Salvatore Attardo, Dean, 903-886-5166, Fax: 903-886-5774, E-mail: salvatore.attardo@tamuc.edu. *Application contact:* Shelby Miller, Graduate Recruiter, 903-468-8123, Fax: 903-886-5774, E-mail: shelby.miller@tamuc.edu.
Website: http://www.tamuc.edu/academics/graduateSchool/programs/humanitiesSocialScienceArts/default.aspx

**Tiffin University,** Program in Humanities, Tiffin, OH 44883-2161. Offers art and visual media (MH); communication (MH); creative writing (MH); English (MH); film studies (MH); humanities (MH); individualized studies (MH). *Program availability:* Part-time, evening/weekend, online only, 100% online, blended/hybrid learning. *Students:* 17 full-time (15 women), 116 part-time (75 women); includes 25 minority (15 Black or African American, non-Hispanic/Latino; 2 Asian, non-Hispanic/Latino; 6 Hispanic/Latino; 2 Two or more races, non-Hispanic/Latino). Average age 36. 84 applicants, 80% accepted, 43 enrolled. In 2016, 42 master's awarded. *Entrance requirements:* For master's, work experience. Additional exam requirements/recommendations for international students: Required—TOEFL (minimum score 550 paper-based; 79 iBT). *Application deadline:* For fall admission, 9/1 for domestic students; for spring admission, 1/9 for domestic students. Applications are processed on a rolling basis. Application fee: $50. Electronic applications accepted. Application fee is waived when completed online. *Expenses:* Contact institution. *Financial support:* Unspecified assistantships available. Financial award applicants required to submit FAFSA. *Unit head:* Dr. Jason Slone, Program Chair, 419-448-5851, Fax: 419-443-5002, E-mail: slonedj@tiffin.edu. *Application contact:* Nikki Hintze, Director of Graduate and Distance Education Academic Advising, 800-968-6446 Ext. 3596, Fax: 419-443-5002, E-mail: hintzenm@tiffin.edu.

**Université de Montréal,** Faculty of Arts and Sciences, Department of Art History and Film Studies, Montréal, QC H3C 3J7, Canada. Offers art history (MA, PhD); film studies (MA, PhD). Programs offered jointly with Concordia University, Université Laval, and Université du Québec à Montréal. *Degree requirements:* For master's, thesis. Electronic applications accepted. *Faculty research:* Western art from the Middle Ages, classic and modern theory, modern and contemporary art, Canadian art.

**Université Laval,** Faculty of Letters, Department of Literature, Programs in Literature and Arts of the Screen and Stage, Québec, QC G1K 7P4, Canada. Offers MA, PhD. *Program availability:* Part-time. Terminal master's awarded for partial completion of doctoral program. *Degree requirements:* For master's, thesis; for doctorate, comprehensive exam, thesis/dissertation. *Entrance requirements:* For master's and doctorate, linguistics exams, knowledge of French, knowledge of a second language. Electronic applications accepted.

**University at Buffalo, the State University of New York,** Graduate School, College of Arts and Sciences, Department of Media Study, Buffalo, NY 14260. Offers film and media study (MAH); media arts production (MFA); media study (PhD); new media design (Certificate); social media (MAH); M Arch/MFA. *Faculty:* 11 full-time (5 women), 3 part-time/adjunct (1 woman). *Students:* 53 full-time (28 women); includes 20 minority (4 Black or African American, non-Hispanic/Latino; 15 Asian, non-Hispanic/Latino; 1 Hispanic/Latino). Average age 26. 82 applicants, 35% accepted, 12 enrolled. In 2016, 14 master's, 1 doctorate, 1 other advanced degree awarded. Terminal master's awarded for partial completion of doctoral program. *Degree requirements:* For master's, thesis, media project; for doctorate, thesis/dissertation, qualifying exam, media project. *Entrance requirements:* For master's, portfolio; for doctorate, GRE, portfolio. Additional exam requirements/recommendations for international students: Required—TOEFL (minimum score 550 paper-based; 79 iBT). *Application deadline:* For fall admission, 1/7 priority date for domestic and international students. Applications are processed on a rolling basis. Application fee: $75. Electronic applications accepted. *Expenses:* $6,673.50 full-time resident tuition and fees, $12,343.50 full-time non-resident tuition and fees. *Financial support:* In 2016–17, 11 students received support, including 11 teaching assistantships with full tuition reimbursements available (averaging $13,733 per year); fellowships, career-related internships or fieldwork, Federal Work-Study, scholarships/grants, health care benefits, and unspecified assistantships also available. Support available to part-time students. Financial award application deadline: 1/7; financial award applicants required to submit FAFSA. *Faculty research:* Digital arts, video, documentary, film, game design, digital poetics, locative media. *Unit head:* Prof. Marc Bohlen, Chair, 716-645-6902, Fax: 716-645-6979, E-mail: mrbohlen@buffalo.edu. *Application contact:* Ann Mangan, Academic Advisor/Graduate Coordinator, 716-645-

0945, Fax: 716-645-6979, E-mail: annmanga@buffalo.edu.
Website: http://mediastudy.buffalo.edu/

**The University of Arizona,** College of Fine Arts, School of Theatre, Film and Television, Tucson, AZ 85721. Offers MFA. *Accreditation:* NAST. *Degree requirements:* For master's, comprehensive exam (for some programs), thesis (for some programs), production monograph. *Entrance requirements:* For master's, 3 letters of recommendation, portfolio. Additional exam requirements/recommendations for international students: Required—TOEFL (minimum score 550 paper-based; 79 iBT). Electronic applications accepted. *Faculty research:* Modern and contemporary theater, cultural studies, musical theater, women and theater.

**The University of British Columbia,** Faculty of Arts and Faculty of Graduate Studies, Department of Theatre and Film, Film Program, Vancouver, BC V6T 1Z2, Canada. Offers film production (MFA); film studies (MA). *Degree requirements:* For master's, variable foreign language requirement, comprehensive exam, thesis (MA); thesis or project (MFA). *Entrance requirements:* For master's, portfolio (MFA). Additional exam requirements/recommendations for international students: Required—TOEFL. Application fee: $100 Canadian dollars ($162 Canadian dollars for international students). *Expenses:* $4,802 per year tuition and fees, $8,436 per year international. *Financial support:* Fellowships, research assistantships, and teaching assistantships available. *Faculty research:* Film theory and violence; American and European cinema; cult cinema; Irish cinema. *Application contact:* Zanna Downes, Graduate Program Staff, 604-822-6037, Fax: 604-822-0508, E-mail: fipr.sec@ubc.ca.
Website: http://theatrefilm.ubc.ca/

**University of California, Berkeley,** Graduate Division, College of Letters and Science, Department of Film and Media, Berkeley, CA 94720-2670. Offers PhD. *Students:* 23 full-time (16 women); includes 5 minority (all Hispanic/Latino), 2 international. 91 applicants, 2 enrolled. In 2016, 2 doctorates awarded. *Degree requirements:* For doctorate, thesis/dissertation, qualifying exam. *Entrance requirements:* Additional exam requirements/recommendations for international students: Required—TOEFL (minimum score 570 paper-based; 90 iBT). *Application deadline:* For fall admission, 12/5 for domestic students. Application fee: $105 ($125 for international students). Electronic applications accepted. *Financial support:* Fellowships, research assistantships, teaching assistantships, institutionally sponsored loans, health care benefits, and unspecified assistantships available. Financial award applicants required to submit FAFSA. *Unit head:* Kristen Whissel, Chair, 510-642-1415, E-mail: rfa@berkeley.edu.
Website: http://filmmedia.berkeley.edu

**University of California, Santa Cruz,** Division of Graduate Studies, Division of the Arts, Department of Film and Digital Media, Santa Cruz, CA 95064. Offers PhD. *Degree requirements:* For doctorate, one foreign language, thesis/dissertation, qualifying exams. *Entrance requirements:* For doctorate, GRE. Additional exam requirements/recommendations for international students: Required—TOEFL (minimum score 550 paper-based; 83 iBT), Recommended—IELTS (minimum score 8). Electronic applications accepted. *Faculty research:* Integrating critical and creative practice, working across media, pursuing new modes of social and political engagement, fostering global cultural citizenship.

**University of Chicago,** Division of the Humanities, Department of Cinema and Media Studies, Chicago, IL 60637. Offers PhD. *Students:* 36 full-time (22 women); includes 5 minority (3 Black or African American, non-Hispanic/Latino; 2 Two or more races, non-Hispanic/Latino), 15 international. 99 applicants, 8% accepted, 5 enrolled. In 2016, 4 doctorates awarded. *Degree requirements:* For doctorate, 2 foreign languages, comprehensive exam, thesis/dissertation. *Entrance requirements:* For doctorate, GRE General Test. Additional exam requirements/recommendations for international students: Required—TOEFL (minimum score 104 iBT), IELTS (minimum score 7). *Application deadline:* For fall admission, 12/15 for domestic and international students. Application fee: $90. Electronic applications accepted. *Financial support:* Fellowships with full tuition reimbursements, teaching assistantships with tuition reimbursements, Federal Work-Study, institutionally sponsored loans, scholarships/grants, and health care benefits available. Financial award application deadline: 12/15; financial award applicants required to submit FAFSA. *Unit head:* Daniel Morgan, Chair, 773-702-3317, E-mail: drmorgan@uchicago.edu. *Application contact:* Michael Beetley, Assistant Dean of Students, Admissions and Fellowships, 773-702-1552, Fax: 773-834-9148, E-mail: humanitiesadmissions@uchicago.edu.
Website: https://cms.uchicago.edu/

**The University of Iowa,** Graduate College, College of Liberal Arts and Sciences, Department of Cinema and Comparative Literature, Program in Film Studies, Iowa City, IA 52242-1316. Offers MA, PhD. *Degree requirements:* For master's, thesis optional, exam; for doctorate, comprehensive exam, thesis/dissertation. *Entrance requirements:* For master's and doctorate, GRE General Test, minimum GPA of 3.0. Additional exam requirements/recommendations for international students: Required—TOEFL (minimum score 550 paper-based; 81 iBT). Electronic applications accepted.

**The University of Kansas,** Graduate Studies, College of Liberal Arts and Sciences, Department of Film and Media Studies, Lawrence, KS 66045. Offers MA, PhD. *Students:* 20 full-time (9 women); includes 5 minority (2 Black or African American, non-Hispanic/Latino; 1 American Indian or Alaska Native, non-Hispanic/Latino; 1 Native Hawaiian or other Pacific Islander, non-Hispanic/Latino; 1 Two or more races, non-Hispanic/Latino), 4 international. Average age 32. 16 applicants, 38% accepted, 4 enrolled. In 2016, 2 doctorates awarded. *Entrance requirements:* For master's, GRE General Test, three recent letters of recommendation, current resume, statement of personal goals, writing sample; for doctorate, GRE General Test, MA in film or related field; three recent letters of recommendation; current resume; statement of personal goals; writing sample; minimum GPA of 3.2 undergraduate, 3.5 graduate. Additional exam requirements/recommendations for international students: Required—TOEFL or IELTS. *Application deadline:* For fall admission, 1/1 priority date for domestic and international students. Application fee: $65 ($85 for international students). Electronic applications accepted. *Financial support:* Fellowships, research assistantships, teaching assistantships, scholarships/grants, and unspecified assistantships available. Financial award application deadline: 1/1; financial award applicants required to submit FAFSA. *Faculty research:* Latin American cinema, Japanese and East Asian cinema, new media/cultural geography of media, film history, film theory and visual culture. *Unit head:* Dr. Michael Baskett, Chair, 785-864-1384, E-mail: eiga@ku.edu. *Application contact:* Karla Conrad, Graduate Secretary, 785-864-1340, E-mail: kmconrad@ku.edu.
Website: http://film.ku.edu/

**University of Miami,** Graduate School, School of Communication, Coral Gables, FL 33124. Offers communication (PhD); communication studies (MA); film studies (MA, PhD); motion pictures (MFA), including production, producing, and screenwriting; print journalism (MA); public relations (MA); Spanish language journalism (MA); television broadcast journalism (MA). *Program availability:* Part-time. *Degree requirements:* For master's, comprehensive exam (for some programs), thesis (for some programs); for doctorate, comprehensive exam, thesis/dissertation. *Entrance requirements:* For master's, GRE General Test; for doctorate, GRE General Test, master's thesis or scholarly research. Additional exam requirements/recommendations for international students: Required—TOEFL (minimum score 600 paper-based; 100 iBT). Electronic

*Film, Television, and Video Theory and Criticism*

optional; for doctorate, thesis/dissertation. *Entrance requirements:* For master's, honours BA or the equivalent in English, minimum B+ in English courses above first year level; for doctorate, MA in English, minimum A- average in graduate work. Additional exam requirements/recommendations for international students: Recommended—TOEFL (minimum score 89 iBT). Electronic applications accepted. *Faculty research:* Gender and genre, Canadian studies, early modern studies, postcolonial studies, nineteenth century studies.

**Yale University,** Graduate School of Arts and Sciences, Department of East Asian Languages and Literatures, New Haven, CT 06520. Offers East Asian languages and literatures (PhD); East Asian languages and literatures and film studies (PhD). *Degree requirements:* For doctorate, 2 foreign languages, thesis/dissertation. *Entrance requirements:* For doctorate, GRE General Test.

**Yale University,** Graduate School of Arts and Sciences, Department of Slavic Languages and Literatures, New Haven, CT 06520. Offers medieval Slavic literature and philology (PhD); Polish literature (PhD); Russian literature (PhD); Slavic languages and literatures and film studies (PhD). *Degree requirements:* For doctorate, 3 foreign languages, thesis/dissertation. *Entrance requirements:* For doctorate, GRE General Test.

**Yale University,** Graduate School of Arts and Sciences, Interdisciplinary Program in Film Studies, New Haven, CT 06520. Offers PhD.

# FLORIDA STATE UNIVERSITY
*College of Motion Picture Arts*

 For more information, visit http://petersons.to/fsu_motionpicturearts

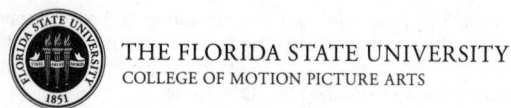

THE FLORIDA STATE UNIVERSITY
COLLEGE OF MOTION PICTURE ARTS

## Programs of Study

The Florida State University (FSU) College of Motion Picture Arts was created in 1989 by the Florida legislature with the expressed mission to prepare men and women for successful careers in the motion picture industry.

Recognized by the Directors Guild of America for its distinguished contribution to American culture, the college enrolls 32 new graduate students per year and pays for the production of their films, allowing the faculty to maintain the high caliber of education necessary for graduates to succeed in an extremely competitive industry.

Instructors are senior industry members and young, accomplished professionals who work as writers, directors, producers, cinematographers, sound designers, or editors in film and television. Many of them have won national and international awards and honors for their work, including Oscars from the Academy of Motion Picture Arts and Sciences.

The college offers a Master of Fine Arts (M.F.A.) program in narrative filmmaking, which prepares students for careers in screenwriting, producing, directing, cinematography, sound, and editing, and an M.F.A. program in writing for the stage and screen. The Production program centered on narrative filmmaking requires the completion of 90 credit hours, and the Screenwriting program requires 66 credit hours. Both programs take place during six consecutive semesters.

During the first semester of study, all students participate in a common curriculum and take a wide range of courses, including screenwriting, producing, directing, cinematography, editing, and sound design. During the second semester, screenwriting students engage in exclusive coursework that focuses on the creation and management of feature-length screenplays while studying abroad in London. Production students engage in production workshops that support the creation of short films. During the last two semesters of the second year, students culminate their programs by creating a thesis film or a feature-length screenplay. Throughout the program, students engage in various seminars, conferences, and visits from industry professionals in the fields of film, theater, and creative writing.

## Research Facilities

Students have 24-hour access to FSU Studios, which are among the largest and best-equipped production facilities in the world devoted to motion picture education. FSU facilities include three soundstages, student production offices, ADR and Foley stages, animation and visual effects studios, dedicated screening rooms, and mix stages. FSU is the only university in the United States—with graduate and undergraduate programs—that provides a full range of motion picture equipment to its students, including grip and camera trucks, generators, dollies, grip and electric equipment, and RED Helium cameras.

## Financial Aid

FSU is the only film school in the country that pays for the production costs of undergraduate and graduate student films, thereby creating a level playing field for students to focus on art, craft, and imagination—instead of fundraising. To ensure that this high caliber of education is available to the most talented student regardless of financial means, the university offers generous scholarships and assistantships, and its tuition costs are among the lowest in the country.

## Cost of Study

In the 2016–17 academic year, graduate tuition was $479.32 per credit hour for Florida residents and close to $1,110.72 for nonresidents. The cost of student productions, including equipment, is included in the tuition rates.

## Living and Housing Costs

The amounts listed in the "Cost of Study" section do not include the cost of food, housing, and transportation. A one-bedroom apartment in Leon County costs approximately $600 per month, and a two-bedroom approximately $700.

## Student Group

Each fall, a new class of 24 production students and 8 screenwriting students is admitted, for a maximum of 64 students in the two-year program. Approximately two-thirds of these students are from outside the state of Florida and come from a wide variety of academic and creative backgrounds.

## Student Outcomes

Thesis films are widely promoted by the College at regional, national, and international film festivals and competitions—including those sponsored by the Academy of Motion Picture Arts and Sciences and Academy of Television Arts and Sciences—and have won more than 4000 awards, recognitions, and selected screenings. Students in the writing program graduate with a portfolio of creative work that includes short- and long-form plays, short and feature-length screenplays, an original television pilot, and two full-length plays and/or screenplays ready for submission to the film and theater industries.

Alumni are unusually involved with the College of Motion Picture Arts and actively work to transition graduates into the industry. Every graduate student has the opportunity to be assigned a mentor who coordinates with faculty and staff members to create career plans for students before they leave the program. This provides 97 percent of the college's graduates with meaningful work in the film and television industry within twelve months of graduation.

## Location

Florida State University is located in Tallahassee, the state capital, with a population of approximately 185,000 people. The northern Florida location has a landscape and climate that are substantially different from that of southern Florida.

Home to the state capital, two major universities, and an array of museums, attractions, and unique experiences, Tallahassee shares a deep-rooted history and culture with unparalleled nature and outdoor recreation. A fusion of cosmopolitan flair and charming personality defines the spirit of Florida's capital city.

## The University

Florida State University is an internationally-recognized teaching and research institution committed to preparing graduates for the ever-expanding opportunities of a global society.

Florida State University's 15 colleges offer more than 275 undergraduate, graduate, doctoral, professional and specialist degree programs,

## Florida State University

including medicine and law, covering a broad array of disciplines critical to society today. The arts programs—dance, film, music, and theater—rank among the finest in the world, offering an arts education comparable to leading conservatories.

With its impressive breadth of leading graduate, professional, and undergraduate programs, Florida State University is a demanding, intellectually stimulating, yet warm and caring environment for students and faculty.

### The Faculty

Bill Carruth, Filmmaker in Residence (Editing). Mr. Carruth is a third-generation film editor with over 40 years' experience in the film industry. He began his career working with Verna Fields on *Paper Moon, Sugarland Express,* and *Jaws,* and from there, as film editor on *Nickelodeon, Saint Jack, FM, Caddyshack, Night Games, What Comes Around, Island of Dr. Moreau, They All Laughed,* and others. He also worked as a sound supervisor editing dialogue, ADR, and effects for feature films such as *The Fan, Maverick, Executive Decision, U.S. Marshals, Assassins, Lethal Weapon 4,* and *Conspiracy Theory,* as well as TV shows and series including *The Division, Purgatory, Atomic Train, Netforce, Into The West, NCIS, JAG, Touched by an Angel, Las Vegas,* and *Crossing Jordan.*

Paul Cohen, Filmmaker in Residence (Distribution and Marketing); B.A., Hofstra University. Mr. Cohen is an independent motion picture executive who has created a number of successful distribution and production companies including Analysis Films, Masada Productions, Moonbeam Productions, and Aries Films. He has acquired and marketed a wide range of successful films often recognized as cinematic gems and contemporary classics. These include Abel Ferrara's *Bad Lieutenant,* starring Harvey Keitel; *Mephisto,* the 1981 Academy Award-winner for Best Foreign Language Film; *My Brilliant Career,* directed by first-timer Gillian Armstrong and starring Judy Davis and Sam Neill; *The Chosen,* starring Maximilian Schell; and Luchino Visconti's *The Innocent.* Mr. Cohen's motion picture selections over the years have garnered Oscar nominations, a Golden Globe, a Spirit Award, Italy's Donatello, and France's Cesar, as well as other award recognitions for their high quality. His cinema acquisitions have played in film festivals across the country and around the world. In addition, Mr. Cohen has served in the capacity of executive producer on a number of independent productions. He serves as the director of The Torchlight Program, established by The Film School to enhance the education of students through instruction in current and emerging business practices of the motion picture industry.

Victor Nunez, Filmmaker in Residence (Directing); M.F.A. (film), UCLA. Regarded as a national treasure in American independent cinema, Nunez is a producer, director, writer, and cinematographer whose credits include *Gal Young Un, Ruby in Paradise,* and the IFC release *Coastlines.* Actor Peter Fonda won the Golden Globe, the New York Film Critics Award, and was nominated for an Academy Award for his portrayal of the title role in Nunez's feature film *Ulee's Gold.* Nunez is a founding board member of the Independent Feature Project and the Sundance Film Institute and a member of the Writers Guild of America.

Valerie Scoon, Filmmaker in Residence (Producing); B.A., (American history and literature), Harvard. Ms. Scoon is a producer and creative executive with extensive industry experience. She worked as the director of development for television and film at Oprah Winfrey's Harpo Pictures where she served as the key creative executive developing such major motion pictures as Spike Lee's *Malcolm X;* Oprah Winfrey's *Beloved* and *Their Eyes Were Watching God;* Frances Hodgson Burnett's classic children's story, *The Secret Garden;* and most recently, *The Great Debaters.* In addition, Ms. Scoon has worked as a creative executive developing feature films at Warner Brothers Studio, a story analyst at Creative Artists Agency, and as the associate director of news and public affairs at PBS. As president and CEO of True Visions Productions, she currently develops and produces films and documentaries for theatrical release.

### Applying

To be considered for admission, applicants must complete an online application that includes a current resume, a statement of purpose (500–1,000 words) describing artistic experiences and creative influences, three letters of recommendation, an official college transcript showing a GPA of 3.0 or higher, a writing sample, a video story pitch, and an optional portfolio of creative work.

The online application is offered through the Florida State University Office of Admissions and is located at http://admissions.fsu.edu/. Approximately 90 students are invited each year to interview with the Film School's Admissions Committee. The application deadline is December 1.

### Correspondence and Information

Gloria McElroy, Staff Director of Admissions and Recruitment
Florida State University
282 Champions Way
University Center A 5100
Tallahassee, Florida 32306
United States
Phone: 850-644-8524
E-mail: gmcelroy@fsu.edu
Website: http://www.film.fsu.edu

# Section 6
# Performing Arts

This section contains a directory of institutions offering graduate work in performing arts, followed by an in-depth entry submitted by an institution that chose to prepare a detailed program description. Additional information about programs listed in the directory but not augmented by an in-depth entry may be obtained by writing directly to the dean of a graduate school or chair of a department at the address given in the directory.

For programs offering related work, see also in this book *Area and Cultural Studies, Art and Art History, Communication and Media,* and *Film, Television, and Video.* In another guide in this series:

**Graduate Programs in Business, Education, Information Studies, Law & Social Work**

See *Leisure Studies and Recreation, Subject Areas (Music Education),* and *Physical Education and Kinesiology*

## CONTENTS

# Dance

**Arizona State University at the Tempe campus,** Herberger Institute for Design and the Arts, School of Film, Dance and Theatre, Department of Dance, Tempe, AZ 85287-0304. Offers dance (MFA); interdisciplinary digital media and performance (MFA). *Degree requirements:* For master's, thesis optional, project, written document and oral defense, interactive Program of Study (iPOS) submitted before completing 50 percent of required credit hours. *Entrance requirements:* For master's, personal statement relating to school's core values, resume, 3 letters of recommendation from professionals in the dance field. Electronic applications accepted.

**Bennington College,** Graduate Programs, MFA in Dance Program, Bennington, VT 05201. Offers MFA. *Program availability:* Part-time. *Degree requirements:* For master's, performances. *Entrance requirements:* Additional exam requirements/recommendations for international students: Recommended—TOEFL. Electronic applications accepted. *Expenses:* Contact institution. *Faculty research:* Exploration of relationship between emergent improvisation and complex systems.

**California Institute of the Arts,** School of Dance, Valencia, CA 91355-2340. Offers MFA, Adv C. *Accreditation:* NASD. *Degree requirements:* For master's, thesis presentation. *Entrance requirements:* For master's, audition, video of choreography. Additional exam requirements/recommendations for international students: Required—TOEFL.

**California State University, Long Beach,** Graduate Studies, College of the Arts, Department of Dance, Long Beach, CA 90840. Offers MA, MFA. *Accreditation:* NASD. *Program availability:* Part-time. *Degree requirements:* For master's, thesis. *Application deadline:* Applications are processed on a rolling basis. Application fee: $5. Electronic applications accepted. *Financial support:* Federal Work-Study, institutionally sponsored loans, scholarships/grants, and traineeships available. Financial award application deadline: 3/2. *Unit head:* Prof. Cyrus Parker-Jeannette, Chair, 562-985-4747, Fax: 562-985-7896, E-mail: cyparker@csulb.edu. *Application contact:* Dr. Colleen Dunagan, Graduate Advisor, 562-985-7040, Fax: 562-985-7896, E-mail: cdunagan@csulb.edu.

**Case Western Reserve University,** School of Graduate Studies, Department of Dance, Cleveland, OH 44106. Offers MA, MFA. *Faculty:* 3 full-time (2 women). *Students:* 7 full-time (2 women); includes 1 minority (Two or more races, non-Hispanic/Latino), 3 international. Average age 25. 12 applicants, 58% accepted, 4 enrolled. *Degree requirements:* For master's, thesis, performance thesis. *Entrance requirements:* For master's, professional video, statement of goals and objectives, audition, interview. Additional exam requirements/recommendations for international students: Required—TOEFL (minimum score 577 paper-based; 90 iBT); Recommended—IELTS (minimum score 7). *Application deadline:* For fall admission, 3/1 priority date for domestic students; for spring admission, 11/1 priority date for domestic students. Application fee: $50. Electronic applications accepted. *Expenses:* Tuition: Full-time $42,576; part-time $1774 per credit hour. *Required fees:* $34. Tuition and fees vary according to course load and program. *Financial support:* Fellowships, teaching assistantships, scholarships/grants, and stipends available. Financial award application deadline: 3/1. *Faculty research:* Dance medicine and science, dance/technology. *Unit head:* Karen Potter, Professor and Chair, 216-368-1491, E-mail: karen.potter@case.edu. *Application contact:* Lori Waugh, Department Assistant, 216-368-2854, Fax: 216-368-4250,
E-mail: lori.waugh@case.edu.
Website: http://dance.case.edu/

**The College at Brockport, State University of New York,** School of Arts and Sciences, Department of Dance, Brockport, NY 14420-2997. Offers dance (MA, MFA), including choreography/performance (MA), dance education (preK-12) (MA), dance studies (MA). *Program availability:* Part-time. *Faculty:* 6 full-time (4 women), 2 part-time/adjunct (both women). *Students:* 16 full-time (all women); includes 2 minority (1 American Indian or Alaska Native, non-Hispanic/Latino; 1 Two or more races, non-Hispanic/Latino), 4 international. 34 applicants, 44% accepted, 7 enrolled. In 2016, 3 master's awarded. *Degree requirements:* For master's, thesis or alternative. *Entrance requirements:* For master's, local writing assessment, audition/interview, minimum GPA of 3.0, letters of recommendation. Additional exam requirements/recommendations for international students: Required—TOEFL (minimum score 550 paper-based; 79 iBT), IELTS (minimum score 6.5). *Application deadline:* For fall admission, 4/15 priority date for domestic and international students. Application fee: $50. Electronic applications accepted. *Expenses:* Contact institution. *Financial support:* In 2016–17, 1 fellowship with full tuition reimbursement (averaging $7,500 per year), 4 teaching assistantships with full tuition reimbursements (averaging $6,000 per year) were awarded; Federal Work-Study, scholarships/grants, and unspecified assistantships also available. Support available to part-time students. Financial award application deadline: 3/15; financial award applicants required to submit FAFSA. *Faculty research:* Choreography and performance, world dance and culture, dance process and theory, dance education, dance science and somatics. *Unit head:* Tamara Carrasco, Graduate Director, 585-395-2413, Fax: 585-395-5134, E-mail: tcarrasc@brockport.edu. *Application contact:* Danielle A. Welch, Graduate Counselor, 585-395-5430, Fax: 585-395-2115, E-mail: dwelch@brockport.edu.
Website: http://www.brockport.edu/dance/

**Eastern Michigan University,** Graduate School, College of Arts and Sciences, School of Music and Dance, Ypsilanti, MI 48197. Offers composition (MM); music education (MM); performance (MM); piano pedagogy (MM). *Accreditation:* NASM. *Program availability:* Part-time, evening/weekend, online learning. *Faculty:* 25 full-time (12 women). *Students:* 12 full-time (5 women), 10 part-time (4 women); includes 1 minority (Asian, non-Hispanic/Latino), 2 international. Average age 28. 16 applicants, 56% accepted, 6 enrolled. In 2016, 6 master's awarded. *Entrance requirements:* Additional exam requirements/recommendations for international students: Required—TOEFL. *Application deadline:* Applications are processed on a rolling basis. Application fee: $45. *Financial support:* Fellowships, research assistantships with full tuition reimbursements, teaching assistantships with full tuition reimbursements, career-related internships or fieldwork, Federal Work-Study, institutionally sponsored loans, scholarships/grants, tuition waivers (partial), and unspecified assistantships available. Support available to part-time students. Financial award applicants required to submit FAFSA. *Unit head:* Dr. Diane Winder, Director, 734-487-4380, Fax: 734-487-6939, E-mail: dwinder@emich.edu. *Application contact:* Dr. David Pierce, Coordinator of Music Advising, 734-487-4380, Fax: 734-487-6939, E-mail: david.pierce@emich.edu.
Website: http://www.emich.edu/musicdance

**Florida State University,** The Graduate School, College of Fine Arts, School of Dance, Tallahassee, FL 32306-2120. Offers American dance studies (MA); dance (MFA); studio and related studies (MA). *Accreditation:* NASD. *Faculty:* 20 full-time (13 women), 1 (woman) part-time/adjunct. *Students:* 25 full-time (19 women); includes 9 minority (6 Black or African American, non-Hispanic/Latino; 1 Asian, non-Hispanic/Latino; 2 Hispanic/Latino). Average age 28. 18 applicants, 72% accepted, 9 enrolled. In 2016, 14

master's awarded. *Degree requirements:* For master's, comprehensive exam (for some programs), thesis (for some programs), 1 foreign language (for MA in American dance studies). *Entrance requirements:* For master's, GRE General Test or minimum GPA of 3.0 (for MA in American dance studies), writing sample, audition and interview (for MFA, MA in studio and related studies). Additional exam requirements/recommendations for international students: Required—TOEFL (minimum score 550 paper-based, 80 iBT), IELTS (minimum score 6.5) or Michigan English Language Assessment Battery (minimum score 77). *Application deadline:* For fall admission, 2/1 priority date for domestic and international students; for spring admission, 11/1 priority date for domestic and international students. Applications are processed on a rolling basis. Application fee: $30. Electronic applications accepted. *Expenses:* Contact institution. *Financial support:* In 2016–17, 23 students received support, including 3 fellowships with full tuition reimbursements available (averaging $16,666 per year), 10 research assistantships with full tuition reimbursements available (averaging $5,000 per year), 13 teaching assistantships with full tuition reimbursements available (averaging $5,000 per year); scholarships/grants, health care benefits, tuition waivers (full), and unspecified assistantships also available. Financial award application deadline: 6/30; financial award applicants required to submit FAFSA. *Faculty research:* Choreography, performance, dance and cultural significance, American dance history, dance technology, critical dance theory. *Unit head:* Prof. Josephine Garibaldi, Associate Professor and Chair, 850-644-1024, Fax: 850-644-1277, E-mail: jgaribaldi@fsu.edu. *Application contact:* Stephanie Mills, Academic Coordinator, 850-644-1023, Fax: 850-644-1277, E-mail: smmills@fsu.edu.
Website: http://dance.fsu.edu/

**The George Washington University,** Columbian College of Arts and Sciences, Department of Theatre and Dance, Washington, DC 20052. Offers classical acting (MFA); dance (MFA); exhibit design (Graduate Certificate); production design (MFA). *Program availability:* Part-time, evening/weekend. *Faculty:* 10 full-time (6 women). *Students:* 31 full-time (20 women), 19 part-time (10 women); includes 13 minority (7 Black or African American, non-Hispanic/Latino; 1 Asian, non-Hispanic/Latino; 3 Hispanic/Latino; 2 Two or more races, non-Hispanic/Latino), 5 international. Average age 33. 66 applicants, 61% accepted, 26 enrolled. In 2016, 19 master's, 2 other advanced degrees awarded. *Degree requirements:* For master's, thesis. *Entrance requirements:* For master's, minimum GPA of 3.0, portfolio. Additional exam requirements/recommendations for international students: Required—TOEFL (minimum score 550 paper-based; 80 iBT). *Application deadline:* For fall admission, 8/1 priority date for domestic students; for spring admission, 10/1 priority date for domestic students. Applications are processed on a rolling basis. Application fee: $75. Electronic applications accepted. *Financial support:* In 2016–17, 2 students received support. Fellowships with tuition reimbursements available, teaching assistantships with tuition reimbursements available, career-related internships or fieldwork, Federal Work-Study, and tuition waivers available. *Unit head:* Dana Burgess, Chair, 202-994-1660, E-mail: dtsb@gwu.edu. *Application contact:* Information Contact, 202-994-8072, E-mail: trdanews@gwu.edu.
Website: http://theatredance.columbian.gwu.edu/

**Hollins University,** Graduate Programs, Program in Dance, Roanoke, VA 24020. Offers MFA. *Program availability:* Part-time. *Degree requirements:* For master's, thesis. *Entrance requirements:* For master's, DVD of selected works, 3 letters of recommendation, bachelor's degree or equivalent dance experience. Additional exam requirements/recommendations for international students: Required—TOEFL (minimum score 550 paper-based; 80 iBT), IELTS (minimum score 6.5). *Application deadline:* For summer admission, 12/1 for domestic and international students. Application fee: $40. Electronic applications accepted. *Expenses:* $902 per credit hour. *Financial support:* Fellowships, institutionally sponsored loans, and scholarships/grants available. Support available to part-time students. Financial award application deadline: 2/2; financial award applicants required to submit FAFSA. *Unit head:* Jeffery Bullock, Director, 540-362-6429, E-mail: hugrad@hollins.edu. *Application contact:* Cathy S. Koon, Manager of Graduate Programs, 540-362-6326, Fax: 540-362-6288, E-mail: ckoon@hollins.edu.
Website: http://www.hollins.edu/academics/graduate-degrees/dance-mfa/

**Jacksonville University,** College of Fine Arts, MFA in Choreography Program, Jacksonville, FL 32211. Offers MFA. *Expenses: Tuition:* Full-time $13,320. One-time fee: $50 part-time. Tuition and fees vary according to course load, degree level, campus/location and program.

**Mills College,** Graduate Studies, Department of Dance, Oakland, CA 94613-1000. Offers MA, MFA. *Program availability:* Part-time. *Faculty:* 4 full-time (2 women), 2 part-time/adjunct (both women). *Students:* 16 full-time (15 women); includes 6 minority (1 Black or African American, non-Hispanic/Latino; 1 Asian, non-Hispanic/Latino; 2 Hispanic/Latino; 2 Two or more races, non-Hispanic/Latino), 3 international. Average age 26. 29 applicants, 69% accepted, 8 enrolled. In 2016, 7 master's awarded. *Degree requirements:* For master's, comprehensive exam, thesis, performance. *Entrance requirements:* For master's, audition, DVD recording of original choreography of up to two choreographic works (for MFA); writing sample with topic related to field of dance studies (for MA). Additional exam requirements/recommendations for international students: Required—TOEFL (minimum score 550 paper-based; 80 iBT) or IELTS (minimum score 6). *Application deadline:* For fall admission, 2/1 priority date for domestic students, 12/15 for international students. Applications are processed on a rolling basis. Application fee: $50. Electronic applications accepted. *Expenses:* Contact institution. *Financial support:* In 2016–17, 28 students received support, including 15 fellowships with partial tuition reimbursements available (averaging $7,873 per year), 13 teaching assistantships with partial tuition reimbursements available (averaging $5,477 per year); scholarships/grants and unspecified assistantships also available. Financial award application deadline: 2/1; financial award applicants required to submit FAFSA. *Faculty research:* Modern techniques, movement for actors, choreography, dance criticism and analysis, dance and literature. *Unit head:* Sheldon Smith, Department Head, 510-430-3260, E-mail: shsmith@mills.edu. *Application contact:* Robynne Lofton, Director of Admissions, 510-430-3309, Fax: 510-430-2159, E-mail: grad-admission@mills.edu.
Website: http://www.mills.edu/dance

**New York University,** Steinhardt School of Culture, Education, and Human Development, Department of Music and Performing Arts Professions, Program in Dance Education, New York, NY 10010. Offers teaching dance in the professions (MA), including American Ballet Theatre ballet pedagogy, teaching dance in the professions; teaching dance, all grades (MA, Advanced Certificate); MA/MA. *Program availability:* Part-time. *Degree requirements:* For master's, thesis (for some programs). *Entrance requirements:* For master's, audition, interview. Additional exam requirements/recommendations for international students: Required—TOEFL (minimum score 100

iBT). Electronic applications accepted. *Faculty research:* Dance cognition and creativity, technology in dance, development of teacher expertise, ballet pedagogy.

**New York University,** Tisch School of the Arts, Department of Dance, New York, NY 10012-1019. Offers MFA. *Entrance requirements:* For master's, audition. Additional exam requirements/recommendations for international students: Required—TOEFL or IELTS. Electronic applications accepted.

**New York University,** Tisch School of the Arts and Graduate School of Arts and Science, Department of Performance Studies, New York, NY 10012-1019. Offers MA, PhD. *Degree requirements:* For doctorate, one foreign language, comprehensive exam, thesis/dissertation, dissertation defense, qualifying exam. *Entrance requirements:* For master's, sample of written work; for doctorate, master's degree, writing sample. Additional exam requirements/recommendations for international students: Required— TOEFL or IELTS. Electronic applications accepted. *Expenses:* Contact institution. *Faculty research:* Performance theory, dance, folklore and festivals, postcolonial theory, anthropology and gender studies.

**Northern Illinois University,** Graduate School, College of Visual and Performing Arts, School of Theatre and Dance, De Kalb, IL 60115-2854. Offers MFA. *Program availability:* Part-time. *Faculty:* 16 full-time (9 women). *Students:* 26 full-time (13 women); includes 2 minority (both Two or more races, non-Hispanic/Latino). Average age 28. 34 applicants, 56% accepted, 19 enrolled. In 2016, 14 master's awarded. *Degree requirements:* For master's, comprehensive exam, final project and defense. *Entrance requirements:* For master's, minimum GPA of 2.75, audition or portfolio. Additional exam requirements/recommendations for international students: Required— TOEFL (minimum score 550 paper-based). *Application deadline:* For fall admission, 4/1 priority date for domestic students, 5/1 for international students; for spring admission, 10/15 priority date for domestic students, 10/1 for international students. Applications are processed on a rolling basis. Application fee: $40. Electronic applications accepted. *Financial support:* In 2016–17, 26 teaching assistantships with full tuition reimbursements were awarded; fellowships with full tuition reimbursements, research assistantships with full tuition reimbursements, career-related internships or fieldwork, Federal Work-Study, scholarships/grants, tuition waivers (full), and staff assistantships also available. Support available to part-time students. Financial award applicants required to submit FAFSA. *Faculty research:* Theatre history, choreography, performance art spectacles, storytelling, computer visualization of the ethical space. *Unit head:* Alexander Gelman, Director, 815-753-8253, Fax: 815-753-8415, E-mail: agelman@niu.edu. *Application contact:* Graduate School Office, 815-753-0395, E-mail: gradsch@niu.edu.
Website: http://www.niu.edu/theatre/

**The Ohio State University,** Graduate School, College of Arts and Sciences, Division of Arts and Humanities, Department of Dance, Columbus, OH 43210. Offers choreography (MFA); dance (MFA, PhD); dance and technology (MFA); dance studies (PhD); history, theory and literature (MFA); lighting and production (MFA); movement analysis, Laban studies, notation and dance documentation (MFA); performance (MFA). *Accreditation:* NASD. *Faculty:* 13. *Students:* 33 full-time (23 women), 5 international. Average age 33. In 2016, 9 master's, 1 doctorate awarded. *Degree requirements:* For master's, thesis optional. *Entrance requirements:* For master's, GRE General Test (for all applicants with cumulative GPA below 3.0), audition; for doctorate, GRE General Test, invitation-only interview. Additional exam requirements/recommendations for international students: Required—Michigan English Language Assessment Battery (minimum score 82); Recommended—TOEFL (minimum score 550 paper-based; 79 iBT), IELTS (minimum score 7). *Application deadline:* For fall admission, 11/15 priority date for domestic and international students; for spring admission, 3/1 for domestic students, 2/1 for international students. Applications are processed on a rolling basis. Application fee: $60 ($70 for international students). Electronic applications accepted. *Financial support:* Fellowships with tuition reimbursements, teaching assistantships with tuition reimbursements, Federal Work-Study, and institutionally sponsored loans available. Support available to part-time students. *Unit head:* Susan Hadley, Chair, 614-292-0984, E-mail: hadley.4@osu.edu. *Application contact:* Amy Schmidt, Academic Program Coordinator, 614-292-8933, E-mail: schmidt.442@osu.edu.
Website: http://dance.osu.edu/

**Saint Mary's College of California,** School of Liberal Arts, MFA Program in Dance, Moraga, CA 94575. Offers dance: creative practice (MFA); dance: design and production (MFA).

**Sam Houston State University,** College of Fine Arts and Mass Communication, Department of Dance, Huntsville, TX 77341. Offers MFA. *Program availability:* Part-time. *Degree requirements:* For master's, comprehensive exam, thesis, project. *Entrance requirements:* For master's, GRE General Test, writing sample, interview, audition, resume, video portfolio, letters of recommendation. Additional exam requirements/recommendations for international students: Required—TOEFL (minimum score 550 paper-based; 79 iBT), IELTS (minimum score 6.5). Electronic applications accepted.

**Sarah Lawrence College,** Graduate Studies, Program in Dance, Bronxville, NY 10708-5999. Offers MFA. *Degree requirements:* For master's, performance. *Entrance requirements:* For master's, audition, minimum B average in undergraduate course work. Additional exam requirements/recommendations for international students: Required—TOEFL. Electronic applications accepted.

**Sarah Lawrence College,** Graduate Studies, Program in Dance/Movement Therapy, Bronxville, NY 10708-5999. Offers MS. *Degree requirements:* For master's, thesis, practicum.

**Smith College,** Graduate and Special Programs, Department of Dance, Northampton, MA 01063. Offers MFA. *Students:* 8 full-time (all women); includes 2 minority (1 Black or African American, non-Hispanic/Latino; 1 Hispanic/Latino). Average age 31. 22 applicants, 23% accepted, 4 enrolled. In 2016, 4 master's awarded. *Degree requirements:* For master's, thesis performance. *Entrance requirements:* For master's, audition. Additional exam requirements/recommendations for international students: Required—TOEFL (minimum score 550 paper-based; 97 iBT), IELTS. *Application deadline:* For fall admission, 12/1 for domestic and international students. Application fee: $60. *Expenses: Tuition:* Full-time $34,560; part-time $1440 per credit. Tuition and fees vary according to course load and program. *Financial support:* In 2016–17, 8 students received support, including 8 teaching assistantships with full tuition reimbursements available (averaging $6,925 per year); institutionally sponsored loans also available. Financial award application deadline: 12/1; financial award applicants required to submit CSS PROFILE or FAFSA. *Unit head:* Rodger Blum, Department Chair, 413-585-3234, E-mail: rblum@smith.edu. *Application contact:* Lester Tome, Graduate Student Adviser, 413-585-3699, E-mail: ltome@smith.edu.
Website: http://www.smith.edu/dance/

**Temple University,** Center for the Performing and Cinematic Arts, Boyer College of Music and Dance, Department of Dance, Philadelphia, PA 19122. Offers MA, MFA, PhD. *Accreditation:* NASD. *Program availability:* Part-time, online learning. *Degree requirements:* For master's, thesis optional, professional project; for doctorate, thesis/dissertation. *Entrance requirements:* For master's and doctorate, minimum GPA of 3.0, audition/interview, academic writing sample, dance questionnaire. Additional exam

requirements/recommendations for international students: Required—TOEFL. Electronic applications accepted. *Faculty research:* Cultural studies, dance technology, aesthetics, choreography, dance research.

**Texas Woman's University,** Graduate School, College of Arts and Sciences, School of the Arts, Department of Dance, Denton, TX 76201. Offers MA, MFA, PhD. *Accreditation:* NASD. *Students:* Average age 37. In 2016, 10 master's, 3 doctorates awarded. *Degree requirements:* For master's, comprehensive exam, thesis, choreography portfolio, professional paper; for doctorate, comprehensive exam, thesis/dissertation. *Entrance requirements:* For master's, audition, 3 letters of recommendation, interview, writing sample, resume, personal essay; for doctorate, interview, 3 letters of reference, personal essay, curriculum vitae, DVD portfolio of artistic work. Additional exam requirements/recommendations for international students: Required—TOEFL (minimum score 550 paper-based; 79 iBT). *Application deadline:* For fall admission, 2/1 priority date for domestic and international students. Applications are processed on a rolling basis. Application fee: $50 ($75 for international students). Electronic applications accepted. *Expenses:* Tuition, state resident: full-time $9046; part-time $251 per credit hour. Tuition, nonresident: full-time $22,922; part-time $614 per credit hour. International tuition: $23,046 full-time. *Required fees:* $2690; $1285 per credit hour. One-time fee: $50. Tuition and fees vary according to course level, course load, program and reciprocity agreements. *Financial support:* Research assistantships, teaching assistantships, career-related internships or fieldwork, Federal Work-Study, institutionally sponsored loans, scholarships/grants, traineeships, health care benefits, tuition waivers (partial), and unspecified assistantships available. Support available to part-time students. Financial award application deadline: 3/1; financial award applicants required to submit FAFSA. *Faculty research:* Performance, choreography, pedagogy, somatic practices, theorizing artistic practice. *Unit head:* Prof. Mary Williford-Shade, Chair/Professor, 940-898-2082, Fax: 940-898-2098, E-mail: dance@twu.edu. *Application contact:* Dr. Samuel Wheeler, Assistant Director of Admissions, 940-898-3188, Fax: 940-898-3081, E-mail: wheelersr@twu.edu.
Website: http://www.twu.edu/dance/

**Tulane University,** School of Liberal Arts, Department of Theatre and Dance, New Orleans, LA 70118-5669. Offers design and technical production (MFA). *Entrance requirements:* For master's, GRE General Test, minimum B average in undergraduate course work. Additional exam requirements/recommendations for international students: Required—TOEFL. Electronic applications accepted. *Expenses: Tuition:* Full-time $50,920; part-time $2829 per credit hour. *Required fees:* $2040; $44.50 per credit hour. $580 per term. Tuition and fees vary according to course load, degree level and program. *Faculty research:* Scene design, stage management, costume design, technical direction, lighting design.

**Université du Québec à Montréal,** Graduate Programs, Program in Dance, Montréal, QC H3C 3P8, Canada. Offers MA. *Program availability:* Part-time. *Degree requirements:* For master's, thesis optional. *Entrance requirements:* For master's, appropriate bachelor's degree or equivalent and proficiency in French.

**The University of Arizona,** College of Fine Arts, School of Dance, Tucson, AZ 85721. Offers MFA. *Accreditation:* NASD. *Entrance requirements:* Additional exam requirements/recommendations for international students: Required—TOEFL (minimum score 550 paper-based; 79 iBT). Electronic applications accepted.

**University of California, Irvine,** Claire Trevor School of the Arts, Department of Dance, Irvine, CA 92697. Offers MFA. *Students:* 19 full-time (16 women); includes 8 minority (2 Asian, non-Hispanic/Latino; 4 Hispanic/Latino; 2 Two or more races, non-Hispanic/Latino), 2 international. Average age 29. 31 applicants, 42% accepted, 7 enrolled. In 2016, 9 master's awarded. *Degree requirements:* For master's, thesis. *Entrance requirements:* For master's, minimum GPA of 3.0. *Application deadline:* For fall admission, 1/15 priority date for domestic students, 1/15 for international students. Applications are processed on a rolling basis. Application fee: $105 ($125 for international students). Electronic applications accepted. *Financial support:* Fellowships, teaching assistantships, institutionally sponsored loans, traineeships, health care benefits, and unspecified assistantships available. Financial award application deadline: 3/1; financial award applicants required to submit FAFSA. *Faculty research:* Dance science, digital technology, history and theory, choreography. *Unit head:* Lisa Marie Naugle, Chair, 949-824-3209, E-mail: lnaugle@uci.edu. *Application contact:* Alan Terricciano, Graduate Advisor, 949-824-5744, Fax: 949-824-4563, E-mail: aterricc@uci.edu.
Website: http://dance.arts.uci.edu/

**University of California, Los Angeles,** Graduate Division, School of the Arts and Architecture, Department of World Arts and Cultures, Los Angeles, CA 90095. Offers culture and performance (MA, PhD); dance (MFA). *Degree requirements:* For master's, 1 foreign language, and comprehensive exam or thesis (MA); comprehensive exam (MFA); for doctorate, one foreign language, thesis/dissertation, oral and written qualifying exams. *Entrance requirements:* For master's, bachelor's degree; minimum undergraduate GPA of 3.0 (or its equivalent if letter grade system not used); audition and interview (MFA); writing sample (MA); for doctorate, master's degree; minimum undergraduate GPA of 3.0 (or its equivalent if letter grade system not used); writing sample. Additional exam requirements/recommendations for international students: Required—TOEFL. Electronic applications accepted.

**University of California, Riverside,** Graduate Division, Department of Dance, Riverside, CA 92521. Offers experimental choreography (MFA). *Entrance requirements:* For master's, stable electronic link (such as Vimeo/YouTube) of a choreographed piece (for MFA program only). Additional exam requirements/recommendations for international students: Required—TOEFL (minimum score 550 paper-based; 80 iBT). Electronic applications accepted. *Expenses:* Tuition, state resident: full-time $16,666. Tuition, nonresident: full-time $31,768. *Required fees:* $11,055.54 per quarter. $3685.18 per quarter. Tuition and fees vary according to campus/location and program. *Faculty research:* Movement analysis, cultural postcolonial gender studies of performance, theories of dance, anthropology of dance, history and reconstruction of dance.

**University of California, San Diego,** Graduate Division, Department of Theatre and Dance, La Jolla, CA 92093. Offers acting (MFA); contemporary dance and performance (MFA); design (MFA); directing (MFA); drama and theatre (PhD); playwriting (MFA); stage management (MFA). PhD offered jointly with University of California, Irvine. *Students:* 75 full-time (42 women). 497 applicants, 6% accepted, 20 enrolled. In 2016, 24 master's, 1 doctorate awarded. *Degree requirements:* For master's, thesis; for doctorate, comprehensive exam, thesis/dissertation. *Entrance requirements:* For master's, GRE General Test (for playwriting only), minimum GPA of 3.5; audition or interview; for doctorate, GRE General Test, minimum GPA of 3.5, audition and/or interview, two samples of critical writing. Additional exam requirements/recommendations for international students: Required—TOEFL (minimum score 550 paper-based; 80 iBT), IELTS (minimum score 7). *Application deadline:* For fall admission, 1/8 for domestic students. Application fee: $105 ($125 for international students). Electronic applications accepted. *Expenses:* Tuition, state resident: full-time $11,220. Tuition, nonresident: full-time $26,322. *Required fees:* $1864. *Financial support:* Fellowships, teaching assistantships, and scholarships/grants available. Financial award applicants required to submit FAFSA. *Faculty research:* Theatre of the

*Dance*

Americas, European theatre, Asian theatre, gender studies, critical theory. *Unit head:* Charles Means, Chair, 858-534-2062, E-mail: chmeans@ucsd.edu. *Application contact:* Marybeth Ward, Graduate Coordinator, 858-534-1046, E-mail: meward@ucsd.edu. *Website:* http://theatre.ucsd.edu/

**University of Colorado Boulder,** Graduate School, College of Arts and Sciences, Department of Theatre and Dance, Boulder, CO 80309. Offers dance (MFA); theatre (MA, PhD). *Faculty:* 16 full-time (8 women). *Students:* 34 full-time (27 women), 1 part-time (0 women); includes 8 minority (3 Black or African American, non-Hispanic/Latino; 1 Asian, non-Hispanic/Latino; 4 Hispanic/Latino). Average age 32. 39 applicants, 51% accepted, 9 enrolled. In 2016, 10 master's, 2 doctorates awarded. Terminal master's awarded for partial completion of doctoral program. *Degree requirements:* For master's, comprehensive exam, thesis; for doctorate, one foreign language, thesis/dissertation. *Entrance requirements:* For master's, GRE General Test (MA), audition (MFA), minimum undergraduate GPA of 2.75. *Application deadline:* For fall admission, 12/15 for domestic students, 12/1 for international students. Application fee: $60 ($80 for international students). Electronic applications accepted. Application fee is waived when completed online. *Financial support:* In 2016–17, 103 students received support, including 27 fellowships (averaging $2,814 per year), 31 teaching assistantships with full and partial tuition reimbursements available (averaging $27,201 per year); institutionally sponsored loans, scholarships/grants, health care benefits, and unspecified assistantships also available. Financial award application deadline: 1/15; financial award applicants required to submit FAFSA. *Faculty research:* Performing arts, drama, dramatic/theatre arts, choreography, dance. *Application contact:* E-mail: wendy.franz@colorado.edu.
*Website:* http://www.colorado.edu/theatredance/

**University of Hawaii at Manoa,** Graduate Division, College of Arts and Humanities, Department of Theatre and Dance, Honolulu, HI 96822. Offers dance (MA, MFA); theatre (MA, MFA, PhD). *Program availability:* Part-time. *Degree requirements:* For master's, one foreign language, thesis optional; for doctorate, one foreign language, comprehensive exam, thesis/dissertation. *Entrance requirements:* For master's and doctorate, GRE General Test. Additional exam requirements/recommendations for international students: Required—TOEFL (minimum score 600 paper-based; 100 iBT), IELTS (minimum score 7). *Faculty research:* Asian theatre, feminist theatre and dance, Russian theatre, Australian theatre.

**University of Illinois at Urbana–Champaign,** Graduate College, College of Fine and Applied Arts, Department of Dance, Champaign, IL 61820. Offers MFA. *Accreditation:* NASD.

**The University of Iowa,** Graduate College, College of Liberal Arts and Sciences, Department of Dance, Iowa City, IA 52242-1316. Offers MFA. *Accreditation:* NASD. *Degree requirements:* For master's, thesis, exam. *Entrance requirements:* For master's, minimum GPA of 3.0. Additional exam requirements/recommendations for international students: Required—TOEFL (minimum score 550 paper-based; 81 iBT). Electronic applications accepted.

**University of Maryland, Baltimore County,** The Graduate School, College of Arts, Humanities and Social Sciences, Department of Education, Program in Teaching, Baltimore, MD 21250. Offers early childhood education (MAT); elementary education (MAT); teaching (MAT), including art, biology, chemistry, choral music, classical foreign language, dance, earth/space science, English, instrumental music, mathematics, modern foreign language, physical science, physics, social studies, theatre. *Program availability:* Part-time, evening/weekend. *Faculty:* 24 full-time (18 women), 25 part-time/adjunct (19 women). *Students:* 41 full-time (34 women), 27 part-time (18 women); includes 26 minority (6 Black or African American, non-Hispanic/Latino; 9 Asian, non-Hispanic/Latino; 7 Hispanic/Latino; 1 Native Hawaiian or other Pacific Islander, non-Hispanic/Latino; 3 Two or more races, non-Hispanic/Latino), 2 international. Average age 30. 54 applicants, 83% accepted, 35 enrolled. In 2016, 50 master's awarded. *Degree requirements:* For master's, comprehensive exam (for some programs), thesis (for some programs). *Entrance requirements:* For master's, PRAXIS Core Examination or GRE (minimum score of 1000), minimum GPA of 3.0. Additional exam requirements/recommendations for international students: Required—TOEFL. *Application deadline:* For fall admission, 6/1 for domestic and international students; for spring admission, 11/1 for domestic and international students. Applications are processed on a rolling basis. Application fee: $50. Electronic applications accepted. *Expenses:* Tuition, state resident: full-time $13,294. Tuition, nonresident: full-time $20,286. *Financial support:* In 2016–17, 8 students received support, including teaching assistantships with tuition reimbursements available (averaging $12,000 per year); career-related internships or fieldwork, Federal Work-Study, scholarships/grants, tuition waivers, and unspecified assistantships also available. Financial award application deadline: 3/15. *Faculty research:* STEM teacher education, culturally sensitive pedagogy, ESOL/bilingual education, early childhood education, language, literacy and culture. *Total annual research expenditures:* $100,000. *Unit head:* Dr. Susan M. Blunck, Graduate Program Director, 410-455-2869, Fax: 410-455-3986, E-mail: blunck@umbc.edu. *Application contact:* Cheryl Johnson, MAT Program Specialist, 410-455-3388, E-mail: blackwel@umbc.edu.
*Website:* http://www.umbc.edu/education/

**University of Maryland, College Park,** Academic Affairs, College of Arts and Humanities, School of Theatre, Dance and Performance Studies, Program in Dance, College Park, MD 20742. Offers MFA. *Accreditation:* NASD. *Degree requirements:* For master's, final project. *Entrance requirements:* For master's, audition/interview, video tapes/writing sample, 3 letters of recommendation. Additional exam requirements/recommendations for international students: Required—TOEFL. Electronic applications accepted. *Faculty research:* Performance and choreography.

**University of Michigan,** Rackham Graduate School, School of Music, Theatre, and Dance, Department of Dance, Ann Arbor, MI 48109-2217. Offers modern dance performance and choreography (MFA). Offered through the Rackham Graduate School. *Accreditation:* NASD. *Entrance requirements:* For master's, audition. Additional exam requirements/recommendations for international students: Required—TOEFL. Electronic applications accepted. *Expenses:* Tuition, state resident: full-time $21,466; part-time $1152 per credit hour. Tuition, nonresident: full-time $43,346; part-time $2367 per credit hour. Part-time tuition and fees vary according to course load, degree level and program.

**University of New Mexico,** Graduate Studies, College of Fine Arts, Department of Theatre and Dance, Albuquerque, NM 87131-2039. Offers dance (MFA); dance history (MA); dramatic writing (MFA); theatre education and outreach (MA). *Accreditation:* NASD; NAST. *Faculty:* 6 full-time (3 women), 2 part-time/adjunct (both women). *Students:* 13 full-time (7 women), 3 part-time (all women); includes 13 minority (1 Black or African American, non-Hispanic/Latino; 1 American Indian or Alaska Native, non-Hispanic/Latino; 9 Hispanic/Latino; 2 Two or more races, non-Hispanic/Latino). Average age 36. 15 applicants, 53% accepted, 7 enrolled. In 2016, 4 master's awarded. *Degree requirements:* For master's, comprehensive exam (for some programs), thesis (for some programs). *Entrance requirements:* For master's, minimum GPA of 3.0; undergraduate major in theatre, dance or closely-related field; 3 letters of recommendation; letter of intent; BA, BFA, BS, or MA in dance movement science or related field, or equivalent experience (for MFA in dance). *Application deadline:* For fall admission, 4/15 for domestic students; for spring admission, 11/10 for domestic students. Application fee: $50. Electronic applications accepted. *Financial support:* Fellowships, research assistantships with partial tuition reimbursements, teaching assistantships with partial tuition reimbursements, Federal Work-Study, health care benefits, tuition waivers (partial), and unspecified assistantships available. Financial award application deadline: 3/1; financial award applicants required to submit FAFSA. *Faculty research:* Theater education and outreach, choreography, dramatic writing, dance history/criticism. *Unit head:* Bill Liotta, Chair, 505-277-4332, Fax: 505-277-8921, E-mail: wliotta@unm.edu. *Application contact:* Christina Squire, Administrator II, 505-277-7362, Fax: 505-277-8921, E-mail: csquire@unm.edu.
*Website:* http://theatredance.unm.edu

**The University of North Carolina at Greensboro,** Graduate School, School of Music, Theatre and Dance, Department of Dance, Greensboro, NC 27412-5001. Offers MA, MFA. *Accreditation:* NASD. *Degree requirements:* For master's, thesis. *Entrance requirements:* For master's, GRE General Test or MAT, audition or video (MFA). Additional exam requirements/recommendations for international students: Required—TOEFL. Electronic applications accepted. *Faculty research:* Consciousness-raising images, perspectives on ballet.

**University of Oklahoma,** Weitzenhoffer Family College of Fine Arts, School of Dance, Norman, OK 73019. Offers ballet (MFA); modern dance (MFA). *Faculty:* 5 full-time (2 women). *Students:* 5 full-time (all women), 1 (woman) part-time; includes 1 minority (Two or more races, non-Hispanic/Latino), 1 international. Average age 41. 5 applicants, 80% accepted, 4 enrolled. In 2016, 3 master's awarded. *Degree requirements:* For master's, thesis. *Entrance requirements:* For master's, BFA in dance, audition, interview, writing sample, letters of recommendation. Additional exam requirements/recommendations for international students: Required—TOEFL (minimum score 79 iBT) or IELTS (minimum score 6.5). *Application deadline:* For fall admission, 4/15 for domestic students, 3/1 for international students. Applications are processed on a rolling basis. Application fee: $50 ($100 for international students). Electronic applications accepted. *Expenses:* Tuition, state resident: full-time $4886; part-time $203.60 per credit hour. Tuition, nonresident: full-time $18,989; part-time $791.20 per credit hour. *Required fees:* $3283; $126.25 per credit hour. $126.50 per semester. *Financial support:* In 2016–17, 4 students received support, including 1 fellowship with full tuition reimbursement available (averaging $8,000 per year), 4 teaching assistantships (averaging $12,091 per year); health care benefits and unspecified assistantships also available. Financial award application deadline: 6/1; financial award applicants required to submit FAFSA. *Faculty research:* Ballet choreography, modern dance choreography, dance history, teaching methods, body science. *Unit head:* Dr. Mary Margaret Holt, Dean/Professor/Director, 405-325-4051, Fax: 405-325-7024, E-mail: marymholt@ou.edu. *Application contact:* Jeremy Lindberg, Associate Professor, 405-325-0567 Ext. 15, Fax: 405-325-7024, E-mail: jlindberg@ou.edu.
*Website:* http://www.ou.edu/finearts/dance

**University of Oregon,** Graduate School, School of Music, Department of Dance, Eugene, OR 97403. Offers MA, MS. *Degree requirements:* For master's, thesis or alternative. *Entrance requirements:* For master's, minimum GPA of 3.0. Additional exam requirements/recommendations for international students: Required—TOEFL. *Faculty research:* Choreography, dance history, dance pedagogy, scientific aspects of dance.

**The University of Texas at Austin,** Graduate School, College of Fine Arts, Department of Theatre and Dance, Austin, TX 78712-1111. Offers acting (MFA); dance (MFA); directing (MFA); drama and theatre for youth (MFA); performance as public practice (MA, MFA, PhD); playwriting (MFA); theatre technology (MFA); theatrical design (MFA). *Degree requirements:* For master's, thesis; for doctorate, variable foreign language requirement, thesis/dissertation. *Entrance requirements:* For master's and doctorate, GRE General Test.

**University of Utah,** Graduate School, College of Fine Arts, School of Dance, Salt Lake City, UT 84112-0280. Offers MFA, Certificate. *Accreditation:* NASD. *Faculty:* 8 full-time (4 women), 8 part-time/adjunct (5 women). *Students:* 17 full-time (10 women), 1 part-time (0 women); includes 2 minority (1 Asian, non-Hispanic/Latino; 1 Hispanic/Latino), 4 international. Average age 28. 13 applicants, 54% accepted, 6 enrolled. In 2016, 7 master's awarded. *Degree requirements:* For master's, thesis, project, oral examination. *Entrance requirements:* For master's, audition, interview, minimum GPA of 3.0. Additional exam requirements/recommendations for international students: Required—TOEFL (minimum score 550 paper-based; 80 iBT). *Application deadline:* For fall admission, 3/1 priority date for domestic and international students. Applications are processed on a rolling basis. Application fee: $55 ($65 for international students). Electronic applications accepted. *Expenses:* Contact institution. *Financial support:* In 2016–17, 20 students received support, including 18 teaching assistantships with full tuition reimbursements (averaging $9,000 per year); fellowships with partial tuition reimbursements available, career-related internships or fieldwork, Federal Work-Study, institutionally sponsored loans, scholarships/grants, health care benefits, and unspecified assistantships also available. Financial award application deadline: 3/1; financial award applicants required to submit FAFSA. *Faculty research:* Choreography, pedagogy, performance, dance for camera, dance technology. *Total annual research expenditures:* $28,926. *Unit head:* Stephen Koester, Chair, 801-581-7327, Fax: 801-581-5442, E-mail: stephen.koester@utah.edu. *Application contact:* Eric Handman, Director of Graduate Studies, 801-587-9813, Fax: 801-581-5442, E-mail: eric.handman@utah.edu.
*Website:* http://www.dance.utah.edu

**University of Washington,** Graduate School, College of Arts and Sciences, Program in Dance, Seattle, WA 98195-1150. Offers MFA. *Degree requirements:* For master's, performance, project, course development. *Entrance requirements:* For master's, 8 years of professional dance experience, resume, performance DVD or VHS tape, 3 letters of reference. Additional exam requirements/recommendations for international students: Required—TOEFL. Electronic applications accepted. *Faculty research:* Choreography, history, anatomy, ethnography, integrated dance, social dance.

**Washington University in St. Louis,** The Graduate School, Department of Performing Arts, St. Louis, MO 63130-4899. Offers dance (MFA); theater and performance studies (MA). *Degree requirements:* For master's, thesis optional. *Entrance requirements:* For master's, GRE General Test, sample of written work. Additional exam requirements/recommendations for international students: Required—TOEFL. Electronic applications accepted. *Faculty research:* Theater and performance studies; dance.

**Wayne State University,** School of Medicine, Office of Biomedical Graduate Programs, Detroit, MI 48202. Offers anatomy and cell biology (MS, PhD); basic medical sciences (MS); biochemistry and molecular biology (MS, PhD); cancer biology (MS, PhD); clinical and translational science (Graduate Certificate); family medicine and public health sciences (MPH, Graduate Certificate), including public health practice; genetic counseling (MS); immunology and microbiology (MS, PhD); medical physics (MS, PhD, Graduate Certificate); medical research (MS); molecular medicine and genomics (MS, PhD), including molecular genetics and genomics; pathology (PhD); pharmacology (MS, PhD); physiology (MS, PhD), including physiology, reproductive sciences (PhD); psychiatry and behavioral neurosciences (PhD), including translational neuroscience;

MD/MPH; MD/PhD; MPH/MA; MSW/MPH. *Program availability:* Part-time, evening/weekend. *Students:* 301 full-time (150 women), 112 part-time (56 women); includes 114 minority (19 Black or African American, non-Hispanic/Latino; 1 American Indian or Alaska Native, non-Hispanic/Latino; 65 Asian, non-Hispanic/Latino; 12 Hispanic/Latino; 17 Two or more races, non-Hispanic/Latino; 62 international. Average age 27. 1,009 applicants, 22% accepted, 161 enrolled. In 2016, 65 master's, 22 doctorates, 8 other advanced degrees awarded. Terminal master's awarded for partial completion of doctoral program. *Degree requirements:* For master's, thesis (for some programs); for doctorate, thesis/dissertation. *Entrance requirements:* For master's, doctorate, and Graduate Certificate, GRE. Additional exam requirements/recommendations for international students: Required—TOEFL (minimum score 550 paper-based; 100 iBT), Michigan English Language Assessment Battery (minimum score 85); Recommended—IELTS (minimum score 6.5), TWE (minimum score 5.5). *Application deadline:* For fall admission, 2/1 for domestic and international students. Applications are processed on a rolling basis. Application fee: $50. Electronic applications accepted. *Expenses:* $20,126 per year resident tuition and fees, $36,434 per year non-resident tuition and fees. *Financial support:* In 2016–17, 197 students received support, including 67 fellowships with full tuition reimbursements available (averaging $24,294 per year), 94 research assistantships with full tuition reimbursements available (averaging $26,850 per year); scholarships/grants, traineeships, and health care benefits also available. *Faculty research:* Cancer biology, neurosciences, vision sciences, molecular biology, pathology, physiology, pharmacology, public health, medical physics. *Unit head:* Dr. Daniel A. Walz, Associate Dean for Biomedical Graduate Programs, 313-577-1455, Fax: 313-577-8796, E-mail: gradprogs@med.wayne.edu. Website: https://www.med.wayne.edu/biomedical-graduate-programs/

**Wilson College,** Graduate Programs, Chambersburg, PA 17201-1285. Offers accounting (M Acc); choreography and visual art (MFA); education (M Ed); healthcare management for sustainability (MHM); humanities (MA), including art and culture, critical/cultural theory, English language and literature, women's studies; management (MSM); nursing (MSN), including nursing education, nursing leadership and management. *Program availability:* Evening/weekend. *Degree requirements:* For master's, project. *Entrance requirements:* For master's, PRAXIS, minimum undergraduate cumulative GPA of 3.0, 2 letters of recommendation, current certification for eligibility to teach in grades K-12, resume, personal interview. Electronic applications accepted.

**York University,** Faculty of Graduate Studies, Faculty of Fine Arts, Program in Dance, Toronto, ON M3J 1P3, Canada. Offers MA, MFA, PhD. *Degree requirements:* For master's, thesis or alternative. Electronic applications accepted.

# Music

**Academy of Art University,** Graduate Programs, School of Music Production and Sound Design for Visual Media, San Francisco, CA 94105-3410. Offers music scoring and composition (MA, MFA); sound design (MA, MFA). *Program availability:* Part-time, 100% online. *Faculty:* 4 full-time (0 women), 22 part-time/adjunct (3 women). *Students:* 97 full-time (46 women), 32 part-time (10 women); includes 21 minority (10 Black or African American, non-Hispanic/Latino; 1 American Indian or Alaska Native, non-Hispanic/Latino; 2 Asian, non-Hispanic/Latino; 6 Hispanic/Latino; 1 Native Hawaiian or other Pacific Islander, non-Hispanic/Latino; 1 Two or more races, non-Hispanic/Latino), 86 international. Average age 29. 31 applicants, 100% accepted, 27 enrolled. In 2016, 38 master's awarded. *Degree requirements:* For master's, final review. *Entrance requirements:* For master's, statement of intent; resume; portfolio/reel; official college transcripts. *Application deadline:* Applications are processed on a rolling basis. Application fee: $50. Electronic applications accepted. *Expenses: Tuition:* Part-time $982 per unit. *Financial support:* Career-related internships or fieldwork, Federal Work-Study, and scholarships/grants available. Financial award application deadline: 8/10; financial award applicants required to submit FAFSA. *Unit head:* 800-544-ARTS, E-mail: info@academyart.edu. *Application contact:* 800-544-ARTS, E-mail: info@academyart.edu.
Website: http://www.academyart.edu/music-for-visual-media/index.html

**American University,** College of Arts and Sciences, Department of Performing Arts, Washington, DC 20016-8053. Offers art management (MA); audio production (Certificate); audio technology (MA); international arts management (Certificate); technology in arts management (Certificate). *Program availability:* Part-time, evening/weekend. *Faculty:* 28 full-time (14 women), 41 part-time/adjunct (15 women). *Students:* 46 full-time (28 women), 21 part-time (9 women); includes 25 minority (18 Black or African American, non-Hispanic/Latino; 3 Hispanic/Latino; 1 Native Hawaiian or other Pacific Islander, non-Hispanic/Latino; 3 Two or more races, non-Hispanic/Latino), 11 international. Average age 29. 115 applicants, 77% accepted, 30 enrolled. In 2016, 44 master's, 7 other advanced degrees awarded. *Degree requirements:* For master's, comprehensive exam, thesis or alternative. *Entrance requirements:* For master's, GRE, minimum GPA of 3.0, statement of purpose, transcripts, 2 letters of recommendation, resume, art portfolio; for Certificate, bachelor's degree, statement of purpose, transcripts, resume, art portfolio. Additional exam requirements/recommendations for international students: Required—TOEFL (minimum score 100 iBT), IELTS, PTE (minimum score 68). *Application deadline:* For fall admission, 2/1 priority date for domestic students; for spring admission, 11/1 priority date for domestic students. Application fee: $55. *Expenses:* $1,579 per credit tuition; $690 mandatory fees. *Financial support:* Unspecified assistantships available. Financial award application deadline: 2/1; financial award applicants required to submit FAFSA. *Unit head:* Dr. Daniel Abraham, Department Chair, 202-885-3427, Fax: 202-885-1092, E-mail: dabraham@american.edu. *Application contact:* Kathleen Clowery, Director, Graduate Admissions, 202-885-3620, Fax: 202-885-1344, E-mail: clowery@american.edu.
Website: http://www.american.edu/cas/performing-arts/

**Andrews University,** School of Graduate Studies, College of Arts and Sciences, Department of Music, Berrien Springs, MI 49104. Offers M Mus, MA. *Accreditation:* NASM. *Faculty:* 10 full-time (4 women). *Students:* 3 full-time (2 women), 13 part-time (9 women); includes 3 minority (1 Black or African American, non-Hispanic/Latino; 2 Hispanic/Latino), 8 international. Average age 28. In 2016, 7 master's awarded. *Degree requirements:* For master's, variable foreign language requirement. *Entrance requirements:* For master's, GRE Subject Test, minimum undergraduate GPA of 2.6. Additional exam requirements/recommendations for international students: Required—TOEFL (minimum score 550 paper-based). *Application deadline:* Applications are processed on a rolling basis. Application fee: $40. *Unit head:* Dr. Lilinna Doukan, Chairman, 269-471-3555. *Application contact:* Justina Clayburn, Supervisor of Graduate Admission, 800-253-2874, Fax: 269-471-6321, E-mail: graduate@andrews.edu.

**Appalachian State University,** Cratis D. Williams Graduate School, School of Music, Boone, NC 28608. Offers music performance (MM); music therapy (MMT). *Accreditation:* NASM. *Program availability:* Part-time. *Degree requirements:* For master's, comprehensive exam, thesis or alternative. *Entrance requirements:* For master's, GRE General Test, 3 letters of reference, audition. Additional exam requirements/recommendations for international students: Required—TOEFL (minimum score 550 paper-based; 79 iBT), IELTS (minimum score 6.5). *Application deadline:* For fall admission, 3/15 for domestic students, 2/1 for international students; for spring admission, 11/1 for domestic students, 7/1 for international students. Applications are processed on a rolling basis. Application fee: $55. Electronic applications accepted. *Expenses:* Tuition, state resident: full-time $4744. Tuition, nonresident: full-time $17,913. Full-time tuition and fees vary according to program. *Financial support:* Fellowships, research assistantships, teaching assistantships, career-related internships or fieldwork, Federal Work-Study, scholarships/grants, tuition waivers (partial), and unspecified assistantships available. Financial award application deadline: 4/1; financial award applicants required to submit FAFSA. *Faculty research:* Music of the Holocaust, Celtic folk music, early nineteenth-century performance practice, hypermeter and phase rhythm, world music, music and psychoneuroimmunology. *Unit head:* Dr. Kathy McKinney, Program Director, 828-262-6444, E-mail: mckinneych@appstate.edu. *Application contact:* Dr. Jennifer Snodgrass, Graduate Program Director, 828-262-6463, E-mail: snodgrassjs@appstate.edu.
Website: http://www.music.appstate.edu

**Aquinas Institute of Theology,** Graduate and Professional Programs, St. Louis, MO 63108. Offers biblical studies (Certificate); church music (MM); health care mission (MAHCM); ministry (M Div); pastoral care (Certificate); pastoral ministry (MAPM); pastoral studies (MAPS); preaching (D Min); spiritual direction (Certificate); theology (M Div, MA); Thomistic studies (Certificate); M Div/MA; MA/PhD; MAPS/MSW. *Accreditation:* ATS (one or more programs are accredited). *Program availability:* Part-time, evening/weekend, online learning. *Degree requirements:* For master's, variable foreign language requirement, comprehensive exam (for some programs), thesis (for some programs); for doctorate, thesis/dissertation. *Entrance requirements:* For master's and Certificate, MAT; for doctorate, 3 years of ministerial experience, 6 hours of graduate course work in homiletics, M Div or the equivalent, minimum GPA of 3.0. Additional exam requirements/recommendations for international students: Required—TOEFL. *Expenses:* Contact institution. *Faculty research:* Theology of preaching, hermeneutics, lay ecclesial ministry, pastoral and practical theology.

**Arizona State University at the Tempe campus,** Herberger Institute for Design and the Arts, School of Film, Dance and Theatre, Tempe, AZ 85287-2002. Offers dance (MFA), including dance, interdisciplinary digital media and performance; theatre (MA, MFA, PhD), including arts entrepreneurship and management (MFA), directing (MFA), dramatic writing (MFA), interdisciplinary digital media and performance (MFA), performance (MFA), performance design (MFA), theatre (MFA), theatre and performance of the Americas (PhD), theatre for youth (MFA, PhD). Terminal master's awarded for partial completion of doctoral program. *Degree requirements:* For master's, comprehensive exam (for some programs), thesis (for some programs), applied project (for some programs); interactive Program of Study (iPOS) submitted before completing 50 percent of required credit hours; for doctorate, comprehensive exam, thesis/dissertation, interactive Program of Study (iPOS) submitted before completing 50 percent of required credit hours. *Entrance requirements:* For master's, GRE or MAT, minimum GPA of 3.0 in last 2 years of work leading to bachelor's degree (depending on program); for doctorate, GRE, minimum GPA of 3.0 or equivalent in last 2 years of work leading to bachelor's degree, 3 letters of recommendation, resume, scholarly writing sample, statement of purpose. Additional exam requirements/recommendations for international students: Required—TOEFL, IELTS, or PTE. Electronic applications accepted.

**Arizona State University at the Tempe campus,** Herberger Institute for Design and the Arts, School of Music, Tempe, AZ 85287-0405. Offers composition (MM, DMA); conducting (DMA); ethnomusicology (MA); interdisciplinary digital media/performance (DMA); music education (MM, PhD); music history and literature (MA); music therapy (MM); performance (MM, DMA). *Accreditation:* NASM. Terminal master's awarded for partial completion of doctoral program. *Degree requirements:* For master's, thesis (for some programs), interactive Program of Study (iPOS) submitted before completing 50 percent of required credit hours; for doctorate, comprehensive exam, thesis/dissertation, interactive Program of Study (iPOS) submitted before completing 50 percent of required credit hours. *Entrance requirements:* For master's, minimum GPA of 3.0 or equivalent in last 2 years of work leading to bachelor's degree, 3 letters of recommendation, resume; for doctorate, GRE or MAT, minimum GPA of 3.0 or equivalent in last 2 years of work leading to bachelor's degree, 3 letters of recommendation, curriculum vitae, statement of intent. Additional exam requirements/recommendations for international students: Required—TOEFL, IELTS, or PTE. Electronic applications accepted.

**Arkansas State University,** Graduate School, College of Fine Arts, Department of Music, State University, AR 72467. Offers music education (MME, SCCT); music performance (MM). *Accreditation:* NASM (one or more programs are accredited). *Program availability:* Part-time. *Degree requirements:* For master's, 2 foreign languages, comprehensive exam, thesis or alternative; for SCCT, comprehensive exam. *Entrance requirements:* For master's, GRE General Test or MAT, university entrance exam, appropriate bachelor's degree, audition, letters of recommendation, teaching experience, official transcripts, immunization records, valid teaching certificate; for SCCT, GRE General Test or MAT, interview, master's degree, official transcript, immunization records, letters of recommendation. Additional exam requirements/recommendations for international students: Required—TOEFL (minimum score 550 paper-based; 79 iBT), IELTS (minimum score 6), PTE (minimum score 56). Electronic applications accepted.

**Austin Peay State University,** College of Graduate Studies, College of Arts and Letters, Department of Music, Clarksville, TN 37044. Offers music education (M Mu); music performance (M Mu). *Accreditation:* NASM. *Program availability:* Part-time. *Faculty:* 15 full-time (7 women), 1 part-time/adjunct (0 women). *Students:* 13 full-time (4 women), 1 part-time (0 women); includes 1 minority (Black or African American, non-Hispanic/Latino), 1 international. Average age 28. 17 applicants, 24% accepted, 4 enrolled. In 2016, 9 master's awarded. *Degree requirements:* For master's, comprehensive exam, thesis optional. *Entrance requirements:* For master's, GRE General Test, diagnostic exams, audition, interview, bachelor's degree, 3 letters of recommendation. Additional exam requirements/recommendations for international students: Required—TOEFL (minimum score 500 paper-based). *Application deadline:* For fall admission, 8/9 priority date for domestic students. Applications are processed on a rolling basis. Application fee: $45 ($50 for international students). Electronic applications accepted. *Expenses:* Tuition, state resident: full-time $8300; part-time $415 per credit hour. Tuition, nonresident: full-time $22,280; part-time $1114 per credit hour. *Required fees:* $1473; $73.65 per credit hour. *Financial support:* Research assistantships with full tuition reimbursements, career-related internships or fieldwork, Federal Work-Study, institutionally sponsored loans, scholarships/grants, and unspecified assistantships available. Support available to part-time students. Financial award application deadline: 4/1; financial award applicants required to submit FAFSA. *Unit head:* Dr. Douglas Rose, Chair, 931-221-7808, Fax: 931-221-7529, E-mail: rosed@apsu.edu. *Application contact:* Brad Averitt, Coordinator of Graduate Admissions, 800-859-4723, Fax: 931-221-7641, E-mail: gradadmissions@apsu.edu. Website: http://www.apsu.edu/music/

**Azusa Pacific University,** School of Music, Azusa, CA 91702-7000. Offers education (M Mus); performance (M Mus). *Accreditation:* NASM. *Program availability:* Part-time, evening/weekend. *Degree requirements:* For master's, recital. *Entrance requirements:* For master's, interview, audition. Additional exam requirements/recommendations for international students: Required—TOEFL (minimum score 550 paper-based).

**Ball State University,** Graduate School, College of Fine Arts, School of Music, Muncie, IN 47306. Offers music (MA, MM, DA, Artist Diploma), including conducting (MM, DA), music education (MA, MM, DA), music history and musicology (MA, MM, DA), music performance (MA, MM, DA), music theory (MA), music theory and composition (DA), piano chamber music/accompanying (MM, DA), piano performance and pedagogy (MM), woodwinds (MM). *Accreditation:* NASM; NCATE (one or more programs are accredited). *Degree requirements:* For doctorate, thesis/dissertation. *Entrance requirements:* For master's, placement tests in history and theory, minimum baccalaureate GPA of 2.75 or 3.0 in latter half of baccalauareate, resume, audition; for doctorate, GRE General Test, minimum graduate GPA of 3.2, interview, audition, resume, three professional letters of reference. Additional exam requirements/recommendations for international students: Required—TOEFL (minimum score 550 paper-based; 79 iBT), IELTS (minimum score 6.5). Electronic applications accepted. *Expenses:* Contact institution.

**The Baptist College of Florida,** Graduate Programs, Graceville, FL 32440-1898. Offers Christian ministry (MA); Christian studies (MA), including Biblical studies; music and worship leadership (MA). *Program availability:* Part-time, 100% online, blended/hybrid learning. *Degree requirements:* For master's, variable foreign language requirement, comprehensive exam (for some programs), thesis (for some programs). *Entrance requirements:* For master's, regionally-accredited undergraduate degree, undergraduate courses in field, minimum GPA of 2.5. Additional exam requirements/recommendations for international students: Required—TOEFL. Electronic applications accepted. *Expenses:* Contact institution. *Faculty research:* Biblical studies, ministry studies.

**Bard College,** Conservatory of Music, The Conductors Institute, Annandale-on-Hudson, NY 12504. Offers MFA. *Entrance requirements:* For master's, resume, 3 letters of recommendation.

**Bard College,** Conservatory of Music, Graduate Program in Vocal Arts, Annandale-on-Hudson, NY 12504. Offers MM. *Entrance requirements:* For master's, portfolio, 3 letters of recommendation, headshot, repertoire list.

**Bard College,** Longy School of Music, Cambridge, MA 02138. Offers chamber ensemble (Artist Diploma); collaborative piano (MM, Artist Diploma, GPD); composition (MM); Dalcroze eurhythmics (MM); early music (MM, Artist Diploma, GPD); instrumental performance (MM, Artist Diploma, GPD); modern American music (MM, GPD); opera performance (MM, GPD); organ performance (MM, Artist Diploma, GPD); piano performance (MM, Artist Diploma, GPD); vocal performance (MM, Artist Diploma, GPD). *Program availability:* Part-time. *Degree requirements:* For master's, thesis (for some programs), recital; for other advanced degree, recital. *Entrance requirements:* For master's and other advanced degree, audition. Additional exam requirements/recommendations for international students: Required—TOEFL (minimum score 550 paper-based; 79 iBT). Electronic applications accepted.

**Baylor University,** Graduate School, School of Music, Waco, TX 76798. Offers church music (MM, DMA); collaborative piano (MM); composition (MM); conducting (MM); music history and literature (MM); music theory (MM); performance (MM); piano pedagogy and performance (MM); M Div/MM. *Accreditation:* NASM. *Students:* 15 full-time (8 women), 59 part-time (26 women); includes 11 minority (2 Black or African American, non-Hispanic/Latino; 2 Asian, non-Hispanic/Latino; 7 Hispanic/Latino), 16 international. In 2016, 24 master's awarded. *Degree requirements:* For master's, variable foreign language requirement, thesis (for some programs). *Entrance requirements:* For master's, GRE General Test. *Application deadline:* For fall admission, 8/1 for domestic students; for spring admission, 12/1 for domestic students. Applications are processed on a rolling basis. Application fee: $25. *Expenses:* Tuition: Full-time $28,494; part-time $1583 per credit hour. *Required fees:* $167 per credit hour. Tuition and fees vary according to course load and program. *Financial support:* In 2016–17, 43 teaching assistantships with full tuition reimbursements (averaging $5,990 per year) were awarded; Federal Work-Study and institutionally sponsored loans also available. *Unit head:* Dr. David Music, Graduate Program Director, 254-710-2360, Fax: 254-710-1191, E-mail: david_music@baylor.edu. *Application contact:* Melinda Coates, Administrative Assistant, 254-710-2360, Fax: 254-710-3870, E-mail: melinda_coats@baylor.edu. Website: http://www.baylor.edu/music/

**Bennington College,** Graduate Programs, MFA in Music Program, Bennington, VT 05201. Offers MFA. *Program availability:* Part-time. *Degree requirements:* For master's, thesis, concert performances. *Entrance requirements:* Additional exam requirements/recommendations for international students: Recommended—TOEFL. Electronic applications accepted. *Expenses:* Contact institution.

**Berklee College of Music,** Berklee Graduate Programs, Boston, MA 02215-3693. Offers contemporary performance (MM), including global jazz, production; global entertainment and music business (MA); music production, technology, and innovation (MM); music therapy (MA); scoring for film, television, and video games (MM). Production; global entertainment and music business; music production, technology, and innovation; and scoring for film, television, and video games programs offered at Valencia, Spain campus. *Program availability:* Part-time, blended/hybrid learning. *Faculty:* 53 full-time (18 women), 39 part-time/adjunct (7 women). *Students:* 159 full-time (51 women), 30 part-time (24 women); includes 35 minority (12 Black or African American, non-Hispanic/Latino; 7 Asian, non-Hispanic/Latino; 12 Hispanic/Latino; 4 Two or more races, non-Hispanic/Latino), 78 international. Average age 26. 774 applicants, 36% accepted, 177 enrolled. In 2016, 137 master's awarded. *Degree requirements:* For master's, thesis, culminating experience project. *Entrance requirements:* Additional exam requirements/recommendations for international students: Required—TOEFL (minimum score 600 paper-based; 100 iBT), IELTS (minimum score 7.5), PTE (minimum score 73). *Application deadline:* For fall admission, 2/1 for domestic and

international students. Application fee: $150. Electronic applications accepted. *Expenses:* Contact institution. *Financial support:* In 2016–17, 161 students received support, including 120 fellowships with full and partial tuition reimbursements available (averaging $18,507 per year), 41 research assistantships (averaging $4,220 per year); career-related internships or fieldwork, scholarships/grants, and tuition waivers (full and partial) also available. Support available to part-time students. Financial award application deadline: 2/1; financial award applicants required to submit CSS PROFILE or FAFSA. *Faculty research:* Neuroscience, integrative medicine, music therapy practice, music cognition, ethnomusicology. *Unit head:* Camille Colatosti, PhD, Dean, Institutional Assessment and Graduate Studies, E-mail: ccolatosti@berklee.edu. *Application contact:* Office of Admissions, 617-747-2221, E-mail: admissions@berklee.edu. Website: https://www.berklee.edu/graduate

**Berklee College of Music,** The Boston Conservatory at Berklee, Boston, MA 02115. Offers bassoon performance (MM); cello performance (MM); choral conducting (MM); clarinet performance (MM); collaborative piano (MM); composition (MM); contemporary music performance (MM); double bass performance (MM); flute performance (MM); harp performance (MM); horn performance (MM); marimba performance (MM); music and autism (Certificate); music education (MM); music education and autism (MM); music performance (ADP); musical theater (MFA); oboe performance (MM); opera performance (MM); orchestral conducting (MM); percussion performance (MM); piano performance (MM); saxophone performance (MM); trombone performance (MM); trumpet performance (MM). *Accreditation:* NASM (one or more programs are accredited). *Program availability:* Part-time. *Faculty:* 87 full-time (35 women), 43 part-time/adjunct (24 women). *Students:* 209 full-time (123 women), 11 part-time (3 women); includes 44 minority (7 Black or African American, non-Hispanic/Latino; 11 Asian, non-Hispanic/Latino; 15 Hispanic/Latino; 1 Native Hawaiian or other Pacific Islander, non-Hispanic/Latino; 10 Two or more races, non-Hispanic/Latino), 67 international. Average age 25. 568 applicants, 41% accepted, 86 enrolled. In 2016, 77 master's, 14 other advanced degrees awarded. *Degree requirements:* For master's, recital or performance; for other advanced degree, recital. *Entrance requirements:* For master's and other advanced degree, audition. Additional exam requirements/recommendations for international students: Required—TOEFL (minimum score 550 paper-based; 79 iBT), IELTS (minimum score 6.5), TOEFL (minimum score 580 paper-based) and IELTS (minimum score 7.0) for MM in music education. *Application deadline:* For fall admission, 12/15 for domestic and international students. Application fee: $110. Electronic applications accepted. *Expenses:* Contact institution. *Financial support:* In 2016–17, 236 students received support. Federal Work-Study and scholarships/grants available. Financial award application deadline: 12/1; financial award applicants required to submit FAFSA. *Unit head:* Camille Colatosti, PhD, Dean, Institutional Assessment and Graduate Studies, E-mail: ccolatosti@berklee.edu. *Application contact:* Director of Admissions, 617-912-9153, Fax: 617-912-9217, E-mail: admissions@bostonconservatory.edu. Website: http://www.bostonconservatory.edu/

**Bethesda University,** Graduate and Professional Programs, Anaheim, CA 92801. Offers biblical studies (MA); music (MA); theology (M Div). *Entrance requirements:* For master's, interview. Additional exam requirements/recommendations for international students: Recommended—TOEFL.

**Binghamton University, State University of New York,** Graduate School, Harpur College of Arts and Sciences, Department of Music, Binghamton, NY 13902-6000. Offers MM. *Accreditation:* NASM. *Program availability:* Part-time. *Faculty:* 12 full-time (2 women), 29 part-time/adjunct (11 women). *Students:* 20 full-time (14 women), 2 part-time (1 woman); includes 5 minority (2 Black or African American, non-Hispanic/Latino; 1 American Indian or Alaska Native, non-Hispanic/Latino; 1 Asian, non-Hispanic/Latino; 1 Two or more races, non-Hispanic/Latino), 8 international. Average age 26. 43 applicants, 67% accepted, 15 enrolled. In 2016, 9 master's awarded. *Degree requirements:* For master's, variable foreign language requirement, comprehensive exam, thesis (for some programs). *Entrance requirements:* For master's, GRE (for music history and literature applicants), portfolio, writing sample. Additional exam requirements/recommendations for international students: Required—TOEFL (minimum score 550 paper-based; 80 iBT). *Application deadline:* For fall admission, 4/1 priority date for domestic and international students; for spring admission, 10/1 priority date for domestic and international students. Application fee: $75. Electronic applications accepted. *Financial support:* In 2016–17, 11 students received support, including 10 teaching assistantships with full tuition reimbursements available (averaging $9,500 per year); career-related internships or fieldwork, Federal Work-Study, institutionally sponsored loans, scholarships/grants, health care benefits, tuition waivers (full and partial), and unspecified assistantships also available. Financial award application deadline: 2/15; financial award applicants required to submit FAFSA. *Unit head:* Christopher Bartlette, Director of Graduate Studies, 607-777-2559, E-mail: cbartlet@binghamton.edu. *Application contact:* Ben Balkaya, Assistant Dean and Director, 607-777-2151, Fax: 607-777-2501, E-mail: balkaya@binghamton.edu.

**Bob Jones University,** Graduate Programs, Greenville, SC 29614. Offers accountancy (MS); Bible (MA); Bible translation (MA); Biblical studies (Certificate); broadcast management (MS); business administration (MBA); church history (MA, PhD); church ministries (MA); church music (MM); cinema and video production (MA); counseling (MS); curriculum and instruction (Ed D); divinity (M Div); dramatic production (MA); educational leadership (MS, Ed D, Ed S); elementary education (M Ed, MAT); English (M Ed, MA, MAT); fine arts (MA); graphic design (MA); history (M Ed, MA); illustration (MA); interpretative speech (MA); mathematics (M Ed, MAT); medical missions (Certificate); ministry (MM, D Min); multi-categorical special education (M Ed, MAT); music (M Ed); New Testament interpretation (PhD); Old Testament interpretation (PhD); orchestral instrument performance (MM); organ performance (MM); pastoral studies (MA); personnel services (MS, Ed S); piano pedagogy (MM); piano performance (MM); platform arts (MA); radio and television broadcasting (MS); rhetoric and public address (MA); secondary education (M Ed); studio art (MA); teaching Bible (MA); theology (MA, PhD); voice performance (MM); youth ministries (MA); M Div/MM.

**Boise State University,** College of Arts and Sciences, Department of Music, Boise, ID 8325-1560. Offers music education (MM); performance (MM). *Accreditation:* NASM. *Program availability:* Part-time. *Faculty:* 14. *Students:* 11 full-time (3 women), 6 part-time (3 women); includes 2 minority (1 Asian, non-Hispanic/Latino; 1 Hispanic/Latino), 2 international. Average age 27. 9 applicants, 78% accepted, 5 enrolled. In 2016, 10 master's awarded. *Degree requirements:* For master's, thesis optional. *Entrance requirements:* For master's, minimum GPA of 3.0, performance demonstration. Additional exam requirements/recommendations for international students: Required—TOEFL (minimum score 550 paper-based; 80 iBT), IELTS (minimum score 6). *Application deadline:* For fall admission, 2/9 priority date for domestic and international students. Application fee: $65 ($95 for international students). Electronic applications accepted. *Expenses:* Tuition, state resident: full-time $6058; part-time $358 per credit hour. Tuition, nonresident: full-time $20,108; part-time $608 per credit hour. *Required fees:* $2108. Tuition and fees vary according to program. *Financial support:* In 2016–17, 6 students received support, including 4 teaching assistantships (averaging $9,352 per year); scholarships/grants and unspecified assistantships also available. Financial award application deadline: 2/9; financial award applicants required to submit FAFSA.

*Unit head:* Dr. Linda Kline Lamar, Chair, 208-426-3665, E-mail: lkline@boisestate.edu. *Application contact:* Dr. Jeanne Belfy, Graduate Program Coordinator, 208-426-1216, E-mail: jbelfy@boisestate.edu. Website: http://music.boisestate.edu/graduate/

**Boston University,** College of Fine Arts, School of Music, Boston, MA 02118. Offers choral conducting (MM); collaborative piano (DMA); composition and theory (DMA); conducting (Performance Diploma); historical performance (MM, Artist Diploma); music education (MM, DMA, CAS); music theory (MM); opera performance (Certificate); performance (MM). *Accreditation:* NASM. *Program availability:* Part-time. *Faculty:* 36 full-time, 21 part-time/adjunct. *Students:* 378 full-time (218 women), 6 part-time (4 women); includes 48 minority (8 Black or African American, non-Hispanic/Latino; 14 Asian, non-Hispanic/Latino; 16 Hispanic/Latino; 10 Two or more races, non-Hispanic/Latino; 190 international. Average age 28. 1,027 applicants, 35% accepted, 111 enrolled. In 2016, 131 master's, 53 doctorates, 11 Artist Diplomas awarded. *Degree requirements:* For master's, thesis; for doctorate, 2 foreign languages, thesis/dissertation. *Entrance requirements:* Additional exam requirements/recommendations for international students: Required—TOEFL (minimum score 84 iBT), IELTS (minimum score 7). *Application deadline:* For fall admission, 12/1 priority date for domestic and international students. Application fee: $95. Electronic applications accepted. *Expenses:* Contact institution. *Financial support:* Fellowships, teaching assistantships, scholarships/grants, and unspecified assistantships available. Financial award application deadline: 12/1. *Unit head:* Shiela Kibbe, Director, 617-353-3341, Fax: 617-353-7455, E-mail: cfamusic@bu.edu. *Application contact:* Shaun Ramsay, Assistant Director, Admissions and Student Affairs, 617-353-3341, E-mail: arts@bu.edu.

**Boston University,** Graduate School of Arts and Sciences, Department of Musicology and Ethnomusicology, Boston, MA 02215. Offers ethnomusicology (PhD); historical musicology (PhD); historical musicology and ethnomusicology (PhD); musicology (MM). *Accreditation:* NASM. *Students:* 15 full-time (8 women), 2 international. Average age 33. 30 applicants, 17% accepted, 3 enrolled. Terminal master's awarded for partial completion of doctoral program. *Degree requirements:* For master's, 2 foreign languages, comprehensive exam, thesis; for doctorate, 2 foreign languages, comprehensive exam, thesis/dissertation. *Entrance requirements:* For master's and doctorate, GRE General Test, musical composition or research paper, 3 letters of recommendation, transcripts, personal statement, curriculum vitae. Additional exam requirements/recommendations for international students: Required—TOEFL (minimum score 550 paper-based; 84 iBT). *Application deadline:* For fall admission, 1/5 for domestic and international students. Application fee: $95. Electronic applications accepted. *Financial support:* In 2016–17, 15 students received support, including 12 fellowships (averaging $21,500 per year); Federal Work-Study, scholarships/grants, health care benefits, and unspecified assistantships also available. Financial award application deadline: 1/5. *Unit head:* Victor Coelho, Director, 617-358-0628, Fax: 617-353-7455, E-mail: blues@bu.edu. *Application contact:* Melissa Riesgo, Administrative Coordinator, 617-353-6888, Fax: 617-353-7455, E-mail: riesgo@bu.edu. Website: http://www.bu.edu/musicology/

**Bowling Green State University,** Graduate College, College of Musical Arts, Bowling Green, OH 43403. Offers composition (MM); contemporary music (DMA), including composition, performance; ethnomusicology (MM); music education (MM), including choral music education, comprehensive music education, instrumental music education; music history (MM); music theory (MM); performance (MM). *Accreditation:* NASM. *Program availability:* Part-time. *Degree requirements:* For master's, thesis or alternative, recitals; for doctorate, comprehensive exam, thesis/dissertation. *Entrance requirements:* For master's, GRE General Test, diagnostic placement exams in music history and theory, audition, interview. Additional exam requirements/recommendations for international students: Required—TOEFL. *Application deadline:* For fall admission, 3/1 priority date for domestic students. Application fee: $30. Electronic applications accepted. *Financial support:* Research assistantships with full tuition reimbursements, teaching assistantships with full tuition reimbursements, career-related internships or fieldwork, Federal Work-Study, and unspecified assistantships available. Financial award applicants required to submit FAFSA. *Faculty research:* Ethnomusicology. *Unit head:* Dr. Richard Kennell, Dean, 419-372-2188. *Application contact:* Dr. Robert Satterlee, Graduate Coordinator, 419-372-2360.

**Brandeis University,** Graduate School of Arts and Sciences, Department of Music, Waltham, MA 02454-9110. Offers composition and theory (MA, MFA, PhD); musicology (MA, MFA, PhD). *Program availability:* Part-time. *Faculty:* 6 full-time (2 women), 14 part-time/adjunct (3 women). *Students:* 28 full-time (9 women), 1 part-time (0 women); includes 6 minority (3 Black or African American, non-Hispanic/Latino; 2 Asian, non-Hispanic/Latino; 1 Hispanic/Latino), 1 international. 64 applicants, 34% accepted, 7 enrolled. In 2016, 5 master's, 3 doctorates awarded. Terminal master's awarded for partial completion of doctoral program. *Degree requirements:* For master's, variable foreign language requirement, comprehensive exam, thesis (for some programs); for doctorate, one foreign language, comprehensive exam, thesis/dissertation, colloquia. *Entrance requirements:* For master's and doctorate, resume, 2 letters of recommendation, transcript(s), statement of purpose, writing sample, examples of original work (for composition and theory applicants). Additional exam requirements/recommendations for international students: Required—TOEFL (minimum score 600 paper-based; 100 iBT); Recommended—IELTS (minimum score 7), TSE (minimum score 68). *Application deadline:* For fall admission, 1/15 priority date for domestic and international students. Application fee: $75. Electronic applications accepted. *Financial support:* In 2016–17, 21 students received support, including 16 fellowships with full tuition reimbursements available (averaging $24,000 per year), 1 teaching assistantship with partial tuition reimbursement available (averaging $3,200 per year); Federal Work-Study, scholarships/grants, health care benefits, and tuition waivers (partial) also available. Support available to part-time students. Financial award application deadline: 4/15; financial award applicants required to submit FAFSA. *Faculty research:* Composition and theory, musicology, music history. *Unit head:* Prof. Mark Berger, Department Chair, 781-736-3211, E-mail: mberger@brandeis.edu. *Application contact:* Mark Kagan, Senior Academic Administrator, 781-736-3311, E-mail: kagan@brandeis.edu. Website: http://www.brandeis.edu/gsas

**Brandon University,** School of Music, Brandon, MB R7A 6A9, Canada. Offers composition (M Mus); music education (M Mus); performance and literature (M Mus), including clarinet, conducting, jazz, low brass, piano, strings, trumpet. *Program availability:* Part-time. *Degree requirements:* For master's, comprehensive exam (for some programs), thesis (for some programs), 2 recitals. *Entrance requirements:* For master's, B Mus. Additional exam requirements/recommendations for international students: Required—TOEFL (minimum score 580 paper-based), IELTS (minimum score 7). Electronic applications accepted. *Expenses:* Contact institution. *Faculty research:* Composition, evaluation and assessment, performance anxiety, philosophy of music, teacher education.

**Brigham Young University,** Graduate Studies, College of Fine Arts and Communications, School of Music, Provo, UT 84602-1001. Offers composition (MM); conducting (MM), including band and orchestral conducting, choral conducting; music education (MA, MM); performance (MM), including keyboard performance, orchestral instrument, vocal performance. *Accreditation:* NASM. *Faculty:* 50 full-time (9 women), 58 part-time/adjunct (33 women). *Students:* 39 full-time (23 women), 8 part-time (7 women); includes 8 minority (1 American Indian or Alaska Native, non-Hispanic/Latino; 5 Asian, non-Hispanic/Latino; 1 Hispanic/Latino; 1 Native Hawaiian or other Pacific Islander, non-Hispanic/Latino). Average age 30. 47 applicants, 47% accepted, 16 enrolled. In 2016, 22 master's awarded. *Degree requirements:* For master's, comprehensive exam (for some programs), thesis (for some programs), recital, project, or composition (for some programs). *Entrance requirements:* For master's, School of Music Entrance Exam, minimum GPA of 3.0, BM. Additional exam requirements/recommendations for international students: Required—TOEFL (minimum score 85 iBT). *Application deadline:* For fall admission, 12/15 priority date for domestic and international students. Application fee: $50. Electronic applications accepted. *Expenses:* Contact institution. *Financial support:* In 2016–17, 44 students received support, including 44 research assistantships (averaging $3,000 per year), 44 teaching assistantships (averaging $3,500 per year); career-related internships or fieldwork, institutionally sponsored loans, scholarships/grants, tuition waivers (partial), and unspecified assistantships also available. Support available to part-time students. Financial award application deadline: 12/15; financial award applicants required to submit FAFSA. *Faculty research:* Algorithmic composition; string quartet repertoire; Summer of Love 50th Anniversary (through lens of music). *Unit head:* Dr. Kirt R. Saville, Director, 801-422-6304, Fax: 801-422-0533, E-mail: kirt_saville@byu.edu. *Application contact:* Dr. A. Claudine Bigelow, Graduate Coordinator, 801-422-1315, Fax: 801-422-0533, E-mail: claudine_bigelow@byu.edu. Website: https://cfac.byu.edu/music/

**Brooklyn College of the City University of New York,** School of Visual, Media and Performing Arts, Conservatory of Music, Brooklyn, NY 11210-2889. Offers composition (MM); music teacher (MA); musicology (MA); performance (MM). *Program availability:* Part-time. *Degree requirements:* For master's, one foreign language, comprehensive exam, thesis. *Entrance requirements:* For master's, placement exam, 36 credits in music, audition, completed composition, writing sample. Additional exam requirements/recommendations for international students: Required—TOEFL (minimum score 550 paper-based; 79 iBT). Electronic applications accepted. *Faculty research:* American music, computer music.

**Brooklyn College of the City University of New York,** School of Visual, Media and Performing Arts, Program in Performance and Interactive Media Arts, Brooklyn, NY 11210-2889. Offers MFA. *Entrance requirements:* For master's, 2 letters of recommendation, resume, portfolio, interview. Additional exam requirements/recommendations for international students: Required—TOEFL (minimum score 550 paper-based; 61 iBT). Electronic applications accepted.

**Brown University,** Graduate School, Department of Music, Providence, RI 02912. Offers computer music and multimedia (PhD); ethnomusicology (PhD). *Degree requirements:* For doctorate, 2 foreign languages, comprehensive exam, thesis/dissertation, departmental qualifying exam. *Entrance requirements:* For doctorate, GRE General Test. *Faculty research:* Ethnomusicology.

**Butler University,** Jordan College of the Arts, Indianapolis, IN 46208-3485. Offers composition (MM); conducting (MM); music education (MM); music history (MM). *Accreditation:* NASM. *Program availability:* Part-time. *Faculty:* 29 full-time (10 women), 36 part-time/adjunct (18 women). *Students:* 16 full-time (5 women), 21 part-time (4 women); includes 7 minority (3 Black or African American, non-Hispanic/Latino; 1 Asian, non-Hispanic/Latino; 1 Hispanic/Latino; 2 Two or more races, non-Hispanic/Latino), 1 international. Average age 26. 41 applicants, 66% accepted, 13 enrolled. In 2016, 16 master's awarded. *Degree requirements:* For master's, variable foreign language requirement, comprehensive exam, thesis (for some programs). *Entrance requirements:* For master's, GRE General Test (for MA in musicology), audition, interview, three letters of recommendation, transcripts, sample works. Additional exam requirements/recommendations for international students: Required—TOEFL (minimum score 550 paper-based; 79 iBT), IELTS (minimum score 6). *Application deadline:* For fall admission, 2/1 for domestic and international students; for spring admission, 12/15 for domestic and international students; for summer admission, 4/15 for domestic and international students. Applications are processed on a rolling basis. Application fee: $0. Electronic applications accepted. *Expenses:* Contact institution. *Financial support:* Scholarships/grants, tuition waivers (full and partial), and unspecified assistantships available. Financial award application deadline: 7/15; financial award applicants required to submit FAFSA. *Faculty research:* Music neuroscience; woodwind pedagogy and repertoire; music of the Renaissance; Johannes Kepler and Johannes Ockeghem; music criticism in early 20th-century Germany and Austria; Arabic choral music; pedagogy of music theory. *Unit head:* Michele Jarvis, Interim Dean, 317-940-9231, E-mail: mjarvis@butler.edu. *Application contact:* Diane Dubord, Graduate Student Services Specialist, 317-940-8107, E-mail: ddubord@butler.edu. Website: http://www.butler.edu/jca/

**California Baptist University,** Program in Music, Riverside, CA 92504-3206. Offers conducting (MM); music education (MM); performance (MM). *Accreditation:* NASM. *Program availability:* Part-time, evening/weekend. *Faculty:* 14 full-time (8 women), 18 part-time/adjunct (7 women). *Students:* 12 full-time (6 women), 8 part-time (6 women); includes 8 minority (2 Black or African American, non-Hispanic/Latino; 3 Asian, non-Hispanic/Latino; 3 Hispanic/Latino), 8 international. Average age 26. 7 applicants, 57% accepted, 3 enrolled. In 2016, 7 master's awarded. *Degree requirements:* For master's, comprehensive exam or thesis. *Entrance requirements:* For master's, minimum undergraduate GPA of 2.75; bachelor's degree in music; three recommendations; comprehensive essay; interview/audition. Additional exam requirements/recommendations for international students: Required—TOEFL (minimum score 80 iBT). *Application deadline:* For fall admission, 8/1 priority date for domestic students, 7/1 for international students; for spring admission, 12/1 priority date for domestic students, 11/1 for international students. Applications are processed on a rolling basis. Application fee: $45. Electronic applications accepted. *Expenses:* Contact institution. *Financial support:* In 2016–17, 8 students received support. Federal Work-Study and scholarships/grants available. Financial award applicants required to submit CSS PROFILE or FAFSA. *Faculty research:* Choral conducting, church music, choir building, hymnology, music technology. *Unit head:* Dr. Joseph Bolin, Dean, School of Music, 951-343-4714, Fax: 951-343-4570, E-mail: jbolin@calbaptist.edu. *Application contact:* Stephanie Fluitt, Graduate Admissions Counselor, 952-343-4696, E-mail: sfluitt@calbaptist.edu. Website: http://www.calbaptist.edu/masterofmusic/

**California Institute of Integral Studies,** School of Consciousness and Transformation, San Francisco, CA 94103. Offers anthropology and social change (MA, PhD); Asian philosophies and cultures (MA); creative inquiry/interdisciplinary arts (MFA); East-West psychology (MA, PhD); integral and transpersonal psychology (PhD); philosophy and religion (PhD), including ecology, spirituality, and religion, philosophy, cosmology, and consciousness, women's spirituality; theater and performance making (MFA); transformative leadership (MA); transformative studies (PhD); women, gender, spirituality and social justice (MA); writing and consciousness (MFA). *Program availability:* Part-time, evening/weekend, 100% online, blended/hybrid learning. *Students:* 390 full-time (256 women), 121 part-time (84 women); includes 135 minority

## Music

(39 Black or African American, non-Hispanic/Latino; 2 American Indian or Alaska Native, non-Hispanic/Latino; 22 Asian, non-Hispanic/Latino; 40 Hispanic/Latino; 2 Native Hawaiian or other Pacific Islander, non-Hispanic/Latino; 30 Two or more races, non-Hispanic/Latino; 51 international. Average age 38. 195 applicants, 92% accepted, 124 enrolled. In 2016, 35 master's, 41 doctorates awarded. Terminal master's awarded for partial completion of doctoral program. *Degree requirements:* For master's, thesis optional; for doctorate, comprehensive exam, thesis/dissertation, 1 foreign language (for Asian philosophies and cultures). *Entrance requirements:* For master's, minimum GPA of 3.0, letters of recommendation, writing sample; for doctorate, master's degree, minimum GPA of 3.0, letters of recommendation, writing sample. Additional exam requirements/recommendations for international students: Required—TOEFL. *Application deadline:* For fall admission, 2/1 priority date for domestic and international students; for spring admission, 10/15 priority date for domestic and international students. Applications are processed on a rolling basis. Application fee: $65. Electronic applications accepted. *Expenses: Tuition:* Full-time $19,728; part-time $1098 per semester hour. *Required fees:* $320; $320 per semester hour. *Financial support:* Research assistantships, teaching assistantships, career-related internships or fieldwork, Federal Work-Study, and scholarships/grants available. Support available to part-time students. Financial award application deadline: 4/15; financial award applicants required to submit FAFSA. *Faculty research:* Ecology and sustainability, philosophy and religion, East-West psychology, integrative health, social and cultural anthropology, transformative leadership. *Application contact:* Ellen Durst, Director of Admissions, 415-575-6100, Fax: 415-575-1268, E-mail: admissions@ciis.edu. Website: http://www.ciis.edu/

**California Institute of the Arts,** School of Music, Valencia, CA 91355-2340. Offers African music (MFA, Adv C); composition (MFA, Adv C); composition/new media (MFA, Adv C); Indonesian music (MFA, Adv C); jazz (MFA, Adv C); North Indian music (MFA, Adv C); performance (MFA, Adv C); performer/composer (MFA, Adv C); voice (MFA, Adv C); world music performance (MFA). *Program availability:* Part-time. *Degree requirements:* For master's, composition or recital. *Entrance requirements:* For master's, audition or portfolio. Additional exam requirements/recommendations for international students: Required—TOEFL. Electronic applications accepted. *Faculty research:* Music composition and twentieth century performance practice, interactive multimedia and computer music, music cognition.

**California State University, East Bay,** Office of Graduate Studies, College of Letters, Arts, and Social Sciences, Department of Music, Hayward, CA 94542-3000. Offers MA. *Accreditation:* NASM. *Program availability:* Part-time. *Students:* 16 full-time (6 women), 5 part-time (3 women); includes 11 minority (3 Black or African American, non-Hispanic/Latino; 1 American Indian or Alaska Native, non-Hispanic/Latino; 2 Asian, non-Hispanic/Latino; 3 Hispanic/Latino; 1 Native Hawaiian or other Pacific Islander, non-Hispanic/Latino; 1 Two or more races, non-Hispanic/Latino), 5 international. Average age 29. 21 applicants, 52% accepted, 5 enrolled. In 2016, 5 master's awarded. *Degree requirements:* For master's, variable foreign language requirement, comprehensive exam, project, recital, or thesis. *Entrance requirements:* For master's, minimum GPA of 3.0 in field; audition or work sample; 2 letters of recommendation. Additional exam requirements/recommendations for international students: Required—TOEFL (minimum score 550 paper-based). *Application deadline:* For fall admission, 3/1 for domestic and international students. Application fee: $55. Electronic applications accepted. *Financial support:* Fellowships, Federal Work-Study, institutionally sponsored loans, and scholarships/grants available. Support available to part-time students. Financial award application deadline: 3/2. *Unit head:* Buddy James, Chair, 510-885-3149, E-mail: buddy.james@csueastbay.edu. *Application contact:* Prof. Peter Marsh, Graduate Advisor, 510-885-3132, Fax: 510-885-3461, E-mail: peter.marsh@csueastbay.edu. Website: http://www20.csueastbay.edu/class/departments/music/

**California State University, Fresno,** Division of Research and Graduate Studies, College of Arts and Humanities, Department of Music, Fresno, CA 93740-8027. Offers music (MA); music education (MA); performance (MA). *Accreditation:* NASM. *Program availability:* Part-time. *Degree requirements:* For master's, thesis or alternative. *Entrance requirements:* For master's, GRE General Test, BA in music, minimum GPA of 3.0. Additional exam requirements/recommendations for international students: Required—TOEFL. *Application deadline:* For fall admission, 5/1 for domestic and international students; for spring admission, 10/1 for domestic and international students. Applications are processed on a rolling basis. Application fee: $55. Electronic applications accepted. *Financial support:* Teaching assistantships, career-related internships or fieldwork, Federal Work-Study, and scholarships/grants available. Support available to part-time students. Financial award application deadline: 3/1; financial award applicants required to submit FAFSA. *Faculty research:* Technology transfer, folk art. *Unit head:* Matthew Darling, Chair, 559-278-2654, Fax: 559-278-6800, E-mail: matthewd@csufresno.edu. *Application contact:* Dr. Teresa Beaman, Graduate Program Coordinator, 559-278-3975, Fax: 559-278-6800, E-mail: teresab@csufresno.edu. Website: http://www.fresnostate.edu/artshum/music/

**California State University, Fullerton,** Graduate Studies, College of the Arts, Department of Music, Fullerton, CA 92834-9480. Offers music education (MA); performance (MM). *Accreditation:* NASM. *Program availability:* Part-time. *Degree requirements:* For master's, comprehensive exam, project or thesis. *Entrance requirements:* For master's, audition, major in music or related field, minimum GPA of 2.5 in last 60 units of course work. Application fee: $55. *Expenses:* Tuition, state resident: full-time $3369; part-time $1953 per unit. Tuition, nonresident: full-time $3915; part-time $2499 per unit. Tuition and fees vary according to course load, degree level and program. *Financial support:* Career-related internships or fieldwork, Federal Work-Study, institutionally sponsored loans, and scholarships/grants available. Support available to part-time students. Financial award application deadline: 3/1; financial award applicants required to submit FAFSA. *Unit head:* Dr. Marc Dickey, Chair, 657-278-3511. *Application contact:* Admissions/Applications, 657-278-2371.

**California State University, Long Beach,** Graduate Studies, College of the Arts, Department of Music, Long Beach, CA 90840. Offers composition (MM); music (MA). *Accreditation:* NASM. *Program availability:* Part-time. *Degree requirements:* For master's, thesis or alternative, departmental qualifying exam. *Application deadline:* For fall admission, 5/1 for domestic students; for spring admission, 12/1 for domestic students. Applications are processed on a rolling basis. Application fee: $55. Electronic applications accepted. *Financial support:* Federal Work-Study, institutionally sponsored loans, and scholarships/grants available. Financial award application deadline: 3/2. *Unit head:* John A. Carnahan, Director, 562-985-4781, Fax: 562-985-2490, E-mail: jcarnaha@csulb.edu. *Application contact:* Dr. Leland Vail, Graduate Advisor, 562-985-4399, Fax: 562-985-2490, E-mail: lvail@csulb.edu.

**California State University, Los Angeles,** Graduate Studies, College of Arts and Letters, Department of Music, Los Angeles, CA 90032-8530. Offers music composition (MM); music education (MA); musicology (MA); performance (MM). *Accreditation:* NASM. *Program availability:* Part-time, evening/weekend. *Degree requirements:* For master's, comprehensive exam, project or thesis. *Entrance requirements:* For master's, audition. Additional exam requirements/recommendations for international students:

Required—TOEFL (minimum score 500 paper-based). Electronic applications accepted. *Faculty research:* Gregorian semiology, Baroque opera.

**California State University, Northridge,** Graduate Studies, College of Arts, Media, and Communication, Department of Music, Northridge, CA 91330. Offers composition (MM); conducting (MM); music education (MA); performance (MM). *Accreditation:* NASM. *Faculty:* 24 full-time (7 women), 66 part-time/adjunct (18 women). *Students:* 35 full-time (18 women), 44 part-time (28 women); includes 23 minority (2 Black or African American, non-Hispanic/Latino; 1 American Indian or Alaska Native, non-Hispanic/Latino; 5 Asian, non-Hispanic/Latino; 11 Hispanic/Latino; 4 Two or more races, non-Hispanic/Latino), 25 international. Average age 28. 162 applicants, 46% accepted, 29 enrolled. *Degree requirements:* For master's, thesis. *Entrance requirements:* For master's, audition, GRE General Test or minimum GPA of 3.0. Additional exam requirements/recommendations for international students: Required—TOEFL. *Application deadline:* For fall admission, 11/30 for domestic students. Application fee: $55. *Expenses:* Tuition, state resident: full-time $4152. *Financial support:* Application deadline: 3/1. *Unit head:* Rick Alviso, Chair, 816-677-4752. *Application contact:* Diane Roscetti Heinen, 818-677-3184, E-mail: diane.roscetti@csun.edu. Website: http://www.csun.edu/music/

**California State University, Sacramento,** Office of Graduate Studies, College of Arts and Letters, Department of English, Sacramento, CA 95819. Offers composition (MA); creative writing (MA); literature (MA); teaching English to speakers of other languages (MA). *Program availability:* Part-time. *Students:* 36 full-time (26 women), 47 part-time (35 women); includes 22 minority (5 Black or African American, non-Hispanic/Latino; 1 American Indian or Alaska Native, non-Hispanic/Latino; 8 Asian, non-Hispanic/Latino; 8 Hispanic/Latino). Average age 30. 54 applicants, 69% accepted, 26 enrolled. In 2016, 29 master's awarded. *Degree requirements:* For master's, thesis, project, or comprehensive exam; TESOL exam; writing proficiency exam. *Entrance requirements:* For master's, portfolio (creative writing); minimum GPA of 3.0 in English and overall during previous 2 years. Additional exam requirements/recommendations for international students: Required—TOEFL (minimum score 600 paper-based; 100 iBT). *Application deadline:* For fall admission, 2/15 for domestic students, 3/1 for international students; for spring admission, 9/30 for international students. Applications are processed on a rolling basis. Application fee: $55. Electronic applications accepted. *Expenses:* $4,302 full-time tuition and fees per semester, $2,796 part-time. *Financial support:* Research assistantships, teaching assistantships, career-related internships or fieldwork, and Federal Work-Study available. Support available to part-time students. Financial award application deadline: 3/1; financial award applicants required to submit FAFSA. *Faculty research:* Teaching composition, remedial writing. *Unit head:* Dr. David Toise, Chair, 916-278-6586, E-mail: dwtoise@csus.edu. *Application contact:* Jose Martinez, Graduate Admissions Supervisor, 916-278-7871, E-mail: martinj@skymail.csus.edu. Website: http://www.csus.edu/engl

**California State University, Sacramento,** Office of Graduate Studies, College of Arts and Letters, Department of Music, Sacramento, CA 95819. Offers MM. *Accreditation:* NASM. *Program availability:* Part-time. *Students:* 18 full-time (8 women), 11 part-time (5 women); includes 6 minority (1 Black or African American, non-Hispanic/Latino; 3 Asian, non-Hispanic/Latino; 1 Hispanic/Latino; 1 Native Hawaiian or other Pacific Islander, non-Hispanic/Latino). Average age 32. 12 applicants, 83% accepted, 9 enrolled. In 2016, 11 master's awarded. *Degree requirements:* For master's, thesis or project, writing proficiency exam. *Entrance requirements:* For master's, GRE, music exam, BA in music or equivalent, minimum GPA of 3.0 during previous 2 years of course work. Additional exam requirements/recommendations for international students: Required—TOEFL (minimum score 550 paper-based; 80 iBT). *Application deadline:* For fall admission, 3/1 for domestic and international students; for spring admission, 9/15 for domestic students, 9/30 for international students. Applications are processed on a rolling basis. Application fee: $55. Electronic applications accepted. *Expenses:* $4,302 full-time tuition and fees per semester, $2,796 part-time. *Financial support:* Research assistantships, teaching assistantships, career-related internships or fieldwork, and Federal Work-Study available. Support available to part-time students. Financial award application deadline: 3/1. *Unit head:* Dr. Ernie Hills, Chair, 916-278-5191, E-mail: hills@csus.edu. *Application contact:* Jose Martinez, Graduate Admissions Supervisor, 916-278-7871, E-mail: martinj@skymail.csus.edu. Website: http://www.csus.edu/music

**California State University, San Bernardino,** Graduate Studies, College of Arts and Letters, Program in English, San Bernardino, CA 92407. Offers creative writing (MFA), including fiction; English composition (MA), including composition. *Program availability:* Part-time, evening/weekend. *Faculty:* 8 full-time (all women). *Students:* 16 full-time (11 women), 56 part-time (39 women); includes 38 minority (6 Black or African American, non-Hispanic/Latino; 1 Asian, non-Hispanic/Latino; 29 Hispanic/Latino; 2 Two or more races, non-Hispanic/Latino), 5 international. 32 applicants, 66% accepted, 21 enrolled. In 2016, 26 master's awarded. *Degree requirements:* For master's, one foreign language, thesis. *Entrance requirements:* Additional exam requirements/recommendations for international students: Required—TOEFL. *Application deadline:* For fall admission, 7/16 for domestic students. Application fee: $55. *Expenses:* Tuition, state resident: full-time $7843; part-time $5011.20 per year. Tuition and fees vary according to course load, degree level, program and reciprocity agreements. *Financial support:* Application deadline: 3/1. *Unit head:* Dr. Sunny Hyon, Chair, 909-537-5834, Fax: 909-537-7086, E-mail: shyon@csusb.edu. *Application contact:* Dr. Francisca Beer, Dean of Graduate Studies, 909-537-5058, Fax: 909-537-5078, E-mail: fbeer@csusb.edu.

**Campbellsville University,** School of Music, Campbellsville, KY 42718-2799. Offers church music (MM); conducting (MM); instrumental performance (MM); music (MA); music education (MM); musicology (MM); pedagogy and performance (MM), including piano and vocal; worship (MA). *Accreditation:* NASM. *Program availability:* Part-time, 100% online, blended/hybrid learning. *Faculty:* 13 full-time (6 women), 10 part-time/adjunct (4 women). *Students:* 1 (woman) full-time, 26 part-time (13 women), 14 international. Average age 30. 17 applicants, 76% accepted, 12 enrolled. In 2016, 10 master's awarded. *Degree requirements:* For master's, comprehensive exam, thesis (for some programs), paper or recital. *Entrance requirements:* For master's, GRE General Test or PRAXIS, minimum GPA of 2.75, college transcripts. Additional exam requirements/recommendations for international students: Required—TOEFL (minimum score 550 paper-based; 79 iBT); Recommended—IELTS (minimum score 6). *Application deadline:* Applications are processed on a rolling basis. Application fee: $25. Electronic applications accepted. Application fee is waived when completed online. *Expenses:* $399 per credit hour. *Financial support:* Application deadline: 6/1; applicants required to submit FAFSA. *Unit head:* Dr. Tony Cunha, Dean, 270-789-5240, Fax: 270-789-5524, E-mail: accunha@campbellsville.edu. *Application contact:* Monica Bamwine, Assistant Director of Graduate Admissions, 270-789-5221, Fax: 270-789-5071, E-mail: mkbamwine@campbellsville.edu. Website: http://www.campbellsville.edu/music

**Capital University,** Conservatory of Music, Columbus, OH 43209-2394. Offers music education (MM), including instrumental emphasis, Kodály emphasis. Program offered only in summer. *Accreditation:* NASM. *Program availability:* Part-time. *Degree*

*requirements:* For master's, comprehensive exam, thesis or alternative, chamber performance exam. *Entrance requirements:* For master's, music theory exam, minimum undergraduate GPA of 3.0. Additional exam requirements/recommendations for international students: Required—TOEFL (minimum score 550 paper-based; 80 iBT). Electronic applications accepted. *Expenses:* Contact institution. *Faculty research:* Folk song research, Kodály method, performance, composition.

**Carleton University,** Faculty of Graduate Studies, Faculty of Arts and Social Sciences, School for Studies in Art and Culture, Program in Music and Culture, Ottawa, ON K1S 5B6, Canada. Offers MA.

**Carnegie Mellon University,** College of Fine Arts, School of Music, Pittsburgh, PA 15213-3891. Offers collaborative piano (MM); composition (MM); instrumental performance (MM); music and technology (MS); music education (MM); vocal performance (MM). *Accreditation:* NASM. *Program availability:* Part-time. *Degree requirements:* For master's, comprehensive exam, recital. *Entrance requirements:* For master's, audition. *Faculty research:* Computer music, music history.

**Case Western Reserve University,** School of Graduate Studies, Department of Music, Program in Historical Musicology, Cleveland, OH 44106. Offers historical musicology (PhD); music history (MA). *Faculty:* 7 full-time (2 women). *Students:* 22 full-time (8 women), 1 part-time (0 women), 2 international. Average age 31. 25 applicants, 12% accepted, 3 enrolled. In 2016, 2 doctorates awarded. *Degree requirements:* For master's, thesis. *Entrance requirements:* Additional exam requirements/recommendations for international students: Required—TOEFL (minimum score 577 paper-based; 90 iBT); Recommended—IELTS (minimum score 7). *Application deadline:* For fall admission, 12/15 for domestic students. Application fee: $50. *Expenses: Tuition:* Full-time $42,576; part-time $1774 per credit hour. *Required fees:* $34. Tuition and fees vary according to course load and program. *Financial support:* Fellowships, teaching assistantships, career-related internships or fieldwork, tuition waivers (full), unspecified assistantships, and stipends available. *Faculty research:* Musicology, historical performance practice. *Unit head:* David J. Rothenberg, Associate Professor/Department Chair, 216-368-6046, Fax: 216-368-6557, E-mail: music@case.edu. *Application contact:* Laura Stauffer, Department Administrator, 216-368-0117, Fax: 216-368-6557, E-mail: music@case.edu.

**Case Western Reserve University,** School of Graduate Studies, Department of Music, Program in Historical Performance Practice, Cleveland, OH 44106. Offers MA, DMA, PhD. *Faculty:* 2 full-time (both women). *Students:* 1 (woman) full-time, all international. Average age 29. 7 applicants, 43% accepted, 3 enrolled. In 2016, 2 doctorates awarded. Terminal master's awarded for partial completion of doctoral program. *Degree requirements:* For master's, one foreign language, comprehensive exam (for some programs), ensemble participation; juried lecture-recital; for doctorate, 2 foreign languages, comprehensive exam (for some programs), thesis/dissertation, ensemble participation; juried lecture-recital. *Entrance requirements:* For master's, GRE, statement of purpose; audio/video recording of a performance; two writing samples; three letters of recommendation; live audition; for doctorate, GRE, statement of purpose; two writing samples; curriculum vitae; three letters of recommendation. Additional exam requirements/recommendations for international students: Required—TOEFL (minimum score 577 paper-based; 90 iBT); Recommended—IELTS (minimum score 7). *Application deadline:* For fall admission, 1/1 priority date for domestic students. Application fee: $50. Electronic applications accepted. *Expenses: Tuition:* Full-time $42,576; part-time $1774 per credit hour. *Required fees:* $34. Tuition and fees vary according to course load and program. *Financial support:* Fellowships, tuition waivers (full and partial), and stipends available. Financial award application deadline: 1/1; financial award applicants required to submit FAFSA. *Faculty research:* Early music, music history and historical performance practice. *Unit head:* David J. Rothenberg, Associate Professor/Department Chair, 216-368-6046, Fax: 216-368-6557, E-mail: music@case.edu. *Application contact:* Laura Stauffer, Department Administrator, 216-368-0117, Fax: 216-368-6557, E-mail: music@case.edu. Website: http://music.case.edu/

**The Catholic University of America,** Benjamin T. Rome School of Music, Washington, DC 20064. Offers cello (Artist Diploma); chamber music (piano) (MM, DMA); composition (MM, DMA), including concert music (MM), stage music (MM); music (MAT); musicology (MA, PhD); orchestral conducting (MM, DMA, Artist Diploma); orchestral instruments/guitar (MM, DMA); piano (Artist Diploma); piano pedagogy (MM, DMA); piano performance (MM, DMA); sacred music (MMSM, DMA); violin (Artist Diploma); vocal accompanying (MM, DMA); vocal pedagogy (MM, DMA); vocal performance (MM, DMA); voice (Artist Diploma); MA/MSLIS. MA/MSLIS offered in partnership with Department of Library and Information Science. *Accreditation:* NASM. *Program availability:* Part-time. *Faculty:* 20 full-time (4 women), 53 part-time/adjunct (21 women). *Students:* 29 full-time (15 women), 71 part-time (31 women); includes 26 minority (7 Black or African American, non-Hispanic/Latino; 13 Asian, non-Hispanic/Latino; 6 Hispanic/Latino), 22 international. Average age 33. 80 applicants, 73% accepted, 24 enrolled. In 2016, 15 master's, 9 doctorates awarded. *Degree requirements:* For master's, variable foreign language requirement, comprehensive exam (for some programs), thesis (for some programs), final recital (for some programs); for doctorate, variable foreign language requirement, comprehensive exam (for some programs), thesis/dissertation (for some programs), final recital (for some programs); for Artist Diploma, variable foreign language requirement, final recital (for some programs). *Entrance requirements:* For master's, music theory and music history placement examinations, statement of purpose, 2 letters of recommendation, minimum undergraduate B average, audition (for all performance degrees), official copy of academic transcript showing completed and conferred BM; for doctorate, music theory and music history placement examinations, 2 letters of recommendation, minimum B average in all previous course work and degrees, official copies of academic transcripts showing completion and conferral of all previous degrees, audition (for all performance degrees); for Artist Diploma, music theory and music history placement examinations, statement of purpose, 2 letters of recommendation, minimum B average in all previous course work and degrees, BM, audition, official copies of academic transcripts showing completion and conferral of all previous degrees. Additional exam requirements/recommendations for international students: Required—TOEFL (minimum score 580 paper-based). *Application deadline:* For fall admission, 7/15 priority date for domestic students, 7/1 for international students; for spring admission, 11/15 priority date for domestic students, 11/1 for international students. Applications are processed on a rolling basis. Application fee: $55. Electronic applications accepted. *Expenses:* $42,850 per year; $1,170 per credit; $200 per semester part-time fees. *Financial support:* Fellowships, research assistantships, teaching assistantships, Federal Work-Study, scholarships/grants, tuition waivers (full and partial), and unspecified assistantships available. Financial award application deadline: 2/1; financial award applicants required to submit FAFSA. *Faculty research:* Composition, sacred music, orchestral instruments, piano and vocal performance, piano and vocal pedagogy. *Total annual research expenditures:* $10,650. *Unit head:* Dr. Grayson Wagstaff, Dean, 202-319-5417, Fax: 202-319-6280, E-mail: cua-music@cua.edu. *Application contact:* Director of Graduate Admissions, 202-319-5057, Fax: 202-319-6533, E-mail: cua-admissions@cua.edu. Website: http://music.cua.edu/

**Central Michigan University,** College of Graduate Studies, College of Communication and Fine Arts, School of Music, Mount Pleasant, MI 48859. Offers composition (MM); conducting (MM); music education (MM); performance (MM). *Accreditation:* NASM. *Program availability:* Part-time. *Degree requirements:* For master's, thesis or alternative. Electronic applications accepted. *Faculty research:* Music education, music composition, conducting, music performance.

**Central Washington University,** Graduate Studies and Research, College of Arts and Humanities, Department of Music, Ellensburg, WA 98926. Offers MM. *Accreditation:* NASM. *Degree requirements:* For master's, thesis or alternative. *Entrance requirements:* For master's, minimum GPA of 3.0. Additional exam requirements/recommendations for international students: Required—TOEFL (minimum score 550 paper-based; 79 iBT) or IELTS (minimum score 6.5). Electronic applications accepted.

**Charlotte Christian College and Theological Seminary,** Graduate Program, Charlotte, NC 28205. Offers urban Christian ministry (MA), including church planting, multi-cultural studies, sacred music, youth ministry. *Program availability:* Part-time, evening/weekend. *Degree requirements:* For master's, thesis. *Entrance requirements:* For master's, MAT, writing sample/essay. Additional exam requirements/recommendations for international students: Required—TOEFL, IELTS. Electronic applications accepted. *Expenses:* Contact institution.

**Claremont Graduate University,** Graduate Programs, School of Arts and Humanities, Department of Music, Claremont, CA 91711-6160. Offers church music (MA, DCM); composition (MA, DMA); historical performance practices (MA, DMA); musicology (MA, PhD); performance (MA, DMA); MBA/PhD. *Program availability:* Part-time. *Faculty:* 3 full-time (1 woman). *Students:* 42 full-time (21 women), 20 part-time (11 women); includes 17 minority (12 Asian, non-Hispanic/Latino; 5 Hispanic/Latino), 16 international. Average age 36. In 2016, 2 master's, 8 doctorates awarded. Terminal master's awarded for partial completion of doctoral program. *Degree requirements:* For master's, one foreign language, comprehensive exam, thesis (for some programs); oral and written qualifying exams, recitals; for doctorate, 2 foreign languages, comprehensive exam, thesis/dissertation (for some programs), oral and written qualifying exams, oral defense of dissertation, recitals. *Entrance requirements:* For master's and doctorate, GRE General Test, auditions, compositions, or papers. Additional exam requirements/recommendations for international students: Required—TOEFL (minimum score 75 iBT). *Application deadline:* For fall admission, 2/1 priority date for domestic and international students. Applications are processed on a rolling basis. Application fee: $80. Electronic applications accepted. *Expenses: Tuition:* Full-time $44,328; part-time $1847 per unit. *Required fees:* $600; $300 per semester. Tuition and fees vary according to course load and program. *Financial support:* Fellowships, research assistantships, teaching assistantships, Federal Work-Study, institutionally sponsored loans, and scholarships/grants available. Support available to part-time students. Financial award application deadline: 2/15; financial award applicants required to submit FAFSA. *Unit head:* Robert Zappulla, Chair, 909-607-9664, Fax: 909-607-3694, E-mail: robert.zappula@cgu.edu. *Application contact:* Amy Sandefur, Assistant Director of Admissions, 909-607-9101, E-mail: amy.sandefur@cgu.edu. Website: https://www.cgu.edu/departments/music/

**Cleveland Institute of Music,** Graduate Programs, Cleveland, OH 44106-1776. Offers MM, DMA, AD, CPS. DMA and MM programs offered jointly with Case Western Reserve University. *Accreditation:* NASM (one or more programs are accredited). *Degree requirements:* For master's, comprehensive exam, recital; for doctorate, comprehensive exam, thesis/dissertation (for some programs), final projects; for other advanced degree, recital. *Entrance requirements:* For master's, theory placement tests, audition; for doctorate, diagnostic exams, theory placement test, audition; for other advanced degree, audition. Additional exam requirements/recommendations for international students: Required—TOEFL (minimum score 550 paper-based). Electronic applications accepted.

**Cleveland State University,** College of Graduate Studies, College of Liberal Arts and Social Sciences, Department of Music, Cleveland, OH 44115. Offers composition (MM); music education (MM). *Accreditation:* NASM. *Program availability:* Part-time, evening/weekend. *Faculty:* 9 full-time (2 women), 19 part-time/adjunct (6 women). *Students:* 9 full-time (3 women), 20 part-time (8 women); includes 6 minority (1 Black or African American, non-Hispanic/Latino; 1 Asian, non-Hispanic/Latino; 2 Hispanic/Latino; 2 Two or more races, non-Hispanic/Latino), 4 international. Average age 26. 34 applicants, 91% accepted, 19 enrolled. In 2016, 10 master's awarded. *Degree requirements:* For master's, comprehensive exam (for some programs), thesis or recital. *Entrance requirements:* For master's, departmental assessment in music history, minimum undergraduate GPA of 2.75, audition on primary instrument, or submission of composition portfolio or written samples (for music education). Additional exam requirements/recommendations for international students: Required—TOEFL (minimum score 550 paper-based; 78 iBT). *Application deadline:* For fall admission, 7/1 priority date for domestic students, 5/15 for international students; for spring admission, 11/15 for domestic students, 11/1 for international students; for summer admission, 4/1 for domestic students, 3/15 for international students. Applications are processed on a rolling basis. Application fee: $40. Electronic applications accepted. *Expenses:* Tuition, state resident: full-time $9565. Tuition, nonresident: full-time $17,980. Tuition and fees vary according to program. *Financial support:* In 2016–17, 14 students received support. Scholarships/grants, tuition waivers (partial), and unspecified assistantships available. Financial award application deadline: 3/15; financial award applicants required to submit FAFSA. *Faculty research:* Performance, music education, music composition. *Total annual research expenditures:* $162,000. *Unit head:* Dr. John Perrine, Chairperson/Associate Professor, 216-687-3959, Fax: 216-687-9279, E-mail: j.m.perrine@csuohio.edu. *Application contact:* Kate Bill, Music Admission Specialist, 216-687-5039, Fax: 216-687-9279, E-mail: m.c.bill@csuohio.edu. Website: http://www.csuohio.edu/music/

**The Colburn School Conservatory of Music,** Graduate Programs, Los Angeles, CA 90012. Offers music (AD); performance (MM).

**Colorado State University,** College of Health and Human Sciences, School of Education, Fort Collins, CO 80523-1588. Offers adult education and training (M Ed); counseling and career development (M Ed); education sciences (PhD); higher education leadership (PhD); organization learning, performance, and change (PhD); organizational learning, performance, and change (M Ed); student affairs in higher education (MS); teaching and learning (M Ed), including principal licensure, teacher licensure. *Accreditation:* ACA; TEAC. *Program availability:* Part-time, online only, 100% online, blended/hybrid learning, face-to-face off-campus courses. *Faculty:* 29 full-time (21 women), 23 part-time/adjunct (11 women). *Students:* 80 full-time (56 women), 541 part-time (353 women); includes 142 minority (26 Black or African American, non-Hispanic/Latino; 2 American Indian or Alaska Native, non-Hispanic/Latino; 22 Asian, non-Hispanic/Latino; 71 Hispanic/Latino; 21 Two or more races, non-Hispanic/Latino), 18 international. Average age 37. 483 applicants, 31% accepted, 137 enrolled. In 2016, 183 master's, 33 doctorates awarded. *Degree requirements:* For master's, thesis optional, professional portfolio; for doctorate, comprehensive exam, thesis/dissertation. *Entrance requirements:* For master's, bachelor's degree; minimum GPA of 3.0 in last degree earned; for doctorate, GRE or GMAT (depending upon specialization), master's degree; minimum GPA of 3.0 in last degree earned. Additional exam requirements/

recommendations for international students: Required—TOEFL (minimum score 550 paper-based; 80 iBT), IELTS (minimum score 6.5), PTE (minimum score 58). *Application deadline:* Applications are processed on a rolling basis. Application fee: $60 ($70 for international students). Electronic applications accepted. *Expenses:* Contact institution. *Financial support:* In 2016–17, 3 students received support, including 7 research assistantships with full tuition reimbursements available (averaging $11,749 per year); 5 teaching assistantships with full tuition reimbursements available (averaging $15,886 per year); fellowships with full tuition reimbursements available, scholarships/grants, and unspecified assistantships also available. Financial award application deadline: 3/1; financial award applicants required to submit FAFSA. *Faculty research:* Higher education leadership; research methods; human resource development; K-16 education; diversity, equity, and inclusion. *Total annual research expenditures:* $499,898. *Unit head:* Dr. Louise Jennings, Co-Director, 970-491-6317, Fax: 970-491-1317, E-mail: louise.jennings@colostate.edu. *Application contact:* Kelli Clark, Graduate Programs Coordinator, 970-491-2093, Fax: 970-491-1317, E-mail: kelli.clark@colostate.edu.
Website: http://www.soe.chhs.colostate.edu/

**Colorado State University,** College of Liberal Arts, Department of English, Fort Collins, CO 80523-1773. Offers creative nonfiction (MA); creative writing (MFA); literature (MA); rhetoric and composition (MA); TESL/TEFL (MA). *Program availability:* Part-time. *Faculty:* 31 full-time (21 women), 25 part-time/adjunct (23 women). *Students:* 71 full-time (54 women), 30 part-time (21 women); includes 7 minority (1 Black or African American, non-Hispanic/Latino; 2 Asian, non-Hispanic/Latino; 2 Hispanic/Latino; 2 Two or more races, non-Hispanic/Latino), 13 international. Average age 29. 177 applicants, 42% accepted, 39 enrolled. In 2016, 33 master's awarded. *Degree requirements:* For master's, thesis (for some programs). *Entrance requirements:* For master's, BA/BS or equivalent with minimum cumulative undergraduate GPA of 3.0, transcripts, writing sample, statement of purpose, 3 letters of recommendation. Additional exam requirements/recommendations for international students: Recommended—TOEFL (minimum score 550 paper-based; 80 iBT), IELTS (minimum score 6.5). *Application deadline:* For spring admission, 9/15 for domestic and international students. Application fee: $60 ($70 for international students). Electronic applications accepted. *Expenses:* Tuition, state resident: full-time $9628. Tuition, nonresident: full-time $23,603. *Required fees:* $2253; $528.14 per credit hour. $264.07 per semester. Tuition and fees vary according to course load and program. *Financial support:* In 2016–17, 39 students received support, including 38 teaching assistantships with full and partial tuition reimbursements available (averaging $14,005 per year); scholarships/grants, health care benefits, and unspecified assistantships also available. Financial award application deadline: 1/1. *Faculty research:* Literary texts in historical and cultural contexts; creation and criticism of fiction, poetry, creative nonfiction and hybrid genres; critical literacies, multimodalities, and technologies including pedagogical theory and practice; linguistics, second language acquisition and TEFL/TESOL; rhetoric and social change. *Total annual research expenditures:* $154,039. *Unit head:* Louann Reid, Professor, 970-491-6428, E-mail: louann.reid@colostate.edu. *Application contact:* Marnie Leonard, Administrative Assistant, 970-491-2403, E-mail: marnie.leonard@colostate.edu.
Website: http://english.colostate.edu/

**Colorado State University,** College of Liberal Arts, School of Music, Theatre and Dance, Fort Collins, CO 80523-1779. Offers choral conducting (MM); collaborative piano (MM); instrumental conducting (MM); music education (MM), including conducting; music performance (MM); music therapy (MM). *Accreditation:* NASM. *Program availability:* Part-time. *Faculty:* 25 full-time (7 women), 9 part-time/adjunct (5 women). *Students:* 54 full-time (31 women), 100 part-time (77 women); includes 16 minority (2 Black or African American, non-Hispanic/Latino; 4 Asian, non-Hispanic/Latino; 8 Hispanic/Latino; 2 Two or more races, non-Hispanic/Latino), 13 international. Average age 30. 77 applicants, 79% accepted, 43 enrolled. In 2016, 69 master's awarded. *Degree requirements:* For master's, comprehensive exam, thesis, recital. *Entrance requirements:* For master's, minimum GPA of 3.0, audition, bachelor's degree, 3 letters of recommendation, transcripts, statement of purpose, curriculum vitae. Additional exam requirements/recommendations for international students: Required—TOEFL (minimum score 550 paper-based; 80 iBT), IELTS (minimum score 6.5). *Application deadline:* For fall admission, 2/15 for domestic and international students. Applications are processed on a rolling basis. Application fee: $60 ($70 for international students). Electronic applications accepted. *Expenses:* Contact institution. *Financial support:* In 2016–17, 25 students received support, including 24 teaching assistantships with full and partial tuition reimbursements available (averaging $8,998 per year); research assistantships, scholarships/grants, traineeships, and unspecified assistantships also available. Financial award application deadline: 2/15; financial award applicants required to submit FAFSA. *Faculty research:* Musical creativity in children with autism spectrum disorder; music therapy; cognitive, sensorimotor, speech and language and psychosocial functioning techniques; study/analysis/ear training strategies. *Total annual research expenditures:* $12,966. *Unit head:* Dr. Daniel Goble, Director, 970-491-5529, E-mail: dan.goble@colostate.edu. *Application contact:* Dr. G. Murray Oliver, Graduate Program Coordinator, 970-491-5193, Fax: 970-491-7541, E-mail: murray.oliver@colostate.edu.
Website: http://smtd.colostate.edu/

**Columbia College Chicago,** Graduate School, MFA Program in Music Composition for the Screen, Chicago, IL 60605-1996. Offers MFA. *Entrance requirements:* For master's, self-assessment essay, work samples, resume, letters of recommendation. Additional exam requirements/recommendations for international students: Required—TOEFL (minimum score 600 paper-based; 100 iBT). Electronic applications accepted. *Expenses:* Contact institution.

**Columbia University,** Graduate School of Arts and Sciences, New York, NY 10027. Offers African-American studies (MA); American studies (MA); anthropology (MA, PhD); art history and archaeology (MA, PhD); astronomy (PhD); biological sciences (PhD); biotechnology (MA); chemical physics (PhD); chemistry (PhD); classical studies (MA, PhD); classics (MA, PhD); climate and society (MA); conservation biology (MA); earth and environmental sciences (PhD); East Asia: regional studies (MA); East Asian languages and cultures (MA, PhD); ecology, evolution and environmental biology (MA), including conservation biology; ecology, evolution, and environmental biology (PhD), including ecology and evolutionary biology, evolutionary primatology; economics (MA, PhD); English and comparative literature (MA, PhD); French and Romance philology (MA, PhD); Germanic languages (MA, PhD); global French studies (MA); global thought (MA); Hispanic cultural studies (MA); history (PhD); history and literature (MA); human rights studies (MA); Islamic studies (MA); Italian (MA, PhD); Japanese pedagogy (MA); Jewish studies (MA); Latin America and the Caribbean: regional studies (MA); Latin American and Iberian cultures (PhD); mathematics (MA, PhD), including finance (MA); medieval and Renaissance studies (MA); Middle Eastern, South Asian, and African studies (MA, PhD); modern art: critical and curatorial studies (MA); modern European studies (MA); museum anthropology (MA); music (DMA, PhD); oral history (MA); philosophical foundations of physics (MA); philosophy (MA, PhD); physics (PhD); political science (PhD); psychology (PhD); quantitative methods in the social sciences (MA); religion (MA, PhD); Russia, Eurasia and East Europe: regional studies (MA); Russian translation (MA); Slavic cultures (MA); Slavic languages (MA, PhD); sociology (MA, PhD); South Asian studies (MA); statistics (MA, PhD); theatre (PhD). Dual-degree programs require admission to both Graduate School of Arts and Sciences

and another Columbia school. *Program availability:* Part-time. Terminal master's awarded for partial completion of doctoral program. *Degree requirements:* For master's, variable foreign language requirement, comprehensive exam (for some programs), thesis (for some programs); for doctorate, variable foreign language requirement, comprehensive exam (for some programs), thesis/dissertation. *Entrance requirements:* For master's and doctorate, GRE General Test, GRE Subject Test (for some programs). Additional exam requirements/recommendations for international students: Required—TOEFL, IELTS. Electronic applications accepted.

**Columbus State University,** Graduate Studies, College of the Arts, Schwob School of Music, Columbus, GA 31907-5645. Offers music (Artist Diploma); music education (MM); music performance (MM). *Accreditation:* NASM; NCATE (one or more programs are accredited). *Program availability:* Part-time. *Faculty:* 25 full-time (10 women), 2 part-time/adjunct (both women). *Students:* 46 full-time (21 women), 11 part-time (2 women); includes 8 minority (3 Black or African American, non-Hispanic/Latino; 1 Asian, non-Hispanic/Latino; 3 Hispanic/Latino; 1 Native Hawaiian or other Pacific Islander, non-Hispanic/Latino), 26 international. Average age 26. 67 applicants, 51% accepted, 28 enrolled. In 2016, 8 master's, 7 Artist Diplomas awarded. *Degree requirements:* For master's, exit exam. *Entrance requirements:* For master's, audition, letters of recommendation, undergraduate degree in music with a minimum GPA of 2.5. Additional exam requirements/recommendations for international students: Required—TOEFL (minimum score 550 paper-based; 79 iBT). *Application deadline:* For fall admission, 6/30 for domestic students, 5/1 for international students; for spring admission, 11/1 for domestic and international students; for summer admission, 3/1 for domestic and international students. Applications are processed on a rolling basis. Application fee: $50. Electronic applications accepted. *Expenses:* Tuition, state resident: full-time $4804; part-time $2412 per semester hour. Tuition, nonresident: full-time $19,218; part-time $9612 per semester hour. *Required fees:* $1850; $1850 per semester hour. Tuition and fees vary according to program. *Financial support:* In 2016–17, 44 students received support, including 32 research assistantships with partial tuition reimbursements available (averaging $3,000 per year); career-related internships or fieldwork, Federal Work-Study, institutionally sponsored loans, scholarships/grants, tuition waivers (partial), and unspecified assistantships also available. Support available to part-time students. Financial award application deadline: 5/1; financial award applicants required to submit FAFSA. *Unit head:* Dr. Edwin Scott Harris, Director, 706-507-8419, E-mail: harris_scott@columbusstate.edu. *Application contact:* Kristin Williams, Director of International and Graduate Recruitment, 706-507-8848, Fax: 706-568-5091, E-mail: williams_kristin@columbusstate.edu.
Website: http://music.columbusstate.edu/

**Concordia University,** School of Graduate Studies, Faculty of Fine Arts, Department of Music, Montréal, QC H3G 1M8, Canada. Offers advanced music performance studies (Diploma). *Degree requirements:* For Diploma, performance, 2 recitals.

**Concordia University Chicago,** College of Graduate and Innovative Programs, Program in Church Music, River Forest, IL 60305-1499. Offers MCM. *Accreditation:* NASM. *Program availability:* Part-time. *Degree requirements:* For master's, composition, recital, or thesis. *Entrance requirements:* For master's, minimum GPA of 2.9, audition. Additional exam requirements/recommendations for international students: Required—TOEFL (minimum score 550 paper-based). Electronic applications accepted. *Faculty research:* Twentieth-century sacred choral music, liturgical context of sacred music after the Council of Trent, dance and music of J.S. Bach.

**Concordia University Chicago,** College of Graduate and Innovative Programs, Program in Music, River Forest, IL 60305-1499. Offers MA. *Program availability:* Part-time. *Degree requirements:* For master's, composition, recital, or thesis. *Entrance requirements:* For master's, minimum GPA of 2.9, audition. Additional exam requirements/recommendations for international students: Required—TOEFL (minimum score 550 paper-based). Electronic applications accepted.

**Concordia University Wisconsin,** Graduate Programs, School of Arts and Sciences, Program in Church Music, Mequon, WI 53097-2402. Offers MCM. *Degree requirements:* For master's, comprehensive exam, thesis or alternative. *Entrance requirements:* For master's, minimum GPA of 3.0. Additional exam requirements/recommendations for international students: Required—TOEFL. *Application deadline:* For fall admission, 8/1 priority date for domestic students; for spring admission, 1/15 for domestic students. Applications are processed on a rolling basis. Application fee: $35 ($125 for international students). *Financial support:* Application deadline: 8/1. *Unit head:* Dr. James Freese, Director, 262-243-4245, E-mail: james.freese@cuw.edu. *Application contact:* Dr. James Freese, Director, 262-243-4245, E-mail: james.freese@cuw.edu.
Website: http://www.cuw.edu/

**Conservatorio de Musica de Puerto Rico,** Program in Musical Performance, San Juan, PR 00907. Offers guitar (Diploma); orchestral instruments (Diploma); piano (Diploma); vocal performance (Diploma). *Entrance requirements:* For degree, 3 letters of recommendation, audition, degree in music, minimum GPA of 2.5.

**Converse College,** School of Education and Graduate Studies, Petrie School of Music, Spartanburg, SC 29302. Offers music education (M Mus); performance (M Mus). *Accreditation:* NASM. *Program availability:* Part-time, evening/weekend. *Degree requirements:* For master's, variable foreign language requirement, comprehensive exam, thesis (for some programs), recitals. *Entrance requirements:* For master's, NTE (music education), audition, 3 letters of recommendation. Additional exam requirements/recommendations for international students: Required—TOEFL. *Application deadline:* For spring admission, 3/1 priority date for domestic and international students. Applications are processed on a rolling basis. Application fee: $40. Electronic applications accepted. *Expenses:* Tuition: Full-time $3600; part-time $400 per credit hour. *Required fees:* $70 per term. *Financial support:* Career-related internships or fieldwork, Federal Work-Study, institutionally sponsored loans, and unspecified assistantships available. Support available to part-time students. Financial award application deadline: 4/15. *Faculty research:* Chamber music, opera, performance, composition, recording. *Unit head:* Patricia S. Foy, Director, 864-596-9172, E-mail: patti.foy@converse.edu. *Application contact:* 864-596-9404, E-mail: graduate@converse.edu.
Website: http://www.converse.edu/academics/school-arts/petrie-school-music

**Cornell University,** Graduate School, Graduate Fields of Arts and Sciences, Field of Music, Ithaca, NY 14853. Offers composition (DMA); musicology (PhD); performance practice (DMA); theory of music (MA). *Degree requirements:* For doctorate, comprehensive exam, thesis/dissertation, 1 foreign language (DMA), 2 foreign languages (PhD). *Entrance requirements:* For doctorate, GRE General Test, 2 music papers (PhD); 2 recent scores with recording and 1 music paper (DMA in composition); 1 music paper, recording and audition (DMA in performance practice). Additional exam requirements/recommendations for international students: Required—TOEFL (minimum score 600 paper-based; 77 iBT). Electronic applications accepted. *Faculty research:* Music history, music theory, performance practice, ethnomusicology, composition.

**Curtis Institute of Music,** Graduate Studies, Philadelphia, PA 19103-6107. Offers opera (MM). *Accreditation:* NASM. *Entrance requirements:* For master's, audition or performance in 2 or more principal roles or 6 major scenes.

**Dalhousie University,** Faculty of Arts and Social Science, Department of Musicology, Halifax, NS B3H 4R2, Canada. Offers MA. *Entrance requirements:* Additional exam requirements/recommendations for international students: Required—TOEFL, IELTS, CANTEST, CAEL, or Michigan English Language Assessment Battery. Electronic applications accepted.

**Dartmouth College,** School of Graduate and Advanced Studies, Department of Music, Hanover, NH 03755. Offers digital music (MA). *Faculty:* 11 full-time (3 women), 20 part-time/adjunct (8 women). *Students:* 6 full-time (2 women); includes 2 minority (both Two or more races, non-Hispanic/Latino), 1 international. Average age 24. 12 applicants, 33% accepted, 3 enrolled. In 2016, 3 master's awarded. *Degree requirements:* For master's, thesis or alternative. *Entrance requirements:* Additional exam requirements/recommendations for international students: Required—TOEFL. *Application deadline:* For fall admission, 2/1 for domestic students. Application fee: $35. Electronic applications accepted. *Financial support:* Fellowships with full tuition reimbursements, career-related internships or fieldwork, institutionally sponsored loans, and tuition waivers (full) available. *Faculty research:* Composition and design of computer music software and related topics. *Unit head:* Michael Casey, Chair, 603-646-9609. *Application contact:* Catherine La Touche, Administrative Assistant, 603-646-2520, Fax: 603-646-2551.
Website: http://music.dartmouth.edu/

**DePaul University,** School of Music, Chicago, IL 60614. Offers composition (MM); jazz studies (MM); music education (MM); music performance (MM); performance (Certificate). *Accreditation:* NASM (one or more programs are accredited). *Program availability:* Part-time, evening/weekend. *Degree requirements:* For master's, comprehensive exam. *Entrance requirements:* For master's, bachelor's degree in music or related field, minimum GPA of 3.0, auditions (performance), scores (composition); for Certificate, master's degree in performance or related field, auditions (for performance majors). Additional exam requirements/recommendations for international students: Required—TOEFL (minimum score 550 paper-based; 80 iBT). Electronic applications accepted. *Expenses:* Contact institution.

**Dominican University of California,** School of Arts, Humanities and Social Sciences, Humanities Program, San Rafael, CA 94901-2298. Offers applied music (MA); art history (MA); creative writing (MA); gender studies (MA); history (MA); literature (MA); philosophy (MA); political theory (MA); religion (MA). *Program availability:* Part-time. *Degree requirements:* For master's, thesis or alternative. *Entrance requirements:* For master's, minimum GPA of 3.0, interview. Additional exam requirements/recommendations for international students: Required—TOEFL (minimum score 550 paper-based; 80 iBT), IELTS (minimum score 6.5). Electronic applications accepted. Application fee is waived when completed online. *Expenses:* Contact institution.

**Duke University,** Graduate School, Department of Music, Durham, NC 27708. Offers music composition (PhD); musicology (PhD); performance practice (PhD). *Program availability:* Part-time. Terminal master's awarded for partial completion of doctoral program. *Degree requirements:* For doctorate, 3 foreign languages, thesis/dissertation. *Entrance requirements:* For doctorate, GRE General Test, paper on musical topic (for musicology); samples of compositions (for music composition). Additional exam requirements/recommendations for international students: Required—TOEFL (minimum score 577 paper-based; 90 iBT) or IELTS (minimum score 7). Electronic applications accepted.

**Duquesne University,** Mary Pappert School of Music, Pittsburgh, PA 15282-0001. Offers music education (MM). *Accreditation:* NASM. *Program availability:* Part-time. *Faculty:* 26 full-time (9 women), 77 part-time/adjunct (22 women). *Students:* 69 full-time (27 women), 16 part-time (6 women); includes 7 minority (3 Black or African American, non-Hispanic/Latino; 1 Asian, non-Hispanic/Latino; 1 Hispanic/Latino; 2 Two or more races, non-Hispanic/Latino), 24 international. Average age 26. 94 applicants, 93% accepted, 29 enrolled. In 2016, 19 master's, 9 ADs awarded. *Degree requirements:* For master's, comprehensive exam, thesis (for some programs), recital (music performance); for AD, recital. *Entrance requirements:* For master's, audition, minimum undergraduate QPA of 3.0 in music, portfolio of original compositions, or music education experience; for AD, audition. Additional exam requirements/recommendations for international students: Required—TOEFL (minimum score 550 paper-based; 79 iBT), IELTS (minimum score 6.5). *Application deadline:* For fall admission, 7/1 for domestic and international students; for spring admission, 12/1 for domestic and international students; for summer admission, 6/1 for domestic students, 5/1 for international students. Applications are processed on a rolling basis. Application fee: $50. Electronic applications accepted. Application fee is waived when completed online. *Expenses:* $1,469 per credit. *Financial support:* In 2016–17, 76 students received support. Scholarships/grants and unspecified assistantships available. Financial award application deadline: 4/1. *Faculty research:* Assessment of music education and professional dispositions; music philosophy; curricular design, pedagogy, and assessment; music composition; music performance. *Unit head:* Dr. Seth Beckman, Dean/Professor, 412-396-6082, Fax: 412-396-1524, E-mail: beckmans@duq.edu. *Application contact:* Katherine Shields, Director of Music Admissions, 412-396-5983, Fax: 412-396-5719, E-mail: shieldsk1@duq.edu.
Website: http://duq.edu/music

**East Carolina University,** Graduate School, College of Fine Arts and Communication, School of Music, Greenville, NC 27858-4353. Offers advanced performance studies (Certificate); music education (MM); music therapy (MM); performance (MM), including accompanying, choral conducting, instrumental conducting, jazz studies, organ, percussion, piano, piano pedagogy, sacred music, strings, Suzuki string pedagogy, vocal pedagogy, voice, woodwind specialist; Suzuki pedagogy (Certificate); theory and composition (MM). *Accreditation:* NASM. *Program availability:* Part-time. *Students:* 29 full-time (15 women), 19 part-time (9 women); includes 4 minority (2 Black or African American, non-Hispanic/Latino; 2 Asian, non-Hispanic/Latino), 1 international. Average age 27. 39 applicants, 100% accepted, 28 enrolled. In 2016, 10 master's awarded. *Degree requirements:* For master's, comprehensive exam, thesis optional. *Entrance requirements:* For master's, GRE General Test or MAT. Additional exam requirements/recommendations for international students: Required—TOEFL. *Application deadline:* For fall admission, 6/1 priority date for domestic students. Applications are processed on a rolling basis. Application fee: $50. *Financial support:* Fellowships, research assistantships, teaching assistantships, and Federal Work-Study available. Support available to part-time students. Financial award application deadline: 6/1. *Unit head:* Christopher Ulffers, Director, 252-328-4270, E-mail: ulffersj@ecu.edu. *Application contact:* Dean of Graduate School, 252-328-6012, Fax: 252-328-6071, E-mail: gradschool@ecu.edu.
Website: http://www.music.ecu.edu/

**East Carolina University,** Graduate School, Thomas Harriot College of Arts and Sciences, Department of English, Greenville, NC 27858-4353. Offers creative writing (MA); English studies (MA); linguistics (MA); literature (MA); multicultural and transnational literatures (MA, Certificate); rhetoric and composition (MA); rhetoric, writing, and professional communication (PhD); teaching English in the two-year college (Certificate); teaching English to speakers of other languages (MA, Certificate); technical and professional communication (MA). *Program availability:* Part-time, evening/weekend. *Students:* 54 full-time (36 women), 95 part-time (77 women); includes 32 minority (19 Black or African American, non-Hispanic/Latino; 3 Asian, non-Hispanic/Latino; 6 Hispanic/Latino; 4 Two or more races, non-Hispanic/Latino), 1 international.

Average age 35. 78 applicants, 96% accepted, 50 enrolled. In 2016, 34 master's, 1 doctorate awarded. *Degree requirements:* For master's, one foreign language, comprehensive exam, thesis optional. *Entrance requirements:* For master's, GRE General Test, MAT (for MA Ed). Additional exam requirements/recommendations for international students: Required—TOEFL. *Application deadline:* For fall admission, 6/1 priority date for domestic students; for spring admission, 10/15 for domestic students. Applications are processed on a rolling basis. Application fee: $50. *Financial support:* Research assistantships with partial tuition reimbursements, teaching assistantships with partial tuition reimbursements, and Federal Work-Study available. Support available to part-time students. Financial award application deadline: 6/1. *Unit head:* Dr. Jeffrey Johnson, Chair, 252-328-6041, E-mail: johnsonj@ecu.edu. *Application contact:* Dean of Graduate School, 252-328-6012, Fax: 252-328-6071, E-mail: gradschool@ecu.edu.
Website: http://www.ecu.edu/cs-cas/engl/graduate/

**Eastern Illinois University,** Graduate School, College of Arts and Humanities, Department of Music, Charleston, IL 61920. Offers MA. *Accreditation:* NASM. *Program availability:* Part-time, evening/weekend, online learning. *Degree requirements:* For master's, comprehensive exam (for some programs), thesis (for some programs). *Entrance requirements:* For master's, personal statement, resume, three letters of recommendation. Additional exam requirements/recommendations for international students: Required—TOEFL (minimum score 500 paper-based; 61 iBT), IELTS (minimum score 6). Electronic applications accepted.

**Eastern Kentucky University,** The Graduate School, College of Arts and Sciences, Department of Music, Richmond, KY 40475-3102. Offers choral conducting (MM); performance (MM); theory/composition (MM). *Accreditation:* NASM. *Program availability:* Part-time. *Degree requirements:* For master's, thesis optional. *Entrance requirements:* For master's, GRE General Test, minimum GPA of 2.5. *Faculty research:* Technology.

**Eastern Michigan University,** Graduate School, College of Arts and Sciences, School of Music and Dance, Ypsilanti, MI 48197. Offers composition (MM); music education (MM); performance (MM); piano pedagogy (MM). *Accreditation:* NASM. *Program availability:* Part-time, evening/weekend, online learning. *Faculty:* 25 full-time (12 women). *Students:* 12 full-time (5 women), 10 part-time (4 women); includes 1 minority (Asian, non-Hispanic/Latino), 2 international. Average age 28. 16 applicants, 56% accepted, 6 enrolled. In 2016, 6 master's awarded. *Entrance requirements:* Additional exam requirements/recommendations for international students: Required—TOEFL. *Application deadline:* Applications are processed on a rolling basis. Application fee: $45. *Financial support:* Fellowships, research assistantships with full tuition reimbursements, teaching assistantships with full tuition reimbursements, career-related internships or fieldwork, Federal Work-Study, institutionally sponsored loans, scholarships/grants, tuition waivers (partial), and unspecified assistantships available. Support available to part-time students. Financial award applicants required to submit FAFSA. *Unit head:* Dr. Diane Winder, Director, 734-487-4380, Fax: 734-487-6939, E-mail: dwinder@emich.edu. *Application contact:* Dr. David Pierce, Coordinator of Music Advising, 734-487-4380, Fax: 734-487-6939, E-mail: david.pierce@emich.edu.
Website: http://www.emich.edu/musicdance

**Eastern Washington University,** Graduate Studies, College of Arts, Letters and Education, Department of Music, Cheney, WA 99004-2431. Offers composition (MA); general (MA); instrumental/vocal performance (MA); jazz pedagogy (MA); music education (MA). *Accreditation:* NASM. *Program availability:* Part-time. *Faculty:* 17 full-time (9 women), 14 part-time/adjunct (5 women). *Students:* 10 full-time (3 women), 6 part-time (2 women); includes 3 minority (1 Hispanic/Latino; 2 Native Hawaiian or other Pacific Islander, non-Hispanic/Latino), 2 international. Average age 31. 13 applicants, 77% accepted, 9 enrolled. In 2016, 9 master's awarded. *Degree requirements:* For master's, comprehensive exam, thesis or alternative. *Entrance requirements:* For master's, GRE General Test, minimum GPA of 3.0. Additional exam requirements/recommendations for international students: Required—TOEFL (minimum score 580 paper-based; 92 iBT), IELTS (minimum score 7), TWE, PTE (minimum score 63). *Application deadline:* For fall admission, 4/1 priority date for domestic students; for spring admission, 1/15 for domestic students. Applications are processed on a rolling basis. Application fee: $75. Electronic applications accepted. *Expenses:* Tuition, state resident: full-time $11,000; part-time $5500 per credit. Tuition, nonresident: full-time $24,000; part-time $12,000 per credit. *Required fees:* $1300. One-time fee: $50 full-time. Part-time tuition and fees vary according to course load, campus/location and program. *Financial support:* In 2016–17, 8 students received support, including 8 teaching assistantships with partial tuition reimbursements available (averaging $10,000 per year); career-related internships or fieldwork, Federal Work-Study, institutionally sponsored loans, scholarships/grants, health care benefits, tuition waivers (partial), and unspecified assistantships also available. Support available to part-time students. Financial award application deadline: 2/1; financial award applicants required to submit FAFSA. *Unit head:* Dr. Sheila Woodward, Director and Chair of Music Education, 509-359-7073, Fax: 509-359-7028. *Application contact:* Dr. Jane Ellsworth, Assistant Professor, 509-359-7076, E-mail: gradprograms@ewu.edu.
Website: http://www.ewu.edu/cale/programs/music.xml

**Emory University,** Laney Graduate School, Department of Music, Atlanta, GA 30322-1100. Offers choral conducting (MM, MSM); organ performance (MM, MSM). Terminal master's awarded for partial completion of doctoral program. *Degree requirements:* For master's, comprehensive exam, recital or worship service. *Entrance requirements:* For master's, GRE General Test, audition, interview. Additional exam requirements/recommendations for international students: Required—TOEFL. Electronic applications accepted. *Faculty research:* Nineteenth century criticism, Heinrich Schenker, Bach aria styles, contemporary passion music, Louis Andriessen, cross-cultural research, organ performance.

**Emporia State University,** Department of Music, Emporia, KS 66801-5415. Offers MM. *Accreditation:* NASM. *Program availability:* Part-time. *Faculty:* 12 full-time (3 women), 4 part-time/adjunct (all women). *Students:* 9 full-time (5 women), 3 part-time (1 woman); includes 1 minority (Black or African American, non-Hispanic/Latino), 6 international. 11 applicants, 100% accepted, 7 enrolled. In 2016, 6 master's awarded. *Degree requirements:* For master's, comprehensive exam or thesis. *Entrance requirements:* For master's, music qualifying exam, appropriate undergraduate degree. Additional exam requirements/recommendations for international students: Required—TOEFL (minimum score 520 paper-based; 68 iBT). *Application deadline:* For fall admission, 8/15 priority date for domestic students. Applications are processed on a rolling basis. Application fee: $30 ($75 for international students). Electronic applications accepted. *Expenses:* Tuition, state resident: full-time $5922; part-time $246.75 per credit hour. Tuition, nonresident: full-time $18,414; part-time $767.25 per credit hour. *Required fees:* $1884; $78.50 per credit hour. *Financial support:* In 2016–17, 5 teaching assistantships with full tuition reimbursements (averaging $7,344 per year) were awarded; Federal Work-Study, institutionally sponsored loans, health care benefits, and unspecified assistantships also available. Financial award application deadline: 3/15; financial award applicants required to submit FAFSA. *Unit head:* Dr. Allan D. Comstock, Chair, 620-341-5431, E-mail: acomstoc@emporia.edu. *Application contact:* Dr. Andrew Houchins, Graduate Coordinator, 620-341-6089, E-mail: ahouchin@emporia.edu.
Website: http://www.emporia.edu/music/

*Music*

**Five Towns College,** Graduate Programs, Dix Hills, NY 11746-6055. Offers childhood education (MS Ed); composition and arranging (DMA); jazz/commercial music (MM); music education (MM, DMA); music history and literature (DMA); music performance (DMA). *Program availability:* Part-time. *Faculty:* 12 full-time (3 women), 6 part-time/adjunct (0 women). *Students:* 18 full-time (7 women), 6 part-time (2 women); includes 9 minority (3 Black or African American, non-Hispanic/Latino; 4 Asian, non-Hispanic/Latino; 1 Hispanic/Latino; 1 Two or more races, non-Hispanic/Latino), 1 international. Average age 35. 63 applicants, 11% accepted, 7 enrolled. In 2016, 4 master's, 2 doctorates awarded. *Degree requirements:* For master's, thesis, exams, major composition or capstone project, recital; for doctorate, comprehensive exam, thesis/dissertation, final oral exam. *Entrance requirements:* For master's, audition (for MM); New York state teaching certification (for MS Ed); personal statement, two letters of recommendation; for doctorate, 3 letters of recommendation, audition, essay. Additional exam requirements/recommendations for international students: Required—TOEFL (minimum score 520 paper-based; 85 iBT); Recommended—IELTS (minimum score 7). *Application deadline:* For fall admission, 9/1 for domestic and international students; for spring admission, 1/25 for domestic and international students. Applications are processed on a rolling basis. Application fee: $50. Electronic applications accepted. *Expenses: Tuition:* Full-time $15,000; part-time $625 per credit. *Required fees:* $600; $150 per semester. Tuition and fees vary according to degree level. *Financial support:* Fellowships with tuition reimbursements, teaching assistantships with tuition reimbursements, and tuition waivers (partial) available. Financial award applicants required to submit FAFSA. *Faculty research:* Teaching methods, teaching strategies and techniques, analysis of modern music, jazz. *Application contact:* Ronnie MacDonald, Director of Admissions, 631-656-2110, Fax: 631-656-2172, E-mail: admissions@ftc.edu.
Website: http://www.ftc.edu

**Florida Atlantic University,** College of Business, Program in Music Business Administration, Boca Raton, FL 33431-0991. Offers MS. *Students:* 3 full-time (all women), 2 part-time (1 woman); includes 1 minority (Hispanic/Latino), 1 international. Average age 46. 1 applicant. *Expenses:* Tuition, state resident: full-time $7392; part-time $369.82 per credit hour. Tuition, nonresident: full-time $19,432; part-time $1024.81 per credit hour. *Unit head:* Dr. Daniel Gropper, Dean, 561-297-3629, Fax: 561-297-3686, E-mail: vhale4@fau.edu. *Application contact:* Dr. Marcy Krugel, Graduate Adviser, 561-297-3940, Fax: 561-297-0801, E-mail: krugel@fau.edu.

**Florida Atlantic University,** Dorothy F. Schmidt College of Arts and Letters, Department of Music, Boca Raton, FL 33431-0991. Offers MM. *Accreditation:* NASM. *Program availability:* Part-time. *Faculty:* 17 full-time (7 women), 12 part-time/adjunct (6 women). *Students:* 18 full-time (8 women); includes 3 minority (1 Black or African American, non-Hispanic/Latino; 1 Asian, non-Hispanic/Latino; 1 Hispanic/Latino), 4 international. Average age 28. 14 applicants, 50% accepted, 7 enrolled. In 2016, 8 master's awarded. *Degree requirements:* For master's, one foreign language, comprehensive exam, thesis (for some programs), lecture/recital or thesis. *Entrance requirements:* For master's, placement evaluations in music history and theory, audition, minimum GPA of 3.0 in last 60 hours of course work. Additional exam requirements/recommendations for international students: Required—TOEFL (minimum score 500 paper-based; 61 iBT), IELTS (minimum score 6). *Application deadline:* For fall admission, 7/1 priority date for domestic students, 2/15 for international students; for spring admission, 11/1 for domestic students, 7/15 for international students. Applications are processed on a rolling basis. Application fee: $30. *Expenses:* Tuition, state resident: full-time $7392; part-time $369.82 per credit hour. Tuition, nonresident: full-time $19,432; part-time $1024.81 per credit hour. *Financial support:* Fellowships with partial tuition reimbursements, teaching assistantships with partial tuition reimbursements, career-related internships or fieldwork, Federal Work-Study, and scholarships/grants available. Financial award application deadline: 5/1. *Faculty research:* Classical guitar history and literature, women composers, Mozart opera, composition, performance. *Unit head:* Dr. Sandra McClain, 561-297-3820, E-mail: smcclai2@fau.edu.
Website: http://www.fau.edu/music/

**Florida International University,** College of Communication, Architecture and The Arts, School of Music, Miami, FL 33199. Offers MM); music education (MS). *Program availability:* Part-time, evening/weekend. *Faculty:* 21 full-time (3 women), 25 part-time/adjunct (5 women). *Students:* 31 full-time (13 women), 18 part-time (8 women); includes 34 minority (7 Black or African American, non-Hispanic/Latino; 1 Asian, non-Hispanic/Latino; 24 Hispanic/Latino; 2 Two or more races, non-Hispanic/Latino), 3 international. Average age 29. 48 applicants, 56% accepted, 16 enrolled. In 2016, 18 master's awarded. *Degree requirements:* For master's, thesis (for some programs). *Entrance requirements:* For master's, GRE (depending on program), statement of intent; 2 letters of recommendation; audition, interview and/or writing sample (depending on area). Additional exam requirements/recommendations for international students: Required—TOEFL (minimum score 550 paper-based; 80 iBT). *Application deadline:* For fall admission, 6/1 for domestic students, 4/1 for international students; for spring admission, 10/1 for domestic students, 9/1 for international students. Applications are processed on a rolling basis. Application fee: $30. Electronic applications accepted. *Expenses:* Tuition, state resident: full-time $8912; part-time $446 per credit hour. Tuition, nonresident: full-time $21,393; part-time $992 per credit hour. *Required fees:* $2185; $195 per semester. Tuition and fees vary according to program. *Financial support:* Institutionally sponsored loans and scholarships/grants available. Financial award application deadline: 3/1; financial award applicants required to submit FAFSA. *Unit head:* Robert Dundas, Interim Chair, 305-348-3587, Fax: 305-348-4073, E-mail: robert.dundas@fiu.edu. *Application contact:* Joel Galand, Graduate Program Director, 305-348-7078, E-mail: galandj@fiu.edu.
Website: http://carta.fiu.edu/music/

**Florida State University,** The Graduate School, College of Arts and Sciences, Department of English, Tallahassee, FL 32312. Offers creative writing (MFA); English (PhD), including creative writing, literature, rhetoric and composition; literature (MA); rhetoric and composition (MA). *Program availability:* Part-time. *Faculty:* 47 full-time (24 women), 2 part-time/adjunct (1 woman). *Students:* 142 full-time (80 women), 31 part-time (23 women); includes 44 minority (17 Black or African American, non-Hispanic/Latino; 1 American Indian or Alaska Native, non-Hispanic/Latino; 12 Asian, non-Hispanic/Latino; 5 Hispanic/Latino; 9 Two or more races, non-Hispanic/Latino), 9 international. Average age 30. 307 applicants, 20% accepted, 38 enrolled. In 2016, 21 master's, 24 doctorates awarded. *Degree requirements:* For master's, one foreign language, 33 hours of coursework including capstone essay, thesis or portfolio (MA); 45 hours of coursework including 9-12 thesis hours (MFA); for doctorate, one foreign language, comprehensive exam, thesis/dissertation, 27 hours of coursework, 24 hours of dissertation work. *Entrance requirements:* For master's and doctorate, GRE General Test, sample of written work, 3 letters of recommendation, resume. Additional exam requirements/recommendations for international students: Required—TOEFL. *Application deadline:* For fall admission, 1/1 priority date for domestic and international students. Application fee: $30. Electronic applications accepted. *Expenses:* Tuition, state resident: full-time $7263; part-time $403.51 per credit hour. Tuition, nonresident: full-time $18,087; part-time $1004.85 per credit hour. *Required fees:* $1365; $75.81 per credit hour. $20 per semester. Tuition and fees vary according to campus/location.

*Financial support:* In 2016–17, 132 students received support, including 5 fellowships with tuition reimbursements available, teaching assistantships with tuition reimbursements available (averaging $13,250 per year); career-related internships or fieldwork, Federal Work-Study, and institutionally sponsored loans also available. Financial award application deadline: 8/1; financial award applicants required to submit FAFSA. *Faculty research:* British and Irish literature, American literature, creative writing, rhetoric and composition, multiethnic transnational literature, history of text technologies. *Unit head:* Dr. Gary Taylor, Chair, 850-644-4230, Fax: 850-644-0811, E-mail: ewalker@fsu.edu. *Application contact:* Ginger Martin, Senior Graduate Academic Coordinator, 850-644-1081, Fax: 850-644-9656, E-mail: vmartin@fsu.edu.
Website: http://english.fsu.edu/

**Florida State University,** The Graduate School, College of Music, Tallahassee, FL 32306. Offers accompanying (MM); arts administration (MA); choral conducting (MM); composition (MM, DM); ethnomusicology (MM); general music (MA); instrumental accompanying (MM); instrumental conducting (MM); jazz studies (MM); music theory (MM, PhD); music therapy (MM); musicology (MM, PhD), including ethnomusicology (PhD), historical musicology; opera (MM); performance (MM, DM); piano pedagogy (MM); piano technology (MA); vocal accompanying (MM). *Accreditation:* NASM. *Program availability:* Part-time. *Faculty:* 79 full-time, 2 part-time/adjunct. *Students:* 324 full-time (156 women); includes 87 minority (26 Black or African American, non-Hispanic/Latino; 1 American Indian or Alaska Native, non-Hispanic/Latino; 32 Asian, non-Hispanic/Latino; 26 Hispanic/Latino; 2 Native Hawaiian or other Pacific Islander, non-Hispanic/Latino). Average age 26. 737 applicants, 42% accepted, 138 enrolled. In 2016, 120 master's, 36 doctorates awarded. *Degree requirements:* For master's, variable foreign language requirement, comprehensive exam (for some programs), thesis (for some programs), departmental qualifying exam; for doctorate, variable foreign language requirement, comprehensive exam (for some programs), thesis/dissertation, departmental qualifying exam. *Entrance requirements:* For master's, GRE General Test (for some programs), audition, minimum GPA of 3.0; for doctorate, GRE General Test (for some programs), audition, master's degree, minimum GPA of 3.0. Additional exam requirements/recommendations for international students: Required—TOEFL (minimum score 590 paper-based; 97 iBT), IELTS (minimum score 7.5). *Application deadline:* For fall admission, 7/1 for domestic and international students; for spring admission, 11/1 for domestic and international students; for summer admission, 3/1 for domestic students. Applications are processed on a rolling basis. Application fee: $30. Electronic applications accepted. *Expenses:* Tuition, state resident: full-time $7263; part-time $403.51 per credit hour. Tuition, nonresident: full-time $18,087; part-time $1004.85 per credit hour. *Required fees:* $1365; $75.81 per credit hour. $20 per semester. Tuition and fees vary according to campus/location. *Financial support:* In 2016–17, 222 students received support, including 2 fellowships with full tuition reimbursements available (averaging $15,000 per year), 14 research assistantships with full and partial tuition reimbursements available (averaging $5,900 per year), 201 teaching assistantships with full and partial tuition reimbursements available (averaging $5,900 per year); career-related internships or fieldwork, scholarships/grants, tuition waivers (full and partial), and unspecified assistantships also available. Support available to part-time students. Financial award application deadline: 2/28; financial award applicants required to submit FAFSA. *Faculty research:* Music therapy in NICU units, music of the Americas, music theory pedagogy, music performance. *Unit head:* Dr. Patricia Flowers, Dean, 850-644-4361, Fax: 850-644-2033, E-mail: pjflowers@fsu.edu. *Application contact:* Kris Watson, Director of Admissions, 850-645-2126, Fax: 850-644-2033, E-mail: krwatson@fsu.edu.
Website: http://www.music.fsu.edu/

**Fuller Theological Seminary,** Graduate Programs, Pasadena, CA 91182. Offers Christian leadership (MACL); clinical psychology (PhD, Psy D); family studies (MA); global leadership (MA); global ministries (D Min); global ministries (Korean language) (D Min); intercultural studies (MA, Th M, PhD); intercultural studies (Korean language) (MA); marital and family therapy (MS); marriage and family enrichment (Certificate); ministry (M Div, D Min); missiology (D Miss); missiology (Korean language) (Th M); theology (MA, Th M, PhD), including evangelism (MA), family life education (MA), pastoral ministry (MA), recovery ministry (MA), worship music ministry (MA), worship, theology, and the arts (MA); youth, family, and culture (MA); theology and ministry (MA).

**Garrett-Evangelical Theological Seminary,** Graduate and Professional Programs, Evanston, IL 60201-3298. Offers Bible and culture (PhD); Christian education (MA); Christian education and congregational studies (PhD); contemporary theology and culture (PhD); divinity (M Div); ethics, church, and society (MA); liturgical studies (PhD); ministry (D Min); music ministry (MA); pastoral care and counseling (MA); pastoral theology, personality, and culture (PhD); spiritual formation and evangelism (MA); theological studies (MTS); M Div/MSW. M Div/MSW offered jointly with Loyola University Chicago. *Accreditation:* ACIPE; ATS (one or more programs are accredited). *Program availability:* Part-time. *Degree requirements:* For master's, thesis (for some programs); for doctorate, thesis/dissertation. *Entrance requirements:* For doctorate, GRE (PhD). Additional exam requirements/recommendations for international students: Required—TOEFL (minimum score 560 paper-based). Electronic applications accepted.

**George Mason University,** College of Visual and Performing Arts, School of Music, Program in Music, Fairfax, VA 22030. Offers composition (MM); conducting (MM); jazz studies (MM); music education (MM); pedagogy (MM); performance (MM). *Accreditation:* NASM. *Faculty:* 20 full-time (8 women), 34 part-time/adjunct (13 women). *Students:* 14 full-time (9 women), 26 part-time (15 women); includes 11 minority (3 Black or African American, non-Hispanic/Latino; 4 Asian, non-Hispanic/Latino; 3 Hispanic/Latino; 1 Native Hawaiian or other Pacific Islander, non-Hispanic/Latino), 2 international. Average age 31. 33 applicants, 70% accepted, 10 enrolled. In 2016, 28 master's awarded. *Degree requirements:* For master's, comprehensive exam. *Entrance requirements:* For master's, expanded goals statement; 2 letters of recommendation; official transcript. Additional exam requirements/recommendations for international students: Required—TOEFL (minimum score 575 paper-based; 88 iBT), IELTS (minimum score 6.5), PTE (minimum score 59). Application fee: $75 ($80 for international students). Electronic applications accepted. *Expenses:* Tuition, state resident: full-time $10,628; part-time $443 per credit. Tuition, nonresident: full-time $29,306; part-time $1221 per credit. *Required fees:* $3096; $129 per credit. Tuition and fees vary according to program. *Financial support:* Career-related internships or fieldwork, Federal Work-Study, scholarships/grants, and unspecified assistantships available. Financial award application deadline: 3/1; financial award applicants required to submit FAFSA. *Unit head:* Dr. Linda Apple Monson, Managing Director, 703-993-3580, Fax: 703-993-1394, E-mail: lmonson@gmu.edu. *Application contact:* Dr. Lisa A. Billingham, Director of Graduate Studies, 703-993-3778, Fax: 703-993-1394, E-mail: lbillin1@gmu.edu.
Website: http://music.gmu.edu

**George Mason University,** College of Visual and Performing Arts, School of Music, Program in Musical Arts, Fairfax, VA 22030. Offers composition (DMA); conducting (DMA); performance (DMA). *Faculty:* 20 full-time (8 women), 34 part-time/adjunct (13 women). *Students:* 13 full-time (5 women), 14 part-time (4 women); includes 6 minority (4 Asian, non-Hispanic/Latino; 2 Hispanic/Latino). Average age 36. 10 applicants, 70% accepted, 4 enrolled. In 2016, 5 doctorates awarded. *Degree requirements:* For

doctorate, one foreign language, comprehensive exam, thesis/dissertation. *Entrance requirements:* For doctorate, GRE, master's degree in music; minimum GPA of 3.0 in master's coursework, 3.25 in courses related to field of study; 3 letters of recommendation; writing sample; audition or portfolio (depending on area of study). Additional exam requirements/recommendations for international students: Required—TOEFL (minimum score 575 paper-based; 88 iBT), IELTS (minimum score 6.5), PTE (minimum score 59). *Application deadline:* For fall admission, 1/15 for domestic students. Application fee: $75 ($80 for international students). Electronic applications accepted. *Expenses:* Tuition, state resident: full-time $10,628; part-time $443 per credit. Tuition, nonresident: full-time $29,306; part-time $1221 per credit. *Required fees:* $3096; $129 per credit. Tuition and fees vary according to program. *Financial support:* In 2016–17, 18 students received support, including 2 research assistantships with tuition reimbursements available (averaging $16,753 per year), 16 teaching assistantships with tuition reimbursements available (averaging $5,601 per year); career-related internships or fieldwork, Federal Work-Study, scholarships/grants, unspecified assistantships, and health care benefits (for full-time research or teaching assistantship recipients) also available. Support available to part-time students. Financial award application deadline: 3/1; financial award applicants required to submit FAFSA. *Unit head:* Dr. Linda Apple Monson, Managing Director, 703-993-3580, Fax: 703-993-1394, E-mail: lmonson@gmu.edu. *Application contact:* Dr. Lisa A. Billingham, Director of Graduate Studies, 703-993-3778, Fax: 703-993-1394, E-mail: lbillin1@gmu.edu.
Website: http://music.gmu.edu

**Georgia Christian University,** School of Music, Atlanta, GA 30360. Offers MA.

**Georgia Institute of Technology,** Graduate Studies, College of Architecture, School of Music, Atlanta, GA 30332-0001. Offers music technology (MS, PhD).

**Georgia Southern University,** Jack N. Averitt College of Graduate Studies, College of Liberal Arts and Social Sciences, Program in Music, Statesboro, GA 30460. Offers composition (MM); conducting (MM); music education (MM); music technology (MM); performance (MM). *Accreditation:* NASM. *Program availability:* Part-time, evening/weekend. *Students:* 15 full-time (5 women), 11 part-time (6 women); includes 6 minority (4 Black or African American, non-Hispanic/Latino; 1 Hispanic/Latino; 1 Two or more races, non-Hispanic/Latino), 3 international. Average age 27. 23 applicants, 87% accepted, 11 enrolled. In 2016, 16 master's awarded. *Degree requirements:* For master's, comprehensive exam, recital or final project. *Entrance requirements:* For master's, minimum GPA of 2.5, audition, letters of recommendation. Additional exam requirements/recommendations for international students: Required—TOEFL (minimum score 550 paper-based; 80 iBT), IELTS (minimum score 6). *Application deadline:* For fall admission, 3/1 priority date for domestic and international students; for spring admission, 10/1 priority date for domestic students, 10/1 for international students. Applications are processed on a rolling basis. Application fee: $50. Electronic applications accepted. *Expenses:* Tuition, state resident: full-time $7236; part-time $277 per semester hour. Tuition, nonresident: full-time $27,118; part-time $1105 per semester hour. *Required fees:* $2092. *Financial support:* In 2016–17, 10 fellowships with full tuition reimbursements (averaging $7,750 per year), 3 teaching assistantships with full tuition reimbursements (averaging $7,750 per year) were awarded; Federal Work-Study, scholarships/grants, tuition waivers (full), and unspecified assistantships also available. Support available to part-time students. Financial award application deadline: 4/15; financial award applicants required to submit FAFSA. *Faculty research:* Performance, conducting, composition, technology, education. *Unit head:* Dr. Greg Harwood, Graduate Director, 912-478-5813, Fax: 912-478-1295, E-mail: gharwood@georgiasouthern.edu.
Website: http://class.georgiasouthern.edu/music/

**Georgia State University,** College of Arts and Sciences, School of Music, Atlanta, GA 30303. Offers choral conducting (MM); jazz studies (MM); music (Certificate); music composition (MM); music education (PhD); orchestral conducting (MM); performance (MM), including orchestral, piano, vocal; piano pedagogy (MM); wind band conducting (MM). *Accreditation:* NASM. *Program availability:* Part-time, evening/weekend. *Faculty:* 40 full-time (13 women). *Students:* 80 full-time (36 women), 10 part-time (4 women); includes 32 minority (19 Black or African American, non-Hispanic/Latino; 5 Asian, non-Hispanic/Latino; 8 Hispanic/Latino), 13 international. Average age 30. 84 applicants, 69% accepted, 42 enrolled. In 2016, 25 master's, 2 other advanced degrees awarded. *Degree requirements:* For master's, comprehensive exam, thesis (for some programs), recital; for doctorate, comprehensive exam, thesis/dissertation; for Certificate, recital. *Entrance requirements:* For master's, GRE (for music education, composition only), BM; for doctorate, GRE, MM; for Certificate, MM. Additional exam requirements/recommendations for international students: Required—TOEFL (minimum score 550 paper-based; 80 iBT). *Application deadline:* For fall admission, 3/1 priority date for domestic and international students; for spring admission, 10/1 priority date for domestic and international students. Applications are processed on a rolling basis. Application fee: $50. Electronic applications accepted. *Expenses:* Tuition, state resident: full-time $6876; part-time $382 per credit hour. Tuition, nonresident: full-time $22,374; part-time $1243 per credit hour. *Required fees:* $2128; $1064 per term. Part-time tuition and fees vary according to course load and program. *Financial support:* In 2016–17, research assistantships with full tuition reimbursements (averaging $4,000 per year) were awarded; Federal Work-Study, scholarships/grants, health care benefits, tuition waivers (partial), and unspecified assistantships also available. Financial award application deadline: 3/1; financial award applicants required to submit FAFSA. *Faculty research:* Male changing voice, nineteenth-century chamber music, improvisation and learning, Garibunda, African-American classical musicians. *Unit head:* William Dwight Coleman, Director, School of Music, 404-413-5953, Fax: 404-413-5910, E-mail: wcoleman@gsu.edu. *Application contact:* Dr. Steven Andrew Harper, Graduate Director, 404-413-5943, Fax: 404-413-5910, E-mail: sharper@gsu.edu.
Website: http://www.music.gsu.edu/

**The Graduate Center, City University of New York,** Graduate Studies, Program in Music, New York, NY 10016-4039. Offers DMA, PhD. *Degree requirements:* For doctorate, 2 foreign languages, thesis/dissertation. *Entrance requirements:* For doctorate, GRE General Test. Additional exam requirements/recommendations for international students: Required—TOEFL. Electronic applications accepted.

**Hardin-Simmons University,** Graduate School, College of Fine Arts, Abilene, TX 79698-0001. Offers church music (MM); music education (MM); music performance (MM); theory and composition (MM). *Accreditation:* NASM. *Program availability:* Part-time. *Faculty:* 9 full-time (3 women), 3 part-time/adjunct (1 woman). *Students:* 4 full-time (2 women), 4 part-time (1 woman); includes 4 minority (1 Black or African American, non-Hispanic/Latino; 2 Hispanic/Latino; 1 Two or more races, non-Hispanic/Latino). Average age 28. In 2016, 2 master's awarded. *Degree requirements:* For master's, one foreign language, comprehensive exam, thesis (for some programs). *Entrance requirements:* For master's, minimum undergraduate GPA of 3.0 in major, 2.7 overall; writing sample; demonstrated knowledge in chosen area. Additional exam requirements/recommendations for international students: Required—TOEFL (minimum score 550 paper-based; 75 iBT). *Application deadline:* For fall admission, 8/15 priority date for domestic students, 4/1 for international students; for spring admission, 1/5 priority date for domestic students, 9/1 for international students. Applications are processed on a

rolling basis. Application fee: $50. Electronic applications accepted. *Expenses: Tuition:* Full-time $12,510; part-time $695 per credit hour. *Required fees:* $325; $110 per semester. *Financial support:* In 2016–17, 6 students received support, including 4 fellowships (averaging $2,700 per year); career-related internships or fieldwork and scholarships/grants also available. Support available to part-time students. Financial award application deadline: 6/30; financial award applicants required to submit FAFSA. *Unit head:* Dr. Lynnette Chambers, Program Director, 325-670-1430, Fax: 325-670-5873, E-mail: lchambers@hsutx.edu. *Application contact:* Dr. Nancy Kucinski, Dean of Graduate Studies, 325-670-1298, Fax: 325-670-1564, E-mail: gradoff@hsutx.edu.
Website: http://www.hsutx.edu/academics/cofa/

**Harvard University,** Graduate School of Arts and Sciences, Department of Music, Cambridge, MA 02138. Offers composition (AM, PhD); musicology (AM); musicology and ethnomusicology (PhD); theory (AM, PhD). *Degree requirements:* For doctorate, 3 foreign languages, thesis/dissertation, composition, analytical paper. *Entrance requirements:* For master's and doctorate, GRE General Test. Additional exam requirements/recommendations for international students: Required—TOEFL.

**Hebrew College,** Program in Jewish Studies, Newton Centre, MA 02459. Offers Jewish liturgical music (Certificate); Jewish music education (Certificate); Jewish studies (MA). *Program availability:* Part-time, evening/weekend, online learning. *Degree requirements:* For master's, one foreign language. *Entrance requirements:* For master's, GRE, interview. Additional exam requirements/recommendations for international students: Required—TOEFL.

**Hebrew Union College–Jewish Institute of Religion,** School of Sacred Music, New York, NY 10012-1186. Offers MSM. *Degree requirements:* For master's, one foreign language, thesis, recital. *Entrance requirements:* For master's, GRE, minimum 2 years of college-level Hebrew, bachelor's degree in music or related area, trained singing voice. Additional exam requirements/recommendations for international students: Required—TOEFL. *Expenses:* Contact institution.

**Hollins University,** Graduate Programs, Program in Liberal Studies, Roanoke, VA 24020. Offers humanities (MALS); interdisciplinary studies (MALS); leadership (MALS); social sciences (MALS); visual and performing arts (MALS). *Program availability:* Part-time, evening/weekend. *Degree requirements:* For master's, thesis. *Entrance requirements:* For master's, three letters of recommendation, interview, bachelor's degree, undergraduate transcripts, statement of educational objectives. Additional exam requirements/recommendations for international students: Required—TOEFL (minimum score 550 paper-based; 80 iBT), IELTS (minimum score 6.5). *Application deadline:* Applications are processed on a rolling basis. Application fee: $40. Electronic applications accepted. *Expenses:* $395 per credit hour. *Financial support:* Fellowships and scholarships/grants available. Support available to part-time students. Financial award application deadline: 7/15; financial award applicants required to submit FAFSA. *Faculty research:* Diversity, gender and women's studies, political science, leadership. *Unit head:* Director, 540-362-6576, Fax: 540-362-6288, E-mail: hugrad@hollins.edu. *Application contact:* Cathy S. Koon, Manager of Graduate Programs, 540-362-6326, Fax: 540-362-6288, E-mail: ckoon@hollins.edu.
Website: http://www.hollins.edu/academics/graduate-degrees/liberal-studies/

**Holy Names University,** Graduate Division, Department of Music, Oakland, CA 94619-1699. Offers Kodaly (Certificate); music education with Kodaly emphasis (MM); piano pedagogy (MM); vocal pedagogy (MM). *Students:* 1 (woman) full-time, 12 part-time (10 women); includes 5 minority (1 Black or African American, non-Hispanic/Latino; 2 Asian, non-Hispanic/Latino; 1 Native Hawaiian or other Pacific Islander, non-Hispanic/Latino; 1 Two or more races, non-Hispanic/Latino). Average age 37. 10 applicants, 60% accepted, 4 enrolled. In 2016, 4 master's, 2 Certificates awarded. *Degree requirements:* For master's, comprehensive exam, recital. *Entrance requirements:* For master's, audition; minimum undergraduate GPA of 2.6 overall, 3.0 in major. Additional exam requirements/recommendations for international students: Required—TOEFL (minimum score 550 paper-based; 79 iBT). *Application deadline:* For fall admission, 8/1 priority date for domestic students, 7/15 for international students; for spring admission, 12/1 priority date for domestic students, 12/1 for international students; for summer admission, 5/1 priority date for domestic students, 5/1 for international students. Applications are processed on a rolling basis. Application fee: $65. Electronic applications accepted. *Expenses: Tuition:* Full-time $17,532; part-time $974 per credit hour. *Required fees:* $500; $250 per credit hour. *Financial support:* Career-related internships or fieldwork, Federal Work-Study, scholarships/grants, and unspecified assistantships available. Support available to part-time students. Financial award application deadline: 3/2; financial award applicants required to submit FAFSA. *Faculty research:* Performance practice with special interest in Baroque, Romantic, and twentieth-century instrumental and vocal music; choral pedagogy; Hungarian music education. *Unit head:* Dr. Steven Hofer, Chair of Music Department, 510-436-1244, E-mail: hofer@hnu.edu. *Application contact:* 800-430-1321, Fax: 510-436-1325, E-mail: graduateadmissions@hnu.edu.

**Hope International University,** School of Graduate and Professional Studies, Programs in Ministry, Fullerton, CA 92831-3138. Offers Christian leadership (MCM); church music (MA); church music (Korean track) (MCM); church planting (MCM); intercultural studies (MCM); worship (MCM). *Program availability:* Part-time, evening/weekend, online learning. *Degree requirements:* For master's, thesis (for some programs), project. *Entrance requirements:* For master's, minimum GPA of 3.0, MCM program requires an undergraduate degree in music, 2 references. Additional exam requirements/recommendations for international students: Required—TOEFL (minimum score 550 paper-based; 86 iBT); Recommended—IELTS (minimum score 6.5). Electronic applications accepted. *Expenses:* Contact institution. *Faculty research:* Church dynamics, growth methodologies.

**Houghton College,** Greatbatch School of Music, Houghton, NY 14744. Offers collaborative performance (MMus); composition (MMus); conducting (MMus); music (MA); performance (MMus); world music with theology and intercultural studies (MA). *Accreditation:* NASM. *Degree requirements:* For master's, comprehensive exam (for some programs), thesis (for some programs), recitals (for some programs). *Entrance requirements:* For master's, B Mus or equivalent. Additional exam requirements/recommendations for international students: Required—TOEFL (minimum score 600 paper-based). Electronic applications accepted. *Faculty research:* Bach Studies; original compositions; professional performance; contemporary women composers; music in Christian worship.

**Howard University,** Graduate School, Division of Fine Arts, Department of Music, Washington, DC 20059-0002. Offers applied music (MM); instrument (MM Ed); jazz studies (MM); organ (MM Ed); piano (MM Ed); voice (MM Ed). *Accreditation:* NASM. *Program availability:* Part-time. *Degree requirements:* For master's, comprehensive exam, thesis or alternative, departmental qualifying exam, recital. *Entrance requirements:* For master's, minimum GPA of 3.0, bachelor's degree in music or music education. Additional exam requirements/recommendations for international students: Required—TOEFL.

**Hunter College of the City University of New York,** Graduate School, School of Arts and Sciences, Department of Music, New York, NY 10065-5085. Offers composition (MA); ethnomusicology (MA); music history (MA); music theory (MA); performance (MA).

*Music*

*Program availability:* Part-time, evening/weekend. *Students:* 33 part-time (16 women); includes 9 minority (2 Black or African American, non-Hispanic/Latino; 3 Asian, non-Hispanic/Latino; 4 Hispanic/Latino), 5 international. Average age 32. 29 applicants, 76% accepted, 15 enrolled. In 2016, 15 master's awarded. *Degree requirements:* For master's, one foreign language, thesis, composition, essay, or recital; proficiency exam. *Entrance requirements:* For master's, undergraduate major in music (minimum 24 credits) or equivalent, sample of work, research paper. Additional exam requirements/recommendations for international students: Required—TOEFL. *Application deadline:* For fall admission, 4/1 for domestic students, 2/1 for international students; for spring admission, 11/1 for domestic students, 9/1 for international students. Applications are processed on a rolling basis. *Financial support:* Fellowships, Federal Work-Study, tuition waivers (partial), and lesson stipends available. Support available to part-time students. Financial award application deadline: 4/15. *Faculty research:* African and African-American music, Bach, Renaissance music, early romantic music, theory of tonal music. *Unit head:* Dr. Suzanne Farrin, Chair, 212-772-5026, Fax: 212-772-5022, E-mail: music@hunter.cuny.edu. *Application contact:* Philip Ewell, Graduate Advisor, 212-396-6253, E-mail: pewell@hunter.cuny.edu.
Website: http://www.hunter.cuny.edu/music/

**Illinois State University,** Graduate School, College of Fine Arts, School of Music, Normal, IL 61790-2200. Offers MM, MM Ed. *Accreditation:* NASM. *Degree requirements:* For master's, thesis or alternative, performance. *Entrance requirements:* For master's, minimum GPA of 3.0 in music, 2.6 overall; auditions. *Faculty research:* Concerts on the quad summer concert series.

**Indiana State University,** College of Graduate and Professional Studies, College of Arts and Sciences, School of Music, Terre Haute, IN 47809. Offers conducting (MM); music education (MM); music performance (MM). *Accreditation:* NASM. *Degree requirements:* For master's, comprehensive exam, thesis, qualifying exam. Electronic applications accepted.

**Indiana University Bloomington,** Jacobs School of Music, Bloomington, IN 47405-7000. Offers MA, MM, MME, MS, DM, DME, PhD, Artist Diploma, Performance Diploma, Spec, MA/MLS, MM/MLS. *Faculty:* 143 full-time (43 women), 1 (woman) part-time/adjunct. *Students:* 777 full-time (390 women), 72 part-time (39 women); includes 139 minority (17 Black or African American, non-Hispanic/Latino; 3 American Indian or Alaska Native, non-Hispanic/Latino; 54 Asian, non-Hispanic/Latino; 45 Hispanic/Latino; 1 Native Hawaiian or other Pacific Islander, non-Hispanic/Latino; 19 Two or more races, non-Hispanic/Latino), 254 international. Average age 28. 1,429 applicants, 42% accepted, 253 enrolled. In 2016, 196 master's, 35 doctorates, 56 other advanced degrees awarded. *Degree requirements:* For master's, comprehensive exam (for some programs); for doctorate, comprehensive exam, thesis/dissertation. *Entrance requirements:* For master's and doctorate, GRE, audition, 3 letters of recommendation. Additional exam requirements/recommendations for international students: Required—TOEFL; Recommended—IELTS. *Application deadline:* For fall admission, 12/1 for domestic and international students; for spring admission, 9/1 for domestic and international students. Application fee: $135 ($145 for international students). Electronic applications accepted. *Expenses:* Contact institution. *Financial support:* Fellowships with full and partial tuition reimbursements, research assistantships with tuition reimbursements, teaching assistantships with full tuition reimbursements, Federal Work-Study, and health care benefits available. Financial award application deadline: 3/1. *Total annual research expenditures:* $8,300. *Unit head:* Gwyn Richards, Dean, 812-855-2435, E-mail: musdean@indiana.edu. *Application contact:* Rebecca Patrick Shipman, Music Admissions, 812-855-7998, E-mail: musicadm@indiana.edu.
Website: http://www.music.indiana.edu/

**Indiana University Bloomington,** University Graduate School, College of Arts and Sciences, Department of Folklore and Ethnomusicology, Bloomington, IN 47405. Offers ethnomusicology (MA, PhD), including folklore. *Faculty:* 15 full-time (5 women), 1 (woman) part-time/adjunct. *Students:* 71 full-time (46 women), 2 part-time (1 woman); includes 15 minority (5 Black or African American, non-Hispanic/Latino; 4 Asian, non-Hispanic/Latino; 4 Hispanic/Latino; 2 Two or more races, non-Hispanic/Latino), 13 international. Average age 32. 40 applicants, 53% accepted, 9 enrolled. In 2016, 7 master's, 6 doctorates awarded. Terminal master's awarded for partial completion of doctoral program. *Degree requirements:* For master's, one foreign language, comprehensive exam, project, thesis, or exam; for doctorate, 2 foreign languages, comprehensive exam, thesis/dissertation. *Entrance requirements:* For master's, GRE General Test (minimum scores: 151 for Verbal, 150 for Quantitative, 4.5 for Analytical), minimum GPA of 3.0, writing sample, curriculum vitae, 3 letters of recommendation, personal statement; for doctorate, GRE General Test (minimum scores: 151 for Verbal, 150 for Quantitative, 4.5 for Analytical), minimum GPA of 3.0, writing sample, curriculum vitae, 3 letters of recommendation, personal statement, MA. Additional exam requirements/recommendations for international students: Required—TOEFL (minimum score 550 paper-based; 79 iBT). *Application deadline:* For fall admission, 12/1 for domestic and international students. Application fee: $55 ($65 for international students). Electronic applications accepted. *Expenses:* $36,500 per year. *Financial support:* In 2016–17, 34 students received support, including 3 fellowships with full tuition reimbursements available (averaging $18,000 per year), 15 research assistantships with full tuition reimbursements available (averaging $15,750 per year), 20 teaching assistantships with full tuition reimbursements available (averaging $15,750 per year); Federal Work-Study, scholarships/grants, health care benefits, tuition waivers, and unspecified assistantships also available. Financial award application deadline: 3/1; financial award applicants required to submit FAFSA. *Faculty research:* Narrative, performance studies, material culture, popular culture, music, public practice. *Unit head:* Dr. John McDowell, Chair, 812-855-0390, Fax: 812-855-4008, E-mail: mcdowell@indiana.edu. *Application contact:* Michelle Melhouse, Graduate Recorder, 812-855-0389, Fax: 812-855-4008, E-mail: mmelhous@indiana.edu.
Website: http://www.indiana.edu/~folklore/

**Indiana University of Pennsylvania,** School of Graduate Studies and Research, College of Fine Arts, Department of Music, Program in Music Performance, Indiana, PA 15705. Offers MA. *Accreditation:* NASM. *Program availability:* Part-time. *Faculty:* 14 full-time (4 women). *Students:* 10 full-time (5 women), 8 part-time (5 women); includes 6 minority (1 Black or African American, non-Hispanic/Latino; 1 Asian, non-Hispanic/Latino; 4 Hispanic/Latino). Average age 25. 15 applicants, 73% accepted, 8 enrolled. In 2016, 8 master's awarded. *Degree requirements:* For master's, thesis optional. *Entrance requirements:* For master's, 2 letters of recommendation, audition. Additional exam requirements/recommendations for international students: Required—TOEFL (minimum score 550 paper-based). *Application deadline:* Applications are processed on a rolling basis. Application fee: $50. Electronic applications accepted. *Expenses:* Tuition, state resident: full-time $8694; part-time $483 per credit. Tuition, nonresident: full-time $13,050; part-time $725 per credit. *Required fees:* $157 per credit. $50 per term. Tuition and fees vary according to course load and program. *Financial support:* In 2016–17, 8 research assistantships with tuition reimbursements (averaging $4,205 per year) were awarded; fellowships with full tuition reimbursements, career-related internships or fieldwork, Federal Work-Study, scholarships/grants, and unspecified assistantships also available. Support available to part-time students. Financial award application deadline: 4/15; financial award applicants required to submit FAFSA. *Unit head:* Dr. Stephanie

Caulder, Chairperson, 724-357-2391, E-mail: scaulder@iup.edu.
Website: http://www.iup.edu/music/grad/default.aspx

**Indiana University–Purdue University Indianapolis,** School of Engineering and Technology, Department of Music and Arts Technology, Indianapolis, IN 46202. Offers music technology (MS, PhD); music therapy (MS). *Accreditation:* NASM. *Program availability:* Part-time, evening/weekend, online learning. *Faculty:* 9 full-time (2 women), 2 part-time/adjunct. *Students:* 9 full-time (1 woman), 12 part-time (4 women); includes 6 minority (4 Black or African American, non-Hispanic/Latino; 2 Hispanic/Latino), 1 international. Average age 31. 19 applicants, 63% accepted, 9 enrolled. In 2016, 15 master's awarded. *Degree requirements:* For master's, thesis optional, internship or final project; for doctorate, thesis/dissertation. *Entrance requirements:* For master's, GRE, interview, audition, minimum GPA of 3.0; for doctorate, GRE, three letters of recommendation; research adviser letter; statement of purpose; writing samples; transcripts; portfolio. Additional exam requirements/recommendations for international students: Required—TOEFL (minimum score 550 paper-based; 79 iBT); Recommended—IELTS (minimum score 6.5). *Application deadline:* For fall admission, 4/15 for domestic students, 3/15 for international students; for spring admission, 11/15 for domestic and international students. Application fee: $55 ($65 for international students). Electronic applications accepted. *Expenses:* Contact institution. *Financial support:* Fellowships, research assistantships, teaching assistantships with full tuition reimbursements, scholarships/grants, tuition waivers, and unspecified assistantships available. Financial award application deadline: 11/15. *Faculty research:* Music-related cross-disciplinary technologies in fine arts, education, business, health care, computer science, and engineering; exploring and creating multi-disciplinary music, dance, and arts performance; developing new recording techniques and emerging technologies. *Total annual research expenditures:* $9,951. *Unit head:* Dr. Debra S. Burns, Chair, Department of Music and Arts Technology, 317-278-2014, E-mail: desburns@iupui.edu. *Application contact:* Tina Everts, Assistant to Chair, 317-274-7088, E-mail: teverts@iupui.edu.
Website: http://www.engr.iupui.edu/departments/mat/

**Indiana University South Bend,** Ernestine M. Raclin School of the Arts, South Bend, IN 46634-7111. Offers communication studies (MA); music (MM), including composition, performance; music performance (AD). *Accreditation:* NASM. *Program availability:* Part-time. *Faculty:* 1 full-time (0 women). *Students:* 2 full-time (1 woman), 11 part-time (3 women); includes 2 minority (1 Black or African American, non-Hispanic/Latino; 1 Hispanic/Latino), 3 international. Average age 32. 23 applicants, 65% accepted, 6 enrolled. In 2016, 4 master's awarded. *Entrance requirements:* For master's, performance audition. Additional exam requirements/recommendations for international students: Required—TOEFL (minimum score 600 paper-based; 90 iBT). *Application deadline:* For fall admission, 7/1 priority date for domestic students; for spring admission, 11/1 for domestic students. Applications are processed on a rolling basis. Application fee: $40 ($60 for international students). Electronic applications accepted. *Expenses:* $276.98 per credit hour in-state; $652.54 per credit hour out-of-state. *Financial support:* Fellowships, teaching assistantships, and Federal Work-Study available. Support available to part-time students. Financial award application deadline: 3/1; financial award applicants required to submit FAFSA. *Faculty research:* Orchestral conducting. *Unit head:* Dr. Marvin V. Curtis, Dean, 574-520-4170, E-mail: mvcurtis@iusb.edu. *Application contact:* Admissions Counselor, 574-520-4839, Fax: 574-520-4834, E-mail: graduate@iusb.edu.
Website: https://www.iusb.edu/arts/

**Inter American University of Puerto Rico, San Germán Campus,** Graduate Studies Center, Program in Music Education, San Germán, PR 00683-5008. Offers music (MA); music teacher education (MA). *Accreditation:* TEAC. *Program availability:* Part-time, evening/weekend.

**Ithaca College,** School of Music, Programs in Music and Music Education, Ithaca, NY 14850. Offers composition (MM); conducting (MM); music education (MM, MS); performance (MM); Suzuki pedagogy (MM). *Accreditation:* NASM. *Program availability:* Part-time. *Faculty:* 57 full-time (19 women), 4 part-time/adjunct (3 women). *Students:* 22 full-time (7 women), 28 part-time (14 women); includes 11 minority (1 Black or African American, non-Hispanic/Latino; 6 Asian, non-Hispanic/Latino; 2 Hispanic/Latino; 2 Two or more races, non-Hispanic/Latino), 7 international. Average age 25. 155 applicants, 36% accepted, 25 enrolled. In 2016, 20 master's awarded. *Degree requirements:* For master's, comprehensive exam (for some programs), thesis (for some programs). *Entrance requirements:* Additional exam requirements/recommendations for international students: Required—TOEFL (minimum score 550 paper-based; 80 iBT). *Application deadline:* For fall admission, 1/15 for domestic and international students; for spring admission, 12/1 for domestic and international students. Applications are processed on a rolling basis. Application fee: $40. Electronic applications accepted. *Expenses:* Contact institution. *Financial support:* In 2016–17, 47 students received support, including 46 teaching assistantships (averaging $9,458 per year); career-related internships or fieldwork, Federal Work-Study, scholarships/grants, and unspecified assistantships also available. Support available to part-time students. Financial award application deadline: 1/15; financial award applicants required to submit CSS PROFILE or FAFSA. *Unit head:* Dr. Les Black, Chair, Graduate Studies in Music, 607-274-7997, E-mail: lblack@ithaca.edu. *Application contact:* Nicole Eversley Bradwell, Director, Office of Admission, 607-274-3124, Fax: 607-274-1263, E-mail: admission@ithaca.edu.
Website: http://www.ithaca.edu/gradprograms/music

**Jacksonville State University,** College of Graduate Studies and Continuing Education, College of Arts and Sciences, Department of Music, Jacksonville, AL 36265-1602. Offers MA. *Accreditation:* NASM. *Program availability:* Part-time, evening/weekend. *Faculty:* 21 full-time (7 women), 6 part-time/adjunct (1 woman). *Students:* 7 full-time (3 women), 6 part-time (1 woman). Average age 27. 15 applicants, 40% accepted, 6 enrolled. In 2016, 5 master's awarded. *Degree requirements:* For master's, comprehensive exam, thesis (for some programs). *Entrance requirements:* For master's, GRE General Test or MAT. Additional exam requirements/recommendations for international students: Required—TOEFL (minimum score 500 paper-based; 61 iBT). *Application deadline:* Applications are processed on a rolling basis. Application fee: $35. Electronic applications accepted. *Financial support:* In 2016–17, 7 students received support. Available to part-time students. Application deadline: 4/1; applicants required to submit FAFSA. *Unit head:* Dr. Thomas McCutchen, Head, 256-782-5560, E-mail: tmccutchen@jsu.edu. *Application contact:* Dr. Jean Pugliese, Associate Dean, 256-782-8278, Fax: 256-782-5321, E-mail: pugliese@jsu.edu.

**James Madison University,** The Graduate School, College of Visual and Performing Arts, Doctor of Musical Arts Program, Harrisonburg, VA 22807. Offers conducting (DMA); performance (DMA). *Program availability:* Part-time. *Students:* 20 full-time (8 women), 16 part-time (9 women); includes 3 minority (all Hispanic/Latino), 12 international. Average age 30. 27 applicants, 78% accepted, 9 enrolled. In 2016, 8 doctorates awarded. Application fee: $55. Electronic applications accepted. *Financial support:* In 2016–17, 18 students received support, including 1 fellowship; Federal Work-Study, unspecified assistantships, and 18 doctoral assistantships (averaging $12,935) also available. Financial award application deadline: 3/1; financial award applicants required to submit FAFSA. *Unit head:* Dr. Jeffrey Bush, Director of the School

of Music, 540-568-3614, E-mail: bushje@jmu.edu. *Application contact:* Lynette D. Michael, Director of Graduate Admissions, 540-568-6131 Ext. 6395, Fax: 540-568-7860, E-mail: michaeld@jmu.edu.
Website: http://www.jmu.edu/music/degree-programs/dma.shtml

**James Madison University,** The Graduate School, College of Visual and Performing Arts, Master of Music Program, Harrisonburg, VA 22802. Offers composition (MM); conducting (MM); music education (MM); performance (MM). *Accreditation:* NASM. *Program availability:* Part-time. *Faculty:* 39 full-time (12 women), 9 part-time/adjunct (3 women). *Students:* 18 full-time (9 women), 3 part-time (0 women); includes 5 minority (1 Black or African American, non-Hispanic/Latino; 3 Hispanic/Latino; 1 Two or more races, non-Hispanic/Latino), 2 international. Average age 30. 38 applicants, 68% accepted, 12 enrolled. In 2016, 10 master's awarded. Application fee: $55. Electronic applications accepted. *Financial support:* In 2016–17, 12 students received support, including 2 teaching assistantships with full tuition reimbursements available (averaging $8,837 per year); fellowships, Federal Work-Study, and 12 assistantships (averaging $7911) also available. Financial award application deadline: 3/1; financial award applicants required to submit FAFSA. *Unit head:* Dr. Jeffrey Bush, Director of the School of Music, 540-568-3614, E-mail: bushje@jmu.edu. *Application contact:* Lynette D. Michael, Director of Graduate Admissions, 540-568-6131 Ext. 6395, Fax: 540-568-7860, E-mail: michaeld@jmu.edu.
Website: http://www.jmu.edu/music/

**The Jewish Theological Seminary,** H. L. Miller Cantorial School and College of Jewish Music, New York, NY 10027-4649. Offers MSM. *Degree requirements:* For master's, one foreign language, comprehensive exam, departmental qualifying exam, recitals. *Entrance requirements:* For master's, music aptitude test, audition, interview, 3 letters of recommendation. Additional exam requirements/recommendations for international students: Required—TOEFL. *Expenses:* Contact institution.

**Johns Hopkins University,** Peabody Conservatory, Baltimore, MD 21218. Offers MA, MM, DMA, AD, GPD. *Degree requirements:* For master's, thesis (for some programs), departmental qualifying exam, recital; for doctorate, 2 foreign languages, thesis/dissertation (for some programs), departmental qualifying exam, recitals; for other advanced degree, recitals. *Entrance requirements:* For master's and other advanced degree, audition; for doctorate, audition, interview. Additional exam requirements/recommendations for international students: Required—TOEFL (minimum score 550 paper-based; 79 iBT). Electronic applications accepted. *Expenses:* Contact institution.

**The Juilliard School,** Graduate Programs, New York, NY 10023-6588. Offers acting (MFA); jazz studies (Artist Diploma); music (MM, DMA, Diploma); music performance (Artist Diploma); opera studies (Artist Diploma); string quartet (Artist Diploma). *Degree requirements:* For master's and other advanced degree, performance jury, recital; for doctorate, one foreign language, thesis/dissertation, performance jury, 3 recitals. *Entrance requirements:* For master's and other advanced degree, audition; for doctorate, audition, interview. Additional exam requirements/recommendations for international students: Required—TOEFL (minimum score 570 paper-based; 89 iBT). *Application deadline:* For fall admission, 12/1 for domestic and international students. Application fee: $110. Electronic applications accepted. *Expenses: Tuition:* Full-time $41,310. *Financial support:* In 2016–17, 308 students received support. Fellowships, research assistantships, teaching assistantships, Federal Work-Study, institutionally sponsored loans, scholarships/grants, and unspecified assistantships available. Support available to part-time students. Financial award application deadline: 3/1; financial award applicants required to submit FAFSA. *Unit head:* Ara Guzelimian, Provost and Dean, 212-799-5204, Fax: 212-724-0263. *Application contact:* Ekaterina Lawson, Director of Admissions and Academic Affairs, 212-799-5000 Ext. 223, Fax: 212-724-6420.

**Kansas State University,** Graduate School, College of Arts and Sciences, School of Music, Theatre and Dance, Manhattan, KS 66506. Offers MA, MM. *Accreditation:* NASM; NAST. *Program availability:* Part-time, online learning. *Faculty:* 38 full-time (16 women). *Students:* 24 full-time (14 women), 9 part-time (8 women); includes 7 minority (1 Black or African American, non-Hispanic/Latino; 1 American Indian or Alaska Native, non-Hispanic/Latino; 4 Hispanic/Latino; 1 Two or more races, non-Hispanic/Latino), 5 international. Average age 30. 33 applicants, 79% accepted, 12 enrolled. In 2016, 26 master's awarded. *Degree requirements:* For master's, thesis optional. *Entrance requirements:* For master's, GRE, audition (in person or recording), interview (for music education). Additional exam requirements/recommendations for international students: Required—TOEFL (minimum score 600 paper-based). *Application deadline:* For fall admission, 2/1 priority date for domestic and international students; for spring admission, 8/1 priority date for domestic and international students. Applications are processed on a rolling basis. Application fee: $50 ($75 for international students). Electronic applications accepted. *Expenses:* Tuition, state resident: full-time $9670. Tuition, nonresident: full-time $21,828. *Required fees:* $862. *Financial support:* In 2016–17, 15 teaching assistantships with full tuition reimbursements (averaging $12,000 per year) were awarded; fellowships, institutionally sponsored loans, scholarships/grants, and tuition waivers (full and partial) also available. Support available to part-time students. Financial award application deadline: 3/1; financial award applicants required to submit FAFSA. *Faculty research:* American music, opera, drama therapy, directing, costume and scenic design, music by women composers. *Total annual research expenditures:* $26,693. *Unit head:* Dr. Jeffrry Ward, Director, 785-532-5740, Fax: 785-532-6899, E-mail: jeff98@ksu.edu. *Application contact:* Dr. Fred Burrack, Director of Graduate Music Programs, 785-532-3429, Fax: 785-532-5740, E-mail: fburrack@ksu.edu.
Website: http://www.k-state.edu/mtd/

**Kent State University,** College of the Arts, Hugh A. Glauser School of Music, Kent, OH 44242-0001. Offers conducting (MM); ethnomusicology (MA); music composition (MA); music education (MM, PhD); music theory (MA); music theory-composition (PhD); performance (MM), including chamber music. *Accreditation:* NASM. *Program availability:* Part-time, online learning. *Faculty:* 33 full-time (12 women). *Students:* 51 full-time (23 women), 167 part-time (120 women); includes 18 minority (8 Black or African American, non-Hispanic/Latino; 1 American Indian or Alaska Native, non-Hispanic/Latino; 1 Asian, non-Hispanic/Latino; 4 Hispanic/Latino; 1 Native Hawaiian or other Pacific Islander, non-Hispanic/Latino; 3 Two or more races, non-Hispanic/Latino), 25 international. Average age 32. 90 applicants, 86% accepted, 51 enrolled. In 2016, 95 master's, 2 doctorates awarded. *Degree requirements:* For master's, comprehensive exam (for some programs), thesis (for some programs), capstone project or thesis (for MM in music education); for doctorate, comprehensive exam, thesis/dissertation. *Entrance requirements:* For master's, transcripts; minimum GPA of 3.0; 3 letters of recommendation; goal statement; resume; writing sample (for MA in ethnomusicology); portfolio of original composition (for MA in composition); audition (for MM in conducting, performance); prior degree, teaching certificate, and 1 year of teaching experience (for MM in music education); for doctorate, writing sample; 3 letters of recommendation; curriculum vitae/resume; transcripts; minimum GPA of 3.0; prior degree in music education, teaching license, statement of purpose, video of teaching sample, 3 years of teaching, and interview (for music education); goal statement and 3 original compositions (for music theory-composition). Additional exam requirements/recommendations for international students: Required—TOEFL (minimum score of 525

paper-based, 71 iBT), IELTS (minimum score of 6), Michigan English Language Assessment Battery (minimum score of 75), or PTE (minimum score of 48). *Application deadline:* Applications are processed on a rolling basis. Application fee: $45 ($70 for international students). Electronic applications accepted. *Expenses:* Tuition, state resident: full-time $10,864; part-time $495 per credit hour. Tuition, nonresident: full-time $18,380; part-time $837 per credit hour. *Financial support:* Unspecified assistantships available. Financial award application deadline: 4/1. *Unit head:* Dr. Ralph Lorenz, Interim Director, 330-672-2172, E-mail: rlorenz@kent.edu. *Application contact:* Michael Chunn, Graduate Coordinator/Trumpet Professor, 330-672-9234, Fax: 330-672-7837, E-mail: mchunn@kent.edu.
Website: http://www.kent.edu/music/

**Lamar University,** College of Graduate Studies, College of Fine Arts and Communication, Mary Morgan Moore Department of Music, Beaumont, TX 77710. Offers MM. *Accreditation:* NASM. *Faculty:* 8 full-time (1 woman). *Students:* 9 full-time (4 women), 4 part-time (0 women); includes 2 minority (both Black and African American, non-Hispanic/Latino), 1 international. Average age 32. 9 applicants, 100% accepted, 3 enrolled. In 2016, 4 master's awarded. *Degree requirements:* For master's, comprehensive exam, thesis optional. *Entrance requirements:* For master's, GRE General Test, theory placement exams, audition. Additional exam requirements/recommendations for international students: Required—TOEFL (minimum score 550 paper-based; 79 iBT), IELTS (minimum score 6.5). *Application deadline:* For fall admission, 8/10 for domestic students, 7/1 for international students; for spring admission, 1/5 for domestic students, 12/1 for international students. Applications are processed on a rolling basis. Application fee: $25 ($50 for international students). Electronic applications accepted. *Expenses:* $8,134 in-state full-time, $5,574 in-state part-time; $15,604 out-of-state full-time, $10,554 out-of-state part-time per year. *Financial support:* Fellowships with tuition reimbursements, teaching assistantships, institutionally sponsored loans, and tuition waivers (partial) available. Support available to part-time students. Financial award application deadline: 4/1; financial award applicants required to submit FAFSA. *Faculty research:* Performance: ensembles and personal. *Unit head:* Dr. Brian Shook, Interim Chair, 409-880-8144, Fax: 409-880-8143. *Application contact:* Deidre Mayer, Interim Director, Admissions and Academic Services, 409-880-8888, Fax: 409-880-7419, E-mail: gradmissions@lamar.edu.
Website: http://fineartscomm.lamar.edu/music

**Lee University,** Program in Music, Cleveland, TN 37320-3450. Offers conducting (MM); music education (MM); music performance (MM); religious studies (MCM); sacred music (MCM). *Accreditation:* NASM. *Program availability:* Part-time. *Faculty:* 21 full-time (5 women), 5 part-time/adjunct (2 women). *Students:* 25 full-time (13 women), 9 part-time (7 women); includes 5 minority (3 Black & African American, non-Hispanic/Latino; 2 Asian, non-Hispanic/Latino), 10 international. Average age 28. 21 applicants, 67% accepted, 8 enrolled. In 2016, 17 master's awarded. *Degree requirements:* For master's, variable foreign language requirement, comprehensive exam, thesis, internship. *Entrance requirements:* For master's, placement exercises in music theory, music history, diction, and piano proficiency, audition, resume, interview, minimum GPA of 2.75, official transcripts, essay, 3 recommendations, immunization forms. Additional exam requirements/recommendations for international students: Required—TOEFL (minimum score 61 iBT). *Application deadline:* For fall admission, 4/1 priority date for domestic and international students; for spring admission, 10/1 priority date for domestic and international students. Applications are processed on a rolling basis. Application fee: $25. Electronic applications accepted. *Expenses: Tuition:* Full-time $11,367; part-time $632 per credit hour. *Required fees:* $35 per term. One-time fee: $25. Tuition and fees vary according to program. *Financial support:* In 2016–17, 30 students received support. Career-related internships or fieldwork, Federal Work-Study, institutionally sponsored loans, scholarships/grants, and unspecified assistantships available. Financial award application deadline: 3/1; financial award applicants required to submit FAFSA. *Unit head:* Dr. Brad J. Moffett, Director, 423-614-8240, Fax: 423-614-8245, E-mail: gradmusic@leeuniversity.edu.
Website: http://www.leeuniversity.edu/academics/graduate/music

**Liberty University,** School of Music, Lynchburg, VA 24515. Offers ethnomusicology (MA); music and worship (MA); music education (MA); worship studies (MA, DWS), including ethnomusicology (MA), leadership (MA). *Accreditation:* NASM. *Program availability:* Part-time, online learning. *Students:* 58 full-time (26 women), 184 part-time (90 women); includes 52 minority (42 Black or African American, non-Hispanic/Latino; 3 Asian, non-Hispanic/Latino; 2 Hispanic/Latino; 5 Two or more races, non-Hispanic/Latino), 8 international. Average age 38. 323 applicants, 24% accepted, 49 enrolled. In 2016, 39 master's, 1 doctorate awarded. *Entrance requirements:* For master's, minimum GPA of 3.0; interview; letter of recommendation; statement of purpose; bachelor's/master's degree in music, worship, or related field, or 5 years of experience. Additional exam requirements/recommendations for international students: Required—TOEFL (minimum score 600 paper-based; 100 iBT). *Application deadline:* Applications are processed on a rolling basis. Application fee: $50. Electronic applications accepted. *Financial support:* Applicants required to submit FAFSA. *Unit head:* Dr. Vernon Whaley, Dean, 434-592-3463, E-mail: vwhaley@liberty.edu. *Application contact:* Jay Bridge, Director of Admissions, 800-424-9595, Fax: 800-628-7977, E-mail: gradadmissions@liberty.edu.
Website: http://www.liberty.edu/academics/music/

**Long Island University–LIU Post,** College of Arts, Communications and Design, Brookville, NY 11548-1300. Offers art (MA); clinical art therapy (MA); clinical art therapy and counseling (MA); digital game design and development (MA); fine arts and design (MFA); interactive multimedia arts (MA); music (MA); theater (MA); theatre (MFA). *Faculty:* 36 full-time (19 women), 144 part-time/adjunct (74 women). *Students:* 123 full-time (91 women), 21 part-time (18 women); includes 25 minority (6 Black or African American, non-Hispanic/Latino; 1 American Indian or Alaska Native, non-Hispanic/Latino; 6 Asian, non-Hispanic/Latino; 11 Hispanic/Latino; 1 Two or more races, non-Hispanic/Latino), 32 international. 175 applicants, 73% accepted, 46 enrolled. In 2016, 68 master's awarded. *Degree requirements:* For master's, variable foreign language requirement, comprehensive exam (for some programs), thesis (for some programs). *Entrance requirements:* For master's, performance audition or portfolio. Additional exam requirements/recommendations for international students: Required—TOEFL (minimum score 550 paper-based; 79 iBT). *Application deadline:* Applications are processed on a rolling basis. Application fee: $50. Electronic applications accepted. *Expenses: Tuition:* Full-time $28,272; part-time $1178 per credit. *Required fees:* $451 per term. Tuition and fees vary according to degree level and program. *Financial support:* In 2016–17, 6 research assistantships with partial tuition reimbursements (averaging $1,020 per year), 14 teaching assistantships with partial tuition reimbursements (averaging $670 per year) were awarded; career-related internships or fieldwork, Federal Work-Study, institutionally sponsored loans, scholarships/grants, tuition waivers (full and partial), and unspecified assistantships also available. Support available to part-time students. Financial award application deadline: 2/15; financial award applicants required to submit FAFSA. *Faculty research:* Game design, new plays, musical theatre, compositions for wind symphony, jazz ensemble, jazz combo and vocal jazz. *Unit head:* Dr. Christine Kerr, Acting Dean, 516-299-2309, E-mail: christine.kerr@liu.edu. *Application contact:* Carol Zerah, Director of Graduate Admissions, 516-299-2900, Fax: 516-299-2137, E-mail: post-enroll@liu.edu.

*Music*

Website: http://www.liu.edu/CWPost/Academics/School-of-Visual-Arts-Communications-and-Digital-Technologies

**Louisiana State University and Agricultural & Mechanical College,** Graduate School, College of Music and Dramatic Arts, School of Music, Baton Rouge, LA 70803. Offers music (MM, DMA, PhD); music education (PhD). *Accreditation:* NASM.

**Loyola University New Orleans,** College of Music and Fine Arts, New Orleans, LA 70118-6195. Offers music therapy (MMT); performance (MM). *Accreditation:* NASM. *Program availability:* Part-time. *Faculty:* 15 full-time (7 women), 7 part-time/adjunct (5 women). *Students:* 37 full-time (25 women), 8 part-time (6 women); includes 16 minority (6 Black or African American, non-Hispanic/Latino; 1 Asian, non-Hispanic/Latino; 6 Hispanic/Latino; 3 Two or more races, non-Hispanic/Latino), 3 international. Average age 28. 55 applicants, 44% accepted, 17 enrolled. In 2016, 5 master's awarded. *Degree requirements:* For master's, comprehensive written and oral exams; thesis (for MMT). *Entrance requirements:* For master's, performance audition, appropriate bachelor's degree, transcripts, minimum GPA of 3.0, 2 letters of recommendation, resume. Additional exam requirements/recommendations for international students: Required—TOEFL (minimum score 550 paper-based; 79 iBT). *Application deadline:* For fall admission, 8/15 priority date for domestic and international students; for spring admission, 1/1 priority date for domestic and international students. Applications are processed on a rolling basis. Application fee: $20. Electronic applications accepted. *Expenses:* $818 per credit hour full-time tuition, $883 fees; $409 per credit hour part-time tuition, $527 fees; $275 graduation fee. *Financial support:* Career-related internships or fieldwork, Federal Work-Study, institutionally sponsored loans, scholarships/grants, unspecified assistantships, and talent-based music scholarships available. Support available to part-time students. Financial award application deadline: 5/1; financial award applicants required to submit FAFSA. *Faculty research:* Music business, music therapy, musicology, music theory, music education. *Unit head:* Dr. Victoria P. Vega, Associate Dean, 504-865-3037, Fax: 504-865-2852, E-mail: vpvega@loyno.edu. *Application contact:* Melissa L. Lightell, Director, Office of Professional and Continuing Studies, 504-865-3530, Fax: 504-865-2787, E-mail: evening@loyno.edu.
Website: http://cmfa.loyno.edu/

**Lynchburg College,** Graduate Studies, MA Program in Music, Lynchburg, VA 24501-3199. Offers MA. *Accreditation:* NASM. *Program availability:* Part-time, evening/weekend. *Students:* 2 part-time (1 woman). In 2016, 4 master's awarded. *Degree requirements:* For master's, comprehensive exam, recital. *Entrance requirements:* For master's, minimum undergraduate GPA of 3.0 (preferred); official transcripts (bachelor's, others as relevant), three letters of recommendation, career goals statement, minimum of 1 year of public or private school teaching experience or 2 years of experience as a conductor or associate conductor, performance portfolio. Additional exam requirements/recommendations for international students: Required—TOEFL (minimum score 550 paper-based; 79 iBT), IELTS (minimum score 6.5). *Application deadline:* For fall admission, 7/31 for domestic students, 6/1 for international students; for spring admission, 11/30 for domestic students, 10/15 for international students. Applications are processed on a rolling basis. Application fee: $30. Electronic applications accepted. Application fee is waived when completed online. *Expenses:* Contact institution. *Financial support:* Federal Work-Study, scholarships/grants, health care benefits, and unspecified assistantships available. Support available to part-time students. Financial award application deadline: 7/31; financial award applicants required to submit FAFSA. *Unit head:* Dr. Jong Kim, Professor/Director of MA in Music, 434-544-8443, E-mail: kim@lynchburg.edu.
Website: http://www.lynchburg.edu/graduate/master-of-arts-in-music/

**Lynn University,** Conservatory of Music, Boca Raton, FL 33431-5598. Offers collaborative piano (MM); composition (MM); performance (MM); professional performance (Certificate). *Accreditation:* NASM. *Program availability:* Part-time, evening/weekend. *Faculty:* 11 full-time (3 women), 20 part-time/adjunct (11 women). *Students:* 32 full-time (14 women), 21 part-time (9 women); includes 8 minority (3 Black or African American, non-Hispanic/Latino; 5 Hispanic/Latino), 29 international. Average age 24. 88 applicants, 93% accepted, 31 enrolled. In 2016, 16 master's, 9 Certificates awarded. *Degree requirements:* For master's, comprehensive exam, completion of program in 4 calendar years, minimum GPA of 3.0. *Entrance requirements:* For master's, bachelor's degree from accredited institution, essay/personal statement, resume, letter of recommendation, official transcripts, audition. Additional exam requirements/recommendations for international students: Required—TOEFL (minimum score 550 paper-based; 80 iBT), IELTS (minimum score 6.5). *Application deadline:* For fall admission, 8/18 for domestic students, 8/4 for international students; for spring admission, 12/15 for domestic students, 12/1 for international students; for summer admission, 4/17 for domestic students, 4/3 for international students. Applications are processed on a rolling basis. Application fee: $50. Electronic applications accepted. *Expenses:* $725 per credit. *Financial support:* In 2016–17, 53 students received support. Federal Work-Study, scholarships/grants, and unspecified assistantships available. Support available to part-time students. Financial award application deadline: 3/1; financial award applicants required to submit FAFSA. *Unit head:* Dr. Jon Robertson, Dean, 561-237-7702, Fax: 561-237-9002, E-mail: jrobertson@lynn.edu. *Application contact:* Steven Pruitt, Director of Graduate Admissions, 561-237-7834, Fax: 561-237-7100, E-mail: admission@lynn.edu.
Website: http://www.lynn.edu/academics/colleges/conservatory

**Manhattan School of Music,** Graduate Programs, New York, NY 10027-4698. Offers composition (MM, DMA); jazz (MM, DMA); music performance (MM, DMA); orchestral performance (MM). *Degree requirements:* For master's, recital; for doctorate, variable foreign language requirement, thesis/dissertation, departmental qualifying exam, recitals. *Entrance requirements:* For master's, audition, pre-screen CD, bachelor's degree; for doctorate, departmental exam, audition, interview, pre-screen CD, master's degree. Additional exam requirements/recommendations for international students: Required—TOEFL (minimum score 550 paper-based; 79 iBT). Electronic applications accepted.

**Manhattan School of Music,** Professional Studies Certificate Program, New York, NY 10027-4698. Offers instrumental music (CPS), including accompanying, brass, composition, guitar, orchestral performance, organ, piano, strings, voice, woodwinds; vocal music (CPS), including accompanying, brass, composition, guitar, orchestral performance, organ, piano, strings, voice, woodwinds. *Degree requirements:* For CPS, recital. *Entrance requirements:* For degree, audition, pre-screen CD. Additional exam requirements/recommendations for international students: Required—TOEFL (minimum score 550 paper-based). Electronic applications accepted.

**Mansfield University of Pennsylvania,** Graduate Studies, Department of Music, Mansfield, PA 16933. Offers band conducting (MA); choral conducting (MA); performance (MA). *Accreditation:* NASM. *Program availability:* Part-time, evening/weekend. *Degree requirements:* For master's, comprehensive exam, thesis optional. *Entrance requirements:* For master's, minimum GPA of 3.0, audition. Additional exam requirements/recommendations for international students: Required—TOEFL (minimum score 550 paper-based). Electronic applications accepted.

**Marshall University,** Academic Affairs Division, College of Arts and Media, Program in Music, Huntington, WV 25755. Offers music (MA), including music composition. *Accreditation:* NASM. *Program availability:* Evening/weekend. *Degree requirements:* For master's, thesis optional.

**McGill University,** Faculty of Graduate and Postdoctoral Studies, Schulich School of Music, Montréal, QC H3A 2T5, Canada. Offers composition (M Mus, D Mus, PhD); music education (MA, PhD); music technology (MA, PhD); musicology (MA, PhD); performance (M Mus); performance studies (D Mus); sound recording (M Mus, PhD); theory (MA, PhD).

**McNally Smith College of Music,** Master of Music in Performance Program, Saint Paul, MN 55101. Offers bass performance (MM); brass and woodwind performance (MM); guitar performance (MM); keyboard performance (MM); percussion performance (MM); string performance (MM); vocal performance (MM). *Accreditation:* NASM. *Program availability:* Part-time, evening/weekend. *Degree requirements:* For master's, comprehensive exam, thesis, final project, final recital. *Entrance requirements:* For master's, audition, performance sample (2 recordings), artist statement, resume/curriculum vitae, 3 reference letters/letters of recommendation, undergraduate transcripts. Additional exam requirements/recommendations for international students: Required—TOEFL (minimum score 70 iBT), IELTS (minimum score 6.5). Electronic applications accepted.

**Memorial University of Newfoundland,** School of Graduate Studies, Interdisciplinary Program in Ethnomusicology, St. John's, NL A1C 5S7, Canada. Offers MA, PhD. *Program availability:* Part-time. *Degree requirements:* For master's, research paper or thesis; for doctorate, one foreign language, comprehensive exam, thesis/dissertation, oral defense of thesis. *Entrance requirements:* For master's, minimum B+ average with B Mus or humanities/social sciences degree; for doctorate, MA in ethnomusicology or a related field. Electronic applications accepted.

**Memorial University of Newfoundland,** School of Graduate Studies, School of Music, St. John's, NL A1C 5S7, Canada. Offers conducting (MMus); performance pedagogy (MMus); performing (MMus). *Entrance requirements:* For master's, diagnostic exams measuring skills and knowledge in musical literacy, B Mus with first-class standing, audition. Electronic applications accepted.

**Mercer University,** Graduate Studies, Macon Campus, Townsend School of Music, Macon, GA 31207. Offers choral conducting (MM); church music (MM); collaborative piano (MM), including instrumental, vocal; instrumental conducting (MM); performance (MM). *Faculty:* 9 full-time (3 women), 3 part-time/adjunct (2 women). *Students:* 12 full-time (6 women), 1 (woman) part-time; includes 3 minority (2 Black or African American, non-Hispanic/Latino; 1 Hispanic/Latino). Average age 25. 25 applicants, 48% accepted, 9 enrolled. In 2016, 11 master's awarded. *Degree requirements:* For master's, comprehensive exam, recitals. *Entrance requirements:* For master's, audition. Additional exam requirements/recommendations for international students: Required—TOEFL (minimum score 550 paper-based; 80 iBT). *Application deadline:* For fall admission, 6/1 for domestic students, 5/11 for international students. Applications are processed on a rolling basis. Application fee: $100. *Expenses:* Contact institution. *Financial support:* In 2016–17, 14 students received support. Tuition waivers (full) and unspecified assistantships available. Financial award application deadline: 6/1; financial award applicants required to submit FAFSA. *Faculty research:* Philosophy of church music, performance practices of the Baroque and classical periods, organ repertoire of the high Baroque, choral and instrumental conducting techniques. *Total annual research expenditures:* $5,000. *Unit head:* Dr. Richard G. Kosowski, Director of Graduate Studies, 478-301-4167, Fax: 478-301-5633, E-mail: keith_cd@mercer.edu. *Application contact:* Director, 912-301-2700.
Website: http://music.mercer.edu

**Messiah College,** Program in Conducting, Mechanicsburg, PA 17055. Offers choral conducting (MM); orchestral conducting (MM); wind conducting (MM). *Accreditation:* NASM. *Program availability:* Part-time, online learning. *Degree requirements:* For master's, advanced conducting project. Electronic applications accepted.

**Miami University,** College of Creative Arts, Department of Music, Oxford, OH 45056. Offers music education (MM); music performance (MM). *Accreditation:* NASM. *Students:* 18 full-time (13 women), 1 (woman) part-time; includes 2 minority (both Hispanic/Latino), 8 international. Average age 26. In 2016, 6 master's awarded. *Expenses:* Tuition, state resident: full-time $12,890; part-time $564 per credit hour. Tuition, nonresident: full-time $29,604; part-time $1260 per credit hour. *Required fees:* $638. Part-time tuition and fees vary according to course load and program. *Unit head:* Dr. Bruce Murray, Chair and Professor, 513-529-3014, E-mail: bruce.murray@miamioh.edu. *Application contact:* Dr. Brenda Mitchell, Associate Professor of Music/Director of Graduate Studies, 513-529-1228, E-mail: mitchebs@miamioh.edu.
Website: http://www.miamioh.edu/music

**Michigan State University,** The Graduate School, College of Music, East Lansing, MI 48824. Offers collaborative piano (M Mus); jazz studies (M Mus); music (PhD); music composition (M Mus, DMA); music conducting (M Mus, DMA); music education (M Mus); music performance (M Mus, DMA); music theory (M Mus); music therapy (M Mus); musicology (MA); piano pedagogy (M Mus). *Accreditation:* NASM. *Entrance requirements:* Additional exam requirements/recommendations for international students: Required—TOEFL. Electronic applications accepted.

**Middle Tennessee State University,** College of Graduate Studies, College of Liberal Arts, School of Music, Murfreesboro, TN 37132. Offers MA. *Accreditation:* NASM. *Program availability:* Part-time, evening/weekend, online learning. *Degree requirements:* For master's, one foreign language, comprehensive exam, thesis optional. *Entrance requirements:* For master's, GRE or MAT. Additional exam requirements/recommendations for international students: Required—TOEFL (minimum score 525 paper-based; 71 iBT) or IELTS (minimum score 6). Electronic applications accepted.

**Middle Tennessee State University,** College of Graduate Studies, College of Mass Communication, Department of Recording Industry, Murfreesboro, TN 37132. Offers recording arts and technologies (MFA). *Program availability:* Part-time, evening/weekend, online learning. *Degree requirements:* For master's, comprehensive exam, thesis or alternative. *Entrance requirements:* For master's, GRE. Additional exam requirements/recommendations for international students: Required—TOEFL (minimum score 525 paper-based; 71 iBT) or IELTS (minimum score 6). *Faculty research:* Digital audio, music production.

**Midwestern Baptist Theological Seminary,** Graduate and Professional Programs, Kansas City, MO 64118-4697. Offers Christian education (MACE); Christian foundations (Graduate Certificate); church music (MCM); counseling (MA); ministry (D Ed Min, D Min); Old or New Testament studies (PhD); theology (M Div). *Accreditation:* ATS. *Program availability:* Part-time, online learning. *Degree requirements:* For doctorate, thesis/dissertation. *Entrance requirements:* For doctorate, MAT. Electronic applications accepted. *Faculty research:* Ministerial studies, Biblical and theological studies, missions, counseling.

**Mills College,** Graduate Studies, Department of Music, Oakland, CA 94613-1000. Offers composition (MA); electronic music and recording media (MFA); music performance and literature (MFA). *Program availability:* Part-time. *Faculty:* 6 full-time (1

woman), 2 part-time/adjunct (1 woman). *Students:* 35 full-time (17 women), 1 part-time (0 women); includes 8 minority (1 Black or African American, non-Hispanic/Latino; 3 Asian, non-Hispanic/Latino; 1 Hispanic/Latino; 3 Two or more races, non-Hispanic/Latino), 9 international. Average age 29. 50 applicants, 80% accepted, 18 enrolled. In 2016, 18 master's awarded. *Degree requirements:* For master's, variable foreign language requirement, thesis, performance or recital. *Entrance requirements:* For master's, portfolio or audition. Additional exam requirements/recommendations for international students: Required—TOEFL (minimum score 550 paper-based; 80 iBT) or IELTS (minimum score 6). *Application deadline:* For fall admission, 1/15 priority date for domestic students, 12/15 for international students; for spring admission, 11/1 priority date for domestic students, 10/1 for international students. Applications are processed on a rolling basis. Application fee: $50. Electronic applications accepted. *Expenses: Tuition:* Full-time $31,620. *Required fees:* $1118. Tuition and fees vary according to course load, degree level and program. *Financial support:* In 2016–17, 56 students received support, including 33 fellowships with tuition reimbursements available (averaging $11,561 per year), 23 teaching assistantships with tuition reimbursements available (averaging $9,881 per year); scholarships/grants also available. Support available to part-time students. Financial award application deadline: 2/1; financial award applicants required to submit FAFSA. *Faculty research:* Composition and songwriting, nineteenth- and twentieth-century Western classical music and opera, interdisciplinary electroacoustic composition and performance, musical instrument building and new instrumental resources, sound installation. *Unit head:* David Bernstein, Head, Center for Contemporary Music, 510-430-2187, Fax: 510-430-3314, E-mail: davidb@mills.edu. *Application contact:* Robynne Lofton, Director of Admissions, 510-430-3295, Fax: 510-430-2159, E-mail: grad-admission@mills.edu.
Website: http://www.mills.edu/music

**Minnesota State University Mankato,** College of Graduate Studies and Research, College of Arts and Humanities, Department of English, Mankato, MN 56001. Offers communication and composition (MA); creative writing (MFA); English studies (MA); teaching English as a second language (MA, Certificate); technical communication (MA, Certificate). *Program availability:* Part-time. *Students:* 59 full-time (44 women), 106 part-time (67 women). *Degree requirements:* For master's, one foreign language, comprehensive exam, thesis or alternative. *Entrance requirements:* For master's, minimum GPA of 3.0 during previous 2 years, writing sample (MFA). Additional exam requirements/recommendations for international students: Required—TOEFL (minimum score 500 paper-based; 61 iBT). *Application deadline:* For fall admission, 7/1 for domestic students, 5/1 for international students. Applications are processed on a rolling basis. Application fee: $40. Electronic applications accepted. *Financial support:* Research assistantships with full tuition reimbursements, teaching assistantships with full tuition reimbursements, career-related internships or fieldwork, Federal Work-Study, and unspecified assistantships available. Financial award application deadline: 3/15; financial award applicants required to submit FAFSA. *Unit head:* Matthew Sewell, Chair, 507-389-2117, E-mail: matthew.sewell@mnsu.edu.
Website: http://english.mnsu.edu/

**Minnesota State University Mankato,** College of Graduate Studies and Research, College of Arts and Humanities, Department of Music, Mankato, MN 56001. Offers choral conducting (MM); music education (MAT); piano performance (MM); wind band conducting (MM). *Accreditation:* NASM. *Students:* 1 full-time (0 women), 7 part-time (4 women). *Degree requirements:* For master's, comprehensive exam, thesis or alternative. *Entrance requirements:* For master's, minimum GPA of 3.0 during previous 2 years, audition or test. Additional exam requirements/recommendations for international students: Required—TOEFL. *Application deadline:* For fall admission, 7/1 priority date for domestic students; for spring admission, 11/1 for domestic students. Applications are processed on a rolling basis. Application fee: $40. Electronic applications accepted. *Financial support:* Research assistantships with full tuition reimbursements, teaching assistantships with full tuition reimbursements, career-related internships or fieldwork, Federal Work-Study, and institutionally sponsored loans available. Support available to part-time students. Financial award application deadline: 3/15. *Unit head:* John Lindberg, Chairperson, E-mail: john.lindberg@mnsu.edu.
Website: http://www.mnsu.edu/music/

**Mississippi College,** Graduate School, College of Arts and Sciences, School of Christian Studies and the Arts, Department of Music, Clinton, MS 39058. Offers applied music performance (MM); conducting (MM); music education (MM); music performance: organ (MM); vocal pedagogy (MM). *Accreditation:* NASM. *Program availability:* Part-time, evening/weekend. *Degree requirements:* For master's, comprehensive exam, recital. *Entrance requirements:* For master's, GRE, minimum GPA of 2.5. Additional exam requirements/recommendations for international students: Recommended—TOEFL, IELTS. Electronic applications accepted.

**Missouri State University,** Graduate College, College of Arts and Letters, Department of Music, Springfield, MO 65897. Offers MM, MS Ed. *Accreditation:* NASM. *Program availability:* Part-time. *Faculty:* 27 full-time (11 women), 1 (woman) part-time/adjunct. *Students:* 25 full-time (16 women), 18 part-time (9 women); includes 5 minority (2 Black or African American, non-Hispanic/Latino; 1 Asian, non-Hispanic/Latino; 2 Hispanic/Latino), 12 international. Average age 28. 35 applicants, 60% accepted, 15 enrolled. In 2016, 22 master's awarded. *Degree requirements:* For master's, comprehensive exam, thesis or alternative. *Entrance requirements:* For master's, GRE, interview/audition (MM), 9-12 teaching certification (MS Ed). Additional exam requirements/recommendations for international students: Required—TOEFL (minimum score 550 paper-based; 79 iBT), IELTS (minimum score 6). *Application deadline:* For fall admission, 7/20 for domestic students, 5/1 for international students; for spring admission, 12/20 for domestic students, 9/1 for international students. Applications are processed on a rolling basis. Application fee: $35 ($50 for international students). Electronic applications accepted. *Expenses: Tuition,* state resident: full-time $5830. Tuition, nonresident: full-time $10,708. *Required fees:* $1130. Tuition and fees vary according to class time, course level, course load and program. *Financial support:* In 2016–17, 9 teaching assistantships with full tuition reimbursements (averaging $8,772 per year) were awarded; Federal Work-Study, institutionally sponsored loans, scholarships/grants, tuition waivers (partial), and unspecified assistantships also available. Financial award application deadline: 3/31; financial award applicants required to submit FAFSA. *Faculty research:* Musical theatre, Ozarks music, carillon, jazz studies. *Unit head:* Dr. Julie Combs, Head, 417-836-5648, Fax: 417-836-7665, E-mail: music@missouristate.edu. *Application contact:* Michael Edwards, Coordinator of Graduate Admissions, 417-836-5330, Fax: 417-836-6200, E-mail: michaeledwards@missouristate.edu.
Website: http://www.missouristate.edu/music/

**Montclair State University,** The Graduate School, College of the Arts, John J. Cali School of Music, Artist's Diploma Program, Montclair, NJ 07043-1624. Offers AD. *Accreditation:* NASM. *Program availability:* Part-time, evening/weekend. *Entrance requirements:* For degree, essay. Additional exam requirements/recommendations for international students: Required—TOEFL (minimum score 83 iBT), IELTS (minimum score 6.5). Electronic applications accepted. *Expenses: Tuition,* state resident: part-time $553 per credit. Tuition, nonresident: part-time $854 per credit. *Required fees:* $91 per credit. Tuition and fees vary according to program.

**Montclair State University,** The Graduate School, College of the Arts, John J. Cali School of Music, Performer's Certificate Program, Montclair, NJ 07043-1624. Offers Performer's Certificate. *Expenses: Tuition,* state resident: part-time $553 per credit. Tuition, nonresident: part-time $854 per credit. *Required fees:* $91 per credit. Tuition and fees vary according to program.

**Montclair State University,** The Graduate School, College of the Arts, John J. Cali School of Music, Program in Music, Montclair, NJ 07043-1624. Offers music education (MA); music therapy (MA); performance (MA); theory/composition (MA). *Program availability:* Part-time, evening/weekend. *Degree requirements:* For master's, thesis. *Entrance requirements:* For master's, GRE General Test, 2 letters of recommendation, essay. Additional exam requirements/recommendations for international students: Required—TOEFL (minimum score 83 iBT), IELTS (minimum score 6.5). Electronic applications accepted. *Expenses: Tuition,* state resident: part-time $553 per credit. Tuition, nonresident: part-time $854 per credit. *Required fees:* $91 per credit. Tuition and fees vary according to program.

**Morehead State University,** Graduate Programs, Caudill College of Arts, Humanities and Social Sciences, Department of Music, Theatre and Dance, Morehead, KY 40351. Offers music education (MM); music performance (MM). *Accreditation:* NASM. *Program availability:* Part-time, evening/weekend. *Degree requirements:* For master's, comprehensive exam, oral and written exams. *Entrance requirements:* For master's, music entrance exam, BA in music with minimum GPA of 3.0, 2.5 overall; audition. Additional exam requirements/recommendations for international students: Required—TOEFL (minimum score 550 paper-based). Electronic applications accepted. *Faculty research:* Musical instrument digital interface (MIDI) applications, tonal concepts of euphonium and baritone horn, digital synthesis, computer-assisted instruction in music, musical composition.

**Morgan State University,** School of Graduate Studies, College of Liberal Arts, Department of Fine and Performing Arts, Baltimore, MD 21251. Offers MA. *Accreditation:* NASM. *Program availability:* Part-time, evening/weekend. *Degree requirements:* For master's, comprehensive exam, thesis. *Entrance requirements:* Additional exam requirements/recommendations for international students: Required—TOEFL (minimum score 550 paper-based).

**Murray State University,** College of Humanities and Fine Arts, Program in Music, Murray, KY 42071. Offers music education (MME). *Accreditation:* NASM. *Program availability:* Part-time. *Entrance requirements:* For master's, GRE General Test or MAT. Additional exam requirements/recommendations for international students: Required—TOEFL.

**Nazareth College of Rochester,** Graduate Studies, Department of Music, Rochester, NY 14618. Offers music education (MS Ed); music performance and pedagogy (MM). *Program availability:* Part-time, evening/weekend. *Students:* 11 part-time (8 women). Average age 25. 7 applicants, 100% accepted, 6 enrolled. *Entrance requirements:* For master's, GRE or MAT (for music education program), audition, minimum GPA of 3.0. Additional exam requirements/recommendations for international students: Required—TOEFL (minimum score 550 paper-based, 79 iBT) or IELTS (6.5). *Application deadline:* For fall admission, 4/1 for domestic students. Applications are processed on a rolling basis. Electronic applications accepted. *Expenses: Tuition:* Part-time $880 per credit hour. Part-time tuition and fees vary according to course load, degree level and program. *Financial support:* Unspecified assistantships available. Financial award application deadline: 3/1; financial award applicants required to submit FAFSA. *Unit head:* Dr. Beverly Smoker, Chairperson, 585-389-2701, Fax: 585-389-2452, E-mail: bsmoker5@naz.edu. *Application contact:* Judith Baker, Director, Graduate Admissions, 585-531-1154, Fax: 585-389-2826, E-mail: gradadmissions@naz.edu.
Website: https://www2.naz.edu/academics/music-degree-program/

**New England Conservatory of Music,** Graduate Program in Music, Boston, MA 02115-5000. Offers MM, DMA, Diploma. *Faculty:* 92 full-time (31 women), 106 part-time/adjunct (37 women). *Students:* 380 full-time (182 women), 26 part-time (14 women); includes 70 minority (4 Black or African American, non-Hispanic/Latino; 37 Asian, non-Hispanic/Latino; 16 Hispanic/Latino; 13 Two or more races, non-Hispanic/Latino), 175 international. Average age 22. 1,369 applicants, 33% accepted, 195 enrolled. In 2016, 167 master's, 7 doctorates awarded. *Degree requirements:* For master's, variable foreign language requirement, comprehensive exam, thesis (for some programs), recital; for doctorate, one foreign language, comprehensive exam, thesis/dissertation, qualifying exams, recital. *Entrance requirements:* For master's and Diploma, audition; for doctorate, music theory and musicology exam, audition. Additional exam requirements/recommendations for international students: Required—TOEFL (minimum score 550 paper-based; 79 iBT). *Application deadline:* For fall admission, 12/1 priority date for domestic and international students; for spring admission, 10/15 for domestic and international students. Applications are processed on a rolling basis. Application fee: $115. Electronic applications accepted. *Expenses: Tuition:* Full-time $44,300. *Financial support:* In 2016–17, 392 students received support. Fellowships with partial tuition reimbursements available, teaching assistantships, Federal Work-Study, scholarships/grants, and tuition waivers (partial) available. Support available to part-time students. Financial award application deadline: 12/1; financial award applicants required to submit FAFSA. *Unit head:* Tom Novak, Provost/Dean of the College, 617-585-1308, Fax: 617-585-1303, E-mail: tom.novak@necmusic.edu. *Application contact:* Alex Powell, Assistant Dean for Admissions, 617-585-1101, Fax: 617-585-1115, E-mail: alex.powell@newenglandconservatory.edu.

**New Jersey City University,** William J. Maxwell College of Arts and Sciences, Department of Music, Dance and Theatre, Jersey City, NJ 07305-1597. Offers music education (MA); performance (MM). *Accreditation:* NASM. *Program availability:* Part-time, evening/weekend. *Degree requirements:* For master's, thesis optional, recital. *Entrance requirements:* Additional exam requirements/recommendations for international students: Required—TOEFL (minimum score 79 iBT).

**New Mexico State University,** College of Arts and Sciences, Department of Music, Las Cruces, NM 88003. Offers conducting (MM); music education (MM); performance (MM). *Accreditation:* NASM. *Program availability:* Part-time. *Faculty:* 16 full-time (6 women), 3 part-time/adjunct (0 women). *Students:* 12 full-time (6 women), 12 part-time (4 women); includes 9 minority (all Hispanic/Latino), 4 international. Average age 31. 17 applicants, 59% accepted, 8 enrolled. In 2016, 6 master's awarded. *Degree requirements:* For master's, comprehensive exam (for some programs), thesis (for some programs), recital. *Entrance requirements:* For master's, diagnostic exam, audition, bachelor's degree or equivalent from an accredited institution. Additional exam requirements/recommendations for international students: Required—TOEFL (minimum score 550 paper-based; 79 iBT), IELTS (minimum score 6.5). *Application deadline:* For fall admission, 7/1 priority date for domestic students; for spring admission, 11/1 for domestic students. Applications are processed on a rolling basis. Application fee: $40 ($50 for international students). Electronic applications accepted. *Expenses: Tuition,* state resident: full-time $4086. Tuition, nonresident: full-time $14,254. *Required fees:* $853. Tuition and fees vary according to course load. *Financial support:* In 2016–17, 10 students received support, including 1 fellowship (averaging $812 per year), 8 teaching assistantships (averaging $13,960 per year); career-related internships or fieldwork, Federal Work-Study, scholarships/grants, traineeships, health care benefits, and unspecified assistantships also available. Support available to part-time students. Financial award application deadline: 3/1. *Faculty research:* Music education, contemporary wind band literature, performance, music history, composition. *Total annual research expenditures:* $6,480. *Unit head:* Dr. Lon W. Chaffin, Department Head, 575-646-2421, Fax: 575-646-8199, E-mail: lchaffin@nmsu.edu. *Application contact:* Dr. James Shearer, Coordinator of Graduate Studies, 575-646-2601, Fax: 575-646-8199, E-mail: jshearer@nmsu.edu. *Website:* http://music.nmsu.edu

**New Orleans Baptist Theological Seminary,** Graduate and Professional Programs, Division of Church Music Ministries, New Orleans, LA 70126-4858. Offers M Div, MMCM, DMA. *Accreditation:* NASM. *Program availability:* Online learning. *Degree requirements:* For doctorate, one foreign language, thesis/dissertation. *Entrance requirements:* For doctorate, GRE General Test. Additional exam requirements/recommendations for international students: Required—TOEFL.

**The New School,** College of Performing Arts, Mannes School of Music, New York, NY 10003. Offers composition (MM, Advanced Diploma); guitar (MM, Advanced Diploma); harpsichord (MM, Advanced Diploma); music theory (MM); orchestral conducting (MM, Advanced Diploma); orchestral instruments (MM, Advanced Diploma); piano (MM, Advanced Diploma); piano and collaborative piano (MM, Advanced Diploma); theory (Advanced Diploma); voice (MM, Advanced Diploma). *Program availability:* Part-time. *Faculty:* 9 full-time (4 women), 2 part-time/adjunct (0 women). *Students:* 206 full-time (124 women), 35 part-time (18 women); includes 38 minority (7 Black or African American, non-Hispanic/Latino; 15 Asian, non-Hispanic/Latino; 12 Hispanic/Latino; 1 Native Hawaiian or other Pacific Islander, non-Hispanic/Latino; 3 Two or more races, non-Hispanic/Latino), 129 international. Average age 25. 835 applicants, 53% accepted, 127 enrolled. In 2016, 91 master's, 18 Advanced Diplomas awarded. *Entrance requirements:* For master's, transcripts, recommendation letter, essay, live audition. Additional exam requirements/recommendations for international students: Required—TOEFL (minimum score 79 iBT), IELTS (minimum score 6.5), PTE (minimum score 53). *Application deadline:* For fall admission, 1/15 priority date for domestic and international students; for spring admission, 11/1 priority date for domestic and international students. Applications are processed on a rolling basis. Application fee: $50. Electronic applications accepted. *Expenses: Tuition:* Full-time $42,610; part-time $1685 per credit. *Required fees:* $276; $138 per semester. Full-time tuition and fees vary according to degree level and program. Part-time tuition and fees vary according to course load and program. *Financial support:* Fellowships, research assistantships, teaching assistantships, Federal Work-Study, scholarships/grants, and unspecified assistantships available. Support available to part-time students. Financial award application deadline: 2/1; financial award applicants required to submit FAFSA. *Unit head:* Richard Kessler, Executive Dean, College of Performing Arts, 212-580-0210 Ext. 4848, E-mail: richardkessler@newschool.edu. *Application contact:* Taryn Wolf, Senior Director of Recruitment and Outreach, 212-229-5150 Ext. 3007, E-mail: performingarts@newschool.edu. *Website:* http://www.newschool.edu/mannes/

**New York University,** Graduate School of Arts and Science, Department of Music, New York, NY 10012-1019. Offers composition and theory (MA, PhD); early music performance (Advanced Certificate); ethnomusicology (MA, PhD). Terminal master's awarded for partial completion of doctoral program. *Degree requirements:* For master's, one foreign language, thesis (for some programs), general exam; for doctorate, 2 foreign languages, thesis/dissertation, general and special exams. *Entrance requirements:* For master's, GRE General Test, bachelor's degree in liberal arts or music; for doctorate, GRE General Test, master's degree in music. Additional exam requirements/recommendations for international students: Required—TOEFL. *Faculty research:* Early music (nineteenth century), Wagner, Verdi, performance practice.

**New York University,** Steinhardt School of Culture, Education, and Human Development, Department of Music and Performing Arts Professions, Program in Music Business, New York, NY 10012. Offers music business (MA); music technology (MA). *Program availability:* Part-time. *Degree requirements:* For master's, thesis (for some programs). *Entrance requirements:* For master's, interview. Additional exam requirements/recommendations for international students: Required—TOEFL (minimum score 100 iBT). Electronic applications accepted. *Faculty research:* Strategic marketing, new technologies, intellectual property, entrepreneurship, globalization, music in video games.

**New York University,** Steinhardt School of Culture, Education, and Human Development, Department of Music and Performing Arts Professions, Program in Music Performance and Composition, New York, NY 10012. Offers instrumental performance (MM), including instrumental performance, jazz instrumental performance; music performance and composition (PhD), including music performance and composition; music theory and composition (MM), including composition for film and multimedia, composition for music theater, computer music composition, music theory and composition, songwriting; piano performance (MM), including collaborative piano, solo piano; vocal pedagogy (Advanced Certificate); vocal performance (MM), including classical voice, musical theatre performance. *Program availability:* Part-time. *Degree requirements:* For master's, thesis (for some programs); for doctorate, thesis/dissertation. *Entrance requirements:* For master's, audition; for doctorate, GRE General Test, audition, interview. Additional exam requirements/recommendations for international students: Required—TOEFL (minimum score 100 iBT). Electronic applications accepted. *Faculty research:* Aesthetics, performance analysis, twentieth century music, music methodologies for arts criticism and analysis.

**New York University,** Steinhardt School of Culture, Education, and Human Development, Department of Music and Performing Arts Professions, Program in Music Technology, New York, NY 10012. Offers MM, PhD. *Program availability:* Part-time. *Degree requirements:* For master's, thesis (for some programs); for doctorate, thesis/dissertation. *Entrance requirements:* For master's, portfolio; for doctorate, essay, 3 letters of recommendation, master's degree. Additional exam requirements/recommendations for international students: Required—TOEFL (minimum score 100 iBT). Electronic applications accepted. *Faculty research:* Pattern processing in music, computer music, acoustics, music perception, interactive music systems.

**New York University,** Tisch School of the Arts, Graduate Musical Theatre Writing Program, New York, NY 10012-1019. Offers MFA. *Degree requirements:* For master's, full-length musical theatre work. *Entrance requirements:* For master's, interview, portfolio. Additional exam requirements/recommendations for international students: Required—TOEFL or IELTS. Electronic applications accepted.

**Norfolk State University,** School of Graduate Studies, School of Liberal Arts, Department of Music, Norfolk, VA 23504. Offers music (MM); music education (MM); performance (MM); theory and composition (MM). *Accreditation:* NASM. *Program availability:* Part-time. *Degree requirements:* For master's, thesis or alternative. *Entrance requirements:* For master's, minimum GPA of 2.7, letters of recommendation. Additional exam requirements/recommendations for international students: Required—TOEFL.

**North Carolina Central University,** College of Liberal Arts, Department of Music, Durham, NC 27707-3129. Offers jazz studies (MM).

**North Dakota State University,** College of Graduate and Interdisciplinary Studies, College of Arts, Humanities and Social Sciences, Challey School of Music, Fargo, ND

58102. Offers conducting (MM, DMA); music education (MM); performance (MM, DMA). *Accreditation:* NASM. *Degree requirements:* For master's, 2 foreign languages, comprehensive exam, thesis or alternative, recitals; for doctorate, 2 foreign languages, comprehensive exam, thesis/dissertation or alternative, recitals. *Entrance requirements:* For master's and doctorate, music history, music theory, performance audition. Additional exam requirements/recommendations for international students: Required—TOEFL (minimum score 525 paper-based; 71 iBT). Electronic applications accepted. *Faculty research:* Performance, conducting.

**Northeastern Illinois University,** College of Graduate Studies and Research, College of Arts and Sciences, Program in Music, Chicago, IL 60625-4699. Offers MA. *Accreditation:* NASM. *Program availability:* Part-time, evening/weekend. *Degree requirements:* For master's, comprehensive exam, thesis optional. *Entrance requirements:* For master's, departmental exam, audition, minimum GPA of 2.75. Additional exam requirements/recommendations for international students: Required—TOEFL (minimum score 550 paper-based; 79 iBT). Electronic applications accepted. *Faculty research:* World music, computers as applied instruments, vocal pedagogy, vocal interpretation, jazz repertory.

**Northern Arizona University,** Graduate College, College of Arts and Letters, School of Music, Flagstaff, AZ 86011. Offers choral conducting (MM); composition (MM); instrumental conducting (MM); instrumental performance (MM); musicology (MM); performance (Certificate); piano accompanying and chamber music (MM); Suzuki violin/viola (MM); theory (MM); vocal performance (MM). *Accreditation:* NASM. *Degree requirements:* For master's, comprehensive exam, thesis (for some programs), departmental exams. *Entrance requirements:* For master's, bachelor's degree in music, minimum GPA of 3.0, audition. Additional exam requirements/recommendations for international students: Required—TOEFL (minimum score 550 paper-based; 80 iBT), IELTS (minimum score 7). Electronic applications accepted. *Expenses:* Tuition, state resident: full-time $8971; part-time $444 per credit hour. Tuition, nonresident: full-time $20,958; part-time $1164 per credit hour. *Required fees:* $1018; $644 per credit hour. Tuition and fees vary according to course load, campus/location and program.

**Northern Illinois University,** Graduate School, College of Visual and Performing Arts, School of Music, De Kalb, IL 60115-2854. Offers MM, Performer's Certificate. *Accreditation:* NASM. *Program availability:* Part-time. *Faculty:* 33 full-time (3 women), 14 part-time/adjunct (3 women). *Students:* 42 full-time (16 women), 29 part-time (15 women); includes 9 minority (4 Black or African American, non-Hispanic/Latino; 2 Asian, non-Hispanic/Latino; 1 Hispanic/Latino; 2 Two or more races, non-Hispanic/Latino), 30 international. Average age 28. 118 applicants, 55% accepted, 28 enrolled. In 2016, 44 master's, 5 other advanced degrees awarded. *Degree requirements:* For master's, comprehensive exam, thesis optional, recital or project; for Performer's Certificate, recitals. *Entrance requirements:* For master's, minimum GPA of 2.75, appropriate bachelor's degree, audition, interview; for Performer's Certificate, minimum GPA of 2.75 (undergraduate), 3.2 (graduate); audition. Additional exam requirements/recommendations for international students: Required—TOEFL (minimum score 550 paper-based). *Application deadline:* For fall admission, 4/1 for domestic students, 5/1 for international students; for spring admission, 11/1 for domestic students, 10/1 for international students. Applications are processed on a rolling basis. Application fee: $40. Electronic applications accepted. *Financial support:* In 2016–17, 2 research assistantships with full tuition reimbursements, 24 teaching assistantships with full tuition reimbursements were awarded; fellowships with full tuition reimbursements, Federal Work-Study, scholarships/grants, tuition waivers (full), and staff assistantships also available. Support available to part-time students. Financial award applicants required to submit FAFSA. *Faculty research:* Impact of music on urban children and acquisition of language skills, music in seventeenth-century Madrid, Finnish music and culture, jazz studies. *Unit head:* Dr. Janet Hathaway, Director, 815-753-1551, Fax: 815-753-1759, E-mail: jhathaway@niu.edu. *Application contact:* Lynn Slater, Coordinator of Admissions and Public Relations, 815-753-1546, E-mail: lslater@niu.edu. *Website:* http://www.niu.edu/music/

**Northern Kentucky University,** Office of Graduate Programs, College of Arts and Sciences, Program in English, Highland Heights, KY 41099. Offers composition and rhetoric (Certificate); creative writing (Certificate); cultural studies and discourses (Certificate); English (MA); professional writing (Certificate). *Program availability:* Part-time, evening/weekend. *Degree requirements:* For master's, comprehensive exam (for some programs), capstone (thesis, portfolio, project, or exams); 30 hours of credit; for Certificate, 18 hours of credit. *Entrance requirements:* For master's, bachelor's degree in English or related field from regionally-accredited institution with minimum GPA of 3.0 in major or cognate area coursework; official transcripts for all undergraduate and graduate work; two letters of reference; for Certificate, official transcripts for all undergraduate and graduate work; bachelor's degree from regionally-accredited institution; minimum undergraduate GPA of 2.5. Additional exam requirements/recommendations for international students: Required—TOEFL (minimum score 79 iBT); Recommended—IELTS (minimum score 6.5). Electronic applications accepted.

**North Park University,** School of Music, Chicago, IL 60625-4895. Offers vocal performance (MM). *Accreditation:* NASM.

**Northwestern State University of Louisiana,** Graduate Studies and Research, School of Creative and Performing Arts, Program in Music, Natchitoches, LA 71497. Offers MM. *Accreditation:* NASM. *Degree requirements:* For master's, comprehensive exam, thesis or alternative. *Entrance requirements:* For master's, GRE General Test, minimum undergraduate GPA of 2.5. Additional exam requirements/recommendations for international students: Required—TOEFL. Electronic applications accepted.

**Northwestern University,** The Graduate School, School of Communication, Department of Performance Studies, Evanston, IL 60208. Offers MA, PhD. Admissions and degrees offered through The Graduate School. *Program availability:* Part-time. Terminal master's awarded for partial completion of doctoral program. *Degree requirements:* For master's, recital; for doctorate, one foreign language, thesis/dissertation, recital. *Entrance requirements:* For master's and doctorate, GRE General Test. Additional exam requirements/recommendations for international students: Required—TOEFL. *Faculty research:* Adaptation/performance of literature, ethnography of performance, critical cultural studies, performance theory, intercultural performance, gender studies.

**Northwestern University,** Henry and Leigh Bienen School of Music, Department of Music Performance, Evanston, IL 60208. Offers brass performance (MM, DMA); conducting (MM, DMA); jazz studies (MM); percussion performance (MM, DMA); performance (MM); piano pedagogy (MME); piano performance (MM, DMA); piano performance and collaborative arts (MM, DMA); piano performance and pedagogy (MM, DMA); string performance (MM, DMA); voice and opera performance (MM, DMA); woodwind performance (MM, DMA). *Accreditation:* NASM. *Degree requirements:* For master's, recital; for doctorate, comprehensive exam, thesis/dissertation, 3 recitals. *Entrance requirements:* For master's, audition, prescreening auditions where required; for doctorate, audition, preliminary tapes. Additional exam requirements/recommendations for international students: Required—TOEFL (minimum score 80 iBT).

**Northwestern University,** Henry and Leigh Bienen School of Music, Department of Music Studies, Evanston, IL 60208. Offers composition (DMA); music education (MME, PhD); music theory and cognition (PhD); musicology (MM, PhD); theory (MM). PhD admissions and degree offered through The Graduate School. *Accreditation:* NASM. *Degree requirements:* For doctorate, comprehensive exam, thesis/dissertation. *Entrance requirements:* For master's, portfolio or research papers; for doctorate, GRE General Test (for PhD), portfolio, research papers. Additional exam requirements/recommendations for international students: Required—TOEFL (minimum score 600 paper-based; 80 iBT). *Faculty research:* Music cognition, cognitive learning, aesthetic education, computer music, technology in education.

**Notre Dame de Namur University,** Division of Academic Affairs, College of Arts and Sciences, Program in Musical Performance, Belmont, CA 94002-1908. Offers MFA, Certificate. *Program availability:* Part-time. *Degree requirements:* For master's, recital, final project. *Entrance requirements:* For master's, audition, appropriate bachelor's degree, minimum GPA of 2.5. Additional exam requirements/recommendations for international students: Required—TOEFL (minimum score 550 paper-based; 79 iBT). Electronic applications accepted.

**Oakland University,** Graduate Study and Lifelong Learning, College of Arts and Sciences, Department of Music, Rochester, MI 48309-4401. Offers music (MM); music education (PhD). *Accreditation:* NASM. *Entrance requirements:* For master's, minimum GPA of 3.0. Additional exam requirements/recommendations for international students: Required—TOEFL (minimum score 550 paper-based). Electronic applications accepted. *Expenses:* Contact institution.

**Oberlin College,** Conservatory of Music, Oberlin, OH 44074-1588. Offers conducting (MM); contemporary chamber music (MM); historical performance (MM); performance (AD); piano technology (AD). *Students:* 16 full-time (5 women). 102 applicants, 23% accepted, 14 enrolled. *Degree requirements:* For master's, 2 recitals. *Entrance requirements:* For master's and AD, audition. Additional exam requirements/recommendations for international students: Recommended—TOEFL, IELTS. *Application deadline:* For fall admission, 12/1 for domestic and international students. Application fee: $100. Electronic applications accepted. *Financial support:* Career-related internships or fieldwork, Federal Work-Study, and scholarships/grants available. Financial award application deadline: 2/15; financial award applicants required to submit CSS PROFILE or FAFSA. *Unit head:* Andrea Kalyn, Dean, 440-775-8200. *Application contact:* Michael Manderen, Director of Conservatory Admissions, 440-775-8413, Fax: 440-775-6972, E-mail: conservatory.admissions@oberlin.edu.
Website: http://new.oberlin.edu/conservatory/

**The Ohio State University,** Graduate School, College of Arts and Sciences, Division of Arts and Humanities, Department of Dance, Columbus, OH 43210. Offers choreography (MFA); dance (MFA, PhD); dance and technology (MFA); dance studies (PhD); history, theory and literature (MFA); lighting and production (MFA); movement analysis, Laban studies, notation and dance documentation (MFA); performance (MFA). *Accreditation:* NASD. *Faculty:* 13. *Students:* 33 full-time (23 women), 5 international. Average age 33. In 2016, 9 master's, 1 doctorate awarded. *Degree requirements:* For master's, thesis optional. *Entrance requirements:* For master's, GRE General Test (for all applicants with cumulative GPA below 3.0), audition; for doctorate, GRE General Test, invitation-only interview. Additional exam requirements/recommendations for international students: Required—Michigan English Language Assessment Battery (minimum score 82); Recommended—TOEFL (minimum score 550 paper-based; 79 iBT), IELTS (minimum score 7). *Application deadline:* For fall admission, 11/15 priority date for domestic and international students; for spring admission, 3/1 for domestic students, 2/1 for international students. Applications are processed on a rolling basis. Application fee: $60 ($70 for international students). Electronic applications accepted. *Financial support:* Fellowships with tuition reimbursements, teaching assistantships with tuition reimbursements, Federal Work-Study, and institutionally sponsored loans available. Support available to part-time students. *Unit head:* Susan Hadley, Chair, 614-292-0984, E-mail: hadley.4@osu.edu. *Application contact:* Amy Schmidt, Academic Program Coordinator, 614-292-8933, E-mail: schmidt.442@osu.edu.
Website: http://dance.osu.edu/

**The Ohio State University,** Graduate School, College of Arts and Sciences, Division of Arts and Humanities, School of Music, Columbus, OH 43210. Offers MA, MM, DMA, PhD. *Accreditation:* NASM. *Program availability:* Part-time. *Faculty:* 47. *Students:* 117 full-time (58 women), 14 part-time (6 women); includes 11 minority (5 Hispanic/Latino; 6 Two or more races, non-Hispanic/Latino), 25 international. Average age 30. In 2016, 23 master's, 25 doctorates awarded. *Degree requirements:* For master's, thesis optional; for doctorate, 2 foreign languages, thesis/dissertation. *Entrance requirements:* For master's, GRE General Test (for all MA applicants and for MM applicants if GPA is below 3.0), pre-screen video audition (for piano and voice); for doctorate, GRE General Test (for all PhD applicants and for DMA applicants if GPA is below 3.0), pre-screen video audition (for piano and voice). Additional exam requirements/recommendations for international students: Required—TOEFL (minimum score 550 paper-based; 79 iBT), Michigan English Language Assessment Battery (minimum score 82); Recommended—IELTS (minimum score 7). *Application deadline:* For fall admission, 12/13 priority date for domestic students, 11/30 priority date for international students; for spring admission, 12/14 for domestic students, 11/12 for international students; for summer admission, 5/15 for domestic students, 4/14 for international students. Applications are processed on a rolling basis. Application fee: $60 ($70 for international students). Electronic applications accepted. *Financial support:* Fellowships with tuition reimbursements, research assistantships with tuition reimbursements, teaching assistantships with tuition reimbursements, Federal Work-Study, institutionally sponsored loans, and unspecified assistantships available. Support available to part-time students. *Unit head:* David Bruenger, Interim Director, 614-292-7664, E-mail: bruenger.1@osu.edu. *Application contact:* Rebecca Harrah, Graduate Studies Coordinator, 614-292-6389, Fax: 614-292-1102, E-mail: mus-grad@osu.edu.
Website: http://music.osu.edu/

**Ohio University,** Graduate College, College of Fine Arts, School of Music, Athens, OH 45701-2979. Offers accompanying (MM); composition (MM); conducting (MM); history/literature (MM); music education (MM); music therapy (MM); performance (MM, Certificate); performance/pedagogy (MM); theory (MM). *Accreditation:* NASM. *Program availability:* Part-time, evening/weekend, online learning. *Degree requirements:* For master's, comprehensive exam, thesis (for some programs), oral exam. *Entrance requirements:* For master's, audition, interview, portfolio, recordings (varies by program). Additional exam requirements/recommendations for international students: Required—TOEFL (minimum score 550 paper-based; 80 iBT) or IELTS (minimum score 6.5). *Application deadline:* For fall admission, 1/1 priority date for domestic and international students. Application fee: $50 ($55 for international students). Electronic applications accepted. *Financial support:* Teaching assistantships with full and partial tuition reimbursements, career-related internships or fieldwork, Federal Work-Study, institutionally sponsored loans, and tuition waivers (full and partial) available. Financial award application deadline: 1/1. *Unit head:* Dr. Christopher Hayes, Director, 740-593-4244, E-mail: hayesc1@ohio.edu. *Application contact:* Dr. Richard Wetzel, Graduate Chair, 740-593-1652, Fax: 740-593-1429, E-mail: wetzel@ohio.edu.
Website: http://www.finearts.ohio.edu/music

**Oklahoma City University,** Wanda L. Bass School of Music, Oklahoma City, OK 73106-1402. Offers composition (MM); conducting (MM); musical theatre (MM); opera performance (MM); performance (MM); vocal coaching (MM). *Accreditation:* NASM. *Program availability:* Part-time. *Faculty:* 25 full-time (9 women), 10 part-time/adjunct (5 women). *Students:* 62 full-time (21 women), 3 part-time (2 women); includes 15 minority (4 Black or African American, non-Hispanic/Latino; 2 American Indian or Alaska Native, non-Hispanic/Latino; 3 Asian, non-Hispanic/Latino; 3 Hispanic/Latino; 3 Two or more races, non-Hispanic/Latino), 14 international. Average age 25. 98 applicants, 70% accepted, 35 enrolled. In 2016, 22 master's awarded. *Degree requirements:* For master's, thesis, departmental qualifying exam, recital. *Entrance requirements:* For master's, audition, bachelor's degree in music from NASM-accredited institution, minimum GPA of 3.0. Additional exam requirements/recommendations for international students: Required—TOEFL (minimum score 550 paper-based; 80 iBT). *Application deadline:* Applications are processed on a rolling basis. Application fee: $50. Electronic applications accepted. *Expenses:* Contact institution. *Financial support:* In 2016–17, 63 students received support. Career-related internships or fieldwork, Federal Work-Study, institutionally sponsored loans, scholarships/grants, and tuition waivers (full and partial) available. Support available to part-time students. Financial award application deadline: 6/1; financial award applicants required to submit FAFSA. *Unit head:* Mark Parker, Dean, 405-208-5474, Fax: 405-208-5971, E-mail: mparker@okcu.edu. *Application contact:* Michael Harrington, Director of Graduate Admission, 800-633-7242, Fax: 405-208-5916, E-mail: gadmissions@okcu.edu.
Website: http://www.okcu.edu/music/

**Oklahoma State University,** College of Arts and Sciences, Department of Music, Stillwater, OK 74078. Offers pedagogy and performance (MM). *Accreditation:* NASM. *Faculty:* 31 full-time (12 women), 5 part-time/adjunct (4 women). *Students:* 10 full-time (4 women), 6 part-time (1 woman); includes 1 minority (Hispanic/Latino), 1 international. Average age 25. 39 applicants, 36% accepted, 10 enrolled. In 2016, 10 master's awarded. *Degree requirements:* For master's, final project, oral exam. *Entrance requirements:* For master's, GRE, audition. Additional exam requirements/recommendations for international students: Required—TOEFL (minimum score 550 paper-based; 79 iBT). *Application deadline:* For fall admission, 3/1 priority date for international students; for spring admission, 8/1 priority date for international students. Applications are processed on a rolling basis. Application fee: $40 ($75 for international students). Electronic applications accepted. *Expenses:* Tuition, state resident: full-time $3775; part-time $209.70 per credit hour. Tuition, nonresident: full-time $14,851; part-time $825.05 per credit hour. *Required fees:* $2027; $112.60 per credit hour. Tuition and fees vary according to campus/location. *Financial support:* In 2016–17, 14 teaching assistantships (averaging $11,411 per year) were awarded; career-related internships or fieldwork, Federal Work-Study, scholarships/grants, health care benefits, tuition waivers (partial), and unspecified assistantships also available. Support available to part-time students. Financial award application deadline: 3/1; financial award applicants required to submit FAFSA. *Faculty research:* Discovery and presentation of music literature of other countries, transportation of ancient music literature to modern notation. *Unit head:* Dr. Howard Potter, Department Head, 405-744-8997, Fax: 405-744-9324, E-mail: osumusic@okstate.edu.
Website: http://music.okstate.edu/

**Open University,** Graduate Programs, Milton Keynes, United Kingdom. Offers business (MBA); education (M Ed); engineering (M Eng); history (MA); music (MA); philosophy (MA).

**Park University,** School of Graduate and Professional Studies, Kansas City, MO 54105. Offers adult education (M Ed); business and government leadership (Graduate Certificate); business, government, and global society (MPA); communication and leadership (MA); creative and life writing (Graduate Certificate); disaster and emergency management (MPA, Graduate Certificate); educational leadership (M Ed); finance (MBA, Graduate Certificate); general business (MBA); global business (Graduate Certificate); healthcare administration (MHA); healthcare services management and leadership (Graduate Certificate); international business (MBA); language and literacy (M Ed), including English for speakers of other languages, special reading teacher/literacy coach; leadership of international healthcare organizations (Graduate Certificate); management information systems (MBA, Graduate Certificate); music performance (ADP, Graduate Certificate), including cello (MM, ADP), piano (MM, ADP), viola (MM, ADP), violin (MM, ADP); nonprofit and community services management (MPA); nonprofit leadership (Graduate Certificate); performance (MM), including cello (MM, ADP), piano (MM, ADP), viola (MM, ADP), violin (MM, ADP); public management (MPA); social work (MSW); teacher leadership (M Ed), including curriculum and assessment, instructional leader. *Program availability:* Part-time, evening/weekend, online learning. *Degree requirements:* For master's, comprehensive exam (for some programs), thesis (for some programs), internship (for some programs); exam (for some programs). *Entrance requirements:* For master's, GRE or GMAT (for some programs), teacher certification (for some M Ed programs), letters of recommendation, essay, resume (for some programs). Additional exam requirements/recommendations for international students: Required—TOEFL (minimum score 550 paper-based; 79 iBT), IELTS (minimum score 6). Electronic applications accepted.

**Penn State University Park,** Graduate School, College of Arts and Architecture, School of Music, University Park, PA 16802. Offers composition-theory (M Mus); conducting (M Mus); music (MA); music education (MME, PhD, Certificate); pedagogy and performance (M Mus); performance (M Mus); piano performance (DMA). *Accreditation:* NASM. *Unit head:* Dr. Barbara O. Korner, Dean, 814-865-2592, Fax: 814-865-2018. *Application contact:* Lori Hawn, Director, Graduate Student Services, 814-865-1795, Fax: 814-863-4627, E-mail: l-gswww@lists.psu.edu.
Website: http://music.psu.edu/

**Pensacola Christian College,** Graduate Studies, Pensacola, FL 32503-2267. Offers business administration (MBA); curriculum and instruction (MS, Ed D, Ed S); dramatics (MFA); educational leadership (MS, Ed D, Ed S); graphic design (MA, MFA); music (MA); nursing (MSN); performance studies (MA); studio art (MA, MFA).

**Phillips Theological Seminary,** Programs in Theology, Tulsa, OK 74116. Offers administration of church agencies (M Div); campus ministry (M Div); church-related social work (M Div); college and seminary teaching (M Div); global mission work (M Div); institutional chaplaincy (M Div); ministerial vocations in Christian education (M Div); ministry (D Min), including parish ministry, pastoral counseling, practices of ministry; ministry and culture (MAMC), including Christian education, congregational leadership, history and practice of Christian spirituality, theology, ethics, and culture; ministry of music (M Div); pastoral care and counseling (M Div); pastoral ministry (M Div); theological studies (MTS). *Accreditation:* ATS. *Program availability:* Part-time, online learning. *Degree requirements:* For master's, thesis (for some programs); for doctorate, thesis/dissertation. *Entrance requirements:* For master's, minimum GPA of 2.5; for doctorate, M Div, minimum GPA of 3.0. *Faculty research:* Biblical studies, historical studies, theology and culture, practical theology, theology and film.

**Pittsburg State University,** Graduate School, College of Arts and Sciences, Department of Music, Pittsburg, KS 66762. Offers conducting (MM), including choral, instrumental - orchestral, instrumental - wind, organ, piano, voice; education (MM), including instrumental, vocal; performance (MM), including harpsichord, percussion, strings, winds. *Accreditation:* NASM. *Students:* 16 (11 women); includes 1 minority (Two or more races, non-Hispanic/Latino), 7 international. In 2016, 7 master's awarded. *Degree requirements:* For master's, thesis or alternative. *Entrance requirements:* Additional exam requirements/recommendations for international students: Required—TOEFL (minimum score 520 paper-based; 68 iBT), IELTS (minimum score 6), PTE (minimum score 47). *Application deadline:* For fall admission, 7/15 for domestic students, 6/1 for international students; for spring admission, 12/15 for domestic students, 10/15 for international students; for summer admission, 5/15 for domestic students, 4/1 for international students. Applications are processed on a rolling basis. Application fee: $35 ($60 for international students). Electronic applications accepted. *Expenses:* Contact institution. *Financial support:* In 2016–17, 5 teaching assistantships with full tuition reimbursements (averaging $5,500 per year) were awarded; career-related internships or fieldwork, Federal Work-Study, and unspecified assistantships also available. Financial award application deadline: 2/1; financial award applicants required to submit FAFSA. *Unit head:* Dr. Susan Marchant, 620-235-4466, E-mail: smarchant@pittstate.edu. *Application contact:* Lisa Allen, Assistant Director of Graduate and Continuing Studies, 620-235-4223, Fax: 620-235-4219, E-mail: lallen@pittstate.edu.

**Point Park University,** Conservatory of Performing Arts, Pittsburgh, PA 15222-1984. Offers theatre arts-acting (MFA). *Degree requirements:* For master's, comprehensive exam (for some programs), thesis or alternative. *Entrance requirements:* For master's, interview, undergraduate degree in related field, theatre experience. Additional exam requirements/recommendations for international students: Required—TOEFL (minimum score 550 paper-based; 79 iBT). Electronic applications accepted.

**Portland State University,** Graduate Studies, College of the Arts, School of Music, Portland, OR 97207-0751. Offers conducting (MMC); music education (MAT, MST); performance (MMP). *Accreditation:* NASM. *Program availability:* Part-time. *Faculty:* 25 full-time (8 women), 52 part-time/adjunct (18 women). *Students:* 31 full-time (13 women), 7 part-time (4 women); includes 5 minority (1 Asian, non-Hispanic/Latino; 4 Two or more races, non-Hispanic/Latino), 5 international. Average age 30. 40 applicants, 65% accepted, 16 enrolled. In 2016, 12 master's awarded. *Degree requirements:* For master's, variable foreign language requirement, exit exam. *Entrance requirements:* For master's, GRE General Test, departmental exam, minimum GPA of 3.0 in upper-division course work or 2.75 overall. Additional exam requirements/recommendations for international students: Required—TOEFL (minimum score 550 paper-based). *Application deadline:* For fall admission, 4/15 priority date for domestic students, 4/15 for international students; for winter admission, 10/1 for domestic and international students; for spring admission, 12/1 for domestic and international students; for summer admission, 1/15 for domestic and international students. Application fee: $65. *Expenses:* Contact institution. *Financial support:* Teaching assistantships, Federal Work-Study, scholarships/grants, and unspecified assistantships available. Support available to part-time students. Financial award application deadline: 3/1; financial award applicants required to submit FAFSA. *Faculty research:* Composition, music analysis, music history, jazz. *Unit head:* Bonnie Miksch, Director, 503-725-3063, Fax: 503-725-8215, E-mail: bonnie@pdx.edu. *Application contact:* Ron Babcock, Graduate Coordinator, 503-725-3181, E-mail: babcocr@pdx.edu.
Website: https://www.pdx.edu/music/

**Pratt Institute,** School of Liberal Arts and Sciences, Program in Performance and Performance Studies, Brooklyn, NY 11205-3899. Offers MFA. *Students:* 18 full-time (13 women); includes 9 minority (5 Black or African American, non-Hispanic/Latino; 1 American Indian or Alaska Native, non-Hispanic/Latino; 2 Hispanic/Latino; 1 Two or more races, non-Hispanic/Latino), 3 international. Average age 32. 39 applicants, 87% accepted, 18 enrolled. *Degree requirements:* For master's, thesis. *Entrance requirements:* Additional exam requirements/recommendations for international students: Required—TOEFL. *Application deadline:* For fall admission, 1/5 for domestic and international students; for spring admission, 10/1 for domestic and international students. Application fee: $50 ($90 for international students). Electronic applications accepted. *Expenses:* $29,646 full-time tuition, $1,938 fees. *Financial support:* Career-related internships or fieldwork, Federal Work-Study, institutionally sponsored loans, scholarships/grants, health care benefits, and unspecified assistantships available. Support available to part-time students. Financial award application deadline: 2/1; financial award applicants required to submit FAFSA. *Unit head:* Andrew W. Barnes, Dean, 718-636-3570, Fax: 718-399-4586, E-mail: awbarnes@pratt.edu. *Application contact:* Natalie Capannelli, Director of Graduate Admissions, 718-636-3551, Fax: 718-399-4242, E-mail: ncapanne@pratt.edu.
Website: https://www.pratt.edu/academics/liberal-arts-and-sciences/performance-and-performance-studies/

**See Display on page 746 and Close-Up on page 769.**

**Princeton University,** Graduate School, Department of Music, Princeton, NJ 08544-1019. Offers composition (PhD); musicology (PhD). *Degree requirements:* For doctorate, variable foreign language requirement, thesis/dissertation. *Entrance requirements:* For doctorate, GRE General Test, sample of written work. Additional exam requirements/recommendations for international students: Required—TOEFL (minimum score 600 paper-based). Electronic applications accepted. *Faculty research:* Computer synthesis, history of Western music, comparative musicology, theory.

**Purchase College, State University of New York,** Conservatory of Music, Purchase, NY 10577-1400. Offers classical composition (MM); instrumental performance (MM); jazz studies (MM); studio composition (MM); voice and opera studies (MM). *Degree requirements:* For master's, thesis or alternative, composition, performance. *Entrance requirements:* For master's, audition. *Application deadline:* For fall admission, 1/15 for domestic students; for spring admission, 10/15 for domestic students. Application fee: $85. Electronic applications accepted. *Expenses:* Tuition, state resident: full-time $10,870; part-time $453 per credit. Tuition, nonresident: full-time $22,210; part-time $925 per credit. *Required fees:* $1737. *Financial support:* Fellowships, teaching assistantships, career-related internships or fieldwork, Federal Work-Study, scholarships/grants, and tuition waivers (partial) available. Support available to part-time students. Financial award application deadline: 3/15; financial award applicants required to submit FAFSA. *Unit head:* James Undercofler, Interim Director, 914-251-6700, Fax: 914-251-6739, E-mail: james.undercofler@purchase.edu. *Application contact:* Sabrina Johnston, Admission Counselor, 914-251-6479, Fax: 914-251-6314, E-mail: admissn@purchase.edu.
Website: https://www.purchase.edu/academics/music/

**Queens College of the City University of New York,** Arts and Humanities Division, Aaron Copland School of Music, Queens, NY 11367-1597. Offers classical performance (MM, Advanced Diploma); jazz studies (MM); music (MA); music (PreK-12) (MS Ed); performance (Advanced Certificate). *Program availability:* Part-time. *Faculty:* 26 full-time (7 women), 67 part-time/adjunct (32 women). *Students:* 17 full-time (4 women), 166 part-time (73 women); includes 58 minority (8 Black or African American, non-Hispanic/Latino; 19 Asian, non-Hispanic/Latino; 23 Hispanic/Latino; 8 Two or more races, non-Hispanic/Latino), 54 international. Average age 30. 197 applicants, 57% accepted, 61 enrolled. In 2016, 97 master's, 16 other advanced degrees awarded. *Degree*

*requirements:* For master's, qualifying exams, recital. *Entrance requirements:* For master's, audition, bachelor's degree in music, minimum GPA of 3.0. Additional exam requirements/recommendations for international students: Required—TOEFL, IELTS. *Application deadline:* For fall admission, 4/1 for domestic students; for spring admission, 11/1 for domestic students. Applications are processed on a rolling basis. Application fee: $125. Electronic applications accepted. *Expenses:* Tuition, state resident: full-time $5065; part-time $425 per credit. Tuition, nonresident: part-time $780 per credit. *Required fees:* $522; $397 per credit. Part-time tuition and fees vary according to course load and program. *Financial support:* Career-related internships or fieldwork, Federal Work-Study, institutionally sponsored loans, and tuition waivers (partial) available. Support available to part-time students. Financial award application deadline: 4/1; financial award applicants required to submit FAFSA. *Unit head:* Dr. Edward Smaldone, Chair/Director, 718-997-3800, E-mail: edward.smaldone@qc.cuny.edu.

**Radford University,** College of Graduate Studies and Research, Program in Music, Radford, VA 24142. Offers MA, MS. *Accreditation:* NASM. *Program availability:* Part-time. *Faculty:* 9 full-time (3 women), 3 part-time/adjunct (1 woman). *Students:* 17 full-time (11 women), 2 part-time (1 woman); includes 4 minority (1 Black or African American, non-Hispanic/Latino; 1 Asian, non-Hispanic/Latino; 1 Hispanic/Latino; 1 Two or more races, non-Hispanic/Latino). Average age 32. 10 applicants, 90% accepted, 9 enrolled. In 2016, 6 master's awarded. *Degree requirements:* For master's, comprehensive exam, thesis or alternative. *Entrance requirements:* For master's, GRE or PRAXIS II (music content knowledge), minimum GPA of 2.75, 3 letters of reference, resume, official transcripts. Additional exam requirements/recommendations for international students: Required—TOEFL (minimum score 550 paper-based; 79 iBT), IELTS (minimum score 6.5). *Application deadline:* For fall admission, 2/15 priority date for domestic students, 12/1 for international students; for spring admission, 7/1 for international students. Applications are processed on a rolling basis. Application fee: $50. Electronic applications accepted. *Expenses:* Tuition, state resident: full-time $7868; part-time $328 per credit hour. Tuition, nonresident: full-time $16,394; part-time $683 per credit hour. *Required fees:* $3090; $130 per credit hour. Tuition and fees vary according to course load and program. *Financial support:* In 2016–17, 15 students received support, including 1 research assistantship (averaging $11,000 per year), 6 teaching assistantships (averaging $9,917 per year); scholarships/grants and unspecified assistantships also available. Support available to part-time students. Financial award application deadline: 3/1; financial award applicants required to submit FAFSA. *Unit head:* Dr. Trish Winter, Coordinator, 540-831-6174, E-mail: pwinter3@radford.edu.
Website: http://www.radford.edu/content/cvpa/home/music.html

**Rice University,** Graduate Programs, Shepherd School of Music, Houston, TX 77251-1892. Offers composition (MM, DMA); conducting (MM); musicology (MM); performance (MM, DMA); theory (MM). *Degree requirements:* For master's, thesis (for some programs), 2 recitals; for doctorate, one foreign language, comprehensive exam, thesis/dissertation, 4 recitals. *Entrance requirements:* For master's, GRE General Test (musicology); for doctorate, GRE General Test. Additional exam requirements/recommendations for international students: Required—TOEFL (minimum score 600 paper-based; 100 iBT), IELTS (minimum score 7). *Faculty research:* Musicology, performance, theory, composition.

**Rider University,** Westminster Choir College, Programs in Music, Lawrenceville, NJ 08648-3001. Offers choral conducting (MM); composition (MM); organ performance (MM); piano accompanying and coaching (MM); piano pedagogy and performance (MM); piano performance (MM); sacred music (MM); vocal pedagogy and performance (MM); vocal training (MVP). *Accreditation:* NASM. *Program availability:* Part-time. *Degree requirements:* For master's, variable foreign language requirement, departmental qualifying exam. *Entrance requirements:* For master's, audition, interview, repertoire list, 2 letters of reference, resume. Additional exam requirements/recommendations for international students: Required—TOEFL (minimum score 525 paper-based). Electronic applications accepted.

**Roosevelt University,** Graduate Division, Chicago College of Performing Arts, The Music Conservatory, Chicago, IL 60605. Offers music (MM); piano pedagogy (Diploma). *Program availability:* Part-time, evening/weekend.

**Rowan University,** Graduate School, College of Performing Arts, Program in Performance, Glassboro, NJ 08028-1701. Offers MM. *Accreditation:* NASM. *Program availability:* Part-time, evening/weekend. *Degree requirements:* For master's, thesis (for some programs). *Entrance requirements:* For master's, GRE General Test. Additional exam requirements/recommendations for international students: Required—TOEFL. Electronic applications accepted.

**Rutgers University–Newark,** Graduate School, Program in Jazz History and Research, Newark, NJ 07102. Offers MA. *Entrance requirements:* For master's, GRE, minimum B average. Electronic applications accepted.

**Rutgers University–New Brunswick,** Mason Gross School of the Arts, Music Department, New Brunswick, NJ 08901. Offers collaborative piano (MM, DMA); conducting: choral (MM, DMA); conducting: instrumental (MM, DMA); conducting: orchestral (MM, DMA); jazz studies (MM); music (DMA, AD); music education (MM, DMA); music performance (MM). *Accreditation:* NASM. *Degree requirements:* For doctorate, one foreign language. *Entrance requirements:* For master's and doctorate, audition. Additional exam requirements/recommendations for international students: Required—TOEFL (minimum score 550 paper-based), IELTS (minimum score 7). Electronic applications accepted. *Faculty research:* Performance, twentieth century music, jazz, music education.

**St. Cloud State University,** School of Graduate Studies, College of Liberal Arts, Department of Music, St. Cloud, MN 56301-4498. Offers conducting and literature (MM); music education (MM); piano pedagogy (MM). *Degree requirements:* For master's, comprehensive exam (for some programs), thesis or alternative. *Entrance requirements:* For master's, GRE General Test, minimum GPA of 2.75. Additional exam requirements/recommendations for international students: Required—TOEFL (minimum score 550 paper-based; 79 iBT), IELTS (minimum score 6.5), Michigan English Language Assessment Battery. Electronic applications accepted.

**Saint John's University,** Saint John's School of Theology and Seminary, Collegeville, MN 56321. Offers divinity (M Div); liturgical music (MA); liturgical studies (MA); pastoral ministry (MA); theology (MA), including church history, liturgy, monastic studies, scripture, spirituality, systematics; M Div/MA. *Program availability:* Part-time, online learning. *Degree requirements:* For master's, one foreign language, comprehensive exam (for some programs), thesis (for some programs). *Entrance requirements:* For master's, GRE General Test or MAT. Electronic applications accepted. *Faculty research:* Religious education, biblical literature.

**Samford University,** School of the Arts, Birmingham, AL 35229. Offers design studies (MS); music (MM); music education (MME). MME program offered in traditional, fifth year non-traditional, and national board cohort formats. *Accreditation:* NASM. *Program availability:* Part-time, evening/weekend, online learning. *Faculty:* 9 full-time (4 women), 3 part-time/adjunct (1 woman). *Students:* 11 full-time (5 women); includes 4 minority (all Black or African American, non-Hispanic/Latino), 1 international. Average age 30. 9 applicants, 100% accepted, 5 enrolled. In 2016, 7 master's awarded. Terminal master's awarded for partial completion of doctoral program. *Degree requirements:* For master's, comprehensive exam, recital. *Entrance requirements:* For master's, audition. Additional exam requirements/recommendations for international students: Required—TOEFL (minimum score 90 iBT). *Application deadline:* For fall admission, 11/15 for domestic and international students; for spring admission, 4/15 for domestic and international students; for summer admission, 8/1 for domestic and international students. Applications are processed on a rolling basis. Application fee: $35. Electronic applications accepted. *Expenses: Tuition:* Full-time $18,530; part-time $789 per credit hour. *Required fees:* $610. Tuition and fees vary according to course load, degree level, program and student level. *Financial support:* In 2016–17, 10 students received support. Federal Work-Study, scholarships/grants, and unspecified assistantships available. Financial award application deadline: 3/1; financial award applicants required to submit FAFSA. *Unit head:* Dr. Joseph Hopkin, Dean of the School of the Arts/Professor, 205-726-2778, Fax: 205-726-2615, E-mail: jhopkins@samford.edu. *Application contact:* Dr. Demondrae L. Thurman, Director of Graduate Studies/Professor of Music, 205-726-2389, Fax: 205-726-2615, E-mail: dthurman@samford.edu. Website: http://www.samford.edu/arts

**Sam Houston State University,** College of Fine Arts and Mass Communication, School of Music, Huntsville, TX 77341. Offers MM. *Accreditation:* NASM. *Program availability:* Part-time. *Degree requirements:* For master's, comprehensive exam, thesis, departmental qualifying exam. *Entrance requirements:* For master's, GRE General Test, letters of recommendation, audition/interview. Additional exam requirements/recommendations for international students: Required—TOEFL (minimum score 550 paper-based; 79 iBT), IELTS (minimum score 6.5). Electronic applications accepted.

**San Diego State University,** Graduate and Research Affairs, College of Professional Studies and Fine Arts, School of Music and Dance, San Diego, CA 92182. Offers composition (acoustic and electronic) (MM); conducting (MM); ethnomusicology (MA); jazz studies (MM); musicology (MA); performance (MM); piano pedagogy (MA); theory (MA). *Degree requirements:* For master's, comprehensive exam (for some programs), thesis (for some programs). *Entrance requirements:* For master's, GRE General Test, bachelor's degree in related field, 2 letters of reference. Additional exam requirements/recommendations for international students: Required—TOEFL. Electronic applications accepted.

**San Francisco Conservatory of Music,** Graduate Division, San Francisco, CA 94102. Offers brass (MM), including bass trombone, horn, tenor trombone, trumpet, tuba; chamber music (MM, Artist Certificate), including cello, piano, preformed string quartet, viola, violin; composition (MM); conducting (MM); guitar (MM); harp (MM); percussion (MM), including marimba, timpani; piano (MM, MM), including harpsichord (MM), historical keyboard (MM), organ (MM). *Faculty:* 26 full-time (7 women), 94 part-time/adjunct (31 women). *Students:* 211 full-time (122 women), 2 part-time (0 women); includes 42 minority (6 Black or African American, non-Hispanic/Latino; 1 American Indian or Alaska Native, non-Hispanic/Latino; 20 Asian, non-Hispanic/Latino; 8 Hispanic/Latino; 1 Native Hawaiian or other Pacific Islander, non-Hispanic/Latino; 6 Two or more races, non-Hispanic/Latino), 83 international. Average age 25. 684 applicants, 39% accepted, 131 enrolled. In 2016, 99 master's, 29 other advanced degrees awarded. *Degree requirements:* For master's and Artist Certificate, variable foreign language requirement, 1-2 recitals, 1-3 juried performances. *Entrance requirements:* For master's and Artist Certificate, recommendations, transcripts, audition. Additional exam requirements/recommendations for international students: Required—TOEFL (minimum score 500 paper-based; 80 iBT). *Application deadline:* For fall admission, 12/1 for domestic and international students; for spring admission, 10/1 for domestic and international students. Application fee: $110. Electronic applications accepted. *Expenses: Tuition:* Full-time $42,400; part-time $1868 per credit. *Required fees:* $1010; $1010 per credit. One-time fee: $50 full-time. Tuition and fees vary according to course load. *Financial support:* In 2016–17, 212 students received support. Federal Work-Study, scholarships/grants, tuition waivers (partial), and unspecified assistantships available. Financial award application deadline: 2/15; financial award applicants required to submit FAFSA. *Unit head:* Kate Sheeran, Provost and Dean, 415-503-6251, Fax: 415-503-6205, E-mail: lnickels@sfcm.edu. *Application contact:* Melissa Cocco-Mitten, Director of Admission, 415-503-6231, Fax: 415-503-6299, E-mail: admit@sfcm.edu. Website: http://www.sfcm.edu/

**San Francisco State University,** Division of Graduate Studies, College of Liberal and Creative Arts, School of Music, San Francisco, CA 94132-1722. Offers chamber music (MM); classical performance (MM); composition (MA); conducting (MM); music education (MA); music history (MA). *Accreditation:* NASM. *Expenses:* Tuition, state resident: full-time $6738. Tuition, nonresident: full-time $15,666. *Required fees:* $1012. Tuition and fees vary according to degree level and program. *Unit head:* Dr. Cyrus Ginwala, Director, 415-405-0486, Fax: 415-338-3294, E-mail: cginwala@sfsu.edu. *Application contact:* Easther Oh, Academic Office Coordinator, 415-338-7613, Fax: 415-338-3294, E-mail: music@sfsu.edu. Website: http://music.sfsu.edu/

**San Jose State University,** Graduate Studies and Research, College of Humanities and the Arts, San Jose, CA 95192-0001. Offers art (MA, MFA), including art history and visual culture (MA), digital media art (MFA), photography (MFA), pictorial art (MFA), spatial art (MFA); computational linguistics (Certificate); English (MA, MFA), including creative writing (MFA); French (MA); humanities and arts (Certificate); linguistics (MA); music (MA); philosophy (MA); professional and technical communication (Certificate); Spanish (MA); teaching English to speakers of other languages (MA); TESOL (Certificate); theatre arts (MA). Electronic applications accepted.

**Savannah College of Art and Design,** Graduate School, Program in Performing Arts, Savannah, GA 31402-3146. Offers MFA. *Faculty:* 13 full-time (5 women), 6 part-time/adjunct (4 women). *Students:* 41 full-time (26 women), 2 part-time (both women); includes 16 minority (13 Black or African American, non-Hispanic/Latino; 1 American Indian or Alaska Native, non-Hispanic/Latino; 2 Hispanic/Latino), 1 international. Average age 26. 92 applicants, 60% accepted, 20 enrolled. In 2016, 28 master's awarded. *Degree requirements:* For master's, thesis. *Entrance requirements:* For master's, GRE (recommended), portfolio (submitted in digital format), audition or writing submission, resume, statement of purpose, two letters of recommendation. Additional exam requirements/recommendations for international students: Required—TOEFL (minimum score 550 paper-based, 85 iBT), IELTS (minimum score 6.5), or ACTFL. *Application deadline:* For fall admission, 4/1 for domestic and international students. Applications are processed on a rolling basis. Application fee: $40. Electronic applications accepted. *Expenses: Tuition:* Full-time $36,045. Tuition and fees vary according to course load. *Financial support:* Career-related internships or fieldwork, Federal Work-Study, and scholarships/grants available. Financial award application deadline: 4/1; financial award applicants required to submit FAFSA. *Unit head:* Mark Tymchyshyn, Chair, Performing Arts. *Application contact:* Jenny Jaquillard, Executive Director of Admissions, Recruitment and Events, 912-525-5100, Fax: 912-525-5985, E-mail: admission@scad.edu. Website: http://www.scad.edu/academics/programs/performing-arts

**School of the Art Institute of Chicago,** Graduate Division, Department of Performance, Chicago, IL 60603-3103. Offers MFA. *Entrance requirements:* Additional

exam requirements/recommendations for international students: Required—TOEFL, IELTS.

**Shenandoah University,** Shenandoah Conservatory, Winchester, VA 22601-5195. Offers church music (MM, Certificate); collaborative piano (MM); composition (MM); conducting (MM); music (Artist Diploma); music education (MME); music therapy (MMT); pedagogy - voice (MM, DMA); performance (MM, DMA); performing arts leadership and management (MS). *Accreditation:* NASM. *Program availability:* Part-time. *Faculty:* 36 full-time (13 women), 12 part-time/adjunct (6 women). *Students:* 70 full-time (40 women), 71 part-time (43 women); includes 25 minority (7 Black or African American, non-Hispanic/Latino; 2 American Indian or Alaska Native, non-Hispanic/Latino; 5 Asian, non-Hispanic/Latino; 11 Hispanic/Latino), 21 international. Average age 31. 121 applicants, 79% accepted, 47 enrolled. In 2016, 29 master's, 7 doctorates, 9 other advanced degrees awarded. *Degree requirements:* For master's, comprehensive exam, minimum GPA of 3.0, internship (MS), recital (MM), research teaching project or thesis (MME), project (MA); for doctorate, comprehensive exam, minimum GPA of 3.0, dissertation or teaching project, recital; for other advanced degree, minimum GPA of 3.0, research project, recital. *Entrance requirements:* For master's, music theory diagnostic exam, bachelor's degree with minimum of GPA of 2.5, performance audition, writing sample, resume, all academic transcripts; for doctorate, music theory diagnostic exam; music history diagnostic exam; vocal diction proficiency exam, master's degree with minimum GPA of 3.25, performance audition, 2 letters of recommendation, writing sample, resume, all academic transcripts; for other advanced degree, bachelor's or master's degree; minimum GPA of 2.5; performance audition (for Artist Diploma). Additional exam requirements/recommendations for international students: Required—TOEFL (minimum score 550 paper-based; 79 iBT), IELTS (minimum score 6.5). *Application deadline:* For fall and spring admission, 1/15 for domestic and international students; for summer admission, 4/15 for domestic and international students. Application fee: $30. Electronic applications accepted. *Expenses:* Contact institution. *Financial support:* In 2016–17, 43 students received support. Scholarships/grants and unspecified assistantships available. Financial award applicants required to submit FAFSA. *Faculty research:* Brahms, Scriabin, arts as inquiry. *Unit head:* Dr. Michael J. Stepniak, Dean, 540-542.6201, Fax: 540-665-5402, E-mail: mstepnia@su.edu. *Application contact:* Andrew Woodall, Executive Director of Recruitment and Advancement, 540-665-4581, Fax: 540-665-4627, E-mail: admit@su.edu. Website: http://www.su.edu/conservatory/

**Shepherd University,** Cornel School of Contemporary Music, Los Angeles, CA 90065. Offers MM. *Entrance requirements:* For master's, official college/university transcripts, bachelor's degree, audition. Electronic applications accepted.

**Silver Lake College of the Holy Family,** Graduate School, Graduate Music Program, Manitowoc, WI 54220-9319. Offers music education-Kodaly emphasis (MM). *Accreditation:* NASM. *Program availability:* Part-time, online learning. *Faculty:* 1 full-time (0 women), 3 part-time/adjunct (1 woman). *Students:* Average age 39. In 2016, 2 master's awarded. *Degree requirements:* For master's, comprehensive exam, thesis, capstone culminating project, comprehensive portfolio, public presentation of skills, or thesis research. *Entrance requirements:* For master's, ACT (preferred) or SAT, minimum undergraduate GPA of 3.0. Additional exam requirements/recommendations for international students: Required—TOEFL (minimum score 550 paper-based; 89 iBT). *Application deadline:* For summer admission, 6/1 for domestic and international students. Applications are processed on a rolling basis. Application fee: $50. Electronic applications accepted. *Expenses:* $540 per credit; $220 comprehensive fee. *Financial support:* Career-related internships or fieldwork, Federal Work-Study, scholarships/grants, and unspecified assistantships available. Support available to part-time students. Financial award application deadline: 6/1; financial award applicants required to submit FAFSA. *Faculty research:* Effects of prenatal music on bonding and stimulation, music and the brain, early childhood music, effective use of smart music for choral and general music areas. *Unit head:* Nancy Sim, Director of Graduate Education Programs, 920-686-6117, Fax: 920-686-6322, E-mail: nancy.sim@sl.edu. *Application contact:* Jamie A. Grant, Executive Director of Enrollment Management, 920-686-6175, Fax: 920-686-6322, E-mail: jamie.grant@sl.edu. Website: http://www.sl.edu/future-students/kod%C3%A1ly-summer-graduate-music

**Southeastern Baptist Theological Seminary,** Graduate and Professional Programs, Wake Forest, NC 27588-1889. Offers advanced biblical studies (M Div); Christian education (M Div, MACE); Christian ethics (PhD); Christian ministry (M Div); Christian planting (M Div); church music (MACM); counseling (MACO); evangelism (PhD); language (M Div); ministry (D Min); New Testament (PhD); Old Testament (PhD); philosophy (PhD); theology (Th M, PhD); women's studies (M Div). *Accreditation:* ACIPE; ATS (one or more programs are accredited). *Degree requirements:* For master's, thesis (for some programs), oral exam; for doctorate, thesis/dissertation, fieldwork. *Entrance requirements:* For master's, Cooperative English Test, minimum GPA of 2.0, M Div or equivalent (Th M); for doctorate, GRE General Test or MAT, Cooperative English Test, M Div or equivalent, 3 years of professional experience.

**Southeastern Louisiana University,** College of Arts, Humanities and Social Sciences, Department of Fine and Performing Arts, Hammond, LA 70402. Offers choral conducting (M Mus); instrumental conducting (M Mus); music performance (M Mus); music theory (M Mus). *Accreditation:* NASM. *Faculty:* 9 full-time (2 women), 5 part-time/adjunct (2 women). *Students:* 18 full-time (8 women); includes 2 minority (1 Black or African American, non-Hispanic/Latino; 1 Asian, non-Hispanic/Latino), 9 international. Average age 28. 11 applicants, 73% accepted, 4 enrolled. In 2016, 11 master's awarded. *Degree requirements:* For master's, comprehensive exam, thesis (for some programs). *Entrance requirements:* For master's, BM; senior recital (for performance program). Additional exam requirements/recommendations for international students: Required—IELTS (minimum score 5.5); Recommended—TOEFL (minimum score 500 paper-based; 61 iBT). *Application deadline:* For fall admission, 7/15 priority date for domestic students, 6/1 priority date for international students; for spring admission, 12/1 priority date for domestic students, 10/1 priority date for international students. Applications are processed on a rolling basis. Application fee: $20 ($30 for international students). Electronic applications accepted. *Expenses:* Tuition, state resident: full-time $6540; part-time $465 per credit hour. Tuition, nonresident: full-time $19,017; part-time $1158 per credit hour. *Required fees:* $1829. *Financial support:* In 2016–17, 11 students received support, including 11 teaching assistantships (averaging $9,664 per year); research assistantships, career-related internships or fieldwork, Federal Work-Study, institutionally sponsored loans, scholarships/grants, traineeships, and unspecified assistantships also available. Support available to part-time students. Financial award application deadline: 5/1; financial award applicants required to submit FAFSA. *Faculty research:* Wind band performance and repertoire for young audiences, pedagogical piano music of contemporary American composers, spectral music composition, intonation and extended woodwind techniques. *Unit head:* Dale Newkirk, Interim Department Head, 985-549-2184, Fax: 985-549-2892, E-mail: dale.newkirk@southeastern.edu. *Application contact:* Amanda Harper, Graduate Admissions Analyst, 985-549-5620, Fax: 985-549-5632, E-mail: admissions@southeastern.edu. Website: http://www.selu.edu/acad_research/depts/arts/

## Music

**Southern Illinois University Carbondale,** Graduate School, College of Liberal Arts, School of Music, Carbondale, IL 62901-4701. Offers MM. *Accreditation:* NASM. *Program availability:* Part-time. *Degree requirements:* For master's, one foreign language, thesis or alternative. *Entrance requirements:* For master's, audition, minimum GPA of 2.7. Additional exam requirements/recommendations for international students: Required—TOEFL. *Faculty research:* Performance practices, historical research, operatic development.

**Southern Illinois University Edwardsville,** Graduate School, College of Arts and Sciences, Department of Music, Program in Music, Edwardsville, IL 62026-0001. Offers music education (MM); music performance (MM). *Accreditation:* NASM. *Program availability:* Part-time. *Degree requirements:* For master's, one foreign language, thesis (for some programs), recital. *Entrance requirements:* Additional exam requirements/ recommendations for international students: Required—TOEFL (minimum score 550 paper-based; 79 iBT), IELTS (minimum score 6.5). Electronic applications accepted.

**Southern Methodist University,** Meadows School of the Arts, Division of Music, Dallas, TX 75275. Offers composition (MM); conducting (MM), including choral, instrumental; music education (MM); music history and literature (MM); performance (MM), including harpsichord, orchestral instrument, organ, piano, voice; piano performance and pedagogy (MM); theory pedagogy (MM). *Accreditation:* NASM. *Program availability:* Part-time. *Degree requirements:* For master's, variable foreign language requirement, comprehensive exam, project, recital, or thesis. *Entrance requirements:* For master's, placement exams in music history and theory, audition, bachelor's degree in music or equivalent; minimum GPA of 3.0; research paper in history, theory, education. Additional exam requirements/recommendations for international students: Required—TOEFL (minimum score 550 paper-based; 80 iBT). Electronic applications accepted. *Faculty research:* Music perception and cognition, computer-based instruction, music medicine and therapy, theoretical and historical analysis-medieval to contemporary.

**Southern Oregon University,** Graduate Studies, Department of Music, Ashland, OR 97520. Offers performance (MM). *Accreditation:* NASM. *Program availability:* Part-time. *Faculty:* 7 full-time (2 women), 11 part-time/adjunct (6 women). *Students:* 9 full-time (4 women); includes 3 minority (1 American Indian or Alaska Native, non-Hispanic/Latino; 2 Asian, non-Hispanic/Latino). Average age 26. 13 applicants, 54% accepted, 4 enrolled. In 2016, 6 master's awarded. *Entrance requirements:* For master's, undergraduate degree with music major, audition, three letters of recommendation. *Application deadline:* For fall admission, 7/31 priority date for domestic and international students; for winter admission, 11/15 priority date for domestic and international students; for spring admission, 1/7 priority date for domestic and international students. Application fee: $60. *Expenses:* Tuition, state resident: full-time $10,719; part-time $397 per credit. Tuition, nonresident: full-time $13,419; part-time $497 per credit. *Required fees:* $548. *Financial support:* In 2016–17, 4 students received support, including 4 research assistantships with partial tuition reimbursements available. *Unit head:* Dr. Vicki Purslow, Graduate Program Coordinator, 541-552-6538, E-mail: purslowv@sou.edu. *Application contact:* Kelly Moutsatson, Director of Admissions, 541-552-6411, Fax: 541-552-8403, E-mail: admissions@sou.edu.

**Southern Utah University,** Program in Music, Cedar City, UT 84720-2498. Offers music education (MM Ed); music technology (MM). *Program availability:* Part-time, 100% online. *Faculty:* 2 full-time (1 woman), 3 part-time/adjunct. *Students:* 13 full-time (4 women), 8 part-time (2 women); includes 1 minority (Hispanic/Latino). Average age 30. 15 applicants, 100% accepted, 14 enrolled. *Entrance requirements:* Additional exam requirements/recommendations for international students: Required—TOEFL (minimum score 550 paper-based; 79 iBT), IELTS (minimum score 6). Application fee: $60 ($65 for international students). *Expenses:* $7,692 per year resident or online full-time; $23,384 per year on-campus non-resident full-time. *Unit head:* Dr. Keith Bradshaw, Department Chair, 435-586-7891, E-mail: bradshaw@suu.edu.

**Southwestern Baptist Theological Seminary,** School of Church Music, Fort Worth, TX 76122-0000. Offers MACM, MAWSHP, MM, DMA, PhD. *Accreditation:* NASM. *Program availability:* Part-time. Terminal master's awarded for partial completion of doctoral program. *Degree requirements:* For master's, comprehensive exam, thesis; for doctorate, comprehensive exam, thesis/dissertation. *Entrance requirements:* For master's, audition; for doctorate, MM or equivalent. Additional exam requirements/ recommendations for international students: Required—TOEFL. Electronic applications accepted.

**Southwestern Oklahoma State University,** College of Arts and Sciences, Department of Music, Weatherford, OK 73096-3098. Offers music education (MM); performance (MM). *Accreditation:* NASM. *Program availability:* Part-time. *Degree requirements:* For master's, comprehensive exam, recital (music performance). *Entrance requirements:* For master's, minimum GPA of 2.5. Additional exam requirements/recommendations for international students: Required—TOEFL.

**Stanford University,** School of Humanities and Sciences, Department of Music, Stanford, CA 94305-2004. Offers composition (DMA); computer-based music theory and acoustics (PhD); music, science, and technology (MA); musicology (PhD). Terminal master's awarded for partial completion of doctoral program. *Degree requirements:* For master's, variable foreign language requirement, thesis or alternative, project; for doctorate, variable foreign language requirement, thesis/dissertation (for some programs), qualifying, special area, and oral exams (PhD); composition project and lecture-demonstration exams (DMA). *Entrance requirements:* For master's and doctorate, GRE General Test, departmental theory/analysis test, samples of work. Additional exam requirements/recommendations for international students: Required—TOEFL. Electronic applications accepted. *Expenses: Tuition:* Full-time $47,331. *Required fees:* $609.

**State University of New York at Fredonia,** School of Music, Fredonia, NY 14063. Offers music education (MM); music performance (MM); music theory/composition (MM); music therapy (MM). *Accreditation:* NASM. *Program availability:* Part-time. *Faculty:* 44 full-time (17 women), 58 part-time/adjunct (31 women). *Students:* 31 full-time (21 women), 14 part-time (11 women); includes 4 minority (2 Asian, non-Hispanic/ Latino; 1 Hispanic/Latino; 1 Two or more races, non-Hispanic/Latino), 12 international. Average age 25. 46 applicants, 72% accepted, 14 enrolled. In 2016, 16 master's awarded. *Degree requirements:* For master's, comprehensive exam (for some programs), thesis or final project/recital. *Entrance requirements:* For master's, audition. Additional exam requirements/recommendations for international students: Required—TOEFL (minimum score 79 iBT), IELTS (minimum score 6.5). *Application deadline:* For fall admission, 4/1 priority date for domestic and international students; for spring admission, 11/1 priority date for domestic students, 11/1 for international students. Applications are processed on a rolling basis. Application fee: $75. Electronic applications accepted. *Expenses:* Tuition, state resident: full-time $10,370; part-time $453 per credit. Tuition, nonresident: full-time $20,190; part-time $925 per credit. *Required fees:* $1619; $67.30 per credit hour. $403.80 per semester. *Financial support:* In 2016–17, 14 students received support, including 4 fellowships (averaging $7,314 per year). Financial award application deadline: 3/15; financial award applicants required to submit FAFSA. *Unit head:* Dr. Melvin Unger, Director, School of Music, 716-673-3151, E-mail: melvin.unger@fredonia.edu. *Application contact:* Dr. Barry Kilpatrick, Admissions Coordinator, School of Music, 716-673-4635, E-mail: barry.kilpatrick@fredonia.edu. Website: http://www.fredonia.edu/music/

**State University of New York at New Paltz,** Graduate School, School of Fine and Performing Arts, Department of Music, New Paltz, NY 12561. Offers music therapy (MS). *Accreditation:* NASM. *Program availability:* Part-time. *Students:* 22 full-time (15 women), 11 part-time (9 women); includes 3 minority (1 Black or African American, non-Hispanic/Latino; 2 Hispanic/Latino), 7 international. 16 applicants, 81% accepted, 9 enrolled. In 2016, 10 master's awarded. *Degree requirements:* For master's, thesis. *Entrance requirements:* For master's, audition, minimum GPA of 3.0. Additional exam requirements/recommendations for international students: Required—TOEFL (minimum score 550 paper-based; 80 iBT), IELTS (minimum score 6.5). *Application deadline:* For fall admission, 5/15 for domestic and international students; for spring admission, 11/15 for domestic and international students. Applications are processed on a rolling basis. Application fee: $50. Electronic applications accepted. *Financial support:* In 2016–17, 4 teaching assistantships with partial tuition reimbursements (averaging $5,000 per year) were awarded. Financial award application deadline: 8/1. *Unit head:* Dr. John Mahoney, Program Director, 845-257-2709, E-mail: mahoneyj@newpaltz.edu. Website: http://www.newpaltz.edu/music/

**State University of New York College at Potsdam,** Crane School of Music, Potsdam, NY 13676. Offers music education (MM); music performance (MM). *Program availability:* Part-time. *Degree requirements:* For master's, variable foreign language requirement, thesis (for some programs). *Entrance requirements:* For master's, audition, minimum GPA of 3.0. Additional exam requirements/recommendations for international students: Required—TOEFL (minimum score 550 paper-based; 80 iBT), IELTS (minimum score 6). Electronic applications accepted.

**Stephen F. Austin State University,** Graduate School, College of Fine Arts, School of Music, Nacogdoches, TX 75962. Offers MA, MM. *Accreditation:* NASM (one or more programs are accredited). *Program availability:* Part-time. *Degree requirements:* For master's, comprehensive exam, thesis optional. *Entrance requirements:* For master's, GRE General Test, audition. Additional exam requirements/recommendations for international students: Required—TOEFL. *Faculty research:* Music classroom methodology, serial music, seventeenth century sacred music, vocal pedagogy, organ duet literature.

**Stony Brook University, State University of New York,** Graduate School, College of Arts and Sciences, Department of Music, Program in Music History/Theory, Stony Brook, NY 11794. Offers MA, PhD. *Students:* 28 full-time (10 women), 3 part-time (0 women); includes 2 minority (both Hispanic/Latino), 4 international. Average age 30. 46 applicants, 37% accepted, 4 enrolled. In 2016, 2 master's, 4 doctorates awarded. *Degree requirements:* For doctorate, thesis/dissertation. *Entrance requirements:* For master's and doctorate, GRE General Test. Additional exam requirements/ recommendations for international students: Required—TOEFL (minimum score 90 iBT). *Application deadline:* For fall admission, 1/15 for domestic students; for spring admission, 10/1 for domestic students. Application fee: $100. Electronic applications accepted. *Expenses:* Contact institution. *Financial support:* In 2016–17, 13 teaching assistantships were awarded. *Unit head:* Dr. Perry Goldstein, Chair, 631-632-7340, E-mail: perry.goldstein@stonybrook.edu. *Application contact:* Monica Gentile, Coordinator, 631-632-7340, Fax: 631-632-7404, E-mail: monica.gentile@stonybrook.edu.

**Stony Brook University, State University of New York,** Graduate School, College of Arts and Sciences, Department of Music, Program in Music Performance, Stony Brook, NY 11794. Offers MM, DMA. *Students:* 194 full-time (93 women), 9 part-time (6 women); includes 36 minority (1 Black or African American, non-Hispanic/Latino; 19 Asian, non-Hispanic/Latino; 9 Hispanic/Latino; 7 Two or more races, non-Hispanic/Latino), 71 international. 293 applicants, 26% accepted, 41 enrolled. In 2016, 13 master's, 39 doctorates awarded. *Degree requirements:* For doctorate, thesis/dissertation. *Entrance requirements:* For master's and doctorate, GRE General Test. Additional exam requirements/recommendations for international students: Required—TOEFL (minimum score 90 iBT). *Application deadline:* For fall admission, 1/15 for domestic students; for spring admission, 10/1 for domestic students. Application fee: $100. Electronic applications accepted. *Expenses:* Contact institution. *Financial support:* In 2016–17, 38 teaching assistantships were awarded. *Unit head:* Dr. Perry Goldstein, Chair, 631-632-7340, E-mail: perry.goldstein@stonybrook.edu. *Application contact:* Monica Gentile, Coordinator, 631-632-7330, Fax: 631-632-7404, E-mail: monica.gentile@stonybrook.edu. Website: http://www.stonybrook.edu/commcms/music/degree_programs/graduate/performance.html

**Syracuse University,** College of Visual and Performing Arts, MM in Music and Performance Program, Syracuse, NY 13244. Offers music and performance (MM), including organ, percussion, piano, strings, voice, wind instruments. *Degree requirements:* For master's, thesis or alternative. *Entrance requirements:* For master's, audition, three letters of recommendation, academic transcript, personal statement/ essay, resume. Additional exam requirements/recommendations for international students: Required—TOEFL (minimum score 100 iBT). *Application deadline:* For fall admission, 2/1 priority date for domestic and international students. Application fee: $75. Electronic applications accepted. *Expenses: Tuition:* Full-time $25,974; part-time $1443 per credit hour. *Required fees:* $802; $50 per course. Tuition and fees vary according to course load and program. *Financial support:* Fellowships with full tuition reimbursements and teaching assistantships with tuition reimbursements available. Financial award application deadline: 1/1; financial award applicants required to submit FAFSA. *Faculty research:* Organ, percussion, piano, strings, voice, wind instruments. *Unit head:* Steven Heyman Jones, Chair, Department of Applied Music and Performance, 315-443-1638, E-mail: sheyman@syr.edu. *Application contact:* Therese West, Information Contact, 315-443-0137, E-mail: admissg@syr.edu. Website: http://vpa.syr.edu/academics/setnor/graduate/performance/

**Syracuse University,** College of Visual and Performing Arts, MM Program in Composition, Syracuse, NY 13244. Offers MM. *Degree requirements:* For master's, thesis or alternative. *Entrance requirements:* For master's, audition, three letters of recommendation, academic transcript, personal statement/essay, resume. Additional exam requirements/recommendations for international students: Required—TOEFL (minimum score 100 iBT). *Application deadline:* For fall admission, 2/1 priority date for domestic and international students. Application fee: $75. Electronic applications accepted. *Expenses: Tuition:* Full-time $25,974; part-time $1443 per credit hour. *Required fees:* $802; $50 per course. Tuition and fees vary according to course load and program. *Financial support:* Fellowships with full tuition reimbursements and teaching assistantships with tuition reimbursements available. Financial award application deadline: 1/1; financial award applicants required to submit FAFSA. *Faculty research:* Research in music, tonal analysis, orchestral repertoire, music literature. *Unit head:* Nicolas Scherzinger, Associate Professor/Chair of the Department of Music Composition, Theory, and History, 315-443-3907, E-mail: nscherzi@syr.edu. *Application contact:* Therese West, Information Contact, 315-443-0137, E-mail: admissg@syr.edu. Website: http://vpa.syr.edu/academics/setnor/graduate/composition/

**Syracuse University,** College of Visual and Performing Arts, MM Program in Conducting, Syracuse, NY 13244. Offers MM. *Accreditation:* NASM. *Degree requirements:* For master's, thesis or alternative. *Entrance requirements:* For master's, audition, interview, three letters of recommendation, transcripts, personal statement, resume. Additional exam requirements/recommendations for international students: Required—TOEFL (minimum score 100 iBT). *Application deadline:* For fall admission, 2/1 priority date for domestic and international students. Application fee: $75. Electronic applications accepted. *Expenses: Tuition:* Full-time $25,974; part-time $1443 per credit hour. *Required fees:* $802; $50 per course. Tuition and fees vary according to course load and program. *Financial support:* Fellowships with full tuition reimbursements, teaching assistantships with tuition reimbursements, Federal Work-Study, and tuition waivers available. Financial award application deadline: 1/1; financial award applicants required to submit FAFSA. *Faculty research:* Choral, orchestral, winds, baton technique and body language, score reading, score study. *Unit head:* Dr. Steven Heyman, Chair, Department of Applied Music and Performance, 315-443-1638, E-mail: sheyman@syr.edu. *Application contact:* Therese West, Information Contact, 315-443-0137, E-mail: admissg@syr.edu.
Website: http://vpa.syr.edu/academics/setnor/graduate/conducting/

**Syracuse University,** College of Visual and Performing Arts, MM Program in Voice Pedagogy, Syracuse, NY 13244. Offers MM. *Degree requirements:* For master's, thesis or alternative. *Entrance requirements:* For master's, audition, three letters of recommendation, academic transcript, personal statement/essay, resume. Additional exam requirements/recommendations for international students: Required—TOEFL (minimum score 100 iBT). *Application deadline:* For fall admission, 2/1 priority date for domestic and international students. Application fee: $75. Electronic applications accepted. *Expenses: Tuition:* Full-time $25,974; part-time $1443 per credit hour. *Required fees:* $802; $50 per course. Tuition and fees vary according to course load and program. *Financial support:* Fellowships with full tuition reimbursements and teaching assistantships with tuition reimbursements available. Financial award application deadline: 1/1; financial award applicants required to submit FAFSA. *Faculty research:* Voice pedagogy, voice science, pedagogical issues, repertoire, diction, career planning methods, voice study, performance, experience in teaching. *Unit head:* Prof. Kathleen Roland-Silverstein, Assistant Professor, Applied Music and Performance, 315-443-5898, E-mail: krolands@syr.edu. *Application contact:* Therese West, Information Contact, 315-443-0137, E-mail: admissg@syr.edu.
Website: http://vpa.syr.edu/academics/setnor/graduate/voice-pedagogy/

**Temple University,** Center for the Performing and Cinematic Arts, Boyer College of Music and Dance, Department of Music, Philadelphia, PA 19122-6096. Offers choral conducting (MM); collaborative piano/chamber music (MM); collaborative piano/opera coaching (MM); composition (MM, PhD); instrumental conducting (MM); music education (MM, PhD); music history (MM); music performance (MM, DMA), including instrumental studies (MM), keyboard (DMA), keyboard studies (MM), voice (DMA), voice and opera (MM); music studies (PhD); music theory (MM, PhD); music therapy (MMT, PhD); musicology (MM, PhD); opera (MM); piano pedagogy (MM); string pedagogy (MM). *Accreditation:* NASM. *Program availability:* Part-time, online learning. Terminal master's awarded for partial completion of doctoral program. *Degree requirements:* For doctorate, thesis/dissertation. *Entrance requirements:* Additional exam requirements/recommendations for international students: Required—TOEFL. Electronic applications accepted.

**Texas A&M University,** College of Liberal Arts, Department of Performance Studies, College Station, TX 77843. Offers MA. *Faculty:* 12. *Students:* 1 (woman) full-time; minority (Black or African American, non-Hispanic/Latino). Average age 25. 6 applicants, 83% accepted. In 2016, 8 master's awarded. *Degree requirements:* For master's, comprehensive exam (for some programs), thesis or alternative. *Entrance requirements:* For master's, GRE General Test. Additional exam requirements/recommendations for international students: Required—TOEFL (minimum score 550 paper-based; 80 iBT), IELTS (minimum score 6), PTE (minimum score 53). *Application deadline:* For fall admission, 12/1 for domestic students; for spring admission, 10/15 for domestic students. Applications are processed on a rolling basis. Application fee: $50 ($90 for international students). Electronic applications accepted. *Expenses:* Contact institution. *Financial support:* Unspecified assistantships available. Financial award application deadline: 3/15; financial award applicants required to submit FAFSA. *Unit head:* Dr. Donnlee Dox, Department Head, 979-458-1870, E-mail: dox@tamu.edu. *Application contact:* Dr. Kirsten Pullen, Director of Graduate Studies, 979-845-2899, Fax: 979-845-5164, E-mail: kpullen@tamu.edu.
Website: http://performancestudies.tamu.edu/

**Texas A&M University–Commerce,** College of Humanities, Social Sciences and Arts, Commerce, TX 75429-3011. Offers applied criminology (MS); applied linguistics (MA, MS); art (MA, MFA); Christianity in history (Graduate Certificate); computational linguistics (Graduate Certificate); creative writing (Graduate Certificate); English (MA, MS, PhD); film studies (Graduate Certificate); history (MA, MS); music (MM); political science (MA, MS); public history (Graduate Certificate); sociology (MS); Spanish (MA); studies in children's and adolescent literature and culture (Graduate Certificate); teaching English to speakers of other languages (Graduate Certificate); theater (MA, MS). *Program availability:* Part-time. *Faculty:* 53 full-time (26 women), 7 part-time/adjunct (2 women). *Students:* 87 full-time (55 women), 528 part-time (362 women); includes 198 minority (86 Black or African American, non-Hispanic/Latino; 2 American Indian or Alaska Native, non-Hispanic/Latino; 8 Asian, non-Hispanic/Latino; 84 Hispanic/Latino; 18 Two or more races, non-Hispanic/Latino), 27 international. Average age 37. 333 applicants, 56% accepted, 149 enrolled. In 2016, 66 master's, 8 doctorates awarded. *Degree requirements:* For master's, one foreign language, comprehensive exam, thesis (for some programs); for doctorate, one foreign language, comprehensive exam, thesis/dissertation, departmental qualifying exam. *Entrance requirements:* For master's and doctorate, GRE General Test. Additional exam requirements/recommendations for international students: Required—TOEFL (minimum score 550 paper-based; 79 iBT), IELTS (minimum score 6). *Application deadline:* Applications are processed on a rolling basis. Application fee: $50. Electronic applications accepted. *Expenses:* Contact institution. *Financial support:* In 2016–17, 255 students received support, including 9 research assistantships with partial tuition reimbursements available (averaging $9,000 per year), 68 teaching assistantships with partial tuition reimbursements available (averaging $9,000 per year); Federal Work-Study, institutionally sponsored loans, scholarships/grants, health care benefits, and unspecified assistantships also available. Financial award application deadline: 5/1; financial award applicants required to submit FAFSA. *Unit head:* Dr. Salvatore Attardo, Dean, 903-886-5166, Fax: 903-886-5774, E-mail: salvatore.attardo@tamuc.edu. *Application contact:* Shelby Miller, Graduate Recruiter, 903-468-8123, Fax: 903-886-5774, E-mail: shelby.miller@tamuc.edu.
Website: http://www.tamuc.edu/academics/graduateSchool/programs/humanitiesSocialScienceArts/default.aspx

**Texas A&M University–Kingsville,** College of Graduate Studies, College of Arts and Sciences, Department of Music, Progam in Music, Kingsville, TX 78363. Offers instrumental performance (MM); vocal performance (MM).

**Texas Christian University,** College of Fine Arts, School of Music, Doctoral Programs in Music, Fort Worth, TX 76129. Offers composition (DMA), including music history; conducting (DMA), including music history, music theory; performance (DMA), including music history, music theory, piano pedagogy; piano pedagogy (DMA). *Accreditation:* NASM. *Faculty:* 38 full-time (6 women), 12 part-time/adjunct (4 women). *Students:* 10 full-time (1 woman), 6 part-time (3 women); includes 1 minority (Two or more races, non-Hispanic/Latino), 4 international. Average age 32. 27 applicants, 30% accepted, 5 enrolled. In 2016, 2 doctorates awarded. *Degree requirements:* For doctorate, comprehensive exam, thesis/dissertation. *Entrance requirements:* For doctorate, GRE General Test. Additional exam requirements/recommendations for international students: Required—TOEFL (minimum score 100 iBT). *Application deadline:* For spring admission, 12/1 for domestic and international students. Application fee: $80. Electronic applications accepted. *Expenses: Tuition:* Full-time $26,640; part-time $1480 per credit hour. *Required fees:* $48. Tuition and fees vary according to program. *Financial support:* In 2016–17, 9 students received support, including 10 research assistantships with full tuition reimbursements available (averaging $10,000 per year); career-related internships or fieldwork, institutionally sponsored loans, scholarships/grants, tuition waivers (full and partial), and unspecified assistantships also available. Financial award application deadline: 12/1; financial award applicants required to submit CSS PROFILE or FAFSA. *Unit head:* Dr. Richard C. Gipson, Director, 817-257-6606, Fax: 817-257-5818, E-mail: r.gipson@tcu.edu. *Application contact:* Donna Smolik, TCU College of Fine Arts Graduate Office, 817-257-7603, Fax: 817-257-5672, E-mail: cfagradinfo@tcu.edu.
Website: http://www.music.tcu.edu

**Texas Christian University,** College of Fine Arts, School of Music, Master's Programs in Music, Fort Worth, TX 76129. Offers conducting (M Mus); music education (MM Ed); music theory (M Mus); musicology (M Mus); performance (M Mus), including piano, strings, voice, winds/percussion; piano pedagogy (M Mus); voice pedagogy (M Mus). *Faculty:* 38 full-time (6 women), 12 part-time/adjunct (4 women). *Students:* 41 full-time (20 women); includes 5 minority (2 Asian, non-Hispanic/Latino; 2 Hispanic/Latino; 1 Two or more races, non-Hispanic/Latino), 11 international. Average age 25. 60 applicants, 45% accepted, 19 enrolled. In 2016, 22 master's awarded. *Degree requirements:* For master's, comprehensive exam. *Entrance requirements:* For master's, GRE General Test. Additional exam requirements/recommendations for international students: Required—TOEFL (minimum score 80 iBT). *Application deadline:* For fall admission, 3/1 for domestic and international students. Application fee: $80. Electronic applications accepted. *Expenses: Tuition:* Full-time $26,640; part-time $1480 per credit hour. *Required fees:* $48. Tuition and fees vary according to program. *Financial support:* In 2016–17, 41 students received support, including 41 research assistantships with full tuition reimbursements available (averaging $6,000 per year); career-related internships or fieldwork, institutionally sponsored loans, scholarships/grants, tuition waivers (full and partial), and unspecified assistantships also available. Financial award application deadline: 3/1; financial award applicants required to submit CSS PROFILE or FAFSA. *Unit head:* Dr. Richard C. Gipson, Director, 817-257-6606, Fax: 817-257-5818, E-mail: music@tcu.edu. *Application contact:* Donna Smolik, TCU College of Fine Arts Graduate Office, 817-257-7603, Fax: 817-257-5672, E-mail: cfagradinfo@tcu.edu.
Website: http://www.music.tcu.edu

**Texas Southern University,** College of Liberal Arts and Behavioral Sciences, Department of Fine Arts, Houston, TX 77004-4584. Offers fine arts (MA); music (MA). *Program availability:* Part-time. *Degree requirements:* For master's, one foreign language, comprehensive exam, recital. *Entrance requirements:* For master's, GRE General Test, minimum GPA of 2.5. Additional exam requirements/recommendations for international students: Required—TOEFL. Electronic applications accepted. *Faculty research:* Music theory, choral music, composition, percussion composition, ethnic musicology.

**Texas State University,** The Graduate College, College of Fine Arts and Communication, Program in Music, San Marcos, TX 78666. Offers MM. *Accreditation:* NASM. *Program availability:* Part-time. *Faculty:* 46 full-time (21 women), 9 part-time/adjunct (3 women). *Students:* 53 full-time (31 women), 10 part-time (6 women); includes 19 minority (2 Black or African American, non-Hispanic/Latino; 17 Hispanic/Latino), 12 international. Average age 28. 63 applicants, 59% accepted, 24 enrolled. In 2016, 25 master's awarded. *Degree requirements:* For master's, comprehensive exam, thesis (for some programs). *Entrance requirements:* For master's, baccalaureate degree from regionally-accredited institution with minimum GPA of 2.75 in last 60 hours of undergraduate course work, resume, 3 letters of recommendation; music portfolio (for composition, theory and history concentrations). Additional exam requirements/recommendations for international students: Required—TOEFL (minimum score 550 paper-based; 78 iBT), IELTS (minimum score 6.5). *Application deadline:* For fall admission, 1/15 priority date for domestic and international students; for spring admission, 10/15 priority date for domestic students, 10/1 for international students; for summer admission, 4/15 for domestic students, 3/15 for international students. Applications are processed on a rolling basis. Application fee: $40 ($90 for international students). Electronic applications accepted. *Expenses:* $4,851 per semester. *Financial support:* In 2016–17, 53 students received support, including 28 teaching assistantships (averaging $6,371 per year); research assistantships, career-related internships or fieldwork, Federal Work-Study, institutionally sponsored loans, scholarships/grants, and unspecified assistantships also available. Support available to part-time students. Financial award application deadline: 3/1; financial award applicants required to submit FAFSA. *Unit head:* Dr. Jason Kwak, Graduate Advisor, 512-245-3390, Fax: 512-245-8181, E-mail: jk45@txstate.edu. *Application contact:* Dr. Andrea Golato, Dean of Graduate School, 512-245-2581, Fax: 512-245-8365, E-mail: gradcollege@txstate.edu.
Website: http://www.finearts.txstate.edu/music/

**Texas State University,** The Graduate College, College of Liberal Arts, Program in Rhetoric and Composition, San Marcos, TX 78666. Offers MA. *Program availability:* Part-time. *Faculty:* 4 full-time (2 women). *Students:* 8 full-time (3 women), 7 part-time (5 women); includes 6 minority (1 Black or African American, non-Hispanic/Latino; 1 Asian, non-Hispanic/Latino; 4 Hispanic/Latino). Average age 31. 8 applicants, 75% accepted, 4 enrolled. In 2016, 6 master's awarded. *Degree requirements:* For master's, comprehensive exam, thesis optional. *Entrance requirements:* For master's, baccalaureate degree from regionally-accredited institution with minimum GPA of 2.75 on last 60 undergraduate semester hours, 3.0 in minimum of 12 hours of undergraduate English courses; 3 letters of recommendation; portfolio. Additional exam requirements/recommendations for international students: Required—TOEFL (minimum score 550 paper-based; 78 iBT), IELTS (minimum score 6.5). *Application deadline:* For fall admission, 1/15 priority date for domestic and international students; for spring admission, 11/1 for domestic students, 10/1 for international students; for summer admission, 4/15 for domestic students, 3/15 for international students. Applications are processed on a rolling basis. Application fee: $40 ($90 for international students). Electronic applications accepted. *Expenses:* $4,851 per semester. *Financial support:* In 2016–17, 10 students received support, including 1 research assistantship (averaging $16,755 per year), 5 teaching assistantships (averaging $16,396 per year); Federal Work-Study, institutionally sponsored loans, scholarships/grants, and unspecified assistantships also available. Support available to part-time students. Financial award application deadline: 3/1; financial award applicants required to submit FAFSA. *Unit* *head:* Dr. Rebecca Jackson, Graduate Advisor, 512-245-8975, E-mail: rj10@txstate.edu. *Application contact:* Dr. Andrea Golato, Dean of Graduate School, 512-245-2581, Fax: 512-245-8365, E-mail: gradcollege@txstate.edu. Website: http://marc.english.txstate.edu/

**Texas Tech University,** Graduate School, J.T. and Margaret Talkington College of Visual and Performing Arts, School of Music, Lubbock, TX 79409-2033. Offers music (MM, DMA); music education (MM Ed). *Accreditation:* NASM. *Program availability:* Part-time. *Faculty:* 55 full-time (20 women), 6 part-time/adjunct (4 women). *Students:* 97 full-time (37 women), 27 part-time (16 women); includes 22 minority (4 Black or African American, non-Hispanic/Latino; 16 Hispanic/Latino; 2 Two or more races, non-Hispanic/Latino), 36 international. Average age 30. 119 applicants, 53% accepted, 37 enrolled. In 2016, 34 master's, 25 doctorates awarded. *Degree requirements:* For master's, thesis or alternative; for doctorate, comprehensive exam (for some programs), thesis/dissertation. *Entrance requirements:* For master's, GRE General Test. Additional exam requirements/recommendations for international students: Required—TOEFL (minimum score 550 paper-based; 79 iBT). *Application deadline:* For fall admission, 6/1 priority date for domestic students, 1/15 priority date for international students; for spring admission, 9/1 priority date for domestic students, 6/15 priority date for international students. Applications are processed on a rolling basis. Application fee: $75. Electronic applications accepted. *Expenses:* $325 per credit hour full-time resident tuition, $733 per credit hour full-time non-resident tuition; $53.75 per credit hour fee plus $608 per term fee. *Financial support:* In 2016–17, 143 students received support, including 125 fellowships (averaging $2,194 per year), 4 research assistantships (averaging $7,011 per year), 101 teaching assistantships (averaging $10,736 per year); Federal Work-Study, institutionally sponsored loans, scholarships/grants, health care benefits, tuition waivers (partial), and unspecified assistantships also available. Financial award application deadline: 4/15; financial award applicants required to submit FAFSA. *Faculty research:* Strategies for music pedagogy in grades K-12, performance practice of traditional music, role of the woman piano virtuoso, vernacular music center, voice health and culture. *Total annual research expenditures:* $23,000. *Unit head:* Prof. William Ballenger, Director, 806-834-1724, Fax: 806-742-2294, E-mail: william.ballenger@ttu.edu. *Application contact:* Emily Gifford, Admissions and Scholarship Coordinator, 806-834-5076, Fax: 806-742-2294, E-mail: emily.gifford@ttu.edu. Website: http://www.depts.ttu.edu/music

**Texas Woman's University,** Graduate School, College of Arts and Sciences, School of the Arts, Department of Music and Drama, Denton, TX 76201. Offers instrumental pedagogy (MA); instrumental performance (MA); music (MA); music education (MA); piano performance (MA); vocal pedagogy (MA); vocal performance (MA). *Accreditation:* NASM. *Program availability:* Part-time. *Students:* 44 full-time (31 women), 29 part-time (21 women); includes 22 minority (4 Black or African American, non-Hispanic/Latino; 3 Asian, non-Hispanic/Latino; 13 Hispanic/Latino; 2 Two or more races, non-Hispanic/Latino), 3 international. Average age 29. In 2016, 18 master's awarded. *Degree requirements:* For master's, comprehensive exam, thesis (for some programs), project recital, professional paper. *Entrance requirements:* For master's, music history/theory placement exam (for music only), audition and/or design portfolio, interview, resume, writing sample (for drama only). Additional exam requirements/recommendations for international students: Required—TOEFL (minimum score 550 paper-based; 79 iBT). *Application deadline:* For fall admission, 7/1 priority date for domestic students, 3/1 for international students; for spring admission, 12/1 priority date for domestic students, 7/1 for international students. Applications are processed on a rolling basis. Application fee: $50 ($75 for international students). Electronic applications accepted. *Expenses:* Tuition, state resident: full-time $9046; part-time $251 per credit hour. Tuition, nonresident: full-time $22,922; part-time $614 per credit hour. *International tuition:* $23,046 full-time. *Required fees:* $2690; $1285 per credit hour. One-time fee: $50. Tuition and fees vary according to course level, course load, program and reciprocity agreements. *Financial support:* Research assistantships, career-related internships or fieldwork, Federal Work-Study, institutionally sponsored loans, scholarships/grants, traineeships, health care benefits, tuition waivers (partial), and unspecified assistantships available. Support available to part-time students. Financial award application deadline: 3/1; financial award applicants required to submit FAFSA. *Faculty research:* Musical development in early childhood, little known or neglected compositions for flute (especially by women composers), relationship of visual art to piano music, pedagogical development of the singing voice, guided imagery and music. *Unit head:* Dr. Pamela Youngblood, Chair, 940-898-2495, Fax: 940-898-2494, E-mail: pyoungblood@twu.edu. *Application contact:* Dr. Samuel Wheeler, Assistant Director of Admissions, 940-898-3188, Fax: 940-898-3081, E-mail: wheelersr@twu.edu.

**Towson University,** Program in Music Performance and Composition, Towson, MD 21252-0001. Offers MM. *Accreditation:* NASM. *Program availability:* Part-time, evening/weekend. *Students:* 11 full-time (7 women), 7 part-time (4 women); includes 8 minority (4 Black or African American, non-Hispanic/Latino; 1 Asian, non-Hispanic/Latino; 1 Hispanic/Latino; 2 Two or more races, non-Hispanic/Latino), 1 international. *Entrance requirements:* For master's, audition, bachelor's degree in music, minimum GPA of 3.0. Additional exam requirements/recommendations for international students: Required—TOEFL (minimum score 550 paper-based). *Application deadline:* Applications are processed on a rolling basis. Application fee: $45. Electronic applications accepted. *Expenses:* Tuition, state resident: full-time $7580; part-time $379 per unit. Tuition, nonresident: full-time $15,700; part-time $785 per unit. *Required fees:* $2480. *Financial support:* Application deadline: 4/1. *Unit head:* Dr. Terry Ewell, Graduate Program Director, 410-704-2824, E-mail: tewell@towson.edu. *Application contact:* Coverley Beidleman, Assistant Director of Graduate Admissions, 410-704-2113, Fax: 410-704-3030, E-mail: grads@towson.edu. Website: http://www.towson.edu/cofac/departments/music/grad/performance/

**Trinity College,** Faculty of Divinity, Toronto, ON M5S 1H8, Canada. Offers ministry (Diploma); ministry for church musicians (Diploma); theology (M Div, MA, MTS, Th M, D Min, PhD, Th D, Diploma, L Th); M Div/MA. *Accreditation:* ATS. *Program availability:* Part-time. *Degree requirements:* For master's, 2 foreign languages, thesis (for some programs); for doctorate, 3 foreign languages, comprehensive exam, thesis/dissertation; for other advanced degree, thesis (for some programs). *Entrance requirements:* For master's, 1 language (modern or ancient), interview; for doctorate, 2 languages (modern and ancient). Additional exam requirements/recommendations for international students: Required—TOEFL, TWE. *Faculty research:* Interreligious dialogue, feminist theology, systematic theology, philosophy of religion, pastoral theology.

**Trinity Lutheran Seminary,** Graduate and Professional Programs, Columbus, OH 43209-2334. Offers African American studies (MTS); Biblical studies (MTS, STM); Christian education (MA); Christian spirituality (STM); church in the world (MTS); church music (MA); divinity (M Div); general theological studies (MTS); mission and evangelism (STM); pastoral leadership and practice (STM); youth and family ministry (MA); MSN/MTS; MTS/JD. *Accreditation:* ACIPE; ATS. *Program availability:* Part-time. *Degree requirements:* For master's, variable foreign language requirement, comprehensive exam (for some programs), thesis (for some programs), field experience (for some programs). *Entrance requirements:* For master's, BA or equivalent (for MA, M Div, MTS); M Div, MTS, or equivalent (for STM); audition (for MACM). Additional exam

requirements/recommendations for international students: Required—TOEFL. Electronic applications accepted. *Expenses:* Contact institution.

**Truman State University,** Graduate School, School of Arts and Letters, Program in Music, Kirksville, MO 63501-4221. Offers MA. *Accreditation:* NASM. *Degree requirements:* For master's, comprehensive exam, thesis or alternative. *Entrance requirements:* For master's, GRE General Test, minimum GPA of 3.0. Additional exam requirements/recommendations for international students: Required—TOEFL (minimum score 550 paper-based). *Application deadline:* For fall admission, 6/1 for domestic and international students; for spring admission, 11/1 for domestic and international students; for summer admission, 4/1 for domestic and international students. Applications are processed on a rolling basis. Application fee: $40. Electronic applications accepted. *Expenses:* Tuition, state resident: full-time $6300; part-time $350 per credit hour. Tuition, nonresident: full-time $10,818; part-time $601 per credit hour. Tuition and fees vary according to course load and program. *Financial support:* Research assistantships with tuition reimbursements, teaching assistantships with tuition reimbursements, career-related internships or fieldwork, and Federal Work-Study available. Financial award application deadline: 5/1; financial award applicants required to submit FAFSA. *Unit head:* Dr. Thomas Hueber, Director, 660-785-4433, Fax: 660-785-7463, E-mail: thueber@truman.edu. *Application contact:* Stephanie Rudolph, Graduate Office Secretary, 660-785-4109, Fax: 660-785-7460, E-mail: sdunn@truman.edu.

**Tufts University,** Graduate School of Arts and Sciences, Department of Music, Medford, MA 02155. Offers composition (MA); ethnomusicology (MA); music theory (MA). *Program availability:* Part-time. *Students:* 11 full-time (5 women); includes 1 minority (Asian, non-Hispanic/Latino). Average age 25. 21 applicants, 52% accepted, 3 enrolled. In 2016, 5 master's awarded. *Degree requirements:* For master's, one foreign language, thesis. *Entrance requirements:* For master's, GRE General Test, writing sample or musical score. Additional exam requirements/recommendations for international students: Required—TOEFL (minimum score 550 paper-based; 80 iBT), IELTS (minimum score 6.5). *Application deadline:* For fall admission, 1/15 for domestic and international students. Applications are processed on a rolling basis. Application fee: $85. Electronic applications accepted. *Expenses:* $49,982 full-time tuition (for MA). *Financial support:* In 2016–17, 10 students received support. Teaching assistantships, Federal Work-Study, scholarships/grants, tuition waivers (full and partial), and unspecified assistantships available. Financial award application deadline: 1/15. *Unit head:* Dr. Stephan Pennington, Graduate Program Director, 617-627-3564. *Application contact:* Office of Graduate Admissions, 617-627-3395, E-mail: gradadmissions@tufts.edu. Website: http://www.tufts.edu/as/music/

**Tulane University,** School of Liberal Arts, Department of Music, New Orleans, LA 70118-5669. Offers MA, MFA. *Degree requirements:* For master's, one foreign language, thesis (for some programs), recital or composition (MA). *Entrance requirements:* For master's, GRE General Test, minimum B average in undergraduate course work. Additional exam requirements/recommendations for international students: Required—TOEFL. Electronic applications accepted. *Expenses:* Full-time $50,920; part-time $2829 per credit hour. *Required fees:* $2040; $44.50 per credit hour. $580 per term. Tuition and fees vary according to course load, degree level and program. *Faculty research:* New Orleans music, composition, piano, voice, music theatre, classical guitar.

**Université de Montréal,** Faculty of Music, Montréal, QC H3C 3J7, Canada. Offers composition (M Mus, D Mus); interpretation (M Mus, D Mus, DESS); music (MA, PhD); orchestral repertoire (DESS). *Degree requirements:* For doctorate, thesis/dissertation, general exam. Electronic applications accepted. *Faculty research:* Semiology, music in Creole areas, computer-assisted composition, Argentinean tango.

**Université Laval,** Faculty of Music, Programs in Music, Québec, QC G1K 7P4, Canada. Offers composition (M Mus); instrumental didactics (M Mus); interpretation (M Mus); music education (M Mus, PhD); musicology (M Mus, PhD). Terminal master's awarded for partial completion of doctoral program. *Degree requirements:* For master's, thesis (for some programs); for doctorate, comprehensive exam, thesis/dissertation. *Entrance requirements:* For master's, English exam, audition, knowledge of French; for doctorate, English exam, knowledge of French, third language. Electronic applications accepted.

**University at Buffalo, the State University of New York,** Graduate School, College of Arts and Sciences, Department of Music, Buffalo, NY 14260. Offers contemporary performance (Advanced Certificate); historical musicology and music theory (PhD); music composition (MA, PhD); music history (MA); music performance (MM); music theory (MA). *Program availability:* Part-time. Terminal master's awarded for partial completion of doctoral program. *Degree requirements:* For master's, variable foreign language requirement, comprehensive exam (for some programs), thesis (for some programs), recitals (for MM); projects and/or thesis (for MA); for doctorate, variable foreign language requirement, comprehensive exam, thesis/dissertation; for Advanced Certificate, recitals. *Entrance requirements:* For master's, audition (for MM), compositions, writing sample(s), essay, letters of recommendation; for doctorate, GRE General Test, compositions, writing sample(s), essay, letters of recommendation; for Advanced Certificate, audition. Additional exam requirements/recommendations for international students: Required—TOEFL (minimum score 550 paper-based; 79 iBT). Electronic applications accepted. *Faculty research:* Music composition, music theory, historical musicology, concert performance, contemporary music.

**The University of Akron,** Graduate School, Buchtel College of Arts and Sciences, School of Music, Program in Accompanying, Akron, OH 44325. Offers MM. *Entrance requirements:* For master's, minimum GPA of 2.75, three letters of recommendation, audition. *Application deadline:* Applications are processed on a rolling basis. Application fee: $45 ($70 for international students). *Expenses:* Tuition, state resident: full-time $8618; part-time $359 per credit hour. Tuition, nonresident: full-time $17,149; part-time $715 per credit hour. *Required fees:* $1652. *Unit head:* Dr. J. Thomas Dukes, Interim Director, 330-972-5761, E-mail: jtdukes@uakron.edu. *Application contact:* Dr. Ann Usher, Graduate Director, 330-972-6923, E-mail: ausher@uakron.edu.

**The University of Akron,** Graduate School, Buchtel College of Arts and Sciences, School of Music, Program in Composition, Akron, OH 44325. Offers MM. *Degree requirements:* For master's, comprehensive exam, thesis optional. *Entrance requirements:* For master's, theory diagnostic exam, minimum GPA of 2.75, three letters of recommendation, sample of scholarly writing, composition portfolio, interview. Additional exam requirements/recommendations for international students: Required—TOEFL (minimum score 550 paper-based; 79 iBT), IELTS. *Application deadline:* Applications are processed on a rolling basis. Application fee: $45 ($70 for international students). Electronic applications accepted. *Expenses:* Tuition, state resident: full-time $8618; part-time $359 per credit hour. Tuition, nonresident: full-time $17,149; part-time $715 per credit hour. *Required fees:* $1652. *Unit head:* Dr. J. Thomas Dukes, Interim Director, 330-972-5761, E-mail: jtdukes@uakron.edu. *Application contact:* Dr. Ann Usher, Graduate Coordinator, 330-972-6923, E-mail: ausher@uakron.edu.

**The University of Akron,** Graduate School, Buchtel College of Arts and Sciences, School of Music, Program in Music Technology, Akron, OH 44325. Offers MM. *Students:* 2 full-time (0 women); includes 1 minority (Asian, non-Hispanic/Latino). Average age 26.

1 applicant, 100% accepted, 1 enrolled. In 2016, 2 master's awarded. *Degree requirements:* For master's, comprehensive exam, thesis optional. *Entrance requirements:* For master's, minimum GPA of 2.75, three letters of recommendation, interview. Additional exam requirements/recommendations for international students: Required—TOEFL (minimum score 550 paper-based; 79 iBT), IELTS (minimum score 6.5). *Application deadline:* Applications are processed on a rolling basis. Application fee: $45 ($70 for international students). Electronic applications accepted. *Expenses:* Tuition, state resident: full-time $8618; part-time $359 per credit hour. Tuition, nonresident: full-time $17,149; part-time $715 per credit hour. *Required fees:* $1652. *Unit head:* Dr. J. Thomas Dukes, Interim Director, 330-972-5761, E-mail: jtdukes@uakron.edu. *Application contact:* Dr. Ann Usher, Graduate Coordinator, 330-972-6923, E-mail: ausher@uakron.edu.

**The University of Akron,** Graduate School, Buchtel College of Arts and Sciences, School of Music, Program in Performance, Akron, OH 44325. Offers MM. *Students:* 31 full-time (16 women); includes 5 minority (1 Asian, non-Hispanic/Latino; 3 Hispanic/Latino; 1 Two or more races, non-Hispanic/Latino), 2 international. Average age 25. 30 applicants, 100% accepted, 16 enrolled. In 2016, 27 master's awarded. *Degree requirements:* For master's, comprehensive exam. *Entrance requirements:* For master's, minimum GPA of 2.75, three letters of recommendation, audition. Additional exam requirements/recommendations for international students: Required—TOEFL (minimum score 550 paper-based; 79 iBT), IELTS (minimum score 6.5). *Application deadline:* Applications are processed on a rolling basis. Application fee: $45 ($70 for international students). Electronic applications accepted. *Expenses:* Tuition, state resident: full-time $8618; part-time $359 per credit hour. Tuition, nonresident: full-time $17,149; part-time $715 per credit hour. *Required fees:* $1652. *Unit head:* Dr. J. Thomas Dukes, Interim Director, 330-972-5761, E-mail: jtdukes@uakron.edu. *Application contact:* Dr. Ann Usher, Graduate Director, 330-972-6923, E-mail: ausher@uakron.edu.

**The University of Akron,** Graduate School, Buchtel College of Arts and Sciences, School of Music, Program in Theory, Akron, OH 44325. Offers MM. *Students:* 2 full-time (0 women), 1 part-time (0 women), 1 international. Average age 36. 1 applicant, 100% accepted, 1 enrolled. In 2016, 1 master's awarded. *Degree requirements:* For master's, comprehensive exam, thesis optional. *Entrance requirements:* For master's, minimum GPA of 2.75, interview, three letters of recommendation. Additional exam requirements/recommendations for international students: Required—TOEFL (minimum score 550 paper-based; 79 iBT), IELTS (minimum score 6.5). *Application deadline:* Applications are processed on a rolling basis. Application fee: $45 ($70 for international students). Electronic applications accepted. *Expenses:* Tuition, state resident: full-time $8618; part-time $359 per credit hour. Tuition, nonresident: full-time $17,149; part-time $715 per credit hour. *Required fees:* $1652. *Unit head:* Dr. J. Thomas Dukes, Interim Director, 330-972-5761, E-mail: jtdukes@uakron.edu. *Application contact:* Dr. Ann Usher, Graduate Director, 330-972-6923, E-mail: ausher@uakron.edu.

**The University of Alabama,** Graduate School, College of Arts and Sciences, Department of English, Tuscaloosa, AL 35487. Offers composition and rhetoric (PhD); creative writing (MFA), including fiction, poetry; literature (MA, PhD); rhetoric and composition (MA); teaching English as a second language (MATESOL). *Faculty:* 38 full-time (20 women). *Students:* 129 full-time (69 women), 6 part-time (5 women); includes 23 minority (12 Black or African American, non-Hispanic/Latino; 1 Asian, non-Hispanic/Latino; 7 Hispanic/Latino; 3 Two or more races, non-Hispanic/Latino), 3 international. Average age 29. 406 applicants, 13% accepted, 35 enrolled. In 2016, 31 master's, 4 doctorates awarded. *Degree requirements:* For master's, one foreign language, comprehensive exam, thesis optional; for doctorate, 2 foreign languages, comprehensive exam, thesis/dissertation. *Entrance requirements:* For master's, GRE (minimum score of 300, except for MFA), minimum GPA of 3.0, critical writing sample; for doctorate, GRE (minimum score of 300), minimum GPA of 3.5 on master's or equivalent graduate work, critical writing sample. Additional exam requirements/recommendations for international students: Required—TOEFL (minimum score 550 paper-based; 79 iBT). *Application deadline:* For fall admission, 12/31 priority date for domestic and international students. Application fee: $50 ($60 for international students). Electronic applications accepted. *Expenses:* Tuition, state resident: full-time $10,470. Tuition, nonresident: full-time $26,950. *Financial support:* In 2016–17, 128 students received support, including 11 fellowships with full tuition reimbursements available (averaging $15,000 per year), 13 research assistantships with full tuition reimbursements available (averaging $13,500 per year), 100 teaching assistantships with full tuition reimbursements available (averaging $13,500 per year); career-related internships or fieldwork, scholarships/grants, health care benefits, and unspecified assistantships also available. Financial award application deadline: 12/31. *Faculty research:* American literature, British literature, composition/rhetoric, applied linguistics, creative writing. *Unit head:* Prof. Joel Brouwer, Department Chair, 205-348-5065, Fax: 205-348-1388, E-mail: joel.brouwer@ua.edu. *Application contact:* Jennifer Fuqua, Graduate Coordinator, 205-348-0766, Fax: 205-348-1388, E-mail: jfuqua@ua.edu.

**The University of Alabama,** Graduate School, College of Arts and Sciences, School of Music, Tuscaloosa, AL 35487. Offers arranging (MM); choral conducting (MM, DMA); church music (MM); composition (MM, DMA); music education (MA, PhD); musicology (MM); performance (MM, DMA); theory (MM); wind conducting (MM, DMA). *Accreditation:* NASM. *Faculty:* 38 full-time (13 women), 1 (woman) part-time/adjunct. *Students:* 57 full-time (20 women), 11 part-time (4 women); includes 15 minority (7 Black or African American, non-Hispanic/Latino; 1 American Indian or Alaska Native, non-Hispanic/Latino; 5 Hispanic/Latino; 2 Two or more races, non-Hispanic/Latino), 9 international. Average age 29. 82 applicants, 60% accepted, 25 enrolled. In 2016, 13 master's, 7 doctorates awarded. *Degree requirements:* For master's, variable foreign language requirement, comprehensive exam (for some programs), thesis (for some programs), recital; for doctorate, variable foreign language requirement, comprehensive exam, thesis/dissertation, oral exam; recital (for some majors). *Entrance requirements:* For master's and doctorate, audition exam, audition in the major instrument or area. Additional exam requirements/recommendations for international students: Required—PTE (minimum score 59), TOEFL (minimum score 550 paper-based, 79 iBT) or IELTS (minimum score 6.5). *Application deadline:* For fall admission, 3/15 priority date for domestic and international students; for winter admission, 9/1 priority date for domestic and international students; for spring admission, 9/1 priority date for domestic and international students. Applications are processed on a rolling basis. Application fee: $50 ($60 for international students). Electronic applications accepted. *Expenses:* Tuition, state resident: full-time $10,470. Tuition, nonresident: full-time $26,950. *Financial support:* In 2016–17, 50 students received support, including 1 fellowship with full tuition reimbursement available (averaging $10,000 per year), 44 teaching assistantships with tuition reimbursements available (averaging $10,161 per year); institutionally sponsored loans, scholarships/grants, health care benefits, and unspecified assistantships also available. Financial award application deadline: 3/15. *Faculty research:* Performance practice, musicology, theory, composition. *Unit head:* Charles G. Snead, Director, 205-348-7110, Fax: 205-348-1473, E-mail: ssnead@music.ua.edu. *Application contact:* Dr. Jon Noffsinger, Director of Graduate Studies, 205-348-1475, Fax: 205-348-1473, E-mail: jnoffsin@ua.edu. Website: http://music.ua.edu/

**The University of Alabama at Birmingham,** College of Arts and Sciences, Program in English, Birmingham, AL 35294. Offers creative writing (MA); literature (MA); rhetoric and composition (MA). *Program availability:* Part-time. *Degree requirements:* For master's, one foreign language, comprehensive exam, thesis or alternative. *Entrance requirements:* For master's, GRE General Test or MAT, minimum GPA of 2.75. Electronic applications accepted. Full-time tuition and fees vary according to course load and program.

**University of Alaska Fairbanks,** College of Liberal Arts, Department of Music, Fairbanks, AK 99775-5660. Offers MM. *Accreditation:* NASM. *Program availability:* Part-time. *Faculty:* 9 full-time (2 women). *Students:* 3 full-time (2 women), 1 part-time (0 women), 2 international. Average age 25. In 2016, 4 master's awarded. *Degree requirements:* For master's, comprehensive exam, thesis or alternative, project, oral defense of project. *Entrance requirements:* For master's, diagnostic examinations in music theory, music history, and music literature, bachelor's degree from accredited institution with minimum cumulative undergraduate and major GPA of 3.0, performance audition. Additional exam requirements/recommendations for international students: Required—TOEFL (minimum score 550 paper-based; 79 iBT), IELTS (minimum score 6.5). *Application deadline:* For fall admission, 6/1 for domestic students, 3/1 for international students; for spring admission, 10/15 for domestic students, 9/1 for international students. Applications are processed on a rolling basis. Application fee: $60. Electronic applications accepted. *Expenses:* Tuition, state resident: full-time $7992; part-time $444 per credit. Tuition, nonresident: full-time $16,326; part-time $907 per credit. *Required fees:* $39 per credit. $322 per semester. Tuition and fees vary according to course level, course load, campus/location, program and reciprocity agreements. *Financial support:* In 2016–17, 3 teaching assistantships with full tuition reimbursements (averaging $5,908 per year) were awarded; fellowships with full tuition reimbursements, Federal Work-Study, scholarships/grants, health care benefits, and unspecified assistantships also available. Support available to part-time students. Financial award application deadline: 7/1; financial award applicants required to submit FAFSA. *Unit head:* Dr. Eduard Zilberkant, Department Chair, 907-474-7555, Fax: 907-474-6420, E-mail: uaf.music@alaska.edu. *Application contact:* Mary Kreta, Director of Admissions, 907-474-7500, Fax: 907-474-7097, E-mail: admissions@uaf.edu. Website: http://www.uaf.edu/music/

**University of Alberta,** Faculty of Graduate Studies and Research, Department of Music, Edmonton, AB T6G 2E1, Canada. Offers applied music (M Mus); choral conducting (M Mus); composition (M Mus); music (PhD); organ and choral conductors (D Mus); piano (D Mus). *Degree requirements:* For master's, one foreign language, thesis; for doctorate, one foreign language, thesis/dissertation. *Entrance requirements:* Additional exam requirements/recommendations for international students: Required—TOEFL (minimum score 550 paper-based). Electronic applications accepted. *Faculty research:* Classical/Indian and West African music, popular music, choral conducting, theory and composition, musicology, applied music.

**The University of Arizona,** College of Fine Arts, School of Music, Program in Music, Tucson, AZ 85721. Offers composition (MM); ethnomusicology (MM); music education (MM, PhD); music theory (MM, PhD); musicology (MM); performance (MM), including conducting - choral, conducting - instrumental, instrumental, keyboard, piano accompanying, piano and dance accompanying, vocal. *Entrance requirements:* Additional exam requirements/recommendations for international students: Required—TOEFL (minimum score 550 paper-based; 79 iBT). Electronic applications accepted. *Faculty research:* Music in general education, psychology of music learning, innovation in string music education, Zarzuela, Franz Liszt's work.

**The University of Arizona,** College of Fine Arts, School of Music, Program in Musical Arts, Tucson, AZ 85721. Offers composition (DMA); conducting (DMA); performance (DMA), including instrumental, keyboard, vocal. *Entrance requirements:* Additional exam requirements/recommendations for international students: Required—TOEFL (minimum score 550 paper-based; 79 iBT). Electronic applications accepted. *Faculty research:* Music in general education, psychology of music learning, innovation in string music education, Zarzuela, Franz Liszt's work.

**The University of Arizona,** College of Humanities, Department of English, Rhetoric, Composition and the Teaching of English Program, Tucson, AZ 85721. Offers MA, PhD. *Accreditation:* NASM. *Degree requirements:* For master's, one foreign language, comprehensive exam; for doctorate, one foreign language, comprehensive exam, thesis/dissertation. *Entrance requirements:* For doctorate, GRE General Test, 3 letters of recommendation, writing sample. Additional exam requirements/recommendations for international students: Required—TOEFL (minimum score 550 paper-based; 79 iBT). Electronic applications accepted.

**University of Arkansas,** Graduate School, J. William Fulbright College of Arts and Sciences, Department of Music, Fayetteville, AR 72701. Offers MM. *Accreditation:* NASM. In 2016, 15 master's awarded. *Entrance requirements:* For master's, GRE General Test. *Application deadline:* For fall admission, 4/1 for international students; for spring admission, 10/1 for international students. Applications are processed on a rolling basis. Application fee: $40 ($50 for international students). Electronic applications accepted. *Financial support:* In 2016–17, 2 research assistantships, 24 teaching assistantships were awarded; fellowships, career-related internships or fieldwork, and Federal Work-Study also available. Support available to part-time students. Financial award application deadline: 4/1; financial award applicants required to submit FAFSA. *Unit head:* Dr. Ronda Mains, Departmental Chair, 479-575-4701, Fax: 479-575-5409, E-mail: rmains@uark.edu. *Application contact:* Dr. Ronda Mains, 479-575-4709, E-mail: rmains@uark.edu. Website: http://music.uark.edu/

**The University of British Columbia,** Faculty of Arts and Faculty of Graduate Studies, School of Music, Vancouver, BC V6T 1Z2, Canada. Offers M Mus, MA, PhD. *Program availability:* Part-time. *Degree requirements:* For master's, recital (M Mus), thesis (MA); for doctorate, one foreign language, comprehensive exam, public performance or composition (DMA), dissertation (PhD). *Entrance requirements:* For master's, audition/performance (M Mus); for doctorate, audition/performance (DMA). Additional exam requirements/recommendations for international students: Required—TOEFL. *Application deadline:* Applications are processed on a rolling basis. Application fee: $100 Canadian dollars ($162 Canadian dollars for international students). Electronic applications accepted. *Expenses:* $4,802 per year tuition and fees, $8,436 per year international. *Financial support:* Fellowships, research assistantships, teaching assistantships, institutionally sponsored loans, scholarships/grants, tuition waivers (partial), and unspecified assistantships available. *Faculty research:* Performance, composition, opera, musicology, ethnomusicology, theory. *Application contact:* Robert Ablenas, Manager, Academic Advising, 604-822-5502, Fax: 604-822-4884, E-mail: music.advisor@ubc.ca. Website: https://music.ubc.ca/

**University of Calgary,** Faculty of Graduate Studies, Faculty of Arts, Department of Music, Calgary, AB T2N 1N4, Canada. Offers M Mus, MA, PhD. *Degree requirements:* For master's, one foreign language, thesis; for doctorate, 2 foreign languages, thesis/dissertation. *Entrance requirements:* For master's, audition (performance), 3 compositions. Additional exam requirements/recommendations for international

## Music

students: Required—TOEFL. Electronic applications accepted. *Faculty research:* Musicology, theory and composition, performance and performance practice, teaching methodology, folk music collection and analyses.

**University of California, Berkeley,** Graduate Division, College of Letters and Science, Department of Music, Berkeley, CA 94720-1500. Offers composition (PhD); ethnomusicology (PhD); musicology (PhD). *Faculty:* 21 full-time, 53 part-time/adjunct. *Students:* 49 full-time (23 women); includes 14 minority (2 Black or African American, non-Hispanic/Latino; 7 Asian, non-Hispanic/Latino; 5 Hispanic/Latino), 9 international. Average age 31. 118 applicants, 7 enrolled. In 2016, 8 doctorates awarded. *Degree requirements:* For doctorate, 2 foreign languages, thesis/dissertation, qualifying exam. *Entrance requirements:* For doctorate, GRE General Test, minimum GPA of 3.0, examples of work, 3 letters of recommendation. Additional exam requirements/recommendations for international students: Required—TOEFL (minimum score 570 paper-based; 90 iBT). *Application deadline:* For fall admission, 12/1 for domestic students. Application fee: $105 ($125 for international students). Electronic applications accepted. *Financial support:* Fellowships with full tuition reimbursements, research assistantships, teaching assistantships with full tuition reimbursements, Federal Work-Study, institutionally sponsored loans, scholarships/grants, health care benefits, and unspecified assistantships available. Financial award applicants required to submit FAFSA. *Faculty research:* Historical musicology, music criticism, computer music. *Unit head:* Prof. Cindy Cox, Chair, 510-642-2678, Fax: 510-642-8480, E-mail: music@berkeley.edu. *Application contact:* Karen Chang, Student Affairs Officer, 510-643-8725, Fax: 510-642-8482, E-mail: musicgradadvisor@berkeley.edu. Website: http://music.berkeley.edu/

**University of California, Davis,** Graduate Studies, Program in Music, Davis, CA 95616. Offers composition (MA, PhD); conducting (MA, PhD); musicology (MA, PhD). Terminal master's awarded for partial completion of doctoral program. *Degree requirements:* For master's, one foreign language, thesis; for doctorate, 2 foreign languages, thesis/dissertation. *Entrance requirements:* For master's, minimum GPA of 3.0; for doctorate, GRE, minimum GPA of 3.0. Additional exam requirements/recommendations for international students: Required—TOEFL (minimum score 550 paper-based). Electronic applications accepted.

**University of California, Davis,** Graduate Studies, Program in Performance Studies, Davis, CA 95616. Offers dramatic art (PhD). *Degree requirements:* For doctorate, 2 foreign languages, thesis/dissertation. *Entrance requirements:* For doctorate, GRE, minimum GPA of 3.25. Additional exam requirements/recommendations for international students: Required—TOEFL (minimum score 550 paper-based). Electronic applications accepted.

**University of California, Irvine,** Claire Trevor School of the Arts, Department of Music, Irvine, CA 92697. Offers accompanying (MFA); choral conducting (MFA); composition and technology (MFA); guitar/lute performance (MFA); instrumental performance (MFA); jazz instrumental/composition (MFA); piano performance (MFA); vocal performance (MFA). *Students:* 5 full-time (2 women), 1 part-time (0 women); includes 25 minority (3 Black or African American, non-Hispanic/Latino; 4 Asian, non-Hispanic/Latino; 12 Hispanic/Latino; 6 Two or more races, non-Hispanic/Latino). Average age 39. 16 applicants, 25% accepted, 3 enrolled. In 2016, 13 master's awarded. *Degree requirements:* For master's, one foreign language, thesis. *Entrance requirements:* For master's, minimum GPA of 3.0. *Application deadline:* For fall admission, 1/15 priority date for domestic students, 1/15 for international students. Applications are processed on a rolling basis. Application fee: $105 ($125 for international students). Electronic applications accepted. *Financial support:* Fellowships, teaching assistantships, institutionally sponsored loans, traineeships, health care benefits, and unspecified assistantships available. Financial award application deadline: 3/1; financial award applicants required to submit FAFSA. *Faculty research:* Composition, instrumental and choral performance, African-American music, Italian Baroque music and performance practice. *Unit head:* Michael Dessen, Chair, 949-824-4281, Fax: 949-824-4914, E-mail: mdessen@uci.edu. *Application contact:* Peter Chang, Department Administrator, 949-824-4281, Fax: 949-824-4914, E-mail: pechang@uci.edu. Website: http://www.arts.uci.edu/ctsa-academic-departments-music

**University of California, Los Angeles,** Graduate Division, College of Letters and Science, Department of Musicology, Los Angeles, CA 90095. Offers MA, PhD. Terminal master's awarded for partial completion of doctoral program. *Degree requirements:* For master's, one foreign language, comprehensive exam, thesis; for doctorate, one foreign language, thesis/dissertation, oral and written qualifying exams. *Entrance requirements:* For master's and doctorate, GRE General Test (recommended), bachelor's degree; minimum undergraduate GPA of 3.0 (or its equivalent if letter grade system not used); writing sample. Additional exam requirements/recommendations for international students: Required—TOEFL. Electronic applications accepted.

**University of California, Los Angeles,** Graduate Division, School of the Arts and Architecture, Department of Ethnomusicology, Los Angeles, CA 90095. Offers MA, PhD. *Degree requirements:* For master's, one foreign language, comprehensive exam; for doctorate, 2 foreign languages, thesis/dissertation, oral and written qualifying exams. *Entrance requirements:* For master's, bachelor's degree; minimum undergraduate GPA of 3.0 (or its equivalent if letter grade system not used); writing sample; for doctorate, master's degree; minimum undergraduate GPA of 3.0 (or its equivalent if letter grade system not used); writing sample. Additional exam requirements/recommendations for international students: Required—TOEFL. Electronic applications accepted.

**University of California, Los Angeles,** Graduate Division, School of the Arts and Architecture, Department of Music, Los Angeles, CA 90095. Offers composition (MA, PhD); performance (MM, DMA). *Degree requirements:* For master's, one foreign language, thesis, final recital (for MM); for doctorate, one foreign language, thesis/dissertation, oral and written qualifying exams; recital (DMA). *Entrance requirements:* For master's, departmental assessment exams, bachelor's degree; minimum undergraduate GPA of 3.0 (or its equivalent if letter grade system not used); portfolio; interview; audition; for doctorate, departmental assessment exams, master's degree; minimum undergraduate GPA of 3.0 (or its equivalent if letter grade system not used); portfolio; interview. Additional exam requirements/recommendations for international students: Required—TOEFL. Electronic applications accepted.

**University of California, Riverside,** Graduate Division, Department of Music, Riverside, CA 92521-0102. Offers composition (PhD); ethnomusicology (MA). Terminal master's awarded for partial completion of doctoral program. *Degree requirements:* For master's, one foreign language, comprehensive exam, thesis (for some programs), oral exams; for doctorate, 2 foreign languages, comprehensive exam, thesis/dissertation, written and oral qualifying examination. *Entrance requirements:* For master's and doctorate, GRE General Test, minimum GPA of 3.0. Additional exam requirements/recommendations for international students: Required—TOEFL (minimum score 550 paper-based; 80 iBT). Electronic applications accepted. *Expenses:* Tuition, state resident: full-time $16,666. Tuition, nonresident: full-time $31,768. *Required fees:* $11,055.54 per quarter. $3685.18 per quarter. Tuition and fees vary according to campus/location and program. *Faculty research:* Composition, ethnomusicology (especially Southeast Asian and Asian-American music), cultural musicology, gender studies, performance practice.

**University of California, San Diego,** Graduate Division, Department of Music, La Jolla, CA 92093. Offers contemporary music performance (DMA); music (MA, PhD). *Students:* 88 full-time (32 women), 2 part-time (1 woman). 139 applicants, 17% accepted, 18 enrolled. In 2016, 7 master's, 8 doctorates awarded. *Degree requirements:* For master's, thesis; for doctorate, comprehensive exam (for some programs), thesis/dissertation (for some programs), 6 credit units of apprentice teaching; major composition (for some programs); major recital (for some programs). *Entrance requirements:* For master's, GRE General Test, musical portfolio; for doctorate, GRE General Test, master's degree; supporting musical portfolio. Additional exam requirements/recommendations for international students: Required—TOEFL (minimum score 550 paper-based; 80 iBT), IELTS (minimum score 7). *Application deadline:* For fall admission, 12/8 for domestic students. Application fee: $105 ($125 for international students). Electronic applications accepted. *Expenses:* Tuition, state resident: full-time $11,220. Tuition, nonresident: full-time $26,322. *Required fees:* $1864. *Financial support:* Fellowships, research assistantships, teaching assistantships, scholarships/grants, unspecified assistantships, and readerships available. Financial award applicants required to submit FAFSA. *Faculty research:* Composition, computer music, integrative studies, performance. *Unit head:* Rand Steiger, Chair, 858-534-3675, E-mail: rand@ucsd.edu. *Application contact:* Taylor Robinette, Graduate Coordinator, 858-534-3279, E-mail: mus-grad@ucsd.edu. Website: http://musicweb.ucsd.edu

**University of California, San Diego,** Graduate Division, Department of Theatre and Dance, La Jolla, CA 92093. Offers acting (MFA); contemporary dance and performance (MFA); design (MFA); directing (MFA); drama and theatre (PhD); playwriting (MFA); stage management (MFA). PhD offered jointly with University of California, Irvine. *Students:* 75 full-time (42 women). 497 applicants, 6% accepted, 20 enrolled. In 2016, 24 master's, 1 doctorate awarded. *Degree requirements:* For master's, thesis; for doctorate, comprehensive exam, thesis/dissertation. *Entrance requirements:* For master's, GRE General Test (for playwriting only), minimum GPA of 3.5; audition or interview; for doctorate, GRE General Test, minimum GPA of 3.5, audition and/or interview, two samples of critical writing. Additional exam requirements/recommendations for international students: Required—TOEFL (minimum score 550 paper-based; 80 iBT), IELTS (minimum score 7). *Application deadline:* For fall admission, 1/8 for domestic students. Electronic applications accepted. *Expenses:* Tuition, state resident: full-time $11,220. Tuition, nonresident: full-time $26,322. *Required fees:* $1864. *Financial support:* Fellowships, teaching assistantships, and scholarships/grants available. Financial award applicants required to submit FAFSA. *Faculty research:* Theatre of the Americas, European theatre, Asian theatre, gender studies, critical theory. *Unit head:* Charles Means, Chair, 858-534-2062, E-mail: chmeans@ucsd.edu. *Application contact:* Marybeth Ward, Graduate Coordinator, 858-534-1046, E-mail: meward@ucsd.edu. Website: http://theatre.ucsd.edu/

**University of California, Santa Barbara,** Graduate Division, College of Letters and Sciences, Division of Humanities and Fine Arts, Department of Music, Santa Barbara, CA 93106-6070. Offers brass (MM); composition (MA, PhD); conducting (MM, DMA); ethnomusicology (MA, PhD); keyboard (MM, DMA); musicology (MA, PhD); piano accompanying (MM); strings (MM, DMA); theory (MA, PhD); voice (MM, DMA); woodwinds (MM); MA/PhD; MM/DMA. *Degree requirements:* For master's, variable foreign language requirement, comprehensive exam (for some programs), thesis (for some programs); for doctorate, variable foreign language requirement, comprehensive exam, thesis/dissertation. *Entrance requirements:* For master's and doctorate, GRE. Additional exam requirements/recommendations for international students: Required—TOEFL (minimum score 550 paper-based; 80 iBT), IELTS (minimum score 7). Electronic applications accepted. *Faculty research:* Music theory, ethnomusicology, musicology, music performance, music composition.

**University of California, Santa Cruz,** Division of Graduate Studies, Division of the Arts, Department of Music, Santa Cruz, CA 95064. Offers ethnomusicology (MA); music (PhD), including cross-cultural and interdisciplinary studies; music composition (MA, DMA), including world music composition (DMA); music composition (DMA), including computer-assisted (algorithmic) composition; performance practice (MA). *Degree requirements:* For master's, one foreign language, thesis, recital; for doctorate, one foreign language, thesis/dissertation, qualifying and final examinations. *Entrance requirements:* For master's, GRE General Test, 3 letters of recommendation, writing or composition sample, 10-20 minute unedited recording; for doctorate, GRE General Test, 3 letters of recommendation, writing sample. Additional exam requirements/recommendations for international students: Required—TOEFL (minimum score 550 paper-based; 83 iBT); Recommended—IELTS (minimum score 8). Electronic applications accepted. *Faculty research:* Western music history, new music, composition, ethnomusicology, musicology.

**University of Central Arkansas,** Graduate School, College of Fine Arts and Communication, Department of Music, Conway, AR 72035-0001. Offers choral conducting (MM); instrumental conducting (MM); music (PC); music education (MM); music theory (MM); performance (MM). *Accreditation:* NASM. *Program availability:* Part-time. *Degree requirements:* For master's, comprehensive exam, thesis optional. *Entrance requirements:* For master's, GRE General Test, minimum GPA of 2.7. Additional exam requirements/recommendations for international students: Required—TOEFL (minimum score 550 paper-based). Electronic applications accepted.

**University of Central Florida,** College of Arts and Humanities, School of Performing Arts, Orlando, FL 32816. Offers music (MA); theatre (MA, MFA), including acting (MFA), theatre for young audiences (MFA). *Accreditation:* NASM; NCATE. *Program availability:* Part-time. *Faculty:* 53 full-time (20 women), 13 part-time/adjunct (6 women). *Students:* 34 full-time (20 women), 18 part-time (10 women); includes 7 minority (5 Hispanic/Latino; 2 Two or more races, non-Hispanic/Latino), 5 international. Average age 31. 55 applicants, 51% accepted, 20 enrolled. In 2016, 18 master's awarded. *Degree requirements:* For master's, comprehensive exam. *Entrance requirements:* For master's, GRE General Test. Additional exam requirements/recommendations for international students: Required—TOEFL. *Application deadline:* For fall admission, 7/15 for domestic students; for spring admission, 12/1 for domestic students. Application fee: $30. Electronic applications accepted. *Expenses:* Tuition, state resident: part-time $288.16 per credit hour. Tuition, nonresident: part-time $1071.31 per credit hour. *Financial support:* In 2016–17, 28 students received support, including 6 fellowships with partial tuition reimbursements available (averaging $7,167 per year), 6 research assistantships with partial tuition reimbursements available (averaging $9,088 per year), 20 teaching assistantships with partial tuition reimbursements available (averaging $8,267 per year); career-related internships or fieldwork, Federal Work-Study, institutionally sponsored loans, tuition waivers (partial), and unspecified assistantships also available. Financial award application deadline: 3/1; financial award applicants required to submit FAFSA. *Unit head:* Dr. Steven Chicurel-Stein, Interim Director, 407-823-2519, Fax: 407-823-3378, E-mail: steven.chicurel@ucf.edu. *Application contact:* Assistant Director, Graduate Admissions, 407-823-2766, Fax: 407-823-6442, E-mail: gradadmissions@ucf.edu. Website: http://performingarts.cah.ucf.edu/

**University of Central Missouri,** The Graduate School, Warrensburg, MO 64093. Offers accountancy (MA); accounting (MBA); applied mathematics (MS); aviation safety (MA);

biology (MS); business administration (MBA); career and technical education leadership (MS); college student personnel administration (MS); communication (MA); computer science (MS); counseling (MS); criminal justice (MS); educational leadership (Ed D); educational technology (MS); elementary and early childhood education (MSE); English (MA); environmental studies (MA); finance (MBA); history (MA); human services/educational technology (Ed S); human services/learning resources (Ed S); human services/professional counseling (Ed S); industrial hygiene (MS); industrial management (MS); information systems (MBA); information technology (MS); kinesiology (MS); library science and information services (MS); literacy education (MSE); marketing (MBA); mathematics (MS); music (MA); occupational safety management (MS); psychology (MS); rural family nursing (MS); school administration (MSE); social gerontology (MS); sociology (MA); special education (MSE); speech language pathology (MS); superintendency (Ed S); teaching (MAT); teaching English as a second language (MA); technology (MS); technology management (PhD); theatre (MA). *Program availability:* Part-time, 100% online, blended/hybrid learning. *Degree requirements:* For master's and Ed S, comprehensive exam (for some programs), thesis (for some programs). *Entrance requirements:* Additional exam requirements/recommendations for international students: Required—TOEFL (minimum score 550 paper-based; 79 iBT). Electronic applications accepted.

**University of Central Oklahoma,** The Jackson College of Graduate Studies, College of Fine Arts and Design, Department of Music, Edmond, OK 73034-5209. Offers jazz (MM), including commercial music production, performance; music (MM). *Accreditation:* NASM. *Program availability:* Part-time. *Degree requirements:* For master's, comprehensive exam, recital or project. *Entrance requirements:* For master's, interview, audition. Additional exam requirements/recommendations for international students: Required—TOEFL (minimum score 550 paper-based; 79 iBT), IELTS (minimum score 6.5). Electronic applications accepted. *Faculty research:* Historical performance, history of music education.

**University of Chicago,** Division of the Humanities, Department of Music, Chicago, IL 60637. Offers composition (PhD); ethnomusicology (PhD); music history and theory (PhD). *Students:* 70 full-time (33 women); includes 9 minority (3 Black or African American, non-Hispanic/Latino; 1 Asian, non-Hispanic/Latino; 3 Hispanic/Latino; 2 Two or more races, non-Hispanic/Latino), 20 international. 103 applicants, 15% accepted, 12 enrolled. In 2016, 10 doctorates awarded. Terminal master's awarded for partial completion of doctoral program. *Degree requirements:* For doctorate, 3 foreign languages, comprehensive exam, thesis/dissertation. *Entrance requirements:* For doctorate, GRE General Test. Additional exam requirements/recommendations for international students: Required—TOEFL (minimum score 104 iBT), IELTS (minimum score 7). *Application deadline:* For fall admission, 12/15 for domestic and international students. Application fee: $90. Electronic applications accepted. *Financial support:* Fellowships with full tuition reimbursements, teaching assistantships with full tuition reimbursements, Federal Work-Study, institutionally sponsored loans, scholarships/grants, and health care benefits available. Financial award application deadline: 12/15; financial award applicants required to submit FAFSA. *Faculty research:* Early music, history of music theory, historical anthropology of music, Jewish music, popular and vernacular music. *Unit head:* Thomas Christensen, Chair, 773-702-8500. *Application contact:* Michael Beetley, Assistant Dean of Students, Admissions and Fellowships, 773-702-1552, Fax: 773-834-9148, E-mail: humanitiesadmissions@uchicago.edu. Website: http://music.uchicago.edu/

**University of Chicago,** Division of the Humanities, Master of Arts Program in the Humanities, Chicago, IL 60637. Offers art history (MA); cinema and media studies (MA); classic languages (MA); comparative literature (MA); creative writing (MA); cultural policy studies (MA); digital humanities (MA); East Asian languages and civilizations (MA); English language and literature (MA); gender and sexuality studies (MA); Germanic studies (MA); linguistics (MA); music (MA); near Eastern languages and civilizations (MA); philosophy (MA); poetics (MA); race, politics and culture (MA); Romance languages and literatures (MA); Slavic languages and literatures (MA); South Asian languages and civilizations (MA); theater and performance studies (MA). *Students:* 80 full-time (43 women), 7 part-time (3 women); includes 20 minority (5 Black or African American, non-Hispanic/Latino; 1 American Indian or Alaska Native, non-Hispanic/Latino; 6 Asian, non-Hispanic/Latino; 5 Hispanic/Latino; 3 Two or more races, non-Hispanic/Latino), 11 international. Average age 26. 706 applicants, 15% accepted, 42 enrolled. In 2016, 92 master's awarded. *Degree requirements:* For master's, thesis. *Entrance requirements:* For master's, GRE General Test. Additional exam requirements/recommendations for international students: Required—TOEFL (minimum score 104 iBT), IELTS (minimum score 7). *Application deadline:* For fall admission, 1/3 for domestic and international students. Application fee: $90. Electronic applications accepted. *Financial support:* In 2016–17, 8 fellowships with partial tuition reimbursements (averaging $12,000 per year) were awarded; Federal Work-Study, institutionally sponsored loans, scholarships/grants, and tuition waivers (partial) also available. Financial award application deadline: 12/15; financial award applicants required to submit FAFSA. *Unit head:* Malynne Sternstein, Co-Director, 773-834-1201, Fax: 773-834-7526. *Application contact:* Program Coordinator, 773-834-1201, Fax: 773-834-7526, E-mail: ma-humanities@uchicago.edu. Website: http://maph.uchicago.edu/

**University of Cincinnati,** Graduate School, College-Conservatory of Music, Division of Composition, Musicology and Theory, Cincinnati, OH 45221. Offers composition (MM, DMA); music history (MM); music theory (MM, DMA); musicology (PhD). *Accreditation:* NASM. *Degree requirements:* For master's, variable foreign language requirement, comprehensive exam, thesis; for doctorate, variable foreign language requirement, comprehensive exam, thesis/dissertation. *Entrance requirements:* For master's and doctorate, GRE General Test, interview. Additional exam requirements/recommendations for international students: Required—TOEFL (minimum score 520 paper-based). Electronic applications accepted. *Expenses: Tuition, area resident:* Full-time $12,790; part-time $389 per credit hour. Tuition, state resident: full-time $13,290; part-time $419 per credit hour. Tuition, nonresident: full-time $24,532; part-time $976 per credit hour. *International tuition:* $24,832 full-time. *Required fees:* $3958; $140 per credit hour. Tuition and fees vary according to course load, degree level, program and reciprocity agreements.

**University of Cincinnati,** Graduate School, College-Conservatory of Music, Division of Ensembles and Conducting, Cincinnati, OH 45221. Offers choral conducting (MM, DMA); orchestral conducting (MM, DMA); wind conducting (MM, DMA). *Accreditation:* NASM. *Degree requirements:* For master's, comprehensive exam, conducting performances; for doctorate, one foreign language, comprehensive exam, thesis/dissertation, conducting performances, lecture recital. *Entrance requirements:* For master's and doctorate, GRE General Test, audition, interview. Additional exam requirements/recommendations for international students: Required—TOEFL (minimum score 520 paper-based). Electronic applications accepted. *Expenses: Tuition, area resident:* Full-time $12,790; part-time $389 per credit hour. Tuition, state resident: full-time $13,290; part-time $419 per credit hour. Tuition, nonresident: full-time $24,532; part-time $976 per credit hour. *International tuition:* $24,832 full-time. *Required fees:* $3958; $140 per credit hour. Tuition and fees vary according to course load, degree level, program and reciprocity agreements.

**University of Cincinnati,** Graduate School, College-Conservatory of Music, Division of Keyboard Studies, Cincinnati, OH 45221. Offers MM, DMA, AD. *Degree requirements:* For master's, comprehensive exam; for doctorate, one foreign language, comprehensive exam, thesis/dissertation. *Entrance requirements:* For master's and doctorate, GRE General Test, audition; for AD, audition. Additional exam requirements/recommendations for international students: Required—TOEFL (minimum score 520 paper-based). Electronic applications accepted. *Expenses: Tuition, area resident:* Full-time $12,790; part-time $389 per credit hour. Tuition, state resident: full-time $13,290; part-time $419 per credit hour. Tuition, nonresident: full-time $24,532; part-time $976 per credit hour. *International tuition:* $24,832 full-time. *Required fees:* $3958; $140 per credit hour. Tuition and fees vary according to course load, degree level, program and reciprocity agreements.

**University of Cincinnati,** Graduate School, College-Conservatory of Music, Division of Performance Studies, Cincinnati, OH 45221. Offers performance (MM, DMA, AD). MM, DMA, and AD are available for every instrument. *Accreditation:* NASM. *Degree requirements:* For master's, comprehensive exam, recitals; for doctorate, one foreign language, comprehensive exam, thesis/dissertation, recitals; for AD, recitals. *Entrance requirements:* For master's and doctorate, GRE General Test, audition. Additional exam requirements/recommendations for international students: Required—TOEFL (minimum score 520 paper-based). Electronic applications accepted. *Expenses: Tuition, area resident:* Full-time $12,790; part-time $389 per credit hour. Tuition, state resident: full-time $13,290; part-time $419 per credit hour. Tuition, nonresident: full-time $24,532; part-time $976 per credit hour. *International tuition:* $24,832 full-time. *Required fees:* $3958; $140 per credit hour. Tuition and fees vary according to course load, degree level, program and reciprocity agreements. *Faculty research:* Performance, guest teaching.

**University of Cincinnati,** Graduate School, College-Conservatory of Music, Division of Theatre Arts, Production and Arts Administration, Cincinnati, OH 45221. Offers arts administration (MA); directing (MFA); theater design and production (MFA); voice and opera (MM, DMA); MBA/MA. *Accreditation:* NAST (one or more programs are accredited). *Degree requirements:* For master's, final project. *Entrance requirements:* For master's, GMAT (MA), audition/interview. Additional exam requirements/recommendations for international students: Required—TOEFL (minimum score 520 paper-based). Electronic applications accepted. *Expenses: Tuition, area resident:* Full-time $12,790; part-time $389 per credit hour. Tuition, state resident: full-time $13,290; part-time $419 per credit hour. Tuition, nonresident: full-time $24,532; part-time $976 per credit hour. *International tuition:* $24,832 full-time. *Required fees:* $3958; $140 per credit hour. Tuition and fees vary according to course load, degree level, program and reciprocity agreements.

**University of Colorado Boulder,** Graduate School, College of Music, Boulder, CO 80309. Offers composition (M Mus, D Mus A); conducting (M Mus); instrumental conducting and literature (D Mus A); literature and performance of choral music (D Mus A); music education (M Mus Ed, PhD), including choral or wind instrument conducting (M Mus Ed), general (M Mus Ed), Kodaly concepts (M Mus Ed), piano pedagogy (M Mus Ed), primary instruments (M Mus Ed), secondary instruments (M Mus Ed), voice pedagogy (M Mus Ed); music theory (M Mus); performance (M Mus, D Mus A); performance and pedagogy (M Mus, D Mus A). *Accreditation:* NASM. *Faculty:* 62 full-time (19 women). *Students:* 163 full-time (77 women), 43 part-time (25 women); includes 26 minority (4 Black or African American, non-Hispanic/Latino; 7 Asian, non-Hispanic/Latino; 9 Hispanic/Latino; 6 Two or more races, non-Hispanic/Latino), 18 international. Average age 30. 458 applicants, 38% accepted, 51 enrolled. In 2016, 39 master's, 27 doctorates awarded. Terminal master's awarded for partial completion of doctoral program. *Degree requirements:* For master's, variable foreign language requirement, comprehensive exam, thesis or alternative, recital; for doctorate, variable foreign language requirement, thesis/dissertation. *Entrance requirements:* For master's, GRE General Test, GRE Subject Test (music literature), minimum undergraduate GPA of 2.75; for doctorate, GRE General Test, GRE Subject Test, audition, sample of research. *Application deadline:* For fall admission, 12/1 for domestic and international students; for spring admission, 10/1 for domestic and international students. Applications are processed on a rolling basis. Application fee: $60 ($80 for international students). Electronic applications accepted. Application fee is waived when completed online. *Financial support:* In 2016–17, 496 students received support, including 234 fellowships (averaging $2,277 per year), 1 research assistantship with full and partial tuition reimbursement available (averaging $6,020 per year), 108 teaching assistantships with full and partial tuition reimbursements available (averaging $22,460 per year); institutionally sponsored loans, scholarships/grants, health care benefits, and unspecified assistantships also available. Financial award application deadline: 3/1; financial award applicants required to submit FAFSA. *Faculty research:* Music, instrumental music, performing arts, chamber music, musicology/music theory. *Total annual research expenditures:* $90,364. *Application contact:* E-mail: gradmusc@colorado.edu. Website: http://music.colorado.edu/

**University of Colorado Denver,** College of Arts and Media, Denver, CO 80217. Offers recording arts (MS), including media forensics, recording arts. *Accreditation:* NASM. *Program availability:* Part-time, evening/weekend. *Faculty:* 34 full-time (12 women), 1 (woman) part-time/adjunct. *Students:* 27 full-time (9 women), 5 part-time (2 women); includes 9 minority (2 Black or African American, non-Hispanic/Latino; 1 Asian, non-Hispanic/Latino; 4 Hispanic/Latino; 2 Two or more races, non-Hispanic/Latino), 2 international. Average age 31. 26 applicants, 92% accepted, 16 enrolled. In 2016, 13 master's awarded. *Degree requirements:* For master's, 34 credits, thesis/portfolio. *Entrance requirements:* For master's, GRE General Test (minimum scores higher than 50th percentile for all sections), minimum undergraduate GPA of 3.0, portfolio, resume, interview, 3 letters of recommendation. Additional exam requirements/recommendations for international students: Required—TOEFL (minimum score 70 iBT). *Application deadline:* For fall admission, 4/1 for domestic students, 3/1 for international students. Application fee: $50 ($75 for international students). Electronic applications accepted. *Expenses:* Contact institution. *Financial support:* In 2016–17, 4 students received support. Federal Work-Study, institutionally sponsored loans, scholarships/grants, traineeships, and unspecified assistantships available. Financial award application deadline: 4/1; financial award applicants required to submit FAFSA. *Faculty research:* Audio forensics, audio pedagogy, concert recordings, digital audio workstations, music law. *Total annual research expenditures:* $10,753. *Unit head:* Laurence D. Kaptain, Dean, College of Arts and Media, 303-556-2279, E-mail: laurence.kaptain@ucdenver.edu. *Application contact:* Lisa Funderburg, Program Assistant, 303-352-3833, E-mail: lisa.funderburg@ucdenver.edu. Website: http://www.ucdenver.edu/academics/colleges/CAM/programs/meis/masterdegree/Pages/index.aspx

**University of Connecticut,** Graduate School, School of Fine Arts, Department of Music, Storrs, CT 06269. Offers conducting (M Mus, DMA); historical musicology (MA); music theory (MA); music theory and history (PhD); performance (M Mus, DMA). *Accreditation:* NASM. Terminal master's awarded for partial completion of doctoral program. *Degree requirements:* For master's, comprehensive exam; for doctorate, thesis/dissertation. *Entrance requirements:* For master's, GRE General Test, GRE

## Music

Subject Test, audition; for doctorate, GRE Subject Test, MAT, audition. Additional exam requirements/recommendations for international students: Required—TOEFL (minimum score 550 paper-based).

**University of Delaware,** College of Arts and Sciences, Department of Music, Newark, DE 19716. Offers composition (MM); music education (MM); performance (MM). *Accreditation:* NASM. *Program availability:* Part-time. *Entrance requirements:* For master's, audition. Additional exam requirements/recommendations for international students: Required—TOEFL. Electronic applications accepted. *Faculty research:* Teaching of music.

**University of Denver,** Division of Arts, Humanities and Social Sciences, Lamont School of Music, Denver, CO 80208. Offers composition (MM); composition - jazz emphasis (MM); conducting (MM, Certificate); jazz studies (Certificate); music theory (MA); musicology (MA); orchestral studies (Certificate); pedagogy (MM); performance (MM, Certificate); performance - jazz emphasis (MM); Suzuki teaching (Certificate). *Accreditation:* NASM. *Program availability:* Part-time. *Faculty:* 32 full-time (9 women), 33 part-time/adjunct (15 women). *Students:* 30 full-time (9 women), 71 part-time (35 women); includes 16 minority (2 Black or African American, non-Hispanic/Latino; 1 American Indian or Alaska Native, non-Hispanic/Latino; 2 Asian, non-Hispanic/Latino; 7 Hispanic/Latino; 4 Two or more races, non-Hispanic/Latino), 16 international. Average age 27. 150 applicants, 81% accepted, 58 enrolled. In 2016, 24 master's, 2 other advanced degrees awarded. *Degree requirements:* For master's, one foreign language, comprehensive exam, recital or project (for performance), thesis (for musicology, music theory, piano pedagogy). *Entrance requirements:* For master's, GRE General Test (for MA only), bachelor's degree, transcripts, personal statement, resume, three letters of recommendation, pre-screen audition (for performance), portfolio (for composition), essay or research paper (for MA only); for Certificate, bachelor's degree, transcripts, personal statement, resume, letters of recommendation, pre-screen video recording or music audition. Additional exam requirements/recommendations for international students: Required—TOEFL (minimum score 550 paper-based; 80 iBT). *Application deadline:* For fall admission; 1/15 priority date for domestic and international students. Applications are processed on a rolling basis. Application fee: $65. Electronic applications accepted. *Expenses:* $29,022 per year full-time. *Financial support:* In 2016–17, 89 students received support, including 25 teaching assistantships with tuition reimbursements available (averaging $6,933 per year); career-related internships or fieldwork, Federal Work-Study, institutionally sponsored loans, scholarships/grants, tuition waivers, and unspecified assistantships also available. Support available to part-time students. Financial award application deadline: 2/15; financial award applicants required to submit FAFSA. *Faculty research:* Performance, jazz studies and commercial music, musicology, music theory, composition, music pedagogy, music recording and production. *Unit head:* Dr. Nancy Cochran, Professor and Director, 303-871-6986, Fax: 303-871-3118, E-mail: nancy.cochran@du.edu. *Application contact:* Stephen Campbell, Director of Admission, 303-871-6973, Fax: 303-871-3118, E-mail: stephen.l.campbell@du.edu.
Website: http://www.du.edu/ahss/lamont/index.html

**University of Florida,** Graduate School, College of The Arts, School of Music, Gainesville, FL 32611. Offers choral conducting (MM); composition (MM, PhD); electronic music (MM); ethnomusicology (MM); instrumental conducting (MM); music (MM, PhD); music education (MM, PhD), including choral conducting (MM), composition (MM), electronic music (MM), ethnomusicology (MM), instrumental conducting (MM), music education (MM), music history and literature (MM), music theory (MM), performance (MM), piano pedagogy (MM); music history and literature (MM, PhD); music theory (MM); performance (MM); sacred music (MM). *Accreditation:* NASM. *Degree requirements:* For master's, variable foreign language requirement, comprehensive exam, thesis, recital; for doctorate, thesis/dissertation. *Entrance requirements:* For master's and doctorate, GRE General Test, audition, minimum GPA of 3.0. Additional exam requirements/recommendations for international students: Required—TOEFL (minimum score 550 paper-based; 80 iBT), IELTS (minimum score 6). Electronic applications accepted.

**University of Georgia,** Franklin College of Arts and Sciences, Hugh Hodgson School of Music, Athens, GA 30602. Offers MA, MM, MM Ed, DMA, PhD. *Accreditation:* NASM. *Degree requirements:* For master's, variable foreign language requirement, thesis (MA); for doctorate, variable foreign language requirement, thesis/dissertation. *Entrance requirements:* For master's and doctorate, GRE General Test. *Application deadline:* For fall admission, 7/1 priority date for domestic students; for spring admission, 11/15 for domestic students. Application fee: $50. Electronic applications accepted. *Financial support:* Fellowships, research assistantships, teaching assistantships, and unspecified assistantships available. *Unit head:* Dr. Dale Monson, Director, 706-542-2776, Fax: 706-542-2773, E-mail: dmonson@uga.edu. *Application contact:* Peter Jutras, Graduate Coordinator, 206-542-2765, E-mail: pjutras@uga.edu.
Website: http://www.music.uga.edu

**University of Hartford,** The Hartt School, West Hartford, CT 06117-1599. Offers choral conducting (MM Ed); composition (MM, DMA, Artist Diploma, Diploma); conducting (MM, DMA, Artist Diploma, Diploma), including choral (MM, Diploma), instrumental (MM, Diploma); early childhood education (MM Ed); instrumental conducting (MM Ed); Kodály (MM Ed); music (CAGS); music education (DMA, PhD); music history (MM); music theory (MM); pedagogy (MM Ed); performance (MM, MM Ed, DMA, Artist Diploma, Diploma); research (MM Ed); technology (MM Ed). *Program availability:* Part-time. *Degree requirements:* For master's, variable foreign language requirement, thesis (for some programs), recital; for doctorate, variable foreign language requirement, thesis/dissertation (for some programs), recital; for other advanced degree, recital. *Entrance requirements:* For master's, audition, letters of recommendation; for doctorate, proficiency exam, audition, interview, research paper; for other advanced degree, audition. Additional exam requirements/recommendations for international students: Required—TOEFL. Electronic applications accepted. *Expenses:* Contact institution.

**University of Hawaii at Manoa,** Graduate Division, College of Arts and Humanities, Department of Music, Honolulu, HI 96822. Offers M Mus, MA, PhD. *Accreditation:* NASM. *Program availability:* Part-time. *Degree requirements:* For master's, variable foreign language requirement, thesis optional; for doctorate, variable foreign language requirement, comprehensive exam, thesis/dissertation. *Entrance requirements:* For master's, GRE General Test, diagnostic exams in acoustics theory; for doctorate, diagnostic exams in music history and theory, GRE General Test. Additional exam requirements/recommendations for international students: Required—TOEFL (minimum score 540 paper-based; 76 iBT), IELTS (minimum score 5). *Faculty research:* Original compositions, nineteenth century German music, Korean and Indonesian music, piano/voice performance, Pacific music.

**University of Houston,** College of Liberal Arts and Social Sciences, Moores School of Music, Houston, TX 77204. Offers accompanying and chamber music (MM); applied music (MM); composition (MM); music education (DMA); music theory (MM); performance (DMA). *Accreditation:* NASM. *Program availability:* Part-time. *Degree requirements:* For master's, one foreign language, comprehensive exam, recital; for doctorate, one foreign language, comprehensive exam, thesis/dissertation. *Entrance requirements:* For master's, audition, resume, 3 letters of recommendation; for doctorate, writing sample, audition, statement of purpose, resume. Additional exam

requirements/recommendations for international students: Required—TOEFL (minimum score 550 paper-based; 79 iBT), IELTS (minimum score 6.5). Electronic applications accepted. *Faculty research:* Twentieth century music, Baroque music, history of music theory, music analysis.

**University of Idaho,** College of Graduate Studies, College of Letters, Arts and Social Sciences, Lionel Hampton School of Music, Moscow, ID 83844. Offers M Mus, MA. *Accreditation:* NASM. *Faculty:* 22 full-time (8 women), 1 part-time. Average age 26. In 2016, 8 master's awarded. *Degree requirements:* For master's, thesis or alternative. *Entrance requirements:* For master's, minimum GPA of 3.0. Additional exam requirements/recommendations for international students: Required—TOEFL. *Application deadline:* For fall admission, 8/1 for domestic students; for spring admission, 12/15 for domestic students. Applications are processed on a rolling basis. Application fee: $60. Electronic applications accepted. *Expenses:* Tuition, state resident: full-time $6460; part-time $414 per credit hour. Tuition, nonresident: full-time $21,268; part-time $1237 per credit hour. *Required fees:* $2070; $60 per credit hour. Full-time tuition and fees vary according to course load and reciprocity agreements. *Financial support:* Research assistantships and teaching assistantships available. Financial award applicants required to submit FAFSA. *Unit head:* Dr. Torrey Lawrence, Director, 208-885-6231, E-mail: music@uidaho.edu. *Application contact:* Sean Scoggin, Director of Graduate Admissions, 208-885-4723, Fax: 208-885-4406, E-mail: graduateadmissions@uidaho.edu.
Website: https://www.uidaho.edu/class/music

**University of Illinois at Urbana–Champaign,** Graduate College, College of Fine and Applied Arts, School of Music, Champaign, IL 61820. Offers music (M Mus, AD, DMA); music education (MME, PhD); musicology (PhD). *Accreditation:* NASM.

**The University of Iowa,** Graduate College, College of Liberal Arts and Sciences, School of Music, Iowa City, IA 52242-1316. Offers MA, MFA, DMA, PhD. *Accreditation:* NASM. *Degree requirements:* For master's, thesis (for some programs), exam; for doctorate, comprehensive exam, thesis/dissertation. *Entrance requirements:* For master's and doctorate, minimum GPA of 3.0. Additional exam requirements/recommendations for international students: Required—TOEFL (minimum score 550 paper-based; 81 iBT). Electronic applications accepted.

**The University of Kansas,** Graduate Studies, School of Music, Program in Music, Lawrence, KS 66045. Offers MM, DMA, PhD. *Program availability:* Part-time. *Students:* 148 full-time (70 women), 10 part-time (5 women); includes 13 minority (2 Black or African American, non-Hispanic/Latino; 3 Asian, non-Hispanic/Latino; 2 Hispanic/Latino; 6 Two or more races, non-Hispanic/Latino), 48 international. Average age 29. 196 applicants, 54% accepted, 44 enrolled. In 2016, 26 master's, 26 doctorates awarded. *Entrance requirements:* For master's, KU Musicology and Music Theory diagnostic exam, minimum GPA of 3.0, resume/curriculum vitae, 3 letters of reference, official transcripts, statement of purpose; for doctorate, GRE (for PhD); KU Musicology and Music Theory diagnostic exam, minimum GPA of 3.0, audition (for DMA), resume/curriculum vitae, 3 letters of reference, official transcripts, statement of purpose. Additional exam requirements/recommendations for international students: Required—TOEFL or IELTS (minimum score 6). *Application deadline:* For fall admission, 12/1 priority date for domestic and international students; for summer admission, 4/15 for domestic students, 2/15 for international students. Application fee: $65 ($85 for international students). Electronic applications accepted. *Financial support:* Fellowships, teaching assistantships, institutionally sponsored loans, scholarships/grants, and unspecified assistantships available. Financial award application deadline: 12/1; financial award applicants required to submit FAFSA. *Faculty research:* Musicology, music theory, composition, performance, conducting. *Unit head:* Dr. Martin Bergee, Associate Dean for Academic Affairs, 785-864-3421, Fax: 785-864-5866, E-mail: music@ku.edu. *Application contact:* Jane Gnojek, Administrative Professional, 785-864-2862, E-mail: jgnojek@ku.edu.
Website: http://www.music.ku.edu

**University of Kentucky,** Graduate School, College of Fine Arts, Program in Music, Lexington, KY 40506-0032. Offers composition (MM, DMA); conducting (MM, DMA); music education (MM, PhD); music theory (MA, PhD); music therapy (MM); musicology (MA, PhD); performance (MM, DMA); sacred music (MM). *Accreditation:* NASM. *Program availability:* Part-time, evening/weekend. *Degree requirements:* For master's, variable foreign language requirement, comprehensive exam, thesis (for some programs); for doctorate, variable foreign language requirement, comprehensive exam, thesis/dissertation. *Entrance requirements:* For master's, GRE General Test, minimum undergraduate GPA of 2.75; for doctorate, GRE General Test, minimum undergraduate GPA of 2.75, graduate 3.0. Additional exam requirements/recommendations for international students: Required—TOEFL (minimum score 550 paper-based). Electronic applications accepted. *Faculty research:* Musicology, music theory, jazz, music education, performance and conducting.

**University of Lethbridge,** School of Graduate Studies, Lethbridge, AB T1K 3M4, Canada. Offers addictions counseling (M Sc); agricultural biotechnology (M Sc); agricultural studies (M Sc, MA); anthropology (MA); archaeology (M Sc, MA); art (MA, MFA); biochemistry (M Sc); biological sciences (M Sc); biomolecular science (PhD); biosystems and biodiversity (PhD); Canadian studies (MA); chemistry (M Sc); computer science (M Sc); computer science and geographical information science (M Sc); counseling (MC); counseling psychology (M Ed); dramatic arts (MA); earth, space, and physical science (PhD); economics (MA); education (MA, PhD); educational leadership (M Ed); English (MA); environmental science (M Sc); evolution and behavior (PhD); exercise science (M Sc); French (MA); French/German (MA); French/Spanish (MA); general education (M Ed); geography (M Sc, MA); German (MA); health sciences (M Sc); individualized multidisciplinary (M Sc, MA); kinesiology (M Sc, MA); management (M Sc), including accounting, finance, human resource management and labor relations, information systems, international management, marketing, policy and strategy; mathematics (M Sc); music (M Mus, MA); Native American studies (MA); neuroscience (M Sc, PhD); new media (MA, MFA); nursing (M Sc, MN); philosophy (MA); physics (M Sc); political science (MA); psychology (M Sc, MA); religious studies (MA); sociology (MA); theatre and dramatic arts (MFA); theoretical and computational science (PhD); urban and regional studies (MA); women and gender studies (MA). *Program availability:* Part-time, evening/weekend. *Degree requirements:* For master's, thesis (for some programs); for doctorate, comprehensive exam, thesis/dissertation. *Entrance requirements:* For master's, GMAT (for M Sc in management), bachelor's degree in related field, minimum GPA of 3.0 during previous 20 graded semester courses, 2 years' teaching or related experience (M Ed); for doctorate, master's degree, minimum graduate GPA of 3.5. Additional exam requirements/recommendations for international students: Required—TOEFL (minimum score 580 paper-based; 93 iBT). Electronic applications accepted. *Faculty research:* Movement and brain plasticity, gibberellin physiology, photosynthesis, carbon cycling, molecular properties of main-group ring components.

**University of Louisiana at Lafayette,** College of the Arts, School of Music, Lafayette, LA 70504. Offers conducting (MM); pedagogy (MM); vocal and instrumental performance (MM). *Accreditation:* NASM. *Degree requirements:* For master's, thesis or alternative. *Entrance requirements:* For master's, GRE General Test, minimum GPA of 2.75. Additional exam requirements/recommendations for international students:

Required—TOEFL (minimum score 550 paper-based). Electronic applications accepted. *Faculty research:* Nineteenth century American music, trumpet pedagogy, fifteenth century Renaissance polyphony, Charles Ives.

**University of Louisville,** Graduate School, School of Music, Louisville, KY 40292-0001. Offers composition (MM); electronic composition (MM); music education (MME); music history and literature (MM); music performance (MM), including choral conducting, instrumental, jazz composition, jazz performance, orchestral conducting, organ performance, piano pedagogy, piano performance, string pedagogy, vocal performance, wind band performance, wind conducting; music theory (MM). *Accreditation:* NASM. *Program availability:* Part-time. *Faculty:* 36 full-time (10 women), 39 part-time/adjunct (18 women). *Students:* 54 full-time (20 women), 5 part-time (3 women); includes 5 minority (2 Black or African American, non-Hispanic/Latino; 1 Hispanic/Latino; 2 Two or more races, non-Hispanic/Latino), 7 international. Average age 25. 62 applicants, 66% accepted, 25 enrolled. In 2016, 31 master's awarded. *Degree requirements:* For master's, variable foreign language requirement, comprehensive exam, thesis (for some programs), recital (for performance), paper or thesis (for music education), major composition (for composition). *Entrance requirements:* For master's, music history and theory entrance exams, jazz history and theory entrance exam (for jazz majors), audition, portfolio. Additional exam requirements/recommendations for international students: Required—TOEFL (minimum score 79 iBT) or IELTS (6.5). Application fee: $60. Electronic applications accepted. *Expenses:* Contact institution. *Financial support:* In 2016–17, 1 fellowship with full tuition reimbursement (averaging $12,000 per year), 12 teaching assistantships with full tuition reimbursements (averaging $12,000 per year) were awarded; Federal Work-Study, scholarships/grants, health care benefits, and unspecified assistantships also available. Financial award application deadline: 3/1. *Faculty research:* Composition, musicology, performance, pedagogy, analysis and theoretical application. *Total annual research expenditures:* $87,500. *Unit head:* Dr. Christopher P. Doane, Dean, 502-852-6907, Fax: 502-852-0520, E-mail: c0doan01@louisville.edu. *Application contact:* Laura Angermeier, Admissions Counselor/Senior Advising Counselor, 502-852-1623, Fax: 502-852-0520, E-mail: leange01@louisville.edu.
Website: http://www.louisville.edu/music/

**University of Maine,** Graduate School, College of Liberal Arts and Sciences, School of Performing Arts, Orono, ME 04469. Offers MM. *Accreditation:* NASM. *Program availability:* Part-time. *Faculty:* 10 full-time (3 women), 9 part-time/adjunct (6 women). *Students:* 5 full-time (1 woman), 5 part-time (2 women), 4 international. Average age 26. 3 applicants, 100% accepted, 2 enrolled. In 2016, 5 master's awarded. *Entrance requirements:* For master's, audition. Additional exam requirements/recommendations for international students: Required—TOEFL. *Application deadline:* For fall admission, 2/1 priority date for domestic students. Applications are processed on a rolling basis. Application fee: $65. Electronic applications accepted. *Expenses:* Tuition, state resident: full-time $7524; part-time $2508 per credit. Tuition, nonresident: full-time $24,498; part-time $8166 per credit. *Required fees:* $1148; $571 per credit. *Financial support:* In 2016–17, 4 students received support, including 4 teaching assistantships with full tuition reimbursements available (averaging $7,300 per year); career-related internships or fieldwork, Federal Work-Study, institutionally sponsored loans, scholarships/grants, and tuition waivers (full and partial) also available. Support available to part-time students. Financial award application deadline: 3/1. *Faculty research:* Percussion music of Carter and Varese; song-settings of the poetry of W.B. Yeats; philosophy of voice; entartete musik: music and composers banned by the Nazis; historic performance practices of the Baroque Era. *Unit head:* Dr. Beth Wiemann, Chair, 207-581-1244, Fax: 207-581-4701. *Application contact:* Scott G. Delcourt, Assistant Vice President for Graduate Studies and Senior Associate Dean, 207-581-3291, Fax: 207-581-3232, E-mail: graduate@maine.edu.
Website: http://umaine.edu/spa/

**The University of Manchester,** School of Arts, Histories and Cultures, Manchester, United Kingdom. Offers anthropology, media and performance (PhD); applied theatre professional (PhD); archaeology (PhD); art history and visual studies (PhD); arts management and cultural policy (PhD); classics and ancient history (PhD); composition (PhD); creative writing (PhD); drama (PhD); economic and social history (PhD); electroacoustic composition (PhD); English and American studies (PhD); history (PhD); humanitarianism and conflict response (PhD); museology (PhD); music (PhD); musicology (PhD); religions and theology (PhD).

**University of Manitoba,** Faculty of Graduate Studies, Marcel A. Desautels Faculty of Music, Winnipeg, MB R3T 2N2, Canada. Offers M Mus.

**University of Maryland, Baltimore County,** The Graduate School, College of Arts, Humanities and Social Sciences, Department of Music, Baltimore, MD 21250. Offers American contemporary music (Postbaccalaureate Certificate). *Accreditation:* NASM. *Program availability:* Part-time. *Faculty:* 3 full-time (2 women). *Students:* 1 (woman) full-time, 1 (woman) part-time. Average age 22. 3 applicants, 67% accepted, 2 enrolled. In 2016, 1 Postbaccalaureate Certificate awarded. *Degree requirements:* For Postbaccalaureate Certificate, solo recital. *Entrance requirements:* For degree, minimum GPA of 3.0, resume, reference letters, DVD of performance, BM. Additional exam requirements/recommendations for international students: Recommended—TOEFL. *Application deadline:* For fall admission, 12/1 for domestic and international students; for winter admission, 1/30 for domestic and international students; for spring admission, 5/15 priority date for domestic students, 4/15 for international students. Applications are processed on a rolling basis. Application fee: $50. Electronic applications accepted. *Expenses:* Contact institution. *Financial support:* Scholarships/grants available. Financial award applicants required to submit FAFSA. *Faculty research:* Music, composition, performance, music technology, contemporary music. *Total annual research expenditures:* $150,000. *Unit head:* Dr. Linda Dusman, Chair, 410-455-5960, E-mail: dusman@umbc.edu. *Application contact:* Dr. Lisa Cella, Director, Certificate Program in American Contemporary Music, 410-455-1405, Fax: 410-455-1181, E-mail: cella@umbc.edu.
Website: http://www.umbc.edu/degrees-certificates/american-contemporary-music/

**University of Maryland, College Park,** Academic Affairs, College of Arts and Humanities, School of Music, Program in Ethnomusicology, College Park, MD 20742. Offers MA. *Degree requirements:* For master's, comprehensive exam, thesis optional, oral defense. *Entrance requirements:* Additional exam requirements/recommendations for international students: Required—TOEFL.

**University of Maryland, College Park,** Academic Affairs, College of Arts and Humanities, School of Music, Program in Music, College Park, MD 20742. Offers M Ed, MA, MM, DMA, Ed D, PhD. *Accreditation:* NASM. *Entrance requirements:* For master's, GRE General Test (for ethnomusicology, historical musicology and music theory), 3 letters of recommendation, audition/interview. Additional exam requirements/recommendations for international students: Required—TOEFL.

**University of Massachusetts Amherst,** Graduate School, College of Humanities and Fine Arts, Department of English, Amherst, MA 01003. Offers American studies (PhD); composition and rhetoric (PhD); creative writing (MFA); English and American literature (MA, PhD). *Program availability:* Part-time. Terminal master's awarded for partial completion of doctoral program. *Degree requirements:* For master's, one foreign language, thesis optional; for doctorate, one foreign language, comprehensive exam, thesis/dissertation. *Entrance requirements:* For master's, manuscript; for doctorate, GRE General Test, manuscript. Additional exam requirements/recommendations for international students: Required—TOEFL (minimum score 550 paper-based; 80 iBT), IELTS (minimum score 6.5). Electronic applications accepted.

**University of Massachusetts Amherst,** Graduate School, College of Humanities and Fine Arts, Department of Music and Dance, Amherst, MA 01003. Offers collaborative piano (MM); composition (MM); conducting (MM); jazz composition/arranging (MM); music education (MM, PhD); music history (MM); music theory (PhD); performance (MM). *Accreditation:* NASM. *Program availability:* Part-time. Terminal master's awarded for partial completion of doctoral program. *Degree requirements:* For master's, thesis or alternative; for doctorate, comprehensive exam, thesis/dissertation. *Entrance requirements:* For master's and doctorate, placement tests, original scores, research, audition or tape. Additional exam requirements/recommendations for international students: Required—TOEFL (minimum score 550 paper-based; 80 iBT), IELTS (minimum score 6.5). Electronic applications accepted.

**University of Massachusetts Lowell,** College of Fine Arts, Humanities and Social Sciences, Department of Music, Lowell, MA 01854. Offers music education (MM). *Accreditation:* NASM. *Program availability:* Part-time. *Degree requirements:* For master's, one foreign language, thesis. *Entrance requirements:* For master's, MAT, audition. Electronic applications accepted.

**University of Memphis,** Graduate School, College of Communication and Fine Arts, Rudi E. Scheidt School of Music, Memphis, TN 38152. Offers composition (M Mu, DMA); conducting (M Mu, DMA); jazz and studio music (M Mu); music education (M Mu, PhD); music theory (DCC); musicology (PhD); Orff-Schulwerk (M Mu); pedagogy (M Mu); performance (M Mu, DMA). *Accreditation:* NASM. *Program availability:* Part-time. *Faculty:* 35 full-time (8 women), 6 part-time/adjunct (2 women). *Students:* 72 full-time (31 women), 47 part-time (24 women); includes 24 minority (11 Black or African American, non-Hispanic/Latino; 4 Asian, non-Hispanic/Latino; 6 Hispanic/Latino; 3 Two or more races, non-Hispanic/Latino), 15 international. Average age 32. 76 applicants, 83% accepted, 33 enrolled. In 2016, 25 master's, 18 doctorates awarded. Terminal master's awarded for partial completion of doctoral program. *Degree requirements:* For master's, variable foreign language requirement, comprehensive exam, thesis or alternative; for doctorate, one foreign language, comprehensive exam, thesis/dissertation, qualifying exam. *Entrance requirements:* For master's, audition; for doctorate, GRE General Test or MAT, proficiency exam, audition, work sample, master's degree. Additional exam requirements/recommendations for international students: Required—TOEFL (minimum score 550 paper-based; 79 iBT). *Application deadline:* For fall admission, 8/1 for domestic students; for spring admission, 12/1 for domestic students. Applications are processed on a rolling basis. Application fee: $35 ($60 for international students). Electronic applications accepted. *Expenses:* $5,231.50 per semester full-time in-state, $9,623.50 full-time out-of-state. *Financial support:* In 2016–17, 73 students received support, including 5 research assistantships with tuition reimbursements available (averaging $9,600 per year), 28 teaching assistantships with tuition reimbursements available (averaging $12,142 per year); Federal Work-Study, scholarships/grants, and unspecified assistantships also available. Financial award application deadline: 2/1; financial award applicants required to submit FAFSA. *Faculty research:* Spanish Renaissance, twentieth-century music, Project OPTIMUS, composition, musical performance, regional music, performance, performance practice, composition. *Unit head:* Dr. John Chiego, Director, 901-678-3773, Fax: 901-678-3096, E-mail: jchiego@memphis.edu. *Application contact:* Dr. Dave Spencer, Assistant Director for Graduate Studies, 901-678-3779, Fax: 901-678-3096, E-mail: dspencer@memphis.edu.
Website: http://www.memphis.edu/music/

**University of Miami,** Graduate School, Frost School of Music, Department of Instrumental Performance, Coral Gables, FL 33124. Offers instrumental conducting (MM, DMA); instrumental performance (MM, DMA, AD); multiple woodwinds (MM, DMA). *Accreditation:* NASM. *Degree requirements:* For master's, thesis, recital paper, recital; for doctorate, thesis/dissertation, essay, 2 research tools, 3 recitals. *Entrance requirements:* For master's and doctorate, GRE General Test, audition. Additional exam requirements/recommendations for international students: Required—TOEFL (minimum score 550 paper-based; 59 iBT). Electronic applications accepted. *Faculty research:* Performance, conducting, composition.

**University of Miami,** Graduate School, Frost School of Music, Department of Keyboard Performance, Coral Gables, FL 33124. Offers accompanying and chamber music (MM, DMA); keyboard performance and pedagogy (MM, DMA); piano performance (MM, DMA, AD). *Accreditation:* NASM. *Degree requirements:* For master's, thesis, recital paper, recital; for doctorate, thesis/dissertation, essay, 2 research tools, 3 recitals. *Entrance requirements:* For master's and doctorate, GRE General Test, audition. Additional exam requirements/recommendations for international students: Required—TOEFL (minimum score 555 paper-based; 59 iBT). Electronic applications accepted.

**University of Miami,** Graduate School, Frost School of Music, Department of Music Media and Industry, Coral Gables, FL 33124. Offers music business and entertainment industries (MM); music engineering (MS). *Accreditation:* NASM. *Degree requirements:* For master's, thesis, internship (MM), research project (MS). *Entrance requirements:* For master's, GRE General Test. Additional exam requirements/recommendations for international students: Required—TOEFL (minimum score 550 paper-based; 59 iBT). Electronic applications accepted. *Faculty research:* Recording rights and property, digital sound design, recording industry, Internet-based music industries.

**University of Miami,** Graduate School, Frost School of Music, Department of Musicology, Coral Gables, FL 33124. Offers MM. *Accreditation:* NASM. *Degree requirements:* For master's, thesis. *Entrance requirements:* For master's, GRE General Test. Additional exam requirements/recommendations for international students: Required—TOEFL (minimum score 550 paper-based; 59 iBT). Electronic applications accepted.

**University of Miami,** Graduate School, Frost School of Music, Department of Music Theory-Composition, Coral Gables, FL 33124. Offers composition (MM, DMA); electronic music (MM); media writing and production (MM); music theory (MM). *Accreditation:* NASM. *Degree requirements:* For master's, thesis; for doctorate, thesis/dissertation, essay. *Entrance requirements:* For master's and doctorate, GRE General Test, portfolio. Additional exam requirements/recommendations for international students: Required—TOEFL (minimum score 550 paper-based; 59 iBT). Electronic applications accepted. *Faculty research:* Composition, commercial music and media music.

**University of Miami,** Graduate School, Frost School of Music, Department of Studio Music and Jazz, Coral Gables, FL 33124. Offers jazz composition (DMA); jazz pedagogy (MM); jazz performance (MM, DMA); studio jazz writing (MM). *Accreditation:* NASM. *Degree requirements:* For master's, thesis. *Entrance requirements:* For master's and doctorate, GRE General Test, portfolio. Additional exam requirements/recommendations for international students: Required—TOEFL (minimum score 550 paper-based; 59 iBT). Electronic applications accepted. *Faculty research:* Jazz performance, jazz conducting, jjazz composition.

## Music

**University of Miami,** Graduate School, Frost School of Music, Department of Vocal Performance, Coral Gables, FL 33124. Offers choral conducting (MM, DMA); vocal pedagogy (DMA); vocal performance (MM, DMA, AD). *Accreditation:* NASM. *Degree requirements:* For master's, 2 foreign languages, thesis, recital paper; for doctorate, thesis/dissertation, essay. *Entrance requirements:* For master's and doctorate, GRE General Test, audition. Additional exam requirements/recommendations for international students: Required—TOEFL (minimum score 550 paper-based; 59 iBT). Electronic applications accepted. *Faculty research:* Opera, musical theatre, performance, directing, pedagogy.

**University of Michigan,** Rackham Graduate School, School of Music, Theatre, and Dance, Program in Composition, Ann Arbor, MI 48109-2217. Offers MA, MM, A Mus D. *Degree requirements:* For doctorate, one foreign language, thesis/dissertation, oral exam, composition. *Entrance requirements:* For master's and doctorate, portfolio. Additional exam requirements/recommendations for international students: Required—TOEFL. *Expenses:* Tuition, state resident: full-time $21,466; part-time $1152 per credit hour. Tuition, nonresident: full-time $43,346; part-time $2367 per credit hour. Part-time tuition and fees vary according to course load, degree level and program.

**University of Michigan,** Rackham Graduate School, School of Music, Theatre, and Dance, Program in Composition and Theory, Ann Arbor, MI 48109-2085. Offers PhD. *Degree requirements:* For doctorate, one foreign language, thesis/dissertation, oral exam, composition. *Entrance requirements:* For doctorate, GRE, portfolio. Additional exam requirements/recommendations for international students: Required—TOEFL. Electronic applications accepted. *Expenses:* Tuition, state resident: full-time $21,466; part-time $1152 per credit hour. Tuition, nonresident: full-time $43,346; part-time $2367 per credit hour. Part-time tuition and fees vary according to course load, degree level and program.

**University of Michigan,** Rackham Graduate School, School of Music, Theatre, and Dance, Program in Conducting, Ann Arbor, MI 48109-2085. Offers MM, A Mus D. *Degree requirements:* For doctorate, one foreign language, thesis/dissertation, 3 concerts, oral exam. *Entrance requirements:* For doctorate, audition, portfolio. Additional exam requirements/recommendations for international students: Required—TOEFL. Electronic applications accepted. *Expenses:* Tuition, state resident: full-time $21,466; part-time $1152 per credit hour. Tuition, nonresident: full-time $43,346; part-time $2367 per credit hour. Part-time tuition and fees vary according to course load, degree level and program.

**University of Michigan,** Rackham Graduate School, School of Music, Theatre, and Dance, Program in Musicology, Ann Arbor, MI 48109-2085. Offers MA, PhD. *Degree requirements:* For doctorate, 2 foreign languages, thesis/dissertation, oral exam. *Entrance requirements:* For master's and doctorate, GRE General Test, writing sample. Additional exam requirements/recommendations for international students: Required—TOEFL. Electronic applications accepted. *Expenses:* Tuition, state resident: full-time $21,466; part-time $1152 per credit hour. Tuition, nonresident: full-time $43,346; part-time $2367 per credit hour. Part-time tuition and fees vary according to course load, degree level and program.

**University of Michigan,** Rackham Graduate School, School of Music, Theatre, and Dance, Program in Music Theory, Ann Arbor, MI 48109-2085. Offers PhD. *Degree requirements:* For doctorate, one foreign language, thesis/dissertation, oral exam. *Entrance requirements:* For doctorate, GRE, writing sample. Additional exam requirements/recommendations for international students: Required—TOEFL. Electronic applications accepted. *Expenses:* Tuition, state resident: full-time $21,466; part-time $1152 per credit hour. Tuition, nonresident: full-time $43,346; part-time $2367 per credit hour. Part-time tuition and fees vary according to course load, degree level and program.

**University of Michigan,** Rackham Graduate School, School of Music, Theatre, and Dance, Program in Performance, Ann Arbor, MI 48109-2085. Offers MM, A Mus D, Spec M. *Degree requirements:* For doctorate, one foreign language, thesis/dissertation, 3 concerts, oral exam. *Entrance requirements:* For doctorate, audition. Additional exam requirements/recommendations for international students: Required—TOEFL. Electronic applications accepted. *Expenses:* Tuition, state resident: full-time $21,466; part-time $1152 per credit hour. Tuition, nonresident: full-time $43,346; part-time $2367 per credit hour. Part-time tuition and fees vary according to course load, degree level and program.

**University of Michigan–Flint,** Graduate Programs, Program in Arts Administration, Flint, MI 48502. Offers museum and visual arts (MA). *Program availability:* Part-time. *Faculty:* 5 full-time (4 women), 3 part-time/adjunct (all women). *Students:* 7 full-time (6 women), 5 part-time (3 women); includes 2 minority (both Black or African American, non-Hispanic/Latino). Average age 39. 11 applicants, 55% accepted, 3 enrolled. In 2016, 3 master's awarded. *Degree requirements:* For master's, thesis, internship. *Entrance requirements:* For master's, bachelor's degree in the arts (visual art, theatre, dance, music, etc.) from regionally-accredited institution; minimum cumulative undergraduate GPA of 3.0. Additional exam requirements/recommendations for international students: Required—TOEFL (minimum score 84 iBT), IELTS (minimum score 6.5). *Application deadline:* For fall admission, 8/1 for domestic students, 5/1 for international students; for winter admission, 11/15 for domestic students, 9/1 for international students. Applications are processed on a rolling basis. Application fee: $55. Electronic applications accepted. *Expenses:* Contact institution. *Financial support:* Federal Work-Study, scholarships/grants, and unspecified assistantships available. Support available to part-time students. Financial award application deadline: 3/1; financial award applicants required to submit FAFSA. *Unit head:* Nicole Broughton, Director, 810-237-6522, E-mail: broughn@umflint.edu. *Application contact:* Bradley T. Maki, Director of Graduate Admissions, 810-762-3171, Fax: 810-766-6789, E-mail: bmaki@umflint.edu.
Website: http://www.umflint.edu/graduateprograms/arts-administration-ma

**University of Minnesota, Duluth,** Graduate School, School of Fine Arts, Department of Music, Duluth, MN 55812-2496. Offers music education (MM); performance (MM). *Accreditation:* NASM. *Program availability:* Part-time. *Degree requirements:* For master's, comprehensive exam, thesis (for some programs), recital (MM in performance). *Entrance requirements:* For master's, audition, minimum GPA of 3.0, sample of written work, interview, bachelor's degree in music, video of teaching. Additional exam requirements/recommendations for international students: Required—TOEFL (minimum score 550 paper-based). *Faculty research:* Band composition, music aesthetics, learning theory, value theory, music advocacy.

**University of Minnesota, Twin Cities Campus,** Graduate School, College of Liberal Arts, School of Music, Minneapolis, MN 55455-0213. Offers MA, MM, DMA, PhD. *Accreditation:* NASM. *Degree requirements:* For master's, comprehensive exam, thesis (for some programs), foreign language (MA), recital (MM); for doctorate, comprehensive exam, 5 recitals (DMA); 2 foreign languages or computer languages, dissertation (PhD). *Entrance requirements:* For master's, GRE (MA); for doctorate, GRE (PhD). Additional exam requirements/recommendations for international students: Required—TOEFL (minimum score 550 paper-based; 79 iBT: 21 writing, 19 reading), IELTS (minimum score 6.5). Electronic applications accepted.

**University of Mississippi,** Graduate School, College of Liberal Arts, University, MS 38677. Offers anthropology (MA); biology (MS, PhD); chemistry (MS, PhD); economics (MA, PhD); English (MA, PhD); experimental psychology (PhD); history (MA, PhD); mathematics (MS, PhD); modern languages (MA); music (MM); philosophy (MA); physics (MA, MS, PhD); political science (MA, PhD); studio art (MFA). *Program availability:* Part-time. *Faculty:* 472 full-time (263 women), 75 part-time/adjunct (35 women). *Students:* 415 full-time (210 women), 57 part-time (20 women); includes 70 minority (35 Black or African American, non-Hispanic/Latino; 13 Asian, non-Hispanic/Latino; 14 Hispanic/Latino; 8 Two or more races, non-Hispanic/Latino), 102 international. Average age 27. *Degree requirements:* For doctorate, thesis/dissertation. *Entrance requirements:* For master's, GRE General Test, minimum GPA of 3.0; for doctorate, GRE General Test. Additional exam requirements/recommendations for international students: Required—TOEFL. *Application deadline:* For fall admission, 4/1 for domestic students; for spring admission, 10/1 for domestic students. Applications are processed on a rolling basis. Application fee: $40. Electronic applications accepted. *Financial support:* Fellowships, research assistantships, teaching assistantships, career-related internships or fieldwork, Federal Work-Study, institutionally sponsored loans, scholarships/grants, and unspecified assistantships available. Financial award application deadline: 3/1; financial award applicants required to submit FAFSA. *Unit head:* Dr. Lee Michael Cohen, Dean, 662-915-7177, Fax: 662-915-5792, E-mail: libarts@olemiss.edu. *Application contact:* Dr. Christy M. Wyandt, Associate Dean of Graduate School, 662-915-7474, Fax: 662-915-7577, E-mail: cwyandt@olemiss.edu. Website: https://www.olemiss.edu

**University of Missouri,** Office of Research and Graduate Studies, College of Arts and Science, School of Music, Columbia, MO 65211. Offers MA, MM. *Accreditation:* NASM. *Faculty:* 35 full-time (17 women), 11 part-time/adjunct (5 women). *Students:* 41 full-time (16 women), 10 part-time (5 women). *Degree requirements:* For master's, 3 foreign languages, thesis. *Entrance requirements:* For master's, minimum GPA of 3.0. Additional exam requirements/recommendations for international students: Required—TOEFL (minimum score 500 paper-based; 61 iBT). *Application deadline:* For fall admission, 12/15 priority date for domestic and international students. Applications are processed on a rolling basis. Application fee: $75 ($90 for international students). Electronic applications accepted. *Expenses:* Tuition, state resident: full-time $6347; part-time $352.60 per credit hour. Tuition, nonresident: full-time $17,379; part-time $965.50 per credit hour. *Required fees:* $1035. Tuition and fees vary according to course load, campus/location and program. *Financial support:* Fellowships with full tuition reimbursements, research assistantships, teaching assistantships with full tuition reimbursements, institutionally sponsored loans, health care benefits, and unspecified assistantships available.
Website: http://music.missouri.edu/

**University of Missouri–Kansas City,** Conservatory of Music and Dance, Kansas City, MO 64110-2499. Offers composition (MM, DMA); conducting (MM, DMA); music (MA); music education (MME, PhD); music history and literature (MM); music theory (MM); music therapy (MA); performance (MM, DMA). PhD (interdisciplinary) offered through the School of Graduate Studies. *Accreditation:* NASM. *Program availability:* Part-time. *Faculty:* 55 full-time (24 women), 39 part-time/adjunct (12 women). *Students:* 165 full-time (67 women), 64 part-time (34 women); includes 21 minority (4 Black or African American, non-Hispanic/Latino; 7 Asian, non-Hispanic/Latino; 7 Hispanic/Latino; 3 Two or more races, non-Hispanic/Latino), 49 international. Average age 28. 368 applicants, 49% accepted, 88 enrolled. In 2016, 49 master's, 26 doctorates awarded. *Degree requirements:* For master's, variable foreign language requirement, comprehensive exam, thesis (for some programs); for doctorate, variable foreign language requirement, comprehensive exam, thesis/dissertation or alternative. *Entrance requirements:* For master's, minimum GPA of 3.0 in major, auditions (for MM in performance); for doctorate, minimum graduate GPA of 3.5, auditions (for DMA in performance), portfolio of compositions. Additional exam requirements/recommendations for international students: Required—TOEFL (minimum score 550 paper-based; 80 iBT). *Application deadline:* For fall admission, 1/15 priority date for domestic students, 1/15 for international students. Application fee: $45 ($50 for international students). *Financial support:* In 2016–17, 32 teaching assistantships with partial tuition reimbursements (averaging $8,238 per year) were awarded; career-related internships or fieldwork, Federal Work-Study, institutionally sponsored loans, scholarships/grants, tuition waivers (partial), and unspecified assistantships also available. Support available to part-time students. Financial award application deadline: 3/1; financial award applicants required to submit FAFSA. *Faculty research:* Electro-acoustic composition, affective music responses, American music theatre, Russian choral music, music therapy and Alzheimer's. *Unit head:* Peter Witte, Dean, 816-235-2731, Fax: 816-235-5265, E-mail: wittep@umkc.edu. *Application contact:* William Everett, Associate Dean for Graduate Studies, 816-235-2857, Fax: 816-235-5264, E-mail: everettw@umkc.edu.
Website: http://conservatory.umkc.edu/

**University of Montana,** Graduate School, College of Visual and Performing Arts, School of Music, Missoula, MT 59812-0002. Offers performance (MM). *Accreditation:* NASM. *Entrance requirements:* For master's, GRE General Test, GRE Subject Test, portfolio.

**University of Nebraska at Omaha,** Graduate Studies, College of Communication, Fine Arts and Media, School of Music, Omaha, NE 68182. Offers MM. *Accreditation:* NASM. *Program availability:* Part-time, evening/weekend. *Faculty:* 10 full-time (4 women). *Students:* 5 full-time (2 women), 17 part-time (9 women); includes 2 minority (1 Hispanic/Latino; 1 Two or more races, non-Hispanic/Latino), 3 international. Average age 29. 17 applicants, 76% accepted, 4 enrolled. In 2016, 10 master's awarded. *Degree requirements:* For master's, comprehensive exam (for some programs), thesis (for some programs). *Entrance requirements:* For master's, departmental diagnostic exam, minimum GPA of 3.0, resume, transcripts. Additional exam requirements/recommendations for international students: Required—TOEFL, IELTS, PTE. *Application deadline:* For fall admission, 6/15 priority date for domestic and international students; for spring admission, 11/15 priority date for domestic and international students; for summer admission, 4/15 for domestic and international students. Applications are processed on a rolling basis. Application fee: $45. Electronic applications accepted. *Financial support:* In 2016–17, 5 students received support, including 5 teaching assistantships with tuition reimbursements available; research assistantships with tuition reimbursements available, career-related internships or fieldwork, Federal Work-Study, scholarships/grants, health care benefits, tuition waivers (partial), and unspecified assistantships also available. Support available to part-time students. Financial award application deadline: 3/1; financial award applicants required to submit FAFSA. *Unit head:* Dr. Washington Garcia, Director, 402-554-2341, E-mail: graduate@unomaha.edu. *Application contact:* Dr. Peter Madsen, Graduate Program Chair, 402-554-2341, E-mail: graduate@unomaha.edu.

**University of Nebraska–Lincoln,** Graduate College, College of Arts and Sciences, Department of English, Lincoln, NE 68588-0333. Offers composition and rhetoric (MA, PhD); creative writing (MA, PhD); literature studies (MA, PhD). *Degree requirements:* For master's, thesis optional; for doctorate, one foreign language, comprehensive exam, thesis/dissertation. *Entrance requirements:* For master's, writing sample; for doctorate, GRE General Test, writing sample. Additional exam requirements/recommendations for international students: Required—TOEFL (minimum score 600 paper-based). Electronic applications accepted. *Faculty research:* Creative writing, composition and rhetoric, women's studies, North American literature, medieval/Renaissance studies.

**University of Nebraska–Lincoln,** Graduate College, College of Fine and Performing Arts, School of Music, Lincoln, NE 68588. Offers composition (MM, DMA); conducting (MM, DMA); music education (MM, PhD); music history (MM); music theory (MM); performance (MM, DMA); piano pedagogy (MM); woodwind specialties (MM). *Accreditation:* NASM. *Degree requirements:* For master's, thesis optional; for doctorate, comprehensive exam, thesis/dissertation. *Entrance requirements:* For master's and doctorate, audition. Additional exam requirements/recommendations for international students: Required—TOEFL. Electronic applications accepted. *Faculty research:* Mozart, Tchaikovsky, Josquin des Prez, practice of J.S. Bach's organ works, instructional strategies in music education.

**University of Nevada, Las Vegas,** Graduate College, College of Fine Arts, School of Music, Las Vegas, NV 89154-5025. Offers K-12 music (Certificate); music (MM); musical arts (DMA). *Accreditation:* NASM. *Program availability:* Part-time. *Faculty:* 24 full-time (7 women), 19 part-time/adjunct (6 women). *Students:* 60 full-time (26 women), 34 part-time (20 women); includes 29 minority (11 Black or African American, non-Hispanic/Latino; 4 Asian, non-Hispanic/Latino; 12 Hispanic/Latino; 1 Native Hawaiian or other Pacific Islander, non-Hispanic/Latino; 1 Two or more races, non-Hispanic/Latino), 12 international. Average age 33. 60 applicants, 78% accepted, 30 enrolled. In 2016, 16 master's, 12 doctorates awarded. *Degree requirements:* For master's, oral and/or written comprehensive exam; for doctorate, one foreign language, comprehensive exam, thesis/dissertation, lecture-recital and document. *Entrance requirements:* For master's, placement examinations, bachelor's degree with minimum GPA 3.0; statement of purpose; 2 letters of recommendation; portfolio of compositions; for doctorate, music history placement exam, music theory and aural skills/sight-singing placement examination, master's degree in music; for Certificate, PRAXIS I Pre-Professional Skills Test, bachelor's degree. Additional exam requirements/recommendations for international students: Required—TOEFL (minimum score 550 paper-based; 80 iBT), IELTS (minimum score 7). *Application deadline:* For fall admission, 5/1 for domestic students; for spring admission, 11/15 for domestic students; for summer admission, 5/15 for domestic students. Application fee: $60 ($95 for international students). Electronic applications accepted. *Expenses:* $269.25 per credit, $792 per 3-credit course; $9,634 per year resident; $23,274 per year non-resident; $7,094 fees non-resident (7 credits or more); $1,307 annual health insurance fee. *Financial support:* In 2016–17, 2 research assistantships with partial tuition reimbursements (averaging $15,000 per year), 41 teaching assistantships with partial tuition reimbursements (averaging $12,911 per year) were awarded; institutionally sponsored loans, scholarships/grants, health care benefits, and unspecified assistantships also available. Financial award application deadline: 3/15. *Faculty research:* Technology in preparing future teachers, professional development for music educators, Roman music history, music of Richard Wagner, Baroque music. Total annual research expenditures: $1,298. *Unit head:* Dr. Sue Mueller, Chair/Professor, 702-895-5776, Fax: 702-895-4239, E-mail: susan.mueller@unlv.edu. *Application contact:* Dr. Jennifer Grim, Graduate Coordinator, 702-895-5849, Fax: 702-895-4239, E-mail: jennifer.grim@unlv.edu.
Website: http://music.unlv.edu/

**University of Nevada, Reno,** Graduate School, College of Liberal Arts, Department of Music, Reno, NV 89557. Offers MA, MM. *Accreditation:* NASM. *Degree requirements:* For master's, thesis optional. *Entrance requirements:* For master's, minimum GPA of 2.75. Additional exam requirements/recommendations for international students: Required—TOEFL (minimum score 500 paper-based; 61 iBT), IELTS (minimum score 6). Electronic applications accepted. *Faculty research:* Performance, conducting, music composition and arranging.

**University of New Hampshire,** Graduate School, College of Liberal Arts, Department of English, Durham, NH 03824. Offers composition (PhD); English education (MST); language and linguistics (MA); literature (MA, PhD); writing (MFA). *Program availability:* Part-time. *Degree requirements:* For master's, one foreign language; for doctorate, 2 foreign languages, thesis/dissertation. *Entrance requirements:* For master's, GRE General Test, sample of written work; for doctorate, GRE General Test, GRE Subject Test, sample of written work. Additional exam requirements/recommendations for international students: Required—TOEFL (minimum score 550 paper-based; 80 iBT). Electronic applications accepted.

**University of New Hampshire,** Graduate School, College of Liberal Arts, Department of Music, Durham, NH 03824. Offers composition (MA); musicology (MA). *Accreditation:* NASM. *Degree requirements:* For master's, one foreign language. *Entrance requirements:* For master's, audition. Additional exam requirements/recommendations for international students: Required—TOEFL (minimum score 550 paper-based; 80 iBT). Electronic applications accepted.

**University of New Mexico,** Graduate Studies, College of Fine Arts, Program in Music, Albuquerque, NM 87131. Offers collaborative piano (M Mu); conducting (M Mu); music education (M Mu); music history and literature (M Mu); performance (M Mu); theory and composition (M Mu). *Accreditation:* NASM. *Program availability:* Part-time. *Faculty:* 33 full-time (12 women), 8 part-time/adjunct (6 women). *Students:* 39 full-time (19 women), 54 part-time (29 women); includes 17 minority (1 Black or African American, non-Hispanic/Latino; 1 American Indian or Alaska Native, non-Hispanic/Latino; 3 Asian, non-Hispanic/Latino; 9 Hispanic/Latino; 3 Two or more races, non-Hispanic/Latino), 17 international. Average age 29. 75 applicants, 76% accepted, 36 enrolled. In 2016, 30 master's awarded. *Degree requirements:* For master's, variable foreign language requirement, comprehensive exam, thesis (for some programs), recital (for some programs). *Entrance requirements:* For master's, placement exams in music history and theory. Additional exam requirements/recommendations for international students: Required—TOEFL (minimum score 550 paper-based). *Application deadline:* For fall admission, 7/1 for domestic students, 5/1 for international students; for spring admission, 11/1 for domestic students, 10/1 for international students. Applications are processed on a rolling basis. Application fee: $50. Electronic applications accepted. *Financial support:* Research assistantships, teaching assistantships with tuition reimbursements, Federal Work-Study, scholarships/grants, and unspecified assistantships available. Support available to part-time students. Financial award application deadline: 2/1; financial award applicants required to submit FAFSA. *Faculty research:* Opera, twentieth-century and contemporary music, performance, conducting. *Unit head:* Dr. Steven Block, Chair, 505-277-2127, Fax: 505-277-4202, E-mail: sblock@unm.edu. *Application contact:* Colleen M. Sheinberg, Graduate Coordinator, 505-277-8401, Fax: 505-277-4202, E-mail: colleens@unm.edu.
Website: http://music.unm.edu/

**University of New Orleans,** Graduate School, College of Liberal Arts, Department of Music, New Orleans, LA 70148. Offers MM. *Accreditation:* NASM. *Program availability:* Evening/weekend. *Degree requirements:* For master's, recital. *Entrance requirements:* For master's, GRE General Test, audition. Additional exam requirements/recommendations for international students: Required—TOEFL (minimum score 550 paper-based; 79 iBT), IELTS (minimum score 6.5). Electronic applications accepted. *Faculty research:* American jazz, Czech music, Hispanic music.

**The University of North Carolina at Chapel Hill,** Graduate School, College of Arts and Sciences, Department of Music, Chapel Hill, NC 27599. Offers MA, PhD. Terminal master's awarded for partial completion of doctoral program. *Degree requirements:* For master's, one foreign language, thesis, theory and keyboard exams; for doctorate, 2 foreign languages, comprehensive exam, thesis/dissertation, theory and keyboard exams. *Entrance requirements:* For master's and doctorate, GRE General Test, department diagnostic exam, minimum GPA of 3.0. Additional exam requirements/recommendations for international students: Required—TOEFL. Electronic applications accepted. *Expenses:* Contact institution. *Faculty research:* Music theory, ethnomusicology, music history.

**The University of North Carolina at Charlotte,** College of Arts and Architecture, Department of Music, Charlotte, NC 28223-0001. Offers vocal pedagogy (Graduate Certificate). *Accreditation:* NASM. *Program availability:* Part-time. *Faculty:* 7 full-time (3 women). In 2016, 2 Graduate Certificates awarded. *Degree requirements:* For Graduate Certificate, thesis or alternative, directed project. *Entrance requirements:* For degree, placement tests in music theory, ear training, and piano; diagnostic vocal pedagogy exam, bachelor's degree in music from accredited university or conservatory; official transcripts; formal audition. Additional exam requirements/recommendations for international students: Required—TOEFL (minimum score 523 paper-based, 70 iBT) or IELTS (6.5). *Application deadline:* For fall admission, 3/1 priority date for domestic and international students; for spring admission, 10/1 priority date for domestic and international students. Applications are processed on a rolling basis. Application fee: $75. Electronic applications accepted. *Expenses:* Tuition, state resident: full-time $4252. Tuition, nonresident: full-time $17,423. *Required fees:* $3026. Tuition and fees vary according to course load and program. *Financial support:* Career-related internships or fieldwork and unspecified assistantships available. Financial award application deadline: 3/1; financial award applicants required to submit FAFSA. *Unit head:* James A. Grymes, Chair, 704-687-0251, E-mail: jagrymes@uncc.edu. *Application contact:* Kathy B. Giddings, Director of Graduate Admissions, 704-687-5503, Fax: 704-687-1668, E-mail: gradadm@uncc.edu.
Website: http://coaa.uncc.edu/academics/department-of-music

**The University of North Carolina at Greensboro,** Graduate School, School of Music, Theatre and Dance, Greensboro, NC 27412-5001. Offers composition (MM); dance (MA, MFA); education (MM); music education (PhD); performance (MM, DMA); theatre (M Ed, MFA), including acting (MFA), design (MFA), directing (MFA), theatre education (M Ed), theatre for youth (MFA); theory (MM). *Accreditation:* NASM. *Degree requirements:* For master's, variable foreign language requirement, thesis (for some programs), recital; for doctorate, comprehensive exam, thesis/dissertation, diagnostic exam, recital. *Entrance requirements:* For master's, GRE General Test, NTE, audition; for doctorate, GRE General Test, GRE Subject Test (music), audition. Additional exam requirements/recommendations for international students: Required—TOEFL. Electronic applications accepted.

**University of North Carolina School of the Arts,** School of Filmmaking, Winston-Salem, NC 27127-2738. Offers creative producing (MFA); film music composition (MFA); screenwriting (MFA). *Entrance requirements:* For master's, audition, performance, portfolio, interview. Additional exam requirements/recommendations for international students: Required—TOEFL. *Application deadline:* For fall admission, 4/1 priority date for domestic students. Applications are processed on a rolling basis. Application fee: $95 ($100 for international students). Electronic applications accepted. *Expenses:* Tuition, state resident: full-time $7996; part-time $444 per credit hour. Tuition, nonresident: full-time $21,403; part-time $1189 per credit hour. *Required fees:* $2769; $153.83 per credit hour. *Financial support:* Fellowships, research assistantships, career-related internships or fieldwork, and Federal Work-Study available. Support available to part-time students. Financial award application deadline: 3/15; financial award applicants required to submit FAFSA. *Unit head:* Susan Ruskin, Dean, 336-770-1334, Fax: 336-770-1339, E-mail: ruskins@uncsa.edu. *Application contact:* Sheeler Lawson, Director of Admissions, 336-770-3290, Fax: 336-770-3370, E-mail: admissions@uncsa.edu.
Website: http://www.uncsa.edu/filmmaking/

**University of North Carolina School of the Arts,** School of Music, Winston-Salem, NC 27127-2738. Offers music (Artist Certificate); music performance (MM), including chamber music performance; vocal performance (MM). *Entrance requirements:* For master's, audition (music performance), interview, original score. Additional exam requirements/recommendations for international students: Required—TOEFL. *Application deadline:* For fall admission, 4/1 priority date for domestic students. Applications are processed on a rolling basis. Application fee: $95 ($100 for international students). Electronic applications accepted. *Expenses:* Tuition, state resident: full-time $7996; part-time $444 per credit hour. Tuition, nonresident: full-time $21,403; part-time $1189 per credit hour. *Required fees:* $2769; $153.83 per credit hour. *Financial support:* Fellowships with partial tuition reimbursements, teaching assistantships with partial tuition reimbursements, career-related internships or fieldwork, and Federal Work-Study available. Financial award application deadline: 3/15; financial award applicants required to submit FAFSA. *Unit head:* Brian Cole, Dean, 336-770-3251, Fax: 336-770-3248, E-mail: coleb@uncsa.edu. *Application contact:* Sheeler Lawson, Director of Admissions, 336-770-3290, Fax: 336-770-3370, E-mail: admissions@uncsa.edu.
Website: http://www.uncsa.edu/music/

**University of North Dakota,** Graduate School, College of Arts and Sciences, Department of Music, Grand Forks, ND 58202. Offers music (MM); music education (PhD). *Accreditation:* NASM. *Program availability:* Part-time. *Degree requirements:* For master's, comprehensive exam, thesis or alternative. *Entrance requirements:* For master's, minimum GPA of 3.0. Additional exam requirements/recommendations for international students: Required—TOEFL (minimum score 550 paper-based; 79 iBT), IELTS (minimum score 6.5). *Application deadline:* For fall admission, 8/1 priority date for domestic students, 5/1 priority date for international students; for spring admission, 12/1 priority date for domestic students, 9/1 priority date for international students. Applications are processed on a rolling basis. Application fee: $35. Electronic applications accepted. *Financial support:* Fellowships with full and partial tuition reimbursements, research assistantships with full and partial tuition reimbursements, teaching assistantships with full tuition reimbursements, Federal Work-Study, institutionally sponsored loans, scholarships/grants, health care benefits, tuition waivers (full and partial), and unspecified assistantships available. Support available to part-time students. Financial award application deadline: 3/15; financial award applicants required to submit FAFSA. *Unit head:* Dr. Michael Wittgraf, Graduate Director, 701-777-2644, Fax: 701-777-3320, E-mail: michael.wittgraf@und.edu. *Application contact:* Debbie Ford, Admissions Specialist, 701-777-0749, Fax: 701-777-3619, E-mail: debra.ford@gradschool.und.edu.
Website: http://arts-sciences.und.edu/music/

**University of Northern Colorado,** Graduate School, College of Performing and Visual Arts, School of Music, Greeley, CO 80639. Offers collaborative keyboard (MM); conducting (MM); instrumental performance (MM); jazz studies (MM); music conducting (DA); music education (MM, DA); music history and literature (MM, MA); music performance (DA); music theory and composition (MM, DA); vocal performance (MM). *Accreditation:* NASM; NCATE (one or more programs are accredited). *Program* availability: Part-time. *Degree requirements:* For master's, comprehensive exam, thesis or alternative; for doctorate, comprehensive exam, thesis/dissertation. *Entrance requirements:* For master's, audition; for doctorate, GRE General Test, audition, 3 letters of recommendation. *Application deadline:* Applications are processed on a rolling basis. Application fee: $50 ($60 for international students). Electronic applications accepted. *Financial support:* Fellowships, research assistantships, teaching assistantships, and unspecified assistantships available. Financial award application deadline: 3/1; financial award applicants required to submit FAFSA. *Unit head:* David Caffey, Director, 970-351-2679. *Application contact:* Linda Sisson, Graduate Student Admission Coordinator, 970-351-1807, Fax: 970-351-2371, E-mail: linda.sisson@unco.edu. Website: http://www.arts.unco.edu/

**University of Northern Iowa,** Graduate College, College of Humanities, Arts and Sciences, School of Music, MA Program in Music, Cedar Falls, IA 50614. Offers MA. *Accreditation:* NASM. *Degree requirements:* For master's, comprehensive exam, thesis or alternative. *Entrance requirements:* For master's, written diagnostic exam in theory, music history, expository writing skills, and in the area of claimed competency, portfolio, tape recordings of compositions, in-person interview, minimum GPA of 3.0. Additional exam requirements/recommendations for international students: Required—TOEFL (minimum score 500 paper-based; 61 iBT). Electronic applications accepted.

**University of Northern Iowa,** Graduate College, College of Humanities, Arts and Sciences, School of Music, MM Program in Composition, Cedar Falls, IA 50614. Offers MM. *Degree requirements:* For master's, comprehensive exam. *Entrance requirements:* For master's, portfolio, recordings of compositions.

**University of Northern Iowa,** Graduate College, College of Humanities, Arts and Sciences, School of Music, MM Program in Conducting, Cedar Falls, IA 50614. Offers MM. *Degree requirements:* For master's, comprehensive exam. *Entrance requirements:* For master's, audition, interview.

**University of Northern Iowa,** Graduate College, College of Humanities, Arts and Sciences, School of Music, MM Program in Music History, Cedar Falls, IA 50614. Offers MM. *Entrance requirements:* For master's, scholarly paper.

**University of Northern Iowa,** Graduate College, College of Humanities, Arts and Sciences, School of Music, MM Program in Performance, Cedar Falls, IA 50614. Offers percussion (MM); piano/organ (MM); strings (MM); voice (MM); woodwind (MM). *Degree requirements:* For master's, comprehensive exam. *Entrance requirements:* For master's, audition.

**University of Northern Iowa,** Graduate College, College of Humanities, Arts and Sciences, School of Music, MM Program in Piano Performance and Pedagogy, Cedar Falls, IA 50614. Offers MM.

**University of North Texas,** Robert B. Toulouse School of Graduate Studies, Denton, TX 76203-5459. Offers accounting (MS); applied anthropology (MA, MS); applied behavior analysis (Certificate); applied geography (MA); applied technology and performance improvement (M Ed, MS); art education (MA); art history (MA); art museum education (Certificate); arts leadership (Certificate); audiology (Au D); behavior analysis (MS); behavioral science (PhD); biochemistry and molecular biology (MS); biology (MA, MS); biomedical engineering (MS); business analysis (MS); chemistry (MS); clinical health psychology (PhD); communication studies (MA, MS); computer engineering (MS); computer science (MS); counseling (M Ed, MS), including clinical mental health counseling (MS), college and university counseling, elementary school counseling, secondary school counseling; creative writing (MA); criminal justice (MS); curriculum and instruction (M Ed); decision sciences (MA, MFA), including fashion design (MFA), innovation studies, interior design (MFA); early childhood studies (MS); economics (MS); educational leadership (M Ed, Ed D); educational psychology (MS, PhD), including family studies (MS), gifted and talented (MS), human development (MS), learning and cognition (MS), research, measurement and evaluation (MS); electrical engineering (MS); emergency management (MPA); engineering technology (MS); English (MA); English as a second language (MA); environmental science (MS); finance (MBA, MS); financial management (MPA); French (MA); health services management (MBA); higher education (M Ed, Ed D); history (MA, MS); hospitality management (MS); human resources management (MPA); information science (MS); information systems (PhD); information technologies (MBA); interdisciplinary studies (MA, MS); international studies (MA); international sustainable tourism (MS); jazz studies (MM); journalism (MA, MJ, Graduate Certificate), including interactive and virtual digital communication (Graduate Certificate), narrative journalism (Graduate Certificate), public relations (Graduate Certificate); kinesiology (MS); linguistics (MA); local government management (MPA); logistics (PhD); logistics and supply chain management (MBA); long-term care, senior housing, and aging services (MA); management (PhD); marketing (MBA); mathematics (MA, MS); mechanical and energy engineering (MS, PhD); music (MA), including ethnomusicology, music theory, musicology, performance; music composition (PhD); music education (MM Ed, PhD); nonprofit management (MPA); operations and supply chain management (MBA); performance (MM, DMA); philosophy (MA); political science (MA); professional and technical communication (MA); radio, television and film (MA, MFA); rehabilitation counseling (Certificate); sociology (MA); Spanish (MA); special education (M Ed); speech-language pathology (MA); strategic management (MBA); studio art (MFA); teaching (M Ed); MBA/MS. *Program availability:* Part-time, evening/weekend, online learning. Terminal master's awarded for partial completion of doctoral program. *Degree requirements:* For master's, variable foreign language requirement, comprehensive exam, thesis (for some programs); for doctorate, variable foreign language requirement, comprehensive exam (for some programs), thesis/dissertation; for other advanced degree, variable foreign language requirement, comprehensive exam (for some programs). *Entrance requirements:* For master's and doctorate, GRE, GMAT. Additional exam requirements/recommendations for international students: Required—TOEFL (minimum score 550 paper-based; 79 iBT). Electronic applications accepted.

**University of Oklahoma,** College of Arts and Sciences, Department of English, Norman, OK 73019. Offers composition and rhetoric (MA, PhD); literary and cultural studies (MA, PhD). *Program availability:* Part-time. *Faculty:* 31 full-time (15 women). *Students:* 26 full-time (16 women), 18 part-time (9 women); includes 9 minority (2 American Indian or Alaska Native, non-Hispanic/Latino; 2 Asian, non-Hispanic/Latino; 3 Hispanic/Latino; 2 Two or more races, non-Hispanic/Latino), 1 international. Average age 32. 38 applicants, 34% accepted, 3 enrolled. In 2016, 7 master's, 7 doctorates awarded. *Degree requirements:* For master's, one foreign language, comprehensive exam (for some programs), thesis (for some programs), exam or thesis; for doctorate, one foreign language, comprehensive exam, thesis/dissertation. *Entrance requirements:* For master's, BA in English or related field; for doctorate, MA in English or related field. Additional exam requirements/recommendations for international students: Required— TOEFL (minimum score 79 iBT) or IELTS (minimum score 6.5). *Application deadline:* For fall admission, 1/5 priority date for domestic and international students. Application fee: $50 ($100 for international students). Electronic applications accepted. *Expenses:* Tuition, state resident: full-time $4886; part-time $203.60 per credit hour. Tuition, nonresident: full-time $18,989; part-time $791.20 per credit hour. *Required fees:* $3283; $126.25 per credit hour. $126.50 per semester. *Financial support:* In 2016–17, 40 students received support, including 5 research assistantships (averaging $13,011 per

year), 32 teaching assistantships (averaging $12,550 per year); fellowships, scholarships/grants, health care benefits, and unspecified assistantships also available. Financial award application deadline: 6/1; financial award applicants required to submit FAFSA. *Faculty research:* American Indian literature and culture; composition and rhetoric; American literature; British literature; postcolonial literature and culture. *Unit head:* Dr. Daniela Garofalo, Professor and Chair, 405-325-4661, Fax: 405-325-0831, E-mail: dg@ou.edu. *Application contact:* Sara Day, Graduate Assistant, 405-325-0831, Fax: 405-325-0831, E-mail: redpanda@ou.edu. Website: http://cas.ou.edu/english

**University of Oklahoma,** Weitzenhoffer Family College of Fine Arts, School of Music, Norman, OK 73019. Offers choral conducting (M Mus), including church music (M Mus, DMA), standard (M Mus, DMA); composition (M Mus, DMA); conducting (M Mus Ed, DMA), including choral, church music (M Mus, DMA), instrumental (M Mus Ed), orchestral (DMA), wind band (DMA); general music education (M Mus Ed), including Kodaly concepts; instrumental (M Mus Ed), including primary instrument, secondary instrument; instrumental conducting (M Mus); music education (PhD); music performance (Graduate Certificate); music theory (M Mus); musicology (M Mus); organ (M Mus, DMA), including church music, organ technology (M Mus); standard; piano (M Mus, DMA), including performance, performance and pedagogy; piano pedagogy (M Mus Ed); voice (M Mus, DMA), including opera (M Mus), performance; wind/percussion/string instruments (M Mus, DMA). *Accreditation:* NASM. *Faculty:* 61 full-time (17 women), 1 part-time/adjunct (0 women). *Students:* 113 full-time (49 women), 68 part-time (32 women); includes 32 minority (5 Black or African American, non-Hispanic/Latino; 4 American Indian or Alaska Native, non-Hispanic/Latino; 7 Asian, non-Hispanic/Latino; 11 Hispanic/Latino; 5 Two or more races, non-Hispanic/Latino), 26 international. Average age 29. 161 applicants, 43% accepted, 50 enrolled. In 2016, 35 master's, 13 doctorates awarded. *Degree requirements:* For master's, variable foreign language requirement, comprehensive exam (for some programs); thesis (for some programs); for doctorate, variable foreign language requirement, comprehensive exam, thesis/dissertation, three recitals and/or workshops (two recitals for DMA in composition); for Graduate Certificate, variable foreign language requirement, two recitals. *Entrance requirements:* For master's, bachelor's degree in music, music education, or the equivalent; transcripts; resume; personal statement; 3 letters of recommendation; audition and/or other practical application materials as appropriate to intended degree; sample of scholarly writing (for M Mus in musicology and M Mus in music theory); for doctorate, master's degree in music, music education, or the equivalent; transcripts; resume; personal statement; 3 letters of recommendation; sample of scholarly writing; audition and/or other practical application materials as appropriate to intended degree; for Graduate Certificate, bachelor's degree in music, music education, or the equivalent; transcripts; resume; personal statement; 3 letters of recommendation; audition. Additional exam requirements/recommendations for international students: Required— TOEFL (minimum score 79 iBT) or IELTS (minimum score 6.5). *Application deadline:* For fall admission, 2/1 for domestic and international students; for spring admission, 10/1 for domestic students, 9/1 for international students; for summer admission, 2/1 for domestic and international students. Applications are processed on a rolling basis. Application fee: $50 ($100 for international students). Electronic applications accepted. *Expenses:* Tuition, state resident: full-time $4886; part-time $203.60 per credit hour. Tuition, nonresident: full-time $18,989; part-time $791.20 per credit hour. *Required fees:* $3283; $126.25 per credit hour. $126.50 per semester. *Financial support:* In 2016–17, 121 students received support, including 3 fellowships with full tuition reimbursements available (averaging $5,000 per year), 31 research assistantships with full tuition reimbursements available (averaging $10,557 per year), 64 teaching assistantships with full tuition reimbursements available (averaging $10,494 per year); health care benefits and unspecified assistantships also available. Financial award application deadline: 6/1; financial award applicants required to submit FAFSA. *Faculty research:* Piano pedagogy, performance practice, music education, musicology, music theory. *Unit head:* Dr. Roland Barrett, Interim Director, 405-325-2081, Fax: 405-325-7574, E-mail: rebarrett@ou.edu. *Application contact:* Jan Russell, Graduate Admissions and Recruiting Advisor, 405-325-5393, Fax: 405-325-7574, E-mail: jrussell@ou.edu. Website: http://www.ou.edu/finearts/music/

**University of Oregon,** Graduate School, School of Music, Program in Music, Eugene, OR 97403. Offers composition (M Mus, DMA, PhD); conducting (M Mus); jazz studies (M Mus); music (MA), including music history, music theory; music history (PhD); music theory (PhD); performance (M Mus, DMA); piano pedagogy (M Mus). *Entrance requirements:* For master's, minimum GPA of 3.0, audition (performance applicants), videotape or interview (conducting applicants); for doctorate, GRE General Test, minimum GPA of 3.0, audition (performance applicants), videotape or interview (conducting applicants). Additional exam requirements/recommendations for international students: Required—TOEFL.

**University of Ottawa,** Faculty of Graduate and Postdoctoral Studies, Faculty of Arts, Department of Music, Ottawa, ON K1N 6N5, Canada. Offers music (M Mus, MA); orchestral studies (Certificate); piano pedagogy research (Certificate). *Degree requirements:* For master's, thesis optional. *Entrance requirements:* For master's, honors degree or equivalent, minimum B+ average. Electronic applications accepted. *Faculty research:* Performance, theory, musicology.

**University of Pennsylvania,** School of Arts and Sciences, Graduate Group in Music, Philadelphia, PA 19104. Offers AM, PhD. *Faculty:* 13 full-time (5 women), 3 part-time/adjunct (0 women). *Students:* 37 full-time (17 women), 2 part-time (both women); includes 4 minority (1 Black or African American, non-Hispanic/Latino; 1 Asian, non-Hispanic/Latino; 2 Two or more races, non-Hispanic/Latino), 14 international. Average age 30. 87 applicants, 11% accepted, 7 enrolled. In 2016, 1 master's, 5 doctorates awarded. Terminal master's awarded for partial completion of doctoral program. *Degree requirements:* For doctorate, thesis/dissertation. *Expenses:* Tuition: Full-time $31,068; part-time $5762 per course. *Required fees:* $3200; $336 per course. Full-time tuition and fees vary according to degree level, program and student level. Part-time tuition and fees vary according to course load, degree level and program. Website: http://www.sas.upenn.edu/graduate-division

**University of Pittsburgh,** Dietrich School of Arts and Sciences, Department of Music, Pittsburgh, PA 15260. Offers composition and theory (PhD); ethnomusicology (PhD); jazz studies (PhD); music (MA); musicology (PhD). *Faculty:* 12 full-time (5 women), 1 part-time/adjunct (0 women). *Students:* 41 full-time (13 women); includes 3 minority (2 Black or African American, non-Hispanic/Latino; 1 Hispanic/Latino), 9 international. 57 applicants, 26% accepted, 9 enrolled. In 2016, 3 master's, 3 doctorates awarded. *Degree requirements:* For master's, comprehensive exam, thesis; for doctorate, one foreign language, comprehensive exam, thesis/dissertation. *Entrance requirements:* For master's and doctorate, GRE General Test, samples of work, 3 letters of reference, minimum GPA of 3.0, bachelor's degree. Additional exam requirements/recommendations for international students: Required—TOEFL (minimum score 90 iBT), IELTS (minimum score 7). *Application deadline:* For fall admission, 1/5 for domestic and international students. Application fee: $50. Electronic applications accepted. Tuition and fees vary according to program. *Financial support:* In 2016–17, 3 fellowships with full tuition reimbursements, 17 teaching assistantships with full tuition reimbursements were awarded; scholarships/grants, health care benefits, and unspecified assistantships also available. Financial award application deadline: 1/5. *Faculty research:* Composition, theory, ethnomusicology, musicology, jazz studies. *Unit head:* Dr. Deane L. Root, Chair, 412-624-7775, Fax: 412-624-4186, E-mail: dlr@pitt.edu. *Application contact:* Dr. Adriana Helbig, Associate Professor, 412-624-4193, E-mail: anh59@pitt.edu. Website: http://www.music.pitt.edu/

**University of Redlands,** College of Arts and Sciences, School of Music, Redlands, CA 92373-0999. Offers MM. *Accreditation:* NASM. *Program availability:* Part-time. *Degree requirements:* For master's, comprehensive exam, thesis, major conducted ensemble. *Entrance requirements:* For master's, GRE, bachelor's degree in music, minimum GPA of 2.75, audition, original scores. Additional exam requirements/recommendations for international students: Required—TOEFL (minimum score 550 paper-based). *Expenses:* Contact institution. *Faculty research:* Performance, composition.

**University of Regina,** Faculty of Graduate Studies and Research, Faculty of Media, Art, and Performance, Department of Music, Regina, SK S4S 0A2, Canada. Offers composition (MMus); conducting (MMus); music theory (MA); musicology (MA); performance (MMus), including piano, organ, voice, and orchestral instruments. *Faculty:* 9 full-time (6 women). *Students:* 3 part-time (2 women). 2 applicants, 50% accepted. *Degree requirements:* For master's, thesis (for some programs), recital, oral exam, jury examinations. *Entrance requirements:* For master's, B Mus or equivalent; recent compositions (composers only); audition; singing ability in French, Italian, German (vocalists only). Additional exam requirements/recommendations for international students: Required—TOEFL (minimum score 580 paper-based; 80 iBT), IELTS (minimum score 6.5), PTE (minimum score 59). *Application deadline:* For fall admission, 1/15 for domestic and international students. Application fee: $100. Electronic applications accepted. *Financial support:* Fellowships, teaching assistantships, and scholarships/grants available. Financial award application deadline: 6/15. *Faculty research:* Renaissance, Baroque, and medieval music; music of the Classical and Romantic eras; analysis of music written since 1900; music theory; history of music theory. *Unit head:* Dr. Brent Ghiglione, Department Head, 306-585-5542, Fax: 306-585-5549, E-mail: brent.ghiglione@uregina.ca.

**University of Rhode Island,** Graduate School, College of Arts and Sciences, Department of Music, Kingston, RI 02881. Offers music education (MM); music performance (MM). *Accreditation:* NASM. *Program availability:* Part-time. *Faculty:* 12 full-time (6 women). *Students:* 6 full-time (3 women), 2 part-time (both women); includes 2 minority (both Black or African American, non-Hispanic/Latino). In 2016, 3 master's awarded. *Entrance requirements:* For master's, 2 letters of recommendation, audition. Additional exam requirements/recommendations for international students: Required—TOEFL. *Application deadline:* For fall admission, 7/15 for domestic students, 2/1 for international students; for spring admission, 11/15 for domestic students, 7/15 for international students; for summer admission, 4/15 for domestic students. Application fee: $65. Electronic applications accepted. *Expenses:* Tuition, state resident: full-time $11,796; part-time $655 per credit. Tuition, nonresident: full-time $24,206; part-time $1345 per credit. *Required fees:* $1546; $44 per credit. One-time fee: $155 full-time; $35 part-time. *Financial support:* In 2016–17, 3 teaching assistantships with tuition reimbursements (averaging $10,310 per year) were awarded; research assistantships also available. Financial award application deadline: 3/15; financial award applicants required to submit FAFSA. *Unit head:* Dr. Mark Conley, Chair, 401-874-2431, E-mail: mconley@uri.edu. *Application contact:* Dr. Joe Parillo, Director of Graduate Studies, 401-874-2431, E-mail: jmparillo@uri.edu. Website: http://www.uri.edu/artsci/mus/

**University of Rochester,** Eastman School of Music, Program in Ethnomusicology, Rochester, NY 14627. Offers MA. *Expenses: Tuition:* Full-time $47,450; part-time $1482 per credit hour. *Required fees:* $528. Tuition and fees vary according to program.

**University of Rochester,** Eastman School of Music, Program in Music Theory Pedagogy, Rochester, NY 14627. Offers MA. *Accreditation:* NASM. *Expenses: Tuition:* Full-time $47,450; part-time $1482 per credit hour. *Required fees:* $528. Tuition and fees vary according to program.

**University of Rochester,** Eastman School of Music, Programs in Music Composition, Rochester, NY 14627. Offers MA, MM, DMA, PhD. *Accreditation:* NASM. *Expenses: Tuition:* Full-time $47,450; part-time $1482 per credit hour. *Required fees:* $528. Tuition and fees vary according to program.

**University of Rochester,** Eastman School of Music, Programs in Musicology, Rochester, NY 14627. Offers PhD. *Expenses: Tuition:* Full-time $47,450; part-time $1482 per credit hour. *Required fees:* $528. Tuition and fees vary according to program.

**University of Rochester,** Eastman School of Music, Programs in Music Theory, Rochester, NY 14627. Offers PhD. *Accreditation:* NASM. *Expenses: Tuition:* Full-time $47,450; part-time $1482 per credit hour. *Required fees:* $528. Tuition and fees vary according to program.

**University of St. Thomas,** Graduate Studies, College of Arts and Sciences, Graduate Programs in Music Education, St. Paul, MN 55105-1096. Offers choral (MA); instrumental (MA); Kodaly (MA); leadership in music education (Ed D); Orff Schulwerk (MA); piano pedagogy (MA). *Accreditation:* NASM; NCATE. *Program availability:* Part-time. *Degree requirements:* For master's, comprehensive exam, thesis, music history theory and diagnostic exam, piano recital (for piano pedagogy students). *Entrance requirements:* For master's, performance assessment hearing, interview. Additional exam requirements/recommendations for international students: Required—TOEFL (minimum score 550 paper-based; 80 iBT). *Application deadline:* For fall admission, 7/1 for domestic and international students; for winter admission, 12/1 for domestic and international students; for spring admission, 4/1 for domestic and international students. Applications are processed on a rolling basis. Application fee: $0. Electronic applications accepted. *Expenses:* Contact institution. *Financial support:* Federal Work-Study, institutionally sponsored loans, and scholarships/grants available. Financial award application deadline: 4/1; financial award applicants required to submit FAFSA. *Faculty research:* Kodaly, choral, piano pedagogy, Orff, instrumental, world music. *Unit head:* Dr. Douglas C. Orzolek, Director, 651-962-5878, Fax: 651-962-5886, E-mail: dcorzolek@stthomas.edu. *Application contact:* Bev Johnson, Program Coordinator, 651-962-5870, Fax: 651-962-5886, E-mail: bhjohnson@stthomas.edu. Website: http://www.stthomas.edu/music/graduate

**University of St. Thomas,** School of Arts and Sciences, Houston, TX 77006-4696. Offers public policy administration (MPPA); sacred music (MSM). *Program availability:* Part-time. *Faculty:* 2 full-time (0 women), 4 part-time/adjunct (all women). *Students:* 9 full-time (6 women), 17 part-time (10 women); includes 16 minority (3 Black or African American, non-Hispanic/Latino; 1 Asian, non-Hispanic/Latino; 12 Hispanic/Latino). Average age 33. 14 applicants, 86% accepted, 9 enrolled. In 2016, 7 master's awarded. *Entrance requirements:* Additional exam requirements/recommendations for international students: Required—TOEFL (minimum score 79 iBT), IELTS (minimum score 6.5), PTE (minimum score 53). *Application deadline:* For fall admission, 7/15 priority date for domestic and international students; for spring admission, 12/1 priority date for domestic and international students; for summer admission, 5/1 priority date for domestic and international students. Applications are processed on a rolling basis.

Application fee: $35. Electronic applications accepted. *Expenses: Tuition:* Full-time $20,934; part-time $1163 per credit hour. *Required fees:* $81 per semester. One-time fee: $100. Part-time tuition and fees vary according to course level, course load, campus/location and program. *Financial support:* In 2016–17, 23 students received support. Federal Work-Study, scholarships/grants, and state work-study, institutional employment available. Support available to part-time students. Financial award application deadline: 4/15; financial award applicants required to submit FAFSA. *Unit head:* Dr. John W. Starner, Jr., Interim Dean, School of Arts and Sciences, 713-525-3527, E-mail: starner@stthom.edu. *Application contact:* Todd Boutte, Director of Graduate Admissions, 713-942-3403, E-mail: bouttet@stthom.edu. Website: http://www.stthom.edu/Academics/School_of_Arts_and_Sciences/Index.aqf

**University of Saskatchewan,** College of Graduate Studies and Research, College of Arts and Science, Department of Music, Saskatoon, SK S7N 5A2, Canada. Offers M Mus, MA. *Degree requirements:* For master's, thesis. *Entrance requirements:* Additional exam requirements/recommendations for international students: Required—TOEFL (minimum score 80 iBT); Recommended—IELTS (minimum score 6.5). Electronic applications accepted.

**University of South Africa,** College of Human Sciences, Pretoria, South Africa. Offers adult education (M Ed); African languages (MA, PhD); African politics (MA, PhD); Afrikaans (MA, PhD); ancient history (MA, PhD); ancient Near Eastern studies (MA, PhD); anthropology (MA, PhD); applied linguistics (MA); Arabic (MA, PhD); archaeology (MA); art history (MA); Biblical archaeology (MA); Biblical studies (M Th, D Th, PhD); Christian spirituality (M Th, D Th); church history (M Th, D Th); classical studies (MA, PhD); clinical psychology (MA); communication (MA, PhD); comparative education (M Ed, Ed D); consulting psychology (D Admin, D Com, PhD); curriculum studies (M Ed, Ed D); development studies (M Admin, MA, D Admin, PhD); didactics (M Ed, Ed D); education (M Tech); education management (M Ed, Ed D); educational psychology (M Ed); English (MA); environmental education (M Ed); French (MA, PhD); German (MA, PhD); Greek (MA); guidance and counseling (M Ed); health studies (MA, PhD), including health sciences education (MA), health services management (MA), medical and surgical nursing science (critical care general) (MA), midwifery and neonatal nursing science (MA), trauma and emergency care (MA); history (MA, PhD); history of education (Ed D); inclusive education (M Ed, Ed D); information and communications technology policy and regulation (MA); information science (MA, MIS, PhD); international politics (MA, PhD); Islamic studies (MA, PhD); Italian (MA, PhD); Judaica (MA, PhD); linguistics (MA, PhD); mathematical education (M Ed); mathematics education (MA); missiology (M Th, D Th); modern Hebrew (MA, PhD); musicology (MA, MMus, D Mus, PhD); natural science education (M Ed); New Testament (M Th, D Th); Old Testament (D Th); pastoral therapy (M Th, D Th); philosophy (MA); philosophy of education (M Ed, Ed D); politics (MA, PhD); Portuguese (MA, PhD); practical theology (M Th, D Th); psychology (MA, MS, PhD); psychology of education (M Ed, Ed D); public health (MA); religious studies (MA, D Th, PhD); Romance languages (MA); Russian (MA, PhD); Semitic languages (MA, PhD); social behavior studies in HIV/AIDS (MA); social science (mental health) (MA); social science in development studies (MA); social science in psychology (MA); social science in social work (MA); social science in sociology (MA); social work (MSW, DSW, PhD); socio-education (M Ed, Ed D); sociolinguistics (MA); sociology (MA, PhD); Spanish (MA, PhD); systematic theology (M Th, D Th); TESOL (teaching English to speakers of other languages) (MA); theological ethics (M Th, D Th); theory of literature (MA, PhD); urban ministries (D Th); urban ministry (M Th).

**University of South Alabama,** College of Arts and Sciences, Department of Music, Mobile, AL 36688. Offers collaborative keyboard (MM); music education (MM); performance (MM). *Faculty:* 6 full-time (1 woman). *Students:* 1 full-time (0 women), 3 part-time (0 women). Average age 29. 4 applicants, 50% accepted, 2 enrolled. In 2016, 5 master's awarded. *Degree requirements:* For master's, comprehensive exam, final project. *Entrance requirements:* For master's, GRE/GMAT, undergraduate degree in music with minimum GPA of 3.0, official transcript, resume, 3 recommendation letters; teaching certificate (for music education). Additional exam requirements/recommendations for international students: Required—TOEFL (minimum score 525 paper-based; 71 iBT). *Application deadline:* For fall admission, 7/1 priority date for domestic students, 6/1 priority date for international students; for spring admission, 12/1 priority date for domestic students, 11/1 priority date for international students; for summer admission, 5/1 priority date for domestic students, 4/1 priority date for international students. Applications are processed on a rolling basis. Application fee: $35. Electronic applications accepted. *Expenses:* Tuition, state resident: full-time $9768; part-time $407 per credit hour. Tuition, nonresident: full-time $19,536; part-time $814 per credit hour. *Financial support:* Fellowships, research assistantships, teaching assistantships, career-related internships or fieldwork, Federal Work-Study, institutionally sponsored loans, scholarships/grants, and unspecified assistantships available. Support available to part-time students. Financial award application deadline: 5/31; financial award applicants required to submit FAFSA. *Unit head:* Dr. Greg Gruner, Chair, Music, 251-460-6804, Fax: 251-460-7328, E-mail: ggruner@southalabama.edu. *Application contact:* Dr. Jeannette Fresne, Graduate Coordinator, Music, 251-460-6697, Fax: 251-460-7328, E-mail: jfresne@southalabama.edu. Website: http://www.southalabama.edu/colleges/music/

**University of South Carolina,** The Graduate School, School of Music, Columbia, SC 29208. Offers composition (MM, DMA); conducting (MM, DMA); jazz studies (MM); music education (MM Ed, PhD); music history (MM); music performance (Certificate); music theory (MM); opera theater (MM); performance (MM, DMA); piano pedagogy (MM, DMA). *Program availability:* Part-time. *Degree requirements:* For master's, 5 foreign languages, comprehensive exam, thesis (for some programs); for doctorate, one foreign language, comprehensive exam, thesis/dissertation; for Certificate, recitals. *Entrance requirements:* For master's and doctorate, GRE General Test or MAT, music diagnostic exam. Additional exam requirements/recommendations for international students: Required—TOEFL (minimum score 570 paper-based). Electronic applications accepted. *Expenses:* Contact institution. *Faculty research:* Music skills in pre-school children, evaluation of school performing ensembles.

**The University of South Dakota,** Graduate School, College of Fine Arts, Department of Music, Vermillion, SD 57069. Offers collaborative piano (MM); conducting (MM); history of musical instruments (MM); music education (MM); music history (MM); music performance (MM). *Accreditation:* NASM. *Degree requirements:* For master's, thesis or alternative. *Entrance requirements:* For master's, minimum GPA of 2.7, audition or performance tape. Additional exam requirements/recommendations for international students: Required—TOEFL (minimum score 550 paper-based; 79 iBT). Electronic applications accepted.

**University of Southern California,** Graduate School, Thornton School of Music, Los Angeles, CA 90089. Offers brass performance (MM, DMA, Graduate Certificate); choral and sacred music (MM, DMA); classical guitar (MM, DMA, Graduate Certificate); composition (MM, DMA); early music (MA, DMA); harp performance (MM, DMA, Graduate Certificate); historical musicology (PhD); jazz studies (MM, DMA, Graduate Certificate); keyboard collaborative arts (MM, DMA, Graduate Certificate); music education (MM, DMA); organ performance (MM, DMA, Graduate Certificate); percussion performance (MM, DMA, Graduate Certificate); piano performance (MM, DMA, Graduate Certificate); scoring for motion pictures and television (Graduate Certificate);

strings performance (MM, DMA, Graduate Certificate); studio jazz guitar (MM, DMA, Graduate Certificate); teaching music (MA); vocal arts (classical voice/opera) (MM, DMA, Graduate Certificate); woodwind performance (MM, DMA, Graduate Certificate). *Accreditation:* NASM. *Program availability:* Part-time, evening/weekend. Terminal master's awarded for partial completion of doctoral program. *Degree requirements:* For master's, variable foreign language requirement, comprehensive exam (for some programs), thesis (for some programs); for doctorate, variable foreign language requirement, comprehensive exam, thesis/dissertation (for some programs). *Entrance requirements:* For master's, GRE (for MA in early music and MM in music education); for doctorate, GRE (for DMA). Additional exam requirements/recommendations for international students: Required—TOEFL (minimum score 560 paper-based; 83 iBT). Electronic applications accepted. *Expenses:* Contact institution. *Faculty research:* Early Modern musical improvisation and composition, maternal sound stimulation of the premature infant, physiological characteristics of jazz guitarists, the musical experience of the very young child, electronic music.

**University of Southern Maine,** College of Arts, Humanities, and Social Sciences, School of Music, Portland, ME 04103. Offers composition (MM); conducting (MM); jazz studies (MM); music education (MM); performance (MM). *Accreditation:* NASM.

**University of Southern Mississippi,** Graduate School, College of Arts and Letters, Department of Theatre, Hattiesburg, MS 39406. Offers costume design (MFA); directing (MFA); lighting and sound design (MFA); performance (MFA); scenic design (MFA). *Accreditation:* NAST. *Program availability:* Part-time. *Degree requirements:* For master's, comprehensive exam, thesis or alternative, creative project. *Entrance requirements:* For master's, GRE General Test, minimum GPA of 3.0. Additional exam requirements/recommendations for international students: Required—TOEFL, IELTS. *Application deadline:* For fall admission, 3/1 priority date for domestic students, 3/1 for international students; for spring admission, 1/10 priority date for domestic and international students. Applications are processed on a rolling basis. Application fee: $60. *Expenses: Tuition, area resident:* Full-time $15,708; part-time $437 per credit hour. *Financial support:* Research assistantships, teaching assistantships with full tuition reimbursements, career-related internships or fieldwork, Federal Work-Study, institutionally sponsored loans, health care benefits, and unspecified assistantships available. Support available to part-time students. Financial award application deadline: 3/15; financial award applicants required to submit FAFSA. *Faculty research:* Technical design, acting. *Unit head:* Louis Rackoff, Chair, 601-266-6907, Fax: 601-266-6423. *Application contact:* Shonna Breland, Manager of Graduate Admissions, 601-266-4369, Fax: 601-266-5138, E-mail: shonna.breland@usm.edu. Website: http://www.usm.edu/theatre

**University of Southern Mississippi,** Graduate School, College of Arts and Letters, School of Music, Hattiesburg, MS 39406. Offers conducting (MM, DMA); history and literature (MM); music education (MME, PhD); performance (MM); performance and pedagogy (DMA); piano accompanying (MM); theory (MM); woodwind performance and pedagogy (MM). *Accreditation:* NASM. *Program availability:* Blended/hybrid learning. Terminal master's awarded for partial completion of doctoral program. *Degree requirements:* For master's, comprehensive exam, thesis (for some programs); for doctorate, comprehensive exam, thesis/dissertation. *Entrance requirements:* For master's, GRE General Test, minimum GPA of 2.75 in last 60 hours; for doctorate, GRE General Test, minimum GPA of 3.5. Additional exam requirements/recommendations for international students: Required—TOEFL, IELTS. *Application deadline:* For fall admission, 6/1 for domestic students; for spring admission, 11/1 for domestic students; for summer admission, 3/1 for domestic students. Applications are processed on a rolling basis. Application fee: $60. *Expenses: Tuition, area resident:* Full-time $15,708; part-time $437 per credit hour. *Financial support:* Fellowships with full tuition reimbursements, research assistantships, teaching assistantships with full tuition reimbursements, Federal Work-Study, institutionally sponsored loans, scholarships/grants, health care benefits, tuition waivers (partial), and unspecified assistantships available. Financial award application deadline: 2/1; financial award applicants required to submit FAFSA. *Faculty research:* Music theory, composition, music performance. *Unit head:* Dr. Richard Kravchak, Director, 601-266-5543, Fax: 601-266-6427. Website: https://www.usm.edu/music

**University of South Florida,** College of Arts and Sciences, Department of English, Tampa, FL 33620-9951. Offers creative writing (MFA), including fiction, poetry; English (MA, PhD), including literature, rhetoric and composition. *Program availability:* Part-time, evening/weekend. *Faculty:* 26 full-time (14 women). *Students:* 73 full-time (50 women), 28 part-time (21 women); includes 17 minority (3 Black or African American, non-Hispanic/Latino; 3 Asian, non-Hispanic/Latino; 9 Hispanic/Latino; 2 Two or more races, non-Hispanic/Latino), 2 international. Average age 33. 114 applicants, 55% accepted, 27 enrolled. In 2016, 12 master's, 10 doctorates awarded. *Degree requirements:* For master's, comprehensive exam (for MFA); thesis or portfolio (for MA); for doctorate, one foreign language, comprehensive exam, thesis/dissertation. *Entrance requirements:* For master's, GRE General Test, minimum undergraduate GPA of 3.5 (for MA), 3.2 (for MFA); three letters of recommendation; personal statement; writing sample from 10 to 20 pages (depending on genre); for doctorate, GRE General Test, minimum graduate GPA of 3.7; three letters of recommendation; 2-3 page personal statement; 2500-word writing sample from English coursework. Additional exam requirements/recommendations for international students: Required—TOEFL (minimum score 550 paper-based; 79 iBT) or IELTS (minimum score 6.5) for MA and PhD; TOEFL (minimum score 600 paper-based) for MFA. *Application deadline:* For fall admission, 1/1 for domestic and international students. Applications are processed on a rolling basis. Application fee: $30. Electronic applications accepted. *Expenses:* Tuition, state resident: full-time $7766; part-time $431.43 per credit hour. Tuition, nonresident: full-time $15,789; part-time $877.17 per credit hour. *Required fees:* $37 per term. *Financial support:* In 2016–17, 20 students received support, including 2 research assistantships (averaging $17,221 per year), 79 teaching assistantships with tuition reimbursements available (averaging $11,576 per year); unspecified assistantships also available. Financial award application deadline: 6/30; financial award applicants required to submit FAFSA. *Faculty research:* British and American literature, rhetoric and composition, world and comparative literatures, creative writing, gender and sexuality studies, women's literature, film and genre studies, literary theory, popular and visual culture, textual and translation studies. *Total annual research expenditures:* $44,400. *Unit head:* Dr. Hunt Hawkins, Professor and Chairperson, 813-974-9492, Fax: 813-974-2270, E-mail: hhawkins@usf.edu. *Application contact:* Dr. Marty Gould, Associate Professor and Graduate Director, 813-974-9474, Fax: 813-974-2270, E-mail: mgould@usf.edu. Website: http://english.usf.edu/

**University of South Florida,** College of The Arts, School of Music, Tampa, FL 33620-9951. Offers music (MM, PhD), including chamber music (MM), choral conducting (MM), composition (MM), electro-acoustic music (MM), instrumental conducting (MM), jazz composition (MM), jazz performance (MM), music education (PhD), performance (MM), piano pedagogy (MM), theory (MM); music education (MA). *Accreditation:* NASM. *Program availability:* Part-time, evening/weekend. *Faculty:* 26 full-time (9 women), 1 part-time/adjunct (0 women). *Students:* 66 full-time (27 women), 19 part-time (6 women); includes 15 minority (6 Black or African American, non-Hispanic/Latino; 2 Asian, non-Hispanic/Latino; 5 Hispanic/Latino; 2 Two or more races, non-Hispanic/Latino), 21

international. Average age 29. 93 applicants, 56% accepted, 38 enrolled. In 2016, 29 master's, 3 doctorates awarded. *Degree requirements:* For master's, comprehensive exam, thesis optional; for doctorate, comprehensive exam, thesis/dissertation. *Entrance requirements:* For master's, minimum GPA of 3.0 in upper-division courses and music courses for bachelor's degree; resume; three letters of recommendation; at least 2 years of K-12 music teaching experience (for MA in music education); audition or interview (for MM); for doctorate, GRE General Test, master's degree from accredited institution with minimum GPA of 3.5, 3.0 in upper-division undergraduate courses; at least 2 years of K-12 music teaching experience; interview with faculty; 3 letters of recommendation; academic writing sample; curriculum vitae; personal goals statement; 15-20 minute video of applicant teaching music. Additional exam requirements/recommendations for international students: Required—TOEFL (minimum score 550 paper-based; 79 iBT) or IELTS (minimum score 6.5). *Application deadline:* For fall admission, 2/15 priority date for domestic students, 2/1 for international students; for spring admission, 10/15 for domestic students, 9/15 for international students; for summer admission, 2/15 for domestic students, 1/15 for international students. Application fee: $30. Electronic applications accepted. *Expenses:* Tuition, state resident: full-time $7766; part-time $431.43 per credit hour. Tuition, nonresident: full-time $15,789; part-time $877.17 per credit hour. *Required fees:* $37 per term. *Financial support:* In 2016–17, 48 students received support, including 1 research assistantship with tuition reimbursement available (averaging $15,724 per year), 46 teaching assistantships with tuition reimbursements available (averaging $10,099 per year); unspecified assistantships also available. Financial award application deadline: 2/15. *Faculty research:* Music education: alternate methods, community collaboration, contemporary changes, early childhood, general music, international perspectives, multicultural issues, technology, teacher behaviors, philosophy, psychology, sociology; music: chamber music, composition, conducting, jazz studies, music performance, music theory, pedagogy, electronic music. *Total annual research expenditures:* $18,982. *Unit head:* Dr. Karen Bryan, Director, 813-974-2311, Fax: 813-974-8721, E-mail: kmbryan@usf.edu. *Application contact:* Dr. William Hayden, Associate Professor and Graduate Program Director, 813-974-1753, Fax: 813-974-8721, E-mail: wphayden@usf.edu. Website: http://music.arts.usf.edu/

**The University of Tennessee,** Graduate School, College of Arts and Sciences, Department of Theatre, Knoxville, TN 37996. Offers costume design (MFA); lighting design (MFA); performance (MFA); scene design (MFA); theatre technology (MFA). *Accreditation:* NAST. *Degree requirements:* For master's, thesis or alternative. *Entrance requirements:* For master's, audition, minimum GPA of 2.7. Additional exam requirements/recommendations for international students: Required—TOEFL. Electronic applications accepted.

**The University of Tennessee,** Graduate School, College of Arts and Sciences, School of Music, Knoxville, TN 37996. Offers accompanying (MM); choral conducting (MM); composition (MM); instrumental conducting (MM); jazz (MM); music education (MM); music theory (MM); musicology (MM); performance (MM); piano pedagogy and literature (MM). *Accreditation:* NASM. *Program availability:* Part-time. *Degree requirements:* For master's, thesis (for some programs). *Entrance requirements:* For master's, audition, minimum GPA of 2.7. Additional exam requirements/recommendations for international students: Required—TOEFL. Electronic applications accepted.

**The University of Tennessee at Chattanooga,** Program in Music, Chattanooga, TN 37403. Offers music education (MM); performance (MM). *Accreditation:* NASM. *Faculty:* 5 full-time (3 women). *Students:* 5 part-time (3 women); includes 1 minority (Black or African American, non-Hispanic/Latino). Average age 29. 1 applicant, 100% accepted. In 2016, 7 master's awarded. *Degree requirements:* For master's, comprehensive exam, thesis or alternative, recital. *Entrance requirements:* For master's, GRE General Test or MAT, bachelor's degree in music, audition for placement. Additional exam requirements/recommendations for international students: Required—TOEFL (minimum score 550 paper-based; 79 iBT), IELTS (minimum score 6). *Application deadline:* For fall admission, 6/15 priority date for domestic students, 7/1 for international students; for spring admission, 11/1 priority date for domestic students, 11/1 for international students. Applications are processed on a rolling basis. Application fee: $35 ($40 for international students). Electronic applications accepted. *Expenses:* $9,876 full-time in-state; $25,994 full-time out-of-state; $450 per credit part-time in-state; $1,345 per credit part-time out-of-state. *Financial support:* Research assistantships, Federal Work-Study, scholarships/grants, and unspecified assistantships available. Financial award application deadline: 7/1; financial award applicants required to submit FAFSA. *Faculty research:* Music education, conducting, opera, vocal instruction, orchestras. *Total annual research expenditures:* $1,400. *Unit head:* Dr. Lee Harris, Department Head, 423-425-4601, Fax: 423-425-4603, E-mail: lee-harris@utc.edu. *Application contact:* Dr. Joanne Romagni, Dean of the Graduate School, 423-425-4478, Fax: 423-425-5223, E-mail: joanne-romagni@utc.edu. Website: http://www.utc.edu/music/

**The University of Texas at Arlington,** Graduate School, College of Liberal Arts, Department of Music, Arlington, TX 76019. Offers education (MM); performance (MM). *Accreditation:* NASM. *Program availability:* Part-time, evening/weekend. *Degree requirements:* For master's, comprehensive exam, thesis optional. *Entrance requirements:* For master's, GRE, 3 letters of recommendation, minimum GPA of 3.0 in last 60 hours of course work. Additional exam requirements/recommendations for international students: Required—TOEFL (minimum score 550 paper-based). *Application deadline:* For fall admission, 6/1 priority date for domestic students. Applications are processed on a rolling basis. Application fee: $35 ($50 for international students). Electronic applications accepted. *Financial support:* Fellowships with full tuition reimbursements, teaching assistantships with partial tuition reimbursements, and scholarships/grants available. *Unit head:* Dr. Rick Bogard, Chair, 817-272-3471, Fax: 817-272-3434, E-mail: bogard@uta.edu. *Application contact:* Dr. Clifton Evans, Graduate Advisor, 817-272-5027, Fax: 817-272-3434, E-mail: cevans@uta.edu. Website: http://www.uta.edu/music

**The University of Texas at Austin,** Graduate School, College of Fine Arts, Sarah and Ernest Butler School of Music, Austin, TX 78712-1111. Offers band and wind conducting (M Music, DMA); brass/woodwind/percussion (MM, DMA); chamber music (MM); choral conducting (MM, DMA); collaborative piano (MM, DMA); composition (MM, DMA), including composition, jazz, jazz (DMA); ethnomusicology (MM, PhD); literature and pedagogy (MM); music and human learning (MM, PhD); music and human learning (DMA), including jazz (MM, DMA), piano pedagogy; musicology (MM, PhD); opera performance (MM, DMA); orchestral conducting (MM, DMA); organ (MM), including sacred music; organ performance (MM, DMA); performance (MM), including jazz (MM, DMA); performance (DMA), including jazz (MM, DMA), piano (DMA), including jazz (MM, DMA); piano literature and pedagogy (MM); piano performance (MM, DMA); string performance (MM, DMA); theory (MM, PhD); vocal performance (MM, DMA); voice (DMA), including opera; voice performance pedagogy (DMA); woodwind, brass, percussion performance (MM, DMA). *Accreditation:* NASM. *Program availability:* Part-time. *Degree requirements:* For master's, one foreign language, comprehensive exam, thesis (for some programs), recital (performance or composition majors); for doctorate, one foreign language, comprehensive exam, thesis/dissertation (for some programs), recital (for performance or composition majors). *Entrance requirements:* For master's and doctorate, GRE General Test (except for performance or composition majors), audition (performance majors). Electronic applications accepted.

**The University of Texas at El Paso,** Graduate School, College of Liberal Arts, Department of Music, El Paso, TX 79968-0001. Offers music education (MM); music performance (MM). *Accreditation:* NASM. *Program availability:* Part-time, evening/weekend. *Degree requirements:* For master's, thesis optional. *Entrance requirements:* For master's, audition, interview, letters of recommendation. Additional exam requirements/recommendations for international students: Required—TOEFL; Recommended—IELTS. Electronic applications accepted.

**The University of Texas at San Antonio,** College of Liberal and Fine Arts, Department of Music, San Antonio, TX 78249-0617. Offers MM. *Accreditation:* NASM. *Program availability:* Part-time. *Faculty:* 21 full-time (7 women), 3 part-time/adjunct (2 women). *Students:* 9 full-time (6 women), 20 part-time (11 women); includes 13 minority (10 Hispanic/Latino; 1 Native Hawaiian or other Pacific Islander, non-Hispanic/Latino; 2 Two or more races, non-Hispanic/Latino). Average age 32. 13 applicants, 62% accepted, 6 enrolled. In 2016, 12 master's awarded. *Degree requirements:* For master's, comprehensive exam, thesis (for some programs). *Entrance requirements:* For master's, GRE, audition, 3 letters of recommendation. Additional exam requirements/recommendations for international students: Required—TOEFL (minimum score 550 paper-based; 79 iBT), IELTS (minimum score 6.5). *Application deadline:* For fall admission, 7/1 for domestic students, 4/1 for international students; for spring admission, 11/1 for domestic students, 9/1 for international students. Application fee: $45 ($80 for international students). *Financial support:* Scholarships/grants and unspecified assistantships available. *Faculty research:* Music cognition and perception, dalcroze eurhythmics in therapy, vocology, music of the Americas, music and film. *Unit head:* Dr. David Frego, Department Chair, 210-458-4357, Fax: 210-458-4381, E-mail: david.frego@utsa.edu.
Website: http://music.utsa.edu

**The University of Texas Rio Grande Valley,** College of Fine Arts, School of Music, Edinburg, TX 78539. Offers ethnomusicology (M Mus); interdisciplinary studies (MAIS); music education (M Mus); performance (M Mus). *Accreditation:* NASM. *Program availability:* Part-time. *Degree requirements:* For master's, comprehensive exam, thesis optional, recital (performance). *Entrance requirements:* For master's, audition for performance area, bachelor's degree in music. Tuition and fees vary according to course load and program. *Faculty research:* Music history, instrumental pedagogy, vocal pedagogy, music education, ethnomusicology.

**The University of the Arts,** College of Performing Arts, School of Music, Program in Jazz Studies, Philadelphia, PA 19102-4944. Offers MM. *Degree requirements:* For master's, recital, thesis/project. *Entrance requirements:* For master's, audition consisting of a performance, interview and written examination to measure aural, theoretical, arranging and historical skills and knowledge; official transcripts from each undergraduate or graduate school attended; three letters of recommendation; one- to two-page statement of professional plans and goals. Additional exam requirements/recommendations for international students: Required—TOEFL (minimum score 580 paper-based, 92 iBT) or IELTS (minimum score 6.5).

**University of the Pacific,** Conservatory of Music, Stockton, CA 95211-0197. Offers music education (MM); music therapy (MA). *Students:* 10 full-time (7 women), 23 part-time (15 women); includes 8 minority (3 Asian, non-Hispanic/Latino; 4 Hispanic/Latino; 1 Two or more races, non-Hispanic/Latino), 4 international. Average age 33. 24 applicants, 129% accepted, 13 enrolled. In 2016, 4 master's awarded. *Entrance requirements:* For master's, GRE General Test. Additional exam requirements/recommendations for international students: Required—TOEFL. *Application deadline:* For fall admission, 3/1 priority date for domestic students; for spring admission, 10/1 priority date for domestic students. Applications are processed on a rolling basis. Application fee: $75. *Financial support:* Teaching assistantships and institutionally sponsored loans available. Support available to part-time students. Financial award application deadline: 3/1; financial award applicants required to submit FAFSA. *Unit head:* Dr. Daniel Ebbers, Interim Dean, 209-946-2415, E-mail: musicdean@pacific.edu. *Application contact:* 209-946-2415, Fax: 209-946-2770.

**The University of Toledo,** College of Graduate Studies, College of Communication and the Arts, Department of Music, Toledo, OH 43606-3390. Offers music (Certificate); music performance (MMP). *Accreditation:* NASM. *Degree requirements:* For master's, comprehensive exam, diagnostic theory exam. *Entrance requirements:* For master's, GRE if GPA less than 2.7, minimum cumulative point-hour ratio of 2.7 for all previous academic work, audition. Additional exam requirements/recommendations for international students: Required—TOEFL (minimum score 550 paper-based; 80 iBT). Electronic applications accepted.

**University of Toronto,** School of Graduate Studies, Faculty of Music, Toronto, ON M5S 1A1, Canada. Offers composition (M Mus, DMA); ethnomusicology (MA, PhD); jazz (M Mus); music education (MA, PhD); musicology/theory (MA, PhD); opera (M Mus); performance (M Mus, DMA). *Program availability:* Part-time. *Degree requirements:* For master's, comprehensive exam (for some programs), oral examination (M Mus in composition), 1 foreign language (MA); for doctorate, recital of original works (DMA), thesis (PhD). *Entrance requirements:* For master's, BM in area of specialization with minimum B average in final 2 years, original compositions (M Mus in composition); for doctorate, master's degree in area of specialization, minimum B+ average, at least 2 extended compositions (DMA). Additional exam requirements/recommendations for international students: Required—TOEFL (minimum score 580 paper-based; 93 iBT), TWE (minimum score 5). Electronic applications accepted.

**University of Utah,** Graduate School, College of Fine Arts, School of Music, Salt Lake City, UT 84112. Offers choral conducting (M Mus, DMA); collaborative piano (M Mus); composition (M Mus, PhD); instrumental conducting (M Mus, DMA); instrumental performance (M Mus, DMA); jazz studies (M Mus); music education (M Mus, PhD); music history and literature (M Mus); musicology (MA); organ performance (M Mus); piano performance (M Mus, DMA); piano performance and pedagogy (M Mus); string performance and pedagogy (M Mus); theory (M Mus); vocal performance (DMA). *Accreditation:* NASM. *Faculty:* 33 full-time (11 women), 53 part-time/adjunct (20 women). *Students:* 83 full-time (44 women), 24 part-time (12 women); includes 27 minority (1 American Indian or Alaska Native, non-Hispanic/Latino; 13 Asian, non-Hispanic/Latino; 6 Hispanic/Latino; 7 Two or more races, non-Hispanic/Latino). Average age 32. 121 applicants, 55% accepted, 31 enrolled. In 2016, 10 master's, 13 doctorates awarded. *Degree requirements:* For master's, variable foreign language requirement, comprehensive exam (for some programs), thesis (for some programs), 1-2 recitals (MM), final oral exam; for doctorate, variable foreign language requirement, comprehensive exam (for some programs), thesis/dissertation, 4 recitals (DMA), thesis/dissertation defense. *Entrance requirements:* For master's, placement exams, minimum GPA of 3.0, audition, bachelor's degree in music; for doctorate, placement exams, minimum GPA of 3.0, audition, master's degree in music. Additional exam requirements/recommendations for international students: Required—TOEFL (minimum score 85 iBT). *Application deadline:* For fall admission, 2/15 for domestic students, 1/15 for international students; for spring admission, 10/1 for domestic students, 9/1 for international students; for summer admission, 3/15 for domestic students, 2/15 for

international students. Applications are processed on a rolling basis. Application fee: $55 ($65 for international students). Electronic applications accepted. *Expenses:* Contact institution. *Financial support:* In 2016–17, 64 students received support, including 56 teaching assistantships with tuition reimbursements available (averaging $10,292 per year); fellowships with tuition reimbursements available, research assistantships with tuition reimbursements available, scholarships/grants, health care benefits, and unspecified assistantships also available. Financial award application deadline: 2/1. *Faculty research:* Music education, conducting, musicology, composition, performance. *Total annual research expenditures:* $25,000. *Unit head:* Miguel Chuaqui, Director, 801-585-3720, E-mail: m.chauqui@utah.edu. *Application contact:* Cassie Wagstaff, Academic Coordinator, 801-585-6972, Fax: 801-581-5683, E-mail: cassandra.wagstaff@utah.edu.
Website: http://www.music.utah.edu/

**University of Valley Forge,** Program in Music Technology, Phoenixville, PA 19460. Offers MM. *Program availability:* Online learning.

**University of Victoria,** Faculty of Graduate Studies, Faculty of Fine Arts, School of Music, Victoria, BC V8W 2Y2, Canada. Offers composition (M Mus); musicology (MA, PhD); musicology with performance (MA); performance (M Mus). *Degree requirements:* For master's, 2 foreign languages, thesis; for doctorate, 2 foreign languages, thesis/dissertation, candidacy exam. *Entrance requirements:* For master's, theory placement test, audition or sample papers and compositions; for doctorate, audition or sample papers and compositions. Additional exam requirements/recommendations for international students: Required—TOEFL (minimum score 575 paper-based), IELTS (minimum score 7). Electronic applications accepted. *Faculty research:* Beethoven, Wagner, metrical structure in tonal music, French baroque, eighteenth-century opera.

**University of Virginia,** College and Graduate School of Arts and Sciences, Department of Music, Charlottesville, VA 22903. Offers MA, PhD. *Faculty:* 16 full-time (2 women), 13 part-time/adjunct (6 women). *Students:* 28 full-time (11 women); includes 5 minority (1 Black or African American, non-Hispanic/Latino; 1 American Indian or Alaska Native, non-Hispanic/Latino; 1 Hispanic/Latino; 2 Two or more races, non-Hispanic/Latino), 1 international. Average age 30. 51 applicants, 14% accepted, 5 enrolled. In 2016, 7 master's, 6 doctorates awarded. *Degree requirements:* For master's, one foreign language, article-length paper; for doctorate, one foreign language, comprehensive exam, thesis/dissertation. *Entrance requirements:* For master's and doctorate, GRE General Test, 2 writing samples or portfolio. Additional exam requirements/recommendations for international students: Required—TOEFL (minimum score 600 paper-based; 90 iBT), IELTS (minimum score 7). *Application deadline:* For fall admission, 1/1 for domestic students, 1/2 for international students. Applications are processed on a rolling basis. Application fee: $60. Electronic applications accepted. *Expenses:* Tuition, state resident: full-time $15,026; part-time $834 per credit hour. Tuition, nonresident: full-time $25,168; part-time $1378 per credit hour. *Required fees:* $2654. *Financial support:* Teaching assistantships available. Financial award applicants required to submit FAFSA. *Unit head:* Matthew Burtner, Chair, 434-924-3052, Fax: 434-924-6033, E-mail: mburtner@virginia.edu. *Application contact:* Michael Puri, Director of Graduate Studies, 434-924-3052, Fax: 434-924-6033, E-mail: mjp3h@virginia.edu.
Website: http://music.virginia.edu/

**University of Washington,** Graduate School, College of Arts and Sciences, School of Music, Concentration in Choral Conducting, Seattle, WA 98195. Offers MM, DMA.

**University of Washington,** Graduate School, College of Arts and Sciences, School of Music, Concentration in Ethnomusicology, Seattle, WA 98195. Offers MA.

**University of Washington,** Graduate School, College of Arts and Sciences, School of Music, Concentration in Music History, Seattle, WA 98195. Offers MA, PhD.

**University of Washington,** Graduate School, College of Arts and Sciences, School of Music, Department of Choral Music, Seattle, WA 98195. Offers choral conducting (MM, DMA).

**The University of Western Ontario,** Faculty of Graduate Studies, Don Wright Faculty of Music, London, ON N6A 5B8, Canada. Offers music (M Mus, PhD); popular music and culture (MA). *Program availability:* Part-time. Terminal master's awarded for partial completion of doctoral program. *Degree requirements:* For master's, 2 foreign languages, thesis (for some programs), recital; for doctorate, 2 foreign languages, thesis/dissertation. *Entrance requirements:* For master's, honors degree in music; minimum A average in proposed area of concentration, B average overall; for doctorate, MA or equivalent. *Faculty research:* Systematic musicology, musicology, theory, music education.

**University of West Georgia,** College of Arts and Humanities, Carrollton, GA 30118. Offers English (MA); history (MA); museum studies (Postbaccalaureate Certificate); music performance (M Mus); music teacher education (M Mus); public history (Postbaccalaureate Certificate). *Program availability:* Part-time, evening/weekend, 100% online, blended/hybrid learning. *Faculty:* 70 full-time (39 women). *Students:* 23 full-time (16 women), 55 part-time (33 women); includes 18 minority (10 Black or African American, non-Hispanic/Latino; 1 American Indian or Alaska Native, non-Hispanic/Latino; 5 Hispanic/Latino; 2 Two or more races, non-Hispanic/Latino), 1 international. Average age 31. 24 applicants, 100% accepted, 23 enrolled. In 2016, 34 master's, 6 other advanced degrees awarded. *Entrance requirements:* Additional exam requirements/recommendations for international students: Required—TOEFL (minimum score 523 paper-based; 69 iBT); Recommended—IELTS (minimum score 6.5). *Application deadline:* For fall admission, 8/1 for domestic students, 6/1 for international students; for spring admission, 11/15 for domestic students, 10/15 for international students; for summer admission, 5/15 for domestic students, 3/30 for international students. Applications are processed on a rolling basis. Application fee: $40. Electronic applications accepted. *Expenses:* Tuition, state resident: full-time $5316; part-time $222 per semester hour. Tuition, nonresident: full-time $20,658; part-time $861 per semester hour. *Required fees:* $1962. Tuition and fees vary according to course load, degree level and program. *Financial support:* Fellowships, research assistantships, teaching assistantships, career-related internships or fieldwork, Federal Work-Study, institutionally sponsored loans, scholarships/grants, and unspecified assistantships available. Support available to part-time students. Financial award application deadline: 4/1; financial award applicants required to submit FAFSA. *Unit head:* Dr. Pauline D. Gagnon, Dean of Arts and Humanities, 678-839-5450, Fax: 678-839-5451, E-mail: pgagnon@westga.edu. *Application contact:* Dr. Toby Ziglar, Assistant Dean of the Graduate School, 678-839-1394, Fax: 678-839-1395, E-mail: graduate@westga.edu.
Website: http://www.westga.edu/coah

**University of Wisconsin–Madison,** Graduate School, College of Letters and Science, School of Music, Program in Composition, Madison, WI 53706-1380. Offers MM, DMA. *Accreditation:* NASM. *Degree requirements:* For doctorate, thesis/dissertation.

**University of Wisconsin–Madison,** Graduate School, College of Letters and Science, School of Music, Program in Conducting, Madison, WI 53706-1380. Offers choral (MM, DMA); instrumental (MM, DMA); orchestral (MM, DMA). *Accreditation:* NASM. *Degree requirements:* For doctorate, thesis/dissertation.

**University of Wisconsin–Madison,** Graduate School, College of Letters and Science, School of Music, Program in Musicology and Ethnomusicology, Madison, WI 53706-1380. Offers ethnomusicology (MA, PhD); historical musicology (PhD); music history

(MA). *Accreditation:* NASM. *Degree requirements:* For doctorate, 2 foreign languages, thesis/dissertation. *Entrance requirements:* For doctorate, GRE General Test.

**University of Wisconsin–Madison,** Graduate School, College of Letters and Science, School of Music, Program in Music Performance, Madison, WI 53706-1380. Offers MM, DMA. *Accreditation:* NASM. *Degree requirements:* For doctorate, one foreign language, thesis/dissertation.

**University of Wisconsin–Madison,** Graduate School, College of Letters and Science, School of Music, Program in Music Theory, Madison, WI 53706-1380. Offers MA, PhD. *Accreditation:* NASM. *Degree requirements:* For master's, thesis, 1 foreign language (MA); for doctorate, 2 foreign languages, thesis/dissertation. *Entrance requirements:* For master's, GRE General Test (MA); for doctorate, GRE General Test.

**University of Wyoming,** College of Arts and Sciences, Department of Music, Laramie, WY 82071. Offers music education (MME); performance (MM). *Accreditation:* NASM. *Degree requirements:* For master's, comprehensive exam, thesis or alternative. *Entrance requirements:* For master's, minimum GPA of 3.0. Additional exam requirements/recommendations for international students: Required—TOEFL (minimum score 540 paper-based). Electronic applications accepted.

**Valdosta State University,** Department of English, Valdosta, GA 31698. Offers literature (MA); rhetoric and composition (MA); studies for language arts teachers (MA). *Program availability:* Part-time, 100% online, blended/hybrid learning. *Degree requirements:* For master's, one foreign language, thesis, comprehensive written and/or oral exams. *Entrance requirements:* For master's, GRE General Test, minimum GPA of 3.0. Additional exam requirements/recommendations for international students: Required—TOEFL (minimum score 523 paper-based); Recommended—IELTS. Electronic applications accepted. *Expenses:* Contact institution. *Faculty research:* American literature, creative writing.

**Vermont College of Fine Arts,** MFA in Music Composition Program, Montpelier, VT 05602. Offers MFA. *Faculty:* 10 part-time/adjunct (1 woman). *Students:* 35 full-time (4 women); includes 5 minority (2 Black or African American, non-Hispanic/Latino; 3 Hispanic/Latino), 3 international. Average age 43. 13 applicants, 77% accepted, 6 enrolled. In 2016, 12 master's awarded. *Degree requirements:* For master's, thesis. *Entrance requirements:* For master's, resume of education and relevant professional experience, three samples of original compositions, official transcripts of all previous undergraduate and graduate coursework, two letters of recommendation, statement of purpose. *Application deadline:* For fall admission, 6/15 for domestic and international students; for spring admission, 12/15 for domestic and international students. Applications are processed on a rolling basis. Application fee: $75. *Expenses:* Contact institution. *Financial support:* Scholarships/grants available. Financial award applicants required to submit FAFSA. *Unit head:* Carol Beatty, Program Director, 866-934-8232 Ext. 8610, E-mail: carol.beatty@vcfa.edu. *Application contact:* Sarah Madru, Assistant Program Director, 802-828-8534, E-mail: sarah.madru@vcfa.edu. Website: http://www.vcfa.edu/music-comp

**Virginia Commonwealth University,** Graduate School, School of the Arts, Department of Music, Richmond, VA 23284-9005. Offers music education (MM). *Accreditation:* NASM. *Degree requirements:* For master's, departmental qualifying exam, recital. *Entrance requirements:* For master's, department examination, audition or tapes, portfolio. Additional exam requirements/recommendations for international students: Required—TOEFL (minimum score 600 paper-based; 100 iBT). *Application deadline:* For fall admission, 4/1 for domestic students. Application fee: $50. Electronic applications accepted. *Financial support:* Fellowships, teaching assistantships, career-related internships or fieldwork, Federal Work-Study, and institutionally sponsored loans available. Support available to part-time students. Financial award application deadline: 3/15. *Faculty research:* Composition, conducting, education, performance. *Unit head:* Darryl Harper, Interim Chair, 804-828-1166, Fax: 804-828-6469, E-mail: dharper2@vcu.edu. *Application contact:* Dr. David A. Greennagel, Graduate Program Director, 804-828-8523, E-mail: djgreennagel@vcu.edu. Website: http://www.vcu.edu/arts/music/dept/index.html

**Washington State University,** College of Arts and Sciences, School of Music, Pullman, WA 99164-5300. Offers MA. *Accreditation:* NASM. *Program availability:* Part-time. *Degree requirements:* For master's, one foreign language, comprehensive exam, thesis (for some programs), oral exam. *Entrance requirements:* For master's, audition, minimum GPA of 3.0, 3 letters of recommendation, composition portfolio and recording (for composition); writing sample and written philosophy (for music education); writing sample (for music history); in-depth audition (for performance). Additional exam requirements/recommendations for international students: Required—TOEFL, IELTS. Electronic applications accepted. *Faculty research:* Composition, education.

**Washington University in St. Louis,** The Graduate School, Department of Music, St. Louis, MO 63130-4899. Offers MA, PhD. Terminal master's awarded for partial completion of doctoral program. *Degree requirements:* For master's, thesis or alternative; for doctorate, thesis/dissertation. *Entrance requirements:* For master's, GRE General Test, departmental exam; for doctorate, departmental exam, GRE General Test. Additional exam requirements/recommendations for international students: Required—TOEFL. Electronic applications accepted. *Faculty research:* Musicology, ethnomusicology; theory.

**Wayne State University,** College of Fine, Performing and Communication Arts, Department of Music, Detroit, MI 48202. Offers composition/theory (MM); conducting (MM); jazz performance (MM); music (MA); music education (MM); orchestral studies (Certificate); performance (MM). *Accreditation:* NASM. *Faculty:* 14. *Students:* 14 full-time (6 women), 8 part-time (3 women); includes 6 minority (3 Black or African American, non-Hispanic/Latino; 2 Hispanic/Latino; 1 Two or more races, non-Hispanic/Latino), 1 international. Average age 27. 23 applicants, 39% accepted, 9 enrolled. In 2016, 7 master's awarded. *Degree requirements:* For master's, thesis (for some programs), oral examination (for some programs), recital with program notes (for some programs). *Entrance requirements:* For master's, diagnostic exam in theory and history, undergraduate degree in same field as desired field of graduate study or equivalent in course work, private study, or experience; audition/interview; for Certificate, undergraduate degree in same field as desired field of graduate study or equivalent in course work, private study, or experience; audition/interview. Additional exam requirements/recommendations for international students: Required—TOEFL (minimum score 550 paper-based; 79 iBT), Michigan English Language Assessment Battery (minimum score 85); Recommended—IELTS (minimum score 6.5), TWE (minimum score 5.5). *Application deadline:* Applications are processed on a rolling basis. Application fee: $50. Electronic applications accepted. *Expenses:* $17,240 per year resident tuition and fees, $34,434 per year non-resident tuition and fees. *Financial support:* In 2016–17, 17 students received support. Career-related internships or fieldwork, institutionally sponsored loans, and scholarships/grants available. Support available to part-time students. Financial award applicants required to submit FAFSA. *Faculty research:* Teacher training, pedagogy, musicology, composition/theory, conducting/performance practice. *Unit head:* Dr. Norah Duncan, Professor and Chair, 313-577-1775, E-mail: norah.duncan@wayne.edu. *Application contact:* E-mail: music@wayne.edu. Website: http://music.wayne.edu/

**Wayne State University,** College of Liberal Arts and Sciences, Department of English, Detroit, MI 48202. Offers English (MA); film and media studies (PhD); literary and cultural studies (PhD); rhetoric and composition studies (PhD). *Faculty:* 30. *Students:* 78 full-time (48 women), 23 part-time (10 women); includes 22 minority (10 Black or African American, non-Hispanic/Latino; 3 Asian, non-Hispanic/Latino; 6 Hispanic/Latino; 3 Two or more races, non-Hispanic/Latino), 7 international. Average age 35. 114 applicants, 33% accepted, 18 enrolled. In 2016, 15 master's, 5 doctorates awarded. Terminal master's awarded for partial completion of doctoral program. *Degree requirements:* For master's, variable foreign language requirement, essay, thesis, or portfolio of work approved by Director of Graduate Studies; for doctorate, one foreign language, comprehensive exam, thesis/dissertation. *Entrance requirements:* For master's, statement of purpose; two academic letters of reference; sample essay from previous English course; for doctorate, GRE General Test, statement of purpose; two academic letters of reference; sample of scholarly or critical writing. Additional exam requirements/recommendations for international students: Required—TOEFL (minimum score 550 paper-based; 79 iBT), TWE (minimum score 5.5), Michigan English Language Assessment Battery (minimum score 85); Recommended—IELTS (minimum score 6.5). *Application deadline:* For fall admission, 1/15 for domestic students. Applications are processed on a rolling basis. Application fee: $50. Electronic applications accepted. *Expenses:* $16,503 per year resident tuition and fees, $33,697 per year non-resident tuition and fees. *Financial support:* In 2016–17, 63 students received support, including 5 fellowships with tuition reimbursements available (averaging $15,800 per year), 30 teaching assistantships with tuition reimbursements available (averaging $17,994 per year); research assistantships with tuition reimbursements available, scholarships/grants, and unspecified assistantships also available. Financial award applicants required to submit FAFSA. *Faculty research:* Literary and cultural studies, film and new media studies, rhetoric and composition studies, linguistics, and creative writing. *Unit head:* Dr. Kenneth Jackson, Chair and Professor, 313-577-7692, E-mail: ai4054@wayne.edu. *Application contact:* Dr. Carolin Maun, Director of Graduate Studies, 313-577-7694, E-mail: caroline.maun@wayne.edu. Website: http://clas.wayne.edu/english/

**Webster University,** Leigh Gerdine College of Fine Arts, Department of Music, St. Louis, MO 63119-3194. Offers church music (MM); composition (MM); jazz studies (MM); music (MA); music education (MM); organ (MM); performance (MM); piano (MM); voice (MM). *Accreditation:* NASM. *Entrance requirements:* Additional exam requirements/recommendations for international students: Required—TOEFL. *Application deadline:* Applications are processed on a rolling basis. Application fee: $25 ($50 for international students). *Expenses: Tuition:* Full-time $21,900; part-time $730 per credit hour. Tuition and fees vary according to campus/location and program. *Financial support:* Teaching assistantships and Federal Work-Study available. Support available to part-time students. Financial award application deadline: 4/1; financial award applicants required to submit FAFSA. *Unit head:* Dr. Jeffrey Carter, Chair, 314-968-7033, E-mail: jeffreycarter67@webster.edu. *Application contact:* Jean Huber, Department Representative, 314-968-7032, E-mail: huberje@webster.edu.

**Wesleyan University,** Graduate Studies, Department of Music, Middletown, CT 06459. Offers composition (MA); ethnomusicology (MA, PhD). *Degree requirements:* For master's, one foreign language, thesis; for doctorate, 2 foreign languages, comprehensive exam, thesis/dissertation. *Entrance requirements:* For master's, undergraduate music major or its equivalent; for doctorate, MA. Additional exam requirements/recommendations for international students: Required—TOEFL. *Application deadline:* For fall admission, 1/15 for domestic and international students. Application fee: $85. Electronic applications accepted. *Financial support:* Tuition waivers (full) and unspecified assistantships available. *Faculty research:* Ethnomusicology, musicology, music theory, composition, performance. *Unit head:* Eric Charry, Director of Graduate Studies/Professor, 860-685-2579, Fax: 860-685-2651, E-mail: echarry@wesleyan.edu. *Application contact:* Deborah Shore, Administrative Assistant, 860-685-2598, Fax: 860-685-2651, E-mail: dshore@wesleyan.edu. Website: http://www.wesleyan.edu/music/

**West Chester University of Pennsylvania,** College of Arts and Humanities, Department of Applied Music, West Chester, PA 19383. Offers performance (MM), including conducting, instrumental, keyboard, voice; piano pedagogy (MM, Certificate). *Program availability:* Part-time, evening/weekend. *Faculty:* 22 full-time (7 women), 4 part-time/adjunct (2 women). *Students:* 17 full-time (6 women), 13 part-time (3 women); includes 2 minority (1 Native Hawaiian or other Pacific Islander, non-Hispanic/Latino; 1 Two or more races, non-Hispanic/Latino), 5 international. Average age 30. 15 applicants, 87% accepted, 9 enrolled. In 2016, 14 master's awarded. *Degree requirements:* For master's, comprehensive exam, thesis optional, recital. *Entrance requirements:* For master's and Certificate, School of Music Graduate Placement Test (GPT), audition, interview. Additional exam requirements/recommendations for international students: Required—TOEFL or IELTS. *Application deadline:* For fall admission, 5/15 for international students; for spring admission, 10/15 for international students. Applications are processed on a rolling basis. Application fee: $50. Electronic applications accepted. *Expenses:* Tuition, state resident: full-time $8694; part-time $483 per credit. Tuition, nonresident: full-time $13,050; part-time $725 per credit. *Required fees:* $2399; $119.05 per credit. Tuition and fees vary according to campus/location and program. *Financial support:* Scholarships/grants and unspecified assistantships available. Financial award application deadline: 2/15; financial award applicants required to submit FAFSA. *Faculty research:* Performance, historical perspective, pedagogy. *Unit head:* Dr. Chris Hanning, Chair, 610-436-4178, Fax: 610-436-2873, E-mail: channing@wcupa.edu. *Application contact:* Dr. M. Gregory Martin, Graduate Coordinator, 610-436-2070, Fax: 610-436-2873, E-mail: mmartin@wcupa.edu. Website: http://www.wcupa.edu/arts-humanities/music/appliedMusic/

**West Chester University of Pennsylvania,** College of Arts and Humanities, Department of Music Education, West Chester, PA 19383. Offers Kodaly methodology (Certificate); music education (MM, Teaching Certificate), including Kodaly methodology (MM), music technology (MM), Orff-Schulwerk (MM), performance (MM); music technology (Certificate); Orff-Schulwerk (Certificate). *Accreditation:* NASM; NCATE. *Program availability:* Part-time. *Faculty:* 3 full-time (1 woman). *Students:* 4 full-time (2 women), 18 part-time (13 women). Average age 29. 14 applicants, 93% accepted, 7 enrolled. In 2016, 10 master's, 3 Certificates awarded. *Degree requirements:* For master's, comprehensive exam, thesis (for some programs), recital (performance option only). *Entrance requirements:* For master's, School of Music Graduate Placement Test (GPT), audition (performance track only), interview; for other advanced degree, School of Music Graduate Placement Test (GPT), audition, interview. Additional exam requirements/recommendations for international students: Required—TOEFL or IELTS. *Application deadline:* For fall admission, 5/15 for international students; for spring admission, 10/15 for international students. Applications are processed on a rolling basis. Application fee: $50. Electronic applications accepted. *Expenses:* Tuition, state resident: full-time $8694; part-time $483 per credit. Tuition, nonresident: full-time $13,050; part-time $725 per credit. *Required fees:* $2399; $119.05 per credit. Tuition and fees vary according to campus/location and program. *Financial support:* Scholarships/grants and unspecified assistantships available. Financial award application deadline: 2/15; financial award applicants required to submit FAFSA. *Faculty research:* Music education in other cultures, educational advocacy and pedagogy, research in music education, special needs learners in music education, developing music listening skills. *Unit head:* Dr. Marci Major, Chair, 610-436-3030, Fax: 610-436-2873, E-mail: mmajor@wcupa.edu. *Application contact:* Dr. M. Gregory Martin, Graduate Coordinator, 610-436-2070, E-mail: mmartin@wcupa.edu. Website: http://www.wcupa.edu/arts-humanities/music/musicEducation/

**West Chester University of Pennsylvania,** College of Arts and Humanities, Department of Music Theory, History and Composition, West Chester, PA 19383. Offers history and literature (MM), including history and literature; music theory, history, and composition (MM). *Program availability:* Part-time, evening/weekend. *Faculty:* 7 full-time (0 women). *Students:* 3 full-time (0 women), 3 part-time (0 women); includes 1 minority (Black or African American, non-Hispanic/Latino). Average age 30. 5 applicants, 60% accepted, 2 enrolled. In 2016, 4 master's awarded. *Degree requirements:* For master's, comprehensive exam, thesis. *Entrance requirements:* For master's, School of Music Graduate Placement Test (GPT), interview. Additional exam requirements/recommendations for international students: Required—TOEFL or IELTS. *Application deadline:* For fall admission, 5/15 for international students; for spring admission, 10/15 for international students. Applications are processed on a rolling basis. Application fee: $50. Electronic applications accepted. *Expenses:* Tuition, state resident: full-time $8694; part-time $483 per credit. Tuition, nonresident: full-time $13,050; part-time $725 per credit. *Required fees:* $2399; $119.05 per credit. Tuition and fees vary according to campus/location and program. *Financial support:* Scholarships/grants and unspecified assistantships available. Financial award application deadline: 2/15; financial award applicants required to submit FAFSA. *Faculty research:* Musicology, eighteenth century European music, advanced compositional techniques, opera history, current trends in theory and composition. *Unit head:* Dr. Robert Maggio, Chair, 610-436-2646, E-mail: musicinfo@wcupa.edu. *Application contact:* Dr. M. Gregory Martin, Graduate Coordinator, 610-436-2070, E-mail: gmartin@wcupa.edu. Website: http://www.wcupa.edu/arts-humanities/music/musicTheory/

**Western Illinois University,** School of Graduate Studies, College of Fine Arts and Communication, School of Music, Macomb, IL 61455-1390. Offers MM. *Accreditation:* NASM. *Program availability:* Part-time. *Students:* 23 full-time (8 women), 2 part-time (1 woman); includes 1 minority (Hispanic/Latino), 9 international. Average age 27. 21 applicants, 71% accepted, 9 enrolled. In 2016, 9 master's awarded. *Degree requirements:* For master's, comprehensive exam, thesis or alternative. *Entrance requirements:* For master's, audition. Additional exam requirements/recommendations for international students: Required—TOEFL (minimum score 500 paper-based; 80 iBT). *Application deadline:* Applications are processed on a rolling basis. Application fee: $30. Electronic applications accepted. *Financial support:* In 2016–17, 21 students received support, including 1 teaching assistantship with full tuition reimbursement available (averaging $8,688 per year); unspecified assistantships also available. Financial award applicants required to submit FAFSA. *Unit head:* Dr. Tammie Walker, Director, 309-298-1544, E-mail: tl-walker4@wiu.edu. *Application contact:* Dr. Nancy Parsons, Associate Provost and Director of Graduate Studies, 309-298-1806, Fax: 309-298-2345, E-mail: grad-office@wiu.edu. Website: http://wiu.edu/music

**Western Michigan University,** Graduate College, College of Fine Arts, School of Music, Kalamazoo, MI 49008. Offers music (MA); music composition (MM); music conducting (MM); music education (MM); music performance (MM); music therapy (MM). *Accreditation:* NASM.

**Western Oregon University,** Graduate Programs, College of Liberal Arts and Sciences, Division of Creative Arts, Monmouth, OR 97361. Offers contemporary music (MM). *Accreditation:* NASM. *Entrance requirements:* Additional exam requirements/recommendations for international students: Required—TOEFL (minimum score 550 paper-based; 79 iBT), IELTS (minimum score 6.5).

**Western Washington University,** Graduate School, College of Fine and Performing Arts, Department of Music, Bellingham, WA 98225-5996. Offers M Mus. *Accreditation:* NASM. *Program availability:* Part-time. *Degree requirements:* For master's, thesis. *Entrance requirements:* For master's, GRE General Test, department placement exams, audition, portfolio, minimum GPA of 3.0 in last 60 semester hours or last 90 quarter hours of course work. Additional exam requirements/recommendations for international students: Required—TOEFL (minimum score 567 paper-based). Electronic applications accepted. *Faculty research:* Baroque opera, historical music of the Silk Road, original composition, 20th century orchestral music, 13th century polyphony.

**West Texas A&M University,** College of Fine Arts and Humanities, School of Music, Program in Music, Canyon, TX 79016-0001. Offers MA. *Accreditation:* NASM. *Program availability:* Part-time. *Degree requirements:* For master's, comprehensive exam, thesis optional. *Entrance requirements:* For master's, GRE General Test. Additional exam requirements/recommendations for international students: Required—TOEFL (minimum score 550 paper-based). *Application deadline:* For fall admission, 8/1 for domestic students, 5/1 for international students; for spring admission, 12/1 for domestic students, 10/30 for international students; for summer admission, 5/1 for domestic students. Applications are processed on a rolling basis. Application fee: $40 ($75 for international students). Electronic applications accepted. *Financial support:* Research assistantships, teaching assistantships with partial tuition reimbursements, career-related internships or fieldwork, Federal Work-Study, institutionally sponsored loans, and tuition waivers (partial) available. Support available to part-time students. Financial award applicants required to submit CSS PROFILE or FAFSA. *Unit head:* Dr. Benjamin Brooks, Associate Professor, 806-651-2862, E-mail: bbrooks@wtamu.edu. Website: http://www.wtamu.edu/academics/music-graduate-program.aspx

**West Texas A&M University,** College of Fine Arts and Humanities, School of Music, Program in Performance, Canyon, TX 79016-0001. Offers MM. *Accreditation:* NASM. *Program availability:* Part-time. *Degree requirements:* For master's, comprehensive exam, thesis optional. *Entrance requirements:* For master's, GRE General Test. Additional exam requirements/recommendations for international students: Required—TOEFL (minimum score 550 paper-based). *Application deadline:* For fall admission, 8/1 for domestic students, 5/1 for international students; for spring admission, 12/1 for domestic students, 10/30 for international students; for summer admission, 5/1 for domestic students. Applications are processed on a rolling basis. Application fee: $40 ($75 for international students). Electronic applications accepted. *Financial support:* Research assistantships, teaching assistantships with partial tuition reimbursements, career-related internships or fieldwork, Federal Work-Study, institutionally sponsored loans, and tuition waivers (partial) available. Support available to part-time students. Financial award applicants required to submit CSS PROFILE or FAFSA. *Unit head:* Dr. Benjamin Brooks, Associate Professor, 806-651-2862, E-mail: bbrooks@wtamu.edu. Website: http://www.wtamu.edu/academics/performance-graduate-program.aspx

**West Virginia University,** College of Creative Arts, School of Music, Morgantown, WV 26506. Offers music composition (MM, DMA); music education (MM, PhD); music history (MM); music industry (MA); music performance (MM, DMA); music theory (MM). *Accreditation:* NASM. *Degree requirements:* For master's, comprehensive exam, thesis (for some programs), recitals; for doctorate, variable foreign language requirement, comprehensive exam, thesis/dissertation, recitals (DMA). *Entrance requirements:* For master's, GRE General Test (music history), minimum GPA of 3.0, audition; for doctorate, GRE General Test (music education), minimum GPA of 3.0, audition. Additional exam requirements/recommendations for international students: Required—TOEFL. *Faculty research:* Jazz history, seventeenth century French court music, nineteenth century composition theory.

**Wichita State University,** Graduate School, College of Fine Arts, School of Music, Wichita, KS 67260. Offers music (MM); music education (MME). *Accreditation:* NASM. *Program availability:* Part-time. *Unit head:* Prof. Russ Widener, Director, 316-978-6435, Fax: 316-978-3625, E-mail: russ.widener@wichita.edu. *Application contact:* Jordan Oleson, Admissions Coordinator, 316-978-3095, Fax: 316-978-3253, E-mail: jordan.oleson@wichita.edu. Website: http://www.wichita.edu/music

**William Paterson University of New Jersey,** College of the Arts and Communication, Wayne, NJ 07470-8420. Offers art (MFA); music (MM); professional communication (MA). *Accreditation:* NASAD. *Program availability:* Part-time, evening/weekend. *Faculty:* 23 full-time (10 women), 26 part-time/adjunct (7 women). *Students:* 44 full-time (21 women), 19 part-time (9 women); includes 17 minority (7 Black or African American, non-Hispanic/Latino; 1 Asian, non-Hispanic/Latino; 8 Hispanic/Latino; 1 Two or more races, non-Hispanic/Latino), 12 international. Average age 30. 81 applicants, 75% accepted, 33 enrolled. In 2016, 22 master's awarded. *Degree requirements:* For master's, comprehensive exam (for some programs), thesis (for some programs). *Entrance requirements:* For master's, GRE, minimum GPA of 2.75; audition; 2 letters of recommendation; portfolio with letter of intent. Additional exam requirements/recommendations for international students: Required—TOEFL (minimum score 550 paper-based; 79 iBT), IELTS (minimum score 6). *Application deadline:* For fall admission, 8/1 for domestic students, 4/1 for international students; for spring admission, 12/1 for domestic students, 11/1 for international students; for summer admission, 5/1 for domestic students, 2/1 for international students. Applications are processed on a rolling basis. Application fee: $50. Electronic applications accepted. *Expenses:* Tuition, state resident: full-time $12,480; part-time $611 per credit. Tuition, nonresident: full-time $20,263; part-time $992 per credit. *Required fees:* $1573; $77 per credit. Tuition and fees vary according to course load, degree level and program. *Financial support:* Career-related internships or fieldwork, Federal Work-Study, scholarships/grants, and unspecified assistantships available. Support available to part-time students. Financial award applicants required to submit FAFSA. *Faculty research:* Early art technologies, communication and social media in families with veterans, new sculpture technologies, musical interactions in music education, learning communities in spatially separated classrooms. *Unit head:* Daryl Moore, Dean, 973-720-2232, E-mail: moored@wpunj.edu. *Application contact:* Christina Aiello, Assistant Director, Graduate Admissions, 973-720-2506, Fax: 973-720-2035, E-mail: aielloc@wpunj.edu. Website: http://www.wpunj.edu/coac

**Winthrop University,** College of Visual and Performing Arts, Department of Music, Rock Hill, SC 29733. Offers conducting (MM); music education (MME); performance (MM). *Accreditation:* NASM. *Program availability:* Part-time. *Degree requirements:* For master's, comprehensive exam (for some programs), oral and written exams, recital (MM). *Entrance requirements:* For master's, GRE General Test, audition, minimum GPA of 3.0, 2 recitals. Additional exam requirements/recommendations for international students: Required—TOEFL (minimum score 550 paper-based; 79 iBT), IELTS (minimum score 6). Electronic applications accepted. *Expenses:* Tuition, state resident: full-time $14,312; part-time $599 per credit hour. Tuition, nonresident: full-time $27,570; part-time $1153 per credit hour.

**Yale University,** Graduate School of Arts and Sciences, Department of Music, New Haven, CT 06520. Offers music history (MA); music theory (MA). Terminal master's awarded for partial completion of doctoral program. *Degree requirements:* For master's, one foreign language; for doctorate, 3 foreign languages, thesis/dissertation. *Entrance requirements:* For doctorate, GRE General Test, GRE Subject Test.

**Yale University,** School of Music, New Haven, CT 06520. Offers MM, MMA, DMA, AD, Certificate. *Accreditation:* NASM. *Faculty:* 28 full-time (9 women), 33 part-time/adjunct (7 women). *Students:* 211 full-time (87 women); includes 43 minority (2 Black or African American, non-Hispanic/Latino; 23 Asian, non-Hispanic/Latino; 8 Hispanic/Latino; 10 Two or more races, non-Hispanic/Latino), 76 international. Average age 23. 1,512 applicants, 10% accepted, 108 enrolled. In 2016, 72 master's, 3 doctorates, 23 ADs awarded. *Degree requirements:* For master's and other advanced degree, one foreign language, recitals; for doctorate, one foreign language, comprehensive exam, thesis/dissertation, oral and written exam, recitals. *Entrance requirements:* For master's and other advanced degree, departmental exams, audition; for doctorate, entrance exam in music history, analysis, and musicianship, audition. Additional exam requirements/recommendations for international students: Required—TOEFL (minimum score 567 paper-based; 86 iBT). *Application deadline:* For fall admission, 12/1 for domestic and international students. Application fee: $150. Electronic applications accepted. *Expenses:* Contact institution. *Financial support:* In 2016–17, 211 students received support, including 211 fellowships (averaging $34,000 per year); Federal Work-Study and scholarships/grants also available. Financial award application deadline: 5/30; financial award applicants required to submit FAFSA. *Faculty research:* Performance, composition, conducting, music history and theory. *Unit head:* Robert Blocker, Dean, 203-432-4160, Fax: 203-432-7542. *Application contact:* Suzanne M. Stringer, Director of Student Services, 203-432-1962, Fax: 203-432-7448, E-mail: suzanne.stringer@yale.edu. Website: http://music.yale.edu/

**York University,** Faculty of Graduate Studies, Faculty of Fine Arts, Program in Music, Toronto, ON M3J 1P3, Canada. Offers composition (MA); music (PhD); musicology and ethnomusicology (MA). *Program availability:* Part-time. *Degree requirements:* For master's, one foreign language, thesis optional; for doctorate, 2 foreign languages, comprehensive exam, thesis/dissertation. *Entrance requirements:* For master's, portfolio. Electronic applications accepted.

**Youngstown State University,** Graduate School, College of Fine and Performing Arts, Dana School of Music, Youngstown, OH 44555-0001. Offers jazz studies (MM); music education (MM); music history and literature (MM); music theory and composition (MM); performance (MM). *Accreditation:* NASM. *Program availability:* Part-time, evening/weekend. *Degree requirements:* For master's, one foreign language, thesis optional, final qualifying exam. *Entrance requirements:* For master's, audition; GRE General Test or minimum GPA of 2.7. Additional exam requirements/recommendations for international students: Required—TOEFL. *Faculty research:* Teaching education, use of computers, conducting.

# Theater

**Academy of Art University,** Graduate Programs, School of Acting, San Francisco, CA 94105-3410. Offers MA, MFA. *Program availability:* Part-time. *Faculty:* 1 (woman) full-time, 17 part-time/adjunct (11 women). *Students:* 19 full-time (14 women), 1 part-time (0 women); includes 5 minority (1 Black or African American, non-Hispanic/Latino; 1 Asian, non-Hispanic/Latino; 1 Hispanic/Latino; 2 Two or more races, non-Hispanic/Latino), 10 international. Average age 28. 12 applicants, 100% accepted, 4 enrolled. In 2016, 6 master's awarded. *Degree requirements:* For master's, final review. *Entrance requirements:* For master's, statement of intent; resume; portfolio/reel; official college transcripts. *Application deadline:* Applications are processed on a rolling basis. Application fee: $50. Electronic applications accepted. *Expenses: Tuition:* Part-time $982 per unit. *Financial support:* Career-related internships or fieldwork, Federal Work-Study, and scholarships/grants available. Financial award application deadline: 8/10; financial award applicants required to submit FAFSA. *Unit head:* 800-544-ARTS, E-mail: info@academyart.edu. *Application contact:* 800-544-ARTS, E-mail: info@academyart.edu.
Website: http://www.academyart.edu/acting-school/index.html

**Academy of Art University,** Graduate Programs, School of Fashion, San Francisco, CA 94105-3410. Offers costume design (MA, MFA); fashion (MA, MFA); fashion journalism (MA); fashion marketing and brand management (MFA); fashion merchandising (MA); fashion merchandising and management (MFA); fashion product development (MFA); textile design (MFA). *Program availability:* Part-time, 100% online. *Faculty:* 27 full-time (17 women), 62 part-time/adjunct (47 women). *Students:* 376 full-time (335 women), 196 part-time (184 women); includes 154 minority (81 Black or African American, non-Hispanic/Latino; 2 American Indian or Alaska Native, non-Hispanic/Latino; 36 Asian, non-Hispanic/Latino; 25 Hispanic/Latino; 1 Native Hawaiian or other Pacific Islander, non-Hispanic/Latino; 9 Two or more races, non-Hispanic/Latino), 306 international. Average age 29. 190 applicants, 100% accepted, 114 enrolled. In 2016, 137 master's awarded. *Degree requirements:* For master's, final review. *Entrance requirements:* For master's, statement of intent; resume; portfolio/reel; official college transcripts. *Application deadline:* Applications are processed on a rolling basis. Application fee: $50. Electronic applications accepted. *Expenses: Tuition:* Part-time $982 per unit. *Financial support:* Career-related internships or fieldwork, Federal Work-Study, and scholarships/grants available. Financial award application deadline: 8/10; financial award applicants required to submit FAFSA. *Unit head:* 800-544-ARTS, E-mail: info@academyart.edu. *Application contact:* 800-544-ARTS, E-mail: info@academyart.edu.
Website: http://www.academyart.edu/fashion-school/index.html

**American Conservatory Theater,** Program in Acting, San Francisco, CA 94108-5800. Offers MFA, Certificate. *Degree requirements:* For master's, thesis (for some programs), stage performance. *Entrance requirements:* For master's, audition, interview, bachelor's degree from an accredited institution, 2 confidential letters of recommendation.

**Arcadia University,** School of Education, Glenside, PA 19038-3295. Offers art education (M Ed); computer education (CAS); curriculum (CAS); curriculum studies (M Ed); early childhood education (M Ed), including individualized, master teacher, research in child development; educational leadership (M Ed, Ed D, CAS); elementary education (M Ed); English education (MA Ed); environmental education (MA Ed); instructional technology (M Ed); language arts (M Ed); library science (M Ed); mathematics education (M Ed, MA Ed); music education (MA Ed); psychology (MA Ed); reading (M Ed, CAS); science education (M Ed, CAS); secondary education (M Ed, CAS); special education (M Ed, Ed D, CAS); theater arts (MA Ed); written communication (MA Ed). *Accreditation:* NASAD. *Program availability:* Part-time, evening/weekend, online learning. *Faculty:* 19 full-time (13 women), 3 part-time/adjunct (all women). *Students:* 22 full-time (16 women), 356 part-time (284 women); includes 84 minority (55 Black or African American, non-Hispanic/Latino; 2 American Indian or Alaska Native, non-Hispanic/Latino; 13 Asian, non-Hispanic/Latino; 11 Hispanic/Latino; 3 Two or more races, non-Hispanic/Latino), 4 international. Average age 34. 145 applicants, 73% accepted, 80 enrolled. In 2016, 95 master's, 11 doctorates awarded. *Application deadline:* Applications are processed on a rolling basis. Application fee: $50. Electronic applications accepted. *Expenses:* Contact institution. *Financial support:* Career-related internships or fieldwork, tuition waivers (partial), and unspecified assistantships available. *Unit head:* John T Groves, Interim Dean of the School of Education, 215-572-2940. *Application contact:* 215-572-2925, Fax: 215-572-2126, E-mail: grad@arcadia.edu.

**Arizona State University at the Tempe campus,** Herberger Institute for Design and the Arts, School of Film, Dance and Theatre, Tempe, AZ 85287-2002. Offers dance (MFA), including dance, interdisciplinary digital media and performance; theatre (MA, MFA, PhD), including arts entrepreneurship and management (MFA), directing (MFA), dramatic writing (MFA), interdisciplinary digital media and performance (MFA), performance (MFA), performance design (MFA), theatre (MFA), theatre and performance of the Americas (PhD), theatre for youth (MFA, PhD). Terminal master's awarded for partial completion of doctoral program. *Degree requirements:* For master's, comprehensive exam (for some programs), thesis (for some programs), applied project (for some programs); interactive Program of Study (iPOS) submitted before completing 50 percent of required credit hours; for doctorate, comprehensive exam, thesis/dissertation, interactive Program of Study (iPOS) submitted before completing 50 percent of required credit hours. *Entrance requirements:* For master's, GRE or MAT, minimum GPA of 3.0 in last 2 years of work leading to bachelor's degree (depending on program); for doctorate, GRE, minimum GPA of 3.0 or equivalent in last 2 years of work leading to bachelor's degree, 3 letters of recommendation, resume, scholarly writing sample, statement of purpose. Additional exam requirements/recommendations for international students: Required—TOEFL, IELTS, or PTE. Electronic applications accepted.

**Baylor University,** Graduate School, College of Arts and Sciences, Department of Theatre Arts, Waco, TX 76798. Offers MA, MFA. *Accreditation:* NAST. *Program availability:* Part-time. *Faculty:* 6 full-time (2 women). *Students:* 7 full-time (4 women); includes 1 minority (Black or African American, non-Hispanic/Latino). Average age 30. 14 applicants, 21% accepted, 3 enrolled. In 2016, 2 master's awarded. *Degree requirements:* For master's, comprehensive exam, thesis. *Entrance requirements:* For master's, GRE General Test. *Application deadline:* For spring admission, 2/15 for domestic students. Applications are processed on a rolling basis. Application fee: $25. Electronic applications accepted. *Expenses: Tuition:* Full-time $28,494; part-time $1583 per credit hour. *Required fees:* $167 per credit hour. Tuition and fees vary according to course load and program. *Financial support:* In 2016–17, 6 students received support, including 2 research assistantships with full tuition reimbursements available (averaging $12,000 per year), 4 teaching assistantships with full tuition reimbursements available (averaging $13,500 per year); Federal Work-Study, institutionally sponsored loans, health care benefits, tuition waivers (full and partial), and unspecified assistantships also

available. Financial award application deadline: 3/15; financial award applicants required to submit FAFSA. *Faculty research:* Military and theatre, Avant-garde Japanese theatre, Horton Foote, Post-War Japan, Modernism in theatre. *Unit head:* Dr. David Jortner, Graduate Program Director, 254-710-6452, Fax: 254-710-1765, E-mail: david_jortner@baylor.edu. *Application contact:* Renee Cluke, Administrative Assistant, 254-710-1861, Fax: 254-710-1765, E-mail: renee_cluke@baylor.edu.
Website: http://www.baylor.edu/Theatre_Arts/

**Berklee College of Music,** The Boston Conservatory at Berklee, Boston, MA 02115. Offers bassoon performance (MM); cello performance (MM); choral conducting (MM); clarinet performance (MM); collaborative piano (MM); composition (MM); contemporary music performance (MM); double bass performance (MM); flute performance (MM); harp performance (MM); horn performance (MM); marimba performance (MM); music and autism (Certificate); music education (MM); music education and autism (MM); music performance (ADP); musical theater (MFA); oboe performance (MM); opera performance (MM); orchestral conducting (MM); percussion performance (MM); piano performance (MM); saxophone performance (MM); trombone performance (MM); trumpet performance (MM). *Accreditation:* NASM (one or more programs are accredited). *Program availability:* Part-time. *Faculty:* 87 full-time (35 women), 43 part-time/adjunct (24 women). *Students:* 209 full-time (123 women), 11 part-time (3 women); includes 44 minority (7 Black or African American, non-Hispanic/Latino; 11 Asian, non-Hispanic/Latino; 15 Hispanic/Latino; 1 Native Hawaiian or other Pacific Islander, non-Hispanic/Latino; 10 Two or more races, non-Hispanic/Latino), 67 international. Average age 25. 568 applicants, 41% accepted, 86 enrolled. In 2016, 77 master's, 14 other advanced degrees awarded. *Degree requirements:* For master's, recital or performance; for other advanced degree, recital. *Entrance requirements:* For master's and other advanced degree, audition. Additional exam requirements/recommendations for international students: Required—TOEFL (minimum score 550 paper-based; 79 iBT), IELTS (minimum score 6.5), TOEFL (minimum score 580 paper-based) and IELTS (minimum score 7.0) for MM in music education. *Application deadline:* For fall admission, 12/15 for domestic and international students. Application fee: $110. Electronic applications accepted. *Expenses:* Contact institution. *Financial support:* In 2016–17, 236 students received support. Federal Work-Study and scholarships/grants available. Financial award application deadline: 12/1; financial award applicants required to submit FAFSA. *Unit head:* Camille Colatosti, PhD, Dean, Institutional Assessment and Graduate Studies, E-mail: ccolatosti@berklee.edu. *Application contact:* Director of Admissions, 617-912-9153, Fax: 617-912-9217, E-mail: admissions@bostonconservatory.edu.
Website: http://www.bostonconservatory.edu/

**Binghamton University, State University of New York,** Graduate School, Harpur College of Arts and Sciences, Department of Theatre, Binghamton, NY 13902-6000. Offers MA. *Program availability:* Part-time. *Faculty:* 9 full-time (4 women), 17 part-time/adjunct (8 women). *Students:* 5 full-time (4 women), 1 (woman) part-time; includes 2 minority (both Asian, non-Hispanic/Latino), 1 international. Average age 32. 2 applicants, 50% accepted. In 2016, 2 master's awarded. *Degree requirements:* For master's, thesis. *Entrance requirements:* For master's, GRE General Test, writing sample, portfolio. Additional exam requirements/recommendations for international students: Required—TOEFL (minimum score 550 paper-based; 80 iBT). *Application deadline:* Applications are processed on a rolling basis. Application fee: $75. Electronic applications accepted. *Financial support:* In 2016–17, 4 students received support. Career-related internships or fieldwork, Federal Work-Study, institutionally sponsored loans, scholarships/grants, health care benefits, and unspecified assistantships available. Financial award application deadline: 2/15; financial award applicants required to submit FAFSA. *Unit head:* Dr. Barbara E. Wolfe, Chairperson, 607-777-2360, E-mail: bwolfe@binghamton.edu. *Application contact:* Ben Balkaya, Assistant Dean and Director, 607-777-2151, Fax: 607-777-2501, E-mail: balkaya@binghamton.edu.
Website: http://www2.binghamton.edu/theatre/

**Bob Jones University,** Graduate Programs, Greenville, SC 29614. Offers accountancy (MS); Bible (MA); Bible translation (MA); Biblical studies (Certificate); broadcast management (MS); business administration (MBA); church history (MA, PhD); church ministries (MA); church music (MM); cinema and video production (MA); counseling (MS); curriculum and instruction (Ed D); divinity (M Div); dramatic production (MA); educational leadership (MS, Ed D, Ed S); elementary education (M Ed, MAT); English (M Ed, MA, MAT); fine arts (MA); graphic design (MA); history (M Ed, MA); illustration (MA); interpretative speech (MA, MAT); mathematics (M Ed, MAT); medical missions (Certificate); ministry (MM, D Min); multi-categorical special education (M Ed, MAT); music (M Ed); New Testament interpretation (PhD); Old Testament interpretation (PhD); orchestral instrument performance (MM); organ performance (MM); pastoral studies (MA); personnel services (MS, Ed S); piano pedagogy (MM); piano performance (MM); platform arts (MA); radio and television broadcasting (MS); rhetoric and public address (MA); secondary education (M Ed); studio art (MA); teaching Bible (MA); theology (MA, PhD); voice performance (MM); youth ministries (MA); M Div/MM.

**Boston University,** College of Fine Arts, School of Theatre, Boston, MA 02215. Offers design (MFA); lighting crafts (Certificate); management (MFA); production (MFA); scenic painting (Certificate). *Faculty:* 16 full-time, 9 part-time/adjunct. *Students:* 48 full-time (28 women), 2 part-time (0 women); includes 7 minority (1 Black or African American, non-Hispanic/Latino; 1 American Indian or Alaska Native, non-Hispanic/Latino; 3 Asian, non-Hispanic/Latino; 1 Hispanic/Latino; 1 Two or more races, non-Hispanic/Latino), 3 international. Average age 27. 142 applicants, 15% accepted, 16 enrolled. In 2016, 14 master's awarded. *Entrance requirements:* For master's, interview, portfolio. Additional exam requirements/recommendations for international students: Required—TOEFL (minimum score 90 iBT), IELTS (minimum score 7). *Application deadline:* For fall admission, 2/1 priority date for domestic and international students. Application fee: $95. Electronic applications accepted. *Expenses:* Contact institution. *Financial support:* In 2016–17, 16 students received support. Fellowships, teaching assistantships, scholarships/grants, unspecified assistantships, and stipends available. Financial award application deadline: 2/1. *Unit head:* Jim Petosa, Director, 617-353-3390. *Application contact:* Mark Krone, Manager, Graduate Admissions and Online Marketing, 617-353-3350, E-mail: arts@bu.edu.

**Bowling Green State University,** Graduate College, College of Arts and Sciences, Department of Theatre and Film, Bowling Green, OH 43403. Offers MA, PhD. *Accreditation:* NAST. *Program availability:* Part-time. Terminal master's awarded for partial completion of doctoral program. *Degree requirements:* For master's, thesis or alternative; for doctorate, comprehensive exam, thesis/dissertation, 9 hour research tool. *Entrance requirements:* For master's and doctorate, GRE General Test. Additional exam requirements/recommendations for international students: Required—TOEFL. *Application deadline:* For fall admission, 1/15 for domestic students. Application fee: $30. Electronic applications accepted. *Financial support:* Fellowships with full tuition reimbursements, research assistantships with full tuition reimbursements, teaching assistantships with full tuition reimbursements, Federal Work-Study, and unspecified assistantships available. Financial award applicants required to submit FAFSA. *Faculty research:* Theatre history, dramatic theory, cultural studies, performance studies, American theatre history. *Unit head:* Dr. Lesa Lockford, Chair, 419-372-2222, Fax: 419-372-7186, E-mail: theatrefilm@bgsu.edu. *Application contact:* Dr. Jonathan Chambers, Graduate Coordinator, 419-372-9618.

**Brandeis University,** Graduate School of Arts and Sciences, Department of Theater Arts, Waltham, MA 02454-9110. Offers acting (MFA). *Faculty:* 7 full-time (5 women), 7 part-time/adjunct (3 women). *Entrance requirements:* For master's, curriculum vitae or resume, 2 letters of recommendation, interview, audition, head shot, artistic resume, transcript(s), statement of purpose. Additional exam requirements/recommendations for international students: Required—TOEFL (minimum score 600 paper-based; 100 iBT); Recommended—IELTS (minimum score 7), TSE (minimum score 68). *Application deadline:* For fall admission, 3/15 for domestic students. Application fee: $75. Electronic applications accepted. *Financial support:* Fellowships with full tuition reimbursements, teaching assistantships with partial tuition reimbursements, Federal Work-Study, scholarships/grants, health care benefits, and tuition waivers (partial) available. Financial award application deadline: 4/15; financial award applicants required to submit FAFSA. *Unit head:* Prof. Marya Lowry, Director of Graduate Studies, 781-736-3340, Fax: 781-736-3408, E-mail: theater@brandeis.edu. *Application contact:* Alicia Hyland, Academic Administrator, 781-736-3340, Fax: 781-736-3408, E-mail: theater@brandeis.edu.
Website: http://www.brandeis.edu/theater

**Brigham Young University,** Graduate Studies, College of Fine Arts and Communications, Department of Theatre and Media Arts, Provo, UT 84602-6404. Offers MA. *Accreditation:* NAST. *Program availability:* Evening/weekend. *Faculty:* 18 full-time (6 women). *Students:* 5 full-time (2 women); includes 1 minority (Asian, non-Hispanic/Latino). Average age 31. In 2016, 6 master's awarded. *Degree requirements:* For master's, comprehensive exam, thesis, 32 hours, oral defense. *Entrance requirements:* For master's, GRE, two samples of scholarly writing, letter of intent, three letters of recommendation. Additional exam requirements/recommendations for international students: Required—TOEFL (minimum score 580 paper-based; 85 iBT). *Application deadline:* For fall admission, 4/1 priority date for domestic and international students. Application fee: $50. Electronic applications accepted. *Expenses: Tuition:* Full-time $6680; part-time $393 per credit. Tuition and fees vary according to course load, program and student's religious affiliation. *Financial support:* In 2016–17, 6 students received support, including 6 teaching assistantships with full and partial tuition reimbursements available; research assistantships, career-related internships or fieldwork, scholarships/grants, and unspecified assistantships also available. Support available to part-time students. *Faculty research:* History, literary and screen theory, curatorial studies, critical race theory, popular culture, performance philosophy, women's studies, and media literacy. *Unit head:* Dr. Megan Sanborn Jones, Graduate Coordinator, 801-422-1321, E-mail: msjones@byu.edu. *Application contact:* Lindsi Michelle Neilson, Graduate Secretary, 801-422-3750, E-mail: lindsi_neilson@byu.edu. Website: http://cfac.byu.edu/departments/tma

**Brooklyn College of the City University of New York,** School of Visual, Media and Performing Arts, Department of Theater, Brooklyn, NY 11210-2889. Offers acting (MFA); design and technical theater (MFA); directing (MFA); performing arts management (MFA); theater history and criticism (MA). *Program availability:* Part-time. *Degree requirements:* For master's, thesis, professional residency. *Entrance requirements:* For master's, audition or interview, 18 credits in theater, 2 letters of recommendation, essay. Additional exam requirements/recommendations for international students: Required—TOEFL. Electronic applications accepted. *Faculty research:* Multiculturalism and the arts, art education, arts collaboration.

**Brown University,** Graduate School, Department of Theatre Arts and Performance Studies, Providence, RI 02912. Offers acting and directing (MFA); playwriting (MFA); theatre and performance studies (PhD). *Degree requirements:* For master's, thesis or alternative. *Entrance requirements:* For master's, GRE General Test.

**California Institute of Integral Studies,** School of Consciousness and Transformation, San Francisco, CA 94103. Offers anthropology and social change (MA, PhD); Asian philosophies and cultures (MA); creative inquiry/interdisciplinary arts (MFA); East-West psychology (MA, PhD); integral and transpersonal psychology (PhD); philosophy and religion (PhD), including ecology, spirituality, and religion, philosophy, cosmology, and consciousness, women's spirituality; theater and performance making (MFA); transformative leadership (MA); transformative studies (PhD); women, gender, spirituality and social justice (MA); writing and consciousness (MFA). *Program availability:* Part-time, evening/weekend, 100% online, blended/hybrid learning. *Students:* 390 full-time (256 women), 121 part-time (84 women); includes 135 minority (39 Black or African American, non-Hispanic/Latino; 2 American Indian or Alaska Native, non-Hispanic/Latino; 22 Asian, non-Hispanic/Latino; 40 Hispanic/Latino; 2 Native Hawaiian or other Pacific Islander, non-Hispanic/Latino; 30 Two or more races, non-Hispanic/Latino), 51 international. Average age 38. 195 applicants, 92% accepted, 124 enrolled. In 2016, 35 master's, 41 doctorates awarded. Terminal master's awarded for partial completion of doctoral program. *Degree requirements:* For master's, thesis optional; for doctorate, comprehensive exam, thesis/dissertation, 1 foreign language (for Asian philosophies and cultures). *Entrance requirements:* For master's, minimum GPA of 3.0, letters of recommendation, writing sample; for doctorate, master's degree, minimum GPA of 3.0, letters of recommendation, writing sample. Additional exam requirements/recommendations for international students: Required—TOEFL. *Application deadline:* For fall admission, 2/1 priority date for domestic and international students; for spring admission, 10/15 priority date for domestic and international students. Applications are processed on a rolling basis. Application fee: $65. Electronic applications accepted. *Expenses: Tuition:* Full-time $19,728; part-time $1098 per semester hour. *Required fees:* $320; $320 per semester hour. *Financial support:* Research assistantships, teaching assistantships, career-related internships or fieldwork, Federal Work-Study, and scholarships/grants available. Support available to part-time students. Financial award application deadline: 4/15; financial award applicants required to submit FAFSA. *Faculty research:* Ecology and sustainability, philosophy and religion, East-West psychology, integrative health, social and cultural anthropology, transformative leadership. *Application contact:* Ellen Durst, Director of Admissions, 415-575-6100, Fax: 415-575-1268, E-mail: admissions@ciis.edu. Website: http://www.ciis.edu/

**California Institute of the Arts,** School of Theater, Valencia, CA 91355-2340. Offers acting (MFA, Adv C); creative producing and management (MFA); design and production (MFA); design and technology (Adv C); directing (MFA); theater management (Adv C). *Degree requirements:* For master's, thesis (for some programs), faculty review, performance or portfolio. *Entrance requirements:* For master's, audition or portfolio, interview. Additional exam requirements/recommendations for international students: Required—TOEFL. Electronic applications accepted.

**California State University, Fullerton,** Graduate Studies, College of the Arts, Department of Theatre and Dance, Fullerton, CA 92834-9480. Offers theatre arts (MFA), including acting. *Accreditation:* NAST. *Program availability:* Part-time. *Degree*

*requirements:* For master's, oral and written exam, project or thesis. *Entrance requirements:* For master's, major in theatre or related field, audition or interview, minimum GPA of 2.5 in last 60 units of course work. Application fee: $55. *Expenses:* Tuition, state resident: full-time $3369; part-time $1953 per unit. Tuition, nonresident: full-time $3915; part-time $2499 per unit. Tuition and fees vary according to course load, degree level and program. *Financial support:* Career-related internships or fieldwork, Federal Work-Study, institutionally sponsored loans, and scholarships/grants available. Support available to part-time students. Financial award application deadline: 3/1; financial award applicants required to submit FAFSA. *Unit head:* Dr. Bruce Goodrich, Chair, 657-278-3649. *Application contact:* Admissions/Applications, 657-278-2371. Website: http://www.fullerton.edu/theatredance

**California State University, Long Beach,** Graduate Studies, College of the Arts, Department of Theatre Arts, Long Beach, CA 90840. Offers acting (MFA); MBA/MFA. *Accreditation:* NAST. *Program availability:* Part-time. *Degree requirements:* For master's, thesis or alternative. *Application deadline:* For fall admission, 7/1 for domestic students; for spring admission, 12/1 for domestic students. Applications are processed on a rolling basis. Application fee: $55. Electronic applications accepted. *Financial support:* Research assistantships, teaching assistantships, Federal Work-Study, institutionally sponsored loans, scholarships/grants, and traineeships available. Financial award application deadline: 3/2. *Unit head:* Jeff Janisheski, Chair, 562-985-7890. *Application contact:* Barbara Matthews, Graduate Advisor, 562-985-4042, Fax: 562-985-2263, E-mail: jmatthew@csulb.edu.

**California State University, Los Angeles,** Graduate Studies, College of Arts and Letters, Department of Theatre Arts and Dance, Los Angeles, CA 90032-8530. Offers theater arts (MA). *Program availability:* Part-time, evening/weekend. *Degree requirements:* For master's, comprehensive exam, project or thesis. *Entrance requirements:* For master's, minimum GPA of 2.5, 30 units of course work in theater. Additional exam requirements/recommendations for international students: Required—TOEFL (minimum score 500 paper-based). Electronic applications accepted. *Faculty research:* Sondheim, Taiwanese theater, Australian theater, absurdism, dramaturgy.

**California State University, Northridge,** Graduate Studies, College of Arts, Media, and Communication, Department of Theatre, Northridge, CA 91330. Offers MA. *Accreditation:* NAST. *Faculty:* 12 full-time (6 women), 15 part-time/adjunct (10 women). *Students:* 6 full-time (4 women), 11 part-time (10 women); includes 5 minority (1 Black or African American, non-Hispanic/Latino; 1 Asian, non-Hispanic/Latino; 3 Hispanic/Latino), 2 international. Average age 34. 10 applicants, 70% accepted, 6 enrolled. *Degree requirements:* For master's, thesis. *Entrance requirements:* For master's, GRE General Test or minimum GPA of 3.0. Additional exam requirements/recommendations for international students: Required—TOEFL. *Application deadline:* For fall admission, 11/30 for domestic students. Application fee: $55. *Expenses:* Tuition, state resident: full-time $4152. *Financial support:* Application deadline: 3/1. *Unit head:* Ah-Jeong Kim, Acting Chair, 818-677-3086. Website: http://www.csun.edu/theatre/

**Carnegie Mellon University,** College of Fine Arts, School of Drama, Pittsburgh, PA 15213-3891. Offers design (MFA); directing (MFA); dramatic writing (MFA); production technology and management (MFA); video and media design (MFA). *Degree requirements:* For master's, thesis (for some programs). *Entrance requirements:* For master's, audition, portfolio review, interview. Additional exam requirements/recommendations for international students: Required—TOEFL. *Faculty research:* Developing voice and speech compact disc.

**Case Western Reserve University,** School of Graduate Studies, Department of Theater, Cleveland, OH 44106. Offers acting (MFA); theater (MA). *Faculty:* 7 full-time (3 women), 1 part-time/adjunct (0 women). *Students:* 8 full-time (3 women), 1 (woman) part-time; includes 3 minority (2 Black or African American, non-Hispanic/Latino; 1 Hispanic/Latino). Average age 26. 1 applicant, 100% accepted, 1 enrolled. In 2016, 8 master's awarded. *Degree requirements:* For master's, comprehensive exam, thesis, oral presentation and defense, portfolio, thesis concert production and presentation (for MFA). *Entrance requirements:* For master's, audition, interview, letter of intent, three recommendations, headshots, resume. Additional exam requirements/recommendations for international students: Required—TOEFL (minimum score 577 paper-based; 90 iBT); Recommended—IELTS (minimum score 7). *Application deadline:* For fall admission, 10/15 priority date for domestic students. Applications are processed on a rolling basis. Electronic applications accepted. *Expenses: Tuition:* Full-time $42,576; part-time $1774 per credit hour. *Required fees:* $34. Tuition and fees vary according to course load and program. *Financial support:* Fellowships, scholarships/grants, tuition waivers (full and partial), and stipends available. Financial award application deadline: 1/15. *Faculty research:* Playwriting; history of theater; participation in professional area theaters in performing, design, acting, coaching; choreography, performance and pedagogy, dance wellness medicine and science. *Unit head:* Jerrold Scott, Professor/Chair/Artistic Director, 216-368-6140, Fax: 216-368-5184, E-mail: jerrold.scott@case.edu. *Application contact:* Scarlett Grala, Department Assistant, 216-368-4868, Fax: 216-368-5184, E-mail: k.grala@case.edu. Website: http://theater.case.edu

**The Catholic University of America,** School of Arts and Sciences, Department of Drama, Washington, DC 20064. Offers acting (MFA); creative teaching through drama (Certificate); directing (MFA); playwriting (MFA); theatre education (MA); theatre history and criticism (MA). *Program availability:* Part-time. *Faculty:* 8 full-time (4 women), 5 part-time/adjunct (1 woman). *Students:* 11 full-time (6 women), 19 part-time (16 women); includes 6 minority (3 Black or African American, non-Hispanic/Latino; 1 Hispanic/Latino; 2 Two or more races, non-Hispanic/Latino). Average age 31. 24 applicants, 79% accepted, 14 enrolled. In 2016, 8 master's awarded. *Degree requirements:* For master's, variable foreign language requirement, comprehensive exam, thesis or alternative. *Entrance requirements:* For master's, GRE General Test, statement of purpose, official copies of academic transcripts, three letters of recommendation. Additional exam requirements/recommendations for international students: Required—TOEFL (minimum score 550 paper-based; 80 iBT). *Application deadline:* For fall admission, 7/15 priority date for domestic students, 7/1 for international students; for spring admission, 11/15 priority date for domestic students, 11/1 for international students. Applications are processed on a rolling basis. Application fee: $55. Electronic applications accepted. *Expenses:* $42,850 per year; $1,170 per credit; $200 per semester part-time fees. *Financial support:* Fellowships, research assistantships, teaching assistantships, Federal Work-Study, scholarships/grants, tuition waivers (full and partial), and unspecified assistantships available. Financial award application deadline: 2/1; financial award applicants required to submit FAFSA. *Faculty research:* Acting, directing, playwriting, costume design, Shakespearean stage history. *Unit head:* Dr. Patrick Tuite, Chair, 202-319-5351, Fax: 202-319-5359, E-mail: tuite@cua.edu. *Application contact:* Director of Graduate Admissions, 202-319-5057, Fax: 202-319-6533, E-mail: cua-admissions@cua.edu. Website: http://drama.cua.edu/

**Central Washington University,** Graduate Studies and Research, College of Arts and Humanities, Department of Theatre Arts, Ellensburg, WA 98926. Offers theatre production (MA); theatre studies (MA). *Program availability:* Part-time. *Degree requirements:* For master's, thesis or alternative. *Entrance requirements:* For master's, minimum GPA of 3.0. Additional exam requirements/recommendations for international students: Required—TOEFL (minimum score 550 paper-based; 79 iBT). Electronic applications accepted.

**Columbia University,** Graduate School of Arts and Sciences, New York, NY 10027. Offers African-American studies (MA); American studies (MA); anthropology (MA, PhD); art history and archaeology (MA, PhD); astronomy (PhD); biological sciences (PhD); biotechnology (MA); chemical physics (PhD); chemistry (PhD); classical studies (MA, PhD); classics (MA, PhD); climate and society (MA); conservation biology (MA); earth and environmental sciences (PhD); East Asia: regional studies (MA); East Asian languages and cultures (MA, PhD); ecology, evolution and environmental biology (MA), including conservation biology; ecology, evolution, and environmental biology (PhD), including ecology and evolutionary biology, evolutionary primatology; economics (MA, PhD); English and comparative literature (MA, PhD); French and Romance philology (MA, PhD); Germanic languages (MA, PhD); global French studies (MA); global thought (MA); Hispanic cultural studies (MA); history (PhD); history and literature (MA); human rights studies (MA); Islamic studies (MA); Italian (MA, PhD); Japanese pedagogy (MA); Jewish studies (MA); Latin America and the Caribbean: regional studies (MA); Latin American and Iberian cultures (PhD); mathematics (MA, PhD), including finance (MA); medieval and Renaissance studies (MA); Middle Eastern, South Asian, and African studies (MA, PhD); modern art: critical and curatorial studies (MA); modern European studies (MA); museum anthropology (MA); music (DMA, PhD); oral history (MA); philosophical foundations of physics (MA); philosophy (MA, PhD); physics (PhD); political science (MA, PhD); psychology (PhD); quantitative methods in the social sciences (MA); religion (MA, PhD); Russia, Eurasia and East Europe: regional studies (MA); Russian translation (MA); Slavic cultures (MA); Slavic languages (MA, PhD); sociology (MA, PhD); South Asian studies (MA); statistics (MA, PhD); theatre (PhD). Dual-degree programs require admission to both Graduate School of Arts and Sciences and another Columbia school. *Program availability:* Part-time. Terminal master's awarded for partial completion of doctoral program. *Degree requirements:* For master's, variable foreign language requirement, comprehensive exam (for some programs), thesis (for some programs); for doctorate, variable foreign language requirement, comprehensive exam (for some programs), thesis/dissertation. *Entrance requirements:* For master's and doctorate, GRE General Test, GRE Subject Test (for some programs). Additional exam requirements/recommendations for international students: Required—TOEFL, IELTS. Electronic applications accepted.

**Columbia University,** School of the Arts, Theatre Arts Program, New York, NY 10027. Offers acting (MFA); directing (MFA); dramaturgy (MFA); playwriting (MFA); stage management (MFA); theater management and producing (MFA); JD/MFA. *Degree requirements:* For master's, thesis, 2 internships. *Entrance requirements:* For master's, 3 letters of recommendation, resume. Additional exam requirements/recommendations for international students: Required—TOEFL (minimum score 600 paper-based; 100 iBT). Electronic applications accepted.

**See Display on page 147 and Close-Up on page 201.**

**Columbus State University,** Graduate Studies, College of the Arts, Department of Theatre, Columbus, GA 31907-5645. Offers theatre education (M Ed, MAT). *Accreditation:* NAST. *Faculty:* 1 full-time (0 women). *Students:* 1 (woman) full-time, 8 part-time (all women); includes 2 minority (1 Black or African American, non-Hispanic/Latino; 1 Two or more races, non-Hispanic/Latino). Average age 31. 2 applicants, 100% accepted, 2 enrolled. In 2016, 1 master's awarded. *Entrance requirements:* For master's, audition, letters of recommendation, minimum GPA of 2.75. Additional exam requirements/recommendations for international students: Required—TOEFL (minimum score 550 paper-based; 79 iBT). *Application deadline:* For fall admission, 6/1 for domestic and international students; for spring admission, 11/1 for domestic and international students; for summer admission, 3/1 for domestic and international students. Applications are processed on a rolling basis. Application fee: $50. Electronic applications accepted. *Expenses:* Tuition, state resident: full-time $4804; part-time $2412 per semester hour. Tuition, nonresident: full-time $19,218; part-time $9612 per semester hour. *Required fees:* $1850; $1850 per semester hour. Tuition and fees vary according to program. *Financial support:* In 2016–17, 1 research assistantship (averaging $3,000 per year) was awarded; scholarships/grants also available. Financial award application deadline: 5/1; financial award applicants required to submit FAFSA. *Unit head:* Dr. Larry Dooley, Department Chair, 706-507-8402, E-mail: dooley_larry@columbusstate.edu. *Application contact:* Kristin Williams, Director of International and Graduate Recruitment, 706-507-8848, Fax: 706-568-5091, E-mail: thornton_katie@colstate.edu.
Website: http://theatre.columbusstate.edu/

**Cornell University,** Graduate School, Graduate Fields of Arts and Sciences, Field of Theatre Arts, Ithaca, NY 14853. Offers drama and the theatre (PhD); theatre history (PhD); theatre theory and aesthetics (PhD). *Degree requirements:* For doctorate, 2 foreign languages, comprehensive exam, thesis/dissertation. *Entrance requirements:* For doctorate, GRE General Test, sample of written work, 3 letters of recommendation. Additional exam requirements/recommendations for international students: Required—TOEFL (minimum score 600 paper-based; 77 iBT). Electronic applications accepted. *Faculty research:* Cultural studies and critical theory, seventeenth to twenty-first century European and American theater, theory of the performing arts, film history and theory, feminism and theater.

**Dell'Arte International School of Physical Theatre,** MFA Program, Blue Lake, CA 95525. Offers ensemble based physical theatre (MFA). *Accreditation:* NAST. *Degree requirements:* For master's, thesis. *Entrance requirements:* For master's, undergraduate degree, audition. Electronic applications accepted. *Faculty research:* Physical theatre, international theatre, ensemble, devised.

**DePaul University,** The Theatre School, Chicago, IL 60614. Offers acting (MFA); arts leadership (MFA); directing (MFA). *Degree requirements:* For master's, comprehensive exam, thesis. *Entrance requirements:* For master's, audition or interview, official transcripts, three letters of recommendation, resume, written statements (for directing program). Additional exam requirements/recommendations for international students: Required—TOEFL (minimum score 550 paper-based; 80 iBT), IELTS (minimum score 6.5). Electronic applications accepted. *Expenses:* Contact institution.

**Eastern Michigan University,** Graduate School, College of Arts and Sciences, School of Communication, Media and Theatre Arts, Programs in Applied Drama/Theatre for the Young, Ypsilanti, MI 48197. Offers MA, MFA. *Program availability:* Part-time, online learning. *Students:* 2 full-time (1 woman), 4 part-time (3 women); includes 1 minority (Black or African American, non-Hispanic/Latino). Average age 37. 11 applicants, 73% accepted, 4 enrolled. In 2016, 3 master's awarded. *Degree requirements:* For master's, thesis optional. *Entrance requirements:* Additional exam requirements/recommendations for international students: Required—TOEFL. *Application deadline:* Applications are processed on a rolling basis. Application fee: $45. *Financial support:* Fellowships, research assistantships with full tuition reimbursements, teaching assistantships with full tuition reimbursements, career-related internships or fieldwork, Federal Work-Study, institutionally sponsored loans, scholarships/grants, tuition waivers (partial), and unspecified assistantships available. Support available to part-time students. Financial award applicants required to submit FAFSA. *Application contact:*

Prof. Patricia Zimmer, Coordinator, 734-487-0331, Fax: 734-487-3443, E-mail: pzimmer@emich.edu.

**Eastern Michigan University,** Graduate School, College of Arts and Sciences, School of Communication, Media and Theatre Arts, Programs in Theatre Arts, Ypsilanti, MI 48197. Offers interpretation/performance studies (MA); theatre arts (MA), including drama/theatre for the young, general. *Program availability:* Part-time, evening/weekend, online learning. *Students:* 4 full-time (all women), 11 part-time (8 women); includes 6 minority (all Black or African American, non-Hispanic/Latino). Average age 26. 14 applicants, 93% accepted, 7 enrolled. In 2016, 10 master's awarded. *Degree requirements:* For master's, thesis or alternative. *Entrance requirements:* Additional exam requirements/recommendations for international students: Required—TOEFL. *Application deadline:* Applications are processed on a rolling basis. Application fee: $45. *Financial support:* Fellowships, research assistantships with full tuition reimbursements, teaching assistantships with full tuition reimbursements, career-related internships or fieldwork, Federal Work-Study, institutionally sponsored loans, scholarships/grants, and unspecified assistantships available. Support available to part-time students. Financial award applicants required to submit FAFSA. *Application contact:* Dr. Lee Stille, Coordinator, 734-487-6846, Fax: 734-487-3443, E-mail: lstille@emich.edu.

**Emerson College,** Graduate Studies, School of the Arts, Department of Performing Arts, Program in Theatre Education, Boston, MA 02116-4624. Offers MA. *Program availability:* Part-time. *Faculty:* 33 full-time (17 women), 2 part-time/adjunct (both women). *Students:* 47 full-time (36 women), 12 part-time (8 women); includes 8 minority (2 Black or African American, non-Hispanic/Latino; 2 Asian, non-Hispanic/Latino; 1 Hispanic/Latino; 3 Two or more races, non-Hispanic/Latino), 1 international. Average age 30. 56 applicants, 93% accepted, 25 enrolled. In 2016, 36 master's awarded. *Entrance requirements:* For master's, GRE General Test. Additional exam requirements/recommendations for international students: Required—TOEFL (minimum score 550 paper-based; 80 iBT), IELTS (minimum score 6.5). *Application deadline:* For fall admission, 2/15 priority date for domestic and international students. Applications are processed on a rolling basis. Application fee: $60 ($75 for international students). Electronic applications accepted. *Financial support:* In 2016–17, 27 students received support, including 27 fellowships with partial tuition reimbursements available (averaging $6,621 per year); research assistantships with partial tuition reimbursements available, Federal Work-Study, scholarships/grants, and unspecified assistantships also available. Financial award application deadline: 3/1; financial award applicants required to submit FAFSA. *Faculty research:* Theater. *Application contact:* Leanda Ferland, Director of Graduate Admission, 617-824-8610, Fax: 617-824-8614, E-mail: gradapp@emerson.edu.
Website: http://www.emerson.edu/graduate_admission

**Florida Atlantic University,** Dorothy F. Schmidt College of Arts and Letters, Department of Theatre and Dance, Boca Raton, FL 33431-0991. Offers acting (MFA); design and technology (MFA). *Faculty:* 8 full-time (3 women), 2 part-time/adjunct (1 woman). *Students:* 12 full-time (6 women); includes 6 minority (1 Black or African American, non-Hispanic/Latino; 4 Hispanic/Latino; 1 Two or more races, non-Hispanic/Latino), 1 international. Average age 29. 16 applicants, 63% accepted, 10 enrolled. *Degree requirements:* For master's, thesis, production. *Entrance requirements:* For master's, GRE General Test, minimum GPA of 3.0 during last 60 hours of undergraduate course work. *Application deadline:* For fall admission, 8/15 priority date for domestic students, 8/15 for international students. Applications are processed on a rolling basis. Application fee: $30. *Expenses:* Tuition, state resident: full-time $7392; part-time $369.82 per credit hour. Tuition, nonresident: full-time $19,432; part-time $1024.81 per credit hour. *Financial support:* Fellowships, teaching assistantships with full tuition reimbursements, career-related internships or fieldwork, Federal Work-Study, and institutionally sponsored loans available. Support available to part-time students. Financial award application deadline: 3/31. *Faculty research:* Contemporary British theatre, Eastern European playwrights, Latin American drama. *Unit head:* Dr. Desmond Gallant, Chair, 561-297-3815, Fax: 561-297-2180, E-mail: dgallant@fau.edu.
Website: http://www.fau.edu/theatre/

**Florida State University,** The Graduate School, College of Fine Arts, School of Theatre, Tallahassee, FL 32396. Offers acting (MFA); costume design (MFA); directing (MFA); technical production (MFA); theatre (MA, PhD); theatre management (MFA). *Accreditation:* NAST. *Faculty:* 17 full-time (8 women). *Students:* 81 full-time (41 women); includes 15 minority (5 Black or African American, non-Hispanic/Latino; 1 Asian, non-Hispanic/Latino; 5 Hispanic/Latino; 4 Two or more races, non-Hispanic/Latino). Average age 25. 125 applicants, 23% accepted, 25 enrolled. In 2016, 21 master's awarded. *Degree requirements:* For master's, one foreign language, comprehensive exam (for some programs), thesis (for some programs); for doctorate, one foreign language, comprehensive exam, thesis/dissertation. *Entrance requirements:* For master's, GRE General Test, writing sample (MA); interview and portfolio (MFA); minimum undergraduate GPA of 3.0; audition (MFA in acting). Additional exam requirements/recommendations for international students: Required—TOEFL. *Application deadline:* For fall admission, 2/15 priority date for domestic and international students. Applications are processed on a rolling basis. Application fee: $30. Electronic applications accepted. *Expenses:* Tuition, state resident: full-time $7263; part-time $403.51 per credit hour. Tuition, nonresident: full-time $18,087; part-time $1004.85 per credit hour. *Required fees:* $1365; $75.81 per credit hour. $20 per semester. Tuition and fees vary according to campus/location. *Financial support:* In 2016–17, 1 fellowship with full tuition reimbursement (averaging $18,000 per year), 30 research assistantships with full tuition reimbursements (averaging $12,000 per year), 24 teaching assistantships with full tuition reimbursements (averaging $12,000 per year) were awarded; career-related internships or fieldwork, Federal Work-Study, institutionally sponsored loans, scholarships/grants, health care benefits, and unspecified assistantships also available. Financial award application deadline: 1/1; financial award applicants required to submit FAFSA. *Faculty research:* Gender theatre, performance theory, computers in theatre, dramaturgy, music theatre performance. *Unit head:* Cameron Jackson, Director, 850-644-7257, Fax: 850-644-7408, E-mail: ccjackson@admin.fsu.edu. *Application contact:* Barbara Thomas, Program Assistant, 850-644-7234, Fax: 850-644-7246, E-mail: bgthomas@admin.fsu.edu.
Website: http://theatre.fsu.edu/

**Fontbonne University,** Graduate Programs, St. Louis, MO 63105-3098. Offers accounting (MBA, MS); art (MA); art (K-12) (MAT); business (MBA); computer science (MS); deaf education (MA); early intervention in deaf education (MA); education (MA), including autism spectrum disorders, curriculum and instruction, diverse learners, early childhood education, reading, special education; elementary education (MAT); family and consumer sciences (MA), including multidisciplinary health communication studies; fine arts (MFA); instructional design and technology (MS); management and leadership (MM); middle school education (MAT); secondary education (MAT); special education (MAT); speech-language pathology (MS); supply chain management (MS); theatre (MA). *Program availability:* Part-time, evening/weekend, online learning. *Faculty:* 32 full-time (24 women), 43 part-time/adjunct (26 women). *Students:* 456 full-time (313 women), 102 part-time (77 women); includes 138 minority (118 Black or African American, non-Hispanic/Latino; 1 American Indian or Alaska Native, non-Hispanic/Latino; 7 Asian, non-Hispanic/Latino; 9 Hispanic/Latino; 3 Two or more races, non-

Hispanic/Latino), 37 international. *Degree requirements:* For master's, comprehensive exam (for some programs), thesis (for some programs). *Entrance requirements:* Additional exam requirements/recommendations for international students: Required—TOEFL (minimum score 500 paper-based; 65 iBT). *Application deadline:* For fall admission, 8/1 for international students; for spring admission, 12/1 for international students. Applications are processed on a rolling basis. Application fee: $25 ($30 for international students). Electronic applications accepted. *Expenses: Tuition:* Full-time $8436; part-time $703 per credit hour. *Required fees:* $18 per credit hour. Tuition and fees vary according to course load. *Financial support:* Teaching assistantships with partial tuition reimbursements and scholarships/grants available. Support available to part-time students. Financial award application deadline: 4/1; financial award applicants required to submit FAFSA. *Unit head:* Dr. Carey Adams, Vice President for Academic Affairs, 314-719-3609, E-mail: cadams@fontbonne.edu. *Application contact:* Lauryn Filip, Coordinator, Graduate Admission and Professional Studies, 314-889-4650, E-mail: admissions@fontbonne.edu.
Website: https://www.fontbonne.edu/academics/graduate-programs/

**Fordham University,** Graduate School of Arts and Sciences, Program in Playwriting, New York, NY 10023. Offers MFA. Program offered jointly with Primary Stages theater company. *Students:* 4 full-time (0 women). 14 applicants, 21% accepted, 2 enrolled. *Entrance requirements:* For master's, 3 letters of recommendation, resume/curriculum vitae, statement of intent, official transcripts, playwriting portfolio, bachelor's degree. Additional exam requirements/recommendations for international students: Required—TOEFL. *Application deadline:* Applications are processed on a rolling basis. Application fee: $70. Electronic applications accepted. *Unit head:* Matthew Maguire, Director, E-mail: mmaguire@fordham.edu. *Application contact:* Bernadette Valentino-Morrison, Director of Graduate Admissions, 718-817-4419, Fax: 718-817-3566, E-mail: valentinomor@fordham.edu.
Website: http://www.fordham.edu/info/21309/playwriting_mfa/2561/playwriting_mfa_application_information

**The George Washington University,** Columbian College of Arts and Sciences, Department of Theatre and Dance, Washington, DC 20052. Offers classical acting (MFA); dance (MFA); exhibit design (Graduate Certificate); production design (MFA). *Program availability:* Part-time, evening/weekend. *Faculty:* 10 full-time (6 women). *Students:* 31 full-time (20 women), 19 part-time (10 women); includes 13 minority (7 Black or African American, non-Hispanic/Latino; 1 Asian, non-Hispanic/Latino; 3 Hispanic/Latino; 2 Two or more races, non-Hispanic/Latino), 5 international. Average age 33. 66 applicants, 61% accepted, 26 enrolled. In 2016, 19 master's, 2 other advanced degrees awarded. *Degree requirements:* For master's, thesis. *Entrance requirements:* For master's, minimum GPA of 3.0, portfolio. Additional exam requirements/recommendations for international students: Required—TOEFL (minimum score 550 paper-based; 80 iBT). *Application deadline:* For fall admission, 8/1 priority date for domestic students; for spring admission, 10/1 priority date for domestic students. Applications are processed on a rolling basis. Application fee: $75. Electronic applications accepted. *Financial support:* In 2016–17, 2 students received support. Fellowships with tuition reimbursements available, teaching assistantships with tuition reimbursements available, career-related internships or fieldwork, Federal Work-Study, and tuition waivers available. *Unit head:* Dana Burgess, Chair, 202-994-1660, E-mail: dtsb@gwu.edu. *Application contact:* Information Contact, 202-994-8072, E-mail: trdanews@gwu.edu.
Website: http://theatredance.columbian.gwu.edu/

**The Graduate Center, City University of New York,** Graduate Studies, Program in Theatre, New York, NY 10016-4039. Offers PhD. *Degree requirements:* For doctorate, 2 foreign languages, thesis/dissertation. *Entrance requirements:* For doctorate, GRE General Test, writing sample. Additional exam requirements/recommendations for international students: Required—TOEFL. Electronic applications accepted.

**Hollins University,** Graduate Programs, Program in Playwriting, Roanoke, VA 24020. Offers new play directing (Certificate); new play performance (Certificate); playwriting (MFA). *Program availability:* Part-time. *Degree requirements:* For master's, comprehensive exam, thesis. *Entrance requirements:* For master's, letters of recommendation, bachelor's degree, undergraduate transcripts, manuscript. Additional exam requirements/recommendations for international students: Required—TOEFL (minimum score 550 paper-based; 80 iBT), IELTS (minimum score 6.5). *Application deadline:* For summer admission, 2/15 priority date for domestic and international students. Application fee: $40. *Expenses:* $830 per credit hour. *Financial support:* Fellowships and scholarships/grants available. Financial award application deadline: 2/15. *Unit head:* Todd Ristau, Director, 540-362-6386, E-mail: tristau@hollins.edu. *Application contact:* Cathy S. Koon, Manager of Graduate Programs, 540-362-6326, Fax: 540-362-6288, E-mail: ckoon@hollins.edu.
Website: http://www.hollins.edu/academics/graduate-degrees/playwriting/

**Hunter College of the City University of New York,** Graduate School, School of Arts and Sciences, Department of Theatre, New York, NY 10065-5085. Offers playwriting (MFA); theatre (MA). *Program availability:* Part-time, evening/weekend. *Students:* 1 (woman) full-time, 28 part-time (15 women); includes 5 minority (2 Black or African American, non-Hispanic/Latino; 1 Asian, non-Hispanic/Latino; 2 Hispanic/Latino), 2 international. Average age 35. 35 applicants, 37% accepted, 10 enrolled. In 2016, 5 master's awarded. *Degree requirements:* For master's, comprehensive exam, thesis. *Entrance requirements:* For master's, GRE General Test. Additional exam requirements/recommendations for international students: Required—TOEFL. *Application deadline:* For fall admission, 4/1 for domestic students, 2/1 for international students; for spring admission, 11/1 for domestic students, 9/1 for international students. *Financial support:* Fellowships, research assistantships, teaching assistantships, career-related internships or fieldwork, Federal Work-Study, and tuition waivers (partial) available. Support available to part-time students. Financial award application deadline: 4/15. *Faculty research:* Modern French mimes, acting techniques, directing, New York avant-garde theater and popular entertainment, playwriting. *Unit head:* Prof. Claudia Orenstein, Chair, 212-772-5149, E-mail: corenste@hunter.cuny.edu. *Application contact:* Milena Solo, Graduate Admissions Director, 212-772-4780, E-mail: admissions@hunter.cuny.edu.
Website: http://www.hunter.cuny.edu/theatre/

**Idaho State University,** Office of Graduate Studies, College of Arts and Letters, Program in Theatre and Dance, Pocatello, ID 83209-8006. Offers theatre (MA). *Accreditation:* NAST. *Program availability:* Part-time. *Degree requirements:* For master's, comprehensive exam, thesis optional, oral and written exam. *Entrance requirements:* For master's, GRE General Test (35th percentile or above on one of the 3 sections). Additional exam requirements/recommendations for international students: Required—TOEFL (minimum score 550 paper-based; 80 iBT). Electronic applications accepted. *Faculty research:* Theatre history, technical theatre.

**Illinois State University,** Graduate School, College of Fine Arts, School of Theatre, Normal, IL 61790-2200. Offers MA, MFA, MS. *Accreditation:* NAST. *Program availability:* Part-time. *Degree requirements:* For master's, variable foreign language requirement, thesis or alternative. *Entrance requirements:* For master's, sample of written work, minimum GPA of 3.0 in last 60 hours of course work. *Faculty research:* Illinois Shakespeare festival.

**Indiana University Bloomington,** University Graduate School, College of Arts and Sciences, Department of Theatre, Drama, and Contemporary Dance, Bloomington, IN 47405. Offers acting (MFA); design and technology (MFA); directing (MFA); playwriting (MFA); theatre history, theory, and literature (MA, PhD). *Accreditation:* NAST. *Faculty:* 12 full-time (5 women), 2 part-time/adjunct (0 women). *Students:* 51 full-time (25 women), 1 part-time (0 women); includes 2 minority (both Hispanic/Latino), 4 international. Average age 30. 40 applicants, 23% accepted, 8 enrolled. In 2016, 10 master's, 3 doctorates awarded. Terminal master's awarded for partial completion of doctoral program. *Degree requirements:* For master's, one foreign language, comprehensive exam, thesis, 30 credit hours; for doctorate, 2 foreign languages, comprehensive exam, thesis/dissertation, 90 credit hours. *Entrance requirements:* For master's, audition, interview, portfolio or script analysis; for doctorate, GRE General Test. Additional exam requirements/recommendations for international students: Required—TOEFL (minimum score 550 paper-based, 80 iBT) or IELTS. *Application deadline:* For fall admission, 1/15 priority date for domestic students, 12/1 for international students. Application fee: $55 ($65 for international students). Electronic applications accepted. *Expenses:* Contact institution. *Financial support:* In 2016–17, 52 students received support, including 3 fellowships with tuition reimbursements available (averaging $18,000 per year), 24 teaching assistantships with tuition reimbursements available (averaging $15,750 per year); health care benefits, tuition waivers, and unspecified assistantships also available. Financial award application deadline: 3/1; financial award applicants required to submit FAFSA. *Faculty research:* American, Western European, world literature; history and theory; theatrical production, design and technology; acting; directing; playwriting. *Unit head:* Jonathan R. Michaelsen, Chairperson and Professor, 812-855-4535, Fax: 812-856-0698, E-mail: theatre@indiana.edu. *Application contact:* Catherine Richards, Academic Secretary, 812-855-4503, Fax: 812-855-0698, E-mail: car@indiana.edu.
Website: http://www.indiana.edu/~thtr/

**The Juilliard School,** Graduate Programs, New York, NY 10023-6588. Offers acting (MFA); jazz studies (Artist Diploma); music (MM, DMA, Diploma); music performance (Artist Diploma); opera studies (Artist Diploma); string quartet (Artist Diploma). *Degree requirements:* For master's and other advanced degree, performance jury, recital; for doctorate, one foreign language, thesis/dissertation, performance jury, 3 recitals. *Entrance requirements:* For master's and other advanced degree, audition; for doctorate, audition, interview. Additional exam requirements/recommendations for international students: Required—TOEFL (minimum score 570 paper-based; 89 iBT). *Application deadline:* For fall admission, 12/1 for domestic and international students. Application fee: $110. Electronic applications accepted. *Expenses: Tuition:* Full-time $41,310. *Financial support:* In 2016–17, 308 students received support. Fellowships, research assistantships, teaching assistantships, Federal Work-Study, institutionally sponsored loans, scholarships/grants, and unspecified assistantships available. Support available to part-time students. Financial award application deadline: 3/1; financial award applicants required to submit FAFSA. *Unit head:* Ara Guzelimian, Provost and Dean, 212-799-5204, Fax: 212-724-0263. *Application contact:* Ekaterina Lawson, Director of Admissions and Academic Affairs, 212-799-5000 Ext. 223, Fax: 212-724-6420.

**Kansas State University,** Graduate School, College of Arts and Sciences, School of Music, Theatre and Dance, Manhattan, KS 66506. Offers MA, MM. *Accreditation:* NASM; NAST. *Program availability:* Part-time, online learning. *Faculty:* 38 full-time (16 women). *Students:* 24 full-time (14 women), 9 part-time (8 women); includes 7 minority (1 Black or African American, non-Hispanic/Latino; 1 American Indian or Alaska Native, non-Hispanic/Latino; 4 Hispanic/Latino; 1 Two or more races, non-Hispanic/Latino), 5 international. Average age 30. 33 applicants, 79% accepted, 12 enrolled. In 2016, 26 master's awarded. *Degree requirements:* For master's, thesis optional. *Entrance requirements:* For master's, GRE, audition (in person or recording), interview (for music education). Additional exam requirements/recommendations for international students: Required—TOEFL (minimum score 600 paper-based). *Application deadline:* For fall admission, 2/1 priority date for domestic and international students; for spring admission, 8/1 priority date for domestic and international students. Applications are processed on a rolling basis. Application fee: $50 ($75 for international students). Electronic applications accepted. *Expenses:* Tuition, state resident: full-time $9670. Tuition, nonresident: full-time $21,828. *Required fees:* $862. *Financial support:* In 2016–17, 15 teaching assistantships with full tuition reimbursements (averaging $12,000 per year) were awarded; fellowships, institutionally sponsored loans, scholarships/grants, and tuition waivers (full and partial) also available. Support available to part-time students. Financial award application deadline: 3/1; financial award applicants required to submit FAFSA. *Faculty research:* American music, opera, drama therapy, directing, costume and scenic design, music by women composers. *Total annual research expenditures:* $26,693. *Unit head:* Dr. Jeffrry Ward, Director, 785-532-5740, Fax: 785-532-6899, E-mail: jeff98@ksu.edu. *Application contact:* Dr. Fred Burrack, Director of Graduate Music Programs, 785-532-3429, Fax: 785-532-5740, E-mail: fburrack@ksu.edu.
Website: http://www.k-state.edu/mtd/

**Kent State University,** College of the Arts, School of Theatre and Dance, Kent, OH 44242-0001. Offers theatre studies (MFA), including acting, design/technology. *Accreditation:* NAST. *Program availability:* Part-time. *Faculty:* 18 full-time (11 women). *Students:* 15 full-time (7 women), 1 (woman) part-time, 1 international. Average age 34. 17 applicants, 53% accepted, 7 enrolled. In 2016, 6 master's awarded. *Degree requirements:* For master's, comprehensive project. *Entrance requirements:* For master's, transcripts, 3 letters of recommendation, goal statement, resume; audition (for acting); portfolio (for design/technology). *Application deadline:* Applications are processed on a rolling basis. Application fee: $45 ($70 for international students). Electronic applications accepted. *Expenses:* Tuition, state resident: full-time $10,864; part-time $495 per credit hour. Tuition, nonresident: full-time $18,380; part-time $837 per credit hour. *Financial support:* Teaching assistantships with full tuition reimbursements, career-related internships or fieldwork, Federal Work-Study, scholarships/grants, and unspecified assistantships available. Financial award application deadline: 5/1. *Unit head:* Eric van Baars, Director and Associate Professor, 330-672-0102, E-mail: fvanbaar@kent.edu. *Application contact:* Yuko Kurahashi, Graduate Coordinator and Associate Professor of Theatre, 330-672-9483, E-mail: ykurahas@kent.edu.
Website: http://www.kent.edu/theatredance

**Long Island University–LIU Post,** College of Arts, Communications and Design, Brookville, NY 11548-1300. Offers art (MA); clinical art therapy (MA); clinical art therapy and counseling (MA); digital game design and development (MA); fine arts and design (MFA); interactive multimedia arts (MA); music (MA); theater (MA); theatre (MFA). *Faculty:* 36 full-time (19 women), 144 part-time/adjunct (74 women). *Students:* 123 full-time (91 women), 21 part-time (18 women); includes 25 minority (6 Black or African American, non-Hispanic/Latino; 1 American Indian or Alaska Native, non-Hispanic/Latino; 6 Asian, non-Hispanic/Latino; 11 Hispanic/Latino; 1 Two or more races, non-Hispanic/Latino), 32 international. 175 applicants, 73% accepted, 46 enrolled. In 2016, 68 master's awarded. *Degree requirements:* For master's, variable foreign language requirement, comprehensive exam (for some programs), thesis (for some programs). *Entrance requirements:* For master's, performance audition or portfolio. Additional exam

## Theater

requirements/recommendations for international students: Required—TOEFL (minimum score 550 paper-based; 79 iBT). *Application deadline:* Applications are processed on a rolling basis. Application fee: $50. Electronic applications accepted. *Expenses: Tuition:* Full-time $28,272; part-time $1178 per credit. *Required fees:* $451 per term. Tuition and fees vary according to degree level and program. *Financial support:* In 2016–17, 6 research assistantships with partial tuition reimbursements (averaging $1,020 per year), 14 teaching assistantships with partial tuition reimbursements (averaging $670 per year) were awarded; career-related internships or fieldwork, Federal Work-Study, institutionally sponsored loans, scholarships/grants, tuition waivers (full and partial), and unspecified assistantships also available. Support available to part-time students. Financial award application deadline: 2/15; financial award applicants required to submit FAFSA. *Faculty research:* Game design, new plays, musical theatre, compositions for wind symphony, jazz ensemble, jazz combo and vocal jazz. *Unit head:* Dr. Christine Kerr, Acting Dean, 516-299-2309, E-mail: christine.kerr@liu.edu. *Application contact:* Carol Zerah, Director of Graduate Admissions, 516-299-2900, Fax: 516-299-2137, E-mail: post-enroll@liu.edu.
Website: http://www.liu.edu/CWPost/Academics/School-of-Visual-Arts-Communications-and-Digital-Technologies

**Louisiana State University and Agricultural & Mechanical College,** Graduate School, College of Music and Dramatic Arts, Department of Theatre, Baton Rouge, LA 70803. Offers acting (MFA); directing (MFA); theatre (PhD); theatre design/technology (MFA). *Accreditation:* NAST.

**Louisiana Tech University,** Graduate School, College of Liberal Arts, Department of Theatre, Ruston, LA 71272. Offers MA. *Unit head:* Prof. Cherrie A. Sciro, Coordinator, 318-257-2930, E-mail: lulu@latech.edu. *Application contact:* Mary Green, Administrative Assistant, 318-257-2924, Fax: 318-257-4487, E-mail: meg@latech.edu.
Website: http://latechuniversitytheatre.com/

**Mary Baldwin University,** Graduate Studies, Program in Shakespeare and Renaissance Literature in Performance, Staunton, VA 24401-3610. Offers acting (M Litt); directing (M Litt); Shakespeare and Renaissance literature in performance (MFA); teaching (M Litt). *Entrance requirements:* For master's, GRE (M Litt).

**Miami University,** College of Creative Arts, Department of Theatre, Oxford, OH 45056. Offers MA. *Accreditation:* NAST. *Students:* 6. In 2016, 8 master's awarded. *Expenses:* Tuition, state resident: full-time $12,890; part-time $564 per credit hour. Tuition, nonresident: full-time $29,604; part-time $1260 per credit hour. *Required fees:* $638. Part-time tuition and fees vary according to course load and program. *Unit head:* Dr. Julia Guichard, Chair and Associate Professor of Theatre, 513-529-1517, E-mail: theatre@miamioh.edu. *Application contact:* Dr. Ann Elizabeth Armstrong, Associate Professor and Director of Graduate Studies, 513-529-8317, E-mail: armstra2@miamioh.edu.
Website: http://www.MiamiOH.edu/theatre

**Michigan State University,** The Graduate School, College of Arts and Letters, Department of Theatre, East Lansing, MI 48824. Offers MA, MFA. *Entrance requirements:* Additional exam requirements/recommendations for international students: Required—TOEFL. Electronic applications accepted.

**Minnesota State University Mankato,** College of Graduate Studies and Research, College of Arts and Humanities, Department of Theatre and Dance, Mankato, MN 56001. Offers theatre arts (MA, MFA). *Students:* 9 full-time (6 women), 3 part-time (1 woman). *Degree requirements:* For master's, one foreign language, comprehensive exam, thesis. *Entrance requirements:* For master's, minimum GPA of 3.0 during previous 2 years, 3 letters of recommendation, resume of theatre work, audition. Additional exam requirements/recommendations for international students: Required—TOEFL. *Application deadline:* For fall admission, 7/1 priority date for domestic students, 5/1 for international students; for spring admission, 11/1 for domestic students, 10/1 for international students. Applications are processed on a rolling basis. Application fee: $40. Electronic applications accepted. *Financial support:* Research assistantships with full tuition reimbursements, teaching assistantships with full tuition reimbursements, career-related internships or fieldwork, Federal Work-Study, institutionally sponsored loans, and unspecified assistantships available. Support available to part-time students. Financial award application deadline: 3/15; financial award applicants required to submit FAFSA. *Unit head:* Dr. Paul J. Hustoles, Chair, 507-389-2118, Fax: 507-389-2922.
Website: http://www.mnsu.edu/theatre/

**Missouri State University,** Graduate College, College of Arts and Letters, Department of Theatre and Dance, Springfield, MO 65897. Offers speech and theatre education (MS Ed). *Accreditation:* NAST. *Program availability:* Part-time. *Faculty:* 9 full-time (5 women). *Students:* 2 part-time (both women). Average age 33. 2 applicants, 50% accepted, 1 enrolled. In 2016, 1 master's awarded. *Degree requirements:* For master's, comprehensive exam, thesis or alternative. *Entrance requirements:* For master's, 9-12 teaching certification (MS Ed). Additional exam requirements/recommendations for international students: Required—TOEFL (minimum score 550 paper-based; 79 iBT), IELTS (minimum score 6). *Application deadline:* For fall admission, 7/20 for domestic students, 5/1 for international students; for spring admission, 12/20 for domestic students, 9/1 for international students. Applications are processed on a rolling basis. Application fee: $35 ($50 for international students). Electronic applications accepted. *Expenses:* Tuition, state resident: full-time $5830. Tuition, nonresident: full-time $10,708. *Required fees:* $1130. Tuition and fees vary according to class time, course level, course load and program. *Financial support:* Federal Work-Study, institutionally sponsored loans, scholarships/grants, and unspecified assistantships available. Financial award application deadline: 3/31; financial award applicants required to submit FAFSA. *Unit head:* Dr. Jeremy Chesman, Interim Department Head, 417-836-4400, Fax: 417-836-4234, E-mail: theatreanddance@missouristate.edu. *Application contact:* Michael Edwards, Coordinator of Graduate Admissions, 417-836-5330, Fax: 417-836-6200, E-mail: michaeledwards@missouristate.edu.
Website: http://theatreanddance.missouristate.edu/

**Montclair State University,** The Graduate School, College of the Arts, MA Program in Theatre, Montclair, NJ 07043-1624. Offers arts management (MA); production/stage management (MA); theatre studies (MA). *Accreditation:* NAST. *Program availability:* Part-time, evening/weekend. *Degree requirements:* For master's, comprehensive exam, thesis or alternative. *Entrance requirements:* For master's, GRE General Test, 2 letters of recommendation. Additional exam requirements/recommendations for international students: Required—TOEFL (minimum score 83 iBT) or IELTS (minimum score 6.5). Electronic applications accepted. *Expenses:* Tuition, state resident: part-time $553 per credit. Tuition, nonresident: part-time $854 per credit. *Required fees:* $91 per credit. Tuition and fees vary according to program. *Faculty research:* Danceturgy, Arab and Muslim images in American drama, Neil LaBute and playwriting, directing, Robert Edmond Jones.

**Naropa University,** Graduate Programs, Program in Theater: Contemporary Performance, Boulder, CO 80302-6697. Offers MFA. *Faculty:* 2 full-time (0 women), 3 part-time/adjunct (2 women). *Students:* 15 full-time (10 women); includes 6 minority (3 Hispanic/Latino; 3 Two or more races, non-Hispanic/Latino), 2 international. Average age 29. 43 applicants, 100% accepted, 9 enrolled. In 2016, 7 master's awarded. *Degree requirements:* For master's, thesis, culminating projects and performances. *Entrance*

*requirements:* For master's, interview/audition; headshot; resume/curriculum vitae with pertinent academic, employment and volunteer activities; transcripts; 2 letters of recommendation; letter of interest. Additional exam requirements/recommendations for international students: Required—TOEFL (minimum score 550 paper-based; 80 iBT). *Application deadline:* For fall admission, 1/15 priority date for domestic and international students. Applications are processed on a rolling basis. Application fee: $60. Electronic applications accepted. *Expenses:* $25,740 for first year. *Financial support:* In 2016–17, 15 students received support. Research assistantships with partial tuition reimbursements available, teaching assistantships with partial tuition reimbursements available, career-related internships or fieldwork, Federal Work-Study, scholarships/grants, tuition waivers (partial), and unspecified assistantships available. Support available to part-time students. Financial award application deadline: 3/1; financial award applicants required to submit FAFSA. *Unit head:* Sue Hammond West, Dean, School of the Arts and Jack Kerouac School, 303-546-3585, E-mail: suewest@naropa.edu. *Application contact:* Office of Admissions, 303-536-3572, Fax: 303-546-3583, E-mail: admissions@naropa.edu.
Website: http://www.naropa.edu/academics/masters/contemporary-performance/index.php

**The New School,** College of Performing Arts, School of Drama, New York, NY 10011. Offers acting (MFA); directing (MFA); playwriting (MFA). *Program availability:* Part-time. *Faculty:* 35 part-time/adjunct (19 women). *Students:* 59 full-time (32 women), 1 (woman) part-time; includes 13 minority (3 Black or African American, non-Hispanic/Latino; 2 Asian, non-Hispanic/Latino; 7 Hispanic/Latino; 1 Two or more races, non-Hispanic/Latino), 5 international. Average age 27. 226 applicants, 17% accepted, 19 enrolled. In 2016, 16 master's awarded. *Degree requirements:* For master's, thesis or alternative, student involvement in theatrical production and presentation. *Entrance requirements:* For master's, official transcripts, recommendation letters, statement of purpose; artistic resume and photograph (for directing and acting); writing sample (for directing); auditions (for acting). Additional exam requirements/recommendations for international students: Required—TOEFL (minimum score 100 iBT), IELTS (minimum score 7), PTE (minimum score 68). *Application deadline:* For fall admission, 1/10 priority date for domestic and international students. Applications are processed on a rolling basis. Application fee: $50. Electronic applications accepted. *Expenses:* Contact institution. *Financial support:* Fellowships, teaching assistantships, career-related internships or fieldwork, Federal Work-Study, scholarships/grants, and unspecified assistantships available. Support available to part-time students. Financial award application deadline: 2/1; financial award applicants required to submit FAFSA. *Unit head:* Pippin Parker, Dean, School of Drama, 212-229-5859 Ext. 2636, E-mail: parkerp@newschool.edu. *Application contact:* Taryn Wolf, Senior Director of Recruitment and Outreach, 212-229-5150 Ext. 3007, E-mail: wolft@newschool.edu.

**New York University,** Steinhardt School of Culture, Education, and Human Development, Department of Music and Performing Arts Professions, Program in Educational Theatre, New York, NY 10012. Offers educational theatre and English 7-12 (MA); educational theatre and social studies 7-12 (MA); educational theatre in colleges and communities (MA, Ed D, PhD); educational theatre, all grades (MA). *Program availability:* Part-time. *Degree requirements:* For master's, thesis (for some programs); for doctorate, thesis/dissertation. *Entrance requirements:* For master's, audition; for doctorate, GRE General Test, interview. Additional exam requirements/recommendations for international students: Required—TOEFL (minimum score 100 iBT). Electronic applications accepted. *Faculty research:* Theatre for young audiences, drama in education, applied theatre, arts education assessment, reflective praxis.

**New York University,** Steinhardt School of Culture, Education, and Human Development, Department of Music and Performing Arts Professions, Program in Music Performance and Composition, New York, NY 10012. Offers instrumental performance (MM), including instrumental performance, jazz instrumental performance; music performance and composition (PhD), including music performance and composition; music theory and composition (MM), including composition for film and multimedia, composition for music theater, computer music composition, music theory and composition, songwriting; piano performance (MM), including collaborative piano, solo piano; vocal pedagogy (Advanced Certificate); vocal performance (MM), including classical voice, musical theatre performance. *Program availability:* Part-time. *Degree requirements:* For master's, thesis (for some programs); for doctorate, thesis/dissertation. *Entrance requirements:* For master's, audition; for doctorate, GRE General Test, audition, interview. Additional exam requirements/recommendations for international students: Required—TOEFL (minimum score 100 iBT). Electronic applications accepted. *Faculty research:* Aesthetics, performance analysis, twentieth century music, music methodologies for arts criticism and analysis.

**New York University,** Tisch School of the Arts and Graduate School of Arts and Science, Department of Performance Studies, New York, NY 10012-1019. Offers MA, PhD. *Degree requirements:* For doctorate, one foreign language, comprehensive exam, thesis/dissertation, dissertation defense, qualifying exam. *Entrance requirements:* For master's, sample of written work; for doctorate, master's degree, writing sample. Additional exam requirements/recommendations for international students: Required—TOEFL or IELTS. Electronic applications accepted. *Expenses:* Contact institution. *Faculty research:* Performance theory, dance, folklore and festivals, postcolonial theory, anthropology and gender studies.

**New York University,** Tisch School of the Arts, Graduate Acting Program, New York, NY 10012-1019. Offers MFA. *Entrance requirements:* For master's, audition. Electronic applications accepted.

**Northern Illinois University,** Graduate School, College of Visual and Performing Arts, School of Theatre and Dance, De Kalb, IL 60115-2854. Offers MFA. *Program availability:* Part-time. *Faculty:* 16 full-time (9 women). *Students:* 26 full-time (13 women); includes 2 minority (both Two or more races, non-Hispanic/Latino). Average age 28. 34 applicants, 56% accepted, 19 enrolled. In 2016, 14 master's awarded. *Degree requirements:* For master's, comprehensive exam, final project and defense. *Entrance requirements:* For master's, minimum GPA of 2.75, audition or portfolio. Additional exam requirements/recommendations for international students: Required—TOEFL (minimum score 550 paper-based). *Application deadline:* For fall admission, 4/1 priority date for domestic students, 5/1 for international students; for spring admission, 10/15 priority date for domestic students, 10/1 for international students. Applications are processed on a rolling basis. Application fee: $40. Electronic applications accepted. *Financial support:* In 2016–17, 26 teaching assistantships with full tuition reimbursements were awarded; fellowships with full tuition reimbursements, research assistantships with full tuition reimbursements, career-related internships or fieldwork, Federal Work-Study, scholarships/grants, tuition waivers (full), and staff assistantships also available. Support available to part-time students. Financial award applicants required to submit FAFSA. *Faculty research:* Theatre history, choreography, performance art spectacles, storytelling, computer visualization of the ethical space. *Unit head:* Alexander Gelman, Director, 815-753-8253, Fax: 815-753-8415, E-mail: agelman@niu.edu. *Application contact:* Graduate School Office, 815-753-0395, E-mail: gradsch@niu.edu.
Website: http://www.niu.edu/theatre/

**Northern Michigan University,** Office of Graduate Education and Research, College of Arts and Sciences, Department of English, Marquette, MI 49855-5301. Offers creative writing (MFA); literature (MA); pedagogy (MA); teaching English to speakers of other languages (Graduate Certificate); theater (MA); writing (MA). *Program availability:* Part-time, evening/weekend. Terminal master's awarded for partial completion of doctoral program. *Degree requirements:* For master's, capstone project: thesis, practicum or portfolio (for MA); thesis (for MFA); for Graduate Certificate, one foreign language. *Entrance requirements:* For master's, minimum GPA of 3.0; bachelor's degree in English or minimum of 30 credit hours in undergraduate English; statement of purpose; resume; critical essay; 3 letters of recommendation; for Graduate Certificate, bachelor's degree. Additional exam requirements/recommendations for international students: Required—TOEFL (minimum score 550 paper-based; 79 iBT), IELTS (minimum score 6.5). Electronic applications accepted. *Faculty research:* Modern Arabic literature, British literature (medieval to contemporary), postcolonial literature, Native and African-American literature, creative writing, critical theory, pedagogy.

**Northwestern University,** The Graduate School, School of Communication, Department of Theatre, Evanston, IL 60208. Offers directing (MFA); stage design (MFA); theatre and drama (PhD). Admissions and degrees offered through The Graduate School. *Degree requirements:* For master's, thesis (MFA). *Entrance requirements:* For master's, GRE General Test. Additional exam requirements/recommendations for international students: Required—TOEFL. *Faculty research:* Critical analysis, theory and history of theatre and drama, philosophy of dance and movement, performance in multicultural contexts, storytelling, computer design process.

**Northwestern University,** The Graduate School, School of Communication, Interdisciplinary PhD Program in Theatre and Drama, Evanston, IL 60208. Offers PhD. Admissions and degree offered through The Graduate School. *Degree requirements:* For doctorate, thesis/dissertation, qualifying and final oral exams. *Entrance requirements:* For doctorate, GRE General Test, sample of written work. Additional exam requirements/recommendations for international students: Required—TOEFL. Electronic applications accepted. *Faculty research:* Theory and history of theatre and drama, performance theory, performance in multicultural contexts, critical analysis drama, theatre historiography.

**The Ohio State University,** Graduate School, College of Arts and Sciences, Division of Arts and Humanities, Department of Theatre, Columbus, OH 43210. Offers acting (MFA); design (MFA); theatre (PhD); theatre studies (MA). *Accreditation:* NAST. *Faculty:* 17. *Students:* 32 full-time (18 women), 1 part-time (0 women). Average age 34. In 2016, 7 master's, 3 doctorates awarded. Terminal master's awarded for partial completion of doctoral program. *Degree requirements:* For master's, thesis (for some programs); for doctorate, one foreign language, thesis/dissertation. *Entrance requirements:* For master's, GRE General Test (for all MA applicants and MFA applicants with GPA below 3.0), audition (for MFA in acting); electronic design portfolio (for MFA in design); sample of published or unpublished research work (for MA); for doctorate, GRE General Test. Additional exam requirements/recommendations for international students: Required—Michigan English Language Assessment Battery (minimum score 82); Recommended—TOEFL (minimum score 550 paper-based; 79 iBT), IELTS (minimum score 7). *Application deadline:* For fall admission, 11/30 priority date for domestic and international students; for spring admission, 3/1 for domestic students, 2/1 for international students. Applications are processed on a rolling basis. Application fee: $60 ($70 for international students). Electronic applications accepted. *Financial support:* Fellowships, teaching assistantships, Federal Work-Study, and institutionally sponsored loans available. Support available to part-time students. Financial award application deadline: 3/1; financial award applicants required to submit FAFSA. *Unit head:* Dr. Janet Parrott, Chair, 614-292-5821, E-mail: parrott.1@osu.edu. *Application contact:* Graduate and Professional Admissions, 614-292-9444, Fax: 614-292-3895, E-mail: gpadmissions@osu.edu. Website: http://theatre.osu.edu/

**Ohio University,** Graduate College, College of Fine Arts, School of Theater, Athens, OH 45701-2979. Offers MA, MFA. *Accreditation:* NAST. *Degree requirements:* For master's, thesis or alternative. *Entrance requirements:* For master's, minimum GPA of 3.0. Additional exam requirements/recommendations for international students: Required—TOEFL (minimum score 550 paper-based; 80 iBT) or IELTS (minimum score 6.5). *Application deadline:* For fall admission, 3/15 priority date for domestic and international students. Application fee: $50 ($55 for international students). Electronic applications accepted. *Financial support:* Research assistantships with full and partial tuition reimbursements, career-related internships or fieldwork, Federal Work-Study, institutionally sponsored loans, scholarships/grants, tuition waivers (partial), and unspecified assistantships available. Financial award application deadline: 3/15; financial award applicants required to submit FAFSA. *Unit head:* Michael Lincoln, Director of Graduate Studies, 740-593-4806, Fax: 740-593-4817, E-mail: lincolnm@ohio.edu. *Application contact:* Barbara M. Fiocchi, Administrative Assistant, 740-593-4818, Fax: 740-593-4817, E-mail: fiocchi@ohio.edu. Website: http://www.finearts.ohio.edu/theater/home.htm

**Oklahoma State University,** College of Arts and Sciences, Department of Theatre, Stillwater, OK 74078. Offers MA. *Accreditation:* NAST. *Faculty:* 11 full-time (6 women), 1 (woman) part-time/adjunct. *Students:* 2 full-time (1 woman), 2 part-time (0 women). Average age 30. 1 applicant, 100% accepted, 1 enrolled. In 2016, 1 master's awarded. *Degree requirements:* For master's, creative component or thesis. *Entrance requirements:* For master's, GRE. Additional exam requirements/recommendations for international students: Required—TOEFL (minimum score 550 paper-based; 79 iBT). *Application deadline:* For fall admission, 3/1 priority date for international students; for spring admission, 8/1 priority date for international students. Applications are processed on a rolling basis. Application fee: $40 ($75 for international students). Electronic applications accepted. *Expenses:* Tuition, state resident: full-time $3775; part-time $209.70 per credit hour. Tuition, nonresident: full-time $14,851; part-time $825.05 per credit hour. *Required fees:* $2027; $112.60 per credit hour. Tuition and fees vary according to campus/location. *Financial support:* In 2016–17, 1 research assistantship (averaging $18,250 per year), 5 teaching assistantships (averaging $15,392 per year) were awarded; career-related internships or fieldwork, Federal Work-Study, scholarships/grants, health care benefits, tuition waivers (partial), and unspecified assistantships also available. Support available to part-time students. Financial award application deadline: 3/1; financial award applicants required to submit FAFSA. *Faculty research:* Historical scene painting and scenic art, Eastern European stage design, stage direction, voice and diction for the actor, stage choreography and dance. *Unit head:* Andrew Kimbrough, Department Head, 405-744-6094, Fax: 405-744-6509, E-mail: andrew.kimbrough@okstate.edu. *Application contact:* Dr. Maria Beach, Graduate Coordinator, 405-744-2966, Fax: 405-744-6509, E-mail: maria.beach@okstate.edu. Website: http://theatre.okstate.edu/

**Pace University,** Dyson College of Arts and Sciences, The Actors Studio MFA Program, New York, NY 10038. Offers acting (MFA); directing (MFA); playwriting (MFA). *Faculty:* 7 full-time (3 women), 11 part-time/adjunct (3 women). *Students:* 113 full-time (67 women); includes 38 minority (20 Black or African American, non-Hispanic/Latino; 1 Asian, non-Hispanic/Latino; 14 Hispanic/Latino; 3 Two or more races, non-Hispanic/Latino), 23 international. Average age 27. In 2016, 34 master's awarded. *Degree requirements:* For master's, thesis. *Entrance requirements:* For master's, artistics resume, 2 letters of recommendation (theater, academic and/or professional), official transcripts; audition (for actors); interview and portfolio (for directors and plawrights). Additional exam requirements/recommendations for international students: Required—TOEFL (minimum score 88 iBT), IELTS (minimum score 7) or PTE (minimum score 60). *Application deadline:* For fall admission, 1/1 for domestic students. Application fee: $70. *Expenses: Tuition:* Part-time $1195 per credit. *Required fees:* $260 per semester. Tuition and fees vary according to degree level, campus/location and program. *Financial support:* Scholarships/grants available. Financial award application deadline: 2/15; financial award applicants required to submit FAFSA. *Unit head:* Andreas Manolikakis, Chair, 212-346-1131, E-mail: actorsstudiomfa@pace.edu. *Application contact:* Susan Ford-Goldschein, Director of Graduate Admissions, 212-346-1531, Fax: 212-346-1585, E-mail: graduateadmission@pace.edu. Website: http://www.pace.edu/dyson/academic-departments-and-programs/asds

**Penn State University Park,** Graduate School, College of Arts and Architecture, School of Theatre, University Park, PA 16802. Offers MFA. *Accreditation:* NAST. *Application contact:* Lori Hawn, Director, Graduate Student Services, 814-865-1795, Fax: 814-863-4627, E-mail: l-gswww@lists.psu.edu. Website: http://theatre.psu.edu/

**Pensacola Christian College,** Graduate Studies, Pensacola, FL 32503-2267. Offers business administration (MBA); curriculum and instruction (MS, Ed D, Ed S); dramatics (MFA); educational leadership (MS, Ed D, Ed S); graphic design (MA, MFA); music (MA); nursing (MSN); performance studies (MA); studio art (MA, MFA).

**Point Park University,** Conservatory of Performing Arts, Pittsburgh, PA 15222-1984. Offers theatre arts-acting (MFA). *Degree requirements:* For master's, comprehensive exam (for some programs), thesis or alternative. *Entrance requirements:* For master's, interview, undergraduate degree in related field, theatre experience. Additional exam requirements/recommendations for international students: Required—TOEFL (minimum score 550 paper-based; 79 iBT). Electronic applications accepted.

**Portland State University,** Graduate Studies, College of the Arts, School of Theatre and Film, Portland, OR 97207-0751. Offers theater (MA, MS). *Accreditation:* NAST. *Faculty:* 19 full-time (11 women), 14 part-time/adjunct (8 women). *Students:* 5 part-time (4 women); includes 2 minority (1 Black or African American, non-Hispanic/Latino; 1 Two or more races, non-Hispanic/Latino). Average age 48. 11 applicants, 100% accepted, 6 enrolled. In 2016, 2 master's awarded. *Degree requirements:* For master's, variable foreign language requirement, thesis or alternative. *Entrance requirements:* For master's, minimum GPA of 3.0 in upper-division course work or 2.75 overall, 24 credits in theater arts. Additional exam requirements/recommendations for international students: Required—TOEFL (minimum score 550 paper-based; 80 iBT). *Application deadline:* For fall admission, 4/1 priority date for domestic students, 3/1 priority date for international students; for winter admission, 9/1 for domestic students; for spring admission, 11/1 for domestic students; for summer admission, 2/1 for domestic students. Applications are processed on a rolling basis. Application fee: $65. *Expenses:* Contact institution. *Financial support:* Teaching assistantships, career-related internships or fieldwork, Federal Work-Study, and unspecified assistantships available. Support available to part-time students. Financial award application deadline: 3/1; financial award applicants required to submit FAFSA. *Faculty research:* Design, acting/directing, scene/costume technology, dramatic literature, theater history. *Total annual research expenditures:* $1,621. *Unit head:* Mark Berrettini, Director, 503-725-4623, Fax: 503-725-4624, E-mail: mberre@pdx.edu. *Application contact:* Katie Sinback, Office Coordinator, 503-725-4622, Fax: 503-725-4624, E-mail: sinback@pdx.edu. Website: https://www.pdx.edu/theater-film/

**Purdue University,** Graduate School, College of Liberal Arts, Department of Theatre, West Lafayette, IN 47907. Offers MFA. *Students:* 19 full-time (11 women); includes 4 minority (1 Black or African American, non-Hispanic/Latino; 2 Hispanic/Latino; 1 Native Hawaiian or other Pacific Islander, non-Hispanic/Latino), 3 international. Average age 28. 25 applicants, 40% accepted, 10 enrolled. In 2016, 8 master's awarded. *Unit head:* Michael McNamara, Admissions Coordinator, 765-496-2386, E-mail: mmcnamara@purdue.edu. *Application contact:* Rosina C. Starks, Graduate Contact, 765-494-3080, E-mail: rstarks@purdue.edu. Website: https://www.cla.purdue.edu/vpa/theatre/

**Regent University,** Graduate School, School of Communication and the Arts, Virginia Beach, VA 23464-9800. Offers communication (MA, PhD), including media and arts management and promotion (MA), political communication (MA), strategic communication (MA); directing for cinema/television (MFA); film and TV (MA), including producing, production, script writing; journalism (MA); producing for cinema/television (MFA); script and screenwriting (MFA); theatre (MA). *Program availability:* Part-time, 100% online, blended/hybrid learning. *Faculty:* 19 full-time (3 women), 51 part-time/adjunct (17 women). *Students:* 92 full-time (52 women), 344 part-time (225 women); includes 163 minority (116 Black or African American, non-Hispanic/Latino; 6 American Indian or Alaska Native, non-Hispanic/Latino; 7 Asian, non-Hispanic/Latino; 25 Hispanic/Latino; 1 Native Hawaiian or other Pacific Islander, non-Hispanic/Latino; 8 Two or more races, non-Hispanic/Latino), 8 international. Average age 37. 368 applicants, 52% accepted, 124 enrolled. In 2016, 91 master's, 7 doctorates awarded. *Degree requirements:* For master's, thesis or alternative; for doctorate, thesis/dissertation. *Entrance requirements:* For master's, transcripts, writing sample, resume, audition (for MFA programs); for doctorate, GRE General Test, resume, writing sample, recommendations, interview, transcripts, personal goals statement. Additional exam requirements/recommendations for international students: Required—TOEFL (minimum score 577 paper-based). *Application deadline:* For fall admission, 3/1 priority date for domestic students; for spring admission, 10/1 priority date for domestic students. Applications are processed on a rolling basis. Application fee: $50. Electronic applications accepted. *Expenses:* $685 per credit (for MA); $895 per credit (for MFA in acting); $885 per credit (for PhD); $250 per semester technology fee. *Financial support:* In 2016–17, 178 students received support, including 2 fellowships (averaging $10,000 per year); career-related internships or fieldwork, scholarships/grants, and unspecified assistantships also available. Support available to part-time students. *Faculty research:* Screenwriting, digital media production, communication, acting, directing. *Unit head:* Dr. Mitch Land, Dean, 757-352-4916, Fax: 757-352-4291, E-mail: mland@regent.edu. *Application contact:* Heidi Cece, Assistant Vice President of Enrollment Management, 800-373-5504, Fax: 757-352-4381, E-mail: admissions@regent.edu. Website: http://www.regent.edu/sca/

**Roosevelt University,** Graduate Division, Chicago College of Performing Arts, Theatre Conservatory, Chicago, IL 60605. Offers directing and dramaturgy (MFA); musical theatre (MA, MFA); theatre (MA); theatre-directing (MFA). MA is a special 3-summer program for high school teachers only. *Degree requirements:* For master's, thesis production/performance. *Entrance requirements:* For master's, audition, interview, minimum GPA of 2.5. *Faculty research:* Brecht, Shakespeare, contemporary and new work, fully mounted theatre.

## Theater

**Rowan University,** Graduate School, College of Education, Department of Language, Literacy, and Sociocultural Education, Program in Theatre Education, Glassboro, NJ 08028-1701. Offers MST. *Accreditation:* NAST. Electronic applications accepted.

**Rowan University,** Graduate School, College of Performing Arts, Department of Theatre and Dance, Glassboro, NJ 08028-1701. Offers theatre arts administration (MA). *Accreditation:* NASAD. Electronic applications accepted.

**Rutgers University–New Brunswick,** Mason Gross School of the Arts, Theater Department, New Brunswick, NJ 08901. Offers acting (MFA); design (MFA); playwriting (MFA); stage management (MFA); technical direction (MFA). *Degree requirements:* For master's, thesis (for some programs), performance project. *Entrance requirements:* For master's, audition, interview, portfolio. Additional exam requirements/recommendations for international students: Required—TOEFL (minimum score 550 paper-based), IELTS (minimum score 7). Electronic applications accepted. *Faculty research:* Faculty of working professional.

**San Diego State University,** Graduate and Research Affairs, College of Professional Studies and Fine Arts, School of Theater, Television and Film, San Diego, CA 92182. Offers television, film, and new media production (MA); theatre arts (MA, MFA). *Accreditation:* NAST. *Program availability:* Part-time. *Degree requirements:* For master's, thesis. *Entrance requirements:* For master's, GRE General Test, 3 letters of recommendation, interview. Additional exam requirements/recommendations for international students: Required—TOEFL. Electronic applications accepted.

**San Francisco State University,** Division of Graduate Studies, College of Liberal and Creative Arts, School of Theatre and Dance, San Francisco, CA 94132-1722. Offers drama (MA); theatre arts (MFA), including design/technical production. *Accreditation:* NAST. *Expenses:* Tuition, state resident: full-time $6738. Tuition, nonresident: full-time $15,666. *Required fees:* $1012. Tuition and fees vary according to degree level and program. *Unit head:* Todd Roehrman, Director, 415-338-2519, Fax: 415-338-6159, E-mail: roehrman@sfsu.edu. *Application contact:* Prof. Joel Schechter, MA Coordinator, 415-338-1331, Fax: 415-338-6159, E-mail: jschech@sfsu.edu. Website: http://www.theatre.sfsu.edu

**San Jose State University,** Graduate Studies and Research, College of Humanities and the Arts, San Jose, CA 95192-0001. Offers art (MA, MFA), including art history and visual culture (MA), digital media art (MFA), photography (MFA), pictorial art (MFA), spatial art (MFA); computational linguistics (Certificate); English (MA, MFA), including creative writing (MFA); French (MA); humanities and arts (Certificate); linguistics (MA); music (MA); philosophy (MA); professional and technical communication (Certificate); Spanish (MA); teaching English to speakers of other languages (MA); TESOL (Certificate); theatre arts (MA). Electronic applications accepted.

**Sarah Lawrence College,** Graduate Studies, Program in Theater, Bronxville, NY 10708-5999. Offers MFA. *Degree requirements:* For master's, portfolio. *Entrance requirements:* For master's, interview, minimum B average in undergraduate course work. Additional exam requirements/recommendations for international students: Required—TOEFL (minimum score 600 paper-based). Electronic applications accepted.

**Savannah College of Art and Design,** Graduate School, Program in Dramatic Writing, Savannah, GA 31402-3146. Offers MFA. *Program availability:* Part-time. *Faculty:* 4 full-time (1 woman), 1 (woman) part-time/adjunct. *Students:* 17 full-time (12 women), 5 part-time (2 women); includes 11 minority (all Black or African American, non-Hispanic/Latino), 4 international. Average age 28. 26 applicants, 58% accepted, 8 enrolled. In 2016, 3 master's awarded. *Degree requirements:* For master's, thesis. *Entrance requirements:* For master's, GRE (recommended), portfolio (submitted in digital format), audition or writing submission, resume, statement of purpose, two letters of recommendation. Additional exam requirements/recommendations for international students: Required—TOEFL (minimum score 550 paper-based, 85 iBT), IELTS (minimum score 6.5), or ACTFL. *Application deadline:* For fall admission, 4/1 for domestic and international students. Applications are processed on a rolling basis. Application fee: $40. Electronic applications accepted. *Expenses: Tuition:* Full-time $36,045. Tuition and fees vary according to course load. *Financial support:* Career-related internships or fieldwork, Federal Work-Study, and scholarships/grants available. Financial award application deadline: 4/1; financial award applicants required to submit FAFSA. *Unit head:* Averie Storck, Academic Program Coordinator. *Application contact:* Jenny Jaquillard, Executive Director of Admissions, Recruitment and Events, 912-525-5100, Fax: 912-525-5985, E-mail: admission@scad.edu. Website: http://www.scad.edu/academics/programs/dramatic-writing

**Savannah College of Art and Design,** Graduate School, Program in Production Design, Savannah, GA 31402-3146. Offers MA, MFA. *Program availability:* Part-time. *Faculty:* 5 full-time (3 women). *Students:* 17 full-time (13 women); includes 3 minority (1 Black or African American, non-Hispanic/Latino; 1 Asian, non-Hispanic/Latino; 1 Hispanic/Latino), 5 international. Average age 28. 27 applicants, 52% accepted, 8 enrolled. In 2016, 4 master's awarded. *Degree requirements:* For master's, final project (for MA); thesis (for MFA). *Entrance requirements:* For master's, GRE (recommended), portfolio (submitted in digital format), audition or writing submission, resume, statement of purpose, two letters of recommendation. Additional exam requirements/recommendations for international students: Required—TOEFL (minimum score 550 paper-based, 85 iBT), IELTS (minimum score 6.5), or ACTFL. *Application deadline:* For fall admission, 4/1 for domestic and international students. Applications are processed on a rolling basis. Application fee: $40. Electronic applications accepted. *Expenses: Tuition:* Full-time $36,045. Tuition and fees vary according to course load. *Financial support:* Career-related internships or fieldwork, Federal Work-Study, and scholarships/grants available. Financial award application deadline: 4/1; financial award applicants required to submit FAFSA. *Unit head:* Gregory Beck, Chair, Production Design and Themed Entertainment. *Application contact:* Jenny Jaquillard, Executive Director of Admissions, Recruitment and Events, 912-525-5100, Fax: 912-525-5985, E-mail: admission@scad.edu. Website: http://www.scad.edu/academics/programs/production-design

**Smith College,** Graduate and Special Programs, Department of Theatre, Northampton, MA 01063. Offers theatre (MFA), including playwriting. *Program availability:* Part-time. *Students:* 2 full-time (both women). Average age 25. 3 applicants, 33% accepted, 1 enrolled. In 2016, 2 master's awarded. *Degree requirements:* For master's, thesis. *Entrance requirements:* For master's, full-length play. Additional exam requirements/recommendations for international students: Required—TOEFL (minimum score 595 paper-based; 97 iBT), IELTS. *Application deadline:* For fall admission, 4/1 for domestic students, 1/15 for international students; for spring admission, 12/1 for domestic students. Application fee: $60. *Expenses: Tuition:* Full-time $34,560; part-time $1440 per credit. Tuition and fees vary according to course load and program. *Financial support:* In 2016–17, 2 students received support. Scholarships/grants available. Support available to part-time students. Financial award application deadline: 1/15; financial award applicants required to submit CSS PROFILE or FAFSA. *Unit head:* Leonard Berkman, Graduate Student Adviser, 413-585-3206, E-mail: lberkman@smith.edu. *Application contact:* Ruth Morgan, Program Assistant, 413-585-3050, Fax: 413-585-3054, E-mail: rmorgan@smith.edu. Website: http://www.smith.edu/theatre/

**Southern Illinois University Carbondale,** Graduate School, College of Liberal Arts, Theater Department, Carbondale, IL 62901-4701. Offers speech/theater (PhD); theater (MFA). *Accreditation:* NAST (one or more programs are accredited). *Program availability:* Part-time. *Degree requirements:* For master's, thesis; for doctorate, thesis/dissertation. *Entrance requirements:* For master's, minimum GPA of 2.7; for doctorate, minimum GPA of 3.25. Additional exam requirements/recommendations for international students: Required—TOEFL. *Faculty research:* Scenography, theater performance, theater history, dramatic criticism, theater technology, playwriting.

**Southern Methodist University,** Meadows School of the Arts, Division of Theatre, Dallas, TX 75275. Offers acting (MFA); design (MFA). *Accreditation:* NAST. *Entrance requirements:* For master's, audition or interview. Additional exam requirements/recommendations for international students: Required—TOEFL (minimum score 550 paper-based; 80 iBT). Electronic applications accepted. *Faculty research:* European lighting techniques.

**Southern Oregon University,** Graduate Studies, Ashland Center for Theatre Studies, Ashland, OR 97520. Offers MTS. *Program availability:* Part-time. *Faculty:* 5 full-time (2 women), 1 part-time/adjunct (0 women). *Students:* 45 full-time (30 women), 3 part-time (2 women); includes 6 minority (2 Hispanic/Latino; 4 Two or more races, non-Hispanic/Latino), 2 international. Average age 40. 23 applicants, 87% accepted, 16 enrolled. In 2016, 20 master's awarded. *Degree requirements:* For master's, thesis (for some programs). *Entrance requirements:* For master's, GRE General Test, minimum cumulative GPA of 3.0 in the last 90 quarter credits (60 semester credits) of undergraduate coursework. Additional exam requirements/recommendations for international students: Required—TOEFL (minimum score 540 paper-based; 76 iBT), IELTS (minimum score 6), ELPT (minimum score 964) or ELS (minimum score 112). *Application deadline:* For fall admission, 7/31 priority date for domestic and international students; for winter admission, 11/15 priority date for domestic and international students; for spring admission, 1/7 priority date for domestic and international students. Applications are processed on a rolling basis. Application fee: $60. Electronic applications accepted. *Expenses:* Tuition, state resident: full-time $10,719; part-time $397 per credit. Tuition, nonresident: full-time $13,419; part-time $497 per credit. *Required fees:* $548. *Financial support:* Career-related internships or fieldwork, institutionally sponsored loans, scholarships/grants, and unspecified assistantships available. *Unit head:* Dr. Eric Levin, Graduate Program Coordinator, 541-552-6364, E-mail: levine@sou.edu. *Application contact:* Kelly Moutsatson, Director of Admissions, 541-552-6411, Fax: 541-552-8403, E-mail: admissions@sou.edu. Website: http://www.sou.edu/acts/

**Stanford University,** School of Humanities and Sciences, Department of Theater and Performance Studies, Stanford, CA 94305-2004. Offers PhD. *Degree requirements:* For doctorate, one foreign language, thesis/dissertation, qualifying exams. *Entrance requirements:* For doctorate, GRE General Test, summary of production experience. Additional exam requirements/recommendations for international students: Required—TOEFL. Electronic applications accepted. *Expenses:* Tuition: Full-time $47,331. *Required fees:* $609.

**Stony Brook University, State University of New York,** Graduate School, College of Arts and Sciences, Department of Theatre Arts, Program in Dramaturgy, Stony Brook, NY 11794. Offers MFA. *Degree requirements:* For master's, one foreign language, thesis. *Entrance requirements:* For master's, GRE General Test. Additional exam requirements/recommendations for international students: Required—TOEFL. *Application deadline:* For fall admission, 1/15 for domestic students; for spring admission, 10/1 for domestic students. Application fee: $100. *Expenses:* Contact institution. *Unit head:* Dr. John Lutterbie, Chair, 631-632-7245, E-mail: john.lutterbie@stonybrook.edu. *Application contact:* Lisa Perez, Coordinator, 631-632-7270, Fax: 631-632-7261, E-mail: lisa.perez@stonybrook.edu.

**Stony Brook University, State University of New York,** Graduate School, College of Arts and Sciences, Department of Theatre Arts, Program in Theatre Arts, Stony Brook, NY 11794. Offers MA. *Program availability:* Evening/weekend. *Students:* 3 full-time (2 women), 1 international. Average age 35. 5 applicants, 80% accepted. In 2016, 2 master's awarded. *Degree requirements:* For master's, one foreign language, thesis. *Entrance requirements:* For master's, GRE General Test. Additional exam requirements/recommendations for international students: Required—TOEFL. *Application deadline:* For fall admission, 1/15 for domestic students; for spring admission, 10/1 for domestic students. Application fee: $100. *Expenses:* Contact institution. *Faculty research:* Theatre arts, theater, dramatic arts, dramatic language and or literature, theatre or film criticism. *Total annual research expenditures:* $4,476. *Unit head:* Dr. John Lutterbie, Chair, 631-632-7245, E-mail: john.lutterbie@stonybrook.edu. *Application contact:* Lisa Perez, Coordinator, 631-632-7270, Fax: 631-632-7258, E-mail: lisa.perez@stonybrook.edu. Website: http://www.stonybrook.edu/commcms/theatre-arts/academics/graduate.html

**Temple University,** Center for the Performing and Cinematic Arts, Division of Theater, Film and Media Arts, Department of Theater, Philadelphia, PA 19122. Offers acting (MFA); design (MFA); directing (MFA); musical theater collaboration (MFA); musical theater studies (MA); playwriting (MFA). *Accreditation:* NAST. *Program availability:* Part-time. *Degree requirements:* For master's, thesis (for some programs). *Entrance requirements:* For master's, minimum GPA of 3.0; audition/interview, portfolio, or samples of written work. Additional exam requirements/recommendations for international students: Required—TOEFL (minimum score 550 paper-based; 79 iBT). Electronic applications accepted. *Expenses:* Contact institution. *Faculty research:* Acting/voice/speech/movement, theatrical design and production, musical theater, directing, playwriting.

**Texas A&M University–Commerce,** College of Humanities, Social Sciences and Arts, Commerce, TX 75429-3011. Offers applied criminology (MS); applied linguistics (MA, MS); art (MA, MFA); Christianity in history (Graduate Certificate); computational linguistics (Graduate Certificate); creative writing (Graduate Certificate); English (MA, MS, PhD); film studies (Graduate Certificate); history (MA, MS); music (MM); political science (MA, MS); public history (Graduate Certificate); sociology (MS); Spanish (MA); studies in children's and adolescent literature and culture (Graduate Certificate); teaching English to speakers of other languages (Graduate Certificate); theater (MA, MS). *Program availability:* Part-time. *Faculty:* 53 full-time (26 women), 7 part-time/adjunct (2 women). *Students:* 87 full-time (55 women), 528 part-time (362 women); includes 198 minority (86 Black or African American, non-Hispanic/Latino; 2 American Indian or Alaska Native, non-Hispanic/Latino; 8 Asian, non-Hispanic/Latino; 84 Hispanic/Latino; 18 Two or more races, non-Hispanic/Latino), 27 international. Average age 37. 333 applicants, 56% accepted, 149 enrolled. In 2016, 66 master's, 8 doctorates awarded. *Degree requirements:* For master's, one foreign language, comprehensive exam, thesis (for some programs); for doctorate, one foreign language, comprehensive exam, thesis/dissertation, departmental qualifying exam. *Entrance requirements:* For master's and doctorate, GRE General Test. Additional exam requirements/recommendations for international students: Required—TOEFL (minimum score 550 paper-based; 79 iBT), IELTS (minimum score 6). *Application deadline:* Applications are processed on a rolling basis. Application fee: $50. Electronic applications accepted. *Expenses:* Contact institution. *Financial support:* In 2016–17, 255 students received support, including 9 research assistantships with partial tuition reimbursements available (averaging $9,000 per year), 68 teaching assistantships with partial tuition

reimbursements available (averaging $9,000 per year); Federal Work-Study, institutionally sponsored loans, scholarships/grants, health care benefits, and unspecified assistantships also available. Financial award application deadline: 5/1; financial award applicants required to submit FAFSA. *Unit head:* Dr. Salvatore Attardo, Dean, 903-886-5166, Fax: 903-886-5774, E-mail: salvatore.attardo@tamuc.edu. *Application contact:* Shelby Miller, Graduate Recruiter, 903-468-8123, Fax: 903-886-5774, E-mail: shelby.miller@tamuc.edu.
Website: http://www.tamuc.edu/academics/graduateSchool/programs/humanitiesSocialScienceArts/default.aspx

**Texas State University,** The Graduate College, College of Fine Arts and Communication, Program in Theatre Arts, San Marcos, TX 78666. Offers design (MFA); directing (MFA); dramatic writing (MFA); theatre history, dramatic criticism and dramaturgy (MA). *Program availability:* Part-time, evening/weekend. *Faculty:* 17 full-time (9 women), 2 part-time/adjunct. *Students:* 18 full-time (8 women), 1 (woman) part-time; includes 3 minority (2 Black or African American, non-Hispanic/Latino; 1 Two or more races, non-Hispanic/Latino). Average age 33. 25 applicants, 44% accepted, 8 enrolled. In 2016, 11 master's awarded. *Degree requirements:* For master's, comprehensive exam, thesis (for some programs). *Entrance requirements:* For master's, GRE General Test (minimum preferred score of 300), baccalaureate degree from regionally-accredited institution with minimum GPA of 2.75 in last 60 hours of undergraduate course work, 2 letters of recommendation, statement of purpose, curriculum vitae/resume; writing sample (for playwriting applicants only); interview (for directing applicants only). Additional exam requirements/recommendations for international students: Required—TOEFL (minimum score 550 paper-based; 78 iBT), IELTS (minimum score 6.5). *Application deadline:* For fall admission, 3/15 for domestic and international students. Applications are processed on a rolling basis. Application fee: $40 ($90 for international students). Electronic applications accepted. *Expenses:* $4,851 per semester. *Financial support:* In 2016–17, 18 teaching assistantships (averaging $13,246 per year) were awarded; research assistantships, Federal Work-Study, institutionally sponsored loans, scholarships/grants, and unspecified assistantships also available. Support available to part-time students. Financial award application deadline: 3/1; financial award applicants required to submit FAFSA. *Unit head:* Dr. Sandra Mayo, Graduate Advisor, 512-245-7889, Fax: 512-245-8440, E-mail: th_gradadvisor@txstate.edu. *Application contact:* Dr. Andrea Golato, Dean of Graduate School, 512-245-2581, Fax: 512-245-8365, E-mail: gradcollege@txstate.edu.
Website: http://www.theatreanddance.txstate.edu/

**Texas Tech University,** Graduate School, J.T. and Margaret Talkington College of Visual and Performing Arts, School of Theatre and Dance, Lubbock, TX 79409-2601. Offers theatre arts (MA, MFA). *Accreditation:* NAST. *Program availability:* Part-time. *Faculty:* 21 full-time (10 women), 4 part-time/adjunct (all women). *Students:* 33 full-time (21 women); includes 2 minority (1 Hispanic/Latino; 1 Two or more races, non-Hispanic/Latino), 2 international. Average age 28. 27 applicants, 52% accepted, 11 enrolled. In 2016, 9 master's awarded. *Degree requirements:* For master's, variable foreign language requirement, comprehensive exam, thesis (for some programs), direct a production (for some programs). *Entrance requirements:* For master's, GRE, samples of artistic work in area of interest and/or interview/audition with faculty (for MFA). Additional exam requirements/recommendations for international students: Required—TOEFL (minimum score 550 paper-based; 79 iBT), IELTS (minimum score 6.5), PTE (minimum score 60). *Application deadline:* For fall admission, 6/1 priority date for domestic students, 1/15 priority date for international students; for spring admission, 9/1 priority date for domestic students, 6/15 priority date for international students. Applications are processed on a rolling basis. Application fee: $75. Electronic applications accepted. *Expenses:* $325 per credit hour full-time resident tuition, $733 per credit hour full-time non-resident tuition; $53.75 per credit hour fee plus $608 per term fee. *Financial support:* In 2016–17, 39 students received support, including 33 fellowships (averaging $3,751 per year), 48 teaching assistantships (averaging $9,703 per year); research assistantships, Federal Work-Study, scholarships/grants, tuition waivers (partial), and unspecified assistantships also available. Financial award application deadline: 4/15; financial award applicants required to submit FAFSA. *Faculty research:* Translation/adaptation, early modern theatre studies, arts in medicine, Bertolt Brecht studies, devised theatre, working with diverse populations including people on the spectrum. *Total annual research expenditures:* $37,336. *Unit head:* Dr. Mark Charney, Director of Theatre and Dance, 806-742-3601, Fax: 806-742-1338, E-mail: mark.charney@ttu.edu. *Application contact:* Cory Norman, Graduate Admissions and Recruitment Coordinator, 806-834-6761, Fax: 806-742-1338, E-mail: cory.norman@ttu.edu.
Website: http://www.depts.ttu.edu/theatreanddance/

**Texas Woman's University,** Graduate School, College of Arts and Sciences, School of the Arts, Department of Music and Drama, Denton, TX 76201. Offers instrumental pedagogy (MA); instrumental performance (MA); music (MA); music education (MA); piano performance (MA); vocal pedagogy (MA); vocal performance (MA). *Accreditation:* NASM. *Program availability:* Part-time. *Students:* 44 full-time (31 women), 29 part-time (21 women); includes 22 minority (4 Black or African American, non-Hispanic/Latino; 3 Asian, non-Hispanic/Latino; 13 Hispanic/Latino; 2 Two or more races, non-Hispanic/Latino), 3 international. Average age 29. In 2016, 18 master's awarded. *Degree requirements:* For master's, comprehensive exam, thesis (for some programs), project recital, professional paper. *Entrance requirements:* For master's, music history/theory placement exam (for music only), audition and/or design portfolio, interview, resume, writing sample (for drama only). Additional exam requirements/recommendations for international students: Required—TOEFL (minimum score 550 paper-based; 79 iBT). *Application deadline:* For fall admission, 7/1 priority date for domestic students, 3/1 for international students; for spring admission, 12/1 priority date for domestic students, 7/1 for international students. Applications are processed on a rolling basis. Application fee: $50 ($75 for international students). Electronic applications accepted. *Expenses:* Tuition, state resident: full-time $9046; part-time $251 per credit hour. Tuition, nonresident: full-time $22,922; part-time $614 per credit hour. *International tuition:* $23,046 full-time. *Required fees:* $2690; $1285 per credit hour. One-time fee: $50. Tuition and fees vary according to course level, course load, program and reciprocity agreements. *Financial support:* Research assistantships, career-related internships or fieldwork, Federal Work-Study, institutionally sponsored loans, scholarships/grants, traineeships, health care benefits, tuition waivers (partial), and unspecified assistantships available. Support available to part-time students. Financial award application deadline: 3/1; financial award applicants required to submit FAFSA. *Faculty research:* Musical development in early childhood, little known or neglected compositions for flute (especially by women composers), relationship of visual art to piano music, pedagogical development of the singing voice, guided imagery and music. *Unit head:* Dr. Pamela Youngblood, Chair, 940-898-2495, Fax: 940-898-2494, E-mail: pyoungblood@twu.edu. *Application contact:* Dr. Samuel Wheeler, Assistant Director of Admissions, 940-898-3188, Fax: 940-898-3081, E-mail: wheelersr@twu.edu.

**Towson University,** Program in Theatre, Towson, MD 21252-0001. Offers MFA. *Accreditation:* NAST. *Students:* 6 full-time (5 women), 1 international. *Degree requirements:* For master's, thesis. *Entrance requirements:* For master's, minimum GPA of 3.0, bachelor's degree, 3 letters of recommendation, artistic statement, current professional resume, 3 references, portfolio, interview. *Application deadline:* For fall

admission, 3/1 for domestic students. Application fee: $45. Electronic applications accepted. *Expenses:* Tuition, state resident: full-time $7580; part-time $379 per unit. Tuition, nonresident: full-time $15,700; part-time $785 per unit. *Required fees:* $2480. *Financial support:* Application deadline: 4/1. *Unit head:* Prof. Naoko Maeshiba, Graduate Program Director, 410-704-2791, E-mail: nmaeshiba@towson.edu. *Application contact:* Coverley Beidleman, Assistant Director of Graduate Admissions, 410-704-2113, Fax: 410-704-3030, E-mail: grads@towson.edu.
Website: http://www.towson.edu/cofac/departments/theatre/gradtheatre/

**Tufts University,** Graduate School of Arts and Sciences, Department of Drama and Dance, Medford, MA 02155. Offers drama (MA, PhD). *Students:* 24 full-time (16 women); includes 2 minority (1 Black or African American, non-Hispanic/Latino; 1 Two or more races, non-Hispanic/Latino), 4 international. Average age 31. 25 applicants, 40% accepted, 4 enrolled. In 2016, 2 master's, 7 doctorates awarded. Terminal master's awarded for partial completion of doctoral program. *Degree requirements:* For master's, one foreign language, thesis; for doctorate, one foreign language, thesis/dissertation, oral exam, written general exam. *Entrance requirements:* For master's and doctorate, GRE General Test, writing sample. Additional exam requirements/recommendations for international students: Required—TOEFL (minimum score 600 paper-based; 80 iBT), IELTS (minimum score 6.5). *Application deadline:* For fall admission, 1/15 for domestic and international students. Applications are processed on a rolling basis. Application fee: $85. Electronic applications accepted. *Expenses:* $49,982 full-time tuition (for MA); $29,936 full-time tuition (for PhD). *Financial support:* In 2016–17, 23 students received support. Fellowships, teaching assistantships, Federal Work-Study, scholarships/grants, tuition waivers (full and partial), and unspecified assistantships available. Financial award application deadline: 1/15. *Unit head:* Dr. Noe Montez, Graduate Program Director. *Application contact:* Office of Graduate Admissions, 617-627-3395, E-mail: gradadmissions@tufts.edu.
Website: http://www.tufts.edu/as/drama/

**Tulane University,** School of Liberal Arts, Department of Theatre and Dance, New Orleans, LA 70118-5669. Offers design and technical production (MFA). *Entrance requirements:* For master's, GRE General Test, minimum B average in undergraduate course work. Additional exam requirements/recommendations for international students: Required—TOEFL. Electronic applications accepted. *Expenses:* Tuition: Full-time $50,920; part-time $2829 per credit hour. *Required fees:* $2040; $44.50 per credit hour. $580 per term. Tuition and fees vary according to course load, degree level and program. *Faculty research:* Scene design, stage management, costume design, technical direction, lighting design.

**Université de Sherbrooke,** Faculty of Letters and Human Sciences, Department of Letters and Communications, Sherbrooke, QC J1K 2R1, Canada. Offers comparative Canadian literature (MA, PhD); French literature (MA, PhD); linguistics (MA); theatre (MA). *Degree requirements:* For master's, thesis or alternative; for doctorate, thesis/dissertation. *Entrance requirements:* For master's, minimum GPA of 2.8; for doctorate, minimum GPA of 3.0.

**Université Laval,** Faculty of Letters, Department of Literature, Programs in Literature and Arts of the Screen and Stage, Québec, QC G1K 7P4, Canada. Offers MA, PhD. *Program availability:* Part-time. Terminal master's awarded for partial completion of doctoral program. *Degree requirements:* For master's, thesis; for doctorate, comprehensive exam, thesis/dissertation. *Entrance requirements:* For master's and doctorate, linguistics exams, knowledge of French, knowledge of a second language. Electronic applications accepted.

**University at Buffalo, the State University of New York,** Graduate School, College of Arts and Sciences, Department of Theatre and Dance, Buffalo, NY 14260. Offers theatre and performance (MA, PhD). *Program availability:* Part-time. *Degree requirements:* For master's, thesis project or written thesis; for doctorate, one foreign language, comprehensive exam, thesis/dissertation. *Entrance requirements:* For master's, statement of purpose; academic writing sample (e.g., scholarly essay, performance or book review); 3 letters of recommendation (sent electronically); portfolio of creative work; resume; completed BA, BFA, or BS; for doctorate, GRE, statement of purpose; academic writing sample (e.g., scholarly essay, performance or book review); 3 letters of recommendation (sent electronically); portfolio of creative work; resume; completed MA. Additional exam requirements/recommendations for international students: Required—TOEFL (minimum score 550 paper-based). Electronic applications accepted. *Faculty research:* Intermediality in theatre and performance; contemporary performance and theory; intersections of technology and performance; performances of authenticity and realness in intermedial theater, reality television, and immersive and pervasive gaming; digital dramaturgy; American theaters of the everyday.

**The University of Akron,** Graduate School, Buchtel College of Arts and Sciences, School of Dance, Theatre, and Arts Administration, Akron, OH 44325. Offers arts administration (MA); theatre arts (MA). *Program availability:* Part-time, evening/weekend. *Faculty:* 3 full-time (1 woman), 22 part-time/adjunct (13 women). *Students:* 16 full-time (13 women), 7 part-time (6 women); includes 4 minority (3 Black or African American, non-Hispanic/Latino; 1 Two or more races, non-Hispanic/Latino), 2 international. Average age 29. 17 applicants, 76% accepted, 11 enrolled. In 2016, 8 master's awarded. *Degree requirements:* For master's, thesis. *Entrance requirements:* For master's, minimum GPA of 2.75, 300-word statement of intent summarizing student background and outlining career goals. Additional exam requirements/recommendations for international students: Required—TOEFL (minimum score 550 paper-based; 79 iBT), IELTS (minimum score 6.5). *Application deadline:* For fall admission, 3/15 for domestic and international students. Application fee: $45 ($70 for international students). Electronic applications accepted. *Expenses:* Tuition, state resident: full-time $8618; part-time $359 per credit hour. Tuition, nonresident: full-time $17,149; part-time $715 per credit hour. *Required fees:* $1652. *Financial support:* In 2016–17, 1 teaching assistantship with full tuition reimbursement was awarded; instructional support assistantships also available. *Faculty research:* Theatre history; technical theatre; set, costume, and design; lighting; playwriting. *Total annual research expenditures:* $5,908. *Unit head:* Dr. J. Thomas Dukes, Interim Director, 330-972-7948, E-mail: jtdukes@uakron.edu. *Application contact:* Elisa Gargarella, Coordinator, Arts Administration, 330-972-8325, E-mail: gelisa@uakron.edu.
Website: http://www.uakron.edu/dtaa/

**The University of Alabama,** Graduate School, College of Arts and Sciences, Department of Theatre and Dance, Tuscaloosa, AL 35487. Offers acting (MFA); costume design (MFA); directing (MFA); scene design/technical production (MFA); stage management (MFA); theatre (MFA); theatre management/administration (MFA). *Accreditation:* NAST. *Faculty:* 16 full-time (8 women). *Students:* 35 full-time (19 women), 1 part-time (0 women); includes 6 minority (3 Black or African American, non-Hispanic/Latino; 3 Hispanic/Latino), 1 international. Average age 29. 22 applicants, 41% accepted, 7 enrolled. In 2016, 11 master's awarded. *Degree requirements:* For master's, thesis project. *Entrance requirements:* For master's, audition and/or portfolio review. *Application deadline:* For fall admission, 4/1 priority date for domestic students, 3/1 priority date for international students. Applications are processed on a rolling basis. Application fee: $50 ($60 for international students). Electronic applications accepted. *Expenses:* Tuition, state resident: full-time $10,470. Tuition, nonresident: full-time $26,950. *Financial support:* In 2016–17, 21 research assistantships with full tuition

## Theater

reimbursements (averaging $13,140 per year), 19 teaching assistantships with full tuition reimbursements (averaging $13,140 per year) were awarded; career-related internships or fieldwork, health care benefits, and unspecified assistantships also available. Financial award application deadline: 4/15. *Faculty research:* Acting, theatre history, directing, design practice and production (scenery, costumes, and lighting), technical direction and production, theatre management. *Total annual research expenditures:* $2,925. *Unit head:* Prof. William Teague, Chair and Professor, 205-348-5283, Fax: 205-348-9048, E-mail: wteague@ua.edu. *Application contact:* Nancy Calvert, Recruiting Contact, 205-348-5283, Fax: 205-348-9048, E-mail: ncalvert@ua.edu.
Website: http://www.as.ua.edu/theatre/

**University of Alberta,** Faculty of Graduate Studies and Research, Department of Drama, Edmonton, AB T6G 2E1, Canada. Offers design (MFA); directing (MFA); drama (MA). *Degree requirements:* For master's, one foreign language, production thesis. *Faculty research:* Dramaturgy, history, theory and criticism, design.

**The University of Arizona,** College of Fine Arts, School of Theatre, Film and Television, Tucson, AZ 85721. Offers MFA. *Accreditation:* NAST. *Degree requirements:* For master's, comprehensive exam (for some programs), thesis (for some programs), production monograph. *Entrance requirements:* For master's, 3 letters of recommendation, portfolio. Additional exam requirements/recommendations for international students: Required—TOEFL (minimum score 550 paper-based; 79 iBT). Electronic applications accepted. *Faculty research:* Modern and contemporary theater, cultural studies, musical theater, women and theater.

**University of Arkansas,** Graduate School, J. William Fulbright College of Arts and Sciences, Department of Theatre, Fayetteville, AR 72701. Offers MA, MFA. In 2016, 9 master's awarded. *Degree requirements:* For master's, thesis optional. *Application deadline:* For fall admission, 4/1 for international students; for spring admission, 10/1 for international students. Applications are processed on a rolling basis. Application fee: $40 ($50 for international students). Electronic applications accepted. *Financial support:* In 2016–17, 9 research assistantships, 11 teaching assistantships were awarded; fellowships with tuition reimbursements, career-related internships or fieldwork, and Federal Work-Study also available. Support available to part-time students. Financial award application deadline: 4/1; financial award applicants required to submit FAFSA. *Unit head:* Dr. Michael Riha, Department Chairperson, 479-575-2953, Fax: 479-575-7602, E-mail: mriha@uark.edu. *Application contact:* Les Wade, 479-575-2293, Fax: 575-7602, E-mail: law018@uark.edu.
Website: http://drama.uark.edu/

**The University of British Columbia,** Faculty of Arts, Creative Writing Program, Vancouver, BC V6T 1Z1, Canada. Offers creative writing (MFA); creative writing and theatre (MFA); film production and creative writing (MFA). *Program availability:* Part-time, online learning. *Degree requirements:* For master's, thesis. *Entrance requirements:* For master's, sample of written work. Additional exam requirements/recommendations for international students: Required—TOEFL. Application fee: $100 Canadian dollars ($162 Canadian dollars for international students). Electronic applications accepted. *Expenses:* $4,802 per year tuition and fees, $8,436 per year international; $592 per credit, $996 per credit international (online). *Financial support:* Fellowships, teaching assistantships, Federal Work-Study, institutionally sponsored loans, and unspecified assistantships available. *Faculty research:* Writing of fiction; poetry, creative nonfiction, plays for stage, screen, television, radio, writing for children and translation, song lyrics and libretto, new media and graphic novel. *Application contact:* Heather Miller, Graduate Program Staff, 604-822-0699, E-mail: crwr.grad@ubc.ca.
Website: http://creativewriting.ubc.ca/

**The University of British Columbia,** Faculty of Arts and Faculty of Graduate Studies, Department of Theatre and Film, Theatre Program, Vancouver, BC V6T 1Z2, Canada. Offers theatre (MA, PhD); theatre design (MFA); theatre directing (MFA). Terminal master's awarded for partial completion of doctoral program. *Degree requirements:* For master's, variable foreign language requirement, comprehensive exam, thesis; for doctorate, one foreign language, comprehensive exam, thesis/dissertation. *Entrance requirements:* For master's, portfolio (MFA); for doctorate, MA or equivalent. Additional exam requirements/recommendations for international students: Required—TOEFL (minimum score 550 paper-based for MFA; 600 for MA and PhD). Application fee: $100 Canadian dollars ($162 Canadian dollars for international students). *Expenses:* $4,802 per year tuition and fees, $8,436 per year international. *Financial support:* Fellowships, research assistantships, and teaching assistantships available. *Faculty research:* Devising theatre; Canadian theatre; multicultural and theatre arts; stage lighting and costume design. *Application contact:* Karen Tong, Graduate Program Staff, 604-822-6342, Fax: 604-822-5985, E-mail: thtr.sec@ubc.ca.
Website: http://theatrefilm.ubc.ca/

**University of Calgary,** Faculty of Graduate Studies, Faculty of Arts, Department of Drama, Calgary, AB T2N 1N4, Canada. Offers design and technical theatre (MFA); directing (MFA); playwriting (MFA); theatre studies (MFA). *Degree requirements:* For master's, thesis. *Entrance requirements:* For master's, bachelor's degree in drama, minimum GPA of 3.0, portfolio (design and playwriting). Additional exam requirements/recommendations for international students: Required—TOEFL. *Faculty research:* Popular theatre, collective creation, technical design, dramaturgy, directing styles.

**University of California, Berkeley,** Graduate Division, College of Letters and Science, Group in Performance Studies, Berkeley, CA 94720-1500. Offers PhD. *Faculty:* 23 full-time. *Students:* 24 full-time (18 women); includes 9 minority (2 Black or African American, non-Hispanic/Latino; 1 American Indian or Alaska Native, non-Hispanic/Latino; 3 Asian, non-Hispanic/Latino; 3 Hispanic/Latino), 5 international. Average age 30. 63 applicants, 2 enrolled. In 2016, 1 doctorate awarded. *Degree requirements:* For doctorate, one foreign language, thesis/dissertation, qualifying exam. *Entrance requirements:* For doctorate, GRE General Test, sample of critical writing, 3 letters of recommendation. Additional exam requirements/recommendations for international students: Required—TOEFL. *Application deadline:* For fall admission, 12/1 for domestic students. Application fee: $105 ($125 for international students). Electronic applications accepted. *Financial support:* Fellowships, research assistantships, teaching assistantships with tuition reimbursements, institutionally sponsored loans, health care benefits, and unspecified assistantships available. Financial award applicants required to submit FAFSA. *Faculty research:* Postcolonial performance; gender, sexuality, and performance; political performance; dramatic literature and theory; race, ethnicity, performance. *Unit head:* Prof. Lisa Wymore, Chair, 510-642-1677, E-mail: tdps@berkely.edu. *Application contact:* Robin Davidson, Graduate Assistant for Admission, 510-642-4050, E-mail: phdprogram@theater.berkeley.edu.
Website: http://tdps.berkeley.edu/

**University of California, Davis,** Graduate Studies, Program in Dramatic Art, Davis, CA 95616. Offers acting (MFA); dramatic art (PhD). *Entrance requirements:* For master's, minimum GPA of 3.0, portfolio. Additional exam requirements/recommendations for international students: Required—TOEFL (minimum score 550 paper-based). Electronic applications accepted. *Faculty research:* Twentieth century performance and culture.

**University of California, Davis,** Graduate Studies, Program in Performance Studies, Davis, CA 95616. Offers dramatic art (PhD). *Degree requirements:* For doctorate, 2 foreign languages, thesis/dissertation. *Entrance requirements:* For doctorate, GRE, minimum GPA of 3.25. Additional exam requirements/recommendations for international students: Required—TOEFL (minimum score 550 paper-based). Electronic applications accepted.

**University of California, Irvine,** Claire Trevor School of the Arts, Department of Drama, Irvine, CA 92697. Offers acting (MFA); design and stage management (MFA); directing (MFA); drama (MFA); drama and theatre (PhD). *Students:* 70 full-time (37 women), 3 part-time (2 women); includes 25 minority (3 Black or African American, non-Hispanic/Latino; 4 Asian, non-Hispanic/Latino; 12 Hispanic/Latino; 6 Two or more races, non-Hispanic/Latino), 1 international. Average age 28. 216 applicants, 12% accepted, 23 enrolled. In 2016, 22 master's, 2 doctorates awarded. *Degree requirements:* For master's, comprehensive exam, thesis; for doctorate, one foreign language, thesis/dissertation. *Entrance requirements:* For master's, audition, interview, or portfolio; minimum GPA of 3.0; for doctorate, GRE, minimum GPA of 3.5, critical writing samples. *Application deadline:* For fall admission, 1/15 priority date for domestic students, 1/15 for international students. Applications are processed on a rolling basis. Application fee: $105 ($125 for international students). Electronic applications accepted. *Financial support:* Fellowships, teaching assistantships, institutionally sponsored loans, traineeships, health care benefits, and unspecified assistantships available. Financial award application deadline: 3/1; financial award applicants required to submit FAFSA. *Faculty research:* Costume, scenery, and lighting design; production; theatre history, literature, and criticism. *Unit head:* Daniel Gary Busby, Department Chair, 949-824-8243, Fax: 949-824-3475, E-mail: dgbusby@uci.edu. *Application contact:* Prof. Stephen F. Barker, Interim Dean, 949-824-5684, Fax: 949-824-2450, E-mail: barker@uci.edu.
Website: http://www.arts.uci.edu/ctsa-academic-departments-drama

**University of California, Los Angeles,** Graduate Division, School of Theater, Film and Television, Department of Theater, Los Angeles, CA 90095. Offers theater (MA, MFA); theater and performance studies (PhD). *Accreditation:* NAST. *Degree requirements:* For master's, comprehensive exam or thesis; for doctorate, one foreign language, thesis/dissertation, oral and written qualifying exams. *Entrance requirements:* For master's, bachelor's degree; minimum undergraduate GPA of 3.0 (or its equivalent if letter grade system not used); portfolio (MFA); writing sample (MA); for doctorate, GRE General Test, bachelor's degree; minimum undergraduate GPA of 3.0 (or its equivalent if letter grade system not used); writing sample. Additional exam requirements/recommendations for international students: Required—TOEFL. Electronic applications accepted. *Expenses:* Contact institution.

**University of California, San Diego,** Graduate Division, Department of Theatre and Dance, La Jolla, CA 92093. Offers acting (MFA); contemporary dance and performance (MFA); design (MFA); directing (MFA); drama and theatre (PhD); playwriting (MFA); stage management (MFA). PhD offered jointly with University of California, Irvine. *Students:* 75 full-time (42 women). 497 applicants, 6% accepted, 20 enrolled. In 2016, 24 master's, 1 doctorate awarded. *Degree requirements:* For master's, thesis; for doctorate, comprehensive exam, thesis/dissertation. *Entrance requirements:* For master's, GRE General Test (for playwriting only), minimum GPA of 3.5; audition or interview; for doctorate, GRE General Test, minimum GPA of 3.5, audition and/or interview, two samples of critical writing. Additional exam requirements/recommendations for international students: Required—TOEFL (minimum score 550 paper-based; 80 iBT), IELTS (minimum score 7). *Application deadline:* For fall admission, 1/8 for domestic students. Application fee: $105 ($125 for international students). Electronic applications accepted. *Expenses:* Tuition, state resident: full-time $11,220. Tuition, nonresident: full-time $26,322. *Required fees:* $1864. *Financial support:* Fellowships, teaching assistantships, and scholarships/grants available. Financial award applicants required to submit FAFSA. *Faculty research:* Theatre of the Americas, European theatre, Asian theatre, gender studies, critical theory. *Unit head:* Charles Means, Chair, 858-534-2062, E-mail: chmeans@ucsd.edu. *Application contact:* Marybeth Ward, Graduate Coordinator, 858-534-1046, E-mail: meward@ucsd.edu.
Website: http://theatre.ucsd.edu/

**University of California, Santa Barbara,** Graduate Division, College of Letters and Sciences, Division of Humanities and Fine Arts, Department of Theater and Dance, Santa Barbara, CA 93106-7060. Offers theater studies (MA, PhD), including European medieval studies (PhD), feminist studies (PhD), theatre studies (PhD); MA/PhD. Terminal master's awarded for partial completion of doctoral program. *Degree requirements:* For master's, comprehensive exam, thesis; for doctorate, one foreign language, comprehensive exam, thesis/dissertation. *Entrance requirements:* For master's and doctorate, GRE. Additional exam requirements/recommendations for international students: Required—TOEFL (minimum score 550 paper-based; 80 iBT), IELTS (minimum score 7). Electronic applications accepted. *Faculty research:* English and American theater and Ancient Greek; Spanish, Latin American and Caribbean performance; Renaissance and Baroque drama and intercultural theory; East Asian performance, gender and nationalism; Korean cultural studies, Russian literature, and Slavic folklore; history of German theater, Shakespeare, and European opera; postcolonialism, performance-based ethnography, globalism and national identity formation in Africa.

**University of California, Santa Cruz,** Division of Graduate Studies, Division of the Arts, Department of Theater Arts, Santa Cruz, CA 95064. Offers Certificate. *Entrance requirements:* Additional exam requirements/recommendations for international students: Required—TOEFL (minimum score 550 paper-based; 83 iBT); Recommended—IELTS (minimum score 8). Electronic applications accepted.

**University of Central Florida,** College of Arts and Humanities, School of Performing Arts, Orlando, FL 32816. Offers music (MA); theatre (MA, MFA), including acting (MFA), theatre for young audiences (MFA). *Accreditation:* NASM; NCATE. *Program availability:* Part-time. *Faculty:* 53 full-time (20 women), 13 part-time/adjunct (6 women). *Students:* 34 full-time (20 women), 18 part-time (10 women); includes 7 minority (5 Hispanic/Latino; 2 Two or more races, non-Hispanic/Latino), 5 international. Average age 31. 55 applicants, 51% accepted, 20 enrolled. In 2016, 18 master's awarded. *Degree requirements:* For master's, comprehensive exam. *Entrance requirements:* For master's, GRE General Test. Additional exam requirements/recommendations for international students: Required—TOEFL. *Application deadline:* For fall admission, 7/15 for domestic students; for spring admission, 12/1 for domestic students. Application fee: $30. Electronic applications accepted. *Expenses:* Tuition, state resident: part-time $288.16 per credit hour. Tuition, nonresident: part-time $1071.31 per credit hour. *Financial support:* In 2016–17, 28 students received support, including 6 fellowships with partial tuition reimbursements available (averaging $7,167 per year), 6 research assistantships with partial tuition reimbursements available (averaging $9,088 per year), 20 teaching assistantships with partial tuition reimbursements available (averaging $8,267 per year); career-related internships or fieldwork, Federal Work-Study, institutionally sponsored loans, tuition waivers (partial), and unspecified assistantships also available. Financial award application deadline: 3/1; financial award applicants required to submit FAFSA. *Unit head:* Dr. Steven Chicurel-Stein, Interim Director, 407-823-2519, Fax: 407-823-3378, E-mail: steven.chicurel@ucf.edu. *Application contact:* Assistant Director, Graduate Admissions, 407-823-2766, Fax: 407-823-6442, E-mail:

gradadmissions@ucf.edu.
Website: http://performingarts.cah.ucf.edu/

**University of Central Missouri,** The Graduate School, Warrensburg, MO 64093. Offers accountancy (MA); accounting (MBA); applied mathematics (MS); aviation safety (MA); biology (MS); business administration (MBA); career and technical education leadership (MS); college student personnel administration (MS); communication (MA); computer science (MS); counseling (MS); criminal justice (MS); educational leadership (Ed D); educational technology (MS); elementary and early childhood education (MSE); English (MA); environmental studies (MA); finance (MBA); history (MA); human services/ educational technology (Ed S); human services/learning resources (Ed S); human services/professional counseling (Ed S); industrial hygiene (MS); industrial management (MS); information systems (MBA); information technology (MS); kinesiology (MS); library science and information services (MS); literacy education (MSE); marketing (MBA); mathematics (MS); music (MA); occupational safety management (MS); psychology (MS); rural family nursing (MS); school administration (MSE); social gerontology (MS); sociology (MA); special education (MSE); speech language pathology (MS); superintendency (Ed S); teaching (MAT); teaching English as a second language (MA); technology (MS); technology management (PhD); theatre (MA). *Program availability:* Part-time, 100% online, blended/hybrid learning. *Degree requirements:* For master's and Ed S, comprehensive exam (for some programs), thesis (for some programs). *Entrance requirements:* Additional exam requirements/recommendations for international students: Required—TOEFL (minimum score 550 paper-based; 79 iBT). Electronic applications accepted.

**University of Chicago,** Division of the Humanities, Master of Arts Program in the Humanities, Chicago, IL 60637. Offers art history (MA); cinema and media studies (MA); classic languages (MA); comparative literature (MA); creative writing (MA); cultural policy studies (MA); digital humanities (MA); East Asian languages and civilizations (MA); English language and literature (MA); gender and sexuality studies (MA); Germanic studies (MA); linguistics (MA); music (MA); near Eastern languages and civilizations (MA); philosophy (MA); poetics (MA); race, politics and culture (MA); Romance languages and literatures (MA); Slavic languages and literatures (MA); South Asian languages and civilizations (MA); theater and performance studies (MA). *Students:* 80 full-time (43 women), 7 part-time (3 women); includes 20 minority (5 Black or African American, non-Hispanic/Latino; 1 American Indian or Alaska Native, non-Hispanic/Latino; 6 Asian, non-Hispanic/Latino; 5 Hispanic/Latino; 3 Two or more races, non-Hispanic/Latino), 11 international. Average age 26. 706 applicants, 15% accepted, 42 enrolled. In 2016, 92 master's awarded. *Degree requirements:* For master's, thesis. *Entrance requirements:* For master's, GRE General Test. Additional exam requirements/ recommendations for international students: Required—TOEFL (minimum score 104 iBT), IELTS (minimum score 7). *Application deadline:* For fall admission, 1/3 for domestic and international students. Application fee: $90. Electronic applications accepted. *Financial support:* In 2016–17, 8 fellowships with partial tuition reimbursements (averaging $12,000 per year) were awarded; Federal Work-Study, institutionally sponsored loans, scholarships/grants, and tuition waivers (partial) also available. Financial award application deadline: 12/15; financial award applicants required to submit FAFSA. *Unit head:* Malynne Sternstein, Co-Director, 773-834-1201, Fax: 773-834-7526. *Application contact:* Program Coordinator, 773-834-1201, Fax: 773-834-7526, E-mail: ma-humanities@uchicago.edu.
Website: http://maph.uchicago.edu/

**University of Cincinnati,** Graduate School, College-Conservatory of Music, Division of Theatre Arts, Production and Arts Administration, Cincinnati, OH 45221. Offers arts administration (MA); directing (MFA); theater design and production (MFA); voice and opera (MM, DMA); MBA/MA. *Accreditation:* NAST (one or more programs are accredited). *Degree requirements:* For master's, final project. *Entrance requirements:* For master's, GMAT (MA), audition/interview. Additional exam requirements/ recommendations for international students: Required—TOEFL (minimum score 520 paper-based). Electronic applications accepted. *Expenses: Tuition, area resident:* Full-time $12,790; part-time $389 per credit hour. *Tuition, state resident:* full-time $13,290; part-time $419 per credit hour. *Tuition, nonresident:* full-time $24,532; part-time $976 per credit hour. *International tuition:* $24,832 full-time. *Required fees:* $3958; $140 per credit hour. Tuition and fees vary according to course load, degree level, program and reciprocity agreements.

**University of Colorado Boulder,** Graduate School, College of Arts and Sciences, Department of Theatre and Dance, Boulder, CO 80309. Offers dance (MFA); theatre (MA, PhD). *Faculty:* 16 full-time (8 women). *Students:* 34 full-time (27 women), 1 part-time (0 women); includes 8 minority (3 Black or African American, non-Hispanic/Latino; 1 Asian, non-Hispanic/Latino; 4 Hispanic/Latino). Average age 32. 39 applicants, 51% accepted, 9 enrolled. In 2016, 10 master's, 2 doctorates awarded. Terminal master's awarded for partial completion of doctoral program. *Degree requirements:* For master's, comprehensive exam, thesis; for doctorate, one foreign language, thesis/dissertation. *Entrance requirements:* For master's, GRE General Test (MA), audition (MFA), minimum undergraduate GPA of 2.75. *Application deadline:* For fall admission, 12/15 for domestic students, 12/1 for international students. Application fee: $60 ($80 for international students). Electronic applications accepted. Application fee is waived when completed online. *Financial support:* In 2016–17, 103 students received support, including 27 fellowships (averaging $2,814 per year), 31 teaching assistantships with full and partial tuition reimbursements available (averaging $27,201 per year); institutionally sponsored loans, scholarships/grants, health care benefits, and unspecified assistantships also available. Financial award application deadline: 1/15; financial award applicants required to submit FAFSA. *Faculty research:* Performing arts, drama, dramatic/theatre arts, choreography, dance. *Application contact:* E-mail: wendy.franz@colorado.edu.
Website: http://www.colorado.edu/theatredance/

**University of Connecticut,** Graduate School, School of Fine Arts, Department of Dramatic Arts, Storrs, CT 06269. Offers acting (MA, MFA); design (MA, MFA); puppetry (MA, MFA); technical direction (MA, MFA). *Degree requirements:* For master's, comprehensive exam. *Entrance requirements:* Additional exam requirements/ recommendations for international students: Required—TOEFL (minimum score 550 paper-based). Electronic applications accepted.

**University of Delaware,** College of Arts and Sciences, Professional Theatre Training Program, Newark, DE 19716. Offers acting (MFA); stage management (MFA); technical production (MFA). Students are matriculated into program once every three years. *Entrance requirements:* For master's, audition, interview. Electronic applications accepted. *Faculty research:* Theatre training, acting, technical production, stage management.

**University of Florida,** Graduate School, College of The Arts, School of Theatre and Dance, Gainesville, FL 32611. Offers theatre (MFA), including acting, costume design, lighting design, scene design. *Accreditation:* NAST. *Program availability:* Online learning. *Degree requirements:* For master's, thesis, creative project. *Entrance requirements:* For master's, GRE General Test, audition/portfolio, bachelor's degree in theatre, interview, minimum GPA 3.0. Additional exam requirements/recommendations for international students: Required—TOEFL (minimum score 550 paper-based; 80 iBT),

IELTS (minimum score 6). Electronic applications accepted. *Faculty research:* Aesthetics of lighting design for the theater, production, history of theatre, criticism.

**University of Georgia,** Franklin College of Arts and Sciences, Department of Theatre and Film Studies, Athens, GA 30602. Offers theatre (MFA, PhD). *Accreditation:* NAST. *Degree requirements:* For master's, comprehensive exam; for doctorate, one foreign language, comprehensive exam, thesis/dissertation. *Entrance requirements:* For master's and doctorate, GRE General Test. Additional exam requirements/ recommendations for international students: Required—TOEFL (minimum score 550 paper-based). *Application deadline:* For fall admission, 7/1 for domestic students, 4/15 for international students; for winter admission, 11/15 for domestic students, 10/15 for international students; for spring admission, 5/1 for domestic students, 2/15 for international students. Application fee: $50. Electronic applications accepted. *Financial support:* Fellowships, research assistantships with full tuition reimbursements, teaching assistantships with full tuition reimbursements, health care benefits, and unspecified assistantships available. Financial award application deadline: 2/15. *Faculty research:* Digital media, African-American theatre, Indian theatre, history of animation, Vaudeville and popular culture history. *Unit head:* Dr. David Z. Saltz, Head, 706-542-2836, Fax: 706-542-2080, E-mail: saltz@uga.edu. *Application contact:* Marla Carlson, Graduate Coordinator, 706-542-2093, E-mail: marlac@uga.edu.
Website: http://www.drama.uga.edu/

**University of Guelph,** Graduate Studies, College of Arts, School of English and Theatre Studies, Program in Drama, Guelph, ON N1G 2W1, Canada. Offers MA. *Program availability:* Part-time. *Degree requirements:* For master's, thesis (for some programs). *Entrance requirements:* For master's, 2 letters of reference, 4 year honours undergraduate degree in English or drama. Additional exam requirements/ recommendations for international students: Required—TOEFL. Electronic applications accepted. *Faculty research:* Canadian theatre, Renaissance, nineteenth- and twentieth-century drama and theatre, Shaw, theatre history, dramatic literature, performance theory.

**University of Hawaii at Manoa,** Graduate Division, College of Arts and Humanities, Department of Theatre and Dance, Honolulu, HI 96822. Offers dance (MA, MFA); theatre (MA, MFA, PhD). *Program availability:* Part-time. *Degree requirements:* For master's, one foreign language, thesis optional; for doctorate, one foreign language, comprehensive exam, thesis/dissertation. *Entrance requirements:* For master's and doctorate, GRE General Test. Additional exam requirements/recommendations for international students: Required—TOEFL (minimum score 600 paper-based; 100 iBT), IELTS (minimum score 7). *Faculty research:* Asian theatre, feminist theatre and dance, Russian theatre, Australian theatre.

**University of Houston,** College of Liberal Arts and Social Sciences, School of Theatre and Dance, Houston, TX 77204. Offers theatre (MA, MFA). *Program availability:* Part-time. *Degree requirements:* For master's, thesis optional. *Entrance requirements:* For master's, GRE General Test, audition/interview (for MFA). Electronic applications accepted.

**University of Idaho,** College of Graduate Studies, College of Letters, Arts and Social Sciences, Department of Theatre Arts, Moscow, ID 83844. Offers theatre arts (MFA). *Faculty:* 8 full-time, 1 part-time/adjunct. *Students:* 24 full-time (11 women). Average age 33. In 2016, 3 master's awarded. *Entrance requirements:* For master's, minimum GPA of 3.0. Additional exam requirements/recommendations for international students: Required—TOEFL. *Application deadline:* For fall admission, 8/1 for domestic students; for spring admission, 12/15 for domestic students. Applications are processed on a rolling basis. Application fee: $60. Electronic applications accepted. *Expenses:* Tuition, state resident: full-time $6460; part-time $414 per credit hour. Tuition, nonresident: full-time $21,268; part-time $1237 per credit hour. *Required fees:* $2070; $60 per credit hour. Full-time tuition and fees vary according to course load and reciprocity agreements. *Financial support:* Research assistantships and teaching assistantships available. Financial award applicants required to submit FAFSA. *Unit head:* Dr. Ann Hoste, Chair, 208-885-5182, E-mail: theatre@uidaho.edu. *Application contact:* Sean Scoggin, Graduate Recruitment Coordinator, 208-885-4723, E-mail: graduateadmissions@uidaho.edu.
Website: https://www.uidaho.edu/class/theatre

**University of Illinois at Urbana–Champaign,** Graduate College, College of Fine and Applied Arts, Department of Theatre, Champaign, IL 61820. Offers MA, MFA, PhD.

**The University of Iowa,** Graduate College, College of Liberal Arts and Sciences, Department of Theatre Arts, Iowa City, IA 52242-1316. Offers MFA. *Accreditation:* NAST. *Degree requirements:* For master's, thesis, exam. *Entrance requirements:* For master's, minimum GPA of 3.0. Additional exam requirements/recommendations for international students: Required—TOEFL (minimum score 550 paper-based; 81 iBT). Electronic applications accepted.

**The University of Kansas,** Graduate Studies, College of Liberal Arts and Sciences, Department of Theatre, Lawrence, KS 66045. Offers theatre (MA, PhD); theatre design (MFA), including scenography. *Program availability:* Part-time. *Students:* 17 full-time (12 women), 3 part-time (all women); includes 6 minority (3 Black or African American, non-Hispanic/Latino; 1 American Indian or Alaska Native, non-Hispanic/Latino; 2 Hispanic/Latino), 3 international. Average age 30. 26 applicants, 73% accepted, 8 enrolled. In 2016, 1 master's, 3 doctorates awarded. *Entrance requirements:* For master's and doctorate, GRE General Test, official transcript, three recent letters of recommendation, current resume, statement of personal goals, writing sample. Additional exam requirements/recommendations for international students: Required—TOEFL. *Application deadline:* For fall admission, 1/1 priority date for domestic and international students. Application fee: $65 ($85 for international students). Electronic applications accepted. *Financial support:* Fellowships, research assistantships, teaching assistantships, Federal Work-Study, scholarships/grants, and unspecified assistantships available. Financial award application deadline: 1/1. *Faculty research:* Theatre history, performance studies, scenography, theatre historiography, cultural studies. *Unit head:* Nicole Hodges Persley, Acting Chair/Director of Graduate Studies, 785-864-2820, E-mail: hodgespersley@ku.edu. *Application contact:* Karen Hummel, Graduate Secretary, 785-864-3511, E-mail: kuthr@ku.edu.
Website: http://www.theatre.ku.edu/

**University of Lethbridge,** School of Graduate Studies, Lethbridge, AB T1K 3M4, Canada. Offers addictions counseling (M Sc); agricultural biotechnology (M Sc); agricultural studies (M Sc, MA); anthropology (MA); archaeology (M Sc, MA); art (MA, MFA); biochemistry (M Sc); biological sciences (M Sc); biomolecular science (PhD); biosystems and biodiversity (PhD); Canadian studies (MA); chemistry (M Sc); computer science (M Sc); computer science and geographical information science (M Sc); counseling (MC); counseling psychology (M Ed); dramatic arts (MA); earth, space, and physical science (PhD); economics (MA); education (MA, PhD); educational leadership (M Ed); English (MA); environmental science (M Sc); evolution and behavior (PhD); exercise science (M Sc); French (MA); French/German (MA); French/Spanish (MA); general education (M Ed); geography (M Sc, MA); German (MA); health sciences (M Sc); individualized multidisciplinary (M Sc, MA); kinesiology (M Sc, MA); management (M Sc), including accounting, finance, human resource management and labor relations, information systems, international management, marketing, policy and strategy; mathematics (M Sc); music (M Mus, MA); Native American studies (MA); neuroscience (M Sc, PhD); new media (MA, MFA); nursing (M Sc, MN); philosophy (MA); physics (M Sc); political science (MA); psychology (M Sc, MA); religious studies (MA); sociology (MA); theatre and dramatic arts (MFA); theoretical and computational science (PhD); urban and regional studies (MA); women and gender studies (MA). *Program availability:* Part-time, evening/weekend. *Degree requirements:* For master's, thesis (for some programs); for doctorate, comprehensive exam, thesis/dissertation. *Entrance requirements:* For master's, GMAT (for M Sc in management), bachelor's degree in related field, minimum GPA of 3.0 during previous 20 graded semester courses, 2 years' teaching or related experience (M Ed); for doctorate, master's degree, minimum graduate GPA of 3.5. Additional exam requirements/recommendations for international students: Required—TOEFL (minimum score 580 paper-based; 93 iBT). Electronic applications accepted. *Faculty research:* Movement and brain plasticity, gibberellin physiology, photosynthesis, carbon cycling, molecular properties of main-group ring components.

**University of Louisville,** Graduate School, College of Arts and Sciences, Department of Theatre Arts, Louisville, KY 40292-0001. Offers design (MFA); performance (MFA). *Accreditation:* NAST. *Program availability:* Part-time. *Faculty:* 11 full-time (5 women), 4 part-time/adjunct (3 women). *Students:* 11 full-time (7 women); includes 6 minority (5 Black or African American, non-Hispanic/Latino; 1 Hispanic/Latino). Average age 28. 6 applicants, 67% accepted, 3 enrolled. In 2016, 2 master's awarded. *Degree requirements:* For master's, variable foreign language requirement, performance project and monograph. *Entrance requirements:* For master's, audition. Additional exam requirements/recommendations for international students: Required—TOEFL. *Application deadline:* For spring admission, 4/15 for domestic and international students. Application fee: $60. Electronic applications accepted. *Expenses:* Contact institution. *Financial support:* In 2016–17, 3 teaching assistantships (averaging $12,000 per year) were awarded; health care benefits also available. Financial award application deadline: 2/15; financial award applicants required to submit FAFSA. *Faculty research:* Social justice, African American theatre, African diaspora theatre, costume history and design, lighting design, scenic design. *Unit head:* Dr. Nefertiti Burton, Chair, 502-852-8444, Fax: 502-852-7235, E-mail: ncburt01@louisville.edu. *Application contact:* Libby Leggett, Director, Graduate Admissions, 502-852-3101, Fax: 502-852-6536, E-mail: gradadm@louisville.edu.
Website: http://louisville.edu/theatrearts/

**The University of Manchester,** School of Arts, Histories and Cultures, Manchester, United Kingdom. Offers anthropology, media and performance (PhD); applied theatre professional (PhD); archaeology (PhD); art history and visual studies (PhD); arts management and cultural policy (PhD); classics and ancient history (PhD); composition (PhD); creative writing (PhD); drama (PhD); economic and social history (PhD); electroacoustic composition (PhD); English and American studies (PhD); history (PhD); humanitarianism and conflict response (PhD); museology (PhD); music (PhD); musicology (PhD); religions and theology (PhD).

**University of Maryland, Baltimore County,** The Graduate School, College of Arts, Humanities and Social Sciences, Department of Education, Program in Teaching, Baltimore, MD 21250. Offers early childhood education (MAT); elementary education (MAT); teaching (MAT), including art, biology, chemistry, choral music, classical foreign language, dance, earth/space science, English, instrumental music, mathematics, modern foreign language, physical science, physics, social studies, theatre. *Program availability:* Part-time, evening/weekend. *Faculty:* 24 full-time (18 women), 25 part-time/adjunct (19 women). *Students:* 41 full-time (34 women), 27 part-time (18 women); includes 26 minority (6 Black or African American, non-Hispanic/Latino; 9 Asian, non-Hispanic/Latino; 7 Hispanic/Latino; 1 Native Hawaiian or other Pacific Islander, non-Hispanic/Latino; 3 Two or more races, non-Hispanic/Latino), 2 international. Average age 30. 54 applicants, 83% accepted, 35 enrolled. In 2016, 50 master's awarded. *Degree requirements:* For master's, comprehensive exam (for some programs), thesis (for some programs). *Entrance requirements:* For master's, PRAXIS Core Examination or GRE (minimum score of 1000), minimum GPA of 3.0. Additional exam requirements/recommendations for international students: Required—TOEFL. *Application deadline:* For fall admission, 6/1 for domestic and international students; for spring admission, 11/1 for domestic and international students. Applications are processed on a rolling basis. Application fee: $50. Electronic applications accepted. *Expenses:* Tuition, state resident: full-time $13,294. Tuition, nonresident: full-time $20,286. *Financial support:* In 2016–17, 8 students received support, including teaching assistantships with tuition reimbursements available (averaging $12,000 per year); career-related internships or fieldwork, Federal Work-Study, scholarships/grants, tuition waivers, and unspecified assistantships also available. Financial award application deadline: 3/15. *Faculty research:* STEM teacher education, culturally sensitive pedagogy, ESOL/bilingual education, early childhood education, language, literacy and culture. *Total annual research expenditures:* $100,000. *Unit head:* Dr. Susan M. Blunck, Graduate Program Director, 410-455-2869, Fax: 410-455-3986, E-mail: blunck@umbc.edu. *Application contact:* Cheryl Johnson, MAT Program Specialist, 410-455-3388, E-mail: blackwel@umbc.edu.
Website: http://www.umbc.edu/education/

**University of Maryland, College Park,** Academic Affairs, College of Arts and Humanities, School of Theatre, Dance and Performance Studies, Theatre Program, College Park, MD 20742. Offers performance (MFA); theatre and performance studies (MA, PhD); theatre design (MFA). *Degree requirements:* For master's, comprehensive exam, thesis optional. *Entrance requirements:* For master's, GRE General Test, portfolio, writing sample, 3 letters of recommendation. Additional exam requirements/recommendations for international students: Required—TOEFL. Electronic applications accepted.

**University of Massachusetts Amherst,** Graduate School, College of Humanities and Fine Arts, Department of Theater, Amherst, MA 01003. Offers costume design (MFA); directing (MFA); dramaturgy (MFA); lighting design (MFA); scenic design (MFA). *Program availability:* Part-time. *Degree requirements:* For master's, thesis. *Entrance requirements:* For master's, GRE (for dramaturgy and costume design only), two critical essays or design portfolios, resume of production experience. Additional exam requirements/recommendations for international students: Required—TOEFL (minimum score 550 paper-based; 80 iBT), IELTS (minimum score 6.5). Electronic applications accepted.

**University of Memphis,** Graduate School, College of Communication and Fine Arts, Department of Theatre and Dance, Memphis, TN 38152. Offers theatre (MFA). *Accreditation:* NAST. *Faculty:* 6 full-time (1 woman). *Students:* 16 full-time (8 women), 3 part-time (2 women); includes 3 minority (2 Black or African American, non-Hispanic/Latino; 1 Two or more races, non-Hispanic/Latino). Average age 35. 22 applicants, 23% accepted, 5 enrolled. In 2016, 8 master's awarded. *Degree requirements:* For master's, comprehensive exam, practicum, internship. *Entrance requirements:* For master's, minimum GPA of 3.0 in major, 2.5 overall, interview/audition. *Application deadline:* For fall admission, 8/1 priority date for domestic students; for spring admission, 12/1 priority date for domestic students. Applications are processed on a rolling basis. Application fee: $35 ($60 for international students). Electronic applications accepted. *Expenses:* $5,231.50 per semester full-time in-state, $9,623.50 full-time out-of-state. *Financial*

support: In 2016–17, 12 students received support, including 9 research assistantships with full tuition reimbursements available (averaging $7,944 per year), 4 teaching assistantships with full tuition reimbursements available (averaging $2,750 per year); career-related internships or fieldwork, Federal Work-Study, institutionally sponsored loans, scholarships/grants, and unspecified assistantships also available. Financial award application deadline: 2/1; financial award applicants required to submit FAFSA. *Faculty research:* Theatre design, production management, Lessac vocal training, movement styles, directing. *Unit head:* Prof. Holly C. Lau, Chair, 901-678-2523, Fax: 901-678-4331, E-mail: hclau@memphis.edu. *Application contact:* Sarah Brown, Director of Graduate Studies, 901-678-2523, Fax: 901-678-5118, E-mail: kshupe@memphis.edu.
Website: http://www.memphis.edu/theatre/

**University of Minnesota, Twin Cities Campus,** Graduate School, College of Liberal Arts, Department of Theatre Arts and Dance, Minneapolis, MN 55455. Offers design technology (MFA); theatre arts (MA, PhD). *Accreditation:* NAST (one or more programs are accredited). Terminal master's awarded for partial completion of doctoral program. *Degree requirements:* For master's, thesis (for some programs), final creative project (MFA), foreign language (MA); for doctorate, one foreign language, thesis/dissertation, oral defense, written exams. *Entrance requirements:* For master's, GRE General Test (for MA), minimum GPA of 3.0 or portfolio; for doctorate, GRE General Test, minimum GPA of 3.0, writing sample, 1 foreign language. Additional exam requirements/recommendations for international students: Required—TOEFL (minimum score 550 paper-based; 79 iBT). Electronic applications accepted. *Faculty research:* Theatre historiography, theatre for social change, dance and performance studies, performance politics of ethnicity, migration, globalization, European avant-garde; theatre design and technology: costume, scenography, lighting, sound, multimedia.

**University of Missouri,** Office of Research and Graduate Studies, College of Arts and Science, Department of Theatre, Columbia, MO 65211. Offers MA, PhD. *Program availability:* Part-time. *Faculty:* 9 full-time (5 women). *Students:* 19 full-time (13 women), 2 part-time (1 woman). *Degree requirements:* For doctorate, thesis/dissertation. *Entrance requirements:* For master's, GRE General Test, minimum GPA of 3.0 overall and in last 60 hours; for doctorate, GRE General Test, minimum GPA of 3.0 overall and in last 60 hours, 3.5 in master's program. Additional exam requirements/recommendations for international students: Required—TOEFL (minimum score 650 paper-based; 114 iBT). *Application deadline:* For fall admission, 1/15 priority date for domestic and international students. Electronic applications accepted. *Expenses:* Tuition, state resident: full-time $6347; part-time $352.60 per credit hour. Tuition, nonresident: full-time $17,379; part-time $965.50 per credit hour. *Required fees:* $1035. Tuition and fees vary according to course load, campus/location and program. *Financial support:* Fellowships with full tuition reimbursements, research assistantships with full tuition reimbursements, teaching assistantships with full tuition reimbursements, institutionally sponsored loans, health care benefits, and unspecified assistantships available.
Website: http://theatre.missouri.edu/gradprogram/index.html

**University of Missouri–Kansas City,** College of Arts and Sciences, Theatre Department, Kansas City, MO 64110-2499. Offers MA, MFA. *Accreditation:* NAST. *Faculty:* 17 full-time (5 women), 9 part-time/adjunct (1 woman). *Students:* 59 full-time (31 women), 7 part-time (5 women); includes 10 minority (3 Black or African American, non-Hispanic/Latino; 7 Hispanic/Latino), 3 international. Average age 27. 46 applicants, 72% accepted, 30 enrolled. In 2016, 33 master's awarded. *Degree requirements:* For master's, thesis. *Entrance requirements:* For master's, audition or portfolio, interview. Additional exam requirements/recommendations for international students: Required—TOEFL (minimum score 550 paper-based; 80 iBT). *Application deadline:* For fall admission, 3/1 priority date for domestic and international students; for spring admission, 11/1 priority date for domestic and international students. Applications are processed on a rolling basis. Application fee: $45 ($50 for international students). Electronic applications accepted. *Financial support:* In 2016–17, 27 teaching assistantships with partial tuition reimbursements (averaging $7,220 per year) were awarded; career-related internships or fieldwork, Federal Work-Study, institutionally sponsored loans, and scholarships/grants also available. Financial award application deadline: 3/1; financial award applicants required to submit FAFSA. *Faculty research:* Contemporary Russian theatre, Shakespeare in performance, subtle energies in actor training, multi-channel sound, renovation of Zuni Pueblo historic Spanish mission. *Unit head:* Tom Mardikes, Chair, 816-235-2784, Fax: 816-235-6562, E-mail: mardikest@umkc.edu. *Application contact:* Cindy Stofiel, Student Affairs Representative, 816-235-6683, Fax: 816-235-6562, E-mail: stofielc@umkc.edu.
Website: http://cas.umkc.edu/theatre/

**University of Montana,** Graduate School, College of Visual and Performing Arts, School of Theatre and Dance, Missoula, MT 59812-0002. Offers design/technology (MFA); theatre (MA). *Accreditation:* NAST (one or more programs are accredited). *Degree requirements:* For master's, thesis or alternative. *Entrance requirements:* For master's, GRE General Test, audition, portfolio, production notebook.

**University of Nebraska–Lincoln,** Graduate College, College of Fine and Performing Arts, Johnny Carson School of Theatre and Film, Lincoln, NE 68588. Offers acting (MFA); costume (MFA); directing (MFA); stage design (MFA). *Accreditation:* NAST. *Degree requirements:* For master's, thesis. *Entrance requirements:* For master's, audition, portfolio. Additional exam requirements/recommendations for international students: Required—TOEFL (minimum score 500 paper-based). Electronic applications accepted. *Faculty research:* American theatre history, British theatre history, modern American drama, contemporary performance, Elizabethan theatre history.

**University of Nevada, Las Vegas,** Graduate College, College of Fine Arts, Department of Theatre, Las Vegas, NV 89154-5036. Offers MA, MFA. *Program availability:* Part-time. *Faculty:* 11 full-time (3 women), 2 part-time/adjunct (1 woman). *Students:* 29 full-time (15 women), 4 part-time (all women); includes 10 minority (4 Black or African American, non-Hispanic/Latino; 5 Hispanic/Latino; 1 Two or more races, non-Hispanic/Latino), 1 international. Average age 32. 40 applicants, 55% accepted, 19 enrolled. In 2016, 21 master's awarded. *Degree requirements:* For master's, comprehensive exam (for some programs), thesis (for some programs), creative project, oral exam. *Entrance requirements:* For master's, sample research paper or research statement; statement of purpose; 2 letters of recommendation. Additional exam requirements/recommendations for international students: Required—TOEFL (minimum score 550 paper-based; 80 iBT), IELTS (minimum score 7). *Application deadline:* For fall admission, 8/1 for domestic students, 5/1 for international students. Application fee: $60 ($95 for international students). Electronic applications accepted. *Expenses:* $269.25 per credit, $792 per 3-credit course; $9,634 per year resident; $23,274 per year non-resident; $7,094 fees non-resident (7 credits or more); $1,307 annual health insurance fee. *Financial support:* In 2016–17, 11 research assistantships with partial tuition reimbursements (averaging $15,000 per year), 17 teaching assistantships with partial tuition reimbursements (averaging $14,882 per year) were awarded; institutionally sponsored loans, scholarships/grants, health care benefits, and unspecified assistantships also available. Financial award application deadline: 3/15. *Faculty research:* Designing scenery, costumes or lighting, directing or stage managing, serving as technical director/consultant, or acting for a production for a regional theatre. *Unit head:* Brackley Frayer,

Chair/Associate Professor, 702-895-3353, Fax: 702-895-0833, E-mail: brackley.frayer@unlv.edu. *Application contact:* Nate Bynum, Graduate Coordinator, 702-895-4248, Fax: 702-895-0833, E-mail: joe.bynum@unlv.edu.
Website: http://theatre.unlv.edu/

**University of New Mexico,** Graduate Studies, College of Fine Arts, Department of Theatre and Dance, Albuquerque, NM 87131-2039. Offers dance (MFA); dance history (MA); dramatic writing (MFA); theatre education and outreach (MA). *Accreditation:* NASD; NAST. *Faculty:* 6 full-time (3 women), 2 part-time/adjunct (both women). *Students:* 13 full-time (7 women), 3 part-time (all women); includes 13 minority (1 Black or African American, non-Hispanic/Latino; 1 American Indian or Alaska Native, non-Hispanic/Latino; 9 Hispanic/Latino; 2 Two or more races, non-Hispanic/Latino). Average age 36. 15 applicants, 53% accepted, 7 enrolled. In 2016, 4 master's awarded. *Degree requirements:* For master's, comprehensive exam (for some programs), thesis (for some programs). *Entrance requirements:* For master's, minimum GPA of 3.0; undergraduate major in theatre, dance or closely-related field; 3 letters of recommendation; letter of intent; BA, BFA, BS, or MA in dance movement science or related field, or equivalent experience (for MFA in dance). *Application deadline:* For fall admission, 4/15 for domestic students; for spring admission, 11/10 for domestic students. Application fee: $50. Electronic applications accepted. *Financial support:* Fellowships, research assistantships with partial tuition reimbursements, teaching assistantships with partial tuition reimbursements, Federal Work-Study, health care benefits, tuition waivers (partial), and unspecified assistantships available. Financial award application deadline: 3/1; financial award applicants required to submit FAFSA. *Faculty research:* Theater education and outreach, choreography, dramatic writing, dance history/criticism. *Unit head:* Bill Liotta, Chair, 505-277-4332, Fax: 505-277-8921, E-mail: wliotta@unm.edu. *Application contact:* Christina Squire, Administrator II, 505-277-7362, Fax: 505-277-8921, E-mail: csquire@unm.edu.
Website: http://theatredance.unm.edu

**University of New Orleans,** Graduate School, College of Liberal Arts, Department of Film and Theatre, New Orleans, LA 70148. Offers design (MFA); film production (MFA); theatre performance (MFA), including acting, directing. *Accreditation:* NAST. *Degree requirements:* For master's, comprehensive exam, thesis. *Entrance requirements:* Additional exam requirements/recommendations for international students: Required—TOEFL (minimum score 550 paper-based; 79 iBT), IELTS (minimum score 6.5). Electronic applications accepted. *Faculty research:* Mass communication theory, nineteenth and twentieth century theater history, film criticism and history.

**The University of North Carolina at Chapel Hill,** Graduate School, College of Arts and Sciences, Department of Dramatic Art, Chapel Hill, NC 27599. Offers acting (MFA); costume production (MFA); technical production (MFA). *Entrance requirements:* For master's, audition or portfolio.

**The University of North Carolina at Charlotte,** Cato College of Education, Interdisciplinary Education Programs, Charlotte, NC 28223-0001. Offers art education (Graduate Certificate); child and family development: early childhood education (MAT); curriculum and instruction (PhD); elementary education (MAT); foreign language education (MAT); middle grades education (MAT); secondary education (MAT); special education (MAT); teaching (Graduate Certificate); teaching English as a second language (MAT); theatre education (Graduate Certificate). *Program availability:* Part-time, 100% online, blended/hybrid learning. *Students:* 78 full-time (59 women), 619 part-time (484 women); includes 255 minority (186 Black or African American, non-Hispanic/Latino; 1 American Indian or Alaska Native, non-Hispanic/Latino; 16 Asian, non-Hispanic/Latino; 37 Hispanic/Latino; 15 Two or more races, non-Hispanic/Latino; 10 international. Average age 33. 380 applicants, 92% accepted, 264 enrolled. In 2016, 93 master's, 8 doctorates, 176 other advanced degrees awarded. *Degree requirements:* For master's, thesis or alternative, research project/portfolio. *Entrance requirements:* For master's, GRE or MAT, bachelor's degree, or its U.S. equivalent, from regionally-accredited college or university; minimum overall GPA of 3.0 on all previous work beyond high school; statement of purpose (essay); at least three recommendation forms; for doctorate, GRE or MAT, bachelor's degree (or its U.S. equivalent) from regionally-accredited college or university; minimum overall GPA of 3.5 in master's degree program; for Graduate Certificate, bachelor's degree from regionally-accredited university; minimum GPA of 2.75 on all post-secondary work attempted; transcripts; personal statement outlining why the applicant seeks admission to the program. Additional exam requirements/recommendations for international students: Required—TOEFL (minimum score 523 paper-based; 70 iBT) or IELTS (6.5). *Application deadline:* For fall admission, 3/1 priority date for domestic and international students; for spring admission, 10/1 priority date for domestic and international students; for summer admission, 4/1 priority date for domestic and international students. Applications are processed on a rolling basis. Application fee: $75. Electronic applications accepted. *Expenses:* Tuition, state resident: full-time $4252. Tuition, nonresident: full-time $17,423. *Required fees:* $3026. Tuition and fees vary according to course load and program. *Financial support:* Career-related internships or fieldwork, institutionally sponsored loans, scholarships/grants, and unspecified assistantships available. Support available to part-time students. Financial award application deadline: 3/1; financial award applicants required to submit FAFSA. *Unit head:* Dr. Ellen McIntyre, Dean, 704-687-8722, E-mail: ellen.mcintyre@uncc.edu. *Application contact:* Kathy B. Giddings, Director of Graduate Admissions, 704-687-5503, Fax: 704-687-1668, E-mail: gradadm@uncc.edu.
Website: http://education.uncc.edu/academic-programs

**The University of North Carolina at Greensboro,** Graduate School, School of Music, Theatre and Dance, Department of Theatre, Greensboro, NC 27412-5001. Offers acting (MFA); design (MFA); directing (MFA); theater education (M Ed); theater for youth (MFA). *Accreditation:* NAST. *Entrance requirements:* For master's, portfolio, interviews. Electronic applications accepted.

**University of North Carolina School of the Arts,** School of Design and Production, Winston-Salem, NC 27127-2738. Offers costume design (MFA); costume technology (MFA); scene design (MFA); scenic art (MFA); sound design (MFA); stage automation (MFA); stage properties (MFA); technical direction (MFA); wig and makeup design (MFA). *Faculty:* 21 full-time (6 women), 4 part-time/adjunct (1 woman). *Students:* 49 full-time (33 women), 1 (woman) part-time; includes 7 minority (2 Black or African American, non-Hispanic/Latino; 4 Hispanic/Latino; 1 Two or more races, non-Hispanic/Latino), 3 international. Average age 27. 37 applicants, 62% accepted, 18 enrolled. *Degree requirements:* For master's, thesis (for some programs), project. *Entrance requirements:* For master's, interview, portfolio. Additional exam requirements/recommendations for international students: Required—TOEFL. *Application deadline:* For fall admission, 4/1 priority date for domestic students. Applications are processed on a rolling basis. Application fee: $95 ($100 for international students). Electronic applications accepted. *Expenses:* Tuition, state resident: full-time $7996; part-time $444 per credit hour. Tuition, nonresident: full-time $21,403; part-time $1189 per credit hour. *Required fees:* $2769; $153.83 per credit hour. *Financial support:* Career-related internships or fieldwork, Federal Work-Study, and unspecified assistantships available. Support available to part-time students. Financial award application deadline: 3/15; financial award applicants required to submit FAFSA. *Unit head:* Michael J. Kelley, Dean, 336-770-1307, Fax: 336-770-3213, E-mail: kelleym@uncsa.edu. *Application contact:*

Sheeler Lawson, Director of Admissions, 336-770-3290, Fax: 336-770-3370, E-mail: admissions@uncsa.edu.
Website: http://www.uncsa.edu/design-production/

**University of Oklahoma,** Weitzenhoffer Family College of Fine Arts, Helmerich School of Drama, Norman, OK 73019. Offers MA. *Faculty:* 7 full-time (3 women), 1 part-time/adjunct (0 women). *Students:* 1 full-time (0 women), 1 (woman) part-time; includes 1 minority (American Indian or Alaska Native, non-Hispanic/Latino). Average age 26. *Degree requirements:* For master's, thesis. *Entrance requirements:* For master's, BFA in Drama. Additional exam requirements/recommendations for international students: Required—TOEFL (minimum score 79 iBT) or IELTS (minimum score 6.5). *Application deadline:* For fall admission, 3/15 for domestic students; for spring admission, 11/1 for domestic and international students. Application fee: $50 ($100 for international students). Electronic applications accepted. *Expenses:* Tuition, state resident: full-time $4886; part-time $203.60 per credit hour. Tuition, nonresident: full-time $18,989; part-time $791.20 per credit hour. *Required fees:* $3283; $126.25 per credit hour. $126.50 per semester. *Financial support:* In 2016–17, 3 teaching assistantships with full tuition reimbursements (averaging $12,818 per year) were awarded; Federal Work-Study, health care benefits, tuition waivers, and unspecified assistantships also available. Financial award application deadline: 6/1; financial award applicants required to submit FAFSA. *Faculty research:* Dramaturgy, theatre history, playwriting. *Unit head:* Dr. Tom Huston Orr, Director, School of Drama, 405-325-4021, Fax: 405-325-0400, E-mail: thorr@ou.edu. *Application contact:* Dr. Kae Koger, Graduate Liaison, E-mail: akoger@ou.edu.
Website: http://www.ou.edu/finearts/drama

**University of Oregon,** Graduate School, College of Arts and Sciences, Department of Theater Arts, Eugene, OR 97403. Offers MA, MFA, MS, PhD. *Degree requirements:* For master's, variable foreign language requirement, thesis or alternative; for doctorate, variable foreign language requirement, thesis/dissertation. *Entrance requirements:* For master's and doctorate, minimum GPA of 3.0. Additional exam requirements/recommendations for international students: Required—TOEFL.

**University of Ottawa,** Faculty of Graduate and Postdoctoral Studies, Faculty of Arts, Department of Theatre, Ottawa, ON K1N 6N5, Canada. Offers directing for theatre (MA). Electronic applications accepted. *Faculty research:* Lamise en scéne.

**University of Pittsburgh,** Dietrich School of Arts and Sciences, Department of Theatre Arts, Pittsburgh, PA 15260. Offers MA, MFA, PhD. *Accreditation:* NAST. *Faculty:* 6 full-time (4 women). *Students:* 17 full-time (13 women); includes 5 minority (2 Black or African American, non-Hispanic/Latino; 3 Hispanic/Latino). Average age 31. 39 applicants, 10% accepted, 4 enrolled. In 2016, 2 master's, 1 doctorate awarded. Terminal master's awarded for partial completion of doctoral program. *Degree requirements:* For master's, thesis optional; for doctorate, one foreign language, comprehensive exam, thesis/dissertation, diagnostic exams. *Entrance requirements:* For master's and doctorate, GRE General Test, samples of written work. Additional exam requirements/recommendations for international students: Required—TOEFL (minimum score 500 paper-based; 90 iBT). *Application deadline:* For fall admission, 1/15 priority date for domestic and international students. Application fee: $50. Electronic applications accepted. Tuition and fees vary according to program. *Financial support:* In 2016–17, 13 students received support, including 8 fellowships with full tuition reimbursements available (averaging $17,800 per year), 5 teaching assistantships with full tuition reimbursements available (averaging $17,100 per year). Financial award application deadline: 1/15; financial award applicants required to submit FAFSA. *Faculty research:* American theatre and popular entertainment, performance pedagogy, theatre historiography, Latin American theatre and performance, performance studies. *Unit head:* Prof. Annmarie Duggan, Chairman, 412-624-7284, Fax: 412-624-6338, E-mail: duggan@pitt.edu. *Application contact:* Margaret Bupp, Graduate Student Services Administrator, 412-624-6568, Fax: 412-624-6338, E-mail: maggiebupp@pitt.edu.
Website: http://www.play.pitt.edu/

**University of Portland,** Department of Performing and Fine Arts, Portland, OR 97203-5798. Offers directing (MFA). *Program availability:* Part-time, evening/weekend. *Degree requirements:* For master's, thesis optional. *Entrance requirements:* For master's, GRE General Test, minimum GPA of 3.0, resume, 3 letters of recommendation, statement of goals, official transcripts. Additional exam requirements/recommendations for international students: Required—TOEFL (minimum score 600 paper-based; 100 iBT), IELTS (minimum score 7.5).

**University of San Diego,** College of Arts and Sciences, The Old Globe and University of San Diego Shiley Graduate Theatre Program, San Diego, CA 92110-2492. Offers MFA. *Faculty:* 4 full-time (1 woman). *Students:* 14 full-time (6 women); includes 5 minority (3 Black or African American, non-Hispanic/Latino; 2 Hispanic/Latino), 2 international. Average age 26. 374 applicants, 2% accepted, 7 enrolled. In 2016, 7 master's awarded. *Entrance requirements:* For master's, audition. Additional exam requirements/recommendations for international students: Required—TOEFL (minimum score 580 paper-based; 83 iBT), TWE. *Application deadline:* For fall admission, 1/5 for domestic and international students. Application fee: $55. *Financial support:* In 2016–17, 13 students received support, including 13 fellowships with full tuition reimbursements available; career-related internships or fieldwork, Federal Work-Study, and institutionally sponsored loans also available. Financial award applicants required to submit FAFSA. *Faculty research:* Voice and dialect coaching, directing, stage combat, movement choreography, acting. *Unit head:* Richard Seer, Graduate Program Director, 619-260-8813, Fax: 619-231-5879. *Application contact:* Monica Mahon, Associate Director of Graduate Admissions, 619-260-4524, Fax: 619-260-4158, E-mail: grads@sandiego.edu.
Website: http://www.graduateacting.com/

**University of Saskatchewan,** College of Graduate Studies and Research, College of Arts and Science, Department of Drama, Saskatoon, SK S7N 5A2, Canada. Offers MA. *Degree requirements:* For master's, thesis. *Entrance requirements:* Additional exam requirements/recommendations for international students: Required—TOEFL (minimum score 80 iBT); Recommended—IELTS (minimum score 6.5). Electronic applications accepted.

**University of South Carolina,** The Graduate School, College of Arts and Sciences, Department of Theatre and Dance, Columbia, SC 29208. Offers theatre (MA, MAT, MFA). MA and MAT offered in cooperation with the College of Education. *Accreditation:* NAST (one or more programs are accredited). *Degree requirements:* For master's, comprehensive exam, thesis. *Entrance requirements:* For master's, GRE General Test, GRE or MAT (MAT), audition, interview (for MFA). Additional exam requirements/recommendations for international students: Required—TOEFL. Electronic applications accepted. *Faculty research:* Computer assisted design, rhetoric of science and technology, Alexander Technique, script analysis, Lessac Method.

**University of South Carolina,** The Graduate School, College of Education, Department of Instruction and Teacher Education, Program in Secondary Education, Columbia, SC 29208. Offers art education (IMA, MAT); business education (IMA, MAT); English (MAT); foreign language (MAT); health education (MAT); mathematics (MAT); science (IMA, MAT); secondary (Ed D); secondary education (MT, PhD); social studies (MAT); theatre and speech (MAT). IMA and MT offered jointly with the subject areas.

## Theater

*Accreditation:* NCATE. *Degree requirements:* For master's, comprehensive exam, thesis (for some programs), foreign language (MA); for doctorate, one foreign language, comprehensive exam, thesis/dissertation. *Entrance requirements:* For master's, GRE General Test or MAT, teaching certificate (IMA, M Ed), interview; for doctorate, GRE General Test or MAT, interview. *Faculty research:* Middle school programs, professional development, school collaboration.

**The University of South Dakota,** Graduate School, College of Fine Arts, Department of Theatre, Vermillion, SD 57069. Offers design/technology (MFA); directing (MFA); theatre (MA). *Accreditation:* NAST. *Degree requirements:* For master's, thesis or alternative. *Entrance requirements:* For master's, GRE (for MA), minimum GPA of 2.7, portfolio. Additional exam requirements/recommendations for international students: Required—TOEFL (minimum score 550 paper-based; 79 iBT). Electronic applications accepted.

**University of Southern California,** Graduate School, School of Dramatic Arts, Los Angeles, CA 90089. Offers acting (MFA); dramatic writing (MFA). *Degree requirements:* For master's, comprehensive exam. *Entrance requirements:* For master's, GRE. Additional exam requirements/recommendations for international students: Required—TOEFL. Electronic applications accepted.

**University of Southern Mississippi,** Graduate School, College of Arts and Letters, Department of Theatre, Hattiesburg, MS 39406. Offers costume design (MFA); directing (MFA); lighting and sound design (MFA); performance (MFA); scenic design (MFA). *Accreditation:* NAST. *Program availability:* Part-time. *Degree requirements:* For master's, comprehensive exam, thesis or alternative, creative project. *Entrance requirements:* For master's, GRE General Test, minimum GPA of 3.0. Additional exam requirements/recommendations for international students: Required—TOEFL, IELTS. *Application deadline:* For fall admission, 3/1 priority date for domestic students, 3/1 for international students; for spring admission, 1/10 priority date for domestic and international students. Applications are processed on a rolling basis. Application fee: $60. *Expenses:* Tuition, area resident: Full-time $15,708; part-time $437 per credit hour. *Financial support:* Research assistantships, teaching assistantships with full tuition reimbursements, career-related internships or fieldwork, Federal Work-Study, institutionally sponsored loans, health care benefits, and unspecified assistantships available. Support available to part-time students. Financial award application deadline: 3/15; financial award applicants required to submit FAFSA. *Faculty research:* Technical design, acting. *Unit head:* Louis Rackoff, Chair, 601-266-6907, Fax: 601-266-6423. *Application contact:* Shonna Breland, Manager of Graduate Admissions, 601-266-4369, Fax: 601-266-5138, E-mail: shonna.breland@usm.edu.
Website: http://www.usm.edu/theatre

**The University of Tennessee,** Graduate School, College of Arts and Sciences, Department of Theatre, Knoxville, TN 37996. Offers costume design (MFA); lighting design (MFA); performance (MFA); scene design (MFA); theatre technology (MFA). *Accreditation:* NAST. *Degree requirements:* For master's, thesis or alternative. *Entrance requirements:* For master's, audition, minimum GPA of 2.7. Additional exam requirements/recommendations for international students: Required—TOEFL. Electronic applications accepted.

**The University of Texas at Austin,** Graduate School, College of Fine Arts, Department of Theatre and Dance, Austin, TX 78712-1111. Offers acting (MFA); dance (MFA); directing (MFA); drama and theatre for youth (MFA); performance as public practice (MA, MFA, PhD); playwriting (MFA); theatre technology (MFA); theatrical design (MFA). *Degree requirements:* For master's, thesis; for doctorate, variable foreign language requirement, thesis/dissertation. *Entrance requirements:* For master's and doctorate, GRE General Test.

**The University of Texas at Austin,** Graduate School, Michener Center for Writers, Austin, TX 78712-1111. Offers fiction (MFA); playwriting (MFA); poetry (MFA); screenwriting (MFA). Electronic applications accepted.

**The University of Texas Rio Grande Valley,** College of Liberal Arts, Department of Communication, Edinburg, TX 78539. Offers communication (MA); communication training and consulting (Graduate Certificate); strategic communication and media relations (Graduate Certificate); theatre (MA). *Accreditation:* NAST. *Program availability:* Part-time, evening/weekend. *Degree requirements:* For master's, comprehensive exam, thesis or alternative. *Entrance requirements:* For master's, minimum GPA of 3.0. Additional exam requirements/recommendations for international students: Required—TOEFL. Tuition and fees vary according to course load and program. *Faculty research:* Rhetorical theory, intercultural and mass communication, American theatre, multicultural theatre and drama, television and film.

**University of the Cumberlands,** Graduate Programs in Education, Williamsburg, KY 40769-1372. Offers all grades (P-12) (M Ed); business and marketing (MA Ed, MAT); counselor education and supervision (Ed D); director of pupil personnel (Certificate); director of special education (Certificate); educational administration and supervision (Ed S); educational leadership (Ed D); elementary education (MA Ed, MAT); instructional leadership - principalship (MA Ed); instructional leadership - school principal (Certificate); middle school education (MA Ed, MAT); reading and writing (MA Ed); school counseling (MA Ed); school superintendent (Certificate); secondary education (MA Ed, MAT); special education (MAT); supervisor of instruction (Certificate); teacher leader (MA Ed). *Program availability:* Part-time, evening/weekend, online learning. *Degree requirements:* For master's, comprehensive exam. Electronic applications accepted.

**University of Toronto,** School of Graduate Studies, Faculty of Arts and Science, Centre for Drama, Theatre and Performance Studies, Toronto, ON M5S 1A1, Canada. Offers MA, PhD. *Program availability:* Part-time. *Entrance requirements:* For master's, minimum B+ average, significant coursework in drama and related disciplines, resume, 2 letters of recommendation. Additional exam requirements/recommendations for international students: Required—TOEFL (minimum score 580 paper-based; 93 iBT), TWE (minimum score 5). Electronic applications accepted.

**University of Victoria,** Faculty of Graduate Studies, Faculty of Fine Arts, Department of Theatre, Victoria, BC V8W 2Y2, Canada. Offers design (MFA); directing (MFA); theatre history (MA). *Degree requirements:* For master's, thesis. *Entrance requirements:* Additional exam requirements/recommendations for international students: Required—TOEFL (minimum score 575 paper-based), IELTS (minimum score 7). Electronic applications accepted.

**University of Virginia,** College and Graduate School of Arts and Sciences, Department of Drama, Charlottesville, VA 22903. Offers MFA. *Faculty:* 18 full-time (10 women), 1 (woman) part-time/adjunct. *Students:* 18 full-time (7 women); includes 5 minority (2 Black or African American, non-Hispanic/Latino; 2 Hispanic/Latino; 1 Two or more races, non-Hispanic/Latino), 1 international. Average age 30. 12 applicants, 100% accepted, 12 enrolled. In 2016, 10 master's awarded. *Degree requirements:* For master's, thesis project. *Entrance requirements:* For master's, GRE General Test, resume; 3 letters of recommendation. Additional exam requirements/recommendations for international students: Required—TOEFL (minimum score 600 paper-based; 90 iBT), IELTS (minimum score 7). *Application deadline:* For fall admission, 2/20 for domestic and international students. Applications are processed on a rolling basis. Application fee:

$60. Electronic applications accepted. *Expenses:* Tuition, state resident: full-time $15,026; part-time $834 per credit hour. Tuition, nonresident: full-time $25,168; part-time $1378 per credit hour. *Required fees:* $2654. *Financial support:* Fellowships and teaching assistantships available. Financial award applicants required to submit FAFSA. *Faculty research:* Acting, scenic design, lighting design, technical direction, costume design/technology. *Unit head:* Colleen Kelly, Chair, 434-924-3326, Fax: 434-924-1447, E-mail: drama@virginia.edu.
Website: http://drama.virginia.edu//

**University of Washington,** Graduate School, College of Arts and Sciences, School of Drama, Seattle, WA 98195. Offers acting (MFA); costume design (MFA); directing (MFA); dramatic theory (PhD); lighting design (MFA); scenic design (MFA); theatre and performance history (PhD). *Degree requirements:* For master's, thesis; for doctorate, one foreign language, comprehensive exam, thesis/dissertation. *Entrance requirements:* For master's, interview, minimum GPA of 3.0, portfolio; for doctorate, GRE General Test, minimum GPA of 3.0, writing sample. Additional exam requirements/recommendations for international students: Required—TOEFL. *Faculty research:* Semiotics, Suzuki actor training, modern American theatre, ethnic American theatre.

**University of Wisconsin–Madison,** Graduate School, College of Letters and Science, Department of Theatre and Drama, Madison, WI 53706-1380. Offers MA, MFA, PhD. *Accreditation:* NAST. *Program availability:* Part-time. *Degree requirements:* For master's, thesis; for doctorate, thesis/dissertation. *Entrance requirements:* For master's and doctorate, GRE. Electronic applications accepted. *Faculty research:* Theories and histories of dance, theatre and performance studies; Russian theatre and dance; postmodern performance; Holocaust drama; race and representation.

**University of Wisconsin–Superior,** Graduate Division, Department of Communicating Arts, Superior, WI 54880-4500. Offers mass communication (MA); speech communication (MA); theater (MA). *Program availability:* Part-time. *Degree requirements:* For master's, comprehensive exam, thesis or alternative, position paper or project. *Entrance requirements:* For master's, minimum GPA of 2.75. Electronic applications accepted. *Faculty research:* Multimedia technology, ethics in journalism, diversity, electronic portfolio assessment.

**Utah State University,** School of Graduate Studies, College of Humanities, Arts and Social Sciences, Department of Theatre Arts, Logan, UT 84322. Offers advanced technical practice (MFA); design (MFA); theatre arts (MA, MFA). *Degree requirements:* For master's, variable foreign language requirement, thesis (for some programs), summer internship (MFA). *Entrance requirements:* For master's, GRE General Test or MAT, portfolio (MFA), minimum GPA of 3.0, interview, BS or 20 semester credit. Additional exam requirements/recommendations for international students: Required—TOEFL. *Faculty research:* Seventeenth and eighteenth century Spanish theatre, Greek and Roman theatre, interpretation of literature for performance.

**Villanova University,** Graduate School of Liberal Arts and Sciences, Department of Theatre, Villanova, PA 19085-1699. Offers MA. *Program availability:* Part-time, evening/weekend. *Faculty:* 7. *Students:* 37 full-time (25 women), 8 part-time (4 women); includes 7 minority (4 Black or African American, non-Hispanic/Latino; 2 Hispanic/Latino; 1 Two or more races, non-Hispanic/Latino). Average age 32. 27 applicants, 96% accepted, 19 enrolled. In 2016, 18 master's awarded. *Degree requirements:* For master's, comprehensive exam. *Entrance requirements:* For master's, GRE, minimum GPA of 3.0, resume, statement of goals, headshot. Additional exam requirements/recommendations for international students: Required—TOEFL. *Application deadline:* For fall admission, 3/1 for domestic students, 5/1 priority date for international students; for spring admission, 11/15 for domestic students, 10/15 priority date for international students; for summer admission, 5/1 for domestic students. Applications are processed on a rolling basis. Application fee: $50. Electronic applications accepted. *Financial support:* Research assistantships, teaching assistantships, scholarships/grants, and unspecified assistantships available. Financial award applicants required to submit FAFSA. *Unit head:* Valerie Joyce, Program Director, 610-519-7174. *Application contact:* Dean, Graduate School of Liberal Arts and Sciences.
Website: http://www1.villanova.edu/villanova/artsci/theatre.html

**Virginia Commonwealth University,** Graduate School, School of the Arts, Department of Theatre, Richmond, VA 23284-9005. Offers costume design (MFA); pedagogy/literature (MFA); pedagogy/performance (MFA); scene design/technical theatre (MFA). *Accreditation:* NAST. *Degree requirements:* For master's, thesis (for some programs). *Entrance requirements:* For master's, audition, portfolio. Additional exam requirements/recommendations for international students: Required—TOEFL (minimum score 600 paper-based; 100 iBT). *Application deadline:* For fall admission, 5/1 priority date for domestic students. Application fee: $50. Electronic applications accepted. *Financial support:* Fellowships, teaching assistantships, career-related internships or fieldwork, Federal Work-Study, and institutionally sponsored loans available. Support available to part-time students. Financial award application deadline: 3/15. *Faculty research:* Dramatic literature, speech. *Unit head:* David S. Leong, Chair, 804-828-1514, Fax: 804-828-6741, E-mail: dsleong@vcu.edu. *Application contact:* Dr. Noreen C. Barnes, Director of Graduate Studies, 804-827-1677, E-mail: nbarnesm@vcu.edu.
Website: http://www.vcu.edu/arts/theatre/dept/programs.shtml

**Virginia Polytechnic Institute and State University,** Graduate School, College of Liberal Arts and Human Sciences, Blacksburg, VA 24061. Offers career and technical education (MS Ed, Ed D, PhD, Ed S); communication (MA); counselor education (MA Ed, Ed D, PhD, Ed S); creative writing (MFA); curriculum and instruction (MA Ed, Ed D, PhD, Ed S); educational leadership and policy studies (MA Ed, Ed D, PhD, Ed S); educational research and evaluation (PhD); English (MA); foreign languages, cultures, and literatures (MA); higher education (PhD); higher education and student affairs (MA Ed); history (MA); human development (MS, PhD); material culture and public humanities (MA); philosophy (MA); political science (MA); rhetoric and writing (PhD); science and technology studies (MS, PhD); social, political, ethical, and cultural thought (PhD); sociology (MS, PhD); theater arts (MFA). *Faculty:* 408 full-time (204 women), 3 part-time/adjunct (2 women). *Students:* 657 full-time (446 women), 457 part-time (292 women); includes 213 minority (114 Black or African American, non-Hispanic/Latino; 3 American Indian or Alaska Native, non-Hispanic/Latino; 29 Asian, non-Hispanic/Latino; 44 Hispanic/Latino; 23 Two or more races, non-Hispanic/Latino), 93 international. Average age 33. 805 applicants, 55% accepted, 328 enrolled. In 2016, 270 master's, 91 doctorates awarded. *Degree requirements:* For master's, comprehensive exam (for some programs), thesis (for some programs); for doctorate, comprehensive exam (for some programs), thesis/dissertation (for some programs). *Entrance requirements:* For master's and doctorate, GRE/GMAT. Additional exam requirements/recommendations for international students: Required—TOEFL (minimum score 80 iBT). *Application deadline:* For fall admission, 8/1 for domestic students, 4/1 for international students; for spring admission, 1/1 for domestic students, 9/1 for international students. Applications are processed on a rolling basis. Application fee: $75. Electronic applications accepted. *Expenses:* Tuition, state resident: full-time $12,467; part-time $692.50 per credit hour. Tuition, nonresident: full-time $25,095; part-time $1394.25 per credit hour. *Required fees:* $2669; $491.50 per semester. Tuition and fees vary according to course load, campus/location and program. *Financial support:* In 2016–17, 21 research assistantships with full tuition reimbursements (averaging $19,817 per year), 237 teaching assistantships with full tuition reimbursements (averaging $15,497 per year)

were awarded. Financial award application deadline: 3/1; financial award applicants required to submit FAFSA. *Total annual research expenditures:* $6.6 million. *Unit head:* Rosemary Blieszner, Interim Dean, 540-231-6779, Fax: 540-231-7157, E-mail: liberalartsdean@vt.edu. *Application contact:* Chelsea Blanchet, Executive Assistant, 540-231-6779, Fax: 540-231-7157, E-mail: bchels1@vt.edu.
Website: http://www.liberalarts.vt.edu/

**Washington University in St. Louis,** The Graduate School, Department of Performing Arts, St. Louis, MO 63130-4899. Offers dance (MFA); theater and performance studies (MA). *Degree requirements:* For master's, thesis optional. *Entrance requirements:* For master's, GRE General Test, sample of written work. Additional exam requirements/recommendations for international students: Required—TOEFL. Electronic applications accepted. *Faculty research:* Theater and performance studies; dance.

**Wayne State University,** College of Fine, Performing and Communication Arts, Department of Theatre and Dance, Detroit, MI 48202. Offers theatre (MFA), including acting, costume design, lighting design, stage management, theatre management, theatre stage design; theatre and dance (MA). Application deadline for MA is June 1. *Accreditation:* NAST. *Program availability:* 100% online, blended/hybrid learning. *Faculty:* 5. *Students:* 32 full-time (17 women), 13 part-time (11 women); includes 14 minority (8 Black or African American, non-Hispanic/Latino; 3 Hispanic/Latino; 3 Two or more races, non-Hispanic/Latino), 1 international. Average age 27. 66 applicants, 36% accepted, 19 enrolled. In 2016, 7 master's awarded. *Degree requirements:* For master's, comprehensive exam, thesis (for some programs), final project (for MFA). *Entrance requirements:* For master's, minimum GPA of 3.0; auditions and head shots (for MFA in acting only); interviews, resume, letters of recommendation, samples of work (except for MFA in acting and MA). Additional exam requirements/recommendations for international students: Required—TOEFL (minimum score 550 paper-based; 79 iBT), TWE (minimum score 5.5), Michigan English Language Assessment Battery (minimum score 85); Recommended—IELTS (minimum score 6.5). *Application deadline:* For fall admission, 1/15 for domestic and international students. Applications are processed on a rolling basis. Application fee: $50. Electronic applications accepted. *Expenses:* $17,240 per year resident tuition and fees, $34,434 per year non-resident tuition and fees. *Financial support:* In 2016–17, 34 students received support, including 32 research assistantships with tuition reimbursements available (averaging $17,994 per year); fellowships with tuition reimbursements available, teaching assistantships with tuition reimbursements available, scholarships/grants, and unspecified assistantships also available. Financial award applicants required to submit FAFSA. *Faculty research:* Dramatic criticism, lighting design, acting, directing, scenography. *Unit head:* Dr. John Wolf, Chair, 313-577-4273, E-mail: fe3828@wayne.edu. *Application contact:* E-mail: theatreanddance@wayne.edu.
Website: http://theatreanddance.wayne.edu/

**Western Illinois University,** School of Graduate Studies, College of Fine Arts and Communication, Department of Theatre and Dance, Macomb, IL 61455-1390. Offers theatre (MFA), including acting, design, directing. *Accreditation:* NAST. *Program availability:* Part-time. *Students:* 15 full-time (4 women), 2 part-time (0 women); includes 3 minority (2 Black or African American, non-Hispanic/Latino; 1 Two or more races, non-Hispanic/Latino). Average age 30. 8 applicants, 38% accepted. In 2016, 4 master's awarded. *Degree requirements:* For master's, comprehensive exam, thesis or alternative, creative project, written exam. *Entrance requirements:* For master's, audition or interview. Additional exam requirements/recommendations for international students: Required—TOEFL (minimum score 550 paper-based; 80 iBT). *Application deadline:* Applications are processed on a rolling basis. Application fee: $30. Electronic applications accepted. *Financial support:* In 2016–17, 15 students received support, including 6 teaching assistantships with full tuition reimbursements available (averaging $8,688 per year); unspecified assistantships also available. Financial award applicants required to submit FAFSA. *Unit head:* Dr. Sharon Evans, Chairperson, 309-298-1618. *Application contact:* Dr. Nancy Parsons, Associate Provost and Director of Graduate Studies, 309-298-1806, Fax: 309-298-2345, E-mail: grad-office@wiu.edu.
Website: http://wiu.edu/theatre/

**West Virginia University,** College of Creative Arts, School of Theatre and Dance, Morgantown, WV 26506. Offers acting (MFA); theatre design/technology (MFA). *Accreditation:* NAST. *Program availability:* Part-time. *Degree requirements:* For master's, thesis, oral defense. *Entrance requirements:* For master's, minimum GPA of 3.0, audition or portfolio. Additional exam requirements/recommendations for international students: Required—TOEFL. *Faculty research:* Professional directing, consulting, design.

**Yale University,** School of Drama, New Haven, CT 06520. Offers acting (MFA, Certificate); design (MFA, Certificate), including costume design, lighting design, projection design, set design; directing (MFA, Certificate); dramaturgy and dramatic criticism (MFA, DFA); playwriting (MFA, Certificate); sound design (MFA, Certificate); stage management (MFA, Certificate); technical design and production (MFA, Certificate); theater management (MFA); MFA/MBA. *Degree requirements:* For master's, comprehensive exam (for some programs), thesis (for some programs); for doctorate, thesis/dissertation, oral and written comprehensive exams. *Entrance requirements:* For master's, GRE (verbal, quantitative, and analytical), in-person audition (for acting); portfolio review (for design). Additional exam requirements/recommendations for international students: Required—TOEFL. Electronic applications accepted.

**York University,** Faculty of Graduate Studies, Faculty of Fine Arts, Program in Theatre, Toronto, ON M3J 1P3, Canada. Offers MFA. *Degree requirements:* For master's, thesis. Electronic applications accepted.

**York University,** Faculty of Graduate Studies, Faculty of Fine Arts, Program in Theatre and Performance Studies, Toronto, ON M3J 1P3, Canada. Offers MA, PhD.

# Therapies—Dance, Drama, and Music

**Antioch University New England,** Graduate School, Department of Applied Psychology, Program in Dance/Movement Therapy and Counseling, Keene, NH 03431-3552. Offers M Ed, MA, PMC. *Degree requirements:* For master's, thesis, internship, practicum. *Entrance requirements:* For master's, previous course work and work experience in psychology, experience in dance or movement. Additional exam requirements/recommendations for international students: Required—TOEFL (minimum score 550 paper-based). Electronic applications accepted. *Expenses:* Contact institution. *Faculty research:* Research attitudes and needs of dance/movement therapists.

**Appalachian State University,** Cratis D. Williams Graduate School, School of Music, Boone, NC 28608. Offers music performance (MM); music therapy (MMT). *Accreditation:* NASM. *Program availability:* Part-time. *Degree requirements:* For master's, comprehensive exam, thesis or alternative. *Entrance requirements:* For master's, GRE General Test, 3 letters of reference, audition. Additional exam requirements/recommendations for international students: Required—TOEFL (minimum score 550 paper-based; 79 iBT), IELTS (minimum score 6.5). *Application deadline:* For fall admission, 3/15 for domestic students, 2/1 for international students; for spring admission, 11/1 for domestic students, 7/1 for international students. Applications are processed on a rolling basis. Application fee: $55. Electronic applications accepted. *Expenses:* Tuition, state resident: full-time $4744. Tuition, nonresident: full-time $17,913. Full-time tuition and fees vary according to program. *Financial support:* Fellowships, research assistantships, teaching assistantships, career-related internships or fieldwork, Federal Work-Study, scholarships/grants, tuition waivers (partial), and unspecified assistantships available. Financial award application deadline: 4/1; financial award applicants required to submit FAFSA. *Faculty research:* Music of the Holocaust, Celtic folk music, early nineteenth-century performance practice, hypermeter and phase rhythm, world music, music and psychoneuroimmunology. *Unit head:* Dr. Kathy McKinney, Program Director, 828-262-6444, E-mail: mckinneych@appstate.edu. *Application contact:* Dr. Jennifer Snodgrass, Graduate Program Director, 828-262-6463, E-mail: snodgrassjs@appstate.edu.
Website: http://www.music.appstate.edu

**Arizona State University at the Tempe campus,** Herberger Institute for Design and the Arts, School of Music, Tempe, AZ 85287-0405. Offers composition (MM, DMA); conducting (DMA); ethnomusicology (MA); interdisciplinary digital media/performance (DMA); music education (MM, PhD); music history and literature (MA); music therapy (MM); performance (MM, DMA). *Accreditation:* NASM. Terminal master's awarded for partial completion of doctoral program. *Degree requirements:* For master's, thesis (for some programs), interactive Program of Study (iPOS) submitted before completing 50 percent of required credit hours; for doctorate, comprehensive exam, thesis/dissertation, interactive Program of Study (iPOS) submitted before completing 50 percent of required credit hours. *Entrance requirements:* For master's, minimum GPA of 3.0 or equivalent in last 2 years of work leading to bachelor's degree, 3 letters of recommendation, resume; for doctorate, GRE or MAT, minimum GPA of 3.0 or equivalent in last 2 years of work leading to bachelor's degree, 3 letters of recommendation, curriculum vitae, statement of intent. Additional exam requirements/recommendations for international students: Required—TOEFL, IELTS, or PTE. Electronic applications accepted.

**Berklee College of Music,** Berklee Graduate Programs, Boston, MA 02215-3693. Offers contemporary performance (MM), including global jazz, production; global entertainment and music business (MA); music production, technology, and innovation (MM); music therapy (MA); scoring for film, television, and video games (MM). Production; global entertainment and music business; music production, technology, and innovation; and scoring for film, television, and video games programs offered at Valencia, Spain campus. *Program availability:* Part-time, blended/hybrid learning. *Faculty:* 53 full-time (18 women), 39 part-time/adjunct (7 women). *Students:* 159 full-time (51 women), 30 part-time (24 women); includes 35 minority (12 Black or African American, non-Hispanic/Latino; 7 Asian, non-Hispanic/Latino; 12 Hispanic/Latino; 4 Two or more races, non-Hispanic/Latino), 78 international. Average age 26. 774 applicants, 36% accepted, 177 enrolled. In 2016, 137 master's awarded. *Degree requirements:* For master's, thesis, culminating experience project. *Entrance requirements:* Additional exam requirements/recommendations for international students: Required—TOEFL (minimum score 600 paper-based; 100 iBT), IELTS (minimum score 7.5), PTE (minimum score 73). *Application deadline:* For fall admission, 2/1 for domestic and international students. Application fee: $150. Electronic applications accepted. *Expenses:* Contact institution. *Financial support:* In 2016–17, 161 students received support, including 120 fellowships with full and partial tuition reimbursements available (averaging $18,507 per year), 41 research assistantships (averaging $4,220 per year); career-related internships or fieldwork, scholarships/grants, and tuition waivers (full and partial) also available. Support available to part-time students. Financial award application deadline: 2/1; financial award applicants required to submit CSS PROFILE or FAFSA. *Faculty research:* Neuroscience, integrative medicine, music therapy practice, music cognition, ethnomusicology. *Unit head:* Camille Colatosti, PhD, Dean, Institutional Assessment and Graduate Studies, E-mail: ccolatosti@berklee.edu. *Application contact:* Office of Admissions, 617-747-2221, E-mail: admissions@berklee.edu.
Website: https://www.berklee.edu/graduate

**California Institute of Integral Studies,** School of Professional Psychology and Health, San Francisco, CA 94103. Offers clinical psychology (Psy D); community mental health (MA); drama therapy (MA); expressive arts therapy (MA); human sexuality (PhD); integral counseling psychology (MA); integrative health studies (MA); psychological studies (MA); somatic psychology (MA). *Program availability:* Part-time, evening/weekend, 100% online, blended/hybrid learning. *Students:* 526 full-time (408 women), 113 part-time (96 women); includes 173 minority (34 Black or African American, non-Hispanic/Latino; 5 American Indian or Alaska Native, non-Hispanic/Latino; 31 Asian, non-Hispanic/Latino; 58 Hispanic/Latino; 1 Native Hawaiian or other Pacific Islander, non-Hispanic/Latino; 44 Two or more races, non-Hispanic/Latino), 52 international. Average age 38. 319 applicants, 85% accepted, 164 enrolled. In 2016, 157 master's, 21 doctorates awarded. *Degree requirements:* For doctorate, comprehensive exam, thesis/dissertation. *Entrance requirements:* For master's, minimum GPA of 3.0, letters of recommendation, writing sample; for doctorate, GRE, MA in psychology or social work with appropriate practical experience for advanced standing, or BA with a minimum GPA of 3.1; letters of recommendation; writing sample. Additional exam requirements/recommendations for international students: Required—TOEFL. *Application deadline:* For fall admission, 2/1 priority date for domestic and international students; for spring admission, 10/15 priority date for domestic and international students. Applications are processed on a rolling basis. Application fee: $65. Electronic applications accepted. *Expenses:* Tuition: Full-time $19,728; part-time $1098 per semester hour. *Required fees:* $320; $320 per semester hour. *Financial support:* Research assistantships with tuition reimbursements, teaching assistantships with tuition reimbursements, career-related internships or fieldwork, Federal Work-Study, and scholarships/grants available. Support available to part-time students. Financial award application deadline: 4/15; financial award applicants required to submit FAFSA. *Faculty research:* Transpersonal psychology, somatic psychology, expressive arts therapy, drama therapy, community mental health, ecopsychology, integrative health, human sexuality. *Application contact:*

Ellen Durst, Director of Admissions, 415-575-6100, Fax: 415-575-1268, E-mail: admissions@ciis.edu.

**Colorado State University,** College of Liberal Arts, School of Music, Theatre and Dance, Fort Collins, CO 80523-1779. Offers choral conducting (MM); collaborative piano (MM); instrumental conducting (MM); music education (MM), including conducting; music performance (MM); music therapy (MM). *Accreditation:* NASM. *Program availability:* Part-time. *Faculty:* 25 full-time (7 women), 9 part-time/adjunct (5 women). *Students:* 54 full-time (31 women), 100 part-time (77 women); includes 16 minority (2 Black or African American, non-Hispanic/Latino; 4 Asian, non-Hispanic/Latino; 8 Hispanic/Latino; 2 Two or more races, non-Hispanic/Latino), 13 international. Average age 30. 77 applicants, 79% accepted, 43 enrolled. In 2016, 69 master's awarded. *Degree requirements:* For master's, comprehensive exam, thesis, recital. *Entrance requirements:* For master's, minimum GPA of 3.0, audition, bachelor's degree, 3 letters of recommendation, transcripts, statement of purpose, curriculum vitae. Additional exam requirements/recommendations for international students: Required—TOEFL (minimum score 550 paper-based; 80 iBT), IELTS (minimum score 6.5). *Application deadline:* For fall admission, 2/15 for domestic and international students. Applications are processed on a rolling basis. Application fee: $60 ($70 for international students). Electronic applications accepted. *Expenses:* Contact institution. *Financial support:* In 2016–17, 25 students received support, including 24 teaching assistantships with full and partial tuition reimbursements available (averaging $8,998 per year); research assistantships, scholarships/grants, traineeships, and unspecified assistantships also available. Financial award application deadline: 2/15; financial award applicants required to submit FAFSA. *Faculty research:* Musical creativity in children with autism spectrum disorder; music therapy; cognitive, sensorimotor, speech and language and psychosocial functioning techniques; study/analysis/ear training strategies. *Total annual research expenditures:* $12,966. *Unit head:* Dr. Daniel Goble, Director, 970-491-5529, E-mail: dan.goble@colostate.edu. *Application contact:* Dr. G. Murray Oliver, Graduate Program Coordinator, 970-491-5193, Fax: 970-491-7541, E-mail: murray.oliver@colostate.edu. Website: http://smtd.colostate.edu/

**Columbia College Chicago,** Graduate School, Department of Creative Arts Therapies, Chicago, IL 60605-1996. Offers dance/movement therapy and counseling (MA, Certificate); drama therapy and counseling (MA); Laban movement analysis (Certificate); movement pattern analysis (Certificate). *Degree requirements:* For master's, thesis, internship. *Entrance requirements:* For master's, self-assessment essay, work sample, interview, letters of recommendation. Additional exam requirements/recommendations for international students: Required—TOEFL (minimum score 600 paper-based; 100 iBT). Electronic applications accepted.

**Concordia University,** School of Graduate Studies, Faculty of Fine Arts, Department of Creative Arts Therapies, Montréal, QC H3G 1M8, Canada. Offers art therapy (MA); drama therapy (MA); music therapy (MA).

**Drexel University,** College of Nursing and Health Professions, Department of Creative Arts Therapies, Specialization in Dance/Movement Therapy, Philadelphia, PA 19104-2875. Offers MA, PMC. *Program availability:* Part-time. *Students:* 32 full-time (29 women), 3 part-time (all women); includes 6 minority (5 Black or African American, non-Hispanic/Latino; 1 Native Hawaiian or other Pacific Islander, non-Hispanic/Latino), 3 international. Average age 26. In 2016, 6 master's awarded. *Degree requirements:* For master's, comprehensive exam, thesis. *Entrance requirements:* For master's, GRE General Test or MAT, audition, interview, minimum GPA of 2.75. *Application deadline:* For fall admission, 3/1 for domestic students. Applications are processed on a rolling basis. Application fee: $50. Electronic applications accepted. *Expenses:* Tuition: Full-time $32,184; part-time $1192 per credit hour. *Required fees:* $280. Tuition and fees vary according to campus/location and program. *Financial support:* Career-related internships or fieldwork, Federal Work-Study, and institutionally sponsored loans available. Support available to part-time students. Financial award application deadline: 5/1; financial award applicants required to submit FAFSA. *Faculty research:* Family nonverbal communication, early intervention, sexual abuse. *Unit head:* Sharon W. Goodill, Director, 215-762-6926, E-mail: sherry.goodill@drexel.edu. *Application contact:* Director of Graduate Admissions, 215-895-6700, Fax: 215-895-5939, E-mail: enroll@drexel.edu.

**Drexel University,** College of Nursing and Health Professions, Department of Creative Arts Therapies, Specialization in Music Therapy, Philadelphia, PA 19104-2875. Offers MA, PMC. *Program availability:* Part-time. *Students:* 20 full-time (14 women), 3 part-time (all women); includes 4 minority (2 Black or African American, non-Hispanic/Latino; 1 Asian, non-Hispanic/Latino; 1 Two or more races, non-Hispanic/Latino), 3 international. Average age 28. In 2016, 11 master's awarded. *Degree requirements:* For master's, comprehensive exam, thesis. *Entrance requirements:* For master's, GRE General Test or MAT, audition, interview, minimum GPA of 2.75. *Application deadline:* For fall admission, 3/1 for domestic students. Applications are processed on a rolling basis. Application fee: $50. Electronic applications accepted. *Expenses:* Tuition: Full-time $32,184; part-time $1192 per credit hour. *Required fees:* $280. Tuition and fees vary according to campus/location and program. *Financial support:* Career-related internships or fieldwork, Federal Work-Study, institutionally sponsored loans, and unspecified assistantships available. Support available to part-time students. Financial award application deadline: 5/1; financial award applicants required to submit FAFSA. *Faculty research:* Early childhood intervention through creative art therapies, rhythm and dementia, music therapy and bulimia, assessment of adolescent suicide. *Unit head:* Paul Nolan, Director, 215-762-6927, Fax: 215-762-6933, E-mail: paul.nolan@drexel.edu. *Application contact:* Director of Graduate Admissions, 215-895-6700, Fax: 215-895-5939, E-mail: enroll@drexel.edu.

**East Carolina University,** Graduate School, College of Fine Arts and Communication, School of Music, Greenville, NC 27858-4353. Offers advanced performance studies (Certificate); music education (MM); music therapy (MM); performance (MM), including accompanying, choral conducting, instrumental conducting, jazz studies, organ, percussion, piano, piano pedagogy, sacred music, strings, Suzuki string pedagogy, vocal pedagogy, voice, woodwind specialist; Suzuki pedagogy (Certificate); theory and composition (MM). *Accreditation:* NASM. *Program availability:* Part-time. *Students:* 29 full-time (15 women), 19 part-time (9 women); includes 4 minority (2 Black or African American, non-Hispanic/Latino; 2 Asian, non-Hispanic/Latino), 1 international. Average age 27. 39 applicants, 100% accepted, 28 enrolled. In 2016, 10 master's awarded. *Degree requirements:* For master's, comprehensive exam, thesis optional. *Entrance requirements:* For master's, GRE General Test or MAT. Additional exam requirements/recommendations for international students: Required—TOEFL. *Application deadline:* For fall admission, 6/1 priority date for domestic students. Applications are processed on a rolling basis. Application fee: $50. *Financial support:* Fellowships, research assistantships, teaching assistantships, and Federal Work-Study available. Support available to part-time students. Financial award application deadline: 6/1. *Unit head:* Christopher Ulffers, Director, 252-328-4270, E-mail: ulffersj@ecu.edu. *Application contact:* Dean of Graduate School, 252-328-6012, Fax: 252-328-6071, E-mail: gradschool@ecu.edu. Website: http://www.music.ecu.edu/

**Florida State University,** The Graduate School, College of Music, Tallahassee, FL 32306. Offers accompanying (MM); arts administration (MA); choral conducting (MM);

composition (MM, DM); ethnomusicology (MM); general music (MA); instrumental accompanying (MM); instrumental conducting (MM); jazz studies (MM); music theory (MM, PhD); music therapy (MM); musicology (MM, PhD), including ethnomusicology (PhD), historical musicology (PhD); opera (MM); performance (MM, DM); piano pedagogy (MM); piano technology (MA); vocal accompanying (MM). *Accreditation:* NASM. *Program availability:* Part-time. *Faculty:* 79 full-time, 2 part-time/adjunct. *Students:* 324 full-time (156 women); includes 87 minority (26 Black or African American, non-Hispanic/Latino; 1 American Indian or Alaska Native, non-Hispanic/Latino; 32 Asian, non-Hispanic/Latino; 26 Hispanic/Latino; 2 Native Hawaiian or other Pacific Islander, non-Hispanic/Latino). Average age 26. 737 applicants, 42% accepted, 138 enrolled. In 2016, 120 master's, 36 doctorates awarded. *Degree requirements:* For master's, variable foreign language requirement, comprehensive exam (for some programs), thesis (for some programs), departmental qualifying exam; for doctorate, variable foreign language requirement, comprehensive exam (for some programs), thesis/dissertation, departmental qualifying exam. *Entrance requirements:* For master's, GRE General Test (for some programs), audition, minimum GPA of 3.0; for doctorate, GRE General Test (for some programs), audition, master's degree, minimum GPA of 3.0. Additional exam requirements/recommendations for international students: Required—TOEFL (minimum score 590 paper-based; 97 iBT), IELTS (minimum score 7.5). *Application deadline:* For fall admission, 7/1 for domestic and international students; for spring admission, 11/1 for domestic and international students; for summer admission, 3/1 for domestic students. Applications are processed on a rolling basis. Application fee: $30. Electronic applications accepted. *Expenses:* Tuition, state resident: full-time $7263; part-time $403.51 per credit hour. Tuition, nonresident: full-time $18,087; part-time $1004.85 per credit hour. *Required fees:* $1365; $75.81 per credit hour. $20 per semester. Tuition and fees vary according to campus/location. *Financial support:* In 2016–17, 222 students received support, including 2 fellowships with full tuition reimbursements available (averaging $15,000 per year), 14 research assistantships with full and partial tuition reimbursements available (averaging $5,900 per year), 201 teaching assistantships with full and partial tuition reimbursements available (averaging $5,900 per year); career-related internships or fieldwork, scholarships/grants, tuition waivers (full and partial), and unspecified assistantships also available. Support available to part-time students. Financial award application deadline: 2/28; financial award applicants required to submit FAFSA. *Faculty research:* Music therapy in NICU units, music of the Americas, music theory pedagogy, music performance. *Unit head:* Dr. Patricia Flowers, Dean, 850-644-4361, Fax: 850-644-2033, E-mail: pjflowers@fsu.edu. *Application contact:* Kris Watson, Director of Admissions, 850-645-2126, Fax: 850-644-2033, E-mail: krwatson@fsu.edu. Website: http://www.music.fsu.edu/

**Georgia College & State University,** Graduate School, College of Health Sciences, Program in Music Therapy, Milledgeville, GA 31061. Offers MMT. *Program availability:* Part-time, evening/weekend. *Students:* 10 full-time (7 women), 4 part-time (all women); includes 4 minority (3 Black or African American, non-Hispanic/Latino; 1 Hispanic/Latino), 1 international. Average age 32. 4 applicants, 100% accepted, 3 enrolled. In 2016, 4 master's awarded. *Degree requirements:* For master's, comprehensive exam, thesis or alternative, minimum GPA of 3.0. *Entrance requirements:* For master's, bachelor's degree in music therapy or equivalent, minimum undergraduate GPA of 2.75, 2 letters of recommendation, essay, interview. *Application deadline:* For fall admission, 7/1 priority date for domestic students; for spring admission, 11/1 priority date for domestic students; for summer admission, 4/1 priority date for domestic students. Applications are processed on a rolling basis. Application fee: $40. Electronic applications accepted. *Expenses:* $338 per credit hour tuition, $1,586 per year full-time fees. *Financial support:* In 2016–17, 3 students received support. Unspecified assistantships available. Support available to part-time students. Financial award application deadline: 3/1; financial award applicants required to submit FAFSA. *Unit head:* Dr. Chesley Mercado, Director, 478-445-2645, Fax: 478-445-2645, E-mail: chesley.mercado@gcsu.edu. *Application contact:* Kate Marshall, Graduate Admissions Coordinator, 478-445-1184, Fax: 478-445-1336, E-mail: grad-admit@gcsu.edu. Website: http://gcsu.edu/health/therapy/music-therapy-mmt

**Immaculata University,** College of Graduate Studies, Program in Music Therapy, Immaculata, PA 19345. Offers MA. *Accreditation:* NASM. *Program availability:* Part-time, evening/weekend. *Degree requirements:* For master's, comprehensive exam, thesis optional. *Entrance requirements:* For master's, GRE General Test or MAT, minimum GPA of 3.0. Additional exam requirements/recommendations for international students: Required—TOEFL. Electronic applications accepted. *Faculty research:* Biofeedback music laboratory, experimental music therapy, virtual arts therapies, sound beam.

**Indiana University–Purdue University Indianapolis,** School of Engineering and Technology, Department of Music and Arts Technology, Indianapolis, IN 46202. Offers music technology (MS, PhD); music therapy (MS). *Accreditation:* NASM. *Program availability:* Part-time, evening/weekend, online learning. *Faculty:* 8 full-time (2 women), 2 part-time/adjunct. *Students:* 9 full-time (1 woman), 12 part-time (4 women); includes 6 minority (4 Black or African American, non-Hispanic/Latino; 2 Hispanic/Latino), 1 international. Average age 31. 19 applicants, 63% accepted, 9 enrolled. In 2016, 15 master's awarded. *Degree requirements:* For master's, thesis optional, internship or final project; for doctorate, thesis/dissertation. *Entrance requirements:* For master's, GRE, interview, audition, minimum GPA of 3.0; for doctorate, GRE, three letters of recommendation; research adviser letter; statement of purpose; writing samples; transcripts; portfolio. Additional exam requirements/recommendations for international students: Required—TOEFL (minimum score 550 paper-based; 79 iBT); Recommended—IELTS (minimum score 6.5). *Application deadline:* For fall admission, 4/15 for domestic students, 3/15 for international students; for spring admission, 11/15 for domestic and international students. Application fee: $55 ($65 for international students). Electronic applications accepted. *Expenses:* Contact institution. *Financial support:* Fellowships, research assistantships, teaching assistantships with full tuition reimbursements, scholarships/grants, tuition waivers, and unspecified assistantships available. Financial award application deadline: 11/15. *Faculty research:* Music-related cross-disciplinary technologies in fine arts, education, business, health care, computer science, and engineering; exploring and creating multi-disciplinary music, dance, and arts performance; developing new recording techniques and emerging technologies. *Total annual research expenditures:* $9,951. *Unit head:* Dr. Debra S. Burns, Chair, Department of Music and Arts Technology, 317-278-2014, E-mail: desburns@iupui.edu. *Application contact:* Tina Everts, Assistant to Chair, 317-274-7088, E-mail: teverts@iupui.edu. Website: http://www.engr.iupui.edu/departments/mat/

**Lesley University,** Graduate School of Arts and Social Sciences, Cambridge, MA 02138-2790. Offers clinical mental health counseling (MA), including holistic counseling, school and community counseling, trauma studies; counseling psychology (MA, CAGS), including professional counseling (MA), school counseling (MA); creative writing (MFA); expressive therapies (MA, PhD, CAGS), including art (MA), clinical mental health counseling (MA), dance (MA), expressive therapies (MA), music (MA); independent studies (CAGS); independent study (MA); intercultural relations (MA, CAGS); interdisciplinary studies (MA), including individualized studies, integrative holistic health, mindfulness studies, peace and conflict transformation, trauma sensitive assessment, intervention, and consultation, women's studies; urban environmental leadership (MA). *Program availability:* Part-time, online learning. *Degree requirements:* For master's, internship, practicum, thesis (for expressive therapies); for doctorate, thesis/dissertation, arts apprenticeship, field placement; for CAGS, thesis, internship (for counseling psychology, expressive therapies). *Entrance requirements:* For master's, MAT (counseling psychology), interview, writing samples, art portfolio; for doctorate, GRE or MAT, interview, master's degree; for CAGS, interview, master's degree. Additional exam requirements/recommendations for international students: Required—TOEFL (minimum score 550 paper-based; 80 iBT). Electronic applications accepted. *Faculty research:* Psychotherapy and culture; psychotherapy and psychological trauma; women's issues in art, teaching and psychotherapy; community-based art, psycho-spiritual inquiry.

**Loyola University New Orleans,** College of Music and Fine Arts, New Orleans, LA 70118-6195. Offers music therapy (MMT); performance (MM). *Accreditation:* NASM. *Program availability:* Part-time. *Faculty:* 15 full-time (7 women), 7 part-time/adjunct (5 women). *Students:* 37 full-time (25 women), 8 part-time (6 women); includes 16 minority (6 Black or African American, non-Hispanic/Latino; 1 Asian, non-Hispanic/Latino; 6 Hispanic/Latino; 3 Two or more races, non-Hispanic/Latino), 3 international. Average age 28. 55 applicants, 44% accepted, 17 enrolled. In 2016, 5 master's awarded. *Degree requirements:* For master's, comprehensive written and oral exams; thesis (for MMT). *Entrance requirements:* For master's, performance audition, appropriate bachelor's degree, transcripts, minimum GPA of 3.0, 2 letters of recommendation, resume. Additional exam requirements/recommendations for international students: Required—TOEFL (minimum score 550 paper-based; 79 iBT). *Application deadline:* For fall admission, 8/15 priority date for domestic and international students; for spring admission, 1/1 priority date for domestic and international students. Applications are processed on a rolling basis. Application fee: $20. Electronic applications accepted. *Expenses:* $818 per credit hour full-time tuition, $883 fees; $409 per credit hour part-time tuition, $527 fees; $275 graduation fee. *Financial support:* Career-related internships or fieldwork, Federal Work-Study, institutionally sponsored loans, scholarships/grants, unspecified assistantships, and talent-based music scholarships available. Support available to part-time students. Financial award application deadline: 5/1; financial award applicants required to submit FAFSA. *Faculty research:* Music business, music therapy, musicology, music theory, music education. *Unit head:* Dr. Victoria P. Vega, Associate Dean, 504-865-3037, Fax: 504-865-2852, E-mail: vpvega@loyno.edu. *Application contact:* Melissa L. Lightell, Director, Office of Professional and Continuing Studies, 504-865-3530, Fax: 504-865-2787, E-mail: evening@loyno.edu.
Website: http://cmfa.loyno.edu/

**Maryville University of Saint Louis,** Walker College of Health Professions, Program in Music Therapy, St. Louis, MO 63141-7299. Offers MMT. *Accreditation:* NASM. *Program availability:* Part-time. *Faculty:* 1 (woman) full-time, 4 part-time/adjunct (all women). *Students:* 9 full-time (all women), 7 part-time (all women); includes 4 minority (1 Black or African American, non-Hispanic/Latino; 2 Hispanic/Latino; 1 Two or more races, non-Hispanic/Latino), 1 international. Average age 27. In 2016, 4 master's awarded. *Entrance requirements:* For master's, music audition, interview, minimum undergraduate GPA of 3.0, 3 letters of recommendation. Additional exam requirements/recommendations for international students: Required—TOEFL (minimum score 550 paper-based). *Application deadline:* Applications are processed on a rolling basis. Electronic applications accepted. *Expenses:* $781 per credit hour. *Financial support:* Application deadline: 3/1; applicants required to submit FAFSA. *Unit head:* Dr. Cynthia Briggs, Director, 314-529-9441, Fax: 314-529-9495, E-mail: cbriggs@maryville.edu. *Application contact:* Jeannie DeLuca, Director, Admissions and Advising, 314-529-9355, Fax: 314-529-9927, E-mail: jdeluca@maryville.edu.
Website: http://www.maryville.edu/hp/music-therapy

**Michigan State University,** The Graduate School, College of Music, East Lansing, MI 48824. Offers collaborative piano (M Mus); jazz studies (M Mus); music (PhD); music composition (M Mus, DMA); music conducting (M Mus, DMA); music education (M Mus); music performance (M Mus, DMA); music theory (M Mus); music therapy (M Mus); musicology (MA); piano pedagogy (M Mus). *Accreditation:* NASM. *Entrance requirements:* Additional exam requirements/recommendations for international students: Required—TOEFL. Electronic applications accepted.

**Molloy College,** Graduate Music Therapy Program, Rockville Centre, NY 11571-5002. Offers MS. *Program availability:* Part-time, evening/weekend. *Faculty:* 4 full-time (3 women), 6 part-time/adjunct (5 women). *Students:* 9 full-time (6 women), 20 part-time (12 women); includes 5 minority (1 Black or African American, non-Hispanic/Latino; 1 Asian, non-Hispanic/Latino; 3 Hispanic/Latino), 5 international. Average age 33. 28 applicants, 39% accepted, 9 enrolled. In 2016, 12 master's awarded. *Entrance requirements:* Additional exam requirements/recommendations for international students: Required—TOEFL (minimum score 550 paper-based; 79 iBT). *Application deadline:* Applications are processed on a rolling basis. Application fee: $60. Electronic applications accepted. *Expenses:* Tuition: Full-time $19,170; part-time $1065 per credit. *Required fees:* $950; $790 per credit. Tuition and fees vary according to course load. *Financial support:* Applicants required to submit FAFSA. *Faculty research:* Validity and reliability evidence for the individual music-centered assessment profile for neurodevelopmental disorders (IMCAP-ND); imitation or mimicry in improvisational music therapy to increase joint attention for children with autism spectrum disorder; randomized control trial of improvisational music therapy's effectiveness for children with autism spectrum disorders. *Unit head:* Suzanne Sorel, Associate Dean/Director of Graduate Music Therapy, 516-323-3322, E-mail: ssorel@molloy.edu. *Application contact:* Jaclyn Machowicz, Assistant Director for Admissions, 516-323-4010, E-mail: jmachowicz@molloy.edu.

**Montclair State University,** The Graduate School, College of the Arts, John J. Cali School of Music, Post Baccalaureate Certificate Program in Music Therapy, Montclair, NJ 07043-1624. Offers Postbaccalaureate Certificate. *Program availability:* Part-time, evening/weekend. *Entrance requirements:* For degree, 2 letters of recommendation, essay. Additional exam requirements/recommendations for international students: Required—TOEFL (minimum score 83 iBT), IELTS (minimum score 6.5). Electronic applications accepted. *Expenses:* Tuition, state resident: part-time $553 per credit. Tuition, nonresident: part-time $854 per credit. *Required fees:* $91 per credit. Tuition and fees vary according to program.

**Montclair State University,** The Graduate School, College of the Arts, John J. Cali School of Music, Program in Music, Montclair, NJ 07043-1624. Offers music education (MA); music therapy (MA); performance (MA); theory/composition (MA). *Program availability:* Part-time, evening/weekend. *Degree requirements:* For master's, thesis. *Entrance requirements:* For master's, GRE General Test, 2 letters of recommendation, essay. Additional exam requirements/recommendations for international students: Required—TOEFL (minimum score 83 iBT), IELTS (minimum score 6.5). Electronic applications accepted. *Expenses:* Tuition, state resident: part-time $553 per credit. Tuition, nonresident: part-time $854 per credit. *Required fees:* $91 per credit. Tuition and fees vary according to program.

**Naropa University,** Graduate Programs, Program in Clinical Mental Health Counseling, Concentration in Somatic Counseling: Dance/Movement Therapy, Boulder, CO 80302-

6697. Offers MA. *Faculty:* 3 full-time (2 women), 8 part-time/adjunct (all women). *Students:* 25 full-time (23 women), 13 part-time (12 women); includes 16 minority (3 Black or African American, non-Hispanic/Latino; 1 American Indian or Alaska Native, non-Hispanic/Latino; 3 Asian, non-Hispanic/Latino; 5 Hispanic/Latino; 4 Two or more races, non-Hispanic/Latino), 1 international. Average age 29. 28 applicants, 71% accepted, 11 enrolled. In 2016, 13 master's awarded. *Degree requirements:* For master's, thesis, internship, clinical practicum. *Entrance requirements:* For master's, BA (preferably in field related to the helping professions); minimum of 100 hours of paid or volunteer experience in mental health field or community facility/service organization; interview; state of interest essay; supplemental essays; 2 letters of recommendation; transcripts. Additional exam requirements/recommendations for international students: Required—TOEFL (minimum score 550 paper-based; 80 iBT). *Application deadline:* For fall admission, 1/15 priority date for domestic and international students. Applications are processed on a rolling basis. Application fee: $60. Electronic applications accepted. *Expenses:* $25,545 for first year. *Financial support:* In 2016–17, 10 students received support, including 1 research assistantship with partial tuition reimbursement available (averaging $3,000 per year); teaching assistantships with partial tuition reimbursements available, career-related internships or fieldwork, Federal Work-Study, scholarships/grants, tuition waivers (partial), and unspecified assistantships also available. Support available to part-time students. Financial award application deadline: 3/1; financial award applicants required to submit FAFSA. *Unit head:* Dr. Deborah Bowman, Dean, Graduate School of Counseling and Psychology, 303-546-3559, E-mail: bowman@naropa.edu. *Application contact:* Office of Admissions, 303-546-3572, Fax: 303-546-3583, E-mail: admissions@naropa.edu.
Website: http://www.naropa.edu/academics/masters/clinical-mental-health-counseling/somatic-counseling/dance-movement-therapy/index.php

**Nazareth College of Rochester,** Graduate Studies, Department of Creative Arts Therapy, Rochester, NY 14618. Offers art therapy (MS); music therapy (MS). *Program availability:* Part-time. *Students:* 36 full-time (32 women), 10 part-time (9 women); includes 3 minority (1 Black or African American, non-Hispanic/Latino; 2 Asian, non-Hispanic/Latino). Average age 25. 64 applicants, 55% accepted, 20 enrolled. *Entrance requirements:* For master's, minimum GPA of 3.0; portfolio review (art therapy); audition (music therapy). Additional exam requirements/recommendations for international students: Required—TOEFL (minimum score 550 paper-based, 79 iBT) or IELTS (6.5). *Application deadline:* For fall admission, 1/15 for domestic students. Electronic applications accepted. *Expenses:* Tuition: Part-time $880 per credit hour. Part-time tuition and fees vary according to course load, degree level and program. *Financial support:* Unspecified assistantships available. Financial award application deadline: 3/1; financial award applicants required to submit FAFSA. *Unit head:* Dr. Bryan Hunter, Chair, Creative Arts Therapy, 585-389-2702, E-mail: bhunter7@naz.edu. *Application contact:* Judith Baker, Director, Transfer and Graduate Admissions, 585-531-1154, Fax: 585-389-2826, E-mail: gradadmissions@naz.edu.

**New York University,** Steinhardt School of Culture, Education, and Human Development, Department of Music and Performing Arts Professions, Program in Drama Therapy, New York, NY 10012. Offers MA. *Program availability:* Part-time. *Degree requirements:* For master's, thesis (for some programs). *Entrance requirements:* For master's, audition, interview. Additional exam requirements/recommendations for international students: Required—TOEFL (minimum score 100 iBT). Electronic applications accepted. *Faculty research:* Meaning of role in drama, therapy, and everyday life; clinical approaches to drama therapy; trauma effects on children.

**New York University,** Steinhardt School of Culture, Education, and Human Development, Department of Music and Performing Arts Professions, Program in Music Therapy, New York, NY 10010. Offers MA. *Program availability:* Part-time. *Degree requirements:* For master's, thesis (for some programs). *Entrance requirements:* For master's, audition, interview. Additional exam requirements/recommendations for international students: Required—TOEFL (minimum score 100 iBT). Electronic applications accepted. *Faculty research:* Music therapy in special education, including autism and emotional disabilities; guided imagery.

**Ohio University,** Graduate College, College of Fine Arts, School of Music, Athens, OH 45701-2979. Offers accompanying (MM); composition (MM); conducting (MM); history/literature (MM); music education (MM); music therapy (MM); performance (MM, Certificate); performance/pedagogy (MM); theory (MM). *Accreditation:* NASM. *Program availability:* Part-time, evening/weekend, online learning. *Degree requirements:* For master's, comprehensive exam, thesis (for some programs), oral exam. *Entrance requirements:* For master's, audition, interview, portfolio, recordings (varies by program). Additional exam requirements/recommendations for international students: Required—TOEFL (minimum score 550 paper-based; 80 iBT) or IELTS (minimum score 6.5). *Application deadline:* For fall admission, 1/1 priority date for domestic and international students. Application fee: $50 ($55 for international students). Electronic applications accepted. *Financial support:* Teaching assistantships with full and partial tuition reimbursements, career-related internships or fieldwork, Federal Work-Study, institutionally sponsored loans, and tuition waivers (full and partial) available. Financial award application deadline: 1/1. *Unit head:* Dr. Christopher Hayes, Director, 740-593-4244, E-mail: hayesc1@ohio.edu. *Application contact:* Dr. Richard Wetzel, Graduate Chair, 740-593-1652, Fax: 740-593-1429, E-mail: wetzel@ohio.edu.
Website: http://www.finearts.ohio.edu/music

**Pratt Institute,** School of Art, Programs in Creative Arts Therapy, Brooklyn, NY 11205-3899. Offers art therapy and creativity development (MPS); dance/movement therapy (MS). *Accreditation:* NASAD (one or more programs are accredited). *Program availability:* Part-time. *Faculty:* 3 full-time (all women), 22 part-time/adjunct (19 women). *Students:* 109 full-time (108 women); includes 38 minority (17 Black or African American, non-Hispanic/Latino; 4 Asian, non-Hispanic/Latino; 14 Hispanic/Latino; 3 Two or more races, non-Hispanic/Latino), 3 international. Average age 29. 149 applicants, 58% accepted, 44 enrolled. In 2016, 47 master's awarded. *Degree requirements:* For master's, thesis. *Entrance requirements:* For master's, letters of recommendation, portfolio. Additional exam requirements/recommendations for international students: Required—TOEFL (minimum score 600 paper-based; 100 iBT). *Application deadline:* For fall admission, 1/5 for domestic and international students; for spring admission, 10/1 for domestic and international students. Applications are processed on a rolling basis. Application fee: $50 ($90 for international students). Electronic applications accepted. *Expenses:* $29,646 full-time tuition, $1,938 fees. *Financial support:* Career-related internships or fieldwork, Federal Work-Study, institutionally sponsored loans, scholarships/grants, health care benefits, and unspecified assistantships available. Support available to part-time students. Financial award application deadline: 2/1; financial award applicants required to submit FAFSA. *Faculty research:* Psychology and aesthetic interaction, art therapy and AIDS, art therapy and autism, art diagnosis. *Unit head:* Dina Schapiro, Assistant Chairperson, 718-399-4267, Fax: 718-636-3597, E-mail: dschapir@pratt.edu. *Application contact:* Natalie Capannelli, Director of Graduate Admissions, 718-636-3551, Fax: 718-399-4242, E-mail: ncapanne@pratt.edu.
Website: https://www.pratt.edu/academics/school-of-art/graduate-school-of-art/creative-arts-therapy/

See Display on page 156 and Close-Up on page 209.

## Therapies—Dance, Drama, and Music

**Saint Mary-of-the-Woods College,** Master of Arts in Music Therapy Program, Saint Mary of the Woods, IN 47876. Offers MA. *Accreditation:* NASM. *Program availability:* Blended/hybrid learning. *Students:* 24 full-time (22 women). Average age 32. *Degree requirements:* For master's, thesis or alternative, qualifying exam, portfolio. *Entrance requirements:* For master's, diagnostic music exam, audition. *Application deadline:* Applications are processed on a rolling basis. Application fee: $0. Electronic applications accepted. *Expenses: Tuition:* Full-time $10,000. *Required fees:* $2000. Full-time tuition and fees vary according to program. *Financial support:* Career-related internships or fieldwork, scholarships/grants, and unspecified assistantships available. *Unit head:* Dr. Tracy Richardson, Director, 812-535-5154, E-mail: trichardson@smwc.edu.

**Shenandoah University,** Shenandoah Conservatory, Winchester, VA 22601-5195. Offers church music (MM, Certificate); collaborative piano (MM); composition (MM); conducting (MM); music (Artist Diploma); music education (MME); music therapy (MMT); pedagogy - voice (MM, DMA); performance (MM, DMA); performing arts leadership and management (MS). *Accreditation:* NASM. *Program availability:* Part-time. *Faculty:* 36 full-time (13 women), 12 part-time/adjunct (6 women). *Students:* 70 full-time (40 women), 71 part-time (43 women); includes 25 minority (7 Black or African American, non-Hispanic/Latino; 2 American Indian or Alaska Native, non-Hispanic/Latino; 5 Asian, non-Hispanic/Latino; 11 Hispanic/Latino), 21 international. Average age 31. 121 applicants, 79% accepted, 47 enrolled. In 2016, 29 master's, 7 doctorates, 9 other advanced degrees awarded. *Degree requirements:* For master's, comprehensive exam, minimum GPA of 3.0, internship (MS), recital (MM), research teaching project or thesis (MME), project (MA); for doctorate, comprehensive exam, minimum GPA of 3.0, dissertation or teaching project, recital; for other advanced degree, minimum GPA of 3.0, research project, recital. *Entrance requirements:* For master's, music theory diagnostic exam, bachelor's degree with minimum of GPA of 2.5, performance audition, writing sample, resume, all academic transcripts; for doctorate, music theory diagnostic exam; music history diagnostic exam; vocal diction proficiency exam, master's degree with minimum GPA of 3.25, performance audition, 2 letters of recommendation, writing sample, resume, all academic transcripts; for other advanced degree, bachelor's or master's degree; minimum GPA of 2.5; performance audition (for Artist Diploma). Additional exam requirements/recommendations for international students: Required—TOEFL (minimum score 550 paper-based; 79 iBT), IELTS (minimum score 6.5). *Application deadline:* For fall and spring admission, 1/15 for domestic and international students; for summer admission, 4/15 for domestic and international students. Application fee: $30. Electronic applications accepted. *Expenses:* Contact institution. *Financial support:* In 2016–17, 43 students received support. Scholarships/grants and unspecified assistantships available. Financial award applicants required to submit FAFSA. *Faculty research:* Brahms, Scriabin, arts as inquiry. *Unit head:* Dr. Michael J. Stepniak, Dean, 540-542.6201, Fax: 540-665-5402, E-mail: mstepnia@su.edu. *Application contact:* Andrew Woodall, Executive Director of Recruitment and Advancement, 540-665-4581, Fax: 540-665-4627, E-mail: admit@su.edu. Website: http://www.su.edu/conservatory/

**Slippery Rock University of Pennsylvania,** Graduate Studies (Recruitment), College of Liberal Arts, Department of Music, Slippery Rock, PA 16057-1383. Offers music therapy (MMT). *Program availability:* Part-time, blended/hybrid learning, interactive online classes and face-to-face intensives. *Faculty:* 2 full-time (1 woman). *Students:* 2 full-time (both women), 9 part-time (7 women); includes 1 minority (Two or more races, non-Hispanic/Latino). Average age 28. 16 applicants, 88% accepted, 11 enrolled. *Degree requirements:* For master's, thesis or alternative. *Entrance requirements:* For master's, bachelor's degree in music therapy with minimum GPA of 3.0, resume, statement of professional goals, video-recording of three songs accompanied on piano and three songs accompanied on guitar, video interview, official transcripts. Additional exam requirements/recommendations for international students: Required—TOEFL (minimum score 550 paper-based; 80 iBT). *Application deadline:* For fall admission, 5/1 priority date for domestic students, 3/1 priority date for international students; for spring admission, 10/1 priority date for domestic students, 9/1 priority date for international students. Applications are processed on a rolling basis. Application fee: $25 ($30 for international students). Electronic applications accepted. *Expenses:* $646.50 per credit in-state, $936.80 per credit out-of-state; $581.45 per online credit in-state, $648.65 per online credit out-of-state. *Financial support:* In 2016–17, 1 student received support. Career-related internships or fieldwork, Federal Work-Study, institutionally sponsored loans, scholarships/grants, tuition waivers (partial), and unspecified assistantships available. Support available to part-time students. Financial award application deadline: 5/1; financial award applicants required to submit FAFSA. *Unit head:* Dr. Susan Hadley, Program Director, 724-738-2063, Fax: 724-738-2263, E-mail: susan.hadley@sru.edu. *Application contact:* Brandi Weber-Mortimer, Director of Graduate Admissions, 724-738-4340, E-mail: graduate.admissions@sru.edu. Website: http://www.sru.edu/academics/colleges-and-departments/cla/departments/music

**State University of New York at New Paltz,** Graduate School, School of Fine and Performing Arts, Department of Music, New Paltz, NY 12561. Offers music therapy (MS). *Accreditation:* NASM. *Program availability:* Part-time. *Students:* 22 full-time (15 women), 11 part-time (9 women); includes 3 minority (1 Black or African American, non-Hispanic/Latino; 2 Hispanic/Latino), 7 international. 16 applicants, 81% accepted, 9 enrolled. In 2016, 10 master's awarded. *Degree requirements:* For master's, thesis. *Entrance requirements:* For master's, audition, minimum GPA of 3.0. Additional exam requirements/recommendations for international students: Required—TOEFL (minimum score 550 paper-based; 80 iBT), IELTS (minimum score 6.5). *Application deadline:* For fall admission, 5/15 for domestic and international students; for spring admission, 11/15 for domestic and international students. Applications are processed on a rolling basis. Application fee: $50. Electronic applications accepted. *Financial support:* In 2016–17, 4 teaching assistantships with partial tuition reimbursements (averaging $5,000 per year) were awarded. Financial award application deadline: 8/1. *Unit head:* Dr. John Mahoney, Program Director, 845-257-2709, E-mail: mahoneyj@newpaltz.edu. Website: http://www.newpaltz.edu/music/

**Temple University,** Center for the Performing and Cinematic Arts, Boyer College of Music and Dance, Department of Music, Philadelphia, PA 19122-6096. Offers choral conducting (MM); collaborative piano/chamber music (MM); collaborative piano/opera coaching (MM); composition (MM, PhD); instrumental conducting (MM); music education (MM, PhD); music history (MM); music performance (MM, DMA), including instrumental studies (MM), keyboard (DMA), keyboard studies (MM), voice (DMA), voice and opera (MM); music studies (PhD); music theory (MM, PhD); music therapy (MMT, PhD); musicology (MM, PhD); opera (MM); piano pedagogy (MM); string pedagogy (MM). *Accreditation:* NASM. *Program availability:* Part-time, online learning. Terminal master's awarded for partial completion of doctoral program. *Degree requirements:* For doctorate, thesis/dissertation. *Entrance requirements:* Additional exam requirements/recommendations for international students: Required—TOEFL. Electronic applications accepted.

**The University of Kansas,** Graduate Studies, School of Music, Program in Music Therapy, Lawrence, KS 66045. Offers MME, PhD. *Program availability:* Part-time.

*Students:* 10 full-time (9 women), 16 part-time (15 women); includes 3 minority (1 Black or African American, non-Hispanic/Latino; 2 Asian, non-Hispanic/Latino), 2 international. Average age 26. 14 applicants, 71% accepted, 6 enrolled. In 2016, 8 master's awarded. *Entrance requirements:* For master's, GRE General Test, minimum undergraduate GPA of 3.0, video, reference letters, transcripts; for doctorate, GRE General Test, MEMT Diagnostic Exam, minimum graduate GPA of 3.5, video, reference letters, transcripts, writing sample, proof of professional experience. Additional exam requirements/recommendations for international students: Required—TOEFL (minimum score 570 paper-based; 92 iBT) or IELTS (minimum score 6). *Application deadline:* For fall admission, 12/1 priority date for domestic and international students. Application fee: $65 ($85 for international students). Electronic applications accepted. *Financial support:* Fellowships, research assistantships, teaching assistantships, institutionally sponsored loans, scholarships/grants, and unspecified assistantships available. Financial award application deadline: 12/1; financial award applicants required to submit FAFSA. *Faculty research:* Orff-based music therapy; music therapy in health, wellness, autism and hospice; changing attitudes toward individuals with disabilities; music therapy in medical settings; music therapy in pediatrics, early intervention. *Unit head:* Dr. Christopher Johnson, Director, 785-864-9633, E-mail: cmj@ku.edu. *Application contact:* Lois Elmer, Administrative Professional for Music, 785-864-4784, Fax: 785-864-9640, E-mail: elmer@ku.edu. Website: http://www.memt.ku.edu

**University of Kentucky,** Graduate School, College of Fine Arts, Program in Music, Lexington, KY 40506-0032. Offers composition (MM, DMA); conducting (MM, DMA); music education (MM, PhD); music theory (MA, PhD); music therapy (MM); musicology (MA, PhD); performance (MM, DMA); sacred music (MM). *Accreditation:* NASM. *Program availability:* Part-time, evening/weekend. *Degree requirements:* For master's, variable foreign language requirement, comprehensive exam, thesis (for some programs); for doctorate, variable foreign language requirement, comprehensive exam, thesis/dissertation. *Entrance requirements:* For master's, GRE General Test, minimum undergraduate GPA of 2.75; for doctorate, GRE General Test, minimum undergraduate GPA of 2.75, graduate 3.0. Additional exam requirements/recommendations for international students: Required—TOEFL (minimum score 550 paper-based). Electronic applications accepted. *Faculty research:* Musicology, music theory, jazz, music education, performance and conducting.

**University of Miami,** Graduate School, Frost School of Music, Department of Music Education and Music Therapy, Coral Gables, FL 33124. Offers music education (MM, PhD, Spec M); music therapy (MM). *Accreditation:* NASM. *Degree requirements:* For master's, thesis; for doctorate, thesis/dissertation, 2 research tools; for Spec M, thesis, research project. *Entrance requirements:* For master's and doctorate, GRE General Test. Additional exam requirements/recommendations for international students: Required—TOEFL (minimum score 550 paper-based; 59 iBT). Electronic applications accepted. *Faculty research:* Motivation, quantitative research, early childhood, instrumental music, elementary music.

**University of Missouri–Kansas City,** Conservatory of Music and Dance, Kansas City, MO 64110-2499. Offers composition (MM, DMA); conducting (MM, DMA); music (MA); music education (MME, PhD); music history and literature (MM); music theory (MM); music therapy (MA); performance (MM, DMA). PhD (interdisciplinary) offered through the School of Graduate Studies. *Accreditation:* NASM. *Program availability:* Part-time. *Faculty:* 55 full-time (24 women), 39 part-time/adjunct (12 women). *Students:* 165 full-time (67 women), 64 part-time (34 women); includes 21 minority (4 Black or African American, non-Hispanic/Latino; 7 Asian, non-Hispanic/Latino; 7 Hispanic/Latino; 3 Two or more races, non-Hispanic/Latino), 49 international. Average age 28. 368 applicants, 49% accepted, 88 enrolled. In 2016, 49 master's, 26 doctorates awarded. *Degree requirements:* For master's, variable foreign language requirement, comprehensive exam, thesis (for some programs); for doctorate, variable foreign language requirement, comprehensive exam, thesis/dissertation or alternative. *Entrance requirements:* For master's, minimum GPA of 3.0 in major, auditions (for MM in performance); for doctorate, minimum graduate GPA of 3.5, auditions (for DMA in performance), portfolio of compositions. Additional exam requirements/recommendations for international students: Required—TOEFL (minimum score 550 paper-based; 80 iBT). *Application deadline:* For fall admission, 1/15 priority date for domestic students, 1/15 for international students. Application fee: $45 ($50 for international students). *Financial support:* In 2016–17, 32 teaching assistantships with partial tuition reimbursements (averaging $8,238 per year) were awarded; career-related internships or fieldwork, Federal Work-Study, institutionally sponsored loans, scholarships/grants, tuition waivers (partial), and unspecified assistantships also available. Support available to part-time students. Financial award application deadline: 3/1; financial award applicants required to submit FAFSA. *Faculty research:* Electro-acoustic composition, affective music responses, American music theatre, Russian choral music, music therapy and Alzheimer's. *Unit head:* Peter Witte, Dean, 816-235-2731, Fax: 816-235-5265, E-mail: wittep@umkc.edu. *Application contact:* William Everett, Associate Dean for Graduate Studies, 816-235-2857, Fax: 816-235-5264, E-mail: everettw@umkc.edu. Website: http://conservatory.umkc.edu/

**University of the Pacific,** Conservatory of Music, Stockton, CA 95211-0197. Offers music education (MM); music therapy (MA). *Students:* 10 full-time (7 women), 23 part-time (15 women); includes 8 minority (3 Asian, non-Hispanic/Latino; 4 Hispanic/Latino; 1 Two or more races, non-Hispanic/Latino), 4 international. Average age 33. 24 applicants, 129% accepted, 13 enrolled. In 2016, 4 master's awarded. *Entrance requirements:* For master's, GRE General Test. Additional exam requirements/recommendations for international students: Required—TOEFL. *Application deadline:* For fall admission, 3/1 priority date for domestic students; for spring admission, 10/1 priority date for domestic students. Applications are processed on a rolling basis. Application fee: $75. *Financial support:* Teaching assistantships and institutionally sponsored loans available. Support available to part-time students. Financial award application deadline: 3/1; financial award applicants required to submit FAFSA. *Unit head:* Dr. Daniel Ebbers, Interim Dean, 209-946-2415, E-mail: musicdean@pacific.edu. *Application contact:* 209-946-2415, Fax: 209-946-2770.

**Western Michigan University,** Graduate College, College of Fine Arts, School of Music, Kalamazoo, MI 49008. Offers music (MA); music composition (MM); music conducting (MM); music education (MM); music performance (MM); music therapy (MM). *Accreditation:* NASM.

**Wilfrid Laurier University,** Faculty of Graduate and Postdoctoral Studies, Faculty of Music, Waterloo, ON N2L 3C5, Canada. Offers MMT. *Entrance requirements:* For master's, 4-year honours BA in music therapy with minimum B average in final year, grade 6 RCM and grade 10 performance ability (for 1-year program); 4-year honours BA in allied area (music or psychology) with minimum B average in final year, grade 6 RCM, grade 10 performance ability (for 2-year program). Additional exam requirements/recommendations for international students: Required—TOEFL (minimum score 89 iBT). Electronic applications accepted. *Faculty research:* Group analytic music therapy, music psychotherapy, low frequency sound wave, aesthetic music therapy.

# ACADEMIC AND PROFESSIONAL PROGRAMS IN THE HUMANITIES

ACADEMIC AND PROFESSIONAL
PROGRAMS IN THE HUMANITIES

# Section 7
# History

This section contains a directory of institutions offering graduate work in history. Additional information about programs listed in the directory may be obtained by writing directly to the dean of a graduate school or chair of a department at the address given in the directory.

For programs offering related work, see also in this book *Area and Cultural Studies, Architecture, Humanities, Political Science and International Affairs,* and *Sociology, Anthropology, and Archaeology.*

## CONTENTS

### Program Directories

# History

**Adams State University,** The Graduate School, Department of History, Government and Philosophy, Alamosa, CO 81101. Offers history (MA).

**Alabama State University,** College of Liberal Arts and Social Sciences, Department of History and Political Science, Montgomery, AL 36101-0271. Offers history (MA). *Program availability:* Part-time. *Degree requirements:* For master's, one foreign language, comprehensive exam, thesis. *Entrance requirements:* For master's, GRE General Test, graduate writing competency test or MAT. Additional exam requirements/recommendations for international students: Recommended—TOEFL (minimum score 500 paper-based). Electronic applications accepted. *Expenses:* Tuition, state resident: full-time $3087; part-time $2744 per credit. Tuition, nonresident: full-time $6174; part-time $5488 per credit. *Required fees:* $2284; $1142 per credit. $571 per semester. Tuition and fees vary according to class time, course level, course load, degree level, program and student level. *Faculty research:* NAACP in Alabama, race relations in Alabama, confrontation at Cassville in 1864.

**American Public University System,** AMU/APU Graduate Programs, Charles Town, WV 25414. Offers accounting (MBA, MS); applied business analytics (MBA, MS); criminal justice (MA), including business administration, emergency and disaster management, general (MA, MS); educational leadership (M Ed); emergency and disaster management (MA); entrepreneurship (MBA); environmental policy and management (MS), including environmental planning, environmental sustainability, fish and wildlife management, general (MA, MS); global environmental management; finance (MBA); general (MBA); government contracting and acquisition (MBA); health care administration (MBA); health information management (MS); history (MA), including American history, ancient and classical history, European history, global history, public history; homeland security (MA), including business administration, counterterrorism studies, criminal justice, cyber, emergency management and public health, intelligence studies, transportation security; homeland security resource allocation (MBA); humanities (MA); information technology (MS), including digital forensics, enterprise software development, information assurance and security, IT project management; information technology management (MBA); intelligence studies (MA), including criminal intelligence, cyber, general (MA, MS), homeland security, intelligence analysis, intelligence collection, intelligence management, intelligence operations, terrorism studies; international relations and conflict resolution (MA), including comparative and security issues, conflict resolution, international and transnational security issues, peacekeeping; legal studies (MA); management (MA), including strategic consulting; marketing (MBA); military history (MA), including American military history, American Revolution, civil war, war since 1945, World War II; military studies (MA), including joint warfare, strategic leadership; national security studies (MA), including cyber, general (MA, MS), homeland security, regional security studies, security and intelligence analysis, terrorism studies; nonprofit management (MBA); political science (MA), including American politics and government, comparative government and development, general (MA, MS), international relations, public policy; psychology (MA); public administration (MPA), including disaster management, environmental policy, health policy, human resources, national security, organizational management, security management; public health (MPH); reverse logistics management (MA); security management (MA); space studies (MS), including aerospace science, general (MA, MS), planetary science; sports and health sciences (MS); sports management (MBA); teaching (M Ed), including autism spectrum disorder, curriculum and instruction for elementary teachers, elementary reading, English language learners, instructional leadership, online learning, special education, STEAM (STEM plus the arts); transportation and logistics management (MA). *Program availability:* Part-time, evening/weekend, online only, 100% online. *Faculty:* 401 full-time (228 women), 1,678 part-time/adjunct (781 women). *Students:* 378 full-time (184 women), 8,455 part-time (3,484 women); includes 2,972 minority (1,552 Black or African American, non-Hispanic/Latino; 52 American Indian or Alaska Native, non-Hispanic/Latino; 211 Asian, non-Hispanic/Latino; 791 Hispanic/Latino; 70 Native Hawaiian or other Pacific Islander, non-Hispanic/Latino; 296 Two or more races, non-Hispanic/Latino), 109 international. Average age 37. In 2016, 3,185 master's awarded. *Degree requirements:* For master's, comprehensive exam or practicum. *Entrance requirements:* For master's, official transcript showing earned bachelor's degree from institution accredited by recognized accrediting body. Additional exam requirements/recommendations for international students: Required—TOEFL (minimum score 550 paper-based), IELTS (minimum score 6.5). *Application deadline:* Applications are processed on a rolling basis. Application fee: $0. Electronic applications accepted. *Expenses: Tuition:* Part-time $350 per credit hour. *Required fees:* $50 per course. *Financial support:* Scholarships/grants available. Financial award applicants required to submit FAFSA. *Unit head:* Dr. Karan Powell, President, 877-468-6268, Fax: 304-724-3780. *Application contact:* Terry Grant, Vice President of Enrollment Management, 877-468-6268, Fax: 304-724-3780, E-mail: info@apus.edu. Website: http://www.apus.edu

**American University,** College of Arts and Sciences, Department of History, Washington, DC 20016-8038. Offers MA, PhD. *Program availability:* Part-time, evening/weekend. *Faculty:* 27 full-time (13 women), 3 part-time/adjunct (1 woman). *Students:* 53 full-time (32 women), 20 part-time (11 women); includes 7 minority (2 Black or African American, non-Hispanic/Latino; 2 Asian, non-Hispanic/Latino; 1 Two or more races, non-Hispanic/Latino), 4 international. Average age 30. 124 applicants, 60% accepted, 22 enrolled. In 2016, 25 master's, 5 doctorates awarded. *Degree requirements:* For master's, comprehensive exam, thesis or alternative; for doctorate, thesis/dissertation. *Entrance requirements:* For master's, GRE, personal statement, transcripts, 2 letters of recommendation, resume, writing sample; for doctorate, GRE, sample of written work, personal statement, transcripts, 3 letters of recommendation, resume. Additional exam requirements/recommendations for international students: Required—TOEFL (minimum score 100 iBT), IELTS (minimum score 7), PTE (minimum score 68). *Application deadline:* For fall admission, 2/1 priority date for domestic students; for spring admission, 11/1 for domestic students. Application fee: $55. Electronic applications accepted. *Expenses:* $1,579 per credit tuition; $690 mandatory fees. *Financial support:* Institutionally sponsored loans and unspecified assistantships available. Financial award application deadline: 2/1; financial award applicants required to submit FAFSA. *Unit head:* Dr. Eric J. Lohr, Department Chair, 202-885-2464, Fax: 202-885-1098, E-mail: elohr@american.edu. *Application contact:* Kathleen Clowery, Associate Director of Graduate Admissions, 202-885-3620, Fax: 202-885-1344, E-mail: clowery@american.edu.
Website: http://www.american.edu/cas/history/

**American University of Beirut,** Graduate Programs, Faculty of Arts and Sciences, Beirut, Lebanon. Offers anthropology (MA); Arab and Middle Eastern history (PhD); Arabic language and literature (MA, PhD); archaeology (MA); art history and curating (MA); biology (MS); cell and molecular biology (PhD); chemistry (MS); clinical psychology (MA); computational sciences (MS); computer science (MS); economics

(MA); education (MA); English language (MA); English literature (MA); environmental policy planning (MS); financial economics (MAFE); geology (MS); history (MA); Islamic studies (MA); mathematics (MS); media studies (MA); Middle Eastern studies (MA); physics (MS); political studies (MA); psychology (MA); public administration (MA); public policy and international affairs (MA); sociology (MA); statistics (MA, MS); theoretical physics (PhD); transnational American studies (MA). *Program availability:* Part-time. *Faculty:* 133 full-time (42 women), 6 part-time/adjunct (2 women). *Students:* 240 full-time (172 women), 227 part-time (166 women). Average age 27. 286 applicants, 67% accepted, 108 enrolled. In 2016, 60 master's, 3 doctorates awarded. Terminal master's awarded for partial completion of doctoral program. *Degree requirements:* For master's, one foreign language, comprehensive exam, thesis (for some programs); for doctorate, one foreign language, comprehensive exam, thesis/dissertation. *Entrance requirements:* For master's, GRE (for some MA, MS programs), letters of recommendation; for doctorate, GRE, letters of recommendation. Additional exam requirements/recommendations for international students: Required—TOEFL (minimum score 600 paper-based; 97 iBT), IELTS (minimum score 7). *Application deadline:* For fall admission, 4/3 for domestic students; for winter admission, 11/3 for domestic students. Application fee: $50. Electronic applications accepted. *Expenses:* Contact institution. *Financial support:* In 2016–17, 4 fellowships (averaging $11,200 per year), 18 research assistantships (averaging $5,400 per year) were awarded; teaching assistantships, career-related internships or fieldwork, Federal Work-Study, institutionally sponsored loans, scholarships/grants, traineeships, health care benefits, tuition waivers (full), and unspecified assistantships also available. Support available to part-time students. *Faculty research:* Development economics, spatial econometrics, health economics, labor economics, energy economics, hydrogeology, geophysics, petrophysics, structural geology, mineralogy, petrology, geochemistry, multilingualism, comparative/world literature, translation studies, book histories/ cultures, biocatalysis, molecular recognition, photocatalysis, photophysical and biophysical chemistry, probe chemistry, machine learning, data science. *Unit head:* Dr. Nadia Maria El Cheikh, Dean, Faculty of Arts and Sciences, 961-1374374 Ext. 3800, Fax: 961-1744461, E-mail: nmcheikh@aub.edu.lb. *Application contact:* Dr. Salim Kanaan, Director, Admissions Office, 961-1350000 Ext. 2590, Fax: 961-1750775, E-mail: sk00@aub.edu.lb. Website: http://www.aub.edu.lb/fas/

**Appalachian State University,** Cratis D. Williams Graduate School, Department of History, Boone, NC 28608. Offers general history (MA). *Program availability:* Part-time, online learning. *Degree requirements:* For master's, one foreign language, comprehensive exam, thesis (for some programs). *Entrance requirements:* For master's, GRE General Test, 3 letters of recommendation. Additional exam requirements/recommendations for international students: Required—TOEFL (minimum score 570 paper-based; 79 iBT), IELTS (minimum score 6.5). *Application deadline:* For fall admission, 3/15 priority date for domestic students, 2/1 for international students; for spring admission, 11/1 for domestic students, 7/1 for international students. Applications are processed on a rolling basis. Application fee: $55. Electronic applications accepted. *Expenses:* Tuition, state resident: full-time $4744. Tuition, nonresident: full-time $17,913. Full-time tuition and fees vary according to program. *Financial support:* Fellowships, research assistantships, teaching assistantships, career-related internships or fieldwork, Federal Work-Study, scholarships/grants, and unspecified assistantships available. Financial award application deadline: 4/1; financial award applicants required to submit FAFSA. *Faculty research:* Women's history, social/cultural history, U.S. history, Latin America, medieval studies. *Unit head:* Dr. Lucinda McCray, Chairperson, 828-262-2282, E-mail: mccraylm@appstate.edu. *Application contact:* Dr. Mary Valante, Graduate Program Director, 828-262-4983, E-mail: valantema@appstate.edu.
Website: http://www.history.appstate.edu

**Arizona State University at the Tempe campus,** College of Liberal Arts and Sciences, School of Historical, Philosophical and Religious Studies, Tempe, AZ 85287-4301. Offers European history (MA, PhD); medieval studies (Graduate Certificate); North American history (MA, PhD); philosophy (MA, PhD); public history (MA); religious studies (MA, PhD); Renaissance studies (Graduate Certificate); scholarly publishing (Graduate Certificate). *Program availability:* Part-time. Terminal master's awarded for partial completion of doctoral program. *Degree requirements:* For master's, thesis or alternative, interactive Program of Study (iPOS) submitted before completing 50 percent of required credit hours; for doctorate, variable foreign language requirement, comprehensive exam, thesis/dissertation, interactive Program of Study (iPOS) submitted before completing 50 percent of required credit hours. *Entrance requirements:* For master's and doctorate, GRE, minimum GPA of 3.0 or equivalent in last 2 years of work leading to bachelor's degree. Additional exam requirements/recommendations for international students: Required—TOEFL, IELTS, or PTE. Electronic applications accepted.

**Arkansas State University,** Graduate School, College of Humanities and Social Sciences, Department of History, State University, AR 72467. Offers history (MA); history education (SCCT); social science education (MSE). *Program availability:* Part-time. *Degree requirements:* For master's, comprehensive exam, thesis or alternative; for SCCT, comprehensive exam. *Entrance requirements:* For master's, GRE General Test or MAT, GMAT, appropriate bachelor's degree, letters of reference, official transcript, valid teaching certificate (for MSE), immunization records; for SCCT, GRE General Test or MAT, interview, master's degree, letters of reference, official transcript, immunization records. Additional exam requirements/recommendations for international students: Required—TOEFL (minimum score 550 paper-based; 79 iBT), IELTS (minimum score 6), PTE (minimum score 56). Electronic applications accepted.

**Arkansas Tech University,** College of Arts and Humanities, Russellville, AR 72801. Offers applied sociology (MS); English (M Ed, MA); history (MA); liberal arts (MLA); multi-media journalism (MA); psychology (MS); teaching English as a second language (MA). *Program availability:* Part-time. *Students:* 56 full-time (42 women), 121 part-time (85 women); includes 23 minority (7 Black or African American, non-Hispanic/Latino; 1 Asian, non-Hispanic/Latino; 11 Hispanic/Latino; 4 Two or more races, non-Hispanic/Latino), 34 international. Average age 32. In 2016, 90 master's awarded. *Degree requirements:* For master's, comprehensive exam (for some programs), thesis (for some programs), project. *Entrance requirements:* For master's, GRE General Test or GMAT. Additional exam requirements/recommendations for international students: Required—TOEFL (minimum score 550 paper-based; 79 iBT), IELTS (minimum score 6). *Application deadline:* For fall admission, 3/1 priority date for domestic students, 5/1 priority date for international students; for spring admission, 10/1 priority date for domestic and international students. Applications are processed on a rolling basis. Application fee: $25 ($75 for international students). Electronic applications accepted. *Expenses:* Tuition, state resident: full-time $4932; part-time $274 per credit hour. Tuition, nonresident: full-time $9864; part-time $548 per credit hour. *Required fees:*

$513 per semester. Tuition and fees vary according to course load. *Financial support:* In 2016–17, research assistantships with full tuition reimbursements (averaging $4,800 per year), teaching assistantships with full tuition reimbursements (averaging $4,800 per year) were awarded; career-related internships or fieldwork, Federal Work-Study, scholarships/grants, health care benefits, and unspecified assistantships also available. Support available to part-time students. Financial award application deadline: 4/15; financial award applicants required to submit FAFSA. *Unit head:* Dr. Jeffrey Woods, Dean, 479-968-0274, Fax: 479-964-0812, E-mail: jwoods@atu.edu. *Application contact:* Dr. Mary B. Gunter, Dean of Graduate College, 479-964-0398, Fax: 479-964-0542, E-mail: gradcollege@atu.edu.
Website: http://www.atu.edu/humanities/

**Armstrong State University,** School of Graduate Studies, Program in History, Savannah, GA 31419-1997. Offers American and European history (MA); public history (MA). *Program availability:* Part-time, evening/weekend. *Faculty:* 6 full-time (1 woman), 1 (woman) part-time/adjunct. *Students:* 5 full-time (3 women), 11 part-time (4 women); includes 2 minority (1 Black or African American, non-Hispanic/Latino; 1 Hispanic/Latino). Average age 37. 17 applicants, 71% accepted, 8 enrolled. In 2016, 3 master's awarded. *Degree requirements:* For master's, one foreign language, comprehensive exam (for some programs), thesis (for some programs), thesis, internship, or advanced fieldwork. *Entrance requirements:* For master's, GRE General Test, minimum GPA of 3.0, letters of recommendation, BA in history or equivalent. Additional exam requirements/recommendations for international students: Required—TOEFL (minimum score 523 paper-based; 70 iBT). *Application deadline:* For fall admission, 6/30 priority date for domestic students, 5/1 priority date for international students; for spring admission, 11/15 priority date for domestic students, 9/15 priority date for international students; for summer admission, 4/15 priority date for domestic students, 9/15 for international students. Applications are processed on a rolling basis. Application fee: $30. Electronic applications accepted. *Expenses:* Tuition, state resident: full-time $1781; part-time $161.93 per credit hour. Tuition, nonresident: full-time $6482; part-time $589.27 per credit hour. *Required fees:* $1224 per unit. $612 per semester. Tuition and fees vary according to course load, campus/location and program. *Financial support:* In 2016–17, research assistantships with full tuition reimbursements (averaging $5,000 per year) were awarded; career-related internships or fieldwork, Federal Work-Study, and unspecified assistantships also available. Support available to part-time students. Financial award application deadline: 3/15; financial award applicants required to submit FAFSA. *Faculty research:* Public history; European, Latin American, African, and United States history. *Unit head:* Dr. Christopher Hendricks, Interim Department Head, 912-344-2725, Fax: 912-344-3451, E-mail: chris.hendricks@armstrong.edu. *Application contact:* McKenzie Peterman, Assistant Director of Graduate Admissions, 912-344-2503, Fax: 912-344-3417, E-mail: graduate@armstrong.edu.
Website: http://www.armstrong.edu/Liberal_Arts/history/history_graduate_program

**Ashland University,** College of Arts and Sciences, Program in American History and Government, Ashland, OH 44805-3702. Offers MAHG. *Program availability:* Part-time. *Degree requirements:* For master's, capstone project or thesis. *Entrance requirements:* For master's, minimum undergraduate GPA of 2.75, 3.0 graduate. *Application deadline:* Applications are processed on a rolling basis. Application fee: $30. Electronic applications accepted. *Expenses:* Contact institution. *Financial support:* Fellowships and research assistantships available. Financial award application deadline: 4/1. *Faculty research:* American founding, United States Civil War, Progressive Era. *Unit head:* Dr. Peter W. Schramm, Chair, 419-289-5411, Fax: 419-289-5425, E-mail: pschramm@ashland.edu. *Application contact:* Christian A. Pascarella, Director, 419-289-5411, Fax: 419-289-5425, E-mail: cpascare@ashland.edu.
Website: http://mahg.ashland.edu

**Auburn University,** Graduate School, College of Liberal Arts, Department of History, Auburn University, AL 36849. Offers MA, PhD, Graduate Certificate. *Program availability:* Part-time. *Faculty:* 28 full-time (13 women), 3 part-time/adjunct (0 women). *Students:* 26 full-time (8 women), 20 part-time (5 women); includes 2 minority (1 Black or African American, non-Hispanic/Latino; 1 Two or more races, non-Hispanic/Latino). Average age 34. 33 applicants, 64% accepted, 9 enrolled. In 2016, 9 master's, 3 doctorates, 4 other advanced degrees awarded. *Degree requirements:* For master's, thesis, oral exam; for doctorate, 2 foreign languages, thesis/dissertation. *Entrance requirements:* For master's, GRE General Test; for doctorate, GRE General Test, master's degree with thesis. *Application deadline:* Applications are processed on a rolling basis. Application fee: $50 ($60 for international students). Electronic applications accepted. *Expenses:* Tuition, state resident: full-time $9072; part-time $504 per credit hour. Tuition, nonresident: full-time $27,216; part-time $1512 per credit hour. *Required fees:* $812 per semester. Tuition and fees vary according to degree level and program. *Financial support:* Teaching assistantships and Federal Work-Study available. Support available to part-time students. Financial award application deadline: 3/15; financial award applicants required to submit FAFSA. *Unit head:* David Lucsko, Chair, 334-844-4360. *Application contact:* Dr. George Flowers, Dean of the Graduate School, 334-844-2125.

**Ball State University,** Graduate School, College of Sciences and Humanities, Department of History, Muncie, IN 47306. Offers MA. *Program availability:* Part-time. *Degree requirements:* For master's, thesis optional. *Entrance requirements:* For master's, minimum baccalaureate GPA of 2.75 or 3.0 in latter half of baccalauareate, resume or curriculum vitae, two letters of recommendation, undergraduate transcripts, writing sample, goal statement. Additional exam requirements/recommendations for international students: Required—TOEFL (minimum score 550 paper-based; 79 iBT), IELTS (minimum score 6.5). Electronic applications accepted. *Faculty research:* European, British, and American history.

**Baylor University,** Graduate School, College of Arts and Sciences, Department of History, Waco, TX 76798. Offers MA, PhD. *Faculty:* 26 full-time (9 women), 2 part-time/adjunct (1 woman). *Students:* 20 full-time (8 women), 3 part-time (1 woman); includes 1 minority (Hispanic/Latino). 20 applicants, 35% accepted, 5 enrolled. In 2016, 4 master's awarded. Terminal master's awarded for partial completion of doctoral program. *Degree requirements:* For master's, one foreign language, comprehensive exam, thesis; for doctorate, one foreign language, comprehensive exam, thesis/dissertation. *Entrance requirements:* For master's and doctorate, GRE General Test, 18 semester hours in history. Additional exam requirements/recommendations for international students: Required—TOEFL. *Application deadline:* For fall admission, 12/30 for domestic and international students. Application fee: $25. Electronic applications accepted. *Expenses:* Tuition: Full-time $28,494; part-time $1583 per credit hour. *Required fees:* $167 per credit hour. Tuition and fees vary according to course load and program. *Financial support:* In 2016–17, 20 students received support, including 2 fellowships with full tuition reimbursements available (averaging $15,500 per year), 10 research assistantships with full tuition reimbursements available (averaging $16,500 per year); tuition waivers (full) and unspecified assistantships also available. Financial award application deadline: 12/30. *Faculty research:* American religion and culture, British religion and culture, American higher education and religion, medieval women and religion. *Unit head:* Dr. Beth Allison Barr, Graduate Program Director, 254-710-3512, Fax: 254-710-2551, E-mail: beth_barr@baylor.edu.
Website: http://www.baylor.edu/history/

**Binghamton University, State University of New York,** Graduate School, Harpur College of Arts and Sciences, Department of History, Binghamton, NY 13902-6000. Offers MA, PhD. *Program availability:* Part-time. *Faculty:* 27 full-time (14 women), 4 part-time/adjunct (2 women). *Students:* 31 full-time (11 women), 40 part-time (22 women); includes 2 minority (1 Black or African American, non-Hispanic/Latino; 1 Asian, non-Hispanic/Latino), 20 international. Average age 31. 60 applicants, 58% accepted, 16 enrolled. In 2016, 6 master's, 7 doctorates awarded. Terminal master's awarded for partial completion of doctoral program. *Degree requirements:* For master's, variable foreign language requirement, comprehensive exam, thesis; for doctorate, variable foreign language requirement, comprehensive exam, thesis/dissertation. *Entrance requirements:* For master's and doctorate, GRE General Test, writing sample. Additional exam requirements/recommendations for international students: Required—TOEFL (minimum score 550 paper-based; 80 iBT). *Application deadline:* For fall admission, 4/1 priority date for domestic and international students; for spring admission, 11/1 priority date for domestic and international students. Application fee: $75. Electronic applications accepted. *Financial support:* In 2016–17, 44 students received support, including 40 teaching assistantships with full tuition reimbursements available (averaging $15,000 per year); career-related internships or fieldwork, Federal Work-Study, institutionally sponsored loans, scholarships/grants, health care benefits, tuition waivers (full and partial), and unspecified assistantships also available. Financial award application deadline: 1/15; financial award applicants required to submit FAFSA. *Unit head:* Heather DeHaan, Chairperson, 607-777-2625, E-mail: hdehaan@binghamton.edu. *Application contact:* Ben Balkaya, Assistant Dean and Director, 607-777-2151, Fax: 607-777-2501, E-mail: balkaya@binghamton.edu.

**Bob Jones University,** Graduate Programs, Greenville, SC 29614. Offers accountancy (MS); Bible (MA); Bible translation (MA); Biblical studies (Certificate); broadcast management (MS); business administration (MBA); church history (MA, PhD); church ministries (MA); church music (MM); cinema and video production (MA); counseling (MS); curriculum and instruction (Ed D); divinity (M Div); dramatic production (MA); educational leadership (MS, Ed D, Ed S); elementary education (M Ed, MAT); English (M Ed, MA, MAT); fine arts (MA); graphic design (MA); history (M Ed, MA); illustration (MA); interpretative speech (MA); mathematics (M Ed, MAT); medical missions (Certificate); ministry (MM, D Min); multi-categorical special education (M Ed, MAT); music (M Ed); New Testament interpretation (PhD); Old Testament interpretation (PhD); orchestral instrument performance (MM); organ performance (MM); pastoral studies (MA); personnel services (MS, Ed S); piano pedagogy (MM); piano performance (MM); platform arts (MA); radio and television broadcasting (MS); rhetoric and public address (MA); secondary education (M Ed); studio art (MA); teaching Bible (MA); theology (MA, PhD); voice performance (MM); youth ministries (MA); M Div/MM.

**Boise State University,** College of Arts and Sciences, Department of History, Boise, ID 83725-1925. Offers applied historical research (MAHR); history (MA). *Program availability:* Part-time. *Faculty:* 12. *Students:* 12 full-time (5 women), 11 part-time (7 women); includes 1 minority (Hispanic/Latino). Average age 38. 19 applicants, 63% accepted, 6 enrolled. In 2016, 7 master's awarded. *Degree requirements:* For master's, thesis (for MA); applied research project (for MAHR). *Entrance requirements:* For master's, GRE General Test, minimum GPA of 3.0. Additional exam requirements/recommendations for international students: Required—TOEFL (minimum score 550 paper-based; 80 iBT), IELTS (minimum score 6). *Application deadline:* For fall admission, 4/1 for domestic and international students; for spring admission, 9/15 for domestic and international students. Application fee: $65 ($95 for international students). Electronic applications accepted. *Expenses:* Tuition, state resident: full-time $6058; part-time $358 per credit hour. Tuition, nonresident: full-time $20,108; part-time $608 per credit hour. *Required fees:* $2108. Tuition and fees vary according to program. *Financial support:* In 2016–17, 10 students received support, including 1 research assistantship (averaging $11,108 per year), 2 teaching assistantships (averaging $4,083 per year); scholarships/grants and unspecified assistantships also available. Financial award application deadline: 1/15; financial award applicants required to submit FAFSA. *Faculty research:* Public history, American social and cultural history, European history, Third World history. *Unit head:* Dr. Nick Miller, Department Chair, 208-426-3902, E-mail: nmiller@boisestate.edu. *Application contact:* Dr. Lisa McClain, Graduate Coordinator, 208-426-1985, E-mail: lisamcclain@boisestate.edu.
Website: http://history.boisestate.edu/

**Boston College,** Graduate School of Arts and Sciences, Department of History, Chestnut Hill, MA 02467-3800. Offers European national studies (MA); history (MA, PhD); medieval studies (MA). *Faculty:* 44 full-time. *Students:* 56 full-time (24 women); includes 6 minority (1 Black or African American, non-Hispanic/Latino; 3 Hispanic/Latino; 2 Two or more races, non-Hispanic/Latino), 3 international. 162 applicants, 34% accepted, 16 enrolled. In 2016, 12 master's, 6 doctorates awarded. Terminal master's awarded for partial completion of doctoral program. *Degree requirements:* For master's, one foreign language, comprehensive exam, thesis optional; for doctorate, 2 foreign languages, comprehensive exam, thesis/dissertation. *Entrance requirements:* For master's and doctorate, GRE General Test, writing sample. Additional exam requirements/recommendations for international students: Required—TOEFL (minimum score 600 paper-based; 100 iBT), IELTS (minimum score 8). *Application deadline:* For fall admission, 1/2 for domestic and international students. Application fee: $75. Electronic applications accepted. Tuition and fees vary according to program. *Financial support:* In 2016–17, fellowships with full tuition reimbursements (averaging $21,400 per year), teaching assistantships with full tuition reimbursements (averaging $21,400 per year) were awarded; Federal Work-Study, scholarships/grants, health care benefits, and unspecified assistantships also available. Support available to part-time students. Financial award application deadline: 3/1; financial award applicants required to submit FAFSA. *Faculty research:* U.S. history, medieval history, early modern European history, modern European history, British and Irish history, Latin American history, Asian history, Middle eastern history, international and global history, transnational history. *Unit head:* Dr. Kevin Kenny, Chairperson, 617-552-1196, E-mail: kevin.kenny@bc.edu. *Application contact:* Dr. Prasannan Pathasarathi, Director of Graduate Studies, 617-552-3781, E-mail: pathasa@bc.edu.
Website: http://www.bc.edu/history

**Boston University,** Graduate School of Arts and Sciences, Department of History, Boston, MA 02215. Offers MA, PhD, JD/MA. *Students:* 42 full-time (18 women), 1 part-time (0 women); includes 5 minority (2 Black or African American, non-Hispanic/Latino; 1 Hispanic/Latino; 2 Two or more races, non-Hispanic/Latino), 2 international. Average age 30. 101 applicants, 16% accepted, 6 enrolled. In 2016, 3 master's, 6 doctorates awarded. Terminal master's awarded for partial completion of doctoral program. *Degree requirements:* For master's, one foreign language, thesis or alternative, major research paper; for doctorate, 2 foreign languages, comprehensive exam, thesis/dissertation. *Entrance requirements:* For master's and doctorate, GRE General Test, 3 letters of recommendation, writing sample, transcripts, personal statement, curriculum vitae, foreign language proficiency. Additional exam requirements/recommendations for international students: Required—TOEFL (minimum score 550 paper-based; 84 iBT). *Application deadline:* For fall admission, 1/15 for domestic and international students. Application fee: $95. Electronic applications accepted. *Financial support:* In 2016–17, 37 students received support, including 7 fellowships with full tuition reimbursements available (averaging $21,500 per year), 5 research assistantships with full tuition

*History*

reimbursements available (averaging $21,500 per year), 17 teaching assistantships with full tuition reimbursements available (averaging $21,500 per year); Federal Work-Study, scholarships/grants, health care benefits, and unspecified assistantships also available. Financial award application deadline: 1/15. *Unit head:* Louis Ferleger, Chairman, 617-353-2550, Fax: 617-353-2556, E-mail: ferleger@bu.edu. *Application contact:* Carrie Mountain, Department Administrator, 617-353-2555, Fax: 617-353-2556, E-mail: cmount@bu.edu.
Website: http://www.bu.edu/history/

**Bowling Green State University,** Graduate College, College of Arts and Sciences, Department of History, Bowling Green, OH 43403. Offers history (MA, MAT, PhD); public history (MA); MA/MA. *Program availability:* Part-time. *Degree requirements:* For master's, thesis or alternative; for doctorate, one foreign language, comprehensive exam, thesis/dissertation. *Entrance requirements:* For master's and doctorate, GRE General Test. Additional exam requirements/recommendations for international students: Required—TOEFL. *Application deadline:* For fall admission, 2/15 priority date for domestic students. Application fee: $30. Electronic applications accepted. *Financial support:* Fellowships with full tuition reimbursements, research assistantships with full tuition reimbursements, teaching assistantships with full tuition reimbursements, Federal Work-Study, and unspecified assistantships available. Financial award applicants required to submit FAFSA. *Faculty research:* Policy history, modern Europe, recent United States history, East Asia, Latin America. *Unit head:* Dr. Amilcar Challu, Chair, 419-372-2769, E-mail: achallu@bgsu.edu. *Application contact:* Dr. Walter Grunden, Graduate Coordinator, 419-372-8639.

**Brandeis University,** Graduate School of Arts and Sciences, Department of History, Waltham, MA 02454-9110. Offers MA, PhD. *Faculty:* 14 full-time (4 women), 4 part-time/adjunct (1 woman). *Students:* 36 full-time (20 women); includes 6 minority (3 Black or African American, non-Hispanic/Latino; 1 Asian, non-Hispanic/Latino; 1 Hispanic/Latino; 1 Two or more races, non-Hispanic/Latino), 6 international. 90 applicants, 22% accepted, 10 enrolled. In 2016, 4 master's, 1 doctorate awarded. Terminal master's awarded for partial completion of doctoral program. *Degree requirements:* For master's, thesis or capstone; seminars; for doctorate, one foreign language, comprehensive exam, thesis/dissertation, regional colloquia; seminars; directed research analyzing primary sources. *Entrance requirements:* For master's and doctorate, GRE General Test, resume, writing sample, 2 letters of recommendation, statement of purpose, transcript(s). Additional exam requirements/recommendations for international students: Required—TOEFL (minimum score 600 paper-based; 100 iBT); Recommended—IELTS (minimum score 7), TSE (minimum score 68). *Application deadline:* For fall admission, 1/15 priority date for domestic students. Application fee: $75. Electronic applications accepted. *Financial support:* In 2016–17, 19 students received support, including 16 fellowships with full tuition reimbursements available (averaging $29,000 per year), 3 teaching assistantships with partial tuition reimbursements available (averaging $3,200 per year); Federal Work-Study, scholarships/grants, health care benefits, and tuition waivers (partial) also available. Financial award application deadline: 4/15; financial award applicants required to submit FAFSA. *Faculty research:* American and European history, world history, regional and national history, medieval history, modern history, international and cultural history. *Unit head:* Dr. David Engerman, Director of Graduate Studies, 781-736-2281, Fax: 781-736-2273, E-mail: engerman@brandeis.edu. *Application contact:* Dona DiLorenzo, Department Senior Academic Administrator, 781-736-2270, Fax: 781-736-2273, E-mail: delorenz@brandeis.edu.
Website: http://www.brandeis.edu/gsas

**Brock University,** Faculty of Graduate Studies, Faculty of Humanities, Program in History, St. Catharines, ON L2S 3A1, Canada. Offers MA. *Program availability:* Part-time. *Degree requirements:* For master's, thesis optional. *Entrance requirements:* For master's, honors degree in history. Additional exam requirements/recommendations for international students: Required—TOEFL (minimum score 550 paper-based; 80 iBT), IELTS (minimum score 6.5), TWE (minimum score 4). Electronic applications accepted.

**Brooklyn College of the City University of New York,** School of Humanities and Social Sciences, Department of History, Brooklyn, NY 11210-2889. Offers MA. *Program availability:* Part-time, evening/weekend. *Degree requirements:* For master's, 30 credits. *Entrance requirements:* For master's, 12 credits in history, minimum GPA of 3.0 in major, 2 letters of recommendation. Additional exam requirements/recommendations for international students: Required—TOEFL (minimum score 650 paper-based; 114 iBT). Electronic applications accepted. *Faculty research:* Modern European, U.S., medieval, women's, Asian, and Caribbean history.

**Brown University,** Graduate School, Department of History, Providence, RI 02912. Offers MA, PhD. *Degree requirements:* For master's, thesis or alternative; for doctorate, variable foreign language requirement, thesis/dissertation, preliminary exam.

**Buffalo State College, State University of New York,** The Graduate School, Faculty of Natural and Social Sciences, Department of History and Social Studies, Buffalo, NY 14222-1095. Offers history (MA); secondary education (MS Ed), including social studies. *Program availability:* Part-time, evening/weekend. *Degree requirements:* For master's, one foreign language, thesis (for some programs), project (MS Ed). *Entrance requirements:* For master's, minimum GPA of 2.75, 30 hours in history (MA), 36 hours in history or social sciences (MS Ed). Additional exam requirements/recommendations for international students: Required—TOEFL (minimum score 550 paper-based).

**Butler University,** College of Liberal Arts and Sciences, Department of History, Indianapolis, IN 46208-3485. Offers MA. *Program availability:* Part-time. *Faculty:* 10 full-time (2 women). *Students:* 2 full-time (1 woman), 3 part-time (2 women), 1 international. Average age 39. 8 applicants, 63% accepted, 4 enrolled. In 2016, 3 master's awarded. *Degree requirements:* For master's, thesis (for some programs). *Entrance requirements:* For master's, GRE General Test. *Application deadline:* For fall admission, 3/1 for domestic and international students; for spring admission, 12/15 for domestic and international students; for summer admission, 4/1 for domestic and international students. Applications are processed on a rolling basis. Application fee: $50. Electronic applications accepted. *Expenses:* Contact institution. *Financial support:* Scholarships/grants and unspecified assistantships available. Financial award application deadline: 7/15; financial award applicants required to submit FAFSA. *Faculty research:* European history, U.S. history, Latin American history, East Asian history, cultural geography. *Unit head:* Dr. Elise Edwards, Chair, 317-940-9743, E-mail: emedwar1@butler.edu. *Application contact:* Diane Dubord, Student Services Specialist, 317-940-8100, Fax: 317-940-8250, E-mail: ddubord@butler.edu.
Website: https://www.butler.edu/history-anthropology/graduate

**California Polytechnic State University, San Luis Obispo,** College of Liberal Arts, Department of History, San Luis Obispo, CA 93407. Offers MA. *Program availability:* Part-time. *Faculty:* 5 full-time (2 women). *Students:* 1 (woman) full-time, 12 part-time (6 women); includes 5 minority (1 Black or African American, non-Hispanic/Latino; 1 Hispanic/Latino; 1 Native Hawaiian or other Pacific Islander, non-Hispanic/Latino; 2 Two or more races, non-Hispanic/Latino). Average age 26. 15 applicants, 47% accepted, 6 enrolled. In 2016, 9 master's awarded. *Degree requirements:* For master's, comprehensive exam (for some programs), thesis (for some programs). *Entrance requirements:* For master's, GRE. Additional exam requirements/recommendations for international students: Required—TOEFL (minimum score 80 iBT). *Application deadline:*

For fall admission, 4/1 for domestic students, 3/1 for international students. Applications are processed on a rolling basis. Application fee: $55. Electronic applications accepted. *Expenses:* Tuition, state resident: full-time $6738; part-time $3906 per year. Tuition, nonresident: full-time $15,666; part-time $8370 per year. *Required fees:* $3603; $3141 per unit. $1047 per term. *Financial support:* Federal Work-Study and scholarships/grants available. Support available to part-time students. Financial award application deadline: 3/2; financial award applicants required to submit FAFSA. *Faculty research:* American history, European history, Asian history, African history, comparative world history. *Unit head:* Dr. Kathleen Murphy, Graduate Coordinator, 805-756-2839, E-mail: ksmurphy@calpoly.edu.
Website: http://cla.calpoly.edu/hist.html

**California State Polytechnic University, Pomona,** Program in History, Pomona, CA 91768-2557. Offers MA. *Program availability:* Part-time, evening/weekend. *Students:* 13 part-time (8 women); includes 8 minority (7 Hispanic/Latino; 1 Two or more races, non-Hispanic/Latino). Average age 32. 8 applicants, 100% accepted, 7 enrolled. In 2016, 9 master's awarded. *Entrance requirements:* Additional exam requirements/recommendations for international students: Required—TOEFL. *Application deadline:* Applications are processed on a rolling basis. Application fee: $55. Electronic applications accepted. *Expenses:* Contact institution. *Financial support:* Application deadline: 3/2; applicants required to submit FAFSA. *Unit head:* Dr. Amanda H. Podany, Graduate Coordinator, 909-869-3875, Fax: 909-869-4724, E-mail: ahpodany@cpp.edu. *Application contact:* Andrew M. Wright, Director of Admissions, 909-869-3139, Fax: 909-869-4529, E-mail: awright@cpp.edu.
Website: http://www.cpp.edu/~class/history/graduate-students/

**California State University, Bakersfield,** Division of Graduate Studies, School of Arts and Humanities, Program in History, Bakersfield, CA 93311. Offers MA. *Students:* 8 full-time (2 women), 10 part-time (5 women); includes 10 minority (1 Black or African American, non-Hispanic/Latino; 7 Hispanic/Latino; 2 Two or more races, non-Hispanic/Latino). Average age 40. 13 applicants, 77% accepted, 9 enrolled. In 2016, 9 master's awarded. *Degree requirements:* For master's, comprehensive exam or thesis. *Entrance requirements:* For master's, 2 letters of recommendation, letter of intent, writing sample, undergraduate transcripts. *Application deadline:* For fall admission, 7/15 for domestic students; for winter admission, 11/1 for domestic students; for spring admission, 2/1 for domestic students. Applications are processed on a rolling basis. Application fee: $55. *Expenses:* Tuition, state resident: full-time $2246; part-time $1302 per semester. *Financial support:* In 2016–17, fellowships (averaging $1,850 per year) were awarded; Federal Work-Study, scholarships/grants, and tuition waivers (full and partial) also available. Financial award application deadline: 3/2; financial award applicants required to submit FAFSA. *Faculty research:* American, European, Latin American, and modern Chinese history. *Unit head:* Dr. Douglas Dodd, Coordinator, 661-654-6815, E-mail: ddodd@csub.edu. *Application contact:* Debbie Blowers, Assistant Director of Admissions and Evaluations, 661-664-3381, E-mail: dblowers@csub.edu.
Website: https://www.csub.edu/history/M.A.%20Program/index.html

**California State University, Chico,** Office of Graduate Studies, College of Humanities and Fine Arts, Department of History, Chico, CA 95929-0722. Offers MA. *Program availability:* Part-time. *Faculty:* 13 full-time (3 women), 10 part-time/adjunct (3 women). *Students:* 6 full-time (2 women); includes 2 minority (1 Hispanic/Latino; 1 Two or more races, non-Hispanic/Latino). 8 applicants, 63% accepted, 3 enrolled. In 2016, 2 master's awarded. *Degree requirements:* For master's, thesis, oral exam. *Entrance requirements:* For master's, GRE General Test, 2 letters of recommendation, statement of purpose, writing sample. Additional exam requirements/recommendations for international students: Required—TOEFL (minimum score 550 paper-based; 80 iBT), IELTS (minimum score 6.5), PTE (minimum score 59). *Application deadline:* For fall admission, 3/1 priority date for domestic students, 3/1 for international students; for spring admission, 9/15 priority date for domestic students, 9/15 for international students. Application fee: $55. Electronic applications accepted. *Financial support:* Teaching assistantships, career-related internships or fieldwork, scholarships/grants, and unspecified assistantships available. Financial award application deadline: 3/1; financial award applicants required to submit FAFSA. *Unit head:* Stephen E. Lewis, Chair, 530-898-5366, Fax: 530-898-6925, E-mail: hist@csuchico.edu. *Application contact:* Judy L. Morris, Graduate Admissions Coordinator, 530-898-5416, Fax: 530-898-3342, E-mail: jlmorris@csuchico.edu.
Website: http://www.csuchico.edu/hist

**California State University, East Bay,** Office of Graduate Studies, College of Letters, Arts, and Social Sciences, Department of History, Hayward, CA 94542-3000. Offers history (MA); public history (MA); teaching (MA). *Program availability:* Part-time, evening/weekend. *Students:* 3 full-time (1 woman), 20 part-time (12 women); includes 9 minority (2 Black or African American, non-Hispanic/Latino; 4 Hispanic/Latino; 1 Two or more races, non-Hispanic/Latino). Average age 37. 28 applicants, 57% accepted, 13 enrolled. In 2016, 8 master's awarded. *Degree requirements:* For master's, one foreign language, comprehensive exam, project, thesis, or exam. *Entrance requirements:* For master's, GRE (strongly recommended), minimum GPA of 3.0 in field, 3.3 in history; 2 letters of recommendation; writing sample. Additional exam requirements/recommendations for international students: Required—TOEFL (minimum score 550 paper-based). *Application deadline:* For fall admission, 5/16 for domestic and international students. Applications are processed on a rolling basis. Application fee: $55. Electronic applications accepted. *Financial support:* Fellowships, teaching assistantships, career-related internships or fieldwork, Federal Work-Study, institutionally sponsored loans, and scholarships/grants available. Support available to part-time students. Financial award application deadline: 3/2; financial award applicants required to submit FAFSA. *Faculty research:* Digital history, American women, early America, Native Americans, medieval colonial India. *Unit head:* Dr. Linda L. Ivey, Chair, 510-885-4015, E-mail: linda.ivey@csueastbay.edu. *Application contact:* Dr. Khal Schneider, Graduate Coordinator, 510-885-3237, Fax: 510-885-4791, E-mail: khal.schneider@csueastbay.edu.
Website: http://www20.csueastbay.edu/class/departments/history/

**California State University, Fresno,** Division of Research and Graduate Studies, College of Social Sciences, Department of History, Fresno, CA 93740-8027. Offers history (MA); history teaching (MA). *Program availability:* Part-time, evening/weekend. *Degree requirements:* For master's, project; thesis or comprehensive examination. *Entrance requirements:* For master's, GRE General Test, minimum GPA of 3.0. Additional exam requirements/recommendations for international students: Required—TOEFL. *Application deadline:* For fall admission, 6/1 for domestic and international students; for spring admission, 11/1 for domestic and international students. Applications are processed on a rolling basis. Application fee: $55. Electronic applications accepted. *Financial support:* Teaching assistantships, career-related internships or fieldwork, Federal Work-Study, scholarships/grants, and unspecified assistantships available. Support available to part-time students. Financial award application deadline: 3/1; financial award applicants required to submit FAFSA. *Faculty research:* International education, classical art history, improving teacher quality. *Unit head:* Michelle DenBeste, Chair, 559-278-2153, Fax: 559-278-5321, E-mail: michelle_denbeste@csufresno.edu. *Application contact:* Dr. Brad Jones, Graduate Program Coordinator, 559-278-2153, Fax: 559-278-5321, E-mail:

brajones@csufresno.edu.
Website: http://www.fresnostate.edu/socialsciences/historydept/

**California State University, Fullerton,** Graduate Studies, College of Humanities and Social Sciences, Department of History, Fullerton, CA 92834-9480. Offers MA. *Program availability:* Part-time. *Degree requirements:* For master's, comprehensive exam, project or thesis. *Entrance requirements:* For master's, undergraduate major in history or related field, minimum GPA of 3.0. Application fee: $55. *Expenses:* Tuition, state resident: full-time $3369; part-time $1953 per unit. Tuition, nonresident: full-time $3915; part-time $2499 per unit. Tuition and fees vary according to course load, degree level and program. *Financial support:* Career-related internships or fieldwork, Federal Work-Study, institutionally sponsored loans, and scholarships/grants available. Support available to part-time students. Financial award application deadline: 3/1; financial award applicants required to submit FAFSA. *Unit head:* Dr. Jochen Burgtorf, Chair, 657-278-3474. *Application contact:* Admissions/Applications, 657-278-2371.

**California State University, Long Beach,** Graduate Studies, College of Liberal Arts, Department of History, Long Beach, CA 90840. Offers Africa and the Middle East (MA). *Program availability:* Part-time, evening/weekend. *Degree requirements:* For master's, one foreign language, comprehensive exam or thesis. *Application deadline:* For fall admission, 3/1 for domestic students. Applications are processed on a rolling basis. Application fee: $55. Electronic applications accepted. *Financial support:* Research assistantships, Federal Work-Study, institutionally sponsored loans, and scholarships/grants available. Financial award application deadline: 3/2. *Faculty research:* All periods of European and American history, recent Asian and African history. *Unit head:* David A. Shefer, Chair, 562-985-4431, Fax: 562-985-5431. *Application contact:* Dr. Houri Berberian, Graduate Advisor, 562-985-4524, Fax: 562-985-4431, E-mail: hberber@csulb.edu.
Website: http://www.csulb.edu/colleges/cla/departments/history/

**California State University, Los Angeles,** Graduate Studies, College of Natural and Social Sciences, Department of History, Los Angeles, CA 90032-8530. Offers MA. *Program availability:* Part-time, evening/weekend. *Degree requirements:* For master's, one foreign language, comprehensive exam or thesis. *Entrance requirements:* For master's, minimum GPA of 3.0, undergraduate major in history. Additional exam requirements/recommendations for international students: Required—TOEFL (minimum score 500 paper-based). Electronic applications accepted. *Faculty research:* Ancient and modern Europe, the Middle East, Latin America, U.S. history: Bill of Rights.

**California State University, Northridge,** Graduate Studies, College of Social and Behavioral Sciences, Department of History, Northridge, CA 91330. Offers MA. *Faculty:* 16 full-time (11 women), 11 part-time/adjunct (6 women). *Students:* 14 full-time (5 women), 33 part-time (13 women); includes 18 minority (2 Asian, non-Hispanic/Latino; 15 Hispanic/Latino; 1 Two or more races, non-Hispanic/Latino), 2 international. Average age 32. 40 applicants, 68% accepted, 22 enrolled. *Degree requirements:* For master's, one foreign language. *Entrance requirements:* For master's, GRE General Test or minimum GPA of 3.0, 2 letters of recommendation. Additional exam requirements/recommendations for international students: Required—TOEFL. *Application deadline:* For fall admission, 5/15 for domestic students; for spring admission, 11/1 for domestic students. Application fee: $55. *Expenses:* Tuition, state resident: full-time $4152. *Financial support:* Fellowships and scholarships/grants available. Financial award application deadline: 3/1. *Unit head:* Dr. Susan Fitzpatrick-Behrens, Chair, 818-677-3566.
Website: http://www.csun.edu/csbs/departments/history/index.html

**California State University, San Marcos,** College of Humanities, Arts, Behavioral and Social Sciences, Program in History, San Marcos, CA 92096-0001. Offers MA. *Degree requirements:* For master's, thesis. *Entrance requirements:* For master's, GRE General Test, three letters of recommendation, minimum GPA of 3.0 overall and in major, academic writing sample. Additional exam requirements/recommendations for international students: Required—TOEFL (minimum score 500 paper-based). *Expenses:* Tuition, state resident: full-time $6738. Tuition, nonresident: full-time $13,434. *Required fees:* $1906. Tuition and fees vary according to campus/location and program.

**California State University, Stanislaus,** College of Humanities and Social Sciences, Program in History (MA), Turlock, CA 95382. Offers history (MA); international relations (MA); secondary school teachers (MA). *Program availability:* Part-time. *Degree requirements:* For master's, comprehensive exam, thesis or alternative. *Entrance requirements:* For master's, GRE, minimum GPA of 3.0, personal statement. Additional exam requirements/recommendations for international students: Required—TOEFL (minimum score 575 paper-based). Electronic applications accepted. *Faculty research:* History of Ancient Greece, history and ecology of the Central Valley, acculturation and gender.

**Carleton University,** Faculty of Graduate Studies, Faculty of Arts and Social Sciences, Department of History, Ottawa, ON K1S 5B6, Canada. Offers MA, PhD. *Degree requirements:* For master's, one foreign language, thesis; for doctorate, one foreign language, thesis/dissertation. *Entrance requirements:* For master's, honors degree; for doctorate, master's degree. Additional exam requirements/recommendations for international students: Required—TOEFL. *Faculty research:* Canadian, American, British, modern French, and modern Russian history; international, medieval, and European intellectual history; women's history.

**Carnegie Mellon University,** Dietrich College of Humanities and Social Sciences, Department of History, Pittsburgh, PA 15213-3891. Offers African and African-American diaspora (PhD); culture and power (PhD); labor, politics and social movements (PhD); technology, environment, science and health (PhD); women, gender and the family (PhD). *Program availability:* Part-time. *Degree requirements:* For doctorate, oral and written comprehensive exams, dissertation defense. *Entrance requirements:* For doctorate, GRE General Test. Additional exam requirements/recommendations for international students: Required—TOEFL. Electronic applications accepted. *Faculty research:* Anthropology and history, African-American history, technology/environment, cultural history analysis.

**Case Western Reserve University,** School of Graduate Studies, Department of History, Cleveland, OH 44106. Offers MA, PhD. *Program availability:* Part-time. *Faculty:* 15 full-time (6 women). *Students:* 25 full-time (11 women), 3 part-time (all women), 2 international. Average age 34. 19 applicants, 16% accepted, 3 enrolled. Terminal master's awarded for partial completion of doctoral program. *Degree requirements:* For master's, thesis; for doctorate, thesis/dissertation. *Entrance requirements:* For master's and doctorate, GRE General Test, statement of objectives; three letters of recommendation; curriculum vitae; writing sample; short essay. Additional exam requirements/recommendations for international students: Required—TOEFL (minimum score 577 paper-based; 90 iBT); Recommended—IELTS (minimum score 7). *Application deadline:* For fall admission, 1/31 priority date for domestic students. Application fee: $50. Electronic applications accepted. *Expenses: Tuition:* Full-time $42,576; part-time $1774 per credit hour. *Required fees:* $34. Tuition and fees vary according to course load and program. *Financial support:* Fellowships, research assistantships, teaching assistantships, career-related internships or fieldwork, tuition waivers (full and partial), and unspecified assistantships available. Financial award

application deadline: 1/31; financial award applicants required to submit FAFSA. *Faculty research:* American social history, social policy history, history of technology, environment, science, medicine. *Unit head:* Kenneth Ledford, Associate Professor and Chair, 216-368-4144, Fax: 216-368-4681, E-mail: kenneth.ledford@case.edu. *Application contact:* Daniel Cohen, Associate Professor, 216-368-4165, Fax: 216-368-4681, E-mail: daniel.a.cohen@case.edu.
Website: http://history.case.edu/

**The Catholic University of America,** School of Arts and Sciences, Department of History, Washington, DC 20064. Offers history (MA, PhD), including early modern Europe, Latin America (MA), Medieval, modern Europe, U.S.; religion and society in the late medieval and early modern world (MA); MA/JD; MSLS/MA. *Program availability:* Part-time. *Faculty:* 14 full-time (6 women), 3 part-time/adjunct (2 women). *Students:* 7 full-time (2 women), 20 part-time (6 women); includes 3 minority (all Two or more races, non-Hispanic/Latino), 2 international. Average age 30. 22 applicants, 45% accepted, 4 enrolled. In 2016, 4 master's, 5 doctorates awarded. Terminal master's awarded for partial completion of doctoral program. *Degree requirements:* For master's, one foreign language, comprehensive exam, thesis optional, 2 languages (for medievalists), one of which must be Latin; for doctorate, 2 foreign languages, comprehensive exam, thesis/dissertation, 3 languages (for medievalists), one of which must be Latin. *Entrance requirements:* For master's and doctorate, GRE General Test, statement of purpose, official copies of academic transcripts, three letters of recommendation, writing sample. Additional exam requirements/recommendations for international students: Required—TOEFL (minimum score 550 paper-based; 80 iBT). *Application deadline:* For fall admission, 7/15 priority date for domestic students, 7/1 for international students; for spring admission, 11/15 priority date for domestic students, 11/1 for international students. Applications are processed on a rolling basis. Application fee: $55. Electronic applications accepted. *Expenses:* $42,850 per year; $1,170 per credit; $200 per semester part-time fees. *Financial support:* Fellowships, research assistantships, teaching assistantships, Federal Work-Study, scholarships/grants, tuition waivers (full and partial), and unspecified assistantships available. Financial award application deadline: 2/1; financial award applicants required to submit FAFSA. *Faculty research:* Medieval history, including the Islamic Middle East, with particular expertise in later medieval religious, social, and economic history and early medieval and late antique history; European and American intellectual history; renaissance, reformation, catholic reformation; US catholic history; history of immigration. *Total annual research expenditures:* $42,594. *Unit head:* Dr. Katherine Jansen, Chair, 202-319-5484, Fax: 202-319-5569, E-mail: jansen@cua.edu. *Application contact:* Director of Graduate Admissions, 202-319-5057, Fax: 202-319-6533, E-mail: cua-admissions@cua.edu.
Website: http://history.cua.edu/

**Central Connecticut State University,** School of Graduate Studies, College of Liberal Arts and Social Sciences, Department of History, New Britain, CT 06050-4010. Offers MA, Certificate. *Program availability:* Part-time, evening/weekend. *Faculty:* 9 full-time (6 women). *Students:* 20 full-time (11 women), 23 part-time (12 women). Average age 32. 26 applicants, 62% accepted, 14 enrolled. In 2016, 5 master's, 4 other advanced degrees awarded. *Degree requirements:* For master's, comprehensive exam, thesis or alternative; for Certificate, qualifying exam. *Entrance requirements:* For master's, minimum undergraduate GPA of 3.0, essays, letters of recommendation. Additional exam requirements/recommendations for international students: Required—TOEFL (minimum score 550 paper-based; 79 iBT). *Application deadline:* For fall admission, 5/1 for domestic and international students; for spring admission, 11/1 for domestic and international students. Applications are processed on a rolling basis. Application fee: $50. Electronic applications accepted. *Expenses: Tuition, area resident:* Full-time $6497; part-time $606 per credit. Tuition, state resident: full-time $9748; part-time $622 per credit. Tuition, nonresident: full-time $18,102; part-time $622 per credit. *Required fees:* $4459; $246 per credit. *Financial support:* In 2016–17, 15 students received support. Career-related internships or fieldwork, Federal Work-Study, scholarships/grants, and unspecified assistantships available. Support available to part-time students. Financial award application deadline: 3/1; financial award applicants required to submit FAFSA. *Faculty research:* American West, African history, Eastern Europe, modern Middle East, East Asia. *Unit head:* Dr. Katherine Hermes, Chair, 860-832-2800, E-mail: hermesk@ccsu.edu. *Application contact:* Patricia Gardner, Associate Director of Graduate Studies, 860-832-2350, Fax: 860-832-2362.
Website: http://www.ccsu.edu/history/

**Central European University,** Department of History, Budapest, Hungary. Offers MA, PhD. *Faculty:* 14 full-time (3 women), 8 part-time/adjunct (2 women). *Students:* 94 full-time (35 women). Average age 28. 191 applicants, 35% accepted, 51 enrolled. In 2016, 30 master's, 4 doctorates awarded. Terminal master's awarded for partial completion of doctoral program. *Degree requirements:* For master's, one foreign language, thesis; for doctorate, one foreign language, comprehensive exam, thesis/dissertation. *Entrance requirements:* For master's and doctorate, essay, statement of purpose, interview. Additional exam requirements/recommendations for international students: Required—TOEFL (minimum score 570 paper-based); Recommended—IELTS (minimum score 6.5). *Application deadline:* For fall admission, 2/4 for domestic and international students. Application fee: $30. Electronic applications accepted. *Expenses: Tuition:* Full-time 13,500 euros. Tuition and fees vary according to degree level, program and student level. *Financial support:* Fellowships, career-related internships or fieldwork, institutionally sponsored loans, scholarships/grants, and tuition waivers (full and partial) available. *Faculty research:* History of central, Southeastern and Eastern Europe and the Eastern Mediterranean from the 16th century to the present. *Unit head:* Dr. Matthias Riedl, Head, 36 1 327-3022, Fax: 361-327-3191, E-mail: history@ceu.edu. *Application contact:* Agnes Bendik, Coordinator, 361-327-3000 Ext. 2591, Fax: 361-235-6145, E-mail: history@ceu.edu.
Website: http://history.ceu.edu/

**Central Michigan University,** College of Graduate Studies, College of Humanities and Social and Behavioral Sciences, Department of History, Mount Pleasant, MI 48859. Offers European history (Graduate Certificate); history (MA); modern history (Graduate Certificate); United States history (Graduate Certificate); MA/PhD. *Program availability:* Part-time. *Degree requirements:* For master's, thesis or alternative. Electronic applications accepted. *Faculty research:* Colonial and revolutionary United States history, modern European history, Latin American and transatlantic history, transnational and comparative history, United States social history.

**Central Washington University,** Graduate Studies and Research, College of Arts and Humanities, Department of History, Ellensburg, WA 98926. Offers MA. *Degree requirements:* For master's, thesis or alternative. *Entrance requirements:* For master's, GRE General Test, minimum GPA of 3.0, writing sample. Additional exam requirements/recommendations for international students: Required—TOEFL (minimum score 550 paper-based; 79 iBT). Electronic applications accepted.

**Centro de Estudios Avanzados de Puerto Rico y el Caribe,** Graduate Program in Puerto Rican and Caribbean Studies, Old San Juan, PR 00902-3970. Offers Puerto Rican and Caribbean history (MA, PhD); Puerto Rican and Caribbean literature (MA, PhD); Puerto Rican studies (MA). *Program availability:* Part-time, evening/weekend. *Degree requirements:* For master's, comprehensive exam, thesis; for doctorate, 2 foreign languages, comprehensive exam, thesis/dissertation. *Entrance requirements:*

## History

For master's and doctorate, interview. *Faculty research:* Literature, history, art, folklore, and culture of Puerto Rico and Caribbean countries.

**Chicago State University,** School of Graduate and Professional Studies, College of Arts and Sciences, Department of Geography, Sociology, History, African-American Studies and Anthropology, Chicago, IL 60628. Offers geographic information systems (MA); geography (MA); history (MA). *Entrance requirements:* For master's, minimum GPA of 3.0.

**The Citadel, The Military College of South Carolina,** Citadel Graduate College, School of Humanities and Social Sciences, Department of History, Charleston, SC 29409. Offers history (MA); history and teaching content (Graduate Certificate). Program offered jointly with The Graduate School of the College of Charleston. *Program availability:* Part-time, evening/weekend. *Faculty:* 4 full-time (0 women). *Students:* 4 part-time (1 woman); includes 1 minority (Black or African American, non-Hispanic/Latino). 13 applicants, 100% accepted, 1 enrolled. In 2016, 2 master's awarded. *Degree requirements:* For master's, variable foreign language requirement, thesis optional. *Entrance requirements:* For master's, GRE (minimum verbal score of 152) taken within the last 5 years, minimum undergraduate GPA of 2.5 (3.0 in major); 3 letters of recommendation; evidence of ability to conduct research and present findings; at least 15 hours of history course work; for Graduate Certificate, no more than 2 page letter of intent that answers specific questions listed on the Department of History website and academic course catalog; 3 references familiar with work; baccalaureate degree in specified fields. Additional exam requirements/recommendations for international students: Required—TOEFL (minimum score 550 paper-based). *Application deadline:* Applications are processed on a rolling basis. Application fee: $40. Electronic applications accepted. *Expenses:* Tuition, state resident: full-time $5121; part-time $569 per credit hour. Tuition, nonresident: full-time $8613; part-time $957 per credit hour. *Required fees:* $90 per term. *Financial support:* Fellowships and unspecified assistantships available. Support available to part-time students. Financial award application deadline: 7/1; financial award applicants required to submit FAFSA. *Unit head:* Dr. Katherine H. Grenier, Department Head, 843-953-5073, E-mail: grenierk@citadel.edu. *Application contact:* Dr. Keith Knapp, Director of Graduate Studies, 843-953-5073, E-mail: knappk@citadel.edu.
Website: http://www.citadel.edu/root/history-masters-program

**City College of the City University of New York,** Graduate School, Division of Humanities and the Arts, Department of History, New York, NY 10031-9198. Offers MA. *Program availability:* Part-time. *Degree requirements:* For master's, one foreign language, comprehensive exam, thesis. *Entrance requirements:* Required—TOEFL (minimum score 600 paper-based; 100 iBT). Electronic applications accepted. Tuition and fees vary according to course load, degree level and program. *Faculty research:* Latin American, European, Asian, urban, and architectural history.

**Claremont Graduate University,** Graduate Programs, School of Arts and Humanities, Department of History, Claremont, CA 91711-6160. Offers Africana history (Certificate); American studies and U.S. history (MA, PhD); archival studies (MA); early modern studies (MA, PhD); European studies (MA, PhD); oral history (MA, PhD); MBA/MA; MBA/PhD. *Faculty:* 5 full-time (3 women), 2 part-time/adjunct (0 women). *Students:* 45 full-time (23 women), 24 part-time (14 women); includes 21 minority (2 Black or African American, non-Hispanic/Latino; 1 American Indian or Alaska Native, non-Hispanic/Latino; 5 Asian, non-Hispanic/Latino; 6 Hispanic/Latino; 1 Native Hawaiian or other Pacific Islander, non-Hispanic/Latino; 6 Two or more races, non-Hispanic/Latino). Average age 38. In 2016, 5 master's, 2 doctorates awarded. Terminal master's awarded for partial completion of doctoral program. *Entrance requirements:* For master's and doctorate, GRE General Test. Additional exam requirements/recommendations for international students: Required—TOEFL (minimum score 75 iBT). *Application deadline:* For fall admission, 2/1 priority date for domestic and international students. Applications are processed on a rolling basis. Application fee: $80. Electronic applications accepted. *Expenses: Tuition:* Full-time $44,328; part-time $1847 per unit. *Required fees:* $600; $300 per semester. Tuition and fees vary according to course load and program. *Financial support:* Fellowships, research assistantships, Federal Work-Study, institutionally sponsored loans, and scholarships/grants available. Support available to part-time students. Financial award application deadline: 2/15; financial award applicants required to submit FAFSA. *Faculty research:* Intellectual and social history, cultural studies, gender studies, Western history, Chicano history. *Unit head:* Joshua Goode, Chair, 909-607-7430, E-mail: joshua.goode@cgu.edu. *Application contact:* Amy Sandefur, Assistant Director of Admissions, 909-607-9101, E-mail: amy.sandefur@cgu.edu.
Website: https://www.cgu.edu/departments/history/

**Clark Atlanta University,** School of Arts and Sciences, Department of History, Atlanta, GA 30314. Offers MA, DAH. *Program availability:* Part-time. *Faculty:* 3 full-time (1 woman). *Students:* 5 part-time (3 women); includes 4 minority (all Black or African American, non-Hispanic/Latino). Average age 41. In 2016, 1 master's, 1 doctorate awarded. *Degree requirements:* For master's, one foreign language, comprehensive exam, thesis; for doctorate, one foreign language, comprehensive exam, thesis/dissertation. *Entrance requirements:* For master's, GRE General Test, minimum GPA of 2.5. Additional exam requirements/recommendations for international students: Required—TOEFL (minimum score 500 paper-based; 61 iBT). *Application deadline:* For fall admission, 4/1 for domestic and international students; for spring admission, 11/1 for domestic and international students. Applications are processed on a rolling basis. Application fee: $40 ($55 for international students). Electronic applications accepted. *Expenses: Tuition:* Full-time $15,498; part-time $861 per credit hour. *Required fees:* $1326; $1326 per credit hour. Tuition and fees vary according to course load. *Financial support:* Scholarships/grants and unspecified assistantships available. Financial award application deadline: 4/30; financial award applicants required to submit FAFSA. *Faculty research:* Education for public service. *Unit head:* Dr. Stephanie Evans, Dean, 404-880-6774, E-mail: sevans@cau.edu. *Application contact:* Graduate Program Admissions, 404-880-8483, E-mail: graduateadmissions@cau.edu.

**Clark University,** Graduate School, Department of History, Program in United States and Atlantic History, Worcester, MA 01610-1477. Offers history of the Atlantic world (PhD); history of the United States (PhD). *Students:* 9 full-time (3 women), 7 part-time (3 women), 1 international. Average age 59. 14 applicants, 43% accepted, 6 enrolled. In 2016, 1 doctorate awarded. *Application deadline:* For fall admission, 1/15 for domestic students. Application fee: $75. *Expenses: Tuition:* Full-time $44,050. *Required fees:* $80. Tuition and fees vary according to course load and program. *Financial support:* In 2016–17, fellowships with tuition reimbursements (averaging $17,000 per year), research assistantships with tuition reimbursements (averaging $17,000 per year), teaching assistantships with tuition reimbursements (averaging $17,000 per year) were awarded. *Faculty research:* American political history, comparative history, American family history. *Unit head:* Dr. Willem Klooster, Professor, 508-421-3768. *Application contact:* Diane Fenner, Department Assistant, 508-793-7288, Fax: 508-793-8816, E-mail: dfenner@clarku.edu.

**Clayton State University,** School of Graduate Studies, College of Arts and Sciences, Program in Education, Morrow, GA 30260-0285. Offers biology (MAT); English (MAT); history (MAT); mathematics (MAT). *Accreditation:* NCATE. *Entrance requirements:* For

master's, GRE, GACE, 2 official copies of transcripts, 3 recommendation letters, statement of purpose. Additional exam requirements/recommendations for international students: Required—TOEFL (minimum score 550 paper-based). Electronic applications accepted. *Expenses:* Tuition, state resident: full-time $3528; part-time $196 per credit hour. Tuition, nonresident: full-time $13,176; part-time $732 per credit hour. *Required fees:* $1454; $1454 per credit hour. $727 per semester. Tuition and fees vary according to campus/location and program.

**Clemson University,** Graduate School, College of Architecture, Arts, and Humanities, Department of History, Clemson, SC 29634. Offers MA. *Program availability:* Part-time. *Faculty:* 25 full-time (10 women), 1 part-time/adjunct (0 women). *Students:* 16 full-time (10 women), 5 part-time (4 women); includes 4 minority (1 Black or African American, non-Hispanic/Latino; 3 Hispanic/Latino). Average age 34. 19 applicants, 42% accepted, 5 enrolled. In 2016, 8 master's awarded. *Degree requirements:* For master's, one foreign language, comprehensive exam, thesis. *Entrance requirements:* For master's, GRE General Test, unofficial transcripts, letters of recommendation, personal statement, sample term paper. Additional exam requirements/recommendations for international students: Required—TOEFL (minimum score 80 iBT), IELTS (minimum score 6.5). *Application deadline:* For fall admission, 1/20 priority date for domestic and international students. Application fee: $80 ($90 for international students). Electronic applications accepted. *Expenses:* $4,841 per semester full-time resident, $9,640 per semester full-time non-resident, $612 per credit hour part-time resident, $1,223 per credit hour part-time non-resident. *Financial support:* In 2016–17, 13 students received support, including 1 fellowship with partial tuition reimbursement available (averaging $1,800 per year); unspecified assistantships also available. Financial award application deadline: 1/20. *Faculty research:* U.S., U.S. South, British, European and non-Western history. *Total annual research expenditures:* $35,625. *Unit head:* Dr. James Burns, Department Chair, 864-656-3153, E-mail: burnsj@clemson.edu. *Application contact:* Dr. Paul Anderson, Graduate Program Coordinator, 864-656-3153, E-mail: pcander@clemson.edu.
Website: https://www.clemson.edu/caah/departments/history/

**Cleveland State University,** College of Graduate Studies, College of Liberal Arts and Social Sciences, Department of History, Cleveland, OH 44115. Offers art history (MA); museum studies (MA). *Program availability:* Part-time, evening/weekend. *Faculty:* 13 full-time (4 women). *Students:* 10 full-time (6 women), 7 part-time (4 women); includes 3 minority (1 Hispanic/Latino; 2 Two or more races, non-Hispanic/Latino). Average age 30. 21 applicants, 90% accepted, 6 enrolled. In 2016, 14 master's awarded. *Degree requirements:* For master's, thesis optional. *Entrance requirements:* For master's, minimum GPA of 3.0, bachelor's degree in history (or related field for art history). Additional exam requirements/recommendations for international students: Required—TOEFL (minimum score 550 paper-based; 78 iBT). *Application deadline:* For fall admission, 7/1 priority date for domestic students, 5/15 for international students; for spring admission, 11/15 for domestic students, 11/1 for international students; for summer admission, 4/1 for domestic students, 3/15 for international students. Applications are processed on a rolling basis. Application fee: $40. Electronic applications accepted. *Expenses:* Tuition, state resident: full-time $9565. Tuition, nonresident: full-time $17,980. Tuition and fees vary according to program. *Financial support:* In 2016–17, 7 students received support, including research assistantships with full tuition reimbursements available (averaging $8,600 per year); career-related internships or fieldwork, tuition waivers (full and partial), and unspecified assistantships also available. Financial award application deadline: 4/15. *Faculty research:* Africa and African diaspora, European history, Middle Eastern history, Latin American/Caribbean history, American history, gender and sexuality. *Unit head:* Dr. Elizabeth A. Lehfeldt, Chairperson, 216-687-3920, Fax: 216-687-5592, E-mail: e.lehfeldt@csuohio.edu. *Application contact:* Dr. Karen Sotiropoulos, Graduate Director, 216-687-3940, E-mail: r.s.shelton@csuohio.edu.
Website: http://www.csuohio.edu/history/

**The College at Brockport, State University of New York,** School of Arts and Sciences, Department of History, Brockport, NY 14420-2997. Offers history (MA), including American and world history, American history, American public history, world history. *Program availability:* Part-time, evening/weekend. *Faculty:* 9 full-time (5 women). *Students:* 8 full-time (5 women), 17 part-time (9 women); includes 1 minority (Black or African American, non-Hispanic/Latino). 17 applicants, 82% accepted, 14 enrolled. In 2016, 15 master's awarded. *Degree requirements:* For master's, thesis or alternative. *Entrance requirements:* For master's, minimum GPA of 3.0, writing sample, letters of recommendation, statement of objectives. Additional exam requirements/recommendations for international students: Required—TOEFL (minimum score 550 paper-based; 79 iBT), IELTS (minimum score 6.5). *Application deadline:* For fall admission, 7/1 priority date for domestic and international students; for spring admission, 11/15 priority date for domestic and international students; for summer admission, 4/15 for domestic and international students. Application fee: $50. Electronic applications accepted. *Expenses:* Contact institution. *Financial support:* In 2016–17, 1 fellowship with tuition reimbursement (averaging $3,750 per year), 2 teaching assistantships with full tuition reimbursements (averaging $6,000 per year) were awarded; Federal Work-Study, scholarships/grants, and unspecified assistantships also available. Support available to part-time students. Financial award application deadline: 3/15; financial award applicants required to submit FAFSA. *Faculty research:* American history, women's history, European history, world history, cultural history. *Unit head:* Dr. Owen Steve Ireland, Chairperson, 585-395-5627, Fax: 585-395-2620, E-mail: oireland@brockport.edu. *Application contact:* Dr. Morag Martin, Graduate Director, 585-395-5690, Fax: 585-395-2620, E-mail: mmartin@brockport.edu.
Website: http://www.brockport.edu/history/grad/

**College of Charleston,** Graduate School, School of Humanities and Social Sciences, Program in History, Charleston, SC 29424-0001. Offers MA. Program offered jointly with The Citadel, The Military College of South Carolina. *Program availability:* Part-time, evening/weekend. *Degree requirements:* For master's, comprehensive exam, thesis optional. *Entrance requirements:* For master's, GRE General Test or MAT, writing sample. Additional exam requirements/recommendations for international students: Required—TOEFL (minimum score 81 iBT). *Application deadline:* For fall admission, 3/1 for domestic students; for spring admission, 10/15 for domestic students. Applications are processed on a rolling basis. Application fee: $45. Electronic applications accepted. *Financial support:* Research assistantships, career-related internships or fieldwork, Federal Work-Study, scholarships/grants, and unspecified assistantships available. Financial award application deadline: 4/1; financial award applicants required to submit FAFSA. *Faculty research:* Modern West Africa, labor history, Southern women's' education, Native Americans, the Atlantic world. *Unit head:* Bill Olejniczak, Director, 843-953-5930, E-mail: olejniczakb@cofc.edu. *Application contact:* Bill Olejniczak, Director, 843-953-5930, E-mail: olejniczakb@cofc.edu.
Website: http://history.cofc.edu/graduate-program/index.php

**College of Staten Island of the City University of New York,** Graduate Programs, Division of Humanities and Social Sciences, Program in History, Staten Island, NY 10314-6600. Offers history of Africa and the Middle East (MA); history of Asia (MA); history of Europe (MA); history of Latin America and the Caribbean (MA); history of the United States (MA). *Program availability:* Part-time, evening/weekend. *Faculty:* 2 full-time. *Students:* 11 part-time. Average age 36. 8 applicants, 25% accepted, 2 enrolled. In

2016, 5 master's awarded. *Degree requirements:* For master's, comprehensive exam (for some programs), 32 credits (total of eight courses); thesis or portfolio. *Entrance requirements:* For master's, bachelor's degree with minimum GPA of 3.0 overall and in undergraduate history courses, two letters of recommendation, letter of interest, research-based writing sample. Additional exam requirements/recommendations for international students: Required—TOEFL (minimum score 550 paper-based; 79 iBT), IELTS (minimum score 6.5). *Application deadline:* For fall admission, 5/10 priority date for domestic and international students; for spring admission, 12/2 priority date for domestic and international students. Applications are processed on a rolling basis. Application fee: $125. Electronic applications accepted. *Expenses:* Tuition, state resident: full-time $10,130; part-time $425 per credit. Tuition, nonresident: full-time $18,720; part-time $780 per credit. *Required fees:* $181.10 per semester. Tuition and fees vary according to program. *Faculty research:* African and African diaspora history, South Asian history, Middle Eastern history, U.S. history, environmental history. *Unit head:* John Dixon, Graduate Program Coordinator, 718-982-3307, E-mail: john.dixon@csi.cuny.edu. *Application contact:* Sasha Spence, Associate Director for Graduate Admissions, 718-982-2019, Fax: 718-982-2500, E-mail: sasha.spence@csi.cuny.edu.
Website: http://www.csi.cuny.edu/catalog/graduate/master-of-arts-in-history-ma.htm

**College of Staten Island of the City University of New York,** Graduate Programs, School of Education, Staten Island, NY 10314-6600. Offers adolescence education (MS Ed), including biology, English, mathematics, social studies; childhood education (MS Ed), including learning and development, literacy education, mathematics education, music education, science education, social foundations of education, social studies education; leadership in education (Post-Master's Certificate); special education (MS Ed); teaching of English to speakers of other languages (MS Ed, Advanced Certificate). *Accreditation:* NCATE. *Faculty:* 25 full-time, 40 part-time/adjunct. *Students:* 32 full-time, 414 part-time. Average age 30. In 2016, 117 master's, 26 Advanced Certificates awarded. *Expenses:* Tuition, state resident: full-time $10,130; part-time $425 per credit. Tuition, nonresident: full-time $18,720; part-time $780 per credit. *Required fees:* $181.10 per semester. Tuition and fees vary according to program. *Unit head:* Dr. Kenneth Gold, 718-982-3737, Fax: 718-982-3743, E-mail: kenneth.gold@csi.cuny.edu. *Application contact:* Sasha Spence, Associate Director for Graduate Admissions, 718-982-2019, Fax: 718-982-2500, E-mail: sasha.spence@csi.cuny.edu.
Website: http://csivc.csi.cuny.edu/education/files

**The College of William and Mary,** Faculty of Arts and Sciences, Lyon Gardiner Tyler Department of History, Williamsburg, VA 23187-8795. Offers MA, PhD. *Faculty:* 24 full-time (8 women), 3 part-time/adjunct (2 women). *Students:* 50 full-time (30 women); includes 2 minority (1 Black or African American, non-Hispanic/Latino; 1 Two or more races, non-Hispanic/Latino), 2 international. Average age 28. 102 applicants, 21% accepted, 18 enrolled. In 2016, 17 master's, 6 doctorates awarded. Terminal master's awarded for partial completion of doctoral program. *Degree requirements:* For master's, one foreign language, comprehensive exam, thesis; for doctorate, one foreign language, comprehensive exam, thesis/dissertation. *Entrance requirements:* For master's and doctorate, GRE General Test, minimum GPA of 3.0. Additional exam requirements/recommendations for international students: Required—TOEFL. *Application deadline:* For fall admission, 12/5 for domestic and international students. Application fee: $45. Electronic applications accepted. *Expenses:* Tuition, state resident: full-time $9000; part-time $500 per credit hour. Tuition, nonresident: full-time $24,686; part-time $1200 per credit hour. *Required fees:* $5258. One-time fee: $400 full-time. *Financial support:* In 2016–17, 32 students received support, including 5 fellowships with full tuition reimbursements available (averaging $25,000 per year), 18 research assistantships with full tuition reimbursements available (averaging $22,100 per year), 9 teaching assistantships with full tuition reimbursements available (averaging $22,100 per year); career-related internships or fieldwork also available. Financial award application deadline: 12/5; financial award applicants required to submit FAFSA. *Faculty research:* Early America and the Atlantic world; comparative and transnational; race and ethnicity; gender and sexuality; imperialism and colonialism. *Total annual research expenditures:* $191,575. *Unit head:* Dr. Frederick Corney, Chair, 757-221-6285, Fax: 757-221-2111, E-mail: fccorn@wm.edu. *Application contact:* Dr. Hiroshi Kitamura, Director of Graduate Studies, 757-221-3724, Fax: 757-221-2111, E-mail: hxkita@wm.edu.
Website: http://www.wm.edu/as/history/gradprogram/index.php

**The College of William and Mary,** School of Education, Program in Curriculum and Instruction, Williamsburg, VA 23187-8795. Offers elementary education (MA Ed); gifted education (MA Ed); literacy leadership (MA Ed); math specialist (MA Ed); secondary education (MA Ed), including English, foreign language, math, science, social studies; special education (MA Ed). *Accreditation:* NCATE. *Program availability:* Part-time. *Faculty:* 30 full-time (21 women), 48 part-time/adjunct (38 women). *Students:* 60 full-time (47 women), 14 part-time (all women); includes 13 minority (1 Black or African American, non-Hispanic/Latino; 1 American Indian or Alaska Native, non-Hispanic/Latino; 2 Asian, non-Hispanic/Latino; 7 Hispanic/Latino; 2 Two or more races, non-Hispanic/Latino). Average age 26. 134 applicants, 79% accepted, 66 enrolled. In 2016, 77 master's awarded. *Degree requirements:* For master's, project. *Entrance requirements:* For master's, GRE, MAT, PRAXIS Core Academic Skills for Educators, minimum GPA of 2.5. Additional exam requirements/recommendations for international students: Required—TOEFL (minimum score 100 iBT), IELTS (minimum score 7). *Application deadline:* For fall admission, 1/15 for domestic and international students; for spring admission, 10/1 for domestic and international students. Application fee: $50. Electronic applications accepted. *Expenses:* $14,258 per year in-state full-time, $275 per credit in-state part-time; $30,500 per year out-of-state full-time, $1,200 per credit out-of-state part-time. *Financial support:* In 2016–17, 30 students received support, including 3 research assistantships (averaging $14,259 per year); scholarships/grants and unspecified assistantships also available. Financial award application deadline: 1/15; financial award applicants required to submit FAFSA. *Faculty research:* Educational technology, professional development and evaluation, inclusive education, rural education, education policy. *Unit head:* Dr. Jeremy D. Stoddard, Department Chair, 757-221-2348, E-mail: jdstod@wm.edu. *Application contact:* Dorothy Smith Osborne, Assistant Dean for Academic Programs and Student Services, 757-221-2317, E-mail: dsosbo@wm.edu.
Website: http://education.wm.edu

**Colorado State University,** College of Liberal Arts, Department of History, Fort Collins, CO 80523-1776. Offers liberal arts (MA); public history (MA), including cultural resource management, historic preservation, museum studies. *Program availability:* Part-time. *Faculty:* 6 full-time (2 women), 1 part-time/adjunct (0 women). *Students:* 25 full-time (14 women), 4 part-time (1 woman); includes 2 minority (1 American Indian or Alaska Native, non-Hispanic/Latino; 1 Hispanic/Latino). Average age 28. 23 applicants, 61% accepted, 13 enrolled. In 2016, 6 master's awarded. *Degree requirements:* For master's, one foreign language, comprehensive exam, thesis (for some programs), minimum final grade of B- in history courses counted toward degree. *Entrance requirements:* For master's, GRE General Test, 21 credits in history, statement of purpose, 3 letters of reference. Additional exam requirements/recommendations for international students: Required—TOEFL, IELTS. *Application deadline:* For fall admission, 2/1 priority date for domestic and international students. Application fee: $60 ($70 for international

students). Electronic applications accepted. *Expenses:* Tuition, state resident: full-time $9628. Tuition, nonresident: full-time $23,603. *Required fees:* $2253; $528.14 per credit hour. $264.07 per semester. Tuition and fees vary according to course load and program. *Financial support:* In 2016–17, 22 students received support, including 1 research assistantship with full tuition reimbursement available (averaging $13,932 per year), 23 teaching assistantships with full tuition reimbursements available (averaging $13,932 per year); fellowships with full tuition reimbursements available and health care benefits also available. Financial award application deadline: 3/1; financial award applicants required to submit FAFSA. *Faculty research:* United states and north America; public and environmental history; modern world; religion; women, gender and sexuality. *Total annual research expenditures:* $281,014. *Unit head:* Dr. Doug Yarrington, Department Chair, 970-491-6801, Fax: 970-491-2941, E-mail: doug.yarrington@colostate.edu. *Application contact:* Diane Margolf, Graduate Studies Committee Chair, 970-491-5671, Fax: 970-491-2941, E-mail: diane.margolf@colostate.edu.
Website: http://history.colostate.edu/

**Columbia University,** Graduate School of Arts and Sciences, New York, NY 10027. Offers African-American studies (MA); American studies (MA); anthropology (MA, PhD); art history and archaeology (MA, PhD); astronomy (PhD); biological sciences (PhD); biotechnology (MA); chemical physics (PhD); chemistry (PhD); classical studies (MA, PhD); classics (MA, PhD); climate and society (MA); conservation biology; earth and environmental sciences (PhD); East Asia: regional studies (MA); East Asian languages and cultures (MA, PhD); ecology, evolution and environmental biology (MA), including conservation biology; ecology, evolution, and environmental biology (PhD), including ecology and evolutionary biology, evolutionary primatology; economics (MA, PhD); English and comparative literature (MA, PhD); French and Romance philology (MA, PhD); Germanic languages (MA, PhD); global French studies (MA); global thought (MA); Hispanic cultural studies (MA); history (PhD); history and literature (MA); human rights studies (MA); Islamic studies (MA); Italian (MA, PhD); Japanese pedagogy (MA); Jewish studies (MA); Latin America and the Caribbean: regional studies (MA); Latin American and Iberian cultures (PhD); mathematics (MA, PhD), including finance (MA); medieval and Renaissance studies (MA); Middle Eastern, South Asian, and African studies (MA, PhD); modern art: critical and curatorial studies (MA); modern European studies (MA); museum anthropology (MA); music (DMA, PhD); oral history (MA); philosophical foundations of physics (MA); philosophy (MA, PhD); physics (PhD); political science (MA, PhD); psychology (PhD); quantitative methods in the social sciences (MA); religion (MA, PhD); Russia, Eurasia and East Europe: regional studies (MA); Russian translation (MA); Slavic cultures (MA); Slavic languages (MA, PhD); sociology (MA, PhD); South Asian studies (MA); statistics (MA, PhD); theatre (PhD). Dual-degree programs require admission to both Graduate School of Arts and Sciences and another Columbia school. *Program availability:* Part-time. Terminal master's awarded for partial completion of doctoral program. *Degree requirements:* For master's, variable foreign language requirement, comprehensive exam (for some programs), thesis (for some programs); for doctorate, variable foreign language requirement, comprehensive exam (for some programs), thesis/dissertation. *Entrance requirements:* For master's and doctorate, GRE General Test, GRE Subject Test (for some programs). Additional exam requirements/recommendations for international students: Required—TOEFL, IELTS. Electronic applications accepted.

**Columbus State University,** Graduate Studies, College of Education and Health Professions, Department of Teacher Education, Columbus, GA 31907-5645. Offers curriculum and instruction in accomplished teaching (M Ed); early childhood education (M Ed, MAT, Ed S); middle grades education (M Ed, MAT, Ed S); secondary education (M Ed, MAT, Ed S), including biology (MAT), chemistry (MAT), earth and space science (MAT), English/language arts, general science (M Ed), history (MAT), mathematics, science (Ed S), social science (M Ed, Ed S); special education (M Ed, MAT, Ed S), including general curriculum (M Ed, MAT); teacher leadership (M Ed). *Accreditation:* NCATE. *Program availability:* Part-time, evening/weekend, 100% online, blended/hybrid learning. *Faculty:* 20 full-time (13 women), 19 part-time/adjunct (16 women). *Students:* 92 full-time (66 women), 212 part-time (179 women); includes 113 minority (104 Black or African American, non-Hispanic/Latino; 1 American Indian or Alaska Native, non-Hispanic/Latino; 2 Asian, non-Hispanic/Latino; 4 Hispanic/Latino; 2 Two or more races, non-Hispanic/Latino), 5 international. Average age 34. 209 applicants, 56% accepted, 79 enrolled. In 2016, 111 master's, 18 other advanced degrees awarded. *Degree requirements:* For Ed S, thesis or alternative. *Entrance requirements:* For master's, GRE General Test, minimum undergraduate GPA of 2.75; for Ed S, GRE General Test, minimum undergraduate GPA of 2.75, graduate 3.0. Additional exam requirements/recommendations for international students: Required—TOEFL (minimum score 550 paper-based; 79 iBT). *Application deadline:* For fall admission, 6/30 for domestic students, 5/1 for international students; for spring admission, 11/1 for domestic and international students; for summer admission, 3/1 for domestic and international students. Applications are processed on a rolling basis. Application fee: $50. Electronic applications accepted. *Expenses:* Tuition, state resident: full-time $4804; part-time $2412 per semester hour. Tuition, nonresident: full-time $19,218; part-time $9612 per semester hour. *Required fees:* $1850; $1850 per semester hour. Tuition and fees vary according to program. *Financial support:* In 2016–17, 60 students received support, including 12 research assistantships with partial tuition reimbursements available (averaging $3,000 per year); career-related internships or fieldwork, Federal Work-Study, institutionally sponsored loans, scholarships/grants, tuition waivers (partial), and unspecified assistantships also available. Support available to part-time students. Financial award application deadline: 5/1; financial award applicants required to submit FAFSA. *Unit head:* Dr. Jan Burcham, Department Chair, 706-507-8519, Fax: 706-568-3134, E-mail: burcham_jan@columbusstate.edu. *Application contact:* Kristin Williams, Director of International and Graduate Recruitment, 706-507-8848, Fax: 706-568-5091, E-mail: williams_kristin@columbusstate.edu.
Website: http://te.columbusstate.edu/

**Columbus State University,** Graduate Studies, College of Letters and Sciences, Department of History and Geography, Columbus, GA 31907-5645. Offers history (MA), including race, ethnicity and society. *Program availability:* Evening/weekend. *Faculty:* 4 full-time (1 woman). *Students:* 6 full-time (3 women), 6 part-time (1 woman); includes 5 minority (3 Black or African American, non-Hispanic/Latino; 1 American Indian or Alaska Native, non-Hispanic/Latino; 1 Hispanic/Latino). Average age 33. 7 applicants, 43% accepted, 2 enrolled. *Degree requirements:* For master's, thesis. *Entrance requirements:* For master's, GRE, minimum GPA of 3.0, writing sample, statement of purpose, two letters of recommendation. Additional exam requirements/recommendations for international students: Required—TOEFL (minimum score 550 paper-based; 79 iBT). *Application deadline:* For fall admission, 6/30 for domestic students, 5/1 for international students; for spring admission, 11/1 for domestic and international students; for summer admission, 3/1 for domestic and international students. Applications are processed on a rolling basis. Application fee: $50. Electronic applications accepted. *Expenses:* Tuition, state resident: full-time $4804; part-time $2412 per semester hour. Tuition, nonresident: full-time $19,218; part-time $9612 per semester hour. *Required fees:* $1850; $1850 per semester hour. Tuition and fees vary according to program. *Financial support:* In 2016–17, 3 students received support, including 1 research assistantship (averaging $3,000 per year); teaching assistantships,

## History

tuition waivers (partial), and unspecified assistantships also available. Financial award application deadline: 5/1; financial award applicants required to submit FAFSA. *Unit head:* Dr. Doug Tompson, Department Chair, 706-507-8356, E-mail: tompson_doug@columbusstate.edu. *Application contact:* Kristin Williams, Director of International and Graduate Recruitment, 706-507-8848, Fax: 706-568-5091, E-mail: williams_kristin@columbusstate.edu.
Website: http://history.columbusstate.edu/

**Concordia University,** School of Graduate Studies, Faculty of Arts and Science, Department of History, Montréal, QC H3G 1M8, Canada. Offers MA, PhD. *Degree requirements:* For master's, one foreign language, thesis optional; for doctorate, one foreign language, comprehensive exam, thesis/dissertation. *Entrance requirements:* For master's, honors degree in history or equivalent. *Faculty research:* Canadian history, European social history, Canadian-American relations.

**Converse College,** School of Education and Graduate Studies, Program in Liberal Arts, Spartanburg, SC 29302. Offers English (MLA); history (MLA); political science (MLA). *Degree requirements:* For master's, capstone paper. *Entrance requirements:* For master's, minimum GPA of 3.0, 2 recommendations. *Application deadline:* For fall admission, 5/1 priority date for domestic students; for spring admission, 1/30 for domestic students. Application fee: $40. *Expenses: Tuition:* Full-time $3600; part-time $400 per credit hour. *Required fees:* $70 per term. *Unit head:* Dr. Kathy Good, Dean of the School of Education and Graduate Studies, 864-596-9082, E-mail: kathy.good@converse.edu. *Application contact:* Dr. Thomas McDaniel, Director of Master of Liberal Arts Program, 864-596-9015, E-mail: tom.mcdaniel@converse.edu.

**Cornell University,** Graduate School, Graduate Fields of Arts and Sciences, Field of History, Ithaca, NY 14853. Offers African history (MA, PhD); American history (MA, PhD); ancient Greek history (PhD); ancient history (MA, PhD); ancient Roman history (PhD); early modern European history (MA, PhD); English history (MA, PhD); French history (MA, PhD); German history (MA, PhD); history of science (MA, PhD); Korean history (PhD); Latin American history (MA, PhD); medieval Chinese history (MA, PhD); medieval history (MA, PhD); modern Chinese history (MA, PhD); modern European history (MA, PhD); modern Japanese history (MA, PhD); modern Middle Eastern history (PhD); premodern Islamic history (MA, PhD); premodern Japanese history (MA, PhD); Renaissance history (MA, PhD); Russian history (MA, PhD); South Asian history (PhD); Southeast Asian history (MA, PhD). Terminal master's awarded for partial completion of doctoral program. *Degree requirements:* For master's; for doctorate, 2 foreign languages, comprehensive exam, thesis/dissertation, 1 year of teaching experience. *Entrance requirements:* For master's and doctorate, GRE General Test, writing sample, 3 letters of recommendation. Additional exam requirements/recommendations for international students: Required—TOEFL (minimum score 550 paper-based; 77 iBT). Electronic applications accepted.

**Dalhousie University,** Faculty of Arts and Social Science, Department of History, Halifax, NS B3H 4R2, Canada. Offers MA, PhD. *Entrance requirements:* Additional exam requirements/recommendations for international students: Required—TOEFL, IELTS, CANTEST, CAEL, or Michigan English Language Assessment Battery. Electronic applications accepted. *Faculty research:* African, British, Russian, Canadian and medieval history.

**DePaul University,** College of Liberal Arts and Social Sciences, Chicago, IL 60614. Offers Arabic (MA); Chinese (MA); English (MA); French (MA); German (MA); history (MA); interdisciplinary studies (MA, MS); international public service (MS); international studies (MA); Italian (MA); Japanese (MA); leadership and policy studies (MS); liberal studies (MA); new media studies (MA); nonprofit management (MNM); public administration (MPA); public health (MPH); public service management (MS); social work (MSW); sociology (MA); Spanish (MA); sustainable urban development (MA); women and gender studies (MA); writing and publishing (MA); writing, rhetoric, and discourse (MA); MA/PhD. *Program availability:* Part-time, evening/weekend, online learning. Terminal master's awarded for partial completion of doctoral program. *Degree requirements:* For master's, variable foreign language requirement, comprehensive exam (for some programs), thesis (for some programs). Electronic applications accepted.

**Dominican University of California,** School of Arts, Humanities and Social Sciences, Humanities Program, San Rafael, CA 94901-2298. Offers applied music (MA); art history (MA); creative writing (MA); gender studies (MA); history (MA); literature (MA); philosophy (MA); political theory (MA); religion (MA). *Program availability:* Part-time. *Degree requirements:* For master's, thesis or alternative. *Entrance requirements:* For master's, minimum GPA of 3.0, interview. Additional exam requirements/recommendations for international students: Required—TOEFL (minimum score 550 paper-based; 80 iBT), IELTS (minimum score 6.5). Electronic applications accepted. Application fee is waived when completed online. *Expenses:* Contact institution.

**Drew University,** Caspersen School of Graduate Studies, Madison, NJ 07940-1493. Offers conflict resolution and leadership (Certificate), including community leadership, moderation, peace building; history and culture (MA, PhD), including American history, book history, British history, European history, Holocaust and genocide (M Litt, MA, D Litt, PhD), intellectual history, Irish history, print culture, public history; K-12 education (MAT), including art, biology, chemistry, elementary education, English, French, Italian, math, secondary education, special education, teacher of students with disabilities; liberal studies (M Litt, D Litt), including history, Holocaust and genocide (M Litt, MA, D Litt, PhD), Irish/Irish-American studies, literature (M Litt, MMH, D Litt, DMH, CMH), religion, spirituality, teaching in the two-year college, writing; medical humanities (MMH, DMH, CMH), including arts, health, healthcare, literature (M Litt, MMH, D Litt, DMH, CMH), scientific research; poetry (MFA). *Program availability:* Part-time, evening/weekend. *Faculty:* 4 full-time (2 women), 31 part-time/adjunct (16 women). *Students:* 62 full-time (41 women), 199 part-time (130 women); includes 38 minority (17 Black or African American, non-Hispanic/Latino; 3 Asian, non-Hispanic/Latino; 17 Hispanic/Latino; 1 Two or more races, non-Hispanic/Latino), 3 international. Average age 27. 93 applicants, 81% accepted, 46 enrolled. In 2016, 39 master's, 27 doctorates, 26 other advanced degrees awarded. Terminal master's awarded for partial completion of doctoral program. *Degree requirements:* For master's and other advanced degree, thesis (for some programs); for doctorate, one foreign language, comprehensive exam (for some programs), thesis/dissertation. *Entrance requirements:* For master's, PRAXIS Core and Subject Area tests (for MAT), resume, transcripts, writing sample, personal statement, letters of recommendation; for doctorate, GRE (PhD in history and culture), resume, transcripts, writing sample, personal statement, letters of recommendation. Additional exam requirements/recommendations for international students: Required—TOEFL (minimum score 587 paper-based; 94 iBT), IELTS (minimum score 7), TWE (minimum score 4). *Application deadline:* For fall admission, 8/1 for domestic students, 6/1 for international students; for spring admission, 12/1 for domestic students, 10/1 for international students. Applications are processed on a rolling basis. Application fee: $35. Electronic applications accepted. Tuition and fees vary according to program. *Financial support:* Fellowships, research assistantships, teaching assistantships, career-related internships or fieldwork, Federal Work-Study, scholarships/grants, and unspecified assistantships available. Support available to part-time students. Financial award applicants required to submit FAFSA. *Application contact:* Leanne Horinko,

Director of Caspersen Admissions, 973-408-3280, E-mail: gradm@drew.edu.
Website: http://www.drew.edu/caspersen

**Duke University,** Graduate School, Department of History, Durham, NC 27708. Offers history (AM, PhD); Latin American studies (PhD); JD/AM. *Degree requirements:* For doctorate, 2 foreign languages, thesis/dissertation. *Entrance requirements:* For doctorate, GRE General Test. Additional exam requirements/recommendations for international students: Required—TOEFL (minimum score 577 paper-based; 90 iBT) or IELTS (minimum score 7). Electronic applications accepted.

**Duquesne University,** Graduate School of Liberal Arts, Department of History, Pittsburgh, PA 15282-0001. Offers historical studies (MA); public history (MA). *Program availability:* Part-time, evening/weekend. *Faculty:* 15 full-time (5 women), 5 part-time/adjunct (3 women). *Students:* 33 full-time (25 women), 3 part-time (1 woman); includes 1 minority (Two or more races, non-Hispanic/Latino). Average age 24. 38 applicants, 89% accepted, 16 enrolled. In 2016, 14 master's awarded. *Degree requirements:* For master's, comprehensive exam (for some programs), thesis optional. *Entrance requirements:* For master's, GRE General Test, writing sample. Additional exam requirements/recommendations for international students: Required—TOEFL. *Application deadline:* For fall admission, 8/15 for domestic students, 5/1 for international students; for spring admission, 11/1 priority date for domestic students. Applications are processed on a rolling basis. Application fee: $0. Electronic applications accepted. *Expenses: Tuition:* Full-time $22,212; part-time $1234 per credit. Tuition and fees vary according to program. *Financial support:* In 2016–17, 30 students received support, including 7 teaching assistantships with full tuition reimbursements available (averaging $8,000 per year); career-related internships or fieldwork, Federal Work-Study, scholarships/grants, tuition waivers (full and partial), and unspecified assistantships also available. Support available to part-time students. Financial award application deadline: 5/1. *Faculty research:* American studies, immigration history, local social history, applied history, Eastern European history. *Unit head:* Dr. John Dwyer, Chair, 412-396-6470, E-mail: dwyer@duq.edu. *Application contact:* Linda Rendulic, Assistant to the Dean, 412-396-6400, Fax: 412-396-5265, E-mail: rendulic@duq.edu.
Website: http://www.duq.edu/academics/schools/liberal-arts/graduate-school/programs/history

**East Carolina University,** Graduate School, Thomas Harriot College of Arts and Sciences, Department of History, Greenville, NC 27858-4353. Offers American history (MA); Atlantic world (MA); European history (MA); history education (MA Ed); maritime studies (MA); military history (MA); public history (MA). *Program availability:* Part-time, evening/weekend. *Students:* 44 full-time (21 women), 48 part-time (27 women); includes 8 minority (1 Black or African American, non-Hispanic/Latino; 5 Hispanic/Latino; 2 Two or more races, non-Hispanic/Latino), 2 international. Average age 29. 46 applicants, 80% accepted, 23 enrolled. In 2016, 24 master's awarded. *Degree requirements:* For master's, one foreign language, comprehensive exam, thesis. *Entrance requirements:* For master's, GRE General Test, GRE Subject Test. Additional exam requirements/recommendations for international students: Required—TOEFL. *Application deadline:* For fall admission, 6/1 priority date for domestic students; for spring admission, 10/15 for domestic students. Applications are processed on a rolling basis. Application fee: $50. *Financial support:* Fellowships, research assistantships with partial tuition reimbursements, teaching assistantships with partial tuition reimbursements, and Federal Work-Study available. Support available to part-time students. Financial award application deadline: 6/1. *Unit head:* Dr. Gerry Prokopowicz, Chair, 252-328-6587, E-mail: prokopowiczg@ecu.edu.
Website: http://www.ecu.edu/cs-cas/history/graduatedegrees.cfm

**Eastern Illinois University,** Graduate School, College of Arts and Humanities, Department of History, Charleston, IL 61920. Offers historical administration (MA); history (MA). *Program availability:* Part-time, evening/weekend. *Degree requirements:* For master's, comprehensive exam (for some programs), thesis (for some programs). *Entrance requirements:* For master's, GMAT or GRE. Additional exam requirements/recommendations for international students: Required—TOEFL (minimum score 500 paper-based; 61 iBT), IELTS (minimum score 6). Electronic applications accepted.

**Eastern Kentucky University,** The Graduate School, College of Arts and Sciences, Department of History, Richmond, KY 40475-3102. Offers MA. *Program availability:* Part-time. *Degree requirements:* For master's, comprehensive exam, thesis optional. *Entrance requirements:* For master's, GRE General Test, GRE Subject Test, minimum GPA of 2.5. *Faculty research:* Twentieth-century U.S. history, Kentucky history, British history, world history, Eastern Europe.

**Eastern Michigan University,** Graduate School, College of Arts and Sciences, Department of History and Philosophy, Program in History, Ypsilanti, MI 48197. Offers MA. *Program availability:* Part-time, evening/weekend, online learning. *Students:* 6 full-time (3 women), 47 part-time (23 women); includes 13 minority (4 Black or African American, non-Hispanic/Latino; 2 Asian, non-Hispanic/Latino; 2 Hispanic/Latino; 5 Two or more races, non-Hispanic/Latino), 1 international. Average age 33. 25 applicants, 80% accepted, 11 enrolled. In 2016, 17 master's awarded. *Degree requirements:* For master's, thesis optional. *Entrance requirements:* Additional exam requirements/recommendations for international students: Required—TOEFL. *Application deadline:* Applications are processed on a rolling basis. Application fee: $45. *Financial support:* Fellowships, research assistantships with full tuition reimbursements, teaching assistantships with full tuition reimbursements, career-related internships or fieldwork, Federal Work-Study, institutionally sponsored loans, scholarships/grants, tuition waivers (partial), and unspecified assistantships available. Support available to part-time students. Financial award applicants required to submit FAFSA. *Application contact:* Dr. Ronald Delph, Director, 734-487-1018, Fax: 734-487-6835, E-mail: rdelph@emich.edu.

**Eastern Washington University,** Graduate Studies, College of Social Sciences, Department of History, Cheney, WA 99004-2431. Offers MA. *Faculty:* 12 full-time (4 women), 2 part-time/adjunct (1 woman). *Students:* 12 full-time (7 women), 2 part-time (both women); includes 1 minority (Hispanic/Latino). Average age 36. 9 applicants, 56% accepted, 3 enrolled. In 2016, 13 master's awarded. *Degree requirements:* For master's, comprehensive exam, thesis optional. *Entrance requirements:* For master's, minimum GPA of 3.0. Additional exam requirements/recommendations for international students: Required—TOEFL (minimum score 580 paper-based; 92 iBT), IELTS (minimum score 7), TWE, PTE (minimum score 63). *Application deadline:* For fall admission, 4/1 priority date for domestic students; for spring admission, 1/15 for domestic students. Applications are processed on a rolling basis. Application fee: $50. *Expenses:* Tuition, state resident: full-time $11,000; part-time $5500 per credit. Tuition, nonresident: full-time $24,000; part-time $12,000 per credit. *Required fees:* $1300. One-time fee: $50 full-time. Part-time tuition and fees vary according to course load, campus/location and program. *Financial support:* In 2016–17, 6 students received support, including teaching assistantships with partial tuition reimbursements available (averaging $7,000 per year); career-related internships or fieldwork, Federal Work-Study, institutionally sponsored loans, scholarships/grants, health care benefits, tuition waivers (partial), and unspecified assistantships also available. Support available to part-time students. Financial award application deadline: 2/1; financial award applicants required to submit FAFSA. *Unit head:* Dr. Liping Zhu, Chair, 509-359-6086, E-mail: lzhu@ewu.edu. *Application contact:* Dr. Michael Conlin, Director of Graduate Programs, 509-359-7851.

**East Stroudsburg University of Pennsylvania,** Graduate and Extended Studies, College of Arts and Sciences, Department of History and Geography, East Stroudsburg, PA 18301-2999. Offers M Ed, MA, MS. *Program availability:* Part-time, evening/ weekend. *Students:* 13 full-time (2 women), 10 part-time (1 woman), 8 international. *Degree requirements:* For master's, comprehensive exam, thesis, thesis defense. *Entrance requirements:* For master's, Commonwealth of Pennsylvania Department of Education certification requirements (M Ed). Additional exam requirements/ recommendations for international students: Recommended—TOEFL (minimum score 560 paper-based; 83 iBT), IELTS. *Application deadline:* For fall admission, 7/31 priority date for domestic students, 6/30 priority date for international students; for spring admission, 11/30 for domestic students, 10/31 for international students. Applications are processed on a rolling basis. Application fee: $50. Electronic applications accepted. *Expenses:* Tuition, state resident: full-time $8694; part-time $5796 per year. Tuition, nonresident: full-time $13,050; part-time $8700 per year. *Required fees:* $2550; $1690 per unit. $845 per semester. Tuition and fees vary according to course load, campus/ location and program. *Financial support:* Research assistantships with tuition reimbursements, Federal Work-Study, and unspecified assistantships available. Support available to part-time students. Financial award application deadline: 3/1; financial award applicants required to submit FAFSA. *Unit head:* Martin Wilson, Graduate Coordinator, 570-422-3536, Fax: 570-422-3937, E-mail: mwilson@esu.edu. *Application contact:* Kevin Quintero, Associate Director, Graduate and Extended Studies, 570-422-3890, Fax: 570-422-2711, E-mail: kquintero@esu.edu.

**East Tennessee State University,** School of Graduate Studies, College of Arts and Sciences, Department of Appalachian Studies, Johnson City, TN 37614. Offers MA, Postbaccalaureate Certificate. *Program availability:* Part-time. *Entrance requirements:* For master's, GRE General Test, minimum undergraduate GPA of 3.0, writing sample, 3 letters of recommendation; for Postbaccalaureate Certificate, minimum undergraduate GPA of 3.0, writing sample. Additional exam requirements/recommendations for international students: Required—TOEFL (minimum score 550 paper-based; 79 iBT). Electronic applications accepted. *Faculty research:* Appalachian culture, history, literature, art, environmental studies; bluegrass, old time, Celtic, and country music; community development and sustainability.

**East Tennessee State University,** School of Graduate Studies, College of Arts and Sciences, Department of History, Johnson City, TN 37614. Offers MA. *Program availability:* Part-time, evening/weekend. *Degree requirements:* For master's, comprehensive exam, thesis optional. *Entrance requirements:* For master's, bachelor's degree in history, minimum GPA of 3.0, three letters of recommendation. Additional exam requirements/recommendations for international students: Required—TOEFL (minimum score 550 paper-based; 79 iBT). Electronic applications accepted. *Faculty research:* Post-World War II German occupation, biographies of Eleanor Copenhaver Anderson and Harry M. Candill, the Miss America Pageant, encyclopedia of colonialism, the new Georgia campaign in the Pacific war.

**Edinboro University of Pennsylvania,** Department of History, Politics, Languages and Cultures, Edinboro, PA 16444. Offers social sciences (MA), including anthropology, history. *Program availability:* Part-time, evening/weekend. *Degree requirements:* For master's, thesis or alternative, competency exam. *Entrance requirements:* For master's, GRE or MAT, minimum QPA of 2.5. Electronic applications accepted.

**Emory & Henry College,** Graduate Programs, Emory, VA 24327-0947. Offers American history (MA Ed); organizational leadership (MCOL); professional studies (M Ed); reading specialist (MA Ed). *Program availability:* Part-time, evening/weekend. *Entrance requirements:* For master's, GRE or PRAXIS I, recommendations, writing sample. Additional exam requirements/recommendations for international students: Recommended—TOEFL.

**Emory University,** Laney Graduate School, Department of History, Atlanta, GA 30322-1100. Offers PhD. *Degree requirements:* For doctorate, 2 foreign languages, comprehensive exam, thesis/dissertation. *Entrance requirements:* For doctorate, GRE General Test, minimum GPA of 3.0. Additional exam requirements/recommendations for international students: Recommended—TOEFL. Electronic applications accepted. *Faculty research:* United States, modern Europe, early modern Europe, medieval Europe, Latin America, Africa.

**Emporia State University,** Program in History, Emporia, KS 66801-5415. Offers American history (MA); world history (MA). *Program availability:* Part-time. *Faculty:* 13 full-time (6 women), 1 part-time/adjunct (0 women). *Students:* 8 full-time (2 women), 17 part-time (9 women); includes 3 minority (1 Black or African American, non-Hispanic/ Latino; 2 Two or more races, non-Hispanic/Latino). 10 applicants, 90% accepted, 5 enrolled. In 2016, 4 master's awarded. *Degree requirements:* For master's, comprehensive exam or thesis. *Entrance requirements:* For master's, 12 credit hours in history, minimum undergraduate GPA of 2.5, writing sample. Additional exam requirements/recommendations for international students: Required—TOEFL (minimum score 520 paper-based; 68 iBT). *Application deadline:* For fall admission, 8/15 priority date for domestic students. Applications are processed on a rolling basis. Application fee: $30 ($75 for international students). Electronic applications accepted. *Expenses:* Tuition, state resident: full-time $5922; part-time $246.75 per credit hour. Tuition, nonresident: full-time $18,414; part-time $767.25 per credit hour. *Required fees:* $1884; $78.50 per credit hour. *Financial support:* In 2016–17, 1 research assistantship with full tuition reimbursement (averaging $7,344 per year), 6 teaching assistantships with full tuition reimbursements (averaging $7,344 per year) were awarded; Federal Work-Study, institutionally sponsored loans, health care benefits, and unspecified assistantships also available. Financial award application deadline: 3/15; financial award applicants required to submit FAFSA. *Faculty research:* Great Plains history. *Unit head:* Dr. Michael Smith, Chair, 620-341-5566, E-mail: msmith3@emporia.edu.

**Fairleigh Dickinson University, Metropolitan Campus,** University College: Arts, Sciences, and Professional Studies, School of History, Political and International Studies, Program in History, Teaneck, NJ 07666-1914. Offers MA.

**Faulkner University,** Great Books Honors College, Montgomery, AL 36109-3398. Offers M Litt.

**Fitchburg State University,** Division of Graduate and Continuing Education, Programs in History and Teaching History (Secondary Level), Fitchburg, MA 01420-2697. Offers MA, MAT, Certificate. *Accreditation:* NCATE. *Program availability:* Part-time, evening/ weekend. *Entrance requirements:* Additional exam requirements/recommendations for international students: Required—TOEFL (minimum score 550 paper-based; 79 iBT). Electronic applications accepted. *Expenses:* Tuition, state resident: full-time $2871; part-time $1914 per year. Tuition, nonresident: full-time $2871; part-time $1914 per year. *Required fees:* $3828. Tuition and fees vary according to program.

**Florida Agricultural and Mechanical University,** Division of Graduate Studies, Research, and Continuing Education, College of Social Sciences, Arts and Humanities, Department of History and Political Science, Program in Applied Social Science, Tallahassee, FL 32307-3200. Offers criminal justice (MASS); history (MASS); political science (MASS); public administration (MASS). *Program availability:* Part-time. *Degree requirements:* For master's, thesis optional. *Entrance requirements:* For master's, GRE General Test, minimum GPA of 3.0. *Faculty research:* Southern history, black history, election trends, Presidential history.

**Florida Atlantic University,** Dorothy F. Schmidt College of Arts and Letters, Department of History, Boca Raton, FL 33431-0991. Offers MA. *Program availability:* Part-time. *Faculty:* 16 full-time (6 women). *Students:* 14 full-time (4 women), 13 part-time (4 women); includes 5 minority (1 Asian, non-Hispanic/Latino; 4 Hispanic/Latino). Average age 32. 18 applicants, 78% accepted, 11 enrolled. In 2016, 7 master's awarded. *Degree requirements:* For master's, one foreign language, thesis optional. *Entrance requirements:* For master's, GRE General Test, minimum GPA of 3.0. Additional exam requirements/recommendations for international students: Required— TOEFL (minimum score 500 paper-based; 61 iBT), IELTS (minimum score 6). *Application deadline:* For fall admission, 6/1 priority date for domestic students, 2/15 for international students; for spring admission, 10/15 for domestic students, 8/15 for international students. Applications are processed on a rolling basis. Application fee: $30. Electronic applications accepted. *Expenses:* Tuition, state resident: full-time $7392; part-time $369.82 per credit hour. Tuition, nonresident: full-time $19,432; part-time $1024.81 per credit hour. *Financial support:* Fellowships, research assistantships, teaching assistantships with tuition reimbursements, career-related internships or fieldwork, Federal Work-Study, and tuition waivers (partial) available. Support available to part-time students. Financial award application deadline: 3/1. *Faculty research:* Twentieth-century America, U.S. urban history, Florida history, history of socialism, Latin America. *Unit head:* Dr. Douglas Kanter, 561-297-3593, E-mail: dkanter1@fau.edu. Website: http://www.fau.edu/history/

**Florida Gulf Coast University,** College of Arts and Sciences, Program in History, Fort Myers, FL 33965-6565. Offers MA. *Program availability:* Part-time, evening/weekend. *Faculty:* 238 full-time (97 women), 158 part-time/adjunct (62 women). *Students:* 7 full-time (5 women), 7 part-time (2 women); includes 1 minority (Two or more races, non-Hispanic/Latino). Average age 28. 4 applicants, 100% accepted, 3 enrolled. In 2016, 5 master's awarded. *Entrance requirements:* Additional exam requirements/ recommendations for international students: Required—TOEFL (minimum score 550 paper-based). *Application deadline:* For fall admission, 2/15 priority date for domestic students; for spring admission, 10/1 for domestic students. Applications are processed on a rolling basis. Application fee: $30. Electronic applications accepted. *Expenses:* Tuition, state resident: full-time $6721. Tuition, nonresident: full-time $28,170. *Required fees:* $1987. Tuition and fees vary according to course load and degree level. *Financial support:* Application deadline: 3/1; applicants required to submit FAFSA. *Unit head:* Scott Rohrer, Head, 239-590-7258, E-mail: srohrer@fgcu.edu. *Application contact:* Patricia Rice, Executive Secretary, 239-590-7196, Fax: 239-590-7200, E-mail: price@fgcu.edu.

**Florida International University,** Steven J. Green School of International and Public Affairs, Department of History, Miami, FL 33199. Offers Atlantic history (PhD); history (MA). *Program availability:* Part-time, evening/weekend. *Faculty:* 21 full-time (14 women), 3 part-time/adjunct (2 women). *Students:* 35 full-time (16 women), 25 part-time (10 women); includes 35 minority (8 Black or African American, non-Hispanic/Latino; 27 Hispanic/Latino), 5 international. Average age 35. 40 applicants, 58% accepted, 16 enrolled. In 2016, 6 master's, 6 doctorates awarded. *Degree requirements:* For master's, one foreign language, thesis optional; for doctorate, 2 foreign languages, comprehensive exam, thesis/dissertation. *Entrance requirements:* For master's, 12 credits of history courses (non-history majors), 2 letters of recommendation, writing sample, minimum GPA of 3.25; for doctorate, GRE General Test (minimum score of 1120), two letters of recommendation, statement of purpose, curriculum vitae, writing sample, minimum GPA of 3.25. Additional exam requirements/recommendations for international students: Required—TOEFL (minimum score 575 paper-based; 90 iBT). *Application deadline:* For fall admission, 1/15 priority date for domestic students, 1/15 for international students. Application fee: $30. Electronic applications accepted. *Expenses:* Tuition, state resident: full-time $8912; part-time $446 per credit hour. Tuition, nonresident: full-time $21,393; part-time $992 per credit hour. *Required fees:* $2185; $195 per semester. Tuition and fees vary according to program. *Financial support:* Institutionally sponsored loans, scholarships/grants, and unspecified assistantships available. Financial award application deadline: 3/1; financial award applicants required to submit FAFSA. *Faculty research:* European social history, American culture, social and labor history, Latin American culture and social history, military history, Diaspora studies. *Unit head:* Dr. Victor Uribe, Chair, 305-348-2961, Fax: 305-348-3561, E-mail: victor.uribe@fiu.edu. *Application contact:* Nanett Rojas, Manager, Admissions Operations, 305-348-7464, E-mail: gradadm@fiu.edu. Website: http://history.fiu.edu/

**Florida State University,** The Graduate School, College of Arts and Sciences, Department of Classics, Tallahassee, FL 32306-1510. Offers ancient history (MA); classical archaeology (MA); classical civilization (MA); classics (PhD), including classical archaeology, classics; Greek (MA); Greek and Latin (MA); Latin (MA). *Faculty:* 17 full-time (7 women), 2 part-time/adjunct (1 woman). *Students:* 47 full-time (29 women); includes 3 minority (1 Black or African American, non-Hispanic/Latino; 1 Asian, non-Hispanic/Latino; 1 Hispanic/Latino). Average age 25. 50 applicants, 40% accepted, 12 enrolled. In 2016, 4 master's, 3 doctorates awarded. Terminal master's awarded for partial completion of doctoral program. *Degree requirements:* For master's, 2 foreign languages, comprehensive exam, thesis or alternative; for doctorate, 4 foreign languages, comprehensive exam, thesis/dissertation. *Entrance requirements:* For master's, GRE General Test, minimum GPA of 3.0; for doctorate, GRE General Test, minimum GPA of 3.5. Additional exam requirements/recommendations for international students: Required—TOEFL (minimum score 550 paper-based; 80 iBT). *Application deadline:* For fall admission, 12/15 priority date for domestic students, 12/15 for international students. Applications are processed on a rolling basis. Application fee: $30. Electronic applications accepted. *Expenses:* Tuition, state resident: full-time $7263; part-time $403.51 per credit hour. Tuition, nonresident: full-time $18,087; part-time $1004.85 per credit hour. *Required fees:* $1365; $75.81 per credit hour. $20 per semester. Tuition and fees vary according to campus/location. *Financial support:* In 2016–17, 45 students received support, including 2 fellowships with full tuition reimbursements available (averaging $18,000 per year), 3 research assistantships with full tuition reimbursements available (averaging $12,000 per year), 25 teaching assistantships with full tuition reimbursements available (averaging $14,000 per year); Federal Work-Study, scholarships/grants, tuition waivers (full), and unspecified assistantships also available. Financial award application deadline: 1/15; financial award applicants required to submit FAFSA. *Faculty research:* Greek and Latin literature, classical archaeology, mythology, ancient history, religion. *Total annual research expenditures:* $100,000. *Unit head:* Dr. Daniel J. Pullen, Chairman, 850-644-0304, Fax: 850-644-4073, E-mail: dpullen@fsu.edu. *Application contact:* Dr. Timothy Stover, Admissions Director, 850-644-4259, Fax: 850-644-4073, E-mail: tstover@fsu.edu. Website: http://classics.fsu.edu/

**Florida State University,** The Graduate School, College of Arts and Sciences, Department of History, Tallahassee, FL 32306. Offers history (MA, MS, PhD); public history (MA). *Program availability:* Part-time. *Faculty:* 29 full-time (11 women). *Students:* 64 full-time (27 women), 21 part-time (5 women); includes 10 minority (2 Black or African American, non-Hispanic/Latino; 2 Asian, non-Hispanic/Latino; 1 Hispanic/Latino; 5 Two or more races, non-Hispanic/Latino), 3 international. Average age 32. 53 applicants, 60% accepted, 15 enrolled. In 2016, 22 master's, 16 doctorates awarded. *Degree requirements:* For master's, one foreign language, comprehensive exam (for some

## History

programs), thesis (for some programs), internships; for doctorate, one foreign language, comprehensive exam, thesis/dissertation. *Entrance requirements:* For master's, GRE General Test, minimum GPA of 3.3, minimum 18 hours of course work in history; for doctorate, GRE General Test, master's degree, minimum graduate GPA of 3.65. Additional exam requirements/recommendations for international students: Required— TOEFL (minimum score 550 paper-based; 80 iBT). *Application deadline:* For fall admission, 12/1 for domestic and international students. Applications are processed on a rolling basis. Application fee: $30. Electronic applications accepted. *Expenses:* Tuition, state resident: full-time $7263; part-time $403.51 per credit hour. Tuition, nonresident: full-time $18,087; part-time $1004.85 per credit hour. *Required fees:* $1365; $75.81 per credit hour. $20 per semester. Tuition and fees vary according to campus/location. *Financial support:* In 2016–17, 49 students received support, including 11 fellowships with full tuition reimbursements available (averaging $16,300 per year), 5 research assistantships with full tuition reimbursements available (averaging $15,000 per year), 5 teaching assistantships with full tuition reimbursements available (averaging $18,000 per year); Federal Work-Study, institutionally sponsored loans, scholarships/grants, tuition waivers (full and partial), and unspecified assistantships also available. Financial award application deadline: 12/1; financial award applicants required to submit FAFSA. *Faculty research:* Napoleon and the French Revolution, modern Europe, early modern Europe, Middle East, Latin America, Hispanic Caribbean, 20th-century Cuba, modern Britain, gender and sexuality, Atlantic world, modern Germany, Medieval Europe, World War II, U.S. 19th century, early U.S., Native American, science, medicine and technology, Russia, East Asia. *Unit head:* Dr. Edward Gray, Chair, 850-644-5888, Fax: 850-644-6402, E-mail: egray@fsu.edu. *Application contact:* Natalie Webster, Academic Program Assistant, 850-644-2610, E-mail: nswebster@fsu.edu. Website: http://history.fsu.edu/

**Fordham University,** Graduate School of Arts and Sciences, Department of History, New York, NY 10458. Offers MA, PhD. *Program availability:* Part-time, evening/weekend. *Faculty:* 32 full-time (14 women). *Students:* 22 full-time (13 women), 28 part-time (11 women); includes 4 minority (2 Black or African American, non-Hispanic/Latino; 2 Asian, non-Hispanic/Latino), 3 international. Average age 33. 86 applicants, 40% accepted, 9 enrolled. In 2016, 9 master's, 4 doctorates awarded. Terminal master's awarded for partial completion of doctoral program. *Degree requirements:* For master's, one foreign language, thesis optional; for doctorate, 2 foreign languages, comprehensive exam, thesis/dissertation. *Entrance requirements:* For master's and doctorate, GRE General Test. Additional exam requirements/recommendations for international students: Required—TOEFL (minimum score 650 paper-based). *Application deadline:* For fall admission, 1/4 priority date for domestic students; for spring admission, 11/1 for domestic students. Application fee: $70. Electronic applications accepted. *Financial support:* In 2016–17, 23 students received support, including 3 fellowships with tuition reimbursements available (averaging $27,622 per year), 16 teaching assistantships with tuition reimbursements available (averaging $16,806 per year); research assistantships with tuition reimbursements available, institutionally sponsored loans, tuition waivers (full and partial), and unspecified assistantships also available. Financial award application deadline: 1/4; financial award applicants required to submit FAFSA. *Unit head:* Dr. Nicholas Paul, Director of Graduate Studies, 718-817-3928, Fax: 718-817-4680, E-mail: npaul@fordham.edu. *Application contact:* Bernadette Valentino-Morrison, Director of Graduate Admissions, 718-817-4419, Fax: 718-817-3566, E-mail: valentinomor@fordham.edu.

**Fort Hays State University,** Graduate School, College of Arts and Sciences, Department of History, Hays, KS 67601-4099. Offers MA. *Degree requirements:* For master's, comprehensive exam, thesis or alternative. *Entrance requirements:* For master's, minimum undergraduate GPA of 3.0. Additional exam requirements/recommendations for international students: Required—TOEFL (minimum score 550 paper-based). Electronic applications accepted. *Faculty research:* Seventeenth century English legal history, Native American history, immigration history, Volga German settlement.

**George Mason University,** College of Education and Human Development, Programs in Curriculum and Instruction, Fairfax, VA 22030. Offers advanced international baccalaureate (M Ed); assistive technology (M Ed); designing digital learning in schools (M Ed); early childhood education (M Ed); early childhood education for diverse learners (M Ed); elementary education (M Ed); English as a second language (M Ed); gifted child education (M Ed); history (M Ed); literacy (M Ed), including PK-12 classroom teachers, reading specialist; literacy leadership for diverse schools (M Ed), including K-12 reading; physical education (M Ed); science K-12 (M Ed); secondary education (M Ed), including biology, chemistry, earth science, English, history/social science, math, physics; special education (M Ed); teacher leadership (M Ed); teaching culturally, linguistically diverse and exceptional learners (M Ed); transformative teaching (M Ed). *Faculty:* 41 full-time (35 women), 53 part-time/adjunct (46 women). *Students:* 155 full-time (127 women), 821 part-time (697 women); includes 267 minority (82 Black or African American, non-Hispanic/Latino; 5 American Indian or Alaska Native, non-Hispanic/Latino; 75 Asian, non-Hispanic/Latino; 88 Hispanic/Latino; 1 Native Hawaiian or other Pacific Islander, non-Hispanic/Latino; 16 Two or more races, non-Hispanic/Latino), 19 international. Average age 33. 513 applicants, 90% accepted, 352 enrolled. In 2016, 347 master's awarded. *Degree requirements:* For master's, comprehensive exam, thesis (for some programs). *Entrance requirements:* For master's, PRAXIS Core (for some programs), minimum GPA of 3.0 in last 60 hours, licensed as teacher or educational administrator, official transcripts, goals statement, 3 recommendation letters, interview or writing sample (depending on program), up to 3 years' teaching experience (depending on program). Additional exam requirements/recommendations for international students: Required—TOEFL (minimum score 575 paper-based; 88 iBT), IELTS (minimum score 6.5), PTE (minimum score 59). *Application deadline:* For spring admission, 11/1 priority date for domestic and international students. Application fee: $75 ($80 for international students). Electronic applications accepted. *Expenses:* Tuition, state resident: full-time $10,628; part-time $443 per credit. Tuition, nonresident: full-time $29,306; part-time $1221 per credit. *Required fees:* $3096; $129 per credit. Tuition and fees vary according to program. *Financial support:* In 2016–17, 1 student received support, including 1 teaching assistantship (averaging $4,060 per year); career-related internships or fieldwork, Federal Work-Study, scholarships/grants, unspecified assistantships, and health care benefits (for full-time research or teaching assistantship recipients) also available. Support available to part-time students. Financial award application deadline: 3/1; financial award applicants required to submit FAFSA. *Faculty research:* Achievement gaps and superintendent decisions, constructivist view of classroom teaching, cost of cheating, creating a critical literacy milieu in kindergarten. *Unit head:* Rebecca Fox, Professor and Academic Program Coordinator, 703-993-4123, E-mail: rfox@gmu.edu. Website: http://gse.gmu.edu/programs/gsemasters

**George Mason University,** College of Humanities and Social Sciences, Department of History and Art History, Program in History, Fairfax, VA 22030. Offers MA, PhD. *Faculty:* 39 full-time (14 women), 17 part-time/adjunct (9 women). *Students:* 51 full-time (27 women), 88 part-time (35 women); includes 10 minority (6 Hispanic/Latino; 4 Two or more races, non-Hispanic/Latino), 1 international. Average age 35. 108 applicants, 57% accepted, 21 enrolled. In 2016, 41 master's, 6 doctorates awarded. *Degree requirements:* For master's, comprehensive exam, translation language exam; for

doctorate, comprehensive exam, thesis/dissertation. *Entrance requirements:* For master's, GRE (waived for students who received their undergraduate degree 10 or more years ago or hold another graduate degree), expanded goals statement; 2 letters of recommendation; resume; official transcript; for doctorate, GRE, expanded goals statement; 3 letters of recommendation; writing sample; official transcripts. Additional exam requirements/recommendations for international students: Required—TOEFL (minimum score 575 paper-based; 88 iBT), IELTS (minimum score 6.5), PTE (minimum score 59). Application fee: $75 ($80 for international students). Electronic applications accepted. *Expenses:* Tuition, state resident: full-time $10,628; part-time $443 per credit. Tuition, nonresident: full-time $29,306; part-time $1221 per credit. *Required fees:* $3096; $129 per credit. Tuition and fees vary according to program. *Financial support:* In 2016–17, 35 students received support, including 1 fellowship (averaging $10,000 per year), 16 research assistantships with tuition reimbursements available (averaging $17,373 per year), 19 teaching assistantships with tuition reimbursements available (averaging $13,049 per year); career-related internships or fieldwork, Federal Work-Study, scholarships/grants, unspecified assistantships, and health care benefits (for full-time research or teaching assistantship recipients) also available. Support available to part-time students. Financial award application deadline: 3/1; financial award applicants required to submit FAFSA. *Faculty research:* History and new media, American history (digital), building digital archives in the 1930's. *Unit head:* Brian Platt, Chair, 703-993-1253, Fax: 703-993-1251, E-mail: bplatt1@gmu.edu. *Application contact:* Emily Gibson, Graduate Program Coordinator, 703-993-1248, Fax: 703-993-1251, E-mail: egibson5@gmu.edu. Website: http://historyarthistory.gmu.edu/programs/la-ma-hist

**Georgetown University,** Graduate School of Arts and Sciences, Department of History, Washington, DC 20057-1305. Offers global history (MA); global, international and comparative history (MA); history (MA, PhD); MA/PhD; MS/MA. MA in global history offered jointly with the history department at King's College London. *Degree requirements:* For master's, thesis (for some programs); for doctorate, 2 foreign languages, comprehensive exam, thesis/dissertation. *Entrance requirements:* For master's and doctorate, GRE General Test. Additional exam requirements/recommendations for international students: Required—TOEFL.

**Georgetown University,** Graduate School of Arts and Sciences, School of Continuing Studies, Washington, DC 20057. Offers American studies (MALS); Catholic studies (MALS); classical civilizations (MALS); emergency and disaster management (MPS); ethics and the professions (MALS); global strategic communications (MPS); hospitality management (MPS); human resources management (MALS); humanities (MALS); individualized study (MALS); integrated marketing communications (MPS); international affairs (MALS); Islam and Muslim-Christian relations (MALS); journalism (MPS); liberal studies (DLS); literature and society (MALS); medieval and early modern European studies (MALS); public relations and corporate communications (MPS); real estate (MPS); religious studies (MPS); social and public policy (MALS); sports industry management (MPS); systems engineering management (MPS); technology management (MPS); the theory and practice of American democracy (MALS); urban and regional planning (MPS); visual culture (MALS). MPS in systems engineering management offered jointly with Stevens Institute of Technology. *Entrance requirements:* Additional exam requirements/recommendations for international students: Required—TOEFL.

**The George Washington University,** Columbian College of Arts and Sciences, Department of History, Washington, DC 20052. Offers MA, PhD. *Program availability:* Part-time, evening/weekend. *Faculty:* 27 full-time (10 women). *Students:* 30 full-time (12 women), 33 part-time (11 women); includes 5 minority (3 Black or African American, non-Hispanic/Latino; 1 Asian, non-Hispanic/Latino; 1 Two or more races, non-Hispanic/Latino), 6 international. Average age 30. 134 applicants, 33% accepted, 13 enrolled. In 2016, 14 master's, 5 doctorates awarded. Terminal master's awarded for partial completion of doctoral program. *Degree requirements:* For master's, one foreign language, comprehensive exam, thesis or alternative; for doctorate, 2 foreign languages, thesis/dissertation, general exam. *Entrance requirements:* For master's and doctorate, GRE General Test, minimum GPA of 3.0. Additional exam requirements/recommendations for international students: Required—TOEFL (minimum score 550 paper-based; 80 iBT). *Application deadline:* For fall admission, 1/15 priority date for domestic and international students; for spring admission, 10/1 priority date for domestic students, 9/1 priority date for international students. Applications are processed on a rolling basis. Application fee: $75. Electronic applications accepted. *Financial support:* In 2016–17, 28 students received support. Fellowships with full tuition reimbursements available, teaching assistantships with tuition reimbursements available, career-related internships or fieldwork, Federal Work-Study, and tuition waivers available. Financial award application deadline: 1/15. *Unit head:* William Becker, Chair, 202-994-6052, E-mail: whbecker@gwu.edu. *Application contact:* Information Contact, 202-994-6230, Fax: 202-994-6231, E-mail: history@gwu.edu. Website: http://www.gwu.edu/~history/

**Georgia College & State University,** Graduate School, College of Arts and Sciences, Department of History, Geography and Philosophy, Milledgeville, GA 31061. Offers history, geography, and philosophy (MA). *Program availability:* Part-time, evening/weekend. *Students:* 4 full-time (2 women), 1 part-time (0 women). Average age 28. 4 applicants, 75% accepted, 3 enrolled. In 2016, 4 master's awarded. *Degree requirements:* For master's, one foreign language, comprehensive exam (for some programs), thesis or alternative, complete program within 5 years of matriculation. *Entrance requirements:* For master's, GRE (minimum scores: verbal 500, quantitative 460 and analytical writing 4.0), 2 letters of reference; transcript; minimum GPA of 3.0; undergraduate degree in history or other liberal arts, or advanced degree in unrelated field; foreign language. *Application deadline:* For fall admission, 4/15 priority date for domestic students, 4/1 priority date for international students; for spring admission, 11/15 priority date for domestic students, 9/1 priority date for international students; for summer admission, 4/1 priority date for domestic students. Applications are processed on a rolling basis. Application fee: $40. Electronic applications accepted. *Expenses:* $288 per credit hour in-state, $1,027 per credit hour out-of-state, $1,990 full-time annual fees. *Financial support:* In 2016–17, 3 students received support. Unspecified assistantships available. Support available to part-time students. Financial award application deadline: 4/15; financial award applicants required to submit FAFSA. *Unit head:* Dr. Stephen Auerbach, Graduate Coordinator for MA in History, 478-445-8276, E-mail: stephen.auerbach@gcsu.edu. *Application contact:* Kate Marshall, Graduate Admissions Coordinator, 478-445-1184, Fax: 478-445-1336, E-mail: gradadmit@gcsu.edu. Website: http://gcsu.edu/artsandsciences/history/history-ma

**Georgia Southern University,** Jack N. Averitt College of Graduate Studies, College of Liberal Arts and Social Sciences, Program in History, Statesboro, GA 30460. Offers history (MA); public history (Graduate Certificate). *Program availability:* Part-time. *Students:* 21 full-time (13 women), 7 part-time (5 women); includes 2 minority (both Hispanic/Latino). Average age 29. 15 applicants, 73% accepted, 10 enrolled. In 2016, 7 master's awarded. *Degree requirements:* For master's, one foreign language, thesis optional, terminal exams. *Entrance requirements:* For master's, GRE General Test, minimum GPA of 3.0, undergraduate major in history or equivalent, letters of reference.

Additional exam requirements/recommendations for international students: Required—TOEFL (minimum score 550 paper-based; 80 iBT), IELTS (minimum score 6). *Application deadline:* For fall admission, 3/1 priority date for domestic and international students; for spring admission, 10/1 priority date for domestic students, 10/1 for international students. Applications are processed on a rolling basis. Application fee: $50. Electronic applications accepted. *Expenses: Tuition,* state resident: full-time $7236; part-time $277 per semester hour. Tuition, nonresident: full-time $27,118; part-time $1105 per semester hour. *Required fees:* $2092. *Financial support:* In 2016–17, 16 students received support, including 14 fellowships with full tuition reimbursements available (averaging $7,750 per year), 1 teaching assistantship with full tuition reimbursement available (averaging $7,750 per year); career-related internships or fieldwork, Federal Work-Study, scholarships/grants, tuition waivers (full), and unspecified assistantships also available. Support available to part-time students. Financial award application deadline: 4/15; financial award applicants required to submit FAFSA. *Faculty research:* Women's/gender history, the American South, military history, public history, modern Europe. *Unit head:* Dr. Timothy Teeter, Graduate Program Director, 912-478-0239, Fax: 912-478-0377, E-mail: tmteeter@georgiasouthern.edu. Website: http://class.georgiasouthern.edu/history/

**Georgia State University,** College of Arts and Sciences, Department of History, Program in History, Atlanta, GA 30302-3083. Offers historic preservation (MA); history (PhD); public history (MA); world history (MA). *Program availability:* Part-time, evening/weekend. Terminal master's awarded for partial completion of doctoral program. *Degree requirements:* For master's, one foreign language, comprehensive exam, thesis optional, continuous enrollment; 6 hours of thesis credits; for doctorate, 2 foreign languages, comprehensive exam, thesis/dissertation, dissertation prospectus and prospectus defense; dissertation defense; residency; continuous enrollment; 6 hours of thesis credits. *Entrance requirements:* For master's, GRE, BA in history; statement of purpose; writing sample; three letters of recommendation; official transcripts; for doctorate, GRE, MA in history; master's thesis; statement of purpose; writing sample; three letters of recommendation; official transcripts; appropriate language skills. Additional exam requirements/recommendations for international students: Required—TOEFL (minimum score 550 paper-based; 80 iBT). *Application deadline:* For fall admission, 3/15 for domestic and international students; for spring admission, 10/15 for domestic and international students. Applications are processed on a rolling basis. Application fee: $50. Electronic applications accepted. *Expenses:* Tuition, state resident: full-time $6876; part-time $382 per credit hour. Tuition, nonresident: full-time $22,374; part-time $1243 per credit hour. *Required fees:* $2128; $1064 per term. Part-time tuition and fees vary according to course load and program. *Financial support:* Research assistantships with tuition reimbursements, teaching assistantships with tuition reimbursements, and scholarships/grants available. Financial award application deadline: 2/15; financial award applicants required to submit FAFSA. *Faculty research:* Nineteenth- and twentieth-century U.S. history, early modern European history, modern European history, world history, public history. *Unit head:* Dr. Michelle Brattain, Chair, 404-413-6352, Fax: 404-413-6384, E-mail: mbrattain@gsu.edu. *Application contact:* Dr. Joe Perry, Director of Graduate Studies, 404-413-6374, Fax: 404-413-6384, E-mail: jbperry@gsu.edu.
Website: http://www.gsu.edu/~wwwhis/

**Georgia State University,** College of Education and Human Development, Department of Middle and Secondary Education, Atlanta, GA 30302-3083. Offers curriculum and instruction (Ed D); English education (MAT); mathematics education (M Ed, MAT); middle level education (MAT); reading, language and literacy education (M Ed, MAT), including reading instruction (M Ed); science education (M Ed, MAT), including biology (MAT), broad field science (MAT), chemistry (MAT), earth science (MAT), physics (MAT); social studies education (M Ed, MAT), including economics (MAT), geography (MAT), history (MAT), political science (MAT); teaching and learning (PhD), including language and literacy, mathematics education, music education, science education, social studies education, teaching and teacher education. *Accreditation:* NCATE. *Program availability:* Part-time, evening/weekend, online learning. *Faculty:* 24 full-time (18 women). *Students:* 145 full-time (91 women), 151 part-time (102 women); includes 141 minority (104 Black or African American, non-Hispanic/Latino; 1 American Indian or Alaska Native, non-Hispanic/Latino; 16 Asian, non-Hispanic/Latino; 12 Hispanic/Latino; 8 Two or more races, non-Hispanic/Latino), 10 international. Average age 36. 115 applicants, 50% accepted, 41 enrolled. In 2016, 94 master's, 22 doctorates awarded. *Degree requirements:* For master's, comprehensive exam (for some programs), thesis or alternative, exit portfolio; for doctorate, comprehensive exam, thesis/dissertation. *Entrance requirements:* For master's, GRE; GACE I (for initial teacher preparation programs), baccalaureate degree or equivalent, resume, goals statement, two letters of recommendation, minimum undergraduate GPA of 2.5; proof of initial teacher certification in the content area (for M Ed); for doctorate, GRE, resume, goals statement, writing sample, two letters of recommendation, minimum graduate GPA of 3.3, interview. Additional exam requirements/recommendations for international students: Required—TOEFL (minimum score 550 paper-based; 79 iBT) or IELTS (minimum score 6.5). *Application deadline:* For fall admission, 1/15 priority date for domestic and international students; for spring admission, 10/1 for domestic and international students. Application fee: $50. Electronic applications accepted. *Expenses:* Tuition, state resident: full-time $6876; part-time $382 per credit hour. Tuition, nonresident: full-time $22,374; part-time $1243 per credit hour. *Required fees:* $2128; $1064 per term. Part-time tuition and fees vary according to course load and program. *Financial support:* In 2016–17, fellowships with full tuition reimbursements (averaging $19,667 per year), research assistantships with full tuition reimbursements (averaging $5,436 per year), teaching assistantships with full tuition reimbursements (averaging $2,779 per year) were awarded; career-related internships or fieldwork, Federal Work-Study, scholarships/grants, health care benefits, tuition waivers (full and partial), and unspecified assistantships also available. Financial award application deadline: 3/15. *Faculty research:* Teacher education in language and literacy, mathematics, science, and social studies in urban middle and secondary school settings; learning technologies in school, community, and corporate settings; multicultural education and education for social justice; urban education; international education. *Unit head:* Dr. Dana L. Fox, Chair, 404-413-8060, Fax: 404-413-8063, E-mail: dfox@gsu.edu. *Application contact:* Bobbie Turner, Administrative Coordinator I, 404-413-8405, Fax: 404-413-8063, E-mail: bnturner@gsu.edu.
Website: http://mse.education.gsu.edu/

**The Graduate Center, City University of New York,** Graduate Studies, Program in History, New York, NY 10016-4039. Offers PhD. *Degree requirements:* For doctorate, one foreign language, thesis/dissertation. *Entrance requirements:* For doctorate, GRE General Test, writing sample (15 pages). Additional exam requirements/recommendations for international students: Required—TOEFL. Electronic applications accepted.

**Hardin-Simmons University,** Graduate School, Cynthia Ann Parker College of Liberal Arts, Department of History, Abilene, TX 79698-0001. Offers MA. *Program availability:* Part-time. *Faculty:* 1 full-time (0 women). *Students:* 2 part-time (0 women). Average age 37. In 2016, 1 master's awarded. *Degree requirements:* For master's, one foreign language, comprehensive exam, thesis or alternative. *Entrance requirements:* For master's, GRE, minimum undergraduate GPA of 3.0 in history, 2.7 overall; 18 upper-level hours of course work in history; letters of recommendation; resume; writing sample.

Additional exam requirements/recommendations for international students: Required—TOEFL (minimum score 550 paper-based; 75 iBT). *Application deadline:* For fall admission, 8/15 priority date for domestic students, 4/1 for international students; for spring admission, 1/5 priority date for domestic students, 9/1 for international students. Applications are processed on a rolling basis. Application fee: $50. Electronic applications accepted. *Expenses: Tuition:* Full-time $12,510; part-time $695 per credit hour. *Required fees:* $325; $110 per semester. *Financial support:* Fellowships and scholarships/grants available. Support available to part-time students. Financial award application deadline: 6/30; financial award applicants required to submit FAFSA. *Faculty research:* Vietnam, diplomatic history, Texas politics, Mexico and NAFTA, classical warfare. *Unit head:* Dr. Mark Beasley, Program Director, 325-670-1279, Fax: 325-670-1526, E-mail: mbeasley@hsutx.edu. *Application contact:* Dr. Nancy Kucinski, Dean of Graduate Studies, 325-670-1298, Fax: 325-670-1564, E-mail: gradoff@hsutx.edu. Website: http://www.hsutx.edu/academics/cap/graduate/history

**Harvard University,** Graduate School of Arts and Sciences, Department of History, Cambridge, MA 02138. Offers African history (PhD); American history (PhD); ancient, medieval, early modern, and modern Europe (PhD), including Central Europe, Russia, Southeastern Europe, Western Europe; diplomatic history (PhD); East Asian history (PhD); economic and social history (PhD); intellectual history (PhD); Latin American history (PhD); Near Eastern history (PhD); oceanic history (PhD). *Degree requirements:* For doctorate, variable foreign language requirement, thesis/dissertation, oral general exam. *Entrance requirements:* For doctorate, GRE General Test, proficiency in 2 languages. Additional exam requirements/recommendations for international students: Required—TOEFL.

**High Point University,** Norcross Graduate School, High Point, NC 27268. Offers business administration (MBA); educational leadership (M Ed); elementary education (M Ed); history (MA); nonprofit management (MA); secondary math (M Ed); special education (M Ed); strategic communication (MA); teaching elementary education k-6 (MAT); teaching secondary mathematics 9-12 (MAT). *Accreditation:* NCATE. *Program availability:* Part-time, evening/weekend. *Degree requirements:* For master's, comprehensive exam (for some programs), thesis (for some programs). *Entrance requirements:* For master's, GMAT (MBA), GRE, MAT, minimum GPA of 3.0. Additional exam requirements/recommendations for international students: Required—TOEFL (minimum score 550 paper-based). Electronic applications accepted.

**Howard University,** Graduate School, Department of History, Washington, DC 20059-0002. Offers African diaspora (MA, PhD); African history (MA, PhD); Latin America and the Caribbean (MA, PhD); public history (MA); United States history (MA, PhD). *Program availability:* Part-time. Terminal master's awarded for partial completion of doctoral program. *Degree requirements:* For master's, one foreign language, thesis optional; for doctorate, 2 foreign languages, comprehensive exam, thesis/dissertation. *Entrance requirements:* For master's, GRE General Test, minimum GPA of 3.0, 3 letters of recommendation; for doctorate, GRE General Test, minimum GPA of 3.5, 3 letters of recommendation. Additional exam requirements/recommendations for international students: Required—TOEFL. Electronic applications accepted. *Faculty research:* Africa diaspora, U.S. diplomatic relations, Caribbean economic history.

**Hunter College of the City University of New York,** Graduate School, School of Arts and Sciences, Department of History, New York, NY 10065-5085. Offers MA. *Students:* 22 part-time (6 women); includes 3 minority (1 Black or African American, non-Hispanic/Latino; 2 Hispanic/Latino). Average age 38. 11 applicants, 36% accepted, 1 enrolled. In 2016, 3 master's awarded. *Degree requirements:* For master's, one foreign language, comprehensive exam, thesis, essay, language exam. *Entrance requirements:* For master's, GRE General Test, minimum of 18 credits in undergraduate history or related field. Additional exam requirements/recommendations for international students: Required—TOEFL. *Application deadline:* For fall admission, 4/1 for domestic students, 2/1 for international students; for spring admission, 11/1 for domestic students, 9/1 for international students. *Financial support:* Federal Work-Study, scholarships/grants, and tuition waivers (partial) available. Support available to part-time students. *Unit head:* Mary Roldan, Chair, 212-772-5480, E-mail: mrol@hunter.cuny.edu. Website: http://www.hunter.cuny.edu/history/

**Idaho State University,** Office of Graduate Studies, College of Arts and Letters, Department of History, Pocatello, ID 83209-8079. Offers historical resources management (MA). *Program availability:* Part-time. *Degree requirements:* For master's, comprehensive exam, thesis optional, internship. *Entrance requirements:* For master's, GRE, 3 letters of recommendation, minimum of 18 upper division history credits. Additional exam requirements/recommendations for international students: Required—TOEFL (minimum score 550 paper-based; 80 iBT). Electronic applications accepted. *Faculty research:* Historical geographic information systems, historical and urban geography, environmental history and environmental policy, United States political history, womens' and gender history.

**Illinois State University,** Graduate School, College of Arts and Sciences, Department of History, Normal, IL 61790-2200. Offers MA, MS. *Degree requirements:* For master's, thesis or alternative. *Entrance requirements:* For master's, GRE General Test, minimum GPA of 2.6 in last 60 hours of course work.

**Indiana State University,** College of Graduate and Professional Studies, College of Arts and Sciences, Department of History, Terre Haute, IN 47809. Offers MA, MS. *Program availability:* Part-time, evening/weekend. *Degree requirements:* For master's, comprehensive exam (for some programs), thesis or alternative. *Entrance requirements:* For master's, GRE, equivalent of minor in geography or geology. Additional exam requirements/recommendations for international students: Required—TOEFL (minimum score 550 paper-based).

**Indiana University Bloomington,** School of Education, Department of Educational Leadership and Policy Studies, Bloomington, IN 47405. Offers educational leadership (MS, Ed D, Ed S); higher education (Ed D, PhD); higher education and student affairs (MS); history and philosophy of education (MS); history, philosophy, and policy in education (PhD), including education policy studies, history of education, philosophy of education; international and comparative education (MS). *Accreditation:* NCATE. *Faculty:* 32 full-time (18 women). *Students:* 223 full-time (140 women), 94 part-time (50 women); includes 80 minority (44 Black or African American, non-Hispanic/Latino; 13 Asian, non-Hispanic/Latino; 18 Hispanic/Latino; 1 Native Hawaiian or other Pacific Islander, non-Hispanic/Latino; 4 Two or more races, non-Hispanic/Latino), 29 international. Average age 34. 309 applicants, 40% accepted, 57 enrolled. In 2016, 60 master's, 18 doctorates, 5 other advanced degrees awarded. *Degree requirements:* For master's, thesis optional; for doctorate, comprehensive exam, thesis/dissertation; for Ed S, comprehensive exam or project. *Entrance requirements:* For master's, doctorate, and Ed S, GRE General Test. Additional exam requirements/recommendations for international students: Required—TOEFL (minimum score 79 iBT). *Application deadline:* For fall admission, 1/15 priority date for domestic students, 12/1 priority date for international students; for spring admission, 9/1 priority date for domestic and international students. Applications are processed on a rolling basis. Application fee: $55 ($65 for international students). Electronic applications accepted. *Financial support:* Fellowships with full and partial tuition reimbursements, research assistantships with full and partial tuition reimbursements, teaching assistantships with full and partial tuition

## History

reimbursements, career-related internships or fieldwork, scholarships/grants, health care benefits, and unspecified assistantships available. *Faculty research:* Culturally engaging campus environments, school choice policy analysis, democracy and education in the national and international context, and principal leadership. *Unit head:* Dr. Dionne Danns, Interim Chair, 812-856-8398. *Application contact:* Maria Jensen, Department Administrator, 812-856-8370, Fax: 812-856-8394, E-mail: jensen5@indiana.edu.
Website: http://education.indiana.edu/about/departments/leadership/index.html

**Indiana University Bloomington,** University Graduate School, College of Arts and Sciences, Department of Art History, Bloomington, IN 47405-7000. Offers MA, PhD, MA/MLS. *Accreditation:* NASAD. *Faculty:* 14 full-time (8 women). *Students:* 24 full-time (19 women), 3 part-time (2 women); includes 1 minority (Asian, non-Hispanic/Latino), 3 international. Average age 33. 41 applicants, 49% accepted, 3 enrolled. In 2016, 7 master's, 4 doctorates awarded. *Degree requirements:* For master's, one foreign language, thesis; for doctorate, 2 foreign languages, comprehensive exam, thesis/dissertation. *Entrance requirements:* For master's, GRE, writing sample, 3 letters of recommendation, transcript; for doctorate, GRE, transcript, writing sample, 3 letters of recommendation. Additional exam requirements/recommendations for international students: Required—TOEFL (minimum score 550 paper-based). *Application deadline:* For fall and spring admission, 1/5 for domestic and international students. Application fee: $55 ($65 for international students). *Financial support:* In 2016–17, 15 students received support, including 2 fellowships with full tuition reimbursements available (averaging $18,000 per year), 11 teaching assistantships with full tuition reimbursements available (averaging $15,750 per year); scholarships/grants, health care benefits, and unspecified assistantships also available. Financial award application deadline: 2/15; financial award applicants required to submit FAFSA. *Faculty research:* Art and social history, consumer culture, feminist art and theory, classical revivals. *Unit head:* Diane Reilly, Chair, 812-855-5277, Fax: 812-855-9557, E-mail: dreilly@indiana.edu. *Application contact:* Alexandra Burlingame, Department Manager, 812-855-9556, Fax: 812-855-9557, E-mail: acburlin@indiana.edu.
Website: http://arthistory.indiana.edu

**Indiana University Bloomington,** University Graduate School, College of Arts and Sciences, Department of History, Bloomington, IN 47405. Offers MA, MAT, PhD, MA/MLS. Terminal master's awarded for partial completion of doctoral program. *Degree requirements:* For master's, one foreign language, thesis optional; for doctorate, variable foreign language requirement, comprehensive exam, thesis/dissertation. *Entrance requirements:* For master's and doctorate, GRE General Test. Additional exam requirements/recommendations for international students: Required—TOEFL. Electronic applications accepted. *Faculty research:* Medieval and early modern Europe, Russia, Latin America, Middle East, Great Britain, United States, Africa, African Diaspora, Europe, eastern Europe, gender and sexuality.

**Indiana University of Pennsylvania,** School of Graduate Studies and Research, College of Humanities and Social Sciences, Department of History, Program in History, Indiana, PA 15705. Offers MA. *Program availability:* Part-time. *Faculty:* 6 full-time (4 women). *Students:* 7 full-time (4 women), 1 part-time (0 women); includes 1 minority (Black or African American, non-Hispanic/Latino). Average age 24. 11 applicants, 73% accepted, 4 enrolled. In 2016, 6 master's awarded. *Degree requirements:* For master's, thesis optional. *Entrance requirements:* For master's, GRE, 2 letters of recommendation. Additional exam requirements/recommendations for international students: Required—TOEFL (minimum score 540 paper-based). *Application deadline:* Applications are processed on a rolling basis. Application fee: $50. Electronic applications accepted. *Expenses:* Tuition, state resident: full-time $8694; part-time $483 per credit. Tuition, nonresident: full-time $13,050; part-time $725 per credit. *Required fees:* $157 per credit. $50 per term. Tuition and fees vary according to course load and program. *Financial support:* In 2016–17, 3 research assistantships with tuition reimbursements (averaging $2,870 per year) were awarded; fellowships, career-related internships or fieldwork, Federal Work-Study, scholarships/grants, and unspecified assistantships also available. Support available to part-time students. Financial award application deadline: 4/15; financial award applicants required to submit FAFSA. *Unit head:* Dr. Jeanine Mazak-Kahne, Graduate Coordinator, 724-357-2436, E-mail: j.mkahne@iup.edu.
Website: http://www.iup.edu/grad/history/default.aspx

**Indiana University–Purdue University Indianapolis,** School of Liberal Arts, Department of History, Indianapolis, IN 46202. Offers history (MA); public history (MA); MA/MLS. *Program availability:* Part-time, evening/weekend. *Degree requirements:* For master's, one foreign language, thesis. *Entrance requirements:* For master's, GRE General Test, minimum GPA of 3.0. Electronic applications accepted.

**Inter American University of Puerto Rico, Metropolitan Campus,** Graduate Programs, Program in History, San Juan, PR 00919-1293. Offers American history (PhD); history (MA, PhD).

**Inter American University of Puerto Rico, Metropolitan Campus,** Graduate Programs, Program in History Education, San Juan, PR 00919-1293. Offers MA.

**Iona College,** School of Arts and Science, Department of History, New Rochelle, NY 10801-1890. Offers MA. *Program availability:* Part-time, evening/weekend. *Faculty:* 1 full-time (0 women). *Students:* 3 full-time (2 women), 9 part-time (3 women); includes 3 minority (1 Black or African American, non-Hispanic/Latino; 2 Hispanic/Latino). Average age 30. 4 applicants, 100% accepted, 2 enrolled. In 2016, 1 master's awarded. *Degree requirements:* For master's, one foreign language, comprehensive exam, 27 credits of coursework and culminating project or 24 credits of coursework and thesis. *Entrance requirements:* For master's, undergraduate major in history or related field, minimum GPA of 3.0. Additional exam requirements/recommendations for international students: Required—TOEFL (minimum score 550 paper-based; 80 iBT), IELTS (minimum score 6.5). *Application deadline:* For fall admission, 8/1 priority date for domestic students, 5/1 priority date for international students; for spring admission, 1/1 priority date for domestic students, 8/1 priority date for international students. Applications are processed on a rolling basis. Application fee: $50. Electronic applications accepted. *Expenses: Tuition:* Full-time $19,692; part-time $1094 per credit. *Required fees:* $245 per term. Tuition and fees vary according to program. *Financial support:* In 2016–17, 9 students received support. Unspecified assistantships available. Financial award application deadline: 4/15; financial award applicants required to submit FAFSA. *Faculty research:* Military history, Asian economies, American diplomacy, Catholic education, Armenian history, the history of violence, French Revolution, medieval religion. *Unit head:* Daniel Thiery, PhD, Chairman, 914-633-2694, E-mail: dthiery@iona.edu. *Application contact:* Katelyn Brunck, Assistant Director of Graduate Admissions, 914-633-2492, Fax: 914-633-2277, E-mail: kbrunck@iona.edu.
Website: http://www.iona.edu/Academics/School-of-Arts-Science/Departments/History/Graduate-Programs.aspx

**Iowa State University of Science and Technology,** Department of History, Ames, IA 50011. Offers history (MA); rural, agricultural, technological, and environmental history (PhD). *Degree requirements:* For master's, thesis or alternative; for doctorate, thesis/dissertation. *Entrance requirements:* For master's and doctorate, GRE General Test. Additional exam requirements/recommendations for international students: Required—

TOEFL (minimum score 600 paper-based; 79 iBT), IELTS (minimum score 7). *Application deadline:* For fall admission, 1/15 priority date for domestic and international students. Application fee: $60 ($90 for international students). Electronic applications accepted. *Application contact:* Jennifer Rivera, Application Contact, 515-294-7266, E-mail: rivera@iastate.edu.
Website: http://www.history.iastate.edu/index.php?

**Jackson State University,** Graduate School, College of Liberal Arts, Department of History and Philosophy, Jackson, MS 39217. Offers history (MA). *Program availability:* Part-time, evening/weekend, 100% online, blended/hybrid learning. *Faculty:* 5 full-time (0 women). *Students:* 9 full-time (6 women), 22 part-time (10 women); includes 26 minority (25 Black or African American, non-Hispanic/Latino; 1 Two or more races, non-Hispanic/Latino), 1 international. Average age 34. 21 applicants, 57% accepted, 8 enrolled. In 2016, 3 master's awarded. *Degree requirements:* For master's, comprehensive exam, thesis or alternative. *Entrance requirements:* For master's, GRE General Test. Additional exam requirements/recommendations for international students: Required—TOEFL (minimum score 520 paper-based; 67 iBT). *Application deadline:* For fall admission, 3/1 priority date for domestic students, 3/1 for international students; for spring admission, 10/1 for domestic and international students. Applications are processed on a rolling basis. Application fee: $25. Electronic applications accepted. *Expenses:* Contact institution. *Financial support:* Career-related internships or fieldwork, Federal Work-Study, scholarships/grants, and unspecified assistantships available. Support available to part-time students. Financial award application deadline: 3/1; financial award applicants required to submit FAFSA. *Unit head:* Dr. Rico Chapman, Interim Chair, 601-979-2490, Fax: 601-979-2192, E-mail: rico.d.chapman@jsums.edu. *Application contact:* Mark Bernhardt, Graduate Program Coordinator, 601-979-2495, Fax: 601-979-4325, E-mail: mark.a.bernhardt@jsums.edu.
Website: http://www.jsums.edu/history/

**Jacksonville State University,** College of Graduate Studies and Continuing Education, College of Arts and Sciences, Department of History, Jacksonville, AL 36265-1602. Offers MA. *Program availability:* Part-time, evening/weekend. *Faculty:* 9 full-time (2 women). *Students:* 8 part-time (3 women). Average age 31. 6 applicants, 67% accepted, 2 enrolled. In 2016, 4 master's awarded. *Degree requirements:* For master's, comprehensive exam, thesis (for some programs). *Entrance requirements:* For master's, GRE General Test or MAT. Additional exam requirements/recommendations for international students: Required—TOEFL (minimum score 500 paper-based; 61 iBT). *Application deadline:* Applications are processed on a rolling basis. Application fee: $35. Electronic applications accepted. *Financial support:* In 2016–17, 1 student received support. Available to part-time students. Application deadline: 4/1; applicants required to submit FAFSA. *Unit head:* Dr. Gordon Harvey, Head, 256-782-5622, E-mail: gharvey@jsu.edu. *Application contact:* Dr. Jean Pugliese, Associate Dean, 256-782-8278, Fax: 256-782-5321, E-mail: pugliese@jsu.edu.

**James Madison University,** The Graduate School, College of Arts and Letters, Program in History, Harrisonburg, VA 22807. Offers local/regional/public history (MA); United States history (MA); world history (MA). *Program availability:* Part-time. *Faculty:* 31 full-time (9 women). *Students:* 19 full-time (6 women), 9 part-time (2 women). Average age 30. 32 applicants, 84% accepted, 13 enrolled. In 2016, 13 master's awarded. *Degree requirements:* For master's, one foreign language, comprehensive exam, thesis. Application fee: $55. Electronic applications accepted. *Financial support:* In 2016–17, 3 teaching assistantships with full tuition reimbursements (averaging $9,284 per year) were awarded; fellowships, Federal Work-Study, and 7 assistantships (averaging $7911) also available. Financial award application deadline: 3/1; financial award applicants required to submit FAFSA. *Unit head:* Dr. Gabrielle Lanier, Department Head, 540-568-6132, E-mail: laniergm@jmu.edu. *Application contact:* Lynette D. Michael, Director of Graduate Admissions, 540-568-6131 Ext. 6395, Fax: 540-568-7860, E-mail: michaeld@jmu.edu.
Website: http://www.jmu.edu/history

**Johns Hopkins University,** Zanvyl Krieger School of Arts and Sciences, Department of History, Baltimore, MD 21218. Offers PhD. *Degree requirements:* For doctorate, variable foreign language requirement, comprehensive exam, thesis/dissertation. *Entrance requirements:* For doctorate, GRE General Test. Additional exam requirements/recommendations for international students: Required—TOEFL (minimum score 600 paper-based; 100 iBT), IELTS. Electronic applications accepted. *Faculty research:* American, European, Latin American, East Asian, and African history.

**Kansas State University,** Graduate School, College of Arts and Sciences, Department of History, Manhattan, KS 66506. Offers MA, PhD. *Program availability:* Part-time. *Faculty:* 20 full-time (8 women). *Students:* 17 full-time (5 women), 21 part-time (3 women); includes 4 minority (1 Black or African American, non-Hispanic/Latino; 1 American Indian or Alaska Native, non-Hispanic/Latino; 2 Two or more races, non-Hispanic/Latino). Average age 37. 25 applicants, 44% accepted, 6 enrolled. In 2016, 2 master's, 5 doctorates awarded. *Degree requirements:* For master's, thesis (for some programs); for doctorate, one foreign language, thesis/dissertation, qualifying exam. *Entrance requirements:* For master's, GRE General Test, minimum undergraduate GPA of 3.0; for doctorate, GRE General Test. Additional exam requirements/recommendations for international students: Required—TOEFL (minimum score 600 paper-based). *Application deadline:* For fall admission, 3/1 priority date for domestic students, 1/1 priority date for international students; for spring admission, 10/15 priority date for domestic students, 8/1 priority date for international students. Application fee: $50 ($75 for international students). Electronic applications accepted. *Expenses:* Tuition, state resident: full-time $9670. Tuition, nonresident: full-time $21,828. *Required fees:* $862. *Financial support:* In 2016–17, 1 research assistantship (averaging $17,000 per year), 13 teaching assistantships with full tuition reimbursements (averaging $15,000 per year) were awarded; career-related internships or fieldwork, Federal Work-Study, institutionally sponsored loans, and scholarships/grants also available. Support available to part-time students. Financial award application deadline: 3/1; financial award applicants required to submit FAFSA. *Faculty research:* Environmental history, religious history, American social history, history of war and society, history of international relations and diplomacy, gender and women's history. *Total annual research expenditures:* $100,609. *Unit head:* Michael Krysko, Associate Professor/Department Chair, 785-532-6730, E-mail: mkrysko@ksu.edu. *Application contact:* Albert Hamscher, Professor/Director of Graduate Admissions, 785-532-0436, Fax: 785-532-2045, E-mail: aham@ksu.edu.
Website: http://www.k-state.edu/history/

**Kent State University,** College of Arts and Sciences, Department of History, Kent, OH 44242-0001. Offers history (MA, PhD), including history (MA), history for teachers (MA). *Program availability:* Part-time. *Faculty:* 13 full-time (4 women). *Students:* 22 full-time (5 women), 5 part-time (2 women); includes 3 minority (1 Black or African American, non-Hispanic/Latino; 1 Hispanic/Latino; 1 Two or more races, non-Hispanic/Latino). Average age 31. 30 applicants, 47% accepted, 8 enrolled. In 2016, 9 master's, 8 doctorates awarded. *Degree requirements:* For master's, one foreign language, thesis (for some programs); for doctorate, one foreign language, comprehensive exam, thesis/dissertation. *Entrance requirements:* For master's and doctorate, GRE General Test, minor in history, minimum GPA of 2.75, statement of intent, writing sample, transcripts, 3 letters of recommendation. Additional exam requirements/recommendations for

international students: Required—TOEFL (minimum score of 525 paper-based, 71 iBT), IELTS (minimum score of 6), Michigan English Language Assessment Battery (minimum score of 75), or PTE (minimum score of 48). *Application deadline:* For fall admission, 2/1 for domestic and international students. Applications are processed on a rolling basis. Application fee: $45 ($70 for international students). Electronic applications accepted. *Expenses:* Tuition, state resident: full-time $10,864; part-time $495 per credit hour. Tuition, nonresident: full-time $18,380; part-time $837 per credit hour. *Financial support:* Teaching assistantships with full tuition reimbursements and unspecified assistantships available. Financial award application deadline: 2/1. *Unit head:* Dr. Brian M. Hayashi, Professor and Chair, 330-672-8914, E-mail: bhayashi@kent.edu. *Application contact:* Kevin Adams, Associate Professor and Graduate Coordinator, 330-672-8902, E-mail: kadams9@kent.edu.
Website: https://www.kent.edu/history/graduate-0

**Lake Forest College,** Graduate Program in Liberal Studies, Lake Forest, IL 60045. Offers American studies (MLS); environmental studies (MLS); history (MLS); Medieval and Renaissance art (MLS); philosophy (MLS); Spanish (MLS); writing (MLS). *Program availability:* Part-time, evening/weekend. *Faculty:* 9 full-time (3 women), 1 part-time/adjunct (0 women). *Students:* 1 full-time (0 women), 38 part-time (20 women); includes 5 minority (1 Black or African American, non-Hispanic/Latino; 2 Asian, non-Hispanic/Latino; 2 Hispanic/Latino). Average age 38. 19 applicants, 53% accepted, 7 enrolled. In 2016, 4 master's awarded. *Degree requirements:* For master's, thesis optional, 8 courses, including at least 3 interdisciplinary seminars. *Entrance requirements:* For master's, transcript, essay, interview. Additional exam requirements/recommendations for international students: Required—TOEFL (minimum score 550 paper-based; 83 iBT); Recommended—IELTS (minimum score 6.5). *Application deadline:* For fall admission, 7/15 priority date for domestic students, 6/1 priority date for international students; for spring admission, 12/1 priority date for domestic students, 10/1 priority date for international students. Applications are processed on a rolling basis. Application fee: $30. *Expenses:* $2,600 per course. *Financial support:* In 2016–17, 2 students received support. Partial tuition grants for full-time teachers available. *Faculty research:* Realigning of the international order; Renaissance women artists; literature of Latin Americans in the U.S.; modern Chinese history; environmental biology. *Unit head:* Prof. D. L. LeMahieu, Director, 847-735-5133, Fax: 847-735-6291, E-mail: lemahieu@lakeforest.edu. *Application contact:* Prof. Carol Gayle, Associate Director, 847-735-5083, Fax: 847-735-6291, E-mail: gayle@lakeforest.edu.
Website: http://www.lakeforest.edu/academics/programs/mls/

**Lakehead University,** Graduate Studies, Department of History, Thunder Bay, ON P7B 5E1, Canada. Offers gerontology (MA); history (MA); women's studies (MA). *Program availability:* Part-time. *Degree requirements:* For master's, one foreign language, thesis. *Entrance requirements:* For master's, minimum B average. Additional exam requirements/recommendations for international students: Required—TOEFL. *Faculty research:* Canadian history, British history, Russian/German history, women's studies.

**Lamar University,** College of Graduate Studies, College of Arts and Sciences, Department of History, Beaumont, TX 77710. Offers MA. *Program availability:* Part-time. *Faculty:* 5 full-time (2 women). *Students:* 4 full-time (2 women), 5 part-time (3 women); includes 2 minority (both Two or more races, non-Hispanic/Latino). Average age 33. 2 applicants, 100% accepted, 1 enrolled. *Degree requirements:* For master's, comprehensive exam (for some programs), thesis (for some programs). *Entrance requirements:* For master's, GRE General Test, minimum GPA of 2.5 in last 60 hours of undergraduate course work. Additional exam requirements/recommendations for international students: Required—TOEFL (minimum score 550 paper-based; 79 iBT), IELTS (minimum score 6.5). *Application deadline:* For fall admission, 8/11 for domestic students, 7/1 for international students; for spring admission, 1/5 for domestic students, 12/1 for international students. Applications are processed on a rolling basis. Application fee: $25 ($50 for international students). Electronic applications accepted. *Expenses:* $8,134 in-state full-time, $5,574 in-state part-time; $15,604 out-of-state full-time, $10,554 out-of-state part-time per year. *Financial support:* Fellowships and teaching assistantships available. Financial award application deadline: 4/1. *Faculty research:* Old South, nineteenth-century reform, twentieth-Century U.S., religion in America's South, Renaissance/early modern Europe. *Unit head:* Dr. Mary L. Scheer, Chair, 409-880-8511, Fax: 409-880-8710. *Application contact:* Deidre Mayer, Interim Director, Admissions and Academic Services, 409-880-8888, Fax: 409-880-7419, E-mail: gradmissions@lamar.edu.
Website: http://artssciences.lamar.edu/history/

**La Salle University,** School of Arts and Sciences, Program in History, Philadelphia, PA 19141-1199. Offers American history (Certificate); European history (Certificate); history (MA); history for educators (MA); public history (MA); teaching advanced placement history (Certificate); world history (Certificate). *Program availability:* Part-time. *Faculty:* 4 full-time (1 woman), 1 (woman) part-time/adjunct. *Students:* 4 full-time (1 woman), 16 part-time (7 women); includes 2 minority (1 Hispanic/Latino; 1 Two or more races, non-Hispanic/Latino). Average age 33. 8 applicants, 75% accepted, 3 enrolled. In 2016, 11 master's awarded. *Degree requirements:* For master's, thesis or comprehensive exam. *Entrance requirements:* For master's, GRE or MAT, 18 hours of undergraduate coursework in history or a related discipline with minimum GPA of 3.0; two letters of recommendation; brief personal statement (250 to 500 words); writing sample (preferably from an undergraduate research paper). Additional exam requirements/recommendations for international students: Required—TOEFL. *Application deadline:* For fall admission, 8/15 priority date for domestic students, 7/15 for international students; for spring admission, 12/15 priority date for domestic students, 11/15 for international students; for summer admission, 4/15 priority date for domestic students, 3/15 for international students. Applications are processed on a rolling basis. Application fee: $35. Electronic applications accepted. Application fee is waived when completed online. *Expenses:* Contact institution. *Financial support:* In 2016–17, 1 student received support. Scholarships/grants available. Support available to part-time students. Financial award application deadline: 8/31; financial award applicants required to submit FAFSA. *Unit head:* Dr. George B. Stow, Director, 215-951-1097, E-mail: grahis@lasalle.edu. *Application contact:* Elizabeth Heenan, Director, Graduate and Adult Enrollment, 215-951-1100, Fax: 215-951-1462, E-mail: heenan@lasalle.edu.
Website: http://www.lasalle.edu/master-history/

**Laurentian University,** School of Graduate Studies and Research, Programme in History, Sudbury, ON P3E 2C6, Canada. Offers European history (MA); history of Northern Ontario (MA); North American history (MA). *Program availability:* Part-time. *Degree requirements:* For master's, thesis or alternative. *Entrance requirements:* For master's, honors degree with minimum second class. *Faculty research:* Franco-Ontarian history, northern Ontarian history, Canadian social history, European social history, Franco-Canadian history.

**Lee University,** Program in Education, Cleveland, TN 37320-3450. Offers art (MAT); curriculum and instruction (M Ed, Ed S); early childhood (MAT); educational leadership (M Ed, Ed S); elementary education (MAT); English and math (MAT); English and science (MAT); English and social studies (MAT); higher education administration (MS); history (MAT); history and economics (MAT); math and science (MAT); math and social studies (MAT); middle grades (MAT); science and social studies (MASW); secondary education (MAT); Spanish (MAT); special education (M Ed, MAT); TESOL (MAT).

*Accreditation:* NCATE. *Program availability:* Part-time. *Faculty:* 13 full-time (6 women), 9 part-time/adjunct (4 women). *Students:* 35 full-time (27 women), 50 part-time (32 women); includes 12 minority (5 Black or African American, non-Hispanic/Latino; 5 Hispanic/Latino; 2 Two or more races, non-Hispanic/Latino), 4 international. Average age 30. 43 applicants, 79% accepted, 28 enrolled. In 2016, 42 master's, 6 other advanced degrees awarded. *Degree requirements:* For master's, variable foreign language requirement, thesis optional, internship. *Entrance requirements:* For master's, MAT or GRE General Test, minimum undergraduate GPA of 2.75, 3 letters of recommendation, interview, writing sample, official transcripts, background check; for Ed S, minimum undergraduate and master's GPA of 2.75, official transcripts for undergraduate and master's degrees. Additional exam requirements/recommendations for international students: Required—TOEFL (minimum score 61 iBT). *Application deadline:* For fall admission, 6/1 priority date for domestic and international students; for spring admission, 11/1 priority date for domestic and international students; for summer admission, 4/1 priority date for domestic and international students. Applications are processed on a rolling basis. Application fee: $25. Electronic applications accepted. *Expenses:* Tuition: Full-time $11,367; part-time $632 per credit hour. *Required fees:* $35 per term. One-time fee: $25. Tuition and fees vary according to program. *Financial support:* In 2016–17, 42 students received support. Career-related internships or fieldwork, Federal Work-Study, institutionally sponsored loans, scholarships/grants, and unspecified assistantships available. Financial award application deadline: 3/1; financial award applicants required to submit FAFSA. *Unit head:* Dr. William Kamm, Director, 423-614-8544, E-mail: wkamm@leeuniversity.edu. *Application contact:* Crystal Keeter, Graduate Education Secretary, 423-614-8544, E-mail: ckeeter@leeuniversity.edu.
Website: http://www.leeuniversity.edu/academics/graduate/education

**Lehigh University,** College of Arts and Sciences, Department of History, Bethlehem, PA 18015. Offers Atlantic world (PhD); British history (PhD); history (MA); industrial and modern America (PhD); public history (MA). *Program availability:* Part-time. *Faculty:* 14 full-time (7 women). *Students:* 18 full-time (7 women), 19 part-time (5 women); includes 2 minority (1 Black or African American, non-Hispanic/Latino; 1 Two or more races, non-Hispanic/Latino), 2 international. Average age 34. 10 applicants, 50% accepted, 3 enrolled. In 2016, 6 master's, 3 doctorates awarded. Terminal master's awarded for partial completion of doctoral program. *Degree requirements:* For master's, comprehensive exam (for some programs), thesis (for some programs), comprehensive exam or thesis; for doctorate, comprehensive exam, thesis/dissertation. *Entrance requirements:* For master's, GRE General Test, recommendations, writing sample; for doctorate, GRE General Test, recommendations, writing samples. Additional exam requirements/recommendations for international students: Required—TOEFL. *Application deadline:* For fall admission, 2/15 priority date for domestic and international students. Applications are processed on a rolling basis. Application fee: $75. Electronic applications accepted. *Expenses:* Contact institution. *Financial support:* In 2016–17, 2 fellowships with full tuition reimbursements (averaging $22,500 per year), 10 teaching assistantships with full tuition reimbursements (averaging $10,000 per year) were awarded; research assistantships, institutionally sponsored loans, scholarships/grants, tuition waivers (full and partial), and unspecified assistantships also available. Financial award application deadline: 1/15. *Faculty research:* Colonial America, modern America, history of technology, Atlantic world, French Atlantic, Spanish Atlantic, British empire, gender, intellectual history, African diaspora history. *Unit head:* Prof. John Pettegrew, Chairman, 610-758-3360, Fax: 610-758-6554, E-mail: jcp5@lehigh.edu. *Application contact:* Dr. John Savage, Graduate Coordinator, 610-758-3363, Fax: 610-758-6554, E-mail: jms8@lehigh.edu.
Website: http://history.cas2.lehigh.edu/

**Lehman College of the City University of New York,** School of Arts and Humanities, Department of History, Bronx, NY 10468-1589. Offers MA. *Program availability:* Part-time, evening/weekend. *Degree requirements:* For master's, comprehensive exam, thesis. *Entrance requirements:* For master's, 18 undergraduate credits in history, minimum GPA of 2.7.

**Liberty University,** College of Arts and Sciences, Lynchburg, VA 24515. Offers English (MA); history (MA); professional writing (MA). *Accreditation:* AACN. *Program availability:* Part-time, online learning. *Students:* 59 full-time (28 women), 58 part-time (26 women); includes 9 minority (2 Black or African American, non-Hispanic/Latino; 1 American Indian or Alaska Native, non-Hispanic/Latino; 1 Asian, non-Hispanic/Latino; 2 Hispanic/Latino; 3 Two or more races, non-Hispanic/Latino), 1 international. Average age 33. 206 applicants, 35% accepted, 52 enrolled. In 2016, 36 master's awarded. *Degree requirements:* For master's, comprehensive exam (for some programs), thesis (for some programs). *Entrance requirements:* For master's, GRE, minimum undergraduate GPA of 3.0, letters of recommendation, statement of purpose. Additional exam requirements/recommendations for international students: Required—TOEFL (minimum score 600 paper-based; 100 iBT). *Application deadline:* For fall admission, 6/1 for domestic students; for spring admission, 11/1 for domestic students. Applications are processed on a rolling basis. Application fee: $50. Electronic applications accepted. *Financial support:* Teaching assistantships with tuition reimbursements and Federal Work-Study available. *Faculty research:* God concept and adult attachment, building marital strength, image of God and gender, breastfeeding behavior among adolescent mothers, osteoporosis. *Unit head:* Dr. Roger Schultz, Dean, 434-592-4031, Fax: 434-522-0430, E-mail: rschultz@liberty.edu. *Application contact:* Dr. Terry Elam, Director of Graduate Admissions, 434-592-3966, Fax: 434-522-0430, E-mail: gradadmissions@liberty.edu.

**Lincoln University,** Graduate Studies, Jefferson City, MO 65101. Offers business administration (MBA), including accounting, management, management information systems, public administration/policy; elementary teaching (M Ed); environmental science (MS); guidance and counseling (M Ed), including community/agency counseling, elementary school, secondary school; higher education (MA); history (MA); integrated agricultural systems (MS); middle school (M Ed); natural sciences (MS); secondary teaching (M Ed); sociology (MA); sociology/criminal justice (MA). *Program availability:* Part-time, evening/weekend, 100% online, blended/hybrid learning. *Students:* 50 full-time (29 women), 68 part-time (39 women); includes 40 minority (37 Black or African American, non-Hispanic/Latino; 1 Asian, non-Hispanic/Latino; 2 Two or more races, non-Hispanic/Latino), 14 international. Average age 33. 75 applicants, 80% accepted, 34 enrolled. In 2016, 51 master's awarded. *Degree requirements:* For master's, comprehensive exam, thesis optional. *Entrance requirements:* For master's, GRE, MAT or GMAT, minimum GPA of 2.75 overall, 3.0 in courses related to specialization; 3 letters of recommendation; minimum C average in English composition; personal statement of purpose. Additional exam requirements/recommendations for international students: Required—TOEFL (minimum score 500 paper-based; 61 iBT), IELTS (minimum score 5.5), Michigan English Language Assessment Battery (minimum score 80). *Application deadline:* For fall admission, 7/1 priority date for domestic students, 5/1 priority date for international students; for spring admission, 11/1 priority date for domestic students, 10/1 priority date for international students; for summer admission, 6/1 priority date for domestic students. Applications are processed on a rolling basis. Application fee: $30. Electronic applications accepted. *Expenses:* Tuition, state resident: full-time $6840; part-time $5130 per year. Tuition, nonresident: full-time $12,720; part-time $9540 per year. *Required fees:* $852; $811 per unit. Tuition and fees vary according to course load. *Financial support:* In 2016–17, 2 fellowships with tuition reimbursements, 8 research assistantships with tuition reimbursements were awarded;

## History

Federal Work-Study, scholarships/grants, and unspecified assistantships also available. Support available to part-time students. Financial award application deadline: 3/1; financial award applicants required to submit FAFSA. *Unit head:* Dr. Rolundus R. Rice, Dean, 573-681-5247, Fax: 573-681-5106, E-mail: gradschool@lincolnu.edu. *Application contact:* Irasema Steck, Administrative Assistant, 573-681-5247, Fax: 573-681-5106, E-mail: gradschool@lincolnu.edu.
Website: http://www.lincolnu.edu/web/graduate-studies/graduate-studies

**Long Island University–LIU Post,** College of Liberal Arts and Sciences, Brookville, NY 11548-1300. Offers applied mathematics (MS); behavior analysis (MA); biology (MS); criminal justice (MS); earth science (MS); English (MA); environmental sustainability (MS); genetic counseling (MS); history (MA); interdisciplinary studies (MA, MS); mathematics for secondary school teachers (MS); mobile GIS application development (Advanced Certificate); political science (MA); psychology (MA). *Program availability:* Part-time, evening/weekend, blended/hybrid learning. *Faculty:* 68 full-time (30 women), 20 part-time/adjunct (13 women). *Students:* 155 full-time (117 women), 125 part-time (82 women); includes 65 minority (17 Black or African American, non-Hispanic/Latino; 14 Asian, non-Hispanic/Latino; 27 Hispanic/Latino; 7 Two or more races, non-Hispanic/Latino), 19 international. 485 applicants, 36% accepted, 77 enrolled. In 2016, 91 master's, 15 other advanced degrees awarded. *Degree requirements:* For master's, comprehensive exam (for some programs), thesis (for some programs). *Entrance requirements:* Additional exam requirements/recommendations for international students: Required—PTE, TOEFL (minimum score 550 paper-based, 75 iBT) or IELTS (6.5). *Application deadline:* Applications are processed on a rolling basis. Application fee: $50. Electronic applications accepted. *Expenses: Tuition:* Full-time $28,272; part-time $1178 per credit. *Required fees:* $451 per term. Tuition and fees vary according to degree level and program. *Financial support:* In 2016–17, 24 teaching assistantships with partial tuition reimbursements (averaging $410 per year) were awarded; fellowships, research assistantships, career-related internships or fieldwork, Federal Work-Study, institutionally sponsored loans, scholarships/grants, tuition waivers (partial), and unspecified assistantships also available. Support available to part-time students. Financial award application deadline: 2/15; financial award applicants required to submit FAFSA. *Faculty research:* Biology, criminal justice, environmental sustainability, mathematics, psychology. *Total annual research expenditures:* $218,000. *Unit head:* Dr. Jeffrey Belnap, Acting Dean, 516-299-2233, Fax: 516-299-4140, E-mail: jeffrey.belnap@liu.edu. *Application contact:* Carol Zerah, Director of Graduate Admissions, 516-299-2900, Fax: 516-299-2137, E-mail: post-enroll@liu.edu.
Website: http://liu.edu/CWPost/Academics/Schools/CLAS

**Louisiana State University and Agricultural & Mechanical College,** Graduate School, College of Humanities and Social Sciences, Department of History, Baton Rouge, LA 70803. Offers MA, PhD.

**Louisiana Tech University,** Graduate School, College of Liberal Arts, Department of History, Ruston, LA 71272. Offers MA. *Program availability:* Part-time, online learning. *Degree requirements:* For master's, thesis or alternative. *Entrance requirements:* For master's, GRE General Test. *Application deadline:* For fall admission, 7/29 for domestic students; for spring admission, 2/3 for domestic students. Application fee: $40. *Financial support:* Fellowships available. Financial award application deadline: 2/1. *Unit head:* Dr. Jeffery R. Hankins, Interim Head, 318-257-2872, Fax: 318-257-3935, E-mail: jhankins@latech.edu. *Application contact:* Marilyn J. Robinson, Assistant to the Dean of the Graduate School, 318-257-2924, Fax: 318-257-4487.
Website: http://liberalarts.latech.edu/shss/history/

**Loyola University Chicago,** Graduate School, Department of History, Chicago, IL 60611. Offers history (PhD); public history (MA). *Program availability:* Part-time, evening/weekend. *Faculty:* 32 full-time (12 women), 7 part-time/adjunct (2 women). *Students:* 45 full-time (25 women), 10 part-time (6 women); includes 8 minority (2 Black or African American, non-Hispanic/Latino; 1 Asian, non-Hispanic/Latino; 4 Hispanic/Latino; 1 Two or more races, non-Hispanic/Latino), 1 international. Average age 31. 89 applicants, 52% accepted, 18 enrolled. In 2016, 16 master's, 3 doctorates awarded. Terminal master's awarded for partial completion of doctoral program. *Degree requirements:* For master's, one foreign language, comprehensive exam, thesis optional, portfolio (for public history program); for doctorate, 2 foreign languages, comprehensive exam, thesis/dissertation. *Entrance requirements:* For master's, GRE General Test, research paper/writing sample; for doctorate, GRE General Test, seminar paper or master's thesis. Additional exam requirements/recommendations for international students: Required—TOEFL (minimum score 550 paper-based), IELTS. *Application deadline:* For fall admission, 5/1 for domestic students; for spring admission, 10/1 for domestic students. Applications are processed on a rolling basis. Application fee: $50. Electronic applications accepted. Application fee is waived when completed online. *Expenses:* Contact institution. *Financial support:* In 2016–17, 20 students received support, including 20 fellowships with full tuition reimbursements available (averaging $5,251 per year), 18 teaching assistantships with full tuition reimbursements available (averaging $17,722 per year); research assistantships with full tuition reimbursements available and Federal Work-Study also available. Financial award application deadline: 1/1; financial award applicants required to submit FAFSA. *Faculty research:* Medieval and early modern Europe, U.S. public history, U.S. urban history, gender history, Britain and Ireland, transnational history. *Unit head:* Dr. Robert O. Bucholz, Chair, 773-508-2232, Fax: 773-508-2153, E-mail: rbuchol@luc.edu. *Application contact:* Dr. Michelle Nickerson, Director, Graduate Programs, 773-508-2228, Fax: 773-508-2153, E-mail: mnickerson@luc.edu.
Website: http://www.luc.edu/history/

**Marquette University,** Graduate School, College of Arts and Sciences, Department of History, Milwaukee, WI 53201-1881. Offers European history (MA, PhD); global studies (MA); United States history (MA, PhD). *Program availability:* Part-time. *Faculty:* 22 full-time (7 women), 2 part-time/adjunct (0 women). *Students:* 29 full-time (10 women), 8 part-time (3 women); includes 2 minority (1 Hispanic/Latino; 1 Two or more races, non-Hispanic/Latino), 2 international. Average age 32. 26 applicants, 85% accepted, 13 enrolled. In 2016, 10 master's, 2 doctorates awarded. *Degree requirements:* For master's, comprehensive exam, essay, 2 classes of research seminars (6 hours); for doctorate, one foreign language, comprehensive exam, thesis/dissertation, 2 research seminars, dissertation seminar. *Entrance requirements:* For master's, GRE General Test, official transcripts from all current and previous colleges/universities except Marquette, one-page statement of purpose, three letters of recommendation from former teachers; for doctorate, GRE General Test, official transcripts from all current and previous colleges/universities except Marquette, one-page statement of purpose, three letters of recommendation from former teachers, writing sample. Additional exam requirements/recommendations for international students: Required—TOEFL. *Application deadline:* For fall admission, 12/31 for domestic and international students. Application fee: $50. Electronic applications accepted. *Financial support:* Fellowships with partial tuition reimbursements, research assistantships with full tuition reimbursements, teaching assistantships with full tuition reimbursements, scholarships/grants, health care benefits, tuition waivers (full and partial), and unspecified assistantships available. Support available to part-time students. Financial award application deadline: 2/15. *Faculty research:* Children's history, Soviet and post-Soviet history, modern Ireland and Britain, Japan and martial arts, American Catholicism. *Unit*

*head:* Dr. James Marten, Chair, 414-288-7901, Fax: 414-288-1578. *Application contact:* Dr. Angela Sorby.
Website: http://www.marquette.edu/history/grad.shtml

**Marshall University,** Academic Affairs Division, College of Liberal Arts, Department of History, Huntington, WV 25755. Offers MA, Certificate. *Degree requirements:* For master's, thesis optional. *Entrance requirements:* For master's, GRE.

**McGill University,** Faculty of Graduate and Postdoctoral Studies, Faculty of Arts, Department of History and Classical Studies, Montréal, QC H3A 2T5, Canada. Offers history (MA, PhD); history of medicine (MA).

**McMaster University,** School of Graduate Studies, Faculty of Humanities, Department of History, Hamilton, ON L8S 4M2, Canada. Offers MA, PhD. *Program availability:* Part-time. *Degree requirements:* For master's, one foreign language, thesis or alternative; for doctorate, one foreign language, comprehensive exam, thesis/dissertation. *Entrance requirements:* For master's, honors BA in history, minimum B+ average. Additional exam requirements/recommendations for international students: Required—TOEFL (minimum score 580 paper-based). *Faculty research:* Canadian, European, British, U.S. history; ancient history.

**Memorial University of Newfoundland,** School of Graduate Studies, Department of History, St. John's, NL A1C 5S7, Canada. Offers MA, PhD. *Program availability:* Part-time. *Degree requirements:* For master's, thesis or comprehensive exam; for doctorate, one foreign language, comprehensive exam, thesis/dissertation, oral defense of thesis. *Entrance requirements:* For master's, honors degree or equivalent; for doctorate, master's degree. Electronic applications accepted. *Faculty research:* Canadian history, maritime history, Newfoundland history, social history, labor history.

**Miami University,** College of Arts and Science, Department of History, Oxford, OH 45056. Offers MA. *Students:* 15 full-time (9 women). Average age 27. In 2016, 4 master's awarded. *Expenses:* Tuition, state resident: full-time $12,890; part-time $564 per credit hour. Tuition, nonresident: full-time $29,604; part-time $1260 per credit hour. *Required fees:* $638. Part-time tuition and fees vary according to course load and program. *Unit head:* Dr. Weitse de Boer, Department Chair, 513-529-5121, E-mail: deboerwt@miamioh.edu. *Application contact:* Dr. Daniel Prior, Director of Graduate Studies, 513-529-7148, E-mail: priordg@miamioh.edu.
Website: http://www.MiamiOH.edu/history/

**Michigan State University,** The Graduate School, College of Social Science, Department of History, East Lansing, MI 48824. Offers history (MA, PhD); history-secondary school teaching (MA). *Entrance requirements:* Additional exam requirements/recommendations for international students: Required—TOEFL. Electronic applications accepted.

**Middle Tennessee State University,** College of Graduate Studies, College of Liberal Arts, Department of History, Program in History, Murfreesboro, TN 37132. Offers MA. *Program availability:* Part-time, evening/weekend, online learning. *Degree requirements:* For master's, one foreign language, comprehensive exam, thesis optional. *Entrance requirements:* For master's, GRE. Additional exam requirements/recommendations for international students: Required—TOEFL (minimum score 525 paper-based; 71 iBT) or IELTS (minimum score 6).

**Midwestern State University,** Billie Doris McAda Graduate School, Prothro-Yeager College of Humanities and Social Sciences, Department of History, Wichita Falls, TX 76308. Offers MA. *Program availability:* Part-time. *Degree requirements:* For master's, one foreign language, thesis. *Entrance requirements:* For master's, GRE General Test. Additional exam requirements/recommendations for international students: Required—TOEFL (minimum score 550 paper-based). Electronic applications accepted. *Faculty research:* Early modern England, Spanish borderlands, Jacksonian era, New Deal, Texas and the Southwest.

**Millersville University of Pennsylvania,** College of Graduate Studies and Adult Learning, College of Arts, Humanities and Social Sciences, Department of History, Millersville, PA 17551-0302. Offers MA. *Program availability:* Part-time. *Faculty:* 11 full-time (6 women), 1 part-time/adjunct (0 women). *Students:* 7 full-time (3 women), 12 part-time (6 women). Average age 34. 7 applicants, 86% accepted, 3 enrolled. In 2016, 4 master's awarded. *Degree requirements:* For master's, comprehensive exam, thesis optional. *Entrance requirements:* For master's, GRE if undergraduate GPA is lower than 2.85, 8-12 page academic writing sample. Additional exam requirements/recommendations for international students: Required—TOEFL (minimum score 600 paper-based), IELTS (minimum score 6). *Application deadline:* Applications are processed on a rolling basis. Application fee: $40. Electronic applications accepted. *Expenses:* $483 per credit resident tuition; $725 per credit non-resident tuition. *Financial support:* In 2016–17, 6 students received support. Unspecified assistantships available. Financial award application deadline: 3/15; financial award applicants required to submit FAFSA. *Faculty research:* Modern and early American history, modern and early European history, genocide and Holocaust studies, women's history, military and diplomacy. *Unit head:* Dr. John M. MacLarnon, III, Department Chair, 717-871-7193, Fax: 717-871-7939, E-mail: john.mcLarnon@millersville.edu. *Application contact:* Dr. Victor S. DeSantis, Dean of College of Graduate Studies and Adult Learning/Associate Provost for Civic and Community Engagement, 717-871-7619, Fax: 717-871-7954, E-mail: victor.desantis@millersville.edu.
Website: http://www.millersville.edu/history/graduate-program.php

**Minnesota State University Mankato,** College of Graduate Studies and Research, College of Social and Behavioral Sciences, Department of History, Mankato, MN 56001. Offers history (MA, MS); social studies (MAT). *Faculty:* 11. *Students:* 2 full-time (both women), 6 part-time (1 woman). *Degree requirements:* For master's, one foreign language, comprehensive exam, thesis or alternative. *Entrance requirements:* For master's, minimum GPA of 3.0, statement of purpose. Additional exam requirements/recommendations for international students: Required—TOEFL (minimum score 600 paper-based). *Application deadline:* For fall admission, 7/1 priority date for domestic students; for spring admission, 11/1 for domestic students. Applications are processed on a rolling basis. Application fee: $40. Electronic applications accepted. *Financial support:* Research assistantships, teaching assistantships with full tuition reimbursements, career-related internships or fieldwork, Federal Work-Study, institutionally sponsored loans, and unspecified assistantships available. Support available to part-time students. Financial award application deadline: 3/15. *Unit head:* Chris Corley, Graduate Coordinator, 507-389-1618, E-mail: christopher.corley@mnsu.edu.
Website: http://sbs.mnsu.edu/history/

**Mississippi College,** Graduate School, College of Arts and Sciences, School of Humanities and Social Sciences, Department of History, Political Science, Administration of Justice, and Paralegal Studies, Clinton, MS 39058. Offers administration of justice (MSS); history (M Ed, MA, MSS); paralegal studies (Certificate); political science (MSS); social sciences (M Ed, MSS). *Program availability:* Part-time. *Degree requirements:* For master's, one foreign language, comprehensive exam, thesis (for some programs). *Entrance requirements:* For master's, GRE or NTE, minimum GPA of 2.5. Additional exam requirements/recommendations for international students: Recommended—TOEFL, IELTS. Electronic applications accepted.

**Mississippi State University,** College of Arts and Sciences, Department of History, Mississippi State, MS 39762. Offers U.S. and European history (MA). *Program availability:* Part-time. *Faculty:* 22 full-time (5 women). *Students:* 43 full-time (14 women), 12 part-time (3 women); includes 10 minority (7 Black or African American, non-Hispanic/Latino; 3 Two or more races, non-Hispanic/Latino), 2 international. Average age 30. 27 applicants, 89% accepted, 19 enrolled. In 2016, 10 master's, 3 doctorates awarded. *Degree requirements:* For master's, one foreign language, comprehensive exam, thesis optional; for doctorate, 2 foreign languages, thesis/dissertation, comprehensive oral and written exam. *Entrance requirements:* For master's, minimum GPA of 3.0 on last two years of undergraduate courses; for doctorate, GRE, writing sample, minimum graduate GPA of 3.0. Additional exam requirements/recommendations for international students: Required—TOEFL (minimum score 550 paper-based). *Application deadline:* For fall admission, 4/1 for domestic students, 5/1 for international students; for spring admission, 11/1 for domestic students, 9/1 for international students. Applications are processed on a rolling basis. Application fee: $60. Electronic applications accepted. *Expenses:* Tuition, state resident: full-time $7670; part-time $852.50 per credit hour. Tuition, nonresident: full-time $20,790; part-time $2310.50 per credit hour. Part-time tuition and fees vary according to course load. *Financial support:* In 2016–17, 1 research assistantship with full tuition reimbursement (averaging $15,269 per year), 36 teaching assistantships with full tuition reimbursements (averaging $11,977 per year) were awarded; Federal Work-Study, institutionally sponsored loans, scholarships/grants, and unspecified assistantships also available. Financial award application deadline: 4/1; financial award applicants required to submit FAFSA. *Faculty research:* U.S. political, diplomatic, military, social, and cultural history; modern Europe; Latin America; Asian history; African history. *Unit head:* Dr. Alan I. Marcus, Department Head, 662-325-7075, Fax: 662-325-1139, E-mail: aimarcus@history.msstate.edu. *Application contact:* Linda Bonner, Senior Admissions Assistant, 662-325-3363, E-mail: lbonner@grad.msstate.edu.
Website: http://www.history.msstate.edu

**Missouri State University,** Graduate College, College of Humanities and Public Affairs, Department of History, Springfield, MO 65897. Offers history (MA); history education (MS Ed); history for teachers (Certificate). *Program availability:* Part-time, 100% online, blended/hybrid learning. *Faculty:* 18 full-time (7 women). *Students:* 6 full-time (1 woman), 33 part-time (11 women); includes 2 minority (1 Black or African American, non-Hispanic/Latino; 1 Asian, non-Hispanic/Latino), 1 international. Average age 34. 20 applicants, 65% accepted, 6 enrolled. In 2016, 8 master's awarded. *Degree requirements:* For master's, comprehensive exam, thesis or alternative. *Entrance requirements:* For master's, minimum GPA of 2.75, 24 hours of undergraduate course work in history (MA), 9-12 teaching certification (MS Ed). Additional exam requirements/recommendations for international students: Required—TOEFL (minimum score 550 paper-based; 79 iBT), IELTS (minimum score 6). *Application deadline:* For fall admission, 7/20 priority date for domestic students, 5/1 for international students; for spring admission, 12/20 priority date for domestic students, 9/1 for international students. Applications are processed on a rolling basis. Application fee: $35 ($50 for international students). Electronic applications accepted. *Expenses:* Tuition, state resident: full-time $5830. Tuition, nonresident: full-time $10,708. *Required fees:* $1130. Tuition and fees vary according to class time, course level, course load and program. *Financial support:* Federal Work-Study, scholarships/grants, and unspecified assistantships available. Support available to part-time students. Financial award application deadline: 3/31; financial award applicants required to submit FAFSA. *Faculty research:* Early modern France, cultural history of modern Britain, Latin American history, women's history, American Civil War in Missouri. *Unit head:* Dr. Kathleen Kennedy, Department Head, 417-836-5511, Fax: 417-836-5523, E-mail: history@missouristate.edu. *Application contact:* Michael Edwards, Coordinator of Graduate Admissions, 417-836-5330, Fax: 417-836-6200, E-mail: michaeledwards@missouristate.edu.
Website: http://history.missouristate.edu/

**Monmouth University,** Graduate Studies, Department of History, West Long Branch, NJ 07764-1898. Offers European history (MA); history of the U.S. (MA); world history (MA). *Program availability:* Part-time, evening/weekend. *Degree requirements:* For master's, comprehensive exam (for some programs), thesis (for some programs). *Entrance requirements:* For master's, minimum GPA of 3.0 in major, 2.5 overall; two letters of recommendation; statement describing historical areas of interest and how graduate study will contribute to professional and academic goals. Additional exam requirements/recommendations for international students: Required—TOEFL (minimum score 550 paper-based; 79 iBT), IELTS (minimum score 6) or Michigan English Language Assessment Battery (minimum score 77). Electronic applications accepted. *Faculty research:* British, German, and French Revolutions; Soviet Union; Africa; English history; U.S. military; women's history.

**Montana State University,** The Graduate School, College of Letters and Science, Department of History, Bozeman, MT 59717. Offers MA, PhD. *Program availability:* Part-time. *Degree requirements:* For master's, comprehensive exam; for doctorate, comprehensive exam, thesis/dissertation. *Entrance requirements:* For master's, GRE General Test, transcripts, 3 letters of recommendation, writing sample, statement of interest; for doctorate, GRE General Test, MA, transcripts, 3 letters of recommendation, writing sample, statement of interest. Additional exam requirements/recommendations for international students: Required—TOEFL (minimum score 550 paper-based). Electronic applications accepted. *Faculty research:* Science, environment, technology, American West, science and technology, environmental history, Asian studies.

**Morgan State University,** School of Graduate Studies, College of Liberal Arts, Department of History and Geography, Baltimore, MD 21251. Offers African-American studies (MA); history (MA, PhD); museum studies and historic preservation (MA). *Program availability:* Part-time, evening/weekend. *Degree requirements:* For master's, comprehensive exam, thesis; for doctorate, comprehensive exam, thesis/dissertation. *Entrance requirements:* For master's, minimum GPA of 2.5; for doctorate, GRE or MAT. Additional exam requirements/recommendations for international students: Required—TOEFL (minimum score 550 paper-based). *Faculty research:* Women's history, African diaspora history, urban history.

**Murray State University,** College of Humanities and Fine Arts, Program in History, Murray, KY 42071. Offers MA. *Program availability:* Part-time. *Degree requirements:* For master's, one foreign language, comprehensive exam, thesis (for some programs). *Entrance requirements:* For master's, GRE General Test. Additional exam requirements/recommendations for international students: Required—TOEFL.

**Nebraska Wesleyan University,** University College, Program in Historical Studies, Lincoln, NE 68504-2796. Offers MA. *Program availability:* Part-time. *Expenses:* Contact institution.

**New Jersey Institute of Technology,** College of Science and Liberal Arts, Newark, NJ 07102. Offers applied mathematics (MS); applied physics (M Sc, PhD); applied statistics (MS, Certificate); biology (MS, PhD); biostatistics (MS); chemistry (MS, PhD); computational biology (MS); environmental and sustainability policy (MS); environmental science (MS, PhD); history (MA, MAT); materials science and engineering (MS, PhD); mathematical and computational finance (MS); mathematics science (PhD); pharmaceutical chemistry (MS); practice of technical communications (Certificate); professional and technical communications (MS). *Program availability:* Part-time, evening/weekend. *Faculty:* 166 full-time (39 women), 87 part-time/adjunct (32 women). *Students:* 196 full-time (71 women), 68 part-time (33 women); includes 55 minority (15 Black or African American, non-Hispanic/Latino; 19 Asian, non-Hispanic/Latino; 15 Hispanic/Latino; 6 Two or more races, non-Hispanic/Latino), 140 international. Average age 28. 504 applicants, 64% accepted, 65 enrolled. In 2016, 81 master's, 18 doctorates, 1 other advanced degree awarded. Terminal master's awarded for partial completion of doctoral program. *Degree requirements:* For master's, thesis optional; for doctorate, thesis/dissertation. *Entrance requirements:* For master's, GRE General Test; for doctorate, GRE General Test, minimum graduate GPA of 3.5. Additional exam requirements/recommendations for international students: Required—TOEFL (minimum score 550 paper-based; 79 iBT). *Application deadline:* For fall admission, 6/1 priority date for domestic students, 5/1 priority date for international students; for spring admission, 11/15 priority date for domestic and international students. Applications are processed on a rolling basis. Application fee: $75. Electronic applications accepted. *Expenses:* Contact institution. *Financial support:* In 2016–17, 106 students received support, including 32 research assistantships (averaging $17,108 per year), 74 teaching assistantships (averaging $21,368 per year); fellowships, scholarships/grants, traineeships, and unspecified assistantships also available. Financial award application deadline: 1/15. *Faculty research:* Biophotonics and bioimaging, morphogenetic patterning, embryogenesis, biological fluid dynamics, applied research in the mathematical sciences. *Unit head:* Dr. Kevin Belfield, Dean, 973-596-3676, Fax: 973-565-0586, E-mail: kevin.d.belfield@njit.edu. *Application contact:* Stephen Eck, Director of Admissions, 973-596-3300, Fax: 973-596-3461, E-mail: admissions@njit.edu.
Website: http://csla.njit.edu/

**New Mexico Highlands University,** Graduate Studies, College of Arts and Sciences, Department of History, Political Science, and Languages and Culture, Las Vegas, NM 87701. Offers public affairs (MA), including historical and cross-cultural perspectives, history/political science, political and governmental processes. *Degree requirements:* For master's, comprehensive exam, thesis or alternative. *Entrance requirements:* Additional exam requirements/recommendations for international students: Required—TOEFL (minimum score 540 paper-based).

**New Mexico State University,** College of Arts and Sciences, Department of History, Las Cruces, NM 88003. Offers history (MA); public history (MA). *Program availability:* Part-time. *Faculty:* 10 full-time (4 women), 1 part-time/adjunct (0 women). *Students:* 18 full-time (8 women), 13 part-time (5 women); includes 13 minority (1 Asian, non-Hispanic/Latino; 11 Hispanic/Latino; 1 Two or more races, non-Hispanic/Latino), 1 international. Average age 35. 12 applicants, 58% accepted, 5 enrolled. In 2016, 8 master's awarded. *Degree requirements:* For master's, one foreign language, comprehensive exam, thesis (for some programs). *Entrance requirements:* For master's, 12 undergraduate history credits, writing sample, minimum GPA of 3.0. Additional exam requirements/recommendations for international students: Required—TOEFL (minimum score 550 paper-based; 79 iBT), IELTS (minimum score 6.5). *Application deadline:* For fall admission, 7/1 priority date for domestic students; for spring admission, 11/1 for domestic students. Applications are processed on a rolling basis. Application fee: $40 ($50 for international students). Electronic applications accepted. *Expenses:* Tuition, state resident: full-time $4086. Tuition, nonresident: full-time $14,254. *Required fees:* $853. Tuition and fees vary according to course load. *Financial support:* In 2016–17, 15 students received support, including 7 teaching assistantships (averaging $16,964 per year); career-related internships or fieldwork, Federal Work-Study, scholarships/grants, traineeships, health care benefits, and unspecified assistantships also available. Support available to part-time students. Financial award application deadline: 3/1. *Faculty research:* European history, U.S. history (early and recent), history of science, public history, east Asian history, U.S. southwestern and border history, New Mexico history, Latin American history. *Total annual research expenditures:* $51,039. *Unit head:* Dr. William Storm, Interim Department Head, 575-646-4601, Fax: 575-646-6096, E-mail: wstorm@nmsu.edu. *Application contact:* Dr. Margaret Malamud, Director of Graduate Studies, 575-646-4310, Fax: 575-646-6096, E-mail: mmalamud@nmsu.edu.
Website: http://history.nmsu.edu

**The New School,** The New School for Social Research, Department of Historical Studies, New York, NY 10003. Offers MA, PhD. *Program availability:* Part-time, evening/weekend. *Faculty:* 5 full-time (2 women). *Students:* 8 full-time (3 women), 2 part-time (1 woman); includes 3 minority (1 Black or African American, non-Hispanic/Latino; 1 Asian, non-Hispanic/Latino; 1 Two or more races, non-Hispanic/Latino). Average age 34. 15 applicants, 93% accepted, 3 enrolled. In 2016, 5 master's, 2 doctorates awarded. Terminal master's awarded for partial completion of doctoral program. *Degree requirements:* For master's, variable foreign language requirement, thesis. *Entrance requirements:* For master's, GRE, two letters of recommendation, writing sample, essays, unofficial transcripts. Additional exam requirements/recommendations for international students: Required—TOEFL (minimum score 100 iBT), IELTS (minimum score 7), PTE (minimum score 68). *Application deadline:* For fall admission, 8/1 priority date for domestic students, 6/1 priority date for international students; for spring admission, 10/15 priority date for domestic and international students. Applications are processed on a rolling basis. Application fee: $50. Electronic applications accepted. *Expenses:* Contact institution. *Financial support:* Research assistantships, Federal Work-Study, scholarships/grants, health care benefits, and tuition waivers (full and partial) available. Support available to part-time students. Financial award application deadline: 3/1; financial award applicants required to submit FAFSA. *Faculty research:* History of capitalism, history of political violence, history and theory, public history. *Unit head:* Dr. William Milberg, Dean, The New School for Social Research, 212-229-5777, E-mail: milbergw@newschool.edu. *Application contact:* Dana Messinger, Director of Graduate Admission, 212-229-5150 Ext. 2300, E-mail: messingd@newschool.edu.
Website: http://www.newschool.edu/nssr/historical-studies/

**The New School,** The New School for Social Research, Department of Sociology, New York, NY 10003. Offers historical studies (PhD); sociology (MA). *Program availability:* Part-time. *Faculty:* 7 full-time (3 women), 12 part-time/adjunct (4 women). *Students:* 92 full-time (50 women), 4 part-time (1 woman); includes 13 minority (2 Black or African American, non-Hispanic/Latino; 2 Asian, non-Hispanic/Latino; 5 Hispanic/Latino; 4 Two or more races, non-Hispanic/Latino), 49 international. Average age 34. 109 applicants, 69% accepted, 9 enrolled. In 2016, 21 master's, 11 doctorates awarded. Terminal master's awarded for partial completion of doctoral program. *Degree requirements:* For master's, comprehensive exam; for doctorate, one foreign language, thesis/dissertation. *Entrance requirements:* For master's and doctorate, GRE, letters of recommendation, writing sample, essays, unofficial transcripts. Additional exam requirements/recommendations for international students: Required—TOEFL (minimum score 100 iBT), IELTS (minimum score 7), PTE (minimum score 68). *Application deadline:* For fall admission, 5/5 priority date for domestic students, 6/1 priority date for international students; for spring admission, 10/15 priority date for domestic and international students. Applications are processed on a rolling basis. Application fee: $50. Electronic applications accepted. *Expenses:* Contact institution. *Financial support:* Fellowships, research assistantships, teaching assistantships, Federal Work-Study, scholarships/grants, and tuition waivers (full and partial) available. Support available to part-time students. Financial award application deadline: 2/1; financial award applicants required to submit FAFSA. *Faculty research:* Social inequalities; culture and politics; law, rights,

*History*

and citizenship; historical and comparative sociology; and cities and publics. *Unit head:* Dr. William Milberg, Dean, The New School for Social Research, 212-229-5777, E-mail: milbergw@newschool.edu. *Application contact:* Dana Messinger, Director of Graduate Admission, 212-229-5150 Ext. 2300, E-mail: socialresearchadmit@newschool.edu. Website: http://www.newschool.edu/

**New York University,** Graduate School of Arts and Science, Department of History, New York, NY 10012-1019. Offers African diaspora (PhD); African history (PhD); archival management (Advanced Certificate); Atlantic history (PhD); French studies/ history (PhD); Hebrew and Judaic studies/history (PhD); history (MA, PhD), including Europe (PhD), Latin America and the Caribbean (PhD), United States (PhD), women's history (MA); Middle Eastern history (MA); Middle Eastern studies/history (PhD); public history (Advanced Certificate); world history (PhD); JD/MA; MA/Advanced Certificate. *Program availability:* Part-time. Terminal master's awarded for partial completion of doctoral program. *Degree requirements:* For master's, seminar paper; for doctorate, one foreign language, thesis/dissertation, oral and written exams; for Advanced Certificate, internship. *Entrance requirements:* For master's, GRE General Test, minimum GPA of 3.0, writing sample; for doctorate, GRE. Additional exam requirements/ recommendations for international students: Required—TOEFL. *Faculty research:* African, East Asian, medieval, early modern, and modern European history; U.S. history; African and African diaspora; Latin American history; Atlantic world.

**New York University,** Graduate School of Arts and Science, Institute for the Study of the Ancient World, New York, NY 10012-1019. Offers PhD. *Degree requirements:* For doctorate, 4 foreign languages, comprehensive exam, thesis/dissertation, fieldwork, teaching experience. *Entrance requirements:* For doctorate, GRE General Test. Electronic applications accepted.

**North Carolina Central University,** College of Liberal Arts, Department of History, Durham, NC 27707-3129. Offers MA. *Program availability:* Part-time, evening/weekend. *Degree requirements:* For master's, one foreign language, comprehensive exam, thesis. *Entrance requirements:* For master's, GRE, minimum GPA of 3.0 in major, 2.5 overall. Additional exam requirements/recommendations for international students: Required— TOEFL.

**North Carolina State University,** Graduate School, College of Humanities and Social Sciences, Department of History, Raleigh, NC 27695. Offers history (MA); public history (MA). *Program availability:* Part-time, evening/weekend. *Degree requirements:* For master's, thesis. *Entrance requirements:* For master's, GRE General Test. Electronic applications accepted. *Faculty research:* History of the United States, Europe, Asia Africa and the Middle East; history of science; intellectual, cultural, social, environmental and political history.

**North Dakota State University,** College of Graduate and Interdisciplinary Studies, College of Arts, Humanities and Social Sciences, Department of History, Philosophy, and Religious Studies, Fargo, ND 58102. Offers history (MA, MS, PhD). *Program availability:* Part-time, evening/weekend. *Degree requirements:* For master's, one foreign language, comprehensive exam, thesis optional; for doctorate, 2 foreign languages, comprehensive exam, thesis/dissertation. *Entrance requirements:* For master's and doctorate, GRE General Test. Additional exam requirements/ recommendations for international students: Required—TOEFL (minimum score 600 paper-based; 100 iBT). Electronic applications accepted. *Faculty research:* Recent U.S., modern English, early modern European, North Dakota, Latin American, and Great Plains history.

**Northeastern Illinois University,** College of Graduate Studies and Research, College of Arts and Sciences, Program in History, Chicago, IL 60625-4699. Offers MA. *Program availability:* Part-time, evening/weekend. *Degree requirements:* For master's, comprehensive exam, thesis optional. *Entrance requirements:* For master's, 24 undergraduate hours in history, minimum GPA of 2.75. Additional exam requirements/ recommendations for international students: Required—TOEFL (minimum score 550 paper-based; 79 iBT). Electronic applications accepted. *Faculty research:* Africa; East Asia; European medieval, early-modern, and modern history; U.S. social, cultural, and intellectual history.

**Northeastern University,** College of Social Sciences and Humanities, Boston, MA 02115. Offers criminology and criminal justice (MSCJ); criminology and justice policy (PhD); economics (MA, PhD); English (MA, PhD); international affairs (MA); law and public policy (PhD); political science (MA, PhD); public administration (MPA); public history (MA); public policy (MPP); security and resilience studies (MS); sociology (MA, PhD); urban and regional policy (MS); urban informatics (MS); world history (MA, PhD); JD/MS. *Program availability:* Online learning. *Faculty:* 234 full-time (114 women), 55 part-time/adjunct (34 women). *Students:* 427 full-time (239 women), 77 part-time (42 women). In 2016, 143 master's, 38 doctorates awarded. *Degree requirements:* For doctorate, variable foreign language requirement, comprehensive exam, thesis/ dissertation. *Entrance requirements:* For master's and doctorate, GRE. Additional exam requirements/recommendations for international students: Required—TOEFL, IELTS. Application fee: $75. Electronic applications accepted. *Expenses:* $1,295 per credit. *Financial support:* Teaching assistantships, career-related internships or fieldwork, scholarships/grants, health care benefits, tuition waivers (full and partial), and unspecified assistantships available. Support available to part-time students. Financial award applicants required to submit FAFSA. *Unit head:* Dr. Uta Poiger, Dean, 617-373-5173. *Application contact:* Amber Crowe, Administrative Coordinator, 617-373-5990, Fax: 617-373-7281, E-mail: gradcssh@northeastern.edu. Website: http://www.northeastern.edu/cssh/graduate

**Northern Arizona University,** Graduate College, College of Arts and Letters, Department of History, Flagstaff, AZ 86011. Offers MA. *Program availability:* Part-time. *Degree requirements:* For master's, thesis (for some programs), thesis or departmental qualifying exam. *Entrance requirements:* For master's, GRE General Test. Additional exam requirements/recommendations for international students: Required—TOEFL (minimum score 550 paper-based; 80 iBT), IELTS (minimum score 7). Electronic applications accepted. *Expenses:* Tuition, state resident: full-time $8971; part-time $444 per credit hour. Tuition, nonresident: full-time $20,958; part-time $1164 per credit hour. *Required fees:* $1018; $644 per credit hour. Tuition and fees vary according to course load, campus/location and program. *Faculty research:* Twentieth-century United States, U.S. trans-Mississippi West, Arizona and the Southwest, women's history, U.S. intellectual history.

**Northern Illinois University,** Graduate School, College of Liberal Arts and Sciences, Department of History, De Kalb, IL 60115-2854. Offers MA, PhD. *Program availability:* Part-time. *Faculty:* 18 full-time (8 women), 2 part-time/adjunct (0 women). *Students:* 13 full-time (7 women), 21 part-time (9 women); includes 6 minority (2 Black or African American, non-Hispanic/Latino; 2 Asian, non-Hispanic/Latino; 2 Hispanic/Latino), 1 international. Average age 32. 26 applicants, 69% accepted, 7 enrolled. In 2016, 9 master's, 4 doctorates awarded. Terminal master's awarded for partial completion of doctoral program. *Degree requirements:* For master's, variable foreign language requirement, comprehensive exam, thesis optional, research seminars; for doctorate, variable foreign language requirement, thesis/dissertation, candidacy exam, dissertation defense, research seminars. *Entrance requirements:* For master's, GRE General Test, minimum GPA of 2.75; for doctorate, GRE General Test, minimum undergraduate GPA

of 2.75, graduate 3.2. Additional exam requirements/recommendations for international students: Required—TOEFL (minimum score 550 paper-based). *Application deadline:* For fall admission, 6/1 for domestic students, 5/1 for international students; for spring admission, 11/1 for domestic students, 10/1 for international students. Applications are processed on a rolling basis. Application fee: $40. Electronic applications accepted. *Financial support:* In 2016–17, 1 research assistantship with full tuition reimbursement, 15 teaching assistantships with full tuition reimbursements were awarded; fellowships with full tuition reimbursements, career-related internships or fieldwork, Federal Work-Study, scholarships/grants, tuition waivers (full), and unspecified assistantships also available. Support available to part-time students. Financial award applicants required to submit FAFSA. *Faculty research:* History of the Carolingian empire, history of early modern Europe, modern Irish history, history of the Ming dynasty. *Unit head:* Dr. James Schmidt, Chair, 815-753-6810, Fax: 815-753-6302, E-mail: jschmidt@niu.edu. *Application contact:* Dr. Anne G. Hanley, Assistant Chair/Director of Graduate Studies, 815-753-6695, E-mail: ahanley@niu.edu. Website: http://www.niu.edu/history/

**Northwestern University,** The Graduate School, Judd A. and Marjorie Weinberg College of Arts and Sciences, Department of History, Evanston, IL 60208. Offers PhD, JD/PhD. Admissions and degrees offered through The Graduate School. *Degree requirements:* For doctorate, variable foreign language requirement, thesis/dissertation, major and minor field exams. *Entrance requirements:* For doctorate, sample of written work. Additional exam requirements/recommendations for international students: Required—TOEFL. Electronic applications accepted. *Faculty research:* Medieval and early modern Europe, Africa, race and slavery, Atlantic history, gender.

**Northwestern University,** School of Professional Studies, Program in Liberal Studies, Evanston, IL 60208. Offers American studies (MA); history (MA); religious and ethical studies (MA).

**Norwich University,** College of Graduate and Continuing Studies, Master of Arts in History Program, Northfield, VT 05663. Offers history (MA), including American history, world history. *Program availability:* Evening/weekend, online only, mostly all online with a week-long residency requirement. *Faculty:* 16 part-time/adjunct (6 women). *Students:* 83 full-time (28 women); includes 6 minority (3 Black or African American, non-Hispanic/ Latino; 1 Asian, non-Hispanic/Latino; 2 Hispanic/Latino). Average age 37. 29 applicants, 93% accepted, 25 enrolled. In 2016, 40 master's awarded. *Degree requirements:* For master's, thesis optional, capstone. *Entrance requirements:* For master's, minimum undergraduate GPA of 2.75. Additional exam requirements/recommendations for international students: Required—TOEFL (minimum score 550 paper-based; 80 iBT), IELTS (minimum score 6.5). *Application deadline:* For fall admission, 8/14 for domestic and international students; for winter admission, 11/13 for domestic and international students; for spring admission, 2/12 for domestic and international students; for summer admission, 6/5 for domestic and international students. Electronic applications accepted. *Expenses:* Contact institution. *Financial support:* In 2016–17, 18 students received support. Scholarships/grants available. Financial award application deadline: 8/4; financial award applicants required to submit FAFSA. *Unit head:* Dr. James Ehrman, Program Director, 802-485-2885, Fax: 802-485-2533, E-mail: jehrman@norwich.edu. *Application contact:* Admissions Advisor, 800-460-5597 Ext. 3372, Fax: 802-485-2533, E-mail: mah@online.norwich.edu. Website: https://online.norwich.edu/degree-programs/masters/master-arts-history/ overview

**Oakland University,** Graduate Study and Lifelong Learning, College of Arts and Sciences, Department of History, Rochester, MI 48309-4401. Offers MA. *Program availability:* Part-time, evening/weekend. *Entrance requirements:* For master's, minimum GPA of 3.0. Additional exam requirements/recommendations for international students: Required—TOEFL (minimum score 550 paper-based). Electronic applications accepted.

**The Ohio State University,** Graduate School, College of Arts and Sciences, Division of Arts and Humanities, Department of History, Columbus, OH 43210. Offers MA, PhD. *Faculty:* 65. *Students:* 94 full-time (36 women), 2 part-time (1 woman); includes 7 minority (all Hispanic/Latino), 10 international. Average age 30. In 2016, 8 master's, 21 doctorates awarded. Terminal master's awarded for partial completion of doctoral program. *Degree requirements:* For master's, thesis optional; for doctorate, variable foreign language requirement, thesis/dissertation. *Entrance requirements:* For master's and doctorate, GRE General Test. Additional exam requirements/recommendations for international students: Required—TOEFL (minimum score 550 paper-based; 79 iBT), GRE General Test (strongly recommended). *Application deadline:* For fall admission, 12/1 priority date for domestic students, 11/30 priority date for international students; for spring admission, 3/1 for domestic students, 2/1 for international students. Applications are processed on a rolling basis. Application fee: $60 ($70 for international students). Electronic applications accepted. *Financial support:* Fellowships with tuition reimbursements, research assistantships with tuition reimbursements, teaching assistantships with tuition reimbursements, Federal Work-Study, institutionally sponsored loans, and unspecified assistantships available. Support available to part-time students. *Unit head:* Dr. Nathan Rosenstein, Chair and Professor, 614-292-7645, E-mail: rosenstein.1@osu.edu. *Application contact:* Graduate and Professional Admissions, 614-292-9444, Fax: 614-292-3895, E-mail: gpadmissions@osu.edu. Website: http://history.osu.edu/

**Ohio University,** Graduate College, College of Arts and Sciences, Department of History, Athens, OH 45701-2979. Offers MA, PhD. *Degree requirements:* For master's, one foreign language, thesis optional; for doctorate, 2 foreign languages, comprehensive exam, thesis/dissertation. *Entrance requirements:* For master's, GRE, minimum GPA of 3.0; for doctorate, GRE, minimum GPA of 3.0, MA. Additional exam requirements/recommendations for international students: Required—TOEFL (minimum score 550 paper-based; 80 iBT) or IELTS (minimum score 6.5). *Application deadline:* For fall admission, 2/1 priority date for domestic and international students. Application fee: $50 ($55 for international students). Electronic applications accepted. *Financial support:* Fellowships with tuition reimbursements, teaching assistantships with tuition reimbursements, Federal Work-Study, and institutionally sponsored loans available. Financial award application deadline: 2/1. *Faculty research:* U.S. foreign relations, modern Europe, Latin America, southeast Asia, U.S. women. *Unit head:* Dr. Katherine Jellison, Interim Department Chair, 740-593-0438, Fax: 740-593-0259, E-mail: barmel@ohio.edu. *Application contact:* Dr. Peter John Brobst, Graduate Chair, 740-593-0221, Fax: 740-593-0259, E-mail: brobst@ohio.edu. Website: http://www.ohio.edu/history/

**Oklahoma State University,** College of Arts and Sciences, Department of History, Stillwater, OK 74078. Offers MA, PhD. *Faculty:* 22 full-time (7 women), 2 part-time/ adjunct (1 woman). *Students:* 8 full-time (7 women), 31 part-time (11 women); includes 4 minority (1 Black or African American, non-Hispanic/Latino; 1 Hispanic/Latino; 2 Two or more races, non-Hispanic/Latino). Average age 35. 17 applicants, 35% accepted, 4 enrolled. In 2016, 8 master's, 4 doctorates awarded. *Degree requirements:* For master's, thesis; for doctorate, comprehensive exam, thesis/dissertation. *Entrance requirements:* For master's and doctorate, GRE. Additional exam requirements/recommendations for international students: Required—TOEFL (minimum score 550 paper-based; 79 iBT). *Application deadline:* For fall admission, 3/1 priority date for international students; for spring admission, 8/1 priority date for international students. Applications are processed

*Peterson's Graduate Programs in the Humanities, Arts & Social Sciences 2018*

on a rolling basis. Application fee: $40 ($75 for international students). Electronic applications accepted. *Expenses:* Tuition, state resident: full-time $3775; part-time $209.70 per credit hour. Tuition, nonresident: full-time $14,851; part-time $825.05 per credit hour. *Required fees:* $2027; $112.60 per credit hour. Tuition and fees vary according to campus/location. *Financial support:* In 2016–17, 18 teaching assistantships (averaging $16,403 per year) were awarded; career-related internships or fieldwork, Federal Work-Study, scholarships/grants, health care benefits, tuition waivers (partial), and unspecified assistantships also available. Support available to part-time students. Financial award application deadline: 3/1; financial award applicants required to submit FAFSA. *Faculty research:* U.S. history, the American West, Native American history, modern European history, women's history. *Unit head:* Dr. Laura Belmonte, Head, 405-744-8182, Fax: 405-744-5400, E-mail: laura.belmonte@okstate.edu. Website: http://history.okstate.edu/

**Old Dominion University,** College of Arts and Letters, Program in History, Norfolk, VA 23529. Offers MA. *Program availability:* Part-time, evening/weekend. *Faculty:* 16 full-time (9 women), 1 part-time/adjunct (0 women). *Students:* 5 full-time (2 women), 29 part-time (16 women); includes 4 minority (1 Black or African American, non-Hispanic/Latino; 3 Two or more races, non-Hispanic/Latino). Average age 32. 41 applicants, 80% accepted, 20 enrolled. In 2016, 11 master's awarded. *Degree requirements:* For master's, comprehensive exam, thesis optional. *Entrance requirements:* For master's, GRE General Test, 24 credits in history with minimum GPA of 3.0. Additional exam requirements/recommendations for international students: Recommended—TOEFL. *Application deadline:* For fall admission, 4/1 for domestic students; for spring admission, 11/1 for domestic students. Applications are processed on a rolling basis. Application fee: $50. Electronic applications accepted. *Expenses:* Tuition, state resident: full-time $8604; part-time $478 per credit hour. Tuition, nonresident: full-time $21,510; part-time $1195 per credit hour. *Required fees:* $66 per semester. Tuition and fees vary according to campus/location, program and reciprocity agreements. *Financial support:* In 2016–17, 6 students received support, including 1 research assistantship (averaging $10,000 per year), 5 teaching assistantships (averaging $10,000 per year); career-related internships or fieldwork, scholarships/grants, and unspecified assistantships also available. Support available to part-time students. Financial award application deadline: 2/15; financial award applicants required to submit FAFSA. *Faculty research:* History: maritime, American, European, modern Asian, and African. *Unit head:* Dr. Michael C. Carhart, Graduate Program Director, 757-683-3949, Fax: 757-683-5644, E-mail: histgpd@odu.edu. *Application contact:* Dr. David C. Earnest, Associate Dean, 757-683-6077, Fax: 757-683-5746, E-mail: dearnest@odu.edu.
Website: http://al.odu.edu/history/

**Open University,** Graduate Programs, Milton Keynes, United Kingdom. Offers business (MBA); education (M Ed); engineering (M Eng); history (MA); music (MA); philosophy (MA).

**Penn State University Park,** Graduate School, College of the Liberal Arts, Department of History, University Park, PA 16802. Offers MA, PhD. *Unit head:* Dr. Susan Welch, Dean, 814-865-7691, Fax: 814-863-2085. *Application contact:* Lori Hawn, Director, Graduate Student Services, 814-865-1795, Fax: 814-863-4627, E-mail: l-gswww@lists.psu.edu.
Website: http://history.psu.edu/

**Pittsburg State University,** Graduate School, College of Arts and Sciences, Department of History, Pittsburg, KS 66762. Offers MA. *Program availability:* Part-time, 100% online, blended/hybrid learning. *Students:* 43 (19 women); includes 8 minority (2 Black or African American, non-Hispanic/Latino; 2 American Indian or Alaska Native, non-Hispanic/Latino; 3 Hispanic/Latino; 1 Two or more races, non-Hispanic/Latino). In 2016, 15 master's awarded. *Degree requirements:* For master's, thesis or alternative. *Entrance requirements:* Additional exam requirements/recommendations for international students: Required—TOEFL (minimum score 520 paper-based; 68 iBT), IELTS (minimum score 6), PTE (minimum score 47). *Application deadline:* For fall admission, 6/1 for international students; for spring admission, 10/15 for international students; for summer admission, 4/1 for international students. Applications are processed on a rolling basis. Application fee: $35 ($60 for international students). Electronic applications accepted. *Expenses:* Contact institution. *Financial support:* In 2016–17, 2 teaching assistantships with full tuition reimbursements (averaging $5,500 per year) were awarded; career-related internships or fieldwork, Federal Work-Study, and unspecified assistantships also available. Financial award application deadline: 2/1; financial award applicants required to submit FAFSA. *Unit head:* Dr. Barbara Bonnekessen, Chairperson, 620-235-4325, E-mail: bbonnekessen@pittstate.edu. *Application contact:* Lisa Allen, Assistant Director of Graduate and Continuing Studies, 620-235-4223, Fax: 620-235-4219, E-mail: lallen@pittstate.edu.

**Pontifical Catholic University of Puerto Rico,** College of Arts and Humanities, Department of History, Ponce, PR 00717-0777. Offers MA. *Entrance requirements:* For master's, GRE General Test, minimum GPA of 2.75, 2 letters of recommendation.

**Portland State University,** Graduate Studies, College of Liberal Arts and Sciences, Department of History, Portland, OR 97207-0751. Offers MA. *Program availability:* Part-time. *Faculty:* 23 full-time (7 women), 1 (woman) part-time/adjunct. *Students:* 16 full-time (9 women), 21 part-time (11 women); includes 6 minority (1 American Indian or Alaska Native, non-Hispanic/Latino; 1 Asian, non-Hispanic/Latino; 2 Hispanic/Latino; 2 Two or more races, non-Hispanic/Latino). Average age 34. 22 applicants, 55% accepted, 5 enrolled. In 2016, 7 master's awarded. *Degree requirements:* For master's, one foreign language, comprehensive exam, thesis and oral and written exams. *Entrance requirements:* For master's, GRE General Test, minimum GPA of 3.5 in upper-division history courses, 2 letters of recommendation, BA/BS in history, statement of intent, writing samples. Additional exam requirements/recommendations for international students: Required—TOEFL (minimum score 550 paper-based; 80 iBT). *Application deadline:* For fall admission, 2/15 for domestic and international students; for winter admission, 9/1 for domestic students, 6/1 for international students; for spring admission, 11/1 for domestic and international students; for summer admission, 2/1 for domestic and international students. Application fee: $65. Electronic applications accepted. *Expenses:* Contact institution. *Financial support:* In 2016–17, 3 research assistantships with full tuition reimbursements (averaging $10,872 per year), 7 teaching assistantships with tuition reimbursements (averaging $5,712 per year) were awarded; career-related internships or fieldwork, Federal Work-Study, scholarships/grants, and unspecified assistantships also available. Support available to part-time students. Financial award application deadline: 3/1; financial award applicants required to submit FAFSA. *Faculty research:* Germany and modern Europe, early modern France and England, Mexico in the 1920's, eighteenth-century France, Reformation, U.S. cultural history. *Unit head:* Dr. Tim Garrison, Chair, 503-725-3978, Fax: 503-725-3953, E-mail: timgarrison@pdx.edu. *Application contact:* Dr. Richard Beyler, Graduate Coordinator, 503-725-3996, Fax: 503-725-3953, E-mail: r.beyler@pdx.edu.
Website: https://www.pdx.edu/history/

**Princeton University,** Graduate School, Department of Classics, Princeton, NJ 08544-1019. Offers classical and hellenic studies (PhD); classical philosophy (PhD); history (the ancient world) (PhD); literature and philology (PhD). *Degree requirements:* For doctorate, thesis/dissertation. *Entrance requirements:* For doctorate, GRE General Test, sample of written work. Additional exam requirements/recommendations for

international students: Required—TOEFL (minimum score 600 paper-based). Electronic applications accepted.

**Princeton University,** Graduate School, Department of History, Princeton, NJ 08544-1019. Offers history (PhD); history of science (PhD). *Degree requirements:* For doctorate, variable foreign language requirement, comprehensive exam, thesis/dissertation. *Entrance requirements:* For doctorate, GRE General Test, sample of written work. Additional exam requirements/recommendations for international students: Required—TOEFL (minimum score 600 paper-based). Electronic applications accepted. *Faculty research:* World comparative, Europe-early modern, modern, late antique, medieval.

**Providence College,** Department of History, Providence, RI 02918. Offers American history (MA); modern European history (MA). *Program availability:* Part-time, evening/weekend. *Faculty:* 6 full-time (1 woman), 4 part-time/adjunct (0 women). *Students:* 13 full-time (6 women), 19 part-time (2 women); includes 1 minority (Two or more races, non-Hispanic/Latino). Average age 33. 14 applicants, 100% accepted, 11 enrolled. In 2016, 20 master's awarded. *Degree requirements:* For master's, comprehensive exam, thesis optional. *Entrance requirements:* Additional exam requirements/recommendations for international students: Required—TOEFL (minimum score 577 paper-based; 90 iBT). *Application deadline:* For fall admission, 7/15 priority date for domestic and international students; for spring admission, 11/15 priority date for domestic and international students; for summer admission, 3/15 priority date for domestic students, 3/15 for international students. Application fee: $55. *Expenses:* Contact institution. *Financial support:* Career-related internships or fieldwork, institutionally sponsored loans, and unspecified assistantships available. Support available to part-time students. Financial award application deadline: 8/1; financial award applicants required to submit FAFSA. *Faculty research:* American history, modern European history, Medieval history, Native American history, religion, slavery, western civilization, labor movements, Japanese and Asian history, early modern Europe.
Website: http://www.providence.edu/academics/Pages/master-arts-history.aspx

**Purdue University,** Graduate School, College of Liberal Arts, Department of History, West Lafayette, IN 47907. Offers MA, PhD. *Program availability:* Part-time. *Faculty:* 32 full-time (14 women), 1 (woman) part-time/adjunct. *Students:* 36 full-time (17 women), 13 part-time (7 women); includes 2 minority (1 Hispanic/Latino; 1 Two or more races, non-Hispanic/Latino), 5 international. Average age 35. 41 applicants, 46% accepted, 11 enrolled. In 2016, 7 master's, 7 doctorates awarded. *Degree requirements:* For master's, thesis optional; for doctorate, one foreign language, thesis/dissertation. *Entrance requirements:* For master's, GRE General Test, minimum undergraduate GPA of 3.0 or equivalent; for doctorate, GRE General Test, minimum undergraduate GPA of 3.0 or equivalent; master's degree with minimum GPA of 3.0 or equivalent. Additional exam requirements/recommendations for international students: Required—TOEFL (minimum score 550 paper-based; 77 iBT), TWE. *Application deadline:* For fall admission, 1/1 priority date for domestic and international students; for spring admission, 9/1 for domestic and international students. Applications are processed on a rolling basis. Application fee: $60 ($75 for international students). Electronic applications accepted. *Financial support:* In 2016–17, 37 students received support. Fellowships with full tuition reimbursements available and teaching assistantships with full tuition reimbursements available available. Support available to part-time students. Financial award application deadline: 1/15; financial award applicants required to submit FAFSA. *Faculty research:* U.S. history, early modern and modern European history, global women's history, U.S. minority history, medieval history. *Unit head:* Dr. R. Douglas Hurt, Head, 765-494-4132, Fax: 765-496-1755. *Application contact:* Fay M. Chan, Graduate Secretary, 765-494-4126, Fax: 765-496-1755, E-mail: chanf@purdue.edu.
Website: http://www.cla.purdue.edu/history/

**Purdue University Northwest,** Graduate Studies Office, School of Liberal Arts and Social Sciences, Department of History and Political Science, Hammond, IN 46323-2094. Offers history (MA). *Program availability:* Part-time, evening/weekend. *Entrance requirements:* Additional exam requirements/recommendations for international students: Required—TOEFL. *Faculty research:* Mid-east, German history, U. S. regional history, U. S. social history, Holocaust.

**Queens College of the City University of New York,** Division of Education, Department of Elementary and Early Childhood Education, Queens, NY 11367-1597. Offers bilingual education (MS Ed); child development psychology (AC); childhood education (MAT, MS Ed); childhood education and special education (MAT); childhood education-bilingual education (MAT, MS Ed, AC); children's literacy (AC); early childhood education (MAT); early childhood education birth-2 (MS Ed, AC); elementary education (MS Ed); literacy birth-grade 6 (AC); literacy technology birth-grade 6 (MS Ed); social studies education grades 1-6 (AC). *Program availability:* Part-time, evening/weekend. *Faculty:* 25 full-time (19 women), 33 part-time/adjunct (28 women). *Students:* 134 full-time (119 women), 374 part-time (349 women); includes 251 minority (55 Black or African American, non-Hispanic/Latino; 1 American Indian or Alaska Native, non-Hispanic/Latino; 82 Asian, non-Hispanic/Latino; 103 Hispanic/Latino; 10 Two or more races, non-Hispanic/Latino), 12 international. Average age 29. 364 applicants, 72% accepted, 224 enrolled. In 2016, 184 master's, 62 other advanced degrees awarded. *Degree requirements:* For master's, research project. *Entrance requirements:* For master's, minimum GPA of 3.0. Additional exam requirements/recommendations for international students: Required—TOEFL, IELTS. *Application deadline:* For fall admission, 4/1 for domestic students. Applications are processed on a rolling basis. Application fee: $125. Electronic applications accepted. *Expenses:* Tuition, state resident: full-time $5065; part-time $425 per credit. Tuition, nonresident: part-time $780 per credit. *Required fees:* $522; $397 per credit. Part-time tuition and fees vary according to course load and program. *Financial support:* Career-related internships or fieldwork available. Financial award application deadline: 4/1; financial award applicants required to submit FAFSA. *Unit head:* Dr. Mary Bushnell Greiner, Chairperson, 718-997-5328, E-mail: mary.greiner@qc.cuny.edu.

**Queens College of the City University of New York,** Division of Social Sciences, Department of History, Queens, NY 11367-1597. Offers MA. *Program availability:* Part-time, evening/weekend. *Faculty:* 26 full-time (14 women), 22 part-time/adjunct (5 women). *Students:* 2 full-time, 50 part-time (16 women); includes 14 minority (2 Black or African American, non-Hispanic/Latino; 11 Hispanic/Latino; 1 Two or more races, non-Hispanic/Latino). Average age 33. 24 applicants, 83% accepted, 7 enrolled. In 2016, 13 master's awarded. *Degree requirements:* For master's, comprehensive exam, thesis optional. *Entrance requirements:* For master's, minimum GPA of 3.0. Additional exam requirements/recommendations for international students: Required—TOEFL (minimum score 90 iBT), IELTS (minimum score 6.5). *Application deadline:* For fall admission, 4/1 for domestic students; for spring admission, 11/1 for domestic students. Applications are processed on a rolling basis. Application fee: $125. Electronic applications accepted. *Expenses:* Tuition, state resident: full-time $5065; part-time $425 per credit. Tuition, nonresident: part-time $780 per credit. *Required fees:* $522; $397 per credit. Part-time tuition and fees vary according to course load and program. *Financial support:* Career-related internships or fieldwork, tuition waivers (partial), and unspecified assistantships available. Financial award application deadline: 4/1; financial award applicants required

*History*

to submit FAFSA. *Unit head:* Dr. Joel W. Allen, Chairperson, 718-997-5350, E-mail: joel.allen@qc.cuny.edu.

**Regent University,** Graduate School, School of Divinity, Virginia Beach, VA 23464-9800. Offers divinity (M Div), including Biblical studies (M Div, MTS, PhD), chaplain ministry, Christian theology (M Div, MTS, PhD), church and ministry (M Div, MA), history of Christianity (M Div, MTS, PhD), inter-cultural studies (M Div, MA), interdisciplinary studies (M Div, MA, MTS), marketplace ministry, worship and media (M Div, MA); leadership and renewal (D Min), including Christian leadership and renewal, clinical pastoral education, community transformation, military ministry, ministry leadership coaching; practical theology (MA), including church and ministry (M Div, MA), inter-cultural studies (M Div, MA), interdisciplinary studies (M Div, MA, MTS), worship and media (M Div, MA); theological studies (MTS, PhD), including Biblical studies (M Div, MTS, PhD), Christian theology (M Div, MTS, PhD), history of Christianity (M Div, MTS, PhD), interdisciplinary studies (M Div, MA, MTS). *Accreditation:* ACIPE; ATS. *Program availability:* Part-time, evening/weekend, 100% online, blended/hybrid learning. *Faculty:* 15 full-time (3 women), 51 part-time/adjunct (6 women). *Students:* 148 full-time (60 women), 787 part-time (321 women); includes 506 minority (416 Black or African American, non-Hispanic/Latino; 1 American Indian or Alaska Native, non-Hispanic/Latino; 23 Asian, non-Hispanic/Latino; 54 Hispanic/Latino; 1 Native Hawaiian or other Pacific Islander, non-Hispanic/Latino; 11 Two or more races, non-Hispanic/Latino), 31 international. Average age 43. 1,020 applicants, 42% accepted, 276 enrolled. In 2016, 127 master's, 25 doctorates awarded. *Degree requirements:* For master's, comprehensive exam, thesis or alternative, internship; for doctorate, thesis/dissertation or alternative. *Entrance requirements:* For master's, minimum undergraduate GPA of 2.75, writing sample, personal goal statement, college transcripts; for doctorate, GRE, minimum graduate GPA of 3.5 (PhD), 3.0 (D Min); clergy recommendations; writing sample; transcripts; resume; interview. Additional exam requirements/recommendations for international students: Required—TOEFL (minimum score 577 paper-based). *Application deadline:* For fall admission, 5/1 priority date for domestic students. Applications are processed on a rolling basis. Application fee: $50. Electronic applications accepted. *Expenses:* Contact institution. *Financial support:* In 2016–17, 602 students received support. Career-related internships or fieldwork, scholarships/grants, and unspecified assistantships available. Support available to part-time students. *Faculty research:* Greek and Hebrew, theology, spiritual formation, global missions and world Christianity, women in ministry leadership. *Unit head:* Dr. Cornelius Bekker, Dean, 757-352-4401, Fax: 757-352-4597, E-mail: clbekker@regent.edu. *Application contact:* Heidi Cece, Assistant Vice President of Enrollment Management, 800-373-5504, Fax: 757-352-4381, E-mail: admissions@regent.edu.
Website: http://www.regent.edu/sod/

**Rhode Island College,** School of Graduate Studies, Faculty of Arts and Sciences, Department of History, Providence, RI 02908-1991. Offers MA. *Program availability:* Part-time, evening/weekend. *Faculty:* 11 full-time (3 women). *Students:* 1 full-time (0 women), 2 part-time (1 woman). Average age 31. In 2016, 1 master's awarded. *Degree requirements:* For master's, oral exam or thesis. *Entrance requirements:* For master's, GRE General and Subject Tests, 3 letters of recommendation, interview. Additional exam requirements/recommendations for international students: Recommended—TOEFL (minimum score 550 paper-based; 79 iBT). *Application deadline:* For fall admission, 3/1 for domestic students; for spring admission, 11/1 for domestic students. Applications are processed on a rolling basis. Application fee: $50. Electronic applications accepted. *Expenses:* Tuition, state resident: full-time $8928; part-time $372 per credit. Tuition, nonresident: full-time $17,376; part-time $724 per credit. *Required fees:* $604; $22 per credit. One-time fee: $74. *Financial support:* In 2016–17, 2 teaching assistantships with full tuition reimbursements (averaging $1,500 per year) were awarded; Federal Work-Study, scholarships/grants, health care benefits, and unspecified assistantships also available. Support available to part-time students. Financial award application deadline: 5/15; financial award applicants required to submit FAFSA. *Unit head:* Dr. David Espinosa, Chair, 401-456-8039. *Application contact:* Graduate Studies, 401-456-8700.
Website: http://www.ric.edu/history/index.php

**Rice University,** Graduate Programs, School of Humanities, Department of History, Houston, TX 77251-1892. Offers MA, PhD. Terminal master's awarded for partial completion of doctoral program. *Degree requirements:* For doctorate, variable foreign language requirement, comprehensive exam, thesis/dissertation, 4 semesters of coursework. *Entrance requirements:* For doctorate, GRE, writing samples, letters of recommendation, personal statement, transcripts. Additional exam requirements/recommendations for international students: Required—TOEFL (minimum score 600 paper-based; 90 iBT) or IELTS (minimum score 7). Electronic applications accepted. *Faculty research:* U.S. Southern, Caribbean, African-American, world, Latin American.

**Roosevelt University,** Graduate Division, College of Arts and Sciences, Department of History, Art, and Philosophy, Chicago, IL 60605. Offers history (MA). *Program availability:* Part-time, evening/weekend. *Degree requirements:* For master's, thesis or alternative. *Faculty research:* American social history, Holocaust, European history, African-American history, popular culture.

**Rowan University,** Graduate School, College of Humanities and Social Sciences, Department of History, Glassboro, NJ 08028-1701. Offers history (MA, CGS).

**Rowan University,** Graduate School, College of Humanities and Social Sciences, Program in History, Glassboro, NJ 08028-1701. Offers MA, CGS. *Degree requirements:* For master's, thesis optional. *Entrance requirements:* For master's, GRE, statement of objectives; current resume; official transcript demonstrating that applicant has earned undergraduate degree from accredited institution with minimum GPA of 3.0; two letters of recommendation from undergraduate professors or other qualified professionals; writing sample. Additional exam requirements/recommendations for international students: Required—TOEFL (minimum score 90 iBT). Electronic applications accepted.

**Rutgers University–Camden,** Graduate School of Arts and Sciences, Program in American and Public History, Camden, NJ 08102. Offers MA. *Program availability:* Part-time, evening/weekend. *Degree requirements:* For master's, comprehensive exam, thesis optional, 30 credits. *Entrance requirements:* For master's, GRE General Test (for full-time applicants), 3 letters of recommendation; history or related undergraduate degree (preferred). Additional exam requirements/recommendations for international students: Required—TOEFL, IELTS. Electronic applications accepted. *Faculty research:* Women's history, military history, Afro-American history, urban history, history of technology.

**Rutgers University–Newark,** Graduate School, Program in History, Newark, NJ 07102. Offers MA, MAT. MA, MAT offered jointly with New Jersey Institute of Technology. *Program availability:* Part-time, evening/weekend. *Degree requirements:* For master's, one foreign language, comprehensive exam, thesis optional. *Entrance requirements:* For master's, GRE, minimum undergraduate B average. *Faculty research:* Global history, American history, American diplomatic and legal history, women's history, history of technology, environment and medicine.

**Rutgers University–New Brunswick,** Graduate School-New Brunswick, Program in History, Piscataway, NJ 08854-8097. Offers African-American history (PhD); early American history (PhD); early modern European history (PhD); east Asian history (PhD); global and comparative history (PhD); history (PhD); history of diplomacy and foreign relations (PhD); history of technology, environment and health (PhD); history of the Atlantic cultures and African diaspora (PhD); Latin American history (PhD); medieval history (PhD); modern European history (PhD); nineteenth and twentieth century American history (PhD); women's and gender history (PhD). *Degree requirements:* For doctorate, thesis/dissertation. *Entrance requirements:* For doctorate, GRE General Test, sample of written work. Electronic applications accepted. *Faculty research:* American history, European history, Afro-American history, women's history, Latin American history.

**St. Cloud State University,** School of Graduate Studies, College of Liberal Arts, Department of History, St. Cloud, MN 56301-4498. Offers MA, MS. *Program availability:* Part-time. *Degree requirements:* For master's, thesis or alternative. *Entrance requirements:* For master's, GRE General Test, GRE Subject Test, minimum GPA of 2.75. Additional exam requirements/recommendations for international students: Required—Michigan English Language Assessment Battery; Recommended—TOEFL (minimum score 550 paper-based), IELTS (minimum score 6.5).

**St. John's University,** St. John's College of Liberal Arts and Sciences, Department of History, Queens, NY 11439. Offers history (MA); modern world history (DA); public history (MA). *Program availability:* Part-time, evening/weekend. *Degree requirements:* For master's, one foreign language, comprehensive exam, thesis optional, colloquia; for doctorate, one foreign language, comprehensive exam, thesis/dissertation, internship, practicum. *Entrance requirements:* For master's, minimum GPA of 3.0, 24 undergraduate credits in history or related field, 2 letters of recommendation, personal statement; for doctorate, minimum GPA of 3.5 in history, 3.0 overall; writing sample; 3 letters of recommendation; personal essay; bachelor's degree; at least 24 undergraduate credits in history or related field. Additional exam requirements/recommendations for international students: Required—TOEFL (minimum score 600 paper-based; 100 iBT), IELTS (minimum score 7). Electronic applications accepted. *Faculty research:* World history, gender, transnationalism, history of technology, cultural history, social history.

**Saint Louis University,** Graduate Education, College of Arts and Sciences and Graduate Education, Department of History, St. Louis, MO 63103. Offers MA, MA-R, PhD. *Program availability:* Part-time. *Degree requirements:* For master's, one foreign language, comprehensive exam, thesis optional, comprehensive oral exam; for doctorate, 2 foreign languages, comprehensive exam, thesis/dissertation, preliminary oral and written exams. *Entrance requirements:* For master's, GRE General Test, letters of recommendation, resume, writing sample; for doctorate, GRE General Test, letters of recommendation, resumé, writing sample, goal statement, transcripts. Additional exam requirements/recommendations for international students: Required—TOEFL (minimum score 525 paper-based). Electronic applications accepted. *Faculty research:* Medieval Europe, Crusades, Byzantine Empire, U.S. West and Borderlands, Early Modern Europe.

**Saint Mary's University,** Faculty of Arts, Department of History, Halifax, NS B3H 3C3, Canada. Offers MA. *Program availability:* Part-time. *Degree requirements:* For master's, one foreign language, comprehensive exam, thesis. *Entrance requirements:* For master's, honors degree. *Expenses:* Contact institution. *Faculty research:* Atlantic Canada, British Empire, history of science, South Africa.

**Salem State University,** School of Graduate Studies, Program in History, Salem, MA 01970-5353. Offers MA, MAT. *Program availability:* Part-time, evening/weekend. *Entrance requirements:* For master's, GRE or MAT. Additional exam requirements/recommendations for international students: Required—TOEFL (minimum score 550 paper-based; 80 iBT) or IELTS (minimum score 5.5).

**Salisbury University,** Department of History, Salisbury, MD 21801-6837. Offers history (MA), including colonial and revolutionary American history, history of the Chesapeake Bay region, United States history in the 19th and 20th centuries, world history. *Program availability:* Part-time, evening/weekend. *Faculty:* 8 full-time (2 women). *Students:* 4 full-time (2 women), 9 part-time (2 women); includes 1 minority (Black or African American, non-Hispanic/Latino). Average age 27. 4 applicants, 100% accepted, 2 enrolled. In 2016, 3 master's awarded. *Degree requirements:* For master's, comprehensive exam, thesis optional. *Entrance requirements:* Additional exam requirements/recommendations for international students: Required—TOEFL (minimum score 550 paper-based, 79 iBT) or IELTS (6.5). *Application deadline:* For fall admission, 4/15 priority date for domestic and international students; for spring admission, 10/15 priority date for domestic and international students. Applications are processed on a rolling basis. Application fee: $65. Electronic applications accepted. *Expenses:* $381 per credit hour resident tuition, $670 per credit hour non-resident tuition; $84 per credit hour fees. *Financial support:* In 2016–17, 2 teaching assistantships with full tuition reimbursements (averaging $8,000 per year) were awarded; career-related internships or fieldwork and scholarships/grants also available. Support available to part-time students. Financial award application deadline: 3/1; financial award applicants required to submit FAFSA. *Faculty research:* Chesapeake studies (regional focus), 20th century U.S. history, African American history, Native American history (minorities/ethnic focus), Afro-Asia (transitional topic). *Unit head:* Dr. Celine Carayon, Graduate Program Director, 410-677-3251, E-mail: cxcarayon@salisbury.edu.
Website: http://www.salisbury.edu/gsr/gradstudies/HISTpage.html

**Sam Houston State University,** College of Humanities and Social Sciences, Department of History, Huntsville, TX 77341. Offers MA. *Program availability:* Part-time, evening/weekend. *Degree requirements:* For master's, comprehensive exam, thesis optional. *Entrance requirements:* For master's, GRE General Test. Additional exam requirements/recommendations for international students: Required—TOEFL (minimum score 550 paper-based; 79 iBT), IELTS (minimum score 6.5). Electronic applications accepted.

**San Diego State University,** Graduate and Research Affairs, College of Arts and Letters, Department of History, San Diego, CA 92182. Offers MA. *Degree requirements:* For master's, one foreign language. *Entrance requirements:* For master's, GRE General Test, bachelor's degree in related field. Additional exam requirements/recommendations for international students: Required—TOEFL. Electronic applications accepted. *Faculty research:* Latin American history, Filipino history.

**San Francisco State University,** Division of Graduate Studies, College of Liberal and Creative Arts, Department of History, San Francisco, CA 94132-1722. Offers MA. *Expenses:* Tuition, state resident: full-time $6738. Tuition, nonresident: full-time $15,666. *Required fees:* $1012. Tuition and fees vary according to degree level and program. *Unit head:* Dr. Trevor R. Getz, Chair, 415-338-1604, Fax: 415-338-6159, E-mail: tgetz@sfsu.edu. *Application contact:* Dr. Sarah Curtis, Graduate Coordinator, 415-338-2250, Fax: 415-338-6159, E-mail: scurtis@sfsu.edu.
Website: http://history.sfsu.edu/

**San Jose State University,** Graduate Studies and Research, College of Social Sciences, San Jose, CA 95192-0001. Offers applications of technology in planning (Certificate); applied anthropology (MA); communication studies (MS); community design and development (Certificate); economics (MA), including applied economics, social sciences; environmental planning (Certificate); geographic information science (Certificate); geography (MA); global citizenship (Certificate); history (MA), including history education, social sciences; Mexican American studies (MA); psychology (MA, MS), including clinical psychology (MS), industrial/organizational psychology (MS), research and experimental psychology (MA); public administration (MA); real estate development (Certificate); social sciences (MPA, MS); sociology (MA); transportation and land use planning (Certificate). *Program availability:* Part-time, evening/weekend. *Entrance requirements:* For master's, minimum GPA of 3.0. Electronic applications accepted.

**Sarah Lawrence College,** Graduate Studies, Program in Women's History, Bronxville, NY 10708-5999. Offers MA. *Program availability:* Part-time. *Degree requirements:* For master's, thesis. *Entrance requirements:* For master's, previous course work in history, minimum B average in undergraduate course work. Additional exam requirements/recommendations for international students: Required—TOEFL (minimum score 600 paper-based). Electronic applications accepted.

**Seton Hall University,** College of Arts and Sciences, Department of History, South Orange, NJ 07079-2697. Offers history (MA), including Catholic history, European history, global history, United States history. *Program availability:* Part-time. *Degree requirements:* For master's, thesis or comprehensive exam. *Entrance requirements:* For master's, GRE. Additional exam requirements/recommendations for international students: Required—TOEFL. Electronic applications accepted. *Faculty research:* Catholic history, European history, global history, United States history, African-American history.

**Shippensburg University of Pennsylvania,** School of Graduate Studies, College of Arts and Sciences, Department of History and Philosophy, Shippensburg, PA 17257-2299. Offers applied history (MA). *Program availability:* Part-time, evening/weekend. *Faculty:* 6 full-time (1 woman), 1 part-time/adjunct (0 women). *Students:* 15 full-time (6 women), 9 part-time (4 women); includes 2 minority (1 Black or African American, non-Hispanic/Latino; 1 Two or more races, non-Hispanic/Latino). Average age 28. 19 applicants, 68% accepted, 8 enrolled. In 2016, 15 master's awarded. *Degree requirements:* For master's, thesis, internship, or student teaching and professional practicum. *Entrance requirements:* For master's, 500-word statement of purpose; interview (if GPA is below 2.75). Additional exam requirements/recommendations for international students: Required—TOEFL (minimum score 550 paper-based, 68 iBT) or IELTS (minimum score 6). *Application deadline:* For fall admission, 2/15 for domestic and international students; for spring admission, 9/15 for domestic and international students; for summer admission, 2/15 for domestic and international students. Applications are processed on a rolling basis. Application fee: $45. Electronic applications accepted. *Expenses:* Tuition, state resident: part-time $483 per credit. Tuition, nonresident: part-time $725 per credit. *Required fees:* $141 per credit. *Financial support:* In 2016–17, 9 students received support. Career-related internships or fieldwork, scholarships/grants, unspecified assistantships, and resident hall director and student payroll positions available. Support available to part-time students. Financial award application deadline: 3/1; financial award applicants required to submit FAFSA. *Unit head:* Dr. John D. Bloom, Associate Professor and Program Coordinator, 717-477-1621, Fax: 717-477-4062, E-mail: jdbloo@ship.edu. *Application contact:* Megan N. Luft, Assistant Dean of Graduate Admissions, 717-477-1231, Fax: 717-477-4016, E-mail: mnluft@ship.edu.
Website: http://www.ship.edu/history/

**Shippensburg University of Pennsylvania,** School of Graduate Studies, College of Education and Human Services, Department of Teacher Education, Shippensburg, PA 17257-2299. Offers curriculum and instruction (M Ed), including biology, early childhood education, elementary and middle level education, elementary education, geography/earth science, history, mathematics, middle school education, modern languages; literacy studies (Certificate); online instruction, learning, and technology (Certificate); reading (M Ed); teaching English as a second language (Certificate). *Accreditation:* NCATE. *Program availability:* Part-time, evening/weekend, 100% online, blended/hybrid learning. *Faculty:* 14 full-time (9 women), 5 part-time/adjunct (all women). *Students:* 11 full-time (10 women), 88 part-time (81 women); includes 8 minority (3 Black or African American, non-Hispanic/Latino; 2 Asian, non-Hispanic/Latino; 3 Hispanic/Latino), 4 international. Average age 32. 57 applicants, 60% accepted, 28 enrolled. In 2016, 18 master's awarded. *Degree requirements:* For master's, comprehensive exam (for some programs), thesis optional, practicum or internship; capstone seminar (for some programs). *Entrance requirements:* For master's, MAT or GRE (if GPA less than 2.75), interview, 3 letters of reference, questionnaire of teaching background and future goals, resume. Additional exam requirements/recommendations for international students: Required—TOEFL (minimum score 550 paper-based, 68 iBT) or IELTS (minimum score 6). *Application deadline:* For fall admission, 4/1 priority date for domestic students, 4/30 for international students; for spring admission, 9/1 priority date for domestic students, 9/30 for international students; for summer admission, 2/1 priority date for domestic students. Applications are processed on a rolling basis. Application fee: $45. Electronic applications accepted. *Expenses:* Tuition, state resident: part-time $483 per credit. Tuition, nonresident: part-time $725 per credit. *Required fees:* $141 per credit. *Financial support:* In 2016–17, 3 students received support. Career-related internships or fieldwork, scholarships/grants, unspecified assistantships, and resident hall director and student payroll positions available. Support available to part-time students. Financial award application deadline: 3/1; financial award applicants required to submit FAFSA. *Unit head:* Dr. Christine A. Royce, Chairperson, 717-477-1688, Fax: 717-477-4046, E-mail: caroyc@ship.edu. *Application contact:* Megan N. Luft, Assistant Dean of Graduate Admissions, 717-477-1231, Fax: 717-477-4016, E-mail: mnluft@ship.edu.
Website: http://www.ship.edu/teacher/

**Simmons College,** College of Arts and Sciences, Boston, MA 02115. Offers elementary education (MAT); English (MA); gender/cultural studies (MA); history (MA); public health (MPH); public policy (MPP). *Program availability:* Part-time. *Faculty:* 19 full-time (12 women), 1 (woman) part-time/adjunct. *Students:* 6 full-time (all women), 38 part-time (27 women); includes 10 minority (4 Black or African American, non-Hispanic/Latino; 1 Asian, non-Hispanic/Latino; 2 Hispanic/Latino; 3 Two or more races, non-Hispanic/Latino), 1 international. Average age 26. 50 applicants, 88% accepted, 17 enrolled. In 2016, 19 master's awarded. Terminal master's awarded for partial completion of doctoral program. *Degree requirements:* For master's, thesis (for some programs). *Entrance requirements:* For master's, GRE. Additional exam requirements/recommendations for international students: Required—TOEFL (minimum score 600 paper-based; 100 iBT). *Application deadline:* For fall admission, 8/1 for domestic and international students; for spring admission, 12/15 for domestic and international students; for summer admission, 5/1 for domestic and international students. Applications are processed on a rolling basis. Application fee: $35. Electronic applications accepted. *Expenses:* $1,050 per credit, $4,200 per course, $52 activity fee per semester. *Financial support:* In 2016–17, 4 fellowships with partial tuition reimbursements, 22 teaching assistantships with partial tuition reimbursements were awarded; scholarships/grants and unspecified assistantships also available. Support available to part-time students. Financial award applicants required to submit FAFSA. *Unit head:* Dr. Renee White, Dean, 617-521-2079. *Application contact:* Patricia Flaherty, Director, Graduate Studies Admission, 617-521-3902, Fax: 617-521-3058, E-mail: gsa@simmons.edu.
Website: http://www.simmons.edu/gradstudies/

**Simon Fraser University,** Office of Graduate Studies and Postdoctoral Fellows, Faculty of Arts and Social Sciences, Department of History, Burnaby, BC V5A 1S6, Canada. Offers MA, PhD. *Faculty:* 24 full-time (11 women). *Students:* 31 full-time (9 women). 29 applicants, 17% accepted, 5 enrolled. In 2016, 6 master's, 1 doctorate awarded. *Degree requirements:* For master's, one foreign language, thesis, language exam; for doctorate, one foreign language, comprehensive exam, thesis/dissertation, language exam. *Entrance requirements:* For master's, minimum GPA of 3.0 (on scale of 4.33) or 3.33 based on last 60 credits of undergraduate courses; for doctorate, minimum GPA of 3.5 (on scale of 4.33). Additional exam requirements/recommendations for international students: Recommended—TOEFL (minimum score 580 paper-based; 93 iBT), IELTS (minimum score 7), TWE (minimum score 5). *Application deadline:* For fall admission, 1/15 for domestic and international students; for spring admission, 10/15 for domestic students. Applications are processed on a rolling basis. Application fee: $90 ($125 for international students). Electronic applications accepted. *Financial support:* In 2016–17, 22 students received support, including 7 fellowships (averaging $6,500 per year), teaching assistantships (averaging $5,608 per year); research assistantships and scholarships/grants also available. Financial award application deadline: 3/15. *Faculty research:* Colonialism and imperialism Asian history, labor history, race, gender and sexuality, political and social history, cultural and urban history. *Unit head:* Dr. Jeremy Brown, Graduate Chair, 778-782-4379, Fax: 778-782-5837, E-mail: hist-grad-chair@sfu.ca. *Application contact:* Ruth Anderson, Graduate Secretary, 604-291-3740, Fax: 778-782-5837, E-mail: histgrad@sfu.ca.
Website: http://www.sfu.ca/history/

**Slippery Rock University of Pennsylvania,** Graduate Studies (Recruitment), College of Liberal Arts, Department of History, Slippery Rock, PA 16057-1383. Offers MA. *Program availability:* Part-time, evening/weekend, online only, 100% online. *Faculty:* 3 full-time (2 women). *Students:* 2 full-time (1 woman), 27 part-time (11 women); includes 1 minority (Hispanic/Latino). Average age 32. 31 applicants, 74% accepted, 12 enrolled. In 2016, 3 master's awarded. *Degree requirements:* For master's, comprehensive exam, thesis (for some programs). *Entrance requirements:* For master's, transcripts (undergraduate/graduate), minimum GPA of 3.0, personal statement. Additional exam requirements/recommendations for international students: Required—TOEFL (minimum score 550 paper-based; 80 iBT). *Application deadline:* For fall admission, 3/1 priority date for domestic students, 5/1 priority date for international students; for spring admission, 11/1 priority date for domestic students, 9/1 priority date for international students. Applications are processed on a rolling basis. Application fee: $25 ($30 for international students). Electronic applications accepted. *Expenses:* $646.50 per credit in-state, $936.80 per credit out-of-state; $581.45 per online credit in-state, $648.65 per online credit out-of-state. *Financial support:* In 2016–17, 2 students received support. Career-related internships or fieldwork, Federal Work-Study, institutionally sponsored loans, scholarships/grants, tuition waivers (partial), and unspecified assistantships available. Support available to part-time students. Financial award application deadline: 5/1; financial award applicants required to submit FAFSA. *Unit head:* Dr. Paula Rieder, Graduate Coordinator, 724-738-4923, Fax: 724-738-4762, E-mail: paula.rieder@sru.edu. *Application contact:* Brandi Weber-Mortimer, Director of Graduate Admissions, 724-738-2051, Fax: 724-738-2146, E-mail: graduate.admissions@sru.edu.
Website: http://www.sru.edu/academics/graduate-programs/history-master-of-arts

**Smith College,** Graduate and Special Programs, Department of History, Northampton, MA 01063. Offers secondary education (MAT), including history education. *Program availability:* Part-time. *Students:* 2 full-time (1 woman), 1 part-time (0 women). Average age 28. 6 applicants, 83% accepted, 3 enrolled. In 2016, 2 master's awarded. *Entrance requirements:* Additional exam requirements/recommendations for international students: Required—TOEFL (minimum score 595 paper-based; 97 iBT), IELTS. *Application deadline:* For fall admission, 4/1 for domestic students, 1/15 for international students; for spring admission, 12/1 for domestic students. Application fee: $60. *Expenses: Tuition:* Full-time $34,560; part-time $1440 per credit. Tuition and fees vary according to course load and program. *Financial support:* In 2016–17, 2 students received support. Scholarships/grants available. Support available to part-time students. Financial award application deadline: 4/1; financial award applicants required to submit CSS PROFILE or FAFSA. *Unit head:* Joshua Birk, Graduate Student Adviser, 413-585-3740, E-mail: jbirk@smith.edu. *Application contact:* Ruth Morgan, Program Assistant, 413-585-3050, Fax: 413-585-3054, E-mail: gradstdy@smith.edu.
Website: http://www.smith.edu/history/

**Sonoma State University,** School of Social Sciences, Department of History, Rohnert Park, CA 94928-3609. Offers MA. *Program availability:* Part-time. *Degree requirements:* For master's, thesis or alternative. *Entrance requirements:* For master's, GRE General Test or GRE Subject Test, minimum GPA of 3.0. Additional exam requirements/recommendations for international students: Required—TOEFL (minimum score 500 paper-based). *Application deadline:* For fall admission, 11/30 for domestic students; for spring admission, 8/31 for domestic students. Application fee: $55. *Expenses:* Tuition, state resident: full-time $6738; part-time $3906 per unit. *Required fees:* $1916; $1916 per year. Tuition and fees vary according to course load, degree level and program. *Financial support:* Fellowships, research assistantships, teaching assistantships, career-related internships or fieldwork, and Federal Work-Study available. Financial award application deadline: 3/2; financial award applicants required to submit FAFSA. *Unit head:* Kathleen Noonan, Chair, 707-664-2313, E-mail: noonan@sonoma.edu.
Website: http://www.sonoma.edu/history/

**Southeastern Louisiana University,** College of Arts, Humanities and Social Sciences, Department of History and Political Science, Hammond, LA 70402. Offers history (MA). *Program availability:* Part-time. *Faculty:* 11 full-time (2 women), 1 part-time/adjunct (0 women). *Students:* 3 full-time (0 women), 30 part-time (9 women); includes 3 minority (1 Black or African American, non-Hispanic/Latino; 2 Hispanic/Latino). Average age 28. 13 applicants, 69% accepted, 6 enrolled. In 2016, 14 master's awarded. *Degree requirements:* For master's, comprehensive exam, thesis optional. *Entrance requirements:* Additional exam requirements/recommendations for international students: Required—TOEFL (minimum score 500 paper-based; 61 iBT). *Application deadline:* For fall admission, 7/15 priority date for domestic students, 6/1 priority date for international students; for spring admission, 12/1 priority date for domestic students, 10/1 priority date for international students. Applications are processed on a rolling basis. Application fee: $20 ($30 for international students). Electronic applications accepted. *Expenses:* Tuition, state resident: full-time $6540; part-time $465 per credit hour. Tuition, nonresident: full-time $19,017; part-time $1158 per credit hour. *Required fees:* $1829. *Financial support:* In 2016–17, 8 teaching assistantships (averaging $8,712 per year) were awarded; research assistantships, career-related internships or fieldwork, Federal Work-Study, institutionally sponsored loans, scholarships/grants, and unspecified assistantships also available. Support available to part-time students. Financial award application deadline: 5/1; financial award applicants required to submit FAFSA. *Faculty research:* American, British and European, and Southern and Louisiana history; American and international politics; philosophy. *Unit head:* Dr. William Robison, Department Head, 985-549-2109, Fax: 985-549-2012, E-mail: wrobison@southeastern.edu. *Application contact:* Amanda Harper, Graduate Admissions Analyst, 985-549-5620, Fax: 985-549-5632, E-mail:

## History

admissions@southeastern.edu.
Website: http://www.southeastern.edu/acad_research/depts/hist_ps/index.html

**Southeast Missouri State University,** School of Graduate Studies, Department of History, Cape Girardeau, MO 63701-4799. Offers heritage interpretation (Certificate); historic preservation (Certificate); history (MA); public history (MA), including heritage education, historic preservation. *Program availability:* Part-time, evening/weekend. *Faculty:* 11 full-time (3 women). *Students:* 8 full-time (2 women), 19 part-time (7 women); includes 2 minority (both Hispanic/Latino). Average age 31. 13 applicants, 92% accepted, 7 enrolled. In 2016, 8 master's awarded. *Degree requirements:* For master's, comprehensive exam (for some programs), thesis or comprehensive exams plus a capstone project/paper (for history); thesis or internship plus advanced project in applied history and comprehensive exams (for public history). *Entrance requirements:* For master's, minimum GPA of 2.75; 24 semester hours of undergraduate credit in history; letter of intent indicating how past experiences have prepared the candidate for graduate study and what the candidate expects to achieve through graduate study; two letters of recommendation; academic or professional writing sample; for Certificate, minimum GPA of 2.75; letter of intent indicating how past experiences have prepared the candidate for graduate study and what the candidate expects to achieve through graduate study; two letters of recommendation; academic or professional writing sample. Additional exam requirements/recommendations for international students: Required—TOEFL (minimum score 550 paper-based; 79 iBT), IELTS (minimum score 6), PTE (minimum score 53). *Application deadline:* For fall admission, 8/1 for domestic students, 6/1 for international students; for spring admission, 11/21 for domestic students, 10/1 for international students; for summer admission, 5/15 for domestic students. Applications are processed on a rolling basis. Application fee: $30 ($40 for international students). Electronic applications accepted. *Expenses:* Tuition, state resident: full-time $3130; part-time $260.80 per credit hour. Tuition, nonresident: full-time $5842; part-time $486.80 per credit hour. *Required fees:* $33.70 per credit hour. *Financial support:* In 2016–17, 5 students received support, including 4 teaching assistantships with full tuition reimbursements available; career-related internships or fieldwork, Federal Work-Study, scholarships/grants, traineeships, tuition waivers (full), and unspecified assistantships also available. Financial award application deadline: 6/30; financial award applicants required to submit FAFSA. *Faculty research:* Medieval Europe; modern Europe including Britain, Germany, France, Russia, and Spain; colonial and nineteenth-century America; twentieth-century America and American West; public history and historic preservation; Latin America. *Unit head:* Dr. Wayne Bowen, Chairperson/Professor of History, 573-651-2179, Fax: 573-651-5114, E-mail: wbowen@semo.edu. *Application contact:* Dr. Vicky McAlister, Graduate Coordinator/Assistant Professor of History, 573-651-2763, Fax: 573-651-5114, E-mail: vmcalister@semo.edu.

**Southern Connecticut State University,** School of Graduate Studies, School of Arts and Sciences, Department of History, New Haven, CT 06515-1355. Offers MA, MS. *Program availability:* Part-time, evening/weekend. *Faculty:* 8 full-time (5 women). *Students:* 12 full-time (4 women), 19 part-time (8 women); includes 3 minority (1 Black or African American, non-Hispanic/Latino; 1 Hispanic/Latino; 1 Two or more races, non-Hispanic/Latino). Average age 32. 18 applicants, 39% accepted, 6 enrolled. In 2016, 16 master's awarded. *Degree requirements:* For master's, one foreign language, thesis. *Entrance requirements:* For master's, interview, undergraduate major or minor in history. *Application deadline:* For fall admission, 7/15 priority date for domestic students. Applications are processed on a rolling basis. Application fee: $50. Electronic applications accepted. *Expenses:* Tuition, state resident: full-time $6497; part-time $519 per credit hour. Tuition, nonresident: full-time $18,102; part-time $535 per credit hour. *Required fees:* $4722; $55 per semester. Tuition and fees vary according to program. *Financial support:* Career-related internships or fieldwork, scholarships/grants, and unspecified assistantships available. Financial award application deadline: 4/15; financial award applicants required to submit FAFSA. *Unit head:* Dr. Troy Paddock, Chairperson, 203-392-5639, Fax: 203-392-5670, E-mail: paddockt1@southernct.edu. *Application contact:* Lisa Galvin, Director of Graduate Admissions, 203-392-5240, Fax: 203-392-5235, E-mail: galvinl1@southernct.edu.

**Southern Illinois University Carbondale,** Graduate School, College of Liberal Arts, Department of History, Carbondale, IL 62901-4701. Offers MA, PhD. *Program availability:* Part-time. *Degree requirements:* For master's, one foreign language, research papers or thesis, written exams; for doctorate, 2 foreign languages, thesis/dissertation. *Entrance requirements:* For master's, GRE General Test, minimum GPA of 3.0; for doctorate, GRE General Test, minimum GPA of 3.25. Additional exam requirements/recommendations for international students: Required—TOEFL. *Faculty research:* American, Asian, European, and Latin American history; global history.

**Southern Illinois University Edwardsville,** Graduate School, College of Arts and Sciences, Department of Historical Studies, Program in History, Edwardsville, IL 62026-0001. Offers MA. *Program availability:* Part-time, evening/weekend. *Degree requirements:* For master's, one foreign language, thesis (for some programs), final exam. *Entrance requirements:* For master's, GRE. Additional exam requirements/recommendations for international students: Required—TOEFL (minimum score 550 paper-based; 79 iBT), IELTS (minimum score 6.5). Electronic applications accepted.

**Southern Methodist University,** Dedman College of Humanities and Sciences, Clements Department of History, Dallas, TX 75275. Offers classical/medieval history (MA); European history (MA); history (PhD); Ibero-American history (MA); United States history (MA). PhD offered jointly with the Clements Center for Southwest Studies. *Program availability:* Part-time. Terminal master's awarded for partial completion of doctoral program. *Degree requirements:* For master's, one foreign language, thesis, oral exam, thesis defense; for doctorate, one foreign language, thesis/dissertation, oral exam, dissertation defense. *Entrance requirements:* For master's and doctorate, GRE General Test, minimum GPA of 3.0, 12 undergraduate hours in advanced level history, writing sample. Additional exam requirements/recommendations for international students: Required—TOEFL. Electronic applications accepted. *Faculty research:* U.S. history, European history, Latin America, Africa/Middle East, China.

**Southern University and Agricultural and Mechanical College,** Graduate School, College of Arts and Humanities, Department of History, Baton Rouge, LA 70813. Offers social sciences (MA). *Program availability:* Part-time. *Degree requirements:* For master's, thesis. *Entrance requirements:* For master's, GRE General Test. Additional exam requirements/recommendations for international students: Required—TOEFL (minimum score 525 paper-based).

**Southwestern Assemblies of God University,** Thomas F. Harrison School of Graduate Studies, Program in History, Waxahachie, TX 75165-5735. Offers MA.

**Spring Hill College,** Graduate Programs, Program in Liberal Arts, Mobile, AL 36608-1791. Offers fine arts (MLA); history and social science (MLA); leadership and ethics (MLA, Postbaccalaureate Certificate); literature (MLA); studio art (Postbaccalaureate Certificate). *Program availability:* Part-time, evening/weekend. *Faculty:* 5 full-time (0 women), 2 part-time/adjunct (1 woman). *Students:* 2 full-time (1 woman), 31 part-time (10 women); includes 4 minority (3 Black or African American, non-Hispanic/Latino; 1 Hispanic/Latino), 3 international. Average age 35. In 2016, 7 master's, 1 other advanced degree awarded. *Degree requirements:* For master's, capstone course, completion of

program within 6 years of initial admittance. *Entrance requirements:* For master's, bachelor's degree with minimum undergraduate GPA of 3.0 or graduate/professional degree. Additional exam requirements/recommendations for international students: Required—TOEFL (minimum score 550 paper-based; 80 iBT), IELTS (minimum score 6.5), CPE or CAE (minimum score C), Michigan English Language Assessment Battery (minimum score 90). *Application deadline:* For fall admission, 8/1 priority date for domestic and international students; for spring admission, 12/1 priority date for domestic and international students. Applications are processed on a rolling basis. Application fee: $25 ($35 for international students). Electronic applications accepted. *Expenses:* Contact institution. *Financial support:* Applicants required to submit FAFSA. *Unit head:* Dr. Thomas J. Hoffman, Director, 251-380-4184, Fax: 251-460-2115, E-mail: thoffman@shc.edu. *Application contact:* Robert Stewart, Vice President of Enrollment, 251-380-3030, Fax: 251-460-2186, E-mail: rstewart@shc.edu.
Website: http://ug.shc.edu/graduate-degrees/master-liberal-arts/

**Stanford University,** School of Humanities and Sciences, Department of History, Stanford, CA 94305-2004. Offers MA, PhD. Terminal master's awarded for partial completion of doctoral program. *Degree requirements:* For doctorate, variable foreign language requirement, thesis/dissertation, oral exam. *Entrance requirements:* For master's and doctorate, GRE General Test. Additional exam requirements/recommendations for international students: Required—TOEFL. Electronic applications accepted. *Expenses: Tuition:* Full-time $47,331. *Required fees:* $609.

**State University of New York at Oswego,** Graduate Studies, College of Liberal Arts and Sciences, Department of History, Oswego, NY 13126. Offers MA. *Program availability:* Part-time. *Degree requirements:* For master's, thesis optional. *Entrance requirements:* For master's, writing sample. Additional exam requirements/recommendations for international students: Required—TOEFL (minimum score 560 paper-based).

**State University of New York College at Cortland,** Graduate Studies, School of Arts and Sciences, Department of History, Cortland, NY 13045. Offers MA. *Program availability:* Part-time, evening/weekend. *Degree requirements:* For master's, one foreign language, comprehensive exam, thesis optional. *Entrance requirements:* Additional exam requirements/recommendations for international students: Required—TOEFL.

**Stephen F. Austin State University,** Graduate School, College of Liberal Arts, Department of History, Nacogdoches, TX 75962. Offers MA. *Program availability:* Part-time, evening/weekend. *Degree requirements:* For master's, comprehensive exam. *Entrance requirements:* For master's, GRE General Test. Additional exam requirements/recommendations for international students: Required—TOEFL. *Faculty research:* U.S.-Third World foreign policy, racial attitudes of antebellum Southern whites, naval warfare in World War II, demography of East Texas, medieval sermons.

**Stony Brook University, State University of New York,** Graduate School, College of Arts and Sciences, Department of History, Stony Brook, NY 11794. Offers MA, PhD. *Program availability:* Evening/weekend. *Faculty:* 30 full-time (15 women), 3 part-time/adjunct (1 woman). *Students:* 49 full-time (20 women), 3 part-time (0 women); includes 6 minority (1 Black or African American, non-Hispanic/Latino; 1 Asian, non-Hispanic/Latino; 3 Hispanic/Latino; 1 Two or more races, non-Hispanic/Latino), 9 international. Average age 33. 37 applicants, 46% accepted, 7 enrolled. In 2016, 5 master's, 9 doctorates awarded. *Degree requirements:* For doctorate, thesis/dissertation. *Entrance requirements:* For master's and doctorate, GRE General Test. Additional exam requirements/recommendations for international students: Required—TOEFL. *Application deadline:* For fall admission, 1/15 for domestic students; for spring admission, 10/1 for domestic students. Application fee: $100. Electronic applications accepted. *Expenses:* Contact institution. *Financial support:* In 2016–17, 2 fellowships, 26 teaching assistantships were awarded; research assistantships also available. *Total annual research expenditures:* $12,073. *Unit head:* Dr. Paul Gootenberg, Chair, 631-632-7507, E-mail: paul.gootenberg@stonybrook.edu. *Application contact:* Roxanne Fernandez, Coordinator, 631-632-7490, Fax: 631-632-7367, E-mail: roxanne.fernandez@stonybrook.edu.
Website: http://www.sunysb.edu/history/

**Sul Ross State University,** College of Arts and Sciences, Department of Behavioral and Social Sciences, Program in History, Alpine, TX 79832. Offers MA. *Program availability:* Part-time, evening/weekend. *Degree requirements:* For master's, thesis optional. *Entrance requirements:* For master's, GRE General Test, minimum GPA of 2.5 in last 60 hours of undergraduate work. *Faculty research:* Borderland/Southwestern studies, British studies, women's history, Native American studies, local history.

**Syracuse University,** Maxwell School of Citizenship and Public Affairs, Programs in History, Syracuse, NY 13244. Offers MA, PhD. *Program availability:* Part-time. Terminal master's awarded for partial completion of doctoral program. *Degree requirements:* For master's, comprehensive exam, thesis or alternative; for doctorate, 2 foreign languages, comprehensive exam, thesis/dissertation. *Entrance requirements:* For master's and doctorate, GRE General Test, sample of written work, resume, personal statement, three letters of recommendation. Additional exam requirements/recommendations for international students: Required—TOEFL (minimum score 100 iBT). *Application deadline:* For fall admission, 1/1 priority date for domestic and international students. Application fee: $75. Electronic applications accepted. *Expenses: Tuition:* Full-time $25,974; part-time $1443 per credit hour. *Required fees:* $802; $50 per course. Tuition and fees vary according to course load and program. *Financial support:* Fellowships with full tuition reimbursements, research assistantships with tuition reimbursements, and teaching assistantships with tuition reimbursements available. Financial award application deadline: 1/1; financial award applicants required to submit FAFSA. *Faculty research:* American, medieval, European, South East Asian, and Russian history. *Unit head:* Dr. Michael Ebner, Associate Professor and Chair, History, 315-443-2594, E-mail: mebner@maxwell.syr.edu. *Application contact:* Erin Borchik, Information Contact, 315-443-2210, E-mail: eborchik@syr.edu.
Website: http://www.maxwell.syr.edu/

**Tarleton State University,** College of Graduate Studies, College of Liberal and Fine Arts, Department of Social Sciences, Stephenville, TX 76402. Offers history (MA). *Program availability:* Part-time, evening/weekend. *Faculty:* 5 full-time (1 woman). *Students:* 9 part-time (7 women); includes 2 minority (both Hispanic/Latino). 6 applicants, 100% accepted, 3 enrolled. In 2016, 2 master's awarded. *Degree requirements:* For master's, variable foreign language requirement, comprehensive exam, thesis optional. *Entrance requirements:* For master's, GRE General Test, minimum GPA of 3.0. Additional exam requirements/recommendations for international students: Required—TOEFL (minimum score 550 paper-based; 80 iBT). *Application deadline:* For fall admission, 8/15 priority date for domestic students; for spring admission, 1/7 for domestic students. Applications are processed on a rolling basis. Application fee: $45 ($145 for international students). Electronic applications accepted. *Expenses:* $3,672 tuition; $2,437 fees. *Financial support:* Research assistantships, teaching assistantships, career-related internships or fieldwork, and Federal Work-Study available. Support available to part-time students. Financial award application deadline: 5/1; financial award applicants required to submit FAFSA. *Unit head:* Dr. Eric Morrow, Department Head, 254-968-9626, E-mail: morrow@tarleton.edu. *Application contact:*

Information Contact, 254-968-9104, Fax: 254-968-9670, E-mail: gradoffice@tarleton.edu.

**Temple University,** College of Liberal Arts, Department of History, Philadelphia, PA 19122-6096. Offers MA, PhD. *Program availability:* Part-time, evening/weekend. Terminal master's awarded for partial completion of doctoral program. *Degree requirements:* For doctorate, one foreign language, thesis/dissertation. *Entrance requirements:* For master's and doctorate, GRE General Test, minimum GPA of 3.0, 3 letters of recommendation. Additional exam requirements/recommendations for international students: Required—TOEFL (minimum score 550 paper-based; 79 iBT). Electronic applications accepted. *Faculty research:* American history, foreign relations, transnational and international history, military history, urban history, environmental history.

**Texas A&M International University,** Office of Graduate Studies and Research, College of Arts and Sciences, Department of Humanities, Laredo, TX 78041-1900. Offers English (MA); Hispanic studies (PhD); history and political thought (MA); language, literature and translation (MA). *Degree requirements:* For master's, comprehensive exam (for some programs), thesis (for some programs). *Entrance requirements:* For master's, GRE General Test. Additional exam requirements/recommendations for international students: Required—TOEFL (minimum score 550 paper-based; 79 iBT).

**Texas A&M International University,** Office of Graduate Studies and Research, College of Arts and Sciences, Department of Public Affairs and Social Research, Laredo, TX 78041-1900. Offers criminal justice (MS); history and political thought (MA); political science (MA); public administration (MPA). *Degree requirements:* For master's, comprehensive exam (for some programs), thesis (for some programs). *Entrance requirements:* For master's, GRE General Test. Additional exam requirements/recommendations for international students: Required—TOEFL (minimum score 550 paper-based; 79 iBT).

**Texas A&M University,** College of Liberal Arts, Department of History, College Station, TX 77843. Offers MA, PhD. *Program availability:* Part-time. *Faculty:* 41. *Students:* 38 full-time (15 women), 24 part-time (4 women); includes 8 minority (7 Hispanic/Latino; 1 Two or more races, non-Hispanic/Latino), 2 international. Average age 33. 56 applicants, 41% accepted, 13 enrolled. In 2016, 4 master's, 7 doctorates awarded. Terminal master's awarded for partial completion of doctoral program. *Degree requirements:* For master's, one foreign language, thesis optional; for doctorate, 2 foreign languages, thesis/dissertation. *Entrance requirements:* For master's and doctorate, GRE General Test. Additional exam requirements/recommendations for international students: Required—TOEFL (minimum score 550 paper-based; 80 iBT), IELTS (minimum score 6), PTE (minimum score 53). *Application deadline:* For fall admission, 12/15 for domestic students. Application fee: $50 ($90 for international students). *Expenses:* Contact institution. *Financial support:* In 2016–17, 46 students received support, including 8 fellowships with tuition reimbursements available (averaging $13,110 per year), 2 research assistantships with tuition reimbursements available (averaging $6,860 per year), 33 teaching assistantships with tuition reimbursements available (averaging $11,106 per year); career-related internships or fieldwork, institutionally sponsored loans, scholarships/grants, traineeships, health care benefits, tuition waivers (full and partial), and unspecified assistantships also available. Support available to part-time students. Financial award application deadline: 3/15; financial award applicants required to submit FAFSA. *Faculty research:* Recent U.S. history, Southwest, border studies, military history, Europe. *Unit head:* Dr. David Vaught, Department Head, 979-845-2571, Fax: 979-862-4314, E-mail: d-vaught@tamu.edu. *Application contact:* Adam Seipp, Director of Graduate Studies, 979-845-5996, Fax: 979-862-4314, E-mail: aseipp@tamu.edu.
Website: http://history.tamu.edu/

**Texas A&M University–Central Texas,** Graduate Studies and Research, Killeen, TX 76549. Offers accounting (MS); business administration (MBA); clinical mental health counseling (MS); criminal justice (MCJ); curriculum and instruction (M Ed); educational administration (M Ed); educational psychology - experimental psychology (MS); history (MA); human resource management (MS); information systems (MS); liberal studies (MS); management and leadership (MS); marriage and family therapy (MS); mathematics (MS); political science (MA); school counseling (M Ed); school psychology (Ed S).

**Texas A&M University–Commerce,** College of Humanities, Social Sciences and Arts, Commerce, TX 75429-3011. Offers applied criminology (MS); applied linguistics (MA, MS); art (MA, MFA); Christianity in history (Graduate Certificate); computational linguistics (Graduate Certificate); creative writing (Graduate Certificate); English (MA, MS, PhD); film studies (Graduate Certificate); history (MA, MS); music (MM); political science (MA, MS); public history (Graduate Certificate); sociology (MS); Spanish (MA); studies in children's and adolescent literature and culture (Graduate Certificate); teaching English to speakers of other languages (Graduate Certificate); theater (MA, MS). *Program availability:* Part-time. *Faculty:* 53 full-time (26 women), 7 part-time/adjunct (2 women). *Students:* 87 full-time (55 women), 528 part-time (362 women); includes 198 minority (86 Black or African American, non-Hispanic/Latino; 2 American Indian or Alaska Native, non-Hispanic/Latino; 8 Asian, non-Hispanic/Latino; 84 Hispanic/Latino; 18 Two or more races, non-Hispanic/Latino), 27 international. Average age 37. 333 applicants, 56% accepted, 149 enrolled. In 2016, 66 master's, 8 doctorates awarded. *Degree requirements:* For master's, one foreign language, comprehensive exam, thesis (for some programs); for doctorate, one foreign language, comprehensive exam, thesis/dissertation, departmental qualifying exam. *Entrance requirements:* For master's and doctorate, GRE General Test. Additional exam requirements/recommendations for international students: Required—TOEFL (minimum score 550 paper-based; 79 iBT), IELTS (minimum score 6). *Application deadline:* Applications are processed on a rolling basis. Application fee: $50. Electronic applications accepted. *Expenses:* Contact institution. *Financial support:* In 2016–17, 255 students received support, including 9 research assistantships with partial tuition reimbursements available (averaging $9,000 per year), 68 teaching assistantships with partial tuition reimbursements available (averaging $9,000 per year); Federal Work-Study, institutionally sponsored loans, scholarships/grants, health care benefits, and unspecified assistantships also available. Financial award application deadline: 5/1; financial award applicants required to submit FAFSA. *Unit head:* Dr. Salvatore Attardo, Dean, 903-886-5166, Fax: 903-886-5774, E-mail: salvatore.attardo@tamuc.edu. *Application contact:* Shelby Miller, Graduate Recruiter, 903-468-8123, Fax: 903-886-5774, E-mail: shelby.miller@tamuc.edu.
Website: http://www.tamuc.edu/academics/graduateSchool/programs/humanitiesSocialScienceArts/default.aspx

**Texas A&M University–Corpus Christi,** College of Graduate Studies, College of Liberal Arts, Corpus Christi, TX 78412-5503. Offers communication (MA); English (MA); history (MA); psychology (MA), including clinical psychology, general psychology; public administration (MPA); studio art (MFA). *Program availability:* Part-time, evening/weekend. *Faculty:* 76 full-time (39 women), 9 part-time/adjunct (4 women). *Students:* 81 full-time (49 women), 102 part-time (71 women); includes 90 minority (8 Black or African American, non-Hispanic/Latino; 2 Asian, non-Hispanic/Latino; 76 Hispanic/Latino; 4 Two or more races, non-Hispanic/Latino), 13 international. Average age 32. 134 applicants,

56% accepted, 57 enrolled. In 2016, 48 master's awarded. *Degree requirements:* For master's, comprehensive exam (for some programs), thesis (for some programs). *Entrance requirements:* For master's, portfolio. Additional exam requirements/recommendations for international students: Required—TOEFL (minimum score 550 paper-based; 79 iBT), IELTS (minimum score 6.5). *Application deadline:* For fall admission, 7/15 for domestic students, 5/1 for international students; for spring admission, 11/15 priority date for domestic students, 9/1 priority date for international students. Applications are processed on a rolling basis. Application fee: $50 ($70 for international students). Electronic applications accepted. *Financial support:* Research assistantships, teaching assistantships, career-related internships or fieldwork, Federal Work-Study, institutionally sponsored loans, scholarships/grants, health care benefits, and unspecified assistantships available. Support available to part-time students. Financial award application deadline: 3/15; financial award applicants required to submit FAFSA. *Unit head:* Dr. Mark Hartlaub, Interim Dean, 361-825-2659, Fax: 361-825-5844, E-mail: mark.hartlaub@tamucc.edu. *Application contact:* Graduate Admissions Coordinator, 361-825-2177, Fax: 361-825-2755, E-mail: gradweb@tamucc.edu.
Website: http://cla.tamucc.edu/

**Texas Christian University,** AddRan College of Liberal Arts, Department of History, Fort Worth, TX 76129. Offers Latin America (MA, PhD); United States (MA, PhD). *Faculty:* 16 full-time (4 women). *Students:* 49 full-time (22 women); includes 6 minority (1 Black or African American, non-Hispanic/Latino; 4 Hispanic/Latino; 1 Two or more races, non-Hispanic/Latino). Average age 34. 24 applicants, 33% accepted, 5 enrolled. In 2016, 6 master's, 4 doctorates awarded. Terminal master's awarded for partial completion of doctoral program. *Degree requirements:* For master's, comprehensive exam, thesis or alternative; for doctorate, one foreign language, comprehensive exam, thesis/dissertation. *Entrance requirements:* For master's and doctorate, GRE General Test. Additional exam requirements/recommendations for international students: Recommended—TOEFL. *Application deadline:* 2/1 for domestic and international students; for summer admission, 2/1 for domestic and international students. Applications are processed on a rolling basis. Application fee: $60. Electronic applications accepted. *Expenses: Tuition:* Full-time $26,640; part-time $1480 per credit hour. *Required fees:* $48. Tuition and fees vary according to program. *Financial support:* In 2016–17, 50 students received support, including 3 fellowships with full tuition reimbursements available (averaging $20,000 per year), 15 research assistantships with full tuition reimbursements available (averaging $17,500 per year), 5 teaching assistantships with full tuition reimbursements available (averaging $17,500 per year); tuition waivers (full) also available. Financial award application deadline: 2/1. *Faculty research:* U.S. South, Latin American history, Atlantic World history, American West. *Total annual research expenditures:* $140,000. *Unit head:* Dr. Jodi Campbell, Associate Professor, 817-257-5882, Fax: 817-257-5650, E-mail: j.campbell@tcu.edu. *Application contact:* Heather Confessore, Administrative Assistant, 817-257-7288, Fax: 817-257-5650, E-mail: h.confessore@tcu.edu.
Website: http://www.his.tcu.edu/graduate.asp

**Texas Southern University,** College of Liberal Arts and Behavioral Sciences, Department of History and Geography, Houston, TX 77004-4584. Offers history (MA). *Program availability:* Part-time, evening/weekend. *Degree requirements:* For master's, comprehensive exam, thesis optional. *Entrance requirements:* For master's, GRE General Test, minimum GPA of 2.5. Additional exam requirements/recommendations for international students: Required—TOEFL. Electronic applications accepted. *Faculty research:* American, Colonial, African, Asian, and African-American history.

**Texas State University,** The Graduate College, College of Liberal Arts, Program in History, San Marcos, TX 78666. Offers M Ed, MA. *Program availability:* Part-time. *Faculty:* 25 full-time (13 women), 4 part-time/adjunct (1 woman). *Students:* 43 full-time (25 women), 32 part-time (14 women); includes 11 minority (1 Black or African American, non-Hispanic/Latino; 1 Asian, non-Hispanic/Latino; 8 Hispanic/Latino; 1 Two or more races, non-Hispanic/Latino). Average age 30. 43 applicants, 65% accepted, 16 enrolled. In 2016, 26 master's awarded. *Degree requirements:* For master's, comprehensive exam, thesis optional. *Entrance requirements:* For master's, GRE General Test (minimum preferred score 156 verbal reasoning/500 old test), baccalaureate degree from regionally-accredited university with minimum GPA of 2.75 on last 60 undergraduate semester hours. Additional exam requirements/recommendations for international students: Required—TOEFL (minimum score 550 paper-based; 78 iBT), IELTS (minimum score 6.5). *Application deadline:* For fall admission, 2/15 priority date for domestic and international students; for spring admission, 10/15 priority date for domestic students, 10/1 for international students; for summer admission, 4/15 for domestic students, 3/15 for international students. Applications are processed on a rolling basis. Application fee: $40 ($90 for international students). Electronic applications accepted. *Expenses:* $4,851 per semester. *Financial support:* In 2016–17, 42 students received support, including 3 research assistantships (averaging $13,397 per year), 31 teaching assistantships (averaging $14,021 per year); Federal Work-Study, institutionally sponsored loans, scholarships/grants, and unspecified assistantships also available. Support available to part-time students. Financial award application deadline: 3/1; financial award applicants required to submit FAFSA. *Unit head:* Dr. Rebecca Montgomery, Graduate Advisor, 512-245-2116, Fax: 512-245-3043, E-mail: rm53@txstate.edu. *Application contact:* Dr. Andrea Golato, Dean of the Graduate College, 512-245-2581, E-mail: gradcollege@txstate.edu.
Website: http://www.txstate.edu/history/

**Texas Tech University,** Graduate School, College of Arts and Sciences, Department of History, Lubbock, TX 79409. Offers MA, PhD. *Program availability:* Part-time, evening/weekend. *Faculty:* 31 full-time (11 women), 6 part-time/adjunct (1 woman). *Students:* 67 full-time (29 women), 21 part-time (2 women); includes 14 minority (1 Black or African American, non-Hispanic/Latino; 1 American Indian or Alaska Native, non-Hispanic/Latino; 1 Asian, non-Hispanic/Latino; 9 Hispanic/Latino; 1 Native Hawaiian or other Pacific Islander, non-Hispanic/Latino; 1 Two or more races, non-Hispanic/Latino), 7 international. Average age 34. 38 applicants, 47% accepted, 15 enrolled. In 2016, 9 master's, 3 doctorates awarded. *Degree requirements:* For master's, one foreign language, comprehensive exam (for some programs), thesis optional; for doctorate, one foreign language, comprehensive exam, thesis/dissertation. *Entrance requirements:* For master's and doctorate, GRE, statement of purpose, 3 letters of reference, writing sample. Additional exam requirements/recommendations for international students: Required—TOEFL (minimum score 550 paper-based; 79 iBT). *Application deadline:* For fall admission, 6/1 priority date for domestic students, 1/15 priority date for international students; for spring admission, 9/1 priority date for domestic students, 6/15 priority date for international students. Applications are processed on a rolling basis. Application fee: $75. Electronic applications accepted. *Expenses:* $300 per credit hour full-time resident tuition, $708 per credit hour full-time non-resident tuition; $50.50 per credit hour fee plus $608 per term fee. *Financial support:* In 2016–17, 69 students received support, including 53 fellowships (averaging $2,561 per year), 60 teaching assistantships (averaging $14,657 per year); research assistantships, scholarships/grants, health care benefits, and unspecified assistantships also available. Financial award application deadline: 3/15; financial award applicants required to submit FAFSA. *Faculty research:* International politics and political culture; U.S. in global context; Texas, borderlands, and the West; race and national identity; gender and sexuality. *Total annual research expenditures:* $7,832. *Unit head:* Dr. Sean P. Cunningham, Chair, 806-742-3744, Fax:

# History

806-742-1060, E-mail: sean.cunningham@ttu.edu. *Application contact:* Dr. Laura Calkins, Director of Graduate Studies, 806-742-3744, Fax: 806-742-1060, E-mail: laura.calkins@ttu.edu.
Website: http://www.history.ttu.edu

**Texas Woman's University,** Graduate School, College of Arts and Sciences, Department of History and Government, Denton, TX 76201. Offers government (MA); history (MA). *Program availability:* Part-time, evening/weekend. *Students:* 4 full-time (1 woman), 23 part-time (21 women); includes 8 minority (2 Black or African American, non-Hispanic/Latino; 1 Asian, non-Hispanic/Latino; 4 Hispanic/Latino; 1 Two or more races, non-Hispanic/Latino), 2 international. Average age 35. In 2016, 7 master's awarded. *Degree requirements:* For master's, comprehensive exam, thesis. *Entrance requirements:* For master's, minimum GPA of 3.25, written statement of purpose, 2 letters of reference. Additional exam requirements/recommendations for international students: Required—TOEFL (minimum score 550 paper-based; 79 iBT). *Application deadline:* For fall admission, 7/1 priority date for domestic students, 3/1 for international students; for spring admission, 12/1 priority date for domestic students, 7/1 for international students. Applications are processed on a rolling basis. Application fee: $50 ($75 for international students). Electronic applications accepted. *Expenses:* Tuition, state resident: full-time $9046; part-time $251 per credit hour. Tuition, nonresident: full-time $22,922; part-time $614 per credit hour. *International tuition:* $23,046 full-time. *Required fees:* $2690; $1285 per credit hour. One-time fee: $50. Tuition and fees vary according to course level, course load, program and reciprocity agreements. *Financial support:* Research assistantships, teaching assistantships, career-related internships or fieldwork, Federal Work-Study, institutionally sponsored loans, scholarships/grants, traineeships, health care benefits, and unspecified assistantships available. Support available to part-time students. Financial award application deadline: 3/1; financial award applicants required to submit FAFSA. *Faculty research:* U.S. history, politics, and law; global history, politics, and law; Latin American and Caribbean history; legal studies; women in history, politics, and law. *Unit head:* Dr. Jonathan Olsen, Chair, 940-898-2156, Fax: 940-898-2130, E-mail: jolsen1@twu.edu. *Application contact:* Dr. Samuel Wheeler, Assistant Director of Admissions, 940-898-3188, Fax: 940-898-3081, E-mail: wheelersr@twu.edu.
Website: http://www.twu.edu/history-government/

**Trinity Western University,** School of Graduate Studies, Program in Interdisciplinary Humanities, Langley, BC V2Y 1Y1, Canada. Offers general humanities (MAIH); specialized (MAIH), including English, history, philosophy. *Program availability:* Part-time. *Degree requirements:* For master's, thesis or alternative, 36 semester hours. *Entrance requirements:* For master's, strong undergraduate degree in humanities or English, history or philosophy. Additional exam requirements/recommendations for international students: Recommended—TOEFL. Electronic applications accepted. *Faculty research:* Literary theory, gender, medieval and early modern literature, philosophy of religion, Thomas Merton's poetics.

**Troy University,** Graduate School, College of Arts and Sciences, Program in History, Troy, AL 36082. Offers American history (MA); European history (MA). *Program availability:* Part-time, evening/weekend. *Faculty:* 5 full-time (2 women). *Students:* 1 full-time (0 women), 17 part-time (6 women); includes 2 minority (1 Black or African American, non-Hispanic/Latino; 1 Native Hawaiian or other Pacific Islander, non-Hispanic/Latino). Average age 30. 28 applicants, 100% accepted, 3 enrolled. *Degree requirements:* For master's, variable foreign language requirement, comprehensive exam, thesis optional. *Entrance requirements:* For master's, GRE (minimum score of 850 on old exam or 290 on new exam), MAT (minimum score of 385), or GMAT (minimum score of 380), bachelor's degree, minimum undergraduate GPA of 2.5 or 3.0 on last 30 semester hours, letter of recommendation. Additional exam requirements/recommendations for international students: Required—TOEFL (minimum score 523 paper-based; 70 iBT), IELTS (minimum score 6); Recommended—TWE. *Application deadline:* For fall admission, 6/1 for international students; for spring admission, 10/15 for international students. Applications are processed on a rolling basis. Application fee: $50. Electronic applications accepted. *Expenses:* Tuition, state resident: full-time $7146; part-time $397 per credit hour. Tuition, nonresident: full-time $14,292; part-time $794 per credit hour. *Required fees:* $802; $50 per semester. Tuition and fees vary according to campus/location and program. *Financial support:* Fellowships, career-related internships or fieldwork, and scholarships/grants available. Support available to part-time students. Financial award applicants required to submit FAFSA. *Unit head:* Dr. Allen E. Jones, Jr., Chairman, 334-340-3512, E-mail: ajones@troy.edu. *Application contact:* Jessica Campbell, Director of Graduate Admissions, 334-670-3178, Fax: 334-670-3733, E-mail: jacord@troy.edu.

**Tufts University,** Graduate School of Arts and Sciences, Department of History, Medford, MA 02155. Offers history (MA, PhD), including global history (PhD); history and museum studies (MA). *Students:* 23 full-time (16 women); includes 4 minority (1 Black or African American, non-Hispanic/Latino; 2 Asian, non-Hispanic/Latino; 1 Two or more races, non-Hispanic/Latino), 5 international. Average age 26. 57 applicants, 42% accepted, 7 enrolled. In 2016, 4 master's awarded. Terminal master's awarded for partial completion of doctoral program. *Degree requirements:* For master's, one foreign language, thesis optional; for doctorate, 2 foreign languages, comprehensive exam, thesis/dissertation. *Entrance requirements:* For master's and doctorate, GRE General Test, writing sample. Additional exam requirements/recommendations for international students: Required—TOEFL (minimum score 550 paper-based; 80 iBT), IELTS (minimum score 6.5). *Application deadline:* For fall admission, 1/15 for domestic and international students. Applications are processed on a rolling basis. Application fee: $85. Electronic applications accepted. *Expenses:* Tuition: $49,982 full-time tuition (for MA); $29,936 full-time tuition (for PhD). *Financial support:* In 2016–17, 20 students received support. Teaching assistantships, Federal Work-Study, scholarships/grants, tuition waivers (full and partial), and unspecified assistantships available. Financial award application deadline: 1/15. *Unit head:* Dr. Steven Marrone, Graduate Program Director. *Application contact:* Office of Graduate Admissions, 617-627-3395, E-mail: gradadmissions@tufts.edu.
Website: http://www.ase.tufts.edu/history/

**Tulane University,** School of Liberal Arts, Department of History, New Orleans, LA 70118-5669. Offers MA, PhD. *Degree requirements:* For master's, one foreign language, thesis; for doctorate, variable foreign language requirement, thesis/dissertation. *Entrance requirements:* For master's, GRE General Test, minimum B average in undergraduate course work; for doctorate, GRE General Test. Additional exam requirements/recommendations for international students: Required—TOEFL. Electronic applications accepted. *Expenses: Tuition:* Full-time $50,920; part-time $2829 per credit hour. *Required fees:* $2040; $44.50 per credit hour. $580 per term. Tuition and fees vary according to course load, degree level and program.

**Union Institute & University,** Master of Arts Program, Cincinnati, OH 45206-1925. Offers creativity studies (MA); health and wellness (MA); history and culture (MA); leadership, public policy, and social issues (MA); literature and writing (MA). *Program availability:* Part-time, online only, 100% online. *Faculty:* 2 full-time (both women), 9 part-time/adjunct (7 women). *Students:* 9 full-time (7 women), 70 part-time (56 women); includes 33 minority (22 Black or African American, non-Hispanic/Latino; 1 American Indian or Alaska Native, non-Hispanic/Latino; 6 Hispanic/Latino; 4 Two or more races,

non-Hispanic/Latino). Average age 40. In 2016, 45 master's awarded. *Degree requirements:* For master's, thesis. *Entrance requirements:* For master's, transcript, essay, 3 letters of recommendation, resume. Additional exam requirements/recommendations for international students: Recommended—TOEFL. *Application deadline:* For spring admission, 3/13 for domestic students. Applications are processed on a rolling basis. Application fee: $50. Electronic applications accepted. *Expenses:* Contact institution. *Financial support:* Career-related internships or fieldwork and tuition waivers available. Financial award applicants required to submit FAFSA. *Unit head:* Elden Golden, Director, 513-487-1153, E-mail: elden.golden@myunion.edu. *Application contact:* Director of Admissions, 800-861-6400.

**Université de Moncton,** Faculty of Arts and Social Sciences, Department of History and Geography, Moncton, NB E1A 3E9, Canada. Offers history (MA). *Degree requirements:* For master's, thesis, proficiency in English and French. *Entrance requirements:* For master's, honors degree in history, minimum GPA of 2.7. Electronic applications accepted. *Faculty research:* Economic and social history (Canada, France, Acadia), sociocultural history, women's history, labor history, history of the press.

**Université de Montréal,** Faculty of Arts and Sciences, Department of History, Montréal, QC H3C 3J7, Canada. Offers MA, PhD. *Degree requirements:* For master's, thesis; for doctorate, thesis/dissertation, general exam. *Entrance requirements:* For doctorate, master's degree in related field. Electronic applications accepted. *Faculty research:* Preindustrial Quebec, Quebec working class, Quebec intellectual, diffusion of scientific thought, history of medicine.

**Université de Sherbrooke,** Faculty of Letters and Human Sciences, Department of Human Sciences, Sherbrooke, QC J1K 2R1, Canada. Offers history (MA); philosophy (MA). *Degree requirements:* For master's, thesis. *Entrance requirements:* For master's, minimum GPA of 2.75. *Faculty research:* Political, social, and urban history; history of women.

**Université du Québec à Montréal,** Graduate Programs, Program in History, Montréal, QC H3C 3P8, Canada. Offers MA, PhD. *Program availability:* Part-time. *Degree requirements:* For master's, thesis; for doctorate, thesis/dissertation. *Entrance requirements:* For master's, appropriate bachelor's degree or equivalent, proficiency in French; for doctorate, appropriate master's degree or equivalent, proficiency in French.

**Université Laval,** Faculty of Letters, Department of History, Programs in History, Québec, QC G1K 7P4, Canada. Offers MA, PhD. Terminal master's awarded for partial completion of doctoral program. *Degree requirements:* For master's, thesis (for some programs); for doctorate, comprehensive exam, thesis/dissertation. *Entrance requirements:* For master's and doctorate, English exam (comprehension of written English), knowledge of French. Electronic applications accepted.

**Université Laval,** Faculty of Letters, Department of Literature, Programs in Ancient Civilization, Québec, QC G1K 7P4, Canada. Offers MA, PhD. *Program availability:* Part-time. Terminal master's awarded for partial completion of doctoral program. *Degree requirements:* For master's, thesis; for doctorate, comprehensive exam, thesis/dissertation. *Entrance requirements:* For master's and doctorate, English test (comprehension of written English), knowledge of French, knowledge of an ancient language. Electronic applications accepted.

**University at Albany, State University of New York,** College of Arts and Sciences, Department of History, Albany, NY 12222-0001. Offers history (MA, PhD); public history (Certificate). *Program availability:* Part-time. *Faculty:* 6 full-time (2 women), 2 part-time/adjunct (both women). *Students:* 26 full-time (6 women), 52 part-time (27 women); includes 4 minority (1 Black or African American, non-Hispanic/Latino; 1 Hispanic/Latino; 2 Two or more races, non-Hispanic/Latino), 4 international. 48 applicants, 69% accepted, 18 enrolled. In 2016, 17 master's, 4 doctorates awarded. *Degree requirements:* For master's, variable foreign language requirement, exam, research paper or thesis; for doctorate, thesis/dissertation. *Entrance requirements:* For master's, minimum GPA of 3.0; for doctorate, GRE General Test, minimum GPA of 3.0. Additional exam requirements/recommendations for international students: Required—TOEFL (minimum score 550 paper-based). *Application deadline:* For fall admission, 3/1 for domestic students, 5/1 for international students; for spring admission, 11/1 for international students. Applications are processed on a rolling basis. Application fee: $75. Electronic applications accepted. *Expenses:* Tuition, state resident: full-time $10,870; part-time $453 per credit hour. Tuition, nonresident: full-time $22,210; part-time $925 per credit hour. *International tuition:* $21,550 full-time. *Required fees:* $1864; $96 per credit hour. *Financial support:* Teaching assistantships and career-related internships or fieldwork available. Financial award application deadline: 3/1. *Faculty research:* American history (all phases); public policy; European history (Medieval to modern); Asian, African, and Latin American history. *Total annual research expenditures:* $783. *Unit head:* Richard Hamm, Chair, 518-442-5300, Fax: 518-442-5301, E-mail: rhamm@albany.edu. *Application contact:* Michael DeRensis, Director, Graduate Admissions, 518-442-3980, Fax: 518-442-3922, E-mail: graduate@albany.edu.
Website: http://www.albany.edu/history/

**University at Buffalo, the State University of New York,** Graduate School, College of Arts and Sciences, Department of History, Buffalo, NY 14214. Offers history (MA, PhD, Advanced Certificate); public history (MA). *Program availability:* Part-time. *Faculty:* 26 full-time (11 women). *Students:* 54 full-time (21 women), 2 part-time (1 woman); includes 9 minority (3 Black or African American, non-Hispanic/Latino; 6 Asian, non-Hispanic/Latino), 5 international. Average age 29. 76 applicants, 47% accepted, 23 enrolled. In 2016, 8 master's, 4 doctorates awarded. Terminal master's awarded for partial completion of doctoral program. *Degree requirements:* For master's, project; for doctorate, one foreign language, comprehensive exam, thesis/dissertation. *Entrance requirements:* For doctorate, GRE General Test. Additional exam requirements/recommendations for international students: Required—TOEFL (minimum score 550 paper-based; 79 iBT). *Application deadline:* For fall admission, 1/5 priority date for domestic and international students; for spring admission, 10/1 priority date for domestic students, 10/1 for international students. Applications are processed on a rolling basis. Application fee: $75. Electronic applications accepted. *Expenses:* $13,347. *Financial support:* In 2016–17, 29 students received support, including 5 fellowships (averaging $14,000 per year), 4 research assistantships (averaging $600 per year), 26 teaching assistantships with full tuition reimbursements available (averaging $16,500 per year); career-related internships or fieldwork, institutionally sponsored loans, scholarships/grants, health care benefits, and conference travel support also available. Financial award application deadline: 1/5; financial award applicants required to submit FAFSA. *Faculty research:* Geographical areas: Africa, Asia, early modern Europe, Latin America and Caribbean, modern Europe (Britain, France, Germany, Spain), North and South Atlantic, world, United States and Colonial America; thematic areas: African-American, gender, imperialism and colonialism, intellectual/cultural/religious, political, public history, medicine/disability/science/knowledge, slavery, transnational/international, urban. *Total annual research expenditures:* $35,000. *Unit head:* Dr. Victoria Wolcott, Chair, 716-645-3435, Fax: 716-645-5954, E-mail: vwwolcott@buffalo.edu. *Application contact:* Sarah Handley-Cousins, Staff Assistant, 716-645-3433, Fax: 716-645-5954, E-mail: handley2@buffalo.edu.
Website: https://www.history.buffalo.edu

**The University of Akron,** Graduate School, Buchtel College of Arts and Sciences, Department of History, Akron, OH 44325. Offers MA, PhD. *Program availability:* Part-time. *Faculty:* 15 full-time (5 women), 4 part-time/adjunct (2 women). *Students:* 13 full-time (6 women), 12 part-time (5 women); includes 2 minority (1 Black or African American, non-Hispanic/Latino; 1 American Indian or Alaska Native, non-Hispanic/Latino). Average age 35. 19 applicants, 74% accepted, 8 enrolled. In 2016, 8 master's, 5 doctorates awarded. *Degree requirements:* For master's, one foreign language, thesis optional, written exams, seminars; for doctorate, 2 foreign languages, comprehensive exam, thesis/dissertation, written exams, oral exams. *Entrance requirements:* For master's, GRE General Test, minimum GPA of 3.0, writing sample, three letters of recommendation, letter of intent; for doctorate, GRE General Test, minimum GPA of 3.5, three letters of recommendation, personal statement, writing sample, evidence of reading knowledge in one foreign language. Additional exam requirements/recommendations for international students: Required—TOEFL (minimum score 580 paper-based; 92 iBT). *Application deadline:* For fall admission, 2/1 priority date for domestic and international students. Application fee: $45 ($70 for international students). Electronic applications accepted. *Expenses:* Tuition, state resident: full-time $8618; part-time $359 per credit hour. Tuition, nonresident: full-time $17,149; part-time $715 per credit hour. *Required fees:* $1652. *Financial support:* In 2016–17, 2 fellowships, 8 teaching assistantships with full tuition reimbursements were awarded. Financial award application deadline: 2/1. *Faculty research:* European, American, and world history. *Total annual research expenditures:* $15,444. *Unit head:* Dr. A. Martin Wainwright, Chair, 330-972-6512, E-mail: amartin@uakron.edu. *Application contact:* Dr. Martha Santos, Graduate Director, 330-972-2686, E-mail: santos@uakron.edu. Website: http://www.uakron.edu/history/

**The University of Alabama,** Graduate School, College of Arts and Sciences, Department of History, Tuscaloosa, AL 35487. Offers MA, PhD. *Faculty:* 27 full-time (12 women). *Students:* 38 full-time (16 women), 3 part-time (0 women); includes 3 minority (2 Black or African American, non-Hispanic/Latino; 1 Hispanic/Latino). Average age 31. 40 applicants, 50% accepted, 12 enrolled. In 2016, 12 master's, 4 doctorates awarded. Terminal master's awarded for partial completion of doctoral program. *Degree requirements:* For master's, one foreign language, thesis optional, oral exam; for doctorate, 2 foreign languages, comprehensive exam, thesis/dissertation, oral exams, written exam. *Entrance requirements:* For master's and doctorate, GRE General Test. *Application deadline:* For fall admission, 5/1 for domestic students. Applications are processed on a rolling basis. Application fee: $50 ($60 for international students). *Expenses:* Tuition, state resident: full-time $10,470. Tuition, nonresident: full-time $26,950. *Financial support:* In 2016–17, 29 students received support, including 6 fellowships with full tuition reimbursements available (averaging $10,000 per year), research assistantships (averaging $10,000 per year), 23 teaching assistantships with full tuition reimbursements available (averaging $10,200 per year); institutionally sponsored loans and unspecified assistantships also available. Financial award application deadline: 1/15. *Faculty research:* United States, modern European, Latin American, military, and southern U.S. history. *Unit head:* Dr. Joshua Rothman, Professor/Department Chair, 205-348-3818, E-mail: jrothman@ua.edu. *Application contact:* Dr. Lisa Lindquist Dorr, Graduate Director, 205-348-1859, E-mail: ldorr@bama.ua.edu.

**The University of Alabama at Birmingham,** College of Arts and Sciences, Program in History, Birmingham, AL 35294. Offers MA. *Program availability:* Part-time. *Degree requirements:* For master's, variable foreign language requirement, thesis or alternative. *Entrance requirements:* For master's, GRE General Test. Additional exam requirements/recommendations for international students: Required—TOEFL, TWE. Electronic applications accepted. Full-time tuition and fees vary according to course load and program. *Faculty research:* History of Europe, United States, Latin America, American South.

**The University of Alabama in Huntsville,** School of Graduate Studies, College of Arts, Humanities, and Social Sciences, Department of History, Huntsville, AL 35899. Offers MA. *Program availability:* Part-time, evening/weekend. *Degree requirements:* For master's, one foreign language, comprehensive exam, thesis or alternative, oral and written exams. *Entrance requirements:* For master's, GRE General Test, minimum GPA of 3.0, bachelor's degree in history or related area. Additional exam requirements/recommendations for international students: Required—TOEFL (minimum score 500 paper-based; 80 iBT), IELTS (minimum score 6.5). Electronic applications accepted. *Expenses:* Tuition, state resident: full-time $9834; part-time $600 per credit hour. Tuition, nonresident: full-time $21,830; part-time $1325 per credit hour. *Faculty research:* Public history, history of the U.S. space program, military history, history of science and technology, women in history.

**University of Alaska Fairbanks,** College of Liberal Arts, Department of Arctic and Northern Studies, Fairbanks, AK 99775-6460. Offers Arctic policy (MA); environmental politics and policy (MA); Northern history (MA). *Program availability:* Part-time. *Students:* 13 full-time (9 women), 15 part-time (11 women); includes 2 minority (1 American Indian or Alaska Native, non-Hispanic/Latino; 1 Two or more races, non-Hispanic/Latino), 5 international. Average age 35. 7 applicants, 43% accepted, 1 enrolled. In 2016, 8 master's awarded. *Degree requirements:* For master's, comprehensive exam, oral defense of project or thesis. *Entrance requirements:* For master's, bachelor's degree from accredited institution with minimum cumulative undergraduate and major GPA of 3.0. Additional exam requirements/recommendations for international students: Required—TOEFL (minimum score 550 paper-based; 79 iBT), IELTS (minimum score 6.5). *Application deadline:* For fall admission, 6/1 for domestic students, 3/1 for international students; for spring admission, 10/15 for domestic students, 9/1 for international students. Applications are processed on a rolling basis. Application fee: $60. Electronic applications accepted. *Expenses:* Tuition, state resident: full-time $7992; part-time $444 per credit. Tuition, nonresident: full-time $16,326; part-time $907 per credit. *Required fees:* $39 per credit. $322 per semester. Tuition and fees vary according to course level, course load, campus/location, program and reciprocity agreements. *Financial support:* In 2016–17, 1 research assistantship with full tuition reimbursement (averaging $7,574 per year), 9 teaching assistantships with full tuition reimbursements (averaging $5,653 per year) were awarded; fellowships with full tuition reimbursements, career-related internships or fieldwork, Federal Work-Study, scholarships/grants, health care benefits, and unspecified assistantships also available. Support available to part-time students. Financial award application deadline: 1/1; financial award applicants required to submit FAFSA. *Total annual research expenditures:* $64,000. *Unit head:* Mary Ehrlander, Director, 907-474-7126, Fax: 907-474-5817, E-mail: fynors@uaf.edu. *Application contact:* Mary Kreta, Director of Admissions, 907-474-7500, Fax: 907-474-7097, E-mail: admissions@uaf.edu. Website: http://www.uaf.edu/northern/

**University of Alberta,** Faculty of Graduate Studies and Research, Department of History and Classics, Edmonton, AB T6G 2E1, Canada. Offers ancient history (PhD); classical archaeology (MA, PhD); classical literature (PhD); classics (MA); history (MA, PhD). *Program availability:* Part-time, evening/weekend. *Degree requirements:* For master's, one foreign language, thesis (for some programs); for doctorate, one foreign language, thesis/dissertation. *Entrance requirements:* For master's, minimum B+ average; for doctorate, minimum A- average. Additional exam requirements/

recommendations for international students: Required—TOEFL (minimum score 580 paper-based). Electronic applications accepted. *Faculty research:* Western Canada, classical archaeology, Britain, Eastern Europe, East Asia.

**The University of Arizona,** College of Social and Behavioral Sciences, Department of History, Tucson, AZ 85721. Offers MA, PhD, Graduate Certificate. *Program availability:* Part-time. Terminal master's awarded for partial completion of doctoral program. *Degree requirements:* For master's, one foreign language, comprehensive exam, thesis optional; for doctorate, 2 foreign languages, comprehensive exam, thesis/dissertation. *Entrance requirements:* For master's, GRE General Test, 3 letters of recommendation, writing sample; for doctorate, GRE General Test, 3 letters of recommendation, statement of purpose, 2 writing samples. Additional exam requirements/recommendations for international students: Required—TOEFL (minimum score 550 paper-based; 79 iBT). Electronic applications accepted. *Faculty research:* Latin American history, European history, U.S. history, women's history, global/environmental history.

**University of Arkansas,** Graduate School, J. William Fulbright College of Arts and Sciences, Department of History, Fayetteville, AR 72701. Offers MA, PhD. *Program availability:* Part-time. In 2016, 7 master's, 7 doctorates awarded. *Degree requirements:* For master's, thesis optional; for doctorate, 2 foreign languages, thesis/dissertation. *Entrance requirements:* For master's, GRE General Test; for doctorate, GRE General Test, GRE Subject Test. *Application deadline:* For fall admission, 4/1 for international students; for spring admission, 10/1 for international students. Applications are processed on a rolling basis. Application fee: $40 ($50 for international students). Electronic applications accepted. *Financial support:* In 2016–17, 9 research assistantships, 9 teaching assistantships were awarded; fellowships with tuition reimbursements, career-related internships or fieldwork, and Federal Work-Study also available. Support available to part-time students. Financial award application deadline: 4/1; financial award applicants required to submit FAFSA. *Unit head:* Dr. Calvin White, Jr., Departmental Chairperson, 479-575-3001, Fax: 479-575-2775, E-mail: calvinwh@uark.edu. *Application contact:* Dr. Jim Gigantino, II, Graduate Coordinator, 479-575-3001, Fax: 479-575-2775, E-mail: jgiganti@uark.edu. Website: http://history.uark.edu/

**The University of British Columbia,** Faculty of Arts, Department of History, Vancouver, BC V6T 1Z1, Canada. Offers MA, PhD. *Faculty:* 33 full-time (11 women). *Students:* 67 full-time (22 women). 114 applicants, 21% accepted, 14 enrolled. In 2016, 9 master's, 4 doctorates awarded. *Degree requirements:* For master's, one foreign language, thesis, six 3-credit courses; for doctorate, one foreign language, comprehensive exam, thesis/dissertation, four or five 3-credit courses. *Entrance requirements:* For master's, four-year bachelor's degree; for doctorate, master's degree (or equivalent) in history, first-class (A) standing in graduate courses, language relevant to dissertation research. Additional exam requirements/recommendations for international students: Required—TOEFL (minimum score 90 iBT). *Application deadline:* For fall admission, 1/10 for domestic and international students. Applications are processed on a rolling basis. Application fee: $100 Canadian dollars ($162 Canadian dollars for international students). Electronic applications accepted. *Expenses:* Tuition, province resident: full-time $4708 Canadian dollars. Tuition, Canadian resident: full-time $4708 Canadian dollars. International tuition: $8271 Canadian dollars full-time. *Required fees:* $884 Canadian dollars. Tuition and fees vary according to program. *Financial support:* In 2016–17, 45 students received support, including 12 fellowships with partial tuition reimbursements available (averaging $18,000 per year), 3 research assistantships with tuition reimbursements available (averaging $3,310 per year), 32 teaching assistantships with tuition reimbursements available (averaging $10,914 per year); scholarships/grants, tuition waivers (partial), and unspecified assistantships also available. Financial award application deadline: 9/19. *Faculty research:* Canadian, British, European, modern Chinese and Japanese history; international relations. *Unit head:* Dr. Eagle Glassheim, Department Head, 604-822-4101, Fax: 604-822-6658, E-mail: eagle.g@ubc.ca. *Application contact:* Dr. Coll Thrush, Graduate Advisor, 604-827-3623, Fax: 604-822-6658, E-mail: coll.thrush@ubc.ca. Website: http://www.history.ubc.ca/

**University of Calgary,** Faculty of Graduate Studies, Faculty of Arts, Department of History, Calgary, AB T2N 1N4, Canada. Offers MA, PhD. *Program availability:* Part-time. *Degree requirements:* For master's, one foreign language, thesis; for doctorate, one foreign language, thesis/dissertation, 3 written comprehensive exams, oral candidacy exam. *Entrance requirements:* For master's, minimum GPA of 3.4, writing sample; for doctorate, sample of written work, master's degree in history. Additional exam requirements/recommendations for international students: Recommended—TOEFL. Electronic applications accepted. *Faculty research:* Military history, Canadian history, Latin American history, gender/women's history, native history.

**University of California, Berkeley,** Graduate Division, College of Letters and Science, Department of History, Berkeley, CA 94720-2550. Offers PhD. *Degree requirements:* For doctorate, variable foreign language requirement, comprehensive exam, thesis/dissertation. *Entrance requirements:* For doctorate, GRE General Test, minimum GPA of 3.0, 3 letters of recommendation, writing sample (not to exceed 10 pages), academic transcripts, 2 essays (statement of purpose, personal statement). Additional exam requirements/recommendations for international students: Required—TOEFL (minimum score 570 paper-based; 68 iBT). Electronic applications accepted. *Faculty research:* African, British, Byzantine, European (Ancient Greece and Rome, Medieval, Early Modern, Late Modern), Asian (China, Japan, South, Southeast), Jewish, Latin American, Middle Eastern, science, and United States history.

**University of California, Berkeley,** Graduate Division, College of Letters and Science, Group in Ancient History and Mediterranean Archaeology, Berkeley, CA 94720-1500. Offers MA, PhD. *Students:* 14 full-time (8 women); includes 2 minority (1 Asian, non-Hispanic/Latino; 1 Hispanic/Latino). Average age 30. 45 applicants, 3 enrolled. In 2016, 1 master's, 3 doctorates awarded. Terminal master's awarded for partial completion of doctoral program. *Degree requirements:* For master's, one foreign language, exam or thesis; for doctorate, 2 foreign languages, thesis/dissertation, qualifying exam. *Entrance requirements:* For master's and doctorate, GRE General Test, minimum GPA of 3.0, 3 letters of recommendation. Additional exam requirements/recommendations for international students: Required—TOEFL (minimum score 570 paper-based; 90 iBT), TWE. *Application deadline:* For fall admission, 12/9 for domestic students. Application fee: $105 ($125 for international students). Electronic applications accepted. *Financial support:* Fellowships, research assistantships, teaching assistantships, career-related internships or fieldwork, institutionally sponsored loans, health care benefits, and unspecified assistantships available. *Unit head:* Prof. Carlos Norena, Chair, 510-643-8741, E-mail: casmaadm@berkeley.edu. *Application contact:* Miguel Valencia, Student Affairs Officer, 510-643-8741, Fax: 510-643-2959, E-mail: casmaadm@berkeley.edu. Website: http://ahma.berkeley.edu

**University of California, Davis,** Graduate Studies, Program in History, Davis, CA 95616. Offers MA, PhD. Terminal master's awarded for partial completion of doctoral program. *Degree requirements:* For master's, one foreign language, comprehensive exam (for some programs), thesis (for some programs); for doctorate, 2 foreign languages, thesis/dissertation. *Entrance requirements:* For master's, GRE General Test, minimum GPA of 3.0, writing sample; for doctorate, GRE General Test, master's degree,

## History

writing sample. Additional exam requirements/recommendations for international students: Required—TOEFL (minimum score 550 paper-based). Electronic applications accepted. *Faculty research:* American social, cultural, and western history; modern and early history; modern European, East Asian, and Latin American history; history of science and medicine; cross-cultural history of women.

**University of California, Irvine,** School of Humanities, Department of History, Irvine, CA 92697. Offers MA, PhD. *Students:* 39 full-time (23 women); includes 14 minority (2 Black or African American, non-Hispanic/Latino; 2 Asian, non-Hispanic/Latino; 5 Hispanic/Latino; 5 Two or more races, non-Hispanic/Latino), 8 international. Average age 32. 52 applicants, 25% accepted, 10 enrolled. In 2016, 6 master's, 12 doctorates awarded. *Degree requirements:* For doctorate, thesis/dissertation. *Entrance requirements:* For master's and doctorate, GRE General Test, minimum GPA of 3.0. Additional exam requirements/recommendations for international students: Required—TOEFL (minimum score 550 paper-based). *Application deadline:* For fall admission, 1/2 priority date for domestic students, 1/2 for international students. Application fee: $105 ($125 for international students). Electronic applications accepted. *Financial support:* Fellowships, research assistantships with full tuition reimbursements, teaching assistantships, institutionally sponsored loans, traineeships, health care benefits, and unspecified assistantships available. Financial award application deadline: 3/1; financial award applicants required to submit FAFSA. *Faculty research:* European, U.S., Latin American, ancient, and East Asian history. *Unit head:* Prof. David Igler, Chair, 949-824-9313, E-mail: digler@uci.edu. *Application contact:* Yuting Wu, Graduate Coordinator, 949-824-5891, E-mail: yutingw6@uci.edu.
Website: http://www.hnet.uci.edu/history/

**University of California, Los Angeles,** Graduate Division, College of Letters and Science, Department of History, Los Angeles, CA 90095. Offers MA, PhD, MLIS/MA. Terminal master's awarded for partial completion of doctoral program. *Degree requirements:* For master's, one foreign language, comprehensive exam; for doctorate, variable foreign language requirement, thesis/dissertation, oral and written qualifying exams. *Entrance requirements:* For doctorate, GRE General Test, bachelor's degree; minimum undergraduate GPA of 3.0, 3.5 graduate (or its equivalent if letter grade system not used). Additional exam requirements/recommendations for international students: Required—TOEFL. Electronic applications accepted.

**University of California, Riverside,** Graduate Division, Department of History, Riverside, CA 92521-0102. Offers archival management (MA); history (PhD). *Program availability:* Part-time. Terminal master's awarded for partial completion of doctoral program. *Degree requirements:* For master's, one foreign language, comprehensive exam, internship report and oral exams, or thesis; for doctorate, 2 foreign languages, thesis/dissertation, qualifying exams. *Entrance requirements:* For master's and doctorate, GRE General Test, minimum GPA of 3.2. Additional exam requirements/recommendations for international students: Required—TOEFL (minimum score 550 paper-based; 80 iBT). Electronic applications accepted. *Expenses:* Tuition, state resident: full-time $16,666. Tuition, nonresident: full-time $31,768. *Required fees:* $11,055.54 per quarter. $3685.18 per quarter. Tuition and fees vary according to campus/location and program. *Faculty research:* Native American history, United States, public history, Europe, Latin America.

**University of California, San Diego,** Graduate Division, Department of History, La Jolla, CA 92093. Offers history (MA, PhD); Judaic studies (MA). *Students:* 93 full-time (38 women), 2 part-time (1 woman). 119 applicants, 19% accepted, 12 enrolled. In 2016, 7 master's, 7 doctorates awarded. *Degree requirements:* For master's, one foreign language, comprehensive exam; for doctorate, one foreign language, comprehensive exam, thesis/dissertation. *Entrance requirements:* For master's, GRE General Test, minimum GPA of 3.0; for doctorate, GRE General Test, writing sample (7-15 pages long), preferably in a history course. Additional exam requirements/recommendations for international students: Required—TOEFL (minimum score 550 paper-based; 80 iBT), IELTS (minimum score 7). *Application deadline:* For fall admission, 1/9 for domestic students. Application fee: $105 ($125 for international students). Electronic applications accepted. *Expenses:* Tuition, state resident: full-time $11,220. Tuition, nonresident: full-time $26,322. *Required fees:* $1864. *Financial support:* Fellowships, research assistantships, teaching assistantships, career-related internships or fieldwork, scholarships/grants, and readerships available. Financial award applicants required to submit FAFSA. *Faculty research:* Ancient history, east Asian history, history of science, Jewish studies, global transnational studies. *Unit head:* Pamela Radcliff, Chair, 858-534-8919, E-mail: pradcliff@ucsd.edu. *Application contact:* Amber Rieder, Graduate Coordinator, 858-822-0664, E-mail: arieder@ucsd.edu.
Website: http://history.ucsd.edu

**University of California, Santa Barbara,** Graduate Division, College of Letters and Sciences, Division of Humanities and Fine Arts, Department of History, Santa Barbara, CA 93106-9410. Offers European medieval studies (PhD); global studies (PhD); public historical studies (PhD); technology and society (PhD); women's studies (PhD); MA/PhD. *Degree requirements:* For doctorate, variable foreign language requirement, comprehensive exam, thesis/dissertation. *Entrance requirements:* For doctorate, GRE. Additional exam requirements/recommendations for international students: Required—TOEFL (minimum score 550 paper-based; 80 iBT), IELTS (minimum score 7). Electronic applications accepted. *Faculty research:* Europe, United States, Latin America, Africa, Middle East, East Asia.

**University of California, Santa Cruz,** Division of Graduate Studies, Division of Humanities, Department of History, Santa Cruz, CA 95064. Offers MA, PhD. *Degree requirements:* For doctorate, variable foreign language requirement, comprehensive exam, thesis/dissertation, qualifying exam. *Entrance requirements:* For master's and doctorate, GRE, writing sample of up to 30 pages. Additional exam requirements/recommendations for international students: Required—TOEFL (minimum score 550 paper-based; 83 iBT); Recommended—IELTS (minimum score 8). Electronic applications accepted. *Faculty research:* Comparative, interdisciplinary approach to history; the Americas, Asia, the Islamic world, and Europe since 1500; society history.

**University of Central Arkansas,** Graduate School, College of Liberal Arts, Department of History, Conway, AR 72035-0001. Offers MA. *Program availability:* Part-time. *Degree requirements:* For master's, one foreign language, comprehensive exam, thesis optional. *Entrance requirements:* For master's, GRE General Test, minimum GPA of 2.7. Additional exam requirements/recommendations for international students: Required—TOEFL (minimum score 550 paper-based). Electronic applications accepted. *Faculty research:* History Day, Russian culture.

**University of Central Florida,** College of Arts and Humanities, Department of History, Orlando, FL 32816. Offers MA. *Program availability:* Part-time, evening/weekend. *Faculty:* 28 full-time (16 women), 21 part-time/adjunct (8 women). *Students:* 31 full-time (10 women), 19 part-time (8 women); includes 11 minority (4 Black or African American, non-Hispanic/Latino; 1 Asian, non-Hispanic/Latino; 6 Hispanic/Latino). Average age 29. 12 applicants, 67% accepted, 7 enrolled. In 2016, 10 master's awarded. *Degree requirements:* For master's, thesis, written exam. *Entrance requirements:* For master's, GRE General Test, minimum GPA of 3.0 in last 60 hours. Additional exam requirements/recommendations for international students: Required—TOEFL. *Application deadline:* For fall admission, 6/1 for domestic students; for spring admission, 12/1 for domestic

students. Application fee: $30. Electronic applications accepted. *Expenses:* Tuition, state resident: part-time $288.16 per credit hour. Tuition, nonresident: part-time $1071.31 per credit hour. *Financial support:* In 2016-17, 12 students received support, including 5 fellowships with partial tuition reimbursements available (averaging $4,800 per year), 6 research assistantships with partial tuition reimbursements available (averaging $6,921 per year), 7 teaching assistantships with partial tuition reimbursements available (averaging $7,166 per year); career-related internships or fieldwork, Federal Work-Study, institutionally sponsored loans, tuition waivers (partial), and unspecified assistantships also available. Financial award application deadline: 3/1; financial award applicants required to submit FAFSA. *Unit head:* Dr. Peter Larson, Interim Chair, 407-823-6466, E-mail: john.sacher@ucf.edu. *Application contact:* Assistant Director, Graduate Admissions, 407-823-2766, Fax: 407-823-6442, E-mail: gradadmissions@ucf.edu.
Website: http://history.cah.ucf.edu/

**University of Central Missouri,** The Graduate School, Warrensburg, MO 64093. Offers accountancy (MA); accounting (MBA); applied mathematics (MS); aviation safety (MA); biology (MS); business administration (MBA); career and technical education leadership (MS); college student personnel administration (MS); communication (MA); computer science (MS); counseling (MS); criminal justice (MS); educational leadership (Ed S); educational technology (MS); elementary and early childhood education (MSE); English (MA); environmental studies (MA); finance (MBA); history (MA); human services/educational technology (Ed S); human services/learning resources (Ed S); human services/professional counseling (Ed S); industrial hygiene (MS); industrial management (MS); information systems (MBA); information technology (MS); kinesiology (MS); library science and information services (MS); literacy education (MSE); marketing (MBA); mathematics (MS); music (MA); occupational safety management (MS); psychology (MS); rural family nursing (MS); school administration (MSE); social gerontology (MS); sociology (MA); special education (MSE); speech language pathology (MS); superintendency (Ed S); teaching (MAT); teaching English as a second language (MA); technology (MS); technology management (PhD); theatre (MA). *Program availability:* Part-time, 100% online, blended/hybrid learning. *Degree requirements:* For master's and Ed S, comprehensive exam (for some programs), thesis (for some programs). *Entrance requirements:* Additional exam requirements/recommendations for international students: Required—TOEFL (minimum score 550 paper-based; 79 iBT). Electronic applications accepted.

**University of Central Oklahoma,** The Jackson College of Graduate Studies, College of Liberal Arts, Department of History, Edmond, OK 73034-5209. Offers history (MA); museum studies (MA). *Program availability:* Part-time. *Degree requirements:* For master's, one foreign language, comprehensive exam (for some programs), thesis (for some programs). *Entrance requirements:* For master's, GRE, writing sample, essay. Additional exam requirements/recommendations for international students: Required—TOEFL (minimum score 550 paper-based; 79 iBT), IELTS (minimum score 6.5). Electronic applications accepted. *Faculty research:* China, Russia, civil war, American naval logistics.

**University of Chicago,** Division of the Social Sciences, Department of History, Chicago, IL 60637. Offers PhD. *Students:* 177 full-time (73 women); includes 47 minority (10 Black or African American, non-Hispanic/Latino; 6 Asian, non-Hispanic/Latino; 19 Hispanic/Latino; 12 Two or more races, non-Hispanic/Latino), 35 international. 371 applicants, 13% accepted, 21 enrolled. In 2016, 28 doctorates awarded. *Degree requirements:* For doctorate, variable foreign language requirement, thesis/dissertation, oral exams in 3 fields. *Entrance requirements:* For doctorate, GRE General Test. Additional exam requirements/recommendations for international students: Required—TOEFL (minimum score 104 iBT), IELTS (minimum score 7). *Application deadline:* For fall admission, 12/15 for domestic and international students. Application fee: $90. Electronic applications accepted. *Financial support:* In 2016-17, 21 students received support, including 21 fellowships with full tuition reimbursements available (averaging $23,000 per year); Federal Work-Study, institutionally sponsored loans, scholarships/grants, and health care benefits also available. Financial award application deadline: 12/15. *Unit head:* Dr. Emilio Kouri, Chair, 773-834-4769, Fax: 773-702-7550, E-mail: kouri@uchicago.edu. *Application contact:* Office of the Dean of Students, 773-702-8415, E-mail: admissions@ssd.uchicago.edu.
Website: http://history.uchicago.edu

**University of Cincinnati,** Graduate School, McMicken College of Arts and Sciences, Department of History, Cincinnati, OH 45221. Offers MA, PhD. Terminal master's awarded for partial completion of doctoral program. *Degree requirements:* For master's, comprehensive exam, thesis optional; for doctorate, comprehensive exam, thesis/dissertation. *Entrance requirements:* For master's, GRE General Test, BA in history; for doctorate, GRE General Test, MA in history. Additional exam requirements/recommendations for international students: Required—TOEFL (minimum score 600 paper-based). Electronic applications accepted. *Expenses: Tuition, area resident:* Full-time $12,790; part-time $389 per credit hour. Tuition, state resident: full-time $13,290; part-time $419 per credit hour. Tuition, nonresident: full-time $24,532; part-time $976 per credit hour. *International tuition:* $24,832 full-time. *Required fees:* $3958; $140 per credit hour. Tuition and fees vary according to course load, degree level, program and reciprocity agreements. *Faculty research:* U.S. cultural and social history, women's history, U.S. and British intellectual history, modern Europe.

**University of Colorado Boulder,** Graduate School, College of Arts and Sciences, Department of History, Boulder, CO 80309. Offers MA, PhD. *Faculty:* 36 full-time (15 women). *Students:* 51 full-time (25 women), 6 part-time (2 women); includes 7 minority (1 Black or African American, non-Hispanic/Latino; 1 American Indian or Alaska Native, non-Hispanic/Latino; 2 Asian, non-Hispanic/Latino; 1 Hispanic/Latino; 2 Two or more races, non-Hispanic/Latino), 3 international. Average age 34. 93 applicants, 41% accepted, 12 enrolled. In 2016, 6 master's, 2 doctorates awarded. Terminal master's awarded for partial completion of doctoral program. *Degree requirements:* For master's, comprehensive exam, thesis optional; for doctorate, one foreign language, thesis/dissertation. *Entrance requirements:* For master's, GRE General Test, minimum undergraduate GPA of 2.75; for doctorate, GRE General Test. *Application deadline:* For fall admission, 12/1 for domestic and international students. Application fee: $60 ($80 for international students). Electronic applications accepted. Application fee is waived when completed online. *Financial support:* In 2016-17, 117 students received support, including 28 fellowships (averaging $8,266 per year), 2 research assistantships with full and partial tuition reimbursements available (averaging $27,267 per year), 35 teaching assistantships with full and partial tuition reimbursements available (averaging $29,001 per year); institutionally sponsored loans, scholarships/grants, health care benefits, and unspecified assistantships also available. Financial award applicants required to submit FAFSA. *Faculty research:* History, social history, cultural history, American history, modern history. *Total annual research expenditures:* $115,796. *Application contact:* E-mail: history@colorado.edu.
Website: http://www.colorado.edu/history/

**University of Colorado Colorado Springs,** College of Letters, Arts and Sciences, Department of History, Colorado Springs, CO 80918. Offers MA. *Program availability:* Part-time, evening/weekend. *Faculty:* 8 full-time (2 women). *Students:* 6 full-time (2 women), 36 part-time (15 women); includes 7 minority (3 Black or African American, non-Hispanic/Latino; 3 Hispanic/Latino; 1 Two or more races, non-Hispanic/Latino). Average age 35. 19 applicants, 89% accepted, 12 enrolled. In 2016, 6 master's awarded. *Degree requirements:* For master's, portfolio of 3-4 research projects, oral exam. *Entrance requirements:* For master's, minimum GPA of 3.0, writing sample. Additional exam requirements/recommendations for international students: Recommended—TOEFL (minimum score 550 paper-based; 80 iBT), IELTS (minimum score 6.5). *Application deadline:* Applications are processed on a rolling basis. Application fee: $60 ($100 for international students). Electronic applications accepted. *Expenses:* Tuition, state resident: full-time $9983. Tuition, nonresident: full-time $20,153. Tuition and fees vary according to course load, degree level, program and reciprocity agreements. *Financial support:* In 2016–17, 12 students received support. Federal Work-Study, scholarships/grants, and unspecified assistantships available. Support available to part-time students. Financial award application deadline: 3/1; financial award applicants required to submit FAFSA. *Faculty research:* Greek and Roman history; late antiquity; historiography; Greek and Latin languages/stylistics; ancient and Renaissance cultural history; early medieval history; Native American Indian ethno history east of the Mississippi; U.S. social history, 1865-1980; traditional West African (Yoruba) religion and syncretism; U.S. religious, political, economic, and cultural history; environmental history of modern India; Latin American history; Mexican history; history of cities, citizenship. *Unit head:* Dr. Christina Jimenez, Chair, 719-255-4079, Fax: 719-255-4068, E-mail: cjimenez@uccs.edu. *Application contact:* Ian Smith, Administrative Assistant, 719-255-4069, Fax: 719-255-4068, E-mail: ismith2@uccs.edu. Website: http://www.uccs.edu/~history/

**University of Colorado Denver,** College of Liberal Arts and Sciences, Department of History, Denver, CO 80217. Offers European history (MA); global history (MA); public history (MA); U.S. history (MA). *Program availability:* Part-time, evening/weekend. *Faculty:* 12 full-time (4 women), 2 part-time/adjunct (0 women). *Students:* 24 full-time (15 women), 16 part-time (10 women); includes 10 minority (1 Asian, non-Hispanic/Latino; 6 Hispanic/Latino; 3 Two or more races, non-Hispanic/Latino). Average age 35. 23 applicants, 70% accepted, 7 enrolled. In 2016, 15 master's awarded. *Degree requirements:* For master's, comprehensive exam, thesis optional, 36 semester hours (12 courses). *Entrance requirements:* For master's, GRE General Test, writing sample, minimum undergraduate GPA of 3.25, three letters of recommendation, statement of purpose addressing any weaknesses in academic record. Additional exam requirements/recommendations for international students: Required—TOEFL (minimum score 537 paper-based; 75 iBT); Recommended—IELTS (minimum score 6.5). *Application deadline:* For fall admission, 1/20 for domestic and international students; for spring admission, 10/1 for domestic and international students. Application fee: $50 ($75 for international students). Electronic applications accepted. *Expenses:* Tuition, state resident: full-time $11,006; part-time $474 per credit. Tuition, nonresident: full-time $28,212; part-time $1264 per credit hour. *Required fees:* $256 per semester. One-time fee: $94.32. Tuition and fees vary according to campus/location and program. *Financial support:* In 2016–17, 8 students received support. Fellowships, research assistantships, teaching assistantships, Federal Work-Study, institutionally sponsored loans, scholarships/grants, and traineeships available. Financial award application deadline: 4/1; financial award applicants required to submit FAFSA. *Faculty research:* Uses of pre-modern Islamic heritage in modern India; relationship between liberal understandings of democracy, crime, and police discretion; relationships between gender, class, health, and welfare in nineteenth and early twentieth century England; U.S. business cultures and their influences on marketing and personnel practices; intersection of business and political ideologies; social and environmental history of the Rocky Mountain West. *Unit head:* Dr. Kariann Akemi Yokota, Associate Chair, 303-315-1784, E-mail: kariann.yokota@ucdenver.edu. *Application contact:* Tabitha Fitzpatrick, Program Assistant, 303-315-1776, E-mail: tabitha.fitzpatrick@ucdenver.edu. Website: http://www.ucdenver.edu/academics/colleges/CLAS/Departments/history/Programs/Masters/Pages/MasterofArts.aspx

**University of Connecticut,** Graduate School, College of Liberal Arts and Sciences, Department of History, Storrs, CT 06269. Offers MA, PhD. Terminal master's awarded for partial completion of doctoral program. *Degree requirements:* For master's, comprehensive exam; for doctorate, thesis/dissertation. *Entrance requirements:* For master's and doctorate, GRE General Test, GRE Subject Test. Additional exam requirements/recommendations for international students: Required—TOEFL (minimum score 550 paper-based). Electronic applications accepted.

**University of Delaware,** College of Arts and Sciences, Department of History, Hagley Program in the History of Technology and Industrialization, Newark, DE 19716. Offers MA, PhD. *Degree requirements:* For master's, thesis optional; for doctorate, comprehensive exam, thesis/dissertation. *Entrance requirements:* For master's and doctorate, interview. Electronic applications accepted.

**University of Denver,** University College, Denver, CO 80208. Offers arts and culture (MA, Certificate); communication management (MS, Certificate), including translation studies (Certificate); world history and culture (Certificate); environmental policy and management (MS); geographic information systems (MS); global affairs (MA, Certificate), including human capital in organizations (Certificate), philanthropic leadership (Certificate), project management (Certificate), strategic innovation and change (Certificate); healthcare leadership (MS); information communications and technology (MS); leadership and organizations (MS); professional creative writing (MA, Certificate), including emergency planning and response (Certificate), organizational security (Certificate); security management (MS, Certificate); strategic human resources (Certificate). *Program availability:* Part-time, evening/weekend, online learning. *Faculty:* 118 part-time/adjunct (62 women). *Students:* 59 full-time (22 women), 1,285 part-time (750 women); includes 316 minority (111 Black or African American, non-Hispanic/Latino; 8 American Indian or Alaska Native, non-Hispanic/Latino; 39 Asian, non-Hispanic/Latino; 123 Hispanic/Latino; 3 Native Hawaiian or other Pacific Islander, non-Hispanic/Latino; 32 Two or more races, non-Hispanic/Latino), 85 international. Average age 35. 703 applicants, 89% accepted, 390 enrolled. In 2016, 428 master's, 138 other advanced degrees awarded. *Degree requirements:* For master's, capstone project. *Entrance requirements:* For master's, transcripts, two letters of recommendation, personal statement, resume. Additional exam requirements/recommendations for international students: Required—TOEFL (minimum score 550 paper-based; 80 iBT). *Application deadline:* For fall admission, 6/21 priority date for domestic students, 5/1 priority date for international students; for winter admission, 9/14 priority date for domestic students, 9/19 priority date for international students; for spring admission, 1/11 priority date for domestic students, 12/12 priority date for international students; for summer admission, 3/29 priority date for domestic students, 3/6 priority date for international students. Applications are processed on a rolling basis. Application fee: $75. Electronic applications accepted. *Expenses:* $7,236 per year full-time. *Financial support:* In 2016–17, 27 students received support, including 1 teaching assistantship (averaging $1,489 per year). Financial award applicants required to submit FAFSA. *Unit head:* Dr. Michael McGuire, Dean, 303-871-3518, Fax: 303-871-3303, E-mail: mmcguire@du.edu. *Application contact:* Information Contact, 303-871-2291, E-mail: ucoladm@du.edu. Website: http://universitycollege.du.edu/

**University of Florida,** Graduate School, College of Liberal Arts and Sciences, Department of History, Gainesville, FL 32611. Offers historic preservation (MA, PhD); history (MA, PhD); Jewish studies (MA); women's and gender studies (PhD); JD/MA; JD/PhD. *Program availability:* Part-time. Terminal master's awarded for partial completion of doctoral program. *Degree requirements:* For master's, variable foreign language requirement, thesis optional, 30 credit hours; for doctorate, variable foreign language requirement, comprehensive exam, thesis/dissertation, 90 credit hours. *Entrance requirements:* For master's and doctorate, GRE General Test, minimum GPA of 3.0. Additional exam requirements/recommendations for international students: Required—TOEFL (minimum score 550 paper-based; 80 iBT), IELTS (minimum score 6). Electronic applications accepted. *Faculty research:* Latin American and Caribbean history, nineteenth century U.S. history, medieval European history, African history and Atlantic world history.

**University of Georgia,** Franklin College of Arts and Sciences, Department of History, Athens, GA 30602. Offers MA, PhD. *Degree requirements:* For master's, one foreign language, thesis; for doctorate, one foreign language, thesis/dissertation. *Entrance requirements:* For master's and doctorate, GRE General Test. *Application deadline:* For fall admission, 7/1 priority date for domestic students; for spring admission, 11/15 for domestic students. Application fee: $50. Electronic applications accepted. *Financial support:* Fellowships, research assistantships, teaching assistantships, and unspecified assistantships available. *Unit head:* Dr. John Morrow, Head, 706-542-2510, E-mail: jmorrow@uga.edu. *Application contact:* Reinaldo L. Roman, Graduate Coordinator, 706-542-2501, E-mail: hiscoord@uga.edu. Website: http://www.uga.edu/history/

**University of Guelph,** Graduate Studies, College of Arts, Department of History, Guelph, ON N1G 2W1, Canada. Offers MA, PhD. MA, PhD offered jointly with University of Waterloo, Wilfrid Laurier University. *Program availability:* Part-time. *Degree requirements:* For master's, one foreign language, thesis (for some programs); for doctorate, one foreign language, thesis/dissertation, 3 qualifying fields. *Entrance requirements:* For master's, minimum B+ average during previous 2 years of course work; for doctorate, minimum A- average in MA. Additional exam requirements/recommendations for international students: Required—TOEFL (minimum score 550 paper-based). Electronic applications accepted. *Faculty research:* Gender and family, Scottish history, rural and urban community studies, eighteenth century England, Canadian legal and social history, modern Europe.

**University of Hawaii at Manoa,** Graduate Division, College of Arts and Humanities, Department of History, Honolulu, HI 96822. Offers MA, PhD. *Program availability:* Part-time. *Degree requirements:* For master's, 2 foreign languages, thesis optional; for doctorate, 2 foreign languages, comprehensive exam, thesis/dissertation. *Entrance requirements:* For master's, GRE, minimum GPA of 3.0, writing sample; for doctorate, GRE, MA, sample of written work. Additional exam requirements/recommendations for international students: Required—TOEFL (minimum score 580 paper-based; 92 iBT), IELTS (minimum score 5). *Faculty research:* Asian, Pacific, world, American and European history.

**University of Houston,** College of Liberal Arts and Social Sciences, Department of History, Houston, TX 77204. Offers MA, PhD. *Program availability:* Part-time. Terminal master's awarded for partial completion of doctoral program. *Degree requirements:* For master's, one foreign language, thesis (for some programs); for doctorate, one foreign language, comprehensive exam, thesis/dissertation. *Entrance requirements:* For master's, GRE General Test, minimum GPA of 3.3; for doctorate, GRE General Test, minimum GPA of 3.67. Additional exam requirements/recommendations for international students: Required—TOEFL. Electronic applications accepted. *Faculty research:* U.S., Latin American, European, social, and women's history.

**University of Houston–Clear Lake,** School of Human Sciences and Humanities, Programs in Humanities and Fine Arts, Houston, TX 77058-1002. Offers history (MA); humanities (MA); literature (MA). *Program availability:* Part-time, evening/weekend, online learning. *Degree requirements:* For master's, thesis or alternative. *Entrance requirements:* For master's, GRE General Test. Additional exam requirements/recommendations for international students: Required—TOEFL (minimum score 550 paper-based). *Faculty research:* Digital media studies, Latin American history, labor history, Chaucer evolution versus creationism debate.

**University of Idaho,** College of Graduate Studies, College of Letters, Arts and Social Sciences, Department of History, Moscow, ID 83844. Offers MA, PhD. *Faculty:* 5 full-time. *Students:* 7 full-time, 5 part-time. Average age 33. In 2016, 3 master's, 1 doctorate awarded. *Degree requirements:* For doctorate, thesis/dissertation. *Entrance requirements:* For master's and doctorate, minimum GPA of 3.0. Additional exam requirements/recommendations for international students: Required—TOEFL. *Application deadline:* For fall admission, 8/1 for domestic students; for spring admission, 12/15 for domestic students. Applications are processed on a rolling basis. Application fee: $60. Electronic applications accepted. *Expenses:* Tuition, state resident: full-time $6460; part-time $414 per credit hour. Tuition, nonresident: full-time $21,268; part-time $1237 per credit hour. *Required fees:* $2070; $60 per credit hour. Full-time tuition and fees vary according to course load and reciprocity agreements. *Financial support:* Research assistantships and teaching assistantships available. Financial award applicants required to submit FAFSA. *Unit head:* Dr. Sean Quinlan, Chair, 208-885-6253, E-mail: history@uidaho.edu. *Application contact:* Sean Scoggin, Graduate Recruitment Coordinator, 208-885-4723, Fax: 208-885-4406, E-mail: graduateadmissions@uidaho.edu. Website: https://www.uidaho.edu/class/history

**University of Illinois at Chicago,** College of Liberal Arts and Sciences, Department of History, Chicago, IL 60607-7128. Offers MA, MAT, PhD. *Program availability:* Part-time, evening/weekend. *Degree requirements:* For master's, one foreign language, comprehensive exam; for doctorate, 2 foreign languages, comprehensive exam, thesis/dissertation. *Entrance requirements:* For master's and doctorate, GRE General Test, previous course work in a foreign language, minimum GPA of 3.0. Additional exam requirements/recommendations for international students: Required—TOEFL. Electronic applications accepted. *Faculty research:* American urban and immigration history, early modern European history, Eastern European history.

**University of Illinois at Springfield,** Graduate Programs, College of Liberal Arts and Sciences, Program in History, Springfield, IL 62703-5407. Offers MA. *Program availability:* Part-time, evening/weekend. *Faculty:* 5 full-time (2 women). *Students:* 10 full-time (4 women), 16 part-time (6 women); includes 2 minority (1 Black or African American, non-Hispanic/Latino; 1 Two or more races, non-Hispanic/Latino). Average age 34. 19 applicants, 58% accepted, 7 enrolled. In 2016, 13 master's awarded. *Degree requirements:* For master's, internship; closure exercise; position paper and historiography; thesis or project. *Entrance requirements:* For master's, BA in history or related field, minimum undergraduate GPA of 3.0, writing sample, statement of purpose. Additional exam requirements/recommendations for international students: Required—TOEFL (minimum score 500 paper-based; 61 iBT). *Application deadline:* Applications are processed on a rolling basis. Application fee: $60 ($75 for international students). Electronic applications accepted. *Expenses:* Tuition, state resident: part-time $329 per credit hour. Tuition, nonresident: part-time $675 per credit hour. *Financial support:* In

## History

2016–17, fellowships with full tuition reimbursements (averaging $9,900 per year), research assistantships with full tuition reimbursements (averaging $9,991 per year), teaching assistantships with full tuition reimbursements (averaging $10,059 per year) were awarded; career-related internships or fieldwork, Federal Work-Study, scholarships/grants, health care benefits, and unspecified assistantships also available. Support available to part-time students. Financial award application deadline: 11/15; financial award applicants required to submit FAFSA. *Unit head:* Dr. David Bertaina, Program Administrator, 217-206-8412, Fax: 217-206-6217, E-mail: dbert3@uis.edu. *Application contact:* Dr. Cecelia Cornell, Associate Vice Chancellor for Graduate Education, 217-206-7230, E-mail: ccorn1@uis.edu.
Website: http://www.uis.edu/history/curriculum/ma/

**University of Illinois at Urbana–Champaign,** Graduate College, College of Liberal Arts and Sciences, Department of History, Champaign, IL 61820. Offers MA, PhD.

**University of Indianapolis,** Graduate Programs, College of Arts and Sciences, Department of History and Political Science, Indianapolis, IN 46227-3697. Offers history (MA); international relations (MA). *Program availability:* Part-time, evening/weekend. *Degree requirements:* For master's, thesis optional. *Entrance requirements:* For master's, GRE Subject Test, minimum GPA of 3.0, 3 letters of recommendation. Additional exam requirements/recommendations for international students: Required—TOEFL (minimum score 550 paper-based). Electronic applications accepted.

**The University of Iowa,** Graduate College, College of Liberal Arts and Sciences, Department of History, Iowa City, IA 52242-1316. Offers MA, PhD. *Degree requirements:* For master's, thesis optional, exam; for doctorate, comprehensive exam, thesis/dissertation. *Entrance requirements:* For master's and doctorate, GRE General Test, minimum GPA of 3.0. Additional exam requirements/recommendations for international students: Required—TOEFL (minimum score 550 paper-based; 81 iBT). Electronic applications accepted.

**The University of Kansas,** Graduate Studies, College of Liberal Arts and Sciences, Department of History, Lawrence, KS 66045. Offers MA, PhD. *Program availability:* Part-time. *Students:* 52 full-time (16 women), 4 part-time (1 woman); includes 5 minority (2 Hispanic/Latino; 3 Two or more races, non-Hispanic/Latino), 6 international. Average age 33. 52 applicants, 31% accepted, 8 enrolled. In 2016, 2 master's, 12 doctorates awarded. *Entrance requirements:* For master's and doctorate, GRE General Test, two-page statement of objectives, writing sample (20-25 pages maximum), three letters of reference, transcripts, curriculum vitae. Additional exam requirements/recommendations for international students: Required—TOEFL or IELTS. *Application deadline:* For fall admission, 1/1 for domestic and international students. Application fee: $65 ($85 for international students). Electronic applications accepted. *Financial support:* Fellowships, research assistantships, teaching assistantships, and unspecified assistantships available. Financial award application deadline: 1/1. *Faculty research:* Environmental history, early American history, modern European history. *Unit head:* Eve Levin, Chair, 785-864-9463, E-mail: evelevin@ku.edu. *Application contact:* Emily Lowrance-Floyd, Graduate Program Administrator, 785-864-9438, E-mail: lowrance@ku.edu.
Website: http://www.history.ku.edu/

**University of Kentucky,** Graduate School, College of Arts and Sciences, Program in History, Lexington, KY 40506-0032. Offers MA, PhD. *Program availability:* Part-time. *Degree requirements:* For master's, one foreign language, comprehensive exam, thesis optional; for doctorate, variable foreign language requirement, comprehensive exam, thesis/dissertation. *Entrance requirements:* For master's, GRE General Test, minimum undergraduate GPA of 2.75; for doctorate, GRE General Test, minimum graduate GPA of 3.0. Additional exam requirements/recommendations for international students: Required—TOEFL (minimum score 550 paper-based). Electronic applications accepted. *Faculty research:* English, British, European history; U.S. social, political and diplomatic history; U.S. early national history; U.S. Southern history; Native American and African-American history.

**University of Louisiana at Lafayette,** College of Liberal Arts, Department of History and Geography, Lafayette, LA 70504. Offers history (MA). *Program availability:* Part-time. *Degree requirements:* For master's, one foreign language, thesis or alternative. *Entrance requirements:* For master's, GRE General Test, minimum GPA of 2.75. Additional exam requirements/recommendations for international students: Required—TOEFL (minimum score 550 paper-based). Electronic applications accepted.

**University of Louisiana at Monroe,** Graduate School, College of Arts, Education, and Sciences, Department of History, Monroe, LA 71209-0001. Offers MA. *Program availability:* Part-time, evening/weekend. *Faculty:* 3 full-time (1 woman). *Students:* 2 full-time (0 women), 3 part-time (2 women). Average age 39. 34 applicants, 26% accepted. In 2016, 7 master's awarded. *Degree requirements:* For master's, thesis (for some programs). *Entrance requirements:* For master's, GRE General Test, minimum undergraduate GPA of 2.5. Additional exam requirements/recommendations for international students: Required—TOEFL (minimum score 500 paper-based; 61 iBT). *Application deadline:* For fall admission, 8/24 priority date for domestic students, 7/1 for international students; for winter admission, 12/14 priority date for domestic students; for spring admission, 1/19 for domestic students, 11/1 for international students. Applications are processed on a rolling basis. Application fee: $20 ($30 for international students). Electronic applications accepted. *Expenses:* Tuition, state resident: full-time $6489. Tuition, nonresident: full-time $18,589. *Required fees:* $8984. Tuition and fees vary according to course level, course load, degree level and program. *Financial support:* Research assistantships, career-related internships or fieldwork, Federal Work-Study, and unspecified assistantships available. Financial award application deadline: 4/1; financial award applicants required to submit FAFSA. *Faculty research:* Early Louisiana settlements, Soviet history, Anglo-American relations, U.S./East European relations. *Unit head:* Dr. Monica Bontty, Head, 318-342-1542, E-mail: bontty@ulm.edu.
Website: http://www.ulm.edu/history/

**University of Louisville,** Graduate School, College of Arts and Sciences, Department of History, Louisville, KY 40292-0001. Offers history (MA); public history (Certificate). *Program availability:* Part-time. *Faculty:* 22 full-time (9 women), 4 part-time/adjunct (3 women). *Students:* 9 full-time (7 women), 13 part-time (8 women); includes 2 minority (1 Black or African American, non-Hispanic/Latino; 1 Two or more races, non-Hispanic/Latino). Average age 33. 16 applicants, 75% accepted, 6 enrolled. In 2016, 5 master's awarded. *Degree requirements:* For master's, variable foreign language requirement, comprehensive exam (for some programs), thesis. *Entrance requirements:* For master's, GRE General Test, statement of purpose, not to exceed 500 words, which describes in reasonably specific terms, academic and career objectives and how they can be advanced through work in program. Additional exam requirements/recommendations for international students: Required—TOEFL. *Application deadline:* For fall admission, 2/15 for domestic and international students; for winter admission, 12/1 for domestic students; for spring admission, 12/1 for domestic and international students. Application fee: $60. Electronic applications accepted. *Expenses:* Contact institution. *Financial support:* In 2016–17, 1 teaching assistantship with full tuition reimbursement (averaging $12,000 per year) was awarded; scholarships/grants also available. Financial award application deadline: 2/15. *Faculty research:* Ancient and Medieval Europe, U.S. social

and constitutional history, U.S. foreign relations and military, public history, Latin American and Borderlands. *Unit head:* Dr. Blake Beattie, Chairperson/Associate Professor, 502-852-6818, Fax: 502-852-0770, E-mail: history@louisville.edu. *Application contact:* Jennifer T. Westerfeld, Associate Professor, 502-852-3756, Fax: 502-852-0770, E-mail: histgrad@louisville.edu.
Website: http://louisville.edu/history/

**University of Maine,** Graduate School, College of Liberal Arts and Sciences, Department of History, Orono, ME 04469. Offers MA, PhD. *Faculty:* 15 full-time (4 women), 7 part-time/adjunct (4 women). *Students:* 24 full-time (10 women), 12 part-time (7 women); includes 2 minority (both Two or more races, non-Hispanic/Latino), 2 international. Average age 37. 14 applicants, 79% accepted, 7 enrolled. In 2016, 2 master's, 4 doctorates awarded. *Degree requirements:* For master's, variable foreign language requirement, thesis optional; for doctorate, one foreign language, comprehensive exam, thesis/dissertation. *Entrance requirements:* For master's and doctorate, GRE General Test. Additional exam requirements/recommendations for international students: Required—TOEFL. *Application deadline:* For fall admission, 1/15 priority date for domestic and international students; for spring admission, 10/15 for domestic students, 10/15 priority date for international students. Applications are processed on a rolling basis. Application fee: $65. Electronic applications accepted. *Expenses:* Tuition, state resident: full-time $7524; part-time $2508 per credit. Tuition, nonresident: full-time $24,498; part-time $8166 per credit. *Required fees:* $1148; $571 per credit. *Financial support:* In 2016–17, 22 students received support, including 9 fellowships (averaging $15,000 per year), 12 teaching assistantships with tuition reimbursements available (averaging $14,600 per year); career-related internships or fieldwork, Federal Work-Study, and tuition waivers (full and partial) also available. Support available to part-time students. Financial award application deadline: 3/1. *Faculty research:* Borderlands, loyalism, trans-Atlantic, environmental, modern U.S. Total annual research expenditures: $45,048. *Unit head:* Dr. Stephen Miller, Chair, 207-581-1905, Fax: 207-581-1817, E-mail: stephen.miller@maine.edu. *Application contact:* Scott G. Delcourt, Assistant Vice President for Graduate Studies and Senior Associate Dean, 207-581-3291, Fax: 207-581-3232, E-mail: graduate@maine.edu.
Website: http://www.umaine.edu/history/

**The University of Manchester,** School of Arts, Histories and Cultures, Manchester, United Kingdom. Offers anthropology, media and performance (PhD); applied theatre professional (PhD); archaeology (PhD); art history and visual studies (PhD); arts management and cultural policy (PhD); classics and ancient history (PhD); composition (PhD); creative writing (PhD); drama (PhD); economic and social history (PhD); electroacoustic composition (PhD); English and American studies (PhD); history (PhD); humanitarianism and conflict response (PhD); museology (PhD); music (PhD); musicology (PhD); religions and theology (PhD).

**University of Manitoba,** Faculty of Graduate Studies, Faculty of Arts, Department of History, Winnipeg, MB R3T 2N2, Canada. Offers archival studies (MA); history (MA, PhD). MA offered jointly with The University of Winnipeg. *Degree requirements:* For master's, thesis; for doctorate, one foreign language, thesis/dissertation.

**University of Maryland, Baltimore County,** The Graduate School, College of Arts, Humanities and Social Sciences, Department of History, Program in Historical Studies, Baltimore, MD 21250. Offers MA. *Program availability:* Part-time, evening/weekend. *Faculty:* 15 full-time (9 women), 2 part-time/adjunct (0 women). *Students:* 15 full-time (9 women), 11 part-time (7 women); includes 4 minority (2 Black or African American, non-Hispanic/Latino; 2 Hispanic/Latino), 1 international. Average age 30. 22 applicants, 86% accepted, 9 enrolled. In 2016, 11 master's awarded. *Degree requirements:* For master's, thesis. *Entrance requirements:* For master's, GRE General Test, minimum GPA of 3.0. Additional exam requirements/recommendations for international students: Required—TOEFL. *Application deadline:* For fall admission, 2/15 priority date for domestic students, 1/1 for international students. Application fee: $50. Electronic applications accepted. *Expenses:* Tuition, state resident: full-time $13,294. Tuition, nonresident: full-time $20,286. *Financial support:* In 2016–17, 7 students received support, including 1 research assistantship with full tuition reimbursement available (averaging $12,560 per year), 6 teaching assistantships with tuition reimbursements available (averaging $12,560 per year); career-related internships or fieldwork, health care benefits, tuition waivers (partial), and unspecified assistantships also available. Financial award application deadline: 2/15; financial award applicants required to submit FAFSA. *Faculty research:* U.S. history, European history, public history, community engagement. Total annual research expenditures: $50,000. *Unit head:* Dr. Michelle R. Scott, Graduate Program Director, 410-455-2035, Fax: 410-455-1045, E-mail: mscott@umbc.edu. *Application contact:* Carla S. Ison, Graduate Program Coordinator, 410-455-2049, Fax: 410-455-1045, E-mail: ison@umbc.edu.
Website: http://www.umbc.edu/history

**University of Maryland, College Park,** Academic Affairs, College of Arts and Humanities, Department of History, College Park, MD 20742. Offers MA, PhD. *Degree requirements:* For master's, comprehensive exam, thesis optional; for doctorate, one foreign language, thesis/dissertation, oral and written exams. *Entrance requirements:* For master's, GRE General Test, minimum GPA of 3.25, writing sample, 3 letters of recommendation, statements of goals and research interests and experiences; for doctorate, GRE General Test, minimum GPA of 3.5. Additional exam requirements/recommendations for international students: Required—TOEFL. Electronic applications accepted. *Faculty research:* Ancient, British, East Asian, Latin American, and diplomatic history; papers of Samuel Gompers; Freedman and Southern Society; Caesarea excavations; Folger Institute.

**University of Maryland, College Park,** Academic Affairs, Program in History, Library, and Information Services, College Park, MD 20742. Offers MA/MLS. *Entrance requirements:* Additional exam requirements/recommendations for international students: Required—TOEFL. Electronic applications accepted.

**University of Massachusetts Amherst,** Graduate School, College of Humanities and Fine Arts, Department of History, Amherst, MA 01003. Offers MA, PhD. *Program availability:* Part-time. Terminal master's awarded for partial completion of doctoral program. *Degree requirements:* For master's, one foreign language, thesis or alternative; for doctorate, one foreign language, comprehensive exam, thesis/dissertation. *Entrance requirements:* For master's and doctorate, GRE General Test, writing sample. Additional exam requirements/recommendations for international students: Required—TOEFL (minimum score 550 paper-based; 80 iBT), IELTS (minimum score 6.5). Electronic applications accepted. *Faculty research:* Ancient and medieval history; global and comparative history; public history; history of science, technology, medicine and the environment; history of women, gender, sexuality and family.

**University of Massachusetts Boston,** College of Liberal Arts, Program in History, Boston, MA 02125-3393. Offers archival methods (MA). *Program availability:* Part-time, evening/weekend. *Faculty:* 17 full-time (10 women), 11 part-time/adjunct (6 women). *Students:* 9 full-time (6 women), 63 part-time (34 women); includes 9 minority (3 Black or African American, non-Hispanic/Latino; 2 Asian, non-Hispanic/Latino; 3 Hispanic/Latino; 1 Two or more races, non-Hispanic/Latino). Average age 35. 40 applicants, 88% accepted, 25 enrolled. In 2016, 22 master's awarded. *Degree requirements:* For master's, thesis, oral exam. *Entrance requirements:* For master's, minimum GPA of 2.75. *Application deadline:* For fall admission, 3/1 for domestic students; for spring admission, 11/1 for domestic students. *Expenses:* Tuition, state resident: full-time $16,863. Tuition, nonresident: full-time $32,913. *Required fees:* $177. *Financial support:* Research assistantships with full tuition reimbursements, teaching assistantships with full tuition reimbursements, career-related internships or fieldwork, Federal Work-Study, and unspecified assistantships available. Support available to part-time students. Financial award application deadline: 3/1; financial award applicants required to submit FAFSA. *Faculty research:* European intellectual history, American labor and social history in nineteenth century, colonial American Revolution, Afro-American Cold War. *Unit head:* Dr. Spencer DiScala, Director, 617-287-6860, E-mail: spencer.discala@umb.edu. *Application contact:* Peggy Roldan Patel, Graduate Admissions Coordinator, 617-287-6400, Fax: 617-287-6236, E-mail: bos.gadm@dpc.umassp.edu.

**University of Memphis,** Graduate School, College of Arts and Sciences, Department of History, Memphis, TN 38152. Offers ancient Egyptian history (MA, PhD). *Program availability:* 100% online. *Faculty:* 20 full-time (8 women), 3 part-time/adjunct (2 women). *Students:* 30 full-time (20 women), 37 part-time (20 women); includes 14 minority (11 Black or African American, non-Hispanic/Latino; 1 Hispanic/Latino; 2 Two or more races, non-Hispanic/Latino), 1 international. Average age 35. 40 applicants, 65% accepted, 17 enrolled. In 2016, 20 master's, 10 doctorates awarded. *Degree requirements:* For master's, comprehensive exam, thesis optional; for doctorate, one foreign language, comprehensive exam, thesis/dissertation, 60 credits plus 12 dissertation credits, 2 research seminars. *Entrance requirements:* For master's, GRE General Test or MAT, 18 undergraduate hours of course work in history with minimum GPA of 3.0, 2 letters of recommendation, writing sample, statement of research interest; for doctorate, GRE General Test, GRE Subject Test, MA in history or related field, three letters of recommendation, writing sample, statement of purpose. Additional exam requirements/recommendations for international students: Required—TOEFL (minimum score 550 paper-based; 79 iBT). *Application deadline:* For fall admission, 1/15 for domestic students; for spring admission, 9/15 for domestic students. Applications are processed on a rolling basis. Application fee: $35 ($60 for international students). Electronic applications accepted. *Expenses:* $5,231.50 per semester full-time in-state, $9,623.50 full-time out-of-state. *Financial support:* In 2016–17, 54 students received support, including 1 research assistantship with full tuition reimbursement available (averaging $12,000 per year), 20 teaching assistantships with full tuition reimbursements available (averaging $17,350 per year); career-related internships or fieldwork, Federal Work-Study, scholarships/grants, and unspecified assistantships also available. Financial award application deadline: 2/1; financial award applicants required to submit FAFSA. *Faculty research:* African/African-American history; U.S. history; ancient Egyptian history; modern European history; women, gender, and family studies. *Unit head:* Dr. Aram Goudsouzian, Chair, 901-678-2516, Fax: 901-678-2720, E-mail: agoudszn@memphis.edu. *Application contact:* Dr. Daniel Unowsky, Coordinator of Graduate Studies, 901-678-3385, Fax: 901-678-2720, E-mail: dunowsky@memphis.edu.
Website: http://history.memphis.edu/

**University of Miami,** Graduate School, College of Arts and Sciences, Department of History, Coral Gables, FL 33124. Offers MA, PhD. *Program availability:* Part-time. Terminal master's awarded for partial completion of doctoral program. *Degree requirements:* For master's, one foreign language, comprehensive exam, thesis optional; for doctorate, one foreign language, comprehensive exam, thesis/dissertation. *Entrance requirements:* For master's and doctorate, GRE General Test, GRE Subject Test. Additional exam requirements/recommendations for international students: Required—TOEFL (minimum score 550 paper-based; 59 iBT). Electronic applications accepted. *Faculty research:* Latin American, European, U.S., and public history.

**University of Michigan,** Rackham Graduate School, College of Literature, Science, and the Arts, Department of History, Ann Arbor, MI 48109. Offers PhD. *Degree requirements:* For doctorate, 2 foreign languages, thesis/dissertation, oral defense of dissertation, preliminary exam. *Entrance requirements:* For doctorate, GRE General Test, writing sample. Additional exam requirements/recommendations for international students: Required—TOEFL. Electronic applications accepted. *Expenses:* Tuition, state resident: full-time $21,466; part-time $1152 per credit hour. Tuition, nonresident: full-time $43,346; part-time $2367 per credit hour. Part-time tuition and fees vary according to course load, degree level and program. *Faculty research:* Europe, Latin America, Africa, Asia, Middle East/Near East, United States, world/global, science/medicine/technology, and topical/thematic history.

**University of Michigan,** Rackham Graduate School, College of Literature, Science, and the Arts, Department of Women's Studies, Ann Arbor, MI 48109. Offers English and women's studies (PhD); history and women's studies (PhD); LGBTQ studies (Certificate); psychology and women's studies (PhD); women's studies (Certificate). *Degree requirements:* For doctorate, variable foreign language requirement, comprehensive exam (for some programs), thesis/dissertation. *Entrance requirements:* For doctorate, GRE General Test, previous undergraduate coursework in women's studies. Electronic applications accepted. *Expenses:* Tuition, state resident: full-time $21,466; part-time $1152 per credit hour. Tuition, nonresident: full-time $43,346; part-time $2367 per credit hour. Part-time tuition and fees vary according to course load, degree level and program. *Faculty research:* LGBTQ studies, sexuality studies, feminist science studies, global feminism, health studies, international studies, cultural studies.

**University of Michigan,** Rackham Graduate School, College of Literature, Science, and the Arts, Doctoral Program in Anthropology and History, Ann Arbor, MI 48109. Offers PhD. *Degree requirements:* For doctorate, 2 foreign languages, thesis/dissertation, oral defense of dissertation, preliminary exam. *Entrance requirements:* For doctorate, GRE General Test, writing sample. Additional exam requirements/recommendations for international students: Required—TOEFL. Electronic applications accepted. *Expenses:* Tuition, state resident: full-time $21,466; part-time $1152 per credit hour. Tuition, nonresident: full-time $43,346; part-time $2367 per credit hour. Part-time tuition and fees vary according to course load, degree level and program. *Faculty research:* Historical anthropology.

**University of Michigan,** Rackham Graduate School, College of Literature, Science, and the Arts, Interdepartmental Program in Greek and Roman History, Ann Arbor, MI 48109. Offers PhD, Certificate. Certificate program only open to students already studying in another PhD program at University of Michigan. *Faculty:* 10 full-time (5 women). *Students:* 10 full-time (5 women). Average age 28. 25 applicants, 12% accepted, 1 enrolled. In 2016, 2 doctorates awarded. *Degree requirements:* For doctorate, 4 foreign languages, comprehensive exam, thesis/dissertation, oral defense of dissertation, dissertation prospectus, preliminary exams, qualifying exams. *Entrance requirements:* For doctorate, GRE, strict minimum of 2 years each of classical Greek and Latin. Additional exam requirements/recommendations for international students: Required—TOEFL (minimum score 560 paper-based). *Application deadline:* For fall admission, 12/15 for domestic and international students. Application fee: $75 ($90 for international students). Electronic applications accepted. *Expenses:* Tuition, state resident: full-time $21,466; part-time $1152 per credit hour. Tuition, nonresident: full-time $43,346; part-time $2367 per credit hour. Part-time tuition and fees vary according

to course load, degree level and program. *Financial support:* In 2016–17, 10 students received support, including 4 fellowships with full tuition reimbursements available (averaging $23,000 per year), 6 teaching assistantships with full tuition reimbursements available (averaging $19,000 per year); career-related internships or fieldwork, Federal Work-Study, institutionally sponsored loans, scholarships/grants, traineeships, health care benefits, tuition waivers (full), and unspecified assistantships also available. Financial award application deadline: 3/15. *Faculty research:* Greek history, Roman history, history of ancient Mediterranean cultures. *Unit head:* Ian Moyer, Associate Professor, 734-763-5855, Fax: 734-763-4959, E-mail: ianmoyer@umich.edu. *Application contact:* Sarah Kandell-Gritzmaker, Student Services Coordinator, 734-615-3181, Fax: 734-763-4959, E-mail: mcravens@umich.edu.
Website: http://www.lsa.umich.edu/ipgrh

**University of Minnesota, Twin Cities Campus,** Graduate School, College of Liberal Arts, Department of Classical and Near Eastern Studies, Minneapolis, MN 55455-0213. Offers ancient and medieval art and archaeology (MA, PhD); classics (MA, PhD); Greek (MA, PhD); Latin (MA, PhD); religions in antiquity (MA). *Program availability:* Part-time. Terminal master's awarded for partial completion of doctoral program. *Degree requirements:* For master's, 2 foreign languages, comprehensive exam, thesis or alternative; for doctorate, variable foreign language requirement, comprehensive exam, thesis/dissertation. *Entrance requirements:* For master's and doctorate, GRE, 3 letters of recommendation, writing sample, copies of transcripts, personal statement. Additional exam requirements/recommendations for international students: Required—TOEFL. Electronic applications accepted. *Faculty research:* Greek and Latin literature, religions in antiquity, ancient Near East.

**University of Minnesota, Twin Cities Campus,** Graduate School, College of Liberal Arts, Department of History, Minneapolis, MN 55455-0213. Offers MA, PhD. *Degree requirements:* For master's, one foreign language, comprehensive exam, thesis or alternative; for doctorate, 2 foreign languages, comprehensive exam, thesis/dissertation. *Entrance requirements:* For doctorate, GRE General Test, writing sample, letters of recommendation. Additional exam requirements/recommendations for international students: Required—TOEFL (minimum score 550 paper-based). Electronic applications accepted. *Faculty research:* Early and modern United States; medieval, early modern and modern Europe; Africa; East and South Asia; Latin America.

**University of Mississippi,** Graduate School, College of Liberal Arts, University, MS 38677. Offers anthropology (MA); biology (MS, PhD); chemistry (MS, PhD); economics (MA, PhD); English (MA, PhD); experimental psychology (PhD); history (MA, PhD); mathematics (MS, PhD); modern languages (MA); music (MM); philosophy (MA); physics (MA, MS, PhD); political science (MA, PhD); studio art (MFA). *Program availability:* Part-time. *Faculty:* 472 full-time (263 women), 75 part-time/adjunct (35 women). *Students:* 415 full-time (210 women), 57 part-time (20 women); includes 70 minority (35 Black or African American, non-Hispanic/Latino; 13 Asian, non-Hispanic/Latino; 14 Hispanic/Latino; 8 Two or more races, non-Hispanic/Latino), 102 international. Average age 27. *Degree requirements:* For doctorate, thesis/dissertation. *Entrance requirements:* For master's, GRE General Test, minimum GPA of 3.0; for doctorate, GRE General Test. Additional exam requirements/recommendations for international students: Required—TOEFL. *Application deadline:* For fall admission, 4/1 for domestic students; for spring admission, 10/1 for domestic students. Applications are processed on a rolling basis. Application fee: $40. Electronic applications accepted. *Financial support:* Fellowships, research assistantships, teaching assistantships, career-related internships or fieldwork, Federal Work-Study, institutionally sponsored loans, scholarships/grants, and unspecified assistantships available. Financial award application deadline: 3/1; financial award applicants required to submit FAFSA. *Unit head:* Dr. Lee Michael Cohen, Dean, 662-915-7177, Fax: 662-915-5792, E-mail: libarts@olemiss.edu. *Application contact:* Dr. Christy M. Wyandt, Associate Dean of Graduate School, 662-915-7474, Fax: 662-915-7577, E-mail: cwyandt@olemiss.edu.
Website: https://www.olemiss.edu

**University of Missouri,** Office of Research and Graduate Studies, College of Arts and Science, Department of History, Columbia, MO 65211. Offers MA, PhD. *Faculty:* 25 full-time (7 women). *Students:* 43 full-time (13 women), 6 part-time (5 women). *Degree requirements:* For master's, thesis; for doctorate, 2 foreign languages, comprehensive exam, thesis/dissertation. *Entrance requirements:* For master's, GRE General Test, minimum GPA of 3.0 in last 60 hours, 3.3 in undergraduate history courses; at least 18 hours in history; BA or BS; for doctorate, GRE General Test, minimum GPA of 3.0; MA in history (strongly preferred); master's thesis or research seminar paper. Additional exam requirements/recommendations for international students: Required—TOEFL (minimum score 500 paper-based; 61 iBT). *Application deadline:* For fall admission, 1/11 priority date for domestic and international students. Applications are processed on a rolling basis. Application fee: $75 ($90 for international students). Electronic applications accepted. *Expenses:* Tuition, state resident: full-time $6347; part-time $352.60 per credit hour. Tuition, nonresident: full-time $17,379; part-time $965.50 per credit hour. *Required fees:* $1035. Tuition and fees vary according to course load, campus/location and program. *Financial support:* Fellowships with full tuition reimbursements, research assistantships with full tuition reimbursements, teaching assistantships with full tuition reimbursements, institutionally sponsored loans, health care benefits, and unspecified assistantships available. *Faculty research:* U.S. history, African-American history, ancient history, Latin American history, Asian history.
Website: http://history.missouri.edu/programs/grad.html

**University of Missouri–Kansas City,** College of Arts and Sciences, Department of History, Kansas City, MO 64110-2499. Offers MA, PhD (interdisciplinary) offered through the School of Graduate Studies. *Program availability:* Part-time. *Faculty:* 16 full-time (7 women). *Students:* 7 full-time (4 women), 23 part-time (9 women); includes 2 minority (1 Asian, non-Hispanic/Latino; 1 Hispanic/Latino). Average age 32. 26 applicants, 54% accepted, 8 enrolled. In 2016, 8 master's awarded. *Degree requirements:* For master's, thesis optional; for doctorate, one foreign language, thesis/dissertation. *Entrance requirements:* For master's, GRE General Test, minimum GPA of 3.0, 2 writing samples, 3 letters of recommendation; for doctorate, GRE General Test. Additional exam requirements/recommendations for international students: Required—TOEFL (minimum score 550 paper-based; 80 iBT). *Application deadline:* For fall admission, 3/15 for domestic and international students; for spring admission, 10/1 priority date for domestic students, 10/1 for international students. Applications are processed on a rolling basis. Application fee: $45 ($50 for international students). Electronic applications accepted. *Financial support:* In 2016–17, 7 teaching assistantships with partial tuition reimbursements (averaging $11,200 per year) were awarded; career-related internships or fieldwork, Federal Work-Study, institutionally sponsored loans, and tuition waivers (full and partial) also available. Support available to part-time students. Financial award application deadline: 3/1; financial award applicants required to submit FAFSA. *Faculty research:* U.S. history, Europe, women and gender, religious studies, history of science. *Unit head:* Dr. John Herron, Chair, 816-235-2546, Fax: 816-235-5723, E-mail: herronj@umkc.edu. *Application contact:* Miriam Forman-Brunell, Master's Advisor, 816-235-5220, Fax: 816-235-5723, E-mail: formanbrunellm@umkc.edu.
Website: http://cas.umkc.edu/history/

## History

**University of Montana,** Graduate School, College of Humanities and Sciences, Department of History, Missoula, MT 59812-0002. Offers MA, PhD. *Degree requirements:* For master's, thesis or additional course work/professional paper. *Entrance requirements:* For master's, GRE General Test. Additional exam requirements/recommendations for international students: Required—TOEFL.

**University of Nebraska at Kearney,** College of Natural and Social Sciences, Department of History, Kearney, NE 68849-0001. Offers MA. *Program availability:* Part-time, evening/weekend, 100% online. *Faculty:* 14 full-time (4 women). *Students:* 7 full-time (5 women), 131 part-time (51 women); includes 10 minority (1 Black or African American, non-Hispanic/Latino; 1 American Indian or Alaska Native, non-Hispanic/Latino; 1 Asian, non-Hispanic/Latino; 3 Hispanic/Latino; 1 Native Hawaiian or other Pacific Islander, non-Hispanic/Latino; 3 Two or more races, non-Hispanic/Latino). Average age 38. 25 applicants, 100% accepted, 17 enrolled. In 2016, 49 master's awarded. *Degree requirements:* For master's, comprehensive exam, thesis optional. *Entrance requirements:* For master's, letters of recommendation, writing sample, letter of interest. Additional exam requirements/recommendations for international students: Recommended—TOEFL (minimum score 550 paper-based; 79 iBT), IELTS (minimum score 6.5). *Application deadline:* For fall admission, 6/15 for domestic and international students; for spring admission, 10/15 for domestic and international students; for summer admission, 3/15 for domestic and international students. Application fee: $45. Electronic applications accepted. *Expenses:* Tuition, state resident: full-time $4064; part-time $225.75 per credit hour. Tuition, nonresident: full-time $8915; part-time $495.25 per credit hour. *Required fees:* $772; $23 per credit hour. Part-time tuition and fees vary according to course load, campus/location, program and reciprocity agreements. *Financial support:* In 2016–17, 5 teaching assistantships with full tuition reimbursements (averaging $10,500 per year) were awarded; career-related internships or fieldwork, scholarships/grants, health care benefits, and unspecified assistantships also available. Support available to part-time students. Financial award application deadline: 2/28; financial award applicants required to submit FAFSA. *Faculty research:* Military history, labor history/labor and the law, state formation and nationalism, American intellectual history, Civil War and Reconstruction, South Asia, Africa, Medieval England, American West, Plains Indians, Soviet Union, cemeteries, gender, history of Christian mission. *Unit head:* Dr. Vernon Volpe, Chair, 308-865-8773, E-mail: volpev@unk.edu. *Application contact:* Amber Alexander, Advisor, Graduate History Program, 308-865-8766, E-mail: alexanderaj@unk.edu. Website: http://unkcms.unk.edu/academics/history/index.php

**University of Nebraska at Omaha,** Graduate Studies, College of Arts and Sciences, Department of History, Omaha, NE 68182. Offers MA. *Program availability:* Part-time, evening/weekend. *Faculty:* 6 full-time (3 women). *Students:* 1 full-time (0 women), 28 part-time (10 women); includes 4 minority (1 American Indian or Alaska Native, non-Hispanic/Latino; 2 Hispanic/Latino; 1 Native Hawaiian or other Pacific Islander, non-Hispanic/Latino). Average age 32. 11 applicants, 64% accepted, 6 enrolled. In 2016, 10 master's awarded. *Degree requirements:* For master's, comprehensive exam, thesis (for some programs). *Entrance requirements:* For master's, minimum GPA of 3.0, 21 hours of course work in history, 2 letters of recommendation, resume, statement of purpose, writing sample, official transcripts. Additional exam requirements/recommendations for international students: Required—TOEFL, IELTS, PTE. *Application deadline:* For fall admission, 7/5 priority date for domestic and international students; for spring admission, 11/15 priority date for domestic and international students. Applications are processed on a rolling basis. Application fee: $45. Electronic applications accepted. *Financial support:* In 2016–17, 6 students received support, including 6 teaching assistantships with tuition reimbursements available; fellowships, research assistantships with tuition reimbursements available, Federal Work-Study, institutionally sponsored loans, scholarships/grants, health care benefits, tuition waivers (partial), and unspecified assistantships also available. Support available to part-time students. Financial award application deadline: 3/1; financial award applicants required to submit FAFSA. *Unit head:* Dr. John Grigg, Chairperson, 402-554-2341, E-mail: graduate@unomaha.edu. *Application contact:* Dr. Jeanne Reames, Graduate Program Chair, 402-554-2341, E-mail: graduate@unomaha.edu.

**University of Nebraska–Lincoln,** Graduate College, College of Arts and Sciences, Department of History, Lincoln, NE 68588. Offers MA, PhD. *Degree requirements:* For master's, thesis optional; for doctorate, one foreign language, comprehensive exam, thesis/dissertation. *Entrance requirements:* For master's and doctorate, GRE General Test, GRE Subject Test, writing sample. Additional exam requirements/recommendations for international students: Required—TOEFL (minimum score 575 paper-based). Electronic applications accepted. *Faculty research:* Military history, indigenous peoples, German history, American history (American West society and culture).

**University of Nevada, Las Vegas,** Graduate College, College of Liberal Arts, Department of History, Las Vegas, NV 89154-5020. Offers MA, PhD. *Program availability:* Part-time. *Faculty:* 18 full-time (8 women). *Students:* 20 full-time (5 women), 24 part-time (18 women); includes 4 minority (1 Black or African American, non-Hispanic/Latino; 1 American Indian or Alaska Native, non-Hispanic/Latino; 2 Two or more races, non-Hispanic/Latino), 1 international. Average age 37. 25 applicants, 44% accepted, 9 enrolled. In 2016, 8 master's, 3 doctorates awarded. *Degree requirements:* For master's, one foreign language, comprehensive exam (for some programs), thesis (for some programs); for doctorate, 2 foreign languages, comprehensive exam, thesis/dissertation, written and oral examinations. *Entrance requirements:* For master's, minimum overall GPA of 3.0, 3.3 in history courses; 2 recommendations; statement of purpose; writing sample; for doctorate, GRE General Test, completion of significant course work at upper-division or graduate level in history; 3 recommendations; minimum overall GPA of 3.75 undergraduate, 3.5 graduate; statement of purpose; writing sample. Additional exam requirements/recommendations for international students: Required—TOEFL (minimum score 550 paper-based; 80 iBT), IELTS (minimum score 7). *Application deadline:* For fall admission, 4/15 for domestic students; for spring admission, 11/1 for domestic students. Application fee: $60 ($95 for international students). Electronic applications accepted. *Expenses:* $269.25 per credit, $792 per 3-credit course; $9,634 per year resident; $23,274 per year non-resident; $7,094 fees non-resident (7 credits or more); $1,307 annual health insurance fee. *Financial support:* In 2016–17, 2 research assistantships with partial tuition reimbursements (averaging $10,000 per year), 18 teaching assistantships with partial tuition reimbursements (averaging $13,667 per year) were awarded; institutionally sponsored loans, scholarships/grants, health care benefits, and unspecified assistantships also available. Financial award application deadline: 3/15. *Faculty research:* North American West, North American culture and society, European culture and society, American urban history, American gender and sexuality. *Total annual research expenditures:* $3,336. *Unit head:* Dr. Paul Werth, Chair/Professor, 702-895-3344, Fax: 702-895-1782, E-mail: paul.werth@unlv.edu. *Application contact:* Dr. William Bauer, Graduate Coordinator, 702-895-0918, Fax: 702-895-1782, E-mail: wbauer@unlv.edu. Website: http://history.unlv.edu/graduate.html

**University of Nevada, Reno,** Graduate School, College of Liberal Arts, Department of History, Reno, NV 89557. Offers MA, PhD. Terminal master's awarded for partial completion of doctoral program. *Degree requirements:* For master's, thesis optional; for doctorate, one foreign language, thesis/dissertation. *Entrance requirements:* For master's, GRE General Test, minimum GPA of 2.75; for doctorate, GRE General Test, minimum GPA of 3.0. Additional exam requirements/recommendations for international students: Required—TOEFL (minimum score 500 paper-based; 61 iBT), IELTS (minimum score 6). Electronic applications accepted. *Faculty research:* History of medicine, science, environmental history, western America, social/cultural history.

**University of New Brunswick Fredericton,** School of Graduate Studies, Faculty of Arts, Department of History, Fredericton, NB E3B 5A3, Canada. Offers MA, PhD. *Program availability:* Part-time. *Degree requirements:* For master's, thesis; for doctorate, thesis/dissertation. *Entrance requirements:* For master's, minimum GPA of 3.0, resume, writing sample, statement of research interests, honors degree in history or equivalent; for doctorate, minimum GPA of 3.0, statement of research interests, writing sample, master's degree in history. Additional exam requirements/recommendations for international students: Required—TWE (minimum score 5.5), TOEFL (minimum paper-based score 600) or IELTS (minimum score 7). Electronic applications accepted. *Faculty research:* Atlantic Canada, military, early modern-modern Europe, colonial North America, women's and gender history, history of medicine.

**University of New Hampshire,** Graduate School, College of Liberal Arts, Department of History, Durham, NH 03824. Offers history (MA, PhD); museum studies (MA). *Program availability:* Part-time. *Degree requirements:* For master's, thesis or alternative; for doctorate, 2 foreign languages, thesis/dissertation. *Entrance requirements:* For master's and doctorate, GRE General Test. Additional exam requirements/recommendations for international students: Required—TOEFL (minimum score 550 paper-based; 80 iBT). Electronic applications accepted.

**University of New Mexico,** Graduate Studies, College of Arts and Sciences, Program in History, Albuquerque, NM 87131-2039. Offers MA, PhD. *Program availability:* Part-time. *Faculty:* 17 full-time (7 women). *Students:* 30 full-time (14 women), 29 part-time (14 women); includes 14 minority (1 Black or African American, non-Hispanic/Latino; 4 American Indian or Alaska Native, non-Hispanic/Latino; 7 Hispanic/Latino; 2 Two or more races, non-Hispanic/Latino), 1 international. Average age 38. 62 applicants, 56% accepted, 13 enrolled. In 2016, 13 master's, 9 doctorates awarded. Terminal master's awarded for partial completion of doctoral program. *Degree requirements:* For master's, one foreign language, comprehensive exam, thesis optional; for doctorate, 2 foreign languages, comprehensive exam, thesis/dissertation. *Entrance requirements:* For master's, GRE, BA in history or equivalent; for doctorate, GRE, MA in history or equivalent. Additional exam requirements/recommendations for international students: Required—TOEFL. *Application deadline:* For fall admission, 12/15 for domestic students; for spring admission, 10/15 for domestic students. Application fee: $50. Electronic applications accepted. *Financial support:* Fellowships, research assistantships, teaching assistantships with full tuition reimbursements, institutionally sponsored loans, scholarships/grants, and health care benefits available. Financial award application deadline: 12/15. *Faculty research:* American Western history, Asian history, environmental history, European history, frontiers and borderlands, gender and sexuality, Latin American history, politics and economy, race and ethnicity, religion, United States history, war and society. *Unit head:* Dr. Charlie Steen, Chair, 505-277-2451, Fax: 505-277-6023, E-mail: csteen@unm.edu. *Application contact:* Yolanda Martinez, Department Administrator, 505-277-2451, Fax: 505-277-6023, E-mail: history@unm.edu. Website: http://www.unm.edu/~hist/

**University of New Orleans,** Graduate School, College of Liberal Arts, Department of History, New Orleans, LA 70148. Offers MA. *Degree requirements:* For master's, one foreign language, thesis (for some programs). *Entrance requirements:* For master's, GRE General Test. Additional exam requirements/recommendations for international students: Required—TOEFL (minimum score 550 paper-based; 79 iBT), IELTS (minimum score 6.5). Electronic applications accepted. *Faculty research:* Recent U.S. political, military, urban, regional, and legal history.

**University of North Alabama,** College of Arts and Sciences, Department of History, Florence, AL 35632-0001. Offers history (MA); public history (MA). *Program availability:* Part-time, 100% online. *Faculty:* 7 full-time (3 women), 2 part-time/adjunct (1 woman). *Students:* 9 full-time (3 women), 13 part-time (6 women); includes 1 minority (Black or African American, non-Hispanic/Latino). Average age 31. 11 applicants, 82% accepted, 6 enrolled. In 2016, 6 master's awarded. *Degree requirements:* For master's, comprehensive exam (for some programs), thesis optional. *Entrance requirements:* For master's, GRE, 3 letters of recommendation, essay, writing sample. Additional exam requirements/recommendations for international students: Required—TOEFL (minimum score 79 iBT), IELTS (minimum score 6), PTE (minimum score 54). *Application deadline:* Applications are processed on a rolling basis. Application fee: $50 ($100 for international students). Electronic applications accepted. *Expenses:* Tuition, state resident: full-time $2799; part-time $1866 per semester. Tuition, nonresident: full-time $5598; part-time $3732 per semester. *Required fees:* $915; $642 per semester. Tuition and fees vary according to course load. *Financial support:* In 2016–17, 6 students received support. Scholarships/grants and unspecified assistantships available. Financial award application deadline: 2/1; financial award applicants required to submit FAFSA. *Unit head:* Dr. Jeffrey Bibbee, Chair, 256-765-4306, E-mail: jrbibbee@una.edu. *Application contact:* Hillary N. Coats, Graduate Admissions Coordinator, 256-765-4447, E-mail: graduate@una.edu. Website: http://www.una.edu/history/

**The University of North Carolina at Chapel Hill,** Graduate School, College of Arts and Sciences, Department of History, Chapel Hill, NC 27599. Offers MA, PhD. Terminal master's awarded for partial completion of doctoral program. *Degree requirements:* For master's, one foreign language, thesis, oral thesis defense; for doctorate, 2 foreign languages, comprehensive exam, thesis/dissertation, oral dissertation defense. *Entrance requirements:* For master's and doctorate, GRE General Test, minimum GPA of 3.0. Electronic applications accepted.

**The University of North Carolina at Charlotte,** College of Liberal Arts and Sciences, Department of History, Charlotte, NC 28223-0001. Offers MA. *Program availability:* Part-time, evening/weekend. *Faculty:* 26 full-time (13 women), 1 part-time/adjunct (0 women). *Students:* 18 full-time (9 women), 22 part-time (10 women); includes 10 minority (4 Black or African American, non-Hispanic/Latino; 1 Asian, non-Hispanic/Latino; 4 Hispanic/Latino; 1 Two or more races, non-Hispanic/Latino). Average age 32. 32 applicants, 97% accepted, 13 enrolled. In 2016, 15 master's awarded. *Degree requirements:* For master's, thesis or comprehensive exam. *Entrance requirements:* For master's, GRE General Test, minimum undergraduate GPA in history or related discipline of 3.0; personal statement (1-2 pages) detailing experiences, interests, and goals in history; three letters of recommendation, at least two of which should be from professors in history or related field; writing sample; curriculum vitae/resume. Additional exam requirements/recommendations for international students: Required—TOEFL (minimum score 523 paper-based, 70 iBT) or IELTS (6.5). *Application deadline:* For fall admission, 2/1 priority date for domestic and international students; for spring admission, 10/1 priority date for domestic and international students. Applications are processed on a rolling basis. Application fee: $75. Electronic applications accepted. *Expenses:* Tuition, state resident: full-time $4252. Tuition, nonresident: full-time $17,423. *Required fees:* $3026. Tuition and fees vary according to course load and

program. *Financial support:* In 2016–17, 15 students received support, including 1 fellowship (averaging $42,000 per year), 2 research assistantships (averaging $9,000 per year), 12 teaching assistantships (averaging $9,916 per year); career-related internships or fieldwork, Federal Work-Study, institutionally sponsored loans, scholarships/grants, and unspecified assistantships also available. Support available to part-time students. Financial award application deadline: 3/1; financial award applicants required to submit FAFSA. *Total annual research expenditures:* $185. *Unit head:* Dr. Jurgen Buchenau, Chair, 704-687-5125, E-mail: jbuchenau@uncc.edu. *Application contact:* Kathy B. Giddings, Director of Graduate Admissions, 704-687-5530, Fax: 704-687-1668, E-mail: gradadm@uncc.edu.
Website: http://history.uncc.edu/

**The University of North Carolina at Greensboro,** Graduate School, College of Arts and Sciences, Department of History, Greensboro, NC 27412-5001. Offers historic preservation (Certificate); history (MA); museum studies (Certificate); U.S. history (PhD). *Program availability:* Part-time. *Entrance requirements:* For master's, GRE General Test. Additional exam requirements/recommendations for international students: Required—TOEFL. Electronic applications accepted. *Faculty research:* Simultaneous discovery in science, progressive social reform, Robert Mayer.

**The University of North Carolina Wilmington,** College of Arts and Sciences, Department of History, Wilmington, NC 28403-3297. Offers MA. *Program availability:* Part-time, online learning. *Faculty:* 17 full-time (6 women). *Students:* 10 full-time (6 women), 30 part-time (21 women); includes 5 minority (2 Black or African American, non-Hispanic/Latino; 1 American Indian or Alaska Native, non-Hispanic/Latino; 2 Two or more races, non-Hispanic/Latino). Average age 31. 38 applicants, 79% accepted, 21 enrolled. In 2016, 9 master's awarded. *Degree requirements:* For master's, comprehensive exam, thesis or alternative. *Entrance requirements:* For master's, GRE General Test, minimum B average in undergraduate work, 3 recommendations, essay, writing sample. Additional exam requirements/recommendations for international students: Required—TOEFL (minimum score 79 iBT), IELTS (minimum score 6.5). *Application deadline:* For fall admission, 3/15 for domestic students. Applications are processed on a rolling basis. Application fee: $60. Electronic applications accepted. *Expenses:* Contact institution. *Financial support:* Teaching assistantships, scholarships/grants, and out-of-state tuition remission available. Financial award application deadline: 3/15; financial award applicants required to submit FAFSA. *Unit head:* Dr. Lynn Mollenauer, Chair, 910-962-3308, Fax: 910-962-7011, E-mail: mollenauerl@uncw.edu. *Application contact:* Dr. W. Taylor Fain, Graduate Director, 910-962-3305, Fax: 910-962-7011, E-mail: fainwt@uncw.edu.
Website: http://www.uncw.edu/hst/graduate/index.html

**University of North Dakota,** Graduate School, College of Arts and Sciences, Department of History, Grand Forks, ND 58202. Offers M Ed, MA, DA, PhD. *Program availability:* Part-time. *Degree requirements:* For master's, comprehensive exam (for some programs), thesis (for some programs), final exam; for doctorate, comprehensive exam, thesis/dissertation, final exam. *Entrance requirements:* For master's, minimum GPA of 3.0; for doctorate, minimum GPA of 3.5. Additional exam requirements/recommendations for international students: Required—TOEFL (minimum score 550 paper-based; 79 iBT), IELTS (minimum score 6.5). *Application deadline:* For fall admission, 8/1 priority date for domestic students, 5/1 priority date for international students; for spring admission, 12/1 priority date for domestic students, 9/1 priority date for international students. Applications are processed on a rolling basis. Application fee: $35. Electronic applications accepted. *Financial support:* Fellowships with full and partial tuition reimbursements, research assistantships with full and partial tuition reimbursements, teaching assistantships with full and partial tuition reimbursements, career-related internships or fieldwork, Federal Work-Study, institutionally sponsored loans, scholarships/grants, health care benefits, tuition waivers (full and partial), and unspecified assistantships available. Support available to part-time students. Financial award application deadline: 3/15; financial award applicants required to submit FAFSA. *Faculty research:* U.S. history, Latin America, Russia, modern Europe, women studies. *Unit head:* Dr. Hans P. Broedel, Graduate Director, 701-777-2693, Fax: 701-777-4636, E-mail: history_und@mail.und.nodak.edu. *Application contact:* Matt Anderson, Admissions Specialist, 701-777-2947, Fax: 701-777-3619, E-mail: matthew.anderson@gradschool.und.edu.
Website: http://arts-sciences.und.edu/history/

**University of Northern British Columbia,** Office of Graduate Studies, Prince George, BC V2N 4Z9, Canada. Offers business administration (Diploma); community health science (M Sc); disability management (MA); education (M Ed); first nations studies (MA); gender studies (MA); history (MA); interdisciplinary studies (MA); international studies (MA); mathematical, computer and physical sciences (M Sc); natural resources and environmental studies (M Sc, MA, MNRES, PhD); political science (MA); psychology (M Sc, PhD); social work (MSW). *Program availability:* Part-time, evening/weekend, online learning. *Degree requirements:* For master's, thesis; for doctorate, thesis/dissertation. *Entrance requirements:* For master's, GRE, minimum B average in undergraduate course work; for doctorate, candidacy exam, minimum A average in graduate course work.

**University of Northern Colorado,** Graduate School, College of Humanities and Social Sciences, Department of History, Greeley, CO 80639. Offers MA. *Program availability:* Part-time. *Degree requirements:* For master's, comprehensive exam, thesis or alternative. *Entrance requirements:* For master's, GRE, 3 letters of recommendation. *Application deadline:* Applications are processed on a rolling basis. Application fee: $50 ($60 for international students). Electronic applications accepted. *Financial support:* Teaching assistantships available. Financial award application deadline: 3/1; financial award applicants required to submit FAFSA. *Unit head:* Fritz Fischer, Chair, 970-351-2263, Fax: 970-351-2199, E-mail: fritz.fischer@unco.edu. *Application contact:* Linda Sisson, Graduate Student Admission Coordinator, 970-351-1807, Fax: 970-351-2371, E-mail: linda.sisson@unco.edu.
Website: http://www.unco.edu/hss/history/

**University of Northern Iowa,** Graduate College, College of Social and Behavioral Sciences, Department of History, Cedar Falls, IA 50614. Offers history (MA); public history (MA). *Program availability:* Part-time. *Degree requirements:* For master's, comprehensive exam (for some programs), thesis or alternative. *Entrance requirements:* For master's, minimum GPA of 3.2. Additional exam requirements/recommendations for international students: Required—TOEFL (minimum score 500 paper-based; 61 iBT). Electronic applications accepted.

**University of North Florida,** College of Arts and Sciences, Department of History, Jacksonville, FL 32224. Offers European history (MA); U.S. history (MA). *Program availability:* Part-time. *Faculty:* 12 full-time (5 women). *Students:* 6 full-time (3 women), 21 part-time (13 women); includes 3 minority (1 Black or African American, non-Hispanic/Latino; 2 Hispanic/Latino). Average age 30. 18 applicants, 56% accepted, 6 enrolled. In 2016, 10 master's awarded. *Degree requirements:* For master's, comprehensive exam, thesis optional. *Entrance requirements:* For master's, GRE General Test, 3 letters of recommendation, minimum GPA of 3.0 in last 60 hours of course work. Additional exam requirements/recommendations for international students: Required—TOEFL (minimum score 500 paper-based; 61 iBT). *Application deadline:* For fall admission, 4/15 priority date for domestic students, 5/1 for

international students; for spring admission, 12/1 priority date for domestic students, 10/1 for international students. Application fee: $30. Electronic applications accepted. Tuition and fees vary according to course load, campus/location and program. *Financial support:* In 2016–17, 2 students received support. Career-related internships or fieldwork, Federal Work-Study, scholarships/grants, tuition waivers (partial), and unspecified assistantships available. Financial award application deadline: 4/1; financial award applicants required to submit FAFSA. *Total annual research expenditures:* $9,969. *Unit head:* Dr. Charles Closmann, Chair, 904-620-1864, Fax: 904-620-1018, E-mail: cclosman@unf.edu. *Application contact:* Dr. Amanda Pascale, Director, The Graduate School, 904-620-1360, Fax: 904-620-1362, E-mail: graduateschool@unf.edu.
Website: http://www.unf.edu/coas/history/

**University of North Georgia,** Department of History, Anthropology and Philosophy, Dahlonega, GA 30597. Offers history (MA), including American history, military history, world history. *Program availability:* Part-time, evening/weekend. *Faculty:* 11 full-time (4 women), 1 part-time/adjunct. *Students:* 4 full-time (0 women), 11 part-time (5 women); includes 1 minority (Two or more races, non-Hispanic/Latino). Average age 32. 12 applicants, 92% accepted, 11 enrolled. In 2016, 2 master's awarded. *Degree requirements:* For master's, thesis optional. *Entrance requirements:* For master's, GRE, 3 recommendations, writing sample, letter of intent, minimum GPA of 2.75. Additional exam requirements/recommendations for international students: Required—TOEFL (minimum score 550 paper-based; 79 iBT), IELTS (minimum score 6.5). *Application deadline:* For fall admission, 4/15 priority date for domestic students, 7/1 priority date for international students. Applications are processed on a rolling basis. Application fee: $40. Electronic applications accepted. *Expenses:* Contact institution. *Financial support:* Unspecified assistantships available. Financial award application deadline: 3/17; financial award applicants required to submit FAFSA. *Unit head:* Dr. Jeff Pardue, Department Head, 678-717-3867. *Application contact:* Melinda Maxwell, Director of Graduate Admissions, 706-864-1543, E-mail: melinda.maxwell@ung.edu.
Website: http://ung.edu/history-anthropology-philosophy/

**University of North Texas,** Robert B. Toulouse School of Graduate Studies, Denton, TX 76203-5459. Offers accounting (MS); applied anthropology (MA, MS); applied behavior analysis (Certificate); applied geography (MA); applied technology and performance improvement (M Ed, MS); art education (MA); art history (MA); art museum education (Certificate); arts leadership (Certificate); audiology (Au D); behavior analysis (MS); behavioral science (PhD); biochemistry and molecular biology (MS); biology (MA, MS); biomedical engineering (MS); business analysis (MS); chemistry (MS); clinical health psychology (PhD); communication studies (MA, MS); computer engineering (MS); computer science (MS); counseling (M Ed, MS), including clinical mental health counseling (MS), college and university counseling, elementary school counseling, secondary school counseling; creative writing (MA); criminal justice (MS); curriculum and instruction (M Ed); decision sciences (MBA); design (MA, MFA), including fashion design (MFA), innovation studies, interior design (MFA); early childhood studies (MS); economics (MS); educational leadership (M Ed, Ed D); educational psychology (MS, PhD), including family studies (MS), gifted and talented (MS), human development (MS), learning and cognition (MS), research, measurement and evaluation (MS); electrical engineering (MS); emergency management (MPA); engineering technology (MS); English (MA); English as a second language (MA); environmental science (MS); finance (MBA, MS); financial management (MPA); French (MA); health services management (MBA); higher education (M Ed, Ed D); history (MA, MS); hospitality management (MS); human resources management (MPA); information science (MS); information systems (PhD); information technologies (MBA); interdisciplinary studies (MA, MS); international studies (MA); international sustainable tourism (MS); jazz studies (MM); journalism (MA, MJ, Graduate Certificate), including interactive and virtual digital communication (Graduate Certificate), narrative journalism (Graduate Certificate), public relations (Graduate Certificate); kinesiology (MS); linguistics (MA); local government management (MPA); logistics (PhD); logistics and supply chain management (MBA); long-term care, senior housing, and aging services (MA); management (PhD); marketing (MBA); mathematics (MA, MS); mechanical and energy engineering (MS, PhD); music (MA), including ethnomusicology, music theory, musicology, performance; music composition (PhD); music education (MM Ed, PhD); nonprofit management (MPA); operations and supply chain management (MBA); performance (MM, DMA); philosophy (MA); political science (MA); professional and technical communication (MA); radio, television and film (MA, MFA); rehabilitation counseling (Certificate); sociology (MA); Spanish (MA); special education (M Ed); speech-language pathology (MA); strategic management (MBA); studio art (MFA); teaching (MFA); MBA/MS. *Program availability:* Part-time, evening/weekend, online learning. Terminal master's awarded for partial completion of doctoral program. *Degree requirements:* For master's, variable foreign language requirement, comprehensive exam (for some programs), thesis (for some programs); for doctorate, variable foreign language requirement, comprehensive exam (for some programs), thesis/dissertation; for other advanced degree, variable foreign language requirement, comprehensive exam (for some programs). *Entrance requirements:* For master's and doctorate, GRE, GMAT. Additional exam requirements/recommendations for international students: Required—TOEFL (minimum score 550 paper-based; 79 iBT). Electronic applications accepted.

**University of Notre Dame,** Graduate School, College of Arts and Letters, Division of Humanities, Department of History, Notre Dame, IN 46556. Offers MA, PhD. *Degree requirements:* For doctorate, one foreign language, thesis/dissertation, candidacy exam. *Entrance requirements:* For doctorate, GRE General Test. Additional exam requirements/recommendations for international students: Required—TOEFL (minimum score 600 paper-based; 80 iBT). Electronic applications accepted. *Faculty research:* U.S., modern European and medieval history; history of European and U.S. religions; U.S. and European intellectual and cultural history; history of Central Europe.

**University of Oklahoma,** College of Arts and Sciences, Department of History, Norman, OK 73019. Offers MA, PhD. *Faculty:* 40 full-time (16 women). *Students:* 29 full-time (10 women), 26 part-time (9 women); includes 7 minority (1 Black or African American, non-Hispanic/Latino; 5 Hispanic/Latino; 1 Two or more races, non-Hispanic/Latino). Average age 31. 29 applicants, 66% accepted, 12 enrolled. In 2016, 8 master's, 5 doctorates awarded. *Degree requirements:* For master's, comprehensive exam (for some programs), thesis (for some programs), 30 hours (for thesis), 34 hours (for non-thesis); for doctorate, one foreign language, comprehensive exam, thesis/dissertation, 90 hours: 30 hours of MA coursework, 31 hours of PhD-level coursework, and 29 dissertation hours. *Entrance requirements:* For master's and doctorate, GRE, 3 letters of reference, preferably from applicant's history professors; statement of purpose; writing sample; minimum GPA of 3.5. Additional exam requirements/recommendations for international students: Required—TOEFL (minimum score 79 iBT) or IELTS (minimum score 6.5). *Application deadline:* For fall admission, 12/1 for domestic and international students. Application fee: $50 ($100 for international students). Electronic applications accepted. *Expenses:* Tuition, state resident: full-time $4886; part-time $203.60 per credit hour. Tuition, nonresident: full-time $18,989; part-time $791.20 per credit hour. *Required fees:* $3283; $126.25 per credit hour. $126.50 per semester. *Financial support:* In 2016–17, 46 students received support, including 4 fellowships with full tuition reimbursements available (averaging $5,750 per year), 10 research assistantships with full tuition reimbursements available (averaging $17,292 per year), 24 teaching assistantships with full tuition reimbursements available (averaging $15,559

## History

per year); health care benefits and unspecified assistantships also available. Financial award application deadline: 6/1; financial award applicants required to submit FAFSA. *Faculty research:* American West, Native American studies, Latin American studies, environmental history, Judaic studies. *Total annual research expenditures:* $68,395. *Unit head:* Dr. James Hart, Jr., Professor/Chair of History, 405-325-6305, Fax: 405-325-4503, E-mail: jshart@ou.edu. *Application contact:* Dr. Judith S. Lewis, Professor of History/Director of Graduate Studies, 405-325-6383, Fax: 405-325-4503, E-mail: judith.s.lewis-1@ou.edu.
Website: http://history.ou.edu

**University of Oregon,** Graduate School, College of Arts and Sciences, Department of History, Eugene, OR 97403. Offers MA, PhD. *Degree requirements:* For master's, one foreign language, thesis or alternative, written exam; for doctorate, 2 foreign languages, thesis/dissertation, oral and written exams. *Entrance requirements:* For master's and doctorate, GRE General Test, minimum GPA of 3.0. Additional exam requirements/recommendations for international students: Required—TOEFL. *Faculty research:* U.S., European, East and Southeast Asian, Latin American, and ancient history.

**University of Ottawa,** Faculty of Graduate and Postdoctoral Studies, Faculty of Arts, Department of History, Ottawa, ON K1N 6N5, Canada. Offers MA, PhD. *Degree requirements:* For master's, 2 foreign languages, thesis or alternative; for doctorate, 2 foreign languages, thesis/dissertation, oral exam. *Entrance requirements:* For master's, honors degree or equivalent, minimum B average; for doctorate, master's degree, minimum B+ average. Electronic applications accepted. *Faculty research:* Canadian history.

**University of Pennsylvania,** School of Arts and Sciences, Graduate Group in Ancient History, Philadelphia, PA 19104. Offers AM, PhD. *Faculty:* 24 full-time (8 women), 3 part-time/adjunct (0 women). *Students:* 15 full-time (3 women), 4 international. Average age 29. 22 applicants, 14% accepted, 2 enrolled. Application fee: $80. *Expenses: Tuition:* Full-time $31,068; part-time $5762 per course. *Required fees:* $3200; $336 per course. Full-time tuition and fees vary according to degree level, program and student level. Part-time tuition and fees vary according to course load, degree level and program.
Website: http://www.sas.upenn.edu/graduate-division

**University of Pennsylvania,** School of Arts and Sciences, Graduate Group in History, Philadelphia, PA 19104. Offers AM, PhD. *Faculty:* 47 full-time (20 women), 8 part-time/adjunct (3 women). *Students:* 74 full-time (38 women), 4 part-time (3 women); includes 11 minority (2 Black or African American, non-Hispanic/Latino; 2 Asian, non-Hispanic/Latino; 6 Hispanic/Latino; 1 Two or more races, non-Hispanic/Latino), 23 international. Average age 30. 247 applicants, 9% accepted, 10 enrolled. In 2016, 17 master's, 14 doctorates awarded. Terminal master's awarded for partial completion of doctoral program. *Expenses: Tuition:* Full-time $31,068; part-time $5762 per course. *Required fees:* $3200; $336 per course. Full-time tuition and fees vary according to degree level, program and student level. Part-time tuition and fees vary according to course load, degree level and program.
Website: http://www.sas.upenn.edu/graduate-division

**University of Pittsburgh,** Dietrich School of Arts and Sciences, Department of History, Pittsburgh, PA 15260. Offers MA, PhD. *Faculty:* 24 full-time (9 women). *Students:* 38 full-time (12 women); includes 3 minority (all Hispanic/Latino), 8 international. Average age 26. 58 applicants, 16% accepted, 4 enrolled. In 2016, 3 master's, 9 doctorates awarded. Terminal master's awarded for partial completion of doctoral program. *Degree requirements:* For master's, one foreign language, thesis, oral exam, seminar paper; for doctorate, 2 foreign languages, comprehensive exam, thesis/dissertation. *Entrance requirements:* For master's and doctorate, GRE General Test, writing sample. Additional exam requirements/recommendations for international students: Required—TOEFL (minimum score 550 paper-based, 90 iBT) or IELTS (minimum score 7.0). *Application deadline:* For fall admission, 1/15 for domestic and international students. Application fee: $50. Electronic applications accepted. Tuition and fees vary according to program. *Financial support:* In 2016–17, 32 students received support, including 13 fellowships with full tuition reimbursements available (averaging $22,000 per year), 18 teaching assistantships with full tuition reimbursements available (averaging $18,000 per year); Federal Work-Study, scholarships/grants, health care benefits, tuition waivers (full and partial), and unspecified assistantships also available. Financial award application deadline: 1/15. *Faculty research:* Europe, Latin America, Atlantic, United States, East Asia. *Unit head:* Dr. Lara Putnam, Chair, 412-648-7452, Fax: 412-648-9074, E-mail: lep12@pitt.edu. *Application contact:* Patty Landon, Graduate Administrator, 412-648-7854, Fax: 412-648-9074, E-mail: pal24@pitt.edu.
Website: http://www.history.pitt.edu

**University of Puerto Rico, Río Piedras Campus,** College of Humanities, Department of History, San Juan, PR 00931-3300. Offers Caribbean history (PhD); history (MA); Puerto Rican history (PhD). *Program availability:* Part-time. *Degree requirements:* For master's, one foreign language, comprehensive exam, thesis; for doctorate, one foreign language, comprehensive exam, thesis/dissertation. *Entrance requirements:* For master's, PAEG or GRE, interview, minimum GPA of 3.0, 2 letters of recommendation; for doctorate, PAEG or GRE, interview, master's degree, minimum GPA of 3.0, 2 letters of recommendation.

**University of Regina,** Faculty of Graduate Studies and Research, Faculty of Arts, Department of History, Regina, SK S4S 0A2, Canada. Offers MA. *Program availability:* Part-time. *Faculty:* 11 full-time (4 women), 1 part-time/adjunct (0 women). *Students:* 5 full-time (3 women), 4 part-time (1 woman). 4 applicants, 75% accepted. In 2016, 3 master's awarded. *Degree requirements:* For master's, thesis. *Entrance requirements:* Additional exam requirements/recommendations for international students: Required—TOEFL (minimum score 580 paper-based; 80 iBT), IELTS (minimum score 6.5), PTE (minimum score 59). *Application deadline:* For fall admission, 3/31 for domestic and international students. Application fee: $100. Electronic applications accepted. *Financial support:* In 2016–17, 2 fellowships (averaging $6,000 per year), 1 teaching assistantship (averaging $2,501 per year) were awarded; scholarships/grants also available. Financial award application deadline: 6/15. *Faculty research:* Canadian, European, Asian, British, and the Americas history. *Unit head:* Dr. Raymond Blake, Department Head, 306-585-5431, Fax: 306-585-4827, E-mail: raymond.blake@uregina.ca. *Application contact:* Dr. Philip Charrier, Graduate Program Coordinator, 306-585-4215, Fax: 306-585-4827, E-mail: philip.charrier@uregina.ca.
Website: http://www.uregina.ca/arts/history

**University of Rhode Island,** Graduate School, College of Arts and Sciences, Department of History, Kingston, RI 02881. Offers archaeology and anthropology (MA); history (MA), including European history, United States history; MLIS/MA. *Program availability:* Part-time. *Faculty:* 16 full-time (7 women). *Students:* 11 full-time (5 women), 3 part-time (2 women). In 2016, 7 master's awarded. *Degree requirements:* For master's, comprehensive exam (for some programs), thesis optional. *Entrance requirements:* For master's, GRE, 2 letters of recommendation. Additional exam requirements/recommendations for international students: Required—TOEFL. *Application deadline:* For fall admission, 7/15 for domestic students, 2/1 for international students; for spring admission, 11/15 for domestic students, 7/15 for international students; for summer admission, 4/15 for domestic students. Application fee: $65.

Electronic applications accepted. *Expenses:* Tuition, state resident: full-time $11,796; part-time $655 per credit. Tuition, nonresident: full-time $24,206; part-time $1345 per credit. *Required fees:* $1546; $44 per credit. One-time fee: $155 full-time; $35 part-time. *Financial support:* In 2016–17, 4 teaching assistantships with tuition reimbursements (averaging $15,036 per year) were awarded. Financial award application deadline: 2/1; financial award applicants required to submit FAFSA. *Unit head:* Dr. Rod Mather, Chair, 401-874-4093, E-mail: rodmather@uri.edu. *Application contact:* Dr. Erik Loomis, Acting Director of Graduate Studies, 401-874-4078, E-mail: eloomis@uri.edu.
Website: http://www.uri.edu/artsci/his/

**University of Rochester,** School of Arts and Sciences, Department of History, Rochester, NY 14627. Offers American history (MA, PhD); European history (MA, PhD); global history (MA, PhD). *Faculty:* 19 full-time (4 women). *Students:* 28 full-time (12 women); includes 2 minority (1 Asian, non-Hispanic/Latino; 1 Two or more races, non-Hispanic/Latino), 2 international. Average age 31. 32 applicants, 28% accepted, 5 enrolled. In 2016, 5 master's, 4 doctorates awarded. Terminal master's awarded for partial completion of doctoral program. *Degree requirements:* For master's, one foreign language, thesis or alternative; for doctorate, 2 foreign languages, thesis/dissertation, comprehensive oral exam, qualifying exam. *Entrance requirements:* For master's and doctorate, GRE General Test, sample of written work. Additional exam requirements/recommendations for international students: Required—TOEFL. *Application deadline:* For fall admission, 1/15 for domestic and international students. Application fee: $60. Electronic applications accepted. *Expenses:* $1,538 per credit. *Financial support:* In 2016–17, 24 students received support, including 7 fellowships (averaging $20,000 per year); tuition waivers (full and partial) also available. Financial award application deadline: 1/15. *Unit head:* Matthew Lenoe, Chair, 585-275-9355, E-mail: matthew.lenoe@rochester.edu. *Application contact:* Alissa Clark, Secretary, 585-275-2053.
Website: http://www.rochester.edu/College/HIS/

**University of Saskatchewan,** College of Graduate Studies and Research, College of Arts and Science, Department of History, Saskatoon, SK S7N 5A2, Canada. Offers MA, PhD. *Program availability:* Part-time. *Degree requirements:* For master's, thesis; for doctorate, comprehensive exam (for some programs), thesis/dissertation. *Entrance requirements:* Additional exam requirements/recommendations for international students: Required—TOEFL (minimum score 80 iBT); Recommended—IELTS (minimum score 6.5). Electronic applications accepted.

**University of South Africa,** College of Human Sciences, Pretoria, South Africa. Offers adult education (M Ed); African languages (MA, PhD); African politics (MA, PhD); Afrikaans (MA, PhD); ancient history (MA, PhD); ancient Near Eastern studies (MA, PhD); anthropology (MA, PhD); applied linguistics (MA); Arabic (MA, PhD); archaeology (MA); art history (MA); Biblical archaeology (MA); Biblical studies (M Th, D Th, PhD); Christian spirituality (M Th, D Th); church history (M Th, D Th); classical studies (MA, PhD); clinical psychology (MA); communication (MA, PhD); comparative education (M Ed, Ed D); consulting psychology (D Admin, D Com, PhD); curriculum studies (M Ed, Ed D); development studies (M Admin, MA, D Admin, PhD); didactics (M Ed, Ed D); education (M Tech); education management (M Ed, Ed D); educational psychology (M Ed); English (MA); environmental education (M Ed); French (MA, PhD); German (MA, PhD); Greek (MA); guidance and counseling (M Ed); health studies (MA, PhD), including health sciences education (MA), health services management (MA), medical and surgical nursing science (critical care general) (MA), midwifery and neonatal nursing science (MA), trauma and emergency care (MA); history (MA, PhD); history of education (Ed D); inclusive education (M Ed, Ed D); information and communications technology policy and regulation (MA); information science (MA, MIS, PhD); international politics (MA, PhD); Islamic studies (MA, PhD); Italian (MA, PhD); Judaica (MA, PhD); linguistics (MA, PhD); mathematical education (M Ed); mathematics education (MA); missiology (M Th, D Th); modern Hebrew (MA, PhD); musicology (MA, MMus, D Mus, PhD); natural science education (M Ed); New Testament (M Th, D Th); Old Testament (D Th); pastoral therapy (M Th, D Th); philosophy (MA); philosophy of education (M Ed, Ed D); politics (MA, PhD); Portuguese (MA, PhD); practical theology (M Th, D Th); psychology (MA, MS, PhD); psychology of education (M Ed, Ed D); public health (MA); religious studies (MA, D Th, PhD); Romance languages (MA); Russian (MA, PhD); Semitic languages (MA); social behavior studies in HIV/AIDS (MA); social science (mental health) (MA); social science in development studies (MA); social science in psychology (MA); social science in social work (MA); social science in sociology (MA); social work (MSW, DSW, PhD); socio-education (M Ed, Ed D); sociolinguistics (MA); sociology (MA, PhD); Spanish (MA, PhD); systematic theology (M Th, D Th); TESOL (teaching English to speakers of other languages) (MA); theological ethics (M Th, D Th); theory of literature (MA, PhD); urban ministries (D Th); urban ministry (M Th).

**University of South Alabama,** College of Arts and Sciences, Department of History, Mobile, AL 36688. Offers MA. *Program availability:* Part-time, evening/weekend. *Faculty:* 6 full-time (5 women). *Students:* 9 full-time (3 women), 4 part-time (2 women). Average age 32. 7 applicants, 57% accepted, 3 enrolled. In 2016, 5 master's awarded. *Degree requirements:* For master's, comprehensive exam, thesis optional, 30 credit hours of course work. *Entrance requirements:* For master's, GRE General Test, 21 hours of course work in history, minimum GPA of 3.0. Additional exam requirements/recommendations for international students: Required—TOEFL (minimum score 525 paper-based; 71 iBT). *Application deadline:* For fall admission, 7/10 priority date for domestic students, 6/15 priority date for international students; for spring admission, 11/20 priority date for domestic students, 11/1 priority date for international students; for summer admission, 4/20 for domestic students. Applications are processed on a rolling basis. Application fee: $35. Electronic applications accepted. *Expenses:* Tuition, state resident: full-time $9768; part-time $407 per credit hour. Tuition, nonresident: full-time $19,536; part-time $814 per credit hour. *Financial support:* Fellowships, research assistantships, teaching assistantships, career-related internships or fieldwork, Federal Work-Study, institutionally sponsored loans, scholarships/grants, and unspecified assistantships available. Support available to part-time students. Financial award application deadline: 3/15; financial award applicants required to submit FAFSA. *Unit head:* Dr. Marsha Hamilton, Interim Chair, History, 251-460-7611, E-mail: mhamilton@southalabama.edu. *Application contact:* Dr. Martha J. Brazy, Graduate Coordinator, History, 251-460-7540, E-mail: mjbrazy@southalabama.edu.
Website: http://www.southalabama.edu/colleges/artsandsci/history/gradprogram.html

**University of South Carolina,** The Graduate School, College of Arts and Sciences, Department of History, Columbia, SC 29208. Offers history (MA, PhD); public history (MA, Certificate), including archive management (MA), historic preservation (MA), museum administration (MA), museum management (Certificate); MLIS/MA. IMA and MAT offered in cooperation with the College of Education. *Program availability:* Part-time. Terminal master's awarded for partial completion of doctoral program. *Degree requirements:* For master's, one foreign language, thesis; for doctorate, one foreign language, thesis/dissertation. *Entrance requirements:* For master's and doctorate, GRE General Test. Additional exam requirements/recommendations for international students: Required—TOEFL. Electronic applications accepted. *Faculty research:* U.S. history; European history; Latin American history; history of science and technology.

**The University of South Dakota,** Graduate School, College of Arts and Sciences, Department of History, Vermillion, SD 57069. Offers MA, JD/MA. *Program availability:*

Part-time. *Degree requirements:* For master's, thesis (for some programs). *Entrance requirements:* For master's, GRE General Test, minimum GPA of 2.7. Additional exam requirements/recommendations for international students: Required—TOEFL (minimum score 550 paper-based; 79 iBT). Electronic applications accepted.

**University of Southern California,** Graduate School, Dana and David Dornsife College of Letters, Arts and Sciences, Department of History, Los Angeles, CA 90089. Offers PhD. *Degree requirements:* For doctorate, 2 foreign languages, comprehensive exam, thesis/dissertation, 60 semester units of acceptable coursework. *Entrance requirements:* For doctorate, GRE General Test. Additional exam requirements/recommendations for international students: Recommended—TOEFL. Electronic applications accepted. *Faculty research:* U.S. North American and Latin American history, California and Western American history (including Borderlands), European history from the early Middle Ages to present, East Asian (Chinese, Japanese, Korean) history, early modern Atlantic world/world history.

**University of Southern Mississippi,** Graduate School, College of Arts and Letters, Department of History, Hattiesburg, MS 39406. Offers MA, MS, PhD. *Program availability:* Part-time. *Degree requirements:* For master's, one foreign language, comprehensive exam, thesis (for some programs); for doctorate, 2 foreign languages, comprehensive exam, thesis/dissertation. *Entrance requirements:* For master's, GRE General Test, minimum GPA of 3.0 in field of study, 2.75 in last 2 years; for doctorate, GRE General Test, minimum GPA of 3.5. Additional exam requirements/recommendations for international students: Required—TOEFL, IELTS. *Application deadline:* For fall admission, 3/1 priority date for domestic students, 3/1 for international students. Applications are processed on a rolling basis. Application fee: $60. *Expenses: Tuition, area resident:* Full-time $15,708; part-time $437 per credit hour. *Financial support:* Fellowships with full tuition reimbursements, research assistantships with full tuition reimbursements, teaching assistantships with full tuition reimbursements, Federal Work-Study, institutionally sponsored loans, scholarships/grants, health care benefits, and unspecified assistantships available. Financial award application deadline: 3/15; financial award applicants required to submit FAFSA. *Faculty research:* Civil War, civil rights, modern European history, war history. *Unit head:* Dr. Kyle F. Zelner, Chair, 601-266-6196, Fax: 601-266-4334.
Website: https://www.usm.edu/history

**University of South Florida,** College of Arts and Sciences, Department of History, Tampa, FL 33620-9951. Offers history (MA, PhD), including American history (MA), ancient history (MA), European history (MA), Latin American history (MA), Medieval history (MA). *Program availability:* Part-time, evening/weekend. *Faculty:* 17 full-time (8 women). *Students:* 39 full-time (9 women), 14 part-time (8 women); includes 7 minority (1 Black or African American, non-Hispanic/Latino; 1 American Indian or Alaska Native, non-Hispanic/Latino; 1 Asian, non-Hispanic/Latino; 4 Hispanic/Latino), 1 international. Average age 35. 34 applicants, 68% accepted, 15 enrolled. In 2016, 8 master's, 2 doctorates awarded. *Degree requirements:* For master's, one foreign language, comprehensive exam, thesis optional; for doctorate, one foreign language, comprehensive exam, thesis/dissertation. *Entrance requirements:* For master's, GRE General Test, minimum GPA of 3.0, two letters of recommendation, 2-page statement of purpose, writing sample; for doctorate, GRE General Test, minimum GPA of 3.5 in master's degree coursework, three letters of recommendation, statement of purpose, writing sample, foreign language proficiency in the field of study. Additional exam requirements/recommendations for international students: Required—TOEFL (minimum score 550 paper-based; 79 iBT) or IELTS (minimum score 6.5). *Application deadline:* For fall admission, 12/1 priority date for domestic students, 12/1 for international students. Applications are processed on a rolling basis. Application fee: $30. Electronic applications accepted. *Expenses:* Tuition, state resident: full-time $7766; part-time $431.43 per credit hour. Tuition, nonresident: full-time $15,789; part-time $877.17 per credit hour. *Required fees:* $37 per term. *Financial support:* In 2016–17, 20 students received support, including 17 teaching assistantships with tuition reimbursements available (averaging $12,750 per year); unspecified assistantships also available. Financial award application deadline: 1/15. *Faculty research:* North American and U.S. history, European history, nineteenth- and twentieth-centuries/modern world, early modern world, ancient history, history of gender/sexuality, Latin American history, history of science and medicine. *Total annual research expenditures:* $195,413. *Unit head:* Dr. Fraser Ottanelli, Professor and Chair, 813-974-6209, Fax: 813-974-6228, E-mail: ottanelli@usf.edu. *Application contact:* Dr. Brian Connolly, Associate Professor and Graduate Program Director, 813-974-1087, Fax: 813-974-6228, E-mail: bconnelly@usf.edu.
Website: http://history.usf.edu

**The University of Tennessee,** Graduate School, College of Arts and Sciences, Department of History, Knoxville, TN 37996. Offers American history (PhD); European history (PhD); history (MA). *Program availability:* Part-time. *Degree requirements:* For master's, thesis or alternative; for doctorate, one foreign language, thesis/dissertation. *Entrance requirements:* For master's and doctorate, GRE General Test, minimum GPA of 2.7. Additional exam requirements/recommendations for international students: Required—TOEFL. Electronic applications accepted.

**The University of Texas at Arlington,** Graduate School, College of Liberal Arts, Department of History, Arlington, TX 76019. Offers history (MA); transatlantic history (PhD). *Program availability:* Part-time, evening/weekend. *Degree requirements:* For master's, one foreign language, comprehensive exam (for some programs), thesis (for some programs); for doctorate, one foreign language, comprehensive exam, thesis/dissertation. *Entrance requirements:* For master's, GRE General Test, minimum GPA of 3.0 in last 60 hours, 3 letters of recommendation; for doctorate, GRE General Test, minimum graduate GPA of 3.5, 3 letters of recommendation, academic writing sample. Additional exam requirements/recommendations for international students: Required—TOEFL (minimum score 550 paper-based). *Application deadline:* For fall admission, 6/15 for domestic students. Applications are processed on a rolling basis. Application fee: $35 ($50 for international students). Electronic applications accepted. *Financial support:* Fellowships with full tuition reimbursements, research assistantships, teaching assistantships, career-related internships or fieldwork, scholarships/grants, and 5-6 full-tuition fellowships, conference travel support available. Financial award application deadline: 5/1; financial award applicants required to submit FAFSA. *Unit head:* Dr. Marvin Dulaney, Chair, 817-272-2861, Fax: 817-272-2852, E-mail: history@uta.edu. *Application contact:* Dr. John Garrigus, Graduate Advisor, 817-272-2861, Fax: 817-272-2852, E-mail: garrigus@uta.edu.
Website: http://www.uta.edu/history/

**The University of Texas at Austin,** Graduate School, College of Liberal Arts, Department of History, Austin, TX 78712-1111. Offers MA, PhD. *Degree requirements:* For doctorate, thesis/dissertation. *Entrance requirements:* For master's and doctorate, GRE General Test. Electronic applications accepted. *Faculty research:* United States, Latin American, European, African, Asian, and Middle Eastern history.

**The University of Texas at Dallas,** School of Arts and Humanities, Richardson, TX 75080. Offers history (MA); humanities (MA, PhD), including aesthetic studies, history of ideas, studies in literature (PhD), studies of literature (MA); Latin American studies (MA). *Program availability:* Part-time, evening/weekend. *Faculty:* 46 full-time (15 women), 5 part-time/adjunct (1 woman). *Students:* 129 full-time (78 women), 127 part-time (81

women); includes 63 minority (12 Black or African American, non-Hispanic/Latino; 4 American Indian or Alaska Native, non-Hispanic/Latino; 13 Asian, non-Hispanic/Latino; 23 Hispanic/Latino; 11 Two or more races, non-Hispanic/Latino), 27 international. Average age 41. 113 applicants, 58% accepted, 38 enrolled. In 2016, 39 master's, 16 doctorates awarded. *Degree requirements:* For master's, one foreign language, portfolio; for doctorate, one foreign language, thesis/dissertation. *Entrance requirements:* For master's and doctorate, minimum GPA of 3.0 in undergraduate course work in field. Additional exam requirements/recommendations for international students: Required—TOEFL (minimum score 550 paper-based). *Application deadline:* For fall admission, 7/15 for domestic students, 5/1 priority date for international students; for spring admission, 11/15 for domestic students, 9/1 priority date for international students. Applications are processed on a rolling basis. Application fee: $50 ($100 for international students). Electronic applications accepted. *Expenses:* Tuition, state resident: full-time $12,418; part-time $690 per semester hour. Tuition, nonresident: full-time $24,150; part-time $1342 per semester hour. Tuition and fees vary according to course load. *Financial support:* In 2016–17, 135 students received support, including 1 fellowship (averaging $2,000 per year), 12 research assistantships with partial tuition reimbursements available (averaging $23,948 per year), 69 teaching assistantships with partial tuition reimbursements available (averaging $15,001 per year); Federal Work-Study, institutionally sponsored loans, scholarships/grants, and unspecified assistantships also available. Support available to part-time students. Financial award application deadline: 4/30; financial award applicants required to submit FAFSA. *Faculty research:* Science and the arts and humanities, intellectual and philosophical history, cultural studies, translation studies. *Total annual research expenditures:* $177,908. *Unit head:* Dr. Dennis M. Kratz, Dean, 972-883-2984, Fax: 972-883-2989, E-mail: dkratz@utdallas.edu. *Application contact:* Dr. John Gooch, Associate Dean of Graduate Studies, 972-883-2756, Fax: 972-883-2989, E-mail: john.gooch@utdallas.edu.
Website: http://www.utdallas.edu/ah/

**The University of Texas at El Paso,** Graduate School, College of Liberal Arts, Department of History, El Paso, TX 79968-0001. Offers border history (MA); borderlands history (PhD); history (MA). *Program availability:* Part-time. *Degree requirements:* For master's, thesis optional; for doctorate, 2 foreign languages, thesis/dissertation. *Entrance requirements:* For master's, GRE, minimum GPA of 3.0, writing sample, letters of recommendation, transcripts; for doctorate, GRE, statement of purpose, writing sample, letters of recommendation, transcripts. Additional exam requirements/recommendations for international students: Required—TOEFL; Recommended—IELTS.

**The University of Texas at San Antonio,** College of Liberal and Fine Arts, Department of History, San Antonio, TX 78249-0617. Offers MA. *Program availability:* Part-time. *Faculty:* 8 full-time (3 women). *Students:* 12 full-time (5 women), 23 part-time (11 women); includes 19 minority (3 Black or African American, non-Hispanic/Latino; 15 Hispanic/Latino; 1 Two or more races, non-Hispanic/Latino). Average age 33. 22 applicants, 77% accepted, 14 enrolled. In 2016, 19 master's awarded. *Degree requirements:* For master's, comprehensive exam, thesis optional, minimum of 30 credit hours. *Entrance requirements:* For master's, GRE, bachelor's degree with 18 credit hours in field of study or in another appropriate field of study (12 of these hours must be at the upper-division level with minimum GPA of 3.0 in last 60 hours), statement of purpose. Additional exam requirements/recommendations for international students: Required—TOEFL (minimum score 550 paper-based; 79 iBT), IELTS (minimum score 6.5). *Application deadline:* For fall admission, 7/1 for domestic students, 4/1 for international students; for spring admission, 11/1 for domestic students, 9/1 for international students. Application fee: $45 ($80 for international students). Electronic applications accepted. *Expenses:* Contact institution. *Financial support:* In 2016–17, 6 students received support, including 3 research assistantships (averaging $1,609 per year); Federal Work-Study also available. *Faculty research:* Borderlands and empires, Latin American history, early American history, Chinese history, Latina/o studies. *Total annual research expenditures:* $74,151. *Unit head:* Dr. Gregg Michel, Department Chair, 210-458-4033, Fax: 210-458-4796, E-mail: gregg.michel@utsa.edu. *Application contact:* Roschelle Kelly, Administrative Associate II, 210-458-5716, E-mail: roschelle.kelly@utsa.edu.
Website: http://colfa.utsa.edu/history/

**The University of Texas at Tyler,** College of Arts and Sciences, Department of History, Tyler, TX 75799-0001. Offers MA. *Program availability:* Part-time, evening/weekend. *Degree requirements:* For master's, one foreign language, comprehensive exam, thesis optional. *Entrance requirements:* For master's, GRE General Test, minimum GPA of 3.0. Additional exam requirements/recommendations for international students: Required—TOEFL. Electronic applications accepted. *Faculty research:* Early and modern U.S. history, early modern and modern European history.

**The University of Texas of the Permian Basin,** Office of Graduate Studies, College of Arts and Sciences, Department of History, Odessa, TX 79762-0001. Offers MA. *Program availability:* Part-time, evening/weekend. *Degree requirements:* For master's, comprehensive exam (for some programs), thesis (for some programs). *Entrance requirements:* For master's, GRE General Test. Additional exam requirements/recommendations for international students: Required—TOEFL (minimum score 550 paper-based).

**The University of Texas Rio Grande Valley,** College of Liberal Arts, Department of History, Edinburg, TX 78539. Offers MA, MAIS. *Program availability:* Part-time, evening/weekend. *Degree requirements:* For master's, comprehensive exam, thesis or alternative. *Entrance requirements:* For master's, GRE General Test, minimum GPA of 3.0. Tuition and fees vary according to course load and program. *Faculty research:* Texas-Mexican legacy, modern America, Southwest, labor, modern Europe.

**The University of Toledo,** College of Graduate Studies, College of Languages, Literature and Social Sciences, Department of History, Toledo, OH 43606-3390. Offers MA, PhD. *Program availability:* Part-time. *Degree requirements:* For master's, comprehensive exam (for some programs), thesis or comprehensive exam; for doctorate, thesis/dissertation, oral and written exams. *Entrance requirements:* For master's and doctorate, GRE General Test, minimum cumulative point-hour ratio of 2.7 for all previous academic work, three letters of recommendation. Additional exam requirements/recommendations for international students: Required—TOEFL (minimum score 550 paper-based; 80 iBT). Electronic applications accepted. *Faculty research:* U.S. diplomatic history, U.S. history, urban history, public history, European history.

**University of Toronto,** School of Graduate Studies, Faculty of Arts and Science, Department of History, Toronto, ON M5S 1A1, Canada. Offers MA, PhD. *Program availability:* Part-time. *Degree requirements:* For master's, one foreign language, thesis or research essay, French language exam; for doctorate, comprehensive exam, thesis/dissertation, oral examination/thesis defense. *Entrance requirements:* For master's, minimum B+ average or GPA of 3.3, 6 full academic year history courses; for doctorate, MA in history, minimum A- average or GPA of 3.7. Additional exam requirements/recommendations for international students: Required—TOEFL (minimum score 580 paper-based; 93 iBT), TWE (minimum score 5). Electronic applications accepted.

**The University of Tulsa,** Graduate School, Kendall College of Arts and Sciences, Department of History, Tulsa, OK 74104-3189. Offers MA, MTA, JD/MA. *Program*

## History

availability: Part-time. *Faculty:* 9 full-time (3 women). *Students:* 7 full-time (3 women), 5 part-time (2 women); includes 3 minority (all American Indian or Alaska Native, non-Hispanic/Latino). Average age 32. 10 applicants, 70% accepted, 6 enrolled. In 2016, 4 master's awarded. *Degree requirements:* For master's, thesis (for some programs), public presentation or oral defense of thesis. *Entrance requirements:* For master's, GRE General Test, writing sample. Additional exam requirements/recommendations for international students: Required—TOEFL (minimum score 577 paper-based; 91 iBT), IELTS (minimum score 6.5). *Application deadline:* Applications are processed on a rolling basis. Application fee: $55. Electronic applications accepted. *Expenses: Tuition:* Full-time $22,230; part-time $1235 per credit hour. *Required fees:* $990 per semester. Tuition and fees vary according to course load. *Financial support:* In 2016–17, 7 students received support, including 2 fellowships with full tuition reimbursements available (averaging $9,025 per year), 5 teaching assistantships with full tuition reimbursements available (averaging $13,410 per year); research assistantships, Federal Work-Study, scholarships/grants, health care benefits, tuition waivers (full and partial), and unspecified assistantships also available. Support available to part-time students. Financial award application deadline: 2/1; financial award applicants required to submit FAFSA. *Faculty research:* United States history, modern European history, Native American History, comparative history. *Total annual research expenditures:* $500. *Unit head:* Dr. Thomas Buoye, Chairperson, 918-631-2825, Fax: 918-631-2057, E-mail: thomas-buoye@utulsa.edu. *Application contact:* Dr. Joseph Bradley, Adviser, 918-631-2819, Fax: 918-631-2057, E-mail: joseph-bradley@utulsa.edu.
Website: http://artsandsciences.utulsa.edu/academics/departments-schools/history/

**The University of Tulsa,** Graduate School, Kendall College of Arts and Sciences, School of Urban Education, Program in Teaching Arts, Tulsa, OK 74104-3189. Offers art (MTA); biology (MTA); English (MTA); history (MTA); mathematics (MTA). *Program availability:* Part-time. *Students:* 1 (woman) full-time. Average age 26. 4 applicants, 50% accepted, 1 enrolled. In 2016, 1 master's awarded. *Entrance requirements:* For master's, GRE General Test. Additional exam requirements/recommendations for international students: Required—TOEFL (minimum score 577 paper-based), IELTS (minimum score 6.5). *Application deadline:* Applications are processed on a rolling basis. Application fee: $55. Electronic applications accepted. *Expenses: Tuition:* Full-time $22,230; part-time $1235 per credit hour. *Required fees:* $990 per semester. Tuition and fees vary according to course load. *Financial support:* In 2016–17, 1 student received support, including 1 teaching assistantship with full tuition reimbursement available (averaging $13,410 per year); fellowships with tuition reimbursements available, research assistantships with tuition reimbursements available, career-related internships or fieldwork, Federal Work-Study, scholarships/grants, health care benefits, tuition waivers (full and partial), and unspecified assistantships also available. Support available to part-time students. Financial award application deadline: 2/1; financial award applicants required to submit FAFSA. *Unit head:* Dr. Sharon Baker, Chair, 918-631-2238, Fax: 918-631-3721, E-mail: sharon-baker@utulsa.edu. *Application contact:* Dr. David Brown, Advisor, 918-631-2719, Fax: 918-631-2133, E-mail: david-brown@utulsa.edu.

**University of Utah,** Graduate School, College of Humanities, Department of History, Salt Lake City, UT 84112. Offers MA, MS, PhD. *Program availability:* Part-time. *Faculty:* 29 full-time (12 women), 5 part-time/adjunct (2 women). *Students:* 19 full-time (11 women), 27 part-time (8 women); includes 11 minority (1 American Indian or Alaska Native, non-Hispanic/Latino; 1 Asian, non-Hispanic/Latino; 5 Hispanic/Latino; 4 Two or more races, non-Hispanic/Latino). Average age 36. 45 applicants, 33% accepted, 14 enrolled. In 2016, 6 master's, 4 doctorates awarded. *Degree requirements:* For master's, one foreign language, comprehensive exam (for some programs), thesis (for some programs); for doctorate, one foreign language, comprehensive exam, thesis/dissertation. *Entrance requirements:* For master's, GRE General Test, minimum GPA of 3.2; for doctorate, GRE General Test, minimum graduate GPA of 3.6. Additional exam requirements/recommendations for international students: Required—TOEFL (minimum score 500 paper-based). *Application deadline:* For fall admission, 1/15 for domestic and international students. Application fee: $55 ($65 for international students). Electronic applications accepted. *Expenses:* Contact institution. *Financial support:* In 2016–17, 16 students received support, including 2 fellowships with full tuition reimbursements available (averaging $17,000 per year), 14 teaching assistantships with full tuition reimbursements available (averaging $16,200 per year). Financial award application deadline: 1/15. *Faculty research:* U.S. history, European history, Asian history, Middle East, Latin America. *Unit head:* Prof. Isabel Moreira, Chair, 801-581-5685, Fax: 801-585-0580, E-mail: isabel.moreira@utah.edu. *Application contact:* Amarilys Scott, Academic Advisor, 801-581-6121, Fax: 801-585-0580, E-mail: amarilys.scott@utah.edu.
Website: http://history.utah.edu

**University of Utah,** Graduate School, College of Humanities, Program in Middle East Studies, Salt Lake City, UT 84112. Offers Arabic (MA, PhD); Hebrew (MA); history (MA, PhD); Persian (MA, PhD); political science (MA, PhD). *Students:* 3 part-time (2 women); includes 1 minority (Asian, non-Hispanic/Latino), 1 international. In 2016, 2 master's awarded. Terminal master's awarded for partial completion of doctoral program. *Degree requirements:* For master's, 2 foreign languages, comprehensive exam, thesis optional; for doctorate, 3 foreign languages, comprehensive exam, thesis/dissertation. *Entrance requirements:* For master's, GRE General Test, minimum GPA of 3.2; for doctorate, GRE General Test, MA in Middle East studies or equivalent, minimum GPA of 3.2. Additional exam requirements/recommendations for international students: Required—TOEFL (minimum score 580 paper-based; 92 iBT); Recommended—IELTS (minimum score 7). *Application deadline:* For fall admission, 1/15 priority date for domestic and international students. Application fee: $55 ($65 for international students). Electronic applications accepted. *Expenses:* Tuition, state resident: full-time $7011; part-time $3918.24 per credit hour. Tuition, nonresident: full-time $22,154; part-time $11,665.42 per credit hour. *Financial support:* In 2016–17, 5 students received support, including 2 teaching assistantships with full tuition reimbursements available (averaging $13,500 per year); fellowships and unspecified assistantships also available. Financial award application deadline: 1/15. *Faculty research:* Islamic studies; Middle Eastern history; political science; Judaic studies; anthropology; Arabic, Persian, Hebrew, and Turkish language and literature. *Unit head:* Johanna Watzinger-Tharp, Director, 801-581-7148, Fax: 801-581-6105, E-mail: j.tharp@utah.edu. *Application contact:* Kellie Hubbard, Academic Advisor, 801-581-5362, Fax: 801-581-6105, E-mail: kellie.hubbard@utah.edu.
Website: http://www.mec.utah.edu

**University of Vermont,** Graduate College, College of Arts and Sciences, Department of History, Burlington, VT 05405. Offers MA. *Degree requirements:* For master's, thesis. *Entrance requirements:* For master's, GRE General Test, sample project. Additional exam requirements/recommendations for international students: Required—TOEFL (minimum score 550 paper-based; 80 iBT). Electronic applications accepted. *Expenses:* Tuition, state resident: full-time $5814. Tuition, nonresident: full-time $14,670. *Faculty research:* American, European, and Asian history.

**University of Victoria,** Faculty of Graduate Studies, Faculty of Humanities, Department of History, Victoria, BC V8W 2Y2, Canada. Offers MA, PhD. *Program availability:* Part-time. *Degree requirements:* For master's, one foreign language, thesis; for doctorate,

one foreign language, comprehensive exam, thesis/dissertation. *Entrance requirements:* Additional exam requirements/recommendations for international students: Required—TOEFL (minimum score 600 paper-based), TWE. Electronic applications accepted. *Faculty research:* Canadian social history, Canadian gender history, Canadian native history, Canadian military history, British Columbian history, Western history, medieval history, world history.

**University of Virginia,** College and Graduate School of Arts and Sciences, Corcoran Department of History, Charlottesville, VA 22903. Offers MA, PhD, JD/MA. *Faculty:* 38 full-time (11 women), 2 part-time (both women); includes 67 full-time (31 women), 2 part-time (both women); includes 4 minority (1 Black or African American, non-Hispanic/Latino; 1 Asian, non-Hispanic/Latino; 2 Hispanic/Latino), 11 international. Average age 28. 179 applicants, 18% accepted, 19 enrolled. In 2016, 12 master's, 12 doctorates awarded. *Degree requirements:* For master's, one foreign language, essay; for doctorate, variable foreign language requirement, comprehensive exam, thesis/dissertation. *Entrance requirements:* For master's and doctorate, GRE General Test, 2 or more letters of recommendation. Additional exam requirements/recommendations for international students: Required—TOEFL (minimum score 600 paper-based; 90 iBT), IELTS (minimum score 7). *Application deadline:* For fall admission, 12/1 for domestic and international students. Applications are processed on a rolling basis. Application fee: $60. Electronic applications accepted. *Expenses:* Tuition, state resident: full-time $15,026; part-time $834 per credit hour. Tuition, nonresident: full-time $25,168; part-time $1378 per credit hour. *Required fees:* $2654. *Financial support:* Fellowships and teaching assistantships available. Financial award application deadline: 12/1; financial award applicants required to submit FAFSA. *Unit head:* Karen Parshall, Chair, 434-924-6397, Fax: 434-924-7891, E-mail: history@virginia.edu. *Application contact:* Robert Stolz, Director of Graduate Studies, 434-924-5954, Fax: 434-924-7891, E-mail: stolz@virginia.edu.
Website: http://history.as.virginia.edu/

**University of Washington,** Graduate School, College of Arts and Sciences, Department of History, Seattle, WA 98195. Offers MA, PhD. *Program availability:* Part-time. *Degree requirements:* For master's, one foreign language, comprehensive exam, thesis optional; for doctorate, one foreign language, comprehensive exam, thesis/dissertation. *Entrance requirements:* For master's and doctorate, GRE, minimum GPA of 3.0. Additional exam requirements/recommendations for international students: Required—TOEFL. Electronic applications accepted. *Faculty research:* United States, Asia, Europe, comparative history.

**University of Waterloo,** Graduate Studies, Faculty of Arts, Department of Classical Studies, Waterloo, ON N2L 3G1, Canada. Offers ancient Mediterranean cultures (MA). *Degree requirements:* For master's, one foreign language. *Faculty research:* Ancient history, philosophy, anthropology, religion, culture.

**University of Waterloo,** Graduate Studies, Faculty of Arts, Department of History, Waterloo, ON N2L 3G1, Canada. Offers MA, PhD. PhD offered jointly with University of Guelph and Wilfrid Laurier University. *Program availability:* Part-time, evening/weekend. *Degree requirements:* For master's, one foreign language, thesis optional; for doctorate, one foreign language, thesis/dissertation. *Entrance requirements:* For master's, honors degree, minimum B+ average, resume; for doctorate, master's degree, minimum A average, resume, writing sample. Additional exam requirements/recommendations for international students: Required—TOEFL, IELTS, PTE. Electronic applications accepted. *Faculty research:* Canadian, British, international, modern, European, and U.S. history; women's history; imperialism and slavery.

**The University of West Alabama,** School of Graduate Studies, College of Education, Departments of Instructional Leadership and Support/Curriculum and Instruction, Program in Secondary Education, Livingston, AL 35470. Offers biology (MAT); English language arts (MAT); high school 6-12 (M Ed); history (MAT); mathematics (MAT); science (MAT); social science (MAT). *Program availability:* Part-time, evening/weekend, 100% online. *Faculty:* 19 full-time (7 women), 7 part-time/adjunct (3 women). *Students:* 236 (159 women); includes 59 minority (53 Black or African American, non-Hispanic/Latino; 2 American Indian or Alaska Native, non-Hispanic/Latino; 1 Asian, non-Hispanic/Latino; 1 Hispanic/Latino; 2 Two or more races, non-Hispanic/Latino). Average age 32. 85 applicants, 88% accepted, 52 enrolled. In 2016, 84 master's awarded. *Degree requirements:* For master's, comprehensive exam, thesis optional. *Entrance requirements:* For master's, GRE General Test, MAT, minimum GPA of 2.75. Additional exam requirements/recommendations for international students: Required—TOEFL (minimum score 500 paper-based; 61 iBT). *Application deadline:* Applications are processed on a rolling basis. Application fee: $40. Electronic applications accepted. *Expenses:* Tuition, state resident: part-time $355 per credit hour. Tuition, nonresident: part-time $710 per credit hour. *Required fees:* $130 per semester. *Financial support:* Teaching assistantships, Federal Work-Study, scholarships/grants, and unspecified assistantships available. Support available to part-time students. Financial award application deadline: 3/1; financial award applicants required to submit FAFSA. *Faculty research:* Integrated arts in the curriculum, moral development of children. *Unit head:* Dr. Jodie Winship, Chair of Curriculum and Instruction, 205-652-5415, Fax: 205-652-3706, E-mail: jwinship@uwa.edu. *Application contact:* Dr. B. J. Kimbrough, Dean of Graduate Studies, 205-652-3647, Fax: 205-652-3706, E-mail: bkimbrough@uwa.edu.
Website: http://www.uwa.edu/highschool612.aspx

**The University of Western Ontario,** Faculty of Graduate Studies, Social Sciences Division, Department of History, London, ON N6A 5B8, Canada. Offers MA, PhD. *Program availability:* Part-time. *Degree requirements:* For master's, one foreign language, thesis (for some programs); for doctorate, one foreign language, thesis/dissertation. *Entrance requirements:* For master's, minimum B+ average on last 10 senior courses; for doctorate, minimum A- average on MA or last year honors degree. Additional exam requirements/recommendations for international students: Required—TOEFL. *Faculty research:* Canadian, U.S., Britain, Modern Europe, British Empire and Commonwealth Latin America.

**University of West Florida,** College of Arts, Social Sciences, and Humanities, Department of History, Pensacola, FL 32514-5750. Offers early American studies (MA); public history (MA); traditional history (MA). *Program availability:* Part-time, evening/weekend. *Degree requirements:* For master's, thesis or alternative. *Entrance requirements:* For master's, GRE (minimum score: verbal 500, writing 3.5) or MAT (minimum score 415), minimum GPA of 3.0, minimum 15 hours of upper-level history courses; official transcripts; letter of intent; writing sample (undergraduate research paper preferred). Additional exam requirements/recommendations for international students: Required—TOEFL (minimum score 550 paper-based). *Application deadline:* For fall admission, 6/1 for domestic and international students; for spring admission, 10/1 for domestic and international students. Applications are processed on a rolling basis. Application fee: $30. *Expenses:* Tuition, state resident: full-time $5316.12. Tuition, nonresident: full-time $11,308. *Required fees:* $583.92. Tuition and fees vary according to course load and program. *Financial support:* Fellowships with partial tuition reimbursements, research assistantships with partial tuition reimbursements, teaching assistantships with partial tuition reimbursements, and unspecified assistantships available. Financial award application deadline: 4/15; financial award applicants required to submit FAFSA. *Unit head:* Dr. Erin Stone, Program Director, 850-474-2685, Fax: 850-857-6015, E-mail: estone@uwf.edu. *Application contact:* Terry McCray, Assistant

Director of Graduate Admissions, 850-473-7718, Fax: 850-473-7714, E-mail: gradadmissions@uwf.edu. Website: http://uwf.edu/history/

**University of West Georgia,** College of Arts and Humanities, Carrollton, GA 30118. Offers English (MA); history (MA); museum studies (Postbaccalaureate Certificate); music performance (M Mus); music teacher education (M Mus); public history (Postbaccalaureate Certificate). *Program availability:* Part-time, evening/weekend, 100% online, blended/hybrid learning. *Faculty:* 70 full-time (39 women). *Students:* 23 full-time (16 women), 55 part-time (33 women); includes 18 minority (10 Black or African American, non-Hispanic/Latino; 1 American Indian or Alaska Native, non-Hispanic/Latino; 5 Hispanic/Latino; 2 Two or more races, non-Hispanic/Latino), 1 international. Average age 31. 24 applicants, 100% accepted, 23 enrolled. In 2016, 34 master's, 6 other advanced degrees awarded. *Entrance requirements:* Additional exam requirements/recommendations for international students: Required—TOEFL (minimum score 523 paper-based; 69 iBT); Recommended—IELTS (minimum score 6.5). *Application deadline:* For fall admission, 8/1 for domestic students, 6/1 for international students; for spring admission, 11/15 for domestic students, 10/15 for international students; for summer admission, 5/15 for domestic students, 3/30 for international students. Applications are processed on a rolling basis. Application fee: $40. Electronic applications accepted. *Expenses:* Tuition, state resident: full-time $5316; part-time $222 per semester hour. Tuition, nonresident: full-time $20,658; part-time $861 per semester hour. *Required fees:* $1962. Tuition and fees vary according to course load, degree level and program. *Financial support:* Fellowships, research assistantships, teaching assistantships, career-related internships or fieldwork, Federal Work-Study, institutionally sponsored loans, scholarships/grants, and unspecified assistantships available. Support available to part-time students. Financial award application deadline: 4/1; financial award applicants required to submit FAFSA. *Unit head:* Dr. Pauline D. Gagnon, Dean of Arts and Humanities, 678-839-5450, Fax: 678-839-5451, E-mail: pgagnon@westga.edu. *Application contact:* Dr. Toby Ziglar, Assistant Dean of the Graduate School, 678-839-1394, Fax: 678-839-1395, E-mail: graduate@westga.edu. Website: http://www.westga.edu/coah

**University of Windsor,** Faculty of Graduate Studies, Faculty of Arts and Social Sciences, Department of History, Windsor, ON N9B 3P4, Canada. Offers MA. *Program availability:* Part-time. *Degree requirements:* For master's, thesis (for some programs). *Entrance requirements:* For master's, minimum B average. Additional exam requirements/recommendations for international students: Required—TOEFL (minimum score 600 paper-based). Electronic applications accepted. *Faculty research:* Gender history, social-history questions about class gender and national identity, divorce in France: 1792-1816, gender and sexuality in Western Europe during the high and later Middle Ages, U.S.-Canadian comparisons in women's history.

**The University of Winnipeg,** Graduate Studies, Department of History, Winnipeg, MB R3B 2E9, Canada. Offers MA. MA program offered jointly with University of Manitoba. *Program availability:* Part-time, evening/weekend. *Degree requirements:* For master's, one foreign language, comprehensive exam or thesis. *Faculty research:* Canadian social history, European diplomacy, Indian history, colonial America, medieval history.

**University of Wisconsin–Eau Claire,** College of Arts and Sciences, Department of History, Eau Claire, WI 54702-4004. Offers public history (MA). *Program availability:* Part-time. *Degree requirements:* For master's, comprehensive exam, thesis optional, oral and written exams. *Entrance requirements:* For master's, minimum GPA of 3.15 during last 2 years, 3.3 in history, or 3.0 overall; research paper; bachelor's degree with minimum of 24 credits in history. Additional exam requirements/recommendations for international students: Required—TOEFL (minimum score 79 iBT).

**University of Wisconsin–Madison,** Graduate School, College of Letters and Science, Department of History, Madison, WI 53706-1380. Offers African history (MA, PhD); Central Asian history (MA, PhD); comparative world history (MA, PhD); East Asian history (MA, PhD); European history (MA, PhD); gender and women's history (MA, PhD); Latin American and Caribbean history (MA, PhD); Middle Eastern history (MA, PhD); South Asian history (MA, PhD); Southeast Asian history (MA, PhD); United States history (MA, PhD). Terminal master's awarded for partial completion of doctoral program. *Degree requirements:* For master's, thesis (for some programs); for doctorate, variable foreign language requirement, thesis/dissertation. *Entrance requirements:* For master's and doctorate, GRE General Test. Additional exam requirements/recommendations for international students: Required—Michigan English Language Assessment Battery or TOEFL. Electronic applications accepted. *Faculty research:* American, African, European, Asian, Latin American, and Middle Eastern history.

**University of Wisconsin–Milwaukee,** Graduate School, College of Letters and Science, Department of History, Milwaukee, WI 53201-0413. Offers global history (PhD); history (MA), including public history, urban historical studies; modern studies (PhD); urban history (PhD). *Program availability:* Part-time. *Students:* 24 full-time (15 women), 26 part-time (10 women); includes 5 minority (1 Black or African American, non-Hispanic/Latino; 1 Asian, non-Hispanic/Latino; 1 Hispanic/Latino; 2 Two or more races, non-Hispanic/Latino). Average age 32. 53 applicants, 66% accepted, 18 enrolled. In 2016, 15 master's awarded. *Degree requirements:* For master's, comprehensive exam, thesis or alternative; for doctorate, thesis/dissertation. *Entrance requirements:* For master's and doctorate, GRE General Test. Additional exam requirements/recommendations for international students: Required—TOEFL (minimum score 550 paper-based; 79 iBT), IELTS (minimum score 6.5). *Application deadline:* For fall admission, 1/1 priority date for domestic students; for spring admission, 9/1 for domestic students. Applications are processed on a rolling basis. Application fee: $56 ($96 for international students). Electronic applications accepted. *Financial support:* In 2016–17, 23 teaching assistantships were awarded; career-related internships or fieldwork and unspecified assistantships also available. Support available to part-time students. Financial award application deadline: 4/15; financial award applicants required to submit FAFSA. *Unit head:* Merry Weisner-Hanks, Department Chair, 414-229-4529, E-mail: merryh@uwm.edu. *Application contact:* General Information Contact, 414-229-4982, Fax: 414-229-6967, E-mail: gradschool@uwm.edu. Website: http://www.uwm.edu/dept/history/

**University of Wisconsin–Stevens Point,** College of Letters and Science, Department of History, Stevens Point, WI 54481-3897. Offers MST. *Degree requirements:* For master's, thesis or alternative.

**University of Wyoming,** College of Arts and Sciences, Department of History, Laramie, WY 82071. Offers MA, MAT. *Program availability:* Part-time. *Degree requirements:* For master's, one foreign language, thesis (for some programs). *Entrance requirements:* For master's, GRE General Test, minimum GPA of 3.0, 12 semester hours of undergraduate course work in history. Additional exam requirements/recommendations for international students: Required—TOEFL. Electronic applications accepted. *Faculty research:* American West, Native American history, nineteenth and twentieth century U.S. history, European history, Asian studies.

**Utah State University,** School of Graduate Studies, College of Humanities, Arts and Social Sciences, Department of History, Logan, UT 84322. Offers MA, MS. *Program availability:* Part-time, evening/weekend. *Degree requirements:* For master's, one foreign language, thesis. *Entrance requirements:* For master's, GRE General Test,

minimum GPA of 3.0. Additional exam requirements/recommendations for international students: Required—TOEFL. Electronic applications accepted. *Faculty research:* U.S. race and ethnicity, early modern and modern Europe, environmental history, western regional history.

**Valparaiso University,** Graduate School and Continuing Education, Programs in Liberal Studies, Concentration in History, Valparaiso, IN 46383. Offers MALS, Post-Master's Certificate, JD/MALS. *Program availability:* Part-time, evening/weekend. *Entrance requirements:* For master's, minimum GPA of 3.0. Additional exam requirements/recommendations for international students: Required—TOEFL (minimum score 550 paper-based; 80 iBT), IELTS (minimum score 6). Electronic applications accepted. *Expenses: Tuition:* Full-time $11,070; part-time $615 per credit hour. *Required fees:* $116 per semester. Tuition and fees vary according to course load, degree level and program. *Faculty research:* Regional Chinese history, British history, Martin Luther, Latin American history, African history.

**Vanderbilt University,** Department of History, Nashville, TN 37240-1001. Offers MA, MAT, PhD. *Faculty:* 40 full-time (11 women). *Students:* 59 full-time (30 women), 1 (woman) part-time; includes 11 minority (2 Black or African American, non-Hispanic/Latino; 1 Asian, non-Hispanic/Latino; 5 Hispanic/Latino; 3 Two or more races, non-Hispanic/Latino), 13 international. Average age 29. 164 applicants, 15% accepted, 12 enrolled. In 2016, 4 master's, 4 doctorates awarded. Terminal master's awarded for partial completion of doctoral program. *Degree requirements:* For doctorate, one foreign language, comprehensive exam, thesis/dissertation, final and qualifying exams. *Entrance requirements:* For doctorate, GRE General Test, sample of written work (recommended). Additional exam requirements/recommendations for international students: Required—TOEFL (minimum score 570 paper-based; 88 iBT). *Application deadline:* For fall admission, 1/15 for domestic and international students. Application fee: $0. Electronic applications accepted. *Expenses: Tuition:* Part-time $1854 per credit hour. *Financial support:* Fellowships with full tuition reimbursements, teaching assistantships with full tuition reimbursements, Federal Work-Study, institutionally sponsored loans, scholarships/grants, and health care benefits available. Financial award application deadline: 1/15; financial award applicants required to submit CSS PROFILE or FAFSA. *Faculty research:* Southern American history, recent U.S. history, intellectual and cultural history, European history, Latin American history. *Unit head:* Dr. Joel Harrington, Chair, 615-322-2575, Fax: 615-343-6002, E-mail: joel.harrington@vanderbilt.edu. *Application contact:* Catherine Molineux, Director of Graduate Studies, 615-322-2575, Fax: 615-343-6002, E-mail: catherine.a.molineux@vanderbilt.edu. Website: http://www.vanderbilt.edu/historydept/graduate.html

**Villanova University,** Graduate School of Liberal Arts and Sciences, Department of History, Villanova, PA 19085-1699. Offers MA. *Program availability:* Part-time, evening/weekend. *Faculty:* 6. *Students:* 33 full-time (14 women), 14 part-time (4 women); includes 3 minority (1 Black or African American, non-Hispanic/Latino; 1 Asian, non-Hispanic/Latino; 1 Hispanic/Latino), 1 international. Average age 27. 24 applicants, 92% accepted, 18 enrolled. In 2016, 18 master's awarded. *Degree requirements:* For master's, comprehensive exam, thesis optional. *Entrance requirements:* For master's, GRE General Test, minimum GPA of 3.0, 3 letters of recommendation, personal statement. Additional exam requirements/recommendations for international students: Required—TOEFL. *Application deadline:* For fall admission, 3/1 for domestic students, 5/1 priority date for international students; for spring admission, 11/15 for domestic students, 10/15 priority date for international students; for summer admission, 5/1 for domestic students. Applications are processed on a rolling basis. Application fee: $50. Electronic applications accepted. *Financial support:* Research assistantships, Federal Work-Study, scholarships/grants, and unspecified assistantships available. Financial award applicants required to submit FAFSA. *Unit head:* Dr. Judith Giesberg, Director, 610-519-4668. Website: http://www1.villanova.edu/villanova/artsci/history/academic-programs/graduate.html

**Virginia Commonwealth University,** Graduate School, College of Humanities and Sciences, Department of History, Richmond, VA 23284-9005. Offers MA. *Program availability:* Part-time. *Degree requirements:* For master's, thesis optional. *Entrance requirements:* For master's, GRE General Test, 30 undergraduate credits in history. Additional exam requirements/recommendations for international students: Required—TOEFL (minimum score 600 paper-based; 100 iBT); Recommended—IELTS (minimum score 6.5). *Application deadline:* For fall admission, 7/1 for domestic students; for spring admission, 12/1 for domestic students. Application fee: $50. Electronic applications accepted. *Financial support:* Research assistantships, teaching assistantships, Federal Work-Study, institutionally sponsored loans, and tuition waivers (full and partial) available. Support available to part-time students. Financial award applicants required to submit FAFSA. *Faculty research:* United States history, history of the South, urban history, African American history, colonial American history, the Civil War, twentieth-century American history, European history, trans-Atlantic history. *Unit head:* Dr. Ryan K. Smith, Graduate Program Director, 804-828-1635, E-mail: rksmith3@vcu.edu. *Application contact:* Dr. Timothy N. Thurber, Director of Graduate Studies, 804-828-4760, Fax: 804-828-7085, E-mail: tnthurber@vcu.edu. Website: http://www.has.vcu.edu/his/

**Virginia Polytechnic Institute and State University,** Graduate School, College of Liberal Arts and Human Sciences, Blacksburg, VA 24061. Offers career and technical education (MS Ed, Ed D, PhD, Ed S); communication (MA); counselor education (MA Ed, Ed D, PhD, Ed S); creative writing (MFA); curriculum and instruction (MA Ed, Ed D, PhD, Ed S); educational leadership and policy studies (MA Ed, Ed D, PhD, Ed S); educational research and evaluation (PhD); English (MA); foreign languages, cultures, and literatures (MA); higher education (PhD); higher education and student affairs (MA Ed); history (MA); human development (MS, PhD); material culture and public humanities (MA); philosophy (MA); political science (MA); rhetoric and writing (PhD); science and technology studies (MS, PhD); social, political, ethical, and cultural thought (PhD); sociology (MS, PhD); theater arts (MFA). *Faculty:* 408 full-time (204 women), 3 part-time/adjunct (2 women). *Students:* 657 full-time (446 women), 457 part-time (292 women); includes 213 minority (114 Black or African American, non-Hispanic/Latino; 3 American Indian or Alaska Native, non-Hispanic/Latino; 29 Asian, non-Hispanic/Latino; 44 Hispanic/Latino; 23 Two or more races, non-Hispanic/Latino), 93 international. Average age 33. 805 applicants, 55% accepted, 328 enrolled. In 2016, 270 master's, 91 doctorates awarded. *Degree requirements:* For master's, comprehensive exam (for some programs), thesis (for some programs); for doctorate, comprehensive exam (for some programs), thesis/dissertation (for some programs). *Entrance requirements:* For master's and doctorate, GRE/GMAT. Additional exam requirements/recommendations for international students: Required—TOEFL (minimum score 80 iBT). *Application deadline:* For fall admission, 8/1 for domestic students, 4/1 for international students; for spring admission, 1/1 for domestic students, 9/1 for international students. Applications are processed on a rolling basis. Application fee: $75. Electronic applications accepted. *Expenses:* Tuition, state resident: full-time $12,467; part-time $692.50 per credit hour. Tuition, nonresident: full-time $25,095; part-time $1394.25 per credit hour. *Required fees:* $2669; $491.50 per semester. Tuition and fees vary according to course load, campus/location and program. *Financial support:* In 2016–17, 21 research

## History

assistantships with full tuition reimbursements (averaging $19,817 per year), 237 teaching assistantships with full tuition reimbursements (averaging $15,497 per year) were awarded. Financial award application deadline: 3/1; financial award applicants required to submit FAFSA. *Total annual research expenditures:* $6.6 million. *Unit head:* Rosemary Blieszner, Interim Dean, 540-231-6779, Fax: 540-231-7157, E-mail: liberalartsdean@vt.edu. *Application contact:* Chelsea Blanchet, Executive Assistant, 540-231-6779, Fax: 540-231-7157, E-mail: bchels1@vt.edu.
Website: http://www.liberalarts.vt.edu/

**Washington State University,** College of Arts and Sciences, Department of History, Pullman, WA 99164. Offers MA, PhD. Program applications must be made through the Pullman campus. *Program availability:* Part-time. *Degree requirements:* For master's, comprehensive exam, thesis optional, oral exam; for doctorate, one foreign language, comprehensive exam, thesis/dissertation, oral and written exam. *Entrance requirements:* For master's and doctorate, GRE General Test, official transcripts from all universities attended; three letters of recommendation; statement of purpose; writing sample; Preferred Fields of Study form; Language Background form. Additional exam requirements/recommendations for international students: Required—TOEFL (minimum score 550 paper-based), IELTS. Electronic applications accepted. *Faculty research:* Public, world, environmental, women's and U.S. history.

**Washington University in St. Louis,** The Graduate School, Department of History, St. Louis, MO 63130-4899. Offers PhD. *Degree requirements:* For doctorate, 2 foreign languages, thesis/dissertation. *Entrance requirements:* For doctorate, GRE General Test. Additional exam requirements/recommendations for international students: Required—TOEFL. Electronic applications accepted. *Faculty research:* Seventeenth-through nineteenth-century America, twentieth-century America, African history, Central Europe, East Asian history, history of American political culture, international urban history, Middle East, Medieval and Early Modern Europe.

**Wayland Baptist University,** Graduate Programs, Programs in Behavioral and Social Sciences, Plainview, TX 79072-6998. Offers counseling (MA); criminal justice (MACJ); government administration (MPA); history (MA); homeland security (MPA); humanities (MAH); justice administration (MPA). *Program availability:* Part-time, evening/weekend, online learning. *Degree requirements:* For master's, comprehensive exam. *Entrance requirements:* For master's, GRE, MAT. Additional exam requirements/recommendations for international students: Required—TOEFL (minimum score 500 paper-based; 61 iBT). Electronic applications accepted.

**Wayne State University,** College of Liberal Arts and Sciences, Department of History, Detroit, MI 48202. Offers Africa (PhD); America (PhD); Asia (PhD); Europe (PhD); gender (PhD); history (MA); labor (PhD); public history (MA); science and technology (PhD); world history (PhD, Graduate Certificate); JD/MA; M Ed/MA; MLIS/MA. Doctoral program admits for fall only. *Program availability:* Evening/weekend. *Faculty:* 18. *Students:* 23 full-time (8 women), 21 part-time (5 women); includes 8 minority (3 Black or African American, non-Hispanic/Latino; 2 Hispanic/Latino; 3 Two or more races, non-Hispanic/Latino). Average age 40. 55 applicants, 38% accepted, 15 enrolled. In 2016, 6 master's, 5 doctorates awarded. *Degree requirements:* For master's, comprehensive exam, thesis (for some programs), final oral exam on thesis or essay and seminar; internship and project (for public history); for doctorate, variable foreign language requirement, comprehensive exam, thesis/dissertation, qualifying exam in 4 fields of history. *Entrance requirements:* For master's, GRE General Test, minimum undergraduate GPA of 3.25 in history, 3.0 overall; at least 18 credits in history and related subjects at the advanced undergraduate level; foreign language; letter of intent; research paper; at least two letters of recommendation from former instructors; for doctorate, GRE General Test, minimum GPA of 3.0, 3.25 in minimum of 18 semester credits in history and related subjects; letter of intent; research paper; at least three letters of recommendation from former professors; for Graduate Certificate, baccalaureate degree from accredited college or university; minimum GPA of 3.0, 3.25 in a minimum of eighteen semester credits in history and related subjects at the advanced undergraduate level. Additional exam requirements/recommendations for international students: Required—TOEFL (minimum score 550 paper-based; 79 iBT), TWE (minimum score 5.5), Michigan English Language Assessment Battery (minimum score 85); Recommended—IELTS (minimum score 6.5). *Application deadline:* For fall admission, 2/1 priority date for domestic and international students; for winter admission, 11/1 for domestic students, 10/1 priority date for international students; for spring admission, 2/1 for domestic students, 1/1 priority date for international students. Application fee: $50. Electronic applications accepted. *Expenses:* $16,503 per year resident tuition and fees, $33,697 per year non-resident tuition and fees. *Financial support:* In 2016–17, 16 students received support, including 2 fellowships with tuition reimbursements available (averaging $18,796 per year), 1 research assistantship with tuition reimbursement available (averaging $21,593 per year), 6 teaching assistantships with tuition reimbursements available (averaging $17,994 per year); scholarships/grants, health care benefits, and unspecified assistantships also available. Financial award applicants required to submit FAFSA. *Faculty research:* African, American, Asian, European, gender, German, labor, science and technology, urban/labor, violence, world. *Unit head:* Dr. Elizabeth V. Faue, Professor/Chair, 313-577-2525, E-mail: evfaue@wayne.edu. *Application contact:* Dr. Eric Ash, Associate Professor and Director of Graduate Studies, 313-577-2525, E-mail: ericash@wayne.edu.
Website: http://clas.wayne.edu/history/

**West Chester University of Pennsylvania,** College of Arts and Humanities, Department of History, West Chester, PA 19383. Offers history (M Ed, MA). *Program availability:* Part-time, evening/weekend. *Faculty:* 4 full-time (0 women). *Students:* 2 full-time (1 woman), 18 part-time (8 women); includes 1 minority (Two or more races, non-Hispanic/Latino). Average age 33. 13 applicants, 92% accepted, 6 enrolled. In 2016, 6 master's awarded. *Degree requirements:* For master's, comprehensive exam, thesis optional. *Entrance requirements:* For master's, statement of professional goals, writing sample, minimum GPA of 3.0 in history, three letters of recommendation. Additional exam requirements/recommendations for international students: Required—TOEFL or IELTS. *Application deadline:* For fall admission, 5/15 for international students; for spring admission, 10/15 for international students. Applications are processed on a rolling basis. Application fee: $50. Electronic applications accepted. *Expenses:* Tuition, state resident: full-time $8694; part-time $483 per credit. Tuition, nonresident: full-time $13,050; part-time $725 per credit. *Required fees:* $2399; $119.05 per credit. Tuition and fees vary according to campus/location and program. *Financial support:* Scholarships/grants and unspecified assistantships available. Financial award application deadline: 2/15; financial award applicants required to submit FAFSA. *Unit head:* Dr. Wayne Hanley, Chair, 610-436-2201, E-mail: whanley@wcupa.edu. *Application contact:* Dr. Brenda Gaydosh, Graduate Coordinator, 610-436-0734, E-mail: bgaydosh@wcupa.edu.
Website: http://www.wcupa.edu/arts-humanities/history/

**Western Carolina University,** Graduate School, College of Arts and Sciences, Department of History, Cullowhee, NC 28723. Offers MA. *Program availability:* Part-time, evening/weekend. *Degree requirements:* For master's, one foreign language, comprehensive exam, thesis or alternative. *Entrance requirements:* For master's, GRE General Test, appropriate undergraduate degree, 3 letters of recommendation. Additional exam requirements/recommendations for international students: Required—

TOEFL (minimum score 550 paper-based; 79 iBT). *Expenses:* Tuition, state resident: full-time $2174. Tuition, nonresident: full-time $7377. *Required fees:* $1442. Part-time tuition and fees vary according to course load. *Faculty research:* Social and economic history of the American South, Islamic world history, German history, social and political protest, medieval social history.

**Western Connecticut State University,** Division of Graduate Studies, Maricostas School of Arts and Sciences, Department of History and Non-Western Cultures, Danbury, CT 06810-6885. Offers MA. *Program availability:* Part-time. *Degree requirements:* For master's, thesis or research project, completion of program in 6 years. *Entrance requirements:* For master's, minimum GPA of 2.5. Additional exam requirements/recommendations for international students: Recommended—TOEFL (minimum score 550 paper-based; 79 iBT), IELTS (minimum score 6). *Faculty research:* History of jazz, music and leisure, African-American musicians.

**Western Illinois University,** School of Graduate Studies, College of Arts and Sciences, Department of History, Macomb, IL 61455-1390. Offers MA. *Program availability:* Part-time. *Students:* 14 full-time (6 women), 12 part-time (5 women); includes 6 minority (3 Black or African American, non-Hispanic/Latino; 1 American Indian or Alaska Native, non-Hispanic/Latino; 1 Hispanic/Latino; 1 Native Hawaiian or other Pacific Islander, non-Hispanic/Latino). Average age 33. 14 applicants, 79% accepted, 7 enrolled. In 2016, 5 master's awarded. *Degree requirements:* For master's, thesis or alternative. *Entrance requirements:* Additional exam requirements/recommendations for international students: Required—TOEFL (minimum score 550 paper-based; 80 iBT). *Application deadline:* Applications are processed on a rolling basis. Application fee: $30. Electronic applications accepted. *Financial support:* In 2016–17, 9 students received support. Unspecified assistantships available. Financial award applicants required to submit FAFSA. *Unit head:* Dr. Jennifer McNabb, Chairperson, 309-298-1053. *Application contact:* Dr. Nancy Parsons, Associate Provost and Director of Graduate Studies, 309-298-1806, Fax: 309-298-2345, E-mail: grad-office@wiu.edu.
Website: http://wiu.edu/history

**Western Kentucky University,** Graduate Studies, Potter College of Arts and Letters, Department of History, Bowling Green, KY 42101. Offers MA, MA Ed. *Program availability:* Part-time, evening/weekend, online learning. *Degree requirements:* For master's, comprehensive exam, thesis optional, final exam. *Entrance requirements:* For master's, GRE General Test, minimum GPA of 2.75. Additional exam requirements/recommendations for international students: Required—TOEFL (minimum score 555 paper-based; 79 iBT). *Faculty research:* United States, Europe, China, India, Latin America.

**Western Michigan University,** Graduate College, College of Arts and Sciences, Department of History, Kalamazoo, MI 49008. Offers MA, PhD. *Degree requirements:* For master's, thesis optional; for doctorate, thesis/dissertation.

**Western Washington University,** Graduate School, College of Humanities and Social Sciences, Department of History, Bellingham, WA 98225-5996. Offers MA. *Program availability:* Part-time. *Degree requirements:* For master's, one foreign language, comprehensive exam, thesis (for some programs). *Entrance requirements:* For master's, GRE General Test, minimum GPA of 3.0 in last 60 semester hours or last 90 quarter hours. Additional exam requirements/recommendations for international students: Required—TOEFL (minimum score 567 paper-based). Electronic applications accepted.

**Westfield State University,** College of Graduate and Continuing Education, Department of Education, Westfield, MA 01086. Offers early childhood education (M Ed); elementary education (M Ed); occupational education (M Ed); reading (M Ed), including reading specialist; secondary education (M Ed), including biology teacher education, chemistry teacher education, general science teacher education, history teacher education, mathematics teacher education, physical education teacher education; special education (M Ed). *Accreditation:* NCATE. *Program availability:* Part-time, evening/weekend. *Faculty:* 16 full-time (7 women), 33 part-time/adjunct (24 women). *Students:* 21 full-time (10 women), 168 part-time (126 women); includes 6 minority (2 Black or African American, non-Hispanic/Latino; 2 Hispanic/Latino; 2 Two or more races, non-Hispanic/Latino), 1 international. Average age 32. 47 applicants, 85% accepted, 30 enrolled. In 2016, 51 master's awarded. *Degree requirements:* For master's, comprehensive exam, practicum. *Entrance requirements:* For master's, GRE General Test or MAT, minimum undergraduate GPA of 2.8. Additional exam requirements/recommendations for international students: Recommended—TOEFL (minimum score 550 paper-based; 79 iBT). *Application deadline:* For fall admission, 6/30 for domestic students; for spring admission, 10/31 for domestic students; for summer admission, 3/31 for domestic students. Applications are processed on a rolling basis. Application fee: $50. Electronic applications accepted. *Expenses:* Tuition, state resident: part-time $318 per semester hour. Tuition, nonresident: part-time $318 per semester hour. *Required fees:* $75 per semester. Tuition and fees vary according to course load and program. *Financial support:* Unspecified assistantships and SOS scholarships for education majors only available. Financial award application deadline: 3/1; financial award applicants required to submit FAFSA. *Faculty research:* Collaborative teacher education, developmental early childhood education. *Unit head:* Dr. Sandra Berkowitz, Department Chair, 413-572-5323, E-mail: sberkowitz@westfield.ma.edu. *Application contact:* Shelly Henrichon, Coordinator of DGCE Admissions, 413-572-8022, Fax: 413-572-5227, E-mail: mhenrichon@westfield.ma.edu.
Website: http://www.westfield.ma.edu/academics/degrees/education-graduate-programs

**West Texas A&M University,** College of Fine Arts and Humanities, Department of History, Canyon, TX 79016-0001. Offers MA. *Program availability:* Part-time, evening/weekend. *Degree requirements:* For master's, comprehensive exam, thesis optional. *Entrance requirements:* For master's, GRE General Test. Additional exam requirements/recommendations for international students: Required—TOEFL (minimum score 550 paper-based). *Application deadline:* For fall admission, 8/1 for domestic students, 5/1 for international students; for spring admission, 12/1 for domestic students, 10/30 for international students; for summer admission, 5/1 for domestic students. Applications are processed on a rolling basis. Application fee: $40 ($75 for international students). Electronic applications accepted. *Financial support:* Research assistantships with partial tuition reimbursements, teaching assistantships with partial tuition reimbursements, career-related internships or fieldwork, Federal Work-Study, institutionally sponsored loans, and tuition waivers (partial) available. Support available to part-time students. Financial award applicants required to submit CSS PROFILE or FAFSA. *Faculty research:* Latin America, Middle and Far East, Southern Asia, Western Europe, United States. *Unit head:* Dr. Kristina Drumheller, Interim Head, 806-651-2427, E-mail: kdrumheller@wtamu.edu.
Website: http://www.wtamu.edu/academics/history.aspx

**West Virginia University,** Eberly College of Arts and Sciences, Department of History, Morgantown, WV 26506. Offers African history (MA, PhD); African-American history (MA, PhD); American history (MA, PhD); Appalachian/regional history (MA, PhD); East Asian history (MA, PhD); European history (MA, PhD); history of science and technology (MA, PhD); Latin American history (MA). *Program availability:* Part-time. *Degree requirements:* For master's, one foreign language, thesis (for some programs), oral exam, thesis defense; for doctorate, one foreign language, comprehensive exam, thesis/dissertation, dissertation defense. *Entrance requirements:* For master's, GRE General Test, minimum GPA of 3.0; for doctorate, GRE General Test. Additional exam requirements/recommendations for international students: Required—TOEFL (minimum score 550 paper-based), IELTS (minimum score 6.5). Electronic applications accepted. *Faculty research:* United States, Appalachia, modern Europe, Africa, colonial and post-colonial societies.

**Wichita State University,** Graduate School, Fairmount College of Liberal Arts and Sciences, Department of History, Wichita, KS 67260. Offers MA. *Program availability:* Part-time. *Unit head:* Dr. Jay Price, Chair, 316-978-3150, Fax: 316-978-3473, E-mail: jay.price@wichita.edu. *Application contact:* Jordan Oleson, Admissions Coordinator, 316-978-3150, Fax: 316-978-3473, E-mail: jordan.oleson@wichita.edu. Website: http://www.wichita.edu/history

**Wilfrid Laurier University,** Faculty of Graduate and Postdoctoral Studies, Faculty of Arts, Department of History, Waterloo, ON N2L 3C5, Canada. Offers MA, PhD. *Program availability:* Part-time. *Degree requirements:* For master's, thesis optional; for doctorate, thesis/dissertation. *Entrance requirements:* For master's, honors BA or the equivalent in history; minimum B+ average in undergraduate course work, exclusive of first year level courses; for doctorate, MA in history, minimum A- average. Additional exam requirements/recommendations for international students: Required—TOEFL (minimum score 89 iBT). Electronic applications accepted. *Faculty research:* Canadian, early modern European, modern European, Scottish, race, class, imperialism, slavery, British, urban and rural, science/medicine/technology, gender/women's/family, international, United States.

**William Paterson University of New Jersey,** College of Humanities and Social Sciences, Wayne, NJ 07470-8420. Offers applied sociology (MA); clinical and counseling psychology (MA); clinical psychology (Psy D); creative and professional writing (MFA); English (MA); history (MA); political science and public policy (MA); public policy and international affairs (MA). *Program availability:* Part-time, evening/weekend. *Faculty:* 35 full-time (19 women), 8 part-time/adjunct (5 women). *Students:* 58 full-time (38 women), 62 part-time (46 women); includes 40 minority (9 Black or African American, non-Hispanic/Latino; 6 Asian, non-Hispanic/Latino; 21 Hispanic/Latino; 4 Two or more races, non-Hispanic/Latino), 4 international. Average age 32. 160 applicants, 55% accepted, 50 enrolled. In 2016, 56 master's awarded. *Degree requirements:* For master's, thesis (for some programs), internship (for some programs). *Entrance requirements:* For master's, GRE/MAT, minimum GPA of 3.0; 2 letters of recommendation; writing sample/personal statement. Additional exam requirements/recommendations for international students: Required—TOEFL (minimum score 550 paper-based; 79 iBT), IELTS (minimum score 6). *Application deadline:* For fall admission, 8/1 for domestic students, 4/1 for international students; for spring admission, 12/1 for domestic students, 11/1 for international students; for summer admission, 5/1 for domestic students, 2/1 for international students. Applications are processed on a rolling basis. Application fee: $50. Electronic applications accepted. *Expenses:* Tuition, state resident: full-time $12,480; part-time $611 per credit. Tuition, nonresident: full-time $20,263; part-time $992 per credit. *Required fees:* $1573; $77 per credit. Tuition and fees vary according to course load, degree level and program. *Financial support:* Career-related internships or fieldwork, Federal Work-Study, scholarships/grants, and unspecified assistantships available. Support available to part-time students. Financial award applicants required to submit FAFSA. *Faculty research:* Relationship violence among adolescents; autism in young children; game theory; gender, governance and empowerment in India; Chinese development policies concerning Africa. *Total annual research expenditures:* $162,900. *Unit head:* Dr. Kara Rabbitt, Dean, 973-720-2180, Fax: 973-720-2955, E-mail: rabbittk@wpunj.edu. *Application contact:* Tinu Adeniran, Associate Director, Graduate Admissions, 973-720-2764, Fax: 973-720-2035, E-mail: adenirant@wpunj.edu. Website: http://www.wpunj.edu/cohss

**Winthrop University,** College of Arts and Sciences, Department of History, Rock Hill, SC 29733. Offers MA. *Program availability:* Part-time. *Degree requirements:* For master's, one foreign language. *Entrance requirements:* For master's, GRE General Test or PRAXIS, 24 hours of history at the undergraduate level. Additional exam requirements/recommendations for international students: Required—TOEFL (minimum score 550 paper-based; 79 iBT), IELTS (minimum score 6). Electronic applications accepted. *Expenses:* Tuition, state resident: full-time $14,312; part-time $599 per credit hour. Tuition, nonresident: full-time $27,570; part-time $1153 per credit hour.

**Worcester State University,** Graduate Studies, Program in History, Worcester, MA 01602-2597. Offers MA. *Program availability:* Part-time. *Faculty:* 6 full-time (4 women), 1 part-time/adjunct (0 women). *Students:* 3 full-time (2 women), 9 part-time (4 women); includes 1 minority (American Indian or Alaska Native, non-Hispanic/Latino). Average age 37. 15 applicants, 73% accepted, 4 enrolled. In 2016, 12 master's awarded. *Degree requirements:* For master's, comprehensive exam (for some programs), thesis (for some programs), portfolio. *Entrance requirements:* For master's, GRE General Test or MAT, 18 undergraduate credits in history, including U.S. history and Western civilizations. Additional exam requirements/recommendations for international students: Required—TOEFL (minimum score 550 paper-based; 79 iBT). *Application deadline:* For fall admission, 6/15 for domestic and international students; for spring admission, 11/1 for domestic and international students; for summer admission, 4/1 for domestic and international students. Applications are processed on a rolling basis. Application fee: $50. Electronic applications accepted. *Expenses:* Tuition, state resident: part-time $150 per credit. Tuition, nonresident: part-time $150 per credit. *Financial support:* Career-related internships or fieldwork, scholarships/grants, and unspecified assistantships available. Financial award application deadline: 3/1; financial award applicants required to submit FAFSA. *Unit head:* Dr. Erika Briesacher, Coordinator, 508-929-8692, Fax: 508-929-8155, E-mail: ebriesacher@worcester.edu. *Application contact:* Sara Grady, Associate Dean, Graduate Studies and Professional Development, 508-929-8787, Fax: 508-929-8100, E-mail: sara.grady@worcester.edu.

**Wright State University,** Graduate School, College of Liberal Arts, Department of History, Dayton, OH 45435. Offers MA. *Degree requirements:* For master's, thesis optional. *Entrance requirements:* For master's, GRE General Test, minimum GPA of 3.0 in history, 2.7 overall. Additional exam requirements/recommendations for international students: Required—TOEFL. Application fee: $25. *Expenses:* Tuition, state resident: full-time $9952; part-time $622 per credit hour. Tuition, nonresident: full-time $16,960; part-time $1060 per credit hour. *Financial support:* Fellowships, research assistantships, teaching assistantships, and unspecified assistantships available. Support available to part-time students. Financial award applicants required to submit FAFSA. *Faculty research:* U.S. religions; women's, Southern, European, and archival history. *Unit head:* Dr. Edward F. Haas, Chair, 937-775-3110, Fax: 937-775-3301, E-mail: edward.haas@wright.edu. *Application contact:* Dr. John W. Sherman, Director, 937-775-4946, Fax: 937-775-3301, E-mail: john.sherman@wright.edu.

**Yale University,** Graduate School of Arts and Sciences, Department of History, New Haven, CT 06520. Offers history (M Phil, MA, PhD); history of science and medicine (MA, PhD). Terminal master's awarded for partial completion of doctoral program. *Degree requirements:* For master's, one foreign language; for doctorate, 2 foreign languages, thesis/dissertation. *Entrance requirements:* For doctorate, GRE General Test.

**York University,** Faculty of Graduate Studies, Faculty of Liberal Arts and Professional Studies, Program in History, Toronto, ON M3J 1P3, Canada. Offers MA, PhD. *Program availability:* Part-time. *Degree requirements:* For master's, thesis or alternative; for doctorate, one foreign language, comprehensive exam, thesis/dissertation, qualifying exam. Electronic applications accepted.

**Youngstown State University,** Graduate School, College of Liberal Arts and Social Sciences, Department of History, Youngstown, OH 44555-0001. Offers MA. *Program availability:* Part-time. *Degree requirements:* For master's, thesis optional, oral and written exams. *Entrance requirements:* For master's, minimum GPA of 2.75. Additional exam requirements/recommendations for international students: Required—TOEFL. *Faculty research:* Holocaust, Marxism, nineteenth- and twentieth-century United States, historic preservation, revolutionary France.

# History of Medicine

**The College at Brockport, State University of New York,** School of Education, Health, and Human Services, Department of Education and Human Development, Brockport, NY 14420-2997. Offers adolescence education (MS Ed), including adolescence biology education, adolescence chemistry education, adolescence earth science education, adolescence English education, adolescence mathematics education, adolescence physics education, adolescence social studies education; bilingual education (MS Ed, AGC); childhood curriculum specialist (MS Ed); inclusive generalist education (MS Ed, AGC, Advanced Certificate), including biology (MS Ed, AGC), chemistry (MS Ed), English (MS Ed, Advanced Certificate), mathematics (MS Ed, Advanced Certificate), science (MS Ed, Advanced Certificate), social studies (MS Ed, Advanced Certificate); literacy education B-12 (MS Ed). *Accreditation:* NCATE. *Faculty:* 14 full-time (9 women), 12 part-time/adjunct (11 women). *Students:* 56 full-time (36 women), 168 part-time (130 women); includes 16 minority (5 Black or African American, non-Hispanic/Latino; 3 Asian, non-Hispanic/Latino; 4 Hispanic/Latino; 4 Two or more races, non-Hispanic/Latino). 93 applicants, 78% accepted, 62 enrolled. In 2016, 74 master's, 1 AGC awarded. *Degree requirements:* For master's, thesis or alternative. *Entrance requirements:* For master's, minimum GPA of 3.0, letters of recommendation, interview (for some programs); statement of objectives, current resume. Additional exam requirements/recommendations for international students: Required—TOEFL (minimum score 550 paper-based; 79 iBT), IELTS (minimum score 6.5). *Application deadline:* For fall admission, 3/15 priority date for domestic and international students; for spring admission, 10/15 priority date for domestic and international students; for summer admission, 3/15 priority date for domestic and international students. Application fee: $80. Electronic applications accepted. *Expenses:* Contact institution. *Financial support:* In 2016–17, 1 fellowship with full tuition reimbursement (averaging $7,500 per year), 1 teaching assistantship with full tuition reimbursement (averaging $6,000 per year) were awarded; Federal Work-Study, scholarships/grants, and unspecified assistantships also available. Support available to part-time students. Financial award application deadline: 3/15; financial award applicants required to submit FAFSA. *Faculty research:* Educational assessment, literacy education, inclusive education, teacher preparation, qualitative methodology. *Unit head:* Dr. Sue Robb, Chairperson, 585-395-5550, Fax: 585-395-2172, E-mail: srobb@brockport.edu. *Application contact:* Anne Walton, Coordinator of Certification and Graduate Advisement, 585-395-2326, Fax: 585-395-2172, E-mail: awalton@brockport.edu. Website: http://www.brockport.edu/ehd/

**McGill University,** Faculty of Graduate and Postdoctoral Studies, Faculty of Arts, Department of History and Classical Studies, Montréal, QC H3A 2T5, Canada. Offers history (MA, PhD); history of medicine (MA).

**McGill University,** Faculty of Graduate and Postdoctoral Studies, Faculty of Medicine, Department of Social Studies in Medicine, Montréal, QC H3A 2T5, Canada. Offers medical anthropology (MA, PhD); medical history (MA, PhD); medical sociology (MA, PhD).

**Oregon State University,** College of Liberal Arts, Program in History of Science, Corvallis, OR 97331. Offers development of the physical, biological, and environmental sciences (MA, MS, PhD); history of science and medicine (MA, MS, PhD); intellectual and social history of science in Europe and the U.S. (MA, MS, PhD). *Program availability:* Part-time. *Faculty:* 16 full-time (7 women), 1 part-time/adjunct (0 women). *Students:* 8 full-time (4 women), 5 part-time (2 women); includes 2 minority (1 Asian, non-Hispanic/Latino; 1 Hispanic/Latino), 1 international. Average age 37. 11 applicants, 27% accepted, 3 enrolled. In 2016, 2 master's, 1 doctorate awarded. *Degree requirements:* For master's, variable foreign language requirement, thesis optional; for doctorate, one foreign language, thesis/dissertation. *Entrance requirements:* For master's and doctorate, GRE. Additional exam requirements/recommendations for international students: Required—TOEFL (minimum score 80 iBT), IELTS (minimum score 6.5). *Application deadline:* For fall admission, 1/1 for domestic and international students. Application fee: $75 ($85 for international students). *Expenses:* Tuition, state resident: full-time $12,150; part-time $450 per credit. Tuition, nonresident: full-time $21,789; part-time $807 per credit. *Required fees:* $1651; $1507 per credit. One-time fee: $350. Tuition and fees vary according to course load, campus/location and program. *Financial support:* Application deadline: 1/1. *Unit head:* Dr. Ben Mutschler, Director. *Application contact:* Dr. Allen Thompson, Director of Graduate Studies/Associate Professor, 541-737-5654, E-mail: allen.thompson@oregonstate.edu. Website: http://liberalarts.oregonstate.edu/history/graduate-history-of-science

**Rutgers University–New Brunswick,** Graduate School-New Brunswick, Program in History, Piscataway, NJ 08854-8097. Offers African-American history (PhD); early American history (PhD); early modern European history (PhD); east Asian history (PhD);

global and comparative history (PhD); history (PhD); history of diplomacy and foreign relations (PhD); history of technology, environment and health (PhD); history of the Atlantic cultures and African diaspora (PhD); Latin American history (PhD); medieval history (PhD); modern European history (PhD); nineteenth and twentieth century American history (PhD); women's and gender history (PhD). *Degree requirements:* For doctorate, thesis/dissertation. *Entrance requirements:* For doctorate, GRE General Test, sample of written work. Electronic applications accepted. *Faculty research:* American history, European history, Afro-American history, women's history, Latin American history.

**The University of Manchester,** Faculty of Life Sciences, Manchester, United Kingdom. Offers adaptive organismal biology (M Phil, PhD); animal biology (M Phil, PhD); biochemistry (M Phil, PhD); bioinformatics (M Phil, PhD); biomolecular sciences (M Phil, PhD); biotechnology (M Phil, PhD); cell biology (M Phil, PhD); cell matrix research (M Phil, PhD); channels and transporters (M Phil, PhD); developmental biology (M Phil, PhD); Egyptology (M Phil, PhD); environmental biology (M Phil, PhD); evolutionary biology (M Phil, PhD); gene expression (M Phil, PhD); genetics (M Phil, PhD); history of science, technology and medicine (M Phil, PhD); immunology (M Phil, PhD); integrative neurobiology and behavior (M Phil, PhD); membrane trafficking (M Phil, PhD);

microbiology (M Phil, PhD); molecular and cellular neuroscience (M Phil, PhD); molecular biology (M Phil, PhD); molecular cancer studies (M Phil, PhD); neuroscience (M Phil, PhD); ophthalmology (M Phil, PhD); optometry (M Phil, PhD); organelle function (M Phil, PhD); pharmacology (M Phil, PhD); physiology (M Phil, PhD); plant sciences (M Phil, PhD); stem cell research (M Phil, PhD); structural biology (M Phil, PhD); systems neuroscience (M Phil, PhD); toxicology (M Phil, PhD).

**University of Minnesota, Twin Cities Campus,** Graduate School, Program in the History of Science, Technology and Medicine, Minneapolis, MN 55455-0213. Offers MA, PhD. *Program availability:* Part-time. *Degree requirements:* For master's, one foreign language, thesis or alternative; for doctorate, 2 foreign languages, thesis/dissertation. *Entrance requirements:* For master's and doctorate, GRE General Test. *Faculty research:* History of infectious diseases, history of public health, history of evolutionary biology, history of infertility, women in science.

**Yale University,** Graduate School of Arts and Sciences, Department of History, Program in the History of Science and Medicine, New Haven, CT 06520. Offers MS, PhD. *Degree requirements:* For doctorate, 2 foreign languages, thesis/dissertation. *Entrance requirements:* For doctorate, GRE General Test.

# History of Science and Technology

**Arizona State University at the Tempe campus,** College of Liberal Arts and Sciences, School of Life Sciences, Tempe, AZ 85287-4601. Offers animal behavior (PhD); applied ethics (biomedical and health ethics) (MA); biology (MS, PhD), including biology, biology and society, complex adaptive systems science (PhD), plant biology and conservation (MS); environmental life sciences (PhD); evolutionary biology (PhD); history and philosophy of science (PhD); human and social dimensions of science and technology (PhD); microbiology (PhD); molecular and cellular biology (PhD); neuroscience (PhD). Terminal master's awarded for partial completion of doctoral program. *Degree requirements:* For master's, thesis (for some programs), interactive Program of Study (iPOS) submitted before completing 50 percent of required credit hours; for doctorate, variable foreign language requirement, comprehensive exam, thesis/dissertation, interactive Program of Study (iPOS) submitted before completing 50 percent of required credit hours. *Entrance requirements:* For master's and doctorate, GRE, minimum GPA of 3.0 or equivalent in last 2 years of work leading to bachelor's degree. Additional exam requirements/recommendations for international students: Required—TOEFL (minimum score 600 paper-based; 100 iBT). Electronic applications accepted.

**Arizona State University at the Tempe campus,** Graduate College, Program in Human and Social Dimensions of Science and Technology, Tempe, AZ 85287-5603. Offers PhD. *Degree requirements:* For doctorate, comprehensive exam, thesis/dissertation, interactive Program of Study (iPOS) submitted before completing 50 percent of required credit hours. *Entrance requirements:* For doctorate, GRE, minimum GPA of 3.0 in the last 2 years of work leading to the bachelor's degree, 3 letters of recommendation, statement of research interests and goals, curriculum vitae or resume, completed academic record form, 10-25 page writing sample. Additional exam requirements/recommendations for international students: Required—TOEFL (minimum score 550 paper-based; 80 iBT), IELTS (minimum score 6.5). Electronic applications accepted.

**Brown University,** Graduate School, Department of Egyptology and Ancient Western Asian Studies, Providence, RI 02912. Offers western Asian studies (PhD); Egyptology (PhD); history of the exact sciences in antiquity (PhD). *Degree requirements:* For doctorate, 2 foreign languages, comprehensive exam, thesis/dissertation. *Entrance requirements:* For doctorate, GRE General Test.

**Carnegie Mellon University,** Dietrich College of Humanities and Social Sciences, Department of History, Pittsburgh, PA 15213-3891. Offers African and African-American diaspora (PhD); culture and power (PhD); labor, politics and social movements (PhD); technology, environment, science and health (PhD); women, gender and the family (PhD). *Program availability:* Part-time. *Degree requirements:* For doctorate, oral and written comprehensive exams, dissertation defense. *Entrance requirements:* For doctorate, GRE General Test. Additional exam requirements/recommendations for international students: Required—TOEFL. Electronic applications accepted. *Faculty research:* Anthropology and history, African-American history, technology/environment, cultural history analysis.

**Cornell University,** Graduate School, Graduate Fields of Arts and Sciences, Field of History, Ithaca, NY 14853. Offers African history (MA, PhD); American history (MA, PhD); ancient Greek history (PhD); ancient history (MA, PhD); ancient Roman history (PhD); early modern European history (MA, PhD); English history (MA, PhD); French history (MA, PhD); German history (MA, PhD); history of science (MA, PhD); Korean history (PhD); Latin American history (MA, PhD); medieval Chinese history (MA, PhD); medieval history (MA, PhD); modern Chinese history (MA, PhD); modern European history (MA, PhD); modern Japanese history (MA, PhD); modern Middle Eastern history (PhD); premodern Islamic history (PhD); premodern Japanese history (MA, PhD); Renaissance history (MA, PhD); Russian history (MA, PhD); South Asian history (PhD); Southeast Asian history (MA, PhD). Terminal master's awarded for partial completion of doctoral program. *Degree requirements:* For master's, thesis; for doctorate, 2 foreign languages, comprehensive exam, thesis/dissertation, 1 year of teaching experience. *Entrance requirements:* For master's and doctorate, GRE General Test, writing sample, 3 letters of recommendation. Additional exam requirements/recommendations for international students: Required—TOEFL (minimum score 550 paper-based; 77 iBT). Electronic applications accepted.

**Cornell University,** Graduate School, Graduate Fields of Arts and Sciences, Field of Science and Technology Studies, Ithaca, NY 14853. Offers history and philosophy of science and technology (MA, PhD); social studies of science and technology (MA, PhD). Terminal master's awarded for partial completion of doctoral program. *Degree requirements:* For master's, one foreign language, thesis; for doctorate, one foreign language, comprehensive exam, thesis/dissertation. *Entrance requirements:* For master's and doctorate, GRE General Test, writing sample, 3 letters of recommendation. Additional exam requirements/recommendations for international students: Required—TOEFL (minimum score 550 paper-based; 77 iBT). Electronic applications accepted. *Faculty research:* History, philosophy, sociology, politics, and policy of science and technology; gender, legal order, environment, and communication.

**Drexel University,** College of Arts and Sciences, Department of History and Politics, Philadelphia, PA 19104-2875. Offers science, technology and society (MS). *Program availability:* Part-time. *Faculty:* 14 full-time (4 women), 4 part-time/adjunct (1 woman). *Students:* 3 full-time (2 women), 3 part-time (1 woman). Average age 31. *Entrance*

*requirements:* For master's, GRE. Additional exam requirements/recommendations for international students: Required—TOEFL. *Application deadline:* For fall admission, 8/21 for domestic students. Applications are processed on a rolling basis. Application fee: $50. Electronic applications accepted. *Expenses: Tuition:* Full-time $32,184; part-time $1192 per credit hour. *Required fees:* $280. Tuition and fees vary according to campus/location and program. *Financial support:* Application deadline: 2/1. *Total annual research expenditures:* $166,650. *Unit head:* Scott F. Knowles, Interim Head, 215-895-2496. *Application contact:* Director of Graduate Admissions, 215-895-6700, Fax: 215-895-5939, E-mail: enroll@drexel.edu.

**Georgia Institute of Technology,** Graduate Studies, Ivan Allen College of Liberal Arts, School of History, Technology, and Society, Atlanta, GA 30332-0001. Offers history and sociology of technology and science (MS, PhD). *Program availability:* Part-time. Terminal master's awarded for partial completion of doctoral program. *Degree requirements:* For master's, research paper; for doctorate, one foreign language, comprehensive exam, thesis/dissertation. *Entrance requirements:* For master's and doctorate, GRE, college transcripts, three letters of recommendation, biographical statement. Additional exam requirements/recommendations for international students: Required—TOEFL (minimum score 550 paper-based; 79 iBT). Electronic applications accepted. *Faculty research:* Industrialization, labor history, modern Europe, social history, sociology of science.

**Harvard University,** Graduate School of Arts and Sciences, Department of the History of Science, Cambridge, MA 02138. Offers AM, PhD. Terminal master's awarded for partial completion of doctoral program. *Degree requirements:* For master's, one foreign language; for doctorate, 2 foreign languages, thesis/dissertation. *Entrance requirements:* For master's and doctorate, GRE General Test. Additional exam requirements/recommendations for international students: Required—TOEFL.

**Indiana University Bloomington,** University Graduate School, College of Arts and Sciences, Department of History and Philosophy of Science, Bloomington, IN 47405-7000. Offers MA, MLS/MA. *Program availability:* Part-time. Terminal master's awarded for partial completion of doctoral program. *Degree requirements:* For master's, one foreign language, thesis optional; for doctorate, 2 foreign languages, thesis/dissertation. *Entrance requirements:* For master's and doctorate, GRE General Test. Additional exam requirements/recommendations for international students: Required—TOEFL. Electronic applications accepted. *Faculty research:* History of scientific ideas, instruments, and institutions; foundations of physics; history of philosophy of science; history and philosophy of biology; early modern science and medicine.

**Johns Hopkins University,** Zanvyl Krieger School of Arts and Sciences, Department of the History of Science and Technology, Baltimore, MD 21218. Offers MA, PhD. Terminal master's awarded for partial completion of doctoral program. *Degree requirements:* For master's, one foreign language, thesis; for doctorate, 2 foreign languages, thesis/dissertation. *Entrance requirements:* For doctorate, GRE General Test. Additional exam requirements/recommendations for international students: Required—TOEFL (minimum score 600 paper-based; 100 iBT), IELTS. Electronic applications accepted. *Faculty research:* History of physical and biological sciences, history of technology, history of medicine (sixteenth-twentieth centuries), environmental science (nineteenth-twentieth century).

**Massachusetts Institute of Technology,** School of Humanities, Arts, and Social Sciences, Program in Science, Technology, and Society, Cambridge, MA 02139. Offers history, anthropology, and science, technology and society (PhD). *Faculty:* 13 full-time (5 women). *Students:* 31 full-time (22 women); includes 5 minority (1 American Indian or Alaska Native, non-Hispanic/Latino; 2 Asian, non-Hispanic/Latino; 2 Hispanic/Latino), 8 international. Average age 31. 160 applicants, 5% accepted, 5 enrolled. In 2016, 3 doctorates awarded. *Degree requirements:* For doctorate, one foreign language, comprehensive exam, thesis/dissertation. *Entrance requirements:* For doctorate, GRE General Test. Additional exam requirements/recommendations for international students: Required—TOEFL, IELTS. *Application deadline:* For fall admission, 12/15 for domestic and international students. Application fee: $75. Electronic applications accepted. *Expenses: Tuition:* Full-time $46,400; part-time $725 per credit. One-time fee: $312 full-time. Full-time tuition and fees vary according to course load and program. *Financial support:* In 2016–17, 30 students received support, including 21 fellowships (averaging $38,600 per year), 1 research assistantship (averaging $39,300 per year), 4 teaching assistantships (averaging $40,200 per year); Federal Work-Study, institutionally sponsored loans, scholarships/grants, traineeships, health care benefits, unspecified assistantships, and resident tutors also available. Support available to part-time students. Financial award application deadline: 5/1; financial award applicants required to submit FAFSA. *Faculty research:* History of science; history of technology; sociology of science and technology; anthropology of science and technology; science, technology, and society. *Total annual research expenditures:* $186,000. *Unit head:* Prof. Jenniger Light, Program Director, 617-253-4062, Fax: 617-258-8118, E-mail: stsprogram@mit.edu. *Application contact:* 617-253-9759, E-mail: hasts@mit.edu. Website: http://sts-program.mit.edu/

**Oregon State University,** College of Liberal Arts, Program in History of Science, Corvallis, OR 97331. Offers development of the physical, biological, and environmental sciences (MA, MS, PhD); history of science and medicine (MA, MS, PhD); intellectual and social history of science in Europe and the U.S. (MA, MS, PhD). *Program availability:* Part-time. *Faculty:* 16 full-time (7 women), 1 part-time/adjunct (0 women). *Students:* 8 full-time (4 women), 5 part-time (2 women); includes 2 minority (1 Asian, non-Hispanic/Latino; 1 Hispanic/Latino), 1 international. Average age 37. 11 applicants, 27% accepted, 3 enrolled. In 2016, 2 master's, 1 doctorate awarded. *Degree requirements:* For master's, variable foreign language requirement, thesis optional; for doctorate, one foreign language, thesis/dissertation. *Entrance requirements:* For master's and doctorate, GRE. Additional exam requirements/recommendations for international students: Required—TOEFL (minimum score 80 iBT), IELTS (minimum score 6.5). *Application deadline:* For fall admission, 1/1 for domestic and international students. Application fee: $75 ($85 for international students). *Expenses:* Tuition, state resident: full-time $12,150; part-time $450 per credit. Tuition, nonresident: full-time $21,789; part-time $807 per credit. *Required fees:* $1651; $1507 per credit. One-time fee: $350. Tuition and fees vary according to course load, campus/location and program. *Financial support:* Application deadline: 1/1. *Unit head:* Dr. Ben Mutschler, Director. *Application contact:* Dr. Allen Thompson, Director of Graduate Studies/Associate Professor, 541-737-5654, E-mail: allen.thompson@oregonstate.edu. Website: http://liberalarts.oregonstate.edu/history/graduate-history-of-science

**Princeton University,** Graduate School, Department of History, Program in History of Science, Princeton, NJ 08544-1019. Offers PhD. *Degree requirements:* For doctorate, 2 foreign languages, thesis/dissertation. *Entrance requirements:* For doctorate, GRE General Test, sample of written work, 3 letters of recommendation. Additional exam requirements/recommendations for international students: Required—TOEFL (minimum score 600 paper-based). Electronic applications accepted. *Faculty research:* Early modern science, history of modern life sciences, history of physical sciences, history of modern technology, science and medicine in European expansion and colonialism.

**Rensselaer Polytechnic Institute,** Graduate School, School of Humanities, Arts, and Social Sciences, Program in Science and Technology Studies, Troy, NY 12180-3590. Offers MS, PhD. *Faculty:* 14 full-time (4 women), 2 part-time/adjunct (0 women). *Students:* 19 full-time (10 women), 1 (woman) part-time. 20 applicants, 60% accepted, 4 enrolled. In 2016, 1 master's, 6 doctorates awarded. Terminal master's awarded for partial completion of doctoral program. *Degree requirements:* For master's, thesis (for some programs); for doctorate, comprehensive exam, thesis/dissertation. *Entrance requirements:* For master's and doctorate, GRE. Additional exam requirements/recommendations for international students: Required—TOEFL (minimum score 600 paper-based; 100 iBT), IELTS (minimum score 7), PTE (minimum score 68). *Application deadline:* For fall admission, 1/1 priority date for domestic and international students; for spring admission, 8/15 priority date for domestic and international students. Applications are processed on a rolling basis. Application fee: $75. Electronic applications accepted. *Expenses:* Tuition: Full-time $49,520; part-time $2060 per credit hour. *Required fees:* $2617. *Financial support:* In 2016–17, research assistantships (averaging $22,000 per year), teaching assistantships (averaging $22,000 per year) were awarded; fellowships also available. Financial award application deadline: 1/1. *Faculty research:* Policy studies, science studies, technology studies. *Unit head:* Dr. Abby Kinchy, Graduate Program Director, 518-276-6980, E-mail: kincha@rpi.edu. *Application contact:* Office of Graduate Admissions, 518-276-6216, E-mail: gradadmissions@rpi.edu. Website: http://www.sts.rpi.edu/pl/graduate-programs-sts

**Rutgers University–New Brunswick,** Graduate School-New Brunswick, Program in History, Piscataway, NJ 08854-8097. Offers African-American history (PhD); early American history (PhD); early modern European history (PhD); east Asian history (PhD); global and comparative history (PhD); history (PhD); history of diplomacy and foreign relations (PhD); history of technology, environment and health (PhD); history of the Atlantic cultures and African diaspora (PhD); Latin American history (PhD); medieval history (PhD); modern European history (PhD); nineteenth and twentieth century American history (PhD); women's and gender history (PhD). *Degree requirements:* For doctorate, thesis/dissertation. *Entrance requirements:* For doctorate, GRE General Test, sample of written work. Electronic applications accepted. *Faculty research:* American history, European history, Afro-American history, women's history, Latin American history.

**University of California, Berkeley,** Graduate Division, College of Letters and Science, Group in Logic and the Methodology of Science, Berkeley, CA 94720-1500. Offers PhD. *Students:* 17 full-time (2 women); includes 13 minority (7 American Indian or Alaska Native, non-Hispanic/Latino; 6 Hispanic/Latino), 17 international. Average age 26. 41 applicants, 2 enrolled. In 2016, 3 doctorates awarded. *Degree requirements:* For doctorate, qualifying exam, oral defense of dissertation. *Entrance requirements:* For doctorate, GRE General Test, minimum GPA of 3.5, 3 letters of recommendation. *Application deadline:* For fall admission, 12/9 for domestic students. Application fee: $105 ($125 for international students). Electronic applications accepted. *Financial support:* Fellowships, research assistantships, teaching assistantships, institutionally sponsored loans, health care benefits, tuition waivers (full and partial), and unspecified assistantships available. *Faculty research:* Set theory, recursion theory, theoretical computer science, philosophy of mathematics, philosophy of language. *Unit head:* Prof. Paolo Mancosu, Chair, 510-642-0665. *Application contact:* Victoria Lee, Student Affairs Officer, 510-642-0665, E-mail: vickyalee@berkeley.edu. Website: http://logic.berkeley.edu/

**University of California, San Diego,** Graduate Division, Program in Science Studies, La Jolla, CA 92093. Offers communication of science (PhD); history of science (PhD); philosophy of science (PhD); sociology of science (PhD). *Students:* 4 full-time (all women). In 2016, 7 doctorates awarded. *Degree requirements:* For doctorate, one foreign language, comprehensive exam, thesis/dissertation, internship. *Entrance requirements:* For doctorate, GRE General Test, 3 letters of recommendation. Additional exam requirements/recommendations for international students: Required—TOEFL (minimum score 550 paper-based; 80 iBT), IELTS (minimum score 7). Electronic applications accepted. *Expenses:* Tuition, state resident: full-time $11,220. Tuition, nonresident: full-time $26,322. *Required fees:* $1864. *Financial support:* Fellowships, research assistantships, teaching assistantships, and scholarships/grants available. Financial award applicants required to submit FAFSA. *Unit head:* Cathy Gere, Director, 858-534-6051, E-mail: cgere@ucsd.edu. *Application contact:* Jennifer Dieli, Program Coordinator, 858-534-0491, E-mail: ssadmin@ucsd.edu. Website: http://sciencestudies.ucsd.edu/

**University of California, San Francisco,** Graduate Division, Program in History of Health Sciences, San Francisco, CA 94143. Offers MA, PhD, MD/PhD. Program admits students biennially. Terminal master's awarded for partial completion of doctoral program. *Degree requirements:* For master's, 2 foreign languages, thesis; for doctorate, 2 foreign languages, thesis/dissertation. *Entrance requirements:* For master's and doctorate, GRE General Test.

**University of Delaware,** College of Arts and Sciences, Department of History, Hagley Program in the History of Technology and Industrialization, Newark, DE 19716. Offers MA, PhD. *Degree requirements:* For master's, thesis optional; for doctorate, comprehensive exam, thesis/dissertation. *Entrance requirements:* For master's and doctorate, interview. Electronic applications accepted.

**The University of Manchester,** Faculty of Life Sciences, Manchester, United Kingdom. Offers adaptive organismal biology (M Phil, PhD); animal biology (M Phil, PhD); biochemistry (M Phil, PhD); bioinformatics (M Phil, PhD); biomolecular sciences (M Phil, PhD); biotechnology (M Phil, PhD); cell biology (M Phil, PhD); cell matrix research (M Phil, PhD); channels and transporters (M Phil, PhD); developmental biology (M Phil, PhD); Egyptology (M Phil, PhD); environmental biology (M Phil, PhD); evolutionary biology (M Phil, PhD); gene expression (M Phil, PhD); genetics (M Phil, PhD); history of science, technology and medicine (M Phil, PhD); immunology (M Phil, PhD); integrative neurobiology and behavior (M Phil, PhD); membrane trafficking (M Phil, PhD); microbiology (M Phil, PhD); molecular and cellular neuroscience (M Phil, PhD); molecular biology (M Phil, PhD); molecular cancer studies (M Phil, PhD); neuroscience (M Phil, PhD); ophthalmology (M Phil, PhD); optometry (M Phil, PhD); organelle function (M Phil, PhD); pharmacology (M Phil, PhD); physiology (M Phil, PhD); plant sciences (M Phil, PhD); stem cell research (M Phil, PhD); structural biology (M Phil, PhD); systems neuroscience (M Phil, PhD); toxicology (M Phil, PhD).

**University of Minnesota, Twin Cities Campus,** College of Science and Engineering, Program in History of Science, Technology and Medicine, Minneapolis, MN 55455-0213. Offers MA, PhD. Terminal master's awarded for partial completion of doctoral program. *Degree requirements:* For master's, one foreign language; for doctorate, 2 foreign languages, thesis/dissertation. *Entrance requirements:* For master's and doctorate, GRE General Test. Additional exam requirements/recommendations for international students: Required—TOEFL. Electronic applications accepted. *Faculty research:* History of physical sciences, biological sciences, technology, and medicine.

**University of Notre Dame,** Graduate School, College of Arts and Letters, Division of Humanities, Program in History and Philosophy of Science, Notre Dame, IN 46556. Offers history and philosophy of science (MA, PhD); theology and science (PhD). *Degree requirements:* For doctorate, 2 foreign languages, comprehensive exam, thesis/dissertation, candidacy exam. *Entrance requirements:* For doctorate, GRE General Test. Additional exam requirements/recommendations for international students: Required—TOEFL (minimum score 600 paper-based; 80 iBT). Electronic applications accepted. *Faculty research:* Philosophy of physics, science and ethics, history and philosophy of biology, history of medicine and technology, history and philosophy of economics.

**University of Oklahoma,** College of Arts and Sciences, Department of History of Science, Norman, OK 73019. Offers history of science, technology and medicine (MA, PhD); MLIS/MA. *Program availability:* Part-time. *Faculty:* 12 full-time (4 women). *Students:* 13 full-time (6 women), 8 part-time (4 women); includes 1 minority (Two or more races, non-Hispanic/Latino), 2 international. Average age 31. 18 applicants, 39% accepted, 5 enrolled. In 2016, 3 master's awarded. Terminal master's awarded for partial completion of doctoral program. *Degree requirements:* For master's, one foreign language, comprehensive exam (for some programs), thesis (for some programs); for doctorate, 2 foreign languages, comprehensive exam, thesis/dissertation. *Entrance requirements:* For master's, GRE General Test, transcripts, statement of purpose, 3 letters of recommendation, writing sample; for doctorate, GRE General Test, MA in the history of science or related field, transcripts, statement of purpose, 3 letters of recommendation, writing sample. Additional exam requirements/recommendations for international students: Required—TOEFL (minimum score 79 iBT) or IELTS (minimum score 6.5). *Application deadline:* For fall admission, 1/15 for domestic and international students. Application fee: $50 ($100 for international students). Electronic applications accepted. *Expenses:* Tuition, state resident: full-time $4886; part-time $203.60 per credit hour. Tuition, nonresident: full-time $18,989; part-time $791.20 per credit hour. *Required fees:* $3283; $126.25 per credit hour. $126.50 per semester. *Financial support:* In 2016–17, 17 students received support, including 2 fellowships with full tuition reimbursements available (averaging $2,883 per year), 2 research assistantships with full tuition reimbursements available (averaging $15,125 per year), 7 teaching assistantships with full tuition reimbursements available (averaging $16,007 per year); career-related internships or fieldwork, Federal Work-Study, institutionally sponsored loans, scholarships/grants, traineeships, and health care benefits also available. Financial award application deadline: 6/1; financial award applicants required to submit FAFSA. *Faculty research:* Premodern science; medicine, public health, and biomedical science; science, the public, and popular culture; science and religion; history of technology. *Total annual research expenditures:* $169,160. *Unit head:* Dr. Hunter Heyck, Professor/Department Chair, 405-325-2213, Fax: 405-325-2363, E-mail: hheyck@ou.edu. *Application contact:* Stella L. Graves Stuart, Graduate Studies Coordinator, 405-325-6026, Fax: 405-325-2363, E-mail: slgstuart@ou.edu. Website: http://cas.ou.edu/hsci

**University of Pennsylvania,** School of Arts and Sciences, Graduate Group in the History and Sociology of Science, Philadelphia, PA 19104. Offers AM, PhD. *Faculty:* 26 full-time (14 women), 8 part-time/adjunct (5 women). *Students:* 25 full-time (15 women); includes 3 minority (1 Black or African American, non-Hispanic/Latino; 1 Asian, non-Hispanic/Latino; 1 Hispanic/Latino), 6 international. Average age 31. 43 applicants, 21% accepted, 5 enrolled. In 2016, 7 doctorates awarded. *Expenses:* Tuition: Full-time $31,068; part-time $5762 per course. *Required fees:* $3200; $336 per course. Full-time tuition and fees vary according to degree level, program and student level. Part-time tuition and fees vary according to course load, degree level and program. *Financial support:* Application deadline: 12/1. Website: http://hss.sas.upenn.edu/hssc

**University of Pittsburgh,** Dietrich School of Arts and Sciences, Department of History and Philosophy of Science, Pittsburgh, PA 15260. Offers PhD. *Faculty:* 8 full-time (2 women). *Students:* 27 full-time (11 women); includes 2 minority (both Two or more races, non-Hispanic/Latino), 9 international. Average age 28. 51 applicants, 12% accepted, 4 enrolled. In 2016, 2 doctorates awarded. Terminal master's awarded for partial completion of doctoral program. *Degree requirements:* For doctorate, one foreign language, comprehensive exam, thesis/dissertation, minimum of 72 credit hours, proficiency in logic. *Entrance requirements:* For doctorate, GRE General Test, curriculum vitae, statement of career objective, 3 letters of recommendation, sample of written work. Additional exam requirements/recommendations for international students: Required—TOEFL (minimum score 577 paper-based; 90 iBT), IELTS (minimum score 7). *Application deadline:* For fall admission, 1/10 for domestic and international students. Application fee: $50. Electronic applications accepted. Tuition and fees vary according to program. *Financial support:* In 2016–17, 23 students received support, including 12 fellowships with full tuition reimbursements available (averaging $24,710 per year), 11 teaching assistantships with full tuition reimbursements available (averaging $24,710 per year); research assistantships, health care benefits, and tuition waivers (full) also available. Financial award application deadline: 1/10. *Faculty research:* History and philosophy of biology, psychology, and neuroscience; history and philosophy of physics; early modern science; cognitive science; philosophy of social science; philosophy of mind and perception. *Unit head:* Sandra Mitchell, Chair, 412-624-5896, Fax: 412-624-6825, E-mail: smitchel@pitt.edu. *Application contact:* Kathy Rivet, Graduate Administrator, 412-624-5774, Fax: 412-624-5377, E-mail: krivet@pitt.edu. Website: http://www.hps.pitt.edu/

**University of Toronto,** School of Graduate Studies, Faculty of Arts and Science, Institute for the History and Philosophy of Science and Technology, Toronto, ON M5S

## History of Science and Technology

1A1, Canada. Offers MA, PhD. *Program availability:* Part-time. *Degree requirements:* For master's, one foreign language, thesis optional, reading ability in French or German; for doctorate, 2 foreign languages, thesis/dissertation, reading knowledge examinations, thesis defense. *Entrance requirements:* For master's, 2 letters of reference, B+ in the final two years of undergraduate work; for doctorate, 2 letters of reference, MA in history and philosophy of science and technology, minimum A- average. Additional exam requirements/recommendations for international students: Required—TOEFL (minimum score 580 paper-based; 93 iBT), TWE (minimum score 5). Electronic applications accepted.

**University of Wisconsin–Madison,** Graduate School, College of Letters and Science, Department of History of Science, Madison, WI 53706-1380. Offers history of medicine (MA); history of science (MA, PhD). Terminal master's awarded for partial completion of doctoral program. *Degree requirements:* For master's, thesis; for doctorate, 2 foreign languages, thesis/dissertation. *Entrance requirements:* For master's and doctorate, GRE General Test. Electronic applications accepted. *Faculty research:* History of biology, physical sciences, technology, medicine.

**Virginia Polytechnic Institute and State University,** Graduate School, College of Liberal Arts and Human Sciences, Blacksburg, VA 24061. Offers career and technical education (MS Ed, Ed D, PhD, Ed S); communication (MA); counselor education (MA Ed, Ed D, PhD, Ed S); creative writing (MFA); curriculum and instruction (MA Ed, Ed D, PhD, Ed S); educational leadership and policy studies (MA Ed, Ed D, PhD, Ed S); educational research and evaluation (PhD); English (MA); foreign languages, cultures, and literatures (MA); higher education (PhD); higher education and student affairs (MA Ed); history (MA); human development (MS, PhD); material culture and public humanities (MA); philosophy (MA); political science (MA); rhetoric and writing (PhD); science and technology studies (MS, PhD); social, political, ethical, and cultural thought (PhD); sociology (MS, PhD); theater arts (MFA). *Faculty:* 408 full-time (204 women), 3 part-time/adjunct (2 women). *Students:* 657 full-time (446 women), 457 part-time (292 women); includes 213 minority (114 Black or African American, non-Hispanic/Latino; 3 American Indian or Alaska Native, non-Hispanic/Latino; 29 Asian, non-Hispanic/Latino; 44 Hispanic/Latino; 23 Two or more races, non-Hispanic/Latino), 93 international. Average age 33. 805 applicants, 55% accepted, 328 enrolled. In 2016, 270 master's, 91 doctorates awarded. *Degree requirements:* For master's, comprehensive exam (for some programs), thesis (for some programs); for doctorate, comprehensive exam (for some programs), thesis/dissertation (for some programs). *Entrance requirements:* For master's and doctorate, GRE/GMAT. Additional exam requirements/recommendations for international students: Required—TOEFL (minimum score 80 iBT). *Application deadline:* For fall admission, 8/1 for domestic students, 4/1 for international students; for spring admission, 1/1 for domestic students, 9/1 for international students. Applications are processed on a rolling basis. Application fee: $75. Electronic applications accepted. *Expenses:* Tuition, state resident: full-time $12,467; part-time $692.50 per credit hour. Tuition, nonresident: full-time $25,095; part-time $1394.25 per credit hour. *Required fees:* $2669; $491.50 per semester. Tuition and fees vary according to course load, campus/location and program. *Financial support:* In 2016–17, 21 research assistantships with full tuition reimbursements (averaging $19,817 per year), 237 teaching assistantships with full tuition reimbursements (averaging $15,497 per year) were awarded. Financial award application deadline: 3/1; financial award applicants required to submit FAFSA. *Total annual research expenditures:* $6.6 million. *Unit head:* Rosemary Blieszner, Interim Dean, 540-231-6779, Fax: 540-231-7157, E-mail: liberalartsdean@vt.edu. *Application contact:* Chelsea Blanchet, Executive Assistant, 540-231-6779, Fax: 540-231-7157, E-mail: bchels1@vt.edu.
Website: http://www.liberalarts.vt.edu/

**Wayne State University,** College of Liberal Arts and Sciences, Department of History, Detroit, MI 48202. Offers Africa (PhD); America (PhD); Asia (PhD); Europe (PhD); gender (PhD); history (MA); labor (PhD); public history (MA); science and technology (PhD); world history (PhD, Graduate Certificate); JD/MA; M Ed/MA; MLIS/MA. Doctoral program admits for fall only. *Program availability:* Evening/weekend. *Faculty:* 18. *Students:* 23 full-time (8 women), 21 part-time (5 women); includes 8 minority (3 Black or African American, non-Hispanic/Latino; 2 Hispanic/Latino; 3 Two or more races, non-Hispanic/Latino). Average age 40. 55 applicants, 38% accepted, 15 enrolled. In 2016, 6 master's, 5 doctorates awarded. *Degree requirements:* For master's, comprehensive exam, thesis (for some programs), final oral exam on thesis or essay and seminar; internship and project (for public history); for doctorate, variable foreign language requirement, comprehensive exam, thesis/dissertation, qualifying exam in 4 fields of history. *Entrance requirements:* For master's, GRE General Test, minimum undergraduate GPA of 3.25 in history, 3.0 overall; at least 18 credits in history and related subjects at the advanced undergraduate level; foreign language; letter of intent; research paper; at least two letters of recommendation from former instructors; for doctorate, GRE General Test, minimum GPA of 3.0, 3.25 in minimum of 18 semester credits in history and related subjects; letter of intent; research paper; at least three letters of recommendation from former professors; for Graduate Certificate, baccalaureate degree from accredited college or university; minimum GPA of 3.0, 3.25 in a minimum of eighteen semester credits in history and related subjects at the advanced undergraduate level. Additional exam requirements/recommendations for international students: Required—TOEFL (minimum score 550 paper-based; 79 iBT), TWE (minimum score 5.5), Michigan English Language Assessment Battery (minimum score 85); Recommended—IELTS (minimum score 6.5). *Application deadline:* For fall admission, 2/1 priority date for domestic and international students; for winter admission, 11/1 for domestic students, 10/1 priority date for international students; for spring admission, 2/1 for domestic students, 1/1 priority date for international students. Application fee: $50. Electronic applications accepted. *Expenses:* $16,503 per year resident tuition and fees, $33,697 per year non-resident tuition and fees. *Financial support:* In 2016–17, 16 students received support, including 2 fellowships with tuition reimbursements available (averaging $18,796 per year), 1 research assistantship with tuition reimbursement available (averaging $21,593 per year), 6 teaching assistantships with tuition reimbursements available (averaging $17,994 per year); scholarships/grants, health care benefits, and unspecified assistantships also available. Financial award applicants required to submit FAFSA. *Faculty research:* African, American, Asian, European, gender, German, labor, science and technology, urban/labor, violence, world. *Unit head:* Dr. Elizabeth V. Faue, Professor/Chair, 313-577-2525, E-mail: evfaue@wayne.edu. *Application contact:* Dr. Eric Ash, Associate Professor and Director of Graduate Studies, 313-577-2525, E-mail: ericash@wayne.edu.
Website: http://clas.wayne.edu/history/

**West Virginia University,** Eberly College of Arts and Sciences, Department of History, Morgantown, WV 26506. Offers African history (MA, PhD); African-American history (MA, PhD); American history (MA, PhD); Appalachian/regional history (MA, PhD); East Asian history (MA, PhD); European history (MA, PhD); history of science and technology (MA, PhD); Latin American history (MA). *Program availability:* Part-time. *Degree requirements:* For master's, one foreign language, thesis (for some programs), oral exam, thesis defense; for doctorate, one foreign language, comprehensive exam, thesis/dissertation, dissertation defense. *Entrance requirements:* For master's, GRE General Test, minimum GPA of 3.0; for doctorate, GRE General Test. Additional exam requirements/recommendations for international students: Required—TOEFL (minimum score 550 paper-based), IELTS (minimum score 6.5). Electronic applications accepted. *Faculty research:* United States, Appalachia, modern Europe, Africa, colonial and post-colonial societies.

**Yale University,** Graduate School of Arts and Sciences, Department of History, Program in the History of Science and Medicine, New Haven, CT 06520. Offers MS, PhD. *Degree requirements:* For doctorate, 2 foreign languages, thesis/dissertation. *Entrance requirements:* For doctorate, GRE General Test.

# Medieval and Renaissance Studies

**Arizona State University at the Tempe campus,** College of Liberal Arts and Sciences, Department of English, Tempe, AZ 85287-0302. Offers applied linguistics (PhD); creative writing (MFA); English (MA, PhD), including comparative literature (MA), linguistics (MA), literature, rhetoric and composition (MA), rhetoric, composition, and linguistics (PhD); film and media studies (MAS), including American media and popular culture; linguistics (Graduate Certificate); teaching English to speakers of other languages (MTESOL); translation studies (Graduate Certificate). Terminal master's awarded for partial completion of doctoral program. *Degree requirements:* For master's, variable foreign language requirement, comprehensive exam (for some programs), thesis (for some programs), interactive Program of Study (iPOS) submitted before completing 50 percent of required credit hours; for doctorate, variable foreign language requirement, comprehensive exam, thesis/dissertation, interactive Program of Study (iPOS) submitted before completing 50 percent of required credit hours. *Entrance requirements:* For master's and doctorate, GRE, minimum GPA of 3.0 or equivalent in last 2 years of work leading to bachelor's degree. Additional exam requirements/recommendations for international students: Required—TOEFL, IELTS, or PTE. Electronic applications accepted.

**Arizona State University at the Tempe campus,** College of Liberal Arts and Sciences, School of Historical, Philosophical and Religious Studies, Tempe, AZ 85287-4301. Offers European history (MA, PhD); medieval studies (Graduate Certificate); North American history (MA, PhD); philosophy (MA, PhD); public history (MA); religious studies (MA, PhD); Renaissance studies (Graduate Certificate); scholarly publishing (Graduate Certificate). *Program availability:* Part-time. Terminal master's awarded for partial completion of doctoral program. *Degree requirements:* For master's, thesis or alternative, interactive Program of Study (iPOS) submitted before completing 50 percent of required credit hours; for doctorate, variable foreign language requirement, comprehensive exam, thesis/dissertation, interactive Program of Study (iPOS) submitted before completing 50 percent of required credit hours. *Entrance requirements:* For master's and doctorate, GRE, minimum GPA of 3.0 or equivalent in last 2 years of work leading to bachelor's degree. Additional exam requirements/recommendations for international students: Required—TOEFL, IELTS, or PTE. Electronic applications accepted.

**The Catholic University of America,** School of Arts and Sciences, Department of History, Washington, DC 20064. Offers history (MA, PhD), including early modern Europe, Latin America (MA), Medieval, modern Europe, U.S.; religion and society in the late medieval and early modern world (MA); MA/JD; MSLS/MA. *Program availability:* Part-time. *Faculty:* 14 full-time (6 women), 3 part-time/adjunct (2 women). *Students:* 7 full-time (2 women), 20 part-time (6 women); includes 3 minority (all Two or more races, non-Hispanic/Latino), 2 international. Average age 30. 22 applicants, 45% accepted, 4 enrolled. In 2016, 4 master's, 5 doctorates awarded. Terminal master's awarded for partial completion of doctoral program. *Degree requirements:* For master's, one foreign language, comprehensive exam, thesis optional, 2 languages (for medievalists), one of which must be Latin; for doctorate, 2 foreign languages, comprehensive exam, thesis/dissertation, 3 languages (for medievalists), one of which must be Latin. *Entrance requirements:* For master's and doctorate, GRE General Test, statement of purpose, official copies of academic transcripts, three letters of recommendation, writing sample. Additional exam requirements/recommendations for international students: Required—TOEFL (minimum score 550 paper-based; 80 iBT). *Application deadline:* For fall admission, 7/15 priority date for domestic students, 7/1 for international students; for spring admission, 11/15 priority date for domestic students, 11/1 for international students. Applications are processed on a rolling basis. Application fee: $55. Electronic applications accepted. *Expenses:* $42,850 per year; $1,170 per credit; $200 per semester part-time fees. *Financial support:* Fellowships, research assistantships, teaching assistantships, Federal Work-Study, scholarships/grants, tuition waivers (full and partial), and unspecified assistantships available. Financial award application deadline: 2/1; financial award applicants required to submit FAFSA. *Faculty research:* Medieval history, including the Islamic Middle East, with particular expertise in later medieval religious, social, and economic history and early medieval and late antique history; European and American intellectual history; renaissance, reformation, catholic reformation; US catholic history; history of immigration. *Total annual research expenditures:* $42,594. *Unit head:* Dr. Katherine Jansen, Chair, 202-319-5484, Fax: 202-319-5569, E-mail: jansen@cua.edu. *Application contact:* Director of Graduate Admissions, 202-319-5057, Fax: 202-319-6533, E-mail: cua-admissions@cua.edu.
Website: http://history.cua.edu/

**The Catholic University of America,** School of Arts and Sciences, Program in Medieval and Byzantine Studies, Washington, DC 20064. Offers Byzantine and Orthodox studies (MA); Medieval and Byzantine studies (PhD, Certificate); the Islamic world (MA); the Medieval West (MA). *Program availability:* Part-time. *Students:* 6 full-time (2 women), 5 part-time (2 women). Average age 31. 13 applicants, 54% accepted, 3 enrolled. In 2016, 2 master's awarded. *Degree requirements:* For master's, one foreign language, comprehensive exam, thesis or alternative; for doctorate, 2 foreign languages, comprehensive exam, thesis/dissertation. *Entrance requirements:* For master's and doctorate, GRE General Test, statement of purpose, official copies of academic transcripts, three letters of recommendation, writing sample; for Certificate, bachelor's degree. Additional exam requirements/recommendations for international students: Required—TOEFL (minimum score 550 paper-based; 80 iBT). *Application*

*deadline:* For fall admission, 7/15 priority date for domestic students, 7/1 for international students; for spring admission, 11/15 priority date for domestic students, 11/1 for international students. Applications are processed on a rolling basis. Application fee: $55. Electronic applications accepted. *Expenses:* $42,850 per year; $1,170 per credit; $200 per semester part-time fees. *Financial support:* Fellowships, research assistantships, teaching assistantships, Federal Work-Study, scholarships/grants, tuition waivers (full and partial), and unspecified assistantships available. Financial award application deadline: 2/1; financial award applicants required to submit FAFSA. *Faculty research:* Scholasticism and medieval theology; early and late medieval history; medieval philosophy; liturgical studies; medieval English literature. *Unit head:* Dr. Lilla Kopar, Director, 202-319-5794, Fax: 202-319-6609, E-mail: kopar@cua.edu. *Application contact:* Director of Graduate Admissions, 202-319-5057, Fax: 202-319-6533, E-mail: cua-admissions@cua.edu.
Website: http://mbs.cua.edu/

**Central European University,** Department of Medieval Studies, Budapest, Hungary. Offers comparative history: interdisciplinary Medieval studies (MA); cultural heritage studies (MA); Medieval studies (MA, PhD). *Faculty:* 12 full-time (3 women), 9 part-time/adjunct (5 women). *Students:* 101 full-time (60 women). Average age 27. 139 applicants, 32% accepted, 41 enrolled. In 2016, 21 master's, 4 doctorates awarded. *Degree requirements:* For master's, one foreign language, thesis; for doctorate, variable foreign language requirement, comprehensive exam, thesis/dissertation. *Entrance requirements:* For master's and doctorate, interview. Additional exam requirements/recommendations for international students: Required—TOEFL (minimum score 570 paper-based); Recommended—IELTS (minimum score 6.5). *Application deadline:* For fall admission, 2/4 for domestic and international students. Application fee: $30. Electronic applications accepted. *Expenses:* Tuition: Full-time 13,500 euros. Tuition and fees vary according to degree level, program and student level. *Financial support:* In 2016–17, 74 students received support. Fellowships, scholarships/grants, health care benefits, and tuition waivers (full and partial) available. *Faculty research:* Late antique and medieval civilization in Europe (c. 300-1550 AD), dealing with different methods of communication, migration of peoples, mobility of objects, texts, and ideas in the larger medieval oikumene, including Asia and North Africa. *Unit head:* Dr. Katalin Szende, Head, 36 1 327-3046, E-mail: ziemannd@ceu.edu. *Application contact:* Zsuzsanna Jaszberenyi, Admissions Officer, 361-324-3009, Fax: 367-327-3211, E-mail: admissions@ceu.edu.
Website: http://medievalstudies.ceu.edu/

**Columbia University,** Graduate School of Arts and Sciences, New York, NY 10027. Offers African-American studies (MA); American studies (MA); anthropology (MA, PhD); art history and archaeology (MA, PhD); astronomy (PhD); biological sciences (PhD); biotechnology (MA); chemical physics (PhD); chemistry (PhD); classical studies (MA, PhD); classics (MA, PhD); climate and society (MA); conservation biology (MA); earth and environmental sciences (PhD); East Asia: regional studies (MA); East Asian languages and cultures (MA, PhD); ecology, evolution and environmental biology (MA), including conservation biology; ecology, evolution, and environmental biology (PhD), including ecology and evolutionary biology, evolutionary primatology; economics (MA, PhD); English and comparative literature (MA, PhD); French and Romance philology (MA, PhD); Germanic languages (MA, PhD); global French studies (MA); global thought (MA); Hispanic cultural studies (MA); history (PhD); history and literature (MA); human rights studies (MA); Islamic studies (MA); Italian (MA, PhD); Japanese pedagogy (MA); Latin America and the Caribbean: regional studies (MA); Latin American and Iberian cultures (PhD); mathematics (MA, PhD), including finance (MA); medieval and Renaissance studies (MA); Middle Eastern, South Asian, and African studies (MA, PhD); modern art: critical and curatorial studies (MA); modern European studies (MA); museum anthropology (MA); music (DMA, PhD); oral history (MA); philosophical foundations of physics (MA); philosophy (MA, PhD); physics (PhD); political science (MA, PhD); psychology (PhD); quantitative methods in the social sciences (MA); religion (MA, PhD); Russia, Eurasia and East Europe: regional studies (MA); Russian translation (MA); Slavic cultures (MA); Slavic languages (MA, PhD); sociology (MA, PhD); South Asian studies (MA); statistics (MA, PhD); theatre (PhD). Dual-degree programs require admission to both Graduate School of Arts and Sciences and another Columbia school. *Program availability:* Part-time. Terminal master's awarded for partial completion of doctoral program. *Degree requirements:* For master's, variable foreign language requirement, comprehensive exam (for some programs), thesis (for some programs); for doctorate, variable foreign language requirement, comprehensive exam (for some programs), thesis/dissertation. *Entrance requirements:* For master's and doctorate, GRE General Test, GRE Subject Test (for some programs). Additional exam requirements/recommendations for international students: Required—TOEFL, IELTS. Electronic applications accepted.

**Cornell University,** Graduate School, Graduate Fields of Arts and Sciences, Field of Archaeology, Ithaca, NY 14853. Offers environmental archaeology (MA); historical archaeology (MA); Latin American archaeology (MA); medieval archaeology (MA); Mediterranean and Near Eastern archaeology (MA); Stone Age archaeology (MA). *Degree requirements:* For master's, one foreign language, thesis. *Entrance requirements:* For master's, GRE General Test, 3 letters of recommendation, sample of written work. Additional exam requirements/recommendations for international students: Required—TOEFL (minimum score 550 paper-based; 77 iBT). Electronic applications accepted. *Faculty research:* Anatolia, Lydia, Sardis, classical and Hellenistic Greece, science in archaeology, North American Indians, Stone Age Africa, Mayan trade.

**Cornell University,** Graduate School, Graduate Fields of Arts and Sciences, Field of English Language and Literature, Ithaca, NY 14853. Offers African-American literature (PhD); American literature after 1865 (PhD); American literature to 1865 (PhD); American studies (PhD); colonial and postcolonial literatures (PhD); creative writing (MFA); cultural studies (PhD); dramatic literature (PhD); English poetry (PhD); English Renaissance to 1660 (PhD); lesbian, bisexual, and gay literary studies (PhD); literary criticism and theory (PhD); Old and Middle English (PhD); prose fiction (PhD); Restoration and the eighteenth-century (PhD); the nineteenth century (PhD); the twentieth century (PhD); women's literature (PhD); MFA/PhD. Terminal master's awarded for partial completion of doctoral program. *Degree requirements:* For master's, one foreign language, thesis; for doctorate, one foreign language, comprehensive exam, thesis/dissertation, teaching experience. *Entrance requirements:* For master's, GRE General Test, 3 letters of recommendation, creative writing sample; for doctorate, GRE General Test, GRE Subject Test (English), 3 letters of recommendation, writing sample. Additional exam requirements/recommendations for international students: Required—TOEFL (minimum score 600 paper-based; 77 iBT). Electronic applications accepted. *Faculty research:* English and American literature, women's writing, ethnic and post-colonial literature, critical theory, medievalism.

**Cornell University,** Graduate School, Graduate Fields of Arts and Sciences, Field of History, Ithaca, NY 14853. Offers African history (MA, PhD); American history (MA, PhD); ancient Greek history (PhD); ancient history (MA, PhD); ancient Roman history (PhD); early modern European history (MA, PhD); English history (MA, PhD); French history (MA, PhD); German history (MA, PhD); history of science (MA, PhD); Korean history (MA, PhD); Latin American history (MA, PhD); medieval Chinese history (MA, PhD); medieval history (MA, PhD); modern Chinese history (MA, PhD); modern European

history (MA, PhD); modern Japanese history (MA, PhD); modern Middle Eastern history (PhD); premodern Islamic history (MA, PhD); premodern Japanese history (MA, PhD); Renaissance history (MA, PhD); Russian history (MA, PhD); South Asian history (PhD); Southeast Asian history (MA, PhD). Terminal master's awarded for partial completion of doctoral program. *Degree requirements:* For master's, thesis; for doctorate, 2 foreign languages, comprehensive exam, thesis/dissertation, 1 year of teaching experience. *Entrance requirements:* For master's and doctorate, GRE General Test, writing sample, 3 letters of recommendation. Additional exam requirements/recommendations for international students: Required—TOEFL (minimum score 550 paper-based; 77 iBT). Electronic applications accepted.

**Cornell University,** Graduate School, Graduate Fields of Arts and Sciences, Field of History of Art, Archaeology and Visual Studies, Ithaca, NY 14853. Offers 19th century art (PhD); African, African American and African diaspora (PhD); American art (PhD); ancient art and archaeology (PhD); Asian American art (PhD); Baroque art (PhD); comparative modernities (PhD); digital art (PhD); East Asian art (PhD); history of photography (PhD); Islamic art (PhD); Latin American art (PhD); medieval art (PhD); modern art (PhD); Renaissance art (PhD); Southeast Asian art (PhD); theory and criticism (PhD); visual studies (PhD). *Degree requirements:* For doctorate, one foreign language, comprehensive exam, thesis/dissertation, general exams in 3 areas. *Entrance requirements:* For doctorate, GRE General Test, sample of written work, 3 letters of recommendation. Additional exam requirements/recommendations for international students: Required—TOEFL (minimum score 550 paper-based; 77 iBT). Electronic applications accepted.

**Cornell University,** Graduate School, Graduate Fields of Arts and Sciences, Field of Medieval Studies, Ithaca, NY 14853. Offers medieval archaeology (PhD); medieval art (PhD); medieval history (PhD); medieval literature (PhD); medieval music (PhD); medieval philology and linguistics (PhD); medieval philosophy (PhD). *Degree requirements:* For doctorate, 3 foreign languages, comprehensive exam, thesis/dissertation, teaching experience. *Entrance requirements:* For doctorate, GRE General Test, 3 letters of recommendation, proficiency in Latin (recommended), 20-page writing sample on a Medieval topic. Additional exam requirements/recommendations for international students: Required—TOEFL (minimum score 600 paper-based; 77 iBT). Electronic applications accepted. *Faculty research:* Interdisciplinary study of medieval culture, languages, literatures, history, archaeology.

**Fordham University,** Graduate School of Arts and Sciences, Program in Medieval Studies, New York, NY 10458. Offers MA, Certificate. *Program availability:* Part-time, evening/weekend. *Students:* 8 full-time (7 women), 5 part-time (3 women); includes 3 minority (2 Black or African American, non-Hispanic/Latino; 1 Asian, non-Hispanic/Latino), 1 international. Average age 27. 36 applicants, 53% accepted, 7 enrolled. In 2016, 6 master's, 2 other advanced degrees awarded. *Degree requirements:* For master's, thesis. *Entrance requirements:* For master's, GRE General Test. Additional exam requirements/recommendations for international students: Required—TOEFL (minimum score 650 paper-based). *Application deadline:* For fall admission, 1/4 priority date for domestic students; for spring admission, 11/1 for domestic students. Applications are processed on a rolling basis. Application fee: $70. Electronic applications accepted. *Financial support:* In 2016–17, 4 students received support. Institutionally sponsored loans, tuition waivers (full and partial), and unspecified assistantships available. Financial award application deadline: 1/4; financial award applicants required to submit FAFSA. *Faculty research:* Medieval literature, history, philosophy, theology, and fine arts; Anglo-Norman. *Unit head:* Dr. Susanne Hafner, Director, 718-817-4655, E-mail: hafner@fordham.edu. *Application contact:* Bernadette Valentino-Morrison, Director of Graduate Admissions, 718-817-4419, Fax: 718-817-3566, E-mail: valentinomor@fordham.edu.

**Georgetown University,** Graduate School of Arts and Sciences, School of Continuing Studies, Washington, DC 20057. Offers American studies (MALS); Catholic studies (MALS); classical civilizations (MALS); emergency and disaster management (MPS); ethics and the professions (MALS); global strategic communications (MPS); hospitality management (MPS); human resources management (MPS); humanities (MALS); individualized study (MALS); integrated marketing communications (MPS); international affairs (MALS); Islam and Muslim-Christian relations (MALS); journalism (MPS); liberal studies (DLS); literature and society (MALS); medieval and early modern European studies (MALS); public relations and corporate communications (MPS); real estate (MPS); religious studies (MALS); social and public policy (MALS); sports industry management (MPS); systems engineering management (MPS); technology management (MPS); the theory and practice of American democracy (MALS); urban and regional planning (MPS); visual culture (MALS). MPS in systems engineering management offered jointly with Stevens Institute of Technology. *Entrance requirements:* Additional exam requirements/recommendations for international students: Required—TOEFL.

**The Graduate Center, City University of New York,** Graduate Studies, Interdisciplinary Studies, New York, NY 10016-4039. Offers language in social context (PhD); medieval studies (PhD); public policy (MA, PhD); urban studies (MA, PhD); women's studies (MA, PhD). Terminal master's awarded for partial completion of doctoral program. *Degree requirements:* For master's, thesis; for doctorate, comprehensive exam, thesis/dissertation. *Entrance requirements:* For master's and doctorate, GRE General Test.

**Harvard University,** Graduate School of Arts and Sciences, Department of English and American Literature and Language, Cambridge, MA 02138. Offers critical theory (PhD); eighteenth-century literature (PhD); literature: nineteenth-century to the present (PhD); medieval literature and language (PhD); modern British and American literature (PhD); Renaissance literature (PhD). Terminal master's awarded for partial completion of doctoral program. *Degree requirements:* For doctorate, 2 foreign languages, thesis/dissertation, oral exam. *Entrance requirements:* For doctorate, GRE General Test, GRE Subject Test, writing sample. Additional exam requirements/recommendations for international students: Required—TOEFL. *Faculty research:* Old and Middle English language and literature, drama, creative writing, transition to Romanticism, history and theory of criticism.

**Indiana University Bloomington,** University Graduate School, College of Arts and Sciences, Department of Germanic Studies, Bloomington, IN 47405-7000. Offers German philology and linguistics (PhD); German studies (MA, PhD), including German (MA), German literature and culture (MA), German literature and linguistics (MA); medieval German studies (PhD); teaching German (MAT). *Faculty:* 13 full-time (4 women), 6 part-time/adjunct (2 women). *Students:* 28 full-time (15 women), 2 part-time (both women), 5 international. Average age 32. 16 applicants, 56% accepted, 4 enrolled. In 2016, 2 master's, 3 doctorates awarded. *Degree requirements:* For master's, one foreign language, project; for doctorate, one foreign language, comprehensive exam, thesis/dissertation. *Entrance requirements:* For master's, GRE General Test, BA in German or equivalent; for doctorate, GRE General Test, MA in German or equivalent. Additional exam requirements/recommendations for international students: Required—TOEFL. *Application deadline:* For fall admission, 12/1 priority date for domestic students, 12/1 for international students; for spring admission, 9/1 priority date for domestic students, 9/1 for international students. Applications are processed on a rolling basis. Application fee: $55 ($65 for international students). Electronic applications

## Medieval and Renaissance Studies

accepted. *Financial support:* Application deadline: 1/15. *Faculty research:* German and other European literature: medieval to modern/postmodern, German and culture studies, Germanic philology, literary theory, literature and the other arts. *Unit head:* William Rasch, Department Chairman, 812-855-7947, Fax: 812-855-8292, E-mail: wrasch@indiana.edu. *Application contact:* Michelle Dunbar, Graduate Secretary, 812-855-7947, E-mail: midunbar@indiana.edu.
Website: http://germanic.indiana.edu/

**Rutgers University–New Brunswick,** Graduate School-New Brunswick, Program in History, Piscataway, NJ 08854-8097. Offers African-American history (PhD); early American history (PhD); early modern European history (PhD); east Asian history (PhD); global and comparative history (PhD); history (PhD); history of diplomacy and foreign relations (PhD); history of technology, environment and health (PhD); history of the Atlantic cultures and African diaspora (PhD); Latin American history (PhD); medieval history (PhD); modern European history (PhD); nineteenth and twentieth century American history (PhD); women's and gender history (PhD). *Degree requirements:* For doctorate, thesis/dissertation. *Entrance requirements:* For doctorate, GRE General Test, sample of written work. Electronic applications accepted. *Faculty research:* American history, European history, Afro-American history, women's history, Latin American history.

**Southern Methodist University,** Dedman College of Humanities and Sciences, Program in Medieval Studies, Dallas, TX 75275. Offers MA. *Program availability:* Part-time. *Degree requirements:* For master's, 2 foreign languages, thesis. *Entrance requirements:* For master's, GRE General Test, minimum GPA of 3.0. Electronic applications accepted. *Faculty research:* Byzantine culture, medieval Europe, Arthurian literature, Chaucer, Romance.

**University of California, Santa Barbara,** Graduate Division, College of Letters and Sciences, Division of Humanities and Fine Arts, Department of English, Santa Barbara, CA 93106-3170. Offers English (PhD), including environment and society, European medieval studies, feminist studies, global studies, technology and society, translation studies, writing studies; MA/PhD. Terminal master's awarded for partial completion of doctoral program. *Degree requirements:* For doctorate, one foreign language, comprehensive exam, thesis/dissertation. *Entrance requirements:* For doctorate, GRE General Test, GRE Subject Test (English literature). Additional exam requirements/recommendations for international students: Required—TOEFL (minimum score 550 paper-based; 80 iBT), IELTS (minimum score 7). Electronic applications accepted. *Faculty research:* Medieval, Romantic and Victorian studies; gender studies and feminist theory; literature and the mind; American literature; literature and new media/information culture.

**University of California, Santa Barbara,** Graduate Division, College of Letters and Sciences, Division of Humanities and Fine Arts, Department of History, Santa Barbara, CA 93106-9410. Offers European medieval studies (PhD); global studies (PhD); public historical studies (PhD); technology and society (PhD); women's studies (PhD); MA/PhD. *Degree requirements:* For doctorate, variable foreign language requirement, comprehensive exam, thesis/dissertation. *Entrance requirements:* For doctorate, GRE. Additional exam requirements/recommendations for international students: Required—TOEFL (minimum score 550 paper-based; 80 iBT), IELTS (minimum score 7). Electronic applications accepted. *Faculty research:* Europe, United States, Latin America, Africa, Middle East, East Asia.

**University of California, Santa Barbara,** Graduate Division, College of Letters and Sciences, Division of Humanities and Fine Arts, Department of History of Art and Architecture, Santa Barbara, CA 93106-2014. Offers art history (PhD), including art history, European medieval studies, feminist studies; MA/PhD. Terminal master's awarded for partial completion of doctoral program. *Degree requirements:* For doctorate, 2 foreign languages, comprehensive exam, thesis/dissertation. *Entrance requirements:* For doctorate, GRE. Additional exam requirements/recommendations for international students: Required—TOEFL (minimum score 550 paper-based; 80 iBT), IELTS (minimum score 7). Electronic applications accepted. *Faculty research:* History of architecture, Renaissance-Italian, Baroque, American, Chinese, Japanese, contemporary, Northern Renaissance.

**University of California, Santa Barbara,** Graduate Division, College of Letters and Sciences, Division of Humanities and Fine Arts, Department of Religious Studies, Santa Barbara, CA 93106-3130. Offers ancient Mediterranean studies (PhD); cognitive science (PhD); European medieval studies (PhD); feminist studies (PhD); global studies (PhD); religious studies (MA, PhD); translation studies (PhD); MA/PhD. Terminal master's awarded for partial completion of doctoral program. *Degree requirements:* For master's, one foreign language, comprehensive exam (for some programs), thesis (for some programs); for doctorate, 2 foreign languages, thesis/dissertation, methodology. *Entrance requirements:* For master's and doctorate, GRE General Test. Additional exam requirements/recommendations for international students: Required—TOEFL (minimum score 550 paper-based; 80 iBT), IELTS (minimum score 7). Electronic applications accepted. *Faculty research:* Area studies; religious traditions; theory and method in the study of religion; religion, culture, and politics; spirituality and religious experience.

**University of California, Santa Barbara,** Graduate Division, College of Letters and Sciences, Division of Humanities and Fine Arts, Department of Spanish and Portuguese, Santa Barbara, CA 93106-4150. Offers Hispanic languages and literatures (PhD), including European medieval studies, feminist studies, Hispanic linguistics, Hispanic literature, Luso-Brazilian literature; Hispanic linguistics (MA); Luso-Brazilian literature (MA); Spanish or Spanish-American literature (MA); MA/PhD. Terminal master's awarded for partial completion of doctoral program. *Degree requirements:* For master's, 2 foreign languages, comprehensive exam (for some programs), thesis optional; for doctorate, 3 foreign languages, comprehensive exam, thesis/dissertation. *Entrance requirements:* For master's and doctorate, GRE. Additional exam requirements/recommendations for international students: Required—TOEFL (minimum score 550 paper-based; 80 iBT), IELTS (minimum score 7). Electronic applications accepted. *Faculty research:* Nineteenth-century Spanish and Portuguese literature, Spanish and Spanish-American literature, nineteenth- and twentieth-century Portuguese and Brazilian literatures, Hispanic linguistics, Catalan language and culture.

**University of California, Santa Barbara,** Graduate Division, College of Letters and Sciences, Division of Humanities and Fine Arts, Department of Theater and Dance, Santa Barbara, CA 93106-7060. Offers theater studies (MA, PhD), including European medieval studies (PhD), feminist studies (PhD), theatre studies (PhD); MA/PhD. Terminal master's awarded for partial completion of doctoral program. *Degree requirements:* For master's, comprehensive exam, thesis; for doctorate, one foreign language, comprehensive exam, thesis/dissertation. *Entrance requirements:* For master's and doctorate, GRE. Additional exam requirements/recommendations for

international students: Required—TOEFL (minimum score 550 paper-based; 80 iBT), IELTS (minimum score 7). Electronic applications accepted. *Faculty research:* English and American theater and Ancient Greek; Spanish, Latin American and Caribbean performance; Renaissance and Baroque drama and intercultural theory; East Asian performance, gender and nationalism; Korean cultural studies, Russian literature, and Slavic folklore; history of German theater, Shakespeare, and European opera; postcolonialism, performance-based ethnography, globalism and national identity formation in Africa.

**University of Chicago,** Division of the Humanities, Department of Romance Languages and Literatures, Chicago, IL 60637. Offers French and Francophone studies (PhD); Hispanic and Luso-Brazilian studies (PhD); Italian studies (PhD); Renaissance and early modern studies (PhD). *Students:* 44 full-time (28 women); includes 9 minority (1 Asian, non-Hispanic/Latino; 7 Hispanic/Latino; 1 Two or more races, non-Hispanic/Latino), 16 international. 45 applicants, 29% accepted, 5 enrolled. In 2016, 4 doctorates awarded. Terminal master's awarded for partial completion of doctoral program. *Degree requirements:* For doctorate, 3 foreign languages, comprehensive exam, thesis/dissertation. *Entrance requirements:* For doctorate, GRE General Test. Additional exam requirements/recommendations for international students: Required—TOEFL (minimum score 104 iBT), IELTS (minimum score 7). *Application deadline:* For fall admission, 12/15 for domestic and international students. Application fee: $90. Electronic applications accepted. *Financial support:* Fellowships with full tuition reimbursements, teaching assistantships with full tuition reimbursements, Federal Work-Study, institutionally sponsored loans, scholarships/grants, and health care benefits available. Financial award application deadline: 12/15; financial award applicants required to submit FAFSA. *Unit head:* Daisy Delogu, Chair, 773-702-4115, E-mail: ddelogu@uchicago.edu. *Application contact:* Michael Beetley, Assistant Dean of Students, Admissions and Fellowships, 773-702-1552, Fax: 773-834-9148, E-mail: humanitiesadmissions@uchicago.edu.
Website: http://rll.uchicago.edu

**University of Connecticut,** Graduate School, College of Liberal Arts and Sciences, Field of Medieval Studies, Storrs, CT 06269. Offers MA, PhD. Terminal master's awarded for partial completion of doctoral program. *Degree requirements:* For master's, comprehensive exam; for doctorate, 3 foreign languages, thesis/dissertation. *Entrance requirements:* For master's and doctorate, GRE General Test, GRE Subject Test. Additional exam requirements/recommendations for international students: Required—TOEFL (minimum score 550 paper-based). Electronic applications accepted.

**University of Guelph,** Graduate Studies, College of Arts, School of English and Theatre Studies, Joint Program in Literary Studies/Theatre Studies in English, Guelph, ON N1G 2W1, Canada. Offers PhD. *Program availability:* Part-time. *Degree requirements:* For doctorate, one foreign language, comprehensive exam, thesis/dissertation. *Entrance requirements:* For doctorate, MA, 3 letters of reference, writing samples, resume, minimum A- average in graduate course work. Additional exam requirements/recommendations for international students: Required—TOEFL. Electronic applications accepted. *Faculty research:* Canadian studies, Early Modern studies, Postcolonial studies, studies in gender and genre, 19th Century studies.

**University of Minnesota, Twin Cities Campus,** Graduate School, College of Liberal Arts, Department of German, Scandinavian, and Dutch, Minneapolis, MN 55455. Offers Germanic studies (MA, PhD), including German, Germanic medieval studies, Scandinavian studies (MA). *Program availability:* Part-time. Terminal master's awarded for partial completion of doctoral program. *Degree requirements:* For doctorate, 2 foreign languages, thesis/dissertation. *Entrance requirements:* For master's, GRE General Test, BA in German, Scandinavian, or equivalent; for doctorate, MA in German, Scandinavian, or equivalent. Additional exam requirements/recommendations for international students: Required—TOEFL (minimum score 550 paper-based; 79 iBT). Electronic applications accepted. *Faculty research:* Cultural studies, literary theory, feminist criticism, film, Germanic medieval studies.

**University of Notre Dame,** Graduate School, College of Arts and Letters, Division of Humanities, Medieval Institute, Notre Dame, IN 46556. Offers MMS, PhD. Terminal master's awarded for partial completion of doctoral program. *Degree requirements:* For master's, 3 foreign languages, comprehensive exam; for doctorate, 3 foreign languages, thesis/dissertation, candidacy exam. *Entrance requirements:* For master's and doctorate, GRE General Test. Additional exam requirements/recommendations for international students: Required—TOEFL (minimum score 600 paper-based; 80 iBT). Electronic applications accepted. *Faculty research:* Medieval history, vernacular literatures, theology, philosophy, Ambrosiana manuscripts and drawings.

**University of Pittsburgh,** Dietrich School of Arts and Sciences, Program in Medieval and Renaissance Studies, Pittsburgh, PA 15260. Offers Certificate. *Program availability:* Part-time. *Faculty:* 40 full-time (17 women). *Students:* 7 full-time (4 women). Average age 24. 4 applicants, 100% accepted, 4 enrolled. *Entrance requirements:* For degree, good academic standing in a University of Pittsburgh graduate degree-granting department. *Application deadline:* Applications are processed on a rolling basis. Application fee: $0. Electronic applications accepted. Tuition and fees vary according to program. *Financial support:* Scholarships/grants available. *Faculty research:* Medieval historical writing, English Renaissance, Medieval and Renaissance architecture. *Unit head:* Prof. Jennifer Waldron, Director, 412-624-6564, Fax: 412-383-6999, E-mail: jwaldron@pitt.edu. *Application contact:* Kathryn Briar Somerville, Graduate Administrator, 412-624-6564, E-mail: kbs47@pitt.edu.
Website: http://www.medren.pitt.edu/

**University of Toronto,** School of Graduate Studies, Faculty of Arts and Science, Centre for Medieval Studies, Toronto, ON M5S 1A1, Canada. Offers MA, PhD. *Program availability:* Part-time. *Degree requirements:* For master's, one foreign language, 4 courses or 3 courses and thesis; for doctorate, 3 foreign languages, thesis/dissertation, proficiency in Latin, German and French. *Entrance requirements:* For master's, letters of reference, minimum B+ average, course work in the Medieval period; for doctorate, letters of reference. Additional exam requirements/recommendations for international students: Required—TOEFL (minimum score 580 paper-based; 93 iBT), TWE (minimum score 5). Electronic applications accepted.

**Yale University,** Graduate School of Arts and Sciences, Interdisciplinary Program in Medieval Studies, New Haven, CT 06520. Offers M Phil, PhD. *Entrance requirements:* For doctorate, GRE General Test.

**Yale University,** Graduate School of Arts and Sciences, Program in Renaissance Studies, New Haven, CT 06520. Offers PhD. *Degree requirements:* For doctorate, 3 foreign languages. *Entrance requirements:* For doctorate, GRE General Test.

# Public History

**American Public University System,** AMU/APU Graduate Programs, Charles Town, WV 25414. Offers accounting (MBA, MS); applied business analytics (MBA, MS); criminal justice (MA), including business administration, emergency and disaster management, general (MA, MS); educational leadership (M Ed); emergency and disaster management (MA); entrepreneurship (MBA); environmental policy and management (MS), including environmental planning, environmental sustainability, fish and wildlife management, general (MA, MS), global environmental management; finance (MBA); general (MBA); government contracting and acquisition (MBA); health care administration (MBA); health information management (MS); history (MA), including American history, ancient and classical history, European history, global history, public history; homeland security (MA), including business administration, counterterrorism studies, criminal justice, cyber, emergency management and public health, intelligence studies, transportation security; homeland security resource allocation (MBA); humanities (MA); information technology (MS), including digital forensics, enterprise software development, information assurance and security, IT project management; information technology management (MBA); intelligence studies (MA), including criminal intelligence, cyber, general (MA, MS), homeland security, intelligence analysis, intelligence collection, intelligence management, intelligence operations, terrorism studies; international relations and conflict resolution (MA), including comparative and security issues, conflict resolution, international and transnational security issues, peacekeeping; legal studies (MA); management (MA), including strategic consulting; marketing (MBA); military history (MA), including American military history, American Revolution, civil war, war since 1945, World War II; military studies (MA), including joint warfare, strategic leadership; national security studies (MA), including cyber, general (MA, MS), homeland security, regional security studies, security and intelligence analysis, terrorism studies; nonprofit management (MBA); political science (MA), including American politics and government, comparative government and development, general (MA, MS), international relations, public policy; psychology (MA); public administration (MPA), including disaster management, environmental policy, health policy, human resources, national security, organizational management, security management; public health (MPH); reverse logistics management (MA); security management (MA); space studies (MS), including aerospace science, general (MA, MS), planetary science; sports and health sciences (MS); sports management (MBA); teaching (M Ed), including autism spectrum disorder, curriculum and instruction for elementary teachers, elementary reading, English language learners, instructional leadership, online learning, special education, STEAM (STEM plus the arts); transportation and logistics management (MA). *Program availability:* Part-time, evening/weekend, online only, 100% online. *Faculty:* 401 full-time (228 women), 1,678 part-time/adjunct (781 women). *Students:* 378 full-time (184 women), 8,455 part-time (3,484 women); includes 2,972 minority (1,552 Black or African American, non-Hispanic/Latino; 52 American Indian or Alaska Native, non-Hispanic/Latino; 211 Asian, non-Hispanic/Latino; 791 Hispanic/Latino; 70 Native Hawaiian or other Pacific Islander, non-Hispanic/Latino; 296 Two or more races, non-Hispanic/Latino), 109 international. Average age 37. In 2016, 3,185 master's awarded. *Degree requirements:* For master's, comprehensive exam or practicum. *Entrance requirements:* For master's, official transcript showing earned bachelor's degree from institution accredited by recognized accrediting body. Additional exam requirements/recommendations for international students: Required—TOEFL (minimum score 550 paper-based), IELTS (minimum score 6.5). *Application deadline:* Applications are processed on a rolling basis. Application fee: $0. Electronic applications accepted. *Expenses: Tuition:* Part-time $350 per credit hour. *Required fees:* $50 per course. *Financial support:* Scholarships/grants available. Financial award applicants required to submit FAFSA. *Unit head:* Dr. Karan Powell, President, 877-468-6268, Fax: 304-724-3780. *Application contact:* Terry Grant, Vice President of Enrollment Management, 877-468-6268, Fax: 304-724-3780, E-mail: info@apus.edu.
Website: http://www.apus.edu

**Arizona State University at the Tempe campus,** College of Liberal Arts and Sciences, School of Historical, Philosophical and Religious Studies, Tempe, AZ 85287-4301. Offers European history (MA, PhD); medieval studies (Graduate Certificate); North American history (MA, PhD); philosophy (MA, PhD); public history (MA); religious studies (MA, PhD); Renaissance studies (Graduate Certificate); scholarly publishing (Graduate Certificate). *Program availability:* Part-time. Terminal master's awarded for partial completion of doctoral program. *Degree requirements:* For master's, thesis or alternative, interactive Program of Study (iPOS) submitted before completing 50 percent of required credit hours; for doctorate, variable foreign language requirement, comprehensive exam, thesis/dissertation, interactive Program of Study (iPOS) submitted before completing 50 percent of required credit hours. *Entrance requirements:* For master's and doctorate, GRE, minimum GPA of 3.0 or equivalent in last 2 years of work leading to bachelor's degree. Additional exam requirements/recommendations for international students: Required—TOEFL, IELTS, or PTE. Electronic applications accepted.

**Armstrong State University,** School of Graduate Studies, Program in History, Savannah, GA 31419-1997. Offers American and European history (MA); public history (MA). *Program availability:* Part-time, evening/weekend. *Faculty:* 6 full-time (1 woman), 1 (woman) part-time/adjunct. *Students:* 5 full-time (3 women), 11 part-time (4 women); includes 2 minority (1 Black or African American, non-Hispanic/Latino; 1 Hispanic/Latino). Average age 37. 17 applicants, 71% accepted, 8 enrolled. In 2016, 3 master's awarded. *Degree requirements:* For master's, one foreign language, comprehensive exam (for some programs), thesis (for some programs), thesis, internship, or advanced fieldwork. *Entrance requirements:* For master's, GRE General Test, minimum GPA of 3.0, letters of recommendation, BA in history or equivalent. Additional exam requirements/recommendations for international students: Required—TOEFL (minimum score 523 paper-based; 70 iBT). *Application deadline:* For fall admission, 6/30 priority date for domestic students, 5/1 priority date for international students; for spring admission, 11/15 priority date for domestic students, 9/15 priority date for international students; for summer admission, 4/15 priority date for domestic students, 9/15 for international students. Applications are processed on a rolling basis. Application fee: $30. Electronic applications accepted. *Expenses:* Tuition, state resident: full-time $1781; part-time $161.93 per credit hour. Tuition, nonresident: full-time $6482; part-time $589.27 per credit hour. *Required fees:* $1224 per unit. $612 per semester. Tuition and fees vary according to course load, campus/location and program. *Financial support:* In 2016–17, research assistantships with full tuition reimbursements (averaging $5,000 per year) were awarded; career-related internships or fieldwork, Federal Work-Study, and unspecified assistantships also available. Support available to part-time students. Financial award application deadline: 3/15; financial award applicants required to submit FAFSA. *Faculty research:* Public history; European, Latin American, African, and United States history. *Unit head:* Dr. Christopher Hendricks, Interim Department Head, 912-344-2725, Fax: 912-344-3451, E-mail: chris.hendricks@armstrong.edu. *Application contact:* McKenzie Peterman, Assistant Director of Graduate Admissions, 912-344-

2503, Fax: 912-344-3417, E-mail: graduate@armstrong.edu.
Website: http://www.armstrong.edu/Liberal_Arts/history/history_graduate_program

**California State University, East Bay,** Office of Graduate Studies, College of Letters, Arts, and Social Sciences, Department of History, Hayward, CA 94542-3000. Offers history (MA); public history (MA); teaching (MA). *Program availability:* Part-time, evening/weekend. *Students:* 3 full-time (1 woman), 20 part-time (12 women); includes 7 minority (2 Black or African American, non-Hispanic/Latino; 4 Hispanic/Latino; 1 Two or more races, non-Hispanic/Latino). Average age 37. 28 applicants, 57% accepted, 13 enrolled. In 2016, 8 master's awarded. *Degree requirements:* For master's, one foreign language, comprehensive exam, project, thesis, or exam. *Entrance requirements:* For master's, GRE (strongly recommended), minimum GPA of 3.0 in field, 3.3 in history; 2 letters of recommendation; writing sample. Additional exam requirements/recommendations for international students: Required—TOEFL (minimum score 550 paper-based). *Application deadline:* For fall admission, 5/16 for domestic and international students. Applications are processed on a rolling basis. Application fee: $55. Electronic applications accepted. *Financial support:* Fellowships, teaching assistantships, career-related internships or fieldwork, Federal Work-Study, institutionally sponsored loans, and scholarships/grants available. Support available to part-time students. Financial award application deadline: 3/2; financial award applicants required to submit FAFSA. *Faculty research:* Digital history, American women, early America, Native Americans, medieval colonial India. *Unit head:* Dr. Linda L. Ivey, Chair, 510-885-4015, E-mail: linda.ivey@csueastbay.edu. *Application contact:* Dr. Khal Schneider, Graduate Coordinator, 510-885-3237, Fax: 510-885-4791, E-mail: khal.schneider@csueastbay.edu.
Website: http://www20.csueastbay.edu/class/departments/history/

**California State University, Sacramento,** Office of Graduate Studies, College of Arts and Letters, Department of History, Sacramento, CA 95819. Offers history (MA); public historical studies (PhD); public history (MA). PhD held jointly with University of California, Santa Barbara. *Program availability:* Part-time. *Students:* 23 full-time (10 women), 38 part-time (15 women); includes 13 minority (2 Black or African American, non-Hispanic/Latino; 1 American Indian or Alaska Native, non-Hispanic/Latino; 3 Asian, non-Hispanic/Latino; 7 Hispanic/Latino). Average age 29. 49 applicants, 84% accepted, 27 enrolled. In 2016, 18 master's awarded. *Degree requirements:* For master's, thesis, project or comprehensive exam; writing proficiency exam. *Entrance requirements:* For master's, minimum GPA of 3.25 in history, 3.0 overall during previous 2 years; BA in history or equivalent. Additional exam requirements/recommendations for international students: Required—TOEFL (minimum score 550 paper-based; 80 iBT). *Application deadline:* For fall admission, 2/3 for domestic students, 3/1 for international students; for spring admission, 9/15 for domestic students, 9/30 for international students. Applications are processed on a rolling basis. Application fee: $55. Electronic applications accepted. *Expenses:* $4,302 full-time tuition and fees per semester, $2,796 part-time. *Financial support:* Career-related internships or fieldwork and Federal Work-Study available. Support available to part-time students. Financial award application deadline: 3/1; financial award applicants required to submit FAFSA. *Unit head:* Dr. Jeffrey Wilson, Chair, 916-278-6136, Fax: 916-278-7476, E-mail: jkwilson@saclink.csus.edu. *Application contact:* Jose Martinez, Outreach and Graduate Diversity Coordinator, 916-278-6470, Fax: 916-278-5669, E-mail: martinj@skymail.csus.edu.
Website: http://www.csus.edu/hist

**The College at Brockport, State University of New York,** School of Arts and Sciences, Department of History, Brockport, NY 14420-2997. Offers history (MA), including American and world history, American history, American public history, world history. *Program availability:* Part-time, evening/weekend. *Faculty:* 9 full-time (5 women). *Students:* 8 full-time (5 women), 17 part-time (9 women); includes 1 minority (Black or African American, non-Hispanic/Latino). 17 applicants, 82% accepted, 11 enrolled. In 2016, 15 master's awarded. *Degree requirements:* For master's, thesis or alternative. *Entrance requirements:* For master's, minimum GPA of 3.0, writing sample, letters of recommendation, statement of objectives. Additional exam requirements/recommendations for international students: Required—TOEFL (minimum score 550 paper-based; 79 iBT), IELTS (minimum score 6.5). *Application deadline:* For fall admission, 7/1 priority date for domestic and international students; for spring admission, 11/15 priority date for domestic and international students; for summer admission, 4/15 for domestic and international students. Application fee: $50. Electronic applications accepted. *Expenses:* Contact institution. *Financial support:* In 2016–17, 1 fellowship with tuition reimbursement (averaging $3,750 per year), 2 teaching assistantships with full tuition reimbursements (averaging $6,000 per year) were awarded; Federal Work-Study, scholarships/grants, and unspecified assistantships also available. Support available to part-time students. Financial award application deadline: 3/15; financial award applicants required to submit FAFSA. *Faculty research:* American history, women's history, European history, world history, cultural history. *Unit head:* Dr. Owen Steve Ireland, Chairperson, 585-395-5627, Fax: 585-395-2620, E-mail: oireland@brockport.edu. *Application contact:* Dr. Morag Martin, Graduate Director, 585-395-5690, Fax: 585-395-2620, E-mail: mmartin@brockport.edu.
Website: http://www.brockport.edu/history/grad/

**Colorado State University,** College of Liberal Arts, Department of History, Fort Collins, CO 80523-1776. Offers liberal arts (MA); public history (MA), including cultural resource management, historic preservation, museum studies. *Program availability:* Part-time. *Faculty:* 6 full-time (2 women), 1 part-time/adjunct (0 women). *Students:* 25 full-time (14 women), 4 part-time (1 woman); includes 2 minority (1 American Indian or Alaska Native, non-Hispanic/Latino; 1 Hispanic/Latino). Average age 28. 23 applicants, 61% accepted, 13 enrolled. In 2016, 6 master's awarded. *Degree requirements:* For master's, one foreign language, comprehensive exam, thesis (for some programs), minimum final grade of B- in history courses counted toward degree. *Entrance requirements:* For master's, GRE General Test, 21 credits in history, statement of purpose, 3 letters of reference. Additional exam requirements/recommendations for international students: Required—TOEFL, IELTS. *Application deadline:* For fall admission, 2/1 priority date for domestic and international students. Application fee: $60 ($70 for international students). Electronic applications accepted. *Expenses:* Tuition, state resident: full-time $9628. Tuition, nonresident: full-time $23,603. *Required fees:* $2253; $528.14 per credit hour. $264.07 per semester. Tuition and fees vary according to course load and program. *Financial support:* In 2016–17, 22 students received support, including 1 research assistantship with full tuition reimbursement available (averaging $13,932 per year), 23 teaching assistantships with full tuition reimbursements available (averaging $13,932 per year); fellowships with full tuition reimbursements available and health care benefits also available. Financial award application deadline: 3/1; financial award applicants required to submit FAFSA. *Faculty research:* United states and north America; public and environmental history; modern world; religion; women, gender and

## Public History

sexuality. *Total annual research expenditures:* $281,014. *Unit head:* Dr. Doug Yarrington, Department Chair, 970-491-6801, Fax: 970-491-2941, E-mail: doug.yarrington@colostate.edu. *Application contact:* Diane Margolf, Graduate Studies Committee Chair, 970-491-5671, Fax: 970-491-2941, E-mail: diane.margolf@colostate.edu.
Website: http://history.colostate.edu/

**Drew University,** Caspersen School of Graduate Studies, Madison, NJ 07940-1493. Offers conflict resolution and leadership (Certificate), including community leadership, moderation, peace building; history and culture (MA, PhD), including American history, book history, British history, European history, Holocaust and genocide (M Litt, MA, D Litt, PhD), intellectual history, Irish history, print culture, public history; K-12 education (MAT), including art, biology, chemistry, elementary education, English, French, Italian, math, secondary education, special education, teacher of students with disabilities; liberal studies (M Litt, D Litt), including history, Holocaust and genocide (M Litt, MA, D Litt, PhD), Irish/Irish-American studies, literature (M Litt, MMH, D Litt, DMH, CMH), religion, spirituality, teaching in the two-year college, writing; medical humanities (MMH, DMH, CMH), including arts, health, healthcare, literature (M Litt, MMH, D Litt, DMH, CMH), scientific research; poetry (MFA). *Program availability:* Part-time, evening/weekend. *Faculty:* 4 full-time (2 women), 31 part-time/adjunct (16 women). *Students:* 62 full-time (41 women), 199 part-time (130 women); includes 38 minority (17 Black or African American, non-Hispanic/Latino; 3 Asian, non-Hispanic/Latino; 17 Hispanic/Latino; 1 Two or more races, non-Hispanic/Latino), 3 international. Average age 27. 93 applicants, 81% accepted, 46 enrolled. In 2016, 39 master's, 27 doctorates, 26 other advanced degrees awarded. Terminal master's awarded for partial completion of doctoral program. *Degree requirements:* For master's and other advanced degree, thesis (for some programs); for doctorate, one foreign language, comprehensive exam (for some programs), thesis/dissertation. *Entrance requirements:* For master's, PRAXIS Core and Subject Area tests (for MAT), resume, transcripts, writing sample, personal statement, letters of recommendation; for doctorate, GRE (PhD in history and culture), resume, transcripts, writing sample, personal statement, letters of recommendation. Additional exam requirements/recommendations for international students: Required—TOEFL (minimum score 587 paper-based; 94 iBT), IELTS (minimum score 7), TWE (minimum score 4). *Application deadline:* For fall admission, 8/1 for domestic students, 6/1 for international students; for spring admission, 12/1 for domestic students, 10/1 for international students. Applications are processed on a rolling basis. Application fee: $35. Electronic applications accepted. Tuition and fees vary according to program. *Financial support:* Fellowships, research assistantships, teaching assistantships, career-related internships or fieldwork, Federal Work-Study, scholarships/grants, and unspecified assistantships available. Support available to part-time students. Financial award applicants required to submit FAFSA. *Application contact:* Leanne Horinko, Director of Caspersen Admissions, 973-408-3280, E-mail: gradm@drew.edu.
Website: http://www.drew.edu/caspersen

**Duquesne University,** Graduate School of Liberal Arts, Department of History, Pittsburgh, PA 15282-0001. Offers historical studies (MA); public history (MA). *Program availability:* Part-time, evening/weekend. *Faculty:* 15 full-time (5 women), 5 part-time/adjunct (3 women). *Students:* 33 full-time (25 women), 3 part-time (1 woman); includes 1 minority (Two or more races, non-Hispanic/Latino). Average age 24. 38 applicants, 89% accepted, 16 enrolled. In 2016, 14 master's awarded. *Degree requirements:* For master's, comprehensive exam (for some programs), thesis optional. *Entrance requirements:* For master's, GRE General Test, writing sample. Additional exam requirements/recommendations for international students: Required—TOEFL. *Application deadline:* For fall admission, 8/15 for domestic students, 5/1 for international students; for spring admission, 11/1 priority date for domestic students. Applications are processed on a rolling basis. Application fee: $0. Electronic applications accepted. *Expenses:* Tuition: Full-time $22,212; part-time $1234 per credit. Tuition and fees vary according to program. *Financial support:* In 2016–17, 30 students received support, including 7 teaching assistantships with full tuition reimbursements available (averaging $8,000 per year); career-related internships or fieldwork, Federal Work-Study, scholarships/grants, tuition waivers (full and partial), and unspecified assistantships also available. Support available to part-time students. Financial award application deadline: 5/1. *Faculty research:* American studies, immigration history, local social history, applied history, Eastern European history. *Unit head:* Dr. John Dwyer, Chair, 412-396-6470, E-mail: dwyer@duq.edu. *Application contact:* Linda Rendulic, Assistant to the Dean, 412-396-6400, Fax: 412-396-5265, E-mail: rendulic@duq.edu.
Website: http://www.duq.edu/academics/schools/liberal-arts/graduate-school/programs/history

**East Carolina University,** Graduate School, Thomas Harriot College of Arts and Sciences, Department of History, Greenville, NC 27858-4353. Offers American history (MA); Atlantic world (MA); European history (MA); history education (MA Ed); maritime studies (MA); military history (MA); public history (MA). *Program availability:* Part-time, evening/weekend. *Students:* 44 full-time (21 women), 48 part-time (27 women); includes 8 minority (1 Black or African American, non-Hispanic/Latino; 5 Hispanic/Latino; 2 Two or more races, non-Hispanic/Latino), 2 international. Average age 29. 46 applicants, 80% accepted, 23 enrolled. In 2016, 24 master's awarded. *Degree requirements:* For master's, one foreign language, comprehensive exam, thesis. *Entrance requirements:* For master's, GRE General Test, GRE Subject Test. Additional exam requirements/recommendations for international students: Required—TOEFL. *Application deadline:* For fall admission, 6/1 priority date for domestic students; for spring admission, 10/15 for domestic students. Applications are processed on a rolling basis. Application fee: $50. *Financial support:* Fellowships, research assistantships with partial tuition reimbursements, teaching assistantships with partial tuition reimbursements, and Federal Work-Study available. Support available to part-time students. Financial award application deadline: 6/1. *Unit head:* Dr. Gerry Prokopowicz, Chair, 252-328-6587, E-mail: prokopowiczg@ecu.edu.
Website: http://www.ecu.edu/cs-cas/history/graduatedegrees.cfm

**Eastern Illinois University,** Graduate School, College of Arts and Humanities, Department of History, Charleston, IL 61920. Offers historical administration (MA); history (MA). *Program availability:* Part-time, evening/weekend. *Degree requirements:* For master's, comprehensive exam (for some programs), thesis (for some programs). *Entrance requirements:* For master's, GMAT or GRE. Additional exam requirements/recommendations for international students: Required—TOEFL (minimum score 500 paper-based; 61 iBT), IELTS (minimum score 6). Electronic applications accepted.

**Florida State University,** The Graduate School, College of Arts and Sciences, Department of History, Tallahassee, FL 32306. Offers history (MA, MS, PhD); public history (MA). *Program availability:* Part-time. *Faculty:* 29 full-time (11 women). *Students:* 64 full-time (27 women), 21 part-time (5 women); includes 10 minority (2 Black or African American, non-Hispanic/Latino; 2 Asian, non-Hispanic/Latino; 1 Hispanic/Latino; 5 Two or more races, non-Hispanic/Latino), 3 international. Average age 32. 53 applicants, 60% accepted, 15 enrolled. In 2016, 22 master's, 16 doctorates awarded. *Degree requirements:* For master's, one foreign language, comprehensive exam (for some programs), thesis (for some programs), internships; for doctorate, one foreign language, comprehensive exam, thesis/dissertation. *Entrance requirements:* For master's, GRE General Test, minimum GPA of 3.3, minimum 18 hours of course work in history; for doctorate, GRE General Test, master's degree, minimum graduate GPA of 3.65. Additional exam requirements/recommendations for international students: Required—TOEFL (minimum score 550 paper-based; 80 iBT). *Application deadline:* For fall admission, 12/1 for domestic and international students. Applications are processed on a rolling basis. Application fee: $30. Electronic applications accepted. *Expenses:* Tuition, state resident: full-time $7263; part-time $403.51 per credit hour. Tuition, nonresident: full-time $18,087; part-time $1004.85 per credit hour. *Required fees:* $1365; $75.81 per credit hour. $20 per semester. Tuition and fees vary according to campus/location. *Financial support:* In 2016–17, 49 students received support, including 11 fellowships with full tuition reimbursements available (averaging $16,300 per year), 5 research assistantships with full tuition reimbursements available (averaging $15,000 per year), 5 teaching assistantships with full tuition reimbursements available (averaging $18,000 per year); Federal Work-Study, institutionally sponsored loans, scholarships/grants, tuition waivers (full and partial), and unspecified assistantships also available. Financial award application deadline: 12/1; financial award applicants required to submit FAFSA. *Faculty research:* Napoleon and the French Revolution, modern Europe, early modern Europe, Middle East, Latin America, Hispanic Caribbean, 20th-century Cuba, modern Britain, gender and sexuality, Atlantic world, modern Germany, Medieval Europe, World War II, U.S. 19th century, early U.S., Native American, science, medicine and technology, Russia, East Asia. *Unit head:* Dr. Edward Gray, Chair, 850-644-5888, Fax: 850-644-6402, E-mail: egray@fsu.edu. *Application contact:* Natalie Webster, Academic Program Assistant, 850-644-2610, E-mail: nswebster@fsu.edu.
Website: http://history.fsu.edu/

**Georgia Southern University,** Jack N. Averitt College of Graduate Studies, College of Liberal Arts and Social Sciences, Program in History, Statesboro, GA 30460. Offers history (MA); public history (Graduate Certificate). *Program availability:* Part-time. *Students:* 21 full-time (13 women), 7 part-time (5 women); includes 2 minority (both Hispanic/Latino). Average age 29. 15 applicants, 73% accepted, 10 enrolled. In 2016, 7 master's awarded. *Degree requirements:* For master's, one foreign language, thesis optional, terminal exams. *Entrance requirements:* For master's, GRE General Test, minimum GPA of 3.0, undergraduate major in history or equivalent, letters of reference. Additional exam requirements/recommendations for international students: Required—TOEFL (minimum score 550 paper-based; 80 iBT), IELTS (minimum score 6). *Application deadline:* For fall admission, 3/1 priority date for domestic and international students; for spring admission, 10/1 priority date for domestic students, 10/1 for international students. Applications are processed on a rolling basis. Application fee: $50. Electronic applications accepted. *Expenses:* Tuition, state resident: full-time $7236; part-time $277 per semester hour. Tuition, nonresident: full-time $27,118; part-time $1105 per semester hour. *Required fees:* $2092. *Financial support:* In 2016–17, 16 students received support, including 14 fellowships with full tuition reimbursements available (averaging $7,750 per year), 1 teaching assistantship with full tuition reimbursement available (averaging $7,750 per year); career-related internships or fieldwork, Federal Work-Study, scholarships/grants, tuition waivers (full), and unspecified assistantships also available. Support available to part-time students. Financial award application deadline: 4/15; financial award applicants required to submit FAFSA. *Faculty research:* Women's/gender history, the American South, military history, public history, modern Europe. *Unit head:* Dr. Timothy Teeter, Graduate Program Director, 912-478-0239, Fax: 912-478-0377, E-mail: tmteeter@georgiasouthern.edu.
Website: http://class.georgiasouthern.edu/history/

**Georgia State University,** College of Arts and Sciences, Department of History, Program in History, Atlanta, GA 30302-3083. Offers historic preservation (MA); history (PhD); public history (MA); world history (MA). *Program availability:* Part-time, evening/weekend. Terminal master's awarded for partial completion of doctoral program. *Degree requirements:* For master's, one foreign language, comprehensive exam, thesis optional, continuous enrollment; 6 hours of thesis credits; for doctorate, 2 foreign languages, comprehensive exam, thesis/dissertation, dissertation prospectus and prospectus defense; dissertation defense; residency; continuous enrollment; 6 hours of thesis credits. *Entrance requirements:* For master's, GRE, BA in history; statement of purpose; writing sample; three letters of recommendation; official transcripts; for doctorate, GRE, MA in history; master's thesis; statement of purpose; writing sample; three letters of recommendation; official transcripts; appropriate language skills. Additional exam requirements/recommendations for international students: Required—TOEFL (minimum score 550 paper-based; 80 iBT). *Application deadline:* For fall admission, 3/15 for domestic and international students; for spring admission, 10/15 for domestic and international students. Applications are processed on a rolling basis. Application fee: $50. Electronic applications accepted. *Expenses:* Tuition, state resident: full-time $6876; part-time $382 per credit hour. Tuition, nonresident: full-time $22,374; part-time $1243 per credit hour. *Required fees:* $2128; $1064 per term. Part-time tuition and fees vary according to course load and program. *Financial support:* Research assistantships with tuition reimbursements, teaching assistantships with tuition reimbursements, and scholarships/grants available. Financial award application deadline: 2/15; financial award applicants required to submit FAFSA. *Faculty research:* Nineteenth- and twentieth-century U.S. history, early modern European history, modern European history, world history, public history. *Unit head:* Dr. Michelle Brattain, Chair, 404-413-6352, Fax: 404-413-6384, E-mail: mbrattain@gsu.edu. *Application contact:* Dr. Joe Perry, Director of Graduate Studies, 404-413-6374, Fax: 404-413-6384, E-mail: jbperry@gsu.edu.
Website: http://www.gsu.edu/~wwwhis/

**Indiana University of Pennsylvania,** School of Graduate Studies and Research, College of Humanities and Social Sciences, Department of History, Indiana, PA 15705. Offers history (MA); public history (MA). *Program availability:* Part-time. *Faculty:* 6 full-time (4 women). *Students:* 7 full-time (4 women), 3 part-time (1 woman); includes 1 minority (Black or African American, non-Hispanic/Latino), 2 international. Average age 26. 11 applicants, 73% accepted, 4 enrolled. In 2016, 6 master's awarded. *Degree requirements:* For master's, thesis optional. *Entrance requirements:* For master's, GRE, 2 letters of recommendation. Additional exam requirements/recommendations for international students: Required—TOEFL (minimum score 540 paper-based). *Application deadline:* Applications are processed on a rolling basis. Application fee: $50. Electronic applications accepted. *Expenses:* Tuition, state resident: full-time $8694; part-time $483 per credit. Tuition, nonresident: full-time $13,050; part-time $725 per credit. *Required fees:* $157 per credit. $50 per term. Tuition and fees vary according to course load and program. *Financial support:* In 2016–17, 6 research assistantships with tuition reimbursements (averaging $3,827 per year) were awarded; fellowships with partial tuition reimbursements, career-related internships or fieldwork, Federal Work-Study, scholarships/grants, and unspecified assistantships also available. Support available to part-time students. Financial award application deadline: 4/15; financial award applicants required to submit FAFSA. *Unit head:* Dr. R. Scott Moore, Chairperson, 724-357-2573, E-mail: rsmoore@iup.edu. *Application contact:* Dr. Jeanine Mazak-Kahne, Graduate Coordinator, 724-357-2436, E-mail: j.mkahne@iup.edu.
Website: http://www.iup.edu/history

**Indiana University–Purdue University Indianapolis,** School of Liberal Arts, Department of History, Indianapolis, IN 46202. Offers history (MA); public history (MA); MA/MLS. *Program availability:* Part-time, evening/weekend. *Degree requirements:* For master's, one foreign language, thesis. *Entrance requirements:* For master's, GRE General Test, minimum GPA of 3.0. Electronic applications accepted.

**James Madison University,** The Graduate School, College of Arts and Letters, Program in History, Harrisonburg, VA 22807. Offers local/regional/public history (MA); United States history (MA); world history (MA). *Program availability:* Part-time. *Faculty:* 31 full-time (9 women). *Students:* 19 full-time (6 women), 9 part-time (2 women). Average age 30. 32 applicants, 84% accepted, 13 enrolled. In 2016, 13 master's awarded. *Degree requirements:* For master's, one foreign language, comprehensive exam, thesis. Application fee: $55. Electronic applications accepted. *Financial support:* In 2016–17, 3 teaching assistantships with full tuition reimbursements (averaging $9,284 per year) were awarded; fellowships, Federal Work-Study, and 7 assistantships (averaging $7911) also available. Financial award application deadline: 3/1; financial award applicants required to submit FAFSA. *Unit head:* Dr. Gabrielle Lanier, Department Head, 540-568-6132, E-mail: laniergm@jmu.edu. *Application contact:* Lynette D. Michael, Director of Graduate Admissions, 540-568-6131 Ext. 6395, Fax: 540-568-7860, E-mail: michaeld@jmu.edu.
Website: http://www.jmu.edu/history

**La Salle University,** School of Arts and Sciences, Program in History, Philadelphia, PA 19141-1199. Offers American history (Certificate); European history (Certificate); history (MA); history for educators (MA); public history (MA); teaching advanced placement history (Certificate); world history (Certificate). *Program availability:* Part-time. *Faculty:* 4 full-time (1 woman), 1 (woman) part-time/adjunct. *Students:* 4 full-time (1 woman), 16 part-time (7 women); includes 2 minority (1 Hispanic/Latino; 1 Two or more races, non-Hispanic/Latino). Average age 33. 8 applicants, 75% accepted, 3 enrolled. In 2016, 11 master's awarded. *Degree requirements:* For master's, thesis or comprehensive exam. *Entrance requirements:* For master's, GRE or MAT, 18 hours of undergraduate coursework in history or a related discipline with minimum GPA of 3.0; two letters of recommendation; brief personal statement (250 to 500 words); writing sample (preferably from an undergraduate research paper). Additional exam requirements/recommendations for international students: Required—TOEFL. *Application deadline:* For fall admission, 8/15 priority date for domestic students, 7/15 for international students; for spring admission, 12/15 priority date for domestic students, 11/15 for international students; for summer admission, 4/15 priority date for domestic students, 3/15 for international students. Applications are processed on a rolling basis. Application fee: $35. Electronic applications accepted. Application fee is waived when completed online. *Expenses:* Contact institution. *Financial support:* In 2016–17, 1 student received support. Scholarships/grants available. Support available to part-time students. Financial award application deadline: 8/31; financial award applicants required to submit FAFSA. *Unit head:* Dr. George B. Stow, Director, 215-951-1097, E-mail: grahis@lasalle.edu. *Application contact:* Elizabeth Heenan, Director, Graduate and Adult Enrollment, 215-951-1100, Fax: 215-951-1462, E-mail: heenan@lasalle.edu. Website: http://www.lasalle.edu/master-history/

**Lehigh University,** College of Arts and Sciences, Department of History, Bethlehem, PA 18015. Offers Atlantic world (PhD); British history (PhD); history (MA); industrial and modern America (PhD); public history (MA). *Program availability:* Part-time. *Faculty:* 14 full-time (7 women). *Students:* 18 full-time (7 women), 19 part-time (5 women); includes 2 minority (1 Black or African American, non-Hispanic/Latino; 1 Two or more races, non-Hispanic/Latino), 2 international. Average age 34. 10 applicants, 50% accepted, 3 enrolled. In 2016, 6 master's, 3 doctorates awarded. Terminal master's awarded for partial completion of doctoral program. *Degree requirements:* For master's, comprehensive exam (for some programs), thesis (for some programs), comprehensive exam or thesis; for doctorate, comprehensive exam, thesis/dissertation. *Entrance requirements:* For master's, GRE General Test, recommendations, writing sample; for doctorate, GRE General Test, recommendations, writing samples. Additional exam requirements/recommendations for international students: Required—TOEFL. *Application deadline:* For fall admission, 2/15 priority date for domestic and international students. Applications are processed on a rolling basis. Application fee: $75. Electronic applications accepted. *Expenses:* Contact institution. *Financial support:* In 2016–17, 2 fellowships with full tuition reimbursements (averaging $22,500 per year), 10 teaching assistantships with full tuition reimbursements (averaging $10,000 per year) were awarded; research assistantships, institutionally sponsored loans, scholarships/grants, tuition waivers (full and partial), and unspecified assistantships also available. Financial award application deadline: 1/15. *Faculty research:* Colonial America, modern America, history of technology, Atlantic world, French Atlantic, Spanish Atlantic, British empire, gender, intellectual history, African diaspora history. *Unit head:* Prof. John Pettegrew, Chairman, 610-758-3360, Fax: 610-758-6554, E-mail: jcp5@lehigh.edu. *Application contact:* Dr. John Savage, Graduate Coordinator, 610-758-3363, Fax: 610-758-6554, E-mail: jms8@lehigh.edu.
Website: http://history.cas2.lehigh.edu/

**Loyola University Chicago,** Graduate School, Department of History, Chicago, IL 60611. Offers history (PhD); public history (MA). *Program availability:* Part-time, evening/weekend. *Faculty:* 32 full-time (12 women), 7 part-time/adjunct (2 women). *Students:* 45 full-time (25 women), 10 part-time (6 women); includes 8 minority (2 Black or African American, non-Hispanic/Latino; 1 Asian, non-Hispanic/Latino; 4 Hispanic/Latino; 1 Two or more races, non-Hispanic/Latino), 1 international. Average age 31. 89 applicants, 52% accepted, 18 enrolled. In 2016, 16 master's, 3 doctorates awarded. Terminal master's awarded for partial completion of doctoral program. *Degree requirements:* For master's, one foreign language, comprehensive exam, thesis optional, portfolio (for public history program); for doctorate, 2 foreign languages, comprehensive exam, thesis/dissertation. *Entrance requirements:* For master's, GRE General Test, research paper/writing sample; for doctorate, GRE General Test, seminar paper or master's thesis. Additional exam requirements/recommendations for international students: Required—TOEFL (minimum score 550 paper-based), IELTS. *Application deadline:* For fall admission, 5/1 for domestic students; for spring admission, 10/1 for domestic students. Applications are processed on a rolling basis. Application fee: $50. Electronic applications accepted. Application fee is waived when completed online. *Expenses:* Contact institution. *Financial support:* In 2016–17, 20 students received support, including 20 fellowships with full tuition reimbursements available (averaging $5,251 per year), 18 teaching assistantships with full tuition reimbursements available (averaging $17,722 per year); research assistantships with full tuition reimbursements available and Federal Work-Study also available. Financial award application deadline: 1/1; financial award applicants required to submit FAFSA. *Faculty research:* Medieval and early modern Europe, U.S. public history, U.S. urban history, gender history, Britain and Ireland, transnational history. *Unit head:* Dr. Robert O. Bucholz, Chair, 773-508-2232, Fax: 773-508-2153, E-mail: rbuchol@luc.edu. *Application contact:* Dr. Michelle Nickerson, Director, Graduate Programs, 773-508-2228, Fax: 773-508-2153, E-mail: mnickerson@luc.edu.
Website: http://www.luc.edu/history/

**Middle Tennessee State University,** College of Graduate Studies, College of Liberal Arts, Department of History, Program in Public History, Murfreesboro, TN 37132. Offers PhD. *Program availability:* Part-time, evening/weekend, online learning. *Degree requirements:* For doctorate, one foreign language, comprehensive exam, thesis/dissertation. *Entrance requirements:* For doctorate, GRE. Additional exam

requirements/recommendations for international students: Required—TOEFL (minimum score 525 paper-based; 71 iBT) or IELTS (minimum score 6).

**New York University,** Graduate School of Arts and Science, Department of History, New York, NY 10012-1019. Offers African diaspora (PhD); African history (PhD); archival management (Advanced Certificate); Atlantic history (PhD); French studies/history (PhD); Hebrew and Judaic studies/history (PhD); history (MA, PhD), including Europe (PhD), Latin America and the Caribbean (PhD), United States (PhD), women's history (MA); Middle Eastern history (MA); Middle Eastern studies/history (PhD); public history (Advanced Certificate); world history (MA); JD/MA; MA/Advanced Certificate. *Program availability:* Part-time. Terminal master's awarded for partial completion of doctoral program. *Degree requirements:* For master's, seminar paper; for doctorate, one foreign language, thesis/dissertation, oral and written exams; for Advanced Certificate, internship. *Entrance requirements:* For master's, GRE General Test, minimum GPA of 3.0, writing sample; for doctorate, GRE. Additional exam requirements/recommendations for international students: Required—TOEFL. *Faculty research:* African, East Asian, medieval, early modern, and modern European history; U.S. history; African and African diaspora; Latin American history; Atlantic world.

**North Carolina State University,** Graduate School, College of Humanities and Social Sciences, Department of History, Program in Public History, Raleigh, NC 27695. Offers MA. *Degree requirements:* For master's, thesis optional. *Entrance requirements:* For master's, GRE General Test. Electronic applications accepted.

**Northeastern University,** College of Social Sciences and Humanities, Boston, MA 02115. Offers criminology and criminal justice (MSCJ); criminology and justice policy (PhD); economics (MA, PhD); English (MA, PhD); international affairs (MA); law and public policy (PhD); political science (MA, PhD); public administration (MPA); public history (MA); public policy (MPP); security and resilience studies (MS); sociology (MA, PhD); urban and regional policy (MS); urban informatics (MS); world history (MA, PhD); JD/MS. *Program availability:* Online learning. *Faculty:* 234 full-time (114 women), 55 part-time/adjunct (34 women). *Students:* 427 full-time (239 women), 77 part-time (42 women). In 2016, 143 master's, 38 doctorates awarded. *Degree requirements:* For doctorate, variable foreign language requirement, comprehensive exam, thesis/dissertation. *Entrance requirements:* For master's and doctorate, GRE. Additional exam requirements/recommendations for international students: Required—TOEFL, IELTS. Application fee: $75. Electronic applications accepted. *Expenses:* $1,295 per credit. *Financial support:* Teaching assistantships, career-related internships or fieldwork, scholarships/grants, health care benefits, tuition waivers (full and partial), and unspecified assistantships available. Support available to part-time students. Financial award applicants required to submit FAFSA. *Unit head:* Dr. Uta Poiger, Dean, 617-373-5173. *Application contact:* Amber Crowe, Administrative Coordinator, 617-373-5990, Fax: 617-373-7281, E-mail: gradcssh@northeastern.edu.
Website: http://www.northeastern.edu/cssh/graduate

**Northern Kentucky University,** Office of Graduate Programs, College of Arts and Sciences, Program in Public History, Highland Heights, KY 41099. Offers MA. *Program availability:* Part-time, evening/weekend. *Degree requirements:* For master's, comprehensive exam, final capstone project. *Entrance requirements:* Additional exam requirements/recommendations for international students: Required—TOEFL (minimum score 550 paper-based; 79 iBT); Recommended—IELTS (minimum score 6.5). Electronic applications accepted. *Faculty research:* Local history.

**Rutgers University–Camden,** Graduate School of Arts and Sciences, Program in American and Public History, Camden, NJ 08102. Offers MA. *Program availability:* Part-time, evening/weekend. *Degree requirements:* For master's, comprehensive exam, thesis optional, 30 credits. *Entrance requirements:* For master's, GRE General Test (for full-time applicants), 3 letters of recommendation; history or related undergraduate degree (preferred). Additional exam requirements/recommendations for international students: Required—TOEFL, IELTS. Electronic applications accepted. *Faculty research:* Women's history, military history, Afro-American history, urban history, history of technology.

**St. John's University,** St. John's College of Liberal Arts and Sciences, Department of History, Queens, NY 11439. Offers history (MA); modern world history (DA); public history (MA). *Program availability:* Part-time, evening/weekend. *Degree requirements:* For master's, one foreign language, comprehensive exam, thesis optional, colloquia; for doctorate, one foreign language, comprehensive exam, thesis/dissertation, internship, practicum. *Entrance requirements:* For master's, minimum GPA of 3.0, 24 undergraduate credits in history or related field, 2 letters of recommendation, personal statement; for doctorate, minimum GPA of 3.5 in history, 3.0 overall; writing sample; 3 letters of recommendation; personal essay; bachelor's degree; at least 24 undergraduate credits in history or related field. Additional exam requirements/recommendations for international students: Required—TOEFL (minimum score 600 paper-based; 100 iBT), IELTS (minimum score 7). Electronic applications accepted. *Faculty research:* World history, gender, transnationalism, history of technology, cultural history, social history.

**Shippensburg University of Pennsylvania,** School of Graduate Studies, College of Arts and Sciences, Department of History and Philosophy, Shippensburg, PA 17257-2299. Offers applied history (MA). *Program availability:* Part-time, evening/weekend. *Faculty:* 6 full-time (1 woman), 1 part-time/adjunct (0 women). *Students:* 15 full-time (6 women), 9 part-time (4 women); includes 2 minority (1 Black or African American, non-Hispanic/Latino; 1 Two or more races, non-Hispanic/Latino). Average age 28. 19 applicants, 68% accepted, 8 enrolled. In 2016, 15 master's awarded. *Degree requirements:* For master's, thesis, internship, or student teaching and professional practicum. *Entrance requirements:* For master's, 500-word statement of purpose; interview (if GPA is below 2.75). Additional exam requirements/recommendations for international students: Required—TOEFL (minimum score 550 paper-based, 68 iBT) or IELTS (minimum score 6). *Application deadline:* For fall admission, 2/15 for domestic and international students; for spring admission, 9/15 for domestic and international students; for summer admission, 2/15 for domestic and international students. Applications are processed on a rolling basis. Application fee: $45. Electronic applications accepted. *Expenses:* Tuition, state resident: part-time $483 per credit. Tuition, nonresident: part-time $725 per credit. *Required fees:* $141 per credit. *Financial support:* In 2016–17, 9 students received support. Career-related internships or fieldwork, scholarships/grants, unspecified assistantships, and resident hall director and student payroll positions available. Support available to part-time students. Financial award application deadline: 3/1; financial award applicants required to submit FAFSA. *Unit head:* Dr. John D. Bloom, Associate Professor and Program Coordinator, 717-477-1621, Fax: 717-477-4062, E-mail: jdbloo@ship.edu. *Application contact:* Megan N. Luft, Assistant Dean of Graduate Admissions, 717-477-1231, Fax: 717-477-4016, E-mail: mnluft@ship.edu.
Website: http://www.ship.edu/history/

**Shippensburg University of Pennsylvania,** School of Graduate Studies, College of Arts and Sciences, Department of Sociology and Anthropology, Shippensburg, PA 17257-2299. Offers organizational development and leadership (MS), including business, higher education structure and policy, historical administration, leadership in society, management information systems, public organizations. *Program availability:*

*Public History*

Part-time, evening/weekend. *Faculty:* 4 full-time (3 women). *Students:* 11 full-time (6 women), 29 part-time (18 women); includes 9 minority (7 Black or African American, non-Hispanic/Latino; 1 Hispanic/Latino; 1 Two or more races, non-Hispanic/Latino). Average age 29. 58 applicants, 67% accepted, 21 enrolled. In 2016, 24 master's awarded. *Degree requirements:* For master's, capstone experience including internship. *Entrance requirements:* For master's, interview (if GPA less than 2.75), current resume, personal goals statement. Additional exam requirements/recommendations for international students: Required—TOEFL (minimum score 550 paper-based, 68 iBT) or IELTS (minimum score 6). *Application deadline:* For fall admission, 4/30 for international students; for spring admission, 9/30 for international students. Applications are processed on a rolling basis. Application fee: $45. Electronic applications accepted. *Expenses:* Tuition, state resident: part-time $483 per credit. Tuition, nonresident: part-time $725 per credit. *Required fees:* $141 per credit. *Financial support:* In 2016–17, 9 students received support. Career-related internships or fieldwork, scholarships/grants, unspecified assistantships, and resident hall director and student payroll positions available. Support available to part-time students. Financial award application deadline: 3/1; financial award applicants required to submit FAFSA. *Unit head:* Dr. Barbara J. Denison, Departmental Chair and Program Coordinator, 717-477-1735, Fax: 717-477-4011, E-mail: bjdeni@ship.edu. *Application contact:* Megan N. Luft, Assistant Dean of Graduate Admissions, 717-477-1231, Fax: 717-477-4016, E-mail: mnluft@ship.edu. Website: http://www.ship.edu/odl

**Sonoma State University,** School of Social Sciences, Program in Cultural Resources Management, Rohnert Park, CA 94928. Offers MA. *Program availability:* Part-time. *Degree requirements:* For master's, thesis. *Entrance requirements:* For master's, minimum GPA of 3.0. Additional exam requirements/recommendations for international students: Required—TOEFL (minimum score 500 paper-based). *Application deadline:* For fall admission, 1/31 for domestic students. Application fee: $55. *Expenses:* Tuition, state resident: full-time $6738; part-time $3906 per unit. *Required fees:* $1916 ($1916 per year. Tuition and fees vary according to course load, degree level and program. *Financial support:* Career-related internships or fieldwork, scholarships/grants, traineeships, and unspecified assistantships available. Financial award application deadline: 3/2; financial award applicants required to submit FAFSA. *Unit head:* Margaret Purser, Chair, Anthropology Department, 707-664-3164, Fax: 707-664-2505, E-mail: margaret.purser@sonoma.edu. Website: http://www.sonoma.edu/anthropology/graduate/master.html

**Southeast Missouri State University,** School of Graduate Studies, Department of History, Cape Girardeau, MO 63701-4799. Offers heritage interpretation (Certificate); historic preservation (Certificate); history (MA); public history (MA), including heritage education, historic preservation. *Program availability:* Part-time, evening/weekend. *Faculty:* 11 full-time (3 women). *Students:* 8 full-time (2 women), 19 part-time (7 women); includes 2 minority (both Hispanic/Latino). Average age 31. 13 applicants, 92% accepted, 7 enrolled. In 2016, 8 master's awarded. *Degree requirements:* For master's, comprehensive exam (for some programs), thesis or comprehensive exams plus a capstone project/paper (for history); thesis or internship plus advanced project in applied history and comprehensive exams (for public history). *Entrance requirements:* For master's, minimum GPA of 2.75; 24 semester hours of undergraduate credit in history; letter of intent indicating how past experiences have prepared the candidate for graduate study and what the candidate expects to achieve through graduate study; two letters of recommendation; academic or professional writing sample; for Certificate, minimum GPA of 2.75; letter of intent indicating how past experiences have prepared the candidate for graduate study and what the candidate expects to achieve through graduate study; two letters of recommendation; academic or professional writing sample. Additional exam requirements/recommendations for international students: Required—TOEFL (minimum score 550 paper-based; 79 iBT), IELTS (minimum score 6), PTE (minimum score 53). *Application deadline:* For fall admission, 8/1 for domestic students, 6/1 for international students; for spring admission, 11/21 for domestic students, 10/1 for international students; for summer admission, 5/15 for domestic students. Applications are processed on a rolling basis. Application fee: $30 ($40 for international students). Electronic applications accepted. *Expenses:* Tuition, state resident: full-time $3130; part-time $260.80 per credit hour. Tuition, nonresident: full-time $5842; part-time $486.80 per credit hour. *Required fees:* $33.70 per credit hour. *Financial support:* In 2016–17, 5 students received support, including 4 teaching assistantships with full tuition reimbursements available; career-related internships or fieldwork, Federal Work-Study, scholarships/grants, traineeships, tuition waivers (full), and unspecified assistantships also available. Financial award application deadline: 6/30; financial award applicants required to submit FAFSA. *Faculty research:* Medieval Europe; modern Europe including Britain, Germany, France, Russia, and Spain; colonial and nineteenth-century America; twentieth-century America and American West; public history and historic preservation; Latin America. *Unit head:* Dr. Wayne Bowen, Chairperson/Professor of History, 573-651-2179, Fax: 573-651-5114, E-mail: wbowen@semo.edu. *Application contact:* Dr. Vicky McAlister, Graduate Coordinator/Assistant Professor of History, 573-651-2763, Fax: 573-651-5114, E-mail: vmcalister@semo.edu.

**Texas A&M University–Commerce,** College of Humanities, Social Sciences and Arts, Commerce, TX 75429-3011. Offers applied criminology (MS); applied linguistics (MA, MS); art (MA, MFA); Christianity in history (Graduate Certificate); computational linguistics (Graduate Certificate); creative writing (Graduate Certificate); English (MA, MS, PhD); film studies (Graduate Certificate); history (MA, MS); music (MM); political science (MA, MS); public history (Graduate Certificate); sociology (MS); Spanish (MA); studies in children's and adolescent literature and culture (Graduate Certificate); teaching English to speakers of other languages (Graduate Certificate); theater (MA, MS). *Program availability:* Part-time. *Faculty:* 53 full-time (26 women), 7 part-time/adjunct (2 women). *Students:* 87 full-time (55 women), 528 part-time (362 women); includes 198 minority (86 Black or African American, non-Hispanic/Latino; 2 American Indian or Alaska Native, non-Hispanic/Latino; 8 Asian, non-Hispanic/Latino; 84 Hispanic/Latino; 18 Two or more races, non-Hispanic/Latino), 27 international. Average age 37. 333 applicants, 56% accepted, 149 enrolled. In 2016, 66 master's, 8 doctorates awarded. *Degree requirements:* For master's, one foreign language, comprehensive exam, thesis (for some programs); for doctorate, one foreign language, comprehensive exam, thesis/dissertation, departmental qualifying exam. *Entrance requirements:* For master's and doctorate, GRE General Test. Additional exam requirements/recommendations for international students: Required—TOEFL (minimum score 550 paper-based; 79 iBT), IELTS (minimum score 6). *Application deadline:* Applications are processed on a rolling basis. Application fee: $50. Electronic applications accepted. *Expenses:* Contact institution. *Financial support:* In 2016–17, 255 students received support, including 9 research assistantships with partial tuition reimbursements available (averaging $9,000 per year), 68 teaching assistantships with partial tuition reimbursements available (averaging $9,000 per year); Federal Work-Study, institutionally sponsored loans, scholarships/grants, health care benefits, and unspecified assistantships also available. Financial award application deadline: 5/1; financial award applicants required to submit FAFSA. *Unit head:* Dr. Salvatore Attardo, Dean, 903-886-5166, Fax: 903-886-5774, E-mail: salvatore.attardo@tamuc.edu. *Application contact:* Shelby Miller, Graduate Recruiter, 903-468-8123, Fax: 903-886-5774, E-mail: shelby.miller@tamuc.edu.

Website: http://www.tamuc.edu/academics/graduateSchool/programs/humanitiesSocialScienceArts/default.aspx

**University at Albany, State University of New York,** College of Arts and Sciences, Department of History, Albany, NY 12222-0001. Offers history (MA, PhD); public history (Certificate). *Program availability:* Part-time. *Faculty:* 6 full-time (2 women), 2 part-time/adjunct (both women). *Students:* 26 full-time (6 women), 52 part-time (27 women); includes 4 minority (1 Black or African American, non-Hispanic/Latino; 1 Hispanic/Latino; 2 Two or more races, non-Hispanic/Latino), 4 international. 48 applicants, 69% accepted, 18 enrolled. In 2016, 17 master's, 4 doctorates awarded. *Degree requirements:* For master's, variable foreign language requirement, exam, research paper or thesis; for doctorate, thesis/dissertation. *Entrance requirements:* For master's, minimum GPA of 3.0; for doctorate, GRE General Test, minimum GPA of 3.0. Additional exam requirements/recommendations for international students: Required—TOEFL (minimum score 550 paper-based). *Application deadline:* For fall admission, 3/1 for domestic students, 5/1 for international students; for spring admission, 11/1 for international students. Applications are processed on a rolling basis. Application fee: $75. Electronic applications accepted. *Expenses:* Tuition, state resident: full-time $10,870; part-time $453 per credit hour. Tuition, nonresident: full-time $22,210; part-time $925 per credit hour. *International tuition:* $21,550 full-time. *Required fees:* $1864; $96 per credit hour. *Financial support:* Teaching assistantships and career-related internships or fieldwork available. Financial award application deadline: 3/1. *Faculty research:* American history (all phases); public policy; European history (Medieval to modern); Asian, African, and Latin American history. *Total annual research expenditures:* $783. *Unit head:* Richard Hamm, Chair, 518-442-5300, Fax: 518-442-5301, E-mail: rhamm@albany.edu. *Application contact:* Michael DeRensis, Director, Graduate Admissions, 518-442-3980, Fax: 518-442-3922, E-mail: graduate@albany.edu. Website: http://www.albany.edu/history/

**University at Buffalo, the State University of New York,** Graduate School, College of Arts and Sciences, Department of History, Buffalo, NY 14214. Offers history (MA, PhD, Advanced Certificate); public history (MA). *Program availability:* Part-time. *Faculty:* 26 full-time (11 women). *Students:* 54 full-time (21 women), 2 part-time (1 woman); includes 9 minority (3 Black or African American, non-Hispanic/Latino; 6 Asian, non-Hispanic/Latino), 5 international. Average age 29. 76 applicants, 47% accepted, 23 enrolled. In 2016, 8 master's, 4 doctorates awarded. Terminal master's awarded for partial completion of doctoral program. *Degree requirements:* For master's, project; for doctorate, one foreign language, comprehensive exam, thesis/dissertation. *Entrance requirements:* For doctorate, GRE General Test. Additional exam requirements/recommendations for international students: Required—TOEFL (minimum score 550 paper-based; 79 iBT). *Application deadline:* For fall admission, 1/5 priority date for domestic and international students; for spring admission, 10/1 priority date for domestic students, 10/1 for international students. Applications are processed on a rolling basis. Application fee: $75. Electronic applications accepted. *Expenses:* $13,347. *Financial support:* In 2016–17, 29 students received support, including 5 fellowships (averaging $14,000 per year), 4 research assistantships (averaging $600 per year), 26 teaching assistantships with full tuition reimbursements available (averaging $16,500 per year); career-related internships or fieldwork, institutionally sponsored loans, scholarships/grants, health care benefits, and conference travel support also available. Financial award application deadline: 1/5; financial award applicants required to submit FAFSA. *Faculty research:* Geographical areas: Africa, Asia, early modern Europe, Latin America and Caribbean, modern Europe (Britain, France, Germany, Spain), North and South Atlantic, world, United States and Colonial America; thematic areas: African-American, gender, imperialism and colonialism, intellectual/cultural/religious, political, public history, medicine/disability/science/knowledge, slavery, transnational/international, urban. *Total annual research expenditures:* $35,000. *Unit head:* Dr. Victoria Wolcott, Chair, 716-645-3435, Fax: 716-645-5954, E-mail: vwwolcot@buffalo.edu. *Application contact:* Sarah Handley-Cousins, Staff Assistant, 716-645-3433, Fax: 716-645-5954, E-mail: handley2@buffalo.edu. Website: https://www.history.buffalo.edu

**University of Arkansas at Little Rock,** Graduate School, College of Arts, Letters, and Sciences, Department of History, Little Rock, AR 72204-1099. Offers public history (MA). *Program availability:* Part-time. *Degree requirements:* For master's, oral exam. *Entrance requirements:* For master's, GRE General Test, minimum GPA of 3.25 in history, 2.7 overall; 15 hours of undergraduate history; two letters of recommendation. *Faculty research:* Historic preservation and restoration, museum studies, archives.

**University of California, Santa Barbara,** Graduate Division, College of Letters and Sciences, Division of Humanities and Fine Arts, Department of History, Santa Barbara, CA 93106-9410. Offers European medieval studies (PhD); global studies (PhD); public historical studies (PhD); technology and society (PhD); women's studies (PhD); MA/PhD. *Degree requirements:* For doctorate, variable foreign language requirement, comprehensive exam, thesis/dissertation. *Entrance requirements:* For doctorate, GRE. Additional exam requirements/recommendations for international students: Required—TOEFL (minimum score 550 paper-based; 80 iBT), IELTS (minimum score 7). Electronic applications accepted. *Faculty research:* Europe, United States, Latin America, Africa, Middle East, East Asia.

**University of Colorado Denver,** College of Liberal Arts and Sciences, Department of History, Denver, CO 80217. Offers European history (MA); global history (MA); public history (MA); U.S. history (MA). *Program availability:* Part-time, evening/weekend. *Faculty:* 12 full-time (4 women), 2 part-time/adjunct (0 women). *Students:* 24 full-time (15 women), 16 part-time (10 women); includes 10 minority (1 Asian, non-Hispanic/Latino; 6 Hispanic/Latino; 3 Two or more races, non-Hispanic/Latino). Average age 35. 23 applicants, 70% accepted, 7 enrolled. In 2016, 15 master's awarded. *Degree requirements:* For master's, comprehensive exam, thesis optional, 36 semester hours (12 courses). *Entrance requirements:* For master's, GRE General Test, writing sample, minimum undergraduate GPA of 3.25, three letters of recommendation, statement of purpose addressing any weaknesses in academic record. Additional exam requirements/recommendations for international students: Required—TOEFL (minimum score 537 paper-based; 75 iBT); Recommended—IELTS (minimum score 6.5). *Application deadline:* For fall admission, 1/20 for domestic and international students; for spring admission, 10/1 for domestic and international students. Application fee: $50 ($75 for international students). Electronic applications accepted. *Expenses:* Tuition, state resident: full-time $11,006; part-time $474 per credit. Tuition, nonresident: full-time $28,212; part-time $1264 per credit hour. *Required fees:* $256 per semester. One-time fee: $94.32. Tuition and fees vary according to campus/location and program. *Financial support:* In 2016–17, 8 students received support. Fellowships, research assistantships, teaching assistantships, Federal Work-Study, institutionally sponsored loans, scholarships/grants, and traineeships available. Financial award application deadline: 4/1; financial award applicants required to submit FAFSA. *Faculty research:* Uses of premodern Islamic heritage in modern India; relationship between liberal understandings of democracy, crime, and police discretion; relationships between gender, class, health, and welfare in nineteenth and early twentieth century England; U.S. business cultures and their influences on marketing and personnel practices; intersection of business and political ideologies; social and environmental history of the Rocky Mountain West. *Unit*

*head:* Dr. Kariann Akemi Yokota, Associate Chair, 303-315-1784, E-mail: kariann.yokota@ucdenver.edu. *Application contact:* Tabitha Fitzpatrick, Program Assistant, 303-315-1776, E-mail: tabitha.fitzpatrick@ucdenver.edu.
Website: http://www.ucdenver.edu/academics/colleges/CLAS/Departments/history/Programs/Masters/Pages/MasterofArts.aspx

**University of Illinois at Springfield,** Graduate Programs, College of Liberal Arts and Sciences, Program in History, Springfield, IL 62703-5407. Offers MA. *Program availability:* Part-time, evening/weekend. *Faculty:* 5 full-time (2 women). *Students:* 10 full-time (4 women), 16 part-time (6 women); includes 2 minority (1 Black or African American, non-Hispanic/Latino; 1 Two or more races, non-Hispanic/Latino). Average age 34. 19 applicants, 58% accepted, 7 enrolled. In 2016, 13 master's awarded. *Degree requirements:* For master's, internship; closure exercise; position paper and historiography; thesis or project. *Entrance requirements:* For master's, BA in history or related field, minimum undergraduate GPA of 3.0, writing sample, statement of purpose. Additional exam requirements/recommendations for international students: Required—TOEFL (minimum score 500 paper-based; 61 iBT). *Application deadline:* Applications are processed on a rolling basis. Application fee: $60 ($75 for international students). Electronic applications accepted. *Expenses:* Tuition, state resident: part-time $329 per credit hour. Tuition, nonresident: part-time $675 per credit hour. *Financial support:* In 2016–17, fellowships with full tuition reimbursements (averaging $9,900 per year), research assistantships with full tuition reimbursements (averaging $9,991 per year), teaching assistantships with full tuition reimbursements (averaging $10,059 per year) were awarded; career-related internships or fieldwork, Federal Work-Study, scholarships/grants, health care benefits, and unspecified assistantships also available. Support available to part-time students. Financial award application deadline: 11/15; financial award applicants required to submit FAFSA. *Unit head:* Dr. David Bertaina, Program Administrator, 217-206-8412, Fax: 217-206-6217, E-mail: dbert3@uis.edu. *Application contact:* Dr. Cecelia Cornell, Associate Vice Chancellor for Graduate Education, 217-206-7230, E-mail: ccorn1@uis.edu.
Website: http://www.uis.edu/history/curriculum/ma/

**University of Louisville,** Graduate School, College of Arts and Sciences, Department of History, Louisville, KY 40292-0001. Offers history (MA); public history (Certificate). *Program availability:* Part-time. *Faculty:* 22 full-time (9 women), 4 part-time/adjunct (3 women). *Students:* 9 full-time (7 women), 13 part-time (8 women); includes 2 minority (1 Black or African American, non-Hispanic/Latino; 1 Two or more races, non-Hispanic/Latino). Average age 33. 16 applicants, 75% accepted, 6 enrolled. In 2016, 5 master's awarded. *Degree requirements:* For master's, variable foreign language requirement, comprehensive exam (for some programs), thesis. *Entrance requirements:* For master's, GRE General Test, statement of purpose, not to exceed 500 words, which describes in reasonably specific terms, academic and career objectives and how they can be advanced through work in program. Additional exam requirements/recommendations for international students: Required—TOEFL. *Application deadline:* For fall admission, 2/15 for domestic and international students; for winter admission, 12/1 for domestic students; for spring admission, 12/1 for domestic and international students. Application fee: $60. Electronic applications accepted. *Expenses:* Contact institution. *Financial support:* In 2016–17, 1 teaching assistantship with full tuition reimbursement (averaging $12,000 per year) was awarded; scholarships/grants also available. Financial award application deadline: 2/15. *Faculty research:* Ancient and Medieval Europe, U.S. social and constitutional history, U.S. foreign relations and military, public history, Latin American and Borderlands. *Unit head:* Dr. Blake Beattie, Chairperson/Associate Professor, 502-852-6818, Fax: 502-852-0770, E-mail: history@louisville.edu. *Application contact:* Jennifer T. Westerfeld, Associate Professor, 502-852-3756, Fax: 502-852-0770, E-mail: histgrad@louisville.edu.
Website: http://louisville.edu/history/

**University of Maryland, Baltimore County,** The Graduate School, College of Arts, Humanities and Social Sciences, School of Public Policy, Baltimore, MD 21250. Offers public policy (MPP, PhD), including economics (PhD), educational policy, emergency services (PhD), environmental policy, evaluation and analytical methods, health policy, policy history (PhD), public management, urban policy. *Program availability:* Part-time, evening/weekend. *Faculty:* 10 full-time (4 women), 1 part-time/adjunct (0 women). *Students:* 48 full-time (23 women), 66 part-time (36 women); includes 23 minority (14 Black or African American, non-Hispanic/Latino; 4 Asian, non-Hispanic/Latino; 3 Hispanic/Latino; 1 Native Hawaiian or other Pacific Islander, non-Hispanic/Latino; 1 Two or more races, non-Hispanic/Latino), 6 international. Average age 37. 49 applicants, 65% accepted, 16 enrolled. In 2016, 15 master's, 6 doctorates awarded. Terminal master's awarded for partial completion of doctoral program. *Degree requirements:* For master's, thesis, policy analysis paper, internship for pre-service; for doctorate, thesis/dissertation, comprehensive and field qualifying exams. *Entrance requirements:* For master's and doctorate, GRE General Test, 3 academic letters of reference, resume, research paper, official transcripts. Additional exam requirements/recommendations for international students: Required—TOEFL (minimum score 550 paper-based; 80 iBT). *Application deadline:* For fall admission, 1/15 priority date for domestic students, 1/1 priority date for international students; for spring admission, 11/1 priority date for domestic students, 5/1 priority date for international students. Applications are processed on a rolling basis. Application fee: $50. Electronic applications accepted. *Expenses:* $733 per credit hour in-state tuition and fees, $1,127 per credit hour out-of-state; $27,321 tuition and fees in-state, $41,899 out-of-state (for MPP); $38,316 tuition and fees in-state, $58,804 out-of-state (PhD). *Financial support:* In 2016–17, 25 students received support, including 2 fellowships with full tuition reimbursements available (averaging $14,000 per year), 23 research assistantships with full tuition reimbursements available (averaging $20,000 per year); career-related internships or fieldwork, Federal Work-Study, scholarships/grants, health care benefits, and unspecified assistantships also available. Financial award application deadline: 1/15; financial award applicants required to submit FAFSA. *Faculty research:* Education policy, health policy, urban policy, public management, evaluation and analytical method. *Unit head:* Dr. Donald F. Norris, Director, 410-455-3201, Fax: 410-455-1172, E-mail: norris@umbc.edu. *Application contact:* Sally F. Helms, Administrator of Academic Affairs, 410-455-3202, Fax: 410-455-1172, E-mail: gradpubpol@umbc.edu.
Website: http://publicpolicy.umbc.edu/

**University of Missouri–St. Louis,** College of Arts and Sciences, Department of History, St. Louis, MO 63121. Offers history (MA); museum studies (MA, Certificate); public history and cultural heritage (Certificate). *Program availability:* Part-time, evening/weekend. *Faculty:* 11 full-time (3 women), 8 part-time/adjunct (0 women). *Students:* 21 full-time (19 women), 35 part-time (11 women); includes 8 minority (5 Black or African American, non-Hispanic/Latino; 2 Asian, non-Hispanic/Latino; 1 Hispanic/Latino), 1 international. Average age 35. 36 applicants, 86% accepted, 20 enrolled. *Degree requirements:* For master's, thesis (for some programs). *Entrance requirements:* For master's, writing sample; minimum GPA of 2.75 (for history), 3.2 (for museum studies). Additional exam requirements/recommendations for international students: Required—TOEFL (minimum score 550 paper-based; 79 iBT), IELTS (minimum score 6.5). *Application deadline:* For fall admission, 3/15 for domestic and international students; for spring admission, 10/15 for domestic and international students. Applications are processed on a rolling basis. Application fee: $50 ($40 for international students). Electronic applications accepted. *Financial support:* Research assistantships with

tuition reimbursements, teaching assistantships with tuition reimbursements, and career-related internships or fieldwork available. Financial award applicants required to submit FAFSA. *Faculty research:* United States, European, East Asian, Latin American, and African history. *Unit head:* Dr. Andrew Hurley, Director of Graduate Studies, 314-516-4805, Fax: 314-516-5781, E-mail: ahurley@umsl.edu. *Application contact:* 314-516-5458, Fax: 314-516-6996, E-mail: gradadm@umsl.edu.
Website: http://www.umsl.edu/~umslhistory

**University of North Alabama,** College of Arts and Sciences, Department of History, Florence, AL 35632-0001. Offers history (MA); public history (MA). *Program availability:* Part-time, 100% online. *Faculty:* 7 full-time (3 women), 2 part-time/adjunct (1 woman). *Students:* 9 full-time (3 women), 13 part-time (6 women); includes 1 minority (Black or African American, non-Hispanic/Latino). Average age 31. 11 applicants, 82% accepted, 6 enrolled. In 2016, 6 master's awarded. *Degree requirements:* For master's, comprehensive exam (for some programs), thesis optional. *Entrance requirements:* For master's, GRE, 3 letters of recommendation, essay, writing sample. Additional exam requirements/recommendations for international students: Required—TOEFL (minimum score 79 iBT), IELTS (minimum score 6), PTE (minimum score 54). *Application deadline:* Applications are processed on a rolling basis. Application fee: $50 ($100 for international students). Electronic applications accepted. *Expenses:* Tuition, state resident: full-time $2799; part-time $1866 per semester. Tuition, nonresident: full-time $5598; part-time $3732 per semester. *Required fees:* $915; $642 per semester. Tuition and fees vary according to course load. *Financial support:* In 2016–17, 6 students received support. Scholarships/grants and unspecified assistantships available. Financial award application deadline: 2/1; financial award applicants required to submit FAFSA. *Unit head:* Dr. Jeffrey Bibbee, Chair, 256-765-4306, E-mail: jrbibbee@una.edu. *Application contact:* Hillary N. Coats, Graduate Admissions Coordinator, 256-765-4447, E-mail: graduate@una.edu.
Website: http://www.una.edu/history

**University of Northern Iowa,** Graduate College, College of Social and Behavioral Sciences, Department of History, Cedar Falls, IA 50614. Offers history (MA); public history (MA). *Program availability:* Part-time. *Degree requirements:* For master's, comprehensive exam (for some programs), thesis or alternative. *Entrance requirements:* For master's, minimum GPA of 3.2. Additional exam requirements/recommendations for international students: Required—TOEFL (minimum score 500 paper-based; 61 iBT). Electronic applications accepted.

**University of South Carolina,** The Graduate School, College of Arts and Sciences, Department of History, Program in Public History, Columbia, SC 29208. Offers archive management (MA); historic preservation (MA); museum administration (MA); museum management (Certificate); MLIS/MA. *Degree requirements:* For master's, one foreign language, thesis, internship. *Entrance requirements:* For master's, GRE General Test, writing sample. Additional exam requirements/recommendations for international students: Required—TOEFL. Electronic applications accepted. *Faculty research:* Museum studies, historic preservation, archives administration.

**The University of Texas at Austin,** Graduate School, College of Liberal Arts, Department of Anthropology, Austin, TX 78712-1111. Offers archaeology (MA, PhD); cultural forms (MA, PhD); linguistic anthropology (MA, PhD); physical anthropology (MA, PhD); social anthropology (MA, PhD). *Program availability:* Part-time. Terminal master's awarded for partial completion of doctoral program. *Degree requirements:* For master's, thesis; for doctorate, one foreign language, thesis/dissertation. *Entrance requirements:* For master's and doctorate, GRE General Test. Additional exam requirements/recommendations for international students: Required—TOEFL. Electronic applications accepted.

**University of West Florida,** College of Arts, Social Sciences, and Humanities, Department of History, Pensacola, FL 32514-5750. Offers early American studies (MA); public history (MA); traditional history (MA). *Program availability:* Part-time, evening/weekend. *Degree requirements:* For master's, thesis or alternative. *Entrance requirements:* For master's, GRE (minimum score: verbal 500, writing 3.5) or MAT (minimum score 415), minimum GPA of 3.0, minimum 15 hours of upper-level history courses; official transcripts; letter of intent; writing sample (undergraduate research paper preferred). Additional exam requirements/recommendations for international students: Required—TOEFL (minimum score 550 paper-based). *Application deadline:* For fall admission, 6/1 for domestic and international students; for spring admission, 10/1 for domestic and international students. Applications are processed on a rolling basis. Application fee: $30. *Expenses:* Tuition, state resident: full-time $5316.12. Tuition, nonresident: full-time $11,308. *Required fees:* $583.92. Tuition and fees vary according to course load and program. *Financial support:* Fellowships with partial tuition reimbursements, research assistantships with partial tuition reimbursements, teaching assistantships with partial tuition reimbursements, and unspecified assistantships available. Financial award application deadline: 4/15; financial award applicants required to submit FAFSA. *Unit head:* Dr. Erin Stone, Program Director, 850-474-2685, Fax: 850-857-6015, E-mail: estone@uwf.edu. *Application contact:* Terry McCray, Assistant Director of Graduate Admissions, 850-473-7718, Fax: 850-473-7714, E-mail: gradadmissions@uwf.edu.
Website: http://uwf.edu/history/

**University of West Georgia,** College of Arts and Humanities, Carrollton, GA 30118. Offers English (MA); history (MA); museum studies (Postbaccalaureate Certificate); music performance (M Mus); music teacher education (M Mus); public history (Postbaccalaureate Certificate). *Program availability:* Part-time, evening/weekend, 100% online, blended/hybrid learning. *Faculty:* 70 full-time (39 women). *Students:* 23 full-time (16 women), 55 part-time (33 women); includes 18 minority (10 Black or African American, non-Hispanic/Latino; 1 American Indian or Alaska Native, non-Hispanic/Latino; 5 Hispanic/Latino; 2 Two or more races, non-Hispanic/Latino), 1 international. Average age 31. 24 applicants, 100% accepted, 23 enrolled. In 2016, 34 master's, 6 other advanced degrees awarded. *Entrance requirements:* Additional exam requirements/recommendations for international students: Required—TOEFL (minimum score 523 paper-based; 69 iBT); Recommended—IELTS (minimum score 6.5). *Application deadline:* For fall admission, 8/1 for domestic students, 6/1 for international students; for spring admission, 11/15 for domestic students, 10/15 for international students; for summer admission, 5/15 for domestic students, 3/30 for international students. Applications are processed on a rolling basis. Application fee: $40. Electronic applications accepted. *Expenses:* Tuition, state resident: full-time $5316; part-time $222 per semester hour. Tuition, nonresident: full-time $20,658; part-time $861 per semester hour. *Required fees:* $1962. Tuition and fees vary according to course load, degree level and program. *Financial support:* Fellowships, research assistantships, teaching assistantships, career-related internships or fieldwork, Federal Work-Study, institutionally sponsored loans, scholarships/grants, and unspecified assistantships available. Support available to part-time students. Financial award application deadline: 4/1; financial award applicants required to submit FAFSA. *Unit head:* Dr. Pauline D. Gagnon, Dean of Arts and Humanities, 678-839-5450, Fax: 678-839-5451, E-mail: pgagnon@westga.edu. *Application contact:* Dr. Toby Ziglar, Assistant Dean of the Graduate School, 678-839-1394, Fax: 678-839-1395, E-mail: graduate@westga.edu.
Website: http://www.westga.edu/coah

## Public History

**University of Wisconsin–Milwaukee,** Graduate School, College of Letters and Science, Department of History, Milwaukee, WI 53201-0413. Offers global history (PhD); history (MA), including public history, urban historical studies; modern studies (PhD); urban history (PhD). *Program availability:* Part-time. *Students:* 24 full-time (15 women), 26 part-time (10 women); includes 5 minority (1 Black or African American, non-Hispanic/Latino; 1 Asian, non-Hispanic/Latino; 1 Hispanic/Latino; 2 Two or more races, non-Hispanic/Latino). Average age 32. 53 applicants, 66% accepted, 18 enrolled. In 2016, 15 master's awarded. *Degree requirements:* For master's, comprehensive exam, thesis or alternative; for doctorate, thesis/dissertation. *Entrance requirements:* For master's and doctorate, GRE General Test. Additional exam requirements/recommendations for international students: Required—TOEFL (minimum score 550 paper-based; 79 iBT), IELTS (minimum score 6.5). *Application deadline:* For fall admission, 1/1 priority date for domestic students; for spring admission, 9/1 for domestic students. Applications are processed on a rolling basis. Application fee: $56 ($96 for international students). Electronic applications accepted. *Financial support:* In 2016–17, 23 teaching assistantships were awarded; career-related internships or fieldwork and unspecified assistantships also available. Support available to part-time students. Financial award application deadline: 4/15; financial award applicants required to submit FAFSA. *Unit head:* Merry Weisner-Hanks, Department Chair, 414-229-4529, E-mail: merryh@uwm.edu. *Application contact:* General Information Contact, 414-229-4982, Fax: 414-229-6967, E-mail: gradschool@uwm.edu.
Website: http://www.uwm.edu/dept/history/

**Wayne State University,** College of Liberal Arts and Sciences, Department of History, Detroit, MI 48202. Offers Africa (PhD); America (PhD); Asia (PhD); Europe (PhD); gender (PhD); history (MA); labor (PhD); public history (MA); science and technology (PhD); world history (PhD, Graduate Certificate); JD/MA; M Ed/MA; MLIS/MA. Doctoral program admits for fall only. *Program availability:* Evening/weekend. *Faculty:* 18. *Students:* 23 full-time (8 women), 21 part-time (5 women); includes 8 minority (3 Black or African American, non-Hispanic/Latino; 2 Hispanic/Latino; 3 Two or more races, non-Hispanic/Latino). Average age 40. 55 applicants, 38% accepted, 15 enrolled. In 2016, 6 master's, 5 doctorates awarded. *Degree requirements:* For master's, comprehensive exam, thesis (for some programs), final oral exam on thesis or essay and seminar; internship and project (for public history); for doctorate, variable foreign language requirement, comprehensive exam, thesis/dissertation, qualifying exam in 4 fields of history. *Entrance requirements:* For master's, GRE General Test, minimum undergraduate GPA of 3.25 in history, 3.0 overall; at least 18 credits in history and related subjects at the advanced undergraduate level; foreign language; letter of intent; research paper; at least two letters of recommendation from former instructors; for doctorate, GRE General Test, minimum GPA of 3.0, 3.25 in minimum of 18 semester credits in history and related subjects; letter of intent; research paper; at least three letters of recommendation from former professors; for Graduate Certificate, baccalaureate degree from accredited college or university; minimum GPA of 3.0, 3.25 in a minimum of eighteen semester credits in history and related subjects at the advanced undergraduate level. Additional exam requirements/recommendations for international students: Required—TOEFL (minimum score 550 paper-based; 79 iBT), TWE (minimum score 5.5), Michigan English Language Assessment Battery (minimum score 85); Recommended—IELTS (minimum score 6.5). *Application deadline:* For fall admission, 2/1 priority date for domestic and international students; for winter admission, 11/1 for domestic students, 10/1 priority date for international students; for spring admission, 2/1 for domestic students, 1/1 priority date for international students. Application fee: $50. Electronic applications accepted. *Expenses:* $16,503 per year resident tuition and fees, $33,697 per year non-resident tuition and fees. *Financial support:* In 2016–17, 16 students received support, including 2 fellowships with tuition reimbursements available (averaging $18,796 per year), 1 research assistantship with tuition reimbursement available (averaging $21,593 per year), 6 teaching assistantships with tuition reimbursements available (averaging $17,994 per year); scholarships/grants, health care benefits, and unspecified assistantships also available. Financial award applicants required to submit FAFSA. *Faculty research:* African, American, Asian, European, gender, German, labor, science and technology, urban/labor, violence, world. *Unit head:* Dr. Elizabeth V. Faue, Professor/Chair, 313-577-2525, E-mail: evfaue@wayne.edu. *Application contact:* Dr. Eric Ash, Associate Professor and Director of Graduate Studies, 313-577-2525, E-mail: ericash@wayne.edu.
Website: http://clas.wayne.edu/history/

# Section 8
# Humanities

This section contains a directory of institutions offering graduate work in humanities. Additional information about programs listed in the directory may be obtained by writing directly to the dean of a graduate school or chair of a department at the address given in the directory.

For programs offering related work, see also in this book *Area and Cultural Studies, Geography, Interdisciplinary Studies, Philosophy, Political Science and International Affairs, Religious Studies,* and *Sociology, Anthropology, and Archaeology.*

## CONTENTS

# Humanities

**American Public University System,** AMU/APU Graduate Programs, Charles Town, WV 25414. Offers accounting (MBA, MS); applied business analytics (MBA, MS); criminal justice (MA), including business administration, emergency and disaster management, general (MA, MS); educational leadership (M Ed); emergency and disaster management (MA); entrepreneurship (MBA); environmental policy and management (MS), including environmental planning, environmental sustainability, fish and wildlife management, general (MA, MS), global environmental management; finance (MBA); general (MBA); government contracting and acquisition (MBA); health care administration (MBA); health information management (MS); history (MA), including American history, ancient and classical history, European history, global history, public history; homeland security (MA), including business administration, counterterrorism studies, criminal justice, cyber, emergency management and public health, intelligence studies, transportation security; homeland security resource allocation (MBA); humanities (MA); information technology (MS), including digital forensics, enterprise software development, information assurance and security, IT project management; information technology management (MBA); intelligence studies (MA), including criminal intelligence, cyber, general (MA, MS), homeland security, intelligence analysis, intelligence collection, intelligence management, intelligence operations, terrorism studies; international relations and conflict resolution (MA), including comparative and security issues, conflict resolution, international and transnational security issues, peacekeeping; legal studies (MA); management (MA), including strategic consulting; marketing (MBA); military history (MA), including American military history, American Revolution, civil war, war since 1945, World War II; military studies (MA), including joint warfare, strategic leadership; national security studies (MA), including cyber, general (MA, MS), homeland security, regional security studies, security and intelligence analysis, terrorism studies; nonprofit management (MBA); political science (MA), including American politics and government, comparative government and development, general (MA, MS), international relations, public policy; psychology (MA); public administration (MPA), including disaster management, environmental policy, health policy, human resources, national security, organizational management, security management; public health (MPH); reverse logistics management (MA); security management (MA); space studies (MS), including aerospace science, general (MA, MS), planetary science; sports and health sciences (MS); sports management (MBA); teaching (M Ed), including autism spectrum disorder, curriculum and instruction for elementary teachers, elementary reading, English language learners, instructional leadership, online learning, special education, STEAM (STEM plus the arts); transportation and logistics management (MA). *Program availability:* Part-time, evening/weekend, online only, 100% online. *Faculty:* 401 full-time (228 women), 1,678 part-time/adjunct (781 women). *Students:* 378 full-time (184 women), 8,455 part-time (3,484 women); includes 2,972 minority (1,552 Black or African American, non-Hispanic/Latino; 52 American Indian or Alaska Native, non-Hispanic/Latino; 211 Asian, non-Hispanic/Latino; 791 Hispanic/Latino; 70 Native Hawaiian or other Pacific Islander, non-Hispanic/Latino; 296 Two or more races, non-Hispanic/Latino), 109 international. Average age 37. In 2016, 3,185 master's awarded. *Degree requirements:* For master's, comprehensive exam or practicum. *Entrance requirements:* For master's, official transcript showing earned bachelor's degree from institution accredited by recognized accrediting body. Additional exam requirements/recommendations for international students: Required—TOEFL (minimum score 550 paper-based), IELTS (minimum score 6.5). *Application deadline:* Applications are processed on a rolling basis. Application fee: $0. Electronic applications accepted. *Expenses: Tuition:* Part-time $350 per credit hour. *Required fees:* $50 per course. *Financial support:* Scholarships/grants available. Financial award applicants required to submit FAFSA. *Unit head:* Dr. Karan Powell, President, 877-468-6268, Fax: 304-724-3780. *Application contact:* Terry Grant, Vice President of Enrollment Management, 877-468-6268, Fax: 304-724-3780, E-mail: info@apus.edu. Website: http://www.apus.edu

**Antioch University New England,** Graduate School, Department of Education, Integrated Learning Program, Keene, NH 03431-3552. Offers early childhood education (M Ed); elementary education (M Ed), including arts and humanities, science and environmental education; special education (M Ed). *Degree requirements:* For master's, internship. *Entrance requirements:* For master's, previous course work or work experience in education. Additional exam requirements/recommendations for international students: Required—TOEFL (minimum score 550 paper-based). Electronic applications accepted. *Expenses:* Contact institution. *Faculty research:* Problem-based learning, place-based education, mathematics education, democratic classrooms, art education.

**Arcadia University,** College of Arts and Sciences, Program in Humanities, Glenside, PA 19038-3295. Offers MAH. *Program availability:* Part-time. *Students:* 11 part-time (8 women); includes 3 minority (2 Black or African American, non-Hispanic/Latino; 1 Two or more races, non-Hispanic/Latino). Average age 37. 2 applicants, 50% accepted. In 2016, 5 master's awarded. *Degree requirements:* For master's, thesis or alternative. *Application deadline:* Applications are processed on a rolling basis. Application fee: $50. *Expenses:* Contact institution. *Financial support:* Unspecified assistantships available. *Unit head:* Dr. Richard Wertime, Coordinator, 215-572-2963. *Application contact:* 215-572-2925, Fax: 215-572-2126, E-mail: grad@arcadia.edu. Website: https://www.arcadia.edu/academics/programs/humanities

**Brandeis University,** Graduate School of Arts and Sciences, Program in Comparative Humanities, Waltham, MA 02454-9110. Offers MA. *Program availability:* Part-time. *Faculty:* 27 full-time (11 women), 1 (woman) part-time/adjunct. *Students:* 6 full-time (3 women), 1 (woman) part-time; includes 1 minority (Two or more races, non-Hispanic/Latino), 1 international. 12 applicants, 67% accepted, 2 enrolled. In 2016, 4 master's awarded. *Degree requirements:* For master's, one foreign language, thesis or alternative, capstone project. *Entrance requirements:* For master's, GRE, transcripts, two letters of recommendation, curriculum vitae or resume, statement of purpose, writing sample. Additional exam requirements/recommendations for international students: Required—TOEFL (minimum score 600 paper-based; 100 iBT); Recommended—IELTS (minimum score 7), TSE (minimum score 68). *Application deadline:* For fall admission, 5/1 for domestic students. Application fee: $55. Electronic applications accepted. *Financial support:* In 2016–17, 6 students received support, including 2 teaching assistantships (averaging $3,200 per year); Federal Work-Study, scholarships/grants, and tuition waivers (partial) also available. Support available to part-time students. Financial award application deadline: 5/1; financial award applicants required to submit FAFSA. *Faculty research:* Humanities, cross-cultural comparison, trans-regional studies. *Unit head:* Dr. Matthew Fraleigh, Director of Graduate Study, 781-736-3200, E-mail: mach@brandeis.edu. *Application contact:* Alyssa F. Ring, Academic Administrator, 781-736-3200, E-mail: mach@brandeis.edu. Website: http://www.brandeis.edu/gsas

**Brigham Young University,** Graduate Studies, College of Humanities, Department of Comparative Arts and Letters, Provo, UT 84602. Offers comparative studies (MA). *Faculty:* 29 full-time (8 women). *Students:* 19 full-time (12 women), 1 part-time (0 women); includes 1 minority (Hispanic/Latino). Average age 29. 12 applicants, 67% accepted, 6 enrolled. In 2016, 5 master's awarded. *Degree requirements:* For master's, 2 foreign languages, comprehensive exam, thesis. *Entrance requirements:* For master's, GRE, minimum GPA of 3.0 in last 60 hours, writing sample, foreign language experience. Additional exam requirements/recommendations for international students: Required—TOEFL (minimum score 580 paper-based; 85 iBT), IELTS (minimum score 7). *Application deadline:* For fall admission, 3/1 for domestic and international students. Application fee: $50. Electronic applications accepted. *Expenses: Tuition:* Full-time $6680; part-time $393 per credit. Tuition and fees vary according to course load, program and student's religious affiliation. *Financial support:* In 2016–17, 19 students received support, including 33 fellowships with partial tuition reimbursements available (averaging $2,566 per year), 4 research assistantships (averaging $1,500 per year), 29 teaching assistantships (averaging $2,658 per year); scholarships/grants, tuition waivers (full and partial), unspecified assistantships, and student instructorships also available. Support available to part-time students. *Faculty research:* Latin American literature and translation, Mormon women artists, documentary photography, Lucan studies, African Mormon women's oral histories. *Unit head:* Dr. Roger Macfarlane, Graduate Coordinator/Professor of Classical Studies, 801-422-9078, Fax: 801-422-0305, E-mail: macfarlane@byu.edu. *Application contact:* Andrea Kristensen, Graduate Program Manager, 801-422-2996, Fax: 801-422-0305, E-mail: andrea_kristensen@byu.edu. Website: http://cal.byu.edu/

**California Institute of Integral Studies,** School of Consciousness and Transformation, San Francisco, CA 94103. Offers anthropology and social change (MA, PhD); Asian philosophies and cultures (MA); creative inquiry/interdisciplinary arts (MFA); East-West psychology (MA, PhD); integral and transpersonal psychology (PhD); philosophy and religion (PhD), including ecology, spirituality, and religion, philosophy, cosmology, and consciousness, women's spirituality; theater and performance making (MFA); transformative leadership (MA); transformative studies (PhD); women, gender, spirituality and social justice (MA); writing and consciousness (MFA). *Program availability:* Part-time, evening/weekend, 100% online, blended/hybrid learning. *Students:* 390 full-time (256 women), 121 part-time (84 women); includes 135 minority (39 Black or African American, non-Hispanic/Latino; 2 American Indian or Alaska Native, non-Hispanic/Latino; 22 Asian, non-Hispanic/Latino; 40 Hispanic/Latino; 2 Native Hawaiian or other Pacific Islander, non-Hispanic/Latino; 30 Two or more races, non-Hispanic/Latino), 51 international. Average age 38. 195 applicants, 92% accepted, 124 enrolled. In 2016, 35 master's, 41 doctorates awarded. Terminal master's awarded for partial completion of doctoral program. *Degree requirements:* For master's, thesis optional; for doctorate, comprehensive exam, thesis/dissertation, 1 foreign language (for Asian philosophies and cultures). *Entrance requirements:* For master's, minimum GPA of 3.0, letters of recommendation, writing sample; for doctorate, master's degree, minimum GPA of 3.0, letters of recommendation, writing sample. Additional exam requirements/recommendations for international students: Required—TOEFL. *Application deadline:* For fall admission, 2/1 priority date for domestic and international students; for spring admission, 10/15 priority date for domestic and international students. Applications are processed on a rolling basis. Application fee: $65. Electronic applications accepted. *Expenses: Tuition:* Full-time $19,728; part-time $1098 per semester hour. *Required fees:* $320; $320 per semester hour. *Financial support:* Research assistantships, teaching assistantships, career-related internships or fieldwork, Federal Work-Study, and scholarships/grants available. Support available to part-time students. Financial award application deadline: 4/15; financial award applicants required to submit FAFSA. *Faculty research:* Ecology and sustainability, philosophy and religion, East-West psychology, integrative health, social and cultural anthropology, transformative leadership. *Application contact:* Ellen Durst, Director of Admissions, 415-575-6100, Fax: 415-575-1268, E-mail: admissions@ciis.edu. Website: http://www.ciis.edu/

**California State University, Dominguez Hills,** College of Arts and Humanities, Program in Arts and Humanities, Carson, CA 90747-0001. Offers MA. *Program availability:* Part-time, evening/weekend. *Degree requirements:* For master's, thesis or alternative. *Entrance requirements:* For master's, minimum GPA of 3.0. Additional exam requirements/recommendations for international students: Required—TOEFL (minimum score 550 paper-based; 80 iBT). *Faculty research:* African-American music, postmodernism, cities of antiquity, Faust, African studies.

**California State University, Dominguez Hills,** College of Extended and International Education, Humanities Program, Carson, CA 90747-0001. Offers MA. *Program availability:* Part-time, evening/weekend, 100% online. *Degree requirements:* For master's, thesis, advancement to candidacy essays. *Entrance requirements:* For master's, minimum GPA of 3.0 in last 60 undergraduate units. Additional exam requirements/recommendations for international students: Required—TOEFL. Electronic applications accepted. *Expenses:* Contact institution. *Faculty research:* Nineteenth- and twentieth-century literature, Arab history, Greek philosophy, ancient history, East Asian history, Soviet cultural history, Native American history and culture, feminist studies.

**Central Michigan University,** College of Graduate Studies, College of Humanities and Social and Behavioral Sciences, Program in Humanities, Mount Pleasant, MI 48859. Offers humanities (MA), including contemporary issues in the humanities: race, class, and gender, images and ideas of self, Native American issues in modern culture, popular culture studies, the rise of industrial society. *Program availability:* Part-time, evening/weekend. *Degree requirements:* For master's, thesis or alternative. Electronic applications accepted. *Faculty research:* Rise of industrial society; images and ideas of self; contemporary issues of race, class, and gender; popular culture; Native American issues in modern culture.

**Claremont Graduate University,** Graduate Programs, School of Arts and Humanities, Claremont, CA 91711-6160. Offers M Phil, MA, MFA, DCM, DMA, PhD, Certificate, MA/PhD, MBA/MA, MBA/PhD. *Program availability:* Part-time. *Faculty:* 28 full-time (15 women), 5 part-time/adjunct (0 women). *Students:* 372 full-time (202 women), 97 part-time (57 women); includes 138 minority (23 Black or African American, non-Hispanic/Latino; 4 American Indian or Alaska Native, non-Hispanic/Latino; 44 Asian, non-Hispanic/Latino; 47 Hispanic/Latino; 2 Native Hawaiian or other Pacific Islander, non-Hispanic/Latino; 18 Two or more races, non-Hispanic/Latino), 54 international. Average age 37. In 2016, 65 master's, 42 doctorates, 3 other advanced degrees awarded. *Degree requirements:* For doctorate, 2 foreign languages, comprehensive exam, thesis/dissertation, oral and written qualifying exams, oral defense of dissertation, recitals. *Entrance requirements:* For master's and doctorate, GRE General Test. Additional exam requirements/recommendations for international students: Required—TOEFL (minimum

score 75 iBT). *Application deadline:* For fall admission, 2/1 priority date for domestic and international students. Applications are processed on a rolling basis. Application fee: $80. Electronic applications accepted. *Expenses: Tuition:* Full-time $44,328; part-time $1847 per unit. *Required fees:* $600; $300 per semester. Tuition and fees vary according to course load and program. *Financial support:* Fellowships, research assistantships, teaching assistantships, Federal Work-Study, institutionally sponsored loans, and scholarships/grants available. Support available to part-time students. Financial award application deadline: 2/15; financial award applicants required to submit FAFSA. *Unit head:* Patrick Mason, Dean, 909-607-8362, E-mail: patrick.mason@cgu.edu. *Application contact:* Amy Sandefur, Assistant Director of Admissions, 909-607-9101, E-mail: amy.sandefur@cgu.edu.
Website: https://www.cgu.edu/school/school-of-arts-and-humanities/

**The Colorado College,** Education Department, Experienced Teacher Program, Colorado Springs, CO 80903-3294. Offers arts and humanities (MAT); integrated natural sciences (MAT); liberal arts (MAT); Southwest studies (MAT). Programs offered during summer only. *Program availability:* Part-time. *Degree requirements:* For master's, thesis, oral exam, 50-page paper. *Expenses:* Contact institution.

**Concordia University,** School of Graduate Studies, Faculty of Arts and Science, Program in Humanities, Montréal, QC H3G 1M8, Canada. Offers PhD. *Degree requirements:* For doctorate, one foreign language, comprehensive exam, thesis/dissertation.

**Dominican University of California,** School of Arts, Humanities and Social Sciences, Humanities Program, San Rafael, CA 94901-2298. Offers applied music (MA); art history (MA); creative writing (MA); gender studies (MA); history (MA); literature (MA); philosophy (MA); political theory (MA); religion (MA). *Program availability:* Part-time. *Degree requirements:* For master's, thesis or alternative. *Entrance requirements:* For master's, minimum GPA of 3.0, interview. Additional exam requirements/recommendations for international students: Required—TOEFL (minimum score 550 paper-based; 80 iBT), IELTS (minimum score 6.5). Electronic applications accepted. Application fee is waived when completed online. *Expenses:* Contact institution.

**Duke University,** Graduate School, Program in Humanities, Durham, NC 27708. Offers AM, JD/AM. *Program availability:* Part-time. *Entrance requirements:* For master's, GRE General Test. Additional exam requirements/recommendations for international students: Required—TOEFL (minimum score 577 paper-based; 90 iBT) or IELTS (minimum score 7). Electronic applications accepted.

**Georgetown University,** Graduate School of Arts and Sciences, School of Continuing Studies, Washington, DC 20057. Offers American studies (MALS); Catholic studies (MALS); classical civilizations (MALS); emergency and disaster management (MPS); ethics and the professions (MALS); global strategic communications (MPS); hospitality management (MPS); human resources management (MPS); humanities (MALS); individualized study (MALS); integrated marketing communications (MPS); international affairs (MALS); Islam and Muslim-Christian relations (MALS); journalism (MPS); liberal studies (DLS); literature and society (MALS); medieval and early modern European studies (MALS); public relations and corporate communications (MPS); real estate (MPS); religious studies (MALS); social and public policy (MALS); sports industry management (MPS); systems engineering management (MPS); technology management (MPS); the theory and practice of American democracy (MALS); urban and regional planning (MPS); visual culture (MALS). MPS in systems engineering management offered jointly with Stevens Institute of Technology. *Entrance requirements:* Additional exam requirements/recommendations for international students: Required—TOEFL.

**Harrison Middleton University,** Graduate Program, Tempe, AZ 85282. Offers education (MA, Ed D); humanities (MA); imaginative literature (MA); interdisciplinary studies (DA); jurisprudence (MA); natural science (MA); philosophy and religion (MA); social science (MA). *Program availability:* Part-time, evening/weekend, online learning. *Degree requirements:* For master's and doctorate, capstone project. *Entrance requirements:* For master's, interview; for doctorate, 2 academic letters of reference, interview, essay. Additional exam requirements/recommendations for international students: Required—TOEFL (minimum score 550 paper-based; 80 iBT). Electronic applications accepted. *Faculty research:* Japanese animation, educational leadership, war art, John Muir's wilderness.

**Hofstra University,** School of Education, Programs in Teacher Education, Hempstead, NY 11549. Offers bilingual education (MA, Advanced Certificate); bilingual extension (Advanced Certificate), including education/speech language pathology; business education (MS Ed); early childhood and childhood education (MS Ed); early childhood education (MA, MS Ed); education technology (Advanced Certificate); elementary education (MA, MS Ed), including science, technology, engineering, and mathematics (STEM) (MA); English education (MS Ed); family and consumer science (MS Ed); fine arts and music education (Advanced Certificate); fine arts education (MS Ed); foreign language and TESOL (MS Ed); foreign language education (MS Ed), including French, German, Russian, Spanish; learning and teaching (Ed D), including applied linguistics, art education, arts and humanities, early childhood education, English education, human development, math education, math, science, and technology, multicultural education, physical education, science education, social studies education, special education; mathematics education (MA, MS Ed); middle school extension (Advanced Certificate), including grades 5-6, grades 7-9; music education (MA, MS Ed); science education (MA, MS Ed), including biology, chemistry, earth science, geology, physics; secondary education (Advanced Certificate); social studies education (MA, MS Ed); teaching languages other than English and TESOL (MS Ed); TESOL (MS Ed, Advanced Certificate). *Program availability:* Part-time, evening/weekend, blended/hybrid learning. *Students:* 139 full-time (97 women), 145 part-time (106 women); includes 60 minority (15 Black or African American, non-Hispanic/Latino; 1 American Indian or Alaska Native, non-Hispanic/Latino; 12 Asian, non-Hispanic/Latino; 31 Hispanic/Latino; 1 Two or more races, non-Hispanic/Latino), 21 international. Average age 29. 255 applicants, 86% accepted, 122 enrolled. In 2016, 101 master's, 4 doctorates, 43 other advanced degrees awarded. *Degree requirements:* For master's, comprehensive exam, thesis (for some programs), exit project, student teaching, fieldwork, electronic portfolio, curriculum project, minimum GPA of 3.0; for doctorate, thesis/dissertation; for Advanced Certificate, 3 foreign languages, comprehensive exam (for some programs), thesis project. *Entrance requirements:* For master's, GRE, MAT, 2 letters of recommendation, portfolio, teacher certification (MA), interview, essay; for doctorate, GMAT, GRE, LSAT, or MAT; for Advanced Certificate, 2 letters of recommendation, essay, interview and/or portfolio, teaching certificate. Additional exam requirements/recommendations for international students: Required—TOEFL (minimum score 550 paper-based; 80 iBT). *Application deadline:* Applications are processed on a rolling basis. Application fee: $75. Electronic applications accepted. *Expenses: Tuition:* Full-time $1240. *Required fees:* $970. Tuition and fees vary according to program. *Financial support:* In 2016–17, 149 students received support, including 58 fellowships with full and partial tuition reimbursements available (averaging $5,309 per year), 5 research assistantships with full and partial tuition reimbursements available (averaging $7,073 per year); career-related internships or fieldwork, Federal Work-Study, institutionally sponsored loans, scholarships/grants, traineeships, tuition waivers (full and partial), and unspecified assistantships also available. Support available to part-time students. Financial award applicants required to

submit FAFSA. *Faculty research:* Educational interventions that foster critical-thinking skills; teachers' attitudes about professional development; threats to teacher quality. *Unit head:* Dr. Eustace Thompson, Chairperson, 516-463-5749, Fax: 516-463-6275, E-mail: eustace.g.thompson@hofstra.edu. *Application contact:* Sunil Samuel, Assistant Vice President of Admissions, 516-463-4723, Fax: 516-463-4664, E-mail: graduateadmission@hofstra.edu.
Website: http://www.hofstra.edu/education/

**Hollins University,** Graduate Programs, Program in Liberal Studies, Roanoke, VA 24020. Offers humanities (MALS); interdisciplinary studies (MALS); leadership (MALS); social sciences (MALS); visual and performing arts (MALS). *Program availability:* Part-time, evening/weekend. *Degree requirements:* For master's, thesis. *Entrance requirements:* For master's, three letters of recommendation, interview, bachelor's degree, undergraduate transcripts, statement of educational objectives. Additional exam requirements/recommendations for international students: Required—TOEFL (minimum score 550 paper-based; 80 iBT), IELTS (minimum score 6.5). *Application deadline:* Applications are processed on a rolling basis. Application fee: $40. Electronic applications accepted. *Expenses:* $395 per credit hour. *Financial support:* Fellowships and scholarships/grants available. Support available to part-time students. Financial award application deadline: 7/15; financial award applicants required to submit FAFSA. *Faculty research:* Diversity, gender and women's studies, political science, leadership. *Unit head:* Director, 540-362-6576, Fax: 540-362-6288, E-mail: hugrad@hollins.edu. *Application contact:* Cathy S. Koon, Manager of Graduate Programs, 540-362-6326, Fax: 540-362-6288, E-mail: ckoon@hollins.edu.
Website: http://www.hollins.edu/academics/graduate-degrees/liberal-studies/

**Hood College,** Graduate School, Program in Humanities, Frederick, MD 21701-8575. Offers MA. *Program availability:* Part-time, evening/weekend. *Faculty:* 6 full-time, 1 part-time/adjunct. *Students:* 3 full-time (all women), 23 part-time (18 women); includes 2 minority (1 Asian, non-Hispanic/Latino; 1 Two or more races, non-Hispanic/Latino), 3 international. Average age 34. 10 applicants, 90% accepted, 8 enrolled. In 2016, 8 master's awarded. *Degree requirements:* For master's, thesis or alternative, capstone or portfolio. *Entrance requirements:* For master's, minimum GPA of 2.75, essay. Additional exam requirements/recommendations for international students: Required—TOEFL (minimum score 575 paper-based; 89 iBT), IELTS (minimum score 6.5). *Application deadline:* For fall admission, 8/15 priority date for domestic students, 8/5 for international students; for spring admission, 12/1 priority date for domestic students, 12/1 for international students; for summer admission, 5/1 priority date for domestic students, 4/15 for international students. Applications are processed on a rolling basis. Application fee: $35. Electronic applications accepted. *Expenses:* $450 per credit hour; $105 comprehensive fee per semester. *Financial support:* Tuition waivers (partial) and unspecified assistantships available. Financial award applicants required to submit FAFSA. *Unit head:* April Boulton, Interim Dean of the Graduate School, 301-696-3600, E-mail: gofurther@hood.edu. *Application contact:* Jan Marcus, Assistant Director of Graduate Admissions, 301-696-3600, E-mail: gofurther@hood.edu.
Website: http://www.hood.edu/graduate

**Illinois Institute of Technology,** Graduate College, Lewis College of Human Sciences, Department of Humanities, Chicago, IL 60616. Offers information architecture (MS); technical communication (PhD); technical communication and information design (MS). *Program availability:* Part-time. *Degree requirements:* For master's, comprehensive exam, thesis or alternative; for doctorate, comprehensive exam, thesis/dissertation. *Entrance requirements:* For master's, GRE General Test (minimum score 144 Quantitative, 153 Verbal, and 4.0 Analytical Writing), minimum undergraduate GPA of 3.0; 2 letters of recommendation from faculty or supervisors; professional statement discussing academic goals; for doctorate, GRE General Test (minimum score 144 Quantitative, 153 Verbal, and 4.0 Analytical Writing), bachelor's or master's degree in a field that, in combination with the 27-credit hour technical core, would provide a solid basis for advanced academic work leading to original research in the field; 3 letters of recommendation from faculty or supervisors; professional statement discussing academic goals. Additional exam requirements/recommendations for international students: Required—TOEFL (minimum score 95 iBT); Recommended—IELTS (minimum score 7). Electronic applications accepted. *Faculty research:* Linguistics, punishment theory, political communication, gender and technology, philosophical and ethical issues in neuroscience.

**Instituto Tecnologico de Santo Domingo,** Graduate School, Area of Humanities and Social Sciences, Santo Domingo, Dominican Republic. Offers accounting (Certificate); adult education (Certificate); applied linguistics (MA); economics (MA); education (M Ed); educational psychology (MA, Certificate); gender and development (MA, Certificate); humanistic studies (MA); international marketing management (Certificate); international relations in the Caribbean basin (Certificate); intervention systems in family therapy (MA); linguistic and literary communication (Certificate); pedagogical support (MA); social science education (M Ed); sustainable human development (MA); terminal illness and death psychology (Certificate); youth and adult education (M Ed).

**Instituto Tecnológico y de Estudios Superiores de Monterrey, Campus Central de Veracruz,** Graduate Programs, Córdoba, Mexico. Offers administration (MA); administration of information technologies (MTI); computer sciences (MCC); education (MEE); educational institution administration (MAD); educational technology (MTE); electronic commerce (MCE); finance (MAF); humanistic studies (MEH); international business for Latin America (MNL); marketing (MMT); science (MCP). *Program availability:* Part-time, evening/weekend, online learning. *Degree requirements:* For master's, thesis (for some programs). *Entrance requirements:* For master's, PAEP College Board. Electronic applications accepted.

**Instituto Tecnológico y de Estudios Superiores de Monterrey, Campus Ciudad de México,** Virtual University Division, Ciudad de Mexico, Mexico. Offers administration of information technologies (MA); computer sciences (MA); education (MA, PhD); educational technology (MA); environmental engineering (MA); environmental systems (MA); humanistic studies (MA); industrial engineering (MA); international business for Latin America (MA); quality systems (MA); quality systems and productivity (MA). *Program availability:* Part-time, evening/weekend, online learning. *Entrance requirements:* For master's and doctorate, Instituto entrance exam. Additional exam requirements/recommendations for international students: Required—TOEFL.

**Instituto Tecnológico y de Estudios Superiores de Monterrey, Campus Ciudad Juárez,** Program in Humanistic Studies, Ciudad Juárez, Mexico. Offers MEH.

**Instituto Tecnológico y de Estudios Superiores de Monterrey, Campus Estado de México,** Professional and Graduate Division, Estado de Mexico, Mexico. Offers administration of information technologies (MITA); architecture (M Arch); business administration (GMBA, MBA); computer sciences (MCS, PhD); education (M Ed); educational institution administration (MAD); educational technology and innovation (PhD); electronic commerce (MEC); environmental systems (MS); finance (MAF); humanistic studies (MHS); information sciences and knowledge management (MISKM); information systems (MS); manufacturing systems (MS); marketing (MEM); quality systems and productivity (MS); science and materials engineering (PhD); telecommunications management (MTM). *Program availability:* Part-time, online learning. *Degree requirements:* For master's, one foreign language, thesis (for some

## Humanities

programs); for doctorate, one foreign language, thesis/dissertation. *Entrance requirements:* For master's, E-PAEP 500, interview; for doctorate, E-PAEP 500, research proposal. Additional exam requirements/recommendations for international students: Required—TOEFL (minimum score 550 paper-based). *Faculty research:* Surface treatments by plasmas, mechanical properties, robotics, graphical computing, mechatronics security protocols.

**Instituto Tecnológico y de Estudios Superiores de Monterrey, Campus Irapuato,** Graduate Programs, Irapuato, Mexico. Offers administration (MBA); administration of information technology (MAIT); administration of telecommunications (MAT); architecture (M Arch); computer science (MCS); education (M Ed); educational administration (MEA); educational innovation and technology (DEIT); educational technology (MET); electronic commerce (MBA); environmental administration and planning (MEAP); environmental systems (MES); finances (MBA); humanistic studies (MHS); international management for Latin American executives (MIMLAE); library and information science (MLIS); manufacturing quality management (MMQM); marketing research (MBA).

**John Carroll University,** Graduate Studies, Program in Humanities, University Heights, OH 44118-4581. Offers MA. *Program availability:* Part-time, evening/weekend. *Degree requirements:* For master's, thesis optional, comprehensive research essay. *Entrance requirements:* For master's, minimum GPA of 2.75, interview. *Application deadline:* For fall admission, 8/15 priority date for domestic students; for spring admission, 1/3 for domestic students. Applications are processed on a rolling basis. Application fee: $25 ($35 for international students). Electronic applications accepted. *Expenses: Tuition:* Full-time $10,425; part-time $695 per credit hour. One-time fee: $200 full-time. Tuition and fees vary according to course load, campus/location and program. *Financial support:* Application deadline: 3/1; applicants required to submit FAFSA. *Faculty research:* Modern French history, modern American Catholic history. *Unit head:* Dr. Maria N. Marsilli, Coordinator, 216-397-4174, Fax: 216-397-4175, E-mail: mmarsilli@jcu.edu. *Application contact:* Jennifer L. Tucker, Records Management Assistant, 216-397-1925, Fax: 216-397-1835, E-mail: jtucker@jcu.edu.

**Laurentian University,** School of Graduate Studies and Research, Programme in Humanities: Interpretation and Values, Sudbury, ON P3E 2C6, Canada. Offers MA. *Program availability:* Part-time. *Faculty research:* Modern Canadian literature; aboriginal languages and cultures; relation between ethics, religion, and the arts; narrative conventions; Renaissance drama and Reformation literature, Biblical and philosophical hermeneutics.

**Loyola University Chicago,** Graduate School, Program in Digital Humanities, Chicago, IL 60660. Offers MA. *Program availability:* Part-time. *Faculty:* 4 full-time (1 woman). *Students:* 2 full-time (both women), 2 part-time (1 woman); includes 1 minority (Hispanic/Latino), 1 international. Average age 31. 4 applicants, 25% accepted. In 2016, 1 master's awarded. *Entrance requirements:* For master's, GRE General Test, BS or BA, transcripts, 2 letters of recommendation, letter of intent. *Expenses: Tuition:* Full-time $18,594. *Required fees:* $848. Tuition and fees vary according to course load, degree level and program. *Financial support:* In 2016–17, 1 student received support, including 1 fellowship with partial tuition reimbursement available (averaging $10,000 per year). Financial award application deadline: 2/1. *Faculty research:* Textual editing, digital humanities, archiving, book history. *Unit head:* Dr. Kyle Roberts, Director, Center for Textual Studies and Digital Humanities, 773-508-2215, Fax: 773-508-2153, E-mail: kroberts2@luc.edu. *Application contact:* Ron Martin, Assistant Director of Enrollment Management, 312-915-8950, Fax: 312-915-8905, E-mail: gradapp@luc.edu. Website: http://luc.edu/ctsdh

**Marshall University,** Academic Affairs Division, College of Liberal Arts, Program in Humanities, Huntington, WV 25755. Offers MA, Certificate. *Program availability:* Part-time, evening/weekend. *Degree requirements:* For master's, thesis, comprehensive assessment. *Entrance requirements:* For master's, GRE General Test, MAT, bachelor's degree in humanities, minimum undergraduate GPA of 3.0.

**Memorial University of Newfoundland,** School of Graduate Studies, Interdisciplinary Programs in Humanities, St. John's, NL A1C 5S7, Canada. Offers M Phil. *Program availability:* Part-time. *Degree requirements:* For master's, comprehensive exam, journal. *Entrance requirements:* For master's, honors bachelor's degree. Electronic applications accepted. *Faculty research:* Western language, philosophy, literature, and history.

**Mount Saint Mary's University,** Graduate Division, Los Angeles, CA 90049. Offers business administration (MBA); counseling psychology (MS); creative writing (MFA); education (MS, Certificate); film and television (MFA); health policy and management (MS); humanities (MA); nursing (MSN, Certificate); physical therapy (DPT); religious studies (MA). *Program availability:* Part-time, evening/weekend. *Faculty:* 50 full-time (35 women), 116 part-time/adjunct (81 women). *Students:* 670 full-time (518 women), 147 part-time (116 women); includes 414 minority (73 Black or African American, non-Hispanic/Latino; 4 American Indian or Alaska Native, non-Hispanic/Latino; 60 Asian, non-Hispanic/Latino; 259 Hispanic/Latino; 7 Native Hawaiian or other Pacific Islander, non-Hispanic/Latino; 11 Two or more races, non-Hispanic/Latino), 4 international. Average age 32. 1,398 applicants, 21% accepted, 242 enrolled. In 2016, 170 master's, 28 doctorates, 35 other advanced degrees awarded. *Entrance requirements:* Additional exam requirements/recommendations for international students: Required—TOEFL. *Application deadline:* For fall admission, 6/30 priority date for domestic and international students; for spring admission, 10/30 priority date for domestic and international students; for summer admission, 3/30 priority date for domestic and international students. Applications are processed on a rolling basis. Application fee: $50. Electronic applications accepted. *Expenses: Tuition:* Full-time $9983; part-time $829 per unit. One-time fee: $135. Tuition and fees vary according to degree level and program. *Financial support:* Career-related internships or fieldwork, Federal Work-Study, institutionally sponsored loans, and tuition waivers (full and partial) available. Support available to part-time students. Financial award application deadline: 3/15; financial award applicants required to submit FAFSA. *Unit head:* Albert Ramos, Director of Graduate Admissions, 213-477-2800, E-mail: gradprograms@msmu.edu. *Application contact:* Shawn Peters, Graduate Admission Counselor, 213-477-2676, E-mail: gradprograms@msmu.edu. Website: http://www.msmu.edu/graduate-programs

**New York University,** Graduate School of Arts and Science, Draper Interdisciplinary Program in Humanities and Social Thought, New York, NY 10012-1019. Offers humanities and social thought (MA); religion (Advanced Certificate); social theory (Advanced Certificate). *Program availability:* Part-time. *Degree requirements:* For master's, thesis, comprehensive exam or essay. *Entrance requirements:* For master's, GRE General Test; for Advanced Certificate, master's degree. Additional exam requirements/recommendations for international students: Required—TOEFL. *Faculty research:* Art world, gender politics, global histories, literary cultures, the city.

**New York University,** Polytechnic School of Engineering, Department of Technology, Culture and Society, New York, NY 10012-1019. Offers integrated digital media (MS, Graduate Certificate). *Program availability:* Part-time, evening/weekend. *Degree requirements:* For master's, comprehensive exam (for some programs), thesis (for some programs). *Entrance requirements:* Additional exam requirements/recommendations for

international students: Required—TOEFL (minimum score 550 paper-based; 80 iBT); Recommended—IELTS (minimum score 6.5). Electronic applications accepted. *Faculty research:* Trade magazine journalism, technical writing, financial reporting, medical and science reporting, industrial advertising and public relations.

**Nova Southeastern University,** College of Arts, Humanities, and Social Sciences, Fort Lauderdale, FL 33314-7796. Offers advanced conflict resolution practice (Graduate Certificate); college student affairs (MS); conflict analysis and resolution (MS, PhD); cross-disciplinary studies (MA); family studies (Graduate Certificate); family systems health care (Graduate Certificate); family therapy (MS, PhD); marriage and family therapy (DMFT); peace studies (Graduate Certificate); qualitative research (Graduate Certificate); solution focused coaching (Graduate Certificate). *Accreditation:* AAMFT/COAMFTE (one or more programs are accredited). *Program availability:* Part-time, evening/weekend, 100% online, blended/hybrid learning. *Faculty:* 29 full-time (18 women), 27 part-time/adjunct (21 women). *Students:* 306 full-time (242 women), 889 part-time (683 women); includes 677 minority (403 Black or African American, non-Hispanic/Latino; 2 American Indian or Alaska Native, non-Hispanic/Latino; 20 Asian, non-Hispanic/Latino; 224 Hispanic/Latino; 1 Native Hawaiian or other Pacific Islander, non-Hispanic/Latino; 27 Two or more races, non-Hispanic/Latino), 53 international. Average age 37. 624 applicants, 61% accepted, 285 enrolled. In 2016, 303 master's, 71 doctorates, 34 other advanced degrees awarded. *Degree requirements:* For master's, thesis optional, comprehensive exams, portfolios (for some programs), table-top exams (for some programs); for doctorate, comprehensive exam, thesis/dissertation, qualifying exams, portfolios (for some programs). *Entrance requirements:* For master's, interview, minimum GPA of 3.0, writing sample; for doctorate, interview, minimum GPA of 3.5, master's degree in related field, writing sample; for Graduate Certificate, minimum GPA of 3.0. Additional exam requirements/recommendations for international students: Required—TOEFL. *Application deadline:* For fall admission, 5/17 priority date for domestic and international students; for winter admission, 12/1 priority date for domestic and international students; for spring admission, 4/1 priority date for domestic and international students. Applications are processed on a rolling basis. Application fee: $50. Electronic applications accepted. *Expenses:* $1,005. *Financial support:* In 2016–17, 170 students received support. Career-related internships or fieldwork, Federal Work-Study, scholarships/grants, and unspecified assistantships available. Financial award application deadline: 4/1; financial award applicants required to submit CSS PROFILE. *Faculty research:* Conflict resolution, family therapy, peace research, international conflict, multi-disciplinary studies, college student affairs, national security affairs, health care conflict resolution, family systems health care, advanced family systems, qualitative research, solution-focused coaching. *Unit head:* Dr. Honggang Yang, Dean, 954-262-3016, Fax: 954-262-3968, E-mail: yangh@nova.edu. *Application contact:* Marcia Arango, Student Recruitment Coordinator, 954-262-3006, Fax: 954-262-3968, E-mail: marango@nsu.nova.edu. Website: http://cahss.nova.edu/

**Old Dominion University,** College of Arts and Letters, Institute for the Humanities, Norfolk, VA 23529. Offers MA. *Program availability:* Part-time, evening/weekend. *Faculty:* 1 full-time (0 women), 1 part-time/adjunct (0 women). *Students:* 10 full-time (5 women), 15 part-time (10 women); includes 10 minority (5 Black or African American, non-Hispanic/Latino; 1 Asian, non-Hispanic/Latino; 2 Hispanic/Latino; 2 Two or more races, non-Hispanic/Latino). Average age 39. 27 applicants, 96% accepted, 22 enrolled. In 2016, 11 master's awarded. *Degree requirements:* For master's, thesis optional, project. *Entrance requirements:* For master's, GRE General Test, minimum GPA of 3.25. *Application deadline:* For fall admission, 6/15 for domestic students; for spring admission, 11/15 for domestic students; for summer admission, 4/15 for domestic students. Applications are processed on a rolling basis. Application fee: $50. Electronic applications accepted. *Expenses:* Tuition, state resident: full-time $8604; part-time $478 per credit hour. Tuition, nonresident: full-time $21,510; part-time $1195 per credit hour. *Required fees:* $66 per semester. Tuition and fees vary according to campus/location, program and reciprocity agreements. *Financial support:* In 2016–17, 3 students received support, including 5 research assistantships (averaging $10,000 per year); career-related internships or fieldwork, scholarships/grants, and unspecified assistantships also available. Financial award application deadline: 3/15; financial award applicants required to submit FAFSA. *Faculty research:* Media studies, cultural studies, gender studies, American literature, philosophy, art history, cultural geography. *Unit head:* Dr. Avi D. Santo, Graduate Program Director, 757-683-3719, Fax: 757-683-6191, E-mail: humgpd@odu.edu. *Application contact:* Dr. David C. Earnest, Associate Dean, 757-683-6077, Fax: 757-683-5746, E-mail: dearnest@odu.edu. Website: http://al.odu.edu/hum/

**Penn State Harrisburg,** Graduate School, School of Humanities, Middletown, PA 17057. Offers American studies (MA, PhD); communications (MA); heritage and museum practice (Certificate); humanities (MA); writing instruction specialist (Certificate). *Program availability:* Evening/weekend. *Unit head:* Dr. Mukund S. Kulkarni, Chancellor, 717-948-6105, Fax: 717-948-6452. *Application contact:* Robert W. Coffman, Jr., Director of Enrollment Management, Admissions, 717-948-6250, Fax: 717-948-6325, E-mail: hbgadmit@psu.edu. Website: https://harrisburg.psu.edu/humanities

**Pepperdine University,** Seaver College, Division of Humanities, Malibu, CA 90263. Offers American studies (MA); writing for screen and television (MFA). *Program availability:* Part-time. *Students:* 9 full-time (7 women), 41 part-time (23 women); includes 12 minority (3 Black or African American, non-Hispanic/Latino; 2 Asian, non-Hispanic/Latino; 5 Hispanic/Latino; 2 Two or more races, non-Hispanic/Latino), 3 international. Average age 31. In 2016, 15 master's awarded. *Degree requirements:* For master's, oral and written exams. *Entrance requirements:* For master's, GRE General Test, writing sample, letters of recommendation. Additional exam requirements/recommendations for international students: Required—TOEFL. *Application deadline:* For fall admission, 2/1 priority date for domestic students. Applications are processed on a rolling basis. Application fee: $65. *Financial support:* Applicants required to submit FAFSA. *Unit head:* Dr. Michael G. Ditmore, Chair/Professor of English, 310-506-4182, Fax: 310-506-7307, E-mail: michael.ditmore@pepperdine.edu. *Application contact:* Hayley Wolf, Director of Admission, 310-506-4392, E-mail: hayley.wolf@pepperdine.edu. Website: http://seaver.pepperdine.edu/humanities/default.htm

**Prescott College,** Graduate Programs, Program in Arts and Humanities, Prescott, AZ 86301. Offers humanities (MA); social justice and human rights (MA); student-directed independent study (MA). *Program availability:* Part-time, online learning. *Faculty:* 3 full-time (0 women). *Students:* 3 full-time (1 woman), 13 part-time (10 women); includes 1 minority (Hispanic/Latino). Average age 42. 28 applicants, 79% accepted, 17 enrolled. In 2016, 20 master's awarded. *Degree requirements:* For master's, thesis, fieldwork or internship, practicum. *Entrance requirements:* For master's, 2 letters of recommendation, resume, essay. Additional exam requirements/recommendations for international students: Required—TOEFL (minimum score 500 paper-based). *Application deadline:* For fall admission, 4/15 priority date for domestic and international students; for spring admission, 9/15 priority date for domestic and international students. Applications are processed on a rolling basis. Application fee: $40. Electronic applications accepted. *Expenses: Tuition:* Full-time $19,680. One-time fee: $260 part-time. *Financial support:* Fellowships, research assistantships, teaching assistantships, career-related internships or fieldwork, Federal Work-Study, institutionally sponsored loans, scholarships/grants, traineeships, health care benefits, tuition waivers, and unspecified assistantships available. Support available to part-time students. Financial award applicants required to submit FAFSA. *Unit head:* Ellen Greenblum, 928-350-3209, E-mail: egreenblum@prescott.edu. *Application contact:* Amber Harris, Assistant Director, Graduate Admissions, 928-615-8446, Fax: 928-776-5242, E-mail: amber.harris@prescott.edu.

**St. Edward's University,** New College, Program in Liberal Arts, Austin, TX 78704. Offers humanities (MLA); liberal arts (MLA, Certificate). *Program availability:* Part-time, evening/weekend. *Students:* 11 full-time (7 women), 28 part-time (20 women); includes 15 minority (2 Black or African American, non-Hispanic/Latino; 1 American Indian or Alaska Native, non-Hispanic/Latino; 1 Asian, non-Hispanic/Latino; 10 Hispanic/Latino; 1 Two or more races, non-Hispanic/Latino), 1 international. Average age 36. 26 applicants, 69% accepted, 8 enrolled. In 2016, 13 master's awarded. *Degree requirements:* For master's, 33 hours of coursework with minimum cumulative GPA of 3.0. *Entrance requirements:* For master's, minimum GPA of 2.75 in last 60 hours of study, interview. Additional exam requirements/recommendations for international students: Required—TOEFL (minimum score 79 iBT), IELTS (minimum score 6). *Application deadline:* For fall admission, 6/1 priority date for domestic and international students; for spring admission, 10/1 priority date for domestic and international students; for summer admission, 3/1 priority date for domestic and international students. Applications are processed on a rolling basis. Application fee: $50. Electronic applications accepted. *Expenses: Tuition:* Full-time $25,092; part-time $1394 per credit hour. *Required fees:* $75 per trimester. Full-time tuition and fees vary according to course load and program. *Unit head:* Dr. Ramsey Fowler, MLA Program Director/Associate Professor of English, 512-448-8736, Fax: 512-448-8492, E-mail: ramseyf@stewards.edu. *Application contact:* Dave Bralower, Director of Graduate Admission, 512-233-1424, Fax: 512-464-8877, E-mail: davidcb@stedwards.edu. Website: http://www.stedwards.edu

**Salve Regina University,** Program in Humanities, Newport, RI 02840-4192. Offers humanitarian assistance (MA); humanities (PhD); public humanities (MA); religion, peace and justice (MA). *Program availability:* Part-time, evening/weekend, online learning. *Degree requirements:* For master's, thesis optional; for doctorate, one foreign language, comprehensive exam, thesis/dissertation. *Entrance requirements:* For master's, GMAT, GRE General Test, or MAT; for doctorate, GRE General Test. Additional exam requirements/recommendations for international students: Required—TOEFL (minimum score 600 paper-based; 100 iBT) or IELTS. Electronic applications accepted.

**Sam Houston State University,** College of Humanities and Social Sciences, Huntsville, TX 77341. Offers MA, MFA, MPA, PhD, SSP. *Program availability:* Part-time, online learning. Terminal master's awarded for partial completion of doctoral program. *Degree requirements:* For master's, comprehensive exam (for some programs), thesis optional, internship, portfolio; for doctorate, comprehensive exam, thesis/dissertation. *Entrance requirements:* For master's, GRE General Test, personal essay, letters of recommendation, writing sample; for doctorate, GRE General Test, GRE Subject Test (advanced psychology), personal essay, letters of recommendation, resume. Additional exam requirements/recommendations for international students: Required—TOEFL (minimum score 550 paper-based; 79 iBT), IELTS (minimum score 6.5). Electronic applications accepted.

**San Francisco State University,** Division of Graduate Studies, College of Liberal and Creative Arts, School of Humanities and Liberal Studies, San Francisco, CA 94132-1722. Offers MA. *Program availability:* Part-time, evening/weekend. *Expenses:* Tuition, state resident: full-time $6738. Tuition, nonresident: full-time $15,666. *Required fees:* $1012. Tuition and fees vary according to degree level and program. *Unit head:* Dr. Christina Ruotolo, Director, 415-338-1099, E-mail: ruotolo@sfsu.edu. *Application contact:* Prof. Laura Garcia-Moreno, Graduate Coordinator, 415-338-1295, E-mail: lgmoreno@sfsu.edu. Website: http://humanities.sfsu.edu/

**Simon Fraser University,** Office of Graduate Studies and Postdoctoral Fellows, Faculty of Arts and Social Sciences, Department of Humanities, Burnaby, BC V5A 1S6, Canada. Offers MA. *Faculty:* 19 full-time (12 women). *Students:* 11 full-time (7 women). 10 applicants, 30% accepted, 1 enrolled. In 2016, 2 master's awarded. *Degree requirements:* For master's, thesis. *Entrance requirements:* Additional exam requirements/recommendations for international students: Required—TOEFL (minimum score 580 paper-based; 93 iBT), IELTS (minimum score 7), TWE (minimum score 5). *Application deadline:* For spring admission, 4/30 for domestic and international students. Application fee: $90 ($125 for international students). Electronic applications accepted. *Financial support:* In 2016–17, 6 students received support, including 4 fellowships (averaging $6,500 per year); research assistantships and teaching assistantships also available. *Faculty research:* Classic and medieval studies, modern thought and culture, Renaissance humanism, Eastern and Western religions. *Unit head:* Dr. Samir Gandesha, Graduate Chair, 778-782-3406, E-mail: hum-grad-chair@sfu.ca. *Application contact:* Carolyn Richard, Graduate Program Assistant and Secretary, 778-782-8934, E-mail: hum-grad-secy@sfu.ca. Website: http://www.humanities.sfu.ca/

**Tiffin University,** Program in Humanities, Tiffin, OH 44883-2161. Offers art and visual media (MH); communication (MH); creative writing (MH); English (MH); film studies (MH); humanities (MH); individualized studies (MH). *Program availability:* Part-time, evening/weekend, online only, 100% online, blended/hybrid learning. *Students:* 17 full-time (15 women), 116 part-time (75 women); includes 25 minority (15 Black or African American, non-Hispanic/Latino; 2 Asian, non-Hispanic/Latino; 6 Hispanic/Latino; 2 Two or more races, non-Hispanic/Latino). Average age 36. 84 applicants, 80% accepted, 43 enrolled. In 2016, 42 master's awarded. *Entrance requirements:* For master's, work experience. Additional exam requirements/recommendations for international students: Required—TOEFL (minimum score 550 paper-based; 79 iBT). *Application deadline:* For fall admission, 9/1 for domestic students; for spring admission, 1/9 for domestic students. Applications are processed on a rolling basis. Application fee: $50. Electronic applications accepted. Application fee is waived when completed online. *Expenses:* Contact institution. *Financial support:* Unspecified assistantships available. Financial award applicants required to submit FAFSA. *Unit head:* Dr. Jason Slone, Program Chair, 419-448-5851, Fax: 419-443-5002, E-mail: slonedj@tiffin.edu. *Application contact:* Nikki Hintze, Director of Graduate and Distance Education Academic Advising, 800-968-6446 Ext. 3596, Fax: 419-443-5002, E-mail: hintzenm@tiffin.edu.

**Trinity Western University,** School of Graduate Studies, Program in Interdisciplinary Humanities, Langley, BC V2Y 1Y1, Canada. Offers general humanities (MAIH); specialized (MAIH), including English, history, philosophy. *Program availability:* Part-time. *Degree requirements:* For master's, thesis or alternative, 36 semester hours. *Entrance requirements:* For master's, strong undergraduate degree in humanities or English, history or philosophy. Additional exam requirements/recommendations for international students: Recommended—TOEFL. Electronic applications accepted. *Faculty research:* Literary theory, gender, medieval and early modern literature, philosophy of religion, Thomas Merton's poetics.

**United Theological Seminary of the Twin Cities,** Graduate Programs, New Brighton, MN 55112-2598. Offers advanced theological studies (Diploma); justice and peace studies (M Div, MA); leadership toward racial justice (M Div, MA, Certificate); Methodist studies (M Div, MA, Certificate); ministry (D Min); ministry renewal and professional development (Certificate); pastoral care and counseling (M Div, MA, MARL); religion and theology (MA); theological and religious studies (Certificate); theology and the arts (M Div, MA); urban ministry (M Div, MA, MARL); women's studies: religion, theology and ministry (M Div, MA). *Accreditation:* ACIPE; ATS. *Program availability:* Part-time, evening/weekend. *Degree requirements:* For master's, thesis; for doctorate, comprehensive exam, thesis/dissertation. *Entrance requirements:* For master's, minimum GPA of 2.75; strong analytical, reflective thinking and writing skills; vocational and academic goals compatible with those of Seminary; for doctorate, M Div or equivalent, minimum GPA of 3.0, 3 years experience in professional ministry; for other advanced degree, BA or equivalent life experience; strong analytical, reflective thinking and writing skills (Certificate); proficiency in English language, previous study of theology at a theological school, recommendation of student's denomination (Diploma). Additional exam requirements/recommendations for international students: Required—TOEFL (minimum score 550 paper-based).

**University at Buffalo, the State University of New York,** Graduate School, College of Arts and Sciences, Program in Interdisciplinary Studies, Buffalo, NY 14260. Offers humanities (MA); natural sciences (MS); social sciences (MS). *Program availability:* Part-time. *Entrance requirements:* Additional exam requirements/recommendations for international students: Required—TOEFL (minimum score 550 paper-based; 79 iBT). *Application deadline:* For fall admission, 2/1 priority date for domestic students, 1/1 priority date for international students; for spring admission, 11/1 priority date for domestic students, 10/1 priority date for international students. Applications are processed on a rolling basis. Electronic applications accepted. *Expenses:* Contact institution. *Financial support:* Fellowships, research assistantships, and teaching assistantships available. *Unit head:* Danielle Lewis, Graduate Interdisciplinary Program Coordinator, 716-645-1457, E-mail: dvegas@buffalo.edu. Website: http://gradidp.buffalo.edu/

**University of California, Santa Cruz,** Division of Graduate Studies, Division of Humanities, Program in the History of Consciousness, Santa Cruz, CA 95064. Offers PhD. *Degree requirements:* For doctorate, one foreign language, thesis/dissertation, qualifying exam. *Entrance requirements:* For doctorate, GRE General Test. Additional exam requirements/recommendations for international students: Required—TOEFL (minimum score 550 paper-based; 83 iBT); Recommended—IELTS (minimum score 8). Electronic applications accepted. *Faculty research:* Interdisciplinary humanities and social sciences, political theory, cultural theory, feminist studies, literary theory.

**University of Chicago,** Division of the Humanities, Master of Arts Program in the Humanities, Chicago, IL 60637. Offers art history (MA); cinema and media studies (MA); classic languages (MA); comparative literature (MA); creative writing (MA); cultural policy studies (MA); digital humanities (MA); East Asian languages and civilizations (MA); English language and literature (MA); gender and sexuality studies (MA); Germanic studies (MA); linguistics (MA); music (MA); near Eastern languages and civilizations (MA); philosophy (MA); poetics (MA); race, politics and culture (MA); Romance languages and literatures (MA); Slavic languages and literatures (MA); South Asian languages and civilizations (MA); theater and performance studies (MA). *Students:* 80 full-time (43 women), 7 part-time (3 women); includes 20 minority (5 Black or African American, non-Hispanic/Latino; 1 American Indian or Alaska Native, non-Hispanic/Latino; 6 Asian, non-Hispanic/Latino; 5 Hispanic/Latino; 3 Two or more races, non-Hispanic/Latino), 11 international. Average age 26. 706 applicants, 15% accepted, 42 enrolled. In 2016, 92 master's awarded. *Degree requirements:* For master's, thesis. *Entrance requirements:* For master's, GRE General Test. Additional exam requirements/recommendations for international students: Required—TOEFL (minimum score 104 iBT), IELTS (minimum score 7). *Application deadline:* For fall admission, 1/3 for domestic and international students. Application fee: $90. Electronic applications accepted. *Financial support:* In 2016–17, 8 fellowships with partial tuition reimbursements (averaging $12,000 per year) were awarded; Federal Work-Study, institutionally sponsored loans, scholarships/grants, and tuition waivers (partial) also available. Financial award application deadline: 12/15; financial award applicants required to submit FAFSA. *Unit head:* Malynne Sternstein, Co-Director, 773-834-1201, Fax: 773-834-7526. *Application contact:* Program Coordinator, 773-834-1201, Fax: 773-834-7526, E-mail: ma-humanities@uchicago.edu. Website: http://maph.uchicago.edu/

**University of Colorado Denver,** College of Liberal Arts and Sciences, Program in Humanities, Denver, CO 80217. Offers community health science (MSS); humanities (MH); international studies (MSS); philosophy and theory (MH); social justice (MSS); society and the environment (MSS); visual studies (MH); women's and gender studies (MSS). *Program availability:* Part-time, evening/weekend. *Faculty:* 3 full-time (1 woman). *Students:* 12 full-time (6 women), 15 part-time (7 women); includes 6 minority (1 American Indian or Alaska Native, non-Hispanic/Latino; 3 Hispanic/Latino; 2 Two or more races, non-Hispanic/Latino). Average age 41. 4 applicants, 100% accepted, 4 enrolled. In 2016, 5 master's awarded. *Degree requirements:* For master's, 36 credit hours, project or thesis. *Entrance requirements:* For master's, writing sample, statement of purpose/letter of intent, three letters of recommendation. Additional exam requirements/recommendations for international students: Required—TOEFL (minimum score 537 paper-based; 75 iBT); Recommended—IELTS (minimum score 6.5). *Application deadline:* For fall admission, 5/15 for domestic students, 5/15 priority date for international students; for spring admission, 10/15 for domestic students, 10/15 priority date for international students; for summer admission, 3/15 for domestic and international students. Application fee: $50 ($75 for international students). Electronic applications accepted. *Expenses:* Tuition, state resident: full-time $11,006; part-time $474 per credit. Tuition, nonresident: full-time $28,212; part-time $1264 per credit hour. *Required fees:* $256 per semester. One-time fee: $94.32. Tuition and fees vary according to campus/location and program. *Financial support:* In 2016–17, 2 students received support. Fellowships, research assistantships, teaching assistantships, Federal Work-Study, institutionally sponsored loans, scholarships/grants, and traineeships available. Financial award application deadline: 4/1; financial award applicants required to submit FAFSA. *Faculty research:* Women and gender in the classical Mediterranean, communication theory and democracy, relationship between psychology and philosophy. *Unit head:* Margaret Woodhull, Director of Humanities, 303-315-3568, E-mail: margaret.woodhull@ucdenver.edu. *Application contact:* Angela Beale, Program Assistant, 303-315-3565, E-mail: mastershs@ucdenver.edu. Website: http://www.ucdenver.edu/academics/colleges/CLAS/Programs/HumanitiesSocialSciences/Programs/Pages/MasterofHumanities.aspx

**University of Dallas,** Braniff Graduate School of Liberal Arts, Program in Humanities, Irving, TX 75062-4736. Offers M Hum, MA. *Program availability:* Part-time. *Degree requirements:* For master's, one foreign language, comprehensive exam, thesis (for some programs). *Entrance requirements:* For master's, GRE General Test. Additional exam requirements/recommendations for international students: Required—TOEFL. *Faculty research:* Classical epic poetry, scholastic poetry, Renaissance drama, nineteenth and twentieth century Continental philosophy.

## Humanities

**University of Houston–Clear Lake,** School of Human Sciences and Humanities, Programs in Humanities and Fine Arts, Houston, TX 77058-1002. Offers history (MA); humanities (MA); literature (MA). *Program availability:* Part-time, evening/weekend, online learning. *Degree requirements:* For master's, thesis or alternative. *Entrance requirements:* For master's, GRE General Test. Additional exam requirements/recommendations for international students: Required—TOEFL (minimum score 550 paper-based). *Faculty research:* Digital media studies, Latin American history, labor history, Chaucer evolution versus creationism debate.

**University of Louisville,** Graduate School, College of Arts and Sciences, Department of Comparative Humanities, Louisville, KY 40292-0001. Offers civic leadership (MA); culture, criticism, and contemporary thought (PhD); linguistics (MA); public arts and letters (PhD); traditional humanities (MA); MA/JD; MA/MBA. *Program availability:* Part-time. *Faculty:* 15 full-time (6 women), 2 part-time/adjunct (both women). *Students:* 49 full-time (32 women), 21 part-time (12 women); includes 11 minority (3 Black or African American, non-Hispanic/Latino; 2 Asian, non-Hispanic/Latino; 1 Hispanic/Latino; 5 Two or more races, non-Hispanic/Latino), 4 international. Average age 38. 21 applicants, 71% accepted, 10 enrolled. In 2016, 3 master's, 2 doctorates awarded. *Degree requirements:* For master's, one foreign language, thesis or alternative, directed study culminating project; for doctorate, 2 foreign languages, comprehensive exam, thesis/dissertation, internship. *Entrance requirements:* For master's, GRE General Test, two letters of recommendation, transcripts from all institutions attended; for doctorate, GRE General Test, three letters of recommendation, statement of intent, scholarly writing sample, transcripts from all institutions attended. Additional exam requirements/recommendations for international students: Recommended—TOEFL. *Application deadline:* For fall admission, 1/15 for domestic and international students. Application fee: $60. Electronic applications accepted. *Expenses:* Contact institution. *Financial support:* In 2016–17, 1 fellowship with full tuition reimbursement (averaging $18,000 per year), 10 teaching assistantships with full tuition reimbursements (averaging $18,000 per year) were awarded. Financial award application deadline: 1/15. *Faculty research:* Literary studies, medieval studies;, religious studies, linguistics, translation studies. *Total annual research expenditures:* $7,733. *Unit head:* Dr. Ann Hall, Chair, 502-852-6805, Fax: 502-852-0078, E-mail: ann.hall@louisville.edu. *Application contact:* Libby Leggett, Director, Graduate Admissions, 502-852-3101, Fax: 502-852-6536, E-mail: gradadm@louisville.edu.
Website: http://louisville.edu/humanities/

**University of Louisville,** Graduate School, College of Arts and Sciences, Department of Philosophy, Louisville, KY 40292-0001. Offers humanities (MA, PhD). *Faculty:* 11 full-time (3 women), 10 part-time/adjunct (4 women). *Students:* 4 part-time (2 women); includes 3 minority (all Black or African American, non-Hispanic/Latino). Average age 39. *Degree requirements:* For master's, one foreign language, thesis or alternative. *Entrance requirements:* For master's, GRE General Test. Additional exam requirements/recommendations for international students: Required—TOEFL (minimum score 550 paper-based; 79 iBT), IELTS (minimum score 6.5). *Application deadline:* Applications are processed on a rolling basis. Application fee: $60. Electronic applications accepted. *Expenses:* Tuition, state resident: full-time $12,246; part-time $681 per credit hour. Tuition, nonresident: full-time $25,486; part-time $1417 per credit hour. *Required fees:* $196. Tuition and fees vary according to program and reciprocity agreements. *Faculty research:* Philosophy of race; feminist philosophy; political philosophy, bioethics, ethics. *Unit head:* Dr. David S. Owen, Chair and Professor, 502-852-0488, Fax: 502-852-0459, E-mail: david.owen@louisville.edu. *Application contact:* Libby Leggett, Director, Graduate Admissions, 502-852-3101, Fax: 502-852-6536, E-mail: gradadm@louisville.edu.
Website: http://louisville.edu/philosophy

**University of South Florida,** College of Arts and Sciences, Department of Humanities and Cultural Studies, Tampa, FL 33620-9951. Offers liberal arts (MA), including Africana studies, American studies, film studies, humanities, social and political thought. *Program availability:* Part-time, evening/weekend. *Faculty:* 6 full-time (1 woman). *Students:* 17 full-time (10 women), 9 part-time (3 women); includes 3 minority (all Black or African American, non-Hispanic/Latino), 2 international. Average age 33. 23 applicants, 83% accepted, 14 enrolled. In 2016, 6 master's awarded. *Degree requirements:* For master's, comprehensive exam, thesis, language (for humanities subconcentration). *Entrance requirements:* For master's, GRE General Test, minimum GPA of 3.0 in upper-division courses, personal statement, writing sample. Additional exam requirements/recommendations for international students: Required—TOEFL (minimum score 550 paper-based; 79 iBT) or IELTS (minimum score 6.5). *Application deadline:* For fall admission, 2/15 priority date for domestic students, 2/15 for international students; for spring admission, 10/15 priority date for domestic students, 9/15 for international students; for summer admission, 2/15 for domestic students, 1/15 for international students. Application fee: $30. Electronic applications accepted. *Expenses:* Tuition, state resident: full-time $7766; part-time $431.43 per credit hour. Tuition, nonresident: full-time $15,789; part-time $877.17 per credit hour. *Required fees:* $37 per term. *Financial support:* In 2016–17, 5 students received support, including 15 teaching assistantships with tuition reimbursements available (averaging $12,437 per year); scholarships/grants also available. Financial award application deadline: 4/1. *Faculty research:* American South, American autobiography, material culture, critical theory, cultural studies, film studies. *Unit head:* Dr. William Cummings, Professor and Chair, 813-974-9380, Fax: 813-974-9409, E-mail: wcummings@usf.edu. *Application contact:* Dr. Brook Sadler, Associate Professor and Graduate Program Director, 813-974-8841, Fax: 813-974-9409, E-mail: brooksadler@usf.edu.
Website: http://humanities.usf.edu/

**The University of Texas at Dallas,** School of Arts and Humanities, Richardson, TX 75080. Offers history (MA); humanities (MA, PhD), including aesthetic studies, history of ideas, studies in literature (PhD), studies of literature (MA); Latin American studies (MA). *Program availability:* Part-time, evening/weekend. *Faculty:* 46 full-time (15 women), 5 part-time/adjunct (1 woman). *Students:* 129 full-time (78 women), 127 part-time (81 women); includes 63 minority (12 Black or African American, non-Hispanic/Latino; 4 American Indian or Alaska Native, non-Hispanic/Latino; 13 Asian, non-Hispanic/Latino; 23 Hispanic/Latino; 11 Two or more races, non-Hispanic/Latino), 27 international. Average age 41. 113 applicants, 58% accepted, 38 enrolled. In 2016, 39 master's, 16 doctorates awarded. *Degree requirements:* For master's, one foreign language, portfolio; for doctorate, one foreign language, thesis/dissertation. *Entrance requirements:* For master's and doctorate, minimum GPA of 3.0 in undergraduate course work in field. Additional exam requirements/recommendations for international students: Required—TOEFL (minimum score 550 paper-based). *Application deadline:* For fall admission, 7/15 for domestic students, 5/1 priority date for international students; for spring admission, 11/15 for domestic students, 9/1 priority date for international students. Applications are processed on a rolling basis. Application fee: $50 ($100 for international students). Electronic applications accepted. *Expenses:* Tuition, state resident: full-time $12,418; part-time $690 per semester hour. Tuition, nonresident: full-time $24,150; part-time $1342 per semester hour. Tuition and fees vary according to course load. *Financial support:* In 2016–17, 135 students received support, including 1 fellowship (averaging $2,000 per year), 12 research assistantships with partial tuition reimbursements available (averaging $23,948 per year), 69 teaching assistantships with partial tuition reimbursements available (averaging $15,001 per year); Federal Work-

Study, institutionally sponsored loans, scholarships/grants, and unspecified assistantships also available. Support available to part-time students. Financial award application deadline: 4/30; financial award applicants required to submit FAFSA. *Faculty research:* Science and the arts and humanities, intellectual and philosophical history, cultural studies, translation studies. *Total annual research expenditures:* $177,908. *Unit head:* Dr. Dennis M. Kratz, Dean, 972-883-2984, Fax: 972-883-2989, E-mail: dkratz@utdallas.edu. *Application contact:* Dr. John Gooch, Associate Dean of Graduate Studies, 972-883-2756, Fax: 972-883-2989, E-mail: john.gooch@utdallas.edu.
Website: http://www.utdallas.edu/ah/

**The University of Texas Medical Branch,** Graduate School of Biomedical Sciences, Program in Medical Humanities, Galveston, TX 77555. Offers MA, PhD. *Degree requirements:* For master's, thesis; for doctorate, thesis/dissertation. *Entrance requirements:* For master's and doctorate, GRE General Test, writing sample. Additional exam requirements/recommendations for international students: Required—TOEFL (minimum score 550 paper-based). Electronic applications accepted.

**University of Utah,** Graduate School, College of Humanities, Environmental Humanities Graduate Program, Salt Lake City, UT 84113. Offers MA, MS. *Faculty:* 11 full-time (5 women). *Students:* 14 full-time (11 women), 1 (woman) part-time; includes 3 minority (1 Asian, non-Hispanic/Latino; 2 Hispanic/Latino). Average age 28. 31 applicants, 23% accepted, 6 enrolled. In 2016, 7 master's awarded. *Degree requirements:* For master's, one foreign language, comprehensive exam (for some programs), thesis (for some programs). *Entrance requirements:* For master's, minimum GPA of 3.0; undergraduate degree. Additional exam requirements/recommendations for international students: Required—TOEFL (minimum score 500 paper-based; 80 iBT). *Application deadline:* For fall admission, 2/1 priority date for domestic and international students. Application fee: $55 ($65 for international students). Electronic applications accepted. *Expenses:* Tuition, state resident: full-time $7011; part-time $3918.24 per credit hour. Tuition, nonresident: full-time $22,154; part-time $11,665.42 per credit hour. *Financial support:* In 2016–17, 13 students received support, including 13 teaching assistantships with full and partial tuition reimbursements available (averaging $15,600 per year); scholarships/grants also available. Financial award application deadline: 2/10. *Faculty research:* Environmental writing, history/philosophy of science, environmental rhetoric and communication, American environmental history, urban environmentalism. *Unit head:* Jeffrey McCarthy, Director, 801-585-7052, Fax: 801-585-5190, E-mail: j.mccarthy@utah.edu. *Application contact:* Cory Pike, Graduate Advisor, 801-581-6156, E-mail: cory.pike@utah.edu.
Website: http://environmental-humanities.utah.edu/

**Virginia Polytechnic Institute and State University,** Graduate School, College of Liberal Arts and Human Sciences, Blacksburg, VA 24061. Offers career and technical education (MS Ed, Ed D, PhD, Ed S); communication (MA); counselor education (MA Ed, Ed D, PhD, Ed S); creative writing (MFA); curriculum and instruction (MA Ed, Ed D, PhD, Ed S); educational leadership and policy studies (MA Ed, Ed D, PhD, Ed S); educational research and evaluation (PhD); English (MA); foreign languages, cultures, and literatures (MA); higher education (PhD); higher education and student affairs (MA Ed); history (MA); human development (MS, PhD); material culture and public humanities (MA); philosophy (MA); political science (MA); rhetoric and writing (PhD); science and technology studies (MS, PhD); social, political, ethical, and cultural thought (PhD); sociology (MS, PhD); theater arts (MFA). *Faculty:* 408 full-time (204 women), 3 part-time/adjunct (2 women). *Students:* 657 full-time (446 women), 457 part-time (292 women); includes 213 minority (114 Black or African American, non-Hispanic/Latino; 3 American Indian or Alaska Native, non-Hispanic/Latino; 29 Asian, non-Hispanic/Latino; 44 Hispanic/Latino; 23 Two or more races, non-Hispanic/Latino), 93 international. Average age 34. 805 applicants, 55% accepted, 328 enrolled. In 2016, 270 master's, 91 doctorates awarded. *Degree requirements:* For master's, comprehensive exam (for some programs), thesis (for some programs); for doctorate, comprehensive exam (for some programs), thesis/dissertation (for some programs). *Entrance requirements:* For master's and doctorate, GRE/GMAT. Additional exam requirements/recommendations for international students: Required—TOEFL (minimum score 80 iBT). *Application deadline:* For fall admission, 8/1 for domestic students, 4/1 for international students; for spring admission, 1/1 for domestic students, 9/1 for international students. Applications are processed on a rolling basis. Application fee: $75. Electronic applications accepted. *Expenses:* Tuition, state resident: full-time $12,467; part-time $692.50 per credit hour. Tuition, nonresident: full-time $25,095; part-time $1394.25 per credit hour. *Required fees:* $2669; $491.50 per semester. Tuition and fees vary according to course load, campus/location and program. *Financial support:* In 2016–17, 21 research assistantships with full tuition reimbursements (averaging $19,817 per year), 237 teaching assistantships with full tuition reimbursements (averaging $15,497 per year) were awarded. Financial award application deadline: 3/1; financial award applicants required to submit FAFSA. *Total annual research expenditures:* $6.6 million. *Unit head:* Rosemary Blieszner, Interim Dean, 540-231-6779, Fax: 540-231-7157, E-mail: liberalartsdean@vt.edu. *Application contact:* Chelsea Blanchet, Executive Assistant, 540-231-6779, Fax: 540-231-7157, E-mail: bchels1@vt.edu.
Website: http://www.liberalarts.vt.edu/

**Wayland Baptist University,** Graduate Programs, Programs in Behavioral and Social Sciences, Plainview, TX 79072-6998. Offers counseling (MA); criminal justice (MACJ); government administration (MPA); history (MA); homeland security (MPA); humanities (MAH); justice administration (MPA). *Program availability:* Part-time, evening/weekend, online learning. *Degree requirements:* For master's, comprehensive exam. *Entrance requirements:* For master's, GRE, MAT. Additional exam requirements/recommendations for international students: Required—TOEFL (minimum score 500 paper-based; 61 iBT). Electronic applications accepted.

**West Chester University of Pennsylvania,** College of Arts and Humanities, West Chester, PA 19383. Offers M Ed, MA, MM, MS, Certificate, Teaching Certificate. *Program availability:* Part-time, evening/weekend. *Faculty:* 76 full-time (31 women), 5 part-time/adjunct (3 women). *Students:* 78 full-time (48 women), 168 part-time (104 women); includes 25 minority (9 Black or African American, non-Hispanic/Latino; 1 Asian, non-Hispanic/Latino; 9 Hispanic/Latino; 1 Native Hawaiian or other Pacific Islander, non-Hispanic/Latino; 5 Two or more races, non-Hispanic/Latino), 7 international. Average age 31. 146 applicants, 90% accepted, 80 enrolled. In 2016, 82 master's, 7 other advanced degrees awarded. *Degree requirements:* For master's and other advanced degree, variable foreign language requirement, comprehensive exam (for some programs), thesis (for some programs). *Entrance requirements:* Additional exam requirements/recommendations for international students: Required—TOEFL or IELTS. *Application deadline:* For fall admission, 5/15 for international students; for spring admission, 10/15 for international students. Applications are processed on a rolling basis. Application fee: $50. Electronic applications accepted. *Expenses:* Tuition, state resident: full-time $8694; part-time $483 per credit. Tuition, nonresident: full-time $13,050; part-time $725 per credit. *Required fees:* $2399; $119.05 per credit. Tuition and fees vary according to campus/location and program. *Financial support:* Scholarships/grants and unspecified assistantships available. Financial award application deadline: 2/15; financial award applicants required to submit FAFSA. *Unit head:* Dr. Timothy V. Blair, Dean of the College of Arts and Humanities, 610-436-2489, E-mail: tblair@wcupa.edu. *Application contact:* Office of Graduate Studies and

Extended Education, 610-436-2943, Fax: 610-436-2763, E-mail: gradstudy@wcupa.edu.
Website: http://www.wcupa.edu/arts-humanities/default.aspx

**Wilson College,** Graduate Programs, Chambersburg, PA 17201-1285. Offers accounting (M Acc); choreography and visual art (MFA); education (M Ed); healthcare management for sustainability (MHM); humanities (MA), including art and culture, critical/cultural theory, English language and literature, women's studies; management (MSM); nursing (MSN), including nursing education, nursing leadership and management. *Program availability:* Evening/weekend. *Degree requirements:* For master's, project. *Entrance requirements:* For master's, PRAXIS, minimum undergraduate cumulative GPA of 3.0, 2 letters of recommendation, current certification for eligibility to teach in grades K-12, resume, personal interview. Electronic applications accepted.

**Wright State University,** Graduate School, College of Liberal Arts, Interdisciplinary Program in Humanities, Dayton, OH 45435. Offers M Hum. *Degree requirements:* For master's, thesis or alternative. *Entrance requirements:* Additional exam requirements/

recommendations for international students: Required—TOEFL. *Application deadline:* For fall admission, 9/1 priority date for domestic students. Applications are processed on a rolling basis. Application fee: $25. *Expenses:* Tuition, state resident: full-time $9952; part-time $622 per credit hour. Tuition, nonresident: full-time $16,960; part-time $1060 per credit hour. *Financial support:* Fellowships, research assistantships, and unspecified assistantships available. Support available to part-time students. Financial award applicants required to submit FAFSA. *Unit head:* Dr. Ava Chamberlain, Director, 937-775-2740, Fax: 937-775-2707, E-mail: ava.chamberlain@wright.edu. *Application contact:* John Kimble, Associate Director of Graduate Admissions and Records, 937-775-2957, Fax: 937-775-2453, E-mail: john.kimble@wright.edu.

**York University,** Faculty of Graduate Studies, Faculty of Liberal Arts and Professional Studies, Program in Humanities, Toronto, ON M3J 1P3, Canada. Offers MA, PhD. *Program availability:* Part-time. *Degree requirements:* For master's, thesis or alternative; for doctorate, comprehensive exam, thesis/dissertation. *Entrance requirements:* Additional exam requirements/recommendations for international students: Required—TOEFL (minimum score 600 paper-based). Electronic applications accepted.

# Liberal Studies

**Abilene Christian University,** Graduate Programs, College of Arts and Sciences, Interdisciplinary Program in the Liberal Arts, Abilene, TX 79699. Offers MLA. *Program availability:* Part-time. In 2016, 1 master's awarded. *Degree requirements:* For master's, comprehensive exam, thesis or alternative. *Entrance requirements:* For master's, GRE General Test. Additional exam requirements/recommendations for international students: Required—TOEFL (minimum score 80 iBT), IELTS (minimum score 6), PTE. *Application deadline:* For fall admission, 4/1 priority date for domestic students; for spring admission, 11/1 for domestic students. Applications are processed on a rolling basis. Application fee: $50. Electronic applications accepted. *Expenses: Tuition:* Full-time $19,890; part-time $1105 per credit hour. Tuition and fees vary according to course load and program. *Financial support:* Federal Work-Study available. Support available to part-time students. Financial award application deadline: 4/1; financial award applicants required to submit FAFSA. *Unit head:* Dr. Joe Cardot, Graduate Advisor, 325-674-2136, Fax: 325-674-6966, E-mail: cardotj@acu.edu. *Application contact:* Corey Patterson, Director of Graduate Admission and Recruiting, 325-674-6566, Fax: 325-674-6717, E-mail: gradinfo@acu.edu.
Website: http://www.acu.edu/graduate/academics/liberal-arts.html

**Alaska Pacific University,** Graduate Programs, Liberal Studies Department, Anchorage, AK 99508-4672. Offers self-designed study (MA).

**Albertus Magnus College,** Master of Arts in Liberal Studies Program, New Haven, CT 06511-1189. Offers MALS. *Program availability:* Part-time, evening/weekend, blended/hybrid learning. *Faculty:* 10 full-time (3 women). *Students:* 3 part-time (1 woman); includes 1 minority (Asian, non-Hispanic/Latino). Average age 41. In 2016, 4 master's awarded. *Degree requirements:* For master's, thesis, completion of all credits within six years from time when student begins program; minimum cumulative GPA of 3.9; final project. *Entrance requirements:* For master's, interview, 500-word essay detailing applicant's intellectual and professional interests, minimum GPA of 2.8, transcripts. Additional exam requirements/recommendations for international students: Required—TOEFL (minimum score 550 paper-based; 80 iBT). *Application deadline:* For fall admission, 8/31 for domestic students; for spring admission, 1/10 for domestic students. Applications are processed on a rolling basis. Application fee: $50. Electronic applications accepted. *Expenses:* Contact institution. *Financial support:* Federal Work-Study and unspecified assistantships available. Support available to part-time students. Financial award application deadline: 8/15; financial award applicants required to submit FAFSA. *Unit head:* Prof. Julia A. Coash, Director, Liberal Studies Program, 203-773-8993, Fax: 203-773-5257, E-mail: jcoash@albertus.edu. *Application contact:* Anthony Reich, Director of Admission, Division of Professional and Graduate Studies, 203-773-5032, Fax: 203-773-5257, E-mail: arreich@albertus.edu.
Website: http://www.albertus.edu/liberal-studies/ma/

**Alvernia University,** School of Graduate Studies, Program in Liberal Studies, Reading, PA 19607-1799. Offers MALS. *Program availability:* Part-time, evening/weekend. *Degree requirements:* For master's, thesis optional. *Entrance requirements:* For master's, MAT or GRE (alumni excluded). Electronic applications accepted.

**Arizona State University at the Tempe campus,** College of Liberal Arts and Sciences, Program in Liberal Studies, Tempe, AZ 85287-6505. Offers MLS. *Program availability:* Part-time, evening/weekend. *Degree requirements:* For master's, thesis or alternative, integrated/capstone project, interactive Program of Study (iPOS) submitted before completing 50 percent of required credit hours. *Entrance requirements:* For master's, minimum GPA of 3.0 or equivalent in last 2 years of work leading to bachelor's degree, resume or biographical statement, personal letter expressing liberal studies concentration interest, official college transcripts, 2 letters of recommendation, interview with program director (recommended). Additional exam requirements/recommendations for international students: Required—TOEFL, IELTS, or PTE. Electronic applications accepted. *Expenses:* Contact institution.

**Arkansas Tech University,** College of Arts and Humanities, Russellville, AR 72801. Offers applied sociology (MS); English (M Ed, MA); history (MA); liberal arts (MLA); multi-media journalism (MA); psychology (MS); teaching English as a second language (MA). *Program availability:* Part-time. *Students:* 56 full-time (42 women), 121 part-time (85 women); includes 23 minority (7 Black or African American, non-Hispanic/Latino; 1 Asian, non-Hispanic/Latino; 11 Hispanic/Latino; 4 Two or more races, non-Hispanic/Latino), 34 international. Average age 32. In 2016, 90 master's awarded. *Degree requirements:* For master's, comprehensive exam (for some programs), thesis (for some programs), project. *Entrance requirements:* For master's, GRE General Test or GMAT. Additional exam requirements/recommendations for international students: Required—TOEFL (minimum score 550 paper-based; 79 iBT), IELTS (minimum score 6). *Application deadline:* For fall admission, 3/1 priority date for domestic students, 5/1 priority date for international students; for spring admission, 10/1 priority date for domestic and international students. Applications are processed on a rolling basis. Application fee: $25 ($75 for international students). Electronic applications accepted. *Expenses:* Tuition, state resident: full-time $4932; part-time $274 per credit hour. Tuition, nonresident: full-time $9864; part-time $548 per credit hour. *Required fees:* $513 per semester. Tuition and fees vary according to course load. *Financial support:* In 2016–17, research assistantships with full tuition reimbursements (averaging $4,800 per year), teaching assistantships with full tuition reimbursements (averaging $4,800 per year) were awarded; career-related internships or fieldwork, Federal Work-Study, scholarships/grants, health care benefits, and unspecified assistantships also available.

Support available to part-time students. Financial award application deadline: 4/15; financial award applicants required to submit FAFSA. *Unit head:* Dr. Jeffrey Woods, Dean, 479-968-0274, Fax: 479-964-0812, E-mail: jwoods@atu.edu. *Application contact:* Dr. Mary B. Gunter, Dean of Graduate College, 479-968-0398, Fax: 479-964-0542, E-mail: gradcollege@atu.edu.
Website: http://www.atu.edu/humanities/

**Auburn University at Montgomery,** College of Public Policy and Justice, Montgomery, AL 36124-4023. Offers MA, MIR, MPA, MPS, MS, MSJPS, PhD, Certificate. *Program availability:* Part-time, evening/weekend. *Degree requirements:* For master's, thesis. *Entrance requirements:* For master's, GRE or MAT. Electronic applications accepted.

**Baker University,** School of Professional and Graduate Studies, Program in Liberal Arts, Baldwin City, KS 66006-0065. Offers MLA. *Program availability:* Part-time, evening/weekend, online learning. *Students:* 4 full-time (all women), 63 part-time (45 women); includes 16 minority (5 Black or African American, non-Hispanic/Latino; 2 Asian, non-Hispanic/Latino; 8 Hispanic/Latino; 1 Two or more races, non-Hispanic/Latino). Average age 39. In 2016, 18 master's awarded. *Degree requirements:* For master's, portfolio of learning. *Entrance requirements:* Additional exam requirements/recommendations for international students: Required—TOEFL (minimum score 600 paper-based; 100 iBT). *Application deadline:* Applications are processed on a rolling basis. Electronic applications accepted. *Financial support:* Applicants required to submit FAFSA. *Unit head:* Dr. Jacob Bucher Posler, Dean of the School of Professional and Graduate Studies, 785-594-8475, E-mail: jacob.bucher@bakeru.edu. *Application contact:* Kelly Belk, Vice President of Enrollment Management, 913-491-4432, E-mail: kelly.belk@learn.bakeru.edu.
Website: https://www.bakeru.edu/spgs/mla/

**Barry University,** College of Arts and Sciences, Interdisciplinary Program, Miami Shores, FL 33161-6695. Offers MA.

**Brooklyn College of the City University of New York,** School of Education, Program in Childhood Education, Brooklyn, NY 11210-2889. Offers bilingual education (MS Ed); liberal arts (MS Ed); mathematics (MS Ed); science and environmental education (MS Ed). *Program availability:* Part-time, evening/weekend. *Entrance requirements:* For master's, LAST, interview, previous course work in education, writing sample, resume, 2 letters of recommendation. Additional exam requirements/recommendations for international students: Required—TOEFL (minimum score 500 paper-based; 61 iBT). Electronic applications accepted. *Faculty research:* Emotional intelligence, multiculturalism, arts immersion, the Holocaust.

**Cardinal Stritch University,** College of Arts and Sciences, Milwaukee, WI 53217-3985. Offers MA, MS. *Program availability:* Part-time, evening/weekend. *Students:* 11 full-time (8 women), 45 part-time (24 women); includes 12 minority (7 Black or African American, non-Hispanic/Latino; 1 American Indian or Alaska Native, non-Hispanic/Latino; 3 Hispanic/Latino; 1 Two or more races, non-Hispanic/Latino), 5 international. Average age 30. 92 applicants, 24% accepted, 13 enrolled. In 2016, 54 master's awarded. *Degree requirements:* For master's, thesis. *Entrance requirements:* Additional exam requirements/recommendations for international students: Required—TOEFL (minimum score 79 iBT), IELTS (minimum score 6.5). *Application deadline:* For fall admission, 7/15 priority date for domestic students; for spring admission, 12/15 priority date for domestic students. Applications are processed on a rolling basis. Application fee: $0. Electronic applications accepted. *Expenses: Tuition:* Full-time $11,890; part-time $765 per credit hour. Tuition and fees vary according to class time, course load, degree level, program and student's religious affiliation. *Financial support:* Research assistantships with partial tuition reimbursements, career-related internships or fieldwork, Federal Work-Study, scholarships/grants, and unspecified assistantships available. Financial award applicants required to submit FAFSA. *Unit head:* Dr. Dan J. Scholz, Dean, 414-410-4162, E-mail: djscholz@stritch.edu. *Application contact:* 800-347-8822 Ext. 4042, E-mail: admissions@stritch.edu.

**Clayton State University,** School of Graduate Studies, College of Arts and Sciences, Program in Liberal Studies, Morrow, GA 30260-0285. Offers MA. *Program availability:* Part-time. *Degree requirements:* For master's, thesis optional. *Entrance requirements:* For master's, official transcripts, 3 letters of recommendation, statement of purpose, on-campus interview. Additional exam requirements/recommendations for international students: Required—TOEFL (minimum score 550 paper-based; 80 iBT). Electronic applications accepted. *Expenses:* Tuition, state resident: full-time $3528; part-time $196 per credit hour. Tuition, nonresident: full-time $13,176; part-time $732 per credit hour. *Required fees:* $1454; $1454 per credit hour. $727 per semester. Tuition and fees vary according to campus/location and program.

**Coastal Carolina University,** Thomas W. and Robin W. Edwards College of Humanities and Fine Arts, Conway, SC 29528-6054. Offers liberal studies (MA); writing (MA). *Program availability:* Part-time, evening/weekend. *Faculty:* 16 full-time (7 women), 1 (woman) part-time/adjunct. *Students:* 23 full-time (15 women), 14 part-time (11 women); includes 7 minority (4 Black or African American, non-Hispanic/Latino; 1 American Indian or Alaska Native, non-Hispanic/Latino; 2 Hispanic/Latino). Average age 34. 24 applicants, 83% accepted, 13 enrolled. In 2016, 13 master's awarded. *Entrance requirements:* For master's, GRE, official transcripts, 3 letters of recommendation, writing sample, minimum GPA of 3.3 in 18 hours of coursework in English or related discipline. Additional exam requirements/recommendations for international students: Required—TOEFL (minimum score 550 paper-based; 79 iBT), IELTS (minimum score

## Liberal Studies

6.5). *Application deadline:* For fall admission, 5/15 priority date for domestic and international students; for spring admission, 11/15 priority date for domestic and international students. Applications are processed on a rolling basis. Application fee: $45. Electronic applications accepted. *Expenses:* Tuition, state resident: full-time $9990; part-time $555 per credit hour. Tuition, nonresident: full-time $18,108; part-time $1006 per credit hour. *Required fees:* $90; $5 per credit hour. *Financial support:* Fellowships, research assistantships, and unspecified assistantships available. Support available to part-time students. Financial award application deadline: 3/1; financial award applicants required to submit FAFSA. *Unit head:* Joseph R. Oestreich, Associate Professor/Coordinator of Graduate Study, 843-349-2433, E-mail: joeo@coastal.edu. *Application contact:* Dr. James O. Luken, Associate Provost/Vice-Dean of the Coastal Environment, 843-349-2235, Fax: 843-349-6444, E-mail: joluken@coastal.edu. Website: http://www.coastal.edu/humanities/

**The College at Brockport, State University of New York,** General Education Division, Program in Liberal Studies, Brockport, NY 14420-2997. Offers MA. *Program availability:* Part-time, 100% online. *Faculty:* 1 part-time/adjunct (0 women). *Students:* 3 full-time (1 woman), 18 part-time (11 women); includes 7 minority (3 Black or African American, non-Hispanic/Latino; 2 Asian, non-Hispanic/Latino; 1 Hispanic/Latino; 1 Two or more races, non-Hispanic/Latino). 17 applicants, 59% accepted, 7 enrolled. In 2016, 11 master's awarded. *Degree requirements:* For master's, portfolio. *Entrance requirements:* For master's, minimum GPA of 3.0, letters of recommendation. Additional exam requirements/recommendations for international students: Required—TOEFL (minimum score 550 paper-based; 79 iBT), IELTS (minimum score 6.5). *Application deadline:* For fall admission, 6/15 priority date for domestic and international students; for spring admission, 10/15 priority date for domestic and international students; for summer admission, 3/15 priority date for domestic and international students. Application fee: $50. Electronic applications accepted. *Expenses:* Contact institution. *Financial support:* Federal Work-Study, scholarships/grants, and unspecified assistantships available. Support available to part-time students. Financial award application deadline: 3/15; financial award applicants required to submit FAFSA. *Unit head:* Dr. Kalathur Rajasethupathy, Director, 585-395-2262, Fax: 585-395-2172, E-mail: kraja@brockport.edu. *Application contact:* Danielle A. Welch, Graduate Admissions Counselor, 585-395-5465, Fax: 585-395-2515. Website: http://www.brockport.edu/graduate/

**College of Staten Island of the City University of New York,** Graduate Programs, Division of Humanities and Social Sciences, Program in Liberal Studies, Staten Island, NY 10314-6600. Offers MA. *Program availability:* Part-time, evening/weekend. *Faculty:* 2 full-time, 2 part-time/adjunct. *Students:* 20 part-time. Average age 42. 20 applicants, 60% accepted, 10 enrolled. In 2016, 10 master's awarded. *Degree requirements:* For master's, comprehensive exam, 30 credits, essay. *Entrance requirements:* For master's, BA or BS with minimum cumulative GPA of 3.0. Additional exam requirements/recommendations for international students: Required—TOEFL (minimum score 550 paper-based; 79 iBT), IELTS (minimum score 6.5). *Application deadline:* For fall admission, 8/15 priority date for domestic and international students; for spring admission, 1/15 priority date for domestic students, 1/15 for international students. Applications are processed on a rolling basis. Application fee: $125. Electronic applications accepted. *Expenses:* Tuition, state resident: full-time $10,130; part-time $425 per credit. Tuition, nonresident: full-time $18,720; part-time $780 per credit. *Required fees:* $181.10 per semester. Tuition and fees vary according to program. *Faculty research:* Latin-American studies, historical and political anthropology, sociological theory, political economy. *Unit head:* Dr. Ismael Garcia Colon, Graduate Program Coordinator, 718-982-3766, E-mail: ismael.garcia@csi.cuny.edu. *Application contact:* Sasha Spence, Associate Director for Graduate Admissions, 718-982-2019, Fax: 718-982-2500, E-mail: sasha.spence@csi.cuny.edu. Website: http://www.csi.cuny.edu/catalog/graduate/master-of-arts-in-liberal-studies-ma.htm

**The Colorado College,** Education Department, Experienced Teacher Program, Colorado Springs, CO 80903-3294. Offers arts and humanities (MAT); integrated natural sciences (MAT); liberal arts (MAT); Southwest studies (MAT). Programs offered during summer only. *Program availability:* Part-time. *Degree requirements:* For master's, thesis, oral exam, 50-page paper. *Expenses:* Contact institution.

**Colorado State University,** College of Liberal Arts, Department of History, Fort Collins, CO 80523-1776. Offers liberal arts (MA); public history (MA), including cultural resource management, historic preservation, museum studies. *Program availability:* Part-time. *Faculty:* 6 full-time (2 women), 1 part-time/adjunct (0 women). *Students:* 25 full-time (14 women), 4 part-time (1 woman); includes 2 minority (1 American Indian or Alaska Native, non-Hispanic/Latino; 1 Hispanic/Latino). Average age 28. 23 applicants, 61% accepted, 13 enrolled. In 2016, 6 master's awarded. *Degree requirements:* For master's, one foreign language, comprehensive exam, thesis (for some programs), minimum final grade of B- in history courses counted toward degree. *Entrance requirements:* For master's, GRE General Test, 21 credits in history, statement of purpose, 3 letters of reference. Additional exam requirements/recommendations for international students: Required—TOEFL, IELTS. *Application deadline:* For fall admission, 2/1 priority date for domestic and international students. Application fee: $60 ($70 for international students). Electronic applications accepted. *Expenses:* Tuition, state resident: full-time $9628. Tuition, nonresident: full-time $23,603. *Required fees:* $2253; $528.14 per credit hour. $264.07 per semester. Tuition and fees vary according to course load and program. *Financial support:* In 2016–17, 22 students received support, including 1 research assistantship with full tuition reimbursement available (averaging $13,932 per year), 23 teaching assistantships with full tuition reimbursements available (averaging $13,932 per year); fellowships with full tuition reimbursements available and health care benefits also available. Financial award application deadline: 3/1; financial award applicants required to submit FAFSA. *Faculty research:* United states and north America; public and environmental history; modern world; religion; women, gender and sexuality. *Total annual research expenditures:* $281,014. *Unit head:* Dr. Doug Yarrington, Department Chair, 970-491-6801, Fax: 970-491-2941, E-mail: doug.yarrington@colostate.edu. *Application contact:* Diane Margolf, Graduate Studies Committee Chair, 970-491-5671, Fax: 970-491-2941, E-mail: diane.margolf@colostate.edu. Website: http://history.colostate.edu/

**Concordia University Chicago,** College of Graduate and Innovative Programs, Program in Liberal Studies, River Forest, IL 60305-1499. Offers MA. *Entrance requirements:* Additional exam requirements/recommendations for international students: Required—TOEFL (minimum score 550 paper-based). Electronic applications accepted.

**Converse College,** School of Education and Graduate Studies, Program in Liberal Arts, Spartanburg, SC 29302. Offers English (MLA); history (MLA); political science (MLA). *Degree requirements:* For master's, capstone paper. *Entrance requirements:* For master's, minimum GPA of 3.0, 2 recommendations. *Application deadline:* For fall admission, 5/1 priority date for domestic students; for spring admission, 1/30 for domestic students. Application fee: $40. *Expenses: Tuition:* Full-time $3600; part-time $400 per credit hour. *Required fees:* $70 per term. *Unit head:* Dr. Kathy Good, Dean of the School of Education and Graduate Studies, 864-596-9082, E-mail:

kathy.good@converse.edu. *Application contact:* Dr. Thomas McDaniel, Director of Master of Liberal Arts Program, 864-596-9015, E-mail: tom.mcdaniel@converse.edu.

**Dallas Baptist University,** Liberal Arts Program, Dallas, TX 75211-9299. Offers art (MLA); Christian studies (MLA); commercial art (MLA); East Asian studies (MLA); English (MLA); English as a second language (MLA); fine arts (MLA); history (MLA); missions (MLA); political science (MLA). *Program availability:* Part-time, evening/weekend, 100% online, blended/hybrid learning. *Application deadline:* Applications are processed on a rolling basis. Application fee: $25. Electronic applications accepted. Application fee is waived when completed online. *Expenses: Tuition:* Full-time $15,408; part-time $856 per credit hour. *Required fees:* $400 per semester. Tuition and fees vary according to course load and degree level. *Faculty research:* Milton and seventeenth-century Puritans, inter-Biblical years, nineteenth-century literature, Latin American and Texas history. *Unit head:* Jared Ingram, Director, 214-333-5584, E-mail: jared@dbu.edu. *Application contact:* Bobby Soto, Director of Admissions, 214-333-5242, E-mail: graduate@dbu.edu. Website: http://www3.dbu.edu/graduate/mla.asp

**Dartmouth College,** School of Graduate and Advanced Studies, Master of Arts in Liberal Studies Program, Hanover, NH 03755. Offers MALS. *Program availability:* Part-time. *Faculty:* 11 full-time (4 women), 12 part-time/adjunct (5 women). *Students:* 46 full-time (35 women), 32 part-time (21 women); includes 9 minority (2 Black or African American, non-Hispanic/Latino; 2 American Indian or Alaska Native, non-Hispanic/Latino; 2 Asian, non-Hispanic/Latino; 3 Hispanic/Latino), 18 international. Average age 30. 114 applicants, 86% accepted, 59 enrolled. In 2016, 42 master's awarded. *Degree requirements:* For master's, thesis. *Entrance requirements:* Additional exam requirements/recommendations for international students: Required—TOEFL. *Application deadline:* For fall admission, 2/15 for domestic students; for winter admission, 7/15 for domestic students; for spring admission, 7/15 for domestic students; for summer admission, 2/15 for domestic students. Application fee: $50. Electronic applications accepted. *Financial support:* Institutionally sponsored loans available. Financial award application deadline: 4/1; financial award applicants required to submit FAFSA. *Unit head:* Ronald Edsforth, Chair, 603-646-1738. *Application contact:* Wole Ojurongbe, Director, 603-646-3592, E-mail: mals.program@dartmouth.edu. Website: http://mals.dartmouth.edu/

See Display on next page and Close-Up on page 345.

**Delta State University,** Graduate Programs, College of Arts and Sciences, Program in Liberal Studies, Cleveland, MS 38733-0001. Offers evolving human voices (MALS); gender and diversity studies (MALS); globalization studies (MALS); Mississippi Delta studies (MALS); philosophy (MALS); religious studies (MALS). *Degree requirements:* For master's, oral and/or written comprehensive exam.

**DePaul University,** College of Liberal Arts and Social Sciences, Chicago, IL 60614. Offers Arabic (MA); Chinese (MA); English (MA); French (MA); German (MA); history (MA); interdisciplinary studies (MA, MS); international public service (MS); international studies (MA); Italian (MA); Japanese (MA); leadership and policy studies (MS); liberal studies (MA); new media studies (MA); nonprofit management (MNM); public administration (MPA); public health (MPH); public service management (MS); social work (MSW); sociology (MA); Spanish (MA); sustainable urban development (MA); women and gender studies (MA); writing and publishing (MA); writing, rhetoric, and discourse (MA); MA/PhD. *Program availability:* Part-time, evening/weekend, online learning. Terminal master's awarded for partial completion of doctoral program. *Degree requirements:* For master's, variable foreign language requirement, comprehensive exam (for some programs), thesis (for some programs). Electronic applications accepted.

**Drew University,** Caspersen School of Graduate Studies, Madison, NJ 07940-1493. Offers conflict resolution and leadership (Certificate), including community leadership, moderation, peace building; history and culture (MA, PhD), including American history, book history, British history, European history, Holocaust and genocide (M Litt, MA, D Litt, PhD), intellectual history, Irish history, print culture, public history; K-12 education (MAT), including art, biology, chemistry, elementary education, English, French, Italian, math, secondary education, special education, teacher of students with disabilities; liberal studies (M Litt, D Litt), including history, Holocaust and genocide (M Litt, MA, D Litt, PhD), Irish/Irish-American studies, literature (M Litt, MMH, D Litt, DMH, CMH), religion, spirituality, teaching in the two-year college, writing; medical humanities (MMH, DMH, CMH), including arts, health, healthcare, literature (M Litt, MMH, D Litt, DMH, CMH), scientific research; poetry (MFA). *Program availability:* Part-time, evening/weekend. *Faculty:* 4 full-time (2 women), 31 part-time/adjunct (16 women). *Students:* 62 full-time (41 women), 199 part-time (130 women); includes 38 minority (17 Black or African American, non-Hispanic/Latino; 3 Asian, non-Hispanic/Latino; 17 Hispanic/Latino; 1 Two or more races, non-Hispanic/Latino), 3 international. Average age 27. 93 applicants, 81% accepted, 46 enrolled. In 2016, 39 master's, 27 doctorates, 26 other advanced degrees awarded. Terminal master's awarded for partial completion of doctoral program. *Degree requirements:* For master's and other advanced degree, thesis (for some programs); for doctorate, one foreign language, comprehensive exam (for some programs), thesis/dissertation. *Entrance requirements:* For master's, PRAXIS Core and Subject Area tests (for MAT), resume, transcripts, writing sample, personal statement, letters of recommendation; for doctorate, GRE (PhD in history and culture), resume, transcripts, writing sample, personal statement, letters of recommendation. Additional exam requirements/recommendations for international students: Required—TOEFL (minimum score 587 paper-based; 94 iBT), IELTS (minimum score 7), TWE (minimum score 4). *Application deadline:* For fall admission, 8/1 for domestic students, 6/1 for international students; for spring admission, 12/1 for domestic students, 10/1 for international students. Applications are processed on a rolling basis. Application fee: $35. Electronic applications accepted. Tuition and fees vary according to program. *Financial support:* Fellowships, research assistantships, teaching assistantships, career-related internships or fieldwork, Federal Work-Study, scholarships/grants, and unspecified assistantships available. Support available to part-time students. Financial award applicants required to submit FAFSA. *Application contact:* Leanne Horinko, Director of Caspersen Admissions, 973-408-3280, E-mail: gradm@drew.edu. Website: http://www.drew.edu/caspersen

**Duke University,** Graduate School, Program in Liberal Studies, Durham, NC 27708. Offers AM. *Program availability:* Part-time, evening/weekend. *Degree requirements:* For master's, thesis or alternative, final project. *Entrance requirements:* For master's, interview. Additional exam requirements/recommendations for international students: Required—IELTS (preferred) or TOEFL. Electronic applications accepted.

**East Tennessee State University,** School of Graduate Studies, School of Continuing Studies and Academic Outreach, Johnson City, TN 37614. Offers MALS, MPS, Postbaccalaureate Certificate. *Program availability:* Part-time, online learning. *Degree requirements:* For master's, comprehensive exam, thesis optional, professional project. *Entrance requirements:* For master's, GRE General Test, minimum GPA of 2.75, professional portfolio, three letters of recommendation, interview, writing sample; for Postbaccalaureate Certificate, minimum GPA of 2.5, three letters of recommendation, interview. Additional exam requirements/recommendations for international students: Required—TOEFL (minimum score 550 paper-based; 79 iBT). Electronic applications accepted. *Faculty research:* Appalachian studies, women's and gender studies, interdisciplinary theory, regional and Southern cultures.

**Excelsior College,** School of Liberal Arts, Albany, NY 12203-5159. Offers liberal studies (MA). *Program availability:* Part-time, evening/weekend, online learning. *Faculty:* 27 part-time/adjunct (18 women). *Students:* 82 part-time (32 women); includes 40 minority (26 Black or African American, non-Hispanic/Latino; 2 American Indian or Alaska Native, non-Hispanic/Latino; 1 Asian, non-Hispanic/Latino; 7 Hispanic/Latino; 4 Two or more races, non-Hispanic/Latino), 1 international. Average age 46. In 2016, 49 master's awarded. *Degree requirements:* For master's, thesis or alternative. *Application deadline:* Applications are processed on a rolling basis. Application fee: $50. Electronic applications accepted. *Expenses:* Tuition: Part-time $645 per credit. *Required fees:* $265 per credit. *Financial support:* Scholarships/grants available. *Unit head:* Dr. George Timmons, Dean, 518-464-8500, Fax: 518-464-8777, E-mail: mlsadmin@excelsior.edu. *Application contact:* Admissions Counselor, 518-464-8500, Fax: 518-464-8777, E-mail: admissions@excelsior.edu.
Website: http://www.excelsior.edu/programs/liberal-arts

**Faulkner University,** Alabama Christian College of Arts and Sciences, Department of Humanities, Montgomery, AL 36109-3398. Offers liberal arts (MLA).

**Florida International University,** College of Arts, Sciences, and Education, Program in Liberal Studies, Miami, FL 33199. Offers MA. *Program availability:* Part-time, evening/weekend. *Faculty:* 1 part-time/adjunct (0 women). *Students:* 8 part-time (6 women); includes 5 minority (2 Black or African American, non-Hispanic/Latino; 3 Hispanic/Latino). Average age 35. In 2016, 2 master's awarded. *Degree requirements:* For master's, thesis optional. *Entrance requirements:* For master's, minimum GPA of 3.0, 2-3 letters of recommendation, writing sample, curriculum vitae. Additional exam requirements/recommendations for international students: Required—TOEFL (minimum score 550 paper-based; 80 iBT). *Application deadline:* For fall admission, 6/1 for domestic students, 4/1 for international students; for spring admission, 10/1 for domestic students, 9/1 for international students. Applications are processed on a rolling basis. Application fee: $30. Electronic applications accepted. *Expenses:* Tuition, state resident: full-time $8912; part-time $446 per credit hour. Tuition, nonresident: full-time $21,393; part-time $992 per credit hour. *Required fees:* $2185; $195 per semester. Tuition and fees vary according to program. *Financial support:* Institutionally sponsored loans and scholarships/grants available. Financial award application deadline: 3/1; financial award applicants required to submit FAFSA. *Unit head:* Dr. Paul Warren, Chair, 305-348-2498, Fax: 305-348-1799, E-mail: paul.warren@fiu.edu. *Application contact:* Nanett Rojas, Assistant Director, Graduate Admissions, 305-348-7464, Fax: 305-348-7441, E-mail: gradadm@fiu.edu.

**Fort Hays State University,** Graduate School, College of Arts and Sciences, Center for Interdisciplinary Studies, Hays, KS 67601-4099. Offers liberal studies (MLS). *Program availability:* Online learning. *Degree requirements:* For master's, comprehensive exam, thesis or alternative. *Entrance requirements:* Additional exam requirements/recommendations for international students: Required—TOEFL (minimum score 550 paper-based). Electronic applications accepted.

**Georgetown University,** Graduate School of Arts and Sciences, School of Continuing Studies, Washington, DC 20057. Offers American studies (MALS); Catholic studies (MALS); classical civilizations (MALS); emergency and disaster management (MPS); ethics and the professions (MALS); global strategic communications (MPS); hospitality management (MPS); human resources management (MPS); humanities (MALS); individualized study (MALS); integrated marketing communications (MPS); international affairs (MALS); Islam and Muslim-Christian relations (MALS); journalism (MPS); liberal studies (DLS); literature and society (MALS); medieval and early modern European studies (MALS); public relations and corporate communications (MPS); real estate

(MPS); religious studies (MALS); social and public policy (MALS); sports industry management (MPS); systems engineering management (MPS); technology management (MPS); the theory and practice of American democracy (MALS); urban and regional planning (MPS); visual culture (MALS). MPS in systems engineering management offered jointly with Stevens Institute of Technology. *Entrance requirements:* Additional exam requirements/recommendations for international students: Required—TOEFL.

**The Graduate Center, City University of New York,** Graduate Studies, Program in Liberal Studies, New York, NY 10016-4039. Offers MA. *Degree requirements:* For master's, thesis. *Entrance requirements:* For master's, GRE General Test. Additional exam requirements/recommendations for international students: Required—TOEFL. Electronic applications accepted.

**Harvard University,** Extension School, Cambridge, MA 02138-3722. Offers applied sciences (CAS); biotechnology (ALM); educational technologies (ALM); educational technology (CET); English for graduate and professional studies (DGP); environmental management (ALM, CEM); information technology (ALM); journalism (ALM); liberal arts (ALM); management (ALM, CM); mathematics for teaching (ALM); museum studies (ALM); premedical studies (Diploma); publication and communication (CPC). *Program availability:* Part-time, evening/weekend. *Degree requirements:* For master's, thesis. *Entrance requirements:* For master's, 3 completed graduate courses with grade of B or higher. Additional exam requirements/recommendations for international students: Required—TOEFL (minimum score 600 paper-based), TWE (minimum score 5). *Expenses:* Contact institution.

**Hawai`i Pacific University,** College of Liberal Arts, Honolulu, HI 96813. Offers MA. *Program availability:* Part-time, evening/weekend. *Faculty:* 22 full-time (6 women), 9 part-time/adjunct (4 women). *Students:* 109 full-time (61 women), 82 part-time (43 women); includes 83 minority (8 Black or African American, non-Hispanic/Latino; 23 Asian, non-Hispanic/Latino; 21 Hispanic/Latino; 2 Native Hawaiian or other Pacific Islander, non-Hispanic/Latino; 29 Two or more races, non-Hispanic/Latino), 27 international. Average age 33. 145 applicants, 86% accepted, 69 enrolled. In 2016, 93 master's awarded. *Entrance requirements:* Additional exam requirements/recommendations for international students: Recommended—TOEFL (minimum score 550 paper-based; 80 iBT), IELTS (minimum score 6), TWE (minimum score 5). *Application deadline:* For fall admission, 2/15 priority date for domestic students; for spring admission, 10/15 priority date for domestic students. Applications are processed on a rolling basis. Application fee: $50. Electronic applications accepted. *Expenses:* Tuition: Full-time $17,190; part-time $955 per credit. *Required fees:* $150; $26 per credit. Tuition and fees vary according to course load and program. *Financial support:* In 2016–17, 37 students received support. Career-related internships or fieldwork, Federal Work-Study, scholarships/grants, tuition waivers, and unspecified assistantships available. Financial award application deadline: 3/1; financial award applicants required to submit FAFSA. *Unit head:* Dr. William Potter, Interim Dean, 808-544-0274, E-mail: wpotter@hpu.edu. *Application contact:* Danny Lam, Assistant Director of Graduate Admissions, 808-544-1135, E-mail: graduate@hpu.edu.
Website: http://www.hpu.edu/CHSS/

**Henderson State University,** Graduate Studies, Ellis College of Arts and Sciences, Arkadelphia, AR 71999-0001. Offers MLA. *Program availability:* Part-time. *Faculty:* 15 full-time (6 women). *Students:* 6 full-time (3 women), 18 part-time (9 women); includes 8 minority (4 Black or African American, non-Hispanic/Latino; 2 Hispanic/Latino; 2 Two or more races, non-Hispanic/Latino). Average age 32. 7 applicants, 86% accepted, 6 enrolled. In 2016, 3 master's awarded. *Degree requirements:* For master's, thesis. *Entrance requirements:* For master's, MAT or GRE, minimum GPA of 2.7, interview, essay. Additional exam requirements/recommendations for international students:

INTERDISCIPLINARY　FLEXIBLE　CREATIVE　INTELLECTUAL

Required—TOEFL (minimum score 600 paper-based); Recommended—IELTS (minimum score 6.5). *Application deadline:* For fall admission, 8/1 priority date for domestic students, 6/30 priority date for international students; for spring admission, 1/1 priority date for domestic students, 11/30 priority date for international students. Applications are processed on a rolling basis. Application fee: $25 ($75 for international students). *Expenses:* Tuition, state resident: full-time $6288; part-time $3144 per credit hour. Tuition, nonresident: full-time $12,888; part-time $6444 per credit hour. *Required fees:* $1429; $1024 per credit hour. Tuition and fees vary according to course load and student level. *Financial support:* In 2016–17, 10 teaching assistantships with partial tuition reimbursements (averaging $4,000 per year) were awarded; scholarships/grants and unspecified assistantships also available. Financial award application deadline: 4/15; financial award applicants required to submit FAFSA. *Unit head:* Megan Hickerson, MLA Director, 870-230-5250, Fax: 870-230-5144, E-mail: hickerm@hsu.edu. *Application contact:* Dr. Ken Taylor, Graduate Dean, 870-230-5126, Fax: 870-230-5479, E-mail: taylorke@hsu.edu.
Website: http://www.hsu.edu/Academics/EllisCollege/MLA/index.html

**Hollins University,** Graduate Programs, Program in Liberal Studies, Roanoke, VA 24020. Offers humanities (MALS); interdisciplinary studies (MALS); leadership (MALS); social sciences (MALS); visual and performing arts (MALS). *Program availability:* Part-time, evening/weekend. *Degree requirements:* For master's, thesis. *Entrance requirements:* For master's, three letters of recommendation, interview, bachelor's degree, undergraduate transcripts, statement of educational objectives. Additional exam requirements/recommendations for international students: Required—TOEFL (minimum score 550 paper-based; 80 iBT), IELTS (minimum score 6.5). *Application deadline:* Applications are processed on a rolling basis. Application fee: $40. Electronic applications accepted. *Expenses:* $395 per credit hour. *Financial support:* Fellowships and scholarships/grants available. Support available to part-time students. Financial award application deadline: 7/15; financial award applicants required to submit FAFSA. *Faculty research:* Diversity, gender and women's studies, political science, leadership. *Unit head:* Director, 540-362-6576, Fax: 540-362-6288, E-mail: hugrad@hollins.edu. *Application contact:* Cathy S. Koon, Manager of Graduate Programs, 540-362-6326, Fax: 540-362-6288, E-mail: ckoon@hollins.edu.
Website: http://www.hollins.edu/academics/graduate-degrees/liberal-studies/

**Houston Baptist University,** School of Humanities, Program in Liberal Arts, Houston, TX 77074-3298. Offers classical learning (MLA); general liberal arts (MLA); research (MLA). *Program availability:* Part-time, evening/weekend. *Students:* 5 full-time (2 women), 27 part-time (18 women); includes 15 minority (8 Black or African American, non-Hispanic/Latino; 1 American Indian or Alaska Native, non-Hispanic/Latino; 1 Asian, non-Hispanic/Latino; 5 Hispanic/Latino). Average age 31. 36 applicants, 28% accepted, 6 enrolled. In 2016, 8 master's awarded. *Entrance requirements:* For master's, minimum GPA of 2.5, essay/personal statement, resume, bachelor's degree transcript. Additional exam requirements/recommendations for international students: Required—TOEFL (minimum score 80 iBT), IELTS (minimum score 6.5). *Application deadline:* For fall admission, 8/1 for domestic students, 6/1 for international students; for spring admission, 1/1 for domestic students, 11/1 for international students; for summer admission, 5/1 for domestic students, 3/1 for international students. Applications are processed on a rolling basis. Application fee: $0 ($100 for international students). Electronic applications accepted. Application fee is waived when completed online. *Expenses:* $1,500 per 3-hour course; $1,275 annual general fee; $1,060 annual technology fee. *Financial support:* In 2016–17, 3 students received support. Federal Work-Study and scholarships/grants available. Support available to part-time students. Financial award application deadline: 4/1; financial award applicants required to submit FAFSA. *Unit head:* Dr. Jodey Hinze, Dean, School of Humanities, E-mail: jhinze@hbu.edu. *Application contact:* Kathy Holston, Administrative Assistant to the Dean, 281-649-3404, E-mail: kholston@hbu.edu.
Website: http://www.hbu.edu/mla

**Indiana University Northwest,** College of Arts and Sciences, Gary, IN 46408. Offers clinical counseling (MS), including drug and alcohol counseling; community development/urban studies (Graduate Certificate); computer information systems (Graduate Certificate); liberal studies (MLS); race-ethnic studies (Graduate Certificate); women's and gender studies (Graduate Certificate). *Program availability:* Part-time, evening/weekend. *Students:* 4 full-time (all women), 18 part-time (10 women); includes 10 minority (9 Black or African American, non-Hispanic/Latino; 1 Hispanic/Latino). Average age 39. 22 applicants, 77% accepted, 13 enrolled. In 2016, 6 master's awarded. *Entrance requirements:* For master's, GRE (recommended for MS), minimum undergraduate GPA of 3.0, bachelor's degree from accredited university (for MS). *Application deadline:* For fall admission, 7/1 priority date for domestic and international students; for spring admission, 12/1 priority date for domestic and international students. Application fee: $40 ($60 for international students). Electronic applications accepted. *Expenses:* $276.98 per credit hour in-state; $652.54 per credit hour out-of-state. *Financial support:* Applicants required to submit FAFSA. *Unit head:* Mark Hoyert, Dean, E-mail: mhoyert@iun.edu.
Website: http://www.iun.edu/coas/

**Indiana University–Purdue University Indianapolis,** School of Liberal Arts, Indianapolis, IN 46202. Offers MA, MS, PhD, Certificate, JD/MA, MA/MA, MA/MLS, MD/MA. *Students:* 115 full-time (72 women), 111 part-time (67 women); includes 41 minority (19 Black or African American, non-Hispanic/Latino; 1 American Indian or Alaska Native, non-Hispanic/Latino; 5 Asian, non-Hispanic/Latino; 14 Hispanic/Latino; 2 Two or more races, non-Hispanic/Latino), 29 international. Average age 33. 187 applicants, 61% accepted, 67 enrolled. In 2016, 91 master's, 1 doctorate, 16 other advanced degrees awarded. Application fee: $55 ($65 for international students). *Unit head:* Dr. William Blomquist, Dean, School of Liberal Arts, 317-274-8448, E-mail: blomquis@iupui.edu. *Application contact:* Candice L. Smith, Coordinator of Academic and Graduate Programs, 317-274-8305, E-mail: canlsmit@iupui.edu.
Website: http://liberalarts.iupui.edu/

**Indiana University South Bend,** College of Liberal Arts and Sciences, South Bend, IN 46634-7111. Offers advanced computer programming (Graduate Certificate); applied informatics (Graduate Certificate); applied mathematics and computer science (MS); behavior modification (Graduate Certificate); computer applications (Graduate Certificate); computer programming (Graduate Certificate); correctional management and supervision (Graduate Certificate); English (MA); health systems management (Graduate Certificate); international studies (Graduate Certificate); liberal studies (MLS); nonprofit management (Graduate Certificate); paralegal studies (Graduate Certificate); professional writing (Graduate Certificate); public affairs (MPA); public management (Graduate Certificate); social and cultural diversity (Graduate Certificate); strategic sustainability leadership (Graduate Certificate); technology for administration (Graduate Certificate). *Program availability:* Part-time, evening/weekend. *Faculty:* 79 full-time (33 women). *Students:* 31 full-time (11 women), 92 part-time (53 women); includes 28 minority (9 Black or African American, non-Hispanic/Latino; 8 Asian, non-Hispanic/Latino; 5 Hispanic/Latino; 6 Two or more races, non-Hispanic/Latino), 19 international. Average age 38. 51 applicants, 84% accepted, 31 enrolled. In 2016, 30 master's, 6 other advanced degrees awarded. *Degree requirements:* For master's, variable foreign

language requirement, thesis (for some programs). *Entrance requirements:* For master's, minimum GPA of 3.0. Additional exam requirements/recommendations for international students: Required—TOEFL (minimum score 550 paper-based; 80 iBT). *Application deadline:* For fall admission, 7/31 priority date for domestic students, 7/1 priority date for international students; for spring admission, 3/31 priority date for domestic students, 11/1 priority date for international students. Applications are processed on a rolling basis. Application fee: $40 ($60 for international students). *Expenses:* $276.98 per credit hour in-state; $652.54 per credit hour out-of-state. *Financial support:* In 2016–17, 5 teaching assistantships were awarded; Federal Work-Study also available. Support available to part-time students. Financial award application deadline: 3/10. *Faculty research:* Artificial intelligence, bioinformatics, English language and literature, creative writing, computer networks. *Total annual research expenditures:* $127,000. *Unit head:* Dr. Elizabeth E. Dunn, Dean, 574-520-4290, E-mail: elizdunn@iusb.edu. *Application contact:* Admissions Counselor, 574-520-4839, Fax: 574-520-4834, E-mail: graduate@iusb.edu.
Website: https://www.iusb.edu/clas/

**Jacksonville State University,** College of Graduate Studies and Continuing Education, College of Arts and Sciences, Department of Liberal Studies, Jacksonville, AL 36265-1602. Offers MA. *Program availability:* Part-time, evening/weekend. *Students:* 6 full-time (3 women), 14 part-time (5 women); includes 6 minority (all Black or African American, non-Hispanic/Latino), 2 international. Average age 33. In 2016, 3 master's awarded. *Degree requirements:* For master's, comprehensive exam, thesis (for some programs). *Entrance requirements:* Additional exam requirements/recommendations for international students: Required—TOEFL (minimum score 500 paper-based; 61 iBT). *Application deadline:* Applications are processed on a rolling basis. Application fee: $35. Electronic applications accepted. *Financial support:* In 2016–17, 7 students received support. Available to part-time students. Application deadline: 4/1; applicants required to submit FAFSA. *Unit head:* Dr. Earl Wade, Dean, 256-782-5649, E-mail: jwade@jsu.edu. *Application contact:* Dr. Jean Pugliese, Associate Dean, 256-782-8278, Fax: 256-782-5321, E-mail: pugliese@jsu.edu.

**Johns Hopkins University,** Zanvyl Krieger School of Arts and Sciences, Advanced Academic Programs, Program in Liberal Arts, Washington, DC 20036. Offers MA, Certificate. *Program availability:* Part-time, evening/weekend, online learning. *Degree requirements:* For master's, thesis. *Entrance requirements:* For master's, minimum GPA of 3.0. Additional exam requirements/recommendations for international students: Required—TOEFL (minimum score 100 iBT). Electronic applications accepted.

**Kean University,** College of Liberal Arts, Union, NJ 07083. Offers MA, Diploma. *Program availability:* Part-time. *Faculty:* 78 full-time (39 women). *Students:* 110 full-time (91 women), 106 part-time (73 women); includes 104 minority (52 Black or African American, non-Hispanic/Latino; 9 Asian, non-Hispanic/Latino; 39 Hispanic/Latino; 1 Native Hawaiian or other Pacific Islander, non-Hispanic/Latino; 3 Two or more races, non-Hispanic/Latino), 2 international. Average age 30. 146 applicants, 49% accepted, 62 enrolled. In 2016, 89 master's, 9 other advanced degrees awarded. *Degree requirements:* For master's, comprehensive exam, thesis, exhibition, practicum, internship; for Diploma, comprehensive exam, thesis, practicum, internship/externship. *Entrance requirements:* Additional exam requirements/recommendations for international students: Required—TOEFL (minimum score 550 paper-based; 79 iBT), IELTS (minimum score 6.5). *Application deadline:* For fall admission, 6/1 for domestic and international students; for spring admission, 12/1 for domestic and international students. Applications are processed on a rolling basis. Application fee: $75. Electronic applications accepted. *Expenses:* Tuition, state resident: full-time $13,156; part-time $640 per credit. Tuition, nonresident: full-time $17,831; part-time $785 per credit. *Required fees:* $3316; $151 per credit. Tuition and fees vary according to course level, course load, degree level and program. *Financial support:* Scholarships/grants and unspecified assistantships available. Financial award applicants required to submit FAFSA. *Unit head:* Dr. Susan Bousequet, Dean, 908-737-0430, Fax: 908-737-0435, E-mail: sbousque@kean.edu. *Application contact:* Amy Hadjusek, Program Assistant, 908-737-7100, E-mail: grad-adm@kean.edu.
Website: http://www.kean.edu/academics/college-liberal-arts

**Kent State University,** College of Arts and Sciences, Center for Comparative and Integrative Programs, Kent, OH 44242-0001. Offers MLS. *Program availability:* Part-time, evening/weekend, online learning. *Faculty:* 11 full-time (2 women). *Students:* 9 part-time (7 women); includes 1 minority (Black or African American, non-Hispanic/Latino). Average age 40. 7 applicants, 43% accepted, 3 enrolled. In 2016, 2 master's awarded. *Degree requirements:* For master's, capstone essay. *Entrance requirements:* For master's, minimum GPA of 3.0, goal statement, 3 letters of recommendation. Additional exam requirements/recommendations for international students: Required—TOEFL (minimum score 600 paper-based, 100 iBT), IELTS (minimum score of 7.0), Michigan English Language Assessment Battery (minimum score of 85), or PTE (minimum score of 68). *Application deadline:* For fall admission, 6/15 for domestic and international students; for spring admission, 11/29 for domestic and international students. Applications are processed on a rolling basis. Application fee: $45 ($70 for international students). Electronic applications accepted. *Expenses:* Tuition, state resident: full-time $10,864; part-time $495 per credit hour. Tuition, nonresident: full-time $18,380; part-time $837 per credit hour. *Financial support:* Career-related internships or fieldwork and Federal Work-Study available. *Unit head:* Dr. David W. Odell-Scott, Associate Dean, 330-672-0271, E-mail: dodellsc@kent.edu. *Application contact:* Richard M. Berrong, Director of Liberal Studies, E-mail: rberrong@kent.edu.
Website: http://www.kent.edu/ccip/graduate-degree-programs

**Lake Forest College,** Graduate Program in Liberal Studies, Lake Forest, IL 60045. Offers American studies (MLS); environmental studies (MLS); history (MLS); Medieval and Renaissance art (MLS); philosophy (MLS); Spanish (MLS); writing (MLS). *Program availability:* Part-time, evening/weekend. *Faculty:* 9 full-time (3 women), 1 part-time/adjunct (0 women). *Students:* 1 full-time (0 women), 38 part-time (20 women); includes 5 minority (1 Black or African American, non-Hispanic/Latino; 2 Asian, non-Hispanic/Latino; 2 Hispanic/Latino). Average age 38. 19 applicants, 53% accepted, 7 enrolled. In 2016, 4 master's awarded. *Degree requirements:* For master's, thesis optional, 8 courses, including at least 3 interdisciplinary seminars. *Entrance requirements:* For master's, transcript, essay, interview. Additional exam requirements/recommendations for international students: Required—TOEFL (minimum score 550 paper-based; 83 iBT); Recommended—IELTS (minimum score 6.5). *Application deadline:* For fall admission, 7/15 priority date for domestic students, 6/1 priority date for international students; for spring admission, 12/1 priority date for domestic students, 10/1 priority date for international students. Applications are processed on a rolling basis. Application fee: $30. *Expenses:* $2,600 per course. *Financial support:* In 2016–17, 2 students received support. Partial tuition grants for full-time teachers available. *Faculty research:* Realigning of the international order; Renaissance women artists; literature of Latin Americans in the U.S.; modern Chinese history; environmental biology. *Unit head:* Prof. D. L. LeMahieu, Director, 847-735-5133, Fax: 847-735-6291, E-mail: lemahieu@lakeforest.edu. *Application contact:* Prof. Carol Gayle, Associate Director, 847-735-5083, Fax: 847-735-6291, E-mail: gayle@lakeforest.edu.
Website: http://www.lakeforest.edu/academics/programs/mls/

**Louisiana State University and Agricultural & Mechanical College,** Graduate School, College of Humanities and Social Sciences, Interdepartmental Program in the Liberal Arts, Baton Rouge, LA 70803. Offers MALA.

**Louisiana State University in Shreveport,** College of Arts and Sciences, Program in Liberal Arts, Shreveport, LA 71115-2399. Offers MA. *Program availability:* Part-time, evening/weekend. *Students:* 5 full-time (2 women), 14 part-time (9 women); includes 6 minority (2 Black or African American, non-Hispanic/Latino; 1 Hispanic/Latino; 3 Two or more races, non-Hispanic/Latino). Average age 36. 10 applicants, 100% accepted, 2 enrolled. In 2016, 6 master's awarded. *Degree requirements:* For master's, comprehensive exam, thesis or alternative. *Entrance requirements:* For master's, interview, minimum GPA of 3.0 during final 2 years of course work, statement of purpose. Additional exam requirements/recommendations for international students: Required—TOEFL (minimum score 550 paper-based; 61 iBT). *Application deadline:* For fall admission, 6/30 for domestic and international students; for spring admission, 11/30 for domestic and international students; for summer admission, 4/30 for domestic and international students. Applications are processed on a rolling basis. Application fee: $20 ($30 for international students). Electronic applications accepted. *Expenses:* Tuition, state resident: full-time $5163; part-time $350 per credit hour. Tuition, nonresident: full-time $15,578; part-time $1038 per credit hour. *Required fees:* $63 per credit hour. Tuition and fees vary according to course load and program. *Financial support:* In 2016–17, 3 students received support, including 2 research assistantships (averaging $3,750 per year). Financial award applicants required to submit FAFSA. *Unit head:* Dr. Helen Taylor, Program Director, 318-797-5211, Fax: 318-797-5358, E-mail: helen.taylor@lsus.edu. *Application contact:* Mary Catherine Harvison, Director of Admissions, 318-797-2400, Fax: 318-797-5286, E-mail: mary.harvison@lsus.edu.

**Loyola University Maryland,** Graduate Programs, Loyola College of Arts and Sciences, Department of Liberal Studies, Baltimore, MD 21210-2699. Offers MA. *Program availability:* Part-time. *Faculty:* 65 full-time (40 women), 26 part-time/adjunct (18 women). *Students:* 18 full-time (15 women); includes 4 minority (2 Black or African American, non-Hispanic/Latino; 1 American Indian or Alaska Native, non-Hispanic/Latino; 1 Two or more races, non-Hispanic/Latino). Average age 33. 4 applicants, 100% accepted, 2 enrolled. In 2016, 4 master's awarded. *Entrance requirements:* For master's, essay, 2 recommendations, transcripts, resume. *Application deadline:* For fall admission, 8/1 priority date for domestic students, 5/1 for international students; for winter admission, 12/1 for domestic students, 9/1 for international students; for spring admission, 5/1 priority date for domestic students, 2/1 for international students. Applications are processed on a rolling basis. Application fee: $60. Electronic applications accepted. *Expenses:* Contact institution. *Financial support:* Application deadline: 4/15; applicants required to submit FAFSA. *Unit head:* Dr. Steven A. Burr, Director of Program Operations/Affiliate Instructor, 410-617-2841, E-mail: liberalstudies@loyola.edu.
Website: http://www.loyola.edu/liberalstudies/

**Madonna University,** Program in Liberal Studies, Livonia, MI 48150-1173. Offers MALS.

**McDaniel College,** Graduate and Professional Studies, Program in Liberal Arts, Westminster, MD 21157-4390. Offers liberal arts (MLA); writing for children and young adults (Postbaccalaureate Certificate). *Program availability:* Part-time, evening/weekend, 100% online. *Faculty:* 2 full-time (both women), 6 part-time/adjunct (4 women). *Students:* 2 full-time (both women), 26 part-time (22 women); includes 3 minority (2 Black or African American, non-Hispanic/Latino; 1 Asian, non-Hispanic/Latino). Average age 41. 22 applicants, 100% accepted. In 2016, 8 master's, 2 other advanced degrees awarded. *Degree requirements:* For master's, final project. *Entrance requirements:* For master's, 3 recommendations. Additional exam requirements/recommendations for international students: Required—TOEFL (minimum score 79 iBT), IELTS (minimum score 6). *Application deadline:* For fall admission, 6/1 priority date for domestic students; for spring admission, 11/1 priority date for domestic students; for summer admission, 3/1 priority date for domestic students. Applications are processed on a rolling basis. Application fee: $75. Electronic applications accepted. *Expenses:* Tuition: Full-time $8370; part-time $465 per credit. *Required fees:* $75 per semester. Tuition and fees vary according to course load, program and reciprocity agreements. *Financial support:* Application deadline: 3/1; applicants required to submit FAFSA. *Unit head:* E-mail: gradadms@mcdaniel.edu. *Application contact:* Crystal L. Perry, Assistant Director, Graduate Enrollment Management, 410-857-2516, Fax: 410-857-2515, E-mail: cperry@mcdaniel.edu.

**Metropolitan State University,** College of Arts and Sciences, St. Paul, MN 55106-5000. Offers computer science (MS); liberal studies (MA); technical communication (MS). *Program availability:* Part-time, evening/weekend. *Entrance requirements:* For master's, minimum GPA of 2.75, resume. Additional exam requirements/recommendations for international students: Required—TOEFL (minimum score 550 paper-based). Electronic applications accepted.

**Mississippi College,** Graduate School, Program in Liberal Studies, Clinton, MS 39058. Offers MLS. *Program availability:* Part-time. *Degree requirements:* For master's, comprehensive exam, thesis optional. *Entrance requirements:* For master's, GRE, minimum GPA of 2.5. Additional exam requirements/recommendations for international students: Recommended—TOEFL, IELTS.

**The New School,** The New School for Social Research, Department of Liberal Studies, New York, NY 10003. Offers MA. *Program availability:* Part-time, evening/weekend. *Faculty:* 5 full-time (2 women), 12 part-time/adjunct (8 women). *Students:* 18 full-time (10 women), 12 part-time (7 women); includes 3 minority (2 Black or African American, non-Hispanic/Latino; 1 Asian, non-Hispanic/Latino), 11 international. Average age 29. 29 applicants, 83% accepted, 5 enrolled. In 2016, 13 master's awarded. *Degree requirements:* For master's, variable foreign language requirement, thesis. *Entrance requirements:* For master's, GRE, letters of recommendation, writing sample, essays, unofficial transcript. Additional exam requirements/recommendations for international students: Required—TOEFL (minimum score 100 iBT), IELTS (minimum score 7), PTE (minimum score 68). *Application deadline:* For fall admission, 5/5 priority date for domestic students, 6/1 priority date for international students; for spring admission, 10/15 priority date for domestic and international students. Applications are processed on a rolling basis. Application fee: $50. Electronic applications accepted. *Expenses:* Contact institution. *Financial support:* Research assistantships, teaching assistantships, Federal Work-Study, and scholarships/grants available. Support available to part-time students. Financial award application deadline: 2/1; financial award applicants required to submit FAFSA. *Faculty research:* Critical media theory and culture; criticism in literature and arts, aesthetics, and gender. *Unit head:* Dr. William Milberg, Dean, The New School for Social Research, 212-229-5777, E-mail: milbergw@newschool.edu. *Application contact:* Dana Messinger, Director of Graduate Admissions, 212-229-5150 Ext. 2300, E-mail: messingd@newschool.edu.
Website: http://www.newschool.edu/nssr/liberal-studies/

**North Carolina State University,** Graduate School, College of Humanities and Social Sciences, Program in Liberal Studies, Raleigh, NC 27695. Offers MA. *Program availability:* Part-time, evening/weekend. *Degree requirements:* For master's, thesis

optional. Electronic applications accepted. *Faculty research:* Humanities, social sciences, sciences.

**North Central College,** School of Graduate and Professional Studies, Program in Liberal Studies, Naperville, IL 60566-7063. Offers culture and society (MALS). *Program availability:* Part-time, evening/weekend. *Faculty:* 8 full-time (5 women), 8 part-time/adjunct (4 women). *Students:* 6 full-time (1 woman), 13 part-time (9 women); includes 5 minority (1 Black or African American, non-Hispanic/Latino; 1 Asian, non-Hispanic/Latino; 3 Hispanic/Latino). Average age 29. 20 applicants, 60% accepted, 8 enrolled. In 2016, 10 master's awarded. *Degree requirements:* For master's, thesis optional, project. *Entrance requirements:* For master's, interview. Additional exam requirements/recommendations for international students: Required—TOEFL (minimum score 550 paper-based; 80 iBT), IELTS (minimum score 6.5). *Application deadline:* For fall admission, 8/15 for domestic students, 7/15 for international students; for winter admission, 12/1 for domestic students, 11/1 for international students; for spring admission, 2/1 for domestic students, 12/1 for international students. Applications are processed on a rolling basis. Application fee: $25. Electronic applications accepted. Application fee is waived when completed online. *Expenses:* Contact institution. *Financial support:* Scholarships/grants available. Support available to part-time students. Financial award applicants required to submit FAFSA. *Unit head:* Dr. Pamela Monaco, Dean of Graduate and Professional Studies, 630-637-5384, E-mail: pjmonaco@noctrl.edu. *Application contact:* Wendy Kulpinski, Director of Graduate and Professional Studies Admission, 630-637-5808, Fax: 630-637-5844, E-mail: wekulpinski@noctrl.edu.
Website: http://northcentralcollege.edu/admission/liberal-studies

**Northern Arizona University,** Graduate College, College of Social and Behavioral Sciences, Program in Sustainable Communities, Flagstaff, AZ 86011. Offers MA. *Program availability:* Part-time. *Degree requirements:* For master's, thesis. *Entrance requirements:* For master's, minimum GPA of 3.0. Additional exam requirements/recommendations for international students: Required—TOEFL (minimum score 550 paper-based; 80 iBT), IELTS (minimum score 7). Electronic applications accepted. *Expenses:* Tuition, state resident: full-time $8971; part-time $444 per credit hour. Tuition, nonresident: full-time $20,958; part-time $1164 per credit hour. *Required fees:* $1018; $644 per credit hour. Tuition and fees vary according to course load, campus/location and program.

**Northern Kentucky University,** Office of Graduate Programs, College of Arts and Sciences, Program in Integrative Studies, Highland Heights, KY 41099. Offers MA. *Program availability:* Part-time, evening/weekend. *Degree requirements:* For master's, thesis or capstone. *Entrance requirements:* For master's, statement of purpose, three letters of reference, resume, minimum GPA of 3.0. Additional exam requirements/recommendations for international students: Required—TOEFL (minimum score 79 iBT); Recommended—IELTS (minimum score 6.5). Electronic applications accepted. *Faculty research:* Industrial/organizational psychology, truancy, athletic health training, motivation, compassion and stress.

**Northwestern University,** School of Professional Studies, Program in Liberal Studies, Evanston, IL 60208. Offers American studies (MA); history (MA); religious and ethical studies (MA).

**Notre Dame of Maryland University,** Graduate Studies, Program in Liberal Studies, Baltimore, MD 21210-2476. Offers MA. *Program availability:* Part-time, evening/weekend. *Degree requirements:* For master's, thesis or alternative. *Entrance requirements:* For master's, minimum GPA of 3.0. Additional exam requirements/recommendations for international students: Required—TOEFL (minimum score 500 paper-based; 61 iBT). Electronic applications accepted.

**Oakland University,** Graduate Study and Lifelong Learning, College of Arts and Sciences, Program in Liberal Studies, Rochester, MI 48309-4401. Offers MA. *Entrance requirements:* For master's, minimum GPA of 3.0. Additional exam requirements/recommendations for international students: Required—TOEFL (minimum score 550 paper-based). Electronic applications accepted.

**Queens College of the City University of New York,** Division of Social Sciences, Program in Liberal Studies, Queens, NY 11367-1597. Offers MA. *Program availability:* Part-time, evening/weekend. *Faculty:* 10 full-time (3 women), 8 part-time/adjunct (2 women). In 2016, 1 master's awarded. *Degree requirements:* For master's, thesis. *Entrance requirements:* For master's, minimum GPA of 3.0. Additional exam requirements/recommendations for international students: Required—TOEFL (minimum score 61 iBT), IELTS (minimum score 5). *Application deadline:* For fall admission, 8/15 for domestic students; for spring admission, 1/15 for domestic students. Applications are processed on a rolling basis. Application fee: $125. Electronic applications accepted. *Expenses:* Tuition, state resident: full-time $5065; part-time $425 per credit. Tuition, nonresident: part-time $780 per credit. *Required fees:* $522; $397 per credit. Part-time tuition and fees vary according to course load and program. *Financial support:* Career-related internships or fieldwork available. Financial award application deadline: 4/1; financial award applicants required to submit FAFSA. *Unit head:* Stephen Grover, 718-997-5270, E-mail: stephen.grover@qc.cuny.edu. *Application contact:* James Jordan, 718-997-5280, E-mail: james.jordan@qc.cuny.edu.

**Reed College,** Graduate Program in Liberal Studies, Portland, OR 97202-8199. Offers MALS. *Program availability:* Part-time-only, evening/weekend. *Faculty:* 13 part-time/adjunct (7 women). *Students:* 23 part-time (13 women); includes 2 minority (both Black or African American, non-Hispanic/Latino). Average age 45. 5 applicants, 20% accepted, 1 enrolled. In 2016, 3 master's awarded. *Degree requirements:* For master's, thesis, oral defense of thesis. *Entrance requirements:* For master's, interview, letters of recommendation, critical essay. Additional exam requirements/recommendations for international students: Recommended—TOEFL. *Application deadline:* For fall admission, 7/1 priority date for domestic students, 5/1 for international students; for spring admission, 12/1 priority date for domestic students, 9/1 for international students; for summer admission, 4/1 for domestic students, 2/1 for international students. Applications are processed on a rolling basis. Application fee: $75. Electronic applications accepted. *Expenses:* $4,690 per one-unit class (4 semester hours). *Financial support:* In 2016–17, 5 students received support. Scholarships/grants and health care benefits available. Support available to part-time students. Financial award application deadline: 5/1; financial award applicants required to submit CSS PROFILE or FAFSA. *Faculty research:* Renaissance space, psychoanalytic tradition, Vladimir Nabokov, Modern Middle East, race in American theatre. *Unit head:* Barbara A. Amen, Director, Graduate Studies, 503-777-7259, Fax: 503-517-7345, E-mail: bamen@reed.edu.
Website: http://www.reed.edu/mals

**Rice University,** Graduate Programs, Susanne M. Glasscock School of Continuing Studies, Houston, TX 77251-1892. Offers MLS. *Program availability:* Part-time, evening/weekend. *Degree requirements:* For master's, thesis or alternative, capstone paper/project. *Entrance requirements:* For master's, bachelor's degree from accredited institution; minimum GPA of 3.0; two letters of recommendation; personal statement; 3 writing samples; current resume. Additional exam requirements/recommendations for international students: Required—TOEFL (minimum score 600 paper-based; 90 iBT). *Expenses:* Contact institution.

## Liberal Studies

**Rollins College,** Hamilton Holt School, Master of Liberal Studies Program, Winter Park, FL 32789. Offers MLS. *Program availability:* Part-time, evening/weekend. *Faculty:* 5 full-time (1 woman), 1 (woman) part-time/adjunct. *Students:* 3 full-time (2 women), 47 part-time (29 women); includes 8 minority (4 Black or African American, non-Hispanic/Latino; 4 Hispanic/Latino), 2 international. Average age 43. 19 applicants, 79% accepted, 14 enrolled. In 2016, 4 master's awarded. *Degree requirements:* For master's, thesis. *Entrance requirements:* For master's, official transcripts, two letters of recommendation, essay. Additional exam requirements/recommendations for international students: Required—TOEFL (minimum score 550 paper-based; 80 iBT). *Application deadline:* For fall admission, 4/1 for domestic students; for spring admission, 12/1 for domestic students. Application fee: $50. *Expenses:* $479 per credit hour. *Financial support:* In 2016–17, 25 students received support. Federal Work-Study, scholarships/grants, and unspecified assistantships available. Support available to part-time students. Financial award applicants required to submit FAFSA. *Unit head:* Dr. Patricia Lancaster, Faculty Director, 407-646-2237, Fax: 407-646-2363. *Application contact:* Carmen Rasnick, Graduate Coordinator, 407-646-2653, Fax: 407-646-1551, E-mail: crasnick@rollins.edu. Website: http://www.rollins.edu/holt/graduate/mls.html

**Rutgers University–Camden,** Graduate School of Arts and Sciences, Program in Liberal Studies, Camden, NJ 08102. Offers MALS. *Program availability:* Part-time, evening/weekend. *Degree requirements:* For master's, thesis, 30 credits. *Entrance requirements:* For master's, 2 letters of recommendation, writing sample, statement of personal, professional and academic goals. Additional exam requirements/recommendations for international students: Required—TOEFL, IELTS. Electronic applications accepted. *Faculty research:* Psychology, English, history, philosophy, religion.

**St. Edward's University,** New College, Program in Liberal Arts, Austin, TX 78704. Offers humanities (MLA); liberal arts (MLA, Certificate). *Program availability:* Part-time, evening/weekend. *Students:* 11 full-time (7 women), 28 part-time (20 women); includes 15 minority (2 Black or African American, non-Hispanic/Latino; 1 American Indian or Alaska Native, non-Hispanic/Latino; 1 Asian, non-Hispanic/Latino; 10 Hispanic/Latino; 1 Two or more races, non-Hispanic/Latino), 1 international. Average age 36. 26 applicants, 69% accepted, 8 enrolled. In 2016, 13 master's awarded. *Degree requirements:* For master's, 33 hours of coursework with minimum cumulative GPA of 3.0. *Entrance requirements:* For master's, minimum GPA of 2.75 in last 60 hours of study, interview. Additional exam requirements/recommendations for international students: Required—TOEFL (minimum score 79 iBT), IELTS (minimum score 6). *Application deadline:* For fall admission, 6/1 priority date for domestic and international students; for spring admission, 10/1 priority date for domestic and international students; for summer admission, 3/1 priority date for domestic and international students. Applications are processed on a rolling basis. Application fee: $50. Electronic applications accepted. *Expenses:* Tuition: Full-time $25,092; part-time $1394 per credit hour. *Required fees:* $75 per trimester. Full-time tuition and fees vary according to course load and program. *Unit head:* Dr. Ramsey Fowler, MLA Program Director/Associate Professor of English, 512-448-8736, Fax: 512-448-8492, E-mail: ramseyf@stewards.edu. *Application contact:* Dave Bralower, Director of Graduate Admission, 512-233-1424, Fax: 512-464-8877, E-mail: davidcb@stedwards.edu. Website: http://www.stedwards.edu

**St. John's College,** Graduate Institute, Annapolis, MD 21401. Offers MALA. *Program availability:* Evening/weekend. *Degree requirements:* For master's, thesis optional. *Entrance requirements:* For master's, bachelor's degree. Additional exam requirements/recommendations for international students: Required—TOEFL (minimum score 650 paper-based; 112 iBT), TWE (minimum score 5). Electronic applications accepted.

**St. John's College,** Graduate Institute in Liberal Education, Program in Liberal Arts, Santa Fe, NM 87505. Offers MA. *Program availability:* Evening/weekend. *Entrance requirements:* For master's, 2 letters of recommendation. Additional exam requirements/recommendations for international students: Required—TOEFL, TWE.

**St. John's University,** St. John's College of Liberal Arts and Sciences, Program in Liberal Studies, Queens, NY 11439. Offers MA. *Program availability:* Part-time, evening/weekend. *Degree requirements:* For master's, capstone project. *Entrance requirements:* For master's, minimum GPA of 3.0, personal essay, 2 letters of recommendation, 6 credit hours in area of concentration, bachelor's degree. Additional exam requirements/recommendations for international students: Required—TOEFL (minimum score 600 paper-based; 100 iBT), IELTS (minimum score 7). Electronic applications accepted.

**St. Norbert College,** Master of Arts in Liberal Studies Program, De Pere, WI 54115-2099. Offers MA. *Program availability:* Part-time-only, evening/weekend. *Faculty:* 4 part-time/adjunct (3 women). *Students:* 14 part-time (11 women); includes 1 minority (Hispanic/Latino). Average age 40. 2 applicants, 100% accepted, 1 enrolled. In 2016, 4 master's awarded. *Degree requirements:* For master's, thesis. *Application deadline:* Applications are processed on a rolling basis. Application fee: $50. Electronic applications accepted. *Expenses:* Tuition: Part-time $675 per credit. Tuition and fees vary according to program. *Financial support:* Applicants required to submit FAFSA. *Unit head:* Dr. Howard Ebert, Director, 920-403-3956, Fax: 920-403-4086, E-mail: howard.ebert@snc.edu. *Application contact:* Dinah Grassel, Program Coordinator, 920-403-3957, Fax: 920-403-4086, E-mail: dinah.grassel@snc.edu. Website: http://www.snc.edu/mls/

**San Diego State University,** Graduate and Research Affairs, College of Arts and Letters, Program in Liberal Arts and Sciences, San Diego, CA 92182. Offers MA. *Program availability:* Part-time, evening/weekend. *Degree requirements:* For master's, thesis. *Entrance requirements:* For master's, GRE General Test. Additional exam requirements/recommendations for international students: Required—TOEFL. Electronic applications accepted.

**San Francisco State University,** Division of Graduate Studies, College of Liberal and Creative Arts, School of Humanities and Liberal Studies, San Francisco, CA 94132-1722. Offers MA. *Program availability:* Part-time, evening/weekend. *Expenses:* Tuition, state resident: full-time $6738. Tuition, nonresident: full-time $15,666. *Required fees:* $1012. Tuition and fees vary according to degree level and program. *Unit head:* Dr. Christina Ruotolo, Director, 415-338-1099, E-mail: ruotolo@sfsu.edu. *Application contact:* Prof. Laura Garcia-Moreno, Graduate Coordinator, 415-338-1295, E-mail: lgmoreno@sfsu.edu. Website: http://humanities.sfsu.edu/

**Simon Fraser University,** Office of Graduate Studies and Postdoctoral Fellows, Faculty of Arts and Social Sciences, Program in Liberal Studies, Vancouver, BC V6B 5K3, Canada. Offers MALS. *Program availability:* Part-time, evening/weekend, online learning. *Faculty:* 15 full-time (7 women). *Students:* 11 full-time (9 women), 39 part-time (28 women). 21 applicants, 86% accepted, 17 enrolled. In 2016, 10 master's awarded. *Degree requirements:* For master's, thesis or alternative. *Entrance requirements:* For master's, minimum GPA of 3.0 (on scale of 4.33) or 3.33 based on last 60 credits of undergraduate courses. Additional exam requirements/recommendations for international students: Recommended—TOEFL (minimum score 580 paper-based; 93 iBT), IELTS (minimum score 7), TWE (minimum score 5). *Application deadline:* For fall admission, 4/30 for domestic and international students; for spring admission, 4/1 for domestic students. Application fee: $90 ($125 for international students). Electronic

applications accepted. *Financial support:* In 2016–17, 2 students received support, including 2 fellowships (averaging $6,250 per year); scholarships/grants also available. *Faculty research:* Humanities, art history and culture, women's studies, literature, philosophy. *Unit head:* Dr. Gary McCarron, Director, 778-782-5152, E-mail: mals-grad-chair@sfu.ca. *Application contact:* Sandra Zink, Graduate Secretary, 778-782-5152, E-mail: glsp@sfu.ca. Website: http://www.gls.sfu.ca/

**Southern Methodist University,** Annette Caldwell Simmons School of Education and Human Development, Program in Liberal Studies, Dallas, TX 75275. Offers MLS.

**Spring Hill College,** Graduate Programs, Program in Liberal Arts, Mobile, AL 36608-1791. Offers fine arts (MLA); history and social science (MLA); leadership and ethics (MLA, Postbaccalaureate Certificate); literature (MLA); studio art (Postbaccalaureate Certificate). *Program availability:* Part-time, evening/weekend. *Faculty:* 5 full-time (0 women), 2 part-time/adjunct (1 woman). *Students:* 2 full-time (1 woman), 31 part-time (10 women); includes 4 minority (3 Black or African American, non-Hispanic/Latino; 1 Hispanic/Latino), 3 international. Average age 35. In 2016, 7 master's, 1 other advanced degree awarded. *Degree requirements:* For master's, capstone course, completion of program within 6 years of initial admittance. *Entrance requirements:* For master's, bachelor's degree with minimum undergraduate GPA of 3.0 or graduate/professional degree. Additional exam requirements/recommendations for international students: Required—TOEFL (minimum score 550 paper-based; 80 iBT), IELTS (minimum score 6.5), CPE or CAE (minimum score C), Michigan English Language Assessment Battery (minimum score 90). *Application deadline:* For fall admission, 8/1 priority date for domestic and international students; for spring admission, 12/1 priority date for domestic and international students. Applications are processed on a rolling basis. Application fee: $25 ($35 for international students). Electronic applications accepted. *Expenses:* Contact institution. *Financial support:* Applicants required to submit FAFSA. *Unit head:* Dr. Thomas J. Hoffman, Director, 251-380-4184, Fax: 251-460-2115, E-mail: thoffman@shc.edu. *Application contact:* Robert Stewart, Vice President of Enrollment, 251-380-3030, Fax: 251-460-2186, E-mail: rstewart@shc.edu. Website: http://ug.shc.edu/graduate-degrees/master-liberal-arts/

**State University of New York College at Old Westbury,** Program in Liberal Studies, Old Westbury, NY 11568-0210. Offers MA. *Program availability:* Part-time, evening/weekend. *Faculty:* 2 full-time (both women). *Students:* 5 full-time (1 woman), 4 part-time (3 women); includes 4 minority (1 Black or African American, non-Hispanic/Latino; 1 Asian, non-Hispanic/Latino; 2 Hispanic/Latino). Average age 38. 10 applicants, 80% accepted, 5 enrolled. In 2016, 1 master's awarded. *Degree requirements:* For master's, thesis project or internship. *Application deadline:* Applications are processed on a rolling basis. Application fee: $50. Electronic applications accepted. *Expenses:* Tuition, state resident: full-time $10,870; part-time $453 per credit. Tuition, nonresident: full-time $22,210; part-time $925 per credit. *Required fees:* $24.35 per credit. $76 per semester. Tuition and fees vary according to course load. *Financial support:* Applicants required to submit FAFSA. *Unit head:* Dr. Amanda Frisken, Associate Professor, American Studies, 516-876-4853, E-mail: friskena@oldwestbury.edu. *Application contact:* Philip D'Angelo, Graduate Admissions Office, 516-876-3073, E-mail: enroll@oldwestbury.edu.

**State University of New York Empire State College,** School for Graduate Studies, Program in Liberal Studies, Saratoga Springs, NY 12866-4391. Offers MA. *Program availability:* Part-time, evening/weekend, online learning. *Degree requirements:* For master's, thesis, final project. *Entrance requirements:* Additional exam requirements/recommendations for international students: Required—TOEFL (minimum score 600 paper-based). Electronic applications accepted.

**Stony Brook University, State University of New York,** School of Professional Development, Stony Brook, NY 11794-443. Offers biology (MAT); chemistry (MAT); coaching (Graduate Certificate); earth science (MAT); educational computing (Graduate Certificate); educational leadership (Advanced Certificate); English (MAT); environmental management (MPS, Graduate Certificate); French (MAT); German (MAT); higher education administration (MA, Certificate); human resource management (MS, Graduate Certificate); industrial management (Graduate Certificate); information systems management (Graduate Certificate); Italian (MAT); liberal studies (MA); mathematics (MAT); operations research (Graduate Certificate); physics (MAT); school district business leadership (Advanced Certificate); social studies (MAT); Spanish (MAT). *Program availability:* Part-time, evening/weekend, online learning. *Faculty:* 4 full-time (3 women), 77 part-time/adjunct (34 women). *Students:* 197 full-time (125 women), 965 part-time (674 women); includes 222 minority (79 Black or African American, non-Hispanic/Latino; 2 American Indian or Alaska Native, non-Hispanic/Latino; 35 Asian, non-Hispanic/Latino; 87 Hispanic/Latino; 1 Native Hawaiian or other Pacific Islander, non-Hispanic/Latino; 18 Two or more races, non-Hispanic/Latino), 5 international. Average age 33. 462 applicants, 87% accepted, 317 enrolled. In 2016, 348 master's, 159 other advanced degrees awarded. *Degree requirements:* For master's, one foreign language, thesis or alternative. *Entrance requirements:* Additional exam requirements/recommendations for international students: Required—TOEFL (minimum score 85 iBT). *Application deadline:* For fall admission, 1/15 for domestic students, 6/1 for international students; for spring admission, 10/1 for domestic and international students. Applications are processed on a rolling basis. Application fee: $100. *Expenses:* Contact institution. *Financial support:* Fellowships, research assistantships, teaching assistantships, and career-related internships or fieldwork available. Support available to part-time students. *Unit head:* Dr. Ken Lindblom, Dean, 631-632-7049, Fax: 631-632-9046, E-mail: kenneth.lindblom@stonybrook.edu. *Application contact:* Melissa Jordan, Assistant Dean, 631-632-7751, E-mail: melissa.jordan@stonybrook.edu. Website: http://www.stonybrook.edu/spd/

**Texas A&M University–Central Texas,** Graduate Studies and Research, Killeen, TX 76549. Offers accounting (MS); business administration (MBA); clinical mental health counseling (MS); criminal justice (MCJ); curriculum and instruction (M Ed); educational administration (M Ed); educational psychology - experimental psychology (MS); history (MA); human resource management (MS); information systems (MS); liberal studies (MS); management and leadership (MS); marriage and family therapy (MS); mathematics (MS); political science (MA); school counseling (M Ed); school psychology (Ed S).

**Texas Christian University,** Master of Liberal Arts Program, Fort Worth, TX 76129. Offers MLA. *Program availability:* Part-time, evening/weekend, 100% online. *Faculty:* 12 part-time/adjunct (1 woman). *Students:* 77 full-time (40 women), 31 part-time (17 women); includes 27 minority (13 Black or African American, non-Hispanic/Latino; 1 Asian, non-Hispanic/Latino; 11 Hispanic/Latino; 1 Native Hawaiian or other Pacific Islander, non-Hispanic/Latino; 1 Two or more races, non-Hispanic/Latino), 4 international. Average age 32. 61 applicants, 98% accepted, 43 enrolled. In 2016, 35 master's awarded. *Entrance requirements:* Additional exam requirements/recommendations for international students: Required—TOEFL (minimum score 550 paper-based; 80 iBT). *Application deadline:* For fall admission, 8/15 for domestic students, 6/1 for international students; for spring admission, 1/15 for domestic students, 11/1 for international students. Applications are processed on a rolling basis. Application fee: $60. Electronic applications accepted. *Expenses:* $850 per semester hour tuition, $112 fee per online course. *Financial support:* In 2016–17, 50 students received support. Scholarships/grants, unspecified assistantships, and employee tuition benefits available. Financial award applicants required to submit FAFSA. *Unit head:* Dr. Bonnie Melhart, Associate Provost/Dean of University Programs, 817-257-7104, Fax: 817-257-7484, E-mail: b.melhart@tcu.edu. *Application contact:* Anita Unger, Graduate Program Coordinator, 817-257-7515, Fax: 817-257-7484, E-mail: a.unger@tcu.edu. Website: http://www.mla.tcu.edu/

**Thomas Edison State University,** Heavin School of Arts and Sciences, Program in Liberal Studies, Trenton, NJ 08608. Offers MALS. *Program availability:* Part-time, online learning. *Degree requirements:* For master's, final project. *Entrance requirements:* For master's, bachelor's degree from a regionally-accredited college or university; minimum 2 letters of recommendation; 3-5 years of related working experience; current resume. Additional exam requirements/recommendations for international students: Required—TOEFL (minimum score 550 paper-based; 79 iBT). Electronic applications accepted.

**Towson University,** Program in Professional Studies, Towson, MD 21252-0001. Offers art history (MA); individualized plan (MA). *Program availability:* Part-time, evening/weekend. *Students:* 10 full-time (6 women), 13 part-time (11 women); includes 5 minority (4 Black or African American, non-Hispanic/Latino; 1 Two or more races, non-Hispanic/Latino). *Degree requirements:* For master's, thesis optional. *Entrance requirements:* For master's, minimum GPA of 3.0, essay. *Application deadline:* Applications are processed on a rolling basis. Application fee: $45. Electronic applications accepted. *Expenses:* Tuition, state resident: full-time $7580; part-time $379 per unit. Tuition, nonresident: full-time $15,700; part-time $785 per unit. *Required fees:* $2480. *Financial support:* Application deadline: 4/1. *Unit head:* Dr. James Smith, Graduate Program Director, 410-704-4620, E-mail: jmsmith@towson.edu. *Application contact:* Coverley Beidleman, Assistant Director of Graduate Admissions, 410-704-2113, Fax: 410-704-3030, E-mail: grads@towson.edu.
Website: http://www.towson.edu/cla/departments/interdisciplinary/grad/professional/

**Tulane University,** Program in Liberal Arts, New Orleans, LA 70118-5669. Offers MLA. *Program availability:* Part-time. *Degree requirements:* For master's, thesis. *Entrance requirements:* For master's, GRE General Test, minimum B average in undergraduate course work. Additional exam requirements/recommendations for international students: Required—TOEFL. *Expenses: Tuition:* Full-time $50,920; part-time $2829 per credit hour. *Required fees:* $2040; $44.50 per credit hour. $580 per term. Tuition and fees vary according to course load, degree level and program.

**University at Albany, State University of New York,** College of Arts and Sciences, Liberal Studies Program, Albany, NY 12222-0001. Offers MALS. *Faculty:* 4 full-time (1 woman), 1 part-time/adjunct (0 women). *Students:* 1 (woman) full-time, 1 part-time (0 women), 1 international. *Entrance requirements:* Additional exam requirements/recommendations for international students: Required—TOEFL (minimum score 550 paper-based). *Application deadline:* For fall admission, 4/1 for domestic students, 5/1 for international students. Applications are processed on a rolling basis. Application fee: $75. Electronic applications accepted. *Expenses:* Tuition, state resident: full-time $10,870; part-time $453 per credit hour. Tuition, nonresident: full-time $22,210; part-time $925 per credit hour. *International tuition:* $21,550 full-time. *Required fees:* $1864; $96 per credit hour. *Financial support:* Application deadline: 4/1. *Unit head:* Dr. Kir Kuiken, Jr., Interim Director, 518-442-4069, E-mail: kkuiken@albany.edu. *Application contact:* Michael DeRensis, Director, Graduate Admissions, 518-442-3980, Fax: 518-442-3922, E-mail: graduate@albany.edu.
Website: http://www.albany.edu/liberal_studies/

**University of Chicago,** Graham School of Continuing Liberal and Professional Studies, Program in Liberal Arts, Chicago, IL 60637. Offers MLA. *Program availability:* Part-time, evening/weekend. *Students:* 4 full-time (2 women), 46 part-time (23 women); includes 13 minority (6 Black or African American, non-Hispanic/Latino; 6 Asian, non-Hispanic/Latino; 1 Hispanic/Latino), 3 international. 22 applicants, 82% accepted, 14 enrolled. *Entrance requirements:* Additional exam requirements/recommendations for international students: Required—TOEFL (minimum score 104 iBT), IELTS (minimum score 7). *Application deadline:* For fall admission, 9/15 for domestic and international students; for spring admission, 3/3 for domestic and international students. Application fee: $75. Electronic applications accepted. *Unit head:* Tim Murphy, Assistant Director, 773-834-3233. *Application contact:* Bonni Van Eck, Admissions Coordinator, E-mail: mla@uchicago.edu.
Website: https://grahamschool.uchicago.edu/credit/master-liberal-arts/index

**University of Delaware,** College of Arts and Sciences, Program in Liberal Studies, Newark, DE 19716. Offers MALS. *Program availability:* Part-time, evening/weekend. *Degree requirements:* For master's, thesis. Electronic applications accepted. *Faculty research:* British Raj, medical and scientific ethics, Jewish-American novelists, intellectual freedom.

**University of Detroit Mercy,** College of Liberal Arts and Education, Detroit, MI 48221. Offers addiction counseling (MA); addiction studies (Certificate); clinical mental health counseling (MA); clinical psychology (MA, PhD); computer and information systems (MS); criminal justice (MA); curriculum and instruction (MA); economics (MA); educational administration (MA); financial economics (MA); industrial/organizational psychology (MA); information assurance (MS); intelligence analysis (MA); liberal studies (MALS); religious studies (MA); school counseling (MA, Certificate); school psychology (Spec); security administration (MS); special education: emotionally impaired/behaviorally disordered (MA); special education: learning disabilities (MA). *Program availability:* Part-time, evening/weekend. *Degree requirements:* For doctorate, departmental qualifying exam. *Faculty research:* Psychology of aging, history of technology, Renaissance humanism, U.S. and Japanese economic relations.

**University of Memphis,** Graduate School, University College, Memphis, TN 38152. Offers human resources (MPS); liberal studies (MALS, Graduate Certificate); strategic leadership (MPS, Graduate Certificate); training and development (MPS). *Program availability:* Part-time, evening/weekend. *Faculty:* 3 full-time (1 woman), 2 part-time/adjunct (0 women). *Students:* 25 full-time (14 women), 98 part-time (71 women); includes 85 minority (76 Black or African American, non-Hispanic/Latino; 1 Asian, non-Hispanic/Latino; 5 Hispanic/Latino; 3 Two or more races, non-Hispanic/Latino), 2 international. Average age 38. 59 applicants, 73% accepted, 29 enrolled. In 2016, 53 master's, 4 other advanced degrees awarded. *Degree requirements:* For master's, comprehensive exam, thesis (for some programs). *Entrance requirements:* For master's, GRE (for MPS), resume, letters of recommendation, personal essay, interview, minimum undergraduate GPA of 2.75 (for MALS); portfolio in lieu of GRE (for MPS applicants with substantial professional work experience); for Graduate Certificate, essay, letter of recommendation. Additional exam requirements/recommendations for international students: Required—TOEFL (minimum score 550 paper-based; 79 iBT). *Application deadline:* For fall admission, 7/1 for domestic students, 5/1 for international students; for spring admission, 11/1 for domestic students, 9/15 for international students. Applications are processed on a rolling basis. Application fee: $35 ($60 for international students). Electronic applications accepted. *Expenses:* $5,231.50 per semester full-time in-state, $9,623.50 full-time out-of-state. *Financial support:* In 2016–17, 123 students received support, including 2 research assistantships with full tuition reimbursements available (averaging $17,000 per year), 3 teaching assistantships with tuition reimbursements available (averaging $11,334 per year); Federal Work-Study, scholarships/grants, and unspecified assistantships also available. Financial award

application deadline: 2/3; financial award applicants required to submit FAFSA. *Faculty research:* Media ethics, history of psychiatry, public relations. *Unit head:* Dr. Dan Lattimore, Dean, 901-678-2991, E-mail: dlattimr@memphis.edu. *Application contact:* Dr. Colin Chapell, Graduate Coordinator, 901-678-4171, Fax: 901-678-2971, E-mail: cbshpell@memphis.edu.
Website: http://www.memphis.edu/univcoll

**University of Miami,** Graduate School, College of Arts and Sciences, Program in Liberal Studies, Coral Gables, FL 33124. Offers MALS. *Program availability:* Part-time, evening/weekend. *Degree requirements:* For master's, thesis or alternative. *Entrance requirements:* For master's, minimum GPA of 3.0. Additional exam requirements/recommendations for international students: Required—TOEFL. Electronic applications accepted. *Expenses:* Contact institution.

**University of Minnesota, Duluth,** Graduate School, College of Liberal Arts, Department of Sociology/Anthropology, Liberal Studies Program, Duluth, MN 55812-2496. Offers MLS. *Program availability:* Part-time, evening/weekend. *Faculty research:* Nature of knowledge, cultural studies, language, literature, sociology.

**University of New Hampshire,** Graduate School, College of Liberal Arts, Program in Liberal Studies, Durham, NH 03824. Offers MALS. *Entrance requirements:* Additional exam requirements/recommendations for international students: Required—TOEFL (minimum score 550 paper-based; 80 iBT). Electronic applications accepted.

**University of North Carolina at Asheville,** Master of Liberal Arts and Sciences Program, Asheville, NC 28804-3299. Offers climate change and society (Graduate Certificate); environmental and cultural sustainability (Graduate Certificate). *Program availability:* Part-time, evening/weekend. *Faculty:* 5 full-time (1 woman), 4 part-time/adjunct (0 women). *Students:* 2 full-time (1 woman), 19 part-time (9 women); includes 2 minority (1 Black or African American, non-Hispanic/Latino; 1 Asian, non-Hispanic/Latino). Average age 43. 18 applicants, 83% accepted, 8 enrolled. In 2016, 19 master's awarded. *Degree requirements:* For master's, thesis. *Entrance requirements:* For master's and Graduate Certificate, essay, 3 letters of recommendation, official transcripts. Additional exam requirements/recommendations for international students: Required—TOEFL (minimum score 85 iBT) or IELTS (6.5). *Application deadline:* For fall admission, 4/15 for domestic students; for spring admission, 11/15 for domestic students. Applications are processed on a rolling basis. Application fee: $75. Electronic applications accepted. *Expenses:* Tuition, state resident: full-time $4818. Tuition, nonresident: full-time $20,820. *Required fees:* $2936. Part-time tuition and fees vary according to course load. *Financial support:* Health care benefits available. Financial award application deadline: 5/1; financial award applicants required to submit FAFSA. *Unit head:* Gerard Voos, Director, Master of Liberal Arts and Sciences Program and the Asheville Graduate Center, 828-232-5040, E-mail: gvoos@unca.edu. *Application contact:* Jordan Dolfi, Program Associate, Master of Liberal Arts and Sciences Program and the Asheville Graduate Center, 828-251-6099, E-mail: jdolfi@unca.edu.
Website: https://mlas.unca.edu/

**The University of North Carolina at Charlotte,** College of Liberal Arts and Sciences, Interdisciplinary Liberal Arts and Sciences Programs, Charlotte, NC 28223-0001. Offers gender, sexuality, and women's studies (Graduate Certificate); gerontology (MA, Graduate Certificate); Latin American studies (MA); liberal studies (MA); organizational science (PhD); public policy (PhD). *Program availability:* Part-time, evening/weekend. *Faculty:* 1 (woman) part-time/adjunct. *Students:* 65 full-time (49 women), 61 part-time (50 women); includes 31 minority (11 Black or African American, non-Hispanic/Latino; 1 American Indian or Alaska Native, non-Hispanic/Latino; 2 Asian, non-Hispanic/Latino; 16 Hispanic/Latino; 1 Two or more races, non-Hispanic/Latino), 15 international. Average age 32. 128 applicants, 41% accepted, 40 enrolled. In 2016, 15 master's, 12 doctorates, 7 other advanced degrees awarded. *Degree requirements:* For master's, comprehensive exam (for some programs), thesis (for some programs), practicum, project; for doctorate, comprehensive exam, thesis/dissertation; for Graduate Certificate, practicum (for gerontology). *Entrance requirements:* For master's, GRE General Test or MAT, bachelor's degree from accredited college or university; official transcripts of all previous academic work attempted beyond high school; minimum overall GPA of 3.0 on applicant's previous work beyond high school; statement of purpose; recommendation letters; for doctorate, GRE or GMAT, statement of purpose discussing interest in program and objectives for pursuing degree, current resume or curriculum vitae, unofficial transcripts; for Graduate Certificate, bachelor's degree from accredited university and either be enrolled in and in good standing in a graduate degree program at UNC Charlotte or have a minimum undergraduate GPA of 3.0. Additional exam requirements/recommendations for international students: Required—TOEFL (minimum score 523 paper-based, 70 iBT) or IELTS (6.5). *Application deadline:* For fall admission, 2/15 for domestic and international students; for spring admission, 10/1 for domestic and international students; for summer admission, 4/1 for domestic and international students. Applications are processed on a rolling basis. Application fee: $75. Electronic applications accepted. *Expenses:* Tuition, state resident: full-time $4252. Tuition, nonresident: full-time $17,423. *Required fees:* $3026. Tuition and fees vary according to course load and program. *Financial support:* In 2016–17, 26 students received support, including 17 research assistantships (averaging $12,840 per year), 7 teaching assistantships (averaging $14,442 per year); career-related internships or fieldwork, institutionally sponsored loans, scholarships/grants, unspecified assistantships, and administrative assistantships also available. Support available to part-time students. Financial award application deadline: 3/1; financial award applicants required to submit FAFSA. *Unit head:* Dr. Nancy A. Gutierrez, Dean, 704-687-0081, E-mail: ngutierr@uncc.edu. *Application contact:* Kathy B. Giddings, Director of Graduate Admissions, 704-687-5503, Fax: 704-687-3279, E-mail: gradadm@uncc.edu.
Website: http://clas.uncc.edu/academics

**The University of North Carolina at Greensboro,** Graduate School, Program in Liberal Studies, Greensboro, NC 27412-5001. Offers MALS. Electronic applications accepted.

**The University of North Carolina Wilmington,** College of Arts and Sciences, Graduate Liberal Studies Program, Wilmington, NC 28403-3297. Offers MA. *Program availability:* Part-time. *Faculty:* 5 full-time (3 women). *Students:* 9 full-time (7 women), 30 part-time (24 women); includes 7 minority (5 Black or African American, non-Hispanic/Latino; 2 Hispanic/Latino). Average age 38. 13 applicants, 85% accepted, 8 enrolled. In 2016, 12 master's awarded. *Degree requirements:* For master's, final project. *Entrance requirements:* For master's, minimum GPA of 3.0 in undergraduate work, essay, 3 letters of recommendation. Additional exam requirements/recommendations for international students: Required—TOEFL (minimum score 79 iBT), IELTS (minimum score 6.5). *Application deadline:* For fall admission, 6/13 for domestic students; for spring admission, 11/5 for domestic students; for summer admission, 3/14 for domestic students. Applications are processed on a rolling basis. Application fee: $60. Electronic applications accepted. *Expenses:* Contact institution. *Financial support:* Scholarships/grants, unspecified assistantships, and out-of-state tuition remission available. Financial award application deadline: 3/15; financial award applicants required to submit FAFSA. *Unit head:* Dr. Patricia Turrisi, 910-962-3299, Fax: 910-962-3542, E-mail: turrisip@uncw.edu. *Application contact:* Dr. Ashley Hudson, Assistant Director, 910-962-2427, Fax: 910-962-3542, E-mail: hudsona@uncw.edu.
Website: http://www.uncw.edu/gls/

## Liberal Studies

**University of Oklahoma,** College of Liberal Studies, Norman, OK 73072. Offers administrative leadership (Graduate Certificate); corrections management (Graduate Certificate); criminal justice (MS); government and military leadership (MA); human and health services administration (MA), including human and health services administration, integrated studies; liberal studies (MPS); organizational leadership (MA); restorative justice administration (Graduate Certificate); volunteer and non-profit leadership (MA). *Program availability:* Part-time, online only, 100% online, blended/hybrid learning. *Faculty:* 13 full-time (7 women), 1 part-time/adjunct (0 women). *Students:* 74 full-time (48 women), 598 part-time (289 women); includes 175 minority (45 Black or African American, non-Hispanic/Latino; 39 American Indian or Alaska Native, non-Hispanic/Latino; 8 Asian, non-Hispanic/Latino; 46 Hispanic/Latino; 1 Native Hawaiian or other Pacific Islander, non-Hispanic/Latino; 36 Two or more races, non-Hispanic/Latino), 2 international. Average age 35. 191 applicants, 95% accepted, 120 enrolled. In 2016, 192 master's, 6 other advanced degrees awarded. *Degree requirements:* For master's, comprehensive exam, thesis optional, 33 credit hours; project/internship (for museum studies); for Graduate Certificate, 12 credit hours. *Entrance requirements:* For master's and Graduate Certificate, minimum GPA of 3.0 in last 60 undergraduate hours; statement of goals; resume. Additional exam requirements/recommendations for international students: Required—TOEFL (minimum score 79 iBT) or IELTS (minimum score 6.5). *Application deadline:* For fall admission, 7/1 for domestic and international students; for winter admission, 12/1 for domestic and international students; for spring admission, 5/1 for domestic and international students. Applications are processed on a rolling basis. Application fee: $50 ($100 for international students). Electronic applications accepted. *Expenses:* Tuition, state resident: full-time $4886; part-time $203.60 per credit hour. Tuition, nonresident: full-time $18,989; part-time $791.20 per credit hour. *Required fees:* $3283; $126.25 per credit hour. $126.50 per semester. *Financial support:* In 2016–17, 124 students received support. Career-related internships or fieldwork, institutionally sponsored loans, scholarships/grants, health care benefits, and tuition waivers available. Support available to part-time students. Financial award application deadline: 6/1; financial award applicants required to submit FAFSA. *Faculty research:* Management and leadership; policing and corrections management; neuro-psychology of addiction; disproportionate minority contact; ethnic identity and nationalism. *Unit head:* Dr. Martha L. Banz, Associate Provost for Continuing Education/Interim Dean, College of Liberal Studies, 405-325-1061, Fax: 405-325-7132, E-mail: mlbanz@ou.edu. *Application contact:* Michelle Shults, Academic Advisement Services Coordinator, 405-325-2928, Fax: 405-325-7132, E-mail: mshults@ou.edu.
Website: http://www.ou.edu/cls/html

**University of Pennsylvania,** School of Arts and Sciences, College of Liberal and Professional Studies, Philadelphia, PA 19104. Offers applied geosciences (MSAG); applied positive psychology (MAP); chemical sciences (MCS); environmental studies (MES); individualized study (MLA); liberal arts (M Phil); medical physics (MMP); organization dynamics (M Phil). *Students:* 143 full-time (75 women), 337 part-time (189 women); includes 90 minority (28 Black or African American, non-Hispanic/Latino; 2 American Indian or Alaska Native, non-Hispanic/Latino; 22 Asian, non-Hispanic/Latino; 26 Hispanic/Latino; 12 Two or more races, non-Hispanic/Latino), 66 international. Average age 35. 618 applicants, 51% accepted, 231 enrolled. In 2016, 161 master's awarded. *Expenses:* Tuition: Full-time $31,068; part-time $5762 per course. *Required fees:* $3200; $336 per course. Full-time tuition and fees vary according to degree level, program and student level. Part-time tuition and fees vary according to course load, degree level and program. *Unit head:* Nora Lewis, Vice Dean, Professional and Liberal Education, 215-898-7326, E-mail: nlewis@sas.upenn.edu.
Website: http://www.sas.upenn.edu/lps/graduate

**University of St. Thomas,** Program in Liberal Arts, Houston, TX 77006-4696. Offers MLA. *Program availability:* Part-time, evening/weekend. *Faculty:* 24 full-time (9 women), 13 part-time/adjunct (7 women). *Students:* 9 full-time (7 women), 50 part-time (41 women); includes 31 minority (10 Black or African American, non-Hispanic/Latino; 2 Asian, non-Hispanic/Latino; 19 Hispanic/Latino). Average age 38. 18 applicants, 100% accepted, 11 enrolled. In 2016, 35 master's awarded. *Degree requirements:* For master's, thesis optional, capstone, minimum cumulative GPA of 3.0. *Entrance requirements:* For master's, 4-year undergraduate degree with minimum GPA of 2.5, essay, 2 letters of recommendation, interview. Additional exam requirements/recommendations for international students: Required—TOEFL (minimum score 100 iBT), IELTS (minimum score 7), PTE (minimum score 68). *Application deadline:* Applications are processed on a rolling basis. Application fee: $35. Electronic applications accepted. *Expenses:* Tuition: Full-time $20,934; part-time $1163 per credit hour. *Required fees:* $81 per semester. One-time fee: $100. Part-time tuition and fees vary according to course level, course load, campus/location and program. *Financial support:* In 2016–17, 15 students received support. Federal Work-Study, scholarships/grants, and state work-study, institutional employment available. Support available to part-time students. Financial award application deadline: 4/15; financial award applicants required to submit FAFSA. *Unit head:* Dr. Ravi Srinivas, Associate Vice President for Academic Affairs/Dean of Extended Programs/MLA Director, 713-525-3804, Fax: 713-525-6924, E-mail: mla@stthom.edu. *Application contact:* Kate Henderson, Program Coordinator, 713-525-3556, Fax: 713-525-6924, E-mail: mla@stthom.edu.
Website: http://www.stthom.edu/Academics/School_of_Arts_and_Sciences/Graduate/Master_of_Liberal_Arts/Index.aqf

**University of Southern Indiana,** Graduate Studies, College of Liberal Arts, Program in Liberal Studies, Evansville, IN 47712-3590. Offers MA. *Program availability:* Part-time, evening/weekend. *Faculty:* 10 full-time (7 women), 1 part-time/adjunct (0 women). *Students:* 1 (woman) full-time, 3 part-time (2 women). Average age 33. *Entrance requirements:* For master's, minimum GPA of 2.5, resume, interview, written statement of interest, three professional references. Additional exam requirements/recommendations for international students: Required—TOEFL (minimum score 550 paper-based; 79 iBT), IELTS (minimum score 6). *Application deadline:* For fall admission, 8/15 priority date for domestic students, 3/1 priority date for international students. Applications are processed on a rolling basis. Application fee: $40. Electronic applications accepted. *Expenses:* Tuition, state resident: full-time $8497. Tuition, nonresident: full-time $16,691. *Required fees:* $500. *Financial support:* In 2016–17, 1 student received support. Federal Work-Study, scholarships/grants, tuition waivers (full and partial), and unspecified assistantships available. Financial award application deadline: 3/1; financial award applicants required to submit FAFSA. *Unit head:* Dr. Tamara Hunt, Program Director, 812-465-1202, E-mail: tlhunt@usi.edu. *Application contact:* Dr. Mayola Rowser, Director, Graduate Studies, 812-465-7015, E-mail: mrowser@usi.edu.
Website: http://www.usi.edu/liberalarts/master-of-arts-in-liberal-studies

**University of South Florida,** College of Arts and Sciences, Department of Humanities and Cultural Studies, Tampa, FL 33620-9951. Offers liberal arts (MA), including Africana studies, American studies, film studies, humanities, social and political thought. *Program availability:* Part-time, evening/weekend. *Faculty:* 6 full-time (1 woman). *Students:* 17 full-time (10 women), 9 part-time (3 women); includes 3 minority (all Black or African American, non-Hispanic/Latino), 2 international. Average age 33. 23 applicants, 83% accepted, 14 enrolled. In 2016, 6 master's awarded. *Degree requirements:* For master's, comprehensive exam, thesis, language (for humanities subconcentration). *Entrance requirements:* For master's, GRE General Test, minimum GPA of 3.0 in upper-division courses, personal statement, writing sample. Additional exam requirements/recommendations for international students: Required—TOEFL (minimum score 550 paper-based; 79 iBT) or IELTS (minimum score 6.5). *Application deadline:* For fall admission, 2/15 priority date for domestic students, 2/15 for international students; for spring admission, 10/15 priority date for domestic students, 9/15 for international students; for summer admission, 2/15 for domestic students, 1/15 for international students. Application fee: $30. Electronic applications accepted. *Expenses:* Tuition, state resident: full-time $7766; part-time $431.43 per credit hour. Tuition, nonresident: full-time $15,789; part-time $877.17 per credit hour. *Required fees:* $37 per term. *Financial support:* In 2016–17, 5 students received support, including 15 teaching assistantships with tuition reimbursements available (averaging $12,437 per year); scholarships/grants also available. Financial award application deadline: 4/1. *Faculty research:* American South, American autobiography, material culture, critical theory, cultural studies, film studies. *Unit head:* Dr. William Cummings, Professor and Chair, 813-974-9380, Fax: 813-974-9409, E-mail: wcummings@usf.edu. *Application contact:* Dr. Brook Sadler, Associate Professor and Graduate Program Director, 813-974-8841, Fax: 813-974-9409, E-mail: brooksadler@usf.edu.
Website: http://humanities.usf.edu/

**University of South Florida, St. Petersburg,** College of Arts and Sciences, St. Petersburg, FL 33701. Offers digital journalism and design (MA); environmental science and policy (MA, MS); Florida studies (MLA); journalism and media studies (MA); liberal studies (MLA); psychology (MA). *Program availability:* Part-time, online learning. *Degree requirements:* For master's, comprehensive exam, thesis or project. *Entrance requirements:* For master's, GRE, LSAT, MCAT (varies by program), letter of intent, 3 letters of recommendation, writing samples, bachelor's degree from regionally-accredited institution with minimum GPA of 3.0 overall or in upper two years. Additional exam requirements/recommendations for international students: Required—TOEFL (minimum score 550 paper-based; 79 iBT); Recommended—IELTS. Electronic applications accepted.

**University of South Florida Sarasota-Manatee,** College of Liberal Arts and Social Sciences, Sarasota, FL 34243. Offers criminal justice (MA); education (MA); educational leadership (M Ed), including curriculum leadership, K-12 public school leadership, non-public/charter school leadership; elementary education (MAT); English education (MA); social work (MSW). *Program availability:* Part-time, 100% online, blended/hybrid learning. *Faculty:* 11 full-time (9 women), 7 part-time/adjunct (5 women). *Students:* 11 full-time (all women), 55 part-time (41 women); includes 18 minority (5 Black or African American, non-Hispanic/Latino; 1 American Indian or Alaska Native, non-Hispanic/Latino; 2 Asian, non-Hispanic/Latino; 10 Hispanic/Latino). Average age 36. 40 applicants, 43% accepted, 17 enrolled. In 2016, 28 master's awarded. *Degree requirements:* For master's, comprehensive exam (for some programs). *Entrance requirements:* Additional exam requirements/recommendations for international students: Required—TOEFL (minimum score 550 paper-based; 79 iBT), IELTS (minimum score 6.5). *Application deadline:* For fall admission, 3/1 priority date for domestic students, 3/1 for international students; for spring admission, 10/1 priority date for domestic students, 10/1 for international students. Applications are processed on a rolling basis. Application fee: $30. Electronic applications accepted. *Expenses:* Contact institution. *Financial support:* In 2016–17, 9 students received support. Career-related internships or fieldwork, institutionally sponsored loans, scholarships/grants, health care benefits, and unspecified assistantships available. Support available to part-time students. Financial award application deadline: 3/1; financial award applicants required to submit FAFSA. *Faculty research:* Educational leadership, secondary education, elementary education, criminal justice, social work. *Unit head:* Dr. Jane Rose, Dean, 941-359-4469, Fax: 941-359-4778, E-mail: jane.rose@sar.usf.edu. *Application contact:* Brandon Avery, Assistant Director, Admissions, 941-359-4331, E-mail: bavery@sar.usf.edu.
Website: http://usfsm.edu/college-of-liberal-arts-sciences/

**The University of Texas at El Paso,** Graduate School, College of Liberal Arts, Master of Arts in Interdisciplinary Studies Program, El Paso, TX 79968-0001. Offers MAIS. *Program availability:* Part-time, evening/weekend. *Entrance requirements:* For master's, GRE, minimum GPA of 3.0, letters of recommendation. Additional exam requirements/recommendations for international students: Required—TOEFL; Recommended—IELTS. Electronic applications accepted.

**University of the Virgin Islands,** College of Liberal Arts and Social Sciences, St. Thomas, VI 00802. Offers M Psych, MPA. *Program availability:* Part-time, evening/weekend. *Faculty:* 7 full-time (5 women), 4 part-time/adjunct (0 women). *Students:* 23 full-time (19 women), 13 part-time (9 women); includes 27 minority (24 Black or African American, non-Hispanic/Latino; 1 Asian, non-Hispanic/Latino; 1 Hispanic/Latino; 1 Two or more races, non-Hispanic/Latino), 6 international. Average age 34. 13 applicants, 85% accepted, 10 enrolled. In 2016, 4 master's awarded. *Degree requirements:* For master's, comprehensive exam, thesis or alternative. *Entrance requirements:* For master's, GRE, minimum GPA of 2.5. Additional exam requirements/recommendations for international students: Required—TOEFL (minimum score 550 paper-based). *Application deadline:* For fall admission, 4/30 for domestic and international students; for spring admission, 10/30 for domestic and international students. Application fee: $30. Electronic applications accepted. *Expenses:* Contact institution. *Financial support:* Career-related internships or fieldwork and scholarships/grants available. Financial award application deadline: 4/15; financial award applicants required to submit FAFSA. *Faculty research:* Ethical issues of arbitration, spiritual leadership, accountability. *Unit head:* Dr. Emily Allen-Williams, Dean, 340-693-1261, Fax: 340-693-1265, E-mail: emily.allenwilliams@uvi.edu. *Application contact:* Dr. Xuri M. Allen, Director of Admissions, 340-693-1224, Fax: 340-693-1167, E-mail: xallen@uvi.edu.

**The University of Toledo,** College of Graduate Studies, College of Languages, Literature and Social Sciences, Master of Liberal Studies Program, Toledo, OH 43606-3390. Offers MLS. *Program availability:* Part-time, evening/weekend. *Degree requirements:* For master's, thesis. *Entrance requirements:* For master's, GRE if cumulative GPA is less than 3.0, minimum cumulative point-hour ratio of 2.7 for all previous academic work, three letters of recommendation, statement of purpose, transcripts from all prior institutions attended. Additional exam requirements/recommendations for international students: Required—TOEFL (minimum score 550 paper-based; 80 iBT). Electronic applications accepted.

**University of Wisconsin–Milwaukee,** Graduate School, College of Letters and Science, Program in Liberal Studies, Milwaukee, WI 53201-0413. Offers MLS. *Students:* 1 (woman) full-time, 10 part-time (7 women); includes 1 minority (Two or more races, non-Hispanic/Latino), 1 international. Average age 41. 11 applicants, 64% accepted, 7 enrolled. *Entrance requirements:* For master's, interview, bachelor's degree. Additional exam requirements/recommendations for international students: Required—TOEFL (minimum score 600 paper-based; 79 iBT), IELTS (minimum score 7). *Application deadline:* Applications are processed on a rolling basis. Application fee: $56 ($96 for international students). Electronic applications accepted. *Financial support:* Fellowships, research assistantships, teaching assistantships, health care benefits, unspecified assistantships, and project assistantships available. Financial award applicants required to submit FAFSA. *Application contact:* General Information Contact, 414-229-4982, Fax: 414-229-6967, E-mail: gradschool@uwm.edu. Website: https://uwm.edu/liberal-studies/

**Ursuline College,** School of Graduate Studies, Program in Liberal Studies, Pepper Pike, OH 44124-4398. Offers MALS. *Program availability:* Part-time. *Faculty:* 1 full-time (0 women). *Students:* 1 (woman) full-time, 7 part-time (6 women); includes 4 minority (3 Black or African American, non-Hispanic/Latino; 1 Two or more races, non-Hispanic/Latino). Average age 50. 2 applicants, 100% accepted, 1 enrolled. *Degree requirements:* For master's, thesis. *Entrance requirements:* For master's, minimum undergraduate GPA of 3.0. Additional exam requirements/recommendations for international students: Required—TOEFL (minimum score 500 paper-based; 80 iBT). *Application deadline:* For fall admission, 8/1 priority date for domestic students. Applications are processed on a rolling basis. Application fee: $25. Electronic applications accepted. *Expenses:* $1,052 per credit hour. *Financial support:* In 2016–17, 2 students received support. Scholarships/grants available. Financial award application deadline: 3/1; financial award applicants required to submit FAFSA. *Faculty research:* The city in history, values and their expressions, the 1960s, globalization. *Unit head:* Dr. Tim Kinsella, Director, 440-646-8389, Fax: 440-684-6088, E-mail: tkinsell@ursuline.edu. *Application contact:* Melanie Steele, Director, Graduate Admissions, 440-646-8119, Fax: 440-684-6138, E-mail: graduateadmissions@ursuline.edu.

**Utica College,** Liberal Studies Program, Utica, NY 13502-4892. Offers MS. *Program availability:* Part-time, evening/weekend, online only, 100% online. *Faculty:* 19 full-time (8 women). *Students:* 1 (woman) full-time, 16 part-time (10 women); includes 4 minority (2 Black or African American, non-Hispanic/Latino; 2 Hispanic/Latino). Average age 32. 11 applicants, 73% accepted, 8 enrolled. In 2016, 5 master's awarded. *Degree requirements:* For master's, comprehensive exam or thesis. *Entrance requirements:* For master's, GRE, minimum GPA of 3.0. Additional exam requirements/recommendations for international students: Required—TOEFL (minimum score 525 paper-based). *Application deadline:* Applications are processed on a rolling basis. Application fee: $50. Electronic applications accepted. *Expenses:* Contact institution. *Financial support:* Career-related internships or fieldwork, scholarships/grants, tuition waivers (partial), and unspecified assistantships available. Support available to part-time students. Financial award application deadline: 3/15; financial award applicants required to submit FAFSA. *Unit head:* Dr. Lawrence Aaronson, Director, Liberal Studies, 315-792-3092, E-mail: laarons@utica.edu. *Application contact:* John D. Rowe, Director of Graduate Admissions, 315-792-3824, Fax: 315-792-3003, E-mail: jrowe@utica.edu.

**Valparaiso University,** Graduate School and Continuing Education, Programs in Liberal Studies, Concentration in Human Behavior and Society, Valparaiso, IN 46383. Offers MALS, Post-Master's Certificate, JD/MALS. *Program availability:* Part-time, evening/weekend. *Entrance requirements:* For master's, minimum GPA of 3.0. Additional exam requirements/recommendations for international students: Required—TOEFL (minimum score 550 paper-based; 80 iBT), IELTS (minimum score 6). Electronic applications accepted. *Expenses: Tuition:* Full-time $11,070; part-time $615 per credit hour. *Required fees:* $116 per semester. Tuition and fees vary according to course load, degree level and program.

**Valparaiso University,** Graduate School and Continuing Education, Programs in Liberal Studies, Individualized Study Program, Valparaiso, IN 46383. Offers MALS, JD/MALS. *Program availability:* Part-time, evening/weekend. *Entrance requirements:* For master's, minimum GPA of 3.0. Additional exam requirements/recommendations for international students: Required—TOEFL (minimum score 550 paper-based; 80 iBT), IELTS (minimum score 6). Electronic applications accepted. *Expenses: Tuition:* Full-time $11,070; part-time $615 per credit hour. *Required fees:* $116 per semester. Tuition and fees vary according to course load, degree level and program.

**Vanderbilt University,** Program in Liberal Arts and Science, Nashville, TN 37240-1001. Offers MLAS. *Program availability:* Part-time. *Students:* 1 (woman) full-time, 39 part-time (20 women); includes 10 minority (5 Black or African American, non-Hispanic/Latino; 1 American Indian or Alaska Native, non-Hispanic/Latino; 1 Asian, non-Hispanic/Latino; 3 Two or more races, non-Hispanic/Latino). Average age 42. 30 applicants, 57% accepted, 12 enrolled. In 2016, 12 master's awarded. *Degree requirements:* For master's, thesis optional. *Entrance requirements:* For master's, GRE General Test. Additional exam requirements/recommendations for international students: Required—TOEFL (minimum score 570 paper-based; 88 iBT). *Application deadline:* For fall admission, 1/15 priority date for domestic students, 1/15 for international students; for spring admission, 11/15 for domestic and international students. Applications are processed on a rolling basis. *Expenses: Tuition:* Part-time $1854 per credit hour. *Financial support:* Institutionally sponsored loans and tuition waivers (partial) available. *Unit head:* Dr. Martin Rapisarda, Associate Dean and Director of Graduate Studies, 615-343-3140, Fax: 615-343-8702, E-mail: martin.rapisarda@vanderbilt.edu. *Application contact:* Lisa Poynter, Coordinator, 615-343-3140, Fax: 615-343-8702, E-mail: lisa.poynter@vanderbilt.edu. Website: http://www.vanderbilt.edu/mlas/

**Villanova University,** Graduate School of Liberal Arts and Sciences, Graduate Liberal Studies Program, Villanova, PA 19085-1699. Offers MA. *Program availability:* Part-time, evening/weekend. *Faculty:* 4. *Students:* 9 full-time (5 women), 5 part-time (2 women); includes 2 minority (1 Black or African American, non-Hispanic/Latino; 1 Two or more races, non-Hispanic/Latino). Average age 38. 4 applicants, 100% accepted, 3 enrolled. In 2016, 5 master's awarded. *Degree requirements:* For master's, comprehensive exam. *Entrance requirements:* For master's, GRE, statement of objectives, 2 letters of recommendation, writing sample. Additional exam requirements/recommendations for international students: Required—TOEFL. *Application deadline:* For fall admission, 5/1 priority date for international students; for spring admission, 10/15 priority date for international students. Applications are processed on a rolling basis. Application fee: $50. Electronic applications accepted. *Financial support:* Research assistantships, scholarships/grants, and unspecified assistantships available. Financial award applicants required to submit FAFSA. *Unit head:* Dr. Marylu Hill, Program Director, 610-519-7325. Website: http://www1.villanova.edu/villanova/artsci/liberalstudies.html

**Virginia Polytechnic Institute and State University,** VT Online, Blacksburg, VA 24061. Offers advanced transportation systems (Certificate); aerospace engineering (MS); agricultural and life sciences (MSLFS); business information systems (Graduate Certificate); career and technical education (MS); civil engineering (MS); computer engineering (M Eng, MS); decision support systems (Graduate Certificate); eLearning leadership (MA); electrical engineering (M Eng, MS); engineering administration (MEA); environmental engineering (Certificate); environmental politics and policy (Graduate Certificate); environmental sciences and engineering (MS); foundations of political analysis (Graduate Certificate); health product risk management (Graduate Certificate); industrial and systems engineering (MS); information policy and society (Graduate Certificate); information security (Graduate Certificate); information technology (MIT); instructional technology (MA); integrative STEM education (MA Ed); liberal arts (Graduate Certificate); life sciences: health product risk management (MS); natural resources (MNR, Graduate Certificate); networking (Graduate Certificate); nonprofit and nongovernmental organization management (Graduate Certificate); ocean engineering (MS); political science (MA); security studies (Graduate Certificate); software development (Graduate Certificate). *Expenses:* Tuition, state resident: full-time $12,467; part-time $692.50 per credit hour. Tuition, nonresident: full-time $25,095; part-time $1394.25 per credit hour. *Required fees:* $2669; $491.50 per semester. Tuition and fees vary according to course load, campus/location and program.

**Wake Forest University,** Graduate School of Arts and Sciences, Liberal Studies Program, Winston-Salem, NC 27106. Offers MALS. *Program availability:* Part-time. *Degree requirements:* For master's, thesis. *Entrance requirements:* Additional exam requirements/recommendations for international students: Required—TOEFL (minimum score 79 iBT). Electronic applications accepted.

**Washburn University,** College of Arts and Sciences, Program in Liberal Studies, Topeka, KS 66621. Offers MLS. *Program availability:* Part-time, evening/weekend. *Degree requirements:* For master's, thesis, 15 seminar hours. *Entrance requirements:* For master's, minimum GPA of 3.0 in the last 60 hours of undergraduate coursework. Additional exam requirements/recommendations for international students: Required—TOEFL (minimum score 80 iBT). *Faculty research:* European architecture/history, British cultural studies movement, American military strategy/history.

**Wesleyan University,** Graduate Liberal Studies Program, Middletown, CT 06459. Offers liberal arts (M Phil); liberal studies (MALS); writing (Graduate Certificate). *Program availability:* Part-time, evening/weekend. *Degree requirements:* For master's, thesis optional; for Graduate Certificate, thesis. *Entrance requirements:* For master's, essay, undergraduate transcripts, two letters of recommendation. Additional exam requirements/recommendations for international students: Required—TOEFL (minimum score 100 iBT), IELTS (minimum score 7). *Application deadline:* For fall admission, 7/10 for domestic students; for spring admission, 11/6 for domestic students; for summer admission, 4/16 for domestic students. Applications are processed on a rolling basis. Application fee: $100. *Expenses:* Contact institution. *Financial support:* Scholarships/grants available. Support available to part-time students. *Faculty research:* Interdisciplinary studies. *Unit head:* Jennifer Curran, Director, 860-685-3338, Fax: 860-685-2901, E-mail: jcurran@wesleyan.edu. *Application contact:* Sarah-Jane Ripa, Associate Director, Student Services and Outreach, 860-685-3345, Fax: 860-685-2901, E-mail: sripa@wesleyan.edu. Website: http://www.wesleyan.edu/masters/

**Western Illinois University,** School of Graduate Studies, College of Arts and Sciences, Program in Liberal Arts and Sciences, Macomb, IL 61455-1390. Offers MLAS. *Program availability:* Part-time. *Students:* 3 full-time (2 women), 4 part-time (3 women); includes 1 minority (Black or African American, non-Hispanic/Latino). Average age 40. 4 applicants, 75% accepted, 2 enrolled. In 2016, 9 master's awarded. *Degree requirements:* For master's, thesis or alternative. *Entrance requirements:* Additional exam requirements/recommendations for international students: Required—TOEFL (minimum score 550 paper-based; 80 iBT). *Application deadline:* Applications are processed on a rolling basis. Application fee: $30. Electronic applications accepted. *Financial support:* In 2016–17, 1 student received support. Unspecified assistantships available. Financial award applicants required to submit FAFSA. *Unit head:* Dr. Aimee Shouse, Program Director, 309-298-2214. *Application contact:* Dr. Nancy Parsons, Associate Provost and Director of Graduate Studies, 309-298-1806, Fax: 309-298-2345, E-mail: grad-office@wiu.edu. Website: http://wiu.edu/cas

**West Virginia University,** Eberly College of Arts and Sciences, Interdisciplinary Program in Liberal Studies, Morgantown, WV 26506. Offers MALS. *Program availability:* Part-time. *Degree requirements:* For master's, thesis or alternative. *Entrance requirements:* For master's, GRE General Test, minimum GPA of 3.0. Additional exam requirements/recommendations for international students: Required—TOEFL.

**Wichita State University,** Graduate School, Fairmount College of Liberal Arts and Sciences, Interdisciplinary Program in Liberal Studies, Wichita, KS 67260. Offers MA. *Program availability:* Part-time. *Unit head:* Dr. Jeffrey Herschfield, Graduate Coordinator, 316-978-3125, E-mail: jeffrey.hershfield@wichita.edu. *Application contact:* Jordan Oleson, Admissions Coordinator, 316-978-3095, Fax: 316-978-3253, E-mail: jordan.oleson@wichita.edu. Website: http://www.wichita.edu/mals

**Widener University,** College of Arts and Sciences, Program in Liberal Studies, Chester, PA 19013-5792. Offers MA. *Program availability:* Part-time, evening/weekend. *Faculty:* 4 full-time (1 woman). *Students:* 1 (woman) part-time. Average age 40. 3 applicants, 100% accepted. In 2016, 2 master's awarded. *Degree requirements:* For master's, thesis, project. *Entrance requirements:* For master's, interview, minimum undergraduate GPA of 3.0. *Application deadline:* Applications are processed on a rolling basis. Application fee: $25 ($300 for international students). *Expenses:* Contact institution. *Financial support:* Federal Work-Study and tuition waivers (full and partial) available. Financial award application deadline: 5/1. *Faculty research:* Contemporary analytical metaphysics, popular culture, British art, American literature, folklore. *Unit head:* Dr. Kenneth Skinner, Director, 610-499-4287, Fax: 610-499-4605, E-mail: kenneth.a.skinner@widener.edu. *Application contact:* Dr. Roberta Nolan, Assistant to Associate Provost for Graduate Studies, 610-499-4125, Fax: 610-499-4676, E-mail: gradmc@mail.widener.edu.

**Winthrop University,** College of Arts and Sciences, Program in Liberal Arts, Rock Hill, SC 29733. Offers MLA. *Program availability:* Part-time. *Entrance requirements:* For master's, interview, minimum GPA of 3.0. Additional exam requirements/recommendations for international students: Required—TOEFL (minimum score 550 paper-based; 79 iBT), IELTS (minimum score 6). Electronic applications accepted. *Expenses:* Tuition, state resident: full-time $14,312; part-time $599 per credit hour. Tuition, nonresident: full-time $27,570; part-time $1153 per credit hour.

# DARTMOUTH COLLEGE
*Master of Arts in Liberal Studies*

 For more information, visit http://petersons.to/dartmouthliberalstudies

## Programs of Study

**Interdisciplinary, immersive, and flexible graduate-level study**—the Master of Arts in Liberal Studies (MALS) program is part of Dartmouth's School of Graduate and Advanced Studies, which offers nineteen graduate programs in the natural sciences, social sciences, and humanities.

MALS at Dartmouth is a highly selective, inclusive, and diverse program and awards the Master of Arts degree in the following concentrations:

- Cultural Studies
- Creative Writing
- Globalization Studies
- General Liberal Studies

Students enter MALS at Dartmouth from different stages in their academic or professional careers. They come from a wide array of backgrounds and include recent college graduates, scholars, doctors, business leaders, and artists, as well as military personnel, writers, educators, and lawyers.

MALS at Dartmouth is designed for individuals who want to engage in self-directed graduate study in the liberal arts at the Ivy League level. The program affords students full access to both Dartmouth's graduate and undergraduate schools in order to pursue comprehensive, interdisciplinary study. Students create an individualized plan-of-study that significantly enhances their academic and professional credentials. During the past few years, students have received prestigious awards such as the Fulbright Fellowship, the J.B. Reynolds Scholarship, and the MacArthur Genius Grant. The unique MALS at Dartmouth interdisciplinary experience prepares graduates to advance in their chosen field, pursue doctoral programs across all disciplines, as well as gain entrance into the professional schools of law, business, and medicine.

Candidates for the MALS at Dartmouth program may attend on a full-time, part-time, or summers-only basis (for teachers and other professionals) or in a combination of these patterns. The Dartmouth College academic year operates on a four-term/quarter system. The program generally takes seven to eight terms (2 years) with full-time attendance, including thesis research and writing; students have six years from the time of entry to complete the requirements and earn their degree.

## The Application Process

The academic program at Dartmouth is intensive, so applications are evaluated carefully. A student's motivation, initiative, maturity, and ability to do graduate-level work are critical. The program typically enrolls 75 to 90 students during the academic year, and approximately 100 to 120 in the summer session.

The MALS at Dartmouth Admissions Committee requires the completion of an application form, three letters of professional/academic reference, a statement of purpose, and academic transcripts; GRE scores are not required. The application is available online through a link on the MALS at Dartmouth website.

An interview is required prior to the application deadline. Skype or telephone interviews are also acceptable for individuals living outside the immediate area. Application deadlines are February 15 (for summer or fall enrollment) and July 15 (for winter or spring entry). Successful applicants must enroll during the academic year for which they were accepted into the program.

## Resources and History Provide Extraordinary Access

Dartmouth College's reach and reputation as a member of the Ivy League provides students opportunities to engage with the world's leaders and intellectuals. The College's extensive facilities are available to all graduate students year-round including the College library's collection of more than a million volumes, the Hopkins Center for the Performing Arts, the Hood Museum, Alumni Gym, and numerous other facilities and services.

Dartmouth also provides many other resources for students to engage in additional areas of academic and personal interest including community activism, international and public affairs, and intellectual forums with guest speakers, debates, discussion groups, and student organizations. Some of these resources include the Montgomery Fellows Program, the Tucker Center, the John Sloan Dickey Center for International Understanding, the Nelson A. Rockefeller Center for Public Policy, the Ethics Institute, the Leslie Center for the Humanities, and the Gender Research Institute at Dartmouth—among many others.

## Cost of Study

For 2017–18, full-time tuition (2 credits) is $12,009 per term (3 months), plus activity and document fees of $110. Room and board are estimated at $6,950 per term, while books and supplies are $350.

## Faculty

For details on the extraordinary faculty members of MALS at Dartmouth, visit http://mals.dartmouth.edu/people.

## Rural Setting Balances the Fast Pace of Academic Life

Dartmouth College is located in Hanover, New Hampshire, a small New England town dating back to a few years before the college's founding in 1769. Situated in the Upper Valley of the Connecticut River between the White Mountains of New Hampshire and the Green Mountains of Vermont, Hanover combines the advantages of a spectacular rural setting with the extraordinary resources of a university.

The Dartmouth College campus is approximately 2.5 hours by car from Boston and 3 hours from Montreal. Surrounding airports include Lebanon, Manchester (75 miles), Burlington (96 miles), Boston-Logan (126 miles) and Bradley International (150 miles) airports. There are Amtrak and Greyhound stations approximately 15 minutes from campus in White River Junction, Vermont. The Dartmouth Coach runs daily from Logan Airport and South Station to Hanover.

## Correspondence and Information

Master of Arts in Liberal Studies
Dartmouth College
116 Wentworth Hall, HB 6092
Hanover, New Hampshire 03755
United States
Phone: 603-646-3592
E-mail: mals.program@dartmouth.edu
Website: http://mals.dartmouth.edu/

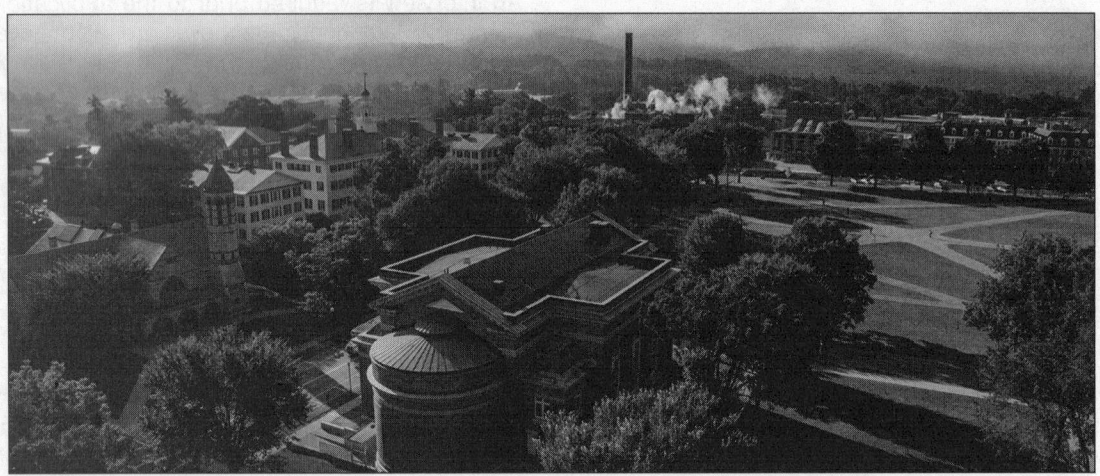

MALS at Dartmouth College in Hanover, NH combines the advantages of a spectacular rural setting with the extraordinary resources of a university.

# Section 9
# Language and Literature

This section contains a directory of institutions offering graduate work in language and literature. Additional information about programs listed in the directory may be obtained by writing directly to the dean of a graduate school or chair of a department at the address given in the directory.

For programs offering related work, see also in this book *Area and Cultural Studies, Communication and Media, Political Science and International Affairs,* and *Sociology, Anthropology, and Archaeology.* In another guide in this series:

**Graduate Programs in Business, Education, Information Studies, Law & Social Work**

See *Special Focus* and *Subject Areas*

## CONTENTS

**Program Directories**

**Display and Close-Up**

**See:**

# Asian Languages

**Cornell University,** Graduate School, Graduate Fields of Arts and Sciences, Field of Linguistics, Ithaca, NY 14853. Offers applied linguistics (MA, PhD); East Asian linguistics (MA, PhD); English linguistics (MA, PhD); general linguistics (MA, PhD); Germanic linguistics (MA, PhD); Indo-European linguistics (MA, PhD); phonetics (MA, PhD); phonological theory (MA, PhD); Romance linguistics (MA, PhD); second language acquisition (MA, PhD); semantics (MA, PhD); Slavic linguistics (MA, PhD); sociolinguistics (MA, PhD); South Asian linguistics (MA, PhD); Southeast Asian linguistics (MA, PhD); syntactic theory (MA, PhD). Terminal master's awarded for partial completion of doctoral program. *Degree requirements:* For master's, one foreign language, thesis; for doctorate, one foreign language, comprehensive exam, thesis/dissertation. *Entrance requirements:* For master's and doctorate, GRE General Test, 2 letters of recommendation. Additional exam requirements/recommendations for international students: Required—TOEFL (minimum score 600 paper-based; 77 iBT). Electronic applications accepted. *Faculty research:* Phonology and phonetics, syntax and semantics, historical linguistics, philosophy of language, language acquisition.

**Harvard University,** Graduate School of Arts and Sciences, Department of East Asian Languages and Civilizations, Cambridge, MA 02138. Offers Chinese (PhD); Japanese (PhD); Korean (PhD); Mongolian (PhD); Vietnamese (PhD). Terminal master's awarded for partial completion of doctoral program. *Degree requirements:* For doctorate, 3 foreign languages, thesis/dissertation, general exams. *Entrance requirements:* For doctorate, GRE General Test. Additional exam requirements/recommendations for international students: Required—TOEFL. *Faculty research:* Central Asian literature, religion, and premodern history.

**Harvard University,** Graduate School of Arts and Sciences, Department of Sanskrit and Indian Studies, Cambridge, MA 02138. Offers Indian philosophy (AM, PhD); Pali (AM, PhD); Sanskrit (AM, PhD); Tibetan (AM, PhD); Urdu (AM, PhD). Terminal master's awarded for partial completion of doctoral program. *Degree requirements:* For master's, 3 foreign languages; for doctorate, 3 foreign languages, thesis/dissertation. *Entrance requirements:* For master's, GRE General Test; for doctorate, GRE General Test, proficiency in French and German. Additional exam requirements/recommendations for international students: Required—TOEFL.

**Indiana University Bloomington,** University Graduate School, College of Arts and Sciences, School of Global and International Studies, Department of East Asian Languages and Cultures, Bloomington, IN 47408. Offers Chinese (MA, PhD); Chinese language pedagogy (MA); East Asian studies (MA); Japanese (MA, PhD); Japanese language pedagogy (MA). *Program availability:* Part-time. *Degree requirements:* For master's, one foreign language, thesis; for doctorate, 2 foreign languages, comprehensive exam, thesis/dissertation. *Entrance requirements:* Additional exam requirements/recommendations for international students: Required—TOEFL (minimum score 93 iBT). Electronic applications accepted. *Faculty research:* Modern East Asian history; politics and society; traditional Chinese thought and society; medieval and premodern Japanese history, literature and society; modern Chinese and Japanese film and literature; Chinese, Japanese, Korean language and linguistics.

**The Ohio State University,** Graduate School, College of Arts and Sciences, Division of Arts and Humanities, Department of East Asian Languages and Literatures, Columbus, OH 43210. Offers Chinese (MA, PhD); Japanese (MA, PhD). *Faculty:* 20. *Students:* 59 full-time (44 women), 1 (woman) part-time; includes 5 minority (all Asian, non-Hispanic/Latino), 36 international. Average age 30. In 2016, 15 master's, 4 doctorates awarded. Terminal master's awarded for partial completion of doctoral program. *Degree requirements:* For master's, thesis optional; for doctorate, thesis/dissertation. *Entrance requirements:* For master's and doctorate, GRE General Test (if applying for financial aid). Additional exam requirements/recommendations for international students: Required—TOEFL (minimum score 577 paper-based; 90 iBT); Recommended—IELTS (minimum score 7.5). *Application deadline:* For fall admission, 11/30 priority date for domestic and international students; for spring admission, 3/1 for domestic students, 2/1 for international students. Applications are processed on a rolling basis. Application fee: $60 ($70 for international students). Electronic applications accepted. *Financial support:* Fellowships, research assistantships, teaching assistantships, Federal Work-Study, institutionally sponsored loans, and unspecified assistantships available. Support available to part-time students. *Unit head:* Dr. Mark Bender, Chair and Professor, 614-688-5737, E-mail: bender.4@osu.edu. *Application contact:* Graduate and Professional Admissions, 614-292-9444, Fax: 614-292-3895, E-mail: gpadmissions@osu.edu. Website: http://deall.osu.edu/

**St. John's College,** Graduate Institute in Liberal Education, Program in Eastern Classics, Santa Fe, NM 87505. Offers MA. *Program availability:* Part-time, evening/weekend. *Entrance requirements:* For master's, 2 letters of recommendation. Additional exam requirements/recommendations for international students: Required—TOEFL, TWE. *Expenses:* Contact institution.

**Stanford University,** School of Humanities and Sciences, Department of East Asian Languages and Cultures, Stanford, CA 94305-2004. Offers Chinese (MA, PhD); Japanese (MA, PhD). Terminal master's awarded for partial completion of doctoral program. *Degree requirements:* For master's, one foreign language, thesis or an annotated translation of a literary or historical text; for doctorate, 2 foreign languages, thesis/dissertation, field exams. *Entrance requirements:* For master's and doctorate, GRE General Test. Additional exam requirements/recommendations for international students: Required—TOEFL. Electronic applications accepted. *Expenses: Tuition:* Full-time $47,331. *Required fees:* $609.

**University of California, Berkeley,** Graduate Division, College of Letters and Science, Department of South and Southeast Asian Studies, Berkeley, CA 94720-1500. Offers Hindi (MA, PhD); Indonesian (MA, PhD); Sanskrit (MA, PhD); Tamil (MA, PhD). *Faculty:* 6 full-time, 14 part-time/adjunct. *Students:* 25 full-time (16 women); includes 6 minority (5 Asian, non-Hispanic/Latino; 1 Hispanic/Latino), 3 international. Average age 34. 31 applicants, 3 enrolled. In 2016, 4 master's, 4 doctorates awarded. Terminal master's awarded for partial completion of doctoral program. *Degree requirements:* For master's, 2 foreign languages, thesis; for doctorate, 2 foreign languages, thesis/dissertation, oral qualifying exam. *Entrance requirements:* For master's and doctorate, GRE General Test, minimum GPA of 3.0, 3 letters of recommendation. *Application deadline:* For fall admission, 12/9 for domestic students. Application fee: $105 ($125 for international students). Electronic applications accepted. *Financial support:* Fellowships, research assistantships, teaching assistantships, institutionally sponsored loans, health care benefits, and unspecified assistantships available. *Unit head:* Prof. Jacob Dalton, Chair, 510-642-4564. *Application contact:* Cassandra Dunn, 510-642-3672, E-mail: cassandrajj@berkeley.edu. Website: http://sseas.berkeley.edu

**University of California, Irvine,** School of Humanities, Department of East Asian Languages and Literatures, Irvine, CA 92697. Offers Chinese (MA, PhD); East Asian languages and literatures (MA, PhD); Japanese (MA, PhD). *Students:* 12 full-time (10 women), 1 part-time (0 women); includes 4 minority (3 Asian, non-Hispanic/Latino; 1 Two or more races, non-Hispanic/Latino), 5 international. Average age 32. 34 applicants, 12% accepted, 2 enrolled. In 2016, 1 doctorate awarded. *Degree requirements:* For doctorate, thesis/dissertation. *Entrance requirements:* For master's and doctorate, GRE General Test, minimum GPA of 3.0. Additional exam requirements/recommendations for international students: Required—TOEFL (minimum score 550 paper-based). *Application deadline:* For fall admission, 1/15 priority date for domestic students, 1/15 for international students. Application fee: $105 ($125 for international students). Electronic applications accepted. *Financial support:* Fellowships with tuition reimbursements, research assistantships with full tuition reimbursements, teaching assistantships with partial tuition reimbursements, institutionally sponsored loans, traineeships, health care benefits, and unspecified assistantships available. Financial award application deadline: 3/1; financial award applicants required to submit FAFSA. *Faculty research:* Chinese, Japanese, and Korean literature and culture; language and textual analysis; historical, social, and cultural dimensions of literary study. *Unit head:* Michael A. Fuller, Chair, 949-824-2802 Ext. 2227, Fax: 949-824-3248, E-mail: mafuller@uci.edu. *Application contact:* Hu Ying, Graduate Faculty Advisor, 949-824-6312, Fax: 949-824-3248, E-mail: huying@uci.edu. Website: http://www.hnet.uci.edu/eastasian/

**University of California, Los Angeles,** Graduate Division, College of Letters and Science, Department of Asian Languages and Cultures, Los Angeles, CA 90095. Offers MA, PhD. Terminal master's awarded for partial completion of doctoral program. *Degree requirements:* For master's, one foreign language, comprehensive exam or thesis; for doctorate, 2 foreign languages, thesis/dissertation, oral and written qualifying exams. *Entrance requirements:* For master's, GRE General Test, bachelor's degree; minimum undergraduate GPA of 3.0 (or its equivalent if letter grade system not used); writing sample; for doctorate, GRE General Test, master's degree; minimum undergraduate GPA of 3.0 (or its equivalent if letter grade system not used); writing sample. Additional exam requirements/recommendations for international students: Required—TOEFL. Electronic applications accepted

**University of California, Santa Barbara,** Graduate Division, College of Letters and Sciences, Division of Humanities and Fine Arts, Department of East Asian Languages and Cultural Studies, Santa Barbara, CA 93106-7075. Offers applied linguistics (PhD); East Asian languages and cultural studies (MA); translation studies (PhD). *Degree requirements:* For master's, one foreign language, comprehensive exam (for some programs), thesis (for some programs); for doctorate, 2 foreign languages, thesis/dissertation, methodology. *Entrance requirements:* For master's and doctorate, GRE General Test. Additional exam requirements/recommendations for international students: Required—TOEFL (minimum score 550 paper-based; 80 iBT), IELTS (minimum score 7). Electronic applications accepted. *Faculty research:* Chinese literature, Chinese film, Japanese society, Japanese literature, East Asian cultural studies.

**University of California, Santa Barbara,** Graduate Division, College of Letters and Sciences, Division of Humanities and Fine Arts, Program in Comparative Literature, Santa Barbara, CA 93106-4130. Offers comparative literature (PhD); East Asian literatures (PhD); feminist studies (PhD); French (PhD); global studies (PhD); translation studies (PhD); MA/PhD. *Degree requirements:* For doctorate, 2 foreign languages, comprehensive exam, thesis/dissertation. *Entrance requirements:* For doctorate, GRE. Additional exam requirements/recommendations for international students: Required—TOEFL (minimum score 550 paper-based; 80 iBT), IELTS (minimum score 7). Electronic applications accepted. *Faculty research:* Comparative literary studies in global context, critical theory, translation studies, media technological studies, trauma studies.

**University of Chicago,** Division of the Humanities, Department of East Asian Languages and Civilizations, Chicago, IL 60637. Offers PhD. *Students:* 32 full-time (18 women); includes 3 minority (all Asian, non-Hispanic/Latino), 16 international. 63 applicants, 13% accepted, 3 enrolled. In 2016, 2 doctorates awarded. Terminal master's awarded for partial completion of doctoral program. *Degree requirements:* For doctorate, 2 foreign languages, comprehensive exam, thesis/dissertation, qualifying exam. *Entrance requirements:* For doctorate, GRE General Test. Additional exam requirements/recommendations for international students: Required—TOEFL (minimum score 104 iBT), IELTS (minimum score 7). *Application deadline:* For fall admission, 12/15 for domestic and international students. Application fee: $90. Electronic applications accepted. *Financial support:* Fellowships with full tuition reimbursements, teaching assistantships with tuition reimbursements, Federal Work-Study, institutionally sponsored loans, scholarships/grants, traineeships, and health care benefits available. Financial award application deadline: 12/15; financial award applicants required to submit FAFSA. *Faculty research:* East Asian literature, material culture, religious and intellectual history, paleography of early China, performance studies. *Unit head:* Dr. Jacob Eyferth, Chair, 773-834-1677, E-mail: eyferth@uchicago.edu. *Application contact:* Michael Beetley, Assistant Dean of Students, Admissions and Fellowships, 773-702-1552, Fax: 773-834-9148, E-mail: humanitiesadmissions@uchicago.edu. Website: http://ealc.uchicago.edu/

**University of Chicago,** Division of the Humanities, Department of South Asian Languages and Civilizations, Chicago, IL 60637. Offers South Asian languages and civilizations (PhD), including Bengali, Hindi, Sanskrit, Tamil, Urdu. *Students:* 29 full-time (17 women); includes 4 minority (1 Black or African American, non-Hispanic/Latino; 1 Asian, non-Hispanic/Latino; 2 Two or more races, non-Hispanic/Latino), 15 international. 39 applicants, 15% accepted, 6 enrolled. In 2016, 2 doctorates awarded. Terminal master's awarded for partial completion of doctoral program. *Degree requirements:* For doctorate, 3 foreign languages, comprehensive exam, thesis/dissertation. *Entrance requirements:* For doctorate, GRE General Test. Additional exam requirements/recommendations for international students: Required—TOEFL (minimum score 104 iBT), IELTS (minimum score 7). *Application deadline:* For fall admission, 12/15 for domestic and international students. Application fee: $90. Electronic applications accepted. *Financial support:* Fellowships with full tuition reimbursements, Federal Work-Study, institutionally sponsored loans, scholarships/grants, and health care benefits available. Financial award application deadline: 12/15; financial award applicants required to submit FAFSA. *Unit head:* Gary Tubb, Chair, 773-834-2825, E-mail: tubb@uchicago.edu. *Application contact:* Michael Beetley, Assistant Dean of Students, Admissions and Fellowships, 773-702-1552, Fax: 773-834-9148, E-mail: humanitiesadmissions@uchicago.edu. Website: http://salc.uchicago.edu

**University of Hawaii at Manoa,** Graduate Division, College of Languages, Linguistics and Literature, Department of East Asian Languages and Literatures, Program in Korean, Honolulu, HI 96822. Offers MA, PhD. *Program availability:* Part-time. *Degree*

*requirements:* For master's, 2 foreign languages, thesis optional; for doctorate, 2 foreign languages, comprehensive exam, thesis/dissertation. *Entrance requirements:* For master's and doctorate, GRE General Test. Additional exam requirements/recommendations for international students: Required—TOEFL (minimum score 560 paper-based; 83 iBT), IELTS (minimum score 5).

**University of Illinois at Urbana–Champaign,** Graduate College, College of Liberal Arts and Sciences, School of Literatures, Cultures and Linguistics, Department of East Asian Languages and Cultures, Champaign, IL 61820. Offers East Asian languages and cultures (PhD); East Asian studies (MA).

**The University of Iowa,** Graduate College, College of Liberal Arts and Sciences, Program in Asian Civilizations, Iowa City, IA 52242-1316. Offers Chinese (MA); Hindi (MA); Sanskrit (MA); South Asian studies (MA). *Degree requirements:* For master's, thesis optional, exam. *Entrance requirements:* For master's, GRE General Test, minimum GPA of 3.0. Additional exam requirements/recommendations for international students: Required—TOEFL (minimum score 590 paper-based; 96 iBT). Electronic applications accepted.

**The University of Kansas,** Graduate Studies, College of Liberal Arts and Sciences, Department of East Asian Languages and Cultures, Lawrence, KS 66045. Offers MA, Graduate Certificate. *Program availability:* Part-time. *Students:* 5 full-time (2 women), 3 part-time (1 woman); includes 1 minority (Two or more races, non-Hispanic/Latino), 3 international. Average age 28. 5 applicants, 40% accepted, 1 enrolled. In 2016, 1 master's awarded. *Entrance requirements:* For master's, GRE, current curriculum vitae, statement of purpose explaining academic objectives, writing sample that demonstrates writing skills and basic research capacity, three letters of recommendation. Additional exam requirements/recommendations for international students: Required—TOEFL. *Application deadline:* For fall admission, 2/1 priority date for domestic and international students. Application fee: $65 ($85 for international students). Electronic applications accepted. *Financial support:* Fellowships, teaching assistantships, and unspecified assistantships available. *Faculty research:* Gender relations in literature, ancient Chinese law, visual culture of modern Japan, Japanese language pedagogy, Chinese paleography, Korean shamanism, folklore, traditional Chinese and Japanese literature, Chinese linguistics and language pedagogy. *Unit head:* Dr. Maggie Childs, Chair, 785-864-9128, E-mail: mgchilds@ku.edu. *Application contact:* Cari Ann Kreienhop, Graduate Programs and Admissions Contact, 785-864-3665, E-mail: ckreienhop@ku.edu.
Website: http://ealc.ku.edu/

**University of Michigan,** Rackham Graduate School, College of Literature, Science, and the Arts, Department of Asian Languages and Cultures, Ann Arbor, MI 48104. Offers PhD. *Faculty:* 24 full-time (10 women). *Students:* 20 full-time (11 women); includes 5 minority (4 Asian, non-Hispanic/Latino; 1 Two or more races, non-Hispanic/Latino), 7 international. Average age 32. 60 applicants, 13% accepted, 5 enrolled. In 2016, 2 doctorates awarded. Terminal master's awarded for partial completion of doctoral program. *Degree requirements:* For doctorate, 2 foreign languages, thesis/dissertation, preliminary exams, oral defense of dissertation. *Entrance requirements:* Additional exam requirements/recommendations for international students: Required—TOEFL (minimum score 560 paper-based; 84 iBT), IELTS (minimum score 6.5). *Application deadline:* For fall admission, 12/1 for domestic and international students. Application fee: $75 ($90 for international students). Electronic applications accepted. *Expenses:* Tuition, state resident: full-time $21,466; part-time $1152 per credit hour. Tuition, nonresident: full-time $43,346; part-time $2367 per credit hour. Part-time tuition and fees vary according to course load, degree level and program. *Financial support:* In 2016–17, 20 students received support. Fellowships with full tuition reimbursements available, teaching assistantships with full tuition reimbursements available, scholarships/grants, health care benefits, and spring/summer stipends available. Financial award application deadline: 12/1. *Faculty research:* Literature, religion, visual culture, history, modern culture. *Unit head:* Prof. Donald S. Lopez, Jr., Chair, 734-615-6571, Fax: 734-647-0157, E-mail: um-alc@umich.edu. *Application contact:* ALC Student Services, 734-734-8286, Fax: 734-647-0157, E-mail: alc-gradservices@umich.edu. Website: http://www.lsa.umich.edu/asian/

**University of Minnesota, Twin Cities Campus,** Graduate School, College of Liberal Arts, Department of Asian Languages and Literatures, Minneapolis, MN 55455-0213. Offers Asian literatures, cultures, and media (PhD). *Degree requirements:* For doctorate, comprehensive exam, thesis/dissertation. *Entrance requirements:* For doctorate, GRE, 3 letters of recommendation. Additional exam requirements/recommendations for international students: Required—TOEFL (minimum score 550 paper-based), IELTS (minimum score 6.5). Electronic applications accepted. *Faculty research:* Gender studies, post-colonial theory, poetics and poetic theory, film studies, post modernist thought.

**University of Oregon,** Graduate School, College of Arts and Sciences, Department of East Asian Languages and Literature, Eugene, OR 97403. Offers Chinese (MA, PhD); Japanese (MA, PhD). *Entrance requirements:* Additional exam requirements/recommendations for international students: Required—TOEFL. *Faculty research:* Linguistics, pedagogy.

**University of Southern California,** Graduate School, Dana and David Dornsife College of Letters, Arts and Sciences, Department of East Asian Languages and Cultures, Los Angeles, CA 90089. Offers classical Chinese literature (MA, PhD); classical Japanese literature (MA, PhD); linguistics (MA, PhD); modern Chinese literature (MA, PhD); modern Japanese literature (MA, PhD); modern Korean literature (MA, PhD). *Degree requirements:* For master's, thesis; for doctorate, 2 foreign languages, comprehensive exam, thesis/dissertation. *Entrance requirements:* For master's and doctorate, GRE, BA in relevant field. Additional exam requirements/recommendations for international students: Required—TOEFL. Electronic applications accepted. *Faculty research:* Gender, visual studies, multimedia, ecocriticism, second language acquisition.

**University of Southern California,** Graduate School, Dana and David Dornsife College of Letters, Arts and Sciences, Department of Linguistics, Los Angeles, CA 90089. Offers East Asian linguistics (PhD); Hispanic linguistics (PhD); linguistics (PhD); Slavic linguistics (PhD). *Degree requirements:* For doctorate, comprehensive exam, thesis/dissertation. *Entrance requirements:* For doctorate, GRE. Additional exam requirements/recommendations for international students: Required—TOEFL (minimum score 100 iBT). Electronic applications accepted. *Faculty research:* Syntax, phonology, phonetics, semantics, sociolinguistics, psycholinguistics.

**The University of Texas at Austin,** Graduate School, College of Liberal Arts, Department of Asian Studies, Austin, TX 78712-1111. Offers Asian cultures and languages (MA, PhD); Asian studies (MA). *Program availability:* Part-time. *Degree requirements:* For master's, thesis; for doctorate, 3 foreign languages, thesis/dissertation. *Entrance requirements:* For master's and doctorate, GRE General Test. Electronic applications accepted. *Faculty research:* Modern Taiwanese fiction, modern Japanese literature, religious studies in South Asia during classical period.

**University of Washington,** Graduate School, College of Arts and Sciences, Department of Asian Languages and Literature, Seattle, WA 98195. Offers Buddhist studies (MA, PhD); Chinese language and literature (MA, PhD); Japanese language and literature (MA, PhD); Korean language and literature (MA, PhD); South Asian language and literature (MA, PhD). *Degree requirements:* For master's, 2 foreign languages, general exam, thesis or 2 research papers; for doctorate, 3 foreign languages, thesis/dissertation, general exam. *Entrance requirements:* For master's, GRE, minimum GPA of 3.0; for doctorate, GRE, master's degree in related field, minimum GPA of 3.0. Additional exam requirements/recommendations for international students: Required—TOEFL. Electronic applications accepted. *Faculty research:* Textual, linguistic, philological, and literary study of languages and literatures of Asia.

**University of Wisconsin–Madison,** Graduate School, College of Letters and Science, Department of Languages and Cultures of Asia, Madison, WI 53706-1380. Offers civilizations and cultures (PhD); languages and cultures of Asia (MA); languages and literatures (PhD); religions of Asia (PhD). *Program availability:* Part-time. Terminal master's awarded for partial completion of doctoral program. *Degree requirements:* For master's, one foreign language, thesis or alternative; for doctorate, 2 foreign languages, thesis/dissertation. *Entrance requirements:* For master's, minimum GPA of 3.0; for doctorate, minimum GPA of 3.25, master's degree. Electronic applications accepted. *Faculty research:* Literature, folklore, religion.

**Washington University in St. Louis,** The Graduate School, Department of East Asian Languages and Cultures, St. Louis, MO 63130-4899. Offers Chinese (MA); Chinese and comparative literature (PhD); Chinese language and literature (PhD); East Asian studies (MA); Japanese (MA); Japanese and comparative literature (PhD); Japanese language and literature (PhD). Terminal master's awarded for partial completion of doctoral program. *Degree requirements:* For master's, thesis optional; for doctorate, thesis/dissertation. *Entrance requirements:* For master's and doctorate, GRE General Test. Additional exam requirements/recommendations for international students: Required—TOEFL. Electronic applications accepted. *Faculty research:* Chinese; Japanese; Chinese fiction, theater, poetry, modern literature; Japanese modern and classical fiction, translation theory.

**Yale University,** Graduate School of Arts and Sciences, Department of East Asian Languages and Literatures, New Haven, CT 06520. Offers East Asian languages and literatures (PhD); East Asian languages and literatures and film studies (PhD). *Degree requirements:* For doctorate, 2 foreign languages, thesis/dissertation. *Entrance requirements:* For doctorate, GRE General Test.

# Celtic Languages

**Harvard University,** Graduate School of Arts and Sciences, Department of Celtic Languages and Literatures, Cambridge, MA 02138. Offers Irish (PhD); Welsh (PhD). *Degree requirements:* For doctorate, thesis/dissertation, proficiency in 2 Celtic languages; reading knowledge of French, German, and Latin. *Entrance requirements:* For doctorate, GRE General Test. Additional exam requirements/recommendations for international students: Required—TOEFL.

# Chinese

**Arizona State University at the Tempe campus,** College of Liberal Arts and Sciences, School of International Letters and Cultures, Program in Chinese, Tempe, AZ 85287-0202. Offers Asian languages and civilizations: Chinese (MA); Chinese (PhD). *Program availability:* Part-time, evening/weekend. Terminal master's awarded for partial completion of doctoral program. *Degree requirements:* For master's, thesis, oral defense, interactive Program of Study (iPOS) submitted no later than beginning of third semester of study; for doctorate, comprehensive exam, thesis/dissertation, interactive Program of Study (iPOS) submitted before completing 50 percent of required credit hours. *Entrance requirements:* For master's, GRE, minimum GPA of 3.0 in the last two years of work leading to the bachelor's degree, BA in Chinese studies (preferred), personal statement, writing sample, 3 letters of recommendation; for doctorate, GRE, minimum GPA of 3.5 in the last two years of work leading to the bachelor's degree,

completion of 3 years of modern Chinese and 1 year of classical Chinese, personal statement, writing sample, 3 letters of recommendation. Additional exam requirements/recommendations for international students: Required—TOEFL (minimum score 550 paper-based; 83 iBT), IELTS (minimum score 6.5). Electronic applications accepted.

**DePaul University,** College of Liberal Arts and Social Sciences, Chicago, IL 60614. Offers Arabic (MA); Chinese (MA); English (MA); French (MA); German (MA); history (MA); interdisciplinary studies (MA, MS); international public service (MS); international studies (MA); Italian (MA); Japanese (MA); leadership and policy studies (MS); liberal studies (MA); new media studies (MA); nonprofit management (MNM); public administration (MPA); public health (MPH); public service management (MS); social work (MSW); sociology (MA); Spanish (MA); sustainable urban development (MA);

women and gender studies (MA); writing and publishing (MA); writing, rhetoric, and discourse (MA); MA/PhD. *Program availability:* Part-time, evening/weekend, online learning. Terminal master's awarded for partial completion of doctoral program. *Degree requirements:* For master's, variable foreign language requirement, comprehensive exam (for some programs), thesis (for some programs). Electronic applications accepted.

**Harvard University,** Graduate School of Arts and Sciences, Department of East Asian Languages and Civilizations, Cambridge, MA 02138. Offers Chinese (PhD); Japanese (PhD); Korean (PhD); Mongolian (PhD); Vietnamese (PhD). Terminal master's awarded for partial completion of doctoral program. *Degree requirements:* For doctorate, 3 foreign languages, thesis/dissertation, general exams. *Entrance requirements:* For doctorate, GRE General Test. Additional exam requirements/recommendations for international students: Required—TOEFL. *Faculty research:* Central Asian literature, religion, and premodern history.

**Hunter College of the City University of New York,** Graduate School, School of Arts and Sciences, Department of Classical and Oriental Studies, New York, NY 10065-5085. Offers teaching Chinese (MA); teaching Latin (MA). *Program availability:* Part-time, evening/weekend. *Degree requirements:* For master's, one foreign language, comprehensive exam. *Entrance requirements:* For master's, undergraduate major in Latin or equivalent with minimum GPA of 3.0, 2.8 overall; interview; 2 letters of recommendation. Additional exam requirements/recommendations for international students: Required—TOEFL. *Application deadline:* For fall admission, 4/1 for domestic students; for spring admission, 11/1 for domestic students. *Financial support:* Federal Work-Study, scholarships/grants, and tuition waivers (partial) available. Support available to part-time students. Financial award application deadline: 4/15. *Faculty research:* Latin poetry, historiography, classical culture, archaeology. *Unit head:* Robert B. Koehl, Chairperson, 212-772-5061, E-mail: rkoehl@hunter.cuny.edu. *Application contact:* Milena Solo, Director of Admissions, 212-772-4480, E-mail: admissions@hunter.cuny.edu.
Website: http://www.hunter.cuny.edu/classics/

**Indiana University Bloomington,** University Graduate School, College of Arts and Sciences, School of Global and International Studies, Department of East Asian Languages and Cultures, Bloomington, IN 47408. Offers Chinese (MA, PhD); Chinese language pedagogy (MA); East Asian studies (MA); Japanese (MA, PhD); Japanese language pedagogy (MA). *Program availability:* Part-time. *Degree requirements:* For master's, one foreign language, thesis; for doctorate, 2 foreign languages, comprehensive exam, thesis/dissertation. *Entrance requirements:* Additional exam requirements/recommendations for international students: Required—TOEFL (minimum score 93 iBT). Electronic applications accepted. *Faculty research:* Modern East Asian history; politics and society; traditional Chinese thought and society; medieval and premodern Japanese history, literature and society; modern Chinese and Japanese film and literature; Chinese, Japanese, Korean language and linguistics.

**Middlebury College,** Language Schools, Chinese School, Middlebury, VT 05753. Offers MA. *Degree requirements:* For master's, one foreign language, teaching practicum. *Entrance requirements:* For master's, placement test, 3 letters of recommendation, writing sample, curriculum vitae, official transcripts of undergraduate coursework. Additional exam requirements/recommendations for international students: Required—TOEFL (minimum score 600 paper-based; 100 iBT), IELTS (minimum score 7.5). Electronic applications accepted. *Expenses:* Contact institution.

**New York University,** Steinhardt School of Culture, Education, and Human Development, Department of Teaching and Learning, Program in Multilingual/Multicultural Studies, New York, NY 10003. Offers bilingual education (MA, PhD, Advanced Certificate); foreign language education (MA); teaching English to speakers of other languages (MA, PhD); teaching foreign languages, 7-12 (MA), including Chinese, French, Italian, Japanese, Spanish; teaching French as a foreign language (MA), including teaching English to speakers of other languages; teaching Spanish as a foreign language (MA), including teaching English to speakers of other languages. *Accreditation:* TEAC. *Program availability:* Part-time, evening/weekend. *Degree requirements:* For master's, thesis (for some programs); for doctorate, thesis/dissertation. *Entrance requirements:* For doctorate, GRE General Test, interview; for Advanced Certificate, master's degree. Additional exam requirements/recommendations for international students: Required—TOEFL (minimum score 100 iBT). Electronic applications accepted. *Faculty research:* Second language acquisition, cross-cultural communication, technology-enhanced language learning, language variation, action learning.

**The Ohio State University,** Graduate School, College of Arts and Sciences, Division of Arts and Humanities, Department of East Asian Languages and Literatures, Columbus, OH 43210. Offers Chinese (MA, PhD); Japanese (MA, PhD). *Faculty:* 20. *Students:* 59 full-time (44 women), 1 (woman) part-time; includes 5 minority (all Asian, non-Hispanic/Latino), 36 international. Average age 30. In 2016, 15 master's, 4 doctorates awarded. Terminal master's awarded for partial completion of doctoral program. *Degree requirements:* For master's, thesis optional; for doctorate, thesis/dissertation. *Entrance requirements:* For master's and doctorate, GRE General Test (if applying for financial aid). Additional exam requirements/recommendations for international students: Required—TOEFL (minimum score 577 paper-based; 90 iBT); Recommended—IELTS (minimum score 7.5). *Application deadline:* For fall admission, 11/30 priority date for domestic and international students; for spring admission, 3/1 for domestic students, 2/1 for international students. Applications are processed on a rolling basis. Application fee: $60 ($70 for international students). Electronic applications accepted. *Financial support:* Fellowships, research assistantships, teaching assistantships, Federal Work-Study, institutionally sponsored loans, and unspecified assistantships available. Support available to part-time students. *Unit head:* Dr. Mark Bender, Chair and Professor, 614-688-5737, E-mail: bender.4@osu.edu. *Application contact:* Graduate and Professional Admissions, 614-292-9444, Fax: 614-292-3895, E-mail: gpadmissions@osu.edu.
Website: http://deall.osu.edu/

**Saginaw Valley State University,** College of Education, Program in Teaching Chinese as a Foreign Language, University Center, MI 48710. Offers MAT. *Program availability:* Part-time, evening/weekend. *Students:* 5 full-time (3 women), 4 international. Average age 30. 4 applicants, 25% accepted, 1 enrolled. In 2016, 4 master's awarded. *Entrance requirements:* For master's, minimum GPA of 3.0. Additional exam requirements/recommendations for international students: Required—TOEFL (minimum score 550 paper-based; 79 iBT). *Application deadline:* For fall admission, 7/15 for international students; for winter admission, 11/15 for international students; for spring admission, 4/15 for international students. Applications are processed on a rolling basis. Application fee: $30 ($90 for international students). Electronic applications accepted. *Expenses:* Tuition, state resident: full-time $9652; part-time $536 per credit hour. Tuition, nonresident: full-time $12,259; part-time $1022 per credit hour. *Required fees:* $263; $14.60 per credit hour. Tuition and fees vary according to degree level. *Financial support:* Federal Work-Study and scholarships/grants available. Support available to part-time students. Financial award application deadline: 4/1; financial award applicants required to submit FAFSA. *Unit head:* Dr. Craig Douglas, Dean, 989-964-4057, Fax: 989-964-4563, E-mail: coeconnect@svsu.edu. *Application contact:* Jenna Briggs,

Director, Graduate and International Admissions, 989-964-6096, Fax: 989-964-2788, E-mail: gradadm@svsu.edu.

**San Francisco State University,** Division of Graduate Studies, College of Liberal and Creative Arts, Department of Modern Languages and Literatures, Program in Chinese, San Francisco, CA 94132-1722. Offers MA. *Application deadline:* Applications are processed on a rolling basis. *Expenses:* Tuition, state resident: full-time $6738. Tuition, nonresident: full-time $15,666. *Required fees:* $1012. Tuition and fees vary according to degree level and program. *Unit head:* Dr. Mohammad Salama, Chair, 415-338-7413, Fax: 415-338-6159, E-mail: mrsalama@sfsu.edu. *Application contact:* Prof. Chris Wen-Chao Li, Program Coordinator and Graduate Advisor, 415-338-1034, Fax: 415-338-6159, E-mail: wenchao@sfsu.edu.
Website: http://chinese.sfsu.edu/

**Stanford University,** School of Humanities and Sciences, Department of East Asian Languages and Cultures, Stanford, CA 94305-2004. Offers Chinese (MA, PhD); Japanese (MA, PhD). Terminal master's awarded for partial completion of doctoral program. *Degree requirements:* For master's, one foreign language, thesis or an annotated translation of a literary or historical text; for doctorate, 2 foreign languages, thesis/dissertation, field exams. *Entrance requirements:* For master's and doctorate, GRE General Test. Additional exam requirements/recommendations for international students: Required—TOEFL. Electronic applications accepted. *Expenses: Tuition:* Full-time $47,331. *Required fees:* $609.

**University of Alberta,** Faculty of Graduate Studies and Research, Department of East Asian Studies, Edmonton, AB T6G 2E1, Canada. Offers Chinese literature (MA); East Asian interdisciplinary studies (MA); Japanese literature (MA). *Program availability:* Part-time. *Degree requirements:* For master's, one foreign language, thesis. *Entrance requirements:* Additional exam requirements/recommendations for international students: Required—TOEFL. Electronic applications accepted. *Faculty research:* Classical Chinese poetry and poetics, Chinese philosophy, modern/contemporary Chinese literature, modern Japanese literature and culture, Japanese women's writing.

**University of California, Berkeley,** Graduate Division, College of Letters and Science, Department of East Asian Languages and Cultures, Berkeley, CA 94720. Offers Chinese language (PhD); Japanese language (PhD). *Students:* 27 full-time (12 women); includes 7 minority (6 Asian, non-Hispanic/Latino; 1 Hispanic/Latino), 8 international. Average age 31. 73 applicants, 3 enrolled. In 2016, 4 doctorates awarded. *Degree requirements:* For doctorate, one foreign language, thesis/dissertation, oral qualifying exam. *Entrance requirements:* For doctorate, GRE General Test, minimum GPA of 3.0, MA thesis, 3 letters of recommendation. *Application deadline:* For fall admission, 12/5 for domestic students. Application fee: $105 ($125 for international students). Electronic applications accepted. *Financial support:* Fellowships, research assistantships, teaching assistantships, Federal Work-Study, institutionally sponsored loans, health care benefits, and unspecified assistantships available. Financial award applicants required to submit FAFSA. *Faculty research:* Chinese and Japanese modern and classical texts, prose, and poetry; Chinese and Japanese linguistics. *Unit head:* Prof. H. Mack Horton, Chair, 510-642-3480, Fax: 510-642-6031, E-mail: ealang@berkeley.edu. *Application contact:* Information Contact, 510-642-3480, E-mail: ealang@berkeley.edu.
Website: http://ealc.berkeley.edu/

**University of California, Irvine,** School of Humanities, Department of East Asian Languages and Literatures, Irvine, CA 92697. Offers Chinese (MA, PhD); East Asian languages and literatures (MA, PhD); Japanese (MA, PhD). *Students:* 12 full-time (10 women), 1 part-time (0 women); includes 4 minority (3 Asian, non-Hispanic/Latino; 1 Two or more races, non-Hispanic/Latino), 5 international. Average age 32. 34 applicants, 12% accepted, 2 enrolled. In 2016, 1 doctorate awarded. *Degree requirements:* For doctorate, thesis/dissertation. *Entrance requirements:* For master's and doctorate, GRE General Test, minimum GPA of 3.0. Additional exam requirements/recommendations for international students: Required—TOEFL (minimum score 550 paper-based). *Application deadline:* For fall admission, 1/15 priority date for domestic students, 1/15 for international students. Application fee: $105 ($125 for international students). Electronic applications accepted. *Financial support:* Fellowships with tuition reimbursements, research assistantships with full tuition reimbursements, teaching assistantships with partial tuition reimbursements, institutionally sponsored loans, traineeships, health care benefits, and unspecified assistantships available. Financial award application deadline: 3/1; financial award applicants required to submit FAFSA. *Faculty research:* Chinese, Japanese, and Korean literature and culture; language and textual analysis; historical, social, and cultural dimensions of literary study. *Unit head:* Michael A. Fuller, Chair, 949-824-2802 Ext. 2227, Fax: 949-824-3248, E-mail: mafuller@uci.edu. *Application contact:* Hu Ying, Graduate Faculty Advisor, 949-824-6312, Fax: 949-824-3248, E-mail: huying@uci.edu.
Website: http://www.hnet.uci.edu/eastasian/

**University of Colorado Boulder,** Graduate School, College of Arts and Sciences, Department of Asian Languages and Civilizations, Boulder, CO 80309. Offers MA, PhD. *Faculty:* 13 full-time (5 women). *Students:* 22 full-time (16 women); includes 6 minority (2 Asian, non-Hispanic/Latino; 2 Hispanic/Latino; 2 Two or more races, non-Hispanic/Latino), 8 international. Average age 29. 33 applicants, 42% accepted, 6 enrolled. In 2016, 11 master's awarded. Terminal master's awarded for partial completion of doctoral program. *Degree requirements:* For master's, comprehensive exam. *Entrance requirements:* For master's, BA in Chinese or Japanese, minimum undergraduate GPA of 3.0. Additional exam requirements/recommendations for international students: Required—TOEFL. *Application deadline:* For fall admission, 1/1 for domestic students, 12/1 for international students; for spring admission, 10/1 for domestic students, 9/1 for international students. Applications are processed on a rolling basis. Application fee: $60 ($80 for international students). Electronic applications accepted. Application fee is waived when completed online. *Financial support:* In 2016–17, 86 students received support, including 39 fellowships (averaging $1,598 per year), 20 teaching assistantships with full and partial tuition reimbursements available (averaging $29,447 per year); institutionally sponsored loans, scholarships/grants, health care benefits, and unspecified assistantships also available. Financial award application deadline: 2/1; financial award applicants required to submit FAFSA. *Faculty research:* Asian languages/literature, Chinese language/literature, literary criticism, religious literature, literary history. *Total annual research expenditures:* $209,262. *Application contact:* E-mail: dalc@colorado.edu.
Website: http://alc.colorado.edu/

**University of Delaware,** College of Arts and Sciences, Department of Foreign Languages and Literatures, Newark, DE 19716. Offers foreign languages and literatures (MA), including French, German, Spanish; foreign languages pedagogy (MA), including French, German, Spanish; technical Chinese translation (MA). *Degree requirements:* For master's, one foreign language, comprehensive exam, thesis optional. *Entrance requirements:* For master's, GRE General Test, letters of recommendation, writing sample. Additional exam requirements/recommendations for international students: Required—TOEFL. Electronic applications accepted. *Faculty research:* Medieval to Modern French and Spanish literature, twentieth-century German, French, Spanish literature by women, computer-assisted instruction.

**University of Hawaii at Manoa,** Graduate Division, College of Languages, Linguistics and Literature, Department of East Asian Languages and Literatures, Program in Chinese, Honolulu, HI 96822. Offers MA, PhD. *Program availability:* Part-time. *Degree requirements:* For master's, 2 foreign languages, thesis optional; for doctorate, 2 foreign languages, comprehensive exam, thesis/dissertation. *Entrance requirements:* For master's and doctorate, GRE General Test. Additional exam requirements/recommendations for international students: Required—TOEFL (minimum score 560 paper-based; 83 iBT), IELTS (minimum score 5).

**University of Hawaii at Manoa,** Graduate Division, School of Pacific and Asian Studies, Program in Asian Studies, Concentration in Chinese Studies, Honolulu, HI 96822. Offers Graduate Certificate. *Program availability:* Part-time. *Degree requirements:* For Graduate Certificate, one foreign language. *Entrance requirements:* For degree, GRE. Additional exam requirements/recommendations for international students: Required—TOEFL (minimum score 560 paper-based; 83 iBT), IELTS (minimum score 5).

**The University of Iowa,** Graduate College, College of Liberal Arts and Sciences, Program in Asian Civilizations, Iowa City, IA 52242-1316. Offers Chinese (MA); Hindi (MA); Sanskrit (MA); South Asian studies (MA). *Degree requirements:* For master's, thesis optional, exam. *Entrance requirements:* For master's, GRE General Test, minimum GPA of 3.0. Additional exam requirements/recommendations for international students: Required—TOEFL (minimum score 590 paper-based; 96 iBT). Electronic applications accepted.

**The University of Manchester,** School of Languages, Linguistics and Cultures, Manchester, United Kingdom. Offers Arab world studies (PhD); Chinese studies (M Phil, PhD); East Asian studies (M Phil, PhD); English language (PhD); French studies (M Phil, PhD); German studies (M Phil, PhD); interpreting studies (PhD); Italian studies (M Phil, PhD); Japanese studies (M Phil, PhD); Latin American cultural studies (M Phil, PhD); linguistics (M Phil, PhD); Middle Eastern studies (M Phil, PhD); Polish studies (M Phil, PhD); Portuguese studies (M Phil, PhD); Russian studies (M Phil, PhD); Spanish studies (M Phil, PhD); translation and intercultural studies (M Phil, PhD).

**University of Massachusetts Amherst,** Graduate School, College of Humanities and Fine Arts, Department of Languages, Literatures, and Cultures, Programs in Asian Languages and Literatures, Amherst, MA 01003. Offers Chinese (MA); Japanese (MA). *Program availability:* Part-time. *Degree requirements:* For master's, thesis, general exam. *Entrance requirements:* For master's, GRE General Test. Additional exam requirements/recommendations for international students: Required—TOEFL (minimum score 550 paper-based; 80 iBT), IELTS (minimum score 6.5). Electronic applications accepted.

**University of Oregon,** Graduate School, College of Arts and Sciences, Department of East Asian Languages and Literature, Eugene, OR 97403. Offers Chinese (MA, PhD); Japanese (MA, PhD). *Entrance requirements:* Additional exam requirements/recommendations for international students: Required—TOEFL. *Faculty research:* Linguistics, pedagogy.

**University of Pittsburgh,** Dietrich School of Arts and Sciences, Department of East Asian Languages and Literatures, Pittsburgh, PA 15260. Offers Chinese (MA); Japanese (MA). *Program availability:* Part-time. *Faculty:* 18 full-time (11 women), 11 part-time/adjunct (all women). *Students:* 5 full-time (4 women); includes 3 minority (all Asian, non-Hispanic/Latino). Average age 26. 18 applicants, 22% accepted, 1 enrolled. In 2016, 2 master's awarded. *Degree requirements:* For master's, one foreign language, thesis, oral comprehensive exam. *Entrance requirements:* For master's, GRE General Test, 2 years of college-level Chinese or Japanese, minimum QPA of 3.0. Additional exam requirements/recommendations for international students: Required—TOEFL (minimum score 600 paper-based; 90 iBT). *Application deadline:* For fall admission, 1/15 for domestic and international students. Application fee: $50. Electronic applications

accepted. Tuition and fees vary according to program. *Financial support:* In 2016–17, 5 students received support, including 5 fellowships with full tuition reimbursements available (averaging $21,812 per year); research assistantships, teaching assistantships, Federal Work-Study, scholarships/grants, tuition waivers (full and partial), and unspecified assistantships also available. Financial award application deadline: 1/15. *Faculty research:* Chinese literature, film, and poetry; Japanese literature, film, and theater; Chinese society and culture; East Asian foreign policy, security studies, and economic history; Japanese performing arts and fine arts translation studies; cultural studies; intellectual history; language and linguistics; second language acquisition; Japanese government; Japanese and Chinese history; ethnomusicology; religious studies. *Unit head:* Dr. Hiroshi Nara, Chair, 412-624-5579, Fax: 412-624-3458, E-mail: hnara@pitt.edu. *Application contact:* Keanna Cash, Graduate Administrator, 412-624-5906, Fax: 412-624-6263, E-mail: kec176@pitt.edu. Website: http://www.deall.pitt.edu/

**University of Washington,** Graduate School, College of Arts and Sciences, Department of Asian Languages and Literature, Seattle, WA 98195. Offers Buddhist studies (MA, PhD); Chinese language and literature (MA, PhD); Japanese language and literature (MA, PhD); Korean language and literature (MA, PhD); South Asian language and literature (MA, PhD). *Degree requirements:* For master's, 2 foreign languages, general exam, thesis or 2 research papers; for doctorate, 3 foreign languages, thesis/dissertation, general exam. *Entrance requirements:* For master's, GRE, minimum GPA of 3.0; for doctorate, GRE, master's degree in related field, minimum GPA of 3.0. Additional exam requirements/recommendations for international students: Required—TOEFL. Electronic applications accepted. *Faculty research:* Textual, linguistic, philological, and literary study of languages and literatures of Asia.

**University of Wisconsin–Madison,** Graduate School, College of Letters and Science, Department of East Asian Languages and Literature, Program in Chinese Literature, Madison, WI 53706-1380. Offers MA, PhD. *Program availability:* Part-time. Terminal master's awarded for partial completion of doctoral program. *Degree requirements:* For master's, one foreign language, seminars, written exam; for doctorate, 3 foreign languages, thesis/dissertation, seminars, preliminary exams, oral exam. *Entrance requirements:* For master's, bachelor's degree or equivalent in Chinese; for doctorate, master's degree or equivalent in Chinese. Electronic applications accepted. *Faculty research:* Chinese historical and modern linguistics, classical Chinese literary and cultural history, modern Chinese literary and cultural history, Chinese paleography.

**Valparaiso University,** Graduate School and Continuing Education, Program in Chinese Studies, Valparaiso, IN 46383. Offers MA, JD/MA. *Program availability:* Part-time, evening/weekend. *Entrance requirements:* For master's, minimum GPA of 3.0, Chinese language proficiency. Additional exam requirements/recommendations for international students: Required—TOEFL (minimum score 550 paper-based; 80 iBT), IELTS (minimum score 6). Electronic applications accepted. *Expenses: Tuition:* Full-time $11,070; part-time $615 per credit hour. *Required fees:* $116 per semester. Tuition and fees vary according to course load, degree level and program.

**Washington University in St. Louis,** The Graduate School, Department of East Asian Languages and Cultures, St. Louis, MO 63130-4899. Offers Chinese (MA); Chinese and comparative literature (PhD); Chinese language and literature (PhD); East Asian studies (MA); Japanese (MA); Japanese and comparative literature (PhD); Japanese language and literature (PhD). Terminal master's awarded for partial completion of doctoral program. *Degree requirements:* For master's, thesis optional; for doctorate, thesis/dissertation. *Entrance requirements:* For master's and doctorate, GRE General Test. Additional exam requirements/recommendations for international students: Required—TOEFL. Electronic applications accepted. *Faculty research:* Chinese; Japanese; Chinese fiction, theater, poetry, modern literature; Japanese modern and classical fiction, translation theory.

# Classics

**American Public University System,** AMU/APU Graduate Programs, Charles Town, WV 25414. Offers accounting (MBA, MS); applied business analytics (MBA, MS); criminal justice (MA), including business administration, emergency and disaster management, general (MA, MS); educational leadership (M Ed); emergency and disaster management (MA); entrepreneurship (MBA); environmental policy and management (MS), including environmental planning, environmental sustainability, fish and wildlife management, general (MA, MS), global environmental management; finance (MBA); general (MBA); government contracting and acquisition (MBA); health care administration (MBA); health information management (MS); history (MA), including American history, ancient and classical history, European history, global history, public history; homeland security (MA), including business administration, counterterrorism studies, criminal justice, cyber, emergency management and public health, intelligence studies, transportation security; homeland security resource allocation (MBA); humanities (MA); information technology (MS), including digital forensics, enterprise software development, information assurance and security, IT project management; information technology management (MBA); intelligence studies (MA), including criminal intelligence, cyber, general (MA, MS), homeland security, intelligence analysis, intelligence collection, intelligence management, intelligence operations, terrorism studies; international relations and conflict resolution (MA), including comparative and security issues, conflict resolution, international and transnational security issues, peacekeeping; legal studies (MA); management (MA), including strategic consulting; marketing (MBA); military history (MA), including American military history, American Revolution, civil war, war since 1945, World War II; military studies (MA), including joint warfare, strategic leadership; national security studies (MA), including cyber, general (MA, MS), homeland security, regional security studies, security and intelligence analysis, terrorism studies; nonprofit management (MBA); political science (MA), including American politics and government, comparative government and development, general (MA, MS), international relations, public policy; psychology (MA); public administration (MPA), including disaster management, environmental policy, health policy, human resources, national security, organizational management, security management; public health (MPH); reverse logistics management (MA); security management (MA); space studies (MS), including aerospace science, general (MA, MS), planetary science; sports and health sciences (MS); sports management (MBA); teaching (M Ed), including autism spectrum disorder, curriculum and instruction for elementary teachers, elementary reading, English language learners, instructional leadership, online learning, special education, STEAM (STEM plus the arts); transportation and logistics management (MA). *Program availability:* Part-time, evening/weekend, online only, 100% online. *Faculty:* 401 full-time (228 women), 1,678 part-time/adjunct (781 women). *Students:* 378 full-time (184 women), 8,455 part-time (3,484

women); includes 2,972 minority (1,552 Black or African American, non-Hispanic/Latino; 52 American Indian or Alaska Native, non-Hispanic/Latino; 211 Asian, non-Hispanic/Latino; 791 Hispanic/Latino; 70 Native Hawaiian or other Pacific Islander, non-Hispanic/Latino; 296 Two or more races, non-Hispanic/Latino), 109 international. Average age 37. In 2016, 3,185 master's awarded. *Degree requirements:* For master's, comprehensive exam or practicum. *Entrance requirements:* For master's, official transcript showing earned bachelor's degree from institution accredited by recognized accrediting body. Additional exam requirements/recommendations for international students: Required—TOEFL (minimum score 550 paper-based), IELTS (minimum score 6.5). *Application deadline:* Applications are processed on a rolling basis. Application fee: $0. Electronic applications accepted. *Expenses: Tuition:* Part-time $350 per credit hour. *Required fees:* $50 per course. *Financial support:* Scholarships/grants available. Financial award applicants required to submit FAFSA. *Unit head:* Dr. Karan Powell, President, 877-468-6268, Fax: 304-724-3780. *Application contact:* Terry Grant, Vice President of Enrollment Management, 877-468-6268, Fax: 304-724-3780, E-mail: info@apus.edu. Website: http://www.apus.edu

**Asbury University,** School of Graduate and Professional Studies, Wilmore, KY 40390-1198. Offers biology: alternative certificate (MA Ed); chemistry: alternative certificate (MA Ed); English (MA Ed); English as a second language (MA Ed); ESL (MA Ed); French (MA Ed); Latin: alternative certificate (MA Ed); mathematics: alternative certificate (MA Ed); reading/writing endorsement (MA Ed); social studies (MA Ed); social work (MSW), including child and family services; Spanish (MA Ed); special education (MA Ed); special education: alternative certificate (MA Ed); teacher as leader endorsement (MA Ed). *Accreditation:* NCATE. *Program availability:* Part-time. *Degree requirements:* For master's, action research project, portfolio. *Entrance requirements:* For master's, PRAXIS/NTE, minimum GPA of 2.75, letters of recommendation. Additional exam requirements/recommendations for international students: Required—TOEFL (minimum score 550 paper-based). Electronic applications accepted.

**Bethel Seminary,** Graduate and Professional Programs, St. Paul, MN 55112-6998. Offers Anglican studies (Certificate); children's and family ministry (MA); Christian studies (Certificate); Christian thought (MA); church planting (Certificate); Greek and Hebrew language (M Div); Greek language (M Div); Hebrew language (M Div); marriage and family therapy (MA, Certificate); mental health counseling (MA); ministry (MA, D Min); ministry practice (Certificate); theological studies (MA, Certificate); transformational leadership (MA); young life youth ministry (Certificate). *Accreditation:* ACIPE. *Program availability:* Part-time, evening/weekend, blended/hybrid learning. *Faculty:* 14 full-time (4 women), 37 part-time/adjunct (17 women). *Students:* 369 full-time (165 women), 147 part-time (43 women); includes 138 minority (48 Black or African

## Classics

American, non-Hispanic/Latino; 45 Asian, non-Hispanic/Latino; 28 Hispanic/Latino; 2 Native Hawaiian or other Pacific Islander, non-Hispanic/Latino; 15 Two or more races, non-Hispanic/Latino), 15 international. 322 applicants, 75% accepted, 174 enrolled. In 2016, 168 master's, 24 doctorates, 6 other advanced degrees awarded. *Degree requirements:* For master's, variable foreign language requirement, thesis (for some programs); for doctorate, thesis/dissertation. *Entrance requirements:* For master's, letters of reference, transcripts, personal statement; for doctorate, M Div, letters of reference, organizational support; for Certificate, letters of reference, family essay, personal statement, and family of origin paper (for marriage and family therapy). Additional exam requirements/recommendations for international students: Required—TOEFL (minimum score 550 paper-based; 87 iBT). *Application deadline:* For fall admission, 8/1 priority date for domestic students, 8/1 for international students; for winter admission, 12/1 priority date for domestic students; for spring admission, 1/1 priority date for domestic students. Applications are processed on a rolling basis. Application fee: $0. Electronic applications accepted. *Expenses:* Contact institution. *Financial support:* In 2016–17, 404 students received support. Teaching assistantships, career-related internships or fieldwork, Federal Work-Study, and scholarships/grants available. Financial award applicants required to submit FAFSA. *Faculty research:* Nature of theology, ethics, Biblical commentaries, nature of God, science and theology. *Unit head:* Dr. David Clark, Vice-President and Dean, 651-638-6659, E-mail: d-clark@bethel.edu. *Application contact:* Jen Niska, Director of Admissions, 651-638-6288, Fax: 651-638-6002, E-mail: seminary-admissions@bethel.edu. Website: https://www.bethel.edu/seminary

**Boston College,** Graduate School of Arts and Sciences, Department of Classics, Chestnut Hill, MA 02467-3800. Offers classics (MA); Greek (MA); Latin (MA). *Program availability:* Part-time. *Students:* 5 full-time (3 women); includes 1 minority (Asian, non-Hispanic/Latino). 12 applicants, 50% accepted, 2 enrolled. In 2016, 1 master's awarded. *Degree requirements:* For master's, one foreign language, thesis optional. *Entrance requirements:* For master's, GRE. Additional exam requirements/recommendations for international students: Required—TOEFL (minimum score 600 paper-based; 100 iBT), IELTS (minimum score 8). *Application deadline:* For fall admission, 2/1 for domestic and international students. Application fee: $75. Electronic applications accepted. Tuition and fees vary according to program. *Financial support:* In 2016–17, 5 students received support, including 2 teaching assistantships with full tuition reimbursements available (averaging $9,200 per year); Federal Work-Study, scholarships/grants, tuition waivers (full and partial), and unspecified assistantships also available. Support available to part-time students. Financial award application deadline: 3/1; financial award applicants required to submit FAFSA. *Faculty research:* Latin, Greek, classical philology, ancient history, modern Greek. *Unit head:* Dr. Gail Hoffman, Chairperson, 617-552-2236, E-mail: hoffmaga@bc.edu. *Application contact:* Gail Rider, Administrative Assistant, 617-552-3661, E-mail: gail.rider@bc.edu.
Website: http://www.bc.edu/classics

**Boston University,** Graduate School of Arts and Sciences, Department of Classical Studies, Boston, MA 02215. Offers MA, PhD, MA/PhD. *Students:* 20 full-time (9 women), 1 part-time (0 women); includes 3 minority (both Two or more races, non-Hispanic/Latino), 2 international. Average age 32. 42 applicants, 26% accepted, 2 enrolled. In 2016, 1 master's, 1 doctorate awarded. Terminal master's awarded for partial completion of doctoral program. *Degree requirements:* For master's, one foreign language, comprehensive exam; for doctorate, 2 foreign languages, comprehensive exam, thesis/dissertation. *Entrance requirements:* For master's and doctorate, GRE General Test, 3 letters of recommendation, transcripts, scholarly writing sample, personal statement. Additional exam requirements/recommendations for international students: Required—TOEFL (minimum score 550 paper-based; 84 iBT). *Application deadline:* For fall admission, 1/15 for domestic and international students; for spring admission, 10/15 for domestic and international students. Application fee: $95. Electronic applications accepted. *Financial support:* In 2016–17, 19 students received support, including 3 fellowships with full tuition reimbursements available (averaging $21,500 per year), research assistantships with full tuition reimbursements available (averaging $21,500 per year), 13 teaching assistantships with full tuition reimbursements available (averaging $21,500 per year); career-related internships or fieldwork, Federal Work-Study, institutionally sponsored loans, and health care benefits also available. Financial award application deadline: 1/15. *Faculty research:* Homer and Hesiod, tragedy and comedy, classical tradition, fifth-century Athenian history, empire literature and history. *Unit head:* Stephen Scully, Chair, 617-353-4572, Fax: 617-353-1610, E-mail: sscully@bu.edu. *Application contact:* Meghan Kelly, Department Administrator, 617-353-2426, Fax: 617-353-1610, E-mail: mekel@bu.edu.
Website: http://www.bu.edu/classics/

**Brandeis University,** Graduate School of Arts and Sciences, Department of Classical Studies, Waltham, MA 02454-9110. Offers MA. *Program availability:* Part-time. *Faculty:* 6 full-time (4 women), 1 part-time/adjunct (0 women). *Students:* 20 full-time (12 women); includes 2 minority (both Hispanic/Latino), 2 international. 31 applicants, 71% accepted, 13 enrolled. In 2016, 11 master's awarded. *Degree requirements:* For master's, variable foreign language requirement, thesis or alternative, capstone course, paper. *Entrance requirements:* For master's, 2 recommendation letters, curriculum vitae or resume, statement of purpose, official transcript(s). Additional exam requirements/recommendations for international students: Required—TOEFL (minimum score 600 paper-based; 100 iBT); Recommended—IELTS (minimum score 7), TSE (minimum score 68). *Application deadline:* For fall admission, 2/15 for domestic students. Applications are processed on a rolling basis. Application fee: $75. Electronic applications accepted. *Financial support:* In 2016–17, 20 students received support, including 20 teaching assistantships with partial tuition reimbursements available (averaging $3,200 per year); scholarships/grants and tuition waivers (partial) also available. Support available to part-time students. Financial award application deadline: 4/15; financial award applicants required to submit FAFSA. *Faculty research:* Languages, literatures, history, and archaeology of ancient Greece and ancient Rome. *Unit head:* Dr. Ann Olga Koloski-Ostrow, Chair, Graduate Program, 781-736-2183, E-mail: aoko@brandeis.edu. *Application contact:* Heidi McAllister, Department Administrator, 781-736-2180, Fax: 781-736-2184, E-mail: hmcallister@brandeis.edu.
Website: http://www.brandeis.edu/gsas

**Brigham Young University,** Graduate Studies, College of Humanities, Department of Comparative Arts and Letters, Provo, UT 84602. Offers comparative studies (MA). *Faculty:* 29 full-time (8 women). *Students:* 19 full-time (12 women), 1 part-time (0 women); includes 1 minority (Hispanic/Latino). Average age 29. 12 applicants, 67% accepted, 6 enrolled. In 2016, 5 master's awarded. *Degree requirements:* For master's, 2 foreign languages, comprehensive exam, thesis. *Entrance requirements:* For master's, GRE, minimum GPA of 3.0 in last 60 hours, writing sample, foreign language experience. Additional exam requirements/recommendations for international students: Required—TOEFL (minimum score 580 paper-based; 85 iBT), IELTS (minimum score 7). *Application deadline:* For fall admission, 3/1 for domestic and international students. Application fee: $50. Electronic applications accepted. *Expenses: Tuition:* Full-time $6680; part-time $393 per credit. Tuition and fees vary according to course load, program and student's religious affiliation. *Financial support:* In 2016–17, 19 students received support, including 33 fellowships with partial tuition reimbursements available (averaging $2,566 per year), 4 research assistantships (averaging $1,500 per year), 29

teaching assistantships (averaging $2,658 per year); scholarships/grants, tuition waivers (full and partial), unspecified assistantships, and student instructorships also available. Support available to part-time students. *Faculty research:* Latin American literature and translation, Mormon women artists, documentary photography, Lucan studies, African Mormon women's oral histories. *Unit head:* Dr. Roger Macfarlane, Graduate Coordinator/Professor of Classical Studies, 801-422-9078, Fax: 801-422-0305, E-mail: macfarlane@byu.edu. *Application contact:* Andrea Kristensen, Graduate Program Manager, 801-422-2996, Fax: 801-422-0305, E-mail: andrea_kristensen@byu.edu. Website: http://cal.byu.edu/

**Brock University,** Faculty of Graduate Studies, Faculty of Humanities, Program in Classics, St. Catharines, ON L2S 3A1, Canada. Offers MA. *Program availability:* Part-time. *Degree requirements:* For master's, one foreign language, major research paper or thesis. *Entrance requirements:* For master's, honors degree, 3 letters of reference, written work (no more than 20 pages). Additional exam requirements/recommendations for international students: Required—TOEFL (minimum score 550 paper-based; 80 iBT), IELTS (minimum score 6.5), TWE (minimum score 4). Electronic applications accepted.

**Brown University,** Graduate School, Department of Classics, Providence, RI 02912. Offers MA, PhD. Terminal master's awarded for partial completion of doctoral program. *Degree requirements:* For master's, one foreign language, thesis; for doctorate, 2 foreign languages, thesis/dissertation. *Entrance requirements:* For master's and doctorate, GRE General Test. *Faculty research:* Philology, archaeology, Sanskrit.

**Bryn Mawr College,** Graduate School of Arts and Sciences, Department of Greek, Latin, and Classical Studies, Bryn Mawr, PA 19010-2899. Offers MA, PhD. *Program availability:* Part-time. *Faculty:* 5 full-time (3 women). *Students:* 17 full-time (11 women), 2 part-time (1 woman). Average age 30. 14 applicants, 36% accepted, 3 enrolled. In 2016, 2 master's awarded. Terminal master's awarded for partial completion of doctoral program. *Degree requirements:* For master's, 2 foreign languages, thesis; for doctorate, 3 foreign languages, comprehensive exam, thesis/dissertation. *Entrance requirements:* For master's and doctorate, GRE General Test, transcripts, three letters of recommendation, statement of interest, resume or curriculum vitae, writing sample. Additional exam requirements/recommendations for international students: Required—TOEFL (minimum score 600 paper-based; 100 iBT), IELTS (minimum score 7). *Application deadline:* For fall admission, 12/15 for domestic and international students. Application fee: $50. Electronic applications accepted. *Expenses: Tuition:* Full-time $40,620; part-time $6770 per unit. Tuition and fees vary according to program. *Financial support:* In 2016–17, 19 students received support, including 11 fellowships with tuition reimbursements available (averaging $16,500 per year), 2 teaching assistantships with tuition reimbursements available (averaging $19,000 per year); Federal Work-Study, scholarships/grants, health care benefits, and tuition waivers also available. Support available to part-time students. Financial award application deadline: 12/15. *Unit head:* Maria Dantis, Graduate Program Administrator, 610-526-5074, E-mail: gsas@brynmawr.edu.

**The Catholic University of America,** School of Arts and Sciences, Department of Greek and Latin, Washington, DC 20064. Offers Greek (MA, Certificate); Greek and Latin (MA, PhD, Certificate); Latin (MA, Certificate). *Program availability:* Part-time. *Faculty:* 5 full-time (1 woman), 3 part-time/adjunct (2 women). *Students:* 3 full-time (2 women), 18 part-time (7 women); includes 2 minority (both Two or more races, non-Hispanic/Latino), 1 international. Average age 35. 10 applicants, 80% accepted, 3 enrolled. In 2016, 3 master's, 1 doctorate awarded. *Degree requirements:* For master's, one foreign language, comprehensive exam; for doctorate, 2 foreign languages, comprehensive exam, thesis/dissertation. *Entrance requirements:* For master's and doctorate, GRE General Test, statement of purpose, official copies of academic transcripts, three letters of recommendation; for Certificate, bachelor's degree. Additional exam requirements/recommendations for international students: Required—TOEFL (minimum score 550 paper-based; 80 iBT). *Application deadline:* For fall admission, 7/15 priority date for domestic students, 7/1 for international students; for spring admission, 11/15 priority date for domestic students, 11/1 for international students. Applications are processed on a rolling basis. Application fee: $55. Electronic applications accepted. *Expenses:* $42,850 per year; $1,170 per credit; $200 per semester part-time fees. *Financial support:* Fellowships, research assistantships, teaching assistantships, Federal Work-Study, scholarships/grants, tuition waivers (full and partial), and unspecified assistantships available. Financial award application deadline: 2/1; financial award applicants required to submit FAFSA. *Faculty research:* Greek and Latin history and literature; classical, late antique and patristic history and literature. *Total annual research expenditures:* $2,618. *Unit head:* Dr. Sarah Ferrario, Chair, 202-319-5216, Fax: 202-319-5297, E-mail: ferrario@cua.edu. *Application contact:* Director of Graduate Admissions, 202-319-5057, Fax: 202-319-6533, E-mail: cua-admissions@cua.edu.
Website: http://greeklatin.cua.edu/

**City College of the City University of New York,** Graduate School, Division of Humanities and the Arts, Department of Classical and Modern Languages and Literatures, New York, NY 10031-9198. Offers Spanish (MA). *Degree requirements:* For master's, one foreign language, comprehensive exam, thesis or alternative. *Entrance requirements:* For master's, minimum GPA of 3.0. Additional exam requirements/recommendations for international students: Required—TOEFL (minimum score 500 paper-based; 61 iBT). Electronic applications accepted. Tuition and fees vary according to course load, degree level and program.

**Columbia University,** Graduate School of Arts and Sciences, New York, NY 10027. Offers African-American studies (MA); American studies (MA); anthropology (MA, PhD); art history and archaeology (MA, PhD); astronomy (PhD); biological sciences (PhD); biotechnology (MA); chemical physics (PhD); chemistry (PhD); classical studies (MA, PhD); classics (MA, PhD); climate and society (MA); conservation biology (MA); earth and environmental sciences (PhD); East Asia: regional studies (MA); East Asian languages and cultures (MA, PhD); ecology, evolution and environmental biology (MA), including conservation biology; ecology, evolution, and environmental biology (PhD), including ecology and evolutionary biology, evolutionary primatology; economics (MA, PhD); English and comparative literature (MA, PhD); French and Romance philology (MA, PhD); Germanic languages (MA, PhD); global French studies (MA); global thought (MA); Hispanic cultural studies (MA); history (PhD); history and literature (MA); human rights studies (MA); Islamic studies (MA); Italian (MA, PhD); Japanese pedagogy (MA); Jewish studies (MA); Latin America and the Caribbean: regional studies (MA); Latin American and Iberian cultures (PhD); mathematics (MA, PhD), including finance (MA); medieval and Renaissance studies (MA); Middle Eastern, South Asian, and African studies (MA, PhD); modern art: critical and curatorial studies (MA); modern European studies (MA); museum anthropology (MA); music (DMA, PhD); oral history (MA); philosophical foundations of physics (MA); philosophy (MA, PhD); physics (PhD); political science (MA, PhD); psychology (PhD); quantitative methods in the social sciences (MA); religion (MA, PhD); Russia, Eurasia and East Europe: regional studies (MA); Russian translation (MA); Slavic cultures (MA); Slavic languages (MA, PhD); sociology (MA, PhD); South Asian studies (MA); statistics (MA, PhD); theatre (PhD). Dual-degree programs require admission to both Graduate School of Arts and Sciences and another Columbia school. *Program availability:* Part-time. Terminal master's awarded for partial completion of doctoral program. *Degree requirements:* For master's, variable foreign language requirement, comprehensive exam (for some programs), thesis (for some programs); for doctorate, variable foreign language requirement, comprehensive exam (for some programs), thesis/dissertation. *Entrance requirements:* For master's and doctorate, GRE General Test, GRE Subject Test (for some programs). Additional exam requirements/recommendations for international students: Required—TOEFL, IELTS. Electronic applications accepted.

**Cornell University,** Graduate School, Graduate Fields of Arts and Sciences, Field of Classics, Ithaca, NY 14853. Offers ancient history (PhD); ancient philosophy (PhD); classical archaeology (PhD); classical literature and philology (PhD); classical myth (PhD); classical rhetoric (PhD); Greek and Latin language and linguistics (PhD); Indo-European linguistics (PhD); medieval and Renaissance Latin literature (PhD). *Degree requirements:* For doctorate, 2 foreign languages, comprehensive exam, thesis/dissertation. *Entrance requirements:* For doctorate, GRE General Test, 3 letters of recommendation, sample of written work. Additional exam requirements/recommendations for international students: Required—TOEFL (minimum score 550 paper-based; 77 iBT). Electronic applications accepted. *Faculty research:* Greek and Roman literature, ancient philosophy, Greek and Roman archaeology, ancient history, Indo-European linguistics.

**Dalhousie University,** Faculty of Arts and Social Science, Department of Classics, Halifax, NS B3H 4R2, Canada. Offers MA, PhD. *Entrance requirements:* Additional exam requirements/recommendations for international students: Required—TOEFL, IELTS, CANTEST, CAEL, or Michigan English Language Assessment Battery. Electronic applications accepted.

**Duke University,** Graduate School, Department of Classical Studies, Durham, NC 27708-0103. Offers PhD. *Degree requirements:* For doctorate, 2 foreign languages, thesis/dissertation. *Entrance requirements:* For doctorate, GRE General Test. Additional exam requirements/recommendations for international students: Required—TOEFL (minimum score 577 paper-based; 90 iBT) or IELTS (minimum score 7). Electronic applications accepted. *Faculty research:* Greek Bronze Age; classical and Roman archaeology; Pompeii and Hadrian; epigraphy, papyrology, and Latin paleography.

**Duquesne University,** School of Education, Department of Instruction and Leadership, Program in Secondary Education, Pittsburgh, PA 15282-0001. Offers biology (MS Ed); chemistry (MS Ed); English (MS Ed); K-12 education (MS Ed), including Latin; mathematics (MS Ed); physics (MS Ed); social studies (MS Ed). *Program availability:* Part-time, evening/weekend. *Faculty:* 5 full-time (4 women). *Students:* 21 full-time (8 women), 4 part-time (0 women); includes 3 minority (2 Black or African American, non-Hispanic/Latino; 1 Two or more races, non-Hispanic/Latino). Average age 28. 12 applicants, 100% accepted, 7 enrolled. In 2016, 19 master's awarded. *Degree requirements:* For master's, thesis optional. *Entrance requirements:* For master's, letters of recommendation, letter of intent, interview, bachelor's degree. Additional exam requirements/recommendations for international students: Required—TOEFL (minimum score 550 paper-based), IELTS (minimum score 7). *Application deadline:* For fall admission, 9/1 for domestic students; for spring admission, 1/1 for domestic students. Applications are processed on a rolling basis. Application fee: $0. Electronic applications accepted. *Expenses: Tuition:* Full-time $22,212; part-time $1234 per credit. Tuition and fees vary according to program. *Financial support:* Research assistantships and Federal Work-Study available. Support available to part-time students. *Unit head:* Dr. Melissa Boston, Associate Professor and Director, 412-396-6109, E-mail: bostonm@duq.edu. *Application contact:* Michael Dolinger, Director of Student and Academic Services, 412-396-6647, Fax: 412-396-5585, E-mail: dolingerm@duq.edu. Website: http://www.duq.edu/academics/schools/education/graduate-programs-education/ms-ed-secondary-education

**Florida State University,** The Graduate School, College of Arts and Sciences, Department of Classics, Tallahassee, FL 32306-1510. Offers ancient history (MA); classical archaeology (MA); classical civilization (MA); classics (PhD), including classical archaeology, classics; Greek (MA); Greek and Latin (MA); Latin (MA). *Faculty:* 17 full-time (7 women), 2 part-time/adjunct (1 woman). *Students:* 47 full-time (29 women); includes 3 minority (1 Black or African American, non-Hispanic/Latino; 1 Asian, non-Hispanic/Latino; 1 Hispanic/Latino). Average age 25. 50 applicants, 40% accepted, 12 enrolled. In 2016, 4 master's, 3 doctorates awarded. Terminal master's awarded for partial completion of doctoral program. *Degree requirements:* For master's, 2 foreign languages, comprehensive exam, thesis or alternative; for doctorate, 4 foreign languages, comprehensive exam, thesis/dissertation. *Entrance requirements:* For master's, GRE General Test, minimum GPA of 3.0; for doctorate, GRE General Test, minimum GPA of 3.5. Additional exam requirements/recommendations for international students: Required—TOEFL (minimum score 550 paper-based; 80 iBT). *Application deadline:* For fall admission, 12/15 priority date for domestic students, 12/15 for international students. Applications are processed on a rolling basis. Application fee: $30. Electronic applications accepted. *Expenses:* Tuition, state resident: full-time $7263; part-time $403.51 per credit hour. Tuition, nonresident: full-time $18,087; part-time $1004.85 per credit hour. *Required fees:* $1365; $75.81 per credit hour. $20 per semester. Tuition and fees vary according to campus/location. *Financial support:* In 2016–17, 45 students received support, including 2 fellowships with full tuition reimbursements available (averaging $18,000 per year), 3 research assistantships with full tuition reimbursements available (averaging $12,000 per year), 25 teaching assistantships with full tuition reimbursements available (averaging $14,000 per year); Federal Work-Study, scholarships/grants, tuition waivers (full), and unspecified assistantships also available. Financial award application deadline: 1/15; financial award applicants required to submit FAFSA. *Faculty research:* Greek and Latin literature, classical archaeology, mythology, ancient history, religion. *Total annual research expenditures:* $100,000. *Unit head:* Dr. Daniel J. Pullen, Chairman, 850-644-0304, Fax: 850-644-4073, E-mail: dpullen@fsu.edu. *Application contact:* Dr. Timothy Stover, Admissions Director, 850-644-4259, Fax: 850-644-4073, E-mail: tstover@fsu.edu. Website: http://classics.fsu.edu/

**Fordham University,** Graduate School of Arts and Sciences, Department of Classical Languages and Literatures, New York, NY 10458. Offers MA, PhD. *Program availability:* Part-time, evening/weekend. *Faculty:* 7 full-time (1 woman). *Students:* 7 full-time (2 women), 4 part-time (2 women), 1 international. Average age 31. 9 applicants, 33% accepted, 1 enrolled. In 2016, 1 master's, 2 doctorates awarded. Terminal master's awarded for partial completion of doctoral program. *Degree requirements:* For master's, one foreign language, comprehensive exam; for doctorate, 2 foreign languages, comprehensive exam, thesis/dissertation. *Entrance requirements:* For master's and doctorate, GRE General Test. Additional exam requirements/recommendations for international students: Required—TOEFL (minimum score 650 paper-based). *Application deadline:* For fall admission, 1/4 priority date for domestic students; for spring admission, 11/1 for domestic students. Application fee: $70. Electronic applications accepted. *Financial support:* In 2016–17, 11 students received support, including 2 fellowships with tuition reimbursements available (averaging $27,000 per year), 4 teaching assistantships with tuition reimbursements available (averaging $21,000 per year); Federal Work-Study, institutionally sponsored loans, scholarships/grants, tuition waivers (full and partial), and unspecified assistantships also available. Support available to part-time students. Financial award application deadline: 1/4; financial award applicants required to submit FAFSA. *Unit head:* Dr. Matthew McGowan,

Chair, 718-817-3140, Fax: 718-817-3134, E-mail: mamcgowan@fordham.edu. *Application contact:* Bernadette Valentino-Morrison, Director of Graduate Admissions, 718-817-4419, Fax: 718-817-3566, E-mail: valentinomor@fordham.edu.

**The Graduate Center, City University of New York,** Graduate Studies, Program in Classics, New York, NY 10016-4039. Offers MA, PhD. *Degree requirements:* For master's, 2 foreign languages, thesis; for doctorate, 2 foreign languages, thesis/dissertation. *Entrance requirements:* For master's and doctorate, GRE General Test. Additional exam requirements/recommendations for international students: Required—TOEFL. Electronic applications accepted.

**The Graduate Center, City University of New York,** Graduate Studies, Program in Comparative Literature, New York, NY 10016-4039. Offers comparative literature (MA, PhD), including classics (PhD), German (PhD), Italian (PhD). PhD offered jointly with New York University. Terminal master's awarded for partial completion of doctoral program. *Degree requirements:* For master's, 2 foreign languages, comprehensive exam, thesis; for doctorate, 3 foreign languages, comprehensive exam, thesis/dissertation. *Entrance requirements:* For master's and doctorate, GRE General Test. Additional exam requirements/recommendations for international students: Required—TOEFL. Electronic applications accepted.

**Harvard University,** Graduate School of Arts and Sciences, Department of the Classics, Cambridge, MA 02138. Offers Byzantine Greek (PhD); classical archaeology (PhD); classical philology (PhD); classical philosophy (PhD); medieval Latin (PhD). *Degree requirements:* For doctorate, 4 foreign languages, thesis/dissertation, preliminary and special exams. *Entrance requirements:* For doctorate, GRE General Test. Additional exam requirements/recommendations for international students: Required—TOEFL.

**Heritage Christian University,** Graduate Programs, Florence, AL 35630. Offers counseling (MM); Greek (MA); ministry (MM); New Testament (MA). *Degree requirements:* For master's, practicum (MM), major research paper (MA). *Entrance requirements:* For master's, MAT or GRE, bachelor's degree in Bible from an accredited college or university, minimum GPA of 2.75, 3 letters of recommendation.

**Hunter College of the City University of New York,** Graduate School, School of Arts and Sciences, Department of Classical and Oriental Studies, Program in Teaching Latin, New York, NY 10065-5085. Offers MA. *Program availability:* Part-time, evening/weekend. *Degree requirements:* For master's, one foreign language. *Entrance requirements:* For master's, undergraduate major in Latin or equivalent with minimum GPA of 3.0; 2 letters of recommendation; personal statement. Additional exam requirements/recommendations for international students: Required—TOEFL. *Application deadline:* For fall admission, 4/28 for domestic students; for spring admission, 11/21 for domestic students. *Financial support:* Federal Work-Study, scholarships/grants, and tuition waivers (partial) available. Support available to part-time students. Financial award application deadline: 4/15. *Faculty research:* Late antique religion and social history, women in antiquity, Horace and lyric poetry, Roman comedy, Latin prose. *Unit head:* Robert B. Koehl, Chair, 212-772-5061, E-mail: rkoehl@hunter.cuny.edu. *Application contact:* Milena Solo, Director of Graduate Admissions, 212-772-4480, E-mail: admissions@hunter.cuny.edu. Website: http://www.hunter.cuny.edu/classics/classics/graduate

**Indiana University Bloomington,** University Graduate School, College of Arts and Sciences, Department of Classical Studies, Bloomington, IN 47405. Offers MA, MAT, PhD. *Program availability:* Part-time. *Degree requirements:* For master's, 2 foreign languages, comprehensive exam; for doctorate, 3 foreign languages, thesis/dissertation. *Entrance requirements:* For master's and doctorate, GRE, minimum GPA of 3.0. Additional exam requirements/recommendations for international students: Required—TOEFL. Electronic applications accepted. *Faculty research:* Roman literature (particularly Empire and late Latin), Greek drama, Homer, history of ideas, papyrology.

**Johns Hopkins University,** Zanvyl Krieger School of Arts and Sciences, Department of Classics, Baltimore, MD 21218. Offers PhD. Terminal master's awarded for partial completion of doctoral program. *Degree requirements:* For doctorate, 4 foreign languages, thesis/dissertation. *Entrance requirements:* For doctorate, GRE General Test. Additional exam requirements/recommendations for international students: Required—TOEFL (minimum score 600 paper-based), IELTS (minimum score 7). Electronic applications accepted. *Faculty research:* Greek culture and mythology, classical sculpture, Early Imperial Roman society.

**Knox Theological Seminary,** Graduate Programs, Master of Arts Programs, Fort Lauderdale, FL 33308. Offers Biblical and theological studies (MA); Christian and classical studies (MA). *Accreditation:* ATS. *Program availability:* Part-time, evening/weekend. *Entrance requirements:* Additional exam requirements/recommendations for international students: Required—TOEFL (minimum score 520 paper-based; 83 iBT), TWE (minimum score 5).

**Marshall University,** Academic Affairs Division, College of Liberal Arts, Program in Latin, Huntington, WV 25755. Offers MA, Certificate. *Entrance requirements:* For master's, GRE General Test.

**McMaster University,** School of Graduate Studies, Faculty of Humanities, Department of Classics, Hamilton, ON L8S 4M2, Canada. Offers MA, PhD. *Degree requirements:* For master's, one foreign language, thesis or alternative; for doctorate, 2 foreign languages, comprehensive exam, thesis/dissertation. *Entrance requirements:* For master's, honors degree, minimum B+ average. Additional exam requirements/recommendations for international students: Required—TOEFL (minimum score 580 paper-based). *Faculty research:* Ancient history, art and archaeology, Latin language and literature, Greek language and literature.

**Memorial University of Newfoundland,** School of Graduate Studies, Department of Classics, St. John's, NL A1C 5S7, Canada. Offers MA. *Program availability:* Part-time. *Degree requirements:* For master's, one foreign language, thesis, language exam, translation exam, research essay. *Entrance requirements:* For master's, honors degree in related field, course work in Greek and Latin. Electronic applications accepted. *Faculty research:* Ancient history, historiography, literature, drama, philosophy, paleography, epigraphy, and textual criticism.

**New York University,** Graduate School of Arts and Science, Department of Classics, New York, NY 10012-1019. Offers classics (MA, PhD); poetics and theory (Advanced Certificate). *Program availability:* Part-time. *Degree requirements:* For master's, 4 foreign languages, exam or specialized project; for doctorate, 4 foreign languages, thesis/dissertation, exams. *Entrance requirements:* For master's, GRE General Test, knowledge of Greek and Latin history and literature, proficiency in Greek and Latin translation; for doctorate, GRE General Test. Additional exam requirements/recommendations for international students: Required—TOEFL. *Faculty research:* Greek and Latin literature, Greek and Roman history, epigraphy, Greek and Roman philosophy, classical archeology.

**The Ohio State University,** Graduate School, College of Arts and Sciences, Division of Arts and Humanities, Department of Classics, Columbus, OH 43210. Offers ancient Greek and Latin (MA); Greek studies (MA); Latin studies (MA, PhD); modern Greek (MA, PhD). *Faculty:* 13. *Students:* 22 full-time (13 women). Average age 28. In 2016, 4 master's, 5 doctorates awarded. *Degree requirements:* For master's, 2 foreign

languages, thesis or alternative; for doctorate, 2 foreign languages, thesis/dissertation. *Entrance requirements:* For master's and doctorate, GRE General Test. Additional exam requirements/recommendations for international students: Required—TOEFL (minimum score 550 paper-based; 79 iBT), Michigan English Language Assessment Battery (minimum score 82); Recommended—IELTS (minimum score 7). *Application deadline:* For fall admission, 11/30 priority date for domestic and international students; for winter admission, 12/1 for domestic students, 11/1 for international students; for spring admission, 3/1 for domestic students, 2/1 for international students. Applications are processed on a rolling basis. Application fee: $60 ($70 for international students). Electronic applications accepted. *Financial support:* Fellowships with tuition reimbursements, research assistantships with tuition reimbursements, teaching assistantships with tuition reimbursements, Federal Work-Study, and institutionally sponsored loans available. Support available to part-time students. *Unit head:* Benjamin Acosta-Hughes, Chair, 614-292-2744, E-mail: acosta-hughes.1@osu.edu. *Application contact:* Graduate and Professional Admissions, 614-292-9444, Fax: 614-292-3895, E-mail: gpadmissions@osu.edu.
Website: http://classics.osu.edu/

**Princeton University,** Graduate School, Department of Classics, Princeton, NJ 08544-1019. Offers classical and hellenic studies (PhD); classical philosophy (PhD); history (the ancient world) (PhD); literature and philology (PhD). *Degree requirements:* For doctorate, thesis/dissertation. *Entrance requirements:* For doctorate, GRE General Test, sample of written work. Additional exam requirements/recommendations for international students: Required—TOEFL (minimum score 600 paper-based). Electronic applications accepted.

**Queen's University at Kingston,** School of Graduate Studies, Faculty of Arts and Sciences, Department of Classics, Kingston, ON K7L 3N6, Canada. Offers classics, Greek, Latin (MA). *Program availability:* Part-time. *Degree requirements:* For master's, one foreign language, thesis (for some programs). *Entrance requirements:* For master's, 3 years of Latin, 2 years of Greek. Additional exam requirements/recommendations for international students: Required—TOEFL. Electronic applications accepted. *Faculty research:* Greek and Latin literature, Greek and Roman history, ancient philosophy, Greek archaeology.

**Rutgers University–New Brunswick,** Graduate School-New Brunswick, Department of Classics, Piscataway, NJ 08854-8097. Offers classics (MA, MAT, PhD); interdisciplinary classical studies and ancient history (MA, PhD). *Program availability:* Part-time, evening/weekend. Terminal master's awarded for partial completion of doctoral program. *Degree requirements:* For master's, 3 foreign languages, comprehensive exam, thesis or alternative; for doctorate, 3 foreign languages, comprehensive exam, thesis/dissertation. *Entrance requirements:* For master's and doctorate, GRE General Test. *Faculty research:* Greek and Latin literature, Greek and Roman social and political history, mythology, religion, ancient philosophy.

**San Francisco State University,** Division of Graduate Studies, College of Liberal and Creative Arts, Department of Classics, San Francisco, CA 94132-1722. Offers MA. *Program availability:* Part-time. *Application deadline:* Applications are processed on a rolling basis. *Expenses:* Tuition, state resident: full-time $6738. Tuition, nonresident: full-time $15,666. *Required fees:* $1012. Tuition and fees vary according to degree level and program. *Unit head:* Dr. David Leitao, Chair, 415-338-2068, Fax: 415-338-2664, E-mail: dleitao@sfsu.edu. *Application contact:* Dr. Gillian McIntosh, Graduate Coordinator, 415-338-1537, Fax: 415-338-2664, E-mail: gillianm@sfsu.edu.
Website: http://classics.sfsu.edu/

**Stanford University,** School of Humanities and Sciences, Department of Classics, Stanford, CA 94305-2004. Offers MA, PhD. *Degree requirements:* For master's, 2 foreign languages, thesis or alternative; for doctorate, 4 foreign languages, thesis/dissertation, general exams. *Entrance requirements:* For master's and doctorate, GRE General Test. Additional exam requirements/recommendations for international students: Required—TOEFL. Electronic applications accepted. *Expenses:* Tuition: Full-time $47,331. *Required fees:* $609.

**Texas Tech University,** Graduate School, College of Arts and Sciences, Department of Classical and Modern Languages and Literatures, Lubbock, TX 79409. Offers applied linguistics (MA); classics (MA); German (MA); languages and cultures (MA); Romance languages (MA); Spanish (PhD); MBA/MA. *Program availability:* Part-time. *Faculty:* 56 full-time (37 women), 4 part-time/adjunct (2 women). *Students:* 80 full-time (39 women), 13 part-time (9 women); includes 20 minority (19 Hispanic/Latino; 1 Two or more races, non-Hispanic/Latino), 49 international. Average age 32. 68 applicants, 68% accepted, 31 enrolled. In 2016, 30 master's, 4 doctorates awarded. *Degree requirements:* For master's, comprehensive exam, thesis or alternative; for doctorate, comprehensive exam, thesis/dissertation. *Entrance requirements:* Additional exam requirements/recommendations for international students: Required—TOEFL (minimum score 550 paper-based; 79 iBT). *Application deadline:* For fall admission, 6/1 priority date for domestic students, 1/15 priority date for international students; for spring admission, 9/1 priority date for domestic students, 6/15 priority date for international students. Applications are processed on a rolling basis. Application fee: $75. Electronic applications accepted. *Expenses:* $300 per credit hour full-time resident tuition, $708 per credit hour full-time non-resident tuition; $50.50 per credit hour fee plus $608 per term fee. *Financial support:* In 2016–17, 78 students received support, including 60 fellowships (averaging $2,488 per year), 76 teaching assistantships (averaging $13,011 per year); research assistantships, Federal Work-Study, scholarships/grants, and unspecified assistantships also available. Financial award application deadline: 4/15; financial award applicants required to submit FAFSA. *Faculty research:* Literature, comparative literature, linguistics, culture, applied linguistics. *Total annual research expenditures:* $36,152. *Unit head:* Dr. Erin Collopy, Chair and Associate Professor, 806-834-8497, Fax: 806-742-3306, E-mail: erin.collopy@ttu.edu. *Application contact:* Carla Burrus, Senior Advisor, 806-834-3282, Fax: 806-742-3306, E-mail: carla.burrus@ttu.edu.
Website: http://www.depts.ttu.edu/classic_modern/

**Tufts University,** Graduate School of Arts and Sciences, Department of Classics, Medford, MA 02155. Offers classical archaeology (MA); classics (MA); classics with teaching licensure (MA). *Program availability:* Part-time. *Students:* 9 full-time (6 women); includes 3 minority (1 Black or African American, non-Hispanic/Latino; 1 Asian, non-Hispanic/Latino; 1 Hispanic/Latino), 3 international. Average age 24. 32 applicants, 53% accepted, 7 enrolled. In 2016, 4 master's awarded. *Degree requirements:* For master's, 2 foreign languages, comprehensive exam, thesis or alternative. *Entrance requirements:* For master's, GRE General Test, writing sample. Additional exam requirements/recommendations for international students: Required—TOEFL (minimum score 550 paper-based; 80 iBT), IELTS (minimum score 6.5). *Application deadline:* For fall admission, 2/15 for domestic and international students; for spring admission, 10/15 for domestic and international students. Applications are processed on a rolling basis. Application fee: $85. Electronic applications accepted. *Expenses:* $49,982 full-time tuition (for MA). *Financial support:* In 2016–17, 9 students received support. Teaching assistantships, Federal Work-Study, scholarships/grants, tuition waivers (full and partial), and unspecified assistantships available. Financial award application deadline: 1/15; financial award applicants required to submit FAFSA. *Unit head:* Dr. Marie-Claire Beaulieu, Graduate Program Director. *Application contact:* Office of Graduate Admissions, 617-627-3395, E-mail: gradadmissions@tufts.edu.
Website: http://www.ase.tufts.edu/classics/

**Tulane University,** School of Liberal Arts, Department of Classical Studies, New Orleans, LA 70118-5669. Offers MA. *Degree requirements:* For master's, 2 foreign languages, thesis or alternative. *Entrance requirements:* For master's, GRE General Test, minimum B average in undergraduate course work. Additional exam requirements/recommendations for international students: Required—TOEFL. Electronic applications accepted. *Expenses:* Tuition: Full-time $50,920; part-time $2829 per credit hour. *Required fees:* $2040; $44.50 per credit hour. $580 per term. Tuition and fees vary according to course load, degree level and program.

**Université de Montréal,** Faculty of Arts and Sciences, Program in Classical Studies, Montréal, QC H3C 3J7, Canada. Offers MA. Electronic applications accepted.

**University at Buffalo, the State University of New York,** Graduate School, College of Arts and Sciences, Department of Classics, Buffalo, NY 14261. Offers classics (MA, PhD); Latin (MA). *Faculty:* 10 full-time (3 women), 2 part-time/adjunct (1 woman). *Students:* 29 full-time (16 women). Average age 25. 23 applicants, 70% accepted, 6 enrolled. In 2016, 4 master's, 7 doctorates awarded. Terminal master's awarded for partial completion of doctoral program. *Degree requirements:* For master's, 3 foreign languages, project; for doctorate, 4 foreign languages, comprehensive exam, thesis/dissertation, general and 2 special exams. *Entrance requirements:* For master's and doctorate, GRE General Test. Additional exam requirements/recommendations for international students: Required—TOEFL. *Application deadline:* For fall admission, 1/15 priority date for domestic and international students. Application fee: $75. Electronic applications accepted. *Expenses:* $13,347. *Financial support:* In 2016–17, 18 students received support, including 3 fellowships with full tuition reimbursements available (averaging $4,000 per year), 18 teaching assistantships with full tuition reimbursements available (averaging $14,200 per year); Federal Work-Study, institutionally sponsored loans, and unspecified assistantships also available. Financial award application deadline: 1/15. *Faculty research:* Greek and Latin literature, historiography, and epigraphy; Greek archaeology, mythology, and ancient philosophy; ancient and Roman religion and women's studies. *Total annual research expenditures:* $37,616. *Unit head:* Dr. Roger Woodard, Chair, 716-645-0464, Fax: 716-645-2225, E-mail: rwoodard@buffalo.edu. *Application contact:* Dr. Bradley Ault, Director of Graduate Studies, 716-645-0458, Fax: 716-645-2225, E-mail: clarbrad@buffalo.edu.
Website: http://www.classics.buffalo.edu/

**University at Buffalo, the State University of New York,** Graduate School, Graduate School of Education, Department of Learning and Instruction, Buffalo, NY 14260. Offers biology education (Ed M, Certificate); chemistry education (Ed M, Certificate); childhood education (Ed M); childhood education with bilingual extension (Ed M); college teaching (Advanced Certificate); curriculum, instruction and the science of learning (PhD); early childhood education (Ed M); early childhood education with bilingual extension (Ed M); earth science education (Ed M, Certificate); education and technology (Ed M); education studies (Ed M); educational technology and new literacies (Certificate); educational technology and new literacies (Advanced Certificate); elementary education (Ed D); English education (Ed M, Certificate); English education studies (Ed M); English for speakers of other languages (Ed M); foreign and second language education (PhD); French education (Ed M, Certificate); German education (Ed M, Certificate); gifted education (Certificate); Latin education (Ed M, Certificate); literacy education studies (Ed M); literacy specialist (Ed M); literacy teaching and learning (Certificate); mathematics education (Ed M, Certificate); music education (Ed M, Certificate); music education studies (Ed M); music learning theory (Advanced Certificate); online education (Advanced Certificate); physics education (Ed M, Certificate); science and the public (Ed M); social studies education (Ed M, Certificate); Spanish education (Ed M, Certificate); special education (PhD); teaching English to speakers of other languages (Ed M). *Program availability:* Part-time, evening/weekend, 100% online. *Faculty:* 28 full-time (21 women), 67 part-time/adjunct (49 women). *Students:* 198 full-time (153 women), 312 part-time (220 women); includes 48 minority (28 Black or African American, non-Hispanic/Latino; 4 American Indian or Alaska Native, non-Hispanic/Latino; 15 Asian, non-Hispanic/Latino; 1 Hispanic/Latino), 66 international. Average age 33. 336 applicants, 86% accepted, 178 enrolled. In 2016, 137 master's, 24 doctorates, 25 other advanced degrees awarded. *Degree requirements:* For master's, comprehensive exam; for doctorate, thesis/dissertation, research analysis exam, research experience. *Entrance requirements:* For master's, letters of reference; for doctorate, GRE General Test or MAT, interview, writing sample, letters of recommendation. Additional exam requirements/recommendations for international students: Required—TOEFL (minimum score 600 paper-based; 96 iBT). *Application deadline:* For fall admission, 2/1 priority date for domestic and international students; for spring admission, 11/15 priority date for domestic students, 10/1 for international students. Applications are processed on a rolling basis. Application fee: $50. Electronic applications accepted. *Financial support:* In 2016–17, 44 fellowships (averaging $4,010 per year), 39 research assistantships with tuition reimbursements (averaging $9,897 per year) were awarded; teaching assistantships, career-related internships or fieldwork, Federal Work-Study, institutionally sponsored loans, scholarships/grants, tuition waivers (full and partial), and unspecified assistantships also available. Financial award application deadline: 2/28; financial award applicants required to submit FAFSA. *Faculty research:* Science assessment, foreign language teaching and learning, early learning, new literacies, gender and education. *Total annual research expenditures:* $534,880. *Unit head:* Dr. Deborah Moore-Russo, Chair, 716-645-4069, Fax: 716-645-3161, E-mail: dam29@buffalo.edu. *Application contact:* Luann Zak, Admissions Assistant, 716-645-2110, Fax: 716-645-7937, E-mail: luannzak@buffalo.edu.
Website: http://gse.buffalo.edu/lai

**University of Alberta,** Faculty of Graduate Studies and Research, Department of History and Classics, Edmonton, AB T6G 2E1, Canada. Offers ancient history (PhD); classical archaeology (MA, PhD); classical literature (PhD); classics (MA); history (MA, PhD). *Program availability:* Part-time, evening/weekend. *Degree requirements:* For master's, one foreign language, thesis (for some programs); for doctorate, one foreign language, thesis/dissertation. *Entrance requirements:* For master's, minimum B+ average; for doctorate, minimum A- average. Additional exam requirements/recommendations for international students: Required—TOEFL (minimum score 580 paper-based). Electronic applications accepted. *Faculty research:* Western Canada, classical archaeology, Britain, Eastern Europe, East Asia.

**The University of Arizona,** College of Humanities, Department of Classics, Tucson, AZ 85721. Offers MA. *Program availability:* Part-time. *Degree requirements:* For master's, one foreign language, comprehensive exam, thesis. *Entrance requirements:* For master's, GRE General Test (minimum combined score of 1000 verbal and quantitative), 2 letters of recommendation. Additional exam requirements/recommendations for international students: Required—TOEFL (minimum score 550 paper-based; 79 iBT). Electronic applications accepted. *Faculty research:* Greek and Roman archaeology, ancient Greek, modern Greek, Latin, Greek and Roman religion, women in antiquity.

**The University of British Columbia,** Faculty of Arts, Department of Classical, Near Eastern and Religious Studies, Program in Classics, Vancouver, BC V6T 1Z1, Canada. Offers classics (MA, PhD). *Program availability:* Part-time. *Degree requirements:* For master's, one foreign language, thesis or comprehensive exam; for doctorate, 2 foreign languages, comprehensive exam, thesis/dissertation. *Entrance requirements:* For doctorate, MA. Additional exam requirements/recommendations for international students: Required—TOEFL, IELTS. *Application deadline:* Applications are processed on a rolling basis. Application fee: $100 Canadian dollars ($162 Canadian dollars for international students). Electronic applications accepted. *Expenses:* $4,802 per year tuition and fees, $8,436 per year international. *Financial support:* Fellowships, teaching assistantships, scholarships/grants, and health care benefits available. Financial award application deadline: 1/1. *Faculty research:* Classical archaeology, ancient historians, late antiquity, ancient prose fiction, epigraphy. *Application contact:* Odessa Cadieux-Rey, Graduate Program Staff, 604-822-2515, Fax: 604-822-9431, E-mail: cners.gradsec@ubc.ca. Website: http://cnrs.gradsec@ubc.ca/

**University of Calgary,** Faculty of Graduate Studies, Faculty of Arts, Department of Greek and Roman Studies, Calgary, AB T2N 1N4, Canada. Offers MA, PhD. *Program availability:* Part-time. *Degree requirements:* For master's, one foreign language; for doctorate, 2 foreign languages, comprehensive exam, thesis/dissertation. *Entrance requirements:* For master's, BA in classics or related field, knowledge of Latin and/or Greek, minimum GPA of 3.7; for doctorate, MA in classics or related field, knowledge of Latin and Greek, GPA 3.7. Additional exam requirements/recommendations for international students: Required—TOEFL. Electronic applications accepted. *Faculty research:* Greek literature, Latin literature, Greek history, Roman history, classical archaeology.

**University of California, Berkeley,** Graduate Division, College of Letters and Science, Department of Classics, Berkeley, CA 94720-1500. Offers classical archaeology (MA, PhD); classics (MA, PhD); Greek (MA); Latin (MA). *Faculty:* 19 full-time, 3 part-time/adjunct. *Students:* 27 full-time (11 women); includes 7 minority (3 Asian, non-Hispanic/Latino; 4 Hispanic/Latino), 2 international. Average age 29. 64 applicants, 4 enrolled. In 2016, 4 master's, 5 doctorates awarded. Terminal master's awarded for partial completion of doctoral program. *Degree requirements:* For master's, one foreign language, exams; for doctorate, 2 foreign languages, thesis/dissertation, qualifying exam. *Entrance requirements:* For master's and doctorate, GRE General Test, minimum GPA of 3.0, 3 letters of recommendation. Additional exam requirements/recommendations for international students: Required—TOEFL (minimum score 570 paper-based; 90 iBT), TWE. *Application deadline:* For fall admission, 12/9 for domestic students. Application fee: $105 ($125 for international students). Electronic applications accepted. *Financial support:* Fellowships, research assistantships, teaching assistantships, Federal Work-Study, institutionally sponsored loans, health care benefits, and unspecified assistantships available. *Faculty research:* Greek and Latin literature, textual criticism, history, archaeology and philosophy. *Unit head:* Prof. Ellen Oliensis, Chair, 510-642-4218, Fax: 510-643-2959. *Application contact:* Cassandra Dunn, 510-642-3672, Fax: 510-643-2959, E-mail: cassandrajj@berkeley.edu. Website: http://classics.berkeley.edu/

**University of California, Irvine,** School of Humanities, Department of Classics, Irvine, CA 92697. Offers MA, PhD. *Students:* 4 full-time (2 women), 1 (woman) part-time; includes 2 minority (1 Hispanic/Latino; 1 Two or more races, non-Hispanic/Latino). Average age 37. In 2016, 1 master's awarded. Terminal master's awarded for partial completion of doctoral program. *Degree requirements:* For master's, one foreign language, thesis or alternative; for doctorate, 2 foreign languages, thesis/dissertation. *Entrance requirements:* For master's and doctorate, GRE General Test, minimum GPA of 3.0. Additional exam requirements/recommendations for international students: Required—TOEFL (minimum score 550 paper-based). *Application deadline:* For fall admission, 1/15 priority date for domestic students, 1/15 for international students. Applications are processed on a rolling basis. Application fee: $105 ($125 for international students). Electronic applications accepted. *Financial support:* Fellowships, research assistantships with full tuition reimbursements, teaching assistantships, institutionally sponsored loans, traineeships, health care benefits, and unspecified assistantships available. Financial award application deadline: 3/1; financial award applicants required to submit FAFSA. *Faculty research:* Greek literature, computer application to Greek literature, Latin literature. *Unit head:* Susan Jarratt, Interim Chair, 949-824-6406, E-mail: sjarratt@uci.edu. *Application contact:* Zina Giannopoulou, Graduate Advisor, 949-824-2641, Fax: 949-824-1966, E-mail: zgiannop@uci.edu. Website: http://www.humanities.uci.edu/classics/

**University of California, Los Angeles,** Graduate Division, College of Letters and Science, Department of Classics, Los Angeles, CA 90095. Offers classics (MA, PhD); Greek (MA); Latin (MA). Terminal master's awarded for partial completion of doctoral program. *Degree requirements:* For master's, 2 foreign languages, comprehensive exam; for doctorate, 2 foreign languages, thesis/dissertation, oral and written qualifying exams. *Entrance requirements:* For doctorate, GRE General Test, bachelor's degree; minimum undergraduate GPA of 3.0 (or its equivalent if letter grade system not used); Greek and Latin. Additional exam requirements/recommendations for international students: Required—TOEFL. Electronic applications accepted.

**University of California, Riverside,** Graduate Division, Tri-Campus Program in Classics, Riverside, CA 92521-0102. Offers PhD. Program offered jointly with University of California, Irvine and University of California, San Diego. *Degree requirements:* For doctorate, 3 foreign languages, comprehensive exam, thesis/dissertation. *Entrance requirements:* For doctorate, GRE, MA in classics. Additional exam requirements/recommendations for international students: Required—TOEFL (minimum score 550 paper-based; 80 iBT). Electronic applications accepted. *Expenses:* Tuition, state resident: full-time $16,666. Tuition, nonresident: full-time $31,768. *Required fees:* $11,055.54 per quarter. $3685.18 per quarter. Tuition and fees vary according to campus/location and program. *Faculty research:* Rhetoric, Greek and Latin drama, Hellenistic poetry, Anglo-Latin literature, Greek and Latin prose.

**University of California, Santa Barbara,** Graduate Division, College of Letters and Sciences, Division of Humanities and Fine Arts, Department of Classics, Santa Barbara, CA 93106-2014. Offers ancient history (PhD); classics (MA, PhD); literature and theory (MA); MA/PhD. Terminal master's awarded for partial completion of doctoral program. *Degree requirements:* For master's, 3 foreign languages, comprehensive exam; for doctorate, 4 foreign languages, comprehensive exam, thesis/dissertation. *Entrance requirements:* For master's and doctorate, GRE. Additional exam requirements/recommendations for international students: Required—TOEFL (minimum score 550 paper-based; 80 iBT), IELTS (minimum score 7). Electronic applications accepted. *Faculty research:* Literary theory and cultural history, gender studies, Greek and Latin literature, Greek and Roman history, Greek and Roman drama and performance.

**University of Chicago,** Division of the Humanities, Department of Classics, Chicago, IL 60637. Offers ancient Greek and Roman philosophy (PhD); ancient Mediterranean world (PhD); classical languages and literatures (PhD); transformations in the classical tradition (PhD). *Students:* 36 full-time (19 women); includes 5 minority (1 American Indian or Alaska Native, non-Hispanic/Latino; 1 Asian, non-Hispanic/Latino; 2 Hispanic/Latino; 1 Two or more races, non-Hispanic/Latino), 4 international. 73 applicants, 18% accepted, 8 enrolled. In 2016, 2 doctorates awarded. Terminal master's awarded for partial completion of doctoral program. *Degree requirements:* For doctorate, 3 foreign languages, comprehensive exam (for some programs), thesis/dissertation. *Entrance requirements:* For doctorate, GRE General Test. Additional exam requirements/

recommendations for international students: Required—TOEFL (minimum score 104 iBT), IELTS (minimum score 7). *Application deadline:* For fall admission, 12/15 for domestic and international students. Application fee: $90. Electronic applications accepted. *Financial support:* Fellowships with full tuition reimbursements, teaching assistantships, Federal Work-Study, institutionally sponsored loans, scholarships/grants, and health care benefits available. Financial award application deadline: 12/15; financial award applicants required to submit FAFSA. *Unit head:* Dr. Mark Payne, Chair, 773-702-2516, E-mail: mpayne@uchicago.edu. *Application contact:* Michael Beetley, Assistant Dean of Students, Admissions and Fellowships, 773-702-1552, Fax: 773-834-9148, E-mail: humanitiesadmissions@uchicago.edu. Website: http://classics.uchicago.edu/

**University of Chicago,** Division of the Humanities, Master of Arts Program in the Humanities, Chicago, IL 60637. Offers art history (MA); cinema and media studies (MA); classic languages (MA); comparative literature (MA); creative writing (MA); cultural policy studies (MA); digital humanities (MA); East Asian languages and civilizations (MA); English language and literature (MA); gender and sexuality studies (MA); Germanic studies (MA); linguistics (MA); music (MA); near Eastern languages and civilizations (MA); philosophy (MA); poetics (MA); race, politics and culture (MA); Romance languages and literatures (MA); Slavic languages and literatures (MA); South Asian languages and civilizations (MA); theater and performance studies (MA). *Students:* 80 full-time (43 women), 7 part-time (3 women); includes 20 minority (5 Black or African American, non-Hispanic/Latino; 1 American Indian or Alaska Native, non-Hispanic/Latino; 6 Asian, non-Hispanic/Latino; 5 Hispanic/Latino; 3 Two or more races, non-Hispanic/Latino), 11 international. Average age 26. 706 applicants, 55% accepted, 42 enrolled. In 2016, 92 master's awarded. *Degree requirements:* For master's, thesis. *Entrance requirements:* For master's, GRE General Test. Additional exam requirements/recommendations for international students: Required—TOEFL (minimum score 104 iBT), IELTS (minimum score 7). *Application deadline:* For fall admission, 1/3 for domestic and international students. Application fee: $90. Electronic applications accepted. *Financial support:* In 2016–17, 8 fellowships with partial tuition reimbursements (averaging $12,000 per year) were awarded; Federal Work-Study, institutionally sponsored loans, scholarships/grants, and tuition waivers (partial) also available. Financial award application deadline: 12/15; financial award applicants required to submit FAFSA. *Unit head:* Malynne Sternstein, Co-Director, 773-834-1201, Fax: 773-834-7526. *Application contact:* Program Coordinator, 773-834-1201, Fax: 773-834-7526, E-mail: ma-humanities@uchicago.edu. Website: http://maph.uchicago.edu/

**University of Cincinnati,** Graduate School, McMicken College of Arts and Sciences, Department of Classics, Cincinnati, OH 45221. Offers MA, PhD. *Program availability:* Part-time. Terminal master's awarded for partial completion of doctoral program. *Degree requirements:* For master's, comprehensive exam (for some programs), thesis (for some programs); for doctorate, 2 foreign languages, comprehensive exam, thesis/dissertation. *Entrance requirements:* For master's and doctorate, GRE. Additional exam requirements/recommendations for international students: Required—TOEFL. Electronic applications accepted. *Expenses: Tuition,* area resident: Full-time $12,790; part-time $389 per credit hour. Tuition, state resident: full-time $13,290; part-time $419 per credit hour. Tuition, nonresident: full-time $24,532; part-time $976 per credit hour. International tuition: $24,832 full-time. *Required fees:* $3958; $140 per credit hour. Tuition and fees vary according to course load, degree level, program and reciprocity agreements. *Faculty research:* Archaeology (bronze age and classical), philosophy (Greek and Latin), ancient history (Greek and Roman).

**University of Colorado Boulder,** Graduate School, College of Arts and Sciences, Department of Classics, Boulder, CO 80309. Offers MA, PhD. *Faculty:* 12 full-time (7 women). *Students:* 24 full-time (12 women); includes 3 minority (2 Hispanic/Latino; 1 Two or more races, non-Hispanic/Latino), 1 international. Average age 26. 76 applicants, 59% accepted, 10 enrolled. In 2016, 8 master's, 2 doctorates awarded. Terminal master's awarded for partial completion of doctoral program. *Degree requirements:* For master's, one foreign language, comprehensive exam, thesis or alternative, oral exam; for doctorate, 4 foreign languages, comprehensive exam, thesis/dissertation. *Entrance requirements:* For master's, minimum undergraduate GPA of 2.75; for doctorate, master's degree in classics or related field. *Application deadline:* For fall admission, 4/1 for domestic and international students. Applications are processed on a rolling basis. Application fee: $60 ($80 for international students). Electronic applications accepted. Application fee is waived when completed online. *Financial support:* In 2016–17, 75 students received support, including 25 fellowships (averaging $3,213 per year), 1 research assistantship with full and partial tuition reimbursement available (averaging $39,708 per year), 17 teaching assistantships with full and partial tuition reimbursements available (averaging $33,761 per year); institutionally sponsored loans, scholarships/grants, health care benefits, and unspecified assistantships also available. Financial award application deadline: 1/2; financial award applicants required to submit FAFSA. *Faculty research:* Classical Greek language/literature, classical Latin language/literature, ancient/classical history, classical/ancient language. *Application contact:* E-mail: classics@colorado.edu. Website: http://www.colorado.edu/classics/

**University of Dallas,** Braniff Graduate School of Liberal Arts, Program in Classics, Irving, TX 75062-4736. Offers MA, MC. *Degree requirements:* For master's, comprehensive exam, thesis (for MA).

**University of Florida,** Graduate School, College of Liberal Arts and Sciences, Department of Classics, Gainesville, FL 32611. Offers classical studies (MA, PhD); Latin (MA, MAT, ML). *Program availability:* Part-time, online learning. *Degree requirements:* For master's, one foreign language, thesis (for some programs); for doctorate, 2 foreign languages, comprehensive exam, thesis/dissertation. *Entrance requirements:* For master's, GRE General Test, minimum GPA of 3.0; for doctorate, GRE General Test, minimum GPA of 3.25 in both graduate and undergraduate work; MA in classical studies or equivalent. Additional exam requirements/recommendations for international students: Required—TOEFL (minimum score 550 paper-based; 80 iBT), IELTS (minimum score 6). Electronic applications accepted. *Faculty research:* Augustan Age Rome, ancient archaeology, Athenian democracy, Roman historiography and satire, Modern Greek studies.

**University of Georgia,** Franklin College of Arts and Sciences, Department of Classics, Athens, GA 30602. Offers classical languages (MA); Greek (MA); Latin (MA). *Degree requirements:* For master's, one foreign language, thesis. *Entrance requirements:* For master's, GRE General Test. *Application deadline:* For fall admission, 7/1 priority date for domestic students; for spring admission, 11/15 for domestic students. Application fee: $50. Electronic applications accepted. *Financial support:* Fellowships, research assistantships, teaching assistantships, and unspecified assistantships available. *Unit head:* Dr. Naomi Norman, Head, 706-542-2187, E-mail: nnorman@uga.edu. *Application contact:* Dr. Sarah Spence, Graduate Coordinator, 706-542-0417, Fax: 706-542-8503, E-mail: sspence@uga.edu. Website: http://www.classics.uga.edu/

**University of Illinois at Urbana–Champaign,** Graduate College, College of Liberal Arts and Sciences, School of Literatures, Cultures and Linguistics, Department of Classics, Champaign, IL 61820. Offers classical philology (PhD); classics (MA); teaching of Latin (MA).

*Classics*

**The University of Iowa,** Graduate College, College of Liberal Arts and Sciences, Department of Classics, Iowa City, IA 52242-1316. Offers classics (MA, PhD); Greek (MA); Latin (MA). *Degree requirements:* For master's, exam; for doctorate, comprehensive exam, thesis/dissertation. *Entrance requirements:* For master's and doctorate, GRE General Test, minimum GPA 3.0. Additional exam requirements/recommendations for international students: Required—TOEFL (minimum score 550 paper-based; 81 iBT). Electronic applications accepted.

**The University of Kansas,** Graduate Studies, College of Liberal Arts and Sciences, Department of Classics, Lawrence, KS 66045. Offers MA. *Students:* 9 full-time (6 women); includes 2 minority (1 Asian, non-Hispanic/Latino; 1 Two or more races, non-Hispanic/Latino). Average age 23. 24 applicants, 79% accepted, 6 enrolled. In 2016, 6 master's awarded. *Entrance requirements:* For master's, GRE (recommended), resume (suggested one-page in length), writing sample (25-page maximum), statement of purpose, three letters of reference, official transcripts. Additional exam requirements/recommendations for international students: Required—TOEFL. *Application deadline:* For fall admission, 1/15 priority date for domestic and international students; for spring admission, 10/25 priority date for domestic and international students. Application fee: $65 ($85 for international students). Electronic applications accepted. *Financial support:* Fellowships, teaching assistantships, career-related internships or fieldwork, Federal Work-Study, scholarships/grants, traineeships, and unspecified assistantships available. Support available to part-time students. Financial award application deadline: 1/15; financial award applicants required to submit FAFSA. *Faculty research:* Greek and Roman gender and sexuality, Roman literature (Cicero, Virgil, Horace, elegy, post-Virgilian epic), Greek literature (archaic epic, tragedy, Second Sophistic), Greek art and archaeology (the Bronze Age), Roman art and archaeology (imperial painting and architecture). *Unit head:* Prof. Tara Welch, Chair, 785-864-2395, E-mail: tswelch@ku.edu. *Application contact:* Cari Ann Kreienhop, Graduate Admissions Contact, 785-864-3665, Fax: 785-864-5566, E-mail: ckreienhop@ku.edu. Website: http://classics.drupal.ku.edu/

**University of Kentucky,** Graduate School, College of Arts and Sciences, Program in Modern and Classical Languages and Literatures, Lexington, KY 40506-0032. Offers MA. *Program availability:* Part-time. *Degree requirements:* For master's, one foreign language, comprehensive exam, thesis optional. *Entrance requirements:* For master's, GRE General Test, minimum undergraduate GPA of 2.75. Additional exam requirements/recommendations for international students: Required—TOEFL (minimum score 550 paper-based). Electronic applications accepted. *Faculty research:* Erasmus, Renaissance Latin, Greek and Roman epic, Greek biography, early Christian literature, classical philosophy.

**The University of Manchester,** School of Arts, Histories and Cultures, Manchester, United Kingdom. Offers anthropology, media and performance (PhD); applied theatre professional (PhD); archaeology (PhD); art history and visual studies (PhD); arts management and cultural policy (PhD); classics and ancient history (PhD); composition (PhD); creative writing (PhD); drama (PhD); economic and social history (PhD); electroacoustic composition (PhD); English and American studies (PhD); history (PhD); humanitarianism and conflict response (PhD); museology (PhD); music (PhD); musicology (PhD); religions and theology (PhD).

**University of Manitoba,** Faculty of Graduate Studies, Faculty of Arts, Department of Classics, Winnipeg, MB R3T 2N2, Canada. Offers MA. *Degree requirements:* For master's, thesis.

**University of Maryland, College Park,** Academic Affairs, College of Arts and Humanities, Department of Classics, College Park, MD 20742. Offers MA. *Degree requirements:* For master's, 2 foreign languages, thesis or alternative. *Entrance requirements:* For master's, writing sample, 3 letters of recommendation. Additional exam requirements/recommendations for international students: Required—TOEFL. Electronic applications accepted. *Faculty research:* Latin, Greek, and Roman culture.

**University of Massachusetts Amherst,** Graduate School, College of Humanities and Fine Arts, Department of Classics, Amherst, MA 01003. Offers Latin and classical humanities (MAT). *Program availability:* Part-time. *Degree requirements:* For master's, thesis or alternative. *Entrance requirements:* For master's, GRE General Test. Additional exam requirements/recommendations for international students: Required—TOEFL (minimum score 550 paper-based; 80 iBT), IELTS (minimum score 6.5). Electronic applications accepted.

**University of Massachusetts Boston,** College of Liberal Arts, Program in Latin and Classical Humanities, Boston, MA 02125-3393. Offers MA. *Faculty:* 9 full-time (8 women), 7 part-time/adjunct (4 women). *Students:* 7 full-time (5 women), 7 part-time (3 women); includes 1 minority (Asian, non-Hispanic/Latino). Average age 28. 8 applicants, 88% accepted, 4 enrolled. In 2016, 6 master's awarded. *Expenses:* Tuition, state resident: full-time $16,863. Tuition, nonresident: full-time $32,913. *Required fees:* $177. *Application contact:* Peggy Roldan Patel, Graduate Admissions Coordinator, 617-287-6400, Fax: 617-287-6236, E-mail: bos.gadm@dpc.umassp.edu.

**University of Michigan,** Rackham Graduate School, College of Literature, Science, and the Arts, Department of Classical Studies, Ann Arbor, MI 48109. Offers classical studies (PhD); teaching Latin (MAT). *Faculty:* 22 full-time (11 women), 6 part-time/adjunct (2 women). *Students:* 27 full-time (10 women); includes 3 minority (1 Hispanic/Latino; 2 Two or more races, non-Hispanic/Latino), 6 international. Average age 28. 54 applicants, 19% accepted, 6 enrolled. In 2016, 4 doctorates awarded. Terminal master's awarded for partial completion of doctoral program. *Degree requirements:* For master's, one foreign language, comprehensive exam; for doctorate, 4 foreign languages, comprehensive exam, thesis/dissertation, oral defense of dissertation, preliminary exams, qualifying exams. *Entrance requirements:* For master's, GRE General Test, 2-3 years of Latin (for the Latin MAT); for doctorate, GRE General Test, strict minimum of 3 years of college-level Latin and 2 years of college-level Greek. Additional exam requirements/recommendations for international students: Required—TOEFL (minimum score 560 paper-based). *Application deadline:* For fall admission, 12/15 for domestic and international students. Application fee: $75 ($90 for international students). Electronic applications accepted. *Expenses:* Tuition, state resident: full-time $21,466; part-time $1152 per credit hour. Tuition, nonresident: full-time $43,346; part-time $2367 per credit hour. Part-time tuition and fees vary according to course load, degree level and program. *Financial support:* In 2016–17, 26 students received support, including 11 fellowships with full tuition reimbursements available (averaging $19,000 per year), 15 teaching assistantships with full tuition reimbursements available (averaging $19,000 per year); career-related internships or fieldwork, Federal Work-Study, institutionally sponsored loans, scholarships/grants, traineeships, tuition waivers (full), unspecified assistantships, and summer stipends, year-round health care also available. Financial award application deadline: 3/15. *Faculty research:* Greek and Latin literature, ancient history, papyrology, archaeology. *Unit head:* Prof. Artemis Leontis, Chair and Professor, 734-764-0360, Fax: 734-763-4959, E-mail: classics@umich.edu. *Application contact:* Sarah Kandell-Gritzmaker, Student Services Coordinator, 734-615-3181, Fax: 734-763-4959, E-mail: skandell@umich.edu. Website: http://www.lsa.umich.edu/classics

**University of Michigan,** Rackham Graduate School, College of Literature, Science, and the Arts, Interdepartmental Program in Greek and Roman History, Ann Arbor, MI 48109. Offers PhD, Certificate. Certificate program only open to students already studying in another PhD program at University of Michigan. *Faculty:* 10 full-time (5 women). *Students:* 10 full-time (5 women). Average age 28. 25 applicants, 12% accepted, 1 enrolled. In 2016, 2 doctorates awarded. *Degree requirements:* For doctorate, 4 foreign languages, comprehensive exam, thesis/dissertation, oral defense of dissertation, dissertation prospectus, preliminary exams, qualifying exams. *Entrance requirements:* For doctorate, GRE, strict minimum of 2 years each of classical Greek and Latin. Additional exam requirements/recommendations for international students: Required—TOEFL (minimum score 560 paper-based). *Application deadline:* For fall admission, 12/15 for domestic and international students. Application fee: $75 ($90 for international students). Electronic applications accepted. *Expenses:* Tuition, state resident: full-time $21,466; part-time $1152 per credit hour. Tuition, nonresident: full-time $43,346; part-time $2367 per credit hour. Part-time tuition and fees vary according to course load, degree level and program. *Financial support:* In 2016–17, 10 students received support, including 4 fellowships with full tuition reimbursements available (averaging $23,000 per year), 6 teaching assistantships with full tuition reimbursements available (averaging $19,000 per year); career-related internships or fieldwork, Federal Work-Study, institutionally sponsored loans, scholarships/grants, traineeships, health care benefits, tuition waivers (full), and unspecified assistantships also available. Financial award application deadline: 3/15. *Faculty research:* Greek history, Roman history, history of ancient Mediterranean cultures. *Unit head:* Ian Moyer, Associate Professor, 734-763-5855, Fax: 734-763-4959, E-mail: ianmoyer@umich.edu. *Application contact:* Sarah Kandell-Gritzmaker, Student Services Coordinator, 734-615-3181, Fax: 734-763-4959, E-mail: mcravens@umich.edu. Website: http://www.lsa.umich.edu/ipgrh

**University of Minnesota, Twin Cities Campus,** Graduate School, College of Liberal Arts, Department of Classical and Near Eastern Studies, Minneapolis, MN 55455-0213. Offers ancient and medieval art and archaeology (MA, PhD); classics (MA, PhD); Greek (MA, PhD); Latin (MA, PhD); religions in antiquity (MA). *Program availability:* Part-time. Terminal master's awarded for partial completion of doctoral program. *Degree requirements:* For master's, 2 foreign languages, comprehensive exam, thesis or alternative; for doctorate, variable foreign language requirement, comprehensive exam, thesis/dissertation. *Entrance requirements:* For master's and doctorate, GRE, 3 letters of recommendation, writing sample, copies of transcripts, personal statement. Additional exam requirements/recommendations for international students: Required—TOEFL. Electronic applications accepted. *Faculty research:* Greek and Latin literature, religions in antiquity, ancient Near East.

**University of Missouri,** Office of Research and Graduate Studies, College of Arts and Science, Department of Classical Studies, Columbia, MO 65211. Offers classical languages (MA, PhD); classical studies (MA, PhD). *Faculty:* 10 full-time (2 women). *Students:* 14 full-time (7 women), 1 part-time (0 women). Average age 29. Terminal master's awarded for partial completion of doctoral program. *Degree requirements:* For master's, one foreign language; for doctorate, 2 foreign languages, comprehensive exam, thesis/dissertation. *Entrance requirements:* For master's, GRE General Test, minimum GPA of 3.0 during last 2 years; BA from accredited college/university; reading knowledge of Greek and/or Latin; for doctorate, GRE General Test, minimum GPA of 3.0; MA with major in Greek, Latin, or classics, or equivalent minimum of 21 hours of graduate work; reading knowledge of Greek, Latin, German, and French (or Italian). Additional exam requirements/recommendations for international students: Required—TOEFL (minimum score 500 paper-based; 61 iBT), IELTS (minimum score 5.5). *Application deadline:* For fall admission, 2/1 priority date for domestic and international students; for winter admission, 11/1 for domestic and international students. Applications are processed on a rolling basis. Application fee: $75 ($90 for international students). Electronic applications accepted. *Expenses:* Tuition, state resident: full-time $6347; part-time $352.60 per credit hour. Tuition, nonresident: full-time $17,379; part-time $965.50 per credit hour. *Required fees:* $1035. Tuition and fees vary according to course load, campus/location and program. *Financial support:* Fellowships with full tuition reimbursements, research assistantships with full tuition reimbursements, teaching assistantships with full tuition reimbursements, institutionally sponsored loans, traineeships, and health care benefits available. *Faculty research:* Studies in the oral tradition, ancient Mediterranean religion, archaeology of the Ancient World, ancient political culture, late antiquity, rhetoric, the Classical Tradition. Website: http://classics.missouri.edu/grad/index.shtml

**University of Nebraska–Lincoln,** Graduate College, College of Arts and Sciences, Department of Classics and Religious Studies, Lincoln, NE 68588. Offers MA. *Degree requirements:* For master's, thesis optional. *Entrance requirements:* For master's, GRE. Additional exam requirements/recommendations for international students: Required—TOEFL (minimum score 550 paper-based). Electronic applications accepted. *Faculty research:* Greek and Latin poetry and prose, Greek and Latin linguistics, patristics, gnosticism, religion of late antiquity.

**University of New Brunswick Fredericton,** School of Graduate Studies, Faculty of Arts, Department of Classics and Ancient History, Fredericton, NB E3B 5A3, Canada. Offers classics (MA). *Program availability:* Part-time. *Degree requirements:* For master's, thesis. *Entrance requirements:* For master's, minimum GPA of 3.0, minimum of 18 credit hours or equivalent in either Greek or Latin. Additional exam requirements/recommendations for international students: Required—TOEFL, TWE. Electronic applications accepted. *Faculty research:* Roman history, Silver Age Latin poetry, stamped roof tiles, Plato, early Christianity, Greek and Roman archaeology, late Antiquity and Byzantium.

**The University of North Carolina at Chapel Hill,** Graduate School, College of Arts and Sciences, Department of Classics, Chapel Hill, NC 27599. Offers classical archaeology (MA, PhD); classics (MA, PhD). Terminal master's awarded for partial completion of doctoral program. *Degree requirements:* For master's, one foreign language, comprehensive exam, thesis; for doctorate, 2 foreign languages, comprehensive exam, thesis/dissertation. *Entrance requirements:* For master's and doctorate, GRE General Test, minimum GPA of 3.0. Electronic applications accepted.

**The University of North Carolina at Greensboro,** Graduate School, College of Arts and Sciences, Department of Classical Studies, Greensboro, NC 27412-5001. Offers Latin (M Ed). *Entrance requirements:* For master's, GRE General Test, MAT, or PRAXIS. Additional exam requirements/recommendations for international students: Required—TOEFL. Electronic applications accepted.

**University of Oregon,** Graduate School, College of Arts and Sciences, Department of Classics, Eugene, OR 97403. Offers classical civilization (MA); classics (MA), including Greek, Latin; Greek (MA); Latin (MA). *Program availability:* Part-time. *Degree requirements:* For master's, 2 foreign languages, thesis or alternative. *Entrance requirements:* For master's, GRE General Test, minimum GPA of 3.0. Additional exam requirements/recommendations for international students: Required—TOEFL. *Faculty research:* Roman religion, Greek philosophy, archaeology, Greek and Roman literature.

**University of Ottawa,** Faculty of Graduate and Postdoctoral Studies, Faculty of Arts, Department of Classics and Religious Studies, Ottawa, ON K1N 6N5, Canada. Offers classical studies (MA); religious studies (PhD). *Degree requirements:* For master's, comprehensive exam, thesis or alternative; for doctorate, comprehensive exam, thesis/

dissertation. *Entrance requirements:* For master's, honors degree or equivalent, minimum B average; for doctorate, master's degree, minimum B+ average. Electronic applications accepted. *Faculty research:* Religions in Canada, including Amerindian and Inuit religions; religion and culture; late antiquity.

**University of Pennsylvania,** School of Arts and Sciences, Graduate Group in Classical Studies, Philadelphia, PA 19104. Offers AM, PhD. *Faculty:* 19 full-time (9 women), 1 part-time/adjunct (0 women). *Students:* 12 full-time (9 women); includes 2 minority (both Two or more races, non-Hispanic/Latino), 3 international. Average age 26. 64 applicants, 14% accepted, 3 enrolled. In 2016, 2 master's, 3 doctorates awarded. Terminal master's awarded for partial completion of doctoral program. Application fee: $70. *Expenses: Tuition:* Full-time $31,068; part-time $5762 per course. *Required fees:* $3200; $336 per course. Full-time tuition and fees vary according to degree level, program and student level. Part-time tuition and fees vary according to course load, degree level and program.

**University of South Africa,** College of Human Sciences, Pretoria, South Africa. Offers adult education (M Ed); African languages (MA, PhD); African politics (MA, PhD); Afrikaans (MA, PhD); ancient history (MA, PhD); ancient Near Eastern studies (MA, PhD); anthropology (MA, PhD); applied linguistics (MA); Arabic (MA, PhD); archaeology (MA); art history (MA); Biblical archaeology (MA); Biblical studies (M Th, D Th, PhD); Christian spirituality (M Th, D Th); church history (M Th, D Th); classical studies (MA, PhD); clinical psychology (MA); communication (MA, PhD); comparative education (M Ed, Ed D); consulting psychology (D Admin, D Com, PhD); curriculum studies (M Ed, Ed D); development studies (M Admin, MA, D Admin, PhD); didactics (M Ed, Ed D); education (M Tech); education management (M Ed, Ed D); educational psychology (M Ed); English (MA); environmental education (M Ed); French (MA, PhD); German (MA, PhD); Greek (MA); guidance and counseling (M Ed); health studies (MA, PhD), including health sciences education (MA), health services management (MA), medical and surgical nursing science (critical care general) (MA), midwifery and neonatal nursing science (MA), trauma and emergency care (MA); history (MA, PhD); history of education (Ed D); inclusive education (M Ed, Ed D); information and communications technology policy and regulation (MA); information science (MA, MIS, PhD); international politics (MA, PhD); Islamic studies (MA, PhD); Italian (MA, PhD); Judaica (MA, PhD); linguistics (MA, PhD); mathematical education (M Ed); mathematics education (MA); missiology (M Th, D Th); modern Hebrew (MA, PhD); musicology (MA, MMus, D Mus); natural science education (M Ed); New Testament (M Th, D Th); Old Testament (D Th); pastoral therapy (M Th, D Th); philosophy (MA); philosophy of education (M Ed, Ed D); politics (MA, PhD); Portuguese (MA, PhD); practical theology (M Th, D Th); psychology (MA, MS, PhD); psychology of education (M Ed, Ed D); public health (MA); religious studies (MA, D Th, PhD); Romance languages (MA); Russian (MA, PhD); Semitic languages (MA, PhD); social behavior studies in HIV/AIDS (MA); social science (mental health) (MA); social science in development studies (MA); social science in psychology (MA); social science in social work (MA); social science in sociology (MA); social work (MSW, DSW, PhD); socio-education (M Ed, Ed D); sociolinguistics (MA); sociology (MA, PhD); Spanish (MA, PhD); systematic theology (M Th, D Th); TESOL (teaching English to speakers of other languages) (MA); theological ethics (M Th, D Th); theory of literature (MA, PhD); urban ministries (D Th); urban ministry (M Th).

**University of Southern California,** Graduate School, Dana and David Dornsife College of Letters, Arts and Sciences, Department of Classics, Los Angeles, CA 90089. Offers MA, PhD. Terminal master's awarded for partial completion of doctoral program. *Degree requirements:* For master's, 2 foreign languages, comprehensive exam, thesis or alternative, Greek and Latin; for doctorate, 2 foreign languages, comprehensive exam, thesis/dissertation, Greek and Latin. *Entrance requirements:* Additional exam requirements/recommendations for international students: Required—TOEFL. Electronic applications accepted. *Faculty research:* Roman literature, Roman history, Greek tragedy, ancient rhetoric and oratory, Greek philosophy.

**The University of Texas at Austin,** Graduate School, College of Liberal Arts, Department of Classics, Austin, TX 78712-1111. Offers MA, PhD. *Degree requirements:* For master's, 2 foreign languages, comprehensive exam, thesis; for doctorate, 4 foreign languages, comprehensive exam, thesis/dissertation. *Entrance requirements:* For master's, GRE General Test, proficiency in classics; for doctorate, GRE General Test, master's degree in classics. Electronic applications accepted.

**University of Toronto,** School of Graduate Studies, Faculty of Arts and Science, Department of Classics, Toronto, ON M5S 1A1, Canada. Offers MA, PhD. *Program availability:* Part-time. *Degree requirements:* For master's, qualifying examinations, sight translation exams in Greek and Latin; for doctorate, thesis/dissertation, qualifying examinations, sight translation exams in Greek and Latin. *Entrance requirements:* For master's, minimum B+ average in final year of an undergraduate program in classics, 3-4 years of course work in Greek and Latin; for doctorate, minimum B+ average with at least one A-; MA in classics. Electronic applications accepted.

**University of Victoria,** Faculty of Graduate Studies, Faculty of Humanities, Department of Greek and Roman Studies, Victoria, BC V8W 2Y2, Canada. Offers MA, PhD. PhD offered by special arrangement. *Program availability:* Part-time. *Degree requirements:* For master's, 3 foreign languages, thesis. *Entrance requirements:* For master's, knowledge of Greek and Latin. Additional exam requirements/recommendations for international students: Required—TOEFL (minimum score 575 paper-based), IELTS (minimum score 7). Electronic applications accepted. *Faculty research:* Roman social history, Roman archaeology and technology, Roman literature, Greek literature, Homer and tragedy, Greek historiography.

**University of Virginia,** College and Graduate School of Arts and Sciences, Department of Classics, Charlottesville, VA 22903. Offers MA, PhD. *Faculty:* 8 full-time (3 women). *Students:* 18 full-time (8 women), 1 international. Average age 27. 37 applicants, 24% accepted, 4 enrolled. In 2016, 4 master's, 1 doctorate awarded. *Degree requirements:* For master's, one foreign language, comprehensive exam, thesis, oral exam; for doctorate, 2 foreign languages, comprehensive exam, thesis/dissertation, oral exam. *Entrance requirements:* For master's and doctorate, GRE General Test, 2 letters of recommendation. Additional exam requirements/recommendations for international students: Required—TOEFL (minimum score 600 paper-based; 90 iBT), IELTS (minimum score 7). *Application deadline:* Applications are processed on a rolling basis. Application fee: $60. Electronic applications accepted. *Expenses:* Tuition, state resident: full-time $15,026; part-time $834 per credit hour. Tuition, nonresident: full-time $25,168; part-time $1378 per credit hour. *Required fees:* $2654. *Financial support:* Fellowships, teaching assistantships, and unspecified assistantships available. Financial award application deadline: 1/3; financial award applicants required to submit FAFSA. *Unit head:* K. Sara Myers, Chair, 434-924-3008, Fax: 434-924-3062, E-mail: classics@virginia.edu. *Application contact:* John Miller, Director of Graduate Studies, 434-924-3008, Fax: 434-924-3062, E-mail: jfm4j@virginia.edu.
Website: http://classics.virginia.edu/

**University of Washington,** Graduate School, College of Arts and Sciences, Department of Washington, Seattle, WA 98195-3110. Offers MA, PhD. *Program availability:* Part-time. *Faculty:* 11 full-time (7 women). *Students:* 19 full-time (11 women), 2 part-time (both women); includes 6 minority (1 Black or African American, non-Hispanic/Latino; 1 American Indian or Alaska Native, non-Hispanic/Latino; 1 Asian, non-Hispanic/Latino; 3

Hispanic/Latino), 4 international. Average age 28. 54 applicants, 50% accepted, 5 enrolled. In 2016, 2 master's, 2 doctorates awarded. Terminal master's awarded for partial completion of doctoral program. *Degree requirements:* For master's, one foreign language, thesis or alternative; for doctorate, 2 foreign languages, comprehensive exam, thesis/dissertation. *Entrance requirements:* For master's, GRE, bachelor's degree in classics, Greek, or Latin; minimum GPA of 3.0; for doctorate, GRE, minimum GPA of 3.0. Additional exam requirements/recommendations for international students: Required—TOEFL (minimum score 82 iBT). *Application deadline:* For fall admission, 1/5 for domestic students. Application fee: $75. Electronic applications accepted. *Financial support:* In 2016–17, 19 students received support, including 3 fellowships with full tuition reimbursements available (averaging $23,148 per year), research assistantships with full tuition reimbursements available (averaging $23,148 per year), 10 teaching assistantships with full tuition reimbursements available (averaging $23,148 per year); Federal Work-Study, institutionally sponsored loans, health care benefits, and tuition waivers (partial) also available. Financial award application deadline: 1/5; financial award applicants required to submit FAFSA. *Faculty research:* Greek and Latin poetry, Greek and Roman cultural institutions, Greek and Latin historiography, Greek tragedy. *Unit head:* Prof. Catherine M. Connors, Chair, 206-543-2266, Fax: 206-543-2267, E-mail: cconnors@uw.edu. *Application contact:* Prof. Deborah Kamen, Graduate Program Coordinator, 206-543-2526, Fax: 206-543-2267, E-mail: dkamen@uw.edu. Website: http://classics.washington.edu

**University of Washington,** Graduate School, College of Arts and Sciences, Department of Philosophy, Seattle, WA 98195. Offers classics and philosophy (PhD); philosophy (MA, PhD). Terminal master's awarded for partial completion of doctoral program. *Degree requirements:* For master's, 3 papers; for doctorate, thesis/dissertation, general exam. *Entrance requirements:* For master's and doctorate, GRE, minimum GPA of 3.0. Additional exam requirements/recommendations for international students: Required—TOEFL. *Faculty research:* History and philosophy of science, epistemology, Aristotle's metaphysics, ethics and politics, causation in modern philosophy.

**The University of Western Ontario,** Faculty of Graduate Studies, Faculty of Arts and Humanities, Department of Classical Studies, London, ON N6A 5B8, Canada. Offers MA. *Program availability:* Part-time. *Degree requirements:* For master's, one foreign language. *Entrance requirements:* For master's, honors degree, minimum B+ average. Additional exam requirements/recommendations for international students: Required—TOEFL. *Faculty research:* Greek literature, Roman history and law, ancient sport, Byzantine literature, Bronze Age archaeology.

**University of Wisconsin–Madison,** Graduate School, College of Letters and Science, Department of Classics, Madison, WI 53706-1380. Offers classics (MA, PhD); Greek (MA); Latin (MA). *Program availability:* Part-time. Terminal master's awarded for partial completion of doctoral program. *Degree requirements:* For master's, 3 foreign languages, oral and written exams; for doctorate, 4 foreign languages, thesis/dissertation, written exams. *Entrance requirements:* For master's, GRE; for doctorate, master's degree. Electronic applications accepted. *Faculty research:* Greek tragedy, Latin elegy, historiography, Homer, Greek lyric poetry.

**University of Wisconsin–Milwaukee,** Graduate School, College of Letters and Science, Department of Foreign Languages and Literature, Milwaukee, WI 53201-0413. Offers classic Greek (MA); classics (MA); comparative literature (MA); foreign language and literature (MA); French (MA); German (MA); Latin (MA); linguistics (MA); Spanish (MA); translation (MA, Certificate). *Program availability:* Part-time. *Students:* 10 full-time (7 women), 19 part-time (16 women); includes 5 minority (2 Black or African American, non-Hispanic/Latino; 2 Hispanic/Latino; 1 Two or more races, non-Hispanic/Latino), 2 international. Average age 31. 41 applicants, 32% accepted, 9 enrolled. In 2016, 21 master's awarded. *Degree requirements:* For master's, 2 foreign languages, thesis or alternative. *Entrance requirements:* Additional exam requirements/recommendations for international students: Required—TOEFL (minimum score 550 paper-based; 79 iBT), IELTS (minimum score 6.5). *Application deadline:* For fall admission, 1/1 priority date for domestic students; for spring admission, 9/1 for domestic students. Applications are processed on a rolling basis. Application fee: $56 ($96 for international students). Electronic applications accepted. *Financial support:* In 2016–17, 1 fellowship, 2 research assistantships, 26 teaching assistantships were awarded; career-related internships or fieldwork, health care benefits, unspecified assistantships, and project assistantships also available. Support available to part-time students. Financial award application deadline: 4/15; financial award applicants required to submit FAFSA. *Unit head:* Kevin Muse, Department Chair, 414-229-5213, E-mail: kmuse@uwm.edu. *Application contact:* General Information Contact, 414-229-4982, Fax: 414-229-6967, E-mail: gradschool@uwm.edu. Website: http://uwm.edu/foreign-languages-literature/

**Vanderbilt University,** Department of Classical Studies, Nashville, TN 37240-1001. Offers classics (MA). *Faculty:* 3 full-time (2 women). In 2016, 1 master's awarded. *Degree requirements:* For master's, 2 foreign languages, thesis. *Entrance requirements:* For master's, GRE General Test. Additional exam requirements/recommendations for international students: Required—TOEFL (minimum score 570 paper-based; 88 iBT). *Application deadline:* For fall admission, 1/15 for domestic and international students. Electronic applications accepted. *Expenses: Tuition:* Part-time $1854 per credit hour. *Financial support:* Fellowships with tuition reimbursements, teaching assistantships with tuition reimbursements, Federal Work-Study, institutionally sponsored loans, scholarships/grants, and health care benefits available. Financial award application deadline: 1/15; financial award applicants required to submit CSS PROFILE or FAFSA. *Faculty research:* Greek and Latin literature and language, Greek and Roman history, classical archaeology, philosophy, religion. *Unit head:* Dr. Barbara Tsakirgis, Director of Graduate Studies, 615-322-2516, Fax: 615-343-7261, E-mail: barbara.tsakirgis@vanderbilt.edu. *Application contact:* Walter B. Bieschke, Program Coordinator for Graduate Admissions, 615-322-0236, Fax: 615-343-9936, E-mail: vandygrad@vanderbilt.edu. Website: http://www.vanderbilt.edu/classics/

**Villanova University,** Graduate School of Liberal Arts and Sciences, Program in Classical Studies, Villanova, PA 19085-1699. Offers Greek/Latin (MA). *Program availability:* Part-time, evening/weekend, blended/hybrid learning. *Degree requirements:* For master's, comprehensive exam, thesis optional. *Entrance requirements:* For master's, minimum GPA of 3.0. Electronic applications accepted.

**Washington University in St. Louis,** The Graduate School, Department of Classics, St. Louis, MO 63130-4899. Offers MA, PhD. Terminal master's awarded for partial completion of doctoral program. *Degree requirements:* For master's, thesis or alternative. *Entrance requirements:* For master's and doctorate, GRE General Test. Additional exam requirements/recommendations for international students: Required—TOEFL. Electronic applications accepted. *Faculty research:* Greek and Latin language and literature; ancient history, philosophy, performance, music, and material culture.

**Yale University,** Graduate School of Arts and Sciences, Department of Classics, New Haven, CT 06520. Offers M Phil, MA, PhD. *Degree requirements:* For doctorate, 2 foreign languages, thesis/dissertation. *Entrance requirements:* For doctorate, GRE General Test.

# Comparative Literature

**American University,** College of Arts and Sciences, Department of Literature, Washington, DC 20016-8047. Offers creative writing (MFA); literature (MA). *Program availability:* Part-time, evening/weekend. *Faculty:* 47 full-time (29 women), 24 part-time/adjunct (15 women). *Students:* 37 full-time (24 women), 20 part-time (11 women); includes 20 minority (9 Black or African American, non-Hispanic/Latino; 1 Asian, non-Hispanic/Latino; 8 Hispanic/Latino; 2 Two or more races, non-Hispanic/Latino), 3 international. Average age 33. 121 applicants, 67% accepted, 20 enrolled. In 2016, 21 master's awarded. *Degree requirements:* For master's, comprehensive exam. *Entrance requirements:* For master's, GRE, writing sample, statement of purpose, transcripts, 2 letters of recommendation, resume. Additional exam requirements/recommendations for international students: Required—TOEFL (minimum score 100 iBT), IELTS (minimum score 7), PTE (minimum score 68). *Application deadline:* For fall admission, 2/1 for domestic students; for spring admission, 11/1 for domestic students. Application fee: $55. *Expenses:* $1,579 per credit tuition; $690 mandatory fees. *Financial support:* Institutionally sponsored loans and unspecified assistantships available. Financial award application deadline: 2/1; financial award applicants required to submit FAFSA. *Unit head:* Dr. David Pike, Department Chair, 202-885-2996, E-mail: dpike@american.edu. *Application contact:* Kathleen Clowery, Associate Director of Graduate Admissions, 202-885-3620, Fax: 202-885-1344, E-mail: clowery@american.edu. Website: http://www.american.edu/cas/literature/

**The American University in Cairo,** School of Humanities and Social Sciences, Cairo, Egypt. Offers Arab and Islamic civilizations (Graduate Diploma); Arabic studies (MA); comparative literary studies (Graduate Diploma); Egyptology and Coptology (MA); English and comparative literature (MA); humanities and social sciences (Graduate Diploma); philosophy (MA); psychology (MA); sociology and anthropology (MA); teaching Arabic as a foreign language (MA); teaching English to speakers of other languages (MA). *Program availability:* Part-time, evening/weekend. *Faculty:* 51 full-time (29 women), 4 part-time/adjunct (2 women). *Students:* 65 full-time (47 women), 179 part-time (138 women), 32 international. Average age 30. 221 applicants, 45% accepted, 54 enrolled. In 2016, 95 master's awarded. *Degree requirements:* For master's, comprehensive exam (for some programs), thesis (for some programs). *Entrance requirements:* Additional exam requirements/recommendations for international students: Required—TOEFL (minimum score 450 paper-based; 45 iBT), IELTS (minimum score 5). *Application deadline:* For fall admission, 2/1 priority date for domestic and international students; for spring admission, 10/15 priority date for domestic and international students. Applications are processed on a rolling basis. Application fee: $80. Electronic applications accepted. *Expenses:* Contact institution. *Financial support:* Fellowships with partial tuition reimbursements, scholarships/grants, tuition waivers (partial), and unspecified assistantships available. Financial award application deadline: 3/10. *Faculty research:* English literature, political science, psychology, sociology, anthropology and Egyptology, teaching English for non-speakers, teaching Arabic as a foreign language, philosophy, Arabic studies. *Unit head:* Dr. Nathaniel Bowditch, Dean, 20-2-2615-1788, E-mail: nbowditch@aucegypt.edu. *Application contact:* Maha Hegazi, Director for Graduate Admissions, 20-2-2615-1462, E-mail: mahahegazi@aucegypt.edu. Website: http://www.aucegypt.edu/huss/Pages/default.aspx

**Arizona State University at the Tempe campus,** College of Liberal Arts and Sciences, Department of English, Tempe, AZ 85287-0302. Offers applied linguistics (PhD); creative writing (MFA); English (MA, PhD), including comparative literature (MA), linguistics (MA), literature, rhetoric and composition (MA), rhetoric, composition, and linguistics (PhD); film and media studies (MAS), including American media and popular culture; linguistics (Graduate Certificate); teaching English to speakers of other languages (MTESOL); translation studies (Graduate Certificate). Terminal master's awarded for partial completion of doctoral program. *Degree requirements:* For master's, variable foreign language requirement, comprehensive exam (for some programs), thesis (for some programs), interactive Program of Study (iPOS) submitted before completing 50 percent of required credit hours; for doctorate, variable foreign language requirement, comprehensive exam, thesis/dissertation, interactive Program of Study (iPOS) submitted before completing 50 percent of required credit hours. *Entrance requirements:* For master's and doctorate, GRE, minimum GPA of 3.0 or equivalent in last 2 years of work leading to bachelor's degree. Additional exam requirements/recommendations for international students: Required—TOEFL, IELTS, or PTE. Electronic applications accepted.

**Binghamton University, State University of New York,** Graduate School, Harpur College of Arts and Sciences, Department of Comparative Literature, Binghamton, NY 13902-6000. Offers MA, PhD. *Program availability:* Part-time. *Faculty:* 9 full-time (7 women), 6 part-time/adjunct (4 women). *Students:* 21 full-time (12 women), 40 part-time (25 women); includes 12 minority (3 Black or African American, non-Hispanic/Latino; 1 American Indian or Alaska Native, non-Hispanic/Latino; 4 Asian, non-Hispanic/Latino; 4 Hispanic/Latino), 30 international. Average age 34. 34 applicants, 94% accepted, 13 enrolled. In 2016, 3 master's, 5 doctorates awarded. Terminal master's awarded for partial completion of doctoral program. *Degree requirements:* For master's, 2 foreign languages, comprehensive exam, thesis or alternative; for doctorate, 2 foreign languages, comprehensive exam, thesis/dissertation. *Entrance requirements:* For master's and doctorate, GRE General Test, writing sample. Additional exam requirements/recommendations for international students: Required—TOEFL (minimum score 550 paper-based; 80 iBT). *Application deadline:* For fall admission, 1/1 priority date for domestic and international students; for spring admission, 10/15 priority date for domestic and international students. Application fee: $75. Electronic applications accepted. *Financial support:* In 2016–17, 25 students received support, including 21 teaching assistantships with full tuition reimbursements available (averaging $14,500 per year); career-related internships or fieldwork, Federal Work-Study, institutionally sponsored loans, scholarships/grants, health care benefits, tuition waivers (full and partial), and unspecified assistantships also available. Financial award applicants required to submit FAFSA. *Unit head:* Dr. Luiza Franco Moreira, Chairperson, 607-777-3673, E-mail: lmoreira@binghamton.edu. *Application contact:* Ben Balkaya, Assistant Dean and Director, 607-777-2151, Fax: 607-777-2501, E-mail: balkaya@binghamton.edu.

**Brigham Young University,** Graduate Studies, College of Humanities, Department of Comparative Arts and Letters, Provo, UT 84602. Offers comparative studies (MA). *Faculty:* 29 full-time (8 women). *Students:* 19 full-time (12 women), 1 part-time (0 women); includes 1 minority (Hispanic/Latino). Average age 29. 12 applicants, 67% accepted, 6 enrolled. In 2016, 5 master's awarded. *Degree requirements:* For master's, 2 foreign languages, comprehensive exam, thesis. *Entrance requirements:* For master's, GRE, minimum GPA of 3.0 in last 60 hours, writing sample, foreign language experience. Additional exam requirements/recommendations for international students: Required—TOEFL (minimum score 580 paper-based; 85 iBT), IELTS (minimum score

7). *Application deadline:* For fall admission, 3/1 for domestic and international students. Application fee: $50. Electronic applications accepted. *Expenses: Tuition:* Full-time $6680; part-time $393 per credit. Tuition and fees vary according to course load, program and student's religious affiliation. *Financial support:* In 2016–17, 19 students received support, including 33 fellowships with partial tuition reimbursements available (averaging $2,566 per year), 4 research assistantships (averaging $1,500 per year), 29 teaching assistantships (averaging $2,658 per year); scholarships/grants, tuition waivers (full and partial), unspecified assistantships, and student instructorships also available. Support available to part-time students. *Faculty research:* Latin American literature and translation, Mormon women artists, documentary photography, Lucan studies, African Mormon women's oral histories. *Unit head:* Dr. Roger Macfarlane, Graduate Coordinator/Professor of Classical Studies, 801-422-9078, Fax: 801-422-0305, E-mail: macfarlane@byu.edu. *Application contact:* Andrea Kristensen, Graduate Program Manager, 801-422-2996, Fax: 801-422-0305, E-mail: andrea_kristensen@byu.edu. Website: http://cal.byu.edu/

**Brock University,** Faculty of Graduate Studies, Faculty of Humanities, Program in Studies in Comparative Literatures and Arts, St. Catharines, ON L2S 3A1, Canada. Offers MA. *Degree requirements:* For master's, thesis optional. *Entrance requirements:* For master's, honors degree. Additional exam requirements/recommendations for international students: Required—TOEFL (minimum score 550 paper-based; 80 iBT), IELTS (minimum score 6.5), TWE (minimum score 4). Electronic applications accepted.

**Brown University,** Graduate School, Department of Comparative Literature, Providence, RI 02912. Offers PhD. *Degree requirements:* For doctorate, 2 foreign languages, thesis/dissertation, preliminary exam. *Entrance requirements:* For doctorate, GRE General Test, GRE Subject Test.

**California State University, Northridge,** Graduate Studies, College of Humanities, Department of English, Northridge, CA 91330. Offers creative writing (MA); literature (MA); rhetoric and composition theory (MA). *Program availability:* Part-time, evening/weekend. *Faculty:* 31 full-time (15 women), 104 part-time/adjunct (34 women). *Students:* 34 full-time (18 women), 60 part-time (34 women); includes 35 minority (4 Black or African American, non-Hispanic/Latino; 4 American Indian or Alaska Native, non-Hispanic/Latino; 2 Asian, non-Hispanic/Latino; 21 Hispanic/Latino; 4 Two or more races, non-Hispanic/Latino), 1 international. Average age 33. 49 applicants, 71% accepted, 22 enrolled. *Degree requirements:* For master's, thesis or alternative. *Entrance requirements:* For master's, writing proficiency test, GRE General Test or minimum GPA of 3.0. Additional exam requirements/recommendations for international students: Required—TOEFL. *Application deadline:* For fall admission, 11/30 for domestic students. Application fee: $55. *Expenses:* Tuition, state resident: full-time $4152. *Financial support:* Teaching assistantships available. Financial award application deadline: 3/1. *Faculty research:* Reading improvement, professional writing, Dickens, Shaw, English as a second language. *Unit head:* Kent Baxter, Chair, 818-677-3431. Website: http://www.csun.edu/english/index.php

**Carleton University,** Faculty of Graduate Studies, Faculty of Arts and Social Sciences, School for Languages, Literatures, and Comparative Literary Studies, Ottawa, ON K1S 5B6, Canada. Offers cultural mediations (PhD). *Entrance requirements:* Additional exam requirements/recommendations for international students: Required—TOEFL. *Faculty research:* Literary history, theory of literature, cross-cultural studies, modernism/postmodernism, comparative Canadian literature.

**Carnegie Mellon University,** Dietrich College of Humanities and Social Sciences, Department of English, Pittsburgh, PA 15213-3891. Offers communication planning and design (M Des); literary and cultural studies (MA, PhD); professional writing (MAPW), including editing and publishing, policy and non-profit communication, public and media relations / corporate communications, science or healthcare communication, technical writing, writing for new media, writing for print media; rhetoric (MA, PhD). *Program availability:* Part-time. Terminal master's awarded for partial completion of doctoral program. *Degree requirements:* For doctorate, 2 foreign languages, comprehensive exam, thesis/dissertation. *Entrance requirements:* For master's and doctorate, GRE General Test. Additional exam requirements/recommendations for international students: Required—TOEFL, TWE. *Faculty research:* Cognitive processes in discourse with emphasis on writing, testing, and evaluation.

**Case Western Reserve University,** School of Graduate Studies, Department of Modern Languages and Literatures and Department of English, Program in World Literature, Cleveland, OH 44106. Offers MA. *Faculty:* 18 full-time (12 women). *Students:* 1 (woman) full-time. Average age 45. 1 applicant, 100% accepted, 1 enrolled. In 2016, 1 master's awarded. *Degree requirements:* For master's, 2 foreign languages, thesis, written exam. *Entrance requirements:* For master's, GRE General Test, sample of written work; project proposal. Additional exam requirements/recommendations for international students: Required—TOEFL (minimum score 577 paper-based; 90 iBT); Recommended—IELTS (minimum score 7). *Application deadline:* For fall admission, 3/1 priority date for domestic students. Applications are processed on a rolling basis. Application fee: $50. Electronic applications accepted. *Expenses: Tuition:* Full-time $42,576; part-time $1774 per credit hour. *Required fees:* $34. Tuition and fees vary according to course load and program. *Financial support:* Fellowships, career-related internships or fieldwork, institutionally sponsored loans, and tuition waivers (partial) available. Financial award application deadline: 3/1; financial award applicants required to submit CSS PROFILE or FAFSA. *Faculty research:* Literary theory and translation, Middle Ages, Renaissance, Baroque, Enlightenment, Romanticism, Modernism. *Unit head:* Prof. Yasuhiro Shirai, Professor in Modern Languages/Chair, 216-368-8976, Fax: 216-368-2216. *Application contact:* Prof. Marie Lathers, Professor of French and Humanities, 216-368-8983, Fax: 216-368-2216, E-mail: marie.lathers@case.edu. Website: http://artsci.case.edu/world-literature/

**Claremont Graduate University,** Graduate Programs, School of Arts and Humanities, Department of English, Claremont, CA 91711-6160. Offers American studies (MA, PhD); critical theory (MA, PhD); early modern studies (MA, PhD); English (M Phil, MA, PhD); literary theory (PhD); literature (MA, PhD); literature and creative writing (MA); literature and film (MA); MBA/MA; MBA/PhD. *Program availability:* Part-time. *Faculty:* 3 full-time (1 woman), 1 part-time/adjunct (0 women). *Students:* 61 full-time (46 women), 20 part-time (14 women); includes 23 minority (4 Black or African American, non-Hispanic/Latino; 1 American Indian or Alaska Native, non-Hispanic/Latino; 9 Asian, non-Hispanic/Latino; 4 Hispanic/Latino; 5 Two or more races, non-Hispanic/Latino), 6 international. Average age 37. In 2016, 10 master's, 8 doctorates awarded. *Entrance requirements:* For master's and doctorate, GRE General Test. Additional exam requirements/recommendations for international students: Required—TOEFL (minimum score 75 iBT). *Application deadline:* For fall admission, 2/1 priority date for domestic and international students. Applications are processed on a rolling basis. Application fee: $80. Electronic applications accepted. *Expenses: Tuition:* Full-time $44,328; part-time

$1847 per unit. *Required fees:* $600; $300 per semester. Tuition and fees vary according to course load and program. *Financial support:* Fellowships, Federal Work-Study, institutionally sponsored loans, and scholarships/grants available. Support available to part-time students. Financial award application deadline: 2/15; financial award applicants required to submit FAFSA. *Faculty research:* American, comparative, and English Renaissance literature; modernism; feminist literature and theory. *Unit head:* Lori Anne Ferrell, Chair, 909-607-2652, E-mail: lorianne.ferrell@cgu.edu. *Application contact:* Amy Sandefur, Assistant Director of Admissions, 909-607-9101, E-mail: amy.sandefur@cgu.edu.
Website: https://www.cgu.edu/departments/english/

**Columbia University,** Graduate School of Arts and Sciences, New York, NY 10027. Offers African-American studies (MA); American studies (MA); anthropology (MA, PhD); art history and archaeology (MA, PhD); astronomy (PhD); biological sciences (PhD); biotechnology (MA); chemical physics (PhD); chemistry (PhD); classical studies (MA, PhD); classics (MA, PhD); climate and society (MA); conservation biology (MA); earth and environmental sciences (PhD); East Asia: regional studies (MA); East Asian languages and cultures (MA, PhD); ecology, evolution and environmental biology (MA), including conservation biology; ecology, evolution, and environmental biology (PhD), including ecology and evolutionary biology, evolutionary primatology; economics (MA, PhD); English and comparative literature (MA, PhD); French and Romance philology (MA, PhD); Germanic languages (MA, PhD); global French studies (MA); global thought (MA); Hispanic cultural studies (MA); history (PhD); history and literature (MA); human rights studies (MA); Islamic studies (MA); Italian (MA, PhD); Japanese pedagogy (MA); Jewish studies (MA); Latin America and the Caribbean: regional studies (MA); Latin American and Iberian cultures (PhD); mathematics (MA, PhD), including finance (MA); medieval and Renaissance studies (MA); Middle Eastern, South Asian, and African studies (MA, PhD); modern art: critical and curatorial studies (MA); modern European studies (MA); museum anthropology (MA); music (DMA, PhD); oral history (MA); philosophical foundations of physics (MA); philosophy (MA, PhD); physics (PhD); political science (MA, PhD); psychology (PhD); quantitative methods in the social sciences (MA); religion (MA, PhD); Russia, Eurasia and East Europe: regional studies (MA); Russian translation (MA); Slavic cultures (MA); Slavic languages (MA, PhD); sociology (MA, PhD); South Asian studies (MA); statistics (MA, PhD); theatre (PhD). Dual-degree programs require admission to both Graduate School of Arts and Sciences and another Columbia school. *Program availability:* Part-time. Terminal master's awarded for partial completion of doctoral program. *Degree requirements:* For master's, variable foreign language requirement, comprehensive exam (for some programs), thesis (for some programs); for doctorate, variable foreign language requirement, comprehensive exam (for some programs), thesis/dissertation. *Entrance requirements:* For master's and doctorate, GRE General Test, GRE Subject Test (for some programs). Additional exam requirements/recommendations for international students: Required—TOEFL, IELTS. Electronic applications accepted.

**Cornell University,** Graduate School, Graduate Fields of Arts and Sciences, Field of Comparative Literature, Ithaca, NY 14853. Offers PhD. *Degree requirements:* For doctorate, 2 foreign languages, comprehensive exam, thesis/dissertation, teaching experience. *Entrance requirements:* For doctorate, GRE General Test, proficiency in 2 foreign literatures, writing sample, 3 letters of recommendation. Additional exam requirements/recommendations for international students: Required—TOEFL (minimum score 550 paper-based; 77 iBT). Electronic applications accepted. *Faculty research:* Critical theory, European studies, Latin American studies, Asian studies.

**Dartmouth College,** School of Graduate and Advanced Studies, Comparative Literature Program, Hanover, NH 03755. Offers MA. *Faculty:* 24 full-time (16 women), 2 part-time/adjunct (1 woman). *Students:* 6 full-time (all women); includes 1 minority (Hispanic/Latino), 4 international. Average age 24. 15 applicants, 80% accepted, 6 enrolled. In 2016, 13 master's awarded. *Degree requirements:* For master's, final paper. *Entrance requirements:* For master's, proficiency in 2 languages. Additional exam requirements/recommendations for international students: Required—TOEFL. *Application deadline:* For fall admission, 2/15 for domestic students. Application fee: $40. Electronic applications accepted. *Financial support:* Fellowships with full tuition reimbursements, teaching assistantships with full tuition reimbursements, career-related internships or fieldwork, institutionally sponsored loans, scholarships/grants, and tuition waivers (full) available. Support available to part-time students. Financial award application deadline: 4/1; financial award applicants required to submit CSS PROFILE or FAFSA. *Unit head:* Dr. Dennis Washburn, Chair, 603-646-1287. *Application contact:* Elizabeth Cassell, Program Administrator, 603-646-0470, E-mail: liz.cassell@dartmouth.edu.
Website: http://complit.dartmouth.edu/

**Duke University,** Graduate School, Program in Literature, Durham, NC 27708. Offers PhD, JD/MA. *Degree requirements:* For doctorate, 2 foreign languages, thesis/dissertation. *Entrance requirements:* For doctorate, GRE General Test, writing sample. Additional exam requirements/recommendations for international students: Required—TOEFL (minimum score 577 paper-based; 90 iBT) or IELTS (minimum score 7).

**East Carolina University,** Graduate School, Thomas Harriot College of Arts and Sciences, Department of English, Greenville, NC 27858-4353. Offers creative writing (MA); English studies (MA); linguistics (MA); literature (MA); multicultural and transnational literatures (MA, Certificate); rhetoric and composition (MA); rhetoric, writing, and professional communication (PhD); teaching English in the two-year college (Certificate); teaching English to speakers of other languages (MA, Certificate); technical and professional communication (MA). *Program availability:* Part-time, evening/weekend. *Students:* 54 full-time (36 women), 95 part-time (77 women); includes 32 minority (19 Black or African American, non-Hispanic/Latino; 3 Asian, non-Hispanic/Latino; 6 Hispanic/Latino; 4 Two or more races, non-Hispanic/Latino), 1 international. Average age 35. 78 applicants, 96% accepted, 50 enrolled. In 2016, 34 master's, 1 doctorate awarded. *Degree requirements:* For master's, one foreign language, comprehensive exam, thesis optional. *Entrance requirements:* For master's, GRE General Test, MAT (for MA Ed). Additional exam requirements/recommendations for international students: Required—TOEFL. *Application deadline:* For fall admission, 6/1 priority date for domestic students; for spring admission, 10/15 for domestic students. Applications are processed on a rolling basis. Application fee: $50. *Financial support:* Research assistantships with partial tuition reimbursements, teaching assistantships with partial tuition reimbursements, and Federal Work-Study available. Support available to part-time students. Financial award application deadline: 6/1. *Unit head:* Dr. Jeffrey Johnson, Chair, 252-328-6041, E-mail: johnsonj@ecu.edu. *Application contact:* Dean of Graduate School, 252-328-6012, Fax: 252-328-6071, E-mail: gradschool@ecu.edu.
Website: http://www.ecu.edu/cs-cas/engl/graduate/

**Emory University,** Laney Graduate School, Department of Comparative Literature, Atlanta, GA 30322-1100. Offers comparative literature (PhD); philosophy (Certificate); psychoanalytic studies (PhD); women's studies (Certificate). *Degree requirements:* For doctorate, 2 foreign languages, comprehensive exam, thesis/dissertation. *Entrance requirements:* For doctorate, GRE General Test, minimum GPA of 3.0. Additional exam requirements/recommendations for international students: Required—TOEFL. Electronic applications accepted. *Faculty research:* Literary theory, psychoanalysis

trauma and testimony, literature and religion, literature and technology, literature and philosophy, politics and global culture, literature and aesthetics.

**Emory University,** Laney Graduate School, Department of Spanish and Portuguese, Atlanta, GA 30322-1100. Offers comparative literature (Certificate); film studies (Certificate); Spanish (PhD); women's studies (Certificate). *Degree requirements:* For doctorate, 2 foreign languages, comprehensive exam, thesis/dissertation. *Entrance requirements:* For doctorate, GRE General Test. Additional exam requirements/recommendations for international students: Required—TOEFL. Electronic applications accepted. *Faculty research:* Spanish literature, Spanish American literature, literary theory, criticism, cultural studies.

**Fairleigh Dickinson University, Metropolitan Campus,** University College: Arts, Sciences, and Professional Studies, Department of English, Philosophy, and Humanities, Program in English and Literature, Teaneck, NJ 07666-1914. Offers MA.

**Florida Atlantic University,** Dorothy F. Schmidt College of Arts and Letters, Department of Languages, Linguistics, and Comparative Literature, Boca Raton, FL 33431-0991. Offers comparative literature (MA); French (MA); linguistics (MA); Spanish (MA). *Program availability:* Part-time. *Faculty:* 22 full-time (13 women). *Students:* 41 full-time (26 women), 16 part-time (12 women); includes 21 minority (9 Black or African American, non-Hispanic/Latino; 1 Asian, non-Hispanic/Latino; 11 Hispanic/Latino), 11 international. Average age 35. 48 applicants, 38% accepted, 11 enrolled. In 2016, 20 master's awarded. *Degree requirements:* For master's, one foreign language, comprehensive exam, thesis optional. *Entrance requirements:* For master's, GRE General Test, minimum GPA of 3.0. Additional exam requirements/recommendations for international students: Required—TOEFL (minimum score 500 paper-based; 61 iBT), IELTS (minimum score 6). *Application deadline:* For fall admission, 7/1 priority date for domestic students, 2/15 for international students; for spring admission, 11/1 for domestic students, 7/15 for international students. Applications are processed on a rolling basis. Application fee: $30. *Expenses:* Tuition, state resident: full-time $7392; part-time $369.82 per credit hour. Tuition, nonresident: full-time $19,432; part-time $1024.81 per credit hour. *Financial support:* Fellowships, research assistantships, teaching assistantships with partial tuition reimbursements, Federal Work-Study, and tuition waivers (partial) available. Support available to part-time students. Financial award application deadline: 4/1. *Faculty research:* Modern European studies, modern Latin America, medieval Europe. *Unit head:* Dr. Marcella Munson, Chair, 561-297-2118, Fax: 561-297-2756, E-mail: mmunson@fau.edu. *Application contact:* Dr. Linda Johnson, Associate Dean, 561-297-0928, Fax: 561-297-2744.
Website: http://www.fau.edu/LLCL/

**Georgetown University,** Graduate School of Arts and Sciences, School of Continuing Studies, Washington, DC 20057. Offers American studies (MALS); Catholic studies (MALS); classical civilizations (MALS); emergency and disaster management (MPS); ethics and the professions (MALS); global strategic communications (MPS); hospitality management (MPS); human resources management (MPS); humanities (MALS); individualized study (MALS); integrated marketing communications (MPS); international affairs (MALS); Islam and Muslim-Christian relations (MALS); journalism (MPS); liberal studies (DLS); literature and society (MALS); medieval and early modern European studies (MALS); public relations and corporate communications (MPS); real estate (MPS); religious studies (MALS); social and public policy (MALS); sports industry management (MPS); systems engineering management (MPS); technology management (MPS); the theory and practice of American democracy (MALS); urban and regional planning (MPS); visual culture (MALS). MPS in systems engineering management offered jointly with Stevens Institute of Technology. *Entrance requirements:* Additional exam requirements/recommendations for international students: Required—TOEFL.

**The Graduate Center, City University of New York,** Graduate Studies, Program in Comparative Literature, New York, NY 10016-4039. Offers comparative literature (MA, PhD), including classics (PhD), German (PhD), Italian (PhD). PhD offered jointly with New York University. Terminal master's awarded for partial completion of doctoral program. *Degree requirements:* For master's, 2 foreign languages, comprehensive exam, thesis; for doctorate, 3 foreign languages, comprehensive exam, thesis/dissertation. *Entrance requirements:* For master's and doctorate, GRE General Test. Additional exam requirements/recommendations for international students: Required—TOEFL. Electronic applications accepted.

**Harrison Middleton University,** Graduate Program, Tempe, AZ 85282. Offers education (MA, Ed D); humanities (MA); imaginative literature (MA); interdisciplinary studies (DA); jurisprudence (MA); natural science (MA); philosophy and religion (MA); social science (MA). *Program availability:* Part-time, evening/weekend, online learning. *Degree requirements:* For master's and doctorate, capstone project. *Entrance requirements:* For master's, interview; for doctorate, 2 academic letters of reference, interview, essay. Additional exam requirements/recommendations for international students: Required—TOEFL (minimum score 550 paper-based; 80 iBT). Electronic applications accepted. *Faculty research:* Japanese animation, educational leadership, war art, John Muir's wilderness.

**Harvard University,** Graduate School of Arts and Sciences, Department of Comparative Literature, Cambridge, MA 02138. Offers comparative literature (PhD); oral literature (PhD). *Degree requirements:* For doctorate, 4 foreign languages, thesis/dissertation, written and oral exams. *Entrance requirements:* For doctorate, GRE General Test, GRE Subject Test (recommended), sample of written work. Additional exam requirements/recommendations for international students: Required—TOEFL.

**Hunter College of the City University of New York,** Graduate School, School of Arts and Sciences, Department of English, Program in Literature, Language, and Theory, New York, NY 10065-5085. Offers MA. *Program availability:* Part-time, evening/weekend. *Students:* 41 part-time (31 women); includes 13 minority (2 Black or African American, non-Hispanic/Latino; 3 Asian, non-Hispanic/Latino; 8 Hispanic/Latino), 1 international. Average age 28. 23 applicants, 87% accepted, 12 enrolled. In 2016, 8 master's awarded. *Degree requirements:* For master's, one foreign language, comprehensive exam, thesis. *Entrance requirements:* For master's, GRE General Test, minimum 18 credits of course work in English, excluding journalism and writing; statement of purpose. Additional exam requirements/recommendations for international students: Required—TOEFL. *Application deadline:* For fall admission, 4/1 for domestic students, 2/1 for international students; for spring admission, 11/1 for domestic students, 9/1 for international students. *Financial support:* Federal Work-Study and tuition waivers (partial) available. Support available to part-time students. Financial award application deadline: 4/15. *Unit head:* Dr. Cristina Alfar, Associate Professor, 212-772-5187, E-mail: calfar@hunter.cuny.edu. *Application contact:* Prof. Amy Robbins, Graduate Advisor, 212-772-5752, E-mail: amy.robbins@hunter.cuny.edu.
Website: http://www.hunter.cuny.edu/english/graduate/majors

**Indiana University Bloomington,** University Graduate School, College of Arts and Sciences, Department of Comparative Literature, Bloomington, IN 47405. Offers MA, MAT, PhD. *Program availability:* Part-time. *Faculty:* 12 full-time (4 women), 24 part-time/adjunct (12 women). *Students:* 32 full-time (19 women); includes 2 minority (1 Hispanic/Latino; 1 Two or more races, non-Hispanic/Latino), 10 international. Average age 33. 20 applicants, 35% accepted, 3 enrolled. In 2016, 4 master's, 3 doctorates awarded.

## Comparative Literature

*Degree requirements:* For master's, 2 foreign languages, comprehensive exam (for some programs), thesis (for some programs); for doctorate, 3 foreign languages, comprehensive exam, thesis/dissertation. *Entrance requirements:* For master's, GRE, proficiency in 1 foreign language, 25-page writing sample, 3 letters of recommendation, transcripts, statement of purpose; for doctorate, GRE, proficiency in 2 foreign languages, 25-page writing sample, 3 letters of recommendation, transcripts, statement of purpose. Additional exam requirements/recommendations for international students: Required—TOEFL (minimum score 550 paper-based; 79 iBT). *Application deadline:* For fall admission, 1/15 for domestic students, 12/1 for international students. Application fee: $55 ($65 for international students). Electronic applications accepted. *Financial support:* Fellowships with full tuition reimbursements, research assistantships with partial tuition reimbursements, teaching assistantships with full tuition reimbursements, Federal Work-Study, tuition waivers (partial), and unspecified assistantships available. Financial award application deadline: 1/15. *Faculty research:* Literary theory, translation, African studies, medieval studies, comparative arts, East-West literary relations. *Unit head:* Prof. Paul Losensky, Chairperson, 812-855-8432, Fax: 812-855-2688, E-mail: plosensk@indiana.edu. *Application contact:* Stephanie Klausing, Graduate Secretary, 812-855-9602, Fax: 812-855-2688, E-mail: sklausin@indiana.edu.
Website: http://www.indiana.edu/~complit/

**Johns Hopkins University,** Zanvyl Krieger School of Arts and Sciences, Humanities Center, Baltimore, MD 21218. Offers comparative literature (PhD); intellectual history (PhD). *Degree requirements:* For doctorate, 2 foreign languages, thesis/dissertation. *Entrance requirements:* For doctorate, GRE General Test, samples of written work. Additional exam requirements/recommendations for international students: Required—TOEFL, IELTS. Electronic applications accepted.

**Louisiana State University and Agricultural & Mechanical College,** Graduate School, College of Humanities and Social Sciences, Interdepartmental Program in Comparative Literature, Baton Rouge, LA 70803. Offers MA, PhD.

**New York University,** Graduate School of Arts and Science, Department of Comparative Literature, New York, NY 10012-1019. Offers MA, PhD. *Program availability:* Part-time. *Degree requirements:* For master's, 2 foreign languages, thesis; for doctorate, 3 foreign languages, thesis/dissertation. *Entrance requirements:* For master's and doctorate, GRE General Test. Additional exam requirements/recommendations for international students: Required—TOEFL. *Faculty research:* European and non-European literature and culture, comparative poetics, cultural studies, Colonial and Post-Colonial literature and theory, philosophical issues and literary theory.

**Northwestern University,** The Graduate School, Judd A. and Marjorie Weinberg College of Arts and Sciences, Program in Comparative Literary Studies, Evanston, IL 60208. Offers PhD. Admissions and degrees offered through The Graduate School. *Program availability:* Part-time. *Degree requirements:* For doctorate, 2 foreign languages, thesis/dissertation, preliminary exams. *Entrance requirements:* For doctorate, GRE General Test, sample of written work. Additional exam requirements/recommendations for international students: Required—TOEFL. *Faculty research:* The novel, modernism, post-colonial literature and theory, literature and the arts, Middle Ages and Renaissance, literature and philosophy.

**Northwestern University,** School of Professional Studies, Program in Literature, Evanston, IL 60208. Offers American literature (MA); British literature (MA); comparative and world literature (MA).

**Penn State University Park,** Graduate School, College of the Liberal Arts, Department of Comparative Literature, University Park, PA 16802. Offers comparative literature (MA, PhD); Russian and comparative literature (MA). *Unit head:* Dr. Susan Welch, Dean, 814-865-7691, Fax: 814-863-2085. *Application contact:* Lori Hawn, Director, Graduate Student Services, 814-865-1795, Fax: 814-863-4627, E-mail: l-gswww@lists.psu.edu.
Website: http://complit.la.psu.edu/

**Princeton University,** Graduate School, Department of Comparative Literature, Princeton, NJ 08544-1019. Offers PhD. *Degree requirements:* For doctorate, variable foreign language requirement, thesis/dissertation. *Entrance requirements:* For doctorate, GRE General Test, GRE Subject Test, sample of written work. Additional exam requirements/recommendations for international students: Required—TOEFL (minimum score 600 paper-based). Electronic applications accepted.

**Purdue University,** Graduate School, College of Liberal Arts, Program in Comparative Literature, West Lafayette, IN 47907. Offers MA, PhD. *Program availability:* Part-time. *Students:* 12 full-time (8 women), 9 part-time (6 women), 16 international. Average age 33. 15 applicants, 7% accepted. In 2016, 1 master's, 3 doctorates awarded. *Degree requirements:* For master's, comprehensive exam (for some programs), thesis optional; for doctorate, comprehensive exam, thesis/dissertation. *Entrance requirements:* For master's, GRE General Test, minimum undergraduate GPA of 3.0 or equivalent; for doctorate, GRE General Test, minimum undergraduate GPA of 3.0 or equivalent; master's degree with minimum GPA of 3.0 or equivalent. Additional exam requirements/recommendations for international students: Required—TOEFL (minimum score 550 paper-based; 77 iBT); Recommended—TWE. *Application deadline:* For fall admission, 1/10 priority date for domestic and international students; for spring admission, 10/1 for domestic and international students. Applications are processed on a rolling basis. Application fee: $60 ($75 for international students). Electronic applications accepted. *Financial support:* In 2016–17, teaching assistantships with tuition reimbursements (averaging $12,000 per year) were awarded; fellowships also available. Support available to part-time students. Financial award application deadline: 4/1; financial award applicants required to submit FAFSA. *Faculty research:* Theory and criticism, philosophy and aesthetics, East Asian literature, postcolonial literature, classics. *Unit head:* Dr. Charles S. Ross, Head, 765-494-3749, E-mail: cross@purdue.edu. *Application contact:* Elsa Schirmer, Graduate Contact, 765-496-9629, Fax: 765-496-1700, E-mail: eschirme@purdue.edu.
Website: https://www.cla.purdue.edu/complit/

**Rutgers University–New Brunswick,** Graduate School-New Brunswick, Program in Comparative Literature, Piscataway, NJ 08854-8097. Offers MA, PhD. *Program availability:* Part-time. Terminal master's awarded for partial completion of doctoral program. *Degree requirements:* For master's, comprehensive exam; for doctorate, 3 foreign languages, thesis/dissertation, written and oral exams. *Entrance requirements:* For doctorate, GRE General Test, GRE Subject Test (recommended). Additional exam requirements/recommendations for international students: Required—TOEFL. Electronic applications accepted. *Faculty research:* Genres and periods, modern literary theory, psychoanalytic approaches to literature, literature and gender, cultural studies.

**San Francisco State University,** Division of Graduate Studies, College of Liberal and Creative Arts, Department of Comparative and World Literature, San Francisco, CA 94132-1722. Offers comparative literature (MA). *Program availability:* Part-time. *Degree requirements:* For master's, one foreign language. *Application deadline:* Applications are processed on a rolling basis. *Expenses:* Tuition, state resident: full-time $6738. Tuition, nonresident: full-time $15,666. *Required fees:* $1012. Tuition and fees vary according to degree level and program. *Unit head:* Dr. Dane Johnson, Interim Chair, 415-338-3072, Fax: 415-338-6159, E-mail: danej@sfsu.edu. *Application contact:* Dr. Shirin Khanmohamadi, Graduate Coordinator, 415-338-7035, Fax: 415-338-6159, E-mail: shirin1@sfsu.edu.
Website: http://complit.sfsu.edu/

**Stanford University,** School of Humanities and Sciences, Department of Comparative Literature, Stanford, CA 94305-2004. Offers PhD. *Degree requirements:* For doctorate, 3 foreign languages, thesis/dissertation. *Entrance requirements:* For doctorate, GRE General Test, GRE Subject Test. Additional exam requirements/recommendations for international students: Required—TOEFL. Electronic applications accepted. *Expenses:* Tuition: Full-time $47,331. *Required fees:* $609.

**Stanford University,** School of Humanities and Sciences, Program in Modern Thought and Literature, Stanford, CA 94305-2004. Offers PhD. *Degree requirements:* For doctorate, 2 foreign languages, thesis/dissertation, qualifying paper, oral exam. *Entrance requirements:* For doctorate, GRE General Test. Additional exam requirements/recommendations for international students: Required—TOEFL. Electronic applications accepted. *Expenses:* Tuition: Full-time $47,331. *Required fees:* $609.

**Stony Brook University, State University of New York,** Graduate School, College of Arts and Sciences, Department of Cultural Studies and Comparative Literature, Stony Brook, NY 11794. Offers comparative literature (MA, PhD); cultural studies (PhD, Certificate). *Program availability:* Evening/weekend. *Faculty:* 12 full-time (4 women). *Students:* 57 full-time (40 women), 4 part-time (all women); includes 7 minority (2 Black or African American, non-Hispanic/Latino; 4 Asian, non-Hispanic/Latino; 1 Hispanic/Latino), 24 international. Average age 34. 58 applicants, 48% accepted, 14 enrolled. In 2016, 3 master's, 1 doctorate, 3 other advanced degrees awarded. Terminal master's awarded for partial completion of doctoral program. *Degree requirements:* For master's, 2 foreign languages, exam; for doctorate, 3 foreign languages, comprehensive exam, thesis/dissertation. *Entrance requirements:* For master's and doctorate, GRE General Test, minimum GPA of 3.5 in major, 3.0 overall. Additional exam requirements/recommendations for international students: Required—TOEFL. *Application deadline:* For fall admission, 1/15 for domestic students; for spring admission, 10/1 for domestic students. Application fee: $100. Electronic applications accepted. *Expenses:* Contact institution. *Financial support:* In 2016–17, 1 research assistantship, 30 teaching assistantships were awarded; fellowships also available. *Faculty research:* Humanities, women's studies, literary criticism, gender studies, philosophy. *Unit head:* Dr. Robert Harvey, Chair, 631-632-7464, E-mail: robert.harvey@stonybrook.edu. *Application contact:* Mary Moran-Luba, Coordinator, 631-632-7460, Fax: 631-632-5707, E-mail: mary.moran-luba@stonybrook.edu.
Website: http://www.stonybrook.edu/commcms/cat/index.html

**Université de Montréal,** Faculty of Arts and Sciences, Department of Comparative Literature, Montréal, QC H3C 3J7, Canada. Offers comparative literature (MA); literature (PhD). *Degree requirements:* For master's, 2 foreign languages, thesis; for doctorate, 3 foreign languages, thesis/dissertation, general exam. *Entrance requirements:* For doctorate, MA with minimum B+ average. Electronic applications accepted.

**Université de Sherbrooke,** Faculty of Letters and Human Sciences, Department of Letters and Communications, Sherbrooke, QC J1K 2R1, Canada. Offers comparative Canadian literature (MA, PhD); French literature (MA, PhD); linguistics (MA); theatre (MA). *Degree requirements:* For master's, thesis or alternative; for doctorate, thesis/dissertation. *Entrance requirements:* For master's, minimum GPA of 2.8; for doctorate, minimum GPA of 3.0.

**Université du Québec à Chicoutimi,** Graduate Programs, Program in Literary Studies, Chicoutimi, QC G7H 2B1, Canada. Offers MA. Program offered jointly with Université du Québec à Rimouski and Université du Québec à Trois-Rivières. *Program availability:* Part-time. *Degree requirements:* For master's, thesis optional. *Entrance requirements:* For master's, appropriate bachelor's degree, proficiency in French.

**Université du Québec à Montréal,** Graduate Programs, Program in Literary Studies, Montréal, QC H3C 3P8, Canada. Offers MA, PhD. *Program availability:* Part-time. *Degree requirements:* For master's, thesis; for doctorate, thesis/dissertation. *Entrance requirements:* For master's, appropriate bachelor's degree or equivalent, proficiency in French; for doctorate, appropriate master's degree or equivalent, proficiency in French.

**Université du Québec à Montréal,** Graduate Programs, Program in Semiology, Montréal, QC H3C 3P8, Canada. Offers PhD. *Program availability:* Part-time. *Degree requirements:* For doctorate, thesis/dissertation. *Entrance requirements:* For doctorate, appropriate master's degree or equivalent, proficiency in French.

**Université du Québec à Rimouski,** Graduate Programs, Program in Literary Studies, Rimouski, QC G5L 3A1, Canada. Offers MA, PhD. Programs offered jointly with Université du Québec à Chicoutimi and Université du Québec à Trois-Rivières. *Program availability:* Part-time. *Degree requirements:* For master's, thesis or alternative. *Entrance requirements:* For master's, appropriate bachelor's degree, proficiency in French.

**Université du Québec à Trois-Rivières,** Graduate Programs, Program in Literary Studies, Trois-Rivières, QC G9A 5H7, Canada. Offers MA. Program offered jointly with Université du Québec à Chicoutimi and Université du Québec à Rimouski. *Program availability:* Part-time. *Degree requirements:* For master's, thesis optional. *Entrance requirements:* For master's, appropriate bachelor's degree, proficiency in French.

**Université Laval,** Faculty of Letters, Department of Literature, Programs in Literary Studies, Québec, QC G1K 7P4, Canada. Offers MA, PhD. *Program availability:* Part-time. Terminal master's awarded for partial completion of doctoral program. *Degree requirements:* For master's, thesis; for doctorate, comprehensive exam, thesis/dissertation. *Entrance requirements:* For master's and doctorate, linguistics exams, knowledge of French, knowledge of a second language. Electronic applications accepted.

**University at Buffalo, the State University of New York,** Graduate School, College of Arts and Sciences, Department of Comparative Literature, Buffalo, NY 14260. Offers MA, PhD. *Program availability:* Part-time. *Faculty:* 7 full-time (2 women). *Students:* 28 full-time (13 women), 12 international. Average age 25. 30 applicants, 20% accepted, 4 enrolled. In 2016, 8 master's, 2 doctorates awarded. Terminal master's awarded for partial completion of doctoral program. *Degree requirements:* For master's, one foreign language, exam or project; for doctorate, 2 foreign languages, comprehensive exam, thesis/dissertation. *Entrance requirements:* For master's and doctorate, GRE General Test, writing sample, 3 letters of recommendation, statement of purpose, undergraduate transcripts. Additional exam requirements/recommendations for international students: Required—TOEFL (minimum score 550 paper-based; 79 iBT). *Application deadline:* For fall admission, 1/15 for domestic and international students. Applications are processed on a rolling basis. Application fee: $75. Electronic applications accepted. *Financial support:* In 2016–17, 16 students received support, including 1 fellowship with full tuition reimbursement available (averaging $4,150 per year), 16 teaching assistantships with full tuition reimbursements available (averaging $14,160 per year); health care benefits also available. Financial award application deadline: 1/15; financial award applicants required to submit FAFSA. *Faculty research:* Theory; interaction between literature and philosophy; European, Francophone, African, American, and South American literature; postmodernism; post colonialism. *Unit head:* Dr. Krzysztof Ziarek, Chair, 716-645-0858, Fax: 716-645-5979, E-mail: kziarek@buffalo.edu. *Application contact:* Dr. Shaun Irlam, Director of Graduate Studies, 716-645-0856, Fax: 716-645-5979, E-mail:

irlam@buffalo.edu.
Website: http://www.complit.buffalo.edu/

**University of Arkansas,** Graduate School, Interdisciplinary Program in Comparative Literature and Cultural Studies, Fayetteville, AR 72701. Offers MA, PhD. *Degree requirements:* For doctorate, 2 foreign languages, comprehensive exam, thesis/dissertation optional. *Entrance requirements:* For doctorate, GRE General Test, official transcripts of all undergraduate and graduate work, three letters of recommendation, writing sample, statement of purpose. Additional exam requirements/recommendations for international students: Required—TOEFL (minimum score 550 paper-based; 80 iBT) or IELTS (minimum score 6.5). Application fee: $40 ($50 for international students). *Financial support:* In 2016–17, 1 research assistantship, 13 teaching assistantships were awarded; fellowships, Federal Work-Study, and institutionally sponsored loans also available. *Faculty research:* Literary and cultural theory, cultural studies, postcolonial theory, gender studies, world literature. *Unit head:* Prof. Luis Restrepo, Director, 479-575-7580, Fax: 479-575-6795, E-mail: lrestr@uark.edu. *Application contact:* Graduate Admissions, 479-575-6246, Fax: 479-575-5908, E-mail: gradinfo@uark.edu.
Website: http://fulbright.uark.edu/programs/comparative-literature-cultural-studies/index.php/

**University of California, Berkeley,** Graduate Division, College of Letters and Science, Department of Comparative Literature, Berkeley, CA 94720-1500. Offers PhD. *Students:* 61 full-time (46 women); includes 14 minority (1 Black or African American, non-Hispanic/Latino; 1 American Indian or Alaska Native, non-Hispanic/Latino; 5 Asian, non-Hispanic/Latino; 7 Hispanic/Latino), 3 international. Average age 31. 82 applicants, 6 enrolled. In 2016, 3 doctorates awarded. *Degree requirements:* For doctorate, 3 foreign languages, thesis/dissertation, qualifying exam. *Entrance requirements:* For doctorate, GRE General Test, fluency in 1 foreign language (2 preferred), minimum GPA of 3.0, writing sample, 3 letters of recommendation. Additional exam requirements/recommendations for international students: Recommended—TOEFL (minimum score 570 paper-based; 90 iBT). *Application deadline:* For fall admission, 12/1 for domestic students. Application fee: $105 ($125 for international students). Electronic applications accepted. *Financial support:* Fellowships, research assistantships, teaching assistantships, institutionally sponsored loans, health care benefits, tuition waivers (full and partial), and unspecified assistantships available. Financial award applicants required to submit FAFSA. *Unit head:* Prof. Miryam Sas, Chair, 510-642-2712, E-mail: complitgrad@berkeley.edu. *Application contact:* 510-642-2629, Fax: 510-642-8852, E-mail: complitgradadmis@berkeley.edu.
Website: http://complit.berkeley.edu/

**University of California, Davis,** Graduate Studies, Graduate Group in Comparative Literature, Davis, CA 95616. Offers PhD. *Degree requirements:* For doctorate, 3 foreign languages, thesis/dissertation. *Entrance requirements:* For doctorate, GRE General Test, minimum GPA of 3.0. Additional exam requirements/recommendations for international students: Required—TOEFL (minimum score 550 paper-based). Electronic applications accepted. *Faculty research:* Literary criticism, literary theory, gender history and literature, genre.

**University of California, Irvine,** School of Humanities, Department of Comparative Literature, Irvine, CA 92697. Offers MA, PhD. *Students:* 36 full-time (18 women), 1 (woman) part-time; includes 7 minority (3 Asian, non-Hispanic/Latino; 1 Hispanic/Latino; 3 Two or more races, non-Hispanic/Latino), 6 international. Average age 33. 62 applicants, 23% accepted, 8 enrolled. In 2016, 4 master's, 1 doctorate awarded. *Degree requirements:* For master's, one foreign language; for doctorate, 2 foreign languages, thesis/dissertation. *Entrance requirements:* For doctorate, GRE General Test, minimum GPA of 3.5, sample of written work, 3 letters of recommendation. Additional exam requirements/recommendations for international students: Required—TOEFL (minimum score 550 paper-based). *Application deadline:* For fall admission, 12/15 for domestic and international students. Application fee: $105 ($125 for international students). Electronic applications accepted. *Financial support:* Fellowships with full tuition reimbursements, research assistantships with full tuition reimbursements, teaching assistantships with partial tuition reimbursements, institutionally sponsored loans, and tuition waivers (partial) available. Financial award application deadline: 3/1; financial award applicants required to submit FAFSA. *Faculty research:* Critical theory, feminist studies, Asian-American studies. *Unit head:* Gabriele Schwab, Department Chair, 949-824-6406, Fax: 949-824-6416, E-mail: gmschwab@uci.edu. *Application contact:* Bindya Baliga, Graduate Coordinator, 949-824-7968, E-mail: bbaliga@uci.edu.

**University of California, Los Angeles,** Graduate Division, College of Letters and Science, Department of Comparative Literature, Los Angeles, CA 90095. Offers MA, PhD. Terminal master's awarded for partial completion of doctoral program. *Degree requirements:* For master's, 2 foreign languages; for doctorate, 2 foreign languages, thesis/dissertation, oral and written qualifying exams. *Entrance requirements:* For doctorate, GRE General Test, bachelor's degree; minimum undergraduate GPA of 3.0, 3.4 in upper-division literature courses (or its equivalent if letter grade system not used); literary proficiency in one foreign language and elementary knowledge of another; writing sample. Additional exam requirements/recommendations for international students: Required—TOEFL. Electronic applications accepted.

**University of California, Riverside,** Graduate Division, Department of Comparative Literature and Foreign Languages, Riverside, CA 92521-0102. Offers comparative literature (MA, PhD). Terminal master's awarded for partial completion of doctoral program. *Degree requirements:* For master's, 3 foreign languages, comprehensive exam; for doctorate, 3 foreign languages, thesis/dissertation, qualifying exams. *Entrance requirements:* For master's and doctorate, GRE General Test, minimum GPA of 3.0. Additional exam requirements/recommendations for international students: Required—TOEFL (minimum score 550 paper-based; 80 iBT). Electronic applications accepted. *Expenses:* Tuition, state resident: full-time $16,666. Tuition, nonresident: full-time $31,768. *Required fees:* $11,055.54 per quarter. $3685.18 per quarter. Tuition and fees vary according to campus/location and program. *Faculty research:* French and German Enlightenment, modern drama and theatre, contemporary critical theory, East-West comparative studies, science fiction and fantasy.

**University of California, Santa Barbara,** Graduate Division, College of Letters and Sciences, Division of Humanities and Fine Arts, Program in Comparative Literature, Santa Barbara, CA 93106-4130. Offers comparative literature (PhD); East Asian literatures (PhD); feminist studies (PhD); French (PhD); global studies (PhD); translation studies (PhD); MA/PhD. *Degree requirements:* For doctorate, 2 foreign languages, comprehensive exam, thesis/dissertation. *Entrance requirements:* For doctorate, GRE. Additional exam requirements/recommendations for international students: Required—TOEFL (minimum score 550 paper-based; 80 iBT), IELTS (minimum score 7). Electronic applications accepted. *Faculty research:* Comparative literary studies in global context, critical theory, translation studies, media technological studies, trauma studies.

**University of California, Santa Cruz,** Division of Graduate Studies, Division of Humanities, Department of Literature, Santa Cruz, CA 95064. Offers MA, PhD. Terminal master's awarded for partial completion of doctoral program. *Degree requirements:* For master's, thesis; for doctorate, one foreign language, thesis/dissertation, qualifying exam. *Entrance requirements:* For master's, GRE General Test, writing sample,

minimum GPA of 3.5; for doctorate, GRE General Test, minimum GPA of 3.5, writing sample. Additional exam requirements/recommendations for international students: Required—TOEFL (minimum score 550 paper-based; 83 iBT); Recommended—IELTS (minimum score 8). Electronic applications accepted. *Faculty research:* Technologies of narrative; trans/post/emergent nationalisms; poetics, poetry, and experimental writing; materialism and material culture; critical theories.

**University of Chicago,** Division of the Humanities, Department of Comparative Literature, Chicago, IL 60637. Offers PhD. *Students:* 26 full-time (12 women); includes 3 minority (2 Hispanic/Latino; 1 Two or more races, non-Hispanic/Latino), 6 international. 65 applicants, 11% accepted, 3 enrolled. In 2016, 3 doctorates awarded. Terminal master's awarded for partial completion of doctoral program. *Degree requirements:* For doctorate, 3 foreign languages, comprehensive exam, thesis/dissertation. *Entrance requirements:* For doctorate, GRE General Test. Additional exam requirements/recommendations for international students: Required—TOEFL (minimum score 104 iBT), IELTS (minimum score 7). *Application deadline:* For fall admission, 12/15 for domestic and international students. Application fee: $90. Electronic applications accepted. *Financial support:* Fellowships with full tuition reimbursements, teaching assistantships with tuition reimbursements, Federal Work-Study, institutionally sponsored loans, scholarships/grants, and health care benefits available. Financial award application deadline: 12/15; financial award applicants required to submit FAFSA. *Unit head:* Francoise Meltzer, Chair, E-mail: mltz@uchicago.edu. *Application contact:* Michael Beetley, Assistant Dean of Students, Admissions and Fellowships, 773-702-1552, Fax: 773-834-9148, E-mail: humanitiesadmissions@uchicago.edu.
Website: http://complit.uchicago.edu/

**University of Chicago,** Division of the Humanities, Master of Arts Program in the Humanities, Chicago, IL 60637. Offers art history (MA); cinema and media studies (MA); classic languages (MA); comparative literature (MA); creative writing (MA); cultural policy studies (MA); digital humanities (MA); East Asian languages and civilizations (MA); English language and literature (MA); gender and sexuality studies (MA); Germanic studies (MA); linguistics (MA); music (MA); near Eastern languages and civilizations (MA); philosophy (MA); poetics (MA); race, politics and culture (MA); Romance languages and literatures (MA); Slavic languages and literatures (MA); South Asian languages and civilizations (MA); theater and performance studies (MA). *Students:* 80 full-time (43 women), 7 part-time (3 women); includes 20 minority (5 Black or African American, non-Hispanic/Latino; 1 American Indian or Alaska Native, non-Hispanic/Latino; 6 Asian, non-Hispanic/Latino; 5 Hispanic/Latino; 3 Two or more races, non-Hispanic/Latino), 11 international. Average age 26. 706 applicants, 15% accepted, 42 enrolled. In 2016, 92 master's awarded. *Degree requirements:* For master's, thesis. *Entrance requirements:* For master's, GRE General Test. Additional exam requirements/recommendations for international students: Required—TOEFL (minimum score 104 iBT), IELTS (minimum score 7). *Application deadline:* For fall admission, 1/3 for domestic and international students. Application fee: $90. Electronic applications accepted. *Financial support:* In 2016–17, 8 fellowships with partial tuition reimbursements (averaging $12,000 per year) were awarded; Federal Work-Study, institutionally sponsored loans, scholarships/grants, and tuition waivers (partial) also available. Financial award application deadline: 12/15; financial award applicants required to submit FAFSA. *Unit head:* Malynne Sternstein, Co-Director, 773-834-1201, Fax: 773-834-7526. *Application contact:* Program Coordinator, 773-834-1201, Fax: 773-834-7526, E-mail: ma-humanities@uchicago.edu.
Website: http://maph.uchicago.edu/

**University of Colorado Boulder,** Graduate School, College of Arts and Sciences, Comparative Literature Program, Boulder, CO 80309. Offers MA, PhD. *Students:* 8 full-time (4 women); includes 3 minority (1 Asian, non-Hispanic/Latino; 2 Hispanic/Latino), 1 international. Average age 31. 11 applicants, 55% accepted, 5 enrolled. In 2016, 6 master's awarded. Terminal master's awarded for partial completion of doctoral program. *Degree requirements:* For master's, 2 foreign languages, comprehensive exam, thesis and alternative; for doctorate, 3 foreign languages, comprehensive exam, thesis/dissertation. *Entrance requirements:* For master's, GRE General Test, minimum undergraduate GPA of 2.75; for doctorate, GRE General Test, MA in related field. *Application deadline:* For fall admission, 3/13 for domestic students, 12/1 for international students. Applications are processed on a rolling basis. Application fee: $60 ($80 for international students). Electronic applications accepted. Application fee is waived when completed online. *Financial support:* In 2016–17, 23 students received support, including 6 fellowships (averaging $351 per year), 8 teaching assistantships with full and partial tuition reimbursements available (averaging $35,377 per year); institutionally sponsored loans, scholarships/grants, health care benefits, and unspecified assistantships also available. Financial award application deadline: 1/1; financial award applicants required to submit FAFSA. *Faculty research:* Enlightenment to modern literature; literary theory and history; philosophy and literature; popular culture studies; reception, translation and interpretation; gender and sexual orientation; nationalism. *Application contact:* E-mail: complit@colorado.edu.
Website: http://complit.colorado.edu/

**University of Dallas,** Braniff Graduate School of Liberal Arts, Institute of Philosophic Studies, Program in Literature, Irving, TX 75062-4736. Offers PhD. *Degree requirements:* For doctorate, 2 foreign languages, comprehensive exam, thesis/dissertation, qualifying exams. *Entrance requirements:* For doctorate, GRE General Test. Additional exam requirements/recommendations for international students: Required—TOEFL. *Faculty research:* Medieval studies, modern literature, Renaissance, Shakespeare.

**University of Georgia,** Franklin College of Arts and Sciences, Department of Comparative Literature, Athens, GA 30602. Offers MA, PhD. *Degree requirements:* For master's, 2 foreign languages, thesis; for doctorate, one foreign language, thesis/dissertation. *Entrance requirements:* For master's and doctorate, GRE General Test. *Application deadline:* For fall admission, 7/1 priority date for domestic students; for spring admission, 11/15 for domestic students. Application fee: $50. Electronic applications accepted. *Financial support:* Fellowships, research assistantships, teaching assistantships, and unspecified assistantships available. *Unit head:* Dr. James H. McGregor, Department Co-Head, 706-542-0420, E-mail: mcgregor@uga.edu. *Application contact:* Dr. Thomas Cerbu, Graduate Coordinator, 706-542-2263, Fax: 706-542-2155, E-mail: tcerbu@uga.edu.
Website: http://www.cmlt.uga.edu/

**University of Guelph,** Graduate Studies, College of Arts, School of English and Theatre Studies, Joint Program in Literary Studies/Theatre Studies in English, Guelph, ON N1G 2W1, Canada. Offers PhD. *Program availability:* Part-time. *Degree requirements:* For doctorate, one foreign language, comprehensive exam, thesis/dissertation. *Entrance requirements:* For doctorate, MA, 3 letters of reference, writing samples, resume, minimum A- average in graduate course work. Additional exam requirements/recommendations for international students: Required—TOEFL. Electronic applications accepted. *Faculty research:* Canadian studies, Early Modern studies, Postcolonial studies, studies in gender and genre, 19th Century studies.

**University of Houston,** College of Liberal Arts and Social Sciences, Department of Modern and Classical Languages, Houston, TX 77204. Offers world cultures and literatures (MA). *Degree requirements:* For master's, one foreign language, thesis

## Comparative Literature

optional. *Entrance requirements:* For master's, GRE General Test, minimum GPA of 3.0 in last 60 hours of course work. Additional exam requirements/recommendations for international students: Required—TOEFL (minimum score 500 paper-based). Electronic applications accepted.

**University of Illinois at Urbana–Champaign,** Graduate College, College of Liberal Arts and Sciences, School of Literatures, Cultures and Linguistics, Program in Comparative and World Literature, Champaign, IL 61820. Offers comparative literature (MA, PhD). *Entrance requirements:* For master's, minimum GPA of 3.0; writing sample.

**University of Maryland, College Park,** Academic Affairs, College of Arts and Humanities, Department of English, Program in Comparative Literature, College Park, MD 20742. Offers MA, PhD. *Degree requirements:* For master's, thesis, oral defense; for doctorate, 3 foreign languages, thesis/dissertation, comprehensive exams in 4 areas. *Entrance requirements:* For master's, GRE General Test, foreign language, writing sample, 3 letters of recommendation; for doctorate, GRE General Test, minimum GPA of 3.0, foreign language, writing sample. Additional exam requirements/recommendations for international students: Required—TOEFL. Electronic applications accepted. *Faculty research:* Renaissance studies, drama, modern literature, postcolonial studies, feminist scholarship.

**University of Massachusetts Amherst,** Graduate School, College of Humanities and Fine Arts, Department of Languages, Literatures, and Cultures, Program in Comparative Literature, Amherst, MA 01003. Offers MA, PhD. *Program availability:* Part-time. Terminal master's awarded for partial completion of doctoral program. *Degree requirements:* For master's, thesis or alternative; for doctorate, comprehensive exam, thesis/dissertation. *Entrance requirements:* For master's and doctorate, GRE General Test, writing samples. Additional exam requirements/recommendations for international students: Required—TOEFL (minimum score 550 paper-based; 80 iBT), IELTS (minimum score 6.5). Electronic applications accepted.

**University of Memphis,** Graduate School, College of Arts and Sciences, Department of English, Memphis, TN 38152. Offers African-American literature (Graduate Certificate); applied linguistics (PhD); composition studies (PhD); creative writing (MFA); English as a second language (MA); linguistics (MA); literary and cultural studies (PhD), including African-American literature; literature (MA); professional writing (MA, PhD); teaching English as a second/foreign language (Graduate Certificate). *Program availability:* Part-time, evening/weekend, 100% online. *Faculty:* 31 full-time (14 women), 1 (woman) part-time/adjunct. *Students:* 86 full-time (44 women), 78 part-time (51 women); includes 36 minority (19 Black or African American, non-Hispanic/Latino; 3 Asian, non-Hispanic/Latino; 10 Hispanic/Latino; 4 Two or more races, non-Hispanic/Latino), 32 international. Average age 35. 68 applicants, 87% accepted, 33 enrolled. In 2016, 39 master's, 17 doctorates, 16 other advanced degrees awarded. Terminal master's awarded for partial completion of doctoral program. *Degree requirements:* For master's, one foreign language, comprehensive exam, thesis optional; for doctorate, 2 foreign languages, comprehensive exam, thesis/dissertation, qualifying exam. *Entrance requirements:* For master's, GRE, minimum undergraduate GPA of 3.0, statement of purpose, two letters of recommendation; for doctorate, GRE, minimum undergraduate and graduate GPA of 3.25, statement of purpose, writing sample, three letters of recommendation. Additional exam requirements/recommendations for international students: Required—TOEFL. *Application deadline:* For fall admission, 1/15 for domestic students; for spring admission, 10/15 for domestic students. Applications are processed on a rolling basis. Application fee: $35 ($60 for international students). Electronic applications accepted. *Expenses:* $5,231.50 per semester full-time in-state, $9,623.50 full-time out-of-state. *Financial support:* In 2016–17, 123 students received support, including 11 research assistantships with full tuition reimbursements available (averaging $17,064 per year); 25 teaching assistantships with full tuition reimbursements available (averaging $17,340 per year); Federal Work-Study, scholarships/grants, and unspecified assistantships also available. Financial award application deadline: 2/1; financial award applicants required to submit FAFSA. *Faculty research:* Applied linguistics, British and American literature, professional writing, composition studies. *Unit head:* Dr. Joshua Phillips, Chair, 901-678-2651, Fax: 901-678-2226, E-mail: jsphllps@memphis.edu. *Application contact:* Dr. Jeffrey Scraba, Coordinator of Graduate Studies, 901-678-4768, Fax: 901-678-2226, E-mail: jscraba@memphis.edu.
Website: http://www.memphis.edu/english

**University of Michigan,** Rackham Graduate School, College of Literature, Science, and the Arts, Department of Comparative Literature, Ann Arbor, MI 48109. Offers PhD. *Faculty:* 16 full-time (9 women). *Students:* 26 full-time (13 women); includes 6 minority (2 Black or African American, non-Hispanic/Latino; 1 Asian, non-Hispanic/Latino; 3 Hispanic/Latino), 10 international. Average age 26. 57 applicants, 18% accepted, 5 enrolled. In 2016, 5 doctorates awarded. *Degree requirements:* For doctorate, 2 foreign languages, thesis/dissertation, 2 languages at advanced level in addition to language of instruction, preliminary exam, topics paper, prospectus, oral defense of dissertation. *Entrance requirements:* For doctorate, GRE General Test. Additional exam requirements/recommendations for international students: Required—TOEFL (minimum score 560 paper-based; 84 iBT), Michigan English Language Assessment Battery, or IELTS (minimum score 6.5). *Application deadline:* For fall admission, 1/7 for domestic and international students. Application fee: $75 ($90 for international students). Electronic applications accepted. *Expenses:* Tuition, state resident: full-time $21,466; part-time $1152 per credit hour. Tuition, nonresident: full-time $43,346; part-time $2367 per credit hour. Part-time tuition and fees vary according to course load, degree level and program. *Financial support:* In 2016–17, 31 students received support, including 10 fellowships with full tuition reimbursements available (averaging $48,257 per year), 1 research assistantship with full tuition reimbursement available (averaging $33,780 per year), 20 teaching assistantships with full tuition reimbursements available (averaging $39,283 per year); scholarships/grants, health care benefits, and unspecified assistantships also available. Financial award application deadline: 4/15. *Faculty research:* Postcolonial theory, cultural studies, critical translation studies, comparative poetics, classical reception studies, gender studies/queer theory, animal studies, medieval literature. *Unit head:* Yopie Prins, Chair, 734-763-2351, Fax: 734-764-8503, E-mail: chair-complit@umich.edu. *Application contact:* Joe Johnson, Student Services Coordinator, 734-647-4894, Fax: 734-764-8503, E-mail: joecjohn@umich.edu.
Website: http://www.lsa.umich.edu/complit/

**University of Minnesota, Twin Cities Campus,** Graduate School, College of Liberal Arts, Department of Cultural Studies and Comparative Literature, Program in Comparative Literature, Minneapolis, MN 55455-0213. Offers PhD. *Degree requirements:* For doctorate, 3 foreign languages, comprehensive exam, thesis/dissertation. *Entrance requirements:* For doctorate, GRE General Test, sample of written work. Additional exam requirements/recommendations for international students: Required—TOEFL. *Faculty research:* Literary theory, emergent literatures, popular culture, postcolonial literature, gender and sexuality.

**University of Missouri,** Office of Research and Graduate Studies, College of Arts and Science, Department of Romance Languages and Literatures, Columbia, MO 65211. Offers French (MA, PhD); literature (MA); Spanish (MA, PhD); teaching (MA). *Faculty:* 25 full-time (15 women). *Students:* 22 full-time (16 women), 15 part-time (10 women); includes 11 minority (3 Black or African American, non-Hispanic/Latino; 6 Hispanic/Latino; 2 Two or more races, non-Hispanic/Latino), 13 international. Average age 35.

Terminal master's awarded for partial completion of doctoral program. *Degree requirements:* For master's, one foreign language; for doctorate, 4 foreign languages, comprehensive exam, thesis/dissertation. *Entrance requirements:* For master's, GRE General Test, minimum GPA of 3.0 in field of major; bachelor's degree; for doctorate, GRE General Test, minimum GPA of 3.0 in field of major; master's degree. Additional exam requirements/recommendations for international students: Required—TOEFL (minimum score 500 paper-based; 61 iBT). *Application deadline:* For fall admission, 2/15 priority date for domestic students; for winter admission, 10/15 for domestic students. Applications are processed on a rolling basis. Application fee: $75 ($90 for international students). Electronic applications accepted. *Expenses:* Tuition, state resident: full-time $6347; part-time $352.60 per credit hour. Tuition, nonresident: full-time $17,379; part-time $965.50 per credit hour. *Required fees:* $1035. Tuition and fees vary according to course load, campus/location and program. *Financial support:* Research assistantships, teaching assistantships with full tuition reimbursements, institutionally sponsored loans, health care benefits, and unspecified assistantships available.
Website: http://romancelanguages.missouri.edu/grad.shtml

**University of Nebraska–Lincoln,** Graduate College, College of Arts and Sciences, Department of English, Lincoln, NE 68588-0333. Offers composition and rhetoric (MA, PhD); creative writing (MA, PhD); literature studies (MA, PhD). *Degree requirements:* For master's, thesis optional; for doctorate, one foreign language, comprehensive exam, thesis/dissertation. *Entrance requirements:* For master's, writing sample; for doctorate, GRE General Test, writing sample. Additional exam requirements/recommendations for international students: Required—TOEFL (minimum score 600 paper-based). Electronic applications accepted. *Faculty research:* Creative writing, composition and rhetoric, women's studies, North American literature, medieval/Renaissance studies.

**University of New Hampshire,** Graduate School, College of Liberal Arts, Department of English, Durham, NH 03824. Offers composition (PhD); English education (MST); language and linguistics (MA); literature (MA, PhD); writing (MFA). *Program availability:* Part-time. *Degree requirements:* For master's, one foreign language; for doctorate, 2 foreign languages, thesis/dissertation. *Entrance requirements:* For master's, GRE General Test, sample of written work; for doctorate, GRE General Test, GRE Subject Test, sample of written work. Additional exam requirements/recommendations for international students: Required—TOEFL (minimum score 550 paper-based; 80 iBT). Electronic applications accepted.

**University of New Mexico,** Graduate Studies, College of Arts and Sciences, Program in Foreign Languages and Literatures, Albuquerque, NM 87131-2039. Offers comparative literature and cultural studies (MA); French (MA); French studies (PhD); German studies (MA). *Program availability:* Part-time. *Faculty:* 9 full-time (5 women). *Students:* 21 full-time (12 women), 10 part-time (6 women); includes 4 minority (3 Hispanic/Latino; 1 Two or more races, non-Hispanic/Latino), 10 international. Average age 30. 17 applicants, 41% accepted, 5 enrolled. In 2016, 9 master's awarded. *Degree requirements:* For master's, one foreign language, thesis optional; for doctorate, 2 foreign languages, thesis/dissertation. *Entrance requirements:* For master's and doctorate, transcript, writing sample, 3 letters of recommendation. Additional exam requirements/recommendations for international students: Required—TOEFL. *Application deadline:* For fall admission, 2/1 priority date for domestic students; for spring admission, 10/1 priority date for domestic students. Application fee: $50. Electronic applications accepted. *Financial support:* Research assistantships, teaching assistantships with tuition reimbursements, Federal Work-Study, health care benefits, and unspecified assistantships available. Financial award application deadline: 3/1; financial award applicants required to submit FAFSA. *Faculty research:* German, Russian, Italian, Japanese, French, comparative literature, culture studies, classics. *Unit head:* Dr. Walter Putnam, Chair, 505-277-4771, Fax: 505-277-3599, E-mail: wputnam@unm.edu. *Application contact:* Jacqueline Ochoa, Application and Graduation Advisor, 505-277-4471, Fax: 505-277-3599, E-mail: jochoa@unm.edu.
Website: http://www.unm.edu/~fll/

**University of Notre Dame,** Graduate School, College of Arts and Letters, Division of Humanities, PhD Program in Literature, Notre Dame, IN 46556. Offers PhD. *Degree requirements:* For doctorate, 3 foreign languages, thesis/dissertation, candidacy exam. *Entrance requirements:* For doctorate, GRE General Test. Additional exam requirements/recommendations for international students: Required—TOEFL (minimum score 600 paper-based; 80 iBT). Electronic applications accepted. *Faculty research:* Interdisciplinary study of literature from a transitional and intercultural perspective; classics, East Asian, French, German, Irish, Italian, Iberian and Latin American (Portuguese, Spanish).

**University of Oregon,** Graduate School, College of Arts and Sciences, Program in Comparative Literature, Eugene, OR 97403. Offers MA, PhD. *Program availability:* Part-time. Terminal master's awarded for partial completion of doctoral program. *Degree requirements:* For master's, 2 foreign languages, field exam; for doctorate, 2 foreign languages, thesis/dissertation, field exam. *Entrance requirements:* For master's, previous course work in English and literature, proficiency in 3 foreign languages, writing sample; for doctorate, previous course work in English and literature, proficiency in 2 foreign languages, writing sample. Additional exam requirements/recommendations for international students: Required—TOEFL. *Faculty research:* Critical theory, historical periods, interdisciplinary approach, Feminist studies.

**University of Pennsylvania,** School of Arts and Sciences, Graduate Group in Comparative Literature and Literary Theory, Philadelphia, PA 19104. Offers comparative literature (AM, PhD); literary theory (AM, PhD). *Faculty:* 38 full-time (14 women), 11 part-time/adjunct (3 women). *Students:* 29 full-time (14 women), 2 part-time (both women); includes 5 minority (2 Black or African American, non-Hispanic/Latino; 3 Hispanic/Latino), 11 international. Average age 30. 111 applicants, 9% accepted, 6 enrolled. In 2016, 4 master's, 4 doctorates awarded. *Entrance requirements:* Additional exam requirements/recommendations for international students: Required—TOEFL. *Expenses:* Tuition: Full-time $31,068; part-time $5762 per course. *Required fees:* $3200; $336 per course. Full-time tuition and fees vary according to degree level, program and student level. Part-time tuition and fees vary according to course load, degree level and program.
Website: http://ccat.sas.upenn.edu/Complit

**University of Puerto Rico, Río Piedras Campus,** College of Humanities, Department of Comparative Literature, San Juan, PR 00931-3300. Offers MA. *Program availability:* Part-time. *Degree requirements:* For master's, comprehensive exam, thesis. *Entrance requirements:* For master's, EXADEP, interview, minimum GPA of 3.0, letter of recommendation.

**University of South Carolina,** The Graduate School, College of Arts and Sciences, Department of Languages, Literatures, and Cultures, Columbia, SC 29208. Offers comparative literature (MA, PhD); foreign languages (MAT), including French, German, Spanish; French (MA); German (MA); Spanish (MA). MAT offered in cooperation with the College of Education. *Program availability:* Part-time. *Degree requirements:* For master's, one foreign language, comprehensive exam, thesis optional; for doctorate, 2 foreign languages, comprehensive exam, thesis/dissertation. *Entrance requirements:* For master's and doctorate, GRE General Test, writing sample. Additional exam requirements/recommendations for international students: Required—TOEFL (minimum score 75 iBT). Electronic applications accepted. *Faculty research:* Modern literature, linguistics, literature and culture, medieval literature, literary theory.

**University of Southern California,** Graduate School, Dana and David Dornsife College of Letters, Arts and Sciences, Comparative Studies in Literature and Culture Doctoral Program, Los Angeles, CA 90089. Offers comparative literature (PhD); comparative media and culture (PhD); Spanish and Latin American studies (PhD). *Degree requirements:* For doctorate, 2 foreign languages, comprehensive exam, thesis/dissertation. *Entrance requirements:* For doctorate, GRE, competence in language other than English (highly recommended). Additional exam requirements/recommendations for international students: Required—TOEFL. Electronic applications accepted. *Faculty research:* Literary theory, Japanese film and contemporary fiction, Francophone literature and cinema, Latin American and Caribbean literature, Spanish literature and film, nineteenth and twentieth century British and American literature.

**University of South Florida,** Innovative Education, Tampa, FL 33620-9951. Offers adult, career and higher education (Graduate Certificate), including college teaching, leadership in developing human resources, leadership in higher education; Africana studies (Graduate Certificate), including diasporas and health disparities, genocide and human rights; aging studies (Graduate Certificate), including gerontology; art research (Graduate Certificate), including museum studies; business foundations (Graduate Certificate); chemical and biomedical engineering (Graduate Certificate), including materials science and engineering, water, health and sustainability; child and family studies (Graduate Certificate), including positive behavior support; civil and industrial engineering (Graduate Certificate), including transportation systems analysis; community and family health (Graduate Certificate), including maternal and child health, social marketing and public health, violence and injury: prevention and intervention, women's health; criminology (Graduate Certificate), including criminal justice administration; educational measurement and research (Graduate Certificate), including evaluation; English (Graduate Certificate), including comparative literary studies, creative writing, professional and technical communication; entrepreneurship (Graduate Certificate); environmental health (Graduate Certificate), including safety management; epidemiology and biostatistics (Graduate Certificate), including applied biostatistics, biostatistics, concepts and tools of epidemiology, epidemiology, epidemiology of infectious diseases; geography, environment and planning (Graduate Certificate), including community development, environmental policy and management, geographical information systems; geology (Graduate Certificate), including hydrogeology; global health (Graduate Certificate), including disaster management, global health and Latin American and Caribbean studies, global health practice, humanitarian assistance, infection control; government and international affairs (Graduate Certificate), including Cuban studies, globalization studies; health policy and management (Graduate Certificate), including health management and leadership, public health policy and programs; hearing specialist: early intervention (Graduate Certificate); industrial and management systems engineering (Graduate Certificate), including systems engineering, technology management; information studies (Graduate Certificate), including school library media specialist; information systems/decision sciences (Graduate Certificate), including analytics and business intelligence; instructional technology (Graduate Certificate), including distance education, Florida digital/virtual educator, instructional design, multimedia design, Web design; internal medicine, bioethics and medical humanities (Graduate Certificate), including biomedical ethics; Latin American and Caribbean studies (Graduate Certificate); mass communications (Graduate Certificate), including multimedia journalism; mathematics and statistics (Graduate Certificate), including mathematics; medicine (Graduate Certificate), including aging and neuroscience, bioinformatics, biotechnology, brain fitness and memory management, clinical investigation, health informatics, health sciences, integrative weight management, intellectual property, medicine and gender, metabolic and nutritional medicine, metabolic cardiology, pharmacy sciences; national and competitive intelligence (Graduate Certificate); psychological and social foundations (Graduate Certificate), including career counseling, college teaching, diversity in education, mental health counseling, school counseling; public affairs (Graduate Certificate), including nonprofit management, public management, research administration; public health (Graduate Certificate), including environmental health, health equity, public health generalist, translational research in adolescent behavioral health; public health practices (Graduate Certificate), including planning for healthy communities; rehabilitation and mental health counseling (Graduate Certificate), including integrative mental health care, marriage and family therapy, rehabilitation technology; secondary education (Graduate Certificate), including ESOL, foreign language education: culture and content, foreign language education: professional; social work (Graduate Certificate), including geriatric social work/clinical gerontology; special education (Graduate Certificate), including autism spectrum disorder, disabilities education: severe/profound; world languages (Graduate Certificate), including teaching English as a second language (TESL) or foreign language. *Expenses:* Tuition, state resident: full-time $7766; part-time $431.43 per credit hour. Tuition, nonresident: full-time $15,789; part-time $877.17 per credit hour. *Required fees:* $37 per term. *Unit head:* Kathy Barnes, Interdisciplinary Programs Coordinator, 813-974-8031, Fax: 813-974-7061, E-mail: barnesk@usf.edu. *Application contact:* Karen Tylinski, Metro Initiatives, 813-974-9943, Fax: 813-974-7061, E-mail: ktylinsk@usf.edu. Website: http://www.usf.edu/innovative-education/

**The University of Texas at Austin,** Graduate School, College of Liberal Arts, Program in Comparative Literature, Austin, TX 78712-1111. Offers MA, PhD. *Degree requirements:* For master's, 2 foreign languages, report or thesis; for doctorate, 3 foreign languages, thesis/dissertation. *Entrance requirements:* For master's and doctorate, GRE General Test. Electronic applications accepted.

**The University of Texas at Dallas,** School of Arts and Humanities, Richardson, TX 75080. Offers history (MA); humanities (MA, PhD), including aesthetic studies, history of ideas, studies in literature (PhD), studies of literature (MA); Latin American studies (MA). *Program availability:* Part-time, evening/weekend. *Faculty:* 46 full-time (15 women), 5 part-time/adjunct (1 woman). *Students:* 129 full-time (78 women), 127 part-time (81 women); includes 63 minority (12 Black or African American, non-Hispanic/Latino; 4 American Indian or Alaska Native, non-Hispanic/Latino; 13 Asian, non-Hispanic/Latino; 23 Hispanic/Latino; 11 Two or more races, non-Hispanic/Latino), 27 international. Average age 41. 113 applicants, 58% accepted, 38 enrolled. In 2016, 39 master's, 16 doctorates awarded. *Degree requirements:* For master's, one foreign language, portfolio; for doctorate, one foreign language, thesis/dissertation. *Entrance requirements:* For master's and doctorate, minimum GPA of 3.0 in undergraduate course work in field. Additional exam requirements/recommendations for international students: Required—TOEFL (minimum score 550 paper-based). *Application deadline:* For fall admission, 7/15 for domestic students, 5/1 priority date for international students; for spring admission, 11/15 for domestic students, 9/1 priority date for international students. Applications are processed on a rolling basis. Application fee: $50 ($100 for international students). Electronic applications accepted. *Expenses:* Tuition, state resident: full-time $12,418; part-time $690 per semester hour. Tuition, nonresident: full-time $24,150; part-time $1342 per semester hour. Tuition and fees vary according to course load. *Financial support:* In 2016–17, 135 students received support, including 1 fellowship (averaging $2,000 per year), 12 research assistantships with partial tuition reimbursements available (averaging $23,948 per year), 69 teaching assistantships with partial tuition reimbursements available (averaging $15,001 per year); Federal Work-Study, institutionally sponsored loans, scholarships/grants, and unspecified assistantships also available. Support available to part-time students. Financial award application deadline: 4/30; financial award applicants required to submit FAFSA. *Faculty research:* Science and the arts and humanities, intellectual and philosophical history, cultural studies, translation studies. *Total annual research expenditures:* $177,908. *Unit head:* Dr. Dennis M. Kratz, Dean, 972-883-2984, Fax: 972-883-2989, E-mail: dkratz@utdallas.edu. *Application contact:* Dr. John Gooch, Associate Dean of Graduate Studies, 972-883-2756, Fax: 972-883-2989, E-mail: john.gooch@utdallas.edu. Website: http://www.utdallas.edu/ah/

**University of Toronto,** School of Graduate Studies, Faculty of Arts and Science, Centre for Comparative Literature, Toronto, ON M5S 1A1, Canada. Offers MA, PhD. *Program availability:* Part-time. *Degree requirements:* For doctorate, thesis/dissertation. *Entrance requirements:* For master's, 2 letters of recommendation, sample of work (short essay on a literary topic preferred), resume, bachelor's degree with a B+ average; for doctorate, 2 letters of recommendation, sample of work (short essay on a literary topic preferred), resume, master's degree with average grade of at least A-. Additional exam requirements/recommendations for international students: Required—TOEFL (minimum score 580 paper-based; 93 iBT), TWE (minimum score 5). Electronic applications accepted.

**University of Utah,** Graduate School, College of Humanities, Department of World Languages and Cultures, Salt Lake City, UT 84112. Offers comparative literary and cultural studies (PhD); French (MA); Spanish (MA, MALP); world languages (MA). *Program availability:* Part-time. *Faculty:* 27 full-time (17 women), 2 part-time/adjunct (both women). *Students:* 37 full-time (29 women), 3 part-time (1 woman); includes 9 minority (2 Asian, non-Hispanic/Latino; 6 Hispanic/Latino; 1 Two or more races, non-Hispanic/Latino), 9 international. Average age 37. 29 applicants, 62% accepted, 15 enrolled. In 2016, 13 master's awarded. Terminal master's awarded for partial completion of doctoral program. *Degree requirements:* For master's, variable foreign language requirement, comprehensive exam (for some programs), thesis (for some programs); for doctorate, 2 foreign languages, comprehensive exam, thesis/dissertation. *Entrance requirements:* For master's, bachelor's degree from regionally-accredited college or university with minimum undergraduate overall GPA of 3.0; for doctorate, MA from regionally-accredited college or university, advanced proficiency in target language. Additional exam requirements/recommendations for international students: Required—TOEFL (minimum score 550 paper-based; 80 iBT). *Application deadline:* For fall admission, 1/15 priority date for domestic students, 12/15 priority date for international students. Application fee: $55 ($65 for international students). Electronic applications accepted. *Expenses:* Tuition, state resident: full-time $7011; part-time $3918.24 per credit hour. Tuition, nonresident: full-time $22,154; part-time $11,665.42 per credit hour. *Financial support:* In 2016–17, 27 students received support, including 27 teaching assistantships with full and partial tuition reimbursements available (averaging $16,500 per year); health care benefits and unspecified assistantships also available. Financial award application deadline: 1/15. *Faculty research:* Literary study, literary theory, linguistics, cultural studies, comparative studies. *Unit head:* Dr. Katharina Gerstenberger, Chair, 801-585-7908, Fax: 801-581-7581, E-mail: katharina.gerstenberger@utah.edu. *Application contact:* Mackenzie Buie, Academic Coordinator, 801-581-7748, Fax: 801-581-7581, E-mail: mackenzie.buie@utah.edu. Website: http://languages.utah.edu/

**University of Washington,** Graduate School, College of Arts and Sciences, Department of Comparative Literature, Seattle, WA 98195. Offers MA, PhD. *Program availability:* Part-time. Terminal master's awarded for partial completion of doctoral program. *Degree requirements:* For master's, 2 foreign languages, thesis optional; for doctorate, 3 foreign languages, thesis/dissertation. *Entrance requirements:* For master's, GRE General Test, BA in comparative literature or equivalent, minimum GPA of 3.0, proficiency in 1 foreign language; for doctorate, GRE General Test, MA in comparative literature or equivalent, minimum GPA of 3.0, proficiency in 2 foreign languages. Additional exam requirements/recommendations for international students: Required—TOEFL. Electronic applications accepted. *Faculty research:* Literature and culture from classical antiquity to twentieth-century, literary theory and criticism.

**The University of Western Ontario,** Faculty of Graduate Studies, Faculty of Arts and Humanities, Department of Modern Languages and Literatures, London, ON N6A 5B8, Canada. Offers comparative literature (MA, PhD); Hispanic studies (MA, PhD). *Program availability:* Part-time. *Degree requirements:* For master's, 2 foreign languages, thesis (for some programs). *Entrance requirements:* For master's, honors degree in Spanish or equivalent, minimum B average. Additional exam requirements/recommendations for international students: Required—TOEFL (comparative literature). *Faculty research:* Spanish golden age, Latin-American, romance, medieval, film.

**University of Wisconsin–Madison,** Graduate School, College of Letters and Science, Department of Comparative Literature, Madison, WI 53706-1380. Offers MA, PhD. *Program availability:* Part-time. Terminal master's awarded for partial completion of doctoral program. *Degree requirements:* For master's, one foreign language, second-year exam; for doctorate, 3 foreign languages, thesis/dissertation, 3 preliminary exams. *Entrance requirements:* For master's, GRE General Test, writing sample; for doctorate, GRE General Test. Electronic applications accepted. *Faculty research:* Literary theory, cultural criticism, classics through early modern literature, postmodernity, gender studies.

**University of Wisconsin–Madison,** Graduate School, College of Letters and Science, Department of East Asian Languages and Literature, Program in Chinese Literature, Madison, WI 53706-1380. Offers MA, PhD. *Program availability:* Part-time. Terminal master's awarded for partial completion of doctoral program. *Degree requirements:* For master's, one foreign language, seminars, written exam; for doctorate, 3 foreign languages, thesis/dissertation, seminars, preliminary exams, oral exam. *Entrance requirements:* For master's, bachelor's degree or equivalent in Chinese; for doctorate, master's degree or equivalent in Chinese. Electronic applications accepted. *Faculty research:* Chinese historical and modern linguistics, classical Chinese literary and cultural history, modern Chinese literary and cultural history, Chinese paleography.

**University of Wisconsin–Madison,** Graduate School, College of Letters and Science, Department of Scandinavian Studies, Madison, WI 53706-1380. Offers area studies (MA); folklore (PhD); literature (MA, PhD); philology (PhD). *Program availability:* Part-time. *Degree requirements:* For master's, 2 foreign languages, exam; for doctorate, thesis/dissertation, exam. *Entrance requirements:* For master's, minimum GPA of 3.25; for doctorate, minimum GPA of 3.5. Electronic applications accepted. *Faculty research:* Historical fiction, Icelandic poetry, nineteenth-century literature, theater, gender studies, folklore.

**University of Wisconsin–Milwaukee,** Graduate School, College of Letters and Science, Department of Foreign Languages and Literature, Milwaukee, WI 53201-0413. Offers classic Greek (MA); classics (MA); comparative literature (MA); foreign language and literature (MA); French (MA); German (MA); Latin (MA); linguistics (MA); Spanish (MA); translation (MA, Certificate). *Program availability:* Part-time. *Students:* 10 full-time (7 women), 19 part-time (16 women); includes 5 minority (2 Black or African American, non-Hispanic/Latino; 2 Hispanic/Latino; 1 Two or more races, non-Hispanic/Latino), 2

*Comparative Literature*

international. Average age 31. 41 applicants, 32% accepted, 9 enrolled. In 2016, 21 master's awarded. *Degree requirements:* For master's, 2 foreign languages, thesis or alternative. *Entrance requirements:* Additional exam requirements/recommendations for international students: Required—TOEFL (minimum score 550 paper-based; 79 iBT), IELTS (minimum score 6.5). *Application deadline:* For fall admission, 1/1 priority date for domestic students; for spring admission, 9/1 for domestic students. Applications are processed on a rolling basis. Application fee: $56 ($96 for international students). Electronic applications accepted. *Financial support:* In 2016–17, 1 fellowship, 2 research assistantships, 26 teaching assistantships were awarded; career-related internships or fieldwork, health care benefits, unspecified assistantships, and project assistantships also available. Support available to part-time students. Financial award application deadline: 4/15; financial award applicants required to submit FAFSA. *Unit head:* Kevin Muse, Department Chair, 414-229-5213, E-mail: kmuse@uwm.edu. *Application contact:* General Information Contact, 414-229-4982, Fax: 414-229-6967, E-mail: gradschool@uwm.edu.
Website: http://uwm.edu/foreign-languages-literature/

**Washington University in St. Louis,** The Graduate School, Department of East Asian Languages and Cultures, St. Louis, MO 63130-4899. Offers Chinese (MA); Chinese and comparative literature (PhD); Chinese language and literature (PhD); East Asian studies (MA); Japanese (MA); Japanese and comparative literature (PhD); Japanese language and literature (PhD). Terminal master's awarded for partial completion of doctoral program. *Degree requirements:* For master's, thesis optional; for doctorate, thesis/dissertation. *Entrance requirements:* For master's and doctorate, GRE General Test. Additional exam requirements/recommendations for international students: Required—TOEFL. Electronic applications accepted. *Faculty research:* Chinese; Japanese; Chinese fiction, theater, poetry, modern literature; Japanese modern and classical fiction, translation theory.

**Washington University in St. Louis,** The Graduate School, Department of Romance Languages and Literatures, Program in French, St. Louis, MO 63130-4899. Offers French and comparative literature (PhD); French language and literature (PhD). Terminal master's awarded for partial completion of doctoral program. *Degree requirements:* For doctorate, thesis/dissertation. *Entrance requirements:* For doctorate, GRE General Test. Additional exam requirements/recommendations for international

students: Required—TOEFL. Electronic applications accepted. *Faculty research:* French language and literature.

**Washington University in St. Louis,** The Graduate School, Department of Romance Languages and Literatures, Program in Spanish, St. Louis, MO 63130-4899. Offers Hispanic languages and literatures (PhD); Spanish and comparative literature (PhD). Terminal master's awarded for partial completion of doctoral program. *Degree requirements:* For doctorate, thesis/dissertation. *Entrance requirements:* For doctorate, GRE General Test. Additional exam requirements/recommendations for international students: Required—TOEFL. Electronic applications accepted. *Faculty research:* Latin American and Iberian literatures and languages, Spanish and comparative literature.

**Washington University in St. Louis,** The Graduate School, Program in Comparative Literature, St. Louis, MO 63130-4899. Offers PhD. Terminal master's awarded for partial completion of doctoral program. *Degree requirements:* For doctorate, thesis/dissertation. *Entrance requirements:* For doctorate, GRE General Test. Additional exam requirements/recommendations for international students: Required—TOEFL. Electronic applications accepted. *Faculty research:* World literature; literary theory; translation studies; global and multicultural theory; comparative drama; comparative arts; studies in literature, politics and society; narrative theory; media ecologies, histories, and poetics.

**Western Kentucky University,** Graduate Studies, Potter College of Arts and Letters, Department of English, Bowling Green, KY 42101. Offers education (MA); English (MA Ed); literature (MA), including American literature, British literature, literary theory, women writers, world literature; teaching English as a second language (MA); writing (MA). *Program availability:* Part-time, evening/weekend. *Degree requirements:* For master's, comprehensive exam, thesis optional, final exam. *Entrance requirements:* For master's, GRE General Test, minimum GPA of 2.75. Additional exam requirements/recommendations for international students: Required—TOEFL (minimum score 555 paper-based; 79 iBT). *Faculty research:* Improving writing, linking teacher knowledge and performance, Victorian women writers, Kentucky women writers, Kentucky poets.

**Yale University,** Graduate School of Arts and Sciences, Department of Comparative Literature, New Haven, CT 06520. Offers PhD. *Degree requirements:* For doctorate, 2 foreign languages, thesis/dissertation. *Entrance requirements:* For doctorate, GRE General Test.

# English

**Abilene Christian University,** Graduate Programs, College of Arts and Sciences, Department of English, Abilene, TX 79699. Offers composition/rhetoric (MA); creative writing (MA); literature (MA). *Program availability:* Part-time. *Faculty:* 16 part-time/adjunct (6 women). *Students:* 8 full-time (6 women), 3 part-time (1 woman). 17 applicants, 53% accepted, 4 enrolled. In 2016, 6 master's awarded. *Degree requirements:* For master's, one foreign language, comprehensive exam (for some programs), thesis (for some programs). *Entrance requirements:* For master's, GRE General Test. Additional exam requirements/recommendations for international students: Required—TOEFL (minimum score 80 iBT), IELTS (minimum score 6), PTE. *Application deadline:* For fall admission, 8/11 for domestic students; for spring admission, 11/1 for domestic students. Applications are processed on a rolling basis. Application fee: $50. Electronic applications accepted. *Expenses: Tuition:* Full-time $19,890; part-time $1105 per credit hour. Tuition and fees vary according to course load and program. *Financial support:* In 2016–17, 11 students received support, including 6 teaching assistantships with partial tuition reimbursements available (averaging $5,800 per year); Federal Work-Study and scholarships/grants also available. Support available to part-time students. Financial award application deadline: 4/1; financial award applicants required to submit FAFSA. *Faculty research:* Feminism, Shakespearean dimensions of new literature, poetic consciousness, deconstruction myths. *Unit head:* Dr. William Carroll, Graduate Director, 325-674-2083, Fax: 325-674-2408, E-mail: william.carroll@acu.edu. *Application contact:* Corey Patterson, Director of Graduate Admission and Recruiting, 325-674-6566, Fax: 325-674-6717, E-mail: gradinfo@acu.edu.
Website: http://www.acu.edu/graduate/academics/english.html

**Acadia University,** Faculty of Arts, Department of English, Wolfville, NS B4P 2R6, Canada. Offers MA. *Degree requirements:* For master's, thesis. *Entrance requirements:* For master's, honors degree in English, minimum A- average. Additional exam requirements/recommendations for international students: Required—TOEFL (minimum score 630 paper-based; 93 iBT), IELTS (minimum score 6.5). *Faculty research:* Renaissance, Canadian, medieval, Victorian, and Romantic literature.

**The American University in Cairo,** School of Humanities and Social Sciences, Cairo, Egypt. Offers Arab and Islamic civilizations (Graduate Diploma); Arabic studies (MA); comparative literary studies (Graduate Diploma); Egyptology and Coptology (MA); English and comparative literature (MA); humanities and social sciences (Graduate Diploma); philosophy (MA); psychology (MA); sociology and anthropology (MA); teaching Arabic as a foreign language (MA); teaching English to speakers of other languages (MA). *Program availability:* Part-time, evening/weekend. *Faculty:* 51 full-time (29 women), 4 part-time/adjunct (2 women). *Students:* 65 full-time (47 women), 179 part-time (138 women), 32 international. Average age 30. 221 applicants, 45% accepted, 54 enrolled. In 2016, 95 master's awarded. *Degree requirements:* For master's, comprehensive exam (for some programs), thesis (for some programs). *Entrance requirements:* Additional exam requirements/recommendations for international students: Required—TOEFL (minimum score 450 paper-based; 45 iBT), IELTS (minimum score 5). *Application deadline:* For fall admission, 2/1 priority date for domestic and international students; for spring admission, 10/15 priority date for domestic and international students. Applications are processed on a rolling basis. Application fee: $80. Electronic applications accepted. *Expenses:* Contact institution. *Financial support:* Fellowships with partial tuition reimbursements, scholarships/grants, tuition waivers (partial), and unspecified assistantships available. Financial award application deadline: 3/10. *Faculty research:* English literature, political science, psychology, sociology, anthropology and Egyptology, teaching English for non-speakers, teaching Arabic as a foreign language, philosophy, Arabic studies. *Unit head:* Dr. Nathaniel Bowditch, Dean, 20-2-2615-1788, E-mail: nbowditch@aucegypt.edu. *Application contact:* Maha Hegazi, Director for Graduate Admissions, 20-2-2615-1462, E-mail: mahahegazi@aucegypt.edu.
Website: http://www.aucegypt.edu/huss/Pages/default.aspx

**American University of Beirut,** Graduate Programs, Faculty of Arts and Sciences, Beirut, Lebanon. Offers anthropology (MA); Arab and Middle Eastern history (PhD); Arabic language and literature (MA, PhD); archaeology (MA); art history and curating

(MA); biology (MS); cell and molecular biology (PhD); chemistry (MS); clinical psychology (MA); computational sciences (MS); computer science (MS); economics (MA); education (MA); English language (MA); English literature (MA); environmental policy planning (MS); financial economics (MAFE); geology (MS); history (MA); Islamic studies (MA); mathematics (MS); media studies (MA); Middle Eastern studies (MA); physics (MS); political studies (MA); psychology (MA); public administration (MA); public policy and international affairs (MA); sociology (MA); statistics (MA, MS); theoretical physics (PhD); transnational American studies (MA). *Program availability:* Part-time. *Faculty:* 133 full-time (42 women), 6 part-time/adjunct (2 women). *Students:* 240 full-time (172 women), 227 part-time (166 women). Average age 27. 286 applicants, 67% accepted, 108 enrolled. In 2016, 60 master's, 3 doctorates awarded. Terminal master's awarded for partial completion of doctoral program. *Degree requirements:* For master's, one foreign language, comprehensive exam, thesis (for some programs); for doctorate, one foreign language, comprehensive exam, thesis/dissertation. *Entrance requirements:* For master's, GRE (for some MA, MS programs), letters of recommendation; for doctorate, GRE, letters of recommendation. Additional exam requirements/recommendations for international students: Required—TOEFL (minimum score 600 paper-based; 97 iBT), IELTS (minimum score 7). *Application deadline:* For fall admission, 4/3 for domestic students; for winter admission, 11/3 for domestic students. Application fee: $50. Electronic applications accepted. *Expenses:* Contact institution. *Financial support:* In 2016–17, 4 fellowships (averaging $11,200 per year), 18 research assistantships (averaging $5,400 per year) were awarded; teaching assistantships, career-related internships or fieldwork, Federal Work-Study, institutionally sponsored loans, scholarships/grants, traineeships, health care benefits, tuition waivers (full), and unspecified assistantships also available. Support available to part-time students. *Faculty research:* Development economics, spatial econometrics, health economics, labor economics, energy economics, hydrogeology, geophysics, petrophysics, structural geology, mineralogy, petrology, geochemistry, multilingualism, comparative/world literature, translation studies, book histories/ cultures, biocatalysis, molecular recognition, photocatalysis, photophysical and biophysical chemistry, probe chemistry, machine learning, data science. *Unit head:* Dr. Nadia Maria El Cheikh, Dean, Faculty of Arts and Sciences, 961-1374374 Ext. 3800, Fax: 961-1744461, E-mail: nmcheikh@aub.edu.lb. *Application contact:* Dr. Salim Kanaan, Director, Admissions Office, 961-1350000 Ext. 2590, Fax: 961-1750775, E-mail: sk00@aub.edu.lb.
Website: http://www.aub.edu.lb/fas/

**Andrews University,** School of Graduate Studies, College of Arts and Sciences, Department of English, Berrien Springs, MI 49104. Offers MA, MAT. *Program availability:* Part-time. *Faculty:* 8 full-time (4 women), 2 part-time/adjunct (1 woman). *Students:* 5 full-time (4 women), 5 part-time (4 women); includes 3 minority (2 Black or African American, non-Hispanic/Latino; 1 Hispanic/Latino), 2 international. Average age 30. In 2016, 5 master's awarded. *Degree requirements:* For master's, one foreign language, thesis optional. *Entrance requirements:* For master's, GRE Subject Test. Additional exam requirements/recommendations for international students: Required—TOEFL (minimum score 550 paper-based). *Application deadline:* For fall admission, 8/15 for domestic students. Applications are processed on a rolling basis. Application fee: $40. *Financial support:* Fellowships, research assistantships, teaching assistantships, career-related internships or fieldwork, and Federal Work-Study available. *Faculty research:* Shakespearean studies. *Unit head:* Dr. Meredith Jones-Gray, Chairperson, 269-471-3298. *Application contact:* Justina Clayburn, Supervisor of Graduate Admission, 800-253-2874, Fax: 269-471-6321, E-mail: graduate@andrews.edu.

**Angelo State University,** College of Graduate Studies and Research, College of Arts and Humanities, Department of English and Modern Languages, San Angelo, TX 76909. Offers English (MA); TESOL (MA). *Program availability:* Part-time, evening/weekend. *Students:* 4 full-time (3 women), 7 part-time (all women); includes 5 minority (1 American Indian or Alaska Native, non-Hispanic/Latino; 4 Hispanic/Latino), 1 international. Average age 27. *Degree requirements:* For master's, comprehensive exam. *Entrance requirements:* For master's, essay. Additional exam requirements/recommendations for international students: Required—TOEFL or IELTS. *Application deadline:* For fall admission, 7/15 priority date for domestic students, 6/10 for international students; for spring admission, 12/1 priority date for domestic students, 11/1 for international students. Applications are processed on a rolling basis. Application fee: $40 ($50 for international students). Electronic applications accepted. *Expenses:* Tuition, state resident: full-time $3726; part-time $2484 per year. Tuition, nonresident: full-time $10,746; part-time $7164 per year. *Required fees:* $2538; $1702 per unit. *Financial support:* Teaching assistantships, Federal Work-Study, scholarships/grants, and unspecified assistantships available. Support available to part-time students. Financial award application deadline: 3/1; financial award applicants required to submit FAFSA. *Unit head:* Dr. Laurence E. Musgrove, Chair, 325-486-6138, Fax: 325-942-2208, E-mail: laurence.musgrove@angelo.edu. *Application contact:* Dr. Laurence E. Musgrove, Chair, 325-486-6138, Fax: 325-942-2208, E-mail: laurence.musgrove@angelo.edu. Website: http://www.angelo.edu/dept/english_modern_languages/

**Appalachian State University,** Cratis D. Williams Graduate School, Department of English, Boone, NC 28608. Offers English (MA). *Program availability:* Part-time, online learning. *Degree requirements:* For master's, one foreign language, comprehensive exam, thesis (for some programs). *Entrance requirements:* For master's, GRE General Test, 3 letters of recommendation. Additional exam requirements/recommendations for international students: Required—TOEFL (minimum score 570 paper-based; 79 iBT), IELTS (minimum score 6.5). *Application deadline:* For fall admission, 3/15 priority date for domestic students, 2/1 for international students; for spring admission, 11/1 for domestic students, 7/1 for international students. Applications are processed on a rolling basis. Application fee: $55. Electronic applications accepted. *Expenses:* Tuition, state resident: full-time $4744. Tuition, nonresident: full-time $17,913. Full-time tuition and fees vary according to program. *Financial support:* Fellowships, research assistantships, teaching assistantships, career-related internships or fieldwork, Federal Work-Study, scholarships/grants, and unspecified assistantships available. Financial award application deadline: 4/1; financial award applicants required to submit FAFSA. *Faculty research:* Contemporary Irish literature, Romantic psychology, cultural practices of everyday life, Gullah linguistics, Renaissance women's writing. *Unit head:* Dr. James Fogelquist, Chair, 828-262-3095, E-mail: fogelquistjd@appstate.edu. *Application contact:* Dr. Susan Staub, Graduate Program Director, 828-262-2335, E-mail: staubsc@appstate.edu.
Website: http://www.english.appstate.edu

**Arcadia University,** College of Arts and Sciences, Department of English, Program in English, Glenside, PA 19038-3295. Offers MA. *Faculty:* 9 full-time (5 women), 1 part-time/adjunct. *Students:* 2 full-time (1 woman), 13 part-time (12 women); includes 3 minority (1 Black or African American, non-Hispanic/Latino; 1 Hispanic/Latino; 1 Two or more races, non-Hispanic/Latino). 11 applicants, 64% accepted, 2 enrolled. In 2016, 18 master's awarded. *Expenses:* Contact institution. *Unit head:* Dr. Richard Wertime, Director of Graduate Studies, 215-572-2963, E-mail: wertimed@arcadia.edu. *Application contact:* 215-572-2925, Fax: 215-572-2126, E-mail: grad@arcadia.edu.

**Arizona State University at the Tempe campus,** College of Liberal Arts and Sciences, Department of English, Tempe, AZ 85287-0302. Offers applied linguistics (PhD); creative writing (MFA); English (MA, PhD), including comparative literature (MA), linguistics (MA), literature, rhetoric and composition (MA), rhetoric, composition, and linguistics (PhD); film and media studies (MAS), including American media and popular culture; linguistics (Graduate Certificate); teaching English to speakers of other languages (MTESOL); translation studies (Graduate Certificate). Terminal master's awarded for partial completion of doctoral program. *Degree requirements:* For master's, variable foreign language requirement, comprehensive exam (for some programs), thesis (for some programs), interactive Program of Study (iPOS) submitted before completing 50 percent of required credit hours; for doctorate, variable foreign language requirement, comprehensive exam, thesis/dissertation, interactive Program of Study (iPOS) submitted before completing 50 percent of required credit hours. *Entrance requirements:* For master's and doctorate, GRE, minimum GPA of 3.0 or equivalent in last 2 years of work leading to bachelor's degree. Additional exam requirements/recommendations for international students: Required—TOEFL, IELTS, or PTE. Electronic applications accepted.

**Arkansas State University,** Graduate School, College of Humanities and Social Sciences, Department of English and Philosophy, State University, AR 72467. Offers English (MA); English education (MSE, SCCT). *Program availability:* Part-time. *Degree requirements:* For master's, variable foreign language requirement, comprehensive exam, thesis or alternative, preliminary exam; for SCCT, comprehensive exam. *Entrance requirements:* For master's, GRE General Test or MAT, appropriate bachelor's degree, official transcript, valid teaching certificate (for MSE), immunization records; for SCCT, GRE General Test or MAT, interview, master's degree, official transcript, immunization records. Additional exam requirements/recommendations for international students: Required—TOEFL (minimum score 550 paper-based; 79 iBT), IELTS (minimum score 6), PTE (minimum score 56). Electronic applications accepted.

**Arkansas Tech University,** College of Arts and Humanities, Russellville, AR 72801. Offers applied sociology (MS); English (M Ed, MA); history (MA); liberal arts (MLA); multi-media journalism (MA); psychology (MS); teaching English as a second language (MA). *Program availability:* Part-time. *Students:* 56 full-time (42 women), 121 part-time (85 women); includes 23 minority (7 Black or African American, non-Hispanic/Latino; 1 Asian, non-Hispanic/Latino; 11 Hispanic/Latino; 4 Two or more races, non-Hispanic/Latino), 34 international. Average age 32. In 2016, 90 master's awarded. *Degree requirements:* For master's, comprehensive exam (for some programs), thesis (for some programs), project. *Entrance requirements:* For master's, GRE General Test or GMAT. Additional exam requirements/recommendations for international students: Required—TOEFL (minimum score 550 paper-based; 79 iBT), IELTS (minimum score 6). *Application deadline:* For fall admission, 3/1 priority date for domestic students, 5/1 priority date for international students; for spring admission, 10/1 priority date for domestic and international students. Applications are processed on a rolling basis. Application fee: $25 ($75 for international students). Electronic applications accepted. *Expenses:* Tuition, state resident: full-time $4932; part-time $274 per credit hour. Tuition, nonresident: full-time $9864; part-time $548 per credit hour. *Required fees:* $513 per semester. Tuition and fees vary according to course load. *Financial support:* In 2016–17, research assistantships with full tuition reimbursements (averaging $4,800 per year), teaching assistantships with full tuition reimbursements (averaging $4,800 per year) were awarded; career-related internships or fieldwork, Federal Work-Study, scholarships/grants, health care benefits, and unspecified assistantships also available. Support available to part-time students. Financial award application deadline: 4/15; financial award applicants required to submit FAFSA. *Unit head:* Dr. Jeffrey Woods, Dean, 479-968-0274, Fax: 479-964-0812, E-mail: jwoods@atu.edu. *Application contact:* Dr. Mary B. Gunter, Dean of Graduate College, 479-968-0398, Fax: 479-964-0542, E-mail: gradcollege@atu.edu.
Website: http://www.atu.edu/humanities/

**Asbury University,** School of Graduate and Professional Studies, Wilmore, KY 40390-1198. Offers biology: alternative certificate (MA Ed); chemistry: alternative certificate (MA Ed); English (MA Ed); English as a second language (MA Ed); ESL (MA Ed); French (MA Ed); Latin: alternative certificate (MA Ed); mathematics: alternative certificate (MA Ed); reading/writing endorsement (MA Ed); social studies (MA Ed); social work (MSW), including child and family services; Spanish (MA Ed); special education (MA Ed); special education: alternative certificate (MA Ed); teacher as leader

endorsement (MA Ed). *Accreditation:* NCATE. *Program availability:* Part-time. *Degree requirements:* For master's, action research project, portfolio. *Entrance requirements:* For master's, PRAXIS/NTE, minimum GPA of 2.75, letters of recommendation. Additional exam requirements/recommendations for international students: Required—TOEFL (minimum score 550 paper-based). Electronic applications accepted.

**Auburn University,** Graduate School, College of Liberal Arts, Department of English, Auburn University, AL 36849. Offers MA, MTPC, PhD, Graduate Certificate. *Program availability:* Part-time. *Faculty:* 61 full-time (31 women), 4 part-time/adjunct (0 women). *Students:* 25 full-time (16 women), 34 part-time (23 women); includes 7 minority (3 Black or African American, non-Hispanic/Latino; 2 Asian, non-Hispanic/Latino; 2 Two or more races, non-Hispanic/Latino), 1 international. Average age 30. 57 applicants, 63% accepted, 19 enrolled. In 2016, 19 master's, 10 doctorates, 2 other advanced degrees awarded. *Degree requirements:* For master's, one foreign language, thesis optional, written exam; for doctorate, 2 foreign languages, thesis/dissertation, oral and written exams. *Entrance requirements:* For master's, GRE General Test, sample of written work; for doctorate, GRE General Test, GRE Subject Test, sample of written work. *Application deadline:* Applications are processed on a rolling basis. Application fee: $50 ($60 for international students). Electronic applications accepted. *Expenses:* Tuition, state resident: full-time $9072; part-time $504 per credit hour. Tuition, nonresident: full-time $27,216; part-time $1512 per credit hour. *Required fees:* $812 per semester. Tuition and fees vary according to degree level and program. *Financial support:* Fellowships, teaching assistantships, and Federal Work-Study available. Support available to part-time students. Financial award application deadline: 3/15; financial award applicants required to submit FAFSA. *Faculty research:* English literature, American literature, linguistics, rhetoric and composition, literary theory. *Unit head:* Dr. Jeremy M. Downes, Chair, 334-844-9079. *Application contact:* Dr. George Flowers, Dean of the Graduate School, 334-844-2125.

**Austin Peay State University,** College of Graduate Studies, College of Arts and Letters, Department of Languages and Literature, Clarksville, TN 37044. Offers English (MA). *Program availability:* Part-time. *Faculty:* 8 full-time (4 women). *Students:* 10 full-time (8 women), 5 part-time (3 women); includes 1 minority (Two or more races, non-Hispanic/Latino). Average age 32. 9 applicants, 78% accepted, 6 enrolled. In 2016, 5 master's awarded. *Degree requirements:* For master's, comprehensive exam, thesis optional. *Entrance requirements:* For master's, GRE General Test, 2 letters of recommendation, minimum undergraduate GPA of 2.9. Additional exam requirements/recommendations for international students: Required—TOEFL (minimum score 500 paper-based). *Application deadline:* For fall admission, 8/9 priority date for domestic students. Applications are processed on a rolling basis. Application fee: $45 ($50 for international students). Electronic applications accepted. *Expenses:* Tuition, state resident: full-time $8300; part-time $415 per credit hour. Tuition, nonresident: full-time $22,280; part-time $1114 per credit hour. *Required fees:* $1473; $73.65 per credit hour. *Financial support:* Research assistantships with full tuition reimbursements, career-related internships or fieldwork, Federal Work-Study, institutionally sponsored loans, scholarships/grants, and unspecified assistantships available. Support available to part-time students. Financial award application deadline: 4/1; financial award applicants required to submit FAFSA. *Faculty research:* American literature, British literature, linguistics, composition, technical writing. *Unit head:* Dr. David Guest, Chair, 931-221-7891, Fax: 931-221-7219, E-mail: guestd@apsu.edu. *Application contact:* Brad Averitt, Coordinator of Graduate Admissions, 800-859-4723, Fax: 931-221-7641, E-mail: gradadmissions@apsu.edu.
Website: http://www.apsu.edu/langlit/

**Ball State University,** Graduate School, College of Sciences and Humanities, Department of English, Muncie, IN 47306. Offers English (MA, PhD), including composition (MA), creative writing (MA), literature, rhetoric and composition; linguistics (MA), including linguistics, teaching English to speakers of other languages (TESOL) and linguistics. *Program availability:* Part-time. *Degree requirements:* For doctorate, variable foreign language requirement, thesis/dissertation. *Entrance requirements:* For master's, GRE General Test, minimum baccalaureate GPA of 2.75 or 3.0 in latter half of baccalaureate, statement of purpose, writing sample, three letters of recommendation; for doctorate, GRE General Test, GRE Subject Test, minimum graduate GPA of 3.2, statement of purpose, writing sample, three letters of recommendation. Additional exam requirements/recommendations for international students: Required—TOEFL (minimum score 550 paper-based; 79 iBT), IELTS (minimum score 6.5). Electronic applications accepted. *Faculty research:* American literature; literary editing; medieval, Renaissance, and eighteenth-century British literature; rhetoric.

**Baylor University,** Graduate School, College of Arts and Sciences, Department of English, Waco, TX 76798. Offers MA, PhD. *Faculty:* 27 full-time (10 women). *Students:* 35 full-time (18 women), 26 part-time (12 women); includes 2 minority (both Two or more races, non-Hispanic/Latino), 1 international. 57 applicants, 12% accepted, 6 enrolled. In 2016, 7 master's, 8 doctorates awarded. Terminal master's awarded for partial completion of doctoral program. *Degree requirements:* For master's, one foreign language, comprehensive exam, thesis (for some programs); for doctorate, 2 foreign languages, comprehensive exam, thesis/dissertation. *Entrance requirements:* For master's and doctorate, GRE (Verbal and Quantitative), 18 hours of upper-level course work in English. Additional exam requirements/recommendations for international students: Required—TOEFL. *Application deadline:* For fall admission, 1/15 priority date for domestic and international students; for spring admission, 11/15 for domestic and international students; for summer admission, 4/15 for domestic and international students. Applications are processed on a rolling basis. Application fee: $75. Electronic applications accepted. *Expenses:* Tuition: Full-time $28,494; part-time $1583 per credit hour. *Required fees:* $167 per credit hour. Tuition and fees vary according to course load and program. *Financial support:* In 2016–17, 70 students received support, including 2 fellowships with full tuition reimbursements available (averaging $17,000 per year), 2 research assistantships with full tuition reimbursements available (averaging $15,000 per year), 45 teaching assistantships with full tuition reimbursements available (averaging $19,500 per year); Federal Work-Study and institutionally sponsored loans also available. Financial award application deadline: 1/15. *Faculty research:* Nineteenth-century British literature, literature and religion, Irish literature, Renaissance studies, rhetoric and composition. *Total annual research expenditures:* $48,400. *Unit head:* Dr. Richard R. Russell, Graduate Program Director, 254-710-1768 Ext. 4815, Fax: 254-710-4815, E-mail: richard_russell@baylor.edu. *Application contact:* Julie Sherrod, Administrative Assistant, 254-710-1768, Fax: 254-710-3870, E-mail: julie_sherrod@baylor.edu.
Website: http://www.baylor.edu/english/

**Bemidji State University,** School of Graduate Studies, Bemidji, MN 56601. Offers biology (MS); education (MS); English (MA, MS); environmental studies (MS); mathematics (MS); mathematics (elementary and middle level education) (MS); special education (M Sp Ed). *Program availability:* Part-time, online learning. *Degree requirements:* For master's, comprehensive exam, thesis (for some programs). *Entrance requirements:* For master's, GRE; GMAT, letters of recommendation, letters of interest. Additional exam requirements/recommendations for international students: Required—TOEFL (minimum score 550 paper-based; 80 iBT). Electronic applications accepted. *Expenses:* Contact institution. *Faculty research:* Human performance, sport, and health:

physical education teacher education, continuum models, spiritual health, intellectual health, resiliency, health priorities; psychology: health psychology, college student drinking behavior, micro-aggressions, infant cognition, false memories, leadership assessment; biology: structure and dynamics of forest communities, aquatic and riverine ecology, interaction between animal populations and aquatic environments, cellular motility.

**Binghamton University, State University of New York,** Graduate School, Harpur College of Arts and Sciences, Department of English, Binghamton, NY 13902-6000. Offers creative writing (MA); English (PhD); English/American literature (MA). *Program availability:* Part-time. *Faculty:* 29 full-time (18 women), 19 part-time/adjunct (9 women). *Students:* 39 full-time (24 women), 49 part-time (28 women); includes 11 minority (3 Black or African American, non-Hispanic/Latino; 1 American Indian or Alaska Native, non-Hispanic/Latino; 5 Asian, non-Hispanic/Latino; 2 Hispanic/Latino), 18 international. Average age 33. 97 applicants, 51% accepted, 20 enrolled. In 2016, 11 master's, 13 doctorates awarded. Terminal master's awarded for partial completion of doctoral program. *Degree requirements:* For master's, one foreign language, thesis; for doctorate, one foreign language, comprehensive exam, thesis/dissertation. *Entrance requirements:* For master's and doctorate, GRE General Test, writing sample. Additional exam requirements/recommendations for international students: Required—TOEFL (minimum score 550 paper-based; 80 iBT). *Application deadline:* For fall admission, 2/15 priority date for domestic and international students; for spring admission, 11/15 priority date for domestic and international students. Application fee: $75. Electronic applications accepted. *Financial support:* In 2016–17, 36 students received support, including 1 fellowship with full tuition reimbursement available (averaging $15,000 per year), 1 research assistantship (averaging $9,000 per year), 30 teaching assistantships with full tuition reimbursements available (averaging $15,000 per year); career-related internships or fieldwork, Federal Work-Study, institutionally sponsored loans, scholarships/grants, health care benefits, tuition waivers (full and partial), and unspecified assistantships also available. Financial award applicants required to submit FAFSA. *Unit head:* Praseeda Gopinath, Graduate Director, 607-777-2033, Fax: 607-777-2408, E-mail: gopinath@binghamton.edu. *Application contact:* Ben Balkaya, Assistant Dean and Director, 607-777-2151, Fax: 607-777-2501, E-mail: balkaya@binghamton.edu.
Website: http://www2.binghamton.edu/english/

**Bob Jones University,** Graduate Programs, Greenville, SC 29614. Offers accountancy (MS); Bible (MA); Bible translation (MA); Biblical studies (Certificate); broadcast management (MS); business administration (MBA); church history (MA, PhD); church ministries (MA); church music (MM); cinema and video production (MA); counseling (MS); curriculum and instruction (Ed D); divinity (M Div); dramatic production (MA); educational leadership (MS, Ed D, Ed S); elementary education (M Ed, MAT); English (M Ed, MA, MAT); fine arts (MA); graphic design (MA); history (M Ed, MA); illustration (MA); interpretative speech (MA, MAT); mathematics (M Ed, MAT); medical missions (Certificate); ministry (MM, D Min); multi-categorical special education (M Ed, MAT); music (M Ed); New Testament interpretation (PhD); Old Testament interpretation (PhD); orchestral instrument performance (MM); organ performance (MM); pastoral studies (MA); personnel services (MS, Ed S); piano pedagogy (MM); piano performance (MM); platform arts (MA); radio and television broadcasting (MS); rhetoric and public address (MA); secondary education (M Ed); studio art (MA); teaching Bible (MA); theology (MA, PhD); voice performance (MM); youth ministries (MA); M Div/MM.

**Boston College,** Graduate School of Arts and Sciences, Department of English, Chestnut Hill, MA 02467-3800. Offers English (MA, PhD); Irish studies (MA, PhD). *Faculty:* 45 full-time. *Students:* 68 full-time (45 women); includes 6 minority (1 Asian, non-Hispanic/Latino; 1 Hispanic/Latino; 4 Two or more races, non-Hispanic/Latino), 4 international. 136 applicants, 50% accepted, 19 enrolled. In 2016, 27 master's, 4 doctorates awarded. Terminal master's awarded for partial completion of doctoral program. *Degree requirements:* For master's, one foreign language, thesis optional; for doctorate, 2 foreign languages, thesis/dissertation. *Entrance requirements:* For master's and doctorate, GRE General Test, GRE Subject Test. Additional exam requirements/recommendations for international students: Required—TOEFL (minimum score 600 paper-based; 100 iBT), IELTS (minimum score 8). *Application deadline:* For fall admission, 1/2 priority date for domestic students, 1/2 for international students. Application fee: $75. Electronic applications accepted. Tuition and fees vary according to program. *Financial support:* In 2016–17, fellowships with full tuition reimbursements (averaging $20,900 per year), teaching assistantships with full tuition reimbursements (averaging $20,900 per year) were awarded; Federal Work-Study, scholarships/grants, health care benefits, tuition waivers (full and partial), and unspecified assistantships also available. Support available to part-time students. Financial award application deadline: 3/1; financial award applicants required to submit FAFSA. *Faculty research:* English and American literature, Irish literature, British literature, early modern and modern literature, critical theory. *Unit head:* Dr. Suzanne Matson, Chairperson, 617-552-3716, E-mail: suzanne.matson@bc.edu. *Application contact:* Dr. Christine Klein, Graduate Program Director, 617-552-3743, E-mail: christine.klein@bc.edu.
Website: http://www.bc.edu/english

**Boston University,** Graduate School of Arts and Sciences, Department of English, Boston, MA 02215. Offers MA, PhD, JD/MA. *Students:* 50 full-time (27 women), 2 part-time (both women); includes 5 minority (1 Black or African American, non-Hispanic/Latino; 4 Hispanic/Latino), 5 international. Average age 27. 150 applicants, 33% accepted, 9 enrolled. In 2016, 7 master's, 7 doctorates awarded. Terminal master's awarded for partial completion of doctoral program. *Degree requirements:* For master's, one foreign language; for doctorate, 2 foreign languages, comprehensive exam, thesis/dissertation, qualifying/oral exam. *Entrance requirements:* For master's, GRE General Test, GRE Subject Test (strongly recommended), 3 letters of recommendation, transcripts, personal statement, scholarly writing sample, curriculum vitae; for doctorate, GRE General Test, GRE Subject Test, 3 letters of recommendation, transcripts, personal statement, scholarly writing sample, curriculum vitae. Additional exam requirements/recommendations for international students: Required—TOEFL (minimum score 550 paper-based; 84 iBT). *Application deadline:* For fall admission, 12/15 for domestic and international students. Application fee: $95. Electronic applications accepted. *Financial support:* In 2016–17, 34 students received support, including 10 fellowships with full tuition reimbursements available (averaging $21,500 per year), research assistantships with full tuition reimbursements available (averaging $21,500 per year), 21 teaching assistantships with full tuition reimbursements available (averaging $21,500 per year); Federal Work-Study, scholarships/grants, health care benefits, and unspecified assistantships also available. Financial award application deadline: 12/15. *Unit head:* Robert Chodat, Chair, 617-353-2509, Fax: 617-353-3653, E-mail: rchodat@bu.edu. *Application contact:* Anne Austin, Administrative Assistant, 617-353-2509, Fax: 617-353-3653, E-mail: akaustin@bu.edu.
Website: http://www.bu.edu/english/

**Bowie State University,** Graduate Programs, Program in English, Bowie, MD 20715-9465. Offers MA. *Program availability:* Part-time, evening/weekend. *Entrance requirements:* For master's, minimum GPA of 2.5, English degree. Electronic applications accepted.

**Bowling Green State University,** Graduate College, College of Arts and Sciences, Department of English, Program in English, Bowling Green, OH 43403. Offers English (MA, PhD); literature (MA); rhetoric and writing (PhD); scientific and technical communication (MA). *Program availability:* Part-time. *Degree requirements:* For master's, thesis or alternative; for doctorate, comprehensive exam, thesis/dissertation, foreign language or proficiency in Old English. *Entrance requirements:* For master's and doctorate, GRE General Test. Additional exam requirements/recommendations for international students: Required—TOEFL. *Application deadline:* For fall admission, 2/15 priority date for domestic students. Applications are processed on a rolling basis. Application fee: $30. Electronic applications accepted. *Financial support:* Fellowships with full tuition reimbursements, research assistantships with full tuition reimbursements, teaching assistantships with full tuition reimbursements, Federal Work-Study, and unspecified assistantships available. Financial award applicants required to submit FAFSA. *Faculty research:* Postmodern literary theory, rhetorical theory, ethnic American literature, literature and culture, composition pedagogy. *Unit head:* Dr. Lawrence Coates, Chair, 419-372-7543, E-mail: coatesl@bgsu.edu. *Application contact:* Dr. Piya Lapinski, Graduate Coordinator, 419-372-6864.

**Bradley University,** The Graduate School, College of Liberal Arts and Sciences, Department of English, Peoria, IL 61625-0002. Offers MA. *Program availability:* Part-time. *Degree requirements:* For master's, comprehensive exam, thesis optional. *Entrance requirements:* For master's, writing sample, 2 letters of recommendation. Additional exam requirements/recommendations for international students: Required—TOEFL (minimum score 550 paper-based; 79 iBT), IELTS (minimum score 6.5). *Application deadline:* For fall admission, 5/15 priority date for domestic and international students; for spring admission, 10/15 priority date for domestic and international students. Applications are processed on a rolling basis. Application fee: $40 ($50 for international students). Electronic applications accepted. *Expenses: Tuition:* Full-time $7650; part-time $850 per credit. *Required fees:* $50 per credit. One-time fee: $100 full-time. *Financial support:* Research assistantships with full and partial tuition reimbursements, teaching assistantships, scholarships/grants, tuition waivers (partial), and unspecified assistantships available. Support available to part-time students. Financial award application deadline: 4/1. *Unit head:* Lee Newton, Chair, 309-677-2471, E-mail: lnewton@bradley.edu. *Application contact:* Kayla Carroll, Director of International Admissions and Student Services, 309-677-2375, E-mail: klcarroll@fsmail.bradley.edu.
Website: http://www.bradley.edu/academic/departments/english/

**Brandeis University,** Graduate School of Arts and Sciences, Department of English, Waltham, MA 02454-9110. Offers English (MA, PhD); English and women's, gender, and sexuality studies (MA). *Program availability:* Part-time. *Faculty:* 18 full-time (9 women), 12 part-time/adjunct (6 women). *Students:* 42 full-time (24 women), 1 part-time (0 women); includes 7 minority (2 Black or African American, non-Hispanic/Latino; 1 Asian, non-Hispanic/Latino; 3 Hispanic/Latino; 1 Two or more races, non-Hispanic/Latino), 8 international. 126 applicants, 28% accepted, 9 enrolled. In 2016, 3 master's, 3 doctorates awarded. Terminal master's awarded for partial completion of doctoral program. *Degree requirements:* For master's, one foreign language, thesis or alternative; for doctorate, 2 foreign languages, thesis/dissertation, field exam, symposium presentation, prospectus defense. *Entrance requirements:* For master's, GRE, resume, sample of work, 2 letters of recommendation, statement of purpose, transcript(s); for doctorate, GRE General Test; GRE Subject Test, resume, sample of work, 2 letters of recommendation, statement of purpose, transcript(s). Additional exam requirements/recommendations for international students: Required—TOEFL (minimum score 600 paper-based; 100 iBT); Recommended—IELTS (minimum score 7), TSE (minimum score 68). *Application deadline:* For fall admission, 1/5 for domestic and international students. Application fee: $75. Electronic applications accepted. *Financial support:* In 2016–17, 23 fellowships with full tuition reimbursements (averaging $24,000 per year), 11 teaching assistantships with partial tuition reimbursements (averaging $3,200 per year) were awarded; Federal Work-Study, scholarships/grants, health care benefits, and tuition waivers (partial) also available. Support available to part-time students. Financial award application deadline: 4/15; financial award applicants required to submit FAFSA. *Faculty research:* Feminist and gender theory, American literature and post-Colonial theory, early modern (Renaissance) English literature, modernism, literature and science, literary theory and philosophy, contemporary poetry. *Unit head:* Dr. John Plotz, Director of Graduate Studies, 781-736-2130, Fax: 781-736-2179, E-mail: chaucer@brandeis.edu. *Application contact:* Lisa Pannella, Department Academic Administrator, 781-736-2130, Fax: 781-736-2179, E-mail: pannella@brandeis.edu.
Website: http://www.brandeis.edu/gsas

**Bridgewater State University,** College of Graduate Studies, College of Humanities and Social Sciences, Department of English, Bridgewater, MA 02325. Offers MA, MAT. *Program availability:* Part-time, evening/weekend. *Degree requirements:* For master's, one foreign language, comprehensive exam, thesis optional. *Entrance requirements:* For master's, GRE General Test.

**Brigham Young University,** Graduate Studies, College of Humanities, Department of English, Provo, UT 84602-1001. Offers creative writing (MFA); literature (MA); rhetoric/composition (MA). *Faculty:* 54 full-time (16 women). *Students:* 75 full-time (52 women), 4 part-time (all women); includes 3 minority (1 Asian, non-Hispanic/Latino; 2 Hispanic/Latino). Average age 25. 44 applicants, 64% accepted, 24 enrolled. In 2016, 21 master's awarded. *Degree requirements:* For master's, variable foreign language requirement, comprehensive exam, thesis. *Entrance requirements:* For master's, GRE General Test, creative portfolio (for MFA). *Application deadline:* For fall admission, 1/15 for domestic and international students. Application fee: $50. Electronic applications accepted. *Expenses: Tuition:* Full-time $6680; part-time $393 per credit. Tuition and fees vary according to course load, program and student's religious affiliation. *Financial support:* In 2016–17, 22 students received support, including 10 research assistantships (averaging $4,000 per year), 62 teaching assistantships (averaging $6,000 per year); career-related internships or fieldwork, institutionally sponsored loans, scholarships/grants, and tuition waivers (partial) also available. Support available to part-time students. Financial award application deadline: 3/15. *Faculty research:* English literature, American literature, rhetoric, creative writing. *Unit head:* Prof. Phillip Snyder, Head, 801-422-2487, Fax: 801-422-0221, E-mail: phillip_snyder@byu.edu. *Application contact:* Danielle N. Steed, Graduate Secretary and English Program Manager, 801-422-8673, Fax: 801-422-0221, E-mail: danielle-steed@byu.edu.
Website: http://english.byu.edu/

**Brock University,** Faculty of Graduate Studies, Faculty of Humanities, Program in English, St. Catharines, ON L2S 3A1, Canada. Offers MA. *Program availability:* Part-time. *Degree requirements:* For master's, thesis optional. *Entrance requirements:* For master's, honours in English. Additional exam requirements/recommendations for international students: Required—TOEFL (minimum score 550 paper-based; 80 iBT), IELTS (minimum score 6.5), TWE (minimum score 4). Electronic applications accepted. *Faculty research:* Literary theory, Canadian literature, Milton and 17th century American literature, 19th century American literature, British Romantic literature and culture.

**Brooklyn College of the City University of New York,** School of Humanities and Social Sciences, Department of English, Brooklyn, NY 11210-2889. Offers creative writing (MFA), including fiction, playwriting, poetry; English (MA). *Program availability:*

Part-time, evening/weekend. *Degree requirements:* For master's, one foreign language, comprehensive exam (for some programs), thesis (for some programs). *Entrance requirements:* For master's, advanced undergraduate courses in English, 2 letters of recommendation, writing sample, statement of purpose. Additional exam requirements/recommendations for international students: Required—TOEFL. Electronic applications accepted. *Faculty research:* Cultural studies, medieval literature, Virginia Woolf.

**Brown University,** Graduate School, Department of English, Providence, RI 02912. Offers English (PhD); literary arts (MFA). *Degree requirements:* For doctorate, thesis/dissertation. *Entrance requirements:* For master's and doctorate, GRE General Test, GRE Subject Test.

**Bucknell University,** Graduate Studies, College of Arts and Sciences, Department of English, Lewisburg, PA 17837. Offers MA. *Program availability:* Part-time. *Degree requirements:* For master's, one foreign language, thesis. *Entrance requirements:* For master's, GRE General Test, GRE Subject Test, minimum GPA of 3.0. Additional exam requirements/recommendations for international students: Required—TOEFL (minimum score 600 paper-based). *Application deadline:* For fall admission, 2/1 priority date for domestic students, 1/1 priority date for domestic students. Application fee: $25. *Expenses: Tuition, area resident:* Part-time $5475 per course. *Financial support:* Research assistantships with full tuition reimbursements and unspecified assistantships available. Financial award application deadline: 2/1. *Unit head:* Dr. G. C. Waldrep, Chair, 570-577-1553. *Application contact:* Gretchen H. Fegley, Coordinator, 570-577-3655, Fax: 570-577-3760, E-mail: gfegley@bucknell.edu.
Website: http://www.bucknell.edu/

**Buffalo State College, State University of New York,** The Graduate School, Faculty of Arts and Humanities, Department of English, Buffalo, NY 14222-1095. Offers English (MA); secondary education (MS Ed), including English. *Program availability:* Part-time, evening/weekend. *Degree requirements:* For master's, thesis or project, 1 foreign language (MS Ed). *Entrance requirements:* For master's, minimum GPA 2.75, 36 hours in English, New York teaching certificate (MS Ed). Additional exam requirements/recommendations for international students: Required—TOEFL (minimum score 550 paper-based).

**Butler University,** College of Liberal Arts and Sciences, Department of English, Indianapolis, IN 46208-3485. Offers creative writing (MFA); English (MA). *Program availability:* Part-time, evening/weekend. *Faculty:* 10 full-time (4 women), 4 part-time/adjunct (2 women). *Students:* 8 full-time (3 women), 48 part-time (28 women); includes 7 minority (4 Black or African American, non-Hispanic/Latino; 1 Hispanic/Latino; 2 Two or more races, non-Hispanic/Latino), 1 international. Average age 33. 44 applicants, 59% accepted, 11 enrolled. In 2016, 9 master's awarded. *Degree requirements:* For master's, thesis (for some programs). *Entrance requirements:* For master's, minimum GPA of 3.0, 350-word statement of purpose, and 7-12 page sample essay (for MA); writing sample in intended genre (12 pages of poetry or 30 pages of prose), statement of interest (1-2 pages), two letters of recommendation, and transcripts from all undergraduate and graduate institutions attended (for MFA). *Application deadline:* For fall admission, 2/15 for domestic and international students; for spring admission, 9/15 for domestic and international students. Applications are processed on a rolling basis. Application fee: $0. Electronic applications accepted. *Expenses:* Contact institution. *Financial support:* In 2016–17, 15 students received support. Scholarships/grants, tuition waivers (full and partial), and unspecified assistantships available. Financial award application deadline: 7/15; financial award applicants required to submit FAFSA. *Faculty research:* Novel, poetry, screenplay and creative nonfiction writing; literary and cultural theory; American literature and culture; British and Postcolonial literature. *Unit head:* Dr. Lee Garver, Director of Graduate Studies, Department of English Language and Literature, 317-940-9859, E-mail: lgarver@butler.edu. *Application contact:* Diane Dubord, Graduate Student Services Specialist, 317-940-8107, Fax: 317-940-8250, E-mail: ddubord@butler.edu.
Website: https://www.butler.edu/english/graduate-studies/ma-english

**California Baptist University,** Program in English, Riverside, CA 92504-3206. Offers English pedagogy (MA); literature (MA); teaching English to speakers of other languages (TESOL) (MA). *Program availability:* Part-time, evening/weekend. *Faculty:* 9 full-time (7 women), 1 (woman) part-time/adjunct. *Students:* 3 full-time (2 women), 26 part-time (19 women); includes 14 minority (4 Black or African American, non-Hispanic/Latino; 1 Asian, non-Hispanic/Latino; 9 Hispanic/Latino), 3 international. Average age 28. 8 applicants, 88% accepted, 6 enrolled. In 2016, 4 master's awarded. *Degree requirements:* For master's, comprehensive exam, project, or thesis. *Entrance requirements:* For master's, GRE (for applicants with a GPA below 2.75) or CSET, minimum undergraduate GPA of 2.75; 18 semester hours of course work in English beyond freshman level; three recommendations; essay; demonstration of writing; interview. Additional exam requirements/recommendations for international students: Required—TOEFL (minimum score 80 iBT). *Application deadline:* For fall admission, 8/1 priority date for domestic students, 7/1 for international students; for spring admission, 12/1 priority date for domestic students, 11/1 for international students. Applications are processed on a rolling basis. Application fee: $45. Electronic applications accepted. *Expenses:* Contact institution. *Financial support:* In 2016–17, 5 students received support. Federal Work-Study and scholarships/grants available. Financial award applicants required to submit CSS PROFILE or FAFSA. *Faculty research:* Classical mythology and folklore, multicultural literature, genre studies, science fiction and fantasy literature, intercultural rhetoric. *Unit head:* Dr. Gayne Anacker, Dean, College of Arts and Sciences, 951-343-4682, E-mail: ganacker@calbaptist.edu. *Application contact:* Dr. Laura Veltman, Director, Master of Arts Program in English, 951-343-4276, Fax: 951-343-4661, E-mail: lveltman@calbaptist.edu.
Website: http://www.calbaptist.edu/maenglish/

**California Polytechnic State University, San Luis Obispo,** College of Liberal Arts, Department of English, San Luis Obispo, CA 93407. Offers MA. *Program availability:* Part-time. *Faculty:* 4 full-time (1 woman). *Students:* 5 full-time (3 women), 14 part-time (9 women); includes 2 minority (both Hispanic/Latino). Average age 28. 7 applicants, 57% accepted, 2 enrolled. In 2016, 10 master's awarded. *Degree requirements:* For master's, one foreign language, comprehensive exam. *Entrance requirements:* For master's, GRE. Additional exam requirements/recommendations for international students: Required—TOEFL (minimum score 80 iBT). *Application deadline:* For fall admission, 4/1 for domestic students, 3/1 for international students. Applications are processed on a rolling basis. Application fee: $55. *Expenses: Tuition, state resident:* full-time $6738; part-time $3906 per year. *Tuition, nonresident:* full-time $15,666; part-time $8370 per year. *Required fees:* $3603; $3141 per unit. $1047 per term. *Financial support:* Fellowships, teaching assistantships, career-related internships or fieldwork, Federal Work-Study, institutionally sponsored loans, and tutorships, writing laboratory assistantships available. Support available to part-time students. Financial award application deadline: 3/2; financial award applicants required to submit FAFSA. *Faculty research:* Feminist literary criticism, literary theory, British and American literature, linguistics, composition theory. *Unit head:* Dr. Dustin Stegner, Graduate Coordinator, 805-756-1277, E-mail: pstegner@calpoly.edu.
Website: http://cla.calpoly.edu/engl.html

**California State Polytechnic University, Pomona,** Program in English, Pomona, CA 91768-2557. Offers MA. *Program availability:* Part-time, evening/weekend. *Students:* 31 full-time (19 women), 45 part-time (32 women); includes 41 minority (3 Black or African American, non-Hispanic/Latino; 2 American Indian or Alaska Native, non-Hispanic/Latino; 10 Asian, non-Hispanic/Latino; 25 Hispanic/Latino; 1 Two or more races, non-Hispanic/Latino), 4 international. Average age 27. 31 applicants, 100% accepted, 26 enrolled. In 2016, 27 master's awarded. *Degree requirements:* For master's, thesis or alternative. *Entrance requirements:* Additional exam requirements/recommendations for international students: Required—TOEFL. *Application deadline:* Applications are processed on a rolling basis. Application fee: $55. Electronic applications accepted. *Expenses:* Contact institution. *Financial support:* Application deadline: 3/2; applicants required to submit FAFSA. *Unit head:* Dr. Lise-Hélène Smith, Graduate Coordinator, 909-869-3979, Fax: 909-869-4896, E-mail: lvtrouilloud@cpp.edu. *Application contact:* Andrew M. Wright, Director of Admissions, 909-869-3130, Fax: 909-869-4529, E-mail: awright@cpp.edu.
Website: http://www.cpp.edu/~class/english-foreign-languages/graduate-programs/

**California State University, Bakersfield,** Division of Graduate Studies, School of Arts and Humanities, Program in English, Bakersfield, CA 93311. Offers MA. *Students:* 7 full-time (5 women), 9 part-time (7 women); includes 7 minority (3 Asian, non-Hispanic/Latino; 4 Hispanic/Latino). Average age 34. 8 applicants, 75% accepted, 4 enrolled. In 2016, 17 master's awarded. *Degree requirements:* For master's, comprehensive exam or thesis. *Entrance requirements:* For master's, GRE General Test, GRE Subject Test (literature), minimum GPA of 2.5 for last 90 quarter units. Additional exam requirements/recommendations for international students: Required—TOEFL (minimum score 550 paper-based). *Application deadline:* Applications are processed on a rolling basis. Application fee: $55. Electronic applications accepted. *Expenses: Tuition, state resident:* full-time $2246; part-time $1302 per semester. *Financial support:* In 2016–17, fellowships (averaging $1,850 per year) were awarded; Federal Work-Study, scholarships/grants, and tuition waivers (full and partial) also available. Financial award application deadline: 3/2; financial award applicants required to submit FAFSA. *Unit head:* Dr. Robert Carlisle, Graduate Studies Coordinator, 661-654-2127, Fax: 661-654-2063, E-mail: rcarlisle@csub.edu. *Application contact:* Debbie Blowers, Assistant Director of Admissions and Evaluations, 661-664-3381, E-mail: dblowers@csub.edu.

**California State University, Chico,** Office of Graduate Studies, College of Humanities and Fine Arts, English Department, Chico, CA 95929-0722. Offers MA. *Faculty:* 13 full-time (9 women), 10 part-time/adjunct (3 women). *Students:* 15 full-time (8 women), 8 part-time (7 women); includes 5 minority (4 Hispanic/Latino; 1 Two or more races, non-Hispanic/Latino). 11 applicants, 73% accepted, 8 enrolled. In 2016, 9 master's awarded. *Degree requirements:* For master's, thesis, project, or comprehensive exam. *Entrance requirements:* For master's, GRE, two letters of recommendation, statement of purpose, writing sample. Additional exam requirements/recommendations for international students: Required—TOEFL (minimum score 550 paper-based; 80 iBT), IELTS (minimum score 6.5), PTE (minimum score 59). *Application deadline:* For fall admission, 3/1 for domestic and international students; for spring admission, 9/15 for domestic and international students. Application fee: $55. Electronic applications accepted. *Financial support:* Teaching assistantships, career-related internships or fieldwork, scholarships/grants, and unspecified assistantships available. *Unit head:* Tracy Butts, Chair, 530-898-5151, Fax: 530-898-4450, E-mail: engl@csuchico.edu. *Application contact:* Judy L. Morris, Graduate Admissions Coordinator, 530-898-5416, Fax: 530-898-3342, E-mail: jlmorris@csuchico.edu.
Website: http://www.csuchico.edu/engl

**California State University, Dominguez Hills,** College of Arts and Humanities, Department of English, Carson, CA 90747-0001. Offers English literature (MA); rhetoric and composition (Certificate); teaching English as a second language (MA, Certificate). *Program availability:* Part-time, evening/weekend. *Degree requirements:* For master's, comprehensive exam (for some programs), thesis or alternative. *Entrance requirements:* For master's, minimum GPA of 3.0 in last 60 units. Additional exam requirements/recommendations for international students: Required—TOEFL (minimum score 550 paper-based). Electronic applications accepted. *Faculty research:* Gender studies, transnationalism, discourse analysis, visual culture, Shakespeare.

**California State University, East Bay,** Office of Graduate Studies, College of Letters, Arts, and Social Sciences, Department of English, Hayward, CA 94542-3000. Offers creative writing (MA); literary studies (MA); teaching English to speakers of other languages (MA). *Program availability:* Part-time. *Students:* 10 full-time (8 women), 35 part-time (24 women); includes 19 minority (4 Black or African American, non-Hispanic/Latino; 3 Asian, non-Hispanic/Latino; 7 Hispanic/Latino; 5 Two or more races, non-Hispanic/Latino), 8 international. Average age 36. 35 applicants, 63% accepted, 13 enrolled. In 2016, 25 master's awarded. *Degree requirements:* For master's, one foreign language, comprehensive exam, thesis optional. *Entrance requirements:* For master's, minimum GPA of 3.0 in field; 2 letters of recommendation; academic or professional writing sample; teaching experience and some degree of bilingualism (preferred for TESOL). Additional exam requirements/recommendations for international students: Required—TOEFL (minimum score 550 paper-based); Recommended—IELTS (minimum score 6.5). *Application deadline:* For fall admission, 6/30 for domestic and international students. Applications are processed on a rolling basis. Application fee: $55. Electronic applications accepted. *Financial support:* Fellowships, teaching assistantships, career-related internships or fieldwork, Federal Work-Study, institutionally sponsored loans, and scholarships/grants available. Support available to part-time students. Financial award application deadline: 3/2; financial award applicants required to submit FAFSA. *Unit head:* Dr. Sarah Nielsen, Acting Chair, 510-885-3151, Fax: 510-885-4797. *Application contact:* Dr. Donna Wiley, Interim Associate Vice President for Academic Programs and Graduate Studies, 510-885-3716, Fax: 510-885-4777, E-mail: donna.wiley@csueastbay.edu.
Website: http://www20.csueastbay.edu/class/departments/english/index.html

**California State University, Fresno,** Division of Research and Graduate Studies, College of Arts and Humanities, Department of English, Fresno, CA 93740-8027. Offers creative writing (MFA); literature (MA); rhetoric and writing studies (MA). *Program availability:* Part-time, evening/weekend. *Degree requirements:* For master's, one foreign language, thesis. *Entrance requirements:* For master's, GRE General Test, minimum GPA of 3.0, writing sample. Additional exam requirements/recommendations for international students: Required—TOEFL. *Application deadline:* For fall admission, 5/1 for domestic and international students; for spring admission, 10/1 for domestic and international students. Applications are processed on a rolling basis. Application fee: $55. Electronic applications accepted. *Financial support:* Teaching assistantships, career-related internships or fieldwork, Federal Work-Study, and scholarships/grants available. Support available to part-time students. Financial award application deadline: 3/1; financial award applicants required to submit FAFSA. *Faculty research:* American literature, Renaissance literature, foreign literature. *Unit head:* Dr. Lisa Weston, Chair, 559-278-2553, Fax: 559-278-7143, E-mail: lisaw@csufresno.edu.
Website: http://www.fresnostate.edu/artshum/english/

**California State University, Fullerton,** Graduate Studies, College of Humanities and Social Sciences, Department of English, Comparative Literature, and Linguistics, Fullerton, CA 92834-9480. Offers English (MA); linguistics (MA). *Program availability:* Part-time. *Degree requirements:* For master's, one foreign language, thesis or alternative, project. *Entrance requirements:* For master's, minimum GPA of 3.0, undergraduate major in linguistics or related field. Application fee: $55. *Expenses:*

## English

Tuition, state resident: full-time $3369; part-time $1953 per unit. Tuition, nonresident: full-time $3915; part-time $2499 per unit. Tuition and fees vary according to course load, degree level and program. *Financial support:* Career-related internships or fieldwork, Federal Work-Study, institutionally sponsored loans, and scholarships/grants available. Support available to part-time students. Financial award application deadline: 3/1; financial award applicants required to submit FAFSA. *Unit head:* Dr. Stephen J. Mexal, Chair, 657-278-3163.

**California State University, Long Beach,** Graduate Studies, College of Liberal Arts, Department of English, Long Beach, CA 90840. Offers creative writing (MFA); English (MA). *Program availability:* Part-time. *Degree requirements:* For master's, one foreign language, comprehensive exam or thesis. *Entrance requirements:* For master's, GRE Subject Test, minimum GPA of 3.0 in English. *Application deadline:* For fall admission, 5/1 for domestic students. Applications are processed on a rolling basis. Application fee: $55. Electronic applications accepted. *Financial support:* Federal Work-Study, institutionally sponsored loans, and scholarships/grants available. Financial award application deadline: 3/2. *Faculty research:* English and American literature, literary theory, linguistics, rhetoric and composition. *Unit head:* Dr. Eileen S. Klink, Chair, 562-985-4223, Fax: 562-985-2369, E-mail: eklink@csulb.edu. *Application contact:* Dr. Beth Lau, Graduate Adviser, 562-985-4252, Fax: 562-985-4223, E-mail: blau@csulb.edu.

**California State University, Los Angeles,** Graduate Studies, College of Arts and Letters, Department of English, Los Angeles, CA 90032-8530. Offers MA, Certificate. *Program availability:* Part-time, evening/weekend. *Degree requirements:* For master's, comprehensive exam or thesis. *Entrance requirements:* Additional exam requirements/recommendations for international students: Required—TOEFL (minimum score 500 paper-based). Electronic applications accepted. *Faculty research:* English and American literature, linguistics, composition.

**California State University, Northridge,** Graduate Studies, College of Humanities, Department of English, Northridge, CA 91330. Offers creative writing (MA); literature (MA); rhetoric and composition theory (MA). *Program availability:* Part-time, evening/weekend. *Faculty:* 31 full-time (15 women), 104 part-time/adjunct (34 women). *Students:* 34 full-time (18 women), 60 part-time (34 women); includes 35 minority (4 Black or African American, non-Hispanic/Latino; 4 American Indian or Alaska Native, non-Hispanic/Latino; 2 Asian, non-Hispanic/Latino; 21 Hispanic/Latino; 4 Two or more races, non-Hispanic/Latino), 1 international. Average age 33. 49 applicants, 71% accepted, 22 enrolled. *Degree requirements:* For master's, thesis or alternative. *Entrance requirements:* For master's, writing proficiency test, GRE General Test or minimum GPA of 3.0. Additional exam requirements/recommendations for international students: Required—TOEFL. *Application deadline:* For fall admission, 11/30 for domestic students. Application fee: $55. *Expenses:* Tuition, state resident: full-time $4152. *Financial support:* Teaching assistantships available. Financial award application deadline: 3/1. *Faculty research:* Reading improvement, professional writing, Dickens, Shaw, English as a second language. *Unit head:* Kent Baxter, Chair, 818-677-3431. Website: http://www.csun.edu/english/index.php

**California State University, Sacramento,** Office of Graduate Studies, College of Arts and Letters, Department of English, Sacramento, CA 95819. Offers composition (MA); creative writing (MA); literature (MA); teaching English to speakers of other languages (MA). *Program availability:* Part-time. *Students:* 36 full-time (26 women), 47 part-time (35 women); includes 22 minority (5 Black or African American, non-Hispanic/Latino; 1 American Indian or Alaska Native, non-Hispanic/Latino; 8 Asian, non-Hispanic/Latino; 8 Hispanic/Latino). Average age 30. 54 applicants, 69% accepted, 26 enrolled. In 2016, 29 master's awarded. *Degree requirements:* For master's, thesis, project, or comprehensive exam; TESOL exam; writing proficiency exam. *Entrance requirements:* For master's, portfolio (creative writing); minimum GPA of 3.0 in English and overall during previous 2 years. Additional exam requirements/recommendations for international students: Required—TOEFL (minimum score 600 paper-based; 100 iBT). *Application deadline:* For fall admission, 2/15 for domestic students, 3/1 for international students; for spring admission, 9/30 for international students. Applications are processed on a rolling basis. Application fee: $55. Electronic applications accepted. *Expenses:* $4,302 full-time tuition and fees per semester, $2,796 part-time. *Financial support:* Research assistantships, teaching assistantships, career-related internships or fieldwork, and Federal Work-Study available. Support available to part-time students. Financial award application deadline: 3/1; financial award applicants required to submit FAFSA. *Faculty research:* Teaching composition, remedial writing. *Unit head:* Dr. David Toise, Chair, 916-278-6586, E-mail: dwtoise@csus.edu. *Application contact:* Jose Martinez, Graduate Admissions Supervisor, 916-278-7871, E-mail: martinj@skymail.csus.edu. Website: http://www.csus.edu/engl

**California State University, San Bernardino,** Graduate Studies, College of Arts and Letters, Program in English, San Bernardino, CA 92407. Offers creative writing (MFA), including fiction; English composition (MA), including composition. *Program availability:* Part-time, evening/weekend. *Faculty:* 8 full-time (all women). *Students:* 16 full-time (11 women), 56 part-time (39 women); includes 38 minority (6 Black or African American, non-Hispanic/Latino; 1 Asian, non-Hispanic/Latino; 29 Hispanic/Latino; 2 Two or more races, non-Hispanic/Latino), 5 international. 32 applicants, 66% accepted, 21 enrolled. In 2016, 26 master's awarded. *Degree requirements:* For master's, one foreign language, thesis. *Entrance requirements:* Additional exam requirements/recommendations for international students: Required—TOEFL. *Application deadline:* For fall admission, 7/16 for domestic students. Application fee: $55. *Expenses:* Tuition, state resident: full-time $7843; part-time $5011.20 per year. Tuition and fees vary according to course load, degree level, program and reciprocity agreements. *Financial support:* Application deadline: 3/1. *Unit head:* Dr. Sunny Hyon, Chair, 909-537-5834, Fax: 909-537-7086, E-mail: shyon@csusb.edu. *Application contact:* Dr. Francisca Beer, Dean of Graduate Studies, 909-537-5058, Fax: 909-537-5078, E-mail: fbeer@csusb.edu.

**California State University, San Marcos,** College of Humanities, Arts, Behavioral and Social Sciences, Program in Literature and Writing Studies, San Marcos, CA 92096-0001. Offers MA. *Program availability:* Part-time, evening/weekend. *Degree requirements:* For master's, one foreign language, thesis. *Entrance requirements:* For master's, GRE General Test, minimum GPA of 3.0, writing sample. *Expenses:* Tuition, state resident: full-time $6738. Tuition, nonresident: full-time $13,434. *Required fees:* $1906. Tuition and fees vary according to campus/location and program. *Faculty research:* Postcolonialism, feminism rhetoric, cultural studies, creative writing, critical theory.

**California State University, Stanislaus,** College of Humanities and Social Sciences, Program in English (MA), Turlock, CA 95382. Offers literature (Certificate); rhetoric and teaching writing (MA); teaching English to speakers of other languages (MA). *Program availability:* Part-time. *Degree requirements:* For master's, comprehensive exam, thesis or alternative. *Entrance requirements:* For master's, GRE, minimum GPA of 3.0, 2 letters of reference, personal statement. Additional exam requirements/recommendations for international students: Required—TOEFL (minimum score 575 paper-based), TWE (minimum score 4). Electronic applications accepted. *Faculty research:* Transnational literacies, Renaissance and medieval literature, abolition writings and slave narratives, qualitative writing.

**Carleton University,** Faculty of Graduate Studies, Faculty of Arts and Social Sciences, Department of English Language and Literature, Ottawa, ON K1S 5B6, Canada. Offers MA, PhD. *Degree requirements:* For master's, thesis optional. *Entrance requirements:* For master's, honors degree. Additional exam requirements/recommendations for international students: Required—TOEFL. *Faculty research:* British, Canadian, American, and Commonwealth literatures; English language and writing; literary criticism; social and historical context of literature.

**Carnegie Mellon University,** Dietrich College of Humanities and Social Sciences, Department of English, Pittsburgh, PA 15213-3891. Offers communication planning and design (M Des); literary and cultural studies (MA, PhD); professional writing (MAPW), including editing and publishing, policy and non-profit communication, public and media relations / corporate communications, science or healthcare communication, technical writing, writing for new media, writing for print media; rhetoric (MA, PhD). *Program availability:* Part-time. Terminal master's awarded for partial completion of doctoral program. *Degree requirements:* For doctorate, 2 foreign languages, comprehensive exam, thesis/dissertation. *Entrance requirements:* For master's and doctorate, GRE General Test. Additional exam requirements/recommendations for international students: Required—TOEFL, TWE. *Faculty research:* Cognitive processes in discourse with emphasis on writing, testing, and evaluation.

**Case Western Reserve University,** School of Graduate Studies, Department of English, Cleveland, OH 44106. Offers MA, PhD. *Program availability:* Part-time. *Faculty:* 21 full-time (12 women), 1 part-time/adjunct (0 women). *Students:* 23 full-time (13 women); includes 1 minority (Black or African American, non-Hispanic/Latino). Average age 30. 40 applicants, 15% accepted, 6 enrolled. In 2016, 3 master's, 5 doctorates awarded. *Degree requirements:* For master's, one foreign language, comprehensive exam, thesis or alternative, written exam; for doctorate, one foreign language, thesis/dissertation, oral and written exams. *Entrance requirements:* For master's and doctorate, GRE General Test, sample of written work, three letters of recommendation. Additional exam requirements/recommendations for international students: Required—TOEFL (minimum score 577 paper-based; 90 iBT); Recommended—IELTS (minimum score 7). *Application deadline:* For fall admission, 1/15 priority date for domestic students. Applications are processed on a rolling basis. Application fee: $50. Electronic applications accepted. *Expenses: Tuition:* Full-time $42,576; part-time $1774 per credit hour. *Required fees:* $34. Tuition and fees vary according to course load and program. *Financial support:* Fellowships, teaching assistantships, institutionally sponsored loans, and tuition waivers (partial) available. Financial award application deadline: 1/15; financial award applicants required to submit FAFSA. *Faculty research:* Sixteenth- to twentieth-century English literature, rhetorical and critical theory, women's studies, genre studies, Renaissance, America modernism, authorship. *Unit head:* Christopher Flint, Associate Professor and Chair, 216-368-3342, Fax: 216-368-4681, E-mail: christopher.flint@case.edu. *Application contact:* Prof. Kurt Koenigsberger, Associate Professor and Graduate Director, 216-368-6994, Fax: 216-368-4367, E-mail: kurt.koenigsberger@case.edu.
Website: http://english.case.edu/

**The Catholic University of America,** School of Arts and Sciences, Department of English Language and Literature, Washington, DC 20064. Offers English (MA, PhD); rhetoric (Certificate). *Program availability:* Part-time. *Faculty:* 14 full-time (6 women). *Students:* 9 full-time (5 women), 34 part-time (20 women); includes 3 minority (2 Hispanic/Latino; 1 Two or more races, non-Hispanic/Latino), 3 international. Average age 29. 29 applicants, 66% accepted, 8 enrolled. In 2016, 7 master's, 8 doctorates awarded. *Degree requirements:* For master's, one foreign language, comprehensive exam; for doctorate, 2 foreign languages, comprehensive exam, thesis/dissertation. *Entrance requirements:* For master's and doctorate, GRE General Test, statement of purpose, official copies of academic transcripts, three letters of recommendation, writing sample. Additional exam requirements/recommendations for international students: Required—TOEFL (minimum score 550 paper-based; 80 iBT). *Application deadline:* For fall admission, 7/15 priority date for domestic students, 7/1 for international students; for spring admission, 11/15 priority date for domestic students, 11/1 for international students. Applications are processed on a rolling basis. Application fee: $55. Electronic applications accepted. *Expenses:* $42,850 per year; $1,170 per credit; $200 per semester part-time fees. *Financial support:* Fellowships, research assistantships, teaching assistantships, Federal Work-Study, scholarships/grants, tuition waivers (full and partial), and unspecified assistantships available. Financial award application deadline: 2/1; financial award applicants required to submit FAFSA. *Faculty research:* Medieval literature, theory and history of rhetoric, Renaissance literature, religion and literature, English and American drama. *Unit head:* Dr. Glen M. Johnson, Chair, 202-319-5488, Fax: 202-319-4188, E-mail: johnsong@cua.edu. *Application contact:* Director of Graduate Admissions, 202-319-5057, Fax: 202-319-6533, E-mail: cua-admissions@cua.edu.
Website: http://english.cua.edu/

**Central Michigan University,** College of Graduate Studies, College of Humanities and Social and Behavioral Sciences, Department of English Language and Literature, Mount Pleasant, MI 48859. Offers English composition and communication (MA); English language and literature (MA), including children's and young adult literature, creative writing, English language and literature; TESOL: teaching English to speakers of other languages (MA). *Program availability:* Part-time, evening/weekend. *Degree requirements:* For master's, thesis or alternative. Electronic applications accepted. *Faculty research:* Composition theory, science fiction history and bibliography, children's and young adult literature, nineteenth century American literature, applied linguistics.

**Central Washington University,** Graduate Studies and Research, College of Arts and Humanities, Department of English, Ellensburg, WA 98926. Offers English (MA); teaching English as a second language (MA). *Program availability:* Part-time. *Degree requirements:* For master's, thesis or alternative. *Entrance requirements:* For master's, GRE General Test, minimum GPA of 3.0, writing sample. Additional exam requirements/recommendations for international students: Required—TOEFL (minimum score 550 paper-based; 79 iBT) or IELTS (minimum score 6.5). Electronic applications accepted.

**Chapman University,** Wilkinson College of Arts, Humanities, and Social Sciences, Department of English, Orange, CA 92866. Offers creative writing (MFA); English (MA). *Program availability:* Part-time, evening/weekend. *Faculty:* 18 full-time (10 women), 17 part-time/adjunct (12 women). *Students:* 39 full-time (24 women), 20 part-time (16 women); includes 50 minority (33 Black or African American, non-Hispanic/Latino; 4 Asian, non-Hispanic/Latino; 10 Hispanic/Latino; 3 Two or more races, non-Hispanic/Latino), 3 international. Average age 29. 88 applicants, 90% accepted, 23 enrolled. In 2016, 31 master's awarded. *Degree requirements:* For master's, thesis. *Entrance requirements:* For master's, GRE (if undergraduate GPA less than 3.0), minimum undergraduate GPA of 2.5. Additional exam requirements/recommendations for international students: Required—TOEFL (minimum score 550 paper-based, 80 iBT), IELTS (6.5), PTE Academic (53), or CAE. *Application deadline:* For fall admission, 2/1 for domestic students. Applications are processed on a rolling basis. Application fee: $60. Electronic applications accepted. *Expenses:* Contact institution. *Financial support:* Fellowships, teaching assistantships, Federal Work-Study, and scholarships/grants available. Financial award applicants required to submit FAFSA. *Unit head:* Mark Axelrod, Director, 714-997-6586, E-mail: axelrod@chapman.edu. *Application contact:*

Shannon McCance, Graduate Admission Counselor, 714-997-6711, E-mail: smccance@chapman.edu.
Website: http://www.chapman.edu/wilkinson/english/

**Chicago State University,** School of Graduate and Professional Studies, College of Arts and Sciences, Department of English, Foreign Languages and Literatures, Chicago, IL 60628. Offers creative writing (MFA); English (MA). *Degree requirements:* For master's, comprehensive exam (for some programs), thesis (for some programs). *Entrance requirements:* For master's, minimum GPA of 3.0.

**The Citadel, The Military College of South Carolina,** Citadel Graduate College, School of Humanities and Social Sciences, Department of English, Fine Arts and Communications, Charleston, SC 29409. Offers English (MA). Program offered jointly with The Graduate School of the College of Charleston. *Program availability:* Part-time, evening/weekend. *Students:* 4 part-time (2 women). 5 applicants, 100% accepted, 2 enrolled. In 2016, 2 master's awarded. *Degree requirements:* For master's, one foreign language, comprehensive exam, thesis optional. *Entrance requirements:* For master's, GRE (minimum combined verbal and quantitative score of 300, 4 on writing assessment section) or MAT (minimum score of 400); GRE Subject Test (for applicants without undergraduate degree in English), minimum undergraduate GPA of 2.5 (3.0 in major); 2 letters of recommendation preferably from former professors; writing sample that demonstrates ability to perform literary analysis and to conduct research; 2-page statement about educational goals and interest in a graduate program in English. Additional exam requirements/recommendations for international students: Required— TOEFL (minimum score 550 paper-based). *Application deadline:* Applications are processed on a rolling basis. Application fee: $40. Electronic applications accepted. *Expenses:* Tuition, state resident: full-time $5121; part-time $569 per credit hour. Tuition, nonresident: full-time $8613; part-time $957 per credit hour. *Required fees:* $90 per term. *Financial support:* Fellowships and unspecified assistantships available. Support available to part-time students. Financial award application deadline: 7/1; financial award applicants required to submit FAFSA. *Unit head:* Dr. David G. Allen, Department Head, 843-953-5134, E-mail: david.allen@citadel.edu. *Application contact:* Dr. James M. Hutchisson, Director of Graduate Studies, 843-953-5139, E-mail: jim.hutchisson@citadel.edu.
Website: http://www.citadel.edu/root/english

**City College of the City University of New York,** Graduate School, Division of Humanities and the Arts, Department of Classical and Modern Languages and Literatures, New York, NY 10031-9198. Offers Spanish (MA). *Degree requirements:* For master's, one foreign language, comprehensive exam, thesis or alternative. *Entrance requirements:* For master's, minimum GPA of 3.0. Additional exam requirements/recommendations for international students: Required—TOEFL (minimum score 500 paper-based; 61 iBT). Electronic applications accepted. Tuition and fees vary according to course load, degree level and program.

**City College of the City University of New York,** Graduate School, Division of Humanities and the Arts, Department of English, Program in Literature, New York, NY 10031-9198. Offers MA. *Degree requirements:* For master's, one foreign language, comprehensive exam, thesis. *Entrance requirements:* For master's, minimum GPA of 3.0. Additional exam requirements/recommendations for international students: Required—TOEFL (minimum score 600 paper-based; 100 iBT). Electronic applications accepted. Tuition and fees vary according to course load, degree level and program.

**Claremont Graduate University,** Graduate Programs, School of Arts and Humanities, Department of English, Claremont, CA 91711-6160. Offers American studies (MA, PhD); critical theory (MA, PhD); early modern studies (MA, PhD); English (M Phil, PhD); literary theory (PhD); literature (MA, PhD); literature and creative writing (MA); literature and film (MA); MBA/MA; MBA/PhD. *Program availability:* Part-time. *Faculty:* 3 full-time (1 woman), 1 part-time/adjunct (0 women). *Students:* 61 full-time (46 women), 20 part-time (14 women); includes 23 minority (4 Black or African American, non-Hispanic/Latino; 1 American Indian or Alaska Native, non-Hispanic/Latino; 9 Asian, non-Hispanic/Latino; 4 Hispanic/Latino; 5 Two or more races, non-Hispanic/Latino), 6 international. Average age 37. In 2016, 10 master's, 8 doctorates awarded. *Entrance requirements:* For master's and doctorate, GRE General Test. Additional exam requirements/recommendations for international students: Required—TOEFL (minimum score 75 iBT). *Application deadline:* For fall admission, 2/1 priority date for domestic and international students. Applications are processed on a rolling basis. Application fee: $80. Electronic applications accepted. *Expenses: Tuition:* Full-time $44,328; part-time $1847 per unit. *Required fees:* $600; $300 per semester. Tuition and fees vary according to course load and program. *Financial support:* Fellowships, Federal Work-Study, institutionally sponsored loans, and scholarships/grants available. Support available to part-time students. Financial award application deadline: 2/15; financial award applicants required to submit FAFSA. *Faculty research:* American, comparative, and English Renaissance literature; modernism; feminist literature and theory. *Unit head:* Lori Anne Ferrell, Chair, 909-607-2652, E-mail: lorianne.ferrell@cgu.edu. *Application contact:* Amy Sandefur, Assistant Director of Admissions, 909-607-9101, E-mail: amy.sandefur@cgu.edu.
Website: https://www.cgu.edu/departments/english/

**Clark Atlanta University,** School of Arts and Sciences, Department of English, Atlanta, GA 30314. Offers MA, DAH. *Program availability:* Part-time. *Faculty:* 7 full-time (3 women). *Students:* 7 full-time (4 women), 21 part-time (15 women); includes 17 minority (all Black or African American, non-Hispanic/Latino), 7 international. Average age 33. 8 applicants, 88% accepted, 6 enrolled. In 2016, 1 master's awarded. *Degree requirements:* For master's, one foreign language, comprehensive exam, thesis; for doctorate, 2 foreign languages, comprehensive exam, thesis/dissertation. *Entrance requirements:* For master's, GRE General Test, minimum GPA of 2.5. Additional exam requirements/recommendations for international students: Required—TOEFL (minimum score 500 paper-based; 61 iBT). *Application deadline:* For fall admission, 4/1 for domestic and international students; for spring admission, 11/1 for domestic and international students. Applications are processed on a rolling basis. Application fee: $40 ($55 for international students). *Expenses: Tuition:* Full-time $15,498; part-time $861 per credit hour. *Required fees:* $1326; $1326 per credit hour. Tuition and fees vary according to course load. *Financial support:* Career-related internships or fieldwork, Federal Work-Study, scholarships/grants, and unspecified assistantships available. Support available to part-time students. Financial award application deadline: 4/30; financial award applicants required to submit FAFSA. *Unit head:* Dr. Georgene Bess Montgomery, Chairperson, 404-880-8174, E-mail: gmontgomery@cau.edu. *Application contact:* Graduate Program Admissions, 404-880-8483, E-mail: graduateadmissions@cau.edu.

**Clarks Summit University,** Graduate Studies, South Abington Township, PA 18411. Offers Bible (MA); counseling (MA, MS); curriculum and instruction (M Ed); educational administration (M Ed); intercultural studies (MA); literature (MA); missions (MA); organizational leadership (MA); reading specialist (M Ed); secondary English/communications (M Ed); social entrepreneurship (MA); worldview studies (MA). MA in missions program available only for Association of Baptists for World Evangelism missionary personnel. *Program availability:* Part-time, evening/weekend, online learning. *Entrance requirements:* Additional exam requirements/recommendations for international students: Required—TOEFL (minimum score 500 paper-based).

**Clark University,** Graduate School, Department of English, Worcester, MA 01610-1477. Offers MA. *Program availability:* Part-time. *Faculty:* 8 full-time (4 women), 10 part-time/adjunct (5 women). *Students:* 20 full-time (13 women), 3 part-time (2 women); includes 3 minority (2 Black or African American, non-Hispanic/Latino; 1 Hispanic/Latino), 12 international. Average age 29. 16 applicants, 88% accepted, 11 enrolled. In 2016, 5 master's awarded. *Degree requirements:* For master's, thesis, oral exam. *Entrance requirements:* For master's, GRE Subject Test. Additional exam requirements/recommendations for international students: Required—TOEFL. *Application deadline:* For fall admission, 1/15 priority date for domestic students. Applications are processed on a rolling basis. Application fee: $75. *Expenses: Tuition:* Full-time $44,050. *Required fees:* $80. Tuition and fees vary according to course load and program. *Financial support:* In 2016–17, research assistantships with tuition reimbursements (averaging $10,500 per year), 5 teaching assistantships with tuition reimbursements (averaging $10,500 per year) were awarded; fellowships, career-related internships or fieldwork, and tuition waivers (partial) also available. Support available to part-time students. Financial award application deadline: 2/15. *Faculty research:* Renaissance literature, American literature, medieval literature, Victorian literature. *Unit head:* Dr. Jay Elliott, Chair, 508-793-7152.
Website: http://www.clarku.edu/departments/english/

**Clemson University,** Graduate School, College of Architecture, Arts, and Humanities, Department of English, Program in English, Clemson, SC 29634. Offers MA. *Program availability:* Part-time. *Faculty:* 66 full-time (32 women), 3 part-time/adjunct (1 woman). *Students:* 11 full-time (6 women), 2 part-time (0 women); includes 1 minority (Two or more races, non-Hispanic/Latino). Average age 31. 18 applicants, 61% accepted, 8 enrolled. In 2016, 12 master's awarded. *Degree requirements:* For master's, one foreign language, thesis. *Entrance requirements:* For master's, GRE General Test, unofficial transcripts, personal statement, writing sample, letters of recommendation. Additional exam requirements/recommendations for international students: Required—TOEFL (minimum score 80 iBT), IELTS (minimum score 6.5). *Application deadline:* For fall admission, 2/1 priority date for domestic and international students. Application fee: $80 ($90 for international students). Electronic applications accepted. *Expenses:* $4,264 per semester full-time resident, $8,485 per semester full-time non-resident, $471 per credit hour part-time resident, $942 per credit hour part-time non-resident. *Financial support:* In 2016–17, 12 students received support, including 7 teaching assistantships with partial tuition reimbursements available (averaging $12,717 per year); unspecified assistantships also available. Financial award application deadline: 2/1. *Faculty research:* English literature, British literature, American literature, literary theory. *Unit head:* Dr. Lee Morrissey, Department Chair, 864-656-3151, E-mail: lmorris@clemson.edu. *Application contact:* Dr. William Stockton, Graduate Program Coordinator, 864-656-3151, E-mail: wstockt@clemson.edu.
Website: http://www.clemson.edu/caah/departments/english/academics/graduate/ma-in-english/index.html

**Cleveland State University,** College of Graduate Studies, College of Liberal Arts and Social Sciences, Department of English, Cleveland, OH 44115. Offers creative writing (MFA), including fiction, non-fiction, playwriting, poetry. *Program availability:* Part-time, evening/weekend. *Faculty:* 14 full-time (8 women), 14 part-time/adjunct (4 women). *Students:* 28 full-time (17 women), 35 part-time (23 women); includes 7 minority (5 Black or African American, non-Hispanic/Latino; 1 Asian, non-Hispanic/Latino; 1 Two or more races, non-Hispanic/Latino), 2 international. Average age 33. 38 applicants, 68% accepted, 9 enrolled. In 2016, 15 master's awarded. *Degree requirements:* For master's, thesis. *Entrance requirements:* For master's, minimum GPA of 2.75, undergraduate concentration in English, writing sample, portfolio. Additional exam requirements/recommendations for international students: Required—TOEFL (minimum score 550 paper-based; 78 iBT). *Application deadline:* For fall admission, 7/15 priority date for domestic students, 5/15 for international students; for spring admission, 12/15 for domestic students, 11/1 for international students; for summer admission, 4/1 for domestic students, 3/15 for international students. Applications are processed on a rolling basis. Application fee: $40. Electronic applications accepted. *Expenses:* Tuition, state resident: full-time $9565. Tuition, nonresident: full-time $17,980. Tuition and fees vary according to program. *Financial support:* In 2016–17, 20 students received support, including 12 teaching assistantships with full tuition reimbursements available (averaging $7,000 per year); tuition waivers (full and partial) and unspecified assistantships also available. Financial award application deadline: 2/1; financial award applicants required to submit FAFSA. *Faculty research:* Literary history and criticism, literature, creative writing. *Total annual research expenditures:* $5,000. *Application contact:* Dr. James J. Marino, Associate Professor/Director of Graduate Studies, 216-687-6874, Fax: 216-687-6943, E-mail: j.marino22@csuohio.edu.
Website: http://www.csuohio.edu/class/english/english

**The College at Brockport, State University of New York,** School of Arts and Sciences, Department of English, Brockport, NY 14420-2997. Offers creative writing (AGC); English (MA), including creative writing, literature. *Program availability:* Part-time. *Faculty:* 8 full-time (3 women). *Students:* 19 full-time (13 women), 15 part-time (9 women); includes 2 minority (1 Black or African American, non-Hispanic/Latino; 1 Hispanic/Latino), 1 international. 24 applicants, 88% accepted, 16 enrolled. In 2016, 11 master's, 2 other advanced degrees awarded. *Degree requirements:* For master's, thesis. *Entrance requirements:* For master's, minimum GPA of 3.0, letters of recommendation, writing sample. Additional exam requirements/recommendations for international students: Required—TOEFL (minimum score 550 paper-based; 79 iBT), IELTS (minimum score 6.5). *Application deadline:* For fall admission, 4/15 priority date for domestic and international students; for spring admission, 11/15 priority date for domestic and international students; for summer admission, 4/15 priority date for domestic and international students. Application fee: $50. Electronic applications accepted. *Expenses:* Contact institution. *Financial support:* In 2016–17, 3 teaching assistantships with full tuition reimbursements (averaging $6,000 per year) were awarded; Federal Work-Study, scholarships/grants, and unspecified assistantships also available. Support available to part-time students. Financial award application deadline: 3/15; financial award applicants required to submit FAFSA. *Faculty research:* British and American literature, creative writing, film studies, children's literature, ancient and modern world literature. *Unit head:* Dr. Jennifer Haytock, Chairperson, 585-395-5832, Fax: 585-395-2391, E-mail: jhaytock@brockport.edu. *Application contact:* Dr. Gregory Garvey, Graduate Program Director, 585-395-5712, Fax: 585-395-5487, E-mail: tgarvey@brockport.edu.
Website: http://www.brockport.edu/english/graduate/

**The College at Brockport, State University of New York,** School of Education, Health, and Human Services, Department of Education and Human Development, Program in Inclusive Generalist Education, Brockport, NY 14420-2997. Offers biology (MS Ed, AGC); chemistry (MS Ed, AGC); English (MS Ed, Advanced Certificate); mathematics (MS Ed, Advanced Certificate); science (MS Ed, Advanced Certificate); social studies (MS Ed, Advanced Certificate). *Students:* 28 full-time (15 women), 19 part-time (10 women); includes 9 minority (2 Black or African American, non-Hispanic/Latino; 3 Asian, non-Hispanic/Latino; 1 Hispanic/Latino; 3 Two or more races, non-Hispanic/Latino). 21 applicants, 52% accepted, 11 enrolled. In 2016, 12 master's, 3 AGCs awarded. *Degree requirements:* For master's, thesis or alternative. *Entrance requirements:* For master's, minimum GPA of 3.0, letters of recommendation, statement

of objectives, academic major (or equivalent) in program discipline, current resume. Additional exam requirements/recommendations for international students: Required—TOEFL (minimum score 550 paper-based; 79 iBT), IELTS (minimum score 6.5). *Application deadline:* For fall admission, 3/15 priority date for domestic and international students; for spring admission, 10/15 priority date for domestic and international students; for summer admission, 3/15 for domestic and international students. Application fee: $80. Electronic applications accepted. *Expenses:* Contact institution. *Financial support:* Federal Work-Study, scholarships/grants, and unspecified assistantships available. Support available to part-time students. Financial award application deadline: 3/15; financial award applicants required to submit FAFSA. *Unit head:* Dr. Sue Robb, Chairperson, 585-395-5935, Fax: 585-395-2171, E-mail: awalton@brockport.edu. *Application contact:* Anne Walton, Coordinator of Certification and Graduate Advisement, 585-395-2326, Fax: 585-395-2172, E-mail: awalton@brockport.edu.
Website: http://www.brockport.edu/ehd/

**College of Charleston,** Graduate School, School of Humanities and Social Sciences, Program in English, Charleston, SC 29424-0001. Offers MA. Program offered jointly with The Citadel, The Military College of South Carolina. *Program availability:* Part-time, evening/weekend. *Degree requirements:* For master's, one foreign language, comprehensive exam, thesis optional. *Entrance requirements:* For master's, GRE General Test or MAT, minimum GPA of 2.5 overall, 3.0 in major; 2 letters of recommendation; writing sample. Additional exam requirements/recommendations for international students: Required—TOEFL (minimum score 81 iBT). *Application deadline:* For fall admission, 5/1 for domestic students; for spring admission, 11/1 for domestic students. Application fee: $45. Electronic applications accepted. *Financial support:* Fellowships, research assistantships, scholarships/grants, and unspecified assistantships available. Financial award application deadline: 4/1; financial award applicants required to submit FAFSA. *Unit head:* Michael Duvall, Director, 843-953-4833, E-mail: duvalljm@cofc.edu. *Application contact:* Michael Duvall, Director, 843-953-4833, E-mail: duvalljm@cofc.edu.
Website: http://english.cofc.edu/graduate-program/index.php

**The College of New Jersey,** Office of Graduate and Advancing Education, School of Humanities and Social Sciences, Department of English, Program in English, Ewing, NJ 08628. Offers MA. *Program availability:* Part-time. *Degree requirements:* For master's, comprehensive exam. *Entrance requirements:* For master's, GRE, minimum GPA of 3.0 in field or 2.75 overall. Additional exam requirements/recommendations for international students: Required—TOEFL. Electronic applications accepted.

**College of Staten Island of the City University of New York,** Graduate Programs, Division of Humanities and Social Sciences, Program in English, Staten Island, NY 10314-6600. Offers MA. *Program availability:* Part-time, evening/weekend. *Faculty:* 2 full-time. *Students:* 35 part-time. Average age 28. 30 applicants, 80% accepted, 17 enrolled. In 2016, 7 master's awarded. *Degree requirements:* For master's, comprehensive exam, minimum overall GPA of 3.0; 2 papers; exam. *Entrance requirements:* For master's, BA with minimum GPA of 3.0 overall or in English courses, 32 undergraduate credits in English, two letters of recommendation, one- to two-page personal statement, minimum of 8-10 page paper written for an English course. Additional exam requirements/recommendations for international students: Required—TOEFL (minimum score 550 paper-based; 79 iBT), IELTS (minimum score 6.5). *Application deadline:* For fall admission, 6/30 for domestic and international students; for spring admission, 11/16 for domestic and international students. Applications are processed on a rolling basis. Application fee: $125. Electronic applications accepted. *Expenses:* Tuition, state resident: full-time $10,130; part-time $425 per credit. Tuition, nonresident: full-time $18,720; part-time $780 per credit. *Required fees:* $181.10 per semester. Tuition and fees vary according to program. *Faculty research:* Renaissance drama, 18th and 19th century British fiction and poetry, 19th and 20th century American literature, 20th century Chinese literature, queer studies. *Unit head:* Dr. Katharine Goodland, Graduate Program Coordinator, 718-982-3639, E-mail: katharine.goodland@csi.cuny.edu. *Application contact:* Sasha Spence, Associate Director for Graduate Admissions, 718-982-2019, Fax: 718-982-2500, E-mail: sasha.spence@csi.cuny.edu.
Website: http://www.csi.cuny.edu/catalog/graduate/master-of-arts-in-english-ma.htm

**College of Staten Island of the City University of New York,** Graduate Programs, School of Education, Staten Island, NY 10314-6600. Offers adolescence education (MS Ed), including biology, English, mathematics, social studies; childhood education (MS Ed), including learning and development, literacy education, mathematics education, music education, science education, social foundations of education, social studies education; leadership in education (Post-Master's Certificate); special education (MS Ed); teaching of English to speakers of other languages (MS Ed, Advanced Certificate). *Accreditation:* NCATE. *Faculty:* 25 full-time, 40 part-time/adjunct. *Students:* 32 full-time, 414 part-time. Average age 30. In 2016, 117 master's, 26 Advanced Certificates awarded. *Expenses:* Tuition, state resident: full-time $10,130; part-time $425 per credit. Tuition, nonresident: full-time $18,720; part-time $780 per credit. *Required fees:* $181.10 per semester. Tuition and fees vary according to program. *Unit head:* Dr. Kenneth Gold, 718-982-3737, Fax: 718-982-3743, E-mail: kenneth.gold@csi.cuny.edu. *Application contact:* Sasha Spence, Associate Director for Graduate Admissions, 718-982-2019, Fax: 718-982-2500, E-mail: sasha.spence@csi.cuny.edu.
Website: http://csivc.csi.cuny.edu/education/files

**The College of William and Mary,** School of Education, Program in Curriculum and Instruction, Williamsburg, VA 23187-8795. Offers elementary education (MA Ed); gifted education (MA Ed); literacy leadership (MA Ed); math specialist (MA Ed); secondary education (MA Ed), including English, foreign language, math, science, social studies; special education (MA Ed). *Accreditation:* NCATE. *Program availability:* Part-time. *Faculty:* 30 full-time (21 women), 48 part-time/adjunct (38 women). *Students:* 60 full-time (47 women), 14 part-time (all women); includes 13 minority (1 Black or African American, non-Hispanic/Latino; 1 American Indian or Alaska Native, non-Hispanic/Latino; 2 Asian, non-Hispanic/Latino; 7 Hispanic/Latino; 2 Two or more races, non-Hispanic/Latino). Average age 26. 134 applicants, 79% accepted, 66 enrolled. In 2016, 77 master's awarded. *Degree requirements:* For master's, project. *Entrance requirements:* For master's, GRE, MAT, PRAXIS Core Academic Skills for Educators, minimum GPA of 2.5. Additional exam requirements/recommendations for international students: Required—TOEFL (minimum score 100 iBT), IELTS (minimum score 7). *Application deadline:* For fall admission, 1/15 for domestic and international students; for spring admission, 10/1 for domestic and international students. Application fee: $50. Electronic applications accepted. *Expenses:* $14,258 per year in-state full-time, $275 per credit in-state part-time; $30,500 per year out-of-state full-time, $1,200 per credit out-of-state part-time. *Financial support:* In 2016–17, 30 students received support, including 3 research assistantships (averaging $14,259 per year); scholarships/grants and unspecified assistantships also available. Financial award application deadline: 1/15; financial award applicants required to submit FAFSA. *Faculty research:* Educational technology, professional development and evaluation, inclusive education, rural education, education policy. *Unit head:* Dr. Jeremy D. Stoddard, Department Chair, 757-221-2348, E-mail: jdstod@wm.edu. *Application contact:* Dorothy Smith Osborne, Assistant Dean for Academic Programs and Student Services, 757-221-2317, E-mail: dsosbo@wm.edu.
Website: http://education.wm.edu

**Colorado State University,** College of Liberal Arts, Department of English, Fort Collins, CO 80523-1773. Offers creative nonfiction (MA); creative writing (MFA); literature (MA); rhetoric and composition (MA); TESL/TEFL (MA). *Program availability:* Part-time. *Faculty:* 31 full-time (21 women), 25 part-time/adjunct (23 women). *Students:* 71 full-time (54 women), 30 part-time (21 women); includes 7 minority (1 Black or African American, non-Hispanic/Latino; 2 Asian, non-Hispanic/Latino; 2 Hispanic/Latino; 2 Two or more races, non-Hispanic/Latino), 13 international. Average age 29. 177 applicants, 42% accepted, 39 enrolled. In 2016, 33 master's awarded. *Degree requirements:* For master's, thesis (for some programs). *Entrance requirements:* For master's, BA/BS or equivalent with minimum cumulative undergraduate GPA of 3.0, transcripts, writing sample, statement of purpose, 3 letters of recommendation. Additional exam requirements/recommendations for international students: Recommended—TOEFL (minimum score 550 paper-based; 80 iBT), IELTS (minimum score 6.5). *Application deadline:* For spring admission, 9/15 for domestic and international students. Application fee: $60 ($70 for international students). Electronic applications accepted. *Expenses:* Tuition, state resident: full-time $9628. Tuition, nonresident: full-time $23,603. *Required fees:* $2253; $528.14 per credit hour. $264.07 per semester. Tuition and fees vary according to course load and program. *Financial support:* In 2016–17, 39 students received support, including 38 teaching assistantships with full and partial tuition reimbursements available (averaging $14,005 per year); scholarships/grants, health care benefits, and unspecified assistantships also available. Financial award application deadline: 1/1. *Faculty research:* Literary texts in historical and cultural contexts; creation and criticism of fiction, poetry, creative nonfiction and hybrid genres; critical literacies, multimodalities, and technologies including pedagogical theory and practice; linguistics, second language acquisition and TEFL/TESOL; rhetoric and social change. *Total annual research expenditures:* $154,039. *Unit head:* Louann Reid, Professor, 970-491-6428, E-mail: louann.reid@colostate.edu. *Application contact:* Marnie Leonard, Administrative Assistant, 970-491-2403, E-mail: marnie.leonard@colostate.edu.
Website: http://english.colostate.edu/

**Columbia University,** Graduate School of Arts and Sciences, New York, NY 10027. Offers African-American studies (MA); American studies (MA); anthropology (MA, PhD); art history and archaeology (MA, PhD); astronomy (PhD); biological sciences (PhD); biotechnology (MA); chemical physics (PhD); chemistry (PhD); classical studies (MA, PhD); classics (MA, PhD); climate and society (MA); conservation biology (MA); earth and environmental sciences (PhD); East Asia: regional studies (MA); East Asian languages and cultures (MA, PhD); ecology, evolution and environmental biology (MA), including conservation biology; ecology, evolution, and environmental biology (PhD), including ecology and evolutionary biology, evolutionary primatology; economics (MA, PhD); English and comparative literature (MA, PhD); French and Romance philology (MA, PhD); Germanic languages (MA, PhD); global French studies (MA); global thought (MA); Hispanic cultural studies (MA); history (PhD); history and literature (MA); human rights studies (MA); Islamic studies (MA); Italian (MA, PhD); Japanese pedagogy (MA); Jewish studies (MA); Latin America and the Caribbean: regional studies (MA); Latin American and Iberian cultures (PhD); mathematics (MA, PhD), including finance (MA); medieval and Renaissance studies (MA); Middle Eastern, South Asian, and African studies (MA, PhD); modern art: critical and curatorial studies (MA); modern European studies (MA); museum anthropology (MA); music (DMA, PhD); oral history (MA); philosophical foundations of physics (MA); philosophy (MA, PhD); physics (PhD); political science (MA, PhD); psychology (PhD); quantitative methods in the social sciences (MA); religion (MA, PhD); Russia, Eurasia and East Europe: regional studies (MA); Russian translation (MA); Slavic cultures (MA); Slavic languages (MA, PhD); sociology (MA, PhD); South Asian studies (MA); statistics (MA, PhD); theatre (PhD). Dual-degree programs require admission to both Graduate School of Arts and Sciences and another Columbia school. *Program availability:* Part-time. Terminal master's awarded for partial completion of doctoral program. *Degree requirements:* For master's, variable foreign language requirement, comprehensive exam (for some programs), thesis (for some programs); for doctorate, variable foreign language requirement, comprehensive exam (for some programs), thesis/dissertation. *Entrance requirements:* For master's and doctorate, GRE General Test, GRE Subject Test (for some programs). Additional exam requirements/recommendations for international students: Required—TOEFL, IELTS. Electronic applications accepted.

**Concordia University,** School of Graduate Studies, Faculty of Arts and Science, Department of English, Program in English Literature, Montréal, QC H3G 1M8, Canada. Offers MA, PhD. *Degree requirements:* For master's, one foreign language, thesis optional. *Entrance requirements:* For master's, honors degree in English, minimum GPA of 3.3 in English literature.

**Converse College,** School of Education and Graduate Studies, Program in Liberal Arts, Spartanburg, SC 29302. Offers English (MLA); history (MLA); political science (MLA). *Degree requirements:* For master's, capstone paper. *Entrance requirements:* For master's, minimum GPA of 3.0, 2 recommendations. *Application deadline:* For fall admission, 5/1 priority date for domestic students; for spring admission, 1/30 for domestic students. Application fee: $40. *Expenses:* Tuition: Full-time $3600; part-time $400 per credit hour. *Required fees:* $70 per term. *Unit head:* Dr. Kathy Good, Dean of the School of Education and Graduate Studies, 864-596-9082, E-mail: kathy.good@converse.edu. *Application contact:* Dr. Thomas McDaniel, Director of Master of Liberal Arts Program, 864-596-9015, E-mail: tom.mcdaniel@converse.edu.

**Converse College,** School of Education and Graduate Studies, Program in Middle Level Education, Spartanburg, SC 29302. Offers language arts/English (MAT); mathematics (MAT); middle level education (M Ed); science (MAT); social studies (MAT). *Expenses:* Tuition: Full-time $3600; part-time $400 per credit hour. *Required fees:* $70 per term. *Application contact:* 864-596-9404, E-mail: graduate@converse.edu.

**Cornell University,** Graduate School, Graduate Fields of Arts and Sciences, Field of English Language and Literature, Ithaca, NY 14853. Offers African-American literature (PhD); American literature after 1865 (PhD); American literature to 1865 (PhD); American studies (PhD); colonial and postcolonial literatures (PhD); creative writing (MFA); cultural studies (PhD); dramatic literature (PhD); English poetry (PhD); English Renaissance to 1660 (PhD); lesbian, bisexual, and gay literary studies (PhD); literary criticism and theory (PhD); Old and Middle English (PhD); prose fiction (PhD); Restoration and the eighteenth-century (PhD); the nineteenth century (PhD); the twentieth century (PhD); women's literature (PhD); MFA/PhD. Terminal master's awarded for partial completion of doctoral program. *Degree requirements:* For master's, one foreign language, thesis; for doctorate, one foreign language, comprehensive exam, thesis/dissertation, teaching experience. *Entrance requirements:* For master's, GRE General Test, 3 letters of recommendation, creative writing sample; for doctorate, GRE General Test, GRE Subject Test (English), 3 letters of recommendation, writing sample. Additional exam requirements/recommendations for international students: Required—TOEFL (minimum score 600 paper-based; 77 iBT). Electronic applications accepted. *Faculty research:* English and American literature, women's writing, ethnic and post-colonial literature, critical theory, medievalism.

**Cornell University,** Graduate School, Graduate Fields of Arts and Sciences, Field of Linguistics, Ithaca, NY 14853. Offers applied linguistics (MA, PhD); East Asian linguistics (MA, PhD); English linguistics (MA, PhD); general linguistics (MA, PhD); Germanic linguistics (MA, PhD); Indo-European linguistics (MA, PhD); phonetics (MA, PhD); phonological theory (MA, PhD); Romance linguistics (MA, PhD); second language acquisition (MA, PhD); semantics (MA, PhD); Slavic linguistics (MA, PhD); sociolinguistics (MA, PhD); South Asian linguistics (MA, PhD); Southeast Asian linguistics (MA, PhD); syntactic theory (MA, PhD). Terminal master's awarded for partial completion of doctoral program. *Degree requirements:* For master's, one foreign language, thesis; for doctorate, one foreign language, comprehensive exam, thesis/dissertation. *Entrance requirements:* For master's and doctorate, GRE General Test, 2 letters of recommendation. Additional exam requirements/recommendations for international students: Required—TOEFL (minimum score 600 paper-based; 77 iBT). Electronic applications accepted. *Faculty research:* Phonology and phonetics, syntax and semantics, historical linguistics, philosophy of language, language acquisition.

**Creighton University,** Graduate School, College of Arts and Sciences, Department of English, Omaha, NE 68178-0001. Offers creative writing (MA, MFA). *Program availability:* Part-time. *Faculty:* 15 full-time (8 women), 1 part-time/adjunct (0 women). *Students:* 6 full-time (5 women), 1 (woman) part-time, 1 international. Average age 27. 31 applicants, 87% accepted, 6 enrolled. In 2016, 5 master's awarded. *Degree requirements:* For master's, thesis optional. *Entrance requirements:* For master's, 10-15 page writing sample, 3 letters of recommendation. Additional exam requirements/recommendations for international students: Required—TOEFL (minimum score 90 iBT). *Application deadline:* For fall admission, 3/15 priority date for domestic and international students. Application fee: $50. Electronic applications accepted. *Expenses: Tuition:* Full-time $14,400; part-time $800 per credit hour. *Required fees:* $158 per semester. Tuition and fees vary according to course load, campus/location, program, reciprocity agreements and student's religious affiliation. *Financial support:* In 2016–17, 5 fellowships with tuition reimbursements (averaging $11,465 per year) were awarded; scholarships/grants, tuition waivers (full and partial), and unspecified assistantships also available. Financial award applicants required to submit FAFSA. *Faculty research:* Henry James letters. *Unit head:* Dr. Robert Whipple, Director, 402-280-2520, E-mail: whippl@creighton.edu. *Application contact:* Lindsay Johnson, Director of Graduate and Adult Recruitment, 402-280-2703, Fax: 402-280-2423, E-mail: gradschool@creighton.edu.

**Dalhousie University,** Faculty of Arts and Social Science, Department of English, Halifax, NS B3H 4R2, Canada. Offers MA, PhD. *Entrance requirements:* Additional exam requirements/recommendations for international students: Required—TOEFL, IELTS, CANTEST, CAEL, or Michigan English Language Assessment Battery. Electronic applications accepted. *Faculty research:* Victorian, Canadian, Renaissance, eighteenth-century, and modern literature.

**DePaul University,** College of Liberal Arts and Social Sciences, Chicago, IL 60614. Offers Arabic (MA); Chinese (MA); English (MA); French (MA); German (MA); history (MA); interdisciplinary studies (MA, MS); international public service (MS); international studies (MA); Italian (MA); Japanese (MA); leadership and policy studies (MS); liberal studies (MA); new media studies (MA); nonprofit management (MNM); public administration (MPA); public health (MPH); public service management (MS); social work (MSW); sociology (MA); Spanish (MA); sustainable urban development (MA); women and gender studies (MA); writing and publishing (MA); writing, rhetoric, and discourse (MA); MA/PhD. *Program availability:* Part-time, evening/weekend, online learning. Terminal master's awarded for partial completion of doctoral program. *Degree requirements:* For master's, variable foreign language requirement, comprehensive exam (for some programs), thesis (for some programs). Electronic applications accepted.

**Dominican University of California,** School of Arts, Humanities and Social Sciences, Humanities Program, San Rafael, CA 94901-2298. Offers applied music (MA); art history (MA); creative writing (MA); gender studies (MA); history (MA); literature (MA); philosophy (MA); political theory (MA); religion (MA). *Program availability:* Part-time. *Degree requirements:* For master's, thesis or alternative. *Entrance requirements:* For master's, minimum GPA of 3.0, interview. Additional exam requirements/recommendations for international students: Required—TOEFL (minimum score 550 paper-based; 80 iBT), IELTS (minimum score 6.5). Electronic applications accepted. Application fee is waived when completed online. *Expenses:* Contact institution.

**Drew University,** Caspersen School of Graduate Studies, Madison, NJ 07940-1493. Offers conflict resolution and leadership (Certificate), including community leadership, moderation, peace building; history and culture (MA, PhD), including American history, book history, British history, European history, Holocaust and genocide (M Litt, MA, D Litt, PhD), intellectual history, Irish history, print culture, public history; K-12 education (MAT), including art, biology, chemistry, elementary education, English, French, Italian, math, secondary education, special education, teacher of students with disabilities; liberal studies (M Litt, D Litt), including history, Holocaust and genocide (M Litt, MA, D Litt, PhD), Irish/Irish-American studies, literature (M Litt, MMH, D Litt, DMH, CMH), religion, spirituality, teaching in the two-year college, writing; medical humanities (MMH, DMH, CMH), including arts, health, healthcare, literature (M Litt, MMH, D Litt, DMH, CMH), scientific research; poetry (MFA). *Program availability:* Part-time, evening/weekend. *Faculty:* 4 full-time (2 women), 31 part-time/adjunct (16 women). *Students:* 62 full-time (41 women), 199 part-time (130 women); includes 38 minority (17 Black or African American, non-Hispanic/Latino; 3 Asian, non-Hispanic/Latino; 17 Hispanic/Latino; 1 Two or more races, non-Hispanic/Latino), 3 international. Average age 27. 93 applicants, 81% accepted, 46 enrolled. In 2016, 39 master's, 27 doctorates, 26 other advanced degrees awarded. Terminal master's awarded for partial completion of doctoral program. *Degree requirements:* For master's and other advanced degree, thesis (for some programs); for doctorate, one foreign language, comprehensive exam (for some programs), thesis/dissertation. *Entrance requirements:* For master's, PRAXIS Core and Subject Area tests (for MAT), resume, transcripts, writing sample, personal statement, letters of recommendation; for doctorate, GRE (PhD in history and culture), resume, transcripts, writing sample, personal statement, letters of recommendation. Additional exam requirements/recommendations for international students: Required—TOEFL (minimum score 587 paper-based; 94 iBT), IELTS (minimum score 7), TWE (minimum score 4). *Application deadline:* For fall admission, 8/1 for domestic students, 6/1 for international students; for spring admission, 12/1 for domestic students, 10/1 for international students. Applications are processed on a rolling basis. Application fee: $35. Electronic applications accepted. Tuition and fees vary according to program. *Financial support:* Fellowships, research assistantships, teaching assistantships, career-related internships or fieldwork, Federal Work-Study, scholarships/grants, and unspecified assistantships available. Support available to part-time students. Financial award applicants required to submit FAFSA. *Application contact:* Leanne Horinko, Director of Caspersen Admissions, 973-408-3280, E-mail: gradm@drew.edu. Website: http://www.drew.edu/caspersen

**Duke University,** Graduate School, Department of English, Durham, NC 27708. Offers PhD, JD/AM. *Degree requirements:* For doctorate, 2 foreign languages, thesis/dissertation. *Entrance requirements:* For doctorate, GRE General Test, writing sample. Additional exam requirements/recommendations for international students: Required—

TOEFL (minimum score 577 paper-based; 90 iBT) or IELTS (minimum score 7). Electronic applications accepted.

**Duquesne University,** Graduate School of Liberal Arts, Department of English, Pittsburgh, PA 15282-0001. Offers MA, PhD. *Program availability:* Part-time, evening/weekend. *Faculty:* 16 full-time (10 women), 8 part-time/adjunct (4 women). *Students:* 43 full-time (30 women), 1 part-time (0 women); includes 1 minority (Black or African American, non-Hispanic/Latino), 2 international. Average age 30. 37 applicants, 73% accepted, 11 enrolled. In 2016, 12 master's, 8 doctorates awarded. Terminal master's awarded for partial completion of doctoral program. *Degree requirements:* For master's, comprehensive exam, thesis or alternative; for doctorate, 2 foreign languages, comprehensive exam, thesis/dissertation. *Entrance requirements:* For master's and doctorate, GRE General Test, bachelor's degree in English, writing sample. Additional exam requirements/recommendations for international students: Required—TOEFL. *Application deadline:* For fall admission, 2/1 priority date for domestic and international students. Applications are processed on a rolling basis. Application fee: $0. Electronic applications accepted. *Expenses: Tuition:* Full-time $22,212; part-time $1234 per credit. Tuition and fees vary according to program. *Financial support:* In 2016–17, 33 students received support, including 7 research assistantships with full tuition reimbursements available (averaging $15,000 per year), 19 teaching assistantships with full tuition reimbursements available (averaging $17,000 per year); Federal Work-Study, scholarships/grants, tuition waivers (full), and unspecified assistantships also available. Support available to part-time students. Financial award application deadline: 5/1. *Unit head:* Dr. Greg Barnhisel, Chair, 412-396-6432, E-mail: barnhiselg@duq.edu. *Application contact:* Linda Rendulic, Assistant to the Dean, 412-396-6400, Fax: 412-396-5265, E-mail: rendulic@duq.edu. Website: http://www.duq.edu/academics/schools/liberal-arts/graduate-school/programs/english

**East Carolina University,** Graduate School, Thomas Harriot College of Arts and Sciences, Department of English, Greenville, NC 27858-4353. Offers creative writing (MA); English studies (MA); linguistics (MA); literature (MA); multicultural and transnational literatures (MA, Certificate); rhetoric and composition (MA); rhetoric, writing, and professional communication (PhD); teaching English in the two-year college (Certificate); teaching English to speakers of other languages (MA, Certificate); technical and professional communication (MA). *Program availability:* Part-time, evening/weekend. *Students:* 54 full-time (36 women), 95 part-time (77 women); includes 32 minority (19 Black or African American, non-Hispanic/Latino; 3 Asian, non-Hispanic/Latino; 6 Hispanic/Latino; 4 Two or more races, non-Hispanic/Latino), 1 international. Average age 35. 78 applicants, 96% accepted, 50 enrolled. In 2016, 34 master's, 1 doctorate awarded. *Degree requirements:* For master's, one foreign language, comprehensive exam, thesis optional. *Entrance requirements:* For master's, GRE General Test, MAT (for MA Ed). Additional exam requirements/recommendations for international students: Required—TOEFL. *Application deadline:* For fall admission, 6/1 priority date for domestic students; for spring admission, 10/15 for domestic students. Applications are processed on a rolling basis. Application fee: $50. *Financial support:* Research assistantships with partial tuition reimbursements, teaching assistantships with partial tuition reimbursements, and Federal Work-Study available. Support available to part-time students. Financial award application deadline: 6/1. *Unit head:* Dr. Jeffrey Johnson, Chair, 252-328-6041, E-mail: johnsonj@ecu.edu. *Application contact:* Dean of Graduate School, 252-328-6012, Fax: 252-328-6071, E-mail: gradschool@ecu.edu. Website: http://www.ecu.edu/cs-cas/engl/graduate/

**Eastern Illinois University,** Graduate School, College of Arts and Humanities, Department of English, Charleston, IL 61920. Offers MA. *Program availability:* Part-time, evening/weekend. *Degree requirements:* For master's, comprehensive exam (for some programs), thesis (for some programs). *Entrance requirements:* For master's, GMAT or GRE. Additional exam requirements/recommendations for international students: Required—TOEFL (minimum score 500 paper-based; 61 iBT), IELTS (minimum score 6). Electronic applications accepted.

**Eastern Kentucky University,** The Graduate School, College of Arts and Sciences, Department of English and Theatre, Richmond, KY 40475-3102. Offers creative writing (MFA); English (MA). *Program availability:* Part-time, evening/weekend. *Degree requirements:* For master's, thesis optional. *Entrance requirements:* For master's, GRE General Test, minimum GPA of 2.5, minor in English with 3.0 GPA. *Faculty research:* Old English, Victorian studies, women's studies, rhetoric, popular culture, novel studies.

**Eastern Michigan University,** Graduate School, College of Arts and Sciences, Department of English Language and Literature, Program in Children's Literature, Ypsilanti, MI 48197. Offers MA. *Program availability:* Part-time, evening/weekend, online learning. *Students:* 2 full-time (1 woman), 9 part-time (8 women); includes 1 minority (Asian, non-Hispanic/Latino). Average age 28. 9 applicants, 89% accepted, 7 enrolled. In 2016, 5 master's awarded. *Entrance requirements:* Additional exam requirements/recommendations for international students: Required—TOEFL. *Application deadline:* Applications are processed on a rolling basis. Application fee: $45. *Financial support:* Fellowships, research assistantships with full tuition reimbursements, teaching assistantships with full tuition reimbursements, and tuition waivers (partial) available. Financial award applicants required to submit FAFSA. *Application contact:* Dr. Annette Wannamaker, Program Coordinator, 734-487-0148, Fax: 734-483-9744, E-mail: awannamak@emich.edu.

**Eastern Michigan University,** Graduate School, College of Arts and Sciences, Department of English Language and Literature, Program in Literature, Ypsilanti, MI 48197. Offers MA. *Program availability:* Part-time, evening/weekend, online learning. *Students:* 3 full-time (2 women), 15 part-time (9 women); includes 2 minority (1 Black or African American, non-Hispanic/Latino; 1 Hispanic/Latino). Average age 33. 14 applicants, 79% accepted, 6 enrolled. In 2016, 9 master's awarded. *Entrance requirements:* Additional exam requirements/recommendations for international students: Required—TOEFL. *Application deadline:* Applications are processed on a rolling basis. Application fee: $45. *Financial support:* Fellowships, research assistantships with full tuition reimbursements, teaching assistantships with full tuition reimbursements, career-related internships or fieldwork, Federal Work-Study, institutionally sponsored loans, scholarships/grants, tuition waivers (partial), and unspecified assistantships available. Support available to part-time students. Financial award applicants required to submit FAFSA. *Application contact:* Dr. Natasa Kovacevic, Program Coordinator, 734-487-0976, Fax: 734-483-9744, E-mail: nkovacev@emich.edu.

**Eastern New Mexico University,** Graduate School, College of Liberal Arts and Sciences, Department of Languages and Literature, Portales, NM 88130. Offers English (MA), including English, literatures and cultures of migration. *Program availability:* Part-time. *Degree requirements:* For master's, one foreign language, thesis, oral and written comprehensive exams. *Entrance requirements:* For master's, minimum GPA of 3.0, foreign language proficiency, interview. Additional exam requirements/recommendations for international students: Required—TOEFL (minimum score 550 paper-based; 79 iBT), IELTS (minimum score 6). Electronic applications accepted.

**Eastern Washington University,** Graduate Studies, College of Arts, Letters and Education, Department of English, Cheney, WA 99004-2431. Offers literature (MA);

rhetoric, composition, and technical communication (MA); teaching English as a second language (MA). *Faculty:* 2 full-time (1 woman), 19 part-time/adjunct (9 women). *Students:* 23 full-time (16 women), 7 part-time (5 women); includes 4 minority (1 Black or African American, non-Hispanic/Latino; 2 Hispanic/Latino; 1 Native Hawaiian or other Pacific Islander, non-Hispanic/Latino), 6 international. Average age 35. 27 applicants, 67% accepted, 13 enrolled. In 2016, 20 master's awarded. *Degree requirements:* For master's, comprehensive exam, thesis or alternative. *Entrance requirements:* For master's, GRE General Test, minimum GPA of 3.0. Additional exam requirements/recommendations for international students: Required—TOEFL (minimum score 580 paper-based; 92 iBT), IELTS (minimum score 7), PTE (minimum score 6). *Application deadline:* For fall admission, 4/1 priority date for domestic students; for spring admission, 1/15 for domestic students. Applications are processed on a rolling basis. Application fee: $50. *Expenses:* Tuition, state resident: full-time $11,000; part-time $5500 per credit. Tuition, nonresident: full-time $24,000; part-time $12,000 per credit. *Required fees:* $1300. One-time fee: $50 full-time. Part-time tuition and fees vary according to course load, campus/location and program. *Financial support:* In 2016–17, 25 teaching assistantships with partial tuition reimbursements (averaging $7,000 per year) were awarded; career-related internships or fieldwork, Federal Work-Study, institutionally sponsored loans, scholarships/grants, health care benefits, tuition waivers (partial), and unspecified assistantships also available. Support available to part-time students. Financial award application deadline: 2/1; financial award applicants required to submit FAFSA. *Unit head:* Dr. Logan Greene, Chair, 509-359-2400, E-mail: lgreene@ewu.edu. *Application contact:* Kathy White, Advisor/Recruiter for Graduate Studies, 509-359-2491, E-mail: gradprograms@ewu.edu. Website: http://www.ewu.edu/CALE/Programs/English.xml

**East Tennessee State University,** School of Graduate Studies, College of Arts and Sciences, Department of Literature and Language, Johnson City, TN 37614. Offers MA, Postbaccalaureate Certificate. *Program availability:* Part-time, evening/weekend. *Degree requirements:* For master's, comprehensive exam, thesis optional. *Entrance requirements:* For master's, GRE General Test, minimum undergraduate GPA of 3.0 in English, writing sample, three letters of recommendation; for Postbaccalaureate Certificate, GRE General Test, speaking and listening assessment, resume, three letters of recommendation. Additional exam requirements/recommendations for international students: Required—TOEFL (minimum score 550 paper-based; 79 iBT). Electronic applications accepted. *Faculty research:* Linguistics and dialectology, English education, critical literary theory, literary biography, environmental literature, modern and ancient languages.

**Emory University,** Laney Graduate School, Department of English, Atlanta, GA 30322-1100. Offers PhD, Graduate Certificate. *Degree requirements:* For doctorate, one foreign language, comprehensive exam, thesis/dissertation. *Entrance requirements:* For doctorate, GRE General Test, minimum GPA of 3.0. Additional exam requirements/recommendations for international students: Required—TOEFL. Electronic applications accepted. *Faculty research:* American literature, Renaissance literature, twentieth-century poetry, Irish literature, cultural studies.

**Emporia State University,** Program in English, Emporia, KS 66801-5415. Offers MA. *Program availability:* Part-time. *Faculty:* 18 full-time (10 women), 4 part-time/adjunct (3 women). *Students:* 19 full-time (10 women), 18 part-time (11 women), 8 international. 20 applicants, 100% accepted, 6 enrolled. In 2016, 7 master's awarded. *Degree requirements:* For master's, comprehensive exam, thesis optional. *Entrance requirements:* For master's, minimum undergraduate GPA of 2.75 in last 60 hours. Additional exam requirements/recommendations for international students: Required—TOEFL (minimum score 550 paper-based; 68 iBT). *Application deadline:* For fall admission, 8/15 for domestic students. Application fee: $30 ($75 for international students). *Expenses:* Tuition, state resident: full-time $5922; part-time $246.75 per credit hour. Tuition, nonresident: full-time $18,414; part-time $767.25 per credit hour. *Required fees:* $1884; $78.50 per credit hour. *Financial support:* In 2016–17, 1 research assistantship with full tuition reimbursement (averaging $7,353 per year), 10 teaching assistantships with full tuition reimbursements (averaging $8,244 per year) were awarded; Federal Work-Study, health care benefits, and unspecified assistantships also available. Financial award application deadline: 2/15; financial award applicants required to submit FAFSA. *Unit head:* Dr. Kevin Rabas, Chair, 620-341-5216, E-mail: krabas@emporia.edu. *Application contact:* Mary Sewell, Admissions Coordinator, 800-950-GRAD, Fax: 620-341-5909, E-mail: msewell@emporia.edu. Website: http://www.emporia.edu/info/degrees-courses/grad/english

**Fairleigh Dickinson University, Metropolitan Campus,** University College: Arts, Sciences, and Professional Studies, Department of English, Philosophy, and Humanities, Program in English and Literature, Teaneck, NJ 07666-1914. Offers MA.

**Fitchburg State University,** Division of Graduate and Continuing Education, Programs in English and Teaching English (Secondary Level), Fitchburg, MA 01420-2697. Offers MA, MAT, Certificate. *Accreditation:* NCATE. *Program availability:* Part-time, evening/weekend. *Entrance requirements:* Additional exam requirements/recommendations for international students: Required—TOEFL (minimum score 550 paper-based; 79 iBT). Electronic applications accepted. *Expenses:* Tuition, state resident: full-time $2871; part-time $1914 per year. Tuition, nonresident: full-time $2871; part-time $1914 per year. *Required fees:* $3828. Tuition and fees vary according to program.

**Florida Atlantic University,** Dorothy F. Schmidt College of Arts and Letters, Department of English, Boca Raton, FL 33431-0991. Offers American literature (MA). *Program availability:* Part-time. *Faculty:* 26 full-time (12 women). *Students:* 32 full-time (15 women), 29 part-time (24 women); includes 9 minority (3 Black or African American, non-Hispanic/Latino; 1 Asian, non-Hispanic/Latino; 3 Hispanic/Latino; 2 Two or more races, non-Hispanic/Latino), 3 international. Average age 31. 62 applicants, 50% accepted, 20 enrolled. In 2016, 23 master's awarded. *Degree requirements:* For master's, one foreign language, thesis. *Entrance requirements:* For master's, GRE General Test, minimum GPA of 3.0, writing samples, 2 letters of recommendation. Additional exam requirements/recommendations for international students: Required—TOEFL (minimum score 500 paper-based; 61 iBT), IELTS (minimum score 6). *Application deadline:* For fall admission, 3/1 for domestic students, 2/15 for international students; for spring admission, 11/1 for domestic students, 7/15 for international students. Applications are processed on a rolling basis. Application fee: $30. Electronic applications accepted. *Expenses:* Tuition, state resident: full-time $7392; part-time $369.82 per credit hour. Tuition, nonresident: full-time $19,432; part-time $1024.81 per credit hour. *Financial support:* Fellowships, teaching assistantships with partial tuition reimbursements, Federal Work-Study, and tuition waivers available. Support available to part-time students. Financial award application deadline: 3/1. *Faculty research:* African-American writers, critical theory, British-American, Asian-American. *Unit head:* Mary Sheffield, 561-297-2974, E-mail: msheffi3@fau.edu. Website: http://www.fau.edu/english/

**Florida Gulf Coast University,** College of Arts and Sciences, Program in English, Fort Myers, FL 33965-6565. Offers MA. *Program availability:* Part-time. *Faculty:* 238 full-time (97 women), 158 part-time/adjunct (62 women). *Students:* 6 full-time (5 women), 19 part-time (13 women); includes 4 minority (1 Black or African American, non-Hispanic/Latino; 2 Hispanic/Latino; 1 Two or more races, non-Hispanic/Latino). Average age 31. 10 applicants, 90% accepted, 5 enrolled. In 2016, 7 master's awarded. *Entrance*

*requirements:* For master's, GRE General Test, minimum GPA of 3.0. Additional exam requirements/recommendations for international students: Required—TOEFL (minimum score 550 paper-based). *Application deadline:* For fall admission, 2/15 for domestic students. Application fee: $30. *Expenses:* Tuition, state resident: full-time $6721. Tuition, nonresident: full-time $28,170. *Required fees:* $1987. Tuition and fees vary according to course load and degree level. *Financial support:* In 2016–17, 2 students received support. Application deadline: 3/1; applicants required to submit FAFSA. *Unit head:* Kimberly Jackson, Interim Chair, 239-590-7423, E-mail: kjackson@fgcu.edu. *Application contact:* Patricia Rice, Executive Secretary, 239-590-7196, Fax: 239-590-7200, E-mail: price@fgcu.edu.

**Florida International University,** College of Arts, Sciences, and Education, Department of English, Miami, FL 33199. Offers creative writing (MFA); English (MA), including literature; linguistics (MA). *Program availability:* Part-time, evening/weekend. *Faculty:* 55 full-time (29 women), 47 part-time/adjunct (29 women). *Students:* 47 full-time (30 women), 35 part-time (19 women); includes 43 minority (6 Black or African American, non-Hispanic/Latino; 36 Hispanic/Latino; 1 Two or more races, non-Hispanic/Latino), 8 international. Average age 31. 59 applicants, 39% accepted, 16 enrolled. In 2016, 27 master's awarded. *Degree requirements:* For master's, thesis. *Entrance requirements:* For master's, GRE General Test, minimum undergraduate GPA of 3.0 (upper-level coursework), letter of intent, two letters of recommendation. Additional exam requirements/recommendations for international students: Required—TOEFL (minimum score 550 paper-based; 80 iBT). *Application deadline:* For fall admission, 2/1 for domestic and international students; for spring admission, 10/1 for domestic students, 9/1 for international students. Applications are processed on a rolling basis. Application fee: $30. Electronic applications accepted. *Expenses:* Tuition, state resident: full-time $8912; part-time $446 per credit hour. Tuition, nonresident: full-time $21,393; part-time $992 per credit hour. *Required fees:* $2185; $195 per semester. Tuition and fees vary according to program. *Financial support:* Institutionally sponsored loans and scholarships/grants available. Financial award application deadline: 3/1; financial award applicants required to submit FAFSA. *Unit head:* Dr. Heather Russell, Chair, 305-348-3369, Fax: 305-348-3878, E-mail: heather.russell@fiu.edu. *Application contact:* Nanett Rojas, Assistant Director, Graduate Admissions, 305-348-7464, Fax: 305-348-7441, E-mail: gradadm@fiu.edu.

**Florida State University,** The Graduate School, College of Arts and Sciences, Department of English, Tallahassee, FL 32312. Offers creative writing (MFA); English (PhD), including creative writing, literature, rhetoric and composition; literature (MA); rhetoric and composition (MA). *Program availability:* Part-time. *Faculty:* 47 full-time (24 women), 2 part-time/adjunct (1 woman). *Students:* 142 full-time (80 women), 31 part-time (23 women); includes 44 minority (17 Black or African American, non-Hispanic/Latino; 1 American Indian or Alaska Native, non-Hispanic/Latino; 12 Asian, non-Hispanic/Latino; 5 Hispanic/Latino; 9 Two or more races, non-Hispanic/Latino), 9 international. Average age 30. 307 applicants, 20% accepted, 38 enrolled. In 2016, 21 master's, 24 doctorates awarded. *Degree requirements:* For master's, one foreign language, 33 hours of coursework including capstone essay, thesis or portfolio (MA); 45 hours of coursework including 9-12 thesis hours (MFA); for doctorate, one foreign language, comprehensive exam, thesis/dissertation, 27 hours of coursework, 24 hours of dissertation work. *Entrance requirements:* For master's and doctorate, GRE General Test, sample of written work, 3 letters of recommendation, resume. Additional exam requirements/recommendations for international students: Required—TOEFL. *Application deadline:* For fall admission, 1/1 priority date for domestic and international students. Application fee: $30. Electronic applications accepted. *Expenses:* Tuition, state resident: full-time $7263; part-time $403.51 per credit hour. Tuition, nonresident: full-time $18,087; part-time $1004.85 per credit hour. *Required fees:* $1365; $75.81 per credit hour. $20 per semester. Tuition and fees vary according to campus/location. *Financial support:* In 2016–17, 132 students received support, including 5 fellowships with tuition reimbursements available, teaching assistantships with tuition reimbursements available (averaging $13,250 per year); career-related internships or fieldwork, Federal Work-Study, and institutionally sponsored loans also available. Financial award application deadline: 8/1; financial award applicants required to submit FAFSA. *Faculty research:* British and Irish literature, American literature, creative writing, rhetoric and composition, multiethnic transnational literature, history of text technologies. *Unit head:* Dr. Gary Taylor, Chair, 850-644-4230, Fax: 850-644-0811, E-mail: ewalker@fsu.edu. *Application contact:* Ginger Martin, Senior Graduate Academic Coordinator, 850-644-1081, Fax: 850-644-9656, E-mail: vmartin@fsu.edu. Website: http://english.fsu.edu/

**Fordham University,** Graduate School of Arts and Sciences, Department of English Language and Literature, New York, NY 10458. Offers MA, PhD. *Program availability:* Part-time, evening/weekend. *Faculty:* 37 full-time (23 women). *Students:* 71 full-time (45 women), 14 part-time (7 women); includes 4 minority (2 Black or African American, non-Hispanic/Latino; 2 Asian, non-Hispanic/Latino), 7 international. Average age 31. 165 applicants, 38% accepted, 23 enrolled. In 2016, 28 master's, 10 doctorates awarded. Terminal master's awarded for partial completion of doctoral program. *Degree requirements:* For master's, one foreign language, comprehensive exam, thesis optional; for doctorate, 2 foreign languages, comprehensive exam, thesis/dissertation. *Entrance requirements:* For master's, GRE General Test; for doctorate, GRE General Test, GRE Subject Test. Additional exam requirements/recommendations for international students: Required—TOEFL (minimum score 650 paper-based). *Application deadline:* For fall admission, 1/4 priority date for domestic students; for spring admission, 11/1 for domestic students. Application fee: $70. Electronic applications accepted. *Financial support:* In 2016–17, 63 students received support, including 1 fellowship with tuition reimbursement available (averaging $25,390 per year), 49 teaching assistantships with tuition reimbursements available (averaging $19,311 per year); institutionally sponsored loans, tuition waivers (full and partial), and unspecified assistantships also available. Financial award application deadline: 1/4; financial award applicants required to submit FAFSA. *Faculty research:* Nineteenth century British and American literature, Shakespeare and early modern drama, Aesthetic Theory, Old Norse, poetics of race and gender, Anglo-Norman. *Unit head:* Dr. Julie Chun Kim, Director, Graduate Studies, 718-817-4017, Fax: 718-817-4013, E-mail: jukim@fordham.edu. *Application contact:* Bernadette Valentino-Morrison, Director of Graduate Admissions, 718-817-4419, Fax: 718-817-3566, E-mail: valentinomor@fordham.edu.

**Fort Hays State University,** Graduate School, College of Arts and Sciences, Department of English, Hays, KS 67601-4099. Offers MA. *Degree requirements:* For master's, comprehensive exam, thesis or alternative. *Entrance requirements:* Additional exam requirements/recommendations for international students: Required—TOEFL (minimum score 550 paper-based). Electronic applications accepted. *Faculty research:* Eisenhower and Hansen papers, Celtic literature and culture, poetry of Robert Frost.

**Gannon University,** School of Graduate Studies, College of Humanities, Education, and Social Sciences, School of Humanities, Program in English, Erie, PA 16541-0001. Offers MA. *Program availability:* Part-time, evening/weekend. *Students:* 7 full-time (4 women), 6 part-time (4 women), 3 international. Average age 30. 20 applicants, 50% accepted, 3 enrolled. In 2016, 5 master's awarded. *Degree requirements:* For master's, thesis. *Entrance requirements:* For master's, undergraduate degree in English.

Additional exam requirements/recommendations for international students: Required—TOEFL (minimum score 79 iBT). *Application deadline:* Applications are processed on a rolling basis. *Application fee:* $25. Electronic applications accepted. Application fee is waived when completed online. *Expenses: Tuition:* Full-time $17,370. *Required fees:* $550. Tuition and fees vary according to course load and program. *Financial support:* Teaching assistantships, Federal Work-Study, and unspecified assistantships available. Financial award application deadline: 7/1; financial award applicants required to submit FAFSA. *Unit head:* Dr. Laura Rutland, Director, 814-871-7532, E-mail: rutland001@gannon.edu. *Application contact:* Bridget Philip, Director of Graduate Admissions, 814-871-7412, E-mail: graduate@gannon.edu.

**Gardner-Webb University,** Graduate School, Department of English, Boiling Springs, NC 28017. Offers English (MA); English education (MA). *Program availability:* Part-time, evening/weekend. *Faculty:* 4 full-time (all women). *Students:* 16 part-time (11 women); includes 1 minority (Black or African American, non-Hispanic/Latino). Average age 29. 27 applicants, 37% accepted, 6 enrolled. In 2016, 6 master's awarded. *Degree requirements:* For master's, comprehensive exam. *Entrance requirements:* For master's, GRE General Test, MAT, or NTE; PRAXIS, minimum GPA of 2.5. *Application deadline:* For fall admission, 8/1 priority date for domestic students. Applications are processed on a rolling basis. *Application fee:* $0. Electronic applications accepted. *Expenses:* Contact institution. *Financial support:* Unspecified assistantships available. *Unit head:* Dr. David Parker, Chair, 704-406-4413, E-mail: dparker@gardner-webb.edu. *Application contact:* Office of Graduate Admissions, 877-498-4723, Fax: 704-406-3895, E-mail: gradinfo@gardner-webb.edu.

**George Mason University,** College of Humanities and Social Sciences, Department of English, Fairfax, VA 22030. Offers creative writing (MFA), including fiction; English (MA, Certificate); linguistics (PhD). *Faculty:* 81 full-time (42 women), 40 part-time/adjunct (28 women). *Students:* 119 full-time (83 women), 111 part-time (87 women); includes 37 minority (9 Black or African American, non-Hispanic/Latino; 1 American Indian or Alaska Native, non-Hispanic/Latino; 7 Asian, non-Hispanic/Latino; 12 Hispanic/Latino; 1 Native Hawaiian or other Pacific Islander, non-Hispanic/Latino; 7 Two or more races, non-Hispanic/Latino), 17 international. Average age 32. 191 applicants, 69% accepted, 61 enrolled. In 2016, 72 master's, 2 doctorates, 17 other advanced degrees awarded. *Degree requirements:* For master's, thesis (for some programs), proficiency in a foreign language by course work or translation test; for doctorate, thesis/dissertation, 2 papers. *Entrance requirements:* For master's, official transcripts; expanded goals statement; writing sample; portfolio; 2 letters of recommendation; for doctorate, GRE, expanded goals statement; 3 letters of recommendation; writing sample; introductory course in linguistics; official transcripts; for Certificate, official transcripts; expanded goals statement; 3 letters of recommendation; writing sample; portfolio (for professional writing and rhetoric); resume (for folklore). Additional exam requirements/recommendations for international students: Required—TOEFL (minimum score 575 paper-based; 88 iBT), IELTS (minimum score 6.5), PTE (minimum score 59). *Application deadline:* For fall admission, 3/15 for domestic and international students. Application fee: $75 ($80 for international students). Electronic applications accepted. *Expenses:* Tuition, state resident: full-time $10,628; part-time $443 per credit. Tuition, nonresident: full-time $29,306; part-time $1221 per credit. *Required fees:* $3096; $129 per credit. Tuition and fees vary according to program. *Financial support:* In 2016–17, 77 students received support, including 1 fellowship (averaging $7,895 per year), 6 research assistantships with tuition reimbursements available (averaging $17,788 per year), 72 teaching assistantships with tuition reimbursements available (averaging $13,102 per year); career-related internships or fieldwork, Federal Work-Study, scholarships/grants, unspecified assistantships, and health care benefits (for full-time research or teaching assistantship recipients) also available. Support available to part-time students. Financial award application deadline: 3/1; financial award applicants required to submit FAFSA. *Faculty research:* Literature, professional writing and editing, writing of fiction or poetry. *Total annual research expenditures:* $123,731. *Unit head:* Debra Lattanzi-Shutika, Chair, 703-993-1170, Fax: 703-993-1161, E-mail: dshutika@gmu.edu. *Application contact:* Alex Walsh, Graduate Admissions Coordinator, 703-993-1185, Fax: 703-993-1161, E-mail: awalsh7@gmu.edu.
Website: http://english.gmu.edu

**Georgetown University,** Graduate School of Arts and Sciences, Department of English, Washington, DC 20057. Offers British and American literature (MA). *Degree requirements:* For master's, thesis or alternative, independent study, oral exam. *Entrance requirements:* For master's, GRE General Test. Additional exam requirements/recommendations for international students: Required—TOEFL.

**The George Washington University,** Columbian College of Arts and Sciences, Department of English, Washington, DC 20052. Offers MA, PhD. *Program availability:* Part-time, evening/weekend. *Faculty:* 35 full-time (18 women). *Students:* 19 full-time (12 women), 26 part-time (18 women); includes 5 minority (2 Black or African American, non-Hispanic/Latino; 1 Asian, non-Hispanic/Latino; 2 Hispanic/Latino), 6 international. Average age 31. 108 applicants, 50% accepted, 15 enrolled. In 2016, 7 master's, 2 doctorates awarded. Terminal master's awarded for partial completion of doctoral program. *Degree requirements:* For master's, one foreign language, comprehensive exam, thesis or alternative; for doctorate, 2 foreign languages, thesis/dissertation, general exam. *Entrance requirements:* For master's and doctorate, GRE General Test, GRE Subject Test, minimum GPA of 3.0, writing sample. Additional exam requirements/recommendations for international students: Required—TOEFL (minimum score 550 paper-based; 80 iBT). *Application deadline:* For fall admission, 1/15 priority date for domestic and international students; for spring admission, 10/1 priority date for domestic students, 9/1 priority date for international students. Applications are processed on a rolling basis. Application fee: $75. Electronic applications accepted. *Financial support:* In 2016–17, 18 students received support. Fellowships with tuition reimbursements available, teaching assistantships with tuition reimbursements available, and Federal Work-Study available. Financial award application deadline: 1/15. *Unit head:* Robert McRuer, Chair, 202-994-1461, E-mail: rmcruer@gwu.edu. *Application contact:* 202-994-6210, Fax: 202-994-6213, E-mail: askccas@gwu.edu.
Website: http://departments.columbian.gwu.edu/english/

**Georgia College & State University,** Graduate School, College of Arts and Sciences, Department of English and Rhetoric, Program in English, Milledgeville, GA 31061. Offers MA. *Program availability:* Part-time. *Students:* 3 full-time (all women), 6 part-time (4 women). Average age 29. 4 applicants, 100% accepted, 3 enrolled. In 2016, 4 master's awarded. *Degree requirements:* For master's, one foreign language, comprehensive exam, thesis optional. *Entrance requirements:* For master's, GRE (minimum score 156 on revised verbal section, 550 on previous version), undergraduate major in English, minimum GPA of 3.0, 2 letters of recommendation, writing samples. *Application deadline:* For fall admission, 7/1 priority date for domestic students, 4/1 priority date for international students; for spring admission, 11/1 priority date for domestic students, 9/1 priority date for international students; for summer admission, 4/1 priority date for domestic students. Applications are processed on a rolling basis. Application fee: $40. Electronic applications accepted. *Expenses:* $288 per credit hour in-state, $1,027 per credit hour out-of-state, $1,990 full-time annual fees. *Financial support:* In 2016–17, 4 students received support. Unspecified assistantships available. Support available to part-time students. Financial award applicants required to submit

FAFSA. *Unit head:* Dr. Jennifer Flaherty, MA Program Coordinator, 478-445-3180, Fax: 478-445-4581, E-mail: jennifer.flaherty@gcsu.edu. *Application contact:* Kate Marshall, Graduate Admissions Coordinator, 478-445-1184, Fax: 478-445-1336, E-mail: grad-admit@gcsu.edu.
Website: http://gcsu.edu/artsandsciences/english/english-ma

**Georgia Southern University,** Jack N. Averitt College of Graduate Studies, College of Liberal Arts and Social Sciences, Program in English, Statesboro, GA 30460. Offers MA. *Program availability:* Part-time. *Students:* Full-time (9 women), 6 part-time (4 women); includes 7 minority (5 Black or African American, non-Hispanic/Latino; 2 Two or more races, non-Hispanic/Latino). Average age 28. 13 applicants, 85% accepted, 6 enrolled. In 2016, 6 master's awarded. *Degree requirements:* For master's, one foreign language, thesis optional, terminal exams. *Entrance requirements:* For master's, GRE General Test, minimum GPA of 3.0, letters of reference. Additional exam requirements/recommendations for international students: Required—TOEFL (minimum score 550 paper-based; 80 iBT), IELTS (minimum score 6). *Application deadline:* For fall admission, 3/1 priority date for domestic and international students; for spring admission, 10/1 priority date for domestic students, 10/1 for international students. Applications are processed on a rolling basis. Application fee: $50. Electronic applications accepted. *Expenses:* Tuition, state resident: full-time $7236; part-time $277 per semester hour. Tuition, nonresident: full-time $27,118; part-time $1105 per semester hour. *Required fees:* $2092. *Financial support:* In 2016–17, 5 students received support, including 4 fellowships with full tuition reimbursements available (averaging $7,750 per year); career-related internships or fieldwork, Federal Work-Study, scholarships/grants, tuition waivers (full), and unspecified assistantships also available. Support available to part-time students. Financial award application deadline: 4/15; financial award applicants required to submit FAFSA. *Faculty research:* Irish literature, Gothic literature, modern British drama, American short story, children's literature. *Unit head:* Dr. Dustin Anderson, Graduate Program Director, 912-478-1354, E-mail: danderson@georgiasouthern.edu.
Website: http://class.georgiasouthern.edu/litphi/

**Georgia State University,** College of Arts and Sciences, Department of English, Atlanta, GA 30302-3083. Offers creative writing (MA, MFA, PhD), including creative writing (PhD), fiction (MA, MFA), poetry (MA, MFA); English (MA, PhD); literary studies (MA, PhD); rhetoric and composition (MA, PhD). *Program availability:* Part-time. *Faculty:* 47 full-time (24 women). *Students:* 123 full-time (73 women), 73 part-time (52 women); includes 28 minority (17 Black or African American, non-Hispanic/Latino; 5 Asian, non-Hispanic/Latino; 2 Hispanic/Latino; 4 Two or more races, non-Hispanic/Latino), 11 international. Average age 37. 164 applicants, 61% accepted, 38 enrolled. In 2016, 15 master's, 9 doctorates awarded. *Degree requirements:* For master's, one foreign language, thesis, 30 hours of coursework plus 6 hours of thesis credit; for doctorate, one foreign language, comprehensive exam, thesis/dissertation, second exam. *Entrance requirements:* For master's and doctorate, GRE. Additional exam requirements/recommendations for international students: Required—TOEFL (minimum score 550 paper-based; 80 iBT). *Application deadline:* For fall admission, 1/15 for domestic and international students. Application fee: $50. Electronic applications accepted. *Expenses:* Tuition, state resident: full-time $6876; part-time $382 per credit hour. Tuition, nonresident: full-time $22,374; part-time $1243 per credit hour. *Required fees:* $2128; $1064 per term. Part-time tuition and fees vary according to course load and program. *Financial support:* In 2016–17, research assistantships with full tuition reimbursements (averaging $6,000 per year), teaching assistantships with full tuition reimbursements (averaging $15,000 per year) were awarded; career-related internships or fieldwork, traineeships, and health care benefits also available. Financial award application deadline: 2/15. *Faculty research:* British and American literature and transnational literatures in English, literary theory and cultural studies, creative writing (fiction and poetry), rhetoric and composition, new media and digital humanities. *Unit head:* Dr. Lynnee Lewis Gaillet, Chair, 404-413-5842, Fax: 404-413-5830, E-mail: lgaillet@gsu.edu.
Website: http://www.english.gsu.edu

**Governors State University,** College of Arts and Sciences, Program in English, University Park, IL 60484. Offers MA. *Program availability:* Part-time. *Faculty:* 91 full-time (43 women), 125 part-time/adjunct (64 women). *Students:* 5 full-time (all women), 7 part-time (4 women); includes 2 minority (1 Black or African American, non-Hispanic/Latino; 1 Hispanic/Latino). Average age 32. 11 applicants, 73% accepted, 8 enrolled. In 2016, 5 master's awarded. *Entrance requirements:* Additional exam requirements/recommendations for international students: Required—TOEFL (minimum score 550 paper-based; 80 iBT), IELTS. *Application deadline:* For fall admission, 4/1 for domestic students. Application fee: $50. Electronic applications accepted. *Expenses:* $307 per credit hour; $38 per term or $76 per credit hour fees. *Financial support:* Application deadline: 5/1; applicants required to submit FAFSA. *Unit head:* Lori Montalbano, Interim Chair, Division of Humanities and Social Science, 708-235-2802, E-mail: lmontalbano@govst.edu. *Application contact:* Yakeea Daniels, Assistant Vice President for Enrollment Services/Director of Admission, 708-534-4510, E-mail: ydaniels@govst.edu.

**The Graduate Center, City University of New York,** Graduate Studies, Program in English, New York, NY 10016-4039. Offers PhD. *Degree requirements:* For doctorate, 2 foreign languages, thesis/dissertation. *Entrance requirements:* For doctorate, GRE General Test, GRE Subject Test, writing sample, curriculum vitae. Additional exam requirements/recommendations for international students: Required—TOEFL. Electronic applications accepted.

**Grambling State University,** School of Graduate Studies and Research, College of Education, Department of Educational Leadership, Grambling, LA 71245. Offers developmental education (MS, Ed D, PMC), including curriculum and instructional design (Ed D), English (MS), guidance and counseling (MS), higher education administration and management (Ed D), mathematics (MS), reading (MS), science (MS), student development and personnel services (Ed D); educational leadership (M Ed). *Program availability:* Part-time, evening/weekend. *Degree requirements:* For master's, comprehensive exam, thesis (for some programs); for doctorate, comprehensive exam, thesis/dissertation. *Entrance requirements:* For master's, GRE, minimum GPA of 2.5 on last degree; for doctorate, GRE (minimum score 1000, 500 on Verbal), master's degree, minimum GPA of 3.0 on last degree. Additional exam requirements/recommendations for international students: Required—TOEFL (minimum score 500 paper-based; 62 iBT). Electronic applications accepted.

**Grand Valley State University,** College of Liberal Arts and Sciences, English Department, Allendale, MI 49401-9403. Offers MA. *Program availability:* Part-time, evening/weekend. *Faculty:* 18 full-time (9 women), 1 (woman) part-time/adjunct. *Students:* 5 full-time (all women), 30 part-time (21 women); includes 3 minority (1 Black or African American, non-Hispanic/Latino; 1 Hispanic/Latino; 1 Two or more races, non-Hispanic/Latino), 3 international. Average age 33. 15 applicants, 80% accepted, 9 enrolled. In 2016, 5 master's awarded. *Degree requirements:* For master's, comprehensive exam (for some programs), thesis (for some programs). *Entrance requirements:* For master's, GRE General Test, brief statement of purpose, original essay (writing sample). Additional exam requirements/recommendations for international students: Required—TOEFL (minimum score 550 paper-based, 80 iBT),

IELTS (6.5), or Michigan English Language Assessment Battery (77). *Application deadline:* Applications are processed on a rolling basis. Application fee: $30. Electronic applications accepted. *Expenses:* $604 per credit hour. *Financial support:* In 2016–17, 7 students received support, including 7 research assistantships with full and partial tuition reimbursements available (averaging $8,000 per year); fellowships and unspecified assistantships also available. *Faculty research:* Literary history, philosophy and literature, feminist issues in literature. *Unit head:* Dr. Corinna McLeod, Chair, 616-331-8576, E-mail: mcleodc@gvsu.edu. *Application contact:* Dr. Jo Miller, Graduate Program Co-Director, 616-331-3552, Fax: 616-331-3430, E-mail: millerj@gvsu.edu.

**Hardin-Simmons University,** Graduate School, Cynthia Ann Parker College of Liberal Arts, Department of English, Abilene, TX 79698-0001. Offers MA. *Program availability:* Part-time. *Faculty:* 5 full-time (2 women). *Students:* 1 full-time (0 women), 4 part-time (3 women); includes 1 minority (Two or more races, non-Hispanic/Latino). Average age 24. In 2016, 2 master's awarded. *Degree requirements:* For master's, one foreign language, comprehensive exam, thesis or alternative. *Entrance requirements:* For master's, minimum undergraduate GPA of 3.0 in English, 2.7 overall; writing sample; letters of recommendation; interview. Additional exam requirements/recommendations for international students: Required—TOEFL (minimum score 550 paper-based; 75 iBT). *Application deadline:* For fall admission, 8/15 priority date for domestic students, 4/1 for international students; for spring admission, 1/5 priority date for domestic students, 9/1 for international students. Applications are processed on a rolling basis. Application fee: $50. Electronic applications accepted. *Expenses:* Tuition: Full-time $12,510; part-time $695 per credit hour. *Required fees:* $325; $110 per semester. *Financial support:* In 2016–17, 4 students received support, including 2 fellowships (averaging $2,200 per year); scholarships/grants also available. Support available to part-time students. Financial award application deadline: 6/30; financial award applicants required to submit FAFSA. *Faculty research:* Milton, Tennyson, American Romantic period, Derek Walcott, women's literature. *Unit head:* Dr. Traci Thompson, Program Director, 325-670-1305, Fax: 325-671-5764, E-mail: tthomp@hsutx.edu. *Application contact:* Dr. Nancy Kucinski, Dean of Graduate Studies, 325-670-1298, Fax: 325-670-1564, E-mail: gradoff@hsutx.edu.
Website: http://www.hsutx.edu/academics/cap/graduate/english

**Harvard University,** Extension School, Cambridge, MA 02138-3722. Offers applied sciences (CAS); biotechnology (ALM); educational technologies (ALM); educational technology (CET); English for graduate and professional studies (DGP); environmental management (ALM, CEM); information technology (ALM); journalism (ALM); liberal arts (ALM); management (ALM, CM); mathematics for teaching (ALM); museum studies (ALM); premedical studies (Diploma); publication and communication (CPC). *Program availability:* Part-time, evening/weekend. *Degree requirements:* For master's, thesis. *Entrance requirements:* For master's, 3 completed graduate courses with grade of B or higher. Additional exam requirements/recommendations for international students: Required—TOEFL (minimum score 600 paper-based), TWE (minimum score 5). *Expenses:* Contact institution.

**Harvard University,** Graduate School of Arts and Sciences, Department of English and American Literature and Language, Cambridge, MA 02138. Offers critical theory (PhD); eighteenth-century literature (PhD); literature: nineteenth-century to the present (PhD); medieval literature and language (PhD); modern British and American literature (PhD); Renaissance literature (PhD). Terminal master's awarded for partial completion of doctoral program. *Degree requirements:* For doctorate, 2 foreign languages, thesis/dissertation, oral exam. *Entrance requirements:* For doctorate, GRE General Test, GRE Subject Test, writing sample. Additional exam requirements/recommendations for international students: Required—TOEFL. *Faculty research:* Old and Middle English language and literature, drama, creative writing, transition to Romanticism, history and theory of criticism.

**Heritage University,** Graduate Programs in Education, Program in Professional Studies, Toppenish, WA 98948-9599. Offers bilingual education/ESL (M Ed); biology (M Ed); English and literature (M Ed); reading/literacy (M Ed); special education (M Ed). *Program availability:* Part-time, evening/weekend. *Degree requirements:* For master's, comprehensive exam (for some programs), thesis (for some programs).

**Hofstra University,** College of Liberal Arts and Sciences, Programs in Creative Writing and English Literature, Hempstead, NY 11549. Offers MFA. *Program availability:* Part-time. *Students:* 13 full-time (7 women), 11 part-time (8 women); includes 4 minority (2 Asian, non-Hispanic/Latino; 2 Hispanic/Latino), 1 international. Average age 31. 26 applicants, 81% accepted, 6 enrolled. In 2016, 16 master's awarded. *Degree requirements:* For master's, thesis optional, minimum GPA of 3.0. *Entrance requirements:* For master's, writing sample, essay, minimum GPA of 3.0 in literature courses. Additional exam requirements/recommendations for international students: Required—TOEFL (minimum score 550 paper-based; 80 iBT). *Application deadline:* Applications are processed on a rolling basis. Application fee: $75. Electronic applications accepted. *Expenses: Tuition:* Full-time $1240. *Required fees:* $970. Tuition and fees vary according to program. *Financial support:* In 2016–17, 13 students received support, including 12 fellowships with full and partial tuition reimbursements available (averaging $4,182 per year), 1 research assistantship with full and partial tuition reimbursement available (averaging $10,463 per year); career-related internships or fieldwork, Federal Work-Study, institutionally sponsored loans, scholarships/grants, tuition waivers (full and partial), and unspecified assistantships also available. Support available to part-time students. Financial award applicants required to submit FAFSA. *Faculty research:* English lyric poetry; Victorian poets and poetics; creative nonfiction; historical research and current politics through the lens of fiction; medieval and monastic studies. *Unit head:* Dr. Stephen Russell, Program Director, 516-463-6284, Fax: 516-463-6395, E-mail: stephen.russell@hofstra.edu. *Application contact:* Sunil Samuel, Assistant Vice President of Admissions, 516-463-4723, Fax: 516-463-4664, E-mail: graduateadmission@hofstra.edu.
Website: http://www.hofstra.edu/hclas

**Hollins University,** Graduate Programs, Program in Children's Literature, Roanoke, VA 24020. Offers children's book writing and illustrating (MFA); children's literature (MA, MFA). Program offered during summer only. *Program availability:* Part-time. *Faculty:* 2 full-time (both women), 8 part-time/adjunct (7 women). *Students:* 40 full-time (38 women), 6 part-time (5 women); includes 6 minority (1 Black or African American, non-Hispanic/Latino; 1 Asian, non-Hispanic/Latino; 3 Hispanic/Latino; 1 Two or more races, non-Hispanic/Latino). Average age 35. 24 applicants, 96% accepted, 10 enrolled. In 2016, 11 master's awarded. *Degree requirements:* For master's, one foreign language, comprehensive exam, thesis. *Entrance requirements:* For master's, transcripts, letters of recommendation, portfolio, personal statement of educational objectives. Additional exam requirements/recommendations for international students: Required—TOEFL (minimum score 550 paper-based; 79 iBT), IELTS (minimum score 6.5). *Application deadline:* For summer admission, 2/15 for domestic and international students. Application fee: $40. Electronic applications accepted. *Expenses:* Contact institution. *Financial support:* Fellowships, Federal Work-Study, and scholarships/grants available. Support available to part-time students. Financial award application deadline: 2/15; financial award applicants required to submit FAFSA. *Faculty research:* Fantasy, children's film, young adult fiction, gender studies, mythology and folk tales, children's poetry, picture books. *Unit head:* Amanda Cockrell, Director, 540-362-6024, Fax: 540-362-6642, E-mail: acockrell@hollins.edu. *Application contact:* Cathy S. Koon, Manager of Graduate Services, 540-362-6326, Fax: 540-362-6288, E-mail: ckoon@hollins.edu.

**Howard University,** Graduate School, Department of English, Washington, DC 20059-0002. Offers MA, PhD. *Program availability:* Part-time. *Degree requirements:* For master's, one foreign language, comprehensive exam, thesis; for doctorate, 2 foreign languages, comprehensive exam, thesis/dissertation, qualifying exam. *Entrance requirements:* For master's, GRE General Test, minimum GPA of 3.0; for doctorate, GRE General Test.

**Humboldt State University,** Academic Programs, College of Arts, Humanities, and Social Sciences, Department of English, Arcata, CA 95521-8299. Offers English (MA), including composition studies and pedagogy, literary and cultural studies, teaching English as a second language. *Degree requirements:* For master's, variable foreign language requirement, thesis or alternative, qualifying exam. *Entrance requirements:* For master's, GRE, minimum GPA of 3.0, 3 letters of recommendation, sample of writing. Additional exam requirements/recommendations for international students: Required—TOEFL (minimum score 500 paper-based). *Expenses:* Tuition, state resident: full-time $6738; part-time $1953 per semester. Tuition, nonresident: full-time $13,434; part-time $3813 per semester. *Required fees:* $1738; $653 per semester. Tuition and fees vary according to program. *Faculty research:* Teaching of writing, literature.

**Idaho State University,** Office of Graduate Studies, College of Arts and Letters, Department of English, Pocatello, ID 83209-8056. Offers English (MA, DA); English and the teaching of English (PhD); TESOL (Post-Master's Certificate). *Program availability:* Part-time. *Degree requirements:* For master's, one foreign language, comprehensive exam, thesis optional; for doctorate, one foreign language, comprehensive exam, thesis/dissertation, 2 papers, 2 teaching internships; for Post-Master's Certificate, 6 credits of elective linguistics, practicum. *Entrance requirements:* For master's, GRE General Test (minimum 50th percentile verbal), general literature exam, minimum GPA of 3.0, 3 letters of recommendation, 5-page writing sample; for doctorate, GRE General Test, GRE Subject Test, minimum GPA of 3.5, writing examples, 3 letters of recommendation, master's degree in English; for Post-Master's Certificate, GRE (minimum 35th percentile on verbal section), bachelor's degree, minimum undergraduate GPA of 3.0 in last 2 years, 3 letters of recommendation, knowledge of second language. Additional exam requirements/recommendations for international students: Required—TOEFL (minimum score 550 paper-based; 80 iBT). Electronic applications accepted. *Faculty research:* American literature, Renaissance literature, composition and rhetoric, Intermountain West studies, ethics.

**Illinois State University,** Graduate School, College of Arts and Sciences, Department of English, Program in English, Normal, IL 61790-2200. Offers English (MA, MS); English studies (PhD). *Degree requirements:* For doctorate, thesis/dissertation, 2 terms of residency. *Entrance requirements:* For master's, GRE General Test, minimum GPA of 3.0 in last 60 hours; for doctorate, GRE General Test.

**Indiana State University,** College of Graduate and Professional Studies, College of Arts and Sciences, Department of English, Terre Haute, IN 47809. Offers British and American literature (MA); English (MA); writing (MA). *Program availability:* Part-time, evening/weekend. *Degree requirements:* For master's, one foreign language, thesis optional. *Entrance requirements:* For master's, minimum GPA of 2.75 in all English courses above freshman level. Additional exam requirements/recommendations for international students: Required—TOEFL (minimum score 550 paper-based). Electronic applications accepted.

**Indiana University Bloomington,** University Graduate School, College of Arts and Sciences, Department of English, Bloomington, IN 47405. Offers creative writing (MA, MFA), including fiction (MFA), poetry (MFA); literature (PhD); rhetoric (PhD). *Faculty:* 51 full-time (23 women). *Students:* 132 full-time (87 women), 2 part-time (1 woman); includes 24 minority (4 Black or African American, non-Hispanic/Latino; 11 Asian, non-Hispanic/Latino; 3 Hispanic/Latino; 6 Two or more races, non-Hispanic/Latino), 8 international. Average age 30. 273 applicants, 18% accepted, 21 enrolled. In 2016, 16 master's, 16 doctorates awarded. *Degree requirements:* For master's, 30-36 credit hours plus one language proficiency (for MA); 60 credit hours plus thesis (for MFA); for doctorate, thesis/dissertation, qualifying exam; 90 credit hours; 2nd language proficiency or one language only if acquired at in-depth level. *Entrance requirements:* For master's, GRE General Test, GRE Subject Test (for all but MFA and MA in creative writing), minimum GPA of 3.5; for doctorate, GRE General Test, GRE Subject Test, minimum GPA of 3.7. Additional exam requirements/recommendations for international students: Required—TOEFL (minimum score 550 paper-based; 79 iBT), IELTS (minimum score 6.5). *Application deadline:* For fall admission, 1/2 priority date for domestic students, 12/1 for international students. Application fee: $55 ($65 for international students). Electronic applications accepted. *Financial support:* In 2016–17, 8 students received support, including 8 fellowships with full and partial tuition reimbursements available (averaging $18,000 per year), 98 teaching assistantships with full tuition reimbursements available (averaging $15,750 per year); health care benefits also available. Financial award application deadline: 2/1. *Unit head:* Dr. Patricia Ingham, Chair, 812-855-0521, Fax: 812-855-9535, E-mail: pingham@indiana.edu. *Application contact:* Rae Greiner, Director of Graduate Studies, 812-855-9536, Fax: 812-855-9535, E-mail: drgreine@indiana.edu.
Website: http://www.indiana.edu/~engweb/

**Indiana University of Pennsylvania,** School of Graduate Studies and Research, College of Humanities and Social Sciences, Department of English, PhD Program in Composition and Teaching English to Speakers of Other Languages, Indiana, PA 15705. Offers PhD. *Program availability:* Part-time. *Faculty:* 20 full-time (9 women). *Students:* 28 full-time (13 women), 78 part-time (52 women); includes 9 minority (3 Black or African American, non-Hispanic/Latino; 1 Asian, non-Hispanic/Latino; 1 Hispanic/Latino; 4 Two or more races, non-Hispanic/Latino), 41 international. Average age 37. 113 applicants, 42% accepted, 13 enrolled. In 2016, 14 doctorates awarded. *Degree requirements:* For doctorate, one foreign language, comprehensive exam, thesis/dissertation. *Entrance requirements:* For doctorate, 2 letters of recommendation. Additional exam requirements/recommendations for international students: Required—TOEFL (minimum score 600 paper-based). *Application deadline:* For fall admission, 2/1 priority date for domestic students; for summer admission, 11/1 priority date for domestic students. Applications are processed on a rolling basis. Application fee: $50. Electronic applications accepted. *Expenses:* Contact institution. *Financial support:* In 2016–17, 18 research assistantships with tuition reimbursements (averaging $6,398 per year), 5 teaching assistantships with partial tuition reimbursements (averaging $11,652 per year) were awarded; fellowships with full tuition reimbursements, career-related internships or fieldwork, Federal Work-Study, scholarships/grants, and unspecified assistantships also available. Support available to part-time students. Financial award application deadline: 4/15; financial award applicants required to submit FAFSA. *Unit head:* Dr. Sharon Deckert, Graduate Coordinator, 724-357-2261, E-mail: sharon.deckert@iup.edu.
Website: http://www.iup.edu/english/grad/composition-tesol-phd/default.aspx

**Indiana University of Pennsylvania,** School of Graduate Studies and Research, College of Humanities and Social Sciences, Department of English, Program in Composition and Literature, Indiana, PA 15705. Offers MA. *Faculty:* 20 full-time (9 women). *Students:* 11 full-time (5 women), 7 part-time (6 women), 5 international. Average age 27. 19 applicants, 84% accepted, 9 enrolled. In 2016, 4 master's awarded. *Application fee:* $50. *Expenses:* Tuition, state resident: full-time $8694; part-time $483 per credit. Tuition, nonresident: full-time $13,050; part-time $725 per credit. *Required fees:* $157 per credit. $50 per term. Tuition and fees vary according to course load and program. *Financial support:* In 2016–17, 4 research assistantships with tuition reimbursements (averaging $1,000 per year) were awarded. *Unit head:* Dr. Todd Thompson, Coordinator, 724-357-2267, E-mail: todd.thompson@iup.edu. Website: http://www.iup.edu/english/grad/composition-literature-ma/

**Indiana University of Pennsylvania,** School of Graduate Studies and Research, College of Humanities and Social Sciences, Department of English, Program in English: Generalist, Indiana, PA 15705. Offers MA. *Program availability:* Part-time. *Faculty:* 20 full-time (9 women). *Degree requirements:* For master's, thesis optional. *Entrance requirements:* Additional exam requirements/recommendations for international students: Required—TOEFL (minimum score 540 paper-based). *Application deadline:* Applications are processed on a rolling basis. Application fee: $50. Electronic applications accepted. *Expenses:* Tuition, state resident: full-time $8694; part-time $483 per credit. Tuition, nonresident: full-time $13,050; part-time $725 per credit. *Required fees:* $157 per credit. $50 per term. Tuition and fees vary according to course load and program. *Financial support:* Research assistantships with tuition reimbursements, career-related internships or fieldwork, Federal Work-Study, scholarships/grants, and unspecified assistantships available. Financial award application deadline: 4/15; financial award applicants required to submit FAFSA. *Unit head:* Dr. Todd Thompson, Coordinator, 724-357-4931, E-mail: todd.thompson@iup.edu. Website: http://www.iup.edu/grad/englishgeneralist/default.aspx

**Indiana University of Pennsylvania,** School of Graduate Studies and Research, College of Humanities and Social Sciences, Department of English, Program in English: Literature, Indiana, PA 15705. Offers MA. *Program availability:* Part-time. *Faculty:* 20 full-time (9 women). *Students:* 9 full-time (4 women), 7 part-time (5 women); includes 1 minority (Two or more races, non-Hispanic/Latino), 6 international. Average age 28. 18 applicants, 61% accepted, 5 enrolled. In 2016, 10 master's awarded. *Degree requirements:* For master's, thesis optional. *Entrance requirements:* For master's, two letters of recommendation. Additional exam requirements/recommendations for international students: Required—TOEFL (minimum score 540 paper-based). *Application deadline:* Applications are processed on a rolling basis. Application fee: $50. Electronic applications accepted. *Expenses:* Tuition, state resident: full-time $8694; part-time $483 per credit. Tuition, nonresident: full-time $13,050; part-time $725 per credit. *Required fees:* $157 per credit. $50 per term. Tuition and fees vary according to course load and program. *Financial support:* Fellowships, research assistantships with tuition reimbursements, teaching assistantships with tuition reimbursements, Federal Work-Study, scholarships/grants, and unspecified assistantships available. Financial award application deadline: 4/15; financial award applicants required to submit FAFSA. *Unit head:* Dr. Todd Thompson, Coordinator, 724-357-4931, E-mail: todd.thompson@iup.edu. Website: http://www.iup.edu/grad/literature/default.aspx

**Indiana University of Pennsylvania,** School of Graduate Studies and Research, College of Humanities and Social Sciences, Department of English, Program in Literature and Criticism, Indiana, PA 15705. Offers PhD. *Program availability:* Part-time. *Faculty:* 20 full-time (9 women). *Students:* 25 full-time (16 women), 110 part-time (62 women); includes 16 minority (6 Black or African American, non-Hispanic/Latino; 2 Asian, non-Hispanic/Latino; 4 Hispanic/Latino; 4 Two or more races, non-Hispanic/Latino), 36 international. Average age 35. 75 applicants, 73% accepted, 17 enrolled. In 2016, 19 doctorates awarded. *Degree requirements:* For doctorate, one foreign language, comprehensive exam, thesis/dissertation. *Entrance requirements:* For doctorate, 2 letters of recommendation. Additional exam requirements/recommendations for international students: Required—TOEFL (minimum score 540 paper-based). *Application deadline:* Applications are processed on a rolling basis. Application fee: $50. Electronic applications accepted. *Expenses:* Tuition, state resident: full-time $8694; part-time $483 per credit. Tuition, nonresident: full-time $13,050; part-time $725 per credit. *Required fees:* $157 per credit. $50 per term. Tuition and fees vary according to course load and program. *Financial support:* In 2016–17, 2 fellowships with full tuition reimbursements (averaging $1,021 per year), 14 research assistantships with tuition reimbursements (averaging $6,733 per year), 5 teaching assistantships with partial tuition reimbursements (averaging $11,652 per year) were awarded; career-related internships or fieldwork, Federal Work-Study, scholarships/grants, and unspecified assistantships also available. Support available to part-time students. Financial award application deadline: 4/15; financial award applicants required to submit FAFSA. *Unit head:* Dr. David Downing, Graduate Coordinator, 724-357-3963, E-mail: david.downing@iup.edu. Website: http://www.iup.edu/english/grad/literature-criticism-phd/default.aspx

**Indiana University–Purdue University Fort Wayne,** College of Arts and Sciences, Department of English and Linguistics, Fort Wayne, IN 46805-1499. Offers English (MA, MAT); TENL (teaching English as a new language) (Certificate). *Program availability:* Part-time. *Degree requirements:* For master's, one foreign language, thesis (for some programs), teaching certificate (for MAT). *Entrance requirements:* For master's, GRE General Test, minimum GPA of 3.0, major or minor in English, 3 letters of recommendation; for Certificate, bachelor's degree with minimum GPA of 2.5. Additional exam requirements/recommendations for international students: Required—TOEFL (minimum score 600 paper-based; 79 iBT). *Faculty research:* Hebrew names and the vernacular Savior in Anglo-Saxon England.

**Indiana University–Purdue University Indianapolis,** School of Liberal Arts, Department of English, Indianapolis, IN 46202. Offers English (MA); teaching English to speakers of other languages (TESOL) (Certificate); teaching writing (Certificate). *Entrance requirements:* For master's, GRE. Additional exam requirements/recommendations for international students: Required—TOEFL.

**Indiana University South Bend,** College of Liberal Arts and Sciences, South Bend, IN 46634-7111. Offers advanced computer programming (Graduate Certificate); applied informatics (Graduate Certificate); applied mathematics and computer science (MS); behavior modification (Graduate Certificate); computer applications (Graduate Certificate); computer programming (Graduate Certificate); correctional management and supervision (Graduate Certificate); English (MA); health systems management (Graduate Certificate); international studies (Graduate Certificate); liberal studies (MLS); nonprofit management (Graduate Certificate); paralegal studies (Graduate Certificate); professional writing (Graduate Certificate); public affairs (MPA); public management (Graduate Certificate); social and cultural diversity (Graduate Certificate); strategic sustainability leadership (Graduate Certificate); technology for administration (Graduate Certificate). *Program availability:* Part-time, evening/weekend. *Faculty:* 79 full-time (33 women). *Students:* 31 full-time (11 women), 92 part-time (53 women); includes 28 minority (9 Black or African American, non-Hispanic/Latino; 8 Asian, non-Hispanic/Latino; 5 Hispanic/Latino; 6 Two or more races, non-Hispanic/Latino), 19 international. Average age 38. 51 applicants, 84% accepted, 31 enrolled. In 2016, 30 master's, 6 other advanced degrees awarded. *Degree requirements:* For master's, variable foreign language requirement, thesis (for some programs). *Entrance requirements:* For

master's, minimum GPA of 3.0. Additional exam requirements/recommendations for international students: Required—TOEFL (minimum score 550 paper-based; 80 iBT). *Application deadline:* For fall admission, 7/31 priority date for domestic students, 7/1 priority date for international students; for spring admission, 3/31 priority date for domestic students, 11/1 priority date for international students. Applications are processed on a rolling basis. Application fee: $40 ($60 for international students). *Expenses:* $276.98 per credit hour in-state; $652.54 per credit hour out-of-state. *Financial support:* In 2016–17, 5 teaching assistantships were awarded; Federal Work-Study also available. Support available to part-time students. Financial award application deadline: 3/10. *Faculty research:* Artificial intelligence, bioinformatics, English language and literature, creative writing, computer networks. *Total annual research expenditures:* $127,000. *Unit head:* Dr. Elizabeth E. Dunn, Dean, 574-520-4290, E-mail: elizdunn@iusb.edu. *Application contact:* Admissions Counselor, 574-520-4839, Fax: 574-520-4834, E-mail: graduate@iusb.edu. Website: https://www.iusb.edu/clas/

**Inter American University of Puerto Rico, Metropolitan Campus,** Graduate Programs, Program in English, San Juan, PR 00919-1293. Offers MA.

**Iona College,** School of Arts and Science, Department of English, New Rochelle, NY 10801-1890. Offers MA. *Program availability:* Part-time. *Faculty:* 4 full-time (all women). *Students:* 2 full-time (1 woman), 3 part-time (all women); includes 2 minority (both Hispanic/Latino). Average age 23. 3 applicants, 100% accepted, 1 enrolled. In 2016, 2 master's awarded. *Degree requirements:* For master's, one foreign language, thesis optional, foreign language competency for use in research. *Entrance requirements:* For master's, minimum GPA of 3.0. Additional exam requirements/recommendations for international students: Required—TOEFL (minimum score 550 paper-based; 80 iBT), IELTS (minimum score 6.5). *Application deadline:* For fall admission, 8/1 priority date for domestic students, 5/1 priority date for international students; for spring admission, 1/1 priority date for domestic students, 9/1 priority date for international students. Applications are processed on a rolling basis. Application fee: $50. Electronic applications accepted. *Expenses:* Tuition: Full-time $19,692; part-time $1094 per credit. *Required fees:* $245 per term. Tuition and fees vary according to program. *Financial support:* Scholarships/grants, tuition waivers (partial), and unspecified assistantships available. Support available to part-time students. Financial award application deadline: 4/15; financial award applicants required to submit FAFSA. *Faculty research:* Victorian fiction, women's studies, nineteenth-century American literature, Irish literature, Shakespeare. *Unit head:* Dean DeFino, PhD, Chair, 914-637-2160, E-mail: ddefino@iona.edu. *Application contact:* Katelyn Brunck, Graduate Admissions, 914-633-2420, Fax: 914-633-2451, E-mail: kbrunck@iona.edu. Website: http://www.iona.edu/Academics/School-of-Arts-Science/Departments/English/Graduate-Programs.aspx

**Iowa State University of Science and Technology,** Department of English, Ames, IA 50011. Offers creative writing (MFA); English (MA); rhetoric and professional communication (PhD). *Degree requirements:* For master's, thesis or alternative; for doctorate, thesis/dissertation. *Entrance requirements:* For master's, GRE General Test, sample of written work, resume, portfolio in creative writing; for doctorate, GRE General Test, sample of written work, resume. Additional exam requirements/recommendations for international students: Required—TOEFL (minimum score 600 paper-based; 100 iBT), IELTS (minimum score 7). *Application deadline:* For fall admission, 1/5 priority date for domestic and international students. Application fee: $60 ($90 for international students). Electronic applications accepted. *Faculty research:* Creative writing, literature, rhetoric, composition and professional communication, teaching English as a second language, applied linguistics. *Application contact:* Teresa Smiley, Application Contact, 515-294-2477, Fax: 515-294-6814, E-mail: englgrad@iastate.edu. Website: http://www.engl.iastate.edu/resources/graduate-studies/

**Jackson State University,** Graduate School, College of Liberal Arts, Department of English and Modern Foreign Languages, Jackson, MS 39217. Offers English (MA); teaching English (MAT). *Program availability:* Part-time, evening/weekend. *Faculty:* 8 full-time (7 women). *Students:* 4 full-time (3 women); includes 1 minority (Black or African American, non-Hispanic/Latino), 1 international. Average age 26. 12 applicants, 75% accepted, 6 enrolled. In 2016, 14 master's awarded. *Degree requirements:* For master's, comprehensive exam, thesis or alternative. *Entrance requirements:* For master's, GRE General Test. Additional exam requirements/recommendations for international students: Required—TOEFL (minimum score 520 paper-based; 67 iBT). *Application deadline:* For fall admission, 3/1 priority date for domestic students, 3/1 for international students; for spring admission, 10/1 for domestic and international students. Applications are processed on a rolling basis. Application fee: $25. Electronic applications accepted. *Expenses:* Contact institution. *Financial support:* Career-related internships or fieldwork, Federal Work-Study, scholarships/grants, and unspecified assistantships available. Support available to part-time students. Financial award application deadline: 3/1; financial award applicants required to submit FAFSA. *Unit head:* Dr. Preselfannie McDaniels, Chair, 601-978-6928, Fax: 601-974-2249, E-mail: preselfannie.w.mcdaniels@jsums.edu. *Application contact:* Dr. Preselfannie McDaniels, Chair, 601-978-6928, Fax: 601-974-2249, E-mail: preselfannie.w.mcdaniels@jsums.edu. Website: http://www.jsums.edu/english/

**Jacksonville State University,** College of Graduate Studies and Continuing Education, College of Arts and Sciences, Department of English, Jacksonville, AL 36265-1602. Offers MA. *Program availability:* Part-time, evening/weekend. *Faculty:* 5 full-time (4 women). *Students:* 1 (woman) full-time, 12 part-time (8 women); includes 2 minority (both Black or African American, non-Hispanic/Latino). Average age 28. 7 applicants, 86% accepted, 5 enrolled. In 2016, 2 master's awarded. *Degree requirements:* For master's, comprehensive exam, thesis (for some programs). *Entrance requirements:* For master's, GRE General Test or MAT. Additional exam requirements/recommendations for international students: Required—TOEFL (minimum score 500 paper-based; 61 iBT). *Application deadline:* Applications are processed on a rolling basis. Application fee: $35. Electronic applications accepted. *Financial support:* In 2016–17, 4 students received support. Available to part-time students. Application deadline: 4/1; applicants required to submit FAFSA. *Unit head:* Dr. Robert Felgar, Head, 256-782-5413, E-mail: bfelgar@jsu.edu. *Application contact:* Dr. Jean Pugliese, Associate Dean, 256-782-8278, Fax: 256-782-5321, E-mail: pugliese@jsu.edu.

**James Madison University,** The Graduate School, College of Arts and Letters, Program in English, Harrisonburg, VA 22802. Offers MA. *Program availability:* Part-time. *Faculty:* 23 full-time (15 women), 1 (woman) part-time/adjunct. *Students:* 11 full-time (9 women), 2 part-time (0 women); includes 1 minority (Two or more races, non-Hispanic/Latino). Average age 30. 9 applicants, 78% accepted, 2 enrolled. In 2016, 3 master's awarded. *Degree requirements:* For master's, one foreign language, thesis. *Application fee:* $55. Electronic applications accepted. *Financial support:* In 2016–17, 9 students received support, including 7 teaching assistantships with full tuition reimbursements available (averaging $9,284 per year); fellowships, Federal Work-Study, and 2 assistantships (averaging $7911) also available. Financial award application deadline: 3/1; financial award applicants required to submit FAFSA. *Unit head:* Dr. Dabney A. Bankert, Department Head, 540-568-6797, E-mail: bankerda@jmu.edu. *Application contact:* Lynette D. Michael, Director of Graduate Admissions, 540-568-6131 Ext. 6395,

## English

Fax: 540-568-7860, E-mail: michaeld@jmu.edu.
Website: http://www.jmu.edu/english

**John Carroll University,** Graduate Studies, Department of English, University Heights, OH 44118-4581. Offers MA. *Program availability:* Part-time, evening/weekend. *Degree requirements:* For master's, comprehensive exam, research essay or thesis. *Entrance requirements:* For master's, GRE General Test, GRE Subject Test, minimum GPA of 3.0, writing sample. Additional exam requirements/recommendations for international students: Required—TOEFL. *Application deadline:* For fall admission, 8/15 priority date for domestic students; for spring admission, 3/15 for domestic students. Applications are processed on a rolling basis. Application fee: $25 ($35 for international students). Electronic applications accepted. *Expenses: Tuition:* Full-time $10,425; part-time $695 per credit hour. One-time fee: $200 full-time. Tuition and fees vary according to course load, campus/location and program. *Financial support:* Teaching assistantships with full tuition reimbursements available. Financial award application deadline: 3/15; financial award applicants required to submit FAFSA. *Faculty research:* Post-colonial literature, African-American literature, Renaissance poetry, Anglo-Saxon literature, American literature. *Unit head:* Dr. Debra J. Rosenthal, Chair, 216-397-4746, Fax: 216-397-1723. *Application contact:* Dr. George Bilgere, Program Coordinator, 216-397-4746, E-mail: gbilgere@jcu.edu.

**Johns Hopkins University,** School of Education, Master's Programs in Education, Baltimore, MD 21218. Offers counseling (MS), including clinical mental health counseling, school counseling; education (MS), including educational studies, gifted education, reading, school administration and supervision, technology for educators; elementary education (MAT); health professions (M Ed); intelligence analysis (MS); organizational leadership (MS); secondary education (MAT), including biology, chemistry, earth/space science, English, physics, social studies; special education (MS), including early childhood special education, general special education studies, mild to moderate disabilities, severe disabilities. *Program availability:* Part-time, evening/weekend, 100% online, blended/hybrid learning. *Students:* 345 full-time (265 women), 1,601 part-time (1,245 women); includes 837 minority (392 Black or African American, non-Hispanic/Latino; 7 American Indian or Alaska Native, non-Hispanic/Latino; 141 Asian, non-Hispanic/Latino; 207 Hispanic/Latino; 7 Native Hawaiian or other Pacific Islander, non-Hispanic/Latino; 83 Two or more races, non-Hispanic/Latino), 55 international. Average age 27. 1,352 applicants, 76% accepted, 819 enrolled. In 2016, 642 master's awarded. *Degree requirements:* For master's, comprehensive exam (for some programs), portfolio, capstone project and/or internship; PRAXIS II (subject area assessments) for initial teacher preparation programs that lead to licensure. *Entrance requirements:* For master's, GRE (for full-time programs only); PRAXIS I/core or state-approved alternative (for initial teacher preparation programs that lead to licensure), minimum of bachelor's degree from regionally- or nationally-accredited institution; minimum GPA of 3.0 in all previous programs of study; official transcripts from all post-secondary institutions attended; essay; curriculum vitae/resume; letters of recommendation (3 for full-time programs, 2 for part-time programs); dispositions survey. Additional exam requirements/recommendations for international students: Required—TOEFL (minimum score 600 paper-based; 100 iBT), IELTS (minimum score 7). *Application deadline:* For fall admission, 4/1 priority date for domestic students, 4/1 for international students; for spring admission, 10/1 priority date for domestic students, 10/1 for international students; for summer admission, 2/1 priority date for domestic students, 2/1 for international students. Applications are processed on a rolling basis. Application fee: $80. Electronic applications accepted. *Expenses:* Contact institution. *Financial support:* Application deadline: 4/1; applicants required to submit FAFSA. *Unit head:* Dr. Christopher C. Morphew, Dean. *Application contact:* Elisabeth Woodward, Director of Admissions, 410-516-9796, Fax: 410-516-9817, E-mail: soe.info@jhu.edu. Website: http://education.jhu.edu

**Johns Hopkins University,** Zanvyl Krieger School of Arts and Sciences, Department of English, Baltimore, MD 21218. Offers English and American literature (PhD). *Degree requirements:* For doctorate, 2 foreign languages, comprehensive exam, thesis/dissertation, 10 seminars, 2 oral exams. *Entrance requirements:* Additional exam requirements/recommendations for international students: Required—TOEFL (minimum score 600 paper-based; 100 iBT), IELTS. Electronic applications accepted. *Faculty research:* Nineteenth-century British, eighteenth-century, Renaissance, American, and cultural studies.

**Kansas State University,** Graduate School, College of Arts and Sciences, Department of English, Manhattan, KS 66506. Offers English (MA); technical writing and professional communication (Graduate Certificate). *Program availability:* Part-time. *Faculty:* 39 full-time (24 women). *Students:* 42 full-time (26 women), 12 part-time (10 women); includes 7 minority (1 Asian, non-Hispanic/Latino; 5 Hispanic/Latino; 1 Two or more races, non-Hispanic/Latino), 1 international. Average age 26. 38 applicants, 76% accepted, 22 enrolled. In 2016, 24 master's awarded. *Degree requirements:* For master's, one foreign language, thesis optional. *Entrance requirements:* For master's, GRE, minimum B average in English. Additional exam requirements/recommendations for international students: Required—TOEFL. *Application deadline:* For fall admission, 2/1 priority date for domestic and international students; for spring admission, 8/1 priority date for domestic and international students. Applications are processed on a rolling basis. Application fee: $50 ($75 for international students). Electronic applications accepted. *Expenses:* Tuition, state resident: full-time $9670. Tuition, nonresident: full-time $21,828. *Required fees:* $862. *Financial support:* In 2016–17, 40 teaching assistantships with full tuition reimbursements (averaging $12,000 per year) were awarded; career-related internships or fieldwork, Federal Work-Study, institutionally sponsored loans, scholarships/grants, and tuition waivers (full) also available. Support available to part-time students. Financial award application deadline: 3/1; financial award applicants required to submit FAFSA. *Faculty research:* Cultural studies, children's literature, American literature, rhetorical and composition theory, British literature. *Unit head:* Karin Westman, Head, 785-532-2190, Fax: 785-532-2192, E-mail: westmank@ksu.edu. *Application contact:* Anne Longmuir, Director of Graduate Studies, 785-532-2169, Fax: 785-532-2192, E-mail: longmuir@ksu.edu. Website: http://www.k-state.edu/english/

**Kent State University,** College of Arts and Sciences, Department of English, Kent, OH 44242-0001. Offers creative writing (MFA); English (MA, PhD); English for teachers (MA); literature and writing (MA); rhetoric and composition (PhD); teaching English as a second language (MA). MFA program offered jointly with Cleveland State University, The University of Akron, and Youngstown State University. *Program availability:* Part-time. *Faculty:* 45 full-time (29 women). *Students:* 111 full-time (75 women), 19 part-time (13 women); includes 8 minority (3 Black or African American, non-Hispanic/Latino; 1 Asian, non-Hispanic/Latino; 2 Hispanic/Latino; 2 Two or more races, non-Hispanic/Latino), 27 international. Average age 30. 98 applicants, 61% accepted, 19 enrolled. In 2016, 30 master's, 8 doctorates awarded. *Degree requirements:* For master's, one foreign language, thesis (for some programs), final portfolio, final exam, or thesis (for MA in teaching English as a second language); for doctorate, one foreign language, comprehensive exam, thesis/dissertation. *Entrance requirements:* For master's and doctorate, GRE General Test, statement of purpose, 3 letters of recommendation, writing sample or undergraduate/graduate paper, transcripts. Additional exam requirements/recommendations for international students: Required—TOEFL (minimum

score of 600 paper-based, 100 iBT), IELTS (minimum score of 7.0), Michigan English Language Assessment Battery (minimum score of 85), or PTE (minimum score of 68). *Application deadline:* For fall admission, 1/15 for domestic and international students. Applications are processed on a rolling basis. Application fee: $45 ($70 for international students). Electronic applications accepted. *Expenses:* Tuition, state resident: full-time $10,864; part-time $495 per credit hour. Tuition, nonresident: full-time $18,380; part-time $837 per credit hour. *Financial support:* Fellowships with full tuition reimbursements, teaching assistantships with full tuition reimbursements, and unspecified assistantships available. Financial award application deadline: 1/15. *Unit head:* Dr. Robert Trogdon, Chair, 330-672-2676, E-mail: rtrogdon@kent.edu. *Application contact:* Kevin Floyd, Professor and Graduate Coordinator, 330-672-1708, E-mail: kfloyd@kent.edu. Website: http://www.kent.edu/english/

**Kutztown University of Pennsylvania,** College of Liberal Arts and Sciences, Program in English, Kutztown, PA 19530-0730. Offers MA. *Program availability:* Part-time, evening/weekend. *Faculty:* 5 full-time (3 women). *Students:* 6 full-time (4 women), 18 part-time (8 women); includes 2 minority (both Black or African American, non-Hispanic/Latino), 1 international. Average age 32. 10 applicants, 90% accepted, 4 enrolled. In 2016, 5 master's awarded. *Degree requirements:* For master's, comprehensive exam, thesis optional. *Entrance requirements:* For master's, brief statement of purpose, short writing example, 3 letters of recommendation. Additional exam requirements/recommendations for international students: Required—TOEFL (minimum score 550 paper-based, 79 iBT) or IELTS (minimum score 6.5). *Application deadline:* For fall admission, 8/1 for domestic and international students; for spring admission, 12/1 for domestic and international students. Application fee: $35. Electronic applications accepted. *Expenses:* Tuition, state resident: full-time $4347; part-time $483 per credit. Tuition, nonresident: full-time $6525; part-time $725 per credit. *Required fees:* $88 per credit. One-time fee: $50 full-time. *Financial support:* Career-related internships or fieldwork, Federal Work-Study, scholarships/grants, and unspecified assistantships available. Financial award application deadline: 3/1; financial award applicants required to submit FAFSA. *Faculty research:* Women science fiction writers, Joyce Cary, myth and symbol, folklore, Victorian revision modes. *Unit head:* Dr. Andrew Vogel, Chairperson, 610-683-4353, Fax: 610-683-4355, E-mail: vogel@kutztown.edu. *Application contact:* Dr. Anne DeLong, Graduate Program Director, 610-683-4344, E-mail: delong@kutztown.edu. Website: https://www.academics/graduate-programs/english.htm

**Lakehead University,** Graduate Studies, Faculty of Social Sciences and Humanities, Department of English, Thunder Bay, ON P7B 5E1, Canada. Offers English (MA); women's studies (MA). *Program availability:* Part-time, evening/weekend. *Degree requirements:* For master's, one foreign language, thesis optional. *Entrance requirements:* For master's, minimum B average. Additional exam requirements/recommendations for international students: Required—TOEFL. *Faculty research:* Rhetoric and literary studies, children's literature, nineteenth- and twentieth-century American literature, modern literature, women's studies.

**Lamar University,** College of Graduate Studies, College of Arts and Sciences, Department of English and Modern Languages, Beaumont, TX 77710. Offers English (MA); teaching Spanish (MA). *Program availability:* Part-time, evening/weekend. *Faculty:* 10 full-time (5 women). *Students:* 7 full-time (all women), 23 part-time (20 women); includes 9 minority (1 Black or African American, non-Hispanic/Latino; 8 Hispanic/Latino), 1 international. Average age 40. 5 applicants, 100% accepted, 2 enrolled. In 2016, 12 master's awarded. *Degree requirements:* For master's, one foreign language, thesis optional, practicum. *Entrance requirements:* For master's, GRE General Test, minimum GPA of 2.5 in last 60 hours of undergraduate course work. Additional exam requirements/recommendations for international students: Required—TOEFL (minimum score 550 paper-based; 79 iBT), IELTS (minimum score 6.5). *Application deadline:* For fall admission, 8/10 for domestic students, 7/1 for international students; for spring admission, 1/5 for domestic students, 12/1 for international students. Applications are processed on a rolling basis. Application fee: $25 ($50 for international students). Electronic applications accepted. *Expenses:* $8,134 in-state full-time, $5,574 in-state part-time; $15,604 out-of-state full-time, $10,554 out-of-state part-time per year. *Financial support:* Teaching assistantships, career-related internships or fieldwork, Federal Work-Study, and institutionally sponsored loans available. Support available to part-time students. Financial award application deadline: 4/1; financial award applicants required to submit FAFSA. *Faculty research:* British, Renaissance, nineteenth-century, and American literature; creative writing; modern literature; African-American literature. *Unit head:* Dr. Jim Sanderson, Chair, 409-880-8558, Fax: 409-880-8591. *Application contact:* Deidre Mayer, Interim Director, Admissions and Academic Services, 409-880-8888, Fax: 409-880-7419, E-mail: gradmissions@lamar.edu. Website: http://artssciences.lamar.edu/english-and-modern-languages

**La Salle University,** School of Arts and Sciences, Program in Education, Philadelphia, PA 19141-1199. Offers autism spectrum disorders (MA, Certificate); bilingual/bicultural studies (MA); classroom management (MA); dual early childhood and special education (MA); dual middle-level science and math and special education (MA); education (MA); English (MA); English as a second language (Certificate); history (MA); instructional coach (Certificate); instructional leadership (MA); reading specialist (MA, Certificate); secondary education (MA); special education (MA, Certificate). *Program availability:* Part-time, evening/weekend. *Faculty:* 5 full-time (4 women), 12 part-time/adjunct (8 women). *Students:* 10 full-time (all women), 98 part-time (74 women); includes 28 minority (13 Black or African American, non-Hispanic/Latino; 1 American Indian or Alaska Native, non-Hispanic/Latino; 1 Asian, non-Hispanic/Latino; 10 Hispanic/Latino; 3 Two or more races, non-Hispanic/Latino). Average age 34. 128 applicants, 84% accepted, 69 enrolled. In 2016, 53 master's awarded. *Degree requirements:* For master's, comprehensive exam. *Entrance requirements:* For master's, MAT or GRE, 2 letters of recommendation; for Certificate, GMAT or GRE, 2 letters of recommendation. Additional exam requirements/recommendations for international students: Required—TOEFL. *Application deadline:* For fall admission, 8/15 priority date for domestic students, 7/15 for international students; for spring admission, 12/15 priority date for domestic students, 11/15 for international students; for summer admission, 4/15 priority date for domestic students, 3/15 for international students. Applications are processed on a rolling basis. Application fee: $35. Electronic applications accepted. Application fee is waived when completed online. *Expenses:* Contact institution. *Financial support:* In 2016–17, 27 students received support. Scholarships/grants available. Support available to part-time students. Financial award application deadline: 8/31; financial award applicants required to submit FAFSA. *Unit head:* Dr. Greer Richardson, Director, 215-951-1806, Fax: 215-951-1843, E-mail: graded@lasalle.edu. *Application contact:* Elizabeth Heenan, Director, Graduate and Adult Enrollment, 215-951-1100, Fax: 215-951-1462, E-mail: heenan@lasalle.edu. Website: http://www.lasalle.edu/grad-education-programs/

**La Sierra University,** College of Arts and Sciences, Department of English and Communication, Riverside, CA 92515. Offers communication (MA), including public relations/advertising, theory emphasis; English (MA), including literary emphasis, writing emphasis. *Program availability:* Part-time. *Degree requirements:* For master's, one foreign language. *Entrance requirements:* For master's, GRE General Test.

**Lee University,** Program in Education, Cleveland, TN 37320-3450. Offers art (MAT); curriculum and instruction (M Ed, Ed S); early childhood (MAT); educational leadership (M Ed, Ed S); elementary education (MAT); English and math (MAT); English and science (MAT); English and social studies (MAT); higher education administration (MS); history (MAT); history and economics (MAT); math and science (MAT); math and social studies (MAT); middle grades (MAT); science and social studies (MASW); secondary education (MAT); Spanish (MAT); special education (M Ed, MAT); TESOL (MAT). *Accreditation:* NCATE. *Program availability:* Part-time. *Faculty:* 13 full-time (6 women), 9 part-time/adjunct (4 women). *Students:* 35 full-time (27 women), 50 part-time (32 women); includes 12 minority (5 Black or African American, non-Hispanic/Latino; 5 Hispanic/Latino; 2 Two or more races, non-Hispanic/Latino), 4 international. Average age 30. 43 applicants, 79% accepted, 28 enrolled. In 2016, 42 master's, 6 other advanced degrees awarded. *Degree requirements:* For master's, variable foreign language requirement, thesis optional, internship. *Entrance requirements:* For master's, MAT or GRE General Test, minimum undergraduate GPA of 2.75, 3 letters of recommendation, interview, writing sample, official transcripts, background check; for Ed S, minimum undergraduate and master's GPA of 2.75, official transcripts for undergraduate and master's degrees. Additional exam requirements/recommendations for international students: Required—TOEFL (minimum score 61 iBT). *Application deadline:* For fall admission, 6/1 priority date for domestic and international students; for spring admission, 11/1 priority date for domestic and international students; for summer admission, 4/1 priority date for domestic and international students. Applications are processed on a rolling basis. Application fee: $25. Electronic applications accepted. *Expenses: Tuition:* Full-time $11,367; part-time $632 per credit hour. *Required fees:* $35 per term. One-time fee: $25. Tuition and fees vary according to program. *Financial support:* In 2016–17, 42 students received support. Career-related internships or fieldwork, Federal Work-Study, institutionally sponsored loans, scholarships/grants, and unspecified assistantships available. Financial award application deadline: 3/1; financial award applicants required to submit FAFSA. *Unit head:* Dr. William Kamm, Director, 423-614-8544, E-mail: wkamm@leeuniversity.edu. *Application contact:* Crystal Keeter, Graduate Education Secretary, 423-614-8544, E-mail: ckeeter@leeuniversity.edu. Website: http://www.leeuniversity.edu/academics/graduate/education

**Lehigh University,** College of Arts and Sciences, Department of English, Bethlehem, PA 18015. Offers MA, PhD. *Program availability:* Part-time. *Faculty:* 20 full-time (10 women). *Students:* 30 full-time (19 women), 2 part-time (both women); includes 2 minority (1 Black or African American, non-Hispanic/Latino; 1 Hispanic/Latino), 1 international. Average age 29. 38 applicants, 34% accepted, 7 enrolled. In 2016, 5 master's, 6 doctorates awarded. Terminal master's awarded for partial completion of doctoral program. *Degree requirements:* For master's, thesis optional; for doctorate, one foreign language, comprehensive exam, thesis/dissertation. *Entrance requirements:* For master's, GRE General Test, minimum GPA of 3.0 in undergraduate English courses; for doctorate, GRE General Test, minimum GPA of 3.5 in MA coursework. Additional exam requirements/recommendations for international students: Required—TOEFL (minimum score 620 paper-based; 96 iBT). *Application deadline:* For fall admission, 1/1 priority date for domestic and international students. Applications are processed on a rolling basis. Application fee: $75. Electronic applications accepted. *Expenses:* $1,420 per credit. *Financial support:* In 2016–17, 33 students received support, including 4 fellowships with full tuition reimbursements available (averaging $26,650 per year), 25 teaching assistantships with full tuition reimbursements available (averaging $21,440 per year); scholarships/grants and tuition waivers (full and partial) also available. Support available to part-time students. Financial award application deadline: 1/1. *Faculty research:* British and American literature, literature and social justice, transatlantic study, rhetoric and composition. *Unit head:* Dr. Dawn Keetley, Chairperson, 610-758-3311, Fax: 610-758-6616, E-mail: dek7@lehigh.edu. *Application contact:* Dr. Jenna Lay, Director of Graduate Studies, 610-758-3308, Fax: 610-758-6616, E-mail: jdl210@lehigh.edu. Website: http://cas.lehigh.edu/casweb/English

**Lehman College of the City University of New York,** School of Arts and Humanities, Department of English, Bronx, NY 10468-1589. Offers MA. *Degree requirements:* For master's, thesis. *Entrance requirements:* For master's, GRE, 18 upper-level credits in U. S. or English literature.

**Liberty University,** College of Arts and Sciences, Lynchburg, VA 24515. Offers English (MA); history (MA); professional writing (MA). *Accreditation:* AACN. *Program availability:* Part-time, online learning. *Students:* 59 full-time (28 women), 58 part-time (26 women); includes 9 minority (2 Black or African American, non-Hispanic/Latino; 1 American Indian or Alaska Native, non-Hispanic/Latino; 1 Asian, non-Hispanic/Latino; 2 Hispanic/Latino; 3 Two or more races, non-Hispanic/Latino), 1 international. Average age 33. 206 applicants, 35% accepted, 52 enrolled. In 2016, 36 master's awarded. *Degree requirements:* For master's, comprehensive exam (for some programs), thesis (for some programs). *Entrance requirements:* For master's, GRE, minimum undergraduate GPA of 3.0, letters of recommendation, statement of purpose. Additional exam requirements/recommendations for international students: Required—TOEFL (minimum score 600 paper-based; 100 iBT). *Application deadline:* For fall admission, 6/1 for domestic students; for spring admission, 11/1 for domestic students. Applications are processed on a rolling basis. Application fee: $50. Electronic applications accepted. *Financial support:* Teaching assistantships with tuition reimbursements and Federal Work-Study available. *Faculty research:* God concept and adult attachment, building marital strength, image of God and gender, breastfeeding behavior among adolescent mothers, osteoporosis. *Unit head:* Dr. Roger Schultz, Dean, 434-592-4031, Fax: 434-522-0430, E-mail: rschultz@liberty.edu. *Application contact:* Dr. Terry Elam, Director of Graduate Admissions, 434-592-3966, Fax: 434-522-0430, E-mail: gradadmissions@liberty.edu.

**Lipscomb University,** College of Education, Nashville, TN 37204-3951. Offers applied behavior analysis (MS, Certificate); educational leadership (M Ed, Ed S); English language learning (M Ed, Ed S); instructional coaching (M Ed, Certificate, Ed S); instructional practice (M Ed); learning organizations and strategic change (Ed D); literacy coaching (Certificate); reading specialty (M Ed, Ed S); special education (M Ed); teaching, learning, and leading (M Ed); technology integration (M Ed, Ed S); technology integration specialist (Certificate). *Accreditation:* NCATE. *Program availability:* Part-time, evening/weekend, 100% online. *Faculty:* 21 full-time (15 women), 38 part-time/adjunct (26 women). *Students:* 111 full-time (80 women), 345 part-time (292 women); includes 104 minority (70 Black or African American, non-Hispanic/Latino; 1 American Indian or Alaska Native, non-Hispanic/Latino; 3 Asian, non-Hispanic/Latino; 20 Hispanic/Latino; 10 Two or more races, non-Hispanic/Latino), 1 international. Average age 33. In 2016, 201 master's, 36 doctorates, 86 other advanced degrees awarded. *Degree requirements:* For master's, comprehensive exam, portfolio, research project and presentation; for doctorate, practical capstone project in experiential setting. *Entrance requirements:* For master's, MAT (minimum score 31) or GRE General Test (minimum score 294), 2 reference letters, goals statement, writing sample, interview; for doctorate, MAT or GRE General Test, 3 reference letters, artifact of demonstrated academic excellence, written personal statements, interview. Additional exam requirements/recommendations for international students: Required—TOEFL (minimum score 570 paper-based; 80 iBT). *Application deadline:* For fall admission, 8/29 priority date for domestic students; for spring admission, 1/15 priority date for domestic students. Applications are processed on a rolling basis. Application fee: $50 ($75 for international

students). Electronic applications accepted. *Expenses:* $934 per hour; $570 per hour (Teach for America). *Financial support:* Scholarships/grants, unspecified assistantships, and partnerships with local school districts available. Financial award applicants required to submit FAFSA. *Faculty research:* Facilitative learning styles, leadership, student assessment, interactive multimedia inclusion, learning organizations and strategic change. *Unit head:* Dr. Deborah Boyd, Director of Graduate Studies, 615-966-6263, E-mail: deborah.boyd@lipscomb.edu. *Application contact:* Amanda Logsdon, Director of Enrollment and Outreach, 615-966-7199, E-mail: amanda.logsdon@lipscomb.edu. Website: http://www.lipscomb.edu/education/graduate-programs

**Long Island University–LIU Brooklyn,** Richard L. Conolly College of Liberal Arts and Sciences, Brooklyn, NY 11201-8423. Offers biology (MS); chemistry (MS); clinical psychology (PhD); communication sciences and disorders (MS); creative writing (MFA); English (MA); media arts (MA, MFA); political science (MA); psychology (MA); social science (MS); sociology (MA); speech-language pathology (MS); United Nations (Advanced Certificate); urban studies (MA); writing and production for television (MFA). *Program availability:* Part-time, evening/weekend. *Faculty:* 90 full-time (35 women), 125 part-time/adjunct (67 women). *Students:* 355 full-time (276 women), 220 part-time (161 women); includes 245 minority (119 Black or African American, non-Hispanic/Latino; 32 Asian, non-Hispanic/Latino; 80 Hispanic/Latino; 1 Native Hawaiian or other Pacific Islander, non-Hispanic/Latino; 13 Two or more races, non-Hispanic/Latino), 85 international. 792 applicants, 41% accepted, 141 enrolled. In 2016, 154 master's, 18 doctorates, 4 other advanced degrees awarded. *Degree requirements:* For master's, comprehensive exam (for some programs), thesis (for some programs); for doctorate, comprehensive exam (for some programs), thesis/dissertation (for some programs). *Entrance requirements:* For master's and doctorate, GRE. Additional exam requirements/recommendations for international students: Recommended—TOEFL (minimum score 550 paper-based; 79 iBT). *Application deadline:* Applications are processed on a rolling basis. Application fee: $50. Electronic applications accepted. *Expenses: Tuition:* Full-time $28,272; part-time $1178 per credit. *Required fees:* $451 per term. Tuition and fees vary according to degree level, program and student level. *Financial support:* In 2016–17, 120 fellowships with full and partial tuition reimbursements (averaging $915 per year), 5 research assistantships with full and partial tuition reimbursements (averaging $2,300 per year), 136 teaching assistantships with full and partial tuition reimbursements (averaging $2,300 per year) were awarded; career-related internships or fieldwork, Federal Work-Study, institutionally sponsored loans, scholarships/grants, tuition waivers (full and partial), and unspecified assistantships also available. Support available to part-time students. Financial award application deadline: 2/15; financial award applicants required to submit FAFSA. *Faculty research:* Nanocrystal polymerization of cellulose using electron microscopy. *Unit head:* Dr. Kevin Lauth, Acting Dean, 718-488-1347, E-mail: kevin.lauth@liu.edu. *Application contact:* Gabrielle Gannon, Director of Graduate Admissions, 718-488-1011, Fax: 718-780-6110, E-mail: bkln-admissions@liu.edu.

**Long Island University–LIU Post,** College of Liberal Arts and Sciences, Brookville, NY 11548-1300. Offers applied mathematics (MS); behavior analysis (MA); biology (MS); criminal justice (MS); earth science (MS); English (MA); environmental sustainability (MS); genetic counseling (MS); history (MA); interdisciplinary studies (MA, MS); mathematics for secondary school teachers (MS); mobile GIS application development (Advanced Certificate); political science (MA); psychology (MA). *Program availability:* Part-time, evening/weekend, blended/hybrid learning. *Faculty:* 68 full-time (30 women), 20 part-time/adjunct (13 women). *Students:* 155 full-time (117 women), 125 part-time (82 women); includes 65 minority (17 Black or African American, non-Hispanic/Latino; 14 Asian, non-Hispanic/Latino; 27 Hispanic/Latino; 7 Two or more races, non-Hispanic/Latino), 19 international. 485 applicants, 36% accepted, 77 enrolled. In 2016, 91 master's, 15 other advanced degrees awarded. *Degree requirements:* For master's, comprehensive exam (for some programs), thesis (for some programs). *Entrance requirements:* Additional exam requirements/recommendations for international students: Required—PTE, TOEFL (minimum score 550 paper-based, 75 iBT) or IELTS (6.5). *Application deadline:* Applications are processed on a rolling basis. Application fee: $50. Electronic applications accepted. *Expenses: Tuition:* Full-time $28,272; part-time $1178 per credit. *Required fees:* $451 per term. Tuition and fees vary according to degree level and program. *Financial support:* In 2016–17, 24 teaching assistantships with partial tuition reimbursements (averaging $410 per year) were awarded; fellowships, research assistantships, career-related internships or fieldwork, Federal Work-Study, institutionally sponsored loans, scholarships/grants, tuition waivers (partial), and unspecified assistantships also available. Support available to part-time students. Financial award application deadline: 2/15; financial award applicants required to submit FAFSA. *Faculty research:* Biology, criminal justice, environmental sustainability, mathematics, psychology. *Total annual research expenditures:* $218,000. *Unit head:* Dr. Jeffrey Belnap, Acting Dean, 516-299-2233, Fax: 516-299-4140, E-mail: jeffrey.belnap@liu.edu. *Application contact:* Carol Zerah, Director of Graduate Admissions, 516-299-2900, Fax: 516-299-2137, E-mail: post-enroll@liu.edu. Website: http://liu.edu/CWPost/Academics/Schools/CLAS

**Louisiana State University and Agricultural & Mechanical College,** Graduate School, College of Humanities and Social Sciences, Department of English, Baton Rouge, LA 70803. Offers creative writing (MFA); English (MA, PhD).

**Louisiana Tech University,** Graduate School, College of Liberal Arts, Department of English, Ruston, LA 71272. Offers English (MA); technical writing (Graduate Certificate). *Program availability:* Part-time. *Degree requirements:* For master's, thesis or alternative. *Entrance requirements:* For master's, GRE General Test. *Application deadline:* For fall admission, 7/29 for domestic students; for spring admission, 2/3 for domestic students. Applications are processed on a rolling basis. Application fee: $40. *Financial support:* Fellowships, research assistantships, teaching assistantships, and career-related internships or fieldwork available. Financial award application deadline: 2/1. *Unit head:* Dr. Susan Roach, Director, School of Literature and Language, 318-257-2718, Fax: 318-257-2719, E-mail: msroach@latech.edu. *Application contact:* Marilyn J. Robinson, Assistant to the Dean of the Graduate School, 318-257-2924, Fax: 318-257-4487. Website: http://liberalarts.latech.edu/literature_language/english/

**Loyola Marymount University,** College of Liberal Arts, Department of English, Program in English, Los Angeles, CA 90045-2659. Offers MA. *Students:* 15 full-time (10 women), 3 part-time (0 women); includes 3 minority (1 Hispanic/Latino; 2 Two or more races, non-Hispanic/Latino). Average age 28. 21 applicants, 81% accepted, 12 enrolled. In 2016, 14 master's awarded. *Degree requirements:* For master's, comprehensive exam. *Entrance requirements:* For master's, GRE, 2 letters of recommendation, 2-page statement of ambition, writing sample (10-15 pages). Additional exam requirements/recommendations for international students: Required—TOEFL (minimum score 600 paper-based; 100 iBT). *Application deadline:* For fall admission, 3/15 for domestic students. Applications are processed on a rolling basis. Application fee: $50. Electronic applications accepted. *Financial support:* In 2016–17, 17 students received support, including 2 research assistantships, 1 teaching assistantship; scholarships/grants and unspecified assistantships also available. Support available to part-time students. Financial award application deadline: 6/30; financial award applicants required to submit FAFSA. *Unit head:* Dr. Dermot Ryan, Director, 310-568-6191, E-mail:

dryan11@lmu.edu. *Application contact:* Chake H. Kouyoumjian, Associate Dean of Graduate Studies, 310-338-2721, E-mail: ckouyoum@lmu.edu. Website: http://bellarmine.lmu.edu/english/graduateprogram/

**Loyola University Chicago,** Graduate School, Department of English, Chicago, IL 60660. Offers MA, PhD. *Program availability:* Part-time, evening/weekend. *Faculty:* 25 full-time (10 women). *Students:* 38 full-time (24 women), 3 part-time (all women); includes 2 minority (both Hispanic/Latino). Average age 29. 67 applicants, 46% accepted, 16 enrolled. In 2016, 9 master's, 5 doctorates awarded. Terminal master's awarded for partial completion of doctoral program. *Degree requirements:* For master's, comprehensive exam, thesis or alternative; for doctorate, one foreign language, comprehensive exam, thesis/dissertation. *Entrance requirements:* For master's, GRE General Test; for doctorate, GRE General Test, GRE Subject Test. Additional exam requirements/recommendations for international students: Required—TOEFL, IELTS. *Application deadline:* For fall admission, 6/1 for domestic students. Applications are processed on a rolling basis. Application fee: $0. Electronic applications accepted. *Expenses:* Tuition: Full-time $18,594. *Required fees:* $848. Part-time tuition and fees vary according to course load, degree level and program. *Financial support:* In 2016–17, 26 students received support, including 5 fellowships with full tuition reimbursements available (averaging $16,000 per year), research assistantships with full tuition reimbursements available (averaging $10,000 per year), 21 teaching assistantships with full tuition reimbursements available (averaging $16,500 per year); Federal Work-Study, institutionally sponsored loans, tuition waivers (partial), and unspecified assistantships also available. Support available to part-time students. Financial award application deadline: 1/15; financial award applicants required to submit FAFSA. *Faculty research:* Medieval and Renaissance studies, Romantic period, Victorian literature, literary history and theory, American studies, modernism and postmodernism, Latino/a literature, post colonialism, transnationalism, textual studies, digital humanities. *Unit head:* Dr. James Knapp, Graduate Program Director, 773-508-2241, Fax: 773-508-8696, E-mail: jknapp3@luc.edu. Website: http://www.luc.edu/english/

**Manhattan College,** Graduate Programs, School of Education and Health, Program in Special Education, Riverdale, NY 10471. Offers adolescence education students with disabilities generalist extension in English or math or social studies - grades 7-12 (MS Ed); bilingual education (Advanced Certificate); dual childhood/students with disabilities - grades 1-6 (MS Ed); students with disabilities - grades 1-6 (MS Ed). *Program availability:* Part-time, evening/weekend. *Faculty:* 3 full-time (all women), 11 part-time/adjunct (7 women). *Students:* 62 full-time (59 women), 4 part-time (all women). Average age 24. 34 applicants, 79% accepted, 24 enrolled. In 2016, 32 master's awarded. *Degree requirements:* For master's, thesis, internship (if not certified). *Entrance requirements:* For master's, GRE, minimum GPA of 3.0. Additional exam requirements/recommendations for international students: Required—TOEFL (minimum score 550 paper-based; 80 iBT), IELTS (minimum score 6). *Application deadline:* For fall admission, 8/10 priority date for domestic students; for spring admission, 1/7 priority date for domestic students. Applications are processed on a rolling basis. Application fee: $75. Electronic applications accepted. Application fee is waived when completed online. *Expenses:* $900 per credit, $105 registration fee, $175 information service fee. *Financial support:* In 2016–17, 52 students received support. Federal Work-Study, scholarships/grants, and unspecified assistantships available. Financial award application deadline: 2/1; financial award applicants required to submit FAFSA. *Unit head:* Dr. Elizabeth Mary Kosky, Director of Childhood and Adolescent Special Education Programs, 718-862-7969, Fax: 718-862-7816, E-mail: elizabeth.kosky@manhattan.edu. *Application contact:* William Bisset, Information Contact, 718-862-8000, E-mail: william.bisset@manhattan.edu.

**Marquette University,** Graduate School, College of Arts and Sciences, Department of English, Milwaukee, WI 53201-1881. Offers American literature (PhD); British and American literature (MA); British literature (PhD). *Program availability:* Part-time. *Faculty:* 30 full-time (17 women), 14 part-time/adjunct (10 women). *Students:* 36 full-time (19 women), 6 part-time (4 women); includes 3 minority (1 Asian, non-Hispanic/Latino; 1 Hispanic/Latino; 1 Two or more races, non-Hispanic/Latino), 1 international. Average age 31. 41 applicants, 41% accepted, 15 enrolled. In 2016, 10 master's, 4 doctorates awarded. Terminal master's awarded for partial completion of doctoral program. *Degree requirements:* For master's, comprehensive exam, thesis or alternative; for doctorate, one foreign language, thesis/dissertation, qualifying exam. *Entrance requirements:* For master's and doctorate, GRE General Test, GRE Subject Test, official transcripts from all current and previous colleges/universities except Marquette, three letters of recommendation, statement of purpose, one or two writing samples. Additional exam requirements/recommendations for international students: Required—TOEFL. *Application deadline:* Applications are processed on a rolling basis. Application fee: $50. Electronic applications accepted. *Financial support:* Fellowships with partial tuition reimbursements, teaching assistantships with full tuition reimbursements, scholarships/grants, health care benefits, tuition waivers (full and partial), and unspecified assistantships available. Support available to part-time students. Financial award application deadline: 2/15. *Faculty research:* Discourse analysis, American literature, British literature, textual criticism, literary history. *Unit head:* Sarah Wadsworth, Chair. *Application contact:* Dr. Angela Sorby. Website: http://www.marquette.edu/english/graduate/index.shtml

**Marshall University,** Academic Affairs Division, College of Liberal Arts, Department of English, Huntington, WV 25755. Offers MA, Graduate Certificate. *Degree requirements:* For master's, one foreign language, thesis optional. *Entrance requirements:* For master's, GRE General Test.

**Mary Baldwin University,** Graduate Studies, Program in Shakespeare and Renaissance Literature in Performance, Staunton, VA 24401-3610. Offers acting (M Litt); directing (M Litt); Shakespeare and Renaissance literature in performance (MFA); teaching (M Litt). *Entrance requirements:* For master's, GRE (M Litt).

**Marygrove College,** Graduate Division, Program in English, Detroit, MI 48221-2599. Offers MA.

**Marymount University,** School of Arts and Sciences, Program in English and the Humanities, Arlington, VA 22207-4299. Offers English and humanities (MA); teaching English at the community college (Certificate). *Program availability:* Part-time, evening/weekend. *Faculty:* 5 full-time (2 women). *Students:* 1 (woman) full-time, 7 part-time (4 women); includes 2 minority (both Two or more races, non-Hispanic/Latino), 1 international. Average age 28. 4 applicants, 75% accepted, 2 enrolled. In 2016, 2 master's, 2 other advanced degrees awarded. *Degree requirements:* For master's, thesis, capstone (final project, practicum). *Entrance requirements:* For master's, 2 letters of recommendation, resume, minimum undergraduate GPA of 3.0 with major in English or other humanities discipline, writing samples of 8-10 pages. Additional exam requirements/recommendations for international students: Required—TOEFL (minimum score 600 paper-based; 96 iBT), IELTS (minimum score 6.5). *Application deadline:* Applications are processed on a rolling basis. Application fee: $40. Electronic applications accepted. *Expenses:* Tuition: Full-time $8460; part-time $940 per credit hour. *Required fees:* $10 per credit hour. One-time fee: $240 part-time. Tuition and fees vary according to program. *Financial support:* In 2016–17, 1 student received support, including 1 teaching assistantship with tuition reimbursement available; career-related internships or fieldwork, Federal Work-Study, scholarships/grants, and unspecified assistantships also available. Support available to part-time students. Financial award applicants required to submit FAFSA. *Unit head:* Dr. David Brown, Director, English and the Humanities, 703-284-5762, Fax: 703-284-3859, E-mail: david.brown@marymount.edu. *Application contact:* Francesca Reed, Director, Graduate Admissions, 703-284-5901, Fax: 703-527-3815, E-mail: grad.admissions@marymount.edu. Website: http://www.marymount.edu/Academics/School-of-Arts-Sciences/Graduate-Programs/English-Humanities-(M-A-)

**McGill University,** Faculty of Graduate and Postdoctoral Studies, Faculty of Arts, Department of English, Montréal, QC H3A 2T5, Canada. Offers MA, PhD. Electronic applications accepted.

**McMaster University,** School of Graduate Studies, Faculty of Humanities, Department of English and Cultural Studies, Hamilton, ON L8S 4M2, Canada. Offers cultural studies and critical theory (MA); English (MA, PhD). *Program availability:* Part-time. *Degree requirements:* For master's, one foreign language, thesis; for doctorate, one foreign language, comprehensive exam, thesis/dissertation. *Entrance requirements:* For master's, honors degree, minimum B+ average in at least 6 full courses of English beyond year 1; for doctorate, MA; minimum A- average in two of three courses. Additional exam requirements/recommendations for international students: Required—TOEFL (minimum score 580 paper-based). *Faculty research:* Literary theory, feminist theory, literature of migration, Bakhting globalization.

**McNeese State University,** Doré School of Graduate Studies, College of Liberal Arts, Department of English and Foreign Languages, Program in English, Lake Charles, LA 70609. Offers MA. *Program availability:* Evening/weekend. *Degree requirements:* For master's, one foreign language, thesis or alternative. *Entrance requirements:* For master's, GRE. *Faculty research:* Textual criticism, seventeenth century literature, American women writers, Romanticism and the origins of diplomacy.

**Memorial University of Newfoundland,** School of Graduate Studies, Department of English, St. John's, NL A1C 5S7, Canada. Offers MA, PhD. *Program availability:* Part-time. *Degree requirements:* For master's, thesis optional; for doctorate, one foreign language, comprehensive exam, thesis/dissertation, oral thesis defense, minimum 3 semesters of full-time study. *Entrance requirements:* For master's, honors degree. Electronic applications accepted. *Faculty research:* American, British, Canadian, and Anglo-Irish literature; Newfoundland literature.

**Mercy College,** School of Liberal Arts, Program in English Literature, Dobbs Ferry, NY 10522-1189. Offers MA. *Program availability:* Part-time, evening/weekend, 100% online, blended/hybrid learning. *Students:* 6 full-time (5 women), 50 part-time (41 women); includes 13 minority (7 Black or African American, non-Hispanic/Latino; 1 American Indian or Alaska Native, non-Hispanic/Latino; 1 Asian, non-Hispanic/Latino; 4 Hispanic/Latino). Average age 35. 29 applicants, 69% accepted, 12 enrolled. In 2016, 22 master's awarded. *Degree requirements:* For master's, comprehensive exam, thesis. *Entrance requirements:* For master's, essay, 2 letters of recommendation, undergraduate transcripts. Additional exam requirements/recommendations for international students: Required—TOEFL (minimum score 600 paper-based; 100 iBT), IELTS (minimum score 8). *Application deadline:* For fall admission, 8/1 for international students. Applications are processed on a rolling basis. Application fee: $40. Electronic applications accepted. *Expenses:* Tuition: Full-time $15,156; part-time $842 per credit hour. *Required fees:* $620; $155 per term. Tuition and fees vary according to course load and program. *Financial support:* Career-related internships or fieldwork, Federal Work-Study, scholarships/grants, and unspecified assistantships available. Support available to part-time students. Financial award applicants required to submit FAFSA. *Unit head:* Dean, School of Liberal Arts, 914-674-7593. *Application contact:* Allison Gurdineer, Senior Director of Admissions, 877-637-2946, Fax: 914-674-7382, E-mail: admissions@mercy.edu. Website: https://www.mercy.edu/degrees-programs/ma-english-literature

**Miami University,** College of Arts and Science, Department of English, Oxford, OH 45056. Offers MA, MAT, PhD. *Students:* 80 full-time (45 women), 45 part-time (36 women); includes 13 minority (5 Black or African American, non-Hispanic/Latino; 3 Hispanic/Latino; 5 Two or more races, non-Hispanic/Latino), 11 international. Average age 31. In 2016, 19 master's, 5 doctorates awarded. *Expenses:* Tuition, state resident: full-time $12,890; part-time $564 per credit hour. Tuition, nonresident: full-time $29,604; part-time $1260 per credit hour. *Required fees:* $638. Part-time tuition and fees vary according to course load and program. *Unit head:* Dr. LuMing Mao, Chair, 513-529-5221, Fax: 513-529-5221, E-mail: maolr@miamioh.edu. *Application contact:* Monica Baxter, Graduate Program Administrative Assistant, 513-529-7530, E-mail: baxterml@miamioh.edu. Website: http://www.MiamiOH.edu/english/

**Michigan State University,** The Graduate School, College of Arts and Letters, Department of English, East Lansing, MI 48824. Offers English (PhD); literature in English (MA). *Entrance requirements:* For master's, GRE General Test, minimum GPA of 3.25, 2 years of foreign language or American Sign Language study, 3 letters of recommendation; for doctorate, GRE General Test, master's degree in English, 2 years of foreign language study, 3 letters of recommendation. Additional exam requirements/recommendations for international students: Required—TOEFL. Electronic applications accepted.

**Middlebury College,** Middlebury Bread Loaf School of English, Middlebury, VT 05753. Offers M Litt, MA. Offered during summer only. *Program availability:* Part-time. *Entrance requirements:* For master's, 2 letters of recommendation; statement of purpose; official transcripts (both undergraduate and graduate); 3-to 10-page writing sample. Electronic applications accepted. *Expenses:* Contact institution.

**Middle Tennessee State University,** College of Graduate Studies, College of Liberal Arts, Department of English, Murfreesboro, TN 37132. Offers MA, PhD. *Program availability:* Part-time, evening/weekend, online learning. *Degree requirements:* For master's, one foreign language, comprehensive exam, thesis optional; for doctorate, one foreign language, comprehensive exam, thesis/dissertation. *Entrance requirements:* For master's and doctorate, GRE. Additional exam requirements/recommendations for international students: Required—TOEFL (minimum score 525 paper-based; 71 iBT) or IELTS (minimum score 6). Electronic applications accepted.

**Midwestern State University,** Billie Doris McAda Graduate School, Prothro-Yeager College of Humanities and Social Sciences, Department of English, Humanities, and Philosophy, Wichita Falls, TX 76308. Offers English (MA); philosophy (PhD). *Program availability:* Part-time, evening/weekend. *Degree requirements:* For master's, one foreign language, thesis optional. *Entrance requirements:* For master's, GRE General Test, MAT or GMAT. Additional exam requirements/recommendations for international students: Required—TOEFL (minimum score 550 paper-based). Electronic applications accepted. *Faculty research:* Mythology, Shakespeare, Oscar Hahn, origins of language, modern American literature.

**Millersville University of Pennsylvania,** College of Graduate Studies and Adult Learning, College of Arts, Humanities and Social Sciences, Department of English, Millersville, PA 17551-0302. Offers English (M Ed, MA); writing (Postbaccalaureate

Certificate). *Program availability:* Part-time, evening/weekend. *Faculty:* 17 full-time (10 women), 1 (woman) part-time/adjunct. *Students:* 7 full-time (5 women), 18 part-time (14 women); includes 6 minority (2 Black or African American, non-Hispanic/Latino; 4 Asian, non-Hispanic/Latino), 1 international. Average age 34. 7 applicants, 100% accepted, 5 enrolled. In 2016, 9 master's awarded. *Degree requirements:* For master's, one foreign language, thesis optional. *Entrance requirements:* For master's, GRE or MAT. Additional exam requirements/recommendations for international students: Required—TOEFL (minimum score 600 paper-based), IELTS (minimum score 6). *Application deadline:* Applications are processed on a rolling basis. Application fee: $40. Electronic applications accepted. *Expenses:* $483 per credit resident tuition; $725 per credit non-resident tuition. *Financial support:* In 2016–17, 3 students received support. Unspecified assistantships available. Financial award application deadline: 3/15; financial award applicants required to submit FAFSA. *Faculty research:* Film studies; critical theory; narrative studies; literacy narratives; multicultural issues surrounding literacy; African American literature and rhetorical traditions; writing pedagogy; public and civic discourse; civic engagement; academic, workplace, and community literacy; grounded theory; critical discourse analysis; rhetorical theory; composition theory; science writing; technical writing; environmental rhetoric; rhetoric of place; public sphere theory. *Unit head:* Dr. Jill R. Craven, Chair, 717-871-7385, Fax: 717-871-7933, E-mail: jill.craven@millersville.edu. *Application contact:* Dr. Victor S. DeSantis, Dean of College of Graduate Studies and Adult Learning/Associate Provost for Civic and Community Engagement, 717-871-7619, Fax: 717-871-7954, E-mail: victor.desantis@millersville.edu.
Website: http://www.millersville.edu/english/

**Mills College,** Graduate Studies, Department of English, Oakland, CA 94613-1000. Offers book art and creative writing (MFA); literature (MA); poetry (MFA); prose (MFA); Spanish creative writing (Certificate); translation (MFA). *Program availability:* Part-time. *Faculty:* 4 full-time (3 women), 4 part-time/adjunct (3 women). *Students:* 47 full-time (38 women), 2 part-time (both women); includes 28 minority (8 Black or African American, non-Hispanic/Latino; 3 Asian, non-Hispanic/Latino; 9 Hispanic/Latino; 8 Two or more races, non-Hispanic/Latino). Average age 32. 78 applicants, 95% accepted, 27 enrolled. In 2016, 29 master's awarded. *Degree requirements:* For master's, comprehensive exam, thesis. *Entrance requirements:* For master's, 15-20 page writing sample. Additional exam requirements/recommendations for international students: Required—TOEFL (minimum score 600 paper-based; 100 iBT), IELTS (minimum score 7). *Application deadline:* For fall admission, 12/15 priority date for domestic students, 12/15 for international students. Applications are processed on a rolling basis. Application fee: $50. Electronic applications accepted. *Expenses: Tuition:* Full-time $31,620. *Required fees:* $1118. Tuition and fees vary according to course load, degree level and program. *Financial support:* In 2016–17, 40 students received support, including 22 fellowships with partial tuition reimbursements available (averaging $9,099 per year), 18 teaching assistantships with tuition reimbursements available (averaging $4,798 per year); research assistantships and scholarships/grants also available. Support available to part-time students. Financial award application deadline: 2/1; financial award applicants required to submit FAFSA. *Faculty research:* Creative writing, African-American literature, Victorian women writers, theories of sexuality, Shakespeare. *Unit head:* Dr. Ajuan Mance, Chair of the English Department, 510-430-2218, E-mail: dcady@mills.edu. *Application contact:* Robynne Lofton, Director of Admissions, 510-430-3295, Fax: 510-430-2159, E-mail: grad-admission@mills.edu.
Website: http://www.mills.edu/english/

**Minnesota State University Mankato,** College of Graduate Studies and Research, College of Arts and Humanities, Department of English, Mankato, MN 56001. Offers communication and composition (MA); creative writing (MFA); English studies (MA); teaching English as a second language (MA, Certificate); technical communication (MA, Certificate). *Program availability:* Part-time. *Students:* 59 full-time (44 women), 106 part-time (67 women). *Degree requirements:* For master's, one foreign language, comprehensive exam, thesis or alternative. *Entrance requirements:* For master's, minimum GPA of 3.0 during previous 2 years, writing sample (MFA). Additional exam requirements/recommendations for international students: Required—TOEFL (minimum score 500 paper-based; 61 iBT). *Application deadline:* For fall admission, 7/1 for domestic students, 5/1 for international students. Applications are processed on a rolling basis. Application fee: $40. Electronic applications accepted. *Financial support:* Research assistantships with full tuition reimbursements, teaching assistantships with full tuition reimbursements, career-related internships or fieldwork, Federal Work-Study, and unspecified assistantships available. Financial award application deadline: 3/15; financial award applicants required to submit FAFSA. *Unit head:* Matthew Sewell, Chair, 507-389-2117, E-mail: matthew.sewell@mnsu.edu.
Website: http://english.mnsu.edu/

**Mississippi College,** Graduate School, College of Arts and Sciences, School of Humanities and Social Sciences, Department of English, Clinton, MS 39058. Offers M Ed, MA. *Program availability:* Part-time, evening/weekend. *Degree requirements:* For master's, one foreign language, comprehensive exam, thesis or alternative. *Entrance requirements:* For master's, GRE or NTE, minimum GPA of 2.5. Additional exam requirements/recommendations for international students: Recommended—TOEFL, IELTS. Electronic applications accepted.

**Mississippi State University,** College of Arts and Sciences, Department of English, Mississippi State, MS 39762. Offers MA. *Program availability:* Part-time. *Faculty:* 27 full-time (13 women). *Students:* 26 full-time (22 women), 2 part-time (1 woman); includes 5 minority (3 Black or African American, non-Hispanic/Latino; 1 Asian, non-Hispanic/Latino; 1 Hispanic/Latino), 1 international. Average age 26. 18 applicants, 83% accepted, 9 enrolled. In 2016, 9 master's awarded. *Degree requirements:* For master's, thesis optional, comprehensive oral or written exam. *Entrance requirements:* For master's, GRE General Test, minimum GPA of 2.75 on last two years of undergraduate courses. Additional exam requirements/recommendations for international students: Required—TOEFL (minimum score 625 paper-based; 106 iBT); Recommended—IELTS (minimum score 8). *Application deadline:* For fall admission, 7/1 for domestic students, 5/1 for international students; for spring admission, 11/1 for domestic students, 9/1 for international students. Applications are processed on a rolling basis. Application fee: $60. Electronic applications accepted. *Expenses:* Tuition, state resident: full-time $7670; part-time $852.50 per credit hour. Tuition, nonresident: full-time $20,790; part-time $2310.50 per credit hour. Part-time tuition and fees vary according to course load. *Financial support:* In 2016–17, 20 teaching assistantships with partial tuition reimbursements (averaging $9,278 per year) were awarded; Federal Work-Study, institutionally sponsored loans, scholarships/grants, and unspecified assistantships also available. Financial award application deadline: 4/1; financial award applicants required to submit FAFSA. *Faculty research:* Literary criticism, linguistics, textual editing, editing "Mississippi Quarterly", Southern literature. *Unit head:* Dr. Daniel Punday, Department Head, 662-325-3644, Fax: 662-325-3645, E-mail: dp1525@msstate.edu. *Application contact:* Lakan Drinker, Admissions and Enrollment Assistant, 662-325-8951, E-mail: ldrinker@grad.msstate.edu.
Website: http://www.english.msstate.edu

**Missouri State University,** Graduate College, College of Arts and Letters, Department of English, Springfield, MO 65897. Offers applied second language acquisition (MASLA); English (MA); English education (MS Ed); teaching English to speakers of other languages (Certificate); writing (MA). MASLA offered with the Department of Modern and Classical Languages. *Program availability:* Part-time, evening/weekend. *Faculty:* 25 full-time (18 women), 5 part-time/adjunct (2 women). *Students:* 47 full-time (34 women), 44 part-time (32 women); includes 4 minority (1 Asian, non-Hispanic/Latino; 3 Two or more races, non-Hispanic/Latino), 17 international. Average age 29. 79 applicants, 63% accepted, 27 enrolled. In 2016, 49 master's awarded. *Degree requirements:* For master's, one foreign language, comprehensive exam, thesis or alternative. *Entrance requirements:* For master's, GRE (for MA), 9-12 teacher certification (MS Ed); minimum GPA of 3.0 (MA); personal statement (200- to 250-word description of reasons and goals behind interest in English graduate studies); at least two letters of recommendation from individuals able to speak of the applicant's academic achievements and potential; writing sample. Additional exam requirements/recommendations for international students: Required—TOEFL (minimum score 550 paper-based; 79 iBT), IELTS (minimum score 6). *Application deadline:* For fall admission, 3/1 priority date for domestic students, 3/1 for international students; for spring admission, 10/1 priority date for domestic students, 10/1 for international students. Applications are processed on a rolling basis. Application fee: $35 ($50 for international students). Electronic applications accepted. *Expenses:* Tuition, state resident: full-time $5830. Tuition, nonresident: full-time $10,708. *Required fees:* $1130. Tuition and fees vary according to class time, course level, course load and program. *Financial support:* In 2016–17, 2 teaching assistantships with full tuition reimbursements (averaging $8,772 per year) were awarded; Federal Work-Study, institutionally sponsored loans, scholarships/grants, and unspecified assistantships also available. Financial award application deadline: 3/31; financial award applicants required to submit FAFSA. *Faculty research:* History of rhetoric, modern poetry, African-American literature, digital writing, teaching English to speakers of other languages. *Unit head:* Dr. W. D. Blackmon, Department Head, 417-836-5107, Fax: 417-836-6940, E-mail: english@missouristate.edu. *Application contact:* Michael Edwards, Coordinator of Graduate Admissions, 417-836-5330, Fax: 417-836-6200, E-mail: michaeledwards@missouristate.edu.
Website: http://english.missouristate.edu/

**Molloy College,** Graduate Education Program, Rockville Centre, NY 11571-5002. Offers adolescent education in biology (MS Ed); adolescent special education (Advanced Certificate); bilingual extension (Advanced Certificate); childhood education (MS Ed); childhood special education (Advanced Certificate); early childhood education (MS Ed); educational technology (MS Ed); English (MS Ed); mathematics (MS Ed); social studies (MS Ed); Spanish (MS Ed); special education on both childhood and adolescent levels (MS Ed); teaching English to speakers of other languages (TESOL) in grades Pre-K to 12 (MS Ed); TESOL (Advanced Certificate). *Accreditation:* NCATE. *Program availability:* Part-time, evening/weekend. *Faculty:* 17 full-time (16 women), 23 part-time/adjunct (19 women). *Students:* 95 full-time (75 women), 221 part-time (177 women); includes 59 minority (14 Black or African American, non-Hispanic/Latino; 6 Asian, non-Hispanic/Latino; 38 Hispanic/Latino; 1 Two or more races, non-Hispanic/Latino), 1 international. Average age 42. 214 applicants, 66% accepted, 125 enrolled. In 2016, 95 master's, 4 Advanced Certificates awarded. *Entrance requirements:* Additional exam requirements/recommendations for international students: Required—TOEFL (minimum score 550 paper-based; 79 iBT). *Application deadline:* Applications are processed on a rolling basis. Application fee: $60. Electronic applications accepted. *Expenses: Tuition:* Full-time $19,170; part-time $1065 per credit. *Required fees:* $950; $790 per credit. Tuition and fees vary according to course load. *Financial support:* Applicants required to submit FAFSA. *Faculty research:* ESL - general education teacher collaboration; special education; school desegregation; American intellectual and social history; families and schools. *Unit head:* Joanne O'Brien, Associate Dean/Director, 516-323-3116, E-mail: jobrien@molloy.edu. *Application contact:* Jaclyn Machowicz, Assistant Director for Admissions, 516-323-4010, E-mail: jmachowicz@molloy.edu.

**Monmouth University,** Graduate Studies, Department of English, West Long Branch, NJ 07764-1898. Offers creative writing (MA); literature (MA); rhetoric and writing (MA). *Program availability:* Part-time, evening/weekend. *Degree requirements:* For master's, comprehensive exam (for some programs), thesis. *Entrance requirements:* For master's, minimum overall GPA of 2.75, fifteen or more credits in literature or related field, essay of 1000 words describing interest and goals, two letters of recommendation, creative writing sample. Additional exam requirements/recommendations for international students: Required—TOEFL (minimum 550 paper-based, 79 internet-based test), IELTS (minimum score 6), Michigan English Language Assessment Battery (minimum score 77) or CAE (minimum score of B2). Electronic applications accepted. *Faculty research:* Renaissance and medieval literature, nineteenth-century American literature, eighteenth-century British literature and women's studies, Old and Middle English, African diaspora and African post-colonial literature.

**Montana State University,** The Graduate School, College of Letters and Science, Department of English, Bozeman, MT 59717. Offers MA. *Program availability:* Part-time. *Degree requirements:* For master's, comprehensive exam. *Entrance requirements:* For master's, GRE General Test, minimum GPA of 3.0, 3 recommendations. Additional exam requirements/recommendations for international students: Required—TOEFL (minimum score 550 paper-based). Electronic applications accepted. *Faculty research:* Writing studies, writing in the disciplines, contemporary literature, Renaissance, Shakespeare, American studies, global studies, urban studies, Victorian literature, popular culture gender and sexuality studies, pedagogy, queer theory, English education, literacy education, literary theory.

**Montclair State University,** The Graduate School, College of Humanities and Social Sciences, Program in English, Montclair, NJ 07043-1624. Offers MA. *Program availability:* Part-time, evening/weekend. *Degree requirements:* For master's, thesis. *Entrance requirements:* For master's, GRE General Test, 2 letters of recommendation, essay. Additional exam requirements/recommendations for international students: Required—TOEFL (minimum score 83 iBT), IELTS (minimum score 6.5). Electronic applications accepted. *Expenses:* Tuition, state resident: part-time $553 per credit. Tuition, nonresident: part-time $854 per credit. *Required fees:* $91 per credit. Tuition and fees vary according to program. *Faculty research:* Shakespeare and aging, nineteenth-century Gothic and Catholicism, African-American poetry and poetics, modern Irish and British culture, Darwin and literary modernism.

**Morehead State University,** Graduate Programs, Caudill College of Arts, Humanities and Social Sciences, Department of English, Morehead, KY 40351. Offers MA. *Program availability:* Part-time, evening/weekend. *Degree requirements:* For master's, comprehensive exam, thesis optional. *Entrance requirements:* For master's, GRE General Test, minimum GPA of 3.0 in English; undergraduate major or minor in English. Additional exam requirements/recommendations for international students: Required—TOEFL (minimum score 500 paper-based). Electronic applications accepted. *Faculty research:* Nineteenth and twentieth century American literature, linguistics, Victorian literature, modern British literature, creative writing.

**Morgan State University,** School of Graduate Studies, College of Liberal Arts, Department of English, Baltimore, MD 21251. Offers MA, PhD. *Program availability:* Part-time. *Degree requirements:* For master's, comprehensive exam, thesis; for

*English*

doctorate, comprehensive exam, thesis/dissertation. *Entrance requirements:* For master's, GRE, minimum GPA of 2.5; for doctorate, GRE. Additional exam requirements/recommendations for international students: Required—TOEFL (minimum score 550 paper-based). *Faculty research:* African and African-American studies, nineteenth century American literature, rhetoric, women's studies, children's literature.

**Mount Mary University,** Graduate Programs, Program in English, Milwaukee, WI 53222-4597. Offers creative writing (MA); professional and new media writing (MA). *Program availability:* Part-time, evening/weekend. *Faculty:* 4 full-time (all women), 2 part-time/adjunct (1 woman). *Students:* 8 full-time (6 women), 16 part-time (13 women); includes 10 minority (5 Black or African American, non-Hispanic/Latino; 1 American Indian or Alaska Native, non-Hispanic/Latino; 1 Hispanic/Latino; 3 Two or more races, non-Hispanic/Latino). Average age 42. 4 applicants, 50% accepted, 2 enrolled. In 2016, 5 master's awarded. *Degree requirements:* For master's, comprehensive exam, thesis or alternative. *Entrance requirements:* For master's, minimum GPA of 2.75. Additional exam requirements/recommendations for international students: Required—TOEFL (minimum score 550 paper-based; 80 iBT); Recommended—IELTS (minimum score 6.5). *Application deadline:* For fall admission, 8/1 for domestic and international students; for spring admission, 12/1 for domestic and international students; for summer admission, 5/1 for domestic and international students. Applications are processed on a rolling basis. Application fee: $45. Electronic applications accepted. *Expenses:* Contact institution. *Financial support:* Career-related internships or fieldwork and Federal Work-Study available. Support available to part-time students. Financial award application deadline: 5/1; financial award applicants required to submit FAFSA. *Unit head:* Ann Angel, Graduate Program Chair, 414-930-3109, E-mail: angela@mtmary.edu. *Application contact:* Kirk Heller de Messer, Director, Graduate Admissions, 414-930-3221, E-mail: hellerk@mtmary.edu.
Website: http://www.mtmary.edu/majors-programs/graduate/english/index.html

**Mount Saint Mary's University,** Graduate Division, Los Angeles, CA 90049. Offers business administration (MBA); counseling psychology (MS); creative writing (MFA); education (MS, Certificate); film and television (MFA); health policy and management (MS); humanities (MA); nursing (MSN, Certificate); physical therapy (DPT); religious studies (MA). *Program availability:* Part-time, evening/weekend. *Faculty:* 50 full-time (35 women), 116 part-time/adjunct (81 women). *Students:* 670 full-time (518 women), 147 part-time (116 women); includes 414 minority (73 Black or African American, non-Hispanic/Latino; 4 American Indian or Alaska Native, non-Hispanic/Latino; 60 Asian, non-Hispanic/Latino; 259 Hispanic/Latino; 7 Native Hawaiian or other Pacific Islander, non-Hispanic/Latino; 11 Two or more races, non-Hispanic/Latino), 4 international. Average age 32. 1,398 applicants, 21% accepted, 242 enrolled. In 2016, 170 master's, 28 doctorates, 35 other advanced degrees awarded. *Entrance requirements:* Additional exam requirements/recommendations for international students: Required—TOEFL. *Application deadline:* For fall admission, 6/30 priority date for domestic and international students; for spring admission, 10/30 priority date for domestic and international students; for summer admission, 3/30 priority date for domestic and international students. Applications are processed on a rolling basis. Application fee: $50. Electronic applications accepted. *Expenses: Tuition:* Full-time $9983; part-time $829 per unit. One-time fee: $135. Tuition and fees vary according to degree level and program. *Financial support:* Career-related internships or fieldwork, Federal Work-Study, institutionally sponsored loans, and tuition waivers (full and partial) available. Support available to part-time students. Financial award application deadline: 3/15; financial award applicants required to submit FAFSA. *Unit head:* Albert Ramos, Director of Graduate Admissions, 213-477-2800, E-mail: gradprograms@msmu.edu. *Application contact:* Shawn Peters, Graduate Admission Counselor, 213-477-2676, E-mail: gradprograms@msmu.edu.
Website: http://www.msmu.edu/graduate-programs/

**Murray State University,** College of Humanities and Fine Arts, Department of English and Philosophy, Program in English, Murray, KY 42071. Offers MA. *Program availability:* Part-time. *Degree requirements:* For master's, comprehensive exam, thesis (for some programs).

**New Mexico Highlands University,** Graduate Studies, College of Arts and Sciences, Department of English, Las Vegas, NM 87701. Offers English (MA), including creative writing, language, rhetoric and composition, literature. *Degree requirements:* For master's, comprehensive exam, thesis. *Entrance requirements:* For master's, minimum undergraduate GPA of 3.0. Additional exam requirements/recommendations for international students: Required—TOEFL (minimum score 540 paper-based). *Faculty research:* Twentieth-century literature, life path writing in homeless shelters, native American philosophy, medieval intellectual and cultural history, creating pedagogical tools for teaching law.

**New Mexico State University,** College of Arts and Sciences, Department of English, Las Cruces, NM 88003. Offers creative writing (MFA); English (MA), including creative writing, English studies for teachers, literature, rhetoric and professional communication; rhetoric and professional communication (PhD). *Program availability:* Part-time. *Faculty:* 19 full-time (9 women), 1 (woman) part-time/adjunct. *Students:* 48 full-time (33 women), 24 part-time (14 women); includes 19 minority (2 Asian, non-Hispanic/Latino; 15 Hispanic/Latino; 2 Two or more races, non-Hispanic/Latino), 6 international. Average age 34. 90 applicants, 32% accepted, 19 enrolled. In 2016, 21 master's, 5 doctorates awarded. *Degree requirements:* For master's, one foreign language, thesis (for some programs); for doctorate, comprehensive exam, thesis/dissertation, internship. *Entrance requirements:* For master's and doctorate, sample of written work. Additional exam requirements/recommendations for international students: Required—TOEFL (minimum score 550 paper-based; 79 iBT), IELTS (minimum score 6.5). *Application deadline:* For fall admission, 2/1 for domestic and international students. Application fee: $40 ($50 for international students). Electronic applications accepted. *Expenses: Tuition,* state resident: full-time $4086. Tuition, nonresident: full-time $14,254. *Required fees:* $853. Tuition and fees vary according to course load. *Financial support:* In 2016–17, 47 students received support, including 42 teaching assistantships (averaging $17,394 per year); career-related internships or fieldwork, Federal Work-Study, scholarships/grants, traineeships, health care benefits, and unspecified assistantships also available. Support available to part-time students. Financial award application deadline: 3/1. *Faculty research:* Composition research, history and theory of rhetoric, technical/professional communication, creative writing, English and American literature. *Total annual research expenditures:* $10,316. *Unit head:* Dr. Barry L. Thatcher, Department Head, 575-646-3931, Fax: 575-646-7725, E-mail: bathatch@nmsu.edu. *Application contact:* Dr. Tracey Eileen Miller-Tomlinson, Director of Graduate Studies, 575-646-2213, Fax: 575-646-7725, E-mail: tomlin@nmsu.edu.
Website: http://english.nmsu.edu

**New York University,** Graduate School of Arts and Science, Program in English and American Literature, New York, NY 10012-1019. Offers MA, PhD. *Degree requirements:* For master's, one foreign language, thesis or alternative, qualifying exams, special project; for doctorate, one foreign language, thesis/dissertation. *Entrance requirements:* For master's, GRE General Test; GRE Subject Test in English (recommended). Additional exam requirements/recommendations for international students: Required—TOEFL.

**North Carolina Agricultural and Technical State University,** School of Graduate Studies, College of Arts and Sciences, Department of English, Greensboro, NC 27411. Offers English (MA); English and African-American literature (MA); English education (MAT, MS). *Program availability:* Part-time, evening/weekend. *Degree requirements:* For master's, comprehensive exam, qualifying exam. *Entrance requirements:* For master's, GRE General Test, minimum GPA of 3.0.

**North Carolina Central University,** College of Liberal Arts, Department of English and Mass Communication, Durham, NC 27707-3129. Offers English (MA). *Program availability:* Part-time, evening/weekend. *Degree requirements:* For master's, one foreign language, comprehensive exam, thesis. *Entrance requirements:* For master's, GRE, minimum GPA of 3.0 in major, 2.5 overall. Additional exam requirements/recommendations for international students: Required—TOEFL.

**North Carolina State University,** Graduate School, College of Humanities and Social Sciences, Department of English, Program in English, Raleigh, NC 27695. Offers MA. *Degree requirements:* For master's, thesis. *Entrance requirements:* For master's, GRE General Test. Electronic applications accepted. *Faculty research:* Creative writing, linguistics, rhetoric and composition, rhetoric and technical communication, film studies.

**North Dakota State University,** College of Graduate and Interdisciplinary Studies, College of Arts, Humanities and Social Sciences, Department of English, Fargo, ND 58102. Offers composition (MA); literature (MA); rhetoric, writing and culture (PhD). *Program availability:* Part-time. *Degree requirements:* For master's, one foreign language, thesis. *Entrance requirements:* Additional exam requirements/recommendations for international students: Required—TOEFL (minimum score 600 paper-based; 100 iBT), IELTS (minimum score 7). Electronic applications accepted. *Faculty research:* American and English literature, women's studies, language attitudes, composition practices, computers and composition.

See Display on page 756 and Close-Up on page 767.

**Northeastern Illinois University,** College of Graduate Studies and Research, College of Arts and Sciences, Programs in English, Chicago, IL 60625-4699. Offers composition/writing (MA); literature (MA). *Program availability:* Part-time, evening/weekend. *Degree requirements:* For master's, comprehensive exam, thesis optional. *Entrance requirements:* For master's, 30 hours of undergraduate course work in literature and composition (literature), BA in English or approval (composition/writing), minimum GPA of 2.75. Additional exam requirements/recommendations for international students: Required—TOEFL (minimum score 550 paper-based; 79 iBT). Electronic applications accepted. *Faculty research:* Arthurian literature, Southern American literature, rhetoric and theories of authorship.

**Northeastern State University,** College of Liberal Arts, Department of Languages and Literature, Tahlequah, OK 74464-2399. Offers English (MA), including literature, rhetoric/composition. *Faculty:* 10 full-time (3 women). *Students:* 9 full-time (6 women), 22 part-time (12 women); includes 6 minority (1 Hispanic/Latino; 5 Two or more races, non-Hispanic/Latino). Average age 31. In 2016, 9 master's awarded. *Degree requirements:* For master's, thesis. *Entrance requirements:* For master's, GRE or MAT, minimum GPA of 2.5. Additional exam requirements/recommendations for international students: Required—TOEFL. *Application deadline:* For fall admission, 6/1 priority date for domestic students. Applications are processed on a rolling basis. Application fee: $25. Electronic applications accepted. *Expenses: Tuition,* state resident: full-time $2816; part-time $216.60 per credit hour. Tuition, nonresident: full-time $6365; part-time $489.60 per credit hour. *Required fees:* $37.40 per credit hour. *Financial support:* Application deadline: 3/1. *Unit head:* Dr. Audell Shelburne, Chair, 918-456-3609, E-mail: shelburn@nsuok.edu. *Application contact:* Josh McCollum, Graduate Coordinator, 918-444-2093, E-mail: mccolluj@nsuok.edu.
Website: http://academics.nsuok.edu/languagesliterature/DegreePrograms/English,MA.aspx

**Northeastern University,** College of Social Sciences and Humanities, Boston, MA 02115. Offers criminology and criminal justice (MSCJ); criminology and justice policy (PhD); economics (MA, PhD); English (MA, PhD); international affairs (MA); law and public policy (PhD); political science (MA, PhD); public administration (MPA); public history (MA); public policy (MPP); security and resilience studies (MS); sociology (MA, PhD); urban and regional policy (MS); urban informatics (MS); world history (MA, PhD); JD/MS. *Program availability:* Online learning. *Faculty:* 234 full-time (114 women), 55 part-time/adjunct (34 women). *Students:* 427 full-time (239 women), 77 part-time (42 women). In 2016, 143 master's, 38 doctorates awarded. *Degree requirements:* For doctorate, variable foreign language requirement, comprehensive exam, thesis/dissertation. *Entrance requirements:* For master's and doctorate, GRE. Additional exam requirements/recommendations for international students: Required—TOEFL, IELTS. Application fee: $75. Electronic applications accepted. *Expenses:* $1,295 per credit. *Financial support:* Teaching assistantships, career-related internships or fieldwork, scholarships/grants, health care benefits, tuition waivers (full and partial), and unspecified assistantships available. Support available to part-time students. Financial award applicants required to submit FAFSA. *Unit head:* Dr. Uta Poiger, Dean, 617-373-5173. *Application contact:* Amber Crowe, Administrative Coordinator, 617-373-5990, Fax: 617-373-7281, E-mail: gradcssh@northeastern.edu.
Website: http://www.northeastern.edu/cssh/graduate

**Northern Arizona University,** Graduate College, College of Arts and Letters, Department of English, Flagstaff, AZ 86011. Offers applied linguistics (PhD); creative writing (MFA), including creative writing; English (MA), including English education, literature, professional writing, rhetoric, writing, and digital media studies; professional writing (Certificate); teaching English as a second language (MA, Certificate). *Program availability:* Part-time. *Degree requirements:* For master's, comprehensive exam (for some programs), thesis (for some programs), departmental qualifying exam; for doctorate, comprehensive exam, thesis/dissertation, departmental qualifying exam. *Entrance requirements:* For master's, minimum GPA of 3.0 or GRE; for doctorate, GRE General Test. Additional exam requirements/recommendations for international students: Required—TOEFL (minimum score 550 paper-based; 80 iBT), IELTS (minimum score 7), TOEFL (minimum score 600 paper-based; 100 iBT) for PhD; TOEFL (minimum score 570 paper-based; 89 iBT) for MA. Electronic applications accepted. *Expenses:* Tuition, state resident: full-time $8971; part-time $444 per credit hour. Tuition, nonresident: full-time $20,958; part-time $1164 per credit hour. *Required fees:* $1018; $644 per credit hour. Tuition and fees vary according to course load, campus/location and program.

**Northern Illinois University,** Graduate School, College of Liberal Arts and Sciences, Department of English, De Kalb, IL 60115-2854. Offers MA, PhD. *Program availability:* Part-time. *Faculty:* 32 full-time (13 women), 2 part-time/adjunct (both women). *Students:* 37 full-time (26 women), 81 part-time (51 women); includes 10 minority (2 Black or African American, non-Hispanic/Latino; 3 Hispanic/Latino; 5 Two or more races, non-Hispanic/Latino), 5 international. Average age 35. 59 applicants, 59% accepted, 15 enrolled. In 2016, 16 master's, 6 doctorates awarded. Terminal master's awarded for partial completion of doctoral program. *Degree requirements:* For master's, variable foreign language requirement, comprehensive exam, thesis optional; for doctorate, variable foreign language requirement, thesis/dissertation, candidacy exam, dissertation defense. *Entrance requirements:* For master's, GRE General Test, minimum GPA of

2.75; for doctorate, GRE General Test, minimum GPA of 2.75 (undergraduate), 3.2 (graduate). Additional exam requirements/recommendations for international students: Required—TOEFL (minimum score 550 paper-based). *Application deadline:* For fall admission, 6/1 for domestic students, 5/1 for international students; for spring admission, 11/1 for domestic students, 10/1 for international students. Applications are processed on a rolling basis. Application fee: $40. Electronic applications accepted. *Financial support:* In 2016–17, 1 research assistantship with full tuition reimbursement, 54 teaching assistantships with full tuition reimbursements were awarded; fellowships with full tuition reimbursements, career-related internships or fieldwork, Federal Work-Study, scholarships/grants, tuition waivers (full), and unspecified assistantships also available. Support available to part-time students. Financial award applicants required to submit FAFSA. *Faculty research:* Nineteenth-century English literature, linguistic programs, portfolio assembly, Mideast literature, old English folklore. *Unit head:* Dr. Kathleen Renk, Chair, 815-753-0615, Fax: 815-753-0606, E-mail: krenk@niu.edu. *Application contact:* Graduate School Office, 815-753-0395, E-mail: gradsch@niu.edu. Website: http://www.engl.niu.edu/

**Northern Kentucky University,** Office of Graduate Programs, College of Arts and Sciences, Program in English, Highland Heights, KY 41099. Offers composition and rhetoric (Certificate); creative writing (Certificate); cultural studies and discourses (Certificate); English (MA); professional writing (Certificate). *Program availability:* Part-time, evening/weekend. *Degree requirements:* For master's, comprehensive exam (for some programs), capstone (thesis, portfolio, project, or exams); 30 hours of credit; for Certificate, 18 hours of credit. *Entrance requirements:* For master's, bachelor's degree in English or related field from regionally-accredited institution with minimum GPA of 3.0 in major or cognate area coursework; official transcripts for all undergraduate and graduate work; two letters of reference; for Certificate, official transcripts for all undergraduate and graduate work; bachelor's degree from regionally-accredited institution; minimum undergraduate GPA of 2.5. Additional exam requirements/recommendations for international students: Required—TOEFL (minimum score 79 iBT); Recommended—IELTS (minimum score 6.5). Electronic applications accepted.

**Northern Michigan University,** Office of Graduate Education and Research, College of Arts and Sciences, Department of English, Marquette, MI 49855-5301. Offers creative writing (MFA); literature (MA); pedagogy (MA); teaching English to speakers of other languages (Graduate Certificate); theater (MA); writing (MA). *Program availability:* Part-time, evening/weekend. Terminal master's awarded for partial completion of doctoral program. *Degree requirements:* For master's, capstone project: thesis, practicum or portfolio (for MA); thesis (for MFA); for Graduate Certificate, one foreign language. *Entrance requirements:* For master's, minimum GPA of 3.0; bachelor's degree in English or minimum of 30 credit hours in undergraduate English; statement of purpose; resume; critical essay; 3 letters of recommendation; for Graduate Certificate, bachelor's degree. Additional exam requirements/recommendations for international students: Required—TOEFL (minimum score 550 paper-based; 79 iBT), IELTS (minimum score 6.5). Electronic applications accepted. *Faculty research:* Modern Arabic literature, British literature (medieval to contemporary), postcolonial literature, Native and African-American literature, creative writing, critical theory, pedagogy.

**Northwestern State University of Louisiana,** Graduate Studies and Research, Department of Language and Communication, Natchitoches, LA 71497. Offers English (MA). *Degree requirements:* For master's, one foreign language, comprehensive exam, thesis or alternative. *Entrance requirements:* For master's, GRE General Test, minimum undergraduate GPA of 2.5. Additional exam requirements/recommendations for international students: Required—TOEFL. Electronic applications accepted.

**Northwestern University,** The Graduate School, Judd A. and Marjorie Weinberg College of Arts and Sciences, Department of English, Evanston, IL 60208. Offers MA, PhD. Admissions and degrees offered through The Graduate School. Terminal master's awarded for partial completion of doctoral program. *Degree requirements:* For master's, thesis; for doctorate, one foreign language, thesis/dissertation, oral and written qualifying exam. *Entrance requirements:* For master's and doctorate, GRE General Test, sample of written work. Additional exam requirements/recommendations for international students: Required—TOEFL. Electronic applications accepted. *Faculty research:* Renaissance literature, theatre and drama, American literature, modern European contemporary literature, poetry, cultural history.

**Northwestern University,** School of Professional Studies, Program in Literature, Evanston, IL 60208. Offers American literature (MA); British literature (MA); comparative and world literature (MA).

**Northwest Missouri State University,** Graduate School, College of Arts and Sciences, Maryville, MO 64468-6001. Offers biology (MS); elementary mathematics specialist (MS Ed); English (MA); English education (MS Ed); English pedagogy (MS Ed); geographic information science (MS, Certificate); history (MS Ed); mathematics (MS); mathematics education (MS Ed); teaching: science (MS Ed). *Program availability:* Part-time. *Students:* 12 full-time (8 women), 69 part-time (31 women). *Degree requirements:* For master's, comprehensive exam. *Entrance requirements:* For master's, GRE General Test, writing sample. Additional exam requirements/recommendations for international students: Required—TOEFL (minimum score 550 paper-based). *Application deadline:* For fall admission, 7/1 for domestic and international students; for spring admission, 11/15 for domestic and international students. Applications are processed on a rolling basis. Application fee: $0 ($50 for international students). Electronic applications accepted. *Expenses:* Tuition, state resident: full-time $3447; part-time $383 per credit hour. Tuition, nonresident: full-time $5724; part-time $636 per credit hour. *Required fees:* $130 per credit hour. *Financial support:* Research assistantships with full tuition reimbursements, teaching assistantships with full tuition reimbursements, and administrative assistantships, tutorial assistantships available. Financial award application deadline: 4/1; financial award applicants required to submit FAFSA. *Unit head:* Dr. Michael Steiner, Dean, 660-562-1197. Website: http://www.nwmissouri.edu/academics/arts/

**Notre Dame de Namur University,** Division of Academic Affairs, College of Arts and Sciences, Program in English, Belmont, CA 94002-1908. Offers MA. *Program availability:* Part-time. *Degree requirements:* For master's, thesis. *Entrance requirements:* For master's, minimum GPA of 2.5, writing sample. Additional exam requirements/recommendations for international students: Required—TOEFL (minimum score 550 paper-based; 79 iBT). Electronic applications accepted.

**Oakland University,** Graduate Study and Lifelong Learning, College of Arts and Sciences, Department of English, Rochester, MI 48309-4401. Offers MA. *Program availability:* Part-time, evening/weekend. *Entrance requirements:* For master's, minimum GPA of 3.0. Additional exam requirements/recommendations for international students: Required—TOEFL (minimum score 550 paper-based). Electronic applications accepted.

**Ohio Dominican University,** Division of Arts and Letters, Program in English, Columbus, OH 43219-2099. Offers MA. *Program availability:* Part-time, evening/weekend, online only, 100% online. *Faculty:* 3 full-time (1 woman). *Students:* 1 (woman) full-time, 27 part-time (23 women); includes 1 minority (Two or more races, non-Hispanic/Latino). Average age 35. 10 applicants, 80% accepted, 7 enrolled. In 2016, 15 master's awarded. *Degree requirements:* For master's, thesis or alternative. *Entrance requirements:* For master's, minimum undergraduate GPA of 3.0, 3 letters of

recommendation, transcripts. Additional exam requirements/recommendations for international students: Required—TOEFL (minimum score 550 paper-based), IELTS (minimum score 6.5). *Application deadline:* For fall admission, 8/15 for domestic students, 6/10 for international students; for spring admission, 1/4 for domestic students, 11/2 for international students; for summer admission, 5/30 for domestic students. Applications are processed on a rolling basis. Application fee: $25. Electronic applications accepted. *Expenses:* $590 per credit hour; $225 fees per semester. *Financial support:* Applicants required to submit FAFSA. *Faculty research:* James Joyce, poetry, African literature. *Unit head:* Dr. Martin Brick, Director, 614-251-4519, E-mail: brickm@ohiodominican.edu. *Application contact:* John W. Naughton, Director for Graduate Admissions, 614-251-4721, Fax: 614-251-6654, E-mail: grad@ohiodominican.edu. Website: http://www.ohiodominican.edu/academics/graduate/ma-in-english

**The Ohio State University,** Graduate School, College of Arts and Sciences, Division of Arts and Humanities, Department of English, Columbus, OH 43210. Offers MA, MFA, PhD. *Faculty:* 65. *Students:* 159 full-time (102 women), 3 part-time (all women); includes 28 minority (10 Black or African American, non-Hispanic/Latino; 18 Asian/Latino; 5 international. Average age 29. In 2016, 20 master's, 11 doctorates awarded. *Degree requirements:* For master's, one foreign language, thesis or written exam; for doctorate, one foreign language, thesis/dissertation. *Entrance requirements:* For master's and doctorate, GRE General Test. Additional exam requirements/recommendations for international students: Required—TOEFL (minimum score 600 paper-based; 100 iBT), IELTS (minimum score 8), Michigan English Language Assessment Battery (minimum score 86). *Application deadline:* For fall admission, 12/6 priority date for domestic students, 11/30 priority date for international students; for spring admission, 3/1 for domestic students, 2/1 for international students. Applications are processed on a rolling basis. Application fee: $60 ($70 for international students). Electronic applications accepted. *Financial support:* Fellowships with tuition reimbursements, research assistantships with tuition reimbursements, teaching assistantships with tuition reimbursements, Federal Work-Study, institutionally sponsored loans, and unspecified assistantships available. Support available to part-time students. *Unit head:* Robyn Warhol, Chair/Arts and Humanities Professor, 614-292-6065, E-mail: warhol.1@osu.edu. *Application contact:* Graduate and Professional Admissions, 614-292-9444, Fax: 614-292-3895, E-mail: gpadmissions@osu.edu. Website: http://english.osu.edu/

**Ohio University,** Graduate College, College of Arts and Sciences, Department of English Language and Literature, Athens, OH 45701-2979. Offers MA, PhD. *Program availability:* Part-time. *Degree requirements:* For master's, one foreign language, thesis or alternative; for doctorate, one foreign language, comprehensive exam, thesis/dissertation, oral exam, public lecture. *Entrance requirements:* For master's, GRE General Test, minimum GPA of 3.0, writing sample; for doctorate, GRE General Test, minimum GPA of 3.0, master's degree in English, writing sample. Additional exam requirements/recommendations for international students: Required—TOEFL (minimum score 550 paper-based; 80 iBT) or IELTS (minimum score 6.5). *Application deadline:* For fall admission, 1/15 for domestic and international students. Application fee: $50 ($55 for international students). Electronic applications accepted. *Financial support:* Teaching assistantships with full tuition reimbursements, Federal Work-Study, institutionally sponsored loans, and unspecified assistantships available. Financial award application deadline: 1/15. *Faculty research:* Environmental literature, post-colonial studies, print culture, film in popular culture, computers in pedagogy. *Unit head:* Dr. Linda Zionkowski, Department Chair, 740-597-2749, Fax: 740-593-2832, E-mail: zionkows@ohio.edu. *Application contact:* Marnie Miller, Student Services Coordinator, 740-593-2800, Fax: 740-593-4625, E-mail: graduate@ohio.edu. Website: http://www.english.ohiou.edu/

**Oklahoma State University,** College of Arts and Sciences, Department of English, Stillwater, OK 74078. Offers creative writing (MFA); English (MA, PhD). *Faculty:* 62 full-time (34 women), 3 part-time/adjunct (1 woman). *Students:* 6 full-time (4 women), 118 part-time (60 women); includes 17 minority (3 Black or African American, non-Hispanic/Latino; 5 American Indian or Alaska Native, non-Hispanic/Latino; 1 Asian, non-Hispanic/Latino; 3 Hispanic/Latino; 5 Two or more races, non-Hispanic/Latino), 20 international. Average age 32. 121 applicants, 34% accepted, 33 enrolled. In 2016, 19 master's, 12 doctorates awarded. *Degree requirements:* For master's, comprehensive exam, thesis; for doctorate, comprehensive exam, thesis/dissertation. *Entrance requirements:* For master's, GRE General Test, minimum GPA of 3.0, writing sample; for doctorate, GRE General Test, minimum GPA of 3.5, writing sample. Additional exam requirements/recommendations for international students: Required—TOEFL (minimum score 550 paper-based; 79 iBT). *Application deadline:* For fall admission, 3/1 priority date for international students; for spring admission, 8/1 priority date for international students. Applications are processed on a rolling basis. Application fee: $40 ($75 for international students). Electronic applications accepted. *Expenses:* Tuition, state resident: full-time $3775; part-time $209.70 per credit hour. Tuition, nonresident: full-time $14,851; part-time $825.05 per credit hour. *Required fees:* $2027; $112.60 per credit hour. Tuition and fees vary according to campus/location. *Financial support:* In 2016–17, 1 research assistantship (averaging $3,106 per year), 106 teaching assistantships (averaging $15,887 per year) were awarded; career-related internships or fieldwork, Federal Work-Study, scholarships/grants, health care benefits, tuition waivers (partial), and unspecified assistantships also available. Support available to part-time students. Financial award application deadline: 3/1; financial award applicants required to submit FAFSA. *Faculty research:* American and British novels, poetry, and autobiography; Native American languages and literature; institutional history of American film, history, and adaptations; rhetoric and theories of human communication; learning strategies of second language learners. *Unit head:* Dr. Richard Frohock, Department Head, 405-744-9474, Fax: 405-744-6326, E-mail: richard.frohock@okstate.edu. Website: http://english.okstate.edu/

**Old Dominion University,** College of Arts and Letters, Doctoral Program in English, Norfolk, VA 23529. Offers PhD. *Program availability:* Part-time, evening/weekend, online learning. *Faculty:* 25 full-time (15 women), 1 (woman) part-time/adjunct. *Students:* 7 full-time (5 women), 51 part-time (36 women); includes 8 minority (6 Black or African American, non-Hispanic/Latino; 1 Hispanic/Latino; 1 Two or more races, non-Hispanic/Latino). Average age 38. 79 applicants, 16% accepted, 11 enrolled. In 2016, 8 doctorates awarded. *Degree requirements:* For doctorate, comprehensive exam, thesis/dissertation, research competency in foreign language, statistics, or new media. *Entrance requirements:* For doctorate, GRE General Test, MA in English or related field with minimum GPA of 3.5, writing sample, resume, goals statement, letter of recommendation. Additional exam requirements/recommendations for international students: Required—TOEFL. *Application deadline:* For fall admission, 2/1 for domestic students. Application fee: $50. Electronic applications accepted. *Expenses:* Tuition, state resident: full-time $8604; part-time $478 per credit hour. Tuition, nonresident: full-time $21,510; part-time $1195 per credit hour. *Required fees:* $66 per semester. Tuition and fees vary according to campus/location, program and reciprocity agreements. *Financial support:* In 2016–17, 13 students received support, including 3 fellowships with full tuition reimbursements available (averaging $15,000 per year), 1 research assistantship with full tuition reimbursement available (averaging $15,000 per year), 9 teaching assistantships with full tuition reimbursements available (averaging $15,000

## English

per year); career-related internships or fieldwork, scholarships/grants, and unspecified assistantships also available. Support available to part-time students. Financial award application deadline: 2/15; financial award applicants required to submit FAFSA. *Faculty research:* New media studies, rhetorical history and theory, digital studies, writing studies, professional writing and document design, linguistics, textual studies, literary studies. *Unit head:* Dr. Kevin Eric DePew, Graduate Program Director, 757-683-4019, Fax: 757-683-3241, E-mail: kdepew@odu.edu. *Application contact:* Dr. David C. Earnest, Associate Dean, 757-683-6077, Fax: 757-683-5746, E-mail: dearnest@odu.edu.
Website: https://www.odu.edu/academics/programs/doctoral/english

**Old Dominion University,** College of Arts and Letters, Master of Arts in English Program, Norfolk, VA 23529. Offers MA. *Program availability:* Part-time, evening/weekend. *Faculty:* 17 full-time (8 women). *Students:* 11 full-time (9 women), 15 part-time (14 women); includes 6 minority (1 Black or African American, non-Hispanic/Latino; 1 American Indian or Alaska Native, non-Hispanic/Latino; 1 Asian, non-Hispanic/Latino; 2 Hispanic/Latino; 1 Two or more races, non-Hispanic/Latino). Average age 32. 56 applicants, 66% accepted, 30 enrolled. In 2016, 13 master's awarded. Terminal master's awarded for partial completion of doctoral program. *Degree requirements:* For master's, comprehensive exam, thesis optional. *Entrance requirements:* For master's, GRE General Test, 24 hours in English, sample of written work, BA. Additional exam requirements/recommendations for international students: Required—TOEFL. *Application deadline:* For fall admission, 3/15 priority date for domestic and international students; for winter admission, 11/1 for domestic students, 10/1 for international students; for spring admission, 11/1 priority date for domestic students, 11/1 for international students. Application fee: $50. Electronic applications accepted. *Expenses:* Tuition, state resident: full-time $8604; part-time $478 per credit hour. Tuition, nonresident: full-time $21,510; part-time $1195 per credit hour. *Required fees:* $66 per semester. Tuition and fees vary according to campus/location, program and reciprocity agreements. *Financial support:* In 2016–17, 2 research assistantships (averaging $10,000 per year), 6 teaching assistantships (averaging $10,000 per year) were awarded; career-related internships or fieldwork and unspecified assistantships also available. Financial award application deadline: 2/15; financial award applicants required to submit FAFSA. *Faculty research:* Literary theory, composition theory, professional writing, rhetoric, British and American literature. *Total annual research expenditures:* $3,451. *Unit head:* Dr. Imtiaz Habib, Graduate Program Director, 757-683-3285, E-mail: ihabib@odu.edu. *Application contact:* Dr. David C. Earnest, Associate Dean, 757-683-6077, Fax: 757-683-5746, E-mail: dearnest@odu.edu.

**Old Dominion University,** Darden College of Education, Programs in Secondary Education, Norfolk, VA 23529. Offers chemistry (MS Ed); English (MS Ed); secondary education (MS Ed). *Accreditation:* NCATE. *Program availability:* Part-time, evening/weekend, online learning. *Faculty:* 13 full-time (7 women), 10 part-time/adjunct (7 women). *Students:* 55 full-time (33 women), 70 part-time (56 women); includes 25 minority (11 Black or African American, non-Hispanic/Latino; 1 American Indian or Alaska Native, non-Hispanic/Latino; 3 Asian, non-Hispanic/Latino; 5 Hispanic/Latino; 5 Two or more races, non-Hispanic/Latino), 1 international. Average age 33. 75 applicants, 71% accepted, 53 enrolled. In 2016, 29 master's awarded. *Degree requirements:* For master's, comprehensive exam, thesis. *Entrance requirements:* For master's, GRE General Test or MAT, PRAXIS I (for licensure), minimum GPA of 2.8, teaching certificate. Additional exam requirements/recommendations for international students: Required—TOEFL. *Application deadline:* For fall admission, 6/1 for domestic and international students; for winter admission, 11/1 for domestic and international students; for spring admission, 3/1 for domestic and international students. Applications are processed on a rolling basis. Application fee: $50. Electronic applications accepted. *Expenses:* Tuition, state resident: full-time $8604; part-time $478 per credit hour. Tuition, nonresident: full-time $21,510; part-time $1195 per credit hour. *Required fees:* $66 per semester. Tuition and fees vary according to campus/location, program and reciprocity agreements. *Financial support:* In 2016–17, 56 students received support, including fellowships (averaging $15,000 per year), research assistantships with tuition reimbursements available (averaging $9,000 per year), teaching assistantships with tuition reimbursements available (averaging $15,000 per year). Financial award application deadline: 2/15; financial award applicants required to submit FAFSA. *Faculty research:* Use of technology, writing project for teachers, geography teaching, reading. *Unit head:* Dr. KaaVonia Hinton, Department Chair, 757-683-5958, Fax: 757-683-5862, E-mail: khintonj@odu.edu. *Application contact:* William Heffelfinger, Director of Graduate Admissions, 757-683-5554, Fax: 757-683-3255, E-mail: gradadmit@odu.edu.
Website: http://education.odu.edu/eci/secondary

**Oregon State University,** College of Liberal Arts, Program in English, Corvallis, OR 97331. Offers literature and culture (MA); rhetoric, writing, and culture (MA). *Program availability:* Part-time. *Faculty:* 26 full-time (10 women), 8 part-time/adjunct (7 women). *Students:* 25 full-time (19 women), 1 part-time (0 women); includes 8 minority (2 Asian, non-Hispanic/Latino; 4 Hispanic/Latino; 2 Two or more races, non-Hispanic/Latino). Average age 25. 65 applicants, 28% accepted, 12 enrolled. In 2016, 10 master's awarded. *Degree requirements:* For master's, thesis. *Entrance requirements:* For master's, GRE (recommended). Additional exam requirements/recommendations for international students: Required—TOEFL (minimum score 80 iBT), IELTS (minimum score 6.5). *Application deadline:* For fall admission, 1/3 for domestic and international students. Application fee: $75 ($85 for international students). *Expenses:* Tuition, state resident: full-time $12,150; part-time $450 per credit. Tuition, nonresident: full-time $21,789; part-time $807 per credit. *Required fees:* $1651; $1507 per credit. One-time fee: $350. Tuition and fees vary according to course load, campus/location and program. *Financial support:* Teaching assistantships and scholarships/grants available. Financial award application deadline: 1/3. *Unit head:* Dr. Peter Betjemann, Director, School of Writing, Literature, and Film. *Application contact:* Dr. Raymond Malewitz, Assistant Professor and Director, 541-737-1656, E-mail: raymond.malewitz@oregonstate.edu.
Website: http://liberalarts.oregonstate.edu/wlf/ma

**Our Lady of the Lake University,** College of Arts and Sciences, Programs in English, San Antonio, TX 78207-4689. Offers literature, creative writing, and social justice (MA); MA/MFA. Program offered jointly with University of the Incarnate Word and St. Mary's University. *Program availability:* Part-time, evening/weekend. *Faculty:* 6 full-time (4 women), 1 (woman) part-time/adjunct. *Students:* 10 full-time (7 women), 10 part-time (all women); includes 17 minority (1 Black or African American, non-Hispanic/Latino; 16 Hispanic/Latino). Average age 35. 10 applicants, 60% accepted, 5 enrolled. In 2016, 1 master's awarded. *Degree requirements:* For master's, comprehensive exam, thesis optional. *Entrance requirements:* For master's, GRE General Test or MAT taken within the last 5 years, bachelor's degree with at least 18 hours of advanced course work in English and/or communication arts with minimum cumulative GPA of 2.5; 2 letters of recommendation; samples of creative and scholarly writing (25 pages total); personal statement. Additional exam requirements/recommendations for international students: Required—TOEFL. *Application deadline:* For fall admission, 6/15 for domestic and international students; for spring admission, 11/15 for domestic and international students; for summer admission, 4/15 for domestic and international students. Applications are processed on a rolling basis. Application fee: $40 ($50 for international students). Electronic applications accepted. Application fee is waived when completed online. *Expenses: Tuition:* Full-time $14,796. Tuition and fees vary according to course load, degree level, campus/location and program. *Financial support:* In 2016–17, 8 students received support. Federal Work-Study, scholarships/grants, unspecified assistantships, and tuition discounts available. Support available to part-time students. Financial award application deadline: 5/1; financial award applicants required to submit FAFSA. *Unit head:* Leah Larson, Chair of the English, Mass Communications and Drama Department, 210-431-6503, E-mail: llarson@ollusa.edu. *Application contact:* Office of Graduate Admissions, 210-431-3995, Fax: 210-431-3945, E-mail: gradadm@ollusa.edu.
Website: http://www.ollusa.edu/s/1190/hybrid/default-hybrid-ollu.aspx?sid-1190&gid-1&pgid-7884

**Pace University,** School of Education, New York, NY 10038. Offers adolescent education (MST), including biology, business education, chemistry, earth science, English, foreign languages, mathematics, physics, social studies, visual arts; childhood education (MST); early childhood development, learning and intervention (MST); educational technology studies (MS); inclusive adolescent education (MST), including biology, business education, chemistry, earth science, English, foreign languages, mathematics, physics, social studies, visual arts; integrated instruction for educational technology (Certificate); integrated instruction for literacy and technology (Certificate); literacy (MS Ed); special education (MS Ed). *Accreditation:* NCATE. *Program availability:* Part-time, evening/weekend, blended/hybrid learning. *Faculty:* 19 full-time (13 women), 86 part-time/adjunct (49 women). *Students:* 115 full-time (97 women), 543 part-time (381 women); includes 280 minority (137 Black or African American, non-Hispanic/Latino; 1 American Indian or Alaska Native, non-Hispanic/Latino; 40 Asian, non-Hispanic/Latino; 87 Hispanic/Latino; 15 Two or more races, non-Hispanic/Latino), 13 international. Average age 30. 181 applicants, 78% accepted, 72 enrolled. In 2016, 193 master's, 9 other advanced degrees awarded. *Degree requirements:* For master's, certification exams. *Entrance requirements:* For master's, GRE, interview, teaching certificate (except for MST). Additional exam requirements/recommendations for international students: Required—TOEFL (minimum score 88 iBT), IELTS or PTE. *Application deadline:* For fall admission, 8/1 priority date for domestic students, 6/1 for international students; for spring admission, 12/1 priority date for domestic students, 10/1 for international students. Applications are processed on a rolling basis. Application fee: $70. Electronic applications accepted. *Expenses:* Contact institution. *Financial support:* In 2016–17, 17 students received support, including 17 research assistantships with partial tuition reimbursements available (averaging $6,020 per year); career-related internships or fieldwork and Federal Work-Study also available. Financial award application deadline: 9/1; financial award applicants required to submit FAFSA. *Faculty research:* STEM education, TESOL, teacher education, special education, language and literary development. *Total annual research expenditures:* $290,153. *Unit head:* Dr. Xiao-Lei Wang, Dean, School of Education, 914-773-3876, E-mail: xwang@pace.edu. *Application contact:* Susan Ford-Goldschein, Director of Graduate Admissions, 212-346-1531, Fax: 212-346-1585, E-mail: graduateadmission@pace.edu.
Website: http://www.pace.edu/school-of-education

**Penn State University Park,** Graduate School, College of the Liberal Arts, Department of English, University Park, PA 16802. Offers MA, MFA, PhD. *Unit head:* Dr. Susan Welch, Dean, 814-865-7691, Fax: 814-863-2085. *Application contact:* Lori Hawn, Director, Graduate Student Services, 814-865-1795, Fax: 814-863-4627, E-mail: l-gswww@lists.psu.edu.
Website: http://english.la.psu.edu/

**Pittsburg State University,** Graduate School, College of Arts and Sciences, Department of English and Modern Languages, Pittsburg, KS 66762. Offers English (MA), including creative writing, literature. *Program availability:* Part-time. *Students:* 18 (12 women); includes 1 minority (Asian, non-Hispanic/Latino). In 2016, 9 master's awarded. *Degree requirements:* For master's, thesis or alternative. *Entrance requirements:* Additional exam requirements/recommendations for international students: Required—TOEFL (minimum score 550 paper-based; 79 iBT), IELTS (minimum score 6.5), PTE (minimum score 53). *Application deadline:* For fall admission, 7/15 for domestic students, 6/1 for international students; for spring admission, 12/15 for domestic students, 10/15 for international students; for summer admission, 5/15 for domestic students, 4/1 for international students. Applications are processed on a rolling basis. Application fee: $35 ($60 for international students). Electronic applications accepted. *Expenses:* Contact institution. *Financial support:* In 2016–17, 10 teaching assistantships with full tuition reimbursements (averaging $8,000 per year) were awarded; career-related internships or fieldwork, Federal Work-Study, and unspecified assistantships also available. Financial award application deadline: 2/1; financial award applicants required to submit FAFSA. *Faculty research:* American fiction, American poetry, British fiction, British poetry, composition theory, creative writing. *Unit head:* Dr. Celia Patterson, Chairperson, 620-235-4689, E-mail: cpatterson@pittstate.edu. *Application contact:* Lisa Allen, Assistant Director of Graduate and Continuing Studies, 620-235-4223, Fax: 620-235-4219, E-mail: lallen@pittstate.edu.

**Portland State University,** Graduate Studies, College of Liberal Arts and Sciences, Department of English, Portland, OR 97207-0751. Offers MA, MFA, MA/MS. *Program availability:* Part-time, evening/weekend. *Faculty:* 34 full-time (18 women), 38 part-time/adjunct (19 women). *Students:* 93 full-time (66 women), 49 part-time (26 women); includes 17 minority (2 Black or African American, non-Hispanic/Latino; 2 American Indian or Alaska Native, non-Hispanic/Latino; 1 Asian, non-Hispanic/Latino; 4 Hispanic/Latino; 1 Native Hawaiian or other Pacific Islander, non-Hispanic/Latino; 7 Two or more races, non-Hispanic/Latino), 2 international. Average age 32. 222 applicants, 30% accepted, 46 enrolled. In 2016, 55 master's awarded. *Degree requirements:* For master's, one foreign language, comprehensive exam (for some programs), thesis (for some programs), oral and written exams. *Entrance requirements:* For master's, GRE (for some programs), statement of purpose, 2 letters of recommendation, transcripts, writing samples. Additional exam requirements/recommendations for international students: Required—TOEFL (minimum score 600 paper-based; 100 iBT). *Application deadline:* For fall admission, 1/3 for domestic and international students; for winter admission, 9/1 for domestic and international students; for spring admission, 11/1 for domestic and international students. Application fee: $65. *Expenses:* Contact institution. *Financial support:* In 2016–17, 18 teaching assistantships with full tuition reimbursements (averaging $7,690 per year) were awarded; career-related internships or fieldwork, Federal Work-Study, scholarships/grants, and unspecified assistantships also available. Support available to part-time students. Financial award application deadline: 3/1; financial award applicants required to submit FAFSA. *Faculty research:* American literature and cultural studies, medieval and British literature, writing prose fiction and poetry, rhetoric and composition, women's literature. *Total annual research expenditures:* $28,767. *Unit head:* Prof. Paul Collins, Chair, 503-725-3521, Fax: 503-725-3561, E-mail: pcollins@pdx.edu. *Application contact:* Matt Swetnam, Program Coordinator, 503-725-3623, Fax: 503-725-3561, E-mail: grdstudy@pdx.edu.
Website: http://www.pdx.edu/english/

**Princeton University,** Graduate School, Department of English, Princeton, NJ 08544-1019. Offers PhD. *Degree requirements:* For doctorate, 2 foreign languages, thesis/dissertation. *Entrance requirements:* For doctorate, GRE General Test, GRE Subject Test, sample of written work. Additional exam requirements/recommendations for international students: Required—TOEFL (minimum score 600 paper-based). Electronic applications accepted.

**Purdue University,** Graduate School, College of Liberal Arts, Department of English, West Lafayette, IN 47907. Offers creative writing (MFA); literature (MA, PhD), including linguistics, literature and philosophy (PhD), rhetoric and composition, theory and cultural studies (PhD). *Program availability:* Part-time. *Faculty:* 57 full-time (26 women), 3 part-time/adjunct (all women). *Students:* 130 full-time (82 women), 50 part-time (28 women); includes 21 minority (6 Black or African American, non-Hispanic/Latino; 5 Asian, non-Hispanic/Latino; 7 Hispanic/Latino; 3 Two or more races, non-Hispanic/Latino), 31 international. Average age 31. 299 applicants, 14% accepted, 29 enrolled. In 2016, 19 master's, 26 doctorates awarded. *Degree requirements:* For master's, one foreign language, comprehensive exam (for some programs), thesis (for some programs); for doctorate, one foreign language, comprehensive exam, thesis/dissertation. *Entrance requirements:* For master's, GRE General Test; GRE Subject Test in English literature (recommended for students applying to literary studies), minimum undergraduate GPA of 3.0 or equivalent; for doctorate, GRE General Test; GRE Subject Test in English literature (recommended for students applying to literary studies), master's degree. Additional exam requirements/recommendations for international students: Required—TOEFL (minimum score 620 paper-based; 77 iBT). *Application deadline:* For fall admission, 1/15 for domestic and international students. Applications are processed on a rolling basis. Application fee: $60 ($75 for international students). Electronic applications accepted. *Financial support:* Fellowships with tuition reimbursements and teaching assistantships with tuition reimbursements available. Support available to part-time students. Financial award application deadline: 1/15; financial award applicants required to submit FAFSA. *Faculty research:* Cultural studies, postmodern narrative, contemporary women writers, composition theory, slave narratives. *Unit head:* Krista L. Ratcliffe, Head, 765-494-6478, E-mail: ratcliffe@purdue.edu. *Application contact:* Jill M. Quirk, Graduate Contact, 765-494-3748, Fax: 765-494-1700, E-mail: griff@purdue.edu. Website: https://www.cla.purdue.edu/english/

**Purdue University,** Graduate School, Program in Philosophy and Literature, West Lafayette, IN 47907. Offers PhD. Program offered jointly with Department of English, School of Languages and Cultures, and Department of Philosophy. *Faculty:* 19 full-time (4 women), 1 part-time/adjunct. *Students:* 36 full-time (5 women), 9 part-time (5 women); includes 4 minority (1 American Indian or Alaska Native, non-Hispanic/Latino; 2 Hispanic/Latino; 1 Two or more races, non-Hispanic/Latino), 6 international. Average age 29. 66 applicants, 14% accepted, 4 enrolled. In 2016, 5 doctorates awarded. *Degree requirements:* For doctorate, one foreign language, comprehensive exam, thesis/dissertation. *Entrance requirements:* For doctorate, GRE, master's degree in either English, philosophy or foreign languages. Additional exam requirements/recommendations for international students: Required—TOEFL. *Application deadline:* For fall admission, 1/10 priority date for domestic students, 1/10 for international students. Application fee: $60 ($75 for international students). Electronic applications accepted. *Financial support:* In 2016–17, teaching assistantships (averaging $1,415 per year) were awarded; fellowships and research assistantships also available. *Unit head:* Dr. Joann L. Miller, Dean, 765-496-7276, E-mail: jlmiller@purdue.edu. *Application contact:* Teresa K. Berninger, Graduate Contact, 765-494-4276, E-mail: tkbernin@purdue.edu.
Website: http://www.cla.purdue.edu/phil-lit/graduate/

**Purdue University Northwest,** Graduate Studies Office, School of Liberal Arts and Social Sciences, Department of English and Philosophy, Hammond, IN 46323-2094. Offers English (MA). *Program availability:* Part-time, evening/weekend, online learning. *Degree requirements:* For master's, comprehensive exam, thesis optional. *Entrance requirements:* Additional exam requirements/recommendations for international students: Required—TOEFL. Electronic applications accepted. *Faculty research:* English literature, American literature, critical theory, women's studies, historical philosophy.

**Queens College of the City University of New York,** Arts and Humanities Division, Department of English, Queens, NY 11367-1597. Offers creative writing and literary translation (MFA); early childhood birth-2nd grade (Advanced Certificate); English (MA). *Program availability:* Part-time. *Faculty:* 51 full-time (26 women), 74 part-time/adjunct (47 women). *Students:* 66 part-time (39 women); includes 29 minority (8 Black or African American, non-Hispanic/Latino; 4 Asian, non-Hispanic/Latino; 14 Hispanic/Latino; 3 Two or more races, non-Hispanic/Latino), 2 international. Average age 31. 88 applicants, 55% accepted, 21 enrolled. In 2016, 29 master's awarded. *Degree requirements:* For master's, thesis, oral exam (English language and literature). *Entrance requirements:* For master's, manuscript (creative writing), minimum GPA of 3.0. Additional exam requirements/recommendations for international students: Required—TOEFL (minimum score 100 iBT), IELTS (minimum score 7). *Application deadline:* For fall admission, 4/1 for domestic students; for spring admission, 11/1 for domestic students. Applications are processed on a rolling basis. Application fee: $125. Electronic applications accepted. *Expenses:* Tuition, state resident: full-time $5065; part-time $425 per credit. Tuition, nonresident: part-time $780 per credit. *Required fees:* $522; $397 per credit. Part-time tuition and fees vary according to course load and program. *Financial support:* Career-related internships or fieldwork available. Financial award application deadline: 4/1; financial award applicants required to submit FAFSA. *Unit head:* Prof. Glenn Burger, Chairperson, 718-997-4600, E-mail: glenn.burger@qc.cuny.edu.

**Queen's University at Kingston,** School of Graduate Studies, Faculty of Arts and Sciences, Department of English Language and Literature, Kingston, ON K7L 3N6, Canada. Offers MA, PhD. *Degree requirements:* For master's, one foreign language, thesis optional; for doctorate, 2 foreign languages, comprehensive exam, thesis/dissertation. *Entrance requirements:* For master's, B.A.H. upper 2nd class standing, 10 full courses in English; for doctorate, M.A. upper 2nd class standing. Additional exam requirements/recommendations for international students: Required—TOEFL, TWE. *Faculty research:* Renaissance, 18th century, post colonial, Canadian, 19th century.

**Radford University,** College of Graduate Studies and Research, Program in English, Radford, VA 24142. Offers MA, MS. *Program availability:* Part-time. *Faculty:* 11 full-time (7 women). *Students:* 16 full-time (10 women), 4 part-time (3 women); includes 1 minority (Native Hawaiian or other Pacific Islander, non-Hispanic/Latino). Average age 26. 11 applicants, 91% accepted, 7 enrolled. In 2016, 12 master's awarded. *Degree requirements:* For master's, comprehensive exam, thesis (for some programs). *Entrance requirements:* For master's, GRE, minimum GPA of 2.75, 2 letters of reference, sample of expository writing, resume, official transcripts. Additional exam requirements/recommendations for international students: Required—TOEFL (minimum score 550 paper-based; 79 iBT), IELTS (minimum score 6.5). *Application deadline:* For fall admission, 2/15 priority date for domestic students, 12/1 for international students; for spring admission, 7/1 for international students. Applications are processed on a rolling basis. Application fee: $50. Electronic applications accepted. *Expenses:* Tuition, state resident: full-time $7868; part-time $328 per credit hour. Tuition, nonresident: full-time $16,394; part-time $683 per credit hour. *Required fees:* $3090; $130 per credit hour. Tuition and fees vary according to course load and program. *Financial support:* In 2016–17, 14 students received support, including 14 teaching assistantships (averaging $10,714 per year); scholarships/grants and unspecified assistantships also available. Support available to part-time students. Financial award application deadline: 3/1;

financial award applicants required to submit FAFSA. *Faculty research:* Effect of translation on the works of James Joyce, life and work of Olive Moore, southern trajectory of the works of Phillis Wheatley after her death, influence of French feminism on the poetry of Anne Bradstreet, postmodern theory and Native American fiction. *Unit head:* Dr. Paul Witkowsky, Coordinator, 540-831-5628, Fax: 540-831-6800, E-mail: english@radford.edu.
Website: http://www.radford.edu/content/chbs/home/english.html

**Rhode Island College,** School of Graduate Studies, Faculty of Arts and Sciences, Department of English, Providence, RI 02908-1991. Offers creative writing (MA, CGS); English (MA); literature (CGS). *Program availability:* Part-time, evening/weekend. *Faculty:* 6 full-time (2 women). *Students:* 5 full-time (2 women), 6 part-time (3 women). Average age 30. In 2016, 4 master's awarded. *Degree requirements:* For master's, thesis (for some programs). *Entrance requirements:* For master's, GRE General Test, 3 letters of recommendation, interview. Additional exam requirements/recommendations for international students: Recommended—TOEFL (minimum score 550 paper-based; 79 iBT). *Application deadline:* For fall admission, 3/1 for domestic students; for spring admission, 11/1 for domestic students. Applications are processed on a rolling basis. Application fee: $50. *Expenses:* Tuition, state resident: full-time $8928; part-time $372 per credit. Tuition, nonresident: full-time $17,376; part-time $724 per credit. *Required fees:* $604; $22 per credit. One-time fee: $74. *Financial support:* In 2016–17, 1 teaching assistantship with full tuition reimbursement (averaging $3,000 per year) was awarded; career-related internships or fieldwork, Federal Work-Study, scholarships/grants, health care benefits, and unspecified assistantships also available. Support available to part-time students. Financial award application deadline: 5/15; financial award applicants required to submit FAFSA. *Unit head:* Dr. Daniel Scott, III, Chair, 401-456-8028. *Application contact:* Graduate Studies, 401-456-8700.
Website: http://www.ric.edu/english/index.php

**Rice University,** Graduate Programs, School of Humanities, Department of English, Houston, TX 77251-1892. Offers MA, PhD. Terminal master's awarded for partial completion of doctoral program. *Degree requirements:* For master's, comprehensive exam, thesis (for some programs); for doctorate, comprehensive exam, thesis/dissertation. *Entrance requirements:* For master's and doctorate, GRE General Test, minimum GPA of 3.0. Additional exam requirements/recommendations for international students: Required—TOEFL (minimum score 600 paper-based; 90 iBT). Electronic applications accepted. *Faculty research:* Traditional periods and genres (excluding Old English), literary criticism and theory, Victorian literature, feminist literature, Renaissance literature, American literature, African-American literature.

**Rivier University,** School of Graduate Studies, Department of English, Nashua, NH 03060. Offers English (MAT); writing and literature (MA). *Program availability:* Part-time, evening/weekend. *Degree requirements:* For master's, comprehensive exam (for some programs). *Entrance requirements:* For master's, GRE Subject Test.

**Roosevelt University,** Graduate Division, College of Arts and Sciences, Department of Literature and Languages, Program in English, Chicago, IL 60605. Offers MA. *Program availability:* Part-time, evening/weekend. *Degree requirements:* For master's, one foreign language, thesis or alternative. *Faculty research:* Eighteenth-century Victorian literature and culture, creative writing, eighteenth through twentieth century literature, American literature and culture.

**Rutgers University–Camden,** Graduate School of Arts and Sciences, Program in English, Camden, NJ 08102. Offers MA. *Program availability:* Part-time, evening/weekend. *Degree requirements:* For master's, comprehensive exam, thesis optional, 30 credits. *Entrance requirements:* For master's, GRE General Test, 3 letters of recommendation, writing sample, statement of personal, professional, and academic goals. Additional exam requirements/recommendations for international students: Required—TOEFL, IELTS. Electronic applications accepted. *Faculty research:* British literature; American literature; women's studies; literary, poetic, and rhetorical theory; creative writing.

**Rutgers University–Newark,** Graduate School, Program in English, Newark, NJ 07102. Offers MA. *Program availability:* Part-time, evening/weekend. *Degree requirements:* For master's, one foreign language, comprehensive exam, thesis optional. *Entrance requirements:* For master's, GRE, minimum undergraduate B average. Electronic applications accepted. *Faculty research:* British and American literature, cultural studies, literary theory, minority literatures.

**Rutgers University–New Brunswick,** Graduate School-New Brunswick, Program of Literatures in English, Piscataway, NJ 08854-8097. Offers PhD. *Degree requirements:* For doctorate, one foreign language, thesis/dissertation, qualifying exam. *Entrance requirements:* For doctorate, GRE General Test, GRE Subject Test, writing sample, 3 letters of recommendation. Additional exam requirements/recommendations for international students: Required—TOEFL. Electronic applications accepted. *Faculty research:* Medieval literature; Renaissance; African American literature; 18th-century British literature; feminism, gender, and sexuality; postcolonial studies.

**St. Cloud State University,** School of Graduate Studies, College of Liberal Arts, Department of English, St. Cloud, MN 56301-4498. Offers English (MA, MS); teaching English as a second language (MA). *Program availability:* Part-time. *Degree requirements:* For master's, thesis or alternative. *Entrance requirements:* For master's, GRE General Test, minimum GPA of 2.75. Additional exam requirements/recommendations for international students: Required—Michigan English Language Assessment Battery; Recommended—TOEFL (minimum score 550 paper-based), IELTS (minimum score 6.5). Electronic applications accepted.

**St. John's University,** St. John's College of Liberal Arts and Sciences, Department of English, Queens, NY 11439. Offers MA, DA. *Program availability:* Part-time, evening/weekend. *Degree requirements:* For master's, comprehensive exam, thesis optional, portfolio; for doctorate, one foreign language, comprehensive exam, thesis/dissertation. *Entrance requirements:* For master's, GRE, minimum GPA of 3.0, 2 letters of recommendation, bachelor's degree; for doctorate, GRE, minimum GPA of 3.5 in literature, 3.0 overall; writing sample; 3 letters of recommendation; essay. Additional exam requirements/recommendations for international students: Required—TOEFL (minimum score 600 paper-based; 100 iBT), IELTS (minimum score 7). Electronic applications accepted. *Faculty research:* Modern comparative drama, literary theories and criticism, nineteenth and early twentieth century American literature, Chaucer, Elizabethan drama.

**Saint Louis University,** Graduate Education, College of Arts and Sciences and Graduate Education, Department of English, St. Louis, MO 63103. Offers MA, MA-R, PhD. *Program availability:* Part-time. *Degree requirements:* For master's, one foreign language, comprehensive exam, thesis optional, comprehensive oral exam; for doctorate, 2 foreign languages, comprehensive exam, thesis/dissertation, preliminary oral and written exams. *Entrance requirements:* For master's, GRE General Test, GRE Subject Test, letters of recommendation, resume, writing sample, interview; for doctorate, GRE General Test, GRE Subject Test, letters of recommendation, resumé, writing sample, interview, goal statement, writing sample. Additional exam requirements/recommendations for international students: Required—TOEFL (minimum score 550 paper-based). *Faculty research:* English literature, American literature, post-colonial literature, composition, literary theory.

*English*

**Saint Louis University–Madrid Campus,** Graduate Programs, Master of Arts in English Program, Madrid, Spain. Offers MA. *Program availability:* Part-time. *Degree requirements:* For master's, one foreign language, comprehensive exam, thesis optional. *Entrance requirements:* For master's, GRE General Test, transcripts, 3 letters of recommendation, writing sample, personal statement, curriculum vitae. Additional exam requirements/recommendations for international students: Required—TOEFL (minimum score 550 paper-based; 80 iBT). Electronic applications accepted. *Faculty research:* English, Irish and American literature; literary theory; translation; linguistics.

**St. Mary's University,** Graduate Studies, Program in English Literature and Language, San Antonio, TX 78228-8507. Offers MA, JD/MA. *Program availability:* Part-time, evening/weekend. *Faculty:* 12 full-time (5 women). *Students:* 5 full-time (3 women), 11 part-time (8 women); includes 8 minority (all Hispanic/Latino), 3 international. Average age 30. 5 applicants, 20% accepted. In 2016, 4 master's awarded. *Degree requirements:* For master's, thesis (for some programs). *Entrance requirements:* For master's, GRE (minimum score within top 35% of verbal section and top 35% of analytical section), minimum GPA of 3.0. Additional exam requirements/recommendations for international students: Required—TOEFL (minimum score 550 paper-based; 80 iBT), IELTS (minimum score 6). *Application deadline:* For fall admission, 7/1 for domestic students; for spring admission, 11/15 for domestic students; for summer admission, 4/1 for domestic students. Applications are processed on a rolling basis. Application fee: $0. Electronic applications accepted. *Expenses:* Tuition: Full-time $15,600; part-time $865 per credit hour. *Required fees:* $148 per semester. *Financial support:* Application deadline: 3/31; applicants required to submit FAFSA. *Faculty research:* Interpersonal communication, rhetorical communication. *Unit head:* Dr. Gwendolyn Diaz, Director of English Literature and Language Graduate Program, 210-436-2007, E-mail: gdiaz@stmarytx.edu. *Application contact:* Kim Thornton, Director, Graduate and Adult Enrollment Services, 210-436-3101, E-mail: kthornton@stmarytx.edu.
Website: https://www.stmarytx.edu/academics/graduate/masters/english-literature/

**Salem State University,** School of Graduate Studies, Program in English, Salem, MA 01970-5353. Offers MA, MAT, MA/MAT. *Program availability:* Part-time, evening/weekend. *Entrance requirements:* For master's, GRE or MAT. Additional exam requirements/recommendations for international students: Required—TOEFL (minimum score 550 paper-based; 80 iBT) or IELTS (minimum score 5.5).

**Salisbury University,** Department of English, Salisbury, MD 21801-6837. Offers English (MA), including creative writing, film, literature, secondary education, TESOL, writing and rhetoric. *Program availability:* Part-time. *Faculty:* 11 full-time (5 women), 1 (woman) part-time/adjunct. *Students:* 11 full-time (9 women), 24 part-time (19 women); includes 1 minority (Black or African American, non-Hispanic/Latino), 4 international. Average age 33. 18 applicants, 67% accepted, 9 enrolled. In 2016, 17 master's awarded. *Degree requirements:* For master's, comprehensive exam, thesis optional. *Entrance requirements:* Additional exam requirements/recommendations for international students: Required—TOEFL (minimum score 550 paper-based, 79 iBT) or IELTS (6.5). *Application deadline:* For fall admission, 8/1 for domestic and international students; for spring admission, 1/1 for domestic and international students. Application fee: $65. Electronic applications accepted. *Expenses:* $381 per credit hour resident tuition, $670 per credit hour non-resident tuition; $84 per credit hour fees. *Financial support:* In 2016–17, 2 students received support, including 11 teaching assistantships with full tuition reimbursements available (averaging $9,395 per year); career-related internships or fieldwork and scholarships/grants also available. Support available to part-time students. Financial award application deadline: 3/1; financial award applicants required to submit FAFSA. *Faculty research:* Literature; linguistics; film studies; rhetoric and composition; TESOL. *Unit head:* Dr. Christopher Vilmar, Graduate Program Director, English, 410-677-6511, E-mail: csvilmar@salisbury.edu.
Website: http://www.salisbury.edu/gsr/gradstudies/ENGpage.html

**Sam Houston State University,** College of Humanities and Social Sciences, Department of English, Huntsville, TX 77341. Offers creative writing, editing, and publishing (MFA); English (MA). *Program availability:* Part-time. *Degree requirements:* For master's, comprehensive exam, thesis optional. *Entrance requirements:* For master's, GRE General Test, creative writing sample, letters of recommendation. Additional exam requirements/recommendations for international students: Required—TOEFL (minimum score 550 paper-based; 79 iBT), IELTS (minimum score 6.5). Electronic applications accepted.

**San Diego State University,** Graduate and Research Affairs, College of Arts and Letters, Department of English and Comparative Literature, San Diego, CA 92182. Offers creative writing (MFA); English (MA). *Degree requirements:* For master's, one foreign language, comprehensive exam (for some programs), thesis (for some programs). *Entrance requirements:* For master's, GRE General Test, minimum GPA of 2.85, writing sample, 3 letters of recommendation. Additional exam requirements/recommendations for international students: Required—TOEFL. Electronic applications accepted.

**San Francisco State University,** Division of Graduate Studies, College of Liberal and Creative Arts, Department of English Language and Literature, Program in Composition, San Francisco, CA 94132-1722. Offers MA, Certificate. *Program availability:* Part-time. *Degree requirements:* For master's, comprehensive exam. *Entrance requirements:* Additional exam requirements/recommendations for international students: Required—TOEFL, TWE. *Application deadline:* Applications are processed on a rolling basis. *Expenses:* Tuition, state resident: full-time $6738. Tuition, nonresident: full-time $15,666. *Required fees:* $1012. Tuition and fees vary according to degree level and program. *Unit head:* Dr. Sugie Goen-Salter, Chair, 415-338-7582, Fax: 415-338-6159, E-mail: sgoen@sfsu.edu. *Application contact:* Prof. Mark Roberge, Graduate Coordinator, 415-338-7457, Fax: 415-338-6159, E-mail: roberge@sfsu.edu.
Website: http://english.sfsu.edu/graduate-composition

**San Francisco State University,** Division of Graduate Studies, College of Liberal and Creative Arts, Department of English Language and Literature, Program in Literature, San Francisco, CA 94132-1722. Offers MA. *Program availability:* Part-time. *Application deadline:* Applications are processed on a rolling basis. *Expenses:* Tuition, state resident: full-time $6738. Tuition, nonresident: full-time $15,666. *Required fees:* $1012. Tuition and fees vary according to degree level and program. *Unit head:* Dr. Sugie Goen-Salter, Chair, 415-338-7582, Fax: 415-338-6159, E-mail: sgoen@sfsu.edu. *Application contact:* Prof. Julie Paulson, Graduate Coordinator, 415-338-3107, Fax: 415-338-6159, E-mail: jpaulson@sfsu.edu.
Website: http://english.sfsu.edu/graduate-literature

**San Jose State University,** Graduate Studies and Research, College of Humanities and the Arts, San Jose, CA 95192-0001. Offers art (MA, MFA), including art history and visual culture (MA), digital media art (MFA), photography (MFA), pictorial art (MFA), spatial art (MFA); computational linguistics (Certificate); English (MA, MFA), including creative writing (MFA); French (MA); humanities and arts (Certificate); linguistics (MA); music (MA); philosophy (MA); professional and technical communication (Certificate); Spanish (MA); teaching English to speakers of other languages (MA); TESOL (Certificate); theatre arts (MA). Electronic applications accepted.

**Seton Hall University,** College of Arts and Sciences, Department of English, South Orange, NJ 07079-2697. Offers literature (MA). *Program availability:* Part-time, evening/weekend. *Degree requirements:* For master's, one foreign language, comprehensive exam, thesis (for some programs). *Entrance requirements:* For master's, minimum of 21 undergraduate credits in English. Additional exam requirements/recommendations for international students: Required—TOEFL. Electronic applications accepted. *Faculty research:* The essay, modern poetry, the novel, medieval poetry, Renaissance drama.

**Sewanee: The University of the South,** Sewanee School of Letters, Sewanee, TN 37383-1000. Offers American and English literature (MA); creative writing (MFA). *Program availability:* Part-time. *Faculty:* 1 full-time (0 women), 10 part-time/adjunct (7 women). *Students:* 54 part-time (31 women); includes 4 minority (1 Black or African American, non-Hispanic/Latino; 3 Two or more races, non-Hispanic/Latino), 1 international. Average age 41. In 2016, 10 master's awarded. *Degree requirements:* For master's, thesis (for some programs). *Entrance requirements:* For master's, writing sample, two letters of recommendation, official transcripts. *Application deadline:* Applications are processed on a rolling basis. Application fee: $40. Electronic applications accepted. *Expenses:* $5,707 tuition and fees for 2 courses (full-time), or $2,941 for one course. *Financial support:* Institutionally sponsored loans and scholarships/grants available. Financial award applicants required to submit FAFSA. *Unit head:* Dr. John M. Grammer, Director, 931-598-1483, Fax: 931-598-3303, E-mail: jgrammer@sewanee.edu. *Application contact:* April R. Alvarez, Coordinator, 931-598-1636, Fax: 931-598-3303.
Website: http://letters.sewanee.edu/

**Simmons College,** College of Arts and Sciences, Boston, MA 02115. Offers elementary education (MAT); English (MA); gender/cultural studies (MA); history (MA); public health (MPH); public policy (MPP). *Program availability:* Part-time. *Faculty:* 15 full-time (12 women), 1 (woman) part-time/adjunct. *Students:* 6 full-time (all women), 38 part-time (27 women); includes 10 minority (4 Black or African American, non-Hispanic/Latino; 1 Asian, non-Hispanic/Latino; 2 Hispanic/Latino; 3 Two or more races, non-Hispanic/Latino), 1 international. Average age 26. 50 applicants, 88% accepted, 17 enrolled. In 2016, 19 master's awarded. Terminal master's awarded for partial completion of doctoral program. *Degree requirements:* For master's, thesis (for some programs). *Entrance requirements:* For master's, GRE. Additional exam requirements/recommendations for international students: Required—TOEFL (minimum score 600 paper-based; 100 iBT). *Application deadline:* For fall admission, 8/1 for domestic and international students; for spring admission, 12/15 for domestic and international students; for summer admission, 5/1 for domestic and international students. Applications are processed on a rolling basis. Application fee: $35. Electronic applications accepted. *Expenses:* $1,050 per credit, $4,200 per course, $52 activity fee per semester. *Financial support:* In 2016–17, 4 fellowships with partial tuition reimbursements, 22 teaching assistantships with partial tuition reimbursements were awarded; scholarships/grants and unspecified assistantships also available. Support available to part-time students. Financial award applicants required to submit FAFSA. *Unit head:* Dr. Renee White, Dean, 617-521-2079. *Application contact:* Patricia Flaherty, Director, Graduate Studies Admission, 617-521-3902, Fax: 617-521-3058, E-mail: gsa@simmons.edu.
Website: http://www.simmons.edu/gradstudies/

**Simon Fraser University,** Office of Graduate Studies and Postdoctoral Fellows, Faculty of Arts and Social Sciences, Department of English, Burnaby, BC V5A 1S6, Canada. Offers English (MA, PhD); teachers of English (MA). *Program availability:* Part-time. *Faculty:* 35 full-time (19 women). *Students:* 54 full-time (39 women). 56 applicants, 32% accepted, 16 enrolled. In 2016, 21 master's, 2 doctorates awarded. *Degree requirements:* For master's, one foreign language, thesis or alternative; for doctorate, one foreign language, thesis/dissertation, field exams. *Entrance requirements:* For master's, minimum GPA of 3.0 (on scale of 4.33) or 3.33 based on last 60 credits of undergraduate courses; for doctorate, minimum GPA of 3.5 (on scale of 4.33). Additional exam requirements/recommendations for international students: Recommended—TOEFL (minimum score 580 paper-based; 93 iBT), IELTS (minimum score 7), TWE (minimum score 5). *Application deadline:* For fall admission, 1/25 for domestic and international students; for spring admission, 2/1 for domestic students. Application fee: $90 ($125 for international students). Electronic applications accepted. *Financial support:* In 2016–17, 40 students received support, including 21 fellowships (averaging $5,571 per year), teaching assistantships (averaging $5,608 per year); research assistantships and scholarships/grants also available. *Faculty research:* Literary criticism, literature and psychoanalysis, Renaissance drama and poetry, Shakespeare, Canadian and American literature. *Unit head:* Dr. Michelle Levy, Graduate Chair, 778-782-5393, E-mail: engl-grad-chair@sfu.ca. *Application contact:* Christa Gruninger, Graduate Secretary, 778-782-4614, Fax: 778-782-3136, E-mail: englgrad@sfu.ca.
Website: http://www.english.sfu.ca/

**Slippery Rock University of Pennsylvania,** Graduate Studies (Recruitment), College of Liberal Arts, Department of English, Slippery Rock, PA 16057-1383. Offers MA. *Program availability:* Part-time, evening/weekend, online only, 100% online. *Faculty:* 3 full-time (2 women). *Students:* 4 full-time (all women), 10 part-time (6 women); includes 2 minority (1 Native Hawaiian or other Pacific Islander, non-Hispanic/Latino; 1 Two or more races, non-Hispanic/Latino). Average age 28. 13 applicants, 85% accepted, 9 enrolled. *Degree requirements:* For master's, comprehensive exam (for some programs), thesis (for some programs). *Entrance requirements:* For master's, official transcripts, essay, two letters of recommendation. Additional exam requirements/recommendations for international students: Required—TOEFL (minimum score 550 paper-based; 80 iBT). *Application deadline:* For fall admission, 3/1 for domestic students, 5/1 for international students; for spring admission, 11/1 for domestic students, 9/1 for international students. Applications are processed on a rolling basis. Application fee: $25 ($30 for international students). Electronic applications accepted. *Expenses:* $646.50 per credit in-state, $936.80 per credit out-of-state; $581.45 per online credit in-state, $648.65 per online credit out-of-state. *Financial support:* In 2016–17, 3 students received support. Career-related internships or fieldwork, Federal Work-Study, institutionally sponsored loans, scholarships/grants, tuition waivers (partial), and unspecified assistantships available. Support available to part-time students. Financial award application deadline: 5/1; financial award applicants required to submit FAFSA. *Unit head:* Dr. Nancy Barta-Smith, Graduate Coordinator, 724-738-2360, Fax: 724-738-2043, E-mail: nancy.barta-smith@sru.edu. *Application contact:* Brandi Weber-Mortimer, Director of Graduate Admissions, 724-738-2051, Fax: 724-738-2146, E-mail: graduate.admissions@sru.edu.
Website: http://www.sru.edu/academics/colleges-and-departments/cola/departments/english

**Sonoma State University,** Department of English, Rohnert Park, CA 94928. Offers American literature (MA); creative writing (MA); English literature (MA); world literature (MA). *Program availability:* Part-time, evening/weekend. *Degree requirements:* For master's, one foreign language, thesis or alternative. *Entrance requirements:* For master's, minimum GPA of 2.5. Additional exam requirements/recommendations for international students: Required—TOEFL (minimum score 500 paper-based). *Application deadline:* For fall admission, 11/30 priority date for domestic students.

Application fee: $55. *Expenses:* Tuition, state resident: full-time $6738; part-time $3906 per unit. *Required fees:* $1916; $1916 per year. Tuition and fees vary according to course load, degree level and program. *Financial support:* Fellowships, teaching assistantships, career-related internships or fieldwork, and Federal Work-Study available. Financial award application deadline: 3/2; financial award applicants required to submit FAFSA. *Unit head:* Brantley L. Bryant, Chair, 707-664-2164, E-mail: brantley.bryant@sonoma.edu. *Application contact:* Dr. Anne Goldman, Chair of Graduate Studies, 707-664-2651, Fax: 707-664-6040, E-mail: goldmana@sonoma.edu. Website: http://www.sonoma.edu/english/programs/ma-program.html

**South Carolina State University,** College of Graduate and Professional Studies, Department of Education, Orangeburg, SC 29117-0001. Offers early childhood education (MAT); education (M Ed); elementary education (M Ed, MAT); English (MAT); general science/biology (MAT); mathematics (MAT); secondary education (M Ed), including biology education, business education, counselor education, English education, home economics education, industrial education, mathematics education, science education, social studies education; special education (M Ed), including emotionally handicapped, learning disabilities, mentally handicapped. *Accreditation:* NCATE. *Program availability:* Part-time, evening/weekend. *Faculty:* 12 full-time (8 women), 3 part-time/adjunct (1 woman). *Students:* 28 full-time (20 women), 20 part-time (17 women); includes 45 minority (44 Black or African American, non-Hispanic/Latino; 1 Two or more races, non-Hispanic/Latino). Average age 31. 22 applicants, 100% accepted, 16 enrolled. In 2016, 9 master's awarded. *Degree requirements:* For master's, thesis optional, departmental qualifying exam. *Entrance requirements:* For master's, GRE General Test, NTE, interview, teaching certificate. *Application deadline:* For fall admission, 6/15 priority date for domestic students, 6/15 for international students; for spring admission, 11/1 for domestic and international students. Application fee: $25. Electronic applications accepted. *Expenses:* Tuition, state resident: full-time $8938; part-time $579 per credit hour. Tuition, nonresident: full-time $19,018; part-time $1139 per credit hour. *Required fees:* $1482; $82 per credit hour. *Financial support:* Fellowships, career-related internships or fieldwork, Federal Work-Study, and scholarships/grants available. Financial award application deadline: 6/1. *Unit head:* Dr. Charlie Spell, Interim Chair, Department of Education, 803-536-8963, Fax: 803-516-4568, E-mail: cspell@scsu.edu. *Application contact:* Curtis Foskey, Coordinator of Graduate Studies, 803-536-8419, Fax: 803-536-8812, E-mail: cfoskey@scsu.edu.

**South Dakota State University,** Graduate School, College of Arts and Science, Department of English, Brookings, SD 57007. Offers MA. *Program availability:* Part-time. *Degree requirements:* For master's, comprehensive exam (for some programs), thesis (for some programs), oral and written exams. *Entrance requirements:* For master's, minimum GPA of 2.75. Additional exam requirements/recommendations for international students: Required—TOEFL (minimum score 600 paper-based; 100 iBT). *Faculty research:* English and American literature topics, regional literature (Midwestern), women's literature, Lakota literature and culture, rhetoric and writing.

**Southeastern Louisiana University,** College of Arts, Humanities and Social Sciences, Department of English, Hammond, LA 70402. Offers creative writing (MA); language and theory (MA); professional writing (MA); publishing studies (MA). *Program availability:* Part-time. *Faculty:* 12 full-time (4 women), 1 part-time/adjunct (0 women). *Students:* 12 full-time (9 women), 15 part-time (10 women); includes 4 minority (1 Black or African American, non-Hispanic/Latino; 2 Hispanic/Latino; 1 Two or more races, non-Hispanic/Latino). Average age 28. 10 applicants, 60% accepted, 4 enrolled. In 2016, 15 master's awarded. *Degree requirements:* For master's, comprehensive exam, thesis optional. *Entrance requirements:* Additional exam requirements/recommendations for international students: Required—TOEFL (minimum score 500 paper-based; 61 iBT), IELTS (minimum score 5.5). *Application deadline:* For fall admission, 7/15 priority date for domestic students, 6/1 priority date for international students; for spring admission, 12/1 priority date for domestic students, 10/1 priority date for international students. Applications are processed on a rolling basis. Application fee: $20 ($30 for international students). Electronic applications accepted. *Expenses:* Tuition, state resident: full-time $6540; part-time $465 per credit hour. Tuition, nonresident: full-time $19,017; part-time $1158 per credit hour. *Required fees:* $1829. *Financial support:* In 2016–17, 16 students received support, including 8 research assistantships (averaging $9,688 per year), 2 teaching assistantships (averaging $9,900 per year); institutionally sponsored loans, scholarships/grants, and unspecified assistantships also available. Support available to part-time students. Financial award application deadline: 5/1; financial award applicants required to submit FAFSA. *Faculty research:* John Ruskin, animal studies, linguistics, film studies. *Unit head:* Dr. David Hanson, Department Head, 985-549-2100, Fax: 985-549-5021, E-mail: dhanson@southeastern.edu. *Application contact:* Amanda Harper, Graduate Admissions Analyst, 985-549-5620, Fax: 985-549-5632, E-mail: admissions@southeastern.edu. Website: http://www.southeastern.edu/acad_research/depts/engl

**Southeast Missouri State University,** School of Graduate Studies, Department of English, Cape Girardeau, MO 63701-4799. Offers teaching English to speakers of other languages (MA). *Program availability:* Part-time, evening/weekend, online learning. *Faculty:* 17 full-time (8 women). *Students:* 52 full-time (33 women), 50 part-time (40 women); includes 3 minority (2 Black or African American, non-Hispanic/Latino; 1 Hispanic/Latino), 33 international. Average age 32. 50 applicants, 84% accepted, 34 enrolled. In 2016, 39 master's awarded. *Degree requirements:* For master's, comprehensive exam (for some programs), thesis optional. *Entrance requirements:* Additional exam requirements/recommendations for international students: Required—TOEFL (minimum score 550 paper-based; 79 iBT), IELTS (minimum score 6), PTE (minimum score 53). *Application deadline:* For fall admission, 8/1 for domestic students, 6/1 for international students; for spring admission, 11/21 for domestic students, 10/1 for international students; for summer admission, 5/15 for domestic students. Applications are processed on a rolling basis. Application fee: $30 ($40 for international students). Electronic applications accepted. *Expenses:* Tuition, state resident: full-time $3130; part-time $260.80 per credit hour. Tuition, nonresident: full-time $5842; part-time $486.80 per credit hour. *Required fees:* $33.70 per credit hour. *Financial support:* In 2016–17, 24 students received support, including 17 teaching assistantships with full tuition reimbursements available; career-related internships or fieldwork, Federal Work-Study, scholarships/grants, traineeships, tuition waivers (full), and unspecified assistantships also available. Financial award application deadline: 6/30; financial award applicants required to submit FAFSA. *Faculty research:* Literature, creative writing, technical writing, secondary English education, teaching English as a second language. *Unit head:* Dr. Susan Kendrick, Department of English Chair, 573-651-2156, Fax: 573-651-5188, E-mail: skendrick@semo.edu. *Application contact:* 573-651-2590, E-mail: admissions@semo.edu. Website: http://www.semo.edu/english/

**Southern Connecticut State University,** School of Graduate Studies, School of Arts and Sciences, Department of English, New Haven, CT 06515-1355. Offers MA, MS, MLS/MS. *Program availability:* Part-time, evening/weekend. *Faculty:* 15 full-time (9 women). *Students:* 37 full-time (26 women), 23 part-time (14 women); includes 9 minority (5 Black or African American, non-Hispanic/Latino; 2 Hispanic/Latino; 2 Two or more races, non-Hispanic/Latino). Average age 32. 30 applicants, 60% accepted, 11 enrolled. In 2016, 12 master's awarded. *Degree requirements:* For master's, one foreign language, thesis or alternative. *Entrance requirements:* For master's, interview. *Application deadline:* For fall admission, 5/1 priority date for domestic students; for spring admission, 12/1 priority date for domestic students. Applications are processed on a rolling basis. Application fee: $50. Electronic applications accepted. *Expenses:* Tuition, state resident: full-time $6497; part-time $519 per credit hour. Tuition, nonresident: full-time $18,102; part-time $535 per credit hour. *Required fees:* $4722; $55 per semester. Tuition and fees vary according to program. *Financial support:* Career-related internships or fieldwork, scholarships/grants, and unspecified assistantships available. Financial award application deadline: 4/15; financial award applicants required to submit FAFSA. *Unit head:* Dr. Michael Shea, Chairperson, 203-392-6741, Fax: 203-392-6731, E-mail: sheam1@southernct.edu. *Application contact:* Lisa Galvin, Director of Graduate Admissions, 203-392-5240, Fax: 203-392-5235, E-mail: galvinl1@southernct.edu.

**Southern Illinois University Carbondale,** Graduate School, College of Liberal Arts, Department of English, Carbondale, IL 62901-4701. Offers composition (MA, PhD), including composition, literature, rhetoric; creative writing (MFA). *Degree requirements:* For master's, one foreign language, thesis; for doctorate, 2 foreign languages, thesis/dissertation. *Entrance requirements:* For master's, GRE General Test, GRE Subject Test, minimum GPA of 2.7; for doctorate, GRE General Test, GRE Subject Test, minimum GPA of 3.25. Additional exam requirements/recommendations for international students: Required—TOEFL. *Faculty research:* British literature, English literature, modern Continental literature, literary criticism and theory, film studies, Irish studies.

**Southern Illinois University Edwardsville,** Graduate School, College of Arts and Sciences, Department of English Language and Literature, Program in Literature, Edwardsville, IL 62026-0001. Offers MA, Postbaccalaureate Certificate. *Program availability:* Part-time. *Degree requirements:* For master's, one foreign language, thesis (for some programs), written papers, oral examination. *Entrance requirements:* Additional exam requirements/recommendations for international students: Required—TOEFL (minimum score 550 paper-based, 79 iBT), IELTS (minimum score 6.5), Michigan Test of English Language Proficiency or PTE. Electronic applications accepted.

**Southern Methodist University,** Dedman College of Humanities and Sciences, Department of English, Dallas, TX 75275. Offers MA, PhD. Terminal master's awarded for partial completion of doctoral program. *Degree requirements:* For master's, one foreign language, comprehensive exam, thesis optional, oral exam; for doctorate, one foreign language, comprehensive exam, thesis/dissertation. *Entrance requirements:* For master's, GRE General Test, minimum GPA of 3.0; for doctorate, GRE General Test, minimum GPA of 3.5, BA in English or other appropriate field. Additional exam requirements/recommendations for international students: Required—TOEFL (minimum score 550 paper-based). Electronic applications accepted. *Faculty research:* British/American literature, critical theory, medieval studies, gender studies, book history.

**Spring Hill College,** Graduate Programs, Program in Liberal Arts, Mobile, AL 36608-1791. Offers fine arts (MLA); history and social science (MLA); leadership and ethics (MLA, Postbaccalaureate Certificate); literature (MLA); studio art (Postbaccalaureate Certificate). *Program availability:* Part-time, evening/weekend. *Faculty:* 5 full-time (0 women), 2 part-time/adjunct (1 woman). *Students:* 2 full-time (1 woman), 31 part-time (10 women); includes 4 minority (3 Black or African American, non-Hispanic/Latino; 1 Hispanic/Latino), 3 international. Average age 35. In 2016, 7 master's, 1 other advanced degree awarded. *Degree requirements:* For master's, capstone course, completion of program within 6 years of initial admittance. *Entrance requirements:* For master's, bachelor's degree with minimum undergraduate GPA of 3.0 or graduate/professional degree. Additional exam requirements/recommendations for international students: Required—TOEFL (minimum score 550 paper-based; 80 iBT), IELTS (minimum score 6.5), CPE or CAE (minimum score C), Michigan English Language Assessment Battery (minimum score 90). *Application deadline:* For fall admission, 8/1 priority date for domestic and international students; for spring admission, 12/1 priority date for domestic and international students. Applications are processed on a rolling basis. Application fee: $25 ($35 for international students). Electronic applications accepted. *Expenses:* Contact institution. *Financial support:* Applicants required to submit FAFSA. *Unit head:* Dr. Thomas J. Hoffman, Director, 251-380-4184, Fax: 251-460-2115, E-mail: thoffman@shc.edu. *Application contact:* Robert Stewart, Vice President of Enrollment, 251-380-3030, Fax: 251-460-2186, E-mail: rstewart@shc.edu. Website: http://ug.shc.edu/graduate-degrees/master-liberal-arts/

**Stanford University,** School of Humanities and Sciences, Department of English, Stanford, CA 94305-2004. Offers MA, PhD. Terminal master's awarded for partial completion of doctoral program. *Degree requirements:* For master's, one foreign language, thesis (for some programs); for doctorate, 2 foreign languages, thesis/dissertation, oral exam. *Entrance requirements:* For master's and doctorate, GRE General Test, GRE Subject Test. Additional exam requirements/recommendations for international students: Required—TOEFL. Electronic applications accepted. *Expenses:* Tuition: Full-time $47,331. *Required fees:* $609.

**State University of New York at New Paltz,** Graduate School, School of Liberal Arts and Sciences, Department of English, New Paltz, NY 12561. Offers MA. *Program availability:* Part-time, evening/weekend. *Students:* 6 full-time (3 women), 30 part-time (18 women); includes 5 minority (2 Black or African American, non-Hispanic/Latino; 1 Asian, non-Hispanic/Latino; 1 Hispanic/Latino; 1 Two or more races, non-Hispanic/Latino). 14 applicants, 79% accepted, 8 enrolled. In 2016, 13 master's awarded. *Degree requirements:* For master's, comprehensive exam, thesis (for some programs), foreign language proficiency exam. *Entrance requirements:* For master's, minimum GPA of 3.0, 10-15 page writing sample. Additional exam requirements/recommendations for international students: Required—TOEFL (minimum score 563 paper-based; 85 iBT), IELTS (minimum score 7). *Application deadline:* For fall admission, 3/15 priority date for domestic students, 3/15 for international students; for spring admission, 10/15 for domestic and international students. Application fee: $50. Electronic applications accepted. *Financial support:* In 2016–17, 1 research assistantship with partial tuition reimbursement (averaging $5,000 per year), 17 teaching assistantships with partial tuition reimbursements (averaging $5,000 per year) were awarded. Financial award application deadline: 8/1. *Faculty research:* Twentieth-century British literature, Hemingway and modernism, British modernist fiction, Faulkner and the Southern Renaissance, revisionary approaches to early twentieth-century literature. *Unit head:* Dr. Nancy Johnson, Chair, 845-257-2720, E-mail: english@newpaltz.edu. *Application contact:* Dr. Cy Mulready, Director of Graduate Studies, 845-257-2739, E-mail: mulreadc@newpaltz.edu. Website: http://www.newpaltz.edu/english/

**State University of New York at Oswego,** Graduate Studies, College of Liberal Arts and Sciences, Department of English, Oswego, NY 13126. Offers MA. *Program availability:* Part-time. *Degree requirements:* For master's, thesis optional. *Entrance requirements:* Additional exam requirements/recommendations for international students: Required—TOEFL (minimum score 560 paper-based).

**State University of New York College at Cortland,** Graduate Studies, School of Arts and Sciences, Department of English, Cortland, NY 13045. Offers MA. *Program availability:* Part-time, evening/weekend. *Degree requirements:* For master's, one foreign language, comprehensive exam, thesis. *Entrance requirements:* For master's, GRE General Test.

**State University of New York College at Potsdam,** School of Arts and Sciences, Department of English and Communication, Potsdam, NY 13676. Offers MA. *Program availability:* Part-time, evening/weekend. *Degree requirements:* For master's, one foreign language, thesis or alternative. *Entrance requirements:* For master's, minimum GPA of 3.0 in last 60 hours of undergraduate course work. Additional exam requirements/recommendations for international students: Required—TOEFL (minimum score 550 paper-based; 80 iBT), IELTS (minimum score 6). Electronic applications accepted.

**Stephen F. Austin State University,** Graduate School, College of Liberal Arts, Department of English and Philosophy, Nacogdoches, TX 75962. Offers English (MA). *Degree requirements:* For master's, comprehensive exam. *Entrance requirements:* For master's, GRE General Test. Additional exam requirements/recommendations for international students: Required—TOEFL. *Faculty research:* Creative writing, Latin American literature, modern American literature, modern British literature, literature for children.

**Stony Brook University, State University of New York,** Graduate School, College of Arts and Sciences, Department of Cultural Studies and Comparative Literature, Stony Brook, NY 11794. Offers comparative literature (MA, PhD); cultural studies (PhD, Certificate). *Program availability:* Evening/weekend. *Faculty:* 12 full-time (4 women). *Students:* 57 full-time (40 women), 4 part-time (all women); includes 7 minority (2 Black or African American, non-Hispanic/Latino; 4 Asian, non-Hispanic/Latino; 1 Hispanic/Latino), 24 international. Average age 34. 58 applicants, 48% accepted, 14 enrolled. In 2016, 3 master's, 1 doctorate, 3 other advanced degrees awarded. Terminal master's awarded for partial completion of doctoral program. *Degree requirements:* For master's, 2 foreign languages, exam; for doctorate, 3 foreign languages, comprehensive exam, thesis/dissertation. *Entrance requirements:* For master's and doctorate, GRE General Test, minimum GPA of 3.5 in major, 3.0 overall. Additional exam requirements/recommendations for international students: Required—TOEFL. *Application deadline:* For fall admission, 1/15 for domestic students; for spring admission, 10/1 for domestic students. Application fee: $100. Electronic applications accepted. *Expenses:* Contact institution. *Financial support:* In 2016–17, 1 research assistantship, 30 teaching assistantships were awarded; fellowships also available. *Faculty research:* Humanities, women's studies, literary criticism, gender studies, philosophy. *Unit head:* Dr. Robert Harvey, Chair, 631-632-7464, E-mail: robert.harvey@stonybrook.edu. *Application contact:* Mary Moran-Luba, Coordinator, 631-632-7460, Fax: 631-632-5707, E-mail: mary.moran-luba@stonybrook.edu.
Website: http://www.stonybrook.edu/commcms/cat/index.html

**Stony Brook University, State University of New York,** Graduate School, College of Arts and Sciences, Department of English, Stony Brook, NY 11794. Offers English (MA, PhD); English education (MAT). MAT offered through the School of Professional Development. *Faculty:* 22 full-time (9 women), 4 part-time/adjunct (3 women). *Students:* 40 full-time (19 women), 11 part-time (8 women); includes 13 minority (1 Black or African American, non-Hispanic/Latino; 3 Asian, non-Hispanic/Latino; 6 Hispanic/Latino; 3 Two or more races, non-Hispanic/Latino), 5 international. Average age 31. 86 applicants, 34% accepted, 9 enrolled. In 2016, 12 master's, 12 doctorates awarded. Terminal master's awarded for partial completion of doctoral program. *Degree requirements:* For doctorate, thesis/dissertation. *Entrance requirements:* For master's and doctorate, GRE General Test. Additional exam requirements/recommendations for international students: Required—TOEFL. *Application deadline:* For fall admission, 1/15 for domestic students; for spring admission, 10/1 for domestic students. Application fee: $100. Electronic applications accepted. *Expenses:* Contact institution. *Financial support:* In 2016–17, 1 research assistantship, 26 teaching assistantships were awarded; fellowships also available. *Faculty research:* Humanities, poetry, literary theory, rhetoric, American literature. *Unit head:* Dr. Celia Marshik, Chair, 631-632-7356, E-mail: celia.marshik@stonybrook.edu. *Application contact:* Theresa Spadola, Coordinator, 631-632-7373, E-mail: theresa.spadola@stonybrook.edu.
Website: http://www.stonybrook.edu/english/

**Sul Ross State University,** College of Arts and Sciences, Department of Languages and Literature, Alpine, TX 79832. Offers English (MA). *Program availability:* Part-time, evening/weekend. *Degree requirements:* For master's, thesis optional. *Entrance requirements:* For master's, GRE General Test, minimum GPA of 2.5 in last 60 hours of undergraduate work. *Faculty research:* Narrative theory, feminist literary criticism, autobiography studies, multiculturalism, biblical narrative.

**Syracuse University,** College of Arts and Sciences, Programs in English, Syracuse, NY 13244. Offers MA, PhD. *Program availability:* Part-time. *Degree requirements:* For doctorate, comprehensive exam, thesis/dissertation. *Entrance requirements:* For master's and doctorate, GRE General Test, transcript from undergraduate/graduate institution, three letters of recommendation, writing sample. Additional exam requirements/recommendations for international students: Required—TOEFL (minimum score 100 iBT). *Application deadline:* For fall admission, 1/9 priority date for domestic and international students. Application fee: $75. Electronic applications accepted. *Expenses: Tuition:* Full-time $25,974; part-time $1443 per credit hour. *Required fees:* $802; $50 per course. Tuition and fees vary according to course load and program. *Financial support:* Fellowships with full tuition reimbursements, teaching assistantships with full tuition reimbursements, and scholarships/grants available. Financial award application deadline: 1/1. *Faculty research:* Critical theory, early modern studies, American studies, literary and filmic periods, reception and book history. *Unit head:* Dorri Beam, Director of Graduate Studies, 315-443-2174, E-mail: drbeam@syr.edu. *Application contact:* Terri Zollo, Graduate Coordinator, 315-443-2174, E-mail: tazollo@syr.edu.
Website: http://english.syr.edu/

**Tarleton State University,** College of Graduate Studies, College of Liberal and Fine Arts, Department of English and Languages, Stephenville, TX 76402. Offers English (MA). *Program availability:* Part-time, evening/weekend, 100% online, blended/hybrid learning. *Faculty:* 3 full-time (1 woman), 1 (woman) part-time/adjunct. *Students:* 3 full-time (2 women), 12 part-time (11 women); includes 2 minority (1 Asian, non-Hispanic/Latino; 1 Two or more races, non-Hispanic/Latino). 9 applicants, 89% accepted, 5 enrolled. In 2016, 8 master's awarded. *Degree requirements:* For master's, comprehensive exam, thesis (for some programs). *Entrance requirements:* For master's, GRE General Test, minimum GPA of 3.0. Additional exam requirements/recommendations for international students: Required—TOEFL (minimum score 550 paper-based; 80 iBT). *Application deadline:* For fall admission, 8/15 priority date for domestic students; for spring admission, 1/7 for domestic students. Applications are processed on a rolling basis. Application fee: $45 ($145 for international students). Electronic applications accepted. *Expenses:* $3,672 tuition; $2,437 fees. *Financial support:* Research assistantships, teaching assistantships, career-related internships or fieldwork, and Federal Work-Study available. Support available to part-time students. Financial award application deadline: 5/1; financial award applicants required to submit FAFSA. *Unit head:* Dr. Jeanelle Barrett, Head, 254-968-9039, Fax: 254-968-1931, E-mail: jbarrett@tarleton.edu. *Application contact:* Information Contact, 254-968-9104,

Fax: 254-968-9670, E-mail: gradoffice@tarleton.edu.
Website: http://www.tarleton.edu/english/graduate/index.html

**Temple University,** College of Liberal Arts, Department of English, Philadelphia, PA 19122-6096. Offers creative writing (MFA); English (MA, PhD). *Program availability:* Part-time. *Degree requirements:* For doctorate, 2 foreign languages, thesis/dissertation. *Entrance requirements:* For master's and doctorate, GRE General Test, minimum GPA of 3.0; 3 letters of recommendation. Additional exam requirements/recommendations for international students: Required—TOEFL (minimum score 620 paper-based; 105 iBT). Electronic applications accepted. *Faculty research:* Early modern British literature, American literature, modernism, critical theory, rhetoric, composition.

**Tennessee Technological University,** College of Graduate Studies, College of Arts and Sciences, Department of English, Cookeville, TN 38505. Offers MA. *Program availability:* Part-time. *Faculty:* 23 full-time (8 women). *Students:* 8 full-time (5 women), 1 (woman) part-time. Average age 28. 6 applicants, 67% accepted, 3 enrolled. In 2016, 2 master's awarded. *Degree requirements:* For master's, comprehensive exam, thesis or alternative. *Entrance requirements:* For master's, GRE General Test. Additional exam requirements/recommendations for international students: Required—TOEFL (minimum score 527 paper-based; 71 iBT), IELTS (minimum score 5.5), PTE (minimum score 48), or TOEIC (Test of English as an International Communication). *Application deadline:* For fall admission, 8/1 for domestic students, 5/1 for international students; for spring admission, 12/1 for domestic students, 10/1 for international students; for summer admission, 5/1 for domestic students, 2/1 for international students. Applications are processed on a rolling basis. Application fee: $35 ($40 for international students). Electronic applications accepted. *Expenses:* Tuition, state resident: full-time $9375; part-time $534 per credit hour. Tuition, nonresident: full-time $22,443; part-time $1260 per credit hour. *Financial support:* In 2016–17, 6 teaching assistantships (averaging $8,000 per year) were awarded; fellowships and research assistantships also available. Financial award application deadline: 4/1. *Unit head:* Dr. Ted Pelton, Chairperson, 931-372-3343, Fax: 931-372-6142, E-mail: tpelton@tntech.edu. *Application contact:* Shelia K. Kendrick, Coordinator of Graduate Studies, 931-372-3808, Fax: 931-372-3497, E-mail: skendrick@tntech.edu.

**Texas A&M International University,** Office of Graduate Studies and Research, College of Arts and Sciences, Department of Humanities, Laredo, TX 78041-1900. Offers English (MA); Hispanic studies (PhD); history and political thought (MA); language, literature and translation (MA). *Degree requirements:* For master's, comprehensive exam (for some programs), thesis (for some programs). *Entrance requirements:* For master's, GRE General Test. Additional exam requirements/recommendations for international students: Required—TOEFL (minimum score 550 paper-based; 79 iBT).

**Texas A&M University,** College of Liberal Arts, Department of English, College Station, TX 77843. Offers MA, PhD. *Faculty:* 40. *Students:* 59 full-time (49 women), 25 part-time (13 women); includes 9 minority (1 Black or African American, non-Hispanic/Latino; 1 Asian, non-Hispanic/Latino; 5 Hispanic/Latino; 2 Two or more races, non-Hispanic/Latino), 27 international. Average age 33. 84 applicants, 42% accepted, 13 enrolled. In 2016, 8 master's, 8 doctorates awarded. Terminal master's awarded for partial completion of doctoral program. *Degree requirements:* For master's, one foreign language, thesis optional; for doctorate, 2 foreign languages, thesis/dissertation. *Entrance requirements:* For master's and doctorate, GRE General Test, sample of written work. Additional exam requirements/recommendations for international students: Required—TOEFL (minimum score 550 paper-based; 80 iBT), IELTS (minimum score 6), PTE (minimum score 53). *Application deadline:* For fall admission, 1/16 for domestic students, 2/1 for international students. Applications are processed on a rolling basis. Application fee: $50 ($90 for international students). Electronic applications accepted. *Expenses:* Contact institution. *Financial support:* In 2016–17, 63 students received support, including 5 fellowships with tuition reimbursements available (averaging $13,360 per year), 9 research assistantships with tuition reimbursements available (averaging $4,622 per year), 49 teaching assistantships with tuition reimbursements available (averaging $9,383 per year); career-related internships or fieldwork, institutionally sponsored loans, scholarships/grants, traineeships, health care benefits, tuition waivers (full and partial), and unspecified assistantships also available. Support available to part-time students. Financial award application deadline: 3/15; financial award applicants required to submit FAFSA. *Faculty research:* American, Renaissance, medieval, textual, and discourse studies. *Unit head:* Dr. Maura Ives, Interim Department Head, 979-845-8319, E-mail: m-ives@tamu.edu. *Application contact:* Director of Graduate Studies, 979-845-9836, Fax: 979-862-2292, E-mail: grad-program@tamuenglish.org.
Website: http://www.english.tamu.edu/

**Texas A&M University–Commerce,** College of Humanities, Social Sciences and Arts, Commerce, TX 75429-3011. Offers applied criminology (MS); applied linguistics (MA, MS); art (MA, MFA); Christianity in history (Graduate Certificate); computational linguistics (Graduate Certificate); creative writing (Graduate Certificate); English (MA, MS, PhD); film studies (Graduate Certificate); history (MA, MS); music (MM); political science (MA, MS); public history (Graduate Certificate); sociology (MA); Spanish (MA); studies in children's and adolescent literature and culture (Graduate Certificate); teaching English to speakers of other languages (Graduate Certificate); theater (MA, MS). *Program availability:* Part-time. *Faculty:* 53 full-time (26 women), 7 part-time/adjunct (2 women). *Students:* 87 full-time (55 women), 528 part-time (362 women); includes 198 minority (86 Black or African American, non-Hispanic/Latino; 2 American Indian or Alaska Native, non-Hispanic/Latino; 8 Asian, non-Hispanic/Latino; 84 Hispanic/Latino; 18 Two or more races, non-Hispanic/Latino), 27 international. Average age 37. 333 applicants, 56% accepted, 149 enrolled. In 2016, 66 master's, 8 doctorates awarded. *Degree requirements:* For master's, one foreign language, comprehensive exam, thesis (for some programs); for doctorate, one foreign language, comprehensive exam, thesis/dissertation, departmental qualifying exam. *Entrance requirements:* For master's and doctorate, GRE General Test. Additional exam requirements/recommendations for international students: Required—TOEFL (minimum score 550 paper-based; 79 iBT), IELTS (minimum score 6). *Application deadline:* Applications are processed on a rolling basis. Application fee: $50. Electronic applications accepted. *Expenses:* Contact institution. *Financial support:* In 2016–17, 255 students received support, including 9 research assistantships with partial tuition reimbursements available (averaging $9,000 per year), 68 teaching assistantships with partial tuition reimbursements available (averaging $9,000 per year); Federal Work-Study, institutionally sponsored loans, scholarships/grants, health care benefits, and unspecified assistantships also available. Financial award application deadline: 5/1; financial award applicants required to submit FAFSA. *Unit head:* Dr. Salvatore Attardo, Dean, 903-886-5166, Fax: 903-886-5774, E-mail: salvatore.attardo@tamuc.edu. *Application contact:* Shelby Miller, Graduate Recruiter, 903-468-8123, Fax: 903-886-5774, E-mail: shelby.miller@tamuc.edu.
Website: http://www.tamuc.edu/academics/graduateSchool/programs/humanitiesSocialScienceArts/default.aspx

**Texas A&M University–Corpus Christi,** College of Graduate Studies, College of Liberal Arts, Program in English, Corpus Christi, TX 78412-5503. Offers MA. *Program availability:* Part-time, evening/weekend. *Students:* 5 full-time (3 women), 20 part-time

(15 women); includes 11 minority (all Hispanic/Latino), 1 international. Average age 31. 11 applicants, 82% accepted, 4 enrolled. In 2016, 8 master's awarded. *Degree requirements:* For master's, comprehensive exam, thesis optional, capstone experience. *Entrance requirements:* For master's, essay (500-1,000 words), writing sample (minimum of 2,000 words), 3 letters of recommendation. Additional exam requirements/recommendations for international students: Required—TOEFL (minimum score 550 paper-based; 79 iBT), IELTS (minimum score 6.5). *Application deadline:* For fall admission, 4/1 priority date for domestic and international students; for spring admission, 11/1 priority date for domestic students, 9/1 priority date for international students; for summer admission, 4/15 for domestic students. Applications are processed on a rolling basis. Application fee: $50 ($70 for international students). Electronic applications accepted. *Financial support:* In 2016-17, 5 students received support. Research assistantships, career-related internships or fieldwork, Federal Work-Study, institutionally sponsored loans, scholarships/grants, health care benefits, and unspecified assistantships available. Support available to part-time students. Financial award application deadline: 3/15; financial award applicants required to submit FAFSA. *Unit head:* Dr. Molly Englehardt, Head, 361-825-3793, E-mail: molly.engelhardt@tamucc.edu. *Application contact:* Graduate Admissions Coordinator, 361-825-2177, Fax: 361-825-2755, E-mail: gradweb@tamucc.edu. Website: http://cla.tamucc.edu/english/pages/graduate.html

**Texas A&M University–Kingsville,** College of Graduate Studies, College of Arts and Sciences, Department of Language and Literature, Kingsville, TX 78363. Offers cultural studies (MA); English (MA, MS); Spanish (MA). *Entrance requirements:* Additional exam requirements/recommendations for international students: Required—TOEFL (minimum score 550 paper-based; 79 iBT); Recommended—IELTS. Electronic applications accepted.

**Texas A&M University–San Antonio,** School of Arts and Sciences, San Antonio, TX 78224. Offers English (MA). *Program availability:* Part-time, evening/weekend. *Degree requirements:* For master's, comprehensive exam, thesis. *Entrance requirements:* For master's, GRE. Additional exam requirements/recommendations for international students: Required—TOEFL (minimum score 550 paper-based; 80 iBT), IELTS (minimum score 6). Electronic applications accepted. *Faculty research:* Twentieth-century British women's literature, twentieth-century American literature, visual studies, children's literature, multi-ethnic literatures.

**Texas A&M University–Texarkana,** Graduate Studies and Research, College of Education and Liberal Arts, Texarkana, TX 75505-5518. Offers adult education (MS); curriculum and instruction (M Ed); education (MS); educational administration (M Ed); English (MA); instructional technology (MS); interdisciplinary studies (MA, MS); special education (MS). *Program availability:* Part-time, evening/weekend. *Degree requirements:* For master's, comprehensive exam (for some programs), thesis optional. *Entrance requirements:* For master's, minimum GPA of 2.5 on last 60 hours of bachelor's degree. Additional exam requirements/recommendations for international students: Required—TOEFL. Electronic applications accepted.

**Texas Christian University,** AddRan College of Liberal Arts, Department of English, Fort Worth, TX 76129. Offers English (MA, PhD); rhetoric and composition (PhD). *Faculty:* 16 full-time (11 women), 1 (woman) part-time/adjunct. *Students:* 58 full-time (43 women); includes 12 minority (4 Black or African American, non-Hispanic/Latino; 5 Hispanic/Latino; 3 Two or more races, non-Hispanic/Latino), 2 international. Average age 30. 34 applicants, 41% accepted, 13 enrolled. In 2016, 5 master's, 6 doctorates awarded. *Degree requirements:* For master's, one foreign language, thesis; for doctorate, one foreign language, comprehensive exam, thesis/dissertation. *Entrance requirements:* For master's and doctorate, GRE General Test. Additional exam requirements/recommendations for international students: Required—TOEFL. *Application deadline:* 1/10 for domestic and international students. Application fee: $60. Electronic applications accepted. *Expenses:* Contact institution. *Financial support:* In 2016-17, 55 students received support, including 4 fellowships with full tuition reimbursements available (averaging $21,000 per year), 4 research assistantships with full tuition reimbursements available, 24 teaching assistantships with full tuition reimbursements available (averaging $17,000 per year); Federal Work-Study, tuition waivers (full and partial), and unspecified assistantships also available. Financial award application deadline: 1/10; financial award applicants required to submit FAFSA. *Faculty research:* Literary studies, rhetoric and composition, new media writing, print culture, women and gender studies. *Total annual research expenditures:* $10,000. *Unit head:* Dr. Mona Narain, Director of Graduate Studies, 817-257-7240, Fax: 817-257-6238, E-mail: m.narain@tcu.edu. *Application contact:* Merry Roberts, English Department Office Manager, 817-257-6890, E-mail: m.roberts@tcu.edu. Website: http://www.eng.tcu.edu/

**Texas Southern University,** College of Liberal Arts and Behavioral Sciences, Department of English, Houston, TX 77004-4584. Offers MA. *Program availability:* Part-time. *Degree requirements:* For master's, one foreign language, comprehensive exam, thesis. *Entrance requirements:* For master's, GRE General Test, minimum GPA of 2.5. Additional exam requirements/recommendations for international students: Required—TOEFL. Electronic applications accepted. *Faculty research:* Linguistics, teaching of English, African-American literature, African literature, developmental English.

**Texas State University,** The Graduate College, College of Liberal Arts, Program in Literature, San Marcos, TX 78666. Offers MA. *Program availability:* Part-time, evening/weekend. *Faculty:* 17 full-time (6 women), 1 (woman) part-time/adjunct. *Students:* 33 full-time (23 women), 17 part-time (13 women); includes 19 minority (1 Black or African American, non-Hispanic/Latino; 1 Asian, non-Hispanic/Latino; 17 Hispanic/Latino), 1 international. Average age 29. 29 applicants, 83% accepted, 11 enrolled. In 2016, 25 master's awarded. *Degree requirements:* For master's, comprehensive exam, thesis optional. *Entrance requirements:* For master's, baccalaureate degree from regionally-accredited university with minimum GPA of 2.75 on last 60 undergraduate semester hours, 3.25 in minimum of 24 hours of undergraduate English including at least 12 advanced hours; minimum of 6 hours in a foreign language; 2 letters of recommendation; writing sample of non-fiction prose. Additional exam requirements/recommendations for international students: Required—TOEFL (minimum score 550 paper-based; 78 iBT), IELTS (minimum score 6.5). *Application deadline:* For fall admission, 1/15 priority date for domestic and international students; for spring admission, 10/15 for domestic students, 10/1 for international students; for summer admission, 4/15 for domestic students, 3/15 for international students. Applications are processed on a rolling basis. Application fee: $40 ($90 for international students). Electronic applications accepted. *Expenses:* $4,851 per semester. *Financial support:* In 2016-17, 34 students received support, including 3 research assistantships (averaging $14,366 per year), 17 teaching assistantships (averaging $15,518 per year); Federal Work-Study, institutionally sponsored loans, and scholarships/grants also available. Support available to part-time students. Financial award application deadline: 3/1; financial award applicants required to submit FAFSA. *Unit head:* Dr. Paul Cohen, Acting Graduate Adviser, 512-245-7685, Fax: 512-245-8546, E-mail: pc06@txstate.edu. *Application contact:* Dr. Andrea Golato, Dean of Graduate School, 512-245-2581, Fax: 512-245-8365, E-mail: gradcollege@txstate.edu. Website: http://ma.english.txstate.edu

**Texas Tech University,** Graduate School, College of Arts and Sciences, Department of English, Lubbock, TX 79409-3091. Offers English (MA, PhD); technical communication (MA); technical communication and rhetoric (PhD). *Program availability:* Part-time, 100% online, blended/hybrid learning. *Faculty:* 60 full-time (37 women), 22 part-time/adjunct (11 women). *Students:* 93 full-time (59 women), 86 part-time (58 women); includes 24 minority (8 Black or African American, non-Hispanic/Latino; 1 American Indian or Alaska Native, non-Hispanic/Latino; 3 Asian, non-Hispanic/Latino; 8 Hispanic/Latino; 4 Two or more races, non-Hispanic/Latino), 11 international. Average age 33. 173 applicants, 30% accepted, 36 enrolled. In 2016, 15 master's, 17 doctorates awarded. Terminal master's awarded for partial completion of doctoral program. *Degree requirements:* For master's, variable foreign language requirement, comprehensive exam, thesis optional; for doctorate, variable foreign language requirement, comprehensive exam, thesis/dissertation. *Entrance requirements:* For master's and doctorate, GRE General Test. Additional exam requirements/recommendations for international students: Required—TOEFL (minimum score 550 paper-based; 79 iBT), IELTS (minimum score 6.5). *Application deadline:* For fall admission, 6/1 priority date for domestic students, 1/15 priority date for international students; for spring admission, 9/1 priority date for domestic students, 6/15 priority date for international students. Applications are processed on a rolling basis. Application fee: $75. Electronic applications accepted. *Expenses:* $300 per credit hour full-time resident tuition, $708 per credit hour full-time non-resident tuition; $50.50 per credit hour fee plus $608 per term fee. *Financial support:* In 2016-17, 116 students received support, including 102 fellowships (averaging $3,457 per year), 6 research assistantships (averaging $13,381 per year), 78 teaching assistantships (averaging $15,273 per year); career-related internships or fieldwork, Federal Work-Study, scholarships/grants, and unspecified assistantships also available. Financial award application deadline: 12/15; financial award applicants required to submit FAFSA. *Faculty research:* American, British, and comparative literature; creative writing; linguistics; film; technical communication and rhetoric. *Total annual research expenditures:* $65,992. *Unit head:* Dr. Bruce Clarke, Professor, 806-834-7652, Fax: 806-742-0989, E-mail: bruce.clarke@ttu.edu. *Application contact:* Dr. Kanika Batra, Director of Graduate Studies, 806-834-1246, Fax: 806-742-0989, E-mail: english.gradadvisor@ttu.edu. Website: http://www.english.ttu.edu/

**Texas Woman's University,** Graduate School, College of Arts and Sciences, Department of English, Speech, and Foreign Languages, Denton, TX 76204-5829. Offers English (MA); rhetoric (PhD). *Program availability:* Part-time. *Students:* 10 full-time (8 women), 41 part-time (34 women); includes 14 minority (5 Black or African American, non-Hispanic/Latino; 3 Asian, non-Hispanic/Latino; 3 Hispanic/Latino; 3 Two or more races, non-Hispanic/Latino). Average age 39. In 2016, 6 master's, 2 doctorates awarded. *Degree requirements:* For master's, comprehensive exam, thesis; for doctorate, comprehensive exam, thesis/dissertation. *Entrance requirements:* For master's, GRE General Test (preferred minimum score 153 [500 old version] verbal, 138 [350 old version] quantitative), 3 letters of reference, minimum GPA of 3.0 on previous upper-division and graduate work; for doctorate, GRE General Test (preferred minimum score 153 [500 old version] verbal, 138 [350 old version] quantitative), writing sample, 3 letters of reference, interview (for graduate assistants), minimum GPA of 3.0 on previous upper-division and graduate work. Additional exam requirements/recommendations for international students: Recommended—TOEFL (minimum score 600 paper-based; 100 iBT). *Application deadline:* For fall admission, 2/1 priority date for domestic students, 2/1 for international students; for spring admission, 11/1 priority date for domestic students, 7/1 for international students. Applications are processed on a rolling basis. Application fee: $50 ($75 for international students). Electronic applications accepted. *Expenses:* Tuition, state resident: full-time $9046; part-time $251 per credit hour. Tuition, nonresident: full-time $22,922; part-time $614 per credit hour. International tuition: $23,046 full-time. *Required fees:* $2690; $1285 per credit hour. One-time fee: $50. Tuition and fees vary according to course level, course load, program and reciprocity agreements. *Financial support:* Research assistantships, teaching assistantships, career-related internships or fieldwork, Federal Work-Study, institutionally sponsored loans, scholarships/grants, traineeships, health care benefits, and unspecified assistantships available. Support available to part-time students. Financial award application deadline: 3/1; financial award applicants required to submit FAFSA. *Faculty research:* British and American literature, rhetoric: historical and applied, composition studies and technology, literary theory and criticism, women's literature and feminist rhetoric. *Unit head:* Dr. Genevieve West, Chair, 940-898-2324, Fax: 940-898-2297, E-mail: gwest@twu.edu. *Application contact:* Dr. Samuel Wheeler, Assistant Director of Admissions, 940-898-3188, Fax: 940-898-3081, E-mail: wheelersr@twu.edu. Website: http://www.twu.edu/english-speech-foreign-languages/

**Tiffin University,** Program in Humanities, Tiffin, OH 44883-2161. Offers art and visual media (MH); communication (MH); creative writing (MH); English (MH); film studies (MH); humanities (MH); individualized studies (MH). *Program availability:* Part-time, evening/weekend, online only, 100% online, blended/hybrid learning. *Students:* 17 full-time (15 women), 116 part-time (75 women); includes 25 minority (15 Black or African American, non-Hispanic/Latino; 2 Asian, non-Hispanic/Latino; 6 Hispanic/Latino; 2 Two or more races, non-Hispanic/Latino). Average age 36. 84 applicants, 80% accepted, 43 enrolled. In 2016, 42 master's awarded. *Entrance requirements:* For master's, work experience. Additional exam requirements/recommendations for international students: Required—TOEFL (minimum score 550 paper-based; 79 iBT). *Application deadline:* For fall admission, 9/1 for domestic students; for spring admission, 1/9 for domestic students. Applications are processed on a rolling basis. Application fee: $50. Electronic applications accepted. Application fee is waived when completed online. *Expenses:* Contact institution. *Financial support:* Unspecified assistantships available. Financial award applicants required to submit FAFSA. *Unit head:* Dr. Jason Slone, Program Chair, 419-448-5851, Fax: 419-443-5002, E-mail: slonedj@tiffin.edu. *Application contact:* Nikki Hintze, Director of Graduate and Distance Education Academic Advising, 800-968-6446 Ext. 3596, Fax: 419-443-5002, E-mail: hintzenm@tiffin.edu.

**Trinity College,** Graduate Programs, Program in English, Hartford, CT 06106-3100. Offers literary studies (MA); writing, rhetoric, and media arts (MA). *Program availability:* Part-time, evening/weekend. *Degree requirements:* For master's, thesis (for some programs). *Entrance requirements:* For master's, minimum GPA of 3.0.

**Trinity Western University,** School of Graduate Studies, Program in Interdisciplinary Humanities, Langley, BC V2Y 1Y1, Canada. Offers general humanities (MAIH); specialized (MAIH), including English, history, philosophy. *Program availability:* Part-time. *Degree requirements:* For master's, thesis or alternative, 36 semester hours. *Entrance requirements:* For master's, strong undergraduate degree in humanities or English, history or philosophy. Additional exam requirements/recommendations for international students: Recommended—TOEFL. Electronic applications accepted. *Faculty research:* Literary theory, gender, medieval and early modern literature, philosophy of religion, Thomas Merton's poetics.

**Truman State University,** Graduate School, School of Arts and Letters, Program in English, Kirksville, MO 63501-4221. Offers MA. *Degree requirements:* For master's, thesis. *Entrance requirements:* For master's, GRE General Test, minimum GPA of 3.0. Additional exam requirements/recommendations for international students: Required—TOEFL (minimum score 550 paper-based). *Application deadline:* For fall admission, 6/1 for domestic and international students; for spring admission, 11/1 for domestic and international students; for summer admission, 4/1 for domestic and international students. Applications are processed on a rolling basis. Application fee: $40. Electronic applications accepted. *Expenses:* Tuition, state resident: full-time $6300; part-time $350 per credit hour. Tuition, nonresident: full-time $10,818; part-time $601 per credit hour. Tuition and fees vary according to course load and program. *Financial support:* Research assistantships with tuition reimbursements, teaching assistantships with tuition reimbursements, career-related internships or fieldwork, and Federal Work-Study available. Financial award application deadline: 5/1; financial award applicants required to submit FAFSA. *Unit head:* Dr. Linda Seidel, Director, 660-785-4491. *Application contact:* Stephanie Rudolph, Graduate Office Secretary, 660-785-4109, Fax: 660-785-7460, E-mail: sdunn@truman.edu.

**Tufts University,** Graduate School of Arts and Sciences, Department of English, Medford, MA 02155. Offers MA, PhD. *Students:* 57 full-time (31 women); includes 9 minority (2 Black or African American, non-Hispanic/Latino; 3 Asian, non-Hispanic/Latino; 1 Hispanic/Latino; 3 Two or more races, non-Hispanic/Latino), 2 international. Average age 31. 68 applicants, 29% accepted, 8 enrolled. In 2016, 7 master's, 9 doctorates awarded. Terminal master's awarded for partial completion of doctoral program. *Degree requirements:* For master's, one foreign language, thesis; for doctorate, 2 foreign languages, thesis/dissertation. *Entrance requirements:* For master's and doctorate, GRE General Test, GRE Subject Test, writing sample. Additional exam requirements/recommendations for international students: Required—TOEFL (minimum score 550 paper-based; 80 iBT), IELTS (minimum score 6.5). *Application deadline:* For fall admission, 1/15 for domestic and international students. Applications are processed on a rolling basis. Application fee: $85. Electronic applications accepted. *Expenses:* $29,936 full-time tuition (for PhD). *Financial support:* In 2016–17, 57 students received support. Fellowships, teaching assistantships, Federal Work-Study, scholarships/grants, tuition waivers (full and partial), and unspecified assistantships available. Financial award application deadline: 1/15. *Unit head:* Dr. Elizabeth Ammons, Graduate Program Director. *Application contact:* Office of Graduate Admissions, 617-627-3395, E-mail: gradadmissions@tufts.edu.
Website: http://www.ase.tufts.edu/english/

**Tulane University,** School of Liberal Arts, Department of English, New Orleans, LA 70118-5669. Offers MA. *Degree requirements:* For master's, one foreign language, thesis or alternative. *Entrance requirements:* For master's, GRE General Test, minimum B average in undergraduate course work. Additional exam requirements/recommendations for international students: Required—TOEFL. Electronic applications accepted. *Expenses: Tuition:* Full-time $50,920; part-time $2829 per credit hour. *Required fees:* $2040; $44.50 per credit hour. $580 per term. Tuition and fees vary according to course load, degree level and program.

**Universidad de las Américas Puebla,** Division of Graduate Studies, School of Humanities, Program in Literature, Puebla, Mexico. Offers MA. *Program availability:* Part-time, evening/weekend. *Degree requirements:* For master's, one foreign language, thesis. *Entrance requirements:* Additional exam requirements/recommendations for international students: Required—TOEFL. *Faculty research:* Women in literature, Mexican and Hispanic literature.

**Université de Montréal,** Faculty of Arts and Sciences, Department of English Studies, Montréal, QC H3C 3J7, Canada. Offers MA, PhD. *Degree requirements:* For doctorate, thesis/dissertation, general exam. *Entrance requirements:* For master's, BA in English with minimum B+ average; for doctorate, MA in English with minimum B+ average. Electronic applications accepted. *Faculty research:* British, Canadian, and American literature.

**Université Laval,** Faculty of Letters, Department of Literature, Programs in Ancient Civilization, Québec, QC G1K 7P4, Canada. Offers MA, PhD. *Program availability:* Part-time. Terminal master's awarded for partial completion of doctoral program. *Degree requirements:* For master's, thesis; for doctorate, comprehensive exam, thesis/dissertation. *Entrance requirements:* For master's and doctorate, English test (comprehension of written English), knowledge of French, knowledge of an ancient language. Electronic applications accepted.

**Université Laval,** Faculty of Letters, Department of Literature, Programs in English Literatures, Québec, QC G1K 7P4, Canada. Offers MA, PhD. *Program availability:* Part-time. Terminal master's awarded for partial completion of doctoral program. *Degree requirements:* For master's, thesis (for some programs); for doctorate, comprehensive exam, thesis/dissertation. *Entrance requirements:* For master's, French exam, knowledge of English; for doctorate, French exam, knowledge of English, knowledge of a third language. Electronic applications accepted.

**University at Albany, State University of New York,** College of Arts and Sciences, Department of English, Albany, NY 12222-0001. Offers MA, PhD. *Faculty:* 11 full-time (4 women), 1 (woman) part-time/adjunct. *Students:* 34 full-time (22 women), 54 part-time (27 women); includes 14 minority (3 Black or African American, non-Hispanic/Latino; 1 Asian, non-Hispanic/Latino; 6 Hispanic/Latino; 4 Two or more races, non-Hispanic/Latino), 19 international. 108 applicants, 39% accepted, 19 enrolled. In 2016, 10 master's, 6 doctorates awarded. *Degree requirements:* For master's, one foreign language; for doctorate, one foreign language, comprehensive exam, thesis/dissertation, residency. *Entrance requirements:* For master's and doctorate, GRE General Test, GRE Subject Test. Additional exam requirements/recommendations for international students: Required—TOEFL (minimum score 550 paper-based). *Application deadline:* For fall admission, 6/15 for domestic students, 1/15 for international students; for spring admission, 11/1 for international students. Applications are processed on a rolling basis. Application fee: $75. Electronic applications accepted. *Expenses:* Tuition, state resident: full-time $10,870; part-time $453 per credit hour. Tuition, nonresident: full-time $22,210; part-time $925 per credit hour. *International tuition:* $21,550 full-time. *Required fees:* $1864; $96 per credit hour. *Financial support:* Fellowships and career-related internships or fieldwork available. Financial award application deadline: 2/15. *Faculty research:* Women playwrights; critical literary theory; poetry and poetics; media history, writing and reporting; creative non-fiction. *Total annual research expenditures:* $51,058. *Unit head:* Randall Craig, Chair, 518-442-4056, Fax: 518-442-4599. *Application contact:* Michael DeRensis, Director, Graduate Admissions, 518-442-3980, Fax: 518-442-3922, E-mail: graduate@albany.edu.
Website: http://www.albany.edu/english/

**University at Buffalo, the State University of New York,** Graduate School, College of Arts and Sciences, Department of English, Buffalo, NY 14260. Offers MA, PhD. *Program availability:* Part-time. Terminal master's awarded for partial completion of doctoral program. *Degree requirements:* For master's, thesis or alternative; for doctorate, thesis/dissertation, departmental qualifying exam. *Entrance requirements:* For master's and doctorate, GRE General Test, sample of written work. Additional exam requirements/recommendations for international students: Required—TOEFL (minimum score 79 iBT). Electronic applications accepted. *Faculty research:* Psychoanalysis, early modern British literature, poetics, nineteenth-century American literature, British and Irish Modernism.

**University at Buffalo, the State University of New York,** Graduate School, Graduate School of Education, Department of Learning and Instruction, Buffalo, NY 14260. Offers

biology education (Ed M, Certificate); chemistry education (Ed M, Certificate); childhood education (Ed M); childhood education with bilingual extension (Ed M); college teaching (Advanced Certificate); curriculum, instruction and the science of learning (PhD); early childhood education (Ed M); early childhood education with bilingual extension (Ed M); earth science education (Ed M, Certificate); education and technology (Ed M); education studies (Ed M); educational technology and new literacies (Certificate); educational technology and new literacies (Advanced Certificate); elementary education (Ed D); English education (Ed M, Certificate); English education studies (Ed M); English for speakers of other languages (Ed M); foreign and second language education (PhD); French education (Ed M, Certificate); German education (Ed M, Certificate); gifted education (Certificate); Latin education (Ed M, Certificate); literacy education studies (Ed M); literacy specialist (Ed M); literacy teaching and learning (Certificate); mathematics education (Ed M, Certificate); music education (Ed M, Certificate); music education studies (Ed M); music learning theory (Advanced Certificate); online education (Advanced Certificate); physics education (Ed M, Certificate); science and the public (Ed M); social studies education (Ed M, Certificate); Spanish education (Ed M, Certificate); special education (PhD); teaching English to speakers of other languages (Ed M). *Program availability:* Part-time, evening/weekend, 100% online. *Faculty:* 28 full-time (21 women), 67 part-time/adjunct (49 women). *Students:* 198 full-time (153 women), 312 part-time (220 women); includes 48 minority (28 Black or African American, non-Hispanic/Latino; 4 American Indian or Alaska Native, non-Hispanic/Latino; 15 Asian, non-Hispanic/Latino; 1 Hispanic/Latino), 66 international. Average age 33. 336 applicants, 86% accepted, 178 enrolled. In 2016, 137 master's, 24 doctorates, 25 other advanced degrees awarded. *Degree requirements:* For master's, comprehensive exam; for doctorate, thesis/dissertation, research analysis exam, research experience. *Entrance requirements:* For master's, letters of reference; for doctorate, GRE General Test or MAT, interview, writing sample, letters of recommendation. Additional exam requirements/recommendations for international students: Required—TOEFL (minimum score 600 paper-based; 96 iBT). *Application deadline:* For fall admission, 2/1 priority date for domestic and international students; for spring admission, 11/15 priority date for domestic students, 10/1 for international students. Applications are processed on a rolling basis. Application fee: $50. Electronic applications accepted. *Financial support:* In 2016–17, 44 fellowships (averaging $4,010 per year), 39 research assistantships with tuition reimbursements (averaging $9,897 per year) were awarded; teaching assistantships, career-related internships or fieldwork, Federal Work-Study, institutionally sponsored loans, scholarships/grants, tuition waivers (full and partial), and unspecified assistantships also available. Financial award application deadline: 2/28; financial award applicants required to submit FAFSA. *Faculty research:* Science assessment, foreign language teaching and learning, early learning, new literacies, gender and education. *Total annual research expenditures:* $534,880. *Unit head:* Dr. Deborah Moore-Russo, Chair, 716-645-4069, Fax: 716-645-3161, E-mail: dam29@buffalo.edu. *Application contact:* Luann Zak, Admissions Assistant, 716-645-2110, Fax: 716-645-7937, E-mail: luannzak@buffalo.edu.
Website: http://gse.buffalo.edu/lai

**The University of Akron,** Graduate School, Buchtel College of Arts and Sciences, Department of English, Program in Literature, Akron, OH 44325. Offers MA. *Degree requirements:* For master's, thesis optional. *Entrance requirements:* For master's, statement of purpose. *Application deadline:* Applications are processed on a rolling basis. *Expenses:* Tuition, state resident: full-time $8618; part-time $359 per credit hour. Tuition, nonresident: full-time $17,149; part-time $715 per credit hour. *Required fees:* $1652. *Financial support:* Fellowships, institutionally sponsored loans, and unspecified assistantships available. *Unit head:* Dr. Sheldon Wrice, Interim Chair, 330-972-6023, E-mail: swrice1@uakron.edu. *Application contact:* Dr. Joseph Ceccio, Director of Graduate Studies, 330-972-7603, E-mail: jceccio@uakron.edu.

**The University of Alabama,** Graduate School, College of Arts and Sciences, Department of English, Tuscaloosa, AL 35487. Offers composition and rhetoric (PhD); creative writing (MFA), including fiction, poetry; literature (MA, PhD); rhetoric and composition (MA); teaching English as a second language (MATESOL). *Faculty:* 38 full-time (20 women). *Students:* 129 full-time (69 women), 6 part-time (5 women); includes 23 minority (12 Black or African American, non-Hispanic/Latino; 1 Asian, non-Hispanic/Latino; 7 Hispanic/Latino; 3 Two or more races, non-Hispanic/Latino), 3 international. Average age 29. 406 applicants, 13% accepted, 35 enrolled. In 2016, 31 master's, 4 doctorates awarded. *Degree requirements:* For master's, one foreign language, comprehensive exam, thesis optional; for doctorate, 2 foreign languages, comprehensive exam, thesis/dissertation. *Entrance requirements:* For master's, GRE (minimum score of 300, except for MFA), minimum GPA of 3.0, critical writing sample; for doctorate, GRE (minimum score of 300), minimum GPA of 3.5 on master's or equivalent graduate work, critical writing sample. Additional exam requirements/recommendations for international students: Required—TOEFL (minimum score 550 paper-based; 79 iBT). *Application deadline:* For fall admission, 12/31 priority date for domestic and international students. Application fee: $50 ($60 for international students). Electronic applications accepted. *Expenses:* Tuition, state resident: full-time $10,470. Tuition, nonresident: full-time $26,950. *Financial support:* In 2016–17, 128 students received support, including 11 fellowships with full tuition reimbursements available (averaging $15,000 per year), 13 research assistantships with full tuition reimbursements available (averaging $13,500 per year), 100 teaching assistantships with full tuition reimbursements available (averaging $13,500 per year); career-related internships or fieldwork, scholarships/grants, health care benefits, and unspecified assistantships also available. Financial award application deadline: 12/31. *Faculty research:* American literature, British literature, composition/rhetoric, applied linguistics, creative writing. *Unit head:* Prof. Joel Brouwer, Department Chair, 205-348-5065, Fax: 205-348-1388, E-mail: joel.brouwer@ua.edu. *Application contact:* Jennifer Fuqua, Graduate Coordinator, 205-348-0766, Fax: 205-348-1388, E-mail: jfuqua@ua.edu.

**The University of Alabama at Birmingham,** College of Arts and Sciences, Program in English, Birmingham, AL 35294. Offers creative writing (MA); literature (MA); rhetoric and composition (MA). *Program availability:* Part-time. *Degree requirements:* For master's, one foreign language, comprehensive exam, thesis or alternative. *Entrance requirements:* For master's, GRE General Test or MAT, minimum GPA of 2.75. Electronic applications accepted. Full-time tuition and fees vary according to course load and program.

**The University of Alabama in Huntsville,** School of Graduate Studies, College of Arts, Humanities, and Social Sciences, Department of English, Huntsville, AL 35899. Offers education (MA); English (MA); technical writing (Certificate); TESOL (Certificate). *Program availability:* Part-time, evening/weekend. *Degree requirements:* For master's, one foreign language, comprehensive exam, thesis or alternative, oral and written exams. *Entrance requirements:* For master's and Certificate, GRE General Test, minimum GPA of 3.0. Additional exam requirements/recommendations for international students: Required—TOEFL (minimum score 500 paper-based; 80 iBT), IELTS (minimum score 6.5). Electronic applications accepted. *Expenses:* Tuition, state resident: full-time $9834; part-time $600 per credit hour. Tuition, nonresident: full-time $21,830; part-time $1325 per credit hour. *Faculty research:* Fiction and identity, Shakespeare, science fiction, eighteenth-century literature, technical writing.

**University of Alaska Anchorage,** College of Arts and Sciences, Department of English, Anchorage, AK 99508. Offers MA. *Program availability:* Part-time. *Degree requirements:* For master's, comprehensive exam, thesis or alternative. *Entrance requirements:* For master's, GRE General Test, GRE Subject Test, portfolio, minimum GPA of 3.5, writing sample. Additional exam requirements/recommendations for international students: Required—TOEFL (minimum score 550 paper-based). *Faculty research:* The rhetoric of essays, American and American Indian literature, linguistics, Shakespeare, literature of war.

**University of Alaska Fairbanks,** College of Liberal Arts, Department of English, Fairbanks, AK 99775-5720. Offers creative writing (MFA); literature (MA); MA/MFA. *Program availability:* Part-time. *Faculty:* 13 full-time (5 women). *Students:* 23 full-time (16 women), 10 part-time (7 women); includes 6 minority (1 Asian, non-Hispanic/Latino; 2 Hispanic/Latino; 3 Two or more races, non-Hispanic/Latino). Average age 31. 52 applicants, 35% accepted, 9 enrolled. In 2016, 7 master's awarded. *Degree requirements:* For master's, comprehensive exam, oral defense of project or thesis. *Entrance requirements:* For master's, GRE General Test, bachelor's degree from accredited institution with minimum cumulative undergraduate and major GPA of 3.0, academic writing sample. Additional exam requirements/recommendations for international students: Required—TOEFL (minimum score 550 paper-based; 79 iBT), IELTS (minimum score 6.5). *Application deadline:* For fall admission, 6/1 for domestic students, 3/1 for international students; for spring admission, 10/15 for domestic students, 9/1 for international students. Applications are processed on a rolling basis. Application fee: $60. Electronic applications accepted. *Expenses:* Tuition, state resident: full-time $7992; part-time $444 per credit. Tuition, nonresident: full-time $16,326; part-time $907 per credit. *Required fees:* $39 per credit. $322 per semester. Tuition and fees vary according to course level, course load, campus/location, program and reciprocity agreements. *Financial support:* In 2016–17, 20 teaching assistantships with full tuition reimbursements (averaging $5,867 per year) were awarded; fellowships with full tuition reimbursements, research assistantships with full tuition reimbursements, Federal Work-Study, scholarships/grants, health care benefits, and unspecified assistantships also available. Support available to part-time students. Financial award application deadline: 7/1; financial award applicants required to submit FAFSA. *Unit head:* Richard Carr, Department Chair, 907-474-7193, Fax: 907-474-5247, E-mail: uaf-english-dept@alaska.edu. *Application contact:* Mary Kreta, Director of Admissions, 907-474-7500, Fax: 907-474-7097, E-mail: admissions@uaf.edu.
Website: http://www.uaf.edu/english

**University of Alberta,** Faculty of Graduate Studies and Research, Department of English and Film Studies, Edmonton, AB T6G 2E1, Canada. Offers English (MA, PhD). *Program availability:* Part-time, evening/weekend. *Degree requirements:* For master's, one foreign language, thesis optional; for doctorate, 2 foreign languages, thesis/dissertation. *Entrance requirements:* For master's, honors BA or equivalent; for doctorate, honors BA and MA. Additional exam requirements/recommendations for international students: Required—TOEFL (minimum score 600 paper-based). Electronic applications accepted. *Faculty research:* Women's writing, postcolonial theory, Victorian literature, Renaissance literature, Canadian literature.

**The University of Arizona,** College of Humanities, Department of English, English Language/Linguistics Program, Tucson, AZ 85721. Offers English (MA, PhD); ESL (MA). *Entrance requirements:* Additional exam requirements/recommendations for international students: Required—TOEFL (minimum score 550 paper-based; 79 iBT); Recommended—IELTS (minimum score 7). Electronic applications accepted.

**University of Arkansas,** Graduate School, J. William Fulbright College of Arts and Sciences, Department of English, Program in English, Fayetteville, AR 72701. Offers MA, PhD. In 2016, 14 master's, 11 doctorates awarded. *Degree requirements:* For master's, thesis; for doctorate, thesis/dissertation. *Entrance requirements:* For master's, GRE General Test; for doctorate, GRE General Test, GRE Subject Test. *Application deadline:* For fall admission, 4/1 for international students; for spring admission, 10/1 for international students. Applications are processed on a rolling basis. Application fee: $40 ($50 for international students). Electronic applications accepted. *Financial support:* In 2016–17, 3 research assistantships, 44 teaching assistantships were awarded; fellowships with tuition reimbursements, career-related internships or fieldwork, and Federal Work-Study also available. Support available to part-time students. Financial award application deadline: 4/1; financial award applicants required to submit FAFSA. *Faculty research:* Creative writing, seventeenth-century literature, twentieth-century literature, American literature. *Unit head:* Dr. Dorothy Stephen, Department Chairperson, 479-575-4301, Fax: 479-575-5919, E-mail: dstephen@uark.edu. *Application contact:* Dr. William Quinn, Graduate Coordinator, 479-575-4301, E-mail: wquinn@uark.edu.
Website: http://www.uark.edu/depts/english/

**The University of British Columbia,** Faculty of Arts and Faculty of Graduate Studies, Department of English, Vancouver, BC V6T 1Z1, Canada. Offers MA, PhD. *Degree requirements:* For master's, thesis or alternative; for doctorate, one foreign language, comprehensive exam, thesis/dissertation. *Entrance requirements:* For master's, BA or equivalent; for doctorate, MA. Additional exam requirements/recommendations for international students: Required—TOEFL, IELTS. Application fee: $100 Canadian dollars ($162 Canadian dollars for international students). Electronic applications accepted. *Expenses:* $4,802 per year tuition and fees, $8,436 per year international. *Financial support:* Fellowships, research assistantships, and teaching assistantships available. *Faculty research:* English, American, Canadian, and Commonwealth post-colonial literature; English language; rhetoric. *Application contact:* Louise Soga, Graduate Program Staff, 604-822-3855, Fax: 604-822-6906, E-mail: english.graduate.program@ubc.ca.
Website: http://www.english.ubc.ca/grad

**The University of British Columbia,** Faculty of Arts, School of Library, Archival and Information Studies, Master of Arts Program in Children's Literature, Vancouver, BC V6T 1Z1, Canada. Offers MA. *Program availability:* Part-time. *Degree requirements:* For master's, thesis. *Entrance requirements:* For master's, minimum GPA of 3.3 in undergraduate upper-division courses. Additional exam requirements/recommendations for international students: Required—TOEFL. Application fee: $100 Canadian dollars ($162 Canadian dollars for international students). Electronic applications accepted. *Expenses:* $4,802 per year tuition and fees, $8,436 per year international. *Financial support:* Fellowships, research assistantships, teaching assistantships, Federal Work-Study, institutionally sponsored loans, scholarships/grants, health care benefits, tuition waivers (partial), and unspecified assistantships available. *Faculty research:* Children's and young adult literature; children's and young adult public library services; Canadian children's and young adult literature; publishing for youth. *Application contact:* Alynne Pols, Graduate Program Staff, 604-822-3459, Fax: 604-822-6006, E-mail: ischool.program@ubc.ca.
Website: http://slais.ubc.ca/

**University of Calgary,** Faculty of Graduate Studies, Faculty of Arts, Department of English, Calgary, AB T2N 1N4, Canada. Offers MA, PhD. *Program availability:* Part-time. *Degree requirements:* For master's, one foreign language, comprehensive exam (for some programs), thesis; for doctorate, one foreign language, thesis/dissertation, candidacy exam. *Entrance requirements:* Additional exam requirements/

recommendations for international students: Required—TOEFL (minimum score 600 paper-based). Electronic applications accepted. *Faculty research:* Various national and period literatures, creative writing, literary theory, gender and women's studies, postcolonial literatures.

**University of California, Berkeley,** Graduate Division, College of Letters and Science, Department of English, Berkeley, CA 94720-1500. Offers PhD. *Students:* 107 full-time (56 women); includes 38 minority (7 Black or African American, non-Hispanic/Latino; 2 American Indian or Alaska Native, non-Hispanic/Latino; 16 Asian, non-Hispanic/Latino; 13 Hispanic/Latino), 11 international. Average age 30. 259 applicants, 9 enrolled. In 2016, 10 doctorates awarded. *Degree requirements:* For doctorate, 2 foreign languages, thesis/dissertation, qualifying exam. *Entrance requirements:* For doctorate, GRE General Test, GRE Subject Test, minimum GPA of 3.0, writing sample, 3 letters of recommendation. *Application deadline:* For fall admission, 12/15 for domestic students. Application fee: $105 ($125 for international students). Electronic applications accepted. *Financial support:* Fellowships, research assistantships, teaching assistantships, Federal Work-Study, institutionally sponsored loans, scholarships/grants, tuition waivers (partial), and unspecified assistantships available. Financial award applicants required to submit FAFSA. *Unit head:* Prof. Samuel Otter, Chair, 510-642-3467. *Application contact:* E-mail: gradadvisor_english@berkeley.edu.
Website: http://english.berkeley.edu/

**University of California, Davis,** Graduate Studies, Program in English, Davis, CA 95616. Offers creative writing (MA); English (MA, PhD). Terminal master's awarded for partial completion of doctoral program. *Degree requirements:* For master's, one foreign language, thesis optional; for doctorate, 2 foreign languages, thesis/dissertation. *Entrance requirements:* For master's and doctorate, GRE General Test, GRE Subject Test, minimum GPA of 3.0, writing sample. Additional exam requirements/recommendations for international students: Required—TOEFL (minimum score 550 paper-based). Electronic applications accepted. *Faculty research:* Feminist theory, ethnic literature, literary theory, history of literature, literature of nature.

**University of California, Irvine,** School of Humanities, Department of English, Program in English, Irvine, CA 92697. Offers English (MA); English and American literature (PhD). *Students:* 49 full-time (20 women); includes 14 minority (1 Black or African American, non-Hispanic/Latino; 4 Asian, non-Hispanic/Latino; 2 Hispanic/Latino; 7 Two or more races, non-Hispanic/Latino), 2 international. Average age 31. 156 applicants, 15% accepted, 4 enrolled. In 2016, 32 master's, 10 doctorates awarded. Terminal master's awarded for partial completion of doctoral program. *Degree requirements:* For master's, one foreign language, comprehensive exam; for doctorate, 2 foreign languages, comprehensive exam, thesis/dissertation. *Entrance requirements:* For doctorate, GRE General Test, GRE Subject Test, minimum GPA of 3.5, sample of written work, 3 letters of recommendation. Additional exam requirements/recommendations for international students: Required—TOEFL (minimum score 550 paper-based). *Application deadline:* For fall admission, 12/1 for domestic and international students. Application fee: $105 ($125 for international students). Electronic applications accepted. *Financial support:* In 2016–17, 59 students received support. Fellowships with full tuition reimbursements available, research assistantships, teaching assistantships with partial tuition reimbursements available, institutionally sponsored loans, health care benefits, tuition waivers (full and partial), and unspecified assistantships available. Financial award application deadline: 3/1; financial award applicants required to submit FAFSA. *Faculty research:* Critical theory, literary history, cultural studies. *Unit head:* Martin Harries, Department Chair, 949-824-6715, Fax: 949-824-2916, E-mail: martin.harries@uci.edu. *Application contact:* Jerome Christensen, Graduate Faculty Advisor, 949-824-9046, Fax: 949-824-2916, E-mail: jchris@uci.edu.

**University of California, Los Angeles,** Graduate Division, College of Letters and Science, Department of English, Los Angeles, CA 90095. Offers MA, PhD. Terminal master's awarded for partial completion of doctoral program. *Degree requirements:* For master's, one foreign language, comprehensive exam, thesis; for doctorate, 2 foreign languages, thesis/dissertation, oral and written qualifying exams. *Entrance requirements:* For doctorate, GRE General Test, GRE Subject Test (literature), bachelor's degree; minimum undergraduate GPA of 3.0, 3.5 in upper-division English courses (or its equivalent if letter grade system not used), 3.7 in graduate courses for applicant with master's degree; writing sample. Additional exam requirements/recommendations for international students: Required—TOEFL. Electronic applications accepted.

**University of California, Riverside,** Graduate Division, Department of English, Riverside, CA 92521-0102. Offers MA, PhD. *Degree requirements:* For master's, one foreign language, comprehensive exam; for doctorate, 2 foreign languages, thesis/dissertation, qualifying exams. *Entrance requirements:* For doctorate, GRE General Test, minimum GPA of 3.5. Additional exam requirements/recommendations for international students: Required—TOEFL (minimum score 550 paper-based; 80 iBT). Electronic applications accepted. *Expenses:* Tuition, state resident: full-time $16,666. Tuition, nonresident: full-time $31,768. *Required fees:* $11,055.54 per quarter. $3685.18 per quarter. Tuition and fees vary according to campus/location and program. *Faculty research:* Critical theory, cultural and film studies, lesbian and gay studies, minority and feminist discourses, rhetoric and composition.

**University of California, San Diego,** Graduate Division, Department of Literature, La Jolla, CA 92093. Offers literature (PhD); writing (MFA). *Students:* 64 full-time (46 women), 2 part-time (1 woman). 223 applicants, 16% accepted, 14 enrolled. In 2016, 7 master's, 10 doctorates awarded. *Degree requirements:* For master's, thesis; for doctorate, one foreign language, comprehensive exam, thesis/dissertation, 3 quarters of teaching assistantship. *Entrance requirements:* For master's, writing sample; for doctorate, GRE General Test, writing sample. Additional exam requirements/recommendations for international students: Required—TOEFL (minimum score 550 paper-based; 80 iBT), IELTS (minimum score 7); Recommended—TSE. *Application deadline:* For fall admission, 11/30 for domestic students. Application fee: $105 ($125 for international students). Electronic applications accepted. *Expenses:* Tuition, state resident: full-time $11,220. Tuition, nonresident: full-time $26,322. *Required fees:* $1864. *Financial support:* Fellowships, research assistantships, teaching assistantships, scholarships/grants, and readerships available. Financial award applicants required to submit FAFSA. *Faculty research:* Chicano/a-Latino/a studies, European studies, film studies and visual culture, Latin American literary and cultural studies, medieval/early modern studies, transnational Africa/African diaspora studies, transnational Asia/Asian diaspora studies. *Unit head:* Yingjin Zhang, Chair, 858-534-5991, E-mail: litchair@ucsd.edu. *Application contact:* Graduate Coordinator, 858-534-3217, E-mail: litgrad@ucsd.edu.
Website: http://literature.ucsd.edu

**University of California, Santa Barbara,** Graduate Division, College of Letters and Sciences, Division of Humanities and Fine Arts, Department of English, Santa Barbara, CA 93106-3170. Offers English (PhD), including environment and society, European medieval studies, feminist studies, global studies, technology and society, translation studies, writing studies; MA/PhD. Terminal master's awarded for partial completion of doctoral program. *Degree requirements:* For doctorate, one foreign language, comprehensive exam, thesis/dissertation. *Entrance requirements:* For doctorate, GRE General Test, GRE Subject Test (English literature). Additional exam requirements/

recommendations for international students: Required—TOEFL (minimum score 550 paper-based; 80 iBT), IELTS (minimum score 7). Electronic applications accepted. *Faculty research:* Medieval, Romantic and Victorian studies; gender studies and feminist theory; literature and the mind; American literature; literature and new media/information culture.

**University of California, Santa Cruz,** Division of Graduate Studies, Division of Humanities, Department of Literature, Santa Cruz, CA 95064. Offers MA, PhD. Terminal master's awarded for partial completion of doctoral program. *Degree requirements:* For master's, thesis; for doctorate, one foreign language, thesis/dissertation, qualifying exam. *Entrance requirements:* For master's, GRE General Test, writing sample, minimum GPA of 3.5; for doctorate, GRE General Test, minimum GPA of 3.5, writing sample. Additional exam requirements/recommendations for international students: Required—TOEFL (minimum score 550 paper-based; 83 iBT); Recommended—IELTS (minimum score 8). Electronic applications accepted. *Faculty research:* Technologies of narrative; trans/post/emergent nationalisms; poetics, poetry, and experimental writing; materialism and material culture; critical theories.

**University of Central Arkansas,** Graduate School, College of Liberal Arts, Department of English, Conway, AR 72035-0001. Offers MA. *Program availability:* Part-time. *Degree requirements:* For master's, comprehensive exam, thesis optional. *Entrance requirements:* For master's, GRE General Test, minimum GPA of 2.7. Additional exam requirements/recommendations for international students: Required—TOEFL (minimum score 550 paper-based). Electronic applications accepted. *Faculty research:* Writing project.

**University of Central Florida,** College of Arts and Humanities, Department of English, Orlando, FL 32816. Offers creative writing (MFA); English (MA, Certificate); texts and technology (PhD). *Program availability:* Part-time, evening/weekend. *Faculty:* 41 full-time (21 women), 12 part-time/adjunct (9 women). *Students:* 76 full-time (53 women), 72 part-time (54 women); includes 23 minority (4 Black or African American, non-Hispanic/Latino; 3 Asian, non-Hispanic/Latino; 14 Hispanic/Latino; 2 Two or more races, non-Hispanic/Latino), 5 international. Average age 33. 142 applicants, 62% accepted, 49 enrolled. In 2016, 31 master's, 7 doctorates, 8 other advanced degrees awarded. *Degree requirements:* For master's, one foreign language, thesis or alternative. *Entrance requirements:* For master's, GRE General Test, minimum GPA of 3.0 in last 60 hours of course work. Additional exam requirements/recommendations for international students: Required—TOEFL. *Application deadline:* For fall admission, 3/30 for domestic students; for spring admission, 11/1 for domestic students. Application fee: $30. Electronic applications accepted. *Expenses:* Tuition, state resident: part-time $288.16 per credit hour. Tuition, nonresident: part-time $1071.31 per credit hour. *Financial support:* In 2016–17, 49 students received support, including 19 fellowships with partial tuition reimbursements available (averaging $5,874 per year), 12 research assistantships with partial tuition reimbursements available (averaging $8,630 per year), 34 teaching assistantships with partial tuition reimbursements available (averaging $9,949 per year); career-related internships or fieldwork, Federal Work-Study, institutionally sponsored loans, tuition waivers (partial), and unspecified assistantships also available. Financial award application deadline: 3/1; financial award applicants required to submit FAFSA. *Unit head:* Dr. Trey Philpotts, Chair, 407-823-1159, E-mail: trey.philpotts@ucf.edu. *Application contact:* Assistant Director, Graduate Admissions, 407-823-2766, Fax: 407-823-6442, E-mail: gradadmissions@ucf.edu. Website: http://www.english.cah.ucf.edu/

**University of Central Missouri,** The Graduate School, Warrensburg, MO 64093. Offers accountancy (MA); accounting (MBA); applied mathematics (MS); aviation safety (MA); biology (MS); business administration (MBA); career and technical education leadership (MS); college student personnel administration (MS); communication (MA); computer science (MS); counseling (MS); criminal justice (MS); educational leadership (Ed D); educational technology (MS); elementary and early childhood education (MSE); English (MA); environmental studies (MA); finance (MBA); history (MA); human services/ educational technology (Ed S); human services/learning resources (Ed S); human services/professional counseling (Ed S); industrial hygiene (MS); industrial management (MS); information systems (MBA); information technology (MS); kinesiology (MS); library science and information services (MS); literacy education (MSE); marketing (MBA); mathematics (MS); music (MA); occupational safety management (MS); psychology (MS); rural family nursing (MS); school administration (MSE); social gerontology (MS); sociology (MA); special education (MSE); speech language pathology (MS); superintendency (Ed S); teaching English as a second language (MA); technology (MS); technology management (PhD); theatre (MA). *Program availability:* Part-time, 100% online, blended/hybrid learning. *Degree requirements:* For master's and Ed S, comprehensive exam (for some programs), thesis (for some programs). *Entrance requirements:* Additional exam requirements/recommendations for international students: Required—TOEFL (minimum score 550 paper-based; 79 iBT). Electronic applications accepted.

**University of Central Oklahoma,** The Jackson College of Graduate Studies, College of Liberal Arts, Department of English, Edmond, OK 73034-5209. Offers creative writing (MA, MFA); traditional studies (MA). *Program availability:* Part-time. *Degree requirements:* For master's, variable foreign language requirement, comprehensive exam (for some programs), thesis (for some programs), portfolio. *Entrance requirements:* For master's, GRE, 18-24 hours of course work in English language and literature; writing sample; essay. Additional exam requirements/recommendations for international students: Required—TOEFL (minimum score 550 paper-based; 79 iBT), IELTS (minimum score 6.5). Electronic applications accepted. *Faculty research:* John Milton, Harriet Beecher Stowe.

**University of Chicago,** Division of the Humanities, Department of English Language and Literature, Chicago, IL 60637. Offers PhD. *Students:* 90 full-time (40 women); includes 12 minority (1 Black or African American, non-Hispanic/Latino; 1 American Indian or Alaska Native, non-Hispanic/Latino; 4 Asian, non-Hispanic/Latino; 5 Hispanic/Latino; 1 Two or more races, non-Hispanic/Latino), 20 international. 267 applicants, 6% accepted, 8 enrolled. In 2016, 6 doctorates awarded. Terminal master's awarded for partial completion of doctoral program. *Degree requirements:* For doctorate, 2 foreign languages, comprehensive exam, thesis/dissertation. *Entrance requirements:* For doctorate, GRE General Test. Additional exam requirements/recommendations for international students: Required—TOEFL (minimum score 104 iBT), IELTS (minimum score 7). *Application deadline:* For fall admission, 12/15 for domestic and international students. Application fee: $90. Electronic applications accepted. *Financial support:* Fellowships with full tuition reimbursements, teaching assistantships with full tuition reimbursements, Federal Work-Study, institutionally sponsored loans, scholarships/grants, and health care benefits available. Financial award application deadline: 12/15; financial award applicants required to submit FAFSA. *Unit head:* Dr. Frances Ferguson, Chair, 773-702-8536, E-mail: ferguso1@uchicago.edu. *Application contact:* Michael Beetley, Assistant Dean of Students, Admissions and Fellowships, 773-702-1552, Fax: 773-834-9148, E-mail: humanitiesadmissions@uchicago.edu. Website: http://english.uchicago.edu/

**University of Chicago,** Division of the Humanities, Master of Arts Program in the Humanities, Chicago, IL 60637. Offers art history (MA); cinema and media studies (MA); classic languages (MA); comparative literature (MA); creative writing (MA); cultural policy studies (MA); digital humanities (MA); East Asian languages and civilizations (MA); English language and literature (MA); gender and sexuality studies (MA); Germanic studies (MA); linguistics (MA); music (MA); near Eastern languages and civilizations (MA); philosophy (MA); poetics (MA); race, politics and culture (MA); Romance languages and literatures (MA); Slavic languages and literatures (MA); South Asian languages and civilizations (MA); theater and performance studies (MA). *Students:* 80 full-time (43 women), 7 part-time (3 women); includes 20 minority (5 Black or African American, non-Hispanic/Latino; 1 American Indian or Alaska Native, non-Hispanic/Latino; 6 Asian, non-Hispanic/Latino; 5 Hispanic/Latino; 3 Two or more races, non-Hispanic/Latino), 11 international. Average age 26. 706 applicants, 15% accepted, 42 enrolled. In 2016, 92 master's awarded. *Degree requirements:* For master's, thesis. *Entrance requirements:* For master's, GRE General Test. Additional exam requirements/ recommendations for international students: Required—TOEFL (minimum score 104 iBT), IELTS (minimum score 7). *Application deadline:* For fall admission, 1/3 for domestic and international students. Application fee: $90. Electronic applications accepted. *Financial support:* In 2016–17, 8 fellowships with partial tuition reimbursements (averaging $12,000 per year) were awarded; Federal Work-Study, institutionally sponsored loans, scholarships/grants, and tuition waivers (partial) also available. Financial award application deadline: 12/15; financial award applicants required to submit FAFSA. *Unit head:* Malynne Sternstein, Co-Director, 773-834-1201, Fax: 773-834-7526. *Application contact:* Program Coordinator, 773-834-1201, Fax: 773-834-7526, E-mail: ma-humanities@uchicago.edu. Website: http://maph.uchicago.edu/

**University of Cincinnati,** Graduate School, McMicken College of Arts and Sciences, Department of English and Comparative Literature, Cincinnati, OH 45221. Offers MA, MAT, PhD. *Program availability:* Part-time. Terminal master's awarded for partial completion of doctoral program. *Degree requirements:* For master's, one foreign language, thesis (for some programs); for doctorate, 2 foreign languages, thesis/dissertation. *Entrance requirements:* For master's, GRE General Test, letters of recommendation (3), writing samples; for doctorate, GRE General Test, GRE Subject Test, letters of recommendation (3), writing samples. Additional exam requirements/ recommendations for international students: Required—TOEFL. Electronic applications accepted. *Expenses:* Tuition, area resident: Full-time $12,790; part-time $389 per credit hour. Tuition, state resident: full-time $13,290; part-time $419 per credit hour. Tuition, nonresident: full-time $24,532; part-time $976 per credit hour. *International tuition:* $24,832 full-time. *Required fees:* $3958; $140 per credit hour. Tuition and fees vary according to course load, degree level, program and reciprocity agreements. *Faculty research:* Literature/theory, creative writing, composition, professional writing/editing, linguistics.

**University of Colorado Boulder,** Graduate School, College of Arts and Sciences, Department of English, Boulder, CO 80309. Offers literature (MA, PhD), including creative writing (MA). *Faculty:* 47 full-time (28 women). *Students:* 95 full-time (58 women), 4 part-time (3 women); includes 21 minority (5 Black or African American, non-Hispanic/Latino; 2 American Indian or Alaska Native, non-Hispanic/Latino; 3 Asian, non-Hispanic/Latino; 9 Hispanic/Latino; 2 Two or more races, non-Hispanic/Latino), 1 international. Average age 30. 406 applicants, 25% accepted, 28 enrolled. In 2016, 26 master's, 4 doctorates awarded. Terminal master's awarded for partial completion of doctoral program. *Degree requirements:* For master's, one foreign language, comprehensive exam, thesis or alternative; for doctorate, 2 foreign languages, comprehensive exam, thesis/dissertation. *Entrance requirements:* For master's, GRE General Test, GRE Subject Test, minimum undergraduate GPA of 3.0; for doctorate, GRE General Test, GRE Subject Test. *Application deadline:* For fall admission, 2/1 for domestic students, 12/1 for international students. Application fee: $60 ($80 for international students). Electronic applications accepted. Application fee is waived when completed online. *Financial support:* In 2016–17, 207 students received support, including 49 fellowships (averaging $2,399 per year), 5 research assistantships with full and partial tuition reimbursements available (averaging $25,901 per year), 62 teaching assistantships with full and partial tuition reimbursements available (averaging $30,862 per year); institutionally sponsored loans, scholarships/grants, health care benefits, and unspecified assistantships also available. Financial award application deadline: 1/1; financial award applicants required to submit FAFSA. *Faculty research:* Literary criticism, English language/literature, literary history, arts/humanities/cultural activities, fiction. *Total annual research expenditures:* $4.3 million. *Application contact:* E-mail: gsengl@colorado.edu. Website: http://english.colorado.edu/

**University of Colorado Boulder,** Graduate School, College of Arts and Sciences, Department of Spanish and Portuguese, Boulder, CO 80309. Offers Hispanic linguistics (MA); medieval and early modern Hispanic literatures (PhD); peninsular and Latin American literature (MA). *Faculty:* 13 full-time (5 women). *Students:* 36 full-time (25 women), 1 (woman) part-time; includes 8 minority (1 American Indian or Alaska Native, non-Hispanic/Latino; 7 Hispanic/Latino), 14 international. Average age 31. 39 applicants, 54% accepted, 8 enrolled. In 2016, 3 master's, 4 doctorates awarded. Terminal master's awarded for partial completion of doctoral program. *Degree requirements:* For master's, one foreign language, comprehensive exam, thesis or alternative; for doctorate, 2 foreign languages, thesis/dissertation. *Entrance requirements:* For master's, minimum undergraduate GPA of 2.75. *Application deadline:* For fall admission, 12/19 for domestic and international students. Applications are processed on a rolling basis. Application fee: $60 ($80 for international students). Electronic applications accepted. Application fee is waived when completed online. *Financial support:* In 2016–17, 127 students received support, including 42 fellowships (averaging $1,111 per year), 32 teaching assistantships with full and partial tuition reimbursements available (averaging $41,562 per year); institutionally sponsored loans, scholarships/grants, health care benefits, and unspecified assistantships also available. Financial award application deadline: 12/15; financial award applicants required to submit FAFSA. *Faculty research:* Literary criticism, Spanish language/literature, Latin American languages/literature, cultural history. *Total annual research expenditures:* $40,070. *Application contact:* E-mail: spanport@colorado.edu. Website: http://spanish.colorado.edu/

**University of Colorado Denver,** College of Liberal Arts and Sciences, Department of English, Denver, CO 80217. Offers applied linguistics (MA); literature (MA); rhetoric and teaching of writing (MA). *Program availability:* Part-time, evening/weekend. *Faculty:* 22 full-time (13 women). *Students:* 18 full-time (12 women), 13 part-time (10 women); includes 3 minority (1 Black or African American, non-Hispanic/Latino; 2 Hispanic/Latino). Average age 31. 19 applicants, 68% accepted, 6 enrolled. In 2016, 10 master's awarded. *Degree requirements:* For master's, variable foreign language requirement, comprehensive exam (for some programs), thesis (for some programs), minimum of 33 credit hours (for literature program), 30 (for rhetoric and teaching of writing and applied linguistics programs). *Entrance requirements:* For master's, GRE General Test, minimum GPA of 3.0 in undergraduate courses, critical writing sample, letters of recommendation, completion of 24 semester hours in English courses (at least 16 at the upper-division level), statement of purpose. Additional exam requirements/ recommendations for international students: Required—TOEFL (minimum score 537 paper-based; 75 iBT); Recommended—IELTS (minimum score 6.5). *Application deadline:* For fall admission, 4/1 for domestic and international students; for spring

admission, 10/1 for domestic and international students; for summer admission, 4/1 for domestic and international students. Application fee: $50 ($75 for international students). Electronic applications accepted. *Expenses:* Tuition, state resident: full-time $11,006; part-time $474 per credit. Tuition, nonresident: full-time $28,212; part-time $1264 per credit hour. *Required fees:* $256 per semester. One-time fee: $94.32. Tuition and fees vary according to campus/location and program. *Financial support:* In 2016–17, 9 students received support. Fellowships, research assistantships, teaching assistantships, Federal Work-Study, institutionally sponsored loans, scholarships/grants, traineeships, and unspecified assistantships available. Financial award application deadline: 4/1; financial award applicants required to submit FAFSA. *Faculty research:* Literature, rhetoric, teaching of writing, applied linguistics. *Unit head:* Prof. Nancy Ciccone, Chair, 303-556-8395, E-mail: nancy.ciccone@ucdenver.edu. *Application contact:* Francine Olivas-Zarate, English Department, 303-556-2584, Fax: 303-556-2959.
Website: http://www.ucdenver.edu/academics/colleges/CLAS/Departments/english/Programs/Masters/Pages/Overview.aspx

**University of Connecticut,** Graduate School, College of Liberal Arts and Sciences, Department of English, Storrs, CT 06269. Offers MA, PhD. Terminal master's awarded for partial completion of doctoral program. *Degree requirements:* For master's, comprehensive exam; for doctorate, thesis/dissertation. *Entrance requirements:* For master's and doctorate, GRE General Test, GRE Subject Test. Additional exam requirements/recommendations for international students: Required—TOEFL (minimum score 550 paper-based). Electronic applications accepted.

**University of Dallas,** Braniff Graduate School of Liberal Arts, Program in English, Irving, TX 75062-4736. Offers MA. *Program availability:* Part-time. *Degree requirements:* For master's, one foreign language. *Entrance requirements:* For master's, GRE General Test. *Faculty research:* Modern literature, Renaissance, Shakespeare, medieval studies.

**University of Dayton,** Department of English, Dayton, OH 45469. Offers literary and cultural studies (MA); teaching English to speakers of other languages (TESOL) (MA); writing and rhetoric (MA). *Program availability:* Part-time. *Faculty:* 22 full-time (11 women). *Students:* 15 full-time (10 women), 2 part-time (1 woman); includes 1 minority (Black or African American, non-Hispanic/Latino), 7 international. Average age 27. 55 applicants, 29% accepted. In 2016, 8 master's awarded. *Degree requirements:* For master's, thesis. *Entrance requirements:* For master's, 24 undergraduate-level semester hours in literature and/or writing; minimum GPA of 3.0; transcripts; personal statement; 8-10 page writing sample; three professional letters of recommendation. Additional exam requirements/recommendations for international students: Required—TOEFL (minimum score 550 paper-based, 80 iBT) or IELTS. *Application deadline:* For fall admission, 6/15 priority date for domestic and international students; for spring admission, 12/15 priority date for domestic and international students. Applications are processed on a rolling basis. Application fee: $0 ($50 for international students). Electronic applications accepted. *Expenses:* $890 per credit hour, $25 registration fee. *Financial support:* In 2016–17, 9 teaching assistantships with full tuition reimbursements (averaging $11,000 per year) were awarded; institutionally sponsored loans and health care benefits also available. Financial award application deadline: 12/15; financial award applicants required to submit FAFSA. *Faculty research:* Gender and Victorian periodicals; literature and human rights; Paul Lawrence Dunbar; the archetype of the Indian princess; Amish country. *Total annual research expenditures:* $35,000. *Unit head:* Dr. Andrew Slade, Chair, 937-229-3434, Fax: 937-229-3563, E-mail: aslade1@udayton.edu. *Application contact:* Dr. Tereza Szeghi, Director of Graduate Studies, 937-229-3443, E-mail: tszeghi1@udayton.edu.
Website: https://www.udayton.edu/artssciences/academics/english/welcome/index.php

**University of Delaware,** College of Arts and Sciences, Department of English, Newark, DE 19716. Offers English and American literature (MA, PhD); MA/PhD. Terminal master's awarded for partial completion of doctoral program. *Degree requirements:* For master's, one foreign language, thesis optional; for doctorate, 2 foreign languages, comprehensive exam, thesis/dissertation, specialty exam. *Entrance requirements:* For master's and doctorate, GRE General Test, GRE Subject Test. Additional exam requirements/recommendations for international students: Required—TOEFL (minimum score 550 paper-based). Electronic applications accepted. *Faculty research:* Significant strengths in American literature and culture, material cultural studies, Renaissance studies, archival studies.

**University of Denver,** Division of Arts, Humanities and Social Sciences, Department of English, Denver, CO 80208. Offers creative writing (PhD); literary studies (MA, PhD). *Program availability:* Part-time. *Faculty:* 19 full-time (8 women), 1 (woman) part-time/adjunct. *Students:* 30 full-time (22 women), 4 part-time (3 women); includes 10 minority (1 Black or African American, non-Hispanic/Latino; 2 Asian, non-Hispanic/Latino; 4 Hispanic/Latino; 3 Two or more races, non-Hispanic/Latino), 1 international. Average age 33. 165 applicants, 13% accepted, 10 enrolled. In 2016, 3 master's, 9 doctorates awarded. *Degree requirements:* For master's, one foreign language, comprehensive exam, thesis; for doctorate, 2 foreign languages, comprehensive exam, thesis/dissertation. *Entrance requirements:* For master's, GRE General Test, GRE Subject Test (advanced literature), bachelor's degree, transcripts, academic essay, statement of intent, three letters of recommendation; for doctorate, GRE General Test, GRE Subject Test (advanced literature), master's degree, transcripts, academic essay, statement of intent, three letters of recommendation, and a writing sample (creative writing program only). Additional exam requirements/recommendations for international students: Required—TOEFL (minimum score 570 paper-based; 88 iBT). *Application deadline:* For fall admission, 1/1 priority date for domestic and international students. Applications are processed on a rolling basis. Application fee: $65. Electronic applications accepted. *Expenses:* $29,022 per year full-time. *Financial support:* In 2016–17, 34 students received support, including 21 teaching assistantships with tuition reimbursements available (averaging $17,500 per year); Federal Work-Study, institutionally sponsored loans, scholarships/grants, and unspecified assistantships also available. Support available to part-time students. Financial award application deadline: 2/15; financial award applicants required to submit FAFSA. *Faculty research:* African diaspora semiotics, Susan Howe's poetics, Renaissance drama and emblematic culture, New England Colonial literature, postmodern literature. *Unit head:* Dr. Clark Davis, Professor and Chair, 303-871-2900, Fax: 303-871-2853, E-mail: cldavis@du.edu. *Application contact:* Dr. Adam Rovner, Associate Professor and Director of Graduate Studies, 303-871-2861, Fax: 303-871-2853, E-mail: adam.rovner@du.edu.
Website: http://www.du.edu/ahss/english

**University of Florida,** Graduate School, College of Liberal Arts and Sciences, Department of English, Gainesville, FL 32611. Offers creative writing (MFA); English (MA, PhD). *Degree requirements:* For master's, one foreign language, comprehensive exam, thesis or alternative; for doctorate, one foreign language, comprehensive exam, thesis/dissertation. *Entrance requirements:* For master's and doctorate, GRE General Test, minimum GPA of 3.0. Additional exam requirements/recommendations for international students: Required—TOEFL (minimum score 550 paper-based; 80 iBT), IELTS (minimum score 6). Electronic applications accepted. *Faculty research:* Modern global literatures in English, film and media studies, cultural studies and critical theory, American literature, English literature.

**University of Georgia,** Franklin College of Arts and Sciences, Department of English, Athens, GA 30602. Offers English (MA, MAT, PhD). *Degree requirements:* For master's, one foreign language, thesis (MA); for doctorate, 2 foreign languages, thesis/dissertation. *Entrance requirements:* For master's and doctorate, GRE General Test. Additional exam requirements/recommendations for international students: Required—TWE. *Application deadline:* For fall admission, 7/1 priority date for domestic students; for spring admission, 11/15 for domestic students. Application fee: $50. Electronic applications accepted. *Financial support:* Fellowships, research assistantships, teaching assistantships, and unspecified assistantships available. *Unit head:* Dr. Michael G. Moran, Head, 706-543-9266, Fax: 706-542-2181, E-mail: mgmoran@uga.edu. *Application contact:* Dr. Michelle Ballif, Graduate Coordinator, 706-542-3110, E-mail: mballif@uga.edu.
Website: http://web.english.uga.edu/

**University of Guam,** Office of Graduate Studies, College of Liberal Arts and Social Sciences, Department of English, Mangilao, GU 96923. Offers MA. *Entrance requirements:* For master's, GRE. Additional exam requirements/recommendations for international students: Required—TOEFL.

**University of Guelph,** Graduate Studies, College of Arts, School of English and Theatre Studies, Program in English, Guelph, ON N1G 2W1, Canada. Offers MA. *Program availability:* Part-time. *Degree requirements:* For master's, thesis (for some programs). *Entrance requirements:* For master's, letters of reference, 4-year honours undergraduate degree in English or drama. Additional exam requirements/recommendations for international students: Required—TOEFL. Electronic applications accepted. *Faculty research:* Post-colonial literature, Canadian literature, children's literature, Scottish literature, American literature, cultural studies.

**University of Hawaii at Manoa,** Graduate Division, College of Languages, Linguistics and Literature, Department of English, Honolulu, HI 96822. Offers MA, PhD. *Program availability:* Part-time. *Degree requirements:* For master's, 2 foreign languages, thesis optional; for doctorate, 2 foreign languages, comprehensive exam, thesis/dissertation. *Entrance requirements:* For master's, GRE General Test; for doctorate, GRE General Test, GRE Subject Test. Additional exam requirements/recommendations for international students: Required—TOEFL (minimum score 600 paper-based; 100 iBT), IELTS (minimum score 7). *Faculty research:* British and American literature, creative writing, cultural studies, rhetoric and composition.

**University of Houston–Clear Lake,** School of Human Sciences and Humanities, Programs in Humanities and Fine Arts, Houston, TX 77058-1002. Offers history (MA); humanities (MA); literature (MA). *Program availability:* Part-time, evening/weekend, online learning. *Degree requirements:* For master's, thesis or alternative. *Entrance requirements:* For master's, GRE General Test. Additional exam requirements/recommendations for international students: Required—TOEFL (minimum score 550 paper-based). *Faculty research:* Digital media studies, Latin American history, labor history, Chaucer evolution versus creationism debate.

**University of Houston–Downtown,** College of Humanities and Social Sciences, Department of English, Houston, TX 77002. Offers rhetoric and composition (MA); technical communication (MS). *Program availability:* Part-time, evening/weekend. *Faculty:* 8 full-time (4 women). *Students:* 9 full-time (4 women), 45 part-time (29 women); includes 31 minority (14 Black or African American, non-Hispanic/Latino; 1 American Indian or Alaska Native, non-Hispanic/Latino; 1 Asian, non-Hispanic/Latino; 15 Hispanic/Latino). Average age 39. 31 applicants, 84% accepted, 23 enrolled. In 2016, 8 master's awarded. *Entrance requirements:* Additional exam requirements/recommendations for international students: Required—TOEFL. *Application deadline:* For fall admission, 4/1 for domestic and international students; for spring admission, 11/15 for domestic and international students. Application fee: $35 ($60 for international students). Electronic applications accepted. *Expenses:* $305.50 in-state, per credit; $663.50 out-of-state, per credit. *Financial support:* Federal Work-Study and scholarships/grants available. Financial award application deadline: 4/1; financial award applicants required to submit FAFSA. *Faculty research:* Environmental rhetoric, instructional design, usability, assessment, presentation slides. *Unit head:* Dr. Michelle Moosally, Chair, 713-221-8254, Fax: 713-226-5205, E-mail: moosallym@uhd.edu. *Application contact:* Ceshia Love, Director of Graduate and International Admissions, 713-221-8093, Fax: 713-223-7408, E-mail: gradadmissions@uhd.edu.
Website: https://www.uhd.edu/academics/humanities/Pages/humanities-index.aspx

**University of Idaho,** College of Graduate Studies, College of Letters, Arts and Social Sciences, Department of English, Moscow, ID 83844. Offers creative writing (MFA); English (MA, MAT); teaching English as a second language (MA). *Faculty:* 14 full-time (7 women). *Students:* 53 full-time, 10 part-time. Average age 31. In 2016, 40 master's awarded. *Entrance requirements:* For master's, minimum GPA of 3.0. Additional exam requirements/recommendations for international students: Required—TOEFL. *Application deadline:* For fall admission, 8/1 for domestic students; for spring admission, 12/15 for domestic students. Applications are processed on a rolling basis. Application fee: $60. Electronic applications accepted. *Expenses:* Tuition, state resident: full-time $6460; part-time $414 per credit hour. Tuition, nonresident: full-time $21,268; part-time $1237 per credit hour. *Required fees:* $2070; $60 per credit hour. Full-time tuition and fees vary according to course load and reciprocity agreements. *Financial support:* Research assistantships and teaching assistantships available. Financial award applicants required to submit FAFSA. *Unit head:* Dr. Scott Slovic, Chair, 208-885-6156, E-mail: englishdept@uidaho.edu. *Application contact:* Sean Scoggin, Graduate Recruitment Coordinator, 208-885-4723, Fax: 208-885-4406, E-mail: graduateadmissions@uidaho.edu.
Website: https://www.uidaho.edu/class/english

**University of Illinois at Chicago,** College of Liberal Arts and Sciences, Department of English, Chicago, IL 60607-7128. Offers MA, PhD. *Program availability:* Part-time, evening/weekend. *Degree requirements:* For doctorate, variable foreign language requirement, thesis/dissertation, written and oral exams. *Entrance requirements:* For master's, GRE General Test; for doctorate, GRE General Test, GRE Subject Test, minimum GPA of 2.0. Additional exam requirements/recommendations for international students: Required—TOEFL. Electronic applications accepted. *Faculty research:* Literary history and theory.

**University of Illinois at Springfield,** Graduate Programs, College of Liberal Arts and Sciences, Department of English and Modern Languages, Springfield, IL 62703-5407. Offers English (MA); teaching English (Graduate Certificate). *Program availability:* Part-time, evening/weekend. *Faculty:* 5 full-time (4 women). *Students:* 8 full-time (4 women), 9 part-time (5 women); includes 1 minority (Asian, non-Hispanic/Latino), 1 international. Average age 31. 11 applicants, 73% accepted, 6 enrolled. In 2016, 4 master's, 1 other advanced degree awarded. *Degree requirements:* For master's, thesis, critical project, or creative project. *Entrance requirements:* For master's, GRE General Test, minimum overall undergraduate GPA of 3.0; analytical writing sample or sample of creative work; two letters of recommendation. Additional exam requirements/recommendations for international students: Required—TOEFL (minimum score 500 paper-based; 61 iBT). *Application deadline:* Applications are processed on a rolling basis. Application fee: $60 ($75 for international students). Electronic applications accepted. *Expenses:* Tuition, state resident: part-time $329 per credit hour. Tuition, nonresident: part-time $675 per credit hour. *Financial support:* In 2016–17, fellowships with full tuition reimbursements (averaging $9,900 per year), research assistantships with full tuition reimbursements (averaging $9,991 per year), teaching assistantships with full tuition reimbursements (averaging $10,059 per year) were awarded; career-related internships or fieldwork, Federal Work-Study, scholarships/grants, health care benefits, and unspecified assistantships also available. Support available to part-time students. Financial award application deadline: 11/15; financial award applicants required to submit FAFSA. *Unit head:* Dr. Tena Helton, Program Administrator, 217-206-7441, Fax: 217-206-6217, E-mail: thelt2@uis.edu. *Application contact:* Dr. Cecelia Cornell, Associate Vice Chancellor for Graduate Education, 217-206-7230, E-mail: ccorn1@uis.edu.

**University of Illinois at Urbana–Champaign,** Graduate College, College of Liberal Arts and Sciences, Department of English, Champaign, IL 61820. Offers creative writing (MFA); English (MA, PhD).

**University of Indianapolis,** Graduate Programs, College of Arts and Sciences, Department of English Language and Literature, Indianapolis, IN 46227-3697. Offers English (MA). *Program availability:* Part-time, evening/weekend. *Entrance requirements:* For master's, GRE Subject Test, minimum GPA of 2.5. Additional exam requirements/recommendations for international students: Required—TOEFL (minimum score 550 paper-based). Electronic applications accepted.

**The University of Iowa,** Graduate College, College of Liberal Arts and Sciences, Department of English, Iowa City, IA 52242-1316. Offers English (PhD); literary studies (MA); nonfiction writing (MFA). *Degree requirements:* For master's, thesis (for some programs), exam; for doctorate, comprehensive exam, thesis/dissertation. *Entrance requirements:* For master's and doctorate, GRE General Test, minimum GPA of 3.0. Additional exam requirements/recommendations for international students: Required—TOEFL (minimum score 640 paper-based; 111 iBT). Electronic applications accepted.

**The University of Kansas,** Graduate Studies, College of Liberal Arts and Sciences, Department of English, Lawrence, KS 66045. Offers creative writing (MFA), including fine arts/creative writing; English (MA, PhD). *Program availability:* Part-time. *Students:* 93 full-time (57 women), 3 part-time (1 woman); includes 14 minority (7 Black or African American, non-Hispanic/Latino; 1 Asian, non-Hispanic/Latino; 3 Hispanic/Latino; 3 Two or more races, non-Hispanic/Latino), 8 international. Average age 30. 143 applicants, 29% accepted, 28 enrolled. In 2016, 9 master's, 3 doctorates awarded. *Entrance requirements:* For master's and doctorate, GRE General Test, two examples of academic writing; resume; statement of approximately 500 words describing interests, training, experience (including teaching experience), academic ability, and goals; three letters of recommendation; official transcripts. Additional exam requirements/recommendations for international students: Required—TOEFL or IELTS. *Application deadline:* For fall admission, 12/31 for domestic and international students. Application fee: $65 ($85 for international students). Electronic applications accepted. *Financial support:* Fellowships, research assistantships, teaching assistantships, and unspecified assistantships available. *Faculty research:* Ecocriticism and science/science fiction writing; gender and sexuality studies; U.S. ethnic literatures, race, and diaspora studies; composition, rhetoric, and language studies; creative writing. *Unit head:* Anna Neill, Chair, 785-864-2521, E-mail: aneill@ku.edu. *Application contact:* Lydia Ash, Graduate Secretary, 785-864-2518, E-mail: lash@ku.edu.
Website: http://www.english.ku.edu

**University of Kentucky,** Graduate School, College of Arts and Sciences, Program in English, Lexington, KY 40506-0032. Offers MA, PhD. *Degree requirements:* For master's, one foreign language, comprehensive exam, thesis optional; for doctorate, one foreign language, comprehensive exam, thesis/dissertation. *Entrance requirements:* For master's, GRE General Test, minimum undergraduate GPA of 2.75; for doctorate, GRE General Test, minimum graduate GPA of 3.0. Additional exam requirements/recommendations for international students: Required—TOEFL (minimum score 550 paper-based). Electronic applications accepted.

**University of La Verne,** Regional and Online Campuses, Graduate Credential Program in Education, California Statewide Campus, La Verne, CA 91750-4443. Offers administration services (preliminary) (Credential); education specialist: mild/moderate (Credential); English (Certificate); multiple subject teaching (Credential); pupil personnel services: school counseling (Credential); single subject teaching (Credential); special education (MS); special emphasis (M Ed). *Accreditation:* NCATE. *Program availability:* Part-time. *Entrance requirements:* For degree, California Basic Educational Skills Test, minimum undergraduate GPA of 2.75, 3 letters of recommendation, interview. *Expenses:* Contact institution.

**University of Lethbridge,** School of Graduate Studies, Lethbridge, AB T1K 3M4, Canada. Offers addictions counseling (M Sc); agricultural biotechnology (M Sc); agricultural studies (M Sc, MA); anthropology (MA); archaeology (M Sc, MA); art (MA, MFA); biochemistry (M Sc); biological sciences (M Sc); biomolecular science (PhD); biosystems and biodiversity (PhD); Canadian studies (MA); chemistry (M Sc); computer science (M Sc); computer science and geographical information science (M Sc); counseling (MC); counseling psychology (M Ed); dramatic arts (MA); earth, space, and physical science (PhD); economics (MA); education (MA); educational leadership (M Ed); English (MA); environmental science (M Sc); evolution and behavior (PhD); exercise science (M Sc); French (MA); French/German (MA); French/Spanish (MA); general education (M Ed); geography (M Sc, MA); German (MA); health sciences (M Sc); individualized multidisciplinary (M Sc, MA); kinesiology (M Sc, MA); management (M Sc), including accounting, finance, human resource management and labor relations, information systems, international management, marketing, policy and strategy; mathematics (M Sc); music (M Mus, MA); Native American studies (MA); neuroscience (M Sc, PhD); new media (MA, MFA); nursing (M Sc, MN); philosophy (MA); physics (M Sc); political science (MA); psychology (M Sc, MA); religious studies (MA); sociology (MA); theatre and dramatic arts (MFA); theoretical and computational science (PhD); urban and regional studies (MA); women and gender studies (MA). *Program availability:* Part-time, evening/weekend. *Degree requirements:* For master's, thesis (for some programs); for doctorate, comprehensive exam, thesis/dissertation. *Entrance requirements:* For master's, GMAT (for M Sc in management), bachelor's degree in related field, minimum GPA of 3.0 during previous 20 graded semester courses, 2 years' teaching or related experience (M Ed); for doctorate, master's degree, minimum graduate GPA of 3.5. Additional exam requirements/recommendations for international students: Required—TOEFL (minimum score 580 paper-based; 93 iBT). Electronic applications accepted. *Faculty research:* Movement and brain plasticity, gibberellin physiology, photosynthesis, carbon cycling, molecular properties of main-group ring components.

**University of Louisiana at Lafayette,** College of Liberal Arts, Department of English, Lafayette, LA 70504. Offers British and American literature (MA), including creative writing, folklore, rhetoric; creative writing (PhD); literature (PhD); rhetoric (PhD). *Program availability:* Part-time. Terminal master's awarded for partial completion of doctoral program. *Degree requirements:* For master's, one foreign language, thesis or alternative; for doctorate, 2 foreign languages, comprehensive exam, thesis/dissertation. *Entrance requirements:* For master's, GRE General Test, minimum GPA of 2.75; for doctorate, GRE General Test, minimum GPA of 3.0. Additional exam requirements/recommendations for international students: Required—TOEFL (minimum score 550

paper-based). Electronic applications accepted. *Faculty research:* Composition theory, Southern literature, medieval literature.

**University of Louisiana at Monroe,** Graduate School, College of Arts, Education, and Sciences, Department of English, Monroe, LA 71209-0001. Offers MA. *Program availability:* Part-time, evening/weekend. *Faculty:* 4 full-time (2 women), 1 part-time/adjunct (0 women). *Students:* 12 full-time (6 women), 1 (woman) part-time; includes 2 minority (1 Hispanic/Latino; 1 Two or more races, non-Hispanic/Latino). Average age 24. 26 applicants, 31% accepted, 6 enrolled. In 2016, 4 master's awarded. *Degree requirements:* For master's, one foreign language, thesis (for some programs). *Entrance requirements:* For master's, GRE General Test (minimum score 900 verbal and quantitative), minimum GPA of 3.0 in English, 2.5 overall. Additional exam requirements/recommendations for international students: Required—TOEFL (minimum score 500 paper-based; 61 iBT) or Michigan English Language Assessment Battery. *Application deadline:* For fall admission, 8/24 priority date for domestic students, 7/1 for international students; for winter admission, 12/14 priority date for domestic students; for spring admission, 1/19 for domestic students, 11/1 for international students. Applications are processed on a rolling basis. Application fee: $20 ($30 for international students). Electronic applications accepted. *Expenses:* Tuition, state resident: full-time $6489. Tuition, nonresident: full-time $18,589. *Required fees:* $8984. Tuition and fees vary according to course level, course load, degree level and program. *Financial support:* Teaching assistantships, career-related internships or fieldwork, Federal Work-Study, institutionally sponsored loans, and unspecified assistantships available. Financial award application deadline: 4/1; financial award applicants required to submit FAFSA. *Faculty research:* Creative writing, American literature, British literature, multicultural literature, literary theory. *Unit head:* Frances Gregory, Associate Director, 318-342-1370, Fax: 318-342-1755, E-mail: gregory@ulm.edu. *Application contact:* Dr. Julia Guernsey-Pitchford, Associate Professor, 318-342-1496, E-mail: pitchford@ulm.edu. Website: http://www.ulm.edu/english

**University of Louisville,** Graduate School, College of Arts and Sciences, Department of English, Louisville, KY 40292. Offers English (MA), including creative writing, literature, rhetoric and composition (MA, PhD); English rhetoric and composition (PhD), including rhetoric and composition (MA, PhD). *Program availability:* Part-time, evening/weekend. *Faculty:* 36 full-time (19 women), 6 part-time/adjunct (3 women). *Students:* 54 full-time (39 women), 17 part-time (12 women); includes 9 minority (3 Black or African American, non-Hispanic/Latino; 1 Asian, non-Hispanic/Latino; 3 Hispanic/Latino; 2 Two or more races, non-Hispanic/Latino), 1 international. Average age 30. 87 applicants, 53% accepted, 20 enrolled. In 2016, 16 master's, 2 doctorates awarded. *Degree requirements:* For master's, one foreign language, thesis optional, culminating project of 25-30 pages; for doctorate, one foreign language, comprehensive exam, thesis/dissertation. *Entrance requirements:* For master's and doctorate, GRE General Test. Additional exam requirements/recommendations for international students: Required—TOEFL (minimum score 600 paper-based) or IELTS (6.5). *Application deadline:* Applications are processed on a rolling basis. Application fee: $60. Electronic applications accepted. *Expenses:* $12,448. *Financial support:* In 2016–17, 3 fellowships with full tuition reimbursements (averaging $20,000 per year), 2 research assistantships (averaging $17,750 per year), 34 teaching assistantships with full tuition reimbursements (averaging $17,750 per year) were awarded; health care benefits and unspecified assistantships also available. Financial award application deadline: 1/5. *Faculty research:* Rhetoric and composition, creative writing, eighteenth- and nineteenth-century British literature, nineteenth-century American literature, critical theory. *Total annual research expenditures:* $124,449. *Unit head:* Dr. Glynis Ridley, Chair, 502-852-6803, E-mail: glynis.ridley@louisville.edu. *Application contact:* Annelise Gray, Senior Program Assistant, 502-852-0505, E-mail: annelise.gray@louisville.edu. Website: http://www.louisville.edu/english/graduate

**University of Maine,** Graduate School, College of Liberal Arts and Sciences, Department of English, Orono, ME 04469. Offers MA. *Program availability:* Part-time, evening/weekend. *Faculty:* 19 full-time (9 women). *Students:* 25 full-time (15 women), 6 part-time (5 women); includes 3 minority (2 Black or African American, non-Hispanic/Latino; 1 Two or more races, non-Hispanic/Latino), 1 international. Average age 29. 27 applicants, 93% accepted, 12 enrolled. In 2016, 13 master's awarded. *Degree requirements:* For master's, one foreign language, thesis optional. *Entrance requirements:* For master's, GRE General Test, minimum GPA of 3.0. Additional exam requirements/recommendations for international students: Required—TOEFL (minimum score 79 iBT). *Application deadline:* For fall admission, 1/15 priority date for domestic and international students. Applications are processed on a rolling basis. Application fee: $65. Electronic applications accepted. *Expenses:* Tuition, state resident: full-time $7524; part-time $2508 per credit. Tuition, nonresident: full-time $24,498; part-time $8166 per credit. *Required fees:* $1148; $571 per credit. *Financial support:* In 2016–17, 23 students received support, including 20 teaching assistantships with full tuition reimbursements available (averaging $14,600 per year); Federal Work-Study, tuition waivers (full and partial), and unspecified assistantships also available. Financial award application deadline: 3/1. *Faculty research:* Creative writing, gender and literature, poetry and poetics, writing studies. *Unit head:* Dr. Laura Cowan, Chair, 207-581-3823, Fax: 207-581-1604. *Application contact:* Scott G. Delcourt, Assistant Vice President for Graduate Studies and Senior Associate Dean, 207-581-3291, Fax: 207-581-3232, E-mail: graduate@maine.edu.
Website: http://english.umaine.edu/

**The University of Manchester,** School of Arts, Histories and Cultures, Manchester, United Kingdom. Offers anthropology, media and performance (PhD); applied theatre professional (PhD); archaeology (PhD); art history and visual studies (PhD); arts management and cultural policy (PhD); classics and ancient history (PhD); composition (PhD); creative writing (PhD); drama (PhD); economic and social history (PhD); electroacoustic composition (PhD); English and American studies (PhD); history (PhD); humanitarianism and conflict response (PhD); museology (PhD); music (PhD); musicology (PhD); religions and theology (PhD).

**University of Manitoba,** Faculty of Graduate Studies, Faculty of Arts, Department of English, Film, and Theatre, Winnipeg, MB R3T 2N2, Canada. Offers English (MA, PhD). *Degree requirements:* For master's, one foreign language, thesis; for doctorate, one foreign language, thesis/dissertation.

**University of Maryland, Baltimore County,** The Graduate School, College of Arts, Humanities and Social Sciences, Program in English: Texts, Technologies, and Literature, Baltimore, MD 21250. Offers MA. *Program availability:* Part-time, evening/weekend. *Faculty:* 13 full-time (11 women). *Students:* 6 full-time (3 women), 11 part-time (7 women); includes 8 minority (5 Black or African American, non-Hispanic/Latino; 1 Asian, non-Hispanic/Latino; 2 Hispanic/Latino). Average age 28. 12 applicants, 83% accepted, 9 enrolled. In 2016, 3 master's awarded. *Degree requirements:* For master's, thesis or portfolio. *Entrance requirements:* For master's, GRE. Additional exam requirements/recommendations for international students: Required—TOEFL. *Application deadline:* For fall admission, 5/1 for domestic students; for spring admission, 5/1 for domestic students. Applications are processed on a rolling basis. Electronic applications accepted. *Expenses:* Tuition, state resident: full-time $13,294. Tuition, nonresident: full-time $20,286. *Financial support:* In 2016–17, 5 students received support. Unspecified assistantships available. Financial award application deadline: 5/1.

*Faculty research:* British and American literature, post colonial and Islamic literature, digital media, electronic literacies, rhetoric and composition. *Unit head:* Dr. Orianne Smith, English Department Chair, 410-455-2384, Fax: 410-455-3010, E-mail: osmith@umbc.edu. *Application contact:* Dr. Lucille McCarthy, Graduate Program Director, 410-455-2384, Fax: 410-455-3010, E-mail: mccarthy@umbc.edu. Website: http://www.umbc.edu/english/ma.html

**University of Maryland, College Park,** Academic Affairs, College of Arts and Humanities, Department of English, Program in English Language and Literature, College Park, MD 20742. Offers MA, PhD. *Degree requirements:* For master's, thesis optional; for doctorate, one foreign language, thesis/dissertation, oral and written exams. *Entrance requirements:* For master's, GRE General Test, minimum GPA of 3.5, writing sample, 3 letters of recommendation; for doctorate, GRE General Test, minimum GPA of 3.7, writing sample. Additional exam requirements/recommendations for international students: Required—TOEFL. Electronic applications accepted.

**University of Massachusetts Amherst,** Graduate School, College of Humanities and Fine Arts, Department of English, Amherst, MA 01003. Offers American studies (PhD); composition and rhetoric (PhD); creative writing (MFA); English and American literature (MA, PhD). *Program availability:* Part-time. Terminal master's awarded for partial completion of doctoral program. *Degree requirements:* For master's, one foreign language, thesis optional; for doctorate, one foreign language, comprehensive exam, thesis/dissertation. *Entrance requirements:* For master's, manuscript; for doctorate, GRE General Test, manuscript. Additional exam requirements/recommendations for international students: Required—TOEFL (minimum score 550 paper-based; 80 iBT), IELTS (minimum score 6.5). Electronic applications accepted.

**University of Massachusetts Boston,** College of Liberal Arts, Program in English, Boston, MA 02125-3393. Offers MA. *Program availability:* Part-time, evening/weekend. *Faculty:* 60 full-time (32 women), 22 part-time/adjunct (10 women). *Students:* 31 full-time (23 women), 28 part-time (15 women); includes 9 minority (3 Black or African American, non-Hispanic/Latino; 3 Hispanic/Latino; 3 Two or more races, non-Hispanic/Latino), 5 international. Average age 32. 36 applicants, 72% accepted, 18 enrolled. In 2016, 26 master's awarded. *Degree requirements:* For master's, one foreign language, final project. *Entrance requirements:* For master's, minimum GPA of 2.75. *Application deadline:* For fall admission, 3/1 for domestic students; for spring admission, 11/1 for domestic students. *Expenses:* Tuition, state resident: full-time $16,863. Tuition, nonresident: full-time $32,913. *Required fees:* $177. *Financial support:* Research assistantships with full tuition reimbursements, teaching assistantships with full tuition reimbursements, career-related internships or fieldwork, Federal Work-Study, and unspecified assistantships available. Support available to part-time students. Financial award application deadline: 3/1; financial award applicants required to submit FAFSA. *Faculty research:* Working class literature, women writers, British fiction, composition theory, modern American literature. *Unit head:* Dr. Pamela Annas, Director, 617-287-6700, E-mail: pamela.annas@umb.edu. *Application contact:* Peggy Roldan Patel, Graduate Admissions Coordinator, 617-287-6400, Fax: 617-287-6236, E-mail: bos.gadm@dpc.umassp.edu.

**University of Memphis,** Graduate School, College of Arts and Sciences, Department of English, Memphis, TN 38152. Offers African-American literature (Graduate Certificate); applied linguistics (PhD); composition studies (PhD); creative writing (MFA); English as a second language (MA); linguistics (MA); literary and cultural studies (PhD), including African-American literature; literature (MA); professional writing (MA, PhD); teaching English as a second/foreign language (Graduate Certificate). *Program availability:* Part-time, evening/weekend, 100% online. *Faculty:* 31 full-time (14 women), 1 (woman) part-time/adjunct. *Students:* 86 full-time (44 women), 78 part-time (51 women); includes 36 minority (19 Black or African American, non-Hispanic/Latino; 3 Asian, non-Hispanic/Latino; 10 Hispanic/Latino; 4 Two or more races, non-Hispanic/Latino), 32 international. Average age 35. 68 applicants, 87% accepted, 33 enrolled. In 2016, 39 master's, 17 doctorates, 16 other advanced degrees awarded. Terminal master's awarded for partial completion of doctoral program. *Degree requirements:* For master's, one foreign language, comprehensive exam, thesis optional; for doctorate, 2 foreign languages, comprehensive exam, thesis/dissertation, qualifying exam. *Entrance requirements:* For master's, GRE, minimum undergraduate GPA of 3.0, statement of purpose, two letters of recommendation; for doctorate, GRE, minimum undergraduate and graduate GPA of 3.25, statement of purpose, writing sample, three letters of recommendation. Additional exam requirements/recommendations for international students: Required—TOEFL. *Application deadline:* For fall admission, 1/15 for domestic students; for spring admission, 10/15 for domestic students. Applications are processed on a rolling basis. Application fee: $35 ($60 for international students). Electronic applications accepted. *Expenses:* $5,231.50 per semester full-time in-state, $9,623.50 full-time out-of-state. *Financial support:* In 2016–17, 123 students received support, including 11 research assistantships with full tuition reimbursements available (averaging $17,064 per year), 25 teaching assistantships with full tuition reimbursements available (averaging $17,340 per year); Federal Work-Study, scholarships/grants, and unspecified assistantships also available. Financial award application deadline: 2/1; financial award applicants required to submit FAFSA. *Faculty research:* Applied linguistics, British and American literature, professional writing, composition studies. *Unit head:* Dr. Joshua Phillips, Chair, 901-678-2651, Fax: 901-678-2226, E-mail: jsphllps@memphis.edu. *Application contact:* Dr. Jeffrey Scraba, Coordinator of Graduate Studies, 901-678-4768, Fax: 901-678-2226, E-mail: jscraba@memphis.edu.
Website: http://www.memphis.edu/english

**University of Miami,** Graduate School, College of Arts and Sciences, Department of English, Coral Gables, FL 33124. Offers creative writing (MFA); English (MA, PhD). *Program availability:* Part-time. Terminal master's awarded for partial completion of doctoral program. *Degree requirements:* For master's, one foreign language, thesis optional; for doctorate, one foreign language, thesis/dissertation. *Entrance requirements:* For master's and doctorate, GRE General Test. Electronic applications accepted. *Faculty research:* Anglo-Irish literature, feminist criticism and theory, Caribbean literature, early modern literature and culture, postcolonial and ethnic studies.

**University of Michigan,** Rackham Graduate School, College of Literature, Science, and the Arts, Department of English Language and Literature, Ann Arbor, MI 48109-1003. Offers creative writing (MFA); English and education (PhD); English and women's studies (PhD); English language and literature (PhD). *Faculty:* 51 full-time (28 women). *Students:* 79 full-time (52 women); includes 19 minority (4 Black or African American, non-Hispanic/Latino; 5 Asian, non-Hispanic/Latino; 7 Hispanic/Latino; 3 Two or more races, non-Hispanic/Latino), 4 international. Average age 29. 358 applicants, 10% accepted, 14 enrolled. In 2016, 7 doctorates awarded. *Degree requirements:* For doctorate, 2 foreign languages, comprehensive exam, thesis/dissertation, oral defense of dissertation, preliminary exam. *Entrance requirements:* For doctorate, GRE General Test, writing sample. Additional exam requirements/recommendations for international students: Required—TOEFL (minimum score 620 paper-based; 106 iBT). *Application deadline:* For fall admission, 12/10 for domestic and international students. Application fee: $75 ($90 for international students). Electronic applications accepted. *Expenses:* Tuition, state resident: full-time $21,466; part-time $1152 per credit hour. Tuition, nonresident: full-time $43,346; part-time $2367 per credit hour. Part-time tuition and fees vary according to course load, degree level and program. *Financial support:* In 2016–

17, 73 students received support. Fellowships with full tuition reimbursements available, teaching assistantships with full tuition reimbursements available, and health care benefits available. Financial award application deadline: 12/10. *Faculty research:* Post colonialism, modernism, early modern, American, British. *Application contact:* Graduate Admissions, 734-763-4139, Fax: 734-763-3128, E-mail: grad.eng.admis@um.cc.umich.edu.
Website: https://www.lsa.umich.edu/english/

**University of Michigan,** Rackham Graduate School, College of Literature, Science, and the Arts, Department of Women's Studies, Ann Arbor, MI 48109. Offers English and women's studies (PhD); history and women's studies (PhD); LGBTQ studies (Certificate); psychology and women's studies (PhD); women's studies (Certificate). *Degree requirements:* For doctorate, variable foreign language requirement, comprehensive exam (for some programs), thesis/dissertation. *Entrance requirements:* For doctorate, GRE General Test, previous undergraduate coursework in women's studies. Electronic applications accepted. *Expenses:* Tuition, state resident: full-time $21,466; part-time $1152 per credit hour. Tuition, nonresident: full-time $43,346; part-time $2367 per credit hour. Part-time tuition and fees vary according to course load, degree level and program. *Faculty research:* LGBTQ studies, sexuality studies, feminist science studies, global feminism, health studies, international studies, cultural studies.

**University of Michigan–Flint,** College of Arts and Sciences, Program in English Language and Literature, Flint, MI 48502-1950. Offers literature (MA); writing and rhetoric (MA). *Program availability:* Part-time. *Faculty:* 26 full-time (17 women), 1 (woman) part-time/adjunct. *Students:* 2 full-time (1 woman), 17 part-time (14 women); includes 5 minority (1 Black or African American, non-Hispanic/Latino; 2 Hispanic/Latino; 2 Two or more races, non-Hispanic/Latino), 1 international. Average age 34. 12 applicants, 83% accepted, 7 enrolled. In 2016, 14 master's awarded. *Degree requirements:* For master's, thesis optional. *Entrance requirements:* For master's, bachelor's degree with major or significant coursework in English or related fields from regionally-accredited institution; minimum overall undergraduate GPA of 3.0. Additional exam requirements/recommendations for international students: Required—TOEFL (minimum score 84 iBT), IELTS (minimum score 6.5). *Application deadline:* For fall admission, 8/1 for domestic students, 5/1 for international students; for winter admission, 11/15 for domestic students, 9/1 for international students; for spring admission, 3/15 for domestic students, 1/1 for international students; for summer admission, 5/15 for domestic students. Applications are processed on a rolling basis. Application fee: $55. Electronic applications accepted. *Expenses:* Contact institution. *Financial support:* Federal Work-Study, scholarships/grants, and unspecified assistantships available. Support available to part-time students. Financial award application deadline: 3/1; financial award applicants required to submit FAFSA. *Unit head:* Dr. Suzanne Knight, Director, 810-762-0145, E-mail: suknight@umflint.edu. *Application contact:* Bradley T. Maki, Director of Graduate Admissions, 810-762-3171, Fax: 810-766-6789, E-mail: bmaki@umflint.edu.
Website: http://www.umflint.edu/graduateprograms/english-language-and-literature-ma

**University of Minnesota, Duluth,** Graduate School, College of Liberal Arts, Department of English, Duluth, MN 55812-2496. Offers MA. *Program availability:* Part-time. *Degree requirements:* For master's, one foreign language, comprehensive exam, 2 extended papers or projects. *Entrance requirements:* For master's, GRE General Test, minimum GPA of 3.0. Additional exam requirements/recommendations for international students: Required—TOEFL. *Faculty research:* British cultural studies, Irish literature, American studies, linguistics, information design.

**University of Minnesota, Twin Cities Campus,** Graduate School, College of Liberal Arts, Department of English, Minneapolis, MN 55455. Offers MA, PhD. Terminal master's awarded for partial completion of doctoral program. *Degree requirements:* For master's, one foreign language, thesis or alternative; for doctorate, 2 foreign languages, thesis/dissertation. *Entrance requirements:* For master's and doctorate, GRE General Test. Additional exam requirements/recommendations for international students: Required—TOEFL (minimum score 620 paper-based, 105 iBT) or IELTS (minimum score 7.5). Electronic applications accepted. *Faculty research:* British and American literature, medieval and early modern literature, postcolonial and contemporary literature, feminist studies, film and cultural studies.

**University of Mississippi,** Graduate School, College of Liberal Arts, University, MS 38677. Offers anthropology (MA); biology (MS, PhD); chemistry (MS, PhD); economics (MA, PhD); English (MA, PhD); experimental psychology (PhD); history (MA, PhD); mathematics (MS, PhD); modern languages (MA); music (MM); philosophy (MA); physics (MA, MS, PhD); political science (MA, PhD); studio art (MFA). *Program availability:* Part-time. *Faculty:* 472 full-time (263 women), 75 part-time/adjunct (35 women). *Students:* 415 full-time (210 women), 57 part-time (20 women); includes 70 minority (35 Black or African American, non-Hispanic/Latino; 13 Asian, non-Hispanic/Latino; 14 Hispanic/Latino; 8 Two or more races, non-Hispanic/Latino), 102 international. Average age 27. *Degree requirements:* For doctorate, thesis/dissertation. *Entrance requirements:* For master's, GRE General Test, minimum GPA of 3.0; for doctorate, GRE General Test. Additional exam requirements/recommendations for international students: Required—TOEFL. *Application deadline:* For fall admission, 4/1 for domestic students; for spring admission, 10/1 for domestic students. Applications are processed on a rolling basis. Application fee: $40. Electronic applications accepted. *Financial support:* Fellowships, research assistantships, teaching assistantships, career-related internships or fieldwork, Federal Work-Study, institutionally sponsored loans, scholarships/grants, and unspecified assistantships available. Financial award application deadline: 3/1; financial award applicants required to submit FAFSA. *Unit head:* Dr. Lee Michael Cohen, Dean, 662-915-7177, Fax: 662-915-5792, E-mail: libarts@olemiss.edu. *Application contact:* Dr. Christy M. Wyandt, Associate Dean of Graduate School, 662-915-7474, Fax: 662-915-7577, E-mail: cwyandt@olemiss.edu.
Website: https://www.olemiss.edu

**University of Missouri,** Office of Research and Graduate Studies, College of Arts and Science, Department of English, Columbia, MO 65211. Offers MA, PhD. *Faculty:* 54 full-time (29 women), 1 (woman) part-time/adjunct. *Students:* 74 full-time (43 women), 13 part-time (7 women). Terminal master's awarded for partial completion of doctoral program. *Degree requirements:* For doctorate, 2 foreign languages, comprehensive exam, thesis/dissertation. *Entrance requirements:* For master's, GRE General Test, minimum GPA of 3.0; for doctorate, GRE General Test, minimum GPA of 3.0; MA in English or equivalent. Additional exam requirements/recommendations for international students: Required—TOEFL (minimum score 500 paper-based; 61 iBT). *Application deadline:* For fall admission, 1/1 priority date for domestic and international students. Applications are processed on a rolling basis. Application fee: $75 ($90 for international students). Electronic applications accepted. *Expenses:* Tuition, state resident: full-time $6347; part-time $352.60 per credit hour. Tuition, nonresident: full-time $17,379; part-time $965.50 per credit hour. *Required fees:* $1035. Tuition and fees vary according to course load, campus/location and program. *Financial support:* Fellowships with full tuition reimbursements, research assistantships with full tuition reimbursements, teaching assistantships with full tuition reimbursements, institutionally sponsored loans, health care benefits, and unspecified assistantships available. *Faculty research:* British and American literature and culture, African Diaspora studies, creative writing, folklore,

*English*

linguistics, rhetoric and composition.
Website: http://english.missouri.edu/graduate.html

**University of Missouri–Kansas City,** College of Arts and Sciences, Department of English Language and Literature, Kansas City, MO 64110-2499. Offers English (MA, PhD). PhD (interdisciplinary) offered through the School of Graduate Studies. *Program availability:* Part-time, evening/weekend. *Faculty:* 19 full-time (12 women), 20 part-time/adjunct (11 women). *Students:* 17 full-time (9 women), 35 part-time (21 women); includes 8 minority (5 Black or African American, non-Hispanic/Latino; 2 Hispanic/Latino; 1 Two or more races, non-Hispanic/Latino). Average age 43. 43 applicants, 49% accepted, 13 enrolled. In 2016, 12 master's awarded. *Degree requirements:* For master's, one foreign language; for doctorate, 2 foreign languages, comprehensive exam, thesis/dissertation. *Entrance requirements:* For master's, GRE General Test, 3 letters of recommendation. Additional exam requirements/recommendations for international students: Required—TOEFL (minimum score 550 paper-based; 80 iBT). *Application deadline:* For fall admission, 1/15 for domestic students, 1/15 priority date for international students. Applications are processed on a rolling basis. Application fee: $45 ($50 for international students). Electronic applications accepted. *Financial support:* In 2016–17, 16 teaching assistantships (averaging $11,625 per year) were awarded; career-related internships or fieldwork, Federal Work-Study, and institutionally sponsored loans also available. Support available to part-time students. Financial award application deadline: 3/1; financial award applicants required to submit FAFSA. *Faculty research:* Creative writing: poetry and prose, computational linguistics, rhetoric and composition, African-American and British literature, print culture. *Unit head:* Dr. Virginia Blanton, Co-Chair, 816-235-2560, Fax: 816-235-1308, E-mail: blantonv@umkc.edu. *Application contact:* Dr. John Cyril Barton, Director of Graduate Studies, 816-235-5206, E-mail: bartonjc@umkc.edu.
Website: http://cas.umkc.edu/english/

**University of Missouri–St. Louis,** College of Arts and Sciences, Department of English, St. Louis, MO 63121. Offers creative writing (MFA); English (MA). *Program availability:* Part-time, evening/weekend. *Faculty:* 17 full-time (6 women), 6 part-time/adjunct (4 women). *Students:* 21 full-time (13 women), 40 part-time (26 women); includes 9 minority (3 Black or African American, non-Hispanic/Latino; 2 Asian, non-Hispanic/Latino; 2 Hispanic/Latino; 2 Two or more races, non-Hispanic/Latino), 3 international. 29 applicants, 90% accepted, 17 enrolled. *Degree requirements:* For master's, thesis optional. *Entrance requirements:* For master's, two letters of recommendation; writing sample (MFA). Additional exam requirements/recommendations for international students: Required—TOEFL (minimum score 550 paper-based; 79 iBT), IELTS (minimum score 6.5). *Application deadline:* For fall admission, 7/1 priority date for domestic and international students; for spring admission, 12/1 priority date for domestic and international students. Applications are processed on a rolling basis. Application fee: $50 ($40 for international students). Electronic applications accepted. *Financial support:* Teaching assistantships with tuition reimbursements available. Financial award applicants required to submit FAFSA. *Faculty research:* Victorian literature, Shakespeare and Renaissance literature, eighteenth-century literature, composition theory. *Unit head:* Dr. Frank Grady, Chair, 314-516-5510, Fax: 314-516-5781, E-mail: fgrady@umsl.edu. *Application contact:* 314-516-5458, Fax: 314-516-5310, E-mail: gradadm@umsl.edu.
Website: http://www.umsl.edu/divisions/artscience/english/

**University of Montana,** Graduate School, College of Humanities and Sciences, Department of English, Program in Literature, Missoula, MT 59812-0002. Offers MA. *Degree requirements:* For master's, thesis optional. *Entrance requirements:* For master's, GRE General Test, sample of written work. Additional exam requirements/recommendations for international students: Required—TOEFL. *Faculty research:* Literary history, cultural studies, criticism and theory, Western studies.

**University of Montevallo,** College of Arts and Sciences, Department of English, Montevallo, AL 35115. Offers MA. *Program availability:* Part-time. *Students:* 1 (woman) full-time, 14 part-time (13 women); includes 3 minority (2 Black or African American, non-Hispanic/Latino; 1 Hispanic/Latino). In 2016, 4 master's awarded. *Degree requirements:* For master's, comprehensive exam, thesis optional. *Entrance requirements:* For master's, GRE General Test, MAT, minimum undergraduate GPA of 2.75 in last 60 hours or 2.5 overall, bachelor's degree in English or equivalent. Additional exam requirements/recommendations for international students: Required—TOEFL (minimum score 550 paper-based). *Application deadline:* For fall admission, 7/15 for domestic students; for spring admission, 11/15 for domestic students. Application fee: $25. *Expenses:* Tuition, state resident: full-time $9936. Tuition, nonresident: full-time $20,592. *Required fees:* $640. *Financial support:* Federal Work-Study, scholarships/grants, and unspecified assistantships available. *Unit head:* Dr. Paul Mahaffey, Chair, 205-665-6420, E-mail: mahaffey@montevallo.edu. *Application contact:* Kevin Thornthwaite, Acting Director, Graduate Studies, 205-665-6350, E-mail: graduate@montevallo.edu.
Website: http://www.montevallo.edu/english/

**University of Nebraska at Kearney,** College of Fine Arts and Humanities, Department of English, Kearney, NE 68849-0001. Offers creative writing (MA); literature (MA); writing (MA). *Program availability:* Part-time, evening/weekend, online learning. *Faculty:* 13 full-time (8 women). *Students:* 2 full-time (1 woman), 10 part-time (9 women); includes 2 minority (1 Black or African American, non-Hispanic/Latino; 1 Hispanic/Latino). Average age 41. 4 applicants, 100% accepted, 3 enrolled. In 2016, 3 master's awarded. *Degree requirements:* For master's, comprehensive exam (for some programs), thesis optional, thesis or exam (for literature option). *Entrance requirements:* For master's, writing sample, three letters of recommendation, letter of interest. Additional exam requirements/recommendations for international students: Recommended—TOEFL (minimum score 550 paper-based; 79 iBT), IELTS (minimum score 6.5). *Application deadline:* For fall admission, 6/15 for domestic and international students; for spring admission, 10/15 for domestic and international students; for summer admission, 3/15 for domestic and international students. Application fee: $45. Electronic applications accepted. *Expenses:* Tuition, state resident: full-time $4064; part-time $225.75 per credit hour. Tuition, nonresident: full-time $8915; part-time $495.25 per credit hour. *Required fees:* $772; $23 per credit hour. Part-time tuition and fees vary according to course load, campus/location, program and reciprocity agreements. *Financial support:* In 2016–17, 2 students received support, including 2 teaching assistantships with full tuition reimbursements available (averaging $11,500 per year); research assistantships, career-related internships or fieldwork, scholarships/grants, and unspecified assistantships also available. Support available to part-time students. Financial award application deadline: 2/28; financial award applicants required to submit FAFSA. *Faculty research:* Narrative theory, popular culture, western and plains literature, women's studies, media studies, children's literature, poetry, speculative fiction, creative writing, comics, composition and rhetoric, renaissance drama, film studies, ecocriticism. *Unit head:* Dr. Martha Kruse, Committee Chair, 308-865-8415, E-mail: krusem@unk.edu. *Application contact:* Linda Johnson, Director, Graduate Admissions and Programs, 308-717-7881, E-mail: gradstudies@unk.edu.
Website: http://www.unk.edu/academics/english/graduate_program.php

**University of Nebraska at Omaha,** Graduate Studies, College of Arts and Sciences, Department of English, Omaha, NE 68182. Offers advanced writing (Certificate); English (MA); teaching English to speakers of other languages (Certificate); technical communication (Certificate). *Program availability:* Part-time, evening/weekend. *Faculty:* 10 full-time (6 women). *Students:* 9 full-time (7 women), 43 part-time (24 women); includes 1 minority (Two or more races, non-Hispanic/Latino), 3 international. Average age 32. 39 applicants, 46% accepted, 14 enrolled. In 2016, 21 master's, 12 other advanced degrees awarded. *Degree requirements:* For master's, comprehensive exam, thesis (for some programs). *Entrance requirements:* For master's, GRE or MAT, minimum GPA of 3.0, transcripts, 3 letters of recommendation, statement of purpose, writing sample; for Certificate, minimum GPA of 3.0, transcripts, statement of purpose. Additional exam requirements/recommendations for international students: Required—TOEFL, IELTS, PTE. *Application deadline:* Applications are processed on a rolling basis. Application fee: $45. Electronic applications accepted. *Financial support:* In 2016–17, 15 students received support, including 15 teaching assistantships with tuition reimbursements available; fellowships, research assistantships, Federal Work-Study, institutionally sponsored loans, scholarships/grants, health care benefits, tuition waivers (partial), and unspecified assistantships also available. Support available to part-time students. Financial award application deadline: 3/1; financial award applicants required to submit FAFSA. *Unit head:* Dr. Tracy Bridgeford, Chairperson, 402-554-2341, E-mail: graduate@unomaha.edu. *Application contact:* Dr. Ramon Guerra, Graduate Program Chair, 402-554-2341, E-mail: graduate@unomaha.edu.

**University of Nebraska–Lincoln,** Graduate College, College of Arts and Sciences, Department of English, Lincoln, NE 68588-0333. Offers composition and rhetoric (MA, PhD); creative writing (MA, PhD); literature studies (MA, PhD). *Degree requirements:* For master's, thesis optional; for doctorate, one foreign language, comprehensive exam, thesis/dissertation. *Entrance requirements:* For master's, writing sample; for doctorate, GRE General Test, writing sample. Additional exam requirements/recommendations for international students: Required—TOEFL (minimum score 600 paper-based). Electronic applications accepted. *Faculty research:* Creative writing, composition and rhetoric, women's studies, North American literature, medieval/Renaissance studies.

**University of Nevada, Las Vegas,** Graduate College, College of Liberal Arts, Department of English, Las Vegas, NV 89154-5011. Offers creative writing (MFA); English (MA, PhD). *Program availability:* Part-time. *Faculty:* 22 full-time (13 women), 1 (woman) part-time/adjunct. *Students:* 61 full-time (28 women), 16 part-time (7 women); includes 20 minority (1 Black or African American, non-Hispanic/Latino; 7 Asian, non-Hispanic/Latino; 7 Hispanic/Latino; 2 Native Hawaiian or other Pacific Islander, non-Hispanic/Latino; 3 Two or more races, non-Hispanic/Latino), 2 international. Average age 33. 144 applicants, 17% accepted, 17 enrolled. In 2016, 19 master's, 4 doctorates awarded. *Degree requirements:* For master's, one foreign language, comprehensive exam (for some programs), thesis, creative thesis; for doctorate, one foreign language, comprehensive exam, thesis/dissertation. *Entrance requirements:* For master's, GRE General Test, GRE Subject Test, writing sample; statement of purpose; 2 letters of recommendation; transcripts from all colleges; for doctorate, GRE General Test, GRE Subject Test, MA in English with minimum GPA 3.5; writing sample; 3 letters of recommendation; statement of purpose. Additional exam requirements/recommendations for international students: Required—TOEFL (minimum score 550 paper-based; 80 iBT), IELTS (minimum score 7). *Application deadline:* For fall admission, 1/15 for domestic students; for spring admission, 11/1 for domestic students. Application fee: $60 ($95 for international students). Electronic applications accepted. *Expenses:* $269.25 per credit; $792 per 3-credit course; $9,634 per year resident; $23,274 per year non-resident; $7,094 fees non-resident (7 credits or more); $1,307 annual health insurance fee. *Financial support:* In 2016–17, 58 teaching assistantships with partial tuition reimbursements (averaging $15,388 per year) were awarded; institutionally sponsored loans, scholarships/grants, health care benefits, and unspecified assistantships also available. Financial award application deadline: 3/15. *Faculty research:* Creative writing, poetry, fiction. *Unit head:* Dr. Gary Totten, Chair/Professor, 702-895-1258, Fax: 702-895-4801, E-mail: gary.totten@unlv.edu. *Application contact:* Christopher Decker, Graduate Coordinator, 702-895-3088, Fax: 702-895-4180, E-mail: christopher.decker@unlv.edu.
Website: http://english.unlv.edu/

**University of Nevada, Reno,** Graduate School, College of Liberal Arts, Department of English, Reno, NV 89557. Offers MA, MATE, PhD. Terminal master's awarded for partial completion of doctoral program. *Degree requirements:* For master's, variable foreign language requirement, thesis optional; for doctorate, variable foreign language requirement, thesis/dissertation. *Entrance requirements:* For master's, GRE General Test, minimum GPA of 2.75; for doctorate, GRE General Test, minimum GPA of 3.0. Additional exam requirements/recommendations for international students: Required—TOEFL (minimum score 500 paper-based; 61 iBT), IELTS (minimum score 6). Electronic applications accepted. *Faculty research:* Translating Persian/Iraqi literature, Shakespearean literature, modern American literature, composition and rhetoric.

**University of New Brunswick Fredericton,** School of Graduate Studies, Faculty of Arts, Department of English, Fredericton, NB E3B 5A3, Canada. Offers MA, PhD. *Program availability:* Part-time. *Degree requirements:* For master's, thesis, 18 credit hours; for doctorate, one foreign language, comprehensive exam, thesis/dissertation. *Entrance requirements:* For master's, BA with minimum GPA of 3.5, honors English (preferred); for doctorate, minimum GPA of 3.7; MA in English. Additional exam requirements/recommendations for international students: Required—TWE (minimum score 4), TOEFL (minimum paper-based score 600) or IELTS (minimum score 7). Electronic applications accepted. *Faculty research:* Creative writing, Canadian and maritime literature, post-Colonial/Commonwealth literature, early modern/Renaissance literature, scholarly editing and textual studies, American literature, British literature, film.

**University of New Hampshire,** Graduate School, College of Liberal Arts, Department of English, Durham, NH 03824. Offers composition (PhD); English education (MST); language and linguistics (MA); literature (MA, PhD); writing (MFA). *Program availability:* Part-time. *Degree requirements:* For master's, one foreign language; for doctorate, 2 foreign languages, thesis/dissertation. *Entrance requirements:* For master's, GRE General Test, sample of written work; for doctorate, GRE General Test, GRE Subject Test, sample of written work. Additional exam requirements/recommendations for international students: Required—TOEFL (minimum score 550 paper-based; 80 iBT). Electronic applications accepted.

**University of New Mexico,** Graduate Studies, College of Arts and Sciences, Program in English, Albuquerque, NM 8713187131. Offers MA, PhD. *Faculty:* 17 full-time (10 women), 1 (woman) part-time/adjunct. *Students:* 38 full-time (26 women), 26 part-time (17 women); includes 14 minority (1 American Indian or Alaska Native, non-Hispanic/Latino; 11 Hispanic/Latino; 2 Two or more races, non-Hispanic/Latino), 5 international. Average age 34. 49 applicants, 31% accepted, 15 enrolled. In 2016, 16 master's, 7 doctorates awarded. *Degree requirements:* For master's, one foreign language, comprehensive exam (for some programs), thesis or alternative, portfolio; for doctorate, 2 foreign languages, comprehensive exam, thesis/dissertation. *Entrance requirements:* For master's, GRE General Test; for doctorate, GRE General Test, GRE Subject Test (literature). *Application deadline:* For fall admission, 1/15 for domestic and international students. Application fee: $50. Electronic applications accepted. *Financial support:* Teaching assistantships with full tuition reimbursements and health care benefits available. Financial award application deadline: 1/15. *Faculty research:* American,

Native American, Chicano, and British and Irish literature; rhetoric and writing; medieval studies. *Unit head:* Dr. Gail Turley Houston, Chair, 505-277-6347, Fax: 505-277-0021, E-mail: ghouston@unm.edu. *Application contact:* N. Ezra Meier, Graduate Advisor, 505-277-4437, Fax: 505-277-0021, E-mail: nezra@unm.edu.
Website: http://english.unm.edu/graduate/index.html

**University of New Orleans,** Graduate School, College of Liberal Arts, Department of English, Program in English, New Orleans, LA 70148. Offers MA. *Program availability:* Part-time, evening/weekend. *Degree requirements:* For master's, one foreign language, thesis (for some programs). *Entrance requirements:* For master's, GRE General Test. Additional exam requirements/recommendations for international students: Required—TOEFL (minimum score 550 paper-based; 79 iBT), IELTS (minimum score 6.5). Electronic applications accepted. *Faculty research:* British and American Literature, professional writing.

**University of North Alabama,** College of Arts and Sciences, Department of English, Florence, AL 35632-0001. Offers MA. *Program availability:* Part-time, evening/weekend. *Faculty:* 11 full-time (8 women). *Students:* 8 full-time (4 women), 10 part-time (8 women); includes 2 minority (1 Asian, non-Hispanic/Latino; 1 Two or more races, non-Hispanic/Latino), 1 international. Average age 31. 14 applicants, 71% accepted, 9 enrolled. In 2016, 4 master's awarded. *Degree requirements:* For master's, comprehensive exam (for some programs), thesis optional. *Entrance requirements:* For master's, GRE, MAT. Additional exam requirements/recommendations for international students: Required—TOEFL (minimum score 79 iBT), IELTS (minimum score 6), PTE (minimum score 54). *Application deadline:* Applications are processed on a rolling basis. Application fee: $50 ($100 for international students). Electronic applications accepted. *Expenses:* Tuition, state resident: full-time $2799; part-time $1866 per semester. Tuition, nonresident: full-time $5598; part-time $3732 per semester. *Required fees:* $915; $642 per semester. Tuition and fees vary according to course load. *Financial support:* In 2016–17, 4 students received support. Scholarships/grants and unspecified assistantships available. Financial award application deadline: 2/1; financial award applicants required to submit FAFSA. *Unit head:* Dr. Cynthia Burkhead, Chair, 256-765-4238, E-mail: english@una.edu. *Application contact:* Hillary N. Coats, Graduate Admissions Coordinator, 256-765-4447, E-mail: graduate@una.edu.
Website: http://www.una.edu/english/

**The University of North Carolina at Chapel Hill,** Graduate School, College of Arts and Sciences, Department of English, Chapel Hill, NC 27599. Offers MA, PhD. *Degree requirements:* For master's, one foreign language, comprehensive exam, thesis; for doctorate, 2 foreign languages, comprehensive exam, thesis/dissertation. *Entrance requirements:* For master's and doctorate, GRE General Test, GRE Subject Test, minimum GPA of 3.0 for last 2 undergraduate years, writing sample. Additional exam requirements/recommendations for international students: Required—TOEFL. Electronic applications accepted. *Faculty research:* African-American, Southern, period, genre, critical theory/culture studies.

**The University of North Carolina at Charlotte,** College of Liberal Arts and Sciences, Department of English, Charlotte, NC 28223-0001. Offers applied linguistics (Graduate Certificate); English (MA); technical and professional writing (Graduate Certificate). *Program availability:* Part-time, evening/weekend. *Faculty:* 30 full-time (16 women), 2 part-time/adjunct (1 woman). *Students:* 28 full-time (22 women), 30 part-time (19 women); includes 13 minority (4 Black or African American, non-Hispanic/Latino; 1 Asian, non-Hispanic/Latino; 8 Hispanic/Latino), 4 international. Average age 30. 33 applicants, 91% accepted, 20 enrolled. In 2016, 30 master's, 1 other advanced degree awarded. *Degree requirements:* For master's, comprehensive exam (for some programs), thesis, comprehensive exam, or project. *Entrance requirements:* For master's, GRE, MAT, minimum undergraduate GPA of 3.0, statement of purpose, recommendation letters; for Graduate Certificate, statement of purpose, three letters of recommendation, writing sample, minimum GPA of 2.75. Additional exam requirements/recommendations for international students: Required—TOEFL (minimum score 523 paper-based, 70 iBT) or IELTS (6.5). *Application deadline:* For fall admission, 3/1 priority date for domestic and international students; for spring admission, 10/1 priority date for domestic and international students; for summer admission, 4/1 priority date for domestic and international students. Applications are processed on a rolling basis. Application fee: $75. Electronic applications accepted. *Expenses:* Tuition, state resident: full-time $4252. Tuition, nonresident: full-time $17,423. *Required fees:* $3026. Tuition and fees vary according to course load and program. *Financial support:* In 2016–17, 17 students received support, including 1 research assistantship (averaging $8,000 per year), 16 teaching assistantships (averaging $8,562 per year); career-related internships or fieldwork, institutionally sponsored loans, scholarships/grants, and unspecified assistantships also available. Support available to part-time students. Financial award application deadline: 3/1; financial award applicants required to submit FAFSA. *Total annual research expenditures:* $61,484. *Unit head:* Dr. Mark West, Chair, 704-687-0618, E-mail: miwest@uncc.edu. *Application contact:* Kathy B. Giddings, Director of Graduate Admissions, 704-687-5503, Fax: 704-687-1668, E-mail: gradadm@uncc.edu.
Website: http://english.uncc.edu/

**The University of North Carolina at Greensboro,** Graduate School, College of Arts and Sciences, Department of English, Program in English, Greensboro, NC 27412-5001. Offers American literature (PhD); English (M Ed, MA); English literature (PhD); rhetoric and composition (PhD). *Degree requirements:* For master's, comprehensive exam, thesis or alternative; for doctorate, variable foreign language requirement, thesis/dissertation, preliminary exam. *Entrance requirements:* For master's, GRE General Test, GRE Subject Test, minimum GPA of 3.0; for doctorate, GRE General Test, GRE Subject Test, critical writing sample, minimum GPA of 3.0. Additional exam requirements/recommendations for international students: Required—TOEFL. Electronic applications accepted.

**The University of North Carolina Wilmington,** College of Arts and Sciences, Department of English, Wilmington, NC 28403-3297. Offers MA. *Program availability:* Part-time. *Faculty:* 21 full-time (10 women). *Students:* 16 full-time (11 women), 6 part-time (all women); includes 2 minority (both Black or African American, non-Hispanic/Latino). Average age 29. 17 applicants, 82% accepted, 8 enrolled. In 2016, 10 master's awarded. *Degree requirements:* For master's, comprehensive exam, thesis optional. *Entrance requirements:* For master's, GRE General Test, minimum B average in undergraduate work, 3 recommendations, statement of interest, writing sample. Additional exam requirements/recommendations for international students: Required—TOEFL (minimum score 79 iBT), IELTS (minimum score 6.5). *Application deadline:* For fall admission, 5/1 for domestic students; for spring admission, 11/1 for domestic students; for summer admission, 5/1 for domestic students. Applications are processed on a rolling basis. Application fee: $60. Electronic applications accepted. *Expenses:* Contact institution. *Financial support:* Teaching assistantships and scholarships/grants available. Financial award application deadline: 3/15; financial award applicants required to submit FAFSA. *Unit head:* Dr. Tiffany Gilbert, Interim Chair, 910-962-7746, Fax: 910-962-7186, E-mail: gilbertt@uncw.edu. *Application contact:* Dr. Meghan Sweeney, Graduate Coordinator, 910-962-3054, Fax: 910-962-7186, E-mail: sweeneym@uncw.edu.
Website: http://www.uncw.edu/english/graduate/index.html

**University of North Dakota,** Graduate School, College of Arts and Sciences, Department of English, Grand Forks, ND 58202. Offers MA, PhD. *Degree requirements:* For master's, one foreign language, comprehensive exam, thesis or alternative; for doctorate, one foreign language, comprehensive exam, thesis/dissertation. *Entrance requirements:* For master's and doctorate, GRE General Test, minimum GPA of 3.0. Additional exam requirements/recommendations for international students: Required—TOEFL (minimum score 550 paper-based; 79 iBT), IELTS (minimum score 6.5). *Application deadline:* For fall admission, 2/1 for domestic and international students. Application fee: $35. Electronic applications accepted. *Financial support:* Fellowships with full and partial tuition reimbursements, research assistantships with full and partial tuition reimbursements, teaching assistantships with full and partial tuition reimbursements, Federal Work-Study, institutionally sponsored loans, scholarships/grants, health care benefits, tuition waivers (full and partial), and unspecified assistantships available. Support available to part-time students. Financial award application deadline: 3/15; financial award applicants required to submit FAFSA. *Faculty research:* Creative writing, rhetorical theory, cinema, American literature, European literature. *Unit head:* Dr. Christopher Nelson, Graduate Director, 701-777-2762, Fax: 701-777-2373, E-mail: chris.nelson@und.edu. *Application contact:* Matt Anderson, Admissions Specialist, 701-777-2947, Fax: 701-777-3619, E-mail: matthew.anderson@gradschool.und.edu.
Website: http://arts-sciences.und.edu/english/

**University of Northern Colorado,** Graduate School, College of Humanities and Social Sciences, Department of English, Greeley, CO 80639. Offers MA. *Program availability:* Part-time. *Degree requirements:* For master's, comprehensive exam. *Entrance requirements:* For master's, GRE General Test, 2 letters of recommendation. *Application deadline:* Applications are processed on a rolling basis. Application fee: $50 ($60 for international students). Electronic applications accepted. *Financial support:* Research assistantships, teaching assistantships, and unspecified assistantships available. Financial award application deadline: 3/1; financial award applicants required to submit FAFSA. *Unit head:* Dr. Marcus Embry, Chair, 970-351-2971, Fax: 970-351-3378. *Application contact:* Linda Sisson, Graduate Student Admission Coordinator, 970-351-1807, Fax: 970-351-2371, E-mail: linda.sisson@unco.edu.
Website: http://www.unco.edu/hss/english/

**University of Northern Iowa,** Graduate College, College of Humanities, Arts and Sciences, Department of Languages and Literatures, MA Program in English, Cedar Falls, IA 50614. Offers creative writing (MA); English (MA); literature (MA). *Program availability:* Part-time, evening/weekend. *Degree requirements:* For master's, one foreign language, comprehensive exam, thesis or alternative, portfolio. *Entrance requirements:* Additional exam requirements/recommendations for international students: Required—TOEFL (minimum score 600 paper-based; 100 iBT). Electronic applications accepted.

**University of North Florida,** College of Arts and Sciences, Department of English, Jacksonville, FL 32224. Offers MA. *Program availability:* Part-time, evening/weekend. *Faculty:* 14 full-time (7 women). *Students:* 18 full-time (10 women), 25 part-time (20 women); includes 5 minority (1 Asian, non-Hispanic/Latino; 2 Hispanic/Latino; 2 Two or more races, non-Hispanic/Latino). Average age 31. 34 applicants, 82% accepted, 19 enrolled. In 2016, 15 master's awarded. *Degree requirements:* For master's, comprehensive exam, thesis optional. *Entrance requirements:* For master's, GRE General Test, minimum GPA of 3.0 in last 60 hours, writing sample. Additional exam requirements/recommendations for international students: Required—TOEFL (minimum score 500 paper-based; 61 iBT). *Application deadline:* For fall admission, 8/1 priority date for domestic students, 5/1 for international students; for spring admission, 12/1 priority date for domestic students, 10/1 for international students; for summer admission, 3/15 priority date for domestic students, 2/1 for international students. Application fee: $30. Electronic applications accepted. Tuition and fees vary according to course load, campus/location and program. *Financial support:* In 2016–17, 10 students received support. Research assistantships, teaching assistantships, Federal Work-Study, and scholarships/grants available. Financial award application deadline: 4/1; financial award applicants required to submit FAFSA. *Unit head:* Dr. Brian A. Striar, Chair, 904-620-1245, Fax: 904-620-3940, E-mail: bstriar@unf.edu. *Application contact:* Dr. Amanda Pascale, Director, The Graduate School, 904-620-1360, Fax: 904-620-1362, E-mail: graduateschool@unf.edu.
Website: http://www.unf.edu/coas/english/

**University of North Texas,** Robert B. Toulouse School of Graduate Studies, Denton, TX 76203-5459. Offers accounting (MS); applied anthropology (MA, MS); applied behavior analysis (Certificate); applied geography (MA); applied technology and performance improvement (M Ed, MS); art education (MA); art history (MA); art museum education (Certificate); arts leadership (Certificate); audiology (Au D); behavior analysis (MS); behavioral science (PhD); biochemistry and molecular biology (MS); biology (MA, MS); biomedical engineering (MS); business analysis (MS); chemistry (MS); clinical health psychology (PhD); communication studies (MA, MS); computer engineering (MS); computer science (MS); counseling (M Ed, MS), including clinical mental health counseling (MS), college and university counseling, elementary school counseling, secondary school counseling; creative writing (MA); criminal justice (MS); curriculum and instruction (M Ed); decision sciences (MBA); design (MA, MFA), including fashion design (MFA), innovation studies, interior design (MFA); early childhood studies (MS); economics (MS); educational leadership (M Ed, Ed D); educational psychology (MS, PhD), including family studies (MS), gifted and talented (MS), human development (MS), learning and cognition (MS), research, measurement and evaluation (MS); electrical engineering (MS); emergency management (MPA); engineering technology (MS); English (MA); English as a second language (MA); environmental science (MS); finance (MBA, MS); financial management (MBA); French (MA); health services management (MBA); higher education (M Ed, Ed D); history (MA, MS); hospitality management (MS); human resources management (MPA); information science (MS); information systems (PhD); information technologies (MBA); interdisciplinary studies (MA, MS); international studies (MA); international sustainable tourism (MS); jazz studies (MM); journalism (MA, MJ, Graduate Certificate), including interactive and virtual digital communication (Graduate Certificate), narrative journalism (Graduate Certificate), public relations (Graduate Certificate); kinesiology (MS); linguistics (MA); local government management (MPA); logistics (PhD); logistics and supply chain management (MBA); long-term care, senior housing, and aging services (MA); management (PhD); marketing (MBA); mathematics (MA, MS); mechanical and energy engineering (MS, PhD); music (MA), including ethnomusicology, music theory, musicology, performance; music composition (PhD); music education (MM Ed, PhD); nonprofit management (MPA); operations and supply chain management (MBA); performance (MM, DMA); philosophy (MA); political science (MA); professional and technical communication (MA); radio, television and film (MA, MFA); rehabilitation counseling (Certificate); sociology (MA); Spanish (MA); special education (M Ed); speech-language pathology (MA); strategic management (MBA); studio art (MFA); teaching (M Ed); MBA/MS. *Program availability:* Part-time, evening/weekend, online learning. Terminal master's awarded for partial completion of doctoral program. *Degree requirements:* For master's, variable foreign language requirement, comprehensive exam (for some programs), thesis (for some programs); for doctorate, variable foreign language requirement, comprehensive exam (for some programs), thesis/dissertation; for other advanced degree, variable foreign

## English

language requirement, comprehensive exam (for some programs). *Entrance requirements:* For master's and doctorate, GRE, GMAT. Additional exam requirements/recommendations for international students: Required—TOEFL (minimum score 550 paper-based; 79 iBT). Electronic applications accepted.

**University of Notre Dame,** Graduate School, College of Arts and Letters, Division of Humanities, Department of English, Notre Dame, IN 46556. Offers creative writing (MFA); English (MA, PhD). *Degree requirements:* For doctorate, one foreign language, thesis/dissertation, candidacy exam. *Entrance requirements:* For master's, GRE General Test, minimum GPA of 3.0; for doctorate, GRE General Test, GRE Subject Test, minimum GPA of 3.0. Additional exam requirements/recommendations for international students: Required—TOEFL (minimum score 600 paper-based; 80 iBT). Electronic applications accepted. *Faculty research:* Early modern studies (medieval/Renaissance), modern British studies (eighteenth-twentieth centuries), American Studies, literature and philosophy, Irish studies.

**University of Oklahoma,** College of Arts and Sciences, Department of English, Norman, OK 73019. Offers composition and rhetoric (MA, PhD); literary and cultural studies (MA, PhD). *Program availability:* Part-time. *Faculty:* 31 full-time (15 women). *Students:* 26 full-time (16 women), 18 part-time (9 women); includes 9 minority (2 American Indian or Alaska Native, non-Hispanic/Latino; 2 Asian, non-Hispanic/Latino; 3 Hispanic/Latino; 2 Two or more races, non-Hispanic/Latino), 1 international. Average age 32. 38 applicants, 34% accepted, 3 enrolled. In 2016, 7 master's, 7 doctorates awarded. *Degree requirements:* For master's, one foreign language, comprehensive exam (for some programs), thesis (for some programs), exam or thesis; for doctorate, one foreign language, comprehensive exam, thesis/dissertation. *Entrance requirements:* For master's, BA in English or related field; for doctorate, MA in English or related field. Additional exam requirements/recommendations for international students: Required—TOEFL (minimum score 79 iBT) or IELTS (minimum score 6.5). *Application deadline:* For fall admission, 1/5 priority date for domestic and international students. Application fee: $50 ($100 for international students). Electronic applications accepted. *Expenses:* Tuition, state resident: full-time $4886; part-time $203.60 per credit hour. Tuition, nonresident: full-time $18,989; part-time $791.20 per credit hour. *Required fees:* $3283; $126.25 per credit hour. $126.50 per semester. *Financial support:* In 2016–17, 40 students received support, including 5 research assistantships (averaging $13,011 per year), 32 teaching assistantships (averaging $12,550 per year); fellowships, scholarships/grants, health care benefits, and unspecified assistantships also available. Financial award application deadline: 6/1; financial award applicants required to submit FAFSA. *Faculty research:* American Indian literature and culture; composition and rhetoric; American literature; British literature; postcolonial literature and culture. *Unit head:* Dr. Daniela Garofalo, Professor and Chair, 405-325-4661, Fax: 405-325-0831, E-mail: dg@ou.edu. *Application contact:* Sara Day, Graduate Assistant, 405-325-0489, Fax: 405-325-0831, E-mail: redpanda@ou.edu.
Website: http://cas.ou.edu/english

**University of Oregon,** Graduate School, College of Arts and Sciences, Department of English, Eugene, OR 97403. Offers MA, PhD. Terminal master's awarded for partial completion of doctoral program. *Degree requirements:* For master's, one foreign language; for doctorate, 2 foreign languages, thesis/dissertation. *Entrance requirements:* For master's, GRE General Test; for doctorate, GRE Subject Test (English literature), minimum GPA of 3.5. Additional exam requirements/recommendations for international students: Required—TOEFL. *Faculty research:* Old and Middle English, women writers, critical theory, literature and the environment, rhetoric and composition.

**University of Ottawa,** Faculty of Graduate and Postdoctoral Studies, Faculty of Arts, Department of English, Ottawa, ON K1N 6N5, Canada. Offers MA, PhD. *Program availability:* Part-time, evening/weekend. *Degree requirements:* For master's, one foreign language, thesis optional; for doctorate, 2 foreign languages, comprehensive exam, thesis/dissertation. *Entrance requirements:* For master's, honors degree or equivalent, minimum B average; for doctorate, master's degree, minimum B+ average. Electronic applications accepted. *Faculty research:* Anglo-Saxon and medieval literature.

**University of Pennsylvania,** School of Arts and Sciences, Graduate Group in English, Philadelphia, PA 19104. Offers AM, PhD. *Faculty:* 43 full-time (19 women), 8 part-time/adjunct (4 women). *Students:* 69 full-time (40 women), 1 part-time (0 women); includes 23 minority (8 Black or African American, non-Hispanic/Latino; 2 Asian, non-Hispanic/Latino; 3 Hispanic/Latino; 4 Two or more races, non-Hispanic/Latino), 10 international. Average age 28. 537 applicants, 4% accepted, 11 enrolled. In 2016, 12 master's, 9 doctorates awarded. Terminal master's awarded for partial completion of doctoral program. *Expenses: Tuition:* Full-time $31,068; part-time $5762 per course. *Required fees:* $3200; $336 per course. Full-time tuition and fees vary according to degree level, program and student level. Part-time tuition and fees vary according to course load, degree level and program.
Website: http://www.english.upenn.edu

**University of Pittsburgh,** Dietrich School of Arts and Sciences, Department of English, Pittsburgh, PA 15260. Offers English (MA, PhD); writing (MFA). *Program availability:* Part-time. *Faculty:* 56 full-time (26 women), 3 part-time/adjunct (1 woman). *Students:* 126 full-time (87 women); includes 41 minority (13 Black or African American, non-Hispanic/Latino; 1 American Indian or Alaska Native, non-Hispanic/Latino; 16 Asian, non-Hispanic/Latino; 11 Hispanic/Latino), 1 international. Average age 30. 333 applicants, 20% accepted, 22 enrolled. In 2016, 13 master's, 7 doctorates awarded. Terminal master's awarded for partial completion of doctoral program. *Degree requirements:* For master's, variable foreign language requirement, thesis; for doctorate, variable foreign language requirement, comprehensive exam, thesis/dissertation. *Entrance requirements:* For master's and doctorate, GRE General Test, writing sample. Additional exam requirements/recommendations for international students: Required—TOEFL (minimum score 550 paper-based; 90 iBT). *Application deadline:* For fall admission, 12/10 for domestic and international students. Application fee: $50. Electronic applications accepted. Tuition and fees vary according to program. *Financial support:* In 2016–17, 18 fellowships with full tuition reimbursements (averaging $22,042 per year), 15 research assistantships with full and partial tuition reimbursements (averaging $14,620 per year), 56 teaching assistantships with full tuition reimbursements (averaging $18,620 per year) were awarded; Federal Work-Study, institutionally sponsored loans, scholarships/grants, health care benefits, tuition waivers (full and partial), and unspecified assistantships also available. Support available to part-time students. Financial award application deadline: 12/10. *Faculty research:* Cultural studies, literary history and theory, film, composition. *Unit head:* Dr. Don Bialostosky, Chair, 412-624-6509, Fax: 412-624-6639, E-mail: dhb2@pitt.edu. *Application contact:* Jesse Daugherty, Graduate Administrator, 412-624-6549, Fax: 412-624-6639, E-mail: engrad@pitt.edu.
Website: http://www.english.pitt.edu

**University of Puerto Rico, Mayagüez Campus,** Graduate Studies, College of Arts and Sciences, Department of English, Mayagüez, PR 00681-9000. Offers English education (MA). *Program availability:* Part-time. *Faculty:* 34 full-time (23 women), 3 part-time/adjunct (2 women). *Students:* 52 full-time (37 women), 3 part-time (all women); includes 50 minority (all Hispanic/Latino). Average age 25. 12 applicants, 67% accepted, 7

enrolled. In 2016, 7 master's awarded. *Degree requirements:* For master's, one foreign language, comprehensive exam, thesis. *Entrance requirements:* For master's, minimum GPA of 3.0; course work in linguistics or language, American literature, British literature, and structure/grammar or syntax. Additional exam requirements/recommendations for international students: Required—TOEFL (minimum score 550 paper-based; 79 iBT). *Application deadline:* For fall admission, 2/15 for domestic and international students; for spring admission, 9/15 for domestic and international students. Applications are processed on a rolling basis. Application fee: $25. Electronic applications accepted. *Expenses: Tuition, area resident:* Full-time $2466. *International tuition:* $7166 full-time. *Required fees:* $210. One-time fee: $5 full-time. Tuition and fees vary according to course level, campus/location, program and student level. *Financial support:* In 2016–17, 46 students received support, including 2 research assistantships with full and partial tuition reimbursements available (averaging $2,200 per year), 46 teaching assistantships with full and partial tuition reimbursements available (averaging $4,145 per year); unspecified assistantships also available. *Faculty research:* Multiliteracies and multimodality theorizing and practice, second language writing, Afro-Puerto Rican studies, modern poetry, Puerto Rican culture and folklore. *Unit head:* Leonardo Flores, PhD, Interim Director, 787-832-4040 Ext. 3064, Fax: 787-265-3847, E-mail: leonardo.flores@upr.edu. *Application contact:* Paulette Almodóvar, Administrative Secretary, 787-265-3847, Fax: 787-265-3847, E-mail: paulette.almodovar@upr.edu.
Website: http://www.uprm.edu./english/

**University of Puerto Rico, Río Piedras Campus,** College of Humanities, Department of English, San Juan, PR 00931-3300. Offers Caribbean linguistics (PhD); Caribbean literature (PhD); English (MA). *Program availability:* Part-time. *Degree requirements:* For master's, one foreign language, comprehensive exam, thesis; for doctorate, residency. *Entrance requirements:* For master's, PAEG or GRE, interview, minimum GPA of 3.0, 2 letters of recommendation; for doctorate, PAEG or GRE, minimum GPA of 3.0, 3 letters of recommendation, interview.

**University of Regina,** Faculty of Graduate Studies and Research, Faculty of Arts, Department of English, Regina, SK S4S 0A2, Canada. Offers creative writing (MA); English (MA, PhD). PhD program is a special case provision. *Program availability:* Part-time. *Faculty:* 21 full-time (9 women), 1 part-time/adjunct (0 women). *Students:* 8 full-time (5 women), 5 part-time (4 women). 12 applicants, 50% accepted. In 2016, 2 master's awarded. *Degree requirements:* For master's, thesis (for some programs); for doctorate, thesis/dissertation. *Entrance requirements:* For master's, writing sample and portfolio of creative material (for creative writing). Additional exam requirements/recommendations for international students: Required—TOEFL (minimum score 600 paper-based; 100 iBT), IELTS (minimum score 7.5), PTE (minimum score 59). *Application deadline:* For fall admission, 4/15 for domestic and international students; for winter admission, 10/15 for domestic and international students; for spring admission, 2/15 for domestic and international students. Application fee: $100. Electronic applications accepted. *Financial support:* In 2016–17, 2 fellowships (averaging $6,000 per year), 1 teaching assistantship (averaging $2,501 per year) were awarded; scholarships/grants also available. Financial award application deadline: 6/15. *Faculty research:* British, American, and Canadian literature; sixteenth-, eighteenth-, nineteenth-, and twentieth-century literature; literary theory. *Unit head:* Dr. Troni Grande, Department Head, 306-585-4570, Fax: 306-585-5429, E-mail: troni.grande@uregina.ca. *Application contact:* Dr. Susan Johnston, Graduate Chair, 306-585-4672, Fax: 306-585-5429, E-mail: susan.johnston@uregina.ca.
Website: http://www.uregina.ca/arts/english

**University of Rhode Island,** Graduate School, College of Arts and Sciences, Department of English, Kingston, RI 02881. Offers American and British literature and culture (PhD); creative writing (PhD); English (MA); film (PhD); gender studies (PhD); MLIS/MA. *Program availability:* Part-time. *Faculty:* 18 full-time (11 women). *Students:* 40 full-time (31 women), 13 part-time (9 women); includes 4 minority (2 Black or African American, non-Hispanic/Latino; 1 Asian, non-Hispanic/Latino; 1 Hispanic/Latino), 4 international. In 2016, 2 master's, 9 doctorates awarded. *Degree requirements:* For master's, comprehensive exam (for some programs), thesis optional; for doctorate, comprehensive exam, thesis/dissertation. *Entrance requirements:* For doctorate, GRE General Test, 3 letters of recommendation, writing sample, curriculum vitae. Additional exam requirements/recommendations for international students: Required—TOEFL (minimum score 91 iBT). *Application deadline:* For fall admission, 1/15 for domestic and international students. Application fee: $65. Electronic applications accepted. *Expenses:* Tuition, state resident: full-time $11,796; part-time $655 per credit. Tuition, nonresident: full-time $24,206; part-time $1345 per credit. *Required fees:* $1546; $44 per credit. One-time fee: $155 full-time; $35 part-time. *Financial support:* In 2016–17, 30 teaching assistantships with tuition reimbursements (averaging $17,264 per year) were awarded. Financial award application deadline: 1/15; financial award applicants required to submit FAFSA. *Unit head:* Dr. Travis Williams, Chair, 401-874-9501, E-mail: tdwilliams@uri.edu. *Application contact:* Dr. David Faflik, Director of Graduate Studies, 401-874-4670, E-mail: faflik@uri.edu.
Website: http://www.uri.edu/artsci/eng/

**University of Rochester,** School of Arts and Sciences, Department of English, Rochester, NY 14627. Offers MA, PhD. *Faculty:* 21 full-time (7 women). *Students:* 65 full-time (40 women), 1 (woman) part-time; includes 5 minority (2 Black or African American, non-Hispanic/Latino; 1 Asian, non-Hispanic/Latino; 2 Hispanic/Latino), 9 international. Average age 28. In 2016, 26 master's, 4 doctorates awarded. Terminal master's awarded for partial completion of doctoral program. *Degree requirements:* For master's, comprehensive exam, thesis optional, final exam; for doctorate, one foreign language, thesis/dissertation, qualifying exam. *Entrance requirements:* Additional exam requirements/recommendations for international students: Required—TOEFL (minimum score 600 paper-based; 100 iBT). *Application deadline:* For fall admission, 1/15 for domestic and international students. Application fee: $60. Electronic applications accepted. *Expenses:* $1,538 per credit. *Faculty research:* All periods and genres of English, American, and Anglophone literature, poetry, fiction, non-fiction, and drama. *Unit head:* Rosemary Kegl, Chair, 585-275-4092. *Application contact:* Carrie Morriss, Graduate Coordinator, 585-275-9256.
Website: http://www.rochester.edu/College/ENG/

**University of St. Thomas,** Graduate Studies, College of Arts and Sciences, Graduate Program in English, St. Paul, MN 55105-1096. Offers MA. *Program availability:* Part-time, evening/weekend. *Degree requirements:* For master's, essay. *Entrance requirements:* For master's, minimum GPA of 3.0, previous course work in literature, sample of written work. Additional exam requirements/recommendations for international students: Required—TOEFL (minimum score 80 iBT). *Application deadline:* For fall admission, 3/1 priority date for domestic students; for spring admission, 10/1 priority date for domestic students; for summer admission, 5/1 priority date for domestic students. Applications are processed on a rolling basis. Application fee: $50. Electronic applications accepted. Application fee is waived when completed online. *Expenses:* Contact institution. *Financial support:* Fellowships with tuition reimbursements, research assistantships, teaching assistantships with tuition reimbursements, institutionally sponsored loans, scholarships/grants, and traineeships available. Support available to part-time students. Financial award application deadline: 3/1; financial award applicants required to submit FAFSA. *Faculty research:* Multicultural literature, literature and

theory, regional writers. *Unit head:* Dr. Alexis Easley, Director, 651-962-5653, Fax: 651-962-5623, E-mail: maeasley@stthomas.edu. *Application contact:* Soren Hoeger-Lerdal, Coordinator, 651-962-5628, Fax: 651-962-5623, E-mail: gradenglish@stthomas.edu. Website: http://www.stthomas.edu/english/graduate/.

**University of Saskatchewan,** College of Graduate Studies and Research, College of Arts and Science, Department of English, Saskatoon, SK S7N 5A2, Canada. Offers MA, PhD. *Degree requirements:* For master's, one foreign language, thesis; for doctorate, one foreign language, comprehensive exam (for some programs), thesis/dissertation. *Entrance requirements:* Additional exam requirements/recommendations for international students: Required—TOEFL (minimum score 80 iBT); Recommended—IELTS (minimum score 6.5). Electronic applications accepted.

**University of South Africa,** College of Human Sciences, Pretoria, South Africa. Offers adult education (M Ed); African languages (MA, PhD); African politics (MA, PhD); Afrikaans (MA, PhD); ancient history (MA, PhD); ancient Near Eastern studies (MA, PhD); anthropology (MA, PhD); applied linguistics (MA); Arabic (MA, PhD); archaeology (MA); art history (MA); Biblical archaeology (MA); Biblical studies (M Th, D Th, PhD); Christian spirituality (M Th, D Th); church history (M Th, D Th); classical studies (MA, PhD); clinical psychology (MA); communication (MA, PhD); comparative education (M Ed, Ed D); consulting psychology (D Admin, D Com, PhD); curriculum studies (M Ed, Ed D); development studies (M Admin, MA, D Admin, PhD); didactics (M Ed, Ed D); education (M Tech); education management (M Ed, Ed D); educational psychology (M Ed); English (MA); environmental education (M Ed); French (MA, PhD); German (MA, PhD); Greek (MA); guidance and counseling (M Ed); health studies (MA, PhD), including health sciences education (MA), health services management (MA), medical and surgical nursing science (critical care general) (MA), midwifery and neonatal nursing science (MA), trauma and emergency care (MA); history (MA, PhD); history of education (Ed D); inclusive education (M Ed, Ed D); information and communications technology policy and regulation (MA); information science (MA, MIS, PhD); international politics (MA, PhD); Islamic studies (MA, PhD); Italian (MA, PhD); Judaica (MA, PhD); linguistics (MA, PhD); mathematical education (M Ed); mathematics education (MA); missiology (M Th, D Th, PhD); modern Hebrew (MA, PhD); musicology (MA, MMus, D Mus, PhD); natural science education (M Ed); New Testament (M Th, D Th); Old Testament (D Th); pastoral therapy (M Th, D Th); philosophy (MA); philosophy of education (M Ed, Ed D); politics (MA, PhD); Portuguese (MA, PhD); practical theology (M Th, D Th); psychology (MA, MS, PhD); psychology of education (M Ed, Ed D); public health (MA); religious studies (MA, D Th, PhD); Romance languages (MA); Russian (MA, PhD); Semitic languages (MA, PhD); social behavior studies in HIV/AIDS (MA); social science (mental health) (MA); social science in development studies (MA); social science in psychology (MA); social science in social work (MA); social science in sociology (MA); social work (MSW, DSW, PhD); socio-education (M Ed, Ed D); sociolinguistics (MA); sociology (MA, PhD); Spanish (MA, PhD); systematic theology (M Th, D Th); TESOL (teaching English to speakers of other languages) (MA); theological ethics (M Th, D Th); theory of literature (MA, PhD); urban ministries (D Th); urban ministry (M Th).

**University of South Alabama,** College of Arts and Sciences, Department of English, Mobile, AL 36688. Offers creative writing (MA); literature (MA). *Program availability:* Part-time, evening/weekend. *Faculty:* 10 full-time (3 women). *Students:* 17 full-time (9 women), 13 part-time (12 women); includes 6 minority (3 Black or African American, non-Hispanic/Latino; 1 Hispanic/Latino; 2 Two or more races, non-Hispanic/Latino). Average age 31. 12 applicants, 58% accepted, 7 enrolled. In 2016, 3 master's awarded. *Degree requirements:* For master's, one foreign language, comprehensive exam, thesis optional. *Entrance requirements:* For master's, GRE General Test, BA in English or 30 hours of course work in English, minimum GPA of 3.0. Additional exam requirements/recommendations for international students: Required—TOEFL (minimum score 535 paper-based; 79 iBT). *Application deadline:* For fall admission, 7/15 priority date for domestic students, 5/15 priority date for international students; for spring admission, 12/1 priority date for domestic students, 11/1 priority date for international students; for summer admission, 5/1 for domestic students. Applications are processed on a rolling basis. Application fee: $35. Electronic applications accepted. *Expenses:* Tuition, state resident: full-time $9768; part-time $407 per credit hour. Tuition, nonresident: full-time $19,536; part-time $814 per credit hour. *Financial support:* Fellowships, research assistantships, teaching assistantships, career-related internships or fieldwork, Federal Work-Study, institutionally sponsored loans, scholarships/grants, and unspecified assistantships available. Support available to part-time students. Financial award application deadline: 4/21; financial award applicants required to submit FAFSA. *Unit head:* Dr. Steven Trout, Chair, English, 251-460-6439, E-mail: strout@southalabama.edu. *Application contact:* Dr. Ellen B. Harrington, Graduate Coordinator, English, 251-460-7326, E-mail: eharrington@southalabama.edu. Website: http://www.southalabama.edu/colleges/artsandsci/english/

**University of South Carolina,** The Graduate School, College of Arts and Sciences, Department of English Language and Literature, Columbia, SC 29208. Offers creative writing (MFA); English (MA, PhD); English education (MAT); MLIS/MA. MAT offered in cooperation with the College of Education. *Program availability:* Part-time. *Degree requirements:* For master's, one foreign language, comprehensive exam, thesis; for doctorate, 2 foreign languages, comprehensive exam, thesis/dissertation. *Entrance requirements:* For master's, GRE General Test (MFA), GRE Subject Test (MA, MAT), sample of written work; for doctorate, GRE General Test, GRE Subject Test, sample of written work. Additional exam requirements/recommendations for international students: Required—TOEFL. Electronic applications accepted. *Faculty research:* American literature, British literature, composition and rhetoric, linguistics, speech communication.

**The University of South Dakota,** Graduate School, College of Arts and Sciences, Department of English, Vermillion, SD 57069. Offers MA, PhD. *Degree requirements:* For master's, comprehensive exam (for some programs), thesis (for some programs); for doctorate, comprehensive exam, thesis/dissertation. *Entrance requirements:* For master's, minimum GPA of 3.0, writing sample; for doctorate, GRE, minimum GPA of 3.0, writing sample. Additional exam requirements/recommendations for international students: Required—TOEFL (minimum score 620 paper-based; 105 iBT). Electronic applications accepted.

**The University of South Dakota,** Graduate School, School of Education, Division of Curriculum and Instruction, Program in Elementary Education, Vermillion, SD 57069. Offers elementary education (MA), including early childhood education, English language learning, reading specialist/literacy coach, science, technology or math (STM). *Accreditation:* NCATE. *Program availability:* Part-time, 100% online, blended/hybrid learning. *Degree requirements:* For master's, comprehensive exam, thesis or alternative. *Entrance requirements:* For master's, GRE General Test, MAT, minimum GPA of 2.7. Additional exam requirements/recommendations for international students: Required—TOEFL (minimum score 550 paper-based; 79 iBT). Electronic applications accepted.

**The University of South Dakota,** Graduate School, School of Education, Division of Curriculum and Instruction, Program in Secondary Education, Vermillion, SD 57069. Offers secondary education (MA), including English language learning, science, technology or math (STM), secondary education plus certification. *Accreditation:* NCATE. *Program availability:* Part-time, online learning. *Degree requirements:* For master's, comprehensive exam, thesis or alternative. *Entrance requirements:* For

master's, GRE General Test, MAT, minimum GPA of 2.7. Additional exam requirements/recommendations for international students: Required—TOEFL (minimum score 550 paper-based; 79 iBT). Electronic applications accepted.

**University of Southern California,** Graduate School, Dana and David Dornsife College of Letters, Arts and Sciences, Department of English, Los Angeles, CA 90089. Offers English (MA, PhD); literature and creative writing (PhD). Terminal master's awarded for partial completion of doctoral program. *Degree requirements:* For doctorate, one foreign language, comprehensive exam, thesis/dissertation. *Entrance requirements:* For doctorate, GRE General Test, GRE Subject Test (English literature). Additional exam requirements/recommendations for international students: Required—TOEFL. Electronic applications accepted. *Faculty research:* Creative writing and literature; early modern studies; gender and sexuality; narrative studies; poetry and poetics; media, film, and popular culture; studies in race and minority literature.

**University of Southern Indiana,** Graduate Studies, College of Liberal Arts, Program in English, Evansville, IN 47712-3590. Offers MA. *Program availability:* Part-time, evening/weekend. *Faculty:* 10 full-time (7 women), 1 part-time/adjunct (0 women). *Students:* 6 full-time (4 women), 12 part-time (8 women). Average age 34. In 2016, 2 master's awarded. *Entrance requirements:* For master's, writing sample, three letters of recommendation. Additional exam requirements/recommendations for international students: Required—TOEFL (minimum score 550 paper-based; 79 iBT), IELTS (minimum score 6). *Application deadline:* For fall admission, 8/1 for domestic and international students; for spring admission, 11/15 for domestic and international students. Applications are processed on a rolling basis. Application fee: $40. Electronic applications accepted. *Expenses:* Tuition, state resident: full-time $8497. Tuition, nonresident: full-time $16,691. *Required fees:* $500. *Financial support:* In 2016–17, 4 students received support. Federal Work-Study, scholarships/grants, and unspecified assistantships available. Financial award application deadline: 3/1; financial award applicants required to submit FAFSA. *Unit head:* Dr. Charles A. Conaway, Program Director, 812-461-5435. *Application contact:* Dr. Mayola Rowser, Director, Graduate Studies, 812-465-7015, E-mail: mrowser@usi.edu. Website: http://www.usi.edu/liberal-arts/master-of-arts-in-english/

**University of Southern Mississippi,** Graduate School, College of Arts and Letters, Department of English, Hattiesburg, MS 39406-0001. Offers creative writing (MA, PhD); English education (MA); literature (MA, PhD). *Degree requirements:* For master's, one foreign language, comprehensive exam, thesis; for doctorate, 2 foreign languages, comprehensive exam, thesis/dissertation. *Entrance requirements:* For master's, GRE General Test, minimum GPA of 3.0 in field of study, 2.75 in last 2 years; for doctorate, GRE General Test, minimum GPA of 3.5. Additional exam requirements/recommendations for international students: Required—TOEFL, IELTS. *Application deadline:* For fall admission, 3/15 priority date for domestic students, 3/15 for international students. Application fee: $60. Electronic applications accepted. *Expenses:* Tuition, area resident: Full-time $15,708; part-time $437 per credit hour. *Financial support:* Fellowships, research assistantships with full tuition reimbursements, teaching assistantships with full tuition reimbursements, Federal Work-Study, institutionally sponsored loans, scholarships/grants, and unspecified assistantships available. Financial award application deadline: 3/15; financial award applicants required to submit FAFSA. *Faculty research:* English and American literature, critical theory and cultural studies, creative writing. *Unit head:* Dr. Luis Iglesias, Chair, 601-266-4060, Fax: 601-266-5757, E-mail: luis.iglesias@usm.edu. *Application contact:* Dr. Monika Gehlawat, Director, Graduate Studies, 601-266-4070, Fax: 601-266-5757, E-mail: monika.gehlawat@usm.edu. Website: https://www.usm.edu/english

**University of South Florida,** College of Arts and Sciences, Department of English, Tampa, FL 33620-9951. Offers creative writing (MFA), including fiction, poetry; English (MA, PhD), including literature, rhetoric and composition. *Program availability:* Part-time, evening/weekend. *Faculty:* 26 full-time (14 women). *Students:* 73 full-time (50 women), 28 part-time (21 women); includes 17 minority (3 Black or African American, non-Hispanic/Latino; 3 Asian, non-Hispanic/Latino; 9 Hispanic/Latino; 2 Two or more races, non-Hispanic/Latino; 2 international. Average age 33. 114 applicants, 55% accepted, 27 enrolled. In 2016, 12 master's, 10 doctorates awarded. *Degree requirements:* For master's, comprehensive exam, thesis (for MFA); thesis or portfolio (for MA); for doctorate, one foreign language, comprehensive exam, thesis/dissertation. *Entrance requirements:* For master's, GRE General Test, minimum undergraduate GPA of 3.5 (for MA), 3.2 (for MFA); three letters of recommendation; personal statement; writing sample from 10 to 20 pages (depending on genre); for doctorate, GRE General Test, minimum graduate GPA of 3.7; three letters of recommendation; 2-3 page personal statement; 2500-word writing sample from English coursework. Additional exam requirements/recommendations for international students: Required—TOEFL (minimum score 550 paper-based; 79 iBT) or IELTS (minimum score 6.5) for MA and PhD; TOEFL (minimum score 600 paper-based) for MFA. *Application deadline:* For fall admission, 1/1 for domestic and international students. Applications are processed on a rolling basis. Application fee: $30. Electronic applications accepted. *Expenses:* Tuition, state resident: full-time $7766; part-time $431.43 per credit hour. Tuition, nonresident: full-time $15,789; part-time $877.17 per credit hour. *Required fees:* $37 per term. *Financial support:* In 2016–17, 20 students received support, including 2 research assistantships (averaging $17,221 per year), 79 teaching assistantships with tuition reimbursements available (averaging $11,576 per year); unspecified assistantships also available. Financial award application deadline: 6/30; financial award applicants required to submit FAFSA. *Faculty research:* British and American literature, rhetoric and composition, world and comparative literatures, creative writing, gender and sexuality studies, women's literature, film and genre studies, literary theory, popular and visual culture, textual and translation studies. *Total annual research expenditures:* $44,400. *Unit head:* Dr. Hunt Hawkins, Professor and Chairperson, 813-974-9492, Fax: 813-974-2270, E-mail: hhawkins@usf.edu. *Application contact:* Dr. Marty Gould, Associate Professor and Graduate Director, 813-974-9474, Fax: 813-974-2270, E-mail: mgould@usf.edu. Website: http://english.usf.edu/

**University of South Florida,** Innovative Education, Tampa, FL 33620-9951. Offers adult, career and higher education (Graduate Certificate), including college teaching, leadership in developing human resources, leadership in higher education; Africana studies (Graduate Certificate), including diasporas and health disparities, genocide and human rights; aging studies (Graduate Certificate), including gerontology; art research (Graduate Certificate), including museum studies; business foundations (Graduate Certificate); chemical and biomedical engineering (Graduate Certificate), including materials science and engineering, water, health and sustainability; child and family studies (Graduate Certificate), including positive behavior support; civil and industrial engineering (Graduate Certificate), including transportation systems analysis; community and family health (Graduate Certificate), including maternal and child health, social marketing and public health, violence and injury: prevention and intervention, women's health; criminology (Graduate Certificate), including criminal justice administration; educational measurement and research (Graduate Certificate), including evaluation; English (Graduate Certificate), including comparative literary studies, creative writing, professional and technical communication; entrepreneurship (Graduate Certificate); environmental health (Graduate Certificate), including safety management;

*English*

epidemiology and biostatistics (Graduate Certificate), including applied biostatistics, biostatistics, concepts and tools of epidemiology, epidemiology, epidemiology of infectious diseases; geography, environment and planning (Graduate Certificate), including community development, environmental policy and management, geographical information systems; geology (Graduate Certificate), including hydrogeology; global health (Graduate Certificate), including disaster management, global health and Latin American and Caribbean studies, global health practice, humanitarian assistance, infection control; government and international affairs (Graduate Certificate), including Cuban studies, globalization studies; health policy and management (Graduate Certificate), including health management and leadership, public health policy and programs; hearing specialist: early intervention (Graduate Certificate); industrial and management systems engineering (Graduate Certificate), including systems engineering, technology management; information studies (Graduate Certificate), including school library media specialist; information systems/decision sciences (Graduate Certificate), including analytics and business intelligence; instructional technology (Graduate Certificate), including distance education, Florida digital/virtual educator, instructional design, multimedia design, Web design; internal medicine, bioethics and medical humanities (Graduate Certificate), including biomedical ethics; Latin American and Caribbean studies (Graduate Certificate); mass communications (Graduate Certificate), including multimedia journalism; mathematics and statistics (Graduate Certificate), including mathematics; medicine (Graduate Certificate), including aging and neuroscience, bioinformatics, biotechnology, brain fitness and memory management, clinical investigation, health informatics, health sciences, integrative weight management, intellectual property, medicine and gender, metabolic and nutritional medicine, metabolic cardiology, pharmacy sciences; national and competitive intelligence (Graduate Certificate); psychological and social foundations (Graduate Certificate), including career counseling, college teaching, diversity in education, mental health counseling, school counseling; public affairs (Graduate Certificate), including nonprofit management, public management, research administration; public health (Graduate Certificate), including environmental health, health equity, public health generalist, translational research in adolescent behavioral health; public health practices (Graduate Certificate), including planning for healthy communities; rehabilitation and mental health counseling (Graduate Certificate), including integrative mental health care, marriage and family therapy, rehabilitation technology; secondary education (Graduate Certificate), including ESOL, foreign language education: culture and content, foreign language education: professional; social work (Graduate Certificate), including geriatric social work/clinical gerontology; special education (Graduate Certificate), including autism spectrum disorder, disabilities education: severe/profound; world languages (Graduate Certificate), including teaching English as a second language (TESL) or foreign language. *Expenses:* Tuition, state resident: full-time $7766; part-time $431.43 per credit hour. Tuition, nonresident: full-time $15,789; part-time $877.17 per credit hour. *Required fees:* $37 per term. *Unit head:* Kathy Barnes, Interdisciplinary Programs Coordinator, 813-974-8031, Fax: 813-974-7061, E-mail: barnesk@usf.edu. *Application contact:* Karen Tylinski, Metro Initiatives, 813-974-9943, Fax: 813-974-7061, E-mail: ktylinsk@usf.edu. Website: http://www.usf.edu/innovative-education/

**The University of Tennessee,** Graduate School, College of Arts and Sciences, Department of English, Knoxville, TN 37996. Offers MA, PhD. *Program availability:* Part-time. *Degree requirements:* For master's, one foreign language, thesis or alternative; for doctorate, one foreign language, thesis/dissertation. *Entrance requirements:* For master's, GRE General Test, minimum GPA of 2.7; for doctorate, GRE General Test, GRE Subject Test, minimum GPA of 2.7. Additional exam requirements/recommendations for international students: Required—TOEFL. Electronic applications accepted.

**The University of Tennessee at Chattanooga,** Program in English, Chattanooga, TN 37403. Offers creative writing (MA); literary study (MA); rhetoric and writing (MA). *Program availability:* Part-time. *Faculty:* 22 full-time (11 women), 1 (woman) part-time/adjunct. *Students:* 16 full-time (11 women), 21 part-time (16 women); includes 3 minority (1 Asian, non-Hispanic/Latino; 1 Hispanic/Latino; 1 Two or more races, non-Hispanic/Latino). Average age 28. 20 applicants, 100% accepted, 17 enrolled. In 2016, 8 master's awarded. *Degree requirements:* For master's, comprehensive exam, thesis. *Entrance requirements:* For master's, minimum GPA of 3.0 in English, two letters of recommendation. Additional exam requirements/recommendations for international students: Required—TOEFL (minimum score 550 paper-based; 79 iBT), IELTS (minimum score 6). *Application deadline:* For fall admission, 6/15 priority date for domestic students, 7/1 for international students; for spring admission, 11/1 priority date for domestic students, 11/1 for international students. Applications are processed on a rolling basis. Application fee: $35 ($40 for international students). Electronic applications accepted. *Expenses:* $9,876 full-time in-state; $25,994 full-time out-of-state; $450 per credit credit in-state; $1,345 per credit part-time out-of-state. *Financial support:* In 2016–17, 4 teaching assistantships were awarded; research assistantships, career-related internships or fieldwork, scholarships/grants, health care benefits, and unspecified assistantships also available. Support available to part-time students. Financial award application deadline: 7/1; financial award applicants required to submit FAFSA. *Faculty research:* Technical writing, African-American literature, Milton, creative writing and poetry, American modernism and gender theory. *Total annual research expenditures:* $6,000. *Unit head:* Dr. Christopher Stuart, Department Head, 423-425-2140, Fax: 423-425-2282, E-mail: chris-stuart@utc.edu. *Application contact:* Dr. Joanne Romagni, Dean of the Graduate School, 423-425-4478, Fax: 423-425-5223, E-mail: joanne-romagni@utc.edu. Website: http://www.utc.edu/english/

**The University of Texas at Arlington,** Graduate School, College of Liberal Arts, Department of English, Arlington, TX 76019. Offers English (MA); literature (PhD). *Program availability:* Part-time, evening/weekend. *Degree requirements:* For master's, thesis or comprehensive exam; for doctorate, one foreign language, comprehensive exam, thesis/dissertation. *Entrance requirements:* For master's, GRE General Test, minimum 5-page writing sample, minimum GPA of 3.0, 3 letters of recommendation; for doctorate, GRE General Test, minimum graduate GPA of 3.5, writing sample, 3 letters of recommendation. Additional exam requirements/recommendations for international students: Required—TOEFL (minimum score 550 paper-based). *Application deadline:* For fall admission, 6/15 for domestic students. Applications are processed on a rolling basis. Application fee: $35 ($50 for international students). *Financial support:* Fellowships with full tuition reimbursements, teaching assistantships, and scholarships/grants available. Financial award application deadline: 5/1; financial award applicants required to submit FAFSA. *Faculty research:* Rhetoric composition, American literature, British literature, cultural studies, women's studies. *Unit head:* Dr. Rechelle Christie, Director, E-mail: rechelle@uta.edu. *Application contact:* Dr. Penelope Ingram, Associate Chair for Graduate Studies, 817-272-2739, E-mail: pingram@uta.edu. Website: http://www.uta.edu/english

**The University of Texas at Austin,** Graduate School, College of Liberal Arts, Department of English, Austin, TX 78712-1111. Offers creative writing (MFA); English (MA, PhD). *Program availability:* Part-time. Terminal master's awarded for partial completion of doctoral program. *Degree requirements:* For master's, 2 foreign languages; for doctorate, variable foreign language requirement. *Entrance*

*requirements:* For master's and doctorate, GRE General Test. Electronic applications accepted.

**The University of Texas at El Paso,** Graduate School, College of Liberal Arts, Department of English, El Paso, TX 79968-0001. Offers bilingual professional writing (Certificate); English and American literature (MA); rhetoric and composition (PhD); rhetoric and writing studies (MA); teaching English (MAT). *Program availability:* Part-time, evening/weekend. *Degree requirements:* For master's, thesis optional. *Entrance requirements:* For master's, GRE General Test, minimum GPA of 3.0. Additional exam requirements/recommendations for international students: Required—TOEFL. Electronic applications accepted. *Faculty research:* Literature, creative writing, literary theory.

**The University of Texas at San Antonio,** College of Liberal and Fine Arts, Department of English, San Antonio, TX 78249-0617. Offers MA, PhD. *Program availability:* Part-time, evening/weekend. *Faculty:* 14 full-time (11 women), 1 (woman) part-time/adjunct. *Students:* 23 full-time (14 women), 41 part-time (31 women); includes 26 minority (1 Black or African American, non-Hispanic/Latino; 22 Hispanic/Latino; 3 Two or more races, non-Hispanic/Latino), 1 international. Average age 32. 29 applicants, 76% accepted, 15 enrolled. In 2016, 8 master's, 2 doctorates awarded. Terminal master's awarded for partial completion of doctoral program. *Degree requirements:* For master's, comprehensive exam, thesis optional; for doctorate, one foreign language, comprehensive exam, thesis/dissertation. *Entrance requirements:* For master's, GRE General Test, minimum GPA of 3.3 on all upper-division English courses, 18 hours of English of which 12 hours must be upper-division English literature; for doctorate, GRE General Test, GRE Subject Test (English literature), 18 hours of upper-division and/or graduate English, minimum GPA of 3.5, statement of purpose, writing sample, 3 letters of recommendation. Additional exam requirements/recommendations for international students: Required—TOEFL (minimum score 550 paper-based; 79 iBT), IELTS (minimum score 6.5). *Application deadline:* For fall admission, 7/1 for domestic students, 4/1 for international students; for spring admission, 11/1 for domestic students, 9/1 for international students. Applications are processed on a rolling basis. Application fee: $45 ($80 for international students). Electronic applications accepted. *Financial support:* Unspecified assistantships available. Financial award application deadline: 2/1. *Faculty research:* Transnational, cross-cultural studies in literature. *Total annual research expenditures:* $8,912. *Unit head:* Dr. Mark Bayer, Department Chair, 210-458-4374, Fax: 210-458-5366, E-mail: mark.bayer@utsa.edu. Website: http://colfa.utsa.edu/English/

**The University of Texas at Tyler,** College of Arts and Sciences, Department of Literature and Languages, Tyler, TX 75799-0001. Offers English (MA); interdisciplinary studies (MAIS). *Program availability:* Part-time, evening/weekend. *Degree requirements:* For master's, one foreign language, comprehensive exam, thesis optional. *Entrance requirements:* For master's, GRE General Test, minimum GPA of 3.0; four semesters or the equivalent of one foreign language. Additional exam requirements/recommendations for international students: Required—TOEFL. Electronic applications accepted. *Faculty research:* Medieval and Tudor drama, Shakespeare, British Romanticism, British and Irish modernism, American realism, Greek drama, nineteenth-century American literature.

**The University of Texas of the Permian Basin,** Office of Graduate Studies, College of Arts and Sciences, Department of Literature and Languages, Program in English, Odessa, TX 79762-0001. Offers MA. *Program availability:* Part-time, evening/weekend. *Degree requirements:* For master's, comprehensive exam (for some programs), thesis (for some programs). *Entrance requirements:* For master's, GRE General Test. Additional exam requirements/recommendations for international students: Required—TOEFL (minimum score 550 paper-based).

**The University of Texas Rio Grande Valley,** College of Liberal Arts, Department of Literatures and Cultural Studies, Edinburg, TX 78539. Offers English (MA); Spanish (MA). MA in Spanish conducted in conjunction with Department of Writing and Language Studies. *Program availability:* Part-time, evening/weekend. *Degree requirements:* For master's, comprehensive exam, thesis optional. *Entrance requirements:* For master's, GRE General Test, minimum GPA of 3.0. Tuition and fees vary according to course load and program. *Faculty research:* Oral vs. literary culture, Borderland literature, Mexican-American literature, topics in British and American literature, discourse analysis.

**The University of Texas Rio Grande Valley,** College of Liberal Arts, Department of Writing and Language Studies, Edinburg, TX 78539. Offers English (MAIS); English as a second language (MA); English: rhetoric, composition and literacy studies (MA). *Program availability:* Part-time. *Degree requirements:* For master's, comprehensive exam, thesis or alternative. *Entrance requirements:* For master's, GRE General Test, minimum GPA of 3.0. Tuition and fees vary according to course load and program. *Faculty research:* Latin American literature, women's literature, Caribbean literature, Latina/o studies, sociolinguistics, applied linguistics, creative writing.

**The University of Toledo,** College of Graduate Studies, College of Languages, Literature and Social Sciences, Department of English Language and Literature, Toledo, OH 43606-3390. Offers English as a second language (MA); teaching of writing (Certificate). *Program availability:* Part-time. *Degree requirements:* For master's, thesis. *Entrance requirements:* For master's, GRE if GPA is less than 3.0, minimum cumulative point-hour ratio of 2.7 for all previous academic work, three letters of recommendation, transcripts from all prior institutions attended, critical essay; for Certificate, statement of purpose, transcripts from all prior institutions attended, 2 letters of recommendation. Additional exam requirements/recommendations for international students: Required—TOEFL (minimum score 550 paper-based; 80 iBT). Electronic applications accepted. *Faculty research:* Literary criticism, linguistics, creative writing, folklore and cultural studies.

**University of Toronto,** School of Graduate Studies, Faculty of Arts and Science, Department of English, Toronto, ON M5S 1A1, Canada. Offers creative writing (MA); English (MA, PhD); JD/MA. *Program availability:* Part-time. *Degree requirements:* For master's, thesis optional; for doctorate, 2 foreign languages, thesis/dissertation. *Entrance requirements:* For master's, minimum B+ average, 2 letters of reference, portfolio (creative writing program); for doctorate, minimum A- average, 2 letters of reference, writing sample. Additional exam requirements/recommendations for international students: Required—TOEFL (minimum score 580 paper-based; 93 iBT), TWE (minimum score 5). Electronic applications accepted.

**The University of Tulsa,** Graduate School, Kendall College of Arts and Sciences, Department of English, Tulsa, OK 74104-3189. Offers English language and literature (MA, PhD); JD/MA. *Program availability:* Part-time, evening/weekend. *Faculty:* 13 full-time (4 women). *Students:* 22 full-time (12 women), 12 part-time (5 women); includes 3 minority (1 American Indian or Alaska Native, non-Hispanic/Latino; 2 Hispanic/Latino), 1 international. Average age 35. 31 applicants, 52% accepted, 7 enrolled. In 2016, 7 master's, 8 doctorates awarded. Terminal master's awarded for partial completion of doctoral program. *Degree requirements:* For master's, independent research project; for doctorate, one foreign language, comprehensive exam, thesis/dissertation. *Entrance requirements:* For master's, GRE General Test, writing sample; for doctorate, GRE General Test, writing sample, list of language proficiencies. Additional exam

requirements/recommendations for international students: Required—TOEFL (minimum score 577 paper-based; 91 iBT), IELTS (minimum score 6.5). *Application deadline:* For fall admission, 1/15 priority date for domestic students, 1/15 for international students. Applications are processed on a rolling basis. Application fee: $55. Electronic applications accepted. *Expenses: Tuition:* Full-time $22,230; part-time $1235 per credit hour. *Required fees:* $990 per semester. Tuition and fees vary according to course load. *Financial support:* In 2016–17, 39 students received support, including 15 fellowships with full tuition reimbursements available (averaging $4,613 per year), 1 research assistantship with full tuition reimbursement available (averaging $13,908 per year), 23 teaching assistantships with full tuition reimbursements available (averaging $13,994 per year); career-related internships or fieldwork, Federal Work-Study, scholarships/grants, health care benefits, tuition waivers (full and partial), and unspecified assistantships also available. Support available to part-time students. Financial award application deadline: 1/15; financial award applicants required to submit FAFSA. *Faculty research:* Twentieth-century literature; modern and contemporary British, Irish, and American literatures; Victorian literature; American studies; cultural and gender studies; African-American literature; women's literature, nineteenth century American literature. *Total annual research expenditures:* $183,618. *Unit head:* Dr. Randall Fuller, Chairperson, 918-631-2812, Fax: 918-631-3033, E-mail: randall-fuller@utulsa.edu. *Application contact:* Dr. Lars Engle, Advisor, 918-631-2807, Fax: 918-631-3033, E-mail: lars-engle@utulsa.edu.
Website: http://artsandsciences.utulsa.edu/academics/departments-schools/english/

**The University of Tulsa,** Graduate School, Kendall College of Arts and Sciences, School of Urban Education, Program in Teaching Arts, Tulsa, OK 74104-3189. Offers art (MTA); biology (MTA); English (MTA); history (MTA); mathematics (MTA). *Program availability:* Part-time. *Students:* 1 (woman) full-time. Average age 26. 4 applicants, 50% accepted, 1 enrolled. In 2016, 1 master's awarded. *Entrance requirements:* For master's, GRE General Test. Additional exam requirements/recommendations for international students: Required—TOEFL (minimum score 577 paper-based), IELTS (minimum score 6.5). *Application deadline:* Applications are processed on a rolling basis. Application fee: $55. Electronic applications accepted. *Expenses: Tuition:* Full-time $22,230; part-time $1235 per credit hour. *Required fees:* $990 per semester. Tuition and fees vary according to course load. *Financial support:* In 2016–17, 1 student received support, including 1 teaching assistantship with full tuition reimbursement available (averaging $13,410 per year); fellowships with tuition reimbursements available, research assistantships with tuition reimbursements available, career-related internships or fieldwork, Federal Work-Study, scholarships/grants, health care benefits, tuition waivers (full and partial), and unspecified assistantships also available. Support available to part-time students. Financial award application deadline: 2/1; financial award applicants required to submit FAFSA. *Unit head:* Dr. Sharon Baker, Chair, 918-631-2238, Fax: 918-631-3721, E-mail: sharon-baker@utulsa.edu. *Application contact:* Dr. David Brown, Advisor, 918-631-2719, Fax: 918-631-2133, E-mail: david-brown@utulsa.edu.

**University of Utah,** Graduate School, College of Humanities, Department of English, Salt Lake City, UT 84112. Offers English (MA, MFA, PhD), including creative writing (MFA, PhD), literature and cultural studies (MA, PhD), rhetoric and composition (MA, PhD). *Faculty:* 28 full-time (11 women), 1 part-time/adjunct (0 women). *Students:* 43 full-time (23 women), 23 part-time (14 women); includes 12 minority (1 Black or African American, non-Hispanic/Latino; 4 Asian, non-Hispanic/Latino; 3 Hispanic/Latino; 4 Two or more races, non-Hispanic/Latino), 3 international. Average age 35. 225 applicants, 17% accepted, 14 enrolled. In 2016, 5 master's, 4 doctorates awarded. Terminal master's awarded for partial completion of doctoral program. *Degree requirements:* For master's, 1 standard-level language; exam (for MA); thesis (for MFA); for doctorate, comprehensive exam, thesis/dissertation, 2 standard-level languages/1 advanced-level language. *Entrance requirements:* For master's and doctorate, GRE General Test, minimum GPA of 3.2. Additional exam requirements/recommendations for international students: Required—TOEFL (minimum score 650 paper-based; 115 iBT); Recommended—IELTS (minimum score 9), TSE. *Application deadline:* For fall admission, 12/15 for domestic and international students. Application fee: $55 ($65 for international students). Electronic applications accepted. *Expenses: Tuition,* state resident: full-time $7011; part-time $3918.24 per credit hour. Tuition, nonresident: full-time $22,154; part-time $11,665.42 per credit hour. *Financial support:* In 2016–17, 39 students received support, including 10 fellowships (averaging $18,000 per year), 29 teaching assistantships with full tuition reimbursements available (averaging $16,500 per year); health care benefits also available. Financial award application deadline: 12/15; financial award applicants required to submit FAFSA. *Faculty research:* Creative writing including poetics and modern poetry, fiction, and experimental forms; nineteenth-and twentieth-century British and American literature; American Studies, the American west, and environmental studies; critical theory and practice; race and gender studies. *Total annual research expenditures:* $126,500. *Unit head:* Prof. Barry L. Weller, Department Chair, 801-581-6168, Fax: 801-585-5167, E-mail: barry.weller@utah.edu. *Application contact:* Prof. Andrew Franta, Director of Graduate Studies, 801-581-7850, Fax: 801-585-5167, E-mail: a.franta@utah.edu.
Website: http://english.utah.edu/

**University of Vermont,** Graduate College, College of Arts and Sciences, Department of English, Burlington, VT 05405. Offers MA. *Degree requirements:* For master's, one foreign language, thesis. *Entrance requirements:* For master's, GRE General Test, writing sample. Additional exam requirements/recommendations for international students: Required—TOEFL (minimum score 550 paper-based; 80 iBT). Electronic applications accepted. *Expenses:* Tuition, state resident: full-time $5814. Tuition, nonresident: full-time $14,670.

**University of Victoria,** Faculty of Graduate Studies, Faculty of Humanities, Department of English, Victoria, BC V8W 2Y2, Canada. Offers MA, PhD. *Program availability:* Part-time. *Degree requirements:* For master's, one foreign language, thesis (for some programs); for doctorate, 2 foreign languages, comprehensive exam, thesis/dissertation, candidacy exam. *Entrance requirements:* For master's, minimum A- average in last 2 years of undergraduate course work, writing sample, resume; for doctorate, minimum A-average in graduate course work, writing sample, resumé. Additional exam requirements/recommendations for international students: Required—TOEFL (minimum score 630 paper-based). Electronic applications accepted. *Faculty research:* Critical theory, nineteenth century literature, postcolonialism/multiculturalism, medieval and Renaissance literature, cultural theory.

**University of Virginia,** College and Graduate School of Arts and Sciences, Department of English Language and Literature, Program in English, Charlottesville, VA 22903. Offers MA, PhD, JD/MA. *Faculty:* 69 full-time (32 women), 3 part-time/adjunct (2 women). *Students:* 83 full-time (52 women), 9 part-time (4 women); includes 10 minority (4 Black or African American, non-Hispanic/Latino; 3 Asian, non-Hispanic/Latino; 3 Two or more races, non-Hispanic/Latino), 7 international. Average age 27. 199 applicants, 30% accepted, 20 enrolled. In 2016, 26 master's, 11 doctorates awarded. *Degree requirements:* For master's, one foreign language, oral exam or thesis; for doctorate, 2 foreign languages, comprehensive exam, thesis/dissertation. *Entrance requirements:* For master's, GRE General Test, GRE Subject Test, 3 letters of recommendation, 2 writing samples; for doctorate, GRE General Test, GRE Subject Test, 3 letters of

recommendation; 2 writing samples. Additional exam requirements/recommendations for international students: Required—TOEFL (minimum score 600 paper-based; 90 iBT), IELTS (minimum score 7). *Application deadline:* For fall admission, 1/1 for domestic students, 1/2 for international students. Applications are processed on a rolling basis. Application fee: $60. Electronic applications accepted. *Expenses:* Tuition, state resident: full-time $15,026; part-time $834 per credit hour. Tuition, nonresident: full-time $25,168; part-time $1378 per credit hour. *Required fees:* $2654. *Financial support:* Fellowships and teaching assistantships available. Financial award applicants required to submit FAFSA. *Unit head:* Stephen Arata, Chair, 434-924-7105, Fax: 434-924-1478, E-mail: sda2e@virginia.edu. *Application contact:* Victoria Olwell, Director of Graduate Studies, 434-924-7105, Fax: 434-924-1478, E-mail: vjo2f@virginia.edu.
Website: http://www.engl.virginia.edu/

**University of Washington,** Graduate School, College of Arts and Sciences, Department of English, Seattle, WA 98195. Offers creative writing (MFA); English as a second language (MAT); English literature and language (MA, MAT, PhD). *Program availability:* Part-time. Terminal master's awarded for partial completion of doctoral program. *Degree requirements:* For master's, one foreign language, thesis (for some programs); for doctorate, one foreign language, thesis/dissertation. *Entrance requirements:* For master's, GRE General Test, GRE Subject Test (MA and MAT in English), minimum GPA of 3.0; for doctorate, GRE General Test, GRE Subject Test. Additional exam requirements/recommendations for international students: Required—TOEFL. Electronic applications accepted. *Faculty research:* English and American literature, critical theory, creative writing, language theory.

**University of Waterloo,** Graduate Studies, Faculty of Arts, Department of English Language and Literature, Waterloo, ON N2L 3G1, Canada. Offers English language and literature (PhD); literary studies (MA); rhetoric and communication design (MA). *Program availability:* Part-time. *Degree requirements:* For master's, one foreign language, thesis optional; for doctorate, 2 foreign languages, thesis/dissertation. *Entrance requirements:* For master's, honors degree, minimum B+ average; for doctorate, master's degree, minimum A- average. Additional exam requirements/recommendations for international students: Required—TOEFL, IELTS, PTE. Electronic applications accepted. *Faculty research:* Shakespeare, American literature, rhetoric, Romantics, moderns.

**The University of Western Ontario,** Faculty of Graduate Studies, Faculty of Arts and Humanities, Department of English, London, ON N6A 5B8, Canada. Offers Canadian literature (MA); English (PhD); English literature (MA). *Degree requirements:* For master's, one foreign language, thesis or alternative; for doctorate, 2 foreign languages, thesis/dissertation, qualifying exam. *Entrance requirements:* For master's, minimum A average in appropriate field; for doctorate, MA or equivalent, minimum A average. Additional exam requirements/recommendations for international students: Required—TOEFL (minimum score 630 paper-based). *Faculty research:* Renaissance, nineteenth-century, modern, and postcolonial literature.

**University of West Florida,** College of Arts, Social Sciences, and Humanities, Department of English, Pensacola, FL 32514-5750. Offers creative writing (MA); literature (MA). *Program availability:* Part-time, evening/weekend. *Degree requirements:* For master's, thesis. *Entrance requirements:* For master's, GRE (minimum score: verbal 500, writing 4.5) or MAT (minimum score 413), official transcripts; two-page statement of purpose; writing sample (2,500 words of literary analysis for literature track or 2,500 words of fiction/non-fiction prose or 10 poems for creative writing track); three letters of recommendation from instructors; 20 hours upper-division undergraduate coursework in English. Additional exam requirements/recommendations for international students: Required—TOEFL (minimum score 550 paper-based). *Application deadline:* For fall admission, 6/1 for domestic and international students; for spring admission, 10/1 for domestic and international students. Applications are processed on a rolling basis. Application fee: $30. *Expenses:* Tuition, state resident: full-time $5316.12. Tuition, nonresident: full-time $11,308. *Required fees:* $583.92. Tuition and fees vary according to course load and program. *Financial support:* Fellowships with partial tuition reimbursements, research assistantships with partial tuition reimbursements, teaching assistantships with partial tuition reimbursements, and unspecified assistantships available. Financial award application deadline: 4/15; financial award applicants required to submit FAFSA. *Faculty research:* Faulkner, Shakespeare, American humor, women's studies, poetry. *Unit head:* Dr. Bob Yeager, Chairperson, 850-474-2923. *Application contact:* Terry McCray, Assistant Director of Graduate Admissions, 850-473-7718, Fax: 850-473-7714, E-mail: gradadmissions@uwf.edu.
Website: http://uwf.edu/cassh/departments/english/

**University of West Georgia,** College of Arts and Humanities, Carrollton, GA 30118. Offers English (MA); history (MA); museum studies (Postbaccalaureate Certificate); music performance (M Mus); music teacher education (M Mus); public history (Postbaccalaureate Certificate). *Program availability:* Part-time, evening/weekend, 100% online, blended/hybrid learning. *Faculty:* 70 full-time (39 women). *Students:* 23 full-time (16 women), 55 part-time (33 women); includes 18 minority (10 Black or African American, non-Hispanic/Latino; 1 American Indian or Alaska Native, non-Hispanic/Latino; 5 Hispanic/Latino; 2 Two or more races, non-Hispanic/Latino), 1 international. Average age 31. 24 applicants, 100% accepted, 23 enrolled. In 2016, 34 master's, 6 other advanced degrees awarded. *Entrance requirements:* Additional exam requirements/recommendations for international students: Required—TOEFL (minimum score 523 paper-based; 69 iBT); Recommended—IELTS (minimum score 6.5). *Application deadline:* For fall admission, 8/1 for domestic students, 6/1 for international students; for spring admission, 11/15 for domestic students, 10/15 for international students; for summer admission, 5/15 for domestic students, 3/30 for international students. Applications are processed on a rolling basis. Application fee: $40. Electronic applications accepted. *Expenses:* Tuition, state resident: full-time $5316; part-time $222 per semester hour. Tuition, nonresident: full-time $20,658; part-time $861 per semester hour. *Required fees:* $1962. Tuition and fees vary according to course load, degree level and program. *Financial support:* Fellowships, research assistantships, teaching assistantships, career-related internships or fieldwork, Federal Work-Study, institutionally sponsored loans, scholarships/grants, and unspecified assistantships available. Support available to part-time students. Financial award application deadline: 4/1; financial award applicants required to submit FAFSA. *Unit head:* Dr. Pauline D. Gagnon, Dean of Arts and Humanities, 678-839-5450, Fax: 678-839-5451, E-mail: pgagnon@westga.edu. *Application contact:* Dr. Toby Ziglar, Assistant Dean of the Graduate School, 678-839-1394, Fax: 678-839-1395, E-mail: graduate@westga.edu.
Website: http://www.westga.edu/coah

**University of Windsor,** Faculty of Graduate Studies, Faculty of Arts and Social Sciences, Department of English Language, Literature and Creative Writing, Windsor, ON N9B 3P4, Canada. Offers English: creative writing and language and literature (MA); English: language and literature (MA). *Program availability:* Part-time. *Degree requirements:* For master's, thesis. *Entrance requirements:* For master's, minimum B average, portfolio. Additional exam requirements/recommendations for international students: Required—TOEFL (minimum score 600 paper-based). Electronic applications accepted. *Faculty research:* Use of gender-related terms in popular culture; international and Aboriginal literatures: expression of cultural identity; critical analysis of authors:

## English

Pope, Munroe, Lady Morgan, Orwell, Thomas; the "feminine" voice in literature and contemporary culture.

**University of Wisconsin–Eau Claire,** College of Arts and Sciences, Program in English, Eau Claire, WI 54702-4004. Offers literature and textual interpretation (MA); writing (MA). *Program availability:* Part-time. *Degree requirements:* For master's, oral defense with thesis. *Entrance requirements:* For master's, minimum GPA of 3.25 in English, 3.0 overall; bachelor's degree with minimum of 24 credits in English. Additional exam requirements/recommendations for international students: Required—TOEFL (minimum score 79 iBT).

**University of Wisconsin–Madison,** Graduate School, College of Letters and Science, Department of English, Madison, WI 53706-1380. Offers applied English linguistics (MA); composition and rhetoric (PhD); creative writing (MFA); English language and linguistics (PhD); literary studies (MA, PhD). *Degree requirements:* For doctorate, thesis/dissertation.

**University of Wisconsin–Milwaukee,** Graduate School, College of Letters and Science, Department of English, Milwaukee, WI 53201-0413. Offers English (MA, PhD), including creative writing, literature and cultural theory, media, cinema and digital studies, professional writing, rhetoric and composition. *Students:* 87 full-time (47 women), 50 part-time (27 women); includes 14 minority (4 Asian, non-Hispanic/Latino; 1 Hispanic/Latino; 9 Two or more races, non-Hispanic/Latino), 7 international. Average age 33. 189 applicants, 48% accepted, 31 enrolled. In 2016, 15 master's, 13 doctorates awarded. *Degree requirements:* For master's, thesis or alternative; for doctorate, one foreign language, thesis/dissertation. *Entrance requirements:* For master's, GRE General Test, GRE Subject Test; for doctorate, GRE. Additional exam requirements/recommendations for international students: Required—TOEFL (minimum score 550 paper-based; 79 iBT), IELTS (minimum score 6.5). *Application deadline:* For fall admission, 1/1 priority date for domestic students; for spring admission, 9/1 for domestic students. Applications are processed on a rolling basis. Application fee: $56 ($96 for international students). Electronic applications accepted. *Financial support:* In 2016–17, 4 fellowships, 1 research assistantship, 84 teaching assistantships were awarded; career-related internships or fieldwork, unspecified assistantships, and project assistantships also available. Support available to part-time students. Financial award application deadline: 4/15; financial award applicants required to submit FAFSA. *Unit head:* Mark Netzloff, Department Chair, 414-229-4511, E-mail: netzloff@uwm.edu. *Application contact:* General Information Contact, 414-229-4982, Fax: 414-229-6967, E-mail: gradschool@uwm.edu.
Website: https://uwm.edu/english/

**University of Wisconsin–Oshkosh,** Graduate Studies, College of Letters and Science, Department of English, Oshkosh, WI 54901. Offers MA. *Program availability:* Part-time. *Degree requirements:* For master's, thesis or alternative. *Entrance requirements:* For master's, GRE. Additional exam requirements/recommendations for international students: Required—TOEFL (minimum score 550 paper-based; 79 iBT). Electronic applications accepted.

**University of Wisconsin–Stevens Point,** College of Letters and Science, Department of English, Stevens Point, WI 54481-3897. Offers MST. *Degree requirements:* For master's, thesis or alternative.

**University of Wyoming,** College of Arts and Sciences, Department of English, Laramie, WY 82071. Offers creative writing (MFA); English (MA). *Program availability:* Part-time. *Degree requirements:* For master's, thesis or alternative, internship. *Entrance requirements:* For master's, GRE General Test, minimum GPA of 3.0. Electronic applications accepted. *Faculty research:* Literature and theory, creative writing, English as a second language, ethnic and women's studies, composition.

**Utah State University,** School of Graduate Studies, College of Humanities, Arts and Social Sciences, Department of English, Logan, UT 84322. Offers American studies (MA, MS), including folklore, western American literature and culture; English (MA, MS), including literature and writing, technical writing. *Program availability:* Part-time, evening/weekend. *Degree requirements:* For master's, thesis or alternative. *Entrance requirements:* For master's, GRE General Test or MAT, minimum GPA of 3.0, recommendation letters, writing samples. Additional exam requirements/recommendations for international students: Required—TOEFL. *Faculty research:* Scottish enlightenment, material culture, composition theory, creative nonfiction, literary criticism.

**Valdosta State University,** Department of English, Valdosta, GA 31698. Offers literature (MA); rhetoric and composition (MA); studies for language arts teachers (MA). *Program availability:* Part-time, 100% online, blended/hybrid learning. *Degree requirements:* For master's, one foreign language, thesis, comprehensive written and/or oral exams. *Entrance requirements:* For master's, GRE General Test, minimum GPA of 3.0. Additional exam requirements/recommendations for international students: Required—TOEFL (minimum score 523 paper-based); Recommended—IELTS. Electronic applications accepted. *Expenses:* Contact institution. *Faculty research:* American literature, creative writing.

**Valparaiso University,** Graduate School and Continuing Education, Program in English Studies, Valparaiso, IN 46383. Offers English studies and communication (MA); teaching of English to speakers of other languages (MA); JD/MA. *Program availability:* Part-time, evening/weekend. *Entrance requirements:* For master's, minimum GPA of 3.0. Additional exam requirements/recommendations for international students: Required—TOEFL (minimum score 550 paper-based; 80 iBT), IELTS (minimum score 6). Electronic applications accepted. *Expenses: Tuition:* Full-time $11,070; part-time $615 per credit hour. *Required fees:* $116 per semester. Tuition and fees vary according to course load, degree level and program.

**Valparaiso University,** Graduate School and Continuing Education, Programs in Liberal Studies, Concentration in English, Valparaiso, IN 46383. Offers MALS, Post-Master's Certificate, JD/MALS. *Program availability:* Part-time, evening/weekend. *Entrance requirements:* For master's, minimum GPA of 3.0. Additional exam requirements/recommendations for international students: Required—TOEFL (minimum score 550 paper-based; 80 iBT), IELTS (minimum score 6). Electronic applications accepted. *Expenses: Tuition:* Full-time $11,070; part-time $615 per credit hour. *Required fees:* $116 per semester. Tuition and fees vary according to course load, degree level and program.

**Vanderbilt University,** Department of English, Nashville, TN 37240-1001. Offers MA, MAT, PhD. *Faculty:* 32 full-time (22 women). *Students:* 35 full-time (27 women); includes 13 minority (9 Black or African American, non-Hispanic/Latino; 2 Asian, non-Hispanic/Latino; 2 Hispanic/Latino), 3 international. Average age 28. 286 applicants, 6% accepted, 5 enrolled. In 2016, 10 master's, 3 doctorates awarded. *Degree requirements:* For master's; for doctorate, one foreign language, comprehensive exam, thesis/dissertation, final and qualifying exams. *Entrance requirements:* For master's and doctorate, GRE General Test, sample of written work. Additional exam requirements/recommendations for international students: Required—TOEFL (minimum score 570 paper-based; 88 iBT). *Application deadline:* For fall admission, 1/15 for domestic and international students. Electronic applications accepted. *Expenses: Tuition:* Part-time $1854 per credit hour. *Financial support:* Fellowships with tuition reimbursements, research assistantships with tuition reimbursements, teaching assistantships with full tuition reimbursements, Federal Work-Study, institutionally sponsored loans, scholarships/grants, and health care benefits available. Financial award application deadline: 1/15; financial award applicants required to submit CSS PROFILE or FAFSA. *Faculty research:* British, American, and Anglophone literature, film, cultural studies, literary theory. *Unit head:* Dr. Dana Nelson, Chair, 615-322-2541, Fax: 615-343-8028, E-mail: dana.d.nelson@vanderbilt.edu. *Application contact:* Vera Kutzinski, Director of Graduate Studies, 615-322-2541, Fax: 615-343-8028, E-mail: vera.kutzinski@vanderbilt.edu.
Website: http://as.vanderbilt.edu/english/graduate/

**Villanova University,** Graduate School of Liberal Arts and Sciences, Department of English, Villanova, PA 19085-1699. Offers MA. *Program availability:* Part-time, evening/weekend. *Faculty:* 5. *Students:* 28 full-time (17 women), 10 part-time (7 women); includes 3 minority (2 Hispanic/Latino; 1 Two or more races, non-Hispanic/Latino), 1 international. Average age 29. 18 applicants, 78% accepted, 11 enrolled. In 2016, 9 master's awarded. *Degree requirements:* For master's, comprehensive exam, thesis optional. *Entrance requirements:* For master's, GRE General Test, minimum GPA of 3.0, writing sample, 3 recommendation letters. Additional exam requirements/recommendations for international students: Required—TOEFL. *Application deadline:* For fall admission, 3/1 priority date for domestic students, 5/1 for international students; for spring admission, 11/15 priority date for domestic students, 10/15 for international students; for summer admission, 5/1 for domestic students. Applications are processed on a rolling basis. Application fee: $50. Electronic applications accepted. *Financial support:* Research assistantships, Federal Work-Study, scholarships/grants, and unspecified assistantships available. Financial award applicants required to submit FAFSA. *Unit head:* Dr. Heather Hicks, Program Director, 610-519-4645.
Website: http://www1.villanova.edu/villanova/artsci/english/gradenglish.html

**Virginia Commonwealth University,** Graduate School, College of Humanities and Sciences, Department of English, Program in English, Richmond, VA 23284-9005. Offers literature (MA). *Program availability:* Part-time. *Entrance requirements:* For master's, GRE General Test. Additional exam requirements/recommendations for international students: Required—TWE, TOEFL (minimum score 600 paper-based; 100 iBT) or IELTS (minimum score 6.5). *Application deadline:* For fall admission, 3/1 for domestic students; for spring admission, 11/15 for domestic students. Applications are processed on a rolling basis. Application fee: $50. Electronic applications accepted. *Financial support:* Federal Work-Study, institutionally sponsored loans, and tuition waivers (full and partial) available. Support available to part-time students. Financial award applicants required to submit FAFSA. *Faculty research:* Literature, writing, rhetoric. *Unit head:* Dr. Joshua M. Eckhardt, Program Director, 804-828-1329, E-mail: jmeckhardt@vcu.edu. *Application contact:* Clint McCown, Director, 804-828-1331, E-mail: jcmccown@vcu.edu.

**Virginia Polytechnic Institute and State University,** Graduate School, College of Liberal Arts and Human Sciences, Blacksburg, VA 24061. Offers career and technical education (MS Ed, Ed D, PhD, Ed S); communication (MA); counselor education (MA Ed, Ed D, PhD, Ed S); creative writing (MFA); curriculum and instruction (MA Ed, Ed D, PhD, Ed S); educational leadership and policy studies (MA Ed, Ed D, PhD, Ed S); educational research and evaluation (PhD); English (MA); foreign languages, cultures, and literatures (MA); higher education (PhD); higher education and student affairs (MA Ed); history (MA); human development (MS, PhD); material culture and public humanities (MA); philosophy (MA); political science (MA); rhetoric and writing (PhD); science and technology studies (MS, PhD); social, political, ethical, and cultural thought (PhD); sociology (MS, PhD); theater arts (MFA). *Faculty:* 408 full-time (204 women), 3 part-time/adjunct (2 women). *Students:* 657 full-time (446 women), 457 part-time (292 women); includes 213 minority (114 Black or African American, non-Hispanic/Latino; 3 American Indian or Alaska Native, non-Hispanic/Latino; 29 Asian, non-Hispanic/Latino; 44 Hispanic/Latino; 23 Two or more races, non-Hispanic/Latino), 93 international. Average age 33. 805 applicants, 55% accepted, 328 enrolled. In 2016, 270 master's, 91 doctorates awarded. *Degree requirements:* For master's, comprehensive exam (for some programs), thesis (for some programs); for doctorate, comprehensive exam (for some programs), thesis/dissertation (for some programs). *Entrance requirements:* For master's and doctorate, GRE/GMAT. Additional exam requirements/recommendations for international students: Required—TOEFL (minimum score 80 iBT). *Application deadline:* For fall admission, 8/1 for domestic students, 4/1 for international students; for spring admission, 1/1 for domestic students, 9/1 for international students. Applications are processed on a rolling basis. Application fee: $75. Electronic applications accepted. *Expenses:* Tuition, state resident: full-time $12,467; part-time $692.50 per credit hour. Tuition, nonresident: full-time $25,095; part-time $1394.25 per credit hour. *Required fees:* $2669; $491.50 per semester. Tuition and fees vary according to course load, campus/location and program. *Financial support:* In 2016–17, 21 research assistantships with full tuition reimbursements (averaging $19,817 per year), 237 teaching assistantships with full tuition reimbursements (averaging $15,497 per year) were awarded. Financial award application deadline: 3/1; financial award applicants required to submit FAFSA. *Total annual research expenditures:* $6.6 million. *Unit head:* Rosemary Blieszner, Interim Dean, 540-231-6779, Fax: 540-231-7157, E-mail: liberalartsdean@vt.edu. *Application contact:* Chelsea Blanchet, Executive Assistant, 540-231-6779, Fax: 540-231-7157, E-mail: bchels1@vt.edu.
Website: http://www.liberalarts.vt.edu/

**Wake Forest University,** Graduate School of Arts and Sciences, Department of English, Winston-Salem, NC 27106. Offers MA. *Program availability:* Part-time. *Degree requirements:* For master's, one foreign language, thesis. *Entrance requirements:* For master's, GRE General Test, writing sample. Additional exam requirements/recommendations for international students: Required—TOEFL (minimum score 79 iBT). Electronic applications accepted. *Faculty research:* Modern and contemporary poetry, feminist criticism and theory, Irish literature, British Commonwealth literature, medieval poetry.

**Washington State University,** College of Arts and Sciences, Department of English, Pullman, WA 99164. Offers MA, PhD. Program applications must be made through the Pullman campus. *Degree requirements:* For master's, one foreign language, comprehensive exam (for some programs), thesis (for some programs), oral exam; for doctorate, 2 foreign languages, comprehensive exam, thesis/dissertation, oral exam, written exam. *Entrance requirements:* For master's and doctorate, GRE General Test, GRE Subject Test, official transcripts; writing sample (approximately 10 pages); three letters of recommendation; statement of purpose (approximately 500 words); undergraduate major in English or other appropriate discipline. Additional exam requirements/recommendations for international students: Required—TOEFL, IELTS. Electronic applications accepted. *Faculty research:* Nationalism and gender in the American West, slavery and exploitation in nineteenth-century Britain, photography and the color line, D.H. Lawrence and Mexico, social movement cultures and the arts.

**Washington University in St. Louis,** The Graduate School, Department of English, St. Louis, MO 63130-4899. Offers English and American literature (PhD); writing (MFA). Terminal master's awarded for partial completion of doctoral program. *Degree requirements:* For master's, thesis or written exam; for doctorate, 2 foreign languages, thesis/dissertation. *Entrance requirements:* For master's and doctorate, GRE General

Test, sample of written work. Additional exam requirements/recommendations for international students: Required—TOEFL. Electronic applications accepted. *Faculty research:* Medieval, early modern, early American, eighteenth-century British, nineteenth-century British, nineteenth-century American, twentieth- and twenty-first century British, and twentieth- and twenty-first century American literature; African American literature and culture; Irish literature; Anglophone Postcolonial literature; gender and sexuality studies; Modernism; poetry and poetics; theory.

**Wayne State University,** College of Liberal Arts and Sciences, Department of English, Detroit, MI 48202. Offers English (MA); film and media studies (PhD); literary and cultural studies (PhD); rhetoric and composition studies (PhD). *Faculty:* 30. *Students:* 78 full-time (48 women), 23 part-time (10 women); includes 22 minority (10 Black or African American, non-Hispanic/Latino; 3 Asian, non-Hispanic/Latino; 6 Hispanic/Latino; 3 Two or more races, non-Hispanic/Latino), 7 international. Average age 35. 114 applicants, 33% accepted, 18 enrolled. In 2016, 15 master's, 5 doctorates awarded. Terminal master's awarded for partial completion of doctoral program. *Degree requirements:* For master's, variable foreign language requirement, essay, thesis, or portfolio of work approved by Director of Graduate Studies; for doctorate, one foreign language, comprehensive exam, thesis/dissertation. *Entrance requirements:* For master's, statement of purpose; two academic letters of reference; sample essay from previous English course; for doctorate, GRE General Test, statement of purpose; two academic letters of reference; sample of scholarly or critical writing. Additional exam requirements/recommendations for international students: Required—TOEFL (minimum score 550 paper-based; 79 iBT), TWE (minimum score 5.5), Michigan English Language Assessment Battery (minimum score 85); Recommended—IELTS (minimum score 6.5). *Application deadline:* For fall admission, 1/15 for domestic students. Applications are processed on a rolling basis. Application fee: $50. Electronic applications accepted. *Expenses:* $16,503 per year resident tuition and fees, $33,697 per year non-resident tuition and fees. *Financial support:* In 2016–17, 63 students received support, including 5 fellowships with tuition reimbursements available (averaging $15,800 per year), 30 teaching assistantships with tuition reimbursements available (averaging $17,994 per year); research assistantships with tuition reimbursements available, scholarships/grants, and unspecified assistantships also available. Financial award applicants required to submit FAFSA. *Faculty research:* Literary and cultural studies, film and new media studies, rhetoric and composition studies, linguistics, and creative writing. *Unit head:* Dr. Kenneth Jackson, Chair and Professor, 313-577-7692, E-mail: ai4054@wayne.edu. *Application contact:* Dr. Carolin Maun, Director of Graduate Studies, 313-577-7694, E-mail: caroline.maun@wayne.edu.
Website: http://clas.wayne.edu/english/

**Weber State University,** Telitha E. Lindquist College of Arts and Humanities, Program in English, Ogden, UT 84408-1001. Offers MA. *Program availability:* Part-time, evening/weekend. *Faculty:* 13 full-time (5 women). *Students:* 6 full-time (4 women), 42 part-time (37 women); includes 5 minority (2 Asian, non-Hispanic/Latino; 1 Hispanic/Latino; 2 Two or more races, non-Hispanic/Latino), 1 international. Average age 33. In 2016, 18 master's awarded. *Degree requirements:* For master's, one foreign language. *Entrance requirements:* For master's, 3 letters of recommendation, 5- to 8-page writing sample. Additional exam requirements/recommendations for international students: Required—TOEFL (minimum score 550 paper-based; 79 iBT). *Application deadline:* For fall admission, 3/15 for domestic students; for spring admission, 3/15 for domestic students; for summer admission, 10/15 for domestic students. Applications are processed on a rolling basis. Application fee: $60 ($90 for international students). Electronic applications accepted. *Expenses:* Contact institution. *Financial support:* In 2016–17, 19 students received support. Scholarships/grants available. Financial award application deadline: 4/1; financial award applicants required to submit FAFSA. *Unit head:* Dr. Mali Subbiah, Program Director, 801-626-6335, Fax: 801-626-7760, E-mail: msubbiah@weber.edu. *Application contact:* Genevieve Bates, Office Specialist, 801-626-7179, Fax: 801-626-7760, E-mail: masterofenglish@weber.edu.
Website: http://weber.edu/maenglish

**West Chester University of Pennsylvania,** College of Arts and Humanities, Department of English, West Chester, PA 19383. Offers English (MA), including creative writing, literature, writing, teaching, and criticism; publishing (Certificate); secondary English (Teaching Certificate). *Program availability:* Part-time, evening/weekend, blended/hybrid learning. *Faculty:* 12 full-time (8 women). *Students:* 21 full-time (14 women), 38 part-time (25 women); includes 3 minority (1 Black or African American, non-Hispanic/Latino; 2 Two or more races, non-Hispanic/Latino). Average age 28. 30 applicants, 97% accepted, 18 enrolled. In 2016, 13 master's, 2 other advanced degrees awarded. *Degree requirements:* For master's, thesis optional; for other advanced degree, capstone internship and e-portfolio (for Certificate). *Entrance requirements:* For master's, minimum GPA of 2.8, two letters of recommendation, writing sample, goals statement, official transcripts; for other advanced degree, undergraduate degree, statement of goals, and two letters of recommendation (for Certificate). Additional exam requirements/recommendations for international students: Required—TOEFL or IELTS. *Application deadline:* For fall admission, 5/15 for international students; for spring admission, 10/15 for international students. Applications are processed on a rolling basis. Application fee: $50. Electronic applications accepted. *Expenses:* Tuition, state resident: full-time $8694; part-time $483 per credit. Tuition, nonresident: full-time $13,050; part-time $725 per credit. *Required fees:* $2399; $119.05 per credit. Tuition and fees vary according to campus/location and program. *Financial support:* Scholarships/grants and unspecified assistantships available. Financial award application deadline: 2/15; financial award applicants required to submit FAFSA. *Faculty research:* Critical theory, cultural studies, literature, rhetoric and composition, creative writing. *Unit head:* Dr. Rodney Mader, Chair, 610-436-2822, Fax: 610-738-0516, E-mail: rmader@wcupa.edu. *Application contact:* Dr. Eleanor Shevlin, Graduate Coordinator for English, 610-436-2745, Fax: 610-738-0516, E-mail: eshevlin@wcupa.edu.
Website: http://www.wcupa.edu/arts-humanities/english/

**Western Carolina University,** Graduate School, College of Arts and Sciences, Department of English, Cullowhee, NC 28723. Offers teaching English as a second language or foreign language (MA). *Program availability:* Part-time, evening/weekend. *Degree requirements:* For master's, one foreign language, comprehensive exam, thesis (for some programs). *Entrance requirements:* For master's, GRE General Test, appropriate undergraduate degree, writing sample, 3 letters of recommendation. Additional exam requirements/recommendations for international students: Required—TOEFL (minimum score 550 paper-based; 79 iBT). *Expenses:* Tuition, state resident: full-time $2174. Tuition, nonresident: full-time $7377. *Required fees:* $1442. Part-time tuition and fees vary according to course load. *Faculty research:* Teaching English to speakers of other languages (TESOL), language assessment, applied linguistics, poetry, folk and fairy tales, post World War II British literature, Appalachian and southern literature.

**Western Connecticut State University,** Division of Graduate Studies, Maricostas School of Arts and Sciences, Department of English, Danbury, CT 06810-6885. Offers literature (MA). *Program availability:* Part-time. *Degree requirements:* For master's, completion of program in 6 years. *Entrance requirements:* For master's, minimum GPA of 2.5, writing sample. Additional exam requirements/recommendations for international students: Recommended—TOEFL (minimum score 550 paper-based; 79 iBT), IELTS

(minimum score 6). *Faculty research:* Developing inquiry in teachers and students, encouraging talent development, analyzing program development and assessment techniques, developing student learning outcomes, encouraging teachers as researchers, assessing the impact of computer technologies.

**Western Illinois University,** School of Graduate Studies, College of Arts and Sciences, Department of English and Journalism, Macomb, IL 61455-1390. Offers English (MA); literary studies (Certificate); professional writing (Certificate); teaching writing (Certificate). *Program availability:* Part-time. *Students:* 9 full-time (7 women), 28 part-time (14 women); includes 1 minority (Hispanic/Latino), 1 international. Average age 31. 16 applicants, 94% accepted, 11 enrolled. In 2016, 11 master's, 2 other advanced degrees awarded. *Degree requirements:* For master's, thesis or alternative. *Entrance requirements:* Additional exam requirements/recommendations for international students: Required—TOEFL (minimum score 575 paper-based; 88 iBT). *Application deadline:* Applications are processed on a rolling basis. Application fee: $30. Electronic applications accepted. *Financial support:* In 2016–17, 17 students received support, including 5 teaching assistantships with full tuition reimbursements available (averaging $8,688 per year). Financial award applicants required to submit FAFSA. *Unit head:* Dr. Mark Mossman, Chairperson, 309-298-1103. *Application contact:* Dr. Nancy Parsons, Associate Provost and Director of Graduate Studies, 309-298-1806, Fax: 309-298-2345, E-mail: grad-office@wiu.edu.
Website: http://wiu.edu/English

**Western Kentucky University,** Graduate Studies, Potter College of Arts and Letters, Department of English, Bowling Green, KY 42101. Offers education (MA); English (MA Ed); literature (MA), including American literature, British literature, literary theory, women writers, world literature; teaching English as a second language (MA); writing (MA). *Program availability:* Part-time, evening/weekend. *Degree requirements:* For master's, comprehensive exam, thesis optional, final exam. *Entrance requirements:* For master's, GRE General Test, minimum GPA of 2.75. Additional exam requirements/recommendations for international students: Required—TOEFL (minimum score 555 paper-based; 79 iBT). *Faculty research:* Improving writing, linking teacher knowledge and performance, Victorian women writers, Kentucky women writers, Kentucky poets.

**Western Michigan University,** Graduate College, College of Arts and Sciences, Department of English, Kalamazoo, MI 49008. Offers creative writing (MFA, PhD); English (MA, PhD); English teaching (MA). *Degree requirements:* For doctorate, one foreign language, thesis/dissertation.

**Western Washington University,** Graduate School, College of Humanities and Social Sciences, Department of English, Bellingham, WA 98225-5996. Offers MA. *Program availability:* Part-time. *Degree requirements:* For master's, one foreign language, comprehensive exam, thesis (for some programs). *Entrance requirements:* For master's, GRE General Test, writing sample, minimum GPA of 3.0 in last 60 semester hours or last 90 quarter hours of course work. Additional exam requirements/recommendations for international students: Required—TOEFL (minimum score 567 paper-based). Electronic applications accepted. *Faculty research:* Literature and technology, film, composition and rhetoric, technical writing, critical and cultural theory.

**Westfield State University,** College of Graduate and Continuing Education, Department of English, Westfield, MA 01086. Offers MA. *Program availability:* Part-time, evening/weekend. *Faculty:* 5 full-time (4 women). *Students:* 4 full-time (2 women), 16 part-time (8 women); includes 1 minority (Hispanic/Latino). Average age 34. 5 applicants, 100% accepted, 5 enrolled. In 2016, 10 master's awarded. *Degree requirements:* For master's, one foreign language, thesis. *Entrance requirements:* For master's, GRE General Test, MAT, minimum undergraduate GPA of 2.8, 3.0 in all English classes; undergraduate course work in English. Additional exam requirements/recommendations for international students: Recommended—TOEFL (minimum score 550 paper-based; 79 iBT). *Application deadline:* For fall admission, 6/30 for domestic students; for spring admission, 10/31 for domestic students; for summer admission, 3/31 for domestic students. Applications are processed on a rolling basis. Application fee: $50. *Expenses:* Tuition, state resident: part-time $318 per semester hour. Tuition, nonresident: part-time $318 per semester hour. *Required fees:* $75 per semester. Tuition and fees vary according to course load and program. *Financial support:* Unspecified assistantships and SOS scholarships for education majors only available. Financial award application deadline: 3/1; financial award applicants required to submit FAFSA. *Unit head:* Dr. Emily Todd, Director, 413-572-5337, E-mail: etodd@westfield.ma.edu. *Application contact:* Shelly Henrichon, Admissions Coordinator, 413-572-8022, Fax: 413-572-5227, E-mail: mhenrichon@westfield.ma.edu.
Website: http://www.westfield.ma.edu/academics/degrees/english-masters-degree

**West Texas A&M University,** College of Fine Arts and Humanities, Department of English, Philosophy and Modern Languages, Canyon, TX 79016-0001. Offers English (MA). *Program availability:* Part-time, evening/weekend. *Degree requirements:* For master's, comprehensive exam, thesis optional. *Entrance requirements:* For master's, GRE General Test. Additional exam requirements/recommendations for international students: Required—TOEFL (minimum score 550 paper-based). *Application deadline:* For fall admission, 8/1 for domestic students, 5/1 for international students; for spring admission, 12/1 for domestic students, 10/30 for international students; for summer admission, 5/1 for domestic students. Applications are processed on a rolling basis. Application fee: $40 ($75 for international students). Electronic applications accepted. *Financial support:* Research assistantships, teaching assistantships with partial tuition reimbursements, Federal Work-Study, and institutionally sponsored loans available. Support available to part-time students. Financial award applicants required to submit CSS PROFILE or FAFSA. *Faculty research:* Medieval studies, composition theory, literary criticism, Evelyn Scott, transformation of literacy in computer mediated communication. *Unit head:* Dr. Stephen Severn, Head, 806-651-2456, E-mail: ssevern@wtamu.edu.
Website: http://www.wtamu.edu/academics/english-philosophy-modern-languages.aspx

**West Virginia University,** Eberly College of Arts and Sciences, Department of English, Morgantown, WV 26506. Offers creative writing (MFA); English (MA, PhD); literary/cultural studies (MA, PhD); writing (MA). *Program availability:* Part-time, evening/weekend. *Degree requirements:* For master's, one foreign language, thesis optional; for doctorate, one foreign language, thesis/dissertation, preliminary exam. *Entrance requirements:* For master's, GRE General Test, minimum GPA of 3.0; for doctorate, GRE General Test, GRE Subject Test, minimum GPA of 3.0. Additional exam requirements/recommendations for international students: Required—TOEFL. Electronic applications accepted. *Faculty research:* American studies, gender studies, media studies, cultural studies.

**Wichita State University,** Graduate School, Fairmount College of Liberal Arts and Sciences, Department of English, Wichita, KS 67260. Offers creative writing (MFA); English (MA). *Program availability:* Part-time, evening/weekend. *Entrance requirements:* For master's, writing sample (MFA). *Unit head:* Dr. Mary Waters, Chair, 316-978-3130, Fax: 316-978-3548, E-mail: mary.waters@wichita.edu. *Application contact:* Jordan Oleson, Admissions Coordinator, 316-978-3095, Fax: 316-978-3253, E-mail: jordan.oleson@wichita.edu.
Website: http://www.wichita.edu/english

*English*

**Wilfrid Laurier University,** Faculty of Graduate and Postdoctoral Studies, Faculty of Arts, Department of English and Film Studies, Waterloo, ON N2L 3C5, Canada. Offers English (MA); English and film (PhD). *Degree requirements:* For master's, thesis optional; for doctorate, thesis/dissertation. *Entrance requirements:* For master's, honours BA or the equivalent in English, minimum B+ in English courses above first year level; for doctorate, MA in English, minimum A- average in graduate work. Additional exam requirements/recommendations for international students: Recommended—TOEFL (minimum score 89 iBT). Electronic applications accepted. *Faculty research:* Gender and genre, Canadian studies, early modern studies, postcolonial studies, nineteenth century studies.

**William Paterson University of New Jersey,** College of Humanities and Social Sciences, Wayne, NJ 07470-8420. Offers applied sociology (MA); clinical and counseling psychology (MA); clinical psychology (Psy D); creative and professional writing (MFA); English (MA); history (MA); political science and public policy (MA); public policy and international affairs (MA). *Program availability:* Part-time, evening/weekend. *Faculty:* 35 full-time (19 women), 8 part-time/adjunct (5 women). *Students:* 58 full-time (38 women), 62 part-time (46 women); includes 40 minority (9 Black or African American, non-Hispanic/Latino; 6 Asian, non-Hispanic/Latino; 21 Hispanic/Latino; 4 Two or more races, non-Hispanic/Latino), 4 international. Average age 32. 160 applicants, 55% accepted, 50 enrolled. In 2016, 56 master's awarded. *Degree requirements:* For master's, thesis (for some programs), internship (for some programs). *Entrance requirements:* For master's, GRE/MAT, minimum GPA of 3.0; 2 letters of recommendation; writing sample/personal statement. Additional exam requirements/recommendations for international students: Required—TOEFL (minimum score 550 paper-based; 79 iBT), IELTS (minimum score 6). *Application deadline:* For fall admission, 8/1 for domestic students, 4/1 for international students; for spring admission, 12/1 for domestic students, 11/1 for international students; for summer admission, 5/1 for domestic students, 2/1 for international students. Applications are processed on a rolling basis. Application fee: $50. Electronic applications accepted. *Expenses:* Tuition, state resident: full-time $12,480; part-time $611 per credit. Tuition, nonresident: full-time $20,263; part-time $992 per credit. *Required fees:* $1573; $77 per credit. Tuition and fees vary according to course load, degree level and program. *Financial support:* Career-related internships or fieldwork, Federal Work-Study, scholarships/grants, and unspecified assistantships available. Support available to part-time students. Financial award applicants required to submit FAFSA. *Faculty research:* Relationship violence among adolescents; autism in young children; game theory; gender, governance and empowerment in India; Chinese development policies concerning Africa. *Total annual research expenditures:* $162,900. *Unit head:* Dr. Kara Rabbitt, Dean, 973-720-2180, Fax: 973-720-2955, E-mail: rabbittk@wpunj.edu. *Application contact:* Tinu Adeniran, Associate Director, Graduate Admissions, 973-720-2764, Fax: 973-720-2035, E-mail: adenirant@wpunj.edu.
Website: http://www.wpunj.edu/cohss

**Wilson College,** Graduate Programs, Chambersburg, PA 17201-1285. Offers accounting (M Acc); choreography and visual art (MFA); education (M Ed); healthcare management for sustainability (MHM); humanities (MA), including art and culture, critical/cultural theory, English language and literature, women's studies; management (MSM); nursing (MSN), including nursing education, nursing leadership and management. *Program availability:* Evening/weekend. *Degree requirements:* For master's, project. *Entrance requirements:* For master's, PRAXIS, minimum undergraduate cumulative GPA of 3.0, 2 letters of recommendation, current certification for eligibility to teach in grades K-12, resume, personal interview. Electronic applications accepted.

**Winona State University,** College of Liberal Arts, Department of English, Winona, MN 55987. Offers MA, MS. *Program availability:* Part-time. *Degree requirements:* For master's, thesis or alternative.

**Winthrop University,** College of Arts and Sciences, Department of English, Rock Hill, SC 29733. Offers MA. *Program availability:* Part-time, evening/weekend. *Degree requirements:* For master's, one foreign language, comprehensive exam, thesis optional. *Entrance requirements:* For master's, GRE General Test, MAT or PRAXIS, 24 undergraduate hours of course work in English. Additional exam requirements/recommendations for international students: Required—TOEFL (minimum score 550 paper-based; 79 iBT). Electronic applications accepted. *Expenses:* Tuition, state resident: full-time $14,312; part-time $599 per credit hour. Tuition, nonresident: full-time $27,570; part-time $1153 per credit hour.

**Wright State University,** Graduate School, College of Liberal Arts, Department of English Language and Literatures, Dayton, OH 45435. Offers English (MA). *Degree requirements:* For master's, thesis optional, portfolio. *Entrance requirements:* For master's, 20 hours in upper-level English. Additional exam requirements/recommendations for international students: Required—TOEFL. *Application deadline:* Applications are processed on a rolling basis. Application fee: $25. *Expenses:* Tuition, state resident: full-time $9952; part-time $622 per credit hour. Tuition, nonresident: full-time $16,960; part-time $1060 per credit hour. *Financial support:* Fellowships, research assistantships, teaching assistantships, and unspecified assistantships available. Support available to part-time students. Financial award applicants required to submit FAFSA. *Faculty research:* American literature, world literature in English, applied linguistics, writing theory and pedagogy. *Unit head:* Dr. Henry S. Limouze, Chair, 937-775-3136, Fax: 937-775-2707, E-mail: henry.limouze@wright.edu. *Application contact:* Dr. Chris Hall, Director, 937-775-2268, Fax: 937-775-2707, E-mail: chris.hall@wright.edu.
Website: http://liberal-arts.wright.edu/english-language-and-literatures

**Xavier University,** College of Arts and Sciences, Department of English, Cincinnati, OH 45207. Offers MA. *Program availability:* Part-time, evening/weekend. *Degree requirements:* For master's, one foreign language, comprehensive exam, thesis optional. *Entrance requirements:* For master's, GRE, writing sample; minimum GPA of 3.2 in undergraduate English courses, 3.0 for all undergraduate coursework; official transcript; intent/purpose statement. Additional exam requirements/recommendations for international students: Required—TOEFL (minimum score 550 paper-based; 79 iBT). Electronic applications accepted. Application fee is waived when completed online. *Expenses:* Contact institution. *Faculty research:* British literature, American literature, linguistics, literary theory, composition studies.

**Yale University,** Graduate School of Arts and Sciences, Department of English Language and Literature, New Haven, CT 06520. Offers MA, PhD. Terminal master's awarded for partial completion of doctoral program. *Degree requirements:* For master's, 2 foreign languages; for doctorate, 3 foreign languages, thesis/dissertation. *Entrance requirements:* For master's and doctorate, GRE General Test, GRE Subject Test.

**York University,** Faculty of Graduate Studies, Faculty of Liberal Arts and Professional Studies, Program in English, Toronto, ON M3J 1P3, Canada. Offers MA, PhD. *Program availability:* Part-time. *Degree requirements:* For master's, thesis or alternative; for doctorate, one foreign language, comprehensive exam, thesis/dissertation. Electronic applications accepted.

**Youngstown State University,** Graduate School, College of Liberal Arts and Social Sciences, Department of English, Youngstown, OH 44555-0001. Offers MA. *Program availability:* Part-time. *Degree requirements:* For master's, portfolio. *Entrance requirements:* For master's, bachelor's degree in English, minimum GPA of 2.7. Additional exam requirements/recommendations for international students: Required—TOEFL. *Faculty research:* Technical communications, multicultural literacy, children's literature, women's literature, film study, linguistics.

# French

**American University,** College of Arts and Sciences, Department of World Languages and Cultures, Washington, DC 20016-8045. Offers Spanish: Latin American studies (MA); teaching English as a foreign language (MA); teaching English to speakers of other languages (MA, Certificate); translation: French (Certificate); translation: Russian (Certificate); translation: Spanish (Certificate). *Program availability:* Part-time, evening/weekend. *Faculty:* 42 full-time (31 women), 27 part-time/adjunct (18 women). *Students:* 41 full-time (31 women), 31 part-time (23 women); includes 14 minority (3 Black or African American, non-Hispanic/Latino; 2 Asian, non-Hispanic/Latino; 7 Hispanic/Latino; 2 Two or more races, non-Hispanic/Latino), 9 international. Average age 32. 73 applicants, 92% accepted, 20 enrolled. In 2016, 24 master's, 6 other advanced degrees awarded. *Degree requirements:* For master's, one foreign language, comprehensive exam, thesis or alternative. *Entrance requirements:* For master's, GRE, writing sample, statement of purpose, transcripts, 2 letters of recommendation, resume; for Certificate, bachelor's degree, statement of purpose, transcripts, resume. Additional exam requirements/recommendations for international students: Required—TOEFL (minimum score 100 iBT), IELTS (minimum score 7), PTE (minimum score 68). *Application deadline:* For fall admission, 2/1 for domestic students; for spring admission, 11/1 for domestic students. Application fee: $55. *Expenses:* $1,579 per credit tuition; $690 mandatory fees. *Financial support:* Institutionally sponsored loans, scholarships/grants, and unspecified assistantships available. Financial award application deadline: 2/1; financial award applicants required to submit FAFSA. *Unit head:* Henry Gerfen, Chair, 202-885-2385, Fax: 202-885-1076, E-mail: gerfen@american.edu. *Application contact:* Kathleen Clowery, Director of Graduate Admissions, 202-885-3620, Fax: 202-885-1344, E-mail: clowery@american.edu.
Website: http://www.american.edu/cas/wlc/

**Arizona State University at the Tempe campus,** College of Liberal Arts and Sciences, School of International Letters and Cultures, Program in French, Tempe, AZ 85287-0202. Offers comparative literature (MA); linguistics (MA); literature (MA). *Program availability:* Part-time, evening/weekend. *Degree requirements:* For master's, thesis or applied project, interactive Program of Study (iPOS) submitted no later than beginning of third semester of study or before completing 50 percent of coursework towards completion of degree. *Entrance requirements:* For master's, GRE, minimum GPA of 3.25 in the last two years of work leading to the bachelor's degree in French major, personal statement, writing sample (preferably written in French), 3 letters of recommendation. Additional exam requirements/recommendations for international students: Required—TOEFL (minimum score 550 paper-based; 83 iBT), IELTS (minimum score 6.5). Electronic applications accepted.

**Asbury University,** School of Graduate and Professional Studies, Wilmore, KY 40390-1198. Offers biology: alternative certificate (MA Ed); chemistry: alternative certificate (MA Ed); English (MA Ed); English as a second language (MA Ed); ESL (MA Ed); French (MA Ed); Latin: alternative certificate (MA Ed); mathematics: alternative certificate (MA Ed); reading/writing endorsement (MA Ed); social studies (MA Ed); social work (MSW), including child and family services; Spanish (MA Ed); special education (MA Ed); special education: alternative certificate (MA Ed); teacher as leader endorsement (MA Ed). *Accreditation:* NCATE. *Program availability:* Part-time. *Degree requirements:* For master's, action research project, portfolio. *Entrance requirements:* For master's, PRAXIS/NTE, minimum GPA of 2.75, letters of recommendation. Additional exam requirements/recommendations for international students: Required—TOEFL (minimum score 550 paper-based). Electronic applications accepted.

**Binghamton University, State University of New York,** Graduate School, Harpur College of Arts and Sciences, Department of Romance Languages and Literatures, Program in French, Binghamton, NY 13902-6000. Offers MA. *Program availability:* Part-time. *Students:* 2 part-time (1 woman). Average age 28. 3 applicants. *Degree requirements:* For master's, one foreign language, comprehensive exam, thesis or alternative. *Entrance requirements:* For master's, GRE General Test. Additional exam requirements/recommendations for international students: Required—TOEFL (minimum score 550 paper-based; 80 iBT). *Application deadline:* For fall admission, 2/15 priority date for domestic and international students; for spring admission, 11/15 priority date for domestic and international students. Application fee: $75. Electronic applications accepted. *Financial support:* In 2016–17, 1 student received support. Career-related internships or fieldwork, Federal Work-Study, institutionally sponsored loans, and unspecified assistantships available. Support available to part-time students. Financial award applicants required to submit FAFSA. *Unit head:* Dr. Dana Stewart, Chairperson, 607-777-2645, E-mail: stewart@binghamton.edu. *Application contact:* Ben Balkaya, Assistant Dean and Director, 607-777-2151, Fax: 607-777-2501, E-mail: balkaya@binghamton.edu.

**Boston College,** Graduate School of Arts and Sciences, Department of Romance Languages and Literatures, Chestnut Hill, MA 02467-3800. Offers French (MA); Italian (MA); Spanish (MA). *Program availability:* Part-time. *Faculty:* 19 full-time. *Students:* 31 full-time (26 women); includes 2 minority (both Hispanic/Latino), 8 international. 34 applicants, 50% accepted, 12 enrolled. In 2016, 12 master's awarded. Terminal master's awarded for partial completion of doctoral program. *Degree requirements:* For master's, one foreign language. *Entrance requirements:* Additional exam requirements/recommendations for international students: Required—TOEFL (minimum score 600 paper-based; 100 iBT), IELTS (minimum score 8). *Application deadline:* For fall admission, 2/1 for domestic and international students. Application fee: $75. Electronic applications accepted. Tuition and fees vary according to program. *Financial support:* In 2016–17, 36 students received support, including fellowships with full tuition reimbursements available (averaging $18,800 per year), teaching assistantships with full tuition reimbursements available (averaging $18,800 per year); Federal Work-Study and unspecified assistantships also available. Support available to part-time students. Financial award application deadline: 3/1; financial award applicants required to submit FAFSA. *Faculty research:* Spanish-American literature, philology, medieval French romance and troubadour lyrics, Golden Age Peninsular literature, secondary language acquisition and pedagogy, Hispanic studies, French language and literature, Italian language and literature. *Unit head:* Dr. Franco Mormando, Chairperson, 617-552-6346, E-mail: franco.mormando@bc.edu. *Application contact:* Dr. Laurie Shepard, Graduate Program Director, 617-552-8269, E-mail: laurie.shepard@bc.edu. Website: http://www.bc.edu/rll

**Boston University,** Graduate School of Arts and Sciences, Department of Romance Studies, Boston, MA 02215. Offers French language and literature (MA, PhD); Hispanic language and literatures (MA, PhD). *Students:* 40 full-time (27 women), 1 part-time (0 women); includes 8 minority (1 Black or African American, non-Hispanic/Latino; 7 Hispanic/Latino), 12 international. Average age 32. 49 applicants, 35% accepted, 6 enrolled. In 2016, 3 master's, 6 doctorates awarded. Terminal master's awarded for partial completion of doctoral program. *Degree requirements:* For master's, one foreign language, comprehensive exam; for doctorate, 2 foreign languages, comprehensive exam, thesis/dissertation. *Entrance requirements:* For master's and doctorate, GRE General Test, sample of written work, 3 letters of recommendation, transcripts, personal statement, summary of related coursework. Additional exam requirements/recommendations for international students: Required—TOEFL (minimum score 550 paper-based; 84 iBT). *Application deadline:* For fall admission, 1/15 for domestic and international students. Application fee: $95. Electronic applications accepted. *Financial support:* In 2016–17, 36 students received support, including 6 fellowships with full tuition reimbursements available (averaging $21,500 per year), 25 teaching assistantships with full tuition reimbursements available (averaging $21,500 per year); Federal Work-Study, scholarships/grants, and health care benefits also available. Financial award application deadline: 1/15. *Unit head:* Odile Cazenave, Chair, 617-353-6225, Fax: 617-353-6246, E-mail: cazenave@bu.edu. *Application contact:* Deanna Wong, Administrative Assistant, 617-353-2641, Fax: 617-353-6246, E-mail: dswong@bu.edu. Website: http://www.bu.edu/rs/

**Bowling Green State University,** Graduate College, College of Arts and Sciences, Department of Romance and Classical Studies, Program in French, Bowling Green, OH 43403. Offers French (MA). *Program availability:* Part-time. *Degree requirements:* For master's, one foreign language, thesis or alternative. *Entrance requirements:* For master's, GRE General Test. Additional exam requirements/recommendations for international students: Required—TOEFL. *Application deadline:* For fall admission, 2/28 priority date for domestic students. Application fee: $30. Electronic applications accepted. *Financial support:* Research assistantships with full tuition reimbursements, teaching assistantships with full tuition reimbursements, Federal Work-Study, and unspecified assistantships available. Financial award applicants required to submit FAFSA. *Faculty research:* Francophone literature, French cinema, business French, nineteenth- and twentieth-century literature. *Unit head:* Dr. Richard Hebein, Chair, 419-372-7153. *Application contact:* Dr. Deborah Shocket, Graduate Coordinator, 419-372-8632.

**Brigham Young University,** Graduate Studies, College of Humanities, Department of French and Italian, Provo, UT 84602. Offers French studies (MA). *Faculty:* 10 full-time (2 women). *Students:* 1 (woman) part-time. Average age 28. In 2016, 2 master's awarded. *Degree requirements:* For master's, one foreign language, thesis. *Entrance requirements:* For master's, GRE General Test, BA in French. Additional exam requirements/recommendations for international students: Required—TOEFL. *Application deadline:* For fall admission, 2/28 for domestic and international students. Application fee: $50. Electronic applications accepted. *Expenses: Tuition:* Full-time $6680; part-time $393 per credit. Tuition and fees vary according to course load, program and student's religious affiliation. *Financial support:* Research assistantships, teaching assistantships, career-related internships or fieldwork, institutionally sponsored loans, scholarships/grants, and tuition waivers (full and partial) available. Support available to part-time students. *Faculty research:* Francophone studies, medieval literature, Provencal literature, existentialism, second language acquisition, cultural studies, the sacred, Renaissance poetry, satire. *Unit head:* Dr. Corry L. Cropper, Department Chair, 801-422-4484, Fax: 801-422-0260, E-mail: corrycropper@gmail.com. *Application contact:* Nicolas G. Unlandt, Graduate Coordinator, 801-422-2895, Fax: 801-422-0260, E-mail: nicolas_unlandt@byu.edu. Website: http://frenital.byu.edu/department.html

**Brooklyn College of the City University of New York,** School of Humanities and Social Sciences, Department of Modern Languages and Literatures, Brooklyn, NY 11210-2889. Offers French (MA); Spanish (MA). *Degree requirements:* For master's, comprehensive exam or research paper. *Entrance requirements:* For master's, 18 credits in advanced courses in Spanish, 2 letters of recommendation. Additional exam requirements/recommendations for international students: Required—TOEFL (minimum score 500 paper-based; 61 iBT). Electronic applications accepted. *Faculty research:* Latin American contemporary novel, Caribbean female contemporary literature, nineteenth- and twentieth-century Spanish novel, twentieth-century Mexican poetry.

**Brown University,** Graduate School, Department of French Studies, Providence, RI 02912. Offers PhD. *Degree requirements:* For doctorate, variable foreign language requirement, thesis/dissertation, preliminary exam.

**California State University, Long Beach,** Graduate Studies, College of Liberal Arts, Department of Romance, German, Russian Languages and Literatures, Program in French and Francophone Studies, Long Beach, CA 90840. Offers MA. *Program availability:* Part-time. *Degree requirements:* For master's, one foreign language, comprehensive exam, thesis optional. *Entrance requirements:* For master's, BA in French. *Application deadline:* For fall admission, 7/1 for domestic students. Applications are processed on a rolling basis. Application fee: $55. Electronic applications accepted. *Financial support:* Federal Work-Study, institutionally sponsored loans, and scholarships/grants available. Financial award application deadline: 3/2. *Faculty research:* Eighteenth-century encyclopedism, development of the novel, La Chanson de Roland. *Unit head:* Markus Muller, Chair, 562-985-4317.

**California State University, Los Angeles,** Graduate Studies, College of Arts and Letters, Department of Modern Languages and Literatures, Los Angeles, CA 90032-8530. Offers French (MA); Spanish (MA). *Program availability:* Part-time, evening/weekend. *Degree requirements:* For master's, comprehensive exam. *Entrance requirements:* Additional exam requirements/recommendations for international students: Required—TOEFL (minimum score 500 paper-based). Electronic applications accepted. *Faculty research:* French literature, language teaching and methodology, Spanish poetry, Spanish American fiction and poetry.

**Carleton University,** Faculty of Graduate Studies, Faculty of Arts and Social Sciences, Department of French, Ottawa, ON K1S 5B6, Canada. Offers MA. *Degree requirements:* For master's, thesis optional. *Entrance requirements:* For master's, honors degree. *Faculty research:* French, French Canadian and Acadian literatures and linguistics, Francophone studies, rhetorical studies.

**Case Western Reserve University,** School of Graduate Studies, Department of Modern Languages and Literatures, Program in French, Cleveland, OH 44106. Offers MA. *Program availability:* Part-time. *Faculty:* 4 full-time (3 women). *Students:* 1 (woman) full-time; minority (Asian, non-Hispanic/Latino). Average age 22. In 2016, 2 master's awarded. Terminal master's awarded for partial completion of doctoral program. *Degree requirements:* For master's, one foreign language, comprehensive exam. *Entrance requirements:* For master's, GRE General Test, writing sample, three letters of recommendation. Additional exam requirements/recommendations for international students: Required—TOEFL (minimum score 577 paper-based; 90 iBT); Recommended—IELTS (minimum score 7). *Application deadline:* For fall admission, 3/1 priority date for domestic students; for spring admission, 11/1 priority date for domestic students. Applications are processed on a rolling basis. Application fee: $50. Electronic applications accepted. *Expenses: Tuition:* Full-time $42,576; part-time $1774 per credit hour. *Required fees:* $34. Tuition and fees vary according to course load and program. *Financial support:* Fellowships, institutionally sponsored loans, and tuition waivers (full) available. Financial award application deadline: 3/1; financial award applicants required to submit CSS PROFILE or FAFSA. *Faculty research:* Eighteenth- and nineteenth-century literature (novel, poetry, drama), literary theory, women's studies, cultural criticism. *Unit head:* Prof. Yasuhiro Shirai, Professor in Modern Languages/Chair, 216-368-8976, Fax: 216-368-4681. *Application contact:* Prof. Marie Lathers, Professor of French and Humanities, 216-368-8983, Fax: 216-368-2216, E-mail: marie.lathers@case.edu. Website: http://dmll.case.edu/graduate/

**Central Connecticut State University,** School of Graduate Studies, College of Liberal Arts and Social Sciences, Department of Modern Languages, New Britain, CT 06050-4010. Offers modern language (MA, Certificate), including French, German (Certificate), Italian, Spanish (MA); Spanish (MS, Certificate). *Program availability:* Part-time, evening/weekend. *Faculty:* 8 full-time (6 women). *Students:* 7 full-time (6 women), 12 part-time (7 women); includes 10 minority (all Hispanic/Latino). Average age 32. 11 applicants, 91% accepted, 4 enrolled. In 2016, 9 master's, 1 other advanced degree awarded. *Degree requirements:* For master's, one foreign language, comprehensive exam, thesis or alternative; for Certificate, qualifying exam. *Entrance requirements:* For master's, minimum undergraduate GPA of 2.7, 24 credits of undergraduate courses in each language in which graduate work will be undertaken. Additional exam requirements/recommendations for international students: Required—TOEFL (minimum score 550 paper-based; 79 iBT). *Application deadline:* For fall admission, 6/1 for domestic students, 5/1 for international students; for spring admission, 11/1 for domestic and international students. Applications are processed on a rolling basis. Application fee: $50. Electronic applications accepted. *Expenses: Tuition, area resident:* Full-time $6497; part-time $606 per credit. Tuition, state resident: full-time $9748; part-time $622 per credit. Tuition, nonresident: full-time $18,102; part-time $622 per credit. *Required fees:* $4459; $246 per credit. *Financial support:* In 2016–17, 6 students received support. Career-related internships or fieldwork, Federal Work-Study, scholarships/grants, and unspecified assistantships available. Support available to part-time students. Financial award application deadline: 3/1; financial award applicants required to submit FAFSA. *Faculty research:* Quebecois literature, Caribbean literature, modern French/Spanish drama, Puerto Rican novel and drama. *Unit head:* Dr. Carmela Pesca, Chair, 860-832-2875, E-mail: pescac@ccsu.edu. *Application contact:* Patricia Gardner, Associate Director of Graduate Studies, 860-832-2350, Fax: 860-832-2362. Website: http://web.ccsu.edu/modlang

**Colorado State University,** College of Liberal Arts, Department of Languages, Literatures and Cultures, Fort Collins, CO 80523-1774. Offers French (MA); German (MA); Spanish (MA). *Program availability:* Part-time. *Faculty:* 7 full-time (6 women), 3 part-time/adjunct (all women). *Students:* 12 full-time (10 women); includes 4 minority (all Hispanic/Latino), 4 international. Average age 34. 7 applicants, 100% accepted, 6 enrolled. In 2016, 6 master's awarded. *Degree requirements:* For master's, one foreign language, comprehensive exam, thesis, teaching portfolio or additional coursework. *Entrance requirements:* For master's, minimum GPA of 3.0, undergraduate major/proficiency in foreign languages, BA/BS in related field, statement of purpose, biographical statement, 3 letters of recommendation, resume, official transcripts, writing sample. Additional exam requirements/recommendations for international students: Required—TOEFL (minimum score 550 paper-based; 80 iBT). *Application deadline:* For fall admission, 2/1 priority date for domestic and international students; for spring admission, 9/15 priority date for domestic and international students. Applications are processed on a rolling basis. Application fee: $60 ($70 for international students). Electronic applications accepted. *Expenses:* Tuition, state resident: full-time $9628. Tuition, nonresident: full-time $23,603. *Required fees:* $2253; $528.14 per credit hour. $264.07 per semester. Tuition and fees vary according to course load and program. *Financial support:* In 2016–17, 10 teaching assistantships with full and partial tuition reimbursements (averaging $13,932 per year) were awarded; career-related internships or fieldwork, scholarships/grants, and unspecified assistantships also available. Financial award application deadline: 3/1; financial award applicants required to submit FAFSA. *Faculty research:* French, German, and Hispanic literatures and cultures; video-assisted language learning; computer-assisted language learners; foreign language teaching methodologies; linguistics. *Unit head:* Dr. Mary Vogl, Department Chair, 970-491-6100, Fax: 970-491-2822, E-mail: mary.vogl@colostate.edu. *Application contact:* Kaity Lewis, Graduate Program Contact, 970-491-6269, Fax: 970-491-2822, E-mail: kaity.lewis@colostate.edu. Website: http://languages.colostate.edu/

**Columbia University,** Graduate School of Arts and Sciences, New York, NY 10027. Offers African-American studies (MA); American studies (MA); anthropology (MA, PhD); art history and archaeology (MA, PhD); astronomy (PhD); biological sciences (PhD); biotechnology (MA); chemical physics (PhD); chemistry (PhD); classical studies (MA, PhD); classics (MA, PhD); climate and society (MA); conservation biology (MA); earth and environmental sciences (PhD); East Asia: regional studies (MA); East Asian languages and cultures (MA, PhD); ecology, evolution and environmental biology (MA), including conservation biology; ecology, evolution, and environmental biology (PhD), including ecology and evolutionary biology, evolutionary primatology; economics (MA, PhD); English and comparative literature (MA, PhD); French and Romance philology (MA, PhD); Germanic languages (MA, PhD); global French studies (MA); global thought (MA); Hispanic cultural studies (MA); history (PhD); history and literature (MA); human rights studies (MA); Islamic studies (MA); Italian (MA, PhD); Japanese pedagogy (MA); Jewish studies (MA); Latin America and the Caribbean: regional studies (MA); Latin American and Iberian cultures (PhD); mathematics (MA, PhD), including finance (MA); medieval and Renaissance studies (MA); Middle Eastern, South Asian, and African studies (MA, PhD); modern art: critical and curatorial studies (MA); modern European studies (MA); museum anthropology (MA); music (DMA, PhD); oral history (MA); philosophical foundations of physics (MA); philosophy (MA, PhD); physics (PhD); political science (MA, PhD); psychology (PhD); quantitative methods in the social sciences (MA); religion (MA, PhD); Russia, Eurasia and East Europe: regional studies (MA); Russian translation (MA); Slavic cultures (MA); Slavic languages (MA, PhD); sociology (MA, PhD); South Asian studies (MA); statistics (MA, PhD); theatre (PhD). Dual-degree programs require admission to both Graduate School of Arts and Sciences and another Columbia school. *Program availability:* Part-time. Terminal master's awarded for partial completion of doctoral program. *Degree requirements:* For master's, variable foreign language requirement, comprehensive exam (for some programs), thesis (for some programs); for doctorate, variable foreign language requirement, comprehensive exam (for some programs), thesis/dissertation. *Entrance requirements:* For master's and doctorate, GRE General Test, GRE Subject Test (for some programs). Additional exam requirements/recommendations for international students: Required— TOEFL, IELTS. Electronic applications accepted.

**Concordia University,** School of Graduate Studies, Faculty of Arts and Science, Department of Études Franlfcaises, Montréal, QC H3G 1M8, Canada. Offers Anglais-Franlfcais en langue et techniques de localization (Certificate); littératures Francophones et résonances médiatiques (MA); translation (Diploma); translation studies (MA). *Degree requirements:* For other advanced degree, one foreign language.

**Cornell University,** Graduate School, Graduate Fields of Arts and Sciences, Field of Romance Studies, Ithaca, NY 14853. Offers French linguistics (PhD); French literature (PhD); Hispanic literature (PhD); Italian linguistics (PhD); Italian literature (PhD); Romance linguistics (PhD); Spanish linguistics (PhD). *Degree requirements:* For doctorate, 2 foreign languages, comprehensive exam, thesis/dissertation. *Entrance requirements:* For doctorate, GRE General Test, sample of written work, 3 letters of recommendation. Additional exam requirements/recommendations for international students: Required—TOEFL (minimum score 550 paper-based; 77 iBT). Electronic applications accepted. *Faculty research:* Literary theory, Hispanic studies, French studies, gender studies.

**Dalhousie University,** Faculty of Arts and Social Science, Department of French, Halifax, NS B3H 4R2, Canada. Offers MA, PhD. *Entrance requirements:* Additional exam requirements/recommendations for international students: Required—TOEFL, IELTS, CANTEST, CAEL, or Michigan English Language Assessment Battery. Electronic applications accepted. *Faculty research:* Literature, linguistics, French civilization, French and Francophone literature of all periods, translation and cultural studies.

**DePaul University,** College of Liberal Arts and Social Sciences, Chicago, IL 60614. Offers Arabic (MA); Chinese (MA); English (MA); French (MA); German (MA); history (MA); interdisciplinary studies (MA, MS); international public service (MS); international studies (MA); Italian (MA); Japanese (MA); leadership and policy studies (MA); liberal studies (MA); new media studies (MA); nonprofit management (MNM); public administration (MPA); public health (MPH); public service management (MS); social work (MSW); sociology (MA); Spanish (MA); sustainable urban development (MA); women and gender studies (MA); writing and publishing (MA); writing, rhetoric, and discourse (MA); MA/PhD. *Program availability:* Part-time, evening/weekend, online learning. Terminal master's awarded for partial completion of doctoral program. *Degree requirements:* For master's, variable foreign language requirement, comprehensive exam (for some programs), thesis (for some programs). Electronic applications accepted.

**Drew University,** Caspersen School of Graduate Studies, Madison, NJ 07940-1493. Offers conflict resolution and leadership (Certificate), including community leadership, moderation, peace building; history and culture (MA, PhD), including American history, book history, British history, European history, Holocaust and genocide (M Litt, MA, D Litt, PhD), intellectual history, Irish history, print culture, public history; K-12 education (MAT), including art, biology, chemistry, elementary education, English, French, Italian, math, secondary education, special education, teacher of students with disabilities; liberal studies (M Litt, D Litt), including history, Holocaust and genocide (M Litt, MA, D Litt, PhD), Irish/Irish-American studies, literature (M Litt, MMH, D Litt, DMH, CMH), religion, spirituality, teaching in the two-year college, writing; medical humanities (MMH, DMH, CMH), including arts, health, healthcare, literature (M Litt, MMH, D Litt, DMH, CMH); scientific research; poetry (MFA). *Program availability:* Part-time, evening/weekend. *Faculty:* 4 full-time (2 women), 31 part-time/adjunct (16 women). *Students:* 62 full-time (41 women), 199 part-time (130 women); includes 38 minority (17 Black or African American, non-Hispanic/Latino; 3 Asian, non-Hispanic/Latino; 17 Hispanic/Latino; 1 Two or more races, non-Hispanic/Latino), 3 international. Average age 27. 93 applicants, 81% accepted, 46 enrolled. In 2016, 39 master's, 27 doctorates, 26 other advanced degrees awarded. Terminal master's awarded for partial completion of doctoral program. *Degree requirements:* For master's and other advanced degree, thesis (for some programs); for doctorate, one foreign language, comprehensive exam (for some programs), thesis/dissertation. *Entrance requirements:* For master's, PRAXIS Core and Subject Area tests (for MAT), resume, transcripts, writing sample, personal statement, letters of recommendation; for doctorate, GRE (PhD in history and culture), resume, transcripts, writing sample, personal statement, letters of recommendation. Additional exam requirements/recommendations for international students: Required— TOEFL (minimum score 587 paper-based; 94 iBT), IELTS (minimum score 7), TWE (minimum score 4). *Application deadline:* For fall admission, 8/1 for domestic students, 6/1 for international students; for spring admission, 12/1 for domestic students, 10/1 for international students. Applications are processed on a rolling basis. Application fee: $35. Electronic applications accepted. Tuition and fees vary according to program. *Financial support:* Fellowships, research assistantships, teaching assistantships, career-related internships or fieldwork, Federal Work-Study, scholarships/grants, and unspecified assistantships available. Support available to part-time students. Financial award applicants required to submit FAFSA. *Application contact:* Leanne Horinko, Director of Caspersen Admissions, 973-408-3280, E-mail: gradm@drew.edu. Website: http://www.drew.edu/caspersen

**Duke University,** Graduate School, Department of Romance Studies, Durham, NC 27708. Offers French (PhD); Italian (PhD); Spanish (PhD); JD/AM. *Degree requirements:* For doctorate, 2 foreign languages, thesis/dissertation. *Entrance requirements:* For doctorate, GRE General Test. Additional exam requirements/recommendations for international students: Required—TOEFL (minimum score 577 paper-based; 90 iBT) or IELTS (minimum score 7). Electronic applications accepted.

**Eastern University,** Loeb School of Education, St. Davids, PA 19087-3696. Offers ESL program specialist (K-12) (Certificate); general supervisor (PreK-12) (Certificate); health and physical education (K-12) (Certificate); middle level (4-8) (Certificate); multicultural education (M Ed); organizational leadership with education (PhD); Pre K-4 (Certificate); Pre K-4 with special education (Certificate); reading (M Ed); reading specialist (K-12) (Certificate); reading supervisor (K-12) (Certificate); school health supervisor (Certificate); school nurse (K-12) (Certificate); secondary biology education (7-12) (Certificate); secondary chemistry education (7-12) (Certificate); secondary communication education (7-12) (Certificate); secondary education (7-12) (Certificate); secondary English education (7-12) (Certificate); secondary math education (7-12) (Certificate); secondary social studies education (7-12) (Certificate); special education (M Ed); special education (7-12) (Certificate); special education (Pre K-8) (Certificate); special education supervisor (N-12) (Certificate); TESOL (M Ed); world language (Certificate), including French, Spanish. *Program availability:* Part-time, evening/

weekend, online learning. *Students:* 41 full-time (32 women), 89 part-time (68 women); includes 54 minority (38 Black or African American, non-Hispanic/Latino; 3 Asian, non-Hispanic/Latino; 11 Hispanic/Latino; 2 Two or more races, non-Hispanic/Latino), 2 international. Average age 37. In 2016, 64 master's awarded. *Entrance requirements:* Additional exam requirements/recommendations for international students: Required— TOEFL. *Application deadline:* Applications are processed on a rolling basis. Application fee: $35. Electronic applications accepted. Application fee is waived when completed online. *Expenses:* $690 per credit. *Unit head:* Michael Dziedziak, Executive Director of Enrollment, 800-452-0996, E-mail: gpsadmissions@eastern.edu. Website: http://www.eastern.edu/academics/programs/loeb-school-education-0

**Emory University,** Laney Graduate School, Department of French and Italian, Atlanta, GA 30322-1100. Offers French (PhD); French and educational studies (PhD). *Degree requirements:* For doctorate, one foreign language, comprehensive exam, thesis/dissertation. *Entrance requirements:* For doctorate, GRE General Test. Additional exam requirements/recommendations for international students: Recommended—TOEFL. Electronic applications accepted. *Faculty research:* French literature through multidisciplinary critical approaches, second language acquisition theory.

**Florida Atlantic University,** College of Education, Department of Teaching and Learning, Boca Raton, FL 33431-0991. Offers curriculum and instruction (M Ed), including art, biology, chemistry, English, French, German, mathematics, music, physics, Pre-K and primary education, reading, social sciences, Spanish; elementary education (M Ed); environmental education (M Ed); reading education (M Ed); social foundations of education (M Ed), including educational psychology, educational technology, multilingual education. *Accreditation:* NCATE. *Program availability:* Part-time, evening/weekend. *Faculty:* 15 full-time (12 women), 2 part-time/adjunct (1 woman). *Students:* 25 full-time (20 women), 41 part-time (37 women); includes 18 minority (9 Black or African American, non-Hispanic/Latino; 2 Asian, non-Hispanic/Latino; 7 Hispanic/Latino), 7 international. Average age 32. 54 applicants, 59% accepted, 18 enrolled. In 2016, 36 master's awarded. *Entrance requirements:* For master's, GRE General Test, minimum GPA of 3.0 in last 2 years of undergraduate course work. Additional exam requirements/recommendations for international students: Required—TOEFL (minimum score 500 paper-based; 61 iBT), IELTS (minimum score 6). *Application deadline:* For fall admission, 7/1 for domestic students, 2/15 for international students; for spring admission, 11/1 for domestic students, 7/15 for international students. Applications are processed on a rolling basis. Application fee: $30. *Expenses:* Tuition, state resident: full-time $7392; part-time $369.82 per credit hour. Tuition, nonresident: full-time $19,432; part-time $1024.81 per credit hour. *Financial support:* Fellowships with partial tuition reimbursements, research assistantships with partial tuition reimbursements, teaching assistantships with partial tuition reimbursements, career-related internships or fieldwork, scholarships/grants, and unspecified assistantships available. *Faculty research:* Technology, teaching English to speakers of other languages, math teaching, electronic portfolio assessment, global perspectives through social studies. *Unit head:* Dr. Barbara Ridener, Chairperson, 561-297-3588, E-mail: bridener@fau.edu. *Application contact:* Dr. Eliah Watlington, Associate Dean, 561-296-8520, Fax: 261-297-2991, E-mail: ewatling@fau.edu. Website: http://www.coe.fau.edu/academicdepartments/tl/

**Florida Atlantic University,** Dorothy F. Schmidt College of Arts and Letters, Department of Languages, Linguistics, and Comparative Literature, Boca Raton, FL 33431-0991. Offers comparative literature (MA); French (MA); linguistics (MA); Spanish (MA). *Program availability:* Part-time. *Faculty:* 22 full-time (13 women). *Students:* 41 full-time (26 women), 16 part-time (12 women); includes 21 minority (9 Black or African American, non-Hispanic/Latino; 1 Asian, non-Hispanic/Latino; 11 Hispanic/Latino), 11 international. Average age 35. 48 applicants, 38% accepted, 11 enrolled. In 2016, 20 master's awarded. *Degree requirements:* For master's, one foreign language, comprehensive exam, thesis optional. *Entrance requirements:* For master's, GRE General Test, minimum GPA of 3.0. Additional exam requirements/recommendations for international students: Required—TOEFL (minimum score 500 paper-based; 61 iBT), IELTS (minimum score 6). *Application deadline:* For fall admission, 7/1 priority date for domestic students, 2/15 for international students; for spring admission, 11/1 for domestic students, 7/15 for international students. Applications are processed on a rolling basis. Application fee: $30. *Expenses:* Tuition, state resident: full-time $7392; part-time $369.82 per credit hour. Tuition, nonresident: full-time $19,432; part-time $1024.81 per credit hour. *Financial support:* Fellowships, research assistantships, teaching assistantships with partial tuition reimbursements, Federal Work-Study, and tuition waivers (partial) available. Support available to part-time students. Financial award application deadline: 4/1. *Faculty research:* Modern European studies, modern Latin America, medieval Europe. *Unit head:* Dr. Marcella Munson, Chair, 561-297-2118, Fax: 561-297-2756, E-mail: mmunson@fau.edu. *Application contact:* Dr. Linda Johnson, Associate Dean, 561-297-0928, Fax: 561-297-2744. Website: http://www.fau.edu/LLCL/

**Florida State University,** The Graduate School, College of Arts and Sciences, Department of Modern Languages and Linguistics, Program in French, Tallahassee, FL 32306. Offers MA, PhD. *Faculty:* 7 full-time (4 women), 1 (woman) part-time/adjunct. *Students:* 19 full-time (10 women); includes 4 minority (3 Black or African American, non-Hispanic/Latino; 1 Asian, non-Hispanic/Latino). Average age 25. 13 applicants, 77% accepted, 9 enrolled. In 2016, 2 master's awarded. Terminal master's awarded for partial completion of doctoral program. *Degree requirements:* For master's, comprehensive exam, thesis optional; for doctorate, 2 foreign languages, thesis/dissertation, reading knowledge of French and 2 other languages. *Entrance requirements:* For master's and doctorate, GRE General Test, minimum GPA of 3.0. Additional exam requirements/recommendations for international students: Required—TOEFL (minimum score 550 paper-based; 80 iBT). *Application deadline:* For fall admission, 1/15 for domestic and international students. Applications are processed on a rolling basis. Application fee: $30. Electronic applications accepted. *Expenses:* Tuition, state resident: full-time $7263; part-time $403.51 per credit hour. Tuition, nonresident: full-time $18,087; part-time $1004.85 per credit hour. *Required fees:* $1365; $75.81 per credit hour. $20 per semester. Tuition and fees vary according to campus/location. *Financial support:* In 2016–17, fellowships with partial tuition reimbursements (averaging $16,500 per year), research assistantships with partial tuition reimbursements (averaging $9,500 per year), 9 teaching assistantships with partial tuition reimbursements (averaging $14,500 per year) were awarded. Financial award application deadline: 1/15; financial award applicants required to submit FAFSA. *Faculty research:* Twentieth-century European novel, Renaissance and Middle Ages literature, second language acquisition. *Unit head:* Dr. Mark Pietralunga, Chair, 850-644-8600, Fax: 850-644-0524, E-mail: mpietralunga@fsu.edu. *Application contact:* Wendy E. Pigott, Graduate Academic Coordinator, 850-644-8397, Fax: 850-644-0524, E-mail: wpigott@fsu.edu. Website: http://www.modlang.fsu.edu/Programs2/French/Graduate-Programs

**George Mason University,** College of Humanities and Social Sciences, Department of Modern and Classical Languages, Fairfax, VA 22030. Offers foreign languages (MA), including French. *Faculty:* 30 full-time (21 women), 44 part-time/adjunct (29 women). *Students:* 4 full-time (all women), 22 part-time (18 women); includes 19 minority (1 Black or African American, non-Hispanic/Latino; 1 Asian, non-Hispanic/Latino; 16 Hispanic/

Latino; 1 Two or more races, non-Hispanic/Latino), 1 international. Average age 36. 11 applicants, 91% accepted, 7 enrolled. In 2016, 7 master's awarded. *Degree requirements:* For master's, comprehensive exam, thesis optional. *Entrance requirements:* For master's, 3 letters of recommendation; official transcripts; goals statement; baccalaureate degree in French or Spanish with minimum GPA of 3.0 (recommended). Additional exam requirements/recommendations for international students: Required—TOEFL (minimum score 575 paper-based; 88 iBT), IELTS (minimum score 6.5), PTE (minimum score 59). *Application deadline:* For fall admission, 4/15 for domestic students. Application fee: $75 ($80 for international students). Electronic applications accepted. *Expenses:* Tuition, state resident: full-time $10,628; part-time $443 per credit. Tuition, nonresident: full-time $29,306; part-time $1221 per credit. *Required fees:* $3096; $129 per credit. Tuition and fees vary according to program. *Financial support:* In 2016–17, 3 students received support, including 3 teaching assistantships with tuition reimbursements available (averaging $10,723 per year); career-related internships or fieldwork, Federal Work-Study, scholarships/grants, unspecified assistantships, and health care benefits (for full-time research or teaching assistantship recipients) also available. Support available to part-time students. Financial award application deadline: 3/1; financial award applicants required to submit FAFSA. *Faculty research:* French Renaissance studies, early Modern (sixteenth- to eighteenth-centuries) literary and cultural studies, history, literature and philosophy, women's studies. *Total annual research expenditures:* $4,138. *Unit head:* Rei Berroa, Chair, 703-993-1220, Fax: 703-993-1245, E-mail: rberroa@gmu.edu. *Application contact:* Jen Barnard, Office Manager, 703-993-1230, Fax: 703-993-1245, E-mail: jbarnard@gmu.edu.
Website: http://mcl.gmu.edu/

**Georgia State University,** College of Arts and Sciences, Department of World Languages and Cultures, Program in French, Atlanta, GA 30302-3083. Offers applied linguistics and pedagogy (MA); French studies (MA); literature and culture (MA). *Program availability:* Part-time. *Degree requirements:* For master's, one foreign language, comprehensive exam, thesis or alternative, Graduate Foreign Language Reading Exam. *Entrance requirements:* For master's, GRE, statement of purpose, writing sample in the target language, 2 letters of recommendation, official transcripts. Additional exam requirements/recommendations for international students: Required—TOEFL (minimum score 79 iBT). *Application deadline:* For fall admission, 3/15 priority date for domestic and international students; for spring admission, 11/15 priority date for domestic and international students. Application fee: $50. Electronic applications accepted. *Expenses:* Tuition, state resident: full-time $6876; part-time $382 per credit hour. Tuition, nonresident: full-time $22,374; part-time $1243 per credit hour. *Required fees:* $2128; $1064 per term. Part-time tuition and fees vary according to course load and program. *Financial support:* Institutionally sponsored loans available. Financial award applicants required to submit FAFSA. *Faculty research:* The nineteenth-century novel, narratology, genetic criticism, poetics, semiotics, and intertextuality; Francophone and transnational studies; early modern travel literature; post/colonial and Diaspora studies; film studies; social and gender studies; eighteenth century French literature and history of ideas; history of civilization; Enlightenment, encyclopedism. *Unit head:* Dr. Fernando Reati, Department Chair, 404-413-5984, Fax: 404-413-5982, E-mail: freati@gsu.edu. *Application contact:* Lita Malveaux, Administrative Academic Specialist, 404-413-5046, Fax: 404-413-5036, E-mail: lmalveaux@gsu.edu.
Website: http://www.gsu.edu/~wwwmcl/

**Georgia State University,** College of Arts and Sciences, Department of World Languages and Cultures, Program in Translation and Interpretation, Atlanta, GA 30302-3083. Offers interpretation (Certificate), including Spanish; translation (Certificate), including French, German, Spanish. *Program availability:* Part-time. *Entrance requirements:* For degree, entrance examination involving translating one passage from English to the target language and one passage from the target language to English, 3 letters of recommendation, resume/curriculum vitae, official transcripts. Additional exam requirements/recommendations for international students: Required—TOEFL (minimum score 79 iBT). *Application deadline:* For fall admission, 3/15 priority date for domestic and international students; for spring admission, 11/15 priority date for domestic and international students. Application fee: $50. Electronic applications accepted. *Expenses:* Tuition, state resident: full-time $6876; part-time $382 per credit hour. Tuition, nonresident: full-time $22,374; part-time $1243 per credit hour. *Required fees:* $2128; $1064 per term. Part-time tuition and fees vary according to course load and program. *Faculty research:* Romance linguistics and translation; theory and practice of translation; medical and legal interpretation. *Unit head:* Dr. Fernando Reati, Chair, 404-413-5984, Fax: 404-413-5982, E-mail: freati@gsu.edu. *Application contact:* Lita Malveaux, Administrative Academic Specialist, 404-413-5046, Fax: 404-413-5036, E-mail: lmalveaux@gsu.edu.
Website: http://wlc.gsu.edu/home/graduate/graduate-certificate/

**The Graduate Center, City University of New York,** Graduate Studies, Program in French, New York, NY 10016-4039. Offers PhD. *Degree requirements:* For doctorate, 2 foreign languages, thesis/dissertation. *Entrance requirements:* For doctorate, GRE General Test. Additional exam requirements/recommendations for international students: Required—TOEFL. Electronic applications accepted.

**Harvard University,** Graduate School of Arts and Sciences, Department of Romance Languages and Literatures, Cambridge, MA 02138. Offers French (AM, PhD); Italian (AM, PhD); Portuguese (AM, PhD); Spanish (AM, PhD). Terminal master's awarded for partial completion of doctoral program. *Degree requirements:* For master's, 2 foreign languages; for doctorate, 2 foreign languages, thesis/dissertation. *Entrance requirements:* For master's and doctorate, GRE General Test, sample of written work. Additional exam requirements/recommendations for international students: Required—TOEFL.

**Howard University,** Graduate School, Department of Modern Languages and Literatures, Washington, DC 20059-0002. Offers French (MA); Spanish (MA). *Program availability:* Part-time. *Degree requirements:* For master's, one foreign language, comprehensive exam, thesis. *Entrance requirements:* For master's, GRE General Test, writing samples in English and French or Spanish. *Faculty research:* African literature in French, Spanish linguistics, Spanish Peninsular literature, Spanish sociolinguistics.

**Hunter College of the City University of New York,** Graduate School, School of Arts and Sciences, Department of Romance Languages, Program in French, New York, NY 10065-5085. Offers MA. *Program availability:* Part-time, evening/weekend. *Students:* 3 part-time (all women); includes 1 minority (Black or African American, non-Hispanic/Latino), 2 international. Average age 28. 3 applicants, 67% accepted, 1 enrolled. In 2016, 2 master's awarded. *Degree requirements:* For master's, 2 foreign languages, comprehensive exam, thesis optional. *Entrance requirements:* For master's, GRE General Test, GRE Subject Test, ability to read, speak, and write French; interview. Additional exam requirements/recommendations for international students: Required—TOEFL. *Application deadline:* For fall admission, 4/1 for domestic students, 2/1 for international students; for spring admission, 11/1 for domestic students, 9/1 for international students. *Financial support:* Fellowships, Federal Work-Study, scholarships/grants, and tuition waivers (partial) available. Support available to part-time students. Financial award application deadline: 4/15. *Faculty research:* Contemporary French theater, Villiers de l 'Isle-Adam, Voltaire, medieval folklore, fin-de-siècle. *Unit*

head: Prof. Marlene Barsoum, Graduate Advisor, 212-650-3511, E-mail: mbarsoum@hunter.cuny.edu. *Application contact:* Milena Solo, Director for Graduate Admissions, 212-772-4480, E-mail: milena.solo@hunter.cuny.edu.
Website: http://www.hunter.cuny.edu/romancelanguages/graduate/ma-requirements

**Illinois State University,** Graduate School, College of Arts and Sciences, Department of Foreign Languages, Literatures and Cultures, Normal, IL 61790-2200. Offers French (MA); French and German (MA); French and Spanish (MA); German (MA); German and Spanish (MA); Spanish (MA). *Degree requirements:* For master's, variable foreign language requirement, comprehensive exam, 1 term of residency. *Entrance requirements:* For master's, GRE General Test, minimum GPA of 2.8 in last 60 hours of course work.

**Indiana University Bloomington,** University Graduate School, College of Arts and Sciences, Department of French and Italian, Bloomington, IN 47405. Offers French (MA, PhD), including French and Francophone studies (MA), French instruction (MA), French linguistics; Italian (MA, PhD). *Program availability:* Part-time. *Faculty:* 23 full-time (10 women). *Students:* 51 full-time (32 women), 6 part-time (3 women); includes 2 minority (1 Black or African American, non-Hispanic/Latino; 1 Hispanic/Latino), 27 international. Average age 31. 28 applicants, 71% accepted, 7 enrolled. In 2016, 8 master's, 4 doctorates awarded. Terminal master's awarded for partial completion of doctoral program. *Degree requirements:* For master's, variable foreign language requirement, comprehensive exam (for some programs), thesis or alternative; for doctorate, variable foreign language requirement, comprehensive exam, thesis/dissertation. *Entrance requirements:* For master's, GRE General Test, BA or equivalent undergraduate preparation in French or Italian; for doctorate, GRE General Test, MA from degree program at IU; MA in the specific field. Additional exam requirements/recommendations for international students: Required—TOEFL (minimum score 550 paper-based; 79 iBT), GRE General Test (recommended). *Application deadline:* For fall admission, 1/15 priority date for domestic students, 12/1 priority date for international students; for spring admission, 9/1 priority date for domestic and international students. Application fee: $55 ($65 for international students). Electronic applications accepted. *Financial support:* In 2016–17, 40 students received support, including 6 fellowships with partial tuition reimbursements available (averaging $18,000 per year), 2 research assistantships with partial tuition reimbursements available (averaging $15,750 per year), 31 teaching assistantships with partial tuition reimbursements available (averaging $15,750 per year); scholarships/grants, health care benefits, and unspecified assistantships also available. Financial award application deadline: 1/15. *Faculty research:* French and Italian literature, French linguistics, including the novel and political theory, literature and fine arts, literary theory, postcolonialism, French-Creole studies, French literature of Africa and its Diaspora, humanism, Medieval folklore and mythology, humor in Medieval and Renaissance literature, emigration, second language acquisition, syntax, sociolinguistics, phonology, lexicography, media and cultural studies, cinema, drama. *Unit head:* Prof. Massimo Scalabrini, Chair, 812-855-8044, Fax: 812-855-8877, E-mail: mscalabar@indiana.edu. *Application contact:* Lauren Anderson, Graduate Student Services Coordinator, 812-855-1088, Fax: 812-855-8877, E-mail: fritgs@indiana.edu.
Website: http://frit.indiana.edu

**Johns Hopkins University,** Zanvyl Krieger School of Arts and Sciences, Department of German and Romance Languages and Literatures, Baltimore, MD 21218. Offers French (PhD); German (PhD); Italian (PhD); Spanish (PhD). *Degree requirements:* For doctorate, 2 foreign languages, thesis/dissertation. *Entrance requirements:* For doctorate, GRE General Test. Additional exam requirements/recommendations for international students: Required—TOEFL (minimum score 600 paper-based; 100 iBT), IELTS. Electronic applications accepted. *Faculty research:* Nineteenth-century French prose and poetry, genetic theory and criticism; twentieth-century Latin American literature and film; medieval and Renaissance Italian literature; gender and queer theory in German literature; the ideology of Baroque and Neobaroque aesthetics.

**Kent State University,** College of Arts and Sciences, Department of Modern and Classical Language Studies, Kent, OH 44242-0001. Offers French (MA), including applied linguistics and pedagogy, literature; Latin (MA), including applied linguistics and pedagogy, literature; Spanish (MA), including applied linguistics and pedagogy, literature; translation (MA), including Arabic, French, German, Japanese, Russian, Spanish; translation studies (PhD); MA/MBA. *Program availability:* Part-time. *Faculty:* 35 full-time (23 women). *Students:* 81 full-time (51 women), 23 part-time (15 women); includes 14 minority (1 Black or African American, non-Hispanic/Latino; 9 Hispanic/Latino; 4 Two or more races, non-Hispanic/Latino), 48 international. Average age 30. 109 applicants, 53% accepted, 33 enrolled. In 2016, 31 master's, 6 doctorates awarded. *Degree requirements:* For master's, variable foreign language requirement, comprehensive exam (for some programs), thesis (for some programs); for doctorate, variable foreign language requirement, comprehensive exam, thesis/dissertation. *Entrance requirements:* For master's, transcripts, goal statement, 3 letters of recommendation, CD/MP3 with oral sample of first and second languages, writing sample of second language; for doctorate, transcripts; MA in translation, a foreign language, or similar field; proficiency in a foreign language; minimum GPA of 3.5 from MA; goal statement; 3 letters of recommendation; essay or writing sample. *Application deadline:* For fall admission, 2/1 for domestic and international students. Applications are processed on a rolling basis. Application fee: $45 ($70 for international students). Electronic applications accepted. *Expenses:* Tuition, state resident: full-time $10,864; part-time $495 per credit hour. Tuition, nonresident: full-time $18,380; part-time $837 per credit hour. *Financial support:* Fellowships with full tuition reimbursements, teaching assistantships with full tuition reimbursements, and unspecified assistantships available. Financial award application deadline: 2/1. *Unit head:* Dr. Keiran Dunne, Professor of French Translation/Chair, 330-672-2150, E-mail: kdunne@kent.edu. *Application contact:* Said Shiyab, Professor of Translation Studies/Graduate Coordinator, 330-672-1864, E-mail: sshiyab@kent.edu.
Website: http://www.kent.edu/mcls/

**Lake Forest College,** Master of Arts in Teaching Program, Lake Forest, IL 60045. Offers elementary education (MAT); K-12 French (MAT); K-12 music (MAT); K-12 Spanish (MAT); K-12 visual art (MAT); secondary biology (MAT); secondary chemistry (MAT); secondary English (MAT); secondary history (MAT); secondary mathematics (MAT). *Degree requirements:* For master's, comprehensive exam, portfolio. *Entrance requirements:* For master's, GRE.

**Louisiana State University and Agricultural & Mechanical College,** Graduate School, College of Humanities and Social Sciences, Department of French Studies, Baton Rouge, LA 70803. Offers French literature and linguistics (MA, PhD).

**McGill University,** Faculty of Graduate and Postdoctoral Studies, Faculty of Arts, Department of French Language and Literature, Montréal, QC H3A 2T5, Canada. Offers MA, PhD.

**McMaster University,** School of Graduate Studies, Faculty of Humanities, Department of French, Hamilton, ON L8S 4M2, Canada. Offers MA. *Program availability:* Part-time, evening/weekend. *Degree requirements:* For master's, thesis or alternative. *Entrance requirements:* For master's, honors degree in French, minimum B+ average. Additional exam requirements/recommendations for international students: Required—TOEFL (minimum score 580 paper-based). *Faculty research:* Medieval literature, eighteenth-

and nineteenth-century literature, twentieth-century French and Francophone literature, linguistics.

**Memorial University of Newfoundland,** School of Graduate Studies, Department of French and Spanish, St. John's, NL A1C 5S7, Canada. Offers French studies (MA). *Program availability:* Part-time. *Degree requirements:* For master's, one foreign language, thesis. *Entrance requirements:* For master's, honors degree (minimum 2nd class standing). Electronic applications accepted. *Faculty research:* French and French-Canadian literature, literary theory, linguistics, philosophy, translation, Francophone culture.

**Miami University,** College of Arts and Science, Department of French and Italian, Oxford, OH 45056. Offers French (MA). *Students:* 7. In 2016, 4 master's awarded. *Expenses:* Tuition, state resident: full-time $12,890; part-time $564 per credit hour. Tuition, nonresident: full-time $29,604; part-time $1260 per credit hour. *Required fees:* $638. Part-time tuition and fees vary according to course load and program. *Unit head:* Dr. Jonathan Strauss, Chair, 513-529-7508, E-mail: strausja@miamioh.edu. *Application contact:* Dr. Elisabeth Hodges, Graduate Director, 513-529-5809, E-mail: hodgesed@miamioh.edu.
Website: http://www.MiamiOH.edu/frenchitalian/

**Michigan State University,** The Graduate School, College of Arts and Letters, Department of French, Classics, and Italian, East Lansing, MI 48824. Offers French (MA); French language and literature (PhD). *Entrance requirements:* Additional exam requirements/recommendations for international students: Required—TOEFL. Electronic applications accepted.

**Middlebury College,** Language Schools, French School, Middlebury, VT 05753-6002. Offers MA, DML. *Degree requirements:* For master's, one foreign language; for doctorate, 2 foreign languages, comprehensive exam, thesis/dissertation, residence abroad, teaching experience. *Entrance requirements:* For master's, online placement test, 3 letters of recommendation, critical essay, transcripts, personal statement; for doctorate, 1st and 2nd language online placement exam, 3 letters of recommendation, critical essay, transcripts, personal statement, MA in first language, oral interview. Electronic applications accepted. *Expenses:* Contact institution.

**Middle Tennessee State University,** College of Graduate Studies, College of Liberal Arts, Department of Foreign Languages and Literatures, Murfreesboro, TN 37132. Offers foreign languages (MAT), including French, German, Spanish. *Program availability:* Part-time, evening/weekend, online learning. *Degree requirements:* For master's, one foreign language, comprehensive exam, thesis optional. *Entrance requirements:* For master's, GRE. Additional exam requirements/recommendations for international students: Required—TOEFL (minimum score 525 paper-based; 71 iBT) or IELTS (minimum score 6). Electronic applications accepted.

**Millersville University of Pennsylvania,** College of Graduate Studies and Adult Learning, College of Arts, Humanities and Social Sciences, Department of Foreign Languages, Program in Languages and Cultures: French Option, Millersville, PA 17551-0302. Offers MA. Program offered in collaboration with West Chester University of Pennsylvania. *Program availability:* Part-time. *Faculty:* 7 full-time (4 women). *Students:* 1 (woman) part-time. Average age 51. *Degree requirements:* For master's, one foreign language, comprehensive exam (for some programs), thesis optional, exam, portfolio, or research project and presentation. *Entrance requirements:* For master's, ACTFL, OPI, OPIc and WPT, baccalaureate degree from regionally-accredited four-year college or university. Additional exam requirements/recommendations for international students: Required—TOEFL (minimum score 600 paper-based), IELTS (minimum score 6). *Application deadline:* Applications are processed on a rolling basis. Application fee: $40. Electronic applications accepted. *Expenses:* $483 per credit resident tuition; $725 per credit non-resident tuition. *Financial support:* Unspecified assistantships available. Financial award application deadline: 3/15; financial award applicants required to submit FAFSA. *Faculty research:* Detective fiction and women's literature. *Unit head:* Dr. Christine M. Gaudry, Associate Professor/Program Contact, 717-871-7152, Fax: 717-871-7935, E-mail: christine.gaudry@millersville.edu. *Application contact:* Dr. Victor S. DeSantis, Dean of College of Graduate Studies and Adult Learning/Associate Provost for Civic and Community Engagement, 717-871-7619, Fax: 717-871-7954, E-mail: victor.desantis@millersville.edu.
Website: http://www.millersville.edu/forlang/

**Minnesota State University Mankato,** College of Graduate Studies and Research, College of Arts and Humanities, Department of World Languages and Cultures, Program in French, Mankato, MN 56001. Offers French (MS); French education (MS). *Students:* 3 full-time (2 women), 1 (woman) part-time. *Degree requirements:* For master's, one foreign language, comprehensive exam, thesis or alternative. *Entrance requirements:* For master's, minimum GPA of 3.0 during previous 2 years. Additional exam requirements/recommendations for international students: Required—TOEFL. *Application deadline:* For fall admission, 7/1 priority date for domestic students; for spring admission, 11/1 for domestic students. Applications are processed on a rolling basis. Application fee: $40. Electronic applications accepted. *Financial support:* Research assistantships, teaching assistantships with full tuition reimbursements, and unspecified assistantships available. Financial award application deadline: 3/15; financial award applicants required to submit FAFSA.

**Montclair State University,** The Graduate School, College of Education and Human Services, MAT Program in Teaching, Montclair, NJ 07043-1624. Offers art (MAT); biology (MAT); chemistry (MAT); earth science (MAT); English (MAT); French (MAT); health and physical education (MAT); health education (MAT); mathematics (MAT); music (MAT); physical education (MAT); physical science (MAT); social studies (MAT); Spanish (MAT); teacher of English as a second language (MAT). *Degree requirements:* For master's, comprehensive exam, thesis or alternative. *Entrance requirements:* For master's, interview, 2 letters of recommendation. Additional exam requirements/recommendations for international students: Required—TOEFL (minimum score 83 iBT), IELTS (minimum score 6.5). Electronic applications accepted. *Expenses:* Tuition, state resident: part-time $553 per credit. Tuition, nonresident: part-time $854 per credit. *Required fees:* $91 per credit. Tuition and fees vary according to program.

**Montclair State University,** The Graduate School, College of Humanities and Social Sciences, Program in French, Montclair, NJ 07043-1624. Offers French literature (MA); French studies (MA). *Program availability:* Part-time, evening/weekend. *Degree requirements:* For master's, comprehensive exam, thesis optional. *Entrance requirements:* Additional exam requirements/recommendations for international students: Required—TOEFL (minimum score 83 iBT), IELTS (minimum score 6.5). Electronic applications accepted. *Expenses:* Tuition, state resident: part-time $553 per credit. Tuition, nonresident: part-time $854 per credit. *Required fees:* $91 per credit. Tuition and fees vary according to program. *Faculty research:* Medieval to twentieth-century French literature, Francophone studies, critical theory, language pedagogy.

**New York University,** Graduate School of Arts and Science, Center for French Civilization and Culture, Department of French, New York, NY 10012-1019. Offers French (PhD); French language and civilization (MA); French literature (MA); Romance languages and literatures (MA). *Program availability:* Part-time. Terminal master's awarded for partial completion of doctoral program. *Degree requirements:* For master's, one foreign language, thesis (for some programs); for doctorate, one foreign language,

thesis/dissertation. *Entrance requirements:* For master's and doctorate, GRE General Test, proficiency in French. Additional exam requirements/recommendations for international students: Required—TOEFL. *Faculty research:* French and Francophone literature, literary theory, and history; rhetoric and poetics; cultural history; theater and cinema.

**New York University,** Graduate School of Arts and Science, Center for French Civilization and Culture, Institute of French Studies, New York, NY 10012-1019. Offers French civilization (PhD); French studies (MA, PhD, Advanced Certificate); French studies and anthropology (PhD); French studies and history (PhD); French studies and journalism (MA); French studies and sociology (PhD); JD/MA; MBA/MA. *Program availability:* Part-time. Terminal master's awarded for partial completion of doctoral program. *Degree requirements:* For master's, one foreign language, comprehensive exam; for doctorate, one foreign language, thesis/dissertation, qualifying exam. *Entrance requirements:* For master's and doctorate, GRE General Test, knowledge of French. Additional exam requirements/recommendations for international students: Required—TOEFL. *Faculty research:* Contemporary French society, politics, economy, and culture; French history since 1789; French cultural studies, French colonialism and the post-colonial world; France and the European community.

**New York University,** Steinhardt School of Culture, Education, and Human Development, Department of Teaching and Learning, Program in Multilingual/Multicultural Studies, New York, NY 10003. Offers bilingual education (MA, PhD, Advanced Certificate); foreign language education (MA); teaching English to speakers of other languages (MA, PhD); teaching foreign languages, 7-12 (MA), including Chinese, French, Italian, Japanese, Spanish; teaching French as a foreign language (MA), including teaching English to speakers of other languages; teaching Spanish as a foreign language (MA), including teaching English to speakers of other languages. *Accreditation:* TEAC. *Program availability:* Part-time, evening/weekend. *Degree requirements:* For master's, thesis (for some programs); for doctorate, thesis/dissertation. *Entrance requirements:* For doctorate, GRE General Test, interview; for Advanced Certificate, master's degree. Additional exam requirements/recommendations for international students: Required—TOEFL (minimum score 100 iBT). Electronic applications accepted. *Faculty research:* Second language acquisition, cross-cultural communication, technology-enhanced language learning, language variation, action learning.

**North Carolina State University,** Graduate School, College of Humanities and Social Sciences, Department of Foreign Languages and Literatures, Program in French Language and Literature, Raleigh, NC 27695. Offers MA. *Degree requirements:* For master's, thesis optional. *Entrance requirements:* For master's, fluency in French. Electronic applications accepted. *Faculty research:* 19th-century visual culture, translation, cinema, modern theater, linguistics.

**Northern Illinois University,** Graduate School, College of Liberal Arts and Sciences, Department of Foreign Languages and Literatures, De Kalb, IL 60115-2854. Offers French (MA); Spanish (MA). *Program availability:* Part-time. *Faculty:* 25 full-time (11 women). *Students:* 3 full-time (0 women), 9 part-time (6 women); includes 8 minority (1 Black or African American, non-Hispanic/Latino; 1 Asian, non-Hispanic/Latino; 6 Hispanic/Latino). Average age 34. 6 applicants, 67% accepted, 1 enrolled. In 2016, 7 master's awarded. *Degree requirements:* For master's, one foreign language, comprehensive exam, thesis or alternative, language proficiency exam. *Entrance requirements:* For master's, GRE General Test, interview, minimum GPA of 2.75, undergraduate major in French or Spanish. Additional exam requirements/recommendations for international students: Required—TOEFL (minimum score 550 paper-based). *Application deadline:* For fall admission, 6/1 for domestic students, 5/1 for international students; for spring admission, 11/1 for domestic students, 10/1 for international students. Applications are processed on a rolling basis. Application fee: $40. Electronic applications accepted. *Financial support:* In 2016–17, 6 teaching assistantships with full tuition reimbursements were awarded; fellowships with full tuition reimbursements, research assistantships with full tuition reimbursements, career-related internships or fieldwork, Federal Work-Study, scholarships/grants, tuition waivers (full), and unspecified assistantships also available. Support available to part-time students. Financial award applicants required to submit FAFSA. *Faculty research:* Francophone women writers, prosodies of French and Italian, early Spanish drama, business German, history of Burmese literature. *Unit head:* Dr. Katharina Barbe, Chair, 815-753-1559, Fax: 815-753-5989, E-mail: kbarbe@niu.edu. *Application contact:* Graduate School Office, 815-753-0395, E-mail: gradsch@niu.edu.
Website: http://www.forlangs.net/

**Northwestern University,** The Graduate School, Judd A. and Marjorie Weinberg College of Arts and Sciences, Department of French and Italian, Evanston, IL 60208. Offers French/Francophone studies (PhD); Italian studies (Graduate Certificate). Admissions and degrees offered through The Graduate School. *Degree requirements:* For doctorate, one foreign language, thesis/dissertation, written and oral exams. *Entrance requirements:* For doctorate, GRE, writing sample, cassette recording. Additional exam requirements/recommendations for international students: Required—TOEFL. *Faculty research:* Francophone studies, eighteenth century contemporary theory.

**The Ohio State University,** Graduate School, College of Arts and Sciences, Division of Arts and Humanities, Department of French and Italian, Columbus, OH 43210. Offers French (MA, PhD); Italian (MA); Italian studies (PhD). *Faculty:* 11. *Students:* 24 full-time (12 women), 9 international. Average age 31. In 2016, 5 master's, 1 doctorate awarded. Terminal master's awarded for partial completion of doctoral program. *Degree requirements:* For master's, variable foreign language requirement, thesis optional; for doctorate, variable foreign language requirement, thesis/dissertation. *Entrance requirements:* For master's and doctorate, GRE General Test. Additional exam requirements/recommendations for international students: Required—TOEFL (minimum score 550 paper-based; 79 iBT), IELTS (minimum score 7), Michigan English Language Assessment Battery (minimum score 82). *Application deadline:* For fall admission, 12/15 priority date for domestic students, 11/30 priority date for international students; for spring admission, 3/1 for domestic students, 2/1 for international students. Applications are processed on a rolling basis. Application fee: $60 ($70 for international students). Electronic applications accepted. *Financial support:* Fellowships with tuition reimbursements, research assistantships with tuition reimbursements, teaching assistantships with tuition reimbursements, Federal Work-Study, institutionally sponsored loans, and unspecified assistantships available. Support available to part-time students. *Faculty research:* Italian and Romance linguistics. *Unit head:* Dr. Jennifer Willging, Chair, 614-292-4938, E-mail: willging.1@osu.edu. *Application contact:* Graduate and Professional Admissions, 614-292-9444, Fax: 614-292-3895, E-mail: gpadmissions@osu.edu.
Website: http://frit.osu.edu/

**Ohio University,** Graduate College, College of Arts and Sciences, Department of Modern Languages, Athens, OH 45701-2979. Offers French (MA); Spanish (MA). *Program availability:* Part-time. *Degree requirements:* For master's, 2 foreign languages, comprehensive exam, thesis optional. *Entrance requirements:* For master's, oral and written samples. Additional exam requirements/recommendations for international students: Required—TOEFL (minimum score 550 paper-based; 80 iBT) or IELTS (minimum score 6.5). *Application deadline:* For fall admission, 1/15 priority date for domestic and international students. Application fee: $50 ($55 for international students). Electronic applications accepted. *Financial support:* Teaching assistantships with tuition reimbursements, Federal Work-Study, institutionally sponsored loans, and tuition waivers (partial) available. Financial award application deadline: 1/15. *Faculty research:* French and Spanish language and literature. *Unit head:* Greg Kessler, 740-593-2748, E-mail: kessler@ohio.edu. Website: http://www.ohio.edu/modlang/

**Penn State University Park,** Graduate School, College of the Liberal Arts, Department of French and Francophone Studies, University Park, PA 16802. Offers French (MA, PhD). *Unit head:* Dr. Susan Welch, Dean, 814-865-7691, Fax: 814-863-2085. *Application contact:* Lori Hawn, Director, Graduate Student Services, 814-865-1795, Fax: 814-863-4627, E-mail: l-gswww@lists.psu.edu. Website: http://french.psu.edu/

**Portland State University,** Graduate Studies, College of Liberal Arts and Sciences, Department of World Languages and Literatures, Portland, OR 97207-0751. Offers French (MA); German (MA); Japanese (MA); Spanish (MA); world literature and language (MA). *Program availability:* Part-time. *Faculty:* 45 full-time (25 women), 39 part-time/adjunct (27 women). *Students:* 22 full-time (13 women), 6 part-time (3 women); includes 8 minority (2 Asian, non-Hispanic/Latino; 6 Hispanic/Latino), 4 international. Average age 31. 19 applicants, 53% accepted, 8 enrolled. In 2016, 18 master's awarded. *Degree requirements:* For master's, one foreign language, thesis (for some programs). *Entrance requirements:* Additional exam requirements/recommendations for international students: Required—TOEFL (minimum score 550 paper-based; 80 iBT), IELTS (minimum score 6.5). *Application deadline:* For fall admission, 4/1 for domestic students, 3/1 for international students; for winter admission, 9/1 for domestic students, 7/1 for international students; for spring admission, 11/1 for domestic and international students. Applications are processed on a rolling basis. Application fee: $65. *Expenses:* Contact institution. *Financial support:* In 2016–17, 18 teaching assistantships with tuition reimbursements (averaging $10,805 per year) were awarded; research assistantships, Federal Work-Study, scholarships/grants, and unspecified assistantships also available. Support available to part-time students. Financial award application deadline: 3/1; financial award applicants required to submit FAFSA. *Faculty research:* Foreign language pedagogy, applied and social linguistics, literary history and criticism. *Total annual research expenditures:* $396,300. *Unit head:* Dr. Gina Greco, Chair, 503-725-5287, E-mail: grecog@pdx.edu. *Application contact:* Kelli Martin, Graduate Admissions Coordinator, 503-725-3243, E-mail: kmarti@pdx.edu. Website: http://www.pdx.edu/wll/

**Princeton University,** Graduate School, Department of French and Italian, Princeton, NJ 08544-1019. Offers French language and literature (PhD). *Degree requirements:* For doctorate, variable foreign language requirement, thesis/dissertation. *Entrance requirements:* For doctorate, GRE General Test, sample of written work. Additional exam requirements/recommendations for international students: Required—TOEFL (minimum score 600 paper-based). Electronic applications accepted.

**Purdue University,** Graduate School, College of Liberal Arts, School of Languages and Cultures, West Lafayette, IN 47907. Offers French (MA, MAT, PhD), including French (MA, PhD), French education (MAT); German (MA, MAT, PhD), including German (MA, PhD), German education (MAT); Japanese pedagogy (MA); Spanish (MA, MAT, PhD), including Spanish (MA, PhD), Spanish education (MAT). *Faculty:* 44 full-time (22 women), 1 (woman) part-time/adjunct. *Students:* 37 full-time (18 women), 41 part-time (30 women); includes 9 minority (1 Asian, non-Hispanic/Latino; 8 Hispanic/Latino), 52 international. Average age 32. 49 applicants, 39% accepted, 14 enrolled. In 2016, 11 master's, 5 doctorates awarded. Terminal master's awarded for partial completion of doctoral program. *Degree requirements:* For master's, one foreign language; for doctorate, 2 foreign languages, thesis/dissertation. *Entrance requirements:* For master's, GRE General Test (minimum score 600, 160 for new scoring), two writing samples, one in English, one in language (French, German, Japanese, or Spanish); sample recording of English and language of study; for doctorate, GRE General Test (minimum score 600, 160 for new scoring), master's degree with minimum GPA of 3.5 or equivalent; two writing samples, one in English, one in language (French, German, Japanese, or Spanish); sample recording of English and language of study. Additional exam requirements/recommendations for international students: Required—TOEFL (minimum score 550 paper-based; 77 iBT); Recommended—TWE. *Application deadline:* For fall admission, 12/12 for domestic and international students; for spring admission, 10/1 for domestic and international students. Applications are processed on a rolling basis. Application fee: $60 ($75 for international students). Electronic applications accepted. *Financial support:* In 2016–17, fellowships with tuition reimbursements (averaging $15,750 per year), teaching assistantships with tuition reimbursements (averaging $13,463 per year) were awarded. Support available to part-time students. Financial award applicants required to submit FAFSA. *Faculty research:* Linguistics, semiotics, literary criticism, pedagogy. *Unit head:* Dr. Madeleine M. Henry, Head, 765-494-3828, E-mail: henry48@purdue.edu. *Application contact:* Joni L. Hipsher, Graduate Contact, 765-494-3841, E-mail: jlhipshe@purdue.edu. Website: http://www.cla.purdue.edu/slc/main/

**Queens College of the City University of New York,** Arts and Humanities Division, Department of European Languages and Literatures, Queens, NY 11367-1597. Offers French (MA); Italian (MA). *Program availability:* Part-time. *Faculty:* 12 full-time (7 women), 16 part-time/adjunct (12 women). *Students:* 3 full-time (2 women), 8 part-time (5 women); includes 2 minority (both Black or African American, non-Hispanic/Latino). Average age 37. 11 applicants, 82% accepted, 6 enrolled. In 2016, 1 master's awarded. *Degree requirements:* For master's, 2 foreign languages, thesis optional, oral exam. *Entrance requirements:* For master's, minimum GPA of 3.0. Additional exam requirements/recommendations for international students: Required—TOEFL (minimum score 61 iBT), IELTS (minimum score 5). *Application deadline:* For fall admission, 4/1 for domestic students; for spring admission, 11/1 for domestic students. Applications are processed on a rolling basis. Application fee: $125. Electronic applications accepted. *Expenses:* Tuition, state resident: full-time $5065; part-time $425 per credit. Tuition, nonresident: part-time $780 per credit. *Required fees:* $522; $397 per credit. Part-time tuition and fees vary according to course load and program. *Financial support:* Career-related internships or fieldwork, Federal Work-Study, institutionally sponsored loans, and tuition waivers (partial) available. Support available to part-time students. Financial award application deadline: 4/1; financial award applicants required to submit FAFSA. *Unit head:* Dr. David Andrew Jones, Chairperson, 718-997-5980, E-mail: david.jones@qc.cuny.edu.

**Queen's University at Kingston,** School of Graduate Studies, Faculty of Arts and Sciences, Department of French Studies, Kingston, ON K7L 3N6, Canada. Offers MA, PhD. *Program availability:* Part-time. *Degree requirements:* For master's, thesis or 4 credits and oral exam; for doctorate, one foreign language, comprehensive exam, thesis/dissertation. *Entrance requirements:* For master's, minimum B+ average; for doctorate, minimum 80% average. Additional exam requirements/recommendations for international students: Required—TOEFL (minimum score 550 paper-based). Electronic applications accepted. *Faculty research:* Reception of Quebec literature in English

Canada, autobiography and postcolonialism, irony in women's writing, critical editions of renaissance authors, aspectual systems and grammatical categories.

**Rider University,** Department of Graduate Education, Leadership and Counseling, Teacher Certification Program, Lawrenceville, NJ 08648-3001. Offers business education (Certificate); elementary education (Certificate); English as a second language (Certificate); English education (Certificate); mathematics education (Certificate); preschool to grade 3 (Certificate); science education (Certificate); social studies education (Certificate); world languages (Certificate), including French, German, Spanish. *Program availability:* Part-time. *Degree requirements:* For Certificate, internship, professional portfolio. *Entrance requirements:* For degree, PRAXIS, resume. Additional exam requirements/recommendations for international students: Required—TOEFL (minimum score 550 paper-based). Electronic applications accepted. *Faculty research:* Conceptual foundations for optimal development of creativity; creative theory, cognitive processes in mathematics learning, teacher collaboration.

**Rutgers University–New Brunswick,** Graduate School-New Brunswick, Program in French, Piscataway, NJ 08854-8097. Offers French (MA, PhD); French studies (MAT). *Program availability:* Part-time, evening/weekend. Terminal master's awarded for partial completion of doctoral program. *Degree requirements:* For master's, one foreign language, written and oral exams (MA); for doctorate, 3 foreign languages, thesis/dissertation, qualifying exam. *Entrance requirements:* For master's and doctorate, GRE General Test. *Faculty research:* Literatures in French, literary history and theory, rhetoric and poetics.

**St. John Fisher College,** Ralph C. Wilson Jr. School of Education, Program in Adolescence Education and Special Education, Rochester, NY 14618-3597. Offers adolescence education: biology with special education (MS Ed); adolescence education: chemistry with special education (MS Ed); adolescence education: English with special education (MS Ed); adolescence education: French with special education (MS Ed); adolescence education: math with special education (MS Ed); adolescence education: physics with special education (MS Ed); adolescence education: social studies with special education (MS Ed); adolescence education: Spanish with special education (MS Ed). *Program availability:* Part-time, evening/weekend. *Faculty:* 7 full-time (6 women), 5 part-time/adjunct (all women). *Students:* 15 full-time (6 women), 9 part-time (6 women); includes 3 minority (2 Black or African American, non-Hispanic/Latino; 1 Hispanic/Latino). Average age 28. 16 applicants, 56% accepted, 6 enrolled. In 2016, 8 master's awarded. *Degree requirements:* For master's, field experiences, student teaching, LAST. *Entrance requirements:* For master's, 2 letters of recommendation, personal statement, current resume. Additional exam requirements/recommendations for international students: Required—TOEFL (minimum score 575 paper-based; 80 iBT). *Application deadline:* Applications are processed on a rolling basis. Application fee: $30. Electronic applications accepted. *Expenses:* $885 per credit hour. *Financial support:* Scholarships/grants available. Financial award applicants required to submit FAFSA. *Faculty research:* Arts and humanities, urban schools, constructivist learning, at-risk students, mentoring. *Unit head:* Dr. Susan Hildenbrand, Program Director, 585-385-7297, E-mail: shildenbrand@sjfc.edu. *Application contact:* Michelle Gosier, Associate Director of Transfer and Graduate Admissions, 585-385-8064, E-mail: mgosier@sjfc.edu.

**Saint Louis University,** Graduate Education, College of Arts and Sciences, Department of Modern and Classical Languages, St. Louis, MO 63103. Offers French (MA); Spanish (MA). *Program availability:* Part-time. *Degree requirements:* For master's, one foreign language, comprehensive exam, thesis/dissertation (Spanish). *Entrance requirements:* For master's, GRE General Test or MAT, letters of recommendation, resume, interview. Additional exam requirements/recommendations for international students: Required—TOEFL (minimum score 525 paper-based). Electronic applications accepted. *Faculty research:* Culture studies, literature studies, foreign language acquisition.

**San Francisco State University,** Division of Graduate Studies, College of Liberal and Creative Arts, Department of Modern Languages and Literatures, Program in French, San Francisco, CA 94132-1722. Offers MA. *Application deadline:* Applications are processed on a rolling basis. *Expenses:* Tuition, state resident: full-time $6738. Tuition, nonresident: full-time $15,666. *Required fees:* $1012. Tuition and fees vary according to degree level and program. *Unit head:* Dr. Mohammad Salama, Chair, 415-338-7413, Fax: 415-338-6159, E-mail: mrsalama@sfsu.edu. *Application contact:* Dr. Berenice Le Marchand, Graduate Advisor, 415-338-7419, Fax: 415-338-6159, E-mail: blemarch@sfsu.edu. Website: http://www.sfsu.edu/~french

**San Jose State University,** Graduate Studies and Research, College of Humanities and the Arts, San Jose, CA 95192-0001. Offers art (MA, MFA), including art history and visual culture (MA), digital media art (MFA), photography (MFA), pictorial art (MFA), spatial art (MFA); computational linguistics (Certificate); English (MA, MFA), including creative writing (MFA); French (MA); humanities and arts (Certificate); linguistics (MA); music (MA); philosophy (MA); professional and technical communication (Certificate); Spanish (MA); teaching English to speakers of other languages (MA); TESOL (Certificate); theatre arts (MA). Electronic applications accepted.

**Simon Fraser University,** Office of Graduate Studies and Postdoctoral Fellows, Faculty of Arts and Social Sciences, Department of French, Burnaby, BC V5A 1S6, Canada. Offers MA. *Faculty:* 13 full-time (9 women). *Students:* 7 full-time (3 women). 7 applicants, 14% accepted, 1 enrolled. In 2016, 5 master's awarded. *Degree requirements:* For master's, one foreign language, thesis or alternative. *Entrance requirements:* For master's, minimum GPA of 3.0 (on scale of 4.33) or 3.33 based on last 60 credits of undergraduate courses. Additional exam requirements/recommendations for international students: Recommended—TOEFL (minimum score 580 paper-based; 93 iBT), IELTS (minimum score 7), TWE (minimum score 5). *Application deadline:* For fall admission, 7/1 for domestic and international students; for winter admission, 11/1 for domestic and international students; for spring admission, 3/1 for domestic and international students. Applications are processed on a rolling basis. Application fee: $90 ($125 for international students). Electronic applications accepted. *Financial support:* In 2016–17, 5 students received support, including 5 fellowships (averaging $6,500 per year), teaching assistantships (averaging $5,608 per year); career-related internships or fieldwork and scholarships/grants also available. *Faculty research:* French linguistics, Creole linguistics, French literature of the Middle Ages and Ancient Regime, modern and contemporary French literature, French Canadian language and literature. *Unit head:* Dr. Jorge Caleron, Graduate Chair, 778-782-5932, E-mail: fren-gradchar@sfu.ca. *Application contact:* Magda Crinu, Graduate Secretary, 778-782-4740, E-mail: fren-grad-secretary@sfu.ca. Website: http://www.sfu.ca/french/

**Smith College,** Graduate and Special Programs, Department of French Language and Literature, Northampton, MA 01063. Offers secondary education (MAT), including French education. *Program availability:* Part-time. In 2016, 1 master's awarded. *Degree requirements:* For master's, one foreign language. *Entrance requirements:* Additional exam requirements/recommendations for international students: Required—TOEFL (minimum score 595 paper-based; 97 iBT), IELTS. *Application deadline:* For fall admission, 4/1 for domestic students, 1/15 for international students; for spring

*French*

admission, 12/1 for domestic students. Application fee: $60. *Expenses: Tuition:* Full-time $34,560; part-time $1440 per credit. Tuition and fees vary according to course load and program. *Financial support:* In 2016–17, 1 student received support. Scholarships/grants available. Support available to part-time students. Financial award application deadline: 4/1; financial award applicants required to submit CSS PROFILE or FAFSA. *Unit head:* Helene Visentin, Chair, 413-585-3359, E-mail: hvisenti@smith.edu. *Application contact:* Ruth Morgan, Program Assistant, 413-585-3050, Fax: 413-585-3054, E-mail: gradstdy@smith.edu. Website: http://www.smith.edu/french

**Southern Oregon University,** Graduate Studies, Department of Foreign Languages and Literatures, Ashland, OR 97520. Offers French language teaching (MA); Spanish language teaching (MA). *Program availability:* Part-time, online learning. *Faculty:* 4 full-time (2 women), 6 part-time/adjunct (3 women). *Students:* 74 full-time (54 women), 18 part-time (14 women); includes 17 minority (2 Black or African American, non-Hispanic/Latino; 1 American Indian or Alaska Native, non-Hispanic/Latino; 1 Asian, non-Hispanic/Latino; 11 Hispanic/Latino; 2 Two or more races, non-Hispanic/Latino), 1 international. Average age 37. 49 applicants, 84% accepted, 37 enrolled. In 2016, 18 master's awarded. *Degree requirements:* For master's, thesis (for some programs). *Entrance requirements:* For master's, GRE General Test, minimum cumulative GPA of 3.0 in the last 90 quarter credits (60 semester credits) of undergraduate coursework. Additional exam requirements/recommendations for international students: Required—TOEFL (minimum score 540 paper-based; 76 iBT), IELTS (minimum score 6), ELPT (minimum score 964) or ELS (minimum score 112). *Application deadline:* For fall admission, 7/31 priority date for domestic and international students; for winter admission, 11/15 priority date for domestic and international students; for spring admission, 1/7 priority date for domestic and international students. Applications are processed on a rolling basis. Application fee: $60. Electronic applications accepted. *Expenses:* Tuition, state resident: full-time $10,719; part-time $397 per credit. Tuition, nonresident: full-time $13,419; part-time $497 per credit. *Required fees:* $548. *Financial support:* Career-related internships or fieldwork, institutionally sponsored loans, scholarships/grants, and unspecified assistantships available. *Unit head:* Dr. Dan Morris, Graduate French Language Program Coordinator, 541-552-6740, E-mail: morris@sou.edu. *Application contact:* Dr. Anne Connor, Graduate Spanish Language Program Coordinator, 541-552-6743, E-mail: connora@sou.edu. Website: http://www.sou.edu/language/

**Stanford University,** School of Humanities and Sciences, Department of French and Italian, Stanford, CA 94305-2004. Offers French (MA, PhD); French and Italian (PhD); Italian (MA, PhD). Terminal master's awarded for partial completion of doctoral program. *Degree requirements:* For master's, one foreign language, written exam; for doctorate, 2 foreign languages, thesis/dissertation, oral exam. *Entrance requirements:* For master's and doctorate, GRE General Test. Additional exam requirements/recommendations for international students: Required—TOEFL. Electronic applications accepted. *Expenses: Tuition:* Full-time $47,331. *Required fees:* $609.

**State University of New York at New Paltz,** Graduate School, School of Education, Department of Secondary Education, New Paltz, NY 12561. Offers adolescence education: biology (MAT, MS Ed); adolescence education: chemistry (MAT, MS Ed); adolescence education: earth science (MAT, MS Ed); adolescence education: English (MAT, MS Ed); adolescence education: French (MAT, MS Ed); adolescence education: social studies (MAT, MS Ed); adolescence education: Spanish (MAT, MS Ed); second language education (MS Ed, AC), including second language education (MS Ed), teaching English language learners (AC). *Accreditation:* NCATE. *Program availability:* Part-time, evening/weekend. *Students:* 60 full-time (36 women), 59 part-time (48 women); includes 28 minority (2 Black or African American, non-Hispanic/Latino; 2 Asian, non-Hispanic/Latino; 22 Hispanic/Latino; 2 Two or more races, non-Hispanic/Latino). 96 applicants, 83% accepted, 54 enrolled. In 2016, 56 master's awarded. *Degree requirements:* For master's, comprehensive exam (for some programs), portfolio. *Entrance requirements:* For master's, minimum GPA of 3.0, New York state teaching certificate (MS Ed). Additional exam requirements/recommendations for international students: Required—TOEFL (minimum score 550 paper-based; 80 iBT), IELTS (minimum score 6.5). *Application deadline:* For fall admission, 3/1 priority date for domestic students, 3/1 for international students; for spring admission, 10/1 priority date for domestic students, 10/1 for international students. Application fee: $50. Electronic applications accepted. *Financial support:* Application deadline: 8/1. *Unit head:* Dr. Laura Dull, Chair, 845-257-2849, E-mail: dullj@newpaltz.edu. *Application contact:* Vika Shock, Director of Graduate Admissions, 845-257-3285, Fax: 845-257-3284, E-mail: gradschool@newpaltz.edu. Website: http://www.newpaltz.edu/secondaryed/

**Stony Brook University, State University of New York,** Graduate School, College of Arts and Sciences, Department of European Languages, Literatures, and Cultures, Program in French, Stony Brook, NY 11794. Offers Romance languages (MA). *Program availability:* Evening/weekend. *Students:* 2 part-time (both women). 2 applicants, 50% accepted, 1 enrolled. *Degree requirements:* For master's, one foreign language. *Entrance requirements:* For master's, GRE General Test. Additional exam requirements/recommendations for international students: Required—TOEFL. *Application deadline:* For fall admission, 1/15 for domestic students; for spring admission, 10/1 for domestic students. Application fee: $100. *Expenses:* Contact institution. *Unit head:* Dr. Prosper Sanou, Coordinator, 631-632-7440, Fax: 631-632-9612, E-mail: prosper.sanou@stonybrook.edu. *Application contact:* Mary Wilmarth, Coordinator, 631-632-7442, Fax: 631-632-9612, E-mail: mary.wilmarth@stonybrook.edu.

**Syracuse University,** College of Arts and Sciences, MA Program in French and Francophone Studies, Syracuse, NY 13244. Offers MA. *Program availability:* Part-time. *Students:* Average age 27. *Degree requirements:* For master's, comprehensive exam, thesis or alternative. *Entrance requirements:* For master's, GRE General Test, writing sample of 5 to 15 pages in French (e.g., paper written for undergraduate French course, honors or senior thesis), personal statement, three letters of recommendation, transcripts. Additional exam requirements/recommendations for international students: Required—TOEFL (minimum score 100 iBT). *Application deadline:* For fall admission, 2/1 priority date for domestic and international students. Application fee: $75. Electronic applications accepted. *Expenses: Tuition:* Full-time $25,974; part-time $1443 per credit hour. *Required fees:* $802; $50 per course. Tuition and fees vary according to course load and program. *Financial support:* Fellowships with full tuition reimbursements, teaching assistantships with tuition reimbursements, scholarships/grants, and tuition waivers available. Financial award application deadline: 1/1; financial award applicants required to submit FAFSA. *Faculty research:* French, Francophone literature, French culture, literary analysis, critical theory. *Unit head:* Jean Jonassaint, Professor, French and Francophone Studies/French Program Coordinator, 315-443-5382, E-mail: jjonassa@syr.edu. Website: http://lang.syr.edu/academics/French/MA-French.html

**Tufts University,** Graduate School of Arts and Sciences, Program in French, Medford, MA 02155. Offers MA. *Students:* 1 applicant. *Degree requirements:* For master's, one foreign language. *Entrance requirements:* For master's, GRE General Test, writing sample. Additional exam requirements/recommendations for international students: Required—TOEFL (minimum score 550 paper-based; 80 iBT), IELTS (minimum score

6.5). *Application deadline:* For fall admission, 2/15 for domestic and international students; for spring admission, 10/15 for domestic and international students. Applications are processed on a rolling basis. Application fee: $85. Electronic applications accepted. *Expenses:* $49,982 full-time tuition (for MA); annual student activity fee of $60; annual health insurance fee of $2,522 (may be waived if proof of outside coverage from U.S. carrier is submitted); comprehensive student health fee of $784 (for students enrolled half-time or more). *Financial support:* Federal Work-Study, scholarships/grants, and tuition waivers (full and partial) available. Support available to part-time students. Financial award application deadline: 1/15. *Unit head:* Dr. Gerard Gasarian, Graduate Program Director. *Application contact:* Office of Graduate Admissions, 617-627-3395, E-mail: gradadmissions@tufts.edu.

**Tulane University,** School of Liberal Arts, Department of French and Italian, New Orleans, LA 70118-5669. Offers French (MA, PhD). *Degree requirements:* For master's, one foreign language, thesis or alternative; for doctorate, 2 foreign languages, thesis/dissertation. *Entrance requirements:* For master's, GRE General Test, minimum B average in undergraduate course work; for doctorate, GRE General Test. Additional exam requirements/recommendations for international students: Required—TOEFL. Electronic applications accepted. *Expenses: Tuition:* Full-time $50,920; part-time $2829 per credit hour. *Required fees:* $2040; $44.50 per credit hour. $580 per term. Tuition and fees vary according to course load, degree level and program.

**Université de Moncton,** Faculty of Arts and Social Sciences, Department of French Studies, Moncton, NB E1A 3E9, Canada. Offers MA, PhD. *Program availability:* Part-time. Terminal master's awarded for partial completion of doctoral program. *Degree requirements:* For master's, thesis, proficiency in French; for doctorate, thesis/dissertation, proficiency in French. *Entrance requirements:* For master's, honors degree in French; for doctorate, MA in French. Electronic applications accepted. *Faculty research:* Language, linguistics, literature, ethnology, Acadian studies.

**Université de Montréal,** Faculty of Arts and Sciences, Department of French Literature, Montréal, QC H3C 3J7, Canada. Offers MA, PhD. *Degree requirements:* For master's, one foreign language, thesis; for doctorate, one foreign language, thesis/dissertation, general exam. Electronic applications accepted. *Faculty research:* Literary history, literary genres, critical edition, creative writing, Quebecois literature.

**Université de Sherbrooke,** Faculty of Letters and Human Sciences, Department of Letters and Communications, Sherbrooke, QC J1K 2R1, Canada. Offers comparative Canadian literature (MA, PhD); French literature (MA, PhD); linguistics (MA); theatre (MA). *Degree requirements:* For master's, thesis or alternative; for doctorate, thesis/dissertation. *Entrance requirements:* For master's, minimum GPA of 2.8; for doctorate, minimum GPA of 3.0.

**Université du Québec à Chicoutimi,** Graduate Programs, Program in Didactics of French-Mother Tongue, Chicoutimi, QC G7H 2B1, Canada. Offers Diploma. *Program availability:* Part-time. *Entrance requirements:* For degree, appropriate bachelor's degree, proficiency in French.

**University at Buffalo, the State University of New York,** Graduate School, College of Arts and Sciences, Department of Romance Languages and Literatures, Buffalo, NY 14260-4620. Offers French (MA, PhD); Spanish (MA, PhD). *Program availability:* Part-time. *Faculty:* 15 full-time (9 women), 6 part-time/adjunct (3 women). *Students:* 33 full-time (24 women), 3 part-time (all women); includes 13 minority (3 Black or African American, non-Hispanic/Latino; 2 Asian, non-Hispanic/Latino; 6 Hispanic/Latino; 2 Two or more races, non-Hispanic/Latino), 9 international. 24 applicants, 58% accepted, 7 enrolled. In 2016, 1 master's, 7 doctorates awarded. Terminal master's awarded for partial completion of doctoral program. *Degree requirements:* For master's, one foreign language, comprehensive exam, thesis (for some programs); for doctorate, 2 foreign languages, comprehensive exam (for some programs), thesis/dissertation. *Entrance requirements:* For doctorate, GRE. Additional exam requirements/recommendations for international students: Required—TOEFL (minimum score 550 paper-based; 79 iBT), IELTS (minimum score 6.5), PTE (minimum score 55). *Application deadline:* For fall admission, 12/31 priority date for domestic and international students; for spring admission, 10/30 for domestic students, 9/1 for international students. Applications are processed on a rolling basis. Application fee: $75. Electronic applications accepted. *Financial support:* In 2016–17, 24 students received support, including 3 fellowships with full tuition reimbursements available (averaging $4,667 per year), 24 teaching assistantships with full tuition reimbursements available (averaging $14,049 per year); Federal Work-Study, institutionally sponsored loans, scholarships/grants, and health care benefits also available. Financial award application deadline: 12/31; financial award applicants required to submit FAFSA. *Faculty research:* Romance linguistics, cultural studies, literary studies, literature, philosophy and poetry. *Unit head:* Dr. Elizabeth Scarlett, Professor of Spanish/Department Chair, 716-645-0873, Fax: 716-645-5981, E-mail: scarlett@buffalo.edu. *Application contact:* Dr. Margarita Vargas, Associate Professor of Spanish/Director of Graduate Studies, 716-645-0859, Fax: 716-645-5981, E-mail: mvargas@buffalo.edu. Website: http://rll.buffalo.edu

**University at Buffalo, the State University of New York,** Graduate School, Graduate School of Education, Department of Learning and Instruction, Buffalo, NY 14260. Offers biology education (Ed M, Certificate); chemistry education (Ed M, Certificate); childhood education (Ed M); childhood education with bilingual extension (Ed M); college teaching (Advanced Certificate); curriculum, instruction and the science of learning (PhD); early childhood education (Ed M); early childhood education with bilingual extension (Ed M); earth science education (Ed M, Certificate); education and technology (Ed M); education studies (Ed M); educational technology and new literacies (Certificate); educational technology and new literacies (Advanced Certificate); elementary education (Ed D); English education (Ed M, Certificate); English education studies (Ed M); English for speakers of other languages (Ed M); foreign and second language education (PhD); French education (Ed M, Certificate); German education (Ed M, Certificate); gifted education (Certificate); Latin education (Ed M, Certificate); literacy education studies (Ed M); literacy specialist (Ed M); literacy teaching and learning (Certificate); mathematics education (Ed M, Certificate); music education (Ed M, Certificate); music education studies (Ed M); music learning theory (Advanced Certificate); online education (Advanced Certificate); physics education (Ed M, Certificate); science and the public (Ed M); social studies education (Ed M, Certificate); Spanish education (Ed M, Certificate); special education (PhD); teaching English to speakers of other languages (Ed M). *Program availability:* Part-time, evening/weekend, 100% online. *Faculty:* 28 full-time (21 women), 67 part-time/adjunct (49 women). *Students:* 198 full-time (153 women), 312 part-time (220 women); includes 48 minority (28 Black or African American, non-Hispanic/Latino; 4 American Indian or Alaska Native, non-Hispanic/Latino; 15 Asian, non-Hispanic/Latino; 1 Hispanic/Latino), 66 international. Average age 33. 336 applicants, 86% accepted, 178 enrolled. In 2016, 137 master's, 24 doctorates, 25 other advanced degrees awarded. *Degree requirements:* For master's, comprehensive exam; for doctorate, thesis/dissertation, research analysis exam, research experience. *Entrance requirements:* For master's, letters of reference; for doctorate, GRE General Test or MAT, interview, writing sample, letters of recommendation. Additional exam requirements/recommendations for international students: Required—TOEFL (minimum score 600 paper-based; 96 iBT). *Application deadline:* For fall admission, 2/1 priority date for domestic and international students; for

spring admission, 11/15 priority date for domestic students, 10/1 for international students. Applications are processed on a rolling basis. Application fee: $50. Electronic applications accepted. *Financial support:* In 2016–17, 44 fellowships (averaging $4,010 per year), 39 research assistantships with tuition reimbursements (averaging $9,897 per year) were awarded; teaching assistantships, career-related internships or fieldwork, Federal Work-Study, institutionally sponsored loans, scholarships/grants, tuition waivers (full and partial), and unspecified assistantships also available. Financial award application deadline: 2/28; financial award applicants required to submit FAFSA. *Faculty research:* Science assessment, foreign language teaching and learning, early learning, new literacies, gender and education. *Total annual research expenditures:* $534,880. *Unit head:* Dr. Deborah Moore-Russo, Chair, 716-645-4069, Fax: 716-645-3161, E-mail: dam29@buffalo.edu. *Application contact:* Luann Zak, Admissions Assistant, 716-645-2110, Fax: 716-645-7937, E-mail: luannzak@buffalo.edu.
Website: http://gse.buffalo.edu/lai

**The University of Alabama,** Graduate School, College of Arts and Sciences, Department of Modern Languages and Classics, Tuscaloosa, AL 35487. Offers French (MA, PhD); French and Spanish (PhD); German (MA); Romance languages (MA, PhD); Spanish (MA, PhD). *Program availability:* Part-time. Faculty: 31 full-time (18 women). *Students:* 49 full-time (32 women), 7 part-time (4 women); includes 9 minority (3 Black or African American, non-Hispanic/Latino; 1 Asian, non-Hispanic/Latino; 4 Hispanic/Latino; 1 Two or more races, non-Hispanic/Latino), 20 international. Average age 31. 29 applicants, 66% accepted, 12 enrolled. In 2016, 11 master's, 6 doctorates awarded. *Degree requirements:* For master's, comprehensive exam, thesis optional; for doctorate, one foreign language, thesis/dissertation, preliminary exam. *Entrance requirements:* For master's and doctorate, minimum GPA of 3.0, writing sample. Additional exam requirements/recommendations for international students: Required—TOEFL or IELTS. *Application deadline:* For fall admission, 7/6 priority date for domestic students, 1/15 priority date for international students; for spring admission, 12/5 priority date for domestic students, 6/1 priority date for international students. Applications are processed on a rolling basis. Application fee: $50 ($60 for international students). Electronic applications accepted. *Expenses:* Tuition, state resident: full-time $10,470. Tuition, nonresident: full-time $26,950. *Financial support:* In 2016–17, 7 students received support, including 1 fellowship, research assistantships with full tuition reimbursements available (averaging $10,291 per year), 6 teaching assistantships with full tuition reimbursements available (averaging $10,291 per year); career-related internships or fieldwork, Federal Work-Study, institutionally sponsored loans, and scholarships/grants also available. Financial award application deadline: 7/14. *Faculty research:* Non-English literature, linguistics, culture, film. *Unit head:* Dr. Douglas Lightfoot, Department Chair, 205-348-5059, E-mail: lightfoot@ua.edu. *Application contact:* Dr. K. Barbara Fischer, Graduate Director/Associate Professor, 205-348-8465, Fax: 205-348-2042, E-mail: bfischer@bama.ua.edu.
Website: http://bama.ua.edu/~mlc

**University of Alberta,** Faculty of Graduate Studies and Research, Department of Modern Languages and Cultural Studies, Edmonton, AB T6G 2E1, Canada. Offers applied linguistics (Germanic, Romance, Slavic) (MA); French language, literatures and linguistics (PhD); French language, literatures, and linguistics (MA); Germanic languages, literatures and linguistics (PhD); Germanic languages, literatures, and linguistics (MA); Italian studies (MA); Slavic languages and literatures (Russian, Ukrainian) (MA, PhD); Slavic linguistics (Russian, Ukrainian) (MA, PhD); Spanish and Latin American studies (MA, PhD); Ukrainian folklore (MA, PhD). *Program availability:* Part-time. *Degree requirements:* For master's, one foreign language, thesis; for doctorate, 2 foreign languages, comprehensive exam, thesis/dissertation. *Entrance requirements:* For master's and doctorate, 1 language other than English. Additional exam requirements/recommendations for international students: Required—Michigan English Language Assessment Battery or TOEFL (minimum score 550 paper-based). Electronic applications accepted. *Faculty research:* Russian/Ukrainian studies; German studies; contemporary Latin American, French and Francophone studies; Italian studies.

**The University of Arizona,** College of Humanities, Department of French and Italian, Tucson, AZ 85721. Offers French (MA). *Program availability:* Part-time. *Entrance requirements:* For master's, 3 letters of reference, writing sample in French, audio recording. Additional exam requirements/recommendations for international students: Required—TOEFL (minimum score 550 paper-based; 79 iBT). Electronic applications accepted. *Faculty research:* French literature (history, criticism, and theory), Francophone literature and culture, second language acquisition and teaching.

**University of Arkansas,** Graduate School, J. William Fulbright College of Arts and Sciences, Department of World Languages, Literature and Cultures, Program in French, Fayetteville, AR 72701. Offers MA. In 2016, 1 master's awarded. *Degree requirements:* For master's, variable foreign language requirement. *Application deadline:* For fall admission, 4/1 for international students; for spring admission, 10/1 for international students. Applications are processed on a rolling basis. Application fee: $40 ($50 for international students). Electronic applications accepted. *Financial support:* In 2016–17, 7 teaching assistantships were awarded; fellowships, research assistantships, career-related internships or fieldwork, and Federal Work-Study also available. Support available to part-time students. Financial award application deadline: 4/1; financial award applicants required to submit FAFSA. *Unit head:* Dr. Steven Bell, Departmental Chair, 479-575-2951, Fax: 479-575-6795, E-mail: sbell@uark.edu. *Application contact:* Dr. Hope Christiansen, Graduate Coordinator, 479-575-2951, Fax: 479-575-6795, E-mail: hopec@uark.edu.
Website: http://www.uark.edu/depts/flaninfo/

**The University of British Columbia,** Faculty of Arts and Faculty of Graduate Studies, Department of French, Hispanic and Italian Studies, Vancouver, BC V6T 1Z1, Canada. Offers French (MA, PhD); Hispanic studies (MA, PhD). *Program availability:* Part-time. *Degree requirements:* For master's, thesis optional; for doctorate, 2 foreign languages, comprehensive exam, thesis/dissertation. *Entrance requirements:* For doctorate, MA. Additional exam requirements/recommendations for international students: Required—TOEFL. *Application deadline:* Applications are processed on a rolling basis. Application fee: $100 Canadian dollars ($162 Canadian dollars for international students). Electronic applications accepted. *Expenses:* $4,802 per year tuition and fees, $8,436 per year international. *Financial support:* Fellowships with tuition reimbursements, research assistantships, teaching assistantships, Federal Work-Study, and tuition waivers (partial) available. Financial award application deadline: 2/1. *Faculty research:* Medieval and Renaissance literature, modern literature, romance philology and linguistics, cultural studies, women's literature. *Application contact:* Carole Schoenfeld, Graduate Program Staff, 604-822-0016, Fax: 604-822-6675, E-mail: fhis.grad@ubc.ca.
Website: http://fhis.ubc.ca/

**University of Calgary,** Faculty of Graduate Studies, Faculty of Arts, Department of French, Italian and Spanish, Calgary, AB T2N 1N4, Canada. Offers French (MA, PhD); Spanish (MA, PhD). PhD offered in special cases only. *Program availability:* Part-time. *Degree requirements:* For master's, one foreign language, thesis, exam; for doctorate, 2 foreign languages, comprehensive exam, thesis/dissertation, candidacy exam. *Entrance requirements:* Additional exam requirements/recommendations for international students: Required—TOEFL (minimum score 550 paper-based; 80 iBT) or IELTS (minimum score 7). Electronic applications accepted. *Faculty research:* French and

French-Canadian language and literature, Hispanic language and literature, comparative literature, language instruction, literary theory.

**University of California, Berkeley,** Graduate Division, College of Letters and Science, Department of French, Berkeley, CA 94720-1500. Offers PhD. *Students:* 24 full-time (13 women); includes 2 minority (1 Black or African American, non-Hispanic/Latino; 1 Asian, non-Hispanic/Latino), 2 international. Average age 29. 36 applicants, 2 enrolled. In 2016, 6 doctorates awarded. *Degree requirements:* For doctorate, one foreign language, thesis/dissertation, qualifying exam. *Entrance requirements:* For doctorate, minimum GPA of 3.0, 3 letters of recommendation. *Application deadline:* For fall admission, 12/1 for domestic students. Application fee: $105 ($125 for international students). Electronic applications accepted. *Financial support:* Fellowships, research assistantships, teaching assistantships, institutionally sponsored loans, health care benefits, and unspecified assistantships available. *Unit head:* Timothy Hampton, Chair, 510-642-2712, Fax: 510-642-8852, E-mail: clfa_aa@berkeley.edu. *Application contact:* Mary Ajideh, 510-642-2714, Fax: 510-642-8852, E-mail: frenchga@berkeley.edu.
Website: http://french.berkeley.edu/

**University of California, Berkeley,** Graduate Division, College of Letters and Science, Group in Romance Languages and Literatures, Berkeley, CA 94720-1500. Offers French (PhD); Italian (PhD); Spanish (PhD). Faculty: 16 full-time. *Students:* 11 full-time (7 women); includes 3 minority (1 Asian, non-Hispanic/Latino; 2 Hispanic/Latino). Average age 33. 12 applicants. In 2016, 4 doctorates awarded. *Degree requirements:* For doctorate, thesis/dissertation, qualifying exam. *Entrance requirements:* For doctorate, GRE General Test, minimum GPA of 3.0, 3 letters of recommendation. Additional exam requirements/recommendations for international students: Required—TOEFL (minimum score 570 paper-based; 90 iBT). *Application deadline:* For fall admission, 12/8 for domestic students. Application fee: $105 ($125 for international students). Electronic applications accepted. *Financial support:* Fellowships with full tuition reimbursements, teaching assistantships with partial tuition reimbursements, health care benefits, and unspecified assistantships available. Financial award applicants required to submit FAFSA. *Unit head:* Ignatio Navarrete, Chair, 510-642-2105. *Application contact:* 510-642-7405.
Website: http://romancelangs.berkeley.edu

**University of California, Davis,** Graduate Studies, Program in French, Davis, CA 95616. Offers PhD. *Program availability:* Part-time. *Degree requirements:* For doctorate, thesis/dissertation. *Entrance requirements:* For doctorate, GRE General Test, minimum GPA of 3.0. Additional exam requirements/recommendations for international students: Required—TOEFL (minimum score 550 paper-based). Electronic applications accepted. *Faculty research:* Art and art criticism, Francophone literature, travel narrative, colonial and postcolonial studies and romance linguistics.

**University of California, Irvine,** School of Humanities, Department of European Languages and Studies, Irvine, CA 92697. Offers French (MA, PhD); German (MA, PhD). *Students:* 5 full-time (3 women), 2 international. Average age 28. 12 applicants, 83% accepted, 3 enrolled. In 2016, 2 doctorates awarded. *Degree requirements:* For doctorate, thesis/dissertation. *Entrance requirements:* For master's and doctorate, GRE General Test, minimum GPA of 3.0. Additional exam requirements/recommendations for international students: Required—TOEFL (minimum score 550 paper-based). *Application deadline:* For fall admission, 1/15 for domestic and international students. Applications are processed on a rolling basis. Application fee: $105 ($125 for international students). Electronic applications accepted. *Financial support:* Fellowships, research assistantships with full tuition reimbursements, teaching assistantships, institutionally sponsored loans, traineeships, health care benefits, and unspecified assistantships available. Financial award application deadline: 3/1; financial award applicants required to submit FAFSA. *Faculty research:* Montaigne, psychoanalysis, feminism and the problem of repression, aesthetics of nationalism and the limits of culture. *Unit head:* Prof. David Pan, Chair, 949-824-6406, Fax: 949-824-6416, E-mail: dtpan@uci.edu. *Application contact:* Bindya Baliga, Graduate Program Coordinator, 949-824-7968, Fax: 949-824-6416, E-mail: bbaliga@uci.edu.
Website: http://www.humanities.uci.edu/els/

**University of California, Los Angeles,** Graduate Division, College of Letters and Science, Department of French and Francophone Studies, Los Angeles, CA 90095. Offers MA, PhD. Terminal master's awarded for partial completion of doctoral program. *Degree requirements:* For master's, one foreign language, comprehensive exam; for doctorate, 2 foreign languages, thesis/dissertation, oral and written qualifying exams. *Entrance requirements:* For doctorate, GRE General Test, bachelor's degree; minimum undergraduate GPA of 3.0 (or its equivalent if letter grade system not used); writing sample in French. Additional exam requirements/recommendations for international students: Required—TOEFL. Electronic applications accepted.

**University of California, Santa Barbara,** Graduate Division, College of Letters and Sciences, Division of Humanities and Fine Arts, Program in Comparative Literature, Santa Barbara, CA 93106-4130. Offers comparative literature (PhD); East Asian literatures (PhD); feminist studies (PhD); French (PhD); global studies (PhD); translation studies (PhD); MA/PhD. *Degree requirements:* For doctorate, 2 foreign languages, comprehensive exam, thesis/dissertation. *Entrance requirements:* For doctorate, GRE. Additional exam requirements/recommendations for international students: Required—TOEFL (minimum score 550 paper-based; 80 iBT), IELTS (minimum score 7). Electronic applications accepted. *Faculty research:* Comparative literary studies in global context, critical theory, translation studies, media technological studies, trauma studies.

**University of Chicago,** Division of the Humanities, Department of Romance Languages and Literatures, Chicago, IL 60637. Offers French and Francophone studies (PhD); Hispanic and Luso-Brazilian studies (PhD); Italian studies (PhD); Renaissance and early modern studies (PhD). *Students:* 44 full-time (28 women); includes 9 minority (1 Asian, non-Hispanic/Latino; 7 Hispanic/Latino; 1 Two or more races, non-Hispanic/Latino), 16 international. 45 applicants, 29% accepted, 5 enrolled. In 2016, 4 doctorates awarded. Terminal master's awarded for partial completion of doctoral program. *Degree requirements:* For doctorate, 3 foreign languages, comprehensive exam, thesis/dissertation. *Entrance requirements:* For doctorate, GRE General Test. Additional exam requirements/recommendations for international students: Required—TOEFL (minimum score 104 iBT), IELTS (minimum score 7). *Application deadline:* For fall admission, 12/15 for domestic and international students. Application fee: $90. Electronic applications accepted. *Financial support:* Fellowships with full tuition reimbursements, teaching assistantships with full tuition reimbursements, Federal Work-Study, institutionally sponsored loans, scholarships/grants, and health care benefits available. Financial award application deadline: 12/15; financial award applicants required to submit FAFSA. *Unit head:* Daisy Delogu, Chair, 773-702-4115, E-mail: ddelogu@uchicago.edu. *Application contact:* Michael Beetley, Assistant Dean of Students, Admissions and Fellowships, 773-702-1552, Fax: 773-834-9148, E-mail: humanitiesadmissions@uchicago.edu.
Website: http://rll.uchicago.edu

**University of Cincinnati,** Graduate School, McMicken College of Arts and Sciences, Department of Romance Languages and Literatures, Program in French, Cincinnati, OH 45221. Offers MA, PhD. Terminal master's awarded for partial completion of doctoral program. *Degree requirements:* For master's, thesis optional; for doctorate, 2 foreign

## French

languages, thesis/dissertation. *Entrance requirements:* For master's, minimum GPA of 3.0. Electronic applications accepted. *Expenses: Tuition, area resident:* Full-time $12,790; part-time $389 per credit hour. Tuition, state resident: full-time $13,290; part-time $419 per credit hour. Tuition, nonresident: full-time $24,532; part-time $976 per credit hour. *International tuition:* $24,832 full-time. *Required fees:* $3958; $140 per credit hour. Tuition and fees vary according to course load, degree level, program and reciprocity agreements.

**University of Colorado Boulder,** Graduate School, College of Arts and Sciences, Department of French and Italian, Boulder, CO 80309. Offers MA, PhD. *Faculty:* 10 full-time (5 women). *Students:* 20 full-time (15 women), 2 part-time (both women); includes 3 minority (all Hispanic/Latino), 3 international. Average age 33. 19 applicants, 42% accepted, 4 enrolled. In 2016, 1 master's, 2 doctorates awarded. Terminal master's awarded for partial completion of doctoral program. *Degree requirements:* For master's, 2 foreign languages, comprehensive exam, thesis or alternative; for doctorate, 3 foreign languages, thesis/dissertation. *Entrance requirements:* For master's, GRE General Test, minimum undergraduate GPA of 3.0; for doctorate, GRE General Test. *Application deadline:* For fall admission, 1/5 for domestic students, 1/15 for international students. Applications are processed on a rolling basis. Application fee: $60 ($80 for international students). Electronic applications accepted. Application fee is waived when completed online. *Financial support:* In 2016–17, 50 students received support, including 3 fellowships (averaging $13,332 per year), 2 research assistantships with full and partial tuition reimbursements available (averaging $27,432 per year), 17 teaching assistantships with full and partial tuition reimbursements available (averaging $37,090 per year); institutionally sponsored loans, scholarships/grants, health care benefits, and unspecified assistantships also available. Financial award application deadline: 2/1; financial award applicants required to submit FAFSA. *Faculty research:* Literary criticism, French language/literature, arts/humanities/cultural activities, culture, fiction. *Application contact:* E-mail: frenital@colorado.edu.
Website: http://www.colorado.edu/FRIT/

**University of Delaware,** College of Arts and Sciences, Department of Foreign Languages and Literatures, Newark, DE 19716. Offers foreign languages and literatures (MA), including French, German, Spanish; foreign languages pedagogy (MA), including French, German, Spanish; technical Chinese translation (MA). *Degree requirements:* For master's, one foreign language, comprehensive exam, thesis optional. *Entrance requirements:* For master's, GRE General Test, letters of recommendation, writing sample. Additional exam requirements/recommendations for international students: Required—TOEFL. Electronic applications accepted. *Faculty research:* Medieval to Modern French and Spanish literature, twentieth-century German, French, Spanish literature by women, computer-assisted instruction.

**University of Florida,** Graduate School, College of Liberal Arts and Sciences, Department of Languages, Literatures and Cultures, Gainesville, FL 32611. Offers French and Francophone studies (MA, PhD); German (MA, PhD), including women's and gender studies (PhD). *Degree requirements:* For master's, comprehensive exam, thesis optional; for doctorate, one foreign language, comprehensive exam, thesis/dissertation. *Entrance requirements:* For master's and doctorate, GRE General Test, minimum GPA of 3.0. Additional exam requirements/recommendations for international students: Required—TOEFL (minimum score 550 paper-based; 80 iBT), IELTS (minimum score 6). Electronic applications accepted. *Faculty research:* Medieval epic, romance, and allegory; Renaissance and Baroque poetry; the eighteenth-century novel; nineteenth-century prose, poetry, and poetics; the twentieth-century novel, theater, and poetry; the literatures of the Francophone world; French and Francophone film; the literatures in Breton and Occitan; criticism and critical theory; applied linguistics; the history of French; phonology; sociolinguistics; the structure of French; French and Haitian Creole linguistics.

**University of Georgia,** Franklin College of Arts and Sciences, Department of Romance Languages, Athens, GA 30602. Offers French (PhD); Italian (MA, PhD); Portuguese (MA, PhD); romance linguistics (MA); Spanish (PhD). *Degree requirements:* For master's, one foreign language; for doctorate, 2 foreign languages, thesis/dissertation. *Entrance requirements:* For master's and doctorate, GRE General Test. *Application deadline:* For fall admission, 7/1 priority date for domestic students; for spring admission, 11/15 for domestic students. Application fee: $50. Electronic applications accepted. *Financial support:* Fellowships, research assistantships, teaching assistantships, and unspecified assistantships available. *Unit head:* Dr. Staccy Casado, Department Head, 706-542-2364, Fax: 706-542-2272, E-mail: sdcasado@uga.edu. *Application contact:* Rachel Gabara, Graduate Coordinator, 706-542-8930, E-mail: romlgradcoord@uga.edu.
Website: http://www.rom.uga.edu/

**University of Guelph,** Graduate Studies, College of Arts, School of Languages and Literatures, Guelph, ON N1G 2W1, Canada. Offers European studies (MA); French studies (MA). *Entrance requirements:* For master's, honours BA or equivalent. Electronic applications accepted. *Faculty research:* Sociolinguistics, poetics and politics of literature, language acquisition.

**University of Hawaii at Manoa,** Graduate Division, College of Languages, Linguistics and Literature, Department of Languages and Literatures of Europe and the Americas, Program in French, Honolulu, HI 96822. Offers MA. *Program availability:* Part-time. *Degree requirements:* For master's, one foreign language, thesis optional. *Entrance requirements:* Additional exam requirements/recommendations for international students: Required—TOEFL (minimum score 580 paper-based; 92 iBT), IELTS (minimum score 5).

**University of Illinois at Chicago,** College of Liberal Arts and Sciences, School of Literatures, Cultural Studies and Linguistics, Department of French and Francophone Studies, Chicago, IL 60607-7128. Offers MA. *Program availability:* Part-time. *Degree requirements:* For master's, one foreign language, thesis optional, exam. *Entrance requirements:* For master's, minimum GPA of 2.75. Additional exam requirements/recommendations for international students: Required—TOEFL. Electronic applications accepted. *Faculty research:* French civilization, feminist theory, French theater, sociology of literature, narrative theory.

**University of Illinois at Urbana–Champaign,** Graduate College, College of Liberal Arts and Sciences, School of Literatures, Cultures and Linguistics, Department of French, Champaign, IL 61820. Offers MA, PhD.

**The University of Iowa,** Graduate College, College of Liberal Arts and Sciences, Department of French and Italian, Iowa City, IA 52242-1316. Offers French (MA, PhD). *Degree requirements:* For master's, thesis optional, exam; for doctorate, comprehensive exam, thesis/dissertation. *Entrance requirements:* For master's and doctorate, GRE General Test, minimum GPA of 3.0. Additional exam requirements/recommendations for international students: Required—TOEFL (minimum score 550 paper-based; 81 iBT). Electronic applications accepted.

**The University of Kansas,** Graduate Studies, College of Liberal Arts and Sciences, Department of French and Italian, Lawrence, KS 66045-7590. Offers French (MA, PhD). *Students:* 11 full-time (9 women); includes 1 minority (Two or more races, non-Hispanic/Latino), 3 international. Average age 29. 10 applicants, 70% accepted, 5 enrolled. In 2016, 6 master's awarded. *Entrance requirements:* For master's and doctorate, GRE,

statement of academic purpose and goals, resume, sample essay, three letters of recommendation, official transcripts. Additional exam requirements/recommendations for international students: Required—TOEFL (minimum score 80 iBT). *Application deadline:* For fall admission, 1/15 priority date for domestic and international students; for spring admission, 11/15 for domestic and international students. Application fee: $65 ($85 for international students). Electronic applications accepted. *Financial support:* Fellowships, teaching assistantships, and unspecified assistantships available. Financial award application deadline: 1/15; financial award applicants required to submit FAFSA. *Faculty research:* French literature and cultural studies; Francophone literature, film. *Unit head:* Dr. Bruce Hayes, Chair, 785-864-9062, E-mail: bhayes@ku.edu. *Application contact:* Cari Ann Kreienhop, Academic Advisor, 785-864-3665, E-mail: ckreienhop@ku.edu.
Website: http://www.frenchitalian.ku.edu/

**University of Lethbridge,** School of Graduate Studies, Lethbridge, AB T1K 3M4, Canada. Offers addictions counseling (M Sc); agricultural biotechnology (M Sc); agricultural studies (M Sc, MA); anthropology (MA); archaeology (M Sc, MA); art (MA, MFA); biochemistry (M Sc); biological sciences (M Sc); biomolecular science (PhD); biosystems and biodiversity (PhD); Canadian studies (MA); chemistry (M Sc); computer science (M Sc); computer science and geographical information science (M Sc); counseling (MC); counseling psychology (M Ed); dramatic arts (MA); earth, space, and physical science (PhD); economics (MA); education (MA, PhD); educational leadership (M Ed); English (MA); environmental science (M Sc); evolution and behavior (PhD); exercise science (M Sc); French (MA); French/German (MA); French/Spanish (MA); general education (M Ed); geography (M Sc, MA); German (MA); health sciences (M Sc); individualized multidisciplinary (M Sc, MA); kinesiology (M Sc, MA); management (M Sc), including accounting, finance, human resource management and labor relations, information systems, international management, marketing, policy and strategy; mathematics (M Sc); music (M Mus, MA); Native American studies (MA); neuroscience (M Sc, PhD); new media (MA, MFA); nursing (M Sc, MN); philosophy (MA); physics (M Sc); political science (MA); psychology (M Sc, MA); religious studies (MA); sociology (MA); theatre and dramatic arts (MFA); theoretical and computational science (PhD); urban and regional studies (MA); women and gender studies (MA). *Program availability:* Part-time, evening/weekend. *Degree requirements:* For master's, thesis (for some programs); for doctorate, comprehensive exam, thesis/dissertation. *Entrance requirements:* For master's, GMAT (for M Sc in management), bachelor's degree in related field, minimum GPA of 3.0 during previous 20 graded semester courses, 2 years' teaching or related experience (M Ed); for doctorate, master's degree, minimum graduate GPA of 3.5. Additional exam requirements/recommendations for international students: Required—TOEFL (minimum score 580 paper-based; 93 iBT). Electronic applications accepted. *Faculty research:* Movement and brain plasticity, gibberellin physiology, photosynthesis, carbon cycling, molecular properties of main-group ring components.

**University of Louisiana at Lafayette,** College of Liberal Arts, Department of Modern Languages, Program in Francophone Studies, Lafayette, LA 70504. Offers PhD. *Degree requirements:* For doctorate, 2 foreign languages, comprehensive exam, thesis/dissertation. *Entrance requirements:* For doctorate, GRE General Test, minimum GPA of 2.75. Additional exam requirements/recommendations for international students: Required—TOEFL (minimum score 550 paper-based). Electronic applications accepted. *Faculty research:* Louisiana folklore, eighteenth-century French literature, contemporary criticism.

**University of Louisiana at Lafayette,** College of Liberal Arts, Department of Modern Languages, Program in French, Lafayette, LA 70504. Offers MA. *Program availability:* Part-time. *Degree requirements:* For master's, 2 foreign languages, thesis or alternative. *Entrance requirements:* For master's, GRE General Test, minimum GPA of 2.75. Additional exam requirements/recommendations for international students: Required—TOEFL (minimum score 550 paper-based). Electronic applications accepted. *Faculty research:* Louisiana studies, nineteenth-century French literature, Francophone studies.

**University of Louisville,** Graduate School, College of Arts and Sciences, Department of Classical and Modern Languages, Louisville, KY 40292-0001. Offers French (MA); Spanish (MA); translation and interpretation (Certificate). *Program availability:* Part-time, evening/weekend. *Students:* 14 full-time (10 women), 16 part-time (13 women); includes 10 minority (3 Black or African American, non-Hispanic/Latino; 2 Asian, non-Hispanic/Latino; 4 Hispanic/Latino; 1 Two or more races, non-Hispanic/Latino), 3 international. Average age 30. 31 applicants, 68% accepted, 14 enrolled. In 2016, 8 master's, 3 other advanced degrees awarded. *Degree requirements:* For master's, one foreign language, thesis (for some programs). *Entrance requirements:* For master's, GRE General Test (recommended), letters of recommendation, transcripts, curriculum vitae, personal statement; for Certificate, GRE, letters of recommendation, transcripts, curriculum vitae, personal statement. Additional exam requirements/recommendations for international students: Required—TOEFL (minimum score 550 paper-based; 79 iBT); Recommended—IELTS (minimum score 6.5). *Application deadline:* Applications are processed on a rolling basis. Application fee: $60. *Expenses:* Tuition, state resident: full-time $12,246; part-time $681 per credit hour. Tuition, nonresident: full-time $25,486; part-time $1417 per credit hour. *Required fees:* $196. Tuition and fees vary according to program and reciprocity agreements. *Financial support:* In 2016–17, 12 teaching assistantships with full tuition reimbursements (averaging $14,000 per year) were awarded; scholarships/grants, health care benefits, and unspecified assistantships also available. Financial award applicants required to submit FAFSA. *Faculty research:* Medieval Spanish literature and culture, Modern Spanish literature and culture, translation and interpreting, film studies, Medieval French literature and culture, Modern, French literature and culture, American Sign Language studies. *Unit head:* Dr. Alan Leidner, Chair, 502-852-0483, Fax: 502-852-8885, E-mail: alan.leidner@louisville.edu. *Application contact:* Travis Henretty, Administrative Assistant, 502-852-6686, Fax: 502-852-8885, E-mail: travis.henretty@louisville.edu.
Website: http://louisville.edu/modernlanguages/

**University of Maine,** Graduate School, College of Liberal Arts and Sciences, Department of Modern Languages and Classics, Orono, ME 04469. Offers French (MA, MAT); Spanish (MAT). *Program availability:* Part-time. *Faculty:* 6 full-time (3 women), 1 (woman) part-time/adjunct. *Students:* 2 full-time (1 woman), 1 (woman) part-time. Average age 41. 2 applicants, 100% accepted, 1 enrolled. In 2016, 5 master's awarded. *Degree requirements:* For master's, one foreign language, thesis (for some programs). *Entrance requirements:* For master's, GRE General Test, Applicants for M.A.T. require PRAXIS II. Additional exam requirements/recommendations for international students: Required—TOEFL. *Application deadline:* For fall admission, 2/1 priority date for domestic and international students. Applications are processed on a rolling basis. Application fee: $65. Electronic applications accepted. *Expenses:* Tuition, state resident: full-time $7524; part-time $2508 per credit. Tuition, nonresident: full-time $24,498; part-time $8166 per credit. *Required fees:* $1148; $571 per credit. *Financial support:* In 2016–17, 2 students received support, including 2 teaching assistantships with tuition reimbursements available (averaging $14,600 per year); Federal Work-Study and tuition waivers (full and partial) also available. Financial award application deadline: 3/1. *Faculty research:* Latin American literature and culture, early modern and modern Spanish literature and culture, North American French linguistics, 20th century Quebec

literature and culture, contemporary French philosophy. *Unit head:* Dr. Jane Smith, Chair, 207-581-2075, Fax: 207-581-1832. *Application contact:* Scott G. Delcourt, Assistant Vice President for Graduate Studies/Senior Associate Dean, 207-581-3291, Fax: 207-581-3232, E-mail: graduate@maine.edu.
Website: https://umaine.edu/mlandc/graduate-programs/

**The University of Manchester,** School of Languages, Linguistics and Cultures, Manchester, United Kingdom. Offers Arab world studies (PhD); Chinese studies (M Phil, PhD); East Asian studies (M Phil, PhD); English language (PhD); French studies (M Phil, PhD); German studies (M Phil, PhD); interpreting studies (PhD); Italian studies (M Phil, PhD); Japanese studies (M Phil, PhD); Latin American cultural studies (M Phil, PhD); linguistics (M Phil, PhD); Middle Eastern studies (M Phil, PhD); Polish studies (M Phil, PhD); Portuguese studies (M Phil, PhD); Russian studies (M Phil, PhD); Spanish studies (M Phil, PhD); translation and intercultural studies (M Phil, PhD).

**University of Manitoba,** Faculty of Graduate Studies, Faculty of Arts, Department of French, Spanish and Italian, Winnipeg, MB R3T 2N2, Canada. Offers French (MA, PhD). *Degree requirements:* For master's, one foreign language, thesis; for doctorate, 2 foreign languages, thesis/dissertation.

**University of Maryland, College Park,** Academic Affairs, College of Arts and Humanities, School of Languages, Literatures, and Cultures, Modern French Studies Program, College Park, MD 20742. Offers PhD. *Entrance requirements:* For doctorate, GRE, letters of recommendation, writing sample. Additional exam requirements/recommendations for international students: Required—TOEFL.

**University of Maryland, College Park,** Academic Affairs, College of Arts and Humanities, School of Languages, Literatures, and Cultures, Program in French Language and Literature, College Park, MD 20742. Offers MA. *Degree requirements:* For master's, one foreign language, comprehensive exam, thesis or alternative. *Entrance requirements:* For master's, GRE General Test, GRE Subject Test, minimum GPA of 3.0, 3 letters of recommendation. Additional exam requirements/recommendations for international students: Required—TOEFL. Electronic applications accepted.

**University of Massachusetts Amherst,** Graduate School, College of Humanities and Fine Arts, Department of Languages, Literatures, and Cultures, Program in French and Francophone Studies, Amherst, MA 01003. Offers French (MAT); French and Francophone studies (MA). *Program availability:* Part-time. *Degree requirements:* For master's, thesis or alternative. *Entrance requirements:* For master's, GRE General Test. Additional exam requirements/recommendations for international students: Required—TOEFL (minimum score 550 paper-based; 80 iBT), IELTS (minimum score 6.5). Electronic applications accepted.

**University of Memphis,** Graduate School, College of Arts and Sciences, Department of Foreign Languages and Literatures, Memphis, TN 38152. Offers romance languages (MA), including French, Spanish. *Program availability:* Part-time. *Faculty:* 11 full-time (6 women). *Students:* 17 full-time (13 women), 5 part-time (4 women); includes 14 minority (2 Black or African American, non-Hispanic/Latino; 12 Hispanic/Latino), 2 international. Average age 33. 12 applicants, 92% accepted, 8 enrolled. In 2016, 4 master's awarded. *Degree requirements:* For master's, 2 foreign languages, comprehensive exam. *Entrance requirements:* For master's, GRE, interview in language of concentration, writing sample, letter of intent, two letters of recommendation. Additional exam requirements/recommendations for international students: Required—TOEFL (minimum score 94 iBT). *Application deadline:* For fall admission, 5/15 for domestic students, 4/5 for international students; for spring admission, 11/30 for domestic students, 10/5 for international students. Applications are processed on a rolling basis. Application fee: $35 ($60 for international students). Electronic applications accepted. *Expenses:* $5,231.50 per semester full-time in-state, $9,623.50 full-time out-of-state. *Financial support:* In 2016–17, 11 students received support, including 15 teaching assistantships with full tuition reimbursements available (averaging $13,534 per year); research assistantships with full tuition reimbursements available, Federal Work-Study, scholarships/grants, and unspecified assistantships also available. Financial award application deadline: 2/1; financial award applicants required to submit FAFSA. *Faculty research:* Latin American studies, Brazilian culture and literature, modernity and postmodernity, Hispanic studies, French studies, French and Hispanic culture and literature, Hispanic linguistics, applied linguistics. *Unit head:* Dr. William Thompson, Chair, 901-678-2507, E-mail: wjthmpsn@memphis.edu. *Application contact:* Dr. Fernando Burgos, Coordinator of Graduate Studies, 901-678-3158, E-mail: fburgos@memphis.edu.
Website: http://www.memphis.edu/fl/

**University of Miami,** Graduate School, College of Arts and Sciences, Department of Modern Languages and Literatures, Coral Gables, FL 33124. Offers romance studies (PhD), including French, Spanish. *Degree requirements:* For doctorate, 2 foreign languages, thesis/dissertation, area exam, qualifying exam. *Entrance requirements:* For doctorate, 1 writing sample in English and 1 writing sample in French or Spanish, minimum GPA of 3.0, oral interview, letters of recommendation. Additional exam requirements/recommendations for international students: Required—TOEFL (minimum score 550 paper-based; 59 iBT). Electronic applications accepted. *Faculty research:* Transatlantic studies, Caribbean studies, comparative literature, gender theory, cultural studies.

**University of Michigan,** Rackham Graduate School, College of Literature, Science, and the Arts, Department of Romance Languages and Literatures, Program in French, Ann Arbor, MI 48109. Offers PhD. *Degree requirements:* For doctorate, 2 foreign languages, thesis/dissertation, oral defense of dissertation, preliminary exams in essay format. *Entrance requirements:* Additional exam requirements/recommendations for international students: Required—TOEFL or Michigan English Language Assessment Battery. Electronic applications accepted. *Expenses:* Tuition: state resident: full-time $21,466; part-time $1152 per credit hour. Tuition, nonresident: full-time $43,346; part-time $2367 per credit hour. Part-time tuition and fees vary according to course load, degree level and program. *Faculty research:* Comparative Romance studies, medieval and early modern studies, postcolonial and minority literatures, culture and materiality, reflection on the nature and function of scholarship.

**University of Minnesota, Twin Cities Campus,** Graduate School, College of Liberal Arts, Department of French and Italian, Minneapolis, MN 55455-0213. Offers French (MA, PhD). *Program availability:* Part-time. *Degree requirements:* For master's, one foreign language, comprehensive exam, thesis optional; for doctorate, one foreign language, thesis/dissertation, individualized exam on topic areas. *Entrance requirements:* For master's and doctorate, GRE, minimum GPA of 3.25 (recommended). Additional exam requirements/recommendations for international students: Required—TOEFL (minimum score 550 paper-based). Electronic applications accepted. *Faculty research:* Francophone literature, cultural studies, feminism, critical theory, medieval studies.

**University of Missouri,** Office of Research and Graduate Studies, College of Arts and Science, Department of Romance Languages and Literatures, Columbia, MO 65211. Offers French (MA, PhD); literature (MA); Spanish (MA, PhD); teaching (MA). *Faculty:* 25 full-time (15 women). *Students:* 22 full-time (16 women), 15 part-time (10 women); includes 11 minority (3 Black or African American, non-Hispanic/Latino; 6 Hispanic/Latino; 2 Two or more races, non-Hispanic/Latino), 13 international. Average age 35. Terminal master's awarded for partial completion of doctoral program. *Degree requirements:* For master's, one foreign language; for doctorate, 4 foreign languages, comprehensive exam, thesis/dissertation. *Entrance requirements:* For master's, GRE General Test, minimum GPA of 3.0 in field of major; bachelor's degree; for doctorate, GRE General Test, minimum GPA of 3.0 in field of major; master's degree. Additional exam requirements/recommendations for international students: Required—TOEFL (minimum score 500 paper-based; 61 iBT). *Application deadline:* For fall admission, 2/15 priority date for domestic students; for winter admission, 10/15 for domestic students. Applications are processed on a rolling basis. Application fee: $75 ($90 for international students). Electronic applications accepted. *Expenses:* Tuition, state resident: full-time $6347; part-time $352.60 per credit hour. Tuition, nonresident: full-time $17,379; part-time $965.50 per credit hour. *Required fees:* $1035. Tuition and fees vary according to course load, campus/location and program. *Financial support:* Research assistantships, teaching assistantships with full tuition reimbursements, institutionally sponsored loans, health care benefits, and unspecified assistantships available.
Website: http://romancelanguages.missouri.edu/grad.shtml

**University of Missouri–Kansas City,** College of Arts and Sciences, Department of Foreign Languages and Literatures, Kansas City, MO 64110-2499. Offers romance languages and literatures (MA), including French, Spanish. *Program availability:* Part-time. *Faculty:* 32 full-time (18 women), 38 part-time/adjunct (32 women). *Students:* 3 full-time (0 women), 13 part-time (9 women); includes 8 minority (all Hispanic/Latino). Average age 35. 12 applicants, 58% accepted, 4 enrolled. In 2016, 7 master's awarded. *Degree requirements:* For master's, 2 foreign languages. *Entrance requirements:* For master's, GRE General Test, minimum GPA of 2.75, 2 letters of recommendation. Additional exam requirements/recommendations for international students: Required—TOEFL (minimum score 550 paper-based; 80 iBT). *Application deadline:* For fall admission, 4/1 priority date for domestic and international students; for spring admission, 11/1 priority date for domestic and international students. Applications are processed on a rolling basis. Application fee: $45 ($50 for international students). Electronic applications accepted. *Financial support:* In 2016–17, 2 teaching assistantships (averaging $12,600 per year) were awarded; Federal Work-Study, institutionally sponsored loans, and tuition waivers (full and partial) also available. Support available to part-time students. Financial award application deadline: 3/1; financial award applicants required to submit FAFSA. *Faculty research:* Literary analyses; psychology and literature; narrative techniques, poetic structure, and style; literature, politics, and society (especially in Latin America). *Unit head:* Dr. K. Scott Baker, Chair, 816-235-2823, Fax: 816-235-1312, E-mail: bakerks@umkc.edu. *Application contact:* 816-235-1311, Fax: 816-235-1312, E-mail: admit@umkc.edu.
Website: http://cas.umkc.edu/foreign

**University of Montana,** Graduate School, College of Humanities and Sciences, Department of Modern and Classical Languages and Literatures, Missoula, MT 59812-0002. Offers French (MA); German (MA); Spanish (MA). *Degree requirements:* For master's, one foreign language. *Entrance requirements:* For master's, GRE General Test. Additional exam requirements/recommendations for international students: Required—TOEFL.

**University of Nebraska–Lincoln,** Graduate College, College of Arts and Sciences, Department of Modern Languages and Literatures, Lincoln, NE 68588. Offers French (MA, PhD); German (MA, PhD); Spanish (MA, PhD). *Degree requirements:* For master's, thesis optional; for doctorate, comprehensive exam, thesis/dissertation. *Entrance requirements:* For master's and doctorate, writing sample in target language. Additional exam requirements/recommendations for international students: Required—TOEFL (minimum score 550 paper-based). Electronic applications accepted. *Faculty research:* French, German, and Spanish language, literature, and culture.

**University of Nevada, Reno,** Graduate School, College of Liberal Arts, Department of Foreign Languages and Literatures, Reno, NV 89557. Offers French (MA); German (MA); Spanish (MA). *Degree requirements:* For master's, one foreign language, thesis optional. *Entrance requirements:* For master's, GRE General Test, minimum GPA of 2.75. Additional exam requirements/recommendations for international students: Required—TOEFL (minimum score 500 paper-based; 61 iBT), IELTS (minimum score 6). *Faculty research:* Thirteenth century mysticism, contemporary Spanish and Latin American poetry and theater, French interrelation between narration and photography, exile literature and Holocaust.

**University of New Mexico,** Graduate Studies, College of Arts and Sciences, Program in Foreign Languages and Literatures, Albuquerque, NM 87131-2039. Offers comparative literature and cultural studies (MA); French (MA); French studies (PhD); German studies (PhD). *Program availability:* Part-time. *Faculty:* 9 full-time (5 women). *Students:* 21 full-time (12 women), 10 part-time (6 women); includes 4 minority (3 Hispanic/Latino; 1 Two or more races, non-Hispanic/Latino), 10 international. Average age 30. 17 applicants, 41% accepted, 5 enrolled. In 2016, 9 master's awarded. *Degree requirements:* For master's, one foreign language, thesis optional; for doctorate, 2 foreign languages, thesis/dissertation. *Entrance requirements:* For master's and doctorate, transcript, writing sample, 3 letters of recommendation. Additional exam requirements/recommendations for international students: Required—TOEFL. *Application deadline:* For fall admission, 2/1 priority date for domestic students; for spring admission, 10/1 priority date for domestic students. Application fee: $50. Electronic applications accepted. *Financial support:* Research assistantships, teaching assistantships with tuition reimbursements, Federal Work-Study, health care benefits, and unspecified assistantships available. Financial award application deadline: 3/1; financial award applicants required to submit FAFSA. *Faculty research:* German, Russian, Italian, Japanese, French, comparative literature, culture studies, classics. *Unit head:* Dr. Walter Putnam, Chair, 505-277-4771, Fax: 505-277-3599, E-mail: wputnam@unm.edu. *Application contact:* Jacqueline Ochoa, Application and Graduation Advisor, 505-277-4471, Fax: 505-277-3599, E-mail: jochoa@unm.edu.
Website: http://www.unm.edu/~fll/

**The University of North Carolina at Chapel Hill,** Graduate School, College of Arts and Sciences, Department of Romance Languages and Literatures, Chapel Hill, NC 27599. Offers French (MA, PhD); Italian (MA, PhD); Portuguese (MA, PhD); Romance languages (MA, PhD); Romance philology (MA, PhD); Spanish (MA, PhD). *Degree requirements:* For master's, one foreign language, comprehensive exam, thesis; for doctorate, 2 foreign languages, comprehensive exam, thesis/dissertation. *Entrance requirements:* For master's and doctorate, GRE General Test, minimum GPA of 3.0. Additional exam requirements/recommendations for international students: Required—TOEFL (minimum score 550 paper-based). Electronic applications accepted.

**The University of North Carolina at Greensboro,** Graduate School, College of Arts and Sciences, Department of Languages, Literatures, and Cultures, Program in French, Greensboro, NC 27412-5001. Offers MA. *Degree requirements:* For master's, one foreign language, comprehensive exam, thesis or alternative. *Entrance requirements:* For master's, GRE General Test, 3-5 minute tape demonstrating foreign language proficiency, composition in French, sample paper in English. Additional exam requirements/recommendations for international students: Required—TOEFL. Electronic applications accepted.

## French

**University of North Texas,** Robert B. Toulouse School of Graduate Studies, Denton, TX 76203-5459. Offers accounting (MS); applied anthropology (MA, MS); applied behavior analysis (Certificate); applied geography (MA); applied technology and performance improvement (M Ed, MS); art education (MA); art history (MA); art museum education (Certificate); arts leadership (Certificate); audiology (Au D); behavior analysis (MS); behavioral science (PhD); biochemistry and molecular biology (MS); biology (MA, MS); biomedical engineering (MS); business analysis (MS); chemistry (MS); clinical health psychology (PhD); communication (MA, MS); computer engineering (MS); computer science (MS); counseling (M Ed, MS), including clinical mental health counseling (MS), college and university counseling, elementary school counseling, secondary school counseling; creative writing (MA); criminal justice (MS); curriculum and instruction (M Ed); decision sciences (MBA); design (MA, MFA), including fashion design (MFA), innovation studies, interior design (MFA); early childhood studies (MS); economics (MS); educational leadership (M Ed, Ed D); educational psychology (MS, PhD), including family studies (MS), gifted and talented (MS), human development (MS), learning and cognition (MS), research, measurement and evaluation (MS); electrical engineering (MS); emergency management (MPA); engineering technology (MS); English (MA); English as a second language (MA); environmental science (MS); finance (MBA, MS); financial management (MPA); French (MA); health services management (MBA); higher education (M Ed, Ed D); history (MA, MS); hospitality management (MS); human resources management (MPA); information science (MS); information systems (PhD); information technologies (MBA); interdisciplinary studies (MA, MS); international studies (MA); international sustainable tourism (MS); jazz studies (MM); journalism (MA, MJ, Graduate Certificate), including interactive and virtual digital communication (Graduate Certificate), narrative journalism (Graduate Certificate), public relations (Graduate Certificate); kinesiology (MS); linguistics (MA); local government management (MPA); logistics (PhD); logistics and supply chain management (MBA); long-term care, senior housing, and aging services (MA); management (PhD); marketing (MBA); mathematics (MA, MS); mechanical and energy engineering (MS, PhD); music (MA), including ethnomusicology, music theory, musicology, performance; music composition (PhD); music education (MM Ed, PhD); nonprofit management (MPA); operations and supply chain management (MBA); performance (MM, DMA); philosophy (MA); political science (MA); professional and technical communication (MA); radio, television and film (MA, MFA); rehabilitation counseling (Certificate); sociology (MA); Spanish (MA); special education (M Ed); speech-language pathology (MA); strategic management (MBA); studio art (MFA); teaching (M Ed) MBA/MS. *Program availability:* Part-time, evening/weekend, online learning. Terminal master's awarded for partial completion of doctoral program. *Degree requirements:* For master's, variable foreign language requirement, comprehensive exam (for some programs), thesis (for some programs); for doctorate, variable foreign language requirement, comprehensive exam (for some programs), thesis/dissertation; for other advanced degree, variable foreign language requirement, comprehensive exam (for some programs). *Entrance requirements:* For master's and doctorate, GRE, GMAT. Additional exam requirements/recommendations for international students: Required—TOEFL (minimum score 550 paper-based; 79 iBT). Electronic applications accepted.

**University of Notre Dame,** Graduate School, College of Arts and Letters, Division of Humanities, Department of Romance Languages and Literatures, Notre Dame, IN 46556. Offers French and Francophone studies (MA); Iberian and Latin American studies (MA); Italian studies (MA); Romance literatures (MA). *Degree requirements:* For master's, 2 foreign languages, comprehensive exam, thesis optional. *Entrance requirements:* For master's, GRE General Test, BA in target language. Additional exam requirements/recommendations for international students: Required—TOEFL (minimum score 600 paper-based; 80 iBT). Electronic applications accepted. *Faculty research:* Literature of discovery and exploration, modern literature, literary criticism, medieval literature, feminist critical theory.

**University of Oklahoma,** College of Arts and Sciences, Department of Modern Languages, Literatures, and Linguistics, Program in French, Norman, OK 73019-2032. Offers MA, PhD, MBA/MA. *Program availability:* Part-time. *Students:* 5 full-time (4 women), 3 part-time (all women); includes 1 minority (Hispanic/Latino), 3 international. Average age 34. 1 applicant, 100% accepted, 1 enrolled. In 2016, 1 master's awarded. Terminal master's awarded for partial completion of doctoral program. *Degree requirements:* For master's, comprehensive exam (for some programs), thesis optional, two languages (one must be French); for doctorate, comprehensive exam (for some programs), thesis/dissertation optional, two languages (one must be French). *Entrance requirements:* For master's, BA (or equivalent) in French, or equivalent hours in the major; for doctorate, MA (or equivalent) in French. Additional exam requirements/recommendations for international students: Required—TOEFL (minimum score 79 iBT) or IELTS (minimum score 6.5). *Application deadline:* For fall admission, 2/1 for domestic and international students; for spring admission, 10/1 for domestic and international students. Application fee: $50 ($100 for international students). Electronic applications accepted. *Expenses:* Tuition, state resident: full-time $4886; part-time $203.60 per credit hour. Tuition, nonresident: full-time $18,989; part-time $791.20 per credit hour. *Required fees:* $3283; $126.25 per credit hour. $126.50 per semester. *Financial support:* In 2016–17, 8 students received support. Fellowships, teaching assistantships with full tuition reimbursements available, scholarships/grants, health care benefits, and unspecified assistantships available. Support available to part-time students. Financial award application deadline: 6/1; financial award applicants required to submit FAFSA. *Faculty research:* Medieval literature and culture, 17th-century literature, 18th-century literature and culture, 19th-century literature and culture, 20th- and 21st-century literature and culture. *Unit head:* Dr. Logan Whalen, Associate Professor of French, E-mail: lwhalen@ou.edu. *Application contact:* Pamela Genova, Professor/Graduate Liaison, E-mail: genova@ou.edu.
Website: http://mlll.publishpath.com/french-ma

**University of Oregon,** Graduate School, College of Arts and Sciences, Department of Romance Languages, Program in French, Eugene, OR 97403. Offers MA. *Program availability:* Part-time. *Degree requirements:* For master's, one foreign language. *Entrance requirements:* For master's, GRE General Test, minimum GPA of 3.0. Additional exam requirements/recommendations for international students: Required—TOEFL.

**University of Ottawa,** Faculty of Graduate and Postdoctoral Studies, Faculty of Arts, Department of Lettres Franlfcaises, Ottawa, ON K1N 6N5, Canada. Offers MA, PhD. *Degree requirements:* For master's, thesis or alternative; for doctorate, thesis/dissertation, oral exam. *Entrance requirements:* For master's, honors degree or equivalent, minimum B average; for doctorate, master's degree, minimum B+ average. Electronic applications accepted. *Faculty research:* Littérature franlfcaise, du Moyen-IfQge á nos jours; littérature québécoise, des origines au XXe sie&,cle; création littéraire.

**University of Pennsylvania,** School of Arts and Sciences, Graduate Group in Romance Languages, Philadelphia, PA 19104. Offers French (AM, PhD); Italian (AM, PhD); Spanish (AM, PhD). *Faculty:* 38 full-time (14 women), 11 part-time/adjunct (3 women). *Students:* 56 full-time (25 women), 3 part-time (2 women); includes 4 minority (all Hispanic/Latino), 34 international. Average age 32. 73 applicants, 33% accepted, 10 enrolled. In 2016, 10 master's, 5 doctorates awarded. Terminal master's awarded for partial completion of doctoral program. Application fee: $70. *Expenses: Tuition:* Full-time $31,068; part-time $5762 per course. *Required fees:* $3200; $336 per course. Full-time tuition and fees vary according to degree level, program and student level. Part-time tuition and fees vary according to course load, degree level and program.
Website: http://www.sas.upenn.edu/graduate-division

**University of Pittsburgh,** Dietrich School of Arts and Sciences, Department of French and Italian, Pittsburgh, PA 15260. Offers French (MA, PhD), including film studies (PhD), French; Italian (MA). *Program availability:* Part-time. *Faculty:* 12 full-time (6 women). *Students:* 24 full-time (16 women); includes 2 minority (both Black or African American, non-Hispanic/Latino), 10 international. Average age 32. 16 applicants, 56% accepted, 6 enrolled. In 2016, 4 master's, 2 doctorates awarded. Terminal master's awarded for partial completion of doctoral program. *Degree requirements:* For master's, one foreign language, comprehensive exam, seminar paper/thesis; for doctorate, one foreign language, comprehensive exam, thesis/dissertation, dissertation defense. *Entrance requirements:* For master's, GRE General Test (for French), phone interview and writing samples in French and English (for French); minimum GPA of 3.0 and writing sample (for Italian); for doctorate, GRE General Test (for French), phone interview and writing samples in French and English (for French). Additional exam requirements/recommendations for international students: Required—TOEFL (minimum score 600 paper-based; 90 iBT). *Application deadline:* For fall admission, 1/10 for domestic and international students. Application fee: $50. Electronic applications accepted. Tuition and fees vary according to program. *Financial support:* In 2016–17, 22 students received support, including 14 fellowships with full tuition reimbursements available (averaging $21,812 per year), 3 teaching assistantships with full tuition reimbursements available (averaging $17,905 per year); Federal Work-Study, traineeships, health care benefits, and tuition waivers (partial) also available. Financial award application deadline: 1/10. *Faculty research:* Literature and politics, constructs of the French nation, literary and cultural theory, French linguistics, gender and sexuality, Dante and his reception, humanism and Renaissance studies, seventeenth- and eighteenth-century Italian literature and culture, Italian theater, Holocaust literature and film, images of Southern Italy in European literature. *Total annual research expenditures:* $5,200. *Unit head:* Dr. Lina Insana, Chair, 412-624-6269, Fax: 412-624-6263, E-mail: insana@pitt.edu. *Application contact:* Keanna Cash, Graduate Administrator, 412-624-5906, Fax: 412-624-6263, E-mail: kec176@pitt.edu.
Website: http://www.frenchanditalian.pitt.edu

**University of Regina,** Faculty of Graduate Studies and Research, Faculty of Arts, Department of French, Regina, SK S4S 0A2, Canada. Offers MA. *Program availability:* Part-time. *Faculty:* 4 full-time (0 women), 2 part-time/adjunct (0 women). *Students:* 18 full-time (9 women). *Degree requirements:* For master's, thesis, seminar presentation. *Entrance requirements:* Additional exam requirements/recommendations for international students: Required—TOEFL (minimum score 580 paper-based; 80 iBT), IELTS (minimum score 6.5), PTE (minimum score 59). *Application deadline:* Applications are processed on a rolling basis. Application fee: $100. Electronic applications accepted. *Financial support:* Fellowships, teaching assistantships, and scholarships/grants available. Financial award application deadline: 6/15. *Faculty research:* French literature, French linguistics, rhetoric, translation and terminology, lexicography. *Unit head:* Dr. Emmanuel Aito, Department Head and Graduate Program Coordinator, 306-337-2576, Fax: 306-585-4827, E-mail: emmanuel.aito@uregina.ca.
Website: http://www.uregina.ca/arts/french

**University of Saskatchewan,** College of Graduate Studies and Research, College of Arts and Science, Department of Languages and Linguistics, Saskatoon, SK S7N 5A2, Canada. Offers MA. *Degree requirements:* For master's, 2 foreign languages, thesis. *Entrance requirements:* Additional exam requirements/recommendations for international students: Required—TOEFL (minimum score 80 iBT); Recommended—IELTS (minimum score 6.5). Electronic applications accepted.

**University of South Africa,** College of Human Sciences, Pretoria, South Africa. Offers adult education (M Ed); African languages (MA, PhD); African politics (MA, PhD); Afrikaans (MA, PhD); ancient history (MA, PhD); ancient Near Eastern studies (MA, PhD); anthropology (MA, PhD); applied linguistics (MA); Arabic (MA, PhD); archaeology (MA); art history (MA); Biblical archaeology (MA); Biblical studies (M Th, D Th, PhD); Christian spirituality (M Th, D Th); church history (M Th, D Th); classical studies (MA, PhD); clinical psychology (MA); communication (MA, PhD); comparative education (M Ed, Ed D); consulting psychology (D Admin, D Com, PhD); curriculum studies (M Ed, Ed D); development studies (M Admin, MA, D Admin, PhD); didactics (M Ed, Ed D); education (M Tech); education management (M Ed, Ed D); educational psychology (M Ed); English (MA); environmental education (M Ed); French (MA, PhD); German (MA, PhD); Greek (MA); guidance and counseling (M Ed); health studies (MA, PhD), including health sciences education (MA), health services management (MA), medical and surgical nursing science (critical care general) (MA), midwifery and neonatal nursing science (MA), trauma and emergency care (MA); history (MA, PhD); history of education (Ed D); inclusive education (M Ed, Ed D); information and communications technology policy and regulation (MA); information science (MA, MIS, PhD); international politics (MA, PhD); Islamic studies (MA, PhD); Italian (MA, PhD); Judaica (MA, PhD); linguistics (MA, PhD); mathematical education (M Ed); mathematics education (MA); missiology (M Th, D Th); modern Hebrew (MA, PhD); musicology (MA, MMus, D Mus, PhD); natural science education (M Ed); New Testament (M Th, D Th); Old Testament (D Th); pastoral therapy (M Th, D Th); philosophy (MA); philosophy of education (M Ed, Ed D); politics (MA, PhD); Portuguese (MA, PhD); practical theology (M Th, D Th); psychology (MA, MS, PhD); psychology of education (M Ed, Ed D); public health (MA); religious studies (MA, D Th, PhD); Romance languages (MA); Russian (MA, PhD); Semitic languages (MA, PhD); social behavior studies in HIV/AIDS (MA); social science (mental health) (MA); social science in development studies (MA); social science in psychology (MA); social science in social work (MA); social science in sociology (MA); social work (MSW, DSW, PhD); socio-education (M Ed, Ed D); sociolinguistics (MA); sociology (MA, PhD); Spanish (MA, PhD); systematic theology (M Th, D Th); TESOL (teaching English to speakers of other languages) (MA); theological ethics (M Th, D Th); theory of literature (MA, PhD); urban ministries (D Th); urban ministry (M Th).

**University of South Carolina,** The Graduate School, College of Arts and Sciences, Department of Languages, Literatures, and Cultures, Columbia, SC 29208. Offers comparative literature (MA, PhD); foreign languages (MAT), including French, German, Spanish; French (MA); German (MA); Spanish (MA). MAT offered in cooperation with the College of Education. *Program availability:* Part-time. *Degree requirements:* For master's, one foreign language, comprehensive exam, thesis optional; for doctorate, 2 foreign languages, comprehensive exam, thesis/dissertation. *Entrance requirements:* For master's and doctorate, GRE General Test, writing sample. Additional exam requirements/recommendations for international students: Required—TOEFL (minimum score 75 iBT). Electronic applications accepted. *Faculty research:* Modern literature, linguistics, literature and culture, medieval literature, literary theory.

**University of South Florida,** College of Arts and Sciences, Department of World Languages, Tampa, FL 33620-9951. Offers French (MA); linguistics (MA); linguistics and applied linguistics studies (PhD); linguistics: English as a second language (MA); Spanish (MA). *Program availability:* Part-time, evening/weekend. *Faculty:* 20 full-time (16 women). *Students:* 38 full-time (28 women), 18 part-time (16 women); includes 19 minority (3 Black or African American, non-Hispanic/Latino; 1 Asian, non-Hispanic/Latino; 14 Hispanic/Latino; 1 Two or more races, non-Hispanic/Latino), 9 international. Average age 34. 36 applicants, 58% accepted, 13 enrolled. In 2016, 26 master's awarded. *Degree requirements:* For master's, one foreign language, comprehensive exam, thesis optional; for doctorate, one foreign language, comprehensive exam, thesis/dissertation. *Entrance requirements:* For master's, GRE General Test, minimum undergraduate GPA of 3.0 and 2-3 letters of recommendation; two-page statement of purpose written in Spanish (for Spanish program); oral interview (for Spanish and French programs); writing sample (for French program); for doctorate, GRE General Test, minimum GPA of 3.5 or international equivalent; master's degree or equivalent academic level; statement of purpose; current curriculum vitae; three letters of recommendation; personal interview with faculty; evidence of research experience or scholarly promise. Additional exam requirements/recommendations for international students: Required—TOEFL (minimum score 600 paper-based; 80 iBT) or IELTS (minimum score 6.5) for MA; TOEFL (minimum score 550 paper-based; 80 iBT) or IELTS (minimum score 6.5) for PhD. *Application deadline:* For fall admission, 1/15 for domestic and international students; for spring admission, 10/15 for domestic students, 9/15 for international students. Application fee: $30. Electronic applications accepted. *Expenses:* Tuition, state resident: full-time $7766; part-time $431.43 per credit hour. Tuition, nonresident: full-time $15,789; part-time $877.17 per credit hour. *Required fees:* $37 per term. *Financial support:* In 2016–17, 4 students received support, including 43 teaching assistantships with tuition reimbursements available (averaging $10,152 per year); tuition waivers (partial) and unspecified assistantships also available. Financial award application deadline: 6/30. *Faculty research:* Second language acquisition, instructional technology, foreign language education, English for speakers of other languages, distance learning. *Total annual research expenditures:* $104,720. *Unit head:* Dr. Stephan Schindler, Chair and Professor, 813-974-2548, Fax: 813-905-9937, E-mail: skschindler@usf.edu. *Application contact:* Patricia Garcia, Academic Program Specialist, 813-974-2548, Fax: 813-905-9937, E-mail: pgarcia@usf.edu. Website: http://languages.usf.edu/

**The University of Tennessee,** Graduate School, College of Arts and Sciences, Department of Modern Foreign Languages and Literatures, Program in French, Knoxville, TN 37996. Offers MA. *Degree requirements:* For master's, one foreign language, thesis or alternative. *Entrance requirements:* For master's, minimum GPA of 2.7. Additional exam requirements/recommendations for international students: Required—TOEFL. Electronic applications accepted.

**The University of Tennessee,** Graduate School, College of Arts and Sciences, Department of Modern Foreign Languages and Literatures, Program in Modern Foreign Languages, Knoxville, TN 37996. Offers applied linguistics (PhD); French (PhD); German (PhD); Italian (PhD); Portuguese (PhD); Russian (PhD); Spanish (PhD). *Degree requirements:* For doctorate, 2 foreign languages, thesis/dissertation. *Entrance requirements:* For doctorate, minimum GPA of 2.7. Additional exam requirements/recommendations for international students: Required—TOEFL. Electronic applications accepted.

**The University of Texas at Arlington,** Graduate School, College of Liberal Arts, Department of Modern Languages, Arlington, TX 76019. Offers French (MA); Spanish (MA). *Program availability:* Part-time, evening/weekend. *Degree requirements:* For master's, 2 foreign languages, comprehensive exam, thesis optional. *Entrance requirements:* For master's, GRE General Test, minimum GPA of 3.0, 3 letters of recommendation. Additional exam requirements/recommendations for international students: Required—TOEFL (minimum score 550 paper-based). *Application deadline:* For fall admission, 6/15 for domestic students. Applications are processed on a rolling basis. Application fee: $35 ($50 for international students). *Financial support:* Fellowships with full tuition reimbursements, research assistantships, teaching assistantships, career-related internships or fieldwork, Federal Work-Study, and scholarships/grants available. Financial award application deadline: 6/1; financial award applicants required to submit FAFSA. *Unit head:* Dr. Antoinette Sol, Chair, 817-272-3161, Fax: 817-272-5408, E-mail: amsol@uta.edu. *Application contact:* Dr. Ignacio Ruiz-Perez, Graduate Advisor, 817-272-3161, Fax: 817-272-5408, E-mail: iruiz@uta.edu. Website: http://www.langlab.uta.edu/modl/

**The University of Texas at Austin,** Graduate School, College of Liberal Arts, Department of French and Italian, Austin, TX 78712-1111. Offers French linguistics (MA, PhD); French studies (MA, PhD); Italian studies (MA, PhD); Romance linguistics (PhD). *Program availability:* Part-time. *Degree requirements:* For master's, one foreign language, thesis; for doctorate, 2 foreign languages, thesis/dissertation. *Entrance requirements:* For master's, GRE General Test, minimum GPA of 3.0, bachelor's degree in French or equivalent; for doctorate, GRE General Test, minimum GPA of 3.0, master's degree in French. Additional exam requirements/recommendations for international students: Required—TOEFL. Electronic applications accepted. *Faculty research:* Nineteenth-century Italian literature, Italian Renaissance, twentieth-century French literature, Francophone literature, fifteenth-century literature and culture.

**The University of Toledo,** College of Graduate Studies, College of Languages, Literature and Social Sciences, Department of Foreign Languages, Toledo, OH 43606-3390. Offers French (MA); German (MA); Spanish (MA). *Program availability:* Part-time. *Degree requirements:* For master's, one foreign language, comprehensive exam, comprehensive reading exam in 1 additional foreign language. *Entrance requirements:* For master's, minimum cumulative point-hour ratio of 2.7 for all previous academic work. Additional exam requirements/recommendations for international students: Required—TOEFL (minimum score 550 paper-based; 80 iBT). Electronic applications accepted.

**University of Toronto,** School of Graduate Studies, Faculty of Arts and Science, Department of French, Toronto, ON M5S 1A1, Canada. Offers French language and literature (MA, PhD). *Program availability:* Part-time. *Degree requirements:* For master's, research essay; for doctorate, one foreign language, thesis/dissertation, field exam. *Entrance requirements:* For master's, 2 letters of reference, writing sample, minimum B+ average overall and in French, undergraduate major in French; for doctorate, 7 courses in French language and literature, minimum A- average, writing sample. Additional exam requirements/recommendations for international students: Required—TOEFL (minimum score 580 paper-based; 93 iBT), TWE (minimum score 5). Electronic applications accepted.

**University of Utah,** Graduate School, College of Humanities, Department of World Languages and Cultures, Salt Lake City, UT 84112. Offers comparative literary and cultural studies (MA, PhD); French (MA); Spanish (MA, MALP); world languages (MA). *Program availability:* Part-time. *Faculty:* 27 full-time (17 women), 2 part-time/adjunct (both women). *Students:* 37 full-time (29 women), 3 part-time (1 woman); includes 9 minority (2 Asian, non-Hispanic/Latino; 6 Hispanic/Latino; 1 Two or more races, non-Hispanic/Latino), 9 international. Average age 37. 29 applicants, 62% accepted, 15 enrolled. In 2016, 13 master's awarded. Terminal master's awarded for partial completion of doctoral program. *Degree requirements:* For master's, variable foreign language requirement, comprehensive exam (for some programs), thesis (for some programs); for doctorate, 2 foreign languages, comprehensive exam, thesis/dissertation. *Entrance requirements:* For master's, bachelor's degree from regionally-accredited college or university with minimum undergraduate overall GPA of 3.0; for doctorate, MA

from regionally-accredited college or university, advanced proficiency in target language. Additional exam requirements/recommendations for international students: Required—TOEFL (minimum score 550 paper-based; 80 iBT). *Application deadline:* For fall admission, 1/15 priority date for domestic students, 12/15 priority date for international students. Application fee: $55 ($65 for international students). Electronic applications accepted. *Expenses:* Tuition, state resident: full-time $7011; part-time $3918.24 per credit hour. Tuition, nonresident: full-time $22,154; part-time $11,665.42 per credit hour. *Financial support:* In 2016–17, 27 students received support, including 27 teaching assistantships with full and partial tuition reimbursements available (averaging $16,500 per year); health care benefits and unspecified assistantships also available. Financial award application deadline: 1/15. *Faculty research:* Literary study, literary theory, linguistics, cultural studies, comparative studies. *Unit head:* Dr. Katharina Gerstenberger, Chair, 801-585-7908, Fax: 801-581-7581, E-mail: katharina.gerstenberger@utah.edu. *Application contact:* Mackenzie Buie, Academic Coordinator, 801-581-7748, Fax: 801-581-7581, E-mail: mackenzie.buie@utah.edu. Website: http://languages.utah.edu/

**University of Victoria,** Faculty of Graduate Studies, Faculty of Humanities, Department of French, Victoria, BC V8W 2Y2, Canada. Offers literature (MA); teaching emphasis (MA). *Program availability:* Part-time, evening/weekend. *Degree requirements:* For master's, 2 foreign languages, thesis optional. *Entrance requirements:* For master's, BA in French. Additional exam requirements/recommendations for international students: Required—TOEFL (minimum score 575 paper-based), IELTS (minimum score 7). Electronic applications accepted. *Faculty research:* French-Canadian literature, stylistics, comparative literature, Francophone literature.

**University of Virginia,** College and Graduate School of Arts and Sciences, Department of French, Charlottesville, VA 22903. Offers MA, PhD. *Faculty:* 22 full-time (16 women), 3 part-time/adjunct (2 women). *Students:* 20 full-time (12 women), 1 (woman) part-time; includes 1 minority (Asian, non-Hispanic/Latino), 8 international. Average age 29. 18 applicants, 56% accepted, 6 enrolled. In 2016, 2 master's, 8 doctorates awarded. *Degree requirements:* For master's, one foreign language, comprehensive exam; for doctorate, one foreign language, comprehensive exam, thesis/dissertation. *Entrance requirements:* For master's and doctorate, GRE General Test, minimum GPA of 3.0 in major and overall; 2 letters of recommendation; writing sample. Additional exam requirements/recommendations for international students: Required—TOEFL (minimum score 600 paper-based; 90 iBT), IELTS (minimum score 7). *Application deadline:* For fall admission, 12/1 for domestic and international students. Applications are processed on a rolling basis. Application fee: $60. Electronic applications accepted. *Expenses:* Tuition, state resident: full-time $15,026; part-time $834 per credit hour. Tuition, nonresident: full-time $25,168; part-time $1378 per credit hour. *Required fees:* $2654. *Financial support:* Fellowships and teaching assistantships available. Financial award applicants required to submit FAFSA. *Unit head:* Ari Blatt, Chair, 434-924-7158, Fax: 434-924-7157, E-mail: ajb6f@virginia.edu. *Application contact:* Amy Ogden, Director of Graduate Studies, 434-924-7158, Fax: 434-924-7157, E-mail: avo2n@virginia.edu. Website: http://french.as.virginia.edu/

**University of Washington,** Graduate School, College of Arts and Sciences, Division of French and Italian Studies, Seattle, WA 98195. Offers French (MA, PhD); Italian (MA). Terminal master's awarded for partial completion of doctoral program. *Degree requirements:* For master's, 2 foreign languages, exam; for doctorate, 3 foreign languages, thesis/dissertation, exam. *Entrance requirements:* For master's and doctorate, GRE General Test, minimum GPA of 3.0. Additional exam requirements/recommendations for international students: Required—TOEFL. Electronic applications accepted. *Faculty research:* Interdisciplinary studies, literary theory and criticism, film, major periods of French and Italian literature, Francophonie.

**University of Waterloo,** Graduate Studies, Faculty of Arts, Department of French Studies, Waterloo, ON N2L 3G1, Canada. Offers French (MA, PhD). *Program availability:* Part-time. *Entrance requirements:* For master's, honors degree, minimum B average, course work and assignments in French, resume. Additional exam requirements/recommendations for international students: Required—TOEFL, IELTS. Electronic applications accepted. *Faculty research:* French and Quebec literature: Middle Ages through twentieth century, phonology of Acadian dialect, computerized scholarly editions of medieval and Renaissance texts.

**The University of Western Ontario,** Faculty of Graduate Studies, Faculty of Arts and Humanities, Department of French Studies, London, ON N6A 5B8, Canada. Offers MA, PhD. *Degree requirements:* For master's, thesis or alternative; for doctorate, one foreign language, thesis/dissertation. *Entrance requirements:* For master's, minimum B average, honors degree, 2 years of teaching experience (MAT); for doctorate, MA or equivalent, minimum B average in French. Additional exam requirements/recommendations for international students: Required—TOEFL. Electronic applications accepted.

**University of Wisconsin–Madison,** Graduate School, College of Letters and Science, Department of French and Italian, Program in French, Madison, WI 53706-1380. Offers MA, PhD. *Program availability:* Part-time. *Degree requirements:* For master's, one foreign language; for doctorate, one foreign language, thesis/dissertation. *Entrance requirements:* For master's and doctorate, GRE. Electronic applications accepted. *Faculty research:* Francophone literature; French literature, culture, linguistics, and language pedagogy.

**University of Wisconsin–Madison,** Graduate School, College of Letters and Science, Department of French and Italian, Program in French Studies, Madison, WI 53706-1380. Offers MFS, Certificate. *Program availability:* Part-time. *Degree requirements:* For master's, one foreign language, thesis, internship; for Certificate, one foreign language, internship. *Entrance requirements:* For master's, GRE. Electronic applications accepted. *Faculty research:* International development, European citizenship, French and business, foreign language education, agricultural economics.

**University of Wisconsin–Milwaukee,** Graduate School, College of Letters and Science, Department of Foreign Languages and Literature, Milwaukee, WI 53201-0413. Offers classic Greek (MA); classics (MA); comparative literature (MA); foreign language and literature (MA); French (MA); German (MA); Latin (MA); linguistics (MA); Spanish (MA); translation (MA, Certificate). *Program availability:* Part-time. *Students:* 10 full-time (7 women), 19 part-time (16 women); includes 5 minority (2 Black or African American, non-Hispanic/Latino; 2 Hispanic/Latino; 1 Two or more races, non-Hispanic/Latino), 2 international. Average age 31. 41 applicants, 32% accepted, 9 enrolled. In 2016, 21 master's awarded. *Degree requirements:* For master's, 2 foreign languages, thesis or alternative. *Entrance requirements:* Additional exam requirements/recommendations for international students: Required—TOEFL (minimum score 550 paper-based; 79 iBT), IELTS (minimum score 6.5). *Application deadline:* For fall admission, 1/1 priority date for domestic students; for spring admission, 9/1 for domestic students. Applications are processed on a rolling basis. Application fee: $56 ($96 for international students). Electronic applications accepted. *Financial support:* In 2016–17, 1 fellowship, 2 research assistantships, 26 teaching assistantships were awarded; career-related internships or fieldwork, health care benefits, unspecified assistantships, and project assistantships also available. Support available to part-time students. Financial award application deadline: 4/15; financial award applicants required to submit FAFSA. *Unit*

*French*

head: Kevin Muse, Department Chair, 414-229-5213, E-mail: kmuse@uwm.edu. *Application contact:* General Information Contact, 414-229-4982, Fax: 414-229-6967, E-mail: gradschool@uwm.edu.
Website: http://uwm.edu/foreign-languages-literature/

**University of Wyoming,** College of Arts and Sciences, Department of Modern and Classical Languages, Program in French, Laramie, WY 82071. Offers MA. *Program availability:* Part-time. *Degree requirements:* For master's, one foreign language, thesis or alternative. *Entrance requirements:* For master's, GRE General Test, minimum GPA of 3.0. *Faculty research:* Poetry, Asian literature, medieval literature, nineteenth- and twentieth century literature.

**Vanderbilt University,** Department of French and Italian, Nashville, TN 37240-1001. Offers French (MA, MAT, PhD). *Faculty:* 12 full-time (6 women). *Students:* 13 full-time (10 women); includes 1 minority (Two or more races, non-Hispanic/Latino), 3 international. Average age 28. 10 applicants, 50% accepted, 5 enrolled. Terminal master's awarded for partial completion of doctoral program. *Degree requirements:* For master's, one foreign language, comprehensive exam; for doctorate, 2 foreign languages, comprehensive exam, thesis/dissertation, final and qualifying exams. *Entrance requirements:* For master's and doctorate, GRE General Test. Additional exam requirements/recommendations for international students: Required—TOEFL (minimum score 570 paper-based; 88 iBT). *Application deadline:* For fall admission, 1/15 for domestic and international students. Electronic applications accepted. *Expenses:* Tuition: Part-time $1854 per credit hour. *Financial support:* Fellowships with tuition reimbursements, teaching assistantships with tuition reimbursements, career-related internships or fieldwork, Federal Work-Study, institutionally sponsored loans, scholarships/grants, and health care benefits available. Financial award application deadline: 1/15; financial award applicants required to submit CSS PROFILE or FAFSA. *Faculty research:* Baudelaire, Rabelais, voyage literature, postcolonial literature, medieval epic. *Unit head:* Dr. Laura Schneider, Chair, 615-322-6900, Fax: 615-343-6909, E-mail: laura.c.schneider@vanderbilt.edu. *Application contact:* Paul Miller, Director of Graduate Studies, 615-322-6900, Fax: 615-343-6909, E-mail: paul.miller@vanderbilt.edu.
Website: http://as.vanderbilt.edu/french-italian/

**Washington University in St. Louis,** The Graduate School, Department of Romance Languages and Literatures, Program in French, St. Louis, MO 63130-4899. Offers French and comparative literature (PhD); French language and literature (PhD). Terminal master's awarded for partial completion of doctoral program. *Degree requirements:* For doctorate, thesis/dissertation. *Entrance requirements:* For doctorate, GRE General Test. Additional exam requirements/recommendations for international students: Required—TOEFL. Electronic applications accepted. *Faculty research:* French language and literature.

**Wayne State University,** College of Liberal Arts and Sciences, Department of Classical and Modern Languages, Literatures, and Cultures, Detroit, MI 48202. Offers classics (MA), including ancient Greek and Latin, ancient studies, classics, Latin; German (MA); language learning (MALL), including Arabic (MA, MALL), French (MA, MALL, PhD), German (MALL, PhD), Italian (MA, MALL), Spanish (MA, MALL, PhD); modern languages (PhD), including French (MA, MALL, PhD), German (MALL, PhD), Spanish (MA, MALL, PhD); Near Eastern languages (MA), including Arabic (MA, MALL), Hebrew; Romance languages (MA), including French (MA, MALL, PhD), Italian (MA, MALL), Spanish (MA, MALL, PhD). *Faculty:* 26. *Students:* 25 full-time (20 women), 14 part-time (8 women); includes 7 minority (2 Black or African American, non-Hispanic/Latino; 1 American Indian or Alaska Native, non-Hispanic/Latino; 1 Asian, non-Hispanic/Latino; 2 Hispanic/Latino; 1 Two or more races, non-Hispanic/Latino), 3 international. Average age 35. 29 applicants, 31% accepted, 5 enrolled. In 2016, 15 master's, 5 doctorates awarded. *Degree requirements:* For master's, variable foreign language requirement, comprehensive exam (for some programs), thesis (for some programs); for doctorate, one foreign language, comprehensive exam, thesis/dissertation. *Entrance requirements:* For master's, GRE (for some programs); for doctorate, GRE. Additional exam requirements/recommendations for international students: Required—TOEFL (minimum score 550 paper-based; 79 iBT), TWE (minimum score 5.5), Michigan English Language Assessment Battery (minimum score 85); Recommended—IELTS (minimum score 6.5).

Application fee: $50. Electronic applications accepted. *Expenses:* $16,503 per year resident tuition and fees, $33,697 per year non-resident tuition and fees. *Financial support:* In 2016–17, 22 students received support, including 4 fellowships with tuition reimbursements available (averaging $13,500 per year), 17 teaching assistantships with tuition reimbursements available (averaging $17,994 per year); research assistantships, scholarships/grants, and unspecified assistantships also available. Financial award applicants required to submit FAFSA. *Faculty research:* Classical and modern literature and culture (Greek, Latin, Arabic, Chinese, French, German, Russian, Spanish) including colonial studies and exile and Holocaust studies; critical theory (French, German, Slavic, Spanish); theoretical and applied linguistics (Arabic, Chinese, French, Spanish); area studies (Arabic, Near Eastern, classical, Islamic, and Judaic studies). *Unit head:* Dr. Anne Duggan, Department Chair, 313-577-6244, Fax: 313-577-6243, E-mail: a.duggan@wayne.edu.
Website: http://clas.wayne.edu/languages/

**West Chester University of Pennsylvania,** College of Arts and Humanities, Department of Languages and Cultures, West Chester, PA 19383. Offers French (Teaching Certificate); German (Teaching Certificate); languages and cultures (MA), including French, German, Spanish; Spanish (Teaching Certificate). *Program availability:* Part-time, evening/weekend, minimal on-campus study. *Faculty:* 12 full-time (9 women). *Students:* 7 full-time (6 women), 26 part-time (23 women); includes 7 minority (all Hispanic/Latino). Average age 31. 14 applicants, 100% accepted, 11 enrolled. In 2016, 8 master's, 2 other advanced degrees awarded. *Degree requirements:* For master's, one foreign language, comprehensive exam, portfolio, exit exam, capstone project; for Teaching Certificate, one foreign language. *Entrance requirements:* For master's and Teaching Certificate, ACTFL OPI and WPT, undergraduate major or equivalent. Additional exam requirements/recommendations for international students: Required—TOEFL or IELTS. *Application deadline:* For fall admission, 5/15 for international students; for spring admission, 10/15 for international students. Applications are processed on a rolling basis. Application fee: $45. Electronic applications accepted. *Expenses:* Tuition, state resident: full-time $8694; part-time $483 per credit. Tuition, nonresident: full-time $13,050; part-time $725 per credit. *Required fees:* $2399; $119.05 per credit. Tuition and fees vary according to campus/location and program. *Financial support:* Scholarships/grants and unspecified assistantships available. Financial award application deadline: 2/15; financial award applicants required to submit FAFSA. *Faculty research:* Language structure, literature, film, culture, pedagogy, technology. *Unit head:* Dr. Jerome Williams, Interim Chair, 610-436-2700, Fax: 610-436-3048, E-mail: isanchez@wcupa.edu. *Application contact:* Dr. Rebecca Pauly, Graduate Coordinator, 610-436-4746, Fax: 610-436-3048, E-mail: mvanliew@wcupa.edu.
Website: http://www.wcupa.edu/arts-humanities/languagesCultures/

**Western Kentucky University,** Graduate Studies, Potter College of Arts and Letters, Department of Modern Languages, Bowling Green, KY 42101. Offers French (MA Ed); German (MA Ed); Spanish (MA Ed).

**West Virginia University,** Eberly College of Arts and Sciences, Department of World Languages, Literatures and Linguistics, Morgantown, WV 26506. Offers French (MA); linguistics (MA); Spanish (MA); teaching English to speakers of other languages (MA). *Program availability:* Part-time. *Degree requirements:* For master's, one foreign language, comprehensive exam (for some programs), thesis optional. *Entrance requirements:* For master's, minimum GPA of 3.0. Electronic applications accepted. *Faculty research:* French, German, and Spanish literature; foreign language pedagogy; English as a second language; cultural studies; linguistics.

**Yale University,** Graduate School of Arts and Sciences, Department of French, New Haven, CT 06520. Offers M Phil, MA, PhD. *Degree requirements:* For doctorate, 3 foreign languages, thesis/dissertation. *Entrance requirements:* For doctorate, GRE General Test.

**York University,** Faculty of Graduate Studies, Glendon Campus, Program in French Studies, Toronto, ON M3J 1P3, Canada. Offers MA, PhD. *Degree requirements:* For master's, thesis or alternative. Electronic applications accepted.

# German

**Arizona State University at the Tempe campus,** College of Liberal Arts and Sciences, School of International Letters and Cultures, Program in German, Tempe, AZ 85287-0202. Offers comparative literature (MA); language and culture (MA); literature (MA). *Degree requirements:* For master's, thesis, applied pedagogical project, or paper portfolio consisting of 2 seminar papers; interactive Program of Study (iPOS) submitted no later than beginning of third semester of study or before completing 50 percent of coursework. *Entrance requirements:* For master's, minimum GPA of 3.0 in the last two years of work leading to the bachelor's degree, personal statement, writing sample (preferably written in German), 3 letters of recommendation. Additional exam requirements/recommendations for international students: Required—TOEFL (minimum score 550 paper-based; 83 iBT), IELTS (minimum score 6.5). Electronic applications accepted.

**Bowling Green State University,** Graduate College, College of Arts and Sciences, Department of German, Russian, and East Asian Languages, Bowling Green, OH 43403. Offers German (MA); MA/MA. *Program availability:* Part-time. *Degree requirements:* For master's, one foreign language, thesis or alternative. *Entrance requirements:* For master's, GRE General Test. Additional exam requirements/recommendations for international students: Required—TOEFL. *Application deadline:* For fall admission, 3/1 priority date for domestic students. Application fee: $30. Electronic applications accepted. *Financial support:* Research assistantships with full tuition reimbursements, teaching assistantships with full tuition reimbursements, Federal Work-Study, institutionally sponsored loans, tuition waivers (partial), and unspecified assistantships available. Financial award applicants required to submit FAFSA. *Unit head:* Dr. Philip Peek, Chair, 419-372-8043, E-mail: peekps@bgsu.edu. *Application contact:* Dr. Geoffrey Howes, Graduate Coordinator, 419-372-7139.

**Brown University,** Graduate School, Department of German Studies, Providence, RI 02912. Offers PhD. *Degree requirements:* For doctorate, 2 foreign languages, thesis/dissertation, preliminary exam. *Entrance requirements:* For doctorate, GRE General Test.

**California State University, Long Beach,** Graduate Studies, College of Liberal Arts, Department of Romance, German, Russian Languages and Literatures, Program in German, Long Beach, CA 90840. Offers MA. *Program availability:* Part-time. *Degree*

requirements: For master's, one foreign language, comprehensive exam or thesis. *Application deadline:* For fall admission, 7/1 for domestic students. Applications are processed on a rolling basis. Application fee: $55. Electronic applications accepted. *Financial support:* Federal Work-Study, institutionally sponsored loans, and scholarships/grants available. Financial award application deadline: 3/2. *Faculty research:* Contemporary German society, Baroque, Goethe, Wagner. *Unit head:* Markus Muller, Chair.

**Central Connecticut State University,** School of Graduate Studies, College of Liberal Arts and Social Sciences, Department of Modern Languages, New Britain, CT 06050-4010. Offers modern language (MA, Certificate), including French, German (Certificate), Italian, Spanish (MA); Spanish (MS, Certificate). *Program availability:* Part-time, evening/weekend. *Faculty:* 8 full-time (6 women). *Students:* 7 full-time (6 women), 12 part-time (7 women); includes 10 minority (all Hispanic/Latino). Average age 32. 11 applicants, 91% accepted, 4 enrolled. In 2016, 9 master's, 1 other advanced degree awarded. *Degree requirements:* For master's, one foreign language, comprehensive exam, thesis or alternative; for Certificate, qualifying exam. *Entrance requirements:* For master's, minimum undergraduate GPA of 2.7, 24 credits of undergraduate courses in each language in which graduate work will be undertaken. Additional exam requirements/recommendations for international students: Required—TOEFL (minimum score 550 paper-based; 79 iBT). *Application deadline:* For fall admission, 6/1 for domestic students, 5/1 for international students; for spring admission, 11/1 for domestic and international students. Applications are processed on a rolling basis. Application fee: $50. Electronic applications accepted. *Expenses: Tuition, area resident:* Full-time $6497; part-time $606 per credit. Tuition, state resident: full-time $9748; part-time $622 per credit. Tuition, nonresident: full-time $18,102; part-time $622 per credit. *Required fees:* $4459; $246 per credit. *Financial support:* In 2016–17, 6 students received support. Career-related internships or fieldwork, Federal Work-Study, scholarships/grants, and unspecified assistantships available. Support available to part-time students. Financial award application deadline: 3/1; financial award applicants required to submit FAFSA. *Faculty research:* Quebecois literature, Caribbean literature, modern French/Spanish drama, Puerto Rican novel and drama. *Unit head:* Dr. Carmela Pesca, Chair, 860-832-2875, E-mail: pescac@ccsu.edu. *Application contact:* Patricia Gardner,

Associate Director of Graduate Studies, 860-832-2350, Fax: 860-832-2362. Website: http://web.ccsu.edu/modlang/

**Colorado State University,** College of Liberal Arts, Department of Languages, Literatures and Cultures, Fort Collins, CO 80523-1774. Offers French (MA); German (MA); Spanish (MA). *Program availability:* Part-time. *Faculty:* 7 full-time (6 women), 3 part-time/adjunct (all women). *Students:* 12 full-time (10 women); includes 4 minority (all Hispanic/Latino), 4 international. Average age 34. 7 applicants, 100% accepted, 6 enrolled. In 2016, 6 master's awarded. *Degree requirements:* For master's, one foreign language, comprehensive exam, thesis, teaching portfolio or additional coursework. *Entrance requirements:* For master's, minimum GPA of 3.0, undergraduate major/proficiency in foreign languages, BA/BS in related field, statement of purpose, biographical statement, 3 letters of recommendation, resume, official transcripts, writing sample. Additional exam requirements/recommendations for international students: Required—TOEFL (minimum score 550 paper-based; 80 iBT). *Application deadline:* For fall admission, 2/1 priority date for domestic and international students; for spring admission, 9/15 priority date for domestic and international students. Applications are processed on a rolling basis. Application fee: $60 ($70 for international students). Electronic applications accepted. *Expenses:* Tuition, state resident: full-time $9628. Tuition, nonresident: full-time $23,603. *Required fees:* $2253; $528.14 per credit hour. $264.07 per semester. Tuition and fees vary according to course load and program. *Financial support:* In 2016–17, 10 teaching assistantships with full and partial tuition reimbursements (averaging $13,932 per year) were awarded; career-related internships or fieldwork, scholarships/grants, and unspecified assistantships also available. Financial award application deadline: 3/1; financial award applicants required to submit FAFSA. *Faculty research:* French, German, and Hispanic literatures and cultures; video-assisted language learning; computer-assisted language learners; foreign language teaching methodologies; linguistics. *Unit head:* Dr. Mary Vogl, Department Chair, 970-491-6100, Fax: 970-491-2822, E-mail: mary.vogl@colostate.edu. *Application contact:* Kaity Lewis, Graduate Program Contact, 970-491-6269, Fax: 970-491-2822, E-mail: kaity.lewis@colostate.edu.
Website: http://languages.colostate.edu/

**Columbia University,** Graduate School of Arts and Sciences, New York, NY 10027. Offers African-American studies (MA); American studies (MA); anthropology (MA, PhD); art history and archaeology (MA, PhD); astronomy (PhD); biological sciences (PhD); biotechnology (MA); chemical physics (PhD); chemistry (PhD); classical studies (MA, PhD); classics (MA, PhD); climate and society (MA); conservation biology (MA); earth and environmental sciences (PhD); East Asia: regional studies (MA); East Asian languages and cultures (MA, PhD); ecology, evolution and environmental biology (MA), including conservation biology; ecology, evolution, and environmental biology (PhD), including ecology and evolutionary biology, evolutionary primatology; economics (MA, PhD); English and comparative literature (MA, PhD); French and Romance philology (MA, PhD); Germanic languages (MA, PhD); global French studies (MA); global thought (MA); Hispanic cultural studies (MA); history (PhD); history and literature (MA); human rights studies (MA); Islamic studies (MA); Italian (MA, PhD); Japanese pedagogy (MA); Jewish studies (MA); Latin America and the Caribbean: regional studies (MA); Latin American and Iberian cultures (PhD); mathematics (MA, PhD), including finance (MA); medieval and Renaissance studies (MA); Middle Eastern, South Asian, and African studies (MA, PhD); modern art: critical and curatorial studies (MA); modern European studies (MA); museum anthropology (MA); music (DMA, PhD); oral history (MA); philosophical foundations of physics (MA); philosophy (MA, PhD); physics (PhD); political science (MA, PhD); psychology (PhD); quantitative methods in the social sciences (MA); religion (MA, PhD); Russia, Eurasia and East Europe: regional studies (MA); Russian translation (MA); Slavic cultures (MA); Slavic languages (MA, PhD); sociology (MA, PhD); South Asian studies (MA); statistics (MA, PhD); theatre (PhD). Dual-degree programs require admission to both Graduate School of Arts and Sciences and another Columbia school. *Program availability:* Part-time. Terminal master's awarded for partial completion of doctoral program. *Degree requirements:* For master's, variable foreign language requirement, comprehensive exam (for some programs), thesis (for some programs); for doctorate, variable foreign language requirement, comprehensive exam (for some programs), thesis/dissertation. *Entrance requirements:* For master's and doctorate, GRE General Test, GRE Subject Test (for some programs). Additional exam requirements/recommendations for international students: Required—TOEFL, IELTS. Electronic applications accepted.

**Cornell University,** Graduate School, Graduate Fields of Arts and Sciences, Field of Germanic Studies, Ithaca, NY 14853. Offers German area studies (MA, PhD); German intellectual history (MA, PhD); Germanic linguistics (MA, PhD); Germanic literature (MA, PhD); old Norse (MA, PhD). Terminal master's awarded for partial completion of doctoral program. *Degree requirements:* For master's, one foreign language, thesis; for doctorate, 2 foreign languages, comprehensive exam, thesis/dissertation. *Entrance requirements:* For master's and doctorate, GRE General Test, fluency in German, writing sample, 2 letters of recommendation. Additional exam requirements/recommendations for international students: Required—TOEFL (minimum score 550 paper-based; 77 iBT). Electronic applications accepted. *Faculty research:* Women's studies, minority literature, literature and intellectual history, theater and film studies, Continental philosophy.

**Cornell University,** Graduate School, Graduate Fields of Arts and Sciences, Field of Linguistics, Ithaca, NY 14853. Offers applied linguistics (MA, PhD); East Asian linguistics (MA, PhD); English linguistics (MA, PhD); general linguistics (MA, PhD); Germanic linguistics (MA, PhD); Indo-European linguistics (MA, PhD); phonetics (MA, PhD); phonological theory (MA, PhD); Romance linguistics (MA, PhD); second language acquisition (MA, PhD); semantics (MA, PhD); Slavic linguistics (MA, PhD); sociolinguistics (MA, PhD); South Asian linguistics (MA, PhD); Southeast Asian linguistics (MA, PhD); syntactic theory (MA, PhD). Terminal master's awarded for partial completion of doctoral program. *Degree requirements:* For master's, one foreign language, thesis; for doctorate, one foreign language, comprehensive exam, thesis/dissertation. *Entrance requirements:* For master's and doctorate, GRE General Test, 2 letters of recommendation. Additional exam requirements/recommendations for international students: Required—TOEFL (minimum score 600 paper-based; 77 iBT). Electronic applications accepted. *Faculty research:* Phonology and phonetics, syntax and semantics, historical linguistics, philosophy of language, language acquisition.

**Dalhousie University,** Faculty of Arts and Social Science, Department of German, Halifax, NS B3H 4R2, Canada. Offers MA. *Entrance requirements:* Additional exam requirements/recommendations for international students: Required—TOEFL, IELTS, CANTEST, CAEL, or Michigan English Language Assessment Battery. Electronic applications accepted. *Faculty research:* Baroque age in Germany, literature and philosophy of German idealism, twentieth-century German culture, aesthetics, reception of the Islamic Orient, reception of Greek and Roman antiquity, realism and ornament.

**DePaul University,** College of Liberal Arts and Social Sciences, Chicago, IL 60614. Offers Arabic (MA); Chinese (MA); English (MA); French (MA); German (MA); history (MA); interdisciplinary studies (MA, MS); international public service (MS); international studies (MA); Italian (MA); Japanese (MA); leadership and policy studies (MA); liberal studies (MA); new media studies (MA); nonprofit management (MNM); public administration (MPA); public health (MPH); public service management (MS); social

work (MSW); sociology (MA); Spanish (MA); sustainable urban development (MA); women and gender studies (MA); writing and publishing (MA); writing, rhetoric, and discourse (MA); MA/PhD. *Program availability:* Part-time, evening/weekend, online learning. Terminal master's awarded for partial completion of doctoral program. *Degree requirements:* For master's, variable foreign language requirement, comprehensive exam (for some programs), thesis (for some programs). Electronic applications accepted.

**Duke University,** Graduate School, Carolina-Duke Graduate Program in German Studies, Durham, NC 27708-0256. Offers PhD. Program offered jointly with The University of North Carolina Chapel Hill. *Program availability:* Part-time. *Degree requirements:* For doctorate, thesis/dissertation. *Entrance requirements:* For doctorate, GRE General Test, writing sample. Additional exam requirements/recommendations for international students: Required—TOEFL (minimum score 577 paper-based; 90 iBT) or IELTS (minimum score 7). Electronic applications accepted.

**Florida Atlantic University,** College of Education, Department of Teaching and Learning, Boca Raton, FL 33431-0991. Offers curriculum and instruction (M Ed), including art, biology, chemistry, English, French, German, mathematics, music, physics, Pre-K and primary education, reading, social sciences, Spanish; elementary education (M Ed); environmental education (M Ed); reading education (M Ed); social foundations of education (M Ed), including educational psychology, educational technology, multilingual education. *Accreditation:* NCATE. *Program availability:* Part-time, evening/weekend. *Faculty:* 15 full-time (12 women), 2 part-time/adjunct (1 woman). *Students:* 25 full-time (20 women), 41 part-time (37 women); includes 18 minority (9 Black or African American, non-Hispanic/Latino; 2 Asian, non-Hispanic/Latino; 7 Hispanic/Latino), 7 international. Average age 32. 54 applicants, 59% accepted, 18 enrolled. In 2016, 36 master's awarded. *Entrance requirements:* For master's, GRE General Test, minimum GPA of 3.0 in last 2 years of undergraduate course work. Additional exam requirements/recommendations for international students: Required—TOEFL (minimum score 500 paper-based; 61 iBT), IELTS (minimum score 6). *Application deadline:* For fall admission, 7/1 for domestic students, 2/15 for international students; for spring admission, 11/1 for domestic students, 7/15 for international students. Applications are processed on a rolling basis. Application fee: $30. *Expenses:* Tuition, state resident: full-time $7392; part-time $369.82 per credit hour. Tuition, nonresident: full-time $19,432; part-time $1024.81 per credit hour. *Financial support:* Fellowships with partial tuition reimbursements, research assistantships with partial tuition reimbursements, teaching assistantships with partial tuition reimbursements, career-related internships or fieldwork, scholarships/grants, and unspecified assistantships available. *Faculty research:* Technology, teaching English to speakers of other languages, math teaching, electronic portfolio assessment, global perspectives through social studies. *Unit head:* Dr. Barbara Ridener, Chairperson, 561-297-3588, E-mail: bridener@fau.edu. *Application contact:* Dr. Eliah Watlington, Associate Dean, 561-296-8520, Fax: 261-297-2991, E-mail: ewatling@fau.edu.
Website: http://www.coe.fau.edu/academicdepartments/tl/

**Florida State University,** The Graduate School, College of Arts and Sciences, Department of Modern Languages and Linguistics, Program in German, Tallahassee, FL 32306. Offers MA. *Faculty:* 4 full-time (3 women), 1 part-time/adjunct (0 women). *Students:* 8 full-time (6 women), 1 (woman) part-time; includes 2 minority (1 Hispanic/Latino; 1 Two or more races, non-Hispanic/Latino). Average age 25. 1 applicant, 100% accepted, 1 enrolled. *Degree requirements:* For master's, thesis optional. *Entrance requirements:* For master's, GRE General Test, minimum GPA of 3.0. Additional exam requirements/recommendations for international students: Required—TOEFL (minimum score 550 paper-based; 80 iBT). *Application deadline:* For fall admission, 2/15 for domestic and international students. Electronic applications accepted. *Expenses:* Tuition, state resident: full-time $7263; part-time $403.51 per credit hour. Tuition, nonresident: full-time $18,087; part-time $1004.85 per credit hour. *Required fees:* $1365; $75.81 per credit hour. $20 per semester. Tuition and fees vary according to campus/location. *Financial support:* In 2016–17, 4 students received support, including research assistantships (averaging $12,000 per year), 8 teaching assistantships with partial tuition reimbursements available (averaging $14,500 per year). Financial award application deadline: 2/1; financial award applicants required to submit FAFSA. *Unit head:* Dr. Christian Weber, Divisional Coordinator, 850-644-8194, Fax: 850-644-0524, E-mail: cweber@fsu.edu. *Application contact:* Wendy E. Pigott, Graduate Academic Coordinator, 850-644-8397, Fax: 850-644-0524, E-mail: wpigott@fsu.edu.
Website: http://www.modlang.fsu.edu/Programs2/German/Graduate-program

**Georgetown University,** Graduate School of Arts and Sciences, Department of German, Washington, DC 20057. Offers MA, PhD, MA/PhD. *Degree requirements:* For master's, 2 foreign languages, research project; for doctorate, 3 foreign languages, thesis/dissertation. *Entrance requirements:* For master's, GRE General Test. Additional exam requirements/recommendations for international students: Required—TOEFL.

**Georgetown University,** Graduate School of Arts and Sciences, Walsh School of Foreign Service, BMW Center for German and European Studies, Washington, DC 20057. Offers MA, MA/JD, MA/PhD. *Degree requirements:* For master's, 2 foreign languages, comprehensive exam. *Entrance requirements:* For master's, GRE General Test. Additional exam requirements/recommendations for international students: Required—TOEFL. Electronic applications accepted. *Faculty research:* Transatlantic relations, European Union, German and European Studies.

**Georgia State University,** College of Arts and Sciences, Department of World Languages and Cultures, Program in Translation and Interpretation, Atlanta, GA 30302-3083. Offers interpretation (Certificate), including Spanish; translation (Certificate), including French, German, Spanish. *Program availability:* Part-time. *Entrance requirements:* For degree, entrance examination involving translating one passage from English to the target language and one passage from the target language to English, 3 letters of recommendation, resume/curriculum vitae, official transcripts. Additional exam requirements/recommendations for international students: Required—TOEFL (minimum score 79 iBT). *Application deadline:* For fall admission, 3/15 priority date for domestic and international students; for spring admission, 11/15 priority date for domestic and international students. Application fee: $50. Electronic applications accepted. *Expenses:* Tuition, state resident: full-time $6876; part-time $382 per credit hour. Tuition, nonresident: full-time $22,374; part-time $1243 per credit hour. *Required fees:* $2128; $1064 per term. Part-time tuition and fees vary according to course load and program. *Faculty research:* Romance linguistics and translation; theory and practice of translation; medical and legal interpretation. *Unit head:* Dr. Fernando Reati, Chair, 404-413-5984, Fax: 404-413-5982, E-mail: freati@gsu.edu. *Application contact:* Lita Malveaux, Administrative Academic Specialist, 404-413-5046, Fax: 404-413-5036, E-mail: lmalveaux@gsu.edu.
Website: http://wlc.gsu.edu/home/graduate/graduate-certificate/

**The Graduate Center, City University of New York,** Graduate Studies, Program in Comparative Literature, New York, NY 10016-4039. Offers comparative literature (MA, PhD), including classics (PhD), German (PhD), Italian (PhD). PhD offered jointly with New York University. Terminal master's awarded for partial completion of doctoral program. *Degree requirements:* For master's, 2 foreign languages, comprehensive exam, thesis; for doctorate, 3 foreign languages, comprehensive exam, thesis/dissertation. *Entrance requirements:* For master's and doctorate, GRE General Test.

## German

Additional exam requirements/recommendations for international students: Required—TOEFL. Electronic applications accepted.

**The Graduate Center, City University of New York,** Graduate Studies, Program in Germanic Languages and Literatures, New York, NY 10016-4039. Offers MA, PhD. *Degree requirements:* For master's, one foreign language, thesis; for doctorate, 2 foreign languages, thesis/dissertation. *Entrance requirements:* For master's and doctorate, GRE General Test.

**Harvard University,** Graduate School of Arts and Sciences, Department of Germanic Languages and Literatures, Cambridge, MA 02138. Offers German (PhD); Scandinavian (PhD). Terminal master's awarded for partial completion of doctoral program. *Degree requirements:* For doctorate, 2 foreign languages, thesis/dissertation, exams. *Entrance requirements:* For doctorate, GRE General Test, German writing sample. Additional exam requirements/recommendations for international students: Required—TOEFL.

**Illinois State University,** Graduate School, College of Arts and Sciences, Department of Foreign Languages, Literatures and Cultures, Normal, IL 61790-2200. Offers French (MA); French and German (MA); French and Spanish (MA); German (MA); German and Spanish (MA); Spanish (MA). *Degree requirements:* For master's, variable foreign language requirement, comprehensive exam, 1 term of residency. *Entrance requirements:* For master's, GRE General Test, minimum GPA of 2.8 in last 60 hours of course work.

**Indiana University Bloomington,** University Graduate School, College of Arts and Sciences, Department of Germanic Studies, Bloomington, IN 47405-7000. Offers German philology and linguistics (PhD); German studies (MA, PhD), including German (MA), German literature and culture (MA), German literature and linguistics (MA); medieval German studies (PhD); teaching German (MAT). *Faculty:* 13 full-time (4 women), 6 part-time/adjunct (2 women). *Students:* 28 full-time (15 women), 2 part-time (both women), 5 international. Average age 32. 16 applicants, 56% accepted, 4 enrolled. In 2016, 2 master's, 3 doctorates awarded. *Degree requirements:* For master's, one foreign language, project; for doctorate, one foreign language, comprehensive exam, thesis/dissertation. *Entrance requirements:* For master's, GRE General Test, BA in German or equivalent; for doctorate, GRE General Test, MA in German or equivalent. Additional exam requirements/recommendations for international students: Required—TOEFL. *Application deadline:* For fall admission, 12/1 priority date for domestic students, 12/1 for international students; for spring admission, 9/1 priority date for domestic students, 9/1 for international students. Applications are processed on a rolling basis. Application fee: $55 ($65 for international students). Electronic applications accepted. *Financial support:* Application deadline: 1/15. *Faculty research:* German and other European literature: medieval to modern/postmodern, German and culture studies, Germanic philology, literary theory, literature and the other arts. *Unit head:* William Rasch, Department Chairman, 812-855-7947, Fax: 812-855-8292, E-mail: wrasch@indiana.edu. *Application contact:* Michelle Dunbar, Graduate Secretary, 812-855-7947, E-mail: midunbar@indiana.edu.
Website: http://germanic.indiana.edu/

**Johns Hopkins University,** Zanvyl Krieger School of Arts and Sciences, Department of German and Romance Languages and Literatures, Baltimore, MD 21218. Offers French (PhD); German (PhD); Italian (PhD); Spanish (PhD). *Degree requirements:* For doctorate, 2 foreign languages, thesis/dissertation. *Entrance requirements:* For doctorate, GRE General Test. Additional exam requirements/recommendations for international students: Required—TOEFL (minimum score 600 paper-based; 100 iBT), IELTS. Electronic applications accepted. *Faculty research:* Nineteenth-century French prose and poetry, genetic theory and criticism; twentieth-century Latin American literature and film; medieval and Renaissance Italian literature; gender and queer theory in German literature; the ideology of Baroque and Neobaroque aesthetics.

**Kent State University,** College of Arts and Sciences, Department of Modern and Classical Language Studies, Kent, OH 44242-0001. Offers French (MA), including applied linguistics and pedagogy, literature; Latin (MA), including applied linguistics and pedagogy, literature; Spanish (MA), including applied linguistics and pedagogy, literature; translation (MA), including Arabic, French, German, Japanese, Russian, Spanish; translation studies (PhD); MA/MBA. *Program availability:* Part-time. *Faculty:* 35 full-time (23 women). *Students:* 81 full-time (51 women), 23 part-time (15 women); includes 14 minority (1 Black or African American, non-Hispanic/Latino; 9 Hispanic/Latino; 4 Two or more races, non-Hispanic/Latino), 48 international. Average age 30. 109 applicants, 53% accepted, 33 enrolled. In 2016, 31 master's, 6 doctorates awarded. *Degree requirements:* For master's, variable foreign language requirement, comprehensive exam (for some programs), thesis (for some programs); for doctorate, variable foreign language requirement, comprehensive exam, thesis/dissertation. *Entrance requirements:* For master's, transcripts, goal statement, 3 letters of recommendation, CD/MP3 with oral sample of first and second languages, writing sample of second language; for doctorate, transcripts; MA in translation, a foreign language, or similar field; proficiency in a foreign language; minimum GPA of 3.5 from MA; goal statement; 3 letters of recommendation; essay or writing sample. *Application deadline:* For fall admission, 2/1 for domestic and international students. Applications are processed on a rolling basis. Application fee: $45 ($70 for international students). Electronic applications accepted. *Expenses:* Tuition, state resident: full-time $10,864; part-time $495 per credit hour. Tuition, nonresident: full-time $18,380; part-time $837 per credit hour. *Financial support:* Fellowships with full tuition reimbursements, teaching assistantships with full tuition reimbursements, and unspecified assistantships available. Financial award application deadline: 2/1. *Unit head:* Dr. Keiran Dunne, Professor of French Translation/Chair, 330-672-2150, E-mail: kdunne@kent.edu. *Application contact:* Said Shiyab, Professor of Translation Studies/Graduate Coordinator, 330-672-1864, E-mail: sshiyab@kent.edu.
Website: http://www.kent.edu/mcls/

**McGill University,** Faculty of Graduate and Postdoctoral Studies, Faculty of Arts, Department of German Studies, Montréal, QC H3A 2T5, Canada. Offers MA, PhD.

**Memorial University of Newfoundland,** School of Graduate Studies, Department of German and Russian, St. John's, NL A1C 5S7, Canada. Offers German language and literature (M Phil, MA). *Program availability:* Part-time. *Degree requirements:* For master's, one foreign language, thesis (for some programs), comprehensive exam (M Phil). *Entrance requirements:* For master's, honors degree (minimum 2nd class standing). Electronic applications accepted. *Faculty research:* German literature from the Middle Ages to the twentieth century, German studies.

**Michigan State University,** The Graduate School, College of Arts and Letters, Department of Linguistics and Germanic, Slavic, Asian, and African Languages, East Lansing, MI 48824. Offers German studies (MA, PhD); linguistics (MA, PhD); teaching English to speakers of other languages (MA). *Program availability:* Part-time, evening/weekend. *Entrance requirements:* For master's, GRE General Test, minimum GPA of 3.2 in last 2 undergraduate years, 2 years of college-level foreign language, 3 letters of recommendation, portfolio (German studies); for doctorate, GRE General Test, minimum graduate GPA of 3.5, 3 letters of recommendation, master's degree or sufficient graduate course work in linguistics or language of study, master's thesis or major research paper. Additional exam requirements/recommendations for international students: Required—TOEFL. Electronic applications accepted.

**Middlebury College,** Language Schools, German School, Middlebury, VT 05753-6002. Offers MA, DML. *Degree requirements:* For master's, one foreign language; for doctorate, 2 foreign languages, comprehensive exam, thesis/dissertation, residence abroad, teaching experience. *Entrance requirements:* For master's, placement exam, 3 letters of recommendation, transcripts, personal statement; for doctorate, 1st and 2nd language placement exams, 3 letters of recommendation, transcripts, personal statement, MA in German. Electronic applications accepted. *Expenses:* Contact institution.

**Middle Tennessee State University,** College of Graduate Studies, College of Liberal Arts, Department of Foreign Languages and Literatures, Murfreesboro, TN 37132. Offers foreign languages (MAT), including French, German, Spanish. *Program availability:* Part-time, evening/weekend, online learning. *Degree requirements:* For master's, one foreign language, comprehensive exam, thesis optional. *Entrance requirements:* For master's, GRE. Additional exam requirements/recommendations for international students: Required—TOEFL (minimum score 525 paper-based; 71 iBT) or IELTS (minimum score 6). Electronic applications accepted.

**Millersville University of Pennsylvania,** College of Graduate Studies and Adult Learning, College of Arts, Humanities and Social Sciences, Department of Foreign Languages, Program in Languages and Cultures: German Option, Millersville, PA 17551-0302. Offers MA. Program offered in collaboration with West Chester University of Pennsylvania. *Program availability:* Part-time. *Faculty:* 7 full-time (4 women). *Students:* 4 part-time (2 women); includes 1 minority (Asian, non-Hispanic/Latino). Average age 30. 1 applicant. In 2016, 1 master's awarded. *Degree requirements:* For master's, comprehensive exam (for some programs), thesis optional, exam, portfolio, or research project and presentation. *Entrance requirements:* For master's, ACTFL, OPI, OPIc and WPT, baccalaureate degree from regionally-accredited four-year college or university. Additional exam requirements/recommendations for international students: Required—TOEFL (minimum score 600 paper-based), IELTS (minimum score 6). *Application deadline:* Applications are processed on a rolling basis. Application fee: $40. Electronic applications accepted. *Expenses:* $483 per credit resident tuition; $725 per credit non-resident tuition. *Financial support:* Unspecified assistantships available. Financial award application deadline: 3/15; financial award applicants required to submit FAFSA. *Faculty research:* Second language acquisition, teaching methodology. *Unit head:* Dr. Susanne J. Nimmrichter, Associate Professor/Program Contact, 717-871-7153, Fax: 717-871-7935, E-mail: susanne.nimmrichter@millersville.edu. *Application contact:* Dr. Victor S. DeSantis, Dean of College of Graduate Studies and Adult Learning/Associate Provost for Civic and Community Engagement, 717-871-7619, Fax: 717-871-7954, E-mail: victor.desantis@millersville.edu.
Website: http://www.millersville.edu/forlang/

**New York University,** Graduate School of Arts and Science, Department of German, New York, NY 10012-1019. Offers German studies and critical thought (MA, PhD). *Program availability:* Part-time. Terminal master's awarded for partial completion of doctoral program. *Degree requirements:* For master's, one foreign language, thesis; for doctorate, 2 foreign languages, thesis/dissertation. *Entrance requirements:* For master's, GRE; for doctorate, GRE, sample of written work. Additional exam requirements/recommendations for international students: Required—TOEFL. *Faculty research:* Eighteenth- to twentieth-century literature, culture and critical thought, film and visual culture, philosophy, critical theory.

**Northwestern University,** The Graduate School, Judd A. and Marjorie Weinberg College of Arts and Sciences, Department of German, Evanston, IL 60208. Offers German literature and critical thought (PhD). Admissions and degrees offered through The Graduate School. *Degree requirements:* For doctorate, one foreign language, thesis/dissertation. *Entrance requirements:* For doctorate, GRE General Test. Additional exam requirements/recommendations for international students: Required—TOEFL. Electronic applications accepted. *Faculty research:* Eighteenth through twentieth century German literature, comparative literature, theory, philosophy, language pedagogy.

**The Ohio State University,** Graduate School, College of Arts and Sciences, Division of Arts and Humanities, Department of Germanic Languages and Literatures, Columbus, OH 43210. Offers MA, PhD. *Faculty:* 11. *Students:* 20 full-time (11 women), 10 international. Average age 28. In 2016, 2 master's, 3 doctorates awarded. *Degree requirements:* For master's, one foreign language, thesis optional; for doctorate, 2 foreign languages, thesis/dissertation. *Entrance requirements:* For master's and doctorate, GRE General Test. Additional exam requirements/recommendations for international students: Required—TOEFL (minimum score 550 paper-based; 79 iBT), Michigan English Language Assessment Battery (minimum score 82); Recommended—IELTS (minimum score 7). *Application deadline:* For fall admission, 12/13 priority date for domestic students, 11/30 priority date for international students; for spring admission, 3/1 for domestic students, 2/1 for international students. Applications are processed on a rolling basis. Application fee: $60 ($70 for international students). Electronic applications accepted. *Financial support:* Fellowships with tuition reimbursements, research assistantships with tuition reimbursements, teaching assistantships with tuition reimbursements, Federal Work-Study, and institutionally sponsored loans available. Support available to part-time students. *Faculty research:* German literature, Germanic philology, linguistics. *Unit head:* Dr. Robert C. Holub, Chair/Professor, 614-292-6985, E-mail: holub.5@osu.edu. *Application contact:* Graduate and Professional Admissions, 614-292-9444, Fax: 614-292-3895, E-mail: gpadmissions@osu.edu.
Website: http://germanic.osu.edu/

**Penn State University Park,** Graduate School, College of the Liberal Arts, Department of Germanic and Slavic Languages and Literatures, University Park, PA 16802. Offers German (MA, PhD). *Faculty research:* Literature, literary theory, culture, language pedagogy. *Unit head:* Dr. Susan Welch, Dean, 814-865-7691, Fax: 814-863-2085. *Application contact:* Lori Hawn, Director, Graduate Student Services, 814-865-1795, Fax: 814-863-4627, E-mail: l-gswww@lists.psu.edu.
Website: http://german.la.psu.edu/

**Portland State University,** Graduate Studies, College of Liberal Arts and Sciences, Department of World Languages and Literatures, Portland, OR 97207-0751. Offers French (MA); German (MA); Japanese (MA); Spanish (MA); world literature and language (MA). *Program availability:* Part-time. *Faculty:* 45 full-time (25 women), 39 part-time/adjunct (27 women). *Students:* 22 full-time (13 women), 6 part-time (3 women); includes 8 minority (2 Asian, non-Hispanic/Latino; 6 Hispanic/Latino), 4 international. Average age 31. 19 applicants, 53% accepted, 8 enrolled. In 2016, 18 master's awarded. *Degree requirements:* For master's, one foreign language, thesis (for some programs). *Entrance requirements:* Additional exam requirements/recommendations for international students: Required—TOEFL (minimum score 550 paper-based; 80 iBT), IELTS (minimum score 6.5). *Application deadline:* For fall admission, 4/1 for domestic students, 3/1 for international students; for winter admission, 9/1 for domestic students, 7/1 for international students; for spring admission, 11/1 for domestic and international students. Applications are processed on a rolling basis. Application fee: $65. *Expenses:* Contact institution. *Financial support:* In 2016–17, 18 teaching assistantships with tuition reimbursements (averaging $10,805 per year) were awarded; research assistantships, Federal Work-Study, scholarships/grants, and unspecified assistantships also available. Support available to part-time students. Financial award application deadline: 3/1; financial award applicants required to submit FAFSA. *Faculty research:* Foreign language pedagogy, applied and social linguistics, literary history and criticism. *Total annual research expenditures:* $396,300. *Unit head:* Dr. Gina Greco, Chair, 503-725-5287, E-mail: grecog@pdx.edu. *Application contact:* Kelli Martin, Graduate Admissions Coordinator, 503-725-3243, E-mail: kmarti@pdx.edu. Website: http://www.pdx.edu/wll/

**Princeton University,** Graduate School, Department of German, Princeton, NJ 08544-1019. Offers PhD. *Degree requirements:* For doctorate, 2 foreign languages, thesis/dissertation. *Entrance requirements:* For doctorate, GRE General Test. Additional exam requirements/recommendations for international students: Required—TOEFL (minimum score 600 paper-based). Electronic applications accepted.

**Purdue University,** Graduate School, College of Liberal Arts, School of Languages and Cultures, West Lafayette, IN 47907. Offers French (MA, MAT, PhD), including French (MA, PhD), French education (MAT); German (MA, MAT, PhD), including German (MA, PhD), German education (MAT); Japanese pedagogy (MA); Spanish (MA, MAT, PhD), including Spanish (MA, PhD), Spanish education (MAT). *Faculty:* 44 full-time (22 women), 1 (woman) part-time/adjunct. *Students:* 37 full-time (18 women), 41 part-time (30 women); includes 9 minority (1 Asian, non-Hispanic/Latino; 8 Hispanic/Latino), 52 international. Average age 32. 49 applicants, 39% accepted, 14 enrolled. In 2016, 11 master's, 5 doctorates awarded. Terminal master's awarded for partial completion of doctoral program. *Degree requirements:* For master's, one foreign language; for doctorate, 2 foreign languages, thesis/dissertation. *Entrance requirements:* For master's, GRE General Test (minimum score 600, 160 for new scoring), two writing samples, one in English, one in language (French, German, Japanese, or Spanish); sample recording of English and language of study; for doctorate, GRE General Test (minimum score 600, 160 for new scoring), master's degree with minimum GPA of 3.5 or equivalent; two writing samples, one in English, one in language (French, German, Japanese, or Spanish); sample recording of English and language of study. Additional exam requirements/recommendations for international students: Required—TOEFL (minimum score 550 paper-based; 77 iBT); Recommended—TWE. *Application deadline:* For fall admission, 12/12 for domestic and international students; for spring admission, 10/1 for domestic and international students. Applications are processed on a rolling basis. Application fee: $60 ($75 for international students). Electronic applications accepted. *Financial support:* In 2016–17, fellowships with tuition reimbursements (averaging $15,750 per year), teaching assistantships with tuition reimbursements (averaging $13,463 per year) were awarded. Support available to part-time students. Financial award applicants required to submit FAFSA. *Faculty research:* Linguistics, semiotics, literary criticism, pedagogy. *Unit head:* Dr. Madeleine M. Henry, Head, 765-494-3828, E-mail: henry48@purdue.edu. *Application contact:* Joni L. Hipsher, Graduate Contact, 765-494-3841, E-mail: jlhipshe@purdue.edu. Website: http://www.cla.purdue.edu/slc/main/

**Queen's University at Kingston,** School of Graduate Studies, Faculty of Arts and Sciences, Program in German, Kingston, ON K7L 3N6, Canada. Offers MA, PhD. *Program availability:* Part-time. *Degree requirements:* For master's, thesis optional; for doctorate, one foreign language, comprehensive exam, thesis/dissertation. *Entrance requirements:* For master's, 7 German courses, honors bachelor's degree in German; for doctorate, MA or equivalent in German. Additional exam requirements/recommendations for international students: Required—TOEFL. Electronic applications accepted. *Faculty research:* Goethe and Weimar classicism, Romanticism, nineteenth- and twentieth-century German literature.

**Rider University,** Department of Graduate Education, Leadership and Counseling, Teacher Certification Program, Lawrenceville, NJ 08648-3001. Offers business education (Certificate); elementary education (Certificate); English as a second language (Certificate); English education (Certificate); mathematics education (Certificate); preschool to grade 3 (Certificate); science education (Certificate); social studies education (Certificate); world languages (Certificate), including French, German, Spanish. *Program availability:* Part-time. *Degree requirements:* For Certificate, internship, professional portfolio. *Entrance requirements:* For degree, PRAXIS, resume. Additional exam requirements/recommendations for international students: Required—TOEFL (minimum score 550 paper-based). Electronic applications accepted. *Faculty research:* Conceptual foundations for optimal development of creativity; creative theory, cognitive processes in mathematics learning, teacher collaboration.

**Rutgers University–New Brunswick,** Graduate School-New Brunswick, Program in German, Piscataway, NJ 08854-8097. Offers German (MAT, PhD); German literature (MA, PhD). *Program availability:* Part-time, evening/weekend. Terminal master's awarded for partial completion of doctoral program. *Degree requirements:* For master's, one foreign language, comprehensive exam, thesis or alternative; for doctorate, 2 foreign languages, comprehensive exam, thesis/dissertation. *Entrance requirements:* For master's and doctorate, GRE General Test. Additional exam requirements/recommendations for international students: Required—TOEFL. Electronic applications accepted. *Faculty research:* Literature and ideology; early German novella; narrative structures, mythology, psychology, and realist literature; German-American cultural history; literary theory and aesthetics; German film.

**San Francisco State University,** Division of Graduate Studies, College of Liberal and Creative Arts, Department of Modern Languages and Literatures, Program in German, San Francisco, CA 94132-1722. Offers MA. *Application deadline:* Applications are processed on a rolling basis. *Expenses:* Tuition, state resident: full-time $6738. Tuition, nonresident: full-time $15,666. *Required fees:* $1012. Tuition and fees vary according to degree level and program. *Unit head:* Dr. Mohammad Salama, Chair, 415-338-7413, Fax: 415-338-6159, E-mail: mrsalama@sfsu.edu. *Application contact:* Dr. Llona Vandergrift, Graduate Advisor, 415-338-1106, Fax: 415-338-6159, E-mail: vdgriff@sfsu.edu. Website: http://german.sfsu.edu/

**Stanford University,** School of Humanities and Sciences, Department of German Studies, Stanford, CA 94305-2004. Offers MA, PhD. *Degree requirements:* For master's, one foreign language, oral exam; for doctorate, 2 foreign languages, thesis/dissertation, oral exam, qualifying paper and exam. *Entrance requirements:* For master's and doctorate, GRE General Test. Additional exam requirements/recommendations for international students: Required—TOEFL. Electronic applications accepted. *Expenses:* Tuition: Full-time $47,331. *Required fees:* $609.

**Texas Tech University,** Graduate School, College of Arts and Sciences, Department of Classical and Modern Languages and Literatures, Lubbock, TX 79409. Offers applied linguistics (MA); classics (MA); German (MA); languages and cultures (MA); Romance languages (MA); Spanish (PhD); MBA/MA. *Program availability:* Part-time. *Faculty:* 56 full-time (37 women), 4 part-time/adjunct (2 women). *Students:* 80 full-time (39 women), 13 part-time (9 women); includes 20 minority (19 Hispanic/Latino; 1 Two or more races, non-Hispanic/Latino), 49 international. Average age 32. 68 applicants, 68% accepted, 31 enrolled. In 2016, 30 master's, 4 doctorates awarded. *Degree requirements:* For master's, comprehensive exam, thesis or alternative; for doctorate, comprehensive exam, thesis/dissertation. *Entrance requirements:* Additional exam requirements/recommendations for international students: Required—TOEFL (minimum score 550 paper-based; 79 iBT). *Application deadline:* For fall admission, 6/1 priority date for domestic students, 1/15 priority date for international students; for spring admission, 9/1 priority date for domestic students, 6/15 priority date for international students. Applications are processed on a rolling basis. Application fee: $75. Electronic applications accepted. *Expenses:* $300 per credit hour full-time resident tuition, $708 per credit hour full-time non-resident tuition; $50.50 per credit hour fee plus $608 per term fee. *Financial support:* In 2016–17, 78 students received support, including 60 fellowships (averaging $2,488 per year), 76 teaching assistantships (averaging $13,011 per year); research assistantships, Federal Work-Study, scholarships/grants, and unspecified assistantships also available. Financial award application deadline: 4/15; financial award applicants required to submit FAFSA. *Faculty research:* Literature, comparative literature, linguistics, culture, applied linguistics. *Total annual research expenditures:* $36,152. *Unit head:* Dr. Erin Collopy, Chair and Associate Professor, 806-834-8497, Fax: 806-742-3306, E-mail: erin.collopy@ttu.edu. *Application contact:* Carla Burrus, Senior Advisor, 806-834-3282, Fax: 806-742-3306, E-mail: carla.burrus@ttu.edu. Website: http://www.depts.ttu.edu/classic_modern/

**Tufts University,** Graduate School of Arts and Sciences, Department of International Literary and Cultural Studies, Medford, MA 02155. Offers German (MA); German with teaching licensure (MA). *Program availability:* Part-time. *Students:* 2 applicants, 50% accepted, 1 enrolled. *Degree requirements:* For master's, one foreign language, oral and written exam. *Entrance requirements:* For master's, GRE General Test. Additional exam requirements/recommendations for international students: Required—TOEFL (minimum score 550 paper-based; 80 iBT), IELTS (minimum score 6.5). *Application deadline:* For fall admission, 3/1 for domestic and international students; for spring admission, 10/15 for domestic and international students. Applications are processed on a rolling basis. Application fee: $85. Electronic applications accepted. *Expenses:* $49,982 full-time tuition (for MA). *Financial support:* Federal Work-Study, scholarships/grants, and tuition waivers (full and partial) available. Support available to part-time students. Financial award application deadline: 1/15. *Unit head:* Dr. Markus Wilczek, Graduate Program Director. *Application contact:* Office of Graduate Admissions, 617-627-3395, E-mail: gradadmissions@tufts.edu. Website: http://ase.tufts.edu/ilcs/

**Université de Montréal,** Faculty of Arts and Sciences, Department of Literatures and Modern Languages, Program in German Studies, Montréal, QC H3C 3J7, Canada. Offers MA. *Degree requirements:* For master's, 2 foreign languages, thesis. Electronic applications accepted.

**University at Buffalo, the State University of New York,** Graduate School, Graduate School of Education, Department of Learning and Instruction, Buffalo, NY 14260. Offers biology education (Ed M, Certificate); chemistry education (Ed M, Certificate); childhood education (Ed M); childhood education with bilingual extension (Ed M); college teaching (Advanced Certificate); curriculum, instruction and the science of learning (PhD); early childhood education (Ed M); early childhood education with bilingual extension (Ed M); earth science education (Ed M, Certificate); education and technology (Ed M); education studies (Ed M); educational technology and new literacies (Certificate); educational technology and new literacies (Advanced Certificate); elementary education (Ed D); English education (Ed M, Certificate); English education studies (Ed M); English for speakers of other languages (Ed M); foreign and second language education (PhD); French education (Ed M, Certificate); German education (Ed M, Certificate); gifted education (Certificate); Latin education (Ed M, Certificate); literacy education studies (Ed M); literacy specialist (Ed M); literacy teaching and learning (Certificate); mathematics education (Ed M, Certificate); music education (Ed M, Certificate); music education studies (Ed M); music learning theory (Advanced Certificate); online education (Advanced Certificate); physics education (Ed M, Certificate); science and the public (Ed M); social studies education (Ed M, Certificate); Spanish education (Ed M, Certificate); special education (PhD); teaching English to speakers of other languages (Ed M). *Program availability:* Part-time, evening/weekend, 100% online. *Faculty:* 28 full-time (21 women), 67 part-time/adjunct (49 women). *Students:* 198 full-time (153 women), 312 part-time (220 women); includes 48 minority (28 Black or African American, non-Hispanic/Latino; 4 American Indian or Alaska Native, non-Hispanic/Latino; 15 Asian, non-Hispanic/Latino; 1 Hispanic/Latino), 66 international. Average age 33. 336 applicants, 86% accepted, 178 enrolled. In 2016, 137 master's, 24 doctorates, 25 other advanced degrees awarded. *Degree requirements:* For master's, comprehensive exam; for doctorate, thesis/dissertation, research analysis exam, research experience. *Entrance requirements:* For master's, letters of reference; for doctorate, GRE General Test or MAT, interview, writing sample, letters of recommendation. Additional exam requirements/recommendations for international students: Required—TOEFL (minimum score 600 paper-based; 96 iBT). *Application deadline:* For fall admission, 2/1 priority date for domestic and international students; for spring admission, 11/15 priority date for domestic students, 10/1 for international students. Applications are processed on a rolling basis. Application fee: $50. Electronic applications accepted. *Financial support:* In 2016–17, 44 fellowships (averaging $4,010 per year), 39 research assistantships with tuition reimbursements (averaging $9,897 per year) were awarded; teaching assistantships, career-related internships or fieldwork, Federal Work-Study, institutionally sponsored loans, scholarships/grants, tuition waivers (full and partial), and unspecified assistantships also available. Financial award application deadline: 2/28; financial award applicants required to submit FAFSA. *Faculty research:* Science assessment, foreign language teaching and learning, early learning, new literacies, gender and education. *Total annual research expenditures:* $534,880. *Unit head:* Dr. Deborah Moore-Russo, Chair, 716-645-4069, Fax: 716-645-3161, E-mail: dam29@buffalo.edu. *Application contact:* Luann Zak, Admissions Assistant, 716-645-2110, Fax: 716-645-7937, E-mail: luannzak@buffalo.edu. Website: http://gse.buffalo.edu/lai

**The University of Alabama,** Graduate School, College of Arts and Sciences, Department of Modern Languages and Classics, Tuscaloosa, AL 35487. Offers French (MA, PhD); French and Spanish (PhD); German (MA); Romance languages (MA, PhD); Spanish (MA, PhD). *Program availability:* Part-time. *Faculty:* 31 full-time (18 women). *Students:* 49 full-time (32 women), 7 part-time (4 women); includes 9 minority (3 Black or African American, non-Hispanic/Latino; 1 Asian, non-Hispanic/Latino; 4 Hispanic/Latino; 1 Two or more races, non-Hispanic/Latino), 20 international. Average age 31. 29 applicants, 66% accepted, 12 enrolled. In 2016, 11 master's, 6 doctorates awarded. *Degree requirements:* For master's, comprehensive exam, thesis optional; for doctorate, one foreign language, thesis/dissertation, preliminary exam. *Entrance requirements:* For master's and doctorate, minimum GPA of 3.0, writing sample. Additional exam requirements/recommendations for international students: Required—TOEFL or IELTS. *Application deadline:* For fall admission, 7/6 priority date for domestic students, 1/15 priority date for international students; for spring admission, 12/5 priority date for domestic students, 6/1 priority date for international students. Applications are processed on a rolling basis. Application fee: $50 ($60 for international students). Electronic applications accepted. *Expenses:* Tuition, state resident: full-time $10,470. Tuition, nonresident: full-time $26,950. *Financial support:* In 2016–17, 7 students received support, including 1 fellowship, research assistantships with full tuition reimbursements available (averaging $10,291 per year), 6 teaching assistantships with full tuition reimbursements available (averaging $10,291 per year); career-related internships or fieldwork, Federal Work-Study, institutionally sponsored loans, and

scholarships/grants also available. Financial award application deadline: 7/14. *Faculty research:* Non-English literature, linguistics, culture, film. *Unit head:* Dr. Douglas Lightfoot, Department Chair, 205-348-5059, E-mail: lightfoot@ua.edu. *Application contact:* Dr. K. Barbara Fischer, Graduate Director/Associate Professor, 205-348-8465, Fax: 205-348-2042, E-mail: bfischer@bama.ua.edu.
Website: http://bama.ua.edu/~mlc

**University of Alberta,** Faculty of Graduate Studies and Research, Department of Modern Languages and Cultural Studies, Edmonton, AB T6G 2E1, Canada. Offers applied linguistics (Germanic, Romance, Slavic) (MA); French language, literatures and linguistics (PhD); French language, literatures, and linguistics (MA); Germanic languages, literatures and linguistics (PhD); Germanic languages, literatures, and linguistics (MA); Italian studies (MA); Slavic languages and literatures (Russian, Ukrainian) (MA, PhD); Slavic linguistics (Russian, Ukrainian) (MA, PhD); Spanish and Latin American studies (MA, PhD); Ukrainian folklore (MA, PhD). *Program availability:* Part-time. *Degree requirements:* For master's, one foreign language, thesis; for doctorate, 2 foreign languages, comprehensive exam, thesis/dissertation. *Entrance requirements:* For master's and doctorate, 1 language other than English. Additional exam requirements/recommendations for international students: Required—Michigan English Language Assessment Battery or TOEFL (minimum score 550 paper-based). Electronic applications accepted. *Faculty research:* Russian/Ukrainian studies; German studies; contemporary Latin American, French and Francophone studies; Italian studies.

**The University of Arizona,** College of Humanities, Department of German Studies, Tucson, AZ 85721. Offers German (MA); transcultural German (PhD). *Degree requirements:* For master's, one foreign language, comprehensive exam, oral exam; for doctorate, 2 foreign languages, comprehensive exam, thesis/dissertation, oral exam, oral defense. *Entrance requirements:* For master's, minimum major GPA of 3.3, 3 letters of recommendation, audio sample, curriculum vitae. Additional exam requirements/recommendations for international students: Required—TOEFL (minimum score 550 paper-based; 79 iBT). Electronic applications accepted. *Faculty research:* Literature, language, and foreign language pedagogy; computer-assisted text analysis.

**University of Arkansas,** Graduate School, J. William Fulbright College of Arts and Sciences, Department of World Languages, Literature and Cultures, Program in German, Fayetteville, AR 72701. Offers MA. In 2016, 12 master's awarded. *Degree requirements:* For master's, variable foreign language requirement. *Application deadline:* For fall admission, 4/1 for international students; for spring admission, 10/1 for international students. Applications are processed on a rolling basis. Application fee: $40 ($50 for international students). Electronic applications accepted. *Financial support:* In 2016–17, 5 teaching assistantships were awarded; fellowships, research assistantships, career-related internships or fieldwork, and Federal Work-Study also available. Support available to part-time students. Financial award application deadline: 4/1; financial award applicants required to submit FAFSA. *Unit head:* Dr. Steven Bell, Graduate Coordinator, 479-575-2951, Fax: 479-575-6795, E-mail: sbell@uark.edu. *Application contact:* Graduate Coordinator.
Website: http://www.uark.edu/depts/flaninfo/

**The University of British Columbia,** Faculty of Arts and Faculty of Graduate Studies, Department of Central, Eastern and Northern European Studies, Vancouver, BC V6T 1Z1, Canada. Offers Germanic studies (MA, PhD). *Program availability:* Part-time. *Degree requirements:* For master's, one foreign language, thesis optional, exam; for doctorate, one foreign language, comprehensive exam, thesis/dissertation. *Entrance requirements:* For master's, BA in German; for doctorate, MA in German. Additional exam requirements/recommendations for international students: Required—TOEFL. *Application deadline:* Applications are processed on a rolling basis. Application fee: $100 Canadian dollars ($162 Canadian dollars for international students). Electronic applications accepted. *Expenses:* $4,802 per year tuition and fees, $8,436 per year international. *Financial support:* Fellowships, research assistantships, teaching assistantships, career-related internships or fieldwork, scholarships/grants, tuition waivers (full and partial), and unspecified assistantships available. Support available to part-time students. Financial award application deadline: 1/1. *Faculty research:* Second language acquisition, media theory, performance theory, gender studies, cultural studies. *Application contact:* Kate Wilczak, Graduate Program Assistant, 604-827-3500, Fax: 604-822-9344, E-mail: cenes.dept@ubc.ca.
Website: http://cenes.ubc.ca/

**University of Calgary,** Faculty of Graduate Studies, Faculty of Arts, Department of Linguistics, Languages and Culture, Calgary, AB T2N 1N4, Canada. Offers German (MA); linguistics (MA, PhD). *Degree requirements:* For master's, one foreign language, thesis; for doctorate, one foreign language, comprehensive exam, thesis/dissertation. *Entrance requirements:* For doctorate, MA. Additional exam requirements/recommendations for international students: Required—TOEFL (minimum score 560 paper-based). Electronic applications accepted. *Faculty research:* Theoretical linguistics, historical linguistics, language acquisition, Amerindian.

**University of California, Berkeley,** Graduate Division, College of Letters and Science, Department of German, Berkeley, CA 94720-1500. Offers PhD. *Students:* 31 full-time (17 women); includes 9 minority (3 Black or African American, non-Hispanic/Latino; 2 Asian, non-Hispanic/Latino; 4 Hispanic/Latino), 4 international. Average age 31. 20 applicants, 3 enrolled. In 2016, 3 doctorates awarded. *Degree requirements:* For doctorate, 2 foreign languages, thesis/dissertation, qualifying exam. *Entrance requirements:* For doctorate, GRE General Test, minimum GPA of 3.0, writing sample, 3 letters of recommendation. *Application deadline:* For fall admission, 12/15 for domestic students. Application fee: $105 ($125 for international students). Electronic applications accepted. *Financial support:* Fellowships, research assistantships, teaching assistantships, Federal Work-Study, institutionally sponsored loans, health care benefits, tuition waivers (full and partial), and unspecified assistantships available. *Faculty research:* German literature/culture, film, Germanic linguistics, second-language acquisition. *Unit head:* Deniz Göktürk, Chair, 510-643-2004, Fax: 510-643-3243. *Application contact:* Andrea Rapport, 510-643-2004, Fax: 510-642-3243, E-mail: germanga@berkeley.edu.
Website: http://german.berkeley.edu

**University of California, Davis,** Graduate Studies, Program in German, Davis, CA 95616. Offers MA, PhD. Terminal master's awarded for partial completion of doctoral program. *Degree requirements:* For master's, comprehensive exam (for some programs), thesis (for some programs); for doctorate, thesis/dissertation. *Entrance requirements:* For master's, GRE; for doctorate, GRE, master's degree or equivalent. Additional exam requirements/recommendations for international students: Required—TOEFL (minimum score 550 paper-based). Electronic applications accepted. *Faculty research:* Sixteenth to twentieth century medieval literature, critical theory, women's studies.

**University of California, Irvine,** School of Humanities, Department of European Languages and Studies, Irvine, CA 92697. Offers French (MA, PhD); German (MA, PhD). *Students:* 5 full-time (3 women), 2 international. Average age 28. 12 applicants, 83% accepted, 3 enrolled. In 2016, 2 doctorates awarded. *Degree requirements:* For doctorate, thesis/dissertation. *Entrance requirements:* For master's and doctorate, GRE General Test, minimum GPA of 3.0. Additional exam requirements/recommendations for

international students: Required—TOEFL (minimum score 550 paper-based). *Application deadline:* For fall admission, 1/15 for domestic and international students. Applications are processed on a rolling basis. Application fee: $105 ($125 for international students). Electronic applications accepted. *Financial support:* Fellowships, research assistantships with full tuition reimbursements, teaching assistantships, institutionally sponsored loans, traineeships, health care benefits, and unspecified assistantships available. Financial award application deadline: 3/1; financial award applicants required to submit FAFSA. *Faculty research:* Montaigne, psychoanalysis, feminism and the problem of repression, aesthetics of nationalism and the limits of culture. *Unit head:* Prof. David Pan, Chair, 949-824-6406, Fax: 949-824-6416, E-mail: dtpan@uci.edu. *Application contact:* Bindya Baliga, Graduate Program Coordinator, 949-824-7968, Fax: 949-824-6416, E-mail: bbaliga@uci.edu.
Website: http://www.humanities.uci.edu/els/

**University of California, Los Angeles,** Graduate Division, College of Letters and Science, Department of Germanic Languages, Program in Germanic Languages, Los Angeles, CA 90095. Offers MA, PhD. Terminal master's awarded for partial completion of doctoral program. *Degree requirements:* For master's, one foreign language, comprehensive exam or thesis; for doctorate, 2 foreign languages, thesis/dissertation, oral and written qualifying exams. *Entrance requirements:* For master's, GRE General Test, bachelor's degree; minimum undergraduate GPA of 3.0 (or its equivalent if letter grade system not used); for doctorate, GRE General Test, master's degree; minimum undergraduate GPA of 3.0 (or its equivalent if letter grade system not used). Additional exam requirements/recommendations for international students: Required—TOEFL. Electronic applications accepted.

**University of Chicago,** Division of the Humanities, Department of Germanic Studies, Chicago, IL 60637. Offers MA, PhD. *Students:* 20 full-time (7 women), 3 international. 16 applicants, 38% accepted, 2 enrolled. In 2016, 5 doctorates awarded. Terminal master's awarded for partial completion of doctoral program. *Degree requirements:* For doctorate, 2 foreign languages, comprehensive exam, thesis/dissertation. *Entrance requirements:* For doctorate, GRE General Test. Additional exam requirements/recommendations for international students: Required—TOEFL (minimum score 104 iBT), IELTS (minimum score 7). *Application deadline:* For fall admission, 12/15 for domestic and international students. Application fee: $90. Electronic applications accepted. *Financial support:* Fellowships with full tuition reimbursements, teaching assistantships with full tuition reimbursements, Federal Work-Study, institutionally sponsored loans, scholarships/grants, traineeships, and health care benefits available. Financial award application deadline: 12/15; financial award applicants required to submit FAFSA. *Unit head:* Dr. Eric Santner, Chair, 773-834-0948, E-mail: esantner@uchicago.edu. *Application contact:* Michael Beetley, Assistant Dean of Students, Admissions and Fellowships, 773-702-1552, Fax: 773-834-9148, E-mail: humanitiesadmissions@uchicago.edu.
Website: http://german.uchicago.edu/

**University of Chicago,** Division of the Humanities, Master of Arts Program in the Humanities, Chicago, IL 60637. Offers art history (MA); cinema and media studies (MA); classic languages (MA); comparative literature (MA); creative writing (MA); cultural policy studies (MA); digital humanities (MA); East Asian languages and civilizations (MA); English language and literature (MA); gender and sexuality studies (MA); Germanic studies (MA); linguistics (MA); music (MA); near Eastern languages and civilizations (MA); philosophy (MA); poetics (MA); race, politics and culture (MA); Romance languages and literatures (MA); Slavic languages and literatures (MA); South Asian languages and civilizations (MA); theater and performance studies (MA). *Students:* 80 full-time (43 women), 7 part-time (3 women); includes 20 minority (5 Black or African American, non-Hispanic/Latino; 1 American Indian or Alaska Native, non-Hispanic/Latino; 6 Asian, non-Hispanic/Latino; 5 Hispanic/Latino; 3 Two or more races, non-Hispanic/Latino), 11 international. Average age 26. 706 applicants, 15% accepted, 42 enrolled. In 2016, 92 master's awarded. *Degree requirements:* For master's, thesis. *Entrance requirements:* For master's, GRE General Test. Additional exam requirements/recommendations for international students: Required—TOEFL (minimum score 104 iBT), IELTS (minimum score 7). *Application deadline:* For fall admission, 1/3 for domestic and international students. Application fee: $90. Electronic applications accepted. *Financial support:* In 2016–17, 8 fellowships with partial tuition reimbursements (averaging $12,000 per year) were awarded; Federal Work-Study, institutionally sponsored loans, scholarships/grants, and tuition waivers (partial) also available. Financial award application deadline: 12/15; financial award applicants required to submit FAFSA. *Unit head:* Malynne Sternstein, Co-Director, 773-834-1201, Fax: 773-834-7526. *Application contact:* Program Coordinator, 773-834-1201, Fax: 773-834-7526, E-mail: ma-humanities@uchicago.edu.
Website: http://maph.uchicago.edu/

**University of Cincinnati,** Graduate School, McMicken College of Arts and Sciences, Department of German Studies, Cincinnati, OH 45221. Offers MA, PhD. *Program availability:* Part-time. Terminal master's awarded for partial completion of doctoral program. *Degree requirements:* For master's, one foreign language, thesis or alternative; for doctorate, 3 foreign languages, thesis/dissertation. *Entrance requirements:* For master's, GRE General Test; for doctorate, GRE General Test, MA in German or equivalent. Additional exam requirements/recommendations for international students: Required—TOEFL (minimum score 560 paper-based). Electronic applications accepted. *Expenses:* Tuition, area resident: Full-time $12,790; part-time $389 per credit hour. Tuition, state resident: full-time $13,290; part-time $419 per credit hour. Tuition, nonresident: full-time $24,532; part-time $976 per credit hour. International tuition: $24,832 full-time. Required fees: $3958; $140 per credit hour. Tuition and fees vary according to course load, degree level, program and reciprocity agreements. *Faculty research:* German literary culture, language and linguistics, medieval and early modern, German-Jewish literature, 20th and 21st century German literature and film.

**University of Colorado Boulder,** Graduate School, College of Arts and Sciences, Department of Germanic and Slavic Languages and Literatures, Boulder, CO 80309. Offers MA. *Faculty:* 11 full-time (4 women). *Students:* 27 full-time (14 women), 1 (woman) part-time; includes 2 minority (1 Asian, non-Hispanic/Latino; 1 Hispanic/Latino), 6 international. Average age 29. 23 applicants, 57% accepted, 9 enrolled. In 2016, 2 master's awarded. Terminal master's awarded for partial completion of doctoral program. *Degree requirements:* For master's, 2 foreign languages, comprehensive exam, thesis or alternative. *Entrance requirements:* For master's, minimum undergraduate GPA of 2.75. *Application deadline:* For fall admission, 2/1 for domestic and international students; for spring admission, 9/15 for domestic and international students. Application fee: $60 ($80 for international students). Electronic applications accepted. Application fee is waived when completed online. *Financial support:* In 2016–17, 75 students received support, including 24 fellowships (averaging $2,447 per year), 17 teaching assistantships with full and partial tuition reimbursements available (averaging $34,919 per year); institutionally sponsored loans, scholarships/grants, health care benefits, and unspecified assistantships also available. Financial award application deadline: 2/1; financial award applicants required to submit FAFSA. *Faculty research:* German language/literature, literary criticism, comparative literature, cultural history, culture. *Total annual research expenditures:* $31,200. *Application contact:* E-mail: gsll@colorado.edu.
Website: http://gsll.colorado.edu/

**University of Delaware,** College of Arts and Sciences, Department of Foreign Languages and Literatures, Newark, DE 19716. Offers foreign languages and literatures (MA), including French, German, Spanish; foreign languages pedagogy (MA), including French, German, Spanish; technical Chinese translation (MA). *Degree requirements:* For master's, one foreign language, comprehensive exam, thesis optional. *Entrance requirements:* For master's, GRE General Test, letters of recommendation, writing sample. Additional exam requirements/recommendations for international students: Required—TOEFL. Electronic applications accepted. *Faculty research:* Medieval to Modern French and Spanish literature, twentieth-century German, French, Spanish literature by women, computer-assisted instruction.

**University of Florida,** Graduate School, College of Liberal Arts and Sciences, Department of Languages, Literatures and Cultures, Gainesville, FL 32611. Offers French and Francophone studies (MA, PhD); German (MA, PhD), including women's and gender studies (PhD). *Degree requirements:* For master's, comprehensive exam, thesis optional; for doctorate, one foreign language, comprehensive exam, thesis/dissertation. *Entrance requirements:* For master's and doctorate, GRE General Test, minimum GPA of 3.0. Additional exam requirements/recommendations for international students: Required—TOEFL (minimum score 550 paper-based; 80 iBT), IELTS (minimum score 6). Electronic applications accepted. *Faculty research:* Medieval epic, romance, and allegory; Renaissance and Baroque poetry; the eighteenth-century novel; nineteenth-century prose, poetry, and poetics; the twentieth-century novel, theater, and poetry; the literatures of the Francophone world; French and Francophone film; the literatures in Breton and Occitan; criticism and critical theory; applied linguistics; the history of French; phonology; sociolinguistics; the structure of French; French and Haitian Creole linguistics.

**University of Georgia,** Franklin College of Arts and Sciences, Department of Germanic and Slavic Studies, Athens, GA 30602. Offers German (MA). *Degree requirements:* For master's, one foreign language, thesis. *Entrance requirements:* For master's, GRE General Test. *Application deadline:* For fall admission, 7/1 priority date for domestic students; for spring admission, 11/15 for domestic students. Application fee: $50. Electronic applications accepted. *Financial support:* Fellowships, research assistantships, teaching assistantships, and unspecified assistantships available. *Unit head:* Dr. Martin H. Kagel, Head, 706-542-2445, Fax: 706-583-0349, E-mail: mkagel@uga.edu. *Application contact:* Dr. Alexander Sager, Graduate Advisor, 706-542-6211, Fax: 706-542-2459, E-mail: asager@uga.edu.
Website: http://www.uga.edu/~gslangs/

**University of Illinois at Chicago,** College of Liberal Arts and Sciences, School of Literatures, Cultural Studies and Linguistics, Department of Germanic Studies, Chicago, IL 60607-7128. Offers MA, PhD. PhD offered jointly with University of Illinois at Urbana–Champaign. *Program availability:* Part-time. Terminal master's awarded for partial completion of doctoral program. *Degree requirements:* For master's, thesis optional, exam; for doctorate, 2 foreign languages, thesis/dissertation. *Entrance requirements:* For master's and doctorate, GRE General Test, minimum GPA of 2.75. Additional exam requirements/recommendations for international students: Required—TOEFL. Electronic applications accepted. *Faculty research:* German literature.

**University of Illinois at Urbana–Champaign,** Graduate College, College of Liberal Arts and Sciences, School of Literatures, Cultures and Linguistics, Department of Germanic Languages and Literatures, Champaign, IL 61820. Offers German (MA, PhD).

**The University of Kansas,** Graduate Studies, College of Liberal Arts and Sciences, Department of Germanic Languages and Literatures, Lawrence, KS 66045. Offers German (MA, PhD). In 2016, 2 master's, 3 doctorates awarded. *Entrance requirements:* Additional exam requirements/recommendations for international students: Required—TOEFL. Application fee: $65 ($85 for international students). *Financial support:* Fellowships, research assistantships, teaching assistantships, Federal Work-Study, institutionally sponsored loans, and unspecified assistantships available. Support available to part-time students. *Faculty research:* Humanism, eighteenth- to twentieth-century literature, Germanic linguistics, German-American studies, German applied linguistics, German philology. *Unit head:* Nina Vyatkina, Chair, 785-864-4813, E-mail: vyatkina@ku.edu. *Application contact:* Cari Ann Kreienhop, Academic Advisor, 785-864-3665, E-mail: ckreienhop@ku.edu.
Website: http://germanic.ku.edu/

**University of Kentucky,** Graduate School, College of Arts and Sciences, Program in German, Lexington, KY 40506-0032. Offers MA. *Degree requirements:* For master's, one foreign language, comprehensive exam, thesis optional. *Entrance requirements:* For master's, GRE General Test, minimum undergraduate GPA of 2.75. Additional exam requirements/recommendations for international students: Required—TOEFL (minimum score 550 paper-based). Electronic applications accepted. *Faculty research:* Medieval studies, literature from Enlightenment to present, literary theory, intellectual history, gender studies.

**University of Lethbridge,** School of Graduate Studies, Lethbridge, AB T1K 3M4, Canada. Offers addictions counseling (M Sc); agricultural biotechnology (M Sc); agricultural studies (M Sc, MA); anthropology (MA); archaeology (M Sc, MA); art (MA, MFA); biochemistry (M Sc); biological sciences (M Sc); biomolecular science (PhD); biosystems and biodiversity (PhD); Canadian studies (MA); chemistry (M Sc); computer science (M Sc); computer science and geographical information science (M Sc); counseling (MC); counseling psychology (M Ed); dramatic arts (MA); earth, space, and physical science (PhD); economics (MA); education (MA, PhD); educational leadership (M Ed); English (MA); environmental science (M Sc); evolution and behavior (PhD); exercise science (M Sc); French (MA); French/German (MA); French/Spanish (MA); general education (M Ed); geography (MA); German (MA); health sciences (M Sc); individualized multidisciplinary (M Sc, MA); kinesiology (M Sc, MA); management (M Sc), including accounting, finance, human resource management and labor relations, information systems, international management, marketing, policy and strategy; mathematics (M Sc); music (M Mus, MA); Native American studies (MA); neuroscience (M Sc, PhD); new media (MA, MFA); nursing (M Sc, MN); philosophy (MA); physics (M Sc); political science (MA); psychology (M Sc, MA); religious studies (MA); sociology (MA); theatre and dramatic arts (MFA); theoretical and computational science (PhD); urban and regional studies (MA); women and gender studies (MA). *Program availability:* Part-time, evening/weekend. *Degree requirements:* For master's, thesis (for some programs); for doctorate, comprehensive exam, thesis/dissertation. *Entrance requirements:* For master's, GMAT (for M Sc in management), bachelor's degree in related field, minimum GPA of 3.0 during previous 20 graded semester courses, 2 years' teaching or related experience (M Ed); for doctorate, master's degree, minimum graduate GPA of 3.5. Additional exam requirements/recommendations for international students: Required—TOEFL (minimum score 580 paper-based; 93 iBT). Electronic applications accepted. *Faculty research:* Movement and brain plasticity, gibberellin physiology, photosynthesis, carbon cycling, molecular properties of main-group ring components.

**The University of Manchester,** School of Languages, Linguistics and Cultures, Manchester, United Kingdom. Offers Arab world studies (PhD); Chinese studies (M Phil, PhD); East Asian studies (M Phil, PhD); English language (PhD); French studies (M Phil, PhD); German studies (M Phil, PhD); interpreting studies (PhD); Italian studies (M Phil, PhD); Japanese studies (M Phil, PhD); Latin American cultural studies (M Phil, PhD); linguistics (M Phil, PhD); Middle Eastern studies (M Phil, PhD); Polish studies (M Phil, PhD); Portuguese studies (M Phil, PhD); Russian studies (M Phil, PhD); Spanish studies (M Phil, PhD); translation and intercultural studies (M Phil, PhD).

**University of Manitoba,** Faculty of Graduate Studies, Faculty of Arts, Department of German and Slavic Studies, Winnipeg, MB R3T 2N2, Canada. Offers German language and literature (MA); Slavic languages and literatures (MA). *Degree requirements:* For master's, one foreign language, thesis or alternative.

**University of Maryland, College Park,** Academic Affairs, College of Arts and Humanities, School of Languages, Literatures, and Cultures, Department of Germanic Studies, College Park, MD 20742. Offers Germanic language and literature (MA, PhD). *Degree requirements:* For master's, one foreign language, thesis optional, exams; for doctorate, 2 foreign languages, comprehensive exam, thesis/dissertation, reading exam, oral defense. *Entrance requirements:* For master's, writing sample, 3 letters of recommendation, interview; for doctorate, MA in German or related discipline. Additional exam requirements/recommendations for international students: Required—TOEFL. Electronic applications accepted. *Faculty research:* Language pedagogy, Germanic philology, medieval culture.

**University of Massachusetts Amherst,** Graduate School, College of Humanities and Fine Arts, Department of Languages, Literatures, and Cultures, Programs in German and Scandinavian Studies, Amherst, MA 01003. Offers MA, PhD. *Program availability:* Part-time. Terminal master's awarded for partial completion of doctoral program. *Degree requirements:* For master's, thesis or alternative; for doctorate, one foreign language, comprehensive exam, thesis/dissertation. *Entrance requirements:* For master's and doctorate, writing sample in English and German. Additional exam requirements/recommendations for international students: Required—TOEFL (minimum score 550 paper-based; 80 iBT), IELTS (minimum score 6.5). Electronic applications accepted.

**University of Michigan,** Rackham Graduate School, College of Literature, Science, and the Arts, Department of Germanic Languages and Literatures, Ann Arbor, MI 48109. Offers German (AM, PhD); German studies (Certificate). *Faculty:* 14 full-time (6 women), 3 part-time/adjunct (2 women). *Students:* 20 full-time (15 women); includes 2 minority (1 Black or African American, non-Hispanic/Latino; 1 Two or more races, non-Hispanic/Latino), 7 international. Average age 30. 24 applicants, 54% accepted, 6 enrolled. In 2016, 1 master's, 1 doctorate awarded. *Degree requirements:* For doctorate, one foreign language, comprehensive exam, thesis/dissertation, oral defense of dissertation, preliminary exam. *Entrance requirements:* For doctorate, GRE General Test. Additional exam requirements/recommendations for international students: Required—TOEFL (minimum score 560 paper-based). *Application deadline:* For fall and winter admission, 1/10 priority date for domestic and international students. Application fee: $75 ($90 for international students). Electronic applications accepted. *Expenses:* Tuition, state resident: full-time $21,466; part-time $1152 per credit hour. Tuition, nonresident: full-time $43,346; part-time $2367 per credit hour. Part-time tuition and fees vary according to course load, degree level and program. *Financial support:* In 2016–17, 11 students received support, including 10 fellowships with full tuition reimbursements available (averaging $21,000 per year), 15 teaching assistantships with full tuition reimbursements available (averaging $19,737 per year); scholarships/grants, health care benefits, and tuition waivers (full) also available. *Faculty research:* German history, German literature, literary theory, film, political and social theory. *Unit head:* Prof. Johannes von Moltke, Chair, 734-764-8018, Fax: 734-763-6557, E-mail: moltke@umich.edu. *Application contact:* Jennifer White, Student Services Coordinator, 734-936-0150, Fax: 734-763-6557, E-mail: jenpatri@umich.edu.
Website: http://www.lsa.umich.edu/german

**University of Minnesota, Twin Cities Campus,** Graduate School, College of Liberal Arts, Department of German, Scandinavian, and Dutch, Minneapolis, MN 55455. Offers Germanic studies (MA, PhD), including German, Germanic medieval studies, Scandinavian studies (MA). *Program availability:* Part-time. Terminal master's awarded for partial completion of doctoral program. *Degree requirements:* For master's, 2 foreign languages, thesis/dissertation. *Entrance requirements:* For master's, GRE General Test, BA in German, Scandinavian, or equivalent; for doctorate, MA in German, Scandinavian, or equivalent. Additional exam requirements/recommendations for international students: Required—TOEFL (minimum score 550 paper-based; 79 iBT). Electronic applications accepted. *Faculty research:* Cultural studies, literary theory, feminist criticism, film, Germanic medieval studies.

**University of Missouri,** Office of Research and Graduate Studies, College of Arts and Science, Department of German and Russian Studies, Columbia, MO 65211. Offers MA. *Faculty:* 20 full-time (6 women). *Students:* 11 full-time (10 women), 6 part-time (4 women). *Entrance requirements:* For master's, GRE General Test, minimum GPA of 3.0. Additional exam requirements/recommendations for international students: Required—TOEFL (minimum score 500 paper-based; 61 iBT). *Application deadline:* For fall admission, 2/1 priority date for domestic and international students. Applications are processed on a rolling basis. Application fee: $75 ($90 for international students). Electronic applications accepted. *Expenses:* Tuition, state resident: full-time $6347; part-time $352.60 per credit hour. Tuition, nonresident: full-time $17,379; part-time $965.50 per credit hour. *Required fees:* $1035. Tuition and fees vary according to course load, campus/location and program. *Financial support:* Teaching assistantships with full tuition reimbursements, institutionally sponsored loans, health care benefits, and unspecified assistantships available. *Faculty research:* German and Russian cultural studies including literature, film, media studies, philosophy, and the history of science.
Website: http://german.missouri.edu/index.html

**University of Montana,** Graduate School, College of Humanities and Sciences, Department of Modern and Classical Languages and Literatures, Missoula, MT 59812-0002. Offers French (MA); German (MA); Spanish (MA). *Degree requirements:* For master's, one foreign language. *Entrance requirements:* For master's, GRE General Test. Additional exam requirements/recommendations for international students: Required—TOEFL.

**University of Nebraska–Lincoln,** Graduate College, College of Arts and Sciences, Department of Modern Languages and Literatures, Lincoln, NE 68588. Offers French (MA, PhD); German (MA, PhD); Spanish (MA, PhD). *Degree requirements:* For master's, thesis optional; for doctorate, comprehensive exam, thesis/dissertation. *Entrance requirements:* For master's and doctorate, writing sample in target language. Additional exam requirements/recommendations for international students: Required—TOEFL (minimum score 550 paper-based). Electronic applications accepted. *Faculty research:* French, German, and Spanish language, literature, and culture.

**University of Nevada, Reno,** Graduate School, College of Liberal Arts, Department of Foreign Languages and Literatures, Reno, NV 89557. Offers French (MA); German (MA); Spanish (MA). *Degree requirements:* For master's, one foreign language, thesis optional. *Entrance requirements:* For master's, GRE General Test, minimum GPA of 2.75. Additional exam requirements/recommendations for international students: Required—TOEFL (minimum score 500 paper-based; 61 iBT), IELTS (minimum score 6). *Faculty research:* Thirteenth century mysticism, contemporary Spanish and Latin

American poetry and theater, French interrelation between narration and photography, exile literature and Holocaust.

**University of New Mexico,** Graduate Studies, College of Arts and Sciences, Program in Foreign Languages and Literatures, Albuquerque, NM 87131-2039. Offers comparative literature and cultural studies (MA); French (MA); French studies (PhD); German studies (MA). *Program availability:* Part-time. *Faculty:* 9 full-time (5 women). *Students:* 21 full-time (12 women), 10 part-time (6 women); includes 4 minority (3 Hispanic/Latino; 1 Two or more races, non-Hispanic/Latino), 10 international. Average age 30. 17 applicants, 41% accepted, 5 enrolled. In 2016, 9 master's awarded. *Degree requirements:* For master's, one foreign language, thesis optional; for doctorate, 2 foreign languages, thesis/dissertation. *Entrance requirements:* For master's and doctorate, transcript, writing sample, 3 letters of recommendation. Additional exam requirements/recommendations for international students: Required—TOEFL. *Application deadline:* For fall admission, 2/1 priority date for domestic students; for spring admission, 10/1 priority date for domestic students. Application fee: $50. Electronic applications accepted. *Financial support:* Research assistantships, teaching assistantships with tuition reimbursements, Federal Work-Study, health care benefits, and unspecified assistantships available. Financial award application deadline: 3/1; financial award applicants required to submit FAFSA. *Faculty research:* German, Russian, Italian, Japanese, French, comparative literature, culture studies, classics. *Unit head:* Dr. Walter Putnam, Chair, 505-277-4771, Fax: 505-277-3599, E-mail: wputnam@unm.edu. *Application contact:* Jacqueline Ochoa, Application and Graduation Advisor, 505-277-4471, Fax: 505-277-3599, E-mail: jochoa@unm.edu. Website: http://www.unm.edu/~fll/

**The University of North Carolina at Chapel Hill,** Graduate School, College of Arts and Sciences, Department of Germanic Languages, Chapel Hill, NC 27599. Offers literature and linguistics (MA, PhD). *Program availability:* Part-time. Terminal master's awarded for partial completion of doctoral program. *Degree requirements:* For master's, comprehensive exam, thesis; for doctorate, one foreign language, comprehensive exam, thesis/dissertation. *Entrance requirements:* For master's and doctorate, GRE General Test, minimum GPA of 3.0. *Faculty research:* Gender and sexuality, literature and politics, German and Jewish culture, medieval through modern literature, Germanic linguistics.

**University of Oklahoma,** College of Arts and Sciences, Department of Modern Languages, Literatures, and Linguistics, Program in German, Norman, OK 73019-2032. Offers MA, MBA/MA. *Program availability:* Part-time. *Students:* 3 full-time (all women). Average age 30. 1 applicant, 100% accepted, 1 enrolled. In 2016, 1 master's awarded. Terminal master's awarded for partial completion of doctoral program. *Degree requirements:* For master's, comprehensive exam, two languages (one must be German); thesis or exam and research papers. *Entrance requirements:* For master's, BA and major or minor in German. Additional exam requirements/recommendations for international students: Required—TOEFL (minimum score 79 iBT) or IELTS (minimum score 6.5). *Application deadline:* For fall admission, 2/1 for domestic and international students; for spring admission, 10/1 for domestic and international students. Application fee: $50 ($100 for international students). Electronic applications accepted. *Expenses:* Tuition, state resident: full-time $4886; part-time $203.60 per credit hour. Tuition, nonresident: full-time $18,989; part-time $791.20 per credit hour. *Required fees:* $3283; $126.25 per credit hour. $126.50 per semester. *Financial support:* In 2016–17, 4 students received support. Fellowships, teaching assistantships with full tuition reimbursements available, scholarships/grants, health care benefits, and unspecified assistantships available. Support available to part-time students. Financial award application deadline: 6/1; financial award applicants required to submit FAFSA. *Faculty research:* Goethe and German-Jewish studies, Arthurian romance, Kafka and turn-of-the-century Austria. *Unit head:* Dr. Karin Schutjer, Professor of German, 405-325-1907, Fax: 405-325-0103, E-mail: kschutjer@ou.edu. *Application contact:* Robert Lemon, Associate Professor/Graduate Section Liaison, 405-325-1551, Fax: 405-325-0103, E-mail: rlemon@ou.edu. Website: http://mlll.publishpath.com/german-ma

**University of Oregon,** Graduate School, College of Arts and Sciences, Department of Germanic Languages and Literatures, Eugene, OR 97403. Offers MA, PhD. *Degree requirements:* For master's, 2 foreign languages, thesis or alternative; for doctorate, 3 foreign languages, thesis/dissertation. *Entrance requirements:* For master's and doctorate, minimum GPA of 3.0. Additional exam requirements/recommendations for international students: Required—TOEFL. *Faculty research:* Medieval language and literature, eighteenth to twentieth century literature and philosophy, literary theory, feminist literature and theory, psychoanalysis and literature.

**University of Pennsylvania,** School of Arts and Sciences, Graduate Group in Germanic Languages, Philadelphia, PA 19104. Offers AM, PhD. *Faculty:* 12 full-time (4 women), 8 part-time/adjunct (1 woman). *Students:* 10 full-time (6 women), 2 international. Average age 29. 1 applicant. In 2016, 2 master's, 1 doctorate awarded. Terminal master's awarded for partial completion of doctoral program. *Expenses:* Tuition: Full-time $31,068; part-time $5762 per course. *Required fees:* $3200; $336 per course. Full-time tuition and fees vary according to degree level, program and student level. Part-time tuition and fees vary according to course load, degree level and program. Website: http://www.sas.upenn.edu/graduate-division

**University of Saskatchewan,** College of Graduate Studies and Research, College of Arts and Science, Department of Languages and Linguistics, Saskatoon, SK S7N 5A2, Canada. Offers MA. *Degree requirements:* For master's, 2 foreign languages, thesis. *Entrance requirements:* Additional exam requirements/recommendations for international students: Required—TOEFL (minimum score 80 iBT); Recommended—IELTS (minimum score 6.5). Electronic applications accepted.

**University of South Africa,** College of Human Sciences, Pretoria, South Africa. Offers adult education (M Ed); African languages (MA, PhD); African politics (MA, PhD); Afrikaans (MA, PhD); ancient history (MA, PhD); ancient Near Eastern studies (MA, PhD); anthropology (MA, PhD); applied linguistics (MA); Arabic (MA, PhD); archaeology (MA); art history (MA); Biblical archaeology (MA); Biblical studies (M Th, D Th, PhD); Christian spirituality (M Th, D Th); church history (M Th, D Th); classical studies (MA, PhD); clinical psychology (MA); communication (MA, PhD); comparative education (M Ed, Ed D); consulting psychology (D Admin, D Com, PhD); curriculum studies (M Ed, Ed D); development studies (M Admin, MA, D Admin, PhD); didactics (M Ed, Ed D); education (M Tech); education management (M Ed, Ed D); educational psychology (M Ed); English (MA); environmental education (M Ed); French (MA, PhD); German (MA, PhD); Greek (MA); guidance and counseling (M Ed); health studies (MA, PhD), including health sciences education (MA), health services management (MA), medical and surgical nursing science (critical care general) (MA), midwifery and neonatal nursing science (MA), trauma and emergency care (MA); history (MA, PhD); history of education (Ed D); inclusive education (M Ed, Ed D); information and communications technology policy and regulation (MA); information science (MA, MIS, PhD); international politics (MA, PhD); Islamic studies (MA, PhD); Italian (MA, PhD); Judaica (MA, PhD); linguistics (MA, PhD); mathematical education (M Ed); mathematics education (MA); missiology (M Th, D Th); modern Hebrew (MA, PhD); musicology (MA, MMus, D Mus, PhD); natural science education (M Ed); New Testament (M Th, D Th); Old Testament (D Th);

pastoral therapy (M Th, D Th); philosophy (MA); philosophy of education (M Ed, Ed D); politics (MA, PhD); Portuguese (MA, PhD); practical theology (M Th, D Th); psychology (MA, MS, PhD); psychology of education (M Ed, Ed D); public health (MA); religious studies (MA, D Th, PhD); Romance languages (MA); Russian (MA, PhD); Semitic languages (MA, PhD); social behavior studies in HIV/AIDS (MA); social science (mental health) (MA); social science in development studies (MA); social science in psychology (MA); social science in social work (MA); social science in sociology (MA); social work (MSW, DSW, PhD); socio-education (M Ed, Ed D); sociolinguistics (MA); sociology (MA, PhD); Spanish (MA, PhD); systematic theology (M Th, D Th); TESOL (teaching English to speakers of other languages) (MA); theological ethics (M Th, D Th); theory of literature (MA, PhD); urban ministries (D Th); urban ministry (M Th).

**University of South Carolina,** The Graduate School, College of Arts and Sciences, Department of Languages, Literatures, and Cultures, Columbia, SC 29208. Offers comparative literature (MA, PhD); foreign languages (MAT), including French, German, Spanish; French (MA); German (MA); Spanish (MA). MAT offered in cooperation with the College of Education. *Program availability:* Part-time. *Degree requirements:* For master's, one foreign language, comprehensive exam, thesis optional; for doctorate, 2 foreign languages, comprehensive exam, thesis/dissertation. *Entrance requirements:* For master's and doctorate, GRE General Test, writing sample. Additional exam requirements/recommendations for international students: Required—TOEFL (minimum score 75 iBT). Electronic applications accepted. *Faculty research:* Modern literature, linguistics, literature and culture, medieval literature, literary theory.

**The University of Tennessee,** Graduate School, College of Arts and Sciences, Department of Modern Foreign Languages and Literatures, Program in German, Knoxville, TN 37996. Offers MA. *Program availability:* Part-time. *Degree requirements:* For master's, one foreign language, thesis or alternative. *Entrance requirements:* For master's, minimum GPA of 2.7. Additional exam requirements/recommendations for international students: Required—TOEFL. Electronic applications accepted.

**The University of Tennessee,** Graduate School, College of Arts and Sciences, Department of Modern Foreign Languages and Literatures, Program in Modern Foreign Languages, Knoxville, TN 37996. Offers applied linguistics (PhD); French (PhD); German (PhD); Italian (PhD); Portuguese (PhD); Russian (PhD); Spanish (PhD). *Degree requirements:* For doctorate, 2 foreign languages, thesis/dissertation. *Entrance requirements:* For doctorate, minimum GPA of 2.7. Additional exam requirements/recommendations for international students: Required—TOEFL. Electronic applications accepted.

**The University of Texas at Austin,** Graduate School, College of Liberal Arts, Department of Germanic Studies, Austin, TX 78712-1111. Offers MA, PhD. *Degree requirements:* For master's, one foreign language, thesis or alternative; for doctorate, 2 foreign languages, thesis/dissertation. *Entrance requirements:* For master's and doctorate, GRE General Test. *Faculty research:* Germanic languages and culture (German, Austrian, Swiss, Dutch, Danish, Norwegian, Swedish, Yiddish), language pedagogy and linguistics.

**The University of Toledo,** College of Graduate Studies, College of Languages, Literature and Social Sciences, Department of Foreign Languages, Toledo, OH 43606-3390. Offers French (MA); German (MA); Spanish (MA). *Program availability:* Part-time. *Degree requirements:* For master's, one foreign language, comprehensive exam, comprehensive reading exam in 1 additional foreign language. *Entrance requirements:* For master's, minimum cumulative point-hour ratio of 2.7 for all previous academic work. Additional exam requirements/recommendations for international students: Required—TOEFL (minimum score 550 paper-based; 80 iBT). Electronic applications accepted.

**University of Toronto,** School of Graduate Studies, Faculty of Arts and Science, Department of Germanic Languages and Literatures, Toronto, ON M5S 1A1, Canada. Offers MA, PhD. *Program availability:* Part-time. *Degree requirements:* For master's, thesis optional, German language competence exam; for doctorate, thesis/dissertation, qualifying exam, thesis defense. *Entrance requirements:* For master's, 7 two-semester courses in German language and literature, 3 letters of recommendation; for doctorate, MA in German, minimum A- average, 3 letters of recommendation, writing sample, resume. Additional exam requirements/recommendations for international students: Required—TOEFL (minimum score 580 paper-based; 93 iBT), TWE (minimum score 5). Electronic applications accepted.

**University of Vermont,** Graduate College, College of Arts and Sciences, Department of German, Burlington, VT 05405. Offers MA. *Degree requirements:* For master's, one foreign language, thesis. *Entrance requirements:* For master's, GRE General Test. Additional exam requirements/recommendations for international students: Required—TOEFL (minimum score 550 paper-based; 80 iBT). Electronic applications accepted. *Expenses:* Tuition, state resident: full-time $5814. Tuition, nonresident: full-time $14,670. *Faculty research:* Medieval, eighteenth-, and nineteenth-century literature; folklore.

**University of Victoria,** Faculty of Graduate Studies, Faculty of Humanities, Department of Germanic and Slavic Studies, Victoria, BC V8W 2Y2, Canada. Offers German studies (MA). *Program availability:* Part-time. *Degree requirements:* For master's, 2 foreign languages, oral defense of thesis. *Entrance requirements:* For master's, BA in German, minimum B+ average in undergraduate course work. Additional exam requirements/recommendations for international students: Required—TOEFL (minimum score 575 paper-based), IELTS (minimum score 7). Electronic applications accepted. *Faculty research:* Nineteenth and twentieth century German literature, literature and music, language acquisition, eighteenth and twentieth century drama and theater, military history.

**University of Virginia,** College and Graduate School of Arts and Sciences, Department of Germanic Languages and Literatures, Charlottesville, VA 22903. Offers German (MA). *Faculty:* 10 full-time (5 women), 1 (woman) part-time/adjunct. *Students:* 2 full-time (0 women). Average age 30. *Degree requirements:* For master's, one foreign language, comprehensive exam, thesis. *Entrance requirements:* For master's, GRE General Test, 3 letters of recommendation, critical writing sample. Additional exam requirements/recommendations for international students: Required—TOEFL (minimum score 600 paper-based; 90 iBT), IELTS (minimum score 7). *Application deadline:* For fall admission, 1/15 for domestic and international students. Applications are processed on a rolling basis. Application fee: $60. Electronic applications accepted. *Expenses:* Tuition, state resident: full-time $15,026; part-time $834 per credit hour. Tuition, nonresident: full-time $25,168; part-time $1378 per credit hour. *Required fees:* $2654. *Financial support:* Applicants required to submit FAFSA. *Unit head:* Jeffrey Grossman, Chair, 434-924-3530, Fax: 434-924-6700, E-mail: jg2t@virginia.edu. *Application contact:* Benjamin Bennett, Graduate Admissions Contact, 434-924-3530, Fax: 434-924-6700, E-mail: bkb@virginia.edu. Website: http://www.german.virginia.edu/

**University of Washington,** Graduate School, College of Arts and Sciences, Department of Germanics, Seattle, WA 98195. Offers MA, PhD. *Program availability:* Part-time. Terminal master's awarded for partial completion of doctoral program. *Degree requirements:* For master's, one foreign language, 2 research papers; for doctorate, 2 foreign languages, thesis/dissertation, 3 research papers. *Entrance requirements:* For master's and doctorate, GRE, minimum GPA of 3.0. Additional exam requirements/

recommendations for international students: Required—TOEFL. Electronic applications accepted. *Faculty research:* Modern German literature, Germanic linguistics and philology, language pedagogy, literary theory, cinema studies.

**University of Waterloo,** Graduate Studies, Faculty of Arts, Department of Germanic and Slavic Studies, Waterloo, ON N2L 3G1, Canada. Offers German (MA, PhD); Russian (MA). *Program availability:* Part-time, evening/weekend. *Degree requirements:* For master's, one foreign language, thesis optional; for doctorate, 2 foreign languages, comprehensive exam, thesis/dissertation. *Entrance requirements:* For master's, honors degree, minimum B average; for doctorate, master's degree, minimum B average. Additional exam requirements/recommendations for international students: Required—TOEFL, IELTS, PTE. Electronic applications accepted. *Faculty research:* Medieval theatre; history and literature; German and Russian literary relations; seventeenth-, eighteenth-, nineteenth-, and twentieth-century German literature.

**University of Wisconsin–Madison,** Graduate School, College of Letters and Science, Department of German, Madison, WI 53706-1380. Offers MA, PhD. *Program availability:* Part-time. Terminal master's awarded for partial completion of doctoral program. *Degree requirements:* For master's, one foreign language, comprehensive exam, thesis optional; for doctorate, 2 foreign languages, comprehensive exam, thesis/dissertation. *Entrance requirements:* For master's and doctorate, GRE. Electronic applications accepted. *Faculty research:* Literature, culture/linguistics, film, Dutch.

**University of Wisconsin–Milwaukee,** Graduate School, College of Letters and Science, Department of Foreign Languages and Literature, Milwaukee, WI 53201-0413. Offers classic Greek (MA); classics (MA); comparative literature (MA); foreign language and literature (MA); French (MA); German (MA); Latin (MA); linguistics (MA); Spanish (MA); translation (MA, Certificate). *Program availability:* Part-time. *Students:* 10 full-time (7 women), 19 part-time (16 women); includes 5 minority (2 Black or African American, non-Hispanic/Latino; 2 Hispanic/Latino; 1 Two or more races, non-Hispanic/Latino), 2 international. Average age 31. 41 applicants, 32% accepted, 9 enrolled. In 2016, 21 master's awarded. *Degree requirements:* For master's, 2 foreign languages, thesis or alternative. *Entrance requirements:* Additional exam requirements/recommendations for international students: Required—TOEFL (minimum score 550 paper-based; 79 iBT), IELTS (minimum score 6.5). *Application deadline:* For fall admission, 1/1 priority date for domestic students; for spring admission, 9/1 for domestic students. Applications are processed on a rolling basis. Application fee: $56 ($96 for international students). Electronic applications accepted. *Financial support:* In 2016–17, 1 fellowship, 2 research assistantships, 26 teaching assistantships were awarded; career-related internships or fieldwork, health care benefits, unspecified assistantships, and project assistantships also available. Support available to part-time students. Financial award application deadline: 4/15; financial award applicants required to submit FAFSA. *Unit head:* Kevin Muse, Department Chair, 414-229-5213, E-mail: kmuse@uwm.edu. *Application contact:* General Information Contact, 414-229-4982, Fax: 414-229-6967, E-mail: gradschool@uwm.edu. Website: http://uwm.edu/foreign-languages-literature/

**University of Wyoming,** College of Arts and Sciences, Department of Modern and Classical Languages, Program in German, Laramie, WY 82071. Offers MA. *Program availability:* Part-time. *Degree requirements:* For master's, one foreign language, thesis or alternative. *Entrance requirements:* For master's, GRE General Test, minimum GPA of 3.0. *Faculty research:* East German literature, German literature, theatre, poetry.

**Vanderbilt University,** Department of Germanic and Slavic Languages, Nashville, TN 37240-1001. Offers German (MA, MAT, PhD). *Faculty:* 5 full-time (2 women). *Students:* 24 full-time (16 women); includes 3 minority (1 Black or African American, non-Hispanic/Latino; 1 Hispanic/Latino; 1 Two or more races, non-Hispanic/Latino), 5 international. Average age 31. 8 applicants, 75% accepted, 4 enrolled. In 2016, 4 doctorates awarded. Terminal master's awarded for partial completion of doctoral program. *Degree requirements:* For master's, one foreign language, comprehensive exam; for doctorate, 2 foreign languages, comprehensive exam, thesis/dissertation, qualifying and final exams. *Entrance requirements:* For master's and doctorate, GRE General Test, sample of written work. Additional exam requirements/recommendations for international students: Required—TOEFL (minimum score 570 paper-based; 88 iBT). *Application deadline:* For fall admission, 1/15 for domestic and international students. Electronic applications accepted. *Expenses:* Tuition: Part-time $1854 per credit hour. *Financial support:* Fellowships with tuition reimbursements, teaching assistantships with tuition reimbursements, career-related internships or fieldwork, Federal Work-Study, institutionally sponsored loans, scholarships/grants, and health care benefits available. Financial award application deadline: 1/15; financial award applicants required to submit CSS PROFILE or FAFSA. *Faculty research:* 1750 to present, Middle Ages, Baroque, language pedagogy, linguistics. *Unit head:* Dr. Lutz Koepnick, Chair, 615-322-2611, Fax: 615-343-7258, E-mail: lutz.koepnick@vanderbilt.edu. *Application contact:* Christoph Zeller, Director of Graduate Studies, 615-875-9065, Fax: 615-343-7258, E-mail: christoph.zeller@vanderbilt.edu. Website: http://www.vanderbilt.edu/german/graduate/

**Washington University in St. Louis,** The Graduate School, Department of Germanic Languages and Literatures, St. Louis, MO 63130-4899. Offers PhD. Terminal master's

awarded for partial completion of doctoral program. *Degree requirements:* For doctorate, thesis/dissertation. *Entrance requirements:* For doctorate, GRE General Test, sample of written work. Additional exam requirements/recommendations for international students: Required—TOEFL. Electronic applications accepted. *Faculty research:* German literature and culture from the Middle Ages through the 21st century; intellectual history; film and media studies; gender studies; Holocaust studies; history of the book; digital humanities.

**Wayne State University,** College of Liberal Arts and Sciences, Department of Classical and Modern Languages, Literatures, and Cultures, Detroit, MI 48202. Offers classics (MA), including ancient Greek and Latin, ancient studies, classics, Latin; German (MA); language learning (MALL), including Arabic (MA, MALL), French (MA, MALL, PhD), German (MALL, PhD), Italian (MA, MALL), Spanish (MA, MALL, PhD); modern languages (PhD), including French (MA, MALL, PhD), German (MALL, PhD), Spanish (MA, MALL, PhD); Near Eastern languages (MA), including Arabic (MA, MALL), Hebrew; Romance languages (MA), including French (MA, MALL, PhD), Italian (MA, MALL), Spanish (MA, MALL, PhD). *Faculty:* 26. *Students:* 25 full-time (20 women), 14 part-time (8 women); includes 7 minority (2 Black or African American, non-Hispanic/Latino; 1 American Indian or Alaska Native, non-Hispanic/Latino; 1 Asian, non-Hispanic/Latino; 2 Hispanic/Latino; 1 Two or more races, non-Hispanic/Latino), 3 international. Average age 35. 29 applicants, 31% accepted, 5 enrolled. In 2016, 15 master's, 5 doctorates awarded. *Degree requirements:* For master's, variable foreign language requirement, comprehensive exam (for some programs), thesis (for some programs); for doctorate, one foreign language, comprehensive exam, thesis/dissertation. *Entrance requirements:* For master's, GRE (for some programs); for doctorate, GRE. Additional exam requirements/recommendations for international students: Required—TOEFL (minimum score 550 paper-based; 79 iBT), TWE (minimum score 5.5), Michigan English Language Assessment Battery (minimum score 85); Recommended—IELTS (minimum score 6.5). Application fee: $50. Electronic applications accepted. *Expenses:* $16,503 per year resident tuition and fees, $33,697 per year non-resident tuition and fees. *Financial support:* In 2016–17, 22 students received support, 4 fellowships with tuition reimbursements available (averaging $13,500 per year), 17 teaching assistantships with tuition reimbursements available (averaging $17,994 per year); research assistantships, scholarships/grants, and unspecified assistantships also available. Financial award applicants required to submit FAFSA. *Faculty research:* Classical and modern literature and culture (Greek, Latin, Arabic, Chinese, French, German, Russian, Spanish) including colonial studies and exile and Holocaust studies; critical theory (French, German, Slavic, Spanish); theoretical and applied linguistics (Arabic, Chinese, French, Spanish); area studies (Arabic, Near Eastern, classical, Islamic, and Judaic studies). *Unit head:* Dr. Anne Duggan, Department Chair, 313-577-6244, Fax: 313-577-6243, E-mail: a.duggan@wayne.edu. Website: http://clas.wayne.edu/languages/

**West Chester University of Pennsylvania,** College of Arts and Humanities, Department of Languages and Cultures, West Chester, PA 19383. Offers French (Teaching Certificate); German (Teaching Certificate); languages and cultures (MA), including French, German, Spanish; Spanish (Teaching Certificate). *Program availability:* Part-time, evening/weekend, minimal on-campus study. *Faculty:* 12 full-time (9 women). *Students:* 7 full-time (6 women), 26 part-time (23 women); includes 7 minority (all Hispanic/Latino). Average age 31. 14 applicants, 100% accepted, 11 enrolled. In 2016, 8 master's, 2 other advanced degrees awarded. *Degree requirements:* For master's, one foreign language, comprehensive exam, portfolio, exit exam, capstone project; for Teaching Certificate, one foreign language. *Entrance requirements:* For master's and Teaching Certificate, ACTFL OPI and WPT, undergraduate major or equivalent. Additional exam requirements/recommendations for international students: Required—TOEFL or IELTS. *Application deadline:* For fall admission, 5/15 for international students; for spring admission, 10/15 for international students. Applications are processed on a rolling basis. Application fee: $45. Electronic applications accepted. *Expenses:* Tuition, state resident: full-time $8694; part-time $483 per credit. Tuition, nonresident: full-time $13,050; part-time $725 per credit. *Required fees:* $2399; $119.05 per credit. Tuition and fees vary according to campus/location and program. *Financial support:* Scholarships/grants and unspecified assistantships available. Financial award application deadline: 2/15; financial award applicants required to submit FAFSA. *Faculty research:* Language structure, literature, film, culture, pedagogy, technology. *Unit head:* Dr. Jerome Williams, Interim Chair, 610-436-2700, Fax: 610-436-3048, E-mail: isanchez@wcupa.edu. *Application contact:* Dr. Rebecca Pauly, Graduate Coordinator, 610-436-4746, Fax: 610-436-3048, E-mail: mvanliew@wcupa.edu. Website: http://www.wcupa.edu/arts-humanities/languagesCultures/

**Western Kentucky University,** Graduate Studies, Potter College of Arts and Letters, Department of Modern Languages, Bowling Green, KY 42101. Offers French (MA Ed); German (MA Ed); Spanish (MA Ed).

**Yale University,** Graduate School of Arts and Sciences, Department of German, New Haven, CT 06520. Offers PhD. Terminal master's awarded for partial completion of doctoral program. *Degree requirements:* For doctorate, 3 foreign languages, thesis/dissertation. *Entrance requirements:* For doctorate, GRE General Test.

# Hispanic and Latin American Languages

**Boston University,** Graduate School of Arts and Sciences, Department of Romance Studies, Boston, MA 02215. Offers French language and literature (MA, PhD); Hispanic language and literatures (MA, PhD). *Students:* 40 full-time (27 women), 1 part-time (0 women); includes 8 minority (1 Black or African American, non-Hispanic/Latino; 7 Hispanic/Latino), 12 international. Average age 32. 49 applicants, 35% accepted, 6 enrolled. In 2016, 3 master's, 6 doctorates awarded. Terminal master's awarded for partial completion of doctoral program. *Degree requirements:* For master's, one foreign language, comprehensive exam; for doctorate, 2 foreign languages, comprehensive exam, thesis/dissertation. *Entrance requirements:* For master's and doctorate, GRE General Test, sample of written work, 3 letters of recommendation, transcripts, personal statement, summary of related coursework. Additional exam requirements/recommendations for international students: Required—TOEFL (minimum score 550 paper-based; 84 iBT). *Application deadline:* For fall admission, 1/15 for domestic and international students. Application fee: $95. Electronic applications accepted. *Financial support:* In 2016–17, 36 students received support, including 6 fellowships with full tuition reimbursements available (averaging $21,500 per year), 25 teaching assistantships with full tuition reimbursements available (averaging $21,500 per year); Federal Work-Study, scholarships/grants, and health care benefits also available. Financial award application deadline: 1/15. *Unit head:* Odile Cazenave, Chair, 617-353-

6225, Fax: 617-353-6246, E-mail: cazenave@bu.edu. *Application contact:* Deanna Wong, Administrative Assistant, 617-353-2641, Fax: 617-353-6246, E-mail: dswong@bu.edu. Website: http://www.bu.edu/rs/

**Brigham Young University,** Graduate Studies, College of Humanities, Department of Spanish and Portuguese, Provo, UT 84602. Offers Portuguese (MA), including Luso-Brazilian literatures, Portuguese linguistics, Portuguese pedagogy; Spanish (MA), including Hispanic linguistics, Hispanic literatures, Spanish pedagogy. *Faculty:* 31 full-time (6 women). *Students:* 20 full-time (9 women), 15 part-time (9 women); includes 12 minority (all Hispanic/Latino). Average age 32. 19 applicants, 79% accepted, 12 enrolled. In 2016, 9 master's awarded. *Degree requirements:* For master's, 2 foreign languages, comprehensive exam, thesis, 1 semester of teaching. *Entrance requirements:* For master's, minimum GPA of 3.5 in Spanish or Portuguese, 3.3 overall. Additional exam requirements/recommendations for international students: Required—TOEFL (minimum score 580 paper-based; 85 iBT). *Application deadline:* For fall admission, 2/1 for domestic and international students. Application fee: $50. Electronic applications accepted. *Expenses:* Contact institution. *Financial support:* In 2016–17, 25 students received support, including 7 research assistantships (averaging $1,895 per

year), 81 teaching assistantships (averaging $3,200 per year); institutionally sponsored loans, scholarships/grants, tuition waivers (partial), and unspecified assistantships also available. Support available to part-time students. *Faculty research:* Mexican prose; Latin American theater, literature, phonetics, and phonology; pedagogy; classical Portuguese literature; Peninsular prose and theater. *Unit head:* Dr. David P. Laraway, Chair, 801-422-3807, Fax: 801-422-0628, E-mail: david_laraway@byu.edu. *Application contact:* Jessica C. Erickson, Graduate Program Manager, 801-422-2196, Fax: 801-422-0628, E-mail: jessica_erickson@byu.edu.
Website: http://spanport.byu.edu/

**California State University, San Marcos,** College of Humanities, Arts, Behavioral and Social Sciences, Program in Spanish, San Marcos, CA 92096-0001. Offers Hispanic cultures and society (MA); Hispanic language and linguistics (MA); Hispanic literatures and literary theory (MA). *Program availability:* Part-time, evening/weekend. *Degree requirements:* For master's, 2 foreign languages, exam. *Entrance requirements:* For master's, GRE General Test, minimum GPA of 3.0 overall and in upper-division Spanish courses, official transcripts, three letters of recommendation, 750-word statement of purpose (in English), academic writing sample (in Spanish). Additional exam requirements/recommendations for international students: Required—TOEFL (minimum score 500 paper-based), TWE (minimum score 4.5). Electronic applications accepted. *Expenses:* Tuition, state resident: full-time $6738. Tuition, nonresident: full-time $13,434. *Required fees:* $1906. Tuition and fees vary according to campus/location and program. *Faculty research:* Applied linguistics, Golden Age Spanish literature, Latin American literature, poetry, Chicano studies.

**Cornell University,** Graduate School, Graduate Fields of Arts and Sciences, Field of Romance Studies, Ithaca, NY 14853. Offers French linguistics (PhD); French literature (PhD); Hispanic literature (PhD); Italian linguistics (PhD); Italian literature (PhD); Romance linguistics (PhD); Spanish linguistics (PhD). *Degree requirements:* For doctorate, 2 foreign languages, comprehensive exam, thesis/dissertation. *Entrance requirements:* For doctorate, GRE General Test, sample of written work, 3 letters of recommendation. Additional exam requirements/recommendations for international students: Required—TOEFL (minimum score 550 paper-based; 77 iBT). Electronic applications accepted. *Faculty research:* Literary theory, Hispanic studies, French studies, gender studies.

**The Graduate Center, City University of New York,** Graduate Studies, Program in Hispanic and Luso-Brazilian Literatures and Languages, New York, NY 10016-4039. Offers PhD. *Degree requirements:* For doctorate, 2 foreign languages, thesis/dissertation. *Entrance requirements:* For doctorate, GRE General Test. Additional exam requirements/recommendations for international students: Required—TOEFL. Electronic applications accepted.

**Indiana University Bloomington,** University Graduate School, College of Arts and Sciences, Department of Spanish and Portuguese, Bloomington, IN 47405. Offers Portuguese (MA, PhD); Spanish (MA, PhD), including Hispanic linguistics, Hispanic literatures. *Faculty:* 22 full-time, 26 part-time/adjunct. *Students:* 84 full-time (47 women); includes 20 minority (19 Hispanic/Latino; 1 Two or more races, non-Hispanic/Latino), 19 international. Average age 30. 72 applicants, 43% accepted, 15 enrolled. In 2016, 7 master's, 8 doctorates awarded. *Degree requirements:* For master's, one foreign language, comprehensive exam, thesis (for Spanish); for doctorate, 2 foreign languages, comprehensive exam, thesis/dissertation. *Entrance requirements:* For master's, GRE General Test, bachelor's degree in Portuguese or Spanish, minimum GPA of 3.0; for doctorate, GRE General Test, master's degree in Portuguese or Spanish, minimum GPA of 3.0. Additional exam requirements/recommendations for international students: Required—TOEFL (minimum score 79 iBT). *Application deadline:* For fall admission, 1/15 priority date for domestic students, 12/1 priority date for international students. Application fee: $55 ($65 for international students). Electronic applications accepted. *Financial support:* Application deadline: 1/15. *Faculty research:* Spanish American literature, Spanish peninsular literature, Hispanic linguistics, Luso-Brazilian studies, Catalan studies. *Unit head:* Steven Wagschal, Chair, 812-855-8498, E-mail: swagscha@indiana.edu. *Application contact:* Patrick Dove, Director of Graduate Studies, 812-855-9194, E-mail: pdove@indiana.edu.
Website: http://www.indiana.edu/~spanport

**Indiana University of Pennsylvania,** School of Graduate Studies and Research, College of Humanities and Social Sciences, Department of Foreign Languages, Program in Spanish/Hispanic Literatures and Cultures, Indiana, PA 15705. Offers MA. Application fee: $50. *Expenses:* Tuition, state resident: full-time $8694; part-time $483 per credit. Tuition, nonresident: full-time $13,050; part-time $725 per credit. *Required fees:* $157 per credit. $50 per term. Tuition and fees vary according to course load and program. *Financial support:* Research assistantships with tuition reimbursements available. *Unit head:* Dr. Sean McDaniel, Chairperson, 724-357-7532, E-mail: mcdaniel@iup.edu.

**Michigan State University,** The Graduate School, College of Arts and Letters, Department of Spanish and Portuguese, East Lansing, MI 48824. Offers applied Spanish linguistics (MA); Hispanic cultural studies (PhD); Hispanic literatures (MA). *Entrance requirements:* Additional exam requirements/recommendations for international students: Required—TOEFL. Electronic applications accepted.

**Queens College of the City University of New York,** Arts and Humanities Division, Department of Hispanic Languages and Literatures, Queens, NY 11367-1597. Offers Spanish (MA). *Program availability:* Part-time. *Faculty:* 11 full-time (7 women), 23 part-time/adjunct (17 women). *Students:* 7 part-time (5 women); all minorities (all Hispanic/Latino). Average age 46. 5 applicants, 100% accepted, 1 enrolled. In 2016, 7 master's awarded. *Degree requirements:* For master's, 3 foreign languages. *Entrance requirements:* For master's, minimum GPA of 3.0. Additional exam requirements/recommendations for international students: Required—TOEFL (minimum score 61 iBT), IELTS (minimum score 5). *Application deadline:* For fall admission, 4/1 for domestic students; for spring admission, 11/1 for domestic students. Applications are processed on a rolling basis. Application fee: $125. Electronic applications accepted. *Expenses:* Tuition, state resident: full-time $5065; part-time $425 per credit. Tuition, nonresident: part-time $780 per credit. *Required fees:* $522; $397 per credit. Part-time tuition and fees vary according to course load and program. *Financial support:* Career-related internships or fieldwork available. Financial award application deadline: 4/1; financial award applicants required to submit FAFSA. *Unit head:* Dr. Jose Martinez-Torrejon, Chair, 718-997-5626.

**Stony Brook University, State University of New York,** Graduate School, College of Arts and Sciences, Department of Hispanic Languages and Literature, Stony Brook, NY 11794. Offers MA, PhD. *Program availability:* Evening/weekend. *Faculty:* 14 full-time (9 women), 5 part-time/adjunct (3 women). *Students:* 33 full-time (21 women), 10 part-time (7 women); includes 19 minority (1 Black or African American, non-Hispanic/Latino; 18 Hispanic/Latino), 14 international. Average age 35. 22 applicants, 36% accepted, 4 enrolled. In 2016, 8 master's, 4 doctorates awarded. *Degree requirements:* For master's, one foreign language, thesis or alternative; for doctorate, 2 foreign languages, thesis/dissertation. *Entrance requirements:* For master's, GRE General Test, BA in Spanish; for doctorate, GRE General Test, MA in Spanish. Additional exam requirements/recommendations for international students: Required—TOEFL. *Application deadline:*

For fall admission, 1/15 for domestic students; for spring admission, 10/1 for domestic students. Application fee: $100. Electronic applications accepted. *Expenses:* Contact institution. *Financial support:* In 2016–17, 20 teaching assistantships were awarded; fellowships, research assistantships, tuition waivers, and unspecified assistantships also available. *Faculty research:* Latin American languages or literature, humanities, Latin American studies, Spanish, race. *Total annual research expenditures:* $10,423. *Unit head:* Dr. Kathleen M. Vernon, Chair, 631-632-9668, Fax: 631-632-9724, E-mail: kathleen.vernon@stonybrook.edu. *Application contact:* Esperanza Fallon, Coordinator, 631-632-6935, Fax: 631-632-9724, E-mail: esperanza.fallon@stonybrook.edu.
Website: http://www.stonybrook.edu/commcms/hispanic/

**Université de Montréal,** Faculty of Arts and Sciences, Department of Literatures and Modern Languages, Montréal, QC H3C 3J7, Canada. Offers German literature (PhD); German studies (MA); Hispanic literature (PhD); Hispanic studies (MA). Terminal master's awarded for partial completion of doctoral program. *Degree requirements:* For master's, 2 foreign languages, thesis; for doctorate, 2 foreign languages, thesis/dissertation, general exam. Electronic applications accepted.

**University of California, Berkeley,** Graduate Division, College of Letters and Science, Department of Spanish and Portuguese, Berkeley, CA 94720-1500. Offers Hispanic languages and literatures (PhD). *Faculty:* 16 full-time (6 women). *Students:* 33 full-time (19 women); includes 17 minority (all Hispanic/Latino), 9 international. Average age 33. 60 applicants, 1 enrolled. In 2016, 2 doctorates awarded. *Degree requirements:* For doctorate, thesis/dissertation, qualifying exam. *Entrance requirements:* For doctorate, GRE General Test, minimum GPA of 3.0, 3 letters of recommendation. Additional exam requirements/recommendations for international students: Required—TOEFL (minimum score 570 paper-based; 90 iBT). *Application deadline:* For fall admission, 12/15 for domestic students. Application fee: $105 ($125 for international students). Electronic applications accepted. *Financial support:* Fellowships with full tuition reimbursements, research assistantships, teaching assistantships with partial tuition reimbursements, institutionally sponsored loans, health care benefits, and unspecified assistantships available. Financial award applicants required to submit FAFSA. *Unit head:* Ignacio Navarrete, Chair, 510-642-0471, E-mail: gspa@berkeley.edu. *Application contact:* 510-642-8037, E-mail: spanga@berkeley.edu.
Website: http://spanish-portuguese.berkeley.edu/

**University of California, Los Angeles,** Graduate Division, College of Letters and Science, Department of Spanish and Portuguese, Program in Hispanic Languages and Literature, Los Angeles, CA 90095. Offers PhD. *Degree requirements:* For doctorate, 2 foreign languages, thesis/dissertation, oral and written qualifying exams. *Entrance requirements:* For doctorate, GRE General Test, master's degree; minimum undergraduate GPA of 3.0 (or its equivalent if letter grade system not used); writing sample. Additional exam requirements/recommendations for international students: Required—TOEFL. Electronic applications accepted.

**University of California, Santa Barbara,** Graduate Division, College of Letters and Sciences, Division of Humanities and Fine Arts, Department of Spanish and Portuguese, Santa Barbara, CA 93106-4150. Offers Hispanic languages and literatures (PhD), including European medieval studies, feminist studies, Hispanic linguistics, Hispanic literature, Luso-Brazilian literature; Hispanic linguistics (MA); Luso-Brazilian literature (MA); Spanish or Spanish-American literature (MA); MA/PhD. Terminal master's awarded for partial completion of doctoral program. *Degree requirements:* For master's, 2 foreign languages, comprehensive exam (for some programs), thesis optional; for doctorate, 3 foreign languages, comprehensive exam, thesis/dissertation. *Entrance requirements:* For master's and doctorate, GRE. Additional exam requirements/recommendations for international students: Required—TOEFL (minimum score 550 paper-based; 80 iBT), IELTS (minimum score 7). Electronic applications accepted. *Faculty research:* Nineteenth-century Spanish and Portuguese literature, Spanish and Spanish-American literature, nineteenth- and twentieth-century Portuguese and Brazilian literatures, Hispanic linguistics, Catalan language and culture.

**University of Colorado Boulder,** Graduate School, College of Arts and Sciences, Department of Spanish and Portuguese, Boulder, CO 80309. Offers Hispanic linguistics (MA); medieval and early modern Hispanic literatures (PhD); peninsular and Latin American literature (MA). *Faculty:* 13 full-time (5 women). *Students:* 36 full-time (25 women), 1 (woman) part-time; includes 8 minority (1 American Indian or Alaska Native, non-Hispanic/Latino; 7 Hispanic/Latino), 14 international. Average age 31. 39 applicants, 54% accepted, 8 enrolled. In 2016, 3 master's, 4 doctorates awarded. Terminal master's awarded for partial completion of doctoral program. *Degree requirements:* For master's, one foreign language, comprehensive exam, thesis or alternative; for doctorate, 2 foreign languages, thesis/dissertation. *Entrance requirements:* For master's, minimum undergraduate GPA of 2.75. *Application deadline:* For fall admission, 12/19 for domestic and international students. Applications are processed on a rolling basis. Application fee: $60 ($80 for international students). Electronic applications accepted. Application fee is waived when completed online. *Financial support:* In 2016–17, 127 students received support, including 42 fellowships (averaging $1,111 per year), 32 teaching assistantships with full and partial tuition reimbursements available (averaging $41,562 per year); institutionally sponsored loans, scholarships/grants, health care benefits, and unspecified assistantships also available. Financial award application deadline: 12/15; financial award applicants required to submit FAFSA. *Faculty research:* Literary criticism, Spanish language/literature, Latin American languages/literature, cultural history. *Total annual research expenditures:* $40,070. *Application contact:* E-mail: spanport@colorado.edu.
Website: http://spanish.colorado.edu/

**University of Illinois at Chicago,** College of Liberal Arts and Sciences, School of Literatures, Cultural Studies and Linguistics, Chicago, IL 60607-7128. Offers French and Francophone studies (MA); Germanic studies (MA); Hispanic and Italian studies (MAT, PhD), including Hispanic linguistics (PhD), Hispanic literary and cultural studies (PhD), teaching of Spanish (MAT); linguistics (MA), including teaching English to speakers of other languages/applied linguistics; Slavic and Baltic languages and literatures (MA), including Slavic studies (MA, PhD); Slavic and Baltic languages and literatures (MA), including Slavic studies (MA, PhD). *Program availability:* Part-time. Terminal master's awarded for partial completion of doctoral program. *Degree requirements:* For master's, one foreign language, exam. *Entrance requirements:* For master's, minimum GPA of 2.75. Additional exam requirements/recommendations for international students: Required—TOEFL. Electronic applications accepted. *Faculty research:* International studies, religious (Catholic, Jewish) studies, moving image arts.

**University of Massachusetts Amherst,** Graduate School, College of Humanities and Fine Arts, Department of Languages, Literatures, and Cultures, Program in Spanish and Portuguese Studies, Amherst, MA 01003. Offers Hispanic literatures, cultures and linguistics (MA, PhD); teaching Spanish (MAT). *Program availability:* Part-time. Terminal master's awarded for partial completion of doctoral program. *Degree requirements:* For master's, one foreign language, thesis or alternative; for doctorate, 2 foreign languages, comprehensive exam, thesis/dissertation. *Entrance requirements:* For master's and doctorate, GRE General Test, sample academic term paper. Additional exam requirements/recommendations for international students: Required—TOEFL (minimum score 550 paper-based; 80 iBT), IELTS (minimum score 6.5). Electronic applications accepted.

**University of Minnesota, Twin Cities Campus,** Graduate School, College of Liberal Arts, Department of Spanish and Portuguese Studies, Minneapolis, MN 55455-0213. Offers Hispanic and Lusophone literatures, cultures and linguistics (PhD); Hispanic linguistics (MA); Hispanic literature (MA); Lusophone literature (MA). *Degree requirements:* For master's, 2 foreign languages, comprehensive exam, thesis or alternative; for doctorate, 2 foreign languages, comprehensive exam, thesis/dissertation. *Entrance requirements:* For master's and doctorate, GRE General Test, samples of written work, 3 letters of recommendation, voice sample, statement of purpose. Additional exam requirements/recommendations for international students: Required—TOEFL (minimum score 550 paper-based; 79 iBT). Electronic applications accepted. *Faculty research:* Sociohistorical approaches to literature and culture, feminist studies, literary theory, ideologies and literature, pragmatics and sociolinguistics.

**The University of North Carolina at Greensboro,** Graduate School, College of Arts and Sciences, Department of Languages, Literatures, and Cultures, Program in Spanish, Greensboro, NC 27412-5001. Offers advanced Spanish language and Hispanic cultural studies (Certificate); Spanish (MA). *Degree requirements:* For master's, one foreign language, comprehensive exam, thesis or alternative. *Entrance requirements:* For master's, GRE General Test, 3-5 minute tape demonstrating foreign language proficiency, composition in Spanish, sample paper in English. Additional exam requirements/recommendations for international students: Required—TOEFL. Electronic applications accepted.

**University of Pittsburgh,** Dietrich School of Arts and Sciences, Department of Hispanic Languages and Literatures, Pittsburgh, PA 15260. Offers MA, PhD. *Faculty:* 10 full-time (2 women). *Students:* 43 full-time (19 women); includes 8 minority (1 American Indian or Alaska Native, non-Hispanic/Latino; 7 Hispanic/Latino), 30 international. Average age 34. 50 applicants, 26% accepted, 6 enrolled. In 2016, 5 master's, 14 doctorates awarded. Terminal master's awarded for partial completion of doctoral program. *Degree requirements:* For master's, 2 foreign languages, comprehensive exam, thesis or alternative, research paper; for doctorate, 2 foreign languages, comprehensive exam, thesis/dissertation. *Entrance requirements:* Additional exam requirements/ recommendations for international students: Required—TOEFL (minimum score 600 paper-based; 90 iBT). *Application deadline:* For fall admission, 1/15 priority date for domestic and international students. Application fee: $50. Electronic applications accepted. Tuition and fees vary according to program. *Financial support:* In 2016–17, 34 students received support, including 6 fellowships with full tuition reimbursements available (averaging $21,692 per year), 25 teaching assistantships with full tuition reimbursements available (averaging $17,905 per year); health care benefits also available. Financial award application deadline: 1/15. *Faculty research:* Latin American, Luso-Brazilian, and peninsular literature; cultural theory; cultural studies; race, ethnicity, and post-colonial studies; gender and sexuality studies; environment and literature; social conflict and violence; Chicano and U.S. Latino literature. *Unit head:* Jerome Branche, Chair, 412-624-5468, E-mail: branche@pitt.edu. *Application contact:* Keanna Cash, Graduate Administrator, 412-624-5906, E-mail: kec176@pitt.edu. Website: http://www.hispanic.pitt.edu

**The University of Texas at Austin,** Graduate School, College of Liberal Arts, Department of Spanish and Portuguese, Austin, TX 78712-1111. Offers Hispanic linguistics (MA, PhD); Hispanic literature (MA, PhD); Ibero-romance philology and linguistics (PhD); Luso-Brazilian literature (MA, PhD). *Degree requirements:* For master's, 2 foreign languages, thesis or alternative; for doctorate, 3 foreign languages, thesis/dissertation. *Entrance requirements:* For master's and doctorate, GRE General Test. Electronic applications accepted.

**University of Washington,** Graduate School, College of Arts and Sciences, Division of Spanish and Portuguese Studies, Seattle, WA 98195. Offers Hispanic literary and cultural studies (MA). *Degree requirements:* For master's, 2 foreign languages, thesis optional, exam. *Entrance requirements:* For master's, GRE General Test, minimum GPA of 3.0. Additional exam requirements/recommendations for international students: Required—TOEFL. Electronic applications accepted. *Faculty research:* Medieval through modern Spanish literature and film, Latin American literature, poetry and essay, pan-Hispanic ballad, Hispanic cultural studies, second language acquisition and applied linguistics.

# Italian

**Binghamton University, State University of New York,** Graduate School, Harpur College of Arts and Sciences, Department of Romance Languages and Literatures, Program in Italian, Binghamton, NY 13902-6000. Offers MA. *Program availability:* Part-time. *Students:* 1 full-time (0 women); minority (Hispanic/Latino). Average age 22. In 2016, 3 master's awarded. *Degree requirements:* For master's, one foreign language, comprehensive exam, thesis or alternative. *Entrance requirements:* For master's, GRE General Test. Additional exam requirements/recommendations for international students: Required—TOEFL (minimum score 550 paper-based; 80 iBT). *Application deadline:* For fall admission, 2/15 priority date for domestic and international students; for spring admission, 11/15 priority date for domestic and international students. Application fee: $75. Electronic applications accepted. *Financial support:* Career-related internships or fieldwork, Federal Work-Study, institutionally sponsored loans, scholarships/grants, health care benefits, and unspecified assistantships available. Financial award applicants required to submit FAFSA. *Unit head:* Dr. Dana Stewart, Chairperson, 607-777-2645, E-mail: stewart@binghamton.edu. *Application contact:* Ben Balkaya, Assistant Dean and Director, 607-777-2151, Fax: 607-777-2501, E-mail: balkaya@binghamton.edu.

**Boston College,** Graduate School of Arts and Sciences, Department of Romance Languages and Literatures, Chestnut Hill, MA 02467-3800. Offers French (MA); Italian (MA); Spanish (MA). *Program availability:* Part-time. *Faculty:* 19 full-time. *Students:* 31 full-time (26 women); includes 2 minority (both Hispanic/Latino), 8 international. 34 applicants, 50% accepted, 12 enrolled. In 2016, 12 master's awarded. Terminal master's awarded for partial completion of doctoral program. *Degree requirements:* For master's, one foreign language. *Entrance requirements:* Additional exam requirements/recommendations for international students: Required—TOEFL (minimum score 600 paper-based; 100 iBT), IELTS (minimum score 8). *Application deadline:* For fall admission, 2/1 for domestic and international students. Application fee: $75. Electronic applications accepted. Tuition and fees vary according to program. *Financial support:* In 2016–17, 36 students received support, including fellowships with full tuition reimbursements available (averaging $18,800 per year), teaching assistantships with full tuition reimbursements available (averaging $18,800 per year); Federal Work-Study and unspecified assistantships also available. Support available to part-time students. Financial award application deadline: 3/1; financial award applicants required to submit FAFSA. *Faculty research:* Spanish-American literature, philology, medieval French romance and troubadour lyrics, Golden Age Peninsular literature, secondary language acquisition and pedagogy, Hispanic studies, French language and literature, Italian language and literature. *Unit head:* Dr. Franco Mormando, Chairperson, 617-552-6346, E-mail: franco.mormando@bc.edu. *Application contact:* Dr. Laurie Shepard, Graduate Program Director, 617-552-8269, E-mail: laurie.shepard@bc.edu. Website: http://www.bc.edu/rll

**Brown University,** Graduate School, Department of Italian Studies, Providence, RI 02912. Offers PhD. Terminal master's awarded for partial completion of doctoral program. *Degree requirements:* For doctorate, 2 foreign languages, thesis/dissertation, preliminary exam.

**Central Connecticut State University,** School of Graduate Studies, College of Liberal Arts and Social Sciences, Department of Modern Languages, New Britain, CT 06050-4010. Offers modern language (MA, Certificate), including French, German (Certificate), Italian, Spanish (MA); Spanish (MS, Certificate). *Program availability:* Part-time, evening/weekend. *Faculty:* 8 full-time (6 women). *Students:* 7 full-time (6 women), 12 part-time (7 women); includes 10 minority (all Hispanic/Latino). Average age 32. 11 applicants, 91% accepted, 4 enrolled. In 2016, 9 master's, 1 other advanced degree awarded. *Degree requirements:* For master's, one foreign language, comprehensive exam, thesis or alternative; for Certificate, qualifying exam. *Entrance requirements:* For master's, minimum undergraduate GPA of 2.7, 24 credits of undergraduate courses in each language in which graduate work will be undertaken. Additional exam requirements/recommendations for international students: Required—TOEFL (minimum score 550 paper-based; 79 iBT). *Application deadline:* For fall admission, 6/1 for domestic students, 5/1 for international students; for spring admission, 11/1 for domestic and international students. Applications are processed on a rolling basis. Application fee: $50. Electronic applications accepted. *Expenses:* Tuition, area resident: Full-time $6497; part-time $606 per credit. Tuition, state resident: full-time $9748; part-time $622 per credit. Tuition, nonresident: full-time $18,102; part-time $622 per credit. *Required fees:* $4459; $246 per credit. *Financial support:* In 2016–17, 6 students received support. Career-related internships or fieldwork, Federal Work-Study, scholarships/grants, and unspecified assistantships available. Support available to part-time students. Financial award application deadline: 3/1; financial award applicants required to submit FAFSA. *Faculty research:* Quebecois literature, Caribbean literature, modern French/Spanish drama, Puerto Rican novel and drama. *Unit head:* Dr. Carmela Pesca, Chair, 860-832-2875, E-mail: pescac@ccsu.edu. *Application contact:* Patricia Gardner, Associate Director of Graduate Studies, 860-832-2350, Fax: 860-832-2362. Website: http://web.ccsu.edu/modlang/

**Columbia University,** Graduate School of Arts and Sciences, New York, NY 10027. Offers African-American studies (MA); American studies (MA); anthropology (MA, PhD); art history and archaeology (MA, PhD); astronomy (PhD); biological sciences (PhD); biotechnology (MA); chemical physics (PhD); chemistry (PhD); classical studies (MA, PhD); classics (MA, PhD); climate and society (MA); conservation biology (MA); earth and environmental sciences (PhD); East Asia: regional studies (MA); East Asian languages and cultures (MA, PhD); ecology, evolution and environmental biology (MA), including conservation biology; ecology, evolution, and environmental biology (PhD), including ecology and evolutionary biology, evolutionary primatology; economics (MA, PhD); English and comparative literature (MA, PhD); French and Romance philology (MA, PhD); Germanic languages (MA, PhD); global French studies (MA); global thought (MA); Hispanic cultural studies (MA); history (PhD); history and literature (MA); human rights studies (MA); Islamic studies (MA); Italian (MA, PhD); Japanese pedagogy (MA); Jewish studies (MA); Latin America and the Caribbean: regional studies (MA); Latin American and Iberian cultures (PhD); mathematics (MA, PhD), including finance (MA); medieval and Renaissance studies (MA); Middle Eastern, South Asian, and African studies (MA, PhD); modern art: critical and curatorial studies (MA); modern European studies (MA); museum anthropology (MA); music (DMA, PhD); oral history (MA); philosophical foundations of physics (MA); philosophy (MA, PhD); physics (PhD); political science (MA, PhD); psychology (PhD); quantitative methods in the social sciences (MA); religion (MA, PhD); Russia, Eurasia and East Europe: regional studies (MA); Russian translation (MA); Slavic cultures (MA); Slavic languages (MA, PhD); sociology (MA, PhD); South Asian studies (MA); statistics (MA, PhD); theatre (PhD). Dual-degree programs require admission to both Graduate School of Arts and Sciences and another Columbia school. *Program availability:* Part-time. Terminal master's awarded for partial completion of doctoral program. *Degree requirements:* For master's, variable foreign language requirement, comprehensive exam (for some programs), thesis (for some programs); for doctorate, variable foreign language requirement, comprehensive exam (for some programs), thesis/dissertation. *Entrance requirements:* For master's and doctorate, GRE General Test, GRE Subject Test (for some programs). Additional exam requirements/recommendations for international students: Required—TOEFL, IELTS. Electronic applications accepted.

**Cornell University,** Graduate School, Graduate Fields of Arts and Sciences, Field of Romance Studies, Ithaca, NY 14853. Offers French linguistics (PhD); French literature (PhD); Hispanic literature (PhD); Italian linguistics (PhD); Italian literature (PhD); Romance linguistics (PhD); Spanish linguistics (PhD). *Degree requirements:* For doctorate, 2 foreign languages, comprehensive exam, thesis/dissertation. *Entrance requirements:* For doctorate, GRE General Test, sample of written work, 3 letters of recommendation. Additional exam requirements/recommendations for international students: Required—TOEFL (minimum score 550 paper-based; 77 iBT). Electronic applications accepted. *Faculty research:* Literary theory, Hispanic studies, French studies, gender studies.

**DePaul University,** College of Liberal Arts and Social Sciences, Chicago, IL 60614. Offers Arabic (MA); Chinese (MA); English (MA); French (MA); German (MA); history (MA); interdisciplinary studies (MA, MS); international public service (MS); international studies (MA); Italian (MA); Japanese (MA); leadership and policy studies (MA); liberal studies (MA); new media studies (MA); nonprofit management (MNM); public administration (MPA); public health (MPH); public service management (MS); social work (MSW); sociology (MA); Spanish (MA); sustainable urban development (MA); women and gender studies (MA); writing and publishing (MA); writing, rhetoric, and discourse (MA); MA/PhD. *Program availability:* Part-time, evening/weekend, online learning. Terminal master's awarded for partial completion of doctoral program. *Degree requirements:* For master's, variable foreign language requirement, comprehensive exam (for some programs), thesis (for some programs). Electronic applications accepted.

## Italian

**Drew University,** Caspersen School of Graduate Studies, Madison, NJ 07940-1493. Offers conflict resolution and leadership (Certificate), including community leadership, moderation, peace building; history and culture (MA, PhD), including American history, book history, British history, European history, Holocaust and genocide (M Litt, MA, D Litt, PhD), intellectual history, Irish history, print culture, public history; K-12 education (MAT), including art, biology, chemistry, elementary education, English, French, Italian, math, secondary education, special education, teacher of students with disabilities; liberal studies (M Litt, D Litt), including history, Holocaust and genocide (M Litt, MA, D Litt, PhD), Irish/Irish-American studies, literature (M Litt, MMH, D Litt, DMH, CMH), religion, spirituality, teaching in the two-year college, writing; medical humanities (MMH, DMH, CMH), including arts, health, healthcare, literature (M Litt, MMH, D Litt, DMH, CMH), scientific research; poetry (MFA). *Program availability:* Part-time, evening/weekend. *Faculty:* 4 full-time (2 women), 31 part-time/adjunct (16 women). *Students:* 62 full-time (41 women), 199 part-time (130 women); includes 38 minority (17 Black or African American, non-Hispanic/Latino; 3 Asian, non-Hispanic/Latino; 17 Hispanic/Latino; 1 Two or more races, non-Hispanic/Latino), 3 international. Average age 27. 93 applicants, 81% accepted, 46 enrolled. In 2016, 39 master's, 27 doctorates, 26 other advanced degrees awarded. Terminal master's awarded for partial completion of doctoral program. *Degree requirements:* For master's and other advanced degree, thesis (for some programs); for doctorate, one foreign language, comprehensive exam (for some programs), thesis/dissertation. *Entrance requirements:* For master's, PRAXIS Core and Subject Area tests (for MAT), resume, transcripts, writing sample, personal statement, letters of recommendation; for doctorate, GRE (PhD in history and culture), resume, transcripts, writing sample, personal statement, letters of recommendation. Additional exam requirements/recommendations for international students: Required—TOEFL (minimum score 587 paper-based; 94 iBT), IELTS (minimum score 7), TWE (minimum score 4). *Application deadline:* For fall admission, 8/1 for domestic students, 6/1 for international students; for spring admission, 12/1 for domestic students, 10/1 for international students. Applications are processed on a rolling basis. Application fee: $35. Electronic applications accepted. Tuition and fees vary according to program. *Financial support:* Fellowships, research assistantships, teaching assistantships, career-related internships or fieldwork, Federal Work-Study, scholarships/grants, and unspecified assistantships available. Support available to part-time students. Financial award applicants required to submit FAFSA. *Application contact:* Leanne Horinko, Director of Caspersen Admissions, 973-408-3280, E-mail: gradm@drew.edu. Website: http://www.drew.edu/caspersen

**Duke University,** Graduate School, Department of Romance Studies, Durham, NC 27708. Offers French (PhD); Italian (PhD); Spanish (PhD); JD/AM. *Degree requirements:* For doctorate, 2 foreign languages, thesis/dissertation. *Entrance requirements:* For doctorate, GRE General Test. Additional exam requirements/recommendations for international students: Required—TOEFL (minimum score 577 paper-based; 90 iBT) or IELTS (minimum score 7). Electronic applications accepted.

**Florida State University,** The Graduate School, College of Arts and Sciences, Department of Modern Languages and Linguistics, Program in Italian Studies, Tallahassee, FL 32306. Offers MA. *Faculty:* 6 full-time (4 women). *Students:* 7 full-time (5 women); includes 3 minority (1 Hispanic/Latino; 2 Two or more races, non-Hispanic/Latino). Average age 24. 5 applicants, 80% accepted, 4 enrolled. *Entrance requirements:* For master's, GRE General Test, minimum GPA of 3.0. Additional exam requirements/recommendations for international students: Required—TOEFL (minimum score 550 paper-based; 80 iBT). *Application deadline:* For fall admission, 2/15 for domestic and international students. Applications are processed on a rolling basis. Application fee: $30. Electronic applications accepted. *Expenses:* Tuition, state resident: full-time $7263; part-time $403.51 per credit hour. Tuition, nonresident: full-time $18,087; part-time $1004.85 per credit hour. *Required fees:* $1365; $75.81 per credit hour. $20 per semester. Tuition and fees vary according to campus/location. *Financial support:* In 2016–17, 7 teaching assistantships with partial tuition reimbursements (averaging $14,000 per year) were awarded. Financial award application deadline: 2/15. *Unit head:* Dr. Mark Pietralunga, Coordinator, 850-644-8392, Fax: 850-644-0524, E-mail: mpietral@fsu.edu. *Application contact:* Wendy E. Pigott, Graduate Academic Coordinator, 850-644-8397, Fax: 850-644-0524, E-mail: wpigott@fsu.edu. Website: http://modlang.ez.fsu.edu/Language-divisions-programs/Italian-Division/Graduate-Program

**The Graduate Center, City University of New York,** Graduate Studies, Program in Comparative Literature, New York, NY 10016-4039. Offers comparative literature (MA, PhD), including classics (PhD), German (PhD), Italian (PhD). PhD offered jointly with New York University. Terminal master's awarded for partial completion of doctoral program. *Degree requirements:* For master's, 2 foreign languages, comprehensive exam, thesis; for doctorate, 3 foreign languages, comprehensive exam, thesis/dissertation. *Entrance requirements:* For master's and doctorate, GRE General Test. Additional exam requirements/recommendations for international students: Required—TOEFL. Electronic applications accepted.

**Harvard University,** Graduate School of Arts and Sciences, Department of Romance Languages and Literatures, Cambridge, MA 02138. Offers French (AM, PhD); Italian (AM, PhD); Portuguese (AM, PhD); Spanish (AM, PhD). Terminal master's awarded for partial completion of doctoral program. *Degree requirements:* For master's, 2 foreign languages; for doctorate, 2 foreign languages, thesis/dissertation. *Entrance requirements:* For master's and doctorate, GRE General Test, sample of written work. Additional exam requirements/recommendations for international students: Required—TOEFL.

**Hunter College of the City University of New York,** Graduate School, School of Arts and Sciences, Department of Romance Languages, Program in Italian, New York, NY 10065-5085. Offers MA. *Students:* 3 part-time (2 women); includes 1 minority (Hispanic/Latino). Average age 34. 2 applicants, 100% accepted, 2 enrolled. *Degree requirements:* For master's, 2 foreign languages, comprehensive exam, thesis optional. *Entrance requirements:* For master's, GRE General Test, GRE Subject Test, ability to read, speak, and write Italian; interview. Additional exam requirements/recommendations for international students: Required—TOEFL. *Application deadline:* For fall admission, 4/1 for domestic students, 2/1 for international students; for spring admission, 11/1 for domestic students, 9/1 for international students. *Financial support:* Federal Work-Study, scholarships/grants, and tuition waivers (partial) available. Support available to part-time students. Financial award application deadline: 4/15. *Faculty research:* Dante, Middle Ages, Renaissance, contemporary Italian novel and poetry, late Renaissance and Baroque. *Unit head:* Dr. Paolo Fasoli, Chairperson and Associate Professor, 212-772-5129, Fax: 212-772-5094, E-mail: pfasoli@hunter.cuny.edu. *Application contact:* Milena Solo, Director for Graduate Admissions, 212-772-4480, E-mail: milena.solo@hunter.cuny.edu. Website: http://www.hunter.cuny.edu/romancelanguages/graduate/ma-requirements

**Indiana University Bloomington,** University Graduate School, College of Arts and Sciences, Department of French and Italian, Bloomington, IN 47405. Offers French (MA, PhD), including French and Francophone studies (MA), French instruction (MA), French linguistics; Italian (MA, PhD). *Program availability:* Part-time. *Faculty:* 23 full-time (10 women). *Students:* 51 full-time (32 women), 6 part-time (3 women); includes 2 minority (1 Black or African American, non-Hispanic/Latino; 1 Hispanic/Latino), 27 international. Average age 31. 28 applicants, 71% accepted, 7 enrolled. In 2016, 8 master's, 4 doctorates awarded. Terminal master's awarded for partial completion of doctoral program. *Degree requirements:* For master's, variable foreign language requirement, comprehensive exam (for some programs), thesis or alternative; for doctorate, variable foreign language requirement, comprehensive exam, thesis/dissertation. *Entrance requirements:* For master's, GRE General Test, BA or equivalent undergraduate preparation in French or Italian; for doctorate, GRE General Test, MA from degree program at IU; MA in the specific field. Additional exam requirements/recommendations for international students: Required—TOEFL (minimum score 550 paper-based; 79 iBT), GRE General Test (recommended). *Application deadline:* For fall admission, 1/15 priority date for domestic students, 12/1 priority date for international students; for spring admission, 9/1 priority date for domestic and international students. Application fee: $55 ($65 for international students). Electronic applications accepted. *Financial support:* In 2016–17, 40 students received support, including 6 fellowships with partial tuition reimbursements available (averaging $18,000 per year), 2 research assistantships with partial tuition reimbursements available (averaging $15,750 per year), 31 teaching assistantships with partial tuition reimbursements available (averaging $15,750 per year); scholarships/grants, health care benefits, and unspecified assistantships also available. Financial award application deadline: 1/15. *Faculty research:* French and Italian literature, French linguistics, including the novel and political theory, literature and fine arts, literary theory, postcolonialism, French-Creole studies, French literature of Africa and its Diaspora, humanism, Medieval folklore and mythology, humor in Medieval and Renaissance literature, emigration, second language acquisition, syntax, sociolinguistics, phonology, lexicography, media and cultural studies, cinema, drama. *Unit head:* Prof. Massimo Scalabrini, Chair, 812-855-8044, Fax: 812-855-8877, E-mail: mscalabar@indiana.edu. *Application contact:* Lauren Anderson, Graduate Student Services Coordinator, 812-855-1088, Fax: 812-855-8877, E-mail: fritgs@indiana.edu. Website: http://frit.indiana.edu

**Johns Hopkins University,** Zanvyl Krieger School of Arts and Sciences, Department of German and Romance Languages and Literatures, Baltimore, MD 21218. Offers French (PhD); German (PhD); Italian (PhD); Spanish (PhD). *Degree requirements:* For doctorate, 2 foreign languages, thesis/dissertation. *Entrance requirements:* For doctorate, GRE General Test. Additional exam requirements/recommendations for international students: Required—TOEFL (minimum score 600 paper-based; 100 iBT), IELTS. Electronic applications accepted. *Faculty research:* Nineteenth-century French prose and poetry, genetic theory and criticism; twentieth-century Latin American literature and film; medieval and Renaissance literature; gender and queer theory in German literature; the ideology of Baroque and Neobaroque aesthetics.

**McGill University,** Faculty of Graduate and Postdoctoral Studies, Faculty of Arts, Department of Italian Studies, Montréal, QC H3A 2T5, Canada. Offers MA, PhD.

**Middlebury College,** Language Schools, Italian School, Middlebury, VT 05753-6002. Offers MA, DML. *Degree requirements:* For master's, one foreign language; for doctorate, 2 foreign languages, comprehensive exam, thesis/dissertation, residence abroad, teaching experience. *Entrance requirements:* For master's, online placement exam, 3 letters of recommendation, writing sample in Italian, transcripts, 200-word essay; for doctorate, 1st and 2nd language online placement exams, 3 letters of recommendation, writing sample in Italian, transcripts, 200-word essay. Electronic applications accepted. *Expenses:* Contact institution.

**New York University,** Graduate School of Arts and Science, Department of Italian Studies, New York, NY 10012-1019. Offers Italian (MA, PhD); Italian studies (MA). *Program availability:* Part-time. Terminal master's awarded for partial completion of doctoral program. *Degree requirements:* For master's, one foreign language, thesis; for doctorate, 3 foreign languages, thesis/dissertation. *Entrance requirements:* For master's and doctorate, GRE General Test. Additional exam requirements/recommendations for international students: Required—TOEFL. *Faculty research:* Dante, early modern literature, fascism and culture, contemporary literature, feminist theory.

**New York University,** Steinhardt School of Culture, Education, and Human Development, Department of Teaching and Learning, Program in Multilingual/Multicultural Studies, New York, NY 10003. Offers bilingual education (MA, PhD, Advanced Certificate); foreign language education (MA); teaching English to speakers of other languages (MA, PhD); teaching foreign languages, 7-12 (MA), including Chinese, French, Italian, Japanese, Spanish; teaching French as a foreign language (MA), including teaching English to speakers of other languages; teaching Spanish as a foreign language (MA), including teaching English to speakers of other languages. *Accreditation:* TEAC. *Program availability:* Part-time, evening/weekend. *Degree requirements:* For master's, thesis (for some programs); for doctorate, thesis/dissertation. *Entrance requirements:* For doctorate, GRE General Test, interview; for Advanced Certificate, master's degree. Additional exam requirements/recommendations for international students: Required—TOEFL (minimum score 100 iBT). Electronic applications accepted. *Faculty research:* Second language acquisition, cross-cultural communication, technology-enhanced language learning, language variation, action learning.

**Northwestern University,** The Graduate School, Judd A. and Marjorie Weinberg College of Arts and Sciences, Department of French and Italian, Evanston, IL 60208. Offers French/Francophone studies (PhD); Italian studies (Graduate Certificate). Admissions and degrees offered through The Graduate School. *Degree requirements:* For doctorate, one foreign language, thesis/dissertation, written and oral exams. *Entrance requirements:* For doctorate, GRE, writing sample, cassette recording. Additional exam requirements/recommendations for international students: Required—TOEFL. *Faculty research:* Francophone studies, eighteenth century contemporary theory.

**The Ohio State University,** Graduate School, College of Arts and Sciences, Division of Arts and Humanities, Department of French and Italian, Columbus, OH 43210. Offers French (MA, PhD); Italian (MA); Italian studies (PhD). *Faculty:* 11. *Students:* 24 full-time (12 women), 9 international. Average age 31. In 2016, 5 master's, 1 doctorate awarded. Terminal master's awarded for partial completion of doctoral program. *Degree requirements:* For master's, variable foreign language requirement, thesis optional; for doctorate, variable foreign language requirement, thesis/dissertation. *Entrance requirements:* For master's and doctorate, GRE General Test. Additional exam requirements/recommendations for international students: Required—TOEFL (minimum score 550 paper-based; 79 iBT), IELTS (minimum score 7), Michigan English Language Assessment Battery (minimum score 82). *Application deadline:* For fall admission, 12/15 priority date for domestic students, 11/30 priority date for international students; for spring admission, 3/1 for domestic students, 2/1 for international students. Applications are processed on a rolling basis. Application fee: $60 ($70 for international students). Electronic applications accepted. *Financial support:* Fellowships with tuition reimbursements, research assistantships with tuition reimbursements, teaching assistantships with tuition reimbursements, Federal Work-Study, institutionally sponsored loans, and unspecified assistantships available. Support available to part-time students. *Faculty research:* Italian and Romance linguistics. *Unit head:* Dr. Jennifer Willging, Chair, 614-292-4938, E-mail: willging.1@osu.edu. *Application contact:* Graduate and Professional Admissions, 614-292-9444, Fax: 614-292-3895, E-mail:

gpadmissions@osu.edu.
Website: http://frit.osu.edu/

**Queens College of the City University of New York,** Arts and Humanities Division, Department of European Languages and Literatures, Queens, NY 11367-1597. Offers French (MA); Italian (MA). *Program availability:* Part-time. *Faculty:* 12 full-time (7 women), 16 part-time/adjunct (12 women). *Students:* 3 full-time (2 women), 8 part-time (5 women); includes 2 minority (both Black or African American, non-Hispanic/Latino). Average age 37. 11 applicants, 82% accepted, 6 enrolled. In 2016, 1 master's awarded. *Degree requirements:* For master's, 2 foreign languages, thesis optional, oral exam. *Entrance requirements:* For master's, minimum GPA of 3.0. Additional exam requirements/recommendations for international students: Required—TOEFL (minimum score 61 iBT), IELTS (minimum score 5). *Application deadline:* For fall admission, 4/1 for domestic students; for spring admission, 11/1 for domestic students. Applications are processed on a rolling basis. Application fee: $125. Electronic applications accepted. *Expenses:* Tuition, state resident: full-time $5065; part-time $425 per credit. Tuition, nonresident: part-time $780 per credit. *Required fees:* $522; $397 per credit. Part-time tuition and fees vary according to course load and program. *Financial support:* Career-related internships or fieldwork, Federal Work-Study, institutionally sponsored loans, and tuition waivers (partial) available. Support available to part-time students. Financial award application deadline: 4/1; financial award applicants required to submit FAFSA. *Unit head:* Dr. David Andrew Jones, Chairperson, 718-997-5980, E-mail: david.jones@qc.cuny.edu.

**Rutgers University–New Brunswick,** Graduate School-New Brunswick, Program in Italian, Piscataway, NJ 08854-8097. Offers Italian (MA, PhD); Italian literature and literary criticism (MA); language, literature and culture (MAT). *Program availability:* Part-time, evening/weekend. Terminal master's awarded for partial completion of doctoral program. *Degree requirements:* For master's, one foreign language, comprehensive exam (for some programs), thesis optional; for doctorate, 2 foreign languages, thesis/dissertation, qualifying exam. *Entrance requirements:* For master's and doctorate, GRE General Test. Additional exam requirements/recommendations for international students: Required—TOEFL. *Faculty research:* Literature.

**San Francisco State University,** Division of Graduate Studies, College of Liberal and Creative Arts, Department of Modern Languages and Literatures, Program in Italian, San Francisco, CA 94132-1722. Offers MA. *Application deadline:* Applications are processed on a rolling basis. *Expenses:* Tuition, state resident: full-time $6738. Tuition, nonresident: full-time $15,666. *Required fees:* $1012. Tuition and fees vary according to degree level and program. *Unit head:* Dr. Mohammad Salama, Chair, 415-338-7413, Fax: 415-338-6159, E-mail: mrsalama@sfsu.edu. *Application contact:* Dr. Christopher Concolino, Program Coordinator, 415-338-3161, Fax: 415-338-6159, E-mail: conco@sfsu.edu.
Website: http://mll.sfsu.edu/italian-program/

**Stanford University,** School of Humanities and Sciences, Department of French and Italian, Stanford, CA 94305-2004. Offers French (MA, PhD); French and Italian (PhD); Italian (MA, PhD). Terminal master's awarded for partial completion of doctoral program. *Degree requirements:* For master's, one foreign language, written exam; for doctorate, 2 foreign languages, thesis/dissertation, oral exam. *Entrance requirements:* For master's and doctorate, GRE General Test. Additional exam requirements/recommendations for international students: Required—TOEFL. Electronic applications accepted. *Expenses: Tuition:* Full-time $47,331. *Required fees:* $609.

**Stony Brook University, State University of New York,** Graduate School, College of Arts and Sciences, Department of European Languages, Literatures, and Cultures, Program in Italian, Stony Brook, NY 11794. Offers MA. *Program availability:* Evening/weekend. *Students:* 1 full-time (0 women), 4 part-time (all women); includes 2 minority (both Hispanic/Latino). 4 applicants, 75% accepted, 3 enrolled. In 2016, 3 master's awarded. *Degree requirements:* For master's, one foreign language. *Entrance requirements:* Additional exam requirements/recommendations for international students: Required—TOEFL. *Application deadline:* For fall admission, 1/15 for domestic students; for spring admission, 10/1 for domestic students. Application fee: $100. Electronic applications accepted. *Expenses:* Contact institution. *Unit head:* Prof. Giuseppe Gazzola, Coordinator, 631-632-7440, Fax: 631-632-9612, E-mail: giuseppe.gazzola@stonybrook.edu. *Application contact:* Mary Wilmarth, Coordinator, 631-632-7442, Fax: 631-632-9612, E-mail: mary.wilmarth@stonybrook.edu.

**University of Alberta,** Faculty of Graduate Studies and Research, Department of Modern Languages and Cultural Studies, Edmonton, AB T6G 2E1, Canada. Offers applied linguistics (Germanic, Romance, Slavic) (MA); French language, literatures and linguistics (PhD); French language, literatures, and linguistics (MA); Germanic languages, literatures and linguistics (PhD); Germanic languages, literatures, and linguistics (MA); Italian studies (MA); Slavic languages and literatures (Russian, Ukrainian) (MA, PhD); Slavic linguistics (Russian, Ukrainian) (MA, PhD); Spanish and Latin American studies (MA, PhD); Ukrainian folklore (MA, PhD). *Program availability:* Part-time. *Degree requirements:* For master's, one foreign language, thesis; for doctorate, 2 foreign languages, comprehensive exam, thesis/dissertation. *Entrance requirements:* For master's and doctorate, 1 language other than English. Additional exam requirements/recommendations for international students: Required—Michigan English Language Assessment Battery or TOEFL (minimum score 550 paper-based). Electronic applications accepted. *Faculty research:* Russian/Ukrainian studies; German studies; contemporary Latin American, French and Francophone studies; Italian studies.

**University of California, Berkeley,** Graduate Division, College of Letters and Science, Department of Italian Studies, Berkeley, CA 94720-1500. Offers PhD. *Faculty:* 9 full-time. *Students:* 13 full-time (11 women); includes 1 minority (Asian, non-Hispanic/Latino), 5 international. Average age 30. 18 applicants, 2 enrolled. In 2016, 2 doctorates awarded. *Degree requirements:* For doctorate, one foreign language, thesis/dissertation, oral and written qualifying exams. *Entrance requirements:* For doctorate, GRE General Test, minimum GPA of 3.0, 3 letters of recommendation. Additional exam requirements/recommendations for international students: Required—TOEFL (minimum score 570 paper-based; 90 iBT). *Application deadline:* For fall admission, 12/16 for domestic students. Application fee: $105 ($125 for international students). Electronic applications accepted. *Financial support:* Fellowships, research assistantships, teaching assistantships, institutionally sponsored loans, scholarships/grants, health care benefits, and unspecified assistantships available. Financial award applicants required to submit FAFSA. *Faculty research:* Literature and culture of Italy in Middle Ages and the Renaissance, literature and culture of Italy in nineteenth and twentieth centuries, Italian film studies, interdisciplinary cultural studies. *Unit head:* Prof. Barbara Spackman, Chair, 510-642-2704, E-mail: issa@berkeley.edu. *Application contact:* Seth Arnopole, Student Affairs Officer, 510-642-9051, Fax: 510-643-6220, E-mail: issag@berkeley.edu.
Website: http://italian.berkeley.edu/

**University of California, Berkeley,** Graduate Division, College of Letters and Science, Group in Romance Languages and Literatures, Berkeley, CA 94720-1500. Offers French (PhD); Italian (PhD); Spanish (PhD). *Faculty:* 16 full-time. *Students:* 11 full-time (7 women); includes 3 minority (1 Asian, non-Hispanic/Latino; 2 Hispanic/Latino). Average age 33. 12 applicants. In 2016, 4 doctorates awarded. *Degree requirements:* For doctorate, thesis/dissertation, qualifying exam. *Entrance requirements:* For

doctorate, GRE General Test, minimum GPA of 3.0, 3 letters of recommendation. Additional exam requirements/recommendations for international students: Required—TOEFL (minimum score 570 paper-based; 90 iBT). *Application deadline:* For fall admission, 12/8 for domestic students. Application fee: $105 ($125 for international students). Electronic applications accepted. *Financial support:* Fellowships with full tuition reimbursements, teaching assistantships with partial tuition reimbursements, health care benefits, and unspecified assistantships available. Financial award applicants required to submit FAFSA. *Unit head:* Ignatio Navarrete, Chair, 510-642-2105. *Application contact:* 510-642-7405.
Website: http://romancelangs.berkeley.edu

**University of California, Los Angeles,** Graduate Division, College of Letters and Science, Department of Italian, Los Angeles, CA 90095. Offers MA, PhD. Terminal master's awarded for partial completion of doctoral program. *Degree requirements:* For master's, one foreign language, comprehensive exam or thesis; for doctorate, 2 foreign languages, thesis/dissertation, oral and written qualifying exams. *Entrance requirements:* For master's, GRE General Test, bachelor's degree; minimum undergraduate GPA of 3.0 (or its equivalent if letter grade system not used); for doctorate, GRE General Test, master's degree; minimum undergraduate GPA of 3.0 (or its equivalent if letter grade system not used). Additional exam requirements/recommendations for international students: Required—TOEFL. Electronic applications accepted.

**University of Chicago,** Division of the Humanities, Department of Romance Languages and Literatures, Chicago, IL 60637. Offers French and Francophone studies (PhD); Hispanic and Luso-Brazilian studies (PhD); Italian studies (PhD); Renaissance and early modern studies (PhD). *Students:* 44 full-time (28 women); includes 9 minority (1 Asian, non-Hispanic/Latino; 7 Hispanic/Latino; 1 Two or more races, non-Hispanic/Latino), 16 international. 45 applicants, 29% accepted, 5 enrolled. In 2016, 4 doctorates awarded. Terminal master's awarded for partial completion of doctoral program. *Degree requirements:* For doctorate, 3 foreign languages, comprehensive exam, thesis/dissertation. *Entrance requirements:* For doctorate, GRE General Test. Additional exam requirements/recommendations for international students: Required—TOEFL (minimum score 104 iBT), IELTS (minimum score 7). *Application deadline:* For fall admission, 12/15 for domestic and international students. Application fee: $90. Electronic applications accepted. *Financial support:* Fellowships with full tuition reimbursements, teaching assistantships with full tuition reimbursements, Federal Work-Study, institutionally sponsored loans, scholarships/grants, and health care benefits available. Financial award application deadline: 12/15; financial award applicants required to submit FAFSA. *Unit head:* Daisy Delogu, Chair, 773-702-4115, E-mail: ddelogu@uchicago.edu. *Application contact:* Michael Beetley, Assistant Dean of Students, Admissions and Fellowships, 773-702-1552, Fax: 773-834-9148, E-mail: humanitiesadmissions@uchicago.edu.
Website: http://rll.uchicago.edu

**University of Georgia,** Franklin College of Arts and Sciences, Department of Romance Languages, Athens, GA 30602. Offers French (PhD); Italian (MA, PhD); Portuguese (MA, PhD); romance linguistics (MA); Spanish (PhD). *Degree requirements:* For master's, one foreign language; for doctorate, 2 foreign languages, thesis/dissertation. *Entrance requirements:* For master's and doctorate, GRE General Test. *Application deadline:* For fall admission, 7/1 priority date for domestic students; for spring admission, 11/15 for domestic students. Application fee: $50. Electronic applications accepted. *Financial support:* Fellowships, research assistantships, teaching assistantships, and unspecified assistantships available. *Unit head:* Dr. Staccy Casado, Department Head, 706-542-2364, Fax: 706-542-2272, E-mail: sdcasado@uga.edu. *Application contact:* Rachel Gabara, Graduate Coordinator, 706-542-8930, E-mail: romlgradcoord@uga.edu.
Website: http://www.rom.uga.edu/

**University of Illinois at Urbana–Champaign,** Graduate College, College of Liberal Arts and Sciences, School of Literatures, Cultures and Linguistics, Department of Spanish, Italian and Portuguese, Champaign, IL 61820. Offers Italian (MA, PhD); Portuguese (MA, PhD); Spanish (MA, PhD).

**The University of Manchester,** School of Languages, Linguistics and Cultures, Manchester, United Kingdom. Offers Arab world studies (PhD); Chinese studies (M Phil, PhD); East Asian studies (M Phil, PhD); English language (PhD); French studies (M Phil, PhD); German studies (M Phil, PhD); interpreting studies (PhD); Italian studies (M Phil, PhD); Japanese studies (M Phil, PhD); Latin American cultural studies (M Phil, PhD); linguistics (M Phil, PhD); Middle Eastern studies (M Phil, PhD); Polish studies (M Phil, PhD); Portuguese studies (M Phil, PhD); Russian studies (M Phil, PhD); Spanish studies (M Phil, PhD); translation and intercultural studies (M Phil, PhD).

**University of Massachusetts Amherst,** Graduate School, College of Humanities and Fine Arts, Department of Languages, Literatures, and Cultures, Program in Italian Studies, Amherst, MA 01003. Offers MAT. *Program availability:* Part-time. *Degree requirements:* For master's, comprehensive exam, thesis or alternative. *Entrance requirements:* For master's, GRE General Test. Additional exam requirements/recommendations for international students: Required—TOEFL (minimum score 550 paper-based; 80 iBT), IELTS (minimum score 6.5). Electronic applications accepted.

**University of Michigan,** Rackham Graduate School, College of Literature, Science, and the Arts, Department of Romance Languages and Literatures, Program in Italian, Ann Arbor, MI 48109. Offers PhD. *Degree requirements:* For doctorate, 2 foreign languages, thesis/dissertation, oral defense of dissertation, preliminary exams in essay format. *Entrance requirements:* Additional exam requirements/recommendations for international students: Required—TOEFL or Michigan English Language Assessment Battery. Electronic applications accepted. *Expenses:* Tuition, state resident: full-time $21,466; part-time $1152 per credit hour. Tuition, nonresident: full-time $43,346; part-time $2367 per credit hour. Part-time tuition and fees vary according to course load, degree level and program. *Faculty research:* Cinema, transnational visual culture, nineteenth-twentieth century Italian literature, medieval and Renaissance literature, medieval Mediterranean literature.

**The University of North Carolina at Chapel Hill,** Graduate School, College of Arts and Sciences, Department of Romance Languages and Literatures, Chapel Hill, NC 27599. Offers French (MA, PhD); Italian (MA, PhD); Portuguese (MA, PhD); Romance languages (MA, PhD); Romance philology (MA, PhD); Spanish (MA, PhD). *Degree requirements:* For master's, one foreign language, comprehensive exam, thesis; for doctorate, 2 foreign languages, comprehensive exam, thesis/dissertation. *Entrance requirements:* For master's and doctorate, GRE General Test, minimum GPA of 3.0. Additional exam requirements/recommendations for international students: Required—TOEFL (minimum score 550 paper-based). Electronic applications accepted.

**University of Notre Dame,** Graduate School, College of Arts and Letters, Division of Humanities, Department of Romance Languages and Literatures, Notre Dame, IN 46556. Offers French and Francophone studies (MA); Iberian and Latin American studies (MA); Italian studies (MA); Romance literatures (MA). *Degree requirements:* For master's, 2 foreign languages, comprehensive exam, thesis optional. *Entrance requirements:* For master's, GRE General Test, BA in target language. Additional exam requirements/recommendations for international students: Required—TOEFL (minimum

## Italian

score 600 paper-based; 80 iBT). Electronic applications accepted. *Faculty research:* Literature of discovery and exploration, modern literature, literary criticism, medieval literature, feminist critical theory.

**University of Oregon,** Graduate School, College of Arts and Sciences, Department of Romance Languages, Program in Italian, Eugene, OR 97403. Offers MA. *Program availability:* Part-time. *Degree requirements:* For master's, variable foreign language requirement. *Entrance requirements:* For master's, GRE General Test, minimum GPA of 3.0. Additional exam requirements/recommendations for international students: Required—TOEFL.

**University of Pennsylvania,** School of Arts and Sciences, Graduate Group in Romance Languages, Philadelphia, PA 19104. Offers French (AM, PhD); Italian (AM, PhD); Spanish (AM, PhD). *Faculty:* 38 full-time (14 women), 11 part-time/adjunct (3 women). *Students:* 56 full-time (25 women), 3 part-time (2 women); includes 4 minority (all Hispanic/Latino), 34 international. Average age 32. 73 applicants, 33% accepted, 10 enrolled. In 2016, 10 master's, 5 doctorates awarded. Terminal master's awarded for partial completion of doctoral program. Application fee: $70. *Expenses: Tuition:* Full-time $31,068; part-time $5762 per course. *Required fees:* $3200; $336 per course. Full-time tuition and fees vary according to degree level, program and student level. Part-time tuition and fees vary according to course load, degree level and program. Website: http://www.sas.upenn.edu/graduate-division

**University of Pittsburgh,** Dietrich School of Arts and Sciences, Department of French and Italian, Pittsburgh, PA 15260. Offers French (MA, PhD), including film studies (PhD); French; Italian (MA). *Program availability:* Part-time. *Faculty:* 12 full-time (6 women). *Students:* 24 full-time (16 women); includes 2 minority (both Black or African American, non-Hispanic/Latino), 10 international. Average age 32. 16 applicants, 56% accepted, 6 enrolled. In 2016, 4 master's, 2 doctorates awarded. Terminal master's awarded for partial completion of doctoral program. *Degree requirements:* For master's, one foreign language, comprehensive exam, seminar paper/thesis; for doctorate, one foreign language, comprehensive exam, thesis/dissertation, dissertation defense. *Entrance requirements:* For master's, GRE General Test (for French), phone interview and writing samples in French and English (for French); minimum GPA of 3.0 and writing sample (for Italian); for doctorate, GRE General Test (for French), phone interview and writing samples in French and English (for French). Additional exam requirements/recommendations for international students: Required—TOEFL (minimum score 600 paper-based; 90 iBT). *Application deadline:* For fall admission, 1/10 for domestic and international students. Application fee: $50. Electronic applications accepted. Tuition and fees vary according to program. *Financial support:* In 2016–17, 22 students received support, including 14 fellowships with full tuition reimbursements available (averaging $21,812 per year), 3 teaching assistantships with full tuition reimbursements available (averaging $17,905 per year); Federal Work-Study, traineeships, health care benefits, and tuition waivers (partial) also available. Financial award application deadline: 1/10. *Faculty research:* Literature and politics, constructs of the French nation, literary and cultural theory, French linguistics, gender and sexuality, Dante and his reception, humanism and Renaissance studies, seventeenth- and eighteenth-century Italian literature and culture, Italian theater, Holocaust literature and film, images of Southern Italy in European literature. *Total annual research expenditures:* $5,200. *Unit head:* Dr. Lina Insana, Chair, 412-624-6269, Fax: 412-624-6263, E-mail: insana@pitt.edu. *Application contact:* Keanna Cash, Graduate Administrator, 412-624-5906, Fax: 412-624-6263, E-mail: kec176@pitt.edu.
Website: http://www.frenchanditalian.pitt.edu

**University of South Africa,** College of Human Sciences, Pretoria, South Africa. Offers adult education (M Ed); African languages (MA, PhD); African politics (MA, PhD); Afrikaans (MA, PhD); ancient history (MA, PhD); ancient Near Eastern studies (MA, PhD); anthropology (MA, PhD); applied linguistics (MA); Arabic (MA, PhD); archaeology (MA); art history (MA); Biblical archaeology (MA); Biblical studies (M Th, D Th, PhD); Christian spirituality (M Th, D Th); church history (M Th, D Th); classical studies (MA, PhD); clinical psychology (MA); communication (MA, PhD); comparative education (M Ed, Ed D); consulting psychology (D Admin, D Com, PhD); curriculum studies (M Ed, Ed D); development studies (M Admin, MA, D Admin, PhD); didactics (M Ed, Ed D); education (M Tech); education management (M Ed, Ed D); educational psychology (M Ed); English (MA); environmental education (M Ed); French (MA, PhD); German (MA, PhD); Greek (MA); guidance and counseling (M Ed); health studies (MA, PhD), including health sciences education (MA), health services management (MA), medical and surgical nursing science (critical care general) (MA), midwifery and neonatal nursing science (MA), trauma and emergency care (MA); history (MA, PhD); history of education (Ed D); inclusive education (M Ed, Ed D); information and communications technology policy and regulation (MA); information science (MA, MIS, PhD); international politics (MA, PhD); Islamic studies (MA, PhD); Italian (MA, PhD); Judaica (MA, PhD); linguistics (MA, PhD); mathematical education (M Ed); mathematics education (MA); missiology (M Th, D Th); modern Hebrew (MA, PhD); musicology (MA, MMus, D Mus, PhD); natural science education (M Ed); New Testament (M Th, D Th); Old Testament (D Th); pastoral therapy (M Th, D Th); philosophy (MA); philosophy of education (M Ed, Ed D); politics (MA, PhD); Portuguese (MA, PhD); practical theology (M Th, D Th); psychology (MA, MS, PhD); psychology of education (M Ed, Ed D); public health (MA); religious studies (MA, D Th, PhD); Romance languages (MA); Russian (MA, PhD); Semitic languages (MA, PhD); social behavior studies in HIV/AIDS (MA); social science (mental health) (MA); social science in development studies (MA); social science in psychology (MA); social science in social work (MA); social science in sociology (MA); social work (MSW, DSW, PhD); socio-education (M Ed, Ed D); sociolinguistics (MA); sociology (MA, PhD); Spanish (MA, PhD); systematic theology (M Th, D Th); TESOL (teaching English to speakers of other languages) (MA); theological ethics (M Th, D Th); theory of literature (MA, PhD); urban ministries (D Th); urban ministry (M Th).

**The University of Tennessee,** Graduate School, College of Arts and Sciences, Department of Modern Foreign Languages and Literatures, Program in Modern Foreign Languages, Knoxville, TN 37996. Offers applied linguistics (PhD); French (PhD); German (PhD); Italian (PhD); Portuguese (PhD); Russian (PhD); Spanish (PhD).

*Degree requirements:* For doctorate, 2 foreign languages, thesis/dissertation. *Entrance requirements:* For doctorate, minimum GPA of 2.7. Additional exam requirements/recommendations for international students: Required—TOEFL. Electronic applications accepted.

**The University of Texas at Austin,** Graduate School, College of Liberal Arts, Department of French and Italian, Austin, TX 78712-1111. Offers French linguistics (MA, PhD); French studies (MA, PhD); Italian studies (MA, PhD); Romance linguistics (PhD). *Program availability:* Part-time. *Degree requirements:* For master's, one foreign language, thesis; for doctorate, 2 foreign languages, thesis/dissertation. *Entrance requirements:* For master's, GRE General Test, minimum GPA of 3.0, bachelor's degree in French or equivalent; for doctorate, GRE General Test, minimum GPA of 3.0, master's degree in French. Additional exam requirements/recommendations for international students: Required—TOEFL. Electronic applications accepted. *Faculty research:* Nineteenth-century Italian literature, Italian Renaissance, twentieth-century French literature, Francophone literature, fifteenth-century literature and culture.

**University of Toronto,** School of Graduate Studies, Faculty of Arts and Science, Department of Italian Studies, Toronto, ON M5S 1A1, Canada. Offers MA, PhD. *Program availability:* Part-time. *Degree requirements:* For doctorate, 2 foreign languages, comprehensive exam, thesis/dissertation, oral defense, language exam(s). *Entrance requirements:* For master's, minimum B average in last 2 years in Italian and in final year overall; 2 letters of recommendation; for doctorate, MA in Italian, minimum A-average. Electronic applications accepted.

**University of Victoria,** Faculty of Graduate Studies, Faculty of Humanities, Department of Hispanic and Italian Studies, Victoria, BC V8W 2Y2, Canada. Offers Hispanic and Italian studies (MA); Hispanic studies (MA). *Degree requirements:* For master's, one foreign language, comprehensive exam, thesis (for some programs). *Entrance requirements:* For master's, undergraduate major in Hispanic studies, minimum B+ average. Additional exam requirements/recommendations for international students: Required—TOEFL (minimum score 575 paper-based), IELTS (minimum score 7). Electronic applications accepted. *Faculty research:* Medieval/Renaissance Spanish and Italian literature, Golden Age literature, Latin American literature.

**University of Washington,** Graduate School, College of Arts and Sciences, Division of French and Italian Studies, Seattle, WA 98195. Offers French (MA, PhD); Italian (MA). Terminal master's awarded for partial completion of doctoral program. *Degree requirements:* For master's, 2 foreign languages, exam; for doctorate, 3 foreign languages, thesis/dissertation, exam. *Entrance requirements:* For master's and doctorate, GRE General Test, minimum GPA of 3.0. Additional exam requirements/recommendations for international students: Required—TOEFL. Electronic applications accepted. *Faculty research:* Interdisciplinary studies, literary theory and criticism, film, major periods of French and Italian literature, Francophonie.

**University of Wisconsin–Madison,** Graduate School, College of Letters and Science, Department of French and Italian, Program in Italian, Madison, WI 53706-1380. Offers MA, PhD. *Program availability:* Part-time. *Degree requirements:* For master's, one foreign language; for doctorate, 2 foreign languages, thesis/dissertation. *Entrance requirements:* For master's and doctorate, GRE. Electronic applications accepted. *Faculty research:* Italian literature, culture, linguistics, cinema, and language.

**Wayne State University,** College of Liberal Arts and Sciences, Department of Classical and Modern Languages, Literatures, and Cultures, Detroit, MI 48202. Offers classics (MA), including ancient Greek and Latin, ancient studies, classics, Latin; German (MA); language learning (MALL), including Arabic (MA, MALL), French (MA, MALL, PhD); German (MALL, PhD); Italian (MA, MALL), Spanish (MA, MALL, PhD); modern languages (PhD), including French (MA, MALL, PhD), German (MALL, PhD), Spanish (MA, MALL, PhD); Near Eastern languages (MA), including Arabic (MA, MALL), Hebrew; Romance languages (MA), including French (MA, MALL), Italian (MA, MALL), Spanish (MA, MALL, PhD). *Faculty:* 26. *Students:* 25 full-time (20 women), 14 part-time (8 women); includes 7 minority (2 Black or African American, non-Hispanic/Latino; 1 American Indian or Alaska Native, non-Hispanic/Latino; 1 Asian, non-Hispanic/Latino; 2 Hispanic/Latino; 1 Two or more races, non-Hispanic/Latino), 3 international. Average age 35. 29 applicants, 31% accepted, 5 enrolled. In 2016, 15 master's, 5 doctorates awarded. *Degree requirements:* For master's, variable foreign language requirement, comprehensive exam (for some programs), thesis (for some programs); for doctorate, one foreign language, comprehensive exam, thesis/dissertation. *Entrance requirements:* For master's, GRE (for some programs); for doctorate, GRE. Additional exam requirements/recommendations for international students: Required—TOEFL (minimum score 550 paper-based; 79 iBT), TWE (minimum score 5.5), Michigan English Language Assessment Battery (minimum score 85); Recommended—IELTS (minimum score 6.5). Application fee: $50. Electronic applications accepted. *Expenses:* $16,503 per year resident tuition and fees, $33,697 per year non-resident tuition and fees. *Financial support:* In 2016–17, 22 students received support, including 4 fellowships with tuition reimbursements available (averaging $13,500 per year), 17 teaching assistantships with tuition reimbursements available (averaging $17,994 per year); research assistantships, scholarships/grants, and unspecified assistantships also available. Financial award applicants required to submit FAFSA. *Faculty research:* Classical and modern literature and culture (Greek, Latin, Arabic, Chinese, French, German, Russian, Spanish) including colonial studies and exile and Holocaust studies; critical theory (French, German, Slavic, Spanish); theoretical and applied linguistics (Arabic, Chinese, French, Spanish); area studies (Arabic, Near Eastern, classical, Islamic, and Judaic studies). *Unit head:* Dr. Anne Duggan, Department Chair, 313-577-6244, Fax: 313-577-6243, E-mail: a.duggan@wayne.edu.
Website: http://clas.wayne.edu/languages/

**Yale University,** Graduate School of Arts and Sciences, Department of Italian Language and Literature, New Haven, CT 06520. Offers PhD. *Degree requirements:* For doctorate, 3 foreign languages, thesis/dissertation. *Entrance requirements:* For doctorate, GRE General Test.

# Japanese

**Arizona State University at the Tempe campus,** College of Liberal Arts and Sciences, School of International Letters and Cultures, Program in Japanese, Tempe, AZ 85287-0202. Offers Asian languages and civilizations: Japanese (MA). *Program availability:* Part-time, evening/weekend. *Degree requirements:* For master's, thesis, oral defense, interactive Program of Study (iPOS) submitted no later than beginning of third semester of study. *Entrance requirements:* For master's, minimum GPA of 3.25 in the last two years of work leading to the bachelor's degree; BA in Japanese or at least 5 semesters

of modern Japanese (preferred); personal statement; writing sample; 3 letters of recommendation. Additional exam requirements/recommendations for international students: Required—TOEFL (minimum score 550 paper-based; 83 iBT), IELTS (minimum score 6.5). Electronic applications accepted.

**Columbia University,** Graduate School of Arts and Sciences, New York, NY 10027. Offers African-American studies (MA); American studies (MA); anthropology (MA, PhD); art history and archaeology (MA, PhD); astronomy (PhD); biological sciences (PhD);

biotechnology (MA); chemical physics (PhD); chemistry (PhD); classical studies (MA, PhD); classics (MA, PhD); climate and society (MA); conservation biology (MA); earth and environmental sciences (PhD); East Asia: regional studies (MA); East Asian languages and cultures (MA, PhD); ecology, evolution and environmental biology (MA), including conservation biology; ecology, evolution, and environmental biology (PhD), including ecology and evolutionary biology, evolutionary primatology; economics (MA, PhD); English and comparative literature (MA, PhD); French and Romance philology (MA, PhD); Germanic languages (MA, PhD); global French studies (MA); global thought (MA); Hispanic cultural studies (MA); history (PhD); history and literature (MA); human rights studies (MA); Islamic studies (MA); Italian (MA, PhD); Japanese pedagogy (MA); Jewish studies (MA); Latin America and the Caribbean: regional studies (MA); Latin American and Iberian cultures (PhD); mathematics (MA, PhD), including finance (MA); medieval and Renaissance studies (MA); Middle Eastern, South Asian, and African studies (MA, PhD); modern art: critical and curatorial studies (MA); modern European studies (MA); museum anthropology (MA); music (DMA, PhD); oral history (MA); philosophical foundations of physics (MA); philosophy (MA, PhD); physics (PhD); political science (MA, PhD); psychology (PhD); quantitative methods in the social sciences (MA); religion (MA, PhD); Russia, Eurasia and East Europe: regional studies (MA); Russian translation (MA); Slavic cultures (MA); Slavic languages (MA, PhD); sociology (MA, PhD); South Asian studies (MA); statistics (MA, PhD); theatre (PhD). Dual-degree programs require admission to both Graduate School of Arts and Sciences and another Columbia school. *Program availability:* Part-time. Terminal master's awarded for partial completion of doctoral program. *Degree requirements:* For master's, variable foreign language requirement, comprehensive exam (for some programs), thesis (for some programs); for doctorate, variable foreign language requirement, comprehensive exam (for some programs), thesis/dissertation. *Entrance requirements:* For master's and doctorate, GRE General Test, GRE Subject Test (for some programs). Additional exam requirements/recommendations for international students: Required—TOEFL, IELTS. Electronic applications accepted.

**DePaul University,** College of Liberal Arts and Social Sciences, Chicago, IL 60614. Offers Arabic (MA); Chinese (MA); English (MA); French (MA); German (MA); history (MA); interdisciplinary studies (MA, MS); international public service (MS); international studies (MA); Italian (MA); Japanese (MA); leadership and policy studies (MS); liberal studies (MA); new media studies (MA); nonprofit management (MNM); public administration (MPA); public health (MPH); public service management (MS); social work (MSW); sociology (MA); Spanish (MA); sustainable urban development (MA); women and gender studies (MA); writing and publishing (MA); writing, rhetoric, and discourse (MA); MA/PhD. *Program availability:* Part-time, evening/weekend, online learning. Terminal master's awarded for partial completion of doctoral program. *Degree requirements:* For master's, variable foreign language requirement, comprehensive exam (for some programs), thesis (for some programs). Electronic applications accepted.

**Harvard University,** Graduate School of Arts and Sciences, Department of East Asian Languages and Civilizations, Cambridge, MA 02138. Offers Chinese (PhD); Japanese (PhD); Korean (PhD); Mongolian (PhD); Vietnamese (PhD). Terminal master's awarded for partial completion of doctoral program. *Degree requirements:* For doctorate, 3 foreign languages, thesis/dissertation, general exams. *Entrance requirements:* For doctorate, GRE General Test. Additional exam requirements/recommendations for international students: Required—TOEFL. *Faculty research:* Central Asian literature, religion, and premodern history.

**Indiana University Bloomington,** University Graduate School, College of Arts and Sciences, School of Global and International Studies, Department of East Asian Languages and Cultures, Bloomington, IN 47408. Offers Chinese (MA, PhD); Chinese language pedagogy (MA); East Asian studies (MA); Japanese (MA, PhD); Japanese language pedagogy (MA). *Program availability:* Part-time. *Degree requirements:* For master's, one foreign language, thesis; for doctorate, 2 foreign languages, comprehensive exam, thesis/dissertation. *Entrance requirements:* Additional exam requirements/recommendations for international students: Required—TOEFL (minimum score 93 iBT). Electronic applications accepted. *Faculty research:* Modern East Asian history; politics and society; traditional Chinese thought and society; medieval and premodern Japanese history, literature and society; modern Chinese and Japanese film and literature; Chinese, Japanese, Korean language and linguistics.

**Kent State University,** College of Arts and Sciences, Department of Modern and Classical Language Studies, Kent, OH 44242-0001. Offers French (MA), including applied linguistics and pedagogy, literature; Latin (MA), including applied linguistics and pedagogy, literature; Spanish (MA), including applied linguistics and pedagogy, literature; translation (MA), including Arabic, French, German, Japanese, Russian, Spanish; translation studies (PhD); MA/MBA. *Program availability:* Part-time. *Faculty:* 35 full-time (23 women). *Students:* 81 full-time (51 women), 23 part-time (15 women); includes 14 minority (1 Black or African American, non-Hispanic/Latino; 9 Hispanic/Latino; 4 Two or more races, non-Hispanic/Latino), 48 international. Average age 30. 109 applicants, 53% accepted, 33 enrolled. In 2016, 31 master's, 6 doctorates awarded. *Degree requirements:* For master's, variable foreign language requirement, comprehensive exam (for some programs), thesis (for some programs); for doctorate, variable foreign language requirement, comprehensive exam, thesis/dissertation. *Entrance requirements:* For master's, transcripts, goal statement, 3 letters of recommendation, CD/MP3 with oral sample of first and second languages, writing sample of second language; for doctorate, transcripts, MA in translation, a foreign language, or similar field; proficiency in a foreign language; minimum GPA of 3.5 from MA; goal statement; 3 letters of recommendation; essay or writing sample. *Application deadline:* For fall admission, 2/1 for domestic and international students. Applications are processed on a rolling basis. Application fee: $45 ($70 for international students). Electronic applications accepted. *Expenses:* Tuition, state resident: full-time $10,864; part-time $495 per credit hour. Tuition, nonresident: full-time $18,380; part-time $837 per credit hour. *Financial support:* Fellowships with full tuition reimbursements, teaching assistantships with full tuition reimbursements, and unspecified assistantships available. Financial award application deadline: 2/1. *Unit head:* Dr. Keiran Dunne, Professor of French Translation/Chair, 330-672-2150, E-mail: kdunne@kent.edu. *Application contact:* Said Shiyab, Professor of Translation Studies/Graduate Coordinator, 330-672-1864, E-mail: sshiyab@kent.edu.
Website: http://www.kent.edu/mcls/

**New York University,** Steinhardt School of Culture, Education, and Human Development, Department of Teaching and Learning, Program in Multilingual/Multicultural Studies, New York, NY 10003. Offers bilingual education (MA, PhD, Advanced Certificate); foreign language education (MA); teaching English to speakers of other languages (MA, PhD); teaching foreign languages, 7-12 (MA), including Chinese, French, Italian, Japanese, Spanish; teaching French as a foreign language (MA), including teaching English to speakers of other languages; teaching Spanish as a foreign language (MA), including teaching English to speakers of other languages. *Accreditation:* TEAC. *Program availability:* Part-time, evening/weekend. *Degree requirements:* For master's, thesis (for some programs); for doctorate, thesis/dissertation. *Entrance requirements:* For doctorate, GRE General Test, interview; for Advanced Certificate, master's degree. Additional exam requirements/recommendations

for international students: Required—TOEFL (minimum score 100 iBT). Electronic applications accepted. *Faculty research:* Second language acquisition, cross-cultural communication, technology-enhanced language learning, language variation, action learning.

**The Ohio State University,** Graduate School, College of Arts and Sciences, Division of Arts and Humanities, Department of East Asian Languages and Literatures, Columbus, OH 43210. Offers Chinese (MA, PhD); Japanese (MA, PhD). *Faculty:* 20. *Students:* 59 full-time (44 women), 1 (woman) part-time; includes 5 minority (all Asian, non-Hispanic/Latino), 36 international. Average age 30. In 2016, 15 master's, 4 doctorates awarded. Terminal master's awarded for partial completion of doctoral program. *Degree requirements:* For master's, thesis optional; for doctorate, thesis/dissertation. *Entrance requirements:* For master's and doctorate, GRE General Test (if applying for financial aid). Additional exam requirements/recommendations for international students: Required—TOEFL (minimum score 577 paper-based; 90 iBT); Recommended—IELTS (minimum score 7.5). *Application deadline:* For fall admission, 11/30 priority date for domestic and international students; for spring admission, 3/1 for domestic students, 2/1 for international students. Applications are processed on a rolling basis. Application fee: $60 ($70 for international students). Electronic applications accepted. *Financial support:* Fellowships, research assistantships, teaching assistantships, Federal Work-Study, institutionally sponsored loans, and unspecified assistantships available. Support available to part-time students. *Unit head:* Dr. Mark Bender, Chair and Professor, 614-688-5737, E-mail: bender.4@osu.edu. *Application contact:* Graduate and Professional Admissions, 614-292-9444, Fax: 614-292-3895, E-mail: gpadmissions@osu.edu. Website: http://deall.osu.edu/

**Portland State University,** Graduate Studies, College of Liberal Arts and Sciences, Department of World Languages and Literatures, Portland, OR 97207-0751. Offers French (MA); German (MA); Japanese (MA); Spanish (MA); world literature and language (MA). *Program availability:* Part-time. *Faculty:* 45 full-time (25 women), 39 part-time/adjunct (27 women). *Students:* 22 full-time (13 women), 6 part-time (3 women); includes 8 minority (2 Asian, non-Hispanic/Latino; 6 Hispanic/Latino), 4 international. Average age 31. 19 applicants, 53% accepted, 8 enrolled. In 2016, 18 master's awarded. *Degree requirements:* For master's, one foreign language, thesis (for some programs). *Entrance requirements:* Additional exam requirements/recommendations for international students: Required—TOEFL (minimum score 550 paper-based; 80 iBT), IELTS (minimum score 6.5). *Application deadline:* For fall admission, 4/1 for domestic students, 3/1 for international students; for winter admission, 9/1 for domestic students, 7/1 for international students; for spring admission, 11/1 for domestic and international students. Applications are processed on a rolling basis. Application fee: $65. *Expenses:* Contact institution. *Financial support:* In 2016–17, 18 teaching assistantships with tuition reimbursements (averaging $10,805 per year) were awarded; research assistantships, Federal Work-Study, scholarships/grants, and unspecified assistantships also available. Support available to part-time students. Financial award application deadline: 3/1; financial award applicants required to submit FAFSA. *Faculty research:* Foreign language pedagogy, applied and social linguistics, literary history and criticism. *Total annual research expenditures:* $396,300. *Unit head:* Dr. Gina Greco, Chair, 503-725-5287, E-mail: grecog@pdx.edu. *Application contact:* Kelli Martin, Graduate Admissions Coordinator, 503-725-3243, E-mail: kmarti@pdx.edu. Website: http://www.pdx.edu/wll/

**Purdue University,** Graduate School, College of Liberal Arts, School of Languages and Cultures, West Lafayette, IN 47907. Offers French (MA, MAT, PhD), including French (MA, PhD), French education (MAT); German (MA, MAT, PhD), including German (MA, PhD), German education (MAT); Japanese pedagogy (MA); Spanish (MA, MAT, PhD), including Spanish (MA, PhD), Spanish education (MAT). *Faculty:* 44 full-time (22 women), 1 (woman) part-time/adjunct. *Students:* 37 full-time (18 women), 41 part-time (30 women); includes 9 minority (1 Asian, non-Hispanic/Latino; 8 Hispanic/Latino), 52 international. Average age 32. 49 applicants, 39% accepted, 14 enrolled. In 2016, 11 master's, 5 doctorates awarded. Terminal master's awarded for partial completion of doctoral program. *Degree requirements:* For master's, one foreign language; for doctorate, 2 foreign languages, thesis/dissertation. *Entrance requirements:* For master's, GRE General Test (minimum score 600, 160 for new scoring), two writing samples, one in English, one in language (French, German, Japanese, or Spanish); sample recording of English and language of study; for doctorate, GRE General Test (minimum score 600, 160 for new scoring), master's degree with minimum GPA of 3.5 or equivalent; two writing samples, one in English, one in language (French, German, Japanese, or Spanish); sample recording of English and language of study. Additional exam requirements/recommendations for international students: Required—TOEFL (minimum score 550 paper-based; 77 iBT); Recommended—TWE. *Application deadline:* For fall admission, 12/12 for domestic and international students; for spring admission, 10/1 for domestic and international students. Applications are processed on a rolling basis. Application fee: $60 ($75 for international students). Electronic applications accepted. *Financial support:* In 2016–17, fellowships with tuition reimbursements (averaging $15,750 per year), teaching assistantships with tuition reimbursements (averaging $13,463 per year) were awarded. Support available to part-time students. Financial award applicants required to submit FAFSA. *Faculty research:* Linguistics, semiotics, literary criticism, pedagogy. *Unit head:* Dr. Madeleine M. Henry, Head, 765-494-3828, E-mail: henry48@purdue.edu. *Application contact:* Joni L. Hipsher, Graduate Contact, 765-494-3841, E-mail: jlhipshe@purdue.edu. Website: http://www.cla.purdue.edu/slc/main/

**San Francisco State University,** Division of Graduate Studies, College of Liberal and Creative Arts, Department of Modern Languages and Literatures, Program in Japanese, San Francisco, CA 94132-1722. Offers MA. *Program availability:* Part-time. *Application deadline:* Applications are processed on a rolling basis. *Expenses:* Tuition, state resident: full-time $6738. Tuition, nonresident: full-time $15,666. *Required fees:* $1012. Tuition and fees vary according to degree level and program. *Unit head:* Dr. Mohammad Salama, Chair, 415-338-7413, Fax: 415-338-6159, E-mail: mrsalama@sfsu.edu. *Application contact:* Dr. Makiko Asano, Program Coordinator, 415-338-1131, Fax: 415-338-6159, E-mail: masano@sfsu.edu. Website: http://mll.sfsu.edu/japanese-program/

**Stanford University,** School of Humanities and Sciences, Department of East Asian Languages and Cultures, Stanford, CA 94305-2004. Offers Chinese (MA, PhD); Japanese (MA, PhD). Terminal master's awarded for partial completion of doctoral program. *Degree requirements:* For master's, one foreign language, thesis or an annotated translation of a literary or historical text; for doctorate, 2 foreign languages, thesis/dissertation, field exams. *Entrance requirements:* For master's and doctorate, GRE General Test. Additional exam requirements/recommendations for international students: Required—TOEFL. Electronic applications accepted. *Expenses: Tuition:* Full-time $47,331. *Required fees:* $609.

**University of Alberta,** Faculty of Graduate Studies and Research, Department of East Asian Studies, Edmonton, AB T6G 2E1, Canada. Offers Chinese literature (MA); East Asian interdisciplinary studies (MA); Japanese literature (MA). *Program availability:* Part-time. *Degree requirements:* For master's, one foreign language, thesis. *Entrance requirements:* Additional exam requirements/recommendations for international students: Required—TOEFL. Electronic applications accepted. *Faculty research:*

## Japanese

Classical Chinese poetry and poetics, Chinese philosophy, modern/contemporary Chinese literature, modern Japanese literature and culture, Japanese women's writing.

**University of California, Berkeley,** Graduate Division, College of Letters and Science, Department of East Asian Languages and Cultures, Berkeley, CA 94720-1500. Offers Chinese language (PhD); Japanese language (PhD). *Students:* 27 full-time (12 women); includes 7 minority (6 Asian, non-Hispanic/Latino; 1 Hispanic/Latino), 8 international. Average age 31. 73 applicants, 3 enrolled. In 2016, 4 doctorates awarded. *Degree requirements:* For doctorate, one foreign language, thesis/dissertation, oral qualifying exam. *Entrance requirements:* For doctorate, GRE General Test, minimum GPA of 3.0, MA thesis, 3 letters of recommendation. *Application deadline:* For fall admission, 12/5 for domestic students. Application fee: $105 ($125 for international students). Electronic applications accepted. *Financial support:* Fellowships, research assistantships, teaching assistantships, Federal Work-Study, institutionally sponsored loans, health care benefits, and unspecified assistantships available. Financial award applicants required to submit FAFSA. *Faculty research:* Chinese and Japanese modern and classical texts, prose, and poetry; Chinese and Japanese linguistics. *Unit head:* Prof. H. Mack Horton, Chair, 510-642-3480, Fax: 510-642-6031, E-mail: ealang@berkeley.edu. *Application contact:* Information Contact, 510-642-3480, E-mail: ealang@berkeley.edu. Website: http://ealc.berkeley.edu/

**University of California, Irvine,** School of Humanities, Department of East Asian Languages and Literatures, Irvine, CA 92697. Offers Chinese (MA, PhD); East Asian languages and literatures (MA, PhD); Japanese (MA, PhD). *Students:* 12 full-time (10 women), 1 part-time (0 women); includes 4 minority (3 Asian, non-Hispanic/Latino; 1 Two or more races, non-Hispanic/Latino), 5 international. Average age 32. 34 applicants, 12% accepted, 2 enrolled. In 2016, 1 doctorate awarded. *Degree requirements:* For doctorate, thesis/dissertation. *Entrance requirements:* For master's and doctorate, GRE General Test, minimum GPA of 3.0. Additional exam requirements/recommendations for international students: Required—TOEFL (minimum score 550 paper-based). *Application deadline:* For fall admission, 1/15 priority date for domestic students, 1/15 for international students. Application fee: $105 ($125 for international students). Electronic applications accepted. *Financial support:* Fellowships with tuition reimbursements, research assistantships with full tuition reimbursements, teaching assistantships with partial tuition reimbursements, institutionally sponsored loans, traineeships, health care benefits, and unspecified assistantships available. Financial award application deadline: 3/1; financial award applicants required to submit FAFSA. *Faculty research:* Chinese, Japanese, and Korean literature and culture; language and textual analysis; historical, social, and cultural dimensions of literary study. *Unit head:* Michael A. Fuller, Chair, 949-824-2802 Ext. 2227, Fax: 949-824-3248, E-mail: mafuller@uci.edu. *Application contact:* Hu Ying, Graduate Faculty Advisor, 949-824-6312, Fax: 949-824-3248, E-mail: huying@uci.edu. Website: http://www.hnet.uci.edu/eastasian/

**University of Colorado Boulder,** Graduate School, College of Arts and Sciences, Department of Asian Languages and Civilizations, Boulder, CO 80309. Offers MA, PhD. *Faculty:* 13 full-time (5 women). *Students:* 22 full-time (16 women); includes 6 minority (2 Asian, non-Hispanic/Latino; 2 Hispanic/Latino; 2 Two or more races, non-Hispanic/Latino), 8 international. Average age 29. 33 applicants, 42% accepted, 6 enrolled. In 2016, 11 master's awarded. Terminal master's awarded for partial completion of doctoral program. *Degree requirements:* For master's, comprehensive exam. *Entrance requirements:* For master's, BA in Chinese or Japanese, minimum undergraduate GPA of 3.0. Additional exam requirements/recommendations for international students: Required—TOEFL. *Application deadline:* For fall admission, 1/1 for domestic students, 12/1 for international students; for spring admission, 10/1 for domestic students, 9/1 for international students. Applications are processed on a rolling basis. Application fee: $60 ($80 for international students). Electronic applications accepted. Application fee is waived when completed online. *Financial support:* In 2016–17, 86 students received support, including 39 fellowships (averaging $1,598 per year), 20 teaching assistantships with full and partial tuition reimbursements available (averaging $29,447 per year); institutionally sponsored loans, scholarships/grants, health care benefits, and unspecified assistantships also available. Financial award application deadline: 2/1; financial award applicants required to submit FAFSA. *Faculty research:* Asian languages/literature, Chinese language/literature, literary criticism, religious literature, literary history. *Total annual research expenditures:* $209,262. *Application contact:* E-mail: dalc@colorado.edu. Website: http://alc.colorado.edu/

**University of Hawaii at Manoa,** Graduate Division, College of Languages, Linguistics and Literature, Department of East Asian Languages and Literatures, Program in Japanese, Honolulu, HI 96822. Offers MA, PhD. *Program availability:* Part-time. *Degree requirements:* For master's, 2 foreign languages, thesis optional; for doctorate, 2 foreign languages, comprehensive exam, thesis/dissertation. *Entrance requirements:* For master's and doctorate, GRE General Test. Additional exam requirements/recommendations for international students: Required—TOEFL (minimum score 560 paper-based; 83 iBT), IELTS (minimum score 5).

**University of Hawaii at Manoa,** Graduate Division, School of Pacific and Asian Studies, Program in Asian Studies, Concentration in Japanese Studies, Honolulu, HI 96822. Offers Graduate Certificate. *Program availability:* Part-time. *Degree requirements:* For Graduate Certificate, one foreign language. *Entrance requirements:* For degree, GRE. Additional exam requirements/recommendations for international students: Required—TOEFL (minimum score 560 paper-based; 83 iBT), IELTS (minimum score 5).

**The University of Manchester,** School of Languages, Linguistics and Cultures, Manchester, United Kingdom. Offers Arab world studies (PhD); Chinese studies (M Phil, PhD); East Asian studies (M Phil, PhD); English language (PhD); French studies (M Phil, PhD); German studies (M Phil, PhD); interpreting studies (PhD); Italian studies (M Phil, PhD); Japanese studies (M Phil, PhD); Latin American cultural studies (M Phil, PhD); linguistics (M Phil, PhD); Middle Eastern studies (M Phil, PhD); Polish studies (M Phil, PhD); Portuguese studies (M Phil, PhD); Russian studies (M Phil, PhD); Spanish studies (M Phil, PhD); translation and intercultural studies (M Phil, PhD).

**University of Massachusetts Amherst,** Graduate School, College of Humanities and Fine Arts, Department of Languages, Literatures, and Cultures, Programs in Asian Languages and Literatures, Amherst, MA 01003. Offers Chinese (MA); Japanese (MA). *Program availability:* Part-time. *Degree requirements:* For master's, thesis, general exam. *Entrance requirements:* For master's, GRE General Test. Additional exam requirements/recommendations for international students: Required—TOEFL (minimum score 550 paper-based; 80 iBT), IELTS (minimum score 6.5). Electronic applications accepted.

**University of Oregon,** Graduate School, College of Arts and Sciences, Department of East Asian Languages and Literature, Eugene, OR 97403. Offers Chinese (MA, PhD); Japanese (MA, PhD). *Entrance requirements:* Additional exam requirements/recommendations for international students: Required—TOEFL. *Faculty research:* Linguistics, pedagogy.

**University of Pittsburgh,** Dietrich School of Arts and Sciences, Department of East Asian Languages and Literatures, Pittsburgh, PA 15260. Offers Chinese (MA); Japanese (MA). *Program availability:* Part-time. *Faculty:* 18 full-time (11 women), 11 part-time/adjunct (all women). *Students:* 5 full-time (4 women); includes 3 minority (all Asian, non-Hispanic/Latino). Average age 26. 18 applicants, 22% accepted, 1 enrolled. In 2016, 2 master's awarded. *Degree requirements:* For master's, one foreign language, thesis, oral comprehensive exam. *Entrance requirements:* For master's, GRE General Test, 2 years of college-level Chinese or Japanese, minimum QPA of 3.0. Additional exam requirements/recommendations for international students: Required—TOEFL (minimum score 600 paper-based; 90 iBT). *Application deadline:* For fall admission, 1/15 for domestic and international students. Application fee: $50. Electronic applications accepted. Tuition and fees vary according to program. *Financial support:* In 2016–17, 5 students received support, including 5 fellowships with full tuition reimbursements available (averaging $21,812 per year); research assistantships, teaching assistantships, Federal Work-Study, scholarships/grants, tuition waivers (full and partial), and unspecified assistantships also available. Financial award application deadline: 1/15. *Faculty research:* Chinese literature, film, and poetry; Japanese literature, film, and theater; Chinese society and culture; East Asian foreign policy, security studies, and economic history; Japanese performing arts and fine arts translation studies; cultural studies; intellectual history; language and linguistics; second language acquisition; Japanese government; Japanese and Chinese history; ethnomusicology; religious studies. *Unit head:* Dr. Hiroshi Nara, Chair, 412-624-5579, Fax: 412-624-3458, E-mail: hnara@pitt.edu. *Application contact:* Keanna Cash, Graduate Administrator, 412-624-5906, Fax: 412-624-6263, E-mail: kec176@pitt.edu. Website: http://www.deall.pitt.edu/

**University of Washington,** Graduate School, College of Arts and Sciences, Department of Asian Languages and Literature, Seattle, WA 98195. Offers Buddhist studies (MA, PhD); Chinese language and literature (MA, PhD); Japanese language and literature (MA, PhD); Korean language and literature (MA, PhD); South Asian language and literature (MA, PhD). *Degree requirements:* For master's, 2 foreign languages, general exam, thesis or 2 research papers; for doctorate, 3 foreign languages, thesis/dissertation, general exam. *Entrance requirements:* For master's, GRE, minimum GPA of 3.0; for doctorate, GRE, master's degree in related field, minimum GPA of 3.0. Additional exam requirements/recommendations for international students: Required—TOEFL. Electronic applications accepted. *Faculty research:* Textual, linguistic, philological, and literary study of languages and literatures of Asia.

**University of Wisconsin–Madison,** Graduate School, College of Letters and Science, Department of East Asian Languages and Literature, Program in Japanese Linguistics, Madison, WI 53706-1380. Offers MA, PhD. *Program availability:* Part-time. Terminal master's awarded for partial completion of doctoral program. *Degree requirements:* For master's, one foreign language, seminars, written exam; for doctorate, 3 foreign languages, thesis/dissertation, seminars, preliminary exams, oral exam. *Entrance requirements:* For master's, GRE General Test, bachelor's degree or equivalent in Japanese; for doctorate, GRE General Test, master's degree or equivalent in Japanese. Electronic applications accepted. *Faculty research:* Modern and historical Japanese linguistics, modern Japanese fiction and poetry, classical Japanese literature, language pedagogy.

**Washington University in St. Louis,** The Graduate School, Department of East Asian Languages and Cultures, St. Louis, MO 63130-4899. Offers Chinese (MA); Chinese and comparative literature (PhD); Chinese language and literature (PhD); East Asian studies (MA); Japanese (MA); Japanese and comparative literature (PhD); Japanese language and literature (PhD). Terminal master's awarded for partial completion of doctoral program. *Degree requirements:* For master's, thesis optional; for doctorate, thesis/dissertation. *Entrance requirements:* For master's and doctorate, GRE General Test. Additional exam requirements/recommendations for international students: Required—TOEFL. Electronic applications accepted. *Faculty research:* Chinese; Japanese; Chinese fiction, theater, poetry, modern literature; Japanese modern and classical fiction, translation theory.

# Near and Middle Eastern Languages

**The American University in Cairo,** School of Humanities and Social Sciences, Cairo, Egypt. Offers Arab and Islamic civilizations (Graduate Diploma); Arabic studies (MA); comparative literary studies (Graduate Diploma); Egyptology and Coptology (MA); English and comparative literature (MA); humanities and social sciences (Graduate Diploma); philosophy (MA); psychology (MA); sociology and anthropology (MA); teaching Arabic as a foreign language (MA); teaching English to speakers of other languages (MA). *Program availability:* Part-time, evening/weekend. *Faculty:* 51 full-time (29 women), 4 part-time/adjunct (2 women). *Students:* 65 full-time (47 women), 179 part-time (138 women), 32 international. Average age 30. 221 applicants, 45% accepted, 54 enrolled. In 2016, 95 master's awarded. *Degree requirements:* For master's, comprehensive exam (for some programs), thesis (for some programs). *Entrance requirements:* Additional exam requirements/recommendations for international students: Required—TOEFL (minimum score 450 paper-based; 45 iBT), IELTS (minimum score 5). *Application deadline:* For fall admission, 2/1 priority date for domestic and international students; for spring admission, 10/15 priority date for domestic and international students. Applications are processed on a rolling basis. Application fee: $80. Electronic applications accepted. *Expenses:* Contact institution. *Financial support:* Fellowships with partial tuition reimbursements, scholarships/grants, tuition waivers (partial), and unspecified assistantships available. Financial award application deadline: 3/10. *Faculty research:* English literature, political science, psychology, sociology, anthropology and Egyptology, teaching English for non-speakers, teaching Arabic as a foreign language, philosophy, Arabic studies. *Unit head:* Dr. Nathaniel Bowditch, Dean, 20-2-2615-1788, E-mail: nbowditch@aucegypt.edu. *Application contact:* Maha Hegazi, Director for Graduate Admissions, 20-2-2615-1462, E-mail: mahahegazi@aucegypt.edu. Website: http://www.aucegypt.edu/huss/Pages/default.aspx

**American University of Beirut,** Graduate Programs, Faculty of Arts and Sciences, Beirut, Lebanon. Offers anthropology (MA); Arab and Middle Eastern history (PhD); Arabic language and literature (MA, PhD); archaeology (MA); art history and curating (MA); biology (MS); cell and molecular biology (PhD); chemistry (MS); clinical psychology (MA); computational sciences (MS); computer science (MS); economics (MA); education (MA); English language (MA); English literature (MA); environmental policy planning (MS); financial economics (MAFE); geology (MS); history (MA); Islamic studies (MA); mathematics (MS); media studies (MA); Middle Eastern studies (MA); physics (MS); political studies (MA); psychology (MA); public administration (MA); public policy and international affairs (MA); sociology (MA); statistics (MA, MS); theoretical physics (PhD); transnational American studies (MA). *Program availability:* Part-time. *Faculty:* 133 full-time (42 women), 6 part-time/adjunct (2 women). *Students:* 240 full-time (172 women), 227 part-time (166 women). Average age 27. 286 applicants, 67% accepted, 108 enrolled. In 2016, 60 master's, 3 doctorates awarded. Terminal master's awarded for partial completion of doctoral program. *Degree requirements:* For master's, one foreign language, comprehensive exam, thesis (for some programs); for doctorate, one foreign language, comprehensive exam, thesis/dissertation. *Entrance requirements:* For master's, GRE (for some MA, MS programs), letters of recommendation; for doctorate, GRE, letters of recommendation. Additional exam requirements/recommendations for international students: Required—TOEFL (minimum score 600 paper-based; 97 iBT), IELTS (minimum score 7). *Application deadline:* For fall admission, 4/3 for domestic students; for winter admission, 11/3 for domestic students. Application fee: $50. Electronic applications accepted. *Expenses:* Contact institution. *Financial support:* In 2016–17, 4 fellowships (averaging $11,200 per year), 18 research assistantships (averaging $5,400 per year) were awarded; teaching assistantships, career-related internships or fieldwork, Federal Work-Study, institutionally sponsored loans, scholarships/grants, traineeships, health care benefits, tuition waivers (full), and unspecified assistantships also available. Support available to part-time students. *Faculty research:* Development economics, spatial econometrics, health economics, labor economics, energy economics, hydrogeology, geophysics, petrophysics, structural geology, mineralogy, petrology, geochemistry, multilingualism, comparative/world literature, translation studies, book histories/ cultures, biocatalysis, molecular recognition, photocatalysis, photophysical and biophysical chemistry, probe chemistry, machine learning, data science. *Unit head:* Dr. Nadia Maria El Cheikh, Dean, Faculty of Arts and Sciences, 961-1374374 Ext. 3800, Fax: 961-1744461, E-mail: nmcheikh@aub.edu.lb. *Application contact:* Dr. Salim Kanaan, Director, Admissions Office, 961-1350000 Ext. 2590, Fax: 961-1750775, E-mail: sk00@aub.edu.lb. Website: http://www.aub.edu.lb/fas/

**Bethel Seminary,** Graduate and Professional Programs, St. Paul, MN 55112-6998. Offers Anglican studies (Certificate); children's and family ministry (MA); Christian studies (Certificate); Christian thought (MA); church planting (Certificate); Greek and Hebrew language (M Div); Greek language (M Div); Hebrew language (M Div); marriage and family therapy (MA, Certificate); mental health counseling (MA); ministry (MA, D Min); ministry practice (Certificate); theological studies (MA, Certificate); transformational leadership (MA); young life youth ministry (Certificate). *Accreditation:* ACIPE. *Program availability:* Part-time, evening/weekend, blended/hybrid learning. *Faculty:* 14 full-time (4 women), 37 part-time/adjunct (17 women). *Students:* 369 full-time (165 women), 147 part-time (43 women); includes 138 minority (48 Black or African American, non-Hispanic/Latino; 45 Asian, non-Hispanic/Latino; 28 Hispanic/Latino; 2 Native Hawaiian or other Pacific Islander, non-Hispanic/Latino; 15 Two or more races, non-Hispanic/Latino), 15 international. 322 applicants, 75% accepted, 174 enrolled. In 2016, 168 master's, 24 doctorates, 6 other advanced degrees awarded. *Degree requirements:* For master's, variable foreign language requirement, thesis (for some programs); for doctorate, thesis/dissertation. *Entrance requirements:* For master's, letters of reference, transcripts, personal statement; for doctorate, M Div, letters of reference, organizational support; for Certificate, letters of reference, family essay, personal statement, and family of origin paper (for marriage and family therapy). Additional exam requirements/recommendations for international students: Required—TOEFL (minimum score 550 paper-based; 87 iBT). *Application deadline:* For fall admission, 8/1 priority date for domestic students, 8/1 for international students; for winter admission, 12/1 priority date for domestic students; for spring admission, 1/1 priority date for domestic students. Applications are processed on a rolling basis. Application fee: $0. Electronic applications accepted. *Expenses:* Contact institution. *Financial support:* In 2016–17, 404 students received support. Teaching assistantships, career-related internships or fieldwork, Federal Work-Study, and scholarships/grants available. Financial award applicants required to submit FAFSA. *Faculty research:* Nature of theology, ethics, Biblical commentaries, nature of God, science and theology. *Unit head:* Dr. David Clark, Vice-President and Dean, 651-638-6659, E-mail: d-clark@bethel.edu. *Application contact:* Jen Niska, Director of Admissions, 651-638-6288, Fax: 651-638-6002, E-mail: seminary-admissions@bethel.edu. Website: https://www.bethel.edu/seminary

**Brandeis University,** Graduate School of Arts and Sciences, Department of Near Eastern and Judaic Studies, Waltham, MA 02454-9110. Offers Near Eastern and Judaic studies (MA, PhD); Near Eastern and Judaic studies and women's, gender, and sexuality studies (MA); teaching of Hebrew (MAT). *Program availability:* Part-time. *Faculty:* 24 full-time (10 women), 6 part-time/adjunct (3 women). *Students:* 44 full-time (18 women), 2 part-time (0 women); includes 7 minority (2 Black or African American, non-Hispanic/Latino; 1 Asian, non-Hispanic/Latino; 4 Hispanic/Latino), 9 international. 67 applicants, 45% accepted, 12 enrolled. In 2016, 9 master's, 3 doctorates awarded. Terminal master's awarded for partial completion of doctoral program. *Degree requirements:* For master's, one foreign language, thesis or alternative, proseminar, capstone; for doctorate, variable foreign language requirement, comprehensive exam, thesis/dissertation. *Entrance requirements:* For master's, GRE (recommended), 2 letters of recommendation, transcript(s), statement of purpose, writing sample, resume; for doctorate, GRE (recommended), 3 letters of recommendation, transcript(s), statement of purpose, writing sample, resume. Additional exam requirements/recommendations for international students: Required—TOEFL (minimum score 600 paper-based; 100 iBT); Recommended—IELTS (minimum score 7), TSE (minimum score 68). *Application deadline:* For fall admission, 1/15 priority date for domestic and international students. Application fee: $75. Electronic applications accepted. *Financial support:* In 2016–17, 28 students received support, including 16 fellowships with full tuition reimbursements available (averaging $24,000 per year), 2 teaching assistantships with partial tuition reimbursements available (averaging $3,200 per year); Federal Work-Study, scholarships/grants, health care benefits, and tuition waivers (full and partial) also available. Support available to part-time students. Financial award application deadline: 4/15; financial award applicants required to submit FAFSA. *Faculty research:* Bible and ancient Near East, Judaic Studies, Israel Studies, modern Middle East, Arabic and Islamic civilizations. *Unit head:* Dr. Jonathan Decter, Department Chair, 781-736-2950, Fax: 781-736-2070, E-mail: decter@brandeis.edu. *Application contact:* Joanne Arnish, Department Administrator, 781-736-2950, Fax: 781-736-2070, E-mail: arnish@brandeis.edu. Website: http://www.brandeis.edu/gsas

**The Catholic University of America,** School of Arts and Sciences, Department of Semitic and Egyptian Languages and Literatures, Washington, DC 20064. Offers ancient Near East (Biblical Hebrew/Aramaic) (MA, PhD); Arabic (PhD); Christian Near East (Biblical Hebrew/Aramaic) (MA); Coptic (MA, PhD); Syriac (MA, PhD). *Program availability:* Part-time. *Faculty:* 3 full-time (0 women), 2 part-time/adjunct (1 woman). *Students:* 18 full-time (2 women), 14 part-time (4 women); includes 4 minority (1 Asian, non-Hispanic/Latino; 1 Hispanic/Latino; 2 Two or more races, non-Hispanic/Latino), 4 international. Average age 36. 11 applicants, 82% accepted, 7 enrolled. In 2016, 3 master's, 2 doctorates awarded. Terminal master's awarded for partial completion of doctoral program. *Degree requirements:* For master's, one foreign language, comprehensive exam; for doctorate, 2 foreign languages, comprehensive exam, thesis/dissertation. *Entrance requirements:* For master's, GRE General Test, statement of purpose, official copies of academic transcripts, three letters of recommendation; for doctorate, GRE General Test, statement of purpose, official copies of academic transcripts, three letters of recommendation, successful completion of MA field. Additional exam requirements/recommendations for international students: Required—TOEFL (minimum score 550 paper-based; 80 iBT). *Application deadline:* For fall admission, 7/15 priority date for domestic students, 7/1 for international students; for spring admission, 11/15 priority date for domestic students, 11/1 for international students. Applications are processed on a rolling basis. Application fee: $55. Electronic applications accepted. *Expenses:* $42,850 per year; $1,170 per credit; $200 per semester part-time fees. *Financial support:* Fellowships, research assistantships, teaching assistantships, Federal Work-Study, scholarships/grants, tuition waivers (full and partial), and unspecified assistantships available. Financial award application deadline: 2/1; financial award applicants required to submit FAFSA. *Faculty research:* Christian history and literature of the Near East, Biblical Hebrew, Arabic Christianity, Coptic, Syriac. *Unit head:* Dr. Andrew D. Gross, Chair, 202-319-5083, Fax: 202-319-4735, E-mail: grossa@cua.edu. *Application contact:* Director of Graduate Admissions, 202-319-5057, Fax: 202-319-6533, E-mail: cua-admissions@cua.edu. Website: http://semitics.cua.edu/

**DePaul University,** College of Liberal Arts and Social Sciences, Chicago, IL 60614. Offers Arabic (MA); Chinese (MA); English (MA); French (MA); German (MA); history (MA); interdisciplinary studies (MA, MS); international public service (MS); international studies (MA); Italian (MA); Japanese (MA); leadership and policy studies (MS); liberal studies (MA); new media studies (MA); nonprofit management (MNM); public administration (MPA); public health (MPH); public service management (MS); social work (MSW); sociology (MA); Spanish (MA); sustainable urban development (MA); women and gender studies (MA); writing and publishing (MA); writing, rhetoric, and discourse (MA); MA/PhD. *Program availability:* Part-time, evening/weekend, online learning. Terminal master's awarded for partial completion of doctoral program. *Degree requirements:* For master's, variable foreign language requirement, comprehensive exam (for some programs), thesis (for some programs). Electronic applications accepted.

**Georgetown University,** Graduate School of Arts and Sciences, Walsh School of Foreign Service, The Center for Contemporary Arab Studies, Washington, DC 20057. Offers MA, Certificate, MA/JD, MA/PhD. *Degree requirements:* For master's, one foreign language, comprehensive exam, thesis or alternative, proficiency in Arabic. *Entrance requirements:* For master's, GRE, minimum GPA of 3.0. Additional exam requirements/recommendations for international students: Required—TOEFL (minimum score 600 paper-based; 100 iBT). Electronic applications accepted. *Faculty research:* Contemporary Arab world.

**Harvard University,** Graduate School of Arts and Sciences, Department of Near Eastern Languages and Civilizations, Cambridge, MA 02138. Offers Akkadian and Sumerian (AM, PhD); Arabic (AM, PhD); Armenian (AM, PhD); biblical history (AM, PhD); Hebrew (AM, PhD); Indo-Muslim culture (AM, PhD); Iranian (AM, PhD); Jewish history and literature (AM, PhD); Persian (AM, PhD); Semitic philology (AM, PhD); Syro-Palestinian archaeology (AM, PhD); Turkish (AM, PhD). *Degree requirements:* For doctorate, variable foreign language requirement, thesis/dissertation, general exams. *Entrance requirements:* For master's, GRE General Test; for doctorate, GRE General Test, proficiency in a Near Eastern language. Additional exam requirements/recommendations for international students: Required—TOEFL.

**Hebrew Union College–Jewish Institute of Religion,** School of Graduate Studies, Program in Hebrew Letters, New York, NY 10012-1186. Offers DHL. *Degree requirements:* For doctorate, one foreign language, thesis/dissertation. *Entrance requirements:* For doctorate, GRE. Additional exam requirements/recommendations for international students: Required—TOEFL. *Expenses:* Contact institution. *Faculty research:* Philosophy and theology, Bible, Hebrew, pastoral care, history and Rabbinics.

**Houston Baptist University,** School of Christian Thought, Program in Biblical Languages, Houston, TX 77074-3298. Offers MA. *Students:* 3 full-time (0 women), 10 part-time (5 women); includes 3 minority (all Black or African American, non-Hispanic/Latino), 1 international. Average age 42. 15 applicants, 67% accepted, 4 enrolled. In 2016, 2 master's awarded. *Entrance requirements:* For master's, bachelor's degree conferred transcript, essay/personal statement, resume. Additional exam requirements/recommendations for international students: Required—TOEFL (minimum score 80 iBT), IELTS (minimum score 6.5). *Application deadline:* For fall admission, 8/1 for domestic students, 6/1 for international students; for spring admission, 1/1 for domestic students, 11/1 for international students; for summer admission, 5/1 for domestic students, 3/1 for international students. Applications are processed on a rolling basis. Application fee: $0 ($100 for international students). Electronic applications accepted. Application fee is waived when completed online. *Expenses:* $1,500 per 3-hour course; $1,275 annual general fee; $1,060 annual technology fee. *Financial support:* Federal Work-Study and scholarships/grants available. Financial award application deadline: 4/1. *Unit head:* Dr. Steven Jones, Chair, Fax: 281-649-3012, E-mail: sljones@hbu.edu. *Application contact:* Celeste Risteski, Administrative Assistant to the Dean, 281-649-3383, Fax: 281-649-3012, E-mail: cristeski@hbu.edu.

**Indiana University Bloomington,** University Graduate School, College of Arts and Sciences, School of Global and International Studies, Department of Near Eastern Languages and Cultures, Bloomington, IN 47405-7000. Offers MA, PhD. *Program availability:* Part-time. Terminal master's awarded for partial completion of doctoral program. *Degree requirements:* For master's, 2 foreign languages, comprehensive exam, thesis or alternative; for doctorate, 3 foreign languages, comprehensive exam, thesis/dissertation. *Entrance requirements:* For master's and doctorate, GRE General Test. Additional exam requirements/recommendations for international students: Required—TOEFL. Electronic applications accepted. *Faculty research:* Classical and modern Arabic literature and linguistics, Biblical and modern Hebrew studies, Persian language and literature, Islamic civilization, Iranian history and language.

**Johns Hopkins University,** Zanvyl Krieger School of Arts and Sciences, Department of Near Eastern Studies, Baltimore, MD 21218. Offers archaeology (PhD); Assyriology (PhD); Egyptology (PhD); Hebrew Bible/Northwest Semitics (PhD). *Degree requirements:* For doctorate, 2 foreign languages, comprehensive exam, thesis/dissertation. *Entrance requirements:* For doctorate, GRE. Additional exam requirements/recommendations for international students: Required—TOEFL (minimum score 600 paper-based; 100 iBT); Recommended—IELTS. Electronic applications accepted. *Faculty research:* Egyptology, Assyriology, Hebrew Bible/Northwest Semitic languages, Demotic Egyptian, archaeology.

## Near and Middle Eastern Languages

**Kent State University,** College of Arts and Sciences, Department of Modern and Classical Language Studies, Kent, OH 44242-0001. Offers French (MA), including applied linguistics and pedagogy, literature; Latin (MA), including applied linguistics and pedagogy, literature; Spanish (MA), including applied linguistics and pedagogy, literature; translation (MA), including Arabic, French, German, Japanese, Russian, Spanish; translation studies (PhD); MA/MBA. *Program availability:* Part-time. *Faculty:* 35 full-time (23 women). *Students:* 81 full-time (51 women), 23 part-time (15 women); includes 14 minority (1 Black or African American, non-Hispanic/Latino; 9 Hispanic/Latino; 4 Two or more races, non-Hispanic/Latino), 48 international. Average age 30. 109 applicants, 53% accepted, 33 enrolled. In 2016, 31 master's, 6 doctorates awarded. *Degree requirements:* For master's, variable foreign language requirement, comprehensive exam (for some programs), thesis (for some programs); for doctorate, variable foreign language requirement, comprehensive exam, thesis/dissertation. *Entrance requirements:* For master's, transcripts, goal statement, 3 letters of recommendation, CD/MP3 with oral sample of first and second languages, writing sample of second language; for doctorate, transcripts; MA in translation, a foreign language, or similar field; proficiency in a foreign language; minimum GPA of 3.5 from MA; goal statement; 3 letters of recommendation; essay or writing sample. *Application deadline:* For fall admission, 2/1 for domestic and international students. Applications are processed on a rolling basis. Application fee: $45 ($70 for international students). Electronic applications accepted. *Expenses:* Tuition, state resident: full-time $10,864; part-time $495 per credit hour. Tuition, nonresident: full-time $18,380; part-time $837 per credit hour. *Financial support:* Fellowships with full tuition reimbursements, teaching assistantships with full tuition reimbursements, and unspecified assistantships available. Financial award application deadline: 2/1. *Unit head:* Dr. Keiran Dunne, Professor of French Translation/Chair, 330-672-2150, E-mail: kdunne@kent.edu. *Application contact:* Said Shiyab, Professor of Translation Studies/Graduate Coordinator, 330-672-1864, E-mail: sshiyab@kent.edu.
Website: http://www.kent.edu/mcls/

**London Metropolitan University,** Graduate Programs, London, United Kingdom. Offers applied psychology (M Sc); architecture (MA); biomedical science (M Sc); blood science (M Sc); cancer pharmacology (M Sc); computer networking and cyber security (M Sc); computing and information systems (M Sc); conference interpreting (MA); counter-terrorism studies (M Sc); creative, digital and professional writing (MA); crime, violence and prevention (M Sc); criminology (M Sc); curating contemporary art (MA); data analytics (M Sc); digital media (MA); early childhood studies (MA); education (MA, Ed D); financial services law, regulation and compliance (LL M); food science (M Sc); forensic psychology (M Sc); health and social care management and policy (M Sc); human nutrition (M Sc); human resource management (MA); human rights and international conflict (MA); information technology (M Sc); intelligence and security studies (M Sc); international oil, gas and energy law (LL M); international relations (MA); interpreting (MA); learning and teaching in higher education (MA); legal practice (LL M); media and entertainment law (LL M); organizational and consumer psychology (M Sc); psychological therapy (M Sc); psychology of mental health (M Sc); public health (M Sc); public policy and management (MPA); security studies (M Sc); social work (M Sc); spatial planning and urban design (MA); sports therapy (M Sc); supporting older children and young people with dyslexia (MA); teaching languages (MA), including Arabic, English; translation (MA); woman and child abuse (MA).

**Middlebury College,** Language Schools, Arabic School, Middlebury, VT 05753-6002. Offers Arabic language pedagogy (MA); Arabic studies (MA). *Degree requirements:* For master's, one foreign language. *Entrance requirements:* For master's, Arabic language oral and written proficiency tests, 3 letters of recommendation, personal statement, transcripts, writing sample in Arabic, Arabic course history, 4 years or equivalent of Arabic language study. Additional exam requirements/recommendations for international students: Required—TOEFL (minimum score 100 iBT). Electronic applications accepted. *Expenses:* Contact institution.

**Middlebury College,** Language Schools, Hebrew School, Middlebury, VT 05753-6002. Offers MA. *Program availability:* Blended/hybrid learning. *Entrance requirements:* For master's, oral interview. Electronic applications accepted. *Expenses:* Contact institution.

**The Ohio State University,** Graduate School, College of Arts and Sciences, Division of Arts and Humanities, Department of Near Eastern Languages and Cultures, Columbus, OH 43210. Offers MA, PhD. *Faculty:* 14. *Students:* 17 full-time (7 women), 6 international. Average age 33. In 2016, 1 master's, 3 doctorates awarded. Terminal master's awarded for partial completion of doctoral program. *Degree requirements:* For master's, thesis optional. *Entrance requirements:* For master's and doctorate, GRE General Test, writing sample. Additional exam requirements/recommendations for international students: Required—TOEFL (minimum score 550 paper-based; 79 iBT), Michigan English Language Assessment Battery (minimum score 82); Recommended—IELTS (minimum score 7). *Application deadline:* For fall admission, 12/14 priority date for domestic students, 11/30 priority date for international students; for winter admission, 12/1 for domestic students, 11/1 for international students; for spring admission, 3/1 for domestic students, 2/1 for international students. Applications are processed on a rolling basis. Application fee: $60 ($70 for international students). Electronic applications accepted. *Financial support:* Fellowships with tuition reimbursements, research assistantships with tuition reimbursements, teaching assistantships with tuition reimbursements, Federal Work-Study, and institutionally sponsored loans available. Support available to part-time students. *Unit head:* Dr. Kevin van Bladel, Chair, 614-292-5643, E-mail: vanbladel.2@osu.edu. *Application contact:* Graduate and Professional Admissions, 614-292-9444, Fax: 614-292-3895, E-mail: gpadmissions@osu.edu.
Website: http://nelc.osu.edu/

**Oral Roberts University,** School of Theology and Missions, Tulsa, OK 74171. Offers biblical literature (MA), including advanced languages, Judaic-Christian studies; Christian counseling (MA), including marriage and family therapy; divinity (M Div); missions (MA); practical theology (MA); theological/historical studies (MA); theology (D Min). *Accreditation:* ATS. *Program availability:* Part-time, online learning. *Degree requirements:* For master's, thesis (for some programs), practicum/internship; for doctorate, thesis/dissertation, applied research project. *Entrance requirements:* For master's, GRE General Test or MAT, minimum GPA of 2.5; for doctorate, M Div, minimum GPA of 3.0, 3 years of full-time ministry experience. Additional exam requirements/recommendations for international students: Required—TOEFL (minimum score 550 paper-based; 79 iBT). Electronic applications accepted.

**University of California, Los Angeles,** Graduate Division, College of Letters and Science, Department of Near Eastern Languages and Cultures, Los Angeles, CA 90034. Offers MA, PhD. *Degree requirements:* For master's, one foreign language, comprehensive exam; for doctorate, 2 foreign languages, thesis/dissertation, oral and written qualifying exams. *Entrance requirements:* For master's, GRE General Test, bachelor's degree; minimum undergraduate GPA of 3.25 (or its equivalent if letter grade system not used); for doctorate, GRE General Test, master's degree; minimum undergraduate GPA of 3.25 (or its equivalent if letter grade system not used). Additional exam requirements/recommendations for international students: Required—TOEFL. Electronic applications accepted.

**University of Chicago,** Division of the Humanities, Department of Near Eastern Languages and Civilizations, Chicago, IL 60637. Offers PhD. *Students:* 119 full-time (43 women); includes 11 minority (3 Asian, non-Hispanic/Latino; 5 Hispanic/Latino; 3 Two or more races, non-Hispanic/Latino), 28 international. 120 applicants, 18% accepted, 15 enrolled. In 2016, 10 doctorates awarded. Terminal master's awarded for partial completion of doctoral program. *Degree requirements:* For doctorate, 2 foreign languages, comprehensive exam, thesis/dissertation. *Entrance requirements:* For doctorate, GRE General Test. Additional exam requirements/recommendations for international students: Required—TOEFL (minimum score 104 iBT), IELTS (minimum score 7). *Application deadline:* For fall admission, 12/15 for domestic and international students. Application fee: $90. Electronic applications accepted. *Financial support:* Fellowships with full tuition reimbursements, teaching assistantships with full tuition reimbursements, Federal Work-Study, institutionally sponsored loans, scholarships/grants, and health care benefits available. Financial award application deadline: 12/15; financial award applicants required to submit FAFSA. *Faculty research:* Archaeology and history of the ancient near East, Middle Eastern history and civilization, Semitic language and literature, Middle Eastern languages and literatures. *Unit head:* Dr. Frank Lewis, Chair, E-mail: flewis@uchicago.edu. *Application contact:* Michael Beetley, Assistant Dean of Students, Admissions and Fellowships, 773-702-1552, Fax: 773-834-9148, E-mail: humanitiesadmissions@uchicago.edu.
Website: http://nelc.uchicago.edu/

**The University of Manchester,** School of Languages, Linguistics and Cultures, Manchester, United Kingdom. Offers Arab world studies (PhD); Chinese studies (M Phil, PhD); East Asian studies (M Phil, PhD); English language (PhD); French studies (M Phil, PhD); German studies (M Phil, PhD); interpreting studies (M Phil, PhD); Italian studies (M Phil, PhD); Japanese studies (M Phil, PhD); Latin American cultural studies (M Phil, PhD); linguistics (M Phil, PhD); Middle Eastern studies (M Phil, PhD); Polish studies (M Phil, PhD); Portuguese studies (M Phil, PhD); Russian studies (M Phil, PhD); Spanish studies (M Phil, PhD); translation and intercultural studies (M Phil, PhD).

**University of Michigan,** Rackham Graduate School, College of Literature, Science, and the Arts, Department of Near Eastern Studies, Ann Arbor, MI 48109. Offers ancient Near Eastern studies (AM, PhD); Arabic for professional purposes (AM); Arabic language and literature (AM, PhD); Armenian studies (AM, PhD); Christianity in late antiquity (AM, PhD); Egyptology (AM, PhD); Hebrew Bible and ancient Israel (AM, PhD); Hebrew literature (AM, PhD); Islamic studies (AM, PhD); Jewish cultural studies (AM, PhD); Jewish mysticism (AM, PhD); Persian and Iranian studies (AM, PhD); Rabbinic literature (AM, PhD); Second Temple Judaism (AM, PhD); teaching Arabic as a foreign language (AM); Turkish studies (AM, PhD). *Faculty:* 27 full-time (8 women). *Students:* 28 full-time (12 women); includes 2 minority (1 Black or African American, non-Hispanic/Latino; 1 Asian, non-Hispanic/Latino), 10 international. Average age 32. 85 applicants, 8% accepted, 3 enrolled. In 2016, 4 master's, 3 doctorates awarded. Terminal master's awarded for partial completion of doctoral program. *Degree requirements:* For master's, 2 foreign languages; for doctorate, 4 foreign languages, comprehensive exam, thesis/dissertation, preliminary exams, oral defense of dissertation. *Entrance requirements:* Additional exam requirements/recommendations for international students: Required—TOEFL (minimum score 560 paper-based; 84 iBT), IELTS (minimum score 6.5). *Application deadline:* For fall admission, 12/1 for domestic and international students. Application fee: $75 ($90 for international students). Electronic applications accepted. *Expenses:* Tuition, state resident: full-time $21,466; part-time $1152 per credit hour. Tuition, nonresident: full-time $43,346; part-time $2367 per credit hour. Part-time tuition and fees vary according to course load, degree level and program. *Financial support:* In 2016–17, 28 students received support. Fellowships with full tuition reimbursements available, teaching assistantships with full tuition reimbursements available, scholarships/grants, health care benefits, unspecified assistantships, and spring/summer stipends available. Financial award application deadline: 12/1. *Faculty research:* Middle and Near Eastern literatures, languages, cultures from ancient times to the present. *Unit head:* Prof. Gottfried Hagen, Chair, 734-764-0314, E-mail: nes-chair@umich.edu. *Application contact:* Student Services, 734-764-0315, E-mail: nes-gradservices@umich.edu.
Website: http://www.lsa.umich.edu/neareast/

**University of South Africa,** College of Human Sciences, Pretoria, South Africa. Offers adult education (M Ed); African languages (MA, PhD); African politics (MA, PhD); Afrikaans (MA, PhD); ancient history (MA, PhD); ancient Near Eastern studies (MA, PhD); anthropology (MA, PhD); applied linguistics (MA); Arabic (MA, PhD); archaeology (MA); art history (MA); Biblical archaeology (MA); Biblical studies (M Th, D Th, PhD); Christian spirituality (M Th, D Th); church history (M Th, D Th); classical studies (MA, PhD); clinical psychology (MA); communication (MA, PhD); comparative education (M Ed, Ed D); consulting psychology (D Admin, D Com, PhD); curriculum studies (M Ed, Ed D); development studies (M Admin, MA, D Admin, PhD); didactics (M Ed, Ed D); education (M Tech); education management (M Ed, Ed D); educational psychology (M Ed); English (MA, PhD); environmental education (M Ed); French (MA, PhD); German (MA, PhD); Greek (MA); guidance and counseling (M Ed); health studies (MA, PhD), including health sciences education (MA), health services management (MA), medical and surgical nursing science (critical care general) (MA), midwifery and neonatal nursing science (MA), trauma and emergency care (MA); history (MA, PhD); history of education (Ed D); inclusive education (M Ed, Ed D); information and communications technology policy and regulation (MA); information science (MA, MIS, PhD); international politics (MA, PhD); Islamic studies (MA, PhD); Italian (MA, PhD); Judaica (MA, PhD); linguistics (MA, PhD); mathematical education (M Ed); mathematics education (MA); missiology (M Th, D Th); modern Hebrew (MA, PhD); musicology (MA, MMus, D Mus, PhD); natural science education (M Ed); New Testament (M Th, D Th); Old Testament (D Th); pastoral therapy (M Th, D Th); philosophy (MA); philosophy of education (M Ed, Ed D); politics (MA, PhD); Portuguese (MA, PhD); practical theology (M Th, D Th); psychology (MA, MS, PhD); psychology of education (M Ed, Ed D); public health (MA); religious studies (MA, D Th, PhD); Romance languages (MA, PhD); Russian (MA, PhD); Semitic languages (MA, PhD); social behavior studies in HIV/AIDS (MA); social science (mental health) (MA); social science in development studies (MA); social science in psychology (MA); social science in social work (MA); social science in sociology (MA); social work (MSW, DSW, PhD); socio-education (M Ed, Ed D); sociolinguistics (MA); sociology (MA, PhD); Spanish (MA, PhD); systematic theology (M Th, D Th); TESOL (teaching English to speakers of other languages) (MA); theological ethics (M Th, D Th); theory of literature (MA, PhD); urban ministries (D Th); urban ministry (M Th).

**The University of Texas at Austin,** Graduate School, College of Liberal Arts, Department of Middle Eastern Studies, Austin, TX 78712-1111. Offers Middle Eastern languages and cultures (MA, PhD); Middle Eastern studies (MA); JD/MA; MA/M Sc; MA/MA; MBA/MA; MPA/MA. *Degree requirements:* For master's, one foreign language, comprehensive exam, thesis; for doctorate, 2 foreign languages, comprehensive exam, thesis/dissertation. *Entrance requirements:* For master's and doctorate, GRE General Test. Additional exam requirements/recommendations for international students: Required—TOEFL. Electronic applications accepted. *Faculty research:* Islamic studies, Persian language and literature, Hebrew language, Jewish studies, Arabic literature and language.

**University of Utah,** Graduate School, College of Humanities, Program in Middle East Studies, Salt Lake City, UT 84112. Offers Arabic (MA, PhD); Hebrew (MA); history (MA, PhD); Persian (MA, PhD); political science (MA, PhD). *Students:* 3 part-time (2 women);

includes 1 minority (Asian, non-Hispanic/Latino), 1 international. In 2016, 2 master's awarded. Terminal master's awarded for partial completion of doctoral program. *Degree requirements:* For master's, 2 foreign languages, comprehensive exam, thesis optional; for doctorate, 3 foreign languages, comprehensive exam, thesis/dissertation. *Entrance requirements:* For master's, GRE General Test, minimum GPA of 3.2; for doctorate, GRE General Test, MA in Middle East studies or equivalent, minimum GPA of 3.2. Additional exam requirements/recommendations for international students: Required—TOEFL (minimum score 580 paper-based; 92 iBT); Recommended—IELTS (minimum score 7). *Application deadline:* For fall admission, 1/15 priority date for domestic and international students. Application fee: $55 ($65 for international students). Electronic applications accepted. *Expenses:* Tuition, state resident: full-time $7011; part-time $3918.24 per credit hour. Tuition, nonresident: full-time $22,154; part-time $11,665.42 per credit hour. *Financial support:* In 2016–17, 5 students received support, including 2 teaching assistantships with full tuition reimbursements available (averaging $13,500 per year); fellowships and unspecified assistantships also available. Financial award application deadline: 1/15. *Faculty research:* Islamic studies; Middle Eastern history; political science; Judaic studies; anthropology; Arabic, Persian, Hebrew, and Turkish language and literature. *Unit head:* Johanna Watzinger-Tharp, Director, 801-581-7148, Fax: 801-581-6105, E-mail: j.tharp@utah.edu. *Application contact:* Kellie Hubbard, Academic Advisor, 801-581-5362, Fax: 801-581-6105, E-mail: kellie.hubbard@utah.edu.
Website: http://www.mec.utah.edu

**University of Wisconsin–Madison,** Graduate School, College of Letters and Science, Department of Hebrew and Semitic Studies, Madison, WI 53706-1380. Offers MA, PhD. Terminal master's awarded for partial completion of doctoral program. *Degree requirements:* For master's, 2 foreign languages; for doctorate, thesis/dissertation. *Entrance requirements:* For master's and doctorate, GRE. Electronic applications accepted. *Faculty research:* Biblical language and literature, Northwest Semitic languages.

**Wayne State University,** College of Liberal Arts and Sciences, Department of Classical and Modern Languages, Literatures, and Cultures, Detroit, MI 48202. Offers classics (MA), including ancient Greek and Latin, ancient studies, classics, Latin; German (MA); language learning (MALL), including Arabic (MA, MALL), French (MA, MALL, PhD), German (MALL, PhD), Italian (MA, MALL), Spanish (MA, MALL, PhD); modern languages (PhD), including French (MA, MALL, PhD), German (MALL, PhD), Spanish

(MA, MALL, PhD); Near Eastern languages (MA), including Arabic (MA, MALL), Hebrew; Romance languages (MA), including French (MA, MALL, PhD), Italian (MA, MALL), Spanish (MA, MALL, PhD). *Faculty:* 26. *Students:* 25 full-time (20 women), 14 part-time (8 women); includes 7 minority (2 Black or African American, non-Hispanic/Latino; 1 American Indian or Alaska Native, non-Hispanic/Latino; 1 Asian, non-Hispanic/Latino; 2 Hispanic/Latino; 1 Two or more races, non-Hispanic/Latino), 3 international. Average age 35. 29 applicants, 31% accepted, 5 enrolled. In 2016, 15 master's, 5 doctorates awarded. *Degree requirements:* For master's, variable foreign language requirement, comprehensive exam (for some programs), thesis (for some programs); for doctorate, one foreign language, comprehensive exam, thesis/dissertation. *Entrance requirements:* For master's, GRE (for some programs); for doctorate, GRE. Additional exam requirements/recommendations for international students: Required—TOEFL (minimum score 550 paper-based; 79 iBT), TWE (minimum score 5.5), Michigan English Language Assessment Battery (minimum score 85); Recommended—IELTS (minimum score 6.5). Application fee: $50. Electronic applications accepted. *Expenses:* $16,503 per year resident tuition and fees, $33,697 per year non-resident tuition and fees. *Financial support:* In 2016–17, 22 students received support, including 4 fellowships with tuition reimbursements available (averaging $13,500 per year), 17 teaching assistantships with tuition reimbursements available (averaging $17,994 per year); research assistantships, scholarships/grants, and unspecified assistantships also available. Financial award applicants required to submit FAFSA. *Faculty research:* Classical and modern literature and culture (Greek, Latin, Arabic, Chinese, French, German, Russian, Spanish) including colonial studies and exile and Holocaust studies; critical theory (French, German, Slavic, Spanish); theoretical and applied linguistics (Arabic, Chinese, French, Spanish); area studies (Arabic, Near Eastern, classical, Islamic, and Judaic studies). *Unit head:* Dr. Anne Duggan, Department Chair, 313-577-6244, Fax: 313-577-6243, E-mail: a.duggan@wayne.edu.
Website: http://clas.wayne.edu/languages/

**Yale University,** Graduate School of Arts and Sciences, Department of Near Eastern Languages and Civilizations, New Haven, CT 06520. Offers Arabic and Islamic studies (MA, PhD); archaeology of the ancient Near East (MA, PhD); Assyriology (MA, PhD); Egyptology (MA, PhD); Graeco-Arabic studies (MA, PhD); Northwest Semitic, Bible, comparative Semitics (MA, PhD). *Degree requirements:* For doctorate, 2 foreign languages, thesis/dissertation. *Entrance requirements:* For doctorate, GRE General Test.

# Portuguese

**Brigham Young University,** Graduate Studies, College of Humanities, Department of Spanish and Portuguese, Provo, UT 84602. Offers Portuguese (MA), including Luso-Brazilian literatures, Portuguese linguistics, Portuguese pedagogy; Spanish (MA), including Hispanic linguistics, Hispanic literatures, Spanish pedagogy. *Faculty:* 31 full-time (6 women). *Students:* 20 full-time (9 women), 15 part-time (9 women); includes 12 minority (all Hispanic/Latino). Average age 32. 19 applicants, 79% accepted, 12 enrolled. In 2016, 9 master's awarded. *Degree requirements:* For master's, 2 foreign languages, comprehensive exam, thesis, 1 semester of teaching. *Entrance requirements:* For master's, minimum GPA of 3.5 in Spanish or Portuguese, 3.3 overall. Additional exam requirements/recommendations for international students: Required—TOEFL (minimum score 580 paper-based; 85 iBT). *Application deadline:* For fall admission, 2/1 for domestic and international students. Application fee: $50. Electronic applications accepted. *Expenses:* Contact institution. *Financial support:* In 2016–17, 25 students received support, including 7 research assistantships (averaging $1,895 per year), 81 teaching assistantships (averaging $3,200 per year); institutionally sponsored loans, scholarships/grants, tuition waivers (partial), and unspecified assistantships also available. Support available to part-time students. *Faculty research:* Mexican prose; Latin American theater, literature, phonetics, and phonology; pedagogy; classical Portuguese literature; Peninsular prose and theater. *Unit head:* Dr. David P. Laraway, Chair, 801-422-3807, Fax: 801-422-0628, E-mail: david_laraway@byu.edu. *Application contact:* Jessica C. Erickson, Graduate Program Manager, 801-422-2196, Fax: 801-422-0628, E-mail: jessica_erickson@byu.edu.
Website: http://spanport.byu.edu/

**Emory University,** Laney Graduate School, Department of Spanish and Portuguese, Atlanta, GA 30322-1100. Offers comparative literature (Certificate); film studies (Certificate); Spanish (PhD); women's studies (Certificate). *Degree requirements:* For doctorate, 2 foreign languages, comprehensive exam, thesis/dissertation. *Entrance requirements:* For doctorate, GRE General Test. Additional exam requirements/recommendations for international students: Required—TOEFL. Electronic applications accepted. *Faculty research:* Spanish literature, Spanish American literature, literary theory, criticism, cultural studies.

**Harvard University,** Graduate School of Arts and Sciences, Department of Romance Languages and Literatures, Cambridge, MA 02138. Offers French (AM, PhD); Italian (AM, PhD); Portuguese (AM, PhD); Spanish (AM, PhD). Terminal master's awarded for partial completion of doctoral program. *Degree requirements:* For master's, 2 foreign languages; for doctorate, 2 foreign languages, thesis/dissertation. *Entrance requirements:* For master's and doctorate, GRE General Test, sample of written work. Additional exam requirements/recommendations for international students: Required—TOEFL.

**Indiana University Bloomington,** University Graduate School, College of Arts and Sciences, Department of Spanish and Portuguese, Bloomington, IN 47405. Offers Portuguese (MA, PhD); Spanish (MA, PhD), including Hispanic linguistics, Hispanic literatures. *Faculty:* 22 full-time, 26 part-time/adjunct. *Students:* 84 full-time (47 women); includes 20 minority (19 Hispanic/Latino; 1 Two or more races, non-Hispanic/Latino), 19 international. Average age 30. 72 applicants, 43% accepted, 15 enrolled. In 2016, 7 master's, 8 doctorates awarded. *Degree requirements:* For master's, one foreign language, comprehensive exam, thesis (for Spanish); for doctorate, 2 foreign languages, comprehensive exam, thesis/dissertation. *Entrance requirements:* For master's, GRE General Test, bachelor's degree in Portuguese or Spanish, minimum GPA of 3.0; for doctorate, GRE General Test, master's degree in Portuguese or Spanish, minimum GPA of 3.0. Additional exam requirements/recommendations for international students: Required—TOEFL (minimum score 79 iBT). *Application deadline:* For fall admission, 1/15 priority date for domestic students, 12/1 priority date for international students. Application fee: $55 ($65 for international students). Electronic applications accepted. *Financial support:* Application deadline: 1/15. *Faculty research:* Spanish American literature, Spanish peninsular literature, Hispanic linguistics, Luso-Brazilian studies, Catalan studies. *Unit head:* Steven Wagschal, Chair, 812-855-8498, E-mail: swagscha@indiana.edu. *Application contact:* Patrick Dove, Director of Graduate

Studies, 812-855-9194, E-mail: pdove@indiana.edu.
Website: http://www.indiana.edu/~spanport/

**Michigan State University,** The Graduate School, College of Arts and Letters, Department of Spanish and Portuguese, East Lansing, MI 48824. Offers applied Spanish linguistics (MA); Hispanic cultural studies (PhD); Hispanic literatures (MA). *Entrance requirements:* Additional exam requirements/recommendations for international students: Required—TOEFL. Electronic applications accepted.

**New York University,** Graduate School of Arts and Science, Department of Spanish and Portuguese Languages and Literatures, New York, NY 10012-1019. Offers Portuguese (MA, PhD); Spanish (PhD); Spanish and Latin American literatures and cultures (MA); Spanish language and translation (MA). *Program availability:* Part-time. *Degree requirements:* For master's, 2 foreign languages, thesis; for doctorate, 2 foreign languages, thesis/dissertation. *Entrance requirements:* For master's, GRE General Test; for doctorate, GRE General Test, master's degree. Additional exam requirements/recommendations for international students: Required—TOEFL. *Faculty research:* Gender and sexuality, transatlantic studies, literacy and cultural theories, Colonial and Post-Colonial studies, autobiography and modern subjectivities.

**Northwestern University,** The Graduate School, Judd A. and Marjorie Weinberg College of Arts and Sciences, Department of Spanish and Portuguese, Evanston, IL 60208. Offers PhD.

**The Ohio State University,** Graduate School, College of Arts and Sciences, Division of Arts and Humanities, Department of Spanish and Portuguese, Columbus, OH 43210. Offers MA, PhD. *Faculty:* 25. *Students:* 63 full-time (35 women), 1 (woman) part-time; includes 9 minority (all Hispanic/Latino), 27 international. Average age 30. In 2016, 9 master's, 14 doctorates awarded. Terminal master's awarded for partial completion of doctoral program. *Degree requirements:* For master's, thesis optional; for doctorate, thesis/dissertation. *Entrance requirements:* For master's and doctorate, GRE General Test, sample of academic writing. Additional exam requirements/recommendations for international students: Required—TOEFL (minimum score 550 paper-based; 79 iBT), Michigan English Language Assessment Battery (minimum score 82); Recommended—IELTS (minimum score 7). *Application deadline:* For fall admission, 12/13 priority date for domestic students, 11/30 priority date for international students; for spring admission, 3/1 for domestic students, 2/1 for international students. Applications are processed on a rolling basis. Application fee: $60 ($70 for international students). Electronic applications accepted. *Financial support:* Fellowships, research assistantships, teaching assistantships, Federal Work-Study, institutionally sponsored loans, and unspecified assistantships available. Support available to part-time students. *Unit head:* Dr. Eugenia Romero, Interim Chair and Professor, 614-247-6179, E-mail: spanport@osu.edu. *Application contact:* Graduate and Professional Admissions, 614-292-9444, Fax: 614-292-3895, E-mail: gpadmissions@osu.edu.
Website: http://sppo.osu.edu/

**Princeton University,** Graduate School, Department of Spanish and Portuguese Languages and Cultures, Princeton, NJ 08544-1019. Offers PhD. *Degree requirements:* For doctorate, variable foreign language requirement, thesis/dissertation. *Entrance requirements:* For doctorate, GRE General Test, sample of written work. Additional exam requirements/recommendations for international students: Required—TOEFL (minimum score 600 paper-based). Electronic applications accepted.

**Tulane University,** School of Liberal Arts, Department of Spanish and Portuguese, New Orleans, LA 70118-5669. Offers Portuguese (MA); Spanish and Portuguese (PhD). *Degree requirements:* For master's, 2 foreign languages; for doctorate, 2 foreign languages, thesis/dissertation. *Entrance requirements:* For master's, GRE General Test, minimum B average in undergraduate course work; for doctorate, GRE General Test. Additional exam requirements/recommendations for international students: Required—TOEFL. Electronic applications accepted. *Expenses:* Tuition: Full-time $50,920; part-time $2829 per credit hour. *Required fees:* $2040; $44.50 per credit hour. $580 per term. Tuition and fees vary according to course load, degree level and program.

## Portuguese

**University of California, Los Angeles,** Graduate Division, College of Letters and Science, Department of Spanish and Portuguese, Program in Portuguese, Los Angeles, CA 90095. Offers MA. *Degree requirements:* For master's, one foreign language, comprehensive exam or thesis. *Entrance requirements:* For master's, GRE General Test, bachelor's degree; minimum undergraduate GPA of 3.0 (or its equivalent if letter grade system not used). Additional exam requirements/recommendations for international students: Required—TOEFL. Electronic applications accepted.

**University of California, Santa Barbara,** Graduate Division, College of Letters and Sciences, Division of Humanities and Fine Arts, Department of Spanish and Portuguese, Santa Barbara, CA 93106-4150. Offers Hispanic languages and literatures (PhD), including European medieval studies, feminist studies, Hispanic linguistics, Hispanic literature, Luso-Brazilian literature; Hispanic linguistics (MA); Luso-Brazilian literature (MA); Spanish or Spanish-American literature (MA); MA/PhD. Terminal master's awarded for partial completion of doctoral program. *Degree requirements:* For master's, 2 foreign languages, comprehensive exam (for some programs), thesis optional; for doctorate, 3 foreign languages, comprehensive exam, thesis/dissertation. *Entrance requirements:* For master's and doctorate, GRE. Additional exam requirements/recommendations for international students: Required—TOEFL (minimum score 550 paper-based; 80 iBT), IELTS (minimum score 7). Electronic applications accepted. *Faculty research:* Nineteenth-century Spanish and Portuguese literature, Spanish and Spanish-American literature, nineteenth- and twentieth-century Portuguese and Brazilian literatures, Hispanic linguistics, Catalan language and culture.

**University of Georgia,** Franklin College of Arts and Sciences, Department of Romance Languages, Athens, GA 30602. Offers French (PhD); Italian (MA, PhD); Portuguese (MA, PhD); romance linguistics (MA); Spanish (PhD). *Degree requirements:* For master's, one foreign language; for doctorate, 2 foreign languages, thesis/dissertation. *Entrance requirements:* For master's and doctorate, GRE General Test. *Application deadline:* For fall admission, 7/1 priority date for domestic students; for spring admission, 11/15 for domestic students. Application fee: $50. Electronic applications accepted. *Financial support:* Fellowships, research assistantships, teaching assistantships, and unspecified assistantships available. *Unit head:* Dr. Staccy Casado, Department Head, 706-542-2364, Fax: 706-542-2272, E-mail: sdcasado@uga.edu. *Application contact:* Rachel Gabara, Graduate Coordinator, 706-542-8930, E-mail: romlgradcoord@uga.edu.
Website: http://www.rom.uga.edu/

**University of Illinois at Urbana–Champaign,** Graduate College, College of Liberal Arts and Sciences, School of Literatures, Cultures and Linguistics, Department of Spanish, Italian and Portuguese, Champaign, IL 61820. Offers Italian (MA, PhD); Portuguese (MA, PhD); Spanish (MA, PhD).

**University of Maryland, College Park,** Academic Affairs, College of Arts and Humanities, School of Languages, Literatures, and Cultures, Spanish Language and Literatures Program, College Park, MD 20742. Offers MA, PhD. *Degree requirements:* For master's, comprehensive exam, thesis optional, scholarly paper; for doctorate, 2 foreign languages, thesis/dissertation. *Entrance requirements:* For master's, minimum GPA of 3.0, interview, sample research paper, minimum of 12 credits in upper-level literature, 3 letters of recommendation; for doctorate, minimum GPA of 3.0, interview, sample research paper, minimum of 12 credits in upper-level literature. Additional exam requirements/recommendations for international students: Required—TOEFL. Electronic applications accepted.

**University of Massachusetts Amherst,** Graduate School, College of Humanities and Fine Arts, Department of Languages, Literatures, and Cultures, Program in Spanish and Portuguese Studies, Amherst, MA 01003. Offers Hispanic literatures, cultures and linguistics (MA, PhD); teaching Spanish (MAT). *Program availability:* Part-time. Terminal master's awarded for partial completion of doctoral program. *Degree requirements:* For master's, one foreign language, thesis or alternative; for doctorate, 2 foreign languages, comprehensive exam, thesis/dissertation. *Entrance requirements:* For master's and doctorate, GRE General Test, sample academic term paper. Additional exam requirements/recommendations for international students: Required—TOEFL (minimum score 550 paper-based; 80 iBT), IELTS (minimum score 6.5). Electronic applications accepted.

**University of Massachusetts Dartmouth,** Graduate School, College of Arts and Sciences, Department of Portuguese, North Dartmouth, MA 02747-2300. Offers Luso-Afro Brazilian studies and theory (PhD); Portuguese (MA). *Program availability:* Part-time. *Faculty:* 5 full-time (2 women), 1 part-time/adjunct (0 women). *Students:* 7 full-time (5 women), 7 part-time (6 women); includes 7 minority (1 Black or African American, non-Hispanic/Latino; 1 Asian, non-Hispanic/Latino; 4 Hispanic/Latino; 1 Two or more races, non-Hispanic/Latino), 3 international. Average age 37. 7 applicants, 43% accepted, 1 enrolled. In 2016, 2 master's, 1 doctorate awarded. Terminal master's awarded for partial completion of doctoral program. *Degree requirements:* For master's, comprehensive exam or project; for doctorate, comprehensive exam, thesis/dissertation. *Entrance requirements:* For master's, GRE (recommended), statement of purpose (minimum of 300 words), resume, 3 letters of recommendation, official transcripts, writing samples in Portuguese (minimum of 10 pages); for doctorate, GRE (recommended), statement of purpose (minimum of 300 words), resume, 3 letters of recommendation, official transcripts, scholarly writing sample (minimum of 10 pages). Additional exam requirements/recommendations for international students: Required—TOEFL (minimum score 533 paper-based; 72 iBT). *Application deadline:* For fall admission, 2/1 priority date for domestic students, 1/1 priority date for international students; for spring admission, 12/1 priority date for domestic students, 11/1 priority date for international students. Application fee: $60. Electronic applications accepted. *Expenses:* Tuition, state resident: full-time $14,994; part-time $624.75 per credit. Tuition, nonresident: full-time $27,068; part-time $1127.83 per credit. *Required fees:* $405; $25.88 per credit. Tuition and fees vary according to course load and reciprocity agreements. *Financial support:* In 2016–17, 9 fellowships (averaging $19,333 per year) were awarded; institutionally sponsored loans and scholarships/grants also available. Support available to part-time students. Financial award application deadline: 3/1; financial award applicants required to submit FAFSA. *Faculty research:* Literature in Luso-Afro-Brazilian studies, literary and cultural theory, studies in ethnicity and migration, bi- and multi-lingualism, gender studies, translation studies. *Total annual research expenditures:* $354,000. *Unit head:* Victor Mendes, Director of Graduate Studies, Department of Portuguese, 508-999-8338, Fax: 508-910-9272, E-mail: vmendes@umassd.edu. *Application contact:* Steven Briggs, Director of Marketing and Recruitment for Graduate Studies, 508-999-8604, Fax: 508-999-8183, E-mail: graduate@umassd.edu.
Website: http://www.umassd.edu/portgrad/

**University of Minnesota, Twin Cities Campus,** Graduate School, College of Liberal Arts, Department of Spanish and Portuguese Studies, Minneapolis, MN 55455-0213. Offers Hispanic and Lusophone literatures, cultures and linguistics (PhD); Hispanic linguistics (MA); Hispanic literature (MA); Lusophone literature (MA). *Degree requirements:* For master's, 2 foreign languages, comprehensive exam, thesis or alternative; for doctorate, 2 foreign languages, comprehensive exam, thesis/dissertation. *Entrance requirements:* For master's and doctorate, GRE General Test, samples of

written work, 3 letters of recommendation, voice sample, statement of purpose. Additional exam requirements/recommendations for international students: Required—TOEFL (minimum score 550 paper-based; 79 iBT). Electronic applications accepted. *Faculty research:* Sociohistorical approaches to literature and culture, feminist studies, literary theory, ideologies and literature, pragmatics and sociolinguistics.

**University of New Mexico,** Graduate Studies, College of Arts and Sciences, Program in Spanish and Portuguese, Albuquerque, NM 87131. Offers Portuguese (MA); Spanish (MA); Spanish and Portuguese (PhD). *Program availability:* Part-time. *Faculty:* 14 full-time (7 women). *Students:* 38 full-time (21 women), 17 part-time (8 women); includes 30 minority (all Hispanic/Latino), 15 international. Average age 33. 43 applicants, 65% accepted, 25 enrolled. In 2016, 13 master's, 3 doctorates awarded. *Degree requirements:* For master's, one foreign language, comprehensive exam, thesis optional; for doctorate, one foreign language, comprehensive exam, thesis/dissertation. *Entrance requirements:* For master's, BA in Spanish or Portuguese, 3 letters of recommendation, letter of intent; for doctorate, GRE, 3 letters of recommendation, letter of intent, sample research paper. Additional exam requirements/recommendations for international students: Required—TOEFL (minimum score 550 paper-based). *Application deadline:* For fall admission, 1/15 priority date for domestic students; for spring admission, 11/15 for domestic students. Applications are processed on a rolling basis. Application fee: $50. Electronic applications accepted. *Financial support:* Research assistantships, teaching assistantships with tuition reimbursements, Federal Work-Study, institutionally sponsored loans, scholarships/grants, health care benefits, and unspecified assistantships available. Support available to part-time students. Financial award application deadline: 3/1; financial award applicants required to submit FAFSA. *Faculty research:* Languages and literatures from the Iberian Peninsula, Latin America and the American Southwest. *Unit head:* Dr. Anthony Cardenas, Chair, 505-277-5907, Fax: 505-277-3885, E-mail: ajcard@unm.edu. *Application contact:* Martha Hurd, Graduate Advisor, 505-277-2974, E-mail: marthah@unm.edu.
Website: http://spanport.unm.edu

**The University of North Carolina at Chapel Hill,** Graduate School, College of Arts and Sciences, Department of Romance Languages and Literatures, Chapel Hill, NC 27599. Offers French (MA, PhD); Italian (MA, PhD); Portuguese (MA, PhD); Romance languages (MA, PhD); Romance philology (MA, PhD); Spanish (MA, PhD). *Degree requirements:* For master's, one foreign language, comprehensive exam, thesis; for doctorate, 2 foreign languages, comprehensive exam, thesis/dissertation. *Entrance requirements:* For master's and doctorate, GRE General Test, minimum GPA of 3.0. Additional exam requirements/recommendations for international students: Required—TOEFL (minimum score 550 paper-based). Electronic applications accepted.

**University of South Africa,** College of Human Sciences, Pretoria, South Africa. Offers adult education (M Ed); African languages (MA, PhD); African politics (MA, PhD); Afrikaans (MA, PhD); ancient history (MA, PhD); ancient Near Eastern studies (MA, PhD); anthropology (MA, PhD); applied linguistics (MA); Arabic (MA, PhD); archaeology (MA); art history (MA); Biblical archaeology (MA); Biblical studies (M Th, D Th, PhD); Christian spirituality (M Th, D Th); church history (M Th, D Th); classical studies (MA, PhD); clinical psychology (MA, PhD); communication (MA, PhD); comparative education (M Ed, Ed D); consulting psychology (D Admin, D Com, PhD); curriculum studies (M Ed, Ed D); development studies (M Admin, MA, D Admin, PhD); didactics (M Ed, Ed D); education (M Tech); education management (M Ed, Ed D); educational psychology (M Ed); English (MA); environmental education (M Ed); French (MA, PhD); German (MA, PhD); Greek (MA); guidance and counseling (M Ed); health studies (MA, PhD), including health sciences education (MA), health services management (MA), medical and surgical nursing science (critical care general) (MA), midwifery and neonatal nursing science (MA), trauma and emergency care (MA); history (MA, PhD); history of education (Ed D); inclusive education (M Ed, Ed D); information and communications technology policy and regulation (MA); information science (MA, MIS, PhD); international politics (MA, PhD); Islamic studies (MA, PhD); Italian (MA, PhD); Judaica (MA, PhD); linguistics (MA, PhD); mathematical education (M Ed); mathematics education (MA); missiology (M Th, D Th); modern Hebrew (MA, PhD); musicology (MA, MMus, D Mus, PhD); natural science education (M Ed); New Testament (M Th, D Th); Old Testament (D Th); pastoral therapy (M Th, D Th); philosophy (MA); philosophy of education (M Ed, Ed D); politics (MA, PhD); Portuguese (MA, PhD); practical theology (M Th, D Th); psychology (MA, MS, PhD); psychology of education (M Ed, Ed D); public health (MA); religious studies (MA, D Th, PhD); Romance languages (MA, PhD); Russian (MA, PhD); Semitic languages (MA, PhD); social behavior studies in HIV/AIDS (MA); social science (mental health) (MA); social science in development studies (MA); social science in psychology (MA); social science in social work (MA); social science in sociology (MA); social work (MSW, DSW, PhD); socio-education (M Ed, Ed D); sociolinguistics (MA); sociology (MA, PhD); Spanish (MA, PhD); systematic theology (M Th, D Th); TESOL (teaching English to speakers of other languages) (MA); theological ethics (M Th, D Th); theory of literature (MA, PhD); urban ministries (D Th); urban ministry (M Th).

**The University of Tennessee,** Graduate School, College of Arts and Sciences, Department of Modern Foreign Languages and Literatures, Program in Modern Foreign Languages, Knoxville, TN 37996. Offers applied linguistics (PhD); French (PhD); German (PhD); Italian (PhD); Portuguese (PhD); Russian (PhD); Spanish (PhD). *Degree requirements:* For doctorate, 2 foreign languages, thesis/dissertation. *Entrance requirements:* For doctorate, minimum GPA of 2.7. Additional exam requirements/recommendations for international students: Required—TOEFL. Electronic applications accepted.

**The University of Texas at Austin,** Graduate School, College of Liberal Arts, Department of Spanish and Portuguese, Austin, TX 78712-1111. Offers Hispanic linguistics (MA, PhD); Hispanic literature (MA, PhD); Ibero-romance philology and linguistics (PhD); Luso-Brazilian literature (MA, PhD). *Degree requirements:* For master's, 2 foreign languages, thesis or alternative; for doctorate, 3 foreign languages, thesis/dissertation. *Entrance requirements:* For master's and doctorate, GRE General Test. Electronic applications accepted.

**University of Toronto,** School of Graduate Studies, Faculty of Arts and Science, Department of Spanish and Portuguese, Toronto, ON M5S 1A1, Canada. Offers MA, PhD. *Program availability:* Part-time. *Degree requirements:* For doctorate, thesis/dissertation. *Entrance requirements:* For master's, minimum B average in final year, 2 letters of reference; for doctorate, minimum A- average, 2 letters of reference, writing sample. Additional exam requirements/recommendations for international students: Required—TWE (minimum score 5), TOEFL, Michigan English Language Assessment Battery, IELTS, or COPE. Electronic applications accepted.

**University of Washington,** Graduate School, College of Arts and Sciences, Division of Spanish and Portuguese Studies, Seattle, WA 98195. Offers Hispanic literary and cultural studies (MA). *Degree requirements:* For master's, 2 foreign languages, thesis optional, exam. *Entrance requirements:* For master's, GRE General Test, minimum GPA of 3.0. Additional exam requirements/recommendations for international students: Required—TOEFL. Electronic applications accepted. *Faculty research:* Medieval through modern Spanish literature and film, Latin American literature, poetry and essay, pan-Hispanic ballad, Hispanic cultural studies, second language acquisition and applied linguistics.

**University of Wisconsin–Madison,** Graduate School, College of Letters and Science, Department of Spanish and Portuguese, Program in Portuguese, Madison, WI 53706-1380. Offers MA, PhD. *Degree requirements:* For master's, one foreign language; for doctorate, 2 foreign languages, thesis/dissertation. *Entrance requirements:* For master's, GRE (recommended), minimum GPA of 3.25 in Spanish or Portuguese; for doctorate, GRE (recommended), minimum graduate GPA of 3.4. Additional exam requirements/recommendations for international students: Required—TOEFL. Electronic applications accepted. *Faculty research:* Portuguese and Brazilian literature.

**University of Wisconsin–Milwaukee,** Graduate School, College of Letters and Science, Department of Spanish and Portuguese, Milwaukee, WI 53201-0413. Offers MA. *Students:* 8 full-time (4 women), 4 part-time (3 women); includes 1 minority (Two or more races, non-Hispanic/Latino), 7 international. Average age 28. 17 applicants, 71% accepted, 7 enrolled. In 2016, 5 master's awarded. *Entrance requirements:* For master's, bachelor's degree. *Application deadline:* Applications are processed on a rolling basis. Application fee: $56 ($96 for international students). Electronic applications accepted. *Financial support:* In 2016–17, 12 teaching assistantships were awarded; fellowships, research assistantships, and unspecified assistantships also available. Financial award applicants required to submit FAFSA. *Faculty research:* Sociolinguistics, Spanish-American literature, Spanish literature, Hispanic culture, Hispanic historiography. *Unit head:* John McCaw, Department Chair, 414-229-4257, E-mail: rjmccaw@uwm.edu. *Application contact:* General Information Contact, 414-229-4982, Fax: 414-229-6967, E-mail: gradschool@uwm.edu.
Website: https://uwm.edu/spanish-portuguese/

**Vanderbilt University,** Department of Spanish and Portuguese, Nashville, TN 37240-1001. Offers Portuguese (MA); Spanish (MA, MAT, PhD); Spanish and Portuguese (PhD). *Faculty:* 13 full-time (6 women). *Students:* 25 full-time (11 women); includes 5 minority (all Hispanic/Latino), 11 international. Average age 31. 39 applicants, 31% accepted, 7 enrolled. In 2016, 2 master's, 3 doctorates awarded. *Degree requirements:* For master's, one foreign language, thesis; for doctorate, 2 foreign languages, thesis/dissertation, final and qualifying exams. *Entrance requirements:* For master's, GRE General Test; for doctorate, GRE General Test, writing sample in Spanish. Additional exam requirements/recommendations for international students: Required—TOEFL (minimum score 570 paper-based; 88 iBT). *Application deadline:* For fall admission, 1/15 for domestic and international students. Electronic applications accepted. *Expenses: Tuition:* Part-time $1854 per credit hour. *Financial support:* Fellowships with tuition reimbursements, teaching assistantships with full tuition reimbursements, Federal Work-Study, institutionally sponsored loans, and health care benefits available. Financial award application deadline: 1/15; financial award applicants required to submit CSS PROFILE or FAFSA. *Faculty research:* Spanish, Portuguese, and Latin American literatures; foreign language pedagogy; Renaissance and Baroque poetry; nineteenth-century Spanish novel. *Unit head:* Dr. Benigno Trigo, Chair, 615-322-6930, Fax: 615-343-7260, E-mail: benigno.trigo@vanderbilt.edu. *Application contact:* Andres Zamora, Director of Graduate Studies, 615-322-6930, Fax: 615-343-7260, E-mail: andres.zamora@vanderbilt.edu.
Website: http://as.vanderbilt.edu/spanish-portuguese/graduate/index.php

**Yale University,** Graduate School of Arts and Sciences, Department of Spanish and Portuguese, New Haven, CT 06520. Offers Latin American literature (PhD); Luso-Brazilian and Spanish/Spanish American literatures (PhD); Spanish peninsular literature (PhD). Terminal master's awarded for partial completion of doctoral program. *Degree requirements:* For doctorate, 3 foreign languages, thesis/dissertation. *Entrance requirements:* For doctorate, GRE General Test.

# Romance Languages

**Boston University,** Graduate School of Arts and Sciences, Department of Romance Studies, Boston, MA 02215. Offers French language and literature (MA, PhD); Hispanic language and literatures (MA, PhD). *Students:* 40 full-time (27 women), 1 part-time (0 women); includes 8 minority (1 Black or African American, non-Hispanic/Latino; 7 Hispanic/Latino), 12 international. Average age 32. 49 applicants, 35% accepted, 6 enrolled. In 2016, 3 master's, 6 doctorates awarded. Terminal master's awarded for partial completion of doctoral program. *Degree requirements:* For master's, one foreign language, comprehensive exam; for doctorate, 2 foreign languages, comprehensive exam, thesis/dissertation. *Entrance requirements:* For master's and doctorate, GRE General Test, sample of written work, 3 letters of recommendation, transcripts, personal statement, summary of related coursework. Additional exam requirements/recommendations for international students: Required—TOEFL (minimum score 550 paper-based; 84 iBT). *Application deadline:* For fall admission, 1/15 for domestic and international students. Application fee: $95. Electronic applications accepted. *Financial support:* In 2016–17, 36 students received support, including 6 fellowships with full tuition reimbursements available (averaging $21,500 per year), 25 teaching assistantships with full tuition reimbursements available (averaging $21,500 per year); Federal Work-Study, scholarships/grants, and health care benefits also available. Financial award application deadline: 1/15. *Unit head:* Odile Cazenave, Chair, 617-353-6225, Fax: 617-353-6246, E-mail: cazenave@bu.edu. *Application contact:* Deanna Wong, Administrative Assistant, 617-353-2641, Fax: 617-353-6246, E-mail: dswong@bu.edu.
Website: http://www.bu.edu/rs/

**Clark Atlanta University,** School of Arts and Sciences, Department of Foreign Languages, Atlanta, GA 30314. Offers Romance languages (MA, DAH). *Program availability:* Part-time. *Faculty:* 2 full-time (1 woman). *Students:* 1 (woman) full-time, 2 part-time (both women); all minorities (all Black or African American, non-Hispanic/Latino). Average age 45. *Degree requirements:* For master's, one foreign language, thesis; for doctorate, 2 foreign languages, comprehensive exam, thesis/dissertation. *Entrance requirements:* For master's, GRE General Test, minimum GPA of 2.5. Additional exam requirements/recommendations for international students: Required—TOEFL (minimum score 500 paper-based; 61 iBT). *Application deadline:* For fall admission, 4/1 for domestic and international students; for spring admission, 11/1 for domestic and international students. Applications are processed on a rolling basis. Application fee: $40 ($55 for international students). *Expenses: Tuition:* Full-time $15,498; part-time $861 per credit hour. *Required fees:* $1326; $1326 per credit hour. Tuition and fees vary according to course load. *Financial support:* Scholarships/grants and unspecified assistantships available. Financial award application deadline: 4/30; financial award applicants required to submit FAFSA. *Unit head:* Dr. Laurent Monye, Chairperson, 404-880-8547, E-mail: lmonye@cau.edu. *Application contact:* Graduate Program Admissions, 404-880-8483, E-mail: graduateadmissions@cau.edu.

**Columbia University,** Graduate School of Arts and Sciences, New York, NY 10027. Offers African-American studies (MA); American studies (MA); anthropology (MA, PhD); art history and archaeology (MA, PhD); astronomy (PhD); biological sciences (PhD); biotechnology (MA); chemical physics (PhD); chemistry (PhD); classical studies (MA, PhD); classics (MA, PhD); climate and society (MA); conservation biology (MA); earth and environmental sciences (PhD); East Asia: regional studies (MA); East Asian languages and cultures (MA, PhD); ecology, evolution and environmental biology (MA), including conservation biology; ecology, evolution, and environmental biology (PhD), including ecology and evolutionary biology, evolutionary primatology; economics (MA, PhD); English and comparative literature (MA, PhD); French and Romance philology (MA, PhD); Germanic languages (MA, PhD); global French studies (MA); global thought (MA); Hispanic cultural studies (MA); history (PhD); history and literature (MA); human rights studies (MA); Islamic studies (MA); Italian (MA, PhD); Japanese pedagogy (MA); Jewish studies (MA); Latin America and the Caribbean: regional studies (MA); Latin American and Iberian cultures (PhD); mathematics (MA, PhD), including finance (MA); medieval and Renaissance studies (MA); Middle Eastern, South Asian, and African studies (MA, PhD); modern art: critical and curatorial studies (MA); modern European studies (MA); museum anthropology (MA); music (DMA, PhD); oral history (MA); philosophical foundations of physics (MA); philosophy (MA, PhD); physics (PhD); political science (MA, PhD); psychology (PhD); quantitative methods in the social sciences (MA); religion (MA, PhD); Russia, Eurasia and East Europe: regional studies (MA); Russian translation (MA); Slavic cultures (MA); Slavic languages (MA, PhD); sociology (MA, PhD); South Asian studies (MA); statistics (MA, PhD); theatre (PhD). Dual-degree programs require admission to both Graduate School of Arts and Sciences and another Columbia school. *Program availability:* Part-time. Terminal master's awarded for partial completion of doctoral program. *Degree requirements:* For master's, variable foreign language requirement, comprehensive exam (for some programs), thesis (for some programs); for doctorate, variable foreign language requirement, comprehensive exam (for some programs), thesis/dissertation. *Entrance requirements:* For master's and doctorate, GRE General Test, GRE Subject Test (for some programs). Additional exam requirements/recommendations for international students: Required—TOEFL, IELTS. Electronic applications accepted.

**Cornell University,** Graduate School, Graduate Fields of Arts and Sciences, Field of Linguistics, Ithaca, NY 14853. Offers applied linguistics (MA, PhD); East Asian linguistics (MA, PhD); English linguistics (MA, PhD); general linguistics (MA, PhD); Germanic linguistics (MA, PhD); Indo-European linguistics (MA, PhD); phonetics (MA, PhD); phonological theory (MA, PhD); Romance linguistics (MA, PhD); second language acquisition (MA, PhD); semantics (MA, PhD); Slavic linguistics (MA, PhD); sociolinguistics (MA, PhD); South Asian linguistics (MA, PhD); Southeast Asian linguistics (MA, PhD); syntactic theory (MA, PhD). Terminal master's awarded for partial completion of doctoral program. *Degree requirements:* For master's, one foreign language, thesis; for doctorate, one foreign language, comprehensive exam, thesis/dissertation. *Entrance requirements:* For master's and doctorate, GRE General Test, 2 letters of recommendation. Additional exam requirements/recommendations for international students: Required—TOEFL (minimum score 600 paper-based; 77 iBT). Electronic applications accepted. *Faculty research:* Phonology and phonetics, syntax and semantics, historical linguistics, philosophy of language, language acquisition.

**Cornell University,** Graduate School, Graduate Fields of Arts and Sciences, Field of Romance Studies, Ithaca, NY 14853. Offers French linguistics (PhD); French literature (PhD); Hispanic literature (PhD); Italian linguistics (PhD); Italian literature (PhD); Romance linguistics (PhD); Spanish linguistics (PhD). *Degree requirements:* For doctorate, 2 foreign languages, comprehensive exam, thesis/dissertation. *Entrance requirements:* For doctorate, GRE General Test, sample of written work, 3 letters of recommendation. Additional exam requirements/recommendations for international students: Required—TOEFL (minimum score 550 paper-based; 77 iBT). Electronic applications accepted. *Faculty research:* Literary theory, Hispanic studies, French studies, gender studies.

**Hunter College of the City University of New York,** Graduate School, School of Arts and Sciences, Department of Romance Languages, New York, NY 10065-5085. Offers French (MA); Italian (MA); Spanish (MA). *Program availability:* Part-time, evening/weekend. *Students:* 1 full-time (0 women), 13 part-time (9 women); includes 8 minority (2 Black or African American, non-Hispanic/Latino; 6 Hispanic/Latino), 3 international. Average age 34. 8 applicants, 63% accepted, 4 enrolled. In 2016, 3 master's awarded. *Degree requirements:* For master's, 2 foreign languages, comprehensive exam, thesis optional. *Entrance requirements:* For master's, GRE General Test, GRE Subject Test, interview, proficiency in chosen language. Additional exam requirements/recommendations for international students: Required—TOEFL. *Application deadline:* For fall admission, 4/1 for domestic students, 2/1 for international students; for spring admission, 11/1 for domestic students, 9/1 for international students. *Financial support:* Fellowships, Federal Work-Study, scholarships/grants, and tuition waivers (partial) available. Support available to part-time students. Financial award application deadline: 4/15. *Unit head:* Dr. Paolo Fasoli, Chair, 212-772-5108, Fax: 212-772-5094. *Application contact:* Milena Solo, Director for Graduate Admissions, 212-772-4480, E-mail: admissions@hunter.cuny.edu.
Website: http://www.hunter.cuny.edu/romancelanguages

**Johns Hopkins University,** Zanvyl Krieger School of Arts and Sciences, Department of German and Romance Languages and Literatures, Baltimore, MD 21218. Offers French (PhD); German (PhD); Italian (PhD); Spanish (PhD). *Degree requirements:* For doctorate, 2 foreign languages, thesis/dissertation. *Entrance requirements:* For doctorate, GRE General Test. Additional exam requirements/recommendations for international students: Required—TOEFL (minimum score 600 paper-based; 100 iBT), IELTS. Electronic applications accepted. *Faculty research:* Nineteenth-century French prose and poetry, genetic theory and criticism; twentieth-century Latin American literature and film; medieval and Renaissance Italian literature; gender and queer theory in German literature; the ideology of Baroque and Neobaroque aesthetics.

**Michigan State University,** The Graduate School, College of Arts and Letters, Department of French, Classics, and Italian, East Lansing, MI 48824. Offers French (MA); French language and literature (PhD). *Entrance requirements:* Additional exam requirements/recommendations for international students: Required—TOEFL. Electronic applications accepted.

**New York University,** Graduate School of Arts and Science, Center for French Civilization and Culture, Department of French, New York, NY 10012-1019. Offers

## Romance Languages

French (PhD); French language and civilization (MA); French literature (MA); Romance languages and literatures (MA). *Program availability:* Part-time. Terminal master's awarded for partial completion of doctoral program. *Degree requirements:* For master's, one foreign language, thesis (for some programs); for doctorate, one foreign language, thesis/dissertation. *Entrance requirements:* For master's and doctorate, GRE General Test, proficiency in French. Additional exam requirements/recommendations for international students: Required—TOEFL. *Faculty research:* French and Francophone literature, literary theory, and history; rhetoric and poetics; cultural history; theater and cinema.

**New York University,** Graduate School of Arts and Science, Department of Spanish and Portuguese Languages and Literatures, New York, NY 10012-1019. Offers Portuguese (MA, PhD); Spanish (PhD); Spanish and Latin American literatures and cultures (MA); Spanish language and translation (MA). *Program availability:* Part-time. *Degree requirements:* For master's, 2 foreign languages, thesis; for doctorate, 2 foreign languages, thesis/dissertation. *Entrance requirements:* For master's, GRE General Test; for doctorate, GRE General Test, master's degree. Additional exam requirements/recommendations for international students: Required—TOEFL. *Faculty research:* Gender and sexuality, transatlantic studies, literacy and cultural theories, Colonial and Post-Colonial studies, autobiography and modern subjectivities.

**Northern Illinois University,** Graduate School, College of Liberal Arts and Sciences, Department of Foreign Languages and Literatures, De Kalb, IL 60115-2854. Offers French (MA); Spanish (MA). *Program availability:* Part-time. *Faculty:* 25 full-time (11 women). *Students:* 3 full-time (0 women), 9 part-time (6 women); includes 8 minority (1 Black or African American, non-Hispanic/Latino; 1 Asian, non-Hispanic/Latino; 6 Hispanic/Latino). Average age 34. 6 applicants, 67% accepted, 1 enrolled. In 2016, 7 master's awarded. *Degree requirements:* For master's, one foreign language, comprehensive exam, thesis or alternative, language proficiency exam. *Entrance requirements:* For master's, GRE General Test, interview, minimum GPA of 2.75, undergraduate major in French or Spanish. Additional exam requirements/recommendations for international students: Required—TOEFL (minimum score 550 paper-based). *Application deadline:* For fall admission, 6/1 for domestic students, 5/1 for international students; for spring admission, 11/1 for domestic students, 10/1 for international students. Applications are processed on a rolling basis. Application fee: $40. Electronic applications accepted. *Financial support:* In 2016–17, 6 teaching assistantships with full tuition reimbursements were awarded; fellowships with full tuition reimbursements, research assistantships with full tuition reimbursements, career-related internships or fieldwork, Federal Work-Study, scholarships/grants, tuition waivers (full), and unspecified assistantships also available. Support available to part-time students. Financial award applicants required to submit FAFSA. *Faculty research:* Francophone women writers, prosodies of French and Italian, early Spanish drama, business German, history of Burmese literature. *Unit head:* Dr. Katharina Barbe, Chair, 815-753-1559, Fax: 815-753-5989, E-mail: kbarbe@niu.edu. *Application contact:* Graduate School Office, 815-753-0395, E-mail: gradsch@niu.edu.
Website: http://www.forlangs.net/

**Queens College of the City University of New York,** Arts and Humanities Division, Department of European Languages and Literatures, Queens, NY 11367-1597. Offers French (MA); Italian (MA). *Program availability:* Part-time. *Faculty:* 12 full-time (7 women), 16 part-time/adjunct (12 women). *Students:* 3 full-time (2 women), 8 part-time (5 women); includes 2 minority (both Black or African American, non-Hispanic/Latino). Average age 37. 11 applicants, 82% accepted, 6 enrolled. In 2016, 1 master's awarded. *Degree requirements:* For master's, 2 foreign languages, thesis optional, oral exam. *Entrance requirements:* For master's, minimum GPA of 3.0. Additional exam requirements/recommendations for international students: Required—TOEFL (minimum score 61 iBT), IELTS (minimum score 5). *Application deadline:* For fall admission, 4/1 for domestic students; for spring admission, 11/1 for domestic students. Applications are processed on a rolling basis. Application fee: $125. Electronic applications accepted. *Expenses:* Tuition, state resident: full-time $5065; part-time $425 per credit. Tuition, nonresident: part-time $780 per credit. *Required fees:* $522; $397 per credit. Part-time tuition and fees vary according to course load and program. *Financial support:* Career-related internships or fieldwork, Federal Work-Study, institutionally sponsored loans, and tuition waivers (partial) available. Support available to part-time students. Financial award application deadline: 4/1; financial award applicants required to submit FAFSA. *Unit head:* Dr. David Andrew Jones, Chairperson, 718-997-5980, E-mail: david.jones@qc.cuny.edu.

**San Diego State University,** Graduate and Research Affairs, College of Arts and Letters, Department of European Studies, San Diego, CA 92182. Offers MA. *Degree requirements:* For master's, one foreign language. *Entrance requirements:* For master's, GRE General Test. Additional exam requirements/recommendations for international students: Required—TOEFL. Electronic applications accepted.

**Stony Brook University, State University of New York,** Graduate School, College of Arts and Sciences, Department of European Languages, Literatures, and Cultures, Program in French, Stony Brook, NY 11794. Offers Romance languages (MA). *Program availability:* Evening/weekend. *Students:* 2 part-time (both women). 2 applicants, 50% accepted, 1 enrolled. *Degree requirements:* For master's, one foreign language. *Entrance requirements:* For master's, GRE General Test. Additional exam requirements/recommendations for international students: Required—TOEFL. *Application deadline:* For fall admission, 1/15 for domestic students; for spring admission, 10/1 for domestic students. Application fee: $100. *Expenses:* Contact institution. *Unit head:* Dr. Prosper Sanou, Coordinator, 631-632-7440, Fax: 631-632-9612, E-mail: prosper.sanou@stonybrook.edu. *Application contact:* Mary Wilmarth, Coordinator, 631-632-7442, Fax: 631-632-9612, E-mail: mary.wilmarth@stonybrook.edu.

**Texas Tech University,** Graduate School, College of Arts and Sciences, Department of Biological Sciences, Lubbock, TX 79409-3131. Offers biology (MS, PhD); environmental sustainability and natural resource management (PSM); microbiology (MS); zoology (MS). *Program availability:* Part-time, blended/hybrid learning. *Faculty:* 42 full-time (16 women), 1 (woman) part-time/adjunct. *Students:* 100 full-time (50 women), 16 part-time (9 women); includes 14 minority (1 Black or African American, non-Hispanic/Latino; 1 American Indian or Alaska Native, non-Hispanic/Latino; 2 Asian, non-Hispanic/Latino; 8 Hispanic/Latino; 2 Two or more races, non-Hispanic/Latino), 53 international. Average age 29. 95 applicants, 37% accepted, 21 enrolled. In 2016, 3 master's, 11 doctorates awarded. *Degree requirements:* For master's, comprehensive exam, thesis or alternative; for doctorate, comprehensive exam, thesis/dissertation. *Entrance requirements:* For master's and doctorate, GRE General Test. Additional exam requirements/recommendations for international students: Required—TOEFL (minimum score 550 paper-based; 79 iBT). *Application deadline:* For fall admission, 6/1 priority date for domestic students, 1/15 priority date for international students; for spring admission, 9/1 priority date for domestic students, 6/15 priority date for international students. Applications are processed on a rolling basis. Application fee: $75. Electronic applications accepted. *Expenses:* $300 per credit hour full-time resident tuition, $708 per credit hour full-time non-resident tuition; $50.50 per credit hour fee plus $608 per term fee. *Financial support:* In 2016–17, 114 students received support, including 82 fellowships (averaging $1,720 per year), 23 research assistantships (averaging $6,310 per year), 100 teaching assistantships (averaging $15,370 per year); Federal Work-

Study and health care benefits also available. Financial award application deadline: 2/15; financial award applicants required to submit FAFSA. *Faculty research:* Biodiversity, genomics and evolution; climate change in arid ecosystems, plant biology and biotechnology; animal communication and behavior; microbiomes, zoonosis and emerging diseases. *Total annual research expenditures:* $1.3 million. *Unit head:* Dr. John Zak, Associate Dean and Interim Chair, 806-834-2682, Fax: 806-742-2963, E-mail: john.zak@ttu.edu. *Application contact:* Dr. Lou Densmore, Graduate Adviser, 806-834-6479, Fax: 806-742-2963, E-mail: lou.densmore@ttu.edu.
Website: http://www.depts.ttu.edu/biology/

**Texas Tech University,** Graduate School, College of Arts and Sciences, Department of Classical and Modern Languages and Literatures, Lubbock, TX 79409. Offers applied linguistics (MA); classics (MA); German (MA); languages and cultures (MA); Romance languages (MA); Spanish (PhD); MBA/MA. *Program availability:* Part-time. *Faculty:* 56 full-time (37 women), 4 part-time/adjunct (2 women). *Students:* 80 full-time (39 women), 13 part-time (9 women); includes 20 minority (19 Hispanic/Latino; 1 Two or more races, non-Hispanic/Latino), 49 international. Average age 32. 68 applicants, 68% accepted, 31 enrolled. In 2016, 30 master's, 4 doctorates awarded. *Degree requirements:* For master's, comprehensive exam, thesis or alternative; for doctorate, comprehensive exam, thesis/dissertation. *Entrance requirements:* Additional exam requirements/recommendations for international students: Required—TOEFL (minimum score 550 paper-based; 79 iBT). *Application deadline:* For fall admission, 6/1 priority date for domestic students, 1/15 priority date for international students; for spring admission, 9/1 priority date for domestic students, 6/15 priority date for international students. Applications are processed on a rolling basis. Application fee: $75. Electronic applications accepted. *Expenses:* $300 per credit hour full-time resident tuition, $708 per credit hour full-time non-resident tuition; $50.50 per credit hour fee plus $608 per term fee. *Financial support:* In 2016–17, 78 students received support, including 60 fellowships (averaging $2,488 per year), 76 teaching assistantships (averaging $13,011 per year); research assistantships, Federal Work-Study, scholarships/grants, and unspecified assistantships also available. Financial award application deadline: 4/15; financial award applicants required to submit FAFSA. *Faculty research:* Literature, comparative literature, linguistics, culture, applied linguistics. *Total annual research expenditures:* $36,152. *Unit head:* Dr. Erin Collopy, Chair and Associate Professor, 806-834-8497, Fax: 806-742-3306, E-mail: erin.collopy@ttu.edu. *Application contact:* Carla Burrus, Senior Advisor, 806-834-3282, Fax: 806-742-3306, E-mail: carla.burrus@ttu.edu.
Website: http://www.depts.ttu.edu/classic_modern/

**University at Buffalo, the State University of New York,** Graduate School, College of Arts and Sciences, Department of Romance Languages and Literatures, Buffalo, NY 14260-4620. Offers French (MA, PhD); Spanish (MA, PhD). *Program availability:* Part-time. *Faculty:* 15 full-time (9 women), 6 part-time/adjunct (3 women). *Students:* 33 full-time (24 women), 3 part-time (all women); includes 13 minority (3 Black or African American, non-Hispanic/Latino; 2 Asian, non-Hispanic/Latino; 6 Hispanic/Latino; 2 Two or more races, non-Hispanic/Latino), 9 international. 24 applicants, 58% accepted, 7 enrolled. In 2016, 1 master's, 7 doctorates awarded. Terminal master's awarded for partial completion of doctoral program. *Degree requirements:* For master's, one foreign language, comprehensive exam, thesis (for some programs); for doctorate, 2 foreign languages, comprehensive exam, thesis (for some programs), thesis/dissertation. *Entrance requirements:* For doctorate, GRE. Additional exam requirements/recommendations for international students: Required—TOEFL (minimum score 550 paper-based; 79 iBT), IELTS (minimum score 6.5), PTE (minimum score 55). *Application deadline:* For fall admission, 12/31 priority date for domestic and international students; for spring admission, 10/30 for domestic students, 9/1 for international students. Applications are processed on a rolling basis. Application fee: $75. Electronic applications accepted. *Financial support:* In 2016–17, 24 students received support, including 3 fellowships with full tuition reimbursements available (averaging $4,667 per year), 24 teaching assistantships with full tuition reimbursements available (averaging $14,049 per year); Federal Work-Study, institutionally sponsored loans, scholarships/grants, and health care benefits also available. Financial award application deadline: 12/31; financial award applicants required to submit FAFSA. *Faculty research:* Romance linguistics, cultural studies, literary studies, literature, philosophy and poetry. *Unit head:* Dr. Elizabeth Scarlett, Professor of Spanish/Department Chair, 716-645-0873, Fax: 716-645-5981, E-mail: scarlett@buffalo.edu. *Application contact:* Dr. Margarita Vargas, Associate Professor of Spanish/Director of Graduate Studies, 716-645-0859, Fax: 716-645-5981, E-mail: mvargas@buffalo.edu.
Website: http://rll.buffalo.edu

**The University of Alabama,** Graduate School, College of Arts and Sciences, Department of Modern Languages and Classics, Tuscaloosa, AL 35487. Offers French (MA, PhD); French and Spanish (PhD); German (MA); Romance languages (MA, PhD); Spanish (MA, PhD). *Program availability:* Part-time. *Faculty:* 31 full-time (18 women). *Students:* 49 full-time (32 women), 7 part-time (4 women); includes 9 minority (3 Black or African American, non-Hispanic/Latino; 1 Asian, non-Hispanic/Latino; 4 Hispanic/Latino; 1 Two or more races, non-Hispanic/Latino), 20 international. Average age 31. 29 applicants, 66% accepted, 12 enrolled. In 2016, 11 master's, 6 doctorates awarded. *Degree requirements:* For master's, comprehensive exam, thesis optional; for doctorate, one foreign language, thesis/dissertation, preliminary exam. *Entrance requirements:* For master's and doctorate, minimum GPA of 3.0, writing sample. Additional exam requirements/recommendations for international students: Required—TOEFL or IELTS. *Application deadline:* For fall admission, 7/6 priority date for domestic students, 1/15 priority date for international students; for spring admission, 12/5 priority date for domestic students, 6/1 priority date for international students. Applications are processed on a rolling basis. Application fee: $50 ($60 for international students). Electronic applications accepted. *Expenses:* Tuition, state resident: full-time $10,470. Tuition, nonresident: full-time $26,950. *Financial support:* In 2016–17, 7 students received support, including 1 fellowship, research assistantships with full tuition reimbursements available (averaging $10,291 per year), 6 teaching assistantships with full tuition reimbursements available (averaging $10,291 per year); career-related internships or fieldwork, Federal Work-Study, institutionally sponsored loans, and scholarships/grants also available. Financial award application deadline: 7/14. *Faculty research:* Non-English literature, linguistics, culture, film. *Unit head:* Dr. Douglas Lightfoot, Department Chair, 205-348-5059, E-mail: lightfoot@ua.edu. *Application contact:* Dr. K. Barbara Fischer, Graduate Director/Associate Professor, 205-348-8465, Fax: 205-348-2042, E-mail: bfischer@bama.ua.edu.
Website: http://bama.ua.edu/~mlc

**University of California, Berkeley,** Graduate Division, College of Letters and Science, Group in Romance Languages and Literatures, Berkeley, CA 94720-1500. Offers French (PhD); Italian (PhD); Spanish (PhD). *Faculty:* 16 full-time. *Students:* 11 full-time (7 women); includes 3 minority (1 Asian, non-Hispanic/Latino; 2 Hispanic/Latino). Average age 33. 12 applicants. In 2016, 4 doctorates awarded. *Degree requirements:* For doctorate, thesis/dissertation, qualifying exam. *Entrance requirements:* For doctorate, GRE General Test, minimum GPA of 3.0, 3 letters of recommendation. Additional exam requirements/recommendations for international students: Required—TOEFL (minimum score 570 paper-based; 90 iBT). *Application deadline:* For fall admission, 12/8 for domestic students. Application fee: $105 ($125 for international

students). Electronic applications accepted. *Financial support:* Fellowships with full tuition reimbursements, teaching assistantships with partial tuition reimbursements, health care benefits, and unspecified assistantships available. Financial award applicants required to submit FAFSA. *Unit head:* Ignatio Navarrete, Chair, 510-642-2105. *Application contact:* 510-642-7405.
Website: http://romancelangs.berkeley.edu

**University of Chicago,** Division of the Humanities, Department of Romance Languages and Literatures, Chicago, IL 60637. Offers French and Francophone studies (PhD); Hispanic and Luso-Brazilian studies (PhD); Italian studies (PhD); Renaissance and early modern studies (PhD). *Students:* 44 full-time (28 women); includes 9 minority (1 Asian, non-Hispanic/Latino; 7 Hispanic/Latino; 1 Two or more races, non-Hispanic/Latino), 16 international. 45 applicants, 29% accepted, 5 enrolled. In 2016, 4 doctorates awarded. Terminal master's awarded for partial completion of doctoral program. *Degree requirements:* For doctorate, 3 foreign languages, comprehensive exam, thesis/dissertation. *Entrance requirements:* For doctorate, GRE General Test. Additional exam requirements/recommendations for international students: Required—TOEFL (minimum score 104 iBT), IELTS (minimum score 7). *Application deadline:* For fall admission, 12/15 for domestic and international students. Application fee: $90. Electronic applications accepted. *Financial support:* Fellowships with full tuition reimbursements, teaching assistantships with full tuition reimbursements, Federal Work-Study, institutionally sponsored loans, scholarships/grants, and health care benefits available. Financial award application deadline: 12/15; financial award applicants required to submit FAFSA. *Unit head:* Daisy Delogu, Chair, 773-702-4115, E-mail: ddelogu@uchicago.edu. *Application contact:* Michael Beetley, Assistant Dean of Students, Admissions and Fellowships, 773-702-1552, Fax: 773-834-9148, E-mail: humanitiesadmissions@uchicago.edu.
Website: http://rll.uchicago.edu

**University of Chicago,** Division of the Humanities, Master of Arts Program in the Humanities, Chicago, IL 60637. Offers art history (MA); cinema and media studies (MA); classic languages (MA); comparative literature (MA); creative writing (MA); cultural policy studies (MA); digital humanities (MA); East Asian languages and civilizations (MA); English language and literature (MA); gender and sexuality studies (MA); Germanic studies (MA); linguistics (MA); music (MA); near Eastern languages and civilizations (MA); philosophy (MA); poetics (MA); race, politics and culture (MA); Romance languages and literatures (MA); Slavic languages and literatures (MA); South Asian languages and civilizations (MA); theater and performance studies (MA). *Students:* 80 full-time (43 women), 7 part-time (3 women); includes 20 minority (5 Black or African American, non-Hispanic/Latino; 1 American Indian or Alaska Native, non-Hispanic/Latino; 6 Asian, non-Hispanic/Latino; 5 Hispanic/Latino; 3 Two or more races, non-Hispanic/Latino), 11 international. Average age 26. 706 applicants, 15% accepted, 42 enrolled. In 2016, 92 master's awarded. *Degree requirements:* For master's, thesis. *Entrance requirements:* For master's, GRE General Test. Additional exam requirements/recommendations for international students: Required—TOEFL (minimum score 104 iBT), IELTS (minimum score 7). *Application deadline:* For fall admission, 1/3 for domestic and international students. Application fee: $90. Electronic applications accepted. *Financial support:* In 2016–17, 8 fellowships with partial tuition reimbursements (averaging $12,000 per year) were awarded; Federal Work-Study, institutionally sponsored loans, scholarships/grants, and tuition waivers (partial) also available. Financial award application deadline: 12/15; financial award applicants required to submit FAFSA. *Unit head:* Malynne Sternstein, Co-Director, 773-834-1201, Fax: 773-834-7526. *Application contact:* Program Coordinator, 773-834-1201, Fax: 773-834-7526, E-mail: ma-humanities@uchicago.edu.
Website: http://maph.uchicago.edu/

**University of Cincinnati,** Graduate School, McMicken College of Arts and Sciences, Department of Romance Languages and Literatures, Cincinnati, OH 45221. Offers French (MA, PhD); Romance languages and literatures (PhD); Spanish (MA, PhD). Terminal master's awarded for partial completion of doctoral program. *Degree requirements:* For master's, 2 foreign languages, comprehensive exam, thesis optional; for doctorate, 3 foreign languages, comprehensive exam, thesis/dissertation. *Entrance requirements:* For master's, minimum GPA of 3.0; for doctorate, MA or equivalent in French or Spanish language and literature. Additional exam requirements/recommendations for international students: Required—TOEFL (minimum score 520 paper-based). Electronic applications accepted. *Expenses: Tuition, area resident:* Full-time $12,790; part-time $389 per credit hour. Tuition, state resident: full-time $13,290; part-time $419 per credit hour. Tuition, nonresident: full-time $24,532; part-time $976 per credit hour. *International tuition:* $24,832 full-time. *Required fees:* $3958; $140 per credit hour. Tuition and fees vary according to course load, degree level, program and reciprocity agreements. *Faculty research:* Teaching methods in Spanish, Spanish theater, Old French, Francophone studies, poetry.

**University of Illinois at Urbana–Champaign,** Graduate College, College of Liberal Arts and Sciences, School of Literatures, Cultures and Linguistics, Program in Romance Linguistics, Champaign, IL 61820. Offers PhD.

**University of Miami,** Graduate School, College of Arts and Sciences, Department of Modern Languages and Literatures, Coral Gables, FL 33124. Offers romance studies (PhD), including French, Spanish. *Degree requirements:* For doctorate, 2 foreign languages, thesis/dissertation, area exam, qualifying exam. *Entrance requirements:* For doctorate, 1 writing sample in English and 1 writing sample in French or Spanish, minimum GPA of 3.0, oral interview, letters of recommendation. Additional exam requirements/recommendations for international students: Required—TOEFL (minimum score 550 paper-based; 59 iBT). Electronic applications accepted. *Faculty research:* Transatlantic studies, Caribbean studies, comparative literature, gender theory, cultural studies.

**University of Missouri,** Office of Research and Graduate Studies, College of Arts and Science, Department of Romance Languages and Literatures, Columbia, MO 65211. Offers French (MA, PhD); literature (MA); Spanish (MA, PhD); teaching (MA). *Faculty:* 25 full-time (15 women). *Students:* 22 full-time (16 women), 15 part-time (10 women); includes 11 minority (3 Black or African American, non-Hispanic/Latino; 6 Hispanic/Latino; 2 Two or more races, non-Hispanic/Latino), 13 international. Average age 35. Terminal master's awarded for partial completion of doctoral program. *Degree requirements:* For master's, one foreign language; for doctorate, 4 foreign languages, comprehensive exam, thesis/dissertation. *Entrance requirements:* For master's, GRE General Test, minimum GPA of 3.0 in field of major; bachelor's degree; for doctorate, GRE General Test, minimum GPA of 3.0 in field of major; master's degree. Additional exam requirements/recommendations for international students: Required—TOEFL (minimum score 500 paper-based; 61 iBT). *Application deadline:* For fall admission, 2/15 priority date for domestic students; for winter admission, 10/15 for domestic students. Applications are processed on a rolling basis. Application fee: $75 ($90 for international students). Electronic applications accepted. *Expenses:* Tuition, state resident: full-time $6347; part-time $352.60 per credit hour. Tuition, nonresident: full-time $17,379; part-time $965.50 per credit hour. *Required fees:* $1035. Tuition and fees vary according to course load, campus/location and program. *Financial support:* Research assistantships, teaching assistantships with full tuition reimbursements, institutionally sponsored loans, health care benefits, and unspecified assistantships available.
Website: http://romancelanguages.missouri.edu/grad.shtml

**University of Missouri–Kansas City,** College of Arts and Sciences, Department of Foreign Languages and Literatures, Kansas City, MO 64110-2499. Offers romance languages and literatures (MA), including French, Spanish. *Program availability:* Part-time. *Faculty:* 32 full-time (18 women), 38 part-time/adjunct (32 women). *Students:* 3 full-time (0 women), 13 part-time (9 women); includes 8 minority (all Hispanic/Latino). Average age 35. 12 applicants, 58% accepted, 4 enrolled. In 2016, 7 master's awarded. *Degree requirements:* For master's, 2 foreign languages. *Entrance requirements:* For master's, GRE General Test, minimum GPA of 2.75, 2 letters of recommendation. Additional exam requirements/recommendations for international students: Required—TOEFL (minimum score 550 paper-based; 80 iBT). *Application deadline:* For fall admission, 4/1 priority date for domestic and international students; for spring admission, 11/1 priority date for domestic and international students. Applications are processed on a rolling basis. Application fee: $45 ($50 for international students). Electronic applications accepted. *Financial support:* In 2016–17, 2 teaching assistantships (averaging $12,600 per year) were awarded; Federal Work-Study, institutionally sponsored loans, and tuition waivers (full and partial) also available. Support available to part-time students. Financial award application deadline: 3/1; financial award applicants required to submit FAFSA. *Faculty research:* Literary analyses; psychology and literature; narrative techniques, poetic structure, and style; literature, politics, and society (especially in Latin America). *Unit head:* Dr. K. Scott Baker, Chair, 816-235-2823, Fax: 816-235-1312, E-mail: bakerks@umkc.edu. *Application contact:* 816-235-1311, Fax: 816-235-1312, E-mail: admit@umkc.edu.
Website: http://cas.umkc.edu/foreign

**University of New Orleans,** Graduate School, College of Liberal Arts, Department of Foreign Languages, New Orleans, LA 70148. Offers MA. *Program availability:* Part-time, evening/weekend. *Degree requirements:* For master's, one foreign language, thesis optional. *Entrance requirements:* For master's, GRE General Test, minimum B average. Additional exam requirements/recommendations for international students: Required—TOEFL (minimum score 550 paper-based; 79 iBT), IELTS (minimum score 6.5). Electronic applications accepted. *Faculty research:* Translation studies, Michelet, Scève, Spanish canzoniero, theories of representation.

**The University of North Carolina at Chapel Hill,** Graduate School, College of Arts and Sciences, Department of Romance Languages and Literatures, Chapel Hill, NC 27599. Offers French (MA, PhD); Italian (MA, PhD); Portuguese (MA, PhD); Romance languages (MA, PhD); Romance philology (MA, PhD); Spanish (MA, PhD). *Degree requirements:* For master's, one foreign language, comprehensive exam, thesis; for doctorate, 2 foreign languages, comprehensive exam, thesis/dissertation. *Entrance requirements:* For master's and doctorate, GRE General Test, minimum GPA of 3.0. Additional exam requirements/recommendations for international students: Required—TOEFL (minimum score 550 paper-based). Electronic applications accepted.

**University of Notre Dame,** Graduate School, College of Arts and Letters, Division of Humanities, Department of Romance Languages and Literatures, Notre Dame, IN 46556. Offers French and Francophone studies (MA); Iberian and Latin American studies (MA); Italian studies (MA); Romance literatures (MA). *Degree requirements:* For master's, 2 foreign languages, comprehensive exam, thesis optional. *Entrance requirements:* For master's, GRE General Test, BA in target language. Additional exam requirements/recommendations for international students: Required—TOEFL (minimum score 600 paper-based; 80 iBT). Electronic applications accepted. *Faculty research:* Literature of discovery and exploration, modern literature, literary criticism, medieval literature, feminist critical theory.

**University of Oregon,** Graduate School, College of Arts and Sciences, Department of Romance Languages, Program in Romance Languages, Eugene, OR 97403. Offers MA, PhD. *Program availability:* Part-time. *Degree requirements:* For master's, 2 foreign languages; for doctorate, 2 foreign languages, thesis/dissertation. *Entrance requirements:* For master's and doctorate, GRE General Test, minimum GPA of 3.0. Additional exam requirements/recommendations for international students: Required—TOEFL.

**University of Pennsylvania,** School of Arts and Sciences, Graduate Group in Romance Languages, Philadelphia, PA 19104. Offers French (AM, PhD); Italian (AM, PhD); Spanish (AM, PhD). *Faculty:* 38 full-time (14 women), 11 part-time/adjunct (3 women). *Students:* 56 full-time (25 women), 3 part-time (2 women); includes 4 minority (all Hispanic/Latino), 34 international. Average age 32. 73 applicants, 33% accepted, 10 enrolled. In 2016, 10 master's, 5 doctorates awarded. Terminal master's awarded for partial completion of doctoral program. Application fee: $70. *Expenses: Tuition:* Full-time $31,068; part-time $5762 per course. *Required fees:* $3200; $336 per course. Full-time tuition and fees vary according to degree level, program and student level. Part-time tuition and fees vary according to course load, degree level and program.
Website: http://www.sas.upenn.edu/graduate-division

**University of South Africa,** College of Human Sciences, Pretoria, South Africa. Offers adult education (M Ed); African languages (MA, PhD); African politics (MA, PhD); Afrikaans (MA, PhD); ancient history (MA, PhD); ancient Near Eastern studies (MA, PhD); anthropology (MA, PhD); applied linguistics (MA); Arabic (MA, PhD); archaeology (MA); art history (MA); Biblical archaeology (MA); Biblical studies (M Th, D Th, PhD); Christian spirituality (M Th, D Th); church history (M Th, D Th); classical studies (MA, PhD); clinical psychology (MA); communication (MA, PhD); comparative education (M Ed, Ed D); consulting psychology (D Admin, D Com, PhD); curriculum studies (M Ed, Ed D); development studies (M Admin, MA, D Admin, PhD); didactics (M Ed, Ed D); education (M Tech); education management (M Ed, Ed D); educational psychology (M Ed); English (MA); environmental education (M Ed); French (MA, PhD); German (MA, PhD); Greek (MA); guidance and counseling (M Ed); health studies (MA, PhD), including health sciences education (MA), health services management (MA), medical and surgical nursing science (critical care general) (MA), midwifery and neonatal nursing science (MA), trauma and emergency care (MA); history (MA, PhD); history of education (Ed D); inclusive education (M Ed, Ed D); information and communications technology policy and regulation (MA); information science (MA, MIS, PhD); international politics (MA, PhD); Islamic studies (MA, PhD); Italian (MA, PhD); Judaica (MA); linguistics (MA, PhD); mathematical education (M Ed); mathematics education (MA); missiology (M Th, D Th); modern Hebrew (MA, PhD); musicology (MA, MMus, D Mus, PhD); natural science education (M Ed); New Testament (M Th, D Th); Old Testament (D Th); pastoral therapy (M Th, D Th); philosophy (MA); philosophy of education (M Ed, Ed D); politics (MA, PhD); Portuguese (MA, PhD); practical theology (M Th, D Th); psychology (MA, MS, PhD); psychology of education (M Ed, Ed D); public health (MA); religious studies (MA, D Th, PhD); Romance languages (MA, PhD); Russian (MA, PhD); Semitic languages (MA, PhD); social behavior studies in HIV/AIDS (MA); social science (mental health) (MA); social science in development studies (MA); social science in psychology (MA); social science in social work (MA); social science in sociology (MA); social work (MSW, DSW, PhD); socio-education (M Ed, Ed D); sociolinguistics (MA); sociology (MA, PhD); Spanish (MA, PhD); systematic theology (M Th, D Th); TESOL (teaching English to speakers of other languages) (MA); theological ethics (M Th, D Th); theory of literature (MA, PhD); urban ministries (D Th); urban ministry (M Th).

## Romance Languages

**The University of Texas at Austin,** Graduate School, College of Liberal Arts, Department of French and Italian, Austin, TX 78712-1111. Offers French linguistics (MA, PhD); French studies (MA, PhD); Italian studies (MA, PhD); Romance linguistics (PhD). *Program availability:* Part-time. *Degree requirements:* For master's, one foreign language, thesis; for doctorate, 2 foreign languages, thesis/dissertation. *Entrance requirements:* For master's, GRE General Test, minimum GPA of 3.0, bachelor's degree in French or equivalent; for doctorate, GRE General Test, minimum GPA of 3.0, master's degree in French. Additional exam requirements/recommendations for international students: Required—TOEFL. Electronic applications accepted. *Faculty research:* Nineteenth-century Italian literature, Italian Renaissance, twentieth-century French literature, Francophone literature, fifteenth-century literature and culture.

**Washington University in St. Louis,** The Graduate School, Department of Romance Languages and Literatures, St. Louis, MO 63130-4899. Offers French (PhD), including French and comparative literature, French language and literature; Spanish (PhD), including Hispanic languages and literatures, Spanish and comparative literature. Terminal master's awarded for partial completion of doctoral program. *Degree requirements:* For doctorate, thesis/dissertation. *Entrance requirements:* For doctorate, GRE General Test. Additional exam requirements/recommendations for international students: Required—TOEFL. Electronic applications accepted. *Faculty research:* French language and literature; Latin American and Iberian literatures and languages, Spanish and comparative literature.

**Wayne State University,** College of Liberal Arts and Sciences, Department of Classical and Modern Languages, Literatures, and Cultures, Detroit, MI 48202. Offers classics (MA), including ancient Greek and Latin, ancient studies, classics, Latin; German (MA); language learning (MALL), including Arabic (MA, MALL), French (MA, MALL, PhD), German (MALL, PhD), Italian (MA, MALL), Spanish (MA, MALL, PhD); modern languages (PhD), including French (MA, MALL, PhD), German (MALL, PhD), Spanish (MA, MALL, PhD); Near Eastern languages (MA), including Arabic (MA, MALL), Hebrew; Romance languages (MA), including French (MA, MALL, PhD), Italian (MA, MALL), Spanish (MA, MALL, PhD). *Faculty:* 26. *Students:* 25 full-time (20 women), 14 part-time (8 women); includes 7 minority (2 Black or African American, non-Hispanic/Latino; 1 American Indian or Alaska Native, non-Hispanic/Latino; 1 Asian, non-Hispanic/Latino; 2 Hispanic/Latino; 1 Two or more races, non-Hispanic/Latino), 3 international. Average age 35. 29 applicants, 31% accepted, 5 enrolled. In 2016, 15 master's, 5 doctorates awarded. *Degree requirements:* For master's, variable foreign language requirement, comprehensive exam (for some programs), thesis (for some programs); for doctorate, one foreign language, comprehensive exam, thesis/dissertation. *Entrance requirements:* For master's, GRE (for some programs); for doctorate, GRE. Additional exam requirements/recommendations for international students: Required—TOEFL (minimum score 550 paper-based; 79 iBT), TWE (minimum score 5.5), Michigan English Language Assessment Battery (minimum score 85); Recommended—IELTS (minimum score 6.5). Application fee: $50. Electronic applications accepted. *Expenses:* $16,503 per year resident tuition and fees, $33,697 per year non-resident tuition and fees. *Financial support:* In 2016–17, 22 students received support, including 4 fellowships with tuition reimbursements available (averaging $13,500 per year), 17 teaching assistantships with tuition reimbursements available (averaging $17,994 per year); research assistantships, scholarships/grants, and unspecified assistantships also available. Financial award applicants required to submit FAFSA. *Faculty research:* Classical and modern literature and culture (Greek, Latin, Arabic, Chinese, French, German, Russian, Spanish) including colonial studies and exile and Holocaust studies; critical theory (French, German, Slavic, Spanish); theoretical and applied linguistics (Arabic, Chinese, French, Spanish); area studies (Arabic, Near Eastern, classical, Islamic, and Judaic studies). *Unit head:* Dr. Anne Duggan, Department Chair, 313-577-6244, Fax: 313-577-6243, E-mail: a.duggan@wayne.edu.
Website: http://clas.wayne.edu/languages/

# Russian

**American University,** College of Arts and Sciences, Department of World Languages and Cultures, Washington, DC 20016-8045. Offers Spanish: Latin American studies (MA); teaching English as a foreign language (MA); teaching English to speakers of other languages (MA, Certificate); translation: French (Certificate); translation: Russian (Certificate); translation: Spanish (Certificate). *Program availability:* Part-time, evening/weekend. *Faculty:* 42 full-time (31 women), 27 part-time/adjunct (18 women). *Students:* 41 full-time (31 women), 31 part-time (23 women); includes 14 minority (3 Black or African American, non-Hispanic/Latino; 2 Asian, non-Hispanic/Latino; 7 Hispanic/Latino; 2 Two or more races, non-Hispanic/Latino), 9 international. Average age 32. 73 applicants, 92% accepted, 20 enrolled. In 2016, 24 master's, 6 other advanced degrees awarded. *Degree requirements:* For master's, one foreign language, comprehensive exam, thesis or alternative. *Entrance requirements:* For master's, GRE, writing sample, statement of purpose, transcripts, 2 letters of recommendation, resume; for Certificate, bachelor's degree, statement of purpose, transcripts, resume. Additional exam requirements/recommendations for international students: Required—TOEFL (minimum score 100 iBT), IELTS (minimum score 7), PTE (minimum score 68). *Application deadline:* For fall admission, 2/1 for domestic students; for spring admission, 11/1 for domestic students. Application fee: $55. *Expenses:* $1,579 per credit tuition; $690 mandatory fees. *Financial support:* Institutionally sponsored loans, scholarships/grants, and unspecified assistantships available. Financial award application deadline: 2/1; financial award applicants required to submit FAFSA. *Unit head:* Henry Gerfen, Chair, 202-885-2385, Fax: 202-885-1076, E-mail: gerfen@american.edu. *Application contact:* Kathleen Clowery, Director of Graduate Admissions, 202-885-3620, Fax: 202-885-1344, E-mail: clowery@american.edu.
Website: http://www.american.edu/cas/wlc/

**Boston College,** Graduate School of Arts and Sciences, Department of Slavic and Eastern Languages and Literatures, Program in Russian, Chestnut Hill, MA 02467-3800. Offers MA, MA/JD, MBA/MA. *Faculty:* 6 full-time. *Students:* 2 full-time (1 woman). 3 applicants, 33% accepted. *Degree requirements:* For master's, 3 foreign languages, comprehensive exam, thesis or alternative. *Entrance requirements:* Additional exam requirements/recommendations for international students: Required—TOEFL (minimum score 600 paper-based; 100 iBT), IELTS (minimum score 8). *Application deadline:* For fall admission, 2/1 for domestic and international students. Application fee: $75. Electronic applications accepted. Tuition and fees vary according to program. *Financial support:* In 2016–17, 2 students received support, including fellowships with full tuition reimbursements available (averaging $9,200 per year), teaching assistantships with full tuition reimbursements available (averaging $9,200 per year); Federal Work-Study also available. Support available to part-time students. Financial award application deadline: 3/1; financial award applicants required to submit FAFSA. *Faculty research:* Structural analysis of language, poetry and semiotic systems. *Unit head:* Dr. Maxin Shrayer, Chairperson, 617-552-3910. *Application contact:* Dr. Michael Connolly, Graduate Program Director, 617-552-3912, E-mail: michael.connolly@bc.edu.
Website: https://www.bc.edu/schools/sl

**Brown University,** Graduate School, Department of Slavic Languages, Providence, RI 02912. Offers Russian language and literature (AM); Slavic linguistics (AM); Slavic studies (PhD). *Degree requirements:* For master's, one foreign language; for doctorate, 2 foreign languages, thesis/dissertation, preliminary exam.

**Columbia University,** Graduate School of Arts and Sciences, New York, NY 10027. Offers African-American studies (MA); American studies (MA); anthropology (MA, PhD); art history and archaeology (MA, PhD); astronomy (PhD); biological sciences (PhD); biotechnology (MA); chemical physics (PhD); chemistry (PhD); classical studies (MA, PhD); classics (MA, PhD); climate and society (MA); conservation biology (MA); earth and environmental sciences (PhD); East Asia: regional studies (MA); East Asian languages and cultures (MA, PhD); ecology, evolution and environmental biology (MA), including conservation biology; ecology, evolution, and environmental biology (PhD), including ecology and evolutionary biology, evolutionary primatology; economics (MA, PhD); English and comparative literature (MA, PhD); French and Romance philology (MA, PhD); Germanic languages (MA, PhD); global French studies (MA); global thought (MA); Hispanic cultural studies (MA); history (PhD); history and literature (MA); human rights studies (MA); Islamic studies (MA); Italian (MA, PhD); Japanese pedagogy (MA); Jewish studies (MA); Latin America and the Caribbean: regional studies (MA); Latin American and Iberian cultures (PhD); mathematics (MA, PhD), including finance (MA); medieval and Renaissance studies (MA); Middle Eastern, South Asian, and African studies (MA, PhD); modern art: critical and curatorial studies (MA); modern European studies (MA); museum anthropology (MA); music (DMA, PhD); oral history (MA); philosophical foundations of physics (MA); philosophy (MA, PhD); physics (PhD); political science (MA, PhD); psychology (PhD); quantitative methods in the social sciences (MA); religion (MA, PhD); Russia, Eurasia and East Europe: regional studies (MA); Russian translation (MA); Slavic cultures (MA); Slavic languages (MA, PhD); sociology (MA, PhD); South Asian studies (MA); statistics (MA, PhD); theatre (PhD). Dual-degree programs require admission to both Graduate School of Arts and Sciences and another Columbia school. *Program availability:* Part-time. Terminal master's awarded for partial completion of doctoral program. *Degree requirements:* For master's, variable foreign language requirement, comprehensive exam (for some programs), thesis (for some programs); for doctorate, variable foreign language requirement, comprehensive exam (for some programs), thesis/dissertation. *Entrance requirements:* For master's and doctorate, GRE General Test, GRE Subject Test (for some programs). Additional exam requirements/recommendations for international students: Required—TOEFL, IELTS. Electronic applications accepted.

**Harvard University,** Graduate School of Arts and Sciences, Department of Slavic Languages and Literatures, Cambridge, MA 02138. Offers Polish (PhD); Russian (PhD); Serbo-Croatian (PhD); Slavic philology (PhD); Ukrainian (PhD). *Degree requirements:* For doctorate, 4 foreign languages, thesis/dissertation. *Entrance requirements:* For doctorate, GRE General Test, writing sample. Additional exam requirements/recommendations for international students: Required—TOEFL.

**Kent State University,** College of Arts and Sciences, Department of Modern and Classical Language Studies, Kent, OH 44242-0001. Offers French (MA), including applied linguistics and pedagogy, literature; Latin (MA), including applied linguistics and pedagogy, literature; Spanish (MA), including applied linguistics and pedagogy, literature; translation (MA), including Arabic, French, German, Japanese, Russian, Spanish; translation studies (PhD); MA/MBA. *Program availability:* Part-time. *Faculty:* 35 full-time (23 women). *Students:* 81 full-time (51 women), 23 part-time (15 women); includes 14 minority (1 Black or African American, non-Hispanic/Latino; 9 Hispanic/Latino; 4 Two or more races, non-Hispanic/Latino), 48 international. Average age 30. 109 applicants, 53% accepted, 33 enrolled. In 2016, 31 master's, 6 doctorates awarded. *Degree requirements:* For master's, variable foreign language requirement, comprehensive exam (for some programs), thesis (for some programs); for doctorate, variable foreign language requirement, comprehensive exam, thesis/dissertation. *Entrance requirements:* For master's, transcripts, goal statement, 3 letters of recommendation, CD/MP3 with oral sample of first and second languages, writing sample of second language; for doctorate, transcripts; MA in translation, a foreign language, or similar field; proficiency in a foreign language; minimum GPA of 3.5 from MA; goal statement; 3 letters of recommendation; essay or writing sample. *Application deadline:* For fall admission, 2/1 for domestic and international students. Applications are processed on a rolling basis. Application fee: $45 ($70 for international students). Electronic applications accepted. *Expenses:* Tuition, state resident: full-time $10,864; part-time $495 per credit hour. Tuition, nonresident: full-time $18,380; part-time $837 per credit hour. *Financial support:* Fellowships with full tuition reimbursements, teaching assistantships with full tuition reimbursements, and unspecified assistantships available. Financial award application deadline: 2/1. *Unit head:* Dr. Keiran Dunne, Professor of French Translation/Chair, 330-672-2150, E-mail: kdunne@kent.edu. *Application contact:* Said Shiyab, Professor of Translation Studies/Graduate Coordinator, 330-672-1864, E-mail: sshiyab@kent.edu.
Website: http://www.kent.edu/mcls/

**McGill University,** Faculty of Graduate and Postdoctoral Studies, Faculty of Arts, Department of Russian and Slavic Studies, Montréal, QC H3A 2T5, Canada. Offers Russian literature (MA, PhD).

**Middlebury College,** Language Schools, Russian School, Middlebury, VT 05753-6002. Offers MA, DML. *Degree requirements:* For master's, one foreign language; for doctorate, 2 foreign languages, comprehensive exam, thesis/dissertation. *Entrance requirements:* For master's, language proficiency exam, placement exam, 3 letters of recommendation, writing sample in Russian, personal statement, transcripts; for doctorate, 1st and 2nd language exams, 3 letters of recommendation, writing sample in Russian, personal statement, transcripts. Electronic applications accepted. *Expenses:* Contact institution.

**New York University,** Graduate School of Arts and Science, Department of Russian and Slavic Studies, New York, NY 10012-1019. Offers Russian literature (MA); Slavic literature (MA). *Program availability:* Part-time. *Degree requirements:* For master's, one foreign language, comprehensive exam, thesis. *Entrance requirements:* For master's,

GRE General Test, minimum 3 years of undergraduate Russian or equivalent. Additional exam requirements/recommendations for international students: Required—TOEFL. *Faculty research:* Modern Russian literature and art, contemporary Russian and East European literature, literary theory, Slavic linguistics, Russian journalism.

**Penn State University Park,** Graduate School, College of the Liberal Arts, Department of Comparative Literature, University Park, PA 16802. Offers comparative literature (MA, PhD); Russian and comparative literature (MA). *Unit head:* Dr. Susan Welch, Dean, 814-865-7691, Fax: 814-863-2085. *Application contact:* Lori Hawn, Director, Graduate Student Services, 814-865-1795, Fax: 814-863-4627, E-mail: l-gswww@lists.psu.edu. Website: http://complit.la.psu.edu/

**Princeton University,** Graduate School, Department of Slavic Languages and Literatures, Princeton, NJ 08544-1019. Offers Russian and Slavic linguistics (PhD); Russian literature (PhD). *Degree requirements:* For doctorate, variable foreign language requirement, thesis/dissertation. *Entrance requirements:* For doctorate, GRE General Test. Additional exam requirements/recommendations for international students: Required—TOEFL (minimum score 600 paper-based). Electronic applications accepted.

**The University of Arizona,** College of Humanities, Department of Russian and Slavic Studies, Tucson, AZ 85721. Offers Russian (MA). *Program availability:* Part-time. *Degree requirements:* For master's, one foreign language, comprehensive exam (for some programs), thesis (for some programs). *Entrance requirements:* For master's, 3 letters of recommendation, audio sample. Additional exam requirements/recommendations for international students: Required—TOEFL (minimum score 550 paper-based; 79 iBT). Electronic applications accepted. *Faculty research:* Russian literature, language/pedagogy, linguistics, Russian culture.

**University of California, Berkeley,** Graduate Division, College of Letters and Science, Department of Slavic Languages and Literatures, Berkeley, CA 94720-1500. Offers Czech (PhD), including Czech linguistics, Czech literature; Polish (PhD), including Polish linguistics, Polish literature; Russian (PhD), including Russian linguistics, Russian literature; Serbo-Croatian (PhD), including Serbo-Croatian linguistics, Serbo-Croatian literature. *Faculty:* 15 full-time. *Students:* 18 full-time (11 women); includes 2 minority (both Asian, non-Hispanic/Latino), 4 international. Average age 30. 26 applicants, 2 enrolled. In 2016, 4 doctorates awarded. Terminal master's awarded for partial completion of doctoral program. *Degree requirements:* For doctorate, thesis/dissertation, oral and written exams. *Entrance requirements:* For doctorate, GRE General Test, minimum GPA of 3.0, 3 letters of recommendation. Additional exam requirements/recommendations for international students: Required—TOEFL (minimum score 570 paper-based). *Application deadline:* For fall admission, 12/21 for domestic students. Application fee: $105 ($125 for international students). Electronic applications accepted. *Financial support:* Fellowships, research assistantships, teaching assistantships, institutionally sponsored loans, health care benefits, and unspecified assistantships available. Financial award applicants required to submit FAFSA. *Unit head:* Eric Naiman, Chair, 510-642-2979, E-mail: issa@berkeley.edu. *Application contact:* Seth Arnopole, Student Affairs Officer, 510-642-9051, Fax: 510-643-6220, E-mail: issag@berkeley.edu. Website: http://slavic.berkeley.edu

**The University of Manchester,** School of Languages, Linguistics and Cultures, Manchester, United Kingdom. Offers Arab world studies (PhD); Chinese studies (M Phil, PhD); East Asian studies (M Phil, PhD); English language (PhD); French studies (M Phil, PhD); German studies (M Phil, PhD); interpreting studies (PhD); Italian studies (M Phil, PhD); Japanese studies (M Phil, PhD); Latin American cultural studies (M Phil, PhD); linguistics (M Phil, PhD); Middle Eastern studies (M Phil, PhD); Polish studies (M Phil, PhD); Portuguese studies (M Phil, PhD); Russian studies (M Phil, PhD); Spanish studies (M Phil, PhD); translation and intercultural studies (M Phil, PhD).

**University of Missouri,** Office of Research and Graduate Studies, College of Arts and Science, Department of German and Russian Studies, Columbia, MO 65211. Offers MA. *Faculty:* 20 full-time (6 women). *Students:* 11 full-time (10 women), 6 part-time (4 women). *Entrance requirements:* For master's, GRE General Test, minimum GPA of 3.0. Additional exam requirements/recommendations for international students: Required—TOEFL (minimum score 500 paper-based; 61 iBT). *Application deadline:* For fall admission, 2/1 priority date for domestic and international students. Applications are processed on a rolling basis. Application fee: $75 ($90 for international students). Electronic applications accepted. *Expenses:* Tuition, state resident: full-time $6347; part-time $352.60 per credit hour. Tuition, nonresident: full-time $17,379; part-time $965.50 per credit hour. *Required fees:* $1035. Tuition and fees vary according to course load, campus/location and program. *Financial support:* Teaching assistantships with full tuition reimbursements, institutionally sponsored loans, health care benefits, and unspecified assistantships available. *Faculty research:* German and Russian cultural studies including literature, film, media studies, philosophy, and the history of science. Website: http://german.missouri.edu/index.html

**University of Oregon,** Graduate School, College of Arts and Sciences, Program in Russian and East European Studies, Eugene, OR 97403. Offers MA. *Program availability:* Part-time. *Degree requirements:* For master's, 2 foreign languages, thesis. *Entrance requirements:* For master's, GRE General Test (recommended), minimum GPA of 3.0. Additional exam requirements/recommendations for international students: Required—TOEFL. *Faculty research:* L. N. Tolstoy's middle years, Russian folklore in eighteenth-century contexts, Bulgarian syntax, medieval Bulgarian texts, contemporary Russian culture film.

**University of South Africa,** College of Human Sciences, Pretoria, South Africa. Offers adult education (M Ed); African languages (MA, PhD); African politics (MA, PhD); Afrikaans (MA, PhD); ancient history (MA, PhD); ancient Near Eastern studies (MA, PhD); anthropology (MA, PhD); applied linguistics (MA); Arabic (MA, PhD); archaeology (MA); art history (MA); Biblical archaeology (MA); Biblical studies (M Th, D Th, PhD); Christian spirituality (M Th, D Th); church history (M Th, D Th); classical studies (MA, PhD); clinical psychology (MA); communication (MA, PhD); comparative education (M Ed, Ed D); consulting psychology (D Admin, D Com, PhD); curriculum studies (M Ed, Ed D); development studies (M Admin, MA, D Admin, PhD); didactics (M Ed, Ed D); education (M Tech); education management (M Ed, Ed D); educational psychology (M Ed); English (MA); environmental education (M Ed); French (MA, PhD); German (MA, PhD); Greek (MA); guidance and counseling (M Ed); health studies (MA, PhD), including health sciences education (MA), health services management (MA), medical and surgical nursing science (critical care general) (MA), midwifery and neonatal nursing science (MA), trauma and emergency care (MA); history (MA, PhD); history of education (Ed D); inclusive education (M Ed, Ed D); information and communications technology policy and regulation (MA); information science (MA, MIS, PhD); international politics (MA, PhD); Islamic studies (MA, PhD); Italian (MA, PhD); Judaica (MA, PhD); linguistics (MA, PhD); mathematical education (M Ed); mathematics education (MA); missiology (M Th, D Th); modern Hebrew (MA, PhD); musicology (MA, MMus, D Mus, PhD); natural science education (M Ed); New Testament (M Th, D Th); Old Testament (D Th); pastoral therapy (M Th, D Th); philosophy (MA); philosophy of education (M Ed, Ed D); politics (MA, PhD); Portuguese (MA, PhD); practical theology (M Th, D Th); psychology (MA, MS, PhD); psychology of education (M Ed, Ed D); public health (MA); religious studies (MA, D Th, PhD); Romance languages (MA); Russian (MA, PhD); Semitic languages (MA, PhD); social behavior studies in HIV/AIDS (MA); social science (mental health) (MA); social science in development studies (MA); social science in psychology (MA); social science in social work (MA); social science in sociology (MA); social work (MSW, DSW, PhD); socio-education (M Ed, Ed D); sociolinguistics (MA); sociology (MA, PhD); Spanish (MA, PhD); systematic theology (M Th, D Th); TESOL (teaching English to speakers of other languages) (MA); theological ethics (M Th, D Th); theory of literature (MA, PhD); urban ministries (D Th); urban ministry (M Th).

**The University of Tennessee,** Graduate School, College of Arts and Sciences, Department of Modern Foreign Languages and Literatures, Program in Modern Foreign Languages, Knoxville, TN 37996. Offers applied linguistics (PhD); French (PhD); German (PhD); Italian (PhD); Portuguese (PhD); Russian (PhD); Spanish (PhD). *Degree requirements:* For doctorate, 2 foreign languages, thesis/dissertation. *Entrance requirements:* For doctorate, minimum GPA of 2.7. Additional exam requirements/recommendations for international students: Required—TOEFL. Electronic applications accepted.

**University of Washington,** Graduate School, College of Arts and Sciences, Department of Slavic Languages and Literatures, Seattle, WA 98195. Offers Russian literature (MA, PhD); Slavic linguistics (MA, PhD). *Degree requirements:* For master's, 2 foreign languages, thesis optional; for doctorate, 3 foreign languages, thesis/dissertation. *Entrance requirements:* For master's and doctorate, GRE General Test, minimum GPA of 3.0. Additional exam requirements/recommendations for international students: Required—TOEFL. Electronic applications accepted. *Faculty research:* Modern and medieval East European languages and literatures, comparative literature, Russian folk literature, Slavic literary theory and criticism, computerized morphology of Russian.

**University of Waterloo,** Graduate Studies, Faculty of Arts, Department of Germanic and Slavic Studies, Waterloo, ON N2L 3G1, Canada. Offers German (MA, PhD); Russian (MA). *Program availability:* Part-time, evening/weekend. *Degree requirements:* For master's, one foreign language, thesis optional; for doctorate, 2 foreign languages, comprehensive exam, thesis/dissertation. *Entrance requirements:* For master's, honors degree, minimum B average; for doctorate, master's degree, minimum B average. Additional exam requirements/recommendations for international students: Required—TOEFL, IELTS, PTE. Electronic applications accepted. *Faculty research:* Medieval theatre; history and literature; German and Russian literary relations; seventeenth-, eighteenth-, nineteenth-, and twentieth-century German literature.

**Yale University,** Graduate School of Arts and Sciences, Department of Slavic Languages and Literatures, New Haven, CT 06520. Offers medieval Slavic literature and philology (PhD); Polish literature (PhD); Russian literature (PhD); Slavic languages and literatures and film studies (PhD). *Degree requirements:* For doctorate, 3 foreign languages, thesis/dissertation. *Entrance requirements:* For doctorate, GRE General Test.

# Scandinavian Languages

**Cornell University,** Graduate School, Graduate Fields of Arts and Sciences, Field of Germanic Studies, Ithaca, NY 14853. Offers German area studies (MA, PhD); German intellectual history (MA, PhD); Germanic linguistics (MA, PhD); Germanic literature (MA, PhD); old Norse (MA, PhD). Terminal master's awarded for partial completion of doctoral program. *Degree requirements:* For master's, one foreign language, thesis; for doctorate, 2 foreign languages, comprehensive exam, thesis/dissertation. *Entrance requirements:* For master's and doctorate, GRE General Test, fluency in German, writing sample, 2 letters of recommendation. Additional exam requirements/recommendations for international students: Required—TOEFL (minimum score 550 paper-based; 77 iBT). Electronic applications accepted. *Faculty research:* Women's studies, minority literature, literature and intellectual history, theater and film studies, Continental philosophy.

**Harvard University,** Graduate School of Arts and Sciences, Department of Germanic Languages and Literatures, Cambridge, MA 02138. Offers German (PhD); Scandinavian (PhD). Terminal master's awarded for partial completion of doctoral program. *Degree requirements:* For doctorate, 2 foreign languages, thesis/dissertation, exams. *Entrance requirements:* For doctorate, GRE General Test, German writing sample. Additional exam requirements/recommendations for international students: Required—TOEFL.

**University of California, Berkeley,** Graduate Division, College of Letters and Science, Department of Scandinavian Languages and Literatures, Berkeley, CA 94720-1500. Offers PhD. *Faculty:* 6 full-time. *Students:* 12 full-time (7 women). Average age 33. 10 applicants, 2 enrolled. In 2016, 2 doctorates awarded. *Degree requirements:* For doctorate, 2 foreign languages, thesis/dissertation, 3 field papers, qualifying exam. *Entrance requirements:* For doctorate, GRE General Test, minimum GPA of 3.0, MA in Scandinavian language or equivalent, 3 letters of recommendation. Additional exam requirements/recommendations for international students: Required—TOEFL (minimum score 570 paper-based; 90 iBT). *Application deadline:* For fall admission, 1/3 for domestic students. Application fee: $105 ($125 for international students). Electronic applications accepted. *Financial support:* Fellowships, research assistantships, teaching assistantships, institutionally sponsored loans, health care benefits, and unspecified assistantships available. *Faculty research:* Modern literatures, old Norse language and literatures, folklore, film. *Unit head:* Prof. Mark Sandberg, Chair, 510-642-4484, E-mail: issa@berkeley.edu. *Application contact:* Seth Arnopole, Student Affairs Officer, 510-642-9051, Fax: 510-643-6220, E-mail: issag@berkeley.edu. Website: http://scandinavian.berkeley.edu

**University of California, Los Angeles,** Graduate Division, College of Letters and Science, Department of Germanic Languages, Program in Scandinavian, Los Angeles, CA 90095. Offers MA. *Degree requirements:* For master's, 3 foreign languages, comprehensive exam. *Entrance requirements:* For master's, GRE General Test, bachelor's degree; minimum undergraduate GPA of 3.0 (or its equivalent if letter grade system not used); writing sample. Additional exam requirements/recommendations for international students: Required—TOEFL. Electronic applications accepted.

**University of Massachusetts Amherst,** Graduate School, College of Humanities and Fine Arts, Department of Languages, Literatures, and Cultures, Programs in German and Scandinavian Studies, Amherst, MA 01003. Offers MA, PhD. *Program availability:* Part-time. Terminal master's awarded for partial completion of doctoral program. *Degree requirements:* For master's, thesis or alternative; for doctorate, one foreign language, comprehensive exam, thesis/dissertation. *Entrance requirements:* For master's and doctorate, writing sample in English and German. Additional exam requirements/recommendations for international students: Required—TOEFL (minimum score 550 paper-based; 80 iBT), IELTS (minimum score 6.5). Electronic applications accepted.

**University of Minnesota, Twin Cities Campus,** Graduate School, College of Liberal Arts, Department of German, Scandinavian, and Dutch, Minneapolis, MN 55455. Offers Germanic studies (MA, PhD), including German, Germanic medieval studies, Scandinavian studies (MA). *Program availability:* Part-time. Terminal master's awarded for partial completion of doctoral program. *Degree requirements:* For doctorate, 2 foreign languages, thesis/dissertation. *Entrance requirements:* For master's, GRE General Test, BA in German, Scandinavian, or equivalent; for doctorate, MA in German, Scandinavian, or equivalent. Additional exam requirements/recommendations for international students: Required—TOEFL (minimum score 550 paper-based; 79 iBT). Electronic

applications accepted. *Faculty research:* Cultural studies, literary theory, feminist criticism, film, Germanic medieval studies.

**University of Washington,** Graduate School, College of Arts and Sciences, Department of Scandinavian Studies, Seattle, WA 98195. Offers MA, PhD. *Degree requirements:* For master's, one foreign language, comprehensive exam, thesis optional; for doctorate, 2 foreign languages, comprehensive exam, thesis/dissertation. *Entrance requirements:* For master's, GRE, BA in Scandinavian or equivalent, minimum GPA of 3.0; for doctorate, GRE, master's degree, minimum GPA of 3.0. Additional exam requirements/recommendations for international students: Required—TOEFL. *Faculty research:* Scandinavian folklore, history, and politics; medieval to modern Scandinavian literature; Scandinavian fiction, poetry, drama, literary history, and theory.

**University of Wisconsin–Madison,** Graduate School, College of Letters and Science, Department of Scandinavian Studies, Madison, WI 53706-1380. Offers area studies (MA); folklore (PhD); literature (MA, PhD); philology (PhD). *Program availability:* Part-time. *Degree requirements:* For master's, 2 foreign languages, exam; for doctorate, thesis/dissertation, exam. *Entrance requirements:* For master's, minimum GPA of 3.25; for doctorate, minimum GPA of 3.5. Electronic applications accepted. *Faculty research:* Historical fiction, Icelandic poetry, nineteenth-century literature, theater, gender studies, folklore.

# Slavic Languages

**Brown University,** Graduate School, Department of Slavic Languages, Providence, RI 02912. Offers Russian language and literature (AM); Slavic linguistics (AM); Slavic studies (PhD). *Degree requirements:* For master's, one foreign language; for doctorate, 2 foreign languages, thesis/dissertation, preliminary exam.

**Columbia University,** Graduate School of Arts and Sciences, New York, NY 10027. Offers African-American studies (MA); American studies (MA); anthropology (MA, PhD); art history and archaeology (MA, PhD); astronomy (PhD); biological sciences (PhD); biotechnology (MA); chemical physics (PhD); chemistry (PhD); classical studies (MA, PhD); classics (MA, PhD); climate and society (MA); conservation biology (MA); earth and environmental sciences (PhD); East Asia: regional studies (MA); East Asian languages and cultures (MA, PhD); ecology, evolution and environmental biology (MA), including conservation biology; ecology, evolution, and environmental biology (PhD), including ecology and evolutionary biology, evolutionary primatology; economics (MA, PhD); English and comparative literature (MA, PhD); French and Romance philology (MA, PhD); Germanic languages (MA, PhD); global French studies (MA); global thought (MA); Hispanic cultural studies (MA); history (PhD); history and literature (MA); human rights studies (MA); Islamic studies (MA); Italian (MA); Japanese pedagogy (MA); Jewish studies (MA); Latin America and the Caribbean: regional studies (MA); Latin American and Iberian cultures (PhD); mathematics (MA, PhD), including finance (MA); medieval and Renaissance studies (MA); Middle Eastern, South Asian, and African studies (MA, PhD); modern art: critical and curatorial studies (MA); modern European studies (MA); museum anthropology (MA); music (DMA, PhD); oral history (MA); philosophical foundations of physics (MA); philosophy (MA, PhD); physics (PhD); political science (MA, PhD); psychology (PhD); quantitative methods in the social sciences (MA, PhD); religion (MA, PhD); Russia, Eurasia and East Europe: regional studies (MA); Russian translation (MA); Slavic cultures (MA); Slavic languages (MA, PhD); sociology (MA, PhD); South Asian studies (MA); statistics (MA, PhD); theatre (PhD). Dual-degree programs require admission to both Graduate School of Arts and Sciences and another Columbia school. *Program availability:* Part-time. Terminal master's awarded for partial completion of doctoral program. *Degree requirements:* For master's, variable foreign language requirement, comprehensive exam (for some programs), thesis (for some programs); for doctorate, variable foreign language requirement, comprehensive exam (for some programs), thesis/dissertation. *Entrance requirements:* For master's and doctorate, GRE General Test, GRE Subject Test (for some programs). Additional exam requirements/recommendations for international students: Required—TOEFL, IELTS. Electronic applications accepted.

**Cornell University,** Graduate School, Graduate Fields of Arts and Sciences, Field of Linguistics, Ithaca, NY 14853. Offers applied linguistics (MA, PhD); East Asian linguistics (MA, PhD); English linguistics (MA, PhD); general linguistics (MA, PhD); Germanic linguistics (MA, PhD); Indo-European linguistics (MA, PhD); phonetics (MA, PhD); phonological theory (MA, PhD); Romance linguistics (MA, PhD); second language acquisition (MA, PhD); semantics (MA, PhD); Slavic linguistics (MA, PhD); sociolinguistics (MA, PhD); South Asian linguistics (MA, PhD); Southeast Asian linguistics (MA, PhD); syntactic theory (MA, PhD). Terminal master's awarded for partial completion of doctoral program. *Degree requirements:* For master's, one foreign language, thesis; for doctorate, one foreign language, comprehensive exam, thesis/dissertation. *Entrance requirements:* For master's and doctorate, GRE General Test, 2 letters of recommendation. Additional exam requirements/recommendations for international students: Required—TOEFL (minimum score 600 paper-based; 77 iBT). Electronic applications accepted. *Faculty research:* Phonology and phonetics, syntax and semantics, historical linguistics, philosophy of language, language acquisition.

**Duke University,** Graduate School, Department of Slavic and Eurasian Studies, Durham, NC 27708. Offers AM, Certificate. *Program availability:* Part-time. *Entrance requirements:* For master's, GRE General Test, writing sample. Additional exam requirements/recommendations for international students: Required—TOEFL (minimum score 577 paper-based; 90 iBT) or IELTS (minimum score 7). Electronic applications accepted.

**Florida State University,** The Graduate School, College of Arts and Sciences, Department of Modern Languages and Linguistics, Program in Slavic Languages/Russian, Tallahassee, FL 32306. Offers Slavic languages and literatures (MA). *Faculty:* 3 full-time (2 women). *Students:* 5 full-time (4 women), 2 part-time (both women); includes 1 minority (Black or African American, non-Hispanic/Latino). Average age 24. 3 applicants, 100% accepted, 3 enrolled. *Degree requirements:* For master's, thesis optional. *Entrance requirements:* For master's, GRE General Test, minimum GPA of 3.0. Additional exam requirements/recommendations for international students: Required—TOEFL (minimum score 550 paper-based; 80 iBT). *Application deadline:* For fall admission, 2/15 for domestic and international students. Applications are processed on a rolling basis. Application fee: $30. Electronic applications accepted. *Expenses:* Tuition, state resident: full-time $7263; part-time $403.51 per credit hour. Tuition, nonresident: full-time $18,087; part-time $1004.85 per credit hour. *Required fees:* $1365; $75.81 per credit hour. $20 per semester. Tuition and fees vary according to campus/location. *Financial support:* In 2016–17, 3 students received support, including 4 teaching assistantships with partial tuition reimbursements available (averaging

$14,000 per year); fellowships and institutionally sponsored loans also available. Financial award application deadline: 2/1; financial award applicants required to submit FAFSA. *Faculty research:* Contemporary literature, emigre literature, Old Russian word formation, political rhetoric, structure of modern Russian. *Total annual research expenditures:* $4,500. *Unit head:* Dr. Robert Romanchuk, Divisional Coordinator, 850-644-8198, Fax: 850-644-0524, E-mail: rromanch@fsu.edu. *Application contact:* Wendy E. Pigott, Graduate Academic Coordinator, 850-644-8397, Fax: 850-644-0524, E-mail: wpigott@fsu.edu.

**Harvard University,** Graduate School of Arts and Sciences, Department of Slavic Languages and Literatures, Cambridge, MA 02138. Offers Polish (PhD); Russian (PhD); Serbo-Croatian (PhD); Slavic philology (PhD); Ukrainian (PhD). *Degree requirements:* For doctorate, 4 foreign languages, thesis/dissertation. *Entrance requirements:* For doctorate, GRE General Test, writing sample. Additional exam requirements/recommendations for international students: Required—TOEFL.

**Indiana University Bloomington,** University Graduate School, College of Arts and Sciences, Department of Slavic Languages and Literatures, Bloomington, IN 47405. Offers MA, MAT, PhD. *Program availability:* Part-time. Terminal master's awarded for partial completion of doctoral program. *Degree requirements:* For master's, variable foreign language requirement; for doctorate, variable foreign language requirement, comprehensive exam, thesis/dissertation. *Entrance requirements:* For master's, GRE General Test. Additional exam requirements/recommendations for international students: Required—TOEFL. Electronic applications accepted. *Faculty research:* Russian stress, Slavic accentology and morphophonemics, Eastern European literature, Bible translation.

**New York University,** Graduate School of Arts and Science, Department of Russian and Slavic Studies, New York, NY 10012-1019. Offers Russian literature (MA); Slavic literature (MA). *Program availability:* Part-time. *Degree requirements:* For master's, one foreign language, comprehensive exam, thesis. *Entrance requirements:* For master's, GRE General Test, minimum 3 years of undergraduate Russian or equivalent. Additional exam requirements/recommendations for international students: Required—TOEFL. *Faculty research:* Modern Russian literature and art, contemporary Russian and East European literature, literary theory, Slavic linguistics, Russian journalism.

**Northwestern University,** The Graduate School, Judd A. and Marjorie Weinberg College of Arts and Sciences, Department of Slavic Languages and Literature, Evanston, IL 60208. Offers PhD. Admissions and degrees offered through The Graduate School. *Program availability:* Part-time. *Degree requirements:* For doctorate, 3 foreign languages, thesis/dissertation. *Entrance requirements:* For doctorate, GRE General Test. Additional exam requirements/recommendations for international students: Required—TOEFL. *Faculty research:* Russian poetry and prose, nineteenth through twentieth centuries, translation and Russian culture, Russian intellectual history, Slavic literature and nationalism, Polish poetry.

**The Ohio State University,** Graduate School, College of Arts and Sciences, Division of Arts and Humanities, Department of Slavic and East European Languages and Cultures, Columbus, OH 43210. Offers Slavic linguistics (MA, PhD); Slavic literature, film, and cultural studies (MA, PhD). *Faculty:* 11. *Students:* 14 full-time (10 women), 1 (woman) part-time. Average age 30. In 2016, 2 master's, 2 doctorates awarded. Terminal master's awarded for partial completion of doctoral program. *Degree requirements:* For master's, variable foreign language requirement, thesis optional; for doctorate, variable foreign language requirement, thesis/dissertation. *Entrance requirements:* For master's and doctorate, GRE General Test, at least 3 years of Russian language study or equivalent. Additional exam requirements/recommendations for international students: Required—TOEFL (minimum score 550 paper-based; 79 iBT), Michigan English Language Assessment Battery (minimum score 82); Recommended—IELTS (minimum score 7). *Application deadline:* For fall admission, 12/12 priority date for domestic students, 11/30 priority date for international students; for spring admission, 3/1 for domestic students, 2/1 for international students. Applications are processed on a rolling basis. Application fee: $60 ($70 for international students). Electronic applications accepted. *Financial support:* Fellowships with tuition reimbursements, teaching assistantships with tuition reimbursements, Federal Work-Study, and institutionally sponsored loans available. Support available to part-time students. *Faculty research:* Polish literature. *Unit head:* Dr. Yana Hashamova, Chair and Professor, 614-292-6733, E-mail: hashamova.1@osu.edu. *Application contact:* Graduate and Professional Admissions, 614-292-9444, Fax: 614-292-3895, E-mail: gpadmissions@osu.edu. Website: http://slavic.osu.edu/

**Princeton University,** Graduate School, Department of Slavic Languages and Literatures, Princeton, NJ 08544-1019. Offers Russian and Slavic linguistics (PhD); Russian literature (PhD). *Degree requirements:* For doctorate, variable foreign language requirement, thesis/dissertation. *Entrance requirements:* For doctorate, GRE General Test. Additional exam requirements/recommendations for international students: Required—TOEFL (minimum score 600 paper-based). Electronic applications accepted.

**Stanford University,** School of Humanities and Sciences, Department of Slavic Languages and Literatures, Stanford, CA 94305-2004. Offers PhD. Terminal master's awarded for partial completion of doctoral program. *Degree requirements:* For doctorate, 3 foreign languages, thesis/dissertation. *Entrance requirements:* For doctorate, GRE General Test. Additional exam requirements/recommendations for international students: Required—TOEFL. Electronic applications accepted. *Expenses:* Tuition: Full-time $47,331. *Required fees:* $609.

**University of Alberta,** Faculty of Graduate Studies and Research, Department of Modern Languages and Cultural Studies, Edmonton, AB T6G 2E1, Canada. Offers applied linguistics (Germanic, Romance, Slavic) (MA); French language, literatures and linguistics (PhD); French language, literatures, and linguistics (MA); Germanic languages, literatures and linguistics (PhD); Germanic languages, literatures, and linguistics (MA); Italian studies (MA); Slavic languages and literatures (Russian, Ukrainian) (MA, PhD); Slavic linguistics (Russian, Ukrainian) (MA, PhD); Spanish and Latin American studies (MA, PhD); Ukrainian folklore (MA, PhD). *Program availability:* Part-time. *Degree requirements:* For master's, one foreign language, thesis; for doctorate, 2 foreign languages, comprehensive exam, thesis/dissertation. *Entrance requirements:* For master's and doctorate, 1 language other than English. Additional exam requirements/recommendations for international students: Required—Michigan English Language Assessment Battery or TOEFL (minimum score 550 paper-based). Electronic applications accepted. *Faculty research:* Russian/Ukrainian studies; German studies; contemporary Latin American, French and Francophone studies; Italian studies.

**University of California, Berkeley,** Graduate Division, College of Letters and Science, Department of Slavic Languages and Literatures, Berkeley, CA 94720-1500. Offers Czech (PhD), including Czech linguistics, Czech literature; Polish (PhD), including Polish linguistics, Polish literature; Russian (PhD), including Russian linguistics, Russian literature; Serbo-Croatian (PhD), including Serbo-Croatian linguistics, Serbo-Croatian literature. *Faculty:* 15 full-time. *Students:* 18 full-time (11 women); includes 2 minority (both Asian, non-Hispanic/Latino), 4 international. Average age 30. 26 applicants, 2 enrolled. In 2016, 4 doctorates awarded. Terminal master's awarded for partial completion of doctoral program. *Degree requirements:* For doctorate, thesis/dissertation, oral and written exams. *Entrance requirements:* For doctorate, GRE General Test, minimum GPA of 3.0, 3 letters of recommendation. Additional exam requirements/recommendations for international students: Required—TOEFL (minimum score 570 paper-based). *Application deadline:* For fall admission, 12/21 for domestic students. Application fee: $105 ($125 for international students). Electronic applications accepted. *Financial support:* Fellowships, research assistantships, teaching assistantships, institutionally sponsored loans, health care benefits, and unspecified assistantships available. Financial award applicants required to submit FAFSA. *Unit head:* Eric Naiman, Chair, 510-642-2979, E-mail: issa@berkeley.edu. *Application contact:* Seth Arnopole, Student Affairs Officer, 510-642-9051, Fax: 510-643-6220, E-mail: issag@berkeley.edu.
Website: http://slavic.berkeley.edu

**University of California, Los Angeles,** Graduate Division, College of Letters and Science, Department of Slavic Languages and Literatures, Los Angeles, CA 90095. Offers MA, PhD. Terminal master's awarded for partial completion of doctoral program. *Degree requirements:* For master's, 2 foreign languages, comprehensive exam; for doctorate, 2 foreign languages, thesis/dissertation, oral and written qualifying exams. *Entrance requirements:* For master's and doctorate, GRE General Test (not required for applicants whose native language not English), bachelor's degree; minimum undergraduate GPA of 3.0 (or its equivalent if letter grade system not used); writing sample. Additional exam requirements/recommendations for international students: Required—TOEFL. Electronic applications accepted.

**University of Chicago,** Division of the Humanities, Master of Arts Program in the Humanities, Chicago, IL 60637. Offers art history (MA); cinema and media studies (MA); classic languages (MA); comparative literature (MA); creative writing (MA); cultural policy studies (MA); digital humanities (MA); East Asian languages and civilizations (MA); English language and literature (MA); gender and sexuality studies (MA); Germanic studies (MA); linguistics (MA); music (MA); near Eastern languages and civilizations (MA); philosophy (MA); poetics (MA); race, politics and culture (MA); Romance languages and literatures (MA); Slavic languages and literatures (MA); South Asian languages and civilizations (MA); theater and performance studies (MA). *Students:* 80 full-time (43 women), 7 part-time (3 women); includes 20 minority (5 Black or African American, non-Hispanic/Latino; 1 American Indian or Alaska Native, non-Hispanic/Latino; 6 Asian, non-Hispanic/Latino; 5 Hispanic/Latino; 3 Two or more races, non-Hispanic/Latino), 11 international. Average age 26. 706 applicants, 15% accepted, 42 enrolled. In 2016, 92 master's awarded. *Degree requirements:* For master's, thesis. *Entrance requirements:* For master's, GRE General Test. Additional exam requirements/recommendations for international students: Required—TOEFL (minimum score 104 iBT), IELTS (minimum score 7). *Application deadline:* For fall admission, 1/3 for domestic and international students. Application fee: $90. Electronic applications accepted. *Financial support:* In 2016–17, 8 fellowships with partial tuition reimbursements (averaging $12,000 per year) were awarded; Federal Work-Study, institutionally sponsored loans, scholarships/grants, and tuition waivers (partial) also available. Financial award application deadline: 12/15; financial award applicants required to submit FAFSA. *Unit head:* Malynne Sternstein, Co-Director, 773-834-1201, Fax: 773-834-7526. *Application contact:* Program Coordinator, 773-834-1201, Fax: 773-834-7526, E-mail: ma-humanities@uchicago.edu.
Website: http://maph.uchicago.edu/

**University of Illinois at Chicago,** College of Liberal Arts and Sciences, School of Literatures, Cultural Studies and Linguistics, Department of Slavic and Baltic Languages and Literatures, Chicago, IL 60607-7128. Offers Slavic studies (MA, PhD). *Program availability:* Evening/weekend. Terminal master's awarded for partial completion of doctoral program. *Degree requirements:* For doctorate, one foreign language, thesis/dissertation. *Entrance requirements:* For master's and doctorate, GRE General Test, minimum GPA of 3.0. Additional exam requirements/recommendations for international students: Required—TOEFL. Electronic applications accepted. *Faculty research:* Twentieth-century Polish literature and culture, Russian and Polish modernisms, nineteenth- and twentieth-century Russian literature, Lithuanian language, Polish-Jewish culture and history, Yiddish literature and language.

**University of Illinois at Urbana–Champaign,** Graduate College, College of Liberal Arts and Sciences, School of Literatures, Cultures and Linguistics, Department of Slavic Languages and Literatures, Champaign, IL 61820. Offers MA, PhD.

**The University of Kansas,** Graduate Studies, College of Liberal Arts and Sciences, Department of Slavic Languages and Literatures, Lawrence, KS 66045. Offers MA, PhD. *Students:* 15 full-time (11 women), 6 international. Average age 31. 11 applicants, 91% accepted, 5 enrolled. In 2016, 3 master's awarded. Terminal master's awarded for partial completion of doctoral program. *Entrance requirements:* For master's and doctorate, GRE, curriculum vitae, statement of academic objectives (500 words), Russian language essay (1-2 pages), writing sample (5000-7000 words), official transcripts. Additional exam requirements/recommendations for international students: Required—TOEFL (minimum score 80 iBT). *Application deadline:* For fall admission, 1/31 priority date for domestic and international students. Application fee: $65 ($85 for international students). Electronic applications accepted. *Financial support:* Fellowships, teaching assistantships, Federal Work-Study, institutionally sponsored loans, scholarships/grants, and unspecified assistantships available. Financial award application deadline: 1/31. *Faculty research:* Russian and south Slavic linguistics, Polish and Russian literature, folklore, Russian intellectual history, Slavic culture. *Unit head:* Stephen M. Dickey, Chair, 785-864-2357, E-mail: smd@ku.edu. *Application contact:* Cari Ann Kreienhop, Senior Academic Advisor, Graduate Programs, 785-864-3665, E-mail: ckreienhop@ku.edu. Website: https://slavic.ku.edu/

**The University of Manchester,** School of Languages, Linguistics and Cultures, Manchester, United Kingdom. Offers Arab world studies (PhD); Chinese studies (M Phil, PhD); East Asian studies (M Phil, PhD); English language (PhD); French studies (M Phil, PhD); German studies (M Phil, PhD); interpreting studies (PhD); Italian studies (M Phil, PhD); Japanese studies (M Phil, PhD); Latin American cultural studies (M Phil, PhD); linguistics (M Phil, PhD); Middle Eastern studies (M Phil, PhD); Polish studies (M Phil, PhD); Portuguese studies (M Phil, PhD); Russian studies (M Phil, PhD); Spanish studies (M Phil, PhD); translation and intercultural studies (M Phil, PhD).

**University of Manitoba,** Faculty of Graduate Studies, Faculty of Arts, Department of German and Slavic Studies, Winnipeg, MB R3T 2N2, Canada. Offers German language and literature (MA); Slavic languages and literatures (MA). *Degree requirements:* For master's, one foreign language, thesis or alternative.

**University of Michigan,** Rackham Graduate School, College of Literature, Science, and the Arts, Department of Slavic Languages and Literatures, Ann Arbor, MI 48109-1275. Offers AM, PhD. *Faculty:* 10 full-time (7 women). *Students:* 11 full-time (8 women), 1 international. Average age 29. 20 applicants, 25% accepted, 2 enrolled. In 2016, 4 doctorates awarded. Terminal master's awarded for partial completion of doctoral program. *Degree requirements:* For doctorate, 3 foreign languages, comprehensive exam, thesis/dissertation, oral defense of dissertation, preliminary exam. *Entrance requirements:* For doctorate, GRE General Test. Additional exam requirements/recommendations for international students: Required—TOEFL (minimum score 560 paper-based). *Application deadline:* For fall admission, 1/15 priority date for domestic and international students. Application fee: $75 ($90 for international students). Electronic applications accepted. *Expenses:* Tuition, state resident: full-time $21,466; part-time $1152 per credit hour. Tuition, nonresident: full-time $43,346; part-time $2367 per credit hour. Part-time tuition and fees vary according to course load, degree level and program. *Financial support:* In 2016–17, 18 students received support, including 11 fellowships with full tuition reimbursements available (averaging $19,740 per year), 6 teaching assistantships with full tuition reimbursements available (averaging $19,737 per year); institutionally sponsored loans, scholarships/grants, health care benefits, and unspecified assistantships also available. Financial award application deadline: 1/15; financial award applicants required to submit FAFSA. *Faculty research:* Russian literature (all periods), Polish literature, South Slavic literatures, Czech literature, Ukrainian literature. *Unit head:* Dr. Mikhail Krutikov, Chair, 734-764-5355, Fax: 734-647-2127, E-mail: krutikov@umich.edu. *Application contact:* Carolyn Dymond, Student Services Coordinator, 734-764-5355, Fax: 734-647-2127, E-mail: slavic@umich.edu. Website: http://lsa.umich.edu/slavic

**University of Pittsburgh,** Dietrich School of Arts and Sciences, Department of Slavic Languages and Literatures, Pittsburgh, PA 15260. Offers film studies (PhD); Russian literature and culture (MA, PhD). *Program availability:* Part-time. *Faculty:* 7 full-time (3 women), 2 part-time/adjunct (0 women). *Students:* 9 full-time (8 women); includes 2 minority (both Asian, non-Hispanic/Latino). Average age 32. 15 applicants, 33% accepted. In 2016, 2 master's, 2 doctorates awarded. Terminal master's awarded for partial completion of doctoral program. *Degree requirements:* For master's, 2 foreign languages, comprehensive exam; for doctorate, 3 foreign languages, comprehensive exam, thesis/dissertation. *Entrance requirements:* For master's and doctorate, GRE General Test. Additional exam requirements/recommendations for international students: Required—TOEFL (minimum score 600 paper-based; 90 iBT). *Application deadline:* For fall admission, 1/15 for domestic and international students; for spring admission, 9/15 for domestic and international students. Application fee: $50. Electronic applications accepted. Tuition and fees vary according to program. *Financial support:* In 2016–17, 9 students received support, including 5 fellowships with full tuition reimbursements available (averaging $22,000 per year), 7 teaching assistantships with full tuition reimbursements available (averaging $18,000 per year); Federal Work-Study, scholarships/grants, health care benefits, and tuition waivers (partial) also available. Support available to part-time students. Financial award application deadline: 1/15. *Faculty research:* Russian cinema, contemporary Russian literature and culture. *Unit head:* Dr. David J. Birnbaum, Chair, 412-624-5712, Fax: 412-624-9714, E-mail: djbpitt@pitt.edu. *Application contact:* Keanna Cash, Graduate Administrator, 412-624-5906, Fax: 412-624-6263, E-mail: kec176@pitt.edu. Website: http://www.slavic.pitt.edu

**University of Southern California,** Graduate School, Dana and David Dornsife College of Letters, Arts and Sciences, Department of Linguistics, Los Angeles, CA 90089. Offers East Asian linguistics (PhD); Hispanic linguistics (PhD); linguistics (PhD); Slavic linguistics (PhD). *Degree requirements:* For doctorate, comprehensive exam, thesis/dissertation. *Entrance requirements:* For doctorate, GRE. Additional exam requirements/recommendations for international students: Required—TOEFL (minimum score 100 iBT). Electronic applications accepted. *Faculty research:* Syntax, phonology, phonetics, semantics, sociolinguistics, psycholinguistics.

**University of Southern California,** Graduate School, Dana and David Dornsife College of Letters, Arts and Sciences, Department of Slavic Languages and Literatures, Los Angeles, CA 90089. Offers MA, PhD. *Degree requirements:* For master's, one foreign language, comprehensive exam, thesis or alternative, 30 units; for doctorate, 3 foreign languages, comprehensive exam, thesis/dissertation, 60 units. *Entrance requirements:* For doctorate, GRE, BA in Russian literature or equivalent. Additional exam requirements/recommendations for international students: Required—TOEFL. Electronic applications accepted. *Faculty research:* Russian avant-garde art, intertextuality in Russian literature, eighteenth-century Russian culture, Russian poetry, Russian music history, twentieth-century Russian literature.

**The University of Texas at Austin,** Graduate School, College of Liberal Arts, Department of Slavic and Eurasian Studies, Austin, TX 78712-1111. Offers applied linguistics/pedagogy (PhD); literature and culture (PhD); Slavic languages (MA); Slavic linguistics (PhD). *Degree requirements:* For master's, 2 foreign languages, thesis; for doctorate, 3 foreign languages, thesis/dissertation. *Entrance requirements:* For master's and doctorate, GRE General Test. Electronic applications accepted. *Faculty research:* Slavic linguistics; applied linguistics; Russian, Czech, and Slavic literature and culture.

**University of Toronto,** School of Graduate Studies, Faculty of Arts and Science, Department of Slavic Languages and Literatures, Toronto, ON M5S 1A1, Canada. Offers MA, PhD. *Program availability:* Part-time. *Degree requirements:* For doctorate, comprehensive exam, thesis/dissertation. *Entrance requirements:* For master's, BA in related area; minimum A- average in Slavic courses taken in final year, writing sample, 2 letters of recommendation; for doctorate, MA in Slavic languages and literatures, minimum A- average, writing sample, 2 letters of recommendation. Additional exam requirements/recommendations for international students: Required—TOEFL (minimum score 580 paper-based; 93 iBT), TWE (minimum score 5). Electronic applications accepted.

## Slavic Languages

**University of Virginia,** College and Graduate School of Arts and Sciences, Department of Slavic Languages and Literatures, Charlottesville, VA 22903. Offers MA, PhD. *Faculty:* 8 full-time (3 women), 1 part-time/adjunct (0 women). *Students:* 11 full-time (10 women), 2 part-time (both women). Average age 28. 15 applicants, 53% accepted, 3 enrolled. In 2016, 1 master's, 1 doctorate awarded. *Degree requirements:* For master's, one foreign language, comprehensive exam, thesis (for some programs); for doctorate, one foreign language, comprehensive exam, thesis/dissertation. *Entrance requirements:* For master's, GRE General Test, 2 letters of recommendation, writing sample in English; for doctorate, GRE General Test, 2 letters of recommendation; writing sample in English. Additional exam requirements/recommendations for international students: Required—TOEFL (minimum score 600 paper-based; 90 iBT), IELTS (minimum score 7). *Application deadline:* Applications are processed on a rolling basis. Application fee: $60. Electronic applications accepted. *Expenses:* Tuition, state resident: full-time $15,026; part-time $834 per credit hour. Tuition, nonresident: full-time $25,168; part-time $1378 per credit hour. *Required fees:* $2654. *Financial support:* Teaching assistantships available. Financial award application deadline: 1/15; financial award applicants required to submit FAFSA. *Unit head:* David Herman, Chair, 434-924-3548, Fax: 434-982-2744, E-mail: herman@virginia.edu. *Application contact:* Edith Clowes, Director of Graduate Studies, 434-924-3548, Fax: 434-982-2744, E-mail: eec3c@virginia.edu.
Website: http://artsandsciences.virginia.edu/slavic/index.html

**University of Washington,** Graduate School, College of Arts and Sciences, Department of Slavic Languages and Literatures, Seattle, WA 98195. Offers Russian literature (MA, PhD); Slavic linguistics (MA, PhD). *Degree requirements:* For master's, 2 foreign languages, thesis optional; for doctorate, 3 foreign languages, thesis/dissertation. *Entrance requirements:* For master's and doctorate, GRE General Test, minimum GPA of 3.0. Additional exam requirements/recommendations for international students: Required—TOEFL. Electronic applications accepted. *Faculty research:* Modern and medieval East European languages and literatures, comparative literature, Russian folk literature, Slavic literary theory and criticism, computerized morphology of Russian.

**University of Wisconsin–Madison,** Graduate School, College of Letters and Science, Department of Slavic Languages and Literature, Madison, WI 53706-1380. Offers MA, PhD. *Program availability:* Part-time. Terminal master's awarded for partial completion of doctoral program. *Degree requirements:* For doctorate, thesis/dissertation. *Entrance requirements:* For master's and doctorate, GRE General Test. Additional exam requirements/recommendations for international students: Required—TOEFL. Electronic applications accepted. *Faculty research:* Polish literature, linguistics, South Slavic literature, second language acquisition, nineteenth- and twentieth-century Russian literature.

**Yale University,** Graduate School of Arts and Sciences, Department of Slavic Languages and Literatures, New Haven, CT 06520. Offers medieval Slavic literature and philology (PhD); Polish literature (PhD); Russian literature (PhD); Slavic languages and literatures and film studies (PhD). *Degree requirements:* For doctorate, 3 foreign languages, thesis/dissertation. *Entrance requirements:* For doctorate, GRE General Test.

# Spanish

**American University,** College of Arts and Sciences, Department of World Languages and Cultures, Washington, DC 20016-8045. Offers Spanish: Latin American studies (MA); teaching English as a foreign language (MA); teaching English to speakers of other languages (MA, Certificate); translation: French (Certificate); translation: Russian (Certificate); translation: Spanish (Certificate). *Program availability:* Part-time, evening/weekend. *Faculty:* 42 full-time (31 women), 27 part-time/adjunct (18 women). *Students:* 41 full-time (31 women), 31 part-time (23 women); includes 14 minority (3 Black or African American, non-Hispanic/Latino; 2 Asian, non-Hispanic/Latino; 7 Hispanic/Latino; 2 Two or more races, non-Hispanic/Latino), 9 international. Average age 32. 73 applicants, 92% accepted, 20 enrolled. In 2016, 24 master's, 6 other advanced degrees awarded. *Degree requirements:* For master's, one foreign language, comprehensive exam, thesis or alternative. *Entrance requirements:* For master's, GRE, writing sample, statement of purpose, transcripts, 2 letters of recommendation, resume; for Certificate, bachelor's degree, statement of purpose, transcripts, resume. Additional exam requirements/recommendations for international students: Required—TOEFL (minimum score 100 iBT), IELTS (minimum score 7), PTE (minimum score 68). *Application deadline:* For fall admission, 2/1 for domestic students; for spring admission, 11/1 for domestic students. Application fee: $55. *Expenses:* $1,579 per credit tuition; $690 mandatory fees. *Financial support:* Institutionally sponsored loans, scholarships/grants, and unspecified assistantships available. Financial award application deadline: 2/1; financial award applicants required to submit FAFSA. *Unit head:* Henry Gerfen, Chair, 202-885-2385, Fax: 202-885-1076, E-mail: gerfen@american.edu. *Application contact:* Kathleen Clowery, Director of Graduate Admissions, 202-885-3620, Fax: 202-885-1344, E-mail: clowery@american.edu.
Website: http://www.american.edu/cas/wlc

**Arizona State University at the Tempe campus,** College of Liberal Arts and Sciences, School of International Letters and Cultures, Program in Spanish, Tempe, AZ 85287-0202. Offers cultural studies (PhD); linguistics (MA), including second language acquisition/applied linguistics, sociolinguistics; literature (PhD); literature and culture (MA). *Program availability:* Part-time. Terminal master's awarded for partial completion of doctoral program. *Degree requirements:* For master's, thesis, oral defense; written comprehensive exam (literature and culture); portfolio review (linguistics); interactive Program of Study (iPOS) submitted before completing 50 percent of required credit hours; for doctorate, comprehensive exam, thesis/dissertation, interactive Program of Study (iPOS) submitted before completing 50 percent of required credit hours. *Entrance requirements:* For master's, GRE (recommended), BA in Spanish or close equivalent from accredited institution with minimum GPA of 3.5, 3 letters of recommendation, personal statement, academic writing sample; for doctorate, GRE (recommended), MA in Spanish or equivalent from accredited institution with minimum GPA of 3.75, 3 letters of recommendation, personal statement, academic writing sample. Additional exam requirements/recommendations for international students: Required—TOEFL (minimum score 550 paper-based; 83 iBT), IELTS (minimum score 6.5). Electronic applications accepted.

**Asbury University,** School of Graduate and Professional Studies, Wilmore, KY 40390-1198. Offers biology: alternative certificate (MA Ed); chemistry: alternative certificate (MA Ed); English (MA Ed); English as a second language (MA Ed); ESL (MA Ed); French (MA Ed); Latin: alternative certificate (MA Ed); mathematics: alternative certificate (MA Ed); reading/writing endorsement (MA Ed); social studies (MA Ed); social work (MSW), including child and family services; Spanish (MA Ed); special education (MA Ed); special education: alternative certificate (MA Ed); teacher as leader endorsement (MA Ed). *Accreditation:* NCATE. *Program availability:* Part-time. *Degree requirements:* For master's, action research project, portfolio. *Entrance requirements:* For master's, PRAXIS/NTE, minimum GPA of 2.75, letters of recommendation. Additional exam requirements/recommendations for international students: Required—TOEFL (minimum score 550 paper-based). Electronic applications accepted.

**Auburn University,** Graduate School, College of Liberal Arts, Department of Foreign Languages and Literatures, Auburn University, AL 36849. Offers MA, MHS. *Program availability:* Part-time. *Faculty:* 31 full-time (22 women), 8 part-time/adjunct (6 women). *Students:* 17 full-time (11 women), 2 part-time (1 woman); includes 2 minority (both Hispanic/Latino), 13 international. Average age 27. 14 applicants, 93% accepted, 12 enrolled. In 2016, 5 master's awarded. *Degree requirements:* For master's, one foreign language, comprehensive exam, thesis (for some programs). *Entrance requirements:* For master's, GRE General Test. *Application deadline:* Applications are processed on a rolling basis. Application fee: $50 ($60 for international students). Electronic applications accepted. *Expenses:* Tuition, state resident: full-time $9072; part-time $504 per credit hour. Tuition, nonresident: full-time $27,216; part-time $1512 per credit hour. *Required fees:* $812 per semester. Tuition and fees vary according to degree level and program. *Financial support:* Fellowships, teaching assistantships, and Federal Work-Study available. Support available to part-time students. Financial award application deadline: 3/15; financial award applicants required to submit FAFSA. *Unit head:* Dr. Lourdes Betanzos, Chair, 334-844-6350, Fax: 334-844-6378. *Application contact:* Dr. George Flowers, Dean of the Graduate School, 334-844-2125.
Website: http://www.cla.auburn.edu/forlang/

**Baylor University,** Graduate School, College of Arts and Sciences, Department of Modern Languages and Cultures, Waco, TX 76798. Offers Spanish (MA). *Faculty:* 13 full-time (7 women). *Students:* 10 full-time (8 women); includes 2 minority (both Two or more races, non-Hispanic/Latino). Average age 30. 12 applicants, 58% accepted, 2 enrolled. In 2016, 7 master's awarded. *Degree requirements:* For master's, 2 foreign languages, comprehensive exam, thesis optional. *Entrance requirements:* For master's, GRE General Test. Additional exam requirements/recommendations for international students: Required—TOEFL. *Application deadline:* For winter admission, 2/1 priority date for domestic students. Application fee: $50. Electronic applications accepted. *Expenses:* Tuition: Full-time $28,494; part-time $1583 per credit hour. *Required fees:* $167 per credit hour. Tuition and fees vary according to course load and program. *Financial support:* In 2016–17, 6 students received support, including teaching assistantships with full tuition reimbursements available (averaging $9,000 per year); scholarships/grants and unspecified assistantships also available. Financial award application deadline: 2/1. *Faculty research:* Spanish post-civil war novel, Latin American detective fiction, nineteenth- and twentieth-century Hispanic women writers, semantics and pragmatics, Miguel de Unamuno. *Unit head:* Dr. Jan E. Evans, Graduate Program Director, 254-710-7361, Fax: 254-710-3799, E-mail: jan_evans@baylor.edu. *Application contact:* Ann Westbrook, Administrative Assistant, 254-710-6027, Fax: 254-710-3870, E-mail: ann_westbrook@baylor.edu.
Website: http://www.baylor.edu/mfl/

**Binghamton University, State University of New York,** Graduate School, Harpur College of Arts and Sciences, Department of Romance Languages and Literatures, Program in Spanish, Binghamton, NY 13902-6000. Offers MA. *Program availability:* Part-time. *Students:* 1 part-time (0 women). Average age 24. 3 applicants, 67% accepted, 1 enrolled. *Degree requirements:* For master's, one foreign language, comprehensive exam, thesis or alternative. *Entrance requirements:* For master's, GRE General Test. Additional exam requirements/recommendations for international students: Required—TOEFL (minimum score 550 paper-based; 80 iBT). *Application deadline:* For fall admission, 2/15 priority date for domestic and international students; for spring admission, 11/15 priority date for domestic and international students. Application fee: $75. Electronic applications accepted. *Financial support:* Career-related internships or fieldwork, Federal Work-Study, institutionally sponsored loans, scholarships/grants, health care benefits, and unspecified assistantships available. Financial award applicants required to submit FAFSA. *Unit head:* Dr. Dana Stewart, Chairperson, 607-777-2645, E-mail: stewart@binghamton.edu. *Application contact:* Ben Balkaya, Assistant Dean and Director, 607-777-2151, Fax: 607-777-2501, E-mail: balkaya@binghamton.edu.

**Boston College,** Graduate School of Arts and Sciences, Department of Romance Languages and Literatures, Chestnut Hill, MA 02467-3800. Offers French (MA); Italian (MA); Spanish (MA). *Program availability:* Part-time. *Faculty:* 19 full-time. *Students:* 31 full-time (26 women); includes 2 minority (both Hispanic/Latino), 8 international. 34 applicants, 50% accepted, 12 enrolled. In 2016, 12 master's awarded. Terminal master's awarded for partial completion of doctoral program. *Degree requirements:* For master's, one foreign language. *Entrance requirements:* Additional exam requirements/recommendations for international students: Required—TOEFL (minimum score 600 paper-based; 100 iBT), IELTS (minimum score 8). *Application deadline:* For fall admission, 2/1 for domestic and international students. Application fee: $75. Electronic applications accepted. Tuition and fees vary according to program. *Financial support:* In 2016–17, 36 students received support, including fellowships with full tuition reimbursements available (averaging $18,800 per year), teaching assistantships with full tuition reimbursements available (averaging $18,800 per year); Federal Work-Study and unspecified assistantships also available. Support available to part-time students. Financial award application deadline: 3/1; financial award applicants required to submit FAFSA. *Faculty research:* Spanish-American literature, philology, medieval French romance and troubadour lyrics, Golden Age Peninsular literature, secondary language acquisition and pedagogy, Hispanic studies, French language and literature, Italian language and literature. *Unit head:* Dr. Franco Mormando, Chairperson, 617-552-6346, E-mail: franco.mormando@bc.edu. *Application contact:* Dr. Laurie Shepard, Graduate Program Director, 617-552-8269, E-mail: laurie.shepard@bc.edu.
Website: http://www.bc.edu/rll

**Bowling Green State University,** Graduate College, College of Arts and Sciences, Department of Romance and Classical Studies, Program in Spanish, Bowling Green, OH 43403. Offers Spanish (MA). *Program availability:* Part-time. *Degree requirements:* For master's, one foreign language, thesis or alternative. *Entrance requirements:* For master's, GRE General Test. Additional exam requirements/recommendations for international students: Required—TOEFL. *Application deadline:* For fall admission, 2/15 priority date for domestic students. Application fee: $30. Electronic applications accepted. *Financial support:* Research assistantships with full tuition reimbursements, teaching assistantships with full tuition reimbursements, Federal Work-Study, and unspecified assistantships available. Financial award applicants required to submit FAFSA. *Faculty research:* U.S. Latino literature and culture, Latin American film and popular culture, applied linguistics, Spanish popular culture. *Unit head:* Dr. Nathan Richardson, Chair, 419-372-8043, E-mail: nrichar@bgsu.edu. *Application contact:* Dr. Amy Robinson, Graduate Coordinator, 419-372-2168, E-mail: ma-spanish@bgsu.edu.

**Brigham Young University,** Graduate Studies, College of Humanities, Department of Spanish and Portuguese, Provo, UT 84602. Offers Portuguese (MA), including Luso-Brazilian literatures, Portuguese linguistics, Portuguese pedagogy; Spanish (MA), including Hispanic linguistics, Hispanic literatures, Spanish pedagogy. *Faculty:* 31 full-time (6 women). *Students:* 20 full-time (9 women), 15 part-time (9 women); includes 12 minority (all Hispanic/Latino). Average age 32. 19 applicants, 79% accepted, 12 enrolled. In 2016, 9 master's awarded. *Degree requirements:* For master's, 2 foreign languages, comprehensive exam, thesis, 1 semester of teaching. *Entrance requirements:* For master's, minimum GPA of 3.5 in Spanish or Portuguese, 3.3 overall. Additional exam requirements/recommendations for international students: Required—TOEFL (minimum score 580 paper-based; 85 iBT). *Application deadline:* For fall admission, 2/1 for domestic and international students. Application fee: $50. Electronic applications accepted. *Expenses:* Contact institution. *Financial support:* In 2016–17, 25 students received support, including 7 research assistantships (averaging $1,895 per year), 81 teaching assistantships (averaging $3,200 per year); institutionally sponsored loans, scholarships/grants, tuition waivers (partial), and unspecified assistantships also available. Support available to part-time students. *Faculty research:* Mexican prose; Latin American theater, literature, phonetics, and phonology; pedagogy; classical Portuguese literature; Peninsular prose and theater. *Unit head:* Dr. David P. Laraway, Chair, 801-422-3807, Fax: 801-422-0628, E-mail: david_laraway@byu.edu. *Application contact:* Jessica C. Erickson, Graduate Program Manager, 801-422-2196, Fax: 801-422-0628, E-mail: jessica_erickson@byu.edu.
Website: http://spanport.byu.edu/

**Brooklyn College of the City University of New York,** School of Humanities and Social Sciences, Department of Modern Languages and Literatures, Brooklyn, NY 11210-2889. Offers French (MA); Spanish (MA). *Degree requirements:* For master's, comprehensive exam or research paper. *Entrance requirements:* For master's, 18 credits in advanced courses in Spanish, 2 letters of recommendation. Additional exam requirements/recommendations for international students: Required—TOEFL (minimum score 500 paper-based; 61 iBT). Electronic applications accepted. *Faculty research:* Latin American contemporary novel, Caribbean female contemporary literature, nineteenth- and twentieth-century Spanish novel, twentieth-century Mexican poetry.

**California State University, Bakersfield,** Division of Graduate Studies, School of Arts and Humanities, Program in Spanish, Bakersfield, CA 93311. Offers MA. *Students:* 6 part-time (3 women); includes 5 minority (all Hispanic/Latino). Average age 34. 4 applicants, 50% accepted, 1 enrolled. *Degree requirements:* For master's, capstone course. *Expenses:* Tuition, state resident: full-time $2246; part-time $1302 per semester. *Financial support:* In 2016–17, fellowships (averaging $1,850 per year) were awarded; Federal Work-Study, scholarships/grants, and tuition waivers (full and partial) also available. Financial award application deadline: 3/2; financial award applicants required to submit FAFSA. *Unit head:* Dr. M. Dustin Knepp, Graduate Coordinator, 661-654-2221, Fax: 661-654-2017. *Application contact:* Debbie Blowers, Assistant Director of Admissions and Evaluations, 661-664-3381, E-mail: dblowers@csub.edu.
Website: https://www.csub.edu/modlang/department/Spanish%20M.A.%20/index.html

**California State University, Fresno,** Division of Research and Graduate Studies, College of Arts and Humanities, Department of Modern and Classical Languages and Literatures, Fresno, CA 93740-8027. Offers Spanish (MA). *Program availability:* Part-time. *Degree requirements:* For master's, one foreign language, thesis or alternative. *Entrance requirements:* For master's, GRE General Test, BA in Spanish, minimum GPA of 3.0. Additional exam requirements/recommendations for international students: Required—TOEFL. *Application deadline:* For fall admission, 5/1 for domestic and international students; for spring admission, 10/1 for domestic and international students. Applications are processed on a rolling basis. Application fee: $55. Electronic applications accepted. *Financial support:* Teaching assistantships, career-related internships or fieldwork, Federal Work-Study, and scholarships/grants available. Support available to part-time students. Financial award application deadline: 3/1; financial award applicants required to submit FAFSA. *Unit head:* Dr. Kristi Eastin, Chair, 559-278-2387, Fax: 559-278-7878, E-mail: keastin@csufresno.edu.
Website: http://www.fresnostate.edu/artshum/mcll/

**California State University, Fullerton,** Graduate Studies, College of Humanities and Social Sciences, Department of Modern Languages and Literatures, Fullerton, CA 92834-9480. Offers Spanish (MA). *Program availability:* Part-time. *Degree requirements:* For master's, comprehensive exam, thesis or alternative. *Entrance requirements:* For master's, minimum GPA of 2.5 in last 60 hours of course work, undergraduate major in a language. Application fee: $55. *Expenses:* Tuition, state resident: full-time $3369; part-time $1953 per unit. Tuition, nonresident: full-time $3915; part-time $2499 per unit. Tuition and fees vary according to course load, degree level and program. *Financial support:* Career-related internships or fieldwork, Federal Work-Study, institutionally sponsored loans, and scholarships/grants available. Support available to part-time students. Financial award application deadline: 3/1; financial award applicants required to submit FAFSA. *Unit head:* Dr. Reyes Fidalgo, Chair, 657-278-4563. *Application contact:* Admissions/Applications, 657-278-2371.

**California State University, Long Beach,** Graduate Studies, College of Liberal Arts, Department of Romance, German, Russian Languages and Literatures, Program in Spanish, Long Beach, CA 90840. Offers MA. *Program availability:* Part-time. *Degree requirements:* For master's, one foreign language, thesis or alternative, research paper. *Entrance requirements:* For master's, BA in Spanish. *Application deadline:* For fall admission, 7/1 for domestic students. Applications are processed on a rolling basis. Application fee: $55. Electronic applications accepted. *Financial support:* Federal Work-Study, institutionally sponsored loans, and scholarships/grants available. Financial award application deadline: 3/2. *Faculty research:* Literary translation, literature and politics, women writers, Latin American poetry, Latin American theatre. *Unit head:* Markus Muller, Chair. *Application contact:* Dr. Bonnie Gasior, Program Director, 562-985-4318, Fax: 562-985-4259, E-mail: bgasior@csulb.edu.

**California State University, Los Angeles,** Graduate Studies, College of Arts and Letters, Department of Modern Languages and Literatures, Los Angeles, CA 90032-8530. Offers French (MA); Spanish (MA). *Program availability:* Part-time, evening/weekend. *Degree requirements:* For master's, comprehensive exam. *Entrance requirements:* Additional exam requirements/recommendations for international students: Required—TOEFL (minimum score 500 paper-based). Electronic applications accepted. *Faculty research:* French literature, language teaching and methodology, Spanish poetry, Spanish American fiction and poetry.

**California State University, Northridge,** Graduate Studies, College of Humanities, Department of Modern and Classical Languages and Literatures, Northridge, CA 91330. Offers Spanish (MA). *Program availability:* Part-time, evening/weekend. *Faculty:* 9 full-time (6 women), 23 part-time/adjunct (6 women). *Students:* 37 full-time (28 women), 26 part-time (22 women); includes 35 minority (6 Asian, non-Hispanic/Latino; 29 Hispanic/Latino), 7 international. Average age 35. 53 applicants, 70% accepted, 26 enrolled. *Degree requirements:* For master's, one foreign language. *Entrance requirements:* For master's, GRE General Test or minimum GPA of 3.0. Additional exam requirements/recommendations for international students: Required—TOEFL. *Application deadline:* For fall admission, 11/30 for domestic students. Application fee: $55. *Expenses:* Tuition, state resident: full-time $4152. *Financial support:* Application deadline: 3/1. *Unit head:* Dr. Brian Castronovo, Chair, 818-677-3467, E-mail: brian.castronovo@csun.edu.
Website: http://www.csun.edu/mcll/

**California State University, San Bernardino,** Graduate Studies, College of Arts and Letters, Program in Spanish, San Bernardino, CA 92407. Offers MA. *Program availability:* Part-time, evening/weekend. *Students:* 5 full-time (all women), 17 part-time (12 women); includes 19 minority (all Hispanic/Latino), 2 international. 6 applicants, 100% accepted, 3 enrolled. *Degree requirements:* For master's, comprehensive exam, advancement to candidacy. *Entrance requirements:* Additional exam requirements/recommendations for international students: Required—TOEFL. *Application deadline:* For fall admission, 7/16 for domestic students. Application fee: $55. *Expenses:* Tuition, state resident: full-time $7843; part-time $5011.20 per year. Tuition and fees vary according to course load, degree level, program and reciprocity agreements. *Financial support:* Institutionally sponsored loans available. *Unit head:* Thomas Davis, Chair, 909-537-5849, Fax: 909-537-7091, E-mail: tomdavis@csusb.edu. *Application contact:* Dr. Francisca Beer, Dean of Graduate Studies, 909-537-5058, E-mail: fbeer@csusb.edu.

**California State University, San Marcos,** College of Humanities, Arts, Behavioral and Social Sciences, Program in Spanish, San Marcos, CA 92096-0001. Offers Hispanic cultures and society (MA); Hispanic language and linguistics (MA); Hispanic literatures and literary theory (MA). *Program availability:* Part-time, evening/weekend. *Degree requirements:* For master's, 2 foreign languages, exam. *Entrance requirements:* For master's, GRE General Test, minimum GPA of 3.0 overall and in upper-division Spanish courses, official transcripts, three letters of recommendation, 750-word statement of purpose (in English), academic writing sample (in Spanish). Additional exam requirements/recommendations for international students: Required—TOEFL (minimum score 500 paper-based), TWE (minimum score 4.5). Electronic applications accepted. *Expenses:* Tuition, state resident: full-time $6738. Tuition, nonresident: full-time $13,434. *Required fees:* $1906. Tuition and fees vary according to campus/location and program. *Faculty research:* Applied linguistics, Golden Age Spanish literature, Latin American literature, poetry, Chicano studies.

**The Catholic University of America,** School of Arts and Sciences, Department of Modern Languages and Literatures, Washington, DC 20064. Offers Hispanic studies (MA, PhD). *Program availability:* Part-time. *Faculty:* 24 full-time (18 women), 3 part-time/adjunct (all women). *Students:* 4 full-time (2 women), 3 part-time (2 women); includes 2 minority (both Hispanic/Latino), 5 international. Average age 37. 4 applicants, 25% accepted. In 2016, 2 master's awarded. *Degree requirements:* For master's, comprehensive exam; for doctorate, one foreign language, comprehensive exam, thesis/dissertation, annotated bibliography; oral defense of the proposal; oral defense of the dissertation. *Entrance requirements:* For master's, GRE General Test, statement of purpose, official copies of academic transcripts, two letters of recommendation, sample of academic writing; for doctorate, GRE General Test, statement of purpose, official copies of academic transcripts, three letters of recommendation, sample of academic writing (20-25-pages long). Additional exam requirements/recommendations for international students: Required—TOEFL (minimum score 550 paper-based; 80 iBT). *Application deadline:* For fall admission, 7/15 priority date for domestic students, 7/1 for international students; for spring admission, 11/15 priority date for domestic students, 11/1 for international students. Applications are processed on a rolling basis. Application fee: $55. Electronic applications accepted. *Expenses:* $42,850 per year; $1,170 per credit; $200 per semester part-time fees. *Financial support:* Fellowships, research assistantships, teaching assistantships, Federal Work-Study, scholarships/grants, tuition waivers (full and partial), and unspecified assistantships available. Financial award application deadline: 2/1; financial award applicants required to submit FAFSA. *Faculty research:* Golden age Spain; 18th-21st-century Latin American and transatlantic studies; modern and contemporary Latin America; theory, criticism, and language teaching methodology. *Total annual research expenditures:* $1,440. *Unit head:* Dr. Margaret Kassen, Chair, 202-319-5240, Fax: 202-319-6077, E-mail: kassen@cua.edu. *Application contact:* Director of Graduate Admissions, 202-319-5057, Fax: 202-319-6533, E-mail: cua-admissions@cua.edu.
Website: http://modernlanguages.cua.edu/

**Central Connecticut State University,** School of Graduate Studies, College of Liberal Arts and Social Sciences, Department of Modern Languages, New Britain, CT 06050-4010. Offers modern language (MA, Certificate), including French, German (Certificate), Italian, Spanish (MA); Spanish (MS, Certificate). *Program availability:* Part-time, evening/weekend. *Faculty:* 8 full-time (6 women). *Students:* 7 full-time (6 women), 12 part-time (7 women); includes 10 minority (all Hispanic/Latino). Average age 32. 11 applicants, 91% accepted, 4 enrolled. In 2016, 9 master's, 1 other advanced degree awarded. *Degree requirements:* For master's, one foreign language, comprehensive exam, thesis or alternative; for Certificate, qualifying exam. *Entrance requirements:* For master's, minimum undergraduate GPA of 2.7, 24 credits of undergraduate courses in each language in which graduate work will be undertaken. Additional exam requirements/recommendations for international students: Required—TOEFL (minimum score 550 paper-based; 79 iBT). *Application deadline:* For fall admission, 6/1 for domestic students, 5/1 for international students; for spring admission, 11/1 for domestic and international students. Applications are processed on a rolling basis. Application fee: $50. Electronic applications accepted. *Expenses:* Tuition, area resident: Full-time $6497; part-time $606 per credit. Tuition, state resident: full-time $9748; part-time $622 per credit. Tuition, nonresident: full-time $18,102; part-time $622 per credit. *Required fees:* $4459; $246 per credit. *Financial support:* In 2016–17, 6 students received support. Career-related internships or fieldwork, Federal Work-Study, scholarships/grants, and unspecified assistantships available. Support available to part-time students. Financial award application deadline: 3/1; financial award applicants required to submit FAFSA. *Faculty research:* Quebecois literature, Caribbean literature, modern French/Spanish drama, Puerto Rican novel and drama. *Unit head:* Dr. Carmela Pesca, Chair, 860-832-2875, E-mail: pescac@ccsu.edu. *Application contact:* Patricia Gardner, Associate Director of Graduate Studies, 860-832-2350, Fax: 860-832-2362.
Website: http://web.ccsu.edu/modlang/

**Central Michigan University,** College of Graduate Studies, College of Humanities and Social and Behavioral Sciences, Department of Foreign Languages, Literatures, and Cultures, Mount Pleasant, MI 48859. Offers Spanish (MA). *Program availability:* Part-time. *Degree requirements:* For master's, thesis or alternative. Electronic applications accepted.

**City College of the City University of New York,** Graduate School, Division of Humanities and the Arts, Department of Classical and Modern Languages and

### Spanish

Literatures, New York, NY 10031-9198. Offers Spanish (MA). *Degree requirements:* For master's, one foreign language, comprehensive exam, thesis or alternative. *Entrance requirements:* For master's, minimum GPA of 3.0. Additional exam requirements/recommendations for international students: Required—TOEFL (minimum score 500 paper-based; 61 iBT). Electronic applications accepted. Tuition and fees vary according to course load, degree level and program.

**Cleveland State University,** College of Graduate Studies, College of Liberal Arts and Social Sciences, Department of World Languages, Literatures, and Cultures, Cleveland, OH 44115. Offers Spanish (MA). *Program availability:* Part-time, evening/weekend. *Faculty:* 6 full-time (3 women), 1 (woman) part-time/adjunct. *Students:* 5 full-time (4 women), 7 part-time (6 women); includes 2 minority (both Hispanic/Latino). Average age 34. 3 applicants, 100% accepted, 1 enrolled. In 2016, 4 master's awarded. *Degree requirements:* For master's, one foreign language, comprehensive exam, thesis optional. *Entrance requirements:* For master's, ACTFL oral proficiency rating, undergraduate major in Spanish or equivalent, essay in Spanish, writing sample, 2 letters of reference. Additional exam requirements/recommendations for international students: Required—TOEFL (minimum score 550 paper-based; 78 iBT). *Application deadline:* For fall admission, 7/1 priority date for domestic students, 5/15 for international students; for spring admission, 11/15 priority date for domestic students, 11/1 for international students; for summer admission, 4/1 for domestic students, 3/15 for international students. Applications are processed on a rolling basis. Application fee: $40. Electronic applications accepted. *Expenses:* Tuition, state resident: full-time $9565. Tuition, nonresident: full-time $17,980. Tuition and fees vary according to program. *Financial support:* In 2016–17, 5 students received support, including 5 teaching assistantships with full tuition reimbursements available (averaging $8,000 per year); Federal Work-Study and unspecified assistantships also available. Financial award application deadline: 4/1. *Faculty research:* Peninsular poetry and prose, sociolinguistics, Latin American and Caribbean literature, Arabic diaspora in Latin America, border literature. *Unit head:* Dr. Antonio Medina-Rivera, Chairperson, 216-523-7175, Fax: 216-687-4650, E-mail: a.medinarivera@csuohio.edu. *Application contact:* Dr. Stephen Gingerich, Graduate Director, 216-687-4677, Fax: 216-687-4650, E-mail: s.gingerich@csuohio.edu.
Website: http://www.csuohio.edu/class/world-languages/world-languages

**Colorado State University,** College of Liberal Arts, Department of Languages, Literatures and Cultures, Fort Collins, CO 80523-1774. Offers French (MA); German (MA); Spanish (MA). *Program availability:* Part-time. *Faculty:* 7 full-time (6 women), 3 part-time/adjunct (all women). *Students:* 12 full-time (10 women); includes 4 minority (all Hispanic/Latino), 4 international. Average age 34. 7 applicants, 100% accepted, 6 enrolled. In 2016, 6 master's awarded. *Degree requirements:* For master's, one foreign language, comprehensive exam, thesis, teaching portfolio or additional coursework. *Entrance requirements:* For master's, minimum GPA of 3.0, undergraduate major/proficiency in foreign languages, BA/BS in related field, statement of purpose, biographical statement, 3 letters of recommendation, resume, official transcripts, writing sample. Additional exam requirements/recommendations for international students: Required—TOEFL (minimum score 550 paper-based; 80 iBT). *Application deadline:* For fall admission, 2/1 priority date for domestic and international students; for spring admission, 9/15 priority date for domestic and international students. Applications are processed on a rolling basis. Application fee: $60 ($70 for international students). Electronic applications accepted. *Expenses:* Tuition, state resident: full-time $9628. Tuition, nonresident: full-time $23,603. *Required fees:* $2253; $528.14 per credit hour. $264.07 per semester. Tuition and fees vary according to course load and program. *Financial support:* In 2016–17, 10 teaching assistantships with full and partial tuition reimbursements (averaging $13,932 per year) were awarded; career-related internships or fieldwork, scholarships/grants, and unspecified assistantships also available. Financial award application deadline: 3/1; financial award applicants required to submit FAFSA. *Faculty research:* French, German, and Hispanic literatures and cultures; video-assisted language learning; computer-assisted language learners; foreign language teaching methodologies; linguistics. *Unit head:* Dr. Mary Vogl, Department Chair, 970-491-6100, Fax: 970-491-2822, E-mail: mary.vogl@colostate.edu. *Application contact:* Kaity Lewis, Graduate Program Contact, 970-491-6269, Fax: 970-491-2822, E-mail: kaity.lewis@colostate.edu.
Website: http://languages.colostate.edu/

**Columbia University,** Graduate School of Arts and Sciences, New York, NY 10027. Offers African-American studies (MA); American studies (MA); anthropology (MA, PhD); art history and archaeology (MA, PhD); astronomy (PhD); biological sciences (PhD); biotechnology (MA); chemical physics (PhD); chemistry (PhD); classical studies (MA, PhD); classics (MA, PhD); climate and society (MA); conservation biology (MA); earth and environmental sciences (PhD); East Asia: regional studies (MA); East Asian languages and cultures (MA, PhD); ecology, evolution and environmental biology (MA), including conservation biology; ecology, evolution, and environmental biology (PhD), including ecology and evolutionary biology, evolutionary primatology; economics (MA, PhD); English and comparative literature (MA, PhD); French and Romance philology (MA, PhD); Germanic languages (MA, PhD); global French studies (MA); global thought (MA); Hispanic cultural studies (MA); history (PhD); history and literature (MA); human rights studies (MA); Islamic studies (MA); Italian (MA, PhD); Japanese pedagogy (MA); Jewish studies (MA); Latin America and the Caribbean: regional studies (MA); Latin American and Iberian cultures (PhD); mathematics (MA, PhD), including finance (MA); medieval and Renaissance studies (MA); Middle Eastern, South Asian, and African studies (MA, PhD); modern art: critical and curatorial studies (MA); modern European studies (MA); museum anthropology (MA); music (DMA, PhD); oral history (MA); philosophical foundations of physics (MA); philosophy (MA, PhD); physics (PhD); political science (MA, PhD); psychology (PhD); quantitative methods in the social sciences (MA); religion (MA, PhD); Russia, Eurasia and East Europe: regional studies (MA); Russian translation (MA); Slavic cultures (MA); Slavic languages (MA, PhD); sociology (MA, PhD); South Asian studies (MA); statistics (MA, PhD); theatre (PhD). Dual-degree programs require admission to both Graduate School of Arts and Sciences and another Columbia school. *Program availability:* Part-time. Terminal master's awarded for partial completion of doctoral program. *Degree requirements:* For master's, variable foreign language requirement, comprehensive exam (for some programs), thesis (for some programs); for doctorate, variable foreign language requirement, comprehensive exam (for some programs), thesis/dissertation. *Entrance requirements:* For master's and doctorate, GRE General Test, GRE Subject Test (for some programs). Additional exam requirements/recommendations for international students: Required—TOEFL, IELTS. Electronic applications accepted.

**Cornell University,** Graduate School, Graduate Fields of Arts and Sciences, Field of Romance Studies, Ithaca, NY 14853. Offers French linguistics (PhD); French literature (PhD); Hispanic literature (PhD); Italian linguistics (PhD); Italian literature (PhD); Romance linguistics (PhD); Spanish linguistics (PhD). *Degree requirements:* For doctorate, 2 foreign languages, comprehensive exam, thesis/dissertation. *Entrance requirements:* For doctorate, GRE General Test, sample of written work, 3 letters of recommendation. Additional exam requirements/recommendations for international students: Required—TOEFL (minimum score 550 paper-based; 77 iBT). Electronic applications accepted. *Faculty research:* Literary theory, Hispanic studies, French studies, gender studies.

**DePaul University,** College of Liberal Arts and Social Sciences, Chicago, IL 60614. Offers Arabic (MA); Chinese (MA); English (MA); French (MA); German (MA); history (MA); interdisciplinary studies (MA, MS); international public service (MS); international studies (MA); Italian (MA); Japanese (MA); leadership and policy studies (MS); liberal studies (MA); new media studies (MA); nonprofit management (MNM); public administration (MPA); public health (MPH); public service management (MS); social work (MSW); sociology (MA); Spanish (MA); sustainable urban development (MA); women and gender studies (MA); writing and publishing (MA); writing, rhetoric, and discourse (MA); MA/PhD. *Program availability:* Part-time, evening/weekend, online learning. Terminal master's awarded for partial completion of doctoral program. *Degree requirements:* For master's, variable foreign language requirement, comprehensive exam (for some programs), thesis (for some programs). Electronic applications accepted.

**Duke University,** Graduate School, Department of Romance Studies, Durham, NC 27708. Offers French (PhD); Italian (PhD); Spanish (PhD); JD/AM. *Degree requirements:* For doctorate, 2 foreign languages, thesis/dissertation. *Entrance requirements:* For doctorate, GRE General Test. Additional exam requirements/recommendations for international students: Required—TOEFL (minimum score 577 paper-based; 90 iBT) or IELTS (minimum score 7). Electronic applications accepted.

**Eastern University,** Loeb School of Education, St. Davids, PA 19087-3696. Offers ESL program specialist (K-12) (Certificate); general supervisor (PreK-12) (Certificate); health and physical education (K-12) (Certificate); middle level (4-8) (Certificate); multicultural education (M Ed); organizational leadership with education (PhD); Pre K-4 (Certificate); Pre K-4 with special education (Certificate); reading (M Ed); reading specialist (K-12) (Certificate); reading supervisor (K-12) (Certificate); school health supervisor (Certificate); school nurse (K-12) (Certificate); secondary biology education (7-12) (Certificate); secondary chemistry education (7-12) (Certificate); secondary communication education (7-12) (Certificate); secondary education (7-12) (Certificate); secondary English education (7-12) (Certificate); secondary math education (7-12) (Certificate); secondary social studies education (7-12) (Certificate); special education (M Ed); special education (7-12) (Certificate); special education (Pre K-8) (Certificate); special education supervisor (N-12) (Certificate); TESOL (M Ed); world language (Certificate), including French, Spanish. *Program availability:* Part-time, evening/weekend, online learning. *Students:* 41 full-time (32 women), 89 part-time (68 women); includes 54 minority (38 Black or African American, non-Hispanic/Latino; 3 Asian, non-Hispanic/Latino; 11 Hispanic/Latino; 2 Two or more races, non-Hispanic/Latino), 2 international. Average age 37. In 2016, 64 master's awarded. *Entrance requirements:* Additional exam requirements/recommendations for international students: Required—TOEFL. *Application deadline:* Applications are processed on a rolling basis. Application fee: $35. Electronic applications accepted. Application fee is waived when completed online. *Expenses:* $690 per credit. *Unit head:* Michael Dziedziak, Executive Director of Enrollment, 800-452-0996, E-mail: gpsadmissions@eastern.edu.
Website: http://www.eastern.edu/academics/programs/loeb-school-education-0

**Emory University,** Laney Graduate School, Department of Spanish and Portuguese, Atlanta, GA 30322-1100. Offers comparative literature (Certificate); film studies (Certificate); Spanish (PhD); women's studies (Certificate). *Degree requirements:* For doctorate, 2 foreign languages, comprehensive exam, thesis/dissertation. *Entrance requirements:* For doctorate, GRE General Test. Additional exam requirements/recommendations for international students: Required—TOEFL. Electronic applications accepted. *Faculty research:* Spanish literature, Spanish American literature, literary theory, criticism, cultural studies.

**Florida Atlantic University,** College of Education, Department of Teaching and Learning, Boca Raton, FL 33431-0991. Offers curriculum and instruction (M Ed), including art, biology, chemistry, English, French, German, mathematics, music, physics, Pre-K and primary education, reading, social sciences, Spanish; elementary education (M Ed); environmental education (M Ed); reading education (M Ed); social foundations of education (M Ed), including educational psychology, educational technology, multilingual education. *Accreditation:* NCATE. *Program availability:* Part-time, evening/weekend. *Faculty:* 15 full-time (12 women), 2 part-time/adjunct (1 woman). *Students:* 25 full-time (20 women), 41 part-time (37 women); includes 18 minority (9 Black or African American, non-Hispanic/Latino; 2 Asian, non-Hispanic/Latino; 7 Hispanic/Latino), 7 international. Average age 32. 54 applicants, 59% accepted, 18 enrolled. In 2016, 36 master's awarded. *Entrance requirements:* For master's, GRE General Test, minimum GPA of 3.0 in last 2 years of undergraduate course work. Additional exam requirements/recommendations for international students: Required—TOEFL (minimum score 500 paper-based; 61 iBT), IELTS (minimum score 6). *Application deadline:* For fall admission, 7/1 for domestic students, 2/15 for international students; for spring admission, 11/1 for domestic students, 7/15 for international students. Applications are processed on a rolling basis. Application fee: $30. *Expenses:* Tuition, state resident: full-time $7392; part-time $369.82 per credit hour. Tuition, nonresident: full-time $19,432; part-time $1024.81 per credit hour. *Financial support:* Fellowships with partial tuition reimbursements, research assistantships with partial tuition reimbursements, teaching assistantships with partial tuition reimbursements, career-related internships or fieldwork, scholarships/grants, and unspecified assistantships available. *Faculty research:* Technology, teaching English to speakers of other languages, math teaching, electronic portfolio assessment, global perspectives through social studies. *Unit head:* Dr. Barbara Ridener, Chairperson, 561-297-3588, E-mail: bridener@fau.edu. *Application contact:* Dr. Eliah Watlington, Associate Dean, 561-296-8520, Fax: 261-297-2991, E-mail: ewatling@fau.edu.
Website: http://www.coe.fau.edu/academicdepartments/tl/

**Florida Atlantic University,** Dorothy F. Schmidt College of Arts and Letters, Department of Languages, Linguistics, and Comparative Literature, Boca Raton, FL 33431-0991. Offers comparative literature (MA); French (MA); linguistics (MA); Spanish (MA). *Program availability:* Part-time. *Faculty:* 22 full-time (13 women). *Students:* 41 full-time (26 women), 16 part-time (12 women); includes 21 minority (9 Black or African American, non-Hispanic/Latino; 1 Asian, non-Hispanic/Latino; 11 Hispanic/Latino), 11 international. Average age 35. 48 applicants, 38% accepted, 11 enrolled. In 2016, 20 master's awarded. *Degree requirements:* For master's, one foreign language, comprehensive exam, thesis optional. *Entrance requirements:* For master's, GRE General Test, minimum GPA of 3.0. Additional exam requirements/recommendations for international students: Required—TOEFL (minimum score 500 paper-based; 61 iBT), IELTS (minimum score 6). *Application deadline:* For fall admission, 7/1 priority date for domestic students, 2/15 for international students; for spring admission, 11/1 for domestic students, 7/15 for international students. Applications are processed on a rolling basis. Application fee: $30. *Expenses:* Tuition, state resident: full-time $7392; part-time $369.82 per credit hour. Tuition, nonresident: full-time $19,432; part-time $1024.81 per credit hour. *Financial support:* Fellowships, research assistantships, teaching assistantships with partial tuition reimbursements, Federal Work-Study, and tuition waivers (partial) available. Support available to part-time students. Financial award application deadline: 4/1. *Faculty research:* Modern European studies, modern Latin America, medieval Europe. *Unit head:* Dr. Marcella Munson, Chair, 561-297-2118, Fax: 561-297-2756, E-mail: mmunson@fau.edu. *Application contact:* Dr. Linda Johnson, Associate Dean, 561-297-0928, Fax: 561-297-2744.
Website: http://www.fau.edu/LLCL/

**Florida International University,** Steven J. Green School of International and Public Affairs, Department of Modern Languages, Miami, FL 33199. Offers Spanish (MA, PhD). Ph D program has fall admissions only. *Program availability:* Part-time, evening/weekend. *Faculty:* 27 full-time (16 women), 23 part-time/adjunct (17 women). *Students:* 20 full-time (10 women), 14 part-time (7 women); includes 24 minority (1 Black or African American, non-Hispanic/Latino; 23 Hispanic/Latino), 10 international. Average age 43. 20 applicants, 20% accepted, 2 enrolled. In 2016, 4 master's, 2 doctorates awarded. *Degree requirements:* For master's, 2 foreign languages, comprehensive exam, thesis or 6 elective credits; for doctorate, 3 foreign languages, comprehensive exam, thesis/dissertation. *Entrance requirements:* For master's, minimum GPA of 3.0, resume, writing sample in Spanish (6-7 pages minimum), 2 letters of recommendation; for doctorate, GRE General Test (minimum score of 1120) or EXADEP (minimum score of 500), minimum GPA of 3.0, letter of intent, resume, writing sample in Spanish (15 pages minimum), 2 letters of recommendation. Additional exam requirements/recommendations for international students: Required—TOEFL (minimum score 550 paper-based; 80 iBT). *Application deadline:* For fall admission, 3/15 for domestic and international students. Application fee: $30. Electronic applications accepted. *Expenses:* Tuition, state resident: full-time $8912; part-time $446 per credit hour. Tuition, nonresident: full-time $21,393; part-time $992 per credit hour. *Required fees:* $2185; $195 per semester. Tuition and fees vary according to program. *Financial support:* Institutionally sponsored loans, scholarships/grants, and health care benefits available. Financial award application deadline: 3/1; financial award applicants required to submit FAFSA. *Faculty research:* Peninsular Spanish literature, Spanish-American literature, cultural studies, film studies, bilingualism. *Unit head:* Dr. Pascale Becel, Chair, 305-348-2851, Fax: 305-348-1085, E-mail: modlang@fiu.edu. *Application contact:* Nanett Rojas, Manager, Admissions Operations, 305-348-7464, Fax: 305-348-7441, E-mail: gradadm@fiu.edu.

**Florida State University,** The Graduate School, College of Arts and Sciences, Department of Modern Languages and Linguistics, Program in Spanish, Tallahassee, FL 32306. Offers MA, PhD. *Faculty:* 15 full-time (8 women), 1 (woman) part-time/adjunct. *Students:* 36 full-time (29 women), 4 part-time (all women); includes 20 minority (2 Black or African American, non-Hispanic/Latino; 1 Asian, non-Hispanic/Latino; 6 Hispanic/Latino; 11 Two or more races, non-Hispanic/Latino). Average age 25. 25 applicants, 84% accepted, 14 enrolled. In 2016, 3 master's awarded. Terminal master's awarded for partial completion of doctoral program. *Degree requirements:* For master's, thesis optional; for doctorate, 2 foreign languages, thesis/dissertation. *Entrance requirements:* For master's and doctorate, GRE General Test, minimum GPA of 3.0. Additional exam requirements/recommendations for international students: Required—TOEFL (minimum score 550 paper-based; 80 iBT). *Application deadline:* For fall admission, 1/15 for domestic and international students. Applications are processed on a rolling basis. Application fee: $30. Electronic applications accepted. *Expenses:* Tuition, state resident: full-time $7263; part-time $403.51 per credit hour. Tuition, nonresident: full-time $18,087; part-time $1004.85 per credit hour. *Required fees:* $1365; $75.81 per credit hour. $20 per semester. Tuition and fees vary according to campus/location. *Financial support:* In 2016–17, fellowships with partial tuition reimbursements (averaging $14,000 per year), research assistantships with partial tuition reimbursements (averaging $12,000 per year), 32 teaching assistantships with partial tuition reimbursements (averaging $17,000 per year) were awarded. Financial award application deadline: 1/15; financial award applicants required to submit FAFSA. *Faculty research:* Latin American theater, Hispanic literature of the United States, twentieth-century Latin American poetry, Spanish-American colonial. *Unit head:* Dr. Jose Gomariz, Divisional Coordinator/Professor, 850-644-3728, Fax: 850-644-0524, E-mail: jgomariz@fsu.edu. *Application contact:* Wendy E. Pigott, Graduate Academic Coordinator, 850-644-8397, Fax: 850-644-0524, E-mail: wpigott@fsu.edu. Website: http://modlang.fsu.edu/Programs2/Spanish/Graduate-program-in-Spanish

**Framingham State University,** Continuing Education, Program in Spanish, Framingham, MA 01701-9101. Offers M Ed.

**Georgetown University,** Graduate School of Arts and Sciences, Department of Spanish and Portuguese, Washington, DC 20057. Offers Spanish (MS, PhD), including Hispanic literature and cultural studies, Spanish linguistics, Spanish literature; MS/PhD. *Degree requirements:* For master's, one foreign language, research project; for doctorate, 3 foreign languages, thesis/dissertation. *Entrance requirements:* Additional exam requirements/recommendations for international students: Required—TOEFL.

**Georgia Southern University,** Jack N. Averitt College of Graduate Studies, College of Liberal Arts and Social Sciences, Program in Spanish, Statesboro, GA 30460. Offers MA. *Program availability:* Part-time, evening/weekend. *Students:* 17 full-time (12 women), 1 (woman) part-time; includes 6 minority (5 Hispanic/Latino; 1 Two or more races, non-Hispanic/Latino), 1 international. Average age 27. 15 applicants, 87% accepted, 11 enrolled. In 2016, 7 master's awarded. *Degree requirements:* For master's, one foreign language, thesis optional. *Entrance requirements:* For master's, GRE, minimum GPA of 3.0, letters of reference. Additional exam requirements/recommendations for international students: Required—TOEFL (minimum score 550 paper-based; 80 iBT), IELTS (minimum score 6). *Application deadline:* For fall admission, 3/1 priority date for domestic and international students; for spring admission, 10/1 priority date for domestic students, 10/1 for international students. Applications are processed on a rolling basis. Application fee: $50. Electronic applications accepted. *Expenses:* Tuition, state resident: full-time $7236; part-time $277 per semester hour. Tuition, nonresident: full-time $27,118; part-time $1105 per semester hour. *Required fees:* $2092. *Financial support:* In 2016–17, 8 students received support, including 7 fellowships with full tuition reimbursements available (averaging $7,750 per year), 3 teaching assistantships with full tuition reimbursements available (averaging $7,750 per year); career-related internships or fieldwork, Federal Work-Study, scholarships/grants, tuition waivers (full), and unspecified assistantships also available. Support available to part-time students. Financial award application deadline: 4/15; financial award applicants required to submit FAFSA. *Faculty research:* Lettrism, twentieth-century France, Spanish medieval studies, Spanish Renaissance studies, Spanish-American colonial period, Mexican studies, Spanish linguistics, foreign language acquisition and education, drama and cinema of Spain and Latin America. *Unit head:* Dr. Eric Kartchner, Department Chair, 912-478-1381, Fax: 912-478-0652, E-mail: ekartchner@georgiasouthern.edu. Website: http://class.georgiasouthern.edu/fl

**Georgia State University,** College of Arts and Sciences, Department of World Languages and Cultures, Program in Spanish, Atlanta, GA 30302-3083. Offers MA. *Degree requirements:* For master's, one foreign language, comprehensive exam, thesis or alternative, Graduate Foreign Language Reading Exam. *Entrance requirements:* For master's, GRE, statement of purpose, writing sample in the target language, 2 letters of recommendation, official transcripts. Additional exam requirements/recommendations for international students: Required—TOEFL (minimum score 79 iBT). *Application deadline:* For fall admission, 3/15 priority date for domestic and international students; for spring admission, 11/15 priority date for domestic and international students. Application fee: $50. Electronic applications accepted. *Expenses:* Tuition, state resident: full-time $6876; part-time $382 per credit hour. Tuition, nonresident: full-time $22,374; part-time $1243 per credit hour. *Required fees:* $2128; $1064 per term. Part-

time tuition and fees vary according to course load and program. *Financial support:* Institutionally sponsored loans available. *Faculty research:* History and literature of colonial Latin America and the early modern Atlantic; contemporary Latin American poetry; interartistic and literary theory and culture; history of ideas in the Spanish Golden Age; interrelation between politics, cultural production in contemporary peninsular literature and film; second language acquisition; receptive skills as means to enhance language acquisition; acquisition of grammatical gender in Spanish as a foreign language. *Unit head:* Dr. Fernando Reati, Department Chair, 404-413-5984, Fax: 404-413-5982, E-mail: freati@gsu.edu. *Application contact:* Lita Malveaux, Administrative Academic Specialist, 404-413-5046, Fax: 404-413-5036, E-mail: lmalveaux@gsu.edu. Website: http://www.gsu.edu/~wwwmcl/

**Georgia State University,** College of Arts and Sciences, Department of World Languages and Cultures, Program in Translation and Interpretation, Atlanta, GA 30302-3083. Offers interpretation (Certificate), including Spanish; translation (Certificate), including French, German, Spanish. *Program availability:* Part-time. *Entrance requirements:* For degree, entrance examination involving translating one passage from English to the target language and one passage from the target language to English, 3 letters of recommendation, resume/curriculum vitae, official transcripts. Additional exam requirements/recommendations for international students: Required—TOEFL (minimum score 79 iBT). *Application deadline:* For fall admission, 3/15 priority date for domestic and international students; for spring admission, 11/15 priority date for domestic and international students. Application fee: $50. Electronic applications accepted. *Expenses:* Tuition, state resident: full-time $6876; part-time $382 per credit hour. Tuition, nonresident: full-time $22,374; part-time $1243 per credit hour. *Required fees:* $2128; $1064 per term. Part-time tuition and fees vary according to course load and program. *Faculty research:* Romance linguistics and translation; theory and practice of translation; medical and legal interpretation. *Unit head:* Dr. Fernando Reati, Chair, 404-413-5984, Fax: 404-413-5982, E-mail: freati@gsu.edu. *Application contact:* Lita Malveaux, Administrative Academic Specialist, 404-413-5046, Fax: 404-413-5036, E-mail: lmalveaux@gsu.edu. Website: http://wlc.gsu.edu/home/graduate/graduate-certificate/

**Harvard University,** Graduate School of Arts and Sciences, Department of Romance Languages and Literatures, Cambridge, MA 02138. Offers French (AM, PhD); Italian (AM, PhD); Portuguese (AM, PhD); Spanish (AM, PhD). Terminal master's awarded for partial completion of doctoral program. *Degree requirements:* For master's, 2 foreign languages; for doctorate, 2 foreign languages, thesis/dissertation. *Entrance requirements:* For master's and doctorate, GRE General Test, sample of written work. Additional exam requirements/recommendations for international students: Required—TOEFL.

**Howard University,** Graduate School, Department of Modern Languages and Literatures, Washington, DC 20059-0002. Offers French (MA); Spanish (MA). *Program availability:* Part-time. *Degree requirements:* For master's, one foreign language, comprehensive exam, thesis. *Entrance requirements:* For master's, GRE General Test, writing samples in English and French or Spanish. *Faculty research:* African literature in French, Spanish linguistics, Spanish Peninsular literature, Spanish sociolinguistics.

**Hunter College of the City University of New York,** Graduate School, School of Arts and Sciences, Department of Romance Languages, Program in Spanish, New York, NY 10065-5085. Offers MA. *Program availability:* Part-time, evening/weekend. *Students:* 1 full-time (0 women), 7 part-time (4 women); includes 6 minority (1 Black or African American, non-Hispanic/Latino; 5 Hispanic/Latino), 1 international. Average age 40. 3 applicants, 33% accepted, 1 enrolled. In 2016, 1 master's awarded. *Degree requirements:* For master's, 2 foreign languages, comprehensive exam, thesis optional. *Entrance requirements:* For master's, GRE General Test, GRE Subject Test, ability to read, speak, and write Spanish; interview. Additional exam requirements/recommendations for international students: Required—TOEFL. *Application deadline:* For fall admission, 4/1 for domestic students, 2/1 for international students; for spring admission, 11/1 for domestic students, 9/1 for international students. *Financial support:* Federal Work-Study and tuition waivers (partial) available. Support available to part-time students. Financial award application deadline: 4/15. *Faculty research:* Galician studies, contemporary Spanish poetry, Lope de Vega, comparative Hispanic literatures, contemporary Hispanic poetry. *Unit head:* Dr. Alicia O. Ramos, Associate Professor and Coordinator, 212-772-5130, E-mail: rosramos@hunter.cuny.edu. *Application contact:* Milena Solo, Director for Graduate Admissions, 212-772-4480, E-mail: admissions@hunter.cuny.edu. Website: http://www.hunter.cuny.edu/romancelanguages/graduate/ma-requirements

**Illinois State University,** Graduate School, College of Arts and Sciences, Department of Foreign Languages, Literatures and Cultures, Normal, IL 61790-2200. Offers French (MA); French and German (MA); French and Spanish (MA); German (MA); German and Spanish (MA); Spanish (MA). *Degree requirements:* For master's, variable foreign language requirement, comprehensive exam, 1 term of residency. *Entrance requirements:* For master's, GRE General Test, minimum GPA of 2.8 in last 60 hours of course work.

**Indiana State University,** College of Graduate and Professional Studies, College of Arts and Sciences, Department of Languages, Literatures, and Linguistics, Terre Haute, IN 47809. Offers applied linguistics/teaching English as a second language (MA); language education (PhD); Spanish/teaching english as a second language (MA); TESL/TEFL (CAS). *Degree requirements:* For master's, comprehensive exam. Electronic applications accepted.

**Indiana University Bloomington,** University Graduate School, College of Arts and Sciences, Department of Spanish and Portuguese, Bloomington, IN 47405. Offers Portuguese (MA, PhD); Spanish (MA, PhD), including Hispanic linguistics, Hispanic literatures. *Faculty:* 22 full-time, 26 part-time/adjunct. *Students:* 84 full-time (47 women); includes 20 minority (19 Hispanic/Latino; 1 Two or more races, non-Hispanic/Latino), 19 international. Average age 30. 72 applicants, 43% accepted, 15 enrolled. In 2016, 7 master's, 8 doctorates awarded. *Degree requirements:* For master's, one foreign language, comprehensive exam, thesis (for Spanish); for doctorate, 2 foreign languages, comprehensive exam, thesis/dissertation. *Entrance requirements:* For master's, GRE General Test, bachelor's degree in Portuguese or Spanish, minimum GPA of 3.0; for doctorate, GRE General Test, master's degree in Portuguese or Spanish, minimum GPA of 3.0. Additional exam requirements/recommendations for international students: Required—TOEFL (minimum score 79 iBT). *Application deadline:* For fall admission, 1/15 priority date for domestic students, 12/1 priority date for international students. Application fee: $55 ($65 for international students). Electronic applications accepted. *Financial support:* Application deadline: 1/15. *Faculty research:* Spanish American literature, Spanish peninsular literature, Hispanic linguistics, Luso-Brazilian studies, Catalan studies. *Unit head:* Steven Wagschal, Chair, 812-855-8498, E-mail: swagscha@indiana.edu. *Application contact:* Patrick Dove, Director of Graduate Studies, 812-855-9194, E-mail: pdove@indiana.edu. Website: http://www.indiana.edu/~spanport/

**Inter American University of Puerto Rico, Metropolitan Campus,** Graduate Programs, Program in Spanish, San Juan, PR 00919-1293. Offers MA. *Program availability:* Part-time, evening/weekend. *Degree requirements:* For master's, one

## Spanish

foreign language, comprehensive exam. *Entrance requirements:* For master's, GRE or EXADEP, interview, minimum GPA of 2.5, 6 credits each of Spanish literature and Hispanic-American literature. Electronic applications accepted.

**Inter American University of Puerto Rico, Metropolitan Campus,** Graduate Programs, Program in Spanish Education, San Juan, PR 00919-1293. Offers MA.

**Inter American University of Puerto Rico, Ponce Campus,** Graduate School, Mercedita, PR 00715-1602. Offers accounting (MBA); biology (M Ed); chemistry (M Ed); criminal justice (MA); elementary education (M Ed); English as a Second Language (M Ed); finance (MBA); history (M Ed); human resources (MBA); marketing (MBA); mathematics (M Ed); Spanish (M Ed). *Entrance requirements:* For master's, minimum GPA of 2.5.

**Iona College,** School of Arts and Science, Department of Education, New Rochelle, NY 10801-1890. Offers adolescence education: biology (MS Ed, MST); adolescence education: English (MS Ed); adolescence education: mathematics (MST); adolescence education: social studies (MS Ed, MST); adolescence education: Spanish (MS Ed); adolescence special education 5-12 (MST); childhood and special education (MST); early childhood and childhood (MST); educational leadership (MS Ed). *Accreditation:* NCATE. *Program availability:* Part-time, evening/weekend. *Faculty:* 7 full-time (6 women), 4 part-time/adjunct (2 women). *Students:* 27 full-time (19 women), 27 part-time (18 women); includes 18 minority (4 Black or African American, non-Hispanic/Latino; 1 Asian, non-Hispanic/Latino; 12 Hispanic/Latino; 1 Two or more races, non-Hispanic/Latino). Average age 26. 6 applicants, 67% accepted, 3 enrolled. In 2016, 25 master's awarded. *Degree requirements:* For master's, thesis or alternative. *Entrance requirements:* For master's, minimum GPA of 3.0, NY State teaching certificate and bachelor's degree (for MS Ed). Additional exam requirements/recommendations for international students: Required—TOEFL (minimum score 550 paper-based; 80 iBT), IELTS (minimum score 6.5). *Application deadline:* For fall admission, 8/1 priority date for domestic students, 5/1 priority date for international students; for spring admission, 1/1 priority date for domestic students, 9/1 priority date for international students. Applications are processed on a rolling basis. Application fee: $50. Electronic applications accepted. *Expenses: Tuition:* Full-time $19,692; part-time $1094 per credit. *Required fees:* $245 per term. Tuition and fees vary according to program. *Financial support:* In 2016–17, 3 students received support. Unspecified assistantships available. Support available to part-time students. Financial award application deadline: 4/15; financial award applicants required to submit FAFSA. *Faculty research:* Engaging teacher educators in scientific process, cross-national comparisons of mathematics teaching, questioning strategies in the classroom, research methods, literacy development. *Unit head:* Margaret Smith, PhD, Chair, 914-633-2210, Fax: 914-633-2608, E-mail: msmith@iona.edu. *Application contact:* Richard McMahon, Coordinator, Graduate School of Education, 914-633-2552, E-mail: rmcmahon@iona.edu. Website: http://www.iona.edu/Academics/School-of-Arts-Science/Departments/Education/Graduate-Programs.aspx

**Ithaca College,** School of Humanities and Sciences, Program in Adolescence Education, Ithaca, NY 14850. Offers biology (MAT); chemistry (MAT); earth science (MAT); English (MAT); French (MAT); mathematics (MAT); physics (MAT); social studies (MAT); Spanish (MAT). *Program availability:* Part-time. *Faculty:* 26 full-time (12 women). *Students:* 11 full-time (4 women). Average age 26. 17 applicants, 94% accepted, 10 enrolled. *Degree requirements:* For master's, thesis or alternative. *Entrance requirements:* Additional exam requirements/recommendations for international students: Required—TOEFL (minimum score 550 paper-based; 80 iBT). *Application deadline:* For fall admission, 2/15 for domestic and international students; for spring admission, 12/1 for domestic and international students. Applications are processed on a rolling basis. Application fee: $40. Electronic applications accepted. *Expenses:* Contact institution. *Financial support:* In 2016–17, 5 students received support, including 5 research assistantships (averaging $13,259 per year); career-related internships or fieldwork, Federal Work-Study, scholarships/grants, and unspecified assistantships also available. Support available to part-time students. Financial award application deadline: 2/15; financial award applicants required to submit CSS PROFILE or FAFSA. *Unit head:* Peter Martin, Chair, 607-274-1076, E-mail: pmartin@ithaca.edu. *Application contact:* Nicole Eversley Bradwell, Director, Office of Admission, 607-274-3124, Fax: 607-274-1263, E-mail: admission@ithaca.edu. Website: http://www.ithaca.edu/gradprograms/education/programs/aded

**Johns Hopkins University,** Zanvyl Krieger School of Arts and Sciences, Department of German and Romance Languages and Literatures, Baltimore, MD 21218. Offers French (PhD); German (PhD); Italian (PhD); Spanish (PhD). *Degree requirements:* For doctorate, 2 foreign languages, thesis/dissertation. *Entrance requirements:* For doctorate, GRE General Test. Additional exam requirements/recommendations for international students: Required—TOEFL (minimum score 600 paper-based; 100 iBT), IELTS. Electronic applications accepted. *Faculty research:* Nineteenth-century French prose and poetry, genetic theory and criticism; twentieth-century Latin American literature and film; medieval and Renaissance Italian literature; gender and queer theory in German literature; the ideology of Baroque and Neobaroque aesthetics.

**Kent State University,** College of Arts and Sciences, Department of Modern and Classical Language Studies, Kent, OH 44242-0001. Offers French (MA), including applied linguistics and pedagogy, literature; Latin (MA), including applied linguistics and pedagogy, literature; Spanish (MA), including applied linguistics and pedagogy, literature; translation (MA), including Arabic, French, German, Japanese, Russian, Spanish; translation studies (PhD); MA/MBA. *Program availability:* Part-time. *Faculty:* 35 full-time (23 women). *Students:* 81 full-time (51 women), 23 part-time (15 women); includes 14 minority (1 Black or African American, non-Hispanic/Latino; 9 Hispanic/Latino; 4 Two or more races, non-Hispanic/Latino), 48 international. Average age 30. 109 applicants, 53% accepted, 33 enrolled. In 2016, 31 master's, 6 doctorates awarded. *Degree requirements:* For master's, variable foreign language requirement, comprehensive exam (for some programs), thesis (for some programs); for doctorate, variable foreign language requirement, comprehensive exam, thesis/dissertation. *Entrance requirements:* For master's, transcripts, goal statement, 3 letters of recommendation, CD/MP3 with oral sample of first and second languages, writing sample of second language; for doctorate, transcripts; MA in translation, a foreign language, or similar field; proficiency in a foreign language; minimum GPA of 3.5 from MA; goal statement; 3 letters of recommendation; essay or writing sample. *Application deadline:* For fall admission, 2/1 for domestic and international students. Applications are processed on a rolling basis. Application fee: $45 ($70 for international students). Electronic applications accepted. *Expenses:* Tuition, state resident: full-time $10,864; part-time $495 per credit hour. Tuition, nonresident: full-time $18,380; part-time $837 per credit hour. *Financial support:* Fellowships with full tuition reimbursements, teaching assistantships with full tuition reimbursements, and unspecified assistantships available. Financial award application deadline: 2/1. *Unit head:* Dr. Keiran Dunne, Professor of French Translation/Chair, 330-672-2150, E-mail: kdunne@kent.edu. *Application contact:* Said Shiyab, Professor of Translation Studies/Graduate Coordinator, 330-672-1864, E-mail: sshiyab@kent.edu. Website: http://www.kent.edu/mcls/

**Lake Forest College,** Graduate Program in Liberal Studies, Lake Forest, IL 60045. Offers American studies (MLS); environmental studies (MLS); history (MLS); Medieval

and Renaissance art (MLS); philosophy (MLS); Spanish (MLS); writing (MLS). *Program availability:* Part-time, evening/weekend. *Faculty:* 9 full-time (3 women), 1 part-time/adjunct (0 women). *Students:* 1 full-time (0 women), 38 part-time (20 women); includes 5 minority (1 Black or African American, non-Hispanic/Latino; 2 Asian, non-Hispanic/Latino; 2 Hispanic/Latino). Average age 38. 19 applicants, 53% accepted, 7 enrolled. In 2016, 4 master's awarded. *Degree requirements:* For master's, thesis optional, 8 courses, including at least 3 interdisciplinary seminars. *Entrance requirements:* For master's, transcript, essay, interview. Additional exam requirements/recommendations for international students: Required—TOEFL (minimum score 550 paper-based; 83 iBT); Recommended—IELTS (minimum score 6.5). *Application deadline:* For fall admission, 7/15 priority date for domestic students, 6/1 priority date for international students; for spring admission, 12/1 priority date for domestic students, 10/1 priority date for international students. Applications are processed on a rolling basis. Application fee: $30. *Expenses:* $2,600 per course. *Financial support:* In 2016–17, 2 students received support. Partial tuition grants for full-time teachers available. *Faculty research:* Realigning of the international order; Renaissance women artists; literature of Latin Americans in the U.S.; modern Chinese history; environmental biology. *Unit head:* Prof. D. L. LeMahieu, Director, 847-735-5133, Fax: 847-735-6291, E-mail: lemahieu@lakeforest.edu. *Application contact:* Prof. Carol Gayle, Associate Director, 847-735-5083, Fax: 847-735-6291, E-mail: gayle@lakeforest.edu. Website: http://www.lakeforest.edu/academics/programs/mls/

**Lake Forest College,** Master of Arts in Teaching Program, Lake Forest, IL 60045. Offers elementary education (MAT); K-12 French (MAT); K-12 music (MAT); K-12 Spanish (MAT); K-12 visual art (MAT); secondary biology (MAT); secondary chemistry (MAT); secondary English (MAT); secondary history (MAT); secondary mathematics (MAT). *Degree requirements:* For master's, comprehensive exam, portfolio. *Entrance requirements:* For master's, GRE.

**Lamar University,** College of Graduate Studies, College of Arts and Sciences, Department of English and Modern Languages, Beaumont, TX 77710. Offers English (MA); teaching Spanish (MA). *Program availability:* Part-time, evening/weekend. *Faculty:* 10 full-time (5 women). *Students:* 7 full-time (all women), 23 part-time (20 women); includes 9 minority (1 Black or African American, non-Hispanic/Latino; 8 Hispanic/Latino), 1 international. Average age 40. 5 applicants, 100% accepted, 2 enrolled. In 2016, 12 master's awarded. *Degree requirements:* For master's, one foreign language, thesis optional, practicum. *Entrance requirements:* For master's, GRE General Test, minimum GPA of 2.5 in last 60 hours of undergraduate course work. Additional exam requirements/recommendations for international students: Required—TOEFL (minimum score 550 paper-based; 79 iBT), IELTS (minimum score 6.5). *Application deadline:* For fall admission, 8/10 for domestic students, 7/1 for international students; for spring admission, 1/5 for domestic students, 12/1 for international students. Applications are processed on a rolling basis. Application fee: $25 ($50 for international students). Electronic applications accepted. *Expenses:* $8,134 in-state full-time, $5,574 in-state part-time; $15,604 out-of-state full-time, $10,554 out-of-state part-time per year. *Financial support:* Teaching assistantships, career-related internships or fieldwork, Federal Work-Study, and institutionally sponsored loans available. Support available to part-time students. Financial award application deadline: 4/1; financial award applicants required to submit FAFSA. *Faculty research:* British, Renaissance, nineteenth-century, and American literature; creative writing; modern literature; African-American literature. *Unit head:* Dr. Jim Sanderson, Chair, 409-880-8558, Fax: 409-880-8591. *Application contact:* Deidre Mayer, Interim Director, Admissions and Academic Services, 409-880-8888, Fax: 409-880-7419, E-mail: gradmissions@lamar.edu. Website: http://artssciences.lamar.edu/english-and-modern-languages

**Lee University,** Program in Education, Cleveland, TN 37320-3450. Offers art (MAT); curriculum and instruction (M Ed, Ed S); early childhood (MAT); educational leadership (M Ed, Ed S); elementary education (MAT); English and math (MAT); English and science (MAT); English and social studies (MAT); higher education administration (MS); history (MAT); history and economics (MAT); math and science (MAT); math and social studies (MAT); middle grades (MAT); science and social studies (MASW); secondary education (MAT); Spanish (MAT); special education (M Ed, MAT); TESOL (MAT). *Accreditation:* NCATE. *Program availability:* Part-time. *Faculty:* 13 full-time (6 women), 9 part-time/adjunct (4 women). *Students:* 35 full-time (27 women), 50 part-time (32 women); includes 12 minority (5 Black or African American, non-Hispanic/Latino; 5 Hispanic/Latino; 2 Two or more races, non-Hispanic/Latino), 4 international. Average age 30. 43 applicants, 79% accepted, 28 enrolled. In 2016, 42 master's, 6 other advanced degrees awarded. *Degree requirements:* For master's, variable foreign language requirement, thesis optional, internship. *Entrance requirements:* For master's, MAT or GRE General Test, minimum undergraduate GPA of 2.75, 3 letters of recommendation, interview, writing sample, official transcripts, background check; for Ed S, minimum undergraduate and master's GPA of 2.75, official transcripts for undergraduate and master's degrees. Additional exam requirements/recommendations for international students: Required—TOEFL (minimum score 61 iBT). *Application deadline:* For fall admission, 6/1 priority date for domestic and international students; for spring admission, 11/1 priority date for domestic and international students; for summer admission, 4/1 priority date for domestic and international students. Applications are processed on a rolling basis. Application fee: $25. Electronic applications accepted. *Expenses: Tuition:* Full-time $11,367; part-time $632 per credit hour. *Required fees:* $35 per term. One-time fee: $25. Tuition and fees vary according to program. *Financial support:* In 2016–17, 42 students received support. Career-related internships or fieldwork, Federal Work-Study, institutionally sponsored loans, scholarships/grants, and unspecified assistantships available. Financial award application deadline: 3/1; financial award applicants required to submit FAFSA. *Unit head:* Dr. William Kamm, Director, 423-614-8544, E-mail: wkamm@leeuniversity.edu. *Application contact:* Crystal Keeter, Graduate Education Secretary, 423-614-8544, E-mail: ckeeter@leeuniversity.edu. Website: http://www.leeuniversity.edu/academics/graduate/education

**Lehman College of the City University of New York,** School of Arts and Humanities, Department of Languages and Literatures, Bronx, NY 10468-1589. Offers Spanish (MA). *Program availability:* Part-time, evening/weekend. *Degree requirements:* For master's, one foreign language.

**Loyola University Chicago,** Graduate School, Department of Modern Languages and Literatures, Chicago, IL 60660. Offers Spanish (MA). *Program availability:* Part-time, evening/weekend. *Faculty:* 8 full-time (6 women), 1 part-time/adjunct (0 women). *Students:* 8 full-time (4 women), 4 part-time (all women); includes 5 minority (1 Asian, non-Hispanic/Latino; 4 Hispanic/Latino), 3 international. Average age 28. 20 applicants, 55% accepted, 6 enrolled. In 2016, 3 master's awarded. *Degree requirements:* For master's, 2 foreign languages, comprehensive exam, thesis or alternative. *Entrance requirements:* Additional exam requirements/recommendations for international students: Required—TOEFL, ACTFL (American Council on the Teaching of Foreign Languages) oral proficiency exam. *Application deadline:* For fall admission, 2/10 for domestic students; for spring admission, 12/1 for domestic students. Application fee: $50. *Expenses: Tuition:* Full-time $18,594. *Required fees:* $848. Part-time tuition and fees vary according to course load, degree level and program. *Financial support:* In 2016–17, 6 students received support, including 3 teaching assistantships with full tuition reimbursements available (averaging $16,000 per year). Financial award

applicants required to submit FAFSA. *Faculty research:* Linguistics, Latin American contemporary narrative, Latin American culture and civilization, Hispanic women's studies, twentieth century peninsular writing, Golden Age, Don Quixote. *Unit head:* Dr. Susan Cavallo, Chair, 773-508-2870, E-mail: scavall@luc.edu. *Application contact:* Dr. D. Scott Hendrickson, Assistant Professor, 773-508-2850, E-mail: dhendrickson@luc.edu.
Website: http://www.luc.edu/modernlang/

**Marquette University,** Graduate School, College of Arts and Sciences, Department of Foreign Languages and Literatures, Milwaukee, WI 53201-1881. Offers Spanish (MA). *Program availability:* Part-time, evening/weekend. *Faculty:* 25 full-time (17 women), 4 part-time/adjunct (2 women). *Students:* 7 full-time (5 women), 1 international. Average age 26. 7 applicants, 86% accepted, 2 enrolled. In 2016, 5 master's awarded. *Degree requirements:* For master's, one foreign language, comprehensive exam. *Entrance requirements:* For master's, official transcripts from all current and previous colleges/universities except Marquette, three letters of recommendation, tape recording of foreign speaking voice. Additional exam requirements/recommendations for international students: Required—TOEFL. *Application deadline:* For fall admission, 12/15 for domestic and international students. Application fee: $50. Electronic applications accepted. *Financial support:* Fellowships, teaching assistantships with full tuition reimbursements, institutionally sponsored loans, scholarships/grants, health care benefits, tuition waivers (full and partial), and unspecified assistantships available. Support available to part-time students. Financial award application deadline: 2/15. *Faculty research:* Latin American literature, Afro-Hispanic literature, descriptive Spanish linguistics, inter-American studies, foreign language education. *Total annual research expenditures:* $22,516. *Unit head:* Dr. Anne Pasero, Chair, 414-288-7063. *Application contact:* Dr. Dinorah Cortes-Velez, Director of Graduate Studies, 414-288-7268, Fax: 414-288-1578.
Website: http://www.marquette.edu/fola/grad_director_intro.shtml

**Michigan State University,** The Graduate School, College of Arts and Letters, Department of Spanish and Portuguese, East Lansing, MI 48824. Offers applied Spanish linguistics (MA); Hispanic cultural studies (PhD); Hispanic literatures (MA). *Entrance requirements:* Additional exam requirements/recommendations for international students: Required—TOEFL. Electronic applications accepted.

**Middlebury College,** Language Schools, Spanish School, Middlebury, VT 05753-6002. Offers MA, DML. *Degree requirements:* For master's, one foreign language; for doctorate, 2 foreign languages, comprehensive exam, thesis/dissertation, residence abroad, teaching experience. *Entrance requirements:* For master's, online placement exam, 3 letters of recommendation, personal statement, transcripts, Spanish essay; for doctorate, 1st and 2nd language placement exams, 3 letters of recommendation, personal statement, transcripts, MA in Spanish. Electronic applications accepted. *Expenses:* Contact institution.

**Middle Tennessee State University,** College of Graduate Studies, College of Liberal Arts, Department of Foreign Languages and Literatures, Murfreesboro, TN 37132. Offers foreign languages (MAT), including French, German, Spanish. *Program availability:* Part-time, evening/weekend, online learning. *Degree requirements:* For master's, one foreign language, comprehensive exam, thesis optional. *Entrance requirements:* For master's, GRE. Additional exam requirements/recommendations for international students: Required—TOEFL (minimum score 525 paper-based; 71 iBT) or IELTS (minimum score 6). Electronic applications accepted.

**Millersville University of Pennsylvania,** College of Graduate Studies and Adult Learning, College of Arts, Humanities and Social Sciences, Department of Foreign Languages, Program in Languages and Cultures: Spanish Option, Millersville, PA 17551-0302. Offers MA. Program offered in collaboration with West Chester University of Pennsylvania. *Program availability:* Part-time. *Faculty:* 7 full-time (4 women). *Students:* 6 part-time (2 women); includes 2 minority (both Hispanic/Latino). Average age 36. 3 applicants, 100% accepted, 2 enrolled. In 2016, 1 master's awarded. *Degree requirements:* For master's, one foreign language, comprehensive exam (for some programs), thesis optional, exam, portfolio, or research project and presentation. *Entrance requirements:* For master's, ACTFL, OPI, OPIc and WPT, baccalaureate degree from regionally-accredited four-year college or university. Additional exam requirements/recommendations for international students: Required—TOEFL (minimum score 600 paper-based), IELTS (minimum score 6). *Application deadline:* Applications are processed on a rolling basis. Application fee: $40. Electronic applications accepted. *Expenses:* $483 per credit resident tuition; $725 per credit non-resident tuition. *Financial support:* Unspecified assistantships available. Financial award application deadline: 3/15; financial award applicants required to submit FAFSA. *Faculty research:* 20th century Spanish and Latin American poetry, comparative poetry (Spanish and American), contemporary Spanish literature, Spanish medieval literature, Spanish sociolinguistics and phonological variation. *Unit head:* Dr. Marco A. Antolin, Associate Professor/Program Contact, 717-871-7150, Fax: 717-871-7935, E-mail: marco.antolin@millersville.edu. *Application contact:* Dr. Victor S. DeSantis, Dean of College of Graduate Studies and Adult Learning/Associate Provost for Civic and Community Engagement, 717-871-7619, Fax: 717-871-7954, E-mail: victor.desantis@millersville.edu.
Website: http://www.millersville.edu/forlang/

**Minnesota State University Mankato,** College of Graduate Studies and Research, College of Arts and Humanities, Department of World Languages and Cultures, Program in Spanish, Mankato, MN 56001. Offers Spanish (MS); Spanish education (MS); Spanish for the professions (MS). *Students:* 6 part-time (5 women). *Degree requirements:* For master's, one foreign language, comprehensive exam, thesis. *Entrance requirements:* For master's, minimum GPA of 3.0 during previous 2 years. *Application deadline:* For fall admission, 7/1 priority date for domestic students; for spring admission, 11/1 for domestic students. Applications are processed on a rolling basis. Application fee: $40. Electronic applications accepted. *Financial support:* Research assistantships with full tuition reimbursements, teaching assistantships with full tuition reimbursements, career-related internships or fieldwork, Federal Work-Study, institutionally sponsored loans, and unspecified assistantships available. Support available to part-time students. Financial award application deadline: 3/15.

**Molloy College,** Graduate Education Program, Rockville Centre, NY 11571-5002. Offers adolescent education in biology (MS Ed); adolescent special education (Advanced Certificate); bilingual extension (Advanced Certificate); childhood education (MS Ed); childhood special education (Advanced Certificate); early childhood education (MS Ed); educational technology (MS Ed); English (MS Ed); mathematics (MS Ed); social studies (MS Ed); Spanish (MS Ed); special education on both childhood and adolescent levels (MS Ed); teaching English to speakers of other languages (TESOL) in grades Pre-K to 12 (MS Ed); TESOL (Advanced Certificate). *Accreditation:* NCATE. *Program availability:* Part-time, evening/weekend. *Faculty:* 17 full-time (16 women), 23 part-time/adjunct (19 women). *Students:* 95 full-time (75 women), 221 part-time (177 women); includes 59 minority (14 Black or African American, non-Hispanic/Latino; 6 Asian, non-Hispanic/Latino; 38 Hispanic/Latino; 1 Two or more races, non-Hispanic/Latino), 1 international. Average age 42. 214 applicants, 66% accepted, 125 enrolled. In 2016, 95 master's, 4 Advanced Certificates awarded. *Entrance requirements:* Additional exam requirements/recommendations for international students: Required—TOEFL

(minimum score 550 paper-based; 79 iBT). *Application deadline:* Applications are processed on a rolling basis. Application fee: $60. Electronic applications accepted. *Expenses: Tuition:* Full-time $19,170; part-time $1065 per credit. *Required fees:* $950; $790 per credit. Tuition and fees vary according to course load. *Financial support:* Applicants required to submit FAFSA. *Faculty research:* ESL - general education teacher collaboration; special education; school desegregation; American intellectual and social history; families and schools. *Unit head:* Joanne O'Brien, Associate Dean/Director, 516-323-3116, E-mail: jobrien@molloy.edu. *Application contact:* Jaclyn Machowicz, Assistant Director for Admissions, 516-323-4010, E-mail: jmachowicz@molloy.edu.

**Montclair State University,** The Graduate School, College of Education and Human Services, MAT Program in Teaching, Montclair, NJ 07043-1624. Offers art (MAT); biology (MAT); chemistry (MAT); earth science (MAT); English (MAT); French (MAT); health and physical education (MAT); health education (MAT); mathematics (MAT); music (MAT); physical education (MAT); physical science (MAT); social studies (MAT); Spanish (MAT); teacher of English as a second language (MAT). *Degree requirements:* For master's, comprehensive exam, thesis or alternative. *Entrance requirements:* For master's, interview, 2 letters of recommendation. Additional exam requirements/recommendations for international students: Required—TOEFL (minimum score 83 iBT), IELTS (minimum score 6.5). Electronic applications accepted. *Expenses:* Tuition, state resident: part-time $553 per credit. Tuition, nonresident: part-time $854 per credit. *Required fees:* $91 per credit. Tuition and fees vary according to program.

**Montclair State University,** The Graduate School, College of Humanities and Social Sciences, Program in Spanish, Montclair, NJ 07043-1624. Offers MA. *Program availability:* Part-time, evening/weekend. *Degree requirements:* For master's, comprehensive exam, thesis or alternative. *Entrance requirements:* For master's, GRE General Test, 2 letters of recommendation, essay. Additional exam requirements/recommendations for international students: Required—TOEFL (minimum score 83 iBT), IELTS (minimum score 6.5). Electronic applications accepted. *Expenses:* Tuition, state resident: part-time $553 per credit. Tuition, nonresident: part-time $854 per credit. *Required fees:* $91 per credit. Tuition and fees vary according to program. *Faculty research:* Contemporary Spanish novel, Spanish poetry of the twentieth century, Golden Age drama, contemporary Spanish film, contemporary Latin American novel, nineteenth-century Latin American literature.

**New Mexico State University,** College of Arts and Sciences, Department of Languages and Linguistics, Las Cruces, NM 88003. Offers Spanish (MA). *Program availability:* Part-time, 100% online. *Faculty:* 12 full-time (6 women). *Students:* 17 full-time (11 women), 66 part-time (52 women); includes 45 minority (all Hispanic/Latino), 8 international. Average age 36. 29 applicants, 79% accepted, 17 enrolled. In 2016, 30 master's awarded. *Degree requirements:* For master's, one foreign language, comprehensive exam, thesis optional, oral and written exams. *Entrance requirements:* For master's, sample of written work in Spanish, 3 letters of reference, language evaluation form (or OPI score), letter of intent. Additional exam requirements/recommendations for international students: Required—TOEFL (minimum score 550 paper-based; 79 iBT), IELTS (minimum score 6.5). *Application deadline:* For fall admission, 1/15 for domestic students; for spring admission, 9/15 for domestic students. Applications are processed on a rolling basis. Application fee: $40 ($50 for international students). Electronic applications accepted. *Expenses:* Tuition, state resident: full-time $4086. Tuition, nonresident: full-time $14,254. *Required fees:* $853. Tuition and fees vary according to course load. *Financial support:* In 2016–17, 18 students received support, including 12 teaching assistantships (averaging $16,497 per year); career-related internships or fieldwork, Federal Work-Study, institutionally sponsored loans, scholarships/grants, traineeships, health care benefits, and unspecified assistantships also available. Support available to part-time students. Financial award application deadline: 3/1. *Faculty research:* Spanish-American literature, U.S. Hispanic and Chicano literature and border culture, Hispanic linguistics, bilingualism, language contact, sociolinguistics, Mexican literature. *Total annual research expenditures:* $6,299. *Unit head:* Dr. Glenn Fetzer, Department Head, 575-646-3408, E-mail: gwfetzer@nmsu.edu. *Application contact:* Dr. Jeff Longwell, Graduate Program Director, 575-646-2726, E-mail: jelongwe@nmsu.edu.
Website: http://www.nmsu.edu/~langling/

**New Mexico State University,** College of Education, Department of Curriculum and Instruction, Las Cruces, NM 88003. Offers bilingual education (MA); curriculum and instruction (Ed D); early childhood education (MA); educational diagnostics (Ed S); language, literacy and culture (MA); learning design and technologies (MA); teaching (MAT), including Spanish; teaching English to speakers of other languages (MA). *Accreditation:* NCATE. *Program availability:* Part-time, evening/weekend, 100% online. *Faculty:* 23 full-time (17 women), 7 part-time/adjunct (5 women). *Students:* 114 full-time (81 women), 219 part-time (159 women); includes 190 minority (16 Black or African American, non-Hispanic/Latino; 2 American Indian or Alaska Native, non-Hispanic/Latino; 5 Asian, non-Hispanic/Latino; 160 Hispanic/Latino; 7 Two or more races, non-Hispanic/Latino), 33 international. Average age 37. 126 applicants, 75% accepted, 65 enrolled. In 2016, 92 master's, 19 doctorates awarded. *Degree requirements:* For master's, comprehensive exam, thesis optional; for doctorate, comprehensive exam, thesis/dissertation. *Entrance requirements:* For master's, minimum cumulative GPA of 3.0; for doctorate, portfolio, minimum cumulative GPA of 3.0. Additional exam requirements/recommendations for international students: Required—TOEFL (minimum score 550 paper-based; 79 iBT), IELTS (minimum score 6.5). *Application deadline:* For fall admission, 12/15 priority date for domestic and international students; for spring admission, 11/1 for domestic students. Applications are processed on a rolling basis. Application fee: $40 ($50 for international students). Electronic applications accepted. *Expenses:* Tuition, state resident: full-time $4086. Tuition, nonresident: full-time $14,254. *Required fees:* $853. Tuition and fees vary according to course load. *Financial support:* In 2016–17, 102 students received support, including 2 fellowships (averaging $4,076 per year), 2 research assistantships (averaging $18,070 per year), 16 teaching assistantships (averaging $16,454 per year); career-related internships or fieldwork, Federal Work-Study, scholarships/grants, traineeships, health care benefits, and unspecified assistantships also available. Support available to part-time students. Financial award application deadline: 3/1. *Faculty research:* STEM education, bilingual and English as a second language education, critical pedagogy/multicultural education, learning design and technology, early childhood education. *Total annual research expenditures:* $29,926. *Unit head:* Dr. David Rutledge, Department Head, 575-646-5411, Fax: 575-646-5436, E-mail: rutledge@nmsu.edu. *Application contact:* Dr. David Rutledge, Associate Department Head for Graduate Programs, 575-646-5411, Fax: 575-646-5436, E-mail: rutledge@nmsu.edu.
Website: http://ci.education.nmsu.edu

**New York University,** Graduate School of Arts and Science, Department of Spanish and Portuguese Languages and Literatures, New York, NY 10012-1019. Offers Portuguese (MA, PhD); Spanish (PhD); Spanish and Latin American literatures and cultures (MA); Spanish language and translation (MA). *Program availability:* Part-time. *Degree requirements:* For master's, 2 foreign languages, thesis; for doctorate, 2 foreign languages, thesis/dissertation. *Entrance requirements:* For master's, GRE General Test; for doctorate, GRE General Test, master's degree. Additional exam requirements/

recommendations for international students: Required—TOEFL. *Faculty research:* Gender and sexuality, transatlantic studies, literacy and cultural theories, Colonial and Post-Colonial studies, autobiography and modern subjectivities.

**New York University,** Steinhardt School of Culture, Education, and Human Development, Department of Teaching and Learning, Program in Multilingual/Multicultural Studies, New York, NY 10003. Offers bilingual education (MA, PhD, Advanced Certificate); foreign language education (MA); teaching English to speakers of other languages (MA, PhD); teaching foreign languages, 7-12 (MA), including Chinese, French, Italian, Japanese, Spanish; teaching French as a foreign language (MA), including teaching English to speakers of other languages; teaching Spanish as a foreign language (MA), including teaching English to speakers of other languages. *Accreditation:* TEAC. *Program availability:* Part-time, evening/weekend. *Degree requirements:* For master's, thesis (for some programs); for doctorate, thesis/dissertation. *Entrance requirements:* For doctorate, GRE General Test, interview; for Advanced Certificate, master's degree. Additional exam requirements/recommendations for international students: Required—TOEFL (minimum score 100 iBT). Electronic applications accepted. *Faculty research:* Second language acquisition, cross-cultural communication, technology-enhanced language learning, language variation, action learning.

**North Carolina State University,** Graduate School, College of Humanities and Social Sciences, Department of Foreign Languages and Literatures, Program in Spanish Language and Literature, Raleigh, NC 27695. Offers MA. *Degree requirements:* For master's, thesis optional. *Entrance requirements:* For master's, fluency in Spanish. Electronic applications accepted. *Faculty research:* Applied linguistics, technology-assisted language instruction, Latin-American literature and culture, 20th and 21st Century Spanish narrative and film, children's literature.

**Northern Arizona University,** Graduate College, College of Arts and Letters, Department of Global Languages and Cultures, Flagstaff, AZ 86011. Offers Spanish (MAT); Spanish education (MAT). *Program availability:* Part-time. *Degree requirements:* For master's, comprehensive exam, thesis optional. *Entrance requirements:* For master's, bachelor's degree in Spanish (coupled with preparation in general or foreign language education courses) or Spanish secondary education, or degree/experience in related field (e.g., bilingual education); minimum GPA of 3.0 or equivalent. Additional exam requirements/recommendations for international students: Required—TOEFL (minimum score 550 paper-based; 80 iBT), IELTS (minimum score 7). Electronic applications accepted. *Expenses:* Tuition, state resident: full-time $8971; part-time $444 per credit hour. Tuition, nonresident: full-time $20,958; part-time $1164 per credit hour. *Required fees:* $1018; $644 per credit hour. Tuition and fees vary according to course load, campus/location and program.

**Northern Illinois University,** Graduate School, College of Liberal Arts and Sciences, Department of Foreign Languages and Literatures, De Kalb, IL 60115-2854. Offers French (MA); Spanish (MA). *Program availability:* Part-time. *Faculty:* 25 full-time (11 women). *Students:* 3 full-time (0 women), 9 part-time (6 women); includes 8 minority (1 Black or African American, non-Hispanic/Latino; 1 Asian, non-Hispanic/Latino; 6 Hispanic/Latino). Average age 34. 6 applicants, 67% accepted, 1 enrolled. In 2016, 7 master's awarded. *Degree requirements:* For master's, one foreign language, comprehensive exam, thesis or alternative, language proficiency exam. *Entrance requirements:* For master's, GRE General Test, interview, minimum GPA of 2.75, undergraduate major in French or Spanish. Additional exam requirements/recommendations for international students: Required—TOEFL (minimum score 550 paper-based). *Application deadline:* For fall admission, 6/1 for domestic students, 5/1 for international students; for spring admission, 11/1 for domestic students, 10/1 for international students. Applications are processed on a rolling basis. Application fee: $40. Electronic applications accepted. *Financial support:* In 2016–17, 6 teaching assistantships with full tuition reimbursements were awarded; fellowships with full tuition reimbursements, research assistantships with full tuition reimbursements, career-related internships or fieldwork, Federal Work-Study, scholarships/grants, tuition waivers (full), and unspecified assistantships also available. Support available to part-time students. Financial award applicants required to submit FAFSA. *Faculty research:* Francophone women writers, prosodies of French and Italian, early Spanish drama, business German, history of Burmese literature. *Unit head:* Dr. Katharina Barbe, Chair, 815-753-1559, Fax: 815-753-5989, E-mail: kbarbe@niu.edu. *Application contact:* Graduate School Office, 815-753-0395, E-mail: gradsch@niu.edu.
Website: http://www.forlangs.net/

**Northwestern University,** The Graduate School, Judd A. and Marjorie Weinberg College of Arts and Sciences, Department of Spanish and Portuguese, Evanston, IL 60208. Offers PhD.

**The Ohio State University,** Graduate School, College of Arts and Sciences, Division of Arts and Humanities, Department of Spanish and Portuguese, Columbus, OH 43210. Offers MA, PhD. *Faculty:* 25. *Students:* 63 full-time (35 women), 1 (woman) part-time; includes 9 minority (all Hispanic/Latino), 27 international. Average age 30. In 2016, 9 master's, 14 doctorates awarded. Terminal master's awarded for partial completion of doctoral program. *Degree requirements:* For master's, thesis optional; for doctorate, thesis/dissertation. *Entrance requirements:* For master's and doctorate, GRE General Test, sample of academic writing. Additional exam requirements/recommendations for international students: Required—TOEFL (minimum score 550 paper-based; 79 iBT), Michigan English Language Assessment Battery (minimum score 82); Recommended—IELTS (minimum score 7). *Application deadline:* For fall admission, 12/13 priority date for domestic students, 11/30 priority date for international students; for spring admission, 3/1 for domestic students, 2/1 for international students. Applications are processed on a rolling basis. Application fee: $60 ($70 for international students). Electronic applications accepted. *Financial support:* Fellowships, research assistantships, teaching assistantships, Federal Work-Study, institutionally sponsored loans, and unspecified assistantships available. Support available to part-time students. *Unit head:* Dr. Eugenia Romero, Interim Chair and Professor, 614-247-6179, E-mail: spanport@osu.edu. *Application contact:* Graduate and Professional Admissions, 614-292-9444, Fax: 614-292-3895, E-mail: gpadmissions@osu.edu.
Website: http://sppo.osu.edu/

**Ohio University,** Graduate College, College of Arts and Sciences, Department of Modern Languages, Athens, OH 45701-2979. Offers French (MA); Spanish (MA). *Program availability:* Part-time. *Degree requirements:* For master's, 2 foreign languages, comprehensive exam, thesis optional. *Entrance requirements:* For master's, oral and written samples. Additional exam requirements/recommendations for international students: Required—TOEFL (minimum score 550 paper-based; 80 iBT) or IELTS (minimum score 6.5). *Application deadline:* For fall admission, 1/15 priority date for domestic and international students. Application fee: $50 ($55 for international students). Electronic applications accepted. *Financial support:* Teaching assistantships with tuition reimbursements, Federal Work-Study, institutionally sponsored loans, and tuition waivers (partial) available. Financial award application deadline: 1/15. *Faculty research:* French and Spanish language and literature. *Unit head:* Greg Kessler, 740-593-2748, E-mail: kessler@ohio.edu.
Website: http://www.ohio.edu/modlang/

**Penn State University Park,** Graduate School, College of the Liberal Arts, Department of Spanish, Italian, and Portuguese, University Park, PA 16802. Offers Spanish (MA, PhD). *Unit head:* Dr. Susan Welch, Dean, 814-865-7691, Fax: 814-863-2085. *Application contact:* Lori Hawn, Director, Graduate Student Services, 814-865-1795, Fax: 814-863-4627, E-mail: l-gswww@lists.psu.edu.
Website: http://sip.la.psu.edu/

**Pontifical Catholic University of Puerto Rico,** College of Arts and Humanities, Department of Hispanic Studies, Ponce, PR 00717-0777. Offers grammar and writing (Professional Certificate); Hispanic studies (MA). *Program availability:* Part-time, evening/weekend. *Degree requirements:* For master's, variable foreign language requirement, comprehensive exam, thesis or alternative. *Entrance requirements:* For master's, GRE General Test, 2 letters of recommendation, interview, minimum GPA of 2.75. Electronic applications accepted.

**Portland State University,** Graduate Studies, College of Liberal Arts and Sciences, Department of World Languages and Literatures, Portland, OR 97207-0751. Offers French (MA); German (MA); Japanese (MA); Spanish (MA); world literature and language (MA). *Program availability:* Part-time. *Faculty:* 45 full-time (25 women), 39 part-time/adjunct (27 women). *Students:* 22 full-time (13 women), 6 part-time (3 women); includes 8 minority (2 Asian, non-Hispanic/Latino; 6 Hispanic/Latino), 4 international. Average age 31. 19 applicants, 53% accepted, 8 enrolled. In 2016, 18 master's awarded. *Degree requirements:* For master's, one foreign language, thesis (for some programs). *Entrance requirements:* Additional exam requirements/recommendations for international students: Required—TOEFL (minimum score 550 paper-based; 80 iBT), IELTS (minimum score 6.5). *Application deadline:* For fall admission, 4/1 for domestic students, 3/1 for international students; for winter admission, 9/1 for domestic students, 7/1 for international students; for spring admission, 11/1 for domestic and international students. Applications are processed on a rolling basis. Application fee: $65. *Expenses:* Contact institution. *Financial support:* In 2016–17, 18 teaching assistantships with tuition reimbursements (averaging $10,805 per year) were awarded; research assistantships, Federal Work-Study, scholarships/grants, and unspecified assistantships also available. Support available to part-time students. Financial award application deadline: 3/1; financial award applicants required to submit FAFSA. *Faculty research:* Foreign language pedagogy, applied and social linguistics, literary history and criticism. *Total annual research expenditures:* $396,300. *Unit head:* Dr. Gina Greco, Chair, 503-725-5287, E-mail: grecog@pdx.edu. *Application contact:* Kelli Martin, Graduate Admissions Coordinator, 503-725-3243, E-mail: kmarti@pdx.edu.
Website: http://www.pdx.edu/wll/

**Princeton University,** Graduate School, Department of Spanish and Portuguese Languages and Cultures, Princeton, NJ 08544-1019. Offers PhD. *Degree requirements:* For doctorate, variable foreign language requirement, thesis/dissertation. *Entrance requirements:* For doctorate, GRE General Test, sample of written work. Additional exam requirements/recommendations for international students: Required—TOEFL (minimum score 600 paper-based). Electronic applications accepted.

**Purdue University,** Graduate School, College of Liberal Arts, School of Languages and Cultures, West Lafayette, IN 47907. Offers French (MA, MAT, PhD), including French (MA, PhD), French education (MAT); German (MA, MAT, PhD), including German (MA, PhD), German education (MAT); Japanese pedagogy (MA); Spanish (MA, MAT, PhD), including Spanish (MA, PhD), Spanish education (MAT). *Faculty:* 44 full-time (22 women), 1 (woman) part-time/adjunct. *Students:* 37 full-time (18 women), 41 part-time (30 women); includes 9 minority (1 Asian, non-Hispanic/Latino; 8 Hispanic/Latino), 52 international. Average age 32. 49 applicants, 39% accepted, 14 enrolled. In 2016, 11 master's, 5 doctorates awarded. Terminal master's awarded for partial completion of doctoral program. *Degree requirements:* For master's, one foreign language; for doctorate, 2 foreign languages, thesis/dissertation. *Entrance requirements:* For master's, GRE General Test (minimum score 600, 160 for new scoring), two writing samples, one in English, one in language (French, German, Japanese, or Spanish); sample recording of English and language of study; for doctorate, GRE General Test (minimum score 600, 160 for new scoring), master's degree with minimum GPA of 3.5 or equivalent; two writing samples, one in English, one in language (French, German, Japanese, or Spanish); sample recording of English and language of study. Additional exam requirements/recommendations for international students: Required—TOEFL (minimum score 550 paper-based; 77 iBT); Recommended—TWE. *Application deadline:* For fall admission, 12/12 for domestic and international students; for spring admission, 10/1 for domestic and international students. Applications are processed on a rolling basis. Application fee: $60 ($75 for international students). Electronic applications accepted. *Financial support:* In 2016–17, fellowships with tuition reimbursements (averaging $15,750 per year), teaching assistantships with tuition reimbursements (averaging $13,463 per year) were awarded. Support available to part-time students. Financial award applicants required to submit FAFSA. *Faculty research:* Linguistics, semiotics, literary criticism, pedagogy. *Unit head:* Dr. Madeleine M. Henry, Head, 765-494-3828, E-mail: henry48@purdue.edu. *Application contact:* Joni L. Hipsher, Graduate Contact, 765-494-3841, E-mail: jlhipshe@purdue.edu.
Website: http://www.cla.purdue.edu/slc/main/

**Queens College of the City University of New York,** Arts and Humanities Division, Department of Hispanic Languages and Literatures, Queens, NY 11367-1597. Offers Spanish (MA). *Program availability:* Part-time. *Faculty:* 11 full-time (7 women), 23 part-time/adjunct (19 women). *Students:* 7 part-time (5 women); all minorities (all Hispanic/Latino). Average age 46. 5 applicants, 100% accepted, 1 enrolled. In 2016, 7 master's awarded. *Degree requirements:* For master's, 3 foreign languages. *Entrance requirements:* For master's, minimum GPA of 3.0. Additional exam requirements/recommendations for international students: Required—TOEFL (minimum score 61 iBT), IELTS (minimum score 5). *Application deadline:* For fall admission, 4/1 for domestic students; for spring admission, 11/1 for domestic students. Applications are processed on a rolling basis. Application fee: $125. Electronic applications accepted. *Expenses:* Tuition, state resident: full-time $5065; part-time $425 per credit. Tuition, nonresident: part-time $780 per credit. *Required fees:* $522; $397 per credit. Part-time tuition and fees vary according to course load and program. *Financial support:* Career-related internships or fieldwork available. Financial award application deadline: 4/1; financial award applicants required to submit FAFSA. *Unit head:* Dr. Jose Martinez-Torrejon, Chair, 718-997-5626.

**Queen's University at Kingston,** School of Graduate Studies, Faculty of Arts and Sciences, Department of Spanish and Italian, Kingston, ON K7L 3N6, Canada. Offers Spanish language and literature (MA). *Program availability:* Part-time. *Degree requirements:* For master's, one foreign language, thesis. *Entrance requirements:* Additional exam requirements/recommendations for international students: Required—TOEFL. Electronic applications accepted. *Faculty research:* Golden Age, nineteenth-and twentieth-century Peninsular novel, literary theory, colonial Latin America, nineteenth-and-twentieth century Latin America.

**Rider University,** Department of Graduate Education, Leadership and Counseling, Teacher Certification Program, Lawrenceville, NJ 08648-3001. Offers business education (Certificate); elementary education (Certificate); English as a second language (Certificate); English education (Certificate); mathematics education (Certificate); preschool to grade 3 (Certificate); science education (Certificate); social studies education (Certificate); world languages (Certificate), including French, German, Spanish. *Program availability:* Part-time. *Degree requirements:* For Certificate, internship, professional portfolio. *Entrance requirements:* For degree, PRAXIS, resume. Additional exam requirements/recommendations for international students: Required—TOEFL (minimum score 550 paper-based). Electronic applications accepted. *Faculty research:* Conceptual foundations for optimal development of creativity; creative theory, cognitive processes in mathematics learning, teacher collaboration.

**Roosevelt University,** Graduate Division, College of Arts and Sciences, Department of Literature and Languages, Program in Spanish, Chicago, IL 60605. Offers MA. *Program availability:* Part-time, evening/weekend. *Degree requirements:* For master's, variable foreign language requirement, thesis or alternative. *Entrance requirements:* For master's, BA in Spanish or the equivalent. *Faculty research:* Latin American narrative, feminism, Hispanic cultures, twentieth-century Hispanic literature, Latino studies.

**Rutgers University–New Brunswick,** Graduate School-New Brunswick, Program in Spanish, Piscataway, NJ 08854-8097. Offers bilingualism and second language acquisition (MA, PhD); Spanish (MA, MAT, PhD); Spanish literature (MA, PhD); translation (MA). *Program availability:* Part-time. *Degree requirements:* For master's, comprehensive exam (for some programs), thesis (for some programs); for doctorate, 2 foreign languages, comprehensive exam, thesis/dissertation. *Entrance requirements:* For master's and doctorate, GRE General Test. Additional exam requirements/recommendations for international students: Required—TOEFL. Electronic applications accepted. *Faculty research:* Hispanic literature, Luso-Brazilian literature, Spanish linguistics, Spanish translation.

**St. John's University,** St. John's College of Liberal Arts and Sciences, Department of Languages and Literatures, Queens, NY 11439. Offers Spanish (MA). *Program availability:* Part-time, evening/weekend. *Degree requirements:* For master's, comprehensive exam, thesis optional. *Entrance requirements:* For master's, 24 credits of undergraduate course work in languages (18 credits in Spanish), minimum GPA of 3.0, bachelor's degree. Additional exam requirements/recommendations for international students: Required—TOEFL (minimum score 600 paper-based; 100 iBT), IELTS (minimum score 7). Electronic applications accepted. *Faculty research:* Paleography; early North American Spanish literature; medieval, Renaissance and Golden Century Spanish literature; journal and book editions.

**Saint Louis University,** Graduate Education, College of Arts and Sciences, Department of Modern and Classical Languages, St. Louis, MO 63103. Offers French (MA); Spanish (MA). *Program availability:* Part-time. *Degree requirements:* For master's, one foreign language, comprehensive exam, thesis/dissertation (Spanish). *Entrance requirements:* For master's, GRE General Test or MAT, letters of recommendation, resume, interview. Additional exam requirements/recommendations for international students: Required—TOEFL (minimum score 525 paper-based). Electronic applications accepted. *Faculty research:* Culture studies, literature studies, foreign language acquisition.

**Saint Louis University–Madrid Campus,** Graduate Programs, Master of Arts in Spanish Program, Madrid, Spain. Offers MA. *Program availability:* Part-time. *Degree requirements:* For master's, one foreign language, comprehensive exam, thesis optional. *Entrance requirements:* For master's, GRE General Test or MAT, 3 letters of recommendation, curriculum vitae, writing sample, interview. Additional exam requirements/recommendations for international students: Required—TOEFL. Electronic applications accepted. *Faculty research:* Spanish and Latin American literature, linguistics, cultural studies, gender studies.

**Saint Xavier University,** Graduate Studies, School of Education, Chicago, IL 60655-3105. Offers counseling (MA); curriculum and instruction (MA); early childhood education (MA); educational administration (MA); elementary education (MA); individualized studies (MA), including educational technology, English as a second language (ESL), ISTEM (integrative science, technology, engineering, and math), science education; music education (MA); reading (MA); secondary education (MA); Spanish education (MA); special education (MA); teaching and leadership (MA). *Accreditation:* NCATE. *Program availability:* Part-time, evening/weekend. *Degree requirements:* For master's, thesis or project. *Entrance requirements:* For master's, minimum GPA of 3.0. *Expenses:* Contact institution.

**Salem State University,** School of Graduate Studies, Program in Spanish, Salem, MA 01970-5353. Offers MAT. *Program availability:* Part-time, evening/weekend. *Entrance requirements:* For master's, GRE or MAT. Additional exam requirements/recommendations for international students: Required—TOEFL (minimum score 550 paper-based; 80 iBT) or IELTS (minimum score 5.5).

**Sam Houston State University,** College of Humanities and Social Sciences, Department of Foreign Languages, Huntsville, TX 77341. Offers Spanish (MA). *Program availability:* Part-time. *Degree requirements:* For master's, comprehensive exam, thesis (for some programs). *Entrance requirements:* For master's, GRE General Test, writing sample, letters of recommendation. Additional exam requirements/recommendations for international students: Required—TOEFL (minimum score 550 paper-based; 79 iBT), IELTS (minimum score 6.5). Electronic applications accepted. *Faculty research:* Pablo Picasso studies, Muslim women, Hispanic literature and art, sociolinguistics, language and the law, medical art and literature (Hispanic emphasis).

**San Diego State University,** Graduate and Research Affairs, College of Arts and Letters, Department of Spanish and Portuguese, San Diego, CA 92182. Offers Spanish (MA). *Degree requirements:* For master's, one foreign language. *Entrance requirements:* For master's, GRE General Test, 3 letters of reference. Additional exam requirements/recommendations for international students: Required—TOEFL. Electronic applications accepted. *Faculty research:* New strategies for teaching foreign languages.

**San Francisco State University,** Division of Graduate Studies, College of Liberal and Creative Arts, Department of Modern Languages and Literatures, Program in Spanish, San Francisco, CA 94132-1722. Offers MA. *Program availability:* Part-time. *Application deadline:* Applications are processed on a rolling basis. Electronic applications accepted. *Expenses:* Tuition, state resident: full-time $6738. Tuition, nonresident: full-time $15,666. *Required fees:* $1012. Tuition and fees vary according to degree level and program. *Financial support:* Unspecified assistantships available. *Unit head:* Dr. Mohammad Salama, Chair, 415-338-7413, Fax: 415-338-6159, E-mail: mrsalama@sfsu.edu. *Application contact:* Prof. Michael Hammer, Program Coordinator, 415-338-1658, Fax: 415-338-6159, E-mail: mhammer@sfsu.edu.
Website: http://mll.sfsu.edu/spanish-program/

**San Jose State University,** Graduate Studies and Research, College of Humanities and the Arts, San Jose, CA 95192-0001. Offers art (MA, MFA), including art history and visual culture (MA), digital media art (MFA), photography (MFA), pictorial art (MFA), spatial art (MFA); computational linguistics (Certificate); English (MA, MFA), including creative writing (MFA); French (MA); humanities and arts (Certificate); linguistics (MA); music (MA); philosophy (MA); professional and technical communication (Certificate); Spanish (MA); teaching English to speakers of other languages (MA); TESOL (Certificate); theatre arts (MA). Electronic applications accepted.

**Smith College,** Graduate and Special Programs, Department of Spanish and Portuguese, Northampton, MA 01063. Offers secondary education (MAT), including Spanish education. *Program availability:* Part-time. *Degree requirements:* For master's, one foreign language. *Entrance requirements:* Additional exam requirements/recommendations for international students: Required—TOEFL (minimum score 595 paper-based; 97 iBT), IELTS. *Application deadline:* For fall admission, 4/1 for domestic students, 1/15 for international students; for spring admission, 12/1 for domestic students. Application fee: $60. *Expenses: Tuition:* Full-time $34,560; part-time $1440 per credit. Tuition and fees vary according to course load and program. *Financial support:* Scholarships/grants available. Support available to part-time students. Financial award application deadline: 4/1; financial award applicants required to submit CSS PROFILE or FAFSA. *Unit head:* Maria Helena Rueda, Chair, 413-585-3451, E-mail: mrueda@smith.edu. *Application contact:* Ruth Morgan, Program Assistant, 413-585-3050, Fax: 413-585-3054, E-mail: gradstdy@smith.edu.
Website: http://www.smith.edu/spp/

**Southern Oregon University,** Graduate Studies, Department of Foreign Languages and Literatures, Ashland, OR 97520. Offers French language teaching (MA); Spanish language teaching (MA). *Program availability:* Part-time, online learning. *Faculty:* 4 full-time (2 women), 6 part-time/adjunct (3 women). *Students:* 74 full-time (54 women), 18 part-time (14 women); includes 17 minority (2 Black or African American, non-Hispanic/Latino; 1 American Indian or Alaska Native, non-Hispanic/Latino; 1 Asian, non-Hispanic/Latino; 11 Hispanic/Latino; 2 Two or more races, non-Hispanic/Latino), 1 international. Average age 37. 49 applicants, 84% accepted, 37 enrolled. In 2016, 18 master's awarded. *Degree requirements:* For master's, thesis (for some programs). *Entrance requirements:* For master's, GRE General Test, minimum cumulative GPA of 3.0 in the last 90 quarter credits (60 semester credits) of undergraduate coursework. Additional exam requirements/recommendations for international students: Required—TOEFL (minimum score 540 paper-based; 76 iBT), IELTS (minimum score 6), ELPT (minimum score 964) or ELS (minimum score 112). *Application deadline:* For fall admission, 7/31 priority date for domestic and international students; for winter admission, 11/15 priority date for domestic and international students; for spring admission, 1/7 priority date for domestic and international students. Applications are processed on a rolling basis. Application fee: $60. Electronic applications accepted. *Expenses:* Tuition, state resident: full-time $10,719; part-time $397 per credit. Tuition, nonresident: full-time $13,419; part-time $497 per credit. *Required fees:* $548. *Financial support:* Career-related internships or fieldwork, institutionally sponsored loans, scholarships/grants, and unspecified assistantships available. *Unit head:* Dr. Dan Morris, Graduate French Language Program Coordinator, 541-552-6740, E-mail: morris@sou.edu. *Application contact:* Dr. Anne Connor, Graduate Spanish Language Program Coordinator, 541-552-6743, E-mail: connora@sou.edu.
Website: http://www.sou.edu/language/

**Stanford University,** School of Humanities and Sciences, Department of Iberian and Latin American Cultures, Stanford, CA 94305-2004. Offers Spanish (MA, PhD). Terminal master's awarded for partial completion of doctoral program. *Degree requirements:* For master's, 2 foreign languages; for doctorate, 3 foreign languages, thesis/dissertation, oral exam. *Entrance requirements:* For master's and doctorate, GRE General Test. Additional exam requirements/recommendations for international students: Required—TOEFL. Electronic applications accepted. *Expenses: Tuition:* Full-time $47,331. *Required fees:* $609.

**State University of New York at New Paltz,** Graduate School, School of Education, Department of Secondary Education, New Paltz, NY 12561. Offers adolescence education: biology (MAT, MS Ed); adolescence education: chemistry (MAT, MS Ed); adolescence education: earth science (MAT, MS Ed); adolescence education: English (MAT, MS Ed); adolescence education: French (MAT, MS Ed); adolescence education: social studies (MAT, MS Ed); adolescence education: Spanish (MAT, MS Ed); second language education (MS Ed, AC), including second language education (MS Ed), teaching English language learners (AC). *Accreditation:* NCATE. *Program availability:* Part-time, evening/weekend. *Students:* 60 full-time (36 women), 59 part-time (48 women); includes 28 minority (2 Black or African American, non-Hispanic/Latino; 2 Asian, non-Hispanic/Latino; 22 Hispanic/Latino; 2 Two or more races, non-Hispanic/Latino). 96 applicants, 83% accepted, 54 enrolled. In 2016, 56 master's awarded. *Degree requirements:* For master's, comprehensive exam (for some programs), portfolio. *Entrance requirements:* For master's, minimum GPA of 3.0, New York state teaching certificate (MS Ed). Additional exam requirements/recommendations for international students: Required—TOEFL (minimum score 550 paper-based; 80 iBT), IELTS (minimum score 6.5). *Application deadline:* For fall admission, 3/1 priority date for domestic students, 3/1 for international students; for spring admission, 10/1 priority date for domestic students, 10/1 for international students. Application fee: $50. Electronic applications accepted. *Financial support:* Application deadline: 8/1. *Unit head:* Dr. Laura Dull, Chair, 845-257-2849, E-mail: dullj@newpaltz.edu. *Application contact:* Vika Shock, Director of Graduate Admissions, 845-257-3285, Fax: 845-257-3284, E-mail: gradschool@newpaltz.edu.
Website: http://www.newpaltz.edu/secondaryed/

**Syracuse University,** College of Arts and Sciences, MA Program in Spanish Literature and Culture, Syracuse, NY 13244. Offers MA. *Program availability:* Part-time. *Students:* Average age 26. In 2016, 6 master's awarded. *Degree requirements:* For master's, comprehensive exam, thesis (for some programs). *Entrance requirements:* For master's, GRE General Test, official transcripts, resume, three letters of recommendation. Additional exam requirements/recommendations for international students: Required—TOEFL (minimum score 100 iBT). *Application deadline:* For fall admission, 2/1 priority date for domestic and international students. Application fee: $75. Electronic applications accepted. *Expenses: Tuition:* Full-time $25,974; part-time $1443 per credit hour. *Required fees:* $802; $50 per course. Tuition and fees vary according to course load and program. *Financial support:* Fellowships with full tuition reimbursements, teaching assistantships with tuition reimbursements, scholarships/grants, and tuition waivers available. Financial award application deadline: 1/1. *Faculty research:* Literature and culture of the Hispanic world, Hispanic linguistics, literatures and cultures of contemporary Spain, methodological approaches and to the orientations of contemporary theory. *Unit head:* Alicia Ríos, Associate Professor/Program Coordinator, 315-443-5385, E-mail: abrios@syr.edu. *Application contact:* Kathryn Clinton, Information Contact, 315-443-5494, E-mail: kclinton@syr.edu.
Website: http://lang.syr.edu/academics/Spanish/MA-Spanish.html

**Temple University,** College of Liberal Arts, Department of Spanish and Portuguese, Philadelphia, PA 19122-6096. Offers Spanish (MA, PhD). *Program availability:* Part-time, evening/weekend. Terminal master's awarded for partial completion of doctoral program. *Degree requirements:* For master's, one foreign language; for doctorate, 2 foreign languages, thesis/dissertation. *Entrance requirements:* For master's and doctorate, GRE General Test, minimum GPA of 3.0, 3 letters of recommendation. Additional exam requirements/recommendations for international students: Required—TOEFL. Electronic applications accepted. *Faculty research:* Spanish literatures and cultures, Latin American literatures and cultures, Lusophone literatures and cultures, Spanish linguistics, literary and linguistic theory.

## Spanish

**Texas A&M University,** College of Liberal Arts, Department of Hispanic Studies, College Station, TX 77843. Offers Hispanic studies (MA, PhD); modern languages (MA), including Spanish. *Faculty:* 15. *Students:* 22 full-time (13 women), 20 part-time (13 women); includes 24 minority (all Hispanic/Latino), 9 international. Average age 41. 12 applicants, 100% accepted, 7 enrolled. In 2016, 2 doctorates awarded. *Entrance requirements:* Additional exam requirements/recommendations for international students: Required—TOEFL (minimum score 550 paper-based; 80 iBT), IELTS (minimum score 6), PTE (minimum score 53). *Application deadline:* For fall admission, 12/15 priority date for domestic and international students. Application fee: $50 ($90 for international students). *Expenses:* Contact institution. *Financial support:* In 2016–17, 23 students received support, including 3 fellowships with tuition reimbursements available (averaging $20,268 per year), 21 teaching assistantships with tuition reimbursements available (averaging $10,841 per year); career-related internships or fieldwork, institutionally sponsored loans, scholarships/grants, traineeships, health care benefits, tuition waivers (full and partial), and unspecified assistantships also available. Support available to part-time students. Financial award application deadline: 3/15; financial award applicants required to submit FAFSA. *Unit head:* Dr. Irene Moyna, Department Head, 979-845-2124, E-mail: moyna@tamu.edu. *Application contact:* Dr. Hilaire Kallendorf, Director of Graduate Studies, 979-458-0621, E-mail: h-kallendorf@tamu.edu.
Website: http://hispanicstudies.tamu.edu/

**Texas A&M University–Commerce,** College of Humanities, Social Sciences and Arts, Commerce, TX 75429-3011. Offers applied criminology (MS); applied linguistics (MA, MS); art (MA, MFA); Christianity in history (Graduate Certificate); computational linguistics (Graduate Certificate); creative writing (Graduate Certificate); English (MA, MS, PhD); film studies (Graduate Certificate); history (MA, MS); music (MM); political science (MA, MS); public history (Graduate Certificate); sociology (MS); Spanish (MA); studies in children's and adolescent literature and culture (Graduate Certificate); teaching English to speakers of other languages (Graduate Certificate); theater (MA, MS). *Program availability:* Part-time. *Faculty:* 53 full-time (26 women), 7 part-time/adjunct (2 women). *Students:* 87 full-time (55 women), 528 part-time (362 women); includes 198 minority (86 Black or African American, non-Hispanic/Latino; 2 American Indian or Alaska Native, non-Hispanic/Latino; 8 Asian, non-Hispanic/Latino; 84 Hispanic/Latino; 18 Two or more races, non-Hispanic/Latino), 27 international. Average age 37. 333 applicants, 56% accepted, 149 enrolled. In 2016, 66 master's, 8 doctorates awarded. *Degree requirements:* For master's, one foreign language, comprehensive exam, thesis (for some programs); for doctorate, one foreign language, comprehensive exam, thesis/dissertation, departmental qualifying exam. *Entrance requirements:* For master's and doctorate, GRE General Test. Additional exam requirements/recommendations for international students: Required—TOEFL (minimum score 550 paper-based; 79 iBT), IELTS (minimum score 6). *Application deadline:* Applications are processed on a rolling basis. Application fee: $50. Electronic applications accepted. *Expenses:* Contact institution. *Financial support:* In 2016–17, 255 students received support, including 9 research assistantships with partial tuition reimbursements available (averaging $9,000 per year), 68 teaching assistantships with partial tuition reimbursements available (averaging $9,000 per year); Federal Work-Study, institutionally sponsored loans, scholarships/grants, health care benefits, and unspecified assistantships also available. Financial award application deadline: 5/1; financial award applicants required to submit FAFSA. *Unit head:* Dr. Salvatore Attardo, Dean, 903-886-5166, Fax: 903-886-5774, E-mail: salvatore.attardo@tamuc.edu. *Application contact:* Shelby Miller, Graduate Recruiter, 903-468-8123, Fax: 903-886-5774, E-mail: shelby.miller@tamuc.edu.
Website: http://www.tamuc.edu/academics/graduateSchool/programs/humanitiesSocialScienceArts/default.aspx

**Texas A&M University–Kingsville,** College of Graduate Studies, College of Arts and Sciences, Department of Language and Literature, Kingsville, TX 78363. Offers cultural studies (MA); English (MA, MS); Spanish (MA). *Entrance requirements:* Additional exam requirements/recommendations for international students: Required—TOEFL (minimum score 550 paper-based; 79 iBT); Recommended—IELTS. Electronic applications accepted.

**Texas State University,** The Graduate College, College of Liberal Arts, Program in Spanish, San Marcos, TX 78666. Offers MA. *Program availability:* Part-time, evening/weekend. *Faculty:* 7 full-time (4 women). *Students:* 6 full-time (2 women), 11 part-time (9 women); includes 15 minority (1 Asian, non-Hispanic/Latino; 14 Hispanic/Latino). Average age 35. 14 applicants, 50% accepted, 3 enrolled. In 2016, 7 master's awarded. *Degree requirements:* For master's, one foreign language, comprehensive exam, thesis optional. *Entrance requirements:* For master's, baccalaureate degree from regionally-accredited university with minimum GPA of 2.75 on last 60 undergraduate semester hours, statement of purpose, resume. Additional exam requirements/recommendations for international students: Required—TOEFL (minimum score 550 paper-based; 78 iBT), IELTS (minimum score 6.5). *Application deadline:* For fall admission, 1/15 priority date for domestic and international students; for spring admission, 10/15 for domestic students, 10/1 for international students. Applications are processed on a rolling basis. Application fee: $40 ($90 for international students). Electronic applications accepted. *Expenses:* $4,851 per semester. *Financial support:* In 2016–17, 8 students received support, including 3 teaching assistantships (averaging $14,002 per year); research assistantships, career-related internships or fieldwork, Federal Work-Study, institutionally sponsored loans, scholarships/grants, and unspecified assistantships also available. Support available to part-time students. Financial award application deadline: 3/1; financial award applicants required to submit FAFSA. *Unit head:* Dr. George Y. Porras, Graduate Advisor, 512-245-2360, Fax: 512-245-8298, E-mail: gradspanish@txstate.edu. *Application contact:* Dr. Andrea Golato, Dean of Graduate School, 512-245-2581, Fax: 512-245-8365, E-mail: gradcollege@txstate.edu.
Website: http://www.modlang.txstate.edu/degrees-programs/spanish-ma.html

**Texas Tech University,** Graduate School, College of Arts and Sciences, Department of Classical and Modern Languages and Literatures, Lubbock, TX 79409. Offers applied linguistics (MA); classics (MA); German (MA); languages and cultures (MA); Romance languages (MA); Spanish (PhD); MBA/MA. *Program availability:* Part-time. *Faculty:* 56 full-time (37 women), 4 part-time/adjunct (2 women). *Students:* 80 full-time (39 women), 13 part-time (9 women); includes 20 minority (19 Hispanic/Latino; 1 Two or more races, non-Hispanic/Latino), 49 international. Average age 32. 68 applicants, 68% accepted, 31 enrolled. In 2016, 30 master's, 4 doctorates awarded. *Degree requirements:* For master's, comprehensive exam, thesis or alternative; for doctorate, comprehensive exam, thesis/dissertation. *Entrance requirements:* Additional exam requirements/recommendations for international students: Required—TOEFL (minimum score 550 paper-based; 79 iBT). *Application deadline:* For fall admission, 6/1 priority date for domestic students, 1/15 priority date for international students; for spring admission, 9/1 priority date for domestic students, 6/15 priority date for international students. Applications are processed on a rolling basis. Application fee: $75. Electronic applications accepted. *Expenses:* $300 per credit hour full-time resident tuition, $708 per credit hour full-time non-resident tuition; $50.50 per credit hour fee plus $608 per term fee. *Financial support:* In 2016–17, 78 students received support, including 60 fellowships (averaging $2,488 per year), 76 teaching assistantships (averaging $13,011 per year); research assistantships, Federal Work-Study, scholarships/grants, and

unspecified assistantships also available. Financial award application deadline: 4/15; financial award applicants required to submit FAFSA. *Faculty research:* Literature, comparative literature, linguistics, culture, applied linguistics. *Total annual research expenditures:* $36,152. *Unit head:* Dr. Erin Collopy, Chair and Associate Professor, 806-834-8497, Fax: 806-742-3306, E-mail: erin.collopy@ttu.edu. *Application contact:* Carla Burrus, Senior Advisor, 806-834-3282, Fax: 806-742-3306, E-mail: carla.burrus@ttu.edu.
Website: http://www.depts.ttu.edu/classic_modern/

**Tulane University,** School of Liberal Arts, Department of Spanish and Portuguese, New Orleans, LA 70118-5669. Offers Portuguese (MA); Spanish and Portuguese (PhD). *Degree requirements:* For master's, 2 foreign languages; for doctorate, 2 foreign languages, thesis/dissertation. *Entrance requirements:* For master's, GRE General Test, minimum B average in undergraduate course work; for doctorate, GRE General Test. Additional exam requirements/recommendations for international students: Required—TOEFL. Electronic applications accepted. *Expenses: Tuition:* Full-time $50,920; part-time $2829 per credit hour. *Required fees:* $2040; $44.50 per credit hour. $580 per term. Tuition and fees vary according to course load, degree level and program.

**Universidad Autonoma de Guadalajara,** Graduate Programs, Guadalajara, Mexico. Offers administrative law and justice (LL M); advertising and corporate communications (MA); architecture (M Arch); business (MBA); computational science (MCC); education (Ed M, Ed D); English-Spanish translation (MA); entrepreneurship and management (MBA); integrated management of digital animation (MA); international business (MIB); international corporate law (LL M); internet technologies (MS); manufacturing systems (MMS); occupational health (MS); philosophy (MA, PhD); power electronics (MS); quality systems (MQS); renewable energy (MS); social evaluation of projects (MBA); strategic market research (MBA); tax law (MA); teaching mathematics (MA).

**Université de Montréal,** Faculty of Arts and Sciences, Department of Literatures and Modern Languages, Program in Hispanic Studies, Montréal, QC H3C 3J7, Canada. Offers MA. *Degree requirements:* For master's, 2 foreign languages, thesis. Electronic applications accepted. *Faculty research:* Spanish literature and culture, Latin American literature and culture.

**Université Laval,** Faculty of Letters, Department of Literature, Programs in Spanish Literatures, Québec, QC G1K 7P4, Canada. Offers MA, PhD. *Program availability:* Part-time. Terminal master's awarded for partial completion of doctoral program. *Degree requirements:* For master's, thesis; for doctorate, comprehensive exam, thesis/dissertation. *Entrance requirements:* For master's and doctorate, linguistics exams, knowledge of French and Spanish. Electronic applications accepted.

**University at Albany, State University of New York,** College of Arts and Sciences, Department of Languages, Literatures, and Cultures, Albany, NY 12222-0001. Offers Spanish (MA, PhD). *Faculty:* 2 full-time (both women). *Students:* 9 full-time (5 women), 29 part-time (17 women); includes 17 minority (3 Black or African American, non-Hispanic/Latino; 14 Hispanic/Latino), 1 international. 21 applicants, 67% accepted, 10 enrolled. In 2016, 13 master's, 2 doctorates awarded. *Degree requirements:* For doctorate, thesis/dissertation. *Entrance requirements:* Additional exam requirements/recommendations for international students: Required—TOEFL (minimum score 550 paper-based). *Application deadline:* For fall admission, 8/1 for domestic students, 5/1 for international students. Application fee: $75. *Expenses:* Tuition, state resident: full-time $10,870; part-time $453 per credit hour. Tuition, nonresident: full-time $22,210; part-time $925 per credit hour. *International tuition:* $21,550 full-time. *Required fees:* $1864; $96 per credit hour. *Unit head:* Maurice Westmoreland, Chair, 518-442-4222, Fax: 518-442-4111, E-mail: mwestmoreland@albany.edu. *Application contact:* Michael DeRensis, Director, Graduate Admissions, 518-442-3980, Fax: 518-442-3922, E-mail: graduate@albany.edu.
Website: http://www.albany.edu/llc/

**University at Buffalo, the State University of New York,** Graduate School, College of Arts and Sciences, Department of Romance Languages and Literatures, Buffalo, NY 14260-4620. Offers French (MA, PhD); Spanish (MA, PhD). *Program availability:* Part-time. *Faculty:* 15 full-time (9 women), 6 part-time/adjunct (3 women). *Students:* 33 full-time (24 women), 3 part-time (all women); includes 13 minority (3 Black or African American, non-Hispanic/Latino; 2 Asian, non-Hispanic/Latino; 6 Hispanic/Latino; 2 Two or more races, non-Hispanic/Latino), 9 international. 24 applicants, 58% accepted, 7 enrolled. In 2016, 1 master's, 7 doctorates awarded. Terminal master's awarded for partial completion of doctoral program. *Degree requirements:* For master's, one foreign language, comprehensive exam, thesis (for some programs); for doctorate, 2 foreign languages, comprehensive exam (for some programs), thesis/dissertation. *Entrance requirements:* For doctorate, GRE. Additional exam requirements/recommendations for international students: Required—TOEFL (minimum score 550 paper-based; 79 iBT), IELTS (minimum score 6.5), PTE (minimum score 55). *Application deadline:* For fall admission, 12/31 priority date for domestic and international students; for spring admission, 10/30 for domestic students, 9/1 for international students. Applications are processed on a rolling basis. Application fee: $75. Electronic applications accepted. *Financial support:* In 2016–17, 24 students received support, including 3 fellowships with full tuition reimbursements available (averaging $4,667 per year), 24 teaching assistantships with full tuition reimbursements available (averaging $14,049 per year); Federal Work-Study, institutionally sponsored loans, scholarships/grants, and health care benefits also available. Financial award application deadline: 12/31; financial award applicants required to submit FAFSA. *Faculty research:* Romance linguistics, cultural studies, literary studies, literature, philosophy and poetry. *Unit head:* Dr. Elizabeth Scarlett, Professor of Spanish/Department Chair, 716-645-0873, Fax: 716-645-5981, E-mail: scarlett@buffalo.edu. *Application contact:* Dr. Margarita Vargas, Associate Professor of Spanish/Director of Graduate Studies, 716-645-0859, Fax: 716-645-5981, E-mail: mvargas@buffalo.edu.
Website: http://rll.buffalo.edu

**University at Buffalo, the State University of New York,** Graduate School, Graduate School of Education, Department of Learning and Instruction, Buffalo, NY 14260. Offers biology education (Ed M, Certificate); chemistry education (Ed M, Certificate); childhood education (Ed M); childhood education with bilingual extension (Ed M); college teaching (Advanced Certificate); curriculum, instruction and the science of learning (PhD); early childhood education (Ed M); early childhood education with bilingual extension (Ed M); earth science education (Ed M, Certificate); education and technology (Ed M); education studies (Ed M); educational technology and new literacies (Certificate); educational technology and new literacies (Advanced Certificate); elementary education (Ed D); English education (Ed M, Certificate); English education studies (Ed M); English for speakers of other languages (Ed M); foreign and second language education (PhD); French education (Ed M, Certificate); German education (Ed M, Certificate); gifted education (Certificate); Latin education (Ed M, Certificate); literacy education studies (Ed M); literacy specialist (Ed M); literacy teaching and learning (Certificate); mathematics education (Ed M, Certificate); music education (Ed M, Certificate); music education studies (Ed M); music learning theory (Advanced Certificate); online education (Advanced Certificate); physics education (Ed M, Certificate); science and the public (Ed M); social studies education (Ed M, Certificate); Spanish education (Ed M, Certificate); special education (PhD); teaching English to speakers of other languages (Ed M). *Program availability:* Part-time, evening/weekend, 100% online. *Faculty:* 28 full-

time (21 women), 67 part-time/adjunct (49 women). *Students:* 198 full-time (153 women), 312 part-time (220 women); includes 48 minority (28 Black or African American, non-Hispanic/Latino; 4 American Indian or Alaska Native, non-Hispanic/Latino; 15 Asian, non-Hispanic/Latino; 1 Hispanic/Latino), 66 international. Average age 33. 336 applicants, 86% accepted, 178 enrolled. In 2016, 137 master's, 24 doctorates, 25 other advanced degrees awarded. *Degree requirements:* For master's, comprehensive exam; for doctorate, thesis/dissertation, research analysis exam, research experience. *Entrance requirements:* For master's, letters of reference; for doctorate, GRE General Test or MAT, interview, writing sample, letters of recommendation. Additional exam requirements/recommendations for international students: Required—TOEFL (minimum score 600 paper-based; 96 iBT). *Application deadline:* For fall admission, 2/1 priority date for domestic and international students; for spring admission, 11/15 priority date for domestic students, 10/1 for international students. Applications are processed on a rolling basis. Application fee: $50. Electronic applications accepted. *Financial support:* In 2016–17, 44 fellowships (averaging $4,010 per year), 39 research assistantships with tuition reimbursements (averaging $9,897 per year) were awarded; teaching assistantships, career-related internships or fieldwork, Federal Work-Study, institutionally sponsored loans, scholarships/grants, tuition waivers (full and partial), and unspecified assistantships also available. Financial award application deadline: 2/28; financial award applicants required to submit FAFSA. *Faculty research:* Science assessment, foreign language teaching and learning, early learning, new literacies, gender and education. *Total annual research expenditures:* $534,880. *Unit head:* Dr. Deborah Moore-Russo, Chair, 716-645-4069, Fax: 716-645-3161, E-mail: dam29@buffalo.edu. *Application contact:* Luann Zak, Admissions Assistant, 716-645-2110, Fax: 716-645-7937, E-mail: luannzak@buffalo.edu.
Website: http://gse.buffalo.edu/lai

**The University of Akron,** Graduate School, Buchtel College of Arts and Sciences, Department of Modern Languages, Akron, OH 44325. Offers Spanish (MA). *Program availability:* Part-time, evening/weekend. *Faculty:* 5 full-time (3 women). *Students:* 1. *Degree requirements:* For master's, one foreign language, comprehensive exam, essay, oral exam, research paper. *Entrance requirements:* For master's, baccalaureate degree in Spanish, minimum GPA of 2.75, interview, proficiency in Spanish, three letters of recommendation, statement of purpose. Additional exam requirements/recommendations for international students: Required—TOEFL (minimum score 550 paper-based; 79 iBT), IELTS (minimum score 6.5). *Application deadline:* Applications are processed on a rolling basis. Application fee: $45 ($70 for international students). Electronic applications accepted. *Expenses:* Tuition, state resident: full-time $8618; part-time $359 per credit hour. Tuition, nonresident: full-time $17,149; part-time $715 per credit hour. *Required fees:* $1652. *Financial support:* Institutionally sponsored loans available. *Faculty research:* Spanish literature and culture from the Golden Age to the present, contemporary Spanish cinema and the plastic arts, contemporary Latin America narrative and poetry, Spanish applied linguistics and pedagogy. *Unit head:* Dr. Maria Zanetta, Chair, 330-972-5872, E-mail: zanetta@uakron.edu. *Application contact:* Dr. Parizad Dejbord-Sawan, Director of Graduate Studies, 330-972-7824, E-mail: parizad@uakron.edu. Website: http://www.uakron.edu/modlang/

**The University of Alabama,** Graduate School, College of Arts and Sciences, Department of Modern Languages and Classics, Tuscaloosa, AL 35487. Offers French (MA, PhD); French and Spanish (PhD); German (MA); Romance languages (MA, PhD); Spanish (MA, PhD). *Program availability:* Part-time. *Faculty:* 31 full-time (18 women). *Students:* 49 full-time (32 women), 7 part-time (4 women); includes 9 minority (3 Black or African American, non-Hispanic/Latino; 1 Asian, non-Hispanic/Latino; 4 Hispanic/Latino; 1 Two or more races, non-Hispanic/Latino), 20 international. Average age 31. 29 applicants, 66% accepted, 12 enrolled. In 2016, 11 master's, 6 doctorates awarded. *Degree requirements:* For master's, comprehensive exam, thesis optional; for doctorate, one foreign language, thesis/dissertation, preliminary exam. *Entrance requirements:* For master's and doctorate, minimum GPA of 3.0, writing sample. Additional exam requirements/recommendations for international students: Required—TOEFL or IELTS. *Application deadline:* For fall admission, 7/6 priority date for domestic students, 1/15 priority date for international students; for spring admission, 12/5 priority date for domestic students, 6/1 priority date for international students. Applications are processed on a rolling basis. Application fee: $50 ($60 for international students). Electronic applications accepted. *Expenses:* Tuition, state resident: full-time $10,470. Tuition, nonresident: full-time $26,950. *Financial support:* In 2016–17, 7 students received support, including 1 fellowship, research assistantships with full tuition reimbursements available (averaging $10,291 per year), 6 teaching assistantships with full tuition reimbursements available (averaging $10,291 per year); career-related internships or fieldwork, Federal Work-Study, institutionally sponsored loans, and scholarships/grants also available. Financial award application deadline: 7/14. *Faculty research:* Non-English literature, linguistics, culture, film. *Unit head:* Dr. Douglas Lightfoot, Department Chair, 205-348-5059, E-mail: lightfoot@ua.edu. *Application contact:* Dr. K. Barbara Fischer, Graduate Director/Associate Professor, 205-348-8465, Fax: 205-348-2042, E-mail: bfischer@bama.ua.edu. Website: http://bama.ua.edu/~mlc

**The University of Arizona,** College of Humanities, Department of Spanish and Portuguese, Tucson, AZ 85721. Offers Spanish (MA, PhD). Terminal master's awarded for partial completion of doctoral program. *Degree requirements:* For master's, one foreign language, comprehensive exam, thesis optional; for doctorate, 3 foreign languages, comprehensive exam, thesis/dissertation. *Entrance requirements:* For master's, GRE General Test, minimum GPA of 3.3, writing sample, 3 letters of recommendation, audio sample; for doctorate, GRE General Test, minimum GPA of 3.4, 3 letters of recommendation, statement of purpose, writing sample, audio sample. Additional exam requirements/recommendations for international students: Required—TOEFL (minimum score 550 paper-based; 79 iBT). Electronic applications accepted. *Faculty research:* Spanish and Latin American literature and linguistics, literary theory.

**University of Arkansas,** Graduate School, J. William Fulbright College of Arts and Sciences, Department of World Languages, Literature and Cultures, Program in Spanish, Fayetteville, AR 72701. Offers MA. In 2016, 6 master's awarded. *Degree requirements:* For master's, one foreign language, comprehensive exam, thesis optional. *Entrance requirements:* Additional exam requirements/recommendations for international students: Required—TOEFL (minimum score 550 paper-based), IELTS (minimum score 6.5). *Application deadline:* For fall admission, 1/15 priority date for domestic students, 4/1 for international students; for spring admission, 9/15 priority date for domestic students, 10/1 for international students. Applications are processed on a rolling basis. Application fee: $40 ($50 for international students). Electronic applications accepted. *Financial support:* In 2016–17, 1 research assistantship, 14 teaching assistantships (averaging $8,200 per year) were awarded; fellowships with tuition reimbursements, career-related internships or fieldwork, and Federal Work-Study also available. Support available to part-time students. Financial award application deadline: 1/15; financial award applicants required to submit FAFSA. *Faculty research:* Medieval and Golden Age poetry, colonial Latin America, contemporary Latin America. *Unit head:* Dr. Steven Bell, Department Chair, 479-575-2951, Fax: 479-575-6795, E-mail: sbell@uark.edu. *Application contact:* Dr. Reina Ruiz, Graduate Coordinator, 479-575-2951, E-mail: rruiz@uark.edu.
Website: http://www.uark.edu/depts/flaninfo/

**University of Calgary,** Faculty of Graduate Studies, Faculty of Arts, Department of French, Italian and Spanish, Calgary, AB T2N 1N4, Canada. Offers French (MA, PhD); Spanish (MA, PhD). PhD offered in special cases only. *Program availability:* Part-time. *Degree requirements:* For master's, one foreign language, thesis, exam; for doctorate, 2 foreign languages, comprehensive exam, thesis/dissertation, candidacy exam. *Entrance requirements:* Additional exam requirements/recommendations for international students: Required—TOEFL (minimum score 550 paper-based; 80 iBT) or IELTS (minimum score 7). Electronic applications accepted. *Faculty research:* French and French-Canadian language and literature, Hispanic language and literature, comparative literature, language instruction, literary theory.

**University of California, Berkeley,** Graduate Division, College of Letters and Science, Group in Romance Languages and Literatures, Berkeley, CA 94720-1500. Offers French (PhD); Italian (PhD); Spanish (PhD). *Faculty:* 16 full-time. *Students:* 11 full-time (7 women); includes 3 minority (1 Asian, non-Hispanic/Latino; 2 Hispanic/Latino). Average age 33. 12 applicants. In 2016, 4 doctorates awarded. *Degree requirements:* For doctorate, thesis/dissertation, qualifying exam. *Entrance requirements:* For doctorate, GRE General Test, minimum GPA of 3.0, 3 letters of recommendation. Additional exam requirements/recommendations for international students: Required—TOEFL (minimum score 570 paper-based; 90 iBT). *Application deadline:* For fall admission, 12/8 for domestic students. Application fee: $105 ($125 for international students). Electronic applications accepted. *Financial support:* Fellowships with full tuition reimbursements, teaching assistantships with partial tuition reimbursements, health care benefits, and unspecified assistantships available. Financial award applicants required to submit FAFSA. *Unit head:* Ignatio Navarrete, Chair, 510-642-2105. *Application contact:* 510-642-7405.
Website: http://romancelangs.berkeley.edu

**University of California, Davis,** Graduate Studies, Program in Spanish, Davis, CA 95616. Offers MA, PhD. Terminal master's awarded for partial completion of doctoral program. *Degree requirements:* For master's, comprehensive exam (for some programs), thesis (for some programs); for doctorate, 2 foreign languages, thesis/dissertation. *Entrance requirements:* For master's, GRE General Test, minimum GPA of 3.0; for doctorate, GRE General Test, master's degree, minimum GPA of 3.0. Additional exam requirements/recommendations for international students: Required—TOEFL (minimum score 550 paper-based). *Faculty research:* Medieval Spanish language and literature, Spanish linguistics, Latin American literature, nineteenth century Peninsular literature.

**University of California, Irvine,** School of Humanities, Department of Spanish and Portuguese, Irvine, CA 92697. Offers Spanish (MA, MAT, PhD). *Students:* 30 full-time (18 women); includes 21 minority (all Hispanic/Latino) 2 international. Average age 38. 14 applicants, 43% accepted, 3 enrolled. In 2016, 1 master's, 3 doctorates awarded. *Degree requirements:* For doctorate, thesis/dissertation. *Entrance requirements:* For master's and doctorate, GRE General Test, minimum GPA of 3.0. Additional exam requirements/recommendations for international students: Required—TOEFL (minimum score 550 paper-based). *Application deadline:* For fall admission, 1/2 priority date for domestic students, 1/2 for international students. Applications are processed on a rolling basis. Application fee: $105 ($125 for international students). Electronic applications accepted. *Financial support:* Fellowships, teaching assistantships, institutionally sponsored loans, traineeships, health care benefits, and unspecified assistantships available. Financial award application deadline: 3/1; financial award applicants required to submit FAFSA. *Faculty research:* Latin American literature, Spanish literature, Spanish linguistics in Creole studies, Hispanic literature in the U.S., Luso-Brazilian literature. *Unit head:* Luis Aviles, Department Chair, 949-824-7268, Fax: 949-824-2803, E-mail: laviles@uci.edu. *Application contact:* Evelyn Flores, Graduate Program Coordinator, 949-824-8793, Fax: 949-824-2803, E-mail: evelynf@uci.edu. Website: http://www.hnet.uci.edu/spanishandportuguese/

**University of California, Los Angeles,** Graduate Division, College of Letters and Science, Department of Spanish and Portuguese, Program in Spanish, Los Angeles, CA 90095. Offers MA. *Degree requirements:* For master's, one foreign language, comprehensive exam or thesis. *Entrance requirements:* For master's, GRE General Test, bachelor's degree; minimum undergraduate GPA of 3.0 (or its equivalent if letter grade system not used). Additional exam requirements/recommendations for international students: Required—TOEFL. Electronic applications accepted.

**University of California, Riverside,** Graduate Division, Department of Hispanic Studies, Riverside, CA 92521-0102. Offers Spanish (MA, PhD). Terminal master's awarded for partial completion of doctoral program. *Degree requirements:* For master's, one foreign language, comprehensive exam; for doctorate, one foreign language, thesis/dissertation, qualifying exams, 1 quarter of teaching experience. *Entrance requirements:* For master's and doctorate, GRE General Test, minimum GPA of 3.0. Additional exam requirements/recommendations for international students: Required—TOEFL (minimum score 550 paper-based; 80 iBT). Electronic applications accepted. *Expenses:* Tuition, state resident: full-time $16,666. Tuition, nonresident: full-time $31,768. *Required fees:* $11,055.54 per quarter. $3685.18 per quarter. Tuition and fees vary according to campus/location and program. *Faculty research:* Spanish literature of the sixteenth-, seventeenth- and twentieth-century; pre-Columbian and colonial Latin American literature; nineteenth- and twentieth-century Latin American literature.

**University of California, Santa Barbara,** Graduate Division, College of Letters and Sciences, Division of Humanities and Fine Arts, Department of Spanish and Portuguese, Santa Barbara, CA 93106-4150. Offers Hispanic languages and literatures (PhD), including European medieval studies, feminist studies, Hispanic linguistics, Hispanic literature, Luso-Brazilian literature; Hispanic linguistics (MA); Luso-Brazilian literature (MA); Spanish or Spanish-American literature (MA); MA/PhD. Terminal master's awarded for partial completion of doctoral program. *Degree requirements:* For master's, 2 foreign languages, comprehensive exam (for some programs), thesis optional; for doctorate, 3 foreign languages, comprehensive exam, thesis/dissertation. *Entrance requirements:* For master's and doctorate, GRE. Additional exam requirements/recommendations for international students: Required—TOEFL (minimum score 550 paper-based; 80 iBT), IELTS (minimum score 7). Electronic applications accepted. *Faculty research:* Nineteenth-century Spanish and Portuguese literature, Spanish and Spanish-American literature, nineteenth- and twentieth-century Portuguese and Brazilian literatures, Hispanic linguistics, Catalan language and culture.

**University of Central Florida,** College of Arts and Humanities, Department of Modern Languages and Literatures, Program in Spanish, Orlando, FL 32816. Offers MA. *Program availability:* Part-time, evening/weekend. *Students:* 5 full-time (all women), 9 part-time (all women); includes 11 minority (all Hispanic/Latino), 1 international. Average age 39. 4 applicants, 50% accepted, 2 enrolled. In 2016, 9 master's awarded. *Degree requirements:* For master's, one foreign language, comprehensive exam, thesis or alternative. *Entrance requirements:* For master's, minimum GPA of 3.0 in last 60 hours. Additional exam requirements/recommendations for international students: Required—TOEFL. *Application deadline:* For fall admission, 7/15 for domestic students; for spring admission, 12/1 for domestic students. Application fee: $30. Electronic applications accepted. *Expenses:* Tuition, state resident: part-time $288.16 per credit hour. Tuition, nonresident: part-time $1071.31 per credit hour. *Financial support:* In 2016–17, 6 students received support, including 2 fellowships (averaging $2,800 per year), 5 teaching assistantships with partial tuition reimbursements available (averaging $9,814 per year); career-related internships or fieldwork, Federal Work-Study, institutionally sponsored loans, tuition waivers (partial), and unspecified assistantships also available. Financial award application deadline: 3/1; financial award applicants required to submit FAFSA. *Unit head:* Dr. Lisa Nalbone, Director, 407-823-2472, E-mail: lisa.nalbone@ucf.edu. *Application contact:* Assistant Director, Graduate Admissions, 407-823-2766, Fax: 407-823-6442, E-mail: gradadmissions@ucf.edu. Website: http://mll.cah.ucf.edu/graduate/index.php#SpanishMA

**University of Chicago,** Division of the Humanities, Department of Romance Languages and Literatures, Chicago, IL 60637. Offers French and Francophone studies (PhD); Hispanic and Luso-Brazilian studies (PhD); Italian studies (PhD); Renaissance and early modern studies (PhD). *Students:* 44 full-time (28 women); includes 9 minority (1 Asian, non-Hispanic/Latino; 7 Hispanic/Latino; 1 Two or more races, non-Hispanic/Latino), 16 international. 45 applicants, 29% accepted, 5 enrolled. In 2016, 4 doctorates awarded. Terminal master's awarded for partial completion of doctoral program. *Degree requirements:* For doctorate, 3 foreign languages, comprehensive exam, thesis/ dissertation. *Entrance requirements:* For doctorate, GRE General Test. Additional exam requirements/recommendations for international students: Required—TOEFL (minimum score 104 iBT), IELTS (minimum score 7). *Application deadline:* For fall admission, 12/ 15 for domestic and international students. Application fee: $90. Electronic applications accepted. *Financial support:* Fellowships with full tuition reimbursements, teaching assistantships with full tuition reimbursements, Federal Work-Study, institutionally sponsored loans, scholarships/grants, and health care benefits available. Financial award application deadline: 12/15; financial award applicants required to submit FAFSA. *Unit head:* Daisy Delogu, Chair, 773-702-4115, E-mail: ddelogu@uchicago.edu. *Application contact:* Michael Beetley, Assistant Dean of Students, Admissions and Fellowships, 773-702-1552, Fax: 773-834-9148, E-mail: humanitiesadmissions@uchicago.edu. Website: http://rll.uchicago.edu

**University of Cincinnati,** Graduate School, McMicken College of Arts and Sciences, Department of Romance Languages and Literatures, Program in Spanish, Cincinnati, OH 45221. Offers MA, PhD. Terminal master's awarded for partial completion of doctoral program. *Degree requirements:* For master's, thesis optional; for doctorate, 2 foreign languages, thesis/dissertation. *Entrance requirements:* For master's, minimum GPA of 3.0. Electronic applications accepted. *Expenses: Tuition, area resident:* Full-time $12,790; part-time $389 per credit hour. Tuition, state resident: full-time $13,290; part-time $419 per credit hour. Tuition, nonresident: full-time $24,532; part-time $976 per credit hour. *International tuition:* $24,832 full-time. *Required fees:* $3958; $140 per credit hour. Tuition and fees vary according to course load, degree level, program and reciprocity agreements. *Faculty research:* Applied linguistics, Spanish essay, Latin American culture, women's studies, poetry.

**University of Colorado Boulder,** Graduate School, College of Arts and Sciences, Department of Spanish and Portuguese, Boulder, CO 80309. Offers Spanish linguistics (MA); medieval and early modern Hispanic literatures (PhD); peninsular and Latin American literature (MA). *Faculty:* 13 full-time (5 women). *Students:* 36 full-time (25 women), 1 (woman) part-time; includes 8 minority (1 American Indian or Alaska Native, non-Hispanic/Latino; 7 Hispanic/Latino), 14 international. Average age 31. 39 applicants, 54% accepted, 8 enrolled. In 2016, 3 master's, 4 doctorates awarded. Terminal master's awarded for partial completion of doctoral program. *Degree requirements:* For master's, one foreign language, comprehensive exam, thesis or alternative; for doctorate, 2 foreign languages, thesis/dissertation. *Entrance requirements:* For master's, minimum undergraduate GPA of 2.75. *Application deadline:* For fall admission, 12/19 for domestic and international students. Applications are processed on a rolling basis. Application fee: $60 ($80 for international students). Electronic applications accepted. Application fee is waived when completed online. *Financial support:* In 2016–17, 127 students received support, including 42 fellowships (averaging $1,111 per year), 32 teaching assistantships with full and partial tuition reimbursements available (averaging $41,562 per year); institutionally sponsored loans, scholarships/grants, health care benefits, and unspecified assistantships also available. Financial award application deadline: 12/15; financial award applicants required to submit FAFSA. *Faculty research:* Literary criticism, Spanish language/literature, Latin American languages/literature, cultural history. *Total annual research expenditures:* $40,070. *Application contact:* E-mail: spanish@colorado.edu. Website: http://spanish.colorado.edu/

**University of Colorado Denver,** College of Liberal Arts and Sciences, Department of Modern Languages, Denver, CO 80217. Offers Spanish (MA). *Program availability:* Part-time. *Faculty:* 8 full-time (4 women). *Students:* 6 full-time (5 women), 8 part-time (6 women); includes 4 minority (all Hispanic/Latino). Average age 34. 6 applicants, 83% accepted, 1 enrolled. In 2016, 6 master's awarded. *Degree requirements:* For master's, comprehensive exam, thesis or alternative, 33 credit hours of course work. *Entrance requirements:* For master's, BA in Spanish from accredited institution, or BA in another discipline plus language skills that meet department's standards; minimum GPA of 2.5, 3.0 in all Spanish courses; written statement in Spanish; oral interview after the application has been submitted; three letters of recommendation. Additional exam requirements/recommendations for international students: Required—TOEFL (minimum score 550 paper-based; 80 iBT). *Application deadline:* For fall admission, 3/15 for domestic students, 2/15 for international students; for spring admission, 10/15 for domestic students, 9/15 for international students; for summer admission, 3/15 for domestic students, 2/15 for international students. Application fee: $50 ($75 for international students). Electronic applications accepted. *Expenses:* Tuition, state resident: full-time $11,006; part-time $474 per credit. Tuition, nonresident: full-time $28,212; part-time $1264 per credit hour. *Required fees:* $256 per semester. One-time fee: $94.32. Tuition and fees vary according to campus/location and program. *Financial support:* In 2016–17, 1 student received support. Fellowships, research assistantships, teaching assistantships, Federal Work-Study, institutionally sponsored loans, scholarships/grants, and traineeships available. Financial award application deadline: 4/ 1; financial award applicants required to submit FAFSA. *Faculty research:* Spanish American literature; sociolinguistics, bilingualism, phonology and historical linguistics; Spanish peninsular literature; applied linguistics, pragmatics and second language acquisition. Website: http://www.ucdenver.edu/academics/colleges/CLAS/Departments/ ModernLanguages/Programs/SpanishMasters/Pages/MasterofArtsSpanish.aspx

**University of Delaware,** College of Arts and Sciences, Department of Foreign Languages and Literatures, Newark, DE 19716. Offers foreign languages and literatures (MA), including French, German, Spanish; foreign languages pedagogy (MA), including French, German, Spanish; technical Chinese translation (MA). *Degree requirements:* For master's, one foreign language, comprehensive exam, thesis optional. *Entrance requirements:* For master's, GRE General Test, letters of recommendation, writing sample. Additional exam requirements/recommendations for international students: Required—TOEFL. Electronic applications accepted. *Faculty research:* Medieval to Modern French and Spanish literature, twentieth-century German, French, Spanish literature by women, computer-assisted instruction.

**University of Florida,** Graduate School, College of Liberal Arts and Sciences, Department of Spanish and Portuguese Studies, Gainesville, FL 32611. Offers Spanish (MA, MAT, PhD). *Program availability:* Part-time. Terminal master's awarded for partial completion of doctoral program. *Degree requirements:* For master's, one foreign language, comprehensive exam, thesis or extended research paper; for doctorate, 2 foreign languages, comprehensive exam, thesis/dissertation, qualifying exam. *Entrance requirements:* For master's and doctorate, GRE General Test, minimum GPA of 3.0. Additional exam requirements/recommendations for international students: Required— TOEFL (minimum score 550 paper-based; 80 iBT), IELTS (minimum score 6). Electronic applications accepted. *Faculty research:* Spanish linguistics; second language acquisition and teaching; Spanish literature, film and culture; Latin American literature, film and culture; Portuguese literature, film and culture.

**University of Georgia,** Franklin College of Arts and Sciences, Department of Romance Languages, Athens, GA 30602. Offers French (PhD); Italian (MA, PhD); Portuguese (MA, PhD); romance linguistics (MA); Spanish (PhD). *Degree requirements:* For master's, one foreign language; for doctorate, 2 foreign languages, thesis/dissertation. *Entrance requirements:* For master's and doctorate, GRE General Test. *Application deadline:* For fall admission, 7/1 priority date for domestic students; for spring admission, 11/15 for domestic students. Application fee: $50. Electronic applications accepted. *Financial support:* Fellowships, research assistantships, teaching assistantships, and unspecified assistantships available. *Unit head:* Dr. Staccy Casado, Department Head, 706-542-2364, Fax: 706-542-2272, E-mail: sdcasado@uga.edu. *Application contact:* Rachel Gabara, Graduate Coordinator, 706-542-8930, E-mail: romlgradcoord@uga.edu. Website: http://www.rom.uga.edu/

**University of Hawaii at Manoa,** Graduate Division, College of Languages, Linguistics and Literature, Department of Languages and Literatures of Europe and the Americas, Program in Spanish, Honolulu, HI 96822. Offers MA. *Program availability:* Part-time. *Degree requirements:* For master's, one foreign language, thesis optional. *Entrance requirements:* For master's, GRE General Test. Additional exam requirements/ recommendations for international students: Required—TOEFL (minimum score 580 paper-based; 92 iBT), IELTS (minimum score 5).

**University of Houston,** College of Liberal Arts and Social Sciences, Department of Hispanic Studies, Houston, TX 77204. Offers Spanish (MA, PhD). *Program availability:* Part-time. *Degree requirements:* For master's, comprehensive exam, thesis optional; for doctorate, 2 foreign languages, comprehensive exam, thesis/dissertation. *Entrance requirements:* For master's and doctorate, GRE. Additional exam requirements/ recommendations for international students: Required—TOEFL (minimum score 550 paper-based; 79 iBT); Recommended—IELTS (minimum score 6.5). Electronic applications accepted.

**University of Houston,** College of Liberal Arts and Social Sciences, Department of Modern and Classical Languages, Houston, TX 77204. Offers world cultures and literatures (MA). *Degree requirements:* For master's, one foreign language, thesis optional. *Entrance requirements:* For master's, GRE General Test, minimum GPA of 3.0 in last 60 hours of course work. Additional exam requirements/recommendations for international students: Required—TOEFL (minimum score 500 paper-based). Electronic applications accepted.

**University of Illinois at Chicago,** College of Liberal Arts and Sciences, School of Literatures, Cultural Studies and Linguistics, Department of Hispanic and Italian Studies, Chicago, IL 60607-7128. Offers Hispanic linguistics (PhD). *Program availability:* Part-time. Terminal master's awarded for partial completion of doctoral program. *Degree requirements:* For master's, one foreign language, departmental qualifying exam. *Entrance requirements:* For master's, GRE General Test, minimum GPA of 2.75, undergraduate major in Spanish. Additional exam requirements/recommendations for international students: Required—TOEFL. Electronic applications accepted. *Faculty research:* Linguistic competence of bilingual speakers as a window to understanding the human faculty of language, neurocognitive processing of language among different speakers and learners, how languages are used within their social contexts.

**University of Illinois at Urbana–Champaign,** Graduate College, College of Liberal Arts and Sciences, School of Literatures, Cultures and Linguistics, Department of Spanish, Italian and Portuguese, Champaign, IL 61820. Offers Italian (MA, PhD); Portuguese (MA, PhD); Spanish (MA, PhD).

**The University of Iowa,** Graduate College, College of Liberal Arts and Sciences, Department of Spanish and Portuguese, Iowa City, IA 52242-1316. Offers Spanish (MA, PhD); Spanish creative writing (MFA). *Degree requirements:* For master's, thesis optional, exam; for doctorate, comprehensive exam, thesis/dissertation. *Entrance requirements:* For master's and doctorate, GRE General Test, minimum GPA of 3.0. Additional exam requirements/recommendations for international students: Required— TOEFL (minimum score 600 paper-based; 100 iBT). Electronic applications accepted.

**The University of Kansas,** Graduate Studies, College of Liberal Arts and Sciences, Department of Spanish and Portuguese, Lawrence, KS 66045. Offers Spanish (MA, PhD). *Students:* 33 full-time (21 women); includes 4 minority (all Hispanic/Latino), 15 international. Average age 31. 26 applicants, 54% accepted, 7 enrolled. In 2016, 4 master's, 3 doctorates awarded. *Entrance requirements:* For master's and doctorate, curriculum vitae, three letters of recommendation, writing sample, personal statement (500-750 words), official transcripts. Additional exam requirements/recommendations for international students: Required—TOEFL. *Application deadline:* For fall admission, 5/15 priority date for domestic students, 12/15 priority date for international students; for spring admission, 10/15 priority date for domestic students, 5/15 priority date for international students. Application fee: $65 ($85 for international students). Electronic applications accepted. *Financial support:* Fellowships, research assistantships, teaching assistantships, and unspecified assistantships available. Financial award application deadline: 1/15. *Faculty research:* Spanish and Latin American cultural studies, Spanish literature, Latin American literature, Hispanic linguistics. *Unit head:* Dr. Santa Arias, Chair, 785-864-3851, E-mail: sarias@ku.edu. *Application contact:* Jill Marietta Mignacca, Graduate Coordinator, 785-864-0279, E-mail: jmig@ku.edu. Website: http://spanport.ku.edu/

**University of Lethbridge,** School of Graduate Studies, Lethbridge, AB T1K 3M4, Canada. Offers addictions counseling (M Sc); agricultural biotechnology (M Sc); agricultural studies (M Sc, MA); anthropology (MA); archaeology (M Sc, MA); art (MA, MFA); biochemistry (M Sc); biological sciences (M Sc); biomolecular science (PhD); biosystems and biodiversity (PhD); Canadian studies (MA); chemistry (M Sc); computer science (M Sc); computer science and geographical information science (M Sc); counseling (MC); counseling psychology (M Ed); dramatic arts (MA); earth, space, and physical science (PhD); economics (MA); education (MA, PhD); educational leadership (M Ed); English (MA); environmental science (M Sc); evolution and behavior (PhD); exercise science (M Sc); French (MA); French/German (MA); French/Spanish (MA); general education (M Ed); geography (MA); German (MA); health sciences (M Sc); individualized multidisciplinary (M Sc, MA); kinesiology (M Sc, MA); management (M Sc), including accounting, finance, human resource management and labor relations, information systems, international management, marketing, policy and strategy; mathematics (M Sc); music (M Mus, MA); Native American studies (MA);

neuroscience (M Sc, PhD); new media (MA, MFA); nursing (M Sc, MN); philosophy (MA); physics (M Sc); political science (MA); psychology (M Sc, MA); religious studies (MA); sociology (MA); theatre and dramatic arts (MFA); theoretical and computational science (PhD); urban and regional studies (MA); women and gender studies (MA). *Program availability:* Part-time, evening/weekend. *Degree requirements:* For master's, thesis (for some programs); for doctorate, comprehensive exam, thesis/dissertation. *Entrance requirements:* For master's, GMAT (for M Sc in management), bachelor's degree in related field, minimum GPA of 3.0 during previous 20 graded semester courses, 2 years' teaching or related experience (M Ed); for doctorate, master's degree, minimum graduate GPA of 3.5. Additional exam requirements/recommendations for international students: Required—TOEFL (minimum score 580 paper-based; 93 iBT). Electronic applications accepted. *Faculty research:* Movement and brain plasticity, gibberellin physiology, photosynthesis, carbon cycling, molecular properties of main-group ring components.

**University of Louisville,** Graduate School, College of Arts and Sciences, Department of Classical and Modern Languages, Louisville, KY 40292-0001. Offers French (MA); Spanish (MA); translation and interpretation (Certificate). *Program availability:* Part-time, evening/weekend. *Students:* 14 full-time (10 women), 16 part-time (13 women); includes 10 minority (3 Black or African American, non-Hispanic/Latino; 2 Asian, non-Hispanic/Latino; 4 Hispanic/Latino; 1 Two or more races, non-Hispanic/Latino), 3 international. Average age 30. 31 applicants, 68% accepted, 14 enrolled. In 2016, 8 master's, 3 other advanced degrees awarded. *Degree requirements:* For master's, one foreign language, thesis (for some programs). *Entrance requirements:* For master's, GRE General Test (recommended), letters of recommendation, transcripts, curriculum vitae, personal statement; for Certificate, GRE, letters of recommendation, transcripts, curriculum vitae, personal statement. Additional exam requirements/recommendations for international students: Required—TOEFL (minimum score 550 paper-based; 79 iBT); Recommended—IELTS (minimum score 6.5). *Application deadline:* Applications are processed on a rolling basis. Application fee: $60. *Expenses:* Tuition, state resident: full-time $12,246; part-time $681 per credit hour. Tuition, nonresident: full-time $25,486; part-time $1417 per credit hour. *Required fees:* $196. Tuition and fees vary according to program and reciprocity agreements. *Financial support:* In 2016–17, 12 teaching assistantships with full tuition reimbursements (averaging $14,000 per year) were awarded; scholarships/grants, health care benefits, and unspecified assistantships also available. Financial award applicants required to submit FAFSA. *Faculty research:* Medieval Spanish literature and culture, Modern Spanish literature and culture, translation and interpreting, film studies, Medieval French literature and culture, Modern French literature and culture, American Sign Language studies. *Unit head:* Dr. Alan Leidner, Chair, 502-852-0483, Fax: 502-852-8885, E-mail: alan.leidner@louisville.edu. *Application contact:* Travis Henretty, Administrative Assistant, 502-852-6686, Fax: 502-852-8885, E-mail: travis.henretty@louisville.edu.
Website: http://louisville.edu/modernlanguages/

**The University of Manchester,** School of Languages, Linguistics and Cultures, Manchester, United Kingdom. Offers Arab world studies (PhD); Chinese studies (M Phil, PhD); East Asian studies (M Phil, PhD); English language (M Phil, PhD); French studies (M Phil, PhD); German studies (M Phil, PhD); interpreting studies (PhD); Italian studies (M Phil, PhD); Japanese studies (M Phil, PhD); Latin American cultural studies (M Phil, PhD); linguistics (M Phil, PhD); Middle Eastern studies (M Phil, PhD); Polish studies (M Phil, PhD); Portuguese studies (M Phil, PhD); Russian studies (M Phil, PhD); Spanish studies (M Phil, PhD); translation and intercultural studies (M Phil, PhD).

**University of Maryland, College Park,** Academic Affairs, College of Arts and Humanities, School of Languages, Literatures, and Cultures, Spanish Language and Literatures Program, College Park, MD 20742. Offers MA, PhD. *Degree requirements:* For master's, comprehensive exam, thesis optional, scholarly paper; for doctorate, 2 foreign languages, thesis/dissertation. *Entrance requirements:* For master's, minimum GPA of 3.0, interview, sample research paper, minimum of 12 credits in upper-level literature, 3 letters of recommendation; for doctorate, minimum GPA of 3.0, interview, sample research paper, minimum of 12 credits in upper-level literature. Additional exam requirements/recommendations for international students: Required—TOEFL. Electronic applications accepted.

**University of Massachusetts Amherst,** Graduate School, College of Humanities and Fine Arts, Department of Languages, Literatures, and Cultures, Program in Spanish and Portuguese Studies, Amherst, MA 01003. Offers Hispanic literatures, cultures and linguistics (MA, PhD); teaching Spanish (MAT). *Program availability:* Part-time. Terminal master's awarded for partial completion of doctoral program. *Degree requirements:* For master's, one foreign language, thesis or alternative; for doctorate, 2 foreign languages, comprehensive exam, thesis/dissertation. *Entrance requirements:* For master's and doctorate, GRE General Test, sample academic term paper. Additional exam requirements/recommendations for international students: Required—TOEFL (minimum score 550 paper-based; 80 iBT), IELTS (minimum score 6.5). Electronic applications accepted.

**University of Memphis,** Graduate School, College of Arts and Sciences, Department of Foreign Languages and Literatures, Memphis, TN 38152. Offers romance languages (MA), including French, Spanish. *Program availability:* Part-time. *Faculty:* 11 full-time (6 women). *Students:* 17 full-time (13 women), 5 part-time (4 women); includes 14 minority (2 Black or African American, non-Hispanic/Latino; 12 Hispanic/Latino), 2 international. Average age 33. 12 applicants, 92% accepted, 8 enrolled. In 2016, 4 master's awarded. *Degree requirements:* For master's, 2 foreign languages, comprehensive exam. *Entrance requirements:* For master's, GRE, interview in language of concentration, writing sample, letter of intent, two letters of recommendation. Additional exam requirements/recommendations for international students: Required—TOEFL (minimum score 94 iBT). *Application deadline:* For fall admission, 5/15 for domestic students, 4/5 for international students; for spring admission, 11/30 for domestic students, 10/5 for international students. Applications are processed on a rolling basis. Application fee: $35 ($60 for international students). Electronic applications accepted. *Expenses:* $5,231.50 per semester full-time in-state, $9,623.50 full-time out-of-state. *Financial support:* In 2016–17, 11 students received support, including 15 teaching assistantships with full tuition reimbursements available (averaging $13,534 per year); research assistantships with full tuition reimbursements available, Federal Work-Study, scholarships/grants, and unspecified assistantships also available. Financial award application deadline: 2/1; financial award applicants required to submit FAFSA. *Faculty research:* Latin American studies, Brazilian culture and literature, modernity and postmodernity, Hispanic studies, French studies, French and Hispanic culture and literature, Hispanic linguistics, applied linguistics. *Unit head:* Dr. William Thompson, Chair, 901-678-2507, E-mail: wjthmpsn@memphis.edu. *Application contact:* Dr. Fernando Burgos, Coordinator of Graduate Studies, 901-678-3158, E-mail: fburgos@memphis.edu.
Website: http://www.memphis.edu/fl/

**University of Miami,** Graduate School, College of Arts and Sciences, Department of Modern Languages and Literatures, Coral Gables, FL 33124. Offers romance studies (PhD), including French, Spanish. *Degree requirements:* For doctorate, 2 foreign languages, thesis/dissertation, area exam, qualifying exam. *Entrance requirements:* For doctorate, 1 writing sample in English and 1 writing sample in French or Spanish,

minimum GPA of 3.0, oral interview, letters of recommendation. Additional exam requirements/recommendations for international students: Required—TOEFL (minimum score 550 paper-based; 59 iBT). Electronic applications accepted. *Faculty research:* Transatlantic studies, Caribbean studies, comparative literature, gender theory, cultural studies.

**University of Miami,** Graduate School, School of Communication, Coral Gables, FL 33124. Offers communication (PhD); communication studies (MA); film studies (MA, PhD); motion pictures (MFA), including production, producing, and screenwriting; print journalism (MA); public relations (MA); Spanish language journalism (MA); television broadcast journalism (MA). *Program availability:* Part-time. *Degree requirements:* For master's, comprehensive exam (for some programs), thesis (for some programs); for doctorate, comprehensive exam, thesis/dissertation. *Entrance requirements:* For master's, GRE General Test; for doctorate, GRE General Test, master's thesis or scholarly research. Additional exam requirements/recommendations for international students: Required—TOEFL (minimum score 600 paper-based; 100 iBT). Electronic applications accepted. *Faculty research:* Communication studies, mass communication, international/interpersonal communication, film studies, journalism.

**University of Michigan,** Rackham Graduate School, College of Literature, Science, and the Arts, Department of Romance Languages and Literatures, Program in Spanish, Ann Arbor, MI 48109-1275. Offers PhD. *Degree requirements:* For doctorate, 2 foreign languages, thesis/dissertation, oral defense of dissertation, preliminary exams in essay format. *Entrance requirements:* Additional exam requirements/recommendations for international students: Required—TOEFL or Michigan English Language Assessment Battery. Electronic applications accepted. *Expenses:* Tuition, state resident: full-time $21,466; part-time $1152 per credit hour. Tuition, nonresident: full-time $43,346; part-time $2367 per credit hour. Part-time tuition and fees vary according to course load, degree level and program. *Faculty research:* Comparative Romance studies, medieval and early modern studies, postcolonial and minority literatures, culture and materiality, reflection on the nature and function of scholarship.

**University of Minnesota, Twin Cities Campus,** Graduate School, College of Liberal Arts, Department of Spanish and Portuguese Studies, Minneapolis, MN 55455-0213. Offers Hispanic and Lusophone literatures, cultures and linguistics (PhD); Hispanic linguistics (MA); Hispanic literature (MA); Lusophone literature (MA). *Degree requirements:* For master's, 2 foreign languages, comprehensive exam, thesis or alternative; for doctorate, 2 foreign languages, comprehensive exam, thesis/dissertation. *Entrance requirements:* For master's and doctorate, GRE General Test, samples of written work, 3 letters of recommendation, voice sample, statement of purpose. Additional exam requirements/recommendations for international students: Required—TOEFL (minimum score 550 paper-based; 79 iBT). Electronic applications accepted. *Faculty research:* Sociohistorical approaches to literature and culture, feminist studies, literary theory, ideologies and literature, pragmatics and sociolinguistics.

**University of Missouri,** Office of Research and Graduate Studies, College of Arts and Science, Department of Romance Languages and Literatures, Columbia, MO 65211. Offers French (MA, PhD); literature (MA); Spanish (MA, PhD); teaching (MA). *Faculty:* 25 full-time (15 women). *Students:* 22 full-time (16 women), 15 part-time (10 women); includes 11 minority (3 Black or African American, non-Hispanic/Latino; 6 Hispanic/Latino; 2 Two or more races, non-Hispanic/Latino), 13 international. Average age 35. Terminal master's awarded for partial completion of doctoral program. *Degree requirements:* For master's, one foreign language; for doctorate, 4 foreign languages, comprehensive exam, thesis/dissertation. *Entrance requirements:* For master's, GRE General Test, minimum GPA of 3.0 in field of major; bachelor's degree; for doctorate, GRE General Test, minimum GPA of 3.0 in field of major; master's degree. Additional exam requirements/recommendations for international students: Required—TOEFL (minimum score 500 paper-based; 61 iBT). *Application deadline:* For fall admission, 2/15 priority date for domestic students; for winter admission, 10/15 for domestic students. Applications are processed on a rolling basis. Application fee: $75 ($90 for international students). Electronic applications accepted. *Expenses:* Tuition, state resident: full-time $6347; part-time $352.60 per credit hour. Tuition, nonresident: full-time $17,379; part-time $965.50 per credit hour. *Required fees:* $1035. Tuition and fees vary according to course load, campus/location and program. *Financial support:* Research assistantships, teaching assistantships with full tuition reimbursements, institutionally sponsored loans, health care benefits, and unspecified assistantships available.
Website: http://romancelanguages.missouri.edu/grad.shtml

**University of Missouri–Kansas City,** College of Arts and Sciences, Department of Foreign Languages and Literatures, Kansas City, MO 64110-2499. Offers romance languages and literatures (MA), including French, Spanish. *Program availability:* Part-time. *Faculty:* 32 full-time (18 women), 38 part-time/adjunct (32 women). *Students:* 3 full-time (0 women), 13 part-time (9 women); includes 8 minority (all Hispanic/Latino). Average age 35. 12 applicants, 58% accepted, 4 enrolled. In 2016, 7 master's awarded. *Degree requirements:* For master's, 2 foreign languages. *Entrance requirements:* For master's, GRE General Test, minimum GPA of 2.75, 2 letters of recommendation. Additional exam requirements/recommendations for international students: Required—TOEFL (minimum score 550 paper-based; 80 iBT). *Application deadline:* For fall admission, 4/1 priority date for domestic and international students; for spring admission, 11/1 priority date for domestic and international students. Applications are processed on a rolling basis. Application fee: $45 ($50 for international students). Electronic applications accepted. *Financial support:* In 2016–17, 2 teaching assistantships (averaging $12,600 per year) were awarded; Federal Work-Study, institutionally sponsored loans, and tuition waivers (full and partial) also available. Support available to part-time students. Financial award application deadline: 3/1; financial award applicants required to submit FAFSA. *Faculty research:* Literary analyses; psychology and literature; narrative techniques, poetic structure, and style; literature, politics, and society (especially in Latin America). *Unit head:* Dr. K. Scott Baker, Chair, 816-235-2823, Fax: 816-235-1312, E-mail: bakerks@umkc.edu. *Application contact:* Admissions, 816-235-1311, Fax: 816-235-1312, E-mail: admit@umkc.edu.
Website: http://cas.umkc.edu/foreign

**University of Montana,** Graduate School, College of Humanities and Sciences, Department of Modern and Classical Languages and Literatures, Missoula, MT 59812-0002. Offers French (MA); German (MA); Spanish (MA). *Degree requirements:* For master's, one foreign language. *Entrance requirements:* For master's, GRE General Test. Additional exam requirements/recommendations for international students: Required—TOEFL.

**University of Nebraska–Lincoln,** Graduate College, College of Arts and Sciences, Department of Modern Languages and Literatures, Lincoln, NE 68588. Offers French (MA, PhD); German (MA, PhD); Spanish (MA, PhD). *Degree requirements:* For master's, thesis optional; for doctorate, comprehensive exam, thesis/dissertation. *Entrance requirements:* For master's and doctorate, writing sample in target language. Additional exam requirements/recommendations for international students: Required—TOEFL (minimum score 550 paper-based). Electronic applications accepted. *Faculty research:* French, German, and Spanish language, literature, and culture.

**University of Nevada, Reno,** Graduate School, College of Liberal Arts, Department of Foreign Languages and Literatures, Reno, NV 89557. Offers French (MA); German

*Spanish*

(MA); Spanish (MA). *Degree requirements:* For master's, one foreign language, thesis optional. *Entrance requirements:* For master's, GRE General Test, minimum GPA of 2.75. Additional exam requirements/recommendations for international students: Required—TOEFL (minimum score 500 paper-based; 61 iBT), IELTS (minimum score 6). *Faculty research:* Thirteenth century mysticism, contemporary Spanish and Latin American poetry and theater, French interrelation between narration and photography, exile literature and Holocaust.

**University of New Hampshire,** Graduate School, College of Liberal Arts, Program in Spanish, Durham, NH 03824. Offers MA. *Degree requirements:* For master's, one foreign language, thesis or alternative. *Entrance requirements:* Additional exam requirements/recommendations for international students: Required—TOEFL (minimum score 550 paper-based; 80 iBT). Electronic applications accepted.

**University of New Mexico,** Graduate Studies, College of Arts and Sciences, Program in Spanish and Portuguese, Albuquerque, NM 87131. Offers Portuguese (MA); Spanish (MA); Spanish and Portuguese (PhD). *Program availability:* Part-time. *Faculty:* 14 full-time (7 women). *Students:* 38 full-time (21 women), 17 part-time (8 women); includes 30 minority (all Hispanic/Latino), 15 international. Average age 33. 43 applicants, 65% accepted, 25 enrolled. In 2016, 13 master's, 3 doctorates awarded. *Degree requirements:* For master's, one foreign language, comprehensive exam, thesis optional; for doctorate, one foreign language, comprehensive exam, thesis/dissertation. *Entrance requirements:* For master's, BA in Spanish or Portuguese, 3 letters of recommendation, letter of intent; for doctorate, GRE, 3 letters of recommendation, letter of intent, sample research paper. Additional exam requirements/recommendations for international students: Required—TOEFL (minimum score 550 paper-based). *Application deadline:* For fall admission, 1/15 priority date for domestic students; for spring admission, 11/15 for domestic students. Applications are processed on a rolling basis. Application fee: $50. Electronic applications accepted. *Financial support:* Research assistantships, teaching assistantships with tuition reimbursements, Federal Work-Study, institutionally sponsored loans, scholarships/grants, health care benefits, and unspecified assistantships available. Support available to part-time students. Financial award application deadline: 3/1; financial award applicants required to submit FAFSA. *Faculty research:* Languages and literatures from the Iberian Peninsula, Latin America and the American Southwest. *Unit head:* Dr. Anthony Cardenas, Chair, 505-277-5907, Fax: 505-277-3885, E-mail: ajcard@unm.edu. *Application contact:* Martha Hurd, Graduate Advisor, 505-277-2974, E-mail: marthah@unm.edu. Website: http://spanport.unm.edu

**The University of North Carolina at Chapel Hill,** Graduate School, College of Arts and Sciences, Department of Romance Languages and Literatures, Chapel Hill, NC 27599. Offers French (MA, PhD); Italian (MA, PhD); Portuguese (MA, PhD); Romance languages (MA, PhD); Romance philology (MA, PhD); Spanish (MA, PhD). *Degree requirements:* For master's, one foreign language, comprehensive exam, thesis; for doctorate, 2 foreign languages, comprehensive exam, thesis/dissertation. *Entrance requirements:* For master's and doctorate, GRE General Test, minimum GPA of 3.0. Additional exam requirements/recommendations for international students: Required—TOEFL (minimum score 550 paper-based). Electronic applications accepted.

**The University of North Carolina at Charlotte,** College of Liberal Arts and Sciences, Department of Languages and Culture Studies, Charlotte, NC 28223-0001. Offers languages and culture studies: translating (MA); translating (Graduate Certificate). *Program availability:* Part-time, evening/weekend. *Faculty:* 14 full-time (8 women). *Students:* 1 (woman) full-time, 8 part-time (6 women); includes 3 minority (all Hispanic/Latino). Average age 39. 3 applicants, 67% accepted, 1 enrolled. In 2016, 4 master's, 3 other advanced degrees awarded. *Degree requirements:* For master's, comprehensive exam, thesis, internship; for Graduate Certificate, internship. *Entrance requirements:* For master's, GRE, baccalaureate degree in Spanish or related field with minimum overall GPA of 2.75; essay that addresses the applicant's motivation for enrolling in program, to include particular areas of research interests and career or professional goals; three letters of reference; oral interview; for Graduate Certificate, GRE or MAT, essay in English that addresses applicant's motivation for seeking enrollment in program; three letters of recommendation; portfolio of best writing samples in both English and Spanish or of translations into each language; oral interview. Additional exam requirements/recommendations for international students: Required—TOEFL (minimum score 523 paper-based, 70 iBT) or IELTS (6.5). *Application deadline:* For fall admission, 3/1 priority date for domestic and international students; for spring admission, 10/1 priority date for domestic and international students. Applications are processed on a rolling basis. Application fee: $75. Electronic applications accepted. *Expenses:* Tuition, state resident: full-time $4252. Tuition, nonresident: full-time $17,423. *Required fees:* $3026. Tuition and fees vary according to course load and program. *Financial support:* In 2016–17, 3 students received support, including 2 research assistantships (averaging $5,000 per year), 1 teaching assistantship (averaging $8,000 per year); career-related internships or fieldwork, institutionally sponsored loans, scholarships/grants, and unspecified assistantships also available. Support available to part-time students. Financial award application deadline: 3/1; financial award applicants required to submit FAFSA. *Total annual research expenditures:* $12,433. *Unit head:* Ann Gonzalez, Chair, 704-687-8761, E-mail: abgonzal@uncc.edu. *Application contact:* Kathy B. Giddings, Director of Graduate Admissions, 704-687-5503, Fax: 704-687-1668, E-mail: gradadm@uncc.edu.
Website: https://languages.uncc.edu/

**The University of North Carolina at Greensboro,** Graduate School, College of Arts and Sciences, Department of Languages, Literatures, and Cultures, Program in Spanish, Greensboro, NC 27412-5001. Offers advanced Spanish language and Hispanic cultural studies (Certificate); Spanish (MA). *Degree requirements:* For master's, one foreign language, comprehensive exam, thesis or alternative. *Entrance requirements:* For master's, GRE General Test, 3-5 minute tape demonstrating foreign language proficiency, composition in Spanish, sample paper in English. Additional exam requirements/recommendations for international students: Required—TOEFL. Electronic applications accepted.

**The University of North Carolina Wilmington,** College of Arts and Sciences, Department of World Languages and Cultures, Wilmington, NC 28403-3297. Offers Spanish (MA). *Program availability:* Part-time, blended/hybrid learning. *Faculty:* 13 full-time (6 women). *Students:* 5 full-time (3 women), 10 part-time (9 women); includes 4 minority (all Hispanic/Latino), 3 international. Average age 31. 12 applicants, 100% accepted, 8 enrolled. In 2016, 3 master's awarded. *Degree requirements:* For master's, one foreign language, comprehensive exam, thesis or alternative. *Entrance requirements:* For master's, 3 letters of recommendation, 2 recorded speaking samples (3-5 minutes), writing sample (both English and Spanish). Additional exam requirements/recommendations for international students: Required—TOEFL (minimum score 79 iBT), IELTS (minimum score 6.5). *Application deadline:* For fall admission, 5/15 for domestic students; for spring admission, 11/1 for domestic students; for summer admission, 4/1 for domestic students. Applications are processed on a rolling basis. Application fee: $60. Electronic applications accepted. *Expenses:* Contact institution. *Financial support:* Teaching assistantships and scholarships/grants available. Financial award application deadline: 3/15; financial award applicants required to submit FAFSA. *Unit head:* Dr. Michelle Scatton-Tessier, Chair, 910-962-4095, Fax: 910-962-7712,

E-mail: scattonm@uncw.edu. *Application contact:* Dr. Brian Chandler, Graduate Coordinator, 910-962-2299, Fax: 910-962-7712, E-mail: chandlerb@uncw.edu. Website: http://www.uncw.edu/fll/spanish/spngraduate.html

**The University of North Carolina Wilmington,** Watson College of Education, Department of Instructional Technology, Foundations and Secondary Education, Wilmington, NC 28403-3297. Offers academically or intellectually gifted (M Ed); English as a second language (M Ed, MAT); instructional technology (MS); physical education and health (M Ed, MAT); secondary education (M Ed, MAT); Spanish (MAT); Spanish education (MASS). *Program availability:* Part-time. *Faculty:* 17 full-time (11 women). *Students:* 36 full-time (22 women), 62 part-time (49 women); includes 17 minority (12 Black or African American, non-Hispanic/Latino; 3 Hispanic/Latino; 2 Two or more races, non-Hispanic/Latino), 5 international. Average age 34. 89 applicants, 89% accepted, 59 enrolled. In 2016, 36 master's awarded. *Degree requirements:* For master's, comprehensive exam (for some programs), thesis (for some programs), thesis or research project. *Entrance requirements:* For master's, GRE or MAT, statement of interest, 3 letters of recommendation, minimum GPA of 3.0 in undergraduate work. Additional exam requirements/recommendations for international students: Required—TOEFL (minimum score 79 iBT), IELTS (minimum score 6.5). *Application deadline:* For fall admission, 5/15 for domestic students; for spring admission, 10/15 for domestic students; for summer admission, 3/15 for domestic students. Applications are processed on a rolling basis. Application fee: $60. Electronic applications accepted. *Expenses:* Contact institution. *Financial support:* Scholarships/grants and unspecified assistantships available. Financial award application deadline: 3/15; financial award applicants required to submit FAFSA. *Unit head:* Dr. Donyell Roseboro, Chair, 910-962-2289, Fax: 910-962-3609, E-mail: roseborod@uncw.edu. *Application contact:* Dr. Mahnaz Moallem, Graduate Coordinator, 910-962-4183, E-mail: moallemm@uncw.edu. Website: http://www.uncw.edu/ed/itfse/

**University of Northern Iowa,** Graduate College, College of Humanities, Arts and Sciences, Department of Languages and Literatures, MA Program in Spanish, Cedar Falls, IA 50614. Offers Spanish (MA); Spanish teaching (MA). *Program availability:* Part-time, evening/weekend. *Degree requirements:* For master's, one foreign language, comprehensive exam, thesis or alternative. *Entrance requirements:* For master's, minimum GPA of 3.0, valid teaching license, documentation of successful teaching experience. Additional exam requirements/recommendations for international students: Required—TOEFL (minimum score 600 paper-based; 100 iBT). Electronic applications accepted.

**University of Northern Iowa,** Graduate College, College of Humanities, Arts and Sciences, Department of Languages and Literatures, MA Program in TESOL/Spanish, Cedar Falls, IA 50614. Offers MA.

**University of North Texas,** Robert B. Toulouse School of Graduate Studies, Denton, TX 76203-5459. Offers accounting (MS); applied anthropology (MA, MS); applied behavior analysis (Certificate); applied geography (MA); applied technology and performance improvement (M Ed, MS); art education (MA); art history (MA); art museum education (Certificate); arts leadership (Certificate); audiology (Au D); behavior analysis (MS); behavioral science (PhD); biochemistry and molecular biology (MS); biology (MA, MS); biomedical engineering (MS); business analysis (MS); chemistry (MS); clinical health psychology (PhD); communication studies (MA, MS); computer engineering (MS); computer science (MS); counseling (M Ed, MS), including clinical mental health counseling (MS), college and university counseling, elementary school counseling, secondary school counseling; creative writing (MA); criminal justice (MS); curriculum and instruction (M Ed); decision sciences (MBA); design (MA, MFA), including fashion design (MFA), innovation studies, interior design (MFA); early childhood studies (MS); economics (MS); educational leadership (M Ed, Ed D); educational psychology (MS, PhD), including family studies (MS), gifted and talented (MS), human development (MS), learning and cognition (MS), research, measurement and evaluation (MS); electrical engineering (MS); emergency management (MPA); engineering technology (MS); English (MA); English as a second language (MA); environmental science (MS); finance (MBA, MS); financial management (MBA); French (MA); health services management (MBA); higher education (M Ed, Ed D); history (MA, MS); hospitality management (MS); human resources management (MPA); information science (MS); information systems (PhD); information technologies (MBA); interdisciplinary studies (MA, MS); international studies (MA); international sustainable tourism (MS); jazz studies (MM); journalism (MA, MJ, Graduate Certificate), including interactive and virtual digital communication (Graduate Certificate), narrative journalism (Graduate Certificate), public relations (Graduate Certificate); kinesiology (MS); linguistics (MA); local government management (MPA); logistics (PhD); logistics and supply chain management (MBA); long-term care, senior housing, and aging services (MA); management (PhD); marketing (MBA); mathematics (MA, MS); mechanical and energy engineering (MS, PhD); music (MA), including ethnomusicology, music theory, musicology, performance; music composition (PhD); music education (MM Ed, PhD); nonprofit management (MPA); operations and supply chain management (MBA); performance (MM, DMA); philosophy (MA); political science (MA); professional and technical communication (MA); radio, television and film (MA, MFA); rehabilitation counseling (Certificate); sociology (MA); Spanish (MA); special education (M Ed); speech-language pathology (MA); strategic management (MBA); studio art (MFA); teaching (M Ed); MBA/MS. *Program availability:* Part-time, evening/weekend, online learning. Terminal master's awarded for partial completion of doctoral program. *Degree requirements:* For master's, variable foreign language requirement, comprehensive exam, thesis (for some programs); for doctorate, variable foreign language requirement, comprehensive exam (for some programs), thesis/dissertation; for other advanced degree, variable foreign language requirement, comprehensive exam (for some programs). *Entrance requirements:* For master's and doctorate, GRE, GMAT. Additional exam requirements/recommendations for international students: Required—TOEFL (minimum score 550 paper-based; 79 iBT). Electronic applications accepted.

**University of Notre Dame,** Graduate School, College of Arts and Letters, Division of Humanities, Department of Romance Languages and Literatures, Notre Dame, IN 46556. Offers French and Francophone studies (MA); Iberian and Latin American studies (MA); Italian studies (MA); Romance literatures (MA). *Degree requirements:* For master's, 2 foreign languages, comprehensive exam, thesis optional. *Entrance requirements:* For master's, GRE General Test, BA in target language. Additional exam requirements/recommendations for international students: Required—TOEFL (minimum score 600 paper-based; 80 iBT). Electronic applications accepted. *Faculty research:* Literature of discovery and exploration, modern literature, literary criticism, medieval literature, feminist critical theory.

**University of Oklahoma,** College of Arts and Sciences, Department of Modern Languages, Literatures, and Linguistics, Program in Spanish, Norman, OK 73019-2032. Offers MA, PhD, MBA/MA. *Program availability:* Part-time. *Students:* 15 full-time (6 women), 10 part-time (9 women); includes 11 minority (all Hispanic/Latino), 7 international. Average age 37. 10 applicants, 40% accepted, 3 enrolled. In 2016, 3 master's, 2 doctorates awarded. Terminal master's awarded for partial completion of doctoral program. *Degree requirements:* For master's, comprehensive exam, thesis optional, 2 languages (Spanish plus one other language); for doctorate, comprehensive exam, thesis/dissertation, 2 languages (Spanish plus one other language). *Entrance*

*requirements:* For master's, BA with at least 6 hours in Spanish literature; for doctorate, MA in any Spanish language-related literatures. Additional exam requirements/recommendations for international students: Required—TOEFL (minimum score 79 iBT) or IELTS (minimum score 6.5). *Application deadline:* For fall admission, 2/1 for domestic and international students; for spring admission, 10/1 for domestic and international students. Application fee: $50 ($100 for international students). Electronic applications accepted. *Expenses:* Tuition, state resident: full-time $4886; part-time $203.60 per credit hour. Tuition, nonresident: full-time $18,989; part-time $791.20 per credit hour. *Required fees:* $3283; $126.25 per credit hour. $126.50 per semester. *Financial support:* In 2016–17, 21 students received support. Fellowships, teaching assistantships with full tuition reimbursements available, scholarships/grants, health care benefits, and unspecified assistantships available. Support available to part-time students. Financial award application deadline: 6/1; financial award applicants required to submit FAFSA. *Faculty research:* 20th- and 21st-century Latin American literatures, colonial literature, 19th-century literature, peninsular golden age literature, medieval literature, modern peninsular literature. *Unit head:* Dr. Robert Lauer, Professor of Spanish, 405-325-1409, Fax: 405-325-5845, E-mail: arlauer@ou.edu. *Application contact:* Marcelo Rioseco, Associate Professor/Graduate Section Liaison, 405-325-1409, Fax: 405-325-2475, E-mail: mrioseco@ou.edu.
Website: http://mlll.publishpath.com/spanish-ma

**University of Oregon,** Graduate School, College of Arts and Sciences, Department of Romance Languages, Program in Spanish, Eugene, OR 97403. Offers MA. *Program availability:* Part-time. *Degree requirements:* For master's, one foreign language. *Entrance requirements:* For master's, GRE General Test, minimum GPA of 3.0. Additional exam requirements/recommendations for international students: Required—TOEFL.

**University of Ottawa,** Faculty of Graduate and Postdoctoral Studies, Faculty of Arts, Department of Modern Languages and Literatures, Ottawa, ON K1N 6N5, Canada. Offers Spanish (MA, PhD). *Program availability:* Part-time, evening/weekend. *Degree requirements:* For master's, one foreign language, thesis or alternative; for doctorate, one foreign language, comprehensive exam, thesis/dissertation. *Entrance requirements:* For master's, BA with honors in Spanish, minimum B average; for doctorate, MA in Spanish or equivalent, minimum B average. Electronic applications accepted. *Faculty research:* Spanish American literature, Mexican literature and film studies, Spanish golden age literature, twentieth-century Spanish literature, Hispanic linguistics with special emphasis on linguistic theory.

**University of Pennsylvania,** School of Arts and Sciences, Graduate Group in Romance Languages, Philadelphia, PA 19104. Offers French (AM, PhD); Italian (AM, PhD); Spanish (AM, PhD). *Faculty:* 38 full-time (14 women), 11 part-time/adjunct (3 women). *Students:* 56 full-time (25 women), 3 part-time (2 women); includes 4 minority (all Hispanic/Latino), 34 international. Average age 32. 73 applicants, 33% accepted, 10 enrolled. In 2016, 10 master's, 5 doctorates awarded. Terminal master's awarded for partial completion of doctoral program. Application fee: $70. *Expenses:* Tuition: Full-time $31,068; part-time $5762 per course. *Required fees:* $3200; $336 per course. Full-time tuition and fees vary according to degree level, program and student level. Part-time tuition and fees vary according to course load, degree level and program.
Website: http://www.sas.upenn.edu/graduate-division

**University of Pittsburgh,** Dietrich School of Arts and Sciences, Program in Hispanic Linguistics, Pittsburgh, PA 15260. Offers Hispanic linguistics (MA); TESOL (PhD). *Faculty:* 6 full-time (2 women). *Students:* 6 full-time (5 women), 1 (woman) part-time; includes 1 minority (Hispanic/Latino), 4 international. Average age 27. In 2016, 1 master's awarded. Terminal master's awarded for partial completion of doctoral program. *Degree requirements:* For master's, one foreign language, thesis optional; for doctorate, 2 foreign languages, comprehensive exam, thesis/dissertation. *Entrance requirements:* For master's and doctorate, GRE General Test, proficiency in Spanish. Additional exam requirements/recommendations for international students: Required—TOEFL (minimum score 600 paper-based; 100 iBT). *Application deadline:* For fall admission, 12/15 priority date for domestic and international students. Application fee: $50. Electronic applications accepted. Tuition and fees vary according to program. *Financial support:* In 2016–17, 6 students received support, including 5 fellowships with full tuition reimbursements available (averaging $17,800 per year), 1 teaching assistantship with full tuition reimbursement available (averaging $17,100 per year). Financial award application deadline: 12/15; financial award applicants required to submit FAFSA. *Faculty research:* Hispanic linguistics, second language acquisition, phonetics, prosody, language variation and change. *Unit head:* Dr. Shelome Gooden, Chair, 412-624-5922, Fax: 412-624-5520, E-mail: sgooden@pitt.edu. *Application contact:* Margaret Bupp, Graduate Student Services Administrator, 412-624-6568, Fax: 412-624-6338, E-mail: maggiebupp@pitt.edu.
Website: http://www.linguistics.pitt.edu

**University of Rhode Island,** Graduate School, College of Arts and Sciences, Department of Modern and Classical Languages and Literatures, Kingston, RI 02881. Offers Spanish (MA). *Program availability:* Part-time. *Faculty:* 29 full-time (18 women), 1 (woman) part-time/adjunct. *Students:* 3 full-time (2 women), 7 part-time (4 women); includes 4 minority (all Hispanic/Latino), 1 international. In 2016, 2 master's awarded. *Degree requirements:* For master's, one foreign language, comprehensive exam, thesis optional. *Entrance requirements:* For master's, 2 letters of recommendation. Additional exam requirements/recommendations for international students: Required—TOEFL. *Application deadline:* For fall admission, 7/15 for domestic students, 2/1 for international students; for spring admission, 11/15 for domestic students, 7/15 for international students. Application fee: $65. Electronic applications accepted. *Expenses:* Tuition, state resident: full-time $11,796; part-time $655 per credit. Tuition, nonresident: full-time $24,206; part-time $1345 per credit. *Required fees:* $1546; $44 per credit. One-time fee: $155 full-time; $35 part-time. *Financial support:* In 2016–17, 3 teaching assistantships with tuition reimbursements (averaging $12,888 per year) were awarded; research assistantships also available. Financial award application deadline: 2/1; financial award applicants required to submit FAFSA. *Unit head:* Dr. Karen de Bruin, Department Chair, 401-874-4697, E-mail: debruin@uri.edu. *Application contact:* Graduate Admission, 401-874-2872, E-mail: gradadm@etal.uri.edu.
Website: http://web.uri.edu/languages/

**University of South Africa,** College of Human Sciences, Pretoria, South Africa. Offers adult education (M Ed); African languages (MA, PhD); African politics (MA, PhD); Afrikaans (MA, PhD); ancient history (MA, PhD); ancient Near Eastern studies (MA, PhD); anthropology (MA, PhD); applied linguistics (MA); Arabic (MA, PhD); archaeology (MA); art history (MA); Biblical archaeology (MA); Biblical studies (M Th, D Th, PhD); Christian spirituality (M Th, D Th); church history (M Th, D Th); classical studies (MA, PhD); clinical psychology (MA); communication (MA, PhD); comparative education (M Ed, Ed D); consulting psychology (D Admin, D Com, PhD); curriculum studies (M Ed, Ed D); development studies (M Admin, MA, D Admin, PhD); didactics (M Ed, Ed D); education (M Tech); education management (M Ed, Ed D); educational psychology (M Ed); English (MA); environmental education (M Ed); French (MA, PhD); German (MA, PhD); Greek (MA); guidance and counseling (M Ed); health studies (MA, PhD), including health sciences education (MA), health services management (MA), medical and surgical nursing science (critical care general) (MA), midwifery and neonatal nursing

science (MA), trauma and emergency care (MA); history (MA, PhD); history of education (Ed D); inclusive education (M Ed, Ed D); information and communications technology policy and regulation (MA); information science (MA, MIS, PhD); international politics (MA, PhD); Islamic studies (MA, PhD); Italian (MA, PhD); Judaica (MA, PhD); linguistics (MA, PhD); mathematical education (M Ed); mathematics education (MA); missiology (M Th, D Th); modern Hebrew (MA, PhD); musicology (MA, MMus, D Mus, PhD); natural science education (M Ed); New Testament (M Th, D Th); Old Testament (D Th); pastoral therapy (M Th, D Th); philosophy (MA); philosophy of education (M Ed, Ed D); politics (MA, PhD); Portuguese (MA, PhD); practical theology (M Th, D Th); psychology (MA, MS, PhD); psychology of education (M Ed, Ed D); public health (MA); religious studies (MA, D Th, PhD); Romance languages (MA); Russian (MA, PhD); Semitic languages (MA, PhD); social behavior studies in HIV/AIDS (MA); social science (mental health) (MA); social science in development studies (MA); social science in psychology (MA); social science in social work (MA); social science in sociology (MA); social work (MSW, DSW, PhD); socio-education (M Ed, Ed D); sociolinguistics (MA); sociology (MA, PhD); Spanish (MA, PhD); systematic theology (M Th, D Th); TESOL (teaching English to speakers of other languages) (MA); theological ethics (M Th, D Th); theory of literature (MA, PhD); urban ministries (D Th); urban ministry (M Th).

**University of South Carolina,** The Graduate School, College of Arts and Sciences, Department of Languages, Literatures, and Cultures, Columbia, SC 29208. Offers comparative literature (MA, PhD); foreign languages (MAT), including French, German, Spanish; French (MA); German (MA); Spanish (MA). MAT offered in cooperation with the College of Education. *Program availability:* Part-time. *Degree requirements:* For master's, one foreign language, comprehensive exam, thesis optional; for doctorate, 2 foreign languages, comprehensive exam, thesis/dissertation. *Entrance requirements:* For master's and doctorate, GRE General Test, writing sample. Additional exam requirements/recommendations for international students: Required—TOEFL (minimum score 75 iBT). Electronic applications accepted. *Faculty research:* Modern literature, linguistics, literature and culture, medieval literature, literary theory.

**University of Southern California,** Graduate School, Dana and David Dornsife College of Letters, Arts and Sciences, Comparative Studies in Literature and Culture Doctoral Program, Los Angeles, CA 90089. Offers comparative literature (PhD); comparative media and culture (PhD); Spanish and Latin American studies (PhD). *Degree requirements:* For doctorate, 2 foreign languages, comprehensive exam, thesis/dissertation. *Entrance requirements:* For doctorate, GRE, competence in language other than English (highly recommended). Additional exam requirements/recommendations for international students: Required—TOEFL. Electronic applications accepted. *Faculty research:* Literary theory, Japanese film and contemporary fiction, Francophone literature and cinema, Latin American and Caribbean literature, Spanish literature and film, nineteenth and twentieth century British and American literature.

**University of South Florida,** College of Arts and Sciences, Department of World Languages, Tampa, FL 33620-9951. Offers French (MA); linguistics (MA); linguistics and applied linguistics studies (PhD); linguistics: English as a second language (MA); Spanish (MA). *Program availability:* Part-time, evening/weekend. *Faculty:* 20 full-time (16 women). *Students:* 38 full-time (28 women), 18 part-time (16 women); includes 19 minority (3 Black or African American, non-Hispanic/Latino; 1 Asian, non-Hispanic/Latino; 14 Hispanic/Latino; 1 Two or more races, non-Hispanic/Latino), 9 international. Average age 34. 36 applicants, 58% accepted, 13 enrolled. In 2016, 26 master's awarded. *Degree requirements:* For master's, one foreign language, comprehensive exam, thesis optional; for doctorate, one foreign language, comprehensive exam, thesis/dissertation. *Entrance requirements:* For master's, GRE General Test, minimum undergraduate GPA of 3.0 and 2-3 letters of recommendation; two-page statement of purpose written in Spanish (for Spanish program); oral interview (for Spanish and French programs); writing sample (for French program); for doctorate, GRE General Test, minimum GPA of 3.5 or international equivalent; master's degree or equivalent academic level; statement of purpose; current curriculum vitae; three letters of recommendation; personal interview with faculty; evidence of research experience or scholarly promise. Additional exam requirements/recommendations for international students: Required—TOEFL (minimum score 600 paper-based; 80 iBT) or IELTS (minimum score 6.5) for MA; TOEFL (minimum score 550 paper-based; 80 iBT) or IELTS (minimum score 6.5) for PhD. *Application deadline:* For fall admission, 1/15 for domestic and international students; for spring admission, 10/15 for domestic students, 9/15 for international students. Application fee: $30. Electronic applications accepted. *Expenses:* Tuition, state resident: full-time $7766; part-time $431.43 per credit hour. Tuition, nonresident: full-time $15,789; part-time $877.17 per credit hour. *Required fees:* $37 per term. *Financial support:* In 2016–17, 4 students received support, including 43 teaching assistantships with tuition reimbursements available (averaging $10,152 per year); tuition waivers (partial) and unspecified assistantships also available. Financial award application deadline: 6/30. *Faculty research:* Second language acquisition, instructional technology, foreign language education, English for speakers of other languages, distance learning. Total annual research expenditures: $104,720. *Unit head:* Dr. Stephan Schindler, Chair and Professor, 813-974-2548, Fax: 813-905-9937, E-mail: skschindler@usf.edu. *Application contact:* Patricia Garcia, Academic Program Specialist, 813-974-2548, Fax: 813-905-9937, E-mail: pgarcia@usf.edu.
Website: http://languages.usf.edu/

**The University of Tennessee,** Graduate School, College of Arts and Sciences, Department of Modern Foreign Languages and Literatures, Program in Modern Foreign Languages, Knoxville, TN 37996. Offers applied linguistics (PhD); French (PhD); German (PhD); Italian (PhD); Portuguese (PhD); Russian (PhD); Spanish (PhD). *Degree requirements:* For doctorate, 2 foreign languages, thesis/dissertation. *Entrance requirements:* For doctorate, minimum GPA of 2.7. Additional exam requirements/recommendations for international students: Required—TOEFL. Electronic applications accepted.

**The University of Tennessee,** Graduate School, College of Arts and Sciences, Department of Modern Foreign Languages and Literatures, Program in Spanish, Knoxville, TN 37996. Offers MA. *Degree requirements:* For master's, one foreign language, thesis or alternative. *Entrance requirements:* For master's, minimum GPA of 2.7. Additional exam requirements/recommendations for international students: Required—TOEFL. Electronic applications accepted.

**The University of Texas at Arlington,** Graduate School, College of Liberal Arts, Department of Modern Languages, Arlington, TX 76019. Offers French (MA); Spanish (MA). *Program availability:* Part-time, evening/weekend. *Degree requirements:* For master's, 2 foreign languages, comprehensive exam, thesis optional. *Entrance requirements:* For master's, GRE General Test, minimum GPA of 3.0, 3 letters of recommendation. Additional exam requirements/recommendations for international students: Required—TOEFL (minimum score 550 paper-based). *Application deadline:* For fall admission, 6/15 for domestic students. Applications are processed on a rolling basis. Application fee: $35 ($50 for international students). *Financial support:* Fellowships with full tuition reimbursements, research assistantships, teaching assistantships, career-related internships or fieldwork, Federal Work-Study, and scholarships/grants available. Financial award application deadline: 6/1; financial award applicants required to submit FAFSA. *Unit head:* Dr. Antoinette Sol, Chair, 817-272-3161, Fax: 817-272-5408, E-mail: amsol@uta.edu. *Application contact:* Dr. Ignacio

*Spanish*

Ruiz-Perez, Graduate Advisor, 817-272-3161, Fax: 817-272-5408, E-mail: iruiz@uta.edu. Website: http://www.langlab.uta.edu/modl/

**The University of Texas at Austin,** Graduate School, College of Liberal Arts, Department of Spanish and Portuguese, Austin, TX 78712-1111. Offers Hispanic linguistics (MA, PhD); Hispanic literature (MA, PhD); Ibero-romance philology and linguistics (PhD); Luso-Brazilian literature (MA, PhD). *Degree requirements:* For master's, 2 foreign languages, thesis or alternative; for doctorate, 3 foreign languages, thesis/dissertation. *Entrance requirements:* For master's and doctorate, GRE General Test. Electronic applications accepted.

**The University of Texas at El Paso,** Graduate School, College of Liberal Arts, Department of Creative Writing, El Paso, TX 79968-0001. Offers creative writing (MFA); creative writing of the Americas (MFA). *Program availability:* Part-time, evening/weekend, online learning. *Degree requirements:* For master's, thesis. *Entrance requirements:* For master's, minimum GPA of 3.0, letters of recommendation, writing sample. Additional exam requirements/recommendations for international students: Recommended—TOEFL, IELTS. Electronic applications accepted.

**The University of Texas at El Paso,** Graduate School, College of Liberal Arts, Department of Languages and Linguistics, El Paso, TX 79968-0001. Offers linguistics (MA); Spanish (MA); teaching English to speakers of other languages (Certificate). *Program availability:* Part-time, evening/weekend. *Degree requirements:* For master's, thesis optional. *Entrance requirements:* For master's, GRE General Test, departmental exam, minimum GPA of 3.0, letters of recommendation. Additional exam requirements/recommendations for international students: Required—TOEFL; Recommended—IELTS. Electronic applications accepted.

**The University of Texas at San Antonio,** College of Liberal and Fine Arts, Department of Modern Languages and Literatures, San Antonio, TX 78249-0617. Offers Spanish (MA). *Program availability:* Part-time. *Faculty:* 5 full-time (2 women). *Students:* 2 full-time (both women), 16 part-time (12 women); includes 16 minority (all Hispanic/Latino), 1 international. Average age 36. 4 applicants, 75% accepted, 2 enrolled. In 2016, 2 master's awarded. *Degree requirements:* For master's, one foreign language, comprehensive exam, thesis optional. *Entrance requirements:* For master's, minimum GPA of 3.0, sample of written and spoken work, letter of recommendation, statement of purpose. Additional exam requirements/recommendations for international students: Required—TOEFL (minimum score 550 paper-based; 79 iBT), IELTS (minimum score 6.5). *Application deadline:* For fall admission, 7/1 for domestic students, 4/1 for international students; for spring admission, 11/1 for domestic students, 9/1 for international students. Applications are processed on a rolling basis. Application fee: $45 ($80 for international students). Electronic applications accepted. *Financial support:* Scholarships/grants available. *Faculty research:* Film studies, religious studies, Spanish literature, Spanish culture, Spanish linguistics. *Unit head:* Dr. Santiago Daydi-Tolson, Department Chair, 210-458-4377, Fax: 210-458-5672, E-mail: santiago.daydiltolson@utsa.edu. *Application contact:* Dr. Malgorzata Oleszkiewicz-Peralba, Graduate Advisor of Record, 210-458-5214, Fax: 210-458-5223, E-mail: malgorzata.oleszkiewicz@utsa.edu. Website: http://colfa.utsa.edu/modern-languages/

**The University of Texas of the Permian Basin,** Office of Graduate Studies, College of Arts and Sciences, Department of Literature and Languages, Odessa, TX 79762-0001. Offers English (MA); Spanish (MA). *Degree requirements:* For master's, comprehensive exam (for some programs), thesis (for some programs). *Entrance requirements:* For master's, GRE General Test. Additional exam requirements/recommendations for international students: Required—TOEFL (minimum score 550 paper-based).

**The University of Texas Rio Grande Valley,** College of Liberal Arts, Department of Literatures and Cultural Studies, Edinburg, TX 78539. Offers English (MA); Spanish (MA). MA in Spanish conducted in conjunction with Department of Writing and Language Studies. *Program availability:* Part-time, evening/weekend. *Degree requirements:* For master's, comprehensive exam, thesis optional. *Entrance requirements:* For master's, GRE General Test, minimum GPA of 3.0. Tuition and fees vary according to course load and program. *Faculty research:* Oral vs. literary culture, Borderland literature, Mexican-American literature, topics in British and American literature, discourse analysis.

**The University of Toledo,** College of Graduate Studies, College of Languages, Literature and Social Sciences, Department of Foreign Languages, Toledo, OH 43606-3390. Offers French (MA); German (MA); Spanish (MA). *Program availability:* Part-time. *Degree requirements:* For master's, one foreign language, comprehensive exam, comprehensive reading exam in 1 additional foreign language. *Entrance requirements:* For master's, minimum cumulative point-hour ratio of 2.7 for all previous academic work. Additional exam requirements/recommendations for international students: Required—TOEFL (minimum score 550 paper-based; 80 iBT). Electronic applications accepted.

**University of Toronto,** School of Graduate Studies, Faculty of Arts and Science, Department of Spanish and Portuguese, Toronto, ON M5S 1A1, Canada. Offers MA, PhD. *Program availability:* Part-time. *Degree requirements:* For doctorate, thesis/dissertation. *Entrance requirements:* For master's, minimum B average in final year, 2 letters of reference; for doctorate, minimum A- average, 2 letters of reference, writing sample. Additional exam requirements/recommendations for international students: Required—TWE (minimum score 5), TOEFL, Michigan English Language Assessment Battery, IELTS, or COPE. Electronic applications accepted.

**University of Utah,** Graduate School, College of Humanities, Department of World Languages and Cultures, Salt Lake City, UT 84112. Offers comparative literary and cultural studies (MA, PhD); French (MA); Spanish (MA, MALP); world languages (MA). *Program availability:* Part-time. *Faculty:* 27 full-time (17 women), 2 part-time/adjunct (both women). *Students:* 37 full-time (29 women), 3 part-time (1 woman); includes 9 minority (2 Asian, non-Hispanic/Latino; 6 Hispanic/Latino; 1 Two or more races, non-Hispanic/Latino), 9 international. Average age 37. 29 applicants, 62% accepted, 15 enrolled. In 2016, 13 master's awarded. Terminal master's awarded for partial completion of doctoral program. *Degree requirements:* For master's, variable foreign language requirement, comprehensive exam (for some programs), thesis (for some programs); for doctorate, 2 foreign languages, comprehensive exam, thesis/dissertation. *Entrance requirements:* For master's, bachelor's degree from regionally-accredited college or university with minimum undergraduate overall GPA of 3.0; for doctorate, MA from regionally-accredited college or university, advanced proficiency in target language. Additional exam requirements/recommendations for international students: Required—TOEFL (minimum score 550 paper-based; 80 iBT). *Application deadline:* For fall admission, 1/15 priority date for domestic students, 12/15 priority date for international students. Application fee: $55 ($65 for international students). Electronic applications accepted. *Expenses:* Tuition, state resident: full-time $7011; part-time $3918.24 per credit hour. Tuition, nonresident: full-time $22,154; part-time $11,665.42 per credit hour. *Financial support:* In 2016–17, 27 students received support, including 27 teaching assistantships with full and partial tuition reimbursements available (averaging $16,500 per year); health care benefits and unspecified assistantships also available. Financial award application deadline: 1/15. *Faculty research:* Literary study, literary theory, linguistics, cultural studies, comparative studies. *Unit head:* Dr. Katharina

Gerstenberger, Chair, 801-585-7908, Fax: 801-581-7581, E-mail: katharina.gerstenberger@utah.edu. *Application contact:* Mackenzie Buie, Academic Coordinator, 801-581-7748, Fax: 801-581-7581, E-mail: mackenzie.buie@utah.edu. Website: http://languages.utah.edu/

**University of Virginia,** College and Graduate School of Arts and Sciences, Department of Spanish, Italian and Portuguese, Charlottesville, VA 22903. Offers Spanish (MA, PhD). *Faculty:* 40 full-time (26 women). *Students:* 32 full-time (21 women); includes 4 minority (all Hispanic/Latino), 7 international. Average age 27. 42 applicants, 36% accepted, 8 enrolled. In 2016, 5 master's, 3 doctorates awarded. *Degree requirements:* For master's, comprehensive exam, thesis; for doctorate, one foreign language, comprehensive exam, thesis/dissertation. *Entrance requirements:* For master's and doctorate, GRE General Test, GRE Subject Test, 2 letters of recommendation. Additional exam requirements/recommendations for international students: Required—TOEFL (minimum score 600 paper-based; 90 iBT), IELTS (minimum score 7). *Application deadline:* For fall admission, 12/1 for domestic and international students. Applications are processed on a rolling basis. Application fee: $60. Electronic applications accepted. *Expenses:* Tuition, state resident: full-time $15,026; part-time $834 per credit hour. Tuition, nonresident: full-time $25,168; part-time $1378 per credit hour. *Required fees:* $2654. *Financial support:* Fellowships and teaching assistantships available. Financial award applicants required to submit FAFSA. *Unit head:* Joel Rini, Chair, 434-924-7159, Fax: 434-924-7160, E-mail: sipinfo@virginia.edu. *Application contact:* David Gies, Director of Graduate Admissions, 434-924-7159, Fax: 434-924-7160, E-mail: sipinfo@virginia.edu. Website: http://spanitalport.virginia.edu/

**University of Washington,** Graduate School, College of Arts and Sciences, Division of Spanish and Portuguese Studies, Seattle, WA 98195. Offers Hispanic literary and cultural studies (MA). *Degree requirements:* For master's, 2 foreign languages, thesis optional, exam. *Entrance requirements:* For master's, GRE General Test, minimum GPA of 3.0. Additional exam requirements/recommendations for international students: Required—TOEFL. Electronic applications accepted. *Faculty research:* Medieval through modern Spanish literature and film, Latin American literature, poetry and essay, pan-Hispanic ballad, Hispanic cultural studies, second language acquisition and applied linguistics.

**The University of Western Ontario,** Faculty of Graduate Studies, Faculty of Arts and Humanities, Department of Modern Languages and Literatures, London, ON N6A 5B8, Canada. Offers comparative literature (MA, PhD); Hispanic studies (MA, PhD). *Program availability:* Part-time. *Degree requirements:* For master's, 2 foreign languages, thesis (for some programs). *Entrance requirements:* For master's, honors degree in Spanish or equivalent, minimum B average. Additional exam requirements/recommendations for international students: Required—TOEFL (comparative literature). *Faculty research:* Spanish golden age, Latin-American, romance, medieval, film.

**University of Wisconsin–Madison,** Graduate School, College of Letters and Science, Department of Spanish and Portuguese, Program in Spanish, Madison, WI 53706-1380. Offers MA, PhD. *Degree requirements:* For master's, one foreign language; for doctorate, 2 foreign languages, thesis/dissertation. *Entrance requirements:* For master's, GRE (recommended), minimum GPA of 3.25 in Spanish or Portuguese; for doctorate, GRE (recommended), minimum graduate GPA of 3.4, writing sample. Additional exam requirements/recommendations for international students: Required—TOEFL. Electronic applications accepted. *Faculty research:* Hispanic linguistics, Spanish and Spanish-American literature.

**University of Wisconsin–Milwaukee,** Graduate School, College of Letters and Science, Department of Foreign Languages and Literature, Milwaukee, WI 53201-0413. Offers classic Greek (MA); classics (MA); comparative literature (MA); foreign language and literature (MA); French (MA); German (MA); Latin (MA); linguistics (MA); Spanish (MA); translation (MA, Certificate). *Program availability:* Part-time. *Students:* 10 full-time (7 women), 19 part-time (16 women); includes 5 minority (2 Black or African American, non-Hispanic/Latino; 2 Hispanic/Latino; 1 Two or more races, non-Hispanic/Latino), 2 international. Average age 31. 41 applicants, 32% accepted, 9 enrolled. In 2016, 21 master's awarded. *Degree requirements:* For master's, 2 foreign languages, thesis or alternative. *Entrance requirements:* Additional exam requirements/recommendations for international students: Required—TOEFL (minimum score 550 paper-based; 79 iBT), IELTS (minimum score 6.5). *Application deadline:* For fall admission, 1/1 priority date for domestic students; for spring admission, 9/1 for domestic students. Applications are processed on a rolling basis. Application fee: $56 ($96 for international students). Electronic applications accepted. *Financial support:* In 2016–17, 1 fellowship, 2 research assistantships, 26 teaching assistantships were awarded; career-related internships or fieldwork, health care benefits, unspecified assistantships, and project assistantships also available. Support available to part-time students. Financial award application deadline: 4/15; financial award applicants required to submit FAFSA. *Unit head:* Kevin Muse, Department Chair, 414-229-5213, E-mail: kmuse@uwm.edu. *Application contact:* General Information Contact, 414-229-4982, Fax: 414-229-6967, E-mail: gradschool@uwm.edu. Website: http://uwm.edu/foreign-languages-literature/

**University of Wisconsin–Milwaukee,** Graduate School, College of Letters and Science, Department of Spanish and Portuguese, Milwaukee, WI 53201-0413. Offers MA. *Students:* 8 full-time (4 women), 4 part-time (3 women); includes 1 minority (Two or more races, non-Hispanic/Latino), 7 international. Average age 28. 17 applicants, 71% accepted, 7 enrolled. In 2016, 5 master's awarded. *Entrance requirements:* For master's, bachelor's degree. *Application deadline:* Applications are processed on a rolling basis. Application fee: $56 ($96 for international students). Electronic applications accepted. *Financial support:* In 2016–17, 12 teaching assistantships were awarded; fellowships, research assistantships, and unspecified assistantships also available. Financial award applicants required to submit FAFSA. *Faculty research:* Sociolinguistics, Spanish-American literature, Spanish literature, Hispanic culture, Hispanic historiography. *Unit head:* John McCaw, Department Chair, 414-229-4257, E-mail: rjmccaw@uwm.edu. *Application contact:* General Information Contact, 414-229-4982, Fax: 414-229-6967, E-mail: gradschool@uwm.edu. Website: https://uwm.edu/spanish-portuguese/

**University of Wyoming,** College of Arts and Sciences, Department of Modern and Classical Languages, Program in Spanish, Laramie, WY 82071. Offers MA. *Program availability:* Part-time. *Degree requirements:* For master's, one foreign language, thesis or alternative. *Entrance requirements:* For master's, GRE General Test, minimum GPA of 3.0. *Faculty research:* Peninsular literature, Latin American literature, theatre, science and literature, linguistics.

**Vanderbilt University,** Department of Spanish and Portuguese, Nashville, TN 37240-1001. Offers Portuguese (MA); Spanish (MA, MAT, PhD); Spanish and Portuguese (PhD). *Faculty:* 13 full-time (6 women). *Students:* 25 full-time (11 women); includes 5 minority (all Hispanic/Latino), 11 international. Average age 31. 39 applicants, 31% accepted, 7 enrolled. In 2016, 2 master's, 3 doctorates awarded. *Degree requirements:* For master's, one foreign language, thesis; for doctorate, 2 foreign languages, thesis/dissertation, final and qualifying exams. *Entrance requirements:* For master's, GRE General Test; for doctorate, GRE General Test, writing sample in Spanish. Additional

exam requirements/recommendations for international students: Required—TOEFL (minimum score 570 paper-based; 88 iBT). *Application deadline:* For fall admission, 1/15 for domestic and international students. Electronic applications accepted. *Expenses: Tuition:* Part-time $1854 per credit hour. *Financial support:* Fellowships with tuition reimbursements, teaching assistantships with full tuition reimbursements, Federal Work-Study, institutionally sponsored loans, and health care benefits available. Financial award application deadline: 1/15; financial award applicants required to submit CSS PROFILE or FAFSA. *Faculty research:* Spanish, Portuguese, and Latin American literatures; foreign language pedagogy; Renaissance and Baroque poetry; nineteenth-century Spanish novel. *Unit head:* Dr. Benigno Trigo, Chair, 615-322-6930, Fax: 615-343-7260, E-mail: benigno.trigo@vanderbilt.edu. *Application contact:* Andres Zamora, Director of Graduate Studies, 615-322-6930, Fax: 615-343-7260, E-mail: andres.zamora@vanderbilt.edu.
Website: http://as.vanderbilt.edu/spanish-portuguese/graduate/index.php

**Washington University in St. Louis,** The Graduate School, Department of Romance Languages and Literatures, Program in Spanish, St. Louis, MO 63130-4899. Offers Hispanic languages and literatures (PhD); Spanish and comparative literature (PhD). Terminal master's awarded for partial completion of doctoral program. *Degree requirements:* For doctorate, thesis/dissertation. *Entrance requirements:* For doctorate, GRE General Test. Additional exam requirements/recommendations for international students: Required—TOEFL. Electronic applications accepted. *Faculty research:* Latin American and Iberian literatures and languages, Spanish and comparative literature.

**Wayne State University,** College of Liberal Arts and Sciences, Department of Classical and Modern Languages, Literatures, and Cultures, Detroit, MI 48202. Offers classics (MA), including ancient Greek and Latin, ancient studies, classics, Latin; German (MA); language learning (MALL), including Arabic (MA, MALL), French (MA, MALL, PhD), German (MALL, PhD), Italian (MA, MALL), Spanish (MA, MALL, PhD); modern languages (PhD), including French (MA, MALL, PhD), German (MALL, PhD), Spanish (MA, MALL, PhD); Near Eastern languages (MA), including Arabic (MA, MALL), Hebrew; Romance languages (MA), including French (MA, MALL, PhD), Italian (MA, MALL), Spanish (MA, MALL, PhD). *Faculty:* 26. *Students:* 25 full-time (20 women), 14 part-time (8 women); includes 7 minority (2 Black or African American, non-Hispanic/Latino; 1 American Indian or Alaska Native, non-Hispanic/Latino; 1 Asian, non-Hispanic/Latino; 2 Hispanic/Latino; 1 Two or more races, non-Hispanic/Latino), 3 international. Average age 35. 29 applicants, 31% accepted, 5 enrolled. In 2016, 15 master's, 5 doctorates awarded. *Degree requirements:* For master's, variable foreign language requirement, comprehensive exam (for some programs), thesis (for some programs); for doctorate, one foreign language, comprehensive exam, thesis/dissertation. *Entrance requirements:* For master's, GRE (for some programs); for doctorate, GRE. Additional exam requirements/recommendations for international students: Required—TOEFL (minimum score 550 paper-based; 79 iBT), TWE (minimum score 5.5), Michigan English Language Assessment Battery (minimum score 85); Recommended—IELTS (minimum score 6.5). Application fee: $50. Electronic applications accepted. *Expenses:* $16,503 per year resident tuition and fees, $33,697 per year non-resident tuition and fees. *Financial support:* In 2016–17, 22 students received support, including 4 fellowships with tuition reimbursements available (averaging $13,500 per year), 17 teaching assistantships with tuition reimbursements available (averaging $17,994 per year); research assistantships, scholarships/grants, and unspecified assistantships also available. Financial award applicants required to submit FAFSA. *Faculty research:* Classical and modern literature and culture (Greek, Latin, Arabic, Chinese, French, German, Russian, Spanish) including colonial studies and exile and Holocaust studies; critical theory (French, German, Slavic, Spanish); theoretical and applied linguistics (Arabic, Chinese, French, Spanish); area studies (Arabic, Near Eastern, classical, Islamic, and Judaic studies). *Unit head:* Dr. Anne Duggan, Department Chair, 313-577-6244, Fax: 313-577-6243, E-mail: a.duggan@wayne.edu.
Website: http://clas.wayne.edu/languages/

**West Chester University of Pennsylvania,** College of Arts and Humanities, Department of Languages and Cultures, West Chester, PA 19383. Offers French (Teaching Certificate); German (Teaching Certificate); languages and cultures (MA), including French, German, Spanish; Spanish (Teaching Certificate). *Program availability:* Part-time, evening/weekend, minimal on-campus study. *Faculty:* 12 full-time (9 women). *Students:* 7 full-time (6 women), 26 part-time (23 women); includes 7 minority (all Hispanic/Latino). Average age 31. 14 applicants, 100% accepted, 11 enrolled. In 2016, 8 master's, 2 other advanced degrees awarded. *Degree requirements:*

For master's, one foreign language, comprehensive exam, portfolio, exit exam, capstone project; for Teaching Certificate, one foreign language. *Entrance requirements:* For master's and Teaching Certificate, ACTFL OPI and WPT, undergraduate major or equivalent. Additional exam requirements/recommendations for international students: Required—TOEFL or IELTS. *Application deadline:* For fall admission, 5/15 for international students; for spring admission, 10/15 for international students. Applications are processed on a rolling basis. Application fee: $45. Electronic applications accepted. *Expenses:* Tuition, state resident: full-time $8694; part-time $483 per credit. Tuition, nonresident: full-time $13,050; part-time $725 per credit. *Required fees:* $2399; $119.05 per credit. Tuition and fees vary according to campus/location and program. *Financial support:* Scholarships/grants and unspecified assistantships available. Financial award application deadline: 2/15; financial award applicants required to submit FAFSA. *Faculty research:* Language structure, literature, film, culture, pedagogy, technology. *Unit head:* Dr. Jerome Williams, Interim Chair, 610-436-2700, Fax: 610-436-3048, E-mail: isanchez@wcupa.edu. *Application contact:* Dr. Rebecca Pauly, Graduate Coordinator, 610-436-4746, Fax: 610-436-3048, E-mail: mvanliew@wcupa.edu.
Website: http://www.wcupa.edu/arts-humanities/languagesCultures/

**Western Kentucky University,** Graduate Studies, Potter College of Arts and Letters, Department of Modern Languages, Bowling Green, KY 42101. Offers French (MA Ed); German (MA Ed); Spanish (MA Ed).

**Western Michigan University,** Graduate College, College of Arts and Sciences, Department of Spanish, Kalamazoo, MI 49008. Offers MA, PhD.

**West Virginia University,** Eberly College of Arts and Sciences, Department of World Languages, Literatures and Linguistics, Morgantown, WV 26506. Offers French (MA); linguistics (MA); Spanish (MA); teaching English to speakers of other languages (MA). *Program availability:* Part-time. *Degree requirements:* For master's, one foreign language, comprehensive exam (for some programs), thesis optional. *Entrance requirements:* For master's, minimum GPA of 3.0. Electronic applications accepted. *Faculty research:* French, German, and Spanish literature; foreign language pedagogy; English as a second language; cultural studies; linguistics.

**Wichita State University,** Graduate School, Fairmount College of Liberal Arts and Sciences, Department of Modern and Classical Languages and Literatures, Wichita, KS 67260. Offers Spanish (MA). *Program availability:* Part-time. *Unit head:* Dr. Wilson Baldridge, Chair, 316-978-3180, Fax: 316-978-3293, E-mail: wilson.baldridge@wichita.edu. *Application contact:* Jordan Oleson, Admissions Coordinator, 316-978-3095, Fax: 316-978-3253, E-mail: jordan.oleson@wichita.edu.
Website: http://www.wichita.edu/mcll

**Worcester State University,** Graduate Studies, Program in Spanish, Worcester, MA 01602-2597. Offers MA. *Program availability:* Part-time. *Faculty:* 3 full-time (1 woman). *Students:* 14 part-time (11 women); includes 7 minority (all Hispanic/Latino). Average age 40. 7 applicants, 86% accepted, 4 enrolled. In 2016, 5 master's awarded. *Degree requirements:* For master's, one foreign language, thesis or comprehensive exam. *Entrance requirements:* For master's, GRE, MAT, BA in Spanish or related field and/or interview with faculty member. Additional exam requirements/recommendations for international students: Required—TOEFL (minimum score 550 paper-based; 79 iBT). *Application deadline:* For fall admission, 6/15 for domestic and international students; for spring admission, 11/1 for domestic and international students; for summer admission, 3/1 for domestic students, 4/1 for international students. Applications are processed on a rolling basis. Application fee: $50. Electronic applications accepted. *Expenses:* Tuition, state resident: part-time $150 per credit. Tuition, nonresident: part-time $150 per credit. *Financial support:* Career-related internships or fieldwork, scholarships/grants, and unspecified assistantships available. Financial award application deadline: 3/1; financial award applicants required to submit FAFSA. *Unit head:* Dr. Ana Perez-Manrique, Program Coordinator, 508-929-8577, E-mail: aperezmanrique@worcester.edu. *Application contact:* Sara Grady, Associate Dean, Graduate Studies and Professional Development, 508-929-8787, Fax: 508-929-8100, E-mail: sara.grady@worcester.edu.

**Yale University,** Graduate School of Arts and Sciences, Department of Spanish and Portuguese, New Haven, CT 06520. Offers Latin American literature (PhD); Luso-Brazilian and Spanish/Spanish American literatures (PhD); Spanish peninsular literature (PhD). Terminal master's awarded for partial completion of doctoral program. *Degree requirements:* For doctorate, 3 foreign languages, thesis/dissertation. *Entrance requirements:* For doctorate, GRE General Test.

# Section 10
# Linguistic Studies

This section contains a directory of institutions offering graduate work in linguistic studies. Additional information about programs listed in the directory may be obtained by writing directly to the dean of a graduate school or chair of a department at the address given in the directory.

For programs offering related work, see also in this book *Area and Cultural Studies, Language and Literature,* and *Sociology, Anthropology, and Archaeology.*

## CONTENTS

### Program Directories

# Linguistics

**Arizona State University at the Tempe campus,** College of Liberal Arts and Sciences, Department of English, Tempe, AZ 85287-0302. Offers applied linguistics (PhD); creative writing (MFA); English (MA, PhD), including comparative literature (MA), linguistics (MA), literature, rhetoric and composition (MA), rhetoric, composition, and linguistics (PhD); film and media studies (MAS), including American media and popular culture; linguistics (Graduate Certificate); teaching English to speakers of other languages (MTESOL); translation studies (Graduate Certificate). Terminal master's awarded for partial completion of doctoral program. *Degree requirements:* For master's, variable foreign language requirement, comprehensive exam (for some programs), thesis (for some programs), interactive Program of Study (iPOS) submitted before completing 50 percent of required credit hours; for doctorate, variable foreign language requirement, comprehensive exam, thesis/dissertation, interactive Program of Study (iPOS) submitted before completing 50 percent of required credit hours. *Entrance requirements:* For master's and doctorate, GRE, minimum GPA of 3.0 or equivalent in last 2 years of work leading to bachelor's degree. Additional exam requirements/recommendations for international students: Required—TOEFL, IELTS, or PTE. Electronic applications accepted.

**Ball State University,** Graduate School, College of Sciences and Humanities, Department of English, Program in Linguistics, Muncie, IN 47306. Offers linguistics (MA); teaching English to speakers of other languages (TESOL) and linguistics (MA). *Program availability:* Part-time. *Entrance requirements:* For master's, GRE General Test, minimum baccalaureate GPA of 2.75 or 3.0 in latter half of baccalaureate, statement of purpose, writing sample, three letters of recommendation. Additional exam requirements/recommendations for international students: Required—TOEFL (minimum score 550 paper-based; 79 iBT), IELTS (minimum score 6.5). Electronic applications accepted. *Faculty research:* Descriptive and theoretical linguistics.

**Biola University,** Cook School of Intercultural Studies, La Mirada, CA 90639-0001. Offers anthropology (MA); applied linguistics (MA); intercultural education (PhD); intercultural studies (MA, PhD); linguistics (Certificate); linguistics and Biblical languages (MA); missiology (D Miss); missions (MA); teaching English to speakers of other languages (MA, Certificate); teaching English to speakers of other languages (online) (MA). *Program availability:* Part-time, 100% online. *Entrance requirements:* For master's, minimum undergraduate GPA of 3.0; for doctorate, master's degree or equivalent, 3 years of cross-cultural experience, minimum graduate GPA of 3.3. Additional exam requirements/recommendations for international students: Required—TOEFL. Electronic applications accepted. *Faculty research:* Linguistics, anthropology, intercultural studies, teaching English to speakers of other languages, missions, missiology.

**Boston College,** Graduate School of Arts and Sciences, Department of Slavic and Eastern Languages and Literatures, Program in Linguistics, Chestnut Hill, MA 02467-3800. Offers MA, MA/JD, MBA/MA. *Faculty:* 6 full-time. *Students:* 2 full-time (1 woman). 3 applicants, 67% accepted, 1 enrolled. *Degree requirements:* For master's, 3 foreign languages, comprehensive exam, thesis or alternative. *Entrance requirements:* Additional exam requirements/recommendations for international students: Required—TOEFL (minimum score 600 paper-based; 100 iBT), IELTS (minimum score 8). *Application deadline:* For fall admission, 2/2 for domestic and international students. Application fee: $75. Electronic applications accepted. Tuition and fees vary according to program. *Financial support:* In 2016–17, 2 students received support, including fellowships with full tuition reimbursements available (averaging $9,200 per year), teaching assistantships with full tuition reimbursements available (averaging $9,200 per year); tuition waivers (full and partial) also available. Financial award application deadline: 3/1. *Unit head:* Dr. Michael Connolly, Chairperson, 617-552-3912. Website: https://www.bc.edu/sl

**Boston University,** Graduate School of Arts and Sciences, Program in Linguistics, Boston, MA 02215. Offers MA, PhD. *Program availability:* Part-time. *Students:* 19 full-time (11 women), 8 part-time (6 women); includes 1 minority (Asian, non-Hispanic/Latino), 3 international. Average age 29. 42 applicants, 62% accepted, 10 enrolled. In 2016, 5 master's, 3 doctorates awarded. Terminal master's awarded for partial completion of doctoral program. *Degree requirements:* For master's, one foreign language; for doctorate, one foreign language, comprehensive exam, thesis/dissertation. *Entrance requirements:* For master's and doctorate, GRE General Test, 3 letters of recommendation, transcripts, personal statement. Additional exam requirements/recommendations for international students: Required—TOEFL (minimum score 550 paper-based; 84 iBT). *Application deadline:* For fall admission, 2/1 priority date for domestic and international students. Application fee: $95. Electronic applications accepted. *Financial support:* In 2016–17, 6 students received support, including 3 teaching assistantships with partial tuition reimbursements available (averaging $12,000 per year); Federal Work-Study, scholarships/grants, and unspecified assistantships also available. Financial award application deadline: 2/1. *Faculty research:* Linguistic theory, experimental phonetics and phonology, morphology, syntax, semantics, pragmatics and information status, prosody sociolinguistics, language acquisition, language documentation and field linguistics, language change and variation, Romance linguistics, sign language linguistics. *Unit head:* Carol Neidle, Director, 617-353-6218, E-mail: carol@bu.edu. *Application contact:* Cameron Samuelson, Administrator, 617-358-4640, Fax: 617-358-4641, E-mail: linggrad@bu.edu. Website: http://ling.bu.edu

**Brandeis University,** Graduate School of Arts and Sciences, Program in Computational Linguistics, Waltham, MA 02454-9110. Offers MA. *Faculty:* 15 full-time (5 women), 2 part-time/adjunct (0 women). *Students:* 31 full-time (15 women), 2 part-time (1 woman); includes 5 minority (1 Asian, non-Hispanic/Latino; 3 Hispanic/Latino; 1 Two or more races, non-Hispanic/Latino), 10 international. 50 applicants, 76% accepted, 12 enrolled. In 2016, 8 master's awarded. *Degree requirements:* For master's, internship in computational linguistics or thesis. *Entrance requirements:* For master's, GRE, statement of purpose, 2 letters of recommendation, transcript(s), resume or curriculum vitae. Additional exam requirements/recommendations for international students: Required—TOEFL (minimum score 650 paper-based; 100 iBT); Recommended—IELTS (minimum score 7), TSE (minimum score 68). *Application deadline:* For fall admission, 2/15 priority date for domestic and international students. Applications are processed on a rolling basis. Application fee: $75. Electronic applications accepted. *Financial support:* In 2016–17, 15 students received support. Federal Work-Study, scholarships/grants, and tuition waivers (partial) available. Financial award application deadline: 4/15; financial award applicants required to submit FAFSA. *Faculty research:* Computational linguistics, statistical natural language processing, machine learning, computer science, speech recognition, automated text analysis. *Unit head:* Dr. James Pustejovsky, Program Chair, 781-736-2701, Fax: 781-736-2741, E-mail: jamesp@brandeis.edu. *Application contact:* Anne Gudaitis, Department Administrator, 781-736-2723, E-mail: gudaitis@brandeis.edu. Website: http://www.brandeis.edu/programs/comp-linguistics/

**Brigham Young University,** Graduate Studies, College of Humanities, Department of Linguistics and English Language, Provo, UT 84602. Offers linguistics (MA); teaching English as a second language (MA). *Program availability:* Part-time. *Faculty:* 23 full-time (4 women), 8 part-time/adjunct (6 women). *Students:* 63 full-time (42 women), 21 part-time (13 women); includes 22 minority (1 American Indian or Alaska Native, non-Hispanic/Latino; 12 Asian, non-Hispanic/Latino; 8 Hispanic/Latino; 1 Native Hawaiian or other Pacific Islander, non-Hispanic/Latino), 14 international. Average age 32. 30 applicants, 77% accepted, 19 enrolled. In 2016, 18 master's awarded. *Degree requirements:* For master's, 2 foreign languages, thesis. *Entrance requirements:* For master's, GRE General Test, minimum GPA of 3.0 in last 60 hours of course work. Additional exam requirements/recommendations for international students: Required—TOEFL (minimum score 580 paper-based; 90 iBT), TWE. *Application deadline:* 1/15 for domestic and international students. Application fee: $50. Electronic applications accepted. *Expenses:* $6,680. *Financial support:* In 2016–17, 53 students received support, including 8 research assistantships with partial tuition reimbursements available (averaging $7,200 per year), 8 teaching assistantships with partial tuition reimbursements available (averaging $2,079 per year); fellowships with partial tuition reimbursements available, career-related internships or fieldwork, scholarships/grants, unspecified assistantships, and travel to conference presentations also available. Financial award application deadline: 7/1. *Faculty research:* Teaching English to speakers of other languages, second language acquisition, computational linguistics, semiotics and semantics, computer-assisted language instruction, forensic linguistics, endangered language documentation. *Unit head:* Dr. Norman Evans, Chair, 801-422-8472, E-mail: norm_evans@byu.edu. *Application contact:* LoriAnne Spear, Graduate Program Manager, 801-422-9010, Fax: 801-422-9010, E-mail: lorianne_spear@byu.edu. Website: http://linguistics.byu.edu/

**Brigham Young University,** Graduate Studies, College of Humanities, Department of Spanish and Portuguese, Provo, UT 84602. Offers Portuguese (MA), including Luso-Brazilian literatures, Portuguese linguistics, Portuguese pedagogy; Spanish (MA), including Hispanic linguistics, Hispanic literatures, Spanish pedagogy. *Faculty:* 31 full-time (6 women). *Students:* 20 full-time (9 women), 15 part-time (9 women); includes 12 minority (all Hispanic/Latino). Average age 32. 19 applicants, 79% accepted, 12 enrolled. In 2016, 9 master's awarded. *Degree requirements:* For master's, 2 foreign languages, comprehensive exam, thesis, 1 semester of teaching. *Entrance requirements:* For master's, minimum GPA of 3.5 in Spanish or Portuguese, 3.3 overall. Additional exam requirements/recommendations for international students: Required—TOEFL (minimum score 580 paper-based; 85 iBT). *Application deadline:* For fall admission, 2/1 for domestic and international students. Application fee: $50. Electronic applications accepted. *Expenses:* Contact institution. *Financial support:* In 2016–17, 25 students received support, including 7 research assistantships (averaging $1,895 per year), 81 teaching assistantships (averaging $3,200 per year); institutionally sponsored loans, scholarships/grants, tuition waivers (partial), and unspecified assistantships also available. Support available to part-time students. *Faculty research:* Mexican prose; Latin American theater, literature, phonetics, and phonology; pedagogy; classical Portuguese literature; Peninsular prose and theater. *Unit head:* Dr. David P. Laraway, Chair, 801-422-3807, Fax: 801-422-0628, E-mail: david_laraway@byu.edu. *Application contact:* Jessica C. Erickson, Graduate Program Manager, 801-422-2196, Fax: 801-422-0628, E-mail: jessica_erickson@byu.edu. Website: http://spanport.byu.edu/

**Brown University,** Graduate School, Department of Cognitive, Linguistic and Psychological Sciences, Providence, RI 02912. Offers cognitive science (Sc M, PhD); linguistics (AM, PhD); psychology (PhD). *Degree requirements:* For master's, one foreign language, thesis or alternative; for doctorate, 2 foreign languages, thesis/dissertation.

**California State University, Fresno,** Division of Research and Graduate Studies, College of Arts and Humanities, Department of Linguistics, Fresno, CA 93740-8027. Offers linguistics (MA), including teaching English as a second language. *Program availability:* Part-time, evening/weekend. *Degree requirements:* For master's, comprehensive exam. *Entrance requirements:* For master's, GRE General Test, minimum GPA of 3.0. Additional exam requirements/recommendations for international students: Required—TOEFL. *Application deadline:* For fall admission, 5/1 for domestic and international students; for spring admission, 10/1 for domestic and international students. Applications are processed on a rolling basis. Application fee: $55. Electronic applications accepted. *Financial support:* Career-related internships or fieldwork, Federal Work-Study, and scholarships/grants available. Support available to part-time students. Financial award application deadline: 3/1; financial award applicants required to submit FAFSA. *Faculty research:* Communication systems, bilingual education, animal communication, conflict resolution, literacy programs. *Unit head:* Brian Agbayani, Chair, 559-278-2441, Fax: 559-278-7299, E-mail: bagbayan@csufresno.edu. *Application contact:* Jidong Chen, Graduate Coordinator, 559-278-2441, Fax: 559-278-7299, E-mail: jchen@csufresno.edu. Website: http://www.fresnostate.edu/artshum/linguistics/

**California State University, Fullerton,** Graduate Studies, College of Humanities and Social Sciences, Department of English, Comparative Literature, and Linguistics, Fullerton, CA 92834-9480. Offers English (MA); linguistics (MA). *Program availability:* Part-time. *Degree requirements:* For master's, one foreign language, thesis or alternative, project. *Entrance requirements:* For master's, minimum GPA of 3.0, undergraduate major in linguistics or related field. Application fee: $55. *Expenses:* Tuition, state resident: full-time $3369; part-time $1953 per unit. Tuition, nonresident: full-time $3915; part-time $2499 per unit. Tuition and fees vary according to course load, degree level and program. *Financial support:* Career-related internships or fieldwork, Federal Work-Study, institutionally sponsored loans, and scholarships/grants available. Support available to part-time students. Financial award application deadline: 3/1; financial award applicants required to submit FAFSA. *Unit head:* Dr. Stephen J. Mexal, Chair, 657-278-3163.

**California State University, Long Beach,** Graduate Studies, College of Liberal Arts, Department of Linguistics, Long Beach, CA 90840. Offers general linguistics (MA); language and culture (MA); special concentration (MA); teaching English to speakers of other languages (MA, Graduate Certificate). *Program availability:* Part-time, evening/weekend. *Degree requirements:* For master's, one foreign language, comprehensive exam, thesis optional. *Application deadline:* For fall admission, 5/1 for domestic students. Applications are processed on a rolling basis. Application fee: $55. Electronic applications accepted. *Financial support:* Teaching assistantships, career-related

internships or fieldwork, Federal Work-Study, institutionally sponsored loans, and scholarships/grants available. Financial award application deadline: 3/2. *Faculty research:* Pedagogy of language instruction, role of language in society, Khmer language instruction. *Unit head:* Alexandra Jaffe, Chair, 562-985-5792, Fax: 562-985-2593.
Website: http://www.csulb.edu/colleges/cla/departments/linguistics/

**California State University, Northridge,** Graduate Studies, College of Humanities, Linguistics Program, Northridge, CA 91330. Offers MA. *Program availability:* Part-time, evening/weekend. *Faculty:* 4 full-time (1 woman), 10 part-time/adjunct. *Students:* 18 full-time (10 women), 12 part-time (9 women); includes 11 minority (1 American Indian or Alaska Native, non-Hispanic/Latino; 4 Asian, non-Hispanic/Latino; 4 Hispanic/Latino; 2 Two or more races, non-Hispanic/Latino), 9 international. Average age 31. 20 applicants, 70% accepted, 8 enrolled. *Degree requirements:* For master's, one foreign language, comprehensive exam, thesis, or project. *Entrance requirements:* For master's, GRE General Test or minimum GPA of 3.0. Additional exam requirements/recommendations for international students: Required—TOEFL (minimum score 563 paper-based; 85 iBT). *Application deadline:* For fall admission, 11/30 for domestic students. Application fee: $55. *Expenses:* Tuition, state resident: full-time $4152. *Financial support:* Application deadline: 3/1. *Faculty research:* Ethnography of communication, stylistics, natural language processing, linguistics and humor, Otomanguean phonology and reconstruction. *Unit head:* Dr. Ana Sanchez Munoz, Chair, 818-677-3453, E-mail: ana.sanchezmunoz@csun.edu.
Website: http://www.csun.edu/linguistics/

**Carleton University,** Faculty of Graduate Studies, Faculty of Arts and Social Sciences, School of Linguistics and Applied Language Studies, Ottawa, ON K1S 5B6, Canada. Offers applied language studies (MA). *Degree requirements:* For master's, thesis optional. *Entrance requirements:* For master's, honors degree. Additional exam requirements/recommendations for international students: Required—TOEFL and/or CAEL. *Faculty research:* Language learning, acquisition and use of first and/or second languages in a variety of professional and academic contexts.

**Carnegie Mellon University,** Dietrich College of Humanities and Social Sciences, Department of Modern Languages, Pittsburgh, PA 15213-3891. Offers second language acquisition (MA, PhD). *Degree requirements:* For doctorate, one foreign language, comprehensive exam, thesis/dissertation. *Entrance requirements:* For doctorate, GRE General Test. Additional exam requirements/recommendations for international students: Required—TOEFL.

**Case Western Reserve University,** School of Graduate Studies, Department of Cognitive Science, Cleveland, OH 44106. Offers cognitive linguistics (MA). *Program availability:* Part-time. *Faculty:* 4 full-time (2 women), 12 part-time/adjunct (4 women). *Students:* 8 full-time (4 women); includes 1 minority (Asian, non-Hispanic/Latino). Average age 27. 4 applicants, 75% accepted, 1 enrolled. *Degree requirements:* For master's, thesis. *Entrance requirements:* For master's, GRE, statement of purpose, three letters of recommendation, writing sample. Additional exam requirements/recommendations for international students: Required—TOEFL (minimum score 577 paper-based; 90 iBT); Recommended—IELTS (minimum score 7). *Application deadline:* For fall admission, 5/1 priority date for domestic students. Application fee: $50. Electronic applications accepted. *Expenses: Tuition:* Full-time $42,576; part-time $1774 per credit hour. *Required fees:* $34. Tuition and fees vary according to course load and program. *Faculty research:* Workings of the human mind in design, art, and technology; interaction of brain and culture in development and evolution; origins of human higher-order cognition; the role of the body and social interaction in shaping human cognition; operation of systems that human beings have invented to guide their thought and action individually and culturally. *Unit head:* Dr. William Deal, Chair, 216-368-2205, E-mail: william.deal@case.edu.
Website: http://cognitivescience.case.edu/

**Concordia University,** School of Graduate Studies, Faculty of Arts and Science, Department of Education, Program in Applied Linguistics, Montréal, QC H3G 1M8, Canada. Offers applied linguistics (MA); teaching English as a second language (Certificate).

**Cornell University,** Graduate School, Graduate Fields of Arts and Sciences, Field of Asian Studies, Ithaca, NY 14853. Offers East Asian linguistics (MA); East Asian studies (MA); South Asian linguistics (MA); South Asian studies (MA); Southeast Asian linguistics (MA); Southeast Asian studies (MA). *Degree requirements:* For master's, one foreign language, thesis. *Entrance requirements:* For master's, GRE General Test, 3 letters of recommendation. Additional exam requirements/recommendations for international students: Required—TOEFL (minimum score 550 paper-based; 77 iBT). Electronic applications accepted. *Faculty research:* East Asian studies, South Asian studies, Southeast Asian studies.

**Cornell University,** Graduate School, Graduate Fields of Arts and Sciences, Field of Linguistics, Ithaca, NY. 14853. Offers applied linguistics (MA, PhD); East Asian linguistics (MA, PhD); English linguistics (MA, PhD); general linguistics (MA, PhD); Germanic linguistics (MA, PhD); Indo-European linguistics (MA, PhD); phonetics (MA, PhD); phonological theory (MA, PhD); Romance linguistics (MA, PhD); second language acquisition (MA, PhD); semantics (MA, PhD); Slavic linguistics (MA, PhD); sociolinguistics (MA, PhD); South Asian linguistics (MA, PhD); Southeast Asian linguistics (MA, PhD); syntactic theory (MA, PhD). Terminal master's awarded for partial completion of doctoral program. *Degree requirements:* For master's, one foreign language, thesis; for doctorate, one foreign language, comprehensive exam, thesis/dissertation. *Entrance requirements:* For master's and doctorate, GRE General Test, 2 letters of recommendation. Additional exam requirements/recommendations for international students: Required—TOEFL (minimum score 600 paper-based; 77 iBT). Electronic applications accepted. *Faculty research:* Phonology and phonetics, syntax and semantics, historical linguistics, philosophy of language, language acquisition.

**East Carolina University,** Graduate School, Thomas Harriot College of Arts and Sciences, Department of English, Greenville, NC 27858-4353. Offers creative writing (MA); English studies (MA); linguistics (MA); literature (MA); multicultural and transnational literatures (MA, Certificate); rhetoric and composition (MA); rhetoric, writing, and professional communication (PhD); teaching English in the two-year college (Certificate); teaching English to speakers of other languages (MA, Certificate); technical and professional communication (MA). *Program availability:* Part-time, evening/weekend. *Students:* 54 full-time (36 women), 95 part-time (77 women); includes 32 minority (19 Black or African American, non-Hispanic/Latino; 3 Asian, non-Hispanic/Latino; 6 Hispanic/Latino; 4 Two or more races, non-Hispanic/Latino), 1 international. Average age 35. 78 applicants, 96% accepted, 50 enrolled. In 2016, 34 master's, 1 doctorate awarded. *Degree requirements:* For master's, one foreign language, comprehensive exam, thesis optional. *Entrance requirements:* For master's, GRE General Test, MAT (for MA Ed). Additional exam requirements/recommendations for international students: Required—TOEFL. *Application deadline:* For fall admission, 6/1 priority date for domestic students; for spring admission, 10/15 for domestic students. Applications are processed on a rolling basis. Application fee: $50. *Financial support:* Research assistantships with partial tuition reimbursements, teaching assistantships with partial tuition reimbursements, and Federal Work-Study available. Support available

to part-time students. Financial award application deadline: 6/1. *Unit head:* Dr. Jeffrey Johnson, Chair, 252-328-6041, E-mail: johnsonj@ecu.edu. *Application contact:* Dean of Graduate School, 252-328-6012, Fax: 252-328-6071, E-mail: gradschool@ecu.edu.
Website: http://www.ecu.edu/cs-cas/engl/graduate/

**Eastern Michigan University,** Graduate School, College of Arts and Sciences, Department of English Language and Literature, Program in English Linguistics, Ypsilanti, MI 48197. Offers MA. *Program availability:* Part-time, evening/weekend, online learning. *Students:* 9 full-time (6 women), 4 part-time (3 women), 3 international. Average age 38. 22 applicants, 64% accepted, 5 enrolled. In 2016, 9 degrees awarded. *Degree requirements:* For master's, thesis (for some programs). *Entrance requirements:* Additional exam requirements/recommendations for international students: Required—TOEFL. *Application deadline:* Applications are processed on a rolling basis. Application fee: $45. *Financial support:* Fellowships with tuition reimbursements, research assistantships with full tuition reimbursements, teaching assistantships with full tuition reimbursements, career-related internships or fieldwork, Federal Work-Study, institutionally sponsored loans, scholarships/grants, tuition waivers (partial), and unspecified assistantships available. Support available to part-time students. Financial award applicants required to submit FAFSA. *Application contact:* Dr. Veronica Grondona, Program Advisor, 734-487-4220, Fax: 734-483-9744, E-mail: vgrondona@emich.edu.

**Florida Atlantic University,** Dorothy F. Schmidt College of Arts and Letters, Department of Languages, Linguistics, and Comparative Literature, Boca Raton, FL 33431-0991. Offers comparative literature (MA); French (MA); linguistics (MA); Spanish (MA). *Program availability:* Part-time. *Faculty:* 22 full-time (13 women). *Students:* 41 full-time (26 women), 16 part-time (12 women); includes 21 minority (9 Black or African American, non-Hispanic/Latino; 1 Asian, non-Hispanic/Latino; 11 Hispanic/Latino), 11 international. Average age 35. 48 applicants, 38% accepted, 11 enrolled. In 2016, 20 master's awarded. *Degree requirements:* For master's, one foreign language, comprehensive exam, thesis optional. *Entrance requirements:* For master's, GRE General Test, minimum GPA of 3.0. Additional exam requirements/recommendations for international students: Required—TOEFL (minimum score 500 paper-based; 61 iBT), IELTS (minimum score 6). *Application deadline:* For fall admission, 7/1 priority date for domestic students, 2/15 for international students; for spring admission, 11/1 for domestic students, 7/15 for international students. Applications are processed on a rolling basis. Application fee: $30. *Expenses:* Tuition, state resident: full-time $7392; part-time $369.82 per credit hour. Tuition, nonresident: full-time $19,432; part-time $1024.81 per credit hour. *Financial support:* Fellowships, research assistantships, teaching assistantships with partial tuition reimbursements, Federal Work-Study, and tuition waivers (partial) available. Support available to part-time students. Financial award application deadline: 4/1. *Faculty research:* Modern European studies, modern Latin America, medieval Europe. *Unit head:* Dr. Marcella Munson, Chair, 561-297-2118, Fax: 561-297-2756, E-mail: mmunson@fau.edu. *Application contact:* Dr. Linda Johnson, Associate Dean, 561-297-0928, Fax: 561-297-2744.
Website: http://www.fau.edu/LLCL/

**Florida International University,** College of Arts, Sciences, and Education, Department of English, Miami, FL 33199. Offers creative writing (MFA); English (MA), including literature; linguistics (MA). *Program availability:* Part-time, evening/weekend. *Faculty:* 55 full-time (29 women), 47 part-time/adjunct (29 women). *Students:* 47 full-time (30 women), 35 part-time (19 women); includes 43 minority (6 Black or African American, non-Hispanic/Latino; 36 Hispanic/Latino; 1 Two or more races, non-Hispanic/Latino), 8 international. Average age 31. 59 applicants, 39% accepted, 16 enrolled. In 2016, 27 master's awarded. *Degree requirements:* For master's, thesis. *Entrance requirements:* For master's, GRE General Test, minimum undergraduate GPA of 3.0 (upper-level coursework), letter of intent, two letters of recommendation. Additional exam requirements/recommendations for international students: Required—TOEFL (minimum score 550 paper-based; 80 iBT). *Application deadline:* For fall admission, 2/1 for domestic and international students; for spring admission, 10/1 for domestic students, 9/1 for international students. Applications are processed on a rolling basis. Application fee: $30. Electronic applications accepted. *Expenses:* Tuition, state resident: full-time $8912; part-time $446 per credit hour. Tuition, nonresident: full-time $21,393; part-time $992 per credit hour. *Required fees:* $2185; $195 per semester. Tuition and fees vary according to program. *Financial support:* Institutionally sponsored loans and scholarships/grants available. Financial award application deadline: 3/1; financial award applicants required to submit FAFSA. *Unit head:* Dr. Heather Russell, Chair, 305-348-3369, Fax: 305-348-3878, E-mail: heather.russell@fiu.edu. *Application contact:* Nanett Rojas, Assistant Director, Graduate Admissions, 305-348-7464, Fax: 305-348-7441, E-mail: gradadm@fiu.edu.

**Gallaudet University,** The Graduate School, Washington, DC 20002-3625. Offers American Sign Language/English bilingual early childhood deaf education: birth to 5 (Certificate); audiology (Au D); clinical psychology (PhD); deaf and hard of hearing infants, toddlers, and their families (Certificate); deaf education (MA, Ed S); deaf history (Certificate); deaf studies (Certificate); educating deaf students with disabilities (Certificate); education: teacher preparation (MA), including deaf education, early childhood education and deaf education, elementary education and deaf education, secondary education and deaf education; educational neuroscience (PhD); hearing, speech and language sciences (MS, PhD); international development (MA); interpretation (MA, PhD), including combined interpreting practice and research (MA), interpreting research (MA); linguistics (MA, PhD); mental health counseling (MA); peer mentoring (Certificate); public administration (MPA); school counseling (MA); school psychology (Psy S); sign language teaching (MA); social work (MSW); speech-language pathology (MS). *Program availability:* Part-time. *Students:* 297 full-time (231 women), 129 part-time (97 women); includes 105 minority (35 Black or African American, non-Hispanic/Latino; 20 Asian, non-Hispanic/Latino; 39 Hispanic/Latino; 11 Two or more races, non-Hispanic/Latino), 22 international. Average age 30. 471 applicants, 52% accepted, 147 enrolled. In 2016, 138 master's, 25 doctorates, 14 other advanced degrees awarded. Terminal master's awarded for partial completion of doctoral program. *Degree requirements:* For master's, comprehensive exam (for some programs), thesis optional; for doctorate, comprehensive exam, thesis/dissertation. *Entrance requirements:* For master's and doctorate, GRE General Test or MAT, letters of recommendation, interviews, goals statement, American Sign Language proficiency interview, written English competency. Additional exam requirements/recommendations for international students: Required—TOEFL. *Application deadline:* For fall admission, 2/15 for domestic students. Applications are processed on a rolling basis. Application fee: $75. Electronic applications accepted. *Expenses: Tuition:* Full-time $17,100; part-time $950 per credit hour. *Required fees:* $3725; $276 per semester. *Financial support:* Fellowships, research assistantships, teaching assistantships, career-related internships or fieldwork, Federal Work-Study, scholarships/grants, tuition waivers (partial), and unspecified assistantships available. Support available to part-time students. Financial award application deadline: 7/1; financial award applicants required to submit FAFSA. *Faculty research:* Signing math dictionaries, telecommunications access, cancer genetics, linguistics, visual language and visual learning, integrated quantum materials, deaf legal discourse, advance recruitment and retention in geosciences. *Unit head:* Dr. Gaurav Mathur, Dean, Graduate School and Continuing Studies, 202-250-2380, Fax: 202-651-5027, E-mail: gaurav.mathur@gallaudet.edu.

## Linguistics

*Application contact:* Wednesday Luria, Coordinator of Prospective Graduate Student Services, 202-651-5400, Fax: 202-651-5295, E-mail: graduate.school@gallaudet.edu.

**George Mason University,** College of Humanities and Social Sciences, Department of English, Fairfax, VA 22030. Offers creative writing (MFA), including fiction; English (MA, Certificate); linguistics (PhD). *Faculty:* 81 full-time (42 women), 40 part-time/adjunct (28 women). *Students:* 119 full-time (83 women), 111 part-time (87 women); includes 37 minority (9 Black or African American, non-Hispanic/Latino; 1 American Indian or Alaska Native, non-Hispanic/Latino; 7 Asian, non-Hispanic/Latino; 12 Hispanic/Latino; 1 Native Hawaiian or other Pacific Islander, non-Hispanic/Latino; 7 Two or more races, non-Hispanic/Latino), 17 international. Average age 32. 191 applicants, 69% accepted, 61 enrolled. In 2016, 72 master's, 2 doctorates, 17 other advanced degrees awarded. *Degree requirements:* For master's, thesis (for some programs), proficiency in a foreign language by course work or translation test; for doctorate, thesis/dissertation, 2 papers. *Entrance requirements:* For master's, official transcripts; expanded goals statement; writing sample; portfolio; 2 letters of recommendation; for doctorate, GRE, expanded goals statement; 3 letters of recommendation; writing sample; introductory course in linguistics; official transcripts; for Certificate, official transcripts; expanded goals statement; 3 letters of recommendation; writing sample; portfolio (for professional writing and rhetoric); resume (for folklore). Additional exam requirements/recommendations for international students: Required—TOEFL (minimum score 575 paper-based; 88 iBT), IELTS (minimum score 6.5), PTE (minimum score 59). *Application deadline:* For fall admission, 3/15 for domestic and international students. Application fee: $75 ($80 for international students). Electronic applications accepted. *Expenses:* Tuition, state resident: full-time $10,628; part-time $443 per credit. Tuition, nonresident: full-time $29,306; part-time $1221 per credit. *Required fees:* $3096; $129 per credit. Tuition and fees vary according to program. *Financial support:* In 2016–17, 77 students received support, including 1 fellowship (averaging $7,895 per year), 6 research assistantships with tuition reimbursements available (averaging $17,788 per year), 72 teaching assistantships with tuition reimbursements available (averaging $13,102 per year); career-related internships or fieldwork, Federal Work-Study, scholarships/grants, unspecified assistantships, and health care benefits (for full-time research or teaching assistantship recipients) also available. Support available to part-time students. Financial award application deadline: 3/1; financial award applicants required to submit FAFSA. *Faculty research:* Literature, professional writing and editing, writing of fiction or poetry. Total annual research expenditures: $123,731. *Unit head:* Debra Lattanzi-Shutika, Chair, 703-993-1170, Fax: 703-993-1161, E-mail: dshutika@gmu.edu. *Application contact:* Alex Walsh, Graduate Admissions Coordinator, 703-993-1185, Fax: 703-993-1161, E-mail: awalsh7@gmu.edu.
Website: http://english.gmu.edu

**Georgetown University,** Graduate School of Arts and Sciences, Department of Linguistics, Washington, DC 20057. Offers language and communication (MA); linguistics (MS, PhD), including applied linguistics, computational linguistics, sociolinguistics, theoretical linguistics. Terminal master's awarded for partial completion of doctoral program. *Degree requirements:* For master's, one foreign language, comprehensive exam; for doctorate, 2 foreign languages, comprehensive exam, thesis/dissertation. *Entrance requirements:* For master's and doctorate, 18 undergraduate credits in a foreign language. Additional exam requirements/recommendations for international students: Required—TOEFL.

**Georgia State University,** College of Arts and Sciences, Department of Applied Linguistics and English as a Second Language, Atlanta, GA 30302. Offers applied linguistics (MA, PhD). *Program availability:* Part-time. *Faculty:* 13 full-time (8 women). *Students:* 45 full-time (28 women), 22 part-time (19 women); includes 15 minority (4 Black or African American, non-Hispanic/Latino; 6 Asian, non-Hispanic/Latino; 1 Hispanic/Latino; 1 Native Hawaiian or other Pacific Islander, non-Hispanic/Latino; 3 Two or more races, non-Hispanic/Latino), 13 international. Average age 38. 96 applicants, 26% accepted, 12 enrolled. In 2016, 21 master's, 2 doctorates awarded. *Degree requirements:* For master's, one foreign language, portfolio; for doctorate, one foreign language, comprehensive exam, thesis/dissertation, qualifying exam. *Entrance requirements:* For master's and doctorate, GRE. Additional exam requirements/recommendations for international students: Required—TWE (minimum score 4), TOEFL (minimum score 600 paper-based; 97 iBT) or IELTS (minimum score 7). *Application deadline:* For fall admission, 1/15 for domestic and international students; for spring admission, 11/15 for domestic and international students. Applications are processed on a rolling basis. Application fee: $50. Electronic applications accepted. *Expenses:* Tuition, state resident: full-time $6876; part-time $382 per credit hour. Tuition, nonresident: full-time $22,374; part-time $1243 per credit hour. *Required fees:* $2128; $1064 per term. Part-time tuition and fees vary according to course load and program. *Financial support:* In 2016–17, fellowships with full tuition reimbursements (averaging $23,500 per year), research assistantships with full tuition reimbursements (averaging $5,000 per year), teaching assistantships with full tuition reimbursements (averaging $8,500 per year) were awarded; scholarships/grants and unspecified assistantships also available. Financial award application deadline: 6/1. *Faculty research:* Corpus linguistics, second language acquisition, second language literacy, assessment, teacher education. *Unit head:* Dr. Diane C. Belcher, Chair, Fax: 404-413-5201, E-mail: dbelcher1@gsu.edu.
Website: http://www2.gsu.edu/~wwwesl/

**Georgia State University,** College of Arts and Sciences, Department of World Languages and Cultures, Program in French, Atlanta, GA 30302-3083. Offers applied linguistics and pedagogy (MA); French studies (MA); literature and culture (MA). *Program availability:* Part-time. *Degree requirements:* For master's, one foreign language, comprehensive exam, thesis or alternative, Graduate Foreign Language Reading Exam. *Entrance requirements:* For master's, GRE, statement of purpose, writing sample in the target language, 2 letters of recommendation, official transcripts. Additional exam requirements/recommendations for international students: Required—TOEFL (minimum score 79 iBT). *Application deadline:* For fall admission, 3/15 priority date for domestic and international students; for spring admission, 11/15 priority date for domestic and international students. Application fee: $50. Electronic applications accepted. *Expenses:* Tuition, state resident: full-time $6876; part-time $382 per credit hour. Tuition, nonresident: full-time $22,374; part-time $1243 per credit hour. *Required fees:* $2128; $1064 per term. Part-time tuition and fees vary according to course load and program. *Financial support:* Institutionally sponsored loans available. Financial award applicants required to submit FAFSA. *Faculty research:* The nineteenth-century novel, narratology, genetic criticism, poetics, semiotics, and intertextuality; Francophone and transnational studies; early modern travel literature; post/colonial and Diaspora studies; film studies; social and gender studies; eighteenth century French literature and history of ideas; history of civilization; Enlightenment, encyclopedism. *Unit head:* Dr. Fernando Reati, Department Chair, 404-413-5984, Fax: 404-413-5982, E-mail: freati@gsu.edu. *Application contact:* Lita Malveaux, Administrative Academic Specialist, 404-413-5046, Fax: 404-413-5036, E-mail: lmalveaux@gsu.edu.
Website: http://www.gsu.edu/~wwwmcl/

**The Graduate Center, City University of New York,** Graduate Studies, Program in Anthropology, New York, NY 10016-4039. Offers anthropological linguistics (PhD); archaeology (PhD); cultural anthropology (PhD); physical anthropology (PhD). *Degree requirements:* For doctorate, one foreign language, thesis/dissertation. *Entrance requirements:* For doctorate, GRE General Test. Additional exam requirements/recommendations for international students: Required—TOEFL. Electronic applications accepted.

**The Graduate Center, City University of New York,** Graduate Studies, Program in Linguistics, New York, NY 10016-4039. Offers MA, PhD. Terminal master's awarded for partial completion of doctoral program. *Degree requirements:* For master's, one foreign language, thesis; for doctorate, 2 foreign languages, thesis/dissertation. *Entrance requirements:* For master's and doctorate, GRE General Test. Additional exam requirements/recommendations for international students: Required—TOEFL. Electronic applications accepted.

**Graduate Institute of Applied Linguistics,** Graduate Programs, Dallas, TX 75236. Offers applied linguistics (MA, Certificate); language development (MA). *Program availability:* Part-time. *Degree requirements:* For master's, one foreign language, comprehensive exam (for some programs), thesis (for some programs). *Entrance requirements:* For master's, GRE. Additional exam requirements/recommendations for international students: Required—TOEFL (minimum score 577 paper-based; 90 iBT). Electronic applications accepted. *Faculty research:* Minority languages, endangered languages, language documentation.

**Grand Valley State University,** College of Liberal Arts and Sciences, Program in Applied Linguistics, Allendale, MI 49401-9403. Offers MA. *Program availability:* Part-time. *Students:* 10 full-time (7 women), 1 part-time, 8 international. Average age 27. 15 applicants, 100% accepted, 11 enrolled. *Degree requirements:* For master's, thesis, project, or capstone. *Entrance requirements:* For master's, minimum GPA of 3.0 or GRE; personal statement; writing sample; 2 letters of recommendation. Additional exam requirements/recommendations for international students: Recommended—TOEFL (minimum score 79 iBT), IELTS (minimum score 6.5). *Application deadline:* Applications are processed on a rolling basis. Application fee: $30. Electronic applications accepted. *Expenses:* $604 per credit hour. *Financial support:* In 2016–17, 2 students received support, including 2 fellowships with full and partial tuition reimbursements available (averaging $8,000 per year). *Unit head:* Dr. Shinian Wu, Director, 616-331-3405, E-mail: wus@gvsu.edu.
Website: http://www.gvsu.edu/linguistics/

**Harvard University,** Graduate School of Arts and Sciences, Department of Linguistics, Cambridge, MA 02138. Offers descriptive linguistics (PhD); historical linguistics (PhD); theoretical linguistics (PhD). *Degree requirements:* For doctorate, 4 foreign languages, thesis/dissertation, field exam, Indo-European language exam, research paper. *Entrance requirements:* For doctorate, GRE General Test. Additional exam requirements/recommendations for international students: Required—TOEFL.

**Hofstra University,** College of Liberal Arts and Sciences, Programs in Forensic Linguistics and Applied Linguistics, Hempstead, NY 11549. Offers applied linguistics (TESOL) (MA); linguistics (MA), including forensic linguistics. *Program availability:* Part-time, blended/hybrid learning. *Students:* 34 full-time (26 women), 3 part-time (2 women); includes 7 minority (3 Black or African American, non-Hispanic/Latino; 4 Hispanic/Latino), 5 international. Average age 26. 38 applicants, 89% accepted, 13 enrolled. In 2016, 26 master's awarded. *Degree requirements:* For master's, thesis, 36 credits, capstone, minimum GPA of 3.0. *Entrance requirements:* For master's, bachelor's degree in related area, interview, 2 letters of recommendation. Additional exam requirements/recommendations for international students: Required—TOEFL (minimum score 550 paper-based; 80 iBT). *Application deadline:* Applications are processed on a rolling basis. Application fee: $75. Electronic applications accepted. *Expenses:* Tuition: Full-time $1240. *Required fees:* $970. Tuition and fees vary according to program. *Financial support:* In 2016–17, 9 students received support, including 6 fellowships with full and partial tuition reimbursements available (averaging $5,942 per year); research assistantships with full and partial tuition reimbursements available, career-related internships or fieldwork, Federal Work-Study, institutionally sponsored loans, scholarships/grants, tuition waivers (full and partial), and unspecified assistantships also available. Support available to part-time students. Financial award applicants required to submit FAFSA. *Faculty research:* Stance in threatening communications, cross-examination techniques in cases of sexual assault, expressions of contrition in parole board hearings, analysis of ordinary meaning in laws using corpus techniques, manifestation of ideologies in immigration legislation; ancient rhetoric, second-language writing instruction, pedagogical grammar of English, English etymology, political oratory. *Unit head:* Dr. George L. Greaney, Program Director, 516-463-5651, E-mail: george.l.greaney@hofstra.edu. *Application contact:* Sunil Samuel, Assistant Vice President of Admissions, 516-463-4723, Fax: 516-463-4664, E-mail: graduateadmission@hofstra.edu.
Website: http://www.hofstra.edu/hclas

**Hofstra University,** School of Education, Programs in Teacher Education, Hempstead, NY 11549. Offers bilingual education (MA, Advanced Certificate); bilingual extension (Advanced Certificate), including education/speech language pathology; business education (MS Ed); early childhood and childhood education (MS Ed); early childhood education (MA, MS Ed); education technology (Advanced Certificate); elementary education (MA, MS Ed), including science, technology, engineering, and mathematics (STEM) (MA); English education (MS Ed); family and consumer science (MS Ed); fine arts and music education (Advanced Certificate); fine arts education (MS Ed); foreign language and TESOL (MS Ed); foreign language education (MS Ed), including French, German, Russian, Spanish; learning and teaching (Ed D), including applied linguistics, art education, arts and humanities, early childhood education, English education, human development, math education, math, science, and technology, multicultural education, physical education, science education, social studies education, special education; mathematics education (MA, MS Ed); middle school extension (Advanced Certificate), including grades 5-6, grades 7-9; music education (MA, MS Ed); science education (MA, MS Ed), including biology, chemistry, earth science, geology, physics; secondary education (Advanced Certificate); social studies education (MA, MS Ed); teaching languages other than English and TESOL (MS Ed); TESOL (MS Ed, Advanced Certificate). *Program availability:* Part-time, evening/weekend, blended/hybrid learning. *Students:* 139 full-time (97 women), 145 part-time (106 women); includes 60 minority (15 Black or African American, non-Hispanic/Latino; 1 American Indian or Alaska Native, non-Hispanic/Latino; 12 Asian, non-Hispanic/Latino; 31 Hispanic/Latino; 1 Two or more races, non-Hispanic/Latino), 21 international. Average age 29. 255 applicants, 86% accepted, 122 enrolled. In 2016, 101 master's, 4 doctorates, 43 other advanced degrees awarded. *Degree requirements:* For master's, comprehensive exam, thesis (for some programs), exit project, student teaching, fieldwork, electronic portfolio, curriculum project, minimum GPA of 3.0; for doctorate, thesis/dissertation; for Advanced Certificate, 3 foreign languages, comprehensive exam (for some programs), thesis project. *Entrance requirements:* For master's, GRE, MAT, 2 letters of recommendation, portfolio, teacher certification (MA), interview, essay; for doctorate, GMAT, GRE, LSAT, or MAT; for Advanced Certificate, 2 letters of recommendation, essay, interview and/or portfolio, teaching certificate. Additional exam requirements/recommendations for international students: Required—TOEFL (minimum score 550 paper-based; 80 iBT). *Application deadline:* Applications are processed on a rolling basis. Application fee: $75. Electronic applications accepted. *Expenses:* Tuition: Full-time $1240. *Required fees:* $970. Tuition and fees vary according to program. *Financial support:* In 2016–17, 149 students received support, including 58 fellowships with full and partial tuition reimbursements available (averaging $5,309 per year), 5 research assistantships with full and partial tuition reimbursements available (averaging $7,073 per year); career-related internships or fieldwork, Federal Work-Study, institutionally sponsored loans, scholarships/grants, traineeships, tuition waivers (full and partial), and unspecified assistantships also available. Support available to part-time students. Financial award applicants required to submit FAFSA. *Faculty research:* Educational interventions that foster critical-thinking skills; teachers' attitudes about professional development; threats to teacher quality. *Unit head:* Dr. Eustace Thompson, Chairperson, 516-463-5749, Fax: 516-463-6275, E-mail: eustace.g.thompson@hofstra.edu. *Application contact:* Sunil Samuel, Assistant Vice President of Admissions, 516-463-4723, Fax: 516-463-4664, E-mail: graduateadmission@hofstra.edu. Website: http://www.hofstra.edu/education/

**Indiana State University,** College of Graduate and Professional Studies, College of Arts and Sciences, Department of Languages, Literatures, and Linguistics, Terre Haute, IN 47809. Offers applied linguistics/teaching English as a second language (MA); language education (PhD); Spanish/teaching english as a second language (MA); TESL/TEFL (CAS). *Degree requirements:* For master's, comprehensive exam. Electronic applications accepted.

**Indiana University Bloomington,** University Graduate School, College of Arts and Sciences, Department of Anthropology, Bloomington, IN 47405. Offers anthropology (MA, PhD), including archaeology (PhD), bioanthropology (PhD), linguistic anthropology (PhD), social-cultural anthropology (PhD). *Faculty:* 35 full-time (23 women). *Students:* 101 full-time (76 women); includes 16 minority (2 Black or African American, non-Hispanic/Latino; 2 American Indian or Alaska Native, non-Hispanic/Latino; 1 Asian, non-Hispanic/Latino; 6 Hispanic/Latino; 5 Two or more races, non-Hispanic/Latino), 15 international. Average age 33. 81 applicants, 15% accepted, 6 enrolled. In 2016, 8 master's, 10 doctorates awarded. *Degree requirements:* For master's, comprehensive exam (for some programs), thesis or alternative; for doctorate, 2 foreign languages, comprehensive exam, thesis/dissertation. *Entrance requirements:* For master's and doctorate, GRE General Test, minimum GPA of 3.0. Additional exam requirements/recommendations for international students: Required—TOEFL (minimum score 550 paper-based, 79 iBT) or IELTS. *Application deadline:* For fall admission, 12/1 for domestic and international students. Application fee: $55 ($65 for international students). Electronic applications accepted. *Expenses:* $3,429 per course non-resident, $990 per course resident. *Financial support:* In 2016–17, 68 students received support, including 22 fellowships with full tuition reimbursements available (averaging $18,000 per year), 4 research assistantships with full tuition reimbursements available (averaging $15,750 per year), 46 teaching assistantships with full tuition reimbursements available (averaging $15,750 per year); Federal Work-Study, scholarships/grants, health care benefits, and unspecified assistantships also available. *Faculty research:* Archaeology in social context; bio anthropology; anthropology of food and ecology; gender studies; communication, media and performance. *Total annual research expenditures:* $170,905. *Unit head:* Dr. Jeanne Sept, Chair, 812-855-2555, Fax: 812-855-4358, E-mail: sept@indiana.edu. *Application contact:* Debra Wilkerson, Administrative Secretary, 812-855-1203, Fax: 812-855-4358, E-mail: dwilkers@indiana.edu. Website: http://www.indiana.edu/~anthro/index.shtml

**Indiana University Bloomington,** University Graduate School, College of Arts and Sciences, Department of French and Italian, Bloomington, IN 47405. Offers French (MA, PhD), including French and Francophone studies (MA), French instruction (MA), French linguistics; Italian (MA, PhD). *Program availability:* Part-time. *Faculty:* 23 full-time (10 women). *Students:* 51 full-time (32 women), 6 part-time (3 women); includes 2 minority (1 Black or African American, non-Hispanic/Latino; 1 Hispanic/Latino), 27 international. Average age 31. 28 applicants, 71% accepted, 7 enrolled. In 2016, 8 master's, 4 doctorates awarded. Terminal master's awarded for partial completion of doctoral program. *Degree requirements:* For master's, variable foreign language requirement, comprehensive exam (for some programs), thesis or alternative; for doctorate, variable foreign language requirement, comprehensive exam, thesis/dissertation. *Entrance requirements:* For master's, GRE General Test, BA or equivalent undergraduate preparation in French or Italian; for doctorate, GRE General Test, MA from degree program at IU; MA in the specific field. Additional exam requirements/recommendations for international students: Required—TOEFL (minimum score 550 paper-based; 79 iBT), GRE General Test (recommended). *Application deadline:* For fall admission, 1/15 priority date for domestic students, 12/1 priority date for international students; for spring admission, 9/1 priority date for domestic and international students. Application fee: $55 ($65 for international students). Electronic applications accepted. *Financial support:* In 2016–17, 40 students received support, including 6 fellowships with partial tuition reimbursements available (averaging $18,000 per year), 2 research assistantships with partial tuition reimbursements available (averaging $15,750 per year), 31 teaching assistantships with partial tuition reimbursements available (averaging $15,750 per year); scholarships/grants, health care benefits, and unspecified assistantships also available. Financial award application deadline: 1/15. *Faculty research:* French and Italian literature, French linguistics, including the novel and political theory, literature and fine arts, literary theory, postcolonialism, French-Creole studies, French literature of Africa and its Diaspora, humanism, Medieval folklore and mythology, humor in Medieval and Renaissance literature, emigration, second language acquisition, syntax, sociolinguistics, phonology, lexicography, media and cultural studies, cinema, drama. *Unit head:* Prof. Massimo Scalabrini, Chair, 812-855-8044, Fax: 812-855-8877, E-mail: mscalabar@indiana.edu. *Application contact:* Lauren Anderson, Graduate Student Services Coordinator, 812-855-1088, Fax: 812-855-8877, E-mail: fritgs@indiana.edu. Website: http://frit.indiana.edu

**Indiana University Bloomington,** University Graduate School, College of Arts and Sciences, Department of Germanic Studies, Bloomington, IN 47405-7000. Offers German philology and linguistics (PhD); German studies (MA, PhD), including German (MA), German literature and culture (MA), German literature and linguistics (MA); medieval German studies (PhD); teaching German (MAT). *Faculty:* 13 full-time (4 women), 6 part-time/adjunct (2 women). *Students:* 28 full-time (15 women), 2 part-time (both women), 5 international. Average age 32. 16 applicants, 56% accepted, 4 enrolled. In 2016, 2 master's, 3 doctorates awarded. *Degree requirements:* For master's, one foreign language, project; for doctorate, one foreign language, comprehensive exam, thesis/dissertation. *Entrance requirements:* For master's, GRE General Test, BA in German or equivalent; for doctorate, GRE General Test, MA in German or equivalent. Additional exam requirements/recommendations for international students: Required—TOEFL. *Application deadline:* For fall admission, 12/1 priority date for domestic students, 12/1 for international students; for spring admission, 9/1 priority date for domestic students, 9/1 for international students. Applications are processed on a rolling basis. Application fee: $55 ($65 for international students). Electronic applications accepted. *Financial support:* Application deadline: 1/15. *Faculty research:* German and other European literature: medieval to modern/postmodern, German and culture studies, Germanic philology, literary theory, literature and the other arts. *Unit head:* William Rasch, Department Chairman, 812-855-7947, Fax: 812-855-8292, E-mail: wrasch@indiana.edu. *Application contact:* Michelle Dunbar, Graduate Secretary, 812-855-7947, E-mail: midunbar@indiana.edu. Website: http://germanic.indiana.edu/

**Indiana University Bloomington,** University Graduate School, College of Arts and Sciences, Department of Linguistics, Bloomington, IN 47405. Offers African languages and linguistics (PhD); computational linguistics (MA, MS, PhD); linguistics (MA, PhD). *Faculty:* 15 full-time (5 women). *Students:* 69 full-time (39 women), 2 part-time (both women); includes 6 minority (2 Black or African American, non-Hispanic/Latino; 1 Asian, non-Hispanic/Latino; 1 Hispanic/Latino; 2 Two or more races, non-Hispanic/Latino), 30 international. Average age 30. 74 applicants, 47% accepted, 12 enrolled. In 2016, 10 master's, 6 doctorates awarded. Terminal master's awarded for partial completion of doctoral program. *Degree requirements:* For master's, one foreign language, thesis optional; for doctorate, one foreign language, comprehensive exam, thesis/dissertation, proficiency in research tool appropriate to research area. *Entrance requirements:* For master's and doctorate, GRE General Test. Additional exam requirements/recommendations for international students: Required—TOEFL (minimum score 580 paper-based; 92 iBT). *Application deadline:* For fall admission, 1/3 for domestic students, 12/1 for international students. Application fee: $55 ($65 for international students). Electronic applications accepted. *Financial support:* In 2016–17, 2 fellowships with full tuition reimbursements, 8 teaching assistantships with full tuition reimbursements were awarded; unspecified assistantships also available. *Faculty research:* African linguistics and language, semantics, phonology, syntactic theory, historical linguistics, phonetics-phonology, syntax, sociolinguistics, computational linguistics. *Unit head:* Dr. Ken de Jong, Chair, 812-855-6456, Fax: 812-855-3594, E-mail: kdejong@indiana.edu. *Application contact:* Margaret Anderson, Secretary, 812-855-6456, Fax: 812-855-5363, E-mail: maraande@indiana.edu. Website: http://www.indiana.edu/~lingdept/

**Instituto Tecnologico de Santo Domingo,** Graduate School, Area of Humanities and Social Sciences, Santo Domingo, Dominican Republic. Offers accounting (Certificate); adult education (Certificate); applied linguistics (MA); economics (MA); education (M Ed); educational psychology (MA, Certificate); gender and development (MA, Certificate); humanistic studies (MA); international marketing management (Certificate); international relations in the Caribbean basin (Certificate); intervention systems in family therapy (MA); linguistic and literary communication (Certificate); pedagogical support (MA); social science education (M Ed); sustainable human development (MA); terminal illness and death psychology (Certificate); youth and adult education (M Ed).

**Iowa State University of Science and Technology,** Program in Applied Linguistics and Technology, Ames, IA 50011. Offers PhD. *Entrance requirements:* For doctorate, GRE, official academic transcripts, resume, three letters of recommendation, writing sample. Additional exam requirements/recommendations for international students: Required—TOEFL (minimum score 640 paper-based; 111 iBT), IELTS (minimum score 7.5). *Application deadline:* For fall admission, 1/5 for domestic and international students. Application fee: $60 ($90 for international students). Electronic applications accepted. *Application contact:* Teresa Smiley, Application Contact, 515-294-2477, Fax: 515-294-6814, E-mail: englgrad@iastate.edu. Website: http://engl.iastate.edu/resources/graduate-studies/

**Iowa State University of Science and Technology,** Program in Teaching English as a Second Language/Applied Linguistics, Ames, IA 50011. Offers MA. *Entrance requirements:* For master's, GRE, official academic transcripts, resume, three letters of recommendation, statement of personal goals, writing sample. Additional exam requirements/recommendations for international students: Required—TOEFL (minimum score 600 paper-based; 100 iBT), IELTS (minimum score 7). *Application deadline:* For fall admission, 1/5 for domestic students. Application fee: $60 ($90 for international students). Electronic applications accepted. *Application contact:* Teresa Smiley, Application Contact, 515-294-2477, Fax: 515-294-6814, E-mail: englgrad@iastate.edu. Website: http://www.public.iastate.edu/~apling/TESL_cert.html

**Kent State University,** College of Arts and Sciences, Department of Modern and Classical Language Studies, Kent, OH 44242-0001. Offers French (MA), including applied linguistics and pedagogy, literature; Latin (MA), including applied linguistics and pedagogy, literature; Spanish (MA), including applied linguistics and pedagogy, literature; translation (MA), including Arabic, French, German, Japanese, Russian, Spanish; translation studies (PhD); MA/MBA. *Program availability:* Part-time. *Faculty:* 35 full-time (23 women). *Students:* 81 full-time (51 women), 23 part-time (15 women); includes 14 minority (1 Black or African American, non-Hispanic/Latino; 9 Hispanic/Latino; 4 Two or more races, non-Hispanic/Latino), 48 international. Average age 30. 109 applicants, 53% accepted, 33 enrolled. In 2016, 31 master's, 6 doctorates awarded. *Degree requirements:* For master's, variable foreign language requirement, comprehensive exam (for some programs), thesis (for some programs); for doctorate, variable foreign language requirement, comprehensive exam, thesis/dissertation. *Entrance requirements:* For master's, transcripts, goal statement, 3 letters of recommendation, CD/MP3 with oral sample of first and second languages, writing sample of second language; for doctorate, transcripts, MA in translation, a foreign language, or similar field; proficiency in a foreign language; minimum GPA of 3.5 from MA; goal statement; 3 letters of recommendation; essay or writing sample. *Application deadline:* For fall admission, 2/1 for domestic and international students. Applications are processed on a rolling basis. Application fee: $45 ($70 for international students). Electronic applications accepted. *Expenses:* Tuition, state resident: full-time $10,864; part-time $495 per credit hour. Tuition, nonresident: full-time $18,380; part-time $837 per credit hour. *Financial support:* Fellowships with full tuition reimbursements, teaching assistantships with full tuition reimbursements, and unspecified assistantships available. Financial award application deadline: 2/1. *Unit head:* Dr. Keiran Dunne, Professor of French Translation/Chair, 330-672-2150, E-mail: kdunne@kent.edu. *Application contact:* Said Shiyab, Professor of Translation Studies/Graduate Coordinator, 330-672-1864, E-mail: sshiyab@kent.edu. Website: http://www.kent.edu/mcls/

**Massachusetts Institute of Technology,** School of Humanities, Arts, and Social Sciences, Department of Linguistics and Philosophy, Linguistics Section, Cambridge, MA 02139. Offers PhD. *Faculty:* 13 full-time (3 women), 1 (woman) part-time/adjunct. *Students:* 32 full-time (14 women); includes 35 minority (1 American Indian or Alaska Native, non-Hispanic/Latino; 31 Asian, non-Hispanic/Latino; 1 Hispanic/Latino; 2 Two or more races, non-Hispanic/Latino), 26 international. Average age 28. 155 applicants, 8% accepted, 9 enrolled. In 2016, 5 doctorates awarded. *Degree requirements:* For doctorate, comprehensive exam, thesis/dissertation, teaching assistantship during two semesters. *Entrance requirements:* Additional exam requirements/recommendations for international students: Required—TOEFL, IELTS. *Application deadline:* For fall admission, 1/2 for domestic and international students. Application fee: $75. Electronic applications accepted. *Expenses:* Tuition: Full-time $46,400; part-time $725 per credit. One-time fee: $312 full-time. Full-time tuition and fees vary according to course load and program. *Financial support:* In 2016–17, 14 fellowships (averaging $36,900 per year), 31 research assistantships (averaging $39,200 per year) were awarded; teaching assistantships, Federal Work-Study, institutionally sponsored loans, scholarships/grants, traineeships, health care benefits, unspecified assistantships, and resident tutors also available. Support available to part-time students. Financial award application deadline: 5/1; financial award applicants required to submit FAFSA. *Faculty research:* Phonology and phonetics, syntax and semantics, morphology, psycholinguistics, language acquisition. *Total annual research expenditures:* $207,000. *Unit head:* Prof.

## Linguistics

David Pesetsky, Linguistics Chair, 617-253-4141, Fax: 617-253-5017. *Application contact:* 617-253-9372, E-mail: lp-admissions@mit.edu. Website: http://web.mit.edu/linguistics/

**McGill University,** Faculty of Graduate and Postdoctoral Studies, Faculty of Arts, Department of Linguistics, Montréal, QC H3A 2T5, Canada. Offers language acquisition (PhD); linguistics (MA, PhD).

**Memorial University of Newfoundland,** School of Graduate Studies, Department of Linguistics, St. John's, NL A1C 5S7, Canada. Offers MA, PhD. *Program availability:* Part-time. *Degree requirements:* For master's, one foreign language, thesis or comprehensive exam; for doctorate, 2 foreign languages, comprehensive exam, thesis/dissertation, oral defense of thesis. *Entrance requirements:* For master's, bachelor's degree in linguistics; for doctorate, master's degree in linguistics. Electronic applications accepted. *Faculty research:* Aboriginal languages of eastern North America, historical/comparative linguistics, languages and dialects of Newfoundland and Labrador.

**Michigan State University,** The Graduate School, College of Arts and Letters, Department of Linguistics and Germanic, Slavic, Asian, and African Languages, East Lansing, MI 48824. Offers German studies (MA, PhD); linguistics (MA, PhD); teaching English to speakers of other languages (MA). *Program availability:* Part-time, evening/weekend. *Entrance requirements:* For master's, GRE General Test, minimum GPA of 3.2 in last 2 undergraduate years, 2 years of college-level foreign language, 3 letters of recommendation, portfolio (German studies); for doctorate, GRE General Test, minimum graduate GPA of 3.5, 3 letters of recommendation, master's degree or sufficient graduate course work in linguistics or language of study, master's thesis or major research paper. Additional exam requirements/recommendations for international students: Required—TOEFL. Electronic applications accepted.

**Michigan State University,** The Graduate School, College of Arts and Letters, Department of Spanish and Portuguese, East Lansing, MI 48824. Offers applied Spanish linguistics (MA); Hispanic cultural studies (PhD); Hispanic literatures (MA). *Entrance requirements:* Additional exam requirements/recommendations for international students: Required—TOEFL. Electronic applications accepted.

**Montclair State University,** The Graduate School, College of Humanities and Social Sciences, Program in Applied Linguistics, Montclair, NJ 07043-1624. Offers MA. *Program availability:* Part-time, evening/weekend. *Degree requirements:* For master's, comprehensive exam. *Entrance requirements:* For master's, GRE General Test, 2 letters of recommendation, essay. Additional exam requirements/recommendations for international students: Required—TOEFL (minimum score 83 iBT), IELTS (minimum score 6.5). Electronic applications accepted. *Expenses:* Tuition, state resident: part-time $553 per credit. Tuition, nonresident: part-time $854 per credit. *Required fees:* $91 per credit. Tuition and fees vary according to program. *Faculty research:* Research on short message service (SMS) text messaging; corpus building and research; research on online, hybrid, and mobile language learning; linguistic code switching and bilingual mental lexical, sentence comprehension; second language acquisition of American Sign Language; cognitive linguistics, phonetics, forensic.

**Montclair State University,** The Graduate School, College of Humanities and Social Sciences, Program in Computational Linguistics, Montclair, NJ 07043-1624. Offers Certificate. *Program availability:* Part-time, evening/weekend. *Entrance requirements:* For degree, 2 letters of recommendation, essay. Additional exam requirements/recommendations for international students: Required—TOEFL (minimum score 83 iBT), IELTS (minimum score 6.5). Electronic applications accepted. *Expenses:* Tuition, state resident: part-time $553 per credit. Tuition, nonresident: part-time $854 per credit. *Required fees:* $91 per credit. Tuition and fees vary according to program. *Faculty research:* Resource light morphology, creativity, idiomatic sentence detection; computational approaches to deception detection; computational approaches to fusional morphology; computational approaches to figurative language.

**New York University,** Graduate School of Arts and Science, Department of Linguistics, New York, NY 10012-1019. Offers MA, PhD. *Program availability:* Part-time. Terminal master's awarded for partial completion of doctoral program. *Degree requirements:* For master's, one foreign language, comprehensive exam, thesis optional; for doctorate, one foreign language, thesis/dissertation, 2 publishable papers. *Entrance requirements:* For master's and doctorate, GRE General Test. Additional exam requirements/recommendations for international students: Required—TOEFL. *Faculty research:* Phonology, syntax, sociolinguistics, cognitive science.

**Northeastern Illinois University,** College of Graduate Studies and Research, College of Arts and Sciences, Program in Linguistics, Chicago, IL 60625-4699. Offers linguistics (MA); TESL (MA). *Program availability:* Part-time, evening/weekend. *Degree requirements:* For master's, one foreign language, comprehensive exam, thesis optional. *Entrance requirements:* For master's, 9 undergraduate hours in a foreign language or equivalent, minimum GPA of 2.75. Additional exam requirements/recommendations for international students: Required—TOEFL (minimum score 550 paper-based; 79 iBT). Electronic applications accepted. *Faculty research:* Acquisition of literacy, Mayan language, Rotuman language, English as a second language methodology, Farsi language.

**Northern Arizona University,** Graduate College, College of Arts and Letters, Department of English, Flagstaff, AZ 86011. Offers applied linguistics (PhD); creative writing (MFA), including creative writing; English (MA), including English education, literature, professional writing, rhetoric, writing, and digital media studies; professional writing (Certificate); teaching English as a second language (MA, Certificate). *Program availability:* Part-time. *Degree requirements:* For master's, comprehensive exam (for some programs), thesis (for some programs), departmental qualifying exam; for doctorate, comprehensive exam, thesis/dissertation, departmental qualifying exam. *Entrance requirements:* For master's, minimum GPA of 3.0 or GRE; for doctorate, GRE General Test. Additional exam requirements/recommendations for international students: Required—TOEFL (minimum score 550 paper-based; 80 iBT), IELTS (minimum score 7), TOEFL (minimum score 600 paper-based; 100 iBT) for PhD; TOEFL (minimum score 570 paper-based; 89 iBT) for MA. Electronic applications accepted. *Expenses:* Tuition, state resident: full-time $8971; part-time $444 per credit hour. Tuition, nonresident: full-time $20,958; part-time $1164 per credit hour. *Required fees:* $1018; $644 per credit hour. Tuition and fees vary according to course load, campus/location and program.

**Northwestern University,** The Graduate School, Judd A. and Marjorie Weinberg College of Arts and Sciences, Department of Linguistics, Evanston, IL 60208. Offers PhD, JD/PhD. Admissions and degrees offered through The Graduate School. *Program availability:* Part-time. Terminal master's awarded for partial completion of doctoral program. *Degree requirements:* For doctorate, 2 foreign languages, thesis/dissertation, 2 qualifying papers. *Entrance requirements:* For doctorate, GRE General Test. Additional exam requirements/recommendations for international students: Required—TOEFL. Electronic applications accepted. *Faculty research:* Theoretical linguistics, empirical approaches to the study of language, language and cognition.

**Oakland University,** Graduate Study and Lifelong Learning, College of Arts and Sciences, Department of Linguistics, Rochester, MI 48309-4401. Offers linguistics (MA); teaching English as a second language (Certificate). *Program availability:* Part-time,

evening/weekend. *Entrance requirements:* For master's, minimum GPA of 3.0. Additional exam requirements/recommendations for international students: Required—TOEFL (minimum score 550 paper-based).

**The Ohio State University,** Graduate School, College of Arts and Sciences, Division of Arts and Humanities, Department of Linguistics, Columbus, OH 43210. Offers MA, PhD. *Faculty:* 16. *Students:* 34 full-time (12 women), 8 international. Average age 30. In 2016, 3 master's, 3 doctorates awarded. Terminal master's awarded for partial completion of doctoral program. *Degree requirements:* For master's, one foreign language, exam or thesis; for doctorate, 2 foreign languages, thesis/dissertation, exam. *Entrance requirements:* For master's and doctorate, GRE General Test. Additional exam requirements/recommendations for international students: Required—TOEFL (minimum score 600 paper-based; 100 iBT), Michigan English Language Assessment Battery (minimum score 86); Recommended—IELTS (minimum score 8). *Application deadline:* For fall admission, 12/1 priority date for domestic students, 11/30 priority date for international students; for spring admission, 3/1 for domestic students, 2/1 for international students. Applications are processed on a rolling basis. Application fee: $60 ($70 for international students). Electronic applications accepted. *Financial support:* Fellowships with tuition reimbursements, research assistantships with tuition reimbursements, teaching assistantships with tuition reimbursements, Federal Work-Study, and institutionally sponsored loans available. Support available to part-time students. *Faculty research:* Experimental phonetics, nonlinear phonology, process morphology (synchronically and diachronically), syntactic theory, Montague semantics. *Unit head:* Dr. Shari R. Speer, Chair, 617-292-5389, E-mail: speer.21@osu.edu. *Application contact:* Graduate and Professional Admissions, 614-292-9444, Fax: 614-292-3895, E-mail: gpadmissions@osu.edu. Website: http://linguistics.osu.edu/

**The Ohio State University,** Graduate School, College of Arts and Sciences, Division of Arts and Humanities, Department of Slavic and East European Languages and Cultures, Columbus, OH 43210. Offers Slavic linguistics (MA, PhD); Slavic literature, film, and cultural studies (MA, PhD). *Faculty:* 11. *Students:* 14 full-time (10 women), 1 (woman) part-time. Average age 30. In 2016, 2 master's, 2 doctorates awarded. Terminal master's awarded for partial completion of doctoral program. *Degree requirements:* For master's, variable foreign language requirement, thesis optional; for doctorate, variable foreign language requirement, thesis/dissertation. *Entrance requirements:* For master's and doctorate, GRE General Test, at least 3 years of Russian language study or equivalent. Additional exam requirements/recommendations for international students: Required—TOEFL (minimum score 550 paper-based; 79 iBT), Michigan English Language Assessment Battery (minimum score 82); Recommended—IELTS (minimum score 7). *Application deadline:* For fall admission, 12/12 priority date for domestic students, 11/30 priority date for international students; for spring admission, 3/1 for domestic students, 2/1 for international students. Applications are processed on a rolling basis. Application fee: $60 ($70 for international students). Electronic applications accepted. *Financial support:* Fellowships with tuition reimbursements, teaching assistantships with tuition reimbursements, Federal Work-Study, and institutionally sponsored loans available. Support available to part-time students. *Faculty research:* Polish literature. *Unit head:* Dr. Yana Hashamova, Chair and Professor, 614-292-6733, E-mail: hashamova.1@osu.edu. *Application contact:* Graduate and Professional Admissions, 614-292-9444, Fax: 614-292-3895, E-mail: gpadmissions@osu.edu. Website: http://slavic.osu.edu/

**Ohio University,** Graduate College, College of Arts and Sciences, Department of Linguistics, Athens, OH 45701-2979. Offers applied linguistics (MA). *Program availability:* Part-time. *Degree requirements:* For master's, one foreign language, thesis or alternative. *Entrance requirements:* For master's, minimum GPA of 3.0. Additional exam requirements/recommendations for international students: Required—TOEFL (minimum score 600 paper-based; 100 iBT) or IELTS (minimum score 7). *Application deadline:* For fall admission, 2/15 priority date for domestic and international students. Application fee: $50 ($55 for international students). Electronic applications accepted. *Financial support:* Fellowships with tuition reimbursements, research assistantships with tuition reimbursements, teaching assistantships with tuition reimbursements, Federal Work-Study, institutionally sponsored loans, tuition waivers (partial), and unspecified assistantships available. Financial award application deadline: 2/15. *Faculty research:* Syntax, language learning, language teaching, computers for teaching, sociolinguistics. *Unit head:* Dr. Chris Thompson, Chair, 740-593-0666, E-mail: thompsoc@ohio.edu. *Application contact:* Dr. Hiroyuki Oshita, Graduate Chair, 740-593-4570, Fax: 740-593-2967, E-mail: oshita@ohio.edu. Website: http://www.ohiou.edu/linguistics/dept/welcome.html

**Old Dominion University,** College of Arts and Letters, Program in Applied Linguistics, Norfolk, VA 23529. Offers sociolinguistics (MA); TESOL (MA). *Program availability:* Part-time. *Faculty:* 4 full-time (all women). *Students:* 5 full-time (3 women), 12 part-time (9 women); includes 2 minority (1 Asian, non-Hispanic/Latino; 1 Two or more races, non-Hispanic/Latino), 1 international. Average age 32. 23 applicants, 91% accepted, 11 enrolled. In 2016, 10 master's awarded. *Degree requirements:* For master's, one foreign language, comprehensive exam, thesis optional, program portfolio. *Entrance requirements:* For master's, GRE General Test, sample of written work; 12 hours in English, 9 on the upper-level; minimum B average; letters of recommendation; resume; essay. Additional exam requirements/recommendations for international students: Required—TOEFL (minimum score 570 paper-based; 88 iBT). *Application deadline:* For fall admission, 3/15 priority date for domestic and international students; for spring admission, 10/1 priority date for domestic and international students. Applications are processed on a rolling basis. Application fee: $50. Electronic applications accepted. *Expenses:* Tuition, state resident: full-time $8604; part-time $478 per credit hour. Tuition, nonresident: full-time $21,510; part-time $1195 per credit hour. *Required fees:* $66 per semester. Tuition and fees vary according to campus/location, program and reciprocity agreements. *Financial support:* In 2016–17, 6 students received support. Career-related internships or fieldwork, institutionally sponsored loans, and unspecified assistantships available. Financial award application deadline: 2/15. *Faculty research:* Discourse analysis, phonology, syntax, second language acquisition, gender, sociolinguistics. *Unit head:* Dr. Bridget Anderson, Graduate Program Director, 757-683-4020, Fax: 757-683-3241, E-mail: linggpd@odu.edu. *Application contact:* Dr. David C. Earnest, Associate Dean, 757-683-6077, Fax: 757-683-5746, E-mail: dearnest@odu.edu. Website: https://www.odu.edu/academics/programs/masters/applied-linguistics

**Penn State University Park,** Graduate School, College of the Liberal Arts, Department of Applied Linguistics, University Park, PA 16802. Offers applied linguistics (PhD); teaching English as a second language (MA). *Unit head:* Dr. Susan Welch, Dean, 814-865-7691, Fax: 814-863-2085. *Application contact:* Lori Hawn, Director, Graduate Student Services, 814-865-1795, Fax: 814-863-4627, E-mail: l-gswww@lists.psu.edu. Website: http://aplng.la.psu.edu/

**Purdue University,** Graduate School, College of Health and Human Sciences, Department of Speech, Language, and Hearing Sciences, West Lafayette, IN 47907. Offers audiology clinic (MS, Au D, PhD); linguistics (MS, PhD); speech and hearing science (MS, PhD); speech-language pathology (MS, PhD). *Accreditation:* ASHA. *Faculty:* 32 full-time (21 women), 9 part-time/adjunct (8 women). *Students:* 106 full-time

(98 women), 7 part-time (6 women); includes 10 minority (1 Black or African American, non-Hispanic/Latino; 4 Asian, non-Hispanic/Latino; 1 Hispanic/Latino; 4 Two or more races, non-Hispanic/Latino), 7 international. Average age 25. 301 applicants, 35% accepted, 48 enrolled. In 2016, 31 master's, 5 doctorates awarded. *Degree requirements:* For master's, comprehensive exam (for some programs), thesis optional; for doctorate, comprehensive exam, thesis/dissertation. *Entrance requirements:* For master's and doctorate, GRE General Test, minimum undergraduate GPA of 3.0 or equivalent. Additional exam requirements/recommendations for international students: Required—TOEFL (minimum score 77 iBT). *Application deadline:* For fall admission, 1/1 priority date for domestic and international students; for spring admission, 8/1 priority date for domestic and international students. Applications are processed on a rolling basis. Application fee: $60 ($75 for international students). Electronic applications accepted. *Financial support:* Fellowships with full tuition reimbursements, research assistantships with full tuition reimbursements, teaching assistantships with full tuition reimbursements, career-related internships or fieldwork, and scholarships/grants available. Support available to part-time students. Financial award application deadline: 2/1; financial award applicants required to submit FAFSA. *Faculty research:* Psychoacoustics, speech perception, speech physiology, stuttering, child language. *Unit head:* Dr. Keith R. Kluender, Head, 765-494-3788, Fax: 765-494-0771, E-mail: kkluender@purdue.edu. *Application contact:* Vickie L. Parker-Black, Graduate Contact, 765-494-3786, Fax: 765-494-0771, E-mail: vpblack@purdue.edu.
Website: http://www.purdue.edu/hhs/slhs/

**Purdue University,** Graduate School, College of Liberal Arts, Department of English, West Lafayette, IN 47907. Offers creative writing (MFA); literature (MA, PhD), including linguistics, literature and philosophy (PhD), rhetoric and composition, theory and cultural studies (PhD). *Program availability:* Part-time. *Faculty:* 57 full-time (26 women), 3 part-time/adjunct (all women). *Students:* 130 full-time (82 women), 50 part-time (28 women); includes 21 minority (6 Black or African American, non-Hispanic/Latino; 5 Asian, non-Hispanic/Latino; 7 Hispanic/Latino; 3 Two or more races, non-Hispanic/Latino), 31 international. Average age 31. 299 applicants, 14% accepted, 29 enrolled. In 2016, 19 master's, 26 doctorates awarded. *Degree requirements:* For master's, one foreign language, comprehensive exam (for some programs), thesis (for some programs); for doctorate, one foreign language, comprehensive exam, thesis/dissertation. *Entrance requirements:* For master's, GRE General Test; GRE Subject Test in English literature (recommended for students applying to literary studies), minimum undergraduate GPA of 3.0 or equivalent; for doctorate, GRE General Test; GRE Subject Test in English literature (recommended for students applying to literary studies), master's degree. Additional exam requirements/recommendations for international students: Required—TOEFL (minimum score 620 paper-based; 77 iBT). *Application deadline:* For fall admission, 1/15 for domestic and international students. Applications are processed on a rolling basis. Application fee: $60 ($75 for international students). Electronic applications accepted. *Financial support:* Fellowships with tuition reimbursements and teaching assistantships with tuition reimbursements available. Support available to part-time students. Financial award application deadline: 1/15; financial award applicants required to submit FAFSA. *Faculty research:* Cultural studies, postmodern narrative, contemporary women writers, composition theory, slave narratives. *Unit head:* Krista L. Ratcliffe, Head, 765-494-6478, E-mail: ratcliffe@purdue.edu. *Application contact:* Jill M. Quirk, Graduate Contact, 765-494-3748, Fax: 765-494-1700, E-mail: griff@purdue.edu.
Website: https://www.cla.purdue.edu/english/

**Purdue University,** Graduate School, College of Liberal Arts, Program in Linguistics, West Lafayette, IN 47907. Offers MS, PhD. *Students:* 12 full-time (9 women), 10 part-time (6 women); includes 3 minority (2 Asian, non-Hispanic/Latino; 1 Two or more races, non-Hispanic/Latino), 5 international. Average age 28. 41 applicants, 17% accepted, 6 enrolled. In 2016, 1 master's, 5 doctorates awarded. *Degree requirements:* For master's, one foreign language, thesis; for doctorate, 3 foreign languages, comprehensive exam, thesis/dissertation. *Entrance requirements:* For master's and doctorate, GRE General Test (minimum score of 500 for verbal and quantitative respectively), minimum undergraduate GPA of 3.4. Additional exam requirements/recommendations for international students: Required—TOEFL (minimum score 620 paper-based; 77 iBT), TWE. *Application deadline:* For fall admission, 1/1 for domestic and international students. Applications are processed on a rolling basis. Application fee: $60 ($75 for international students). Electronic applications accepted. *Financial support:* Fellowships, research assistantships, and teaching assistantships available. Support available to part-time students. Financial award applicants required to submit FAFSA. *Faculty research:* Sign languages, sociolinguistics and African American English, computational linguistics, indigenous languages, theoretical linguistics. *Unit head:* Alejandro Cuza-Blanco, Head, 765-496-1685, E-mail: acuza@purdue.edu. *Application contact:* Elsa Schirmer, Graduate Contact, 765-496-9629, E-mail: eschirme@purdue.edu.
Website: http://www.cla.purdue.edu/linguistics/

**Queens College of the City University of New York,** Arts and Humanities Division, Department of Linguistics and Communication Disorders, Queens, NY 11367-1597. Offers applied linguistics (MA); English language teaching (Advanced Certificate); speech-language pathology (MA); teaching English to speakers of other languages (MS Ed); TESOL (MS Ed); TESOL and bilingual education (MS Ed). *Accreditation:* ASHA. *Program availability:* Part-time. *Faculty:* 22 full-time (16 women), 19 part-time/adjunct (13 women). *Students:* 44 full-time (42 women), 123 part-time (107 women); includes 64 minority (11 Black or African American, non-Hispanic/Latino; 20 Asian, non-Hispanic/Latino; 31 Hispanic/Latino; 2 Two or more races, non-Hispanic/Latino), 4 international. Average age 28. 390 applicants, 25% accepted, 81 enrolled. In 2016, 71 master's, 30 other advanced degrees awarded. *Entrance requirements:* For master's, minimum GPA of 3.0. Additional exam requirements/recommendations for international students: Required—TOEFL, IELTS. *Application deadline:* For fall admission, 4/1 for domestic students. Applications are processed on a rolling basis. Application fee: $125. Electronic applications accepted. *Expenses:* Tuition, state resident: full-time $5065; part-time $425 per credit. Tuition, nonresident: part-time $780 per credit. *Required fees:* $522; $397 per credit. Part-time tuition and fees vary according to course load and program. *Financial support:* Career-related internships or fieldwork available. Financial award application deadline: 4/1; financial award applicants required to submit FAFSA. *Unit head:* Dr. Robert Vago, Chairperson, 718-997-2875, E-mail: robert.vago@qc.cuny.edu.

**Rice University,** Graduate Programs, School of Humanities, Department of Linguistics, Houston, TX 77251-1892. Offers MA, PhD. Terminal master's awarded for partial completion of doctoral program. *Degree requirements:* For master's, one foreign language, thesis; for doctorate, 2 foreign languages, thesis/dissertation, 3 research papers. *Entrance requirements:* For master's and doctorate, GRE General Test, minimum GPA of 3.0. Additional exam requirements/recommendations for international students: Required—TOEFL (minimum score 600 paper-based; 90 iBT). Electronic applications accepted. *Faculty research:* Typology, fieldwork and language description, cognitive grammar, historical linguistics, corpus linguistics.

**Rutgers University–New Brunswick,** Graduate School-New Brunswick, Department of Linguistics, Piscataway, NJ 08854-8097. Offers PhD. *Degree requirements:* For doctorate, thesis/dissertation, 2 qualifying papers. *Entrance requirements:* For

doctorate, GRE General Test, 3 letters of recommendation, writing sample. Additional exam requirements/recommendations for international students: Recommended—TOEFL. Electronic applications accepted. *Faculty research:* Theoretical linguistics, syntax, semantics, phonology, computational linguistics, phoenetics.

**San Diego State University,** Graduate and Research Affairs, College of Arts and Letters, Department of Linguistics and Oriental Languages, San Diego, CA 92182. Offers applied linguistics and English as a second language (CAL); computational linguistics (MA); English as a second language/applied linguistics (MA); general linguistics (MA). *Degree requirements:* For master's, one foreign language, comprehensive exam, thesis optional. *Entrance requirements:* For master's, GRE General Test, 2 letters of recommendation. Additional exam requirements/recommendations for international students: Required—TOEFL (minimum score 570 paper-based). Electronic applications accepted. *Faculty research:* Cross-cultural linguistic studies of semantics.

**San Francisco State University,** Division of Graduate Studies, College of Liberal and Creative Arts, Department of English Language and Literature, Program in Linguistics, San Francisco, CA 94132-1722. Offers MA. *Program availability:* Part-time. *Degree requirements:* For master's, 2 foreign languages, thesis (for some programs). *Application deadline:* Applications are processed on a rolling basis. *Expenses:* Tuition, state resident: full-time $6738. Tuition, nonresident: full-time $15,666. *Required fees:* $1012. Tuition and fees vary according to degree level and program. *Faculty research:* Mental lexicon, endangered languages, language and gender, linguistics, discourse analysis. *Unit head:* Dr. Sugie Goen-Salter, Chair, 415-338-7582, Fax: 415-338-6159, E-mail: sgoen@sfsu.edu. *Application contact:* Prof. Troi Carleton, Graduate Coordinator, 415-338-3156, Fax: 415-338-6159, E-mail: troi@sfsu.edu.
Website: http://english.sfsu.edu/graduate-linguistics

**San Jose State University,** Graduate Studies and Research, College of Humanities and the Arts, San Jose, CA 95192-0001. Offers art (MA, MFA), including art history and visual culture (MA), digital media art (MFA), photography (MFA), pictorial art (MFA), spatial art (MFA); computational linguistics (Certificate); English (MA, MFA), including creative writing (MFA); French (MA); humanities and arts (Certificate); linguistics (MA); music (MA); philosophy (MA); professional and technical communication (Certificate); Spanish (MA); teaching English to speakers of other languages (MA); TESOL (Certificate); theatre arts (MA). Electronic applications accepted.

**Simon Fraser University,** Office of Graduate Studies and Postdoctoral Fellows, Faculty of Arts and Social Sciences, Department of Linguistics, Burnaby, BC V5A 1S6, Canada. Offers MA, PhD. *Faculty:* 17 full-time (9 women). *Students:* 22 full-time (15 women). 66 applicants, 27% accepted, 7 enrolled. In 2016, 4 master's, 2 doctorates awarded. *Degree requirements:* For master's, one foreign language, thesis; for doctorate, 2 foreign languages, thesis/dissertation, qualifying papers. *Entrance requirements:* For master's, minimum GPA of 3.0 (on scale of 4.33) or 3.33 based on last 60 credits of undergraduate courses; for doctorate, minimum GPA of 3.5 (on scale of 4.33). Additional exam requirements/recommendations for international students: Recommended—TOEFL (minimum score 580 paper-based; 93 iBT), IELTS (minimum score 7), TWE (minimum score 5). *Application deadline:* For fall admission, 1/15 for domestic and international students. Application fee: $90 ($125 for international students). Electronic applications accepted. *Financial support:* In 2016–17, 14 students received support, including 9 fellowships (averaging $6,500 per year), teaching assistantships (averaging $5,608 per year); research assistantships and scholarships/grants also available. *Faculty research:* History of linguistics, syntactic theory, relational grammar, experimental phonetics, pragmatics. *Unit head:* Dr. Yue Wang, Graduate Chair, 778-782-6924, E-mail: ling-grad-chair@sfu.ca. *Application contact:* Judi Levang, Graduate Secretary, 778-782-4725, E-mail: linggsec@sfu.ca.
Website: http://www.sfu.ca/linguistics.html

**Southern Illinois University Carbondale,** Graduate School, College of Liberal Arts, Department of Linguistics, Carbondale, IL 62901. Offers linguistics (MA); teaching English to speakers of other languages (MA). *Degree requirements:* For master's, one foreign language. *Entrance requirements:* For master's, minimum GPA of 3.0. Additional exam requirements/recommendations for international students: Required—TOEFL (minimum score 90 iBT). *Faculty research:* Theory and methods, second language acquisition, pidgin and Creole languages, cognitive grammar.

**Stanford University,** School of Humanities and Sciences, Department of Linguistics, Stanford, CA 94305-2004. Offers MA, PhD. *Degree requirements:* For master's, one foreign language, thesis; for doctorate, 2 foreign languages, thesis/dissertation, oral exam, qualifying papers. *Entrance requirements:* For master's and doctorate, GRE General Test. Additional exam requirements/recommendations for international students: Required—TOEFL. Electronic applications accepted. *Expenses: Tuition:* Full-time $47,331. *Required fees:* $609.

**Stony Brook University, State University of New York,** Graduate School, College of Arts and Sciences, Department of Linguistics, Program in Linguistics, Stony Brook, NY 11794. Offers MA, PhD. *Faculty:* 23 full-time (12 women), 8 part-time/adjunct (7 women). *Students:* 39 full-time (24 women); includes 5 minority (1 American Indian or Alaska Native, non-Hispanic/Latino; 2 Asian, non-Hispanic/Latino; 2 Hispanic/Latino), 23 international. Average age 31. 53 applicants, 36% accepted, 9 enrolled. In 2016, 2 master's, 2 doctorates awarded. *Degree requirements:* For doctorate, thesis/dissertation. *Entrance requirements:* For doctorate, GRE. Additional exam requirements/recommendations for international students: Required—TOEFL (minimum score 90 iBT). *Application deadline:* For fall admission, 1/15 for domestic students; for spring admission, 10/1 for domestic students. Application fee: $100. Electronic applications accepted. *Expenses:* Contact institution. *Financial support:* Fellowships, research assistantships, and teaching assistantships available. *Unit head:* Dr. Richard Larson, Chair, 631-632-7776, E-mail: richard.larson@stonybrook.edu. *Application contact:* Michelle Carbone, Coordinator, 631-632-7774, Fax: 631-632-9789, E-mail: michelle.carbone@stonybrook.edu.

**Syracuse University,** College of Arts and Sciences, MA Program in Linguistic Studies, Syracuse, NY 13244. Offers linguistic studies (MA), including information representation and retrieval, language acquisition, language teaching (TESOL), language, culture, and society, linguistic theory, logic and language. *Program availability:* Part-time. *Students:* Average age 25. *Degree requirements:* For master's, comprehensive exam, thesis or alternative. *Entrance requirements:* For master's, GRE General Test, personal statement detailing interest in field of linguistics and possible concentration areas, transcripts, three recommendation letters. Additional exam requirements/recommendations for international students: Required—TOEFL (minimum score 100 iBT). *Application deadline:* For fall admission, 1/15 priority date for domestic and international students. Application fee: $75. Electronic applications accepted. *Expenses: Tuition:* Full-time $25,974; part-time $1443 per credit hour. *Required fees:* $802; $50 per course. Tuition and fees vary according to course load and program. *Financial support:* Fellowships with full tuition reimbursements, teaching assistantships with tuition reimbursements, and scholarships/grants available. Financial award application deadline: 1/1. *Faculty research:* Information representation and retrieval, language acquisition, linguistic theory, logic and language, teaching languages. *Unit head:* Dr. Gerald R. Greenberg, Director, 315-443-1414, E-mail: ggreenbe@syr.edu. *Application*

## Linguistics

*contact:* Amanda Brown, Linguistics Graduate Advisor, 315-443-2244, E-mail: abrown08@syr.edu.
Website: http://lang.syr.edu/academics/Linguistics/MA-Linguistics.html

**Syracuse University,** College of Arts and Sciences, MS Program in Computational Linguistics, Syracuse, NY 13244. Offers MS. Program held jointly with School of Information Studies and the L.C. Smith College of Engineering and Computer Science. *Program availability:* Part-time. *Students:* Average age 27. *Degree requirements:* For master's, thesis or alternative, internship. *Entrance requirements:* For master's, GRE, resume, personal statement, transcripts, three letters of recommendation. Additional exam requirements/recommendations for international students: Required—TOEFL (minimum score 100 iBT). *Application deadline:* For fall admission, 2/1 for domestic students, 2/1 priority date for international students; for summer admission, 2/1 for domestic students, 2/1 priority date for international students. Application fee: $75. Electronic applications accepted. *Expenses: Tuition:* Full-time $25,974; part-time $1443 per credit hour. *Required fees:* $802; $50 per course. Tuition and fees vary according to course load and program. *Financial support:* Fellowships with full tuition reimbursements, research assistantships with tuition reimbursements, teaching assistantships with tuition reimbursements, and scholarships/grants available. Financial award application deadline: 1/1; financial award applicants required to submit FAFSA. *Faculty research:* Human interaction with computers, logic and language, artificial intelligence, theory of classification and subject representation, structured programming and formal methods. *Unit head:* Dr. Jaklin Kornfilt, Professor of Linguistics, 315-443-5375, E-mail: kornfilt@syr.edu.
Website: http://thecollege.syr.edu/

**Teachers College, Columbia University,** Department of Arts and Humanities, New York, NY 10027. Offers applied linguistics (MA, Ed D); art and art education (Ed M, MA, Ed D, Ed DCT); arts administration (MA); bilingual and bicultural education (MA); global competence (Certificate); history and education (Ed D, PhD); music and music education (Ed DCT); philosophy and education (MA, Ed D, PhD); social studies education (Ed M, PhD); teaching English to speakers of other languages (Ed M); teaching of English and English education (Ed M, MA, Ed D, PhD), including English education (Ed M, Ed D, PhD), teaching of English (MA); teaching of social studies (MA); TESOL (MA, Ed D). *Program availability:* Part-time, evening/weekend. *Students:* 429 full-time (329 women), 467 part-time (332 women); includes 268 minority (62 Black or African American, non-Hispanic/Latino; 1 American Indian or Alaska Native, non-Hispanic/Latino; 108 Asian, non-Hispanic/Latino; 76 Hispanic/Latino; 21 Two or more races, non-Hispanic/Latino), 212 international. 1,068 applicants, 53% accepted, 272 enrolled. Terminal master's awarded for partial completion of doctoral program. *Expenses: Tuition:* Full-time $36,288; part-time $1512 per credit. *Required fees:* $438 per semester. One-time fee: $510 full-time. Full-time tuition and fees vary according to course load. *Financial support:* Fellowships, research assistantships, teaching assistantships, career-related internships or fieldwork, Federal Work-Study, institutionally sponsored loans, tuition waivers (full and partial), and unspecified assistantships available. Support available to part-time students. *Unit head:* Prof. William Gaudelli, Department Chair, 212-678-3150, E-mail: wg74@columbia.edu. *Application contact:* David Estrella, Director of Admissions, 212-678-3305, Fax: 212-678-4171, E-mail: estrella@tc.columbia.edu.
Website: http://www.tc.edu/a%26h/

**Texas A&M University–Commerce,** College of Humanities, Social Sciences and Arts, Commerce, TX 75429-3011. Offers applied criminology (MS); applied linguistics (MA, MS); art (MA, MFA); Christianity in history (Graduate Certificate); computational linguistics (Graduate Certificate); creative writing (Graduate Certificate); English (MA, MS, PhD); film studies (Graduate Certificate); history (MA, MS); music (MM); political science (MA, MS); public history (Graduate Certificate); sociology (MS); Spanish (MA); studies in children's and adolescent literature and culture (Graduate Certificate); teaching English to speakers of other languages (Graduate Certificate); theater (MA, MS). *Program availability:* Part-time. *Faculty:* 53 full-time (26 women), 7 part-time/adjunct (2 women). *Students:* 87 full-time (55 women), 528 part-time (362 women); includes 198 minority (86 Black or African American, non-Hispanic/Latino; 2 American Indian or Alaska Native, non-Hispanic/Latino; 8 Asian, non-Hispanic/Latino; 84 Hispanic/Latino; 18 Two or more races, non-Hispanic/Latino), 27 international. Average age 37. 333 applicants, 56% accepted, 149 enrolled. In 2016, 66 master's, 8 doctorates awarded. *Degree requirements:* For master's, one foreign language, comprehensive exam, thesis (for some programs); for doctorate, one foreign language, comprehensive exam, thesis/dissertation, departmental qualifying exam. *Entrance requirements:* For master's and doctorate, GRE General Test. Additional exam requirements/recommendations for international students: Required—TOEFL (minimum score 550 paper-based; 79 iBT), IELTS (minimum score 6). *Application deadline:* Applications are processed on a rolling basis. Application fee: $50. Electronic applications accepted. *Expenses:* Contact institution. *Financial support:* In 2016–17, 255 students received support, including 9 research assistantships with partial tuition reimbursements available (averaging $9,000 per year), 68 teaching assistantships with partial tuition reimbursements available (averaging $9,000 per year); Federal Work-Study, institutionally sponsored loans, scholarships/grants, health care benefits, and unspecified assistantships also available. Financial award application deadline: 5/1; financial award applicants required to submit FAFSA. *Unit head:* Dr. Salvatore Attardo, Dean, 903-886-5166, Fax: 903-886-5774, E-mail: salvatore.attardo@tamuc.edu. *Application contact:* Shelby Miller, Graduate Recruiter, 903-468-8123, Fax: 903-886-5774, E-mail: shelby.miller@tamuc.edu.
Website: http://www.tamuc.edu/academics/graduateSchool/programs/humanitiesSocialScienceArts/default.aspx

**Texas Tech University,** Graduate School, College of Arts and Sciences, Department of Classical and Modern Languages and Literatures, Lubbock, TX 79409. Offers applied linguistics (MA); classics (MA); German (MA); languages and cultures (MA); Romance languages (MA); Spanish (PhD); MBA/MA. *Program availability:* Part-time. *Faculty:* 56 full-time (37 women), 4 part-time/adjunct (2 women). *Students:* 80 full-time (39 women), 13 part-time (9 women); includes 20 minority (19 Hispanic/Latino; 1 Two or more races, non-Hispanic/Latino), 49 international. Average age 32. 68 applicants, 68% accepted, 31 enrolled. In 2016, 30 master's, 4 doctorates awarded. *Degree requirements:* For master's, comprehensive exam, thesis or alternative; for doctorate, comprehensive exam, thesis/dissertation. *Entrance requirements:* Additional exam requirements/recommendations for international students: Required—TOEFL (minimum score 550 paper-based; 79 iBT). *Application deadline:* For fall admission, 6/1 priority date for domestic students, 1/15 priority date for international students; for spring admission, 9/1 priority date for domestic students, 6/15 priority date for international students. Applications are processed on a rolling basis. Application fee: $75. Electronic applications accepted. *Expenses:* $300 per credit hour full-time resident tuition; $708 per credit hour full-time non-resident tuition; $50.50 per credit hour fee plus $608 per term fee. *Financial support:* In 2016–17, 78 students received support, including 60 fellowships (averaging $2,488 per year), 76 teaching assistantships (averaging $13,011 per year); research assistantships, Federal Work-Study, scholarships/grants, and unspecified assistantships also available. Financial award application deadline: 4/15; financial award applicants required to submit FAFSA. *Faculty research:* Literature, comparative literature, linguistics, culture, applied linguistics. *Total annual research*

*expenditures:* $36,152. *Unit head:* Dr. Erin Collopy, Chair and Associate Professor, 806-834-8497, Fax: 806-742-3306, E-mail: erin.collopy@ttu.edu. *Application contact:* Carla Burrus, Senior Advisor, 806-834-3282, Fax: 806-742-3306, E-mail: carla.burrus@ttu.edu.
Website: http://www.depts.ttu.edu/classic_modern/

**Trinity Western University,** School of Graduate Studies, Program in Linguistics, Langley, BC V2Y 1Y1, Canada. Offers MA. *Degree requirements:* For master's, essay (for non-thesis students). *Entrance requirements:* For master's, minimum GPA of 2.7, 3.0 in last two years; 12 seminar hours; linguistic prerequisites; 1 foreign language. Additional exam requirements/recommendations for international students: Required—TOEFL (minimum score 600 paper-based). Electronic applications accepted. *Expenses:* Contact institution. *Faculty research:* Syntax, phonology, tone, historical and comparative, discourse analysis.

**Universidad de las Américas Puebla,** Division of Graduate Studies, School of Humanities, Program in Applied Linguistics, Puebla, Mexico. Offers linguistics (MA). *Program availability:* Part-time, evening/weekend. *Degree requirements:* For master's, one foreign language, thesis. *Entrance requirements:* Additional exam requirements/recommendations for international students: Required—TOEFL. *Faculty research:* English linguistics, teaching English to speakers of other languages.

**Université de Montréal,** Faculty of Arts and Sciences, Department of Linguistics and Translation, Montréal, QC H3C 3J7, Canada. Offers linguistics (MA, PhD); translation (MA, PhD, DESS). *Degree requirements:* For master's, thesis, general exam; for doctorate, thesis/dissertation, general exam. Electronic applications accepted.

**Université de Sherbrooke,** Faculty of Letters and Human Sciences, Department of Letters and Communications, Sherbrooke, QC J1K 2R1, Canada. Offers comparative Canadian literature (MA, PhD); French literature (MA, PhD); linguistics (MA); theatre (MA). *Degree requirements:* For master's, thesis or alternative; for doctorate, thesis/dissertation. *Entrance requirements:* For master's, minimum GPA of 2.8; for doctorate, minimum GPA of 3.0.

**Université du Québec à Chicoutimi,** Graduate Programs, Program in Linguistics, Chicoutimi, QC G7H 2B1, Canada. Offers MA. *Program availability:* Part-time. *Degree requirements:* For master's, thesis. *Entrance requirements:* For master's, appropriate bachelor's degree, proficiency in French.

**Université du Québec à Montréal,** Graduate Programs, Program in Linguistics, Montréal, QC H3C 3P8, Canada. Offers MA, PhD. *Program availability:* Part-time. *Degree requirements:* For master's, thesis optional; for doctorate, thesis/dissertation. *Entrance requirements:* For master's, appropriate bachelor's degree or equivalent, proficiency in French; for doctorate, appropriate master's degree or equivalent, proficiency in French.

**Université Laval,** Faculty of Letters, Department of Languages, Linguistics and Translations, Programs in Linguistics, Québec, QC G1K 7P4, Canada. Offers MA, PhD. Terminal master's awarded for partial completion of doctoral program. *Degree requirements:* For master's, thesis (for some programs); for doctorate, comprehensive exam, thesis/dissertation. *Entrance requirements:* For master's, English test (comprehension of written English), knowledge of French; for doctorate, English exam (comprehension of written English), knowledge of French. Electronic applications accepted.

**University at Buffalo, the State University of New York,** Graduate School, College of Arts and Sciences, Department of Linguistics, Buffalo, NY 14260-1030. Offers interdisciplinary computational linguistics (MS); linguistics (MA, PhD). *Faculty:* 13 full-time (2 women). *Students:* 52 full-time (26 women), 5 part-time (3 women); includes 3 minority (2 American Indian or Alaska Native, non-Hispanic/Latino; 1 Asian, non-Hispanic/Latino), 22 international. Average age 30. 47 applicants, 85% accepted, 8 enrolled. In 2016, 8 master's, 5 doctorates awarded. Terminal master's awarded for partial completion of doctoral program. *Degree requirements:* For master's, exam, project, or thesis; for doctorate, thesis/dissertation, qualifying paper. *Entrance requirements:* For master's and doctorate, GRE General Test. Additional exam requirements/recommendations for international students: Required—TOEFL (minimum score 600 paper-based; 100 iBT). *Application deadline:* For fall admission, 4/1 for domestic students, 3/1 for international students. Application fee: $75. Electronic applications accepted. *Expenses:* $10,870 per academic year full-time resident tuition, $453 per credit hour part-time; $22,210 per academic year full-time non-resident tuition, $925 per credit hour part-time; $1,238.50 fees. *Financial support:* In 2016–17, 27 students received support, including 9 fellowships with full tuition reimbursements available (averaging $6,000 per year), 4 research assistantships with full tuition reimbursements available (averaging $15,226 per year), 23 teaching assistantships with full tuition reimbursements available (averaging $14,110 per year); scholarships/grants also available. Financial award application deadline: 12/15; financial award applicants required to submit FAFSA. *Faculty research:* Typology, psycholinguistics/experimental linguistics, syntax, semantics, language documentation. *Total annual research expenditures:* $319,594. *Unit head:* Dr. Jean-Pierre Koenig, Professor/Chair, 716-645-2177, Fax: 716-645-3825, E-mail: jpkoenig@buffalo.edu. *Application contact:* Jodi L. Reiner, Secretary, 716-645-3794, Fax: 716-645-3825, E-mail: jlreiner@buffalo.edu.
Website: http://www.linguistics.buffalo.edu

**University of Alaska Fairbanks,** College of Liberal Arts, Program in Linguistics, Fairbanks, AK 99775-6280. Offers applied linguistics (MA), including language documentation, second language acquisition teacher education. *Program availability:* Part-time. *Faculty:* 2 full-time (both women). *Students:* 5 full-time (3 women), 21 part-time (17 women); includes 7 minority (all American Indian or Alaska Native, non-Hispanic/Latino), 1 international. Average age 37. 6 applicants, 83% accepted, 4 enrolled. In 2016, 12 master's awarded. *Degree requirements:* For master's, one foreign language, comprehensive exam, oral defense of project or thesis. *Entrance requirements:* For master's, bachelor's degree from accredited institution with minimum cumulative undergraduate and major GPA of 3.0. Additional exam requirements/recommendations for international students: Required—TOEFL (minimum score 550 paper-based; 79 iBT), IELTS (minimum score 6.5). *Application deadline:* For fall admission, 6/1 for domestic students, 3/1 for international students; for spring admission, 10/15 for domestic students, 9/1 for international students. Applications are processed on a rolling basis. Application fee: $60. Electronic applications accepted. *Expenses: Tuition,* state resident: full-time $7992; part-time $444 per credit. *Tuition,* nonresident: full-time $16,326; part-time $907 per credit. *Required fees:* $39 per credit. $322 per semester. Tuition and fees vary according to course level, course load, campus/location, program and reciprocity agreements. *Financial support:* In 2016–17, 3 teaching assistantships with full tuition reimbursements (averaging $5,908 per year) were awarded; fellowships with full tuition reimbursements, research assistantships with full tuition reimbursements, career-related internships or fieldwork, Federal Work-Study, scholarships/grants, health care benefits, and unspecified assistantships also available. Support available to part-time students. Financial award application deadline: 7/1; financial award applicants required to submit FAFSA. *Faculty research:* Second language acquisition/teaching, Inupiaq, Athabaskan languages, language maintenance and shift, phonology, morphology. *Total annual research expenditures:* $23,000. *Unit head:* Dr. Siri Tuttle, Program Head, 907-474-7876, Fax: 907-474-6586, E-mail:

fyling@uaf.edu. *Application contact:* Mary Kreta, Director of Admissions, 907-474-7500, Fax: 907-474-7097, E-mail: admissions@uaf.edu.
Website: http://www.uaf.edu/linguist/

**University of Alberta,** Faculty of Graduate Studies and Research, Department of Linguistics, Edmonton, AB T6G 2E1, Canada. Offers experimental linguistics (M Sc, PhD). *Degree requirements:* For master's, thesis (for some programs); for doctorate, thesis/dissertation. *Entrance requirements:* For master's, BA in linguistics; for doctorate, M Sc or MA in linguistics. Additional exam requirements/recommendations for international students: Required—TOEFL. *Faculty research:* Experimental phonetics, psycholinguistics, phonology, endangered languages, language acquisition.

**University of Alberta,** Faculty of Graduate Studies and Research, Department of Modern Languages and Cultural Studies, Edmonton, AB T6G 2E1, Canada. Offers applied linguistics (Germanic, Romance, Slavic) (MA); French language, literatures and linguistics (PhD); French language, literatures, and linguistics (MA); Germanic languages, literatures and linguistics (PhD); Germanic languages, literatures, and linguistics (MA); Italian studies (MA); Slavic languages and literatures (Russian, Ukrainian) (MA, PhD); Slavic linguistics (Russian, Ukrainian) (MA, PhD); Spanish and Latin American studies (MA, PhD); Ukrainian folklore (MA, PhD). *Program availability:* Part-time. *Degree requirements:* For master's, one foreign language, thesis; for doctorate, 2 foreign languages, comprehensive exam, thesis/dissertation. *Entrance requirements:* For master's and doctorate, 1 language other than English. Additional exam requirements/recommendations for international students: Required—Michigan English Language Assessment Battery or TOEFL (minimum score 550 paper-based). Electronic applications accepted. *Faculty research:* Russian/Ukrainian studies; German studies; contemporary Latin American, French and Francophone studies; Italian studies.

**The University of Arizona,** College of Social and Behavioral Sciences, Department of Linguistics, Tucson, AZ 85721. Offers human language technology (MS); linguistics and anthropology (PhD); Native American linguistics (MA). PhD in linguistics and anthropology offered jointly with Department of Anthropology. Terminal master's awarded for partial completion of doctoral program. *Degree requirements:* For master's, one foreign language, thesis; for doctorate, one foreign language, comprehensive exam, thesis/dissertation. *Entrance requirements:* For master's, GRE General Test, 3 letters of recommendation, writing sample, resume; for doctorate, GRE General Test, 3 letters of recommendation, statement of purpose, writing sample, resume. Additional exam requirements/recommendations for international students: Required—TOEFL (minimum score 550 paper-based; 79 iBT). Electronic applications accepted. *Faculty research:* Semantic, syntactic, morphological, and phonological theories of natural languages; native languages of the American Southwest, psycholinguistics and computational linguistics.

**The University of Arizona,** College of Social and Behavioral Sciences, Program in Human Language Technology, Tucson, AZ 85721. Offers MS. *Entrance requirements:* Additional exam requirements/recommendations for international students: Required—TOEFL (minimum score 550 paper-based; 79 iBT), GRE.

**The University of British Columbia,** Faculty of Arts and Faculty of Graduate Studies, Department of Linguistics, Vancouver, BC V6T 1Z4, Canada. Offers MA, PhD. *Program availability:* Part-time. *Degree requirements:* For master's, one foreign language, thesis optional; for doctorate, 2 foreign languages, thesis/dissertation, 2 qualifying papers. *Entrance requirements:* Additional exam requirements/recommendations for international students: Required—TOEFL. Application fee: $100 Canadian dollars ($162 Canadian dollars for international students). Electronic applications accepted. *Expenses:* $4,802 per year tuition and fees, $8,436 per year international. *Financial support:* Fellowships, research assistantships, teaching assistantships, institutionally sponsored loans, and tuition waivers (full) available. Financial award application deadline: 10/1. *Faculty research:* Linguistic theory (phonology, syntax, semantics), Native American languages, African languages, first language acquisition, experimental phonetics. *Application contact:* Shaine Meghji, Graduate Program Staff, 604-822-0415, Fax: 604-822-9687, E-mail: shaine.meghji@ubc.ca.
Website: http://linguistics.ubc.ca/

**University of Calgary,** Faculty of Graduate Studies, Faculty of Arts, Department of Linguistics, Languages and Culture, Calgary, AB T2N 1N4, Canada. Offers German (MA); linguistics (MA, PhD). *Degree requirements:* For master's, one foreign language, thesis; for doctorate, one foreign language, comprehensive exam, thesis/dissertation. *Entrance requirements:* For doctorate, MA. Additional exam requirements/recommendations for international students: Required—TOEFL (minimum score 560 paper-based). Electronic applications accepted. *Faculty research:* Theoretical linguistics, historical linguistics, language acquisition, Amerindian.

**University of California, Berkeley,** Graduate Division, College of Letters and Science, Department of Linguistics, Berkeley, CA 94720-1500. Offers PhD. *Students:* 32 full-time (17 women); includes 6 minority (1 American Indian or Alaska Native, non-Hispanic/Latino; 3 Asian, non-Hispanic/Latino; 2 Hispanic/Latino), 4 international. Average age 29. 155 applicants, 6 enrolled. In 2016, 7 doctorates awarded. *Degree requirements:* For doctorate, thesis/dissertation, qualifying exam. *Entrance requirements:* For doctorate, GRE General Test, minimum GPA of 3.0, 3 letters of recommendation. Additional exam requirements/recommendations for international students: Required—TOEFL (minimum score 570 paper-based; 90 iBT). *Application deadline:* For fall admission, 12/6 for domestic students. Application fee: $105 ($125 for international students). Electronic applications accepted. *Financial support:* Fellowships, research assistantships, teaching assistantships, institutionally sponsored loans, health care benefits, and unspecified assistantships available. *Unit head:* Prof. Andrew Garrett, Chair, 510-643-7224, E-mail: linginfo@berkeley.edu. *Application contact:* Belén Flores, Student Affairs Officer, 510-643-7224, Fax: 510-643-5688, E-mail: linginfo@berkeley.edu.
Website: http://www.linguistics.berkeley.edu/

**University of California, Davis,** Graduate Studies, Graduate Group in Linguistics, Davis, CA 95616. Offers applied linguistics (MA, PhD); linguistics (MA). *Degree requirements:* For master's, one foreign language, comprehensive exam (for some programs), thesis (for some programs); for doctorate, thesis/dissertation. *Entrance requirements:* For master's and doctorate, GRE General Test, minimum GPA of 3.0. Additional exam requirements/recommendations for international students: Required—TOEFL (minimum score 550 paper-based). Electronic applications accepted. *Faculty research:* Grammatical analysis and theory, sociolinguistics, historical linguistics, Romance linguistics, neurolinguistics.

**University of California, Los Angeles,** Graduate Division, College of Letters and Science, Department of Applied Linguistics and Teaching English as a Second Language, Program in Applied Linguistics, Los Angeles, CA 90095. Offers MA, PhD. *Degree requirements:* For master's, one foreign language, thesis; for doctorate, one foreign language, thesis/dissertation, oral and written qualifying exams. *Entrance requirements:* For master's and doctorate, bachelor's degree; minimum undergraduate GPA of 3.0 (or its equivalent if letter grade system not used); research paper. Additional exam requirements/recommendations for international students: Required—TOEFL. Electronic applications accepted.

**University of California, Los Angeles,** Graduate Division, College of Letters and Science, Department of Linguistics, Los Angeles, CA 90095. Offers MA, PhD. Terminal

master's awarded for partial completion of doctoral program. *Degree requirements:* For master's, one foreign language, comprehensive exam or thesis; for doctorate, thesis/dissertation, oral and written qualifying exams. *Entrance requirements:* For doctorate, bachelor's degree; minimum undergraduate GPA of 3.0 (or its equivalent if letter grade system not used); writing sample. Additional exam requirements/recommendations for international students: Required—TOEFL. Electronic applications accepted.

**University of California, San Diego,** Graduate Division, Department of Linguistics, La Jolla, CA 92093. Offers PhD. *Students:* 20 full-time (12 women), 1 (woman) part-time. 85 applicants, 20% accepted, 5 enrolled. In 2016, 7 doctorates awarded. *Degree requirements:* For doctorate, one foreign language, comprehensive exam, thesis/dissertation, apprentice teaching. *Entrance requirements:* For doctorate, GRE General Test, writing samples, letters of recommendation. Additional exam requirements/recommendations for international students: Required—TOEFL (minimum score 550 paper-based; 80 iBT), IELTS (minimum score 7). *Application deadline:* For fall admission, 11/30 for domestic students. Application fee: $105 ($125 for international students). Electronic applications accepted. *Expenses:* Tuition, state resident: full-time $11,220. Tuition, nonresident: full-time $26,322. *Required fees:* $1864. *Financial support:* Fellowships and teaching assistantships available. Financial award applicants required to submit FAFSA. *Faculty research:* Computational linguistics, computational psycholinguistics, experimental syntax, language acquisition and sign languages, language and the brain, speech production and perception. *Unit head:* Sharon Rose, Chair, 858-534-1159, E-mail: sxrose@ucsd.edu. *Application contact:* Alycia Randol, Graduate Coordinator, 858-534-1145, E-mail: arandol@ucsd.edu.
Website: http://ling.ucsd.edu

**University of California, Santa Barbara,** Graduate Division, College of Letters and Sciences, Division of Humanities and Fine Arts, Department of East Asian Languages and Cultural Studies, Santa Barbara, CA 93106-7075. Offers applied linguistics (PhD); East Asian languages and cultural studies (MA); translation studies (PhD). *Degree requirements:* For master's, one foreign language, comprehensive exam (for some programs), thesis (for some programs); for doctorate, 2 foreign languages, thesis/dissertation, methodology. *Entrance requirements:* For master's and doctorate, GRE General Test. Additional exam requirements/recommendations for international students: Required—TOEFL (minimum score 550 paper-based; 80 iBT), IELTS (minimum score 7). Electronic applications accepted. *Faculty research:* Chinese literature, Chinese film, Japanese society, Japanese literature, East Asian cultural studies.

**University of California, Santa Barbara,** Graduate Division, College of Letters and Sciences, Division of Humanities and Fine Arts, Department of Linguistics, Santa Barbara, CA 93106-9580. Offers PhD, MA/PhD. Terminal master's awarded for partial completion of doctoral program. *Degree requirements:* For doctorate, one foreign language, comprehensive exam, thesis/dissertation, qualifying paper. *Entrance requirements:* For doctorate, GRE. Additional exam requirements/recommendations for international students: Required—TOEFL (minimum score 550 paper-based; 80 iBT), IELTS (minimum score 7). Electronic applications accepted. *Faculty research:* Language documentation, discourse, typology, language and cognition, sociocultural linguistics.

**University of California, Santa Barbara,** Graduate Division, College of Letters and Sciences, Division of Humanities and Fine Arts, Department of Spanish and Portuguese, Santa Barbara, CA 93106-4150. Offers Hispanic languages and literatures (PhD), including European medieval studies, feminist studies, Hispanic linguistics, Hispanic literature, Luso-Brazilian literature; Hispanic linguistics (MA); Luso-Brazilian literature (MA); Spanish or Spanish-American literature (MA); MA/PhD. Terminal master's awarded for partial completion of doctoral program. *Degree requirements:* For master's, 2 foreign languages, comprehensive exam (for some programs), thesis optional; for doctorate, 3 foreign languages, comprehensive exam, thesis/dissertation. *Entrance requirements:* For master's and doctorate, GRE. Additional exam requirements/recommendations for international students: Required—TOEFL (minimum score 550 paper-based; 80 iBT), IELTS (minimum score 7). Electronic applications accepted. *Faculty research:* Nineteenth-century Spanish and Portuguese literature, Spanish and Spanish-American literature, nineteenth- and twentieth-century Portuguese and Brazilian literatures, Hispanic linguistics, Catalan language and culture.

**University of California, Santa Cruz,** Division of Graduate Studies, Division of Humanities, Department of Linguistics, Santa Cruz, CA 95064. Offers MA, PhD. Terminal master's awarded for partial completion of doctoral program. *Degree requirements:* For master's, one foreign language, research paper; for doctorate, one foreign language, thesis/dissertation, qualifying exam. *Entrance requirements:* For master's and doctorate, GRE General Test. Additional exam requirements/recommendations for international students: Required—TOEFL (minimum score 550 paper-based; 83 iBT); Recommended—IELTS (minimum score 8). Electronic applications accepted. *Faculty research:* Theoretical and descriptive linguistics: syntax, semantics and phonology.

**University of Chicago,** Division of the Humanities, Department of Linguistics, Chicago, IL 60637. Offers anthropology and linguistics (PhD); linguistics (PhD). *Students:* 46 full-time (22 women); includes 11 minority (1 Black or African American, non-Hispanic/Latino; 1 American Indian or Alaska Native, non-Hispanic/Latino; 4 Asian, non-Hispanic/Latino; 5 Hispanic/Latino), 13 international. 103 applicants, 13% accepted, 9 enrolled. In 2016, 4 doctorates awarded. Terminal master's awarded for partial completion of doctoral program. *Degree requirements:* For doctorate, 3 foreign languages, thesis/dissertation. *Entrance requirements:* For doctorate, GRE General Test. Additional exam requirements/recommendations for international students: Required—TOEFL (minimum score 104 iBT), IELTS (minimum score 7). *Application deadline:* For fall admission, 12/15 for domestic and international students. Application fee: $90. Electronic applications accepted. *Financial support:* Fellowships with full tuition reimbursements, teaching assistantships with full tuition reimbursements, Federal Work-Study, institutionally sponsored loans, scholarships/grants, and health care benefits available. Financial award application deadline: 12/15; financial award applicants required to submit FAFSA. *Unit head:* Dr. Lenore Grenoble, Chair, 773-702-0927, E-mail: grenoble@uchicago.edu. *Application contact:* Michael Beetley, Assistant Dean of Students, Admissions and Fellowships, 773-702-1552, Fax: 773-834-9148, E-mail: humanitiesadmissions@uchicago.edu.
Website: http://linguistics.uchicago.edu/

**University of Chicago,** Division of the Humanities, Master of Arts Program in the Humanities, Chicago, IL 60637. Offers art history (MA); cinema and media studies (MA); classic languages (MA); comparative literature (MA); creative writing (MA); cultural policy studies (MA); digital humanities (MA); East Asian languages and civilizations (MA); English language and literature (MA); gender and sexuality studies (MA); Germanic studies (MA); linguistics (MA); music (MA); near Eastern languages and civilizations (MA); philosophy (MA); poetics (MA); race, politics and culture (MA); Romance languages and literatures (MA); Slavic languages and literatures (MA); South Asian languages and civilizations (MA); theater and performance studies (MA). *Students:* 80 full-time (43 women), 7 part-time (3 women); includes 20 minority (5 Black or African American, non-Hispanic/Latino; 1 American Indian or Alaska Native, non-Hispanic/Latino; 6 Asian, non-Hispanic/Latino; 5 Hispanic/Latino; 3 Two or more races,

## Linguistics

non-Hispanic/Latino), 11 international. Average age 26. 706 applicants, 15% accepted, 42 enrolled. In 2016, 92 master's awarded. *Degree requirements:* For master's, thesis. *Entrance requirements:* For master's, GRE General Test. Additional exam requirements/recommendations for international students: Required—TOEFL (minimum score 104 iBT), IELTS (minimum score 7). *Application deadline:* For fall admission, 1/3 for domestic and international students. Application fee: $90. Electronic applications accepted. *Financial support:* In 2016–17, 8 fellowships with partial tuition reimbursements (averaging $12,000 per year) were awarded; Federal Work-Study, institutionally sponsored loans, scholarships/grants, and tuition waivers (partial) are available. Financial award application deadline: 12/15; financial award applicants required to submit FAFSA. *Unit head:* Malynne Sternstein, Co-Director, 773-834-1201, Fax: 773-834-7526. *Application contact:* Program Coordinator, 773-834-1201, Fax: 773-834-7526, E-mail: ma-humanities@uchicago.edu.
Website: http://maph.uchicago.edu/

**University of Colorado Boulder,** Graduate School, College of Arts and Sciences, Department of Linguistics, Boulder, CO 80309. Offers MA, PhD. *Faculty:* 10 full-time (6 women). *Students:* 50 full-time (35 women), 9 part-time (5 women); includes 9 minority (4 Asian, non-Hispanic/Latino; 3 Hispanic/Latino; 2 Two or more races, non-Hispanic/Latino), 15 international. Average age 29. 104 applicants, 37% accepted, 14 enrolled. In 2016, 27 master's, 3 doctorates awarded. Terminal master's awarded for partial completion of doctoral program. *Degree requirements:* For master's, comprehensive exam, thesis optional; for doctorate, one foreign language, thesis/dissertation. *Entrance requirements:* For master's, GRE General Test, minimum undergraduate GPA of 2.75; for doctorate, GRE General Test. *Application deadline:* For fall admission, 1/2 for domestic students, 12/1 for international students. Applications are processed on a rolling basis. Application fee: $60 ($80 for international students). Electronic applications accepted. Application fee is waived when completed online. *Financial support:* In 2016–17, 94 students received support, including 21 fellowships (averaging $2,395 per year), 4 research assistantships with full and partial tuition reimbursements available (averaging $28,206 per year), 23 teaching assistantships with full and partial tuition reimbursements available (averaging $29,250 per year); institutionally sponsored loans, scholarships/grants, health care benefits, and unspecified assistantships also available. Financial award application deadline: 1/15; financial award applicants required to submit FAFSA. *Faculty research:* Linguistics/philology, phonology, semantics, syntax, artificial intelligence/cybernetics. *Total annual research expenditures:* $739,711. *Application contact:* E-mail: linguist@colorado.edu.
Website: http://www.colorado.edu/linguistics/

**University of Colorado Denver,** College of Liberal Arts and Sciences, Department of English, Denver, CO 80217. Offers applied linguistics (MA); literature (MA); rhetoric and teaching of writing (MA). *Program availability:* Part-time, evening/weekend. *Faculty:* 22 full-time (13 women). *Students:* 18 full-time (12 women), 13 part-time (10 women); includes 3 minority (1 Black or African American, non-Hispanic/Latino; 2 Hispanic/Latino). Average age 31. 19 applicants, 68% accepted, 6 enrolled. In 2016, 10 master's awarded. *Degree requirements:* For master's, variable foreign language requirement, comprehensive exam (for some programs), thesis (for some programs), minimum of 33 credit hours (for literature program), 30 (for rhetoric and teaching of writing and applied linguistics programs). *Entrance requirements:* For master's, GRE General Test, minimum GPA of 3.0 in undergraduate courses, critical writing sample, letters of recommendation, completion of 24 semester hours in English courses (at least 16 at the upper-division level), statement of purpose. Additional exam requirements/recommendations for international students: Required—TOEFL (minimum score 537 paper-based; 75 iBT); Recommended—IELTS (minimum score 6.5). *Application deadline:* For fall admission, 4/1 for domestic and international students; for spring admission, 10/1 for domestic and international students; for summer admission, 4/1 for domestic and international students. Application fee: $50 ($75 for international students). Electronic applications accepted. *Expenses:* Tuition, state resident: full-time $11,006; part-time $474 per credit. Tuition, nonresident: full-time $28,212; part-time $1264 per credit hour. *Required fees:* $256 per semester. One-time fee: $94.32. Tuition and fees vary according to campus/location and program. *Financial support:* In 2016–17, 9 students received support. Fellowships, research assistantships, teaching assistantships, Federal Work-Study, institutionally sponsored loans, scholarships/grants, traineeships, and unspecified assistantships available. Financial award application deadline: 4/1; financial award applicants required to submit FAFSA. *Faculty research:* Literature, rhetoric, teaching of writing, applied linguistics. *Unit head:* Prof. Nancy Ciccone, Chair, 303-556-8395, E-mail: nancy.ciccone@ucdenver.edu. *Application contact:* Francine Olivas-Zarate, English Department, 303-556-2584, Fax: 303-556-2959.
Website: http://www.ucdenver.edu/academics/colleges/CLAS/Departments/english/Programs/Masters/Pages/Overview.aspx

**University of Connecticut,** Graduate School, College of Liberal Arts and Sciences, Department of Linguistics, Storrs, CT 06269. Offers MA, PhD. *Degree requirements:* For doctorate, thesis/dissertation. *Entrance requirements:* For doctorate, GRE General Test. Additional exam requirements/recommendations for international students: Required—TOEFL (minimum score 550 paper-based). Electronic applications accepted.

**University of Delaware,** College of Arts and Sciences, Department of Linguistics and Cognitive Science, Newark, DE 19716. Offers linguistics (PhD); linguistics and cognitive science (MA). *Degree requirements:* For doctorate, one foreign language, comprehensive exam, thesis/dissertation, publishable research papers. *Entrance requirements:* For master's, GRE General Test; for doctorate, GRE General Test, writing sample. Additional exam requirements/recommendations for international students: Required—TOEFL (minimum score 600 paper-based). Electronic applications accepted. *Faculty research:* East Asian, Austronesian and Romance languages, phonology, phonetics, syntax, cognitive science, semantics, psycholinguistics, language acquisition, endangered languages.

**University of Florida,** Graduate School, College of Liberal Arts and Sciences, Department of Linguistics, Gainesville, FL 32611. Offers linguistics (MA, PhD); teaching English as a second language (Certificate). *Program availability:* Part-time. Terminal master's awarded for partial completion of doctoral program. *Degree requirements:* For master's, one foreign language, comprehensive exam, thesis (for some programs); for doctorate, 2 foreign languages, comprehensive exam, thesis/dissertation. *Entrance requirements:* For master's and doctorate, GRE General Test, minimum GPA of 3.0. Additional exam requirements/recommendations for international students: Required—TOEFL (minimum score 550 paper-based; 80 iBT), IELTS (minimum score 6). Electronic applications accepted. *Faculty research:* Language documentation, psycholinguistics and neuro-linguistics, theoretical linguistics, sociolinguistics second language acquisition.

**University of Georgia,** Franklin College of Arts and Sciences, Program in Linguistics, Athens, GA 30602. Offers MA, PhD. *Degree requirements:* For master's, one foreign language, thesis; for doctorate, 2 foreign languages, comprehensive exam, thesis/dissertation. *Entrance requirements:* For master's and doctorate, GRE General Test. *Application deadline:* For fall admission, 7/1 priority date for domestic students; for spring admission, 11/15 for domestic students. Application fee: $50. Electronic applications accepted. *Expenses:* Contact institution. *Financial support:* Fellowships,

research assistantships, teaching assistantships, Federal Work-Study, and institutionally sponsored loans available. Financial award application deadline: 2/15. *Faculty research:* Applied linguistics, English linguistics, dialectology, lexicography, discourse analysis. *Unit head:* Dr. Jared Stephen Klein, Director, 706-542-9261, Fax: 706-542-2897, E-mail: jklein@uga.edu. *Application contact:* Dr. Jonathan Evans, Graduate Coordinator, 706-542-5099, E-mail: jdmevans@uga.edu.
Website: http://www.uga.edu/linguistics

**University of Hawaii at Manoa,** Graduate Division, College of Languages, Linguistics and Literature, Department of Linguistics, Honolulu, HI 96822. Offers MA, PhD. *Program availability:* Part-time. Terminal master's awarded for partial completion of doctoral program. *Degree requirements:* For master's, 2 foreign languages, thesis optional; for doctorate, 2 foreign languages, comprehensive exam, thesis/dissertation. *Entrance requirements:* For master's and doctorate, GRE General Test. Additional exam requirements/recommendations for international students: Required—TOEFL (minimum score 600 paper-based; 100 iBT), IELTS (minimum score 7). *Faculty research:* Languages of the Pacific and Asia.

**University of Houston,** College of Liberal Arts and Social Sciences, Department of English, Houston, TX 77204. Offers applied English linguistics (MA); creative writing (MFA); creative writing and literature (MA, PhD); English (MA, PhD). *Degree requirements:* For master's, one foreign language, comprehensive exam (for some programs), thesis (MFA); for doctorate, 2 foreign languages, comprehensive exam, thesis/dissertation. *Entrance requirements:* For master's, GRE General Test, minimum GPA of 3.0 in last 60 hours of course work; for doctorate, GRE General Test, GRE Subject Test (literature), writing sample. Additional exam requirements/recommendations for international students: Required—TOEFL (minimum score 550 paper-based; 79 iBT). Electronic applications accepted.

**University of Illinois at Chicago,** College of Liberal Arts and Sciences, School of Literatures, Cultural Studies and Linguistics, Department of Linguistics, Chicago, IL 60607-7128. Offers MA. *Program availability:* Part-time. *Degree requirements:* For master's, one foreign language, comprehensive exam, thesis (for some programs). *Entrance requirements:* For master's, minimum GPA of 3.0. Additional exam requirements/recommendations for international students: Required—TOEFL. Electronic applications accepted. *Faculty research:* Second language acquisition, methodology of second language teaching, lexicography, language, sex and gender.

**University of Illinois at Urbana–Champaign,** Graduate College, College of Liberal Arts and Sciences, School of Literatures, Cultures and Linguistics, Department of Linguistics, Champaign, IL 61820. Offers linguistics (MA, PhD); teaching of English as a second language (MA).

**University of Illinois at Urbana–Champaign,** Graduate College, College of Liberal Arts and Sciences, School of Literatures, Cultures and Linguistics, Program in Romance Linguistics, Champaign, IL 61820. Offers PhD.

**The University of Iowa,** Graduate College, College of Liberal Arts and Sciences, Department of Linguistics, Iowa City, IA 52242-1316. Offers MA, PhD. *Degree requirements:* For master's, thesis optional, exam; for doctorate, comprehensive exam, thesis/dissertation. *Entrance requirements:* For master's and doctorate, GRE General Test, minimum GPA of 3.0. Additional exam requirements/recommendations for international students: Required—TOEFL (minimum score 550 paper-based; 81 iBT). Electronic applications accepted.

**The University of Kansas,** Graduate Studies, College of Liberal Arts and Sciences, Department of Linguistics, Lawrence, KS 66045. Offers MA, PhD. *Students:* 28 full-time (15 women); includes 1 minority (Asian, non-Hispanic/Latino), 14 international. Average age 27. 65 applicants, 29% accepted, 8 enrolled. In 2016, 3 master's, 3 doctorates awarded. Terminal master's awarded for partial completion of doctoral program. *Entrance requirements:* For master's and doctorate, GRE General Test, curriculum vitae, statement of purpose, 3 letters of recommendation. Additional exam requirements/recommendations for international students: Required—TOEFL. *Application deadline:* For fall admission, 1/1 for domestic and international students. Application fee: $65 ($85 for international students). Electronic applications accepted. *Financial support:* Fellowships, research assistantships, teaching assistantships, scholarships/grants, and unspecified assistantships available. Financial award application deadline: 1/1. *Faculty research:* Phonetics and phonology, syntax and semantics, psycholinguistics, neurolinguistics, first and second language acquisition. *Unit head:* Joan A. Sereno, Chair, 785-864-2619, E-mail: sereno@ku.edu. *Application contact:* Corinna Johnson, Office Manager, 785-864-3450, E-mail: cljohns@ku.edu.
Website: http://www.linguistics.ku.edu/

**University of Louisville,** Graduate School, College of Arts and Sciences, Department of Comparative Humanities, Louisville, KY 40292-0001. Offers civic leadership (MA); culture, criticism, and contemporary thought (PhD); linguistics (MA); public arts and letters (PhD); traditional humanities (MA); MA/JD; MA/MBA. *Program availability:* Part-time. *Faculty:* 15 full-time (6 women), 2 part-time/adjunct (both women). *Students:* 49 full-time (32 women), 21 part-time (12 women); includes 11 minority (3 Black or African American, non-Hispanic/Latino; 2 Asian, non-Hispanic/Latino; 1 Hispanic/Latino; 5 Two or more races, non-Hispanic/Latino), 4 international. Average age 38. 21 applicants, 71% accepted, 10 enrolled. In 2016, 3 master's, 2 doctorates awarded. *Degree requirements:* For master's, one foreign language, thesis or alternative, directed study culminating project; for doctorate, 2 foreign languages, comprehensive exam, thesis/dissertation, internship. *Entrance requirements:* For master's, GRE General Test, two letters of recommendation, transcripts from all institutions attended; for doctorate, GRE General Test, three letters of recommendation, statement of intent, scholarly writing sample, transcripts from all institutions attended. Additional exam requirements/recommendations for international students: Recommended—TOEFL. *Application deadline:* For fall admission, 1/15 for domestic and international students. Application fee: $60. Electronic applications accepted. *Expenses:* Contact institution. *Financial support:* In 2016–17, 1 fellowship with full tuition reimbursement (averaging $18,000 per year), 10 teaching assistantships with full tuition reimbursements (averaging $18,000 per year) were awarded. Financial award application deadline: 1/15. *Faculty research:* Literary studies, medieval studies;, religious studies, linguistics, translation studies. *Total annual research expenditures:* $7,733. *Unit head:* Dr. Ann Hall, Chair, 502-852-6805, Fax: 502-852-0078, E-mail: ann.hall@louisville.edu. *Application contact:* Libby Leggett, Director, Graduate Admissions, 502-852-3101, Fax: 502-852-6536, E-mail: gradadm@louisville.edu.
Website: http://louisville.edu/humanities/

**The University of Manchester,** School of Languages, Linguistics and Cultures, Manchester, United Kingdom. Offers Arab world studies (PhD); Chinese studies (M Phil, PhD); East Asian studies (M Phil, PhD); English language (PhD); French studies (M Phil, PhD); German studies (M Phil, PhD); interpreting studies (PhD); Italian studies (M Phil, PhD); Japanese studies (M Phil, PhD); Latin American cultural studies (M Phil, PhD); linguistics (M Phil, PhD); Middle Eastern studies (M Phil, PhD); Polish studies (M Phil, PhD); Portuguese studies (M Phil, PhD); Russian studies (M Phil, PhD); Spanish studies (M Phil, PhD); translation and intercultural studies (M Phil, PhD).

**University of Manitoba,** Faculty of Graduate Studies, Faculty of Arts, Department of Linguistics, Winnipeg, MB R3T 2N2, Canada. Offers MA, PhD.

**University of Maryland, Baltimore County,** The Graduate School, College of Arts, Humanities and Social Sciences, Department of Modern Languages and Linguistics, Program in Intercultural Communication, Baltimore, MD 21250. Offers MA. *Program availability:* Part-time, evening/weekend. *Faculty:* 16 full-time (9 women). *Students:* 12 full-time (5 women), 2 part-time (both women); includes 2 minority (1 Black or African American, non-Hispanic/Latino; 1 Hispanic/Latino), 6 international. Average age 27. 15 applicants, 80% accepted, 8 enrolled. In 2016, 8 master's awarded. *Degree requirements:* For master's, one foreign language, comprehensive exam (for some programs), thesis (for some programs). *Entrance requirements:* For master's, GRE General Test, minimum GPA of 3.0, 3 letters of recommendation, self-evaluation and statement of support, resume, writing sample in modern language. Additional exam requirements/recommendations for international students: Required—TOEFL (minimum score 550 paper-based, 80 iBT) or IELTS. *Application deadline:* For fall admission, 1/31 for domestic and international students. Application fee: $50. Electronic applications accepted. *Expenses:* Tuition, state resident: full-time $13,294. Tuition, nonresident: full-time $20,286. *Financial support:* In 2016–17, 7 students received support, including 5 teaching assistantships with full tuition reimbursements available (averaging $12,560 per year); Federal Work-Study, scholarships/grants, health care benefits, and tuition waivers (full) also available. Financial award application deadline: 1/31; financial award applicants required to submit FAFSA. *Faculty research:* Comparative television research-cross-cultural; cultural studies; social developments in Latin America; intercultural communication; French civilization and cultural studies; language, gender and sexuality; sociolinguistics; African linguistics; immigrants in U.S. and Latin American societies. *Unit head:* Dr. Edward Larkey, Interim Director, 410-455-2104, Fax: 410-455-1025, E-mail: larkey@umbc.edu.
Website: http://www.umbc.edu/mll/incc/

**University of Maryland, College Park,** Academic Affairs, College of Arts and Humanities, Department of Linguistics, College Park, MD 20742. Offers MA, PhD. *Degree requirements:* For master's, thesis or alternative; for doctorate, thesis/dissertation. *Entrance requirements:* For master's, GRE General Test, minimum GPA of 3.0, sample of work, 3 letters of recommendation; for doctorate, GRE General Test, minimum GPA of 3.0, sample of work. Additional exam requirements/recommendations for international students: Required—TOEFL. Electronic applications accepted. *Faculty research:* Psycholinguistics, computational linguistics.

**University of Massachusetts Amherst,** Graduate School, College of Humanities and Fine Arts, Department of Linguistics, Amherst, MA 01003. Offers MA, PhD. *Program availability:* Part-time. *Degree requirements:* For master's, thesis or alternative; for doctorate, comprehensive exam, thesis/dissertation. *Entrance requirements:* For doctorate, GRE General Test, writing sample. Additional exam requirements/recommendations for international students: Required—TOEFL (minimum score 550 paper-based; 80 iBT), IELTS (minimum score 6.5). Electronic applications accepted.

**University of Massachusetts Boston,** College of Liberal Arts, Program in Applied Linguistics, Boston, MA 02125-3393. Offers applied linguistics (PhD). *Program availability:* Part-time, evening/weekend. *Faculty:* 9 full-time (6 women), 6 part-time/adjunct (all women). *Students:* 15 full-time (14 women), 135 part-time (91 women); includes 36 minority (10 Black or African American, non-Hispanic/Latino; 1 American Indian or Alaska Native, non-Hispanic/Latino; 7 Asian, non-Hispanic/Latino; 11 Hispanic/Latino; 7 Two or more races, non-Hispanic/Latino), 7 international. Average age 35. 63 applicants, 68% accepted, 35 enrolled. In 2016, 48 master's awarded. *Degree requirements:* For master's, one foreign language, comprehensive exam. *Entrance requirements:* For master's, minimum GPA of 2.75. *Application deadline:* For fall admission, 2/1 for domestic students; for spring admission, 10/15 for domestic students. *Expenses:* Tuition, state resident: full-time $16,863. Tuition, nonresident: full-time $32,913. *Required fees:* $177. *Financial support:* Research assistantships with full tuition reimbursements, teaching assistantships with full tuition reimbursements, career-related internships or fieldwork, Federal Work-Study, and unspecified assistantships available. Support available to part-time students. Financial award application deadline: 3/1; financial award applicants required to submit FAFSA. *Faculty research:* Multicultural theory and curriculum development, foreign language pedagogy, language and culture, applied psycholinguistics, bilingual education. *Unit head:* Dr. Donaldo Macedo, Director, 617-287-5760, E-mail: donalde.macedo@umb.edu. *Application contact:* Peggy Roldan Patel, Graduate Admissions Coordinator, 617-287-6400, Fax: 617-287-6236, E-mail: bos.gadm@dpc.umassp.edu.

**University of Memphis,** Graduate School, College of Arts and Sciences, Department of English, Memphis, TN 38152. Offers African-American literature (Graduate Certificate); applied linguistics (PhD); composition studies (PhD); creative writing (MFA); English as a second language (MA); linguistics (MA); literary and cultural studies (PhD), including African-American literature; literature (MA); professional writing (MA, PhD); teaching English as a second/foreign language (Graduate Certificate). *Program availability:* Part-time, evening/weekend, 100% online. *Faculty:* 31 full-time (14 women), 1 (woman) part-time/adjunct. *Students:* 86 full-time (44 women), 78 part-time (51 women); includes 36 minority (19 Black or African American, non-Hispanic/Latino; 3 Asian, non-Hispanic/Latino; 10 Hispanic/Latino; 4 Two or more races, non-Hispanic/Latino), 32 international. Average age 35. 68 applicants, 87% accepted, 33 enrolled. In 2016, 39 master's, 17 doctorates, 16 other advanced degrees awarded. Terminal master's awarded for partial completion of doctoral program. *Degree requirements:* For master's, one foreign language, comprehensive exam, thesis optional; for doctorate, 2 foreign languages, comprehensive exam, thesis/dissertation, qualifying exam. *Entrance requirements:* For master's, GRE, minimum undergraduate GPA of 3.0, statement of purpose, two letters of recommendation; for doctorate, GRE, minimum undergraduate and graduate GPA of 3.25, statement of purpose, writing sample, three letters of recommendation. Additional exam requirements/recommendations for international students: Required—TOEFL. *Application deadline:* For fall admission, 1/15 for domestic students; for spring admission, 10/15 for domestic students. Applications are processed on a rolling basis. Application fee: $35 ($60 for international students). Electronic applications accepted. *Expenses:* $5,231.50 per semester full-time in-state, $9,623.50 full-time out-of-state. *Financial support:* In 2016–17, 123 students received support, including 11 research assistantships with full tuition reimbursements available (averaging $17,064 per year), 25 teaching assistantships with full tuition reimbursements available (averaging $17,340 per year); Federal Work-Study, scholarships/grants, and unspecified assistantships also available. Financial award application deadline: 2/1; financial award applicants required to submit FAFSA. *Faculty research:* Applied linguistics, British and American literature, professional writing, composition studies. *Unit head:* Dr. Joshua Phillips, Chair, 901-678-2651, Fax: 901-678-2226, E-mail: jsphllps@memphis.edu. *Application contact:* Dr. Jeffrey Scraba, Coordinator of Graduate Studies, 901-678-4768, Fax: 901-678-2226, E-mail: jscraba@memphis.edu.
Website: http://www.memphis.edu/english

**University of Michigan,** Rackham Graduate School, College of Literature, Science, and the Arts, Department of Anthropology, Ann Arbor, MI 48109. Offers anthropological archaeology (PhD); biological anthropology (PhD); linguistic anthropology (PhD); sociocultural anthropology (PhD). *Faculty:* 41 full-time (18 women), 5 part-time/adjunct (2 women). *Students:* 149 full-time (89 women); includes 41 minority (3 Black or African American, non-Hispanic/Latino; 3 American Indian or Alaska Native, non-Hispanic/ Latino; 16 Asian, non-Hispanic/Latino; 14 Hispanic/Latino; 5 Two or more races, non-Hispanic/Latino), 16 international. Average age 28. 209 applicants, 9% accepted, 13 enrolled. In 2016, 17 doctorates awarded. *Degree requirements:* For doctorate, one foreign language, comprehensive exam, thesis/dissertation, preliminary examination, oral defense of dissertation. *Entrance requirements:* For doctorate, GRE General Test. Additional exam requirements/recommendations for international students: Required—TOEFL (minimum score 560 paper-based; 84 iBT). *Application deadline:* For fall admission, 12/15 for domestic and international students. Application fee: $75 ($90 for international students). Electronic applications accepted. *Expenses:* Tuition, state resident: full-time $21,466; part-time $1152 per credit hour. Tuition, nonresident: full-time $43,346; part-time $2367 per credit hour. Part-time tuition and fees vary according to course load, degree level and program. *Financial support:* In 2016–17, 76 students received support, including 54 fellowships with full tuition reimbursements available (averaging $19,350 per year), 9 research assistantships with full tuition reimbursements available (averaging $19,350 per year), 30 teaching assistantships with full tuition reimbursements available (averaging $19,350 per year); institutionally sponsored loans, scholarships/grants, traineeships, health care benefits, tuition waivers (full), and unspecified assistantships also available. Financial award application deadline: 3/1; financial award applicants required to submit FAFSA. *Faculty research:* Sociocultural, linguistic, biological and archaeological anthropology. *Unit head:* Dr. Andrew Shryock, Chair, 734-764-7274, Fax: 734-763-6077. *Application contact:* Katia Kitchen, Graduate Program Assistant, 734-936-7933, Fax: 734-763-6077, E-mail: kitchenk@umich.edu. Website: http://www.lsa.umich.edu/anthro

**University of Michigan,** Rackham Graduate School, College of Literature, Science, and the Arts, Department of Linguistics, Ann Arbor, MI 48109. Offers PhD. *Faculty:* 18 full-time (8 women). *Students:* 26 full-time (14 women); includes 4 minority (2 Black or African American, non-Hispanic/Latino; 2 Two or more races, non-Hispanic/Latino), 6 international. Average age 29. 136 applicants, 7% accepted, 5 enrolled. In 2016, 2 doctorates awarded. *Degree requirements:* For doctorate, 2 foreign languages, thesis/dissertation, oral defense of dissertation. *Entrance requirements:* Additional exam requirements/recommendations for international students: Required—TOEFL (minimum score 600 paper-based; 100 iBT), IELTS (minimum score 7.5), Michigan English Language Assessment Battery. *Application deadline:* For fall admission, 12/7 for domestic and international students. Application fee: $75 ($90 for international students). Electronic applications accepted. *Expenses:* Tuition, state resident: full-time $21,466; part-time $1152 per credit hour. Tuition, nonresident: full-time $43,346; part-time $2367 per credit hour. Part-time tuition and fees vary according to course load, degree level and program. *Financial support:* In 2016–17, 26 students received support, including 7 fellowships with full tuition reimbursements available (averaging $19,350 per year), 2 research assistantships with full tuition reimbursements available (averaging $19,350 per year), 16 teaching assistantships with full tuition reimbursements available (averaging $19,350 per year); health care benefits and tuition waivers (full) also available. Financial award application deadline: 12/7. *Faculty research:* Broad-based approach to linguistics as a cognitive and social science including theoretical, experimental and computational approaches. *Unit head:* Prof. Robin Queen, Professor/Chair, 734-764-0353, Fax: 734-936-3406, E-mail: linguistics@umich.edu. *Application contact:* Dr. Jennifer Nguyen, Senior Student Services Assistant, 734-936-3403, Fax: 734-936-3406, E-mail: linggradadmissions@umich.edu.
Website: http://www.lsa.umich.edu/linguistics/

**University of Minnesota, Twin Cities Campus,** Graduate School, College of Liberal Arts, Institute of Linguistics, English as a Second Language, and Slavic Languages and Literatures (ILES), Program in Linguistics, Minneapolis, MN 55455-0213. Offers MA, PhD. Terminal master's awarded for partial completion of doctoral program. *Degree requirements:* For master's, one foreign language, comprehensive exam, thesis; for doctorate, 2 foreign languages, comprehensive exam, thesis/dissertation. *Entrance requirements:* For master's and doctorate, GRE General Test, 3 letters of recommendation, unit questionnaire. Additional exam requirements/recommendations for international students: Required—TOEFL (minimum score 550 paper-based; 79 iBT). Electronic applications accepted. *Faculty research:* Pragmatics and language processing, syntactic theory, language policy and planning, contact linguistics, language and cognition.

**University of Montana,** Graduate School, College of Humanities and Sciences, Department of Anthropology, Missoula, MT 59812-0002. Offers anthropology (MA, PhD); applied anthropology (PhD); applied medical anthropology (MA); cultural heritage (MA, PhD); forensic anthropology (MA); linguistic anthropology (MA). *Degree requirements:* For master's, thesis (for some programs). *Entrance requirements:* For master's, GRE General Test. Additional exam requirements/recommendations for international students: Required—TOEFL. *Faculty research:* Historical preservation, plateau-plains archaeology and ethnohistory.

**University of Montana,** Graduate School, College of Humanities and Sciences, Program in Linguistics, Missoula, MT 59812-0002. Offers MA. *Entrance requirements:* For master's, GRE General Test. Additional exam requirements/recommendations for international students: Required—TOEFL.

**University of New Hampshire,** Graduate School, College of Liberal Arts, Department of English, Durham, NH 03824. Offers composition (PhD); English education (MST); language and linguistics (MA); literature (MA, PhD); writing (MFA). *Program availability:* Part-time. *Degree requirements:* For master's, one foreign language; for doctorate, 2 foreign languages, thesis/dissertation. *Entrance requirements:* For master's, GRE General Test, sample of written work; for doctorate, GRE General Test, GRE Subject Test, sample of written work. Additional exam requirements/recommendations for international students: Required—TOEFL (minimum score 550 paper-based; 80 iBT). Electronic applications accepted.

**University of New Mexico,** Graduate Studies, College of Arts and Sciences, Program in Linguistics, Albuquerque, NM 87131-2039. Offers MA, PhD. *Program availability:* Part-time. *Faculty:* 8 full-time (5 women). *Students:* 14 full-time (9 women), 46 part-time (28 women); includes 12 minority (4 American Indian or Alaska Native, non-Hispanic/Latino; 4 Hispanic/Latino; 4 Two or more races, non-Hispanic/Latino), 18 international. Average age 36. 57 applicants, 30% accepted, 11 enrolled. In 2016, 8 master's, 3 doctorates awarded. *Degree requirements:* For master's, comprehensive exam, thesis optional; for doctorate, one foreign language, comprehensive exam, thesis/dissertation, statistics through analysis of variance; knowledge of structure of a non-Indo European language. *Entrance requirements:* For master's, minimum GPA of 3.0, 3 letters of recommendation, letter of intent; for doctorate, MA in linguistics or equivalent, paper of publishable quality, 3 letters of recommendation, letter of intent. Additional exam requirements/recommendations for international students: Required—TOEFL (minimum score 550 paper-based; 79 iBT), IELTS (minimum score 7). *Application deadline:* For fall admission, 12/15 priority date for domestic and international students. Applications are processed on a rolling basis. Application fee: $50. Electronic applications accepted. *Financial support:* Fellowships with full tuition reimbursements, research assistantships, teaching assistantships with tuition reimbursements, Federal Work-Study, health care benefits, and tuition waivers (full and partial) available. Financial award application deadline: 1/15; financial award applicants required to submit FAFSA. *Faculty research:* Cognitive-functional linguistics, signed language linguistics, Native American languages

## Linguistics

of the Southwest, language acquisition, language in interaction (discourse, prosody). *Total annual research expenditures:* $121,296. *Unit head:* Dr. Caroline Smith, Chair, 505-277-6353, Fax: 505-277-6355, E-mail: caroline@unm.edu. *Application contact:* Jessica Slocum, Administrative Assistant III, 505-277-6353, Fax: 505-277-6355, E-mail: jslocum@unm.edu.
Website: http://www.unm.edu/~linguist/

**University of New Mexico,** Graduate Studies, College of Education, Program in Educational Linguistics, Albuquerque, NM 87131-2039. Offers PhD. *Program availability:* Part-time. *Faculty:* 1 (woman) full-time. *Students:* 12 full-time (3 women), 15 part-time (11 women); includes 4 minority (1 American Indian or Alaska Native, non-Hispanic/Latino; 1 Asian, non-Hispanic/Latino; 1 Hispanic/Latino; 1 Two or more races, non-Hispanic/Latino), 14 international. Average age 41. 13 applicants, 8% accepted, 1 enrolled. In 2016, 2 doctorates awarded. *Degree requirements:* For doctorate, comprehensive exam, thesis/dissertation. *Entrance requirements:* For doctorate, master's degree in linguistics or complementary field (recommended). Additional exam requirements/recommendations for international students: Required—TOEFL (minimum score 550 paper-based; 79 iBT). *Application deadline:* For fall admission, 12/1 for domestic and international students. Application fee: $50. Electronic applications accepted. *Financial support:* Teaching assistantships, career-related internships or fieldwork, institutionally sponsored loans, scholarships/grants, and unspecified assistantships available. Support available to part-time students. Financial award application deadline: 1/15; financial award applicants required to submit FAFSA. *Faculty research:* Bilingualism, language maintenance and loss, bilingual deaf education, Spanish dialectical studies, English as a second language, writing/composition, Native American language issues, language and thought, language policy studies, global English issues, assessment. *Unit head:* Dr. Holbrook Mahn, Graduate Director, 505-277-5887, Fax: 505-277-8362, E-mail: hmahn@unm.edu. *Application contact:* Mary Gurule Vernon, Administrator, 505-277-5282, Fax: 505-277-8362, E-mail: mgurule2@unm.edu.
Website: https://coe.unm.edu/departments-programs/llss/educational-linguistics/index.html

**The University of North Carolina at Chapel Hill,** Graduate School, College of Arts and Sciences, Department of Germanic Languages, Chapel Hill, NC 27599. Offers literature and linguistics (MA, PhD). *Program availability:* Part-time. Terminal master's awarded for partial completion of doctoral program. *Degree requirements:* For master's, comprehensive exam, thesis; for doctorate, one foreign language, comprehensive exam, thesis/dissertation. *Entrance requirements:* For master's and doctorate, GRE General Test, minimum GPA of 3.0. *Faculty research:* Gender and sexuality, literature and politics, German and Jewish culture, medieval through modern literature, Germanic linguistics.

**The University of North Carolina at Chapel Hill,** Graduate School, College of Arts and Sciences, Department of Linguistics, Chapel Hill, NC 27599. Offers MA. *Degree requirements:* For master's, one foreign language, comprehensive exam, thesis. *Entrance requirements:* For master's, GRE General Test, minimum GPA of 3.0. Additional exam requirements/recommendations for international students: Required—TOEFL (minimum score 79 iBT). Electronic applications accepted. *Faculty research:* Phonetics, phonology, morphology, syntax, semantics, historical linguistics, language acquisition, Mayan linguistics.

**The University of North Carolina at Charlotte,** College of Liberal Arts and Sciences, Department of English, Charlotte, NC 28223-0001. Offers applied linguistics (Graduate Certificate); English (MA); technical and professional writing (Graduate Certificate). *Program availability:* Part-time, evening/weekend. *Faculty:* 30 full-time (16 women), 2 part-time/adjunct (1 woman). *Students:* 28 full-time (22 women), 30 part-time (19 women); includes 13 minority (4 Black or African American, non-Hispanic/Latino; 1 Asian, non-Hispanic/Latino; 8 Hispanic/Latino), 4 international. Average age 30. 33 applicants, 91% accepted, 20 enrolled. In 2016, 30 master's, 1 other advanced degree awarded. *Degree requirements:* For master's, comprehensive exam (for some programs), thesis, comprehensive exam, or project. *Entrance requirements:* For master's, GRE, MAT, minimum undergraduate GPA of 3.0, statement of purpose, recommendation letters; for Graduate Certificate, statement of purpose, three letters of recommendation, writing sample, minimum GPA of 2.75. Additional exam requirements/recommendations for international students: Required—TOEFL (minimum score 523 paper-based, 70 iBT) or IELTS (6.5). *Application deadline:* For fall admission, 3/1 priority date for domestic and international students; for spring admission, 10/1 priority date for domestic and international students; for summer admission, 4/1 priority date for domestic and international students. Applications are processed on a rolling basis. Application fee: $75. Electronic applications accepted. *Expenses:* Tuition, state resident: full-time $4252. Tuition, nonresident: full-time $17,423. *Required fees:* $3026. Tuition and fees vary according to course load and program. *Financial support:* In 2016–17, 17 students received support, including 1 research assistantship (averaging $8,000 per year), 16 teaching assistantships (averaging $8,562 per year); career-related internships or fieldwork, institutionally sponsored loans, scholarships/grants, and unspecified assistantships also available. Support available to part-time students. Financial award application deadline: 3/1; financial award applicants required to submit FAFSA. *Total annual research expenditures:* $61,484. *Unit head:* Dr. Mark West, Chair, 704-687-0618, E-mail: miwest@uncc.edu. *Application contact:* Kathy B. Giddings, Director of Graduate Admissions, 704-687-5503, Fax: 704-687-1668, E-mail: gradadm@uncc.edu.
Website: http://english.uncc.edu/

**University of North Dakota,** Graduate School, College of Arts and Sciences, Program in Linguistics, Grand Forks, ND 58202. Offers MA. *Degree requirements:* For master's, one foreign language, thesis, final examination. *Entrance requirements:* For master's, minimum GPA of 3.0. Additional exam requirements/recommendations for international students: Required—TOEFL (minimum score 550 paper-based; 79 iBT), IELTS (minimum score 6.5). *Application deadline:* For fall admission, 3/1 priority date for domestic and international students. Applications are processed on a rolling basis. Application fee: $35. Electronic applications accepted. *Financial support:* Fellowships with full and partial tuition reimbursements, research assistantships with full and partial tuition reimbursements, teaching assistantships with full and partial tuition reimbursements, Federal Work-Study, institutionally sponsored loans, tuition waivers (full and partial), and unspecified assistantships available. Support available to part-time students. Financial award application deadline: 3/15; financial award applicants required to submit FAFSA. *Faculty research:* Practice-based field studies. *Unit head:* Dr. John Clifton, Graduate Director, 701-777-2011. *Application contact:* Matt Anderson, Admissions Associate, 701-777-2947, Fax: 701-777-3619, E-mail: matthew.anderson@gradschool.und.edu.
Website: http://www.und.edu/dept/linguistics/lingma.htm

**University of North Texas,** Robert B. Toulouse School of Graduate Studies, Denton, TX 76203-5459. Offers accounting (MS); applied anthropology (MA, MS); applied behavior analysis (Certificate); applied geography (MA); applied technology and performance improvement (M Ed, MS); art education (MA); art history (MA); art museum education (Certificate); arts leadership (Certificate); audiology (Au D); behavior analysis (MS); behavioral science (PhD); biochemistry and molecular biology (MS); biology (MA, MS); biomedical engineering (MS); business analysis (MS); chemistry (MS); clinical health psychology (PhD); communication studies (MA, MS); computer engineering (MS); computer science (MS); counseling (M Ed, MS), including clinical mental health counseling (MS), college and university counseling, elementary school counseling, secondary school counseling; creative writing (MA); criminal justice (MS); curriculum and instruction (M Ed); decision sciences (MBA); design (MA, MFA), including fashion design (MFA), innovation studies, interior design (MFA); early childhood studies (MS); economics (MS); educational leadership (M Ed, Ed D); educational psychology (MS, PhD), including family studies (MS), gifted and talented (MS), human development (MS), learning and cognition (MS), research, measurement and evaluation (MS); electrical engineering (MS); emergency management (MPA); engineering technology (MS); English (MA); English as a second language (MA); environmental science (MS); finance (MBA, MS); financial management (MPA); French (MA); health services management (MBA); higher education (M Ed, Ed D); history (MA, MS); hospitality management (MS); human resources management (MPA); information science (MS); information systems (PhD); information technologies (MBA); interdisciplinary studies (MA, MS); international studies (MA); international sustainable tourism (MS); jazz studies (MM); journalism (MA, MJ, Graduate Certificate), including interactive and virtual digital communication (Graduate Certificate), narrative journalism (Graduate Certificate), public relations (Graduate Certificate); kinesiology (MS); linguistics (MA); local government management (MPA); logistics (PhD); logistics and supply chain management (MBA); long-term care, senior housing, and aging services (MA); management (PhD); marketing (MBA); mathematics (MA, MS); mechanical and energy engineering (MS, PhD); music (MA), including ethnomusicology, music theory, musicology, performance; music composition (PhD); music education (MM Ed, PhD); nonprofit management (MPA); operations and supply chain management (MBA); performance (MM, DMA); philosophy (MA); political science (MA); professional and technical communication (MA); radio, television and film (MA, MFA); rehabilitation counseling (Certificate); sociology (MA); Spanish (MA); special education (M Ed); speech-language pathology (MA); strategic management (MBA); studio art (MFA); teaching (M Ed); MBA/MS. *Program availability:* Part-time, evening/weekend, online learning. Terminal master's awarded for partial completion of doctoral program. *Degree requirements:* For master's, variable foreign language requirement, comprehensive exam (for some programs), thesis (for some programs); for doctorate, variable foreign language requirement, comprehensive exam (for some programs), thesis/dissertation; for other advanced degree, variable foreign language requirement, comprehensive exam (for some programs). *Entrance requirements:* For master's and doctorate, GRE, GMAT. Additional exam requirements/recommendations for international students: Required—TOEFL (minimum score 550 paper-based; 79 iBT). Electronic applications accepted.

**University of Oregon,** Graduate School, College of Arts and Sciences, Department of Linguistics, Eugene, OR 97403. Offers MA, PhD. Terminal master's awarded for partial completion of doctoral program. *Degree requirements:* For master's, 2 foreign languages; for doctorate, thesis/dissertation. *Entrance requirements:* For master's and doctorate, GRE General Test, minimum GPA of 3.0. Additional exam requirements/recommendations for international students: Required—TOEFL. *Faculty research:* Functional syntax, discourse, empirical methods.

**University of Ottawa,** Faculty of Graduate and Postdoctoral Studies, Faculty of Arts, Department of Linguistics, Ottawa, ON K1N 6N5, Canada. Offers MA, PhD. *Degree requirements:* For master's, one foreign language, thesis or alternative; for doctorate, 2 foreign languages, comprehensive exam, thesis/dissertation. *Entrance requirements:* For master's, honors degree or equivalent, minimum B average; for doctorate, master's degree, minimum B+ average. Electronic applications accepted. *Faculty research:* Empirical linguistics, formal linguistics.

**University of Pennsylvania,** Graduate School of Education, Division of Educational Linguistics, Program in Educational Linguistics, Philadelphia, PA 19104. Offers PhD. *Program availability:* Part-time-only. *Students:* 15 full-time (12 women), 2 part-time (0 women); includes 5 minority (3 Asian, non-Hispanic/Latino; 2 Hispanic/Latino), 4 international. Average age 30. 96 applicants, 2% accepted, 2 enrolled. *Expenses:* Tuition: Full-time $31,068; part-time $5762 per course. *Required fees:* $3200; $336 per course. Full-time tuition and fees vary according to degree level, program and student level. Part-time tuition and fees vary according to course load, degree level and program. *Financial support:* In 2016–17, 55 students received support.

**University of Pennsylvania,** School of Arts and Sciences, Graduate Group in Linguistics, Philadelphia, PA 19104. Offers AM, PhD. *Faculty:* 20 full-time (4 women), 1 part-time/adjunct. *Students:* 38 full-time (22 women), 1 (woman) part-time; includes 3 minority (1 Black or African American, non-Hispanic/Latino; 2 Asian, non-Hispanic/Latino), 20 international. Average age 28. 162 applicants, 5% accepted, 6 enrolled. In 2016, 1 master's, 5 doctorates awarded. Terminal master's awarded for partial completion of doctoral program. *Entrance requirements:* For master's, GRE General Test. *Expenses:* Tuition: Full-time $31,068; part-time $5762 per course. *Required fees:* $3200; $336 per course. Full-time tuition and fees vary according to degree level, program and student level. Part-time tuition and fees vary according to course load, degree level and program.
Website: http://www.ling.upenn.edu/graduate/

**University of Puerto Rico, Río Piedras Campus,** College of Humanities, Department of Hispanic Studies, San Juan, PR 00931-3300. Offers Hispanic linguistics (PhD); Hispanic studies (MA); Latin American literature (PhD); Puerto Rican literature (PhD); Spanish literature (PhD). *Program availability:* Part-time. *Degree requirements:* For master's, one foreign language, comprehensive exam, thesis; for doctorate, one foreign language, comprehensive exam, thesis/dissertation. *Entrance requirements:* For master's, PAEG or GRE, interview, minimum GPA of 3.0, letter of recommendation (2); for doctorate, PAEG or GRE, interview, master's degree, minimum GPA of 3.0, letter of recommendation (2). *Faculty research:* Poetry of Luis Palés Matos, short stories in Puerto Rico, language in the social process, "Decima Popular", Anglicism.

**University of Puerto Rico, Río Piedras Campus,** College of Humanities, Department of Linguistics, San Juan, PR 00931-3300. Offers MA. *Program availability:* Part-time. *Degree requirements:* For master's, one foreign language, comprehensive exam, thesis. *Entrance requirements:* For master's, PAEG or GRE, interview, minimum GPA of 3.0, letter of recommendation (2).

**University of Regina,** Faculty of Graduate Studies and Research, Faculty of Arts, Program in Linguistics, Regina, SK S4S 0A2, Canada. Offers MA. Offered as a special case program. *Program availability:* Part-time. *Faculty:* 9 full-time (2 women), 4 part-time/adjunct (0 women). *Degree requirements:* For master's, thesis. *Entrance requirements:* Additional exam requirements/recommendations for international students: Required—TOEFL (minimum score 580 paper-based), IELTS (minimum score 6.5), PTE (minimum score 59). *Application deadline:* Applications are processed on a rolling basis. Application fee: $100. Electronic applications accepted. *Financial support:* Fellowships, teaching assistantships, and scholarships/grants available. Financial award application deadline: 6/15. *Faculty research:* Advanced phonology, advanced morphology, advanced syntax, advanced semantics, diachronic linguistics. *Unit head:* Dr. Arok Wolvengrey, Graduate Studies Advisor/Coordinator, 306-790-5950 Ext. 3310, Fax: 306-790-5994, E-mail: awolvengrey@fnuniv.ca.

**University of Rochester,** School of Arts and Sciences, Department of Linguistics, Rochester, NY 14627. Offers computational linguistics (MS); language documentation (MA); linguistics (MA). *Program availability:* Part-time, evening/weekend. *Faculty:* 4 full-time (1 woman). *Students:* 1 full-time (0 women), 2 part-time (0 women), 1 international. Average age 37. 22 applicants, 32% accepted, 2 enrolled. In 2016, 1 master's awarded. *Entrance requirements:* For master's, GRE, official transcripts, three letters of recommendation. Additional exam requirements/recommendations for international students: Required—TOEFL (minimum score 580 paper-based). *Application deadline:* For fall admission, 1/15 for domestic and international students. Application fee: $60. Electronic applications accepted. *Expenses:* $1,538 per credit hour. *Financial support:* Tuition waivers (partial) available. *Unit head:* Jeffery Runner, Chair, 585-275-2626, E-mail: jeffrey.runner@rochester.edu. *Application contact:* Erica Dayton, Administrative Assistant, 585-275-8053.
Website: http://www.ling.rochester.edu/

**University of South Africa,** College of Human Sciences, Pretoria, South Africa. Offers adult education (M Ed); African languages (MA, PhD); African politics (MA, PhD); Afrikaans (MA, PhD); ancient history (MA, PhD); ancient Near Eastern studies (MA, PhD); anthropology (MA, PhD); applied linguistics (MA); Arabic (MA, PhD); archaeology (MA); art history (MA); Biblical archaeology (MA); Biblical studies (M Th, D Th, PhD); Christian spirituality (M Th, D Th); church history (M Th, D Th); classical studies (MA, PhD); clinical psychology (MA); communication (MA, PhD); comparative education (M Ed, Ed D); consulting psychology (D Admin, D Com, PhD); curriculum studies (M Ed, Ed D); development studies (M Admin, MA, D Admin, PhD); didactics (M Ed, Ed D); education (M Tech); education management (M Ed, Ed D); educational psychology (M Ed); English (MA); environmental education (M Ed); French (MA, PhD); German (MA, PhD); Greek (MA); guidance and counseling (M Ed); health studies (MA, PhD), including health sciences education (MA), health services management (MA), medical and surgical nursing science (critical care general) (MA), midwifery and neonatal nursing science (MA), trauma and emergency care (MA); history (MA, PhD); history of education (Ed D); inclusive education (M Ed, Ed D); information and communications technology policy and regulation (MA); information science (MA, MIS, PhD); international politics (MA, PhD); Islamic studies (MA, PhD); Italian (MA, PhD); Judaica (MA, PhD); linguistics (MA, PhD); mathematical education (M Ed); mathematics education (MA); missiology (M Th, D Th); modern Hebrew (MA); musicology (MA, MMus, D Mus, PhD); natural science education (M Ed); New Testament (M Th, D Th); Old Testament (D Th); pastoral therapy (M Th, D Th); philosophy (MA); philosophy of education (M Ed, Ed D); politics (MA, PhD); Portuguese (MA, PhD); practical theology (M Th, D Th); psychology (MA, MS, PhD); psychology of education (M Ed, Ed D); public health (MA); religious studies (MA, D Th, PhD); Romance languages (MA); Russian (MA, PhD); Semitic languages (MA, PhD); social behavior studies in HIV/AIDS (MA); social science (mental health) (MA); social science in development studies (MA); social science in psychology (MA); social science in social work (MA); social science in sociology (MA); social work (MSW, DSW, PhD); socio-education (M Ed, Ed D); sociolinguistics (MA); sociology (MA, PhD); Spanish (MA, PhD); systematic theology (M Th, D Th); TESOL (teaching English to speakers of other languages) (MA); theological ethics (M Th, D Th); theory of literature (MA, PhD); urban ministries (D Th); urban ministry (M Th).

**University of South Carolina,** The Graduate School, College of Arts and Sciences, Linguistics Program, Columbia, SC 29208. Offers linguistics (MA, PhD); teaching English to speakers of other languages (Certificate). *Program availability:* Part-time. Terminal master's awarded for partial completion of doctoral program. *Degree requirements:* For master's, one foreign language, comprehensive exam, thesis optional; for doctorate, 3 foreign languages, comprehensive exam, thesis/dissertation. *Entrance requirements:* For master's and Certificate, GRE General Test, minimum GPA of 3.0; for doctorate, GRE General Test, minimum GPA of 3.5. Additional exam requirements/recommendations for international students: Required—TOEFL. Electronic applications accepted. *Faculty research:* Second language acquisition, sociolinguistics, syntax, historical linguistics and phonology.

**University of Southern California,** Graduate School, Dana and David Dornsife College of Letters, Arts and Sciences, Department of East Asian Languages and Cultures, Los Angeles, CA 90089. Offers classical Chinese literature (MA, PhD); classical Japanese literature (MA, PhD); linguistics (MA, PhD); modern Chinese literature (MA, PhD); modern Japanese literature (MA, PhD); modern Korean literature (MA, PhD). *Degree requirements:* For master's, thesis; for doctorate, 2 foreign languages, comprehensive exam, thesis/dissertation. *Entrance requirements:* For master's and doctorate, GRE, BA in relevant field. Additional exam requirements/recommendations for international students: Required—TOEFL. Electronic applications accepted. *Faculty research:* Gender, visual studies, multimedia, ecocriticism, second language acquisition.

**University of Southern California,** Graduate School, Dana and David Dornsife College of Letters, Arts and Sciences, Department of Linguistics, Los Angeles, CA 90089. Offers East Asian linguistics (PhD); Hispanic linguistics (PhD); linguistics (PhD); Slavic linguistics (PhD). *Degree requirements:* For doctorate, comprehensive exam, thesis/dissertation. *Entrance requirements:* For doctorate, GRE. Additional exam requirements/recommendations for international students: Required—TOEFL (minimum score 100 iBT). Electronic applications accepted. *Faculty research:* Syntax, phonology, phonetics, semantics, sociolinguistics, psycholinguistics.

**University of South Florida,** College of Arts and Sciences, Department of World Languages, Tampa, FL 33620-9951. Offers French (MA); linguistics (MA); linguistics and applied linguistics studies (PhD); linguistics: English as a second language (PhD); Spanish (MA). *Program availability:* Part-time, evening/weekend. *Faculty:* 20 full-time (16 women). *Students:* 38 full-time (28 women), 18 part-time (16 women); includes 19 minority (3 Black or African American, non-Hispanic/Latino; 1 Asian, non-Hispanic/Latino; 14 Hispanic/Latino; 1 Two or more races, non-Hispanic/Latino), 9 international. Average age 34. 36 applicants, 58% accepted, 13 enrolled. In 2016, 26 master's awarded. *Degree requirements:* For master's, one foreign language, comprehensive exam, thesis optional; for doctorate, one foreign language, comprehensive exam, thesis/dissertation. *Entrance requirements:* For master's, GRE General Test, minimum undergraduate GPA of 3.0 and 2-3 letters of recommendation; two-page statement of purpose written in Spanish (for Spanish program); oral interview (for Spanish and French programs); writing sample (for French program); for doctorate, GRE General Test, minimum GPA of 3.5 or international equivalent; master's degree or equivalent academic level; statement of purpose; current curriculum vitae; three letters of recommendation; personal interview with faculty; evidence of research experience or scholarly promise. Additional exam requirements/recommendations for international students: Required—TOEFL (minimum score 600 paper-based; 80 iBT) or IELTS (minimum score 6.5) for MA; TOEFL (minimum score 550 paper-based; 80 iBT) or IELTS (minimum score 6.5) for PhD. *Application deadline:* For fall admission, 1/15 for domestic and international students; for spring admission, 10/15 for domestic students, 9/15 for international students. Application fee: $30. Electronic applications accepted. *Expenses:* Tuition, state resident: full-time $7766; part-time $431.43 per credit hour. Tuition, nonresident: full-time $15,789; part-time $877.17 per credit hour. *Required fees:* $37 per term. *Financial support:* In 2016-17, 4 students received support, including 43 teaching assistantships with tuition reimbursements available (averaging $10,152 per year); tuition waivers (partial) and unspecified assistantships also available. Financial

award application deadline: 6/30. *Faculty research:* Second language acquisition, instructional technology, foreign language education, English for speakers of other languages, distance learning. *Total annual research expenditures:* $104,720. *Unit head:* Dr. Stephan Schindler, Chair and Professor, 813-974-2548, Fax: 813-905-9937, E-mail: skschindler@usf.edu. *Application contact:* Patricia Garcia, Academic Program Specialist, 813-974-2548, Fax: 813-905-9937, E-mail: pgarcia@usf.edu.
Website: http://languages.usf.edu/

**The University of Tennessee,** Graduate School, College of Arts and Sciences, Department of Modern Foreign Languages and Literatures, Program in Modern Foreign Languages, Knoxville, TN 37996. Offers applied linguistics (PhD); French (PhD); German (PhD); Italian (PhD); Portuguese (PhD); Russian (PhD); Spanish (PhD). *Degree requirements:* For doctorate, 2 foreign languages, thesis/dissertation. *Entrance requirements:* For doctorate, minimum GPA of 2.7. Additional exam requirements/recommendations for international students: Required—TOEFL. Electronic applications accepted.

**The University of Texas at Arlington,** Graduate School, College of Liberal Arts, Department of Linguistics and TESOL, Program in Linguistics, Arlington, TX 76019. Offers MA, PhD. *Program availability:* Part-time, evening/weekend. Terminal master's awarded for partial completion of doctoral program. *Degree requirements:* For master's, one foreign language, comprehensive exam (for some programs), thesis optional; for doctorate, 2 foreign languages, comprehensive exam, thesis/dissertation, qualifying exam, dissertation proposal defense, professional development. *Entrance requirements:* For master's, GRE General Test, minimum undergraduate GPA of 3.0, 9 credits of undergraduate foundation courses; for doctorate, GRE General Test, 30 hours of graduate work in linguistics or a related discipline, minimum GPA of 3.5. Additional exam requirements/recommendations for international students: Required—TOEFL (minimum score 550 paper-based). *Application deadline:* For fall admission, 6/15 for domestic students. Applications are processed on a rolling basis. Application fee: $35 ($50 for international students). Electronic applications accepted. *Financial support:* Fellowships, research assistantships, teaching assistantships with full tuition reimbursements, career-related internships or fieldwork, and institutionally sponsored loans available. Financial award application deadline: 3/1; financial award applicants required to submit FAFSA. *Faculty research:* Field linguistics, discourse analysis, text linguistics, phonology, teaching English as a second language. *Unit head:* Dr. Laurel Stvan, Chair, 817-272-3133, Fax: 817-272-2731, E-mail: stvan@uta.edu. *Application contact:* Dr. Laurel Stvan, Graduate Advisor, 817-272-3133, Fax: 817-272-2731.
Website: http://ling.uta.edu/

**The University of Texas at Austin,** Graduate School, College of Liberal Arts, Department of French and Italian, Austin, TX 78712-1111. Offers French linguistics (MA, PhD); French studies (MA, PhD); Italian studies (MA, PhD); Romance linguistics (PhD). *Program availability:* Part-time. *Degree requirements:* For master's, one foreign language, thesis; for doctorate, 2 foreign languages, thesis/dissertation. *Entrance requirements:* For master's, GRE General Test, minimum GPA of 3.0, bachelor's degree in French or equivalent; for doctorate, GRE General Test, minimum GPA of 3.0, master's degree in French. Additional exam requirements/recommendations for international students: Required—TOEFL. Electronic applications accepted. *Faculty research:* Nineteenth-century Italian literature, Italian Renaissance, twentieth-century French literature, Francophone literature, fifteenth-century literature and culture.

**The University of Texas at Austin,** Graduate School, College of Liberal Arts, Department of Linguistics, Austin, TX 78712-1111. Offers MA, PhD. *Degree requirements:* For master's, one foreign language, thesis; for doctorate, 2 foreign languages, thesis/dissertation. *Entrance requirements:* For master's and doctorate, GRE General Test. Electronic applications accepted. *Faculty research:* Theoretical linguistics, sociolinguistics, documentary and descriptive linguistics, computational linguistics.

**The University of Texas at Austin,** Graduate School, College of Liberal Arts, Department of Slavic and Eurasian Studies, Austin, TX 78712-1111. Offers applied linguistics/pedagogy (PhD); literature and culture (PhD); Slavic languages (MA); Slavic linguistics (PhD). *Degree requirements:* For master's, 2 foreign languages, thesis; for doctorate, 3 foreign languages, thesis/dissertation. *Entrance requirements:* For master's and doctorate, GRE General Test. Electronic applications accepted. *Faculty research:* Slavic linguistics; applied linguistics; Russian, Czech, and Slavic literature and culture.

**The University of Texas at Austin,** Graduate School, College of Liberal Arts, Department of Spanish and Portuguese, Austin, TX 78712-1111. Offers Hispanic linguistics (MA, PhD); Hispanic literature (MA, PhD); Ibero-romance philology and linguistics (PhD); Luso-Brazilian literature (MA, PhD). *Degree requirements:* For master's, 2 foreign languages, thesis or alternative; for doctorate, 3 foreign languages, thesis/dissertation. *Entrance requirements:* For master's and doctorate, GRE General Test. Electronic applications accepted.

**The University of Texas at El Paso,** Graduate School, College of Liberal Arts, Department of Languages and Linguistics, El Paso, TX 79968-0001. Offers linguistics (MA); Spanish (MA); teaching English to speakers of other languages (Certificate). *Program availability:* Part-time, evening/weekend. *Degree requirements:* For master's, thesis optional. *Entrance requirements:* For master's, GRE General Test, departmental exam, minimum GPA of 3.0, letters of recommendation. Additional exam requirements/recommendations for international students: Required—TOEFL; Recommended—IELTS. Electronic applications accepted.

**University of Toronto,** School of Graduate Studies, Faculty of Arts and Science, Department of Linguistics, Toronto, ON M5S 1A1, Canada. Offers MA, PhD. *Program availability:* Part-time. *Degree requirements:* For master's, 2 foreign languages; for doctorate, thesis/dissertation, oral thesis proposal. *Entrance requirements:* For master's, BA in linguistics; for doctorate, MA in linguistics. Electronic applications accepted.

**University of Utah,** Graduate School, College of Humanities, Department of Linguistics, Salt Lake City, UT 84112-0492. Offers MA, PhD. *Faculty:* 10 full-time (5 women), 2 part-time/adjunct (1 woman). *Students:* 7 full-time (4 women), 6 part-time (2 women); includes 4 minority (1 Asian, non-Hispanic/Latino; 3 Hispanic/Latino), 2 international. Average age 31. 43 applicants, 19% accepted, 7 enrolled. In 2016, 12 master's, 3 doctorates awarded. *Degree requirements:* For master's, 2 foreign languages, comprehensive exam, thesis; for doctorate, 2 foreign languages, comprehensive exam, thesis/dissertation. *Entrance requirements:* For master's and doctorate, GRE General Test, minimum undergraduate GPA of 3.0. Additional exam requirements/recommendations for international students: Required—TOEFL (minimum score 600 paper-based; 100 iBT). *Application deadline:* For fall admission, 1/15 for domestic students, 12/1 for international students. Application fee: $55 ($65 for international students). Electronic applications accepted. *Expenses:* Tuition, state resident: full-time $7011; part-time $3918.24 per credit hour. Tuition, nonresident: full-time $22,154; part-time $11,665.42 per credit hour. *Financial support:* In 2016-17, 2 students received support, including 5 teaching assistantships with full tuition reimbursements available (averaging $16,413 per year); fellowships with full tuition reimbursements available, scholarships/grants, health care benefits, and unspecified assistantships also available. Financial award application deadline: 2/1. *Faculty research:* Phonology, second language acquisition, semantics, syntax, second language pedagogy. *Unit head:* Dr.

## Linguistics

Edward Rubin, Chair, 801-581-8047, Fax: 801-585-7351, E-mail: e.rubin@utah.edu. *Application contact:* Kacey Campbell, Academic Advisor, 801-581-3929, Fax: 801-585-7351, E-mail: kacey.campbell@utah.edu. Website: http://www.linguistics.utah.edu

**University of Victoria,** Faculty of Graduate Studies, Faculty of Humanities, Department of Linguistics, Victoria, BC V8W 2Y2, Canada. Offers applied linguistics (MA); linguistics (MA, PhD). *Program availability:* Part-time. *Degree requirements:* For master's, one foreign language, thesis, colloquium; for doctorate, 2 foreign languages, comprehensive exam, thesis/dissertation, candidacy exam. *Entrance requirements:* For master's, GRE; for doctorate, GRE, sample of written work. Additional exam requirements/recommendations for international students: Required—TOEFL. Electronic applications accepted. *Faculty research:* Grammatical theory, syntactic analysis, morphology, Western Amerindian languages, Salishan, applied linguistics.

**University of Virginia,** College and Graduate School of Arts and Sciences, Program in Linguistics, Charlottesville, VA 22903. Offers MA. *Students:* 6 full-time (4 women), 1 part-time (0 women), 3 international. Average age 23. 11 applicants, 91% accepted, 7 enrolled. In 2016, 7 master's awarded. *Degree requirements:* For master's, one foreign language, comprehensive exam, thesis optional, reading knowledge of French or German. *Entrance requirements:* For master's, GRE General Test. Additional exam requirements/recommendations for international students: Required—TOEFL (minimum score 600 paper-based; 90 iBT), IELTS (minimum score 7). *Application deadline:* For fall admission, 2/15 for domestic and international students. Applications are processed on a rolling basis. Application fee: $60. Electronic applications accepted. *Expenses:* Tuition, state resident: full-time $15,026; part-time $834 per credit hour. Tuition, nonresident: full-time $25,168; part-time $1378 per credit hour. Required fees: $2654. *Financial support:* Teaching assistantships available. Financial award applicants required to submit FAFSA. *Unit head:* Lise Dobrin, Program Director, 434-924-7048, E-mail: ld4n@virginia.edu. Website: http://artsandsciences.virginia.edu/linguistics/

**University of Washington,** Graduate School, College of Arts and Sciences, Department of Linguistics, Seattle, WA 98195. Offers computational linguistics (MA); linguistics (MA, PhD); Romance linguistics (MA, PhD). *Program availability:* Part-time. Terminal master's awarded for partial completion of doctoral program. *Degree requirements:* For master's, one foreign language, thesis; for doctorate, 2 foreign languages, thesis/dissertation. *Entrance requirements:* For master's, GRE General Test, minimum GPA of 3.0; for doctorate, GRE, minimum GPA of 3.0. Additional exam requirements/recommendations for international students: Required—TOEFL. Electronic applications accepted. *Faculty research:* Syntax, phonology, semantics, phonetics, sociolinguistics.

**University of Washington,** Graduate School, College of Arts and Sciences, Department of Slavic Languages and Literatures, Seattle, WA 98195. Offers Russian literature (MA, PhD); Slavic linguistics (MA, PhD). *Degree requirements:* For master's, 2 foreign languages, thesis optional; for doctorate, 3 foreign languages, thesis/dissertation. *Entrance requirements:* For master's and doctorate, GRE General Test, minimum GPA of 3.0. Additional exam requirements/recommendations for international students: Required—TOEFL. Electronic applications accepted. *Faculty research:* Modern and medieval East European languages and literatures, comparative literature, Russian folk literature, Slavic literary theory and criticism, computerized morphology of Russian.

**University of Wisconsin–Madison,** Graduate School, College of Letters and Science, Department of East Asian Languages and Literature, Program in Japanese Linguistics, Madison, WI 53706-1380. Offers MA, PhD. *Program availability:* Part-time. Terminal master's awarded for partial completion of doctoral program. *Degree requirements:* For master's, one foreign language, seminars, written exam; for doctorate, 3 foreign languages, thesis/dissertation, seminars, preliminary exams, oral exam. *Entrance requirements:* For master's, GRE General Test, bachelor's degree or equivalent in Japanese; for doctorate, GRE General Test, master's degree or equivalent in Japanese. Electronic applications accepted. *Faculty research:* Modern and historical Japanese linguistics, modern Japanese fiction and poetry, classical Japanese literature, language pedagogy.

**University of Wisconsin–Madison,** Graduate School, College of Letters and Science, Department of English, Madison, WI 53706-1380. Offers applied English linguistics (MA); composition and rhetoric (PhD); creative writing (MFA); English language and linguistics (PhD); literary studies (MA, PhD). *Degree requirements:* For doctorate, thesis/dissertation.

**University of Wisconsin–Madison,** Graduate School, College of Letters and Science, Department of Linguistics, Madison, WI 53706-1380. Offers MA, PhD. *Program availability:* Part-time. Terminal master's awarded for partial completion of doctoral program. *Degree requirements:* For master's, 2 foreign languages; for doctorate, 3 foreign languages, thesis/dissertation. Electronic applications accepted. *Faculty research:* Formal linguistics, acoustic phonetics, American studies, Indo-European linguistics.

**University of Wisconsin–Milwaukee,** Graduate School, College of Letters and Science, Department of Foreign Languages and Literature, Milwaukee, WI 53201-0413. Offers classic Greek (MA); classics (MA); comparative literature (MA); foreign language and literature (MA); French (MA); German (MA); Latin (MA); linguistics (MA); Spanish (MA); translation (MA, Certificate). *Program availability:* Part-time. *Students:* 10 full-time (7 women), 19 part-time (16 women); includes 5 minority (2 Black or African American, non-Hispanic/Latino; 2 Hispanic/Latino; 1 Two or more races, non-Hispanic/Latino), 2 international. Average age 31. 41 applicants, 32% accepted, 9 enrolled. In 2016, 21 master's awarded. *Degree requirements:* For master's, 2 foreign languages, thesis or alternative. *Entrance requirements:* Additional exam requirements/recommendations for international students: Required—TOEFL (minimum score 550 paper-based; 79 iBT), IELTS (minimum score 6.5). *Application deadline:* For fall admission, 1/1 priority date for domestic students; for spring admission, 9/1 for domestic students. Applications are processed on a rolling basis. Application fee: $56 ($96 for international students). Electronic applications accepted. *Financial support:* In 2016–17, 1 fellowship, 2 research assistantships, 26 teaching assistantships were awarded; career-related internships or fieldwork, health care benefits, unspecified assistantships, and project assistantships also available. Support available to part-time students. Financial award application deadline: 4/15; financial award applicants required to submit FAFSA. *Unit head:* Kevin Muse, Department Chair, 414-229-5213, E-mail: kmuse@uwm.edu. *Application contact:* General Information Contact, 414-229-4982, Fax: 414-229-6967, E-mail: gradschool@uwm.edu. Website: http://uwm.edu/foreign-languages-literature/

**University of Wisconsin–Milwaukee,** Graduate School, College of Letters and Science, Department of Linguistics, Milwaukee, WI 53201-0413. Offers linguistics (MA, PhD), including teaching English to speakers of other languages (MA); teaching English to speakers of other languages, adult- and university-level (Graduate Certificate). *Students:* 19 full-time (10 women), 6 part-time (5 women), 15 international. Average age 34. 75 applicants, 36% accepted, 10 enrolled. In 2016, 6 master's, 4 doctorates, 4 other advanced degrees awarded. *Unit head:* Hamid Ouali, Department Chair, 414-229-1113, E-mail: ouali@uwm.edu. *Application contact:* General Information Contact, 414-229-4982, Fax: 414-229-6967, E-mail: gradschool@uwm.edu. Website: http://www4.uwm.edu/letsci/linguistics/

**Virginia International University,** School of Education, Fairfax, VA 22030. Offers applied linguistics (MS); education (M Ed); teaching English to speakers of other languages (MA). *Program availability:* Part-time, online learning. *Entrance requirements:* For master's, bachelor's degree. Additional exam requirements/recommendations for international students: Required—TOEFL (minimum score 550 paper-based; 80 iBT), IELTS (minimum score 6). Electronic applications accepted.

**Wayne State University,** College of Liberal Arts and Sciences, Interdisciplinary Program in Linguistics, Detroit, MI 48202. Offers MA. *Students:* 16 full-time (6 women), 4 part-time (2 women); includes 3 minority (1 Asian, non-Hispanic/Latino; 1 Hispanic/Latino; 1 Two or more races, non-Hispanic/Latino), 10 international. Average age 28. 28 applicants, 57% accepted, 7 enrolled. In 2016, 6 master's awarded. *Degree requirements:* For master's, one foreign language, thesis, essay, oral defense. *Entrance requirements:* For master's, minimum one year of foreign language; at least one course in linguistics; statement of purpose. Additional exam requirements/recommendations for international students: Required—TOEFL (minimum score 550 paper-based; 79 iBT), TWE (minimum score 5.5), Michigan English Language Assessment Battery (minimum score 85); Recommended—IELTS (minimum score 6.5). *Application deadline:* For fall admission, 6/1 priority date for domestic students, 5/1 priority date for international students; for winter admission, 10/1 priority date for domestic students, 9/1 priority date for international students; for spring admission, 2/1 priority date for domestic students, 1/1 priority date for international students. Applications are processed on a rolling basis. Application fee: $50. Electronic applications accepted. *Expenses:* $16,503 per year resident tuition and fees, $33,697 per year non-resident tuition and fees. *Financial support:* Scholarships/grants available. Financial award applicants required to submit FAFSA. *Faculty research:* Discourse/pragmatics, first language acquisition, historical linguistics, morphology, phonetics/phonology, psycholinguistics, second language acquisition, semantics, sociolinguistics, syntax. *Unit head:* Dr. Ljiljana Progovac, Professor/Director, Linguistics Program, 313-577-7553, E-mail: progovac@wayne.edu. *Application contact:* Dr. Stephen Chrisomalis, Graduate Student Advisor, 313-577-9922, E-mail: chrisomalis@wayne.edu. Website: http://clas.wayne.edu/linguistics/

**Wesley Biblical Seminary,** Graduate Programs, Jackson, MS 39206. Offers apologetics (MA); Biblical languages (M Div); Biblical literature (MA); Christian studies (MA); context and mission (M Div); honors research (M Div); interpretation (M Div); ministry (M Div); spiritual formation (M Div); teaching (M Div); theology (MA). *Accreditation:* ATS. *Program availability:* Part-time. *Degree requirements:* For master's, thesis. *Entrance requirements:* Additional exam requirements/recommendations for international students: Required—TOEFL. Electronic applications accepted. *Faculty research:* Patristics, missiology, culture, hermeneutics.

**West Virginia University,** Eberly College of Arts and Sciences, Department of World Languages, Literatures and Linguistics, Morgantown, WV 26506. Offers French (MA); linguistics (MA); Spanish (MA); teaching English to speakers of other languages (MA). *Program availability:* Part-time. *Degree requirements:* For master's, one foreign language, comprehensive exam (for some programs), thesis optional. *Entrance requirements:* For master's, minimum GPA of 3.0. Electronic applications accepted. *Faculty research:* French, German, and Spanish literature; foreign language pedagogy; English as a second language; cultural studies; linguistics.

**Yale University,** Graduate School of Arts and Sciences, Department of Linguistics, New Haven, CT 06520. Offers PhD. *Degree requirements:* For doctorate, 2 foreign languages, thesis/dissertation. *Entrance requirements:* For doctorate, GRE General Test.

**York University,** Faculty of Graduate Studies, Faculty of Liberal Arts and Professional Studies, Program in Linguistics and Applied Linguistics, Toronto, ON M3J 1P3, Canada. Offers MA, PhD. *Degree requirements:* For master's, thesis.

# Translation and Interpretation

**American University of Sharjah,** Graduate Programs, Sharjah, United Arab Emirates. Offers accounting (MS); business (EMBA, MBA); chemical engineering (MS Ch E); civil engineering (MSCE); computer engineering (MS); electrical engineering (MSEE); engineering systems management (MS); mathematics (MS); mechanical engineering (MSME); mechatronics engineering (MS); teaching English to speakers of other languages (MA); translation and interpreting (MA); urban planning (MUP). *Program availability:* Part-time, evening/weekend. *Degree requirements:* For master's, thesis (for some programs). *Entrance requirements:* For master's, GMAT (for MBA). Additional exam requirements/recommendations for international students: Required—TOEFL (minimum score 550 paper-based; 80 iBT), TWE (minimum score 5); Recommended—IELTS (minimum score 6.5). Electronic applications accepted. *Faculty research:* Water pollution, management and waste water treatment, energy and sustainability, air pollution, Islamic finance, family business and small and medium enterprises.

**Arizona State University at the Tempe campus,** College of Liberal Arts and Sciences, Department of English, Tempe, AZ 85287-0302. Offers applied linguistics (PhD); creative writing (MFA); English (MA, PhD), including comparative literature (MA), linguistics (MA), literature, rhetoric and composition (MA), rhetoric, composition, and linguistics (PhD); film and media studies (MAS), including American media and popular culture; linguistics (Graduate Certificate); teaching English to speakers of other languages (MTESOL); translation studies (Graduate Certificate). Terminal master's awarded for partial completion of doctoral program. *Degree requirements:* For master's, variable foreign language requirement, comprehensive exam (for some programs), thesis (for some programs), interactive Program of Study (iPOS) submitted before completing 50 percent of required credit hours; for doctorate, variable foreign language requirement, comprehensive exam, thesis/dissertation, interactive Program of Study (iPOS) submitted before completing 50 percent of required credit hours. *Entrance requirements:* For master's and doctorate, GRE, minimum GPA of 3.0 or equivalent in last 2 years of work leading to bachelor's degree. Additional exam requirements/recommendations for international students: Required—TOEFL, IELTS, or PTE. Electronic applications accepted.

**Babel University Professional School of Translation,** Program in Translation, Honolulu, HI 96815. Offers MS. *Program availability:* Part-time, evening/weekend, online learning. *Degree requirements:* For master's, comprehensive exam, thesis. *Entrance requirements:* For master's, translation exam. Additional exam requirements/recommendations for international students: Recommended—TOEFL (minimum score 550 paper-based).

**Binghamton University, State University of New York,** Graduate School, Harpur College of Arts and Sciences, Translation Research and Instruction Program, Binghamton, NY 13902-6000. Offers PhD, Certificate. *Program availability:* Part-time. *Students:* 25 full-time (16 women), 26 part-time (16 women); includes 2 minority (both Hispanic/Latino), 39 international. Average age 35. 30 applicants, 87% accepted, 11 enrolled. In 2016, 4 doctorates, 3 other advanced degrees awarded. *Degree requirements:* For doctorate, one foreign language, comprehensive exam, thesis/dissertation; for Certificate, one foreign language, comprehensive exam. *Entrance requirements:* For doctorate and Certificate, GRE General Test, writing sample. Additional exam requirements/recommendations for international students: Required—TOEFL (minimum score 550 paper-based; 80 iBT). *Application deadline:* Applications are processed on a rolling basis. Application fee: $75. Electronic applications accepted. *Financial support:* In 2016–17, 9 students received support, including 4 teaching assistantships with full tuition reimbursements available (averaging $14,500 per year); career-related internships or fieldwork, Federal Work-Study, institutionally sponsored loans, scholarships/grants, health care benefits, and unspecified assistantships also available. Financial award applicants required to submit FAFSA. *Unit head:* Dr. Michael Pettid, Director, 607-777-3862, E-mail: mpettid@binghamton.edu. *Application contact:* Ben Balkaya, Assistant Dean and Director, 607-777-2151, Fax: 607-777-2501, E-mail: balkaya@binghamton.edu.

**Columbia University,** Graduate School of Arts and Sciences, New York, NY 10027. Offers African-American studies (MA); American studies (MA); anthropology (MA, PhD); art history and archaeology (MA, PhD); astronomy (PhD); biological sciences (PhD); biotechnology (MA); chemical physics (PhD); chemistry (PhD); classical studies (MA, PhD); classics (MA, PhD); climate and society (MA); conservation biology (MA); earth and environmental sciences (PhD); East Asia: regional studies (MA); East Asian languages and cultures (MA, PhD); ecology, evolution and environmental biology (MA), including conservation biology; ecology, evolution, and environmental biology (PhD), including ecology and evolutionary biology, evolutionary primatology; economics (MA, PhD); English and comparative literature (MA, PhD); French and Romance philology (MA, PhD); Germanic languages (MA, PhD); global French studies (MA); global thought (MA); Hispanic cultural studies (MA); history (PhD); history and literature (MA); human rights studies (MA); Islamic studies (MA); Italian (MA, PhD); Japanese pedagogy (MA); Jewish studies (MA); Latin America and the Caribbean: regional studies (MA); Latin American and Iberian cultures (PhD), including finance (MA); mathematics (MA, PhD), including finance (MA); medieval and Renaissance studies (MA); Middle Eastern, South Asian, and African studies (MA, PhD); modern art: critical and curatorial studies (MA); modern European studies (MA); museum anthropology (MA); music (DMA, PhD); oral history (MA); philosophical foundations of physics (MA); philosophy (MA, PhD); physics (PhD); political science (MA, PhD); psychology (PhD); quantitative methods in the social sciences (MA); religion (MA, PhD); Russia, Eurasia and East Europe: regional studies (MA); Russian translation (MA); Slavic cultures (MA); Slavic languages (MA, PhD); sociology (MA, PhD); South Asian studies (MA); statistics (MA, PhD); theatre (PhD). Dual-degree programs require admission to both Graduate School of Arts and Sciences and another Columbia school. *Program availability:* Part-time. Terminal master's awarded for partial completion of doctoral program. *Degree requirements:* For master's, variable foreign language requirement, comprehensive exam (for some programs), thesis (for some programs); for doctorate, variable foreign language requirement, comprehensive exam (for some programs), thesis/dissertation. *Entrance requirements:* For master's and doctorate, GRE General Test, GRE Subject Test (for some programs). Additional exam requirements/recommendations for international students: Required—TOEFL, IELTS. Electronic applications accepted.

**Concordia University,** School of Graduate Studies, Faculty of Arts and Science, Department of Études Franlfcaises, Montréal, QC H3G 1M8, Canada. Offers Anglais-Franlfcais en langue et techniques de localization (Certificate); littératures Francophones et résonances médiatiques (MA); translation (Diploma); translation studies (MA). *Degree requirements:* For other advanced degree, one foreign language.

**Gallaudet University,** The Graduate School, Washington, DC 20002-3625. Offers American Sign Language/English bilingual early childhood deaf education: birth to 5 (Certificate); audiology (Au D); clinical psychology (PhD); deaf and hard of hearing infants, toddlers, and their families (Certificate); deaf education (MA, Ed S); deaf history (Certificate); deaf studies (Certificate); educating deaf students with disabilities (Certificate); education: teacher preparation (MA), including deaf education, early childhood education and deaf education, elementary education and deaf education, secondary education and deaf education; educational neuroscience (PhD); hearing, speech and language sciences (MS, PhD); international development (MA); interpretation (MA, PhD), including combined interpreting practice and research (MA), interpreting research (MA); linguistics (MA, PhD); mental health counseling (MA); peer mentoring (Certificate); public administration (MPA); school counseling (MA); school psychology (Psy S); sign language teaching (MA); social work (MSW); speech-language pathology (MS). *Program availability:* Part-time. *Students:* 297 full-time (231 women), 129 part-time (97 women); includes 105 minority (35 Black or African American, non-Hispanic/Latino; 20 Asian, non-Hispanic/Latino; 39 Hispanic/Latino; 11 Two or more races, non-Hispanic/Latino), 22 international. Average age 30. 471 applicants, 52% accepted, 147 enrolled. In 2016, 138 master's, 25 doctorates, 14 other advanced degrees awarded. Terminal master's awarded for partial completion of doctoral program. *Degree requirements:* For master's, comprehensive exam (for some programs), thesis optional; for doctorate, comprehensive exam, thesis/dissertation. *Entrance requirements:* For master's and doctorate, GRE General Test or MAT, letters of recommendation, interviews, goals statement, American Sign Language proficiency interview, written English competency. Additional exam requirements/recommendations for international students: Required—TOEFL. *Application deadline:* For fall admission, 2/15 for domestic students. Applications are processed on a rolling basis. Application fee: $75. Electronic applications accepted. *Expenses: Tuition:* Full-time $17,100; part-time $950 per credit hour. *Required fees:* $3725; $276 per semester. *Financial support:* Fellowships, research assistantships, teaching assistantships, career-related internships or fieldwork, Federal Work-Study, scholarships/grants, tuition waivers (partial), and unspecified assistantships available. Support available to part-time students. Financial award application deadline: 7/1; financial award applicants required to submit FAFSA. *Faculty research:* Signing math dictionaries, telecommunications

access, cancer genetics, linguistics, visual language and visual learning, integrated quantum materials, deaf legal discourse, advance recruitment and retention in geosciences. *Unit head:* Dr. Gaurav Mathur, Dean, Graduate School and Continuing Studies, 202-250-2380, Fax: 202-651-5027, E-mail: gaurav.mathur@gallaudet.edu. *Application contact:* Wednesday Luria, Coordinator of Prospective Graduate Student Services, 202-651-5400, Fax: 202-651-5295, E-mail: graduate.school@gallaudet.edu.

**Georgia State University,** College of Arts and Sciences, Department of World Languages and Cultures, Program in Translation and Interpretation, Atlanta, GA 30302-3083. Offers interpretation (Certificate), including Spanish; translation (Certificate), including French, German, Spanish. *Program availability:* Part-time. *Entrance requirements:* For degree, entrance examination involving translating one passage from English to the target language and one passage from the target language to English, 3 letters of recommendation, resume/curriculum vitae, official transcripts. Additional exam requirements/recommendations for international students: Required—TOEFL (minimum score 79 iBT). *Application deadline:* For fall admission, 3/15 priority date for domestic and international students; for spring admission, 11/15 priority date for domestic and international students. Application fee: $50. Electronic applications accepted. *Expenses:* Tuition, state resident: full-time $6876; part-time $382 per credit hour. Tuition, nonresident: full-time $22,374; part-time $1243 per credit hour. *Required fees:* $2128; $1064 per term. Part-time tuition and fees vary according to course load and program. *Faculty research:* Romance linguistics and translation; theory and practice of translation; medical and legal interpretation. *Unit head:* Dr. Fernando Reati, Chair, 404-413-5984, Fax: 404-413-5982, E-mail: freati@gsu.edu. *Application contact:* Lita Malveaux, Administrative Academic Specialist, 404-413-5046, Fax: 404-413-5036, E-mail: lmalveaux@gsu.edu.
Website: http://wlc.gsu.edu/home/graduate/graduate-certificate/

**Kent State University,** College of Arts and Sciences, Department of Modern and Classical Language Studies, Kent, OH 44242-0001. Offers French (MA), including applied linguistics and pedagogy, literature; Latin (MA), including applied linguistics and pedagogy, literature; Spanish (MA), including applied linguistics and pedagogy, literature; translation (MA), including Arabic, French, German, Japanese, Russian, Spanish; translation studies (PhD); MA/MBA. *Program availability:* Part-time. *Faculty:* 35 full-time (23 women). *Students:* 81 full-time (51 women), 23 part-time (15 women); includes 14 minority (1 Black or African American, non-Hispanic/Latino; 9 Hispanic/Latino; 4 Two or more races, non-Hispanic/Latino), 48 international. Average age 30. 109 applicants, 53% accepted, 33 enrolled. In 2016, 31 master's, 6 doctorates awarded. *Degree requirements:* For master's, variable foreign language requirement, comprehensive exam (for some programs), thesis (for some programs); for doctorate, variable foreign language requirement, comprehensive exam, thesis/dissertation. *Entrance requirements:* For master's, transcripts, goal statement, 3 letters of recommendation, CD/MP3 with oral sample of first and second languages, writing sample of second language; for doctorate, transcripts, MA in translation, a foreign language, or similar field; proficiency in a foreign language; minimum GPA of 3.5 from MA; goal statement; 3 letters of recommendation; essay or writing sample. *Application deadline:* For fall admission, 2/1 for domestic and international students. Applications are processed on a rolling basis. Application fee: $45 ($70 for international students). Electronic applications accepted. *Expenses:* Tuition, state resident: full-time $10,864; part-time $495 per credit hour. Tuition, nonresident: full-time $18,380; part-time $837 per credit hour. *Financial support:* Fellowships with full tuition reimbursements, teaching assistantships with full tuition reimbursements, and unspecified assistantships available. Financial award application deadline: 2/1. *Unit head:* Dr. Keiran Dunne, Professor of French Translation/Chair, 330-672-2150, E-mail: kdunne@kent.edu. *Application contact:* Said Shiyab, Professor of Translation Studies/Graduate Coordinator, 330-672-1864, E-mail: sshiyab@kent.edu.
Website: http://www.kent.edu/mcls/

**La Salle University,** School of Arts and Sciences, Hispanic Institute, Philadelphia, PA 19141-1199. Offers bilingual/bicultural studies (MA); ESL program specialist (Certificate); interpretation: English/Spanish-Spanish/English (Certificate); teaching English to speakers of other languages (MA); translation and interpretation (MA); translation: English/Spanish-Spanish/English (Certificate). *Program availability:* Part-time, evening/weekend. *Faculty:* 2 full-time (1 woman), 6 part-time/adjunct (3 women). *Students:* 1 (woman) full-time, 26 part-time (18 women); includes 15 minority (5 Black or African American, non-Hispanic/Latino; 10 Hispanic/Latino), 1 international. Average age 37. 17 applicants, 76% accepted, 7 enrolled. In 2016, 7 master's, 4 other advanced degrees awarded. *Degree requirements:* For master's, one foreign language, project or thesis. *Entrance requirements:* For master's, GRE, MAT, or GMAT, professional resume; two letters of recommendation; for Certificate, GRE, MAT, or GMAT, professional resume; two letters of recommendation; evidence of an advanced level in Spanish. Additional exam requirements/recommendations for international students: Required—TOEFL. *Application deadline:* For fall admission, 8/15 priority date for domestic students, 7/15 for international students; for spring admission, 12/15 priority date for domestic students, 11/15 for international students; for summer admission, 4/15 priority date for domestic students, 3/15 for international students. Applications are processed on a rolling basis. Application fee: $35. Electronic applications accepted. Application fee is waived when completed online. *Expenses:* Contact institution. *Financial support:* In 2016–17, 3 students received support. Scholarships/grants available. Support available to part-time students. Financial award application deadline: 8/31; financial award applicants required to submit FAFSA. *Faculty research:* Puerto Rican literature, cross-cultural communication, English as a second language methodology, Spanish language. *Unit head:* Guadalupe Da Costa Montesinos, Director, 215-951-1209, Fax: 215-991-3506, E-mail: montesin@lasalle.edu. *Application contact:* Elizabeth Heenan, Director, Graduate and Adult Enrollment, 215-951-1100, Fax: 215-951-1462, E-mail: heenan@lasalle.edu.
Website: http://www.lasalle.edu/hispanic-institute/

**London Metropolitan University,** Graduate Programs, London, United Kingdom. Offers applied psychology (M Sc); architecture (M Sc); biomedical science (M Sc); blood science (M Sc); cancer pharmacology (M Sc); computer networking and cyber security (M Sc); computing and information systems (M Sc); conference interpreting (M Sc); counter-terrorism studies (M Sc); creative, digital and professional writing (MA); crime, violence and prevention (M Sc); criminology (M Sc); curating contemporary art (MA); data analytics (M Sc); digital media (MA); early childhood studies (MA); education (MA, Ed D); financial services law, regulation and compliance (LL M); food science (M Sc); forensic psychology (M Sc); health and social care management and policy (M Sc); human nutrition (M Sc); human resource management (MA); human rights and international conflict (MA); information technology (M Sc); intelligence and security studies (M Sc); international oil, gas and energy law (LL M); international relations (MA); interpreting (MA); learning and teaching in higher education (MA); legal practice (LL M); media and entertainment law (LL M); organizational and consumer psychology (M Sc); psychological therapy (M Sc); psychology of mental health (M Sc); public health (M Sc); public policy and management (MPA); security studies (M Sc); social work (M Sc); spatial planning and urban design (MA); sports therapy (M Sc); supporting older children and young people with dyslexia (MA); teaching languages (MA), including Arabic, English; translation (MA); woman and child abuse (MA).

## Translation and Interpretation

**Marygrove College,** Graduate Division, Program in Modern Language Translation, Detroit, MI 48221-2599. Offers Certificate.

**Middlebury Institute of International Studies at Monterey,** Graduate School of Translation, Interpretation and Language Education, Program in Translation and Interpretation, Monterey, CA 93940-2691. Offers conference interpretation (MA); translation (MA); translation and interpretation (MA); translation and localization management (MA). *Degree requirements:* For master's, one foreign language, thesis or alternative, exams. *Entrance requirements:* For master's, minimum GPA of 3.0, proficiency in a foreign language. Additional exam requirements/recommendations for international students: Required—TOEFL (minimum score 600 paper-based; 100 iBT). Electronic applications accepted. *Expenses: Tuition:* Full-time $38,250; part-time $1820 per credit. *Required fees:* $78 per semester. *Faculty research:* Assessment and testing in translation and interpretation, translation and interpretation pedagogy and curricula, integration of translation technology, language policy and planning.

**Mills College,** Graduate Studies, Department of English, Oakland, CA 94613-1000. Offers book art and creative writing (MFA); literature (MA); poetry (MFA); prose (MFA); Spanish creative writing (Certificate); translation (MFA). *Program availability:* Part-time. *Faculty:* 4 full-time (3 women), 4 part-time/adjunct (3 women). *Students:* 47 full-time (38 women), 2 part-time (both women); includes 28 minority (8 Black or African American, non-Hispanic/Latino; 3 Asian, non-Hispanic/Latino; 9 Hispanic/Latino; 8 Two or more races, non-Hispanic/Latino). Average age 32. 78 applicants, 95% accepted, 27 enrolled. In 2016, 29 master's awarded. *Degree requirements:* For master's, comprehensive exam, thesis. *Entrance requirements:* For master's, 15-20 page writing sample. Additional exam requirements/recommendations for international students: Required—TOEFL (minimum score 600 paper-based; 100 iBT), IELTS (minimum score 7). *Application deadline:* For fall admission, 12/15 priority date for domestic students, 12/15 for international students. Applications are processed on a rolling basis. Application fee: $50. Electronic applications accepted. *Expenses: Tuition:* Full-time $31,620. *Required fees:* $1118. Tuition and fees vary according to course load, degree level and program. *Financial support:* In 2016–17, 40 students received support, including 22 fellowships with partial tuition reimbursements available (averaging $9,099 per year), 18 teaching assistantships with tuition reimbursements available (averaging $4,798 per year); research assistantships and scholarships/grants also available. Support available to part-time students. Financial award application deadline: 2/1; financial award applicants required to submit FAFSA. *Faculty research:* Creative writing, African-American literature, Victorian women writers, theories of sexuality, Shakespeare. *Unit head:* Dr. Ajuan Mance, Chair of the English Department, 510-430-2218, E-mail: dcady@mills.edu. *Application contact:* Robynne Lofton, Director of Admissions, 510-430-3295, Fax: 510-430-2159, E-mail: grad-admission@mills.edu. Website: http://www.mills.edu/english/

**Montclair State University,** The Graduate School, College of Humanities and Social Sciences, Translation and Interpreting in Spanish Certificate Program, Montclair, NJ 07043-1624. Offers Certificate. *Expenses:* Tuition, state resident: part-time $553 per credit. Tuition, nonresident: part-time $854 per credit. *Required fees:* $91 per credit. Tuition and fees vary according to program.

**New York University,** School of Continuing and Professional Studies, Center for Foreign Languages, Translation and Interpretation, New York, NY 10012-1019. Offers translation (MS), including Chinese to English, English to Spanish, French to English, Spanish to English. *Program availability:* Part-time, evening/weekend. *Degree requirements:* For master's, thesis. *Entrance requirements:* For master's, GRE or GMAT (only upon request), bachelor's degree, resume with relevant professional work, internship or volunteer experience, two letters of recommendation, statement of purpose. Additional exam requirements/recommendations for international students: Required—TOEFL (minimum score 600 paper-based; 100 iBT), IELTS (minimum score 7). Electronic applications accepted.

**Rochester Institute of Technology,** Graduate Enrollment Services, National Technical Institute for the Deaf, American Sign Language and Interpreting Education Department, MS Program in Health Care Interpretation, Rochester, NY 14623-5603. Offers MS. Program offered in collaboration with College of Health Sciences and Technology. *Program availability:* Part-time, blended/hybrid learning. *Students:* 4 full-time (all women), 4 part-time (all women); includes 3 minority (2 Black or African American, non-Hispanic/Latino; 1 Two or more races, non-Hispanic/Latino). Average age 38. *Degree requirements:* For master's, final capstone project. *Entrance requirements:* For master's, ASL interpretation video sample, ASL/English certification or state licensure, two recommendation letters, audio gram (for deaf or hard-of-hearing applicants), personal statement, transcript with minimum GPA of 3.0. *Application deadline:* For summer admission, 1/15 priority date for domestic and international students. Applications are processed on a rolling basis. Electronic applications accepted. *Expenses:* $724 per credit hour. *Financial support:* In 2016–17, 1 student received support. Research assistantships with partial tuition reimbursements available, teaching assistantships with partial tuition reimbursements available, career-related internships or fieldwork, scholarships/grants, and unspecified assistantships available. Support available to part-time students. Financial award applicants required to submit FAFSA. *Faculty research:* Interpreter's ethics, decision-making in community interpreting, healthcare interpreting, ethical reasoning skills of interpreters, reflective practice of supervision with interpreters. *Unit head:* Kathleen Miraglia, Department Chair, 585-475-5441, E-mail: kamnss@rit.edu. *Application contact:* Diane Ellison, Assistant Vice President, Graduate Enrollment Services, 585-475-2229, Fax: 585-475-7164, E-mail: gradinfo@rit.edu. Website: http://www.ntid.rit.edu/aslie/mshci/overview

**Rutgers University–New Brunswick,** Graduate School-New Brunswick, Program in Spanish, Piscataway, NJ 08854-8097. Offers bilingualism and second language acquisition (MA, PhD); Spanish (MA, MAT, PhD); Spanish literature (MA, PhD); translation (MA). *Program availability:* Part-time. *Degree requirements:* For master's, comprehensive exam (for some programs), thesis (for some programs); for doctorate, 2 foreign languages, comprehensive exam, thesis/dissertation. *Entrance requirements:* For master's and doctorate, GRE General Test. Additional exam requirements/recommendations for international students: Required—TOEFL. Electronic applications accepted. *Faculty research:* Hispanic literature, Luso-Brazilian literature, Spanish linguistics, Spanish translation.

**Texas A&M International University,** Office of Graduate Studies and Research, College of Arts and Sciences, Department of Humanities, Laredo, TX 78041-1900. Offers English (MA); Hispanic studies (PhD); history and political thought (MA); language, literature and translation (MA). *Degree requirements:* For master's, comprehensive exam (for some programs), thesis (for some programs). *Entrance requirements:* For master's, GRE General Test. Additional exam requirements/recommendations for international students: Required—TOEFL (minimum score 550 paper-based; 79 iBT).

**Universidad Autonoma de Guadalajara,** Graduate Programs, Guadalajara, Mexico. Offers administrative law and justice (LL M); advertising and corporate communications (MA); architecture (M Arch); business (MBA); computational science (MCC); education (Ed M, Ed D); English-Spanish translation (MA); entrepreneurship and management (MBA); integrated management of digital animation (MA); international business (MIB);

international corporate law (LL M); internet technologies (MS); manufacturing systems (MMS); occupational health (MS); philosophy (MA, PhD); power electronics (MS); quality systems (MQS); renewable energy (MS); social evaluation of projects (MBA); strategic market research (MBA); tax law (MA); teaching mathematics (MA).

**Université de Montréal,** Faculty of Arts and Sciences, Department of Linguistics and Translation, Montréal, QC H3C 3J7, Canada. Offers linguistics (MA, PhD); translation (MA, PhD, DESS). *Degree requirements:* For master's, thesis, general exam; for doctorate, thesis/dissertation, general exam. Electronic applications accepted.

**Université Laval,** Faculty of Letters, Department of Languages, Linguistics and Translations, Programs in Terminology and Translation, Québec, QC G1K 7P4, Canada. Offers MA, Diploma. *Program availability:* Part-time. *Degree requirements:* For master's, thesis (for some programs). *Entrance requirements:* For master's and Diploma, knowledge of French and English. Electronic applications accepted.

**University of California, Santa Barbara,** Graduate Division, College of Letters and Sciences, Division of Humanities and Fine Arts, Department of East Asian Languages and Cultural Studies, Santa Barbara, CA 93106-7075. Offers applied linguistics (PhD); East Asian languages and cultural studies (MA); translation studies (PhD). *Degree requirements:* For master's, one foreign language, comprehensive exam (for some programs), thesis (for some programs); for doctorate, 2 foreign languages, thesis/dissertation, methodology. *Entrance requirements:* For master's and doctorate, GRE General Test. Additional exam requirements/recommendations for international students: Required—TOEFL (minimum score 550 paper-based; 80 iBT), IELTS (minimum score 7). Electronic applications accepted. *Faculty research:* Chinese literature, Chinese film, Japanese society, Japanese literature, East Asian cultural studies.

**University of California, Santa Barbara,** Graduate Division, College of Letters and Sciences, Division of Humanities and Fine Arts, Department of English, Santa Barbara, CA 93106-3170. Offers English (PhD), including environment and society, European medieval studies, feminist studies, global studies, technology and society, translation studies, writing studies; MA/PhD. Terminal master's awarded for partial completion of doctoral program. *Degree requirements:* For doctorate, one foreign language, comprehensive exam, thesis/dissertation. *Entrance requirements:* For doctorate, GRE General Test, GRE Subject Test (English literature). Additional exam requirements/recommendations for international students: Required—TOEFL (minimum score 550 paper-based; 80 iBT), IELTS (minimum score 7). Electronic applications accepted. *Faculty research:* Medieval, Romantic and Victorian studies; gender studies and feminist theory; literature and the mind; American literature; literature and new media/information culture.

**University of California, Santa Barbara,** Graduate Division, College of Letters and Sciences, Division of Humanities and Fine Arts, Department of Religious Studies, Santa Barbara, CA 93106-3130. Offers ancient Mediterranean studies (PhD); cognitive science (PhD); European medieval studies (PhD); feminist studies (PhD); global studies (PhD); religious studies (MA, PhD); translation studies (PhD); MA/PhD. Terminal master's awarded for partial completion of doctoral program. *Degree requirements:* For master's, one foreign language, comprehensive exam (for some programs), thesis (for some programs); for doctorate, 2 foreign languages, thesis/dissertation, methodology. *Entrance requirements:* For master's and doctorate, GRE General Test. Additional exam requirements/recommendations for international students: Required—TOEFL (minimum score 550 paper-based; 80 iBT), IELTS (minimum score 7). Electronic applications accepted. *Faculty research:* Area studies; religious traditions; theory and method in the study of religion; religion, culture, and politics; spirituality and religious experience.

**University of California, Santa Barbara,** Graduate Division, College of Letters and Sciences, Division of Humanities and Fine Arts, Program in Comparative Literature, Santa Barbara, CA 93106-4130. Offers comparative literature (PhD); East Asian literatures (PhD); feminist studies (PhD); French (PhD); global studies (PhD); translation studies (PhD); MA/PhD. *Degree requirements:* For doctorate, 2 foreign languages, comprehensive exam, thesis/dissertation. *Entrance requirements:* For doctorate, GRE. Additional exam requirements/recommendations for international students: Required—TOEFL (minimum score 550 paper-based; 80 iBT), IELTS (minimum score 7). Electronic applications accepted. *Faculty research:* Comparative literary studies in global context, critical theory, translation studies, media technological studies, trauma studies.

**University of Delaware,** College of Arts and Sciences, Department of Foreign Languages and Literatures, Newark, DE 19716. Offers foreign languages and literatures (MA), including French, German, Spanish; foreign languages pedagogy (MA), including French, German, Spanish; technical Chinese translation (MA). *Degree requirements:* For master's, one foreign language, comprehensive exam, thesis optional. *Entrance requirements:* For master's, GRE General Test, letters of recommendation, writing sample. Additional exam requirements/recommendations for international students: Required—TOEFL. Electronic applications accepted. *Faculty research:* Medieval to Modern French and Spanish literature, twentieth-century German, French, Spanish literature by women, computer-assisted instruction.

**University of Denver,** University College, Denver, CO 80208. Offers arts and culture (MA, Certificate); communication management (MS, Certificate), including translation studies (Certificate), world history and culture (Certificate); environmental policy and management (MS); geographic information systems (MS); global affairs (MA, Certificate), including human capital in organizations (Certificate), philanthropic leadership (Certificate), project management (Certificate), strategic innovation and change (Certificate); healthcare leadership (MS); information communications and technology (MS); leadership and organizations (MS); professional creative writing (MA, Certificate), including emergency planning and response (Certificate), organizational security (Certificate); security management (MS, Certificate); strategic human resources (Certificate). *Program availability:* Part-time, evening/weekend, online learning. *Faculty:* 118 part-time/adjunct (62 women). *Students:* 59 full-time (22 women), 1,285 part-time (750 women); includes 316 minority (111 Black or African American, non-Hispanic/Latino; 8 American Indian or Alaska Native, non-Hispanic/Latino; 39 Asian, non-Hispanic/Latino; 123 Hispanic/Latino; 3 Native Hawaiian or other Pacific Islander, non-Hispanic/Latino; 32 Two or more races, non-Hispanic/Latino), 85 international. Average age 35. 703 applicants, 89% accepted, 390 enrolled. In 2016, 428 master's, 138 other advanced degrees awarded. *Degree requirements:* For master's, capstone project. *Entrance requirements:* For master's, transcripts, two letters of recommendation, personal statement, resume. Additional exam requirements/recommendations for international students: Required—TOEFL (minimum score 550 paper-based; 80 iBT). *Application deadline:* For fall admission, 6/21 priority date for domestic students, 5/1 priority date for international students; for winter admission, 9/14 priority date for domestic students, 9/19 priority date for international students; for spring admission, 1/11 priority date for domestic students, 12/12 priority date for international students; for summer admission, 3/29 priority date for domestic students, 3/6 priority date for international students. Applications are processed on a rolling basis. Application fee: $75. Electronic applications accepted. *Expenses:* $7,236 per year full-time. *Financial support:* In 2016–17, 27 students received support, including 1 teaching assistantship (averaging $1,489 per year). Financial award applicants required to submit FAFSA. *Unit head:* Dr. Michael McGuire, Dean, 303-871-3518, Fax: 303-871-3303,

E-mail: mmguire@du.edu. *Application contact:* Information Contact, 303-871-2291, E-mail: ucoladm@du.edu. Website: http://universitycollege.du.edu/

**University of Illinois at Urbana–Champaign,** Graduate College, College of Liberal Arts and Sciences, School of Literatures, Cultures and Linguistics, Center for Translation Studies, Champaign, IL 61820. Offers translation and interpreting (MA). *Program availability:* Part-time, online learning. *Entrance requirements:* For master's, BA or BS in languages, linguistics, international studies, area studies, or a related field; three letters of recommendation; resume or curriculum vitae; official transcripts.

**The University of Manchester,** School of Languages, Linguistics and Cultures, Manchester, United Kingdom. Offers Arab world studies (PhD); Chinese studies (M Phil, PhD); East Asian studies (M Phil, PhD); English language (PhD); French studies (M Phil, PhD); German studies (M Phil, PhD); interpreting studies (PhD); Italian studies (M Phil, PhD); Japanese studies (M Phil, PhD); Latin American cultural studies (M Phil, PhD); linguistics (M Phil, PhD); Middle Eastern studies (M Phil, PhD); Polish studies (M Phil, PhD); Portuguese studies (M Phil, PhD); Russian studies (M Phil, PhD); Spanish studies (M Phil, PhD); translation and intercultural studies (M Phil, PhD).

**The University of North Carolina at Charlotte,** College of Liberal Arts and Sciences, Department of Languages and Culture Studies, Charlotte, NC 28223-0001. Offers languages and culture studies: translating (MA); translating (Graduate Certificate). *Program availability:* Part-time, evening/weekend. *Faculty:* 14 full-time (8 women). *Students:* 1 (woman) full-time, 8 part-time (6 women); includes 3 minority (all Hispanic/Latino). Average age 39. 3 applicants, 67% accepted, 1 enrolled. In 2016, 4 master's, 3 other advanced degrees awarded. *Degree requirements:* For master's, comprehensive exam, thesis, internship; for Graduate Certificate, internship. *Entrance requirements:* For master's, GRE, baccalaureate degree in Spanish or related field with minimum overall GPA of 2.75; essay that addresses the applicant's motivation for enrolling in program, to include particular areas of research interests and career or professional goals; three letters of reference; oral interview; for Graduate Certificate, GRE or MAT, essay in English that addresses applicant's motivation for seeking enrollment in program; three letters of recommendation; portfolio of best writing samples in both English and Spanish or of translations into each language; oral interview. Additional exam requirements/recommendations for international students: Required—TOEFL (minimum score 523 paper-based, 70 iBT) or IELTS (6.5). *Application deadline:* For fall admission, 3/1 priority date for domestic and international students; for spring admission, 10/1 priority date for domestic and international students. Applications are processed on a rolling basis. Application fee: $75. Electronic applications accepted. *Expenses:* Tuition, state resident: full-time $4252. Tuition, nonresident: full-time $17,423. *Required fees:* $3026. Tuition and fees vary according to course load and program. *Financial support:* In 2016–17, 3 students received support, including 2 research assistantships (averaging $5,000 per year), 1 teaching assistantship (averaging $8,000 per year); career-related internships or fieldwork, institutionally sponsored loans, scholarships/grants, and unspecified assistantships also available. Support available to part-time students. Financial award application deadline: 3/1; financial award applicants required to submit FAFSA. *Total annual research expenditures:* $12,433. *Unit head:* Ann Gonzalez, Chair, 704-687-8761, E-mail: abgonzal@uncc.edu. *Application contact:* Kathy B. Giddings, Director of Graduate Admissions, 704-687-5503, Fax: 704-687-1668, E-mail: gradadm@uncc.edu. Website: https://languages.uncc.edu/

**University of North Florida,** College of Education and Human Services, Department of Exceptional, Deaf, and Interpreter Education, Jacksonville, FL 32224. Offers American Sign Language (MS); American Sign Language/English interpreting (M Ed); applied behavior analysis (M Ed); autism (M Ed); deaf education (M Ed); disability services (M Ed); exceptional student education (M Ed). *Accreditation:* NCATE. *Program availability:* Part-time, evening/weekend. *Faculty:* 11 full-time (9 women), 6 part-time/adjunct (all women). *Students:* 32 full-time (29 women), 50 part-time (40 women); includes 14 minority (5 Black or African American, non-Hispanic/Latino; 2 Asian, non-Hispanic/Latino; 5 Hispanic/Latino; 2 Two or more races, non-Hispanic/Latino), 4 international. Average age 33. 28 applicants, 46% accepted, 7 enrolled. In 2016, 42 master's awarded. *Entrance requirements:* For master's, GRE General Test, minimum GPA of 3.0 in last 60 hours, interview, 3 letters of recommendation. Additional exam requirements/recommendations for international students: Required—TOEFL (minimum score 500 paper-based). *Application deadline:* For fall admission, 3/31 priority date for domestic students, 5/1 for international students; for spring admission, 12/1 priority date for domestic students, 10/1 for international students; for summer admission, 3/31 priority date for domestic students, 2/1 for international students. Application fee: $30. Electronic applications accepted. Tuition and fees vary according to course load, campus/location and program. *Financial support:* In 2016–17, 7 students received support, including 2 research assistantships (averaging $2,639 per year); teaching assistantships, career-related internships or fieldwork, Federal Work-Study, scholarships/grants, tuition waivers (partial), and unspecified assistantships also available. Support available to part-time students. Financial award application deadline: 4/1; financial award applicants required to submit FAFSA. *Faculty research:* Transportation, energy, communications, healthcare, nano-science and engineering, unmanned aircraft systems, biomedical applications. *Total annual research expenditures:* $706,370. *Unit head:* Dr. Janice Seabrooks-Blackmore, Chair, 904-620-2930, Fax: 904-620-3895, E-mail: janice.seabrooks-blackmore@unf.edu. *Application contact:* Dr. Amanda Pascale, Director, The Graduate School, 904-620-1360, Fax: 904-620-1362, E-mail: graduateschool@unf.edu. Website: http://www.unf.edu/coehs/edie/

**University of Ottawa,** Faculty of Graduate and Postdoctoral Studies, Faculty of Arts, Institute of Canadian Studies, Ottawa, ON K1N 6N5, Canada. Offers economics (PhD); English (PhD); geography (PhD); history (PhD); lettres Franlfcaises (PhD); linguistics (PhD); philosophy (PhD); political science (PhD); psychology (PhD); religious studies (PhD); translation studies (PhD). *Degree requirements:* For doctorate, comprehensive exam, thesis/dissertation.

**University of Ottawa,** Faculty of Graduate and Postdoctoral Studies, Faculty of Arts, School of Translation and Interpretation, Ottawa, ON K1N 6N5, Canada. Offers interpreting (MA); Spanish translation (MA); translation (MA); translation studies (PhD). *Degree requirements:* For master's, one foreign language, thesis or alternative, research paper; for doctorate, thesis/dissertation, doctoral exam. *Entrance requirements:* For master's, school-administered exam, honors degree or equivalent, minimum B average; for doctorate, master's degree, minimum B+ average. Electronic applications accepted. *Faculty research:* Theory of translation, Spanish translation, conference interpreting, legal translation, translation-oriented lexicology and terminology.

**University of Puerto Rico, Río Piedras Campus,** College of Humanities, Program in Translation, San Juan, PR 00931-3300. Offers MA, Certificate. *Program availability:* Part-time, evening/weekend. *Degree requirements:* For master's, 2 foreign languages, comprehensive exam, thesis. *Entrance requirements:* For master's, PAEG, minimum GPA of 3.0, graduate-level knowledge of 2 languages (English, French, or Spanish), letter of recommendation.

**University of Rochester,** School of Arts and Sciences, Interdisciplinary Program in Literary Translation Studies, Rochester, NY 14627. Offers MA, Graduate Certificate. *Program availability:* Part-time. *Students:* 1 (woman) full-time. Average age 26. 8 applicants, 75% accepted, 1 enrolled. In 2016, 2 master's awarded. *Degree requirements:* For master's, one foreign language, comprehensive exam, thesis optional. *Entrance requirements:* For master's, official transcripts, three letters of recommendation, personal statement. Additional exam requirements/recommendations for international students: Required—TOEFL (minimum score 600 paper-based; 100 iBT). *Application deadline:* For fall admission, 2/1 for domestic and international students. Applications are processed on a rolling basis. Application fee: $60. Electronic applications accepted. *Expenses: Tuition:* Full-time $47,450; part-time $1482 per credit hour. *Required fees:* $528. Tuition and fees vary according to program. *Financial support:* In 2016–17, 1 student received support. Tuition waivers (partial) available. Financial award application deadline: 2/5. *Unit head:* Jennifer Grotz, Literary Translation Advisor, 585-275-4092, E-mail: jennifer.grotz@rochester.edu. *Application contact:* Jennifer Sherwood, Assistant Director of Multidisciplinary Studies Center, 585-276-5305, E-mail: jennifer.sherwood@rochester.edu. Website: http://www.rochester.edu/college/translation/graduate/index.html

**University of Wisconsin–Milwaukee,** Graduate School, College of Letters and Science, Department of Foreign Languages and Literature, Milwaukee, WI 53201-0413. Offers classic Greek (MA); classics (MA); comparative literature (MA); foreign language and literature (MA); French (MA); German (MA); Latin (MA); linguistics (MA); Spanish (MA); translation (MA, Certificate). *Program availability:* Part-time. *Students:* 10 full-time (7 women), 19 part-time (16 women); includes 5 minority (2 Black or African American, non-Hispanic/Latino; 2 Hispanic/Latino; 1 Two or more races, non-Hispanic/Latino), 2 international. Average age 31. 41 applicants, 32% accepted, 9 enrolled. In 2016, 21 master's awarded. *Degree requirements:* For master's, 2 foreign languages, thesis or alternative. *Entrance requirements:* Additional exam requirements/recommendations for international students: Required—TOEFL (minimum score 550 paper-based; 79 iBT), IELTS (minimum score 6.5). *Application deadline:* For fall admission, 1/1 priority date for domestic students; for spring admission, 9/1 for domestic students. Applications are processed on a rolling basis. Application fee: $56 ($96 for international students). Electronic applications accepted. *Financial support:* In 2016–17, 1 fellowship, 2 research assistantships, 26 teaching assistantships were awarded; career-related internships or fieldwork, health care benefits, unspecified assistantships, and project assistantships also available. Support available to part-time students. Financial award application deadline: 4/15; financial award applicants required to submit FAFSA. *Unit head:* Kevin Muse, Department Chair, 414-229-5213, E-mail: kmuse@uwm.edu. *Application contact:* General Information Contact, 414-229-4982, Fax: 414-229-6967, E-mail: gradschool@uwm.edu. Website: http://uwm.edu/foreign-languages-literature/

**Wesley Biblical Seminary,** Graduate Programs, Jackson, MS 39206. Offers apologetics (MA); Biblical languages (M Div); Biblical literature (MA); Christian studies (MA); context and mission (M Div); honors research (M Div); interpretation (M Div); ministry (M Div); spiritual formation (M Div); teaching (M Div); theology (MA). *Accreditation:* ATS. *Program availability:* Part-time. *Degree requirements:* For master's, thesis. *Entrance requirements:* Additional exam requirements/recommendations for international students: Required—TOEFL. Electronic applications accepted. *Faculty research:* Patristics, missiology, culture, hermeneutics.

**York University,** Faculty of Graduate Studies, Glendon Campus, Program in Translation, Toronto, ON M3J 1P3, Canada. Offers MA. *Degree requirements:* For master's, thesis or alternative. *Entrance requirements:* For master's, professional translating experience. Electronic applications accepted.

# Section 11
# Philosophy and Ethics

This section contains a directory of institutions offering graduate work in philosophy and ethics. Additional information about programs listed in the directory may be obtained by writing directly to the dean of a graduate school or chair of a department at the address given in the directory.

For programs offering related work, see also in this book *Area and Cultural Studies, History, Humanities, Religious Studies,* and *Social Sciences.*

## CONTENTS

### Program Directories

# Ethics

**American University,** College of Arts and Sciences, Department of Philosophy and Religion, Washington, DC 22016-8056. Offers ethics, peace, and global affairs (MA); philosophy (MA). *Program availability:* Part-time, evening/weekend. *Faculty:* 12 full-time (7 women), 13 part-time/adjunct (8 women). *Students:* 13 full-time (9 women), 8 part-time (2 women); includes 5 minority (3 Black or African American, non-Hispanic/Latino; 1 Hispanic/Latino; 1 Two or more races, non-Hispanic/Latino). Average age 30. 45 applicants, 76% accepted, 10 enrolled. In 2016, 8 master's awarded. *Degree requirements:* For master's, one foreign language, comprehensive exam, thesis (for some programs). *Entrance requirements:* For master's, GRE, writing sample, statement of purpose, transcripts, 2 letters of recommendation, resume. Additional exam requirements/recommendations for international students: Required—TOEFL (minimum score 100 iBT), IELTS (minimum score 7), PTE (minimum score 68). *Application deadline:* For fall admission, 2/1 priority date for domestic students; for spring admission, 11/1 for domestic students. Application fee: $55. *Expenses:* $1,579 per credit tuition; $690 mandatory fees. *Financial support:* Research assistantships, teaching assistantships, scholarships/grants, and unspecified assistantships available. Financial award application deadline: 2/1; financial award applicants required to submit FAFSA. *Unit head:* Dr. Ellen Feder, Department Chair, 202-885-2931, Fax: 202-885-1094, E-mail: efeder@american.edu. *Application contact:* Kathleen Clowery, Associate Director, Graduate Admissions, 202-885-3620, Fax: 202-885-1344, E-mail: clowery@american.edu.
Website: http://www.american.edu/cas/philrel/

**American University,** School of International Service, Washington, DC 20016-8071. Offers comparative and regional studies (Certificate); cross-cultural communication (Certificate); development management (MS); ethics, peace, and global affairs (MA); European studies (Certificate); global environmental policy (MA, Certificate); global information technology (Certificate); international affairs (MA), including comparative and international disability policy, comparative and regional studies, international economic relations, international politics, natural resources and sustainable development, U.S. foreign policy; international arts management (Certificate); international communication (MA, Certificate); international development (MA); international economic policy (Certificate); international economic relations (Certificate); international economics (MA); international media (MA); international peace and conflict resolution (MA, Certificate); international politics (Certificate); international relations (MA, PhD); international service (MIS); peacebuilding (Certificate); social enterprise (MA); the Americas (Certificate); United States foreign policy (Certificate); JD/MA. *Program availability:* Part-time, evening/weekend, 100% online. *Faculty:* 116 full-time (53 women), 57 part-time/adjunct (19 women). *Students:* 575 full-time (360 women), 491 part-time (277 women); includes 287 minority (100 Black or African American, non-Hispanic/Latino; 6 American Indian or Alaska Native, non-Hispanic/Latino; 58 Asian, non-Hispanic/Latino; 92 Hispanic/Latino; 1 Native Hawaiian or other Pacific Islander, non-Hispanic/Latino; 30 Two or more races, non-Hispanic/Latino), 151 international. Average age 29. 1,504 applicants, 84% accepted, 403 enrolled. In 2016, 374 master's, 3 doctorates, 1 other advanced degree awarded. Terminal master's awarded for partial completion of doctoral program. *Degree requirements:* For master's, one foreign language, comprehensive exam, thesis or alternative; for doctorate, one foreign language, comprehensive exam, thesis/dissertation. *Entrance requirements:* For master's, GRE; GMAT or GRE (for MA in social enterprise), transcripts, resume, 2 letters of recommendation, statement of purpose; for doctorate, GRE, transcripts, resume, 3 letters of recommendation, statement of purpose. Additional exam requirements/recommendations for international students: Required—TOEFL (minimum score 600 paper-based, 100 iBT), IELTS (minimum score 7 ), or PTE (minimum score of 68). Application fee: $55. Electronic applications accepted. *Expenses:* $1,579 per credit tuition; $1,930 mandatory fees. *Financial support:* Research assistantships, teaching assistantships, institutionally sponsored loans, scholarships/grants, and unspecified assistantships available. Financial award application deadline: 1/15; financial award applicants required to submit FAFSA. *Unit head:* Dr. James Goldgeier, Dean, 202-885-1603, Fax: 202-885-2494, E-mail: goldgeier@american.edu. *Application contact:* Jia Jiang, Associate Director, Graduate Education Enrollment, 202-885-1689, Fax: 202-885-1109, E-mail: jiang@american.edu.
Website: http://www.american.edu/sis/

**Anabaptist Mennonite Biblical Seminary,** Graduate and Professional Programs, Elkhart, IN 46517-1999. Offers chaplaincy (M Div); Christian faith formation (M Div); Christian formation (MA); Christian spiritual formation (Certificate); divinity (M Div); pastoral ministry (M Div); pastoral theology for financial professionals (Certificate); peace studies (M Div), including environmental sustainability leadership (M Div, MA); theological studies (M Div, Certificate), including peace studies (M Div), theology and ethics (M Div); theology and peace studies (MA), including conflict transformation, environmental sustainability leadership (M Div, MA), international development administration; United Methodist leadership (M Div). Conflict transformation and environmental sustainability leadership concentrations offered in cooperation with Goshen College; international development administration offered in cooperation with Andrews University. *Accreditation:* ACIPE; ATS. *Program availability:* Part-time, 100% online, blended/hybrid learning. *Faculty:* 14 full-time (6 women), 17 part-time/adjunct (8 women). *Students:* 38 full-time (14 women), 60 part-time (33 women); includes 15 minority (4 Black or African American, non-Hispanic/Latino; 5 Asian, non-Hispanic/Latino; 5 Hispanic/Latino; 1 Two or more races, non-Hispanic/Latino), 15 international. Average age 35. 43 applicants, 70% accepted, 29 enrolled. In 2016, 16 master's, 2 other advanced degrees awarded. *Degree requirements:* For master's, variable foreign language requirement, comprehensive exam (for some programs), thesis optional, senior interview. *Entrance requirements:* For master's, undergraduate degree transcripts, 3 letters of reference, essay. Additional exam requirements/recommendations for international students: Required—TOEFL (minimum score 90 iBT); Recommended—IELTS (minimum score 7). *Application deadline:* For fall admission, 6/1 priority date for domestic students, 5/1 priority date for international students. Applications are processed on a rolling basis. Application fee: $25. Electronic applications accepted. *Expenses:* Tuition: Full-time $13,950; part-time $5640 per year. *Required fees:* $900; $300 per unit. $50 per term. *Financial support:* In 2016–17, 40 students received support. Career-related internships or fieldwork, scholarships/grants, unspecified assistantships, and church matching grants available. Support available to part-time students. Financial award application deadline: 4/15; financial award applicants required to submit FAFSA. *Faculty research:* Biblical studies, peace studies, theology, ethics, creation care or environmental ethics, church history, church leadership, mission, ministry, preaching, pastoral leadership, social justice, peacemaking, Jesus Christ, Christianity, Anabaptism, Mennonite, Scripture, Bible, Old Testament, New Testament, spirituality, clinical pastoral education, teaching, faith formation, pastoral care, Koine Greek, Hebrew, Aramaic, Syriac, Ugaritic. *Unit head:* Sara Wenger Shenk, President, 800-964-2627, Fax: 574-295-0092. *Application contact:*

Daniel Grimes, Director of Admissions, 574-296-6266, Fax: 574-295-0092, E-mail: admissions@ambs.edu.
Website: http://www.ambs.edu/

**Arizona State University at the Tempe campus,** College of Liberal Arts and Sciences, School of Life Sciences, Tempe, AZ 85287-4601. Offers animal behavior (PhD); applied ethics (biomedical and health ethics) (MA); biology (MS, PhD), including biology, biology and society, complex adaptive systems science (PhD), plant biology and conservation (MS); environmental life sciences (PhD); evolutionary biology (PhD); history and philosophy of science (PhD); human and social dimensions of science and technology (PhD); microbiology (PhD); molecular and cellular biology (PhD); neuroscience (PhD). Terminal master's awarded for partial completion of doctoral program. *Degree requirements:* For master's, thesis (for some programs), interactive Program of Study (iPOS) submitted before completing 50 percent of required credit hours; for doctorate, variable foreign language requirement, comprehensive exam, thesis/dissertation, interactive Program of Study (iPOS) submitted before completing 50 percent of required credit hours. *Entrance requirements:* For master's and doctorate, GRE, minimum GPA of 3.0 or equivalent in last 2 years of work leading to bachelor's degree. Additional exam requirements/recommendations for international students: Required—TOEFL (minimum score 600 paper-based; 100 iBT). Electronic applications accepted.

**Arizona State University at the Tempe campus,** New College of Interdisciplinary Arts and Sciences, Phoenix, AZ 85069-7100. Offers applied ethics and the professions (MA); communication studies (MA); interdisciplinary studies (MA); psychology (MS); social justice and human rights (MA). *Program availability:* Part-time, evening/weekend. *Degree requirements:* For master's, thesis (for some programs), interactive Program of Study (iPOS) submitted before completing 50 percent of required credit hours. *Entrance requirements:* For master's, GRE, minimum GPA of 3.0 or equivalent in last 2 years of work leading to bachelor's degree. Additional exam requirements/recommendations for international students: Required—TOEFL, IELTS, or PTE. Electronic applications accepted.

**Arizona State University at the Tempe campus,** School of Letters and Sciences, Program in Applied Ethics, Tempe, AZ 85287-4503. Offers biomedical and health ethics (MA); ethics and emerging technologies (MA); public administration, policy and ethics (MA); science, technology and ethics (MA). *Program availability:* Part-time, evening/weekend. *Degree requirements:* For master's, thesis or alternative, applied project, interactive Program of Study (iPOS) submitted before completing 50 percent of required credit hours. *Entrance requirements:* For master's, GRE (for ethics and emerging technologies concentration), minimum GPA of 3.0 or equivalent in last 2 years of work leading to bachelor's degree, 2 letters of recommendation, resume, personal statement of interest and qualifications. Additional exam requirements/recommendations for international students: Required—TOEFL (minimum score 550 paper-based; 80 iBT). Electronic applications accepted.

**Azusa Pacific University,** Haggard Graduate School of Theology, Program in Theological Studies, Concentration in Religion: Theology and Ethics, Azusa, CA 91702-7000. Offers MA. *Accreditation:* ATS.

**Boston University,** School of Theology, Boston, MA 02118. Offers chaplaincy (M Div); choral conducting (MSM); church and the arts (M Div); constructive theology and ethics (PhD), including constructive theology, theological ethics; ecological theology and ethics (MTS); global and community engagement (M Div); history and hermeneutics (PhD), including Biblical studies, church history, liturgical studies, mission studies; organ (MSM); pastoral ministry (M Div); practical theology (PhD), including church and society, congregation and community, evangelism and missiology, homiletics, leadership and administration, pastoral theology and psychology, religious education, spirituality studies, worship; religion and conflict transformation (MTS); religion and science (MTS); religion and the academy (M Div); spirituality studies (MTS); theology (MTS, STM); transcultural studies (MTS); transformational leadership (D Min); M Div/MSM; M Div/MSW; MTS/MSW. PhD in history and hermeneutics: mission studies offered in collaboration with Gordon-Conwell Theological Seminary. *Accreditation:* ACIPE; ATS. *Program availability:* Part-time, blended/hybrid learning. *Faculty:* 34 full-time (14 women), 7 part-time/adjunct (3 women). *Students:* 260 full-time (131 women), 69 part-time (30 women); includes 69 minority (36 Black or African American, non-Hispanic/Latino; 10 Asian, non-Hispanic/Latino; 16 Hispanic/Latino; 7 Two or more races, non-Hispanic/Latino), 53 international. Average age 35. 234 applicants, 71% accepted, 106 enrolled. In 2016, 78 master's, 9 doctorates awarded. *Degree requirements:* For master's, comprehensive exam (for some programs), thesis optional, contextual education; for doctorate, 2 foreign languages, comprehensive exam, thesis/dissertation. *Entrance requirements:* For master's, minimum GPA of 3.0; for doctorate, GRE General Test, minimum GPA of 3.3. Additional exam requirements/recommendations for international students: Required—TOEFL (minimum score 570 paper-based; 89 iBT). *Application deadline:* For fall admission, 1/15 priority date for domestic and international students; for spring admission, 10/15 priority date for domestic and international students. Applications are processed on a rolling basis. Application fee: $95. Electronic applications accepted. *Expenses:* $19,500 per year tuition; $156 per semester student service fee; $54 per semester community service fee; $199 per semester health and wellness fee. *Financial support:* In 2016–17, 252 students received support, including 78 fellowships with full tuition reimbursements available (averaging $4,537 per year), 32 research assistantships (averaging $6,000 per year), 32 teaching assistantships with full and partial tuition reimbursements available (averaging $20,000 per year); career-related internships or fieldwork, Federal Work-Study, institutionally sponsored loans, scholarships/grants, traineeships, health care benefits, tuition waivers (full and partial), and unspecified assistantships also available. Support available to part-time students. Financial award application deadline: 7/15; financial award applicants required to submit FAFSA. *Faculty research:* Practical theology, Biblical studies, theology and ethical, history of Christianity. *Total annual research expenditures:* $2.5 million. *Unit head:* Rev. Dr. Mary Elizabeth Moore, Dean, 617-353-3050, Fax: 617-353-3061, E-mail: memoore@bu.edu. *Application contact:* Rev. Anastasia Kidd, Director of Admissions and College Relations, 617-353-3036, Fax: 617-358-0140, E-mail: sthadmis@bu.edu.
Website: http://www.bu.edu/sth

**Chicago Theological Seminary,** Graduate and Professional Programs, Chicago, IL 60637-1507. Offers Bible, culture and hermeneutics (PhD); preaching (D Min); religion and health (D Min); religious studies (MA); spirituality and spiritual direction (D Min); theology (M Div); theology, ethics and the human sciences (PhD); M Div/MSW. *Accreditation:* ACIPE; ATS. *Program availability:* Part-time. *Degree requirements:* For master's, thesis; for doctorate, 2 foreign languages, comprehensive exam, thesis/dissertation. *Entrance requirements:* For doctorate, GRE General Test. Additional exam requirements/recommendations for international students: Required—TOEFL. *Faculty* *research:* Bible, culture and hermeneutics, theology, gender and sexuality, black faith and life, spirituality and psychology, practical theology.

**Claremont Graduate University,** Graduate Programs, School of Arts and Humanities, Department of Religion, Claremont, CA 91711-6160. Offers Hebrew Bible (MA, PhD); history of Christianity and religions of North America (MA, PhD); New Testament (MA, PhD); philosophy of religion and theology (MA, PhD); theology, ethics and culture (MA, PhD); women's studies in religion (MA, PhD); MA/PhD; MBA/PhD. *Program availability:* Part-time. *Faculty:* 7 full-time (4 women), 2 part-time/adjunct (0 women). *Students:* 121 full-time (46 women), 13 part-time (6 women); includes 28 minority (10 Black or African American, non-Hispanic/Latino; 1 American Indian or Alaska Native, non-Hispanic/Latino; 6 Asian, non-Hispanic/Latino; 7 Hispanic/Latino; 1 Native Hawaiian or other Pacific Islander, non-Hispanic/Latino; 3 Two or more races, non-Hispanic/Latino), 19 international. Average age 39. In 2016, 11 master's, 21 doctorates awarded. Terminal master's awarded for partial completion of doctoral program. *Entrance requirements:* For master's and doctorate, GRE General Test. Additional exam requirements/recommendations for international students: Required—TOEFL (minimum score 75 iBT). *Application deadline:* For fall admission, 2/1 priority date for domestic and international students. Applications are processed on a rolling basis. Application fee: $80. Electronic applications accepted. *Expenses: Tuition:* Full-time $44,328; part-time $1847 per unit. *Required fees:* $600; $300 per semester. Tuition and fees vary according to course load and program. *Financial support:* Fellowships, research assistantships, teaching assistantships, Federal Work-Study, institutionally sponsored loans, and scholarships/grants available. Support available to part-time students. Financial award application deadline: 2/15; financial award applicants required to submit FAFSA. *Unit head:* Ruqayya Kahn, Chair, 909-607-0488, E-mail: ruqayya.kahn@cgu.edu. *Application contact:* Amy Sandefur, Assistant Director of Admissions, 909-607-9101, E-mail: amy.sandefur@cgu.edu. Website: https://www.cgu.edu/departments/religion/

**Claremont Lincoln University,** Graduate Programs, Claremont, CA 91711. Offers ethical leadership (MA); interfaith action (MA); social impact (MA).

**Claremont School of Theology,** Graduate and Professional Programs, Program in Religion, Claremont, CA 91711-3199. Offers practical theology (PhD), including religious education and formation, spiritual care and counseling; religion (MA, PhD), including comparative theology and philosophy (PhD), Hebrew Bible and Jewish studies (PhD), New Testament and Christian origins (PhD), process studies (PhD), religion, ethics, and society (PhD). *Accreditation:* ACIPE; ATS. Terminal master's awarded for partial completion of doctoral program. *Degree requirements:* For master's, thesis; for doctorate, 2 foreign languages, thesis/dissertation. *Entrance requirements:* For doctorate, GRE General Test. Additional exam requirements/recommendations for international students: Required—TOEFL. *Application deadline:* For fall admission, 1/15 for domestic and international students. Application fee: $50. Electronic applications accepted. *Expenses: Tuition:* Full-time $21,120. Tuition and fees vary according to course level, course load and degree level. *Financial support:* Research assistantships, teaching assistantships, career-related internships or fieldwork, Federal Work-Study, institutionally sponsored loans, scholarships/grants, and tuition waivers (full and partial) available. Support available to part-time students. Financial award application deadline: 4/1; financial award applicants required to submit FAFSA. *Unit head:* Sheryl A. Kujawa-Holbrook, Vice President for Academic Affairs/Dean, 909-447-2520, Fax: 909-447-6274, E-mail: skujawaholbrook@cst.edu. *Application contact:* Director of Admissions, 866-274-6500, Fax: 909-447-6389, E-mail: admission@cst.edu. Website: https://cst.edu/academics/m-a/

**Columbia University,** Graduate School of Business, MBA Program, New York, NY 10027. Offers accounting (MBA); decision, risk, and operations (MBA); entrepreneurship (MBA); finance and economics (MBA); healthcare and pharmaceutical management (MBA); human resource management (MBA); international business (MBA); leadership and ethics (MBA); management (MBA); marketing (MBA); media (MBA); private equity (MBA); real estate (MBA); social enterprise (MBA); value investing (MBA); DDS/MBA; JD/MBA; MBA/MIA; MBA/MPH; MBA/MS; MD/MBA. *Entrance requirements:* For master's, GMAT, 2 letters of recommendation. Additional exam requirements/recommendations for international students: Required—TOEFL. Electronic applications accepted. *Expenses:* Contact institution. *Faculty research:* Human decision making and behavioral research; real estate market and mortgage defaults; financial crisis and corporate governance; international business; security analysis and accounting.

**Duke University,** The Fuqua School of Business, The Duke MBA-Daytime Program, Durham, NC 27708-0586. Offers academic excellence in finance (Certificate); business administration (MBA); decision sciences (MBA); energy and environment (MBA); energy finance (MBA); entrepreneurship and innovation (MBA); finance (MBA); financial analysis (MBA); health sector management (Certificate); leadership and ethics (MBA); management (MBA); marketing (MBA); operations management (MBA); social entrepreneurship (MBA); strategy (MBA). *Faculty:* 88 full-time (19 women), 50 part-time/adjunct (9 women). *Students:* 897 full-time (310 women); includes 174 minority (39 Black or African American, non-Hispanic/Latino; 3 American Indian or Alaska Native, non-Hispanic/Latino; 75 Asian, non-Hispanic/Latino; 51 Hispanic/Latino; 1 Native Hawaiian or other Pacific Islander, non-Hispanic/Latino; 5 Two or more races, non-Hispanic/Latino), 343 international. Average age 28. In 2016, 440 master's awarded. *Entrance requirements:* For master's, GMAT or GRE, transcripts, essays, resume, recommendation letters, interview. *Application deadline:* For fall admission, 9/13 for domestic and international students; for winter admission, 10/13 for domestic and international students; for spring admission, 1/4 for domestic and international students; for summer admission, 3/20 for domestic and international students. Application fee: $225. Electronic applications accepted. *Expenses:* $66,717 (first-year tuition and fees). *Financial support:* In 2016–17, 415 students received support. Institutionally sponsored loans and scholarships/grants available. Financial award applicants required to submit FAFSA. *Unit head:* Russ Morgan, Senior Associate Dean for Full-time Programs, 919-660-2931, Fax: 919-684-8742, E-mail: ruskin.morgan@duke.edu. *Application contact:* Sharon Thompson, Assistant Dean, Office of Admissions, 919-660-7705, Fax: 919-681-8026, E-mail: admissions-info@fuqua.duke.edu. Website: http://www.fuqua.duke.edu/daytime-mba/

**Emory University,** Candler School of Theology, Atlanta, GA 30322. Offers formation and witness (M Div); history, scripture and tradition (MTS); leadership in church and community (M Div); modern religious thought and experience (MTS); pastoral counseling (Th D); religion and race (M Div); religion, health and science (M Div); scripture and interpretation (M Div); society and personality (M Div); theology (Th M); theology and ethics (M Div); theology and the arts (M Div); traditions of the church (M Div); women and religion (M Div); JD/M Div; JD/MTS; M Div/MBA; M Div/MPH; MBA/MTS; MTS/MPH. *Accreditation:* ACIPE. *Program availability:* Part-time. *Degree requirements:* For master's, thesis optional; for doctorate, comprehensive exam, thesis/dissertation. *Entrance requirements:* For master's, minimum undergraduate GPA of 3.0; for doctorate, GRE, M Div, 8 units of course work in clinical pastoral education. Additional exam requirements/recommendations for international students: Required—TOEFL (minimum score 600 paper-based; 95 iBT). Electronic applications accepted. *Expenses:* Contact institution. *Faculty research:* Biblical studies, church history, ethics, ministry practice, pastoral care.

**Fordham University,** Graduate School of Arts and Sciences, Program in Ethics and Society, New York, NY 10458. Offers ethics and society (MA); health care ethics (Certificate). *Program availability:* Part-time. *Students:* 8 full-time (7 women), 5 part-time (3 women); includes 3 minority (2 Black or African American, non-Hispanic/Latino; 1 Asian, non-Hispanic/Latino), 1 international. Average age 34. 39 applicants, 28% accepted, 7 enrolled. In 2016, 6 master's awarded. *Entrance requirements:* Additional exam requirements/recommendations for international students: Required—TOEFL. *Application deadline:* For fall admission, 1/4 priority date for domestic students; for spring admission, 10/31 for domestic students. Applications are processed on a rolling basis. Application fee: $70. Electronic applications accepted. *Financial support:* In 2016–17, 1 student received support. Teaching assistantships, Federal Work-Study, institutionally sponsored loans, scholarships/grants, tuition waivers (partial), and unspecified assistantships available. Financial award application deadline: 1/4. *Unit head:* Dr. Bryan Pilkington, Director of Academic Programs, Fordham University Center for Ethics Education, 718-817-3775, Fax: 212-759-2009, E-mail: afried@fordham.edu. *Application contact:* Bernadette Valentino-Morrison, Director of Graduate Admissions, 718-817-4419, Fax: 718-817-3566, E-mail: valentinomor@fordham.edu.

**Freed-Hardeman University,** Program in Business Administration, Henderson, TN 38340-2399. Offers accounting (MBA); corporate responsibility (MBA); leadership (MBA). *Accreditation:* ACBSP. *Program availability:* Part-time, evening/weekend, online learning. *Entrance requirements:* For master's, GMAT. Additional exam requirements/recommendations for international students: Required—TOEFL (minimum score 500 paper-based).

**George Mason University,** College of Humanities and Social Sciences, Department of Philosophy, Fairfax, VA 22030. Offers ethics and public affairs (MA). *Faculty:* 12 full-time (3 women), 7 part-time/adjunct (0 women). *Students:* 3 full-time (2 women), 11 part-time (3 women); includes 3 minority (1 Hispanic/Latino; 2 Two or more races, non-Hispanic/Latino). Average age 35. 6 applicants, 83% accepted, 2 enrolled. In 2016, 4 master's awarded. *Degree requirements:* For master's, thesis optional. *Entrance requirements:* For master's, 3 letters of recommendation; official transcript; expanded goals statement; writing sample; resume. Additional exam requirements/recommendations for international students: Required—TOEFL (minimum score 575 paper-based; 88 iBT), IELTS (minimum score 6.5), PTE (minimum score 59). *Application deadline:* For fall admission, 3/1 for domestic students. Electronic applications accepted. *Expenses:* Tuition, state resident: full-time $10,628; part-time $443 per credit. Tuition, nonresident: full-time $29,306; part-time $1221 per credit. *Required fees:* $3096; $129 per credit. Tuition and fees vary according to program. *Financial support:* In 2016–17, 2 students received support, including 1 research assistantship with tuition reimbursement available (averaging $6,500 per year), 1 teaching assistantship with tuition reimbursement available (averaging $7,000 per year); career-related internships or fieldwork, Federal Work-Study, scholarships/grants, unspecified assistantships, and health care benefits (for full-time research or teaching assistantship recipients) also available. Financial award application deadline: 3/1; financial award applicants required to submit FAFSA. *Faculty research:* Cultural studies, political theory philosophy, social and political philosophy, feminist theory, analytical and Continental philosophy, philosophy of science. *Total annual research expenditures:* $36,365. *Unit head:* Ted Kinnaman, Chair/Associate Professor, 703-993-4328, Fax: 703-993-1297, E-mail: tkinnama@gmu.edu. *Application contact:* Rose Cherubin, Associate Professor and Graduate Coordinator, 703-993-1332, Fax: 703-993-1297, E-mail: rcherubi@gmu.edu. Website: http://philosophy.gmu.edu/

**Georgetown University,** Graduate School of Arts and Sciences, School of Continuing Studies, Washington, DC 20057. Offers American studies (MALS); Catholic studies (MALS); classical civilizations (MALS); emergency and disaster management (MPS); ethics and the professions (MALS); global strategic communications (MPS); hospitality management (MPS); human resources management (MPS); humanities (MALS); individualized study (MALS); integrated marketing communications (MPS); international affairs (MALS); Islam and Muslim-Christian relations (MALS); journalism (MPS); liberal studies (DLS); literature and society (MALS); medieval and early modern European studies (MALS); public relations and corporate communications (MPS); real estate (MPS); religious studies (MALS); social and public policy (MALS); sports industry management (MPS); systems engineering management (MPS); technology management (MPS); the theory and practice of American democracy (MALS); urban and regional planning (MPS); visual culture (MALS). MPS in systems engineering management offered jointly with Stevens Institute of Technology. *Entrance requirements:* Additional exam requirements/recommendations for international students: Required—TOEFL.

**Graduate Theological Union,** Graduate Programs, Berkeley, CA 94709-1212. Offers art and religion (MA, PhD, Th D); biblical languages (MA); biblical studies (MA); Biblical studies (PhD, Th D); Buddhist studies (MA); Christian spirituality (MA, PhD, Th D); cultural and historical studies of religions (MA, PhD, Th D); ethics and social theory (PhD, Th D); history (MA, PhD, Th D); homiletics (MA, PhD, Th D); interdisciplinary studies (PhD, Th D); Jewish studies (MA, PhD, Th D, Certificate); liturgical studies (MA, PhD, Th D); Near Eastern religions (PhD, Th D); Orthodox Christian studies (MA); religion and psychology (MA, PhD, Th D); religion and society/ethics and social theory (MA); systematic and philosophical theology (MA, PhD, Th D). PhD programs in Jewish studies and Near Eastern religions offered jointly with University of California, Berkeley. *Accreditation:* ATS. Terminal master's awarded for partial completion of doctoral program. *Degree requirements:* For master's, one foreign language, thesis; for doctorate, one foreign language, comprehensive exam, thesis/dissertation. *Entrance requirements:* For master's, GRE General Test; for doctorate, GRE General Test, MA or M Div. Additional exam requirements/recommendations for international students: Required—TOEFL. Electronic applications accepted.

**John Brown University,** Soderquist College of Business, Siloam Springs, AR 72761-2121. Offers international business (MBA); leadership and ethics (MBA, MS). *Accreditation:* ACBSP. *Program availability:* Part-time, evening/weekend, online only, 100% online, blended/hybrid learning. *Faculty:* 4 full-time (2 women), 26 part-time/adjunct (7 women). *Students:* 42 full-time (27 women), 246 part-time (129 women); includes 65 minority (25 Black or African American, non-Hispanic/Latino; 7 American Indian or Alaska Native, non-Hispanic/Latino; 6 Asian, non-Hispanic/Latino; 15 Hispanic/Latino; 12 Two or more races, non-Hispanic/Latino), 6 international. Average age 33. 145 applicants, 80% accepted, 88 enrolled. In 2016, 114 master's awarded. *Entrance requirements:* For master's, MAT, GMAT or GRE if undergraduate GPA is less than 3.0, recommendation forms from three people, 200-word essay describing professional plans and reason for seeking acceptance. Additional exam requirements/recommendations for international students: Required—TOEFL (minimum score 550 paper-based; 79 iBT). *Application deadline:* Applications are processed on a rolling basis. Application fee: $35 ($100 for international students). Electronic applications accepted. *Expenses: Tuition:* Full-time $13,000; part-time $6500 per credit hour. Part-time tuition and fees vary according to course load and program. *Financial support:* Fellowships with full tuition reimbursements, scholarships/grants, and unspecified assistantships available. Financial award applicants required to submit FAFSA. *Faculty research:* Ethical leadership. *Unit head:* Kai Togami, Program Director, 479-524-7370,

*Ethics*

E-mail: ktogami@jbu.edu. *Application contact:* Kent Shaffer, Graduate Business Representative, 479-631-4665, E-mail: kents@jbu.edu. Website: http://www.jbu.edu/grad/business/

**Kennesaw State University,** Siegel Institute for Leadership, Ethics and Character, Kennesaw, GA 30144. Offers leadership and ethics (Graduate Certificate). *Program availability:* Part-time, evening/weekend, online learning. *Entrance requirements:* Additional exam requirements/recommendations for international students: Required—TOEFL (minimum score 550 paper-based; 80 iBT), IELTS (minimum score 6.5). Electronic applications accepted.

**Lancaster Theological Seminary,** Graduate and Professional Programs, Lancaster, PA 17603-2812. Offers biblical studies (MAR); Christian education (MAR); Christianity and the arts (MAR); church history (MAR); congregational life (MAR); lay leadership (Certificate); theological studies (M Div); theology (D Min); theology and ethics (MAR). *Accreditation:* ACIPE; ATS. *Degree requirements:* For doctorate, thesis/dissertation.

**Lebanon Valley College,** Program in Business Administration, Annville, PA 17003-1400. Offers business administration (MBA); healthcare management (MBA); leadership and ethics (MBA). *Program availability:* Part-time, evening/weekend, 100% online, blended/hybrid learning. *Faculty:* 8 full-time (1 woman), 8 part-time/adjunct (1 woman). *Students:* 17 full-time (12 women), 79 part-time (42 women); includes 14 minority (2 Black or African American, non-Hispanic/Latino; 3 Asian, non-Hispanic/Latino; 8 Hispanic/Latino; 1 Two or more races, non-Hispanic/Latino), 5 international. Average age 34. 23 applicants, 87% accepted, 18 enrolled. In 2016, 49 master's awarded. *Degree requirements:* For master's, capstone course. *Entrance requirements:* For master's, GMAT, 3 years of work experience, resume, professional statement (application form, resume, personal statement, transcripts). Additional exam requirements/recommendations for international students: Required—TOEFL (minimum score 80 iBT), IELTS (minimum score 6.5) or STEP Eiken (grade 1). *Application deadline:* Applications are processed on a rolling basis. Application fee: $0. *Expenses:* $635 per credit hour. *Financial support:* Career-related internships or fieldwork and scholarships/grants available. Financial award application deadline: 3/1; financial award applicants required to submit FAFSA. *Faculty research:* Business intelligence systems, business education as an international aid tool, leadership, business success. *Unit head:* Dr. David Setley, Associate Professor/Chair of Business Administration/Director of the MBA Program, 717-867-6104, Fax: 717-867-6018, E-mail: setley@lvc.edu. *Application contact:* Christine M. Martin, Enrollment and Operations Specialist, 717-867-6486, Fax: 717-867-6013, E-mail: cmartin@lvc.edu. Website: http://www.lvc.edu/academics/graduate-studies/master-of-buisness-administration/

**Lee University,** Programs in Religion, Cleveland, TN 37320-3450. Offers biblical studies (MA); ministry studies/leadership (MA); ministry studies/worship (MA); ministry studies/youth and family (MA); theological studies (MA), including ethics, religion. *Program availability:* Part-time, 100% online. *Faculty:* 13 full-time (2 women), 2 part-time/adjunct (0 women). *Students:* 57 full-time (19 women), 92 part-time (28 women); includes 72 minority (16 Black or African American, non-Hispanic/Latino; 2 Asian, non-Hispanic/Latino; 53 Hispanic/Latino; 1 Two or more races, non-Hispanic/Latino), 4 international. Average age 37. 19 applicants, 79% accepted, 12 enrolled. In 2016, 9 master's awarded. *Degree requirements:* For master's, variable foreign language requirement, comprehensive exam (for some programs), thesis (for some programs). *Entrance requirements:* For master's, GRE or MAT (for biblical/theological studies only), minimum GPA of 3.0, 3 letters of recommendation, interview, official transcripts, essay. Additional exam requirements/recommendations for international students: Required—TOEFL (minimum score 61 iBT). *Application deadline:* For fall admission, 4/1 priority date for domestic and international students; for spring admission, 10/1 priority date for domestic and international students. Applications are processed on a rolling basis. Application fee: $25. Electronic applications accepted. *Expenses:* Contact institution. *Financial support:* In 2016–17, 25 students received support, including 7 teaching assistantships (averaging $2,031 per year); career-related internships or fieldwork, Federal Work-Study, institutionally sponsored loans, scholarships/grants, and unspecified assistantships also available. Financial award application deadline: 3/1; financial award applicants required to submit FAFSA. *Faculty research:* Spiritual and discipleship formation, leadership, Biblical studies, theological studies, ethics. *Unit head:* Dr. Lisa Long, Director, 423-303-5100, E-mail: llong@leeuniversity.edu. Website: http://www.leeuniversity.edu/academics/graduate/

**Loyola University Chicago,** Quinlan School of Business, MBA Programs, Chicago, IL 60611. Offers accounting (MBA); business administration (EMBA); business ethics (MBA); economics (MBA); entrepreneurship (MBA); finance (MBA); healthcare management (MBA); human resources management (MBA); international business (MBA); management (MBA); marketing (MBA); operation management (MBA); risk management (MBA); supply chain management (MBA). *Program availability:* Part-time, evening/weekend. *Faculty:* 79 full-time (22 women), 10 part-time/adjunct (6 women). *Students:* 309 full-time (151 women), 65 part-time (31 women); includes 82 minority (25 Black or African American, non-Hispanic/Latino; 27 Asian, non-Hispanic/Latino; 27 Hispanic/Latino; 3 Two or more races, non-Hispanic/Latino), 49 international. Average age 30. 371 applicants, 53% accepted, 114 enrolled. In 2016, 216 master's awarded. *Entrance requirements:* For master's, GMAT or GRE, official transcripts, two letters of recommendation, statement of purpose, resume. Additional exam requirements/recommendations for international students: Required—TOEFL (minimum score 90 iBT) or IELTS (minimum score 6.5). *Application deadline:* For fall admission, 7/15 for domestic and international students; for winter admission, 10/1 for domestic and international students; for spring admission, 1/15 for domestic and international students; for summer admission, 4/1 for domestic and international students. Applications are processed on a rolling basis. Application fee: $50. Electronic applications accepted. Application fee is waived when completed online. *Expenses:* $4,488 per course. *Financial support:* In 2016–17, 83 students received support. Federal Work-Study, scholarships/grants, health care benefits, and unspecified assistantships available. Support available to part-time students. *Faculty research:* Social enterprise and responsibility, emerging markets, supply chain management, risk management. *Unit head:* Katherine Acles, Assistant Dean for Graduate Programs, 312-915-6124, Fax: 312-915-7207, E-mail: kacles@luc.edu. *Application contact:* Lauren Griffin, Enrollment Advisor, Quinlan School of Business Graduate Programs, 312-915-6124, Fax: 312-915-7207, E-mail: lgriffin3@luc.edu.

**Lutheran Theological Seminary Saskatoon,** Graduate and Professional Programs, Saskatoon, SK S7N 0X3, Canada. Offers Biblical studies (MTS); church history (MTS); ethics/church and society (MTS); history of Christianity (STM); New Testament (STM); Old Testament (STM); pastoral studies (STM); pastoral theology (MTS); systematic theology (MTS); systematic theology and philosophy of religion (STM); theology (M Div, D Div). STM programs offered jointly with College of Emmanuel and St. Chad and St. Andrew's College. *Accreditation:* ATS. *Program availability:* Part-time. *Degree requirements:* For master's, thesis.

**Marquette University,** Graduate School, College of Arts and Sciences, Department of Philosophy, Milwaukee, WI 53201-1881. Offers ancient philosophy (PhD); British empiricism and analytic philosophy (PhD); Christian philosophy (PhD); early modern European philosophy (PhD); ethics (PhD); German philosophy (PhD); history of philosophy (MA); medieval philosophy (PhD); phenomenology and existentialism (PhD); philosophy of religion (PhD); social and applied philosophy (MA); JD/MA. *Program availability:* Part-time. *Faculty:* 23 full-time (7 women), 8 part-time/adjunct (1 woman). *Students:* 38 full-time (12 women), 10 part-time (1 woman); includes 2 minority (1 Asian, non-Hispanic/Latino; 1 Hispanic/Latino), 2 international. Average age 31. 59 applicants, 44% accepted, 9 enrolled. In 2016, 4 master's, 6 doctorates awarded. Terminal master's awarded for partial completion of doctoral program. *Degree requirements:* For master's, variable foreign language requirement, comprehensive exam, thesis or alternative; for doctorate, 2 foreign languages, thesis/dissertation, written and oral qualifying exams. *Entrance requirements:* For master's and doctorate, GRE General Test, official transcripts from all current and previous colleges/universities except Marquette, statement of purpose, at least three letters of recommendation, sample of philosophical writing. Additional exam requirements/recommendations for international students: Required—TOEFL (minimum score 530 paper-based). *Application deadline:* For fall admission, 2/15 for domestic and international students. Applications are processed on a rolling basis. Application fee: $50. Electronic applications accepted. *Financial support:* Fellowships with partial tuition reimbursements, research assistantships with full tuition reimbursements, teaching assistantships with full tuition reimbursements, scholarships/grants, health care benefits, tuition waivers (full and partial), and unspecified assistantships available. Support available to part-time students. Financial award application deadline: 2/15. *Faculty research:* Aristotle, Augustine, Descartes, Hegel, Heidegger. *Total annual research expenditures:* $236,274. *Unit head:* Dr. John Jones, Chair. *Application contact:* Dr. Theresa Tobin, Associate Professor, 414-288-6948. Website: http://www.marquette.edu/phil/grad.shtml

**New England College of Business and Finance,** Program in Business Ethics and Compliance, Boston, MA 02111-2645. Offers MS. *Program availability:* Online learning.

**Northwestern University,** School of Professional Studies, Program in Liberal Studies, Evanston, IL 60208. Offers American studies (MA); history (MA); religious and ethical studies (MA).

**Oregon State University,** College of Liberal Arts, Program in Applied Ethics, Corvallis, OR 97331. Offers biomedical ethics (MA); environmental ethics (MA); ethics and religion (MA); global justice, peace, and war (MA); social justice (MA). *Program availability:* Part-time. *Faculty:* 12 full-time (4 women), 1 (woman) part-time/adjunct. *Students:* 10 full-time (7 women), 1 part-time (0 women); includes 3 minority (1 American Indian or Alaska Native, non-Hispanic/Latino; 2 Hispanic/Latino), 1 international. Average age 29. 9 applicants, 67% accepted, 6 enrolled. In 2016, 1 master's awarded. *Entrance requirements:* For master's, writing sample of 5-7 pages. Additional exam requirements/recommendations for international students: Required—TOEFL (minimum score 80 iBT), IELTS (minimum score 6.5). *Application deadline:* For fall admission, 1/15 priority date for domestic and international students. Application fee: $75 ($85 for international students). *Expenses:* Tuition, state resident: full-time $12,150; part-time $450 per credit. Tuition, nonresident: full-time $21,789; part-time $807 per credit. Required fees: $1651; $1507 per credit. One-time fee: $350. Tuition and fees vary according to course load, campus/location and program. *Unit head:* Dr. Ben Mutschler, Director. *Application contact:* Dr. Allen Thompson, Director of Graduate Studies, 541-737-5654, E-mail: allen.thompson@oregonstate.edu. Website: http://liberalarts.oregonstate.edu/shpr/philosophy

**Phillips Theological Seminary,** Programs in Theology, Tulsa, OK 74116. Offers administration of church agencies (M Div); campus ministry (M Div); church-related social work (M Div); college and seminary teaching (M Div); global mission work (M Div); institutional chaplaincy (M Div); ministerial vocations in Christian education (M Div); ministry (D Min), including parish ministry, pastoral counseling, practices of ministry; ministry and culture (MAMC), including Christian education, congregational leadership, history and practice of Christian spirituality, theology, ethics, and culture; ministry of music (M Div); pastoral care and counseling (M Div); pastoral ministry (M Div); theological studies (MTS). *Accreditation:* ATS. *Program availability:* Part-time, online learning. *Degree requirements:* For master's, thesis (for some programs); for doctorate, thesis/dissertation. *Entrance requirements:* For master's, minimum GPA of 2.5; for doctorate, M Div, minimum GPA of 3.0. *Faculty research:* Biblical studies, historical studies, theology and culture, practical theology, theology and film.

**Pontifical John Paul II Institute for Studies on Marriage and Family,** Graduate Programs, Washington, DC 20064. Offers biotechnology and ethics (MTS); marriage and family (MTS, STD, STL); theology (PhD).

**Santa Clara University,** Jesuit School of Theology, Berkeley, CA 94709. Offers Biblical languages (MABL); Biblical studies (MTS); Christian spirituality (MTS); church history (MTS); cultural and historical studies of Catholicism (MTS); ethics and social theory/religion and society (MTS); history of art and religion (MTS); liturgical studies (MTS); pastoral ministry (M Div); systematic and philosophical theology (MTS); theology (MA, MTS, Th M, STD, STB, STL); M Div/MA. *Program availability:* Part-time, evening/weekend, 100% online. *Faculty:* 20 full-time (5 women), 6 part-time/adjunct (3 women). *Students:* 125 full-time (29 women), 9 part-time (5 women); includes 71 minority (22 Black or African American, non-Hispanic/Latino; 27 Asian, non-Hispanic/Latino; 19 Hispanic/Latino; 2 Native Hawaiian or other Pacific Islander, non-Hispanic/Latino; 1 Two or more races, non-Hispanic/Latino). Average age 36. 93 applicants, 92% accepted, 56 enrolled. In 2016, 55 master's, 5 doctorates awarded. *Entrance requirements:* For master's, GRE, 2 letters of recommendation, resume, transcripts; for doctorate, GRE, master's degree or equivalent, resume, statement of purpose, transcripts, 2 letters of recommendation, research paper. Additional exam requirements/recommendations for international students: Required—TOEFL. *Application deadline:* For fall admission, 3/1 priority date for domestic students; for spring admission, 10/1 priority date for domestic students. Applications are processed on a rolling basis. Application fee: $50 ($0 for international students). Electronic applications accepted. *Expenses:* Contact institution. *Financial support:* Scholarships/grants and unspecified assistantships available. Financial award application deadline: 3/1; financial award applicants required to submit FAFSA. *Faculty research:* Religion and culture, interreligious dialogue, social ethics and restorative justice, Ignatian spirituality. *Unit head:* Alison Benders, Associate Dean, 510-549-5055, E-mail: ambenders@scu.edu. *Application contact:* Barbara Godoy, Assistant Dean of Enrollment Management, 510-549-5016, E-mail: bgodoy@scu.edu. Website: http://www.scu.edu/jst/

**Schreiner University,** MBA Program, Kerrville, TX 78028-5697. Offers ethical leadership (MBA). *Program availability:* Part-time, online learning. *Entrance requirements:* For master's, 3 recommendations; personal essay; transcripts; resume. Additional exam requirements/recommendations for international students: Required—TOEFL. Electronic applications accepted. *Expenses:* Contact institution.

**Southeastern Baptist Theological Seminary,** Graduate and Professional Programs, Wake Forest, NC 27588-1889. Offers advanced biblical studies (M Div); Christian education (M Div, MACE); Christian ethics (PhD); Christian ministry (M Div); Christian planting (M Div); church music (MACM); counseling (MACO); evangelism (PhD); language (M Div); ministry (D Min); New Testament (PhD); Old Testament (PhD); philosophy (PhD); theology (Th M, PhD); women's studies (M Div). *Accreditation:* ACIPE; ATS (one or more programs are accredited). *Degree requirements:* For master's, thesis (for some programs), oral exam; for doctorate, thesis/dissertation, fieldwork. *Entrance requirements:* For master's, Cooperative English Test, minimum GPA of 2.0, M Div or equivalent (Th M); for doctorate, GRE General Test or MAT, Cooperative English Test, M Div or equivalent, 3 years of professional experience.

**Southern Methodist University,** Dedman College of Humanities and Sciences, Graduate Program in Religious Studies, Dallas, TX 75275-0133. Offers Hebrew Bible/Old Testament (PhD); history of the Christian tradition (PhD); New Testament (PhD); religion and culture (PhD); religious ethics (PhD); religious studies (MA); systematics theology (PhD). Terminal master's awarded for partial completion of doctoral program. *Degree requirements:* For master's, one foreign language, thesis, oral and written exams; for doctorate, variable foreign language requirement, thesis/dissertation, oral and written exams. *Entrance requirements:* For master's and doctorate, GRE General Test, minimum GPA of 3.0, course work in religion. Additional exam requirements/recommendations for international students: Required—TOEFL (minimum score 550 paper-based; 79 iBT). Electronic applications accepted. *Faculty research:* Theology, religious ethics, Biblical studies, history of Christianity, religion and culture.

**Southern New Hampshire University,** School of Business, Manchester, NH 03106-1045. Offers accounting (MBA, MS, Graduate Certificate); accounting finance (MS); accounting/auditing (MS); accounting/forensic accounting (MS); accounting/taxation (MS); athletic administration (MBA, Graduate Certificate); business administration (IMBA, MBA, Certificate, Graduate Certificate), including accounting (Certificate), business administration (MBA), business information systems (Graduate Certificate), human resource management (Certificate); corporate social responsibility (MBA); entrepreneurship (MBA); finance (MBA, MS, Graduate Certificate); finance/corporate finance (MS); finance/investments and securities (MS); forensic accounting (MBA); healthcare informatics (MBA); healthcare management (MBA); human resource management (Graduate Certificate); information technology (MS, Graduate Certificate); information technology management (MBA); international business (Graduate Certificate); international business and information technology (Graduate Certificate); international finance (Graduate Certificate); international sport management (Graduate Certificate); justice studies (MBA); leadership of nonprofit organizations (Graduate Certificate); management (MS); marketing (MBA, MS, Graduate Certificate); operations and project management (MBA); operations and supply chain management (MBA, Graduate Certificate); organizational leadership (MS); project management (MBA, Graduate Certificate); Six Sigma (MBA); Six Sigma quality (Graduate Certificate); social media marketing (MBA); sport management (MBA, MS, Graduate Certificate); sustainability and environmental compliance (MBA); workplace conflict management (MBA); MBA/Certificate. *Accreditation:* ACBSP. *Program availability:* Part-time, evening/weekend, online learning. Terminal master's awarded for partial completion of doctoral program. *Degree requirements:* For master's, one foreign language, comprehensive exam (for some programs), thesis or alternative. *Entrance requirements:* For master's, minimum GPA of 2.5. Additional exam requirements/recommendations for international students: Required—TOEFL (minimum score 500 paper-based). Electronic applications accepted.

**Spring Hill College,** Graduate Programs, Program in Liberal Arts, Mobile, AL 36608-1791. Offers fine arts (MLA); history and social science (MLA); leadership and ethics (MLA, Postbaccalaureate Certificate); literature (MLA); studio art (Postbaccalaureate Certificate). *Program availability:* Part-time, evening/weekend. *Faculty:* 5 full-time (0 women), 2 part-time/adjunct (1 woman). *Students:* 2 full-time (1 woman), 31 part-time (10 women); includes 4 minority (3 Black or African American, non-Hispanic/Latino; 1 Hispanic/Latino), 3 international. Average age 35. In 2016, 7 master's, 1 other advanced degree awarded. *Degree requirements:* For master's, capstone course, completion of program within 6 years of initial admittance. *Entrance requirements:* For master's, bachelor's degree with minimum undergraduate GPA of 3.0 or graduate/professional degree. Additional exam requirements/recommendations for international students: Required—TOEFL (minimum score 550 paper-based; 80 iBT), IELTS (minimum score 6.5), CPE or CAE (minimum score C), Michigan English Language Assessment Battery (minimum score 90). *Application deadline:* For fall admission, 8/1 priority date for domestic and international students; for spring admission, 12/1 priority date for domestic and international students. Applications are processed on a rolling basis. Application fee: $25 ($35 for international students). Electronic applications accepted. *Expenses:* Contact institution. *Financial support:* Applicants required to submit FAFSA. *Unit head:* Dr. Thomas J. Hoffman, Director, 251-380-4184, Fax: 251-460-2115, E-mail: thoffman@shc.edu. *Application contact:* Robert Stewart, Vice President of Enrollment, 251-380-3030, Fax: 251-460-2186, E-mail: rstewart@shc.edu.
Website: http://ug.shc.edu/graduate-degrees/master-liberal-arts/

**Stevens Institute of Technology,** Graduate School, College of Arts and Letters, Program in Policy and Innovation, Hoboken, NJ 07030. Offers MA (Graduate Certificate. *Program availability:* Part-time, evening/weekend. *Students:* 2 applicants, 100% accepted. *Degree requirements:* For master's, thesis optional, minimum B average in major field and overall; for Graduate Certificate, minimum B average. *Entrance requirements:* Additional exam requirements/recommendations for international students: Required—TOEFL (minimum score 74 iBT), IELTS (minimum score 6). *Application deadline:* For fall admission, 6/1 for domestic students, 4/15 for international students; for spring admission, 11/30 for domestic students, 11/1 for international students. Applications are processed on a rolling basis. Application fee: $65. Electronic applications accepted. *Expenses:* Contact institution. *Financial support:* Fellowships, research assistantships, teaching assistantships, career-related internships or fieldwork, Federal Work-Study, scholarships/grants, and unspecified assistantships available. Financial award application deadline: 2/15; financial award applicants required to submit FAFSA. *Unit head:* Andrew Russell, Director, 201-216-5400, Fax: 201-216-8245, E-mail: arussell@stevens.edu. *Application contact:* Graduate Admission, 888-783-8367, Fax: 888-511-1306, E-mail: graduate@stevens.edu.
Website: https://www.stevens.edu/college-arts-and-letters/graduate-programs

**Suffolk University,** College of Arts and Sciences, Department of Philosophy, Boston, MA 02108-2770. Offers administration of higher education (M Ed, CAGS); ethics and public policy (MS). *Program availability:* Part-time, evening/weekend. *Faculty:* 4 full-time (0 women), 2 part-time/adjunct (0 women). *Students:* 22 full-time (16 women), 29 part-time (24 women); includes 10 minority (1 Black or African American, non-Hispanic/Latino; 6 Hispanic/Latino; 3 Two or more races, non-Hispanic/Latino), 1 international. Average age 28. 56 applicants, 75% accepted, 19 enrolled. In 2016, 34 master's awarded. *Degree requirements:* For master's, internship or thesis; practicum (for M Ed). *Entrance requirements:* For master's, GRE General Test, MAT, GMAT, statement of professional goals, official transcripts, 2 letters of recommendation, resume. Additional exam requirements/recommendations for international students: Required—TOEFL (minimum score 550 paper-based; 80 iBT). *Application deadline:* For fall admission, 3/15 priority date for domestic and international students; for spring admission, 10/15 priority date for domestic and international students. Applications are processed on a rolling basis. Application fee: $50. Electronic applications accepted. *Expenses:* Contact institution. *Financial support:* In 2016–17, 38 students received support, including 30 fellowships (averaging $6,556 per year); career-related internships or fieldwork, Federal Work-Study, institutionally sponsored loans, and unspecified assistantships also available. Support available to part-time students. Financial award application deadline: 4/1; financial award applicants required to submit FAFSA. *Faculty research:* Predicting

competent Head Start preschoolers, cultural differences, school counseling technology, sibling attachment in divorce cases, consequences of ethical breaches by human resource professionals. *Unit head:* Dr. Greg Fried, Chair of Philosophy Department, 617-573-8109, E-mail: gfried@suffolk.edu. *Application contact:* Mara Marzocchi, Associate Director of Graduate Admissions, 617-573-8302, Fax: 617-305-1733, E-mail: grad.admission@suffolk.edu.
Website: http://www.suffolk.edu/college/graduate/69296.php

**Texas State University,** The Graduate College, College of Liberal Arts, Applied Philosophy and Ethics Program, San Marcos, TX 78666. Offers MA. *Faculty:* 15 full-time (7 women), 4 part-time/adjunct (2 women). *Students:* 15 full-time (3 women), 12 part-time (4 women); includes 16 minority (5 Black or African American, non-Hispanic/Latino; 10 Hispanic/Latino; 1 Two or more races, non-Hispanic/Latino), 1 international. Average age 30. 16 applicants, 75% accepted, 9 enrolled. In 2016, 7 master's awarded. *Degree requirements:* For master's, comprehensive exam, thesis optional. *Entrance requirements:* For master's, baccalaureate degree from regionally-accredited university with minimum GPA of 3.0 on last 60 undergraduate semester hours, statement of purpose, 2 letters of recommendation, writing sample. Additional exam requirements/recommendations for international students: Required—TOEFL (minimum score 550 paper-based; 78 iBT), IELTS (minimum score 6.5). *Application deadline:* For fall admission, 3/1 priority date for domestic and international students; for spring admission, 10/15 for domestic students, 10/1 for international students; for summer admission, 4/15 for domestic students, 3/15 for international students. Applications are processed on a rolling basis. Application fee: $40 ($90 for international students). Electronic applications accepted. *Expenses:* $4,851 per semester. *Financial support:* In 2016–17, 19 students received support, including 1 research assistantship (averaging $13,502 per year), 13 teaching assistantships (averaging $13,721 per year); scholarships/grants also available. Support available to part-time students. Financial award application deadline: 3/1; financial award applicants required to submit FAFSA. *Unit head:* Dr. Audrey Mckinney, Graduate Advisor, 512-245-2047, Fax: 512-245-8336, E-mail: am04@txstate.edu. *Application contact:* Dr. Andrea Golato, Dean of Graduate School, 512-245-2581, Fax: 512-245-8365, E-mail: gradcollege@txstate.edu.

**Université de Sherbrooke,** Faculty of Theology and Religious Studies, Sherbrooke, QC J1K 2R1, Canada. Offers applied ethics (Diploma); human science of religions (MA); intercultural training (Diploma); philosophy (MA, PhD); spiritual anthropology (Diploma); theology (MA, PhD, Diploma). *Program availability:* Part-time, evening/weekend, online learning. Terminal master's awarded for partial completion of doctoral program. *Entrance requirements:* For master's, bachelor's degree in related discipline; for doctorate, master's degree in related discipline. *Faculty research:* Faith and culture interrelation.

**Université du Québec à Chicoutimi,** Graduate Programs, Program in Ethics, Chicoutimi, QC G7H 2B1, Canada. Offers Diploma. *Entrance requirements:* For degree, appropriate bachelor's degree, proficiency in French.

**Université du Québec à Rimouski,** Graduate Programs, Program in Ethics, Rimouski, QC G5L 3A1, Canada. Offers MA, Diploma. *Program availability:* Part-time. *Degree requirements:* For master's, thesis. *Entrance requirements:* For master's, appropriate bachelor's degree, proficiency in French.

**Université Laval,** Faculty of Theology and Religious Sciences, Program in Applied Ethics, Québec, QC G1K 7P4, Canada. Offers DESS. *Program availability:* Part-time. *Entrance requirements:* For degree, knowledge of French. Electronic applications accepted.

**University of Baltimore,** Graduate School, Yale Gordon College of Arts and Sciences, Program in Legal and Ethical Studies, Baltimore, MD 21201-5779. Offers MA. *Program availability:* Part-time, evening/weekend. *Degree requirements:* For master's, thesis optional. *Entrance requirements:* For master's, minimum GPA of 3.0. Additional exam requirements/recommendations for international students: Required—TOEFL (minimum score 550 paper-based). Electronic applications accepted. *Faculty research:* Morality in law and economics, religion in lawmaking, comparative legal history, law and social change, critical issues in Constitutional law, theories of justice.

**University of Chicago,** Divinity School, PhD Program, Chicago, IL 60637. Offers anthropology and sociology of religions (PhD); Bible (PhD); history of Christianity (PhD); history of Judaism (PhD); history of religions (PhD); Islamic studies (PhD); philosophy of religions (PhD); religion, literature, and visual culture (PhD); religions in America (PhD); religious ethics (PhD); theology (PhD). *Students:* 161 full-time (47 women), 1 (woman) part-time; includes 22 minority (6 Black or African American, non-Hispanic/Latino; 10 Asian, non-Hispanic/Latino; 2 Hispanic/Latino; 4 Two or more races, non-Hispanic/Latino), 26 international. 171 applicants, 16% accepted, 15 enrolled. *Degree requirements:* For doctorate, 2 foreign languages, comprehensive exam, thesis/dissertation. *Entrance requirements:* For doctorate, GRE General Test. Additional exam requirements/recommendations for international students: Required—TOEFL (minimum score 600 paper-based; 104 iBT), IELTS (minimum score 7). *Application deadline:* For fall admission, 12/15 for domestic and international students. Application fee: $75. Electronic applications accepted. *Financial support:* In 2016–17, 20 fellowships with full tuition reimbursements (averaging $24,000 per year) were awarded; Federal Work-Study, institutionally sponsored loans, scholarships/grants, and health care benefits also available. Financial award application deadline: 12/15; financial award applicants required to submit FAFSA. *Faculty research:* Constructive studies (philosophy of religion, religious ethics, and theology); historical studies (Bible, history of Christianity, and history of Judaism); religion and the human sciences (anthropology and sociology of religion, history of religions, and religion, literature, and visual culture); Islamic studies; religions in America. *Unit head:* Dr. Richard A. Rosengarten, Dean/Associate Professor of Religion and Literature, 773-702-8200. *Application contact:* John W. Howell, Coordinator for Recruiting and Admissions, 773-702-8249, Fax: 773-834-4581, E-mail: divinityadmissions@uchicago.edu.
Website: http://divinity.uchicago.edu/doctoral-program-phd

**University of Detroit Mercy,** College of Business Administration, Detroit, MI 48221. Offers business administration (MBA); business fundamentals (Certificate); business turnaround management (Certificate); ethical leadership and change management (Certificate); finance (Certificate); forensic accounting (Certificate); JD/MBA; MBA/MHSA. *Program availability:* Part-time, evening/weekend, 100% online, blended/hybrid learning. *Entrance requirements:* For master's, GMAT, resume, letter of recommendation, transcripts; for Certificate, resume, letter of recommendation, transcripts. Electronic applications accepted. Application fee is waived when completed online. *Expenses:* Contact institution. *Faculty research:* Ethics, international finance, trade policy, leadership, information technology.

**University of Maryland, Baltimore,** Graduate School, Program in Research Ethics, Baltimore, MD 21201. Offers Certificate. *Program availability:* Part-time, online learning. *Students:* 13 part-time (10 women), 10 international. Average age 38. 16 applicants, 56% accepted, 3 enrolled. In 2016, 6 Certificates awarded. *Entrance requirements:* Additional exam requirements/recommendations for international students: Required—TOEFL (minimum score 80 iBT); Recommended—IELTS (minimum score 7). *Application deadline:* For fall admission, 7/10 priority date for domestic students, 1/15 for international students. Applications are processed on a rolling basis. Application fee:

*Ethics*

$75. Electronic applications accepted. *Expenses:* $566 per credit in-state; $766 per credit out-of-state. *Financial support:* Application deadline: 3/1; applicants required to submit FAFSA. *Unit head:* Dr. Bruce E. Jarrell, Graduate School Dean, 410-706-2304, Fax: 410-706-0500, E-mail: bjarrell@som.umaryland.edu. *Application contact:* Dr. Henry Silverman, Program Director, 410-328-4881, E-mail: hsilverm@medicine.umaryland.edu. Website: http://www.graduate.umaryland.edu/research-ethics/

**The University of North Carolina at Charlotte,** College of Liberal Arts and Sciences, Department of Philosophy, Charlotte, NC 28223-0001. Offers ethics and applied philosophy (MA, Graduate Certificate). *Program availability:* Part-time. *Faculty:* 11 full-time (4 women). *Students:* 3 full-time (0 women), 12 part-time (4 women); includes 3 minority (2 Black or African American, non-Hispanic/Latino; 1 Two or more races, non-Hispanic/Latino). Average age 32. 8 applicants, 100% accepted, 4 enrolled. In 2016, 2 master's awarded. *Degree requirements:* For master's, thesis or internship. *Entrance requirements:* For master's, GRE or MAT, statement of purpose outlining why applicant seeks admission to program; three recommendations; one official transcript from all colleges or universities attended; philosophical writing sample; for Graduate Certificate, personal statement outlining why the applicant seeks admission to the program; two academic letters of recommendation, in addition to the recommendation forms required by the graduate school, which address the student's philosophical skills and/or ethical reasoning. Additional exam requirements/recommendations for international students: Required—TOEFL (minimum score 523 paper-based, 70 iBT) or IELTS (6.5). *Application deadline:* For fall admission, 3/1 priority date for domestic and international students; for spring admission, 10/1 priority date for domestic and international students; for summer admission, 4/1 priority date for domestic and international students. Applications are processed on a rolling basis. Application fee: $75. Electronic applications accepted. *Expenses:* Tuition, state resident: full-time $4252. Tuition, nonresident: full-time $17,423. *Required fees:* $3026. Tuition and fees vary according to course load and program. *Financial support:* In 2016–17, 7 students received support, including 1 fellowship (averaging $42,000 per year), 5 teaching assistantships (averaging $4,100 per year); career-related internships or fieldwork, institutionally sponsored loans, scholarships/grants, unspecified assistantships, and administrative assistantships also available. Support available to part-time students. Financial award application deadline: 3/1; financial award applicants required to submit FAFSA. *Total annual research expenditures:* $4,880. *Unit head:* Dr. Shannon Sullivan, Chair, 704-687-5418. *Application contact:* Kathy B. Giddings, Director of Graduate Admissions, 704-687-5503, Fax: 704-687-1668, E-mail: gradadm@uncc.edu. Website: http://philosophy.uncc.edu/

**University of North Florida,** College of Arts and Sciences, Department of Philosophy, Jacksonville, FL 32224. Offers applied ethics (Graduate Certificate); practical philosophy and applied ethics (MA). *Program availability:* Part-time, evening/weekend. *Faculty:* 8 full-time (3 women). *Students:* 6 full-time (0 women), 2 part-time (0 women); includes 1 minority (Asian, non-Hispanic/Latino). Average age 33. 8 applicants, 75% accepted, 4 enrolled. In 2016, 5 master's awarded. *Entrance requirements:* For master's, GRE General Test, minimum GPA of 3.0 in last 60 hours, 3 letters of recommendation, writing sample. Additional exam requirements/recommendations for international students: Required—TOEFL (minimum score 500 paper-based; 61 iBT). *Application deadline:* For fall admission, 8/1 priority date for domestic students, 5/1 for international students. Application fee: $30. Electronic applications accepted. Tuition and fees vary according to course load, campus/location and program. *Financial support:* In 2016–17, 1 student received support. Research assistantships, teaching assistantships, Federal Work-Study, scholarships/grants, tuition waivers, and unspecified assistantships available. Financial award application deadline: 4/1; financial award applicants required to submit FAFSA. *Faculty research:* Late modern philosophy, pragmatism, religion and American culture, hermeneutics, philosophy of mind. *Total annual research expenditures:* $31,261. *Unit head:* Mitchell Haney, Chair, 904-620-1187, Fax: 904-620-1840, E-mail: mhaney@unf.edu. *Application contact:* Dr. Amanda Pascale, Director, The Graduate School, 904-620-1360, Fax: 904-620-1362, E-mail: graduateschool@unf.edu. Website: http://www.unf.edu/coas/philosophy/

**University of Pennsylvania,** Wharton School, Legal Studies and Business Ethics Department, Philadelphia, PA 19104. Offers MBA, PhD. *Expenses: Tuition:* Full-time $31,068; part-time $5762 per course. *Required fees:* $3200; $336 per course. Full-time tuition and fees vary according to degree level, program and student level. Part-time tuition and fees vary according to course load, degree level and program.

**University of St. Thomas,** Graduate Studies, School of Law, Minneapolis, MN 55403-2015. Offers law (JD); organizational ethics and compliance (LL M, MSL); U.S. law (LL M); JD/LL M; JD/MA; JD/MBA; JD/MSW. *Accreditation:* ABA. *Degree requirements:* For doctorate, mentor externship, public service. *Entrance requirements:* For doctorate, LSAT, 2 letters of recommendation. Additional exam requirements/recommendations for international students: Required—TOEFL (minimum score 550 paper-based), IELTS (minimum score 6.5), or Michigan English Language Assessment Battery (minimum score 80). *Application deadline:* For fall admission, 7/1 priority date for domestic and international students. Applications are processed on a rolling basis. Application fee: $0. Electronic applications accepted. *Expenses: Tuition:* Full-time $19,354; part-time $1320 per credit. One-time fee: $214. Tuition and fees vary according to course load, degree level, program and reciprocity agreements. *Financial support:* Scholarships/grants available. Financial award application deadline: 7/1; financial award applicants required to submit FAFSA. *Faculty research:* Constitutional law (executive powers and First Amendment); banking, securities, and financial markets; law, religion, and jurisprudence; international law, development and dispute resolution; formation of professional identity, values, and skills. *Unit head:* Robert K. Vischer, Dean, 651-962-4838, Fax: 651-962-4881, E-mail: rkvischer@stthomas.edu. *Application contact:* Cari Haaland, Assistant Dean for Admissions, 651-962-4872, Fax: 651-962-4876, E-mail: lawschool@stthomas.edu. Website: http://www.stthomas.edu/law/

**University of South Africa,** College of Human Sciences, Pretoria, South Africa. Offers adult education (M Ed); African languages (MA, PhD); African politics (MA, PhD); Afrikaans (MA, PhD); ancient history (MA, PhD); ancient Near Eastern studies (MA, PhD); anthropology (MA, PhD); applied linguistics (MA); Arabic (MA, PhD); archaeology (MA); art history (MA); Biblical archaeology (MA); Biblical studies (M Th, D Th, PhD); Christian spirituality (M Th, D Th); church history (M Th, D Th); classical studies (MA, PhD); clinical psychology (MA); communication (MA, PhD); comparative education (M Ed, Ed D); consulting psychology (D Admin, D Com, PhD); curriculum studies (M Ed, Ed D); development studies (M Admin, MA, D Admin, PhD); didactics (M Ed, Ed D); education (M Tech); education management (M Ed, Ed D); educational psychology (M Ed); English (MA); environmental education (M Ed); French (MA, PhD); German (MA, PhD); Greek (MA); guidance and counseling (M Ed); health studies (MA, PhD), including health sciences education (MA), health services management (MA), medical and surgical nursing science (critical care general) (MA), midwifery and neonatal nursing science (MA), trauma and emergency care (MA); history (MA, PhD); history of education (Ed D); inclusive education (M Ed, Ed D); information and communications technology policy and regulation (MA); information science (MA, MIS, PhD); international politics (MA, PhD); Islamic studies (MA, PhD); Italian (MA, PhD); Judaica (MA, PhD); linguistics (MA, PhD); mathematical education (M Ed); mathematics education (MA); missiology (M Th, D Th); modern Hebrew (MA, PhD); musicology (MA, MMus, D Mus, PhD); natural science education (M Ed); New Testament (M Th, D Th); Old Testament (D Th); pastoral therapy (M Th, D Th); philosophy (MA); philosophy of education (M Ed, Ed D); politics (MA, PhD); Portuguese (MA, PhD); practical theology (M Th, D Th); psychology (MA, MS, PhD); psychology of education (M Ed, Ed D); public health (MA); religious studies (MA, D Th, PhD); Romance languages (MA); Russian (MA, PhD); Semitic languages (MA, PhD); social behavior studies in HIV/AIDS (MA); social science (mental health) (MA); social science in development studies (MA); social science in psychology (MA); social science in social work (MA); social science in sociology (MA); social work (MSW, DSW, PhD); socio-education (M Ed, Ed D); sociolinguistics (MA); sociology (MA, PhD); Spanish (MA, PhD); systematic theology (M Th, D Th); TESOL (teaching English to speakers of other languages) (MA); theological ethics (M Th, D Th); theory of literature (MA, PhD); urban ministries (D Th); urban ministry (M Th).

**The University of Tennessee at Chattanooga,** Engineering Management and Technology Program, Chattanooga, TN 37403. Offers construction management (Graduate Certificate); engineering management (MS); fundamentals of engineering management (Graduate Certificate); leadership and ethics (Graduate Certificate); logistics and supply chain management (Graduate Certificate); power systems management (Graduate Certificate); project and technology management (Graduate Certificate); quality management (Graduate Certificate). *Program availability:* 100% online, blended/hybrid learning. *Faculty:* 6 full-time (1 woman). *Students:* 14 full-time (3 women), 49 part-time (11 women); includes 17 minority (10 Black or African American, non-Hispanic/Latino; 2 Asian, non-Hispanic/Latino; 3 Hispanic/Latino; 2 Two or more races, non-Hispanic/Latino), 8 international. Average age 33. 29 applicants, 93% accepted, 15 enrolled. In 2016, 36 master's, 7 other advanced degrees awarded. *Degree requirements:* For master's, thesis. *Entrance requirements:* For master's, GRE General Test, letters of recommendation; minimum undergraduate GPA of 2.7 overall or 3.0 in final two years. Additional exam requirements/recommendations for international students: Required—TOEFL (minimum score 550 paper-based; 79 iBT), IELTS (minimum score 6). *Application deadline:* For fall admission, 6/15 priority date for domestic students, 7/1 for international students; for spring admission, 11/1 priority date for domestic students, 11/1 for international students. Applications are processed on a rolling basis. Application fee: $35 ($40 for international students). Electronic applications accepted. *Expenses:* $9,876 full-time in-state; $25,994 full-time out-of-state; $450 per credit part-time in-state; $1,345 per credit part-time out-of-state. *Financial support:* In 2016–17, 4 research assistantships were awarded; teaching assistantships, career-related internships or fieldwork, scholarships/grants, and unspecified assistantships also available. Support available to part-time students. Financial award application deadline: 7/1; financial award applicants required to submit FAFSA. *Faculty research:* Plant layout design, lean manufacturing, Six Sigma, value management, product development. *Unit head:* Dr. Neslihan Alp, Department Head, 423-425-4032, Fax: 423-425-5818, E-mail: neslihan-alp@utc.edu. *Application contact:* Dr. Joanne Romagni, Dean of the Graduate School, 423-425-4478, Fax: 423-425-5223, E-mail: joanne-romagni@utc.edu. Website: http://www.utc.edu/college-engineering-computer-science/programs/engineering-management-and-technology/index.php#li03

**Valparaiso University,** Graduate School and Continuing Education, Programs in Humane Education, Valparaiso, IN 46383. Offers M Ed, MA, MALS, Graduate Certificate. Program offered in collaboration with Institute for Humane Education. *Program availability:* Part-time, evening/weekend. *Degree requirements:* For master's, thesis, project. *Entrance requirements:* For master's, minimum GPA of 3.0, two letters of reference, official transcripts, personal statement, interview. Additional exam requirements/recommendations for international students: Required—TOEFL (minimum score 550 paper-based; 80 iBT), IELTS (minimum score 6). Electronic applications accepted. *Expenses: Tuition:* Full-time $11,070; part-time $615 per credit hour. *Required fees:* $116 per semester. Tuition and fees vary according to course load, degree level and program.

**Valparaiso University,** Graduate School and Continuing Education, Programs in Liberal Studies, Concentration in Ethics and Values, Valparaiso, IN 46383. Offers MALS, Post-Master's Certificate, JD/MALS. *Program availability:* Part-time, evening/weekend. *Entrance requirements:* For master's, minimum GPA of 3.0. Additional exam requirements/recommendations for international students: Required—TOEFL (minimum score 550 paper-based; 80 iBT), IELTS (minimum score 6). Electronic applications accepted. *Expenses: Tuition:* Full-time $11,070; part-time $615 per credit hour. *Required fees:* $116 per semester. Tuition and fees vary according to course load, degree level and program.

**Viterbo University,** Master of Arts in Servant Leadership Program, La Crosse, WI 54601-4797. Offers ethical leadership in organizations (Certificate); servant leadership (MA). *Program availability:* Part-time, evening/weekend. *Degree requirements:* For master's, 30 credits (15 credits of Servant Leadership core courses and any combination of 15 elective credits). *Entrance requirements:* For master's, letter of reference, statement of goals, baccalaureate degree, transcript, interview. Additional exam requirements/recommendations for international students: Required—TOEFL (minimum score 525 paper-based). Electronic applications accepted. *Expenses:* Contact institution. *Faculty research:* Organizational culture, community building, ethical decision-making, leadership theory and practice.

**West Chester University of Pennsylvania,** College of Arts and Humanities, Department of Philosophy, West Chester, PA 19383. Offers business ethics (Certificate); health care ethics (Certificate); philosophy (MA); philosophy: applied ethics (MA). *Program availability:* Part-time, evening/weekend. *Faculty:* 8 full-time (4 women). *Students:* 1 full-time (0 women), 13 part-time (1 woman). Average age 44. 4 applicants, 75% accepted, 2 enrolled. In 2016, 3 master's awarded. *Degree requirements:* For master's, comprehensive exam, thesis optional, 30 credits. *Entrance requirements:* For master's, GRE or writing sample, three letters of reference, minimum undergraduate GPA of 2.8; for Certificate, undergraduate transcripts, minimum undergraduate GPA of 2.8. Additional exam requirements/recommendations for international students: Required—TOEFL or IELTS. *Application deadline:* For fall admission, 5/15 for international students; for spring admission, 10/15 for international students. Applications are processed on a rolling basis. Application fee: $50. Electronic applications accepted. *Expenses:* Tuition, state resident: full-time $8694; part-time $483 per credit. Tuition, nonresident: full-time $13,050; part-time $725 per credit. *Required fees:* $2399; $119.05 per credit. Tuition and fees vary according to campus/location and program. *Financial support:* Scholarships/grants and unspecified assistantships available. Financial award application deadline: 2/15; financial award applicants required to submit FAFSA. *Faculty research:* Ethics: theory and application; social and political, feminist, continental, Asian, post-colonial, American pragmatism, analytic philosophy. *Unit head:* Dr. Helen Daley Schroepfer, Chair, 610-436-2841, E-mail: hschroepfer@wcupa.edu. *Application contact:* Dr. Joan Woolfrey, Graduate Coordinator, 610-436-0731, E-mail: jwoolfrey@wcupa.edu. Website: http://www.wcupa.edu/arts-humanities/philosophy/

**Xavier University,** Williams College of Business, Master of Business Administration Program, Cincinnati, OH 45207. Offers business administration (Exec MBA, MBA); business intelligence (MBA); finance (MBA); health industry (MBA); international business (MBA); marketing (MBA); values-based leadership (MBA); MBA/MHSA; MSN/MBA. *Accreditation:* AACSB. *Program availability:* Part-time, evening/weekend. *Degree requirements:* For master's, capstone course. *Entrance requirements:* For master's, GMAT or GRE, official transcript; resume. Additional exam requirements/

recommendations for international students: Required—TOEFL (minimum score 550 paper-based; 79 iBT). Electronic applications accepted. Application fee is waived when completed online. *Expenses:* Contact institution.

# Philosophy

**Acadia University,** Faculty of Arts, Program in Social and Political Thought, Wolfville, NS B4P 2R6, Canada. Offers MA. *Degree requirements:* For master's, thesis. *Entrance requirements:* Additional exam requirements/recommendations for international students: Required—TOEFL (minimum score 580 paper-based; 93 iBT), IELTS (minimum score 6.5).

**American University,** College of Arts and Sciences, Department of Philosophy and Religion, Washington, DC 22016-8056. Offers ethics, peace, and global affairs (MA); philosophy (MA). *Program availability:* Part-time, evening/weekend. *Faculty:* 12 full-time (7 women), 13 part-time/adjunct (8 women). *Students:* 13 full-time (9 women), 8 part-time (2 women); includes 5 minority (3 Black or African American, non-Hispanic/Latino; 1 Hispanic/Latino; 1 Two or more races, non-Hispanic/Latino). Average age 30. 45 applicants, 76% accepted, 10 enrolled. In 2016, 8 master's awarded. *Degree requirements:* For master's, one foreign language, comprehensive exam, thesis (for some programs). *Entrance requirements:* For master's, GRE, writing sample, statement of purpose, transcripts, 2 letters of recommendation, resume. Additional exam requirements/recommendations for international students: Required—TOEFL (minimum score 100 iBT), IELTS (minimum score 7), PTE (minimum score 68). *Application deadline:* For fall admission, 2/1 priority date for domestic students; for spring admission, 11/1 for domestic students. Application fee: $55. *Expenses:* $1,579 per credit tuition; $690 mandatory fees. *Financial support:* Research assistantships, teaching assistantships, scholarships/grants, and unspecified assistantships available. Financial award application deadline: 2/1; financial award applicants required to submit FAFSA. *Unit head:* Dr. Ellen Feder, Department Chair, 202-885-2931, Fax: 202-885-1094, E-mail: efeder@american.edu. *Application contact:* Kathleen Clowery, Associate Director, Graduate Admissions, 202-885-3620, Fax: 202-885-1344, E-mail: clowery@american.edu.
Website: http://www.american.edu/cas/philrel/

**The American University in Cairo,** School of Humanities and Social Sciences, Cairo, Egypt. Offers Arab and Islamic civilizations (Graduate Diploma); Arabic studies (MA); comparative literary studies (Graduate Diploma); Egyptology and Coptology (MA); English and comparative literature (MA); humanities and social sciences (Graduate Diploma); philosophy (MA); psychology (MA); sociology and anthropology (MA); teaching Arabic as a foreign language (MA); teaching English to speakers of other languages (MA). *Program availability:* Part-time, evening/weekend. *Faculty:* 51 full-time (29 women), 4 part-time/adjunct (2 women). *Students:* 65 full-time (47 women), 179 part-time (138 women), 32 international. Average age 30. 221 applicants, 45% accepted, 54 enrolled. In 2016, 95 master's awarded. *Degree requirements:* For master's, comprehensive exam (for some programs), thesis (for some programs). *Entrance requirements:* Additional exam requirements/recommendations for international students: Required—TOEFL (minimum score 450 paper-based; 45 iBT), IELTS (minimum score 5). *Application deadline:* For fall admission, 2/1 priority date for domestic and international students; for spring admission, 10/15 priority date for domestic and international students. Applications are processed on a rolling basis. Application fee: $80. Electronic applications accepted. *Expenses:* Contact institution. *Financial support:* Fellowships with partial tuition reimbursements, scholarships/grants, tuition waivers (partial), and unspecified assistantships available. Financial award application deadline: 3/10. *Faculty research:* English literature, political science, psychology, sociology, anthropology and Egyptology, teaching English for non-speakers, teaching Arabic as a foreign language, philosophy, Arabic studies. *Unit head:* Dr. Nathaniel Bowditch, Dean, 20-2-2615-1788, E-mail: nbowditch@aucegypt.edu. *Application contact:* Maha Hegazi, Director for Graduate Admissions, 20-2-2615-1462, E-mail: mahahegazi@aucegypt.edu.
Website: http://www.aucegypt.edu/huss/Pages/default.aspx

**Arizona State University at the Tempe campus,** College of Liberal Arts and Sciences, School of Historical, Philosophical and Religious Studies, Tempe, AZ 85287-4301. Offers European history (MA, PhD); medieval studies (Graduate Certificate); North American history (MA, PhD); philosophy (MA, PhD); public history (MA); religious studies (MA, PhD); Renaissance studies (Graduate Certificate); scholarly publishing (Graduate Certificate). *Program availability:* Part-time. Terminal master's awarded for partial completion of doctoral program. *Degree requirements:* For master's, thesis or alternative, interactive Program of Study (iPOS) submitted before completing 50 percent of required credit hours; for doctorate, variable foreign language requirement, comprehensive exam, thesis/dissertation, interactive Program of Study (iPOS) submitted before completing 50 percent of required credit hours. *Entrance requirements:* For master's and doctorate, GRE, minimum GPA of 3.0 or equivalent in last 2 years of work leading to bachelor's degree. Additional exam requirements/recommendations for international students: Required—TOEFL, IELTS, or PTE. Electronic applications accepted.

**Baylor University,** Graduate School, College of Arts and Sciences, Department of Philosophy, Waco, TX 76798. Offers MA, PhD. *Faculty:* 16 full-time (3 women). *Students:* 30 full-time (8 women); includes 4 minority (2 Asian, non-Hispanic/Latino; 2 Hispanic/Latino). 54 applicants, 13% accepted, 5 enrolled. In 2016, 6 master's, 5 doctorates awarded. Terminal master's awarded for partial completion of doctoral program. *Degree requirements:* For master's, comprehensive exam; for doctorate, comprehensive exam, thesis/dissertation. *Entrance requirements:* For master's and doctorate, GRE General Test. Additional exam requirements/recommendations for international students: Required—TOEFL. *Application deadline:* For fall admission, 1/2 for domestic and international students. Application fee: $50. Electronic applications accepted. *Expenses:* Contact institution. *Financial support:* In 2016–17, 30 students received support, including 30 teaching assistantships with full tuition reimbursements available (averaging $20,000 per year); scholarships/grants, health care benefits, tuition waivers (full), and unspecified assistantships also available. Financial award application deadline: 1/2. *Faculty research:* Epistemology, metaphysics, philosophy of religion, moral psychology, Kierkegaard. *Unit head:* Dr. Alexander Robert Pruss, Graduate Program Director, 254-710-3458, Fax: 254-710-3838, E-mail: alexander_pruss@baylor.edu. *Application contact:* Marilyn McKinney, Administrative Assistant, 254-710-4237, Fax: 254-710-3838, E-mail: marilyn_mckinney@baylor.edu.
Website: http://www.baylor.edu/philosophy/

**Binghamton University, State University of New York,** Graduate School, Harpur College of Arts and Sciences, Department of Philosophy, Binghamton, NY 13902-6000. Offers MA, PhD. *Program availability:* Part-time. *Faculty:* 14 full-time (6 women), 2 part-time/adjunct (0 women). *Students:* 1 applicant. Terminal master's awarded for partial completion of doctoral program. *Degree requirements:* For master's, 2 foreign languages, comprehensive exam (for some programs), thesis or alternative; for doctorate, one foreign language, thesis/dissertation. *Entrance requirements:* For master's and doctorate, GRE General Test, writing sample. Additional exam requirements/recommendations for international students: Required—TOEFL (minimum score 550 paper-based; 80 iBT). *Application deadline:* For fall admission, 2/1 for domestic and international students; for spring admission, 10/15 for domestic and international students. Application fee: $75. Electronic applications accepted. *Financial support:* Career-related internships or fieldwork, Federal Work-Study, institutionally sponsored loans, scholarships/grants, health care benefits, tuition waivers (full and partial), and unspecified assistantships available. Financial award applicants required to submit FAFSA. *Unit head:* Anja Karnein, Graduate Director, 607-777-2778, E-mail: akarnein@binghamton.edu. *Application contact:* Ben Balkaya, Assistant Dean and Director, 607-777-2151, Fax: 607-777-2501, E-mail: balkaya@binghamton.edu.
Website: http://www2.binghamton.edu/philosophy/

**Binghamton University, State University of New York,** Graduate School, Harpur College of Arts and Sciences, Philosophy, Interpretation and Culture Program, Binghamton, NY 13902-6000. Offers MA, PhD. *Program availability:* Part-time. *Students:* 12 full-time (8 women); includes 3 minority (1 Black or African American, non-Hispanic/Latino; 1 Asian, non-Hispanic/Latino; 1 Hispanic/Latino), 5 international. Average age 44. In 2016, 2 doctorates awarded. *Degree requirements:* For doctorate, thesis/dissertation. *Entrance requirements:* Additional exam requirements/recommendations for international students: Required—TOEFL. Application fee: $75. *Financial support:* In 2016–17, 5 students received support. Fellowships, career-related internships or fieldwork, Federal Work-Study, institutionally sponsored loans, scholarships/grants, health care benefits, and unspecified assistantships available. Financial award applicants required to submit FAFSA. *Unit head:* Dr. Nkiru Nzegwu, Graduate Coordinator, 607-777-3082, E-mail: panap@binghamton.edu. *Application contact:* Ben Balkaya, Assistant Dean and Director, 607-777-2151, Fax: 607-777-2501, E-mail: balkaya@binghamton.edu.

**Binghamton University, State University of New York,** Graduate School, Harpur College of Arts and Sciences, Program in Social, Political, Ethical and Legal Philosophy, Binghamton, NY 13902-6000. Offers MA, PhD. *Program availability:* Part-time. *Faculty:* 14 full-time (6 women), 2 part-time/adjunct (0 women). *Students:* 15 full-time (3 women), 23 part-time (9 women); includes 7 minority (1 Black or African American, non-Hispanic/Latino; 1 Asian, non-Hispanic/Latino; 5 Hispanic/Latino), 7 international. Average age 32. 53 applicants, 40% accepted, 8 enrolled. In 2016, 4 master's, 4 doctorates awarded. Terminal master's awarded for partial completion of doctoral program. *Degree requirements:* For master's, comprehensive exam, thesis or alternative; for doctorate, one foreign language, thesis/dissertation. *Entrance requirements:* For master's and doctorate, GRE General Test, writing sample. Additional exam requirements/recommendations for international students: Required—TOEFL (minimum score 550 paper-based; 80 iBT). *Application deadline:* For fall admission, 2/1 for domestic and international students; for spring admission, 10/15 for domestic and international students. Application fee: $75. Electronic applications accepted. *Financial support:* In 2016–17, 22 students received support, including 23 teaching assistantships with full tuition reimbursements available (averaging $15,000 per year); career-related internships or fieldwork, Federal Work-Study, institutionally sponsored loans, scholarships/grants, health care benefits, tuition waivers (full and partial), and unspecified assistantships also available. Financial award applicants required to submit FAFSA. *Unit head:* Dr. Christopher M. Knapp, Chairperson, 607-777-4163, E-mail: c.morgan-knapp@binghamton.edu. *Application contact:* Ben Balkaya, Assistant Dean and Director, 607-777-2151, Fax: 607-777-2501, E-mail: balkaya@binghamton.edu.
Website: http://philosophy.binghamton.edu

**Boston College,** Graduate School of Arts and Sciences, Department of Philosophy, Chestnut Hill, MA 02467-3800. Offers MA, PhD. *Faculty:* 29 full-time. *Students:* 84 full-time (16 women); includes 6 minority (5 Hispanic/Latino; 1 Two or more races, non-Hispanic/Latino), 14 international. 172 applicants, 60% accepted, 26 enrolled. In 2016, 19 master's, 5 doctorates awarded. Terminal master's awarded for partial completion of doctoral program. *Degree requirements:* For master's, one foreign language, thesis optional; for doctorate, 2 foreign languages, thesis/dissertation. *Entrance requirements:* For master's and doctorate, GRE General Test. Additional exam requirements/recommendations for international students: Required—TOEFL (minimum score 600 paper-based; 100 iBT), IELTS (minimum score 8). *Application deadline:* For fall admission, 1/2 for domestic and international students. Application fee: $75. Tuition and fees vary according to program. *Financial support:* In 2016–17, fellowships with full tuition reimbursements (averaging $21,400 per year), research assistantships (averaging $21,400 per year), teaching assistantships with full tuition reimbursements (averaging $21,400 per year) were awarded; Federal Work-Study, scholarships/grants, health care benefits, and unspecified assistantships also available. Support available to part-time students. Financial award application deadline: 3/1; financial award applicants required to submit FAFSA. *Faculty research:* History of philosophy, metaphysics, ethics, Continental philosophy, ancient philosophy, philosophy of science, social theory. *Unit head:* Dr. Gary Gurtler, Chairperson, 617-552-3872, E-mail: gurtlerg@bc.edu. *Application contact:* Dr. Jean-Luc Solere, Graduate Program Director, 617-552-4670, E-mail: jeanluc.solere@bc.edu.
Website: http://www.bc.edu/philosophy

**Boston College,** Graduate School of Arts and Sciences, Department of Theology, Chestnut Hill, MA 02467-3800. Offers philosophy and theology (MA); theology (PhD). *Accreditation:* ATS. *Faculty:* 36 full-time. *Students:* 60 full-time. 92 applicants, 22% accepted, 14 enrolled. In 2016, 2 master's, 10 doctorates awarded. Terminal master's awarded for partial completion of doctoral program. *Degree requirements:* For master's, one foreign language, thesis optional; for doctorate, thesis/dissertation. *Entrance requirements:* For master's and doctorate, GRE General Test. Additional exam requirements/recommendations for international students: Required—TOEFL (minimum

*Philosophy*

score 600 paper-based; 100 iBT), IELTS (minimum score 8). *Application deadline:* For fall admission, 1/2 for domestic and international students. Application fee: $75. Electronic applications accepted. Tuition and fees vary according to program. *Financial support:* In 2016–17, fellowships with full tuition reimbursements (averaging $21,000 per year), research assistantships with full tuition reimbursements (averaging $21,000 per year), teaching assistantships with full tuition reimbursements (averaging $21,000 per year) were awarded; Federal Work-Study, scholarships/grants, and health care benefits also available. Support available to part-time students. Financial award application deadline: 3/1; financial award applicants required to submit FAFSA. *Faculty research:* Historical theology, history of Christianity, systematic theology, Biblical studies, theological ethics, comparative theology. *Unit head:* Dr. Richard Gaillardetz, Chairperson, 617-552-3873, E-mail: gaillard@bc.edu. *Application contact:* Dr. John Darr, Graduate Program Director, 617-552-3884, E-mail: darr@bc.edu. Website: http://www.bc.edu/theology

**Boston University,** Graduate School of Arts and Sciences, Department of Philosophy, Boston, MA 02215. Offers MA, PhD, JD/MA. *Students:* 54 full-time (14 women), 3 part-time (1 woman); includes 6 minority (1 Black or African American, non-Hispanic/Latino; 2 Asian, non-Hispanic/Latino; 2 Hispanic/Latino; 1 Two or more races, non-Hispanic/Latino), 13 international. Average age 30. 169 applicants, 14% accepted, 7 enrolled. In 2016, 10 master's, 2 doctorates awarded. Terminal master's awarded for partial completion of doctoral program. *Degree requirements:* For master's, one foreign language, thesis; for doctorate, one foreign language, comprehensive exam, thesis/dissertation. *Entrance requirements:* For master's and doctorate, GRE General Test, 3 letters of recommendation, transcripts, personal statement, scholarly writing sample. Additional exam requirements/recommendations for international students: Required—TOEFL (minimum score 550 paper-based; 84 iBT). *Application deadline:* For fall admission, 2/1 for domestic and international students. Application fee: $95. Electronic applications accepted. *Financial support:* In 2016–17, 41 students received support, including 15 fellowships with full tuition reimbursements available (averaging $21,500 per year), research assistantships with full tuition reimbursements available (averaging $21,000 per year), 22 teaching assistantships with full tuition reimbursements available (averaging $21,000 per year); Federal Work-Study, scholarships/grants, and health care benefits also available. Financial award application deadline: 2/1. *Unit head:* C. Allen Speight, Chair, 617-353-3067, Fax: 617-353-6805, E-mail: casp8@bu.edu. *Application contact:* Laura Hubbard, Senior Program Coordinator, 617-353-2571, Fax: 617-353-6805, E-mail: casphilo@bu.edu.
Website: http://www.bu.edu/philo/

**Bowling Green State University,** Graduate College, College of Arts and Sciences, Department of Philosophy, Bowling Green, OH 43403. Offers applied philosophy (PhD); institutional theory and history (PhD); philosophy (MA). *Program availability:* Part-time. Terminal master's awarded for partial completion of doctoral program. *Degree requirements:* For master's, thesis or alternative; for doctorate, comprehensive exam, thesis/dissertation, foreign language or research tool. *Entrance requirements:* For master's and doctorate, GRE General Test. Additional exam requirements/recommendations for international students: Required—TOEFL. *Application deadline:* For fall admission, 2/1 priority date for domestic students. Application fee: $30. Electronic applications accepted. *Financial support:* Fellowships with full tuition reimbursements, research assistantships with full tuition reimbursements, teaching assistantships with full tuition reimbursements, Federal Work-Study, and unspecified assistantships available. Financial award applicants required to submit FAFSA. *Faculty research:* Moral philosophy and ethics, political and social philosophy, decision theory, applied ethics, public policy. *Unit head:* Dr. David Shoemaker, Chair, 419-372-6983. *Application contact:* Dr. Dan Jacobson, Graduate Coordinator, 419-372-7218.

**Brandeis University,** Graduate School of Arts and Sciences, Department of Philosophy, Waltham, MA 02454-9110. Offers MA. *Program availability:* Part-time. *Faculty:* 11 full-time (3 women). *Students:* 17 full-time (4 women); includes 4 minority (1 Black or African American, non-Hispanic/Latino; 2 Hispanic/Latino; 1 Two or more races, non-Hispanic/Latino), 1 international. 78 applicants, 44% accepted, 6 enrolled. In 2016, 9 master's awarded. *Degree requirements:* For master's, thesis or alternative, proseminar; symbolic logic; paper. *Entrance requirements:* For master's, GRE, official transcript(s), 3 recommendation letters, resume, statement of purpose, writing sample. Additional exam requirements/recommendations for international students: Required—TOEFL (minimum score 600 paper-based; 100 iBT); Recommended—IELTS (minimum score 7), TSE (minimum score 68). *Application deadline:* For fall admission, 2/15 priority date for domestic and international students. Application fee: $75. Electronic applications accepted. *Financial support:* In 2016–17, 17 students received support, including 20 teaching assistantships with partial tuition reimbursements available (averaging $3,200 per year); Federal Work-Study, scholarships/grants, and tuition waivers (partial) also available. Support available to part-time students. Financial award application deadline: 4/15; financial award applicants required to submit FAFSA. *Faculty research:* Metaphysics and epistemology, ethics, social and political philosophy, philosophy of language, logic, philosophy of mind and cognitive science, early modern philosophy, aesthetics, philosophy of law. *Unit head:* Dr. Jerry Samet, Department Chair, 781-736-2788, Fax: 781-736-8562, E-mail: samet@brandeis.edu. *Application contact:* Julie Seeger, Department Administrator, 781-736-2789, Fax: 781-736-8562, E-mail: jseeger@brandeis.edu.
Website: http://www.brandeis.edu/departments/philosophy/

**Brock University,** Faculty of Graduate Studies, Faculty of Humanities, Program in Philosophy, St. Catharines, ON L2S 3A1, Canada. Offers MA. *Program availability:* Part-time. *Degree requirements:* For master's, thesis optional. *Entrance requirements:* For master's, honors BA in philosophy. Additional exam requirements/recommendations for international students: Required—TOEFL (minimum score 550 paper-based; 80 iBT), IELTS (minimum score 6.5), TWE (minimum score 4). Electronic applications accepted. *Faculty research:* Contemporary continental philosophy, Chinese and comparative philosophy, Indian philosophy, ethics.

**Brown University,** Graduate School, Department of Philosophy, Providence, RI 02912. Offers PhD. *Degree requirements:* For doctorate, variable foreign language requirement, thesis/dissertation. *Entrance requirements:* For doctorate, GRE General Test.

**California Institute of Integral Studies,** School of Consciousness and Transformation, San Francisco, CA 94103. Offers anthropology and social change (MA, PhD); Asian philosophies and cultures (MA); creative inquiry/interdisciplinary arts (MFA); East-West psychology (MA, PhD); integral and transpersonal psychology (PhD); philosophy and religion (PhD), including ecology, spirituality, and religion, philosophy, cosmology, and consciousness, women's spirituality; theater and performance making (MFA); transformative leadership (MA); transformative studies (PhD); women, gender, spirituality and social justice (MA); writing and consciousness (MFA). *Program availability:* Part-time, evening/weekend, 100% online, blended/hybrid learning. *Students:* 390 full-time (256 women), 121 part-time (84 women); includes 135 minority (39 Black or African American, non-Hispanic/Latino; 2 American Indian or Alaska Native, non-Hispanic/Latino; 22 Asian, non-Hispanic/Latino; 40 Hispanic/Latino; 2 Native Hawaiian or other Pacific Islander, non-Hispanic/Latino; 30 Two or more races, non-Hispanic/Latino), 51 international. Average age 38. 195 applicants, 92% accepted, 124 enrolled. In 2016, 35 master's, 41 doctorates awarded. Terminal master's awarded for partial completion of doctoral program. *Degree requirements:* For master's, thesis optional; for doctorate, comprehensive exam, thesis/dissertation, 1 foreign language (for Asian philosophies and cultures). *Entrance requirements:* For master's, minimum GPA of 3.0, letters of recommendation, writing sample; for doctorate, master's degree, minimum GPA of 3.0, letters of recommendation, writing sample. Additional exam requirements/recommendations for international students: Required—TOEFL. *Application deadline:* For fall admission, 2/1 priority date for domestic students; for spring admission, 10/15 priority date for domestic and international students. Applications are processed on a rolling basis. Application fee: $65. Electronic applications accepted. *Expenses:* Tuition: Full-time $19,728; part-time $1098 per semester hour. *Required fees:* $320; $320 per semester hour. *Financial support:* Research assistantships, teaching assistantships, career-related internships or fieldwork, Federal Work-Study, and scholarships/grants available. Support available to part-time students. Financial award application deadline: 4/15; financial award applicants required to submit FAFSA. *Faculty research:* Ecology and sustainability, philosophy and religion, East-West psychology, integrative health, social and cultural anthropology, transformative leadership. *Application contact:* Ellen Durst, Director of Admissions, 415-575-6100, Fax: 415-575-1268, E-mail: admissions@ciis.edu.
Website: http://www.ciis.edu/

**California State University, Long Beach,** Graduate Studies, College of Liberal Arts, Department of Philosophy, Long Beach, CA 90840. Offers MA. *Program availability:* Part-time. *Degree requirements:* For master's, comprehensive exam or thesis. *Application deadline:* For fall admission, 7/1 for domestic students. Applications are processed on a rolling basis. Application fee: $55. Electronic applications accepted. *Financial support:* Federal Work-Study, institutionally sponsored loans, and scholarships/grants available. Financial award application deadline: 3/2. *Faculty research:* Philosophy of science, ethics. *Unit head:* Nellie Wieland, Chair, 562-985-4331, E-mail: philos@csulb.edu. *Application contact:* Dr. Cory Wright, Graduate Advisor, 562-985-4245, Fax: 562-985-4331, E-mail: cdwright@csulb.edu.

**California State University, Los Angeles,** Graduate Studies, College of Arts and Letters, Department of Philosophy, Los Angeles, CA 90032-8530. Offers MA, Graduate Certificate. *Program availability:* Part-time, evening/weekend. *Degree requirements:* For master's, comprehensive exam. *Entrance requirements:* Additional exam requirements/recommendations for international students: Required—TOEFL (minimum score 500 paper-based). Electronic applications accepted. *Faculty research:* Aesthetics, philosophy of language, ethics, philosophy of science, history of philosophy.

**Carleton University,** Faculty of Graduate Studies, Faculty of Arts and Social Sciences, Department of Philosophy, Ottawa, ON K1S 5B6, Canada. Offers MA. *Degree requirements:* For master's, thesis optional. *Entrance requirements:* For master's, honors degree. Additional exam requirements/recommendations for international students: Required—TOEFL. *Faculty research:* Application of philosophical theory to issues of current concern, history of philosophy, contemporary philosophy in North America and Europe.

**Carnegie Mellon University,** Dietrich College of Humanities and Social Sciences, Department of Philosophy, Pittsburgh, PA 15213-3891. Offers logic, computation and methodology (MS, PhD); philosophy (MA, PhD); pure and applied logic (PhD). *Program availability:* Part-time. *Degree requirements:* For master's, thesis; for doctorate, comprehensive exam, thesis/dissertation. *Entrance requirements:* For master's and doctorate, GRE General Test. Additional exam requirements/recommendations for international students: Required—TOEFL. Electronic applications accepted. *Faculty research:* Philosophy of science, artificial intelligence.

**The Catholic University of America,** School of Philosophy, Washington, DC 20064. Offers MA, PhD, Ph L, MA/JD. MA/JD offered in combination with Columbus School of Law. *Program availability:* Part-time. *Faculty:* 22 full-time (5 women), 4 part-time/adjunct (0 women). *Students:* 57 full-time (8 women), 70 part-time (12 women); includes 10 minority (3 Asian, non-Hispanic/Latino; 6 Hispanic/Latino; 1 Two or more races, non-Hispanic/Latino), 8 international. Average age 32. 75 applicants, 53% accepted, 25 enrolled. In 2016, 11 master's, 4 doctorates awarded. *Degree requirements:* For master's, one foreign language, thesis, oral exam; for doctorate, 2 foreign languages, comprehensive exam, thesis/dissertation, oral exam. *Entrance requirements:* For master's, GRE General Test, statement of purpose, official copies of academic transcripts, three letters of recommendation, writing sample; for doctorate, GRE General Test, statement of purpose, official copies of academic transcripts, three letters of recommendation. Additional exam requirements/recommendations for international students: Required—TOEFL (minimum score 550 paper-based; 80 iBT). *Application deadline:* For fall admission, 7/15 priority date for domestic students, 7/1 for international students; for spring admission, 11/15 priority date for domestic students, 11/1 for international students. Applications are processed on a rolling basis. Application fee: $55. Electronic applications accepted. *Expenses:* $42,850 per year; $1,170 per credit; $200 per semester part-time fees. *Financial support:* Fellowships, research assistantships, teaching assistantships, Federal Work-Study, scholarships/grants, tuition waivers (full and partial), and unspecified assistantships available. Financial award application deadline: 2/1; financial award applicants required to submit FAFSA. *Faculty research:* Ancient philosophy (Plato, Aristotle, Neo-Platonism), medieval philosophy (Aquinas, Scotus, Ockham, medieval Islamic), 19th- and 20th-century German philosophy (especially Kant, Hegel, Husserl and Heidegger), metaphysics, ethics, political philosophy. *Total annual research expenditures:* $21,734. *Unit head:* Dr. John McCarthy, Dean, 202-319-6649, Fax: 202-319-4731, E-mail: mccartjc@cua.edu. *Application contact:* Director of Graduate Admissions, 202-319-5057, Fax: 202-319-6533, E-mail: cua-admissions@cua.edu.
Website: http://philosophy.cua.edu/

**Central European University,** Department of Philosophy, Budapest, Hungary. Offers MA, PhD. *Faculty:* 8 full-time (2 women), 3 part-time/adjunct (1 woman). *Students:* 47 full-time (14 women). Average age 28. 153 applicants, 18% accepted, 16 enrolled. In 2016, 14 master's, 6 doctorates awarded. *Degree requirements:* For master's, one foreign language, thesis; for doctorate, one foreign language, comprehensive exam, thesis/dissertation. *Entrance requirements:* For master's and doctorate, interview. Additional exam requirements/recommendations for international students: Required—TOEFL (minimum score 570 paper-based); Recommended—IELTS (minimum score 6.5). *Application deadline:* For fall admission, 2/4 for domestic and international students. Application fee: $30. Electronic applications accepted. *Expenses:* Tuition: Full-time 13,500 euros. Tuition and fees vary according to degree level, program and student level. *Financial support:* In 2016–17, 45 students received support. Fellowships, teaching assistantships, scholarships/grants, health care benefits, and tuition waivers (full and partial) available. *Faculty research:* Questions of metaphysics, both in a contemporary and historical perspective issues about the freedom of the will; ancient metaphysics and philosophy of nature modality in early modern philosophy; the philosophy of mind; perception; political philosophy; cognitive science; ethics and met ethics. *Unit head:* Dr. Hanoch Ben-Yami, Head of Department, 36 1 327-3806, Fax: 361-327-3072, E-mail: philosophy@ceu.edu. *Application contact:* Zsuzsanna Jaszberenyi, Admissions Officer, 361-324-3009, Fax: 367-327-3211, E-mail: admissions@ceu.edu.
Website: http://philosophy.ceu.edu

**Claremont Graduate University,** Graduate Programs, School of Arts and Humanities, Department of Philosophy, Claremont, CA 91711-6160. Offers MA, PhD, MA/PhD, MBA/MA, MBA/PhD. *Program availability:* Part-time. *Faculty:* 3 full-time (1 woman). *Students:* 21 full-time (4 women), 2 part-time (1 woman); includes 6 minority (1 Black or African American, non-Hispanic/Latino; 1 Asian, non-Hispanic/Latino; 4 Hispanic/Latino). Average age 40. In 2016, 10 master's, 1 doctorate awarded. *Degree requirements:* For doctorate, research folio. *Entrance requirements:* For master's and doctorate, GRE General Test. Additional exam requirements/recommendations for international students: Required—TOEFL (minimum score 75 iBT). *Application deadline:* For fall admission, 2/1 priority date for domestic and international students. Applications are processed on a rolling basis. Application fee: $80. Electronic applications accepted. *Expenses:* Tuition: Full-time $44,328; part-time $1847 per unit. *Required fees:* $600; $300 per semester. Tuition and fees vary according to course load and program. *Financial support:* Fellowships, research assistantships, Federal Work-Study, institutionally sponsored loans, and scholarships/grants available. Support available to part-time students. Financial award application deadline: 2/15; financial award applicants required to submit FAFSA. *Faculty research:* Ancient philosophy, philosophy of science, probability theory, philosophical logic, philosophy of logic. *Unit head:* Masahiro Yamada, Chair, 909-607-0471, E-mail: masahiro.yamada@cgu.edu. *Application contact:* Amy Sandefur, Assistant Director of Admissions, 909-607-9101, E-mail: amy.sandefur@cgu.edu.
Website: https://www.cgu.edu/departments/philosophy/

**Clarks Summit University,** Graduate Studies, South Abington Township, PA 18411. Offers Bible (MA); counseling (MA, MS); curriculum and instruction (M Ed); educational administration (M Ed); intercultural studies (MA); literature (MA); missions (MA); organizational leadership (MA); reading specialist (M Ed); secondary English/communications (M Ed); social entrepreneurship (MA); worldview studies (MA). MA in missions program available only for Association of Baptists for World Evangelism missionary personnel. *Program availability:* Part-time, evening/weekend, online learning. *Entrance requirements:* Additional exam requirements/recommendations for international students: Required—TOEFL (minimum score 500 paper-based).

**Cleveland State University,** College of Graduate Studies, College of Liberal Arts and Social Sciences, Department of Philosophy and Comparative Religion, Cleveland, OH 44115. Offers bioethics (MA, Certificate), including bioethics (MA); philosophy (MA), including philosophy. *Program availability:* Part-time, evening/weekend. *Faculty:* 4 full-time (all women), 2 part-time/adjunct (1 woman). *Students:* 3 full-time (0 women), 2 part-time (1 woman); includes 1 minority (Asian, non-Hispanic/Latino). Average age 35. 11 applicants, 100% accepted, 4 enrolled. In 2016, 5 master's, 1 other advanced degree awarded. *Degree requirements:* For master's, comprehensive exam, thesis optional, 32 credit hours of coursework; for Certificate, 12 credit hours of coursework. *Entrance requirements:* For master's and Certificate, BA, BS, or equivalent degree with minimum GPA of 2.75. Additional exam requirements/recommendations for international students: Required—TOEFL (minimum score 550 paper-based; 78 iBT). *Application deadline:* For fall admission, 7/1 priority date for domestic students, 5/15 priority date for international students; for spring admission, 11/15 for domestic students, 11/1 for international students; for summer admission, 4/1 for domestic students, 3/15 for international students. Applications are processed on a rolling basis. Application fee: $40. Electronic applications accepted. *Expenses:* Tuition, state resident: full-time $9565. Tuition, nonresident: full-time $17,980. Tuition and fees vary according to program. *Financial support:* In 2016–17, 5 students received support, including 5 teaching assistantships with full tuition reimbursements available (averaging $4,000 per year); health care benefits, tuition waivers (full), and unspecified assistantships also available. Support available to part-time students. *Faculty research:* Ethics, early modern philosophy, bioethics, social and political philosophy, history of women philosophers. *Unit head:* Dr. Mary Ellen Waithe, Chairperson, 216-687-3900, Fax: 216-523-7482, E-mail: m.waithe@csuohio.edu. *Application contact:* Deborah L. Brown, Interim Assistant Director, Graduate Admissions, 216-523-7572, Fax: 216-687-5400, E-mail: d.l.brown@csuohio.edu.
Website: http://www.csuohio.edu/class/philosophy-religion/philosophy-religion

**Collège Dominicain de Philosophie et de Théologie,** Graduate Programs, Faculty of Philosophy, Ottawa, ON K1R 7G3, Canada. Offers MA Ph, PhD. *Degree requirements:* For master's, thesis; for doctorate, 2 foreign languages, thesis/dissertation, candidacy exam. *Entrance requirements:* For master's, honors degree in philosophy, minimum B average in undergraduate course work; for doctorate, master's degree in philosophy, minimum A average in graduate course work. *Faculty research:* Ethics, philosophy of Kant.

**Colorado State University,** College of Liberal Arts, Department of Philosophy, Fort Collins, CO 80523-1781. Offers MA. *Program availability:* Part-time. *Faculty:* 9 full-time (3 women). *Students:* 10 full-time (2 women), 11 part-time (3 women); includes 3 minority (all Hispanic/Latino). Average age 27. 53 applicants, 34% accepted, 7 enrolled. In 2016, 10 master's awarded. *Degree requirements:* For master's, comprehensive exam (for some programs), thesis or alternative, 30-33 credit hours of coursework. *Entrance requirements:* For master's, minimum undergraduate GPA of 3.25. Additional exam requirements/recommendations for international students: Required—TOEFL (minimum score 550 paper-based; 80 iBT), IELTS, PTE. *Application deadline:* For fall admission, 2/15 for domestic and international students. Application fee: $60 ($70 for international students). Electronic applications accepted. *Expenses:* Tuition, state resident: full-time $9628. Tuition, nonresident: full-time $23,603. *Required fees:* $2253; $528.14 per credit hour. $264.07 per semester. Tuition and fees vary according to course load and program. *Financial support:* In 2016–17, 13 students received support, including 13 teaching assistantships with full tuition reimbursements available (averaging $13,932 per year); fellowships with full tuition reimbursements available and health care benefits also available. Financial award application deadline: 2/15. *Faculty research:* Applied ethics (environmental, animal and bioethics), non-Western and comparative philosophy, metaphysics and epistemology. *Unit head:* Dr. John Didier, Department Chair, 970-491-6315, Fax: 970-491-4900, E-mail: john.didier@colostate.edu. *Application contact:* Gaylene Wolfe, Graduate Coordinator, 970-491-6315, Fax: 970-491-4900, E-mail: gaylene.wolfe@colostate.edu.
Website: http://philosophy.colostate.edu/

**Columbia University,** Graduate School of Arts and Sciences, New York, NY 10027. Offers African-American studies (MA); American studies (MA); anthropology (MA, PhD); art history and archaeology (MA, PhD); astronomy (PhD); biological sciences (PhD); biotechnology (MA); chemical physics (PhD); chemistry (PhD); classical studies (MA, PhD); classics (MA, PhD); climate and society (MA); conservation biology (MA); earth and environmental sciences (PhD); East Asia: regional studies (MA); East Asian languages and cultures (MA, PhD); ecology, evolution and environmental biology (MA), including conservation biology; ecology, evolution, and environmental biology (PhD), including ecology and evolutionary biology, evolutionary primatology; economics (MA, PhD); English and comparative literature (MA, PhD); French and Romance philology (MA, PhD); Germanic languages (MA, PhD); global French studies (MA); global thought (MA); Hispanic cultural studies (MA); history (PhD); history and literature (MA); human rights studies (MA); Islamic studies (MA); Italian (MA, PhD); Japanese pedagogy (MA); Jewish studies (MA); Latin America and the Caribbean: regional studies (MA); Latin

American and Iberian cultures (PhD); mathematics (MA, PhD), including finance (MA); medieval and Renaissance studies (MA); Middle Eastern, South Asian, and African studies (MA, PhD); modern art: critical and curatorial studies (MA); modern European studies (MA); museum anthropology (MA); music (DMA, PhD); oral history (MA); philosophical foundations of physics (MA); philosophy (MA, PhD); physics (PhD); political science (MA); psychology (PhD); quantitative methods in the social sciences (MA); religion (MA, PhD); Russia, Eurasia and East Europe: regional studies (MA); Russian translation (MA); Slavic cultures (MA); Slavic languages (MA, PhD); sociology (MA, PhD); South Asian studies (MA); statistics (MA, PhD); theatre (PhD). Dual-degree programs require admission to both Graduate School of Arts and Sciences and another Columbia school. *Program availability:* Part-time. Terminal master's awarded for partial completion of doctoral program. *Degree requirements:* For master's, variable foreign language requirement, comprehensive exam (for some programs), thesis (for some programs); for doctorate, variable foreign language requirement, comprehensive exam (for some programs), thesis/dissertation. *Entrance requirements:* For master's and doctorate, GRE General Test, GRE Subject Test (for some programs). Additional exam requirements/recommendations for international students: Required—TOEFL, IELTS. Electronic applications accepted.

**Concordia University,** School of Graduate Studies, Faculty of Arts and Science, Department of Philosophy, Montréal, QC H3G 1M8, Canada. Offers MA. *Degree requirements:* For master's, comprehensive exam, thesis or alternative. *Entrance requirements:* For master's, honors degree in philosophy or equivalent. *Faculty research:* Anglo-American analytic thought, Continental thought, pragmatic thought.

**Cornell University,** Graduate School, Graduate Fields of Arts and Sciences, Field of Philosophy, Ithaca, NY 14853. Offers PhD. *Degree requirements:* For doctorate, comprehensive exam, thesis/dissertation, teaching experience. *Entrance requirements:* For doctorate, sample of written work in philosophy, 2 letters of recommendation. Additional exam requirements/recommendations for international students: Required—TOEFL (minimum score 550 paper-based; 77 iBT). Electronic applications accepted.

**Dalhousie University,** Faculty of Arts and Social Science, Department of Philosophy, Halifax, NS B3H 4R2, Canada. Offers MA, PhD. *Entrance requirements:* For doctorate, MA in philosophy. Additional exam requirements/recommendations for international students: Required—TOEFL, IELTS, CANTEST, CAEL, or Michigan English Language Assessment Battery. Electronic applications accepted. *Faculty research:* Ethical and political philosophy; epistemology; philosophy of language, history, and logic; bioethics; feminist theory.

**Dallas Theological Seminary,** Graduate Programs, Dallas, TX 75204-6499. Offers adult education (Th M); apologetics (Th M); Bible backgrounds (Th M); Bible translation (Th M); Biblical and theological studies (Certificate); biblical counseling (MA); biblical exegesis and linguistics (MA); biblical exposition (PhD); biblical studies (MA); Biblical theology (Th M); children's education (Th M); Christian education (MA, D Min); Christian leadership (MA); cross-cultural ministries (MA); educational administration (Th M); educational leadership (Th M); evangelism and discipleship (Th M); exposition of Biblical books (Th M); family life education (Th M); general studies (Th M); Hebrew and cognate studies (Th M); hermeneutics (Th M); historical theology (Th M); homiletics (Th M); intercultural ministries (Th M); Jesus studies (Th M); leadership studies (Th M); media and communication (MA); media arts (Th M); ministry (D Min); ministry with women (Th M); New Testament studies (Th M, PhD); Old Testament studies (Th M, PhD); parachurch ministries (Th M); pastoral care and counseling (Th M); pastoral theology and practice (Th M); philosophy (Th M); sacred theology (STM); spiritual formation (Th M); systematic theology (Th M); teaching in Christian institutions (Th M); theological studies (PhD); urban ministries (Th M); worship studies (Th M); youth education (Th M). *Program availability:* Part-time, online learning. *Degree requirements:* For master's, variable foreign language requirement, thesis (for some programs); for doctorate, 2 foreign languages, thesis/dissertation. *Entrance requirements:* For master's, GRE or MAT (if minimum undergraduate cumulative GPA is below 2.5 or undergraduate degree is unaccredited). Additional exam requirements/recommendations for international students: Required—TOEFL (minimum score 575 paper-based; 85 iBT), TWE. Electronic applications accepted.

**Delta State University,** Graduate Programs, College of Arts and Sciences, Program in Liberal Studies, Cleveland, MS 38733-0001. Offers evolving human voices (MALS); gender and diversity studies (MALS); globalization studies (MALS); Mississippi Delta studies (MALS); philosophy (MALS); religious studies (MALS). *Degree requirements:* For master's, oral and/or written comprehensive exam.

**Dominican School of Philosophy and Theology,** Graduate Programs, Berkeley, CA 94708. Offers philosophy (MA); theology (M Div, MA, MTS, Certificate); M Div/MA; MA/MA. *Accreditation:* ATS. *Program availability:* Part-time. *Degree requirements:* For master's, one foreign language, thesis. *Entrance requirements:* For master's, GRE General Test (for MA), minimum GPA of 3.0 (for MA), 2.3 (for M Div); academic writing sample (for MA); statement of purpose, official transcripts, letters of recommendation. Additional exam requirements/recommendations for international students: Required—TOEFL (minimum score 570 paper-based; 80 iBT), IELTS. Electronic applications accepted.

**Dominican University of California,** School of Arts, Humanities and Social Sciences, Humanities Program, San Rafael, CA 94901-2298. Offers applied music (MA); art history (MA); creative writing (MA); gender studies (MA); history (MA); literature (MA); philosophy (MA); political theory (MA); religion (MA). *Program availability:* Part-time. *Degree requirements:* For master's, thesis or alternative. *Entrance requirements:* For master's, minimum GPA of 3.0, interview. Additional exam requirements/recommendations for international students: Required—TOEFL (minimum score 550 paper-based; 80 iBT), IELTS (minimum score 6.5). Electronic applications accepted. Application fee is waived when completed online. *Expenses:* Contact institution.

**Duke University,** Graduate School, Department of Philosophy, Durham, NC 27708. Offers PhD, JD/AM, JD/PhD. *Degree requirements:* For doctorate, one foreign language, thesis/dissertation. *Entrance requirements:* For doctorate, GRE General Test. Additional exam requirements/recommendations for international students: Required—TOEFL (minimum score 577 paper-based; 90 iBT) or IELTS (minimum score 7). Electronic applications accepted.

**Duquesne University,** Graduate School of Liberal Arts, Department of Philosophy, Pittsburgh, PA 15282-0001. Offers MA, PhD. *Program availability:* Part-time, evening/weekend. *Faculty:* 18 full-time (5 women), 4 part-time/adjunct (2 women). *Students:* 54 full-time (13 women); includes 4 minority (all Hispanic/Latino), 16 international. Average age 30. 93 applicants, 57% accepted, 10 enrolled. In 2016, 7 master's, 6 doctorates awarded. Terminal master's awarded for partial completion of doctoral program. *Degree requirements:* For master's, one foreign language; for doctorate, 2 foreign languages, comprehensive exam, thesis/dissertation. *Entrance requirements:* For master's, GRE General Test, bachelor's degree in philosophy, minimum GPA of 3.5; for doctorate, GRE General Test, master's degree in philosophy, minimum GPA of 3.75. Additional exam requirements/recommendations for international students: Required—TOEFL. *Application deadline:* For fall admission, 2/15 for domestic and international students. Application fee: $0. Electronic applications accepted. *Expenses:* Tuition: Full-time $22,212; part-time $1234 per credit. Tuition and fees vary according to program.

## Philosophy

*Financial support:* In 2016–17, 28 students received support, including 18 teaching assistantships with full tuition reimbursements available (averaging $18,000 per year); Federal Work-Study, scholarships/grants, tuition waivers (partial), and unspecified assistantships also available. Financial award application deadline: 5/1. *Faculty research:* Phenomenology, twentieth-century Continental philosophy, history of philosophy. *Unit head:* Dr. Ronald Polansky, Chair, 412-396-6500, E-mail: polansky@duq.edu. *Application contact:* Linda Rendulic, Assistant to the Dean, 412-396-6400, Fax: 412-396-5265, E-mail: rendulic@duq.edu.
Website: http://www.duq.edu/academics/schools/liberal-arts/graduate-school/programs/philosophy

**Eastern Michigan University,** Graduate School, College of Arts and Sciences, Department of History and Philosophy, Program in Philosophy, Ypsilanti, MI 48197. Offers MA. *Program availability:* Part-time, evening/weekend, online learning. *Students:* 8 full-time (2 women), 8 part-time (2 women); includes 3 minority (1 Black or African American, non-Hispanic/Latino; 1 Hispanic/Latino; 1 Two or more races, non-Hispanic/Latino). Average age 32. 12 applicants, 100% accepted, 9 enrolled. *Degree requirements:* For master's, thesis optional. *Entrance requirements:* Additional exam requirements/recommendations for international students: Required—TOEFL. *Application deadline:* Applications are processed on a rolling basis. Application fee: $45. *Financial support:* Fellowships, research assistantships with full tuition reimbursements, teaching assistantships with full tuition reimbursements, career-related internships or fieldwork, Federal Work-Study, institutionally sponsored loans, traineeships, and unspecified assistantships available. Support available to part-time students. Financial award applicants required to submit FAFSA. *Application contact:* Dr. William John Koolage, Coordinator, 734-487-1018, Fax: 734-487-6835, E-mail: wkoolage@emich.edu.

**Emory University,** Laney Graduate School, Department of Comparative Literature, Atlanta, GA 30322-1100. Offers comparative literature (PhD); philosophy (Certificate); psychoanalytic studies (PhD); women's studies (Certificate). *Degree requirements:* For doctorate, 2 foreign languages, comprehensive exam, thesis/dissertation. *Entrance requirements:* For doctorate, GRE General Test, minimum GPA of 3.0. Additional exam requirements/recommendations for international students: Required—TOEFL. Electronic applications accepted. *Faculty research:* Literary theory, psychoanalysis trauma and testimony, literature and religion, literature and technology, literature and philosophy, politics and global culture, literature and aesthetics.

**Emory University,** Laney Graduate School, Department of Philosophy, Atlanta, GA 30322-1100. Offers PhD. *Degree requirements:* For doctorate, 2 foreign languages, comprehensive exam, thesis/dissertation. *Entrance requirements:* For doctorate, GRE General Test, minimum GPA of 3.0. Additional exam requirements/recommendations for international students: Required—TOEFL. Electronic applications accepted. *Faculty research:* History of philosophy, German idealism, twentieth century Continental philosophy, ethics, social theory.

**Florida State University,** The Graduate School, College of Arts and Sciences, Department of Philosophy, Tallahassee, FL 32306-1500. Offers history and philosophy of science (MA); philosophy (MA, PhD). *Faculty:* 15 full-time (3 women), 2 part-time/adjunct (1 woman). *Students:* 53 full-time (11 women), 4 part-time (3 women); includes 11 minority (2 Black or African American, non-Hispanic/Latino; 2 Asian, non-Hispanic/Latino; 3 Hispanic/Latino; 4 Two or more races, non-Hispanic/Latino), 3 international. Average age 29. 80 applicants, 35% accepted, 15 enrolled. In 2016, 6 master's, 2 doctorates awarded. Terminal master's awarded for partial completion of doctoral program. *Degree requirements:* For master's, one foreign language, comprehensive exam, thesis or alternative; for doctorate, one foreign language, comprehensive exam, thesis/dissertation. *Entrance requirements:* For master's and doctorate, GRE General Test. Additional exam requirements/recommendations for international students: Required—TOEFL (minimum score 550 paper-based; 80 iBT). *Application deadline:* For fall admission, 3/31 priority date for domestic and international students; for winter admission, 10/19 for domestic and international students; for spring admission, 11/1 priority date for domestic and international students; for summer admission, 3/1 priority date for domestic and international students. Applications are processed on a rolling basis. Application fee: $30. Electronic applications accepted. *Expenses:* Tuition, state resident: full-time $7263; part-time $403.51 per credit hour. Tuition, nonresident: full-time $18,087; part-time $1004.85 per credit hour. *Required fees:* $1365; $75.81 per credit hour. $20 per semester. Tuition and fees vary according to campus/location. *Financial support:* In 2016–17, 4 students received support, including 53 teaching assistantships with partial tuition reimbursements available (averaging $15,841 per year); Federal Work-Study, scholarships/grants, and health care benefits also available. Financial award application deadline: 1/3; financial award applicants required to submit FAFSA. *Faculty research:* Philosophy of biology, Greek philosophy, ethics, action theory, philosophy of mind, metaphysics. *Unit head:* Dr. John Piers Rawling, Chairman, 850-644-1483, Fax: 850-644-3832, E-mail: prawling@fsu.edu. *Application contact:* 850-644-1483, Fax: 850-644-3832, E-mail: philosophy@admin.fsu.edu.
Website: http://philosophy.fsu.edu/

**Fordham University,** Graduate School of Arts and Sciences, Department of Philosophy, New York, NY 10458. Offers MA, PhD. *Program availability:* Part-time, evening/weekend. *Faculty:* 31 full-time (10 women). *Students:* 56 full-time (12 women), 13 part-time (1 woman); includes 6 minority (1 Black or African American, non-Hispanic/Latino; 1 American Indian or Alaska Native, non-Hispanic/Latino; 4 Asian, non-Hispanic/Latino), 6 international. Average age 30. 232 applicants, 17% accepted, 15 enrolled. In 2016, 14 master's, 5 doctorates awarded. Terminal master's awarded for partial completion of doctoral program. *Degree requirements:* For master's, one foreign language, comprehensive exam; for doctorate, 2 foreign languages, comprehensive exam, thesis/dissertation. *Entrance requirements:* For master's and doctorate, GRE General Test. Additional exam requirements/recommendations for international students: Required—TOEFL (minimum score 650 paper-based). *Application deadline:* For fall admission, 1/4 priority date for domestic students; for spring admission, 11/1 for domestic students. Application fee: $70. Electronic applications accepted. *Financial support:* In 2016–17, 45 students received support, including 3 fellowships with tuition reimbursements available (averaging $21,605 per year), 1 research assistantship with tuition reimbursement available (averaging $25,390 per year), 26 teaching assistantships with tuition reimbursements available (averaging $23,644 per year); institutionally sponsored loans, tuition waivers (full and partial), and unspecified assistantships also available. Support available to part-time students. Financial award application deadline: 1/4. *Faculty research:* Contemporary Continental philosophy (including German idealism), philosophy of religion, medieval philosophy, ethics, epistemology. *Unit head:* Dr. John Drummond, Department Chair, 718-817-3332, Fax: 718-817-3300, E-mail: drummond@fordham.edu. *Application contact:* Bernadette Valentino-Morrison, Director of Graduate Admissions, 718-817-4419, Fax: 718-817-3566, E-mail: valentinomor@fordham.edu.

**Franciscan University of Steubenville,** Graduate Programs, Department of Philosophy, Steubenville, OH 43952-1763. Offers MA. *Program availability:* Part-time. *Degree requirements:* For master's, one foreign language, thesis. *Entrance requirements:* For master's, minimum undergraduate GPA of 3.0. Additional exam

requirements/recommendations for international students: Required—TOEFL. Electronic applications accepted. Application fee is waived when completed online.

**George Mason University,** College of Humanities and Social Sciences, Department of Philosophy, Fairfax, VA 22030. Offers ethics and public affairs (MA). *Faculty:* 12 full-time (3 women), 7 part-time/adjunct (0 women). *Students:* 3 full-time (2 women), 11 part-time (3 women); includes 3 minority (1 Hispanic/Latino; 2 Two or more races, non-Hispanic/Latino). Average age 35. 6 applicants, 83% accepted, 2 enrolled. In 2016, 4 master's awarded. *Degree requirements:* For master's, thesis optional. *Entrance requirements:* For master's, 3 letters of recommendation; official transcript; expanded goals statement; writing sample; resume. Additional exam requirements/recommendations for international students: Required—TOEFL (minimum score 575 paper-based; 88 iBT), IELTS (minimum score 6.5), PTE (minimum score 59). *Application deadline:* For fall admission, 3/1 for domestic students. Application fee: $75 ($80 for international students). Electronic applications accepted. *Expenses:* Tuition, state resident: full-time $10,628; part-time $443 per credit. Tuition, nonresident: full-time $29,306; part-time $1221 per credit. *Required fees:* $3096; $129 per credit. Tuition and fees vary according to program. *Financial support:* In 2016–17, 2 students received support, including 1 research assistantship with tuition reimbursement available (averaging $6,500 per year), 1 teaching assistantship with tuition reimbursement available (averaging $7,000 per year); career-related internships or fieldwork, Federal Work-Study, scholarships/grants, unspecified assistantships, and health care benefits (for full-time research or teaching assistantship recipients) also available. Financial award application deadline: 3/1; financial award applicants required to submit FAFSA. *Faculty research:* Cultural studies, political theory philosophy, social and political philosophy, feminist theory, analytical and Continental philosophy, philosophy of science. *Total annual research expenditures:* $36,365. *Unit head:* Ted Kinnaman, Chair/Associate Professor, 703-993-4328, Fax: 703-993-1297, E-mail: tkinnama@gmu.edu. *Application contact:* Rose Cherubin, Associate Professor and Graduate Coordinator, 703-993-1332, Fax: 703-993-1297, E-mail: rcherubi@gmu.edu.
Website: http://philosophy.gmu.edu/

**Georgetown University,** Graduate School of Arts and Sciences, Department of Philosophy, Washington, DC 20057. Offers bioethics (MA); philosophy (PhD); JD/MA; JD/PhD; MD/PhD. *Degree requirements:* For master's, thesis or alternative; for doctorate, 2 foreign languages, comprehensive exam, thesis/dissertation. *Entrance requirements:* For master's and doctorate, GRE General Test. Additional exam requirements/recommendations for international students: Required—TOEFL.

**The George Washington University,** Columbian College of Arts and Sciences, Department of Philosophy, Washington, DC 20052. Offers philosophy and social policy (MA). *Faculty:* 12 full-time (4 women). *Students:* 5 full-time (1 woman), 1 part-time. Average age 26. 25 applicants, 80% accepted, 6 enrolled. *Degree requirements:* For master's, comprehensive exam, thesis or alternative. *Entrance requirements:* For master's, GRE General Test, interview, minimum GPA of 3.0. Additional exam requirements/recommendations for international students: Required—TOEFL (minimum score 600 paper-based; 100 iBT). *Application deadline:* For fall admission, 4/1 priority date for domestic and international students; for spring admission, 10/1 priority date for domestic students, 9/1 priority date for international students. Applications are processed on a rolling basis. Application fee: $60. Electronic applications accepted. *Financial support:* Fellowships with tuition reimbursements, Federal Work-Study, and institutionally sponsored loans available. Financial award application deadline: 1/15. *Unit head:* Tad Zawidzki, Chair, 202-994-6444, E-mail: zawidzki@gwu.edu. *Application contact:* Amanda McLaughlin, Executive Aide, 202-994-6265, Fax: 202-994-8683, E-mail: philosop@gwu.edu.
Website: https://philosophy.columbian.gwu.edu/

**Georgia State University,** College of Arts and Sciences, Department of Philosophy, Atlanta, GA 30302-4089. Offers MA, MA/JD. *Program availability:* Part-time. *Faculty:* 17 full-time (4 women). *Students:* 55 full-time (15 women), 2 part-time (0 women); includes 10 minority (3 Asian, non-Hispanic/Latino; 4 Hispanic/Latino; 3 Two or more races, non-Hispanic/Latino), 8 international. Average age 26. 129 applicants, 29% accepted, 24 enrolled. In 2016, 27 master's awarded. *Degree requirements:* For master's, thesis (for some programs). *Entrance requirements:* For master's, GRE, writing sample, 3 letters of recommendation. Additional exam requirements/recommendations for international students: Required—TOEFL (minimum score 550 paper-based; 80 iBT). *Application deadline:* For fall admission, 2/1 priority date for domestic and international students. Applications are processed on a rolling basis. Application fee: $50. Electronic applications accepted. *Expenses:* Tuition, state resident: full-time $6876; part-time $382 per credit hour. Tuition, nonresident: full-time $22,374; part-time $1243 per credit hour. *Required fees:* $2128; $1064 per term. Part-time tuition and fees vary according to course load and program. *Financial support:* In 2016–17, fellowships with full tuition reimbursements (averaging $15,000 per year), research assistantships with full tuition reimbursements (averaging $6,000 per year), teaching assistantships with full tuition reimbursements (averaging $10,000 per year) were awarded; health care benefits also available. Financial award application deadline: 8/1; financial award applicants required to submit FAFSA. *Faculty research:* Social and political philosophy, neurophilosophy (empirical philosophy of mind), Kant and post-Kantian German philosophy. *Unit head:* Dr. George Rainbolt, Chair, 404-413-6109, Fax: 404-413-6124, E-mail: grainbolt@gsu.edu. *Application contact:* Dr. Tim O'Keefe, Director of Graduate Studies, 404-413-6108, Fax: 404-413-6124, E-mail: tokeefe@gsu.edu.
Website: http://www2.gsu.edu/~wwwphi/

**Gonzaga University,** College of Arts and Sciences, Spokane, WA 99258. Offers philosophy (MA); theology and leadership (MA). *Program availability:* Part-time, online with two required campus visits. *Faculty:* 9 full-time (3 women). *Students:* 31 part-time (17 women); includes 5 minority (2 Black or African American, non-Hispanic/Latino; 1 American Indian or Alaska Native, non-Hispanic/Latino; 1 Asian, non-Hispanic/Latino; 1 Hispanic/Latino), 1 international. Average age 39. *Degree requirements:* For master's, comprehensive exam. *Entrance requirements:* For master's, GRE General Test or MAT, minimum GPA of 3.0, official transcripts, two to three letters of recommendation, personal statement, writing sample, resume/curriculum vitae. Additional exam requirements/recommendations for international students: Required—TOEFL (minimum score 88 iBT), IELTS (minimum score 6.5), or verification from Gonzaga University ISSS office or an official recommendation from Gonzaga's ELC. *Application deadline:* For fall admission, 7/15 priority date for domestic students; for spring admission, 11/1 for domestic students; for summer admission, 4/3 for domestic students. Applications are processed on a rolling basis. Application fee: $50. Electronic applications accepted. *Expenses:* $830 per credit (for philosophy); $700 per credit (for theology and leadership). *Financial support:* In 2016–17, 27 students received support. Teaching assistantships, scholarships/grants, tuition waivers, and unspecified assistantships available. Support available to part-time students. Financial award applicants required to submit FAFSA. *Unit head:* Dr. Elisabeth Mermann-Jozwiak, Dean, 509-313-6603, Fax: 509-313-6684, E-mail: mermann-jozwiak@gonzaga.edu. *Application contact:* Carolyn Von Muller, Assistant to the Dean, 509-313-5522, E-mail: vonmuller@gonzaga.edu.
Website: http://www.gonzaga.edu/Academics/Colleges-and-Schools/College-of-Arts-and-Sciences

**The Graduate Center, City University of New York,** Graduate Studies, Program in Philosophy, New York, NY 10016-4039. Offers MA, PhD. Terminal master's awarded for partial completion of doctoral program. *Degree requirements:* For master's, thesis; for doctorate, one foreign language, comprehensive exam, thesis/dissertation. *Entrance requirements:* For master's, GRE General Test; for doctorate, GRE General Test, 3 letters of recommendation, writing sample. Additional exam requirements/ recommendations for international students: Required—TOEFL. Electronic applications accepted.

**Harrison Middleton University,** Graduate Program, Tempe, AZ 85282. Offers education (MA, Ed D); humanities (MA); imaginative literature (MA); interdisciplinary studies (DA); jurisprudence (MA); natural science (MA); philosophy and religion (MA); social science (MA). *Program availability:* Part-time, evening/weekend, online learning. *Degree requirements:* For master's and doctorate, capstone project. *Entrance requirements:* For master's, interview; for doctorate, 2 academic letters of reference, interview, essay. Additional exam requirements/recommendations for international students: Required—TOEFL (minimum score 550 paper-based; 80 iBT). Electronic applications accepted. *Faculty research:* Japanese animation, educational leadership, war art, John Muir's wilderness.

**Harvard University,** Graduate School of Arts and Sciences, Department of Philosophy, Cambridge, MA 02138. Offers classical philosophy (PhD); philosophy (PhD). *Degree requirements:* For doctorate, 2 foreign languages, thesis/dissertation, final exams. *Entrance requirements:* For doctorate, GRE General Test. Additional exam requirements/recommendations for international students: Required—TOEFL.

**Harvard University,** Graduate School of Arts and Sciences, Department of Sanskrit and Indian Studies, Cambridge, MA 02138. Offers Indian philosophy (AM, PhD); Pali (AM, PhD); Sanskrit (AM, PhD); Tibetan (AM, PhD); Urdu (AM, PhD). Terminal master's awarded for partial completion of doctoral program. *Degree requirements:* For master's, 3 foreign languages; for doctorate, 3 foreign languages, thesis/dissertation. *Entrance requirements:* For master's, GRE General Test; for doctorate, GRE General Test, proficiency in French and German. Additional exam requirements/recommendations for international students: Required—TOEFL.

**Harvard University,** Graduate School of Arts and Sciences, Department of the Classics, Cambridge, MA 02138. Offers Byzantine Greek (PhD); classical archaeology (PhD); classical philology (PhD); classical philosophy (PhD); medieval Latin (PhD). *Degree requirements:* For doctorate, 4 foreign languages, thesis/dissertation, preliminary and special exams. *Entrance requirements:* For doctorate, GRE General Test. Additional exam requirements/recommendations for international students: Required—TOEFL.

**Houston Baptist University,** School of Humanities, Program in Philosophy, Houston, TX 77074-3298. Offers MA. *Students:* 5 full-time (0 women), 10 part-time (1 woman); includes 5 minority (2 Black or African American, non-Hispanic/Latino; 1 American Indian or Alaska Native, non-Hispanic/Latino; 1 Asian, non-Hispanic/Latino; 1 Hispanic/ Latino). Average age 34. 16 applicants, 56% accepted, 2 enrolled. In 2016, 2 master's awarded. *Entrance requirements:* For master's, bachelor's degree conferred transcript, resume, essay/personal statement. Additional exam requirements/recommendations for international students: Required—TOEFL (minimum score 80 iBT), IELTS (minimum score 6.5). *Application deadline:* For fall admission, 8/1 for domestic students, 6/1 for international students; for spring admission, 1/1 for domestic students, 11/1 for international students; for summer admission, 5/1 for domestic students, 3/1 for international students. Applications are processed on a rolling basis. Application fee: $0 ($100 for international students). Electronic applications accepted. Application fee is waived when completed online. *Expenses:* $1,500 per 3-hour course; $1,275 annual general fee; $1,060 annual technology fee. *Financial support:* Federal Work-Study and scholarships/grants available. Financial award application deadline: 4/1. *Unit head:* Russell Hemati, Chair, E-mail: rhemati@hbu.edu. *Application contact:* Allyson Cates, Director of Admissions, Graduate School, 281-649-3099, Fax: 281-649-3390, E-mail: acates@hbu.edu.

**Howard University,** Graduate School, Department of Philosophy, Washington, DC 20059-0002. Offers MA. *Program availability:* Part-time. *Degree requirements:* For master's, one foreign language, comprehensive exam, thesis. *Entrance requirements:* For master's, GRE General Test. Additional exam requirements/recommendations for international students: Required—TOEFL. *Faculty research:* African and African-American philosophy, social and political philosophy, ethics, philosophy of culture, applied philosophy.

**Indiana University Bloomington,** School of Education, Department of Educational Leadership and Policy Studies, Bloomington, IN 47405. Offers educational leadership (MS, Ed D, Ed S); higher education (Ed D, PhD); higher education and student affairs (MS); history and philosophy of education (MS); history, philosophy, and policy in education (PhD), including education policy studies, history of education, philosophy of education; international and comparative education (MS). *Accreditation:* NCATE. *Faculty:* 32 full-time (18 women). *Students:* 223 full-time (140 women), 94 part-time (50 women); includes 80 minority (44 Black or African American, non-Hispanic/Latino; 13 Asian, non-Hispanic/Latino; 18 Hispanic/Latino; 1 Native Hawaiian or other Pacific Islander, non-Hispanic/Latino; 4 Two or more races, non-Hispanic/Latino), 29 international. Average age 34. 309 applicants, 40% accepted, 57 enrolled. In 2016, 60 master's, 18 doctorates, 5 other advanced degrees awarded. *Degree requirements:* For master's, thesis optional; for doctorate, comprehensive exam, thesis/dissertation; for Ed S, comprehensive exam or project. *Entrance requirements:* For master's, doctorate, and Ed S, GRE General Test. Additional exam requirements/recommendations for international students: Required—TOEFL (minimum score 79 iBT). *Application deadline:* For fall admission, 1/15 priority date for domestic students, 12/1 priority date for international students; for spring admission, 9/1 priority date for domestic and international students. Applications are processed on a rolling basis. Application fee: $55 ($65 for international students). Electronic applications accepted. *Financial support:* Fellowships with full and partial tuition reimbursements, research assistantships with full and partial tuition reimbursements, teaching assistantships with full and partial tuition reimbursements, career-related internships or fieldwork, scholarships/grants, health care benefits, and unspecified assistantships available. *Faculty research:* Culturally engaging campus environments, school choice policy analysis, democracy and education in the national and international context, and principal leadership. *Unit head:* Dr. Dionne Danns, Interim Chair, 812-856-8398. *Application contact:* Maria Jensen, Department Administrator, 812-856-8370, Fax: 812-856-8394, E-mail: jensen5@indiana.edu.
Website: http://education.indiana.edu/about/departments/leadership/index.html

**Indiana University Bloomington,** University Graduate School, College of Arts and Sciences, Department of Philosophy, Bloomington, IN 47405. Offers MA, PhD. Terminal master's awarded for partial completion of doctoral program. *Degree requirements:* For master's, variable foreign language requirement, thesis optional; for doctorate, comprehensive exam, thesis/dissertation, qualifying paper. *Entrance requirements:* For master's and doctorate, GRE General Test, writing sample. Additional exam requirements/recommendations for international students: Required—TOEFL. Electronic applications accepted. *Faculty research:* Algebraic logic, cognitive science,

history of modern philosophy, ancient and Jewish philosophy, medieval logic and semantics, epistemology, ethics, history, philosophy of mind, philosophy of language.

**Indiana University–Purdue University Indianapolis,** School of Liberal Arts, Department of Philosophy, Indianapolis, IN 46202. Offers American philosophy (Certificate); bioethics (Certificate); philosophy (MA); philosophy/bioethics (MA); JD/MA; MD/MA. *Program availability:* Part-time. *Faculty:* 10 full-time (0 women). *Students:* 3 full-time (2 women), 9 part-time (5 women); includes 1 minority (Two or more races, non-Hispanic/Latino). Average age 39. 12 applicants, 83% accepted, 4 enrolled. In 2016, 4 master's, 1 other advanced degree awarded. *Degree requirements:* For master's, thesis optional. *Entrance requirements:* For master's, GRE, writing sample, transcripts, three letters of recommendation, personal statement; for Certificate, letter of recommendation, transcripts, statement of purpose. Additional exam requirements/recommendations for international students: Required—TOEFL, PTE, IUPUI ESL Exam. *Application deadline:* For fall admission, 3/1 priority date for domestic and international students; for spring admission, 11/15 for domestic and international students. Application fee: $60 ($65 for international students). Electronic applications accepted. *Expenses:* Contact institution. *Financial support:* In 2016–17, 3 students received support, including 5 fellowships with full tuition reimbursements available (averaging $10,000 per year), 3 research assistantships with full tuition reimbursements available (averaging $9,500 per year); Federal Work-Study, health care benefits, and unspecified assistantships also available. Financial award application deadline: 1/15. *Faculty research:* American philosophy, pierce bioethics, metaphysics, ethical theory, philosophy of science, early modern philosophy (esp. Kant). *Unit head:* Dr. Timothy Lyons, Chair, 317-278-7768, E-mail: tdlyons@iupui.edu. *Application contact:* Dr. Chad Carmichael, Associate Professor, 317-278-5825, E-mail: crcarmic@iupui.edu.
Website: http://liberalarts.iupui.edu/philosophy/index.php/programs/

**Institute for Christian Studies,** Graduate Programs, Toronto, ON M5T 1R4, Canada. Offers education (M Phil F, PhD); history of philosophy (M Phil F, PhD); philosophical aesthetics (M Phil F, PhD); philosophy of religion (M Phil F, PhD); political theory (M Phil F, PhD); systematic philosophy (M Phil F, PhD); theology (M Phil F, PhD); worldview studies (MWS). *Program availability:* Part-time, online learning. *Degree requirements:* For master's, one foreign language, thesis; for doctorate, 2 foreign languages, thesis/dissertation. *Entrance requirements:* For master's and doctorate, philosophy background. Additional exam requirements/recommendations for international students: Required—TOEFL (minimum score 600 paper-based). *Faculty research:* Human rights, anthropology of self, medieval discourse, gender and body, post-modern thought; biblical hermeneutics, creational aesthetics, ecumenism, epistemology, political theory and public policy, relational psychotherapy.

**Institute for Doctoral Studies in the Visual Arts,** PhD Program in Visual Art: Philosophy, Aesthetics, and Art Theory, Portland, ME 04102. Offers aesthetics (PhD); art theory (PhD); philosophy (PhD). *Program availability:* Online learning. *Faculty:* 3 full-time, 7 part-time/adjunct. *Students:* 56 full-time. *Degree requirements:* For doctorate, comprehensive exam, thesis/dissertation, dissertation defense. *Entrance requirements:* For doctorate, curriculum vitae, writing sample, portfolio, interview. *Application deadline:* Applications are processed on a rolling basis. Application fee: $56. Electronic applications accepted. Application fee is waived when completed online. *Financial support:* Fellowships, teaching assistantships, and scholarships/grants available. Financial award applicants required to submit FAFSA. *Faculty research:* Visual culture, cultural studies, feminism, contemporary art. *Application contact:* Molly M. Davis, Director of Administration/Co-Director of Admissions, 207-771-8887, E-mail: info@idsva.edu.
Website: https://www.idsva.edu

**Johns Hopkins University,** Zanvyl Krieger School of Arts and Sciences, Department of Philosophy, Baltimore, MD 21218. Offers MA, PhD. *Degree requirements:* For doctorate, thesis/dissertation. *Entrance requirements:* For master's and doctorate, GRE General Test. Additional exam requirements/recommendations for international students: Required—TOEFL. Electronic applications accepted. *Faculty research:* Historical and analytical research on range of philosophical topics.

**Kent State University,** College of Arts and Sciences, Department of Philosophy, Kent, OH 44242-0001. Offers MA. *Program availability:* Part-time. *Faculty:* 9 full-time (3 women). *Students:* 8 full-time (0 women), 1 part-time (0 women); includes 1 minority (Two or more races, non-Hispanic/Latino). Average age 30. 9 applicants, 78% accepted, 4 enrolled. In 2016, 5 master's awarded. *Degree requirements:* For master's, thesis optional, 2 seminars, first-year paper. *Entrance requirements:* For master's, GRE, 3 letters of recommendation, statement of purpose, transcripts. Additional exam requirements/recommendations for international students: Required—TOEFL (minimum score of 600 paper-based, 100 iBT), IELTS (minimum score of 7.0), Michigan English Language Assessment Battery (minimum score of 85), or PTE (minimum score of 68). *Application deadline:* For fall admission, 2/1 for domestic and international students. Applications are processed on a rolling basis. Application fee: $45 ($70 for international students). Electronic applications accepted. *Expenses:* Tuition, state resident: full-time $10,864; part-time $495 per credit hour. Tuition, nonresident: full-time $18,380; part-time $837 per credit hour. *Financial support:* Research assistantships, teaching assistantships with full tuition reimbursements, health care benefits, and unspecified assistantships available. Financial award application deadline: 2/1. *Unit head:* Dr. Deborah R. Barnbaum, Professor and Chair, 330-672-4363, E-mail: dbarnbau@kent.edu. *Application contact:* Dr. Michael Byron, Professor and Graduate Coordinator, 330-672-0273, E-mail: mbyron@kent.edu.
Website: http://www.kent.edu/philosophy

**Lake Forest College,** Graduate Program in Liberal Studies, Lake Forest, IL 60045. Offers American studies (MLS); environmental studies (MLS); history (MLS); Medieval and Renaissance art (MLS); philosophy (MLS); Spanish (MLS); writing (MLS). *Program availability:* Part-time, evening/weekend. *Faculty:* 9 full-time (3 women), 1 part-time/ adjunct (0 women). *Students:* 1 full-time (0 women), 38 part-time (20 women); includes 5 minority (1 Black or African American, non-Hispanic/Latino; 2 Asian, non-Hispanic/ Latino; 2 Hispanic/Latino). Average age 38. 19 applicants, 53% accepted, 7 enrolled. In 2016, 4 master's awarded. *Degree requirements:* For master's, thesis optional, 8 courses, including at least 3 interdisciplinary seminars. *Entrance requirements:* For master's, transcript, essay, interview. Additional exam requirements/recommendations for international students: Required—TOEFL (minimum score 550 paper-based; 83 iBT); Recommended—IELTS (minimum score 6.5). *Application deadline:* For fall admission, 7/15 priority date for domestic students, 6/1 priority date for international students; for spring admission, 12/1 priority date for domestic students, 10/1 priority date for international students. Applications are processed on a rolling basis. Application fee: $30. *Expenses:* $2,600 per course. *Financial support:* In 2016–17, 2 students received support. Partial tuition grants for full-time teachers available. *Faculty research:* Realigning of the international order; Renaissance women artists; literature of Latin Americans in the U.S.; modern Chinese history; environmental biology. *Unit head:* Dr. D. L. LeMahieu, Director, 847-735-5133, Fax: 847-735-6291, E-mail: lemahieu@lakeforest.edu. *Application contact:* Prof. Carol Gayle, Associate Director, 847-735-5083, Fax: 847-735-6291, E-mail: gayle@lakeforest.edu.
Website: http://www.lakeforest.edu/academics/programs/mls/

## Philosophy

**Lincoln Christian University,** Graduate Programs, Lincoln, IL 62656-2167. Offers Biblical studies (MA); church history/historical theology (MA); intercultural studies (MA); ministry (MA); organizational leadership (MA); philosophy and apologetics (MA); spiritual formation (MA); theology (MA). MA in spiritual formation offered in Normal, IL. *Program availability:* Online learning. *Faculty:* 22 full-time (6 women), 27 part-time/adjunct (9 women). *Students:* 89 full-time (45 women), 225 part-time (91 women). Average age 39. *Entrance requirements:* For master's, minimum cumulative GPA of 2.5 in undergraduate degree studies. Additional exam requirements/recommendations for international students: Required—TOEFL (minimum score 550 paper-based); Recommended—IELTS (minimum score 6). *Application deadline:* For fall admission, 8/1 for domestic students, 3/1 for international students; for spring admission, 11/15 for domestic students, 11/1 for international students. *Application fee:* $25 ($50 for international students). Application fee is waived when completed online. *Expenses: Tuition:* Full-time $7812; part-time $5208 per credit hour. *Required fees:* $1000; $1000 per credit hour. One-time fee: $150. Full-time tuition and fees vary according to campus/location and program. *Financial support:* Applicants required to submit FAFSA. *Application contact:* Lindsey Clark, Associate Director of Graduate and Seminary Enrollment, 217-732-3168 Ext. 2398, E-mail: lclark@lincolnchristian.edu.
Website: https://lincolnchristian.edu/academics/programs/masters/

**Louisiana State University and Agricultural & Mechanical College,** Graduate School, College of Humanities and Social Sciences, Department of Philosophy and Religious Studies, Baton Rouge, LA 70803. Offers philosophy (MA).

**Loyola Marymount University,** College of Liberal Arts, Department of Philosophy, Program in Philosophy, Los Angeles, CA 90045-2659. Offers MA. *Students:* 12 full-time (1 woman), 1 part-time (0 women); includes 3 minority (all Hispanic/Latino), 2 international. Average age 31. 20 applicants, 90% accepted, 6 enrolled. In 2016, 10 master's awarded. *Entrance requirements:* For master's, GRE, writing sample (10-15 pages), 2 letters of recommendation, personal statement (4 pages). Additional exam requirements/recommendations for international students: Required—TOEFL (minimum score 600 paper-based; 100 iBT). *Application deadline:* For fall admission, 3/15 for domestic students; for spring admission, 11/1 for domestic students. Application fee: $50. Electronic applications accepted. *Financial support:* In 2016–17, 13 students received support, including 6 research assistantships, 4 teaching assistantships; unspecified assistantships also available. Financial award application deadline: 6/30; financial award applicants required to submit FAFSA. *Unit head:* Dr. Thomas M. Ward, Graduate Program Director, 310-338-4287, E-mail: tward9@lmu.edu. *Application contact:* Chake H. Kouyoumjian, Associate Dean of Graduate Studies, 310-338-2721, E-mail: ckouyoum@lmu.edu.
Website: http://bellarmine.lmu.edu/philosophy/graduateprogram/

**Loyola University Chicago,** Graduate School, Department of Philosophy, Chicago, IL 60611. Offers MA, PhD. *Program availability:* Part-time, evening/weekend. *Faculty:* 26 full-time (9 women). *Students:* 58 full-time (14 women), 6 part-time (0 women); includes 14 minority (1 Black or African American, non-Hispanic/Latino; 7 Asian, non-Hispanic/Latino; 6 Hispanic/Latino), 5 international. Average age 31. 117 applicants, 24% accepted, 16 enrolled. In 2016, 13 master's, 2 doctorates awarded. Terminal master's awarded for partial completion of doctoral program. *Degree requirements:* For master's, comprehensive exam (for some programs), thesis (for some programs), oral exam; for doctorate, one foreign language, thesis/dissertation, oral exam. *Entrance requirements:* For master's and doctorate, GRE General Test. Additional exam requirements/recommendations for international students: Required—TOEFL (minimum score 79 iBT). *Application deadline:* For fall admission, 1/15 priority date for domestic and international students. Applications are processed on a rolling basis. Application fee: $50. Electronic applications accepted. Application fee is waived when completed online. *Expenses: Tuition:* Full-time $18,594. *Required fees:* $848. Part-time tuition and fees vary according to course load, degree level and program. *Financial support:* In 2016–17, 22 students received support, including 4 fellowships with full tuition reimbursements available (averaging $16,000 per year), 19 teaching assistantships with full tuition reimbursements available (averaging $18,000 per year); institutionally sponsored loans, health care benefits, unspecified assistantships, and McNair Scholar Merit Funding also available. Financial award application deadline: 1/15; financial award applicants required to submit FAFSA. *Faculty research:* Social philosophy, ethics/social political, bioethics, analytic philosophy, contemporary continental philosophy. *Unit head:* Dr. Mark Waymack, Chair, 773-508-2738, Fax: 773-508-2292, E-mail: mwaymac@luc.edu. *Application contact:* Dr. Hanne Jacobs, Graduate Program Director, 773-508-8479, Fax: 773-508-2292, E-mail: hjacobs@luc.edu.
Website: http://www.luc.edu/philosophy/

**Marquette University,** Graduate School, College of Arts and Sciences, Department of Philosophy, Milwaukee, WI 53201-1881. Offers ancient philosophy (PhD); British empiricism and analytic philosophy (PhD); Christian philosophy (PhD); early modern European philosophy (PhD); ethics (PhD); German philosophy (PhD); history of philosophy (MA); medieval philosophy (PhD); phenomenology and existentialism (PhD); philosophy of religion (PhD); social and applied philosophy (MA); JD/MA. *Program availability:* Part-time. *Faculty:* 23 full-time (7 women), 8 part-time/adjunct (1 woman). *Students:* 38 full-time (12 women), 10 part-time (1 woman); includes 2 minority (1 Asian, non-Hispanic/Latino; 1 Hispanic/Latino), 2 international. Average age 31. 59 applicants, 44% accepted, 9 enrolled. In 2016, 4 master's, 6 doctorates awarded. Terminal master's awarded for partial completion of doctoral program. *Degree requirements:* For master's, variable foreign language requirement, comprehensive exam, thesis or alternative; for doctorate, 2 foreign languages, thesis/dissertation, written and oral qualifying exams. *Entrance requirements:* For master's and doctorate, GRE General Test, official transcripts from all current and previous colleges/universities except Marquette, statement of purpose, at least three letters of recommendation, sample of philosophical writing. Additional exam requirements/recommendations for international students: Required—TOEFL (minimum score 530 paper-based). *Application deadline:* For fall admission, 2/15 for domestic and international students. Applications are processed on a rolling basis. Application fee: $50. Electronic applications accepted. *Financial support:* Fellowships with partial tuition reimbursements, research assistantships with full tuition reimbursements, teaching assistantships with full tuition reimbursements, scholarships/grants, health care benefits, tuition waivers (full and partial), and unspecified assistantships available. Support available to part-time students. Financial award application deadline: 2/15. *Faculty research:* Aristotle, Augustine, Descartes, Hegel, Heidegger. *Total annual research expenditures:* $236,274. *Unit head:* Dr. John Jones, Chair. *Application contact:* Dr. Theresa Tobin, Associate Professor, 414-288-6948.
Website: http://www.marquette.edu/phil/grad.shtml

**Massachusetts Institute of Technology,** School of Humanities, Arts, and Social Sciences, Department of Linguistics and Philosophy, Philosophy Section, Cambridge, MA 02139. Offers PhD. *Faculty:* 12 full-time (2 women). *Students:* 32 full-time (14 women); includes 7 minority (1 Black or African American, non-Hispanic/Latino; 6 Hispanic/Latino), 7 international. Average age 28. 217 applicants, 6% accepted, 5 enrolled. In 2016, 3 doctorates awarded. *Degree requirements:* For doctorate, comprehensive exam, thesis/dissertation, teaching requirement. *Entrance requirements:* For doctorate, GRE General Test. Additional exam requirements/recommendations for international students: Required—TOEFL, IELTS. *Application deadline:* For fall

admission, 1/2 for domestic and international students. Application fee: $75. Electronic applications accepted. *Expenses: Tuition:* Full-time $46,400; part-time $725 per credit. One-time fee: $312 full-time. Full-time tuition and fees vary according to course load and program. *Financial support:* In 2016–17, 7 fellowships (averaging $39,400 per year), 10 research assistantships (averaging $39,800 per year), 10 teaching assistantships (averaging $40,100 per year) were awarded; Federal Work-Study, institutionally sponsored loans, scholarships/grants, traineeships, health care benefits, unspecified assistantships, and resident tutors also available. Support available to part-time students. Financial award application deadline: 5/1; financial award applicants required to submit FAFSA. *Faculty research:* Metaphysics, philosophy of mind, philosophy of language, ethics, feminist philosophy. *Unit head:* Prof. Alex Byrne, Philosophy Chair, 617-253-4141, Fax: 617-253-5017. *Application contact:* 617-253-9372, E-mail: lp-admissions@mit.edu.
Website: http://web.mit.edu/philosophy/

**McGill University,** Faculty of Graduate and Postdoctoral Studies, Faculty of Arts, Department of Philosophy, Montréal, QC H3A 2T5, Canada. Offers bioethics (MA); philosophy (PhD).

**McMaster University,** School of Graduate Studies, Faculty of Humanities, Department of Philosophy, Hamilton, ON L8S 4M2, Canada. Offers MA, PhD. *Program availability:* Part-time. *Degree requirements:* For master's, thesis; for doctorate, one foreign language, thesis/dissertation. *Entrance requirements:* For master's, honors degree in philosophy; minimum average B+; for doctorate, master's degree in philosophy. Additional exam requirements/recommendations for international students: Required—TOEFL (minimum score 580 paper-based). *Faculty research:* Twentieth-century European philosophy, twentieth-century Anglo-American philosophy, political philosophy, ethics, argumentation.

**Memorial University of Newfoundland,** School of Graduate Studies, Department of Philosophy, St. John's, NL A1C 5S7, Canada. Offers MA, PhD. *Program availability:* Part-time. *Degree requirements:* For master's, thesis; for doctorate, comprehensive exam, thesis/dissertation. *Entrance requirements:* For master's, first-class undergraduate degree in philosophy; for doctorate, MA in philosophy or equivalent. Electronic applications accepted. *Faculty research:* History of philosophy, philosophy of science, phenomenology and existentialism, contemporary metaphysics.

**Miami University,** College of Arts and Science, Department of Philosophy, Oxford, OH 45056. Offers MA. *Students:* 7. In 2016, 7 master's awarded. *Expenses:* Tuition, state resident: full-time $12,890; part-time $564 per credit hour. Tuition, nonresident: full-time $29,604; part-time $1260 per credit hour. *Required fees:* $638. Part-time tuition and fees vary according to course load and program. *Unit head:* Dr. Emily Zakin, Chair, 513-529-2428, E-mail: zakinea@miamioh.edu. *Application contact:* Dr. Pascal Massie, Associate Professor and Director of the Graduate Program, 513-529-2458, E-mail: massiep@miamioh.edu.
Website: http://www.MiamiOH.edu/philosophy/

**Michigan State University,** The Graduate School, College of Arts and Letters, Department of Philosophy, East Lansing, MI 48824. Offers MA, PhD. *Entrance requirements:* Additional exam requirements/recommendations for international students: Required—TOEFL. Electronic applications accepted.

**Midwestern State University,** Billie Doris McAda Graduate School, Prothro-Yeager College of Humanities and Social Sciences, Department of English, Humanities, and Philosophy, Wichita Falls, TX 76308. Offers English (MA); philosophy (MA). *Program availability:* Part-time, evening/weekend. *Degree requirements:* For master's, one foreign language, thesis optional. *Entrance requirements:* For master's, GRE General Test, MAT or GMAT. Additional exam requirements/recommendations for international students: Required—TOEFL (minimum score 550 paper-based). Electronic applications accepted. *Faculty research:* Mythology, Shakespeare, Oscar Hahn, origins of language, modern American literature.

**Mount St. Mary's University,** Program in Philosophical Studies, Emmitsburg, MD 21727-7799. Offers MA. *Program availability:* Part-time. *Faculty:* 3 full-time (0 women). *Students:* 1 full-time (0 women), 1 part-time (0 women). Average age 38. In 2016, 5 master's awarded. *Degree requirements:* For master's, one foreign language, thesis. *Entrance requirements:* For master's, undergraduate degree, minimum cumulative undergraduate GPA of 3.0. Additional exam requirements/recommendations for international students: Required—TOEFL (minimum score 550 paper-based; 83 iBT). *Application deadline:* For fall admission, 8/1 for domestic students; for spring admission, 12/1 for domestic students. *Expenses:* $500 per credit hour. *Financial support:* Unspecified assistantships available. Financial award applicants required to submit FAFSA. *Unit head:* Dr. Christopher Anadale, Director, 301-447-5307 Ext. 4307, E-mail: anadale@msmary.edu.
Website: http://www.msmary.edu/College_of_liberal_arts/Graduate-Programs/MAPS.html

**The New School,** The New School for Social Research, Department of Philosophy, New York, NY 10003. Offers philosophy (M Phil, MA); psychoanalysis (PhD). *Program availability:* Part-time. *Faculty:* 5 full-time (1 woman), 12 part-time/adjunct (4 women). *Students:* 132 full-time (42 women), 25 part-time (5 women); includes 25 minority (2 Black or African American, non-Hispanic/Latino; 1 Asian, non-Hispanic/Latino; 15 Hispanic/Latino; 7 Two or more races, non-Hispanic/Latino), 42 international. Average age 32. 167 applicants, 70% accepted, 27 enrolled. In 2016, 31 master's, 12 doctorates awarded. Terminal master's awarded for partial completion of doctoral program. *Degree requirements:* For master's, one foreign language, comprehensive exam, thesis; for doctorate, one foreign language, comprehensive exam, thesis/dissertation. *Entrance requirements:* For master's, GRE, letters of recommendation, writing sample, essays, unofficial transcript; for doctorate, letters of recommendation, writing sample, essays, unofficial transcript. Additional exam requirements/recommendations for international students: Required—TOEFL (minimum score 100 iBT), IELTS (minimum score 7), PTE (minimum score 68). *Application deadline:* For fall admission, 8/1 priority date for domestic and international students; for spring admission, 10/15 priority date for domestic and international students. Applications are processed on a rolling basis. Application fee: $50. Electronic applications accepted. *Expenses:* Contact institution. *Financial support:* Fellowships, research assistantships, teaching assistantships, Federal Work-Study, and scholarships/grants available. Support available to part-time students. Financial award application deadline: 2/1; financial award applicants required to submit FAFSA. *Faculty research:* History of Western philosophical thought and the European philosophical tradition, particularly contemporary Continental philosophy. *Total annual research expenditures:* $60,000. *Unit head:* Dr. William Milberg, Dean, The New School for Social Research, 212-229-5777, E-mail: milbergw@newschool.edu. *Application contact:* Dana Messinger, Director of Graduate Admission, 212-229-5150 Ext. 2300, E-mail: socialresearchadmit@newschool.edu.
Website: http://www.newschool.edu/nssr/philosophy/

**New York University,** Graduate School of Arts and Science, Department of Philosophy, New York, NY 10012-1019. Offers MA, PhD, JD/MA, JD/PhD, MD/MA. *Program availability:* Part-time. *Degree requirements:* For master's, thesis or alternative; for doctorate, one foreign language, thesis/dissertation. *Entrance requirements:* For master's and doctorate, GRE General Test, sample of written work. Additional exam requirements/recommendations for international students: Required—TOEFL. *Faculty research:* Philosophy of mind and language, metaphysics, ethics and political philosophy.

**Northern Illinois University,** Graduate School, College of Liberal Arts and Sciences, Department of Philosophy, De Kalb, IL 60115-2854. Offers MA. *Program availability:* Part-time. *Faculty:* 12 full-time (2 women), 1 part-time/adjunct (0 women). *Students:* 24 full-time (6 women), 9 part-time (4 women); includes 6 minority (2 Black or African American, non-Hispanic/Latino; 2 Hispanic/Latino; 2 Two or more races, non-Hispanic/Latino), 3 international. Average age 27. 71 applicants, 65% accepted, 13 enrolled. In 2016, 14 master's awarded. *Degree requirements:* For master's, comprehensive exam, thesis optional. *Entrance requirements:* For master's, GRE General Test, minimum GPA of 2.75, writing sample, major or minor in philosophy. Additional exam requirements/recommendations for international students: Required—TOEFL (minimum score 550 paper-based). *Application deadline:* For fall admission, 3/1 priority date for domestic students, 5/1 for international students; for spring admission, 11/1 for domestic students, 10/1 for international students. Applications are processed on a rolling basis. Application fee: $40. Electronic applications accepted. *Financial support:* In 2016–17, 13 teaching assistantships with full tuition reimbursements were awarded; fellowships with full tuition reimbursements, research assistantships with full tuition reimbursements, Federal Work-Study, scholarships/grants, tuition waivers (full), and unspecified assistantships also available. Support available to part-time students. Financial award applicants required to submit FAFSA. *Faculty research:* Epistemology, philosophy of biology, animal rights, philosophy of war, international ethics. *Unit head:* Dr. David J. Buller, Chair, 815-753-6299, Fax: 815-753-6302, E-mail: buller@niu.edu. *Application contact:* Dr. Geoff Pynn, Graduate Advisor, 815-753-6414, E-mail: askphilosophy@niu.edu. Website: http://www.niu.edu/phil/

**Northwestern University,** The Graduate School, Judd A. and Marjorie Weinberg College of Arts and Sciences, Department of Philosophy, Evanston, IL 60208. Offers ancient philosophy (PhD); philosophy (PhD). Admissions and degrees offered through The Graduate School. *Degree requirements:* For doctorate, 2 foreign languages, thesis/dissertation. *Entrance requirements:* For doctorate, GRE General Test, sample of written work. Additional exam requirements/recommendations for international students: Required—TOEFL. Electronic applications accepted. *Faculty research:* Phenomenology, philosophy of science, history of philosophy, ethics, social and political philosophy, epistemology.

**The Ohio State University,** Graduate School, College of Arts and Sciences, Division of Arts and Humanities, Department of Philosophy, Columbus, OH 43210. Offers MA, PhD. *Faculty:* 18. *Students:* 32 full-time (11 women). Average age 28. In 2016, 5 doctorates awarded. Terminal master's awarded for partial completion of doctoral program. *Degree requirements:* For master's, thesis optional; for doctorate, thesis/dissertation. *Entrance requirements:* For doctorate, GRE General Test, writing sample. Additional exam requirements/recommendations for international students: Required—TOEFL (minimum score 600 paper-based; 100 iBT); Recommended—IELTS (minimum score 8). *Application deadline:* For fall admission, 12/15 priority date for domestic students, 12/1 priority date for international students; for spring admission, 3/1 for domestic students, 2/1 for international students. Applications are processed on a rolling basis. Application fee: $60 ($70 for international students). Electronic applications accepted. *Financial support:* Fellowships with tuition reimbursements, research assistantships with tuition reimbursements, teaching assistantships with tuition reimbursements, Federal Work-Study, institutionally sponsored loans, and unspecified assistantships available. Support available to part-time students. *Unit head:* Dr. Justin D'Arms, Chair and Professor, 614-292-7914, E-mail: philosophy@osu.edu. *Application contact:* Graduate and Professional Admissions, 614-292-9444, Fax: 614-292-3895, E-mail: gpadmissions@osu.edu. Website: http://philosophy.osu.edu/

**Ohio University,** Graduate College, College of Arts and Sciences, Department of Philosophy, Athens, OH 45701-2979. Offers MA. *Program availability:* Part-time. *Degree requirements:* For master's, thesis. *Entrance requirements:* For master's, 28 hours in philosophy including logic, ancient and modern philosophy; minimum GPA of 3.0; sample of philosophical writing. Additional exam requirements/recommendations for international students: Required—TOEFL (minimum score 550 paper-based; 80 iBT) or IELTS (minimum score 6.5). *Application deadline:* For fall admission, 3/1 priority date for domestic and international students; for winter admission, 4/1 for domestic and international students; for spring admission, 9/1 for domestic and international students. Applications are processed on a rolling basis. Application fee: $50 ($55 for international students). Electronic applications accepted. *Financial support:* Teaching assistantships with tuition reimbursements, Federal Work-Study, institutionally sponsored loans, tuition waivers (partial), and unspecified assistantships available. Financial award application deadline: 3/1. *Faculty research:* Ethics, phenomenology, applied ethics, Aristotle, Kant, epistemology. *Unit head:* Dr. John W. Bender, Chair, 740-593-4599, Fax: 740-593-4597, E-mail: bender@ohio.edu. *Application contact:* Dr. Mark LeBar, Graduate Chair, 740-593-4599, Fax: 740-593-4597, E-mail: bender@ohio.edu. Website: http://www.philosophy.ohiou.edu/

**Oklahoma State University,** College of Arts and Sciences, Department of Philosophy, Stillwater, OK 74078. Offers MA. *Faculty:* 20 full-time (4 women), 1 part-time/adjunct (0 women). *Students:* 5 full-time (0 women), 5 part-time (1 woman); includes 2 minority (1 Black or African American, non-Hispanic/Latino; 1 Hispanic/Latino), 1 international. Average age 30. 7 applicants, 86% accepted, 5 enrolled. In 2016, 1 master's awarded. *Degree requirements:* For master's, comprehensive exam, thesis. *Entrance requirements:* For master's, GRE, 2 letters of recommendation. Additional exam requirements/recommendations for international students: Required—TOEFL (minimum score 550 paper-based; 79 iBT). *Application deadline:* For fall admission, 3/1 priority date for international students; for spring admission, 8/1 priority date for international students. Applications are processed on a rolling basis. Application fee: $40 ($75 for international students). Electronic applications accepted. *Expenses:* Tuition, state resident: full-time $3775; part-time $209.70 per credit hour. Tuition, nonresident: full-time $14,851; part-time $825.05 per credit hour. *Required fees:* $2027; $112.60 per credit hour. Tuition and fees vary according to campus/location. *Financial support:* In 2016–17, 8 teaching assistantships (averaging $16,251 per year) were awarded; career-related internships or fieldwork, Federal Work-Study, scholarships/grants, health care benefits, tuition waivers (partial), and unspecified assistantships also available. Support available to part-time students. Financial award application deadline: 3/1; financial award applicants required to submit FAFSA. *Faculty research:* Theoretical and applied ethics, history and philosophy of science, east/west comparative philosophy, social/political/legal philosophy, truth and theory of knowledge. *Unit head:* Dr. Scott Gelfand, Department Head, 405-744-9238, Fax: 405-744-4635, E-mail: scott.gelfand@okstate.edu. *Application contact:* Dr. Eric Reitan, Professor and Graduate Advisor, 405-744-7753, E-mail: eric.reitan@okstate.edu. Website: http://philosophy.okstate.edu

**Open University,** Graduate Programs, Milton Keynes, United Kingdom. Offers business (MBA); education (M Ed); engineering (M Eng); history (MA); music (MA); philosophy (MA).

**Penn State University Park,** Graduate School, College of the Liberal Arts, Department of Philosophy, University Park, PA 16802. Offers MA, PhD. *Unit head:* Dr. Susan Welch,

Dean, 814-865-7691, Fax: 814-863-2085. *Application contact:* Lori Hawn, Director, Graduate Student Services, 814-865-1795, Fax: 814-863-4627, E-mail: l-gswww@lists.psu.edu. Website: http://philosophy.la.psu.edu/

**Princeton University,** Graduate School, Department of Classics, Princeton, NJ 08544-1019. Offers classical and hellenic studies (PhD); classical philosophy (PhD); history (the ancient world) (PhD); literature and philology (PhD). *Degree requirements:* For doctorate, thesis/dissertation. *Entrance requirements:* For doctorate, GRE General Test, sample of written work. Additional exam requirements/recommendations for international students: Required—TOEFL (minimum score 600 paper-based). Electronic applications accepted.

**Princeton University,** Graduate School, Department of Philosophy, Princeton, NJ 08544-1019. Offers classical philosophy (PhD); philosophy (PhD); philosophy of science (PhD). *Degree requirements:* For doctorate, variable foreign language requirement, thesis/dissertation. *Entrance requirements:* For doctorate, GRE General Test, sample of written work. Additional exam requirements/recommendations for international students: Required—TOEFL (minimum score 600 paper-based). Electronic applications accepted.

**Princeton University,** Graduate School, Department of Politics, Princeton, NJ 08544-1019. Offers political philosophy (PhD); politics (PhD). *Degree requirements:* For doctorate, comprehensive exam, thesis/dissertation, teaching experience. *Entrance requirements:* For doctorate, GRE General Test, sample of written work, letters of recommendation. Additional exam requirements/recommendations for international students: Required—TOEFL (minimum score 600 paper-based). Electronic applications accepted. *Faculty research:* American politics, comparative politics, formal and quantitative methods, international relations, public law, political theory.

**Purdue University,** Graduate School, College of Liberal Arts, Department of Philosophy, West Lafayette, IN 47907. Offers MA, PhD. *Program availability:* Part-time. *Faculty:* 19 full-time (4 women), 1 part-time/adjunct (0 women). *Students:* 36 full-time (5 women), 9 part-time (5 women); includes 4 minority (1 American Indian or Alaska Native, non-Hispanic/Latino; 2 Hispanic/Latino; 1 Two or more races, non-Hispanic/Latino), 6 international. Average age 29. 66 applicants, 14% accepted, 4 enrolled. In 2016, 2 master's, 5 doctorates awarded. Terminal master's awarded for partial completion of doctoral program. *Degree requirements:* For master's, thesis optional; for doctorate, comprehensive exam, thesis/dissertation. *Entrance requirements:* For master's and doctorate, GRE General Test, minimum undergraduate GPA of 3.4 or equivalent. Additional exam requirements/recommendations for international students: Required—TOEFL (minimum score 550 paper-based; 100 iBT). *Application deadline:* For fall admission, 1/2 for domestic and international students; for spring admission, 12/1 for domestic and international students. Applications are processed on a rolling basis. Application fee: $60 ($75 for international students). Electronic applications accepted. *Financial support:* Fellowships with tuition reimbursements, research assistantships with tuition reimbursements, and teaching assistantships with tuition reimbursements available. Support available to part-time students. Financial award application deadline: 1/15; financial award applicants required to submit FAFSA. *Faculty research:* Continental philosophy, ethics and social philosophy, analytic philosophy, history of philosophy, logic. *Unit head:* Rodney J. Bertolet, Head, 765-494-4275, E-mail: bertolet@purdue.edu. *Application contact:* Vickie Sanders, Graduate Contact, 765-494-4275, E-mail: sanders@purdue.edu. Website: http://www.cla.purdue.edu/philosophy/

**Purdue University,** Graduate School, Program in Philosophy and Literature, West Lafayette, IN 47907. Offers PhD. Program offered jointly with Department of English, School of Languages and Cultures, and Department of Philosophy. *Faculty:* 19 full-time (4 women), 1 part-time/adjunct. *Students:* 36 full-time (5 women), 9 part-time (5 women); includes 4 minority (1 American Indian or Alaska Native, non-Hispanic/Latino; 2 Hispanic/Latino; 1 Two or more races, non-Hispanic/Latino), 6 international. Average age 29. 66 applicants, 14% accepted, 4 enrolled. In 2016, 5 doctorates awarded. *Degree requirements:* For doctorate, one foreign language, comprehensive exam, thesis/dissertation. *Entrance requirements:* For doctorate, GRE, master's degree in either English, philosophy or foreign languages. Additional exam requirements/recommendations for international students: Required—TOEFL. *Application deadline:* For fall admission, 1/10 priority date for domestic students, 1/10 for international students. Application fee: $60 ($75 for international students). Electronic applications accepted. *Financial support:* In 2016–17, teaching assistantships (averaging $1,415 per year) were awarded; fellowships and research assistantships also available. *Unit head:* Dr. Joann L. Miller, Dean, 765-496-7276, E-mail: jlmiller@purdue.edu. *Application contact:* Teresa K. Berninger, Graduate Contact, 765-494-4276, E-mail: tkbernin@purdue.edu. Website: http://www.cla.purdue.edu/phil-lit/graduate/

**Queen's University at Kingston,** School of Graduate Studies, Faculty of Arts and Sciences, Department of Philosophy, Kingston, ON K7L 3N6, Canada. Offers MA, PhD. *Program availability:* Part-time. *Degree requirements:* For master's, thesis; for doctorate, comprehensive exam, thesis/dissertation. *Entrance requirements:* Additional exam requirements/recommendations for international students: Required—TOEFL. Electronic applications accepted. *Faculty research:* Ethics, social and political philosophy, philosophy of language, epistemology, metaphysics.

**Regis College,** Graduate and Professional Programs, Toronto, ON M5S 2Z5, Canada. Offers eastern Christian studies (Certificate); Ignatian spirituality (Diploma); ministry (D Min); ministry and spirituality (MAMS); philosophical studies (Diploma); retreat direction (Certificate); sacred theology (STM, STD, STB, STL); spiritual direction (Diploma); theological studies (MTS, Diploma); theology (M Div, MA, Th M, PhD, Th D); M Div/MA. *Accreditation:* ATS (one or more programs are accredited). Terminal master's awarded for partial completion of doctoral program. *Degree requirements:* For master's, 2 foreign languages, thesis; for doctorate, 3 foreign languages, comprehensive exam, thesis/dissertation. *Entrance requirements:* For doctorate, minimum GPA of 3.7. Additional exam requirements/recommendations for international students: Required—TOEFL (minimum score 580 paper-based; 93 iBT), TWE (minimum score 5).

**Rice University,** Graduate Programs, School of Humanities, Department of Philosophy, Houston, TX 77251-1892. Offers MA, PhD. Terminal master's awarded for partial completion of doctoral program. *Degree requirements:* For master's, one foreign language; for doctorate, one foreign language, comprehensive exam, thesis/dissertation. *Entrance requirements:* For master's and doctorate, GRE General Test, minimum GPA of 3.0. Additional exam requirements/recommendations for international students: Required—TOEFL (minimum score 600 paper-based; 90 iBT). Electronic applications accepted. *Faculty research:* Metaphysics, philosophy of law, philosophy of science, medical ethics, philosophy of language.

**Rutgers University–New Brunswick,** Graduate School-New Brunswick, Program in Philosophy, Piscataway, NJ 08854-8097. Offers PhD. *Degree requirements:* For doctorate, comprehensive exam, thesis/dissertation. *Entrance requirements:* For doctorate, GRE General Test, writing sample. Electronic applications accepted. *Faculty research:* Philosophy of mind, epistemology, philosophy of language, philosophy of science, metaphysics.

## Philosophy

**Saint Louis University,** Graduate Education, College of Arts and Sciences and Graduate Education, Department of Philosophy, St. Louis, MO 63103. Offers MA, MA-R, PhD. *Program availability:* Part-time. *Degree requirements:* For master's, one foreign language, thesis, comprehensive oral and written exams; for doctorate, 2 foreign languages, thesis/dissertation, preliminary exams, comprehensive oral and written exams. *Entrance requirements:* For master's, GRE General Test, letters of recommendation, resume, writing sample, interview; for doctorate, GRE General Test, letters of recommendation, resumé, writing sample, interview, goal statement, transcripts. Additional exam requirements/recommendations for international students: Required—TOEFL (minimum score 550 paper-based). Electronic applications accepted. *Faculty research:* Medieval philosophy, philosophy of religion, political philosophy, ethics, epistemology.

**Saint Mary's University,** Faculty of Arts, Department of Philosophy, Halifax, NS B3H 3C3, Canada. Offers MA. *Degree requirements:* For master's, thesis. *Entrance requirements:* For master's, 3 letters of recommendation, 2 samples of written work. Additional exam requirements/recommendations for international students: Required—TOEFL. *Faculty research:* History of philosophy, analytic philosophy, ethics, social philosophy, logic.

**San Diego State University,** Graduate and Research Affairs, College of Arts and Letters, Department of Philosophy, San Diego, CA 92182. Offers MA. *Program availability:* Part-time. *Entrance requirements:* For master's, GRE General Test. Additional exam requirements/recommendations for international students: Required—TOEFL. Electronic applications accepted. *Faculty research:* Ancient philosophy, modern philosophy, philosophy of technology, logic, philosophy of mind.

**San Francisco State University,** Division of Graduate Studies, College of Liberal and Creative Arts, Department of Philosophy, San Francisco, CA 94132-1722. Offers MA. *Program availability:* Part-time. *Application deadline:* Applications are processed on a rolling basis. *Expenses:* Tuition, state resident: full-time $6738. Tuition, nonresident: full-time $15,666. *Required fees:* $1012. Tuition and fees vary according to degree level and program. *Unit head:* Dr. Anita Silvers, Acting Chair, 415-338-1596, Fax: 415-338-6159, E-mail: asilvers@sfsu.edu. *Application contact:* Prof. David Landy, Graduate Coordinator, 415-338-3126, Fax: 415-338-6159, E-mail: landy@sfsu.edu.
Website: http://www.philosophy.sfsu.edu/

**San Jose State University,** Graduate Studies and Research, College of Humanities and the Arts, San Jose, CA 95192-0001. Offers art (MA, MFA), including art history and visual culture (MA), digital media art (MFA), photography (MFA), pictorial art (MFA), spatial art (MFA); computational linguistics (Certificate); English (MA, MFA), including creative writing (MFA); French (MA); humanities and arts (Certificate); linguistics (MA); music (MA); philosophy (MA); professional and technical communication (Certificate); Spanish (MA); teaching English to speakers of other languages (MA); TESOL (Certificate); theatre arts (MA). Electronic applications accepted.

**Simon Fraser University,** Office of Graduate Studies and Postdoctoral Fellows, Faculty of Arts and Social Sciences, Department of Philosophy, Burnaby, BC V5A 1S6, Canada. Offers MA, PhD. *Faculty:* 13 full-time (4 women). *Students:* 24 full-time (9 women). 64 applicants, 22% accepted, 12 enrolled. In 2016, 9 master's awarded. *Degree requirements:* For master's, thesis or alternative; for doctorate, comprehensive exam, thesis/dissertation. *Entrance requirements:* For master's, minimum GPA of 3.0 (on scale of 4.33) or 3.33 based on last 60 credits of undergraduate courses; for doctorate, minimum GPA of 3.5 (on scale of 4.33). Additional exam requirements/recommendations for international students: Recommended—TOEFL (minimum score 580 paper-based; 93 iBT), IELTS (minimum score 7), TWE (minimum score 5). *Application deadline:* For fall admission, 1/15 for domestic and international students. Application fee: $90 ($125 for international students). Electronic applications accepted. *Financial support:* In 2016–17, 10 students received support, including 8 fellowships (averaging $6,094 per year), teaching assistantships (averaging $5,608 per year); research assistantships and scholarships/grants also available. *Faculty research:* Ethics; philosophy of mind; philosophy of science; epistemology and metaphysics; history of early modern, ancient, and analytic philosophy and logic. *Unit head:* Dr. Kathleen Akins, Graduate Chair, 778-782-3328, Fax: 778-782-4443, E-mail: phil-grad-chair@sfu.ca. *Application contact:* Linda Sheldon, Graduate Secretary, 778-782-4443, Fax: 778-782-4443, E-mail: philsec@sfu.ca.
Website: http://www.sfu.ca/philosophy/

**Southeastern Baptist Theological Seminary,** Graduate and Professional Programs, Wake Forest, NC 27588-1889. Offers advanced biblical studies (M Div); Christian education (M Div, MACE); Christian ethics (PhD); Christian ministry (M Div); Christian planting (M Div); church music (MACM); counseling (MACO); evangelism (PhD); language (M Div); ministry (D Min); New Testament (PhD); Old Testament (PhD); philosophy (PhD); theology (Th M, PhD); women's studies (M Div). *Accreditation:* ACIPE; ATS (one or more programs are accredited). *Degree requirements:* For master's, thesis (for some programs), oral exam; for doctorate, thesis/dissertation, fieldwork. *Entrance requirements:* For master's, Cooperative English Test, minimum GPA of 2.0, M Div or equivalent (Th M); for doctorate, GRE General Test or MAT, Cooperative English Test, M Div or equivalent, 3 years of professional experience.

**The Southern Baptist Theological Seminary,** School of Theology, Louisville, KY 40280-0004. Offers applied theology (D Min); biblical and theological studies (M Div); biblical counseling (M Div, MA, D Min); biblical spirituality (D Min); Christian ministry (M Div); expository preaching (D Min); pastoral studies (M Div); theological studies (MA); theology (Th M, PhD); worldview and apologetics (M Div). *Program availability:* Part-time, evening/weekend, online learning. *Degree requirements:* For master's, 2 foreign languages, thesis; for doctorate, 4 foreign languages, thesis/dissertation. *Entrance requirements:* For master's, GRE General Test, MAT, M Div; for doctorate, GRE General Test, MAT, interview, M Div, field essay. Additional exam requirements/recommendations for international students: Required—TOEFL, TWE. *Faculty research:* Biblical studies, contemporary theology, church history, pastoral care, ministry/missions studies.

**Southern Evangelical Seminary,** Graduate Programs, Matthews, NC 28105. Offers apologetics (MA, D Min, Certificate); Christian education (MA); church ministry (MA, Certificate); divinity (Certificate), including apologetics (M Div, Certificate); Islamic studies (MA, Certificate); Jewish studies (MA); philosophy (MA); philosophy of religion (PhD); religion (MA); theology (M Div), including apologetics (M Div, Certificate), Biblical studies; youth ministry (MA). *Program availability:* Part-time, evening/weekend, online learning. *Degree requirements:* For master's, thesis (for some programs); for doctorate, 2 foreign languages, comprehensive exam (for some programs), thesis/dissertation. *Entrance requirements:* Additional exam requirements/recommendations for international students: Required—TOEFL (minimum score 600 paper-based).

**Southern Illinois University Carbondale,** Graduate School, College of Liberal Arts, Department of Philosophy, Carbondale, IL 62901-4701. Offers MA, PhD. *Degree requirements:* For master's, one foreign language, thesis; for doctorate, 2 foreign languages, thesis/dissertation. *Entrance requirements:* For master's, GRE General Test, minimum GPA of 2.7; for doctorate, GRE General Test, minimum GPA of 3.25. Additional exam requirements/recommendations for international students: Required—

TOEFL. *Faculty research:* Continental philosophy, American philosophy, philosophy of mind, Asian philosophy.

**Stanford University,** School of Humanities and Sciences, Department of Philosophy, Stanford, CA 94305-2004. Offers MA, PhD. Terminal master's awarded for partial completion of doctoral program. *Degree requirements:* For master's, oral exam; for doctorate, thesis/dissertation, oral exam. *Entrance requirements:* For master's and doctorate, GRE General Test. Additional exam requirements/recommendations for international students: Required—TOEFL. Electronic applications accepted. *Expenses:* Tuition: Full-time $47,331. *Required fees:* $609.

**Stony Brook University, State University of New York,** Graduate School, College of Arts and Sciences, Department of Philosophy, Stony Brook, NY 11794-3750. Offers MA, PhD, Advanced Certificate. *Program availability:* Evening/weekend. *Faculty:* 16 full-time (5 women), 1 (woman) part-time/adjunct. *Students:* 59 full-time (18 women), 6 part-time (0 women); includes 11 minority (2 Black or African American, non-Hispanic/Latino; 1 American Indian or Alaska Native, non-Hispanic/Latino; 1 Asian, non-Hispanic/Latino; 2 Hispanic/Latino; 5 Two or more races, non-Hispanic/Latino), 15 international. Average age 31. 135 applicants, 41% accepted, 7 enrolled. In 2016, 12 master's, 6 doctorates awarded. *Degree requirements:* For doctorate, one foreign language, thesis/dissertation. *Entrance requirements:* For master's and doctorate, GRE General Test. Additional exam requirements/recommendations for international students: Required—TOEFL (minimum score 90 iBT). *Application deadline:* For fall admission, 1/15 for domestic students; for spring admission, 10/1 for domestic students. Application fee: $100. Electronic applications accepted. *Expenses:* Contact institution. *Financial support:* In 2016–17, 1 research assistantship, 25 teaching assistantships were awarded; fellowships also available. *Faculty research:* Humanities, philosophy, philosophy of religion, race, Asian-Americans. *Unit head:* Dr. Mary C. Rawlinson, Chair, 631-632-7590, E-mail: mary.rawlinson@stonybrook.edu. *Application contact:* Kathleen-Anna Amella, Coordinator, 631-632-7580, Fax: 631-632-7522, E-mail: kathleen-anna.amella@stonybrook.edu.
Website: http://www.sunysb.edu/philosophy/

**Syracuse University,** College of Arts and Sciences, Programs in Philosophy, Syracuse, NY 13244. Offers MA, PhD. *Program availability:* Part-time. *Students:* Average age 30. *Degree requirements:* For master's, thesis or alternative; for doctorate, thesis/dissertation. *Entrance requirements:* For master's and doctorate, GRE, transcripts from previous institutions, three letters of recommendation, personal statement, writing sample. Additional exam requirements/recommendations for international students: Required—TOEFL (minimum score 100 iBT). *Application deadline:* For fall admission, 1/1 priority date for domestic and international students. Application fee: $75. Electronic applications accepted. *Expenses: Tuition:* Full-time $25,974; part-time $1443 per credit hour. *Required fees:* $802; $50 per course. Tuition and fees vary according to course load and program. *Financial support:* Fellowships with full tuition reimbursements, teaching assistantships with tuition reimbursements, and scholarships/grants available. Financial award application deadline: 1/1. *Faculty research:* Ethics, metaphysics, epistemology, philosophy of language. *Unit head:* Dr. Ben Bradley, Department Chair/Professor of Philosophy, 315-443-5813, E-mail: wbradley@syr.edu. *Application contact:* Lisa Farnsworth, Secretary/Office Coordinator, 315-443-2245, E-mail: lfarmswo@syr.edu.
Website: http://philosophy.syr.edu/

**Teachers College, Columbia University,** Department of Arts and Humanities, New York, NY 10027. Offers applied linguistics (MA, Ed D); art and art education (Ed M, MA, Ed D, Ed DCT); arts administration (MA); bilingual and bicultural education (MA); global competence (Certificate); history and education (Ed D, PhD); music and music education (Ed DCT); philosophy and education (MA, Ed D, PhD); social studies education (Ed M, PhD); teaching English to speakers of other languages (Ed M); teaching of English and English education (Ed M, MA, Ed D, PhD), including English education (Ed M, Ed D, PhD), teaching of English (MA); teaching of social studies (MA); TESOL (MA, Ed D). *Program availability:* Part-time, evening/weekend. *Students:* 429 full-time (329 women), 467 part-time (332 women); includes 268 minority (62 Black or African American, non-Hispanic/Latino; 1 American Indian or Alaska Native, non-Hispanic/Latino; 108 Asian, non-Hispanic/Latino; 76 Hispanic/Latino; 21 Two or more races, non-Hispanic/Latino), 212 international. 1,068 applicants, 53% accepted, 272 enrolled. Terminal master's awarded for partial completion of doctoral program. *Expenses: Tuition:* Full-time $36,288; part-time $1512 per credit. *Required fees:* $438 per semester. One-time fee: $510 full-time. Full-time tuition and fees vary according to course load. *Financial support:* Fellowships, research assistantships, teaching assistantships, career-related internships or fieldwork, Federal Work-Study, institutionally sponsored loans, tuition waivers (full and partial), and unspecified assistantships available. Support available to part-time students. *Unit head:* Prof. William Gaudelli, Department Chair, 212-678-3150, E-mail: wg74@columbia.edu. *Application contact:* David Estrella, Director of Admissions, 212-678-3305, Fax: 212-678-4171, E-mail: estrella@tc.columbia.edu.
Website: http://www.tc.edu/a%26h/

**Temple University,** College of Liberal Arts, Department of Philosophy, Philadelphia, PA 19122-6096. Offers MA, PhD. *Program availability:* Part-time. Terminal master's awarded for partial completion of doctoral program. *Degree requirements:* For master's, thesis or alternative; for doctorate, one foreign language, thesis/dissertation. *Entrance requirements:* For master's and doctorate, GRE General Test, minimum GPA of 3.0, 3 letters of recommendation. Additional exam requirements/recommendations for international students: Required—TOEFL (minimum score 550 paper-based; 79 iBT). Electronic applications accepted. *Faculty research:* History of philosophy, European philosophy, aesthetics, analytic philosophy, pragmatism.

**Texas A&M University,** College of Liberal Arts, Department of Philosophy, College Station, TX 77843. Offers MA, PhD. *Program availability:* Part-time. *Faculty:* 20. *Students:* 26 full-time (7 women), 4 part-time (3 women); includes 8 minority (2 Asian, non-Hispanic/Latino; 6 Hispanic/Latino), 4 international. Average age 31. 6 applicants, 100% accepted, 6 enrolled. In 2016, 3 master's, 2 doctorates awarded. Terminal master's awarded for partial completion of doctoral program. *Degree requirements:* For master's, thesis optional; for doctorate, comprehensive exam, thesis/dissertation. *Entrance requirements:* For master's, GRE General Test, letter of recommendation, resume, writing sample; for doctorate, GRE General Test, letters of recommendation, resume, writing sample. Additional exam requirements/recommendations for international students: Required—TOEFL (minimum score 550 paper-based; 80 iBT), IELTS (minimum score 6), PTE (minimum score 53). *Application deadline:* For fall admission, 1/15 for domestic and international students. Application fee: $50 ($90 for international students). Electronic applications accepted. *Expenses:* Contact institution. *Financial support:* In 2016–17, 30 students received support, including 5 fellowships with tuition reimbursements available (averaging $13,774 per year), 8 research assistantships with tuition reimbursements available (averaging $3,701 per year), 25 teaching assistantships with tuition reimbursements available (averaging $8,764 per year); career-related internships or fieldwork, institutionally sponsored loans, scholarships/grants, traineeships, health care benefits, tuition waivers (full and partial), and unspecified assistantships also available. Support available to part-time students. Financial award application deadline: 3/15; financial award applicants required to submit

FAFSA. *Faculty research:* American philosophy, applied ethics, philosophy of mind, philosophy of religion, history and philosophy of logic. *Unit head:* Dr. Theodore George, Interim Head, 979-845-5605, E-mail: t-george@tamu.edu. *Application contact:* Dr. Clare Palmer, Director of Graduate Program, 979-862-1435, E-mail: c.palmer@tamu.edu. Website: http://philosophy.tamu.edu

**Texas State University,** The Graduate College, College of Liberal Arts, Applied Philosophy and Ethics Program, San Marcos, TX 78666. Offers MA. *Faculty:* 15 full-time (7 women), 4 part-time/adjunct (2 women). *Students:* 15 full-time (3 women), 12 part-time (4 women); includes 16 minority (5 Black or African American, non-Hispanic/Latino; 10 Hispanic/Latino; 1 Two or more races, non-Hispanic/Latino), 1 international. Average age 30. 16 applicants, 75% accepted, 9 enrolled. In 2016, 7 master's awarded. *Degree requirements:* For master's, comprehensive exam, thesis optional. *Entrance requirements:* For master's, baccalaureate degree from regionally-accredited university with minimum GPA of 3.0 on last 60 undergraduate semester hours, statement of purpose, 2 letters of recommendation, writing sample. Additional exam requirements/recommendations for international students: Required—TOEFL (minimum score 550 paper-based; 78 iBT), IELTS (minimum score 6.5). *Application deadline:* For fall admission, 3/1 priority date for domestic and international students; for spring admission, 10/15 for domestic students, 10/1 for international students; for summer admission, 4/15 for domestic students, 3/15 for international students. Applications are processed on a rolling basis. Application fee: $40 ($90 for international students). Electronic applications accepted. *Expenses:* $4,851 per semester. *Financial support:* In 2016–17, 19 students received support, including 1 research assistantship (averaging $13,502 per year), 13 teaching assistantships (averaging $13,721 per year); scholarships/grants also available. Support available to part-time students. Financial award application deadline: 3/1; financial award applicants required to submit FAFSA. *Unit head:* Dr. Audrey Mckinney, Graduate Advisor, 512-245-2047, Fax: 512-245-8336, E-mail: am04@txstate.edu. *Application contact:* Dr. Andrea Golato, Dean of Graduate School, 512-245-2581, Fax: 512-245-8365, E-mail: gradcollege@txstate.edu.

**Texas Tech University,** Graduate School, College of Arts and Sciences, Department of Philosophy, Lubbock, TX 79409-3092. Offers MA. *Program availability:* Part-time. *Faculty:* 13 full-time (2 women), 1 part-time/adjunct (0 women). *Students:* 16 full-time (2 women); includes 2 minority (1 Asian, non-Hispanic/Latino; 1 Hispanic/Latino), 3 international. Average age 26. 33 applicants, 61% accepted, 8 enrolled. In 2016, 8 master's awarded. *Degree requirements:* For master's, thesis or alternative. *Entrance requirements:* For master's, GRE General Test. Additional exam requirements/recommendations for international students: Required—TOEFL (minimum score 550 paper-based; 79 iBT). *Application deadline:* For fall admission, 6/1 priority date for domestic students, 1/15 priority date for international students; for spring admission, 9/1 priority date for domestic students, 6/15 priority date for international students. Applications are processed on a rolling basis. Application fee: $75. Electronic applications accepted. *Expenses:* $300 per credit hour full-time resident tuition, $708 per credit hour full-time non-resident tuition; $50.50 per credit hour fee plus $608 per term fee. *Financial support:* In 2016–17, 18 students received support, including 9 fellowships (averaging $2,902 per year), 16 teaching assistantships (averaging $12,466 per year); research assistantships, Federal Work-Study, and scholarships/grants also available. Financial award application deadline: 4/15; financial award applicants required to submit FAFSA. *Faculty research:* Aesthetics, ethics, history of philosophy, philosophy of mind, philosophy of science. *Total annual research expenditures:* $2,000. *Unit head:* Dr. Mark O. Webb, Professor and Chair, 806-742-3275, Fax: 806-742-0730, E-mail: mark.webb@ttu.edu. *Application contact:* Dr. Daniel O. Nathan, Director of Graduate Studies, 806-742-0373 Ext. 340, Fax: 806-742-0730, E-mail: daniel.nathan@ttu.edu. Website: http://www.philosophy.ttu.edu/

**Trinity Western University,** School of Graduate Studies, Program in Interdisciplinary Humanities, Langley, BC V2Y 1Y1, Canada. Offers general humanities (MAIH); specialized (MAIH), including English, history, philosophy. *Program availability:* Part-time. *Degree requirements:* For master's, thesis or alternative, 36 semester hours. *Entrance requirements:* For master's, strong undergraduate degree in humanities or English, history or philosophy. Additional exam requirements/recommendations for international students: Recommended—TOEFL. Electronic applications accepted. *Faculty research:* Literary theory, gender, medieval and early modern literature, philosophy of religion, Thomas Merton's poetics.

**Tufts University,** Graduate School of Arts and Sciences, Department of Philosophy, Medford, MA 02155. Offers MA. *Students:* 25 full-time (8 women); includes 2 minority (1 Hispanic/Latino; 1 Two or more races, non-Hispanic/Latino), 8 international. Average age 26. 119 applicants, 21% accepted, 9 enrolled. In 2016, 13 master's awarded. *Degree requirements:* For master's, comprehensive exam, departmental qualifying exam. *Entrance requirements:* For master's, GRE General Test, writing sample. Additional exam requirements/recommendations for international students: Required—TOEFL (minimum score 550 paper-based; 80 iBT), IELTS (minimum score 6.5). *Application deadline:* For fall admission, 1/15 for domestic and international students. Applications are processed on a rolling basis. Application fee: $85. Electronic applications accepted. *Expenses:* $49,982 full-time tuition (for MA). *Financial support:* In 2016–17, 23 students received support. Teaching assistantships, Federal Work-Study, scholarships/grants, tuition waivers (full and partial), and unspecified assistantships available. Financial award application deadline: 1/15. *Unit head:* Dr. Patrick Forber, Graduate Program Director. *Application contact:* Office of Graduate Admissions, 617-627-3395, E-mail: gradadmissions@tufts.edu. Website: http://ase.tufts.edu/philosophy/

**Tulane University,** School of Liberal Arts, Department of Philosophy, New Orleans, LA 70118-5669. Offers MA, PhD. *Degree requirements:* For master's, thesis or alternative; for doctorate, one foreign language, thesis/dissertation. *Entrance requirements:* For master's, GRE General Test, minimum B average in undergraduate course work; for doctorate, GRE General Test. Additional exam requirements/recommendations for international students: Required—TOEFL. Electronic applications accepted. *Expenses:* Tuition: Full-time $50,920; part-time $2829 per credit hour. *Required fees:* $2040; $44.50 per credit hour. $580 per term. Tuition and fees vary according to course load, degree level and program.

**Universidad Autonoma de Guadalajara,** Graduate Programs, Guadalajara, Mexico. Offers administrative law and justice (LL M); advertising and corporate communications (MA); architecture (M Arch); business (MBA); computational science (MCC); education (Ed M, Ed D); English-Spanish translation (MA); entrepreneurship and management (MBA); integrated management of digital animation (MA); international business (MIB); international corporate law (LL M); internet technologies (MS); manufacturing systems (MMS); occupational health (MS); philosophy (MA, PhD); power electronics (MS); quality systems (MQS); renewable energy (MS); social evaluation of projects (MBA); strategic market research (MBA); tax law (MA); teaching mathematics (MA).

**Université de Montréal,** Faculty of Arts and Sciences, Department of Philosophy, Montréal, QC H3C 3J7, Canada. Offers MA, PhD. *Degree requirements:* For master's, 2 foreign languages, thesis; for doctorate, thesis/dissertation, general exam. Electronic applications accepted. *Faculty research:* Ancient and modern philosophy; logic and philosophy of language, ethics, and politics; contemporary Continental philosophy.

**Université de Sherbrooke,** Faculty of Letters and Human Sciences, Department of Human Sciences, Sherbrooke, QC J1K 2R1, Canada. Offers history (MA); philosophy (MA). *Degree requirements:* For master's, thesis. *Entrance requirements:* For master's, minimum GPA of 2.75. *Faculty research:* Political, social, and urban history; history of women.

**Université de Sherbrooke,** Faculty of Theology and Religious Studies, Sherbrooke, QC J1K 2R1, Canada. Offers applied ethics (Diploma); human science of religions (MA); intercultural training (Diploma); philosophy (MA, PhD); spiritual anthropology (Diploma); theology (MA, PhD, Diploma). *Program availability:* Part-time, evening/weekend, online learning. Terminal master's awarded for partial completion of doctoral program. *Entrance requirements:* For master's, bachelor's degree in related discipline; for doctorate, master's degree in related discipline. *Faculty research:* Faith and culture interrelation.

**Université du Québec à Montréal,** Graduate Programs, Program in Philosophy, Montréal, QC H3C 3P8, Canada. Offers MA, PhD. PhD offered jointly with Université du Québec à Trois-Rivières. *Program availability:* Part-time. *Degree requirements:* For master's, thesis; for doctorate, thesis/dissertation. *Entrance requirements:* For master's, appropriate bachelor's degree or equivalent, proficiency in French; for doctorate, appropriate master's degree or equivalent, proficiency in French.

**Université du Québec à Trois-Rivières,** Graduate Programs, Program in Philosophy, Trois-Rivières, QC G9A 5H7, Canada. Offers MA, PhD. PhD offered jointly with Université du Québec à Montréal. *Program availability:* Part-time. *Degree requirements:* For master's, thesis; for doctorate, thesis/dissertation. *Entrance requirements:* For master's, appropriate bachelor's degree, proficiency in French; for doctorate, appropriate master's degree, proficiency in French.

**Université Laval,** Faculty of Philosophy, Programs in Philosophy, Québec, QC G1K 7P4, Canada. Offers MA, PhD. Terminal master's awarded for partial completion of doctoral program. *Degree requirements:* For master's, thesis; for doctorate, comprehensive exam, thesis/dissertation. *Entrance requirements:* For master's and doctorate, French exam. Electronic applications accepted.

**University at Albany, State University of New York,** College of Arts and Sciences, Department of Philosophy, Albany, NY 12222-0001. Offers MA, PhD. *Faculty:* 4 full-time (2 women). *Students:* 16 full-time (4 women), 17 part-time (5 women); includes 3 minority (1 Black or African American, non-Hispanic/Latino; 1 American Indian or Alaska Native, non-Hispanic/Latino; 1 Asian, non-Hispanic/Latino), 2 international. 12 applicants, 75% accepted, 3 enrolled. In 2016, 4 master's, 4 doctorates awarded. *Degree requirements:* For master's, one foreign language, thesis; for doctorate, thesis/dissertation. *Entrance requirements:* For master's and doctorate, GRE General Test. Additional exam requirements/recommendations for international students: Required—TOEFL (minimum score 550 paper-based). *Application deadline:* For fall admission, 2/15 for domestic students, 5/1 for international students; for spring admission, 11/1 for international students. Applications are processed on a rolling basis. Application fee: $75. Electronic applications accepted. *Expenses:* Tuition, state resident: full-time $10,870; part-time $453 per credit hour. Tuition, nonresident: full-time $22,210; part-time $925 per credit hour. *International tuition:* $21,550 full-time. *Required fees:* $1864; $96 per credit hour. *Financial support:* Fellowships available. Financial award application deadline: 3/15. *Faculty research:* Philosophical logic, ethics, ancient philosophy/metaphysics, aesthetics, biomedical ethics. *Unit head:* P. D. Magnus, Chair, 518-442-4250, Fax: 518-442-4259, E-mail: pmagnus@albany.edu. *Application contact:* Michael DeRensis, Director, Graduate Admissions, 518-442-3980, Fax: 518-442-3922, E-mail: graduate@albany.edu. Website: http://www.albany.edu/philosophy/

**University at Buffalo, the State University of New York,** Graduate School, College of Arts and Sciences, Department of Philosophy, Buffalo, NY 14260. Offers MA, PhD. Terminal master's awarded for partial completion of doctoral program. *Degree requirements:* For master's, variable foreign language requirement, thesis or alternative; for doctorate, variable foreign language requirement, comprehensive exam, thesis/dissertation. *Entrance requirements:* For master's and doctorate, GRE General Test, minimum GPA of 3.0. Additional exam requirements/recommendations for international students: Required—TOEFL (minimum score 550 paper-based; 79 iBT). Electronic applications accepted. *Faculty research:* Logic, metaphysics (historical and contemporary), aesthetics, epistemology, ethics (historical and contemporary), ontology, social and political.

**University of Alberta,** Faculty of Graduate Studies and Research, Department of Philosophy, Edmonton, AB T6G 2E1, Canada. Offers MA, PhD. *Program availability:* Part-time. *Degree requirements:* For master's, thesis; for doctorate, thesis/dissertation. *Entrance requirements:* Additional exam requirements/recommendations for international students: Required—TOEFL (minimum score 550 paper-based). Electronic applications accepted. *Faculty research:* Philosophy of science, cognitive science, social and political philosophy, philosophy of language and logic, environmental aesthetics.

**The University of Arizona,** College of Social and Behavioral Sciences, Department of Philosophy, Tucson, AZ 85721. Offers MA, PhD. *Program availability:* Part-time. Terminal master's awarded for partial completion of doctoral program. *Degree requirements:* For master's, exams, qualifying paper; for doctorate, thesis/dissertation, preliminary exams. *Entrance requirements:* For doctorate, GRE General Test, 3 letters of recommendation, writing sample. Additional exam requirements/recommendations for international students: Required—TOEFL (minimum score 550 paper-based; 79 iBT). Electronic applications accepted. *Faculty research:* Law, social, and political philosophy; epistemology; philosophy of mind; cognitive science.

**University of Arkansas,** Graduate School, J. William Fulbright College of Arts and Sciences, Department of Philosophy, Fayetteville, AR 72701. Offers MA, PhD. *Program availability:* Part-time. In 2016, 2 master's, 3 doctorates awarded. *Degree requirements:* For master's, thesis; for doctorate, 2 foreign languages, thesis/dissertation. *Application deadline:* For fall admission, 4/1 for international students; for spring admission, 10/1 for international students. Applications are processed on a rolling basis. Application fee: $40 ($50 for international students). Electronic applications accepted. *Financial support:* In 2016–17, 1 research assistantship, 10 teaching assistantships were awarded; fellowships with tuition reimbursements, career-related internships or fieldwork, and Federal Work-Study also available. Support available to part-time students. Financial award application deadline: 4/1; financial award applicants required to submit FAFSA. *Unit head:* Dr. Edward Minar, Departmental Chairperson, 479-575-3551, Fax: 479-575-2642, E-mail: eminar@uark.edu. *Application contact:* Dr. Erick Funkhouser, Graduate Coordinator, 479-575-7441, E-mail: efunkho@uark.edu. Website: http://www.uark.edu/depts/philinfo/

**The University of British Columbia,** Faculty of Arts and Faculty of Graduate Studies, Department of Philosophy, Vancouver, BC V6T 1Z1, Canada. Offers MA, PhD. *Accreditation:* NCATE. *Program availability:* Part-time. *Degree requirements:* For master's, thesis (for some programs); for doctorate, comprehensive exam, thesis/dissertation. *Entrance requirements:* For master's, bachelor's degree with minimum GPA of 3.0 in 3rd- and 4th-year coursework; 3 credits in formal logic; 6 credits at the upper-level in the history of philosophy and in metaphysics, epistemology, or philosophy; 3 credits at the upper-level in ethics or value theory; for doctorate, MA, honors BA with

first class standing, or BA with first class standing in philosophy. Additional exam requirements/recommendations for international students: Required—TOEFL, IELTS, Michigan English Language Assessment Battery (minimum score 81). Application fee: $100 Canadian dollars ($162 Canadian dollars for international students). Electronic applications accepted. *Expenses:* $4,802 per year tuition and fees, $8,436 per year international. *Financial support:* Fellowships, research assistantships, teaching assistantships, Federal Work-Study, and tuition waivers (full) available. *Faculty research:* Ethics and applied ethics, metaphysics and epistemology, history of philosophy, philosophy of science, philosophy of biology, philosophy of mind, philosophy of cognitive science. *Application contact:* Graduate Program Staff, 604-822-8837, Fax: 604-822-8782, E-mail: phil.gradsec@ubc.ca.
Website: http://philosophy.ubc.ca/

**University of Calgary,** Faculty of Graduate Studies, Faculty of Arts, Department of Philosophy, Calgary, AB T2N 1N4, Canada. Offers MA, PhD. *Program availability:* Part-time. *Degree requirements:* For master's, comprehensive exam (for some programs), thesis (for some programs); for doctorate, thesis/dissertation, candidacy exam. *Entrance requirements:* Additional exam requirements/recommendations for international students: Required—TOEFL (minimum score 550 paper-based). Electronic applications accepted. *Faculty research:* Ethics and political philosophy, metaphysics, philosophy of mind, philosophy of language.

**University of California, Berkeley,** Graduate Division, College of Letters and Science, Department of Philosophy, Berkeley, CA 94720-1500. Offers PhD. *Students:* 38 full-time (10 women); includes 3 minority (1 Black or African American, non-Hispanic/Latino; 1 American Indian or Alaska Native, non-Hispanic/Latino; 1 Asian, non-Hispanic/Latino), 13 international. Average age 29. 306 applicants, 6 enrolled. In 2016, 7 doctorates awarded. *Degree requirements:* For doctorate, thesis/dissertation, qualifying exam. *Entrance requirements:* For doctorate, GRE General Test, minimum GPA of 3.0, writing sample, 3 letters of recommendation. *Application deadline:* For fall admission, 1/5 for domestic students. Application fee: $105 ($125 for international students). Electronic applications accepted. *Financial support:* Fellowships, research assistantships, teaching assistantships, institutionally sponsored loans, health care benefits, and unspecified assistantships available. *Unit head:* Prof. Hannah Ginsbourg, Chair, 510-642-2722, E-mail: phildept@berkeley.edu. *Application contact:* Information Contact, 510-642-2722, E-mail: phildept@berkeley.edu.
Website: http://philosophy.berkeley.edu/

**University of California, Davis,** Graduate Studies, Program in Philosophy, Davis, CA 95616. Offers MA, PhD. Terminal master's awarded for partial completion of doctoral program. *Degree requirements:* For doctorate, thesis/dissertation. *Entrance requirements:* For master's and doctorate, GRE General Test, minimum GPA of 3.0. Additional exam requirements/recommendations for international students: Required—TOEFL (minimum score 550 paper-based). Electronic applications accepted. *Faculty research:* Moral and political philosophy, philosophy of language, metaphysics, philosophy of science, history of philosophy.

**University of California, Irvine,** School of Humanities, Department of Philosophy, Irvine, CA 92697. Offers MA, PhD. *Students:* 19 full-time (3 women); includes 6 minority (2 Hispanic/Latino; 4 Two or more races, non-Hispanic/Latino). Average age 29. 50 applicants, 20% accepted, 2 enrolled. In 2016, 3 master's, 4 doctorates awarded. *Degree requirements:* For master's, thesis; for doctorate, thesis/dissertation. *Entrance requirements:* For master's and doctorate, GRE General Test, minimum GPA of 3.0. Additional exam requirements/recommendations for international students: Required—TOEFL (minimum score 550 paper-based). *Application deadline:* For fall admission, 1/15 priority date for domestic students, 1/15 for international students. Applications are processed on a rolling basis. Application fee: $105 ($125 for international students). Electronic applications accepted. *Financial support:* Fellowships with tuition reimbursements, teaching assistantships with partial tuition reimbursements, institutionally sponsored loans, traineeships, health care benefits, and unspecified assistantships available. Financial award application deadline: 3/1; financial award applicants required to submit FAFSA. *Faculty research:* Philosophy of action and decision theory, philosophy of language, philosophy of mathematics, virtue ethics, modern and contemporary Continental philosophy. *Unit head:* Aaron James, Department Chair, E-mail: aaron.james@uci.edu. *Application contact:* Kirsten S. Alonso, Department Coordinator, 949-824-6525, Fax: 949-824-6520, E-mail: kalonso@uci.edu.
Website: http://www.hnet.uci.edu/philosophy/

**University of California, Irvine,** School of Social Sciences, Department of Logic and Philosophy of Science, Irvine, CA 92697. Offers philosophy (PhD). *Students:* 28 full-time (9 women); includes 3 minority (1 Asian, non-Hispanic/Latino; 2 Two or more races, non-Hispanic/Latino), 9 international. Average age 26. 63 applicants, 32% accepted, 12 enrolled. In 2016, 2 doctorates awarded. *Entrance requirements:* For doctorate, GRE, minimum GPA of 3.0. Additional exam requirements/recommendations for international students: Required—TOEFL (minimum score 550 paper-based). *Application deadline:* For fall admission, 1/15 for domestic and international students. Application fee: $105 ($125 for international students). *Financial support:* Fellowships, research assistantships with full tuition reimbursements, teaching assistantships, institutionally sponsored loans, traineeships, health care benefits, and unspecified assistantships available. Financial award application deadline: 3/1. *Unit head:* P. Kyle Stanford, Chair, 949-824-6398, Fax: 949-824-8388, E-mail: stanford@uci.edu. *Application contact:* John Manchak, Graduate Program Director, 949-824-7374, E-mail: jmanchak@uci.edu.
Website: http://www.lps.uci.edu/

**University of California, Los Angeles,** Graduate Division, College of Letters and Science, Department of Philosophy, Los Angeles, CA 90095. Offers MA, PhD. Terminal master's awarded for partial completion of doctoral program. *Degree requirements:* For master's, one foreign language, comprehensive exam; for doctorate, one foreign language, thesis/dissertation, oral and written qualifying exams, 3 quarters of teaching experience. *Entrance requirements:* For doctorate, GRE General Test, bachelor's degree; minimum undergraduate GPA of 3.0 (or its equivalent if letter grade system not used); writing sample. Additional exam requirements/recommendations for international students: Required—TOEFL. Electronic applications accepted.

**University of California, Riverside,** Graduate Division, Department of Philosophy, Riverside, CA 92521-0102. Offers MA, PhD. Terminal master's awarded for partial completion of doctoral program. *Degree requirements:* For master's, logic exam, professional paper; for doctorate, one foreign language, thesis/dissertation, logic exam, proposition papers, qualifying exams. *Entrance requirements:* For master's, GRE General Test, minimum GPA of 3.2; for doctorate, GRE General Test, master's degree in philosophy, minimum GPA of 3.2. Additional exam requirements/recommendations for international students: Required—TOEFL (minimum score 550 paper-based; 80 iBT). Electronic applications accepted. *Expenses:* Tuition, state resident: full-time $16,666. Tuition, nonresident: full-time $31,768. *Required fees:* $11,055.54 per quarter. $3685.18 per quarter. Tuition and fees vary according to campus/location and program. *Faculty research:* Moral philosophy, philosophy of science, history of philosophy, philosophy of language, Continental philosophy.

**University of California, San Diego,** Graduate Division, Department of Philosophy, La Jolla, CA 92093. Offers PhD. *Students:* 37 full-time (10 women), 3 part-time (2 women).

212 applicants, 12% accepted, 7 enrolled. In 2016, 10 doctorates awarded. *Degree requirements:* For doctorate, thesis/dissertation, 3 quarters of teaching assistantship; original essay. *Entrance requirements:* For doctorate, GRE General Test, writing sample. Additional exam requirements/recommendations for international students: Required—TOEFL (minimum score 550 paper-based; 80 iBT), IELTS (minimum score 7). *Application deadline:* For fall admission, 1/26 for domestic students. Application fee: $105 ($125 for international students). Electronic applications accepted. *Expenses:* Tuition, state resident: full-time $11,220. Tuition, nonresident: full-time $26,322. *Required fees:* $1864. *Financial support:* Fellowships, teaching assistantships, and scholarships/grants available. Financial award applicants required to submit FAFSA. *Faculty research:* Philosophy of science, ethics and social-political philosophy, history of philosophy, epistemology and metaphysics, philosophy of mind and language. *Unit head:* Jonathan Cohen, Chair, 858-534-6812, E-mail: joncohen@aardvark.ucsd.edu. *Application contact:* Anna Shonle, Graduate Coordinator, 858-534-3076, E-mail: ashonle@ucsd.edu.
Website: http://philosophy.ucsd.edu/

**University of California, Santa Barbara,** Graduate Division, College of Letters and Sciences, Division of Humanities and Fine Arts, Department of Philosophy, Santa Barbara, CA 93106-9580. Offers PhD, MA/PhD. Terminal master's awarded for partial completion of doctoral program. *Degree requirements:* For doctorate, thesis/dissertation. *Entrance requirements:* For doctorate, GRE. Additional exam requirements/recommendations for international students: Required—TOEFL (minimum score 550 paper-based; 80 iBT), IELTS (minimum score 7). Electronic applications accepted. *Faculty research:* Epistemology, philosophy of language, philosophy of mind, history of philosophy, logic.

**University of California, Santa Cruz,** Division of Graduate Studies, Division of Humanities, Department of Philosophy, Santa Cruz, CA 95064. Offers MA, PhD. *Degree requirements:* For doctorate, thesis/dissertation, qualifying exam. *Entrance requirements:* For master's, GRE, 3 letters of recommendation; for doctorate, GRE, official transcripts, 3 letters of recommendation. Additional exam requirements/recommendations for international students: Required—TOEFL (minimum score 550 paper-based; 83 iBT); Recommended—IELTS (minimum score 8). Electronic applications accepted. *Faculty research:* Philosophy of science.

**University of Chicago,** Division of the Humanities, Department of Philosophy, Chicago, IL 60637. Offers ancient philosophy (PhD); philosophy (PhD). *Students:* 50 full-time (14 women); includes 5 minority (3 Asian, non-Hispanic/Latino; 2 Hispanic/Latino), 22 international. 145 applicants, 9% accepted, 7 enrolled. In 2016, 7 doctorates awarded. Terminal master's awarded for partial completion of doctoral program. *Degree requirements:* For doctorate, variable foreign language requirement, thesis/dissertation. *Entrance requirements:* For doctorate, GRE General Test. Additional exam requirements/recommendations for international students: Required—TOEFL (minimum score 104 iBT), IELTS (minimum score 7). *Application deadline:* For fall admission, 12/15 for domestic and international students. Application fee: $90. Electronic applications accepted. *Financial support:* Fellowships with full tuition reimbursements, teaching assistantships with full tuition reimbursements, Federal Work-Study, institutionally sponsored loans, scholarships/grants, and health care benefits available. Financial award application deadline: 12/15; financial award applicants required to submit FAFSA. *Faculty research:* Kant, history of analytic philosophy, ancient philosophy, philosophy of mind, philosophy of action. *Unit head:* Dr. Gabriel Lear, Chair, 773-702-5078, E-mail: grlear@uchicago.edu. *Application contact:* Michael Beetley, Assistant Dean of Students, Admissions and Fellowships, 773-702-1552, Fax: 773-834-9148, E-mail: humanitiesadmissions@uchicago.edu.
Website: http://philosophy.uchicago.edu/

**University of Chicago,** Division of the Humanities, Master of Arts Program in the Humanities, Chicago, IL 60637. Offers art history (MA); cinema and media studies (MA); classic languages (MA); comparative literature (MA); creative writing (MA); cultural policy studies (MA); digital humanities (MA); East Asian languages and civilizations (MA); English language and literature (MA); gender and sexuality studies (MA); Germanic studies (MA); linguistics (MA); music (MA); near Eastern languages and civilizations (MA); philosophy (MA); poetics (MA); race, politics and culture (MA); Romance languages and literatures (MA); Slavic languages and literatures (MA); South Asian languages and civilizations (MA); theater and performance studies (MA). *Students:* 80 full-time (43 women), 7 part-time (3 women); includes 20 minority (5 Black or African American, non-Hispanic/Latino; 1 American Indian or Alaska Native, non-Hispanic/Latino; 6 Asian, non-Hispanic/Latino; 5 Hispanic/Latino; 3 Two or more races, non-Hispanic/Latino), 11 international. Average age 26. 706 applicants, 15% accepted, 42 enrolled. In 2016, 92 master's awarded. *Degree requirements:* For master's, thesis. *Entrance requirements:* For master's, GRE General Test. Additional exam requirements/recommendations for international students: Required—TOEFL (minimum score 104 iBT), IELTS (minimum score 7). *Application deadline:* For fall admission, 1/3 for domestic and international students. Application fee: $90. Electronic applications accepted. *Financial support:* In 2016–17, 8 fellowships with partial tuition reimbursements (averaging $12,000 per year) were awarded; Federal Work-Study, institutionally sponsored loans, scholarships/grants, and tuition waivers (partial) also available. Financial award application deadline: 12/15; financial award applicants required to submit FAFSA. *Unit head:* Malynne Sternstein, Co-Director, 773-834-1201, Fax: 773-834-7526. *Application contact:* Program Coordinator, 773-834-1201, Fax: 773-834-7526, E-mail: ma-humanities@uchicago.edu.
Website: http://maph.uchicago.edu/

**University of Cincinnati,** Graduate School, McMicken College of Arts and Sciences, Department of Philosophy, Cincinnati, OH 45221. Offers MA, PhD. Terminal master's awarded for partial completion of doctoral program. *Degree requirements:* For master's, thesis; for doctorate, one foreign language, comprehensive exam, thesis/dissertation. *Entrance requirements:* For master's and doctorate, GRE General Test, BA in philosophy or equivalent experience. Additional exam requirements/recommendations for international students: Required—TOEFL. Electronic applications accepted. *Expenses: Tuition, area resident:* Full-time $12,790; part-time $389 per credit hour. Tuition, state resident: full-time $13,290; part-time $419 per credit hour. Tuition, nonresident: full-time $24,532; part-time $976 per credit hour. *International tuition:* $24,832 full-time. *Required fees:* $3958; $140 per credit hour. Tuition and fees vary according to course load, degree level, program and reciprocity agreements.

**University of Colorado Boulder,** Graduate School, College of Arts and Sciences, Department of Philosophy, Boulder, CO 80309. Offers MA, PhD. *Faculty:* 19 full-time (4 women). *Students:* 39 full-time (10 women), 1 part-time (0 women); includes 7 minority (4 Black or African American, non-Hispanic/Latino; 1 Asian, non-Hispanic/Latino; 2 Hispanic/Latino), 5 international. Average age 30. 155 applicants, 23% accepted, 10 enrolled. In 2016, 8 master's, 2 doctorates awarded. Terminal master's awarded for partial completion of doctoral program. *Degree requirements:* For master's, comprehensive exam, thesis; for doctorate, one foreign language, thesis/dissertation, logic and qualifying papers, oral exam. *Entrance requirements:* For master's, GRE General Test, writing sample, minimum undergraduate GPA of 2.75; for doctorate, GRE General Test. *Application deadline:* For fall admission, 1/7 for domestic students, 12/1 for international students. Applications are processed on a rolling basis. Application fee:

$60 ($80 for international students). Electronic applications accepted. Application fee is waived when completed online. *Financial support:* In 2016–17, 105 students received support, including 19 fellowships (averaging $8,815 per year), 6 research assistantships with full and partial tuition reimbursements available (averaging $36,884 per year), 26 teaching assistantships with full and partial tuition reimbursements available (averaging $37,063 per year); institutionally sponsored loans, scholarships/grants, health care benefits, and unspecified assistantships also available. Financial award application deadline: 1/17; financial award applicants required to submit FAFSA. *Faculty research:* Philosophy, ethics, history of philosophy, political philosophy, history of science and technology. *Total annual research expenditures:* $195,466. *Application contact:* E-mail: phildept@colorado.edu.
Website: http://www.colorado.edu/philosophy/

**University of Connecticut,** Graduate School, College of Liberal Arts and Sciences, Department of Philosophy, Storrs, CT 06269. Offers MA, PhD. Terminal master's awarded for partial completion of doctoral program. *Degree requirements:* For master's, comprehensive exam; for doctorate, 2 foreign languages, thesis/dissertation. *Entrance requirements:* For master's and doctorate, GRE General Test. Additional exam requirements/recommendations for international students: Required—TOEFL (minimum score 550 paper-based). Electronic applications accepted.

**University of Dallas,** Braniff Graduate School of Liberal Arts, Institute of Philosophic Studies, Doctoral Program in Philosophy, Irving, TX 75062-4736. Offers PhD. *Degree requirements:* For doctorate, 2 foreign languages, comprehensive exam, thesis/dissertation, qualifying exams. *Entrance requirements:* For doctorate, GRE General Test. *Faculty research:* Aesthetics, postmodernism, Hegel, ethics, Aristotle.

**University of Dallas,** Braniff Graduate School of Liberal Arts, Master's Program in Philosophy, Irving, TX 75062-4736. Offers MA. *Degree requirements:* For master's, one foreign language, comprehensive exam, thesis. *Entrance requirements:* For master's, GRE General Test. Additional exam requirements/recommendations for international students: Required—TOEFL. *Faculty research:* Aesthetics, postmodernism, Hegel, ethics, Aristotle.

**University of Florida,** Graduate School, College of Liberal Arts and Sciences, Department of Philosophy, Gainesville, FL 32611. Offers MA, PhD. *Program availability:* Part-time. *Degree requirements:* For doctorate, one foreign language, comprehensive exam, thesis/dissertation. *Entrance requirements:* For master's and doctorate, GRE General Test, minimum GPA of 3.0. Additional exam requirements/recommendations for international students: Required—TOEFL (minimum score 550 paper-based; 80 iBT), IELTS (minimum score 6). Electronic applications accepted. *Faculty research:* Philosophy of mind, metaphysics, philosophy of science, ancient philosophy, philosophical logic.

**University of Georgia,** Franklin College of Arts and Sciences, Department of Philosophy, Athens, GA 30602. Offers MA, PhD. *Program availability:* Part-time. *Degree requirements:* For master's, one foreign language, thesis; for doctorate, one foreign language, thesis/dissertation. *Entrance requirements:* For master's and doctorate, GRE General Test. Additional exam requirements/recommendations for international students: Required—TOEFL. *Application deadline:* For fall admission, 5/1 priority date for domestic and international students; for spring admission, 11/15 for domestic students. Application fee: $50. Electronic applications accepted. *Financial support:* Teaching assistantships with partial tuition reimbursements and unspecified assistantships available. Financial award application deadline: 1/1. *Unit head:* Dr. Victoria M. Davion, Head, 706-542-2823, Fax: 706-542-2839, E-mail: vdavion@uga.edu. *Application contact:* Christine J. Cuomo, Graduate Coordinator, 706-583-2823, E-mail: cuomo@uga.edu.
Website: http://www.phil.uga.edu/

**University of Guelph,** Graduate Studies, College of Arts, Department of Philosophy, Guelph, ON N1G 2W1, Canada. Offers MA, PhD. PhD offered jointly with McMaster University, Wilfrid Laurier University. *Program availability:* Part-time. *Degree requirements:* For master's, thesis (for some programs); for doctorate, one foreign language, thesis/dissertation. *Entrance requirements:* For master's, minimum B-average during previous 2 years of course work; for doctorate, minimum B average. Additional exam requirements/recommendations for international students: Required—TOEFL (minimum score 550 paper-based). Electronic applications accepted. *Faculty research:* Philosophy of science, ethics, modern philosophy, social philosophy, Continental philosophy.

**University of Hawaii at Manoa,** Graduate Division, College of Arts and Humanities, Department of Philosophy, Honolulu, HI 96822. Offers MA, PhD. *Program availability:* Part-time. *Degree requirements:* For master's, variable foreign language requirement, thesis optional, culminating exam; for doctorate, variable foreign language requirement, comprehensive exam, thesis/dissertation, final oral presentation. *Entrance requirements:* For master's and doctorate, GRE General Test. Additional exam requirements/recommendations for international students: Required—TOEFL (minimum score 600 paper-based; 100 iBT), IELTS (minimum score 7). *Faculty research:* Renaissance philosophy, Indian philosophy, logic, ethics, philosophy of science, philosophy of mathematics, Chinese philosophy.

**University of Houston,** College of Liberal Arts and Social Sciences, Department of Philosophy, Houston, TX 77204. Offers MA. *Degree requirements:* For master's, thesis (for some programs), thesis or additional course requirements. *Entrance requirements:* For master's, GRE General Test, minimum of 18 hours of course work in philosophy; minimum GPA of 3.3 in last 60 hours. Additional exam requirements/recommendations for international students: Required—TOEFL (minimum score 550 paper-based; 79 iBT). Electronic applications accepted. *Faculty research:* Skepticism, nominalism, history of philosophy, cognitive science.

**University of Idaho,** College of Graduate Studies, College of Letters, Arts and Social Sciences, Department of Politics and Philosophy, Moscow, ID 83844. Offers political science (MA, PhD); public administration (MPA). *Faculty:* 9 full-time. *Students:* 8 full-time, 12 part-time. Average age 35. In 2016, 7 master's awarded. *Entrance requirements:* For master's, minimum GPA of 3.0. Additional exam requirements/recommendations for international students: Required—TOEFL. *Expenses:* Tuition, state resident: full-time $6460; part-time $414 per credit hour. Tuition, nonresident: full-time $21,268; part-time $1237 per credit hour. *Required fees:* $2070; $60 per credit hour. Full-time tuition and fees vary according to course load and reciprocity agreements. *Unit head:* Dr. Brian Ellison, Chair, 208-885-6328, E-mail: politicsphilosophy@uidaho.edu. *Application contact:* Sean Scoggin, Graduate Recruitment Coordinator, 208-885-4723, E-mail: graduateadmissions@uidaho.edu.
Website: https://www.uidaho.edu/class/politics-and-philosophy

**University of Illinois at Chicago,** College of Liberal Arts and Sciences, Department of Philosophy, Chicago, IL 60607-7128. Offers MA, PhD. Terminal master's awarded for partial completion of doctoral program. *Degree requirements:* For doctorate, thesis/dissertation, preliminary exams. *Entrance requirements:* For master's and doctorate, minimum GPA of 2.75. Additional exam requirements/recommendations for international students: Required—TOEFL. Electronic applications accepted. *Faculty research:* Philosophy of science, philosophy of language, epistemology and metaphysics, ethics, aesthetics.

**University of Illinois at Urbana–Champaign,** Graduate College, College of Liberal Arts and Sciences, Department of Philosophy, Champaign, IL 61820. Offers MA, PhD, PhD/JD.

**The University of Iowa,** Graduate College, College of Liberal Arts and Sciences, Department of Philosophy, Iowa City, IA 52242-1316. Offers PhD. *Degree requirements:* For doctorate, comprehensive exam, thesis/dissertation. *Entrance requirements:* For doctorate, GRE General Test, minimum GPA of 3.0. Additional exam requirements/recommendations for international students: Required—TOEFL (minimum score 550 paper-based; 81 iBT). Electronic applications accepted.

**The University of Kansas,** Graduate Studies, College of Liberal Arts and Sciences, Department of Philosophy, Lawrence, KS 66045. Offers MA, PhD. *Program availability:* Part-time. *Students:* 32 full-time (11 women), 1 (woman) part-time; includes 2 minority (1 Hispanic/Latino; 1 Two or more races, non-Hispanic/Latino), 6 international. Average age 31. 26 applicants, 62% accepted, 7 enrolled. In 2016, 4 master's, 3 doctorates awarded. Terminal master's awarded for partial completion of doctoral program. *Entrance requirements:* For master's and doctorate, GRE, curriculum vitae or resume, statement of purpose, writing sample, three letters of recommendation, official academic transcripts. Additional exam requirements/recommendations for international students: Required—TOEFL. *Application deadline:* For fall admission, 5/1 for domestic and international students. Application fee: $65 ($85 for international students). Electronic applications accepted. *Financial support:* Fellowships, teaching assistantships, Federal Work-Study, scholarships/grants, and unspecified assistantships available. Financial award application deadline: 2/1. *Faculty research:* Theoretical and applied ethics, social and political philosophy, history of philosophy, analytic philosophy, philosophy of mind and language. *Unit head:* John Symons, Chair, 785-864-1948, E-mail: johnsymons@ku.edu. *Application contact:* Cari Ann Kreienhop, Graduate Program Coordinator, 785-864-3665, E-mail: ckreienhop@ku.edu.
Website: http://www.philosophy.ku.edu

**University of Kentucky,** Graduate School, College of Arts and Sciences, Program in Philosophy, Lexington, KY 40506-0032. Offers MA, PhD. *Degree requirements:* For master's, one foreign language, comprehensive exam, thesis; for doctorate, one foreign language, comprehensive exam, thesis/dissertation. *Entrance requirements:* For master's, GRE General Test, minimum undergraduate GPA of 2.75; for doctorate, GRE General Test, minimum graduate GPA of 3.0. Additional exam requirements/recommendations for international students: Required—TOEFL (minimum score 550 paper-based). Electronic applications accepted. *Faculty research:* History of philosophy, history and philosophy of science, ethics, social and political philosophy.

**University of Lethbridge,** School of Graduate Studies, Lethbridge, AB T1K 3M4, Canada. Offers addictions counseling (M Sc); agricultural biotechnology (M Sc); agricultural studies (M Sc, MA); anthropology (MA); archaeology (M Sc, MA); art (MA, MFA); biochemistry (M Sc); biological sciences (M Sc); biomolecular science (PhD); biosystems and biodiversity (PhD); Canadian studies (MA); chemistry (M Sc); computer science (M Sc); computer science and geographical information science (M Sc); counseling (MC); counseling psychology (M Ed); dramatic arts (MA); earth, space, and physical science (PhD); economics (MA); education (MA, PhD); educational leadership (M Ed); English (MA); environmental science (M Sc); evolution and behavior (PhD); exercise science (M Sc); French (MA); French/German (MA); French/Spanish (MA); general education (M Ed); geography (M Sc, MA); German (MA); health sciences (M Sc); individualized multidisciplinary (M Sc, MA); kinesiology (M Sc, MA); management (M Sc), including accounting, finance, human resource management and labor relations, information systems, international management, marketing, policy and strategy; mathematics (M Sc); music (M Mus, MA); Native American studies (MA); neuroscience (M Sc, PhD); new media (MA, MFA); nursing (M Sc, MN); philosophy (MA); physics (M Sc); political science (MA); psychology (M Sc, MA); religious studies (MA); sociology (MA); theatre and dramatic arts (MFA); theoretical and computational science (PhD); urban and regional studies (MA); women and gender studies (MA). *Program availability:* Part-time, evening/weekend. *Degree requirements:* For master's, thesis (for some programs); for doctorate, comprehensive exam, thesis/dissertation. *Entrance requirements:* For master's, GMAT (for M Sc in management), bachelor's degree in related field, minimum GPA of 3.0 during previous 20 graded semester courses, 2 years' teaching or related experience (M Ed); for doctorate, master's degree, minimum graduate GPA of 3.5. Additional exam requirements/recommendations for international students: Required—TOEFL (minimum score 580 paper-based; 93 iBT). Electronic applications accepted. *Faculty research:* Movement and brain plasticity, gibberellin physiology, photosynthesis, carbon cycling, molecular properties of main-group ring components.

**University of Louisville,** Graduate School, College of Arts and Sciences, Department of Philosophy, Louisville, KY 40292-0001. Offers humanities (MA, PhD). *Faculty:* 11 full-time (3 women), 10 part-time/adjunct (4 women). *Students:* 4 part-time (2 women); includes 3 minority (all Black or African American, non-Hispanic/Latino). Average age 39. *Degree requirements:* For master's, one foreign language, thesis or alternative. *Entrance requirements:* For master's, GRE General Test. Additional exam requirements/recommendations for international students: Required—TOEFL (minimum score 550 paper-based; 79 iBT), IELTS (minimum score 6.5). *Application deadline:* Applications are processed on a rolling basis. Application fee: $60. Electronic applications accepted. *Expenses:* Tuition, state resident: full-time $12,246; part-time $681 per credit hour. Tuition, nonresident: full-time $25,486; part-time $1417 per credit hour. *Required fees:* $196. Tuition and fees vary according to program and reciprocity agreements. *Faculty research:* Philosophy of race; feminist philosophy; political philosophy, bioethics, ethics. *Unit head:* Dr. David S. Owen, Chair and Professor, 502-852-0488, Fax: 502-852-0459, E-mail: david.owen@louisville.edu. *Application contact:* Libby Leggett, Director, Graduate Admissions, 502-852-3101, Fax: 502-852-6536, E-mail: gradadm@louisville.edu.
Website: http://louisville.edu/philosophy

**The University of Manchester,** School of Social Sciences, Manchester, United Kingdom. Offers ethnographic documentary (M Phil); interdisciplinary study of culture (PhD); philosophy (PhD); politics (PhD); social anthropology (PhD); social anthropology with visual media (PhD); social change (PhD); social statistics (PhD); sociology (PhD); visual anthropology (M Phil).

**University of Manitoba,** Faculty of Graduate Studies, Faculty of Arts, Department of Philosophy, Winnipeg, MB R3T 2N2, Canada. Offers MA. *Degree requirements:* For master's, variable foreign language requirement, thesis or alternative.

**University of Maryland, College Park,** Academic Affairs, College of Arts and Humanities, Department of Philosophy, College Park, MD 20742. Offers MA, PhD. *Degree requirements:* For master's, thesis optional; for doctorate, thesis/dissertation, 2 semesters of undergraduate teaching, qualification in symbolic logic. *Entrance requirements:* For master's, GRE General Test, minimum GPA of 3.0, philosophy paper, writing sample, 3 letters of recommendation; for doctorate, GRE General Test, minimum GPA of 3.0, philosophy paper, writing sample. Electronic applications accepted. *Faculty research:* Contemporary British and American philosophy, the relationship between philosophy and other disciplines, ethical and conceptual issues in public policy.

## Philosophy

**University of Massachusetts Amherst,** Graduate School, College of Humanities and Fine Arts, Department of Philosophy, Amherst, MA 01003. Offers MA, PhD. *Program availability:* Part-time. Terminal master's awarded for partial completion of doctoral program. *Degree requirements:* For master's, thesis optional; for doctorate, comprehensive exam, thesis/dissertation. *Entrance requirements:* For master's and doctorate, GRE General Test, writing sample, 3 letters of recommendation. Additional exam requirements/recommendations for international students: Required—TOEFL (minimum score 550 paper-based; 80 iBT), IELTS (minimum score 6.5). Electronic applications accepted.

**University of Memphis,** Graduate School, College of Arts and Sciences, Department of Philosophy, Memphis, TN 38152. Offers MA, PhD. *Program availability:* Part-time, evening/weekend. *Faculty:* 6 full-time (2 women), 2 part-time/adjunct (1 woman). *Students:* 18 full-time (3 women), 13 part-time (5 women); includes 10 minority (5 Black or African American, non-Hispanic/Latino; 2 Hispanic/Latino; 3 Two or more races, non-Hispanic/Latino), 2 international. Average age 31. 45 applicants, 18% accepted, 8 enrolled. In 2016, 15 master's, 6 doctorates awarded. Terminal master's awarded for partial completion of doctoral program. *Degree requirements:* For master's, comprehensive exam, thesis optional, 33 hours of class work; for doctorate, 2 foreign languages, comprehensive exam, thesis/dissertation, 72 hours of class work. *Entrance requirements:* For master's, GRE General Test, minimum GPA of 2.5, 18 hours of undergraduate course work in philosophy, 3 letters of recommendation, writing sample; for doctorate, GRE General Test, minimum GPA of 3.0, bachelor's degree in philosophy, 3 letters of recommendation, writing sample. Additional exam requirements/recommendations for international students: Required—TOEFL (minimum score 550 paper-based; 79 iBT). *Application deadline:* For fall admission, 1/5 priority date for domestic students. Applications are processed on a rolling basis. Application fee: $35 ($60 for international students). Electronic applications accepted. *Expenses:* $5,231.50 per semester full-time in-state, $9,623.50 full-time out-of-state. *Financial support:* In 2016–17, 9 students received support, including 23 teaching assistantships with full tuition reimbursements available (averaging $29,232 per year); fellowships with full tuition reimbursements available, research assistantships with full tuition reimbursements available, Federal Work-Study, scholarships/grants, tuition waivers (full), and unspecified assistantships also available. Financial award application deadline: 2/1; financial award applicants required to submit FAFSA. *Faculty research:* Continental philosophy, ethics, analytic philosophy, feminist theory, Africana philosophy. *Unit head:* Dr. Mary Beth Mader, Chair, 901-678-2535, Fax: 901-678-4365, E-mail: mmader@memphis.edu. *Application contact:* Dr. Timothy Roche, Director of Graduate Studies, 901-678-4365, E-mail: troche@memphis.edu.
Website: http://www.memphis.edu/philosophy/

**University of Miami,** Graduate School, College of Arts and Sciences, Department of Philosophy, Coral Gables, FL 33124. Offers MA, PhD. *Program availability:* Part-time. Terminal master's awarded for partial completion of doctoral program. *Degree requirements:* For master's, thesis or alternative; for doctorate, comprehensive exam, thesis/dissertation. *Entrance requirements:* For master's, GRE General Test; for doctorate, GRE General Test, minimum GPA of 3.0, 3 letters of recommendation, writing sample. Additional exam requirements/recommendations for international students: Required—TOEFL. Electronic applications accepted. *Faculty research:* Ethics, epistemology, pragmatism, philosophy of science, metaphysics.

**University of Michigan,** Rackham Graduate School, College of Literature, Science, and the Arts, Department of Philosophy, Ann Arbor, MI 48109. Offers AM, PhD. *Faculty:* 24 full-time (7 women), 1 part-time/adjunct (0 women). *Students:* 43 full-time (17 women); includes 15 minority (5 Asian, non-Hispanic/Latino; 5 Hispanic/Latino; 1 Two or more races, non-Hispanic/Latino), 9 international. Average age 29. 261 applicants, 7% accepted, 5 enrolled. In 2016, 4 doctorates awarded. Terminal master's awarded for partial completion of doctoral program. *Degree requirements:* For doctorate, thesis/dissertation, oral defense of dissertation. *Entrance requirements:* For master's and doctorate, 3 letters of recommendation, writing sample. Additional exam requirements/recommendations for international students: Required—TOEFL (minimum score 560 paper-based; 84 iBT). *Application deadline:* For fall admission, 12/8 for domestic and international students. Application fee: $75 ($90 for international students). Electronic applications accepted. *Expenses:* Contact institution. *Financial support:* In 2016–17, 39 students received support, including fellowships with full tuition reimbursements available (averaging $23,000 per year); teaching assistantships with full tuition reimbursements available (averaging $23,000 per year); health care benefits also available. Financial award application deadline: 12/8. *Faculty research:* Ethics, metaphysics, philosophy of language and mind, political and social philosophy, philosophy of science. *Unit head:* Elizabeth S. Anderson, Chair, 734-764-6285, Fax: 734-763-8071, E-mail: phil-chair@umich.edu. *Application contact:* Jean McKee, Graduate Program Coordinator, 734-764-3260, Fax: 734-763-8071, E-mail: phil-admissions@umich.edu.
Website: http://www.lsa.umich.edu/philosophy/

**University of Minnesota, Twin Cities Campus,** Graduate School, College of Liberal Arts, Department of Philosophy, Minneapolis, MN 55455-0213. Offers MA, PhD. *Program availability:* Part-time. Terminal master's awarded for partial completion of doctoral program. *Degree requirements:* For master's, comprehensive exam, thesis or 3 papers; oral exam; for doctorate, comprehensive exam, thesis/dissertation. *Entrance requirements:* For master's and doctorate, GRE. Additional exam requirements/recommendations for international students: Required—TOEFL (minimum score 550 paper-based), IELTS (minimum score 6.5), or Michigan English Language Assessment Battery (minimum score 80). Electronic applications accepted. *Faculty research:* Philosophy of science; ethics and social/political philosophy; logic, language, and mind.

**University of Mississippi,** Graduate School, College of Liberal Arts, University, MS 38677. Offers anthropology (MA); biology (MS, PhD); chemistry (MS, PhD); economics (MA, PhD); English (MA, PhD); experimental psychology (PhD); history (MA, PhD); mathematics (MS, PhD); modern languages (MA); music (MM); philosophy (MA); physics (MA, MS, PhD); political science (MA, PhD); studio art (MFA). *Program availability:* Part-time. *Faculty:* 472 full-time (263 women), 75 part-time/adjunct (35 women). *Students:* 415 full-time (210 women), 57 part-time (20 women); includes 70 minority (35 Black or African American, non-Hispanic/Latino; 13 Asian, non-Hispanic/Latino; 14 Hispanic/Latino; 8 Two or more races, non-Hispanic/Latino), 102 international. Average age 27. *Degree requirements:* For doctorate, thesis/dissertation. *Entrance requirements:* For master's, GRE General Test, minimum GPA of 3.0; for doctorate, GRE General Test. Additional exam requirements/recommendations for international students: Required—TOEFL. *Application deadline:* For fall admission, 4/1 for domestic students; for spring admission, 10/1 for domestic students. Applications are processed on a rolling basis. Application fee: $40. Electronic applications accepted. *Financial support:* Fellowships, research assistantships, teaching assistantships, career-related internships or fieldwork, Federal Work-Study, institutionally sponsored loans, scholarships/grants, and unspecified assistantships available. Financial award application deadline: 3/1; financial award applicants required to submit FAFSA. *Unit head:* Dr. Lee Michael Cohen, Dean, 662-915-7177, Fax: 662-915-5792, E-mail: libarts@olemiss.edu. *Application contact:* Dr. Christy M. Wyandt, Associate Dean of

Graduate School, 662-915-7474, Fax: 662-915-7577, E-mail: cwyandt@olemiss.edu.
Website: https://www.olemiss.edu

**University of Missouri,** Office of Research and Graduate Studies, College of Arts and Science, Department of Philosophy, Columbia, MO 65211. Offers PhD. *Faculty:* 14 full-time (2 women). *Students:* 23 full-time (2 women), 5 part-time (2 women). Terminal master's awarded for partial completion of doctoral program. *Degree requirements:* For doctorate, one foreign language, comprehensive exam, thesis/dissertation. *Entrance requirements:* For doctorate, GRE General Test (minimum score 650 verbal, 700 quantitative), minimum GPA of 3.0, 3.9 in major. Additional exam requirements/recommendations for international students: Required—TOEFL (minimum score 500 paper-based; 61 iBT). *Application deadline:* For fall admission, 1/15 priority date for domestic and international students. Applications are processed on a rolling basis. Application fee: $75 ($90 for international students). Electronic applications accepted. *Expenses:* Tuition, state resident: full-time $6347; part-time $352.60 per credit hour. Tuition, nonresident: full-time $17,379; part-time $965.50 per credit hour. *Required fees:* $1035. Tuition and fees vary according to course load, campus/location and program. *Financial support:* Fellowships with full tuition reimbursements, research assistantships with full tuition reimbursements, teaching assistantships with full tuition reimbursements, institutionally sponsored loans, health care benefits, and unspecified assistantships available. Financial award application deadline: 2/1. *Faculty research:* Epistemology, political philosophy, philosophy of biology, decision/game/rational choice theory, ethics, philosophy of mind and psychology, Indian philosophy, metaphysics, action theory.
Website: http://philosophy.missouri.edu/graduate.html

**University of Missouri–St. Louis,** College of Arts and Sciences, Department of Philosophy, St. Louis, MO 63121. Offers MA. *Program availability:* Part-time, evening/weekend. *Faculty:* 10 full-time (2 women), 1 (woman) part-time/adjunct. *Students:* 9 full-time (2 women), 8 part-time (2 women); includes 3 minority (1 Black or African American, non-Hispanic/Latino; 2 Hispanic/Latino), 1 international. 26 applicants, 73% accepted, 6 enrolled. *Entrance requirements:* For master's, writing sample, 3 letters of recommendation, personal statement. Additional exam requirements/recommendations for international students: Required—TOEFL (minimum score 550 paper-based; 79 iBT), IELTS (minimum score 6.5). *Application deadline:* For fall admission, 7/1 priority date for domestic and international students; for spring admission, 12/1 priority date for domestic and international students. Applications are processed on a rolling basis. Application fee: $50 ($40 for international students). Electronic applications accepted. *Financial support:* Research assistantships with tuition reimbursements and teaching assistantships with tuition reimbursements available. Financial award application deadline: 2/15; financial award applicants required to submit FAFSA. *Faculty research:* Ethics, philosophy and history of science, philosophical social science, aesthetics. *Unit head:* Dr. Eric Wiland, Graduate Program Director, 314-516-5495, Fax: 314-516-5816, E-mail: wiland@umsl.edu. *Application contact:* 314-516-5458, Fax: 314-516-6996, E-mail: gradadm@umsl.edu.
Website: http://www.umsl.edu/~philo/

**University of Montana,** Graduate School, College of Humanities and Sciences, Department of Philosophy, Missoula, MT 59812-0002. Offers MA. *Degree requirements:* For master's, thesis or additional course work/professional paper. *Entrance requirements:* For master's, GRE General Test. Additional exam requirements/recommendations for international students: Required—TOEFL (minimum score 525 paper-based). *Faculty research:* Philosophy of law, natural science, feminism, and technology; environmental, business, and medical ethics.

**University of Nebraska–Lincoln,** Graduate College, College of Arts and Sciences, Department of Philosophy, Lincoln, NE 68588. Offers MA, PhD. *Degree requirements:* For master's, thesis optional; for doctorate, comprehensive exam, thesis/dissertation. *Entrance requirements:* For master's and doctorate, GRE General Test, writing sample. Additional exam requirements/recommendations for international students: Required—TOEFL (minimum score 600 paper-based). Electronic applications accepted. *Faculty research:* Ethics, epistemology, metaphysics, cognitive science, history of philosophy.

**University of Nevada, Reno,** Graduate School, College of Liberal Arts, Department of Philosophy, Reno, NV 89557. Offers MA. *Degree requirements:* For master's, thesis optional. *Entrance requirements:* For master's, GRE General Test, minimum GPA of 2.75. Additional exam requirements/recommendations for international students: Required—TOEFL (minimum score 500 paper-based; 61 iBT), IELTS (minimum score 6). Electronic applications accepted. *Faculty research:* Ancient philosophy (Aristotle), ethics, political theory, violence, Continental philosophy.

**University of New Mexico,** Graduate Studies, College of Arts and Sciences, Program in Philosophy, Albuquerque, NM 87131-2039. Offers MA, PhD. *Program availability:* Part-time. *Faculty:* 8 full-time (2 women), 1 part-time/adjunct (0 women). *Students:* 9 full-time (1 woman), 23 part-time (5 women); includes 8 minority (1 Black or African American, non-Hispanic/Latino; 1 Asian, non-Hispanic/Latino; 2 Hispanic/Latino; 4 Two or more races, non-Hispanic/Latino), 4 international. Average age 34. 57 applicants, 32% accepted, 10 enrolled. In 2016, 5 master's, 5 doctorates awarded. Terminal master's awarded for partial completion of doctoral program. *Degree requirements:* For master's, thesis (for some programs); for doctorate, one foreign language, comprehensive exam, thesis/dissertation. *Entrance requirements:* For master's and doctorate, GRE. Additional exam requirements/recommendations for international students: Required—TOEFL. *Application deadline:* For fall admission, 3/1 for domestic and international students; for spring admission, 11/1 for domestic and international students. Application fee: $50. Electronic applications accepted. *Financial support:* Fellowships with tuition reimbursements, research assistantships, and teaching assistantships with tuition reimbursements available. Financial award application deadline: 3/1; financial award applicants required to submit FAFSA. *Faculty research:* Continental philosophy, Indian philosophy, history of philosophy, ethics, phenomenology and existentialism, philosophy of art and literature. *Unit head:* Dr. Richard Hayes, Chair, 505-277-2405, Fax: 505-277-6362, E-mail: rhayes@unm.edu. *Application contact:* Mercedes Nysus, Administrative Assistant II, 505-277-2405, Fax: 505-277-6362, E-mail: thinker@unm.edu.
Website: http://philosophy.unm.edu/

**The University of North Carolina at Chapel Hill,** Graduate School, College of Arts and Sciences, Department of Philosophy, Chapel Hill, NC 27599. Offers MA, PhD. *Degree requirements:* For master's, comprehensive exam, thesis; for doctorate, comprehensive exam, thesis/dissertation. *Entrance requirements:* For master's and doctorate, GRE General Test, minimum GPA of 3.0.

**The University of North Carolina at Charlotte,** College of Liberal Arts and Sciences, Department of Philosophy, Charlotte, NC 28223-0001. Offers ethics and applied philosophy (MA, Graduate Certificate). *Program availability:* Part-time. *Faculty:* 11 full-time (4 women). *Students:* 3 full-time (0 women), 12 part-time (4 women); includes 3 minority (2 Black or African American, non-Hispanic/Latino; 1 Two or more races, non-Hispanic/Latino). Average age 32. 8 applicants, 100% accepted, 4 enrolled. In 2016, 2 master's awarded. *Degree requirements:* For master's, thesis or internship. *Entrance requirements:* For master's, GRE or MAT, statement of purpose outlining why applicant seeks admission to program; three recommendations; one official transcript from all colleges or universities attended; philosophical writing sample; for Graduate Certificate,

personal statement outlining why the applicant seeks admission to the program; two academic letters of recommendation, in addition to the recommendation forms required by the graduate school, which address the student's philosophical skills and/or ethical reasoning. Additional exam requirements/recommendations for international students: Required—TOEFL (minimum score 523 paper-based, 70 iBT) or IELTS (6.5). *Application deadline:* For fall admission, 3/1 priority date for domestic and international students; for spring admission, 10/1 priority date for domestic and international students; for summer admission, 4/1 priority date for domestic and international students. Applications are processed on a rolling basis. Application fee: $75. Electronic applications accepted. *Expenses:* Tuition, state resident: full-time $4252. Tuition, nonresident: full-time $17,423. *Required fees:* $3026. Tuition and fees vary according to course load and program. *Financial support:* In 2016–17, 7 students received support, including 1 fellowship (averaging $42,000 per year), 5 teaching assistantships (averaging $4,100 per year); career-related internships or fieldwork, institutionally sponsored loans, scholarships/grants, unspecified assistantships, and administrative assistantships also available. Support available to part-time students. Financial award application deadline: 3/1; financial award applicants required to submit FAFSA. *Total annual research expenditures:* $4,880. *Unit head:* Dr. Shannon Sullivan, Chair, 704-687-5418. *Application contact:* Kathy B. Giddings, Director of Graduate Admissions, 704-687-5503, Fax: 704-687-1668, E-mail: gradadm@uncc.edu.
Website: http://philosophy.uncc.edu/

**University of North Florida,** College of Arts and Sciences, Department of Philosophy, Jacksonville, FL 32224. Offers applied ethics (Graduate Certificate); practical philosophy and applied ethics (MA). *Program availability:* Part-time, evening/weekend. *Faculty:* 8 full-time (3 women). *Students:* 6 full-time (0 women), 2 part-time (0 women); includes 1 minority (Asian, non-Hispanic/Latino). Average age 33. 8 applicants, 75% accepted, 4 enrolled. In 2016, 5 master's awarded. *Entrance requirements:* For master's, GRE General Test, minimum GPA of 3.0 in last 60 hours, 3 letters of recommendation, writing sample. Additional exam requirements/recommendations for international students: Required—TOEFL (minimum score 500 paper-based; 61 iBT). *Application deadline:* For fall admission, 8/1 priority date for domestic students, 5/1 for international students. Application fee: $30. Electronic applications accepted. Tuition and fees vary according to course load, campus/location and program. *Financial support:* In 2016–17, 1 student received support. Research assistantships, teaching assistantships, Federal Work-Study, scholarships/grants, tuition waivers, and unspecified assistantships available. Financial award application deadline: 4/1; financial award applicants required to submit FAFSA. *Faculty research:* Late modern philosophy, pragmatism, religion and American culture, hermeneutics, philosophy of mind. *Total annual research expenditures:* $31,261. *Unit head:* Mitchell Haney, Chair, 904-620-1187, Fax: 904-620-1840, E-mail: mhaney@unf.edu. *Application contact:* Dr. Amanda Pascale, Director, The Graduate School, 904-620-1360, Fax: 904-620-1362, E-mail: graduateschool@unf.edu.
Website: http://www.unf.edu/coas/philosophy/

**University of North Georgia,** Department of History, Anthropology and Philosophy, Dahlonega, GA 30597. Offers history (MA), including American history, military history, world history. *Program availability:* Part-time, evening/weekend. *Faculty:* 11 full-time (4 women), 1 part-time/adjunct. *Students:* 4 full-time (0 women), 11 part-time (5 women); includes 1 minority (Two or more races, non-Hispanic/Latino). Average age 32. 12 applicants, 92% accepted, 11 enrolled. In 2016, 2 master's awarded. *Degree requirements:* For master's, thesis optional. *Entrance requirements:* For master's, GRE, 3 recommendations, writing sample, letter of intent, minimum GPA of 2.75. Additional exam requirements/recommendations for international students: Required—TOEFL (minimum score 550 paper-based; 79 iBT), IELTS (minimum score 6.5). *Application deadline:* For fall admission, 4/15 priority date for domestic students, 7/1 priority date for international students. Applications are processed on a rolling basis. Application fee: $40. Electronic applications accepted. *Expenses:* Contact institution. *Financial support:* Unspecified assistantships available. Financial award application deadline: 3/17; financial award applicants required to submit FAFSA. *Unit head:* Dr. Jeff Pardue, Department Head, 678-717-3867. *Application contact:* Melinda Maxwell, Director of Graduate Admissions, 706-864-1543, E-mail: melinda.maxwell@ung.edu.
Website: http://ung.edu/history-anthropology-philosophy/

**University of North Texas,** Robert B. Toulouse School of Graduate Studies, Denton, TX 76203-5459. Offers accounting (MS); applied anthropology (MA, MS); applied behavior analysis (Certificate); applied geography (MA); applied technology and performance improvement (M Ed, MS); art education (MA); art history (MA); art museum education (Certificate); arts leadership (Certificate); audiology (Au D); behavior analysis (MS); behavioral science (PhD); biochemistry and molecular biology (MS); biology (MA, MS); biomedical engineering (MS); business analysis (MS); chemistry (MS); clinical health psychology (PhD); communication studies (MA, MS); computer engineering (MS); computer science (MS); counseling (M Ed, MS), including clinical mental health counseling (MS), college and university counseling, elementary school counseling, secondary school counseling; creative writing (MA); criminal justice (MS); curriculum and instruction (M Ed); decision sciences (MBA); design (MA, MFA), including fashion design (MFA), innovation studies, interior design (MFA); early childhood studies (MS); economics (MS); educational leadership (M Ed, Ed D); educational psychology (MS, PhD), including family studies (MS), gifted and talented (MS), human development (MS), learning and cognition (MS), research, measurement and evaluation (MS); electrical engineering (MS); emergency management (MPA); engineering technology (MS); English (MA); English as a second language (MA); environmental science (MS); finance (MBA, MS); financial management (MPA); French (MA); health services management (MBA); higher education (M Ed, Ed D); history (MA, MS); hospitality management (MS); human resources management (MPA); information science (MS); information systems (PhD); information technologies (MBA); interdisciplinary studies (MA, MS); international studies (MA); international sustainable tourism (MS); jazz studies (MM); journalism (MA, MJ, Graduate Certificate), including interactive and virtual digital communication (Graduate Certificate), narrative journalism (Graduate Certificate), public relations (Graduate Certificate); kinesiology (MS); linguistics (MA); local government management (MPA); logistics (PhD); logistics and supply chain management (MBA); long-term care, senior housing, and aging services (MA); management (PhD); marketing (MBA); mathematics (MA, MS); mechanical and energy engineering (MS, PhD); music (MA), including ethnomusicology, music theory, musicology, performance; music composition (PhD); music education (MM Ed, PhD); nonprofit management (MPA); operations and supply chain management (MBA); performance (MM, DMA); philosophy (MA); political science (MA); professional and technical communication (MA); radio, television and film (MA, MFA); rehabilitation counseling (Certificate); sociology (MA); Spanish (MA); special education (M Ed); speech-language pathology (MA); strategic management (MBA); studio art (MFA); teaching (M Ed); MBA/MS. *Program availability:* Part-time, evening/weekend, online learning. Terminal master's awarded for partial completion of doctoral program. *Degree requirements:* For master's, variable foreign language requirement, comprehensive exam (for some programs), thesis (for some programs); for doctorate, variable foreign language requirement, comprehensive exam (for some programs), thesis/dissertation; for other advanced degree, variable foreign language requirement, comprehensive exam (for some programs). *Entrance requirements:* For master's and doctorate, GRE, GMAT. Additional exam requirements/

recommendations for international students: Required—TOEFL (minimum score 550 paper-based; 79 iBT). Electronic applications accepted.

**University of Notre Dame,** Graduate School, College of Arts and Letters, Division of Humanities, Department of Philosophy, Notre Dame, IN 46556. Offers PhD. *Degree requirements:* For doctorate, 2 foreign languages, thesis/dissertation, candidacy exam. *Entrance requirements:* For doctorate, GRE General Test. Additional exam requirements/recommendations for international students: Required—TOEFL (minimum score 600 paper-based; 80 iBT). Electronic applications accepted. *Faculty research:* History of philosophy, ethics, philosophy of science and logic, philosophy of religion, Continental philosophy, metaphysics.

**University of Oklahoma,** College of Arts and Sciences, Department of Philosophy, Norman, OK 73019-2006. Offers MA, PhD. *Program availability:* Part-time. *Faculty:* 15 full-time (5 women). *Students:* 23 full-time (7 women), 9 part-time (1 woman); includes 4 minority (1 Asian, non-Hispanic/Latino; 3 Hispanic/Latino), 3 international. Average age 29. 33 applicants, 30% accepted, 8 enrolled. In 2016, 5 master's, 5 doctorates awarded. Terminal master's awarded for partial completion of doctoral program. *Degree requirements:* For doctorate, comprehensive exam, thesis/dissertation. *Entrance requirements:* Additional exam requirements/recommendations for international students: Required—TOEFL (minimum score 79 iBT) or IELTS (minimum score 6.5). *Application deadline:* For fall admission, 1/15 for domestic and international students; for spring admission, 8/31 for domestic and international students. Application fee: $50 ($100 for international students). Electronic applications accepted. *Expenses:* Tuition, state resident: full-time $4886; part-time $203.60 per credit hour. Tuition, nonresident: full-time $18,989; part-time $791.20 per credit hour. *Required fees:* $3283; $126.25 per credit hour. $126.50 per semester. *Financial support:* In 2016–17, 27 students received support, including 4 fellowships with full tuition reimbursements available (averaging $3,375 per year), 2 research assistantships with full tuition reimbursements available (averaging $16,000 per year), 20 teaching assistantships with full tuition reimbursements available (averaging $16,620 per year); scholarships/grants, health care benefits, and unspecified assistantships also available. Financial award application deadline: 6/1; financial award applicants required to submit FAFSA. *Faculty research:* Metaphysics, epistemology, ethics, philosophy of religion, history of philosophy. *Unit head:* Dr. Wayne Riggs, Associate Professor, 405-325-5950, E-mail: wriggs@ou.edu. *Application contact:* Martin Montminy, Professor, 405-325-6324, E-mail: montminy@ou.edu.
Website: http://philosophy.ou.edu/

**University of Oregon,** Graduate School, College of Arts and Sciences, Department of Philosophy, Eugene, OR 97403. Offers MA, PhD. Terminal master's awarded for partial completion of doctoral program. *Degree requirements:* For master's, one foreign language, thesis or alternative; for doctorate, one foreign language, thesis/dissertation. *Entrance requirements:* For master's and doctorate, GRE General Test. Additional exam requirements/recommendations for international students: Required—TOEFL. *Faculty research:* Social and political philosophy, feminist philosophy, American philosophy, aesthetics, philosophy of mind.

**University of Ottawa,** Faculty of Graduate and Postdoctoral Studies, Faculty of Arts, Department of Philosophy, Ottawa, ON K1N 6N5, Canada. Offers MA, PhD. *Degree requirements:* For master's, thesis or alternative; for doctorate, comprehensive exam, thesis/dissertation. *Entrance requirements:* For master's, honors degree or equivalent, minimum B average; for doctorate, master's degree, minimum B+ average. Electronic applications accepted. *Faculty research:* History of philosophy (ancient, medieval, modern and contemporary); metaphysics/epistemology; value theory: political philosophy, ethics.

**University of Pennsylvania,** School of Arts and Sciences, Graduate Group in Philosophy, Philadelphia, PA 19104. Offers AM, PhD, JD/PhD. *Faculty:* 15 full-time (4 women), 2 part-time/adjunct. *Students:* 31 full-time (8 women), 2 part-time (1 woman); includes 4 minority (1 Asian, non-Hispanic/Latino; 2 Hispanic/Latino; 1 Two or more races, non-Hispanic/Latino), 14 international. Average age 31. 94 applicants, 17% accepted, 6 enrolled. In 2016, 4 master's, 5 doctorates awarded. Terminal master's awarded for partial completion of doctoral program. *Expenses: Tuition:* Full-time $31,068; part-time $5762 per course. *Required fees:* $3200; $336 per course. Full-time tuition and fees vary according to degree level, program and student level. Part-time tuition and fees vary according to course load, degree level and program. *Financial support:* Application deadline: 12/1.
Website: http://www.sas.upenn.edu/graduate-division

**University of Pittsburgh,** Dietrich School of Arts and Sciences, Department of History and Philosophy of Science, Pittsburgh, PA 15260. Offers PhD. *Faculty:* 8 full-time (2 women). *Students:* 27 full-time (11 women); includes 2 minority (both Two or more races, non-Hispanic/Latino), 9 international. Average age 28. 51 applicants, 12% accepted, 4 enrolled. In 2016, 2 doctorates awarded. Terminal master's awarded for partial completion of doctoral program. *Degree requirements:* For doctorate, one foreign language, comprehensive exam, thesis/dissertation, minimum of 72 credit hours, proficiency in logic. *Entrance requirements:* For doctorate, GRE General Test, curriculum vitae, statement of career objective, 3 letters of recommendation, sample of written work. Additional exam requirements/recommendations for international students: Required—TOEFL (minimum score 577 paper-based; 90 iBT), IELTS (minimum score 7). *Application deadline:* For fall admission, 1/10 for domestic and international students. Application fee: $50. Electronic applications accepted. Tuition and fees vary according to program. *Financial support:* In 2016–17, 23 students received support, including 12 fellowships with full tuition reimbursements available (averaging $24,710 per year), 11 teaching assistantships with full tuition reimbursements available (averaging $24,710 per year); research assistantships, health care benefits, and tuition waivers (full) also available. Financial award application deadline: 1/10. *Faculty research:* History and philosophy of biology, psychology, and neuroscience; history and philosophy of physics; early modern science; cognitive science; philosophy of social science; philosophy of mind and perception. *Unit head:* Sandra Mitchell, Chair, 412-624-5896, Fax: 412-624-6825, E-mail: smitchel@pitt.edu. *Application contact:* Kathy Rivet, Graduate Administrator, 412-624-5774, Fax: 412-624-5377, E-mail: krivet@pitt.edu.
Website: http://www.hps.pitt.edu/

**University of Pittsburgh,** Dietrich School of Arts and Sciences, Department of Philosophy, Pittsburgh, PA 15260. Offers PhD. *Faculty:* 20 full-time (4 women). *Students:* 44 full-time (15 women); includes 5 minority (2 Asian, non-Hispanic/Latino; 2 Hispanic/Latino; 1 Two or more races, non-Hispanic/Latino), 18 international. 180 applicants, 11% accepted, 6 enrolled. In 2016, 6 doctorates awarded. Terminal master's awarded for partial completion of doctoral program. *Degree requirements:* For doctorate, one foreign language, comprehensive exam, thesis/dissertation, minimum of 72 credit hours, proficiency in logic. *Entrance requirements:* For doctorate, GRE General Test, curriculum vitae, statement of purpose, 3 letters of recommendation, sample of written work. Additional exam requirements/recommendations for international students: Required—TOEFL (minimum score 577 paper-based; 90 iBT), IELTS (minimum score 7). *Application deadline:* For fall admission, 1/10 for domestic and international students. Application fee: $50. Electronic applications accepted. Tuition and fees vary according to program. *Financial support:* In 2016–17, 41 students received support, including 16 fellowships with full tuition reimbursements available (averaging $24,710 per year), 3

## Philosophy

research assistantships with full tuition reimbursements available (averaging $26,702 per year), 20 teaching assistantships with full tuition reimbursements available (averaging $24,710 per year); Federal Work-Study, scholarships/grants, health care benefits, and tuition waivers (full and partial) also available. Financial award application deadline: 1/10. *Faculty research:* Metaphysics and epistemology, logic and philosophy of science, history of Western philosophy, moral and political philosophy, philosophy of mind and language. *Unit head:* Dr. Robert Batterman, Chairman, 412-624-5775, Fax: 412-624-5377, E-mail: rbatterm@pitt.edu. *Application contact:* Kathy Rivet, Graduate Administrator, 412-624-5774, Fax: 412-624-5377, E-mail: krivet@pitt.edu. Website: http://www.philosophy.pitt.edu/

**University of Puerto Rico, Río Piedras Campus,** College of Humanities, Department of Philosophy, San Juan, PR 00931-3300. Offers MA. *Program availability:* Part-time. *Degree requirements:* For master's, one foreign language, comprehensive exam, thesis. *Entrance requirements:* For master's, PAEG or GRE, interview, minimum GPA of 3.0, letter of recommendation (2).

**University of Regina,** Faculty of Graduate Studies and Research, Faculty of Arts, Department of Philosophy, Regina, SK S4S 0A2, Canada. Offers MA. Offered as a special case program. *Program availability:* Part-time. *Faculty:* 8 full-time (2 women), 2 part-time/adjunct (0 women). *Students:* 1 applicant. In 2016, 1 master's awarded. *Degree requirements:* For master's, thesis. *Entrance requirements:* Additional exam requirements/recommendations for international students: Required—TOEFL (minimum score 580 paper-based; 80 iBT), IELTS (minimum score 6.5), PTE (minimum score 59). *Application deadline:* Applications are processed on a rolling basis. Application fee: $100. Electronic applications accepted. *Financial support:* Fellowships, teaching assistantships, and scholarships/grants available. Financial award application deadline: 6/15. *Faculty research:* Ethics, politics, religion, history, critical thinking. *Unit head:* Dr. Eldon Soifer, Department Head, 306-585-4301, Fax: 306-585-4827, E-mail: eldon.soifer@uregina.ca.
Website: http://www.uregina.ca/arts/philosophy-classics

**University of Regina,** Faculty of Graduate Studies and Research, Faculty of Arts, Program in Social and Political Thought, Regina, SK S4S 0A2, Canada. Offers MA. *Program availability:* Part-time. *Faculty:* 11 full-time (4 women). *Students:* 6 full-time (2 women), 6 part-time (2 women). 12 applicants, 33% accepted. *Degree requirements:* For master's, thesis. *Entrance requirements:* Additional exam requirements/ recommendations for international students: Required—TOEFL (minimum score 580 paper-based; 80 iBT), IELTS (minimum score 6.5), PTE (minimum score 59). *Application deadline:* For fall admission, 3/30 for domestic and international students. Application fee: $100. Electronic applications accepted. *Financial support:* In 2016–17, 2 fellowships (averaging $6,000 per year), 2 teaching assistantships (averaging $2,501 per year) were awarded; scholarships/grants also available. Financial award application deadline: 6/15. *Faculty research:* Liberalism and freedom, neo-conservatism, Aristotle's ethics, Kant's ethical theory and political philosophy, Hegel's philosophy of right. *Unit head:* Dr. Lee Ward, Graduate Coordinator, 306-359-1259, E-mail: lee.ward@uregina.ca. *Application contact:* Doreen Thompson, Administrative Assistant, 306-585-4332, E-mail: doreen.thompson@uregina.ca.

**University of Rochester,** School of Arts and Sciences, Department of Philosophy, Rochester, NY 14627. Offers PhD. *Students:* 20 full-time (1 woman); includes 4 minority (all Hispanic/Latino). Average age 28. 61 applicants, 18% accepted, 3 enrolled. In 2016, 1 doctorate awarded. Terminal master's awarded for partial completion of doctoral program. *Degree requirements:* For doctorate, thesis/ dissertation, qualifying exam. *Entrance requirements:* For doctorate, GRE General Test, sample of written work, three or more confidential letters of recommendation, list of all prior courses in philosophy. Additional exam requirements/recommendations for international students: Required—TOEFL (minimum score 600 paper-based; 100 iBT). *Application deadline:* For fall admission, 1/15 for domestic and international students. Application fee: $60. Electronic applications accepted. *Expenses:* $1,538 per credit. *Financial support:* In 2016–17, 15 students received support, including 3 fellowships with full tuition reimbursements available (averaging $18,000 per year); tuition waivers (full) also available. Financial award application deadline: 4/15. *Faculty research:* Epistemology, ethics, metaphysics, political philosophy, philosophy of science. *Unit head:* Randall Curren, Chair, 585-275-8112, E-mail: randall.curren@rochester.edu. *Application contact:* Cheryl Kingston, Administrative Assistant, 585-275-4105, E-mail: cheryl.kingston@rochester.edu.
Website: http://www.rochester.edu/College/PHL/

**University of St. Thomas,** Center for Thomistic Studies, Houston, TX 77006-4696. Offers philosophy (MA, PhD). *Program availability:* Part-time. *Faculty:* 6 full-time (1 woman). *Students:* 8 full-time (3 women), 26 part-time (3 women); includes 5 minority (1 Asian, non-Hispanic/Latino; 4 Hispanic/Latino), 2 international. Average age 34. 6 applicants, 100% accepted, 5 enrolled. Terminal master's awarded for partial completion of doctoral program. *Degree requirements:* For master's, one foreign language, comprehensive exam, thesis (for some programs); for doctorate, 2 foreign languages, comprehensive exam, thesis/dissertation. *Entrance requirements:* For master's, GRE, bachelor's degree with minimum GPA of 3.0 and at least 18 hours of undergraduate philosophy coursework, 3 letters of recommendation from professional educators, writing sample; for doctorate, GRE, MA in philosophy, 3 letters of recommendation from professional educators, writing sample, fulfillment of Latin language requirement (if not available at time of admission, must be completed no later than the third semester of doctoral study). Additional exam requirements/recommendations for international students: Required—TOEFL (minimum score 550 paper-based; 79 iBT), IELTS (minimum score 6.5), PTE (minimum score 53). *Application deadline:* For fall admission, 2/1 priority date for domestic and international students. Applications are processed on a rolling basis. Application fee: $35. Electronic applications accepted. *Expenses: Tuition:* Full-time $20,934; part-time $1163 per credit hour. *Required fees:* $81 per semester. One-time fee: $100. Part-time tuition and fees vary according to course level, course load, campus/location and program. *Financial support:* In 2016–17, 18 students received support. Fellowships with tuition reimbursements available, teaching assistantships, Federal Work-Study, scholarships/grants, unspecified assistantships, and state work-study, institutional employment available. Support available to part-time students. Financial award application deadline: 2/1; financial award applicants required to submit FAFSA. *Faculty research:* Biomedical ethics, Islamic philosophy, metaphysics, virtue ethics, semiotics. *Unit head:* Dr. Thomas Osborne, Director, 713-942-3483, Fax: 713-942-3464, E-mail: osborntm@stthom.edu. *Application contact:* Valerie Hall, Administrative Assistant II, 713-525-3591, Fax: 713-942-3464, E-mail: hallvl@stthom.edu.
Website: http://www.stthom.edu/Academics/School_of_Arts_and_Sciences/Graduate/ Philosophy/Philosophy_MA_PhD.aqf

**University of Saskatchewan,** College of Graduate Studies and Research, College of Arts and Science, Department of Philosophy, Saskatoon, SK S7N 5A2, Canada. Offers MA. *Degree requirements:* For master's, thesis. *Entrance requirements:* Additional exam requirements/recommendations for international students: Required—TOEFL (minimum score 80 iBT); Recommended—IELTS (minimum score 6.5). Electronic applications accepted.

**University of South Africa,** College of Human Sciences, Pretoria, South Africa. Offers adult education (M Ed); African languages (MA, PhD); African politics (MA, PhD); Afrikaans (MA, PhD); ancient history (MA, PhD); ancient Near Eastern studies (MA, PhD); anthropology (MA, PhD); applied linguistics (MA); Arabic (MA, PhD); archaeology (MA); art history (MA); Biblical archaeology (MA); Biblical studies (M Th, D Th, PhD); Christian spirituality (M Th, D Th); church history (M Th, D Th); classical studies (MA, PhD); clinical psychology (MA); communication (MA, PhD); comparative education (M Ed, Ed D); consulting psychology (D Admin, D Com, PhD); curriculum studies (M Ed, Ed D); development studies (M Admin, MA, D Admin, PhD); didactics (M Ed, Ed D); education (M Tech); education management (M Ed, Ed D); educational psychology (M Ed); English (MA); environmental education (M Ed); French (MA, PhD); German (MA, PhD); Greek (MA); guidance and counseling (M Ed); health studies (MA, PhD); including health sciences education (MA), health services management (MA), medical and surgical nursing science (critical care general) (MA), midwifery and neonatal nursing science (MA), trauma and emergency care (MA); history (MA, PhD); history of education (Ed D); inclusive education (M Ed, Ed D); information and communications technology policy and regulation (MA); information science (MA, MIS, PhD); international politics (MA, PhD); Islamic studies (MA, PhD); Italian (MA, PhD); Judaica (MA, PhD); linguistics (MA, PhD); mathematical education (M Ed); mathematics education (MA); missiology (M Th, D Th); modern Hebrew (MA, PhD); musicology (MA, MMus, D Mus, PhD); natural science education (M Ed); New Testament (M Th, D Th); Old Testament (D Th); pastoral therapy (M Th, D Th); philosophy (MA); philosophy of education (M Ed, Ed D); politics (MA, PhD); Portuguese (MA, PhD); practical theology (M Th, D Th); psychology (MA, MS, PhD); psychology of education (M Ed, Ed D); public health (MA); religious studies (MA, D Th, PhD); Romance languages (MA); Russian (MA, PhD); Semitic languages (MA, PhD); social behavior studies in HIV/AIDS (MA); social science (mental health) (MA); social science in development studies (MA); social science in psychology (MA); social science in social work (MA); social science in sociology (MA); social work (MSW, DSW, PhD); socio-education (M Ed, Ed D); sociolinguistics (MA); sociology (MA, PhD); Spanish (MA, PhD); systematic theology (M Th, D Th); TESOL (teaching English to speakers of other languages) (MA); theological ethics (M Th, D Th); theory of literature (MA, PhD); urban ministries (D Th); urban ministry (M Th).

**University of South Carolina,** The Graduate School, College of Arts and Sciences, Department of Philosophy, Columbia, SC 29208. Offers MA, PhD. *Program availability:* Part-time. *Degree requirements:* For master's, one foreign language, comprehensive exam, thesis optional; for doctorate, one foreign language, comprehensive exam, thesis/ dissertation, candidacy exam. *Entrance requirements:* For master's and doctorate, GRE General Test, 18 hours in philosophy, 3 letters of recommendation, writing sample. Additional exam requirements/recommendations for international students: Required— TOEFL (minimum score 590 paper-based). Electronic applications accepted. *Faculty research:* History of philosophy, ethics, philosophy of science, social philosophy.

**University of Southern California,** Graduate School, Dana and David Dornsife College of Letters, Arts and Sciences, School of Philosophy, Los Angeles, CA 90089. Offers MA, PhD, MA/JD. *Degree requirements:* For doctorate, one foreign language, thesis/ dissertation, area exam, qualifying exam. *Entrance requirements:* For doctorate, GRE General Test. Additional exam requirements/recommendations for international students: Required—TOEFL. Electronic applications accepted. *Faculty research:* Logic, epistemology, ethics/metaethics, philosophy of language, philosophy of law.

**University of South Florida,** College of Arts and Sciences, Department of Humanities and Cultural Studies, Tampa, FL 33620-9951. Offers liberal arts (MA), including Africana studies, American studies, film studies, humanities, social and political thought. *Program availability:* Part-time, evening/weekend. *Faculty:* 6 full-time (1 woman). *Students:* 17 full-time (10 women), 9 part-time (3 women); includes 3 minority (all Black or African American, non-Hispanic/Latino), 2 international. Average age 33. 23 applicants, 83% accepted, 14 enrolled. In 2016, 6 master's awarded. *Degree requirements:* For master's, comprehensive exam, thesis, language (for humanities subconcentration). *Entrance requirements:* For master's, GRE General Test, minimum GPA of 3.0 in upper-division courses, personal statement, writing sample. Additional exam requirements/ recommendations for international students: Required—TOEFL (minimum score 550 paper-based; 79 iBT) or IELTS (minimum score 6.5). *Application deadline:* For fall admission, 2/15 priority date for domestic students, 2/15 for international students; for spring admission, 10/15 priority date for domestic students, 9/15 for international students; for summer admission, 2/15 for domestic students, 1/15 for international students. Application fee: $30. Electronic applications accepted. *Expenses:* Tuition, state resident: full-time $7766; part-time $431.43 per credit hour. Tuition, nonresident: full-time $15,789; part-time $877.17 per credit hour. *Required fees:* $37 per term. *Financial support:* In 2016–17, 5 students received support, including 15 teaching assistantships with tuition reimbursements available (averaging $12,437 per year); scholarships/grants also available. Financial award application deadline: 4/1. *Faculty research:* American South, American autobiography, material culture, critical theory, cultural studies, film studies. *Unit head:* Dr. William Cummings, Professor and Chair, 813-974-9380, Fax: 813-974-9409, E-mail: wcummings@usf.edu. *Application contact:* Dr. Brook Sadler, Associate Professor and Graduate Program Director, 813-974-8841, Fax: 813-974-9409, E-mail: brooksadler@usf.edu.
Website: http://humanities.usf.edu/

**University of South Florida,** College of Arts and Sciences, Department of Philosophy, Tampa, FL 33620-9951. Offers philosophy (MA, PhD), including philosophy and religion. *Program availability:* Part-time, evening/weekend. *Faculty:* 12 full-time (2 women). *Students:* 43 full-time (9 women), 12 part-time (4 women); includes 8 minority (1 Black or African American, non-Hispanic/Latino; 2 Asian, non-Hispanic/Latino; 4 Hispanic/Latino; 1 Two or more races, non-Hispanic/Latino). Average age 32. 27 applicants, 56% accepted, 6 enrolled. In 2016, 3 master's, 10 doctorates awarded. Terminal master's awarded for partial completion of doctoral program. *Degree requirements:* For master's, comprehensive exam, thesis optional; for doctorate, comprehensive exam, thesis/ dissertation. *Entrance requirements:* For master's and doctorate, GRE General Test, minimum GPA of 3.0, three letters of recommendation, 10-page philosophy writing sample, statement of philosophical interests. Additional exam requirements/ recommendations for international students: Required—TOEFL (minimum score 550 paper-based; 79 iBT) or IELTS (minimum score 6.5). *Application deadline:* For fall admission, 2/15 for domestic and international students; for spring admission, 10/15 for domestic students, 8/1 for international students. Application fee: $30. Electronic applications accepted. *Expenses:* Tuition, state resident: full-time $7766; part-time $431.43 per credit hour. Tuition, nonresident: full-time $15,789; part-time $877.17 per credit hour. *Required fees:* $37 per term. *Financial support:* In 2016–17, 15 students received support, including 32 teaching assistantships with tuition reimbursements available (averaging $11,025 per year); unspecified assistantships also available. Financial award application deadline: 1/1. *Faculty research:* Medieval philosophy, early modern philosophy (seventeenth-, eighteenth-, and twentieth-century Continental philosophy), feminist philosophy, social philosophy, ethics, philosophy of science. *Total annual research expenditures:* $93,216. *Unit head:* Dr. Roger Ariew, Professor and Chairperson, 813-974-8207, Fax: 813-974-5914, E-mail: rariew@usf.edu. *Application contact:* Dr. Joanne Waugh, Associate Professor, 813-974-5571, Fax: 813-974-5914, E-mail: jwaugh@usf.edu.
Website: http://philosophy.usf.edu/

**The University of Tennessee,** Graduate School, College of Arts and Sciences, Department of Philosophy, Knoxville, TN 37996. Offers medical ethics (MA, PhD); philosophy (MA, PhD); religious studies (MA). *Program availability:* Part-time. *Degree requirements:* For master's, thesis or alternative; for doctorate, one foreign language, thesis/dissertation. *Entrance requirements:* For master's and doctorate, GRE General Test, minimum GPA of 2.7. Additional exam requirements/recommendations for international students: Required—TOEFL. Electronic applications accepted.

**The University of Texas at Austin,** Graduate School, College of Liberal Arts, Department of Philosophy, Austin, TX 78712-1111. Offers PhD. *Program availability:* Part-time. Terminal master's awarded for partial completion of doctoral program. *Degree requirements:* For doctorate, one foreign language, thesis/dissertation. *Entrance requirements:* For doctorate, GRE General Test. Electronic applications accepted. *Faculty research:* Ancient philosophy, cognitive science, Continental philosophy, history and philosophy of science.

**The University of Texas at El Paso,** Graduate School, College of Liberal Arts, Department of Philosophy, El Paso, TX 79968-0001. Offers MA. *Degree requirements:* For master's, thesis, oral examination. *Entrance requirements:* For master's, GRE, 2 letters of recommendation.

**The University of Texas at San Antonio,** College of Liberal and Fine Arts, Department of Philosophy and Classics, San Antonio, TX 78249-0617. Offers MA. *Program availability:* Part-time. *Faculty:* 8 full-time (3 women). *Students:* 3 full-time (1 woman), 14 part-time (2 women); includes 7 minority (6 Hispanic/Latino; 1 Two or more races, non-Hispanic/Latino), 1 international. Average age 31. 6 applicants, 100% accepted, 5 enrolled. In 2016, 1 master's awarded. *Degree requirements:* For master's, comprehensive exam, thesis. *Entrance requirements:* For master's, GRE. Additional exam requirements/recommendations for international students: Required—TOEFL (minimum score 550 paper-based; 79 iBT). *Application deadline:* For fall admission, 7/1 for domestic students, 3/1 for international students; for spring admission, 11/1 for domestic students, 9/1 for international students. Application fee: $45 ($80 for international students). Electronic applications accepted. *Expenses:* Contact institution. *Financial support:* In 2016–17, 6 students received support. Career-related internships or fieldwork, scholarships/grants, and unspecified assistantships available. Financial award applicants required to submit FAFSA. *Faculty research:* Metaphysics, epistemology, ethics. *Total annual research expenditures:* $463. *Unit head:* Dr. Eve Browning, Department Chair, 210-458-6031, Fax: 210-458-6035, E-mail: eve.browning@utsa.edu. *Application contact:* Jill Hernandez, Graduate Advisor of Record, 210-458-6031, Fax: 210-458-6035, E-mail: jill.hernandez@utsa.edu.

**The University of Toledo,** College of Graduate Studies, College of Languages, Literature and Social Sciences, Department of Philosophy, Toledo, OH 43606-3390. Offers MA. *Program availability:* Part-time. *Degree requirements:* For master's, comprehensive exam, thesis, exam. *Entrance requirements:* For master's, minimum cumulative point-hour ratio of 2.7 for all previous academic work, three letters of recommendation. Additional exam requirements/recommendations for international students: Required—TOEFL (minimum score 550 paper-based; 80 iBT). Electronic applications accepted. *Faculty research:* History of philosophy, ethics, social/political philosophy, philosophy of science, European philosophy.

**University of Toronto,** School of Graduate Studies, Faculty of Arts and Science, Department of Philosophy, Toronto, ON M5S 1A1, Canada. Offers MA, PhD. *Program availability:* Part-time. *Degree requirements:* For doctorate, one foreign language, thesis/dissertation. *Entrance requirements:* For master's, GRE, 6 courses in philosophy; minimum A- average in philosophy courses, B overall; 2 letters of reference; writing sample; for doctorate, GRE, MA in philosophy, minimum A- average, 2 letters of reference, writing sample. Additional exam requirements/recommendations for international students: Required—TOEFL (minimum score 600 paper-based), TWE (minimum score 5). Electronic applications accepted.

**University of Utah,** Graduate School, College of Humanities, Department of Philosophy, Salt Lake City, UT 84112. Offers MA, MS, PhD. *Program availability:* Part-time. *Faculty:* 17 full-time (9 women), 3 part-time/adjunct (0 women). *Students:* 15 full-time (5 women), 6 part-time (1 woman); includes 2 minority (both Hispanic/Latino), 2 international. Average age 33. 38 applicants, 11% accepted, 4 enrolled. In 2016, 2 master's, 3 doctorates awarded. *Degree requirements:* For master's, comprehensive exam, thesis or alternative; for doctorate, comprehensive exam, thesis/dissertation, qualifying oral exam. *Entrance requirements:* For master's, GRE General Test, minimum undergraduate GPA of 3.0; for doctorate, GRE General Test. Additional exam requirements/recommendations for international students: Required—TOEFL (minimum score 650 paper-based). *Application deadline:* For fall admission, 1/15 priority date for domestic and international students. Application fee: $55 ($65 for international students). Electronic applications accepted. *Expenses:* Tuition, state resident: full-time $7011; part-time $3918.24 per credit hour. Tuition, nonresident: full-time $22,154; part-time $11,665.42 per credit hour. *Financial support:* In 2016–17, 13 students received support, including 2 fellowships with full tuition reimbursements available (averaging $1,750 per year); teaching assistantships with full tuition reimbursements available, Federal Work-Study, institutionally sponsored loans, scholarships/grants, health care benefits, and unspecified assistantships also available. Financial award application deadline: 2/15; financial award applicants required to submit FAFSA. *Faculty research:* Philosophy of biology, philosophy of science, applied ethics, practical reasoning, political philosophy, philosophy of cognitive science. *Total annual research expenditures:* $15,000. *Unit head:* Dr. Eric Hutton, Chair, 801-585-3765, Fax: 801-585-5195, E-mail: matt.haber@utah.edu. *Application contact:* Connie Gladden Corbett, Academic Advisor, 801-581-8162, Fax: 801-585-5195, E-mail: c.corbett@utah.edu. Website: http://www.hum.utah.edu/philosophy/

**University of Victoria,** Faculty of Graduate Studies, Faculty of Humanities, Department of Philosophy, Victoria, BC V8W 2Y2, Canada. Offers MA. *Program availability:* Part-time, evening/weekend. *Degree requirements:* For master's, thesis. *Entrance requirements:* For master's, writing sample. Additional exam requirements/recommendations for international students: Required—TOEFL (minimum score 575 paper-based), IELTS (minimum score 7). *Faculty research:* Ethics, metaphysics, philosophy of mind, history of philosophy, political philosophy.

**University of Virginia,** College and Graduate School of Arts and Sciences, Department of Philosophy, Charlottesville, VA 22903. Offers MA, PhD, JD/MA. *Faculty:* 15 full-time (5 women). *Students:* 25 full-time (7 women); includes 2 minority (both Asian, non-Hispanic/Latino), 7 international. Average age 28. 137 applicants, 9% accepted, 7 enrolled. In 2016, 4 doctorates awarded. *Degree requirements:* For master's, 2 papers; for doctorate, thesis/dissertation, 2 papers. *Entrance requirements:* For master's, GRE General Test, GRE Subject Test, 3 letters of recommendation, writing sample; for doctorate, GRE General Test, GRE Subject Test, 3 letters of recommendation; writing sample. Additional exam requirements/recommendations for international students: Required—TOEFL (minimum score 600 paper-based; 90 iBT), IELTS. *Application deadline:* For fall admission, 1/1 for domestic students, 1/5 for international students. Applications are processed on a rolling basis. Application fee: $60. Electronic applications accepted. *Expenses:* Tuition, state resident: full-time $15,026; part-time $834 per credit hour. Tuition, nonresident: full-time $25,168; part-time $1378 per credit

hour. *Required fees:* $2654. *Financial support:* Fellowships and teaching assistantships available. Financial award applicants required to submit FAFSA. *Unit head:* Talbot Brewer, Chair, 434-924-7701, Fax: 434-924-6927, E-mail: tbrewer@virginia.edu. *Application contact:* Antonia LoLordo, Director of Graduate Admissions, 434-924-7701, Fax: 434-924-6927, E-mail: lolordo@virginia.edu. Website: http://philosophy.virginia.edu/

**University of Washington,** Graduate School, College of Arts and Sciences, Department of Philosophy, Seattle, WA 98195. Offers classics and philosophy (PhD); philosophy (MA, PhD). Terminal master's awarded for partial completion of doctoral program. *Degree requirements:* For master's, 3 papers; for doctorate, thesis/dissertation, general exam. *Entrance requirements:* For master's and doctorate, GRE, minimum GPA of 3.0. Additional exam requirements/recommendations for international students: Required—TOEFL. *Faculty research:* History and philosophy of science, epistemology, Aristotle's metaphysics, ethics and politics, causation in modern philosophy.

**University of Waterloo,** Graduate Studies, Faculty of Arts, Department of Philosophy, Waterloo, ON N2L 3G1, Canada. Offers MA, PhD. *Degree requirements:* For master's, thesis or alternative; for doctorate, one foreign language, thesis/dissertation. *Entrance requirements:* For master's, honors degree, minimum B+ average, writing sample, resume; for doctorate, master's degree, minimum A- average, resume. Additional exam requirements/recommendations for international students: Required—TOEFL, IELTS, PTE. Electronic applications accepted. *Faculty research:* Logic, ethics, social/political, cognitive science, philosophy of science.

**The University of Western Ontario,** Faculty of Graduate Studies, Faculty of Arts and Humanities, Department of Philosophy, London, ON N6A 5B8, Canada. Offers MA, PhD. *Degree requirements:* For master's, 1 competency exam; for doctorate, comprehensive exam, thesis/dissertation, 2 competency exams. *Entrance requirements:* For master's, honors degree. Additional exam requirements/recommendations for international students: Required—TOEFL (minimum score 600 paper-based). Electronic applications accepted. *Faculty research:* Philosophy of science, history of philosophy, philosophy of law, ethics, epistemology.

**University of Windsor,** Faculty of Graduate Studies, Faculty of Arts and Social Sciences, Department of Philosophy, Windsor, ON N9B 3P4, Canada. Offers MA. *Program availability:* Part-time. *Degree requirements:* For master's, thesis. *Entrance requirements:* For master's, minimum B average. Additional exam requirements/recommendations for international students: Required—TOEFL (minimum score 600 paper-based). Electronic applications accepted. *Faculty research:* Informal logic, contemporary Continental philosophy, epistemology.

**University of Wisconsin–Madison,** Graduate School, College of Letters and Science, Department of Philosophy, Madison, WI 53706-1380. Offers MA, PhD. *Program availability:* Part-time. Terminal master's awarded for partial completion of doctoral program. *Degree requirements:* For master's, thesis, preliminary exams; for doctorate, thesis/dissertation, preliminary exams. *Entrance requirements:* For doctorate, GRE, BA in philosophy or related area. Additional exam requirements/recommendations for international students: Required—TOEFL. Electronic applications accepted. *Faculty research:* History of philosophy, logic, philosophy of science, philosophy of mind, metaphysics.

**University of Wisconsin–Milwaukee,** Graduate School, College of Letters and Science, Department of Philosophy, Milwaukee, WI 53201-0413. Offers MA. *Program availability:* Part-time. *Students:* 18 full-time (3 women); includes 2 minority (1 Black or African American, non-Hispanic/Latino; 1 Two or more races, non-Hispanic/Latino), 2 international. Average age 28. 73 applicants, 12% accepted, 9 enrolled. In 2016, 10 master's awarded. *Degree requirements:* For master's, thesis or alternative. *Entrance requirements:* For master's, GRE General Test. Additional exam requirements/recommendations for international students: Required—TOEFL (minimum score 550 paper-based; 79 iBT), IELTS (minimum score 6.5). *Application deadline:* For fall admission, 1/1 priority date for domestic students; for spring admission, 9/1 for domestic students. Applications are processed on a rolling basis. Application fee: $56 ($96 for international students). Electronic applications accepted. *Financial support:* In 2016–17, 2 fellowships, 19 teaching assistantships were awarded; career-related internships or fieldwork, unspecified assistantships, and project assistantships also available. Support available to part-time students. Financial award application deadline: 4/15; financial award applicants required to submit FAFSA. *Unit head:* Richard J. Tierney, Chair, 414-229-5217, E-mail: rtierney@uwm.edu. *Application contact:* Carla Bagnoli, General Information Contact, 414-229-5215, Fax: 414-229-6967, E-mail: cbagnoli@uwm.edu. Website: http://www.uwm.edu/dept/philosophy/

**University of Wyoming,** College of Arts and Sciences, Department of Philosophy, Laramie, WY 82071. Offers MA. *Program availability:* Part-time. *Degree requirements:* For master's, thesis, logic proficiency, first-year paper. *Entrance requirements:* For master's, GRE General Test, minimum GPA of 3.0. Additional exam requirements/recommendations for international students: Required—TOEFL (minimum score 525 paper-based). Electronic applications accepted. *Faculty research:* Philosophy of science, political and ethical theory, philosophy of language, epistemology, philosophy of mind, early modern philosophy.

**Vanderbilt University,** Department of Philosophy, Nashville, TN 37240-1001. Offers MA, PhD. *Faculty:* 15 full-time (4 women). *Students:* 26 full-time (17 women); includes 9 minority (1 Black or African American, non-Hispanic/Latino; 2 Asian, non-Hispanic/Latino; 3 Hispanic/Latino; 3 Two or more races, non-Hispanic/Latino). Average age 29. 156 applicants, 4% accepted, 5 enrolled. In 2016, 2 master's, 7 doctorates awarded. Terminal master's awarded for partial completion of doctoral program. *Degree requirements:* For doctorate, one foreign language, comprehensive exam, thesis/dissertation, final and qualifying exams. *Entrance requirements:* For doctorate, GRE General Test, writing sample. Additional exam requirements/recommendations for international students: Required—TOEFL (minimum score 570 paper-based; 88 iBT). *Application deadline:* For fall admission, 1/15 for domestic and international students. Electronic applications accepted. *Expenses:* Tuition: Part-time $1854 per credit hour. *Financial support:* Fellowships with full tuition reimbursements, teaching assistantships with full tuition reimbursements, Federal Work-Study, institutionally sponsored loans, scholarships/grants, and health care benefits available. Financial award application deadline: 1/15; financial award applicants required to submit CSS PROFILE or FAFSA. *Faculty research:* Ancient, medieval, and modern philosophy; philosophy of science; ethics; philosophy of language; philosophy of religion. *Unit head:* Dr. Robert Talisse, Chair, 615-343-5349, Fax: 615-343-7259, E-mail: robert.talisse@vanderbilt.edu. *Application contact:* Julian Wuerth, Director of Graduate Studies, 615-322-2637, Fax: 615-343-7259, E-mail: julian.wuerth@vanderbilt.edu. Website: http://www.vanderbilt.edu/AnS/philosophy/

**Villanova University,** Graduate School of Liberal Arts and Sciences, Department of Philosophy, Villanova, PA 19085-1699. Offers PhD. *Program availability:* Part-time, evening/weekend. *Faculty:* 5. *Students:* 52 full-time (22 women); includes 10 minority (1 Black or African American, non-Hispanic/Latino; 3 Asian, non-Hispanic/Latino; 5 Hispanic/Latino; 1 Two or more races, non-Hispanic/Latino), 5 international. Average age 31. 92 applicants, 7% accepted, 6 enrolled. In 2016, 10 doctorates awarded.

## Philosophy

*Degree requirements:* For doctorate, 2 foreign languages, comprehensive exam, thesis/dissertation. *Entrance requirements:* For doctorate, GRE, 3 recommendation letters, writing sample, curriculum vitae. Additional exam requirements/recommendations for international students: Required—TOEFL. *Application deadline:* For fall admission, 1/10 priority date for domestic and international students. Application fee: $50. *Financial support:* Research assistantships, teaching assistantships, scholarships/grants, and unspecified assistantships available. Financial award applicants required to submit FAFSA. *Unit head:* Dr. Yannik Thiem, Program Director, 610-519-5313. Website: http://www1.villanova.edu/villanova/artsci/philosophy/academic-programs/doctorate.html

**Virginia Polytechnic Institute and State University,** Graduate School, College of Liberal Arts and Human Sciences, Blacksburg, VA 24061. Offers career and technical education (MS Ed, Ed D, PhD, Ed S); communication (MA); counselor education (MA Ed, Ed D, PhD, Ed S); creative writing (MFA); curriculum and instruction (MA Ed, Ed D, PhD, Ed S); educational leadership and policy studies (MA Ed, Ed D, PhD, Ed S); educational research and evaluation (PhD); English (MA); foreign languages, cultures, and literatures (MA); higher education (PhD); higher education and student affairs (MA Ed); history (MA); human development (MS, PhD); material culture and public humanities (MA); philosophy (MA); political science (MA); rhetoric and writing (PhD); science and technology studies (MS, PhD); sociology (MS, PhD); theater arts (MFA). *Faculty:* 408 full-time (204 women), 3 part-time/adjunct (2 women). *Students:* 657 full-time (446 women), 457 part-time (292 women); includes 213 minority (114 Black or African American, non-Hispanic/Latino; 3 American Indian or Alaska Native, non-Hispanic/Latino; 29 Asian, non-Hispanic/Latino; 44 Hispanic/Latino; 23 Two or more races, non-Hispanic/Latino), 93 international. Average age 33. 805 applicants, 55% accepted, 328 enrolled. In 2016, 270 master's, 91 doctorates awarded. *Degree requirements:* For master's, comprehensive exam (for some programs), thesis (for some programs); for doctorate, comprehensive exam (for some programs), thesis/dissertation (for some programs). *Entrance requirements:* For master's and doctorate, GRE/GMAT. Additional exam requirements/recommendations for international students: Required—TOEFL (minimum score 80 iBT). *Application deadline:* For fall admission, 8/1 for domestic students, 4/1 for international students; for spring admission, 1/1 for domestic students, 9/1 for international students. Applications are processed on a rolling basis. Application fee: $75. Electronic applications accepted. *Expenses:* Tuition, state resident: full-time $12,467; part-time $692.50 per credit hour. Tuition, nonresident: full-time $25,095; part-time $1394.25 per credit hour. *Required fees:* $2669; $491.50 per semester. Tuition and fees vary according to course load, campus/location and program. *Financial support:* In 2016–17, 21 research assistantships with full tuition reimbursements (averaging $19,817 per year), 237 teaching assistantships with full tuition reimbursements (averaging $15,497 per year) were awarded. Financial award application deadline: 3/1; financial award applicants required to submit FAFSA. *Total annual research expenditures:* $6.6 million. *Unit head:* Rosemary Blieszner, Interim Dean, 540-231-6779, Fax: 540-231-7157, E-mail: liberalartsdean@vt.edu. *Application contact:* Chelsea Blanchet, Executive Assistant, 540-231-6779, Fax: 540-231-7157, E-mail: bchels1@vt.edu. Website: http://www.liberalarts.vt.edu/

**Washington University in St. Louis,** The Graduate School, Department of Philosophy, St. Louis, MO 63130-4899. Offers philosophy (PhD); philosophy-neuroscience-psychology (PhD). *Degree requirements:* For doctorate, thesis/dissertation. *Entrance requirements:* For doctorate, GRE General Test, sample of written work. Additional exam requirements/recommendations for international students: Required—TOEFL. Electronic applications accepted. *Faculty research:* Ethics; social, political philosophy; history of philosophy; philosophy of law; philosophy of science, of mind and of language; theory of knowledge; aesthetics.

**Wayne State University,** College of Liberal Arts and Sciences, Department of Philosophy, Detroit, MI 48202. Offers MA, PhD. *Faculty:* 9. *Students:* 11 full-time (1 woman), 3 part-time (0 women); includes 2 minority (both Hispanic/Latino), 1 international. Average age 30. 34 applicants, 29% accepted, 4 enrolled. In 2016, 3 master's, 2 doctorates awarded. Terminal master's awarded for partial completion of doctoral program. *Degree requirements:* For master's, comprehensive exam, thesis (for some programs), essay or thesis; for doctorate, one foreign language, comprehensive exam, thesis/dissertation, oral exam, classroom lectures under supervision of Philosophy Department. *Entrance requirements:* For master's, GRE if upper-division GPA is below 2.75 (or 3.0 if from unaccredited college), writing sample; personal statement; three letters of recommendation; prerequisite courses in logic, value theory, and the history of philosophy; for doctorate, minimum undergraduate upper-division GPA of 3.0, undergraduate major or substantial work in philosophy, writing sample, personal statement, three letters of recommendation. Additional exam requirements/recommendations for international students: Required—TOEFL (minimum score 550 paper-based), TWE (minimum score 5.5), Michigan English Language Assessment Battery (minimum score 85); Recommended—IELTS (minimum score 6.5). *Application deadline:* For fall admission, 2/1 priority date for domestic and international students; for winter admission, 10/1 priority date for domestic students, 9/1 priority date for international students. Applications are processed on a rolling basis. Application fee: $50. Electronic applications accepted. *Expenses:* $16,503 per year resident tuition and fees, $33,697 per year non-resident tuition and fees. *Financial support:* In 2016–17, 11 students received support, including 2 fellowships with tuition reimbursements available (averaging $13,500 per year), 1 research assistantship with tuition reimbursement available (averaging $21,594 per year), 6 teaching assistantships with tuition reimbursements available (averaging $17,994 per year); scholarships/grants and unspecified assistantships also available. Financial award applicants required to submit FAFSA. *Faculty research:* Epistemology, ethics and value theory, history and philosophy, metaphysics, philosophy of logic, language, and mathematics. *Unit head:* Dr. John Corvino, Professor and Chair, 313-577-2475, E-mail: j.corvino@wayne.edu. *Application contact:* Dr. Eric Hiddleston, Director of Graduate Admissions/Graduate Advisor, E-mail: eric.hiddleston@wayne.edu. Website: http://clas.wayne.edu/Philosophy

**West Chester University of Pennsylvania,** College of Arts and Humanities, Department of Philosophy, West Chester, PA 19383. Offers business ethics (Certificate); health care ethics (Certificate); philosophy (MA); philosophy: applied ethics (MA). *Program availability:* Part-time, evening/weekend. *Faculty:* 8 full-time (4 women). *Students:* 1 full-time (0 women), 13 part-time (1 woman). Average age 44. 4 applicants, 75% accepted, 2 enrolled. In 2016, 3 master's awarded. *Degree requirements:* For master's, comprehensive exam, thesis optional, 30 credits. *Entrance requirements:* For master's, GRE or writing sample, three letters of reference, minimum undergraduate GPA of 2.8; for Certificate, undergraduate transcripts, minimum undergraduate GPA of 2.8. Additional exam requirements/recommendations for international students: Required—TOEFL or IELTS. *Application deadline:* For fall admission, 5/15 for international students; for spring admission, 10/15 for international students. Applications are processed on a rolling basis. Application fee: $50. Electronic applications accepted. *Expenses:* Tuition, state resident: full-time $8694; part-time $483 per credit. Tuition, nonresident: full-time $13,050; part-time $725 per credit. *Required fees:* $2399; $119.05 per credit. Tuition and fees vary according to campus/location and program. *Financial support:* Scholarships/grants and unspecified assistantships available. Financial award application deadline: 2/15; financial award applicants required to submit FAFSA. *Faculty research:* Ethics: theory and application; social and political, feminist, continental, Asian, post-colonial, American pragmatism, analytic philosophy. *Unit head:* Dr. Helen Daley Schroepfer, Chair, 610-436-2841, E-mail: hschroepfer@wcupa.edu. *Application contact:* Dr. Joan Woolfrey, Graduate Coordinator, 610-436-0731, E-mail: jwoolfrey@wcupa.edu. Website: http://www.wcupa.edu/arts-humanities/philosophy/

**Western Michigan University,** Graduate College, College of Arts and Sciences, Department of Philosophy, Kalamazoo, MI 49008. Offers MA. *Degree requirements:* For master's, thesis optional.

**Wilfrid Laurier University,** Faculty of Graduate and Postdoctoral Studies, Faculty of Arts, Department of Philosophy, Waterloo, ON N2L 3C5, Canada. Offers agency (MA); community (MA); self (MA). *Entrance requirements:* For master's, honours BA in philosophy or equivalent with minimum B+ average in philosophy and in final year. Additional exam requirements/recommendations for international students: Required—TOEFL (minimum score 89 iBT). Electronic applications accepted. *Faculty research:* Self, agency, community.

**Yale University,** Graduate School of Arts and Sciences, Department of Philosophy, New Haven, CT 06520. Offers PhD. *Degree requirements:* For doctorate, 2 foreign languages, thesis/dissertation. *Entrance requirements:* For doctorate, GRE General Test.

**York University,** Faculty of Graduate Studies, Faculty of Liberal Arts and Professional Studies, Program in Philosophy, Toronto, ON M3J 1P3, Canada. Offers MA, PhD. *Program availability:* Part-time. *Degree requirements:* For master's, thesis or alternative; for doctorate, one foreign language, thesis/dissertation. Electronic applications accepted.

# Section 12
# Religious Studies

This section contains a directory of institutions offering graduate work in religious studies. Additional information about programs listed in the directory may be obtained by writing directly to the dean of a graduate school or chair of a department at the address given in the directory.

For programs offering related work, see also in this book *Area and Cultural Studies, History, Humanities,* and *Philosophy.* In another guide in this series:

**Graduate Programs in Business, Education, Information Studies, Law & Social Work**

See *Subject Areas (Religious Education)*

## CONTENTS

### Program Directories

# Missions and Missiology

**Abilene Christian University,** Graduate Programs, College of Biblical Studies, Graduate School of Theology, Program in Divinity, Abilene, TX 79699. Offers ministry (M Div); missions (M Div). *Accreditation:* ATS. *Program availability:* Part-time, evening/weekend, blended/hybrid learning. *Students:* 38 full-time (7 women), 18 part-time (7 women); includes 13 minority (11 Black or African American, non-Hispanic/Latino; 1 Asian, non-Hispanic/Latino; 1 Hispanic/Latino), 6 international. 49 applicants, 67% accepted, 17 enrolled. In 2016, 5 master's awarded. *Degree requirements:* For master's, comprehensive exam, e-portfolio review. *Entrance requirements:* Additional exam requirements/recommendations for international students: Required—TOEFL (minimum score 80 iBT), IELTS (minimum score 6), PTE. *Application deadline:* For fall admission, 8/11 for domestic students; for spring admission, 11/1 for domestic students. Applications are processed on a rolling basis. Application fee: $50. Electronic applications accepted. *Expenses:* $618 per credit hour. *Financial support:* In 2016–17, 6 students received support. Scholarships/grants available. Financial award application deadline: 4/1; financial award applicants required to submit FAFSA. *Unit head:* Dr. Kelli Gibson, Graduate Advisor, 325-674-3709, Fax: 325-674-6716, E-mail: kelli.gibson@acu.edu. *Application contact:* Corey Patterson, Director of Graduate Admission and Recruiting, 325-674-6566, Fax: 325-674-6717, E-mail: gradinfo@acu.edu.
Website: http://www.acu.edu/graduate/academics/divinity.html

**Abilene Christian University,** Graduate Programs, College of Biblical Studies, Graduate School of Theology, Program in Global Service, Abilene, TX 79699. Offers MA. *Program availability:* Part-time. *Students:* 4 full-time (2 women), 9 part-time (3 women); includes 1 minority (Two or more races, non-Hispanic/Latino). 7 applicants, 100% accepted, 4 enrolled. In 2016, 1 master's awarded. *Degree requirements:* For master's, comprehensive exam, thesis. *Entrance requirements:* Additional exam requirements/recommendations for international students: Required—TOEFL (minimum score 80 iBT), IELTS (minimum score 6), PTE. *Application deadline:* For fall admission, 4/1 priority date for domestic students; for spring admission, 11/1 for domestic students. Applications are processed on a rolling basis. Application fee: $50. Electronic applications accepted. *Expenses:* $618 per credit hour. *Financial support:* In 2016–17, 2 students received support. Teaching assistantships, career-related internships or fieldwork, and scholarships/grants available. Financial award application deadline: 4/1; financial award applicants required to submit FAFSA. *Faculty research:* Animism, contextualization, missions education. *Unit head:* Dr. Chris Flanders, Graduate Adviser, 325-674-3742, Fax: 325-674-6180, E-mail: chris.flanders@acu.edu. *Application contact:* Corey Patterson, Director of Graduate Admission and Recruiting, 325-674-6566, Fax: 325-674-6717, E-mail: gradinfo@acu.edu.
Website: http://www.acu.edu/online/academics/global-service.html

**Anderson University,** School of Theology, Anderson, IN 46012-3495. Offers missions (MA); theology (M Div, MTS, D Min). *Accreditation:* ACIPE; ATS. *Program availability:* Part-time. *Degree requirements:* For master's, variable foreign language requirement, thesis (for some programs); for doctorate, thesis/dissertation. *Faculty research:* Small-church/bivocational ministry, women in ministry.

**Asbury Theological Seminary,** Graduate and Professional Programs, Wilmore, KY 40390-1199. Offers M Div, MA, MAAS, MACE, MACL, MACM, MACP, MAMFC, MAMHC, MAPC, MASF, MAYM, Th M, D Min, PhD, Certificate. *Accreditation:* ATS. *Program availability:* Part-time, online learning. Terminal master's awarded for partial completion of doctoral program. *Degree requirements:* For master's, thesis (for some programs); for doctorate, thesis/dissertation, qualifying exam. *Entrance requirements:* For master's, minimum GPA of 2.75; for doctorate, minimum GPA of 3.0. Additional exam requirements/recommendations for international students: Required—TOEFL, IELTS. Electronic applications accepted.

**Assemblies of God Theological Seminary,** Graduate and Professional Programs, Springfield, MO 65802. Offers Biblical interpretation and theology (PhD); Christian ministries (MA); divinity (M Div); intercultural studies (MA, PhD); ministry (D Min); missiology (DAIS); pastoral studies (MPL); theological studies (MA, Th M). *Accreditation:* ATS. *Program availability:* Part-time, evening/weekend, 100% online. *Degree requirements:* For master's, variable foreign language requirement; for doctorate, thesis/dissertation. *Entrance requirements:* For master's, minimum GPA of 2.5; for doctorate, GRE (for PhD in Bible theology), minimum GPA of 3.0. Additional exam requirements/recommendations for international students: Required—TOEFL (minimum score 550 paper-based; 80 iBT). Electronic applications accepted.

**Bethel Seminary,** Graduate and Professional Programs, St. Paul, MN 55112-6998. Offers Anglican studies (Certificate); children's and family ministry (MA); Christian studies (Certificate); Christian thought (MA); church planting (Certificate); Greek and Hebrew language (M Div); Greek language (M Div); Hebrew language (M Div); marriage and family therapy (MA, Certificate); mental health counseling (MA); ministry (MA, D Min); ministry practice (Certificate); theological studies (MA, Certificate); transformational leadership (MA); young life youth ministry (Certificate). *Accreditation:* ACIPE. *Program availability:* Part-time, evening/weekend, blended/hybrid learning. *Faculty:* 14 full-time (4 women), 37 part-time/adjunct (17 women). *Students:* 369 full-time (165 women), 147 part-time (43 women); includes 138 minority (48 Black or African American, non-Hispanic/Latino; 45 Asian, non-Hispanic/Latino; 28 Hispanic/Latino; 2 Native Hawaiian or other Pacific Islander, non-Hispanic/Latino; 15 Two or more races, non-Hispanic/Latino), 15 international. 322 applicants, 75% accepted, 174 enrolled. In 2016, 168 master's, 24 doctorates, 6 other advanced degrees awarded. *Degree requirements:* For master's, variable foreign language requirement, thesis (for some programs); for doctorate, thesis/dissertation. *Entrance requirements:* For master's, letters of reference, transcripts, personal statement; for doctorate, M Div, letters of reference, organizational support; for Certificate, letters of reference, family essay, personal statement, and family of origin paper (for marriage and family therapy). Additional exam requirements/recommendations for international students: Required—TOEFL (minimum score 550 paper-based; 87 iBT). *Application deadline:* For fall admission, 8/1 priority date for domestic students, 8/1 for international students; for winter admission, 12/1 priority date for domestic students; for spring admission, 1/1 priority date for domestic students. Applications are processed on a rolling basis. Application fee: $0. Electronic applications accepted. *Expenses:* Contact institution. *Financial support:* In 2016–17, 404 students received support. Teaching assistantships, career-related internships or fieldwork, Federal Work-Study, and scholarships/grants available. Financial award applicants required to submit FAFSA. *Faculty research:* Nature of theology, ethics, Biblical commentaries, nature of God, science and theology. *Unit head:* Dr. David Clark, Vice-President and Dean, 651-638-6659, E-mail: d-clark@bethel.edu. *Application contact:* Jen Niska, Director of Admissions, 651-638-6288, Fax: 651-638-6002, E-mail: seminary-admissions@bethel.edu.
Website: https://www.bethel.edu/seminary

**Biblical Theological Seminary,** Graduate and Professional Programs, Hatfield, PA 19440-2499. Offers advanced missional leadership (D Min); advanced pastoral studies (Certificate); biblical counseling (Certificate); biblical studies (MA, Certificate); counseling (MA); ministry (M Div, MA); missional theology (MA). *Accreditation:* ATS. *Program availability:* Part-time, evening/weekend. *Faculty:* 9 full-time (1 woman), 21 part-time/adjunct (4 women). *Students:* 145 full-time (54 women), 111 part-time (44 women); includes 98 minority (57 Black or African American, non-Hispanic/Latino; 1 American Indian or Alaska Native, non-Hispanic/Latino; 35 Asian, non-Hispanic/Latino; 4 Hispanic/Latino; 1 Two or more races, non-Hispanic/Latino), 67 international. Average age 39. 165 applicants, 64% accepted, 95 enrolled. In 2016, 47 master's, 7 doctorates awarded. *Degree requirements:* For master's, variable foreign language requirement, thesis optional; for doctorate, thesis/dissertation. *Entrance requirements:* Additional exam requirements/recommendations for international students: Required—TOEFL (minimum score 550 paper-based; 80 iBT). *Application deadline:* Applications are processed on a rolling basis. Application fee: $30. Electronic applications accepted. *Expenses:* Tuition: Full-time $12,360; part-time $6180 per credit. *Required fees:* $75; $75 per credit. $50 per semester. *Financial support:* In 2016–17, 170 students received support. Career-related internships or fieldwork, institutionally sponsored loans, and scholarships/grants available. Support available to part-time students. Financial award application deadline: 8/30; financial award applicants required to submit FAFSA. *Faculty research:* Theology, culture, Biblical interpretation. *Application contact:* Rev. Michael Heath, Student Advancement Counselor, 215-368-5000 Ext. 152, Fax: 215-368-7002, E-mail: mheath@biblical.edu.
Website: http://www.biblical.edu/

**Biola University,** Cook School of Intercultural Studies, La Mirada, CA 90639-0001. Offers anthropology (MA); applied linguistics (MA); intercultural education (PhD); intercultural studies (MA, PhD); linguistics (Certificate); linguistics and Biblical languages (MA); missiology (D Miss); missions (MA); teaching English to speakers of other languages (MA, Certificate); teaching English to speakers of other languages (online) (MA). *Program availability:* Part-time, 100% online. *Entrance requirements:* For master's, minimum undergraduate GPA of 3.0; for doctorate, master's degree or equivalent, 3 years of cross-cultural experience, minimum graduate GPA of 3.3. Additional exam requirements/recommendations for international students: Required—TOEFL. Electronic applications accepted. *Faculty research:* Linguistics, anthropology, intercultural studies, teaching English to speakers of other languages, missions, missiology.

**Biola University,** Talbot School of Theology, La Mirada, CA 90639-0001. Offers adult/family ministry (MACE); Bible exposition (MA, Th M); Biblical and theological studies (Certificate); biblical and theological studies/diversified (MA); children's ministry (MACE); Christian education (M Div); cross-cultural education ministry (MACE); educational studies (Ed D, PhD); evangelism and discipleship (M Div); general Christian education (MACE); Messianic Jewish studies (M Div, Certificate); missions and intercultural studies (M Div); New Testament (MA, Th M); Old Testament (MA); Old Testament and Semitics (Th M); pastoral and general ministry (M Div); pastoral care and counseling (M Div, MACML); philosophy (MA); preaching and pastoral ministry (MACML); spiritual formation (M Div, Certificate); spiritual formation and soul care (MA); sports ministry (MACML); theology (MA, Th M, D Min, Certificate); youth ministry (MACE). *Accreditation:* ATS. *Program availability:* Part-time, evening/weekend. *Entrance requirements:* For master's, bachelor's degree from accredited college or university; minimum GPA of 2.6 (for M Div), 3.0 (for MA); for doctorate, M Div or MA. Additional exam requirements/recommendations for international students: Required—TOEFL (minimum score 600 paper-based; 88 iBT). Electronic applications accepted. *Faculty research:* New Testament, Old Testament, spiritual formation, Christian education, theological studies, Christian ministry, preaching and pastoral ministry, language and literature, bible exposition, Christian leadership.

**Boston University,** School of Theology, Boston, MA 02118. Offers chaplaincy (M Div); choral conducting (MSM); church and the arts (M Div); constructive theology and ethics (PhD), including constructive theology, theological ethics; ecological theology and ethics (MTS); global and community engagement (M Div); history and hermeneutics (PhD), including Biblical studies, church history, liturgical studies, mission studies; organ (MSM); pastoral ministry (M Div); practical theology (PhD), including church and society, congregation and community, evangelism and missiology, homiletics, leadership and administration, pastoral theology and psychology, religious education, spirituality studies, worship; religion and conflict transformation (MTS); religion and science (MTS); religion and the academy (M Div); spirituality studies (MTS); theology (MTS, STM); transcultural studies (MTS); transformational leadership (D Min); M Div/MSM; M Div/MSW; MTS/MSW. PhD in history and hermeneutics: mission studies offered in collaboration with Gordon-Conwell Theological Seminary. *Accreditation:* ACIPE; ATS. *Program availability:* Part-time, blended/hybrid learning. *Faculty:* 34 full-time (14 women), 7 part-time/adjunct (3 women). *Students:* 260 full-time (131 women), 69 part-time (30 women); includes 69 minority (36 Black or African American, non-Hispanic/Latino; 10 Asian, non-Hispanic/Latino; 16 Hispanic/Latino; 7 Two or more races, non-Hispanic/Latino), 53 international. Average age 35. 234 applicants, 71% accepted, 106 enrolled. In 2016, 78 master's, 9 doctorates awarded. *Degree requirements:* For master's, comprehensive exam (for some programs), thesis optional, contextual education; for doctorate, 2 foreign languages, comprehensive exam, thesis/dissertation. *Entrance requirements:* For master's, minimum GPA of 3.0; for doctorate, GRE General Test, minimum GPA of 3.3. Additional exam requirements/recommendations for international students: Required—TOEFL (minimum score 570 paper-based; 89 iBT). *Application deadline:* For fall admission, 1/15 priority date for domestic and international students; for spring admission, 10/15 priority date for domestic and international students. Applications are processed on a rolling basis. Application fee: $95. Electronic applications accepted. *Expenses:* $19,500 per year tuition; $156 per semester student service fee; $54 per semester community service fee; $199 per semester health and wellness fee. *Financial support:* In 2016–17, 252 students received support, including 78 fellowships with full tuition reimbursements available (averaging $4,537 per year), 32 research assistantships (averaging $6,000 per year), 32 teaching assistantships with full and partial tuition reimbursements available (averaging $20,000 per year); career-related internships or fieldwork, Federal Work-Study, institutionally sponsored loans, scholarships/grants, traineeships, health care benefits, tuition waivers (full and partial), and unspecified assistantships also available. Support available to part-time students. Financial award application deadline: 7/15; financial award applicants required to submit FAFSA. *Faculty research:* Practical theology, Biblical studies, theology and ethical, history of Christianity. *Total annual research expenditures:* $2.5 million. *Unit head:* Rev. Dr. Mary Elizabeth Moore, Dean, 617-353-3050, Fax: 617-353-3061, E-mail: memoore@bu.edu. *Application contact:* Rev. Anastasia Kidd, Director of Admissions and College Relations, 617-353-3036, Fax: 617-358-0140, E-mail: sthadmis@bu.edu. Website: http://www.bu.edu/sth

**Briercrest Seminary,** Graduate Programs, Program in Christian Ministries, Caronport, SK S0H 0S0, Canada. Offers leadership (MA); marriage and family counseling (MA); missions (MA); pastoral counseling (MA); worship (MA); youth and family ministry (MA). *Program availability:* Part-time. *Degree requirements:* For master's, comprehensive exam, thesis optional. *Entrance requirements:* Additional exam requirements/ recommendations for international students: Required—TOEFL (minimum score 550 paper-based).

**Calvin Theological Seminary,** Graduate and Professional Programs, Grand Rapids, MI 49546-4387. Offers Bible and theology (MA); divinity (M Div), including ancient near eastern languages and literature, contextual ministry, evangelism and teaching, history of Christianity, new church development, New Testament, Old Testament, pastoral care and leadership, preaching and worship, theological studies, youth and family ministries; educational ministry (MA); historical theology (PhD); missions and evangelism (MA); pastoral care (MA); philosophical and moral theology (PhD); systematic theology (PhD); theological studies (MTS); theology (Th M); worship (MA); youth and family ministries (MA). *Accreditation:* ACIPE; ATS. *Program availability:* Part-time. *Degree requirements:* For master's, variable foreign language requirement, thesis (for some programs); for doctorate, 4 foreign languages, comprehensive exam, thesis/dissertation. *Entrance requirements:* For doctorate, GRE General Test, Hebrew, Greek, and a modern foreign language. Additional exam requirements/recommendations for international students: Required—TOEFL (minimum score 550 paper-based), TWE (minimum score 4). Electronic applications accepted. *Faculty research:* Recent Trinity theory, Christian anthropology, Proverbs, reformed confessions, Paul's view of law.

**Catholic Theological Union,** Graduate and Professional Programs, Chicago, IL 60615-5698. Offers biblical spirituality (Certificate); cross-cultural ministries (D Min); cross-cultural missions (Certificate); divinity (M Div); liturgical studies (Certificate); liturgy (D Min); pastoral studies (MAPS, Certificate); spiritual formation (Certificate); spirituality (D Min); theology (MA); M Div/MA; M Div/MSW; M Div/PhD. M Div/PhD offered jointly with University of Chicago; M Div/MSW with Loyola University Chicago and University of Chicago. *Accreditation:* ACIPE. *Program availability:* Part-time, evening/weekend. *Degree requirements:* For master's, one foreign language, comprehensive exam (for some programs), thesis (for some programs); for doctorate, thesis/dissertation. *Entrance requirements:* For doctorate, master's degree, 5 years of active ministry. *Faculty research:* Doctrine, sacraments, ethics, Bible.

**Central Baptist Theological Seminary,** Graduate and Professional Programs, Shawnee, KS 66226. Offers missional church studies (MA); theological studies (MA); theology (M Div, Diploma). *Accreditation:* ACIPE; ATS (one or more programs are accredited). *Program availability:* Part-time. *Degree requirements:* For master's, thesis optional. *Entrance requirements:* Additional exam requirements/recommendations for international students: Required—TOEFL (minimum score 547 paper-based; 77 iBT). Electronic applications accepted.

**Charlotte Christian College and Theological Seminary,** Graduate Program, Charlotte, NC 28205. Offers urban Christian ministry (MA), including church planting, multi-cultural studies, sacred music, youth ministry. *Program availability:* Part-time, evening/weekend. *Degree requirements:* For master's, thesis. *Entrance requirements:* For master's, MAT, writing sample/essay. Additional exam requirements/ recommendations for international students: Required—TOEFL, IELTS. Electronic applications accepted. *Expenses:* Contact institution.

**Clarks Summit University,** Baptist Bible Seminary, South Abington Township, PA 18411. Offers Biblical apologetics (MA); church education (M Div, M Min); church planting (M Div, M Min); global ministry (M Div, M Min); leadership in communication (D Min); leadership in counseling and spiritual development (D Min); leadership in global ministry (D Min); leadership in pastoral ministry (D Min); leadership in theological studies (D Min); military chaplaincy (M Div); ministry (PhD); organizational leadership (M Min); outreach pastor (M Div, M Min); pastoral counseling (M Div, M Min); pastoral leadership (M Div, M Min); theology (Th M); worship ministries leadership (M Div, M Min); youth pastor (M Div, M Min). *Program availability:* Part-time, evening/weekend, online learning. Terminal master's awarded for partial completion of doctoral program. *Degree requirements:* For master's, 2 foreign languages, thesis, oral exam (for M Div); for doctorate, 2 foreign languages, comprehensive exam (for some programs), thesis/ dissertation, oral exam. *Entrance requirements:* For doctorate, Greek and Hebrew entrance exams (for PhD). Electronic applications accepted.

**Clarks Summit University,** Graduate Studies, South Abington Township, PA 18411. Offers Bible (MA); counseling (MA, MS); curriculum and instruction (M Ed); educational administration (M Ed); intercultural studies (MA); literature (MA); missions (MA); organizational leadership (MA); reading specialist (M Ed); secondary English/ communications (M Ed); social entrepreneurship (MA); worldview studies (MA). MA in missions program available only for Association of Baptists for World Evangelism missionary personnel. *Program availability:* Part-time, evening/weekend, online learning. *Entrance requirements:* Additional exam requirements/recommendations for international students: Required—TOEFL (minimum score 500 paper-based).

**Columbia International University,** Seminary and School of Ministry, Columbia, SC 29230-3122. Offers academic ministries (M Div); Bible and theology (Certificate); bible exposition (M Div, MABE); Biblical ministry (Certificate); chaplaincy (M Div); intercultural studies (MAIS); leadership (D Min); member care (D Min); missions (D Min); preaching (D Min); theological studies (MA). *Accreditation:* ATS (one or more programs are accredited). *Program availability:* Part-time, evening/weekend. *Degree requirements:* For doctorate, comprehensive exam, thesis/dissertation. *Entrance requirements:* For doctorate, 3 years of ministerial experience, M Div. Additional exam requirements/ recommendations for international students: Required—TOEFL. Electronic applications accepted.

**Dallas Baptist University,** Graduate School of Ministry, Program in Christian Ministry, Dallas, TX 75211-9299. Offers chaplaincy (MA); Christian ministry and education (MA); counseling ministry (MA); family ministry (MA); general ministry (MA); heritage and missions (MA); leading the nonprofit organization (MA); ministry leadership (MA); professional life coaching (MA); urban ministry (MA); worship ministry (MA). *Program availability:* Part-time, evening/weekend, 100% online, blended/hybrid learning. *Application deadline:* Applications are processed on a rolling basis. Application fee: $25. Electronic applications accepted. Application fee is waived when completed online. *Expenses: Tuition:* Full-time $15,408; part-time $856 per credit hour. *Required fees:* $400 per semester. Tuition and fees vary according to course load and degree level. *Unit head:* Dr. Tom Vann, Director, 214-333-5805, E-mail: tomv@dbu.edu. *Application contact:* Bobby Soto, Director of Admissions, 214-333-5242, E-mail: graduate@dbu.edu. Website: http://www3.dbu.edu/gsom/Christian-Ministry/

**Dallas Baptist University,** Graduate School of Ministry, Program in Global Leadership, Dallas, TX 75211-9299. Offers church planting (MA); East Asian Studies (MA); English as a second language (MA); general studies (MA); global communication (MA); global studies (MA); international business (MA); leading the nonprofit organization (MA); missions (MA); small group ministry (MA); urban ministry (MA). *Program availability:*

Part-time, evening/weekend. *Application deadline:* Applications are processed on a rolling basis. Application fee: $25. Electronic applications accepted. Application fee is waived when completed online. *Expenses: Tuition:* Full-time $15,408; part-time $856 per credit hour. *Required fees:* $400 per semester. Tuition and fees vary according to course load and degree level. *Unit head:* Dr. Bob Garrett, Director, 214-333-5508, E-mail: bobg@dbu.edu. *Application contact:* Bobby Soto, Director of Admissions, 214-333-5242, E-mail: graduate@dbu.edu. Website: http://www3.dbu.edu/gsom/global-leadership

**Dallas Baptist University,** Liberal Arts Program, Dallas, TX 75211-9299. Offers art (MLA); Christian studies (MLA); commercial art (MLA); East Asian studies (MLA); English (MLA); English as a second language (MLA); fine arts (MLA); history (MLA); missions (MLA); political science (MLA). *Program availability:* Part-time, evening/ weekend, 100% online, blended/hybrid learning. *Application deadline:* Applications are processed on a rolling basis. Application fee: $25. Electronic applications accepted. Application fee is waived when completed online. *Expenses: Tuition:* Full-time $15,408; part-time $856 per credit hour. *Required fees:* $400 per semester. Tuition and fees vary according to course load and degree level. *Faculty research:* Milton and seventeenth-century Puritans, inter-Biblical years, nineteenth-century literature, Latin American and Texas history. *Unit head:* Jared Ingram, Director, 214-333-5584, E-mail: jaredi@dbu.edu. *Application contact:* Bobby Soto, Director of Admissions, 214-333-5242, E-mail: graduate@dbu.edu. Website: http://www3.dbu.edu/mla/index

**Dallas Baptist University,** Professional Development Program, Dallas, TX 75211-9299. Offers accounting (MA); church leadership (MA); communication (MA); counseling (MA); criminal justice (MA); English as a second language (MA); finance (MA); higher education (MA); leadership studies (MA); management (MA); management information systems (MA); marketing (MA); missions (MA); professional life coaching (MA); training and development (MA). *Program availability:* Part-time, evening/weekend, 100% online, blended/hybrid learning. *Application deadline:* Applications are processed on a rolling basis. Application fee: $25. Electronic applications accepted. Application fee is waived when completed online. *Expenses: Tuition:* Full-time $15,408; part-time $856 per credit hour. *Required fees:* $400 per semester. Tuition and fees vary according to course load and degree level. *Unit head:* Jared Ingram, Director, 214-333-5584, E-mail: jaredi@dbu.edu. *Application contact:* Bobby Soto, Director of Admissions, 214-333-5242, E-mail: graduate@dbu.edu. Website: http://www3.dbu.edu/graduate/mapd.asp

**Dallas Theological Seminary,** Graduate Programs, Dallas, TX 75204-6499. Offers adult education (Th M); apologetics (Th M); Bible backgrounds (Th M); Bible translation (Th M); Biblical and theological studies (Certificate); biblical counseling (MA); biblical exegesis and linguistics (MA); biblical exposition (PhD); biblical studies (MA); Biblical theology (Th M); children's education (Th M); Christian education (MA, D Min); Christian leadership (MA); cross-cultural ministries (MA); educational administration (Th M); educational leadership (Th M); evangelism and discipleship (Th M); exposition of Biblical books (Th M); family life education (Th M); general studies (Th M); Hebrew and cognate studies (Th M); hermeneutics (Th M); historical theology (Th M); homiletics (Th M); intercultural ministries (Th M); Jesus studies (Th M); leadership studies (Th M); media and communication (MA); media arts (Th M); ministry (D Min); ministry with women (Th M); New Testament studies (Th M, PhD); Old Testament studies (Th M, PhD); parachurch ministries (Th M); pastoral care and counseling (Th M); pastoral theology and practice (Th M); philosophy (Th M); sacred theology (STM); spiritual formation (Th M); systematic theology (Th M); teaching in Christian institutions (Th M); theological studies (PhD); urban ministries (Th M); worship studies (Th M); youth education (Th M). *Program availability:* Part-time, online learning. *Degree requirements:* For master's, variable foreign language requirement, thesis (for some programs); for doctorate, 2 foreign languages, thesis/dissertation. *Entrance requirements:* For master's, GRE or MAT (if minimum undergraduate cumulative GPA is below 2.5 or undergraduate degree is unaccredited). Additional exam requirements/recommendations for international students: Required—TOEFL (minimum score 575 paper-based; 85 iBT), TWE. Electronic applications accepted.

**Evangelical Seminary,** Graduate and Professional Programs, Myerstown, PA 17067-1212. Offers Biblical studies (MAR); congregational ministry (M Div); global and contextual studies (M Div, MAR); historical and theological studies (MAR); interdisciplinary studies (MAR); marriage and family counseling (MA); marriage and family therapy (MA); New Testament (MAR); Old Testament (MAR); spiritual formation (MAR); teaching ministry (M Div); youth ministry (M Div). *Accreditation:* ATS (one or more programs are accredited). *Program availability:* Part-time, online learning. *Degree requirements:* For master's, 2 foreign languages. *Entrance requirements:* For master's, minimum GPA of 2.5. Additional exam requirements/recommendations for international students: Required—TOEFL (minimum score 550 paper-based). *Faculty research:* Literary form and structure within the Hebrew and Greek scriptures, Wesley studies, esoteric biblical languages, the Mosaic law and the Christian, ethics.

**Faulkner University,** College of Biblical Studies, Montgomery, AL 36109-3398. Offers ministry (MABS); missions (MABS); New Testament (MABS); Old Testament (MABS); youth and family ministry (MABS).

**Fresno Pacific University,** Biblical Seminary, Program in Urban Mission, Fresno, CA 93702-4709. Offers MA. *Entrance requirements:* For master's, minimum GPA of 2.5.

**Fuller Theological Seminary,** Graduate Programs, Pasadena, CA 91182. Offers Christian leadership (MACL); clinical psychology (PhD, Psy D); family studies (MA); global leadership (MA); global ministries (D Min); global ministries (Korean language) (D Min); intercultural studies (MA, Th M, PhD); intercultural studies (Korean language) (MA); marital and family therapy (MS); marriage and family enrichment (Certificate); ministry (M Div, D Min); missiology (D Miss); missiology (Korean language) (Th M); theology (MA, Th M, PhD), including evangelism (MA), family life education (MA), pastoral ministry (MA), recovery ministry (MA), worship music ministry (MA), worship, theology, and the arts (MA), youth, family, and culture (MA); theology and ministry (MA).

**Gardner-Webb University,** School of Divinity, Boiling Springs, NC 28017. Offers biblical studies (M Div); Christian education and formation (M Div); intercultural studies (M Div); ministry (D Min); missiology (M Div); pastoral care and counseling (M Div); pastoral care and counseling/member care for missionaries (D Min); pastoral studies (M Div); M Div/MA; M Div/MBA. *Accreditation:* ACIPE. *Program availability:* Part-time. *Faculty:* 12 full-time (2 women), 3 part-time/adjunct (1 woman). *Students:* 115 full-time (59 women), 68 part-time (27 women); includes 86 minority (80 Black or African American, non-Hispanic/Latino; 5 Asian, non-Hispanic/Latino; 1 Hispanic/Latino). Average age 40. 86 applicants, 44% accepted, 16 enrolled. In 2016, 40 master's, 3 doctorates awarded. *Entrance requirements:* For master's, minimum GPA of 2.6; for doctorate, minimum GPA of 2.75. Additional exam requirements/recommendations for international students: Required—TOEFL (minimum score 500 paper-based; 61 iBT). *Application deadline:* Applications are processed on a rolling basis. Electronic applications accepted. *Expenses:* Contact institution. *Financial support:* Fellowships, institutionally sponsored loans, and unspecified assistantships available. Support available to part-time students. Financial award application deadline: 5/15. *Faculty research:* Jewish-Christian dialogue, Islam. *Unit head:* Dr. Robert W. Canoy, Sr., Dean,

## Missions and Missiology

704-406-4400, Fax: 704-406-3935, E-mail: rcanoy@gardner-webb.edu. *Application contact:* Kheresa Harmon, Director of Admissions, 704-406-3205, Fax: 704-406-3895, E-mail: kharmon@gardner-webb.edu.
Website: http://gardner-webb.edu/academic-programs-and-resources/colleges-and-schools/divinity/index

**Georgia Christian University,** School of Divinity, Atlanta, GA 30360. Offers Christian education (MA); divinity (M Div); ministry (D Min); mission studies and world Christianity (MA); theological studies (MA).

**Global University,** Graduate School of Theology, Springfield, MO 65804. Offers bible and theology (D Min); biblical language (M Div); biblical studies (MA); Christian ministry (M Div, D Min); ministerial studies (MA), including education, leadership, missions, New Testament, Old Testament. *Program availability:* Part-time, evening/weekend, online learning. *Degree requirements:* For master's, thesis (for some programs). *Entrance requirements:* For master's, minimum undergraduate GPA of 3.0. Electronic applications accepted. *Faculty research:* Higher education, cross-cultural missions.

**Gordon-Conwell Theological Seminary,** Graduate and Professional Programs, South Hamilton, MA 01982. Offers Biblical languages (MABL); church history (MACH); counseling (MACO); ministry (D Min); missions/evangelism (MAME); New Testament (MANT); Old Testament (MAOT); religion (MAR); theology (M Div, MATH, Th M, Th D). *Accreditation:* ACIPE; ATS (one or more programs are accredited). *Program availability:* Part-time, evening/weekend. *Degree requirements:* For master's, one foreign language, thesis optional; for doctorate, 2 foreign languages, thesis/dissertation. *Entrance requirements:* For master's, minimum GPA of 2.5; for doctorate, minimum GPA of 3.0.

**Grace Mission University,** Graduate School, Fullerton, CA 92833. Offers M Div, MACE, MAICS, D Miss.

**Grace Theological Seminary,** Graduate and Professional Programs, Winona Lake, IN 46590-9907. Offers biblical studies (Certificate); chaplaincy (M Div); exegetical studies (M Div); intercultural studies (M Div, MA, D Min); local church ministry (MA), including camp administration, women's leadership; pastoral counseling (M Div); pastoral studies (M Div, D Min); theology (Diploma). *Accreditation:* ATS. *Program availability:* Part-time, online learning. *Degree requirements:* For master's, thesis optional; for doctorate, 2 foreign languages, thesis/dissertation. *Entrance requirements:* For master's, MAT, minimum GPA of 2.5. Electronic applications accepted. *Faculty research:* Biblical theology, language, and church ministries.

**Grand Rapids Theological Seminary of Cornerstone University,** Graduate Programs, Grand Rapids, MI 49525-5897. Offers biblical counseling (MA); Biblical counseling (M Div); chaplaincy (M Div); Christian education (M Div, MA); intercultural studies (M Div, MA); New Testament (MA, Th M); Old Testament (MA, Th M); pastoral studies (M Div); systematic theology (MA); theology (Th M). *Accreditation:* ATS. *Program availability:* Part-time, online learning. *Entrance requirements:* Additional exam requirements/recommendations for international students: Required—TOEFL (minimum score 577 paper-based; 90 iBT). Electronic applications accepted.

**Hope International University,** School of Graduate and Professional Studies, Programs in Ministry, Fullerton, CA 92831-3138. Offers Christian leadership (MCM); church music (MA); church music (Korean track) (MCM); church planting (MCM); intercultural studies (MCM); worship (MCM). *Program availability:* Part-time, evening/weekend, online learning. *Degree requirements:* For master's, thesis (for some programs), project. *Entrance requirements:* For master's, minimum GPA of 3.0, MCM program requires an undergraduate degree in music, 2 references. Additional exam requirements/recommendations for international students: Required—TOEFL (minimum score 550 paper-based; 86 iBT); Recommended—IELTS (minimum score 6.5). Electronic applications accepted. *Expenses:* Contact institution. *Faculty research:* Church dynamics, growth methodologies.

**Huntington University,** Graduate School, Huntington, IN 46750-1299. Offers counseling (MA), including licensed mental health counselor; early adolescent education (M Ed); education (M Ed); global missions leadership (MA); global youth ministry (MA); TESOL education (M Ed); youth ministry leadership (MA). *Program availability:* Part-time, online learning. *Degree requirements:* For master's, comprehensive exam (for some programs), thesis (for some programs). *Entrance requirements:* For master's, GRE (for counseling and education students only); for doctorate, GRE (for occupational therapy students). Additional exam requirements/recommendations for international students: Required—TOEFL (minimum score 85 iBT), IELTS (minimum score 6.5). Electronic applications accepted. *Faculty research:* Leadership, educational technology trends, evangelism, youth ministry, mental health.

**Liberty University,** School of Divinity, Lynchburg, VA 24515. Offers Biblical studies (M Div); church history (MAR, Th M); discipleship and church ministry (M Div, MAR, MCM); evangelism and church planting (M Div, MAR, MCM); global studies (M Div, MCM, MGS); homiletics (M Div, MAR, Th M, D Min); leadership (M Div, D Min); marketplace chaplaincy (M Div, MCM); ministry (D Min); pastoral counseling (M Div, MA, MAR, D Min), including addictions and recovery (MA), crisis response and trauma (MA), discipleship and church ministries (MA), leadership (MA), life coaching (MA), marketplace chaplaincy (MA), marriage and family (MA), military resilience (MA); pastoral ministries (M Div, MCM); religious education (MRE); theology (M Div, MAR, MTS); theology and apologetics (PhD); worship (M Div, MAR, MCM, D Min). *Program availability:* Part-time, online learning. *Students:* 2,140 full-time (615 women), 3,020 part-time (906 women); includes 1,312 minority (1,016 Black or African American, non-Hispanic/Latino; 9 American Indian or Alaska Native, non-Hispanic/Latino; 100 Asian, non-Hispanic/Latino; 90 Hispanic/Latino; 7 Native Hawaiian or other Pacific Islander, non-Hispanic/Latino; 90 Two or more races, non-Hispanic/Latino), 158 international. Average age 42. 3,651 applicants, 37% accepted, 909 enrolled. In 2016, 1,551 master's, 39 doctorates, 168 other advanced degrees awarded. *Degree requirements:* For master's, 2 foreign languages, thesis (for some programs); for doctorate, 2 foreign languages, thesis/dissertation. *Entrance requirements:* For master's, minimum undergraduate GPA of 2.0; for doctorate, GRE General Test or MAT, minimum graduate GPA of 3.0. Additional exam requirements/recommendations for international students: Required—TOEFL (minimum score 600 paper-based; 100 iBT). *Application deadline:* For fall admission, 6/1 for domestic students; for spring admission, 11/1 for domestic students. Applications are processed on a rolling basis. Application fee: $50. Electronic applications accepted. *Expenses:* Contact institution. *Financial support:* Teaching assistantships with tuition reimbursements, career-related internships or fieldwork, and Federal Work-Study available. Financial award applicants required to submit FAFSA. *Unit head:* Dr. Ed Hindson, Dean, 434-592-4140, Fax: 434-522-0415, E-mail: ehindson@liberty.edu. *Application contact:* Jay Bridge, Director of Graduate Admissions, 800-424-9595, Fax: 800-628-7977, E-mail: gradadmissions@liberty.edu.
Website: https://www.liberty.edu/divinity/

**Luther Seminary,** Graduate and Professional Programs, St. Paul, MN 55108-1445. Offers aging and health (MA); Biblical preaching (D Min); children, youth and family (M Div, MA); congregational mission and leadership (M Th, MA, D Min); history of Christianity (M Th, MA); missions and world religions (M Th); New Testament (M Th, MA); Old Testament (M Th, MA); pastoral care: clinical pastoral theology (M Th); pastoral theology and ministry (M Th); systematic theology (M Th, MA). *Accreditation:*

ACIPE; ATS. *Program availability:* Part-time, online learning. *Degree requirements:* For master's, thesis or alternative; for doctorate, 2 foreign languages, thesis/dissertation. *Entrance requirements:* For master's, minimum GPA of 3.0; for doctorate, GRE General Test. Additional exam requirements/recommendations for international students: Required—TOEFL, IELTS. Electronic applications accepted. *Faculty research:* Theology, psychology (pastoral care), church history, Bible.

**Milligan College,** Emmanuel Christian Seminary at Milligan College, Milligan College, TN 37682. Offers Christian care and counseling (M Div); Christian education (M Div); Christian ministries (MACM, Graduate Certificate); Christian ministry (M Div); Christian theology (M Div, MAR); church history (MAR); church history/historical theology (M Div); general studies (M Div); ministry (D Min); New Testament (M Div, MAR); Old Testament (M Div, MAR); urban ministry (M Div); world missions (M Div). *Accreditation:* ACIPE; ATS. *Program availability:* Part-time, blended/hybrid learning. *Faculty:* 9 full-time (1 woman), 11 part-time/adjunct (0 women). *Students:* 55 full-time (16 women), 44 part-time (17 women); includes 7 minority (6 Black or African American, non-Hispanic/Latino; 1 Hispanic/Latino), 6 international. Average age 33. In 2016, 21 master's, 3 doctorates awarded. *Degree requirements:* For master's, 2 foreign languages, thesis or alternative, portfolio; for doctorate, thesis/dissertation. *Entrance requirements:* For master's, undergraduate degree and supporting transcripts, essay/personal statement, professional recommendations, interview; for doctorate, M Div or equivalent, essay/personal statement, professional recommendations. Additional exam requirements/recommendations for international students: Required—TOEFL (minimum score 550 paper-based, 79 iBT) or IELTS (6.5). *Application deadline:* For fall admission, 8/1 for domestic students, 6/1 for international students; for spring admission, 12/15 for domestic students, 8/1 for international students. Applications are processed on a rolling basis. Application fee: $30 ($0 for international students). Electronic applications accepted. *Expenses:* $470 per hour tuition; $325 per semester tech/activity fees. *Financial support:* In 2016–17, 124 students received support. Scholarships/grants and unspecified assistantships available. Financial award application deadline: 12/1; financial award applicants required to submit FAFSA. *Faculty research:* Theology of Old Testament prophets; performance criticism of New Testament texts; practical theology and spiritual formation for Christian leaders; church history and missions; constructive theology, art and imagination. *Unit head:* Dr. Rollin Ramsaran, Academic Dean, Emmanuel Christian Seminary, 423-461-1524, Fax: 423-926-6198, E-mail: raramsaran@milligan.edu. *Application contact:* Lauren Gullett, Director of Admissions and Recruitment for Emmanuel Christian Seminary, 423-461-1535, Fax: 423-926-6198, E-mail: lwgullett@milligan.edu.
Website: http://ecs.milligan.edu/

**Northwest Nazarene University,** Program in Religion, Nampa, ID 83686-5897. Offers missional leadership (M Div, MA); pastoral ministry (MA); spiritual formation (M Div, MA); youth, children, and family ministry (M Div, MA). *Program availability:* Part-time, online only, 100% online. *Faculty:* 11 full-time (3 women), 18 part-time/adjunct (0 women). *Students:* 65 full-time (23 women), 25 part-time (11 women); includes 11 minority (4 Black or African American, non-Hispanic/Latino; 1 American Indian or Alaska Native, non-Hispanic/Latino; 2 Asian, non-Hispanic/Latino; 3 Hispanic/Latino; 1 Native Hawaiian or other Pacific Islander, non-Hispanic/Latino; 1 international. Average age 39. 37 applicants, 76% accepted, 24 enrolled. In 2016, 40 master's awarded. *Entrance requirements:* For master's, minimum GPA of 2.5; 8 semester or 12 quarter credits of Bible, theology and/or Western philosophy. Additional exam requirements/recommendations for international students: Required—TOEFL (minimum score 85 iBT). *Application deadline:* For fall admission, 7/31 for domestic students, 7/1 for international students; for spring admission, 2/1 for domestic students, 1/5 for international students. Applications are processed on a rolling basis. Application fee: $50. Electronic applications accepted. *Expenses:* Contact institution. *Financial support:* In 2016–17, 3 students received support. Scholarships/grants available. *Unit head:* Dr. Jay Akkerman, Director, Graduate Studies, 208-467-8437, Fax: 208-467-8252. *Application contact:* Vicki Funk, Program Coordinator, 208-467-8432, Fax: 208-467-8252, E-mail: vlfunk@nnu.edu.
Website: http://www.nnu.edu/ministry/

**Northwest University,** College of Ministry, Kirkland, WA 98033. Offers ministry (MIM); missional leadership (MA); theology and culture (MA). *Program availability:* Part-time, evening/weekend, online learning. *Degree requirements:* For master's, comprehensive exam (for some programs), thesis (for some programs). *Entrance requirements:* Additional exam requirements/recommendations for international students: Required—TOEFL (minimum score 550 paper-based; 75 iBT). Electronic applications accepted.

**Nyack College,** Alliance Theological Seminary, Nyack, NY 10960. Offers Biblical literature (MA), including New Testament, Old Testament; Biblical studies (MA); Christian ministry (MPS); intercultural studies (MA); ministry (D Min), including Christian leadership in the global context; theology and missions (M Div); urban ministry (MPS). *Accreditation:* ATS. *Program availability:* Part-time, evening/weekend, 100% online, blended/hybrid learning. *Students:* 275 full-time (111 women), 370 part-time (175 women); includes 505 minority (177 Black or African American, non-Hispanic/Latino; 128 Asian, non-Hispanic/Latino; 190 Hispanic/Latino; 10 Two or more races, non-Hispanic/Latino), 32 international. Average age 43. In 2016, 117 master's, 14 doctorates awarded. *Degree requirements:* For master's, comprehensive exam (for some programs), thesis optional, internship; for doctorate, thesis/dissertation. *Entrance requirements:* For master's, transcripts, Christian experience statement, recommendations; for doctorate, transcripts, documented three years of ministry experience subsequent to 1st graduate theological degree, reference letters, formal academic paper. Additional exam requirements/recommendations for international students: Required—TOEFL (minimum score 550 paper-based; 80 iBT). *Application deadline:* Applications are processed on a rolling basis. Application fee: $30. Electronic applications accepted. *Expenses:* $575 per credit (for master's-level). *Financial support:* Career-related internships or fieldwork, Federal Work-Study, and scholarships/grants available. Financial award applicants required to submit FAFSA. *Unit head:* Dr. Ronald Walborn, Dean, 845-770-5715, Fax: 845-358-1663. *Application contact:* Julian Williams, Associate Director of Admissions, 800-541-6891, Fax: 845-348-3912, E-mail: admissions.ats@nyack.edu.
Website: http://www.nyack.edu/ats

**Oral Roberts University,** School of Theology and Missions, Tulsa, OK 74171. Offers biblical literature (MA), including advanced languages, Judaic-Christian studies; Christian counseling (MA), including marriage and family therapy; divinity (M Div); missions (MA); practical theology (MA); theological/historical studies (MA); theology (D Min). *Accreditation:* ATS. *Program availability:* Part-time, online learning. *Degree requirements:* For master's, thesis (for some programs), practicum/internship; for doctorate, thesis/dissertation, applied research project. *Entrance requirements:* For master's, GRE General Test or MAT, minimum GPA of 2.5; for doctorate, M Div, minimum GPA of 3.0, 3 years of full-time ministry experience. Additional exam requirements/recommendations for international students: Required—TOEFL (minimum score 550 paper-based; 79 iBT). Electronic applications accepted.

**Phillips Theological Seminary,** Programs in Theology, Tulsa, OK 74116. Offers administration of church agencies (M Div); campus ministry (M Div); church-related social work (M Div); college and seminary teaching (M Div); global mission work (M Div);

institutional chaplaincy (M Div); ministerial vocations in Christian education (M Div); ministry (D Min), including parish ministry, pastoral counseling, practices of ministry; ministry and culture (MAMC), including Christian education, congregational leadership, history and practice of Christian spirituality, theology, ethics, and culture; ministry of music (M Div); pastoral care and counseling (M Div); pastoral ministry (M Div); theological studies (MTS). *Accreditation:* ATS. *Program availability:* Part-time, online learning. *Degree requirements:* For master's, thesis (for some programs); for doctorate, thesis/dissertation. *Entrance requirements:* For master's, minimum GPA of 2.5; for doctorate, M Div, minimum GPA of 3.0. *Faculty research:* Biblical studies, historical studies, theology and culture, practical theology, theology and film.

**Providence University College & Theological Seminary,** Theological Seminary, Otterburne, MB R0A 1G0, Canada. Offers children's ministry (Certificate); Christian studies (MA, Certificate); counseling (MA); cross-cultural discipleship (Certificate); divinity (M Div); educational studies (MA), including counseling psychology, educational ministries, student development, teaching English to speakers of other languages, training teachers of English to speakers of other languages; global studies (MA); lay counseling (Diploma); ministry (D Min); teaching English to speakers of other languages (Certificate); theological studies (MA); training teacher of English to speakers of other languages (Certificate); youth ministry (Certificate). *Accreditation:* ATS. *Program availability:* Part-time. *Degree requirements:* For master's, variable foreign language requirement, thesis (for some programs); for doctorate, thesis/dissertation. *Entrance requirements:* Additional exam requirements/recommendations for international students: Recommended—TOEFL (minimum score 550 paper-based). *Faculty research:* Studies in Isaiah, theology of sin.

**Reformed Theological Seminary–Jackson Campus,** Graduate and Professional Programs, Jackson, MS 39209-3004. Offers Bible, theology, and missions (Certificate); Biblical exegesis (M Div); biblical studies (MA); Christian education (MA); counseling (M Div); marriage and family therapy (MA); ministry (D Min); missions (M Div, MA, D Min); theological studies (MA). *Accreditation:* AAMFT/COAMFTE (one or more programs are accredited); ATS (one or more programs are accredited). *Degree requirements:* For master's, thesis (for some programs), fieldwork; for doctorate, 2 foreign languages, thesis/dissertation. *Entrance requirements:* For master's, minimum GPA of 2.6; for doctorate, minimum GPA of 3.0. Additional exam requirements/recommendations for international students: Required—TOEFL.

**Regent University,** Graduate School, School of Divinity, Virginia Beach, VA 23464-9800. Offers divinity (M Div), including Biblical studies (M Div, MTS, PhD), chaplain ministry, Christian theology (M Div, MTS, PhD), church and ministry (M Div, MA), history of Christianity (M Div, MTS, PhD), inter-cultural studies (M Div, MA), interdisciplinary studies (M Div, MA, MTS), marketplace ministry, worship and media (M Div, MA); leadership and renewal (D Min), including Christian leadership and renewal, clinical pastoral education, community transformation, military ministry, ministry leadership coaching; practical theology (MA), including church and ministry (M Div, MA), inter-cultural studies (M Div, MA), interdisciplinary studies (M Div, MA, MTS), worship and media (M Div, MA); theological studies (MTS, PhD), including Biblical studies (M Div, MTS, PhD), Christian theology (M Div, MTS, PhD), history of Christianity (M Div, MTS, PhD), interdisciplinary studies (M Div, MA, MTS). *Accreditation:* ACIPE; ATS. *Program availability:* Part-time, evening/weekend, 100% online, blended/hybrid learning. *Faculty:* 15 full-time (3 women), 51 part-time/adjunct (6 women). *Students:* 148 full-time (60 women), 787 part-time (321 women); includes 506 minority (416 Black or African American, non-Hispanic/Latino; 1 American Indian or Alaska Native, non-Hispanic/Latino; 23 Asian, non-Hispanic/Latino; 54 Hispanic/Latino; 1 Native Hawaiian or other Pacific Islander, non-Hispanic/Latino; 11 Two or more races, non-Hispanic/Latino), 31 international. Average age 43. 1,020 applicants, 42% accepted, 276 enrolled. In 2016, 127 master's, 25 doctorates awarded. *Degree requirements:* For master's, comprehensive exam, thesis or alternative, internship; for doctorate, thesis/dissertation or alternative. *Entrance requirements:* For master's, minimum undergraduate GPA of 2.75, writing sample, personal goal statement, college transcripts; for doctorate, GRE, minimum graduate GPA of 3.5 (PhD), 3.0 (D Min); clergy recommendations; writing sample; transcripts; resume; interview. Additional exam requirements/recommendations for international students: Required—TOEFL (minimum score 577 paper-based). *Application deadline:* For fall admission, 5/1 priority date for domestic students. Applications are processed on a rolling basis. Application fee: $50. Electronic applications accepted. *Expenses:* Contact institution. *Financial support:* In 2016–17, 602 students received support. Career-related internships or fieldwork, scholarships/grants, and unspecified assistantships available. Support available to part-time students. *Faculty research:* Greek and Hebrew, theology, spiritual formation, global missions and world Christianity, women in ministry leadership. *Unit head:* Dr. Cornelius Bekker, Dean, 757-352-4401, Fax: 757-352-4597, E-mail: clbekker@regent.edu. *Application contact:* Heidi Cece, Assistant Vice President of Enrollment Management, 800-373-5504, Fax: 757-352-4381, E-mail: admissions@regent.edu.
Website: http://www.regent.edu/sod/

**Rochester College,** Center for Missional Leadership, Rochester Hills, MI 48307-2764. Offers MRE.

**Saint Paul University,** Faculty of Human Sciences, Program in Mission and Interreligious Studies, Ottawa, ON K1S 1C4, Canada. Offers MA. *Degree requirements:* For master's, one foreign language, thesis. *Entrance requirements:* For master's, honors BA in mission, minimum B average. *Faculty research:* Theology of mission; mission and sociology; history of mission; faith, religion, and culture; world religions; practice of mission; religious anthropology; sociocultural anthropology.

**Simpson University,** A.W. Tozer Theological Seminary, Redding, CA 96003-8606. Offers ministry leadership (MA). *Program availability:* Part-time, evening/weekend, 100% online, blended/hybrid learning. *Faculty:* 9 part-time/adjunct (0 women). *Students:* 9 full-time (2 women), 30 part-time (7 women); includes 9 minority (1 Black or African American, non-Hispanic/Latino; 3 Asian, non-Hispanic/Latino; 4 Hispanic/Latino; 1 Two or more races, non-Hispanic/Latino), 1 international. Average age 36. In 2016, 12 master's awarded. *Entrance requirements:* For master's, GRE General Test (if undergraduate GPA less than 2.5), Christian statement, one spiritual assessment, one academic recommendation. Additional exam requirements/recommendations for international students: Required—TOEFL (minimum score 583 paper-based; 94 iBT). *Application deadline:* For fall admission, 8/1 for domestic and international students; for spring admission, 12/1 for domestic and international students; for summer admission, 4/1 for domestic and international students. Applications are processed on a rolling basis. Application fee: $35. Electronic applications accepted. *Expenses:* $426 per credit. *Financial support:* Scholarships/grants available. Support available to part-time students. Financial award application deadline: 7/1; financial award applicants required to submit FAFSA. *Unit head:* Dr. Patrick Blewett, Dean, 530-226-4144, Fax: 530-226-4871, E-mail: pblewett@simpsonu.edu. *Application contact:* Stacy Burgess, Director of Admissions for Adult and Graduate Studies, 530-226-4961, Fax: 530-226-4861, E-mail: admissions@simpsonu.edu.
Website: http://www.simpsonu.edu/tozer

**Southeastern Baptist Theological Seminary,** Graduate and Professional Programs, Wake Forest, NC 27588-1889. Offers advanced biblical studies (M Div); Christian education (M Div, MACE); Christian ethics (PhD); Christian ministry (M Div); Christian planting (M Div); church music (MACM); counseling (MACO); evangelism (PhD); language (M Div); ministry (D Min); New Testament (PhD); Old Testament (PhD); philosophy (PhD); theology (Th M, PhD); women's studies (M Div). *Accreditation:* ACIPE; ATS (one or more programs are accredited). *Degree requirements:* For master's, thesis (for some programs), oral exam; for doctorate, thesis/dissertation, fieldwork. *Entrance requirements:* For master's, Cooperative English Test, minimum GPA of 2.0, M Div or equivalent (Th M); for doctorate, GRE General Test or MAT, Cooperative English Test, M Div or equivalent, 3 years of professional experience.

**Southern Adventist University,** School of Religion, Collegedale, TN 37315-0370. Offers Biblical and theological studies (MA); church leadership and management (M Min); church ministry and homiletics (M Min); evangelism and world mission (M Min); religious studies (MA). *Program availability:* Part-time. *Degree requirements:* For master's, comprehensive exam, thesis (for some programs). *Entrance requirements:* For master's, GRE. Additional exam requirements/recommendations for international students: Required—TOEFL (minimum score 600 paper-based). *Faculty research:* Biblical archaeology.

**The Southern Baptist Theological Seminary,** Billy Graham School of Missions, Evangelism and Ministry, Louisville, KY 40280-0004. Offers ministry (D Min); missiology (MA, D Miss); missions and evangelism (M Div, Th M, PhD); theological studies (MA). *Accreditation:* ATS. *Program availability:* Part-time, evening/weekend, online learning. *Degree requirements:* For master's, 2 foreign languages; for doctorate, 4 foreign languages, thesis/dissertation. *Entrance requirements:* For doctorate, GRE General Test, MAT, M Div. Additional exam requirements/recommendations for international students: Required—TOEFL, TWE. *Faculty research:* Assimilation of church congregants, effective methodologies of evangelism, expectations of church members, spiritual warfare literature, formative church discipline.

**Southern Evangelical Seminary,** Graduate Programs, Matthews, NC 28105. Offers apologetics (MA, D Min, Certificate); Christian education (MA); church ministry (MA, Certificate); divinity (Certificate), including apologetics (M Div, Certificate); Islamic studies (MA, Certificate); Jewish studies (MA); philosophy (MA); philosophy of religion (PhD); religion (MA); theology (M Div), including apologetics (M Div, Certificate), Biblical studies; youth ministry (MA). *Program availability:* Part-time, evening/weekend, online learning. *Degree requirements:* For master's, thesis (for some programs); for doctorate, 2 foreign languages, comprehensive exam (for some programs), thesis/dissertation. *Entrance requirements:* Additional exam requirements/recommendations for international students: Required—TOEFL (minimum score 600 paper-based).

**Southwestern Assemblies of God University,** Thomas F. Harrison School of Graduate Studies, Program in Theological Studies, Waxahachie, TX 75165-5735. Offers Bible and theology (MS); Biblical studies (M Div); counseling (M Div); cross cultural missions (M Div); practical theology (M Div); theological studies (M Div). *Program availability:* Online learning. *Degree requirements:* For master's, comprehensive written and oral exams. *Entrance requirements:* For master's, GRE General Test, minimum GPA of 2.5. Electronic applications accepted.

**Southwestern Baptist Theological Seminary,** Roy Fish School of Evangelism and Missions, Fort Worth, TX 76122-0000. Offers cross-cultural missions (MTS); evangelism (M Div); evangelism and missions (D Min); international church planting (M Div); Islamic studies (M Div, MA Islamic); missiology (MA Miss); missions (M Div); North American church planting (M Div); North American evangelism and international missions (D Min); theology (Th M); world Christian studies (PhD).

**Southwestern Christian University,** Program in Ministry, Bethany, OK 73008-0340. Offers church planting (M Min); church revitalization and renewal (M Min); intercultural studies (M Min); leadership (M Min); life coaching (M Min); pastoral ministries (M Min); work place ministries (M Min). *Program availability:* Part-time. *Degree requirements:* For master's, thesis. *Entrance requirements:* For master's, minimum GPA of 2.5. Additional exam requirements/recommendations for international students: Required—TOEFL (minimum score 500 paper-based). Electronic applications accepted.

**Taylor College and Seminary,** Graduate and Professional Programs, Edmonton, AB T6J 4T3, Canada. Offers Christian studies (Diploma); intercultural studies (MA, Diploma), including intercultural studies (Diploma), TESOL; theology (M Div, MTS). *Accreditation:* ATS. *Program availability:* Part-time, online learning. *Degree requirements:* For master's, thesis optional. *Entrance requirements:* Additional exam requirements/recommendations for international students: Required—TOEFL (minimum score 550 paper-based; 80 iBT), IELTS (minimum score 6.5). *Faculty research:* Biblical studies, administration and organization, world religions, ethics, missiology.

**Theological University of the Caribbean,** Graduate Programs, Saint Just, PR 00978-0901. Offers childhood and adolescent education (MA); counseling and pastoral care (MA); ministry (D Min); missions (MA).

**Trinity Bible College and Graduate School,** Graduate School, Ellendale, ND 58436. Offers global theology (MA); missional leadership (MA).

**Trinity International University,** Trinity Evangelical Divinity School, Deerfield, IL 60015-1284. Offers academic ministry (M Div); Biblical and Near Eastern archaeology and languages (MA); chaplaincy and ministry care (M Div); Christian studies (Certificate); church and parachurch ministry (M Div); church history (MA, Th M); counseling (Th M); educational ministries (MA); educational ministry (Th M); educational studies (PhD); intercultural studies (MA, PhD); leadership and management (D Min); mental health counseling (MA); military chaplaincy (D Min); ministry (MA); missions (Th M); missions and evangelism (D Min); New Testament (MA, Th M); Old Testament (Th M); Old Testament and Semitic languages (MA); pastoral ministry and care (D Min); pastoral theology (Th M); preaching and teaching (D Min); spiritual formation and education (D Min); systematic theology (MA, Th M); theological studies (MA, PhD); urban ministry (MA). *Program availability:* Part-time, online learning. *Students:* 578 full-time (141 women), 711 part-time (202 women). *Degree requirements:* For master's, comprehensive exam, thesis, fieldwork; for doctorate, comprehensive exam (for some programs), thesis/dissertation; for Certificate, comprehensive exam, integrative papers. *Entrance requirements:* For master's, GRE, MAT, minimum cumulative undergraduate GPA of 3.0; for doctorate, GRE, minimum cumulative graduate GPA of 3.2; for Certificate, GRE, MAT, minimum undergraduate GPA of 2.5. Additional exam requirements/recommendations for international students: Required—TOEFL (minimum score 580 paper-based), TWE (minimum score 4). *Application deadline:* For fall admission, 7/15 priority date for domestic and international students. Applications are processed on a rolling basis. Application fee: $25. Electronic applications accepted. *Expenses: Tuition, area resident:* Full-time $19,898. *Required fees:* $200. *Financial support:* Fellowships with partial tuition reimbursements, teaching assistantships with partial tuition reimbursements, career-related internships or fieldwork, Federal Work-Study, scholarships/grants, and tuition waivers (partial) available. Financial award application deadline: 4/1; financial award applicants required to submit FAFSA. *Unit head:* Dr. Tite Tienou, Academic Dean, 847-317-8086, Fax: 847-317-8014, E-mail: ttienou@teds.edu. *Application contact:* Ron Campbell, Director of Admissions, 800-345-8337, Fax: 847-317-8097, E-mail: rcampbel@tiu.edu.
Website: https://divinity.tiu.edu/

**Trinity Lutheran Seminary,** Graduate and Professional Programs, Columbus, OH 43209-2334. Offers African American studies (MTS); Biblical studies (MTS, STM); Christian education (MA); Christian spirituality (STM); church in the world (MTS); church music (MA); divinity (M Div); general theological studies (MTS); mission and evangelism (STM); pastoral leadership and practice (STM); youth and family ministry (MA); MSN/MTS; MTS/JD. *Accreditation:* ACIPE; ATS. *Program availability:* Part-time. *Degree requirements:* For master's, variable foreign language requirement, comprehensive exam (for some programs), thesis (for some programs), field experience (for some programs). *Entrance requirements:* For master's, BA or equivalent (for MA, M Div, MTS); M Div, MTS, or equivalent (for STM); audition (for MACM). Additional exam requirements/recommendations for international students: Required—TOEFL. Electronic applications accepted. *Expenses:* Contact institution.

**Trinity School for Ministry,** Graduate Programs, Ambridge, PA 15003-2397. Offers Anglican studies (Diploma); basic Christian studies (Diploma); divinity (M Div); ministry (D Min); mission and evangelism (MAME, Diploma); religion (MAR); youth ministry (Diploma). *Program availability:* Part-time. *Degree requirements:* For master's, thesis optional; for doctorate, thesis/dissertation. *Entrance requirements:* Additional exam requirements/recommendations for international students: Required—TOEFL. *Faculty research:* Pauline Epistles, contemporary theology, history of Anglican liturgy, book of Ruth, biblical theology.

**Tyndale University College & Seminary,** Graduate Programs, Toronto, ON M2M 3S4, Canada. Offers Biblical studies (M Div); Christian foundations (MTS); Christian studies (Diploma); counseling (M Div); educational ministry (M Div); missions (M Div, Diploma); pastoral and Chinese ministry (M Div); pastoral ministry (M Div); Pentecostal studies (MTS); spiritual formation (M Div, Diploma); theological studies (M Div); theology (Th M); worship and liturgy (M Div, MTS); youth and family ministry (M Div). *Accreditation:* ATS. *Program availability:* Part-time, online learning. *Entrance requirements:* For master's and Diploma, minimum C+ average in undergraduate course work. Additional exam requirements/recommendations for international students: Required—TOEFL (minimum score 570 paper-based), TWE (minimum score 5). Electronic applications accepted. *Faculty research:* Canadian church history, Chinese church history, Old Testament, counseling ministries (narrative therapy), world religions.

**University of South Africa,** College of Human Sciences, Pretoria, South Africa. Offers adult education (M Ed); African languages (MA, PhD); African politics (MA, PhD); Afrikaans (MA, PhD); ancient history (MA, PhD); ancient Near Eastern studies (MA, PhD); anthropology (MA, PhD); applied linguistics (MA); Arabic (MA, PhD); archaeology (MA); art history (MA); Biblical archaeology (MA); Biblical studies (M Th, D Th, PhD); Christian spirituality (M Th, D Th); church history (M Th, D Th); classical studies (MA, PhD); clinical psychology (MA); communication (MA, PhD); comparative education (M Ed, Ed D); consulting psychology (D Admin, D Com, PhD); curriculum studies (M Ed, Ed D); development studies (M Admin, MA, D Admin, PhD); didactics (M Ed, Ed D); education (M Tech); education management (M Ed, Ed D); educational psychology (M Ed); English (MA); environmental education (M Ed); French (MA, PhD); German (MA, PhD); Greek (MA); guidance and counseling (M Ed); health studies (MA, PhD), including health sciences education (MA), health services management (MA), medical and surgical nursing science (critical care general) (MA), midwifery and neonatal nursing science (MA), trauma and emergency care (MA); history (MA, PhD); history of education (Ed D); inclusive education (M Ed, Ed D); information and communications technology policy and regulation (MA); information science (MA, MIS, PhD); international politics (MA, PhD); Islamic studies (MA, PhD); Italian (MA, PhD); Judaica (MA, PhD); linguistics (MA, PhD); mathematical education (M Ed); mathematics education (MA); missiology (M Th, D Th); modern Hebrew (MA, PhD); musicology (MA, MMus, D Mus, PhD); natural science education (M Ed); New Testament (M Th, D Th); Old Testament (D Th); pastoral therapy (M Th, D Th); philosophy (MA); philosophy of education (M Ed, Ed D); politics (MA, PhD); Portuguese (MA, PhD); practical theology (M Th, D Th); psychology (MA, MS, PhD); psychology of education (M Ed, Ed D); public health (MA); religious studies (MA, D Th, PhD); Romance languages (MA); Russian (MA, PhD); Semitic languages (MA, PhD); social behavior studies in HIV/AIDS (MA); social science (mental health) (MA); social science in development studies (MA); social science in psychology (MA); social science in social work (MA); social science in sociology (MA); social work (MSW, DSW, PhD); socio-education (M Ed, Ed D); sociolinguistics (MA); sociology (MA, PhD); Spanish (MA, PhD); systematic theology (M Th, D Th); TESOL (teaching English to speakers of other languages) (MA); theological ethics (M Th, D Th); theory of literature (MA, PhD); urban ministries (D Th); urban ministry (M Th).

**Villanova University,** Villanova School of Business, Master of Science in Church Management Program, Villanova, PA 19085. Offers MSCM. *Program availability:* Part-time-only, online only, 100% online, residence week at beginning of program. *Faculty:* 108 full-time (39 women), 32 part-time/adjunct (8 women). *Students:* 85 part-time (37 women); includes 23 minority (8 Black or African American, non-Hispanic/Latino; 5 Asian, non-Hispanic/Latino; 9 Hispanic/Latino; 1 Two or more races, non-Hispanic/Latino), 5 international. Average age 50. *Degree requirements:* For master's, minimum GPA of 3.0. *Entrance requirements:* For master's, current resume, official academic transcripts, two letters of recommendation, personal essay. Additional exam requirements/recommendations for international students: Required—TOEFL (minimum score 550 paper-based; 100 iBT). *Application deadline:* For fall admission, 5/10 for domestic and international students. Applications are processed on a rolling basis. Application fee: $50. Electronic applications accepted. *Expenses:* Contact institution. *Financial support:* Scholarships/grants available. Support available to part-time students. Financial award application deadline: 6/30; financial award applicants required to submit FAFSA. *Faculty research:* Business analytics; creativity, innovation and entrepreneurship; global leadership; real estate; church management; business ethics; marketing and consumer insights. *Unit head:* Dr. Charles Zech, Faculty Director, 610-519-4371, E-mail: charles.zech@villanova.edu. *Application contact:* James Gallo, Staff Director, 610-519-6015, E-mail: james.gallo@villanova.edu.
Website: http://www.villanova.edu/business/graduate/church/

**Wesley Biblical Seminary,** Graduate Programs, Jackson, MS 39206. Offers apologetics (MA); Biblical languages (M Div); Biblical literature (MA); Christian studies (MA); context and mission (M Div); honors research (M Div); interpretation (M Div); ministry (M Div); spiritual formation (M Div); teaching (M Div); theology (MA). *Accreditation:* ATS. *Program availability:* Part-time. *Degree requirements:* For master's, thesis. *Entrance requirements:* Additional exam requirements/recommendations for international students: Required—TOEFL. Electronic applications accepted. *Faculty research:* Patristics, missiology, culture, hermeneutics.

**Westminster Theological Seminary,** Graduate and Professional Programs, Philadelphia, PA 19118. Offers apologetics (Th M); Biblical and urban studies (Certificate); Biblical counseling (MA); biblical studies (MAR); Christian studies (Certificate); church history (Th M); counseling (M Div); general studies (M Div, MAR); hermeneutics and Bible interpretations (PhD); historical and theological studies (PhD); historical theology (Th M); New Testament (Th M); Old Testament (Th M); pastoral counseling (D Min); pastoral ministry (M Div, D Min); systematic theology (Th M); theological studies (MAR); urban missions (M Div, MA, MAR, D Min). *Accreditation:* ATS. *Program availability:* Part-time. Terminal master's awarded for partial completion of doctoral program. *Degree requirements:* For master's, thesis (for some programs); for doctorate, 4 foreign languages, comprehensive exam (for some programs), thesis/dissertation. *Entrance requirements:* For doctorate, GRE General Test. Additional exam requirements/recommendations for international students: Required—TOEFL, TWE.

**Wheaton College,** Graduate School, Department of Evangelism, Wheaton, IL 60187-5593. Offers evangelism and leadership (MA); missional church movements (MA). *Program availability:* Part-time. *Faculty:* 1 full-time (0 women). *Students:* 2 full-time (0 women), 5 part-time (1 woman); includes 1 minority (Hispanic/Latino). Average age 34. 5 applicants, 100% accepted, 4 enrolled. In 2016, 13 master's awarded. *Degree requirements:* For master's, thesis or alternative. *Entrance requirements:* For master's, GRE or MAT. Additional exam requirements/recommendations for international students: Required—TOEFL (minimum score 550 paper-based; IELTS (minimum score 6.5). *Application deadline:* For fall admission, 3/1 priority date for domestic students, 1/1 for international students; for spring admission, 11/1 for domestic students. Applications are processed on a rolling basis. Application fee: $30. Electronic applications accepted. *Expenses: Tuition:* Full-time $19,080; part-time $795 per credit hour. Tuition and fees vary according to degree level and program. *Financial support:* Career-related internships or fieldwork, Federal Work-Study, scholarships/grants, and unspecified assistantships available. Financial award application deadline: 3/1; financial award applicants required to submit FAFSA. *Unit head:* Dr. Ed Stetzer, Chair, 630-752-5806, E-mail: evangelism.leadership@wheaton.edu. *Application contact:* Dusty Di Santo, Director of Graduate Admissions, 630-752-5195, Fax: 630-752-7047, E-mail: graduate.admissions@wheaton.edu.
Website: http://www.wheaton.edu/graduate-school/degrees/evangelism-and-leadership

**Wheaton College,** Graduate School, Department of Intercultural Studies, Wheaton, IL 60187-5593. Offers intercultural studies (MA); intercultural studies/teaching English as a second language (MA); missions (MA); teaching English as a second language (Certificate). *Program availability:* Part-time. *Faculty:* 5 full-time (2 women), 2 part-time/adjunct (both women). *Students:* 25 full-time (20 women), 15 part-time (9 women); includes 8 minority (1 Black or African American, non-Hispanic/Latino; 6 Asian, non-Hispanic/Latino; 1 Hispanic/Latino), 8 international. Average age 32. 35 applicants, 94% accepted, 20 enrolled. In 2016, 23 master's awarded. *Degree requirements:* For master's, thesis or alternative. *Entrance requirements:* For master's, GRE General Test, MAT. Additional exam requirements/recommendations for international students: Required—TOEFL (minimum score 550 paper-based; 80 iBT), IELTS (minimum score 6.5), TOEFL (minimum score 600 paper-based; 90 iBT) or IELTS (minimum score 7.5) for MA in TESOL. *Application deadline:* For fall admission, 5/1 for domestic students, 1/1 for international students; for spring admission, 11/1 for domestic students. Applications are processed on a rolling basis. Application fee: $30. Electronic applications accepted. *Expenses: Tuition:* Full-time $19,080; part-time $795 per credit hour. Tuition and fees vary according to degree level and program. *Financial support:* Career-related internships or fieldwork, scholarships/grants, and unspecified assistantships available. Financial award application deadline: 3/1; financial award applicants required to submit FAFSA. *Unit head:* Dr. Robert Gallagher, Chair, 630-752-5948, E-mail: intercultural.studies@wheaton.edu. *Application contact:* Dusty Di Santo, Director of Graduate Admissions, 630-752-5195, Fax: 630-752-5047, E-mail: graduate.admissions@wheaton.edu.
Website: http://www.wheaton.edu/academics/departments/intr

# Pastoral Ministry and Counseling

**Abilene Christian University,** Graduate Programs, College of Biblical Studies, Graduate School of Theology, Program in Divinity, Abilene, TX 79699. Offers divinity (M Div); missions (M Div). *Accreditation:* ATS. *Program availability:* Part-time, evening/weekend, blended/hybrid learning. *Students:* 38 full-time (7 women), 18 part-time (7 women); includes 13 minority (11 Black or African American, non-Hispanic/Latino; 1 Asian, non-Hispanic/Latino; 1 Hispanic/Latino), 6 international. 49 applicants, 67% accepted, 17 enrolled. In 2016, 5 master's awarded. *Degree requirements:* For master's, comprehensive exam, e-portfolio review. *Entrance requirements:* Additional exam requirements/recommendations for international students: Required—TOEFL (minimum score 80 iBT), IELTS (minimum score 6), PTE. *Application deadline:* For fall admission, 8/11 for domestic students; for spring admission, 11/1 for domestic students. Applications are processed on a rolling basis. Application fee: $50. Electronic applications accepted. *Expenses:* $618 per credit hour. *Financial support:* In 2016–17, 6 students received support. Scholarships/grants available. Financial award application deadline: 4/1; financial award applicants required to submit FAFSA. *Unit head:* Dr. Kelli Gibson, Graduate Advisor, 325-674-3709, Fax: 325-674-6716, E-mail: kelli.gibson@acu.edu. *Application contact:* Corey Patterson, Director of Graduate Admission and Recruiting, 325-674-6566, Fax: 325-674-6717,

E-mail: gradinfo@acu.edu.
Website: http://www.acu.edu/graduate/academics/divinity.html

**Abilene Christian University,** Graduate Programs, College of Biblical Studies, Graduate School of Theology, Program in Ministry, Abilene, TX 79699. Offers D Min. *Program availability:* Part-time. *Students:* 2 full-time (both women), 16 part-time (1 woman); includes 1 minority (Hispanic/Latino), 1 international. 7 applicants, 71% accepted, 5 enrolled. In 2016, 2 doctorates awarded. *Degree requirements:* For doctorate, one foreign language, comprehensive exam, thesis/dissertation. *Entrance requirements:* Additional exam requirements/recommendations for international students: Required—TOEFL (minimum score 80 iBT), IELTS (minimum score 6), PTE. *Application deadline:* For summer admission, 1/31 for domestic students. Applications are processed on a rolling basis. Application fee: $50. *Expenses:* Contact institution. *Financial support:* In 2016–17, 13 students received support. Scholarships/grants available. Financial award application deadline: 4/1; financial award applicants required to submit FAFSA. *Faculty research:* Church growth, ministry evaluation, leadership. *Unit head:* Dr. Carson Reed, Graduate Director, 325-674-3732, Fax: 325-674-6716, E-mail: carson.reed@acu.edu. *Application contact:* Corey Patterson, Director of Graduate Admission and Recruiting, 325-674-6566, Fax: 325-674-6717,

E-mail: gradinfo@acu.edu.
Website: http://www.acu.edu/graduate/academics/doctor-of-ministry.html

**Abilene Christian University,** Graduate Programs, College of Biblical Studies, Graduate School of Theology, Programs in Christian Ministry, Abilene, TX 79699. Offers MACM. *Program availability:* Part-time, online learning. *Students:* 31 full-time (5 women), 33 part-time (2 women); includes 27 minority (24 Black or African American, non-Hispanic/Latino; 3 Hispanic/Latino), 3 international. 56 applicants, 46% accepted, 29 enrolled. In 2016, 5 master's awarded. *Degree requirements:* For master's, comprehensive exam, thesis. *Entrance requirements:* Additional exam requirements/recommendations for international students: Required—TOEFL (minimum score 80 iBT), IELTS (minimum score 6), PTE. *Application deadline:* For fall admission, 8/11 for domestic students; for spring admission, 11/1 for domestic students. Applications are processed on a rolling basis. *Application fee:* $50. Electronic applications accepted. *Expenses:* $618 per credit hour. *Financial support:* In 2016–17, 6 students received support. Scholarships/grants available. Financial award application deadline: 4/1; financial award applicants required to submit FAFSA. *Faculty research:* Program innovation, instruments for educational evaluation. *Unit head:* Dr. Melinda Thompson, Graduate Advisor, 325-674-3706, Fax: 325-674-6180, E-mail: melinda.thomson@acu.edu. *Application contact:* Corey Patterson, Director of Graduate Admission and Recruiting, 325-674-6566, Fax: 325-674-6717, E-mail: gradinfo@acu.edu.
Website: http://www.acu.edu/graduate/academics/christian-ministry.html

**Ambrose University,** Ambrose Seminary, Calgary, AB T3H 0L5, Canada. Offers Biblical/theological studies (MA), including New Testament, Old Testament, theology; Christian studies (MCS, Diploma); intercultural ministries (M Div, MA); leadership (Certificate); leadership and ministry (MA), including chaplaincy, leadership; pastoral ministry (M Div). *Accreditation:* ATS (one or more programs are accredited). *Program availability:* Part-time, blended/hybrid learning. *Faculty:* 14 full-time (3 women), 4 part-time/adjunct (1 woman). *Students:* 76 applicants, 74% accepted, 35 enrolled. In 2016, 21 master's, 1 other advanced degree awarded. *Degree requirements:* For master's, variable foreign language requirement, thesis (for some programs), internship (for M Div, MA in leadership and ministry, MA in intercultural ministries); thesis (for MA in Biblical/theological studies). *Entrance requirements:* For master's, undergraduate degree from other accredited university or bible college, minimum GPA of 2.0. Additional exam requirements/recommendations for international students: Required—PTE (minimum score 58), TOEFL (minimum score 560 paper-based, 83 iBT) or IELTS (minimum score 6.5). *Application deadline:* For fall admission, 8/1 for domestic students, 4/15 for international students; for winter admission, 12/1 for domestic students, 11/15 for international students. Applications are processed on a rolling basis. Application fee: $70 ($100 for international students). Electronic applications accepted. *Expenses: Tuition:* Full-time $11,850 Canadian dollars; part-time $395 Canadian dollars per credit hour. *Required fees:* $810 Canadian dollars; $27 Canadian dollars per credit hour. $50 Canadian dollars per semester. Tuition and fees vary according to course load and program. *Financial support:* Career-related internships or fieldwork and scholarships/grants available. Support available to part-time students. Financial award application deadline: 3/30. *Faculty research:* Evangelicalism and sociology, missiological trends, chaplaincy, intertestamental studies, postmodernism. *Unit head:* Dr. Jo-Ann Badley, Dean of Theology, 403-410-2000 Ext. 3994, Fax: 403-571-2556, E-mail: jbadley@ambrose.edu. *Application contact:* Andreas Striefler, Enrollment Advisor, 403-410-2970, Fax: 403-571-2556, E-mail: enrolment@ambrose.edu.
Website: https://ambrose.edu/seminary

**American Baptist Seminary of the West,** Graduate and Professional Programs, Berkeley, CA 94704-3029. Offers community leadership (MA); theology (M Div, MA). MA program in theology offered jointly with Graduate Theological Union. *Accreditation:* ACIPE; ATS (one or more programs are accredited). *Program availability:* Part-time, evening/weekend, online learning. *Entrance requirements:* Additional exam requirements/recommendations for international students: Required—TOEFL (minimum score 550 paper-based). Electronic applications accepted.

**Amridge University,** Graduate and Professional Programs, Montgomery, AL 36117. Offers Biblical studies (MA, PhD); Christian ministry (MS); family therapy (D Min); human services (MS); leadership and management (MS); marriage and family therapy (M Div, MA, PhD); ministerial leadership (M Div, MS); New Testament studies (MA); Old Testament studies (MA); professional counseling (M Div, MA, PhD); theology (M Div, D Min). *Program availability:* Part-time, evening/weekend, online learning. *Faculty:* 22 full-time (3 women), 10 part-time/adjunct (6 women). *Students:* 81 full-time (49 women), 225 part-time (137 women); includes 81 minority (80 Black or African American, non-Hispanic/Latino; 1 Hispanic/Latino). Average age 41. 122 applicants, 100% accepted, 79 enrolled. *Degree requirements:* For master's, one foreign language, comprehensive exam (for some programs), thesis (for some programs); for doctorate, one foreign language, comprehensive exam (for some programs), thesis/dissertation (for some programs). *Entrance requirements:* For master's, official transcript showing an earned 4-year BA or BS from regionally- or nationally-accredited institution; for doctorate, official transcript showing earned graduate degree from regionally- or nationally-accredited institution; writing sample (e.g. career monograph, published journal article, term paper from master's degree or doctoral dissertation); interview. Additional exam requirements/recommendations for international students: Required—TOEFL (minimum score 79 iBT). *Application deadline:* Applications are processed on a rolling basis. Application fee: $50. Electronic applications accepted. *Expenses: Tuition:* Full-time $12,870; part-time $715 per credit hour. *Required fees:* $1300; $650 per semester. *Financial support:* In 2016–17, 45 students received support. Federal Work-Study and scholarships/grants available. Support available to part-time students. Financial award applicants required to submit FAFSA. *Faculty research:* Technology and mental healthcare, resilience in black families, theology and congregational ministry. *Unit head:* Laina Costanza, Vice President, Student Affairs, 888-790-8080 Ext. 1, Fax: 334-387-3878, E-mail: cc@amridgeuniversity.edu. *Application contact:* Brooks Housley, Student Affairs Coordinator, 888-790-8080 Ext. 1, Fax: 334-387-3878, E-mail: admissions@amridgeuniversity.edu.

**Anabaptist Mennonite Biblical Seminary,** Graduate and Professional Programs, Elkhart, IN 46517-1999. Offers chaplaincy (M Div); Christian faith formation (M Div); Christian formation (MA); Christian spiritual formation (Certificate); divinity (M Div); pastoral ministry (M Div); pastoral theology for financial professionals (Certificate); peace studies (M Div), including environmental sustainability leadership (M Div, MA); theological studies (M Div, Certificate), including peace studies (M Div), theology and ethics (M Div); theology and peace studies (MA), including conflict transformation, environmental sustainability leadership (M Div, MA), international development administration; United Methodist leadership (M Div). Conflict transformation and environmental sustainability leadership concentrations offered in cooperation with Goshen College; international development administration offered in cooperation with Andrews University. *Accreditation:* ACIPE; ATS. *Program availability:* Part-time, 100% online, blended/hybrid learning. *Faculty:* 14 full-time (6 women), 17 part-time/adjunct (8 women). *Students:* 38 full-time (14 women), 60 part-time (33 women); includes 15 minority (4 Black or African American, non-Hispanic/Latino; 5 Asian, non-Hispanic/Latino; 5 Hispanic/Latino; 1 Two or more races, non-Hispanic/Latino), 15 international.

Average age 35. 43 applicants, 70% accepted, 29 enrolled. In 2016, 16 master's, 2 other advanced degrees awarded. *Degree requirements:* For master's, variable foreign language requirement, comprehensive exam (for some programs), thesis optional, senior interview. *Entrance requirements:* For master's, undergraduate degree transcripts, 3 letters of reference, essay. Additional exam requirements/recommendations for international students: Required—TOEFL (minimum score 90 iBT); Recommended—IELTS (minimum score 7). *Application deadline:* For fall admission, 6/1 priority date for domestic students, 5/1 priority date for international students. Applications are processed on a rolling basis. Application fee: $25. Electronic applications accepted. *Expenses: Tuition:* Full-time $13,950; part-time $5640 per year. *Required fees:* $900; $300 per unit. $50 per term. *Financial support:* In 2016–17, 40 students received support. Career-related internships or fieldwork, scholarships/grants, unspecified assistantships, and church matching grants available. Support available to part-time students. Financial award application deadline: 4/15; financial award applicants required to submit FAFSA. *Faculty research:* Biblical studies, peace studies, theology, ethics, creation care or environmental ethics, church history, church leadership, mission, ministry, preaching, pastoral leadership, social justice, peacemaking, Jesus Christ, Christianity, Anabaptism, Mennonite, Scripture, Bible, Old Testament, New Testament, spirituality, clinical pastoral education, teaching, faith formation, pastoral care, Koine Greek, Hebrew, Aramaic, Syriac, Ugaritic. *Unit head:* Sara Wenger Shenk, President, 800-964-2627, Fax: 574-295-0092. *Application contact:* Daniel Grimes, Director of Admissions, 574-296-6266, Fax: 574-295-0092, E-mail: admissions@ambs.edu.
Website: http://www.ambs.edu/

**Anderson University,** David T. Clamp Graduate School of Christian Ministry, Anderson, SC 29621-4035. Offers Biblical preaching (D Min); ministry (M Min). *Program availability:* Online learning. *Degree requirements:* For master's, capstone course, ministry project. *Entrance requirements:* For master's, 3 references. *Financial support:* Tuition waivers available. Financial award application deadline: 3/1; financial award applicants required to submit FAFSA. *Unit head:* Dr. Michael Duduit, Dean, 864-328-1809, E-mail: ministry@andersonuniversity.edu. *Application contact:* Mallory Knight, Graduate Admission Counselor, 864-231-2182, Fax: 864-231-2115, E-mail: malloryknight@andersonuniversity.edu.
Website: https://www.andersonuniversity.edu/christian-studies/david-t-clamp-graduate-school-christian-ministry

**Andrews University,** School of Graduate Studies, Seventh-day Adventist Theological Seminary, Berrien Springs, MI 49104. Offers ministry (M Div, D Min); pastoral ministry (MA); religious education (MA, Ed D, PhD, Ed S); theology (M Th, Th D); youth ministry (MA). *Faculty:* 40 full-time (5 women), 12 part-time/adjunct (2 women). *Students:* 477 full-time (69 women), 530 part-time (83 women); includes 498 minority (237 Black or African American, non-Hispanic/Latino; 3 American Indian or Alaska Native, non-Hispanic/Latino; 53 Asian, non-Hispanic/Latino; 198 Hispanic/Latino; 2 Native Hawaiian or other Pacific Islander, non-Hispanic/Latino; 5 Two or more races, non-Hispanic/Latino), 234 international. Average age 40. In 2016, 194 master's, 52 doctorates awarded. *Degree requirements:* For master's, thesis optional; for doctorate, variable foreign language requirement, thesis/dissertation. *Entrance requirements:* For master's, GRE Subject Test, minimum GPA of 2.0. Additional exam requirements/recommendations for international students: Required—TOEFL (minimum score 550 paper-based). *Application deadline:* Applications are processed on a rolling basis. Application fee: $40. *Financial support:* Fellowships, research assistantships, teaching assistantships, career-related internships or fieldwork, Federal Work-Study, and institutionally sponsored loans available. *Faculty research:* Biblical archaeology, biblical studies, biblical language learning methods, church growth. *Unit head:* Dr. Jiri Moskala, Dean, 269-471-3537. *Application contact:* Justina Clayburn, Director, 800-253-2874, Fax: 269-471-6321.

**Appalachian Bible College,** Graduate Program, Mount Hope, WV 25880. Offers ministry (MA). *Program availability:* Part-time, online learning. *Entrance requirements:* For master's, ABHE Bible Content Exam, bachelor's degree, 3 references, minimum undergraduate cumulative GPA of 2.75. Additional exam requirements/recommendations for international students: Required—TOEFL (minimum score 550 paper-based). Application fee: $25. Electronic applications accepted. One-time fee: $25 part-time. Tuition and fees vary according to course level, degree level and program. *Unit head:* Dr. John Rinehart, Dean of Graduate Studies, 304-877-6428. *Application contact:* Benjamin Cale, Director of Admissions, 304-877-6428 Ext. 311, Fax: 304-877-5082, E-mail: benjamin.cale@abc.edu.

**Aquinas Institute of Theology,** Graduate and Professional Programs, St. Louis, MO 63108. Offers biblical studies (Certificate); church music (MM); health care mission (MAHCM); ministry (M Div); pastoral care (Certificate); pastoral ministry (MAPM); pastoral studies (MAPS); preaching (D Min); spiritual direction (Certificate); theology (M Div, MA); Thomistic studies (Certificate); M Div/MA; MA/PhD; MAPS/MSW. *Accreditation:* ATS (one or more programs are accredited). *Program availability:* Part-time, evening/weekend, online learning. *Degree requirements:* For master's, variable foreign language requirement, comprehensive exam (for some programs), thesis (for some programs); for doctorate, thesis/dissertation. *Entrance requirements:* For master's and Certificate, MAT; for doctorate, 3 years of ministerial experience, 6 hours of graduate course work in homiletics, M Div or the equivalent, minimum GPA of 3.0. Additional exam requirements/recommendations for international students: Required—TOEFL. *Expenses:* Contact institution. *Faculty research:* Theology of preaching, hermeneutics, lay ecclesial ministry, pastoral and practical theology.

**Argosy University, Sarasota,** College of Psychology and Behavioral Sciences, Sarasota, FL 34235. Offers community counseling (MA); counseling psychology (Ed D); counselor education and supervision (Ed D); forensic psychology (MA); marriage and family therapy (MA); mental health counseling (MA); pastoral community counseling (Ed D).

**Asbury Theological Seminary,** Graduate and Professional Programs, Wilmore, KY 40390-1199. Offers M Div, MA, MAAS, MACE, MACL, MACM, MACP, MAMFC, MAMHC, MAPC, MASF, MAYM, Th M, D Min, PhD, Certificate. *Accreditation:* ATS. *Program availability:* Part-time, online learning. Terminal master's awarded for partial completion of doctoral program. *Degree requirements:* For master's, thesis (for some programs); for doctorate, thesis/dissertation, qualifying exam. *Entrance requirements:* For master's, minimum GPA of 2.75; for doctorate, minimum GPA of 3.0. Additional exam requirements/recommendations for international students: Required—TOEFL, IELTS. Electronic applications accepted.

**Ashland Theological Seminary,** Graduate Programs, Ashland, OH 44805. Offers Biblical studies (MA); Christian ministries (MACM), including Black church studies (MACM, D Min), general Christian ministries, leadership, spiritual formation (MACM, D Min); clinical mental health counseling (MA); counseling (MAC); historical and theological studies (MA), including Anabaptism and Pietism, Christian theology, church history, New Testament, Old Testament; ministry (D Min), including Black church studies (MACM, D Min), chaplaincy (M Div, D Min), independent design, spiritual formation (MACM, D Min), transformational leadership; pastoral ministry (M Div), including chaplaincy (M Div, D Min), general ministry. MAC program offered in Detroit, MI. *Accreditation:* ATS. *Program availability:* Part-time. *Degree requirements:* For

## Pastoral Ministry and Counseling

master's, 2 foreign languages, comprehensive exam (for some programs), thesis (for some programs); for doctorate, thesis/dissertation. *Entrance requirements:* For master's, bachelor's degree from accredited institution with a minimum undergraduate GPA of 2.75; for doctorate, M Div, minimum undergraduate GPA of 3.0. Additional exam requirements/recommendations for international students: Required—TOEFL (minimum score 500 paper-based; 65 iBT). *Application deadline:* For fall admission, 8/30 for domestic students. Applications are processed on a rolling basis. Application fee: $35. Electronic applications accepted. *Expenses: Tuition:* Full-time $15,120; part-time $630 per semester hour. Tuition and fees vary according to program. *Financial support:* Research assistantships, teaching assistantships, career-related internships or fieldwork, institutionally sponsored loans, scholarships/grants, and unspecified assistantships available. Support available to part-time students. Financial award application deadline: 5/15; financial award applicants required to submit FAFSA. *Faculty research:* Semitic languages and linguistics, rhetorical and social-scientific criticism, Anabaptist studies, inner spiritual healing, African-American clergy in film and literature. *Unit head:* Dr. Mark Harden, President, 419-289-5160, Fax: 419-289-5969, E-mail: mharden@ashland.edu. *Application contact:* Dr. Mark Harden, President, 419-289-5160, Fax: 419-289-5969, E-mail: mharden@ashland.edu.

**Assemblies of God Theological Seminary,** Graduate and Professional Programs, Springfield, MO 65802. Offers Biblical interpretation and theology (PhD); Christian ministries (MA); divinity (M Div); intercultural studies (MA, PhD); ministry (D Min); missiology (DAIS); pastoral studies (MPL); theological studies (MA, Th M). *Accreditation:* ATS. *Program availability:* Part-time, evening/weekend, 100% online. *Degree requirements:* For master's, variable foreign language requirement; for doctorate, thesis/dissertation. *Entrance requirements:* For master's, minimum GPA of 2.5; for doctorate, GRE (for PhD in Bible theology), minimum GPA of 3.0. Additional exam requirements/recommendations for international students: Required—TOEFL (minimum score 550 paper-based; 80 iBT). Electronic applications accepted.

**Atlantic School of Theology,** Graduate and Professional Programs, Halifax, NS B3H 3B5, Canada. Offers ministry (M Div); theological studies (Graduate Certificate). *Accreditation:* ATS. *Program availability:* Part-time, online learning. *Degree requirements:* For master's, thesis (for some programs). *Entrance requirements:* For master's and Graduate Certificate, minimum B average in undergraduate course work. *Faculty research:* Ethics and biology; death, dying and pastoral care; theology and the economy; adult education; John and anti-Judaism.

**Atlantic University,** Spiritual Guidance Mentor Program, Virginia Beach, VA 23451-2061. Offers Certificate. *Entrance requirements:* For degree, 500-word essay. *Application deadline:* For fall admission, 8/13 for domestic students; for spring admission, 11/13 for domestic students; for summer admission, 4/9 for domestic students. Application fee: $35. *Expenses:* Contact institution. *Application contact:* Rachel Alvidrez, Educational Services Manager, 757-631-8101, Fax: 757-631-8096, E-mail: info@atlanticuniv.edu.
Website: https://www.atlanticuniv.edu/academics/programs/spiritual-mentor-certificate/

**Austin Presbyterian Theological Seminary,** Graduate and Professional Programs, Austin, TX 78705-5797. Offers divinity (M Div); ministry (D Min); ministry practice (MA); theological studies (MA); youth ministry (MA); M Div/MSSW. M Div/MSSW offered in collaboration with The University of Texas at Austin School of Social Work. *Accreditation:* ACIPE; ATS. *Faculty:* 20 full-time (6 women), 5 part-time/adjunct (1 woman). *Students:* 88 full-time (50 women), 74 part-time (41 women). In 2016, 44 master's, 4 doctorates awarded. *Degree requirements:* For master's, Greek, Hebrew (for M Div); for doctorate, thesis/dissertation. *Entrance requirements:* For master's, references (for M Div). Additional exam requirements/recommendations for international students: Required—TOEFL (minimum score 550 paper-based; 79 iBT). *Application deadline:* For fall admission, 5/1 for domestic students, 1/1 for international students; for summer admission, 2/2 for domestic students. Applications are processed on a rolling basis. Electronic applications accepted. *Expenses: Tuition:* Full-time $13,200; part-time $220 per credit. *Required fees:* $120; $120 per credit. $25 per semester. One-time fee: $175 full-time; $120 part-time. Tuition and fees vary according to degree level and program. *Financial support:* Fellowships, career-related internships or fieldwork, institutionally sponsored loans, and scholarships/grants available. Support available to part-time students. Financial award application deadline: 3/1; financial award applicants required to submit FAFSA. *Faculty research:* Mystical theology, religious pluralism, narrative preaching, social ethics, pastoral care and healing. *Unit head:* Dr. David Jensen, Academic Dean, 512-404-4821, Fax: 512-479-0738, E-mail: dean@austinseminary.edu. *Application contact:* Dr. Jack Barden, Vice President for Admissions, 512-404-4827, Fax: 512-472-7089, E-mail: admissions@austinseminary.edu.

**Ave Maria University,** Graduate Programs, Ave Maria, FL 34142. Offers pastoral theology (MTS); theology (MA, PhD). Terminal master's awarded for partial completion of doctoral program. *Degree requirements:* For master's, one foreign language, thesis; for doctorate, 3 foreign languages, comprehensive exam, thesis/dissertation. *Entrance requirements:* For master's, GRE; for doctorate, GRE, M Div or equivalent; MA or MTS in religion, theology, or philosophy; bachelor's degree with strong background in religion, theology, and/or philosophy.

**Azusa Pacific University,** College of Liberal Arts and Sciences, Program in Transformational Urban Leadership, Azusa, CA 91702-7000. Offers MA.

**Azusa Pacific University,** Haggard Graduate School of Theology, Program in Divinity, Azusa, CA 91702-7000. Offers M Div.

**Azusa Pacific University,** Haggard Graduate School of Theology, Program in Pastoral Studies, Concentration in Church Leadership and Development, Azusa, CA 91702-7000. Offers MAPS.

**Azusa Pacific University,** Haggard Graduate School of Theology, Program in Pastoral Studies, Concentration in Worship Leadership, Azusa, CA 91702-7000. Offers MAPS.

**Bakke Graduate University,** Programs in Pastoral Ministry and Business, Dallas, TX 75243-7039. Offers business administration (MBA); church and ministry multiplication (D Min); global urban leadership (MA); leadership (D Min); ministry in complex contexts (D Min); social and civic entrepreneurship (MA); theology of work (D Min); theology reflection (D Min); transformational leadership (DTL); urban youth ministry (D Min). *Program availability:* Part-time, online learning. *Degree requirements:* For master's, thesis; for doctorate, thesis/dissertation. *Entrance requirements:* For master's, 2 years of ministry experience, BA in Biblical studies or theology; for doctorate, 3 years of ministry experience, M Div. Additional exam requirements/recommendations for international students: Required—TOEFL. Electronic applications accepted. *Faculty research:* Theological systems, church management, worship.

**Baptist Bible College,** Graduate School of Theology, Springfield, MO 65803-3498. Offers biblical counseling (MA); biblical studies (MA); church ministry (MA); intercultural studies (MA); theology (M Div). *Program availability:* Part-time. *Entrance requirements:* Additional exam requirements/recommendations for international students: Required—TOEFL. Electronic applications accepted.

**The Baptist College of Florida,** Graduate Programs, Graceville, FL 32440-1898. Offers Christian ministry (MA); Christian studies (MA), including Biblical studies; music

and worship leadership (MA). *Program availability:* Part-time, 100% online, blended/hybrid learning. *Degree requirements:* For master's, variable foreign language requirement, comprehensive exam (for some programs), thesis (for some programs). *Entrance requirements:* For master's, regionally-accredited undergraduate degree, undergraduate courses in field, minimum GPA of 2.5. Additional exam requirements/recommendations for international students: Required—TOEFL. Electronic applications accepted. *Expenses:* Contact institution. *Faculty research:* Biblical studies, ministry studies.

**Baptist Theological Seminary at Richmond,** Graduate and Professional Programs, Richmond, VA 23228. Offers Biblical interpretation (M Div); Christian education formation (M Div); Christian ministry (MCM); justice and peacebuilding (M Div); ministry (D Min); religious freedom (M Div); theological studies (MTS, Graduate Certificate); theology (M Div); youth and student ministries (M Div); M Div/MBA; M Div/MS; M Div/MSW. *Accreditation:* ATS. *Program availability:* Part-time, 100% online, blended/hybrid learning. *Faculty:* 5 full-time (1 woman), 11 part-time/adjunct (2 women). *Students:* 42 full-time (23 women), 34 part-time (19 women); includes 11 minority (all Black or African American, non-Hispanic/Latino), 2 international. Average age 46. In 2016, 8 master's, 2 doctorates awarded. *Degree requirements:* For master's and Graduate Certificate, thesis optional; for doctorate, comprehensive exam, thesis/dissertation, field study, independent study. *Entrance requirements:* For master's, BA/BS, minimum GPA of 2.2, 2 references, resume, official transcripts, writing sample; for doctorate, MAT (minimum score of 400), M Div with minimum GPA of 2.75, 3 years of full-time ministry experience, 3 references, resume, official transcripts, writing sample, personal statement. Additional exam requirements/recommendations for international students: Required—TOEFL (minimum score 550 paper-based), IELTS (minimum score 5.5). *Application deadline:* For fall admission, 7/1 for domestic students, 5/1 for international students; for winter admission, 12/15 for domestic students, 9/1 for international students; for spring admission, 1/15 for domestic students, 10/1 for international students. Applications are processed on a rolling basis. Application fee: $35. Electronic applications accepted. *Expenses:* $19,800 for 12 credit hours for both semesters; $1,650 per 3 semester hour course. *Financial support:* In 2016–17, 46 students received support, including 11 teaching assistantships (averaging $3,300 per year); scholarships/grants also available. Financial award application deadline: 2/1. *Faculty research:* Biblical studies, pastoral care, church history, theology, ministry. *Unit head:* Dr. Ronald W. Crawford, President, 804-204-1201, Fax: 804-355-8182, E-mail: rcrawford@btsr.edu. *Application contact:* Melissa Fallen, Director of Admissions and Recruitment, 804-204-1208, E-mail: admissions@btsr.edu.
Website: http://www.btsr.edu/programs/degree-programs/

**Barry University,** College of Arts and Sciences, Department of Theology and Philosophy, Miami Shores, FL 33161-6695. Offers ministry (D Min); pastoral ministry for Hispanics (MA); pastoral theology (MA); practical theology (MA). *Accreditation:* ATS. *Program availability:* Part-time, evening/weekend. *Degree requirements:* For master's, comprehensive exam, thesis optional; for doctorate, thesis/dissertation. *Entrance requirements:* For master's, GRE General Test or MAT, minimum GPA of 3.0. Electronic applications accepted. *Faculty research:* Fundamental morals, bioethics, social ethics, liturgical and sacramental theology, biblical studies.

**Bethany Global University,** Graduate Programs, Bloomington, MN 55438. Offers intercultural ministry education (MA); intercultural ministry leadership (MA); intercultural ministry studies (MA). *Program availability:* Part-time, evening/weekend, online only, 100% online. *Faculty:* 1 full-time (0 women), 5 part-time/adjunct (0 women). *Students:* 39 part-time (13 women). *Degree requirements:* For master's, thesis (for some programs). *Entrance requirements:* For master's, bachelor's degree, Christian testimony. Additional exam requirements/recommendations for international students: Required—TOEFL. Electronic applications accepted. *Expenses:* $300 per credit hour. *Faculty research:* Cross cultural training. *Unit head:* Dr. Jim Raymo, Director, 952-829-4680, E-mail: jim.raymo@bethanygu.edu. *Application contact:* Dr. Jim Raymo, Director, 952-829-4680, E-mail: jim.raymo@bethanygu.edu.
Website: https://bethanygu.edu/programs/graduate/

**Bethany Theological Seminary,** Graduate and Professional Programs, Richmond, IN 47374-4019. Offers biblical studies (MA Th); ministry studies (M Div); peace studies (M Div, MA Th); theological studies (MA Th, CATS); youth ministry (M Div). *Accreditation:* ACIPE; ATS. *Program availability:* Part-time, online learning. *Degree requirements:* For master's, thesis (for some programs). *Entrance requirements:* For master's, letters of reference. Additional exam requirements/recommendations for international students: Required—TOEFL (minimum score 550 paper-based).

**Bethel College,** Adult and Graduate Programs, Program in Ministries, Mishawaka, IN 46545-5591. Offers M Min. *Program availability:* Part-time, evening/weekend, 100% online, blended/hybrid learning. *Faculty:* 7 part-time/adjunct (0 women). *Students:* 7 full-time (4 women), 34 part-time (18 women); includes 8 minority (4 Black or African American, non-Hispanic/Latino; 2 Hispanic/Latino; 2 Two or more races, non-Hispanic/Latino), 1 international. Average age 37. 12 applicants, 83% accepted, 10 enrolled. In 2016, 6 master's awarded. *Degree requirements:* For master's, thesis or alternative. *Entrance requirements:* Additional exam requirements/recommendations for international students: Required—TOEFL (minimum score 540 paper-based). *Application deadline:* For fall admission, 5/1 for international students; for spring admission, 10/1 for international students. Applications are processed on a rolling basis. Application fee: $0. Electronic applications accepted. *Expenses: Tuition:* Full-time $6750; part-time $3375 per credit hour. *Required fees:* $75 per semester. Tuition and fees vary according to course load and program. *Financial support:* Career-related internships or fieldwork available. Financial award applicants required to submit FAFSA. *Unit head:* Steve Ganger, Director, 574-807-7507, E-mail: gangers@bethelcollege.edu.

**Bethel Seminary,** Graduate and Professional Programs, St. Paul, MN 55112-6998. Offers Anglican studies (Certificate); children's and family ministry (MA); Christian studies (Certificate); Christian thought (MA); church planting (Certificate); Greek and Hebrew language (M Div); Greek language (M Div); Hebrew language (M Div); marriage and family therapy (MA, Certificate); mental health counseling (MA); ministry (MA, D Min); ministry practice (Certificate); theological studies (MA, Certificate); transformational leadership (MA); young life youth ministry (Certificate). *Accreditation:* ACIPE. *Program availability:* Part-time, evening/weekend, blended/hybrid learning. *Faculty:* 14 full-time (4 women), 37 part-time/adjunct (17 women). *Students:* 369 full-time (165 women), 147 part-time (43 women); includes 138 minority (88 Black or African American, non-Hispanic/Latino; 45 Asian, non-Hispanic/Latino; 28 Hispanic/Latino; 2 Native Hawaiian or other Pacific Islander, non-Hispanic/Latino; 15 Two or more races, non-Hispanic/Latino), 15 international. 322 applicants, 75% accepted, 174 enrolled. In 2016, 168 master's, 24 doctorates, 6 other advanced degrees awarded. *Degree requirements:* For master's, variable foreign language requirement, thesis (for some programs); for doctorate, thesis/dissertation. *Entrance requirements:* For master's, letters of reference, transcripts, personal statement; for doctorate, M Div, letters of reference, organizational support; for Certificate, letters of reference, family essay, personal statement, and family of origin paper (for marriage and family therapy). Additional exam requirements/recommendations for international students: Required—TOEFL (minimum score 550 paper-based; 87 iBT). *Application deadline:* For fall admission, 8/1 priority date for domestic students, 8/1 for international students; for winter admission, 12/1 priority date for domestic students; for spring admission, 1/1 priority date for domestic students. Applications are processed on a rolling basis. Application fee: $0. Electronic applications accepted. *Expenses:* Contact institution. *Financial support:* In 2016–17, 404 students received support. Teaching assistantships, career-related internships or fieldwork, Federal Work-Study, and scholarships/grants available. Financial award applicants required to submit FAFSA. *Faculty research:* Nature of theology, ethics, Biblical commentaries, nature of God, science and theology. *Unit head:* Dr. David Clark, Vice-President and Dean, 651-638-6659, E-mail: d-clark@bethel.edu. *Application contact:* Jen Niska, Director of Admissions, 651-638-6288, Fax: 651-638-6002, E-mail: seminary-admissions@bethel.edu. Website: https://www.bethel.edu/seminary

**Biblical Theological Seminary,** Graduate and Professional Programs, Hatfield, PA 19440-2499. Offers advanced missional leadership (D Min); advanced pastoral studies (Certificate); biblical counseling (Certificate); biblical studies (MA, Certificate); counseling (MA); ministry (M Div, MA); missional theology (MA). *Accreditation:* ATS. *Program availability:* Part-time, evening/weekend. *Faculty:* 9 full-time (1 woman), 21 part-time/adjunct (4 women). *Students:* 145 full-time (54 women), 111 part-time (44 women); includes 98 minority (57 Black or African American, non-Hispanic/Latino; 1 American Indian or Alaska Native, non-Hispanic/Latino; 35 Asian, non-Hispanic/Latino; 4 Hispanic/Latino; 1 Two or more races, non-Hispanic/Latino), 67 international. Average age 39. 165 applicants, 64% accepted, 95 enrolled. In 2016, 47 master's, 7 doctorates awarded. *Degree requirements:* For master's, variable foreign language requirement, thesis optional; for doctorate, thesis/dissertation. *Entrance requirements:* Additional exam requirements/recommendations for international students: Required—TOEFL (minimum score 550 paper-based; 80 iBT). *Application deadline:* Applications are processed on a rolling basis. Application fee: $30. Electronic applications accepted. *Expenses:* Tuition: Full-time $12,360; part-time $6180 per credit. *Required fees:* $75; $75 per credit. $50 per semester. *Financial support:* In 2016–17, 170 students received support. Career-related internships or fieldwork, institutionally sponsored loans, and scholarships/grants available. Support available to part-time students. Financial award application deadline: 8/30; financial award applicants required to submit FAFSA. *Faculty research:* Theology, culture, Biblical interpretation. *Application contact:* Rev. Michael Heath, Student Advancement Counselor, 215-368-5000 Ext. 152, Fax: 215-368-7002, E-mail: mheath@biblical.edu. Website: http://www.biblical.edu/

**Biola University,** Talbot School of Theology, La Mirada, CA 90639-0001. Offers adult/family ministry (MACE); Bible exposition (MA, Th M); Biblical and theological studies (Certificate); biblical and theological studies/diversified (MA); children's ministry (MACE); Christian education (MACE); cross-cultural education ministry (MACE); educational studies (Ed D, PhD); evangelism and discipleship (M Div); general Christian education (MACE); Messianic Jewish studies (M Div, Certificate); missions and intercultural studies (M Div); New Testament (MA, Th M); Old Testament (MA); Old Testament and Semitics (Th M); pastoral and general ministry (M Div); pastoral care and counseling (M Div, MACML); philosophy (MA); preaching and pastoral ministry (MACML); spiritual formation (M Div, Certificate); spiritual formation and soul care (MA); sports ministry (MACML); theology (MA, Th M, D Min, Certificate); youth ministry (MACE). *Accreditation:* ATS. *Program availability:* Part-time, evening/weekend. *Entrance requirements:* For master's, bachelor's degree from accredited college or university; minimum GPA of 2.6 (for M Div), 3.0 (for MA); for doctorate, M Div or MA. Additional exam requirements/recommendations for international students: Required—TOEFL (minimum score 600 paper-based; 88 iBT). Electronic applications accepted. *Faculty research:* New Testament, Old Testament, spiritual formation, Christian education, theological studies, Christian ministry, preaching and pastoral ministry, language and literature, bible exposition, Christian leadership.

**Bob Jones University,** Graduate Programs, Greenville, SC 29614. Offers accountancy (MS); Bible (MA); Bible translation (MA); Biblical studies (Certificate); broadcast management (MS); business administration (MBA); church history (MA, PhD); church ministries (MA); church music (MM); cinema and video production (MA); counseling (MS); curriculum and instruction (Ed D); divinity (M Div); dramatic production (MA); educational leadership (MS, Ed D, Ed S); elementary education (M Ed, MAT); English (M Ed, MA, MAT); fine arts (MA); graphic design (MA); history (M Ed, MA); illustration (MA); interpretative speech (MA); mathematics (M Ed, MAT); medical missions (Certificate); ministry (MM, D Min); multi-categorical special education (M Ed, MAT); music (M Ed); New Testament interpretation (PhD); Old Testament interpretation (PhD); orchestral instrument performance (MM); organ performance (MM); pastoral studies (MA); personnel services (MS, Ed S); piano pedagogy (MM); piano performance (MM); platform arts (MA); radio and television broadcasting (MS); rhetoric and public address (MA); secondary education (M Ed); studio art (MA); teaching Bible (MA); theology (MA, PhD); voice performance (MM); youth ministries (MA); M Div/MM.

**Boston College,** School of Theology and Ministry, Chestnut Hill, MA 02467-3800. Offers church leadership (MA); divinity (M Div); pastoral ministry (MA), including Hispanic ministry, liturgy and worship, pastoral care and counseling, spirituality; religious education (MA, M Ed); sacred theology (STD, STL); social justice/social ministry (MA); spiritual direction (MA); theological studies (MTS); theology (Th M, PhD); youth ministry (MA); MA/MA; MS/MA; MSW/MA. *Accreditation:* TEAC. *Program availability:* Part-time. *Degree requirements:* For doctorate, one foreign language, thesis/dissertation. *Entrance requirements:* For doctorate, GRE. Additional exam requirements/recommendations for international students: Required—TOEFL (minimum score 550 paper-based). Electronic applications accepted. Tuition and fees vary according to program. *Faculty research:* Philosophy and practice of religious education, pastoral psychology, liturgical and spiritual theology, spiritual formation for the practice of ministry.

**Boston University,** School of Theology, Boston, MA 02118. Offers chaplaincy (M Div); choral conducting (MSM); church and the arts (M Div); constructive theology and ethics (PhD), including constructive theology, theological ethics; ecological theology and ethics (MTS); global and community engagement (M Div); history and hermeneutics (PhD), including Biblical studies, church history, liturgical studies, mission studies; organ (MSM); pastoral ministry (M Div); practical theology (PhD), including church and society, congregation and community, evangelism and missiology, homiletics, leadership and administration, pastoral theology and psychology, religious education, spirituality studies, worship; religion and conflict transformation (MTS); religion and science (MTS); religion and the academy (M Div); spirituality studies (MTS); theology (MTS, STM); transcultural studies (MTS); transformational leadership (D Min); M Div/MSM; M Div/MSW; MTS/MSW. PhD in history and hermeneutics: mission studies offered in collaboration with Gordon-Conwell Theological Seminary. *Accreditation:* ACIPE; ATS. *Program availability:* Part-time, blended/hybrid learning. *Faculty:* 34 full-time (14 women), 7 part-time/adjunct (3 women). *Students:* 260 full-time (131 women), 69 part-time (30 women); includes 69 minority (36 Black or African American, non-Hispanic/Latino; 10 Asian, non-Hispanic/Latino; 16 Hispanic/Latino; 7 Two or more races, non-Hispanic/Latino), 53 international. Average age 35. 234 applicants, 71% accepted, 106 enrolled. In 2016, 78 master's, 9 doctorates awarded. *Degree requirements:* For master's, comprehensive exam (for some programs), thesis optional, contextual education; for doctorate, 2 foreign languages, comprehensive exam, thesis/dissertation. *Entrance requirements:* For master's, minimum GPA 3.0; for doctorate, GRE General

Test, minimum GPA of 3.3. Additional exam requirements/recommendations for international students: Required—TOEFL (minimum score 570 paper-based; 89 iBT). *Application deadline:* For fall admission, 1/15 priority date for domestic and international students; for spring admission, 10/15 priority date for domestic and international students. Applications are processed on a rolling basis. Application fee: $95. Electronic applications accepted. *Expenses:* $19,500 per year tuition; $156 per semester student service fee; $54 per semester community service fee; $199 per semester health and wellness fee. *Financial support:* In 2016–17, 252 students received support, including 78 fellowships with full tuition reimbursements available (averaging $4,537 per year), 32 research assistantships (averaging $6,000 per year), 32 teaching assistantships with full and partial tuition reimbursements available (averaging $20,000 per year); career-related internships or fieldwork, Federal Work-Study, institutionally sponsored loans, scholarships/grants, traineeships, health care benefits, tuition waivers (full and partial), and unspecified assistantships also available. Support available to part-time students. Financial award application deadline: 7/15; financial award applicants required to submit FAFSA. *Faculty research:* Practical theology, Biblical studies, theology and ethical, history of Christianity. *Total annual research expenditures:* $2.5 million. *Unit head:* Rev. Dr. Mary Elizabeth Moore, Dean, 617-353-3050, Fax: 617-353-3061, E-mail: memoore@bu.edu. *Application contact:* Rev. Anastasia Kidd, Director of Admissions and College Relations, 617-353-3036, Fax: 617-358-0140, E-mail: sthadmis@bu.edu. Website: http://www.bu.edu/sth

**Briercrest Seminary,** Graduate Programs, Program in Christian Ministries, Caronport, SK S0H 0S0, Canada. Offers leadership (MA); marriage and family counseling (MA); missions (MA); pastoral counseling (MA); worship (MA); youth and family ministry (MA). *Program availability:* Part-time. *Degree requirements:* For master's, comprehensive exam, thesis optional. *Entrance requirements:* Additional exam requirements/recommendations for international students: Required—TOEFL (minimum score 550 paper-based).

**Briercrest Seminary,** Graduate Programs, Program in Theology, Caronport, SK S0H 0S0, Canada. Offers Biblical studies (M Div); leadership and management (M Div); New Testament (MATS); Old Testament (MATS); pastoral counseling (M Div); pastoral ministry (M Div); theological studies (M Div); theology (MATS); worship (M Div); youth and family ministry (M Div). *Accreditation:* ATS. *Program availability:* Part-time. *Degree requirements:* For master's, comprehensive exam, thesis optional. *Entrance requirements:* Additional exam requirements/recommendations for international students: Required—TOEFL (minimum score 550 paper-based).

**Brite Divinity School,** Graduate and Professional Programs, Fort Worth, TX 76109. Offers Biblical interpretation (PhD); divinity (M Div); ministry (D Min); pastoral theology (PhD); theological studies (MTS, CTS); theology (Th M); theology and ministry (MA). *Accreditation:* ACIPE; ATS (one or more programs are accredited); SACS/CC. *Program availability:* Part-time, evening/weekend. *Faculty:* 18 full-time (6 women), 4 part-time/adjunct (1 woman). *Entrance requirements:* For master's, minimum GPA of 2.5. Additional exam requirements/recommendations for international students: Required—TOEFL. *Application deadline:* For fall admission, 3/1 for domestic students; for spring admission, 12/1 for domestic students. Applications are processed on a rolling basis. Application fee: $0. *Financial support:* Career-related internships or fieldwork and unspecified assistantships available. Financial award application deadline: 3/1. *Unit head:* Dr. D. Newell Williams, President, 817-257-7231. *Application contact:* Dr. Valerie Forstman, Director of Admissions, 817-257-7513, E-mail: v.forstman@tcu.edu. Website: http://www.brite.edu/academics/degrees/

**Cairn University,** Department of Counseling, Langhorne, PA 19047-2990. Offers MS. *Program availability:* Part-time, evening/weekend. *Faculty:* 3 full-time (1 woman), 4 part-time/adjunct (all women). *Students:* 20 full-time (15 women), 58 part-time (35 women); includes 29 minority (18 Black or African American, non-Hispanic/Latino; 1 Asian, non-Hispanic/Latino; 8 Hispanic/Latino; 2 Two or more races, non-Hispanic/Latino), 3 international. Average age 37. 30 applicants, 80% accepted, 22 enrolled. In 2016, 19 master's awarded. *Entrance requirements:* Additional exam requirements/recommendations for international students: Required—TOEFL (minimum score 550 paper-based). *Application deadline:* Applications are processed on a rolling basis. Application fee: $25. Electronic applications accepted. Application fee is waived when completed online. *Expenses:* $655 per semester credit. *Financial support:* Scholarships/grants available. Support available to part-time students. Financial award applicants required to submit FAFSA. *Unit head:* Dr. Jeff Black, Chair, 215-702-4347, E-mail: jblack@cairn.edu. *Application contact:* Gwen Dorsey, Enrollment Counselor, Graduate Counseling, 800-572-2472, Fax: 215-702-4248, E-mail: gdorsey@cairn.edu. Website: http://www.cairn.edu/academics/counseling

**California Baptist University,** Program in Counseling Ministry, Riverside, CA 92504-3206. Offers professional ministry (MA); research in counseling ministry (MA). *Program availability:* Part-time, evening/weekend. *Faculty:* 4 full-time (1 woman), 1 (woman) part-time/adjunct. *Students:* 3 full-time (2 women), 9 part-time (8 women); includes 4 minority (1 Black or African American, non-Hispanic/Latino; 3 Hispanic/Latino). Average age 36. 4 applicants, 100% accepted, 2 enrolled. In 2016, 4 master's awarded. *Degree requirements:* For master's, comprehensive exam, additional professional ministry practicum or research thesis. *Entrance requirements:* For master's, GRE (minimum score of 300 for applicants with a GPA below 2.75), minimum undergraduate GPA of 2.75; official transcripts; three recommendations; comprehensive essay; interview; three prerequisite classes completed with minimum C grade. Additional exam requirements/recommendations for international students: Required—TOEFL (minimum score 80 iBT). *Application deadline:* For fall admission, 8/1 priority date for domestic students, 7/1 for international students; for spring admission, 12/1 priority date for domestic students, 11/1 for international students. Applications are processed on a rolling basis. Application fee: $45. Electronic applications accepted. *Expenses:* Contact institution. *Financial support:* In 2016–17, 2 students received support. Federal Work-Study and scholarships/grants available. Financial award applicants required to submit CSS PROFILE or FAFSA. *Faculty research:* Social psychology, clinical psychology, psychology of religion, child development, marriage and family therapy. *Unit head:* Dr. Jacqueline Gustafson, Dean, School of Behavioral Sciences, 951-343-4487, E-mail: jcraig@calbaptist.edu. *Application contact:* Dr. Nathan Lewis, Program Director of Counseling Ministry, 951-343-4348, E-mail: nlewis@calbaptist.edu. Website: http://www.calbaptist.edu/macounseling

**California Baptist University,** Program in Counseling Ministry and Counseling Psychology (Dual Master's), Riverside, CA 92504-3206. Offers MA/MS. *Program availability:* Part-time, evening/weekend. *Faculty:* 18 full-time (11 women), 10 part-time/adjunct (7 women). *Students:* 14 full-time (11 women), 2 part-time (1 woman); includes 12 minority (2 Black or African American, non-Hispanic/Latino; 1 Asian, non-Hispanic/Latino; 9 Hispanic/Latino). Average age 31. 11 applicants, 45% accepted, 5 enrolled. *Entrance requirements:* Additional exam requirements/recommendations for international students: Required—TOEFL (minimum score 80 iBT). *Application deadline:* For fall admission, 8/1 priority date for domestic students, 7/1 for international students; for spring admission, 12/1 priority date for domestic students, 11/1 for international students. Applications are processed on a rolling basis. Application fee: $45. Electronic applications accepted. *Expenses:* Contact institution. *Financial support:* In 2016–17, 2 students received support. Federal Work-Study and scholarships/grants available.

*Pastoral Ministry and Counseling*

Financial award applicants required to submit CSS PROFILE or FAFSA. *Faculty research:* Law enforcement psychology, neuroethology, organizational neuroscience, integration of theology and behavioral science, cognitive development/cross-cultural psychology. *Unit head:* Dr. Jacqueline Gustafson, Dean, School of Behavioral Sciences, 951-343-4487, E-mail: jcraig@calbaptist.edu. *Application contact:* Mischa Routon, Director of Counseling Psychology Program, 951-343-4206, Fax: 877-228-8877, E-mail: mrouton@calbaptist.edu.
Website: http://www.calbaptist.edu/mft

**Calvary University,** Graduate School and Seminary, Kansas City, MO 64147. Offers Bible and theology (MS); Biblical counseling (MA); education (MS), including administration and leadership, Christian education, curriculum and instruction, elementary education; organization development (MS); pastoral studies (M Div). *Program availability:* Part-time, evening/weekend. *Faculty:* 6 full-time (2 women), 2 part-time/adjunct (1 woman). *Students:* 11 full-time (3 women), 29 part-time (15 women); includes 12 minority (4 Black or African American, non-Hispanic/Latino; 1 American Indian or Alaska Native, non-Hispanic/Latino; 6 Asian, non-Hispanic/Latino; 1 Native Hawaiian or other Pacific Islander, non-Hispanic/Latino). Average age 39. In 2016, 19 master's awarded. *Degree requirements:* For master's, variable foreign language requirement, comprehensive exam, thesis or alternative. *Entrance requirements:* For master's, minimum GPA of 2.5, BA or BS, doctrine agreement. Additional exam requirements/recommendations for international students: Required—TOEFL (minimum score 550 paper-based). *Application deadline:* Applications are processed on a rolling basis. Application fee: $0. Electronic applications accepted. *Expenses:* Tuition: Full-time $7200; part-time $4800 per credit. *Required fees:* $640; $520 per credit. $140 per semester. One-time fee: $100. Tuition and fees vary according to program. *Financial support:* In 2016–17, 8 students received support. Scholarships/grants available. Financial award application deadline: 11/5; financial award applicants required to submit FAFSA. *Unit head:* Dr. Thomas Baurain, Director of Seminary, 816-322-0110 Ext. 1502, Fax: 816-331-4474, E-mail: thomas.baurain@calvary.edu. *Application contact:* Ann Rogers, Admissions Office Assistant, 800-326-3960 Ext. 1321, Fax: 816-331-4474, E-mail: admissions@calvary.edu.
Website: http://www.calvary.edu

**Calvin Theological Seminary,** Graduate and Professional Programs, Grand Rapids, MI 49546-4387. Offers Bible and theology (MA); divinity (M Div), including ancient near eastern languages and literature, contextual ministry, evangelism and teaching, history of Christianity, new church development, New Testament, Old Testament, pastoral care and leadership, preaching and worship, theological studies, youth and family ministries; educational ministry (MA); historical theology (PhD); missions and evangelism (MA); pastoral care (MA); philosophical and moral theology (PhD); systematic theology (PhD); theological studies (MTS); theology (Th M); worship (MA); youth and family ministries (MA). *Accreditation:* ACIPE; ATS. *Program availability:* Part-time. *Degree requirements:* For master's, variable foreign language requirement, thesis (for some programs); for doctorate, 4 foreign languages, comprehensive exam, thesis/dissertation. *Entrance requirements:* For doctorate, GRE General Test, Hebrew, Greek, and a modern foreign language. Additional exam requirements/recommendations for international students: Required—TOEFL (minimum score 550 paper-based), TWE (minimum score 4). Electronic applications accepted. *Faculty research:* Recent Trinity theory, Christian anthropology, Proverbs, reformed confessions, Paul's view of law.

**Campbell University,** Graduate and Professional Programs, Divinity School, Buies Creek, NC 27506. Offers Christian ministry (MA); divinity (M Div); ministry (D Min); JD/M Div; M Div/MA; M Div/MBA. *Accreditation:* ATS. *Degree requirements:* For doctorate, final project. *Entrance requirements:* For master's, minimum GPA of 2.5; for doctorate, MAT, M Div, minimum graduate GPA of 3.0. Additional exam requirements/recommendations for international students: Required—TOEFL (minimum score 580 paper-based). *Expenses:* Contact institution. *Faculty research:* New Testament, theology, spiritual formation, Old Testament, Christian leadership.

**Canadian Southern Baptist Seminary,** Graduate Programs, Cochrane, AB T4C 2G1, Canada. Offers Biblical studies (MBS); Christian ministry (MCMin); Christian studies (MCS); ministry (M Div). *Accreditation:* ATS. *Program availability:* Part-time, 100% online, blended/hybrid learning. *Faculty:* 3 full-time (0 women), 8 part-time/adjunct (1 woman). *Students:* 24 full-time (9 women), 18 part-time (2 women); includes 4 minority (1 Black or African American, non-Hispanic/Latino; 3 Asian, non-Hispanic/Latino), 11 international. Average age 29. 17 applicants, 76% accepted, 11 enrolled. In 2016, 10 master's awarded. *Entrance requirements:* Additional exam requirements/recommendations for international students: Required—TOEFL (minimum score 560 paper-based; 83 iBT); Recommended—IELTS. *Application deadline:* For fall admission, 7/1 priority date for domestic students, 3/1 priority date for international students; for winter admission, 11/15 priority date for domestic students. Applications are processed on a rolling basis. Application fee: $50 ($150 for international students). *Expenses:* Tuition: Full-time $6900 Canadian dollars; part-time $345 Canadian dollars per credit hour. *Required fees:* $20 Canadian dollars per credit hour. $35 Canadian dollars per semester. Tuition and fees vary according to course load. *Financial support:* Scholarships/grants available. Financial award application deadline: 7/1. *Unit head:* Dr. Steve Booth, Academic Dean, 403-932-6622 Ext. 232, E-mail: steve.booth@csbs.ca. *Application contact:* Kathleen McNaughton, Registrar, 403-932-6622 Ext. 221, E-mail: kathleen.mcnaughton@csbs.ca.

**Cardinal Stritch University,** College of Arts and Sciences, Department of Religious Studies, Milwaukee, WI 53217-3985. Offers ministry (MA); religious studies (MA). *Program availability:* Part-time, evening/weekend. *Students:* 8 part-time (4 women); includes 2 minority (both Black or African American, non-Hispanic/Latino). Average age 43. 10 applicants, 100% accepted, 1 enrolled. In 2016, 8 master's awarded. *Degree requirements:* For master's, comprehensive exam, thesis, research project. *Entrance requirements:* For master's, interview, minimum GPA of 2.75. Additional exam requirements/recommendations for international students: Required—TOEFL (minimum score 79 iBT), IELTS (minimum score 6.5). *Application deadline:* For fall admission, 7/15 priority date for domestic students; for spring admission, 12/15 priority date for domestic students. Applications are processed on a rolling basis. Electronic applications accepted. *Expenses:* Tuition: Full-time $11,890; part-time $765 per credit hour. Tuition and fees vary according to class time, course load, degree level, program and student's religious affiliation. *Financial support:* Research assistantships with partial tuition reimbursements, career-related internships or fieldwork, Federal Work-Study, and scholarships/grants available. Financial award applicants required to submit FAFSA. *Unit head:* Dr. Michelle Gilgannon, Chair, 414-410-4047, E-mail: mlgilgannon@stritch.edu. *Application contact:* Graduate Admissions, 800-347-8822 Ext. 4042, E-mail: admissions@stritch.edu.

**Carolina Christian College,** Program in Religious Education, Winston-Salem, NC 27102-0777. Offers Christian education (MRE); pastoral care (MRE). *Entrance requirements:* For master's, bachelor's degree from accredited institution, minimum undergraduate "B" average.

**Catholic Theological Union,** Graduate and Professional Programs, Chicago, IL 60615-5698. Offers biblical spirituality (Certificate); cross-cultural ministries (D Min); cross-cultural missions (Certificate); divinity (M Div); liturgical studies (Certificate); liturgy

(D Min); pastoral studies (MAPS, Certificate); spiritual formation (Certificate); spirituality (D Min); theology (MA); M Div/MA; M Div/MSW; M Div/PhD. M Div/PhD offered jointly with University of Chicago; M Div/MSW with Loyola University Chicago and University of Chicago. *Accreditation:* ACIPE. *Program availability:* Part-time, evening/weekend. *Degree requirements:* For master's, one foreign language, comprehensive exam (for some programs), thesis (for some programs); for doctorate, thesis/dissertation. *Entrance requirements:* For doctorate, master's degree, 5 years of active ministry. *Faculty research:* Doctrine, sacraments, ethics, Bible.

**The Catholic University of America,** School of Theology and Religious Studies, Washington, DC 20064. Offers M Cat, M Div, MA, D Min, PhD, STD, Certificate, STB, STL, MSLS/MA, STB/M Div. MSLA/MA offered in conjunction with Department of Library and Information Science. *Program availability:* Part-time. *Faculty:* 40 full-time (2 women), 8 part-time/adjunct (2 women). *Students:* 156 full-time (11 women), 193 part-time (51 women); includes 61 minority (9 Black or African American, non-Hispanic/Latino; 1 American Indian or Alaska Native, non-Hispanic/Latino; 13 Asian, non-Hispanic/Latino; 24 Hispanic/Latino; 14 Two or more races, non-Hispanic/Latino), 51 international. Average age 36. 168 applicants, 65% accepted, 58 enrolled. In 2016, 96 master's, 20 doctorates awarded. Terminal master's awarded for partial completion of doctoral program. *Degree requirements:* For master's, variable foreign language requirement, comprehensive exam (for some programs), thesis (for some programs); for doctorate, variable foreign language requirement, comprehensive exam, thesis/dissertation. *Entrance requirements:* For master's and doctorate, GRE General Test, statement of purpose, official copies of academic transcripts, three letters of recommendation. Additional exam requirements/recommendations for international students: Required—TOEFL (minimum score 550 paper-based; 80 iBT). *Application deadline:* For fall admission, 7/15 priority date for domestic students, 7/1 for international students; for spring admission, 11/15 priority date for domestic students, 11/1 for international students. Applications are processed on a rolling basis. Application fee: $55. Electronic applications accepted. *Expenses:* $42,850 per year; $1,170 per credit; $200 per semester part-time fees. *Financial support:* Fellowships, research assistantships, teaching assistantships, Federal Work-Study, scholarships/grants, tuition waivers (full and partial), and unspecified assistantships available. Financial award application deadline: 2/1; financial award applicants required to submit FAFSA. *Faculty research:* Historical and systematic theology, religious education and Catechetics, moral theology and ethics, Biblical studies, liturgical studies and sacramental theology, religion and culture. *Total annual research expenditures:* $194,166. *Unit head:* Very Rev. Mark Morozowich, Dean, 202-319-5684, Fax: 202-319-4967, E-mail: morozowich@cua.edu. *Application contact:* Director of Graduate Admissions, 202-319-5057, Fax: 202-319-6533, E-mail: cua-admissions@cua.edu.
Website: http://trs.cua.edu/

**Cedarville University,** Graduate Programs, Cedarville, OH 45314. Offers business administration (MBA); curriculum (M Ed); educational administration (M Ed); family nurse practitioner (MSN); global health ministries (MSN); instruction (M Ed); ministry (M Min); pharmacy (Pharm D). *Program availability:* Part-time, evening/weekend, online learning. *Degree requirements:* For master's, thesis. *Entrance requirements:* For master's, GRE, 2 professional recommendations; for doctorate, PCAT, professional recommendation from a practicing pharmacist or current employer/supervisor, resume, essay, interview. Additional exam requirements/recommendations for international students: Required—TOEFL (minimum score 550 paper-based; 80 iBT). Electronic applications accepted. *Expenses:* Contact institution.

**Chaminade University of Honolulu,** Office of Professional and Continuing Education, Program in Pastoral Theology, Honolulu, HI 96816-1578. Offers diaconate education (MPT); pastoral counseling and spiritual direction (MPT); pastoral theology (MPT). *Program availability:* Part-time, evening/weekend, blended/hybrid learning. *Faculty:* 3 full-time (0 women), 1 part-time/adjunct (0 women). *Students:* 23 full-time (6 women); includes 13 minority (1 Black or African American, non-Hispanic/Latino; 5 Asian, non-Hispanic/Latino; 3 Hispanic/Latino; 4 Native Hawaiian or other Pacific Islander, non-Hispanic/Latino). Average age 53. 1 applicant, 100% accepted, 1 enrolled. *Degree requirements:* For master's, capstone course. *Entrance requirements:* For master's, minimum GPA of 2.5, resume, 2 letters of recommendation, letter of intent, article reflection essay. Additional exam requirements/recommendations for international students: Required—TOEFL (minimum score 550 paper-based; 79 iBT). *Application deadline:* Applications are processed on a rolling basis. Application fee: $40. Electronic applications accepted. *Expenses:* Contact institution. *Financial support:* Applicants required to submit FAFSA. *Unit head:* Dr. David Coleman, Director, 808-739-8341, E-mail: paul.fitzpatrick@chaminade.edu. *Application contact:* 808-735-4755, E-mail: gradserv@chaminade.edu.
Website: http://www.chaminade.edu/mpt

**Charlotte Christian College and Theological Seminary,** Graduate Program, Charlotte, NC 28205. Offers urban Christian ministry (MA), including church planting, multi-cultural studies, sacred music, youth ministry. *Program availability:* Part-time, evening/weekend. *Degree requirements:* For master's, thesis. *Entrance requirements:* For master's, MAT, writing sample/essay. Additional exam requirements/recommendations for international students: Required—TOEFL, IELTS. Electronic applications accepted. *Expenses:* Contact institution.

**Chicago Theological Seminary,** Graduate and Professional Programs, Chicago, IL 60637-1507. Offers Bible, culture and hermeneutics (PhD); preaching (D Min); religion and health (D Min); religious studies (MA); spirituality and spiritual direction (D Min); theology (M Div); theology, ethics and the human sciences (PhD); M Div/MSW. *Accreditation:* ACIPE; ATS. *Program availability:* Part-time. *Degree requirements:* For master's, thesis; for doctorate, 2 foreign languages, comprehensive exam, thesis/dissertation. *Entrance requirements:* For doctorate, GRE General Test. Additional exam requirements/recommendations for international students: Required—TOEFL. *Faculty research:* Bible, culture and hermeneutics, theology, gender and sexuality, black faith and life, spirituality and psychology, practical theology.

**Christian Theological Seminary,** Graduate and Professional Programs, Indianapolis, IN 46208-3301. Offers educational and arts ministries (MA); marriage and family therapy (MA); pastoral care and counseling (D Min); psychotherapy and faith (MA); theological studies (MTS); theology (M Div). *Accreditation:* AAMFT/COAMFTE (one or more programs are accredited); ACIPE; ATS. *Program availability:* Part-time. Terminal master's awarded for partial completion of doctoral program. *Degree requirements:* For master's, comprehensive exam (for some programs), thesis (for some programs), missionary and cross-cultural experience (for M Div); for doctorate, comprehensive exam, thesis/dissertation. *Entrance requirements:* For doctorate, M Div. Additional exam requirements/recommendations for international students: Recommended—TOEFL. Electronic applications accepted. *Faculty research:* Faith formation, peer learning post graduation.

**Christ the King Seminary,** Graduate and Professional Programs, East Aurora, NY 14052. Offers divinity (M Div); pastoral ministry (MA); theology (MA). *Accreditation:* ATS. *Program availability:* Part-time, evening/weekend. *Degree requirements:* For master's, comprehensive exam, thesis. *Entrance requirements:* For master's, previous course work in philosophy and religious studies.

**Cincinnati Christian University,** Graduate School, Program in Counseling, Cincinnati, OH 45204-3200. Offers MAC. *Degree requirements:* For master's, thesis or alternative, integration paper. *Entrance requirements:* For master's, GRE General Test, interview, minimum undergraduate GPA of 3.0. Additional exam requirements/recommendations for international students: Required—TOEFL. Electronic applications accepted. *Expenses:* Contact institution.

**City Vision University,** Program in Technology and Ministry, Kansas City, MO 64109-1845. Offers MS. *Program availability:* Online learning. *Degree requirements:* For master's, capstone project.

**Claremont Lincoln University,** Graduate Programs, Claremont, CA 91711. Offers ethical leadership (MA); interfaith action (MA); social impact (MA).

**Claremont School of Theology,** Graduate and Professional Programs, Master of Divinity Program, Claremont, CA 91711-3199. Offers interfaith chaplaincy (M Div); Islamic chaplaincy (M Div); ministerial leadership (M Div). *Accreditation:* ACIPE; ATS. *Program availability:* Part-time, 100% online, blended/hybrid learning. *Entrance requirements:* Additional exam requirements/recommendations for international students: Required—TOEFL. *Application deadline:* For fall admission, 5/1 for domestic students, 4/1 for international students; for winter admission, 11/1 for domestic and international students; for spring admission, 11/1 priority date for domestic students, 11/1 for international students. Applications are processed on a rolling basis. Application fee: $50. Electronic applications accepted. *Expenses: Tuition:* Full-time $21,120. Tuition and fees vary according to course level, course load and degree level. *Financial support:* Research assistantships, teaching assistantships, career-related internships or fieldwork, Federal Work-Study, institutionally sponsored loans, scholarships/grants, and tuition waivers (full and partial) available. Support available to part-time students. Financial award application deadline: 4/1; financial award applicants required to submit FAFSA. *Unit head:* Sheryl A. Kujawa-Holbrook, Vice President for Academic Affairs/Dean, 909-447-2520, Fax: 909-447-6274, E-mail: skujawaholbrook@cst.edu. *Application contact:* Director of Admissions, 866-274-6500, Fax: 909-447-6389, E-mail: admission@cst.edu. Website: https://cst.edu/academics/m-div/

**Claremont School of Theology,** Graduate and Professional Programs, Program in Ministry, Claremont, CA 91711-3199. Offers practical theology of conflict, healing and transformation in Korean contexts (D Min); spiritual renewal, contemplative practice, and strategic leadership (D Min). *Accreditation:* ACIPE. *Program availability:* 100% online, blended/hybrid learning. *Degree requirements:* For doctorate, thesis/dissertation. *Entrance requirements:* For doctorate, GRE General Test. Additional exam requirements/recommendations for international students: Required—TOEFL. *Application deadline:* For fall admission, 4/15 for domestic and international students. Application fee: $50. Electronic applications accepted. *Expenses: Tuition:* Full-time $21,120. Tuition and fees vary according to course level, course load and degree level. *Financial support:* Teaching assistantships, career-related internships or fieldwork, Federal Work-Study, institutionally sponsored loans, scholarships/grants, and tuition waivers (full and partial) available. Support available to part-time students. Financial award application deadline: 4/1. *Unit head:* Sheryl A. Kujawa-Holbrook, Vice President for Academic Affairs/Dean, 909-447-2520, Fax: 909-447-6274, E-mail: skujawaholbrook@cst.edu. *Application contact:* Director of Admissions, 866-274-6500, Fax: 909-447-6389, E-mail: admission@cst.edu. Website: https://cst.edu/academics/d-min/

**Claremont School of Theology,** Graduate and Professional Programs, Program in Religion, Claremont, CA 91711-3199. Offers practical theology (PhD), including religious education and formation, spiritual care and counseling; religion (MA, PhD), including comparative theology and philosophy (PhD), Hebrew Bible and Jewish studies (PhD), New Testament and Christian origins (PhD), process studies (PhD), religion, ethics, and society (PhD). *Accreditation:* ACIPE; ATS. Terminal master's awarded for partial completion of doctoral program. *Degree requirements:* For master's, thesis; for doctorate, 2 foreign languages, thesis/dissertation. *Entrance requirements:* For doctorate, GRE General Test. Additional exam requirements/recommendations for international students: Required—TOEFL. *Application deadline:* For fall admission, 1/15 for domestic and international students. Application fee: $50. Electronic applications accepted. *Expenses: Tuition:* Full-time $21,120. Tuition and fees vary according to course level, course load and degree level. *Financial support:* Research assistantships, teaching assistantships, career-related internships or fieldwork, Federal Work-Study, institutionally sponsored loans, scholarships/grants, and tuition waivers (full and partial) available. Support available to part-time students. Financial award application deadline: 4/1; financial award applicants required to submit FAFSA. *Unit head:* Sheryl A. Kujawa-Holbrook, Vice President for Academic Affairs/Dean, 909-447-2520, Fax: 909-447-6274, E-mail: skujawaholbrook@cst.edu. *Application contact:* Director of Admissions, 866-274-6500, Fax: 909-447-6389, E-mail: admission@cst.edu. Website: https://cst.edu/academics/m-a/

**Clarks Summit University,** Baptist Bible Seminary, South Abington Township, PA 18411. Offers Biblical apologetics (MA); church education (M Div, M Min); church planting (M Div, M Min); global ministry (M Div, M Min); leadership in communication (D Min); leadership in counseling and spiritual development (D Min); leadership in global ministry (D Min); leadership in pastoral ministry (D Min); leadership in theological studies (D Min); military chaplaincy (M Div); ministry (PhD); organizational leadership (M Min); outreach pastor (M Div, M Min); pastoral counseling (M Div, M Min); pastoral leadership (M Div, M Min); theology (Th M); worship ministries leadership (M Div, M Min); youth pastor (M Div, M Min). *Program availability:* Part-time, evening/weekend, online learning. Terminal master's awarded for partial completion of doctoral program. *Degree requirements:* For master's, 2 foreign languages, thesis, oral exam (for M Div); for doctorate, 2 foreign languages, comprehensive exam (for some programs), thesis/dissertation, oral exam. *Entrance requirements:* For doctorate, Greek and Hebrew entrance exams (for PhD). Electronic applications accepted.

**Columbia International University,** Seminary and School of Ministry, Columbia, SC 29230-3122. Offers academic ministries (M Div); Bible and theology (Certificate); bible exposition (M Div, MABE); Biblical ministry (Certificate); chaplaincy (M Div); intercultural studies (MAIS); leadership (D Min); member care (D Min); missions (D Min); preaching (D Min); theological studies (MA). *Accreditation:* ATS (one or more programs are accredited). *Program availability:* Part-time, evening/weekend. *Degree requirements:* For doctorate, comprehensive exam, thesis/dissertation. *Entrance requirements:* For doctorate, 3 years of ministerial experience, M Div. Additional exam requirements/recommendations for international students: Required—TOEFL. Electronic applications accepted.

**Concordia University, Nebraska,** Graduate Programs in Education, Program in Family Life Ministry, Seward, NE 68434-1556. Offers MS. *Program availability:* Part-time, evening/weekend. *Degree requirements:* For master's, thesis or alternative. *Entrance requirements:* For master's, GRE, MAT, or NTE, minimum GPA of 3.0, BS in education or equivalent.

**Corban University,** Graduate School, Program in Counseling, Salem, OR 97301-9392. Offers MA. *Degree requirements:* For master's, internship, practicum.

**Corban University,** Graduate School, School of Ministry, Salem, OR 97301-9392. Offers Biblical languages (M Div); Biblical leadership (Certificate); Christian leadership

(MA); Church ministry (M Div); ministry (D Min). *Program availability:* Part-time, evening/weekend. *Degree requirements:* For master's, thesis. *Entrance requirements:* Additional exam requirements/recommendations for international students: Required—TOEFL (minimum score 550 paper-based), IELTS (minimum score 6).

**Covenant Theological Seminary,** Graduate and Professional Programs, St. Louis, MO 63141-8697. Offers M Div, MA, MAC, MAEM, Th M, D Min, Certificate. *Accreditation:* ATS (one or more programs are accredited). *Program availability:* Part-time, evening/weekend, online learning. *Degree requirements:* For master's, 2 foreign languages, thesis (for some programs); for doctorate, 2 foreign languages, thesis/dissertation; for Certificate, 2 foreign languages. *Entrance requirements:* For doctorate and Certificate, M Div. Additional exam requirements/recommendations for international students: Required—TOEFL (minimum score 550 paper-based). Electronic applications accepted.

**Criswell College,** Graduate School of the Bible, Dallas, TX 75246-1537. Offers biblical studies (M Div); Christian leadership (MA); counseling (MA); Jewish studies (MA); ministry (MA); theological and biblical studies (MA). *Program availability:* Part-time. *Degree requirements:* For master's, 2 foreign languages, thesis optional. *Entrance requirements:* For master's, GRE General Test, minimum GPA of 2.5. Electronic applications accepted. *Faculty research:* Emphasis on biblical languages (Hebrew and Greek), expository preaching and evangelism in the local church.

**Dallas Baptist University,** Gary Cook School of Leadership, Program in Leadership Studies, Dallas, TX 75211-9299. Offers leadership studies (PhD), including business, general leadership, higher education, ministry. *Program availability:* Part-time. *Degree requirements:* For doctorate, thesis/dissertation. *Application deadline:* Applications are processed on a rolling basis. Application fee: $25. Electronic applications accepted. Application fee is waived when completed online. *Expenses: Tuition:* Full-time $15,408; part-time $856 per credit hour. *Required fees:* $400 per semester. Tuition and fees vary according to course load and degree level. *Unit head:* Dr. Jack Goodyear, Director, 214-333-5595, E-mail: jackg@dbu.edu. *Application contact:* Bobby Soto, Director of Admissions, 214-333-5242, E-mail: graduate@dbu.edu. Website: http://www3.dbu.edu/leadership/phdLeadership.asp

**Dallas Baptist University,** Graduate School of Ministry, Program in Children's Ministry, Dallas, TX 75211-9299. Offers general (MA); special needs children ministry (MA). *Program availability:* Part-time, evening/weekend, 100% online, blended/hybrid learning. *Application deadline:* Applications are processed on a rolling basis. Application fee: $25. Electronic applications accepted. Application fee is waived when completed online. *Expenses: Tuition:* Full-time $15,408; part-time $856 per credit hour. *Required fees:* $400 per semester. Tuition and fees vary according to course load and degree level. *Unit head:* Dr. Shelly Melia, Director, 214-333-5246, E-mail: shelly@dbu.edu. *Application contact:* Bobby Soto, Director of Admissions, 214-333-5242, E-mail: graduate@dbu.edu. Website: http://www3.dbu.edu/gsom/Childrens-Ministry/

**Dallas Baptist University,** Graduate School of Ministry, Program in Christian Counseling, Dallas, TX 75211-9299. Offers MA. *Program availability:* Part-time, evening/weekend. *Application deadline:* Applications are processed on a rolling basis. Application fee: $25. Electronic applications accepted. Application fee is waived when completed online. *Expenses: Tuition:* Full-time $15,408; part-time $856 per credit hour. *Required fees:* $400 per semester. Tuition and fees vary according to course load and degree level. *Unit head:* Dr. Dana Wicker, Director, 214-333-5883, E-mail: dana@dbu.edu. *Application contact:* Bobby Soto, Director of Admissions, 214-333-5242, E-mail: graduate@dbu.edu. Website: http://www.dbu.edu/ministry/degree-programs/ma-christian-counseling

**Dallas Baptist University,** Graduate School of Ministry, Program in Christian Ministry, Dallas, TX 75211-9299. Offers chaplaincy (MA); Christian ministry and education (MA); counseling ministry (MA); family ministry (MA); general ministry (MA); heritage and missions (MA); leading the nonprofit organization (MA); ministry leadership (MA); professional life coaching (MA); urban ministry (MA); worship ministry (MA). *Program availability:* Part-time, evening/weekend, 100% online, blended/hybrid learning. *Application deadline:* Applications are processed on a rolling basis. Application fee: $25. Electronic applications accepted. Application fee is waived when completed online. *Expenses: Tuition:* Full-time $15,408; part-time $856 per credit hour. *Required fees:* $400 per semester. Tuition and fees vary according to course load and degree level. *Unit head:* Dr. Tom Vann, Director, 214-333-5805, E-mail: tomv@dbu.edu. *Application contact:* Bobby Soto, Director of Admissions, 214-333-5242, E-mail: graduate@dbu.edu. Website: http://www3.dbu.edu/gsom/Christian-Ministry/

**Dallas Baptist University,** Graduate School of Ministry, Program in Discipleship, Dallas, TX 75211-9299. Offers discipleship for the family (MA); discipleship through communications (MA); local church discipleship (MA). *Program availability:* Part-time, evening/weekend, 100% online, blended/hybrid learning. *Application deadline:* Applications are processed on a rolling basis. Application fee: $25. Electronic applications accepted. Application fee is waived when completed online. *Expenses: Tuition:* Full-time $15,408; part-time $856 per credit hour. *Required fees:* $400 per semester. Tuition and fees vary according to course load and degree level. *Unit head:* Dr. Chris Shirley, Director, 214-333-5256, E-mail: chrissh@dbu.edu. *Application contact:* Bobby Soto, Director of Admissions, 214-333-5242, E-mail: graduate@dbu.edu. Website: http://www.dbu.edu/ministry/degree-programs/m-a-in-christian-education

**Dallas Baptist University,** Graduate School of Ministry, Program in Family Ministry, Dallas, TX 75211-9299. Offers Christian counseling (MA); general (MA); leadership (MA); special needs family ministry (MA). *Program availability:* Part-time, evening/weekend, 100% online, blended/hybrid learning. *Application deadline:* Applications are processed on a rolling basis. Application fee: $25. Electronic applications accepted. Application fee is waived when completed online. *Expenses: Tuition:* Full-time $15,408; part-time $856 per credit hour. *Required fees:* $400 per semester. Tuition and fees vary according to course load and degree level. *Unit head:* Dr. Shelly Melia, Director, 214-333-5943, E-mail: shelly@dbu.edu. *Application contact:* Bobby Soto, Director of Admissions, 214-333-5242, E-mail: graduate@dbu.edu. Website: http://www.dbu.edu/ministry/degree-programs/m-a-in-family-ministry

**Dallas Baptist University,** Graduate School of Ministry, Program in Global Leadership, Dallas, TX 75211-9299. Offers church planting (MA); East Asian Studies (MA); English as a second language (MA); general studies (MA); global communication (MA); global studies (MA); international business (MA); leading the nonprofit organization (MA); missions (MA); small group ministry (MA); urban ministry (MA). *Program availability:* Part-time, evening/weekend. *Application deadline:* Applications are processed on a rolling basis. Application fee: $25. Electronic applications accepted. Application fee is waived when completed online. *Expenses: Tuition:* Full-time $15,408; part-time $856 per credit hour. *Required fees:* $400 per semester. Tuition and fees vary according to course load and degree level. *Unit head:* Dr. Bob Garrett, Director, 214-333-5508, E-mail: bobg@dbu.edu. *Application contact:* Bobby Soto, Director of Admissions, 214-333-5242, E-mail: graduate@dbu.edu. Website: http://www3.dbu.edu/gsom/global-leadership/

## Pastoral Ministry and Counseling

**Dallas Baptist University,** Graduate School of Ministry, Program in Student Ministry, Dallas, TX 75211-9299. Offers MA. *Program availability:* Part-time, evening/weekend, 100% online, blended/hybrid learning. *Application deadline:* Applications are processed on a rolling basis. Application fee: $25. Electronic applications accepted. Application fee is waived when completed online. *Expenses: Tuition:* Full-time $15,408; part-time $856 per credit hour. *Required fees:* $400 per semester. Tuition and fees vary according to course load and degree level. *Unit head:* Dr. Chris Shirley, Director, 214-333-5256, E-mail: crissh@dbu.edu. *Application contact:* Bobby Soto, Director of Admissions, 214-333-5242, E-mail: graduate@dbu.edu. Website: http://www3.dbu.edu/gsom/student-ministry/

**Dallas Baptist University,** Graduate School of Ministry, Program in Theological Studies, Dallas, TX 75211-9299. Offers Christian heritage (MA); Christian ministry (MA); Christian scriptures (MA). *Program availability:* Part-time, evening/weekend. *Application deadline:* Applications are processed on a rolling basis. Application fee: $25. Electronic applications accepted. Application fee is waived when completed online. *Expenses: Tuition:* Full-time $15,408; part-time $856 per credit hour. *Required fees:* $400 per semester. Tuition and fees vary according to course load and degree level. *Unit head:* Dr. Jim Lemons, Director, 214-333-5366, E-mail: jiml@dbu.edu. *Application contact:* Bobby Soto, Director of Admissions, 214-333-5242, E-mail: graduate@dbu.edu. Website: http://www3.dbu.edu/gsom/Theological-Studies/

**Dallas Baptist University,** Graduate School of Ministry, Worship Studies Program, Dallas, TX 75211-9299. Offers worship leadership (MA); worship theology (MA). *Program availability:* Part-time, evening/weekend, 100% online, blended/hybrid learning. *Application deadline:* Applications are processed on a rolling basis. Application fee: $25. Electronic applications accepted. Application fee is waived when completed online. *Expenses: Tuition:* Full-time $15,408; part-time $856 per credit hour. *Required fees:* $400 per semester. Tuition and fees vary according to course load and degree level. *Unit head:* Dr. Robert R. Brooks, Director, 214-333-5494, E-mail: bobb@dbu.edu. *Application contact:* Bobby Soto, Director of Admissions, 214-333-5242, E-mail: graduate@dbu.edu. Website: http://www.dbu.edu/ministry/degree-programs/m-a-in-worship-studies

**Dallas Baptist University,** Professional Development Program, Dallas, TX 75211-9299. Offers accounting (MA); church leadership (MA); communication (MA); counseling (MA); criminal justice (MA); English as a second language (MA); finance (MA); higher education (MA); leadership studies (MA); management (MA); management information systems (MA); marketing (MA); missions (MA); professional life coaching (MA); training and development (MA). *Program availability:* Part-time, evening/weekend, 100% online, blended/hybrid learning. *Application deadline:* Applications are processed on a rolling basis. Application fee: $25. Electronic applications accepted. Application fee is waived when completed online. *Expenses: Tuition:* Full-time $15,408; part-time $856 per credit hour. *Required fees:* $400 per semester. Tuition and fees vary according to course load and degree level. *Unit head:* Jared Ingram, Director, 214-333-5584, E-mail: jaredi@dbu.edu. *Application contact:* Bobby Soto, Director of Admissions, 214-333-5242, E-mail: graduate@dbu.edu. Website: http://www3.dbu.edu/graduate/mapd.asp

**Dallas Theological Seminary,** Graduate Programs, Dallas, TX 75204-6499. Offers adult education (Th M); apologetics (Th M); Bible backgrounds (Th M); Bible translation (Th M); Biblical and theological studies (Certificate); biblical counseling (MA); biblical exegesis and linguistics (MA); biblical exposition (PhD); biblical studies (MA); Biblical theology (Th M); children's education (Th M); Christian education (MA, D Min); Christian leadership (MA); cross-cultural ministries (MA); educational administration (Th M); educational leadership (Th M); evangelism and discipleship (Th M); exposition of Biblical books (Th M); family life education (Th M); general studies (MA); Hebrew and cognate studies (Th M); hermeneutics (Th M); historical theology (Th M); homiletics (Th M); intercultural ministries (Th M); Jesus studies (Th M); leadership studies (Th M); media and communication (MA); media arts (Th M); ministry (D Min); ministry with women (Th M); New Testament studies (Th M, PhD); Old Testament studies (Th M, PhD); parachurch ministries (Th M); pastoral care and counseling (Th M); pastoral theology and practice (Th M); philosophy (Th M); sacred theology (STM); spiritual formation (Th M); systematic theology (Th M); teaching in Christian institutions (Th M); theological studies (PhD); urban ministries (Th M); worship studies (Th M); youth education (Th M). *Program availability:* Part-time, online learning. *Degree requirements:* For master's, variable foreign language requirement, thesis (for some programs); for doctorate, 2 foreign languages, thesis/dissertation. *Entrance requirements:* For master's, GRE or MAT (if minimum undergraduate cumulative GPA is below 2.5 or undergraduate degree is unaccredited). Additional exam requirements/recommendations for international students: Required—TOEFL (minimum score 575 paper-based; 85 iBT), TWE. Electronic applications accepted.

**Denver Seminary,** Graduate and Professional Programs, Littleton, CO 80120. Offers apologetics (Certificate); biblical studies (MA); Christian formation and soul care (MA, Certificate); Christian studies (MA, Certificate); church and parachurch leadership (D Min); counseling licensure (MA); counseling ministry (MA); intercultural ministry (Certificate); leadership (MA, Certificate); marriage and family counseling (D Min); pastoral ministry (D Min); philosophy of religion (MA); spiritual guidance (Certificate); theology (M Div, Certificate); worship (Certificate); youth and family ministry (MA). *Accreditation:* ACA; ACIPE; ATS (one or more programs are accredited). *Program availability:* Part-time, evening/weekend, online learning. *Degree requirements:* For master's, 2 foreign languages, thesis (for some programs); for doctorate, 2 foreign languages, thesis/dissertation. *Entrance requirements:* For doctorate, M Div, 3 years of ministry experience. Additional exam requirements/recommendations for international students: Required—TOEFL (minimum score 575 paper-based; 90 iBT). Electronic applications accepted.

**Eastern Mennonite University,** Eastern Mennonite Seminary, Harrisonburg, VA 22802-2462. Offers church leadership (MA); divinity (M Div); ministry studies (Certificate); religion (MA); theological studies (Certificate). *Accreditation:* ATS. *Program availability:* Part-time. *Degree requirements:* For master's, thesis (for some programs), supervised field education (for M Div). *Entrance requirements:* For master's, minimum GPA of 2.5. Additional exam requirements/recommendations for international students: Required—TOEFL (minimum score 550 paper-based). *Expenses:* Contact institution. *Faculty research:* Spiritual direction and culture of call, leadership coaching: an approach to leadership in a culture of call, clarity of call in the probationary process for United Methodist clergy in Virginia, EMS women's experiences of culture of call efforts, practices of excellent and fruitful Mennonite pastoral ministry.

**Eastern Mennonite University,** Master of Arts in Counseling Program, Harrisonburg, VA 22802-2462. Offers MA, M Div/MA. *Accreditation:* ACA (one or more programs are accredited); ACIPE. *Program availability:* Part-time. *Degree requirements:* For master's, practicum, internship. *Entrance requirements:* For master's, minimum GPA of 3.0. Additional exam requirements/recommendations for international students: Required—TOEFL (minimum score 550 paper-based). Electronic applications accepted. *Expenses:* Contact institution. *Faculty research:* Career and gender, empathy and consciousness, emotion theory, education models.

**Eastern University,** Palmer Theological Seminary, St. Davids, PA 19087-3696. Offers Biblical studies and theology (MTS); Christian counseling (MTS); Christian faith and public policy (MTS); divinity (M Div); general studies (MTS); leadership of missional church renewal (D Min); theological studies (MTS); M Div/MA; M Div/MSW. *Accreditation:* ACIPE; ATS; MSA/CIHE. *Program availability:* Part-time, online learning. *Students:* 93 full-time (43 women), 135 part-time (66 women); includes 120 minority (105 Black or African American, non-Hispanic/Latino; 2 Asian, non-Hispanic/Latino; 12 Hispanic/Latino; 1 Two or more races, non-Hispanic/Latino), 4 international. Average age 47. In 2016, 42 master's, 9 doctorates awarded. *Entrance requirements:* Additional exam requirements/recommendations for international students: Required—TOEFL (minimum score 550 paper-based; 79 iBT). *Application deadline:* Applications are processed on a rolling basis. Application fee: $30. Electronic applications accepted. Application fee is waived when completed online. *Expenses:* $370 - $520 per credit (based on program and number of credits per semester). *Unit head:* Michael Dziedziak, Executive Director of Enrollment, 800-452-0996, E-mail: semadmis@eastern.edu. Website: http://palmerseminary.edu/

**East Texas Baptist University,** School of Christian Studies, Marshall, TX 75670-1498. Offers Christian ministry (MACM), including business leadership, spiritual guidance, sports and recreation ministry; religion (MA). *Program availability:* Part-time, evening/weekend. *Faculty:* 3 full-time (1 woman), 1 part-time/adjunct (0 women). *Students:* 5 full-time (2 women), 3 part-time (0 women); includes 1 minority (Black or African American, non-Hispanic/Latino). Average age 24. 8 applicants, 50% accepted, 4 enrolled. In 2016, 4 master's awarded. *Degree requirements:* For master's, thesis optional. *Entrance requirements:* Additional exam requirements/recommendations for international students: Recommended—TOEFL (minimum score 550 paper-based; 79 iBT). *Application deadline:* For fall admission, 8/17 for domestic students; for spring admission, 1/10 for domestic students; for summer admission, 5/2 for domestic students. Applications are processed on a rolling basis. Application fee: $50. Electronic applications accepted. *Expenses:* $735 per credit hour tuition; $150 per semester fees (6 or more hours enrolled); $75 per semester fees (1-5 hours enrolled). *Financial support:* In 2016–17, 4 students received support. Federal Work-Study, scholarships/grants, unspecified assistantships, and staff grants available. Financial award applicants required to submit FAFSA. *Unit head:* Dr. Warren Johnson, Director, 903-923-2182, Fax: 903-923-2077, E-mail: christianstudiesma@etbu.edu. *Application contact:* Den Murley, Director of Graduate Admissions, 903-923-2079, Fax: 903-934-8115, E-mail: dmurley@etbu.edu. Website: https://www.etbu.edu/christian-studies/masters-degrees/

**Ecumenical Theological Seminary,** Program in Ministry, Detroit, MI 48201. Offers D Min. *Accreditation:* ACIPE.

**Emory University,** Candler School of Theology, Atlanta, GA 30322. Offers formation and witness (M Div); history, scripture and tradition (MTS); leadership in church and community (M Div); modern religious thought and experience (MTS); pastoral counseling (Th D); religion and race (M Div); religion, health and science (M Div); scripture and interpretation (M Div); society and personality (M Div); theology (Th M); theology and ethics (M Div); theology and the arts (M Div); traditions of the church (M Div); women and religion (M Div); JD/M Div; JD/MTS; M Div/MBA; M Div/MPH; MBA/MTS; MTS/MPH. *Accreditation:* ACIPE. *Program availability:* Part-time. *Degree requirements:* For master's, thesis optional; for doctorate, comprehensive exam, thesis/dissertation. *Entrance requirements:* For master's, minimum undergraduate GPA of 3.0; for doctorate, GRE, M Div, 8 units of course work in clinical pastoral education. Additional exam requirements/recommendations for international students: Required—TOEFL (minimum score 600 paper-based; 95 iBT). Electronic applications accepted. *Expenses:* Contact institution. *Faculty research:* Biblical studies, church history, ethics, ministry practice, pastoral care.

**Evangelical Seminary,** Graduate and Professional Programs, Myerstown, PA 17067-1212. Offers Biblical studies (MAR); congregational ministry (M Div); global and contextual studies (M Div, MAR); historical and theological studies (MAR); interdisciplinary studies (MAR); marriage and family counseling (M Div); marriage and family therapy (MA); New Testament (MAR); Old Testament (MAR); spiritual formation (MAR); teaching ministry (M Div); youth ministry (M Div). *Accreditation:* ATS (one or more programs are accredited). *Program availability:* Part-time, online learning. *Degree requirements:* For master's, 2 foreign languages. *Entrance requirements:* For master's, minimum GPA of 2.5. Additional exam requirements/recommendations for international students: Required—TOEFL (minimum score 550 paper-based). *Faculty research:* Literary form and structure within the Hebrew and Greek scriptures, Wesley studies, esoteric biblical languages, the Mosaic law and the Christian, ethics.

**Fairfield University,** Graduate School of Education and Allied Professions, Fairfield, CT 06824. Offers applied behavior analysis (ATC); applied psychology (MA); clinical mental health counseling (MA, CAS); educational technology (MA); elementary education (MA, CAS); family studies (MA); integration of spirituality and religion in counseling (ATC); marriage and family therapy (MA); reading and language development (Sixth Year Certificate); school counseling (MA, CAS); school psychology (MA, CAS); school-based marriage and family therapy (ATC); secondary education (MA); special education (MA, CAS); substance abuse counseling (ATC); teaching (Certificate); teaching and foundations (MA, CAS); TESOL, world languages, and bilingual education (MA, CAS). *Accreditation:* NCATE. *Program availability:* Part-time, evening/weekend. *Faculty:* 19 full-time (15 women), 38 part-time/adjunct (26 women). *Students:* 153 full-time (132 women), 302 part-time (252 women); includes 97 minority (24 Black or African American, non-Hispanic/Latino; 12 Asian, non-Hispanic/Latino; 55 Hispanic/Latino; 6 Two or more races, non-Hispanic/Latino), 6 international. Average age 32. 283 applicants, 61% accepted, 97 enrolled. In 2016, 130 master's awarded. *Degree requirements:* For master's, comprehensive exam. *Entrance requirements:* For master's, minimum GPA of 3.0, 2 recommendations, resume. Additional exam requirements/recommendations for international students: Required—TOEFL (minimum score 550 paper-based; 84 iBT) or IELTS (minimum score 7.5). *Application deadline:* For fall admission, 2/15 for international students; for spring admission, 10/1 for international students. Application fee: $60. Electronic applications accepted. *Expenses:* $725 per credit hour. *Financial support:* In 2016–17, 42 students received support. Career-related internships or fieldwork and unspecified assistantships available. Support available to part-time students. Financial award applicants required to submit FAFSA. *Faculty research:* Reading and literacy, writing, social justice and inequality in education, addictions and mental health issues, therapeutic relationships and clinical supervision. *Unit head:* Dr. Robert D. Hannafin, Dean, 203-254-4250, Fax: 203-254-4241, E-mail: rhannafin@fairfield.edu. *Application contact:* Marianne Gumpper, Director of Graduate Admission, 203-254-4184, Fax: 203-254-4073, E-mail: gradadmis@fairfield.edu. Website: http://www.fairfield.edu/gseap

**Faith Baptist Bible College and Theological Seminary,** Graduate Program, Ankeny, IA 50023. Offers Biblical studies (MA); pastoral studies (M Div); pastoral training (MA); religion (MA); theological studies (MA). *Program availability:* Part-time. *Faculty:* 3 full-time (0 women), 4 part-time/adjunct (0 women). *Students:* 18 full-time (2 women), 30 part-time (5 women); includes 5 minority (1 Black or African American, non-Hispanic/Latino; 2 Asian, non-Hispanic/Latino; 1 Hispanic/Latino; 1 Two or more races, non-

Hispanic/Latino). Average age 33. In 2016, 13 master's awarded. *Degree requirements:* For master's, thesis or alternative. *Entrance requirements:* Additional exam requirements/recommendations for international students: Required—TOEFL (minimum score 550 paper-based; 79 iBT), IELTS (minimum score 6.5). *Application deadline:* For fall admission, 8/1 priority date for domestic students, 8/1 for international students; for spring admission, 12/15 for domestic and international students. Applications are processed on a rolling basis. Application fee: $25. Electronic applications accepted. *Financial support:* Career-related internships or fieldwork and scholarships/grants available. Support available to part-time students. Financial award application deadline: 3/1; financial award applicants required to submit FAFSA. *Faculty research:* Baptist theology, American church history. *Unit head:* Rev. Jim Tillotson, President, 515-964-0601, E-mail: tillotsonj@faith.edu. *Application contact:* Jonathan Balasa, Seminary Admissions Representative, 888-FAITH4U, Fax: 515-964-1638, E-mail: seminaryrep@faith.edu. Website: http://www.faith.edu/

**Faulkner University,** College of Biblical Studies, Montgomery, AL 36109-3398. Offers ministry (MABS); missions (MABS); New Testament (MABS); Old Testament (MABS); youth and family ministry (MABS).

**Fordham University,** Graduate School of Religion and Religious Education, New York, NY 10458. Offers pastoral counseling and spiritual care (MA); pastoral ministry/spirituality/pastoral counseling (D Min); religion and religious education (MA); religious education (MS, PhD, PD); spiritual direction (Certificate). *Program availability:* Part-time. Terminal master's awarded for partial completion of doctoral program. *Degree requirements:* For master's, research paper; for doctorate, comprehensive exam, thesis/dissertation. *Entrance requirements:* For doctorate, MAT. Electronic applications accepted. *Expenses:* Contact institution. *Faculty research:* Spirituality and spiritual direction, pastoral care and counseling, adult family and community, growth and young adult.

**Freed-Hardeman University,** School of Biblical Studies, Program in Ministry, Henderson, TN 38340-2399. Offers M Min. *Program availability:* Part-time. *Degree requirements:* For master's, comprehensive exam, internship. *Entrance requirements:* For master's, GRE General Test or MAT. Additional exam requirements/recommendations for international students: Required—TOEFL (minimum score 500 paper-based).

**Fresno Pacific University,** Biblical Seminary, Program in Christian Ministry, Fresno, CA 93702-4709. Offers MA. *Program availability:* Part-time. *Entrance requirements:* For master's, minimum GPA of 2.5. Additional exam requirements/recommendations for international students: Required—TOEFL (minimum score 550 paper-based). *Expenses:* Contact institution.

**Fuller Theological Seminary,** Graduate Programs, Pasadena, CA 91182. Offers Christian leadership (MACL); clinical psychology (PhD, Psy D); family studies (MA); global leadership (MA); global ministries (D Min); global ministries (Korean language) (D Min); intercultural studies (MA, Th M, PhD); intercultural studies (Korean language) (MA); marital and family therapy (MS); marriage and family enrichment (Certificate); ministry (M Div, D Min); missiology (D Miss); missiology (Korean language) (Th M); theology (MA, Th M, PhD), including evangelism (MA), family life education (MA), pastoral ministry (MA), recovery ministry (MA), worship music ministry (MA), worship, theology, and the arts (MA), youth, family, and culture (MA); theology and ministry (MA).

**Gannon University,** School of Graduate Studies, College of Humanities, Education, and Social Sciences, School of Humanities, Program in Pastoral Studies, Erie, PA 16541-0001. Offers pastoral studies (MA); theological studies (Certificate). *Program availability:* Part-time, evening/weekend. *Students:* 1 (woman) full-time, 2 part-time (both women). Average age 34. 2 applicants, 100% accepted, 1 enrolled. *Degree requirements:* For master's, comprehensive exam, thesis or alternative, research project, internship, written evaluation. *Entrance requirements:* Additional exam requirements/recommendations for international students: Required—TOEFL (minimum score 79 iBT). *Application deadline:* Applications are processed on a rolling basis. Application fee: $25. Electronic applications accepted. Application fee is waived when completed online. *Expenses:* Tuition: Full-time $17,370. *Required fees:* $550. Tuition and fees vary according to course load and program. *Financial support:* Federal Work-Study available. Financial award application deadline: 7/1; financial award applicants required to submit FAFSA. *Unit head:* Fr. Jason Glover, Director, 814-871-5495, E-mail: glover001@gannon.edu. *Application contact:* Bridget Philip, Director of Graduate Admissions, 814-871-7412, E-mail: graduate@gannon.edu.

**Gardner-Webb University,** School of Divinity, Boiling Springs, NC 28017. Offers biblical studies (M Div); Christian education and formation (M Div); intercultural studies (M Div); ministry (D Min); missiology (M Div); pastoral care and counseling (M Div); pastoral care and counseling/member care for missionaries (D Min); pastoral studies (M Div); M Div/MA; M Div/MBA. *Accreditation:* ACIPE. *Program availability:* Part-time. *Faculty:* 12 full-time (2 women), 3 part-time/adjunct (1 woman). *Students:* 115 full-time (59 women), 68 part-time (27 women); includes 86 minority (80 Black or African American, non-Hispanic/Latino; 5 Asian, non-Hispanic/Latino; 1 Hispanic/Latino). Average age 40. 86 applicants, 44% accepted, 16 enrolled. In 2016, 40 master's, 3 doctorates awarded. *Entrance requirements:* For master's, minimum GPA of 2.6; for doctorate, minimum GPA of 2.75. Additional exam requirements/recommendations for international students: Required—TOEFL (minimum score 500 paper-based; 61 iBT). *Application deadline:* Applications are processed on a rolling basis. Electronic applications accepted. *Expenses:* Contact institution. *Financial support:* Fellowships, institutionally sponsored loans, and unspecified assistantships available. Support available to part-time students. Financial award application deadline: 5/15. *Faculty research:* Jewish-Christian dialogue, Islam. *Unit head:* Dr. Robert W. Canoy, Sr., Dean, 704-406-4400, Fax: 704-406-3935, E-mail: rcanoy@gardner-webb.edu. *Application contact:* Kheresa Harmon, Director of Admissions, 704-406-3205, Fax: 704-406-3895, E-mail: kharmon@gardner-webb.edu. Website: http://gardner-webb.edu/academic-programs-and-resources/colleges-and-schools/divinity/index

**Garrett-Evangelical Theological Seminary,** Graduate and Professional Programs, Evanston, IL 60201-3298. Offers Bible and culture (PhD); Christian education (MA); Christian education and congregational studies (PhD); contemporary theology and culture (PhD); divinity (M Div); ethics, church, and society (MA); liturgical studies (PhD); ministry (D Min); music ministry (MA); pastoral care and counseling (MA); pastoral theology, personality, and culture (PhD); spiritual formation and evangelism (MA); theological studies (MTS); M Div/MSW. M Div/MSW offered jointly with Loyola University Chicago. *Accreditation:* ACIPE; ATS (one or more programs are accredited). *Program availability:* Part-time. *Degree requirements:* For master's, thesis (for some programs); for doctorate, thesis/dissertation. *Entrance requirements:* For doctorate, GRE (PhD). Additional exam requirements/recommendations for international students: Required—TOEFL (minimum score 560 paper-based). Electronic applications accepted.

**Gateway Seminary,** Graduate and Professional Programs, Ontario, CA 91761-8642. Offers divinity (M Div); early childhood education (Certificate); education leadership (MAEL, Diploma); ministry (D Min); theological studies (MTS); theology (Th M); youth ministry (Certificate). *Accreditation:* ACIPE. *Program availability:* Part-time, evening/

weekend. *Degree requirements:* For master's, thesis (for some programs); for doctorate, 2 foreign languages, thesis/dissertation. *Entrance requirements:* For doctorate, MAT. Additional exam requirements/recommendations for international students: Required—TOEFL (minimum score 550 paper-based). Electronic applications accepted.

**General Theological Seminary,** Graduate and Professional Programs, New York, NY 10011-4977. Offers Anglican studies (STM, Th D, Certificate); ascetical theology (Certificate); biblical studies (Certificate); congregational development (Certificate); divinity (M Div); historical and theological studies (Certificate); spiritual direction (MASD, STM, Certificate); theology (MA). *Accreditation:* ACIPE; ATS. *Program availability:* Part-time, evening/weekend. Terminal master's awarded for partial completion of doctoral program. *Degree requirements:* For master's, thesis; for doctorate, 2 foreign languages, thesis/dissertation. *Entrance requirements:* For master's, GRE General Test; for doctorate, GRE, M Div or MA. Additional exam requirements/recommendations for international students: Required—TOEFL. *Faculty research:* Liturgy, New Testament, ethics, history, ecumenical relations.

**Geneva College,** Program in Leadership Studies, Beaver Falls, PA 15010-3599. Offers business management (MS); ministry leadership (MS); non-profit leadership (MS); organizational management (MS); project management (MS). *Program availability:* Online only, 100% online. *Faculty:* 1 (woman) full-time, 10 part-time/adjunct (3 women). *Students:* 56 full-time (45 women), 9 part-time (6 women); includes 15 minority (12 Black or African American, non-Hispanic/Latino; 1 Asian, non-Hispanic/Latino; 2 Hispanic/Latino). Average age 45. 13 applicants, 77% accepted, 7 enrolled. In 2016, 38 master's awarded. *Degree requirements:* For master's, thesis or alternative, capstone leadership studies project. *Entrance requirements:* For master's, undergraduate degree from regionally-accredited college or university, one to three years of experience in the workplace, minimum GPA of 3.0 (preferred), resume, essay, two recommendations. Additional exam requirements/recommendations for international students: Required—TOEFL. *Application deadline:* For fall admission, 9/21 for domestic students; for spring admission, 2/23 for domestic students; for summer admission, 7/22 for domestic students. Applications are processed on a rolling basis. Electronic applications accepted. *Expenses:* $640 per credit. *Financial support:* In 2016-17, 50 students received support. Scholarships/grants available. Financial award application deadline: 8/1; financial award applicants required to submit FAFSA. *Faculty research:* Servant leadership, leadership essentials. *Unit head:* John D. Gallo, Dean of Graduate, Adult and Online Programs, 800-576-3111, Fax: 724-847-6839, E-mail: msol@geneva.edu. *Application contact:* Lynsey Auell, Graduate Enrollment Representative, 800-576-3111, Fax: 724-847-6839, E-mail: msol@geneva.edu. Website: http://www.geneva.edu/graduate/leadership-studies

**George Fox University,** Portland Seminary, Portland, OR 97223. Offers Biblical studies (M Div, MA); chaplaincy (M Div); Christian history and theology (M Div, MA); creation care (M Div, MA); intercultural studies (M Div, MA); leadership (M Div, MA); leadership and global perspectives (D Min); leadership and spiritual formation (D Min); semiotics and future studies (D Min); spiritual direction (MA, Certificate); spiritual direction supervision (M Div, MA, Certificate); spiritual formation and discipleship (M Div, MA, Certificate). *Accreditation:* ACIPE; ATS. *Program availability:* Part-time, evening/weekend, online learning. *Entrance requirements:* For master's, resume, three references (one pastoral, one academic or professional, one personal), one official transcript from each college or university attended; for doctorate, resume, 3 references (1 professional, 1 academic, 1 personal), one official transcript from each college or university attended. Additional exam requirements/recommendations for international students: Required—TOEFL (minimum score 577 paper-based; 90 iBT). Electronic applications accepted. *Expenses:* Contact institution.

**Georgia Christian University,** School of Divinity, Atlanta, GA 30360. Offers Christian education (MA); divinity (M Div); ministry (D Min); mission studies and world Christianity (MA); theological studies (MA).

**Global University,** Graduate School of Theology, Springfield, MO 65804. Offers bible and theology (D Min); biblical language (M Div); biblical studies (MA); Christian ministry (M Div, D Min); ministerial studies (MA), including education, leadership, missions, New Testament, Old Testament. *Program availability:* Part-time, evening/weekend, online learning. *Degree requirements:* For master's, thesis (for some programs). *Entrance requirements:* For master's, minimum undergraduate GPA of 3.0. Electronic applications accepted. *Faculty research:* Higher education, cross-cultural missions.

**Gordon-Conwell Theological Seminary,** Graduate and Professional Programs, South Hamilton, MA 01982. Offers Biblical languages (MABL); church history (MACH); counseling (MACO); ministry (D Min); missions/evangelism (MAME); New Testament (MANT); Old Testament (MAOT); religion (MAR); theology (M Div, MATH, Th M, Th D). *Accreditation:* ACIPE; ATS (one or more programs are accredited). *Program availability:* Part-time, evening/weekend. *Degree requirements:* For master's, one foreign language, thesis optional; for doctorate, 2 foreign languages, thesis/dissertation. *Entrance requirements:* For master's, minimum GPA of 2.5; for doctorate, minimum GPA of 3.0.

**Grace Theological Seminary,** Graduate and Professional Programs, Winona Lake, IN 46590-9907. Offers biblical studies (Certificate); chaplaincy (M Div); exegetical studies (M Div); intercultural studies (M Div, MA, D Min); local church ministry (MA), including camp administration, women's leadership; pastoral counseling (M Div); pastoral studies (M Div, D Min); theology (Diploma). *Accreditation:* ATS. *Program availability:* Part-time, online learning. *Degree requirements:* For master's, thesis optional; for doctorate, 2 foreign languages, thesis/dissertation. *Entrance requirements:* For master's, MAT, minimum GPA of 2.5. Electronic applications accepted. *Faculty research:* Biblical theology, language, and church ministries.

**Grace University,** College of Graduate Studies, Counseling Program, Omaha, NE 68108. Offers MA. *Entrance requirements:* For master's, minimum undergraduate GPA of 3.0.

**Grand Canyon University,** College of Doctoral Studies, Phoenix, AZ 85017-1097. Offers data analytics (DBA); general psychology (PhD), including cognition and instruction, industrial and organizational psychology, integrating technology, learning, and psychology, performance psychology; management (DBA); marketing (DBA); organizational leadership (Ed D), including behavioral health, Christian ministry, health care administration, organizational development. *Degree requirements:* For doctorate, comprehensive exam, thesis/dissertation. *Entrance requirements:* For doctorate, minimum GPA of 3.4 on earned advanced degree from regionally-accredited institution; transcripts; goals statement. Application fee: $0. *Unit head:* Michael Berger, Dean, 602-639-7255. *Application contact:* Michael Berger, Dean, 602-639-7255. Website: https://www.gcu.edu/college-of-doctoral-studies.php

**Grand Rapids Theological Seminary of Cornerstone University,** Graduate Programs, Grand Rapids, MI 49525-5897. Offers biblical counseling (MA); Biblical counseling (M Div); chaplaincy (M Div); Christian education (MA); intercultural studies (M Div, MA); New Testament (MA, Th M); Old Testament (MA, Th M); pastoral studies (M Div); systematic theology (MA); theology (Th M). *Accreditation:* ATS. *Program availability:* Part-time, online learning. *Entrance requirements:* Additional exam requirements/recommendations for international students: Required—TOEFL (minimum score 577 paper-based; 90 iBT). Electronic applications accepted.

## Pastoral Ministry and Counseling

**Greenville College,** Program in Leadership and Ministry, Greenville, IL 62246-0159. Offers MA. *Program availability:* Part-time. *Degree requirements:* For master's, 6 hours of research/practicum in applied ministry. *Entrance requirements:* For master's, 1 year of work experience in Christian ministry, interview. Additional exam requirements/recommendations for international students: Required—TOEFL (minimum score 525 paper-based). Electronic applications accepted.

**Hampton University,** School of Education and Human Development, Program in Counseling, Hampton, VA 23668. Offers college student development (MA); community agency counseling (MA); counseling (Ed S); counselor education and supervision (PhD); pastoral counseling (MA); school counseling (MA). *Accreditation:* ACA; NCATE. *Program availability:* Part-time, evening/weekend, online learning. *Faculty:* 4 full-time (2 women). *Students:* 37 full-time (34 women), 17 part-time (16 women); includes 49 minority (all Black or African American, non-Hispanic/Latino), 1 international. Average age 32. 55 applicants, 53% accepted, 19 enrolled. In 2016, 20 master's awarded. *Degree requirements:* For master's, comprehensive exam; for doctorate, comprehensive exam, thesis/dissertation. *Entrance requirements:* For master's, GRE General Test, personal statement, two letters of recommendation; for doctorate, GRE General Test, personal statement, writing sample, three letters of recommendation; for Ed S, personal statement, two letters of recommendation. Additional exam requirements/recommendations for international students: Required—TOEFL (minimum score 525 paper-based) or IELTS (6.5). *Application deadline:* For fall admission, 6/1 priority date for domestic students, 4/1 priority date for international students; for winter admission, 9/1 priority date for international students; for spring admission, 11/1 priority date for domestic students, 9/1 for international students; for summer admission, 4/1 priority date for domestic students, 2/1 priority date for international students. Applications are processed on a rolling basis. Application fee: $35. Electronic applications accepted. *Expenses: Tuition:* Full-time $10,776; part-time $548 per credit hour. *Required fees:* $35; $35 per credit hour. Tuition and fees vary according to course load and program. *Financial support:* Fellowships, research assistantships, teaching assistantships, career-related internships or fieldwork, Federal Work-Study, institutionally sponsored loans, and scholarships/grants available. Support available to part-time students. Financial award application deadline: 6/30; financial award applicants required to submit FAFSA. *Faculty research:* Personality development, temperament, post-traumatic stress disorder, continuum of normal to abnormal personality. *Unit head:* Dr. Spencer R. Baker, Chair, 757-637-2232, E-mail: spencer.baker@hamptonu.edu. Website: http://edhd.hamptonu.edu/counseling/

**Harding School of Theology,** Graduate Programs, Memphis, TN 38117-5499. Offers Christian ministry (MA); counseling (MA); ministry (M Div, D Min); religion (MA). *Accreditation:* ATS. *Program availability:* Part-time, online learning. *Degree requirements:* For master's, variable foreign language requirement, thesis (for some programs); for doctorate, one foreign language, thesis/dissertation. *Entrance requirements:* For master's, minimum GPA of 2.7; for doctorate, minimum GPA of 3.0. Additional exam requirements/recommendations for international students: Required—TOEFL (minimum score 550 paper-based; 79 iBT). Electronic applications accepted.

**Harding University,** College of Bible and Ministry, Master of Ministry Program, Searcy, AR 72149-0001. Offers M Min. *Program availability:* Part-time, evening/weekend, online learning. *Faculty:* 14 part-time/adjunct (1 woman). *Students:* 1 full-time (0 women), 19 part-time (2 women); includes 3 minority (all Black or African American, non-Hispanic/Latino). Average age 42. 3 applicants, 100% accepted, 3 enrolled. In 2016, 3 master's awarded. *Degree requirements:* For master's, 3 practica (1 hour each), portfolio, capstone project. *Entrance requirements:* For master's, 16 hours of course work in Bible, minimum GPA of 2.75. Additional exam requirements/recommendations for international students: Required—TOEFL (minimum score 550 paper-based; 79 iBT). *Application deadline:* For fall admission, 8/1 priority date for domestic and international students; for spring admission, 12/1 priority date for domestic students, 12/15 priority date for international students. Applications are processed on a rolling basis. Application fee: $25. Electronic applications accepted. Tuition and fees vary according to degree level and program. *Financial support:* In 2016–17, 18 students received support. Scholarships/grants and unspecified assistantships available. *Unit head:* Dr. Bill Richardson, Director/Associate Professor, 501-279-4252, Fax: 501-279-4081, E-mail: mmin@harding.edu. *Application contact:* Aleshia O'Neal, Information Contact, 501-279-5290, E-mail: aoneal@harding.edu.

**Hardin-Simmons University,** Graduate School, Logsdon School of Theology, Logsdon Seminary, Program in Family Ministry, Abilene, TX 79698-0001. Offers MA. *Program availability:* Part-time. *Faculty:* 2 full-time (0 women). *Students:* 15 full-time (12 women), 11 part-time (8 women); includes 8 minority (1 Asian, non-Hispanic/Latino; 7 Hispanic/Latino), 1 international. Average age 31. In 2016, 11 master's awarded. *Degree requirements:* For master's, comprehensive exam, clinical experience, project. *Entrance requirements:* For master's, minimum undergraduate GPA of 3.0 in major, 2.7 overall; 6 hours each of course work in psychology and Old and New Testament; interview; writing sample; references. Additional exam requirements/recommendations for international students: Required—TOEFL (minimum score 555 paper-based; 75 iBT). *Application deadline:* For fall admission, 8/15 priority date for domestic students, 4/1 for international students; for spring admission, 1/5 priority date for domestic students, 9/1 for international students. Applications are processed on a rolling basis. Application fee: $50. Electronic applications accepted. *Expenses: Tuition:* Full-time $12,510; part-time $695 per credit hour. *Required fees:* $325; $110 per semester. *Financial support:* In 2016–17, 24 students received support. Fellowships, career-related internships or fieldwork, and scholarships/grants available. Support available to part-time students. Financial award application deadline: 6/30; financial award applicants required to submit FAFSA. *Unit head:* Dr. Randall Maurer, Director, 325-670-1599, Fax: 325-670-1406, E-mail: rmaurer@hsutx.edu. *Application contact:* Dr. Nancy Kucinski, Dean of Graduate Studies, 325-670-1298, Fax: 325-670-1564, E-mail: gradoff@hsutx.edu. Website: http://www.logsdonseminary.org/index.php/academics/mafm

**Hardin-Simmons University,** Graduate School, Logsdon School of Theology, Logsdon Seminary, Program in Ministry, Abilene, TX 79698-0001. Offers D Min. *Program availability:* Part-time. *Faculty:* 7 full-time (0 women). *Students:* 33 part-time (1 woman); includes 7 minority (4 Black or African American, non-Hispanic/Latino; 1 Asian, non-Hispanic/Latino; 2 Hispanic/Latino). Average age 44. In 2016, 3 doctorates awarded. *Degree requirements:* For doctorate, ministry project. *Entrance requirements:* For doctorate, GRE or MAT, M Div or equivalent, minimum graduate GPA of 3.0, minimum 3 years' ministry experience, active current ministry involvement, interview, 4 letters of recommendation, church endorsement. *Application deadline:* For fall admission, 4/30 for domestic students. Application fee: $50. *Expenses: Tuition:* Full-time $12,510; part-time $695 per credit hour. *Required fees:* $325; $110 per semester. *Financial support:* In 2016–17, 18 students received support. Application deadline: 6/30; applicants required to submit FAFSA. *Unit head:* Dr. Larry Baker, Director, 325-671-2110, Fax: 325-670-1406, E-mail: lbaker@hsutx.edu. *Application contact:* Dr. Nancy Kucinski, Dean of Graduate Studies, 325-670-1298, Fax: 325-670-1564, E-mail: gradoff@hsutx.edu. Website: http://www.logsdonseminary.org/index.php/academics/doctor-of-ministry

**Hartford Seminary,** Graduate Programs, Hartford, CT 06105-2279. Offers Islamic studies (MA); ministry (D Min); religious studies (MA); spirituality (Certificate). *Accreditation:* ATS (one or more programs are accredited). *Program availability:* Part-time, evening/weekend, online learning. *Degree requirements:* For master's, thesis optional, oral exam; for doctorate, thesis/dissertation, oral exam. *Entrance requirements:* For master's, M Div. Additional exam requirements/recommendations for international students: Required—TOEFL (minimum score 550 paper-based; 80 iBT). *Faculty research:* Liturgy and social justice, professional leadership in ministry, congregational studies, Christian-Muslim relations, American religion.

**Heritage Christian University,** Graduate Programs, Florence, AL 35630. Offers counseling (MM); Greek (MA); ministry (MM); New Testament (MA). *Degree requirements:* For master's, practicum (MM), major research paper (MA). *Entrance requirements:* For master's, MAT or GRE, bachelor's degree in Bible from an accredited college or university, minimum GPA of 2.75, 3 letters of recommendation.

**Holmes Institute,** Graduate Program, Golden, CO 80401. Offers consciousness studies (MS). *Program availability:* Online learning. *Degree requirements:* For master's, comprehensive exam, 2 spiritual retreats per year, internship (1 per term), 2 spiritual conferences. *Entrance requirements:* For master's, 2 letters of recommendation, interview, official transcripts of an accredited bachelor's degree. Additional exam requirements/recommendations for international students: Required—TOEFL (minimum score 530 paper-based).

**Holy Names University,** Graduate Division, Department of Counseling Psychology, Oakland, CA 94619-1699. Offers counseling and forensic counseling (MA); counseling psychology (MA); forensic psychology (MA). *Program availability:* Part-time, evening/weekend. *Students:* 37 full-time (all women), 37 part-time (32 women); includes 55 minority (37 Black or African American, non-Hispanic/Latino; 6 Asian, non-Hispanic/Latino; 9 Hispanic/Latino; 2 Native Hawaiian or other Pacific Islander, non-Hispanic/Latino; 1 Two or more races, non-Hispanic/Latino), 3 international. Average age 33. 28 applicants, 82% accepted, 18 enrolled. In 2016, 33 master's awarded. *Degree requirements:* For master's, comprehensive paper, seminars. *Entrance requirements:* For master's, minimum undergraduate GPA of 2.6 overall, 3.0 in major. Additional exam requirements/recommendations for international students: Required—TOEFL (minimum score 550 paper-based; 79 iBT). *Application deadline:* For fall admission, 8/1 priority date for domestic students, 7/15 for international students; for spring admission, 12/1 priority date for domestic students, 12/1 for international students; for summer admission, 5/1 priority date for domestic students, 5/1 for international students. Applications are processed on a rolling basis. Application fee: $65. Electronic applications accepted. Application fee is waived when completed online. *Expenses:* Contact institution. *Financial support:* Career-related internships or fieldwork, Federal Work-Study, scholarships/grants, and unspecified assistantships available. Support available to part-time students. Financial award application deadline: 3/2; financial award applicants required to submit FAFSA. *Faculty research:* Cognitive psychology, anger management, grief and grief counseling, post-modernism and psychotherapy, spirituality and psychology. *Unit head:* Dr. Perri Franskoviak, Program Director, 510-436-1465, E-mail: franskoviak@hnu.edu. *Application contact:* 510-436-1351, Fax: 510-436-1325, E-mail: graduateadmissions@hnu.edu.

**Houston Baptist University,** School of Christian Thought, Program in Christian Leadership, Houston, TX 77074-3298. Offers MA. *Program availability:* Evening/weekend. *Students:* 1 part-time (0 women); minority (Black or African American, non-Hispanic/Latino). Average age 29. 3 applicants. *Entrance requirements:* For master's, bachelor's degree conferred transcript, resume, essay/personal statement. Additional exam requirements/recommendations for international students: Required—TOEFL (minimum score 80 iBT), IELTS (minimum score 6.5). *Application deadline:* For fall admission, 8/1 for domestic students, 6/1 for international students; for spring admission, 1/1 for domestic students, 11/1 for international students; for summer admission, 5/1 for domestic students, 3/1 for international students. Applications are processed on a rolling basis. Application fee: $0 ($100 for international students). Electronic applications accepted. Application fee is waived when completed online. *Expenses:* $1,500 per 3-hour course; $1,275 annual general fee; $1,060 annual technology fee. *Financial support:* Federal Work-Study and scholarships/grants available. Financial award application deadline: 4/1; financial award applicants required to submit FAFSA. *Unit head:* Dr. Jeffrey Green, Interim Dean, Fax: 281-649-3012, E-mail: jgreen@hbu.edu. *Application contact:* Celeste Risteski, Administrative Assistant to the Dean, 281-649-3383, Fax: 281-649-3012, E-mail: cristeski@hbu.edu.

**Houston Graduate School of Theology,** Graduate Programs, Houston, TX 77092. Offers counseling (MA); pastoral ministry (M Div, D Min); theology (MA). *Accreditation:* ATS (one or more programs are accredited). *Program availability:* Part-time, evening/weekend. *Degree requirements:* For master's, thesis (for some programs); for doctorate, thesis/dissertation. *Entrance requirements:* For doctorate, GRE General Test or MAT, M Div or equivalent. Additional exam requirements/recommendations for international students: Required—TOEFL (minimum score 550 paper-based). *Faculty research:* Hermeneutics, spirituality, religion of Eastern Europe.

**Howard Payne University,** Program in Youth Ministry, Brownwood, TX 76801-2715. Offers MA. *Program availability:* Part-time. *Faculty:* 2 full-time (0 women), 1 part-time/adjunct (0 women). *Students:* 2 full-time (0 women), 2 part-time (0 women). Average age 28. 5 applicants, 100% accepted, 4 enrolled. In 2016, 6 master's awarded. *Degree requirements:* For master's, three 2-hour internships/mentorships. *Entrance requirements:* For master's, undergraduate degree from accredited university; leveling courses (for students who do not have undergraduate coursework in Old Testament, New Testament, and youth ministry). Additional exam requirements/recommendations for international students: Required—TOEFL (minimum score 79 iBT). *Application deadline:* For fall admission, 7/1 for domestic students; for spring admission, 12/1 for domestic students. Applications are processed on a rolling basis. Application fee: $0. Electronic applications accepted. *Financial support:* Application deadline: 3/15; applicants required to submit FAFSA. *Unit head:* Dr. Gary Gramling, Director, 325-649-8404, E-mail: ggramling@hputx.edu. *Application contact:* Kristian Simpson, Administrative Assistant for Christian Studies Graduate Programs, 325-649-8039, E-mail: ksimpson@hputx.edu. Website: http://www.hputx.edu/academics/schools/school-of-christian-studies/graduate-programs/ma-youth-ministry/

**Huntington University,** Graduate School, Huntington, IN 46750-1299. Offers counseling (MA), including licensed mental health counselor; early adolescent education (M Ed); education (M Ed); global missions leadership (MA); global youth ministry (MA); TESOL education (M Ed); youth ministry leadership (MA). *Program availability:* Part-time, online learning. *Degree requirements:* For master's, comprehensive exam (for some programs), thesis (for some programs). *Entrance requirements:* For master's, GRE (for counseling and education students only); for doctorate, GRE (for occupational therapy students). Additional exam requirements/recommendations for international students: Required—TOEFL (minimum score 85 iBT), IELTS (minimum score 6.5). Electronic applications accepted. *Faculty research:* Leadership, educational technology trends, evangelism, youth ministry, mental health.

**Iliff School of Theology,** Graduate and Professional Programs, Denver, CO 80210-4798. Offers biblical studies (MA); church history (MA); religion (MA); religion and social change (MA); specialized ministry (MASM), including justice and peace, pastoral theology and care, religions leadership; theology (M Div, MTS, D Min, PhD), including Biblical studies (PhD), religion and psychological studies (PhD), religion and social change (PhD), theology, philosophy and culture (PhD); theology/ethics (MA). PhD offered jointly with University of Denver. *Accreditation:* ACIPE; ATS. *Program availability:* Part-time, evening/weekend. *Degree requirements:* For master's, one foreign language, thesis (for some programs); for doctorate, 2 foreign languages, comprehensive exam, thesis/dissertation. *Entrance requirements:* For master's, minimum GPA of 3.0, writing sample, references; for doctorate, GRE General Test, minimum GPA of 3.0, writing sample, letters of recommendation. Additional exam requirements/recommendations for international students: Required—TOEFL (minimum score 550 paper-based). Electronic applications accepted. *Faculty research:* Pastoral care, history, church music, contemporary church, biblical studies.

**Indiana Wesleyan University,** Graduate School, Wesley Seminary, Program in Ministry, Marion, IN 46953-4974. Offers children, youth and family ministry (MA); ministerial leadership (MA). *Accreditation:* ATS. *Program availability:* Part-time, online learning. *Degree requirements:* For master's, one foreign language, capstone practicum and/or project. *Entrance requirements:* Additional exam requirements/recommendations for international students: Required—TOEFL. Electronic applications accepted. *Expenses:* Contact institution. *Faculty research:* History of worship innovation, history of New Testament afterlife traditions, second century mantanism, cross-cultural ministry, church health and growth, leadership in Christian organizations, managing change in the church, effective youth ministry, women in ministry, Biblical hermeneutics.

**Inter American University of Puerto Rico, Metropolitan Campus,** Graduate Programs, Program in Pastoral Theology, San Juan, PR 00919-1293. Offers PhD.

**Interdenominational Theological Center,** Graduate and Professional Programs, Atlanta, GA 30314-4112. Offers Christian education (MACE); ministry (D Min); pastoral counseling (Th D); theology (M Div); M Div/MACE. D Min and Th D programs offered in collaboration with the Atlanta Theological Association. *Accreditation:* ACIPE; ATS (one or more programs are accredited). *Program availability:* Part-time, evening/weekend, blended/hybrid learning. *Faculty:* 15 full-time (6 women), 12 part-time/adjunct (5 women). *Students:* 119 full-time (45 women), 137 part-time (60 women); includes 249 minority (248 Black or African American, non-Hispanic/Latino; 1 Two or more races, non-Hispanic/Latino), 2 international. *Degree requirements:* For doctorate, thesis/dissertation. *Entrance requirements:* For doctorate, master's degree. *Application deadline:* For fall admission, 7/1 for domestic and international students; for spring admission, 10/1 for domestic and international students. Applications are processed on a rolling basis. Application fee: $50. Electronic applications accepted. *Expenses: Tuition:* Full-time $13,000; part-time $9324 per credit. *Required fees:* $938; $938 per credit. Full-time tuition and fees vary according to course load. *Financial support:* Research assistantships, career-related internships or fieldwork, and Federal Work-Study available. Support available to part-time students. Financial award application deadline: 6/15; financial award applicants required to submit FAFSA. *Unit head:* Edward Lorenza Wheeler, President, 404-527-7702, Fax: 404-527-7770. *Application contact:* Michelle Davis, Office of Admission and Recruitment, 404-527-7793, E-mail: lmdavis@itc.edu. Website: http://www.itc.edu/academics/degreeprograms/

**International Baptist College and Seminary,** Program in Ministry, Chandler, AZ 85286. Offers M Min, D Min.

**Johnson University,** Graduate and Professional Programs, Knoxville, TN 37998-1001. Offers biblical interpretation (Graduate Certificate); business administration (MBA); Christian ministries (Graduate Certificate); clinical mental health counseling (MA); educational technology (MA); intercultural studies (MA); leadership (MBA); leadership studies (PhD); New Testament (MA); nonprofit management (MBA); school counseling (MA); spiritual formation and leadership (Graduate Certificate); strategic ministry (MA); teacher education (MA). *Program availability:* Part-time, evening/weekend, 100% online, blended/hybrid learning. *Faculty:* 26 full-time (10 women), 32 part-time/adjunct (9 women). *Students:* 126 full-time (46 women), 170 part-time (65 women); includes 33 minority (13 Black or African American, non-Hispanic/Latino; 1 American Indian or Alaska Native, non-Hispanic/Latino; 4 Asian, non-Hispanic/Latino; 8 Hispanic/Latino; 7 Two or more races, non-Hispanic/Latino), 21 international. Average age 35. In 2016, 106 master's, 3 doctorates awarded. *Degree requirements:* For master's, variable foreign language requirement, comprehensive exam, thesis (for some programs), internships; for doctorate, variable foreign language requirement, comprehensive exam, thesis/dissertation, internships. *Entrance requirements:* For master's, PRAXIS (for MA in teacher education); MAT (for counseling); GRE or GMAT (for MBA), interview, 3 references, transcripts, essay, minimum GPA of 2.5 or 3.0 (depending on program); for doctorate, GRE or MAT (taken not less than 5 years prior), interview, 3 references, transcripts, essay, minimum GPA of 3.0; for Graduate Certificate, interview, 3 references, transcripts, essay, minimum GPA of 3.0. Additional exam requirements/recommendations for international students: Required—TOEFL (minimum score 527 paper-based; 71 iBT). *Application deadline:* For fall admission, 7/1 for domestic; for spring admission, 11/1 for domestic students; for summer admission, 4/1 for domestic students. Application fee: $50. Electronic applications accepted. *Expenses:* Contact institution. *Financial support:* Scholarships/grants available. Financial award application deadline: 4/15; financial award applicants required to submit FAFSA. *Unit head:* Richard Clark, Vice President for External Relations, 865-251-2327, E-mail: rclark@johnsonu.edu. *Application contact:* Lisa Tarwater, Director of Graduate Admissions, 865-251-3400, E-mail: ltarwater@johnsonu.edu.

**John Wesley University,** Graduate Programs, High Point, NC 27265. Offers Christian leadership (D Min); organizational management (MBA); theological studies (MTS). *Program availability:* 100% online. *Faculty:* 1 full-time (0 women), 9 part-time/adjunct (3 women). *Students:* 21 full-time (13 women), 3 part-time (all women). *Entrance requirements:* For master's, GMAT or GRE (taken within last five years), bachelor's degree, minimum GPA of 3.0, resume, two letters of recommendation, autobiographical essay, immunizations. Application fee: $50. Electronic applications accepted. *Expenses: Tuition:* Full-time $3780; part-time $2520 per semester. *Required fees:* $365; $365 per semester. Tuition and fees vary according to degree level. *Application contact:* Rosalie Seitz, Admissions, 336-821-2474, Fax: 336-889-2261, E-mail: admissions@johnwesley.edu.

**Judson University,** Master of Leadership in Ministry Program, Elgin, IL 60123-1498. Offers MLM. *Program availability:* Evening/weekend, online only, blended/hybrid learning. *Faculty:* 3 full-time (1 woman), 5 part-time/adjunct (2 women). *Students:* 1 (woman) part-time; includes 3 minority (all Black or African American, non-Hispanic/Latino). Average age 37. *Degree requirements:* For master's, thesis or alternative. *Entrance requirements:* For master's, prior ministry experience (professional or volunteer); undergraduate degree in a ministry-related field (preferred). *Application deadline:* Applications are processed on a rolling basis. Application fee: $35. Electronic applications accepted. *Expenses:* Contact institution. *Financial support:* In 2016–17, 5 students received support. Scholarships/grants available. Financial award application deadline: 10/31; financial award applicants required to submit FAFSA. *Faculty research:* Volunteer development, ministry team development, ministry with military teams, intergenerational leadership. *Unit head:* Dr. Keith Krispin, Jr., Director, 847-628-1057, E-mail: kkrispin@judsonu.edu. *Application contact:* Debbie Sanders, Assistant,

Department of Christian Ministries, 847-628-1124, E-mail: deborah.sanders@judsonu.edu. Website: http://www.judsonu.edu/Graduate/Master_of_Leadership_in_Ministry/Overview/

**The King's University,** Graduate and Professional Programs, Southlake, TX 76092. Offers Biblical studies (Graduate Certificate); Christian ministry (Graduate Certificate); ministry (M Div, MPT, D Min).

**Kingswood University,** Program in Pastoral Theology, Sussex, NB E4E 5L2, Canada. Offers MA.

**Knox Theological Seminary,** Graduate Programs, Program in Ministry, Fort Lauderdale, FL 33308. Offers D Min. *Program availability:* Part-time. *Degree requirements:* For doctorate, thesis/dissertation. *Entrance requirements:* For doctorate, M Div or equivalent. Additional exam requirements/recommendations for international students: Required—TOEFL, TWE (minimum score 5).

**Lancaster Bible College,** Capital Bible Seminary, Lancaster, PA 17601. Offers biblical studies (MA, Certificate); Christian counseling and discipleship (MA, Certificate); ministry (MA); theology (M Div). *Program availability:* Part-time, evening/weekend. *Degree requirements:* For master's, 2 foreign languages, comprehensive exam, thesis (for some programs). *Entrance requirements:* For master's, GRE General Test, Greek exam for those with 2 years of Greek, proficiency exam in theology, previous course work in Biblical studies. Additional exam requirements/recommendations for international students: Required—TOEFL (minimum score 550 paper-based). *Faculty research:* Dead Sea Scrolls, spiritual gifts, hermeneutics.

**Lancaster Bible College,** Graduate School, Lancaster, PA 17601-5036. Offers adult ministries (MA); Bible (MA); children and family ministry (MA); church planting (MA); consulting resource teacher (M Ed); elementary school counseling (M Ed); leadership (PhD); leadership studies (MA); marriage and family counseling (MA); mental health counseling (MA); pastoral studies (MA); secondary school counseling (M Ed); sports ministry (MA); student ministry (MA); town and country ministry (MA). *Program availability:* Part-time, evening/weekend. *Degree requirements:* For master's, comprehensive exam (for some programs), thesis (for some programs). *Entrance requirements:* For master's, bachelor's degree with a minimum of 30 credits of course work in Bible, minimum undergraduate GPA of 3.0, interview. Additional exam requirements/recommendations for international students: Required—TOEFL.

**La Salle University,** School of Arts and Sciences, Program in Counseling and Family Therapy, Philadelphia, PA 19141-1199. Offers industrial/organizational management and human resources (MA); marriage and family therapy (MA); pastoral counseling (MA); professional clinical counseling (MA). *Accreditation:* ACA; APA. *Program availability:* Part-time, evening/weekend. *Faculty:* 8 full-time (3 women), 20 part-time/adjunct (13 women). *Students:* 77 full-time (55 women), 180 part-time (147 women); includes 84 minority (44 Black or African American, non-Hispanic/Latino; 5 Asian, non-Hispanic/Latino; 31 Hispanic/Latino; 4 Two or more races, non-Hispanic/Latino), 5 international. Average age 30. 156 applicants, 76% accepted, 48 enrolled. In 2016, 106 master's awarded. *Degree requirements:* For master's, comprehensive exam. *Entrance requirements:* For master's, GRE or MAT (waived for applicants that already possess a master's degree in any field or for applicants that have a cumulative GPA of 3.5 or higher), minimum of 15 hours in psychology, counseling, or marriage and family studies; minimum GPA of 3.0; three letters of recommendation; personal statement; work experience (paid or volunteer). Additional exam requirements/recommendations for international students: Required—TOEFL. *Application deadline:* For fall admission, 8/15 priority date for domestic students, 7/15 for international students; for spring admission, 12/15 priority date for domestic students, 11/15 for international students; for summer admission, 4/15 priority date for domestic students, 3/15 for international students. Applications are processed on a rolling basis. Application fee: $35. Electronic applications accepted. Application fee is waived when completed online. *Expenses:* Contact institution. *Financial support:* In 2016–17, 37 students received support. Scholarships/grants and unspecified assistantships available. Support available to part-time students. Financial award application deadline: 8/31; financial award applicants required to submit FAFSA. *Faculty research:* Cognitive therapy, attribution theory, work habits, single parent families, treatment of addictions. *Unit head:* Dr. Donna A. Tonrey, Director, 215-951-1767, Fax: 215-951-1843, E-mail: psyma@lasalle.edu. *Application contact:* Elizabeth Heenan, Director, Graduate and Adult Enrollment, 215-951-1100, Fax: 215-951-1462, E-mail: heenan@lasalle.edu. Website: http://www.lasalle.edu/counseling-family-therapy/

**La Sierra University,** School of Religion, Riverside, CA 92515. Offers pastoral ministry (M Div); religion (MA); religious education (MA); religious studies (MA). *Program availability:* Part-time. *Degree requirements:* For master's, one foreign language, thesis or alternative. *Entrance requirements:* For master's, GRE General Test, minimum GPA of 3.0.

**Lee University,** Programs in Religion, Cleveland, TN 37320-3450. Offers biblical studies (MA); ministry studies/leadership (MA); ministry studies/worship (MA); ministry studies/youth and family (MA); theological studies (MA), including ethics, religion. *Program availability:* Part-time, 100% online. *Faculty:* 13 full-time (2 women), 2 part-time/adjunct (0 women). *Students:* 57 full-time (19 women), 92 part-time (28 women); includes 72 minority (16 Black or African American, non-Hispanic/Latino; 2 Asian, non-Hispanic/Latino; 53 Hispanic/Latino; 1 Two or more races, non-Hispanic/Latino), 4 international. Average age 37. 19 applicants, 79% accepted, 12 enrolled. In 2016, 9 master's awarded. *Degree requirements:* For master's, variable foreign language requirement, comprehensive exam (for some programs), thesis (for some programs). *Entrance requirements:* For master's, GRE or MAT (for biblical/theological studies only), minimum GPA of 3.0, 3 letters of recommendation, interview, official transcripts, essay. Additional exam requirements/recommendations for international students: Required—TOEFL (minimum score 61 iBT). *Application deadline:* For fall admission, 4/1 priority date for domestic and international students; for spring admission, 10/1 priority date for domestic and international students. Applications are processed on a rolling basis. Application fee: $25. Electronic applications accepted. *Expenses:* Contact institution. *Financial support:* In 2016–17, 25 students received support, including 7 teaching assistantships (averaging $2,031 per year); career-related internships or fieldwork, Federal Work-Study, institutionally sponsored loans, scholarships/grants, and unspecified assistantships also available. Financial award application deadline: 3/1; financial award applicants required to submit FAFSA. *Faculty research:* Spiritual and discipleship formation, leadership, Biblical studies, theological studies, ethics. *Unit head:* Dr. Lisa Long, Director, 423-303-5100, E-mail: llong@leeuniversity.edu. Website: http://www.leeuniversity.edu/academics/graduate/

**Liberty University,** School of Behavioral Sciences, Lynchburg, VA 24515. Offers clinical mental health counseling (MA); counselor education and supervision (PhD); human services counseling (MA), including addictions and recovery, business, child and family law, Christian ministries, criminal justice, crisis response and trauma, executive leadership, health and wellness, life coaching, marriage and family, military resilience; marriage and family therapy (MA); military resilience (Certificate); professional counseling (MA). *Program availability:* Part-time, online learning. *Students:* 2,041 full-time (1,612 women), 4,970 part-time (3,875 women); includes 1,991 minority (1,678

## Pastoral Ministry and Counseling

Black or African American, non-Hispanic/Latino; 33 American Indian or Alaska Native, non-Hispanic/Latino; 48 Asian, non-Hispanic/Latino; 80 Hispanic/Latino; 8 Native Hawaiian or other Pacific Islander, non-Hispanic/Latino; 144 Two or more races, non-Hispanic/Latino; 127 international. Average age 39. 5,496 applicants, 41% accepted, 1257 enrolled. In 2016, 2,813 master's, 11 doctorates, 20 other advanced degrees awarded. *Application deadline:* Applications are processed on a rolling basis. Application fee: $50. Electronic applications accepted. *Financial support:* Applicants required to submit FAFSA. *Unit head:* Dr. Ronald Hawkins, Founding Dean, School of Behavioral Sciences. *Application contact:* Jay Bridge, Director of Admissions, 800-424-9595, Fax: 800-628-7977, E-mail: gradadmissions@liberty.edu.

**Liberty University,** School of Divinity, Lynchburg, VA 24515. Offers Biblical studies (M Div); church history (MAR, Th M); discipleship and church ministry (M Div, MAR, MCM); evangelism and church planting (M Div, MAR, MCM); global studies (M Div, MCM, MGS); homiletics (M Div, MAR, Th M, D Min); leadership (M Div, D Min); marketplace chaplaincy (M Div, MCM); ministry (D Min); pastoral counseling (M Div, MA, MAR, D Min), including addictions and recovery (MA), crisis response and trauma (MA), discipleship and church ministries (MA), leadership (MA), life coaching (MA), marketplace chaplaincy (MA), marriage and family (MA), military resilience (MA), pastoral counseling (MA); pastoral ministries (M Div, MCM); religious education (MRE); theology (M Div, MAR, MTS); theology and apologetics (PhD); worship (M Div, MAR, MCM, D Min). *Program availability:* Part-time, online learning. *Students:* 2,140 full-time (615 women), 3,020 part-time (906 women); includes 1,312 minority (1,016 Black or African American, non-Hispanic/Latino; 9 American Indian or Alaska Native, non-Hispanic/Latino; 100 Asian, non-Hispanic/Latino; 90 Hispanic/Latino; 7 Native Hawaiian or other Pacific Islander, non-Hispanic/Latino; 90 Two or more races, non-Hispanic/Latino; 158 international. Average age 42. 3,651 applicants, 37% accepted, 909 enrolled. In 2016, 1,551 master's, 39 doctorates, 168 other advanced degrees awarded. *Degree requirements:* For master's, 2 foreign languages, thesis (for some programs); for doctorate, 2 foreign languages, thesis/dissertation. *Entrance requirements:* For master's, minimum undergraduate GPA of 2.0; for doctorate, GRE General Test or MAT, minimum graduate GPA of 3.0. Additional exam requirements/recommendations for international students: Required—TOEFL (minimum score 600 paper-based; 100 iBT). *Application deadline:* For fall admission, 6/1 for domestic students; for spring admission, 11/1 for domestic students. Applications are processed on a rolling basis. Application fee: $50. Electronic applications accepted. *Expenses:* Contact institution. *Financial support:* Teaching assistantships with tuition reimbursements, career-related internships or fieldwork, and Federal Work-Study available. Financial award applicants required to submit FAFSA. *Unit head:* Dr. Ed Hindson, Dean, 434-592-4140, Fax: 434-522-0415, E-mail: ehindson@liberty.edu. *Application contact:* Jay Bridge, Director of Graduate Admissions, 800-424-9595, Fax: 800-628-7977, E-mail: gradadmissions@liberty.edu.
Website: https://www.liberty.edu/divinity/

**Liberty University,** School of Music, Lynchburg, VA 24515. Offers ethnomusicology (MA); music and worship (MA); music education (MA); worship studies (MA, DWS), including ethnomusicology (MA), leadership (MA). *Accreditation:* NASM. *Program availability:* Part-time, online learning. *Students:* 58 full-time (26 women), 184 part-time (90 women); includes 52 minority (42 Black or African American, non-Hispanic/Latino; 3 Asian, non-Hispanic/Latino; 2 Hispanic/Latino; 5 Two or more races, non-Hispanic/Latino), 8 international. Average age 38. 323 applicants, 24% accepted, 49 enrolled. In 2016, 39 master's, 1 doctorate awarded. *Entrance requirements:* For master's, minimum GPA of 3.0; interview; letter of recommendation; statement of purpose; bachelor's/master's degree in music, worship, or related field, or 5 years of experience. Additional exam requirements/recommendations for international students: Required—TOEFL (minimum score 600 paper-based; 100 iBT). *Application deadline:* Applications are processed on a rolling basis. Application fee: $50. Electronic applications accepted. *Financial support:* Applicants required to submit FAFSA. *Unit head:* Dr. Vernon Whaley, Dean, 434-592-3463, E-mail: vwhaley@liberty.edu. *Application contact:* Jay Bridge, Director of Admissions, 800-424-9595, Fax: 800-628-7977, E-mail: gradadmissions@liberty.edu.
Website: http://www.liberty.edu/academics/music/

**Lincoln Christian Seminary,** Graduate and Professional Programs, Lincoln, IL 62656-2167. Offers Bible and theology (MA); Christian ministries (MA); counseling (MA); divinity (M Div); leadership ministry (D Min); religious education (MRE). *Accreditation:* ACIPE; ATS. *Program availability:* Part-time. *Degree requirements:* For master's, 2 foreign languages, thesis; for doctorate, thesis/dissertation. *Entrance requirements:* For master's, minimum GPA of 2.5; for doctorate, M Div or equivalent. Additional exam requirements/recommendations for international students: Required—TOEFL (minimum score 550 paper-based). Electronic applications accepted.

**Lincoln Christian University,** Graduate Programs, Lincoln, IL 62656-2167. Offers Biblical studies (MA); church history/historical theology (MA); intercultural studies (MA); ministry (MA); organizational leadership (MA); philosophy and apologetics (MA); spiritual formation (MA); theology (MA). MA in spiritual formation offered in Normal, IL. *Program availability:* Online learning. *Faculty:* 22 full-time (6 women), 27 part-time/adjunct (9 women). *Students:* 89 full-time (45 women), 225 part-time (91 women). Average age 39. *Entrance requirements:* For master's, minimum cumulative GPA of 2.5 in undergraduate degree studies. Additional exam requirements/recommendations for international students: Required—TOEFL (minimum score 550 paper-based); Recommended—IELTS (minimum score 6). *Application deadline:* For fall admission, 8/1 for domestic students, 3/1 for international students; for spring admission, 11/15 for domestic students, 11/1 for international students. Application fee: $25 ($50 for international students). Application fee is waived when completed online. *Expenses:* Tuition: Full-time $7812; part-time $5208 per credit hour. *Required fees:* $1000; $1000 per credit hour. One-time fee: $150. Full-time tuition and fees vary according to campus/location and program. *Financial support:* Applicants required to submit FAFSA. *Application contact:* Lindsey Clark, Associate Director of Graduate and Seminary Enrollment, 217-732-3168 Ext. 2398, E-mail: lclark@lincolnchristian.edu.
Website: https://lincolnchristian.edu/academics/programs/masters/

**Lipscomb University,** Hazelip School of Theology, Nashville, TN 37204-3951. Offers Christian practice (MA); missional and spiritual formation (D Min); student ministry (Certificate); theology (M Div). *Program availability:* Part-time, evening/weekend, online learning. *Faculty:* 13 full-time (0 women), 4 part-time/adjunct (1 woman). *Students:* 52 full-time (12 women), 90 part-time (18 women); includes 17 minority (13 Black or African American, non-Hispanic/Latino; 2 Hispanic/Latino; 2 Two or more races, non-Hispanic/Latino), 4 international. Average age 38. In 2016, 16 master's, 8 doctorates awarded. *Degree requirements:* For master's, 2 foreign languages, comprehensive exam (for some programs), thesis optional; for doctorate, comprehensive exam, thesis/dissertation. *Entrance requirements:* For master's, 3 references, transcripts, goals statement; for doctorate, 3 references, transcripts, documentation of full-time participation in ministry, writing sample, interview. Additional exam requirements/recommendations for international students: Required—TOEFL (minimum score 570 paper-based; 80 iBT). *Application deadline:* For fall admission, 8/1 priority date for domestic students; for spring admission, 12/15 for domestic students. Applications are processed on a rolling basis. Application fee: $50 ($75 for international students).

Electronic applications accepted. *Expenses:* $898 per hour (for master's programs), $333 per hour (for D Min). *Financial support:* Scholarships/grants and unspecified assistantships available. Financial award application deadline: 3/1; financial award applicants required to submit FAFSA. *Faculty research:* Status of Churches of Christ in foreign nations, Hebrew grammar, marriage and family. *Unit head:* Frank Guertin, Director, 615-966-5709, Fax: 615-966-5352, E-mail: frank.guertin@lipscomb.edu. *Application contact:* Kellye McCool, Coordinator of Student Services, 615-966-5458, Fax: 615-966-6052, E-mail: kellye.mccool@lipscomb.edu.
Website: http://www.lipscomb.edu/hst

**Loras College,** Graduate Division, Program in Theology and Ministry, Dubuque, IA 52004-0178. Offers ministry (MA); theology (MA). *Program availability:* Part-time, evening/weekend. *Degree requirements:* For master's, comprehensive exam (for some programs), thesis (for some programs). *Entrance requirements:* For master's, bachelor's degree or undergraduate minor in religious studies or equivalent, minimum undergraduate GPA of 2.75.

**Louisiana College,** Caskey School of Divinity, Pineville, LA 71359-0001. Offers biblical and theological studies (MA); pastoral ministry (MA).

**Loyola Marymount University,** College of Liberal Arts, Department of Theological Studies, Program in Pastoral Theology, Los Angeles, CA 90045-8400. Offers MA. *Program availability:* Part-time, evening/weekend. *Students:* 21 full-time (17 women), 28 part-time (11 women); includes 33 minority (2 Black or African American, non-Hispanic/Latino; 11 Asian, non-Hispanic/Latino; 17 Hispanic/Latino; 3 Two or more races, non-Hispanic/Latino), 9 international. Average age 38. 9 applicants, 89% accepted, 5 enrolled. In 2016, 19 master's awarded. *Degree requirements:* For master's, comprehensive exam, thesis or alternative. *Entrance requirements:* For master's, GRE General Test or MAT (recommended), 2 letters of recommendation, personal statement. Additional exam requirements/recommendations for international students: Required—TOEFL (minimum score 600 paper-based; 100 iBT). Application fee: $50. Electronic applications accepted. *Financial support:* In 2016–17, 44 students received support, including 1 research assistantship; scholarships/grants and unspecified assistantships also available. Support available to part-time students. Financial award application deadline: 6/30; financial award applicants required to submit FAFSA. *Unit head:* Dr. Daniel Smith-Christopher, Graduate Director, 310-338-2875, E-mail: dchristopher@lmu.edu. *Application contact:* Chake H. Kouyoumjian, Associate Dean of Graduate Studies, 310-338-2721, E-mail: ckouyoum@lmu.edu.
Website: http://bellarmine.lmu.edu/theologicalstudies/graduateprograms/

**Loyola University Chicago,** Institute of Pastoral Studies, Chicago, IL 60611. Offers Christian spirituality (MA), including spiritual direction; church management (Certificate); counseling for ministry (MA); health care ministry leadership (Certificate); health care mission leadership (MA); pastoral counseling (MA, Certificate); pastoral studies (M Div, MA); religious education (Certificate); social justice (MA, Certificate); spiritual direction (Certificate); M Div/MA; M Div/MSW; MSW/MA. MSW/MA offered with School of Social Work. *Accreditation:* ACIPE. *Program availability:* Part-time, evening/weekend, 100% online, blended/hybrid learning. *Faculty:* 11 full-time (4 women), 25 part-time/adjunct (11 women). *Students:* 79 full-time (58 women), 120 part-time (76 women); includes 54 minority (22 Black or African American, non-Hispanic/Latino; 1 American Indian or Alaska Native, non-Hispanic/Latino; 6 Asian, non-Hispanic/Latino; 23 Hispanic/Latino; 2 Two or more races, non-Hispanic/Latino), 23 international. Average age 42. 116 applicants, 83% accepted, 71 enrolled. In 2016, 63 master's, 4 other advanced degrees awarded. *Degree requirements:* For master's, thesis optional, project. *Entrance requirements:* Additional exam requirements/recommendations for international students: Required—TOEFL (minimum score 550 paper-based; 79 iBT), IELTS (minimum score 6.5). *Application deadline:* Applications are processed on a rolling basis. Application fee: $50. Electronic applications accepted. Application fee is waived when completed online. *Expenses:* Contact institution. *Financial support:* In 2016–17, 84 students received support. Career-related internships or fieldwork, Federal Work-Study, institutionally sponsored loans, scholarships/grants, tuition waivers (partial), and unspecified assistantships available. Support available to part-time students. Financial award application deadline: 3/1; financial award applicants required to submit FAFSA. *Faculty research:* Catholic theology, skills of religious ministry, family ministries, spirituality and divorced men. *Unit head:* Dr. Brian J. Schmisek, Dean, 312-915-7400, Fax: 312-915-7410, E-mail: bschmisek@luc.edu. *Application contact:* Dr. M. Therese Lysaught, Associate Dean, 312-915-7485, Fax: 312-915-7410, E-mail: mlysaught@luc.edu.
Website: http://www.luc.edu/ips/

**Lutheran School of Theology at Chicago,** Graduate and Professional Programs, Chicago, IL 60615-5199. Offers ministry (MAM, D Min); theological studies (MATS, PhD); theology (M Div). *Accreditation:* ACIPE; ATS (one or more programs are accredited). *Program availability:* Part-time. Terminal master's awarded for partial completion of doctoral program. *Degree requirements:* For master's, variable foreign language requirement; for doctorate, variable foreign language requirement, comprehensive exam, thesis/dissertation. *Entrance requirements:* For doctorate, GRE, M Div or equivalent, 3 years of professional experience (D Min).

**Lutheran Theological Seminary at Gettysburg,** Graduate and Professional Programs, Gettysburg, PA 17325-1795. Offers divinity (M Div); ministerial studies (MAMS); outdoor ministry (MAR); parish ministry (D Min); theology (STM). *Accreditation:* ACIPE; ATS (one or more programs are accredited). *Program availability:* Part-time, online learning. *Degree requirements:* For master's, thesis (for some programs). Electronic applications accepted.

**The Lutheran Theological Seminary at Philadelphia,** Graduate School, Philadelphia, PA 19119-1794. Offers divinity (M Div); ministry (D Min); public leadership (MA); religion (MAR); social ministry and church (Certificate); theology (STM, PhD). *Accreditation:* ACIPE. *Program availability:* Part-time, evening/weekend. *Degree requirements:* For master's, one foreign language, comprehensive exam (for some programs), thesis (for some programs); for doctorate, thesis/dissertation. *Entrance requirements:* For master's, minimum undergraduate GPA of 2.8; for doctorate, minimum GPA of 3.0. Additional exam requirements/recommendations for international students: Required—TOEFL (minimum score 550 paper-based; 89 iBT), TWE. Electronic applications accepted.

**Lutheran Theological Seminary Saskatoon,** Graduate and Professional Programs, Saskatoon, SK S7N 0X3, Canada. Offers Biblical studies (MTS); church history (MTS); ethics/church and society (MTS); history of Christianity (STM); New Testament (STM); Old Testament (STM); pastoral studies (STM); pastoral theology (MTS); systematic theology (MTS); systematic theology and philosophy of religion (STM); theology (M Div, D Div). STM programs offered jointly with College of Emmanuel and St. Chad and St. Andrew's College. *Accreditation:* ATS. *Program availability:* Part-time. *Degree requirements:* For master's, thesis.

**Luther Rice College & Seminary,** Graduate Programs, Lithonia, GA 30038-2454. Offers apologetics (MA); Bible languages (M Div); Biblical counseling (MA); Christian ministry (M Div, D Min); Christian studies (MA); leadership (MA). *Program availability:* Part-time, evening/weekend, online learning. *Degree requirements:* For doctorate, thesis/dissertation. *Entrance requirements:* For master's, bachelor's degree or equivalent; for doctorate, M Div. Additional exam requirements/recommendations for international students: Required—TOEFL (minimum score 550 paper-based). Electronic applications accepted.

**Luther Seminary,** Graduate and Professional Programs, St. Paul, MN 55108-1445. Offers aging and health (MA); Biblical preaching (D Min); children, youth and family (M Div, MA); congregational mission and leadership (M Th, MA, D Min); history of Christianity (M Th, MA); missions and world religions (M Th); New Testament (M Th, MA); Old Testament (M Th, MA); pastoral care: clinical pastoral theology (M Th); pastoral theology and ministry (M Th); systematic theology (M Th, MA). *Accreditation:* ACIPE; ATS. *Program availability:* Part-time, online learning. *Degree requirements:* For master's, thesis or alternative; for doctorate, 2 foreign languages, thesis/dissertation. *Entrance requirements:* For master's, minimum GPA of 3.0; for doctorate, GRE General Test. Additional exam requirements/recommendations for international students: Required—TOEFL, IELTS. Electronic applications accepted. *Faculty research:* Theology, psychology (pastoral care), church history, Bible.

**Madonna University,** Program in Religious Studies, Livonia, MI 48150-1173. Offers pastoral ministry (MA).

**Maple Springs Baptist Bible College and Seminary,** Graduate and Professional Programs, Capitol Heights, MD 20743. Offers biblical studies (MA, Certificate); Christian counseling (MA); church administration (MA); divinity (M Div); ministry (D Min); religious education (MRE).

**Maranatha Baptist University,** Program in Biblical Counseling, Watertown, WI 53094. Offers MA. *Program availability:* Part-time. *Entrance requirements:* For master's, BA or BS. Additional exam requirements/recommendations for international students: Recommended—TOEFL. *Application deadline:* Applications are processed on a rolling basis. Application fee: $50. *Expenses:* Tuition: Full-time $6300; part-time $3150 per credit. *Required fees:* $210; $35 per course. Tuition and fees vary according to course load and degree level. *Financial support:* Scholarships/grants and tuition waivers (full and partial) available. Support available to part-time students. Financial award applicants required to submit FAFSA. *Unit head:* Dr. Larry Oats, Dean of Maranatha Baptist Seminary, 920-206-2324, Fax: 920-261-9109, E-mail: larry.oats@mbu.edu. *Application contact:* Dr. Jim Harrison, Director of Admissions, 920-206-2327, Fax: 920-261-9109, E-mail: admissions@mbbc.edu.
Website: https://www.mbu.edu/seminary/academics/programs/biblical-counseling/

**Martin University,** Graduate School of Urban Ministry, Indianapolis, IN 46218-3867. Offers urban ministry studies (MA). *Program availability:* Part-time, evening/weekend. *Degree requirements:* For master's, Greek, oral and written comprehensive exam or thesis. *Faculty research:* How to bridge the gap between black theology and the black church.

**Marymount University,** School of Education and Human Services, Program in Counseling, Arlington, VA 22207-4299. Offers clinical mental health counseling (MA); pastoral counseling (MA); school counseling (MA). *Accreditation:* ACA. *Program availability:* Part-time, evening/weekend. *Faculty:* 29 full-time (21 women), 7 part-time/adjunct (all women). *Students:* 84 full-time (74 women), 57 part-time (51 women); includes 55 minority (28 Black or African American, non-Hispanic/Latino; 2 American Indian or Alaska Native, non-Hispanic/Latino; 3 Asian, non-Hispanic/Latino; 17 Hispanic/Latino; 5 Two or more races, non-Hispanic/Latino), 2 international. Average age 30. 83 applicants, 77% accepted, 45 enrolled. In 2016, 39 master's awarded. *Degree requirements:* For master's, thesis or alternative, capstone/internship. *Entrance requirements:* For master's, GRE, 2 letters of recommendation, interview, resume, personal statement. Additional exam requirements/recommendations for international students: Required—TOEFL (minimum score 600 paper-based; 96 iBT), IELTS (minimum score 6.5). *Application deadline:* For fall admission, 1/15 priority date for domestic and international students; for spring admission, 10/5 for domestic and international students. Applications are processed on a rolling basis. Application fee: $40. Electronic applications accepted. *Expenses:* Tuition: Full-time $8460; part-time $940 per credit hour. *Required fees:* $10 per credit hour. One-time fee: $240 part-time. Tuition and fees vary according to program. *Financial support:* In 2016–17, 15 students received support, including 8 research assistantships with tuition reimbursements available, 4 teaching assistantships with tuition reimbursements available; career-related internships or fieldwork, Federal Work-Study, scholarships/grants, and unspecified assistantships also available. Support available to part-time students. Financial award applicants required to submit FAFSA. *Unit head:* Dr. Lisa Jackson-Cherry, Chair, Counseling, 703-284-1633, Fax: 703-284-5708, E-mail: lisa.jackson-cherry@marymount.edu. *Application contact:* Francesca Reed, Director, Graduate Admissions, 703-284-5901, Fax: 703-527-3815, E-mail: grad.admissions@marymount.edu.
Website: http://www.marymount.edu/Academics/School-of-Education-Human-Services/Graduate-Programs/Counseling-(M-A-)

**The Master's University,** The Master's Seminary, Santa Clarita, CA 91321-1200. Offers biblical counseling (MABC); New Testament (Th D); Old Testament (Th D); preaching (D Min); theology (M Div, M Th, Th D). *Program availability:* Part-time. *Degree requirements:* For master's, 2 foreign languages, thesis; for doctorate, 4 foreign languages, thesis/dissertation. *Entrance requirements:* For master's, minimum GPA of 2.75; for doctorate, Th M, minimum GPA of 3.5. Additional exam requirements/recommendations for international students: Required—TOEFL (minimum score 550 paper-based).

**McCormick Theological Seminary,** Graduate and Professional Programs, Chicago, IL 60615. Offers ministry (D Min); theological studies (MATS, Certificate); theology (M Div); M Div/MSW. M Div/MSW offered jointly with Loyola University Chicago, University of Chicago, and University of Illinois at Chicago. *Accreditation:* ACIPE; ATS (one or more programs are accredited). *Program availability:* Part-time, evening/weekend. *Degree requirements:* For master's, thesis (for some programs); for doctorate, thesis/dissertation. *Entrance requirements:* For master's, minimum GPA of 3.0; for doctorate, M Div, minimum 3 years in pastorate. *Faculty research:* Faith formation, families, biblical literature, Dead Sea scrolls, women in antiquity.

**McMaster University,** McMaster Divinity College, Hamilton, ON L8S 4M2, Canada. Offers biblical studies (M Div); Biblical studies (MA, MTS, Diploma); Christian interpretation/history (M Div, MA, MTS, Diploma); Christian ministry (M Div, MA, MTS, Diploma); Christian Studies (Certificate); Christian theology (PhD). Affiliated with the Toronto School of Theology. *Program availability:* Part-time. *Degree requirements:* For master's, one foreign language, thesis optional; for doctorate, 3 foreign languages, comprehensive exam, thesis/dissertation; for other advanced degree, 2 foreign languages, thesis. *Entrance requirements:* For master's, minimum B average in undergraduate course work, 3 letters of reference; for doctorate, minimum B+ average in bachelor's and master's, appropriate modern/ancient language, interview; for other advanced degree, 6 units of related Biblical language, minimum B+ average in undergraduate course work, minimum 15 units of course work in related area of study, 3 letters of recommendation. Additional exam requirements/recommendations for international students: Required—TOEFL (minimum score 550 paper-based). *Faculty research:* Ethics, Biblical studies, language studies, church history, Christian ministry.

**Meadville Lombard Theological School,** Graduate and Professional Programs, Chicago, IL 60637-1602. Offers divinity (M Div); ministry (D Min); religion (MA); M Div/MSW. M Div/MSW offered jointly with University of Chicago. *Accreditation:* ACIPE; ATS. *Program availability:* Part-time, online learning. *Entrance requirements:* For master's, bachelor's degree; for doctorate, bachelor's and masters degrees, 3 years of ministry.

**Mercer University,** Graduate Studies, Cecil B. Day Campus, James and Carolyn McAfee School of Theology, Atlanta, GA 30341. Offers Christian ministry (MACM); Christian spirituality (D Min); divinity (M Div); preaching (D Min); M Div/MBA; M Div/MS. *Program availability:* Faculty: 14 full-time (7 women), 5 part-time/adjunct (0 women). *Students:* 106 full-time (65 women), 84 part-time (35 women); includes 100 minority (89 Black or African American, non-Hispanic/Latino; 2 American Indian or Alaska Native, non-Hispanic/Latino; 1 Asian, non-Hispanic/Latino; 5 Hispanic/Latino; 1 Native Hawaiian or other Pacific Islander, non-Hispanic/Latino; 2 Two or more races, non-Hispanic/Latino), 1 international. Average age 37. 66 applicants, 71% accepted, 40 enrolled. In 2016, 53 master's, 2 doctorates awarded. *Degree requirements:* For master's, variable foreign language requirement, thesis (for some programs), minimum GPA of 2.5; for doctorate, thesis/dissertation, fieldwork, seminars. *Entrance requirements:* For master's and doctorate, regionally-accredited bachelor's degree with liberal arts core or proof of equivalent degree from foreign university; transcripts; letters of recommendation; resume; essays; writing sample; interview; background check. Additional exam requirements/recommendations for international students: Required—TOEFL (minimum score 550 paper-based; 79 iBT). *Application deadline:* For fall admission, 7/1 for domestic and international students; for spring admission, 11/15 for domestic and international students. Applications are processed on a rolling basis. Application fee: $50. Electronic applications accepted. *Expenses:* $410 per hour (for master's), $375 per hour (for D Min). *Financial support:* In 2016–17, 70 students received support. Career-related internships or fieldwork, Federal Work-Study, institutionally sponsored loans, and scholarships/grants available. Support available to part-time students. Financial award application deadline: 10/1; financial award applicants required to submit FAFSA. *Faculty research:* Biblical studies, Baptist heritage, Christian heritage, theology, pastoral care, ethics, global missions, academic research. *Unit head:* Dr. Jeffrey Willetts, Dean, 678-547-6470, Fax: 678-547-6478, E-mail: willetts_jg@mercer.edu. *Application contact:* L. Nikki Hardeman, Director of Admissions, 678-547-6357, Fax: 678-547-6478, E-mail: hardeman_ln@mercer.edu.
Website: http://www.mercer.edu/theology

**Mid-America Christian University,** Program in Counseling, Oklahoma City, OK 73170-4504. Offers marital and family therapy (MS); pastoral/spiritual direction (MS); professional counselor (MS). *Entrance requirements:* For master's, MAT, bachelor's degree from a regionally accredited college or university, minimum overall cumulative GPA of 2.75 of bachelor course work. Additional exam requirements/recommendations for international students: Required—TOEFL (minimum score 550 paper-based).

**Midwestern Baptist Theological Seminary,** Graduate and Professional Programs, Kansas City, MO 64118-4697. Offers Christian education (MACE); Christian foundations (Graduate Certificate); church music (MCM); counseling (MA); ministry (D Ed Min, D Min); Old or New Testament studies (PhD); theology (M Div). *Accreditation:* ATS. *Program availability:* Part-time, online learning. *Degree requirements:* For doctorate, thesis/dissertation. *Entrance requirements:* For doctorate, MAT. Electronic applications accepted. *Faculty research:* Ministerial studies, Biblical and theological studies, missions, counseling.

**Milligan College,** Area of Social Learning, Milligan College, TN 37682. Offers clinical mental health counseling (MSC); counseling ministry (Graduate Certificate); school counseling (MSC). *Program availability:* Part-time. *Faculty:* 3 full-time (all women), 2 part-time/adjunct (0 women). *Students:* 25 full-time (22 women), 3 part-time (2 women); includes 2 minority (1 Black or African American, non-Hispanic/Latino; 1 Two or more races, non-Hispanic/Latino), 1 international. Average age 31. 29 applicants, 72% accepted, 14 enrolled. In 2016, 15 master's awarded. *Degree requirements:* For master's, thesis or alternative. *Entrance requirements:* For master's, GRE General Test if undergraduate degree is less than 3.0, undergraduate degree and supporting transcripts, essay/personal statement, professional recommendations, interview. Additional exam requirements/recommendations for international students: Required—TOEFL (minimum score 550 paper-based, 79 iBT) or IELTS (6.5). *Application deadline:* For fall admission, 8/1 for domestic students, 6/1 for international students. Applications are processed on a rolling basis. Application fee: $30. Electronic applications accepted. *Expenses:* $430 per hour tuition; $325 per semester tech/activity fees. *Financial support:* Scholarships/grants available. Financial award application deadline: 12/1; financial award applicants required to submit FAFSA. *Faculty research:* Parent-child interaction therapy/autism; childhood sexual abuse/trauma; poverty and homelessness; social justice advocacy and competence; school-based mental health. *Unit head:* Dr. Christine Browning, Director of Master of Science in Counseling Program, 423-461-3513, Fax: 423-461-8777, E-mail: cmbrowning@milligan.edu. *Application contact:* Jenni Duran, Graduate Admissions Recruiter, Healthcare Programs, 423-461-8424, Fax: 423-461-8789, E-mail: jduran@milligan.edu.
Website: http://www.Milligan.edu/GPS

**Milligan College,** Emmanuel Christian Seminary at Milligan College, Milligan College, TN 37682. Offers Christian care and counseling (M Div); Christian education (M Div); Christian ministries (MACM, Graduate Certificate); Christian ministry (M Div); Christian theology (M Div, MAR); church history (MAR); church history/historical theology (M Div); general studies (M Div); ministry (D Min); New Testament (M Div, MAR); Old Testament (M Div, MAR); urban ministry (M Div); world missions (M Div). *Accreditation:* ACIPE; ATS. *Program availability:* Part-time, blended/hybrid learning. *Faculty:* 9 full-time (1 woman), 11 part-time/adjunct (0 women). *Students:* 55 full-time (16 women), 44 part-time (17 women); includes 7 minority (6 Black or African American, non-Hispanic/Latino; 1 Hispanic/Latino), 6 international. Average age 33. In 2016, 21 master's, 3 doctorates awarded. *Degree requirements:* For master's, 2 foreign languages, thesis or alternative, portfolio; for doctorate, thesis/dissertation. *Entrance requirements:* For master's, undergraduate degree and supporting transcripts, essay/personal statement, professional recommendations, interview; for doctorate, M Div or equivalent, essay/personal statement, professional recommendations. Additional exam requirements/recommendations for international students: Required—TOEFL (minimum score 550 paper-based, 79 iBT) or IELTS (6.5). *Application deadline:* For fall admission, 8/1 for domestic students, 6/1 for international students; for spring admission, 12/15 for domestic students, 8/1 for international students. Applications are processed on a rolling basis. Application fee: $30 ($0 for international students). Electronic applications accepted. *Expenses:* $470 per hour tuition; $325 per semester tech/activity fees. *Financial support:* In 2016–17, 124 students received support. Scholarships/grants and unspecified assistantships available. Financial award application deadline: 12/1; financial award applicants required to submit FAFSA. *Faculty research:* Theology of Old Testament prophets; performance criticism of New Testament texts; practical theology and spiritual formation for Christian leaders; church history and missions; constructive theology, art and imagination. *Unit head:* Dr. Rollin Ramsaran, Academic Dean, Emmanuel Christian Seminary, 423-461-1524, Fax: 423-926-6198, E-mail: raramsaran@milligan.edu. *Application contact:* Lauren Gullett, Director of Admissions and Recruitment for Emmanuel Christian Seminary, 423-461-1535, Fax: 423-926-6198,

## Pastoral Ministry and Counseling

E-mail: lwgullett@milligan.edu.
Website: http://ecs.milligan.edu/

**Missouri Baptist University,** Graduate Programs, St. Louis, MO 63141-8660. Offers business administration (MBA); Christian ministries (MACM); counseling (MAC); education (MSE); education administration (MEA); educational leadership (MSE, Ed S); teaching (MAT).

**Moody Bible Institute,** Graduate School, Chicago, IL 60610-3284. Offers biblical studies (MABS, Graduate Certificate); intercultural studies (MAIS, Graduate Certificate); ministry (M Div, M Min); spiritual formation and discipleship (MASF, Graduate Certificate); urban studies (MA, Graduate Certificate). *Program availability:* Part-time. *Degree requirements:* For master's, 2 foreign languages, fieldwork (MABS); colloquium, field research project (MA Min). *Entrance requirements:* For master's, 30 hours in Bible/theology, 2 years of ministry experience (MA Min).

**Moravian Theological Seminary,** Graduate and Certificate Programs, Bethlehem, PA 18018-6614. Offers chaplaincy (MACH); clinical counseling (MACC); divinity (M Div); formative spirituality (M Div, MATS, Graduate Certificate); spiritual direction (Graduate Certificate). *Accreditation:* ACIPE; ATS (one or more programs are accredited). *Program availability:* Part-time. *Faculty:* 8 full-time (3 women), 10 part-time/adjunct (6 women). *Students:* 26 full-time (12 women), 68 part-time (51 women); includes 17 minority (11 Black or African American, non-Hispanic/Latino; 5 Hispanic/Latino; 1 Two or more races, non-Hispanic/Latino), 1 international. Average age 48. 37 applicants, 73% accepted, 25 enrolled. In 2016, 20 master's, 8 other advanced degrees awarded. *Degree requirements:* For master's, thesis (for some programs). *Entrance requirements:* For master's, reference forms, essay, denominational endorsement (M Div); for Graduate Certificate, reference forms, essay. Additional exam requirements/recommendations for international students: Required—TOEFL (minimum score 550 paper-based; 79 iBT). *Application deadline:* For fall admission, 4/1 priority date for international students; for spring admission, 9/1 priority date for international students. Applications are processed on a rolling basis. Application fee: $50. Electronic applications accepted. *Expenses:* Tuition: Full-time $13,680; part-time $7596 per year. *Required fees:* $430; $430 per unit. Tuition and fees vary according to course load. *Financial support:* In 2016–17, 71 students received support. Career-related internships or fieldwork, Federal Work-Study, and scholarships/grants available. Support available to part-time students. Financial award application deadline: 5/1; financial award applicants required to submit FAFSA. *Faculty research:* Intercultural pedagogy, wisdom school spiritual direction, gender and sexuality, Moravian history and theology, holistic clinical counseling. *Unit head:* Rev. Dr. Frank L. Crouch, Dean and Vice President, 610-861-1516, E-mail: crouchf@moravian.edu. *Application contact:* Rev. Dr. David H. DeRemer, Director of Enrollment, 610-861-1512, Fax: 610-861-1569, E-mail: deremerd@moravian.edu. Website: http://moravianseminary.edu

**Mount Marty College,** Graduate Studies Division, Yankton, SD 57078-3724. Offers business administration (MBA); nurse anesthesia (MS); nursing (MSN); pastoral ministries (MPM). *Accreditation:* AANA/CANAEP (one or more programs are accredited). *Degree requirements:* For master's, thesis or alternative. *Entrance requirements:* For master's, GRE General Test, minimum GPA of 3.0. Electronic applications accepted. *Faculty research:* Clinical anesthesia, professional characteristics, motivations of applicants.

**Mount St. Joseph University,** Graduate Program in Religious Studies, Cincinnati, OH 45233-1670. Offers religious studies (MA); spirituality and wellness (Certificate). *Program availability:* Part-time, evening/weekend. *Faculty:* 3 full-time (1 woman), 4 part-time/adjunct (2 women). *Students:* 1 (woman) full-time, 6 part-time (4 women); includes 2 minority (1 Black or African American, non-Hispanic/Latino; 1 Hispanic/Latino). Average age 42. In 2016, 5 master's awarded. *Degree requirements:* For master's, comprehensive exam, 36 hours of credit, pastoral PRAXIS component (3 credit hours), integrating project (3 credit hours). *Entrance requirements:* For master's, undergraduate transcript with minimum overall GPA of 3.0, 3 letters of recommendation from professional colleagues, 3-page essay, interview with the Graduate Admissions Committee, current work resume. Additional exam requirements/recommendations for international students: Required—TOEFL (minimum score 560 paper-based; 83 iBT). *Application deadline:* Applications are processed on a rolling basis. Electronic applications accepted. *Expenses:* $580 per credit hour. *Financial support:* In 2016–17, 5 students received support. Scholarships/grants available. Financial award applicants required to submit FAFSA. *Faculty research:* Contextual/cultural/systematic theology, historical/spiritual theology, business/economics ethics, social justice, Biblical/cultural/pastoral theology. *Unit head:* Dr. John Trokan, Associate Professor of Religious and Pastoral Studies/Director of Graduate Program, 513-244-4272, Fax: 513-244-4222, E-mail: john.trokan@msj.edu. *Application contact:* Mary Brigham, Assistant Director of Graduate Recruitment, 513-244-4233, Fax: 513-244-4629, E-mail: mary.brigham@msj.edu. Website: http://www.msj.edu/academics/graduate-programs/religious-studies-programs/

**Nashotah House Theological Seminary,** Graduate Programs, Nashotah, WI 53058-9793. Offers Anglican studies (Certificate); Biblical studies (STM); Christian spirituality (STM); church history (STM); liturgy (STM); ministry (M Div, MM); pastoral ministry (MPM); theological studies (MTS); theology (STM, D Min). *Accreditation:* ACIPE; ATS (one or more programs are accredited). *Program availability:* Part-time. *Faculty:* 8 full-time (0 women), 6 part-time/adjunct (0 women). *Students:* 78 full-time (14 women), 5 part-time (2 women); includes 3 minority (2 Black or African American, non-Hispanic/Latino; 1 Asian, non-Hispanic/Latino). Average age 37. *Degree requirements:* For master's, thesis optional. *Entrance requirements:* For master's and Certificate, GRE General Test or MAT, interview, 3 recommendations. Additional exam requirements/recommendations for international students: Required—TOEFL. *Application deadline:* For fall admission, 6/15 for domestic students. Applications are processed on a rolling basis. Application fee: $500 per credit hour. *Financial support:* Teaching assistantships, career-related internships or fieldwork, scholarships/grants, and tuition waivers (partial) available. Support available to part-time students. Financial award application deadline: 1/15; financial award applicants required to submit FAFSA. *Faculty research:* Formation for parochial ministry, ancient Semitic epigraphy. *Unit head:* Very Rev. Steven A. Peay, Dean/President, 262-646-6512, Fax: 262-646-6504, E-mail: speay@nashotah.edu. *Application contact:* Fr. Dr. Rick Hartley, Associate Dean of Students/Registrar, 262-646-6547, Fax: 262-646-6504, E-mail: rhartley@nashotah.edu. Website: https://www.nashotah.edu/programs

**Neumann University,** Program in Pastoral Clinical Mental Health Counseling, Aston, PA 19014-1298. Offers pastoral care specialist (Certificate); pastoral clinical mental health counseling (MS); pastoral clinical mental health counseling certificate of advanced study (Certificate); pastoral counseling (PhD); spiritual formation and direction (CSD); spiritual formation and direction supervision certificate of advanced study (Certificate). *Program availability:* Part-time, evening/weekend. *Faculty:* 7 full-time (5 women), 3 part-time/adjunct (2 women). *Students:* 15 full-time (14 women), 90 part-time (64 women); includes 15 minority (10 Black or African American, non-Hispanic/Latino; 1 Asian, non-Hispanic/Latino; 2 Hispanic/Latino; 2 Two or more races, non-Hispanic/Latino). Average age 47. 61 applicants, 52% accepted, 27 enrolled. In 2016, 22 master's, 1 doctorate awarded. *Degree requirements:* For doctorate, comprehensive exam, thesis/dissertation. *Entrance requirements:* For master's and other advanced degree, official transcripts from all institutions attended, letter of intent, three official letters of recommendation; for doctorate, MAT, master's degree, official transcripts from all institutions attended, resume or curriculum vitae, letter of intent, two official letters of recommendation. Additional exam requirements/recommendations for international students: Required—TOEFL (minimum score 70 iBT). *Application deadline:* For fall admission, 8/1 for domestic students; for spring admission, 12/1 for domestic students. Applications are processed on a rolling basis. Application fee: $0. Electronic applications accepted. *Expenses:* $670 per credit tuition (for master's and Certificate); $830 per credit (for PhD in pastoral counseling). *Financial support:* Scholarships/grants and health care benefits available. Support available to part-time students. Financial award application deadline: 3/15; financial award applicants required to submit FAFSA. *Unit head:* Sr. Suzanne Mayer, Director of Pastoral Clinical Mental Health Counseling Program, 610-361-2292, Fax: 610-358-4525, E-mail: mayers@neumann.edu. *Application contact:* Dr. Erika Davis, Director of Adult and Graduate Admissions, 800-9-NEUMANN Ext. 5208, Fax: 610-361-2548, E-mail: GradAdultAdmiss@neumann.edu.

**New Brunswick Theological Seminary,** Graduate and Professional Programs, New Brunswick, NJ 08901-1196. Offers pastoral care and counseling (D Min). *Accreditation:* ACIPE; ATS. *Program availability:* Part-time, evening/weekend. *Degree requirements:* For master's, variable foreign language requirement, thesis (for some programs); for doctorate, thesis/dissertation. *Entrance requirements:* For master's, BA/BS with minimum GPA of 3.0 (for MA), 2.5 (for M Div); for doctorate, M Div. Additional exam requirements/recommendations for international students: Required—TOEFL (minimum score 550 paper-based; 79 iBT); Recommended—IELTS (minimum score 6). Electronic applications accepted.

**New Orleans Baptist Theological Seminary,** Graduate and Professional Programs, Division of Pastoral Ministries, New Orleans, LA 70126-4858. Offers M Div, MAMFC, D Min, PhD. *Accreditation:* ACIPE. *Program availability:* Online learning. *Degree requirements:* For master's, 2 foreign languages, thesis (for some programs); for doctorate, 3 foreign languages, comprehensive exam, thesis/dissertation. *Entrance requirements:* For master's and doctorate, GRE General Test. Additional exam requirements/recommendations for international students: Required—TOEFL.

**Northern Seminary,** Graduate and Professional Programs, Lombard, IL 60148-5698. Offers Biblical studies (M Div); Christian community development (D Min); Christian ministry (MACM); contextual theology (D Min); New Testament (MANT); New Testament context (D Min); theology (M Div); theology and mission (MA); urban leadership (MA); worship (MAW). *Program availability:* Part-time, evening/weekend. *Faculty:* 6 full-time (1 woman), 33 part-time/adjunct (8 women). *Students:* 126 full-time (34 women), 80 part-time (32 women); includes 89 minority (73 Black or African American, non-Hispanic/Latino; 6 Asian, non-Hispanic/Latino; 8 Hispanic/Latino; 2 Two or more races, non-Hispanic/Latino), 3 international. Average age 44. In 2016, 18 master's, 14 doctorates awarded. *Degree requirements:* For master's, thesis (for some programs); for doctorate, thesis/dissertation. *Entrance requirements:* For master's, writing test, all official transcripts, letter of reference from church, 3 letters of reference, autobiographical statement (400 words or more); for doctorate, M Div, 3 years in the ministry post-M Div, 3 letters of reference. Additional exam requirements/recommendations for international students: Required—TOEFL (minimum score 550 paper-based). *Application deadline:* For fall admission, 8/25 for domestic students, 2/1 for international students; for winter admission, 12/10 for domestic students, 2/1 for international students; for spring admission, 3/15 for domestic students, 2/1 for international students. Applications are processed on a rolling basis. Application fee: $35. Electronic applications accepted. *Expenses:* Contact institution. *Financial support:* In 2016–17, 3 teaching assistantships with partial tuition reimbursements were awarded; Federal Work-Study and scholarships/grants also available. Support available to part-time students. Financial award application deadline: 9/1; financial award applicants required to submit FAFSA. *Faculty research:* Theology and mission, worship studies, church history, evangelism, Christian ministry, urban leadership, New Testament. *Unit head:* Dr. William Shiell, President, 630-620-2101, Fax: 630-620-2190. *Application contact:* Greg Armstrong, Director of Admissions, 630-620-2175, Fax: 630-620-2190, E-mail: admissions@seminary.edu.

**North Greenville University,** T. Walter Brashier Graduate School, Greer, SC 29651. Offers Christian ministry (MCM, D Min); education (M Ed, MAT); financial planning (MBA); human resources (MBA). *Program availability:* Part-time, evening/weekend, online learning. *Degree requirements:* For master's, comprehensive exam (for some programs), thesis or alternative, capstone course. *Entrance requirements:* For master's, minimum GPA of 2.25 overall, 2.5 in major; for doctorate, MAT. Additional exam requirements/recommendations for international students: Required—TOEFL (minimum score 550 paper-based). Electronic applications accepted. *Faculty research:* Organizational behavior, church growth, homiletics, human resources, business strategy.

**North Park Theological Seminary,** Graduate and Professional Programs, Program in Christian Ministry, Chicago, IL 60625-4895. Offers MACM, MA/MBA, MA/MM.

**North Park Theological Seminary,** Graduate and Professional Programs, Program in Christian Studies, Chicago, IL 60625-4895. Offers adult ministry (Certificate); camping and retreat ministry (Certificate); children and family ministry (Certificate); Christian formation (Certificate); faith and health (Certificate); intercultural studies (Certificate); justice ministry (Certificate); leadership and administration (Certificate); spiritual direction (Certificate); youth ministry (Certificate). *Accreditation:* ACIPE. *Program availability:* Part-time. *Entrance requirements:* For degree, minimum GPA of 2.5. Additional exam requirements/recommendations for international students: Required—TOEFL.

**Northwest Nazarene University,** Program in Religion, Nampa, ID 83686-5897. Offers missional leadership (M Div, MA); pastoral ministry (MA); spiritual formation (M Div, MA); youth, children, and family ministry (M Div, MA). *Program availability:* Part-time, online only, 100% online. *Faculty:* 11 full-time (3 women), 18 part-time/adjunct (0 women). *Students:* 65 full-time (23 women), 25 part-time (11 women); includes 11 minority (4 Black or African American, non-Hispanic/Latino; 1 American Indian or Alaska Native, non-Hispanic/Latino; 2 Asian, non-Hispanic/Latino; 3 Hispanic/Latino; 1 Native Hawaiian or other Pacific Islander, non-Hispanic/Latino), 1 international. Average age 39. 37 applicants, 76% accepted, 24 enrolled. In 2016, 40 master's awarded. *Entrance requirements:* For master's, minimum GPA of 2.5; 8 semester or 12 quarter credits of Bible, theology and/or Western philosophy. Additional exam requirements/recommendations for international students: Required—TOEFL (minimum score 85 iBT). *Application deadline:* For fall admission, 7/31 for domestic students, 7/1 for international students; for spring admission, 2/1 for domestic students, 1/5 for international students. Applications are processed on a rolling basis. Application fee: $50. Electronic applications accepted. *Expenses:* Contact institution. *Financial support:* In 2016–17, 3 students received support. Scholarships/grants available. *Unit head:* Dr. Jay Akkerman, Director, Graduate Studies, 208-467-8437, Fax: 208-467-8252. *Application contact:* Vicki Funk, Program Coordinator, 208-467-8432, Fax: 208-467-8252, E-mail: vlfunk@nnu.edu. Website: http://www.nnu.edu/ministry/

**Northwest University,** College of Ministry, Kirkland, WA 98033. Offers ministry (MIM); missional leadership (MA); theology and culture (MA). *Program availability:* Part-time, evening/weekend, online learning. *Degree requirements:* For master's, comprehensive exam (for some programs), thesis (for some programs). *Entrance requirements:* Additional exam requirements/recommendations for international students: Required—TOEFL (minimum score 550 paper-based; 75 iBT). Electronic applications accepted.

**Nyack College,** Alliance Theological Seminary, Nyack, NY 10960. Offers Biblical literature (MA), including New Testament, Old Testament; Biblical studies (MA); Christian ministry (MPS); intercultural studies (MA); ministry (D Min), including Christian leadership in the global context; theology and missions (M Div); urban ministry (MPS). *Accreditation:* ATS. *Program availability:* Part-time, evening/weekend, 100% online, blended/hybrid learning. *Students:* 275 full-time (111 women), 370 part-time (175 women); includes 505 minority (177 Black or African American, non-Hispanic/Latino; 128 Asian, non-Hispanic/Latino; 190 Hispanic/Latino; 10 Two or more races, non-Hispanic/Latino), 32 international. Average age 43. In 2016, 117 master's, 14 doctorates awarded. *Degree requirements:* For master's, comprehensive exam (for some programs), thesis optional, internship; for doctorate, thesis/dissertation. *Entrance requirements:* For master's, transcripts, Christian experience statement, recommendations; for doctorate, transcripts, documented three years of ministry experience subsequent to 1st graduate theological degree, reference letters, formal academic paper. Additional exam requirements/recommendations for international students: Required—TOEFL (minimum score 550 paper-based; 80 iBT). *Application deadline:* Applications are processed on a rolling basis. Application fee: $30. Electronic applications accepted. *Expenses:* $575 per credit (for master's-level). *Financial support:* Career-related internships or fieldwork, Federal Work-Study, and scholarships/grants available. Financial award applicants required to submit FAFSA. *Unit head:* Dr. Ronald Walborn, Dean, 845-770-5715, Fax: 845-358-1663. *Application contact:* Julian Williams, Associate Director of Admissions, 800-541-6891, Fax: 845-348-3912, E-mail: admissions.ats@nyack.edu.
Website: http://www.nyack.edu/ats

**Oakwood University,** Program in Pastoral Studies, Huntsville, AL 35896. Offers MA. *Entrance requirements:* For master's, Biblical Literacy Entrance Test (BLET), minimum cumulative GPA of 2.5, 2 letters of recommendation, current resume, 3 years of pastoral or local church leadership experience. Additional exam requirements/recommendations for international students: Required—TOEFL (minimum score 500 paper-based).

**Oblate School of Theology,** Graduate and Professional Programs, San Antonio, TX 78216-6693. Offers African-American pastoral leadership (D Min); divinity (M Div); pastoral leadership (D Min); pastoral ministry (MAP Min); pastoral studies (Certificate); spiritual formation in the local community (D Min); spirituality (MA Sp, PhD); spirituality and ministry (D Min); theology (MA Th); U.S. Hispanic/Latino ministry (D Min); M Div/ MA Th. *Accreditation:* ACIPE; ATS (one or more programs are accredited). *Program availability:* Part-time, online learning. *Faculty:* 24 full-time (8 women), 4 part-time/ adjunct (0 women). *Students:* 76 full-time (10 women), 51 part-time (32 women); includes 56 minority (8 Black or African American, non-Hispanic/Latino; 9 Asian, non-Hispanic/Latino; 39 Hispanic/Latino), 41 international. Average age 40. In 2016, 31 master's, 3 doctorates awarded. *Degree requirements:* For master's, comprehensive exam (for some programs), thesis (for some programs), practicum; for doctorate, one foreign language, comprehensive exam, thesis/dissertation, paper, practicum. *Entrance requirements:* For master's, MAT, interview, course work in theology or religious studies, minimum GPA of 2.5; for doctorate, M Div, MA Th, or MA Sp. Additional exam requirements/recommendations for international students: Required—TOEFL (minimum score 71 iBT). *Application deadline:* For fall admission, 6/15 priority date for domestic and international students; for winter admission, 11/30 for domestic and international students; for spring admission, 11/30 for domestic and international students; for summer admission, 4/1 for domestic and international students. Applications are processed on a rolling basis. Application fee: $65. *Expenses:* Contact institution. *Financial support:* In 2016–17, 25 students received support. Scholarships/grants available. Support available to part-time students. Financial award application deadline: 8/1; financial award applicants required to submit FAFSA. *Unit head:* Dr. R. Scott Woodward, Academic Dean, 210-341-1366, Fax: 210-341-4519, E-mail: rsw@ost.edu. *Application contact:* Mario A. Porter, Registrar, 210-341-1366 Ext. 226, Fax: 210-341-4519, E-mail: registrar@ost.edu.

**Ohio Christian University,** Graduate Programs, Circleville, OH 43113-9487. Offers accounting (MBA); business administration (MBA); digital marketing (MBA); finance (MBA); healthcare management (MBA); human resources (MBA); management (MM); organizational leadership (MBA); pastoral care and counseling (MAM); practical theology (MAM).

**Oral Roberts University,** School of Theology and Missions, Tulsa, OK 74171. Offers biblical literature (MA), including advanced languages, Judaic-Christian studies; Christian counseling (MA), including marriage and family therapy; divinity (M Div); missions (MA); practical theology (MA); theological/historical studies (MA); theology (D Min). *Accreditation:* ATS. *Program availability:* Part-time, online learning. *Degree requirements:* For master's, thesis (for some programs), practicum/internship; for doctorate, thesis/dissertation, applied research project. *Entrance requirements:* For master's, GRE General Test or MAT, minimum GPA of 2.5; for doctorate, M Div, minimum GPA of 3.0, 3 years of full-time ministry experience. Additional exam requirements/recommendations for international students: Required—TOEFL (minimum score 550 paper-based; 79 iBT). Electronic applications accepted.

**Ottawa University,** Graduate Studies-Arizona, Program in Professional Counseling, Ottawa, KS 66067-3399. Offers Christian counseling (MA); expressive arts therapy (MA); marriage and family therapy (MA); treatment of trauma, abuse and deprivation (MA). Programs offered in Mesa, Phoenix, Tempe and West Valley, AZ. *Program availability:* Part-time, evening/weekend, online learning. *Degree requirements:* For master's, comprehensive exam, thesis or alternative, field experience, practicum. *Entrance requirements:* For master's, minimum undergraduate GPA of 3.0; course work in theories of personality, abnormal psychology, and human growth and development. Additional exam requirements/recommendations for international students: Required—TOEFL (minimum score 550 paper-based).

**Pacific Rim Christian University,** Program in Christian Ministry, Honolulu, HI 96819. Offers MA.

**Pentecostal Theological Seminary,** Graduate and Professional Programs, Cleveland, TN 37320-3330. Offers biblical studies (MTS); church ministries (MA); counseling (MA); discipleship and Christian formation (MA); ministry (D Min); Pentecostal theology (MTS); theology (M Div). *Accreditation:* ACIPE; ATS. *Program availability:* Part-time. *Degree requirements:* For master's, variable foreign language requirement, thesis (for some programs), internship. *Faculty research:* Biblical exegesis.

**Pepperdine University,** Seaver College, Division of Religion, Malibu, CA 90263. Offers ministry (MS); religion (M Div, MA). *Program availability:* Part-time, evening/weekend. *Students:* 5 full-time (2 women), 13 part-time (4 women); includes 7 minority (3 Black or African American, non-Hispanic/Latino; 2 Asian, non-Hispanic/Latino; 2 Hispanic/ Latino). Average age 32. In 2016, 7 master's awarded. *Entrance requirements:* For master's, GRE General Test, letters of recommendation, writing sample. Additional exam requirements/recommendations for international students: Required—TOEFL. *Application deadline:* For fall admission, 2/1 priority date for domestic students. Applications are processed on a rolling basis. Application fee: $65. Electronic applications accepted. *Financial support:* Applicants required to submit FAFSA. *Unit head:* Dr. Timothy Willis, Chair/Professor, 310-506-4352, Fax: 310-506-7271, E-mail: timothy.willis@pepperdine.edu. *Application contact:* Hayley Wolf, Director of Admission, 310-506-4392, E-mail: hayley.wolf@pepperdine.edu.
Website: http://seaver.pepperdine.edu/religion/graduate/mareligion/

**Phillips Theological Seminary,** Programs in Theology, Doctor of Ministry Program, Tulsa, OK 74116. Offers parish ministry (D Min); pastoral counseling (D Min); practices of ministry (D Min). *Accreditation:* ATS. *Program availability:* Part-time. *Degree requirements:* For doctorate, thesis/dissertation. *Entrance requirements:* For doctorate, M Div, minimum GPA of 3.0, 3 years of post-M Div pastoral experience. *Expenses:* Contact institution. *Faculty research:* Politics and theology, media and theology, ecology and theology.

**Phoenix Seminary,** Graduate Programs, Phoenix, AZ 85018. Offers Biblical and theological studies (Graduate Diploma); Biblical communication (M Div); Biblical leadership (MA); Christian counseling (Graduate Diploma); counseling and family (M Div); leadership development (M Div); ministry (D Min); professional counseling (MA). *Accreditation:* ATS (one or more programs are accredited). *Program availability:* Part-time, evening/weekend. *Degree requirements:* For master's, 2 foreign languages, comprehensive exam; for doctorate, 2 foreign languages, thesis/dissertation. *Entrance requirements:* For master's, undergraduate degree with minimum GPA of 2.5; for doctorate, M Div (94 hours) with minimum GPA of 3.0. Additional exam requirements/ recommendations for international students: Required—TOEFL (minimum score 587 paper-based; 92 iBT), TWE (minimum score 4.5).

**Piedmont International University,** Graduate School, Winston-Salem, NC 27101-5197. Offers Biblical studies (PhD); curriculum and instruction (M Ed); divinity (M Div); educational leadership (M Ed); leadership (MA, PhD); ministry (MA Min, D Min); non-language track (MABS); PhD preparation track (MABS). *Program availability:* Part-time, online learning. Terminal master's awarded for partial completion of doctoral program. *Degree requirements:* For master's, 2 foreign languages, comprehensive exam, thesis or alternative; for doctorate, 2 foreign languages, comprehensive exam. *Entrance requirements:* For master's, GRE General Test; for doctorate, Hebrew and Greek proficiency, MA. Additional exam requirements/recommendations for international students: Required—TOEFL (minimum score 500 paper-based; 60 iBT). Electronic applications accepted. *Faculty research:* Theological and biblical studies.

**Pittsburgh Theological Seminary,** Graduate and Professional Programs, Pittsburgh, PA 15206-2596. Offers divinity (M Div); theological studies (MA); theology (Th M); theology and ministry (MA, D Min); JD/M Div; M Div/MS; M Div/MSW. M Div/MSW offered jointly with University of Pittsburgh; JD/M Div with Duquesne University; M Div/ MSPPM with Carnegie Mellon University. *Accreditation:* ATS (one or more programs are accredited). *Program availability:* Part-time, evening/weekend. *Faculty:* 16 full-time (5 women), 6 part-time/adjunct (2 women). *Students:* 153 full-time (56 women), 47 part-time (28 women); includes 57 minority (49 Black or African American, non-Hispanic/ Latino; 3 Asian, non-Hispanic/Latino; 3 Hispanic/Latino; 1 Native Hawaiian or other Pacific Islander, non-Hispanic/Latino; 1 Two or more races, non-Hispanic/Latino), 9 international. Average age 35. 57 applicants, 93% accepted, 44 enrolled. In 2016, 34 master's, 16 doctorates awarded. *Degree requirements:* For master's, one foreign language, comprehensive exam (for some programs), thesis (for some programs); for doctorate, thesis/dissertation. *Entrance requirements:* For master's, bachelor's degree with minimum GPA of 2.7, interview, references; for doctorate, interview, references. Additional exam requirements/recommendations for international students: Required—TOEFL (minimum score 570 paper-based; 89 iBT). *Application deadline:* For fall admission, 6/30 priority date for domestic students, 12/1 for international students; for winter admission, 10/15 priority date for domestic students; for spring admission, 1/15 priority date for domestic students. Applications are processed on a rolling basis. Application fee: $50. Electronic applications accepted. *Expenses: Tuition:* Full-time $11,520; part-time $358 per credit. *Required fees:* $300. One-time fee: $125. *Financial support:* In 2016–17, 104 students received support. Career-related internships or fieldwork, scholarships/grants, and institutional work-study available. Financial award application deadline: 5/1; financial award applicants required to submit FAFSA. *Unit head:* Dr. Heathear H. Vacek, Dean of Faculty and Vice President for Academic Affairs, 412-924-1374, Fax: 412-924-1774, E-mail: hvacek@pts.edu. *Application contact:* Dr. Heather Vacek, Dean of Faculty and Vice President for Academic Affairs, 412-924-1374, Fax: 412-924-1774, E-mail: hvacek@pts.edu.
Website: http://www.pts.edu/

**Point Loma Nazarene University,** School of Theology and Christian Ministry, San Diego, CA 92106-2899. Offers M Min. *Program availability:* Part-time, online only, nine-week quads with eight weeks of online coursework and a one-week intensive. *Faculty:* 1 part-time/adjunct (0 women). *Students:* 13 part-time (5 women); includes 5 minority (1 American Indian or Alaska Native, non-Hispanic/Latino; 4 Hispanic/Latino). Average age 41. 6 applicants, 83% accepted, 3 enrolled. In 2016, 7 master's awarded. *Degree requirements:* For master's, thesis optional. *Entrance requirements:* For master's, letters of recommendation, essay, transcripts, interview. Additional exam requirements/ recommendations for international students: Recommended—TOEFL. *Application deadline:* For fall admission, 8/30 priority date for domestic students; for spring admission, 4/4 priority date for domestic students; for summer admission, 6/20 priority date for domestic students. Applications are processed on a rolling basis. Application fee: $0. Electronic applications accepted. *Expenses:* $275 per credit. *Financial support:* Scholarships/grants available. Financial award application deadline: 6/5; financial award applicants required to submit FAFSA. *Faculty research:* Theology, Christian education, church administration. *Unit head:* Dr. Mark Maddix, Dean, 619-849-2234, E-mail: markmaddix@pointloma.edu. *Application contact:* Claire Buckley, Director of Graduate Admissions, 866-692-4723, E-mail: gradinfo@pointloma.edu.
Website: http://www.pointloma.edu/experience/academics/schools-departments/school-theology-christian-ministry/programs/master-ministry

**Providence University College & Theological Seminary,** Theological Seminary, Otterburne, MB R0A 1G0, Canada. Offers children's ministry (Certificate); Christian studies (MA, Certificate); counseling (MA); cross-cultural discipleship (Certificate); divinity (M Div); educational studies (MA), including counseling psychology, educational ministries, student development, teaching English to speakers of other languages, training teachers of English to speakers of other languages; global studies (MA); lay counseling (Diploma); ministry (D Min); teaching English to speakers of other languages (Certificate); theological studies (MA); training teacher of English to speakers of other languages (Certificate); youth ministry (Certificate). *Accreditation:* ATS. *Program availability:* Part-time. *Degree requirements:* For master's, variable foreign language requirement, thesis (for some programs); for doctorate, thesis/dissertation. *Entrance requirements:* Additional exam requirements/recommendations for international students: Recommended—TOEFL (minimum score 550 paper-based). *Faculty research:* Studies in Isaiah, theology of sin.

**Randall University,** Department of Bible Studies, Moore, OK 73160-1208. Offers ministry (MA). *Program availability:* Part-time, evening/weekend. *Degree requirements:*

For master's, thesis optional. *Entrance requirements:* Additional exam requirements/recommendations for international students: Recommended—TOEFL (minimum score 500 paper-based).

**Reformed Theological Seminary–Charlotte Campus,** Graduate and Professional Programs, Charlotte, NC 28226-6318. Offers biblical studies (MA); ministry (D Min); pastoral ministry (M Div); theological studies (MA). *Program availability:* Part-time. *Degree requirements:* For master's, comprehensive exam; for doctorate, thesis/dissertation. *Entrance requirements:* For master's, minimum GPA of 2.6; for doctorate, minimum GPA of 3.0. Additional exam requirements/recommendations for international students: Required—TOEFL (minimum score 550 paper-based). Electronic applications accepted.

**Reformed Theological Seminary–Jackson Campus,** Graduate and Professional Programs, Jackson, MS 39209-3004. Offers Bible, theology, and missions (Certificate); Biblical exegesis (M Div); biblical studies (MA); Christian education (MA); counseling (M Div); marriage and family therapy (MA); ministry (D Min); missions (M Div, MA, D Min); theological studies (MA). *Accreditation:* AAMFT/COAMFTE (one or more programs are accredited); ATS (one or more programs are accredited). *Degree requirements:* For master's, thesis (for some programs), fieldwork; for doctorate, 2 foreign languages, thesis/dissertation. *Entrance requirements:* For master's, minimum GPA of 2.6; for doctorate, minimum GPA of 3.0. Additional exam requirements/recommendations for international students: Required—TOEFL.

**Reformed Theological Seminary–Orlando Campus,** Graduate Programs, Oviedo, FL 32765. Offers Bible (Certificate); biblical studies (MA); counseling (MA); missions (Certificate); reformed expository preaching (D Min); reformed theology and ministry (D Min); theological studies (MA); theology (M Div, Certificate). *Program availability:* Part-time, online learning. *Faculty:* 12 full-time (0 women), 11 part-time/adjunct (2 women). *Students:* 340. *Application deadline:* Applications are processed on a rolling basis. Application fee: $75. Electronic applications accepted. *Expenses: Tuition:* Full-time $17,325. *Required fees:* $160. Tuition and fees vary according to course load. *Unit head:* Dr. Scott R. Swain, President, 407-278-4406, Fax: 407-366-9425. *Application contact:* Winston J. Miller, Director of Admissions, 800-752-4382, Fax: 407-366-9425, E-mail: applications.orlando@rts.edu.

**Regent University,** Graduate School, School of Divinity, Virginia Beach, VA 23464-9800. Offers divinity (M Div), including Biblical studies (M Div, MTS, PhD), chaplain ministry, Christian theology (M Div, MTS, PhD), church and ministry (M Div, MA), history of Christianity (M Div, MTS, PhD), inter-cultural studies (M Div, MA), interdisciplinary studies (M Div, MA, MTS), marketplace ministry, worship and media (M Div, MA); leadership and renewal (D Min), including Christian leadership and renewal, clinical pastoral education, community transformation, military ministry, ministry leadership coaching; practical theology (MA), including church and ministry (M Div, MA), inter-cultural studies (M Div, MA), interdisciplinary studies (M Div, MA, MTS), worship and media (M Div, MA); theological studies (MTS, PhD), including Biblical studies (M Div, MTS, PhD), Christian theology (M Div, MTS, PhD), history of Christianity (M Div, MTS, PhD), interdisciplinary studies (M Div, MA, MTS). *Accreditation:* ACIPE; ATS. *Program availability:* Part-time, evening/weekend, 100% online, blended/hybrid learning. *Faculty:* 15 full-time (3 women), 51 part-time/adjunct (6 women). *Students:* 148 full-time (60 women), 787 part-time (321 women); includes 506 minority (416 Black or African American, non-Hispanic/Latino; 1 American Indian or Alaska Native, non-Hispanic/Latino; 23 Asian, non-Hispanic/Latino; 54 Hispanic/Latino; 1 Native Hawaiian or other Pacific Islander, non-Hispanic/Latino; 11 Two or more races, non-Hispanic/Latino), 31 international. Average age 43. 1,020 applicants, 42% accepted, 276 enrolled. In 2016, 127 master's, 25 doctorates awarded. *Degree requirements:* For master's, comprehensive exam, thesis or alternative, internship; for doctorate, thesis/dissertation or alternative. *Entrance requirements:* For master's, minimum undergraduate GPA of 2.75, writing sample, personal goal statement, college transcripts; for doctorate, GRE, minimum graduate GPA of 3.5 (PhD), 3.0 (D Min); clergy recommendations; writing sample; transcripts; resume; interview. Additional exam requirements/recommendations for international students: Required—TOEFL (minimum score 577 paper-based). *Application deadline:* For fall admission, 5/1 priority date for domestic students. Applications are processed on a rolling basis. Application fee: $50. Electronic applications accepted. *Expenses:* Contact institution. *Financial support:* In 2016–17, 602 students received support. Career-related internships or fieldwork, scholarships/grants, and unspecified assistantships available. Support available to part-time students. *Faculty research:* Greek and Hebrew, theology, spiritual formation, global missions and world Christianity, women in ministry leadership. *Unit head:* Dr. Cornelius Bekker, Dean, 757-352-4401, Fax: 757-352-4597, E-mail: clbekker@regent.edu. *Application contact:* Heidi Cece, Assistant Vice President of Enrollment Management, 800-373-5504, Fax: 757-352-4381, E-mail: admissions@regent.edu.
Website: http://www.regent.edu/sod/

**Regent University,** Graduate School, School of Psychology and Counseling, Virginia Beach, VA 23464-9800. Offers clinical mental health counseling (MA); clinical psychology (Psy D); counseling and psychological studies (PhD); counseling studies (CAGS); counselor education and supervision (PhD); general psychology (MS); marriage, couple, and family counseling (MA); pastoral counseling (MA); school counseling (MA); M Div/MA; M Ed/MA; MBA/MA. *Accreditation:* ACA; APA (one or more programs are accredited). *Program availability:* Part-time, evening/weekend, 100% online, blended/hybrid learning. *Faculty:* 28 full-time (17 women), 45 part-time/adjunct (26 women). *Students:* 295 full-time (240 women), 331 part-time (252 women); includes 244 minority (186 Black or African American, non-Hispanic/Latino; 4 American Indian or Alaska Native, non-Hispanic/Latino; 11 Asian, non-Hispanic/Latino; 29 Hispanic/Latino; 14 Two or more races, non-Hispanic/Latino), 10 international. Average age 36. 1,192 applicants, 29% accepted, 235 enrolled. In 2016, 156 master's, 41 doctorates, 1 other advanced degree awarded. *Degree requirements:* For master's, thesis or alternative, internship, practicum, written competency exam; for doctorate, thesis/dissertation or alternative. *Entrance requirements:* For master's, GRE General Test (including writing exam) or MAT, minimum undergraduate GPA of 3.0, resume, transcripts, writing sample, personal goals statement; for doctorate, GRE General Test (including writing exam), minimum undergraduate GPA of 3.0, graduate 3.5; writing sample; 3 recommendations; resume; college transcripts; personal goals statement. Additional exam requirements/recommendations for international students: Required—TOEFL (minimum score 577 paper-based). *Application deadline:* For fall admission, 4/1 priority date for domestic students; for spring admission, 11/1 priority date for domestic students. Applications are processed on a rolling basis. Application fee: $50. Electronic applications accepted. *Expenses:* Contact institution. *Financial support:* In 2016–17, 446 students received support, including 5 fellowships (averaging $4,000 per year), 10 research assistantships (averaging $3,200 per year); career-related internships or fieldwork, scholarships/grants, and unspecified assistantships also available. Support available to part-time students. *Faculty research:* Marriage enrichment, clinical psychology, troubled youth, faith and learning, trauma. *Unit head:* Dr. William Hathaway, Dean, 757-352-4294, Fax: 757-352-4282, E-mail: willhat@regent.edu. *Application contact:* Heidi Cece, Assistant Vice President of Enrollment Management, 800-373-5504, Fax: 757-352-4381, E-mail: admissions@regent.edu.
Website: http://www.regent.edu/spc/

**Regis College,** Graduate and Professional Programs, Toronto, ON M5S 2Z5, Canada. Offers eastern Christian studies (Certificate); Ignatian spirituality (Diploma); ministry (D Min); ministry and spirituality (MAMS); philosophical studies (Diploma); retreat direction (Certificate); sacred theology (STM, STD, STB, STL); spiritual direction (Diploma); theological studies (MTS, Diploma); theology (M Div, MA, Th M, PhD, Th D); M Div/MA. *Accreditation:* ATS (one or more programs are accredited). Terminal master's awarded for partial completion of doctoral program. *Degree requirements:* For master's, 2 foreign languages, thesis; for doctorate, 3 foreign languages, comprehensive exam, thesis/dissertation. *Entrance requirements:* For doctorate, minimum GPA of 3.7. Additional exam requirements/recommendations for international students: Required—TOEFL (minimum score 580 paper-based; 93 iBT), TWE (minimum score 5).

**Richmont Graduate University,** School of Ministry, Atlanta, GA 30339. Offers ministry (MA); spiritual direction (Graduate Certificate); spiritual formation and direction (MA). *Program availability:* Part-time, evening/weekend, 100% online, blended/hybrid learning. *Degree requirements:* For master's, thesis optional. *Entrance requirements:* For master's, transcripts, recommendation, personal statement, resume. *Application deadline:* For fall admission, 5/1 priority date for domestic students. Applications are processed on a rolling basis. Application fee: $50. Electronic applications accepted. *Expenses:* Contact institution. *Financial support:* Scholarships/grants, tuition waivers (partial), and unspecified assistantships available. Financial award application deadline: 5/1; financial award applicants required to submit FAFSA. *Faculty research:* Integration of Biblical/theological studies; personal and spiritual formation, leadership enrichment; Biblical interpretation; leadership; spiritual formation. *Unit head:* Dr. Michael Stewart, Dean, 404-835-6129, Fax: 404-239-9460, E-mail: mstewart@richmont.edu. *Application contact:* Scottie Blackburn, Admissions Counselor, 404-835-6118, Fax: 404-239-9460, E-mail: sblackburn@richmont.edu.
Website: http://richmont.edu/academics/school-of-ministry/

**Sacred Heart Major Seminary,** School of Theology, Detroit, MI 48206-1799. Offers pastoral studies (MAPS); theology (M Div, MA). *Accreditation:* ACIPE; ATS. *Program availability:* Part-time, evening/weekend. *Degree requirements:* For master's, one foreign language, thesis optional, integrating project. *Entrance requirements:* For master's, GRE, previous course work in philosophy and theology. *Faculty research:* Local church history, patristics, spirituality, religious education.

**St. Ambrose University,** College of Arts and Sciences, Program in Pastoral Theology, Davenport, IA 52803-2898. Offers MP Th. *Program availability:* Part-time. *Degree requirements:* For master's, integration project. *Entrance requirements:* For master's, minimum GPA of 2.6, prior pastoral experience, 9 credits of course work in theology. Additional exam requirements/recommendations for international students: Required—TOEFL. Electronic applications accepted. *Expenses:* Contact institution. *Faculty research:* Theological education, ecclesiology, spirituality and liturgy, medical ethics.

**St. Augustine's Seminary of Toronto,** Graduate and Professional Programs, Scarborough, ON M1M 1M3, Canada. Offers divinity (M Div); lay ministry (Diploma); religious education (MRE); theological studies (MTS, Diploma). *Accreditation:* ATS. *Program availability:* Part-time, evening/weekend. *Entrance requirements:* Additional exam requirements/recommendations for international students: Required—TOEFL (minimum score 580 paper-based), TWE (minimum score 5).

**St. Bernard's School of Theology and Ministry,** Graduate and Professional Programs, Rochester, NY 14618. Offers pastoral studies (MA, Certificate); theological studies (MA); theology (M Div). *Accreditation:* ATS (one or more programs are accredited). *Program availability:* Part-time, evening/weekend. *Faculty:* 4 full-time (3 women), 4 part-time/adjunct (1 woman). *Students:* 1 (woman) full-time, 102 part-time (59 women); includes 6 minority (1 Black or African American, non-Hispanic/Latino; 3 Asian, non-Hispanic/Latino; 2 Hispanic/Latino). *Degree requirements:* For master's, variable foreign language requirement, thesis (for some programs). *Entrance requirements:* For master's, minimum GPA of 2.5. *Application deadline:* Applications are processed on a rolling basis. Application fee: $75. *Expenses: Tuition:* Full-time $10,644; part-time $3548 per year. *Required fees:* $40 per semester. *Financial support:* In 2016–17, 30 students received support. Fellowships, research assistantships, teaching assistantships, career-related internships or fieldwork, scholarships/grants, and tuition waivers (partial) available. Support available to part-time students. Financial award application deadline: 4/1; financial award applicants required to submit FAFSA. *Unit head:* Rev. George Heyman, President, 585-271-3657 Ext. 292, Fax: 585-271-2045, E-mail: george.heyman@stbernards.edu. *Application contact:* Mark R. Capellazzi, Director of Recruitment and Financial Aid, 585-271-3657 Ext. 289, Fax: 585-271-2045, E-mail: admissions@stbernards.edu.
Website: http://www.stbernards.edu/

**St. Catherine University,** Graduate Programs, Program in Theology, St. Paul, MN 55105. Offers catechetical ministry (Certificate); pastoral ministry (Certificate); spiritual direction (Certificate); theology (MA). *Program availability:* Part-time. *Degree requirements:* For master's, comprehensive exam, thesis (for some programs). *Entrance requirements:* For master's, MAT, minimum GPA of 3.0. Additional exam requirements/recommendations for international students: Required—Michigan English Language Assessment Battery or TOEFL (minimum score 600 paper-based; 100 iBT). *Expenses:* Contact institution. *Faculty research:* Feminist scholarship, historical theology, symbols, rites of purification, spirituality.

**St. John's Seminary,** Graduate and Professional Programs, Camarillo, CA 93012-2598. Offers divinity (M Div); pastoral ministry (MAPM); theology (MA). *Accreditation:* ATS. *Program availability:* Part-time. *Degree requirements:* For master's, comprehensive exam (for some programs), thesis optional, comprehensive integration paper (MAPM). *Entrance requirements:* For master's, GRE General Test, minimum GPA of 3.5 (MA), 2.5 (MAPM). Additional exam requirements/recommendations for international students: Required—TOEFL (minimum score 550 paper-based; 79 iBT). Electronic applications accepted. *Faculty research:* Biblical studies, moral theology, church history, systematic theology, spiritual theology.

**Saint John's University,** Saint John's School of Theology and Seminary, Collegeville, MN 56321. Offers divinity (M Div); liturgical music (MA); liturgical studies (MA); pastoral ministry (MA); theology (MA), including church history, liturgy, monastic studies, scripture, spirituality, systematics; M Div/MA. *Program availability:* Part-time, online learning. *Degree requirements:* For master's, one foreign language, comprehensive exam (for some programs), thesis (for some programs). *Entrance requirements:* For master's, GRE General Test or MAT. Electronic applications accepted. *Faculty research:* Religious education, biblical literature.

**Saint Joseph's College of Maine,** Master of Arts in Pastoral Theology Program, Standish, ME 04084. Offers MA. *Program availability:* Part-time, online learning. *Entrance requirements:* For master's, baccalaureate degree with minimum cumulative GPA of 2.5.

**St. Joseph's Seminary,** Graduate and Professional Programs, Yonkers, NY 10704. Offers Catholic philosophical studies (MA); divinity (M Div); pastoral studies (MAPS); theology (MA). *Accreditation:* ATS. *Degree requirements:* For master's, one foreign language, thesis. *Entrance requirements:* For master's, 27 credits in philosophy and 9 in theology.

**Saint Paul University,** Faculty of Canon Law, Ottawa, ON K1S 1C4, Canada. Offers canon law (MCL, JCD, PhD, Graduate Certificate, JCL); canonical practice (Graduate Certificate); ecclesiastical administration (Graduate Certificate). *Program availability:* Part-time. *Degree requirements:* For master's, one foreign language; for doctorate, one foreign language, comprehensive exam, thesis/dissertation; for other advanced degree, one foreign language, comprehensive exam and seminar paper (JCL). *Entrance requirements:* For master's, appropriate bachelor's degree, 18 credits in theology; for doctorate, JCL or MCL; for other advanced degree, B Th or equivalent (JCL), appropriate bachelor's degree, 18 credits in theology. *Faculty research:* Questions related to Church law.

**Saint Paul University,** Faculty of Human Sciences, Program in Counseling and Spirituality, Ottawa, ON K1S 1C4, Canada. Offers individual or marital/couple counseling (MA); spiritual care (MA). *Program availability:* Part-time. *Degree requirements:* For master's, research project or thesis. *Entrance requirements:* For master's, honors BA in human sciences, minimum B average, 12 theology credits.

**Saints Cyril and Methodius Seminary,** Graduate and Professional Programs, Orchard Lake, MI 48324. Offers pastoral ministry (MAPM); religious education (MARE); theology (M Div, MA). *Program availability:* Part-time.

**St. Stephen's College,** Programs in Theology, Edmonton, AB T6G 2J6, Canada. Offers ministry (D Min); pastoral counseling (MA); social transformation ministry (MA); spirituality and liturgy (MA); theological studies (MTS); theology (M Th). *Program availability:* Part-time, evening/weekend, online learning. Terminal master's awarded for partial completion of doctoral program. *Degree requirements:* For master's, thesis; for doctorate, thesis/dissertation. *Entrance requirements:* Additional exam requirements/recommendations for international students: Required—TOEFL. Electronic applications accepted. *Faculty research:* Methodology for theological education, practice and supervision for ministry.

**St. Thomas University,** School of Theology and Ministry, Institute for Pastoral Ministries, Miami Gardens, FL 33054-6459. Offers pastoral ministries (MA, Certificate); practical theology (PhD). *Program availability:* Part-time, evening/weekend. *Degree requirements:* For master's, comprehensive exam; for doctorate, comprehensive exam, thesis/dissertation. *Entrance requirements:* For master's, interview, minimum GPA of 3.0 or GRE; for doctorate, GRE, MA in theology. Additional exam requirements/recommendations for international students: Required—TOEFL (minimum score 550 paper-based; 79 iBT). Electronic applications accepted.

**Saint Vincent Seminary,** School of Theology, Latrobe, PA 15650-2690. Offers Catholic philosophical studies (MA); ecclesial ministry (MA); ministry (M Div); monastic studies (MA); sacred scripture (MA); systematic theology (MA). *Accreditation:* ATS. *Program availability:* Part-time, evening/weekend. *Faculty:* 6 full-time (2 women), 16 part-time/adjunct (2 women). *Students:* 44 full-time (0 women), 1 part-time (0 women); includes 5 minority (1 American Indian or Alaska Native, non-Hispanic/Latino; 2 Asian, non-Hispanic/Latino; 1 Hispanic/Latino; 1 Two or more races, non-Hispanic/Latino), 7 international. Average age 33. 12 applicants, 100% accepted, 12 enrolled. In 2016, 12 master's awarded. *Degree requirements:* For master's, one foreign language, comprehensive exam, thesis optional, public presentation. *Entrance requirements:* For master's, minimum GPA of 2.5. Additional exam requirements/recommendations for international students: Required—TOEFL (minimum score 550 paper-based; 79 iBT). *Application deadline:* For fall admission, 8/15 for domestic and international students. Applications are processed on a rolling basis. Application fee: $34. *Expenses: Tuition:* Full-time $26,320; part-time $874 per credit. *Financial support:* In 2016–17, 45 students received support. Scholarships/grants available. Support available to part-time students. Financial award application deadline: 8/15. *Faculty research:* Church history, preaching, psychology of religion, Biblical studies, moral theology. *Unit head:* Very Rev. Edward M. Mazich, OSB, President/Rector, 724-805-2845, Fax: 724-532-5052, E-mail: edward.mazich@stvincent.edu. *Application contact:* Rev. Patrick T. Cronauer, OSB, Academic Dean, 724-805-2324, Fax: 724-805-2880, E-mail: patrick.cronauer@stvincent.edu.
Website: http://www.saintvincentseminary.edu

**Santa Clara University,** College of Arts and Sciences, Santa Clara, CA 95053. Offers pastoral ministries (MA). *Program availability:* Part-time, evening/weekend. *Faculty:* 3 full-time (1 woman), 5 part-time/adjunct (1 woman). *Students:* 12 full-time (9 women), 50 part-time (35 women); includes 34 minority (1 Black or African American, non-Hispanic/Latino; 6 Asian, non-Hispanic/Latino; 24 Hispanic/Latino; 1 Native Hawaiian or other Pacific Islander, non-Hispanic/Latino; 2 Two or more races, non-Hispanic/Latino), 2 international. Average age 46. 8 applicants, 88% accepted, 5 enrolled. In 2016, 7 master's awarded. *Degree requirements:* For master's, comprehensive exam, thesis optional. *Entrance requirements:* For master's, 2 letters of recommendation, statement of purpose, transcripts. Additional exam requirements/recommendations for international students: Required—TOEFL (minimum score 90 iBT) or IELTS (6.5). *Application deadline:* For fall admission, 7/1 for domestic students; for winter admission, 10/1 for domestic students; for spring admission, 2/14 for domestic students. Applications are processed on a rolling basis. Application fee: $50. Electronic applications accepted. *Expenses:* $545 per unit. *Financial support:* Fellowships, research assistantships, teaching assistantships, career-related internships or fieldwork, Federal Work-Study, scholarships/grants, traineeships, health care benefits, tuition waivers, and unspecified assistantships available. Support available to part-time students. Financial award applicants required to submit FAFSA. *Unit head:* Gary Macy, Director, Graduate Program in Pastoral Ministries, 408-554-2357, E-mail: gmacy@scu.edu. *Application contact:* Saralynn Ferrara, Associate Director, 408-554-4322, E-mail: sferrara@scu.edu.
Website: https://www.scu.edu/cas/academics/graduate-program-in-pastoral-ministries/

**Santa Clara University,** Jesuit School of Theology, Berkeley, CA 94709. Offers Biblical languages (MABL); Biblical studies (MTS); Christian spirituality (MTS); church history (MTS); cultural and historical studies of Catholicism (MTS); ethics and social theory/religion and society (MTS); history of art and religion (MTS); liturgical studies (MTS); pastoral ministry (M Div); systematic and philosophical theology (MTS); theology (MA, MTS, Th M, STD, STB, STL); M Div/MA. *Program availability:* Part-time, evening/weekend, 100% online. *Faculty:* 20 full-time (5 women), 6 part-time/adjunct (3 women). *Students:* 125 full-time (29 women), 9 part-time (5 women); includes 71 minority (22 Black or African American, non-Hispanic/Latino; 27 Asian, non-Hispanic/Latino; 19 Hispanic/Latino; 2 Native Hawaiian or other Pacific Islander, non-Hispanic/Latino; 1 Two or more races, non-Hispanic/Latino). Average age 36. 93 applicants, 92% accepted, 56 enrolled. In 2016, 55 master's, 5 doctorates awarded. *Entrance requirements:* For master's, GRE, 2 letters of recommendation, resume, transcripts; for doctorate, GRE, master's degree or equivalent, resume, statement of purpose, transcripts, 2 letters of recommendation, research paper. Additional exam requirements/recommendations for international students: Required—TOEFL. *Application deadline:* For fall admission, 3/1 priority date for domestic students; for spring admission, 10/1 priority date for domestic students. Applications are processed on a rolling basis. Application fee: $50 ($0 for international students). Electronic applications accepted. *Expenses:* Contact institution. *Financial support:* Scholarships/grants and unspecified assistantships available. Financial award application deadline: 3/1; financial award applicants required to submit FAFSA. *Faculty research:* Religion and culture, interreligious dialogue, social ethics and restorative justice, Ignatian spirituality. *Unit head:* Alison Benders, Associate Dean, 510-549-5055, E-mail: ambenders@scu.edu. *Application contact:* Barbara Godoy, Assistant Dean of Enrollment Management, 510-549-5016, E-mail: bgodoy@scu.edu.
Website: http://www.scu.edu/jst/

**Seattle University,** School of Theology and Ministry, Program in Pastoral Studies, Seattle, WA 98122-1090. Offers MAPS. *Program availability:* Part-time, evening/weekend. *Faculty:* 11 full-time (6 women), 14 part-time/adjunct (6 women). *Students:* 3 full-time (all women), 20 part-time (14 women); includes 5 minority (1 Black or African American, non-Hispanic/Latino; 1 Asian, non-Hispanic/Latino; 2 Hispanic/Latino; 1 Two or more races, non-Hispanic/Latino), 2 international. Average age 48. 6 applicants, 67% accepted, 3 enrolled. In 2016, 6 master's awarded. *Degree requirements:* For master's, project. *Entrance requirements:* For master's, minimum GPA of 2.75 (3.0 for international students); two years of experience in some form of education, ministry, or service as a profession or volunteer; recommendations; interview with admissions committee. *Application deadline:* For fall admission, 7/1 priority date for domestic students. Application fee: $55. *Financial support:* In 2016–17, 11 students received support. Application deadline: 4/1; applicants required to submit FAFSA. *Unit head:* Dr. Mark Markuly, Director, 206-296-5330, Fax: 206-296-5329, E-mail: markulym@seattleu.edu. *Application contact:* Catherine Kehoe Fallon, Admissions Coordinator, 206-296-5333, Fax: 206-296-5329, E-mail: fallon@seattleu.edu.
Website: https://www.seattleu.edu/stm/degrees/maps/

**Seattle University,** School of Theology and Ministry, Program in Transformational Leadership, Seattle, WA 98122-1090. Offers MATL. *Faculty:* 11 full-time (6 women), 14 part-time/adjunct (6 women). *Students:* 4 full-time (2 women), 21 part-time (16 women); includes 4 minority (1 Black or African American, non-Hispanic/Latino; 1 Hispanic/Latino; 2 Two or more races, non-Hispanic/Latino), 2 international. Average age 42. 3 applicants, 100% accepted, 3 enrolled. In 2016, 9 master's awarded. *Degree requirements:* For master's, project. *Entrance requirements:* For master's, minimum GPA of 2.75 (3.0 for international students); two years of experience in some form of education, ministry, or service as a profession or volunteer; recommendations; interview with admissions committee. *Application deadline:* For fall admission, 7/1 priority date for domestic students. Application fee: $55. *Financial support:* In 2016–17, 18 students received support. Application deadline: 4/1; applicants required to submit FAFSA. *Unit head:* Dr. Mark Markuly, Dean, 206-296-5330, Fax: 206-296-5329, E-mail: stm@seattleu.edu. *Application contact:* Jean Adler Stean, Assistant Director of Admissions and Student Services, 206-296-5333, Fax: 206-296-5329, E-mail: fallon@seattleu.edu.
Website: http://www.seattleu.edu/stm/degrees/matl/

**Selma University,** Graduate Programs, Selma, AL 36701-5299. Offers Bible and Christian education (MA); Bible and pastoral ministry (MA).

**Seton Hall University,** Immaculate Conception Seminary School of Theology, South Orange, NJ 07079-2697. Offers Christian spirituality (Certificate); great spiritual books (Certificate); pastoral ministry (M Div, MA, Certificate); scripture studies (Certificate); Seminary's Theological Education for Parish Services (STEPS) (Certificate); theology (MA). *Program availability:* Part-time, evening/weekend. *Degree requirements:* For master's, comprehensive exam (for some programs), thesis (for some programs), final project (for some programs); 1 foreign language (for MA in theology research option). *Entrance requirements:* For master's, GRE General Test or MAT. Additional exam requirements/recommendations for international students: Required—TOEFL (minimum score 600 paper-based; 100 iBT). Electronic applications accepted. *Expenses:* Contact institution. *Faculty research:* Pauline literature, history of Biblical interpretation and theological exegesis, spirituality of St. Edith Stein, Thomism, history of Catholicism in America.

**Shasta Bible College,** Program in Biblical Counseling, Redding, CA 96002. Offers biblical counseling and Christian family life education (MA). *Program availability:* Part-time. *Degree requirements:* For master's, comprehensive exam (for some programs), thesis or alternative. *Entrance requirements:* For master's, minimum GPA of 2.5. Additional exam requirements/recommendations for international students: Required—TOEFL (minimum score 550 paper-based).

**Shasta Bible College,** Program in Christian Ministry, Redding, CA 96002. Offers MA. *Program availability:* Part-time, online learning. *Entrance requirements:* Additional exam requirements/recommendations for international students: Required—TOEFL (minimum score 550 paper-based).

**Shepherds Theological Seminary,** Graduate Programs, Cary, NC 27518. Offers Biblical literature and languages (MA); church ministry (MA); ministry (MTS); New Testament (M Div); Old Testament (M Div); theology (M Div). *Degree requirements:* For master's, thesis. Application fee: $40. *Expenses: Tuition:* Full-time $5400; part-time $300 per credit hour. Tuition and fees vary according to program. *Application contact:* Lucy Burggraff, Registrar, 919-573-1572, Fax: 919-573-1438, E-mail: lburggraff@shepherds.edu.
Website: https://shepherds.edu/academic-programs/

**Shiloh University,** Graduate Programs, Kalona, IA 52247. Offers Christian ministries (M Div); leadership of church and spiritual formation (D Min); theological studies (MA). *Program availability:* Part-time, evening/weekend, online only, 100% online. *Faculty:* 2 full-time (0 women), 12 part-time/adjunct (2 women). *Students:* 7 full-time (3 women), 29 part-time (10 women); includes 8 minority (4 Black or African American, non-Hispanic/Latino; 3 Hispanic/Latino; 1 Native Hawaiian or other Pacific Islander, non-Hispanic/Latino), 1 international. Average age 50. 29 applicants, 86% accepted, 17 enrolled. In 2016, 2 master's awarded. *Degree requirements:* For master's, variable foreign language requirement, thesis optional; for doctorate, comprehensive exam, thesis/dissertation. *Entrance requirements:* For master's, bachelor's degree or educational equivalent from accredited school with minimum GPA of 2.5 on undergraduate work; for doctorate, M Div or equivalent with minimum GPA of 2.5 on graduate work; three years of ministry experience. Additional exam requirements/recommendations for international students: Recommended—TOEFL (minimum score 540 paper-based; 76 iBT), IELTS (minimum score 6.5). *Application deadline:* For fall admission, 7/3 priority date for domestic and international students; for spring admission, 11/6 priority date for domestic and international students; for summer admission, 3/4 priority date for domestic and international students. Applications are processed on a rolling basis. Application fee: $0. Electronic applications accepted. *Expenses:* $167 per credit hour; certain international applicants receive discounted rate depending on country of residence. *Financial support:* In 2016–17, 2 students received support. Scholarships/grants available. Financial award applicants required to submit FAFSA. *Faculty research:* New testament theology, Pauline literature, relational theology. *Unit head:* Christopher Reeves, President, 319-656-2447, Fax: 319-656-2448, E-mail: chris.reeves@shilohuniversity.edu. *Application contact:* Andrew Thompson, Admissions Coordinator, 319-656-2447, Fax: 319-656-2448, E-mail: admissions@shilohuniversity.edu.
Website: http://www.shilohuniversity.edu/academics/

**Simpson University,** A.W. Tozer Theological Seminary, Redding, CA 96003-8606. Offers ministry leadership (MA). *Program availability:* Part-time, evening/weekend, 100% online, blended/hybrid learning. *Faculty:* 9 part-time/adjunct (0 women). *Students:*

## Pastoral Ministry and Counseling

9 full-time (2 women), 30 part-time (7 women); includes 9 minority (1 Black or African American, non-Hispanic/Latino; 3 Asian, non-Hispanic/Latino; 4 Hispanic/Latino; 1 Two or more races, non-Hispanic/Latino), 1 international. Average age 36. In 2016, 12 master's awarded. *Entrance requirements:* For master's, GRE General Test (if undergraduate GPA less than 2.5), Christian statement, one spiritual recommendation, one academic recommendation. Additional exam requirements/recommendations for international students: Required—TOEFL (minimum score 583 paper-based; 94 iBT). *Application deadline:* For fall admission, 8/1 for domestic and international students; for spring admission, 12/1 for domestic and international students; for summer admission, 4/1 for domestic and international students. Applications are processed on a rolling basis. Application fee: $35. Electronic applications accepted. *Expenses:* $426 per credit. *Financial support:* Scholarships/grants available. Support available to part-time students. Financial award application deadline: 7/1; financial award applicants required to submit FAFSA. *Unit head:* Dr. Patrick Blewett, Dean, 530-226-4144, Fax: 530-226-4871, E-mail: pblewett@simpsonu.edu. *Application contact:* Stacy Burgess, Director of Admissions for Adult and Graduate Studies, 530-226-4961, Fax: 530-226-4861, E-mail: admissions@simpsonu.edu.
Website: http://www.simpsonu.edu/tozer

**Sioux Falls Seminary,** Graduate and Professional Programs, Master of Divinity Program, Sioux Falls, SD 57105-1599. Offers marriage and family therapy (M Div); pastoral care and counseling (M Div). Program also offered in Omaha, NE. *Accreditation:* ACIPE. *Program availability:* Part-time, online learning. *Application deadline:* For fall admission, 8/1 priority date for domestic students; for spring admission, 1/1 priority date for domestic students. Applications are processed on a rolling basis. Application fee: $25. *Financial support:* Career-related internships or fieldwork and scholarships/grants available. Support available to part-time students. *Unit head:* Larry Caldwell, Chief Academic Officer/Dean, 605-336-6588, Fax: 605-335-9090, E-mail: lcaldwell@sfseminary.edu. *Application contact:* Dustin Brouwer, Director of Enrollment Management, 605-336-6588, Fax: 605-335-9090, E-mail: dbrouwer@sfseminary.edu.
Website: http://sfseminary.edu/prospective-students/programs/master-of-divinity/

**Sioux Falls Seminary,** Graduate and Professional Programs, Program in Counseling, Sioux Falls, SD 57105-1599. Offers MA. *Program availability:* Part-time. *Entrance requirements:* For master's, minimum GPA of 2.5. *Application deadline:* For fall admission, 8/1 priority date for domestic students; for spring admission, 1/1 priority date for domestic students. Applications are processed on a rolling basis. Application fee: $25. *Unit head:* Gretchen Hartmann, Director, 605-336-6588, Fax: 605-335-9090. *Application contact:* Dustin Brouwer, Director of Enrollment Management, 605-336-6588, Fax: 605-335-9090, E-mail: dbrouwer@sfseminary.edu.
Website: http://sfseminary.edu/prospective-students/programs/ma-counseling/

**Southeastern University,** Barnett College of Ministry and Theology, Lakeland, FL 33801-6099. Offers ministerial leadership (MA, D Min); theological studies (MA); theology (M Div). *Program availability:* Evening/weekend, online learning. *Degree requirements:* For master's, thesis/project. *Expenses: Tuition:* Full-time $9450; part-time $6300 per credit. *Required fees:* $500; $250 per semester. One-time fee: $150. Tuition and fees vary according to degree level, campus/location and program. *Unit head:* Dean, 863-667-5000.
Website: http://www.seu.edu/ministry/

**The Southern Baptist Theological Seminary,** Billy Graham School of Missions, Evangelism and Ministry, Louisville, KY 40280-0004. Offers ministry (D Min); missiology (MA, D Miss); missions and evangelism (M Div, Th M, PhD); theological studies (MA). *Accreditation:* ATS. *Program availability:* Part-time, evening/weekend, online learning. *Degree requirements:* For master's, 2 foreign languages; for doctorate, 4 foreign languages, thesis/dissertation. *Entrance requirements:* For doctorate, GRE General Test, MAT, M Div. Additional exam requirements/recommendations for international students: Required—TOEFL, TWE. *Faculty research:* Assimilation of church congregants, effective methodologies of evangelism, expectations of church members, spiritual warfare literature, formative church discipline.

**The Southern Baptist Theological Seminary,** School of Theology, Louisville, KY 40280-0004. Offers applied theology (D Min); biblical and theological studies (M Div); biblical counseling (M Div, MA, D Min); biblical spirituality (D Min); Christian ministry (M Div); expository preaching (D Min); pastoral studies (M Div); theological studies (MA); theology (Th M, PhD); worldview and apologetics (M Div). *Program availability:* Part-time, evening/weekend, online learning. *Degree requirements:* For master's, 2 foreign languages, thesis; for doctorate, 4 foreign languages, thesis/dissertation. *Entrance requirements:* For master's, GRE General Test, MAT, M Div; for doctorate, GRE General Test, MAT, interview, M Div, field essay. Additional exam requirements/recommendations for international students: Required—TOEFL, TWE. *Faculty research:* Biblical studies, contemporary theology, church history, pastoral care, ministry/missions studies.

**Southern Evangelical Seminary,** Graduate Programs, Matthews, NC 28105. Offers apologetics (MA, D Min, Certificate); Christian education (MA); church ministry (MA, Certificate); divinity (Certificate), including apologetics (M Div, Certificate); Islamic studies (MA, Certificate); Jewish studies (MA); philosophy (MA); philosophy of religion (PhD); religion (MA); theology (M Div), including apologetics (M Div, Certificate), Biblical studies; youth ministry (MA). *Program availability:* Part-time, evening/weekend, online learning. *Degree requirements:* For master's, thesis (for some programs); for doctorate, 2 foreign languages, comprehensive exam (for some programs), thesis/dissertation. *Entrance requirements:* Additional exam requirements/recommendations for international students: Required—TOEFL (minimum score 600 paper-based).

**Southern Wesleyan University,** Program in Christian Ministries, Central, SC 29630-1020. Offers M Min. *Program availability:* Part-time, evening/weekend. *Entrance requirements:* For master's, GRE General Test or MAT, biographical paper; 12 semester credit hours of undergraduate work in religion, Bible, or ethics; 2 years of full-time Christian ministry experience. Additional exam requirements/recommendations for international students: Required—TOEFL (minimum score 500 paper-based).

**South University,** Graduate Programs, Doctor of Ministry Program, Savannah, GA 31406. Offers D Min.

**South University,** Program in Ministry, Novi, MI 48377. Offers D Min.

**Southwestern Assemblies of God University,** Thomas F. Harrison School of Graduate Studies, Program in Theological Studies, Waxahachie, TX 75165-5735. Offers Bible and theology (MS); Biblical studies (M Div); counseling (M Div); cross cultural missions (M Div); practical theology (M Div); theological studies (M Div). *Program availability:* Online learning. *Degree requirements:* For master's, comprehensive written and oral exams. *Entrance requirements:* For master's, GRE General Test, minimum GPA of 2.5. Electronic applications accepted.

**Southwestern Baptist Theological Seminary,** School of Preaching, Fort Worth, TX 76122-0000. Offers Th M, D Min, PhD, Certificate.

**Southwestern Baptist Theological Seminary,** School of Theology, Fort Worth, TX 76122-0000. Offers ministry (D Min); theology (PhD). *Accreditation:* ACIPE; ATS (one or more programs are accredited). *Program availability:* Part-time, evening/weekend.

Terminal master's awarded for partial completion of doctoral program. *Degree requirements:* For master's, 2 foreign languages, thesis (for some programs); for doctorate, 2 foreign languages, comprehensive exam, thesis/dissertation, oral exams. *Entrance requirements:* For doctorate, GRE, M Div or equivalent. Additional exam requirements/recommendations for international students: Required—TOEFL. Electronic applications accepted.

**Southwestern Christian University,** Program in Ministry, Bethany, OK 73008-0340. Offers church planting (M Min); church revitalization and renewal (M Min); intercultural studies (M Min); leadership (M Min); life coaching (M Min); pastoral ministries (M Min); work place ministries (M Min). *Program availability:* Part-time. *Degree requirements:* For master's, thesis. *Entrance requirements:* For master's, minimum GPA of 2.5. Additional exam requirements/recommendations for international students: Required—TOEFL (minimum score 500 paper-based). Electronic applications accepted.

**Spring Arbor University,** School of Arts and Sciences, Spring Arbor, MI 49283-9799. Offers communication (MA); spiritual formation and leadership (MA). *Program availability:* Part-time, online learning. *Degree requirements:* For master's, thesis (for some programs). *Entrance requirements:* For master's, GRE (minimum score of 40th percentile and taken within last 5 years); bachelor's degree from regionally-accredited college or university, minimum GPA of 3.0 for at least the last two years of the bachelor's degree, at least two recommendations from professional/academic individuals. Additional exam requirements/recommendations for international students: Required—TOEFL (minimum score 600 paper-based). *Expenses:* Contact institution.

**Spring Hill College,** Graduate Programs, Program in Theology, Mobile, AL 36608-1791. Offers faith companioning (Postbaccalaureate Certificate); pastoral ministry (Postbaccalaureate Certificate); pastoral studies (MPS); spiritual direction (Postbaccalaureate Certificate); theological studies (MTS); theology (MA). *Program availability:* Part-time, evening/weekend. *Faculty:* 6 full-time (0 women), 2 part-time/adjunct (both women). *Students:* 1 full-time (0 women), 37 part-time (18 women); includes 7 minority (2 Black or African American, non-Hispanic/Latino; 1 American Indian or Alaska Native, non-Hispanic/Latino; 2 Asian, non-Hispanic/Latino; 2 Hispanic/Latino), 2 international. Average age 46. In 2016, 6 master's, 11 other advanced degrees awarded. *Degree requirements:* For master's, variable foreign language requirement, comprehensive exam, thesis (for some programs), completion of program within 6 calendar years of initial enrollment (MTS, MPS); completion of program within 4 1/2 calendar years of formal acceptance (MA). *Entrance requirements:* For master's, bachelor's degree with minimum undergraduate GPA of 3.0; six hours of undergraduate theology, religious studies, or unquestioned equivalency. Additional exam requirements/recommendations for international students: Required—TOEFL (minimum score 550 paper-based; 80 iBT), IELTS (minimum score 6.5), CPE or CAE (minimum score C), Michigan English Language Assessment Battery (minimum score 90). *Application deadline:* For fall admission, 8/1 priority date for domestic and international students; for spring admission, 12/1 priority date for domestic and international students. Applications are processed on a rolling basis. Application fee: $25 ($35 for international students). Electronic applications accepted. *Expenses: Tuition:* Full-time $8200; part-time $490 per credit hour. Tuition and fees vary according to program. *Financial support:* Applicants required to submit FAFSA. *Unit head:* Dr. Timothy R. Carmody, Director, 251-380-4665, Fax: 251-460-2194, E-mail: carmody@shc.edu. *Application contact:* Robert Stewart, Vice President of Enrollment, 251-380-3030, Fax: 251-460-2186, E-mail: rstewart@shc.edu.
Website: http://ug.shc.edu/graduate-degrees/master-arts-theological-studies/

**SUM Bible College & Theological Seminary,** Graduate Programs, Oakland, CA 94603. Offers biblical studies (MA); Christian leadership (MA); theology (M Div). *Entrance requirements:* For master's, minimum GPA of 2.5, currently active in ministry.

**Theological University of the Caribbean,** Graduate Programs, Saint Just, PR 00978-0901. Offers childhood and adolescent education (MA); counseling and pastoral care (MA); ministry (D Min); missions (MA).

**Trevecca Nazarene University,** Graduate Religion Programs, Nashville, TN 37210-2877. Offers biblical and theological studies (MA); Christian ministry (MA); pastoral counseling (MA). *Program availability:* Part-time, online learning. *Faculty:* 6 full-time (1 woman), 6 part-time/adjunct (0 women). *Students:* 63 full-time (32 women), 22 part-time (10 women); includes 32 minority (24 Black or African American, non-Hispanic/Latino; 1 Asian, non-Hispanic/Latino; 6 Hispanic/Latino; 1 Two or more races, non-Hispanic/Latino), 1 international. Average age 41. In 2016, 9 master's awarded. *Degree requirements:* For master's, thesis. *Entrance requirements:* For master's, minimum GPA of 2.7, official transcript from regionally accredited institution, letter of recommendation. Additional exam requirements/recommendations for international students: Required—TOEFL (minimum score 550 paper-based; 80 iBT). *Application deadline:* Applications are processed on a rolling basis. Application fee: $0. Electronic applications accepted. *Expenses:* $350 per credit hour. *Financial support:* Applicants required to submit FAFSA. *Unit head:* Dr. Tim Green, Dean, School of Theology and Christian Ministry/Director, Graduate Religion Program, 615-248-1378, Fax: 615-248-7417. *Application contact:* 844-TNU-GRAD, E-mail: sgcsadmissions@trevecca.edu.
Website: http://www.trevecca.edu/gradreligion

**Trinity College,** Faculty of Divinity, Toronto, ON M5S 1H8, Canada. Offers ministry (Diploma); ministry for church musicians (Diploma); theology (M Div, MA, MTS, Th M, D Min, PhD, D Th, Diploma, L Th); M Div/MA. *Accreditation:* ATS. *Program availability:* Part-time. *Degree requirements:* For master's, 2 foreign languages, thesis (for some programs); for doctorate, 3 foreign languages, comprehensive exam, thesis/dissertation; for other advanced degree, thesis (for some programs). *Entrance requirements:* For master's, 1 language (modern or ancient), interview; for doctorate, 2 languages (modern and ancient). Additional exam requirements/recommendations for international students: Required—TOEFL, TWE. *Faculty research:* Interreligious dialogue, feminist theology, systematic theology, philosophy of religion, pastoral theology.

**Trinity International University,** Trinity Evangelical Divinity School, Deerfield, IL 60015-1284. Offers academic ministry (M Div); Biblical and Near Eastern archaeology and languages (MA); chaplaincy and ministry care (MA); Christian studies (Certificate); church and parachurch ministry (M Div); church history (MA, Th M); counseling (Th M); educational ministries (MA); educational ministry (Th M); educational studies (PhD); intercultural studies (MA, PhD); leadership and management (D Min); mental health counseling (MA); military chaplaincy (D Min); ministry (MA); missions (Th M); missions and evangelism (D Min); New Testament (MA, Th M); Old Testament (Th M); Old Testament and Semitic languages (MA); pastoral ministry and care (D Min); pastoral theology (Th M); preaching and teaching (D Min); spiritual formation and education (D Min); systematic theology (MA, Th M); theological studies (MA, PhD); urban ministry (MA). *Program availability:* Part-time, online learning. *Students:* 578 full-time (141 women), 711 part-time (202 women). *Degree requirements:* For master's, comprehensive exam, thesis, fieldwork; for doctorate, comprehensive exam (for some programs), thesis/dissertation; for Certificate, comprehensive exam, integrative papers. *Entrance requirements:* For master's, GRE, MAT, minimum cumulative undergraduate GPA of 3.0; for doctorate, GRE, minimum cumulative graduate GPA of 3.2; for Certificate, GRE, MAT, minimum undergraduate GPA of 2.5. Additional exam requirements/recommendations for international students: Required—TOEFL (minimum score 580 paper-based), TWE (minimum score 4). *Application deadline:* For fall admission, 7/15 priority date for domestic and international students. Applications are processed on a rolling basis. Application fee: $25. Electronic applications accepted. *Expenses: Tuition, area resident:* Full-time $19,898. *Required fees:* $200. *Financial support:* Fellowships with partial tuition reimbursements, teaching assistantships with partial tuition reimbursements, career-related internships or fieldwork, Federal Work-Study, scholarships/grants, and tuition waivers (partial) available. Financial award application deadline: 4/1; financial award applicants required to submit FAFSA. *Unit head:* Dr. Tite Tienou, Academic Dean, 847-317-8086, Fax: 847-317-8014, E-mail: ttienou@teds.edu. *Application contact:* Ron Campbell, Director of Admissions, 800-345-8337, Fax: 847-317-8097, E-mail: rcampbel@tiu.edu. Website: https://divinity.tiu.edu/

**Trinity Lutheran Seminary,** Graduate and Professional Programs, Columbus, OH 43209-2334. Offers African American studies (MTS); Biblical studies (MTS, STM); Christian education (MA); Christian spirituality (STM); church in the world (MTS); church music (MA); divinity (M Div); general theological studies (MTS); mission and evangelism (STM); pastoral leadership and practice (STM); youth and family ministry (MA); MSN/MTS; MTS/JD. *Accreditation:* ACIPE; ATS. *Program availability:* Part-time. *Degree requirements:* For master's, variable foreign language requirement, comprehensive exam (for some programs), thesis (for some programs), field experience (for some programs). *Entrance requirements:* For master's, BA or equivalent (for MA, M Div, MTS); M Div, MTS, or equivalent (for STM); audition (for MACM). Additional exam requirements/recommendations for international students: Required—TOEFL. Electronic applications accepted. *Expenses:* Contact institution.

**Trinity School for Ministry,** Graduate Programs, Ambridge, PA 15003-2397. Offers Anglican studies (Diploma); basic Christian studies (Diploma); divinity (M Div); ministry (D Min); mission and evangelism (MAME, Diploma); religion (MAR); youth ministry (Diploma). *Program availability:* Part-time. *Degree requirements:* For master's, thesis optional; for doctorate, thesis/dissertation. *Entrance requirements:* Additional exam requirements/recommendations for international students: Required—TOEFL. *Faculty research:* Pauline Epistles, contemporary theology, history of Anglican liturgy, book of Ruth, biblical theology.

**Trinity Western University,** ACTS Seminaries, Langley, BC V2Y 1Y1, Canada. Offers Christian studies (MA); cross cultural ministry (MA); theology (M Div, M Th, MAMFT, MLE, MTS, D Min). *Program availability:* Part-time. *Degree requirements:* For master's, thesis (for some programs), internship. *Entrance requirements:* For doctorate, M Div or equivalent. Additional exam requirements/recommendations for international students: Required—TOEFL. *Expenses:* Contact institution. *Faculty research:* Theology of leadership.

**Tyndale University College & Seminary,** Graduate Programs, Toronto, ON M2M 3S4, Canada. Offers Biblical studies (M Div); Christian foundations (MTS); Christian studies (Diploma); counseling (M Div); educational ministry (M Div); missions (M Div, Diploma); pastoral and Chinese ministry (M Div); pastoral ministry (M Div); Pentecostal studies (MTS); spiritual formation (M Div, Diploma); theological studies (M Div); theology (Th M); worship and liturgy (M Div, MTS); youth and family ministry (M Div). *Accreditation:* ATS. *Program availability:* Part-time, online learning. *Entrance requirements:* For master's and Diploma, minimum C+ average in undergraduate course work. Additional exam requirements/recommendations for international students: Required—TOEFL (minimum score 570 paper-based), TWE (minimum score 5). Electronic applications accepted. *Faculty research:* Canadian church history, Chinese church history, Old Testament, counseling ministries (narrative therapy), world religions.

**Unification Theological Seminary,** Graduate Program, Main Campus, Barrytown, NY 12507. Offers divinity (M Div); ministry (D Min); religious education (MRE), including interfaith peacebuilding (MA, MRE); religious studies (MA), including interfaith peacebuilding (MA, MRE), non-profit leadership, theological studies, unification studies. *Program availability:* Part-time, evening/weekend. *Faculty:* 3 full-time (1 woman), 3 part-time/adjunct (0 women). *Students:* 27 full-time (8 women); includes 15 minority (11 Black or African American, non-Hispanic/Latino; 2 Asian, non-Hispanic/Latino; 1 Hispanic/Latino; 1 Two or more races, non-Hispanic/Latino), 6 international. Average age 50. In 2016, 12 master's, 5 doctorates awarded. *Degree requirements:* For master's, variable foreign language requirement, thesis (for some programs); for doctorate, thesis/dissertation. *Entrance requirements:* For master's, bachelor's degree; for doctorate, M Div or equivalency. Additional exam requirements/recommendations for international students: Required—TOEFL (minimum score 450 paper-based; 45 iBT). *Application deadline:* For fall admission, 3/15 priority date for domestic and international students; for spring admission, 9/15 priority date for domestic and international students. Applications are processed on a rolling basis. Application fee: $30. Electronic applications accepted. *Expenses:* Contact institution. *Financial support:* In 2016–17, 2 students received support. Scholarships/grants available. Financial award application deadline: 6/15; financial award applicants required to submit FAFSA. *Faculty research:* Church leadership, church history, world religions, ecumenism, interfaith peace building, service-learning. *Unit head:* Dr. Kathy Winings, Vice-President for Academic Affairs, 845-752-3000 Ext. 228, Fax: 845-752-3014, E-mail: academics@uts.edu. *Application contact:* Henry Christopher, Director of Admissions, 212-563-6647 Ext. 105, Fax: 845-752-3014, E-mail: h.christopher@uts.edu. Website: http://www.uts.edu

**Union University,** School of Theology and Missions, Jackson, TN 38305-3697. Offers Christian studies (MCS); expository preaching (D Min). *Program availability:* Part-time, evening/weekend, online learning. Electronic applications accepted. *Expenses: Tuition:* Full-time $10,300. *Required fees:* $20.

**United Theological Seminary,** Graduate and Professional Programs, Dayton, OH 45426. Offers Christian ministries (MA); ministry (M Div, D Min); theological studies (MTS). *Accreditation:* ATS. *Program availability:* Part-time, evening/weekend, online learning. *Degree requirements:* For master's, thesis (for some programs); for doctorate, thesis/dissertation, final exam. *Entrance requirements:* For master's, minimum GPA of 2.5, interview, 5 letters of recommendation; for doctorate, minimum GPA of 3.0, 2 letters of recommendation, interview. Additional exam requirements/recommendations for international students: Required—TOEFL (minimum score 550 paper-based). *Application deadline:* For fall admission, 8/1 for domestic students, 1/15 for international students; for spring admission, 1/1 for domestic students. Applications are processed on a rolling basis. Application fee: $60. Electronic applications accepted. *Expenses: Tuition:* Full-time $13,630; part-time $6815 per semester. Tuition and fees vary according to program. *Financial support:* Career-related internships or fieldwork, Federal Work-Study, and scholarships/grants available. Financial award application deadline: 4/1; financial award applicants required to submit CSS PROFILE or FAFSA. *Unit head:* Dr. David Watson, Academic Dean/Vice President for Academic Affairs, 937-529-2257, E-mail: dwatson@united.edu. *Application contact:* Kathleen Boston, Admissions Associate, 937-529-2225 Ext. 4237, E-mail: utsadmis@united.edu.

**United Theological Seminary of the Twin Cities,** Graduate Programs, New Brighton, MN 55112-2598. Offers advanced theological studies (Diploma); justice and peace studies (M Div, MA); leadership toward racial justice (M Div, MA, Certificate); Methodist studies (M Div, MA, Certificate); ministry (D Min); ministry renewal and professional

development (Certificate); pastoral care and counseling (M Div, MA, MARL); religion and theology (MA); theological and religious studies (Certificate); theology and the arts (M Div, MA); urban ministry (M Div, MA, MARL); women's studies: religion, theology and ministry (M Div, MA). *Accreditation:* ACIPE; ATS. *Program availability:* Part-time, evening/weekend. *Degree requirements:* For master's, thesis; for doctorate, comprehensive exam, thesis/dissertation. *Entrance requirements:* For master's, minimum GPA of 2.75; strong analytical, reflective thinking and writing skills; vocational and academic goals compatible with those of Seminary; for doctorate, M Div or equivalent, minimum GPA of 3.0, 3 years experience in professional ministry; for other advanced degree, BA or equivalent life experience; strong analytical, reflective thinking and writing skills (Certificate); proficiency in English language, previous study of theology at a theological school, recommendation of student's denomination (Diploma). Additional exam requirements/recommendations for international students: Required—TOEFL (minimum score 550 paper-based).

**University of Chicago,** Divinity School, Program in Ministry, Chicago, IL 60637. Offers M Div. *Students:* 36 full-time (13 women), 3 part-time (2 women); includes 8 minority (6 Black or African American, non-Hispanic/Latino; 2 Asian, non-Hispanic/Latino), 2 international. 50 applicants, 74% accepted, 14 enrolled. *Degree requirements:* For master's, one foreign language, thesis, field education. *Entrance requirements:* For master's, GRE General Test. Additional exam requirements/recommendations for international students: Required—TOEFL (minimum score 600 paper-based; 104 iBT), IELTS (minimum score 7). *Application deadline:* For fall admission, 1/15 priority date for domestic and international students. Application fee: $75. Electronic applications accepted. *Expenses:* Contact institution. *Financial support:* Career-related internships or fieldwork, Federal Work-Study, institutionally sponsored loans, and scholarships/grants available. Support available to part-time students. Financial award application deadline: 1/15; financial award applicants required to submit FAFSA. *Faculty research:* Constructive studies (philosophy of religion, religious ethics, and theology); historical studies (Bible, history of Christianity, and history of Judaism); religion and the human sciences (anthropology and sociology of religion, history of religions, and religion, literature, and visual culture); Islamic studies; religions in America. *Unit head:* Dr. Cynthia G. Lindner, Director of Ministry Studies/Clinical Professor of Preaching and Pastoral Care, 773-702-8280, E-mail: clindner@uchicago.edu. *Application contact:* John W. Howell, Coordinator for Recruiting and Admissions, 773-702-8249, Fax: 773-834-4581, E-mail: divinityadmissions@uchicago.edu. Website: http://divinity.uchicago.edu/ministry-program-mdiv

**University of Dallas,** Institute for Religious and Pastoral Studies, Irving, TX 75062-4736. Offers MCSL, MPM, MRE, MTS. *Accreditation:* ACIPE. *Program availability:* Part-time, evening/weekend, online learning. *Faculty research:* Scripture, pastoral theology, ecclesiology, systematic theology, theological anthropology.

**University of Dayton,** Department of Religious Studies, Dayton, OH 45469. Offers pastoral ministry (MA); theological studies (MA); theology (PhD). *Program availability:* Part-time. *Faculty:* 19 full-time (7 women), 6 part-time/adjunct (2 women). *Students:* 48 full-time (17 women), 8 part-time (4 women); includes 6 minority (1 Black or African American, non-Hispanic/Latino; 3 Asian, non-Hispanic/Latino; 2 Hispanic/Latino), 1 international. Average age 33. 62 applicants, 48% accepted. In 2016, 15 master's, 5 doctorates awarded. *Degree requirements:* For master's, thesis or alternative; for doctorate, one foreign language, comprehensive exam, thesis/dissertation, ecclesiastical Latin. *Entrance requirements:* For master's, minimum undergraduate GPA of 3.0, 3 letters of recommendation, personal statement, official transcript(s); for doctorate, GRE General Test (minimum score 600 verbal previous scale, 160 current scale), minimum GPA of 3.5, academic writing sample, 3 letters of recommendation, official transcript(s). Additional exam requirements/recommendations for international students: Required—TOEFL (minimum score 550 paper-based; 80 iBT). *Application deadline:* For fall admission, 2/2 priority date for domestic and international students. Applications are processed on a rolling basis. Application fee: $0 ($50 for international students). Electronic applications accepted. *Expenses:* $603 per fall/spring credit hour, $420 per summer credit hour (for MA); $722 per credit hour (for PhD); $25 per term registration fee. *Financial support:* In 2016–17, 36 students received support, including 4 fellowships with full tuition reimbursements available (averaging $17,600 per year), 7 research assistantships with full tuition reimbursements available (averaging $11,000 per year), 16 teaching assistantships with full tuition reimbursements available (averaging $17,952 per year); scholarships/grants, health care benefits, and unspecified assistantships also available. Support available to part-time students. Financial award application deadline: 2/2; financial award applicants required to submit FAFSA. *Faculty research:* Practical/constructive theology, theological ethics, U.S. Catholic/Christian life and thought, methodologies in Biblical studies, religion and science. *Unit head:* Dr. Daniel Thompson, Chair, 937-229-4321, Fax: 937-229-4330. *Application contact:* Amy Doorley, Graduate Program Coordinator, 937-229-4321, Fax: 937-229-4330, E-mail: adoorley1@udayton.edu. Website: http://www.udayton.edu/artssciences/academics/religiousstudies/welcome/index.php

**University of Fort Lauderdale,** Graduate Program, Lauderhill, FL 33313. Offers MS. *Degree requirements:* For master's, thesis.

**University of Northwestern–St. Paul,** Master of Divinity Program, St. Paul, MN 55113-1598. Offers M Div. *Program availability:* Part-time, evening/weekend, online learning. *Application deadline:* Applications are processed on a rolling basis. Electronic applications accepted. *Application contact:* College of Adult and Graduate Studies Admissions, 651-631-5200, E-mail: gradstudies@unwsp.edu. Website: https://www.unwsp.edu/web/graduate-studies/master-of-divinity

**University of Portland,** Department of Theology, Portland, OR 97203-5798. Offers pastoral ministry (MA). *Program availability:* Part-time. *Entrance requirements:* For master's, GRE or MAT, 3 letters of recommendation, minimum GPA of 3.0. Additional exam requirements/recommendations for international students: Required—TOEFL (minimum score 550 paper-based; 80 iBT), IELTS (minimum score 7).

**University of Saint Mary of the Lake–Mundelein Seminary,** Graduate and Professional Programs, Mundelein, IL 60060. Offers liturgical studies (MA); ministry (D Min); pastoral studies (MA); theology (M Div). *Accreditation:* ATS (one or more programs are accredited). *Faculty:* 60 full-time (6 women), 21 part-time/adjunct (9 women). *Students:* 266 full-time (8 women); includes 10 minority (2 Black or African American, non-Hispanic/Latino; 3 Asian, non-Hispanic/Latino; 5 Hispanic/Latino), 78 international. 99 applicants, 81% accepted, 80 enrolled. In 2016, 34 master's awarded. *Degree requirements:* For doctorate, 2 foreign languages, comprehensive exam, thesis/dissertation. *Entrance requirements:* For master's and doctorate, bachelor's degree. Additional exam requirements/recommendations for international students: Required—TOEFL (minimum score 550 paper-based). *Application deadline:* For fall admission, 8/1 for domestic and international students. Applications are processed on a rolling basis. Application fee: $0. Electronic applications accepted. *Expenses: Tuition:* Full-time $25,366. *Required fees:* $300. Full-time tuition and fees vary according to program. *Financial support:* Career-related internships or fieldwork available. *Unit head:* Very Rev. Thomas A. Baima, Dean of the Graduate School, 847-566-6401. *Application contact:* Very Rev. John Kartje, Rector-President, 847-566-6401, Fax: 847-932-3305.

*Pastoral Ministry and Counseling*

**University of St. Michael's College,** Faculty of Theology, Toronto, ON M5S 1J4, Canada. Offers Catholic leadership (MA); eastern Christian studies (Diploma); religious education (Diploma); theological studies (Diploma); theology (M Div, MA, MRE, MTS, D Min, PhD, Th D); theology and Jewish studies (MA). Th D offered jointly with University of Toronto. *Accreditation:* ATS (one or more programs are accredited). *Program availability:* Part-time. *Degree requirements:* For master's, thesis (for some programs), 1 foreign language (MA), 2 foreign languages (Th M); for doctorate, 3 foreign languages, comprehensive exam, thesis/dissertation; for other advanced degree, thesis optional. *Entrance requirements:* For master's, M Div or BA, course work in an ancient or modern language, minimum GPA of 3.3; for doctorate, MA in theology, Th M, or M Div with thesis, minimum GPA of 3.7; for other advanced degree, minimum GPA of 2.7. Additional exam requirements/recommendations for international students: Required—TOEFL (minimum score 600 paper-based). Electronic applications accepted. *Expenses:* Contact institution. *Faculty research:* Patristics, eastern Christianity, ecology and theology, ecumenism, Jewish Christian studies.

**University of St. Thomas,** Graduate Studies, The Saint Paul Seminary School of Divinity, St. Paul, MN 55105. Offers pastoral ministry (MAPM); religious education (MARE); theology (MA). *Accreditation:* ACIPE; ATS. *Program availability:* Part-time, evening/weekend. *Degree requirements:* For master's, one foreign language, comprehensive exam (for some programs), thesis (for some programs). *Entrance requirements:* For master's, GRE, 3 letters of recommendation, interview. Additional exam requirements/recommendations for international students: Required—TOEFL (minimum score 550 paper-based). *Application deadline:* For fall admission, 6/1 priority date for domestic students. Applications are processed on a rolling basis. Application fee: $40. Electronic applications accepted. *Expenses:* Contact institution. *Financial support:* Fellowships, research assistantships, institutionally sponsored loans, and scholarships/grants available. Support available to part-time students. Financial award application deadline: 4/1; financial award applicants required to submit FAFSA. *Faculty research:* Theological education. *Unit head:* Rev. Msgr. Aloysius R. Callaghan, Rector/Vice President, 651-962-5052, Fax: 651-962-5790, E-mail: arcallaghan@stthomas.edu. *Application contact:* Rev. Peter Williams, Vice Rector for Formation, 651-962-5775, Fax: 651-962-5790, E-mail: will2750@stthomas.edu.
Website: http://www.stthomas.edu/spssod/

**University of St. Thomas,** School of Theology, Houston, TX 77024. Offers divinity (M Div); pastoral studies (MAPS); theological studies (MA). *Accreditation:* ATS. *Program availability:* Part-time. *Faculty:* 8 full-time (2 women), 5 part-time/adjunct (0 women). *Students:* 89 full-time (1 woman), 70 part-time (24 women); includes 62 minority (5 Black or African American, non-Hispanic/Latino; 22 Asian, non-Hispanic/Latino; 33 Hispanic/Latino; 2 Two or more races, non-Hispanic/Latino), 20 international. Average age 37. 50 applicants, 100% accepted, 37 enrolled. In 2016, 32 master's awarded. *Degree requirements:* For master's, variable foreign language requirement, comprehensive exam. *Entrance requirements:* For master's, BA, BS or equivalent; personal essay (for some programs); undergraduate philosophy or theology courses; 2 letters of recommendation. Additional exam requirements/recommendations for international students: Required—TOEFL (minimum score 550 paper-based; 79 iBT), IELTS (minimum score 6.5), PTE (minimum score 53). *Application deadline:* Applications are processed on a rolling basis. Application fee: $10. Electronic applications accepted. *Expenses:* Contact institution. *Financial support:* In 2016–17, 4 students received support. Scholarships/grants available. Support available to part-time students. Financial award application deadline: 4/15; financial award applicants required to submit FAFSA. *Unit head:* Dr. Sandra C. Magie, Dean, 713-686-4345 Ext. 242, Fax: 713-683-8673, E-mail: smagie@stthom.edu. *Application contact:* Connie M. Henry, Office Manager, 713-686-4345 Ext. 231, Fax: 713-683-8673, E-mail: sms@stthom.edu.
Website: http://www.stthom.edu/Academics/School_of_Theology_at_St_Marys_Seminary/Index.aqf

**University of South Africa,** College of Human Sciences, Pretoria, South Africa. Offers adult education (M Ed); African languages (MA, PhD); African politics (MA, PhD); Afrikaans (MA, PhD); ancient history (MA, PhD); ancient Near Eastern studies (MA, PhD); anthropology (MA, PhD); applied linguistics (MA); Arabic (MA, PhD); archaeology (MA); art history (MA); Biblical archaeology (MA); Biblical studies (M Th, D Th, PhD); Christian spirituality (M Th, D Th); church history (M Th, D Th, PhD); classical studies (MA, PhD); clinical psychology (MA); communication (MA, PhD); comparative education (M Ed, Ed D); consulting psychology (D Admin, D Com, PhD); curriculum studies (M Ed, Ed D); development studies (M Admin, D Admin, PhD); didactics (M Ed, Ed D); education (M Tech); education management (M Ed, Ed D); educational psychology (M Ed); English (MA); environmental education (M Ed); French (MA, PhD); German (MA, PhD); Greek (MA); guidance and counseling (M Ed); health studies (MA, PhD), including health sciences education (MA), health services management (MA), medical and surgical nursing science (critical care general) (MA), midwifery and neonatal nursing science (MA), trauma and emergency care (MA); history (MA, PhD); history of education (Ed D); inclusive education (M Ed, Ed D); information and communications technology policy and regulation (MA); information science (MA, MIS, PhD); international politics (MA, PhD); Islamic studies (MA, PhD); Italian (MA, PhD); Judaica (MA, PhD); linguistics (MA, PhD); mathematical education (M Ed); mathematics education (MA); missiology (M Th, D Th); modern Hebrew (MA, PhD); musicology (MA, MMus, D Mus, PhD); natural science education (M Ed); New Testament (M Th, D Th); Old Testament (D Th); pastoral therapy (M Th, D Th); philosophy (MA); philosophy of education (M Ed, Ed D); politics (MA, PhD); Portuguese (MA, PhD); practical theology (M Th, D Th); psychology (MA, MS, PhD); psychology of education (M Ed, Ed D); public health (MA); religious studies (MA, D Th, PhD); Romance languages (MA); Russian (MA, PhD); Semitic languages (MA, PhD); social behavior studies in HIV/AIDS (MA); social science (mental health) (MA); social science in development studies (MA); social science in psychology (MA); social science in social work (MA); social science in sociology (MA); social work (MSW, DSW, PhD); socio-education (M Ed, Ed D); sociolinguistics (MA); sociology (MA, PhD); Spanish (MA, PhD); systematic theology (M Th, D Th); TESOL (teaching English to speakers of other languages) (MA); theological ethics (M Th, D Th); theory of literature (MA, PhD); urban ministries (D Th); urban ministry (M Th).

**University of the Incarnate Word,** School of Graduate Studies and Research, College of Humanities, Arts, and Social Sciences, San Antonio, TX 78209-6397. Offers pastoral ministry (MA). *Program availability:* Part-time, evening/weekend. *Faculty:* 3 full-time (all women), 1 part-time/adjunct (0 women). *Students:* 2 part-time (0 women); includes 1 minority (Hispanic/Latino). In 2016, 3 master's awarded. *Degree requirements:* For master's, thesis or alternative. *Entrance requirements:* For master's, GRE/MAT or three letters of recommendation and personal statement of ministerial and educational goals. Additional exam requirements/recommendations for international students: Required—TOEFL (minimum score 560 paper-based; 83 iBT). *Application deadline:* Applications are processed on a rolling basis. Application fee: $20. Electronic applications accepted. *Expenses: Tuition:* Full-time $7965; part-time $885 per credit hour. *Required fees:* $40 per credit hour. Tuition and fees vary according to course load, degree level, campus/location, program and student level. *Financial support:* Research assistantships, scholarships/grants, tuition waivers, and unspecified assistantships available. Financial award applicants required to submit FAFSA. *Faculty research:* Migration patterns in southeast Asia, cultural explorations of identity in border regions, pollution control in historical contexts, cultural exchanges within the Middle East, water and culture. *Unit*

*head:* Dr. Kevin Vichcales, Dean, 210-829-2759, Fax: 210-829-3830, E-mail: vichcale@uiwtx.edu. *Application contact:* Johnny Garcia, Graduate Admissions Counselor, 210-829-6005, Fax: 210-829-3921, E-mail: admis@uiwtx.edu.
Website: http://www.uiw.edu/hass/index.htm

**Ursuline College,** School of Graduate Studies, Theological and Pastoral Studies Program, Pepper Pike, OH 44124-4398. Offers MA. *Program availability:* Part-time. *Faculty:* 3 full-time (all women). *Students:* 1 (woman) full-time, 5 part-time (4 women); includes 5 minority (all Black or African American, non-Hispanic/Latino). Average age 55. 3 applicants, 67% accepted, 1 enrolled. *Degree requirements:* For master's, thesis. *Entrance requirements:* For master's, GRE when GPA under 3.0, minimum undergraduate GPA of 3.0, interview. Additional exam requirements/recommendations for international students: Required—TOEFL (minimum score 550 paper-based; 80 iBT). *Application deadline:* For fall admission, 8/1 priority date for domestic students. Applications are processed on a rolling basis. Application fee: $25. Electronic applications accepted. *Expenses:* $1,052 per credit hour. *Financial support:* In 2016–17, 6 students received support. Scholarships/grants available. Financial award application deadline: 3/1; financial award applicants required to submit FAFSA. *Faculty research:* Household codes of Ephesians, cosmology of Ephesians, early Christian families, the use of theological reflection in integrative education for ministry, premillennial dispensationalism and the politics of the religious right in the United States. *Unit head:* Dr. Linda Martin, Director, 440-646-8191, Fax: 440-684-6088, E-mail: lmartin@ursuline.edu. *Application contact:* Melanie Steele, Director, Graduate Admissions, 440-646-8146, Fax: 440-684-6138, E-mail: graduateadmissions@ursuline.edu.

**Virginia Beach Theological Seminary,** Graduate Programs, Virginia Beach, VA 23464. Offers Biblical studies (MBS, Th M); chaplaincy (MBS); ministry (M Div). *Program availability:* Online learning. *Faculty:* 5 full-time (0 women), 2 part-time/adjunct (0 women). *Students:* 7 full-time (0 women), 29 part-time (3 women). *Entrance requirements:* For master's, GRE, interview, minimum cumulative GPA of 2.4, church endorsement, 3 recommendations. Electronic applications accepted. *Expenses: Tuition:* Full-time $7920; part-time $330 per credit hour. *Required fees:* $265 per semester. *Financial support:* Scholarships/grants available. *Application contact:* Edward Estes, Director of Admissions, 757-479-3706, E-mail: eestes@vbts.edu.
Website: http://www.vbts.edu/academics/

**Virginia University of Lynchburg,** Graduate Programs, Lynchburg, VA 24501-6417. Offers Christian ministry (M Div); ministry (D Min). *Program availability:* Online learning. *Faculty:* 6 full-time (0 women), 4 part-time/adjunct (all women). *Students:* 64 full-time (25 women), 4 part-time (2 women). *Expenses: Tuition:* Full-time $8200; part-time $4100 per credit hour. *Required fees:* $400. Tuition and fees vary according to campus/location and program. *Application contact:* Houston Walthall, Admissions Director, 434-528-5276 Ext. 1130, Fax: 434-528-4257, E-mail: hwalthall@vul.edu.

**Viterbo University,** Master of Arts in Servant Leadership Program, La Crosse, WI 54601-4797. Offers ethical leadership in organizations (Certificate); servant leadership (MA). *Program availability:* Part-time, evening/weekend. *Degree requirements:* For master's, 30 credits (15 credits of Servant Leadership core courses and any combination of 15 elective credits). *Entrance requirements:* For master's, letter of reference, statement of goals, baccalaureate degree, transcript, interview. Additional exam requirements/recommendations for international students: Required—TOEFL (minimum score 525 paper-based). Electronic applications accepted. *Expenses:* Contact institution. *Faculty research:* Organizational culture, community building, ethical decision-making, leadership theory and practice.

**Walsh University,** Graduate Programs, Master of Arts in Theology Program, North Canton, OH 44720-3396. Offers parish administration (MA); pastoral ministry (MA); religious education (MA). *Program availability:* Part-time, evening/weekend. *Faculty:* 4 full-time (0 women). *Students:* 5 full-time (2 women), 10 part-time (3 women); includes 1 minority (Black or African American, non-Hispanic/Latino), 1 international. Average age 41. 6 applicants, 67% accepted, 4 enrolled. In 2016, 7 master's awarded. *Degree requirements:* For master's, thesis or alternative, culminating assignment. *Entrance requirements:* For master's, MAT or GRE (minimum scores: Verbal 145, Quantitative 146, Combined 291, Writing 3.0), minimum GPA of 3.0. Additional exam requirements/recommendations for international students: Required—TOEFL. *Application deadline:* For fall admission, 7/15 for domestic students. Applications are processed on a rolling basis. Application fee: $25. Electronic applications accepted. Application fee is waived when completed online. *Expenses:* $332 per credit hour tuition. *Financial support:* Research assistantships available. Financial award application deadline: 12/31; financial award applicants required to submit FAFSA. *Faculty research:* Cardinal Newman, phenomenological method, Flavius Josephus, post-conciliar moral teaching. *Unit head:* Dr. Bradley Beach, Chair, 330-244-4732, Fax: 330-244-4955, E-mail: bbeach@walsh.edu. *Application contact:* Audra Dice, Graduate Admissions Counselor, 330-490-7181, Fax: 330-244-4925, E-mail: adice@walsh.edu.

**Wayland Baptist University,** Graduate Programs, Programs in Religion, Plainview, TX 79072-6998. Offers Christian ministry (MCM); divinity (M Div); religion (MA). *Program availability:* Part-time, evening/weekend, online learning. *Degree requirements:* For master's, comprehensive exam. *Entrance requirements:* For master's, GRE or MAT, minimum GPA of 3.0; letter of endorsement from Christian congregation, one academic and one personal letter of recommendation (for M Div). Additional exam requirements/recommendations for international students: Required—TOEFL (minimum score 500 paper-based; 61 iBT). Electronic applications accepted.

**Wesley Biblical Seminary,** Graduate Programs, Jackson, MS 39206. Offers apologetics (MA); Biblical languages (M Div); Biblical literature (MA); Christian studies (MA); context and mission (M Div); honors research (M Div); interpretation (M Div); ministry (M Div); spiritual formation (M Div); teaching (M Div); theology (MA). *Accreditation:* ATS. *Program availability:* Part-time. *Degree requirements:* For master's, thesis. *Entrance requirements:* Additional exam requirements/recommendations for international students: Required—TOEFL. Electronic applications accepted. *Faculty research:* Patristics, missiology, culture, hermeneutics.

**Western Seminary,** Graduate Programs, Program in Counseling, Portland, OR 97215-3367. Offers counseling (MA, Certificate); pastoral counseling (M Div); M Div/MA. *Program availability:* Part-time, evening/weekend. *Degree requirements:* For master's, practicum. *Entrance requirements:* Additional exam requirements/recommendations for international students: Required—TOEFL. *Expenses:* Contact institution.

**Western Seminary,** Graduate Programs, Program in Intercultural Studies, Portland, OR 97215-3367. Offers MA, D Miss, Certificate, G Dip. *Program availability:* Part-time, evening/weekend. *Degree requirements:* For master's, practicum; for doctorate, 2 foreign languages, thesis/dissertation. *Entrance requirements:* Additional exam requirements/recommendations for international students: Required—TOEFL.

**Western Seminary,** Graduate Programs, Program in Ministry and Leadership, Portland, OR 97215-3367. Offers chaplaincy (MA); coaching (MA); Jewish ministry (MA); pastoral care to women (MA); youth ministry (MA). *Degree requirements:* For master's, practicum. *Entrance requirements:* Additional exam requirements/recommendations for international students: Required—TOEFL.

**Western Seminary–Sacramento Campus,** Graduate Certificate Programs, Sacramento, CA 95821. Offers Bible (Graduate Certificate); coaching (Graduate Certificate); pastoral care to women (Graduate Certificate); theology (Graduate Certificate); youth and family (Graduate Certificate). *Program availability:* Online learning. *Entrance requirements:* For degree, essays, undergraduate transcripts, 4 recommendations. Additional exam requirements/recommendations for international students: Required—TOEFL.

**Western Seminary–Sacramento Campus,** Graduate Diploma Programs, Sacramento, CA 95821. Offers Bible and theology (Graduate Diploma); ministry (Graduate Diploma); pastoral care to women (Graduate Diploma). *Entrance requirements:* For degree, essays, undergraduate transcripts, 4 recommendations. Additional exam requirements/recommendations for international students: Required—TOEFL.

**Western Seminary–Sacramento Campus,** Program in Ministry and Leadership, Sacramento, CA 95821. Offers MA. *Entrance requirements:* For master's, essays, undergraduate transcripts, 4 recommendations. Additional exam requirements/recommendations for international students: Required—TOEFL.

**Western Seminary–San Jose Campus,** Graduate Programs, Los Gatos, CA 95032-4520. Offers Bible and theology (Graduate Diploma); Bible, camp and conference ministry (CGS); Biblical and theological studies (MA), including exegetical track, theological track; coaching (CGS); expositional ministry (M Div); marital and family therapy (MA); ministry (Graduate Diploma); ministry and leadership (MA), including camp and conference ministry, coaching, pastoral care to women, youth ministry; pastoral care to women (CGS, Graduate Diploma); pastoral ministry (M Div); theology (CGS); youth and family (CGS). *Program availability:* Part-time, evening/weekend, online learning. *Entrance requirements:* For master's, minimum GPA of 3.0. Electronic applications accepted.

**Western Theological Seminary,** Graduate and Professional Programs, Holland, MI 49423-3622. Offers divinity (M Div); ministry (D Min); theology (M Th, MA); urban pastoral ministry (Graduate Certificate); M Div/MSW. *Accreditation:* ACIPE; ATS. *Program availability:* Part-time, 100% online, blended/hybrid learning. *Degree requirements:* For doctorate, thesis/dissertation. *Entrance requirements:* Additional exam requirements/recommendations for international students: Required—TOEFL. Electronic applications accepted.

**Westminster Theological Seminary,** Graduate and Professional Programs, Philadelphia, PA 19118. Offers apologetics (Th M); Biblical and urban studies (Certificate); Biblical counseling (MA); biblical studies (MAR); Christian studies (Certificate); church history (Th M); counseling (M Div); general studies (M Div, MAR); hermeneutics and Bible interpretations (PhD); historical and theological studies (PhD); historical theology (Th M); New Testament (Th M); Old Testament (Th M); pastoral counseling (D Min); pastoral ministry (M Div, D Min); systematic theology (Th M); theological studies (MAR); urban missions (M Div, MA, MAR, D Min). *Accreditation:* ATS. *Program availability:* Part-time. Terminal master's awarded for partial completion of doctoral program. *Degree requirements:* For master's, thesis (for some programs); for doctorate, 4 foreign languages, comprehensive exam (for some programs), thesis/dissertation. *Entrance requirements:* For doctorate, GRE General Test. Additional exam requirements/recommendations for international students: Required—TOEFL, TWE.

**Wheaton College,** Graduate School, Department of Psychology, Wheaton, IL 60187-5593. Offers clinical mental health counseling (MA); clinical psychology (Psy D); counseling ministries (MA); marriage and family therapy (MA). *Accreditation:* APA (one or more programs are accredited). *Faculty:* 14 full-time (7 women), 9 part-time/adjunct (5 women). *Students:* 130 full-time (97 women), 17 part-time (13 women); includes 38 minority (13 Black or African American, non-Hispanic/Latino; 1 American Indian or Alaska Native, non-Hispanic/Latino; 9 Asian, non-Hispanic/Latino; 8 Hispanic/Latino; 7 Two or more races, non-Hispanic/Latino), 17 international. Average age 28. 115 applicants, 80% accepted, 58 enrolled. In 2016, 70 master's, 9 doctorates awarded. Terminal master's awarded for partial completion of doctoral program. *Degree requirements:* For master's, thesis or alternative; for doctorate, thesis/dissertation, internship. *Entrance requirements:* For master's, GRE General Test, 18 hours of course work in psychology; for doctorate, GRE General Test. Additional exam requirements/recommendations for international students: Required—TOEFL (minimum score 550 paper-based; 80 iBT), IELTS (minimum score 6.5), TOEFL (minimum score 600 paper-based; 90 iBT) or IELTS (minimum score 7.5) for PsyD. *Application deadline:* For fall admission, 3/1 priority date for domestic students, 1/1 for international students. Applications are processed on a rolling basis. Application fee: $30. *Expenses: Tuition:* Full-time $19,080; part-time $795 per credit hour. Tuition and fees vary according to degree level and program. *Financial support:* In 2016–17, 3 research assistantships (averaging $4,800 per year) were awarded; career-related internships or fieldwork, Federal Work-Study, scholarships/grants, and unspecified assistantships also available. Financial award application deadline: 3/1; financial award applicants required to submit FAFSA. *Unit head:* Dr. Terri Watson, Associate Dean of Psychology, 630-752-5104, E-mail: psychology@wheaton.edu. *Application contact:* Dusty Di Santo, Director of Graduate Admissions, 630-752-5195, Fax: 630-752-7047, E-mail: graduate.admissions@wheaton.edu. Website: http://www.wheaton.edu/academics/departments/psychology

**Wilfrid Laurier University,** Waterloo Lutheran Seminary, Waterloo, ON N2L 3C5, Canada. Offers divinity (M Div); multifaith spiritual care and counseling (Diploma); pastoral leadership (D Min); spiritual care and counseling (D Min); theology (M Th, MTS); M Div/MTS/MSW. *Accreditation:* ATS. *Program availability:* Part-time. *Degree requirements:* For master's, one foreign language, thesis (for some programs); for doctorate, thesis/dissertation. *Entrance requirements:* For master's, two letters of reference; for doctorate, M Div, two letters of reference. Additional exam requirements/recommendations for international students: Required—TOEFL (minimum score 573 paper-based; 89 iBT), IELTS (minimum score 7). Electronic applications accepted. *Expenses:* Contact institution. *Faculty research:* Biblical study, church history, systematic theology.

**Xavier University,** College of Arts and Sciences, Department of Theology, Cincinnati, OH 45207. Offers health care mission integration (MA); theology (MA), including religious education, social and pastoral ministry, theology. *Program availability:* Part-time, evening/weekend. *Degree requirements:* For master's, final paper (or thesis) and defense or comprehension exam. *Entrance requirements:* For master's, MAT or GRE, 2 letters of recommendation; statement of reasons and goals for enrolling in program (1,000-2,000 words); resume; transcript. Additional exam requirements/recommendations for international students: Required—TOEFL (minimum score 550 paper-based; 79 iBT). Electronic applications accepted. Application fee is waived when completed online. *Expenses:* Contact institution. *Faculty research:* Scripture, ethics, constructive theology, historical theology.

**Xavier University of Louisiana,** Graduate School, Institute for Black Catholic Studies, New Orleans, LA 70125. Offers pastoral theology (Th M). *Program availability:* Part-time. *Degree requirements:* For master's, comprehensive exam, practicum. *Entrance requirements:* For master's, GRE General Test, MAT, minimum GPA of 2.5. Additional exam requirements/recommendations for international students: Required—TOEFL.

# Religion

**Abilene Christian University,** Graduate Programs, College of Biblical Studies, Graduate School of Theology, Program in Ancient and Oriental Christianity, Abilene, TX 79699. Offers MA. *Program availability:* Part-time. *Students:* 1 full-time (0 women). 3 applicants. In 2016, 1 master's awarded. *Degree requirements:* For master's, comprehensive exam, thesis. *Entrance requirements:* Additional exam requirements/recommendations for international students: Required—TOEFL (minimum score 80 iBT), IELTS (minimum score 6). *Application deadline:* For fall admission, 8/11 for domestic students; for spring admission, 11/1 for domestic students. Application fee: $50. *Expenses:* $618 per credit hour. *Financial support:* Application deadline: 4/1; applicants required to submit FAFSA. *Unit head:* Dr. Jeff Childers, Graduate Advisor, 325-674-3797, Fax: 325-674-6180, E-mail: jeff.childers@acu.edu. *Application contact:* Corey Patterson, Director of Graduate Admission and Recruiting, 325-674-6566, Fax: 325-674-6717, E-mail: gradinfo@acu.edu. Website: http://www.acu.edu/graduate/academics/ancient-and-oriental-christianity.html

**Abilene Christian University,** Graduate Programs, College of Biblical Studies, Graduate School of Theology, Program in Modern and American Christianity, Abilene, TX 79699. Offers MA. *Program availability:* Part-time. *Students:* 2 part-time (1 woman). In 2016, 1 master's awarded. *Degree requirements:* For master's, comprehensive exam, thesis. *Entrance requirements:* Additional exam requirements/recommendations for international students: Required—TOEFL (minimum score 80 iBT), IELTS (minimum score 6), PTE. *Application deadline:* For fall admission, 8/11 for domestic students; for spring admission, 11/1 for domestic students. Applications are processed on a rolling basis. Application fee: $50. Electronic applications accepted. *Expenses:* $618 per credit hour. *Financial support:* In 2016–17, 1 student received support. Scholarships/grants available. Financial award application deadline: 4/1; financial award applicants required to submit FAFSA. *Unit head:* Dr. Douglas Foster, Graduate Advisor, 325-674-3795, Fax: 325-674-6180, E-mail: doug.foster@acu.edu. *Application contact:* Corey Patterson, Director of Graduate Admission and Recruiting, 325-674-6566, Fax: 325-674-6717, E-mail: gradinfo@acu.edu. Website: http://www.acu.edu/graduate/academics/modern-and-american-christianity.html

**Ambrose University,** Ambrose Seminary, Calgary, AB T3H 0L5, Canada. Offers Biblical/theological studies (MA), including New Testament, Old Testament, theology; Christian studies (MCS, Diploma); intercultural ministries (M Div, MA); leadership (Certificate); leadership and ministry (MA), including chaplaincy, leadership; pastoral ministry (M Div). *Accreditation:* ATS (one or more programs are accredited). *Program availability:* Part-time, blended/hybrid learning. *Faculty:* 14 full-time (3 women), 4 part-time/adjunct (1 woman). *Students:* 76 applicants, 74% accepted, 35 enrolled. In 2016, 21 master's, 1 other advanced degree awarded. *Degree requirements:* For master's, variable foreign language requirement, thesis (for some programs), internship (for M Div, MA in leadership and ministry, MA in intercultural ministries); thesis (for MA in Biblical/theological studies). *Entrance requirements:* For master's, undergraduate degree from other accredited university or bible college, minimum GPA of 2.0. Additional exam requirements/recommendations for international students: Required—PTE (minimum score 58), TOEFL (minimum score 560 paper-based, 83 iBT) or IELTS (minimum score 6.5). *Application deadline:* For fall admission, 8/1 for domestic students, 4/15 for international students; for winter admission, 12/1 for domestic students, 11/15 for international students. Applications are processed on a rolling basis. Application fee: $70 ($100 for international students). Electronic applications accepted. *Expenses: Tuition:* Full-time $11,850 Canadian dollars; part-time $395 Canadian dollars per credit hour. *Required fees:* $810 Canadian dollars; $27 Canadian dollars per credit hour. $50 Canadian dollars per semester. Tuition and fees vary according to course load and program. *Financial support:* Career-related internships or fieldwork and scholarships/grants available. Support available to part-time students. Financial award application deadline: 3/30. *Faculty research:* Evangelicalism and sociology, missiological trends, chaplaincy, intertestamental studies, postmodernism. *Unit head:* Dr. Jo-Ann Badley, Dean of Theology, 403-410-2000 Ext. 3994, Fax: 403-571-2556, E-mail: jbadley@ambrose.edu. *Application contact:* Andreas Striefler, Enrollment Advisor, 403-410-2970, Fax: 403-571-2556, E-mail: enrolment@ambrose.edu. Website: https://ambrose.edu/seminary

**The American University of Rome,** Graduate School, Rome, Italy. Offers religious studies (MA); sustainable cultural heritage (MA). *Degree requirements:* For master's, thesis, internship. *Entrance requirements:* For master's, bachelor's degree in the liberal arts, humanities or social sciences; minimum GPA of 2.75. Additional exam requirements/recommendations for international students: Required—TOEFL (minimum score 550 paper-based; 80 iBT), IELTS (minimum score 6.5). Electronic applications accepted. *Faculty research:* Sustainable cultural heritage, archaeology in Europe and Italy.

**Amridge University,** Graduate and Professional Programs, Montgomery, AL 36117. Offers Biblical studies (MA, PhD); Christian ministry (MS); family therapy (D Min); human services (MS); leadership and management (MS); marriage and family therapy (M Div, MA, PhD); ministerial leadership (M Div, MS); New Testament studies (MA); Old Testament studies (MA); professional counseling (M Div, MA, PhD); theology (M Div, D Min). *Program availability:* Part-time, evening/weekend, online learning. *Faculty:* 22 full-time (3 women), 10 part-time/adjunct (6 women). *Students:* 81 full-time (49 women), 225 part-time (137 women); includes 81 minority (80 Black or African American, non-Hispanic/Latino; 1 Hispanic/Latino). Average age 41. 122 applicants, 100% accepted, 79 enrolled. *Degree requirements:* For master's, one foreign language, comprehensive exam (for some programs), thesis (for some programs); for doctorate, one foreign language, comprehensive exam (for some programs), thesis/dissertation (for some programs). *Entrance requirements:* For master's, official transcript showing an earned 4-year BA or BS from regionally- or nationally-accredited institution; for doctorate, official transcript showing earned graduate degree from regionally- or nationally-accredited institution; writing sample (e.g. career monograph, published journal article, term paper from master's degree or doctoral dissertation); interview. Additional exam requirements/recommendations for international students: Required—TOEFL (minimum score 79 iBT). *Application deadline:* Applications are processed on a rolling basis. Application fee: $50. Electronic applications accepted. *Expenses: Tuition:* Full-time $12,870; part-time $715 per credit hour. *Required fees:* $1300; $650 per semester. *Financial support:* In 2016–17, 45 students received support. Federal Work-Study and scholarships/grants available. Support available to part-time students. Financial award applicants required to submit FAFSA. *Faculty research:* Technology and mental healthcare, resilience in black families, theology and congregational ministry. *Unit head:* Laina Costanza, Vice President, Student Affairs, 888-790-8080 Ext. 1, Fax: 334-387-3878, E-mail: cc@amridgeuniversity.edu. *Application contact:* Brooks Housley, Student Affairs Coordinator, 888-790-8080 Ext. 1, Fax: 334-387-3878, E-mail: admissions@amridgeuniversity.edu.

**Arizona State University at the Tempe campus,** College of Liberal Arts and Sciences, School of Historical, Philosophical and Religious Studies, Tempe, AZ 85287-4301. Offers European history (MA, PhD); medieval studies (Graduate Certificate); North American history (MA, PhD); philosophy (MA, PhD); public history (MA); religious studies (MA, PhD); Renaissance studies (Graduate Certificate); scholarly publishing (Graduate Certificate). *Program availability:* Part-time. Terminal master's awarded for partial completion of doctoral program. *Degree requirements:* For master's, thesis or alternative, interactive Program of Study (iPOS) submitted before completing 50 percent of required credit hours; for doctorate, variable foreign language requirement, comprehensive exam, thesis/dissertation, interactive Program of Study (iPOS) submitted before completing 50 percent of required credit hours. *Entrance requirements:* For master's and doctorate, GRE, minimum GPA of 3.0 or equivalent in last 2 years of work leading to bachelor's degree. Additional exam requirements/recommendations for international students: Required—TOEFL, IELTS, or PTE. Electronic applications accepted.

**The Baptist College of Florida,** Graduate Programs, Graceville, FL 32440-1898. Offers Christian ministry (MA); Christian studies (MA), including Biblical studies; music and worship leadership (MA). *Program availability:* Part-time, 100% online, blended/hybrid learning. *Degree requirements:* For master's, variable foreign language requirement, comprehensive exam (for some programs), thesis (for some programs). *Entrance requirements:* For master's, regionally-accredited undergraduate degree, undergraduate courses in field, minimum GPA of 2.5. Additional exam requirements/recommendations for international students: Required—TOEFL. Electronic applications accepted. *Expenses:* Contact institution. *Faculty research:* Biblical studies, ministry studies.

**Baptist Theological Seminary at Richmond,** Graduate and Professional Programs, Richmond, VA 23228. Offers Biblical interpretation (M Div); Christian education formation (M Div); Christian ministry (MCM); justice and peacebuilding (M Div); ministry (D Min); religious freedom (M Div); theological studies (MTS, Graduate Certificate); theology (M Div); youth and student ministries (M Div); M Div/MBA; M Div/MS; M Div/MSW. *Accreditation:* ATS. *Program availability:* Part-time, 100% online, blended/hybrid learning. *Faculty:* 5 full-time (1 woman), 11 part-time/adjunct (2 women). *Students:* 42 full-time (23 women), 34 part-time (19 women); includes 11 minority (all Black or African American, non-Hispanic/Latino), 2 international. Average age 46. In 2016, 8 master's, 2 doctorates awarded. *Degree requirements:* For master's and Graduate Certificate, thesis optional; for doctorate, comprehensive exam, thesis/dissertation, field study, independent study. *Entrance requirements:* For master's, BA/BS, minimum GPA of 2.2, 2 references, resume, official transcripts, writing sample; for doctorate, MAT (minimum score of 400), M Div with minimum GPA of 2.75, 3 years of full-time ministry experience, 3 references, resume, official transcripts, writing sample, personal statement. Additional exam requirements/recommendations for international students: Required—TOEFL (minimum score 550 paper-based), IELTS (minimum score 5.5). *Application deadline:* For fall admission, 7/1 for domestic students, 5/1 for international students; for winter admission, 12/15 for domestic students, 9/1 for international students; for spring admission, 1/15 for domestic students, 10/1 for international students. Applications are processed on a rolling basis. Application fee: $35. Electronic applications accepted. *Expenses:* $19,800 per 12 credit hours for both semesters; $1,650 per 3 semester hour course. *Financial support:* In 2016–17, 46 students received support, including 11 teaching assistantships (averaging $3,300 per year); scholarships/grants also available. Financial award application deadline: 2/1. *Faculty research:* Biblical studies, pastoral care, church history, theology, ministry. *Unit head:* Dr. Ronald W. Crawford, President, 804-204-1201, Fax: 804-355-8182, E-mail: rcrawford@btsr.edu. *Application contact:* Melissa Fallen, Director of Admissions and Recruitment, 804-204-1208, E-mail: admissions@btsr.edu.
Website: http://www.btsr.edu/programs/degree-programs/

**Baylor University,** Graduate School, College of Arts and Sciences, Department of Religion, Waco, TX 76798. Offers MA, PhD. *Faculty:* 18 full-time (4 women). *Students:* 49 full-time (15 women), 8 part-time (1 woman); includes 8 minority (2 Black or African American, non-Hispanic/Latino; 3 Asian, non-Hispanic/Latino; 1 Hispanic/Latino; 2 Two or more races, non-Hispanic/Latino), 3 international. 63 applicants, 19% accepted, 8 enrolled. In 2016, 1 master's, 5 doctorates awarded. Terminal master's awarded for partial completion of doctoral program. *Degree requirements:* For master's, one foreign language, thesis; for doctorate, 2 foreign languages, thesis/dissertation. *Entrance requirements:* For master's and doctorate, GRE General Test. Additional exam requirements/recommendations for international students: Required—TOEFL. *Application deadline:* For fall admission, 12/1 for domestic and international students. Application fee: $50. Electronic applications accepted. *Expenses: Tuition:* Full-time $28,494; part-time $1583 per credit hour. *Required fees:* $167 per credit hour. Tuition and fees vary according to course load and program. *Financial support:* In 2016–17, 39 students received support. Fellowships with full tuition reimbursements available, research assistantships with full tuition reimbursements available, teaching assistantships with full tuition reimbursements available, Federal Work-Study, institutionally sponsored loans, scholarships/grants, and unspecified assistantships available. *Unit head:* Dr. James D. Nogalski, Graduate Program Director, 254-710-1592, Fax: 254-710-3740, E-mail: james_nogalski@baylor.edu. *Application contact:* Coco DiMauro, Academic and Student Support Associate, 254-710-3742, Fax: 254-710-3740, E-mail: coco_dimauro@baylor.edu. Website: http://www.baylor.edu/religion/

**Bethany Theological Seminary,** Graduate and Professional Programs, Richmond, IN 47374-4019. Offers biblical studies (MA Th); ministry studies (M Div); peace studies (M Div, MA Th); theological studies (MA Th, CATS); youth ministry (M Div). *Accreditation:* ACIPE; ATS. *Program availability:* Part-time, online learning. *Degree requirements:* For master's, thesis (for some programs). *Entrance requirements:* For master's, letters of reference. Additional exam requirements/recommendations for international students: Required—TOEFL (minimum score 550 paper-based).

**Bethel Seminary,** Graduate and Professional Programs, St. Paul, MN 55112-6998. Offers Anglican studies (Certificate); children's and family ministry (MA); Christian studies (Certificate); Christian thought (MA); church planting (Certificate); Greek and Hebrew language (M Div); Greek language (M Div); Hebrew language (M Div); marriage and family therapy (MA, Certificate); mental health counseling (MA); ministry (MA, D Min); ministry practice (Certificate); theological studies (MA, Certificate); transformational leadership (MA); young life youth ministry (Certificate). *Accreditation:* ACIPE. *Program availability:* Part-time, evening/weekend, blended/hybrid learning. *Faculty:* 14 full-time (4 women), 37 part-time/adjunct (17 women). *Students:* 369 full-time (165 women), 147 part-time (43 women); includes 138 minority (48 Black or African American, non-Hispanic/Latino; 45 Asian, non-Hispanic/Latino; 28 Hispanic/Latino; 2 Native Hawaiian or other Pacific Islander, non-Hispanic/Latino; 15 Two or more races, non-Hispanic/Latino), 15 international. 322 applicants, 75% accepted, 174 enrolled. In 2016, 168 master's, 24 doctorates, 6 other advanced degrees awarded. *Degree requirements:* For master's, variable foreign language requirement, thesis (for some programs); for doctorate, thesis/dissertation. *Entrance requirements:* For master's, letters of reference, transcripts, personal statement; for doctorate, M Div, letters of reference, organizational support; for Certificate, letters of reference, family essay, personal statement, and family of origin paper (for marriage and family therapy). Additional exam requirements/recommendations for international students: Required—TOEFL (minimum score 550 paper-based; 87 iBT). *Application deadline:* For fall admission, 8/1 priority date for domestic students, 8/1 for international students; for winter admission, 12/1 priority date for domestic students; for spring admission, 1/1 priority date for domestic students. Applications are processed on a rolling basis. Application fee: $0. Electronic applications accepted. *Expenses:* Contact institution. *Financial support:* In 2016–17, 404 students received support. Teaching assistantships, career-related internships or fieldwork, Federal Work-Study, and scholarships/grants available. Financial award applicants required to submit FAFSA. *Faculty research:* Nature of theology, ethics, Biblical commentaries, nature of God, science and theology. *Unit head:* Dr. David Clark, Vice-President and Dean, 651-638-6659, E-mail: d-clark@bethel.edu. *Application contact:* Jen Niska, Director of Admissions, 651-638-6288, Fax: 651-638-6002, E-mail: seminary-admissions@bethel.edu.
Website: https://www.bethel.edu/seminary

**Bethesda University,** Graduate and Professional Programs, Anaheim, CA 92801. Offers biblical studies (MA); music (MA); theology (M Div). *Entrance requirements:* For master's, interview. Additional exam requirements/recommendations for international students: Recommended—TOEFL.

**Beulah Heights University,** Graduate School, Atlanta, GA 30316. Offers biblical studies (MA); leadership studies (MA). *Entrance requirements:* Additional exam requirements/recommendations for international students: Required—TOEFL (minimum score 500 paper-based). Electronic applications accepted.

**Biola University,** School of Arts and Sciences, La Mirada, CA 90639-0001. Offers Christian apologetics (MA, Certificate); science and religion (MA); speech language pathology (MA). *Program availability:* Part-time, evening/weekend, online learning. *Entrance requirements:* For master's, minimum GPA of 3.0, bachelor's degree from accredited college or university (in science-related field for science and religion program). Additional exam requirements/recommendations for international students: Required—TOEFL (minimum score 600 paper-based; 100 iBT). Electronic applications accepted. *Faculty research:* Apologetics, science and religion, intelligent design.

**Biola University,** Talbot School of Theology, La Mirada, CA 90639-0001. Offers adult/family ministry (MACE); Bible exposition (MA, Th M); Biblical and theological studies (Certificate); biblical and theological studies/diversified (MA); children's ministry (MACE); Christian education (M Div); cross-cultural education ministry (MACE); educational studies (Ed D, PhD); evangelism and discipleship (M Div); general Christian education (MACE); Messianic Jewish studies (M Div, Certificate); missions and intercultural studies (M Div); New Testament (MA, Th M); Old Testament (MA); Old Testament and Semitics (Th M); pastoral and general ministry (M Div); pastoral care and counseling (M Div, MACML); philosophy (MA); preaching and pastoral ministry (MACML); spiritual formation (M Div, Certificate); spiritual formation and soul care (MA); sports ministry (MACML); theology (MA, Th M, D Min, Certificate); youth ministry (MACE). *Accreditation:* ATS. *Program availability:* Part-time, evening/weekend. *Entrance requirements:* For master's, bachelor's degree from accredited college or university; minimum GPA of 2.6 (for M Div), 3.0 (for MA); for doctorate, M Div or MA. Additional exam requirements/recommendations for international students: Required—TOEFL (minimum score 600 paper-based; 88 iBT). Electronic applications accepted. *Faculty research:* New Testament, Old Testament, spiritual formation, Christian education, theological studies, Christian ministry, preaching and pastoral ministry, language and literature, bible exposition, Christian leadership.

**Bob Jones University,** Graduate Programs, Greenville, SC 29614. Offers accountancy (MS); Bible (MA); Bible translation (MA); Biblical studies (Certificate); broadcast management (MS); business administration (MBA); church history (MA, PhD); church ministries (MA); church music (MM); cinema and video production (MA); counseling (MS); curriculum and instruction (Ed D); divinity (M Div); dramatic production (MA); educational leadership (MS, Ed D, Ed S); elementary education (M Ed, MAT); English (M Ed, MA, MAT); fine arts (MA); graphic design (MA); history (M Ed, MA); illustration (MA); interpretative speech (MA); mathematics (M Ed, MAT); medical missions (Certificate); ministry (MM, D Min); multi-categorical special education (M Ed, MAT); music (M Ed); New Testament interpretation (PhD); Old Testament interpretation (PhD); orchestral instrument performance (MM); organ performance (MM); pastoral studies (MA); personnel services (MS, Ed S); piano pedagogy (MM); piano performance (MM); platform arts (MA); radio and television broadcasting (MS); rhetoric and public address (MA); secondary education (M Ed); studio art (MA); teaching Bible (MA); theology (MA, PhD); voice performance (MM); youth ministries (MA); M Div/MM.

**Boston University,** Graduate School of Arts and Sciences, Graduate Division of Religious Studies, Boston, MA 02215. Offers MA, PhD. *Students:* 52 full-time (24 women), 6 part-time (1 woman); includes 11 minority (3 Black or African American, non-Hispanic/Latino; 4 Asian, non-Hispanic/Latino; 3 Hispanic/Latino; 1 Two or more races, non-Hispanic/Latino), 6 international. Average age 32. 78 applicants, 18% accepted, 8 enrolled. In 2016, 5 master's, 10 doctorates awarded. Terminal master's awarded for partial completion of doctoral program. *Degree requirements:* For master's, one foreign language, comprehensive exam, thesis; for doctorate, 2 foreign languages, comprehensive exam, thesis/dissertation. *Entrance requirements:* For master's and doctorate, GRE General Test, 3 letters of recommendation, transcripts, personal statement, academic writing sample. Additional exam requirements/recommendations for international students: Required—TOEFL (minimum score 550 paper-based; 84 iBT). *Application deadline:* For fall admission, 1/15 for domestic and international students. Application fee: $95. Electronic applications accepted. *Financial support:* In 2016–17, 52 students received support, including 22 fellowships with full tuition reimbursements available (averaging $21,500 per year), 3 research assistantships with full tuition reimbursements available (averaging $21,500 per year), 9 teaching assistantships with full tuition reimbursements available (averaging $21,500 per year); career-related internships or fieldwork, Federal Work-Study, scholarships/grants, health care benefits, and unspecified assistantships also available. Financial award application deadline: 1/15. *Unit head:* Adam Seligman, Director, 617-358-0262, Fax: 617-358-3087, E-mail: seligman@bu.edu. *Application contact:* Karen Nardella, Department Administrator, 617-353-2636, Fax: 617-358-3087, E-mail: kcn@bu.edu.
Website: http://www.bu.edu/gdrs/

**Boston University,** School of Theology, Boston, MA 02118. Offers chaplaincy (M Div); choral conducting (MSM); church and the arts (M Div); constructive theology and ethics (PhD), including constructive theology, theological ethics; ecological theology and ethics (MTS); global and community engagement (M Div); history and hermeneutics (PhD), including Biblical studies, church history, liturgical studies, mission studies; organ (MSM); pastoral ministry (M Div); practical theology (PhD), including church and society, congregation and community, evangelism and missiology, homiletics, leadership and administration, pastoral theology and psychology, religious education, spirituality studies, worship; religion and conflict transformation (MTS); religion and science (MTS); religion and the academy (M Div); spirituality studies (MTS); theology (MTS, STM); transcultural studies (MTS); transformational leadership (D Min); M Div/MSM; M Div/MSW; MTS/MSW. PhD in history and hermeneutics: mission studies offered in collaboration with Gordon-Conwell Theological Seminary. *Accreditation:* ACIPE; ATS. *Program availability:* Part-time, blended/hybrid learning. *Faculty:* 34 full-time (14 women), 7 part-time/adjunct (3 women). *Students:* 260 full-time (131 women), 69 part-time (30 women); includes 69 minority (36 Black or African American, non-Hispanic/Latino; 10 Asian, non-Hispanic/Latino; 16 Hispanic/Latino; 7 Two or more races, non-Hispanic/Latino), 53 international. Average age 35. 234 applicants, 71% accepted, 106 enrolled. In 2016, 78 master's, 9 doctorates awarded. *Degree requirements:* For master's, comprehensive exam (for some programs), thesis optional, contextual education; for doctorate, 2 foreign languages, comprehensive exam, thesis/dissertation. *Entrance requirements:* For master's, minimum GPA of 3.0; for doctorate, GRE General Test, minimum GPA of 3.3. Additional exam requirements/recommendations for international students: Required—TOEFL (minimum score 570 paper-based; 89 iBT). *Application deadline:* For fall admission, 1/15 priority date for domestic and international students; for spring admission, 10/15 priority date for domestic and international students. Applications are processed on a rolling basis. Application fee: $95. Electronic applications accepted. *Expenses:* $19,500 per year tuition; $156 per semester student service fee; $54 per semester community service fee; $199 per semester health and wellness fee. *Financial support:* In 2016–17, 252 students received support, including 78 fellowships with full tuition reimbursements available (averaging $4,537 per year), 32 research assistantships (averaging $6,000 per year), 32 teaching assistantships with full and partial tuition reimbursements available (averaging $20,000 per year); career-related internships or fieldwork, Federal Work-Study, institutionally sponsored loans, scholarships/grants, traineeships, health care benefits, tuition waivers (full and partial), and unspecified assistantships also available. Support available to part-time students. Financial award application deadline: 7/15; financial award applicants required to submit FAFSA. *Faculty research:* Practical theology, Biblical studies, theology and ethical, history of Christianity. *Total annual research expenditures:* $2.5 million. *Unit head:* Rev. Dr. Mary Elizabeth Moore, Dean, 617-353-3050, Fax: 617-353-3061, E-mail: memoore@bu.edu. *Application contact:* Rev. Anastasia Kidd, Director of Admissions and College Relations, 617-353-3036, Fax: 617-358-0140, E-mail: sthadmis@bu.edu. Website: http://www.bu.edu/sth

**Briercrest Seminary,** Graduate Programs, Program in Christian Ministries, Caronport, SK S0H 0S0, Canada. Offers leadership (MA); marriage and family counseling (MA); missions (MA); pastoral counseling (MA); worship (MA); youth and family ministry (MA). *Program availability:* Part-time. *Degree requirements:* For master's, comprehensive exam, thesis optional. *Entrance requirements:* Additional exam requirements/recommendations for international students: Required—TOEFL (minimum score 550 paper-based).

**Briercrest Seminary,** Graduate Programs, Program in Theology, Caronport, SK S0H 0S0, Canada. Offers Biblical studies (M Div); leadership and management (M Div); New Testament (MATS); Old Testament (MATS); pastoral counseling (M Div); pastoral ministry (M Div); theological studies (M Div); theology (MATS); worship (M Div); youth and family ministry (M Div). *Accreditation:* ATS. *Program availability:* Part-time. *Degree requirements:* For master's, comprehensive exam, thesis optional. *Entrance requirements:* Additional exam requirements/recommendations for international students: Required—TOEFL (minimum score 550 paper-based).

**Brown University,** Graduate School, Department of Religious Studies, Providence, RI 02912. Offers Asian religious traditions (PhD); religion and critical thought (PhD); religions of the ancient Mediterranean (PhD). *Degree requirements:* For doctorate, 2 foreign languages, thesis/dissertation. *Entrance requirements:* For doctorate, GRE General Test.

**Bryn Athyn College of the New Church,** Academy of the New Church Theological School, Bryn Athyn, PA 19009-0717. Offers divinity (M Div); religious studies (MA). *Program availability:* Part-time, online learning. *Degree requirements:* For master's, variable foreign language requirement, thesis. *Entrance requirements:* Additional exam requirements/recommendations for international students: Required—TOEFL.

**Cairn University,** School of Divinity, Langhorne, PA 19047-2990. Offers divinity (M Div); religion (MA); theology (Th M). *Program availability:* Part-time, evening/weekend, 100% online, blended/hybrid learning. *Faculty:* 6 full-time (0 women), 3 part-time/adjunct (0 women). *Students:* 24 full-time (2 women), 54 part-time (13 women); includes 29 minority (19 Black or African American, non-Hispanic/Latino; 4 Asian, non-Hispanic/Latino; 5 Hispanic/Latino; 1 Two or more races, non-Hispanic/Latino), 1 international. Average age 37. 29 applicants, 97% accepted, 26 enrolled. In 2016, 31 master's awarded. *Entrance requirements:* Additional exam requirements/recommendations for international students: Required—TOEFL (minimum score 550 paper-based). *Application deadline:* Applications are processed on a rolling basis. Application fee: $25. Electronic applications accepted. Application fee is waived when completed online. *Expenses:* $515 per semester credit. *Financial support:* Scholarships/grants available. Support available to part-time students. Financial award applicants required to submit FAFSA. *Unit head:* Dr. Jonathan L. Master, Dean, 215-702-4358, Fax: 215-702-4359, E-mail: divinity@cairn.edu. *Application contact:* Abigail Simon, Assistant Director, Graduate Admissions, 800-572-2472, Fax: 215-702-4248, E-mail: asimon@cairn.edu. Website: http://www.cairn.edu/academics/divinity

**California Institute of Integral Studies,** School of Consciousness and Transformation, San Francisco, CA 94103. Offers anthropology and social change (MA, PhD); Asian philosophies and cultures (MA); creative inquiry/interdisciplinary arts (MFA); East-West psychology (MA, PhD); integral and transpersonal psychology (PhD); philosophy and religion (PhD), including ecology, spirituality, and religion, philosophy, cosmology, and consciousness, women's spirituality; theater and performance making (MFA); transformative leadership (MA); transformative studies (PhD); women, gender, spirituality and social justice (MA); writing and consciousness (MFA). *Program availability:* Part-time, evening/weekend, 100% online, blended/hybrid learning. *Students:* 390 full-time (256 women), 121 part-time (84 women); includes 135 minority (39 Black or African American, non-Hispanic/Latino; 2 American Indian or Alaska Native, non-Hispanic/Latino; 22 Asian, non-Hispanic/Latino; 40 Hispanic/Latino; 2 Native Hawaiian or other Pacific Islander, non-Hispanic/Latino; 30 Two or more races, non-Hispanic/Latino), 51 international. Average age 38. 195 applicants, 92% accepted, 124 enrolled. In 2016, 35 master's, 41 doctorates awarded. Terminal master's awarded for partial completion of doctoral program. *Degree requirements:* For master's, thesis optional; for doctorate, comprehensive exam, thesis/dissertation, 1 foreign language (for

Asian philosophies and cultures). *Entrance requirements:* For master's, minimum GPA of 3.0, letters of recommendation, writing sample; for doctorate, master's degree, minimum GPA of 3.0, letters of recommendation, writing sample. Additional exam requirements/recommendations for international students: Required—TOEFL. *Application deadline:* For fall admission, 2/1 priority date for domestic and international students; for spring admission, 10/15 priority date for domestic and international students. Applications are processed on a rolling basis. Application fee: $65. Electronic applications accepted. *Expenses:* Tuition: Full-time $19,728; part-time $1098 per semester hour. *Required fees:* $320; $320 per semester hour. *Financial support:* Research assistantships, teaching assistantships, career-related internships or fieldwork, Federal Work-Study, and scholarships/grants available. Support available to part-time students. Financial award application deadline: 4/15; financial award applicants required to submit FAFSA. *Faculty research:* Ecology and sustainability, philosophy and religion, East-West psychology, integrative health, social and cultural anthropology, transformative leadership. *Application contact:* Ellen Durst, Director of Admissions, 415-575-6100, Fax: 415-575-1268, E-mail: admissions@ciis.edu. Website: http://www.ciis.edu/

**California State University, Long Beach,** Graduate Studies, College of Liberal Arts, Department of Religious Studies, Long Beach, CA 90840. Offers MA. *Program availability:* Part-time, evening/weekend. *Entrance requirements:* Additional exam requirements/recommendations for international students: Required—TOEFL. *Application deadline:* For fall admission, 3/15 for domestic students, 7/1 for international students; for spring admission, 12/1 for international students. Applications are processed on a rolling basis. Application fee: $55. Electronic applications accepted. *Financial support:* Application deadline: 3/2; applicants required to submit FAFSA. *Unit head:* David Tabb Stewert, Chair, 562-985-5341, Fax: 562-985-5540, E-mail: religious-studies@csulb.edu. *Application contact:* Dr. Carlos R. Piar, Graduate Advisor, 562-985-8727, Fax: 562-985-5540, E-mail: crpiar@csulb.edu.

**Calvin Theological Seminary,** Graduate and Professional Programs, Grand Rapids, MI 49546-4387. Offers Bible and theology (MA); divinity (M Div), including ancient near eastern languages and literature, contextual ministry, evangelism and teaching, history of Christianity, new church development, New Testament, Old Testament, pastoral care and leadership, preaching and worship, theological studies, youth and family ministries; educational ministry (MA); historical theology (PhD); missions and evangelism (MA); pastoral care (MA); philosophical and moral theology (PhD); systematic theology (PhD); theological studies (MTS); theology (Th M); worship (MA); youth and family ministries (MA). *Accreditation:* ACIPE; ATS. *Program availability:* Part-time. *Degree requirements:* For master's, variable foreign language requirement, thesis (for some programs); for doctorate, 4 foreign languages, comprehensive exam, thesis/dissertation. *Entrance requirements:* For doctorate, GRE General Test, Hebrew, Greek, and a modern foreign language. Additional exam requirements/recommendations for international students: Required—TOEFL (minimum score 550 paper-based), TWE (minimum score 4). Electronic applications accepted. *Faculty research:* Recent Trinity theory, Christian anthropology, Proverbs, reformed confessions, Paul's view of law.

**Canadian Southern Baptist Seminary,** Graduate Programs, Cochrane, AB T4C 2G1, Canada. Offers Biblical studies (MBS); Christian ministry (MCMin); Christian studies (MCS); ministry (M Div). *Accreditation:* ATS. *Program availability:* Part-time, 100% online, blended/hybrid learning. *Faculty:* 3 full-time (0 women), 8 part-time/adjunct (1 woman). *Students:* 24 full-time (9 women), 18 part-time (2 women); includes 4 minority (1 Black or African American, non-Hispanic/Latino; 3 Asian, non-Hispanic/Latino), 11 international. Average age 29. 17 applicants, 76% accepted, 11 enrolled. In 2016, 10 master's awarded. *Entrance requirements:* Additional exam requirements/recommendations for international students: Required—TOEFL (minimum score 560 paper-based; 83 iBT); Recommended—IELTS. *Application deadline:* For fall admission, 7/1 priority date for domestic students, 3/1 priority date for international students; for winter admission, 11/15 priority date for domestic students. Applications are processed on a rolling basis. Application fee: $50 ($150 for international students). *Expenses:* Tuition: Full-time $6900 Canadian dollars; part-time $345 Canadian dollars per credit hour. *Required fees:* $20 Canadian dollars per credit hour. $35 Canadian dollars per semester. Tuition and fees vary according to course load. *Financial support:* Scholarships/grants available. Financial award application deadline: 7/1. *Unit head:* Dr. Steve Booth, Academic Dean, 403-932-6622 Ext. 232, E-mail: steve.booth@csbs.ca. *Application contact:* Kathleen McNaughton, Registrar, 403-932-6622 Ext. 221, E-mail: kathleen.mcnaughton@csbs.ca.

**Cardinal Stritch University,** College of Arts and Sciences, Department of Religious Studies, Milwaukee, WI 53217-3985. Offers ministry (MA); religious studies (MA). *Program availability:* Part-time, evening/weekend. *Students:* 8 part-time (4 women); includes 2 minority (both Black or African American, non-Hispanic/Latino). Average age 43. 10 applicants, 100% accepted, 1 enrolled. In 2016, 8 master's awarded. *Degree requirements:* For master's, comprehensive exam, thesis, research project. *Entrance requirements:* For master's, interview, minimum GPA of 2.75. Additional exam requirements/recommendations for international students: Required—TOEFL (minimum score 79 iBT), IELTS (minimum score 6.5). *Application deadline:* For fall admission, 7/15 priority date for domestic students; for spring admission, 12/15 priority date for domestic students. Applications are processed on a rolling basis. Electronic applications accepted. *Expenses:* Tuition: Full-time $11,890; part-time $765 per credit hour. Tuition and fees vary according to class time, course load, degree level, program and student's religious affiliation. *Financial support:* Research assistantships with partial tuition reimbursements, career-related internships or fieldwork, Federal Work-Study, and scholarships/grants available. Financial award applicants required to submit FAFSA. *Unit head:* Dr. Michelle Gilgannon, Chair, 414-410-4047, E-mail: mlgilgannon@stritch.edu. *Application contact:* Graduate Admissions, 800-347-8822 Ext. 4042, E-mail: admissions@stritch.edu.

**The Catholic University of America,** School of Arts and Sciences, Program in Early Christian Studies, Washington, DC 20064. Offers MA, PhD. *Program availability:* Part-time. *Faculty:* 1 full-time (0 women). *Students:* 1 full-time (0 women), 2 part-time (both women). Average age 31. 6 applicants, 17% accepted. In 2016, 1 master's, 2 doctorates awarded. *Degree requirements:* For master's, one foreign language, comprehensive exam; for doctorate, 2 foreign languages, comprehensive exam, thesis/dissertation. *Entrance requirements:* For master's and doctorate, GRE General Test, statement of purpose, official copies of academic transcripts, three letters of recommendation, writing sample. Additional exam requirements/recommendations for international students: Required—TOEFL (minimum score 550 paper-based; 80 iBT). *Application deadline:* For fall admission, 7/15 priority date for domestic students, 7/1 for international students; for spring admission, 11/15 priority date for domestic students, 11/1 for international students. Applications are processed on a rolling basis. Application fee: $55. Electronic applications accepted. *Expenses:* $42,850 per year; $1,170 per credit; $200 per semester part-time fees. *Financial support:* Fellowships, research assistantships, teaching assistantships, Federal Work-Study, scholarships/grants, tuition waivers (full and partial), and unspecified assistantships available. Financial award application deadline: 2/1; financial award applicants required to submit FAFSA. *Faculty research:* Asceticism and Christian culture, languages and literatures of the Christian Near East, early Christian spirituality, Greek and Latin patristics, late ancient philosophy. *Unit head:*

# Religion

Dr. William E. Klingshirn, Director, 202-319-5795, Fax: 202-319-6609, E-mail: klingshirn@cua.edu. *Application contact:* Director of Graduate Admissions, 202-319-5057, Fax: 202-319-6533, E-mail: cua-admissions@cua.edu. Website: http://earlychristianity.cua.edu/

**The Catholic University of America,** School of Theology and Religious Studies, Washington, DC 20064. Offers M Cat, M Div, M Div, MA, D Min, PhD, STD, Certificate, STB, STL, MSLS/MA, STB/M Div. MSLA/MA offered in conjunction with Department of Library and Information Science. *Program availability:* Part-time. *Faculty:* 40 full-time (2 women), 8 part-time/adjunct (2 women). *Students:* 156 full-time (11 women), 193 part-time (51 women); includes 61 minority (9 Black or African American, non-Hispanic/Latino; 1 American Indian or Alaska Native, non-Hispanic/Latino; 13 Asian, non-Hispanic/Latino; 24 Hispanic/Latino; 14 Two or more races, non-Hispanic/Latino), 51 international. Average age 36. 168 applicants, 65% accepted, 58 enrolled. In 2016, 96 master's, 20 doctorates awarded. Terminal master's awarded for partial completion of doctoral program. *Degree requirements:* For master's, variable foreign language requirement, comprehensive exam (for some programs), thesis (for some programs); for doctorate, variable foreign language requirement, comprehensive exam, thesis/dissertation. *Entrance requirements:* For master's and doctorate, GRE General Test, statement of purpose, official copies of academic transcripts, three letters of recommendation. Additional exam requirements/recommendations for international students: Required—TOEFL (minimum score 550 paper-based; 80 iBT). *Application deadline:* For fall admission, 7/15 priority date for domestic students, 7/1 for international students; for spring admission, 11/15 priority date for domestic students, 11/1 for international students. Applications are processed on a rolling basis. Application fee: $55. Electronic applications accepted. *Expenses:* $42,850 per year; $1,170 per credit; $200 per semester part-time fees. *Financial support:* Fellowships, research assistantships, teaching assistantships, Federal Work-Study, scholarships/grants, tuition waivers (full and partial), and unspecified assistantships available. Financial award application deadline: 2/1; financial award applicants required to submit FAFSA. *Faculty research:* Historical and systematic theology, religious education and Catechetics, moral theology and ethics, Biblical studies, liturgical studies and sacramental theology, religion and culture. *Total annual research expenditures:* $194,166. *Unit head:* Very Rev. Mark Morozowich, Dean, 202-319-5684, Fax: 202-319-4967, E-mail: morozowich@cua.edu. *Application contact:* Director of Graduate Admissions, 202-319-5057, Fax: 202-319-6533, E-mail: cua-admissions@cua.edu. Website: http://trs.cua.edu/

**Charlotte Christian College and Theological Seminary,** Graduate Program, Charlotte, NC 28205. Offers urban Christian ministry (MA), including church planting, multi-cultural studies, sacred music, youth ministry. *Program availability:* Part-time, evening/weekend. *Degree requirements:* For master's, thesis. *Entrance requirements:* For master's, MAT, writing sample/essay. Additional exam requirements/recommendations for international students: Required—TOEFL, IELTS. Electronic applications accepted. *Expenses:* Contact institution.

**Chicago Theological Seminary,** Graduate and Professional Programs, Chicago, IL 60637-1507. Offers Bible, culture and hermeneutics (PhD); preaching (D Min); religion and health (D Min); religious studies (MA); spirituality and spiritual direction (D Min); theology (M Div); theology, ethics and the human sciences (PhD); M Div/MSW. *Accreditation:* ACIPE; ATS. *Program availability:* Part-time. *Degree requirements:* For master's, thesis; for doctorate, 2 foreign languages, comprehensive exam, thesis/dissertation. *Entrance requirements:* For doctorate, GRE General Test. Additional exam requirements/recommendations for international students: Required—TOEFL. *Faculty research:* Bible, culture and hermeneutics, theology, gender and sexuality, black faith and life, spirituality and psychology, practical theology.

**Christian Brothers University,** School of Arts, Memphis, TN 38104-5581. Offers Catholic studies (MACS); educational leadership (MSEL); teacher-leadership (M Ed); teaching (MAT). *Program availability:* Part-time, evening/weekend. *Entrance requirements:* For master's, GRE, GMAT, PRAXIS II. *Expenses:* Contact institution.

**Christian Theological Seminary,** Graduate and Professional Programs, Indianapolis, IN 46208-3301. Offers educational and arts ministries (MA); marriage and family therapy (MA); pastoral care and counseling (D Min); psychotherapy and faith (MA); theological studies (MTS); theology (M Div). *Accreditation:* AAMFT/COAMFTE (one or more programs are accredited); ACIPE; ATS. *Program availability:* Part-time. Terminal master's awarded for partial completion of doctoral program. *Degree requirements:* For master's, comprehensive exam (for some programs), thesis (for some programs), missionary and cross-cultural experience (for M Div); for doctorate, comprehensive exam, thesis/dissertation. *Entrance requirements:* For doctorate, M Div. Additional exam requirements/recommendations for international students: Recommended—TOEFL. Electronic applications accepted. *Faculty research:* Faith formation, peer learning post graduation.

**Cincinnati Christian University,** Graduate School, Cincinnati, OH 45204-3200. Offers biblical studies (MA); church history (MA); counseling (MAC); divinity (M Div); ministry (M Min); practical ministries (MA); theological studies (MA). *Program availability:* Part-time. *Degree requirements:* For master's, variable foreign language requirement, thesis (for some programs), oral exam (for M Div). *Entrance requirements:* Additional exam requirements/recommendations for international students: Required—TOEFL. Electronic applications accepted.

**Claremont Graduate University,** Graduate Programs, School of Arts and Humanities, Department of Religion, Claremont, CA 91711-6160. Offers Hebrew Bible (MA, PhD); history of Christianity and religions of North America (MA, PhD); New Testament (MA, PhD); philosophy of religion and theology (MA, PhD); theology, ethics and culture (MA, PhD); women's studies in religion (MA, PhD); MA/PhD; MBA/PhD. *Program availability:* Part-time. *Faculty:* 7 full-time (4 women), 2 part-time/adjunct (0 women). *Students:* 121 full-time (46 women), 13 part-time (6 women); includes 28 minority (10 Black or African American, non-Hispanic/Latino; 1 American Indian or Alaska Native, non-Hispanic/Latino; 6 Asian, non-Hispanic/Latino; 7 Hispanic/Latino; 1 Native Hawaiian or other Pacific Islander, non-Hispanic/Latino; 3 Two or more races, non-Hispanic/Latino), 19 international. Average age 39. In 2016, 11 master's, 21 doctorates awarded. Terminal master's awarded for partial completion of doctoral program. *Entrance requirements:* For master's and doctorate, GRE General Test. Additional exam requirements/recommendations for international students: Required—TOEFL (minimum score 75 iBT). *Application deadline:* For fall admission, 2/1 priority date for domestic and international students. Applications are processed on a rolling basis. Application fee: $80. Electronic applications accepted. *Expenses:* Tuition: Full-time $44,328; part-time $1847 per unit. *Required fees:* $600; $300 per semester. Tuition and fees vary according to course load and program. *Financial support:* Fellowships, research assistantships, teaching assistantships, Federal Work-Study, institutionally sponsored loans, and scholarships/grants available. Support available to part-time students. Financial award application deadline: 2/15; financial award applicants required to submit FAFSA. *Unit head:* Ruqayya Kahn, Chair, 909-607-0488, E-mail: ruqayya.kahn@cgu.edu. *Application contact:* Amy Sandefur, Assistant Director of Admissions, 909-607-9101, E-mail: amy.sandefur@cgu.edu. Website: https://www.cgu.edu/departments/religion/

**Claremont Lincoln University,** Graduate Programs, Claremont, CA 91711. Offers ethical leadership (MA); interfaith action (MA); social impact (MA).

**Claremont School of Theology,** Graduate and Professional Programs, Program in Religion, Claremont, CA 91711-3199. Offers practical theology (PhD), including religious education and formation, spiritual care and counseling; religion (MA, PhD), including comparative theology and philosophy (PhD), Hebrew Bible and Jewish studies (PhD), New Testament and Christian origins (PhD), process studies (PhD), religion, ethics, and society (PhD). *Accreditation:* ACIPE; ATS. Terminal master's awarded for partial completion of doctoral program. *Degree requirements:* For master's, thesis; for doctorate, 2 foreign languages, thesis/dissertation. *Entrance requirements:* For doctorate, GRE General Test. Additional exam requirements/recommendations for international students: Required—TOEFL. *Application deadline:* For fall admission, 1/15 for domestic and international students. Application fee: $50. Electronic applications accepted. *Expenses:* Tuition: Full-time $21,120. Tuition and fees vary according to course level, course load and degree level. *Financial support:* Research assistantships, teaching assistantships, career-related internships or fieldwork, Federal Work-Study, institutionally sponsored loans, scholarships/grants, and tuition waivers (full and partial) available. Support available to part-time students. Financial award application deadline: 4/1; financial award applicants required to submit FAFSA. *Unit head:* Sheryl A. Kujawa-Holbrook, Vice President for Academic Affairs/Dean, 909-447-2520, Fax: 909-447-6274, E-mail: skujawaholbrook@cst.edu. *Application contact:* Director of Admissions, 866-274-6500, Fax: 909-447-6389, E-mail: admission@cst.edu. Website: https://cst.edu/academics/m-a/

**Clarks Summit University,** Baptist Bible Seminary, South Abington Township, PA 18411. Offers Biblical apologetics (MA); church education (M Div, M Min); church planting (M Div, M Min); global ministry (M Div, M Min); leadership in communication (D Min); leadership in counseling and spiritual development (D Min); leadership in global ministry (D Min); leadership in pastoral ministry (D Min); leadership in theological studies (D Min); military chaplaincy (M Div); ministry (PhD); organizational leadership (M Min); outreach pastor (M Div, M Min); pastoral counseling (M Div, M Min); pastoral leadership (M Div, M Min); theology (Th M); worship ministries leadership (M Div, M Min); youth pastor (M Div, M Min). *Program availability:* Part-time, evening/weekend, online learning. Terminal master's awarded for partial completion of doctoral program. *Degree requirements:* For master's, 2 foreign languages, thesis, oral exam (for M Div); for doctorate, 2 foreign languages, comprehensive exam (for some programs), thesis/dissertation, oral exam. *Entrance requirements:* For doctorate, Greek and Hebrew entrance exams (for PhD). Electronic applications accepted.

**Columbia University,** Graduate School of Arts and Sciences, New York, NY 10027. Offers African-American studies (MA); American studies (MA); anthropology (MA, PhD); art history and archaeology (MA, PhD); astronomy (PhD); biological sciences (PhD); biotechnology (MA); chemical physics (PhD); chemistry (PhD); classical studies (MA, PhD); classics (MA, PhD); climate and society (MA); conservation biology (MA); earth and environmental sciences (PhD); East Asia: regional studies (MA); East Asian languages and cultures (MA, PhD); ecology, evolution and environmental biology (MA), including conservation biology; ecology, evolution, and environmental biology (PhD), including ecology and evolutionary biology, evolutionary primatology; economics (MA, PhD); English and comparative literature (MA, PhD); French and Romance philology (MA, PhD); Germanic languages (MA, PhD); global French studies (MA); global thought (MA); Hispanic cultural studies (MA); history (PhD); history and literature (MA); human rights studies (MA); Islamic studies (MA); Italian (MA, PhD); Japanese pedagogy (MA); Jewish studies (MA); Latin America and the Caribbean: regional studies (MA); Latin American and Iberian cultures (PhD); mathematics (MA, PhD), including finance (MA); medieval and Renaissance studies (MA); Middle Eastern, South Asian, and African studies (MA, PhD); modern art: critical and curatorial studies (MA); modern European studies (MA); museum anthropology (MA); music (DMA, PhD); oral history (MA); philosophical foundations of physics (MA); philosophy (MA, PhD); physics (PhD); political science (MA, PhD); psychology (PhD); quantitative methods in the social sciences (MA); religion (MA, PhD); Russia, Eurasia and East Europe: regional studies (MA); Russian translation (MA); Slavic cultures (MA); Slavic languages (MA, PhD); sociology (MA, PhD); South Asian studies (MA, PhD); statistics (MA, PhD); theatre (PhD). Dual-degree programs require admission to both Graduate School of Arts and Sciences and another Columbia school. *Program availability:* Part-time. Terminal master's awarded for partial completion of doctoral program. *Degree requirements:* For master's, variable foreign language requirement, comprehensive exam (for some programs), thesis (for some programs); for doctorate, variable foreign language requirement, comprehensive exam (for some programs), thesis/dissertation. *Entrance requirements:* For master's and doctorate, GRE General Test, GRE Subject Test (for some programs). Additional exam requirements/recommendations for international students: Required—TOEFL, IELTS. Electronic applications accepted.

**Concordia University,** School of Graduate Studies, Faculty of Arts and Science, Department of Religion, MA Program in Religion, Montréal, QC H3G 1M8, Canada. Offers MA. *Degree requirements:* For master's, comprehensive exam, thesis optional.

**Concordia University,** School of Graduate Studies, Faculty of Arts and Science, Department of Religion, Program in Religion, Montréal, QC H3G 1M8, Canada. Offers PhD. Program offered jointly with Universityé du Quebec à Montréal. *Degree requirements:* For doctorate, one foreign language, comprehensive exam, thesis/dissertation.

**Concordia University Chicago,** College of Graduate and Innovative Programs, Program in Religion, River Forest, IL 60305-1499. Offers MA. *Program availability:* Part-time, evening/weekend. *Degree requirements:* For master's, comprehensive exam, thesis. *Entrance requirements:* For master's, minimum GPA 2.9. Additional exam requirements/recommendations for international students: Required—TOEFL (minimum score 550 paper-based). Electronic applications accepted. *Faculty research:* Dead Sea Scrolls, cultural construction of gender in early modern Europe, Luther, Luther's theology of the cross, gospels of Mark and John.

**Concordia University Irvine,** School of Theology, Irvine, CA 92612-3299. Offers Christian leadership (MA); research in theology (MA); theology and culture (MA). *Program availability:* Part-time, evening/weekend. *Degree requirements:* For master's, project/thesis or vicarage. *Entrance requirements:* For master's, official college transcript(s), statement of intent, 2 references, interview. Additional exam requirements/recommendations for international students: Required—TOEFL. Electronic applications accepted. *Expenses:* Contact institution.

**Concordia University of Edmonton,** Program in Biblical and Christian Studies, Edmonton, AB T5B 4E4, Canada. Offers MA.

**Cornell University,** Graduate School, Graduate Fields of Arts and Sciences, Field of Asian Literature, Religion and Culture, Ithaca, NY 14853. Offers Asian religions (MA, PhD); Chinese philosophy (PhD); classical Chinese literature (PhD); classical Japanese literature (PhD); East Asian literature and culture (PhD); Korean literature (PhD); modern Chinese literature (PhD); modern Japanese literature (PhD); South Asian literature and culture (PhD); Southeast Asian literature and culture (PhD). *Degree requirements:* For doctorate, comprehensive exam, thesis/dissertation. *Entrance requirements:* For doctorate, GRE General Test, academic writing sample, 3 letters of recommendation. Additional exam requirements/recommendations for international students: Required—TOEFL (minimum score 600 paper-based; 77 iBT). Electronic applications accepted.

**Dallas Baptist University,** Liberal Arts Program, Dallas, TX 75211-9299. Offers art (MLA); Christian studies (MLA); commercial art (MLA); East Asian studies (MLA); English (MLA); English as a second language (MLA); fine arts (MLA); history (MLA); missions (MLA); political science (MLA). *Program availability:* Part-time, evening/weekend, 100% online, blended/hybrid learning. *Application deadline:* Applications are processed on a rolling basis. *Application fee:* $25. Electronic applications accepted. Application fee is waived when completed online. *Expenses:* Tuition: Full-time $15,408; part-time $856 per credit hour. *Required fees:* $400 per semester. Tuition and fees vary according to course load and degree level. *Faculty research:* Milton and seventeenth-century Puritans, inter-Biblical years, nineteenth-century literature, Latin American and Texas history. *Unit head:* Jared Ingram, Director, 214-333-5584, E-mail: jaredi@dbu.edu. *Application contact:* Bobby Soto, Director of Admissions, 214-333-5242, E-mail: graduate@dbu.edu.
Website: http://www3.dbu.edu/graduate/mla.asp

**Dallas Theological Seminary,** Graduate Programs, Dallas, TX 75204-6499. Offers adult education (Th M); apologetics (Th M); Bible backgrounds (Th M); Bible translation (Th M); Biblical and theological studies (Certificate); biblical counseling (MA); biblical exegesis and linguistics (MA); biblical exposition (PhD); biblical studies (MA); Biblical theology (Th M); children's education (Th M); Christian education (MA, D Min); Christian leadership (MA); cross-cultural ministries (MA); educational administration (Th M); educational leadership (Th M); evangelism and discipleship (Th M); exposition of Biblical books (Th M); family life education (Th M); general studies (Th M); Hebrew and cognate studies (Th M); hermeneutics (Th M); historical theology (Th M); homiletics (Th M); intercultural ministries (Th M); Jesus studies (Th M); leadership studies (Th M); media and communication (MA); media arts (Th M); ministry (D Min); ministry with women (Th M); New Testament studies (Th M, PhD); Old Testament studies (Th M, PhD); parachurch ministries (Th M); pastoral care and counseling (Th M); pastoral theology and practice (Th M); philosophy (Th M); sacred theology (STM); spiritual formation (Th M); systematic theology (Th M); teaching in Christian institutions (Th M); theological studies (PhD); urban ministries (Th M); worship studies (Th M); youth education (Th M). *Program availability:* Part-time, online learning. *Degree requirements:* For master's, variable foreign language requirement, thesis (for some programs); for doctorate, 2 foreign languages, thesis/dissertation. *Entrance requirements:* For master's, GRE and MAT (if minimum undergraduate cumulative GPA is below 2.5 or undergraduate degree is unaccredited). Additional exam requirements/recommendations for international students: Required—TOEFL (minimum score 575 paper-based; 85 iBT), TWE. Electronic applications accepted.

**Delta State University,** Graduate Programs, College of Arts and Sciences, Program in Liberal Studies, Cleveland, MS 38733-0001. Offers evolving human voices (MALS); gender and diversity studies (MALS); globalization studies (MALS); Mississippi Delta studies (MALS); philosophy (MALS); religious studies (MALS). *Degree requirements:* For master's, oral and/or written comprehensive exam.

**Denver Seminary,** Graduate and Professional Programs, Littleton, CO 80120. Offers apologetics (Certificate); biblical studies (MA); Christian formation and soul care (MA, Certificate); Christian studies (MA, Certificate); church and parachurch leadership (D Min); counseling licensure (MA); counseling ministry (MA); intercultural ministry (Certificate); leadership (MA, Certificate); marriage and family counseling (D Min); pastoral ministry (D Min); philosophy of religion (MA); spiritual guidance (Certificate); theology (M Div, Certificate); worship (Certificate); youth and family ministry (MA). *Accreditation:* ACA; ACIPE; ATS (one or more programs are accredited). *Program availability:* Part-time, evening/weekend, online learning. *Degree requirements:* For master's, 2 foreign languages, thesis (for some programs); for doctorate, 2 foreign languages, thesis/dissertation. *Entrance requirements:* For doctorate, M Div, 3 years of ministry experience. Additional exam requirements/recommendations for international students: Required—TOEFL (minimum score 575 paper-based; 90 iBT). Electronic applications accepted.

**Dominican University of California,** School of Arts, Humanities and Social Sciences, Humanities Program, San Rafael, CA 94901-2298. Offers applied music (MA); art history (MA); creative writing (MA); gender studies (MA); history (MA); literature (MA); philosophy (MA); political theory (MA); religion (MA). *Program availability:* Part-time. *Degree requirements:* For master's, thesis or alternative. *Entrance requirements:* For master's, minimum GPA of 3.0, interview. Additional exam requirements/recommendations for international students: Required—TOEFL (minimum score 550 paper-based; 80 iBT), IELTS (minimum score 6.5). Electronic applications accepted. Application fee is waived when completed online. *Expenses:* Contact institution.

**Drew University,** Caspersen School of Graduate Studies, Madison, NJ 07940-1493. Offers conflict resolution and leadership (Certificate), including community leadership, moderation, peace building; history and culture (MA, PhD), including American history, book history, British history, European history, Holocaust and genocide (M Litt, MA, D Litt, PhD), intellectual history, Irish history, print culture, public history; K-12 education (MAT), including art, biology, chemistry, elementary education, English, French, Italian, math, secondary education, special education, teacher of students with disabilities; liberal studies (M Litt, D Litt), including history, Holocaust and genocide (M Litt, MA, D Litt, PhD), Irish/Irish-American studies, literature (M Litt, MMH, D Litt, DMH, CMH), religion, spirituality, teaching in the two-year college, writing; medical humanities (MMH, DMH, CMH), including arts, health, healthcare, literature (M Litt, MMH, D Litt, DMH, CMH), scientific research; poetry (MFA). *Program availability:* Part-time, evening/weekend. *Faculty:* 4 full-time (2 women), 31 part-time/adjunct (16 women). *Students:* 62 full-time (41 women), 199 part-time (130 women); includes 38 minority (17 Black or African American, non-Hispanic/Latino; 3 Asian, non-Hispanic/Latino; 17 Hispanic/Latino; 1 Two or more races, non-Hispanic/Latino), 3 international. Average age 27. 93 applicants, 81% accepted, 46 enrolled. In 2016, 39 master's, 27 doctorates, 26 other advanced degrees awarded. Terminal master's awarded for partial completion of doctoral program. *Degree requirements:* For master's and other advanced degree, thesis (for some programs); for doctorate, one foreign language, comprehensive exam (for some programs), thesis/dissertation. *Entrance requirements:* For master's, PRAXIS Core and Subject Area tests (for MAT), resume, transcripts, writing sample, personal statement, letters of recommendation; for doctorate, GRE (PhD in history and culture), resume, transcripts, writing sample, personal statement, letters of recommendation. Additional exam requirements/recommendations for international students: Required—TOEFL (minimum score 587 paper-based; 94 iBT), IELTS (minimum score 7), TWE (minimum score 4). *Application deadline:* For fall admission, 8/1 for domestic students, 6/1 for international students; for spring admission, 12/1 for domestic students, 10/1 for international students. Applications are processed on a rolling basis. Application fee: $35. Electronic applications accepted. Tuition and fees vary according to program. *Financial support:* Fellowships, research assistantships, teaching assistantships, career-related internships or fieldwork, Federal Work-Study, scholarships/grants, and unspecified assistantships available. Support available to part-time students. Financial award applicants required to submit FAFSA. *Application contact:* Leanne Horinko,

Director of Caspersen Admissions, 973-408-3280, E-mail: gradm@drew.edu. Website: http://www.drew.edu/caspersen

**Duke University,** Graduate School, Department of Religion, Durham, NC 27708. Offers MA, PhD, JD/MA. *Program availability:* Part-time. Terminal master's awarded for partial completion of doctoral program. *Degree requirements:* For master's, one foreign language, thesis or alternative; for doctorate, 2 foreign languages, thesis/dissertation. *Entrance requirements:* For master's and doctorate, GRE General Test. Additional exam requirements/recommendations for international students: Required—TOEFL (minimum score 577 paper-based; 90 iBT) or IELTS (minimum score 7). Electronic applications accepted.

**Earlham School of Religion,** Graduate Programs, Richmond, IN 47374-5360. Offers religion (MA); theology (M Div, M Min). *Accreditation:* ACIPE; ATS. *Program availability:* Part-time, online learning. *Faculty:* 8 full-time (2 women), 2 part-time/adjunct (1 woman). *Students:* 38 full-time (17 women), 18 part-time (14 women). *Degree requirements:* For master's, variable foreign language requirement, comprehensive exam (for some programs), thesis (for some programs), internship (M Div). *Entrance requirements:* For master's, 3 references, academic writing sample, official college transcripts. Additional exam requirements/recommendations for international students: Required—TOEFL (minimum score 550 paper-based; 82 iBT), IELTS (minimum score 7). *Application deadline:* For fall admission, 7/15 priority date for domestic students; for winter admission, 12/15 priority date for domestic students. Applications are processed on a rolling basis. Application fee: $35. Electronic applications accepted. *Expenses:* Tuition: Full-time $14,823; part-time $1647 per course. *Required fees:* $200 per semester. *Financial support:* Scholarships/grants and tuition waivers (full and partial) available. Financial award application deadline: 4/15; financial award applicants required to submit FAFSA. *Faculty research:* Digitizing Quaker texts, vital Quaker ministry, research in Quaker studies and other seminary areas. *Unit head:* Jay W. Marshall, Dean, 800-432-1377, Fax: 765-983-1688, E-mail: marshja@earlham.edu. *Application contact:* Matthew Hisrich, Director of Recruitment and Admissions, 765-983-1523, Fax: 765-983-1688, E-mail: hisrima@earlham.edu. Website: http://esr.earlham.edu/academic-programs

**Eastern Mennonite University,** Eastern Mennonite Seminary, Harrisonburg, VA 22802-2462. Offers church leadership (MA); divinity (M Div); ministry studies (Certificate); religion (MA); theological studies (Certificate). *Accreditation:* ATS. *Program availability:* Part-time. *Degree requirements:* For master's, thesis (for some programs), supervised field education (for M Div). *Entrance requirements:* For master's, minimum GPA of 2.5. Additional exam requirements/recommendations for international students: Required—TOEFL (minimum score 550 paper-based). *Expenses:* Contact institution. *Faculty research:* Spiritual direction and culture of call, leadership coaching: an approach to leadership in a culture of call, clarity of call in the probationary process for United Methodist clergy in Virginia, EMS women's experiences of culture of call efforts, practices of excellent and fruitful Mennonite pastoral ministry.

**East Texas Baptist University,** School of Christian Studies, Marshall, TX 75670-1498. Offers Christian ministry (MACM), including business leadership, spiritual guidance, sports and recreation ministry; religion (MA). *Program availability:* Part-time, evening/weekend. *Faculty:* 3 full-time (1 woman), 1 part-time/adjunct (0 women). *Students:* 5 full-time (2 women), 3 part-time (0 women); includes 1 minority (Black or African American, non-Hispanic/Latino). Average age 24. 8 applicants, 50% accepted, 4 enrolled. In 2016, 4 master's awarded. *Degree requirements:* For master's, thesis optional. *Entrance requirements:* Additional exam requirements/recommendations for international students: Recommended—TOEFL (minimum score 550 paper-based; 79 iBT). *Application deadline:* For fall admission, 8/17 for domestic students; for spring admission, 1/10 for domestic students; for summer admission, 5/2 for domestic students. Applications are processed on a rolling basis. Application fee: $50. Electronic applications accepted. *Expenses:* $735 per credit hour tuition; $150 per semester fees (6 or more hours enrolled); $75 per semester fees (1-5 hours enrolled). *Financial support:* In 2016–17, 4 students received support. Federal Work-Study, scholarships/grants, unspecified assistantships, and staff grants available. Financial award applicants required to submit FAFSA. *Unit head:* Dr. Warren Johnson, Director, 903-923-2182, Fax: 903-923-2077, E-mail: christianstudiesma@etbu.edu. *Application contact:* Den Murley, Director of Graduate Admissions, 903-923-2079, Fax: 903-934-8115, E-mail: dmurley@etbu.edu.
Website: https://www.etbu.edu/christian-studies/masters-degrees/

**Elms College,** Religious Studies Department, Chicopee, MA 01013-2839. Offers MAAT. *Program availability:* Part-time, evening/weekend. *Faculty:* 3 full-time (0 women), 3 part-time/adjunct (1 woman). *Students:* 3 part-time (2 women). Average age 59. In 2016, 3 master's awarded. *Degree requirements:* For master's, thesis. *Entrance requirements:* For master's, minimum GPA of 3.0. Additional exam requirements/recommendations for international students: Required—TOEFL. *Application deadline:* For fall admission, 7/1 priority date for domestic students; for spring admission, 11/1 priority date for domestic students. Applications are processed on a rolling basis. Application fee: $30. *Expenses:* Tuition: Full-time $13,392. *Required fees:* $200. *Financial support:* Tuition waivers (partial) available. Financial award applicants required to submit FAFSA. *Unit head:* Dr. Martin Pion, Director of Religious Studies, 413-265-3581, Fax: 413-594-3951, E-mail: pionm@elms.edu. *Application contact:* Dr. Elizabeth Teahan Hukowicz, Dean, School of Graduate and Professional Studies, 413-265-2360, Fax: 413-265-2459, E-mail: hukowicze@elms.edu.

**Emory University,** Laney Graduate School, Division of Religion, Atlanta, GA 30322-1100. Offers PhD. *Degree requirements:* For doctorate, 2 foreign languages, comprehensive exam, thesis/dissertation. *Entrance requirements:* For doctorate, GRE General Test, minimum GPA of 3.0. Additional exam requirements/recommendations for international students: Required—TOEFL. Electronic applications accepted. *Faculty research:* Systematic and historical theology, Biblical studies.

**Faith Baptist Bible College and Theological Seminary,** Graduate Program, Ankeny, IA 50023. Offers Biblical studies (MA); pastoral studies (M Div); pastoral training (MA); religion (MA); theological studies (MA). *Program availability:* Part-time. *Faculty:* 3 full-time (0 women), 4 part-time/adjunct (0 women). *Students:* 18 full-time (2 women), 30 part-time (5 women); includes 5 minority (1 Black or African American, non-Hispanic/Latino; 2 Asian, non-Hispanic/Latino; 1 Hispanic/Latino; 1 Two or more races, non-Hispanic/Latino). Average age 33. In 2016, 13 master's awarded. *Degree requirements:* For master's, thesis or alternative. *Entrance requirements:* Additional exam requirements/recommendations for international students: Required—TOEFL (minimum score 550 paper-based; 79 iBT), IELTS (minimum score 6.5). *Application deadline:* For fall admission, 8/1 priority date for domestic students, 8/1 for international students; for spring admission, 12/15 for domestic and international students. Applications are processed on a rolling basis. Application fee: $25. Electronic applications accepted. *Financial support:* Career-related internships or fieldwork and scholarships/grants available. Support available to part-time students. Financial award application deadline: 3/1; financial award applicants required to submit FAFSA. *Faculty research:* Baptist theology, American church history. *Unit head:* Rev. Jim Tillotson, President, 515-964-0601, E-mail: tillotsonj@faith.edu. *Application contact:* Jonathan Balasa, Seminary Admissions Representative, 888-FAITH4U, Fax: 515-964-1638, E-mail: seminaryrep@faith.edu.
Website: http://www.faith.edu/

## Religion

**Florida International University,** Steven J. Green School of International and Public Affairs, Department of Religious Studies, Miami, FL 33199. Offers MA, MA/PhD. *Program availability:* Part-time, evening/weekend. *Faculty:* 11 full-time (2 women), 21 part-time/adjunct (8 women). *Students:* 16 full-time (5 women), 9 part-time (6 women); includes 12 minority (4 Black or African American, non-Hispanic/Latino; 1 Asian, non-Hispanic/Latino; 7 Hispanic/Latino), 7 international. Average age 33. 12 applicants, 75% accepted, 8 enrolled. In 2016, 11 master's awarded. *Degree requirements:* For master's, thesis or alternative. *Entrance requirements:* For master's, minimum GPA of 3.0, 2 letters of recommendation. Additional exam requirements/recommendations for international students: Required—TOEFL (minimum score 550 paper-based; 80 iBT). *Application deadline:* For fall admission, 2/15 for domestic and international students; for spring admission, 10/1 for domestic students, 9/1 for international students. Application fee: $30. Electronic applications accepted. *Expenses:* Tuition, state resident: full-time $8912; part-time $446 per credit hour. Tuition, nonresident: full-time $21,393; part-time $992 per credit hour. *Required fees:* $2185; $195 per semester. Tuition and fees vary according to program. *Financial support:* Institutionally sponsored loans and scholarships/grants available. Financial award application deadline: 3/1; financial award applicants required to submit FAFSA. *Unit head:* Dr. Erik Larson, Chair, 305-348-3518, Fax: 305-348-1879, E-mail: larsone@fiu.edu. *Application contact:* Nanett Rojas, Manager, Admissions Operations, 305-348-7464, Fax: 305-348-7441, E-mail: nanett.rojas@fiu.edu.

**Florida State University,** The Graduate School, College of Arts and Sciences, Department of Religion, Tallahassee, FL 32306-1520. Offers humanities (PhD), including religion; religion (MA, PhD). *Faculty:* 18 full-time (4 women), 4 part-time/adjunct (2 women). *Students:* 74 full-time (20 women), 5 part-time (1 woman); includes 10 minority (2 Black or African American, non-Hispanic/Latino; 2 Asian, non-Hispanic/Latino; 6 Two or more races, non-Hispanic/Latino). Average age 26. 45 applicants, 49% accepted, 16 enrolled. In 2016, 7 master's, 6 doctorates awarded. Terminal master's awarded for partial completion of doctoral program. *Degree requirements:* For master's, one foreign language, comprehensive exam (for some programs), thesis (for some programs); for doctorate, 2 foreign languages, thesis/dissertation. *Entrance requirements:* For master's, GRE General Test, minimum GPA of 3.0; for doctorate, GRE General Test, MA in religion. Additional exam requirements/recommendations for international students: Required—TOEFL (minimum score 550 paper-based; 80 iBT). *Application deadline:* For fall admission, 12/15 for domestic and international students. Application fee: $30. Electronic applications accepted. *Expenses:* Tuition, state resident: full-time $7263; part-time $403.51 per credit hour. Tuition, nonresident: full-time $18,087; part-time $1004.85 per credit hour. *Required fees:* $1365; $75.81 per credit hour. $20 per semester. Tuition and fees vary according to campus/location. *Financial support:* In 2016–17, 63 students received support, including 5 fellowships with partial tuition reimbursements available (averaging $15,000 per year), 26 research assistantships with partial tuition reimbursements available (averaging $10,500 per year), 32 teaching assistantships with partial tuition reimbursements available (averaging $12,000 per year); institutionally sponsored loans, tuition waivers (partial), and unspecified assistantships also available. Financial award application deadline: 3/15; financial award applicants required to submit FAFSA. *Faculty research:* American religious history, comparative religious ethics, religions of Western antiquity, Asian religions and culture, history and ethnography of religion. *Unit head:* Dr. Aline Kalbian, Chair, 850-644-1020, Fax: 850-644-7225, E-mail: akalbian@fsu.edu. *Application contact:* Dr. Matthew Goff, Director of Graduate Studies, 850-644-1020, Fax: 850-644-7225, E-mail: mgoff@fsu.edu. Website: http://www.religion.fsu.edu

**Fordham University,** Graduate School of Religion and Religious Education, New York, NY 10458. Offers pastoral counseling and spiritual care (MA); pastoral ministry/spirituality/pastoral counseling (D Min); religion and religious education (MA); religious education (MS, PhD, PD); spiritual direction (Certificate). *Program availability:* Part-time. Terminal master's awarded for partial completion of doctoral program. *Degree requirements:* For master's, research paper; for doctorate, comprehensive exam, thesis/dissertation. *Entrance requirements:* For doctorate, MAT. Electronic applications accepted. *Expenses:* Contact institution. *Faculty research:* Spirituality and spiritual direction, pastoral care and counseling, adult family and community, growth and young adult.

**General Theological Seminary,** Graduate and Professional Programs, New York, NY 10011-4977. Offers Anglican studies (STM, Th D, Certificate); ascetical theology (Certificate); biblical studies (Certificate); congregational development (Certificate); divinity (M Div); historical and theological studies (Certificate); spiritual direction (MASD, STM, Certificate); theology (MA). *Accreditation:* ACIPE; ATS. *Program availability:* Part-time, evening/weekend. Terminal master's awarded for partial completion of doctoral program. *Degree requirements:* For master's, thesis; for doctorate, 2 foreign languages, thesis/dissertation. *Entrance requirements:* For master's, GRE General Test; for doctorate, GRE, M Div or MA. Additional exam requirements/recommendations for international students: Required—TOEFL. *Faculty research:* Liturgy, New Testament, ethics, history, ecumenical relations.

**George Mason University,** College of Humanities and Social Sciences, Interdisciplinary Studies Program, Fairfax, VA 22030. Offers community college teaching (MAIS); computational social science (MAIS); energy and sustainability (MAIS); folklore studies (MAIS); individualized studies (MAIS); neuroethics (MAIS); religion, culture, and values (MAIS); social entrepreneurship (MAIS); social justice and human rights (MAIS); war and the military in society (MAIS); women and gender studies (MAIS). *Faculty:* 10 full-time (3 women), 9 part-time/adjunct (4 women). *Students:* 25 full-time (21 women), 70 part-time (48 women); includes 31 minority (15 Black or African American, non-Hispanic/Latino; 5 Asian, non-Hispanic/Latino; 7 Hispanic/Latino; 4 Two or more races, non-Hispanic/Latino), 3 international. Average age 33. 52 applicants, 92% accepted, 23 enrolled. In 2016, 40 master's awarded. *Degree requirements:* For master's, project or thesis. *Entrance requirements:* For master's, 3 letters of recommendation; writing sample; official transcript; resume. Additional exam requirements/recommendations for international students: Required—TOEFL (minimum score 575 paper-based; 88 iBT), IELTS (minimum score 6.5), PTE (minimum score 59). *Application deadline:* For fall admission, 3/1 for domestic students. Application fee: $75 ($80 for international students). Electronic applications accepted. *Expenses:* Tuition, state resident: full-time $10,628; part-time $443 per credit. Tuition, nonresident: full-time $29,306; part-time $1221 per credit. *Required fees:* $3096; $129 per credit. Tuition and fees vary according to program. *Financial support:* In 2016–17, 8 students received support, including 3 research assistantships with tuition reimbursements available (averaging $9,629 per year), 5 teaching assistantships with tuition reimbursements available (averaging $12,814 per year); career-related internships or fieldwork, Federal Work-Study, scholarships/grants, unspecified assistantships, and health care benefits (for full-time research or teaching assistantship recipient) also available. Support available to part-time students. Financial award application deadline: 3/1; financial award applicants required to submit FAFSA. *Faculty research:* Combined English and folklore, religious and cultural studies (Christianity and Muslim society). *Unit head:* Meredith H. Lair, Director, 703-993-2159, Fax: 703-993-1251, E-mail: mlair@gmu.edu. *Application contact:* Morgan Fisher, Graduate Coordinator, 703-993-8762, E-mail: mfisherb@gmu.edu. Website: http://mais.gmu.edu

**Georgetown University,** Graduate School of Arts and Sciences, School of Continuing Studies, Washington, DC 20057. Offers American studies (MALS); Catholic studies (MALS); classical civilizations (MALS); emergency and disaster management (MPS); ethics and the professions (MALS); global strategic communications (MPS); hospitality management (MPS); human resources management (MPS); humanities (MALS); individualized study (MALS); integrated marketing communications (MPS); international affairs (MALS); Islam and Muslim-Christian relations (MALS); journalism (MPS); liberal studies (DLS); literature and society (MALS); medieval and early modern European studies (MALS); public relations and corporate communications (MPS); real estate (MPS); religious studies (MALS); social and public policy (MALS); sports industry management (MPS); systems engineering management (MPS); technology management (MPS); the theory and practice of American democracy (MALS); urban and regional planning (MPS); visual culture (MALS). MPS in systems engineering management offered jointly with Stevens Institute of Technology. *Entrance requirements:* Additional exam requirements/recommendations for international students: Required—TOEFL.

**The George Washington University,** Columbian College of Arts and Sciences, Department of Religion, Washington, DC 20052. Offers Islam (MA), including Hinduism and Islam. *Program availability:* Part-time, evening/weekend. *Faculty:* 8 full-time (3 women). *Students:* 9 full-time (6 women), 4 part-time (2 women); includes 3 minority (1 Black or African American, non-Hispanic/Latino; 2 Asian, non-Hispanic/Latino), 6 international. Average age 31. 22 applicants, 68% accepted, 7 enrolled. In 2016, 5 master's awarded. *Degree requirements:* For master's, one foreign language, comprehensive exam, thesis. *Entrance requirements:* For master's, GRE General Test, interview, minimum GPA of 3.0. Additional exam requirements/recommendations for international students: Required—TOEFL (minimum score 550 paper-based; 80 iBT). *Application deadline:* For fall admission, 4/1 priority date for domestic students, 1/15 priority date for international students; for spring admission, 10/1 priority date for domestic students, 9/1 priority date for international students. Applications are processed on a rolling basis. Application fee: $75. Electronic applications accepted. *Financial support:* In 2016–17, 1 student received support. Federal Work-Study and tuition waivers available. *Unit head:* Dr. Robert Eisen, Chair, 202-994-4780, Fax: 202-994-9379, E-mail: eisen@gwu.edu. *Application contact:* Information Contact, 202-994-6325, Fax: 202-994-9379, E-mail: religion@gwu.edu. Website: http://religion.columbian.gwu.edu/

**Georgia State University,** College of Arts and Sciences, Department of Religious Studies, Atlanta, GA 30302-4089. Offers MA. *Program availability:* Part-time. *Faculty:* 9 full-time (4 women). *Students:* 19 full-time (13 women), 5 part-time (3 women); includes 13 minority (7 Black or African American, non-Hispanic/Latino; 2 Hispanic/Latino; 4 Two or more races, non-Hispanic/Latino). Average age 40. 20 applicants, 90% accepted, 9 enrolled. In 2016, 8 master's awarded. *Degree requirements:* For master's, thesis optional. *Entrance requirements:* For master's, GRE. Additional exam requirements/recommendations for international students: Required—TOEFL (minimum score 79 iBT). *Application deadline:* For fall admission, 2/1 priority date for domestic and international students. Application fee: $50. Electronic applications accepted. *Expenses:* Tuition, state resident: full-time $6876; part-time $382 per credit hour. Tuition, nonresident: full-time $22,374; part-time $1243 per credit hour. *Required fees:* $2128; $1064 per term. Part-time tuition and fees vary according to course load and program. *Financial support:* In 2016–17, research assistantships with full tuition reimbursements (averaging $5,000 per year), teaching assistantships with full tuition reimbursements (averaging $6,000 per year) were awarded; career-related internships or fieldwork, health care benefits, and unspecified assistantships also available. Financial award application deadline: 2/1; financial award applicants required to submit FAFSA. *Faculty research:* Comparative/world religions; religion in the Americas; religion, gender and sexuality; religion and public policy/non-profit management; religion, ethics and politics. *Unit head:* Dr. Kathryn McClymond, Chairperson, 404-413-6119, Fax: 404-413-6124, E-mail: kmcclymond@gsu.edu. *Application contact:* Dr. Molly Bassett, Director of Graduate Studies, 404-413-6134, E-mail: mbassett@gsu.edu. Website: http://religiousstudies.gsu.edu/graduate/

**Gordon-Conwell Theological Seminary,** Graduate and Professional Programs, South Hamilton, MA 01982. Offers Biblical languages (MABL); church history (MACH); counseling (MACO); ministry (D Min); missions/evangelism (MAME); New Testament (MANT); Old Testament (MAOT); religion (MAR); theology (M Div, MATH, Th M, Th D). *Accreditation:* ACIPE; ATS (one or more programs are accredited). *Program availability:* Part-time, evening/weekend. *Degree requirements:* For master's, one foreign language, thesis optional; for doctorate, 2 foreign languages, thesis/dissertation. *Entrance requirements:* For master's, minimum GPA of 2.5; for doctorate, minimum GPA of 3.0.

**Grace College of Divinity,** Graduate Program, Fayetteville, NC 28314. Offers MCL.

**Graceland University,** Community of Christ Seminary, Independence, MO 64050. Offers MAR. *Program availability:* Part-time. *Students:* 14 full-time (7 women), 20 part-time (12 women); includes 1 minority (Native Hawaiian or other Pacific Islander, non-Hispanic/Latino), 5 international. 39 applicants, 64% accepted, 19 enrolled. In 2016, 1 master's awarded. *Degree requirements:* For master's, thesis optional, portfolio. *Entrance requirements:* For master's, minimum cumulative GPA of 3.0. Additional exam requirements/recommendations for international students: Required—TOEFL. *Application deadline:* For fall admission, 8/15 priority date for domestic students; for winter admission, 10/15 priority date for domestic students; for spring admission, 4/15 priority date for domestic students. Applications are processed on a rolling basis. Application fee: $50. Electronic applications accepted. *Expenses:* Contact institution. *Financial support:* Scholarships/grants available. Financial award application deadline: 12/15; financial award applicants required to submit FAFSA. *Faculty research:* Theology, scripture. *Unit head:* Dr. Matthew Frizzell, Dean, 641-784-5276, E-mail: mfrizzel@graceland.edu. *Application contact:* Sharon Ward, Administrative Assistant, 816-423-4676, Fax: 816-423-4753, E-mail: ward@graceland.edu. Website: http://www.graceland.edu/seminary

**Graduate Theological Union,** Graduate Programs, Berkeley, CA 94709-1212. Offers art and religion (MA, PhD, Th D); biblical languages (MA); biblical studies (MA); Biblical studies (PhD, Th D); Buddhist studies (MA); Christian spirituality (MA, PhD, Th D); cultural and historical studies of religions (MA, PhD, Th D); ethics and social theory (PhD, Th D); history (MA, PhD, Th D); homiletics (MA, PhD, Th D); interdisciplinary studies (PhD, Th D); Jewish studies (MA, PhD, Th D, Certificate); liturgical studies (MA, PhD, Th D); Near Eastern religions (PhD, Th D); Orthodox Christian studies (MA); religion and psychology (MA, PhD, Th D); religion and society/ethics and social theory (MA); systematic and philosophical theology (MA, PhD, Th D). PhD programs in Jewish studies and Near Eastern religions offered jointly with University of California, Berkeley. *Accreditation:* ATS. Terminal master's awarded for partial completion of doctoral program. *Degree requirements:* For master's, one foreign language, thesis; for doctorate, one foreign language, comprehensive exam, thesis/dissertation. *Entrance requirements:* For master's, GRE General Test; for doctorate, GRE General Test, MA or M Div. Additional exam requirements/recommendations for international students: Required—TOEFL. Electronic applications accepted.

**Grand Rapids Theological Seminary of Cornerstone University,** Graduate Programs, Grand Rapids, MI 49525-5897. Offers biblical counseling (MA); Biblical counseling (M Div); chaplaincy (M Div); Christian education (M Div, MA); intercultural studies (M Div, MA); New Testament (MA, Th M); Old Testament (MA, Th M); pastoral studies (M Div, MA); systematic theology (MA); theology (Th M). *Accreditation:* ATS. *Program availability:* Part-time, online learning. *Entrance requirements:* Additional exam requirements/recommendations for international students: Required—TOEFL (minimum score 577 paper-based; 90 iBT). Electronic applications accepted.

**Harding School of Theology,** Graduate Programs, Memphis, TN 38117-5499. Offers Christian ministry (MA); counseling (MA); ministry (M Div, D Min); religion (MA). *Accreditation:* ATS. *Program availability:* Part-time, online learning. *Degree requirements:* For master's, variable foreign language requirement, thesis (for some programs); for doctorate, one foreign language, thesis/dissertation. *Entrance requirements:* For master's, minimum GPA of 2.7; for doctorate, minimum GPA of 3.0. Additional exam requirements/recommendations for international students: Required—TOEFL (minimum score 550 paper-based; 79 iBT). Electronic applications accepted.

**Hardin-Simmons University,** Graduate School, Logsdon School of Theology, Program in Religion, Abilene, TX 79698-0001. Offers MA. *Program availability:* Part-time. *Faculty:* 7 full-time (1 woman), 20 part-time/adjunct (2 women). *Students:* 4 part-time (1 woman); includes 1 minority (Hispanic/Latino). Average age 34. *Degree requirements:* For master's, one foreign language, comprehensive exam, thesis or alternative. *Entrance requirements:* For master's, minimum undergraduate GPA of 3.0 in major, 2.7 overall; 18 hours of course work in religious studies; interview. Additional exam requirements/recommendations for international students: Required—TOEFL (minimum score 550 paper-based; 75 iBT). *Application deadline:* For fall admission, 8/15 priority date for domestic students, 4/1 for international students; for spring admission, 1/5 priority date for domestic students, 9/1 for international students. Applications are processed on a rolling basis. Application fee: $50. Electronic applications accepted. *Expenses:* Tuition: Full-time $12,510; part-time $695 per credit hour. *Required fees:* $325; $110 per semester. *Financial support:* In 2016–17, 4 students received support. Fellowships and scholarships/grants available. Support available to part-time students. Financial award application deadline: 6/30; financial award applicants required to submit FAFSA. *Faculty research:* Archaeology research in Christian origins, Hebrew grammar, history of Christian education, training of ministers into the twenty-first century, role of women in the Old Testament, contemporary ethical issues. *Unit head:* Dr. Dan Stiver, Program Director, 325-670-1398, Fax: 325-670-1406, E-mail: dstiver@hsutx.edu. *Application contact:* Dr. Nancy Kucinski, Dean of Graduate Studies, 325-670-1298, Fax: 325-670-1564, E-mail: gradoff@hsutx.edu.
Website: http://www.logsdonseminary.org/academics/religion/

**Harrison Middleton University,** Graduate Program, Tempe, AZ 85282. Offers education (MA, Ed D); humanities (MA); imaginative literature (MA); interdisciplinary studies (DA); jurisprudence (MA); natural science (MA); philosophy and religion (MA); social science (MA). *Program availability:* Part-time, evening/weekend, online learning. *Degree requirements:* For master's and doctorate, capstone project. *Entrance requirements:* For master's, interview; for doctorate, 2 academic letters of reference, interview, essay. Additional exam requirements/recommendations for international students: Required—TOEFL (minimum score 550 paper-based; 80 iBT). Electronic applications accepted. *Faculty research:* Japanese animation, educational leadership, war art, John Muir's wilderness.

**Hartford Seminary,** Graduate Programs, Hartford, CT 06105-2279. Offers Islamic studies (MA); ministry (D Min); religious studies (MA); spirituality (Certificate). *Accreditation:* ATS (one or more programs are accredited). *Program availability:* Part-time, evening/weekend, online learning. *Degree requirements:* For master's, thesis optional, oral exam; for doctorate, thesis/dissertation, oral exam. *Entrance requirements:* For doctorate, experience in ministry, M Div. Additional exam requirements/recommendations for international students: Required—TOEFL (minimum score 550 paper-based; 80 iBT). *Faculty research:* Liturgy and social justice, professional leadership in ministry, congregational studies, Christian-Muslim relations, American religion.

**Harvard University,** Graduate School of Arts and Sciences, Committee on the Study of Religion, Cambridge, MA 02138. Offers PhD. Program offered jointly with Harvard Divinity School. *Degree requirements:* For doctorate, 2 foreign languages, thesis/dissertation. *Entrance requirements:* For doctorate, GRE General Test. Additional exam requirements/recommendations for international students: Required—TOEFL.

**Heritage Christian University,** Graduate Programs, Florence, AL 35630. Offers counseling (MM); Greek (MA); ministry (MM); New Testament (MA). *Degree requirements:* For master's, practicum (MM), major research paper (MA). *Entrance requirements:* For master's, MAT or GRE, bachelor's degree in Bible from an accredited college or university, minimum GPA of 2.75, 3 letters of recommendation.

**Hope International University,** School of Graduate and Professional Studies, Programs in Ministry, Fullerton, CA 92831-3138. Offers Christian leadership (MCM); church music (MA); church music (Korean track) (MCM); church planting (MCM); intercultural studies (MCM); worship (MCM). *Program availability:* Part-time, evening/weekend, online learning. *Degree requirements:* For master's, thesis (for some programs), project. *Entrance requirements:* For master's, minimum GPA of 3.0, MCM program requires an undergraduate degree in music, 2 references. Additional exam requirements/recommendations for international students: Required—TOEFL (minimum score 550 paper-based; 86 iBT); Recommended—IELTS (minimum score 6.5). Electronic applications accepted. *Expenses:* Contact institution. *Faculty research:* Church dynamics, growth methodologies.

**Iliff School of Theology,** Graduate and Professional Programs, Denver, CO 80210-4798. Offers biblical studies (MA); church history (MA); religion (MA); religion and social change (MA); specialized ministry (MASM), including justice and peace, pastoral theology and care, religions leadership; theology (M Div, MTS, D Min, PhD), including Biblical studies (PhD), religion and psychological studies (PhD), religion and social change (PhD), theology, philosophy and culture (PhD); theology/ethics (MA). PhD offered jointly with University of Denver. *Accreditation:* ACIPE; ATS. *Program availability:* Part-time, evening/weekend. *Degree requirements:* For master's, one foreign language, thesis (for some programs); for doctorate, 2 foreign languages, comprehensive exam, thesis/dissertation. *Entrance requirements:* For master's, minimum GPA of 3.0, writing sample, references; for doctorate, GRE General Test, minimum GPA of 3.0, writing sample, letters of recommendation. Additional exam requirements/recommendations for international students: Required—TOEFL (minimum score 550 paper-based). Electronic applications accepted. *Faculty research:* Pastoral care, history, church music, contemporary church, biblical studies.

**Indiana University Bloomington,** University Graduate School, College of Arts and Sciences, Department of Religious Studies, Bloomington, IN 47405-7005. Offers MA, PhD. *Program availability:* Part-time. *Faculty:* 20 full-time (8 women). *Students:* 31 full-time (13 women); includes 4 minority (1 Black or African American, non-Hispanic/Latino; 1 Asian, non-Hispanic/Latino; 1 Hispanic/Latino; 1 Two or more races, non-Hispanic/Latino), 7 international. Average age 33. 74 applicants, 15% accepted, 5 enrolled. In 2016, 2 master's, 2 doctorates awarded. Terminal master's awarded for partial completion of doctoral program. *Degree requirements:* For master's, one foreign language, thesis or alternative; for doctorate, 2 foreign languages, thesis/dissertation.

*Entrance requirements:* For master's, GRE General Test; for doctorate, GRE, MA, writing sample. Additional exam requirements/recommendations for international students: Required—TOEFL. *Application deadline:* For fall admission, 12/15 for domestic students, 12/1 for international students. Application fee: $55 ($65 for international students). Electronic applications accepted. *Financial support:* In 2016–17, 20 students received support, including 7 fellowships with full tuition reimbursements available (averaging $18,700 per year), 16 teaching assistantships with full tuition reimbursements available (averaging $15,750 per year); research assistantships with full tuition reimbursements available, scholarships/grants, and health care benefits also available. Financial award application deadline: 2/1. *Faculty research:* Ancient Mediterranean and near eastern religions; religions of Americas; Islamic studies; Buddhist studies; religion, literature, and cultural imagination. *Unit head:* Prof. Winnifred Sullivan, Chair, 812-855-3531, Fax: 812-855-4687, E-mail: wfsulliv@indiana.edu. *Application contact:* Connie May, Graduate Secretary, 812-855-3531, Fax: 812-855-4687, E-mail: deptsec@indiana.edu.
Website: http://www.indiana.edu/~relstud/

**The Jewish Theological Seminary,** The Graduate School, New York, NY 10027-4649. Offers ancient Judaism (MA, DHL, PhD); Bible and ancient Semitic languages (MA, DHL, PhD); interdepartmental studies (MA); Jewish art and visual culture (MA); Jewish gender and women's studies (MA); Jewish history (MA, DHL, PhD); Jewish literature (MA, DHL, PhD); Jewish philosophy (DHL); Jewish thought (MA, PhD); liturgy (MA, DHL, PhD); medieval Jewish studies (MA, DHL, PhD); Midrash (DHL); Midrash and scriptural interpretation (MA, PhD); modern Jewish studies (MA, DHL, PhD); Talmud and rabbinics (MA, DHL, PhD); MA/MSW. MA/MSW offered jointly with Columbia University. *Accreditation:* ACIPE. *Program availability:* Part-time. Terminal master's awarded for partial completion of doctoral program. *Degree requirements:* For master's, one foreign language, comprehensive exam (for some programs), thesis (for some programs); for doctorate, 3 foreign languages, comprehensive exam (for some programs), thesis/dissertation. *Entrance requirements:* For master's, GRE or MAT, 3 letters of recommendation, writing sample; for doctorate, GRE or MAT, 3 letters of recommendation, writing research sample. Additional exam requirements/recommendations for international students: Required—TOEFL.

**John Carroll University,** Graduate Studies, Department of Theology and Religious Studies, University Heights, OH 44118-4581. Offers MA. *Program availability:* Part-time, evening/weekend. *Degree requirements:* For master's, comprehensive exam, research essay or thesis, foreign language proficiency. *Entrance requirements:* For master's, GRE General Test or MAT, minimum GPA of 2.5. Additional exam requirements/recommendations for international students: Required—TOEFL. *Application deadline:* For fall admission, 8/30 priority date for domestic students; for spring admission, 1/11 priority date for domestic students. Applications are processed on a rolling basis. Application fee: $25 ($35 for international students). Electronic applications accepted. *Expenses:* Tuition: Full-time $10,425; part-time $695 per credit hour. One-time fee: $200 full-time. Tuition and fees vary according to course load, campus/location and program. *Financial support:* Teaching assistantships with full tuition reimbursements, scholarships/grants, tuition waivers (partial), and unspecified assistantships available. Support available to part-time students. Financial award application deadline: 3/1; financial award applicants required to submit FAFSA. *Faculty research:* Ethics, women's studies, contemporary theology, Bible studies, Latin American theology. *Unit head:* Dr. Sheila E. McGinn, Chair, 216-397-4700, Fax: 216-397-4518, E-mail: trs@jcu.edu. *Application contact:* Jennifer L. Tucker, Records Management Assistant, 216-397-1925, Fax: 216-397-1835, E-mail: jtucker@jcu.edu.
Website: http://www.jcu.edu/religion/Gr_prog.htm

**Kentucky Christian University,** Graduate School, Grayson, KY 41143-2205. Offers Biblical studies (MA); Christian leadership (MA). *Program availability:* Part-time. *Degree requirements:* For master's, comprehensive exam (for some programs), thesis optional. *Entrance requirements:* For master's, minimum cumulative GPA of 2.75 in major or 2.5 overall; 6 additional hours in Bible (for non-Biblical undergraduate majors). Additional exam requirements/recommendations for international students: Required—TOEFL (minimum score 550 paper-based). Electronic applications accepted.

**Knox Theological Seminary,** Graduate Programs, Master of Arts Programs, Fort Lauderdale, FL 33308. Offers Biblical and theological studies (MA); Christian and classical studies (MA). *Accreditation:* ATS. *Program availability:* Part-time, evening/weekend. *Entrance requirements:* Additional exam requirements/recommendations for international students: Required—TOEFL (minimum score 520 paper-based; 83 iBT), TWE (minimum score 5).

**Lancaster Theological Seminary,** Graduate and Professional Programs, Lancaster, PA 17603-2812. Offers biblical studies (MAR); Christian education (MAR); Christianity and the arts (MAR); church history (MAR); congregational life (MAR); lay leadership (Certificate); theological studies (M Div); theology (D Min); theology and ethics (MAR). *Accreditation:* ACIPE; ATS. *Degree requirements:* For doctorate, thesis/dissertation.

**La Sierra University,** School of Religion, Riverside, CA 92515. Offers pastoral ministry (M Div); religion (MA); religious education (MA); religious studies (MA). *Program availability:* Part-time. *Degree requirements:* For master's, one foreign language, thesis or alternative. *Entrance requirements:* For master's, GRE General Test, minimum GPA of 3.0.

**Lee University,** Programs in Religion, Cleveland, TN 37320-3450. Offers biblical studies (MA); ministry studies/leadership (MA); ministry studies/worship (MA); ministry studies/youth and family (MA); theological studies (MA), including ethics, religion. *Program availability:* Part-time, 100% online. *Faculty:* 13 full-time (2 women), 2 part-time/adjunct (0 women). *Students:* 57 full-time (19 women), 92 part-time (28 women); includes 72 minority (16 Black or African American, non-Hispanic/Latino; 2 Asian, non-Hispanic/Latino; 53 Hispanic/Latino; 1 Two or more races, non-Hispanic/Latino), 4 international. Average age 37. 19 applicants, 79% accepted, 12 enrolled. In 2016, 9 master's awarded. *Degree requirements:* For master's, variable foreign language requirement, comprehensive exam (for some programs), thesis (for some programs). *Entrance requirements:* For master's, GRE or MAT (for biblical/theological studies only), minimum GPA of 3.0, 3 letters of recommendation, interview, official transcripts, essay. Additional exam requirements/recommendations for international students: Required—TOEFL (minimum score 61 iBT). *Application deadline:* For fall admission, 4/1 priority date for domestic and international students; for spring admission, 10/1 priority date for domestic and international students. Applications are processed on a rolling basis. Application fee: $25. Electronic applications accepted. *Expenses:* Contact institution. *Financial support:* In 2016–17, 25 students received support, including 7 teaching assistantships (averaging $2,031 per year); career-related internships or fieldwork, Federal Work-Study, institutionally sponsored loans, scholarships/grants, and unspecified assistantships also available. Financial award application deadline: 3/1; financial award applicants required to submit FAFSA. *Faculty research:* Spiritual and discipleship formation, leadership, Biblical studies, theological studies, ethics. *Unit head:* Dr. Lisa Long, Director, 423-303-5100, E-mail: llong@leeuniversity.edu.
Website: http://www.leeuniversity.edu/academics/graduate/

**Liberty University,** School of Divinity, Lynchburg, VA 24515. Offers Biblical studies (M Div); church history (MAR, Th M); discipleship and church ministry (M Div, MAR,

## Religion

MCM); evangelism and church planting (M Div, MAR, MCM); global studies (M Div, MCM, MGS); homiletics (M Div, MAR, Th M, D Min); leadership (M Div, D Min); marketplace chaplaincy (M Div, MCM); ministry (D Min); pastoral counseling (M Div, MA, MAR, D Min), including addictions and recovery (MA), crisis response and trauma (MA), discipleship and church ministries (MA), leadership (MA), life coaching (MA), marketplace chaplaincy (MA), marriage and family (MA), military resilience (MA), pastoral counseling (MA); pastoral ministries (M Div, MCM); religious education (MRE); theology (M Div, MAR, MTS); theology and apologetics (PhD); worship (M Div, MAR, MCM, D Min). *Program availability:* Part-time, online learning. *Students:* 2,140 full-time (615 women), 3,020 part-time (906 women); includes 1,312 minority (1,016 Black or African American, non-Hispanic/Latino; 9 American Indian or Alaska Native, non-Hispanic/Latino; 100 Asian, non-Hispanic/Latino; 90 Hispanic/Latino; 7 Native Hawaiian or other Pacific Islander, non-Hispanic/Latino; 90 Two or more races, non-Hispanic/Latino), 158 international. Average age 42. 3,651 applicants, 37% accepted, 909 enrolled. In 2016, 1,551 master's, 39 doctorates, 168 other advanced degrees awarded. *Degree requirements:* For master's, 2 foreign languages, thesis (for some programs); for doctorate, 2 foreign languages, thesis/dissertation. *Entrance requirements:* For master's, minimum undergraduate GPA of 2.0; for doctorate, GRE General Test or MAT, minimum graduate GPA of 3.0. Additional exam requirements/recommendations for international students: Required—TOEFL (minimum score 600 paper-based; 100 iBT). *Application deadline:* For fall admission, 6/1 for domestic students; for spring admission, 11/1 for domestic students. Applications are processed on a rolling basis. Application fee: $50. Electronic applications accepted. *Expenses:* Contact institution. *Financial support:* Teaching assistantships with tuition reimbursements, career-related internships or fieldwork, and Federal Work-Study available. Financial award applicants required to submit FAFSA. *Unit head:* Dr. Ed Hindson, Dean, 434-592-4140, Fax: 434-522-0415, E-mail: ehindson@liberty.edu. *Application contact:* Jay Bridge, Director of Graduate Admissions, 800-424-9595, Fax: 800-628-7977, E-mail: gradadmissions@liberty.edu.
Website: https://www.liberty.edu/divinity/

**Lincoln Christian University,** Graduate Programs, Lincoln, IL 62656-2167. Offers Biblical studies (MA); church history/historical theology (MA); intercultural studies (MA); ministry (MA); organizational leadership (MA); philosophy and apologetics (MA); spiritual formation (MA); theology (MA). MA in spiritual formation offered in Normal, IL. *Program availability:* Online learning. *Faculty:* 22 full-time (6 women), 27 part-time/adjunct (9 women). *Students:* 89 full-time (45 women), 225 part-time (91 women). Average age 39. *Entrance requirements:* For master's, minimum cumulative GPA of 2.5 in undergraduate degree studies. Additional exam requirements/recommendations for international students: Required—TOEFL (minimum score 550 paper-based); Recommended—IELTS (minimum score 6). *Application deadline:* For fall admission, 8/1 for domestic students, 3/1 for international students; for spring admission, 11/15 for domestic students, 11/1 for international students. Application fee: $25 ($50 for international students). Application fee is waived when completed online. *Expenses:* Tuition: Full-time $7812; part-time $5208 per credit hour. *Required fees:* $1000; $1000 per credit hour. One-time fee: $150. Full-time tuition and fees vary according to campus/location and program. *Financial support:* Applicants required to submit FAFSA. *Application contact:* Lindsey Clark, Associate Director of Graduate and Seminary Enrollment, 217-732-3168 Ext. 2398, E-mail: lclark@lincolnchristian.edu.
Website: https://lincolnchristian.edu/academics/programs/masters/

**Loma Linda University,** School of Religion, Program in Religion and Society, Loma Linda, CA 92350. Offers MA. *Degree requirements:* For master's, comprehensive exam, thesis optional. *Entrance requirements:* Additional exam requirements/recommendations for international students: Required—TOEFL. Electronic applications accepted.

**Louisville Presbyterian Theological Seminary,** Graduate and Professional Programs, Louisville, KY 40205-1798. Offers Bible (MAR); divinity (M Div); ministry (D Min); religious thought (MAR); JD/M Div; M Div/MBA; M Div/MSSW. JD/M Div, M Div/MBA, and M Div/MSSW offered jointly with University of Louisville. *Accreditation:* AAMFT/COAMFTE (one or more programs are accredited); ACIPE; ATS (one or more programs are accredited). *Program availability:* Part-time (9 women), 8 part-time/adjunct (5 women). *Students:* 99 full-time (54 women), 53 part-time (34 women); includes 42 minority (31 Black or African American, non-Hispanic/Latino; 3 Asian, non-Hispanic/Latino; 6 Hispanic/Latino; 2 Two or more races, non-Hispanic/Latino), 2 international. Average age 40. In 2016, 27 master's, 17 doctorates awarded. *Degree requirements:* For master's, 2 foreign languages, thesis (for some programs); for doctorate, thesis/dissertation. *Entrance requirements:* For doctorate, M Div. Additional exam requirements/recommendations for international students: Required—TOEFL (minimum score 550 paper-based). *Application deadline:* For fall admission, 6/1 priority date for domestic students, 2/1 priority date for international students; for spring admission, 11/1 priority date for domestic students. Applications are processed on a rolling basis. Application fee: $50. Electronic applications accepted. *Expenses:* Tuition: Full-time $11,400; part-time $380 per credit hour. *Required fees:* $286; $286 per credit hour. $143 per semester. *Financial support:* Career-related internships or fieldwork, Federal Work-Study, institutionally sponsored loans, and scholarships/grants available. Financial award application deadline: 2/1. *Unit head:* Dr. Susan R. Garrett, Dean, 502-895-3411, Fax: 502-895-1096, E-mail: sgarrett@lpts.edu. *Application contact:* Rev. Emily Miller, Director of Admissions, 502-895-3411, Fax: 502-895-1096, E-mail: emiller@lpts.edu.
Website: http://www.lpts.edu/

**Lutheran Theological Seminary at Gettysburg,** Graduate and Professional Programs, Gettysburg, PA 17325-1795. Offers divinity (M Div); ministerial studies (MAMS); outdoor ministry (MAR); parish ministry (D Min); theology (STM). *Accreditation:* ACIPE; ATS (one or more programs are accredited). *Program availability:* Part-time, online learning. *Degree requirements:* For master's, thesis (for some programs). Electronic applications accepted.

**The Lutheran Theological Seminary at Philadelphia,** Graduate School, Philadelphia, PA 19119-1794. Offers divinity (M Div); ministry (D Min); public leadership (MA); religion (MAR); social ministry and church (Certificate); theology (STM, PhD). *Accreditation:* ACIPE. *Program availability:* Part-time, evening/weekend. *Degree requirements:* For master's, one foreign language, comprehensive exam (for some programs), thesis (for some programs); for doctorate, thesis/dissertation. *Entrance requirements:* For master's, minimum undergraduate GPA of 2.8; for doctorate, minimum GPA of 3.0. Additional exam requirements/recommendations for international students: Required—TOEFL (minimum score 550 paper-based; 89 iBT), TWE. Electronic applications accepted.

**Lutheran Theological Seminary Saskatoon,** Graduate and Professional Programs, Saskatoon, SK S7N 0X3, Canada. Offers Biblical studies (MTS); church history (MTS); ethics/church and society (MTS); history of Christianity (STM); New Testament (STM); Old Testament (STM); pastoral studies (STM); pastoral theology (MTS); systematic theology (MTS); systematic theology and philosophy of religion (STM); theology (M Div, D Div). STM programs offered jointly with College of Emmanuel and St. Chad and St. Andrew's College. *Accreditation:* ATS. *Program availability:* Part-time. *Degree requirements:* For master's, thesis.

**Luther Rice College & Seminary,** Graduate Programs, Lithonia, GA 30038-2454. Offers apologetics (MA); Bible languages (M Div); Biblical counseling (MA); Christian ministry (M Div, D Min); Christian studies (MA); leadership (MA). *Program availability:* Part-time, evening/weekend, online learning. *Degree requirements:* For doctorate, thesis/dissertation. *Entrance requirements:* For master's, bachelor's degree or equivalent; for doctorate, M Div. Additional exam requirements/recommendations for international students: Required—TOEFL (minimum score 550 paper-based). Electronic applications accepted.

**Maranatha Baptist University,** Master of Arts in English Bible Program, Watertown, WI 53094. Offers MA. *Program availability:* Part-time, 100% online. *Entrance requirements:* For master's, BA or BS. Application fee: $50. *Expenses:* Tuition: Full-time $6300; part-time $3150 per credit. *Required fees:* $210; $35 per course. Tuition and fees vary according to course load and degree level. *Unit head:* Dr. Larry Oats, Dean of Maranatha Baptist Seminary, 920-206-2324, Fax: 920-261-9109, E-mail: larry.oats@mbu.edu. *Application contact:* Dr. Jim Harrison, Director of Admissions, 920-206-2327, Fax: 920-261-9109, E-mail: admissions@mbu.edu.

**McGill University,** Faculty of Graduate and Postdoctoral Studies, Faculty of Religious Studies, Montréal, QC H3A 2T5, Canada. Offers MA, STM, PhD. *Accreditation:* ATS.

**McMaster University,** School of Graduate Studies, Faculty of Social Sciences, Department of Religious Studies, Hamilton, ON L8S 4M2, Canada. Offers MA, PhD. *Program availability:* Part-time. *Degree requirements:* For master's, one foreign language, thesis; for doctorate, 2 foreign languages, comprehensive exam, thesis/dissertation. *Entrance requirements:* For master's, minimum B+ average. Additional exam requirements/recommendations for international students: Required—TOEFL (minimum score 580 paper-based). *Faculty research:* Hellenistic Judaism, religious biographies in Asia, medieval India, synoptic gospels, ritual and belief systems.

**Memorial University of Newfoundland,** School of Graduate Studies, Department of Religious Studies, St. John's, NL A1C 5S7, Canada. Offers MA. *Program availability:* Part-time. *Degree requirements:* For master's, one foreign language, thesis. *Entrance requirements:* For master's, honors degree in religious studies or equivalent. Electronic applications accepted. *Faculty research:* Biblical studies, Christian thought and history, world religions, ethics, contemporary spirituality.

**Milligan College,** Emmanuel Christian Seminary at Milligan College, Milligan College, TN 37682. Offers Christian care and counseling (M Div); Christian education (M Div); Christian ministries (MACM, Graduate Certificate); Christian ministry (M Div); Christian theology (M Div, MAR); church history/historical theology (M Div); general studies (M Div); ministry (D Min); New Testament (M Div, MAR); Old Testament (M Div, MAR); urban ministry (M Div); world missions (M Div). *Accreditation:* ACIPE; ATS. *Program availability:* Part-time, blended/hybrid learning. *Faculty:* 9 full-time (1 woman), 11 part-time/adjunct (0 women). *Students:* 55 full-time (16 women), 44 part-time (17 women); includes 7 minority (6 Black or African American, non-Hispanic/Latino; 1 Hispanic/Latino), 6 international. Average age 33. In 2016, 21 master's, 3 doctorates awarded. *Degree requirements:* For master's, 2 foreign languages, thesis or alternative; for doctorate, thesis/dissertation. *Entrance requirements:* For master's, undergraduate degree and supporting transcripts, essay/personal statement, professional recommendations, interview; for doctorate, M Div or equivalent, essay/personal statement, professional recommendations. Additional exam requirements/recommendations for international students: Required—TOEFL (minimum score 550 paper-based, 79 iBT) or IELTS (6.5). *Application deadline:* For fall admission, 8/1 for domestic students, 6/1 for international students; for spring admission, 12/15 for domestic students, 8/1 for international students. Applications are processed on a rolling basis. Application fee: $30 ($0 for international students). Electronic applications accepted. *Expenses:* $470 per hour tuition; $325 per semester tech/activity fees. *Financial support:* In 2016–17, 124 students received support. Scholarships/grants and unspecified assistantships available. Financial award application deadline: 12/1; financial award applicants required to submit FAFSA. *Faculty research:* Theology of Old Testament prophets; performance criticism of New Testament texts; practical theology and spiritual formation for Christian leaders; church history and missions; constructive theology, art and imagination. *Unit head:* Dr. Rollin Ramsaran, Academic Dean, Emmanuel Christian Seminary, 423-461-1524, Fax: 423-926-6198, E-mail: rraramsaran@milligan.edu. *Application contact:* Lauren Gullett, Director of Admissions and Recruitment for Emmanuel Christian Seminary, 423-461-1535, Fax: 423-926-6198, E-mail: lwgullett@milligan.edu.
Website: http://ecs.milligan.edu/

**Missouri State University,** Graduate College, College of Humanities and Public Affairs, Department of Religious Studies, Springfield, MO 65897. Offers MA, Certificate. *Program availability:* Part-time. *Faculty:* 11 full-time (3 women). *Students:* 5 full-time (1 woman), 9 part-time (2 women); includes 2 minority (1 Black or African American, non-Hispanic/Latino; 1 Hispanic/Latino), 1 international. Average age 29. 9 applicants, 78% accepted, 4 enrolled. In 2016, 7 master's awarded. *Degree requirements:* For master's, one foreign language, comprehensive exam, thesis or alternative. *Entrance requirements:* For master's, GRE, minimum GPA of 3.2. Additional exam requirements/recommendations for international students: Required—TOEFL (minimum score 550 paper-based; 79 iBT), IELTS (minimum score 6). *Application deadline:* For fall admission, 7/20 priority date for domestic students, 5/1 for international students; for spring admission, 12/20 priority date for domestic students, 9/1 for international students. Applications are processed on a rolling basis. Application fee: $35 ($50 for international students). Electronic applications accepted. *Expenses:* Tuition, state resident: full-time $5830. Tuition, nonresident: full-time $10,708. *Required fees:* $1130. Tuition and fees vary according to class time, course level, course load and program. *Financial support:* Federal Work-Study, institutionally sponsored loans, scholarships/grants, and unspecified assistantships available. Financial award application deadline: 3/31; financial award applicants required to submit FAFSA. *Faculty research:* Apocalyptic literature, Protestantism in American society, contemporary Hinduism, Christian history. *Unit head:* Dr. Stephen Berkwitz, Department Head, 417-836-4147, Fax: 417-836-4757, E-mail: religiousstudies@missouristate.edu. *Application contact:* Michael Edwards, Coordinator of Graduate Admissions, 417-836-5330, Fax: 417-836-6200, E-mail: michaeledwards@missouristate.edu.
Website: http://www.missouristate.edu/relst/

**Moody Theological Seminary–Michigan,** Graduate Programs, Plymouth, MI 48170. Offers Bible (Graduate Certificate); Christian education (MA); counseling psychology (MA); divinity (M Div); theological studies (MA). *Program availability:* Part-time, evening/weekend. *Degree requirements:* For master's, one foreign language, thesis. *Faculty research:* Judaism, cults, world religions.

**Mount St. Joseph University,** Graduate Program in Religious Studies, Cincinnati, OH 45233-1670. Offers religious studies (MA); spirituality and wellness (Certificate). *Program availability:* Part-time, evening/weekend. *Faculty:* 3 full-time (1 woman), 4 part-time/adjunct (2 women). *Students:* 1 (woman) full-time, 6 part-time (4 women); includes 2 minority (1 Black or African American, non-Hispanic/Latino; 1 Hispanic/Latino). Average age 42. In 2016, 5 master's awarded. *Degree requirements:* For master's, comprehensive exam, 36 hours of credit, pastoral PRAXIS component (3 credit hours), integrating project (3 credit hours). *Entrance requirements:* For master's, undergraduate

transcript with minimum overall GPA of 3.0, 3 letters of recommendation from professional colleagues, 3-page essay, interview with the Graduate Admissions Committee, current work resume. Additional exam requirements/recommendations for international students: Required—TOEFL (minimum score 560 paper-based; 83 iBT). *Application deadline:* Applications are processed on a rolling basis. Electronic applications accepted. *Expenses:* $580 per credit hour. *Financial support:* In 2016–17, 5 students received support. Scholarships/grants available. Financial award applicants required to submit FAFSA. *Faculty research:* Contextual/cultural/systematic theology, historical/spiritual theology, business/economics ethics, social justice, Biblical/cultural/pastoral theology. *Unit head:* Dr. John Trokan, Associate Professor of Religious and Pastoral Studies/Director of Graduate Program, 513-244-4272, Fax: 513-244-4222, E-mail: john.trokan@msj.edu. *Application contact:* Mary Brigham, Assistant Director of Graduate Recruitment, 513-244-4233, Fax: 513-244-4629, E-mail: mary.brigham@msj.edu.
Website: http://www.msj.edu/academics/graduate-programs/religious-studies-programs/

**Mount Saint Mary's University,** Graduate Division, Los Angeles, CA 90049. Offers business administration (MBA); counseling psychology (MS); creative writing (MFA); education (MS, Certificate); film and television (MFA); health policy and management (MS); humanities (MA); nursing (MSN, Certificate); physical therapy (DPT); religious studies (MA). *Program availability:* Part-time, evening/weekend. *Faculty:* 50 full-time (35 women), 116 part-time/adjunct (81 women). *Students:* 670 full-time (518 women), 147 part-time (116 women); includes 414 minority (73 Black or African American, non-Hispanic/Latino; 4 American Indian or Alaska Native, non-Hispanic/Latino; 60 Asian, non-Hispanic/Latino; 259 Hispanic/Latino; 7 Native Hawaiian or other Pacific Islander, non-Hispanic/Latino; 11 Two or more races, non-Hispanic/Latino), 4 international. Average age 32. 1,398 applicants, 21% accepted, 242 enrolled. In 2016, 170 master's, 28 doctorates, 35 other advanced degrees awarded. *Entrance requirements:* Additional exam requirements/recommendations for international students: Required—TOEFL. *Application deadline:* For fall admission, 6/30 priority date for domestic and international students; for spring admission, 10/30 priority date for domestic and international students; for summer admission, 3/30 priority date for domestic and international students. Applications are processed on a rolling basis. Application fee: $50. Electronic applications accepted. *Expenses: Tuition:* Full-time $9983; part-time $829 per unit. One-time fee: $135. Tuition and fees vary according to degree level and program. *Financial support:* Career-related internships or fieldwork, Federal Work-Study, institutionally sponsored loans, and tuition waivers (full and partial) available. Support available to part-time students. Financial award application deadline: 3/15; financial award applicants required to submit FAFSA. *Unit head:* Albert Ramos, Director of Graduate Admissions, 213-477-2800, E-mail: gradprograms@msmu.edu. *Application contact:* Shawn Peters, Graduate Admission Counselor, 213-477-2676, E-mail: gradprograms@msmu.edu.
Website: http://www.msmu.edu/graduate-programs/

**Naropa University,** Graduate Programs, Program in Religious Studies, Boulder, CO 80302-6697. Offers MA. *Faculty:* 6 full-time (3 women), 5 part-time/adjunct (2 women). *Students:* 12 full-time (5 women), 3 part-time (all women); includes 2 minority (both Two or more races, non-Hispanic/Latino), 3 international. Average age 36. 13 applicants, 100% accepted, 7 enrolled. In 2016, 3 master's awarded. *Degree requirements:* For master's, comprehensive exam, thesis. *Entrance requirements:* For master's, interview; transcripts; letter of interest; resume/curriculum vitae with pertinent academic, employment and volunteer activity; 2 letters of recommendation. Additional exam requirements/recommendations for international students: Required—TOEFL (minimum score 550 paper-based; 80 iBT). *Application deadline:* For fall admission, 1/15 priority date for domestic and international students. Applications are processed on a rolling basis. Application fee: $60. Electronic applications accepted. *Expenses:* $20,570 for first year. *Financial support:* In 2016–17, 7 students received support, including 2 teaching assistantships with partial tuition reimbursements available (averaging $2,250 per year); research assistantships with partial tuition reimbursements available, career-related internships or fieldwork, Federal Work-Study, scholarships/grants, tuition waivers (partial), and unspecified assistantships also available. Support available to part-time students. Financial award application deadline: 3/1; financial award applicants required to submit FAFSA. *Unit head:* Dr. Elaine Yuen, Chair, Department of Wisdom Traditions, 303-245-4718, E-mail: eyuen@naropa.edu. *Application contact:* Office of Admissions, 303-546-3572, Fax: 303-546-3583, E-mail: admissions@naropa.edu.
Website: http://www.naropa.edu/academics/masters/religious-studies/index.php

**Naropa University,** Graduate Programs, Program in Religious Studies with Language, Boulder, CO 80302-6697. Offers MA. Program allows for addition of two years of Sanskrit and/or Tibetan language. *Faculty:* 6 full-time (3 women), 7 part-time/adjunct (3 women). *Students:* 9 full-time (2 women), 4 part-time (0 women); includes 2 minority (both Hispanic/Latino), 1 international. Average age 29. 13 applicants, 100% accepted, 6 enrolled. In 2016, 7 master's awarded. *Degree requirements:* For master's, comprehensive exam, thesis. *Entrance requirements:* For master's, interview; transcripts; resume/curriculum vitae with pertinent academic, employment and volunteer activity; 2 letters of recommendation; letter of interest. Additional exam requirements/recommendations for international students: Required—TOEFL (minimum score 550 paper-based; 80 iBT). *Application deadline:* For fall admission, 1/15 priority date for domestic and international students. Applications are processed on a rolling basis. Application fee: $60. Electronic applications accepted. *Expenses:* $22,560 for first year of study. *Financial support:* In 2016–17, 5 students received support, including 2 teaching assistantships with partial tuition reimbursements available (averaging $1,575 per year); research assistantships with partial tuition reimbursements available, career-related internships or fieldwork, Federal Work-Study, scholarships/grants, tuition waivers (partial), and unspecified assistantships also available. Support available to part-time students. Financial award application deadline: 3/1; financial award applicants required to submit FAFSA. *Unit head:* Dr. Elaine Yuen, Chair, Department of Wisdom Traditions, 303-245-4718, E-mail: eyuen@naropa.edu. *Application contact:* Office of Admissions, 303-546-3572, Fax: 303-546-3583, E-mail: admissions@naropa.edu.
Website: http://www.naropa.edu/academics/masters/religious-studies/index.php

**Nashotah House Theological Seminary,** Graduate Programs, Nashotah, WI 53058-9793. Offers Anglican studies (Certificate); Biblical studies (STM); Christian spirituality (STM); church history (STM); liturgy (STM); ministry (M Div, MM); pastoral ministry (MPM); theological studies (MTS); theology (STM, D Min). *Accreditation:* ACIPE; ATS (one or more programs are accredited). *Program availability:* Part-time. *Faculty:* 8 full-time (0 women), 6 part-time/adjunct (0 women). *Students:* 78 full-time (14 women), 5 part-time (2 women); includes 3 minority (2 Black or African American, non-Hispanic/Latino; 1 Asian, non-Hispanic/Latino). Average age 37. *Degree requirements:* For master's, thesis optional. *Entrance requirements:* For master's and Certificate, GRE General Test or MAT, interview, 3 recommendations. Additional exam requirements/recommendations for international students: Required—TOEFL. *Application deadline:* For fall admission, 6/15 for domestic students. Applications are processed on a rolling basis. Application fee: $0. Electronic applications accepted. *Expenses:* $500 per credit hour. *Financial support:* Teaching assistantships, career-related internships or fieldwork, scholarships/grants, and tuition waivers (partial) available. Support available to part-time students. Financial award application deadline: 1/15; financial award applicants required to submit FAFSA. *Faculty research:* Formation for parochial ministry,

ancient Semitic epigraphy. *Unit head:* Very Rev. Steven A. Peay, Dean/President, 262-646-6512, Fax: 262-646-6504, E-mail: speay@nashotah.edu. *Application contact:* Fr. Dr. Rick Hartley, Associate Dean of Students/Registrar, 262-646-6547, Fax: 262-646-6504, E-mail: rhartley@nashotah.edu.
Website: https://www.nashotah.edu/programs

**New Saint Andrews College,** Graduate School, Moscow, ID 83843. Offers classical Christian studies (Graduate Certificate); theology and letters (MA). *Program availability:* Part-time, blended/hybrid learning. *Faculty:* 12 part-time/adjunct (0 women). *Students:* 12 full-time (3 women), 8 part-time (5 women), 1 international. Average age 25. 15 applicants, 53% accepted, 7 enrolled. In 2016, 3 master's awarded. *Degree requirements:* For master's, comprehensive exam (for some programs), thesis (for some programs), final oral exam. *Entrance requirements:* For master's, GRE, 2 letters of recommendation; for Graduate Certificate, GRE, bachelor's degree, essays, 2 letters of recommendation. *Application deadline:* For fall admission, 12/1 for domestic students. Applications are processed on a rolling basis. Application fee: $50. Electronic applications accepted. *Expenses: Tuition:* Full-time $7200; part-time $475 per credit. One-time fee: $160. *Faculty research:* Hebrew, theology, literature. *Unit head:* Benjamin Merkle, Academic Dean, 208-882-1566 Ext. 104, E-mail: bmerkle@nsa.edu. *Application contact:* Brenda Schlect, Director of Admissions, 208-882-1566 Ext. 113, Fax: 208-882-4293, E-mail: admissions@nsa.edu.
Website: http://www.nsa.edu/academics/graduate-school/

**New York University,** Graduate School of Arts and Science, Draper Interdisciplinary Program in Humanities and Social Thought, New York, NY 10012-1019. Offers humanities and social thought (MA); religion (Advanced Certificate); social theory (Advanced Certificate). *Program availability:* Part-time. *Degree requirements:* For master's, thesis, comprehensive exam or essay. *Entrance requirements:* For master's, GRE General Test; for Advanced Certificate, master's degree. Additional exam requirements/recommendations for international students: Required—TOEFL. *Faculty research:* Art world, gender politics, global histories, literary cultures, the city.

**New York University,** Graduate School of Arts and Science, Program in Religious Studies, New York, NY 10012-1019. Offers MA. *Program availability:* Part-time. *Degree requirements:* For master's, one foreign language, thesis. *Entrance requirements:* For master's, GRE General Test. Additional exam requirements/recommendations for international students: Required—TOEFL. *Faculty research:* Biblical and rabbinic Judaism, New Testament and early Christianity, comparative mysticism, gender and embodiment, East Asian religions.

**Northern Seminary,** Graduate and Professional Programs, Lombard, IL 60148-5698. Offers Biblical studies (M Div); Christian community development (D Min); Christian ministry (MACM); contextual theology (D Min); New Testament (MANT); New Testament context (D Min); theology (M Div); theology and mission (MA); urban leadership (MA); worship (MAW). *Program availability:* Part-time, evening/weekend. *Faculty:* 6 full-time (1 woman), 33 part-time/adjunct (8 women). *Students:* 126 full-time (34 women), 80 part-time (32 women); includes 89 minority (73 Black or African American, non-Hispanic/Latino; 6 Asian, non-Hispanic/Latino; 8 Hispanic/Latino; 2 Two or more races, non-Hispanic/Latino), 3 international. Average age 44. In 2016, 18 master's, 14 doctorates awarded. *Degree requirements:* For master's, thesis (for some programs); for doctorate, thesis/dissertation. *Entrance requirements:* For master's, writing test, all official transcripts, letter of reference from church, 3 letters of reference, autobiographical statement (400 words or more); for doctorate, M Div, 3 years in the ministry post-M Div, 3 letters of reference. Additional exam requirements/recommendations for international students: Required—TOEFL (minimum score 550 paper-based). *Application deadline:* For fall admission, 8/25 for domestic students, 2/1 for international students; for winter admission, 12/10 for domestic students, 2/1 for international students; for spring admission, 3/15 for domestic students, 2/1 for international students. Applications are processed on a rolling basis. Application fee: $35. Electronic applications accepted. *Expenses:* Contact institution. *Financial support:* In 2016–17, 3 teaching assistantships with partial tuition reimbursements were awarded; Federal Work-Study and scholarships/grants also available. Support available to part-time students. Financial award application deadline: 9/1; financial award applicants required to submit FAFSA. *Faculty research:* Theology and mission, worship studies, church history, evangelism, Christian ministry, urban leadership, New Testament. *Unit head:* Dr. William Shiell, President, 630-620-2101, Fax: 630-620-2190. *Application contact:* Greg Armstrong, Director of Admissions, 630-620-2175, Fax: 630-620-2190, E-mail: admissions@seminary.edu.

**Northwestern University,** The Graduate School, Judd A. and Marjorie Weinberg College of Arts and Sciences, Department of Religious Studies, Evanston, IL 60208. Offers PhD.

**Northwestern University,** School of Professional Studies, Program in Liberal Studies, Evanston, IL 60208. Offers American studies (MA); history (MA); religious and ethical studies (MA).

**Northwest Nazarene University,** Program in Religion, Nampa, ID 83686-5897. Offers missional leadership (M Div, MA); pastoral ministry (MA); spiritual formation (M Div, MA); youth, children, and family ministry (M Div, MA). *Program availability:* Part-time, online only, 100% online. *Faculty:* 11 full-time (3 women), 18 part-time/adjunct (0 women). *Students:* 65 full-time (23 women), 25 part-time (11 women); includes 11 minority (4 Black or African American, non-Hispanic/Latino; 1 American Indian or Alaska Native, non-Hispanic/Latino; 2 Asian, non-Hispanic/Latino; 3 Hispanic/Latino; 1 Native Hawaiian or other Pacific Islander, non-Hispanic/Latino), 1 international. Average age 39. 37 applicants, 76% accepted, 24 enrolled. In 2016, 40 master's awarded. *Entrance requirements:* For master's, minimum GPA of 2.5; 8 semester or 12 quarter credits of Bible, theology and/or Western philosophy. Additional exam requirements/recommendations for international students: Required—TOEFL (minimum score 85 iBT). *Application deadline:* For fall admission, 7/31 for domestic students, 7/1 for international students; for spring admission, 2/1 for domestic students, 1/5 for international students. Applications are processed on a rolling basis. Application fee: $50. Electronic applications accepted. *Expenses:* Contact institution. *Financial support:* In 2016–17, 3 students received support. Scholarships/grants available. *Unit head:* Dr. Jay Akkerman, Director, Graduate Studies, 208-467-8437, Fax: 208-467-8252. *Application contact:* Vicki Funk, Program Coordinator, 208-467-8432, Fax: 208-467-8252, E-mail: vlfunk@nnu.edu.
Website: http://www.nnu.edu/ministry/

**Nyack College,** College of Bible and Christian Ministry, Nyack, NY 10960. Offers ancient Judaism and Christian origins (MA). *Program availability:* Part-time, evening/weekend, 100% online, blended/hybrid learning. *Students:* 2 full-time (1 woman), 6 part-time (0 women); includes 5 minority (2 Black or African American, non-Hispanic/Latino; 2 Hispanic/Latino; 1 Two or more races, non-Hispanic/Latino). Average age 39. In 2016, 2 master's awarded. *Degree requirements:* For master's, 2 foreign languages, comprehensive exam. *Entrance requirements:* For master's, GRE, proficiency exam in Biblical Hebrew, essay, Christian experience statement, pastoral reference, academic references, writing sample. Additional exam requirements/recommendations for international students: Required—TOEFL (minimum score 550 paper-based; 80 iBT). *Application deadline:* Applications are processed on a rolling basis. Application fee: $30.

## Religion

Electronic applications accepted. *Expenses:* $575 per credit. *Financial support:* Applicants required to submit FAFSA. *Unit head:* Dr. Steven Notley, Director, 646-378-6148, E-mail: steven.notley@nyack.edu. *Application contact:* 800-541-6891, Fax: 845-348-3912, E-mail: admissions.grad@nyack.edu.

**Oblate School of Theology,** Graduate and Professional Programs, San Antonio, TX 78216-6693. Offers African-American pastoral leadership (D Min); divinity (M Div); pastoral leadership (D Min); pastoral ministry (MAP Min); pastoral studies (Certificate); spiritual formation in the local community (D Min); spirituality (MA Sp, PhD); spirituality and ministry (D Min); theology (MA Th); U.S. Hispanic/Latino ministry (D Min); M Div/ MA Th. *Accreditation:* ACIPE; ATS (one or more programs are accredited). *Program availability:* Part-time, online learning. *Faculty:* 24 full-time (8 women), 4 part-time/ adjunct (0 women). *Students:* 76 full-time (10 women), 51 part-time (32 women); includes 56 minority (8 Black or African American, non-Hispanic/Latino; 9 Asian, non-Hispanic/Latino; 39 Hispanic/Latino), 41 international. Average age 40. In 2016, 31 master's, 3 doctorates awarded. *Degree requirements:* For master's, comprehensive exam (for some programs), thesis (for some programs), practicum; for doctorate, one foreign language, comprehensive exam, thesis/dissertation, paper, practicum. *Entrance requirements:* For master's, MAT, interview, course work in theology or religious studies, minimum GPA of 2.5; for doctorate, M Div, MA Th, or MA Sp. Additional exam requirements/recommendations for international students: Required—TOEFL (minimum score 71 iBT). *Application deadline:* For fall admission, 6/15 priority date for domestic and international students; for winter admission, 11/30 for domestic and international students; for spring admission, 11/30 for domestic and international students; for summer admission, 4/1 for domestic and international students. Applications are processed on a rolling basis. Application fee: $65. *Expenses:* Contact institution. *Financial support:* In 2016–17, 25 students received support. Scholarships/grants available. Support available to part-time students. Financial award application deadline: 8/1; financial award applicants required to submit FAFSA. *Unit head:* Dr. R. Scott Woodward, Academic Dean, 210-341-1366, Fax: 210-341-4519, E-mail: rsw@ost.edu. *Application contact:* Mario A. Porter, Registrar, 210-341-1366 Ext. 226, Fax: 210-341-4519, E-mail: registrar@ost.edu.

**Olivet Nazarene University,** Graduate School, Division of Religion, Bourbonnais, IL 60914. Offers biblical literature (MA); religion (MA); theology (MA). *Program availability:* Part-time. *Degree requirements:* For master's, thesis or alternative.

**Oregon State University,** College of Liberal Arts, Program in Applied Ethics, Corvallis, OR 97331. Offers biomedical ethics (MA); environmental ethics (MA); ethics and religion (MA); global justice, peace, and war (MA); social justice (MA). *Program availability:* Part-time. *Faculty:* 12 full-time (4 women), 1 (woman) part-time/adjunct. *Students:* 10 full-time (7 women), 1 part-time (1 woman); includes 3 minority (1 American Indian or Alaska Native, non-Hispanic/Latino; 2 Hispanic/Latino), 1 international. Average age 29. 9 applicants, 67% accepted, 6 enrolled. In 2016, 1 master's awarded. *Entrance requirements:* For master's, writing sample of 5-7 pages. Additional exam requirements/recommendations for international students: Required—TOEFL (minimum score 80 iBT), IELTS (minimum score 6.5). *Application deadline:* For fall admission, 1/15 priority date for domestic and international students. Application fee: $85 for international students). *Expenses:* Tuition, state resident: full-time $12,150; part-time $450 per credit. Tuition, nonresident: full-time $21,789; part-time $807 per credit. *Required fees:* $1651; $1507 per credit. One-time fee: $350. Tuition and fees vary according to course load, campus/location and program. *Unit head:* Dr. Ben Mutschler, Director. *Application contact:* Dr. Allen Thompson, Director of Graduate Studies, 541-737-5654, E-mail: allen.thompson@oregonstate.edu.
Website: http://liberalarts.oregonstate.edu/shpr/philosophy

**Oxford Graduate School,** Graduate Programs, Dayton, TN 37321-6736. Offers family life education (M Litt); integration of religion and society (D Phil); organizational leadership (M Litt). *Faculty:* 10 full-time (2 women), 22 part-time/adjunct (7 women). *Students:* 105 full-time (40 women). *Entrance requirements:* For master's, official transcripts, three letters of recommendation, bachelor's degree or its equivalent, minimum undergraduate GPA of 3.0, minimum of 3 years of professional experience; for doctorate, official transcripts, three letters of recommendation, master's degree with minimum GPA of 3.0, minimum of 5 years of professional experience. *Expenses:* $7,875 per year (for D Phil); $6,000 per year (for M Litt). *Application contact:* Gwen Ballant, Director of Admissions, 423-775-6596, Fax: 423-775-6599, E-mail: oxfordgraduateschool@ogs.edu.

**Pacific School of Religion,** Graduate and Professional Programs, Berkeley, CA 94709-1323. Offers M Div, MA, MTS, D Min, PhD, Th D, CAPS, CMS, CSS, CTS. MA, PhD, Th D offered jointly with Graduate Theological Union; D Min with Church Divinity School of the Pacific. *Accreditation:* ACIPE; ATS (one or more programs are accredited). *Program availability:* Part-time. *Degree requirements:* For master's, one foreign language, thesis (for some programs); for doctorate, thesis/dissertation. *Entrance requirements:* For master's, minimum GPA of 3.0; for doctorate, M Div, minimum GPA of 3.0 (D Min); for other advanced degree, M Div, minimum GPA of 3.0 (CAPS). Additional exam requirements/recommendations for international students: Required—TOEFL (minimum score 550 paper-based). Electronic applications accepted. *Faculty research:* Medical ethics, gay/lesbian studies in religion, Asian-American religion, race, culture and theology, theology in context.

**Pepperdine University,** Seaver College, Division of Religion, Malibu, CA 90263. Offers ministry (MS); religion (M Div, MA). *Program availability:* Part-time, evening/weekend. *Students:* 5 full-time (2 women), 13 part-time (4 women); includes 7 minority (3 Black or African American, non-Hispanic/Latino; 2 Asian, non-Hispanic/Latino; 2 Hispanic/ Latino). Average age 32. In 2016, 7 master's awarded. *Entrance requirements:* For master's, GRE General Test, letters of recommendation, writing sample. Additional exam requirements/recommendations for international students: Required—TOEFL. *Application deadline:* For fall admission, 2/1 priority date for domestic students. Applications are processed on a rolling basis. Application fee: $65. Electronic applications accepted. *Financial support:* Applicants required to submit FAFSA. *Unit head:* Dr. Timothy Willis, Chair/Advisor, 310-506-4352, Fax: 310-506-7271, E-mail: timothy.willis@pepperdine.edu. *Application contact:* Hayley Wolf, Director of Admission, 310-506-4392, E-mail: hayley.wolf@pepperdine.edu.
Website: http://seaver.pepperdine.edu/religion/graduate/marreligion/

**Princeton Theological Seminary,** Graduate and Professional Programs, Princeton, NJ 08542-0803. Offers M Div, MA, Th M, D Min, PhD. *Accreditation:* ACIPE; ATS. *Program availability:* Part-time. Terminal master's awarded for partial completion of doctoral program. *Degree requirements:* For doctorate, 2 foreign languages, thesis/dissertation, comprehensive exam (PhD), French and German. *Entrance requirements:* For doctorate, GRE General Test. Additional exam requirements/recommendations for international students: Required—TOEFL. Electronic applications accepted.

**Princeton University,** Graduate School, Department of Religion, Princeton, NJ 08544-1019. Offers PhD. *Degree requirements:* For doctorate, variable foreign language requirement, comprehensive exam, thesis/dissertation. *Entrance requirements:* For doctorate, GRE General Test. Additional exam requirements/recommendations for international students: Required—TOEFL (minimum score 600 paper-based). Electronic applications accepted.

**Queen's University at Kingston,** School of Graduate Studies, Faculty of Arts and Sciences, Department of Religious Studies, Kingston, ON K7L 3N6, Canada. Offers MA. *Degree requirements:* For master's, one foreign language, essay. *Entrance requirements:* For master's, honors BA in religious studies or equivalent. Additional exam requirements/recommendations for international students: Required—TOEFL (minimum score 600 paper-based). *Faculty research:* Modernity, culture, feminism, world religions, traditions.

**Reformed Theological Seminary–Charlotte Campus,** Graduate and Professional Programs, Charlotte, NC 28226-6318. Offers biblical studies (MA); ministry (D Min); pastoral ministry (M Div); theological studies (MA). *Program availability:* Part-time. *Degree requirements:* For master's, comprehensive exam; for doctorate, thesis/ dissertation. *Entrance requirements:* For master's, minimum GPA of 2.6; for doctorate, minimum GPA of 3.0. Additional exam requirements/recommendations for international students: Required—TOEFL (minimum score 550 paper-based). Electronic applications accepted.

**Reformed Theological Seminary–Houston Campus,** Graduate Program, Houston, TX 77024. Offers MA. Electronic applications accepted.

**Reformed Theological Seminary–Jackson Campus,** Graduate and Professional Programs, Jackson, MS 39209-3004. Offers Bible, theology, and missions (Certificate); Biblical exegesis (M Div); biblical studies (MA); Christian education (MA); counseling (M Div); marriage and family therapy (MA); ministry (D Min); missions (M Div, MA, D Min); theological studies (MA). *Accreditation:* AAMFT/COAMFTE (one or more programs are accredited); ATS (one or more programs are accredited). *Degree requirements:* For master's, thesis (for some programs), fieldwork; for doctorate, 2 foreign languages, thesis/dissertation. *Entrance requirements:* For master's, minimum GPA of 2.6; for doctorate, minimum GPA of 3.0. Additional exam requirements/ recommendations for international students: Required—TOEFL.

**Reformed Theological Seminary–Washington D.C.,** Graduate and Professional Programs, McLean, VA 22102. Offers Bible (M Div); biblical studies (MA); practical theology (M Div); religion (MA); theology (M Div). *Program availability:* Part-time, evening/weekend. *Faculty:* 4 full-time (0 women), 10 part-time/adjunct (2 women). *Students:* 5 full-time (0 women), 86 part-time (7 women); includes 25 minority (4 Black or African American, non-Hispanic/Latino; 18 Asian, non-Hispanic/Latino; 3 Hispanic/ Latino), 1 international. Average age 35. 73 applicants, 95% accepted, 67 enrolled. In 2016, 8 master's awarded. *Degree requirements:* For master's, integrative paper. *Entrance requirements:* For master's, minimum undergraduate GPA of 2.6. Additional exam requirements/recommendations for international students: Required—TOEFL (minimum score 550 paper-based), TWE. *Application deadline:* Applications are processed on a rolling basis. Application fee: $75. Electronic applications accepted. *Expenses:* $495 per credit hour; $60-$80 student activity fee (fall/spring only); $200 graduation fee. *Financial support:* In 2016–17, 116 students received support. Scholarships/grants and tuition waivers (partial) available. Support available to part-time students. Financial award application deadline: 5/1. *Faculty research:* Theology, Biblical studies, cultural studies. *Unit head:* Dr. John S. Redd, Jr., President, 703-448-3393 Ext. 5107, E-mail: sredd@rts.edu. *Application contact:* Geoff M. Sackett, Director of Admissions, 703-448-3393 Ext. 5104, E-mail: gsackett@rts.edu.
Website: http://www.rts.edu/

**Regent University,** Graduate School, Robertson School of Government, Virginia Beach, VA 23464-9800. Offers government (MA), including American government, healthcare policy and ethics (MA, MPA), international relations, law and public policy, national security studies, political communication, political theory, religion and politics; public administration (MPA), including emergency management and homeland security, federal government, general public administration, healthcare policy and ethics (MA, MPA), law, nonprofit administration and faith-based organizations, public leadership and management, servant leadership. *Program availability:* Part-time, evening/weekend, 100% online, blended/hybrid learning. *Faculty:* 8 full-time (1 woman), 19 part-time/ adjunct (3 women). *Students:* 40 full-time (27 women), 119 part-time (69 women); includes 73 minority (47 Black or African American, non-Hispanic/Latino; 3 Asian, non-Hispanic/Latino; 15 Hispanic/Latino; 8 Two or more races, non-Hispanic/Latino), 6 international. Average age 35. 253 applicants, 41% accepted, 70 enrolled. In 2016, 34 master's awarded. *Degree requirements:* For master's, thesis optional, internship. *Entrance requirements:* For master's, GRE General Test or LSAT, personal essay, writing sample, resume, college transcripts. Additional exam requirements/ recommendations for international students: Required—TOEFL (minimum score 577 paper-based). *Application deadline:* For fall admission, 5/1 priority date for domestic students; for spring admission, 11/1 priority date for domestic students. Applications are processed on a rolling basis. Application fee: $50. Electronic applications accepted. *Expenses:* $650 per credit (MA/MPA); $250 per semester technology fee. *Financial support:* In 2016–17, 78 students received support. Career-related internships or fieldwork, scholarships/grants, and unspecified assistantships available. Support available to part-time students. *Faculty research:* International relations and politics, public administration, leadership and ethics, Biblical law, Constitutional law and Supreme Court. *Unit head:* Dr. Eric Patterson, Dean, 757-352-4616, Fax: 757-352-4735, E-mail: epatterson@regent.edu. *Application contact:* Heidi Cece, Assistant Vice President of Enrollment Management, 800-373-5504, Fax: 757-352-4381, E-mail: admissions@regent.edu.
Website: http://www.regent.edu/rsg/

**Regent University,** Graduate School, School of Divinity, Virginia Beach, VA 23464-9800. Offers divinity (M Div), including Biblical studies (M Div, MTS, PhD), chaplain ministry, Christian theology (M Div, MTS, PhD), church and ministry (M Div, MA), history of Christianity (M Div, MTS, PhD), inter-cultural studies (M Div, MA), interdisciplinary studies (M Div, MA, MTS), marketplace ministry, worship and media (M Div, MA); leadership and renewal (D Min), including Christian leadership and renewal, clinical pastoral education, community transformation, military ministry, ministry leadership coaching; practical theology (MA), including church and ministry (M Div, MA), inter-cultural studies (M Div, MA), interdisciplinary studies (M Div, MA, MTS), worship and media (M Div, MA); theological studies (MTS, PhD), including Biblical studies (M Div, MTS, PhD), Christian theology (M Div, MTS, PhD), history of Christianity (M Div, MTS, PhD), interdisciplinary studies (M Div, MA, MTS). *Accreditation:* ACIPE; ATS. *Program availability:* Part-time, evening/weekend, 100% online, blended/hybrid learning. *Faculty:* 15 full-time (3 women), 51 part-time/adjunct (6 women). *Students:* 148 full-time (60 women), 787 part-time (321 women); includes 506 minority (416 Black or African American, non-Hispanic/Latino; 1 American Indian or Alaska Native, non-Hispanic/ Latino; 23 Asian, non-Hispanic/Latino; 54 Hispanic/Latino; 1 Native Hawaiian or other Pacific Islander, non-Hispanic/Latino; 11 Two or more races, non-Hispanic/Latino), 31 international. Average age 43. 1,020 applicants, 42% accepted, 276 enrolled. In 2016, 127 master's, 25 doctorates awarded. *Degree requirements:* For master's, comprehensive exam, thesis or alternative, internship; for doctorate, thesis/dissertation or alternative. *Entrance requirements:* For master's, minimum undergraduate GPA of 2.75, writing sample, personal goal statement, college transcripts; for doctorate, GRE, minimum graduate GPA of 3.5 (PhD), 3.0 (D Min); clergy recommendations; writing sample; transcripts; resume; interview. Additional exam requirements/recommendations for international students: Required—TOEFL (minimum score 577 paper-based).

*Application deadline:* For fall admission, 5/1 priority date for domestic students. Applications are processed on a rolling basis. Application fee: $50. Electronic applications accepted. *Expenses:* Contact institution. *Financial support:* In 2016–17, 602 students received support. Career-related internships or fieldwork, scholarships/grants, and unspecified assistantships available. Support available to part-time students. *Faculty research:* Greek and Hebrew, theology, spiritual formation, global missions and world Christianity, women in ministry leadership. *Unit head:* Dr. Cornelius Bekker, Dean, 757-352-4401, Fax: 757-352-4597, E-mail: clbekker@regent.edu. *Application contact:* Heidi Cece, Assistant Vice President of Enrollment Management, 800-373-5504, Fax: 757-352-4381, E-mail: admissions@regent.edu.
Website: http://www.regent.edu/sod/

**Rice University,** Graduate Programs, School of Humanities, Department of Religious Studies, Houston, TX 77251-1892. Offers African religions (PhD); African-American religions (PhD); contemplative studies (PhD); ghosticism, esotericism, mysticism (PhD); Islam (PhD); Jewish thought and philosophy (PhD); modern Christianity in thought and popular culture (PhD); psychology of religion (PhD); the Bible and beyond (PhD). *Degree requirements:* For doctorate, 2 foreign languages, comprehensive exam, thesis/dissertation. *Entrance requirements:* For doctorate, GRE, letters of recommendation, writing sample. Additional exam requirements/recommendations for international students: Required—TOEFL (minimum score 600 paper-based; 90 iBT). Electronic applications accepted. *Faculty research:* Origins and historical development of Islam, history of Christianity, the study of comparative religion, African-American religion, religion and culture.

**The Robert E. Webber Institute for Worship Studies,** Doctor of Worship Studies Program, Orange Park, FL 32073. Offers DWS. *Degree requirements:* For doctorate, thesis/dissertation, practicum.

**The Robert E. Webber Institute for Worship Studies,** Master of Worship Studies Program, Orange Park, FL 32073. Offers MWS. *Degree requirements:* For master's, internship.

**Rutgers University–New Brunswick,** Graduate School-New Brunswick, Department of Religion, Piscataway, NJ 08854-8097. Offers religious studies (MA, Graduate Certificate). *Entrance requirements:* For master's and Graduate Certificate, GRE, personal statement, two letters of recommendation, official transcripts. Electronic applications accepted.

**St. Bonaventure University,** School of Graduate Studies, School of Franciscan Studies, St. Bonaventure, NY 14778-2284. Offers MA, Adv C. *Program availability:* Part-time. *Faculty:* 3 full-time (0 women). In 2016, 2 other advanced degrees awarded. *Degree requirements:* For master's, comprehensive exam, thesis optional. *Entrance requirements:* For master's, letter of intent, bachelor's degree, transcripts, letters of recommendation. Additional exam requirements/recommendations for international students: Required—TOEFL (minimum score 550 paper-based; 79 iBT). *Application deadline:* For fall admission, 3/15 priority date for domestic students, 2/1 priority date for international students. Applications are processed on a rolling basis. Application fee: $0. Electronic applications accepted. *Expenses:* Contact institution. *Financial support:* Federal Work-Study, scholarships/grants, health care benefits, and unspecified assistantships available. Support available to part-time students. Financial award application deadline: 4/15; financial award applicants required to submit FAFSA. *Unit head:* Fr. David Couturier, OFM, Dean, 716-375-2160, E-mail: dcouturi@sbu.edu. *Application contact:* Bruce Campbell, Director of Graduate Admissions, 716-375-2429, Fax: 716-375-4015, E-mail: gradsch@sbu.edu.
Website: http://www.sbu.edu/

**Saint Charles Borromeo Seminary, Overbrook,** Graduate and Professional Programs, Program of Catholic Studies, Wynnewood, PA 19096. Offers MA. *Program availability:* Part-time, evening/weekend. *Degree requirements:* For master's, comprehensive exam. *Entrance requirements:* For master's, 18 undergraduate credits in theology and/or philosophy or the equivalent. Additional exam requirements/recommendations for international students: Required—TOEFL.

**Saint John's Seminary,** Graduate Programs, Brighton, MA 02135. Offers M Div, MA Th, MAM.

**St. Joseph's Seminary,** Graduate and Professional Programs, Yonkers, NY 10704. Offers Catholic philosophical studies (MA); divinity (M Div); pastoral studies (MAPS); theology (MA). *Accreditation:* ATS. *Degree requirements:* For master's, one foreign language, thesis. *Entrance requirements:* For master's, 27 credits in philosophy and 9 in theology.

**Saint Mary's University,** Faculty of Arts, Department of Religious Studies, Halifax, NS B3H 3C3, Canada. Offers theology and religious studies (MA).

**Salve Regina University,** Program in Humanities, Newport, RI 02840-4192. Offers humanitarian assistance (MA); humanities (PhD); public humanities (MA); religion, peace and justice (MA). *Program availability:* Part-time, evening/weekend, online learning. *Degree requirements:* For master's, thesis optional; for doctorate, one foreign language, comprehensive exam, thesis/dissertation. *Entrance requirements:* For master's, GMAT, GRE General Test, or MAT; for doctorate, GRE General Test. Additional exam requirements/recommendations for international students: Required—TOEFL (minimum score 600 paper-based; 100 iBT) or IELTS. Electronic applications accepted.

**Santa Clara University,** Jesuit School of Theology, Berkeley, CA 94709. Offers Biblical languages (MABL); Biblical studies (MTS); Christian spirituality (MTS); church history (MTS); cultural and historical studies of Catholicism (MTS); ethics and social theory/religion and society (MTS); history of art and religion (MTS); liturgical studies (MTS); pastoral ministry (M Div); systematic and philosophical theology (MTS); theology (MA, MTS, Th M, STD, STB, STL); M Div/MA. *Program availability:* Part-time, evening/weekend, 100% online. *Faculty:* 20 full-time (5 women), 6 part-time/adjunct (3 women). *Students:* 125 full-time (29 women), 9 part-time (5 women); includes 71 minority (22 Black or African American, non-Hispanic/Latino; 27 Asian, non-Hispanic/Latino; 19 Hispanic/Latino; 2 Native Hawaiian or other Pacific Islander, non-Hispanic/Latino; 1 Two or more races, non-Hispanic/Latino). Average age 36. 93 applicants, 92% accepted, 56 enrolled. In 2016, 55 master's, 5 doctorates awarded. *Entrance requirements:* For master's, GRE, 2 letters of recommendation, resume, transcripts; for doctorate, GRE, master's degree or equivalent, resume, statement of purpose, transcripts, 2 letters of recommendation, research paper. Additional exam requirements/recommendations for international students: Required—TOEFL. *Application deadline:* For fall admission, 3/1 priority date for domestic students; for spring admission, 10/1 priority date for domestic students. Applications are processed on a rolling basis. Application fee: $50 ($0 for international students). Electronic applications accepted. *Expenses:* Contact institution. *Financial support:* Scholarships/grants and unspecified assistantships available. Financial award application deadline: 3/1; financial award applicants required to submit FAFSA. *Faculty research:* Religion and culture, interreligious dialogue, social ethics and restorative justice, Ignatian spirituality. *Unit head:* Alison Benders, Associate Dean, 510-549-5055, E-mail: ambenders@scu.edu. *Application contact:* Barbara Godoy, Assistant Dean of Enrollment Management, 510-549-5016, E-mail: bgodoy@scu.edu.
Website: http://www.scu.edu/jst/

**Seattle Pacific University,** Master of Arts in Theology Program, Seattle, WA 98119-1997. Offers Asian American ministry (MA); business and applied theology (MA); Christian leadership (MA); Christian scripture (MA); Christian studies (Graduate Certificate); reconciliation and intercultural studies (MA); theology (MA). *Degree requirements:* For master's, internship or thesis. *Entrance requirements:* For master's, two letters of recommendation; personal statement; bachelor's degree from regionally-accredited college or university or its equivalent; official copy of transcripts from college or university that granted the bachelor's degree and any institution attended since that time; minimum GPA of 3.0. Additional exam requirements/recommendations for international students: Required—TOEFL (minimum score 550 paper-based). Electronic applications accepted.

**The Seattle School of Theology and Psychology,** Graduate Programs, Seattle, WA 98121. Offers Christian studies (MA); counseling psychology (MA); divinity (M Div). *Program availability:* Part-time. *Entrance requirements:* For master's, MAT.

**Selma University,** Graduate Programs, Selma, AL 36701-5299. Offers Bible and Christian education (MA); Bible and pastoral ministry (MA).

**Seton Hall University,** College of Arts and Sciences, Department of Religion, South Orange, NJ 07079-2697. Offers Jewish-Christian studies (MA). *Program availability:* Part-time, evening/weekend. *Degree requirements:* For master's, thesis optional. *Entrance requirements:* For master's, interview or suitable correspondence with department chair. Additional exam requirements/recommendations for international students: Required—TOEFL. Electronic applications accepted. *Faculty research:* Jewish-Christian issues, Biblical studies, Holocaust studies.

**Seton Hall University,** Immaculate Conception Seminary School of Theology, South Orange, NJ 07079-2697. Offers Christian spirituality (Certificate); great spiritual books (Certificate); pastoral ministry (M Div, MA, Certificate); scripture studies (Certificate); Seminary's Theological Education for Parish Services (STEPS) (Certificate); theology (MA). *Program availability:* Part-time, evening/weekend. *Degree requirements:* For master's, comprehensive exam (for some programs), thesis (for some programs), final project (for some programs); 1 foreign language (for MA in theology research option). *Entrance requirements:* For master's, GRE General Test or MAT. Additional exam requirements/recommendations for international students: Required—TOEFL (minimum score 600 paper-based; 100 iBT). Electronic applications accepted. *Expenses:* Contact institution. *Faculty research:* Pauline literature, history of Biblical interpretation and theological exegesis, spirituality of St. Edith Stein, Thomism, history of Catholicism in America.

**Sioux Falls Seminary,** Graduate and Professional Programs, Program in Christian Leadership, Sioux Falls, SD 57105-1599. Offers MA. *Program availability:* Online learning. Application fee: $25. *Unit head:* Larry Caldwell, Chief Academic Officer/Dean, 605-336-6588, Fax: 605-335-9090, E-mail: lcaldwell@sfseminary.edu. *Application contact:* Dustin Brouwer, Director of Enrollment Management, 605-336-6188, Fax: 605-335-9090, E-mail: dbrouwer@sfseminary.edu.
Website: http://sfseminary.edu/prospective-students/programs/ma-christian-leadership/

**Southern Adventist University,** School of Religion, Collegedale, TN 37315-0370. Offers Biblical and theological studies (MA); church leadership and management (M Min); church ministry and homiletics (M Min); evangelism and world mission (M Min); religious studies (MA). *Program availability:* Part-time. *Degree requirements:* For master's, comprehensive exam, thesis (for some programs). *Entrance requirements:* For master's, GRE. Additional exam requirements/recommendations for international students: Required—TOEFL (minimum score 600 paper-based). *Faculty research:* Biblical archaeology.

**The Southern Baptist Theological Seminary,** School of Theology, Louisville, KY 40280-0004. Offers applied theology (D Min); biblical and theological studies (M Div); biblical counseling (M Div, MA, D Min); biblical spirituality (D Min); Christian ministry (M Div); expository preaching (D Min); pastoral studies (M Div); theological studies (MA); theology (Th M, PhD); worldview and apologetics (M Div). *Program availability:* Part-time, evening/weekend, online learning. *Degree requirements:* For master's, 2 foreign languages, thesis; for doctorate, 4 foreign languages, thesis/dissertation. *Entrance requirements:* For master's, GRE General Test, MAT, M Div; for doctorate, GRE General Test, MAT, interview, M Div, field essay. Additional exam requirements/recommendations for international students: Required—TOEFL, TWE. *Faculty research:* Biblical studies, contemporary theology, church history, pastoral care, ministry/missions studies.

**Southern California Seminary,** Graduate and Professional Programs, El Cajon, CA 92019. Offers Biblical studies (MABS); counseling psychology (MACP); marriage and family therapy (MAMFT); psychology (Psy D); religious studies (MRS); theology (M Div). *Program availability:* Part-time, evening/weekend, online learning. *Degree requirements:* For master's, thesis (for some programs); for doctorate, thesis/dissertation. *Entrance requirements:* For doctorate, master's degree in psychology. Additional exam requirements/recommendations for international students: Required—TOEFL (minimum score 550 paper-based). Electronic applications accepted.

**Southern Evangelical Seminary,** Graduate Programs, Matthews, NC 28105. Offers apologetics (MA, D Min, Certificate); Christian education (MA); church ministry (MA, Certificate); divinity (Certificate), including apologetics (M Div, Certificate); Islamic studies (MA, Certificate); Jewish studies (MA); philosophy (MA); philosophy of religion (PhD); religion (MA); theology (M Div), including apologetics (M Div, Certificate), Biblical studies; youth ministry (MA). *Program availability:* Part-time, evening/weekend, online learning. *Degree requirements:* For master's, thesis (for some programs); for doctorate, 2 foreign languages, comprehensive exam (for some programs), thesis/dissertation. *Entrance requirements:* Additional exam requirements/recommendations for international students: Required—TOEFL (minimum score 600 paper-based).

**Southern Methodist University,** Dedman College of Humanities and Sciences, Graduate Program in Religious Studies, Dallas, TX 75275-0133. Offers Hebrew Bible/Old Testament (PhD); history of the Christian tradition (PhD); New Testament (PhD); religion and culture (PhD); religious ethics (PhD); religious studies (MA); systematics theology (PhD). Terminal master's awarded for partial completion of doctoral program. *Degree requirements:* For master's, one foreign language, thesis, oral and written exams; for doctorate, variable foreign language requirement, thesis/dissertation, oral and written exams. *Entrance requirements:* For master's and doctorate, GRE General Test, minimum GPA of 3.0, course work in religion. Additional exam requirements/recommendations for international students: Required—TOEFL (minimum score 550 paper-based; 79 iBT). Electronic applications accepted. *Faculty research:* Theology, religious ethics, Biblical studies, history of Christianity, religion and culture.

**Southwestern Assemblies of God University,** Thomas F. Harrison School of Graduate Studies, Program in Theological Studies, Waxahachie, TX 75165-5735. Offers Bible and theology (MS); Biblical studies (M Div); counseling (M Div); cross cultural missions (M Div); practical theology (M Div); theological studies (M Div). *Program availability:* Online learning. *Degree requirements:* For master's, comprehensive written and oral exams. *Entrance requirements:* For master's, GRE General Test, minimum GPA of 2.5. Electronic applications accepted.

## Religion

**Stanford University,** School of Humanities and Sciences, Department of Religious Studies, Stanford, CA 94305-2004. Offers PhD. Terminal master's awarded for partial completion of doctoral program. *Degree requirements:* For doctorate, 2 foreign languages, thesis/dissertation, qualifying exam. *Entrance requirements:* For doctorate, GRE General Test. Additional exam requirements/recommendations for international students: Required—TOEFL. Electronic applications accepted. *Expenses: Tuition:* Full-time $47,331. *Required fees:* $609.

**SUM Bible College & Theological Seminary,** Graduate Programs, Oakland, CA 94603. Offers biblical studies (MA); Christian leadership (MA); theology (M Div). *Entrance requirements:* For master's, minimum GPA of 2.5, currently active in ministry.

**Syracuse University,** College of Arts and Sciences, Programs in Religion, Syracuse, NY 13244. Offers MA, PhD. *Program availability:* Part-time. *Students:* Average age 33. Terminal master's awarded for partial completion of doctoral program. *Degree requirements:* For master's, one foreign language, comprehensive exam, thesis optional; for doctorate, 2 foreign languages, comprehensive exam, thesis/dissertation. *Entrance requirements:* For master's and doctorate, GRE General Test, transcripts from all previous institutions; three letters of recommendation; personal statement of not more than 1000 words, including choice of concentration and religious culture to study at SU. Additional exam requirements/recommendations for international students: Required—TOEFL (minimum score 100 iBT). *Application deadline:* For fall admission, 1/10 priority date for domestic and international students. Application fee: $75. Electronic applications accepted. *Expenses: Tuition:* Full-time $25,974; part-time $1443 per credit hour. *Required fees:* $802; $50 per course. Tuition and fees vary according to course load and program. *Financial support:* Fellowships with full tuition reimbursements, teaching assistantships with tuition reimbursements, scholarships/grants, and tuition waivers available. Financial award application deadline: 1/1; financial award applicants required to submit FAFSA. *Faculty research:* Modern theology, religion and aesthetics, gender politics in Islam, global Hinduism, research and writing in religion and society. *Unit head:* Dr. Joanne Waghorne, Professor/Director of Graduate Studies in Religion, 315-443-5715, E-mail: jpwaghor@syr.edu. *Application contact:* Deborah Pratt, Recruiting Contact, 315-443-3863, E-mail: dpratt@syr.edu. Website: http://religion.syr.edu/

**Temple University,** College of Liberal Arts, Department of Religion, Philadelphia, PA 19122-6096. Offers MA, PhD. *Program availability:* Part-time. *Degree requirements:* For doctorate, variable foreign language requirement, thesis/dissertation. *Entrance requirements:* For master's and doctorate, GRE General Test, minimum GPA of 3.0, 3 letters of recommendation. Additional exam requirements/recommendations for international students: Required—TOEFL (minimum score 600 paper-based; 100 iBT). Electronic applications accepted. *Faculty research:* Buddhism, gender/sexuality, Hebrew Bible, Islam, world religions.

**Trevecca Nazarene University,** Graduate Religion Programs, Nashville, TN 37210-2877. Offers biblical and theological studies (MA); Christian ministry (MA); pastoral counseling (MA). *Program availability:* Part-time, online learning. *Faculty:* 6 full-time (1 woman), 6 part-time/adjunct (0 women). *Students:* 63 full-time (32 women), 22 part-time (10 women); includes 32 minority (24 Black or African American, non-Hispanic/Latino; 1 Asian, non-Hispanic/Latino; 6 Hispanic/Latino; 1 Two or more races, non-Hispanic/Latino), 1 international. Average age 41. In 2016, 9 master's awarded. *Degree requirements:* For master's, thesis. *Entrance requirements:* For master's, minimum GPA of 2.7, official transcript from regionally accredited institution, letter of recommendation. Additional exam requirements/recommendations for international students: Required—TOEFL (minimum score 550 paper-based; 80 iBT). *Application deadline:* Applications are processed on a rolling basis. Application fee: $0. Electronic applications accepted. *Expenses:* $350 per credit hour. *Financial support:* Applicants required to submit FAFSA. *Unit head:* Dr. Tim Green, Dean, School of Theology and Christian Ministry/Director, Graduate Religion Program, 615-248-1378, Fax: 615-248-7417. *Application contact:* 844-TNU-GRAD, E-mail: sgcsadmissions@trevecca.edu. Website: http://www.trevecca.edu/gradreligion

**Trinity International University Florida,** Divinity School, Davie, FL 33324. Offers MA, Certificate.

**Trinity School for Ministry,** Graduate Programs, Ambridge, PA 15003-2397. Offers Anglican studies (Diploma); basic Christian studies (Diploma); divinity (M Div); ministry (D Min); mission and evangelism (MAME, Certificate); religion (MAR); youth ministry (Diploma). *Program availability:* Part-time. *Degree requirements:* For master's, thesis optional; for doctorate, thesis/dissertation. *Entrance requirements:* Additional exam requirements/recommendations for international students: Required—TOEFL. *Faculty research:* Pauline Epistles, contemporary theology, history of Anglican liturgy, book of Ruth, biblical theology.

**Unification Theological Seminary,** Graduate Program, Main Campus, Barrytown, NY 12507. Offers divinity (M Div); ministry (D Min); religious education (MRE), including interfaith peacebuilding (MA, MRE); religious studies (MA), including interfaith peacebuilding (MA, MRE), non-profit leadership, theological studies, unification studies. *Program availability:* Part-time, evening/weekend. *Faculty:* 3 full-time (1 woman), 3 part-time/adjunct (0 women). *Students:* 27 full-time (8 women); includes 15 minority (11 Black or African American, non-Hispanic/Latino; 2 Asian, non-Hispanic/Latino; 1 Hispanic/Latino; 1 Two or more races, non-Hispanic/Latino), 6 international. Average age 50. In 2016, 12 master's, 5 doctorates awarded. *Degree requirements:* For master's, variable foreign language requirement, thesis (for some programs); for doctorate, thesis/dissertation. *Entrance requirements:* For master's, bachelor's degree; for doctorate, M Div or equivalency. Additional exam requirements/recommendations for international students: Required—TOEFL (minimum score 450 paper-based; 45 iBT). *Application deadline:* For fall admission, 3/15 priority date for domestic and international students; for spring admission, 9/15 priority date for domestic and international students. Applications are processed on a rolling basis. Application fee: $30. Electronic applications accepted. *Expenses:* Contact institution. *Financial support:* In 2016–17, 2 students received support. Scholarships/grants available. Financial award application deadline: 6/15; financial award applicants required to submit FAFSA. *Faculty research:* Church leadership, church history, world religions, ecumenism, interfaith peace building, service-learning. *Unit head:* Dr. Kathy Winings, Vice-President for Academic Affairs, 845-752-3000 Ext. 228, Fax: 845-752-3014, E-mail: academics@uts.edu. *Application contact:* Henry Christopher, Director of Admissions, 212-563-6647 Ext. 105, Fax: 845-752-3014, E-mail: h.christopher@uts.edu. Website: http://www.uts.edu

**Union University,** School of Theology and Missions, Jackson, TN 38305-3697. Offers Christian studies (MCS); expository preaching (D Min). *Program availability:* Part-time, evening/weekend, online learning. Electronic applications accepted. *Expenses: Tuition:* Full-time $10,300. *Required fees:* $20.

**United Theological Seminary of the Twin Cities,** Graduate Programs, New Brighton, MN 55112-2598. Offers advanced theological studies (Diploma); justice and peace studies (M Div, MA); leadership toward racial justice (M Div, MA, Certificate); Methodist studies (M Div, MA, Certificate); ministry (D Min); ministry renewal and professional development (Certificate); pastoral care and counseling (M Div, MA, MARL); religion and theology (MA); theological and religious studies (Certificate); theology and the arts

(M Div, MA); urban ministry (M Div, MA, MARL); women's studies: religion, theology and ministry (M Div, MA). *Accreditation:* ACIPE; ATS. *Program availability:* Part-time, evening/weekend. *Degree requirements:* For master's, thesis; for doctorate, comprehensive exam, thesis/dissertation. *Entrance requirements:* For master's, minimum GPA of 2.75; strong analytical, reflective thinking and writing skills; vocational and academic goals compatible with those of Seminary; for doctorate, M Div or equivalent, minimum GPA of 3.0, 3 years experience in professional ministry; for other advanced degree, BA or equivalent life experience; strong analytical, reflective thinking and writing skills (Certificate); proficiency in English language, previous study of theology at a theological school, recommendation of student's denomination (Diploma). Additional exam requirements/recommendations for international students: Required—TOEFL (minimum score 550 paper-based).

**Université de Montréal,** Faculty of Theology and Sciences of Religions, Montréal, QC H3C 3J7, Canada. Offers health, spirituality and bioethics (DESS); practical theology (MA, PhD); religious sciences (MA, PhD); theology (MA, D Th, PhD, L Th); theology-Biblical studies (PhD). *Degree requirements:* For master's, one foreign language; for doctorate, 2 foreign languages, thesis/dissertation, general exam. Electronic applications accepted.

**Université de Sherbrooke,** Faculty of Theology and Religious Studies, Sherbrooke, QC J1K 2R1, Canada. Offers applied ethics (Diploma); human science of religions (MA); intercultural training (Diploma); philosophy (MA, PhD); spiritual anthropology (Diploma); theology (MA, PhD, Diploma). *Program availability:* Part-time, evening/weekend, online learning. Terminal master's awarded for partial completion of doctoral program. *Entrance requirements:* For master's, bachelor's degree in related discipline; for doctorate, master's degree in related discipline. *Faculty research:* Faith and culture interrelation.

**Université du Québec à Montréal,** Graduate Programs, Program in Religious Sciences, Montréal, QC H3C 3P8, Canada. Offers MA, PhD. MA offered jointly with Concordia University. *Program availability:* Part-time. *Degree requirements:* For master's, thesis; for doctorate, thesis/dissertation. *Entrance requirements:* For master's, appropriate bachelor's degree or equivalent, proficiency in French; for doctorate, appropriate master's degree or equivalent, proficiency in French.

**Université Laval,** Faculty of Theology and Religious Sciences, Programs in Human Sciences of Religion, Québec, QC G1K 7P4, Canada. Offers MA, PhD. Terminal master's awarded for partial completion of doctoral program. *Degree requirements:* For master's, thesis (for some programs); for doctorate, comprehensive exam, thesis/dissertation. *Entrance requirements:* For master's, knowledge of French, comprehension of a second language; for doctorate, knowledge of French and English. Electronic applications accepted.

**The University of British Columbia,** Faculty of Arts, Department of Classical, Near Eastern and Religious Studies, Program in Religious Studies, Vancouver, BC V6T 1Z1, Canada. Offers MA, PhD. *Program availability:* Part-time. *Degree requirements:* For master's, 2 foreign languages, comprehensive exam, thesis optional; for doctorate, 2 foreign languages, comprehensive exam, thesis/dissertation. *Entrance requirements:* For doctorate, MA. Additional exam requirements/recommendations for international students: Required—TOEFL, IELTS. *Application deadline:* Applications are processed on a rolling basis. Application fee: $100 Canadian dollars ($162 Canadian dollars for international students). Electronic applications accepted. *Expenses:* $4,802 per year tuition and fees, $8,436 per year international. *Financial support:* Fellowships, teaching assistantships, scholarships/grants, and health care benefits available. Financial award application deadline: 1/1. *Faculty research:* Hebrew Bible in ancient Near Eastern context, Christian scriptures in Greco-Roman context, mystical aspects of religion, the feminine in western traditions, modern Jewish experience. *Application contact:* Odessa Cadieux-Rey, Graduate Program Staff, 604-822-2515, Fax: 604-822-9431, E-mail: cners.gradsec@ubc.ca. Website: http://cnrs.ubc.ca/

**University of Calgary,** Faculty of Graduate Studies, Faculty of Arts, Department of Religious Studies, Calgary, AB T2N 1N4, Canada. Offers MA, PhD. *Program availability:* Part-time. *Degree requirements:* For master's, one foreign language, thesis; for doctorate, 2 foreign languages, thesis/dissertation, candidacy exam. *Entrance requirements:* For master's, minimum GPA of 3.3; for doctorate, minimum GPA of 3.5. Additional exam requirements/recommendations for international students: Required—TOEFL (minimum score 550 paper-based). *Faculty research:* Eastern religions, Western religions, nature of religion.

**University of California, Berkeley,** Graduate Division, College of Letters and Science, Group in Buddhist Studies, Berkeley, CA 94720-1500. Offers PhD. *Faculty:* 9 full-time. *Students:* 8 full-time (4 women), 1 international. Average age 31. 15 applicants, 1 enrolled. In 2016, 1 doctorate awarded. *Degree requirements:* For doctorate, 4 foreign languages, thesis/dissertation, dissertation defense, qualifying exam. *Entrance requirements:* For doctorate, GRE General Test, MA in Japanese, Chinese, or Sanskrit; minimum GPA of 3.0; 3 letters of recommendation. *Application deadline:* For fall admission, 12/5 for domestic students. Application fee: $105 ($125 for international students). Electronic applications accepted. *Financial support:* Fellowships, research assistantships, teaching assistantships, institutionally sponsored loans, health care benefits, and unspecified assistantships available. *Unit head:* Prof. Robert Sharf, Chair, 510-642-3480, E-mail: gbs@berkeley.edu. *Application contact:* Information Contact, 510-642-3480, E-mail: gbs@berkeley.edu. Website: http://buddhiststudies.berkeley.edu/

**University of California, Riverside,** Graduate Division, Department of Religious Studies, Riverside, CA 92521. Offers MA, PhD. Terminal master's awarded for partial completion of doctoral program. *Degree requirements:* For master's, one foreign language, comprehensive exam; for doctorate, 2 foreign languages, comprehensive exam. *Entrance requirements:* For master's, GRE, 3 letters of recommendation from academic references, statement of purpose, personal history, scholarly acuity and interest in the critical questions of the discipline of religious studies; for doctorate, GRE General Test, 3 letters of recommendation from academic references; statement of purpose; personal history; basic and advanced courses in religious studies, beginning work in foreign language and ability to work across methods, traditions, and disciplines. Additional exam requirements/recommendations for international students: Required—TOEFL (minimum score 550 paper-based; 80 iBT); Recommended—IELTS (minimum score 7). Electronic applications accepted. *Expenses:* Tuition, state resident: full-time $16,666. Tuition, nonresident: full-time $31,768. *Required fees:* $11,055.54 per quarter. $3685.18 per quarter. Tuition and fees vary according to campus/location and program. *Faculty research:* American religions, southeast Asian religions, transnational Buddhism, modern Hinduism, queer theory, Sikh studies.

**University of California, Santa Barbara,** Graduate Division, College of Letters and Sciences, Division of Humanities and Fine Arts, Department of Religious Studies, Santa Barbara, CA 93106-3130. Offers ancient Mediterranean studies (PhD); cognitive science (PhD); European medieval studies (PhD); feminist studies (PhD); global studies (PhD); religious studies (MA, PhD); translation studies (PhD); MA/PhD. Terminal master's awarded for partial completion of doctoral program. *Degree requirements:* For master's, one foreign language, comprehensive exam (for some programs), thesis (for some programs); for doctorate, 2 foreign languages, thesis/dissertation, methodology. *Entrance requirements:* For master's and doctorate, GRE General Test. Additional exam requirements/recommendations for international students: Required—TOEFL (minimum score 550 paper-based; 80 iBT), IELTS (minimum score 7). Electronic applications accepted. *Faculty research:* Area studies; religious traditions; theory and method in the study of religion; religion, culture, and politics; spirituality and religious experience.

**University of California, Santa Barbara,** Graduate Division, College of Letters and Sciences, Division of Social Sciences, Department of Global Studies, Santa Barbara, CA 93106-7065. Offers global culture, ideology, and religion (MA, PhD); global government, human rights, and civil society (MA, PhD); political economy, sustainable development, and the environment (MA, PhD). *Degree requirements:* For master's, one foreign language, thesis, 2 years of a second language; for doctorate, one foreign language, thesis/dissertation, reading proficiency in at least one language other than English. *Entrance requirements:* For master's, GRE, 2 years of a second language with minimum B grade in the final term, statement of purpose, resume or curriculum vitae, 3 letters of recommendation, transcripts (from all post-secondary institutions attended), writing sample (15-20 pages); for doctorate, GRE, statement of purpose, personal achievements/contributions statement, resume or curriculum vitae, 3 letters of recommendation, transcripts from all post-secondary institutions attended, writing sample (15-20 pages). Additional exam requirements/recommendations for international students: Required—TOEFL (minimum score 600 paper-based; 94 iBT), IELTS (minimum score 7). Electronic applications accepted.

**University of Chicago,** Divinity School, Master of Arts in Religious Studies Program, Chicago, IL 60637. Offers MA. *Program availability:* Part-time. *Students:* 1 (woman) full-time, 3 part-time (1 woman), 1 international. 4 applicants, 50% accepted, 1 enrolled. *Degree requirements:* For master's, oral examination. *Entrance requirements:* For master's, GRE General Test. Additional exam requirements/recommendations for international students: Required—TOEFL (minimum score 600 paper-based; 104 iBT), IELTS (minimum score 7). *Application deadline:* For fall admission, 7/8 for domestic and international students; for winter admission, 10/15 for domestic and international students; for spring admission, 1/20 for domestic and international students. Applications are processed on a rolling basis. Application fee: $75. Electronic applications accepted. *Expenses:* Contact institution. *Financial support:* Federal Work-Study, institutionally sponsored loans, and scholarships/grants available. Support available to part-time students. Financial award applicants required to submit FAFSA. *Faculty research:* Constructive studies (philosophy of religion, religious ethics, and theology); historical studies (Bible, history of Christianity, and history of Judaism); religion and the human sciences (anthropology and sociology of religion, history of religions, and religion, literature, and visual culture); Islamic studies; religions in America. *Unit head:* Teresa Hord Owens, Dean of Students, 773-702-8217. *Application contact:* John W. Howell, Coordinator for Recruiting and Admissions, 773-702-8249, Fax: 773-834-4581, E-mail: divinityadmissions@uchicago.edu.
Website: http://divinity.uchicago.edu/master-arts-religious-studies-amrs

**University of Chicago,** Divinity School, Master of Arts Program, Chicago, IL 60637. Offers MA. *Students:* 94 full-time (49 women), 6 part-time (4 women); includes 11 minority (2 Black or African American, non-Hispanic/Latino; 5 Asian, non-Hispanic/Latino; 4 Hispanic/Latino), 9 international. 146 applicants, 83% accepted, 43 enrolled. *Degree requirements:* For master's, one foreign language, 15 courses with minimum B-grade. *Entrance requirements:* For master's, GRE General Test. Additional exam requirements/recommendations for international students: Required—TOEFL (minimum score 600 paper-based; 104 iBT), IELTS (minimum score 7). *Application deadline:* For fall admission, 1/8 priority date for domestic and international students. Application fee: $75. Electronic applications accepted. *Financial support:* Federal Work-Study, institutionally sponsored loans, and scholarships/grants available. Support available to part-time students. Financial award application deadline: 1/8; financial award applicants required to submit FAFSA. *Faculty research:* Constructive studies (philosophy of religion, religious ethics, and theology); historical studies (Bible, history of Christianity, and history of Judaism); religion and the human sciences (anthropology and sociology of religion, history of religions, and religion, literature, and visual culture); Islamic studies; religions in America. *Unit head:* Dr. Sarah E. Hammerschlag, Director/Assistant Professor of Religion and Literature, 773-702-8200. *Application contact:* John W. Howell, Coordinator for Recruiting and Admissions, 773-702-8249, Fax: 773-834-4581, E-mail: divinityadmissions@uchicago.edu.
Website: http://divinity.uchicago.edu/master-arts-ma

**University of Chicago,** Divinity School, PhD Program, Chicago, IL 60637. Offers anthropology and sociology of religions (PhD); Bible (PhD); history of Christianity (PhD); history of Judaism (PhD); history of religions (PhD); Islamic studies (PhD); philosophy of religions (PhD); religion, literature, and visual culture (PhD); religions in America (PhD); religious ethics (PhD); theology (PhD). *Students:* 161 full-time (47 women), 1 (woman) part-time; includes 22 minority (6 Black or African American, non-Hispanic/Latino; 10 Asian, non-Hispanic/Latino; 2 Hispanic/Latino; 4 Two or more races, non-Hispanic/Latino), 26 international. 171 applicants, 16% accepted, 15 enrolled. *Degree requirements:* For doctorate, 2 foreign languages, comprehensive exam, thesis/dissertation. *Entrance requirements:* For doctorate, GRE General Test. Additional exam requirements/recommendations for international students: Required—TOEFL (minimum score 600 paper-based; 104 iBT), IELTS (minimum score 7). *Application deadline:* For fall admission, 12/15 for domestic and international students. Application fee: $75. Electronic applications accepted. *Financial support:* In 2016–17, 20 fellowships with full tuition reimbursements (averaging $24,000 per year) were awarded; Federal Work-Study, institutionally sponsored loans, scholarships/grants, and health care benefits also available. Financial award application deadline: 12/15; financial award applicants required to submit FAFSA. *Faculty research:* Constructive studies (philosophy of religion, religious ethics, and theology); historical studies (Bible, history of Christianity, and history of Judaism); religion and the human sciences (anthropology and sociology of religion, history of religions, and religion, literature, and visual culture); Islamic studies; religions in America. *Unit head:* Dr. Richard A. Rosengarten, Dean/Associate Professor of Religion and Literature, 773-702-8200. *Application contact:* John W. Howell, Coordinator for Recruiting and Admissions, 773-702-8249, Fax: 773-834-4581, E-mail: divinityadmissions@uchicago.edu.
Website: http://divinity.uchicago.edu/doctoral-program-phd

**University of Colorado Boulder,** Graduate School, College of Arts and Sciences, Department of Religious Studies, Boulder, CO 80309. Offers MA. *Faculty:* 9 full-time (3 women). *Students:* 21 full-time (7 women); includes 2 minority (1 Asian, non-Hispanic/Latino; 1 Hispanic/Latino), 3 international. Average age 29. 21 applicants, 90% accepted, 12 enrolled. In 2016, 7 master's awarded. Terminal master's awarded for partial completion of doctoral program. *Degree requirements:* For master's, one foreign language, comprehensive exam, thesis. *Entrance requirements:* For master's, minimum undergraduate GPA of 2.75. *Application deadline:* For fall admission, 1/15 for domestic students, 12/15 for international students; for spring admission, 10/15 for domestic students, 9/15 for international students. Applications are processed on a rolling basis. Application fee: $60 ($80 for international students). Electronic applications accepted. Application fee is waived when completed online. *Financial support:* In 2016–17, 55 students received support, including 13 fellowships (averaging $4,596 per year), 16

teaching assistantships with full and partial tuition reimbursements available (averaging $25,350 per year); institutionally sponsored loans, scholarships/grants, health care benefits, and unspecified assistantships also available. Financial award application deadline: 1/15; financial award applicants required to submit FAFSA. *Faculty research:* Religious studies, comparative religion, religious history, area studies (arts/humanities), arts/humanities/cultural activities. *Total annual research expenditures:* $53,469. *Application contact:* E-mail: rlst@colorado.edu.
Website: http://www.colorado.edu/ReligiousStudies

**University of Denver,** Division of Arts, Humanities and Social Sciences, Department of Religious Studies, Denver, CO 80208. Offers critical theory and religion (MA); lived religion (MA); philosophy of religion (MA); religion and international studies (MA); sacred texts (MA). *Faculty:* 8 full-time (4 women), 3 part-time/adjunct (2 women). *Students:* 1 (woman) full-time, 14 part-time (4 women); includes 3 minority (1 Hispanic/Latino; 2 Two or more races, non-Hispanic/Latino). Average age 30. 14 applicants, 64% accepted, 6 enrolled. In 2016, 3 master's awarded. *Degree requirements:* For master's, variable foreign language requirement, comprehensive exam, thesis. *Entrance requirements:* For master's, GRE General Test, bachelor's degree, transcripts, personal statement, writing sample, three letters of recommendation. Additional exam requirements/recommendations for international students: Required—TOEFL (minimum score 550 paper-based; 80 iBT). *Application deadline:* For fall admission, 2/15 priority date for domestic and international students. Applications are processed on a rolling basis. Application fee: $65. Electronic applications accepted. *Expenses:* $29,022 per year full-time. *Financial support:* In 2016–17, 13 students received support. Federal Work-Study, scholarships/grants, and unspecified assistantships available. Financial award application deadline: 2/15; financial award applicants required to submit FAFSA. *Unit head:* Dr. Ginni Ishimatsu, Interim Chair, 303-871-2751, Fax: 303-871-2750, E-mail: gishimat@du.edu. *Application contact:* Dr. Carl Raschke, Professor and Graduate Advisor, 303-871-3117, Fax: 303-871-2750, E-mail: rlgs@du.edu.
Website: http://www.du.edu/ahss/religiousstudies

**University of Denver,** Josef Korbel School of International Studies, Denver, CO 80208. Offers conflict resolution (MA); global business and corporate social responsibility (Certificate); global finance, trade and economic integration (MA); global health affairs (Certificate); homeland security (Certificate); humanitarian assistance (Certificate); international administration (MA); international development (MA); international human rights (MA); international security (MA); international studies (MA, PhD); public policy studies (MPP); religion and international affairs (Certificate). *Program availability:* Part-time. *Faculty:* 46 full-time (16 women), 28 part-time/adjunct (8 women). *Students:* 368 full-time (204 women), 26 part-time (10 women); includes 82 minority (15 Black or African American, non-Hispanic/Latino; 2 American Indian or Alaska Native, non-Hispanic/Latino; 11 Asian, non-Hispanic/Latino; 43 Hispanic/Latino; 11 Two or more races, non-Hispanic/Latino), 38 international. Average age 27. 764 applicants, 82% accepted, 138 enrolled. In 2016, 197 master's, 10 doctorates, 28 other advanced degrees awarded. *Degree requirements:* For master's, one foreign language, thesis (for some programs); for doctorate, one foreign language, comprehensive exam, thesis/dissertation, two extended research papers. *Entrance requirements:* For master's, GRE General Test, bachelor's degree, transcripts, two letters of recommendation, statement of purpose, resume or curriculum vitae; for doctorate, GRE General Test, master's degree, transcripts, three letters of recommendation, statement of purpose, resume or curriculum vitae, writing sample; for Certificate, bachelor's degree, transcripts, two letters of recommendation, statement of purpose, resume or curriculum vitae. Additional exam requirements/recommendations for international students: Required—TOEFL (minimum score 587 paper-based; 95 iBT). *Application deadline:* For fall admission, 1/15 priority date for domestic and international students; for winter admission, 11/1 for domestic and international students. Applications are processed on a rolling basis. Application fee: $65. Electronic applications accepted. *Expenses:* $43,458 per year full-time. *Financial support:* In 2016–17, 244 students received support, including 1 research assistantship with tuition reimbursement available (averaging $7,250 per year), 5 teaching assistantships with tuition reimbursements available (averaging $2,842 per year); career-related internships or fieldwork, Federal Work-Study, institutionally sponsored loans, scholarships/grants, and unspecified assistantships also available. Support available to part-time students. Financial award application deadline: 2/15; financial award applicants required to submit FAFSA. *Faculty research:* Human rights and international security, international politics and economics, economic-social and political development, international technology analysis and management. *Unit head:* Dr. Christopher R. Hill, Dean, 303-871-2359, Fax: 303-871-2456, E-mail: christopher.r.hill@du.edu. *Application contact:* Admissions Contact, E-mail: korbeladm@du.edu.
Website: http://www.du.edu/korbel

**University of Florida,** Graduate School, College of Liberal Arts and Sciences, Department of Religion, Gainesville, FL 32611. Offers Jewish studies (MA); religion (MA, PhD); tropical conservation and development (MA, PhD); women's and gender studies (MA, PhD). *Program availability:* Part-time. *Degree requirements:* For master's, one foreign language, thesis optional; for doctorate, one foreign language, comprehensive exam, thesis/dissertation. *Entrance requirements:* For master's, GRE General Test, minimum GPA of 3.0. Additional exam requirements/recommendations for international students: Required—TOEFL (minimum score 550 paper-based; 80 iBT), IELTS (minimum score 6). Electronic applications accepted. *Faculty research:* Religion in America, Christian thought, Islam, religions of India, comparative religion.

**University of Georgia,** Franklin College of Arts and Sciences, Department of Religion, Athens, GA 30602. Offers MA. *Degree requirements:* For master's, one foreign language, thesis. *Entrance requirements:* For master's, GRE General Test. *Application deadline:* For fall admission, 7/1 priority date for domestic students; for spring admission, 11/15 for domestic students. Application fee: $50. Electronic applications accepted. *Financial support:* Fellowships, research assistantships, teaching assistantships, and unspecified assistantships available. *Unit head:* Dr. Sandy D. Martin, Head, 706-542-1485, Fax: 706-542-6724, E-mail: martin@uga.edu. *Application contact:* Dr. Carolyn Medine, Graduate Coordinator, 706-543-0308, Fax: 706-542-6724, E-mail: medine@uga.edu.
Website: http://www.uga.edu/~religion/

**University of Hawaii at Manoa,** Graduate Division, College of Arts and Humanities, Department of Religion, Honolulu, HI 96822. Offers MA. *Program availability:* Part-time. *Degree requirements:* For master's, one foreign language, thesis optional. *Entrance requirements:* For master's, GRE General Test. Additional exam requirements/recommendations for international students: Required—TOEFL (minimum score 600 paper-based; 100 iBT), IELTS (minimum score 7). *Faculty research:* Buddhism, East Asian religion, South Asian religion, Polynesian religion, Western religions.

**University of Illinois at Urbana–Champaign,** Graduate College, College of Liberal Arts and Sciences, School of Literatures, Cultures and Linguistics, Department of Religion, Champaign, IL 61820. Offers religious studies (MA). *Degree requirements:* For master's, one foreign language, comprehensive exam, thesis optional.

**The University of Iowa,** Graduate College, College of Liberal Arts and Sciences, Department of Religious Studies, Iowa City, IA 52242-1316. Offers MA, PhD. Terminal master's awarded for partial completion of doctoral program. *Degree requirements:* For

## Religion

master's, thesis optional, exam; for doctorate, comprehensive exam, thesis/dissertation. *Entrance requirements:* For master's and doctorate, GRE General Test, minimum GPA of 3.0. Additional exam requirements/recommendations for international students: Required—TOEFL (minimum score 550 paper-based; 81 iBT). Electronic applications accepted. *Faculty research:* Eastern and Western religion.

**The University of Kansas,** Graduate Studies, College of Liberal Arts and Sciences, Department of Religious Studies, Lawrence, KS 66045. Offers MA, Graduate Certificate. *Program availability:* Part-time. *Students:* 10 full-time (4 women), 2 part-time (1 woman); includes 2 minority (both Black or African American, non-Hispanic/Latino), 2 international. Average age 26. 5 applicants, 100% accepted, 5 enrolled. In 2016, 3 master's awarded. *Entrance requirements:* For master's, official transcripts, three letters of recommendation, essay of interest and purpose, resume. Additional exam requirements/recommendations for international students: Required—TOEFL. *Application deadline:* For fall admission, 2/1 for domestic and international students. Application fee: $65 ($85 for international students). Electronic applications accepted. *Financial support:* Fellowships, teaching assistantships, scholarships/grants, and unspecified assistantships available. Financial award application deadline: 1/1. *Faculty research:* Hinduism, Chinese Buddhism, Islam, Biblical literatures, American and indigenous people's religion. *Unit head:* Daniel B. Stevenson, Chair, 785-864-7258, E-mail: dbsteve@ku.edu. *Application contact:* Graduate Admission Contact, 785-864-4341, E-mail: rstudies@ku.edu.
Website: https://religiousstudies.ku.edu/

**University of Lethbridge,** School of Graduate Studies, Lethbridge, AB T1K 3M4, Canada. Offers addictions counseling (M Sc); agricultural biotechnology (M Sc); agricultural studies (M Sc, MA); anthropology (MA); archaeology (M Sc, MA); art (MA, MFA); biochemistry (M Sc); biological sciences (M Sc); biomolecular science (PhD); biosystems and biodiversity (PhD); Canadian studies (MA); chemistry (M Sc); computer science (M Sc); computer science and geographical information science (M Sc); counseling (MC); counseling psychology (M Ed); dramatic arts (MA); earth, space, and physical science (PhD); economics (MA); education (MA, PhD); educational leadership (M Ed); English (MA); environmental science (M Sc); evolution and behavior (PhD); exercise science (M Sc); French (MA); French/German (MA); French/Spanish (MA); general education (M Ed); geography (M Sc, MA); German (MA); health sciences (M Sc); individualized multidisciplinary (M Sc, MA); kinesiology (M Sc, MA); management (M Sc), including accounting, finance, human resource management and labor relations, information systems, international management, marketing, policy and strategy; mathematics (M Sc); music (M Mus, MA); Native American studies (MA); neuroscience (M Sc, PhD); new media (MA, MFA); nursing (M Sc, MN); philosophy (MA); physics (M Sc); political science (MA); psychology (M Sc, MA); religious studies (MA); sociology (MA); theatre and dramatic arts (MFA); theoretical and computational science (PhD); urban and regional studies (MA); women and gender studies (MA). *Program availability:* Part-time, evening/weekend. *Degree requirements:* For master's, thesis (for some programs); for doctorate, comprehensive exam, thesis/dissertation. *Entrance requirements:* For master's, GMAT (for M Sc in management), bachelor's degree in related field, minimum GPA of 3.0 during previous 20 graded semester courses, 2 years' teaching or related experience (M Ed); for doctorate, master's degree, minimum graduate GPA of 3.5. Additional exam requirements/recommendations for international students: Required—TOEFL (minimum score 580 paper-based; 93 iBT). Electronic applications accepted. *Faculty research:* Movement and brain plasticity, gibberellin physiology, photosynthesis, carbon cycling, molecular properties of main-group ring components.

**The University of Manchester,** School of Arts, Histories and Cultures, Manchester, United Kingdom. Offers anthropology, media and performance (PhD); applied theatre professional (PhD); archaeology (PhD); art history and visual studies (PhD); arts management and cultural policy (PhD); classics and ancient history (PhD); composition (PhD); creative writing (PhD); drama (PhD); economic and social history (PhD); electroacoustic composition (PhD); English and American studies (PhD); history (PhD); humanitarianism and conflict response (PhD); museology (PhD); music (PhD); musicology (PhD); religions and theology (PhD).

**University of Manitoba,** Faculty of Graduate Studies, Faculty of Arts, Department of Religion, Winnipeg, MB R3T 2N2, Canada. Offers MA, PhD. MA offered jointly with The University of Winnipeg. *Degree requirements:* For master's, one foreign language, thesis or alternative.

**University of Michigan,** Rackham Graduate School, College of Literature, Science, and the Arts, Department of Near Eastern Studies, Ann Arbor, MI 48109. Offers ancient Near Eastern studies (AM, PhD); Arabic for professional purposes (AM); Arabic language and literature (AM, PhD); Armenian studies (AM, PhD); Christianity in late antiquity (AM, PhD); Egyptology (AM, PhD); Hebrew Bible and ancient Israel (AM, PhD); Hebrew literature (AM, PhD); Islamic studies (AM, PhD); Jewish cultural studies (AM, PhD); Jewish mysticism (AM, PhD); Persian and Iranian studies (AM, PhD); Rabbinic literature (AM, PhD); Second Temple Judaism (AM, PhD); teaching Arabic as a foreign language (AM); Turkish studies (AM, PhD). *Faculty:* 27 full-time (8 women). *Students:* 28 full-time (12 women); includes 2 minority (1 Black or African American, non-Hispanic/Latino; 1 Asian, non-Hispanic/Latino), 10 international. Average age 32. 85 applicants, 8% accepted, 3 enrolled. In 2016, 4 master's, 3 doctorates awarded. Terminal master's awarded for partial completion of doctoral program. *Degree requirements:* For master's, 2 foreign languages; for doctorate, 4 foreign languages, comprehensive exam, thesis/dissertation, preliminary exams, oral defense of dissertation. *Entrance requirements:* Additional exam requirements/recommendations for international students: Required—TOEFL (minimum score 560 paper-based; 84 iBT), IELTS (minimum score 6.5). *Application deadline:* For fall admission, 12/1 for domestic and international students. Application fee: $75 ($90 for international students). Electronic applications accepted. *Expenses:* Tuition, state resident: full-time $21,466; part-time $1152 per credit hour. Tuition, nonresident: full-time $43,346; part-time $2367 per credit hour. Part-time tuition and fees vary according to course load, degree level and program. *Financial support:* In 2016–17, 28 students received support. Fellowships with full tuition reimbursements available, teaching assistantships with full tuition reimbursements available, scholarships/grants, health care benefits, unspecified assistantships, and summer stipends available. Financial award application deadline: 12/1. *Faculty research:* Middle and Near Eastern literatures, languages, cultures from ancient times to the present. *Unit head:* Prof. Gottfried Hagen, Chair, 734-764-0314, E-mail: neschair@umich.edu. *Application contact:* Student Services, 734-764-0315, E-mail: nes-gradservices@umich.edu.
Website: http://www.lsa.umich.edu/neareast/

**University of Minnesota, Twin Cities Campus,** Graduate School, College of Liberal Arts, Department of Classical and Near Eastern Studies, Minneapolis, MN 55455-0213. Offers ancient and medieval art and archaeology (MA, PhD); classics (MA, PhD); Greek (MA, PhD); Latin (MA, PhD); religions in antiquity (MA). *Program availability:* Part-time. Terminal master's awarded for partial completion of doctoral program. *Degree requirements:* For master's, 2 foreign languages, comprehensive exam, thesis or alternative; for doctorate, variable foreign language requirement, comprehensive exam, thesis/dissertation. *Entrance requirements:* For master's and doctorate, GRE, 3 letters of recommendation, writing sample, copies of transcripts, personal statement. Additional

exam requirements/recommendations for international students: Required—TOEFL. Electronic applications accepted. *Faculty research:* Greek and Latin literature, religions in antiquity, ancient Near East.

**University of Missouri,** Office of Research and Graduate Studies, College of Arts and Science, Department of Religious Studies, Columbia, MO 65211. Offers MA. *Faculty:* 10 full-time (4 women), 1 (woman) part-time/adjunct. *Students:* 2 full-time (both women), 3 part-time (1 woman). *Entrance requirements:* For master's, GRE General Test, minimum GPA of 3.0. Additional exam requirements/recommendations for international students: Required—TOEFL (minimum score 550 paper-based; 80 iBT). *Application deadline:* For fall admission, 2/1 priority date for domestic students. Application fee: $75 ($90 for international students). Electronic applications accepted. *Expenses:* Tuition, state resident: full-time $6347; part-time $352.60 per credit hour. Tuition, nonresident: full-time $17,379; part-time $965.50 per credit hour. *Required fees:* $1035. Tuition and fees vary according to course load, campus/location and program. *Financial support:* Fellowships with full tuition reimbursements, research assistantships, teaching assistantships with full tuition reimbursements, institutionally sponsored loans, health care benefits, and unspecified assistantships available. *Faculty research:* American religious history, Biblical studies, history of Christianity, religion and society, religions of East Asia, religions of indigenous peoples, religions of South Asia, women and religion. Website: http://religiousstudies.missouri.edu/programs/grad/

**The University of North Carolina at Chapel Hill,** Graduate School, College of Arts and Sciences, Department of Religious Studies, Chapel Hill, NC 27599. Offers MA, PhD. Terminal master's awarded for partial completion of doctoral program. *Degree requirements:* For master's, one foreign language, comprehensive exam, thesis; for doctorate, 2 foreign languages, comprehensive exam, thesis/dissertation. *Entrance requirements:* For master's and doctorate, GRE General Test, minimum GPA of 3.0. Additional exam requirements/recommendations for international students: Required—TOEFL. Electronic applications accepted. *Faculty research:* Religion.

**The University of North Carolina at Charlotte,** College of Liberal Arts and Sciences, Department of Religious Studies, Charlotte, NC 28223-0001. Offers MA. *Program availability:* Part-time. *Faculty:* 8 full-time (3 women). *Students:* 3 full-time (2 women), 8 part-time (4 women); includes 2 minority (1 Black or African American, non-Hispanic/Latino; 1 Hispanic/Latino). Average age 28. 6 applicants, 100% accepted, 4 enrolled. In 2016, 2 master's awarded. *Degree requirements:* For master's, thesis or comprehensive exam. *Entrance requirements:* For master's, GRE or MAT, official transcripts of all previous academic work attempted beyond high school; at least three letters of reference from persons familiar with the applicant's academic prowess and qualifications; essay (statement of purpose). Additional exam requirements/recommendations for international students: Required—TOEFL (minimum score 523 paper-based, 70 iBT) or IELTS (6.5). *Application deadline:* For fall admission, 5/1 for domestic and international students; for spring admission, 10/1 for domestic and international students. Applications are processed on a rolling basis. Application fee: $75. Electronic applications accepted. *Expenses:* Tuition, state resident: full-time $4252. Tuition, nonresident: full-time $17,423. *Required fees:* $3026. Tuition and fees vary according to course load and program. *Financial support:* In 2016–17, 3 students received support, including 3 teaching assistantships (averaging $9,000 per year); career-related internships or fieldwork, institutionally sponsored loans, scholarships/grants, and unspecified assistantships also available. Support available to part-time students. Financial award application deadline: 3/1; financial award applicants required to submit FAFSA. *Total annual research expenditures:* $73,517. *Unit head:* Dr. Joanne Robinson, Chair, 704-687-5198, E-mail: joanne.robinson@uncc.edu. *Application contact:* Kathy B. Giddings, Director of Graduate Admissions, 704-687-5503, Fax: 704-687-1668, E-mail: gradadm@uncc.edu.
Website: http://religiousstudies.uncc.edu/

**University of Notre Dame,** Graduate School, College of Arts and Letters, Division of Humanities, Program in Early Christian Studies, Notre Dame, IN 46556. Offers MA. *Degree requirements:* For master's, 3 foreign languages, comprehensive exam. *Entrance requirements:* For master's, GRE General Test. Additional exam requirements/recommendations for international students: Required—TOEFL (minimum score 600 paper-based; 80 iBT). Electronic applications accepted. *Faculty research:* Early Christian theology, worship and scriptural interpretation; late antique and Byzantine history; art and culture; Greek and Latin literature.

**University of Ottawa,** Faculty of Graduate and Postdoctoral Studies, Faculty of Arts, Department of Classics and Religious Studies, Ottawa, ON K1N 6N5, Canada. Offers classical studies (MA); religious studies (PhD). *Degree requirements:* For master's, comprehensive exam, thesis or alternative; for doctorate, comprehensive exam, thesis/dissertation. *Entrance requirements:* For master's, honors degree or equivalent, minimum B average; for doctorate, master's degree, minimum B+ average. Electronic applications accepted. *Faculty research:* Religions in Canada, including Amerindian and Inuit religions; religion and culture; late antiquity.

**University of Pennsylvania,** School of Arts and Sciences, Graduate Group in Religious Studies, Philadelphia, PA 19104. Offers PhD. *Faculty:* 18 full-time (8 women), 9 part-time/adjunct (3 women). *Students:* 12 full-time (3 women), 6 part-time (3 women); includes 3 minority (2 Asian, non-Hispanic/Latino; 1 Hispanic/Latino), 6 international. Average age 34. 34 applicants, 9% accepted. In 2016, 2 doctorates awarded. *Expenses:* Tuition: Full-time $31,068; part-time $5762 per course. *Required fees:* $3200; $336 per course. Full-time tuition and fees vary according to degree level, program and student level. Part-time tuition and fees vary according to course load, degree level and program. *Financial support:* In 2016–17, 10 students received support. Website: http://www.sas.upenn.edu/religious_studies/graduate

**University of Regina,** Faculty of Graduate Studies and Research, Faculty of Arts, Department of Religious Studies, Regina, SK S4S 0A2, Canada. Offers MA. *Program availability:* Part-time. *Faculty:* 7 full-time (2 women), 1 part-time/adjunct (0 women). *Students:* 2 full-time (1 woman), 1 part-time (0 women). 3 applicants. *Degree requirements:* For master's, thesis. *Entrance requirements:* Additional exam requirements/recommendations for international students: Required—TOEFL (minimum score 580 paper-based; 80 iBT), IELTS (minimum score 6.5), PTE (minimum score 59). *Application deadline:* Applications are processed on a rolling basis. Application fee: $100. Electronic applications accepted. *Financial support:* In 2016–17, 2 teaching assistantships (averaging $2,501 per year) were awarded; fellowships and scholarships/grants also available. Financial award application deadline: 6/15. *Faculty research:* Comparative religion; religious traditions; thematic and methodological studies; advanced studies in Christianity, Islam, and ancient religions. *Unit head:* Dr. Kevin Bond, Acting Department Head, 306-585-4335, Fax: 306-585-4815, E-mail: kevin.bond@uregina.ca.
Website: http://www.uregina.ca/arts/religious-studies

**University of St. Thomas,** Center for Faith and Culture, Houston, TX 77006-4696. Offers MA. *Program availability:* Part-time. *Faculty:* 2 full-time (0 women), 1 part-time/adjunct (0 women). *Students:* 1 full-time (0 women), 15 part-time (9 women); includes 8 minority (4 Black or African American, non-Hispanic/Latino; 2 Asian, non-Hispanic/Latino; 2 Hispanic/Latino). Average age 44. 2 applicants, 100% accepted. In 2016, 3 master's awarded. *Degree requirements:* For master's, service learning and leadership

practicum, integrating presentation. *Entrance requirements:* For master's, bachelor's degree with minimum GPA of 2.75 or advanced degree; 3 letters of recommendation (professional or academic only); essay on student goals and expectations; interview with CFC admissions committee; writing sample; favorable review by admissions committee. Additional exam requirements/recommendations for international students: Required—TOEFL (minimum score 550 paper-based; 100 iBT), IELTS (minimum score 6.5), PTE (minimum score 53). *Application deadline:* For fall admission, 7/1 for domestic students, 6/1 for international students; for spring admission, 11/1 for domestic students, 10/1 for international students. Applications are processed on a rolling basis. Application fee: $35. Electronic applications accepted. *Expenses:* Contact institution. *Financial support:* In 2016–17, 11 students received support. Federal Work-Study, scholarships/grants, and state work-study, institutional employment available. Support available to part-time students. Financial award application deadline: 4/15; financial award applicants required to submit FAFSA. *Unit head:* Fr. Donald S. Nesti, Director, 713-942-5066, E-mail: cfc@stthom.edu. *Application contact:* Dr. Adam Martinez, Program Director, 713-942-5066, E-mail: cfc@stthom.edu.
Website: http://www.stthom.edu/Academics/Centers_of_Excellence/Center_for_Faith_Culture/Index.aqf

**University of St. Thomas,** Graduate Studies, College of Arts and Sciences, Master of Arts Program in Catholic Studies, St. Paul, MN 55105-1096. Offers MA. *Program availability:* Part-time, evening/weekend. *Degree requirements:* For master's, thesis. *Entrance requirements:* For master's, bachelor's degree with minimum GPA of 3.0, writing sample, personal essay, 3 letters of recommendation. Additional exam requirements/recommendations for international students: Required—TOEFL (minimum score 550 paper-based). *Application deadline:* For fall admission, 3/1 for domestic and international students; for spring admission, 11/1 for domestic and international students. Electronic applications accepted. *Expenses: Tuition:* Full-time $19,354; part-time $1320 per credit. One-time fee: $214. Tuition and fees vary according to course load, degree level, program and reciprocity agreements. *Financial support:* Fellowships with full tuition reimbursements, research assistantships, and tuition waivers (partial) available. *Unit head:* Dr. John F. Boyle, Director, 651-962-5714, Fax: 651-962-5710, E-mail: jfboyle@stthomas.edu. *Application contact:* Maureen Huss, Coordinator, Center for Catholic Studies, 651-962-5704, Fax: 651-962-5710, E-mail: huss1887@stthomas.edu.
Website: http://www.stthomas.edu/catholicstudies/masters/

**University of Saskatchewan,** College of Graduate Studies and Research, College of Arts and Science, Department of Religion and Culture, Saskatoon, SK S7N 5A2, Canada. Offers MA. *Degree requirements:* For master's, thesis. *Entrance requirements:* Additional exam requirements/recommendations for international students: Required—TOEFL (minimum score 80 iBT); Recommended—IELTS (minimum score 6.5). Electronic applications accepted.

**University of South Africa,** College of Human Sciences, Pretoria, South Africa. Offers adult education (M Ed); African languages (MA, PhD); African politics (MA, PhD); Afrikaans (MA, PhD); ancient history (MA, PhD); ancient Near Eastern studies (MA, PhD); anthropology (MA, PhD); applied linguistics (MA); Arabic (MA, PhD); archaeology (MA); art history (MA); Biblical archaeology (MA); Biblical studies (M Th, D Th, PhD); Christian spirituality (M Th, D Th); church history (M Th, D Th); classical studies (MA, PhD); clinical psychology (MA); communication (MA, PhD); comparative education (M Ed, Ed D); consulting psychology (D Admin, D Com, PhD); curriculum studies (M Ed, Ed D); development studies (M Admin, MA, D Admin, PhD); didactics (M Ed, Ed D); education (M Tech); education management (M Ed, Ed D); educational psychology (M Ed); English (MA); environmental education (M Ed); French (MA, PhD); German (MA, PhD); Greek (MA); guidance and counseling (M Ed); health studies (MA, PhD), including health sciences education (MA), health services management (MA), medical and surgical nursing science (critical care general) (MA), midwifery and neonatal nursing science (MA), trauma and emergency care (MA); history (MA, PhD); history of education (Ed D); inclusive education (M Ed, Ed D); information and communications technology policy and regulation (MA); information science (MA, MIS, PhD); international politics (MA, PhD); Islamic studies (MA, PhD); Italian (MA, PhD); Judaica (MA, PhD); linguistics (MA, PhD); mathematical education (M Ed); mathematics education (MA); missiology (M Th, D Th); modern Hebrew (MA, PhD); musicology (MA, MMus, D Mus, PhD); natural science education (M Ed); New Testament (M Th, D Th); Old Testament (D Th); pastoral therapy (M Th, D Th); philosophy (MA); philosophy of education (M Ed, Ed D); politics (MA, PhD); Portuguese (MA, PhD); practical theology (M Th, D Th); psychology (MA, MS, PhD); psychology of education (M Ed, Ed D); public health (MA); religious studies (MA, D Th, PhD); Romance languages (MA); Russian (MA, PhD); Semitic languages (MA, PhD); social behavior studies in HIV/AIDS (MA); social science (mental health) (MA); social science in development studies (MA); social science in psychology (MA); social science in social work (MA); social science in sociology (MA); social work (MSW, DSW, PhD); socio-education (M Ed, Ed D); sociolinguistics (MA); sociology (MA, PhD); Spanish (MA, PhD); systematic theology (M Th, D Th); TESOL (teaching English to speakers of other languages) (MA); theological ethics (M Th, D Th); theory of literature (MA, PhD); urban ministries (D Th); urban ministry (M Th).

**University of South Carolina,** The Graduate School, College of Arts and Sciences, Department of Religious Studies, Columbia, SC 29208. Offers MA. *Program availability:* Part-time. *Degree requirements:* For master's, one foreign language, comprehensive exam, thesis. *Entrance requirements:* For master's, GRE General Test or MAT. Additional exam requirements/recommendations for international students: Required—TOEFL. Electronic applications accepted. *Faculty research:* Biblical and Near Eastern studies, theology and religious thought, religion and culture, South Asian religions, Islamic studies.

**University of South Florida,** College of Arts and Sciences, Department of Philosophy, Tampa, FL 33620-9951. Offers philosophy (MA, PhD), including philosophy and religion. *Program availability:* Part-time, evening/weekend. *Faculty:* 12 full-time (2 women). *Students:* 43 full-time (9 women), 12 part-time (4 women); includes 8 minority (1 Black or African American, non-Hispanic/Latino; 2 Asian, non-Hispanic/Latino; 4 Hispanic/Latino; 1 Two or more races, non-Hispanic/Latino). Average age 32. 27 applicants, 56% accepted, 6 enrolled. In 2016, 3 master's, 10 doctorates awarded. Terminal master's awarded for partial completion of doctoral program. *Degree requirements:* For master's, comprehensive exam, thesis optional; for doctorate, comprehensive exam, thesis/dissertation. *Entrance requirements:* For master's and doctorate, GRE General Test, minimum GPA of 3.0, three letters of recommendation, 10-page philosophy writing sample, statement of philosophical interests. Additional exam requirements/recommendations for international students: Required—TOEFL (minimum score 550 paper-based; 79 iBT) or IELTS (minimum score 6.5). *Application deadline:* For fall admission, 2/15 for domestic and international students; for spring admission, 10/15 for domestic students, 8/1 for international students. Application fee: $30. Electronic applications accepted. *Expenses:* Tuition, state resident: full-time $7766; part-time $431.43 per credit hour. Tuition, nonresident: full-time $15,789; part-time $877.17 per credit hour. *Required fees:* $37 per term. *Financial support:* In 2016–17, 15 students received support, including 32 teaching assistantships with tuition reimbursements available (averaging $11,025 per year); unspecified assistantships also available. Financial award application deadline: 1/1. *Faculty research:* Medieval philosophy, early

modern philosophy (seventeenth-, eighteenth-, and twentieth-century Continental philosophy), feminist philosophy, social philosophy, ethics, philosophy of science. *Total annual research expenditures:* $93,216. *Unit head:* Dr. Roger Ariew, Professor and Chairperson, 813-974-8207, Fax: 813-974-5914, E-mail: rariew@usf.edu. *Application contact:* Dr. Joanne Waugh, Associate Professor, 813-974-5571, Fax: 813-974-5914, E-mail: jwaugh@usf.edu.
Website: http://philosophy.usf.edu/

**University of South Florida,** College of Arts and Sciences, Department of Religious Studies, Tampa, FL 33620-9951. Offers MA. *Program availability:* Part-time, evening/weekend. *Faculty:* 3 full-time (0 women). *Students:* 6 full-time (4 women); includes 2 minority (1 Black or African American, non-Hispanic/Latino; 1 Hispanic/Latino). Average age 29. 7 applicants, 57% accepted, 3 enrolled. In 2016, 4 master's awarded. *Degree requirements:* For master's, comprehensive exam, thesis optional. *Entrance requirements:* For master's, GRE General Test (recommended), minimum GPA of 3.0, three letters of recommendation, 1-3 page personal statement of intellectual interest, writing sample. Additional exam requirements/recommendations for international students: Required—TOEFL (minimum score 550 paper-based; 79 iBT) or IELTS (minimum score 6.5). *Application deadline:* For fall admission, 2/15 priority date for domestic and international students; for spring admission, 10/15 priority date for domestic students, 9/15 priority date for international students. Applications are processed on a rolling basis. Application fee: $30. Electronic applications accepted. *Expenses:* Tuition, state resident: full-time $7766; part-time $431.43 per credit hour. Tuition, nonresident: full-time $15,789; part-time $877.17 per credit hour. *Required fees:* $37 per term. *Financial support:* In 2016–17, 2 students received support, including 7 teaching assistantships with tuition reimbursements available (averaging $9,751 per year); unspecified assistantships also available. Financial award applicants required to submit FAFSA. *Faculty research:* Biblical studies, Biblical archaeology, Christianity, Judaism, Mysticism, philosophy of religion, Buddhism, Daoism, Confucianism, Hinduism, Chinese medicine, Vedic religion, Hinduism, religion in culture and society, African religion, African-American religion, Afro-Caribbean religion. *Total annual research expenditures:* $13,053. *Unit head:* Dr. James Cavendish, Professor and Interim Chairperson, 813-974-2758, Fax: 813-974-1853, E-mail: jcavendi@usf.edu. *Application contact:* Dr. Cass Fisher, Associate Professor and Graduate Program Director, 813-974-0445, Fax: 813-974-1853, E-mail: cass@usf.edu.
Website: http://religious-studies.usf.edu/

**The University of Tennessee,** Graduate School, College of Arts and Sciences, Department of Philosophy, Knoxville, TN 37996. Offers medical ethics (MA, PhD); philosophy (MA, PhD); religious studies (MA). *Program availability:* Part-time. *Degree requirements:* For master's, thesis or alternative; for doctorate, one foreign language, thesis/dissertation. *Entrance requirements:* For master's and doctorate, GRE General Test, minimum GPA of 2.7. Additional exam requirements/recommendations for international students: Required—TOEFL. Electronic applications accepted.

**University of the Cumberlands,** Program in Christian Studies, Williamsburg, KY 40769-1372. Offers MA. *Program availability:* Part-time, evening/weekend, online learning. *Entrance requirements:* For master's, GRE or MAT. Additional exam requirements/recommendations for international students: Required—TOEFL. Electronic applications accepted.

**University of the West,** Department of Psychology, Rosemead, CA 91770. Offers Buddhist psychology (MA); multicultural counseling (MA). *Program availability:* Part-time, evening/weekend. *Degree requirements:* For master's, fieldwork; comprehensive exam or thesis. *Application deadline:* For fall admission, 3/15 for domestic and international students; for winter admission, 4/1 for domestic and international students; for spring admission, 11/15 for domestic and international students. Applications are processed on a rolling basis. Application fee: $50 ($100 for international students). *Expenses: Tuition:* Full-time $9324; part-time $4662 per year. *Required fees:* $900; $640 per unit. $320 per semester. Tuition and fees vary according to program. *Financial support:* Applicants required to submit FAFSA. *Unit head:* Dr. Hiroshi Sasaki, Chair, 626-571-8811 Ext. 113, Fax: 626-571-1413, E-mail: hiroshis@uwest.edu. *Application contact:* Rica Toribio, Director of Enrollment Services, 626-571-8811 Ext. 311, Fax: 626-571-1413, E-mail: ricat@uwest.edu.

**University of the West,** Department of Religious Studies, Rosemead, CA 91770. Offers religious studies (MA, PhD), including Buddhism (PhD), Buddhist studies (MA), comparative religions (PhD), comparative religious studies (MA). *Program availability:* Part-time, evening/weekend. *Degree requirements:* For master's, thesis or comprehensive exam, competency in language associated with Buddhist Canon literature; for doctorate, 2 foreign languages, comprehensive exam, thesis/dissertation. *Entrance requirements:* For master's and doctorate, BA in religious studies, theology, philosophy or equivalent from an accredited university; official transcript; three letters of recommendation; essay. Additional exam requirements/recommendations for international students: Required—TOEFL, IELTS. *Application deadline:* For fall admission, 3/15 for domestic and international students; for spring admission, 11/15 for domestic and international students. Applications are processed on a rolling basis. Application fee: $50. *Expenses: Tuition:* Full-time $9324; part-time $4662 per year. *Required fees:* $900; $640 per unit. $320 per semester. Tuition and fees vary according to program. *Financial support:* Fellowships, scholarships/grants, and tuition waivers (partial) available. *Unit head:* Dr. Jane Iwamura, Chair, 626-571-8811 Ext. 342, Fax: 626-571-1413, E-mail: janei@uwest.edu. *Application contact:* Rica Toribio, Director of Enrollment Services, 626-571-8811 Ext. 311, Fax: 626-571-1413, E-mail: ricat@uwest.edu.

**University of Toronto,** School of Graduate Studies, Faculty of Arts and Science, Centre for the Study of Religion, Toronto, ON M5S 1A1, Canada. Offers MA, PhD. *Program availability:* Part-time. *Degree requirements:* For master's, one foreign language, research paper, language examination; for doctorate, 2 foreign languages, thesis/dissertation, language examinations, general examinations, oral examination. *Entrance requirements:* For master's, BA in religion or a related field; minimum A-average in final year, 3 letters of recommendation, resume; for doctorate, MA in religion, minimum average of A- in MA courses with no individual grade below a B, 3 letters of recommendation, resume, brief writing sample. Additional exam requirements/recommendations for international students: Required—TOEFL (minimum score 580 paper-based; 93 iBT), TWE (minimum score 5). Electronic applications accepted.

**University of Valley Forge,** Program in Christian Leadership, Phoenixville, PA 19460. Offers MA. *Degree requirements:* For master's, project.

**University of Valley Forge,** Program in Worship Studies, Phoenixville, PA 19460. Offers MA.

**University of Virginia,** College and Graduate School of Arts and Sciences, Department of Religious Studies, Charlottesville, VA 22903. Offers religion, politics and global society (MA); religious studies (MA, PhD). *Faculty:* 24 full-time (9 women), 1 (woman) part-time/adjunct. *Students:* 69 full-time (25 women); includes 8 minority (1 Black or African American, non-Hispanic/Latino; 2 Asian, non-Hispanic/Latino; 3 Hispanic/Latino; 2 Two or more races, non-Hispanic/Latino), 10 international. Average age 31. 137 applicants, 32% accepted, 16 enrolled. In 2016, 9 master's, 7 doctorates awarded. *Degree requirements:* For master's, one foreign language, thesis optional; for doctorate,

2 foreign languages, comprehensive exam, thesis/dissertation. *Entrance requirements:* For master's and doctorate, GRE General Test, 3 letters of recommendation. Additional exam requirements/recommendations for international students: Required—TOEFL (minimum score 600 paper-based; 90 iBT), IELTS (minimum score 7). *Application deadline:* For fall admission, 12/1 for domestic students, 12/3 for international students. Applications are processed on a rolling basis. Application fee: $60. Electronic applications accepted. *Expenses:* Tuition, state resident: full-time $15,026; part-time $834 per credit hour. Tuition, nonresident: full-time $25,168; part-time $1378 per credit hour. *Required fees:* $2654. *Financial support:* Fellowships and teaching assistantships available. Financial award applicants required to submit FAFSA. *Unit head:* Kurtis Schaeffer, Chair, 434-924-6705, Fax: 434-924-1467, E-mail: ks6bb@virginia.edu. *Application contact:* Matthew Hedstrom, Director of Graduate Studies, 434-924-6705, Fax: 434-924-1467, E-mail: msh6q@virginia.edu.
Website: http://religiousstudies.virginia.edu/

**University of Washington,** Graduate School, College of Arts and Sciences, Department of Asian Languages and Literature, Seattle, WA 98195. Offers Buddhist studies (MA, PhD); Chinese language and literature (MA, PhD); Japanese language and literature (MA, PhD); Korean language and literature (MA, PhD); South Asian language and literature (MA, PhD). *Degree requirements:* For master's, 2 foreign languages, general exam, thesis or 2 research papers; for doctorate, 3 foreign languages, thesis/dissertation, general exam. *Entrance requirements:* For master's, GRE, minimum GPA of 3.0; for doctorate, GRE, master's degree in related field, minimum GPA of 3.0. Additional exam requirements/recommendations for international students: Required—TOEFL. Electronic applications accepted. *Faculty research:* Textual, linguistic, philological, and literary study of languages and literatures of Asia.

**University of Washington,** Graduate School, College of Arts and Sciences, Henry M. Jackson School of International Studies, Comparative Religion Program, Seattle, WA 98195. Offers MAIS. *Degree requirements:* For master's, 2 foreign languages. *Entrance requirements:* For master's, GRE General Test, minimum GPA of 3.0 in last two years. Additional exam requirements/recommendations for international students: Required—TOEFL (minimum score 500 paper-based; 92 iBT), IELTS (minimum score 7). Electronic applications accepted.

**University of Waterloo,** Graduate Studies, Faculty of Arts, Department of Religious Studies, Waterloo, ON N2L 3G1, Canada. Offers religious diversity in North America (PhD). *Degree requirements:* For doctorate, thesis/dissertation. *Entrance requirements:* Additional exam requirements/recommendations for international students: Required—TOEFL, IELTS, PTE. Electronic applications accepted. *Faculty research:* Religious diversity in North America.

**The University of Winnipeg,** Graduate Studies, Department of Religious Studies, Winnipeg, MB R3B 2E9, Canada. Offers MA. Program offered jointly with University of Manitoba. *Program availability:* Part-time. *Faculty research:* Religion and culture, social ethics, religious liberalism, history of Canaanite and Israelite religion, literary criticism of the Hebrew Bible.

**Vancouver School of Theology,** Graduate and Professional Programs, Vancouver, BC V6T 1L4, Canada. Offers public and pastoral leadership (MA); public and pastoral leadership in spiritual care (MA); theological studies (MATS, Diploma); theology (M Div, Th M). *Accreditation:* ATS. *Program availability:* Part-time, online learning. *Degree requirements:* For master's, comprehensive exam (for some programs), thesis (for some programs); for Diploma, one foreign language, thesis. *Entrance requirements:* Additional exam requirements/recommendations for international students: Required—TOEFL (minimum score 80 iBT); Recommended—IELTS (minimum score 6.5). *Application deadline:* Applications are processed on a rolling basis. Application fee: $75 Canadian dollars. Electronic applications accepted. *Expenses: Tuition:* Part-time $281 per credit hour. Part-time tuition and fees vary according to degree level, campus/location and program. *Financial support:* Fellowships, research assistantships with partial tuition reimbursements, teaching assistantships with partial tuition reimbursements, career-related internships or fieldwork, scholarships/grants, and tuition waivers (partial) available. Support available to part-time students. Financial award application deadline: 3/30. *Faculty research:* Old Testament studies, pastoral theology, New Testament studies, field education, church history, systematic theology, spirituality. *Unit head:* Rev. Dr. Richard Topping, Principal, 604-822-9808, Fax: 604-822-9212. *Application contact:* Anita Fast, Registrar, 604-822-9563, Fax: 604-822-9212, E-mail: afast@vst.edu.
Website: http://vst.edu/ccl/about/degree-programs/graduate-degrees

**Vanderbilt University,** Department of Religion, Nashville, TN 37240-1001. Offers MA, PhD. *Faculty:* 30 full-time (10 women). *Students:* 65 full-time (35 women); includes 17 minority (13 Black or African American, non-Hispanic/Latino; 1 Asian, non-Hispanic/Latino; 2 Hispanic/Latino; 1 Two or more races, non-Hispanic/Latino), 5 international. Average age 33. 152 applicants, 15% accepted, 9 enrolled. In 2016, 2 master's, 13 doctorates awarded. *Degree requirements:* For master's, one foreign language, thesis; for doctorate, 2 foreign languages, thesis/dissertation, final and qualifying exams. *Entrance requirements:* For master's and doctorate, GRE General Test. Additional exam requirements/recommendations for international students: Required—TOEFL (minimum score 570 paper-based; 88 iBT). *Application deadline:* For fall admission, 12/15 for domestic and international students. Electronic applications accepted. *Expenses: Tuition:* Part-time $1854 per credit hour. *Financial support:* Fellowships with tuition reimbursements, teaching assistantships with tuition reimbursements, Federal Work-Study, institutionally sponsored loans, health care benefits, and tuition waivers (full and partial) available. Support available to part-time students. Financial award application deadline: 1/15; financial award applicants required to submit CSS PROFILE or FAFSA. *Faculty research:* Hebrew Bible, New Testament, church history, theology, ethics. *Unit head:* Dr. James Byrd, Jr., Chair and Director of Graduate Studies, 615-343-9977, Fax: 615-343-9957, E-mail: james.p.byrd@vanderbilt.edu. *Application contact:* Karen Eardley, Administrative Assistant, 615-343-3977, Fax: 615-343-9957, E-mail: karen.eardley@vanderbilt.edu.
Website: http://divinity.vanderbilt.edu/degrees/graduate/index.php

**Vanguard University of Southern California,** Graduate Programs in Religion, Costa Mesa, CA 92626-9601. Offers leadership studies (MA); theological studies (MTS). *Program availability:* Part-time, evening/weekend. *Degree requirements:* For master's, comprehensive exam (for some programs), thesis (for some programs). *Entrance requirements:* For master's, minimum GPA of 3.0 (MA), 2.5 (MTS). Additional exam requirements/recommendations for international students: Required—TOEFL (minimum score 550 paper-based; 79 iBT). Electronic applications accepted. *Expenses:* Contact institution. *Faculty research:* Narrative theology, ecumenism and Pentecost, leadership studies.

**Virginia University of Lynchburg,** Graduate Programs, Lynchburg, VA 24501-6417. Offers Christian ministry (M Div); ministry (D Min). *Program availability:* Online learning. *Faculty:* 6 full-time (0 women), 4 part-time/adjunct (all women). *Students:* 64 full-time (25 women), 4 part-time (2 women). *Expenses: Tuition:* Full-time $8200; part-time $4100 per credit hour. *Required fees:* $400. Tuition and fees vary according to campus/location and program. *Application contact:* Houston Walthall, Admissions Director, 434-528-5276 Ext. 1130, Fax: 434-528-4257, E-mail: hwalthall@vul.edu.

**Wake Forest University,** Graduate School of Arts and Sciences, Department of Religion, Winston-Salem, NC 27106. Offers MA. *Accreditation:* ACIPE. *Program availability:* Part-time. *Degree requirements:* For master's, one foreign language, thesis. *Entrance requirements:* For master's, GRE General Test. Additional exam requirements/recommendations for international students: Required—TOEFL (minimum score 79 iBT). Electronic applications accepted. *Faculty research:* Christian origins, biblical archaeology, psychology and religion, religion and literature.

**Washington Adventist University,** Program in Religion, Takoma Park, MD 20912. Offers MAR. *Program availability:* Part-time. *Entrance requirements:* Additional exam requirements/recommendations for international students: Required—TOEFL (minimum score 550 paper-based), IELTS (minimum score 5).

**Washington University in St. Louis,** The Graduate School, Department of Jewish, Islamic, and Near Eastern Languages and Cultures, St. Louis, MO 63130-4899. Offers Islamic and Near Eastern studies (MA); Jewish studies (MA). *Degree requirements:* For master's, one foreign language, thesis (for some programs). *Entrance requirements:* For master's, GRE General Test. Additional exam requirements/recommendations for international students: Required—TOEFL. Electronic applications accepted. *Faculty research:* Islamic and Near Eastern studies (Islamic history; Arabic language and literature, modern Middle East history); Jewish studies (Hebrew Bible, Rabbinic literature, Jewish history, modern Hebrew literature).

**Wayland Baptist University,** Graduate Programs, Programs in Religion, Plainview, TX 79072-6998. Offers Christian ministry (MCM); divinity (M Div); religion (MA). *Program availability:* Part-time, evening/weekend, online learning. *Degree requirements:* For master's, comprehensive exam. *Entrance requirements:* For master's, GRE or MAT, minimum GPA of 3.0; letter of endorsement from Christian congregation, one academic and one personal letter of recommendation (for M Div). Additional exam requirements/recommendations for international students: Required—TOEFL (minimum score 500 paper-based; 61 iBT). Electronic applications accepted.

**Wesley Biblical Seminary,** Graduate Programs, Jackson, MS 39206. Offers apologetics (MA); Biblical languages (M Div); Biblical literature (MA); Christian studies (MA); context and mission (M Div); honors research (M Div); interpretation (M Div); ministry (M Div); spiritual formation (M Div); teaching (M Div); theology (MA). *Accreditation:* ATS. *Program availability:* Part-time. *Degree requirements:* For master's, thesis. *Entrance requirements:* Additional exam requirements/recommendations for international students: Required—TOEFL. Electronic applications accepted. *Faculty research:* Patristics, missiology, culture, hermeneutics.

**Western Michigan University,** Graduate College, College of Arts and Sciences, Department of Comparative Religion, Kalamazoo, MI 49008. Offers MA, Graduate Certificate. *Degree requirements:* For master's, one foreign language, thesis optional.

**Western Seminary,** Graduate Programs, Program in Biblical and Theological Studies, Portland, OR 97215-3367. Offers biblical and theological studies (MA, G Dip); biblical studies (Certificate); theology (Th M). *Accreditation:* ATS. *Program availability:* Part-time, evening/weekend. *Degree requirements:* For master's, thesis or alternative, practicum. *Entrance requirements:* Additional exam requirements/recommendations for international students: Required—TOEFL.

**Westminster Seminary California,** Programs in Theology, Escondido, CA 92027-4128. Offers Biblical studies (MA); historical theology (MA); theological studies (M Div, MA). *Accreditation:* ATS. *Program availability:* Part-time, evening/weekend. *Degree requirements:* For master's, 2 foreign languages, thesis (for some programs). *Entrance requirements:* For master's, 2 letters of reference. Additional exam requirements/recommendations for international students: Required—TOEFL (minimum score 570 paper-based; 89 iBT), TWE (minimum score 4.5). *Faculty research:* Neo-paganism, New Testament background, eschatology, Protestant scholasticism, Ezekiel.

**Westminster Theological Seminary,** Graduate and Professional Programs, Philadelphia, PA 19118. Offers apologetics (Th M); Biblical and urban studies (Certificate); Biblical counseling (MA); biblical studies (MAR); Christian studies (Certificate); church history (Th M); counseling (M Div); general studies (M Div, MAR); hermeneutics and Bible interpretations (PhD); historical and theological studies (PhD); historical theology (Th M); New Testament (Th M); Old Testament (Th M); pastoral counseling (D Min); pastoral ministry (M Div, D Min); systematic theology (Th M); theological studies (MAR); urban missions (M Div, MA, MAR, D Min). *Accreditation:* ATS. *Program availability:* Part-time. Terminal master's awarded for partial completion of doctoral program. *Degree requirements:* For master's, thesis (for some programs); for doctorate, 4 foreign languages, comprehensive exam (for some programs), thesis/dissertation. *Entrance requirements:* For doctorate, GRE General Test. Additional exam requirements/recommendations for international students: Required—TOEFL, TWE.

**Wilfrid Laurier University,** Faculty of Graduate and Postdoctoral Studies, Faculty of Arts, Department of Religion and Culture, Waterloo, ON N2L 3C5, Canada. Offers religion and culture (MA); religious diversity of North America (PhD). *Program availability:* Part-time. *Degree requirements:* For master's, thesis optional; for doctorate, thesis/dissertation. *Entrance requirements:* For master's, honors BA or the equivalent in religious studies or other interdisciplinary social science or humanities program, minimum B average in overall undergraduate course work, B+ average in the undergraduate major; for doctorate, MA in religious studies, minimum A- average. Additional exam requirements/recommendations for international students: Required—TOEFL (minimum score 89 iBT). Electronic applications accepted. *Faculty research:* Religious diversity in North America.

**WON Institute of Graduate Studies,** Won Buddhist Studies Program, Glenside, PA 19038. Offers MWBS. *Program availability:* Part-time. *Degree requirements:* For master's, comprehensive exam, comprehensive ordination exam or thesis. *Entrance requirements:* For master's, bachelor's degree or one-year preparatory course in Won Buddhist studies. Additional exam requirements/recommendations for international students: Required—TOEFL (minimum score 550 paper-based; 79 iBT). *Application deadline:* For fall admission, 8/1 for domestic students; for spring admission, 12/1 for domestic students. Applications are processed on a rolling basis. Application fee: $75. *Financial support:* Application deadline: 8/1. *Faculty research:* Environmental ethics, the concept of religion. *Unit head:* Rev. Dr. Sanghyeon Cheon, Chair, 215-884-8942, E-mail: wbschair@woninstitute.edu. *Application contact:* Jennifer Cake, Enrollment Management Counselor, 215-884-8942 Ext. 219, E-mail: jennifer.cake@woninstitute.edu.
Website: https://www.woninstitute.edu/academics/master-of-won-buddhism-degree/

**Wycliffe College,** Division of Advanced Degree Studies, Toronto, ON M5S 1H7, Canada. Offers MA, Th M, D Min, PhD, Th D. PhD, D Min, MA offered jointly with Toronto School of Theology; Th D, Th M with University of Toronto. *Accreditation:* ATS (one or more programs are accredited). *Program availability:* Part-time. Terminal master's awarded for partial completion of doctoral program. *Degree requirements:* For master's, 2 foreign languages, thesis (for some programs); for doctorate, 3 foreign languages, thesis/dissertation. *Entrance requirements:* Additional exam requirements/recommendations for international students: Required—TOEFL (minimum score 600 paper-based). *Expenses:* Contact institution. *Faculty research:* Old and New Testament, doctrine, ethics, philosophy, history.

**Wycliffe College,** Division of Basic Degree Studies, Toronto, ON M5S 1H7, Canada. Offers Christian Studies (Diploma); theology (M Div, M Rel, MTS). M Div, M Rel, MTS offered jointly with University of Toronto. *Accreditation:* ATS. *Program availability:* Part-time. *Degree requirements:* For master's, one foreign language, thesis. *Entrance requirements:* Additional exam requirements/recommendations for international students: Required—TOEFL (minimum score 580 paper-based).

**Yale University,** Graduate School of Arts and Sciences, Department of Religious Studies, New Haven, CT 06520. Offers PhD. *Degree requirements:* For doctorate, 2 foreign languages, thesis/dissertation. *Entrance requirements:* For doctorate, GRE General Test.

**Yeshiva Derech Chaim,** Graduate Program, Brooklyn, NY 11218. Offers PhD. *Accreditation:* AARTS.

# Theology

**Abilene Christian University,** Graduate Programs, College of Biblical Studies, Graduate School of Theology, Program in Divinity, Abilene, TX 79699. Offers ministry (M Div); missions (M Div). *Accreditation:* ATS. *Program availability:* Part-time, evening/weekend, blended/hybrid learning. *Students:* 38 full-time (7 women), 18 part-time (7 women); includes 13 minority (11 Black or African American, non-Hispanic/Latino; 1 Asian, non-Hispanic/Latino; 1 Hispanic/Latino), 6 international. 49 applicants, 67% accepted. In 2016, 5 master's awarded. *Degree requirements:* For master's, comprehensive exam, e-portfolio review. *Entrance requirements:* Additional exam requirements/recommendations for international students: Required—TOEFL (minimum score 80 iBT), IELTS (minimum score 6), PTE. *Application deadline:* For fall admission, 8/11 for domestic students; for spring admission, 11/1 for domestic students. Applications are processed on a rolling basis. Application fee: $50. Electronic applications accepted. *Expenses:* $618 per credit hour. *Financial support:* In 2016–17, 6 students received support. Scholarships/grants available. Financial award application deadline: 4/1; financial award applicants required to submit FAFSA. *Unit head:* Dr. Kelli Gibson, Graduate Advisor, 325-674-3709, Fax: 325-674-6716, E-mail: kelli.gibson@acu.edu. *Application contact:* Corey Patterson, Director of Graduate Admission and Recruiting, 325-674-6566, Fax: 325-674-6717, E-mail: gradinfo@acu.edu.
Website: http://www.acu.edu/graduate/academics/divinity.html

**Abilene Christian University,** Graduate Programs, College of Biblical Studies, Graduate School of Theology, Program in New Testament, Abilene, TX 79699. Offers MA. *Accreditation:* ATS. *Program availability:* Part-time. *Students:* 5 full-time (1 woman). 4 applicants, 100% accepted, 3 enrolled. In 2016, 1 master's awarded. *Degree requirements:* For master's, comprehensive exam, thesis. *Entrance requirements:* Additional exam requirements/recommendations for international students: Required—TOEFL (minimum score 80 iBT), IELTS (minimum score 6), PTE. *Application deadline:* For fall admission, 8/11 for domestic students; for spring admission, 11/1 for domestic students. Applications are processed on a rolling basis. Application fee: $50. Electronic applications accepted. *Expenses:* $618 per credit hour. *Financial support:* In 2016–17, 1 student received support. Scholarships/grants available. Financial award application deadline: 4/1; financial award applicants required to submit FAFSA. *Unit head:* Dr. Richard Wright, Graduate Advisor, 325-674-3708, Fax: 325-674-6180, E-mail: richard.wright@acu.edu. *Application contact:* Corey Patterson, Director of Graduate Admission and Recruiting, 325-674-6566, Fax: 325-674-6717, E-mail: gradinfo@acu.edu.
Website: http://www.acu.edu/graduate/academics/new-testament.html

**Abilene Christian University,** Graduate Programs, College of Biblical Studies, Graduate School of Theology, Program in Old Testament, Abilene, TX 79699. Offers MA. *Accreditation:* ATS. *Program availability:* Part-time. *Students:* 2 part-time (0 women). 2 applicants. In 2016, 2 master's awarded. *Degree requirements:* For master's, comprehensive exam, thesis. *Entrance requirements:* Additional exam requirements/recommendations for international students: Required—TOEFL (minimum score 80 iBT), IELTS (minimum score 6), PTE. *Application deadline:* For fall admission, 8/11 for domestic students; for spring admission, 11/1 for domestic students. Applications are processed on a rolling basis. Application fee: $50. Electronic applications accepted. *Expenses:* $618 per credit hour. *Financial support:* Scholarships/grants available. Financial award application deadline: 4/1; financial award applicants required to submit FAFSA. *Unit head:* Dr. Mark Hamilton, Graduate Advisor, 325-674-3765, Fax: 325-674-6180, E-mail: mark.hamilton@acu.edu. *Application contact:* Corey Patterson, Director of Graduate Admission and Recruiting, 325-674-6566, Fax: 325-674-6717, E-mail: gradinfo@acu.edu.
Website: http://www.acu.edu/graduate/academics/old-testament.html

**Abilene Christian University,** Graduate Programs, College of Biblical Studies, Graduate School of Theology, Program in Theology, Abilene, TX 79699. Offers MA. *Accreditation:* ATS. *Program availability:* Part-time. *Students:* 4 full-time (0 women), 2 part-time (1 woman); includes 1 minority (Hispanic/Latino). 15 applicants, 47% accepted, 3 enrolled. In 2016, 1 master's awarded. *Degree requirements:* For master's, comprehensive exam, thesis. *Entrance requirements:* Additional exam requirements/recommendations for international students: Required—TOEFL (minimum score 80 iBT), IELTS (minimum score 6), PTE. *Application deadline:* For fall admission, 8/11 for domestic students; for spring admission, 11/1 for domestic students. Applications are processed on a rolling basis. Application fee: $50. Electronic applications accepted. *Expenses:* $618 per credit hour. *Financial support:* In 2016–17, 3 students received support. Application deadline: 4/1; applicants required to submit FAFSA. *Unit head:* Dr. Frederick Aquino, Graduate Advisor, 325-674-3789, Fax: 325-674-6180, E-mail: frederick.aquino@acu.edu. *Application contact:* Corey Patterson, Director of Graduate Admission and Recruiting, 325-674-6566, Fax: 325-674-6717, E-mail: gradinfo@acu.edu.
Website: http://www.acu.edu/graduate/academics/theology.html

**Acadia University,** Divinity College, Wolfville, NS B4P 2R6, Canada. Offers divinity (M Div); theology (MA, D Min), including Biblical studies (MA), church history (MA), theology (MA). *Accreditation:* ATS. *Program availability:* Part-time. *Degree requirements:* For master's, variable foreign language requirement, thesis (for some programs); for doctorate, one foreign language, comprehensive exam, thesis/dissertation. *Entrance requirements:* For doctorate, minimum GPA of 3.0, 3 years ministry experience. Additional exam requirements/recommendations for international students: Required—TOEFL. *Expenses:* Contact institution. *Faculty research:* Biblical canon, Jesus, Dead Sea Scrolls, Baptist studies, Old Testament-Septuagint.

**Ambrose University,** Ambrose Seminary, Calgary, AB T3H 0L5, Canada. Offers Biblical/theological studies (MA), including New Testament, Old Testament, theology; Christian studies (MCS, Diploma); intercultural ministries (M Div, MA); leadership (Certificate); leadership and ministry (MA), including chaplaincy, leadership; pastoral ministry (M Div). *Accreditation:* ATS (one or more programs are accredited). *Program availability:* Part-time, blended/hybrid learning. *Faculty:* 14 full-time (3 women), 4 part-time/adjunct (1 woman). *Students:* 76 applicants, 74% accepted, 35 enrolled. In 2016, 21 master's, 1 other advanced degree awarded. *Degree requirements:* For master's, variable foreign language requirement, thesis (for some programs), internship (for M Div, MA in leadership and ministry, MA in intercultural ministries); thesis (for MA in Biblical/theological studies). *Entrance requirements:* For master's, undergraduate degree from other accredited university or bible college, minimum GPA of 2.0. Additional exam requirements/recommendations for international students: Required—PTE (minimum score 58), TOEFL (minimum score 560 paper-based, 83 iBT) or IELTS (minimum score 6.5). *Application deadline:* For fall admission, 8/1 for domestic students, 4/15 for international students; for winter admission, 12/1 for domestic students, 11/15 for international students. Applications are processed on a rolling basis. Application fee: $70 ($100 for international students). Electronic applications accepted. *Expenses:* Tuition: Full-time $11,850 Canadian dollars; part-time $395 Canadian dollars per credit hour. *Required fees:* $810 Canadian dollars; $27 Canadian dollars per credit hour. $50 Canadian dollars per semester. Tuition and fees vary according to course load and program. *Financial support:* Career-related internships or fieldwork and scholarships/grants available. Support available to part-time students. Financial award application deadline: 3/30. *Faculty research:* Evangelicalism and sociology, missiological trends, chaplaincy, intertestamental studies, postmodernism. *Unit head:* Dr. Jo-Ann Badley, Dean of Theology, 403-410-2000 Ext. 3994, Fax: 403-571-2556, E-mail: jbadley@ambrose.edu. *Application contact:* Andreas Striefler, Enrollment Advisor, 403-410-2970, Fax: 403-571-2556, E-mail: enrolment@ambrose.edu.
Website: https://ambrose.edu/seminary

**American Baptist Seminary of the West,** Graduate and Professional Programs, Berkeley, CA 94704-3029. Offers community leadership (MA); theology (M Div, MA). MA program in theology offered jointly with Graduate Theological Union. *Accreditation:* ACIPE; ATS (one or more programs are accredited). *Program availability:* Part-time, evening/weekend, online learning. *Entrance requirements:* Additional exam requirements/recommendations for international students: Required—TOEFL (minimum score 550 paper-based). Electronic applications accepted.

**American Jewish University,** Ziegler School of Rabbinic Studies, Bel Air, CA 90077-1599. Offers MARS. *Degree requirements:* For master's, one foreign language. *Entrance requirements:* For master's, GRE General Test, interview. Additional exam requirements/recommendations for international students: Required—TOEFL.

**Amridge University,** Graduate and Professional Programs, Montgomery, AL 36117. Offers Biblical studies (MA, PhD); Christian ministry (MS); family therapy (D Min); human services (MS); leadership and management (MS); marriage and family therapy (M Div, MA, PhD); ministerial leadership (M Div, MS); New Testament studies (MA); Old Testament studies (MA); professional counseling (M Div, MA, PhD); theology (M Div, D Min). *Program availability:* Part-time, evening/weekend, online learning. *Faculty:* 22 full-time (3 women), 10 part-time/adjunct (6 women). *Students:* 81 full-time (49 women), 225 part-time (137 women); includes 81 minority (80 Black or African American, non-Hispanic/Latino; 1 Hispanic/Latino). Average age 41. 122 applicants, 100% accepted, 79 enrolled. *Degree requirements:* For master's, one foreign language, comprehensive exam (for some programs), thesis (for some programs); for doctorate, one foreign language, comprehensive exam (for some programs), thesis/dissertation (for some programs). *Entrance requirements:* For master's, official transcript showing an earned 4-year BA or BS from regionally- or nationally-accredited institution; for doctorate, official transcript showing earned graduate degree from regionally- or nationally-accredited institution; writing sample (e.g. career monograph, published journal article, term paper from master's degree or doctoral dissertation); interview. Additional exam requirements/recommendations for international students: Required—TOEFL (minimum score 79 iBT). *Application deadline:* Applications are processed on a rolling basis. Application fee: $50. Electronic applications accepted. *Expenses:* Tuition: Full-time $12,870; part-time $715 per credit hour. *Required fees:* $1300; $650 per semester. *Financial support:* In 2016–17, 45 students received support. Federal Work-Study and scholarships/grants available. Support available to part-time students. Financial award applicants required to submit FAFSA. *Faculty research:* Technology and mental healthcare, resilience in black families, theology and congregational ministry. *Unit head:* Laina Costanza, Vice President, Student Affairs, 888-790-8080 Ext. 1, Fax: 334-387-3878, E-mail: cc@amridgeuniversity.edu. *Application contact:* Brooks Housley, Student Affairs Coordinator, 888-790-8080 Ext. 1, Fax: 334-387-3878, E-mail: admissions@amridgeuniversity.edu.

**Anabaptist Mennonite Biblical Seminary,** Graduate and Professional Programs, Elkhart, IN 46517-1999. Offers chaplaincy (M Div); Christian faith formation (M Div); Christian formation (MA); Christian spiritual formation (Certificate); divinity (M Div); pastoral ministry (M Div); pastoral theology for financial professionals (Certificate); peace studies (M Div), including environmental sustainability leadership (M Div, MA); theological studies (M Div, Certificate), including peace studies (M Div), theology and ethics (M Div); theology and peace studies (MA), including conflict transformation, environmental sustainability leadership (M Div, MA), international development administration; United Methodist leadership (M Div). Conflict transformation and environmental sustainability leadership concentrations offered in cooperation with Goshen College; international development administration offered in cooperation with Andrews University. *Accreditation:* ACIPE; ATS. *Program availability:* Part-time, 100% online, blended/hybrid learning. *Faculty:* 14 full-time (6 women), 17 part-time/adjunct (8 women). *Students:* 38 full-time (14 women), 60 part-time (33 women); includes 15 minority (4 Black or African American, non-Hispanic/Latino; 5 Asian, non-Hispanic/Latino; 5 Hispanic/Latino; 1 Two or more races, non-Hispanic/Latino), 15 international. Average age 35. 43 applicants, 70% accepted, 29 enrolled. In 2016, 16 master's, 2 other advanced degrees awarded. *Degree requirements:* For master's, variable foreign language requirement, comprehensive exam (for some programs), thesis optional, senior interview. *Entrance requirements:* For master's, undergraduate degree transcripts, 3 letters of reference, essay. Additional exam requirements/recommendations for international students: Required—TOEFL (minimum score 90 iBT); Recommended—IELTS (minimum score 7). *Application deadline:* For fall admission, 6/1 priority date for domestic students, 5/1 priority date for international students. Applications are processed on a rolling basis. Application fee: $25. Electronic applications accepted. *Expenses:* Tuition: Full-time $13,950; part-time $5640 per year.

## Theology

Required fees: $900; $300 per unit. $50 per term. Financial support: In 2016–17, 40 students received support. Career-related internships or fieldwork, scholarships/grants, unspecified assistantships, and church matching grants available. Support available to part-time students. Financial award application deadline: 4/15; financial award applicants required to submit FAFSA. Faculty research: Biblical studies, peace studies, theology, ethics, creation care or environmental ethics, church history, church leadership, mission, ministry, preaching, pastoral leadership, social justice, peacemaking, Jesus Christ, Christianity, Anabaptism, Mennonite, Scripture, Bible, Old Testament, New Testament, spirituality, clinical pastoral education, teaching, faith formation, pastoral care, Koine Greek, Hebrew, Aramaic, Syriac, Ugaritic. Unit head: Sara Wenger Shenk, President, 800-964-2627, Fax: 574-295-0092. Application contact: Daniel Grimes, Director of Admissions, 574-296-6266, Fax: 574-295-0092, E-mail: admissions@ambs.edu.
Website: http://www.ambs.edu/

**Anderson University,** School of Theology, Anderson, IN 46012-3495. Offers missions (MA); theology (M Div, MTS, D Min). Accreditation: ACIPE; ATS. Program availability: Part-time. Degree requirements: For master's, variable foreign language requirement, thesis (for some programs); for doctorate, thesis/dissertation. Faculty research: Small-church/bivocational ministry, women in ministry.

**Andrews University,** School of Graduate Studies, Seventh-day Adventist Theological Seminary, Berrien Springs, MI 49104. Offers ministry (M Div, D Min); pastoral ministry (MA); religious education (MA, Ed D, PhD, Ed S); theology (M Th, Th D); youth ministry (MA). Faculty: 40 full-time (5 women), 12 part-time/adjunct (2 women). Students: 477 full-time (69 women), 530 part-time (83 women); includes 498 minority (237 Black or African American, non-Hispanic/Latino; 3 American Indian or Alaska Native, non-Hispanic/Latino; 53 Asian, non-Hispanic/Latino; 198 Hispanic/Latino; 2 Native Hawaiian or other Pacific Islander, non-Hispanic/Latino; 5 Two or more races, non-Hispanic/Latino), 234 international. Average age 40. In 2016, 194 master's, 52 doctorates awarded. Degree requirements: For master's, thesis optional; for doctorate, variable foreign language requirement, thesis/dissertation. Entrance requirements: For master's, GRE Subject Test, minimum GPA of 2.0. Additional exam requirements/recommendations for international students: Required—TOEFL (minimum score 550 paper-based). Application deadline: Applications are processed on a rolling basis. Application fee: $40. Financial support: Fellowships, research assistantships, teaching assistantships, career-related internships or fieldwork, Federal Work-Study, and institutionally sponsored loans available. Faculty research: Biblical archaeology, biblical studies, biblical language learning methods, church growth. Unit head: Dr. Jiri Moskala, Dean, 269-471-3537. Application contact: Justina Clayburn, Director, 800-253-2874, Fax: 269-471-6321.

**Apex School of Theology,** Graduate Programs, Durham, NC 27703. Offers M Div, MACC, MCE, D Min. Faculty research: Sociology, educational sciences, economics.

**Aquinas Institute of Theology,** Graduate and Professional Programs, St. Louis, MO 63108. Offers biblical studies (Certificate); church music (MM); health care mission (MAHCM); ministry (M Div); pastoral care (Certificate); pastoral ministry (MAPM); pastoral studies (MAPS); preaching (D Min); spiritual direction (Certificate); theology (M Div, MA); Thomistic studies (Certificate); M Div/MA; MA/PhD; MAPS/MSW. Accreditation: ATS (one or more programs are accredited). Program availability: Part-time, evening/weekend, online learning. Degree requirements: For master's, variable foreign language requirement, comprehensive exam (for some programs), thesis (for some programs); for doctorate, thesis/dissertation. Entrance requirements: For master's and Certificate, MAT; for doctorate, 3 years of ministerial experience, 6 hours of graduate course work in homiletics, M Div or the equivalent, minimum GPA of 3.0. Additional exam requirements/recommendations for international students: Required—TOEFL. Expenses: Contact institution. Faculty research: Theology of preaching, hermeneutics, lay ecclesial ministry, pastoral and practical theology.

**Arlington Baptist College,** Program in Biblical and Theological Studies, Arlington, TX 76012-3425. Offers MA. Entrance requirements: For master's, official transcript, letter of reference from pastor, two letters of recommendation, essay. Additional exam requirements/recommendations for international students: Required—TOEFL. Electronic applications accepted.

**Asbury Theological Seminary,** Graduate and Professional Programs, Wilmore, KY 40390-1199. Offers M Div, MA, MAAS, MACE, MACL, MACM, MACP, MAMFC, MAMHC, MAPC, MASF, MAYM, Th M, D Min, PhD, Certificate. Accreditation: ATS. Program availability: Part-time, online learning. Terminal master's awarded for partial completion of doctoral program. Degree requirements: For master's, thesis (for some programs); for doctorate, thesis/dissertation, qualifying exam. Entrance requirements: For master's, minimum GPA of 2.75; for doctorate, minimum GPA of 3.0. Additional exam requirements/recommendations for international students: Required—TOEFL, IELTS. Electronic applications accepted.

**Ashland Theological Seminary,** Graduate Programs, Ashland, OH 44805. Offers Biblical studies (MA); Christian ministries (MACM), including Black church studies (MACM, D Min), general Christian ministries, leadership, spiritual formation (MACM, D Min); clinical mental health counseling (MA); counseling (MAC); historical and theological studies (MA), including Anabaptism and Pietism, Christian theology, church history, New Testament, Old Testament; ministry (D Min), including Black church studies (MACM, D Min), chaplaincy (M Div, D Min), independent design, spiritual formation (MACM, D Min), transformational leadership; pastoral ministry (M Div), including chaplaincy (M Div, D Min), general ministry. MAC program offered in Detroit, MI. Accreditation: ATS. Program availability: Part-time. Degree requirements: For master's, 2 foreign languages, comprehensive exam (for some programs), thesis (for some programs); for doctorate, thesis/dissertation. Entrance requirements: For master's, bachelor's degree from accredited institution with a minimum undergraduate GPA of 2.75; for doctorate, M Div, minimum undergraduate GPA of 3.0. Additional exam requirements/recommendations for international students: Required—TOEFL (minimum score 500 paper-based; 65 iBT). Application deadline: For fall admission, 8/30 for domestic students. Applications are processed on a rolling basis. Application fee: $35. Electronic applications accepted. Expenses: Tuition: Full-time $15,120; part-time $630 per semester hour. Tuition and fees vary according to program. Financial support: Research assistantships, teaching assistantships, career-related internships or fieldwork, institutionally sponsored loans, scholarships/grants, and unspecified assistantships available. Support available to part-time students. Financial award application deadline: 5/15; financial award applicants required to submit FAFSA. Faculty research: Semitic languages and linguistics, rhetorical and social-scientific criticism, Anabaptist studies, inner spiritual healing, African-American clergy in film and literature. Unit head: Dr. Mark Harden, President, 419-289-5160, Fax: 419-289-5969, E-mail: mharden@ashland.edu. Application contact: Dr. Mark Harden, President, 419-289-5160, Fax: 419-289-5969, E-mail: mharden@ashland.edu.

**Assemblies of God Theological Seminary,** Graduate and Professional Programs, Springfield, MO 65802. Offers Biblical interpretation and theology (PhD); Christian ministries (MA); divinity (M Div); intercultural studies (MA, PhD); ministry (D Min); missiology (DAIS); pastoral studies (MPL); theological studies (MA, Th M). Accreditation: ATS. Program availability: Part-time, evening/weekend, 100% online.

Degree requirements: For master's, variable foreign language requirement; for doctorate, thesis/dissertation. Entrance requirements: For master's, minimum GPA of 2.5; for doctorate, GRE (for PhD in Bible theology), minimum GPA of 3.0. Additional exam requirements/recommendations for international students: Required—TOEFL (minimum score 550 paper-based; 80 iBT). Electronic applications accepted.

**The Athenaeum of Ohio,** Graduate Programs, Cincinnati, OH 45230-5900. Offers M Div, MA, MA Th, MABS, Certificate, M Div/MA Th, M Div/MABS. Program availability: Part-time, evening/weekend. Students: 64 full-time (0 women), 57 part-time (31 women); includes 10 minority (1 Black or African American, non-Hispanic/Latino; 4 Asian, non-Hispanic/Latino; 4 Hispanic/Latino; 1 Two or more races, non-Hispanic/Latino), 3 international. In 2016, 45 master's awarded. Degree requirements: For master's, one foreign language, comprehensive exam (for some programs), thesis or alternative. Entrance requirements: For master's, bachelor's degree, minimum GPA of 3.0. Application deadline: For fall admission, 4/15 priority date for domestic students; for winter admission, 11/1 priority date for domestic students. Applications are processed on a rolling basis. Application fee: $30. Expenses: Tuition: Full-time $10,080; part-time $5040 per credit. One-time fee: $30. Financial support: Scholarships/grants available. Support available to part-time students. Financial award application deadline: 8/1. Unit head: Fr. David J. Endres, Dean, 513-231-2223, Fax: 513-231-3254, E-mail: dendres@athenaeum.edu. Application contact: Nicholas Jobe, Registrar, 513-231-2223, Fax: 513-231-3254, E-mail: njobe@athenaeum.edu.
Website: http://www.athenaeum.edu/

**Atlantic School of Theology,** Graduate and Professional Programs, Halifax, NS B3H 3B5, Canada. Offers ministry (M Div); theological studies (Graduate Certificate). Accreditation: ATS. Program availability: Part-time, online learning. Degree requirements: For master's, thesis (for some programs). Entrance requirements: For master's and Graduate Certificate, minimum B average in undergraduate course work. Faculty research: Ethics and biology; death, dying and pastoral care; theology and the economy; adult education; John and anti-Judaism.

**Austin Graduate School of Theology,** Program in Theological Studies, Austin, TX 78752. Offers MATS. Program availability: Part-time. Faculty: 4 full-time (0 women), 4 part-time/adjunct (0 women). Students: 9 full-time (2 women), 12 part-time (4 women). Degree requirements: For master's, 2 foreign languages, comprehensive exam, faculty forums. Entrance requirements: For master's, 3 letters of reference, essay, minimum cumulative GPA of 2.5, bachelor's degree, official transcripts. Additional exam requirements/recommendations for international students: Required—TOEFL (minimum score 550 paper-based; 80 iBT). Application deadline: For fall admission, 7/1 priority date for domestic and international students; for spring admission, 10/1 priority date for domestic and international students. Applications are processed on a rolling basis. Application fee: $25. Electronic applications accepted. Application fee is waived when completed online. Expenses: Tuition: Full-time $6300; part-time $4200 per credit. Required fees: $350; $350 per credit. $175 per semester. Financial support: Federal Work-Study and scholarships/grants available. Support available to part-time students. Financial award application deadline: 7/1. Faculty research: Revelation, synoptic problem, Acadian, Biblical archaeology, worship. Unit head: Dr. Keith Stanglin, Graduate Student Advisor, 512-476-2772, Fax: 512-476-3919, E-mail: stanglin@austingrad.edu. Application contact: Dawn Bond, Director of Admissions/Registrar, 512-476-2772 Ext. 103, Fax: 512-476-3919, E-mail: dbond@austingrad.edu.
Website: http://www.austingrad.edu/academics_mats.html

**Austin Presbyterian Theological Seminary,** Graduate and Professional Programs, Austin, TX 78705-5797. Offers divinity (M Div); ministry (D Min); ministry practice (MA); theological studies (MA); youth ministry (MA); M Div/MSSW. M Div/MSSW offered in collaboration with The University of Texas at Austin School of Social Work. Accreditation: ACIPE; ATS. Faculty: 20 full-time (6 women), 5 part-time/adjunct (1 woman). Students: 88 full-time (50 women), 74 part-time (41 women). In 2016, 44 master's, 4 doctorates awarded. Degree requirements: For master's, Greek, Hebrew (for M Div); for doctorate, thesis/dissertation. Entrance requirements: For master's, references (for M Div). Additional exam requirements/recommendations for international students: Required—TOEFL (minimum score 550 paper-based; 79 iBT). Application deadline: For fall admission, 5/1 for domestic students, 1/1 for international students; for summer admission, 2/2 for domestic students. Applications are processed on a rolling basis. Electronic applications accepted. Expenses: Tuition: Full-time $13,200; part-time $220 per credit. Required fees: $120; $120 per credit. $25 per semester. One-time fee: $175 full-time; $120 part-time. Tuition and fees vary according to degree level and program. Financial support: Fellowships, career-related internships or fieldwork, institutionally sponsored loans, and scholarships/grants available. Support available to part-time students. Financial award application deadline: 3/1; financial award applicants required to submit FAFSA. Faculty research: Mystical theology, religious pluralism, narrative preaching, social ethics, pastoral care and healing. Unit head: Dr. David Jensen, Academic Dean, 512-404-4821, Fax: 512-479-0738, E-mail: dean@austinseminary.edu. Application contact: Dr. Jack Barden, Vice President for Admissions, 512-404-4827, Fax: 512-472-7089, E-mail: admissions@austinseminary.edu.

**Ave Maria University,** Graduate Programs, Ave Maria, FL 34142. Offers pastoral theology (MTS); theology (MA, PhD). Terminal master's awarded for partial completion of doctoral program. Degree requirements: For master's, one foreign language, thesis; for doctorate, 3 foreign languages, comprehensive exam, thesis/dissertation. Entrance requirements: For master's, GRE; for doctorate, GRE, M Div or equivalent; MA or MTS in religion, theology, or philosophy; bachelor's degree with strong background in religion, theology, and/or philosophy.

**Azusa Pacific University,** Haggard Graduate School of Theology, Program in Ministry, Azusa, CA 91702-7000. Offers D Min. Accreditation: ATS.

**Azusa Pacific University,** Haggard Graduate School of Theology, Program in Theological Studies, Concentration in Religion: Biblical Studies, Azusa, CA 91702-7000. Offers MAR. Accreditation: ATS.

**Azusa Pacific University,** Haggard Graduate School of Theology, Program in Theological Studies, Concentration in Religion: Theology and Ethics, Azusa, CA 91702-7000. Offers MA. Accreditation: ATS.

**Bakke Graduate University,** Programs in Pastoral Ministry and Business, Dallas, TX 75243-7039. Offers business administration (MBA); church and ministry multiplication (D Min); global urban leadership (MA); leadership (D Min); ministry in complex contexts (D Min); social and civic entrepreneurship (MA); theology of work (D Min); theology reflection (D Min); transformational leadership (DTL); urban youth ministry (D Min). Program availability: Part-time, online learning. Degree requirements: For master's, thesis; for doctorate, thesis/dissertation. Entrance requirements: For master's, 2 years of ministry experience, BA in Biblical studies or theology; for doctorate, 3 years of ministry experience, M Div. Additional exam requirements/recommendations for international students: Required—TOEFL. Electronic applications accepted. Faculty research: Theological systems, church management, worship.

**Baptist Bible College,** Graduate School of Theology, Springfield, MO 65803-3498. Offers biblical counseling (MA); biblical studies (MA); church ministry (MA); intercultural studies (MA); theology (M Div). Program availability: Part-time. Entrance requirements:

Additional exam requirements/recommendations for international students: Required—TOEFL. Electronic applications accepted.

**The Baptist College of Florida,** Graduate Programs, Graceville, FL 32440-1898. Offers Christian ministry (MA); Christian studies (MA), including Biblical studies; music and worship leadership (MA). *Program availability:* Part-time, 100% online, blended/hybrid learning. *Degree requirements:* For master's, variable foreign language requirement, comprehensive exam (for some programs), thesis (for some programs). *Entrance requirements:* For master's, regionally-accredited undergraduate degree, undergraduate courses in field, minimum GPA of 2.5. Additional exam requirements/recommendations for international students: Required—TOEFL. Electronic applications accepted. *Expenses:* Contact institution. *Faculty research:* Biblical studies, ministry studies.

**Baptist Missionary Association Theological Seminary,** Graduate and Professional Programs, Jacksonville, TX 75766-5407. Offers M Div, MAR. *Accreditation:* ATS. *Program availability:* Part-time. *Degree requirements:* For master's, variable foreign language requirement, thesis optional. *Entrance requirements:* Additional exam requirements/recommendations for international students: Required—TOEFL (minimum score 550 paper-based). Electronic applications accepted. *Faculty research:* Education, Biblical studies.

**Baptist Theological Seminary at Richmond,** Graduate and Professional Programs, Richmond, VA 23228. Offers Biblical interpretation (M Div); Christian education formation (M Div); Christian ministry (MCM); justice and peacebuilding (M Div); ministry (D Min); religious freedom (M Div); theological studies (MTS, Graduate Certificate); theology (M Div); youth and student ministries (M Div); M Div/MBA; M Div/MS; M Div/MSW. *Accreditation:* ATS. *Program availability:* Part-time, 100% online, blended/hybrid learning. *Faculty:* 5 full-time (1 woman), 11 part-time/adjunct (2 women). *Students:* 42 full-time (23 women), 34 part-time (19 women); includes 11 minority (all Black or African American, non-Hispanic/Latino), 2 international. Average age 46. In 2016, 8 master's, 2 doctorates awarded. *Degree requirements:* For master's and Graduate Certificate, thesis optional; for doctorate, comprehensive exam, thesis/dissertation, field study, independent study. *Entrance requirements:* For master's, BA/BS, minimum GPA of 2.2, 2 references, resume, official transcripts, writing sample; for doctorate, MAT (minimum score of 400), M Div with minimum GPA of 2.75, 3 years of full-time ministry experience, 3 references, resume, official transcripts, writing sample, personal statement. Additional exam requirements/recommendations for international students: Required—TOEFL (minimum score 550 paper-based), IELTS (minimum score 5.5). *Application deadline:* For fall admission, 7/1 for domestic students, 5/1 for international students; for winter admission, 12/15 for domestic students, 9/1 for international students; for spring admission, 1/15 for domestic students, 10/1 for international students. Applications are processed on a rolling basis. Application fee: $35. Electronic applications accepted. *Expenses:* $19,800 per 12 credit hours for both semesters; $1,650 per 3 semester hour course. *Financial support:* In 2016–17, 46 students received support, including 11 teaching assistantships (averaging $3,300 per year); scholarships/grants also available. Financial award application deadline: 2/1. *Faculty research:* Biblical studies, pastoral care, church history, theology, ministry. *Unit head:* Dr. Ronald W. Crawford, President, 804-204-1201, Fax: 804-355-8182, E-mail: rcrawford@btsr.edu. *Application contact:* Melissa Fallen, Director of Admissions and Recruitment, 804-204-1208, E-mail: admissions@btsr.edu.
Website: http://www.btsr.edu/programs/degree-programs/

**Barclay College,** Master of Arts Program, Haviland, KS 67059-0288. Offers MA. *Program availability:* Online learning. *Degree requirements:* For master's, comprehensive exam, capstone project. *Entrance requirements:* Additional exam requirements/recommendations for international students: Required—TOEFL. Electronic applications accepted.

**Barry University,** College of Arts and Sciences, Department of Theology and Philosophy, Miami Shores, FL 33161-6695. Offers ministry (D Min); pastoral ministry for Hispanics (MA); pastoral theology (MA); practical theology (MA). *Accreditation:* ATS. *Program availability:* Part-time, evening/weekend. *Degree requirements:* For master's, comprehensive exam, thesis optional; for doctorate, thesis/dissertation. *Entrance requirements:* For master's, GRE General Test or MAT, minimum GPA of 3.0. Electronic applications accepted. *Faculty research:* Fundamental morals, bioethics, social ethics, liturgical and sacramental theology, biblical studies.

**Baylor University,** George W. Truett Theological Seminary, Waco, TX 76798. Offers M Div, MACM, MTS, D Min, JD/M Div, M Div/MBA, M Div/MM, M Div/MS Ed, M Div/MSW, MTS/MSW. *Program availability:* Part-time. *Faculty:* 20 full-time (2 women), 18 part-time/adjunct (5 women). *Students:* 258 full-time (89 women), 79 part-time (25 women); includes 95 minority (50 Black or African American, non-Hispanic/Latino; 10 Asian, non-Hispanic/Latino; 23 Hispanic/Latino; 12 Two or more races, non-Hispanic/Latino), 20 international. Average age 30. 157 applicants, 82% accepted, 84 enrolled. In 2016, 81 master's, 7 doctorates awarded. *Degree requirements:* For master's, 2 foreign languages, thesis or alternative; for doctorate, comprehensive exam, thesis/dissertation, 12 hours of seminars, 12 hours of directed study (including 2 annotated bibliographies reflecting at least 4800 pages of reading, 10 meetings with a field supervisor, 20 meetings with a faculty supervisor, and 3 major learning events). *Entrance requirements:* For master's, 4 recommendations, 2 essays, transcripts from all colleges/universities attended to include conferred undergraduate degree or equivalent, minimum GPA of 2.7, evidence of Christian commitment and leadership; for doctorate, 4 recommendations, 3 essays, writing sample, church recommendation, interview, transcripts from all colleges/universities attended to include conferred M Div or equivalent, minimum GPA of 3.0, 3 years of ministry experience subsequent to M Div. Additional exam requirements/recommendations for international students: Required—TOEFL (minimum score 550 paper-based; 80 iBT), IELTS (minimum score 6.5). *Application deadline:* For fall admission, 5/1 for domestic students, 6/10 for international students; for spring admission, 11/15 for domestic students, 10/10 for international students; for summer admission, 4/1 for domestic students, 3/10 for international students. Applications are processed on a rolling basis. Application fee: $35. Electronic applications accepted. Application fee is waived when completed online. *Expenses:* $902 per hour tuition; $960 per semester fees. *Financial support:* In 2016–17, 328 students received support, including 33 research assistantships with partial tuition reimbursements available (averaging $3,474 per year); teaching assistantships, career-related internships or fieldwork, Federal Work-Study, institutionally sponsored loans, scholarships/grants, traineeships, health care benefits, tuition waivers, and unspecified assistantships also available. Support available to part-time students. Financial award application deadline: 8/1; financial award applicants required to submit FAFSA. *Faculty research:* Shift within church-world exchange, thinking about sports as Christians, reformation of worship, pastoral theology of prayer. *Total annual research expenditures:* $1.1 million. *Unit head:* Dr. Todd D. Still, Dean, 254-710-3755, Fax: 254-710-3753, E-mail: todd_still@baylor.edu. *Application contact:* Carley Joy Collier, Administrative Associate, Admissions Services, 254-710-7334, Fax: 254-710-7233, E-mail: carley_lund@baylor.edu.
Website: http://www.baylor.edu/truett

**Bethany Theological Seminary,** Graduate and Professional Programs, Richmond, IN 47374-4019. Offers biblical studies (MA Th); ministry studies (M Div); peace studies (M Div, MA Th); theological studies (MA Th, CATS); youth ministry (M Div). *Accreditation:* ACIPE; ATS. *Program availability:* Part-time, online learning. *Degree requirements:* For master's, thesis (for some programs). *Entrance requirements:* For master's, letters of reference. Additional exam requirements/recommendations for international students: Required—TOEFL (minimum score 550 paper-based).

**Bethel College,** Adult and Graduate Programs, Program in Theological Studies, Mishawaka, IN 46545-5591. Offers MATS. *Program availability:* Part-time, evening/weekend, 100% online, blended/hybrid learning. *Faculty:* 7 part-time/adjunct (0 women). *Students:* 1 full-time (0 women), 6 part-time (1 woman); includes 2 minority (1 Black or African American, non-Hispanic/Latino; 1 Hispanic/Latino). Average age 35. 1 applicant. In 2016, 1 master's awarded. *Entrance requirements:* Additional exam requirements/recommendations for international students: Required—TOEFL (minimum score 540 paper-based). *Application deadline:* For fall admission, 5/1 for international students; for spring admission, 10/1 for international students. Applications are processed on a rolling basis. Application fee: $0. Electronic applications accepted. *Expenses:* Tuition: Full-time $6750; part-time $3375 per credit hour. *Required fees:* $75 per semester. Tuition and fees vary according to course load and program. *Financial support:* Career-related internships or fieldwork available. Financial award applicants required to submit FAFSA. *Unit head:* Steve Ganger, Director, 574-807-7507, E-mail: steve.ganger@bethelcollege.edu.

**Bethel Seminary,** Graduate and Professional Programs, St. Paul, MN 55112-6998. Offers Anglican studies (Certificate); children's and family ministry (MA); Christian studies (Certificate); Christian thought (MA); church planting (Certificate); Greek and Hebrew language (M Div); Greek language (M Div); Hebrew language (M Div); marriage and family therapy (MA, Certificate); mental health counseling (MA); ministry (MA, D Min); ministry practice (Certificate); theological studies (MA, Certificate); transformational leadership (MA); young life youth ministry (Certificate). *Accreditation:* ACIPE. *Program availability:* Part-time, evening/weekend, blended/hybrid learning. *Faculty:* 14 full-time (4 women), 37 part-time/adjunct (17 women). *Students:* 369 full-time (165 women), 147 part-time (43 women); includes 138 minority (48 Black or African American, non-Hispanic/Latino; 45 Asian, non-Hispanic/Latino; 28 Hispanic/Latino; 2 Native Hawaiian or other Pacific Islander, non-Hispanic/Latino; 15 Two or more races, non-Hispanic/Latino), 15 international. 322 applicants, 75% accepted, 174 enrolled. In 2016, 168 master's, 24 doctorates, 6 other advanced degrees awarded. *Degree requirements:* For master's, variable foreign language requirement, thesis (for some programs); for doctorate, thesis/dissertation. *Entrance requirements:* For master's, letters of reference, transcripts, personal statement; for doctorate, M Div, letters of reference, organizational support; for Certificate, letters of reference, family essay, personal statement, and family of origin paper (for marriage and family therapy). Additional exam requirements/recommendations for international students: Required—TOEFL (minimum score 550 paper-based; 87 iBT). *Application deadline:* For fall admission, 8/1 priority date for domestic students, 8/1 for international students; for winter admission, 12/1 priority date for domestic students; for spring admission, 1/1 priority date for domestic students. Applications are processed on a rolling basis. Application fee: $0. Electronic applications accepted. *Expenses:* Contact institution. *Financial support:* In 2016–17, 404 students received support. Teaching assistantships, career-related internships or fieldwork, Federal Work-Study, and scholarships/grants available. Financial award applicants required to submit FAFSA. *Faculty research:* Nature of theology, ethics, Biblical commentaries, nature of God, science and theology. *Unit head:* Dr. David Clark, Vice-President and Dean, 651-638-6659, E-mail: d-clark@bethel.edu. *Application contact:* Jen Niska, Director of Admissions, 651-638-6288, Fax: 651-638-6002, E-mail: seminary-admissions@bethel.edu.
Website: https://www.bethel.edu/seminary

**Bethesda University,** Graduate and Professional Programs, Anaheim, CA 92801. Offers biblical studies (MA); music (MA); theology (M Div). *Entrance requirements:* For master's, interview. Additional exam requirements/recommendations for international students: Recommended—TOEFL.

**Beth HaMedrash Shaarei Yosher Institute,** Graduate Programs, Brooklyn, NY 11204. *Accreditation:* AARTS.

**Beth Hatalmud Rabbinical College,** Graduate Programs, Brooklyn, NY 11214. *Accreditation:* AARTS.

**Beth Medrash Govoha,** Graduate Programs, Lakewood, NJ 08701-2797. *Accreditation:* AARTS.

**Bethune-Cookman University,** School of Graduate Studies, Daytona Beach, FL 32114-3099. Offers transformative leadership (MS). *Program availability:* Online learning. *Degree requirements:* For master's, thesis. *Entrance requirements:* For master's, GRE or MAT, minimum GPA of 2.75 in the last 60 semester hours; 3 letters of recommendation. Additional exam requirements/recommendations for international students: Required—TOEFL (minimum score 550 paper-based). Electronic applications accepted. *Faculty research:* Civic engagement, communication ethics, service learning in higher education women in leadership.

**Bexley Seabury Seminary,** Graduate Programs, Chicago, IL 60637. Offers Anglican studies (Diploma); congregational development (D Min); preaching (D Min); theology (M Div). *Accreditation:* ACIPE. *Program availability:* Part-time. *Faculty:* 2 full-time (1 woman), 10 part-time/adjunct (3 women). *Students:* 45 part-time (20 women); includes 6 minority (2 Black or African American, non-Hispanic/Latino; 2 American Indian or Alaska Native, non-Hispanic/Latino; 2 Hispanic/Latino), 2 international. *Degree requirements:* For master's, thesis; for doctorate, thesis/dissertation; for Diploma, thesis (for some programs). *Entrance requirements:* For master's, interview, sample of written work. *Application deadline:* Applications are processed on a rolling basis. Application fee: $25. *Expenses:* Tuition: Full-time $14,160; part-time $3540 per course. One-time fee: $150. *Financial support:* Career-related internships or fieldwork, institutionally sponsored loans, and scholarships/grants available. Financial award application deadline: 5/1; financial award applicants required to submit FAFSA. *Faculty research:* Liturgical interpretations of baptism, Trinitarian theology, congregational development, post modern Biblical criticism-Matthew. *Unit head:* Roger A. Ferlo, President, 773-380-6782, E-mail: rferlo@bexleyseabury.edu. *Application contact:* Jaime Briceno, Recruiter and Digital Missioner, 773-380-7045, Fax: 773-380-5788, E-mail: jbriceno@bexleyseabury.edu.
Website: https://www.bexleyseabury.edu/academic-programs/

**Biblical Theological Seminary,** Graduate and Professional Programs, Hatfield, PA 19440-2499. Offers advanced missional leadership (D Min); advanced pastoral studies (Certificate); biblical counseling (Certificate); biblical studies (MA, Certificate); counseling (MA); ministry (M Div, MA); missional theology (MA). *Accreditation:* ATS. *Program availability:* Part-time, evening/weekend. *Faculty:* 9 full-time (1 woman), 21 part-time/adjunct (4 women). *Students:* 145 full-time (54 women), 111 part-time (44 women); includes 98 minority (57 Black or African American, non-Hispanic/Latino; 1 American Indian or Alaska Native, non-Hispanic/Latino; 35 Asian, non-Hispanic/Latino; 4 Hispanic/Latino; 1 Two or more races, non-Hispanic/Latino), 67 international. Average age 39. 165 applicants, 64% accepted, 95 enrolled. In 2016, 47 master's, 7 doctorates awarded. *Degree requirements:* For master's, variable foreign language requirement, thesis optional; for doctorate, thesis/dissertation. *Entrance requirements:* Additional

exam requirements/recommendations for international students: Required—TOEFL (minimum score 550 paper-based; 80 iBT). *Application deadline:* Applications are processed on a rolling basis. Application fee: $30. Electronic applications accepted. *Expenses: Tuition:* Full-time $12,360; part-time $6180 per credit. *Required fees:* $75; $75 per credit. $50 per semester. *Financial support:* In 2016–17, 170 students received support. Career-related internships or fieldwork, institutionally sponsored loans, and scholarships/grants available. Support available to part-time students. Financial award application deadline: 8/30; financial award applicants required to submit FAFSA. *Faculty research:* Theology, culture, Biblical interpretation. *Application contact:* Rev. Michael Heath, Student Advancement Counselor, 215-368-5000 Ext. 152, Fax: 215-368-7002, E-mail: mheath@biblical.edu.
Website: http://www.biblical.edu/

**Biola University,** Talbot School of Theology, La Mirada, CA 90639-0001. Offers adult/family ministry (MACE); Bible exposition (MA, Th M); Biblical and theological studies (Certificate); biblical and theological studies/diversified (MA); children's ministry (MACE); Christian education (M Div); cross-cultural education ministry (MACE); educational studies (Ed D, PhD); evangelism and discipleship (M Div); general Christian education (MACE); Messianic Jewish studies (M Div, Certificate); missions and intercultural studies (M Div); New Testament (MA, Th M); Old Testament (MA); Old Testament and Semitics (Th M); pastoral and general ministry (M Div); pastoral care and counseling (M Div, MACML); philosophy (MA); preaching and pastoral ministry (MACML); spiritual formation (M Div, Certificate); spiritual formation and soul care (MA); sports ministry (MACML); theology (MA, Th M, D Min, Certificate); youth ministry (MACE). *Accreditation:* ATS. *Program availability:* Part-time, evening/weekend. *Entrance requirements:* For master's, bachelor's degree from accredited college or university; minimum GPA of 2.6 (for M Div), 3.0 (for MA); for doctorate, M Div or MA. Additional exam requirements/recommendations for international students: Required—TOEFL (minimum score 600 paper-based; 88 iBT). Electronic applications accepted. *Faculty research:* New Testament, Old Testament, spiritual formation, Christian education, theological studies, Christian ministry, preaching and pastoral ministry, language and literature, bible exposition, Christian leadership.

**Bob Jones University,** Graduate Programs, Greenville, SC 29614. Offers accountancy (MS); Bible (MA); Bible translation (MA); Biblical studies (Certificate); broadcast management (MS); business administration (MBA); church history (MA, PhD); church ministries (MA); church music (MM); cinema and video production (MA); counseling (MS); curriculum and instruction (Ed D); divinity (M Div); dramatic production (MA); educational leadership (MS, Ed D, Ed S); elementary education (M Ed, MAT); English (M Ed, MA, MAT); fine arts (MA); graphic design (MA); history (M Ed, MA); illustration (MA); interpretative speech (MA); mathematics (M Ed, MAT); medical missions (Certificate); ministry (MM, D Min); multi-categorical special education (M Ed, MAT); music (M Ed); New Testament interpretation (PhD); Old Testament interpretation (PhD); orchestral instrument performance (MM); organ performance (MM); pastoral studies (MA); personnel services (MS, Ed S); piano pedagogy (MM); piano performance (MM); platform arts (MA); radio and television broadcasting (MS); rhetoric and public address (MA); secondary education (M Ed); studio art (MA); teaching Bible (MA); theology (MA, PhD); voice performance (MM); youth ministries (MA); M Div/MM.

**Boston College,** Graduate School of Arts and Sciences, Department of Theology, Chestnut Hill, MA 02467-3800. Offers philosophy and theology (MA); theology (PhD). *Accreditation:* ATS. *Faculty:* 36 full-time. *Students:* 60 full-time. 92 applicants, 22% accepted, 14 enrolled. In 2016, 2 master's, 10 doctorates awarded. Terminal master's awarded for partial completion of doctoral program. *Degree requirements:* For master's, one foreign language, thesis optional; for doctorate, thesis/dissertation. *Entrance requirements:* For master's and doctorate, GRE General Test. Additional exam requirements/recommendations for international students: Required—TOEFL (minimum score 600 paper-based; 100 iBT), IELTS (minimum score 8). *Application deadline:* For fall admission, 1/2 for domestic and international students. Application fee: $75. Electronic applications accepted. Tuition and fees vary according to program. *Financial support:* In 2016–17, fellowships with full tuition reimbursements (averaging $21,000 per year), research assistantships with full tuition reimbursements (averaging $21,000 per year), teaching assistantships with full tuition reimbursements (averaging $21,000 per year) were awarded; Federal Work-Study, scholarships/grants, and health care benefits also available. Support available to part-time students. Financial award application deadline: 3/1; financial award applicants required to submit FAFSA. *Faculty research:* Historical theology, history of Christianity, systematic theology, Biblical studies, theological ethics, comparative theology. *Unit head:* Dr. Richard Gaillardetz, Chairperson, 617-552-3873, E-mail: gaillard@bc.edu. *Application contact:* Dr. John Darr, Graduate Program Director, 617-552-3884, E-mail: darr@bc.edu.
Website: http://www.bc.edu/theology

**Boston College,** School of Theology and Ministry, Chestnut Hill, MA 02467-3800. Offers church leadership (MA); divinity (M Div); pastoral ministry (MA), including Hispanic ministry, liturgy and worship, pastoral care and counseling, spirituality; religious education (MA, PhD); sacred theology (STD, STL); social justice/social ministry (MA); spiritual direction (MA); theological studies (MTS); theology (Th M, PhD); youth ministry (MA); MA/MA; MS/MA; MSW/MA. *Accreditation:* TEAC. *Program availability:* Part-time. *Degree requirements:* For doctorate, one foreign language, thesis/dissertation. *Entrance requirements:* For doctorate, GRE. Additional exam requirements/recommendations for international students: Required—TOEFL (minimum score 550 paper-based). Electronic applications accepted. Tuition and fees vary according to program. *Faculty research:* Philosophy and practice of religious education, pastoral psychology, liturgical and spiritual theology, spiritual formation for the practice of ministry.

**Boston University,** School of Theology, Boston, MA 02118. Offers chaplaincy (M Div); choral conducting (MSM); church and the arts (M Div); constructive theology and ethics (PhD), including constructive theology, theological ethics; ecological theology and ethics (MTS); global and community engagement (M Div); history and hermeneutics (PhD), including Biblical studies, church history, liturgical studies, mission studies; organ (MSM); pastoral ministry (M Div); practical theology (PhD), including church and society, congregation and community, evangelism and missiology, homiletics, leadership and administration, pastoral theology and psychology, religious education, spirituality studies, worship; religion and conflict transformation (MTS); religion and science (MTS); religion and the academy (M Div); spirituality studies (MTS); theology (MTS, STM); transcultural studies (MTS); transformational leadership (D Min); M Div/MSM; M Div/MSW; MTS/MSW. PhD in history and hermeneutics: mission studies offered in collaboration with Gordon-Conwell Theological Seminary. *Accreditation:* ACIPE; ATS. *Program availability:* Part-time, blended/hybrid learning. *Faculty:* 34 full-time (14 women), 7 part-time/adjunct (3 women). *Students:* 260 full-time (131 women), 69 part-time (30 women); includes 69 minority (36 Black or African American, non-Hispanic/Latino; 10 Asian, non-Hispanic/Latino; 16 Hispanic/Latino; 7 Two or more races, non-Hispanic/Latino), 53 international. Average age 35. 234 applicants, 71% accepted, 106 enrolled. In 2016, 78 master's, 9 doctorates awarded. *Degree requirements:* For master's, comprehensive exam (for some programs), thesis optional, contextual education; for doctorate, 2 foreign languages, comprehensive exam, thesis/dissertation. *Entrance requirements:* For master's, minimum GPA of 3.0; for doctorate, GRE General Test, minimum GPA of 3.3. Additional exam requirements/recommendations for

international students: Required—TOEFL (minimum score 570 paper-based; 89 iBT). *Application deadline:* For fall admission, 1/15 priority date for domestic and international students; for spring admission, 10/15 priority date for domestic and international students. Applications are processed on a rolling basis. Application fee: $95. Electronic applications accepted. *Expenses:* $19,500 per year tuition; $156 per semester student service fee; $54 per semester community service fee; $199 per semester health and wellness fee. *Financial support:* In 2016–17, 252 students received support, including 78 fellowships with full tuition reimbursements available (averaging $4,537 per year), 32 research assistantships (averaging $6,000 per year), 32 teaching assistantships with full and partial tuition reimbursements available (averaging $20,000 per year); career-related internships or fieldwork, Federal Work-Study, institutionally sponsored loans, scholarships/grants, traineeships, health care benefits, tuition waivers (full and partial), and unspecified assistantships also available. Support available to part-time students. Financial award application deadline: 7/15; financial award applicants required to submit FAFSA. *Faculty research:* Practical theology, Biblical studies, theology and ethical, history of Christianity. *Total annual research expenditures:* $2.5 million. *Unit head:* Rev. Dr. Mary Elizabeth Moore, Dean, 617-353-3050, Fax: 617-353-3061, E-mail: memoore@bu.edu. *Application contact:* Rev. Anastasia Kidd, Director of Admissions and College Relations, 617-353-3036, Fax: 617-358-0140, E-mail: sthadmis@bu.edu.
Website: http://www.bu.edu/sth

**Briercrest Seminary,** Graduate Programs, Program in Theology, Caronport, SK S0H 0S0, Canada. Offers Biblical studies (M Div); leadership and management (M Div); New Testament (MATS); Old Testament (MATS); pastoral counseling (M Div); pastoral ministry (M Div); theological studies (M Div); theology (MATS); worship (M Div); youth and family ministry (M Div). *Accreditation:* ATS. *Program availability:* Part-time. *Degree requirements:* For master's, comprehensive exam, thesis optional. *Entrance requirements:* Additional exam requirements/recommendations for international students: Required—TOEFL (minimum score 550 paper-based).

**Brite Divinity School,** Graduate and Professional Programs, Fort Worth, TX 76109. Offers Biblical interpretation (PhD); divinity (M Div); ministry (D Min); pastoral theology (PhD); theological studies (MTS, CTS); theology (Th M); theology and ministry (MA). *Accreditation:* ACIPE; ATS (one or more programs are accredited); SACS/CC. *Program availability:* Part-time, evening/weekend. *Faculty:* 18 full-time (6 women), 4 part-time/adjunct (1 woman). *Entrance requirements:* For master's, minimum GPA of 2.5. Additional exam requirements/recommendations for international students: Required—TOEFL. *Application deadline:* For fall admission, 3/1 for domestic students; for spring admission, 12/1 for domestic students. Applications are processed on a rolling basis. Application fee: $0. *Financial support:* Career-related internships or fieldwork and unspecified assistantships available. Financial award application deadline: 3/1. *Unit head:* Dr. D. Newell Williams, President, 817-257-7231. *Application contact:* Dr. Valerie Forstman, Director of Admissions, 817-257-7513, E-mail: v.forstman@tcu.edu.
Website: http://www.brite.edu/academics/degrees/

**Bryn Athyn College of the New Church,** Academy of the New Church Theological School, Bryn Athyn, PA 19009-0717. Offers divinity (M Div); religious studies (MA). *Program availability:* Part-time, online learning. *Degree requirements:* For master's, variable foreign language requirement, thesis. *Entrance requirements:* Additional exam requirements/recommendations for international students: Required—TOEFL.

**Byzantine Catholic Seminary of Saints Cyril and Methodius,** Graduate and Professional Programs, Pittsburgh, PA 15214. Offers M Div, MAT.

**Cairn University,** School of Divinity, Langhorne, PA 19047-2990. Offers divinity (M Div); religion (MA); theology (Th M). *Program availability:* Part-time, evening/weekend, 100% online, blended/hybrid learning. *Faculty:* 6 full-time (0 women), 3 part-time/adjunct (0 women). *Students:* 24 full-time (2 women), 54 part-time (13 women); includes 29 minority (19 Black or African American, non-Hispanic/Latino; 4 Asian, non-Hispanic/Latino; 5 Hispanic/Latino; 1 Two or more races, non-Hispanic/Latino), 1 international. Average age 37. 29 applicants, 97% accepted, 26 enrolled. In 2016, 31 master's awarded. *Entrance requirements:* Additional exam requirements/recommendations for international students: Required—TOEFL (minimum score 550 paper-based). *Application deadline:* Applications are processed on a rolling basis. Application fee: $25. Electronic applications accepted. Application fee is waived when completed online. *Expenses:* $515 per semester credit. *Financial support:* Scholarships/grants available. Support available to part-time students. Financial award applicants required to submit FAFSA. *Unit head:* Dr. Jonathan L. Master, Dean, 215-702-4358, Fax: 215-702-4359, E-mail: divinity@cairn.edu. *Application contact:* Abigail Simon, Assistant Director, Graduate Admissions, 800-572-2472, Fax: 215-702-4248, E-mail: asimon@cairn.edu.
Website: http://www.cairn.edu/academics/divinity

**California Institute of Integral Studies,** School of Consciousness and Transformation, San Francisco, CA 94103. Offers anthropology and social change (MA, PhD); Asian philosophies and cultures (MA); creative inquiry/interdisciplinary arts (MFA); East-West psychology (MA, PhD); integral and transpersonal psychology (PhD); philosophy and religion (PhD), including ecology, spirituality, and religion, philosophy, cosmology, and consciousness, women's spirituality; theater and performance making (MFA); transformative leadership (MA); transformative studies (PhD); women, gender, spirituality and social justice (MA); writing and consciousness (MFA). *Program availability:* Part-time, evening/weekend, 100% online, blended/hybrid learning. *Students:* 390 full-time (256 women), 121 part-time (84 women); includes 135 minority (39 Black or African American, non-Hispanic/Latino; 2 American Indian or Alaska Native, non-Hispanic/Latino; 22 Asian, non-Hispanic/Latino; 40 Hispanic/Latino; 2 Native Hawaiian or other Pacific Islander, non-Hispanic/Latino; 30 Two or more races, non-Hispanic/Latino), 51 international. Average age 38. 195 applicants, 92% accepted, 124 enrolled. In 2016, 35 master's, 41 doctorates awarded. Terminal master's awarded for partial completion of doctoral program. *Degree requirements:* For master's, thesis optional; for doctorate, comprehensive exam, thesis/dissertation, 1 foreign language (for Asian philosophies and cultures). *Entrance requirements:* For master's, minimum GPA of 3.0, letters of recommendation, writing sample; for doctorate, master's degree, minimum GPA of 3.0, letters of recommendation, writing sample. Additional exam requirements/recommendations for international students: Required—TOEFL. *Application deadline:* For fall admission, 2/1 priority date for domestic and international students; for spring admission, 10/15 priority date for domestic and international students. Applications are processed on a rolling basis. Application fee: $65. Electronic applications accepted. *Expenses: Tuition:* Full-time $19,728; part-time $1098 per semester hour. *Required fees:* $320; $320 per semester hour. *Financial support:* Research assistantships, teaching assistantships, career-related internships or fieldwork, Federal Work-Study, and scholarships/grants available. Support available to part-time students. Financial award application deadline: 4/15; financial award applicants required to submit FAFSA. *Faculty research:* Ecology and sustainability, philosophy and religion, East-West psychology, integrative health, social and cultural anthropology, transformative leadership. *Application contact:* Ellen Durst, Director of Admissions, 415-575-6100, Fax: 415-575-1268, E-mail: admissions@ciis.edu.
Website: http://www.ciis.edu/

**California Lutheran University,** Graduate Studies, Pacific Lutheran Theological Seminary, Thousand Oaks, CA 91360-2787. Offers M Div, MA, MCM, MTS, PhD, Th D,

Certificate, M Div/MA. MA, Th D, PhD offered jointly with Graduate Theological Union; PhD with University of California, Berkeley. *Accreditation:* ACIPE. *Program availability:* Part-time. *Faculty:* 6 full-time (5 women), 2 part-time/adjunct (0 women). *Students:* 45 full-time (24 women), 1 (woman) part-time; includes 10 minority (1 Black or African American, non-Hispanic/Latino; 1 Hispanic/Latino; 8 Two or more races, non-Hispanic/Latino), 1 international. Average age 34. 29 applicants, 86% accepted, 19 enrolled. In 2016, 10 master's, 3 other advanced degrees awarded. *Degree requirements:* For master's, variable foreign language requirement, thesis or alternative. *Application deadline:* For fall admission, 8/1 priority date for domestic students; for spring admission, 1/1 priority date for domestic students. Applications are processed on a rolling basis. Application fee: $25. Electronic applications accepted. *Financial support:* In 2016–17, 104 students received support. Teaching assistantships, career-related internships or fieldwork, Federal Work-Study, institutionally sponsored loans, and scholarships/grants available. Support available to part-time students. Financial award application deadline: 3/15; financial award applicants required to submit FAFSA. *Faculty research:* Theology and genetics, power and prayer, liturgy and ethics, Christianity and Confucianism, religion and abuse. *Unit head:* Alica Vargas, Dean, 510-559-2732, E-mail: avargas@plts.edu. *Application contact:* 805-493-3325, Fax: 805-493-3861, E-mail: clugrad@callutheran.edu.

**Calvary University,** Graduate School and Seminary, Kansas City, MO 64147. Offers Bible and theology (MS); Biblical counseling (MA); education (MS), including administration and leadership, Christian education, curriculum and instruction, elementary education; organization development (MS); pastoral studies (M Div). *Program availability:* Part-time, evening/weekend. *Faculty:* 6 full-time (2 women), 2 part-time/adjunct (1 woman). *Students:* 11 full-time (3 women), 29 part-time (15 women); includes 12 minority (4 Black or African American, non-Hispanic/Latino; 1 American Indian or Alaska Native, non-Hispanic/Latino; 6 Asian, non-Hispanic/Latino; 1 Native Hawaiian or other Pacific Islander, non-Hispanic/Latino). Average age 39. In 2016, 19 master's awarded. *Degree requirements:* For master's, variable foreign language requirement, comprehensive exam, thesis or alternative. *Entrance requirements:* For master's, minimum GPA of 2.5, BA or BS, doctrine agreement. Additional exam requirements/recommendations for international students: Required—TOEFL (minimum score 550 paper-based). *Application deadline:* Applications are processed on a rolling basis. Application fee: $0. Electronic applications accepted. *Expenses:* Tuition: Full-time $7200; part-time $4800 per credit. *Required fees:* $640; $520 per credit. $140 per semester. One-time fee: $100. Tuition and fees vary according to program. *Financial support:* In 2016–17, 8 students received support. Scholarships/grants available. Financial award application deadline: 11/5; financial award applicants required to submit FAFSA. *Unit head:* Dr. Thomas Baurain, Director of Seminary, 816-322-0110 Ext. 1502, Fax: 816-331-4474, E-mail: thomas.baurain@calvary.edu. *Application contact:* Ann Rogers, Admissions Office Assistant, 800-326-3960 Ext. 1321, Fax: 816-331-4474, E-mail: admissions@calvary.edu.
Website: http://www.calvary.edu

**Calvin Theological Seminary,** Graduate and Professional Programs, Grand Rapids, MI 49546-4387. Offers Bible and theology (MA); divinity (M Div), including ancient near eastern languages and literature, contextual ministry, evangelism and teaching, history of Christianity, new church development, New Testament, Old Testament, pastoral care and leadership, preaching and worship, theological studies, youth and family ministries; educational ministry (MA); historical theology (PhD); missions and evangelism (MA); pastoral care (MA); philosophical and moral theology (PhD); systematic theology (PhD); theological studies (MTS); theology (Th M); worship (MA); youth and family ministries (MA). *Accreditation:* ACIPE; ATS. *Program availability:* Part-time. *Degree requirements:* For master's, variable foreign language requirement, thesis (for some programs); for doctorate, 4 foreign languages, comprehensive exam, thesis/dissertation. *Entrance requirements:* For doctorate, GRE General Test, Hebrew, Greek, and a modern foreign language. Additional exam requirements/recommendations for international students: Required—TOEFL (minimum score 550 paper-based), TWE (minimum score 4). Electronic applications accepted. *Faculty research:* Recent Trinity theory, Christian anthropology, Proverbs, reformed confessions, Paul's view of law.

**Campbellsville University,** School of Theology, Campbellsville, KY 42718-2799. Offers marriage and family therapy (MMFT); theology (M Th). *Program availability:* Part-time, evening/weekend, 100% online, blended/hybrid learning. *Faculty:* 12 full-time (2 women), 5 part-time/adjunct (1 woman). *Students:* 5 full-time (2 women), 83 part-time (41 women); includes 33 minority (27 Black or African American, non-Hispanic/Latino; 1 American Indian or Alaska Native, non-Hispanic/Latino; 4 Hispanic/Latino; 1 Two or more races, non-Hispanic/Latino), 1 international. Average age 43. 60 applicants, 62% accepted, 30 enrolled. In 2016, 31 master's awarded. *Degree requirements:* For master's, comprehensive exam, thesis optional. *Entrance requirements:* For master's, GRE General Test, minimum GPA of 3.0 in major, 2.75 overall; 18 hours of undergraduate coursework in Christian studies; college transcripts; letters of recommendation. Additional exam requirements/recommendations for international students: Recommended—TOEFL (minimum score 550 paper-based; 79 iBT), IELTS (minimum score 6). *Application deadline:* Applications are processed on a rolling basis. Application fee: $25. Electronic applications accepted. Application fee is waived when completed online. *Expenses:* $399 per credit hour. *Financial support:* Application deadline: 6/1; applicants required to submit FAFSA. *Faculty research:* Clergy needing graduate theology education, trinity and Christian faith, Old Testament David narratives, leadership principles on Christian university integration of Christian principles in counseling process, church history. *Unit head:* Dr. John E. Hurtgen, Dean, 270-789-5077, Fax: 270-789-5050, E-mail: jehurtgen@campbellsville.edu. *Application contact:* Monica Bamwine, Assistant Director of Graduate Admissions, 270-789-5221, Fax: 270-789-5071, E-mail: mkbamwine@campbellsville.edu.
Website: http://www.campbellsville.edu/

**Campbell University,** Graduate and Professional Programs, Divinity School, Buies Creek, NC 27506. Offers Christian ministry (MA); divinity (M Div); ministry (D Min); JD/M Div; M Div/MA; M Div/MBA. *Accreditation:* ATS. *Degree requirements:* For doctorate, final project. *Entrance requirements:* For master's, minimum GPA of 2.5; for doctorate, MAT, M Div, minimum graduate GPA of 3.0. Additional exam requirements/recommendations for international students: Required—TOEFL (minimum score 580 paper-based). *Expenses:* Contact institution. *Faculty research:* New Testament, theology, spiritual formation, Old Testament, Christian leadership.

**Canadian Southern Baptist Seminary,** Graduate Programs, Cochrane, AB T4C 2G1, Canada. Offers Biblical studies (MBS); Christian ministry (MCMin); Christian studies (MCS); ministry (M Div). *Accreditation:* ATS. *Program availability:* Part-time, 100% online, blended/hybrid learning. *Faculty:* 3 full-time (0 women), 8 part-time/adjunct (1 woman). *Students:* 24 full-time (9 women), 18 part-time (2 women); includes 4 minority (1 Black or African American, non-Hispanic/Latino; 3 Asian, non-Hispanic/Latino), 11 international. Average age 29. 17 applicants, 76% accepted, 11 enrolled. In 2016, 10 master's awarded. *Entrance requirements:* Additional exam requirements/recommendations for international students: Required—TOEFL (minimum score 560 paper-based; 83 iBT); Recommended—IELTS. *Application deadline:* For fall admission, 7/1 priority date for domestic students, 3/1 priority date for international students; for winter admission, 11/15 priority date for domestic students. Applications are processed

on a rolling basis. Application fee: $50 ($150 for international students). *Expenses:* Tuition: Full-time $6900 Canadian dollars; part-time $345 Canadian dollars per credit hour. *Required fees:* $20 Canadian dollars per credit hour. $35 Canadian dollars per semester. Tuition and fees vary according to course load. *Financial support:* Scholarships/grants available. Financial award application deadline: 7/1. *Unit head:* Dr. Steve Booth, Academic Dean, 403-932-6622 Ext. 232, E-mail: steve.booth@csbs.ca. *Application contact:* Kathleen McNaughton, Registrar, 403-932-6622 Ext. 221, E-mail: kathleen.mcnaughton@csbs.ca.

**Carey Theological College,** Graduate Programs, Vancouver, BC V6T 1J6, Canada. Offers M Div, MASF, D Min. *Accreditation:* ATS. *Program availability:* Part-time. *Degree requirements:* For doctorate, thesis/dissertation. *Entrance requirements:* For master's, undergraduate degree with minimum GPA of 2.7; for doctorate, M Div with minimum GPA of 3.5. Additional exam requirements/recommendations for international students: Required—TOEFL (minimum score 577 paper-based; 90 iBT). Electronic applications accepted. *Faculty research:* Missional church, new monasticism, women in leadership, spiritual formation, applied theology.

**Carson-Newman University,** Program in Applied Theology, Jefferson City, TN 37760. Offers MAAT. *Program availability:* Part-time, evening/weekend. *Degree requirements:* For master's, thesis optional, completeion of degree within five years of admission into program. *Entrance requirements:* For master's, GRE (minimum score of 290), minimum GPA of 3.0. Additional exam requirements/recommendations for international students: Recommended—TOEFL (minimum score 79 iBT), IELTS (minimum score 6.5), TSE (minimum score 53). *Expenses:* Tuition: Full-time $10,142; part-time $461 per credit hour. *Required fees:* $300; $150 per semester. One-time fee: $150.

**Catholic Distance University,** Graduate Programs, Charles Town, WV 25414. Offers religious studies (MRS); theology (MA). *Program availability:* Part-time, evening/weekend, online learning. *Degree requirements:* For master's, comprehensive exam, capstone paper or project.

**Catholic Theological Union,** Graduate and Professional Programs, Chicago, IL 60615-5698. Offers biblical spirituality (Certificate); cross-cultural ministries (D Min); cross-cultural missions (Certificate); divinity (M Div); liturgical studies (Certificate); liturgy (D Min); pastoral studies (MAPS, Certificate); spiritual formation (Certificate); spirituality (D Min); theology (MA); M Div/MA; M Div/MSW; M Div/PhD. M Div/PhD offered jointly with University of Chicago; M Div/MSW with Loyola University Chicago and University of Chicago. *Accreditation:* ACIPE. *Program availability:* Part-time, evening/weekend. *Degree requirements:* For master's, one foreign language, comprehensive exam (for some programs), thesis (for some programs); for doctorate, thesis/dissertation. *Entrance requirements:* For doctorate, master's degree, 5 years of active ministry. *Faculty research:* Doctrine, sacraments, ethics, Bible.

**The Catholic University of America,** School of Canon Law, Washington, DC 20064. Offers Canon law (JCD, JCL); church administration (MCA); JD/JCL. JD/JCL offered jointly with Columbus School of Law. *Program availability:* Part-time. *Faculty:* 8 full-time (1 woman), 2 part-time/adjunct (0 women). *Students:* 25 full-time (2 women), 49 part-time (7 women); includes 9 minority (1 Black or African American, non-Hispanic/Latino; 2 Asian, non-Hispanic/Latino; 5 Hispanic/Latino; 1 Two or more races, non-Hispanic/Latino), 11 international. Average age 38. 26 applicants, 88% accepted, 21 enrolled. In 2016, 25 master's, 2 doctorates awarded. *Degree requirements:* For master's, one foreign language, comprehensive exam, thesis, fluency in canonical Latin; for doctorate, 2 foreign languages, thesis/dissertation, fluency in canonical Latin. *Entrance requirements:* For master's, GRE General Test, statement of purpose, official copies of academic transcripts, two letters of recommendation; for doctorate, GRE General Test, minimum A- average, JCL. Additional exam requirements/recommendations for international students: Required—TOEFL (minimum score 550 paper-based; 80 iBT). *Application deadline:* For fall admission, 7/15 priority date for domestic students, 7/1 for international students; for spring admission, 11/15 priority date for domestic students, 11/1 for international students. Applications are processed on a rolling basis. Application fee: $55. Electronic applications accepted. *Expenses:* $1,650 per credit hour. *Financial support:* Fellowships, research assistantships, teaching assistantships, Federal Work-Study, scholarships/grants, tuition waivers (full and partial), and unspecified assistantships available. Financial award application deadline: 2/1; financial award applicants required to submit FAFSA. *Faculty research:* Ecclesiology and the Sacrament of Orders, procedural law, temporal goods, matrimonial jurisprudence, sacramental and liturgical law. *Unit head:* Msgr. Ronny Jenkins, Dean, 202-319-5492, Fax: 202-319-4187, E-mail: cua-canonlaw@cua.edu. *Application contact:* Director of Graduate Admissions, 202-319-5057, Fax: 202-319-6533, E-mail: cua-admissions@cua.edu.
Website: http://canonlaw.cua.edu

**The Catholic University of America,** School of Theology and Religious Studies, Washington, DC 20064. Offers M Cat, M Div, MA, D Min, PhD, STD, Certificate, STB, STL, MSLS/MA, STB/M Div. MSLA/MA offered in conjunction with Department of Library and Information Science. *Program availability:* Part-time. *Faculty:* 40 full-time (2 women), 8 part-time/adjunct (2 women). *Students:* 156 full-time (11 women), 193 part-time (51 women); includes 61 minority (9 Black or African American, non-Hispanic/Latino; 1 American Indian or Alaska Native, non-Hispanic/Latino; 13 Asian, non-Hispanic/Latino; 24 Hispanic/Latino; 14 Two or more races, non-Hispanic/Latino), 51 international. Average age 36. 168 applicants, 65% accepted, 58 enrolled. In 2016, 96 master's, 20 doctorates awarded. Terminal master's awarded for partial completion of doctoral program. *Degree requirements:* For master's, variable foreign language requirement, comprehensive exam (for some programs), thesis (for some programs); for doctorate, variable foreign language requirement, comprehensive exam, thesis/dissertation. *Entrance requirements:* For master's and doctorate, GRE General Test, statement of purpose, official copies of academic transcripts, three letters of recommendation. Additional exam requirements/recommendations for international students: Required—TOEFL (minimum score 550 paper-based; 80 iBT). *Application deadline:* For fall admission, 7/15 priority date for domestic students, 7/1 for international students; for spring admission, 11/15 priority date for domestic students, 11/1 for international students. Applications are processed on a rolling basis. Application fee: $55. Electronic applications accepted. *Expenses:* $42,850 per year; $1,170 per credit; $200 per semester part-time fees. *Financial support:* Fellowships, research assistantships, teaching assistantships, Federal Work-Study, scholarships/grants, tuition waivers (full and partial), and unspecified assistantships available. Financial award application deadline: 2/1; financial award applicants required to submit FAFSA. *Faculty research:* Historical and systematic theology, religious education and Catechetics, moral theology and ethics, Biblical studies, liturgical studies and sacramental theology, religion and culture. *Total annual research expenditures:* $194,166. *Unit head:* Very Rev. Mark Morozowich, Dean, 202-319-5684, Fax: 202-319-4967, E-mail: morozowich@cua.edu. *Application contact:* Director of Graduate Admissions, 202-319-5057, Fax: 202-319-6533, E-mail: cua-admissions@cua.edu.
Website: http://trs.cua.edu/

**Central Baptist Theological Seminary,** Graduate and Professional Programs, Shawnee, KS 66226. Offers missional church studies (MA); theological studies (MA); theology (M Div, Diploma). *Accreditation:* ACIPE; ATS (one or more programs are accredited). *Program availability:* Part-time. *Degree requirements:* For master's, thesis optional. *Entrance requirements:* Additional exam requirements/recommendations for

*Theology*

international students: Required—TOEFL (minimum score 547 paper-based; 77 iBT). Electronic applications accepted.

**Central Yeshiva Tomchei Tmimim-Lubavitch,** Graduate Programs, Brooklyn, NY 11230. Offers Jewish/Judaic studies (MA); Talmudic studies (MA). *Accreditation:* AARTS.

**Chaminade University of Honolulu,** Office of Professional and Continuing Education, Program in Pastoral Theology, Honolulu, HI 96816-1578. Offers diaconate education (MPT); pastoral counseling and spiritual direction (MPT); pastoral theology (MPT). *Program availability:* Part-time, evening/weekend, blended/hybrid learning. *Faculty:* 3 full-time (0 women), 1 part-time/adjunct (0 women). *Students:* 23 full-time (6 women); includes 13 minority (1 Black or African American, non-Hispanic/Latino; 5 Asian, non-Hispanic/Latino; 3 Hispanic/Latino; 4 Native Hawaiian or other Pacific Islander, non-Hispanic/Latino). Average age 53. 1 applicant, 100% accepted, 1 enrolled. *Degree requirements:* For master's, capstone course. *Entrance requirements:* For master's, minimum GPA of 2.5, resume, 2 letters of recommendation, letter of intent, article reflection essay. Additional exam requirements/recommendations for international students: Required—TOEFL (minimum score 550 paper-based; 79 iBT). *Application deadline:* Applications are processed on a rolling basis. Application fee: $40. Electronic applications accepted. *Expenses:* Contact institution. *Financial support:* Applicants required to submit FAFSA. *Unit head:* Dr. David Coleman, Director, 808-739-8341, E-mail: paul.fitzpatrick@chaminade.edu. *Application contact:* 808-735-4755, E-mail: gradserv@chaminade.edu.
Website: http://www.chaminade.edu/mpt

**Charlotte Christian College and Theological Seminary,** Graduate Program, Charlotte, NC 28205. Offers urban Christian ministry (MA), including church planting, multi-cultural studies, sacred music, youth ministry. *Program availability:* Part-time, evening/weekend. *Degree requirements:* For master's, thesis. *Entrance requirements:* For master's, MAT, writing sample/essay. Additional exam requirements/recommendations for international students: Required—TOEFL, IELTS. Electronic applications accepted. *Expenses:* Contact institution.

**Chicago Theological Seminary,** Graduate and Professional Programs, Chicago, IL 60637-1507. Offers Bible, culture and hermeneutics (PhD); preaching (D Min); religion and health (D Min); religious studies (MA); spirituality and spiritual direction (D Min); theology (M Div); theology, ethics and the human sciences (PhD); M Div/MSW. *Accreditation:* ACIPE; ATS. *Program availability:* Part-time. *Degree requirements:* For master's, thesis; for doctorate, 2 foreign languages, comprehensive exam, thesis/dissertation. *Entrance requirements:* For doctorate, GRE General Test. Additional exam requirements/recommendations for international students: Required—TOEFL. *Faculty research:* Bible, culture and hermeneutics, theology, gender and sexuality, black faith and life, spirituality and psychology, practical theology.

**Christendom College,** Graduate School, Alexandria, VA 22312. Offers theological studies (MA), including catechetics, consecrated life, moral theology, spirituality, systematic theology. *Program availability:* Part-time, evening/weekend, 100% online, blended/hybrid learning. *Faculty:* 2 full-time (0 women), 9 part-time/adjunct (3 women). *Students:* 5 full-time (2 women), 126 part-time (53 women). Average age 30. 10 applicants, 100% accepted, 8 enrolled. In 2016, 25 master's awarded. *Degree requirements:* For master's, one foreign language, comprehensive exam, thesis or alternative. *Application deadline:* For fall admission, 6/1 priority date for domestic students; for spring admission, 11/1 priority date for domestic students. Applications are processed on a rolling basis. Application fee: $100. Electronic applications accepted. *Expenses:* Tuition: Part-time $380 per credit. *Unit head:* Dr. Robert J. Matava, Dean, 703-658-4304. *Application contact:* Virginia Norris, Director of Admissions, 703-658-4304, E-mail: graduate.school@christendom.edu.
Website: http://graduate.christendom.edu/

**Christian Theological Seminary,** Graduate and Professional Programs, Indianapolis, IN 46208-3301. Offers educational and arts ministries (MA); marriage and family therapy (MA); pastoral care and counseling (D Min); psychotherapy and faith (MA); theological studies (MTS); theology (M Div). *Accreditation:* AAMFT/COAMFTE (one or more programs are accredited); ACIPE; ATS. *Program availability:* Part-time. Terminal master's awarded for partial completion of doctoral program. *Degree requirements:* For master's, comprehensive exam (for some programs), thesis (for some programs), missionary and cross-cultural experience (for M Div); for doctorate, comprehensive exam, thesis/dissertation. *Entrance requirements:* For doctorate, M Div. Additional exam requirements/recommendations for international students: Recommended—TOEFL. Electronic applications accepted. *Faculty research:* Faith formation, peer learning post graduation.

**Christ the King Seminary,** Graduate and Professional Programs, East Aurora, NY 14052. Offers divinity (M Div); pastoral ministry (MA); theology (MA). *Accreditation:* ATS. *Program availability:* Part-time, evening/weekend. *Degree requirements:* For master's, comprehensive exam, thesis. *Entrance requirements:* For master's, previous course work in philosophy and religious studies.

**Church Divinity School of the Pacific,** Graduate and Professional Programs, Berkeley, CA 94709-1217. Offers M Div, MA, MTS, D Min, Certificate. MA program offered jointly with Graduate Theological Union. *Accreditation:* ACIPE; ATS (one or more programs are accredited). *Program availability:* Part-time. *Degree requirements:* For master's, one foreign language, thesis (for some programs); for doctorate, thesis/dissertation. *Entrance requirements:* For master's and Certificate, GRE General Test, letters of reference; for doctorate, letters of reference. Additional exam requirements/recommendations for international students: Required—TOEFL. Electronic applications accepted.

**Cincinnati Christian University,** Graduate School, Cincinnati, OH 45204-3200. Offers biblical studies (MA); church history (MA); counseling (MAC); divinity (M Div); ministry (M Min); practical ministries (MA); theological studies (MA). *Program availability:* Part-time. *Degree requirements:* For master's, variable foreign language requirement, thesis (for some programs), oral exam (for M Div). *Entrance requirements:* Additional exam requirements/recommendations for international students: Required—TOEFL. Electronic applications accepted.

**Claremont Graduate University,** Graduate Programs, School of Arts and Humanities, Department of Religion, Claremont, CA 91711-6160. Offers Hebrew Bible (MA, PhD); history of Christianity and religions of North America (MA, PhD); New Testament (MA, PhD); philosophy of religion and theology (MA, PhD); theology, ethics and culture (MA, PhD); women's studies in religion (MA, PhD); MA/PhD; MBA/PhD. *Program availability:* Part-time. *Faculty:* 7 full-time (4 women), 2 part-time/adjunct (0 women). *Students:* 121 full-time (46 women), 13 part-time (6 women); includes 28 minority (10 Black or African American, non-Hispanic/Latino; 1 American Indian or Alaska Native, non-Hispanic/Latino; 6 Asian, non-Hispanic/Latino; 7 Hispanic/Latino; 1 Native Hawaiian or other Pacific Islander, non-Hispanic/Latino; 3 Two or more races, non-Hispanic/Latino), 19 international. Average age 39. In 2016, 11 master's, 21 doctorates awarded. Terminal master's awarded for partial completion of doctoral program. *Entrance requirements:* For master's and doctorate, GRE General Test. Additional exam requirements/recommendations for international students: Required—TOEFL (minimum score 75 iBT). *Application deadline:* For fall admission, 2/1 priority date for domestic and

international students. Applications are processed on a rolling basis. Application fee: $80. Electronic applications accepted. *Expenses: Tuition:* Full-time $44,328; part-time $1847 per unit. *Required fees:* $600; $300 per semester. Tuition and fees vary according to course load and program. *Financial support:* Fellowships, research assistantships, teaching assistantships, Federal Work-Study, institutionally sponsored loans, and scholarships/grants available. Support available to part-time students. Financial award application deadline: 2/15; financial award applicants required to submit FAFSA. *Unit head:* Ruqayya Kahn, Chair, 909-607-0488, E-mail: ruqayya.kahn@cgu.edu. *Application contact:* Amy Sandefur, Assistant Director of Admissions, 909-607-9101, E-mail: amy.sandefur@cgu.edu.
Website: https://www.cgu.edu/departments/religion/

**Claremont School of Theology,** Graduate and Professional Programs, Master of Divinity Program, Claremont, CA 91711-3199. Offers interfaith chaplaincy (M Div); Islamic chaplaincy (M Div); ministerial leadership (M Div). *Accreditation:* ACIPE; ATS. *Program availability:* Part-time, 100% online, blended/hybrid learning. *Entrance requirements:* Additional exam requirements/recommendations for international students: Required—TOEFL. *Application deadline:* For fall admission, 5/1 for domestic students, 4/1 for international students; for winter admission, 11/1 for domestic and international students; for spring admission, 11/1 priority date for domestic students, 11/1 for international students. Applications are processed on a rolling basis. Application fee: $50. Electronic applications accepted. *Expenses: Tuition:* Full-time $21,120. Tuition and fees vary according to course level, course load and degree level. *Financial support:* Research assistantships, teaching assistantships, career-related internships or fieldwork, Federal Work-Study, institutionally sponsored loans, scholarships/grants, and tuition waivers (full and partial) available. Support available to part-time students. Financial award application deadline: 4/1; financial award applicants required to submit FAFSA. *Unit head:* Sheryl A. Kujawa-Holbrook, Vice President for Academic Affairs/Dean, 909-447-2520, Fax: 909-447-6274, E-mail: skujawaholbrook@cst.edu. *Application contact:* Director of Admissions, 866-274-6500, Fax: 909-447-6389, E-mail: admission@cst.edu.
Website: https://cst.edu/academics/m-div/

**Claremont School of Theology,** Graduate and Professional Programs, Program in Religion, Claremont, CA 91711-3199. Offers practical theology (PhD), including religious education and formation, spiritual care and counseling; religion (MA, PhD), including comparative theology and philosophy (PhD), Hebrew Bible and Jewish studies (PhD), New Testament and Christian origins (PhD), process studies (PhD), religion, ethics, and society (PhD). *Accreditation:* ACIPE; ATS. Terminal master's awarded for partial completion of doctoral program. *Degree requirements:* For master's, thesis; for doctorate, 2 foreign languages, thesis/dissertation. *Entrance requirements:* For doctorate, GRE General Test. Additional exam requirements/recommendations for international students: Required—TOEFL. *Application deadline:* For fall admission, 1/15 for domestic and international students. Application fee: $50. Electronic applications accepted. *Expenses:* Tuition: Full-time $21,120. Tuition and fees vary according to course level, course load and degree level. *Financial support:* Research assistantships, teaching assistantships, career-related internships or fieldwork, Federal Work-Study, institutionally sponsored loans, scholarships/grants, and tuition waivers (full and partial) available. Support available to part-time students. Financial award application deadline: 4/1; financial award applicants required to submit FAFSA. *Unit head:* Sheryl A. Kujawa-Holbrook, Vice President for Academic Affairs/Dean, 909-447-2520, Fax: 909-447-6274, E-mail: skujawaholbrook@cst.edu. *Application contact:* Director of Admissions, 866-274-6500, Fax: 909-447-6389, E-mail: admission@cst.edu.
Website: https://cst.edu/academics/m-a/

**Clarks Summit University,** Baptist Bible Seminary, South Abington Township, PA 18411. Offers Biblical apologetics (MA); church education (M Div, M Min); church planting (M Div, M Min); global ministry (M Div, M Min); leadership in communication (D Min); leadership in counseling and spiritual development (D Min); leadership in global ministry (D Min); leadership in pastoral ministry (D Min); leadership in theological studies (D Min); military chaplaincy (M Div); ministry (PhD); organizational leadership (M Min); outreach pastor (M Div, M Min); pastoral counseling (M Div, M Min); pastoral leadership (M Div, M Min); theology (Th M); worship ministries leadership (M Div, M Min); youth pastor (M Div, M Min). *Program availability:* Part-time, evening/weekend, online learning. Terminal master's awarded for partial completion of doctoral program. *Degree requirements:* For master's, 2 foreign languages, thesis, oral exam (for M Div); for doctorate, 2 foreign languages, comprehensive exam (for some programs), thesis/dissertation, oral exam. *Entrance requirements:* For doctorate, Greek and Hebrew entrance exams (for PhD). Electronic applications accepted.

**Clarks Summit University,** Graduate Studies, South Abington Township, PA 18411. Offers Bible (MA); counseling (MA, MS); curriculum and instruction (M Ed); educational administration (M Ed); intercultural studies (MA); literature (MA); missions (MA); organizational leadership (MA); reading specialist (M Ed); secondary English/communications (M Ed); social entrepreneurship (MA); worldview studies (MA). MA in missions program available only for Association of Baptists for World Evangelism missionary personnel. *Program availability:* Part-time, evening/weekend, online learning. *Entrance requirements:* Additional exam requirements/recommendations for international students: Required—TOEFL (minimum score 500 paper-based).

**Colgate Rochester Crozer Divinity School,** Graduate and Professional Programs, Rochester, NY 14620-2530. Offers divinity (M Div, MA, Certificate); peace building and interfaith dialogue (D Min); prophetic preaching (D Min); transformative leadership (D Min). *Accreditation:* ACIPE; ATS (one or more programs are accredited). *Program availability:* Part-time, evening/weekend. *Faculty:* 6 full-time (3 women), 8 part-time/adjunct (3 women). *Students:* 85 full-time, 29 part-time; includes 66 minority (56 Black or African American, non-Hispanic/Latino; 6 Asian, non-Hispanic/Latino; 4 Hispanic/Latino). Average age 43. 33 applicants, 91% accepted, 27 enrolled. In 2016, 12 master's, 3 doctorates awarded. *Degree requirements:* For master's, thesis (for some programs), supervised ministry year (for M Div); for doctorate, thesis/dissertation. *Entrance requirements:* For master's, BA/BS, personal statement, 4 recommendations; for doctorate, M Div, 3 years' professional experience, writing sample, personal statement, curriculum vitae, 4 recommendations. Additional exam requirements/recommendations for international students: Required—TOEFL (minimum score 600 paper-based; 93 iBT). *Application deadline:* For fall admission, 7/1 priority date for domestic students, 3/1 for international students; for spring admission, 12/1 priority date for domestic students, 9/1 for international students. Applications are processed on a rolling basis. Application fee: $35. Electronic applications accepted. *Expenses:* Contact institution. *Financial support:* In 2016–17, 43 students received support. Scholarships/grants available. Financial award application deadline: 9/1; financial award applicants required to submit FAFSA. *Faculty research:* Book of Jeremiah, postcolonial Asian feminist biblical interpretation, Charles Wesley, Christian ethics, black church studies. *Unit head:* Marvin A. McMickle, PhD, President, 585-271-1320 Ext. 680, Fax: 585-271-8013. *Application contact:* Rev. Melissa M. Morral, Vice President for Enrollment Services, 585-340-9633, Fax: 585-340-9644, E-mail: mmorral@crcds.edu.
Website: http://www.crcds.edu

**Collège Dominicain de Philosophie et de Théologie,** Graduate Programs, Faculty of Theology, Ottawa, ON K1R 7G3, Canada. Offers M Th, MA Th, PhD, Th D, L Th.

*Program availability:* Part-time, evening/weekend. *Degree requirements:* For master's, 2 foreign languages, research paper; for doctorate, 2 foreign languages, thesis/dissertation, candidacy exam. *Entrance requirements:* For master's, B Th or equivalent, minimum A- average in undergraduate course work; for doctorate, MA Th or equivalent, minimum A- average in graduate course work. *Faculty research:* Exegese, bioethics, history of church, New Testament.

**College of Emmanuel and St. Chad,** Bachelor of Theology Program, Saskatoon, SK S7N 0W6, Canada. Offers B Th. *Program availability:* Part-time, online learning. *Degree requirements:* For B Th, internship. *Entrance requirements:* For degree, 1 year of university-level work or equivalent. Additional exam requirements/recommendations for international students: Required—TOEFL. *Application deadline:* For fall admission, 5/31 priority date for domestic students. Applications are processed on a rolling basis. Application fee: $75. *Expenses: Tuition:* Part-time $975 per course. Part-time tuition and fees vary according to degree level and program. *Financial support:* Career-related internships or fieldwork and bursaries available. Support available to part-time students. Financial award application deadline: 9/30. *Faculty research:* Pauline studies, New Testament, ethics, congregational development, trauma and spirituality. *Unit head:* Rev. Dr. Iain Luke, Principal, 306-975-1555, Fax: 306-934-2683, E-mail: iain.luke@usask.ca. *Application contact:* Lisa McInnis, Registrar, 306-975-1550, Fax: 306-934-2683, E-mail: esc.registrar@usask.ca.

**College of Emmanuel and St. Chad,** Graduate Programs, Saskatoon, SK S7N 0W6, Canada. Offers M Div, MTS, STM, D Min, L Th. STM and D Min programs offered jointly with Lutheran Theological Seminary and St. Andrew's College. *Program availability:* Part-time. *Degree requirements:* For master's, thesis optional. *Entrance requirements:* For master's, M Div or MTS (STM). Additional exam requirements/recommendations for international students: Required—TOEFL. *Application deadline:* For fall admission, 5/31 priority date for domestic students. Applications are processed on a rolling basis. Application fee: $75. *Expenses: Tuition:* Part-time $975 per course. Part-time tuition and fees vary according to degree level and program. *Financial support:* Career-related internships or fieldwork and bursaries available. Support available to part-time students. Financial award application deadline: 9/30. *Faculty research:* New Testament, systematics, Christian education, theology, ethics. *Unit head:* Rev. Dr. Iain Luke, Principal, 306-975-1555, Fax: 306-934-2683, E-mail: iain.luke@usask.ca. *Application contact:* Lisa McInnis, Registrar, 306-975-1550, Fax: 306-934-2683.

**College of Saint Elizabeth,** Department of Theology and Philosophy, Morristown, NJ 07960-6989. Offers theology (MA). *Program availability:* Part-time. *Degree requirements:* For master's, thesis or alternative. *Entrance requirements:* For master's, GRE, baccalaureate degree from accredited institution, personal interview with coordinator and another faculty member, minimum cumulative GPA of 3.0. Additional exam requirements/recommendations for international students: Required—TOEFL (minimum score 550 paper-based; 79 iBT), IELTS (minimum score 6.5). Electronic applications accepted. Application fee is waived when completed online. *Expenses:* Contact institution.

**Columbia International University,** Seminary and School of Ministry, Columbia, SC 29230-3122. Offers academic ministries (M Div); Bible and theology (Certificate); bible exposition (M Div, MABE); Biblical ministry (Certificate); chaplaincy (M Div); intercultural studies (MAIS); leadership (D Min); member care (D Min); missions (D Min); preaching (D Min); theological studies (MA). *Accreditation:* ATS (one or more programs are accredited). *Program availability:* Part-time, evening/weekend. *Degree requirements:* For doctorate, comprehensive exam, thesis/dissertation. *Entrance requirements:* For doctorate, 3 years of ministerial experience, M Div. Additional exam requirements/recommendations for international students: Required—TOEFL. Electronic applications accepted.

**Columbia Theological Seminary,** Graduate and Professional Programs, Decatur, GA 30031-0520. Offers M Div, MATS, Th M, D Min, Th D. Th D program offered jointly with Emory University; D Min with Interdenominational Theological Center. *Accreditation:* ACIPE; ATS (one or more programs are accredited). Terminal master's awarded for partial completion of doctoral program. *Degree requirements:* For master's, variable foreign language requirement, thesis (for some programs); for doctorate, one foreign language, thesis/dissertation. *Entrance requirements:* For doctorate, M Div or equivalent, 3 years practice of ministry. Additional exam requirements/recommendations for international students: Required—TOEFL.

**Concordia Lutheran Seminary,** Graduate and Professional Programs, Edmonton, AB T5B 4E3, Canada. Offers M Div, Graduate Certificate. *Accreditation:* ATS (one or more programs are accredited). *Program availability:* Part-time. *Degree requirements:* For master's, thesis or alternative. *Entrance requirements:* For master's, GRE General Test. Additional exam requirements/recommendations for international students: Required—TOEFL. *Faculty research:* Lutheran Pietism, Christianity and culture, missiology, Christian worship, homiletics.

**Concordia Seminary,** Graduate Programs, St. Louis, MO 63105-3199. Offers M Div, MA, STM, D Min, PhD, Certificate. *Accreditation:* ACIPE; ATS (one or more programs are accredited). Terminal master's awarded for partial completion of doctoral program. *Degree requirements:* For master's, variable foreign language requirement, comprehensive exam (for some programs), thesis (for some programs); for doctorate, 4 foreign languages, thesis/dissertation. *Entrance requirements:* For master's, GRE General Test, previous course work in public speaking, Greek, Hebrew, Old Testament, New Testament, and Christian Doctrine (for M Div); for doctorate, GRE General Test, theological essay in English (foreign students only). Additional exam requirements/recommendations for international students: Required—TOEFL. *Faculty research:* Family counseling, educational administration, contemporary theology, pastoral office, humanism and education.

**Concordia Theological Seminary,** Graduate and Professional Programs, Fort Wayne, IN 46825-4996. Offers M Div, MA, STM, D Min, PhD. *Accreditation:* ATS. *Program availability:* Part-time. *Degree requirements:* For master's, variable foreign language requirement, thesis (for some programs); for doctorate, comprehensive exam, thesis/dissertation, oral exam. *Entrance requirements:* For master's, GRE General Test (for M Div), minimum GPA of 2.25 (for M Div).

**Concordia University,** School of Graduate Studies, Faculty of Arts and Science, Department of Theological Studies, Montréal, QC H3G 1M8, Canada. Offers MA. *Degree requirements:* For master's, one foreign language, research papers or thesis. *Entrance requirements:* For master's, minimum B average in theology. *Faculty research:* Interpretation theory, theological methodology.

**Concordia University Irvine,** School of Theology, Irvine, CA 92612-3299. Offers Christian leadership (MA); research in theology (MA); theology and culture (MA). *Program availability:* Part-time, evening/weekend. *Degree requirements:* For master's, project/thesis or vicarage. *Entrance requirements:* For master's, official college transcript(s), statement of intent, 2 references, interview. Additional exam requirements/recommendations for international students: Required—TOEFL. Electronic applications accepted. *Expenses:* Contact institution.

**Concordia University of Edmonton,** Program in Biblical and Christian Studies, Edmonton, AB T5B 4E4, Canada. Offers MA.

**Corban University,** Graduate School, School of Ministry, Salem, OR 97301-9392. Offers Biblical languages (M Div); Biblical leadership (Certificate); Christian leadership (MA); Church ministry (M Div); ministry (D Min). *Program availability:* Part-time, evening/weekend. *Degree requirements:* For master's, thesis. *Entrance requirements:* Additional exam requirements/recommendations for international students: Required—TOEFL (minimum score 550 paper-based), IELTS (minimum score 6).

**Covenant Theological Seminary,** Graduate and Professional Programs, St. Louis, MO 63141-8697. Offers M Div, MA, MAC, MAEM, Th M, D Min, Certificate. *Accreditation:* ATS (one or more programs are accredited). *Program availability:* Part-time, evening/weekend, online learning. *Degree requirements:* For master's, 2 foreign languages, thesis (for some programs); for doctorate, 2 foreign languages, thesis/dissertation; for Certificate, 2 foreign languages. *Entrance requirements:* For doctorate and Certificate, M Div. Additional exam requirements/recommendations for international students: Required—TOEFL (minimum score 550 paper-based). Electronic applications accepted.

**Creighton University,** Graduate School, College of Arts and Sciences, Department of Theology, Omaha, NE 68178-0001. Offers MA. *Program availability:* Part-time, evening/weekend, blended/hybrid learning. *Faculty:* 18 full-time (6 women), 2 part-time/adjunct (1 woman). *Students:* 2 full-time (1 woman), 23 part-time (14 women); includes 3 minority (2 American Indian or Alaska Native, non-Hispanic/Latino; 1 Hispanic/Latino), 2 international. Average age 43. 7 applicants, 57% accepted, 1 enrolled. In 2016, 17 master's awarded. *Degree requirements:* For master's, thesis (for some programs). *Entrance requirements:* For master's, GRE General Test, 9 hours of theology course work, 3 letters of recommendation. Additional exam requirements/recommendations for international students: Required—TOEFL (minimum score 90 iBT). *Application deadline:* For fall admission, 3/1 for domestic and international students; for winter admission, 10/1 for domestic students, 5/1 for international students; for spring admission, 4/1 for domestic students, 10/1 for international students; for summer admission, 3/1 for domestic and international students. Applications are processed on a rolling basis. Application fee: $50. Electronic applications accepted. *Expenses: Tuition:* Full-time $14,400; part-time $800 per credit hour. *Required fees:* $158 per semester. Tuition and fees vary according to course load, campus/location, program, reciprocity agreements and student's religious affiliation. *Financial support:* Scholarships/grants and tuition waivers (partial) available. Support available to part-time students. Financial award applicants required to submit FAFSA. *Unit head:* Dr. Richard Miller, Director, 402-280-3618, E-mail: richardmiller@creighton.edu. *Application contact:* Lindsay Johnson, Director of Graduate and Adult Recruitment, 402-280-2703, Fax: 402-280-2423, E-mail: gradschool@creighton.edu.

**Criswell College,** Graduate School of the Bible, Dallas, TX 75246-1537. Offers biblical studies (M Div); Christian leadership (MA); counseling (MA); Jewish studies (MA); ministry (MA); theological and biblical studies (MA). *Program availability:* Part-time. *Degree requirements:* For master's, 2 foreign languages, thesis optional. *Entrance requirements:* For master's, GRE General Test, minimum GPA of 2.5. Electronic applications accepted. *Faculty research:* Emphasis on biblical languages (Hebrew and Greek), expository preaching and evangelism in the local church.

**Crown College,** Adult and Graduate Studies, St. Bonifacius, MN 55375-9001. Offers Christian studies (MA); instructional leadership (MA); international leadership (MA); ministry leadership (MA); organizational leadership (MA). *Program availability:* Part-time, evening/weekend, online learning. *Degree requirements:* For master's, thesis optional. *Entrance requirements:* For master's, 12 credits in foundational studies, minimum GPA of 2.5 and bachelor's degree from regionally-accredited college. Additional exam requirements/recommendations for international students: Required—TOEFL (minimum score 550 paper-based; 80 iBT). Electronic applications accepted.

**Dallas Baptist University,** Graduate School of Ministry, Program in Theological Studies, Dallas, TX 75211-9299. Offers Christian heritage (MA); Christian ministry (MA); Christian scriptures (MA). *Program availability:* Part-time, evening/weekend. *Application deadline:* Applications are processed on a rolling basis. Application fee: $25. Electronic applications accepted. Application fee is waived when completed online. *Expenses: Tuition:* Full-time $15,408; part-time $856 per credit hour. *Required fees:* $400 per semester. Tuition and fees vary according to course load and degree level. *Unit head:* Dr. Jim Lemons, Director, 214-333-5366, E-mail: jiml@dbu.edu. *Application contact:* Bobby Soto, Director of Admissions, 214-333-5242, E-mail: graduate@dbu.edu. Website: http://www3.dbu.edu/gsom/Theological-Studies/

**Dallas Theological Seminary,** Graduate Programs, Dallas, TX 75204-6499. Offers adult education (Th M); apologetics (Th M); Bible backgrounds (Th M); Bible translation (Th M); Biblical and theological studies (Certificate); biblical counseling (MA); biblical exegesis and linguistics (MA); biblical exposition (PhD); biblical studies (MA); Biblical theology (Th M); children's education (Th M); Christian education (MA, D Min); Christian leadership (MA); cross-cultural ministries (MA); educational administration (Th M); educational leadership (Th M); evangelism and discipleship (Th M); exposition of Biblical books (Th M); family life education (Th M); general studies (Th M); Hebrew and cognate studies (Th M); hermeneutics (Th M); historical theology (Th M); homiletics (Th M); intercultural ministries (Th M); Jesus studies (Th M); leadership studies (Th M); media and communication (MA); media arts (Th M); ministry (D Min); ministry with women (Th M); New Testament studies (Th M, PhD); Old Testament studies (Th M, PhD); parachurch ministries (Th M); pastoral care and counseling (Th M); pastoral theology and practice (Th M); philosophy (Th M); sacred theology (STM); spiritual formation (Th M); systematic theology (Th M); teaching in Christian institutions (Th M); theological studies (PhD); urban ministries (Th M); worship studies (Th M); youth education (Th M). *Program availability:* Part-time, online learning. *Degree requirements:* For master's, variable foreign language requirement, thesis (for some programs); for doctorate, 2 foreign languages, thesis/dissertation. *Entrance requirements:* For master's, GRE or MAT (if minimum undergraduate cumulative GPA is below 2.5 or undergraduate degree is unaccredited). Additional exam requirements/recommendations for international students: Required—TOEFL (minimum score 575 paper-based; 85 iBT), TWE. Electronic applications accepted.

**Denver Seminary,** Graduate and Professional Programs, Littleton, CO 80120. Offers apologetics (Certificate); biblical studies (MA); Christian formation and soul care (MA, Certificate); Christian studies (MA, Certificate); church and parachurch leadership (D Min); counseling licensure (MA); counseling ministry (MA); intercultural ministry (Certificate); leadership (MA, Certificate); marriage and family counseling (D Min); pastoral ministry (D Min); philosophy of religion (MA); spiritual guidance (Certificate); theology (M Div, Certificate); worship (Certificate); youth and family ministry (MA). *Accreditation:* ACA; ACIPE; ATS (one or more programs are accredited). *Program availability:* Part-time, evening/weekend, online learning. *Degree requirements:* For master's, 2 foreign languages, thesis (for some programs); for doctorate, 2 foreign languages, thesis/dissertation. *Entrance requirements:* For doctorate, M Div, 3 years of ministry experience. Additional exam requirements/recommendations for international students: Required—TOEFL (minimum score 575 paper-based; 90 iBT). Electronic applications accepted.

**Dominican House of Studies, Pontifical Faculty of the Immaculate Conception,** Graduate and Professional Programs in Theology, Washington, DC 20017-1585. Offers moral theology (STL); sacred scripture (STL); systematic theology (STL); theology

## Theology

(M Div, MA, STB); Thomistic studies (MA, STD, STL). *Accreditation:* ATS (one or more programs are accredited). *Program availability:* Part-time. *Faculty:* 18 full-time (1 woman), 6 part-time/adjunct (3 women). *Students:* 75 full-time (7 women), 9 part-time (3 women); includes 5 minority (2 Asian, non-Hispanic/Latino; 3 Hispanic/Latino), 13 international. Average age 33. *Degree requirements:* For master's, thesis, thesis defense; for other advanced degree, comprehensive exam (for some programs), thesis (for some programs), lecture. *Entrance requirements:* For master's, 18 credits of philosophy, reading knowledge of Latin, BA with minimum GPA of 3.0; for other advanced degree, 36 credits of philosophy, BA with minimum GPA of 3.25 (for STB). Additional exam requirements/recommendations for international students: Required—TOEFL (minimum score 550 paper-based; 79 iBT). *Application deadline:* For fall admission, 7/1 for domestic and international students; for spring admission, 12/1 for domestic and international students. Applications are processed on a rolling basis. Application fee: $50. *Expenses: Tuition:* Full-time $16,080; part-time $2010 per credit hour. *Required fees:* $280; $280 per credit hour. $140 per semester. One-time fee: $350. *Financial support:* Career-related internships or fieldwork and Federal Work-Study available. Support available to part-time students. Financial award application deadline: 6/30; financial award applicants required to submit FAFSA. *Faculty research:* Sacred scripture, moral theology, systematic theology, philosophy, languages. *Unit head:* Rev. Thomas Petri, OP, Vice-President/Academic Dean, 202-495-3832, Fax: 202-495-3873, E-mail: dean@dhs.edu. *Application contact:* Rev. Albert Trudel, Registrar, 202-495-3836, Fax: 202-495-3873, E-mail: registrar@dhs.edu.

**Dominican School of Philosophy and Theology,** Graduate Programs, Berkeley, CA 94708. Offers philosophy (MA); theology (M Div, MA, MTS, Certificate); M Div/MA; MA/MA. *Accreditation:* ATS. *Program availability:* Part-time. *Degree requirements:* For master's, one foreign language, thesis. *Entrance requirements:* For master's, GRE General Test (for MA), minimum GPA of 3.0 (for MA), 2.3 (for M Div); academic writing sample (for MA); statement of purpose, official transcripts, letters of recommendation. Additional exam requirements/recommendations for international students: Required—TOEFL (minimum score 570 paper-based; 80 iBT), IELTS. Electronic applications accepted.

**Drew University,** Caspersen School of Graduate Studies, Madison, NJ 07940-1493. Offers conflict resolution and leadership (Certificate), including community leadership, moderation, peace building; history and culture (MA, PhD), including American history, book history, British history, European history, Holocaust and genocide (M Litt, MA, D Litt, PhD); intellectual history, Irish history, print culture, public history; K-12 education (MAT), including art, biology, chemistry, elementary education, English, French, Italian, math, secondary education, special education, teacher of students with disabilities; liberal studies (M Litt, D Litt), including history, Holocaust and genocide (M Litt, MA, D Litt, PhD), Irish/Irish-American studies, literature (M Litt, MMH, D Litt, DMH, CMH), religion, spirituality, teaching in the two-year college, writing; medical humanities (MMH, DMH, CMH), including arts, health, healthcare, literature (M Litt, MMH, D Litt, DMH, CMH), scientific research; poetry (MFA). *Program availability:* Part-time, evening/weekend. *Faculty:* 4 full-time (2 women), 31 part-time/adjunct (16 women). *Students:* 62 full-time (41 women), 199 part-time (130 women); includes 38 minority (17 Black or African American, non-Hispanic/Latino; 3 Asian, non-Hispanic/Latino; 17 Hispanic/Latino; 1 Two or more races, non-Hispanic/Latino), 3 international. Average age 27. 93 applicants, 81% accepted, 46 enrolled. In 2016, 39 master's, 27 doctorates, 26 other advanced degrees awarded. Terminal master's awarded for partial completion of doctoral program. *Degree requirements:* For master's and other advanced degree, thesis (for some programs); for doctorate, one foreign language, comprehensive exam (for some programs), thesis/dissertation. *Entrance requirements:* For master's, PRAXIS Core and Subject Area tests (for MAT), resume, transcripts, writing sample, personal statement, letters of recommendation; for doctorate, GRE (PhD in history and culture), resume, transcripts, writing sample, personal statement, letters of recommendation. Additional exam requirements/recommendations for international students: Required—TOEFL (minimum score 587 paper-based; 94 iBT), IELTS (minimum score 7), TWE (minimum score 4). *Application deadline:* For fall admission, 8/1 for domestic students, 6/1 for international students; for spring admission, 12/1 for domestic students, 10/1 for international students. Applications are processed on a rolling basis. Application fee: $35. Electronic applications accepted. Tuition and fees vary according to program. *Financial support:* Fellowships, research assistantships, teaching assistantships, career-related internships or fieldwork, Federal Work-Study, scholarships/grants, and unspecified assistantships available. Support available to part-time students. Financial award applicants required to submit FAFSA. *Application contact:* Leanne Horinko, Director of Caspersen Admissions, 973-408-3280, E-mail: gradm@drew.edu. Website: http://www.drew.edu/caspersen

**Drew University,** Theological School, Madison, NJ 07940-1493. Offers M Div, MA, MA Min, STM, D Min, PhD, Certificate. *Accreditation:* ACIPE; ATS. *Program availability:* Part-time, online learning. *Faculty:* 21 full-time (9 women), 20 part-time/adjunct (9 women). *Students:* 208 full-time (100 women), 147 part-time (62 women); includes 134 minority (94 Black or African American, non-Hispanic/Latino; 2 American Indian or Alaska Native, non-Hispanic/Latino; 17 Asian, non-Hispanic/Latino; 16 Hispanic/Latino; 5 Two or more races, non-Hispanic/Latino), 87 international. Average age 40. 201 applicants, 78% accepted, 94 enrolled. In 2016, 58 master's, 33 doctorates awarded. *Degree requirements:* For doctorate, thesis/dissertation. *Entrance requirements:* For master's, resume, transcripts, writing sample, personal statement, letters of recommendation. Additional exam requirements/recommendations for international students: Required—TOEFL (minimum score 580 paper-based; 88 iBT), IELTS, TWE. *Application deadline:* For fall admission, 8/1 for domestic students, 4/1 for international students; for spring admission, 12/1 for domestic students, 10/1 for international students. Applications are processed on a rolling basis. Application fee: $35. Electronic applications accepted. *Expenses:* Contact institution. *Financial support:* Fellowships, career-related internships or fieldwork, Federal Work-Study, institutionally sponsored loans, and scholarships/grants available. Support available to part-time students. Financial award application deadline: 2/15; financial award applicants required to submit FAFSA. *Faculty research:* Biblical studies, constructive theology, ecology and religion, gender and religion, race/ethnicity and religion. *Unit head:* Dr. Javier Viera, Dean of the Theological School, 973-408-3418, E-mail: jviera@drew.edu. *Application contact:* Dr. Kevin D. Miller, Director of Theological Admissions, 973-408-3111, E-mail: kmiller@drew.edu. Website: http://www.drew.edu/theological/

**Duke University,** Divinity School, Durham, NC 27708-0586. Offers M Div, MACP, MACS, MTS, Th M, D Min, Th D, JD/MTS, M Div/MSW. *Accreditation:* ACIPE; ATS. *Program availability:* Part-time, online learning. Terminal master's awarded for partial completion of doctoral program. *Degree requirements:* For master's, thesis (for some programs); for doctorate, 2 foreign languages, comprehensive exam (for some programs), thesis/dissertation. *Entrance requirements:* For master's, 5 letters of reference, bachelor's degree from regionally-accredited college or university prior to intended date of enrollment, minimum GPA of 2.75, commitment to some form of ordained or lay ministry; for doctorate, GRE, M Div, MTS or comparable master's degree from institution accredited by ATS; bachelor's degree from regionally-accredited college or university prior to intended date of enrollment; 4 letters of reference; 2-page statement of purpose; one sample of academic writing. Additional exam requirements/

recommendations for international students: Required—TOEFL (minimum score 580 paper-based; 93 iBT). Electronic applications accepted. *Expenses:* Contact institution. *Faculty research:* Biblical studies, historical church studies, theological studies, church ministry studies.

**Duquesne University,** Graduate School of Liberal Arts, Department of Theology, Pittsburgh, PA 15282-0001. Offers pastoral ministry (MA); religious education (MA); systematic theology (PhD); theology (MA). *Program availability:* Part-time, evening/weekend, blended/hybrid learning. *Faculty:* 17 full-time (6 women). *Students:* 46 full-time (10 women), 9 part-time (8 women); includes 9 minority (2 Black or African American, non-Hispanic/Latino; 4 Hispanic/Latino; 3 Two or more races, non-Hispanic/Latino), 16 international. Average age 41. 21 applicants, 62% accepted, 7 enrolled. In 2016, 48 master's, 5 doctorates awarded. Terminal master's awarded for partial completion of doctoral program. *Degree requirements:* For master's, comprehensive exam; for doctorate, 2 foreign languages, comprehensive exam, thesis/dissertation. *Entrance requirements:* For master's and doctorate, GRE General Test. Additional exam requirements/recommendations for international students: Required—TOEFL. *Application deadline:* For fall admission, 2/1 for domestic and international students. Application fee: $0. Electronic applications accepted. *Expenses: Tuition:* Full-time $22,212; part-time $1234 per credit. Tuition and fees vary according to program. *Financial support:* In 2016–17, 36 students received support, including 17 teaching assistantships with full tuition reimbursements available (averaging $17,000 per year); career-related internships or fieldwork, scholarships/grants, tuition waivers (partial), and unspecified assistantships also available. Support available to part-time students. Financial award application deadline: 5/1. *Unit head:* Dr. Marinus Iwuchukwu, Chair, 412-396-1014, E-mail: iwuchukwum@duq.edu. *Application contact:* Linda Rendulic, Assistant to the Dean, 412-396-6400, Fax: 412-396-5265, E-mail: rendulic@duq.edu.

**Earlham School of Religion,** Graduate Programs, Richmond, IN 47374-5360. Offers religion (MA); theology (M Div, M Min). *Accreditation:* ATS. *Program availability:* Part-time, online learning. *Faculty:* 8 full-time (2 women), 2 part-time/adjunct (1 woman). *Students:* 38 full-time (17 women), 18 part-time (14 women). *Degree requirements:* For master's, variable foreign language requirement, comprehensive exam (for some programs), thesis (for some programs), internship (M Div). *Entrance requirements:* For master's, 3 references, academic writing sample, official college transcripts. Additional exam requirements/recommendations for international students: Required—TOEFL (minimum score 550 paper-based; 82 iBT), IELTS (minimum score 7). *Application deadline:* For fall admission, 7/15 priority date for domestic students; for winter admission, 12/15 priority date for domestic students. Applications are processed on a rolling basis. Application fee: $35. Electronic applications accepted. *Expenses: Tuition:* Full-time $14,823; part-time $1647 per course. *Required fees:* $200 per semester. *Financial support:* Scholarships/grants and tuition waivers (full and partial) available. Financial award application deadline: 4/15; financial award applicants required to submit FAFSA. *Faculty research:* Digitizing Quaker texts, vital Quaker ministry, research in Quaker studies and other seminary areas. *Unit head:* Jay W. Marshall, Dean, 800-432-1377, Fax: 765-983-1688, E-mail: marshja@earlham.edu. *Application contact:* Matthew Hisrich, Director of Recruitment and Admissions, 765-983-1523, Fax: 765-983-1688, E-mail: hisrima@earlham.edu.
Website: http://esr.earlham.edu/academic-programs

**Eastern Mennonite University,** Eastern Mennonite Seminary, Harrisonburg, VA 22802-2462. Offers church leadership (MA); divinity (M Div); ministry studies (Certificate); religion (MA); theological studies (Certificate). *Accreditation:* ATS. *Program availability:* Part-time. *Degree requirements:* For master's, thesis (for some programs), supervised field education (for M Div). *Entrance requirements:* For master's, minimum GPA of 2.5. Additional exam requirements/recommendations for international students: Required—TOEFL (minimum score 550 paper-based). *Expenses:* Contact institution. *Faculty research:* Spiritual direction and culture of call, leadership coaching: an approach to leadership in a culture of call, clarity of call in the probationary process for United Methodist clergy in Virginia, EMS women's experiences of culture of call efforts, practices of excellent and fruitful Mennonite pastoral ministry.

**Eastern University,** Palmer Theological Seminary, St. Davids, PA 19087-3696. Offers Biblical studies and theology (MTS); Christian counseling (MTS); Christian faith and public policy (MTS); divinity (M Div); general studies (MTS); leadership of missional church renewal (D Min); theological studies (MTS); M Div/MA; M Div/MSW. *Accreditation:* ACIPE; ATS; MSA/CIHE. *Program availability:* Part-time, online learning. *Students:* 93 full-time (43 women), 135 part-time (66 women); includes 120 minority (105 Black or African American, non-Hispanic/Latino; 2 Asian, non-Hispanic/Latino; 12 Hispanic/Latino; 1 Two or more races, non-Hispanic/Latino), 4 international. Average age 47. In 2016, 42 master's, 9 doctorates awarded. *Entrance requirements:* Additional exam requirements/recommendations for international students: Required—TOEFL (minimum score 550 paper-based; 79 iBT). *Application deadline:* Applications are processed on a rolling basis. Application fee: $30. Electronic applications accepted. Application fee is waived when completed online. *Expenses:* $370 - $520 per credit (based on program and number of credits per semester). *Unit head:* Michael Dziedziak, Executive Director of Enrollment, 800-452-0996, E-mail: semadmis@eastern.edu. Website: http://palmerseminary.edu/

**Ecumenical Theological Seminary,** Professional Program, Detroit, MI 48201. Offers M Div. *Accreditation:* ACIPE; ATS.

**Eden Theological Seminary,** Graduate and Professional Programs, St. Louis, MO 63119-3192. Offers M Div, MAPS, MTS, D Min. *Accreditation:* ACIPE; ATS. *Degree requirements:* For master's, comprehensive exam (for some programs), thesis (for some programs), 2 oral exams; for doctorate, professional essay, supervised in-service projects. *Entrance requirements:* For master's, interview, minimum GPA of 2.7; for doctorate, interview, minimum GPA of 3.0. Additional exam requirements/recommendations for international students: Required—TOEFL (minimum score 550 paper-based). Electronic applications accepted. *Faculty research:* Psalms, pastoral ethics, historical Jesus, leadership roles, congregational life.

**Emory University,** Candler School of Theology, Atlanta, GA 30322. Offers formation and witness (M Div); history, scripture and tradition (MTS); leadership in church and community (M Div); modern religious thought and experience (MTS); pastoral counseling (Th D); religion and race (M Div); religion, health and science (M Div); scripture and interpretation (M Div); society and personality (M Div); theology (Th M); theology and ethics (M Div); theology and the arts (M Div); traditions of the church (M Div); women and religion (M Div); JD/M Div; JD/MTS; M Div/MBA; M Div/MPH; MBA/MTS; MTS/MPH. *Accreditation:* ACIPE. *Program availability:* Part-time. *Degree requirements:* For master's, thesis optional; for doctorate, comprehensive exam, thesis/dissertation. *Entrance requirements:* For master's, minimum undergraduate GPA of 3.0; for doctorate, GRE, M Div, 8 units of course work in clinical pastoral education. Additional exam requirements/recommendations for international students: Required—TOEFL (minimum score 600 paper-based; 95 iBT). Electronic applications accepted. *Expenses:* Contact institution. *Faculty research:* Biblical studies, church history, ethics, ministry practice, pastoral care.

**Episcopal Divinity School,** Graduate and Professional Programs, Cambridge, MA 02138-3494. Offers M Div, MATS, D Min, CTS. *Accreditation:* ACIPE; ATS (one or more programs are accredited). *Program availability:* Part-time. *Degree requirements:* For master's, thesis optional; for doctorate, thesis/dissertation, project. *Entrance requirements:* For master's, GRE General Test or MAT, 2 interviews, 4 letters of recommendation, 1500-word autobiographical statement; for doctorate, interview, M Div or equivalent, 3 letters of recommendation, 1500-word autobiographical statement; for CTS, GRE General Test, MAT, or advanced degree; interview; 2 letters of recommendation, 1000-word autobiographical statement. Additional exam requirements/recommendations for international students: Required—TOEFL. *Faculty research:* Anglican, global, and ecumenical studies; congregational studies; feminist liberation theologies.

**Erskine Theological Seminary,** Graduate and Professional Programs, Due West, SC 29639-0668. Offers M Div, MAPM, MATS, Th M, D Min. *Accreditation:* ATS. *Program availability:* Part-time, evening/weekend. *Degree requirements:* For doctorate, thesis/dissertation. *Entrance requirements:* For master's, Myers-Briggs Type Indicator, Taylor Johnson Temperament Analysis, Ministry Specialties Test (MACM), minimum GPA of 3.0, interview with committee (MACM); for doctorate, minimum GPA of 3.0 during M Div. Additional exam requirements/recommendations for international students: Required—TOEFL (minimum score 550 paper-based). Electronic applications accepted. *Faculty research:* Church administration, biblical studies.

**Evangelical Seminary,** Graduate and Professional Programs, Myerstown, PA 17067-1212. Offers Biblical studies (MAR); congregational ministry (M Div); global and contextual studies (M Div, MAR); historical and theological studies (MAR); interdisciplinary studies (MAR); marriage and family counseling (M Div); marriage and family therapy (MA); New Testament (MAR); Old Testament (MAR); spiritual formation (MAR); teaching ministry (M Div); youth ministry (M Div). *Accreditation:* ATS (one or more programs are accredited). *Program availability:* Part-time, online learning. *Degree requirements:* For master's, 2 foreign languages. *Entrance requirements:* For master's, minimum GPA of 2.5. Additional exam requirements/recommendations for international students: Required—TOEFL (minimum score 550 paper-based). *Faculty research:* Literary form and structure within the Hebrew and Greek scriptures, Wesley studies, esoteric biblical languages, the Mosaic law and the Christian, ethics.

**Evangelical Seminary of Puerto Rico,** Graduate and Professional Programs, San Juan, PR 00925-2207. Offers M Div, MAR, D Min. *Accreditation:* ATS. *Program availability:* Part-time. *Degree requirements:* For master's, comprehensive exam. *Entrance requirements:* For doctorate, 3 years experience in ministry service. Additional exam requirements/recommendations for international students: Required—TOEFL. *Faculty research:* Protestantism in Puerto Rico.

**Faith Baptist Bible College and Theological Seminary,** Graduate Program, Ankeny, IA 50023. Offers Biblical studies (MA); pastoral studies (M Div); pastoral training (MA); religion (MA); theological studies (MA). *Program availability:* Part-time. *Faculty:* 3 full-time (0 women), 4 part-time/adjunct (0 women). *Students:* 18 full-time (2 women), 30 part-time (5 women); includes 5 minority (1 Black or African American, non-Hispanic/Latino; 2 Asian, non-Hispanic/Latino; 1 Hispanic/Latino; 1 Two or more races, non-Hispanic/Latino). Average age 33. In 2016, 13 master's awarded. *Degree requirements:* For master's, thesis or alternative. *Entrance requirements:* Additional exam requirements/recommendations for international students: Required—TOEFL (minimum score 550 paper-based; 79 iBT), IELTS (minimum score 6.5). *Application deadline:* For fall admission, 8/1 priority date for domestic students, 8/1 for international students; for spring admission, 12/15 for domestic and international students. Applications are processed on a rolling basis. Application fee: $25. Electronic applications accepted. *Financial support:* Career-related internships or fieldwork and scholarships/grants available. Support available to part-time students. Financial award application deadline: 3/1; financial award applicants required to submit FAFSA. *Faculty research:* Baptist theology, American church history. *Unit head:* Rev. Jim Tillotson, President, 515-964-0601, E-mail: tillotsonj@faith.edu. *Application contact:* Jonathan Balasa, Seminary Admissions Representative, 888-FAITH4U, Fax: 515-964-1638, E-mail: seminaryrep@faith.edu.
Website: http://www.faith.edu/

**Faith Evangelical College & Seminary,** Graduate and Professional Programs, Tacoma, WA 98407. Offers M Div, MACM, MTS, D Min. *Program availability:* Part-time, evening/weekend, online learning. *Degree requirements:* For master's, thesis optional; for doctorate, thesis/dissertation. *Entrance requirements:* For master's, minimum undergraduate GPA of 2.7; for doctorate, minimum graduate GPA of 3.0. Additional exam requirements/recommendations for international students: Required—TOEFL (minimum score 550 paper-based).

**Faith Theological Seminary,** Graduate Programs, Baltimore, MD 21212. Offers M Div, D Min, Th D.

**Faulkner University,** College of Biblical Studies, Montgomery, AL 36109-3398. Offers ministry (MABS); missions (MABS); New Testament (MABS); Old Testament (MABS); youth and family ministry (MABS).

**Fordham University,** Graduate School of Arts and Sciences, Department of Theology, New York, NY 10458. Offers MA, PhD. *Program availability:* Part-time, evening/weekend. *Faculty:* 22 full-time (7 women). *Students:* 50 full-time (17 women), 10 part-time (1 woman); includes 8 minority (3 Black or African American, non-Hispanic/Latino; 1 American Indian or Alaska Native, non-Hispanic/Latino; 4 Asian, non-Hispanic/Latino), 1 international. Average age 37. 99 applicants, 30% accepted, 11 enrolled. In 2016, 10 master's, 4 doctorates awarded. Terminal master's awarded for partial completion of doctoral program. *Degree requirements:* For master's, one foreign language, comprehensive exam; for doctorate, 2 foreign languages, comprehensive exam, thesis/dissertation. *Entrance requirements:* For master's and doctorate, GRE General Test. Additional exam requirements/recommendations for international students: Required—TOEFL (minimum score 650 paper-based). *Application deadline:* For fall admission, 1/4 priority date for domestic students; for spring admission, 11/1 for domestic students. Application fee: $70. Electronic applications accepted. *Financial support:* In 2016–17, 45 students received support, including 2 fellowships with tuition reimbursements available (averaging $25,960 per year), 33 teaching assistantships with tuition reimbursements available (averaging $21,887 per year); institutionally sponsored loans, tuition waivers (full and partial), and unspecified assistantships also available. Support available to part-time students. Financial award application deadline: 1/4. *Faculty research:* History of Christian tradition, contemporary systematic theology, theological/feminist ethics, American Catholicism, Biblical exegesis and theology. *Unit head:* Dr. Patrick Hornbeck, Chair, 718-817-3240, E-mail: ttilley@fordham.edu. *Application contact:* Bernadette Valentino-Morrison, Director of Graduate Admissions, 718-817-4419, Fax: 718-817-3566, E-mail: valentinomor@fordham.edu.

**Franciscan School of Theology,** Graduate and Professional Programs, Oceanside, CA 92057. Offers M Div, MA, MAMC, MTS. *Accreditation:* ATS (one or more programs are accredited). *Program availability:* Part-time. *Degree requirements:* For master's, one foreign language, thesis. *Entrance requirements:* For master's, GRE General Test (MA). Additional exam requirements/recommendations for international students: Required—TOEFL (minimum score 550 paper-based). *Faculty research:* Church history, multicultural ministries, ethics and morality, catechesis, biblical studies.

**Franciscan University of Steubenville,** Graduate Programs, Department of Theology, Steubenville, OH 43952-1763. Offers theology and Christian ministry (MA). *Program availability:* Part-time, online learning. *Degree requirements:* For master's, comprehensive exam. *Entrance requirements:* For master's, minimum undergraduate GPA of 3.0. Additional exam requirements/recommendations for international students: Required—TOEFL. Electronic applications accepted. Application fee is waived when completed online.

**Freed-Hardeman University,** School of Biblical Studies, Program in Divinity, Henderson, TN 38340-2399. Offers M Div. *Program availability:* Part-time. *Degree requirements:* For master's, comprehensive exam. *Entrance requirements:* For master's, GRE General Test or MAT. Additional exam requirements/recommendations for international students: Required—TOEFL (minimum score 500 paper-based).

**Freed-Hardeman University,** School of Biblical Studies, Program in New Testament, Henderson, TN 38340-2399. Offers MA. *Program availability:* Part-time. *Degree requirements:* For master's, one foreign language, comprehensive exam, thesis. *Entrance requirements:* For master's, GRE General Test or MAT. Additional exam requirements/recommendations for international students: Required—TOEFL (minimum score 500 paper-based).

**Fresno Pacific University,** Biblical Seminary, Program in Divinity, Fresno, CA 93702-4709. Offers M Div. *Accreditation:* ATS. *Entrance requirements:* For master's, minimum GPA of 2.5. *Expenses:* Contact institution.

**Fresno Pacific University,** Biblical Seminary, Programs in New Testament, Old Testament, and Theology, Fresno, CA 93702-4709. Offers New Testament (MA); Old Testament (MA); theology (MA). *Accreditation:* ATS. *Program availability:* Part-time. *Entrance requirements:* Additional exam requirements/recommendations for international students: Required—TOEFL (minimum score 550 paper-based).

**Fuller Theological Seminary,** Graduate Programs, Pasadena, CA 91182. Offers Christian leadership (MACL); clinical psychology (PhD, Psy D); family studies (MA); global leadership (MA); global ministries (D Min); global ministries (Korean language) (D Min); intercultural studies (MA, Th M, PhD); intercultural studies (Korean language) (MA); marital and family therapy (MS); marriage and family enrichment (Certificate); ministry (M Div, D Min); missiology (D Miss); missiology (Korean language) (Th M); theology (MA, Th M, PhD), including evangelism (MA), family life education (MA), pastoral ministry (MA), recovery ministry (MA), worship music ministry (MA), worship, theology, and the arts (MA), youth, family, and culture (MA); theology and ministry (MA). *Program availability:* Part-time. *Degree requirements:* For master's, thesis (for some programs); for doctorate, thesis/dissertation. *Entrance requirements:* For doctorate, GRE (PhD). Additional exam requirements/recommendations for international students: Required—TOEFL (minimum score 560 paper-based). Electronic applications accepted.

**Gannon University,** School of Graduate Studies, College of Humanities, Education, and Social Sciences, School of Humanities, Program in Pastoral Studies, Erie, PA 16541-0001. Offers pastoral studies (MA); theological studies (Certificate). *Program availability:* Part-time, evening/weekend. *Students:* 1 (woman) full-time, 2 part-time (both women). Average age 34. 2 applicants, 100% accepted, 1 enrolled. *Degree requirements:* For master's, comprehensive exam, thesis or alternative, research project, internship, written evaluation. *Entrance requirements:* Additional exam requirements/recommendations for international students: Required—TOEFL (minimum score 79 iBT). *Application deadline:* Applications are processed on a rolling basis. Application fee: $25. Electronic applications accepted. Application fee is waived when completed online. *Expenses:* Tuition: Full-time $17,370. *Required fees:* $550. Tuition and fees vary according to course load and program. *Financial support:* Federal Work-Study available. Financial award application deadline: 7/1; financial award applicants required to submit FAFSA. *Unit head:* Fr. Jason Glover, Director, 814-871-5495, E-mail: glover001@gannon.edu. *Application contact:* Bridget Philip, Director of Graduate Admissions, 814-871-7412, E-mail: graduate@gannon.edu.

**Gardner-Webb University,** School of Divinity, Boiling Springs, NC 28017. Offers biblical studies (M Div); Christian education and formation (M Div); intercultural studies (M Div); ministry (D Min); missiology (M Div); pastoral care and counseling (M Div); pastoral care and counseling/member care for missionaries (D Min); pastoral studies (M Div); M Div/MA; M Div/MBA. *Accreditation:* ACIPE. *Program availability:* Part-time. *Faculty:* 12 full-time (2 women), 3 part-time/adjunct (1 woman). *Students:* 115 full-time (59 women), 68 part-time (27 women); includes 86 minority (80 Black or African American, non-Hispanic/Latino; 5 Asian, non-Hispanic/Latino; 1 Hispanic/Latino). Average age 40. 86 applicants, 44% accepted, 16 enrolled. In 2016, 40 master's, 3 doctorates awarded. *Entrance requirements:* For master's, minimum GPA of 2.6; for doctorate, minimum GPA of 2.75. Additional exam requirements/recommendations for international students: Required—TOEFL (minimum score 500 paper-based; 61 iBT). *Application deadline:* Applications are processed on a rolling basis. Electronic applications accepted. *Expenses:* Contact institution. *Financial support:* Fellowships, institutionally sponsored loans, and unspecified assistantships available. Support available to part-time students. Financial award application deadline: 5/15. *Faculty research:* Jewish-Christian dialogue, Islam. *Unit head:* Dr. Robert W. Canoy, Sr., Dean, 704-406-4400, Fax: 704-406-3935, E-mail: rcanoy@gardner-webb.edu. *Application contact:* Kheresa Harmon, Director of Admissions, 704-406-3205, Fax: 704-406-3895, E-mail: kharmon@gardner-webb.edu.
Website: http://gardner-webb.edu/academic-programs-and-resources/colleges-and-schools/divinity/index

**Garrett-Evangelical Theological Seminary,** Graduate and Professional Programs, Evanston, IL 60201-3298. Offers Bible and culture (PhD); Christian education (MA); Christian education and congregational studies (PhD); contemporary theology and culture (PhD); divinity (M Div); ethics, church, and society (MA); liturgical studies (PhD); ministry (D Min); music ministry (MA); pastoral care and counseling (MA); pastoral theology, personality, and culture (PhD); spiritual formation and evangelism (MA); theological studies (MTS); M Div/MSW. M Div/MSW offered jointly with Loyola University Chicago. *Accreditation:* ACIPE; ATS (one or more programs are accredited). *Program availability:* Part-time. *Degree requirements:* For master's, thesis (for some programs); for doctorate, thesis/dissertation. *Entrance requirements:* For doctorate, GRE (PhD). Additional exam requirements/recommendations for international students: Required—TOEFL (minimum score 560 paper-based). Electronic applications accepted.

**Gateway Seminary,** Graduate and Professional Programs, Ontario, CA 91761-8642. Offers divinity (M Div); early childhood education (Certificate); education leadership (MAEL, Diploma); ministry (D Min); theological studies (MTS); theology (Th M); youth ministry (Certificate). *Accreditation:* ACIPE. *Program availability:* Part-time, evening/weekend. *Degree requirements:* For master's, thesis (for some programs); for doctorate, 2 foreign languages, thesis/dissertation. *Entrance requirements:* For doctorate, MAT. Additional exam requirements/recommendations for international students: Required—TOEFL (minimum score 550 paper-based). Electronic applications accepted.

**General Theological Seminary,** Graduate and Professional Programs, New York, NY 10011-4977. Offers Anglican studies (STM, Th D, Certificate); ascetical theology (Certificate); biblical studies (Certificate); congregational development (Certificate); divinity (M Div); historical and theological studies (Certificate); spiritual direction (MASD, STM, Certificate); theology (M Div). *Accreditation:* ACIPE; ATS. *Program availability:* Part-time, evening/weekend. Terminal master's awarded for partial completion of doctoral program. *Degree requirements:* For master's, thesis; for doctorate, 2 foreign languages, thesis/dissertation. *Entrance requirements:* For master's, GRE General Test; for doctorate, GRE, M Div or MA. Additional exam requirements/recommendations for international students: Required—TOEFL. *Faculty research:* Liturgy, New Testament, ethics, history, ecumenical relations.

**George Fox University,** Portland Seminary, Portland, OR 97223. Offers Biblical studies (M Div, MA); chaplaincy (M Div); Christian history and theology (M Div, MA); creation care (M Div, MA); intercultural studies (M Div, MA); leadership (M Div, MA); leadership and global perspectives (D Min); leadership and spiritual formation (D Min); semiotics and future studies (D Min); spiritual direction (MA, Certificate); spiritual direction supervision (M Div, MA, Certificate); spiritual formation and discipleship (M Div, MA, Certificate). *Accreditation:* ACIPE; ATS. *Program availability:* Part-time, evening/weekend, online learning. *Entrance requirements:* For master's, resume, three references (one pastoral, one academic or professional, one personal), one official transcript from each college or university attended; for doctorate, resume, 3 references (1 professional, 1 academic, 1 personal), one official transcript from each college or university attended. Additional exam requirements/recommendations for international students: Required—TOEFL (minimum score 577 paper-based; 90 iBT). Electronic applications accepted. *Expenses:* Contact institution.

**Georgetown University,** Graduate School of Arts and Sciences, Department of Theology, Washington, DC 20057. Offers PhD.

**Georgia Christian University,** School of Divinity, Atlanta, GA 30360. Offers Christian education (MA); divinity (M Div); ministry (D Min); mission studies and world Christianity (MA); theological studies (MA).

**Georgian Court University,** School of Arts and Sciences, Lakewood, NJ 08701-2697. Offers applied behavior analysis (MA); clinical mental health counseling (MA); holistic health studies (MA, Certificate); homeland security (MS, Certificate); mercy spirituality (Certificate); parish business management (Certificate); professional counselor (Certificate); school psychology (MA, Certificate); theology (MA, Certificate). *Program availability:* Part-time, evening/weekend. *Faculty:* 19 full-time (11 women), 6 part-time/adjunct (3 women). *Students:* 90 full-time (75 women), 107 part-time (79 women); includes 34 minority (9 Black or African American, non-Hispanic/Latino; 20 Hispanic/Latino; 5 Two or more races, non-Hispanic/Latino), 1 international. Average age 34. 187 applicants, 49% accepted, 60 enrolled. In 2016, 66 master's, 17 other advanced degrees awarded. *Degree requirements:* For master's, comprehensive exam (for some programs), thesis (for some programs). *Entrance requirements:* For master's, GRE, GMAT, or NTE/PRAXIS, 3 letters of recommendation. Additional exam requirements/recommendations for international students: Required—TOEFL (minimum score 550 paper-based). *Application deadline:* For fall admission, 8/15 for domestic students, 5/1 for international students; for spring admission, 1/15 for domestic students, 10/1 for international students. Applications are processed on a rolling basis. Application fee: $40. Electronic applications accepted. *Expenses: Tuition:* Full-time $15,079; part-time $839 per credit. *Required fees:* $968; $496 per credit. Tuition and fees vary according to campus/location and program. *Financial support:* Scholarships/grants, health care benefits, and unspecified assistantships available. Financial award application deadline: 4/15; financial award applicants required to submit FAFSA. *Unit head:* Dr. Mary Chinery, Dean, 732-987-2493, Fax: 732-987-2007, E-mail: mchinery@georgian.edu. *Application contact:* Patrick Givens, Director of Graduate and Professional Studies Admissions, 732-987-2736, Fax: 732-987-2000, E-mail: gps@georgian.edu. Website: http://georgian.edu/academics/school-of-arts-sciences/

**Global University,** Graduate School of Theology, Springfield, MO 65804. Offers bible and theology (D Min); biblical language (M Div); biblical studies (MA); Christian ministry (M Div, D Min); ministerial studies (MA), including education, leadership, missions, New Testament, Old Testament. *Program availability:* Part-time, evening/weekend, online learning. *Degree requirements:* For master's, thesis (for some programs). *Entrance requirements:* For master's, minimum undergraduate GPA of 3.0. Electronic applications accepted. *Faculty research:* Higher education, cross-cultural missions.

**Gonzaga University,** College of Arts and Sciences, Spokane, WA 99258. Offers philosophy (MA); theology and leadership (MA). *Program availability:* Part-time, online with two required campus visits. *Faculty:* 9 full-time (3 women). *Students:* 31 part-time (17 women); includes 5 minority (2 Black or African American, non-Hispanic/Latino; 1 American Indian or Alaska Native, non-Hispanic/Latino; 1 Asian, non-Hispanic/Latino; 1 Hispanic/Latino), 1 international. Average age 39. *Degree requirements:* For master's, comprehensive exam. *Entrance requirements:* For master's, GRE General Test or MAT, minimum GPA of 3.0, official transcripts, two to three letters of recommendation, personal statement, writing sample, resume/curriculum vitae. Additional exam requirements/recommendations for international students: Required—TOEFL (minimum score 88 iBT), IELTS (minimum score 6.5), or verification from Gonzaga University ISSS office or an official recommendation from Gonzaga's ELC. *Application deadline:* For fall admission, 7/15 priority date for domestic students; for spring admission, 11/1 for domestic students; for summer admission, 4/3 for domestic students. Applications are processed on a rolling basis. Application fee: $50. Electronic applications accepted. *Expenses:* $830 per credit (for philosophy); $700 per credit (for theology and leadership). *Financial support:* In 2016–17, 27 students received support. Teaching assistantships, scholarships/grants, tuition waivers, and unspecified assistantships available. Support available to part-time students. Financial award applicants required to submit FAFSA. *Unit head:* Dr. Elisabeth Mermann-Jozwiak, Dean, 509-313-6603, Fax: 509-313-6684, E-mail: merrmann-jozwiak@gonzaga.edu. *Application contact:* Carolyn Von Muller, Assistant to the Dean, 509-313-5522, E-mail: vonmuller@gonzaga.edu. Website: http://www.gonzaga.edu/Academics/Colleges-and-Schools/College-of-Arts-and-Sciences

**Gordon-Conwell Theological Seminary,** Graduate and Professional Programs, South Hamilton, MA 01982. Offers Biblical languages (MABL); church history (MACH); counseling (MACO); ministry (D Min); missions/evangelism (MAME); New Testament (MANT); Old Testament (MAOT); religion (MAR); theology (M Div, MATH, Th M, Th D). *Accreditation:* ACIPE; ATS (one or more programs are accredited). *Program availability:* Part-time, evening/weekend. *Degree requirements:* For master's, one foreign language, thesis optional; for doctorate, 2 foreign languages, thesis/dissertation. *Entrance requirements:* For master's, minimum GPA of 2.5; for doctorate, minimum GPA of 3.0.

**Graceland University,** Community of Christ Seminary, Independence, MO 64050. Offers MAR. *Program availability:* Part-time. *Students:* 14 full-time (7 women), 20 part-time (12 women); includes 1 minority (Native Hawaiian or other Pacific Islander, non-Hispanic/Latino), 5 international. 39 applicants, 64% accepted, 19 enrolled. In 2016, 1 master's awarded. *Degree requirements:* For master's, thesis optional, portfolio. *Entrance requirements:* For master's, minimum cumulative GPA of 3.0. Additional exam requirements/recommendations for international students: Required—TOEFL. *Application deadline:* For fall admission, 8/15 priority date for domestic students; for winter admission, 10/15 priority date for domestic students; for spring admission, 4/15 priority date for domestic students. Applications are processed on a rolling basis. Application fee: $50. Electronic applications accepted. *Expenses:* Contact institution. *Financial support:* Scholarships/grants available. Financial award application deadline: 12/15; financial award applicants required to submit FAFSA. *Faculty research:* Theology, scripture. *Unit head:* Dr. Matthew Frizzell, Dean, 641-784-5276, E-mail: mfrizzel@graceland.edu. *Application contact:* Sharon Ward, Administrative Assistant,

816-423-4676, Fax: 816-423-4753, E-mail: ward@graceland.edu. Website: http://www.graceland.edu/seminary

**Grace School of Theology,** Graduate Programs, Conroe, TX 77384-4894. Offers M Div, MABS, MM, Th M.

**Grace Theological Seminary,** Graduate and Professional Programs, Winona Lake, IN 46590-9907. Offers biblical studies (Certificate); chaplaincy (M Div); exegetical studies (M Div); intercultural studies (M Div, MA, D Min); local church ministry (MA), including camp administration, women's leadership; pastoral counseling (M Div); pastoral studies (M Div, D Min); theology (Diploma). *Accreditation:* ATS. *Program availability:* Part-time, online learning. *Degree requirements:* For master's, thesis optional; for doctorate, 2 foreign languages, thesis/dissertation. *Entrance requirements:* For master's, MAT, minimum GPA of 2.5. Electronic applications accepted. *Faculty research:* Biblical theology, language, and church ministries.

**Grace University,** College of Graduate Studies, Bible Department, Omaha, NE 68108. Offers MA. *Degree requirements:* For master's, thesis optional. *Entrance requirements:* For master's, minimum undergraduate GPA of 3.0. Electronic applications accepted.

**Graduate Theological Union,** Graduate Programs, Berkeley, CA 94709-1212. Offers art and religion (MA, PhD, Th D); biblical languages (MA); biblical studies (MA); Biblical studies (PhD, Th D); Buddhist studies (MA); Christian spirituality (MA, PhD, Th D); cultural and historical studies of religions (MA, PhD, Th D); ethics and social theory (PhD, Th D); history (MA, PhD, Th D); homiletics (MA, PhD, Th D); interdisciplinary studies (PhD, Th D); Jewish studies (MA, PhD, Th D, Certificate); liturgical studies (MA, PhD, Th D); Near Eastern religions (PhD, Th D); Orthodox Christian studies (MA); religion and psychology (MA, PhD, Th D); religion and society/ethics and social theory (MA); systematic and philosophical theology (MA, PhD, Th D). PhD programs in Jewish studies and Near Eastern religions offered jointly with University of California, Berkeley. *Accreditation:* ATS. Terminal master's awarded for partial completion of doctoral program. *Degree requirements:* For master's, one foreign language, thesis; for doctorate, one foreign language, comprehensive exam, thesis/dissertation. *Entrance requirements:* For master's, GRE General Test; for doctorate, GRE General Test, MA or M Div. Additional exam requirements/recommendations for international students: Required—TOEFL. Electronic applications accepted.

**Grand Rapids Theological Seminary of Cornerstone University,** Graduate Programs, Grand Rapids, MI 49525-5897. Offers biblical counseling (MA); Biblical counseling (M Div); chaplaincy (M Div); Christian education (M Div, MA); intercultural studies (M Div, MA); New Testament (MA, Th M); Old Testament (MA, Th M); pastoral studies (M Div); systematic theology (MA); theology (Th M). *Accreditation:* ATS. *Program availability:* Part-time, online learning. *Entrance requirements:* Additional exam requirements/recommendations for international students: Required—TOEFL (minimum score 577 paper-based; 90 iBT). Electronic applications accepted.

**Harding School of Theology,** Graduate Programs, Memphis, TN 38117-5499. Offers Christian ministry (MA); counseling (MA); ministry (M Div, D Min); religion (MA). *Accreditation:* ATS. *Program availability:* Part-time, online learning. *Degree requirements:* For master's, variable foreign language requirement, thesis (for some programs); for doctorate, one foreign language, thesis/dissertation. *Entrance requirements:* For master's, minimum GPA of 2.7; for doctorate, minimum GPA of 3.0. Additional exam requirements/recommendations for international students: Required—TOEFL (minimum score 550 paper-based; 79 iBT). Electronic applications accepted.

**Hardin-Simmons University,** Graduate School, Logsdon School of Theology, Abilene, TX 79698-0001. Offers M Div, MA, D Min. *Program availability:* Part-time, evening/weekend. *Faculty:* 16 full-time (1 woman), 20 part-time/adjunct (2 women). *Students:* 69 full-time (23 women), 86 part-time (18 women); includes 50 minority (19 Black or African American, non-Hispanic/Latino; 5 Asian, non-Hispanic/Latino; 26 Hispanic/Latino), 8 international. Average age 36. In 2016, 25 master's, 3 doctorates awarded. *Entrance requirements:* Additional exam requirements/recommendations for international students: Required—TOEFL (minimum score 550 paper-based; 75 iBT). *Application deadline:* For fall admission, 8/15 priority date for domestic students, 4/1 for international students; for spring admission, 1/5 priority date for domestic students, 9/1 for international students. Applications are processed on a rolling basis. Application fee: $50. Electronic applications accepted. *Expenses: Tuition:* Full-time $12,510; part-time $695 per credit hour. *Required fees:* $325; $110 per semester. *Financial support:* In 2016–17, 146 students received support. Fellowships and scholarships/grants available. Support available to part-time students. Financial award application deadline: 6/30; financial award applicants required to submit FAFSA. *Unit head:* Dr. Don Williford, Dean, 325-670-1491, Fax: 325-671-2157, E-mail: willifrd@hsutx.edu. *Application contact:* Dr. Nancy Kucinski, Dean of Graduate Studies, 325-670-1298, Fax: 325-670-1564, E-mail: gradoff@hsutx.edu. Website: http://www.hsutx.edu/academics/logsdon

**Hardin-Simmons University,** Graduate School, Logsdon School of Theology, Logsdon Seminary, Program in Theology, Abilene, TX 79698-0001. Offers M Div. *Accreditation:* ATS. *Program availability:* Part-time. *Faculty:* 7 full-time (1 woman), 20 part-time/adjunct (2 women). *Students:* 54 full-time (11 women), 38 part-time (8 women); includes 34 minority (15 Black or African American, non-Hispanic/Latino; 3 Asian, non-Hispanic/Latino; 16 Hispanic/Latino), 7 international. Average age 38. In 2016, 14 master's awarded. *Entrance requirements:* Additional exam requirements/recommendations for international students: Required—TOEFL (minimum score 550 paper-based; 75 iBT). *Application deadline:* For fall admission, 8/15 priority date for domestic students, 4/1 for international students; for spring admission, 1/5 priority date for domestic students, 9/1 for international students. Applications are processed on a rolling basis. Application fee: $50. Electronic applications accepted. *Expenses: Tuition:* Full-time $12,510; part-time $695 per credit hour. *Required fees:* $325; $110 per semester. *Financial support:* In 2016–17, 100 students received support. Fellowships, career-related internships or fieldwork, and scholarships/grants available. Support available to part-time students. Financial award application deadline: 6/30; financial award applicants required to submit FAFSA. *Faculty research:* Hebrew grammar, history of Christian education, training of ministers into the twenty-first century, role of women in the Old Testament, contemporary ethical issues, Ricouer in contemporary theology. *Unit head:* Dr. Kenneth Lyle, Program Director, 325-670-5858, Fax: 325-670-5895, E-mail: klyle@hsutx.edu. *Application contact:* Dr. Nancy Kucinski, Dean of Graduate Studies, 325-670-1298, Fax: 325-670-1564, E-mail: gradoff@hsutx.edu. Website: http://www.logsdonseminary.org/index.php/academics/mdiv

**Hartford Seminary,** Graduate Programs, Hartford, CT 06105-2279. Offers Islamic studies (MA); ministry (D Min); religious studies (MA); spirituality (Certificate). *Accreditation:* ATS (one or more programs are accredited). *Program availability:* Part-time, evening/weekend, online learning. *Degree requirements:* For master's, thesis optional, oral exam; for doctorate, thesis/dissertation, oral exam. *Entrance requirements:* For doctorate, experience in ministry, M Div. Additional exam requirements/recommendations for international students: Required—TOEFL (minimum score 550 paper-based; 80 iBT). *Faculty research:* Liturgy and social justice, professional leadership in ministry, congregational studies, Christian-Muslim relations, American religion.

**Harvard University,** Harvard Divinity School, Cambridge, MA 02138. Offers M Div, MTS, Th M. *Accreditation:* ACIPE; ATS. *Degree requirements:* For master's, one foreign language, thesis (for some programs). *Entrance requirements:* For master's, GRE General Test. Additional exam requirements/recommendations for international students: Required—TOEFL. Electronic applications accepted. *Expenses:* Contact institution. *Faculty research:* Theology, women's studies, history, comparative religion, ministry studies.

**Hebrew College,** Rabbinical School, Newton Centre, MA 02459. Offers MA. *Entrance requirements:* For master's, interview. Additional exam requirements/recommendations for international students: Required—TOEFL.

**Hebrew Union College–Jewish Institute of Religion,** Rabbinical School, New York, NY 10012-1186. Offers MAHL. *Degree requirements:* For master's, one foreign language. *Entrance requirements:* For master's, GRE, language exam, minimum GPA of 3.0, minimum 2 years of college-level Hebrew. Additional exam requirements/recommendations for international students: Required—TOEFL. *Faculty research:* Philosophy and theology, Bible, Hebrew, pastoral care, history and Rabbinics.

**Hebrew Union College–Jewish Institute of Religion,** School of Graduate Studies, Program in Pastoral Counseling, New York, NY 10012-1186. Offers D Min. *Accreditation:* ACIPE. *Degree requirements:* For doctorate, thesis/dissertation. *Entrance requirements:* For doctorate, M Div (or higher), ordination/certification for ministry. Additional exam requirements/recommendations for international students: Required—TOEFL. *Expenses:* Contact institution. *Faculty research:* Philosophy and theology, Bible, Hebrew, pastoral care, history and Rabbinics.

**Heritage College and Seminary,** Graduate and Professional Programs, Cambridge, ON N3C 3T2, Canada. Offers general (M Div); intercultural studies (M Div); pastoral (M Div); research (M Div); theological studies (MTS, CTS). *Faculty:* 1 full-time (0 women), 5 part-time/adjunct (1 woman). *Students:* 22 full-time (1 woman), 106 part-time (30 women). *Expenses: Tuition:* Full-time $4800 Canadian dollars; part-time $320 Canadian dollars per credit hour. *Required fees:* $110 Canadian dollars; $65 Canadian dollars per term. One-time fee: $50 Canadian dollars. Tuition and fees vary according to course load and program. *Unit head:* Head, 519-651-2869. *Application contact:* Theresa Beach, Registrar/Director of Admissions, 800-465-1961.

**Holy Apostles College and Seminary,** Department of Theology, Cromwell, CT 06416-2005. Offers bioethics (MA, Certificate, Post Master's Certificate); church history (MA, Certificate, Post Master's Certificate); dogmatic theology (MA, Certificate, Post Master's Certificate); liturgical music (MA, Certificate, Post Master's Certificate); liturgy (MA, Certificate, Post Master's Certificate); moral theology (MA, Certificate, Post Master's Certificate); philosophical theology (MA, Certificate, Post Master's Certificate); religious education (MA, Certificate, Post Master's Certificate); sacred scripture (MA, Post Master's Certificate); sacred scriptures (Certificate); theology (M Div). *Program availability:* Part-time, evening/weekend, online learning. *Degree requirements:* For master's, one foreign language, comprehensive exam, thesis optional; for other advanced degree, culminating exam. *Entrance requirements:* For master's, minimum undergraduate GPA 3.0; for other advanced degree, minimum graduate GPA of 3.0. Electronic applications accepted. *Faculty research:* Roman Catholic theology, philosophy.

**Holy Cross Greek Orthodox School of Theology,** Theological Programs, Brookline, MA 02445-7496. Offers M Div, MTS, Th M. *Accreditation:* ATS. *Program availability:* Part-time. *Degree requirements:* For master's, 2 foreign languages, thesis (for some programs). *Entrance requirements:* For master's, GRE General Test, interview, official transcripts, letters of recommendation, health report and immunization verification. Additional exam requirements/recommendations for international students: Required—TOEFL (minimum score 550 paper-based; 80 iBT). *Application deadline:* For fall admission, 6/1 for domestic students; for spring admission, 11/1 for domestic students. Applications are processed on a rolling basis. Application fee: $50. *Financial support:* Research assistantships, teaching assistantships, Federal Work-Study, scholarships/grants, and tuition waivers (partial) available. Financial award application deadline: 4/1; financial award applicants required to submit FAFSA. *Faculty research:* Spirituality, liturgies, ecumenism, church history. *Unit head:* James C. Skedros, Dean, 617-850-1254, Fax: 617-850-1460. *Application contact:* Fr. Gregory Floor, Director of Admissions, 617-850-1285, Fax: 617-850-1460, E-mail: gfloor@hchc.edu.

**Hood Theological Seminary,** Graduate and Professional Programs, Salisbury, NC 28144. Offers M Div, MTS, D Min. *Accreditation:* ATS. *Program availability:* Part-time, evening/weekend, online learning. *Degree requirements:* For master's, thesis optional; for doctorate, thesis/dissertation. *Application deadline:* For fall admission, 7/15 for domestic students; for spring admission, 11/30 for domestic students. Application fee: $30. *Expenses: Tuition:* Part-time $500 per credit hour. Part-time tuition and fees vary according to degree level. *Financial support:* Federal Work-Study, scholarships/grants, and resident assistantships available. Financial award application deadline: 7/1; financial award applicants required to submit FAFSA. *Faculty research:* Old Testament human sexuality, preaching and the vulnerable, socio-historical issues, Pauline studies, multiculturalism/African-American studies. *Unit head:* Vergel L. Lattimore, President, 704-636-6823, Fax: 704-636-7699, E-mail: president@hoodseminary.edu. *Application contact:* Reginald Boyd, Jr., Director of Recruitment and Admissions, 704-636-6455, Fax: 704-636-7685, E-mail: admissions@hoodseminary.edu.

**Houston Baptist University,** School of Christian Thought, Program in Apologetics, Houston, TX 77074-3298. Offers cultural apologetics (MA); philosophical apologetics (MA). *Program availability:* Online learning. *Students:* 7 full-time (3 women), 60 part-time (27 women); includes 10 minority (2 Black or African American, non-Hispanic/Latino; 2 Asian, non-Hispanic/Latino; 4 Hispanic/Latino; 2 Two or more races, non-Hispanic/Latino), 2 international. Average age 40. 54 applicants, 72% accepted, 21 enrolled. In 2016, 2 master's awarded. *Entrance requirements:* For master's, bachelor's degree conferred transcript, essay/personal statement, resume. Additional exam requirements/recommendations for international students: Required—TOEFL (minimum score 80 iBT), IELTS (minimum score 6.5). *Application deadline:* For fall admission, 8/1 for domestic students, 6/1 for international students; for spring admission, 1/1 for domestic students, 11/1 for international students; for summer admission, 5/1 for domestic students, 3/1 for international students. Applications are processed on a rolling basis. Application fee: $0 ($100 for international students). Electronic applications accepted. Application fee is waived when completed online. *Expenses:* $1,500 per 3-hour course; $1,275 annual general fee; $1,060 annual technology fee. *Financial support:* Federal Work-Study and scholarships/grants available. Financial award application deadline: 4/1. *Unit head:* Dr. Philip Tallon, Director, 281-649-3403, E-mail: ptallon@hbu.edu. *Application contact:* Celeste Risteski, Administrative Assistant to the Dean, 281-649-3383, Fax: 281-649-3012, E-mail: cristeski@hbu.edu.

**Houston Baptist University,** School of Christian Thought, Program in Divinity, Houston, TX 77074-3298. Offers Biblical languages (M Div); English languages (M Div). *Students:* 3 full-time (1 woman), 14 part-time (5 women); includes 5 minority (4 Black or African American, non-Hispanic/Latino; 1 Hispanic/Latino). Average age 37. 30 applicants, 77% accepted, 17 enrolled. *Entrance requirements:* For master's, bachelor's degree conferred transcript, resume, essay/personal statement. Additional exam requirements/recommendations for international students: Required—TOEFL (minimum

score 80 iBT), IELTS (minimum score 6.5). *Application deadline:* For fall admission, 8/1 for domestic students, 6/1 for international students; for spring admission, 1/1 for domestic students, 11/1 for international students; for summer admission, 5/1 for domestic students, 3/1 for international students. Applications are processed on a rolling basis. Application fee: $0 ($100 for international students). Electronic applications accepted. Application fee is waived when completed online. *Expenses:* $1,500 per 3-hour course; $1,275 annual general fee; $1,060 annual technology fee. *Financial support:* Federal Work-Study and scholarships/grants available. Financial award application deadline: 4/1; financial award applicants required to submit FAFSA. *Unit head:* Dr. Jeffrey Green, Interim Dean, Fax: 281-649-3012, E-mail: jgreen@hbu.edu. *Application contact:* Celeste Risteski, Administrative Assistant to the Dean, 281-649-3383, Fax: 281-649-3012, E-mail: cristeski@hbu.edu.

**Houston Baptist University,** School of Christian Thought, Program in Theological Studies, Houston, TX 77074-3298. Offers MA. *Program availability:* Part-time, evening/weekend. *Students:* 8 full-time (1 woman), 39 part-time (14 women); includes 24 minority (14 Black or African American, non-Hispanic/Latino; 6 Asian, non-Hispanic/Latino; 2 Hispanic/Latino; 2 Two or more races, non-Hispanic/Latino), 1 international. Average age 35. 40 applicants, 58% accepted, 14 enrolled. In 2016, 10 master's awarded. *Degree requirements:* For master's, thesis optional. *Entrance requirements:* For master's, bachelor's degree conferred transcript, resume, essay/personal statement. Additional exam requirements/recommendations for international students: Required—TOEFL (minimum score 80 iBT), IELTS (minimum score 6.5). *Application deadline:* For fall admission, 8/1 for domestic students, 6/1 for international students; for spring admission, 1/1 for domestic students, 11/1 for international students; for summer admission, 5/1 for domestic students, 3/1 for international students. Applications are processed on a rolling basis. Application fee: $0 ($100 for international students). Electronic applications accepted. Application fee is waived when completed online. *Expenses:* $1,500 per 3-hour course; $1,275 annual general fee; $1,060 annual technology fee. *Financial support:* Federal Work-Study and scholarships/grants available. Financial award application deadline: 4/1; financial award applicants required to submit FAFSA. *Unit head:* Dr. Jeffrey Green, Interim Dean, Fax: 281-649-3012, E-mail: jgreen@hbu.edu. *Application contact:* Celeste Risteski, Administrative Assistant to the Dean, 281-649-3383, Fax: 281-649-3012, E-mail: cristeski@hbu.edu.

**Houston Graduate School of Theology,** Graduate Programs, Houston, TX 77092. Offers counseling (MA); pastoral ministry (M Div, D Min); theology (MA). *Accreditation:* ATS (one or more programs are accredited). *Program availability:* Part-time, evening/weekend. *Degree requirements:* For master's, thesis (for some programs); for doctorate, thesis/dissertation. *Entrance requirements:* For doctorate, GRE General Test or MAT, M Div or equivalent. Additional exam requirements/recommendations for international students: Required—TOEFL (minimum score 550 paper-based). *Faculty research:* Hermeneutics, spirituality, religion of Eastern Europe.

**Howard Payne University,** Program in Theology and Ministry, Brownwood, TX 76801-2715. Offers MA. *Program availability:* Part-time. *Faculty:* 3 full-time (0 women), 2 part-time/adjunct (0 women). *Students:* 4 full-time (1 woman), 9 part-time (0 women); includes 1 minority (Hispanic/Latino). Average age 30. 9 applicants, 89% accepted, 5 enrolled. In 2016, 3 master's awarded. *Degree requirements:* For master's, three 2-hour internships/mentorships. *Entrance requirements:* For master's, undergraduate degree from accredited university; leveling courses (for students without undergraduate coursework in Old Testament, New Testament, and theology). Additional exam requirements/recommendations for international students: Required—TOEFL (minimum score 79 iBT). *Application deadline:* For fall admission, 7/1 for domestic students; for spring admission, 12/1 for domestic students. Applications are processed on a rolling basis. Application fee: $0. Electronic applications accepted. *Financial support:* Applicants required to submit FAFSA. *Unit head:* Dr. Gary Gramling, Director of Graduate Programs/Professor of Christian Studies, 325-649-8404, E-mail: ggramling@hputx.edu. *Application contact:* Kristian Simpson, Administrative Assistant for Christian Studies Graduate Programs, 325-649-8039, E-mail: ksimpson@hputx.edu. Website: http://www.hputx.edu/academics/schools/school-of-christian-studies/graduate-programs/ma-theology-and-ministry/

**Howard University,** School of Divinity, Washington, DC 20017. Offers M Div, MARS, D Min. *Accreditation:* ACIPE; ATS. *Program availability:* Part-time, evening/weekend. *Degree requirements:* For master's, thesis; for doctorate, thesis/dissertation. *Entrance requirements:* For master's and doctorate, minimum GPA of 3.0. Electronic applications accepted. *Faculty research:* African-American religious experience, women in ministry, ecumenics, biblical studies.

**Iliff School of Theology,** Graduate and Professional Programs, Denver, CO 80210-4798. Offers biblical studies (MA); church history (MA); religion (MA); religion and social change (MA); specialized ministry (MASM), including justice and peace, pastoral theology and care, religions leadership; theology (M Div, MTS, D Min, PhD), including Biblical studies (PhD), religion and psychological studies (PhD), religion and social change (PhD), theology, philosophy and culture (PhD); theology/ethics (MA). PhD offered jointly with University of Denver. *Accreditation:* ACIPE; ATS. *Program availability:* Part-time, evening/weekend. *Degree requirements:* For master's, one foreign language, thesis (for some programs); for doctorate, 2 foreign languages, comprehensive exam, thesis/dissertation. *Entrance requirements:* For master's, minimum GPA of 3.0, writing sample, references; for doctorate, GRE General Test, minimum GPA of 3.0, writing sample, letters of recommendation. Additional exam requirements/recommendations for international students: Required—TOEFL (minimum score 550 paper-based). Electronic applications accepted. *Faculty research:* Pastoral care, history, church music, contemporary church, biblical studies.

**Indiana Wesleyan University,** Graduate School, Wesley Seminary, Master of Divinity Program, Marion, IN 46953-4974. Offers M Div. *Accreditation:* ATS. *Program availability:* Online learning.

**Institute for Christian Studies,** Graduate Programs, Toronto, ON M5T 1R4, Canada. Offers education (M Phil F, PhD); history of philosophy (M Phil F, PhD); philosophical aesthetics (M Phil F, PhD); philosophy of religion (M Phil F, PhD); political theory (M Phil F, PhD); systematic philosophy (M Phil F, PhD); theology (M Phil F, PhD); worldview studies (MWS). *Program availability:* Part-time, online learning. *Degree requirements:* For master's, one foreign language, thesis; for doctorate, 2 foreign languages, thesis/dissertation. *Entrance requirements:* For master's and doctorate, philosophy background. Additional exam requirements/recommendations for international students: Required—TOEFL (minimum score 600 paper-based). *Faculty research:* Human rights, anthropology of self, medieval discourse, gender and body, post-modern thought; biblical hermeneutics, creational aesthetics, ecumenism, epistemology, political theory and public policy, relational psychotherapy.

**Inter American University of Puerto Rico, Metropolitan Campus,** Graduate Programs, Program in Theological Studies, San Juan, PR 00919-1293. Offers PhD. *Accreditation:* ATS.

**Interdenominational Theological Center,** Graduate and Professional Programs, Atlanta, GA 30314-4112. Offers Christian education (MACE); ministry (D Min); pastoral counseling (Th D); theology (M Div); M Div/MACE. D Min and Th D programs offered in collaboration with the Atlanta Theological Association. *Accreditation:* ACIPE; ATS (one or more programs are accredited). *Program availability:* Part-time, evening/weekend, blended/hybrid learning. *Faculty:* 15 full-time (6 women), 12 part-time/adjunct (5 women). *Students:* 119 full-time (45 women), 137 part-time (60 women); includes 249 minority (248 Black or African American, non-Hispanic/Latino; 1 Two or more races, non-Hispanic/Latino), 2 international. *Degree requirements:* For doctorate, thesis/dissertation. *Entrance requirements:* For doctorate, master's degree. *Application deadline:* For fall admission, 7/1 for domestic and international students; for spring admission, 10/1 for domestic and international students. Applications are processed on a rolling basis. Application fee: $50. Electronic applications accepted. *Expenses: Tuition:* Full-time $13,000; part-time $9324 per credit. *Required fees:* $938; $938 per credit. Full-time tuition and fees vary according to course load. *Financial support:* Research assistantships, career-related internships or fieldwork, and Federal Work-Study available. Support available to part-time students. Financial award application deadline: 6/15; financial award applicants required to submit FAFSA. *Unit head:* Edward Lorenza Wheeler, President, 404-527-7702, Fax: 404-527-7770. *Application contact:* Michelle Davis, Office of Admission and Recruitment, 404-527-7793, E-mail: lmdavis@itc.edu. Website: http://www.itc.edu/academics/degreeprograms/

**International Baptist College and Seminary,** Program in Biblical Studies, Chandler, AZ 85286. Offers MA.

**The Jewish Theological Seminary,** The Graduate School, New York, NY 10027-4649. Offers ancient Judaism (MA, DHL, PhD); Bible and ancient Semitic languages (MA, DHL, PhD); interdepartmental studies (MA); Jewish art and visual culture (MA); Jewish gender and women's studies (MA); Jewish history (MA, DHL, PhD); Jewish literature (MA, DHL, PhD); Jewish philosophy (DHL); Jewish thought (MA, PhD); liturgy (MA, DHL, PhD); medieval Jewish studies (MA, DHL, PhD); Midrash (DHL); Midrash and scriptural interpretation (MA, PhD); modern Jewish studies (MA, DHL, PhD); Talmud and rabbinics (MA, DHL, PhD); MA/MSW. MA/MSW offered jointly with Columbia University. *Accreditation:* ACIPE. *Program availability:* Part-time. Terminal master's awarded for partial completion of doctoral program. *Degree requirements:* For master's, one foreign language, comprehensive exam (for some programs), thesis (for some programs); for doctorate, 3 foreign languages, comprehensive exam (for some programs), thesis/dissertation. *Entrance requirements:* For master's, GRE or MAT, 3 letters of recommendation, writing sample; for doctorate, GRE or MAT, 3 letters of recommendation, writing research sample. Additional exam requirements/recommendations for international students: Required—TOEFL.

**The Jewish Theological Seminary,** The Rabbinical School, New York, NY 10027-4649. Offers MA, Rabbi. *Accreditation:* ACIPE. *Degree requirements:* For master's and Rabbi, one foreign language, competency exams. *Entrance requirements:* For master's and Rabbi, GRE, interview, writing sample. Additional exam requirements/recommendations for international students: Required—TOEFL. *Expenses:* Contact institution.

**John Carroll University,** Graduate Studies, Department of Theology and Religious Studies, University Heights, OH 44118-4581. Offers MA. *Program availability:* Part-time, evening/weekend. *Degree requirements:* For master's, comprehensive exam, research essay or thesis, foreign language proficiency. *Entrance requirements:* For master's, GRE General Test or MAT, minimum GPA of 2.5. Additional exam requirements/recommendations for international students: Required—TOEFL. *Application deadline:* For fall admission, 8/30 priority date for domestic students; for spring admission, 1/11 priority date for domestic students. Applications are processed on a rolling basis. Application fee: $25 ($35 for international students). Electronic applications accepted. *Expenses: Tuition:* Full-time $10,425; part-time $695 per credit hour. One-time fee: $200 full-time. Tuition and fees vary according to course load, campus/location and program. *Financial support:* Teaching assistantships with full tuition reimbursements, scholarships/grants, tuition waivers (partial), and unspecified assistantships available. Support available to part-time students. Financial award application deadline: 3/1; financial award applicants required to submit FAFSA. *Faculty research:* Ethics, women's studies, contemporary theology, Bible studies, Latin American theology. *Unit head:* Dr. Sheila E. McGinn, Chair, 216-397-4700, Fax: 216-397-4518, E-mail: trs@jcu.edu. *Application contact:* Jennifer L. Tucker, Records Management Assistant, 216-397-1925, Fax: 216-397-1835, E-mail: jtucker@jcu.edu. Website: http://www.jcu.edu/religion/Gr_prog.htm

**John Paul the Great Catholic University,** School of Theology, Escondido, CA 92025. Offers biblical theology (MA).

**Johnson University,** Graduate and Professional Programs, Knoxville, TN 37998-1001. Offers biblical interpretation (Graduate Certificate); business administration (MBA); Christian ministries (Graduate Certificate); clinical mental health counseling (MA); educational technology (MA); intercultural studies (MA); leadership (MBA); leadership studies (PhD); New Testament (MA); nonprofit management (MBA); school counseling (MA); spiritual formation and leadership (Graduate Certificate); strategic ministry (MA); teacher education (MA). *Program availability:* Part-time, evening/weekend, 100% online, blended/hybrid learning. *Faculty:* 26 full-time (10 women), 32 part-time/adjunct (9 women). *Students:* 126 full-time (46 women), 170 part-time (65 women); includes 33 minority (13 Black or African American, non-Hispanic/Latino; 1 American Indian or Alaska Native, non-Hispanic/Latino; 4 Asian, non-Hispanic/Latino; 8 Hispanic/Latino; 7 Two or more races, non-Hispanic/Latino), 21 international. Average age 35. In 2016, 106 master's, 3 doctorates awarded. *Degree requirements:* For master's, variable foreign language requirement, comprehensive exam, thesis (for some programs), internships; for doctorate, variable foreign language requirement, comprehensive exam, thesis/dissertation, internships. *Entrance requirements:* For master's, PRAXIS (for MA in teacher education); MAT (for counseling); GRE or GMAT (for MBA), interview, 3 references, transcripts, essay, minimum GPA of 2.5 or 3.0 (depending on program); for doctorate, GRE or MAT (taken not less than 5 years prior), interview, 3 references, transcripts, essay, minimum GPA of 3.0; for Graduate Certificate, interview, 3 references, transcripts, essay, minimum GPA of 3.0. Additional exam requirements/recommendations for international students: Required—TOEFL (minimum score 527 paper-based; 71 iBT). *Application deadline:* For fall admission, 7/1 for domestic students; for spring admission, 11/1 for domestic students; for summer admission, 4/1 for domestic students. Application fee: $50. Electronic applications accepted. *Expenses:* Contact institution. *Financial support:* Scholarships/grants available. Financial award application deadline: 4/15; financial award applicants required to submit FAFSA. *Unit head:* Richard Clark, Vice President for External Relations, 865-251-2327, E-mail: rclark@johnsonu.edu. *Application contact:* Lisa Tarwater, Director of Graduate Admissions, 865-251-3400, E-mail: ltarwater@johnsonu.edu.

**John Wesley University,** Graduate Programs, High Point, NC 27265. Offers Christian leadership (D Min); organizational leadership (MBA); theological studies (MTS). *Program availability:* 100% online. *Faculty:* 1 full-time (0 women), 9 part-time/adjunct (3 women). *Students:* 21 full-time (13 women), 3 part-time (all women). *Entrance requirements:* For master's, GMAT or GRE (taken within last five years), bachelor's degree, minimum GPA of 3.0, resume, two letters of recommendation, autobiographical essay, immunizations. Application fee: $50. Electronic applications accepted. *Expenses: Tuition:* Full-time $3780; part-time $2520 per semester. *Required fees:* $365; $365 per semester. Tuition and fees vary according to degree level. *Application contact:* Rosalie

Seitz, Admissions, 336-821-2474, Fax: 336-889-2261, E-mail: admissions@johnwesley.edu.

**Kehilath Yakov Rabbinical Seminary,** Graduate Programs, Ossining, NY 10562. *Accreditation:* AARTS.

**Kenrick-Glennon Seminary,** Graduate and Professional Programs, St. Louis, MO 63119-4330. Offers M Div, MA. *Accreditation:* ATS. *Degree requirements:* For master's, thesis optional.

**Kentucky Christian University,** Graduate School, Grayson, KY 41143-2205. Offers Biblical studies (MA); Christian leadership (MA). *Program availability:* Part-time. *Degree requirements:* For master's, comprehensive exam (for some programs), thesis optional. *Entrance requirements:* For master's, minimum cumulative GPA of 2.75 in major or 2.5 overall; 6 additional hours in Bible (for non-Biblical undergraduate majors). Additional exam requirements/recommendations for international students: Required—TOEFL (minimum score 550 paper-based). Electronic applications accepted.

**The King's University,** Graduate and Professional Programs, Southlake, TX 76092. Offers Biblical studies (Graduate Certificate); Christian ministry (Graduate Certificate); ministry (M Div, MPT, D Min).

**Kingswood University,** Program in Pastoral Theology, Sussex, NB E4E 5L2, Canada. Offers MA.

**Knox College,** College of Theology, Toronto, ON M5S 2E6, Canada. Offers M Div, MRE, MTS, Th M, D Min, Th D. Applicants for D Min, Th M, and Th D must apply to Toronto School of Theology; MRE, M Div, MTS, Th D, and Th M programs offered jointly with University of Toronto. *Accreditation:* ATS. *Program availability:* Part-time. *Degree requirements:* For master's, one foreign language, thesis (for some programs); for doctorate, 2 foreign languages, thesis/dissertation. *Entrance requirements:* For doctorate, M Div. Additional exam requirements/recommendations for international students: Required—TOEFL (minimum score 580 paper-based), TWE (minimum score 5). *Faculty research:* Nineteenth century theologians.

**Knox Theological Seminary,** Graduate Programs, Master of Arts Programs, Fort Lauderdale, FL 33308. Offers Biblical and theological studies (MA); Christian and classical studies (MA). *Accreditation:* ATS. *Program availability:* Part-time, evening/weekend. *Entrance requirements:* Additional exam requirements/recommendations for international students: Required—TOEFL (minimum score 520 paper-based; 83 iBT), TWE (minimum score 5).

**Knox Theological Seminary,** Graduate Programs, Program in Divinity, Fort Lauderdale, FL 33308. Offers M Div. *Accreditation:* ATS. *Program availability:* Part-time, evening/weekend, online only, blended/hybrid learning. *Entrance requirements:* Additional exam requirements/recommendations for international students: Required—TOEFL (minimum score 520 paper-based; 83 iBT), TWE (minimum score 5).

**Lakeland University,** Graduate Studies Division, Program in Theology, Plymouth, WI 53073. Offers MAT.

**Lancaster Bible College,** Capital Bible Seminary, Lancaster, PA 17601. Offers biblical studies (MA, Certificate); Christian counseling and discipleship (MA, Certificate); ministry (MA); theology (M Div). *Program availability:* Part-time, evening/weekend. *Degree requirements:* For master's, 2 foreign languages, comprehensive exam, thesis (for some programs). *Entrance requirements:* For master's, GRE General Test, Greek exam for those with 2 years of Greek, proficiency exam in theology, previous course work in Biblical studies. Additional exam requirements/recommendations for international students: Required—TOEFL (minimum score 550 paper-based). *Faculty research:* Dead Sea Scrolls, spiritual gifts, hermeneutics.

**Lancaster Bible College,** Graduate School, Lancaster, PA 17601-5036. Offers adult ministries (MA); Bible (MA); children and family ministry (MA); church planting (MA); consulting resource teacher (M Ed); elementary school counseling (M Ed); leadership (PhD); leadership studies (MA); marriage and family counseling (MA); mental health counseling (MA); pastoral studies (MA); secondary school counseling (M Ed); sports ministry (MA); student ministry (MA); town and country ministry (MA). *Program availability:* Part-time, evening/weekend. *Degree requirements:* For master's, comprehensive exam (for some programs), thesis (for some programs). *Entrance requirements:* For master's, bachelor's degree with a minimum of 30 credits of course work in Bible, minimum undergraduate GPA of 3.0, interview. Additional exam requirements/recommendations for international students: Required—TOEFL.

**Lancaster Theological Seminary,** Graduate and Professional Programs, Lancaster, PA 17603-2812. Offers biblical studies (MAR); Christian education (MAR); Christianity and the arts (MAR); church history (MAR); congregational life (MAR); lay leadership (Certificate); theological studies (M Div); theology (D Min); theology and ethics (MAR). *Accreditation:* ACIPE; ATS. *Degree requirements:* For doctorate, thesis/dissertation.

**Lee University,** Programs in Religion, Cleveland, TN 37320-3450. Offers biblical studies (MA); ministry studies/leadership (MA); ministry studies/worship (MA); ministry studies/youth and family (MA); theological studies (MA), including ethics, religion. *Program availability:* Part-time, 100% online. *Faculty:* 13 full-time (2 women), 2 part-time/adjunct (0 women). *Students:* 57 full-time (19 women), 92 part-time (28 women); includes 72 minority (16 Black or African American, non-Hispanic/Latino; 2 Asian, non-Hispanic/Latino; 53 Hispanic/Latino; 1 Two or more races, non-Hispanic/Latino), 4 international. Average age 37. 19 applicants, 79% accepted, 12 enrolled. In 2016, 9 master's awarded. *Degree requirements:* For master's, variable foreign language requirement, comprehensive exam (for some programs), thesis (for some programs). *Entrance requirements:* For master's, GRE or MAT (for biblical/theological studies only), minimum GPA of 3.0, 3 letters of recommendation, interview, official transcripts, essay. Additional exam requirements/recommendations for international students: Required—TOEFL (minimum score 61 iBT). *Application deadline:* For fall admission, 4/1 priority date for domestic and international students; for spring admission, 10/1 priority date for domestic and international students. Applications are processed on a rolling basis. Application fee: $25. Electronic applications accepted. *Expenses:* Contact institution. *Financial support:* In 2016–17, 25 students received support, including 7 teaching assistantships (averaging $2,031 per year); career-related internships or fieldwork, Federal Work-Study, institutionally sponsored loans, scholarships/grants, and unspecified assistantships also available. Financial award application deadline: 3/1; financial award applicants required to submit FAFSA. *Faculty research:* Spiritual and discipleship formation, leadership, Biblical studies, theological studies, ethics. *Unit head:* Dr. Lisa Long, Director, 423-303-5100, E-mail: llong@leeuniversity.edu. *Application contact:* E-mail: llong@leeuniversity.edu. Website: http://www.leeuniversity.edu/academics/graduate/

**Lenoir-Rhyne University,** Graduate Programs, Lutheran Theological Southern Seminary, Hickory, NC 28601. Offers M Div, MACM, MAR, STM. *Accreditation:* ACIPE. *Program availability:* Part-time. *Degree requirements:* For master's, comprehensive exam (for some programs), thesis (for some programs). *Entrance requirements:* Additional exam requirements/recommendations for international students: Recommended—TOEFL. *Expenses:* Contact institution. *Faculty research:* Theology in the twenty-first century, Biblical interpretation.

**Lexington Theological Seminary,** Graduate and Professional Programs, Lexington, KY 40508-3218. Offers M Div, MA, MAPS, D Min, M Div/MSW. M Div/MSW offered jointly with University of Kentucky. *Accreditation:* ACIPE; ATS. *Program availability:* Part-time, evening/weekend. *Degree requirements:* For master's, thesis; for doctorate, thesis/dissertation. *Entrance requirements:* Additional exam requirements/recommendations for international students: Required—TOEFL (minimum score 600 paper-based). *Faculty research:* History of biblical interpretation, biblical apocalyptic, psalms, history of Stone-Campbell traditions.

**Liberty University,** School of Divinity, Lynchburg, VA 24515. Offers Biblical studies (M Div); church history (MAR, Th M); discipleship and church ministry (M Div, MAR, MCM); evangelism and church planting (M Div, MAR, MCM); global studies (M Div, MCM, MGS); homiletics (M Div, MAR, Th M, D Min); leadership (M Div, D Min); marketplace chaplaincy (M Div, MCM); ministry (D Min); pastoral counseling (M Div, MA, MAR, D Min), including addictions and recovery (MA), crisis response and trauma (MA), discipleship and church ministries (MA), leadership (MA), life coaching (MA), marketplace chaplaincy (MA), marriage and family (MA), military resilience (MA), pastoral counseling (MA); pastoral ministries (M Div, MCM); religious education (MRE); theology (M Div, MAR, MTS); theology and apologetics (PhD); worship (M Div, MAR, MCM, D Min). *Program availability:* Part-time, online learning. *Students:* 2,140 full-time (615 women), 3,020 part-time (906 women); includes 1,312 minority (1,016 Black or African American, non-Hispanic/Latino; 9 American Indian or Alaska Native, non-Hispanic/Latino; 100 Asian, non-Hispanic/Latino; 90 Hispanic/Latino; 7 Native Hawaiian or other Pacific Islander, non-Hispanic/Latino; 90 Two or more races, non-Hispanic/Latino; 158 international. Average age 42. 3,651 applicants, 37% accepted, 909 enrolled. In 2016, 1,551 master's, 39 doctorates, 168 other advanced degrees awarded. *Degree requirements:* For master's, 2 foreign languages, thesis (for some programs); for doctorate, 2 foreign languages, thesis/dissertation. *Entrance requirements:* For master's, minimum undergraduate GPA of 2.0; for doctorate, GRE General Test or MAT, minimum graduate GPA of 3.0. Additional exam requirements/recommendations for international students: Required—TOEFL (minimum score 600 paper-based; 100 iBT). *Application deadline:* For fall admission, 6/1 for domestic students; for spring admission, 11/1 for domestic students. Applications are processed on a rolling basis. Application fee: $50. Electronic applications accepted. *Expenses:* Contact institution. *Financial support:* Teaching assistantships with tuition reimbursements, career-related internships or fieldwork, and Federal Work-Study available. Financial award applicants required to submit FAFSA. *Unit head:* Dr. Ed Hindson, Dean, 434-592-4140, Fax: 434-522-0415, E-mail: ehindson@liberty.edu. *Application contact:* Jay Bridge, Director of Graduate Admissions, 800-424-9595, Fax: 800-628-7977, E-mail: gradadmissions@liberty.edu.
Website: https://www.liberty.edu/divinity/

**Lincoln Christian Seminary,** Graduate and Professional Programs, Lincoln, IL 62656-2167. Offers Bible and theology (MA); Christian ministries (MA); counseling (MA); divinity (M Div); leadership ministry (D Min); religious education (MRE). *Accreditation:* ACIPE; ATS. *Program availability:* Part-time. *Degree requirements:* For master's, 2 foreign languages, thesis; for doctorate, thesis/dissertation. *Entrance requirements:* For master's, minimum GPA of 2.5; for doctorate, M Div or equivalent. Additional exam requirements/recommendations for international students: Required—TOEFL (minimum score 550 paper-based). Electronic applications accepted.

**Lincoln Christian University,** Graduate Programs, Lincoln, IL 62656-2167. Offers Biblical studies (MA); church history/historical theology (MA); intercultural studies (MA); ministry (MA); organizational leadership (MA); philosophy and apologetics (MA); spiritual formation (MA); theology (MA). MA in spiritual formation offered in Normal, IL. *Program availability:* Online learning. *Faculty:* 22 full-time (6 women), 27 part-time/adjunct (9 women). *Students:* 89 full-time (45 women), 225 part-time (91 women). Average age 39. *Entrance requirements:* For master's, minimum cumulative GPA of 2.5 in undergraduate degree studies. Additional exam requirements/recommendations for international students: Required—TOEFL (minimum score 550 paper-based); Recommended—IELTS (minimum score 6). *Application deadline:* For fall admission, 8/1 for domestic students, 3/1 for international students; for spring admission, 11/15 for domestic students, 11/1 for international students. Application fee: $25 ($50 for international students). Application fee is waived when completed online. *Expenses: Tuition:* Full-time $7812; part-time $5208 per credit hour. *Required fees:* $1000; $1000 per credit hour. One-time fee: $150. Full-time tuition and fees vary according to campus/location and program. *Financial support:* Applicants required to submit FAFSA. *Application contact:* Lindsey Clark, Associate Director of Graduate and Seminary Enrollment, 217-732-3168 Ext. 2398, E-mail: lclark@lincolnchristian.edu.
Website: https://lincolnchristian.edu/academics/programs/masters/

**Lipscomb University,** Hazelip School of Theology, Nashville, TN 37204-3951. Offers Christian practice (MA); missional and spiritual formation (D Min); student ministry (Certificate); theology (M Div). *Program availability:* Part-time, evening/weekend, online learning. *Faculty:* 13 full-time (0 women), 4 part-time/adjunct (1 woman). *Students:* 52 full-time (12 women), 90 part-time (18 women); includes 17 minority (13 Black or African American, non-Hispanic/Latino; 2 Hispanic/Latino; 2 Two or more races, non-Hispanic/Latino), 4 international. Average age 38. In 2016, 16 master's, 8 doctorates awarded. *Degree requirements:* For master's, 2 foreign languages, comprehensive exam (for some programs), thesis optional; for doctorate, comprehensive exam, thesis/dissertation. *Entrance requirements:* For master's, 3 references, transcripts, goals statement; for doctorate, 3 references, transcripts, documentation of full-time participation in ministry, writing sample, interview. Additional exam requirements/recommendations for international students: Required—TOEFL (minimum score 570 paper-based; 80 iBT). *Application deadline:* For fall admission, 8/1 priority date for domestic students; for spring admission, 12/15 for domestic students. Applications are processed on a rolling basis. Application fee: $50 ($75 for international students). Electronic applications accepted. *Expenses:* $898 per hour (for master's programs), $333 per hour (for D Min). *Financial support:* Scholarships/grants and unspecified assistantships available. Financial award application deadline: 3/1; financial award applicants required to submit FAFSA. *Faculty research:* Status of Churches of Christ in foreign nations, Hebrew grammar, marriage and family. *Unit head:* Frank Guertin, Director, 615-966-5709, Fax: 615-966-5352, E-mail: frank.guertin@lipscomb.edu. *Application contact:* Kellye McCool, Coordinator of Student Services, 615-966-5458, Fax: 615-966-6052, E-mail: kellye.mccool@lipscomb.edu.
Website: http://www.lipscomb.edu/hst

**Logos Evangelical Seminary,** Graduate Programs, El Monte, CA 91731. Offers M Div, MA, Th M, D Min, PhD, Diploma. *Accreditation:* ATS (one or more programs are accredited). *Program availability:* Part-time, 100% online. *Faculty:* 13 full-time (4 women), 11 part-time/adjunct (3 women). *Students:* 78 full-time (31 women), 107 part-time (57 women); includes 111 minority (all Asian, non-Hispanic/Latino), 74 international. Average age 48. 58 applicants, 95% accepted, 47 enrolled. In 2016, 26 master's, 16 doctorates, 3 other advanced degrees awarded. Terminal master's awarded for partial completion of doctoral program. *Degree requirements:* For master's, variable foreign language requirement, comprehensive exam (for some programs), thesis (for some programs); for doctorate, variable foreign language requirement, comprehensive exam (for some programs), thesis/dissertation. *Entrance requirements:* For master's, Biblical Language proficiency exam (for Th M), MA in Biblical studies with minimum GPA of 3.33, 1.5 years of Biblical language studies, 2 recommendations, and

1 research paper (for Th M); for doctorate, Biblical Language proficiency exam and research language exam (for PhD), M Div or its equivalent with minimum GPA of 3.0, at least three years of experience in full-time ministry after receiving M Div, and recommendations by two church leaders (for D Min). Additional exam requirements/recommendations for international students: Required—TOEFL (minimum score 470 paper-based; 52 iBT); Recommended—IELTS. *Application deadline:* For fall admission, 6/15 for domestic students, 5/15 for international students; for spring admission, 12/15 for domestic students, 10/15 for international students. Applications are processed on a rolling basis. Application fee: $75. Electronic applications accepted. *Expenses: Tuition:* Full-time $8624; part-time $308 per unit. *Required fees:* $50 per term. Tuition and fees vary according to degree level. *Faculty research:* Biblical hermeneutics, historical theology, Biblical studies, parenting of teens and young adults, marriage and family. *Unit head:* Rev. Ekron Chen, PhD, Academic Dean, 626-571-5110 Ext. 120, Fax: 626-571-5119, E-mail: ekron@les.edu. *Application contact:* Becky Perng, Admission Specialist, 626-571-5110 Ext. 112, Fax: 626-571-5119, E-mail: admission@les.edu.
Website: https://www.les.edu/language/en/

**Loras College,** Graduate Division, Program in Theology and Ministry, Dubuque, IA 52004-0178. Offers ministry (MA); theology (MA). *Program availability:* Part-time, evening/weekend. *Degree requirements:* For master's, comprehensive exam (for some programs), thesis (for some programs). *Entrance requirements:* For master's, bachelor's degree or undergraduate minor in religious studies or equivalent, minimum undergraduate GPA of 2.75.

**Louisiana College,** Caskey School of Divinity, Pineville, LA 71359-0001. Offers biblical and theological studies (MA); pastoral ministry (MA).

**Louisville Presbyterian Theological Seminary,** Graduate and Professional Programs, Louisville, KY 40205-1798. Offers Bible (MAR); divinity (M Div); ministry (D Min); religious thought (MAR); JD/M Div; M Div/MBA; M Div/MSSW. JD/M Div, M Div/MBA, and M Div/MSSW offered jointly with University of Louisville. *Accreditation:* AAMFT/COAMFTE (one or more programs are accredited); ACIPE; ATS (one or more programs are accredited). *Program availability:* Part-time. *Faculty:* 18 full-time (9 women), 8 part-time/adjunct (5 women). *Students:* 99 full-time (54 women), 53 part-time (34 women); includes 42 minority (31 Black or African American, non-Hispanic/Latino; 3 Asian, non-Hispanic/Latino; 6 Hispanic/Latino; 2 Two or more races, non-Hispanic/Latino), 2 international. Average age 40. In 2016, 27 master's, 17 doctorates awarded. *Degree requirements:* For master's, 2 foreign languages, thesis (for some programs); for doctorate, thesis/dissertation. *Entrance requirements:* For doctorate, M Div. Additional exam requirements/recommendations for international students: Required—TOEFL (minimum score 550 paper-based). *Application deadline:* For fall admission, 6/1 priority date for domestic students, 2/1 priority date for international students; for spring admission, 11/1 priority date for domestic students. Applications are processed on a rolling basis. Application fee: $50. Electronic applications accepted. *Expenses: Tuition:* Full-time $11,400; part-time $380 per credit hour. *Required fees:* $286; $286 per credit hour. $143 per semester. *Financial support:* Career-related internships or fieldwork, Federal Work-Study, institutionally sponsored loans, and scholarships/grants available. Financial award application deadline: 2/1. *Unit head:* Dr. Susan R. Garrett, Dean, 502-895-3411, Fax: 502-895-1096, E-mail: sgarrett@lpts.edu. *Application contact:* Rev. Emily Miller, Director of Admissions, 502-895-3411, Fax: 502-895-1096, E-mail: emiller@lpts.edu.
Website: http://www.lpts.edu/

**Lourdes University,** Graduate School, Sylvania, OH 43560-2898. Offers business (MBA); leadership (M Ed); nurse anesthesia (MSN); nurse educator (MSN); nurse leader (MSN); organizational leadership (MOL); reading (M Ed); teaching and curriculum (M Ed); theology (MA). *Program availability:* Evening/weekend. *Entrance requirements:* Additional exam requirements/recommendations for international students: Required—TOEFL.

**Loyola Marymount University,** College of Liberal Arts, Department of Theological Studies, Program in Theology, Los Angeles, CA 90045-8400. Offers MA. *Accreditation:* ATS. *Students:* 18 full-time (11 women), 15 part-time (6 women); includes 10 minority (1 Black or African American, non-Hispanic/Latino; 3 Asian, non-Hispanic/Latino; 6 Hispanic/Latino), 7 international. Average age 45. 15 applicants, 80% accepted, 5 enrolled. In 2016, 12 master's awarded. *Degree requirements:* For master's, comprehensive exam, thesis or alternative. *Entrance requirements:* For master's, GRE or MAT (recommended), 2 letters of recommendation, personal statement. Additional exam requirements/recommendations for international students: Required—TOEFL (minimum score 600 paper-based; 100 iBT). Application fee: $50. Electronic applications accepted. *Financial support:* In 2016–17, 25 students received support, including 2 research assistantships; Federal Work-Study, scholarships/grants, and unspecified assistantships also available. Support available to part-time students. Financial award application deadline: 6/30; financial award applicants required to submit FAFSA. *Unit head:* Dr. Daniel Smith-Christopher, Graduate Director, 310-338-2875, E-mail: dchristopher@lmu.edu. *Application contact:* Chake H. Kouyoumjian, Associate Dean of Graduate Studies, 310-338-2721, E-mail: ckouyoum@lmu.edu.
Website: http://bellarmine.lmu.edu/theologicalstudies/graduateprograms/

**Loyola University Chicago,** Graduate School, Department of Theology, Chicago, IL 60660. Offers MA, PhD. *Program availability:* Part-time, evening/weekend. *Faculty:* 23 full-time (9 women). *Students:* 46 full-time (14 women), 6 part-time (3 women); includes 6 minority (2 Black or African American, non-Hispanic/Latino; 3 Hispanic/Latino; 1 Native Hawaiian or other Pacific Islander, non-Hispanic/Latino), 7 international. Average age 33. 44 applicants, 50% accepted, 10 enrolled. In 2016, 7 master's, 6 doctorates awarded. Terminal master's awarded for partial completion of doctoral program. *Degree requirements:* For master's, comprehensive exam; for doctorate, 2 foreign languages, comprehensive exam, thesis/dissertation. *Entrance requirements:* For master's, GRE General Test, minimum GPA of 3.0, 9 hours of course work in theology; for doctorate, GRE General Test, minimum GPA of 3.0, master's degree or equivalent. Additional exam requirements/recommendations for international students: Required—TOEFL, IELTS. *Application deadline:* For fall admission, 1/15 for domestic and international students; for spring admission, 12/1 for domestic and international students. Application fee: $50. Electronic applications accepted. Application fee is waived when completed online. *Expenses: Tuition:* Full-time $18,594. *Required fees:* $848. Part-time tuition and fees vary according to course load, degree level and program. *Financial support:* In 2016–17, 12 students received support, including 12 research assistantships (averaging $18,000 per year); fellowships, teaching assistantships, and institutionally sponsored loans also available. Financial award application deadline: 1/15; financial award applicants required to submit FAFSA. *Faculty research:* Systematics, historical theology, constructive theology, scripture, theological ethics. *Unit head:* Dr. Robert Di Vito, Chair, 773-508-8453, Fax: 773-508-2386, E-mail: rdivito@luc.edu. *Application contact:* Dr. Sandra Sullivan-Dunbar, Graduate Program Director, 773-508-2481, Fax: 312-915-8905, E-mail: ssull1@luc.edu.
Website: http://luc.edu/theology/

**Loyola University Chicago,** Institute of Pastoral Studies, Chicago, IL 60611. Offers Christian spirituality (MA), including spiritual direction; church management (Certificate); counseling for ministry (MA); health care ministry leadership (Certificate); health care mission leadership (MA); pastoral counseling (MA, Certificate); pastoral studies (M Div,

## Theology

MA); religious education (Certificate); social justice (MA, Certificate); spiritual direction (Certificate); M Div/MA; M Div/MSW; MSW/MA. MSW/MA offered with School of Social Work. *Accreditation:* ACIPE. *Program availability:* Part-time, evening/weekend, 100% online, blended/hybrid learning. *Faculty:* 11 full-time (4 women), 25 part-time/adjunct (11 women). *Students:* 79 full-time (58 women), 120 part-time (76 women); includes 54 minority (22 Black or African American, non-Hispanic/Latino; 1 American Indian or Alaska Native, non-Hispanic/Latino; 6 Asian, non-Hispanic/Latino; 23 Hispanic/Latino; 2 Two or more races, non-Hispanic/Latino), 23 international. Average age 42. 116 applicants, 83% accepted, 71 enrolled. In 2016, 63 master's, 4 other advanced degrees awarded. *Degree requirements:* For master's, thesis optional, project. *Entrance requirements:* Additional exam requirements/recommendations for international students: Required—TOEFL (minimum score 550 paper-based; 79 iBT), IELTS (minimum score 6.5). *Application deadline:* Applications are processed on a rolling basis. Application fee: $50. Electronic applications accepted. Application fee is waived when completed online. *Expenses:* Contact institution. *Financial support:* In 2016–17, 84 students received support. Career-related internships or fieldwork, Federal Work-Study, institutionally sponsored loans, scholarships/grants, tuition waivers (partial), and unspecified assistantships available. Support available to part-time students. Financial award application deadline: 3/1; financial award applicants required to submit FAFSA. *Faculty research:* Catholic theology, skills of religious ministry, family ministries, spirituality and divorced men. *Unit head:* Dr. Brian J. Schmisek, Dean, 312-915-7400, Fax: 312-915-7410, E-mail: bschmisek@luc.edu. *Application contact:* Dr. M. Therese Lysaught, Associate Dean, 312-915-7485, Fax: 312-915-7410, E-mail: mlysaught@luc.edu.
Website: http://www.luc.edu/ips/

**Loyola University Maryland,** Graduate Programs, Loyola College of Arts and Sciences, Department of Theology, Baltimore, MD 21210-2699. Offers MTS. *Faculty:* 65 full-time (40 women), 26 part-time/adjunct (18 women). *Students:* 5 full-time (4 women), 10 part-time (5 women); includes 5 minority (4 Black or African American, non-Hispanic/Latino; 1 Hispanic/Latino). Average age 39. 21 applicants, 62% accepted, 9 enrolled. In 2016, 7 master's awarded. *Entrance requirements:* Additional exam requirements/recommendations for international students: Required—TOEFL, IELTS. *Application deadline:* For fall admission, 5/1 for domestic students. Application fee: $60. Electronic applications accepted. *Expenses:* Contact institution. *Financial support:* In 2016–17, 5 students received support. Scholarships/grants available. Financial award application deadline: 4/15; financial award applicants required to submit FAFSA. *Unit head:* Daniel McClain, 410-617-5649.
Website: http://www.loyola.edu/academic/theology/graduate.aspx

**Loyola University New Orleans,** Loyola Institute for Ministry, New Orleans, LA 70118-6195. Offers pastoral studies (MPS); religious education (MRE); theology and ministry (Certificate). *Program availability:* Part-time, evening/weekend, online learning. *Faculty:* 3 full-time (1 woman), 4 part-time/adjunct (2 women). *Students:* 23 full-time (16 women), 119 part-time (77 women); includes 20 minority (7 Black or African American, non-Hispanic/Latino; 1 Asian, non-Hispanic/Latino; 11 Hispanic/Latino; 1 Two or more races, non-Hispanic/Latino). Average age 46. 37 applicants, 92% accepted, 25 enrolled. In 2016, 38 master's awarded. *Entrance requirements:* For master's, minimum GPA of 2.5, resume, 2 letters of recommendation, work experience, 3-page statement of purpose. Additional exam requirements/recommendations for international students: Required—TOEFL (minimum score 550 paper-based; 79 iBT). *Application deadline:* For fall admission, 8/15 for domestic and international students; for spring admission, 1/1 for domestic and international students. Applications are processed on a rolling basis. Application fee: $20. Electronic applications accepted. Application fee is waived when completed online. *Expenses:* $818 per credit hour full-time tuition, $883 fees; $409 per credit hour part-time tuition, $527 fees; $275 graduation fee. *Financial support:* Career-related internships or fieldwork, scholarships/grants, health care benefits, and tuition waivers (partial) available. Support available to part-time students. Financial award application deadline: 5/1; financial award applicants required to submit FAFSA. *Faculty research:* Practical theology, ministry education, small Christian communities, religion and ecology, Christian spirituality. *Unit head:* Dr. Tom Ryan, Director, 504-865-2069, Fax: 504-865-2066, E-mail: tfryan@loyno.edu. *Application contact:* Diane Blair, Manager of Admissions, 504-865-3728, Fax: 504-865-2066, E-mail: lim@loyno.edu.
Website: http://lim.loyno.edu/

**Lubbock Christian University,** Graduate Biblical Studies, Lubbock, TX 79407-2099. Offers Bible and ministry (MS); biblical interpretation (MA). *Program availability:* Part-time. *Degree requirements:* For master's, one foreign language, thesis (for some programs). *Entrance requirements:* For master's, GRE General Test or MAT. *Faculty research:* Commentary on John, commentary on First and Second Thessalonians, mission teams, church leadership, family systems.

**Lutheran School of Theology at Chicago,** Graduate and Professional Programs, Chicago, IL 60615-5199. Offers ministry (MAM, D Min); theological studies (MATS, PhD); theology (M Div). *Accreditation:* ACIPE; ATS (one or more programs are accredited). *Program availability:* Part-time. Terminal master's awarded for partial completion of doctoral program. *Degree requirements:* For master's, variable foreign language requirement; for doctorate, variable foreign language requirement, comprehensive exam, thesis/dissertation. *Entrance requirements:* For doctorate, GRE, M Div or equivalent, 3 years of professional experience (D Min).

**Lutheran Theological Seminary at Gettysburg,** Graduate and Professional Programs, Gettysburg, PA 17325-1795. Offers divinity (M Div); ministerial studies (MAMS); outdoor ministry (MAR); parish ministry (D Min); theology (STM). *Accreditation:* ACIPE; ATS (one or more programs are accredited). *Program availability:* Part-time, online learning. *Degree requirements:* For master's, thesis (for some programs). Electronic applications accepted.

**The Lutheran Theological Seminary at Philadelphia,** Graduate School, Philadelphia, PA 19119-1794. Offers divinity (M Div); ministry (D Min); public leadership (MA); religion (MAR); social ministry and church (Certificate); theology (STM, PhD). *Accreditation:* ACIPE. *Program availability:* Part-time, evening/weekend. *Degree requirements:* For master's, one foreign language, comprehensive exam (for some programs), thesis (for some programs); for doctorate, thesis/dissertation. *Entrance requirements:* For master's, minimum undergraduate GPA of 2.8; for doctorate, minimum GPA of 3.0. Additional exam requirements/recommendations for international students: Required—TOEFL (minimum score 550 paper-based; 89 iBT), TWE. Electronic applications accepted.

**Lutheran Theological Seminary Saskatoon,** Graduate and Professional Programs, Saskatoon, SK S7N 0X3, Canada. Offers Biblical studies (MTS); church history (MTS); ethics/church and society (MTS); history of Christianity (STM); New Testament (STM); Old Testament (STM); pastoral studies (STM); pastoral theology (MTS); systematic theology (MTS); systematic theology and philosophy of religion (STM); theology (M Div, D Div). STM programs offered jointly with College of Emmanuel and St. Chad and St. Andrew's College. *Accreditation:* ATS. *Program availability:* Part-time. *Degree requirements:* For master's, thesis.

**Luther Rice College & Seminary,** Graduate Programs, Lithonia, GA 30038-2454. Offers apologetics (MA); Bible languages (M Div); Biblical counseling (MA); Christian ministry (M Div, D Min); Christian studies (MA); leadership (MA). *Program availability:* Part-time, evening/weekend, online learning. *Degree requirements:* For doctorate, thesis/dissertation. *Entrance requirements:* For master's, bachelor's degree or equivalent; for doctorate, M Div. Additional exam requirements/recommendations for international students: Required—TOEFL (minimum score 550 paper-based). Electronic applications accepted.

**Luther Seminary,** Graduate and Professional Programs, St. Paul, MN 55108-1445. Offers aging and health (MA); Biblical preaching (D Min); children, youth and family (M Div, MA); congregational mission and leadership (M Th, MA, D Min); history of Christianity (M Th, MA); missions and world religions (M Th); New Testament (M Th, MA); Old Testament (M Th, MA); pastoral care: clinical pastoral theology (M Th); pastoral theology and ministry (M Th); systematic theology (M Th, MA). *Accreditation:* ACIPE; ATS. *Program availability:* Part-time, online learning. *Degree requirements:* For master's, thesis or alternative; for doctorate, 2 foreign languages, thesis/dissertation. *Entrance requirements:* For master's, minimum GPA of 3.0; for doctorate, GRE General Test. Additional exam requirements/recommendations for international students: Required—TOEFL, IELTS. Electronic applications accepted. *Faculty research:* Theology, psychology (pastoral care), church history, Bible.

**Machzikei Hadath Rabbinical College,** Graduate Programs, Brooklyn, NY 11204-1805. Offers First Talmudic Degree. *Accreditation:* AARTS.

**Madonna University,** Program in Religious Studies, Livonia, MI 48150-1173. Offers pastoral ministry (MA).

**Malone University,** Graduate Program in Theological Studies, Canton, OH 44709. Offers MA. *Program availability:* Part-time, evening/weekend. *Entrance requirements:* For master's, minimum GPA of 3.0. Additional exam requirements/recommendations for international students: Required—TOEFL (minimum score 550 paper-based; 79 iBT). *Expenses:* Contact institution. *Faculty research:* Sacramental nature of the Biblical canon, theological anthropology, narrative criticism of the New Testament, Old Testament prophets, rhetorical criticism of the New Testament.

**Maple Springs Baptist Bible College and Seminary,** Graduate and Professional Programs, Capitol Heights, MD 20743. Offers biblical studies (MA, Certificate); Christian counseling (MA); church administration (MA); divinity (M Div); ministry (D Min); religious education (MRE).

**Maranatha Baptist University,** Master of Divinity Program, Watertown, WI 53094. Offers M Div. *Program availability:* Part-time. *Degree requirements:* For master's, 2 foreign languages. *Entrance requirements:* Additional exam requirements/recommendations for international students: Required—TOEFL. *Application deadline:* Applications are processed on a rolling basis. Application fee: $50. *Expenses: Tuition:* Full-time $6300; part-time $3150 per credit. *Required fees:* $210; $35 per course. Tuition and fees vary according to course load and degree level. *Financial support:* Scholarships/grants and tuition waivers (full and partial) available. Support available to part-time students. *Faculty research:* Church history, counseling techniques, Bible structure, ancient language. *Unit head:* Dr. Larry Oats, Dean of Maranatha Baptist Seminary, 920-206-2324, Fax: 920-261-9109, E-mail: larry.oats@mbu.edu. *Application contact:* Dr. Jim Harrison, Director of Admissions, 920-206-2327, Fax: 920-261-9109, E-mail: admissions@mbu.edu.
Website: http://www.mbu.edu/seminary/academics/programs/master-of-divinity/

**Maranatha Baptist University,** Program in Biblical Studies, Watertown, WI 53094. Offers MA. *Program availability:* Part-time. *Degree requirements:* For master's, one foreign language. *Entrance requirements:* For master's, BA or BS. *Application deadline:* Applications are processed on a rolling basis. Application fee: $50. *Expenses: Tuition:* Full-time $6300; part-time $3150 per credit. *Required fees:* $210; $35 per course. Tuition and fees vary according to course load and degree level. *Financial support:* Scholarships/grants and tuition waivers (full and partial) available. Support available to part-time students. *Faculty research:* Bible structure, counseling techniques, church history. *Unit head:* Dr. Larry Oats, Dean of Maranatha Baptist Seminary, 920-206-2324, Fax: 920-261-9109, E-mail: larry.oats@mbu.edu. *Application contact:* Dr. Jim Harrison, Director of Admissions, 920-206-2327, Fax: 920-261-9109, E-mail: admissions@mbu.edu.
Website: http://www.mbu.edu/seminary/academics/programs/biblical-studies/

**Marquette University,** Graduate School, College of Arts and Sciences, Department of Theology, Milwaukee, WI 53201-1881. Offers MA, PhD. *Program availability:* Part-time, evening/weekend. *Faculty:* 30 full-time (10 women), 7 part-time/adjunct (0 women). *Students:* 48 full-time (9 women), 28 part-time (9 women); includes 17 minority (1 Black or African American, non-Hispanic/Latino; 10 Asian, non-Hispanic/Latino; 5 Hispanic/Latino; 1 Two or more races, non-Hispanic/Latino), 2 international. Average age 34. 74 applicants, 45% accepted, 16 enrolled. In 2016, 3 master's, 16 doctorates awarded. Terminal master's awarded for partial completion of doctoral program. *Degree requirements:* For master's, one foreign language, comprehensive exam, thesis or alternative; for doctorate, 2 foreign languages, comprehensive exam, thesis/dissertation. *Entrance requirements:* For master's, GRE General Test, official transcripts from all current and previous colleges/universities except Marquette, three letters of recommendation, short personal statement; for doctorate, GRE General Test, official transcripts from all current and previous colleges/universities except Marquette, three letters of recommendation, short personal statement, academic writing sample. Additional exam requirements/recommendations for international students: Required—TOEFL (minimum score 530 paper-based). *Application deadline:* For fall admission, 12/15 for domestic and international students. Application fee: $50. Electronic applications accepted. *Financial support:* Fellowships, teaching assistantships, scholarships/grants, health care benefits, tuition waivers (full and partial), and unspecified assistantships available. Support available to part-time students. Financial award application deadline: 2/15. *Faculty research:* Old Testament theology, New Testament theology, church history, Christian ethics. *Unit head:* Dr. Susan Wood, Chair. *Application contact:* Dr. Joshua Burns.
Website: http://www.marquette.edu/theology/graduate.shtml

**Marylhurst University,** Applied Pastoral Theology Program, Marylhurst, OR 97036-0261. Offers MA. *Program availability:* Part-time, evening/weekend. *Students:* 3 (1 woman). Average age 50. In 2016, 5 master's awarded. *Degree requirements:* For master's, thesis. *Entrance requirements:* For master's, transcripts from all universities attended, 3 letters of recommendation, resume, personal statement, autobiography, interview. Additional exam requirements/recommendations for international students: Required—TOEFL (minimum score 79 iBT), IELTS (minimum score 6.5). *Application deadline:* Applications are processed on a rolling basis. Application fee: $0. Electronic applications accepted. *Expenses:* Contact institution. *Financial support:* Scholarships/grants available. Support available to part-time students. Financial award applicants required to submit FAFSA. *Faculty research:* Pastoral care, scripture, world religions. *Unit head:* Dr. Jerry Roussell, Jr., Chair, E-mail: jroussell@marylhurst.edu. *Application contact:* Maruksa Lynch, Graduate Admissions Counselor, 800-699-6322, E-mail: admissions@marylhurst.edu.
Website: http://www.marylhurst.edu

**Marylhurst University,** Divinity Program, Marylhurst, OR 97036-0261. Offers M Div. *Program availability:* Part-time, evening/weekend. *Students:* 22 (16 women). Average

age 46. In 2016, 4 master's awarded. *Entrance requirements:* For master's, MAT (if GPA is below 3.0), official transcript from institution where degree was earned, recommendations, resume. Additional exam requirements/recommendations for international students: Required—TOEFL (minimum iBT score of 79), PTE, or IELTS (6.9). *Application deadline:* Applications are processed on a rolling basis. Application fee: $0. Electronic applications accepted. *Expenses:* Contact institution. *Financial support:* Scholarships/grants available. Support available to part-time students. Financial award applicants required to submit FAFSA. *Faculty research:* Scripture-Biblical studies, theology, history, ministry, spirituality. *Unit head:* Dr. Jerry Roussell, Jr., Chair, 503-636-8141, E-mail: jroussell@marylhurst.edu. *Application contact:* Maruska Lynch, Graduate Admissions Counselor, 503-699-6322, Fax: 503-699-6320, E-mail: admissions@marylhurst.edu.

**The Master's University,** The Master's Seminary, Santa Clarita, CA 91321-1200. Offers biblical counseling (MABC); New Testament (Th D); Old Testament (Th D); preaching (D Min); theology (M Div, M Th, Th D). *Program availability:* Part-time. *Degree requirements:* For master's, 2 foreign languages, thesis; for doctorate, 4 foreign languages, thesis/dissertation. *Entrance requirements:* For master's, minimum GPA of 2.75; for doctorate, Th M, minimum GPA of 3.5. Additional exam requirements/recommendations for international students: Required—TOEFL (minimum score 550 paper-based).

**McCormick Theological Seminary,** Graduate and Professional Programs, Chicago, IL 60615. Offers ministry (D Min); theological studies (MATS, Certificate); theology (M Div); M Div/MSW. M Div/MSW offered jointly with Loyola University Chicago, University of Chicago, and University of Illinois at Chicago. *Accreditation:* ACIPE; ATS (one or more programs are accredited). *Program availability:* Part-time, evening/weekend. *Degree requirements:* For master's, thesis (for some programs); for doctorate, thesis/dissertation. *Entrance requirements:* For master's, minimum GPA of 3.0; for doctorate, M Div, minimum 3 years in pastorate. *Faculty research:* Faith formation, families, biblical literature, Dead Sea scrolls, women in antiquity.

**McGill University,** Faculty of Graduate and Postdoctoral Studies, Faculty of Religious Studies, Montréal, QC H3A 2T5, Canada. Offers MA, STM, PhD. *Accreditation:* ATS.

**McMaster University,** McMaster Divinity College, Hamilton, ON L8S 4M2, Canada. Offers biblical studies (M Div); Biblical studies (MA, MTS, Diploma); Christian interpretation/history (M Div, MA, MTS, Diploma); Christian ministry (M Div, MA, MTS, Diploma); Christian Studies (Certificate); Christian theology (PhD). Affiliated with the Toronto School of Theology. *Program availability:* Part-time. *Degree requirements:* For master's, one foreign language, thesis optional; for doctorate, 3 foreign languages, comprehensive exam, thesis/dissertation; for other advanced degree, 2 foreign languages, thesis. *Entrance requirements:* For master's, minimum B average in undergraduate course work, 3 letters of reference; for doctorate, minimum B+ average in bachelor's and master's, appropriate modern/ancient language, interview; for other advanced degree, 6 units of related Biblical language, minimum B+ average in undergraduate course work, minimum 15 units of course work in related area of study, 3 letters of recommendation. Additional exam requirements/recommendations for international students: Required—TOEFL (minimum score 550 paper-based). *Faculty research:* Ethics, Biblical studies, language studies, church history, Christian ministry.

**Meadville Lombard Theological School,** Graduate and Professional Programs, Chicago, IL 60637-1602. Offers divinity (M Div); ministry (D Min); religion (MA); M Div/MSW. M Div/MSW offered jointly with University of Chicago. *Accreditation:* ACIPE; ATS. *Program availability:* Part-time, online learning. *Entrance requirements:* For master's, bachelor's degree; for doctorate, bachelor's and masters degrees, 3 years of ministry.

**Memphis Theological Seminary,** Graduate and Professional Programs, Memphis, TN 38104-4395. Offers M Div, MAR, D Min. *Accreditation:* ATS. *Program availability:* Part-time. *Degree requirements:* For doctorate, thesis/dissertation. *Entrance requirements:* For doctorate, M Div, 3 years in ministry.

**Mercer University,** Graduate Studies, Cecil B. Day Campus, James and Carolyn McAfee School of Theology, Atlanta, GA 30341. Offers Christian ministry (MACM); Christian spirituality (D Min); divinity (M Div); preaching (D Min); M Div/MBA; M Div/MS. *Program availability:* Part-time. *Faculty:* 14 full-time (7 women), 5 part-time/adjunct (0 women). *Students:* 106 full-time (65 women), 84 part-time (35 women); includes 100 minority (89 Black or African American, non-Hispanic/Latino; 2 American Indian or Alaska Native, non-Hispanic/Latino; 1 Asian, non-Hispanic/Latino; 5 Hispanic/Latino; 1 Native Hawaiian or other Pacific Islander, non-Hispanic/Latino; 2 Two or more races, non-Hispanic/Latino), 1 international. Average age 37. 66 applicants, 71% accepted, 40 enrolled. In 2016, 53 master's, 2 doctorates awarded. *Degree requirements:* For master's, variable foreign language requirement, thesis (for some programs), minimum GPA of 2.5; for doctorate, thesis/dissertation, fieldwork, seminars. *Entrance requirements:* For master's and doctorate, regionally-accredited bachelor's degree with liberal arts core or proof of equivalent degree from foreign university; transcripts; letters of recommendation; resume; essays; writing sample; interview; background check. Additional exam requirements/recommendations for international students: Required—TOEFL (minimum score 550 paper-based; 79 iBT). *Application deadline:* For fall admission, 7/1 for domestic and international students; for spring admission, 11/15 for domestic and international students. Applications are processed on a rolling basis. Application fee: $50. Electronic applications accepted. *Expenses:* $410 per hour (for master's), $375 per hour (for D Min). *Financial support:* In 2016–17, 70 students received support. Career-related internships or fieldwork, Federal Work-Study, institutionally sponsored loans, and scholarships/grants available. Support available to part-time students. Financial award application deadline: 10/1; financial award applicants required to submit FAFSA. *Faculty research:* Biblical studies, Baptist heritage, Christian heritage, theology, pastoral care, ethics, global missions, academic research. *Unit head:* Dr. Jeffrey Willetts, Dean, 678-547-6478, E-mail: willetts_jg@mercer.edu. *Application contact:* L. Nikki Hardeman, Director of Admissions, 678-547-6357, Fax: 678-547-6478, E-mail: hardeman_ln@mercer.edu. Website: http://www.mercer.edu/theology

**Mesivta of Eastern Parkway–Yeshiva Zichron Meilech,** Graduate Programs, Brooklyn, NY 11218-5559. *Accreditation:* AARTS.

**Mesivta Torah Vodaath Rabbinical Seminary,** Graduate Programs, Brooklyn, NY 11218-5299. *Accreditation:* AARTS.

**Mesivtha Tifereth Jerusalem of America,** Graduate Programs, New York, NY 10002-6301. *Accreditation:* AARTS.

**Methodist Theological School in Ohio,** Graduate and Professional Programs, Delaware, OH 43015-8004. Offers M Div, MACE, MACM, MTS, D Min. *Accreditation:* ACIPE; ATS. *Program availability:* Part-time. *Entrance requirements:* For master's, 3 letters of recommendation. Additional exam requirements/recommendations for international students: Required—TOEFL (minimum score 577 paper-based; 90 iBT).

**Mid-America Baptist Theological Seminary,** Graduate and Professional Programs, Cordova, TN 38016. Offers M Div, MACE, MCE, MM, D Min, PhD. *Degree requirements:* For doctorate, 4 foreign languages, thesis/dissertation. *Entrance requirements:* For doctorate, MAT. Additional exam requirements/recommendations for

international students: Required—TOEFL (minimum score 600 paper-based). Electronic applications accepted.

**Mid-America Baptist Theological Seminary Northeast Branch,** Program in Theology, Schenectady, NY 12303-3463. Offers M Div. *Program availability:* Part-time, evening/weekend. *Entrance requirements:* Additional exam requirements/recommendations for international students: Required—TOEFL. Electronic applications accepted.

**Mid-America Reformed Seminary,** Graduate Programs, Dyer, IN 46311. Offers M Div, MTS. *Accreditation:* ATS. *Entrance requirements:* Additional exam requirements/recommendations for international students: Required—TOEFL (minimum score 550 paper-based).

**Midwestern Baptist Theological Seminary,** Graduate and Professional Programs, Kansas City, MO 64118-4697. Offers Christian education (MACE); Christian foundations (Graduate Certificate); church music (MCM); counseling (MA); ministry (D Ed Min, D Min); Old or New Testament studies (PhD); theology (M Div). *Accreditation:* ATS. *Program availability:* Part-time, online learning. *Degree requirements:* For doctorate, thesis/dissertation. *Entrance requirements:* For doctorate, MAT. Electronic applications accepted. *Faculty research:* Ministerial studies, Biblical and theological studies, missions, counseling.

**Milligan College,** Emmanuel Christian Seminary at Milligan College, Milligan College, TN 37682. Offers Christian care and counseling (M Div); Christian education (M Div); Christian ministries (MACM, Graduate Certificate); Christian ministry (M Div); Christian theology (M Div, MAR); church history (MAR); church history/historical theology (M Div); general studies (M Div); ministry (D Min); New Testament (M Div, MAR); Old Testament (M Div, MAR); urban ministry (M Div); world missions (M Div). *Accreditation:* ACIPE; ATS. *Program availability:* Part-time, blended/hybrid learning. *Faculty:* 9 full-time (1 woman), 11 part-time/adjunct (0 women). *Students:* 55 full-time (16 women), 44 part-time (17 women); includes 7 minority (6 Black or African American, non-Hispanic/Latino; 1 Hispanic/Latino), 6 international. Average age 33. In 2016, 21 master's, 3 doctorates awarded. *Degree requirements:* For master's, 2 foreign languages, thesis or alternative, portfolio; for doctorate, thesis/dissertation. *Entrance requirements:* For master's, undergraduate degree and supporting transcripts, essay/personal statement, professional recommendations, interview; for doctorate, M Div or equivalent, essay/personal statement, professional recommendations. Additional exam requirements/recommendations for international students: Required—TOEFL (minimum score 550 paper-based, 79 iBT) or IELTS (6.5). *Application deadline:* For fall admission, 8/1 for domestic students, 6/1 for international students; for spring admission, 12/15 for domestic students, 8/1 for international students. Applications are processed on a rolling basis. Application fee: $30 ($0 for international students). Electronic applications accepted. *Expenses:* $470 per hour tuition; $325 per semester tech/activity fees. *Financial support:* In 2016–17, 124 students received support. Scholarships/grants and unspecified assistantships available. Financial award application deadline: 12/1; financial award applicants required to submit FAFSA. *Faculty research:* Theology of Old Testament prophets; performance criticism of New Testament texts; practical theology and spiritual formation for Christian leaders; church history and missions; constructive theology, art and imagination. *Unit head:* Dr. Rollin Ramsaran, Academic Dean, Emmanuel Christian Seminary, 423-461-1524, Fax: 423-926-6198, E-mail: raramsaran@milligan.edu. *Application contact:* Lauren Gullett, Director of Admissions and Recruitment for Emmanuel Christian Seminary, 423-461-1535, Fax: 423-926-6198, E-mail: lwgullett@milligan.edu. Website: http://ecs.milligan.edu/

**Mirrer Yeshiva,** Graduate Programs, Brooklyn, NY 11223-2010. *Accreditation:* AARTS.

**Moody Bible Institute,** Graduate School, Chicago, IL 60610-3284. Offers biblical studies (MABS, Graduate Certificate); intercultural studies (MAIS, Graduate Certificate); ministry (M Div, M Min); spiritual formation and discipleship (MASF, Graduate Certificate); urban studies (MA, Graduate Certificate). *Program availability:* Part-time. *Degree requirements:* For master's, 2 foreign languages; fieldwork (MABS); colloquium, field research project (MA Min). *Entrance requirements:* For master's, 30 hours in Bible/theology, 2 years of ministry experience (MA Min).

**Moody Theological Seminary–Michigan,** Graduate Programs, Plymouth, MI 48170. Offers Bible (Graduate Certificate); Christian education (MA); counseling psychology (MA); divinity (M Div); theological studies (MA). *Program availability:* Part-time, evening/weekend. *Degree requirements:* For master's, one foreign language, thesis. *Faculty research:* Judaism, cults, world religions.

**Moravian Theological Seminary,** Graduate and Certificate Programs, Bethlehem, PA 18018-6614. Offers chaplaincy (MACH); clinical counseling (MACC); divinity (M Div); formative spirituality (M Div, MATS, Graduate Certificate); spiritual direction (Graduate Certificate). *Accreditation:* ACIPE; ATS (one or more programs are accredited). *Program availability:* Part-time. *Faculty:* 8 full-time (3 women), 10 part-time/adjunct (6 women). *Students:* 26 full-time (12 women), 68 part-time (51 women); includes 17 minority (11 Black or African American, non-Hispanic/Latino; 5 Hispanic/Latino; 1 Two or more races, non-Hispanic/Latino), 1 international. Average age 48. 37 applicants, 73% accepted, 25 enrolled. In 2016, 20 master's, 8 other advanced degrees awarded. *Degree requirements:* For master's, thesis (for some programs). *Entrance requirements:* For master's, reference forms, essay, denominational endorsement (M Div); for Graduate Certificate, reference forms, essay. Additional exam requirements/recommendations for international students: Required—TOEFL (minimum score 550 paper-based; 79 iBT). *Application deadline:* For fall admission, 4/1 priority date for international students; for spring admission, 9/1 priority date for international students. Applications are processed on a rolling basis. Application fee: $50. Electronic applications accepted. *Expenses:* Tuition: Full-time $13,680; part-time $7596 per year. *Required fees:* $430; $430 per unit. Tuition and fees vary according to course load. *Financial support:* In 2016–17, 71 students received support. Career-related internships or fieldwork, Federal Work-Study, and scholarships/grants available. Support available to part-time students. Financial award application deadline: 5/1; financial award applicants required to submit FAFSA. *Faculty research:* Intercultural pedagogy, wisdom school spiritual direction, gender and sexuality, Moravian history and theology, holistic clinical counseling. *Unit head:* Rev. Dr. Frank L. Crouch, Dean and Vice President, 610-861-1516, E-mail: crouchf@moravian.edu. *Application contact:* Rev. Dr. David H. DeRemer, Director of Enrollment, 610-861-1512, Fax: 610-861-1569, E-mail: deremerd@moravian.edu. Website: http://moravianseminary.edu

**Mount Angel Seminary,** Program in Theology, Saint Benedict, OR 97373. Offers M Div, MA. *Accreditation:* ACIPE; ATS. *Program availability:* Part-time. *Degree requirements:* For master's, thesis optional.

**Mount St. Joseph University,** Graduate Program in Religious Studies, Cincinnati, OH 45233-1670. Offers religious studies (MA); spirituality and wellness (Certificate). *Program availability:* Part-time, evening/weekend. *Faculty:* 3 full-time (1 woman), 4 part-time/adjunct (2 women). *Students:* 1 (woman) full-time, 6 part-time (4 women); includes 2 minority (1 Black or African American, non-Hispanic/Latino; 1 Hispanic/Latino). Average age 42. In 2016, 5 master's awarded. *Degree requirements:* For master's, comprehensive exam, 36 hours of credit, pastoral PRAXIS component (3 credit hours), integrating project (3 credit hours). *Entrance requirements:* For master's, undergraduate transcript with minimum overall GPA of 3.0, 3 letters of recommendation from professional colleagues, 3-page essay, interview with the Graduate Admissions Committee, current work resume. Additional exam requirements/recommendations for international students: Required—TOEFL (minimum score 560 paper-based; 83 iBT). *Application deadline:* Applications are processed on a rolling basis. Electronic applications accepted. *Expenses:* $580 per credit hour. *Financial support:* In 2016–17, 5 students received support. Scholarships/grants available. Financial award applicants required to submit FAFSA. *Faculty research:* Contextual/cultural/systematic theology, historical/spiritual theology, business/economics ethics, social justice, Biblical/cultural/pastoral theology. *Unit head:* Dr. John Trokan, Associate Professor of Religious and Pastoral Studies/Director of Graduate Program, 513-244-4272, Fax: 513-244-4222, E-mail: john.trokan@msj.edu. *Application contact:* Mary Brigham, Assistant Director of Graduate Recruitment, 513-244-4233, Fax: 513-244-4629, E-mail: mary.brigham@msj.edu. Website: http://www.msj.edu/academics/graduate-programs/religious-studies-programs/

**Mount St. Mary's University,** Graduate Seminary, Emmitsburg, MD 21727-7799. Offers M Div, MA. *Accreditation:* ATS. *Faculty:* 12 full-time (2 women), 6 part-time/adjunct (2 women). *Students:* 115 full-time (10 women); includes 8 minority (1 Black or African American, non-Hispanic/Latino; 1 Asian, non-Hispanic/Latino; 6 Hispanic/Latino), 7 international. Average age 29. 49 applicants, 86% accepted, 36 enrolled. In 2016, 28 master's awarded. *Degree requirements:* For master's, one foreign language, comprehensive exam, thesis, language proficiency exams. *Entrance requirements:* For master's, 18 credits of course work in philosophy. Additional exam requirements/recommendations for international students: Required—TOEFL (minimum score 550 paper-based; 83 iBT). *Application deadline:* For fall admission, 8/1 for domestic and international students. Application fee: $0. *Expenses:* $23,250 per year full-time tuition; $760 per credit hour part-time tuition; $280 per year facility fee. *Financial support:* Applicants required to submit FAFSA. *Unit head:* Rev. Andrew R. Baker, Vice President/Rector, 301-447-5295, Fax: 301-447-5636, E-mail: baker@msmary.edu. *Application contact:* Susan Nield, Seminary Admissions, 301-447-7423, Fax: 301-447-7402, E-mail: nield@msmary.edu. Website: http://www.msmary.edu/seminary/

**Mount Vernon Nazarene University,** Program in Ministry, Mount Vernon, OH 43050-9500. Offers M Min. *Program availability:* Part-time, evening/weekend. *Degree requirements:* For master's, project. *Faculty research:* Pastoral effectiveness and professional development.

**Multnomah University,** Multnomah Biblical Seminary, Portland, OR 97220-5898. Offers M Div, MABS, MACL, MATS, Th M, D Min. *Accreditation:* ATS. *Program availability:* Part-time. *Faculty:* 9 full-time (3 women), 6 part-time/adjunct (0 women). *Students:* 95 full-time (27 women), 56 part-time (10 women); includes 26 minority (3 Black or African American, non-Hispanic/Latino; 1 American Indian or Alaska Native, non-Hispanic/Latino; 8 Asian, non-Hispanic/Latino; 8 Hispanic/Latino; 2 Native Hawaiian or other Pacific Islander, non-Hispanic/Latino; 4 Two or more races, non-Hispanic/Latino), 2 international. Average age 35. 75 applicants, 79% accepted, 50 enrolled. In 2016, 51 master's awarded. *Degree requirements:* For master's, variable foreign language requirement, thesis (for some programs). *Entrance requirements:* For master's, interview; for doctorate, interview, M Div equivalency. Additional exam requirements/recommendations for international students: Required—TOEFL (minimum score 550 paper-based). *Application deadline:* For fall and spring admission, 12/1 priority date for domestic and international students. Applications are processed on a rolling basis. Application fee: $40. *Expenses: Tuition:* Full-time $10,000; part-time $6000 per semester. *Required fees:* $230; $120 per semester. Tuition and fees vary according to course load, degree level and program. *Financial support:* Career-related internships or fieldwork and scholarships/grants available. Support available to part-time students. Financial award application deadline: 7/1; financial award applicants required to submit FAFSA. *Faculty research:* Grief theology, intercultural studies, New Testament, theology and culture, historical theology, Biblical theology. *Unit head:* Dr. Derek Chinn, Dean, 503-252-6731, Fax: 503-254-6444, E-mail: dchinn@multnomah.edu. *Application contact:* Mindy Kate Hasenkamp, Director of Admissions, 503-251-6483, Fax: 503-254-1268, E-mail: admiss@multnomah.edu.

**Naropa University,** Graduate Programs, Program in Divinity, Boulder, CO 80302-6697. Offers M Div. *Faculty:* 5 full-time (3 women), 5 part-time/adjunct (2 women). *Students:* 11 full-time (6 women), 14 part-time (5 women); includes 6 minority (2 Asian, non-Hispanic/Latino; 2 Hispanic/Latino; 1 Native Hawaiian or other Pacific Islander, non-Hispanic/Latino; 1 Two or more races, non-Hispanic/Latino). Average age 37. 14 applicants, 93% accepted, 7 enrolled. In 2016, 8 master's awarded. *Degree requirements:* For master's, comprehensive exam, thesis, clinical pastoral education or fieldwork placement. *Entrance requirements:* For master's, resume/curriculum vitae with pertinent academic, employment and volunteer activity; 2 letters of recommendation; letter of interest; transcripts; phone interview. Additional exam requirements/recommendations for international students: Required—TOEFL (minimum score 550 paper-based; 80 iBT). *Application deadline:* For fall admission, 1/15 priority date for domestic and international students. Applications are processed on a rolling basis. Application fee: $60. Electronic applications accepted. *Expenses:* $22,570 for first year. *Financial support:* In 2016–17, 11 students received support. Research assistantships with partial tuition reimbursements available, teaching assistantships with partial tuition reimbursements available, career-related internships or fieldwork, Federal Work-Study, scholarships/grants, and unspecified assistantships available. Support available to part-time students. Financial award application deadline: 3/1; financial award applicants required to submit FAFSA. *Unit head:* Dr. Elaine Yuen, Chair, Department of Wisdom Traditions, 303-245-4718, E-mail: eyuen@naropa.edu. *Application contact:* Office of Admissions, 303-546-3572, Fax: 303-546-3583, E-mail: admissions@naropa.edu. Website: http://www.naropa.edu/academics/masters/divinity/index.php

**Nashotah House Theological Seminary,** Graduate Programs, Nashotah, WI 53058-9793. Offers Anglican studies (Certificate); Biblical studies (STM); Christian spirituality (STM); church history (STM); liturgy (STM); ministry (M Div, MM); pastoral ministry (MPM); theological studies (MTS); theology (STM, D Min). *Accreditation:* ACIPE; ATS (one or more programs are accredited). *Program availability:* Part-time. *Faculty:* 8 full-time (0 women), 6 part-time/adjunct (0 women). *Students:* 78 full-time (14 women), 5 part-time (2 women); includes 3 minority (2 Black or African American, non-Hispanic/Latino; 1 Asian, non-Hispanic/Latino). Average age 37. *Degree requirements:* For master's, thesis optional. *Entrance requirements:* For master's and Certificate, GRE General Test or MAT, interview, 3 recommendations. Additional exam requirements/recommendations for international students: Required—TOEFL. *Application deadline:* For fall admission, 6/15 for domestic students. Applications are processed on a rolling basis. Application fee: $0. Electronic applications accepted. *Expenses:* $500 per credit hour. *Financial support:* Teaching assistantships, career-related internships or fieldwork, scholarships/grants, and tuition waivers (partial) available. Support available to part-time students. Financial award application deadline: 1/15; financial award applicants required to submit FAFSA. *Faculty research:* Formation for parochial ministry, ancient Semitic epigraphy. *Unit head:* Very Rev. Steven A. Peay, Dean/President, 262-646-6512, Fax: 262-646-6504, E-mail: speay@nashotah.edu. *Application contact:* Fr. Dr. Rick Hartley, Associate Dean of Students/Registrar, 262-646-6547,

Fax: 262-646-6504, E-mail: rhartley@nashotah.edu. Website: https://www.nashotah.edu/programs

**Nazarene Theological Seminary,** Graduate and Professional Programs, Kansas City, MO 64131-1263. Offers Christian formation and discipleship (MA); intercultural studies (MA); theological studies (MA); theology (M Div, D Min). *Accreditation:* ACIPE; ATS. *Program availability:* Part-time. *Faculty:* 11 full-time (2 women), 26 part-time/adjunct (4 women). *Students:* 105 full-time (33 women), 155 part-time (45 women); includes 22 minority (7 Black or African American, non-Hispanic/Latino; 1 American Indian or Alaska Native, non-Hispanic/Latino; 1 Asian, non-Hispanic/Latino; 9 Hispanic/Latino; 4 Two or more races, non-Hispanic/Latino), 29 international. *Degree requirements:* For master's, comprehensive exam (for some programs), thesis (for some programs); for doctorate, thesis/dissertation. *Entrance requirements:* For master's, three references; for doctorate, three references, interview. Additional exam requirements/recommendations for international students: Required—TOEFL (minimum score 550 paper-based; 80 iBT). *Application deadline:* For fall admission, 3/1 for domestic and international students; for spring admission, 11/1 for domestic and international students. Applications are processed on a rolling basis. Application fee: $50. Electronic applications accepted. *Expenses:* $525 per credit hour. *Financial support:* Teaching assistantships, institutionally sponsored loans, and scholarships/grants available. Support available to part-time students. Financial award application deadline: 3/1; financial award applicants required to submit FAFSA. *Unit head:* Dr. Josh Sweeden, Dean of the Faculty, 816-268-5412, Fax: 816-268-5500, E-mail: jsweeden@nts.edu. *Application contact:* Pamala J. Asher, Registrar/Director of Admissions, 816-268-5442, Fax: 816-268-5500, E-mail: pjasher@nts.edu.

**Ner Israel Rabbinical College,** Graduate Programs, Baltimore, MD 21208. Offers MTL, DTL, Professional Certificate. *Accreditation:* AARTS.

**Ner Israel Yeshiva College of Toronto,** Graduate Programs, Thornhill, ON L4J 8A7, Canada. *Accreditation:* AARTS.

**New Brunswick Theological Seminary,** Graduate and Professional Programs, New Brunswick, NJ 08901-1196. Offers pastoral care and counseling (D Min). *Accreditation:* ACIPE; ATS. *Program availability:* Part-time, evening/weekend. *Degree requirements:* For master's, variable foreign language requirement, thesis (for some programs); for doctorate, thesis/dissertation. *Entrance requirements:* For master's, BA/BS with minimum GPA of 3.0 (for MA), 2.5 (for M Div); for doctorate, M Div. Additional exam requirements/recommendations for international students: Required—TOEFL (minimum score 550 paper-based; 79 iBT); Recommended—IELTS (minimum score 6). Electronic applications accepted.

**Newman Theological College,** Theology Programs, Edmonton, AB T6V 1H3, Canada. Offers M Div, M Th, MTS. *Accreditation:* ATS. *Program availability:* Part-time. *Faculty:* 16 full-time (3 women), 7 part-time/adjunct (0 women). *Students:* 34 full-time (2 women), 16 part-time (10 women). 22 applicants, 100% accepted, 19 enrolled. In 2016, 8 master's awarded. *Degree requirements:* For master's, comprehensive exam, thesis. *Entrance requirements:* For master's, bachelor's degree. Additional exam requirements/recommendations for international students: Required—TOEFL (minimum score 560 paper-based; 86 iBT), IELTS (minimum score 6.5). *Application deadline:* For fall admission, 8/21 priority date for domestic students; for winter admission, 11/22 priority date for domestic students; for spring admission, 4/21 priority date for domestic students. Applications are processed on a rolling basis. Application fee: $45 ($250 for international students). *Expenses:* $639 per course. *Financial support:* Tuition bursaries available. Support available to part-time students. Financial award application deadline: 5/31. *Faculty research:* New Testament world and Inter-Testament period, philosophy of Jacques Maritain, aesthetics of the sublime, Resurrection of the Body, the Trinity and immutability, medical-assisted death. *Unit head:* Sr. Zoe Bernatsky, Academic Dean/Vice President, 780-392-2450 Ext. 2213, Fax: 780-462-4013, E-mail: zoe.bernatsky@newman.edu. *Application contact:* Maria Saulnier, Registrar, 780-392-2451, Fax: 780-462-4013, E-mail: registrar@newman.edu. Website: http://www.newman.edu/

**Newman University,** Graduate Theology Program, Wichita, KS 67213-2097. Offers theological studies (MTS); theology (MA). *Program availability:* Part-time, online learning. *Degree requirements:* For master's, 2 foreign languages, comprehensive exam (for some programs), thesis (for some programs). *Entrance requirements:* For master's, letter of recommendation from pastor; bachelor's degree in theology or related field (MA), in any field (MTS). Additional exam requirements/recommendations for international students: Required—TOEFL (minimum score 600 paper-based; 100 iBT). *Expenses:* Contact institution.

**New Orleans Baptist Theological Seminary,** Graduate and Professional Programs, Division of Biblical Studies, New Orleans, LA 70126-4858. Offers M Div, MA, PhD. *Accreditation:* ACIPE; ATS (one or more programs are accredited). *Degree requirements:* For master's, 2 foreign languages, comprehensive exam (for some programs), thesis (for some programs); for doctorate, 4 foreign languages, comprehensive exam, thesis/dissertation. *Entrance requirements:* For doctorate, GRE General Test.

**New Orleans Baptist Theological Seminary,** Graduate and Professional Programs, Division of Theological and Historical Studies, New Orleans, LA 70126-4858. Offers M Div, MA, D Min, PhD. *Accreditation:* ACIPE; ATS (one or more programs are accredited). *Program availability:* Online learning. *Degree requirements:* For master's, 2 foreign languages, comprehensive exam (for some programs), thesis (for some programs); for doctorate, 3 foreign languages, comprehensive exam, thesis/dissertation. *Entrance requirements:* For doctorate, GRE General Test. Additional exam requirements/recommendations for international students: Required—TOEFL.

**New Saint Andrews College,** Graduate School, Moscow, ID 83843. Offers classical Christian studies (Graduate Certificate); theology and letters (MA). *Program availability:* Part-time, blended/hybrid learning. *Faculty:* 12 part-time/adjunct (0 women). *Students:* 12 full-time (3 women), 8 part-time (5 women), 1 international. Average age 25. 15 applicants, 53% accepted, 7 enrolled. In 2016, 3 master's awarded. *Degree requirements:* For master's, comprehensive exam (for some programs), thesis (for some programs), final oral exam. *Entrance requirements:* For master's, GRE, 2 letters of recommendation; for Graduate Certificate, GRE, bachelor's degree, essays, 2 letters of recommendation. *Application deadline:* For fall admission, 12/1 for domestic students. Applications are processed on a rolling basis. Application fee: $50. Electronic applications accepted. *Expenses: Tuition:* Full-time $7200; part-time $475 per credit. One-time fee: $160. *Faculty research:* Hebrew, theology, literature. *Unit head:* Benjamin Merkle, Academic Dean, 208-882-1566 Ext. 104, E-mail: bmerkle@nsa.edu. *Application contact:* Brenda Schlect, Director of Admissions, 208-882-1566 Ext. 113, Fax: 208-882-4293, E-mail: admissions@nsa.edu. Website: http://www.nsa.edu/academics/graduate-school/

**New York Theological Seminary,** Graduate and Professional Programs, New York, NY 10115. Offers M Div, MPS, MSW, D Min. MSW offered jointly with Fordham University. *Accreditation:* ACIPE; ATS (one or more programs are accredited). *Program availability:* Part-time. *Degree requirements:* For doctorate, thesis/dissertation. *Entrance requirements:* For doctorate, M Div, 3 years of ministry experience, interview. Additional exam requirements/recommendations for international students: Required—TOEFL.

*Faculty research:* Women in leadership; crime and punishment; church history; culture, politics and theology.

**Northeastern Seminary at Roberts Wesleyan College,** Graduate and Professional Programs, Rochester, NY 14624. Offers ministry (D Min); theological studies (MA); theology (M Div); theology and social justice (MA); transformational leadership (MA); M Div/MSW. M Div/MSW offered jointly with Roberts Wesleyan College. *Accreditation:* ATS. *Program availability:* Evening/weekend. *Faculty:* 6 full-time (2 women), 23 part-time/adjunct (4 women). *Students:* 81 full-time (42 women), 40 part-time (9 women); includes 34 minority (28 Black or African American, non-Hispanic/Latino; 1 American Indian or Alaska Native, non-Hispanic/Latino; 2 Asian, non-Hispanic/Latino; 3 Hispanic/Latino). *Degree requirements:* For master's, thesis (for some programs); for doctorate, one foreign language, thesis/dissertation. *Entrance requirements:* For doctorate, M Div, 3 years of full-time ministry experience. Additional exam requirements/recommendations for international students: Required—TOEFL (minimum score 550 paper-based). *Application deadline:* For fall admission, 8/1 priority date for domestic and international students; for spring admission, 12/15 priority date for domestic and international students. Applications are processed on a rolling basis. Application fee: $35. Electronic applications accepted. One-time fee: $400 full-time. Tuition and fees vary according to course load. *Financial support:* Teaching assistantships with partial tuition reimbursements, career-related internships or fieldwork, institutionally sponsored loans, scholarships/grants, and tuition waivers (partial) available. Financial award applicants required to submit FAFSA. *Faculty research:* Historical theology, spiritual formation, biblical theology, counseling education. *Unit head:* Douglas Cullum, Dean, 585-594-6331, Fax: 585-594-6801. *Application contact:* Douglas Cullum, Dean, 585-594-6331, Fax: 585-594-6801.

**Northern Seminary,** Graduate and Professional Programs, Lombard, IL 60148-5698. Offers Biblical studies (M Div); Christian community development (D Min); Christian ministry (MACM); contextual theology (D Min); New Testament (MANT); New Testament context (D Min); theology (M Div); theology and mission (MA); urban leadership (MA); worship (MAW). *Program availability:* Part-time, evening/weekend. *Faculty:* 6 full-time (1 woman), 33 part-time/adjunct (8 women). *Students:* 126 full-time (34 women), 80 part-time (32 women); includes 89 minority (73 Black or African American, non-Hispanic/Latino; 6 Asian, non-Hispanic/Latino; 8 Hispanic/Latino; 2 Two or more races, non-Hispanic/Latino), 3 international. Average age 44. In 2016, 18 master's, 14 doctorates awarded. *Degree requirements:* For master's, thesis (for some programs); for doctorate, thesis/dissertation. *Entrance requirements:* For master's, writing test, all official transcripts, letter of reference from church, 3 letters of reference, autobiographical statement (400 words or more); for doctorate, M Div, 3 years in the ministry post-M Div, 3 letters of reference. Additional exam requirements/recommendations for international students: Required—TOEFL (minimum score 550 paper-based). *Application deadline:* For fall admission, 8/25 for domestic students, 2/1 for international students; for winter admission, 12/10 for domestic students, 2/1 for international students; for spring admission, 3/15 for domestic students, 2/1 for international students. Applications are processed on a rolling basis. Application fee: $35. Electronic applications accepted. *Expenses:* Contact institution. *Financial support:* In 2016–17, 3 teaching assistantships with partial tuition reimbursements were awarded; Federal Work-Study and scholarships/grants also available. Support available to part-time students. Financial award application deadline: 9/1; financial award applicants required to submit FAFSA. *Faculty research:* Theology and mission, worship studies, church history, evangelism, Christian ministry, urban leadership, New Testament. *Unit head:* Dr. William Shiell, President, 630-620-2101, Fax: 630-620-2190. *Application contact:* Greg Armstrong, Director of Admissions, 630-620-2175, Fax: 630-620-2190, E-mail: admissions@seminary.edu.

**North Park Theological Seminary,** Graduate and Professional Programs, Professional Program, Chicago, IL 60625-4895. Offers M Div, M Div/MBA, M Div/MM. M Div/MBA offered jointly with North Park University. *Accreditation:* ACIPE; ATS. *Program availability:* Part-time. *Entrance requirements:* Additional exam requirements/recommendations for international students: Required—TOEFL.

**North Park Theological Seminary,** Graduate and Professional Programs, Program in Christian Formation, Chicago, IL 60625-4895. Offers MA, MA/MM. *Accreditation:* ATS.

**North Park Theological Seminary,** Graduate and Professional Programs, Program in Preaching, Chicago, IL 60625-4895. Offers D Min. Program offered jointly with Chicago Theological Seminary, Lutheran School of Theology at Chicago, McCormick Theological Seminary, Seabury-Western Theological Seminary. *Accreditation:* ACIPE; ATS. *Degree requirements:* For doctorate, thesis/dissertation. *Entrance requirements:* For doctorate, 3 years of preaching experience.

**North Park Theological Seminary,** Graduate and Professional Programs, Program in Theological Studies, Chicago, IL 60625-4895. Offers MATS, MATS/MBA, MATS/MM. MATS/MBA offered jointly with North Park University. *Accreditation:* ACIPE; ATS. *Program availability:* Part-time. *Degree requirements:* For master's, comprehensive exam or thesis. *Entrance requirements:* For master's, minimum GPA of 2.5. Additional exam requirements/recommendations for international students: Required—TOEFL.

**Northwest Nazarene University,** Program in Religion, Nampa, ID 83686-5897. Offers missional leadership (M Div, MA); pastoral ministry (MA); spiritual formation (M Div, MA); youth, children, and family ministry (M Div, MA). *Program availability:* Part-time, online only, 100% online. *Faculty:* 11 full-time (3 women), 18 part-time/adjunct (0 women). *Students:* 65 full-time (23 women), 25 part-time (11 women); includes 11 minority (4 Black or African American, non-Hispanic/Latino; 1 American Indian or Alaska Native, non-Hispanic/Latino; 2 Asian, non-Hispanic/Latino; 3 Hispanic/Latino; 1 Native Hawaiian or other Pacific Islander, non-Hispanic/Latino), 1 international. Average age 39. 37 applicants, 76% accepted, 24 enrolled. In 2016, 40 master's awarded. *Entrance requirements:* For master's, minimum GPA of 2.5; 8 semester or 12 quarter credits of Bible, theology and/or Western philosophy. Additional exam requirements/recommendations for international students: Required—TOEFL (minimum score 85 iBT). *Application deadline:* For fall admission, 7/31 for domestic students, 7/1 for international students; for spring admission, 2/1 for domestic students, 1/5 for international students. Applications are processed on a rolling basis. Application fee: $50. Electronic applications accepted. *Expenses:* Contact institution. *Financial support:* In 2016–17, 3 students received support. Scholarships/grants available. *Unit head:* Dr. Jay Akkerman, Director, Graduate Studies, 208-467-8437, Fax: 208-467-8252. *Application contact:* Vicki Funk, Program Coordinator, 208-467-8432, Fax: 208-467-8252, E-mail: vlfunk@nnu.edu.
Website: http://www.nnu.edu/ministry/

**Northwest University,** College of Ministry, Kirkland, WA 98033. Offers ministry (MIM); missional leadership (MA); theology and culture (MA). *Program availability:* Part-time, evening/weekend, online learning. *Degree requirements:* For master's, comprehensive exam (for some programs), thesis (for some programs). *Entrance requirements:* Additional exam requirements/recommendations for international students: Required—TOEFL (minimum score 550 paper-based; 75 iBT). Electronic applications accepted.

**Notre Dame Seminary,** Graduate School of Theology, New Orleans, LA 70118-4391. Offers M Div, MA. *Accreditation:* ACIPE; ATS. *Program availability:* Part-time. *Degree requirements:* For master's, one foreign language, comprehensive exam, thesis.

*Entrance requirements:* For master's, GRE. Additional exam requirements/recommendations for international students: Required—TOEFL.

**Nyack College,** Alliance Theological Seminary, Nyack, NY 10960. Offers Biblical literature (MA), including New Testament, Old Testament; Biblical studies (MA); Christian ministry (MPS); intercultural studies (MA); ministry (D Min), including Christian leadership in the global context; theology and missions (M Div); urban ministry (MPS). *Accreditation:* ATS. *Program availability:* Part-time, evening/weekend, 100% online, blended/hybrid learning. *Students:* 275 full-time (111 women), 370 part-time (175 women); includes 505 minority (177 Black or African American, non-Hispanic/Latino; 128 Asian, non-Hispanic/Latino; 190 Hispanic/Latino; 10 Two or more races, non-Hispanic/Latino), 32 international. Average age 43. In 2016, 117 master's, 14 doctorates awarded. *Degree requirements:* For master's, comprehensive exam (for some programs), thesis optional, internship; for doctorate, thesis/dissertation. *Entrance requirements:* For master's, transcripts, Christian experience statement, recommendations; for doctorate, transcripts, documented three years of ministry experience subsequent to 1st graduate theological degree, reference letters, formal academic paper. Additional exam requirements/recommendations for international students: Required—TOEFL (minimum score 550 paper-based; 80 iBT). *Application deadline:* Applications are processed on a rolling basis. Application fee: $30. Electronic applications accepted. *Expenses:* $575 per credit (for master's-level). *Financial support:* Career-related internships or fieldwork, Federal Work-Study, and scholarships/grants available. Financial award applicants required to submit FAFSA. *Unit head:* Dr. Ronald Walborn, Dean, 845-770-5715, Fax: 845-358-1663. *Application contact:* Julian Williams, Associate Director of Admissions, 800-541-6891, Fax: 845-348-3912, E-mail: admissions.ats@nyack.edu.
Website: http://www.nyack.edu/ats

**Oakland City University,** Chapman Seminary, Oakland City, IN 47660-1099. Offers M Div, D Min. *Program availability:* Part-time. *Degree requirements:* For doctorate, thesis/dissertation. *Entrance requirements:* For doctorate, GRE, MAT, letters of recommendation. Additional exam requirements/recommendations for international students: Required—TOEFL. *Expenses:* Contact institution. *Faculty research:* Pastoral ministry, Christian education, missions.

**Oblate School of Theology,** Graduate and Professional Programs, San Antonio, TX 78216-6693. Offers African-American pastoral leadership (D Min); divinity (M Div); pastoral leadership (D Min); pastoral ministry (MAP Min); pastoral studies (Certificate); spiritual formation in the local community (D Min); spirituality (MA Sp, PhD); spirituality and ministry (D Min); theology (MA Th); U.S. Hispanic/Latino ministry (D Min); M Div/MA Th. *Accreditation:* ACIPE; ATS (one or more programs are accredited). *Program availability:* Part-time, online learning. *Faculty:* 24 full-time (8 women), 4 part-time/adjunct (0 women). *Students:* 76 full-time (10 women), 51 part-time (32 women); includes 56 minority (8 Black or African American, non-Hispanic/Latino; 9 Asian, non-Hispanic/Latino; 39 Hispanic/Latino), 41 international. Average age 40. In 2016, 31 master's, 3 doctorates awarded. *Degree requirements:* For master's, comprehensive exam (for some programs), thesis (for some programs), practicum; for doctorate, one foreign language, comprehensive exam, thesis/dissertation, paper, practicum. *Entrance requirements:* For master's, MAT, interview, course work in theology or religious studies, minimum GPA of 2.5; for doctorate, M Div, MA Th, or MA Sp. Additional exam requirements/recommendations for international students: Required—TOEFL (minimum score 71 iBT). *Application deadline:* For fall admission, 6/15 priority date for domestic and international students; for winter admission, 11/30 for domestic and international students; for spring admission, 11/30 for domestic and international students; for summer admission, 4/1 for domestic and international students. Applications are processed on a rolling basis. Application fee: $65. *Expenses:* Contact institution. *Financial support:* In 2016–17, 25 students received support. Scholarships/grants available. Support available to part-time students. Financial award application deadline: 8/1; financial award applicants required to submit FAFSA. *Unit head:* Dr. R. Scott Woodward, Academic Dean, 210-341-1366, Fax: 210-341-4519, E-mail: rsw@ost.edu. *Application contact:* Mario A. Porter, Registrar, 210-341-1366 Ext. 226, Fax: 210-341-4519, E-mail: registrar@ost.edu.

**Ohio Christian University,** Graduate Programs, Circleville, OH 43113-9487. Offers accounting (MBA); business administration (MBA); digital marketing (MBA); finance (MBA); healthcare management (MBA); human resources (MBA); management (MM); organizational leadership (MBA); pastoral care and counseling (MAM); practical theology (MAM).

**Ohio Dominican University,** Division of Arts and Letters, Program in Theology, Columbus, OH 43219-2099. Offers MA. *Program availability:* Part-time, evening/weekend. *Faculty:* 1 full-time, 2 part-time/adjunct (1 woman). *Students:* 23 part-time (9 women); includes 3 minority (2 Black or African American, non-Hispanic/Latino; 1 Hispanic/Latino), 1 international. Average age 44. 12 applicants, 75% accepted, 8 enrolled. In 2016, 2 master's awarded. *Degree requirements:* For master's, thesis or alternative. *Entrance requirements:* For master's, 3 letters of recommendation, interview, essay. Additional exam requirements/recommendations for international students: Required—TOEFL (minimum score 550 paper-based), IELTS (minimum score 6.5). *Application deadline:* For fall admission, 8/15 for domestic students, 6/10 for international students; for spring admission, 1/4 for domestic students, 11/2 for international students; for summer admission, 5/30 for domestic students. Applications are processed on a rolling basis. Application fee: $25. Electronic applications accepted. *Expenses:* $590 per credit hour; $225 fees per semester. *Financial support:* Applicants required to submit FAFSA. *Unit head:* Dr. Barbara Finan, Program Director, 614-251-4578, E-mail: finanb@ohiodominican.edu. *Application contact:* John W. Naughton, Director for Graduate Admissions, 614-251-4615, Fax: 614-251-6654, E-mail: grad@ohiodominican.edu.
Website: http://www.ohiodominican.edu/academics/graduate/ma-theology

**Ohr Hameir Theological Seminary,** Graduate Programs, Cortlandt Manor, NY 10567. *Accreditation:* AARTS.

**Oklahoma Christian University,** Graduate School of Theology, Oklahoma City, OK 73136-1100. Offers scripture (MTS); theology (M Div, MACM, MTS). *Program availability:* Part-time. *Faculty:* 8 full-time (0 women). *Students:* 12 full-time (0 women), 30 part-time (4 women). Average age 32. 12 applicants, 100% accepted, 10 enrolled. In 2016, 8 master's awarded. *Degree requirements:* For master's, variable foreign language requirement, comprehensive exam, thesis (for some programs). *Entrance requirements:* For master's, bachelor's degree, minimum GPA of 3.0. Additional exam requirements/recommendations for international students: Recommended—TOEFL (minimum score 550 paper-based; 79 iBT), IELTS (minimum score 6.5). *Application deadline:* For fall admission, 8/15 priority date for domestic and international students; for spring admission, 1/3 priority date for domestic and international students. Applications are processed on a rolling basis. Application fee: $25. Electronic applications accepted. *Expenses:* $460 per credit hour tuition, $200 administrative fee per semester. *Financial support:* In 2016–17, 38 students received support. Scholarships/grants available. Financial award application deadline: 8/15; financial award applicants required to submit FAFSA. *Faculty research:* Old Testament studies, New Testament studies, church history, Hellenistic Greek and Linguistics, Semitic Languages. *Unit head:* Dr. Charles Rix, Dean, 405-425-5379, E-mail:

## Theology

charles.rix@oc.edu. *Application contact:* Josh Bailey, Program Director, 405-425-5389, Fax: 405-425-5076, E-mail: josh.bailey@oc.edu.

**Oklahoma Wesleyan University,** Professional Studies Division, Bartlesville, OK 74006-6299. Offers nursing administration (MSN); nursing education (MSN); strategic leadership (MS); theology and apologetics (MS).

**Olivet Nazarene University,** Graduate School, Department of Practical Ministries, Bourbonnais, IL 60914. Offers MPM. *Program availability:* Part-time. *Degree requirements:* For master's, thesis or alternative.

**Olivet Nazarene University,** Graduate School, Division of Religion, Bourbonnais, IL 60914. Offers biblical literature (MA); religion (MA); theology (MA). *Program availability:* Part-time. *Degree requirements:* For master's, thesis or alternative.

**Oral Roberts University,** School of Theology and Missions, Tulsa, OK 74171. Offers biblical literature (MA), including advanced languages, Judaic-Christian studies; Christian counseling (MA), including marriage and family therapy; divinity (M Div); missions (MA); practical theology (MA); theological/historical studies (MA); theology (D Min). *Accreditation:* ATS. *Program availability:* Part-time, online learning. *Degree requirements:* For master's, thesis (for some programs), practicum/internship; for doctorate, thesis/dissertation, applied research project. *Entrance requirements:* For master's, GRE General Test or MAT, minimum GPA of 2.5; for doctorate, M Div, minimum GPA of 3.0, 3 years of full-time ministry experience. Additional exam requirements/recommendations for international students: Required—TOEFL (minimum score 550 paper-based; 79 iBT). Electronic applications accepted.

**Pacific School of Religion,** Graduate and Professional Programs, Berkeley, CA 94709-1323. Offers M Div, MA, MTS, D Min, PhD, Th D, CAPS, CMS, CSS, CTS. MA, PhD, Th D offered jointly with Graduate Theological Union; D Min with Church Divinity School of the Pacific. *Accreditation:* ACIPE; ATS (one or more programs are accredited). *Program availability:* Part-time. *Degree requirements:* For master's, one foreign language, thesis (for some programs); for doctorate, thesis/dissertation. *Entrance requirements:* For master's, minimum GPA of 3.0; for doctorate, M Div, minimum GPA of 3.0 (D Min); for other advanced degree, M Div, minimum GPA of 3.0 (CAPS). Additional exam requirements/recommendations for international students: Required—TOEFL (minimum score 550 paper-based). Electronic applications accepted. *Faculty research:* Medical ethics, gay/lesbian studies in religion, Asian-American religion, race, culture and theology, theology in context.

**Palm Beach Atlantic University,** School of Ministry, West Palm Beach, FL 33416-4708. Offers Christian studies (MA); ministry (M Div). *Program availability:* Part-time. *Faculty:* 10 part-time/adjunct (2 women). *Students:* 36 full-time (12 women), 1 part-time (0 women); includes 10 minority (2 Black or African American, non-Hispanic/Latino; 7 Hispanic/Latino; 1 Two or more races, non-Hispanic/Latino), 1 international. Average age 28. 26 applicants, 88% accepted, 16 enrolled. In 2016, 7 master's awarded. *Degree requirements:* For master's, one foreign language, comprehensive exam (for some programs), thesis optional, 8 credits of biblical language (for M Div). *Entrance requirements:* For master's, minimum GPA of 2.75; writing samples. Additional exam requirements/recommendations for international students: Required—TOEFL (minimum score 550 paper-based; 79 iBT). *Application deadline:* Applications are processed on a rolling basis. Application fee: $50. Electronic applications accepted. *Expenses: Tuition:* Full-time $6600; part-time $550 per credit hour. Full-time tuition and fees vary according to degree level, campus/location and program. *Financial support:* In 2016–17, 25 students received support. Scholarships/grants, unspecified assistantships, and employee education grants available. Financial award application deadline: 5/1; financial award applicants required to submit FAFSA. *Faculty research:* Ethics, apologetics, spiritual formation, theology. *Unit head:* Dr. Jonathan Grenz, Director of the M Div Program, 561-803-2622. *Application contact:* Graduate Admissions, 888-468-6722, E-mail: grad@pba.edu.
Website: http://www.pba.edu/school-of-ministry

**Payne Theological Seminary,** Program in Theology, Wilberforce, OH 45384-3474. Offers M Div. *Accreditation:* ACIPE; ATS. *Program availability:* Part-time, evening/weekend, online learning.

**Pentecostal Theological Seminary,** Graduate and Professional Programs, Cleveland, TN 37320-3330. Offers biblical studies (MTS); church ministries (MA); counseling (MA); discipleship and Christian formation (MA); ministry (D Min); Pentecostal theology (MTS); theology (M Div). *Accreditation:* ACIPE; ATS. *Program availability:* Part-time. *Degree requirements:* For master's, variable foreign language requirement, thesis (for some programs), internship. *Faculty research:* Biblical exegesis.

**Pfeiffer University,** Program in Practical Theology, Misenheimer, NC 28109-0960. Offers MA. *Program availability:* Part-time, evening/weekend. *Entrance requirements:* For master's, minimum GPA of 2.75.

**Phillips Theological Seminary,** Programs in Theology, Tulsa, OK 74116. Offers administration of church agencies (M Div); campus ministry (M Div); church-related social work (M Div); college and seminary teaching (M Div); global mission work (M Div); institutional chaplaincy (M Div); ministerial vocations in Christian education (M Div); ministry (D Min), including parish ministry, pastoral counseling, practices of ministry; ministry and culture (MAMC), including Christian education, congregational leadership, history and practice of Christian spirituality, theology, ethics, and culture; ministry of music (M Div); pastoral care and counseling (M Div); pastoral ministry (M Div); theological studies (MTS). *Accreditation:* ATS. *Program availability:* Part-time, online learning. *Degree requirements:* For master's, thesis (for some programs); for doctorate, thesis/dissertation. *Entrance requirements:* For master's, minimum GPA of 2.5; for doctorate, M Div, minimum GPA of 3.0. *Faculty research:* Biblical studies, historical studies, theology and culture, practical theology, theology and film.

**Phoenix Seminary,** Graduate Programs, Phoenix, AZ 85018. Offers Biblical and theological studies (Graduate Diploma); Biblical communication (M Div); Biblical leadership (MA); Christian counseling (Graduate Diploma); counseling and family (M Div); leadership development (M Div); ministry (D Min); professional counseling (MA). *Accreditation:* ATS (one or more programs are accredited). *Program availability:* Part-time, evening/weekend. *Degree requirements:* For master's, 2 foreign languages, comprehensive exam; for doctorate, 2 foreign languages, thesis/dissertation. *Entrance requirements:* For master's, undergraduate degree with minimum GPA of 2.5; for doctorate, M Div (94 hours) with minimum GPA of 3.0. Additional exam requirements/recommendations for international students: Required—TOEFL (minimum score 587 paper-based; 92 iBT), TWE (minimum score 4.5).

**Piedmont International University,** Graduate School, Winston-Salem, NC 27101-5197. Offers Biblical studies (PhD); curriculum and instruction (M Ed); divinity (M Div); educational leadership (M Ed); leadership (MA, PhD); ministry (MA Min, D Min); non-language track (MABS); PhD preparation track (MABS). *Program availability:* Part-time, online learning. Terminal master's awarded for partial completion of doctoral program. *Degree requirements:* For master's, 2 foreign languages, comprehensive exam, thesis or alternative; for doctorate, 2 foreign languages, comprehensive exam. *Entrance requirements:* For master's, GRE General Test; for doctorate, Hebrew and Greek proficiency, MA. Additional exam requirements/recommendations for international

students: Required—TOEFL (minimum score 500 paper-based; 60 iBT). Electronic applications accepted. *Faculty research:* Theological and biblical studies.

**Piedmont International University,** Temple Baptist Seminary, Winston-Salem, NC 27101-5197. Offers M Div, D Min. *Program availability:* Part-time, evening/weekend, online learning. *Degree requirements:* For master's, comprehensive exam; for doctorate, comprehensive exam, thesis/dissertation. *Entrance requirements:* For master's, bachelor's degree or equivalent from accredited or recognized college or university with minimum GPA of 2.75 and one of the following: aptitude for graduate studies evidenced by the transcript record, the GRE, or ministry achievement; for doctorate, appropriate master's degree with minimum GPA of 3.0 including 6 semester hours each of Greek, Hebrew, and Biblical introduction (Old Testament and New Testament) and 12 semester hours of systematic theology. Additional exam requirements/recommendations for international students: Required—TOEFL (minimum score 500 paper-based; 60 iBT).

**Pittsburgh Theological Seminary,** Graduate and Professional Programs, Pittsburgh, PA 15206-2596. Offers divinity (M Div); theological studies (MA); theology (Th M); theology and ministry (MA, D Min); JD/M Div; M Div/MS; M Div/MSW. M Div/MSW offered jointly with University of Pittsburgh; JD/M Div with Duquesne University; M Div/MSPPM with Carnegie Mellon University. *Accreditation:* ATS (one or more programs are accredited). *Program availability:* Part-time, evening/weekend. *Faculty:* 16 full-time (5 women), 6 part-time/adjunct (2 women). *Students:* 153 full-time (56 women), 47 part-time (28 women); includes 57 minority (49 Black or African American, non-Hispanic/Latino; 3 Asian, non-Hispanic/Latino; 3 Hispanic/Latino; 1 Native Hawaiian or other Pacific Islander, non-Hispanic/Latino; 1 Two or more races, non-Hispanic/Latino), 9 international. Average age 35. 57 applicants, 93% accepted, 44 enrolled. In 2016, 34 master's, 16 doctorates awarded. *Degree requirements:* For master's, one foreign language, comprehensive exam (for some programs), thesis (for some programs); for doctorate, thesis/dissertation. *Entrance requirements:* For master's, bachelor's degree with minimum GPA of 2.7, interview, references; for doctorate, interview, references. Additional exam requirements/recommendations for international students: Required—TOEFL (minimum score 570 paper-based; 89 iBT). *Application deadline:* For fall admission, 6/30 priority date for domestic students, 12/1 for international students; for winter admission, 10/15 priority date for domestic students; for spring admission, 1/15 priority date for domestic students. Applications are processed on a rolling basis. Application fee: $50. Electronic applications accepted. *Expenses: Tuition:* Full-time $11,520; part-time $358 per credit. *Required fees:* $300. One-time fee: $125. *Financial support:* In 2016–17, 104 students received support. Career-related internships or fieldwork, scholarships/grants, and institutional work-study available. Financial award application deadline: 5/1; financial award applicants required to submit FAFSA. *Unit head:* Dr. Heathear H. Vacek, Dean of Faculty and Vice President for Academic Affairs, 412-924-1374, Fax: 412-924-1774, E-mail: hvacek@pts.edu. *Application contact:* Dr. Heather Vacek, Dean of Faculty and Vice President for Academic Affairs, 412-924-1374, Fax: 412-924-1774, E-mail: hvacek@pts.edu.
Website: http://www.pts.edu/

**Point Loma Nazarene University,** School of Theology and Christian Ministry, San Diego, CA 92106-2899. Offers M Min. *Program availability:* Part-time, online only, nine-week quads with eight weeks of online coursework and a one-week intensive. *Faculty:* 1 part-time/adjunct (0 women). *Students:* 13 part-time (5 women); includes 5 minority (1 American Indian or Alaska Native, non-Hispanic/Latino; 4 Hispanic/Latino). Average age 41. 6 applicants, 83% accepted, 3 enrolled. In 2016, 7 master's awarded. *Degree requirements:* For master's, thesis optional. *Entrance requirements:* For master's, letters of recommendation, essay, transcripts, interview. Additional exam requirements/recommendations for international students: Recommended—TOEFL. *Application deadline:* For fall admission, 8/30 priority date for domestic students; for spring admission, 4/4 priority date for domestic students; for summer admission, 6/20 priority date for domestic students. Applications are processed on a rolling basis. Application fee: $0. Electronic applications accepted. *Expenses:* $275 per credit. *Financial support:* Scholarships/grants available. Financial award application deadline: 6/5; financial award applicants required to submit FAFSA. *Faculty research:* Theology, Christian education, church administration. *Unit head:* Dr. Mark Maddix, Dean, 619-849-2234, E-mail: markmaddix@pointloma.edu. *Application contact:* Claire Buckley, Director of Graduate Admissions, 866-692-4723, E-mail: gradinfo@pointloma.edu.
Website: http://www.pointloma.edu/experience/academics/schools-departments/school-theology-christian-ministry/programs/master-ministry

**Pontifical Catholic University of Puerto Rico,** College of Arts and Humanities, Department of Theology and Philosophy, Ponce, PR 00717-0777. Offers M Div.

**Pontifical College Josephinum,** School of Theology, Columbus, OH 43235. Offers M Div, MA. All students are sponsored/selected by their diocese. *Accreditation:* ATS. *Program availability:* Part-time. *Degree requirements:* For master's, 3 foreign languages, comprehensive exam, thesis. *Entrance requirements:* For master's, GRE General Test, 15 credit hours of course work in philosophy, 6 credit hours of course work in scripture. Additional exam requirements/recommendations for international students: Required—TOEFL (minimum score 600 paper-based).

**Pontifical John Paul II Institute for Studies on Marriage and Family,** Graduate Programs, Washington, DC 20064. Offers biotechnology and ethics (MTS); marriage and family (MTS, STD, STL); theology (PhD).

**Pope St. John XXIII National Seminary,** Graduate Program, Weston, MA 02493-2618. Offers M Div. *Accreditation:* ATS.

**Princeton Theological Seminary,** Graduate and Professional Programs, Princeton, NJ 08542-0803. Offers M Div, MA, Th M, D Min, PhD. *Accreditation:* ACIPE; ATS. *Program availability:* Part-time. Terminal master's awarded for partial completion of doctoral program. *Degree requirements:* For doctorate, 2 foreign languages, thesis/dissertation, comprehensive exam (PhD), French and German. *Entrance requirements:* For doctorate, GRE General Test. Additional exam requirements/recommendations for international students: Required—TOEFL. Electronic applications accepted.

**Providence College,** Department of Theology, Providence, RI 02918. Offers Biblical studies (MA); theology (MA, MTS). *Program availability:* Part-time, evening/weekend. *Faculty:* 7 full-time (2 women), 2 part-time/adjunct (0 women). *Students:* 8 full-time (2 women), 13 part-time (4 women); includes 1 minority (Black or African American, non-Hispanic/Latino), 5 international. Average age 38. 9 applicants, 100% accepted, 7 enrolled. In 2016, 6 master's awarded. *Degree requirements:* For master's, comprehensive exam, thesis. *Entrance requirements:* For master's, GRE (for MA). Additional exam requirements/recommendations for international students: Required—TOEFL (minimum score 577 paper-based; 90 iBT). *Application deadline:* For fall admission, 7/15 priority date for domestic and international students; for spring admission, 11/15 priority date for domestic and international students; for summer admission, 3/15 priority date for domestic students, 3/15 for international students. Application fee: $55. *Expenses:* Contact institution. *Financial support:* Career-related internships or fieldwork, institutionally sponsored loans, and unspecified assistantships available. Support available to part-time students. Financial award application deadline: 8/1; financial award applicants required to submit FAFSA.
Website: http://www.providence.edu/theology/Pages/default.aspx

**Providence University College & Theological Seminary,** Theological Seminary, Otterburne, MB R0A 1G0, Canada. Offers children's ministry (Certificate); Christian studies (MA, Certificate); counseling (MA); cross-cultural discipleship (Certificate); divinity (M Div); educational studies (MA), including counseling psychology, educational ministries, student development, teaching English to speakers of other languages, training teachers of English to speakers of other languages; global studies (MA); lay counseling (Diploma); ministry (D Min); teaching English to speakers of other languages (Certificate); theological studies (MA); training teacher of English to speakers of other languages (Certificate); youth ministry (Certificate). *Accreditation:* ATS. *Program availability:* Part-time. *Degree requirements:* For master's, variable foreign language requirement, thesis (for some programs); for doctorate, thesis/dissertation. *Entrance requirements:* Additional exam requirements/recommendations for international students: Recommended—TOEFL (minimum score 550 paper-based). *Faculty research:* Studies in Isaiah, theology of sin.

**Queen's University at Kingston,** Queen's School of Religion, Kingston, ON K7L 3N6, Canada. Offers M Div, MTS, Certificate. *Program availability:* Part-time. *Degree requirements:* For master's, thesis (for some programs). *Entrance requirements:* For master's, minimum undergraduate B average. Additional exam requirements/ recommendations for international students: Required—TOEFL (minimum score 580 paper-based). *Faculty research:* Early Christian group formations, pastoral care and spiritual direction, feminist theology, public religion, interpretation of Biblical texts using psychologies of shame and trauma.

**Rabbinical Academy Mesivta Rabbi Chaim Berlin,** Graduate Program, Brooklyn, NY 11230-4715. Offers Advanced Talmudic Degree, Second Talmudic Degree. *Accreditation:* AARTS. *Degree requirements:* For other advanced degree, 2 foreign languages. *Entrance requirements:* For degree, must be a graduate of a rabbinical school.

**Rabbinical College Beth Shraga,** Graduate Programs, Monsey, NY 10952-3035. *Accreditation:* AARTS.

**Rabbinical College Bobover Yeshiva B'nei Zion,** Graduate Programs, Brooklyn, NY 11219. *Accreditation:* AARTS.

**Rabbinical College of Long Island,** Graduate Programs, Long Beach, NY 11561-3305. *Accreditation:* AARTS.

**Rabbinical Seminary of America,** Graduate Programs, Flushing, NY 11367. School offers a master's and first professional degree. *Accreditation:* AARTS.

**Reconstructionist Rabbinical College,** Graduate Programs, Wyncote, PA 19095-1898. Offers Jewish studies (MAJS); rabbinics (MAHL, DHL); women's studies (Certificate). Certificate offered jointly with Temple University. *Program availability:* Part-time. *Degree requirements:* For master's, one foreign language, thesis (MAJS), completion of rabbinical program (MAHL); for doctorate, one foreign language. *Entrance requirements:* For master's, GRE General Test; placement examinations in Hebrew and Judaism (MAHL); for doctorate, GRE General Test, placement examinations in Hebrew and Judaism. *Faculty research:* Bible, Hebrew Semitic texts, contemporary Judaism.

**Reformed Episcopal Seminary,** Graduate Program, Blue Bell, PA 19422. Offers M Div. *Accreditation:* ATS. *Entrance requirements:* For master's, personal reference letter, pastor's reference letter, transcript.

**Reformed Presbyterian Theological Seminary,** Graduate and Professional Programs, Pittsburgh, PA 15208-2594. Offers M Div, MTS, D Min. *Accreditation:* ATS. *Program availability:* Part-time, evening/weekend. Electronic applications accepted. *Faculty research:* Prayer.

**Reformed Theological Seminary–Atlanta Campus,** Graduate Programs, Marietta, GA 30067. Offers M Div, MABS, MAR, D Min, Certificate.

**Reformed Theological Seminary–Charlotte Campus,** Graduate and Professional Programs, Charlotte, NC 28226-6318. Offers biblical studies (MA); ministry (D Min); pastoral ministry (M Div); theological studies (MA). *Program availability:* Part-time. *Degree requirements:* For master's, comprehensive exam; for doctorate, thesis/ dissertation. *Entrance requirements:* For master's, minimum GPA of 2.6; for doctorate, minimum GPA of 3.0. Additional exam requirements/recommendations for international students: Required—TOEFL (minimum score 550 paper-based). Electronic applications accepted.

**Reformed Theological Seminary–Jackson Campus,** Graduate and Professional Programs, Jackson, MS 39209-3004. Offers Bible, theology, and missions (Certificate); Biblical exegesis (M Div); biblical studies (MA); Christian education (MA); counseling (M Div); marriage and family therapy (MA); ministry (D Min); missions (M Div, MA, D Min); theological studies (MA). *Accreditation:* AAMFT/COAMFTE (one or more programs are accredited); ATS (one or more programs are accredited). *Degree requirements:* For master's, thesis (for some programs), fieldwork; for doctorate, 2 foreign languages, thesis/dissertation. *Entrance requirements:* For master's, minimum GPA of 2.6; for doctorate, minimum GPA of 3.0. Additional exam requirements/ recommendations for international students: Required—TOEFL.

**Reformed Theological Seminary–Orlando Campus,** Graduate Programs, Oviedo, FL 32765. Offers Bible (Certificate); biblical studies (MA); counseling (MA); missions (Certificate); reformed expository preaching (D Min); reformed theology and ministry (D Min); theological studies (MA); theology (M Div, Certificate). *Program availability:* Part-time, online learning. *Faculty:* 12 full-time (0 women), 11 part-time/adjunct (2 women). *Students:* 340. *Application deadline:* Applications are processed on a rolling basis. Application fee: $75. Electronic applications accepted. *Expenses:* Tuition: Full-time $17,325. *Required fees:* $160. Tuition and fees vary according to course load. *Unit head:* Dr. Scott R. Swain, President, 407-278-4406, Fax: 407-366-9425. *Application contact:* Winston J. Miller, Director of Admissions, 800-752-4382, Fax: 407-366-9425, E-mail: applications.orlando@rts.edu.

**Reformed Theological Seminary–Washington D.C.,** Graduate and Professional Programs, McLean, VA 22102. Offers Bible (M Div); biblical studies (MA); practical theology (M Div); religion (MA); theology (M Div). *Program availability:* Part-time, evening/weekend. *Faculty:* 4 full-time (0 women), 10 part-time/adjunct (2 women). *Students:* 5 full-time (0 women), 86 part-time (7 women); includes 25 minority (4 Black or African American, non-Hispanic/Latino; 18 Asian, non-Hispanic/Latino; 3 Hispanic/ Latino), 1 international. Average age 35. 73 applicants, 95% accepted, 67 enrolled. In 2016, 8 master's awarded. *Degree requirements:* For master's, integrative paper. *Entrance requirements:* For master's, minimum undergraduate GPA of 2.6. Additional exam requirements/recommendations for international students: Required—TOEFL (minimum score 550 paper-based), TWE. *Application deadline:* Applications are processed on a rolling basis. Application fee: $75. Electronic applications accepted. *Expenses:* $495 per credit hour; $60-$80 student activity fee (fall/spring only); $200 graduation fee. *Financial support:* In 2016–17, 116 students received support. Scholarships/grants and tuition waivers (partial) available. Support available to part-time students. Financial award application deadline: 5/1. *Faculty research:* Theology, Biblical studies, cultural studies. *Unit head:* Dr. John S. Redd, Jr., President, 703-448-3393 Ext. 5107, E-mail: sredd@rts.edu. *Application contact:* Geoff M. Sackett, Director of Admissions, 703-448-3393 Ext. 5104, E-mail: gsackett@rts.edu.
Website: http://www.rts.edu/

**Regent College,** Program in Theology, Vancouver, BC V6T 2E4, Canada. Offers Christian history and theology (M Div, MATS); Christian studies (MATS, G Dip); Christianity, church and culture (M Div, MATS); scripture (M Div, MATS); theology (Th M). *Accreditation:* ATS (one or more programs are accredited). *Program availability:* Part-time. *Faculty:* 16 full-time (2 women), 23 part-time/adjunct (6 women). *Students:* 187 full-time (53 women), 268 part-time (103 women). 173 applicants, 65% accepted, 102 enrolled. *Degree requirements:* For master's, one foreign language, comprehensive exam (for some programs), thesis (for some programs). *Entrance requirements:* For master's, minimum GPA of 2.8 (MATS, M Div), 3.3 (Th M); for G Dip, minimum GPA of 2.8. Additional exam requirements/recommendations for international students: Required—TOEFL (minimum score 575 paper-based; 90 iBT), IELTS (minimum score 6.5). *Application deadline:* For fall admission, 2/1 priority date for domestic students, 1/1 priority date for international students; for winter admission, 7/2 priority date for domestic and international students; for spring admission, 2/1 for domestic students, 1/1 for international students. Applications are processed on a rolling basis. Application fee: $60 Canadian dollars. Electronic applications accepted. *Expenses:* $13,000 CAD (for Graduate Diploma and Th M); $32,000 CAD (for MA in theological studies); $49,000 CAD (for M Div). *Financial support:* Teaching assistantships, career-related internships or fieldwork, scholarships/grants, and health care benefits available. Financial award application deadline: 3/1. *Faculty research:* Integration of theology with culture, Biblical studies. *Unit head:* Dr. Jeff Greenman, President, 604-221-3318, Fax: 604-224-3097, E-mail: presidentsoffice@regent-college.edu. *Application contact:* Admissions, 604-224-3245, Fax: 604-224-3097, E-mail: admissions@regent-college.edu.

**Regent University,** Graduate School, School of Divinity, Virginia Beach, VA 23464-9800. Offers divinity (M Div), including Biblical studies (M Div, MTS, PhD), chaplain ministry, Christian theology (M Div, MTS, PhD), church and ministry (M Div, MA), history of Christianity (M Div, MTS, PhD), inter-cultural studies (M Div, MA), interdisciplinary studies (M Div, MA, MTS), marketplace ministry, worship and media (M Div, MA); leadership and renewal (D Min), including Christian leadership and renewal, clinical pastoral education, community transformation, military ministry, ministry leadership coaching; practical theology (MA), including church and ministry (M Div, MA), inter-cultural studies (M Div, MA), interdisciplinary studies (M Div, MA, MTS), worship and media (M Div, MA); theological studies (MTS, PhD), including Biblical studies (M Div, MTS, PhD), Christian theology (M Div, MTS, PhD), history of Christianity (M Div, MTS, PhD), interdisciplinary studies (M Div, MA, MTS). *Accreditation:* ACIPE; ATS. *Program availability:* Part-time, evening/weekend, 100% online, blended/hybrid learning. *Faculty:* 15 full-time (3 women), 51 part-time/adjunct (6 women). *Students:* 148 full-time (60 women), 787 part-time (321 women); includes 506 minority (416 Black or African American, non-Hispanic/Latino; 1 American Indian or Alaska Native, non-Hispanic/ Latino; 23 Asian, non-Hispanic/Latino; 54 Hispanic/Latino; 1 Native Hawaiian or other Pacific Islander, non-Hispanic/Latino; 11 Two or more races, non-Hispanic/Latino), 31 international. Average age 43. 1,020 applicants, 42% accepted, 276 enrolled. In 2016, 127 master's, 25 doctorates awarded. *Degree requirements:* For master's, comprehensive exam, thesis or alternative, internship; for doctorate, thesis/dissertation or alternative. *Entrance requirements:* For master's, minimum undergraduate GPA of 2.75, writing sample, personal goal statement, college transcripts; for doctorate, GRE, minimum graduate GPA of 3.5 (PhD), 3.0 (D Min); clergy recommendations; writing sample; transcripts; resume; interview. Additional exam requirements/recommendations for international students: Required—TOEFL (minimum score 577 paper-based). *Application deadline:* For fall admission, 5/1 priority date for domestic students. Applications are processed on a rolling basis. Application fee: $50. Electronic applications accepted. *Expenses:* Contact institution. *Financial support:* In 2016–17, 602 students received support. Career-related internships or fieldwork, scholarships/ grants, and unspecified assistantships available. Support available to part-time students. *Faculty research:* Greek and Hebrew, theology, spiritual formation, global missions and world Christianity, women in ministry leadership. *Unit head:* Dr. Cornelius Bekker, Dean, 757-352-4401, Fax: 757-352-4597, E-mail: clbekker@regent.edu. *Application contact:* Heidi Cece, Assistant Vice President of Enrollment Management, 800-373-5504, Fax: 757-352-4381, E-mail: admissions@regent.edu.
Website: http://www.regent.edu/sod/

**Regis College,** Graduate and Professional Programs, Toronto, ON M5S 2Z5, Canada. Offers eastern Christian studies (Certificate); Ignatian spirituality (Diploma); ministry (D Min); ministry and spirituality (MAMS); philosophical studies (Diploma); retreat direction (Certificate); sacred theology (STM, STD, STB, STL); spiritual direction (Diploma); theological studies (MTS, Diploma); theology (M Div, MA, Th M, PhD, Th D); M Div/MA. *Accreditation:* ATS (one or more programs are accredited). Terminal master's awarded for partial completion of doctoral program. *Degree requirements:* For master's, 2 foreign languages, thesis; for doctorate, 3 foreign languages, comprehensive exam, thesis/dissertation. *Entrance requirements:* For doctorate, minimum GPA of 3.7. Additional exam requirements/recommendations for international students: Required—TOEFL (minimum score 580 paper-based; 93 iBT), TWE (minimum score 5).

**Sacred Heart Major Seminary,** School of Theology, Detroit, MI 48206-1799. Offers pastoral studies (MAPS); theology (M Div, MA). *Accreditation:* ACIPE; ATS. *Program availability:* Part-time, evening/weekend. *Degree requirements:* For master's, one foreign language, thesis optional, integrating project. *Entrance requirements:* For master's, GRE, previous course work in philosophy and theology. *Faculty research:* Local church history, patristics, spirituality, religious education.

**Sacred Heart School of Theology,** Graduate and Professional Programs, Hales Corners, WI 53130-0429. Offers priestly formation (Certificate); theology (M Div, MA). *Accreditation:* ACIPE; ATS. *Program availability:* Part-time. *Degree requirements:* For master's, essay or comprehensive exam. *Entrance requirements:* For master's, MAT, 6 hours of course work each in philosophy and theology, letter of recommendation. Additional exam requirements/recommendations for international students: Required—TOEFL.

**St. Andrew's College,** Graduate Programs in Theology, Saskatoon, SK S7N 0W3, Canada. Offers M Div, MTS, STM, D Min, Diploma. *Accreditation:* ATS. *Entrance requirements:* Additional exam requirements/recommendations for international students: Required—TOEFL.

**St. Andrew's College in Winnipeg,** Graduate Programs, Winnipeg, MB R3T 2M7, Canada. Offers M Div. *Faculty research:* Church history, doctrine, liturgical theology.

**St. Augustine's Seminary of Toronto,** Graduate and Professional Programs, Scarborough, ON M1M 1M3, Canada. Offers divinity (M Div); lay ministry (Diploma); religious education (MRE); theological studies (MTS, Diploma). *Accreditation:* ATS. *Program availability:* Part-time, evening/weekend. *Entrance requirements:* Additional exam requirements/recommendations for international students: Required—TOEFL (minimum score 580 paper-based), TWE (minimum score 5).

**St. Bernard's School of Theology and Ministry,** Graduate and Professional Programs, Rochester, NY 14618. Offers pastoral studies (MA, Certificate); theological studies (MA); theology (M Div). *Accreditation:* ATS (one or more programs are accredited). *Program availability:* Part-time, evening/weekend. *Faculty:* 4 full-time (3 women), 4 part-time/adjunct (1 woman). *Students:* 1 (woman) full-time, 102 part-time (59

women); includes 6 minority (1 Black or African American, non-Hispanic/Latino; 3 Asian, non-Hispanic/Latino; 2 Hispanic/Latino). *Degree requirements:* For master's, variable foreign language requirement, thesis (for some programs). *Entrance requirements:* For master's, minimum GPA of 2.5. *Application deadline:* Applications are processed on a rolling basis. Application fee: $75. *Expenses: Tuition:* Full-time $10,644; part-time $3548 per year. *Required fees:* $40 per semester. *Financial support:* In 2016–17, 30 students received support. Fellowships, research assistantships, teaching assistantships, career-related internships or fieldwork, scholarships/grants, and tuition waivers (partial) available. Support available to part-time students. Financial award application deadline: 4/1; financial award applicants required to submit FAFSA. *Unit head:* Rev. George Heyman, President, 585-271-3657 Ext. 292, Fax: 585-271-2045, E-mail: george.heyman@stbernards.edu. *Application contact:* Mark R. Capellazzi, Director of Recruitment and Financial Aid, 585-271-3657 Ext. 289, Fax: 585-271-2045, E-mail: admissions@stbernards.edu.
Website: http://www.stbernards.edu/

**St. Catherine University,** Graduate Programs, Program in Theology, St. Paul, MN 55105. Offers catechetical ministry (Certificate); pastoral ministry (Certificate); spiritual direction (Certificate); theology (MA). *Program availability:* Part-time. *Degree requirements:* For master's, comprehensive exam, thesis (for some programs). *Entrance requirements:* For master's, MAT, minimum GPA of 3.0. Additional exam requirements/recommendations for international students: Required—Michigan English Language Assessment Battery or TOEFL (minimum score 600 paper-based; 100 iBT). *Expenses:* Contact institution. *Faculty research:* Feminist scholarship, historical theology, symbols, rites of purification, spirituality.

**Saint Charles Borromeo Seminary, Overbrook,** Graduate and Professional Programs, Division of Theology, Wynnewood, PA 19096. Offers M Div, MA. *Degree requirements:* For master's, comprehensive exam, research papers. *Entrance requirements:* For master's, M Div. Additional exam requirements/recommendations for international students: Required—TOEFL.

**St. John's Seminary,** Graduate and Professional Programs, Camarillo, CA 93012-2598. Offers divinity (M Div); pastoral ministry (MAPM); theology (MA). *Accreditation:* ATS. *Program availability:* Part-time. *Degree requirements:* For master's, comprehensive exam (for some programs), thesis optional, comprehensive integration paper (MAPM). *Entrance requirements:* For master's, GRE General Test, minimum GPA of 3.5 (MA), 2.5 (MAPM). Additional exam requirements/recommendations for international students: Required—TOEFL (minimum score 550 paper-based; 79 iBT). Electronic applications accepted. *Faculty research:* Biblical studies, moral theology, church history, systematic theology, spiritual theology.

**Saint John's Seminary,** Graduate Programs, Brighton, MA 02135. Offers M Div, MA Th, MAM.

**St. John's University,** St. John's College of Liberal Arts and Sciences, Department of Theology and Religious Studies, Queens, NY 11439. Offers theology (MA). *Accreditation:* ACIPE. *Program availability:* Part-time, evening/weekend. *Entrance requirements:* For master's, comprehensive exam, thesis optional, portfolio. *Entrance requirements:* For master's, minimum GPA of 3.0; bachelor's degree in related area; 12 undergraduate credits in theology, philosophy or related subjects. Additional exam requirements/recommendations for international students: Required—TOEFL (minimum score 600 paper-based; 100 iBT), IELTS (minimum score 7). Electronic applications accepted. *Faculty research:* Systematic theology, moral theory, Biblical studies, pastoral theology, church history.

**Saint John's University,** Saint John's School of Theology and Seminary, Collegeville, MN 56321. Offers divinity (M Div); liturgical music (MA); liturgical studies (MA); pastoral ministry (MA); theology (MA), including church history, liturgy, monastic studies, scripture, spirituality, systematics; M Div/MA. *Program availability:* Part-time, online learning. *Degree requirements:* For master's, one foreign language, comprehensive exam (for some programs), thesis (for some programs). *Entrance requirements:* For master's, GRE General Test or MAT. Electronic applications accepted. *Faculty research:* Religious education, biblical literature.

**St. Joseph's Seminary,** Graduate and Professional Programs, Yonkers, NY 10704. Offers Catholic philosophical studies (MA); divinity (M Div); pastoral studies (MAPS); theology (MA). *Accreditation:* ATS. *Degree requirements:* For master's, one foreign language, thesis. *Entrance requirements:* For master's, 27 credits in philosophy and 9 in theology.

**Saint Leo University,** Graduate Studies in Theology, Saint Leo, FL 33574-6665. Offers MA, Certificate. *Program availability:* Part-time, evening/weekend, 100% online, blended/hybrid learning. *Faculty:* 10 full-time (0 women), 10 part-time/adjunct (3 women). *Students:* 253 full-time (91 women); includes 54 minority (35 Black or African American, non-Hispanic/Latino; 1 Asian, non-Hispanic/Latino; 13 Hispanic/Latino; 1 Native Hawaiian or other Pacific Islander, non-Hispanic/Latino; 4 Two or more races, non-Hispanic/Latino; 3 international. Average age 50. 115 applicants, 83% accepted, 55 enrolled. In 2016, 73 master's, 2 other advanced degrees awarded. *Entrance requirements:* For master's, official transcripts, letter of recommendation, bachelor's degree from regionally-accredited university with minimum GPA of 3.0. Additional exam requirements/recommendations for international students: Required—TOEFL (minimum score 550 paper-based; 80 iBT). *Application deadline:* For fall admission, 7/1 priority date for domestic and international students; for spring admission, 11/1 priority date for domestic and international students. Applications are processed on a rolling basis. Application fee: $80. Electronic applications accepted. *Expenses:* $480 per semester hour. *Financial support:* In 2016–17, 3 students received support. Scholarships/grants and health care benefits available. Financial award application deadline: 3/1; financial award applicants required to submit FAFSA. *Faculty research:* Patristic theology, theology and economics, ethics of war and peace, ecclesiology, Catholic-Jewish relations. *Unit head:* Dr. Randall Woodard, Director, Graduate Theology, 352-588-8239, Fax: 352-588-8404, E-mail: randall.woodard@saintleo.edu. *Application contact:* Jennifer Shelley, Senior Associate Director of Graduate Admission, 800-707-8846, Fax: 352-588-7873, E-mail: grad.admissions@saintleo.edu.
Website: http://www.saintleo.edu/academics/graduate/theology.aspx

**Saint Louis University,** Graduate Education, College of Arts and Sciences, Department of Theological Studies, St. Louis, MO 63103. Offers historical theology (MA, PhD); theology (MA). *Program availability:* Part-time. *Degree requirements:* For master's, comprehensive exam; for doctorate, 4 foreign languages, comprehensive exam, thesis/dissertation, preliminary exams. *Entrance requirements:* For master's, GRE General Test, letters of recommendation, resume; for doctorate, GRE General Test, letters of recommendation, resumé, interview, transcripts, goal statement. Additional exam requirements/recommendations for international students: Required—TOEFL (minimum score 550 paper-based). Electronic applications accepted. *Faculty research:* Biblical and early church studies, medieval and renaissance studies, modern and American Christianity, comparative and interreligious studies, moral and ethical theology.

**Saint Mary Seminary and Graduate School of Theology,** Graduate and Professional Programs, Wickliffe, OH 44092-2527. Offers M Div, MA, D Min. *Accreditation:* ATS. *Program availability:* Part-time. *Degree requirements:* For master's, comprehensive

exam, symposium; for doctorate, thesis/dissertation, final project, symposium. *Entrance requirements:* For master's, GRE General Test, previous course work in religion; for doctorate, M Div or equivalent, 3 years in full-time ministry, interviews, ministry profile report. *Faculty research:* Pastoral ministry, theology of ministry, ecclesiology, American Catholics.

**St. Mary's Seminary and University,** Ecumenical Institute of Theology, Baltimore, MD 21210-1994. Offers church ministries (MA); theology (MA Th, Certificate). *Accreditation:* ATS. *Program availability:* Part-time, evening/weekend. *Degree requirements:* For master's, thesis or alternative, comprehensive exam or colloquium. *Expenses:* Contact institution. *Faculty research:* Scripture and ethics, theology and literature, early Christianity and Judaism, medical and social ethics.

**St. Mary's Seminary and University,** School of Theology, Baltimore, MD 21210-1994. Offers M Div, MA Th, STD, STB, STL. *Accreditation:* ATS (one or more programs are accredited). *Program availability:* Part-time. Terminal master's awarded for partial completion of doctoral program. *Degree requirements:* For master's, comprehensive exam; for other advanced degree, one foreign language, thesis. *Entrance requirements:* For master's, Computerized Adaptive Placement Assessment and Support System.

**Saint Mary's University,** Faculty of Arts, Department of Religious Studies, Halifax, NS B3H 3C3, Canada. Offers theology and religious studies (MA).

**St. Mary's University,** Graduate Studies, Program in Theology, San Antonio, TX 78228-8507. Offers MA. *Program availability:* Part-time, evening/weekend. *Faculty:* 4 full-time (0 women), 2 part-time/adjunct (0 women). *Students:* 3 full-time (all women), 17 part-time (10 women); includes 13 minority (1 Asian, non-Hispanic/Latino; 12 Hispanic/Latino), 1 international. Average age 37. 24 applicants, 29% accepted, 5 enrolled. In 2016, 3 master's awarded. *Degree requirements:* For master's, comprehensive exam, thesis optional, 10 clock hours (Graduate Learning Community Experience). *Entrance requirements:* For master's, undergraduate transcripts, writing sample. Additional exam requirements/recommendations for international students: Required—TOEFL (minimum score 550 paper-based; 80 iBT), IELTS (minimum score 6). *Application deadline:* For fall admission, 7/1 for domestic students; for spring admission, 11/15 for domestic students; for summer admission, 4/1 for domestic students. Applications are processed on a rolling basis. Application fee: $0. Electronic applications accepted. *Expenses: Tuition:* Full-time $15,600; part-time $865 per credit hour. *Required fees:* $148 per semester. *Financial support:* Research assistantships, career-related internships or fieldwork, Federal Work-Study, institutionally sponsored loans, scholarships/grants, health care benefits, and unspecified assistantships available. Financial award application deadline: 3/31; financial award applicants required to submit FAFSA. *Faculty research:* Catholic social teaching, recovery of the Jewishness of Jesus and of Christian beginnings, pneumatology of Old and New Testament, ethics of war and nonviolence, inter-religious dialogue. *Unit head:* Dr. Andrew Getz, Graduate Theology Program Director, 210-431-4348, E-mail: agetz@stmarytx.edu.
Website: https://www.stmarytx.edu/academics/graduate/masters/theology/

**Saint Meinrad School of Theology,** Master of Arts (Catholic Philosophical Studies) Program, Saint Meinrad, IN 47577. Offers MA. *Accreditation:* ATS. *Faculty:* 7 full-time (2 women), 2 part-time/adjunct (0 women). *Students:* 17 full-time (0 women), 2 international. Average age 32. In 2016, 8 master's awarded. *Degree requirements:* For master's, thesis. *Entrance requirements:* Additional exam requirements/recommendations for international students: Required—TOEFL (minimum score 550 paper-based; 80 iBT). *Application deadline:* For fall admission, 7/31 for domestic and international students; for winter admission, 11/15 for domestic and international students. Applications are processed on a rolling basis. Electronic applications accepted. *Expenses: Tuition:* Full-time $25,137; part-time $475 per credit hour. *Required fees:* $2900; $34 per course. *Financial support:* Federal Work-Study and scholarships/grants available. Financial award applicants required to submit FAFSA. *Unit head:* Dr. Robert Alvis, Academic Dean, 812-357-6543, Fax: 812-357-6816, E-mail: ralvis@saintmeinrad.edu. *Application contact:* Dr. John Schlachter, Director of Admissions, 812-357-6142, Fax: 812-357-6816, E-mail: jschlachter@saintmeinrad.edu.
Website: http://www.saintmeinrad.edu/priesthood-formation/academic-formation/pre-theologyma/

**Saint Meinrad School of Theology,** Master of Arts (Theology) Program, Saint Meinrad, IN 47577. Offers MA. *Accreditation:* ATS. *Program availability:* Part-time, evening/weekend. *Faculty:* 19 full-time (2 women), 6 part-time/adjunct (1 woman). *Students:* 1 full-time, 27 part-time (10 women), 1 international. Average age 45. In 2016, 15 master's awarded. *Degree requirements:* For master's, comprehensive exam, three capstone essays or one research paper. *Entrance requirements:* Additional exam requirements/recommendations for international students: Required—TOEFL (minimum score 550 paper-based; 80 iBT). *Application deadline:* For fall admission, 7/31 for domestic and international students; for winter admission, 11/15 for domestic and international students. Applications are processed on a rolling basis. Application fee: $30. Electronic applications accepted. *Expenses: Tuition:* Full-time $25,137; part-time $475 per credit hour. *Required fees:* $2900; $34 per course. *Financial support:* Federal Work-Study, institutionally sponsored loans, and scholarships/grants available. Support available to part-time students. Financial award application deadline: 7/31; financial award applicants required to submit FAFSA. *Unit head:* Sr. Jeana Visel, OSB, Director of Graduate Theology Programs, 812-357-6721, Fax: 812-357-6816. *Application contact:* Dr. John Schlachter, Director of Admissions, 812-357-6142, Fax: 812-357-6816, E-mail: apply@saintmeinrad.edu.

**Saint Meinrad School of Theology,** Master of Divinity Program, Saint Meinrad, IN 47577. Offers M Div. *Accreditation:* ATS. *Faculty:* 19 full-time (2 women), 6 part-time/adjunct (1 woman). *Students:* 106 full-time (0 women); includes 7 minority (1 Black or African American, non-Hispanic/Latino; 3 Asian, non-Hispanic/Latino; 3 Hispanic/Latino), 22 international. Average age 31. In 2016, 20 master's awarded. *Entrance requirements:* Additional exam requirements/recommendations for international students: Required—TOEFL (minimum score 550 paper-based; 80 iBT). *Application deadline:* For fall admission, 7/31 for domestic and international students; for winter admission, 11/15 for domestic and international students. Applications are processed on a rolling basis. Application fee: $0. Electronic applications accepted. *Expenses: Tuition:* Full-time $25,137; part-time $475 per credit hour. *Required fees:* $2900; $34 per course. *Financial support:* Federal Work-Study, institutionally sponsored loans, and scholarships/grants available. Support available to part-time students. Financial award application deadline: 7/31; financial award applicants required to submit FAFSA. *Unit head:* Dr. Robert Alvis, Academic Dean, 812-357-6543, Fax: 812-357-6816, E-mail: ralvis@saintmeinrad.edu. *Application contact:* Dr. John Schlachter, Director of Admissions, 812-357-6142, Fax: 812-357-6816, E-mail: apply@saintmeinrad.edu.
Website: http://www.saintmeinrad.edu/priesthood-formation/academic-formation/master-of-divinity/

**St. Norbert College,** Master of Theological Studies Program, De Pere, WI 54115-2099. Offers MTS. *Program availability:* Part-time-only, evening/weekend. *Faculty:* 7 part-time/adjunct (3 women). *Students:* 45 part-time (31 women); includes 10 minority (9 Hispanic/Latino; 1 Two or more races, non-Hispanic/Latino). Average age 51. 4 applicants, 100% accepted, 4 enrolled. In 2016, 2 master's awarded. *Degree requirements:* For master's, comprehensive exam, thesis. *Entrance requirements:* For master's, minimum of 6 credits of course work in theology/religious studies, BA from accredited institution. *Application deadline:* Applications are processed on a rolling basis. Application fee: $50. Electronic applications accepted. *Expenses: Tuition:* Part-time $675 per credit. Tuition and fees vary according to program. *Financial support:* In 2016–17, 10 students received support. Scholarships/grants available. Support available to part-time students. *Faculty research:* Practical theology, Karl Rahner, women in the Bible and Christian ethics. *Unit head:* Dr. Howard Ebert, Director, 920-403-3956, Fax: 920-403-4086, E-mail: howard.ebert@snc.edu. *Application contact:* Dinah Grassel, Program Coordinator, 920-403-3957, Fax: 920-403-4086, E-mail: dinah.grassel@snc.edu. Website: http://www.snc.edu/mts/

**St. Patrick's Seminary & University,** School of Theology, Menlo Park, CA 94025-3596. Offers M Div, MA, STB. STB offered jointly with St. Mary's Seminary and University. *Accreditation:* ATS (one or more programs are accredited). *Program availability:* Part-time. *Degree requirements:* For master's, comprehensive exam, thesis or alternative. *Entrance requirements:* For master's, GRE General Test, minimum GPA of 3.0, interview. Additional exam requirements/recommendations for international students: Required—TOEFL (minimum score 550 paper-based; 80 iBT), TWE. *Faculty research:* Systematic theology, sacred scripture, moral theology, liturgy.

**Saint Paul School of Theology,** Graduate and Professional Programs, Overland Park, KS 66211. Offers M Div, MA, MTS, D Min. *Accreditation:* ACIPE; ATS. *Program availability:* Part-time. *Degree requirements:* For doctorate, thesis/dissertation. *Entrance requirements:* For master's, minimum GPA of 2.75; for doctorate, minimum GPA of 3.0. Additional exam requirements/recommendations for international students: Required—TOEFL. *Faculty research:* Religion and aging; leadership development; feminist, African-American, and liberation theology; rural ministry; worship and the arts.

**Saint Paul University,** Faculty of Canon Law, Ottawa, ON K1S 1C4, Canada. Offers canon law (MCL, JCD, PhD, Graduate Certificate, JCL); canonical practice (Graduate Certificate); ecclesiastical administration (Graduate Certificate). *Program availability:* Part-time. *Degree requirements:* For master's, one foreign language; for doctorate, one foreign language, comprehensive exam, thesis/dissertation; for other advanced degree, one foreign language, comprehensive exam and seminar paper (JCL). *Entrance requirements:* For master's, appropriate bachelor's degree, 18 credits in theology; for doctorate, JCL or MCL; for other advanced degree, B Th or equivalent (JCL), appropriate bachelor's degree, 18 credits in theology. *Faculty research:* Questions related to Church law.

**Saint Paul University,** Faculty of Human Sciences, Program in Counseling and Spirituality, Ottawa, ON K1S 1C4, Canada. Offers individual or marital/couple counseling (MA); spiritual care (MA). *Program availability:* Part-time. *Degree requirements:* For master's, research project or thesis. *Entrance requirements:* For master's, honors BA in human sciences, minimum B average, 12 theology credits.

**Saint Paul University,** Faculty of Theology, Ottawa, ON K1S 1C4, Canada. Offers MA Th, MP Th, MRE, D Min, D Th, PhD, L Th. *Accreditation:* ATS. *Degree requirements:* For master's and L Th, one foreign language; for doctorate, one foreign language, comprehensive exam, thesis/dissertation. *Entrance requirements:* For master's, B Th; for doctorate, MA Th, L Th, MP Th, M Div. *Faculty research:* Biblical studies, systematic and historical theology, ethics, spirituality, Eastern Christian studies, applied theology.

**St. Peter's Seminary,** Department of Theology, London, ON N6A 3Y1, Canada. Offers M Div, MTS. *Accreditation:* ATS.

**Saints Cyril and Methodius Seminary,** Graduate and Professional Programs, Orchard Lake, MI 48324. Offers pastoral ministry (MAPM); religious education (MARE); theology (M Div, MA). *Program availability:* Part-time.

**St. Stephen's College,** Programs in Theology, Edmonton, AB T6G 2J6, Canada. Offers ministry (D Min); pastoral counseling (MA); social transformation ministry (MA); spirituality and liturgy (MA); theological studies (MTS); theology (M Th). *Program availability:* Part-time, evening/weekend, online learning. Terminal master's awarded for partial completion of doctoral program. *Degree requirements:* For master's, thesis; for doctorate, thesis/dissertation. *Entrance requirements:* Additional exam requirements/recommendations for international students: Required—TOEFL. Electronic applications accepted. *Faculty research:* Methodology for theological education, practice and supervision for ministry.

**St. Thomas University,** School of Theology and Ministry, Institute for Pastoral Ministries, Miami Gardens, FL 33054-6459. Offers pastoral ministries (MA, Certificate); practical theology (PhD). *Program availability:* Part-time, evening/weekend. *Degree requirements:* For master's, comprehensive exam; for doctorate, comprehensive exam, thesis/dissertation. *Entrance requirements:* For master's, interview, minimum GPA of 3.0 or GRE; for doctorate, GRE, MA in theology. Additional exam requirements/recommendations for international students: Required—TOEFL (minimum score 550 paper-based; 79 iBT). Electronic applications accepted.

**St. Tikhon's Orthodox Theological Seminary,** Divinity Program, South Canaan, PA 18459. Offers M Div. *Accreditation:* ATS. *Program availability:* Part-time. *Faculty:* 8 full-time (1 woman), 6 part-time/adjunct (0 women). *Students:* 29 full-time (1 woman); includes 1 minority (Black or African American, non-Hispanic/Latino), 2 international. Average age 35. 16 applicants, 100% accepted, 12 enrolled. In 2016, 15 master's awarded. *Degree requirements:* For master's, thesis optional. *Entrance requirements:* For master's, reference letters, official transcripts. Additional exam requirements/recommendations for international students: Required—TOEFL (minimum score 560 paper-based; 87 iBT), IELTS (minimum score 5.5). *Application deadline:* For fall admission, 7/30 for domestic students, 6/30 for international students. Applications are processed on a rolling basis. Application fee: $15. *Expenses:* Contact institution. *Financial support:* Scholarships/grants and tuition waivers (full and partial) available. *Faculty research:* Church history, patristics, scripture, spirituality. *Unit head:* Steven Voytovich, Dean/Director of Admissions, 570-561-1818 Ext. 101, Fax: 570-937-4139, E-mail: steven.voytovich@stots.edu. Website: http://www.stots.edu/master_of_divinity.html

**St. Vincent de Paul Regional Seminary,** Graduate and Professional Programs, Boynton Beach, FL 33436-4899. Offers theology (M Div, MA Th). *Accreditation:* ATS. *Program availability:* Part-time. *Degree requirements:* For master's, comprehensive exam (for some programs), thesis optional. *Entrance requirements:* For master's, GRE General Test, MAT. Additional exam requirements/recommendations for international students: Required—TOEFL.

**Saint Vincent Seminary,** School of Theology, Latrobe, PA 15650-2690. Offers Catholic philosophical studies (MA); ecclesial ministry (MA); ministry (M Div); monastic studies (MA); sacred scripture (MA); systematic theology (MA). *Accreditation:* ATS. *Program availability:* Part-time, evening/weekend. *Faculty:* 6 full-time (2 women), 16 part-time/adjunct (2 women). *Students:* 44 full-time (0 women), 1 part-time (0 women); includes 5 minority (1 American Indian or Alaska Native, non-Hispanic/Latino; 2 Asian, non-Hispanic/Latino; 1 Hispanic/Latino; 1 Two or more races, non-Hispanic/Latino), 7 international. Average age 33. 12 applicants, 100% accepted, 12 enrolled. In 2016, 12 master's awarded. *Degree requirements:* For master's, one foreign language, comprehensive exam, thesis optional, public presentation. *Entrance requirements:* For

master's, minimum GPA of 2.5. Additional exam requirements/recommendations for international students: Required—TOEFL (minimum score 550 paper-based; 79 iBT). *Application deadline:* For fall admission, 8/15 for domestic and international students. Applications are processed on a rolling basis. Application fee: $34. *Expenses: Tuition:* Full-time $26,320; part-time $874 per credit. *Financial support:* In 2016–17, 45 students received support. Scholarships/grants available. Support available to part-time students. Financial award application deadline: 8/15. *Faculty research:* Church history, preaching, psychology of religion, Biblical studies, moral theology. *Unit head:* Very Rev. Edward M. Mazich, OSB, President/Rector, 724-805-2845, Fax: 724-532-5052, E-mail: edward.mazich@stvincent.edu. *Application contact:* Rev. Patrick T. Cronauer, OSB, Academic Dean, 724-805-2324, Fax: 724-805-2880, E-mail: patrick.cronauer@stvincent.edu. Website: http://www.saintvincentseminary.edu

**St. Vladimir's Orthodox Theological Seminary,** Graduate School of Theology, Crestwood, NY 10707-1699. Offers theology (M Div, M Th, MA, D Min). MA in general theological studies and M Div offered jointly with St. Nersess Seminary. *Accreditation:* ATS. *Program availability:* Part-time. *Faculty:* 8 full-time (1 woman), 21 part-time/adjunct (2 women). *Students:* 71 full-time (6 women), 4 part-time (0 women); includes 8 minority (2 Black or African American, non-Hispanic/Latino; 6 Asian, non-Hispanic/Latino), 15 international. Average age 29. 41 applicants, 95% accepted, 37 enrolled. In 2016, 26 master's awarded. *Degree requirements:* For master's, one foreign language, thesis, fieldwork; for doctorate, thesis/dissertation, fieldwork. *Entrance requirements:* For doctorate, M Div, minimum GPA of 3.0. Additional exam requirements/recommendations for international students: Required—TOEFL (minimum score 96 iBT). *Application deadline:* For fall admission, 5/1 priority date for domestic and international students. Applications are processed on a rolling basis. Application fee: $50. Electronic applications accepted. *Expenses: Tuition:* Full-time $12,000; part-time $500 per credit. *Required fees:* $375; $300 per semester. Part-time tuition and fees vary according to course load and campus/location. *Financial support:* In 2016–17, 75 students received support. Fellowships, research assistantships, teaching assistantships, and scholarships/grants available. Financial award application deadline: 4/1; financial award applicants required to submit FAFSA. *Faculty research:* Patristics, New Testament, hospital ministry. *Unit head:* Rev. Dr. John Behr, Dean, 914-961-8313, Fax: 914-961-4507, E-mail: jbehr@svots.edu. *Application contact:* Gabrielle Russin, Student Affairs Administrator, 914-961-8313 Ext. 348, Fax: 914-961-4507, E-mail: grussin@svots.edu.

**Samford University,** Beeson School of Divinity, Birmingham, AL 35229. Offers M Div, MATS, D Min, JD/M Div, JD/MATS, M Div/M Ed, M Div/MBA, M Div/MM, M Div/MSW, MATS/MSW. *Program availability:* Part-time. *Faculty:* 14 full-time (1 woman), 1 part-time/adjunct (0 women). *Students:* 159 full-time (28 women), 8 part-time (4 women); includes 24 minority (19 Black or African American, non-Hispanic/Latino; 1 Asian, non-Hispanic/Latino; 2 Hispanic/Latino; 2 Two or more races, non-Hispanic/Latino), 2 international. Average age 29. 65 applicants, 94% accepted, 45 enrolled. In 2016, 36 master's, 8 doctorates awarded. *Degree requirements:* For master's, 2 foreign languages, thesis optional; for doctorate, thesis/dissertation. *Entrance requirements:* For master's, minimum GPA of 2.5; for doctorate, minimum GPA of 3.0. Additional exam requirements/recommendations for international students: Required—TOEFL (minimum score 550 paper-based; 80 iBT). *Application deadline:* For fall admission, 2/15 for domestic and international students; for spring admission, 10/1 for domestic and international students. Application fee: $35. Electronic applications accepted. *Expenses:* $13,628. *Financial support:* In 2016–17, 140 students received support. Federal Work-Study, institutionally sponsored loans, scholarships/grants, and tuition waivers (full and partial) available. Financial award application deadline: 2/15; financial award applicants required to submit FAFSA. *Faculty research:* Pastoral Epistles, theology of the Protestant Reformation, The Reformation and preaching, Romans, theology of Deuteronomy. *Unit head:* Dr. Timothy George, Dean, 205-726-2632, E-mail: tfgeorge@samford.edu. *Application contact:* Sherri S. Brown, Director of Admission, 205-726-2066, Fax: E-mail: sbrown5@samford.edu. Website: http://www.beesondivinity.com/

**San Francisco Theological Seminary,** Graduate and Professional Programs, San Anselmo, CA 94960. Offers M Div, MA, MATS, D Min, PhD, Th D, M Div/MA. MA, Th D, PhD, M Div/MA offered jointly with Graduate Theological Union. *Accreditation:* ACIPE; ATS (one or more programs are accredited). *Program availability:* Part-time. *Degree requirements:* For master's, one foreign language, thesis (for some programs); for doctorate, thesis/dissertation. *Entrance requirements:* For master's, minimum GPA of 3.0; for doctorate, M Div. Additional exam requirements/recommendations for international students: Required—TOEFL.

**Santa Clara University,** Jesuit School of Theology, Berkeley, CA 94709. Offers Biblical languages (MABL); Biblical studies (MTS); Christian spirituality (MTS); church history (MTS); cultural and historical studies of Catholicism (MTS); ethics and social theory/religion and society (MTS); history of art and religion (MTS); liturgical studies (MTS); pastoral ministry (M Div); systematic and philosophical theology (MTS); theology (MA, MTS, Th M, STD, STB, STL); M Div/MA. *Program availability:* Part-time, evening/weekend, 100% online. *Faculty:* 20 full-time (5 women), 6 part-time/adjunct (3 women). *Students:* 125 full-time (29 women), 9 part-time (5 women); includes 71 minority (22 Black or African American, non-Hispanic/Latino; 27 Asian, non-Hispanic/Latino; 19 Hispanic/Latino; 2 Native Hawaiian or other Pacific Islander, non-Hispanic/Latino; 1 Two or more races, non-Hispanic/Latino). Average age 36. 93 applicants, 92% accepted, 56 enrolled. In 2016, 55 master's, 5 doctorates awarded. *Entrance requirements:* For master's, GRE, 2 letters of recommendation, resume, transcripts; for doctorate, GRE, master's degree or equivalent, resume, statement of purpose, transcripts, 2 letters of recommendation, research paper. Additional exam requirements/recommendations for international students: Required—TOEFL. *Application deadline:* For fall admission, 3/1 priority date for domestic students; for spring admission, 10/1 priority date for domestic students. Applications are processed on a rolling basis. Application fee: $50 ($0 for international students). Electronic applications accepted. *Expenses:* Contact institution. *Financial support:* Scholarships/grants and unspecified assistantships available. Financial award application deadline: 3/1; financial award applicants required to submit FAFSA. *Faculty research:* Religion and culture, interreligious dialogue, social ethics and restorative justice, Ignatian spirituality. *Unit head:* Alison Benders, Associate Dean, 510-549-5055, E-mail: ambenders@scu.edu. *Application contact:* Barbara Godoy, Assistant Dean of Enrollment Management, 510-549-5016, E-mail: bgodoy@scu.edu. Website: http://www.scu.edu/jst/

**Seattle Pacific University,** Master of Arts in Theology Program, Seattle, WA 98119-1997. Offers Asian American ministry (MA); business and applied theology (MA); Christian leadership (MA); Christian scripture (MA); Christian studies (Graduate Certificate); reconciliation and intercultural studies (MA); theology (MA). *Degree requirements:* For master's, internship or thesis. *Entrance requirements:* For master's, two letters of recommendation; personal statement; bachelor's degree from regionally-accredited college or university or its equivalent; official copy of transcripts from college or university that granted the bachelor's degree and any institution attended since that time; minimum GPA of 3.0. Additional exam requirements/recommendations for international students: Required—TOEFL (minimum score 550 paper-based). Electronic applications accepted.

*Theology*

**Seattle Pacific University,** The Master of Divinity Program, Seattle, WA 98119-1997. Offers M Div. *Entrance requirements:* For master's, two letters of recommendation; personal statement; BA; official transcript; minimum GPA of 3.0. Additional exam requirements/recommendations for international students: Required—TOEFL (minimum score 550 paper-based).

**The Seattle School of Theology and Psychology,** Graduate Programs, Seattle, WA 98121. Offers Christian studies (MA); counseling psychology (MA); divinity (M Div). *Program availability:* Part-time. *Entrance requirements:* For master's, MAT.

**Seattle University,** School of Theology and Ministry, Program in Divinity, Seattle, WA 98122-1090. Offers M Div, D Min. *Accreditation:* ATS. *Program availability:* Part-time, evening/weekend. *Faculty:* 11 full-time (6 women), 14 part-time/adjunct (6 women). *Students:* 13 full-time (11 women), 54 part-time (34 women); includes 21 minority (11 Black or African American, non-Hispanic/Latino; 1 American Indian or Alaska Native, non-Hispanic/Latino; 6 Asian, non-Hispanic/Latino; 4 Hispanic/Latino), 2 international. Average age 45. 18 applicants, 56% accepted, 8 enrolled. In 2016, 9 master's, 1 doctorate awarded. *Entrance requirements:* For master's, minimum GPA of 2.75 (3.0 for international students); two years of experience in some form of education, ministry, or service as a profession or volunteer; recommendations; interview with admissions committee. *Application deadline:* For fall admission, 7/1 priority date for domestic students. *Financial support:* In 2016–17, 43 students received support. Career-related internships or fieldwork and Federal Work-Study available. Support available to part-time students. Financial award applicants required to submit FAFSA. *Unit head:* Dr. Mark Markuly, Dean, 206-296-5330, Fax: 206-296-5329, E-mail: markulym@seattleu.edu. *Application contact:* Catherine Kehoe Fallon, Admissions Coordinator, 206-296-5333, Fax: 206-296-5329, E-mail: fallon@seattleu.edu. Website: https://www.seattleu.edu/stm/degrees/mdiv/

**Seattle University,** School of Theology and Ministry, Program in Transforming Spirituality, Seattle, WA 98122-1090. Offers MATS, Certificate. *Accreditation:* ATS. *Program availability:* Part-time, evening/weekend. *Faculty:* 11 full-time (6 women), 14 part-time/adjunct (6 women). *Students:* 2 full-time (both women), 11 part-time (9 women); includes 3 minority (1 American Indian or Alaska Native, non-Hispanic/Latino; 1 Hispanic/Latino; 1 Two or more races, non-Hispanic/Latino), 2 international. Average age 50. 3 applicants, 67% accepted, 2 enrolled. In 2016, 3 master's, 1 Certificate awarded. *Degree requirements:* For master's, project. *Entrance requirements:* For master's, minimum GPA of 2.75 (3.0 for international students); two years of experience in some form of education, ministry, or service as a profession or volunteer; recommendations; interview with admissions committee. *Application deadline:* For fall admission, 7/1 for domestic students. Application fee: $55. *Financial support:* In 2016–17, 6 students received support. Career-related internships or fieldwork and Federal Work-Study available. Support available to part-time students. Financial award application deadline: 4/1; financial award applicants required to submit FAFSA. *Unit head:* Dr. Mark Markuly, Director, 206-296-5330, Fax: 206-296-5329, E-mail: markulym@seattleu.edu. *Application contact:* Jean Adler Stean, Assistant Director of Admissions and Student Services, 206-296-5333, Fax: 206-296-5329, E-mail: steanj@seattleu.edu.
Website: http://www.seattleu.edu/stm/degrees/mats/

**Seminary of the Southwest,** Graduate and Professional Programs, Austin, TX 78768-2247. Offers M Div, MAC, MAR, MCPC, MSF, Advanced Diploma. *Accreditation:* ACIPE; ATS (one or more programs are accredited). *Program availability:* Part-time, evening/weekend. *Faculty:* 10 full-time (4 women), 13 part-time/adjunct (5 women). *Students:* 59 full-time (28 women), 58 part-time (44 women); includes 22 minority (11 Black or African American, non-Hispanic/Latino; 1 American Indian or Alaska Native, non-Hispanic/Latino; 4 Hispanic/Latino; 6 Two or more races, non-Hispanic/Latino). Average age 46. 47 applicants, 98% accepted, 43 enrolled. In 2016, 20 master's, 4 other advanced degrees awarded. *Degree requirements:* For master's, thesis (for some programs). *Entrance requirements:* For master's, GRE, MAT, interview; for Advanced Diploma, interview. Additional exam requirements/recommendations for international students: Recommended—TOEFL. *Application deadline:* For fall admission, 6/30 priority date for domestic and international students; for spring admission, 12/1 priority date for domestic and international students. Applications are processed on a rolling basis. Application fee: $50. *Expenses:* $14,400 per year; $600 per credit; $1,800 per course. *Financial support:* In 2016–17, 110 students received support. Career-related internships or fieldwork and scholarships/grants available. Support available to part-time students. Financial award application deadline: 6/15; financial award applicants required to submit FAFSA. *Unit head:* Rev. Dr. Cynthia Briggs Kittredge, Dean and President, 512-472-4133 Ext. 332, Fax: 512-472-3098, E-mail: cynthia.kittredge@ssw.edu. *Application contact:* Hope Benko, Director of Enrollment Management, 512-472-4133 Ext. 375, Fax: 512-472-3098, E-mail: hope.benko@ssw.edu.

**Seton Hall University,** Immaculate Conception Seminary School of Theology, South Orange, NJ 07079-2697. Offers Christian spirituality (Certificate); great spiritual books (Certificate); pastoral ministry (M Div, MA, Certificate); scripture studies (Certificate); Seminary's Theological Education for Parish Services (STEPS) (Certificate); theology (MA). *Program availability:* Part-time, evening/weekend. *Degree requirements:* For master's, comprehensive exam (for some programs), thesis (for some programs), final project (for some programs); 1 foreign language (for MA in theology research option). *Entrance requirements:* For master's, GRE General Test or MAT. Additional exam requirements/recommendations for international students: Required—TOEFL (minimum score 600 paper-based; 100 iBT). Electronic applications accepted. *Expenses:* Contact institution. *Faculty research:* Pauline literature, history of Biblical interpretation and theological exegesis, spirituality of St. Edith Stein, Thomism, history of Catholicism in America.

**Sewanee: The University of the South,** School of Theology, Sewanee, TN 37383. Offers M Div, MA, STM, D Min. *Accreditation:* ACIPE. *Program availability:* Part-time. *Faculty:* 10 full-time (3 women), 12 part-time/adjunct (2 women). *Students:* 72 full-time (28 women), 5 part-time (3 women); includes 5 minority (3 Black or African American, non-Hispanic/Latino; 1 American Indian or Alaska Native, non-Hispanic/Latino; 1 Two or more races, non-Hispanic/Latino), 5 international. Average age 37. In 2016, 29 master's, 7 doctorates awarded. *Degree requirements:* For master's, thesis (for some programs); for doctorate, thesis/dissertation. *Entrance requirements:* For master's, M Div (for STM); for doctorate, M Div. Additional exam requirements/recommendations for international students: Required—TOEFL. *Application deadline:* For fall admission, 7/15 for domestic and international students. Applications are processed on a rolling basis. Application fee: $0. Electronic applications accepted. *Expenses:* $16,512 per year full-time tuition, $688 per credit hour part-time tuition. *Financial support:* Institutionally sponsored loans and scholarships/grants available. Support available to part-time students. Financial award application deadline: 4/30. *Unit head:* Very Rev. Dr. J. Neil Alexander, Dean, 931-598-1288, Fax: 931-598-1412, E-mail: deansot@sewanee.edu. *Application contact:* Rev. Annwn H. Myers, Associate Dean for Recruiting and Admission, 931-598-1373, E-mail: amyers@sewanee.edu.
Website: http://theology.sewanee.edu/

**Shaw University,** Divinity School, Raleigh, NC 27601-2399. Offers M Div, MACE. *Accreditation:* ATS. *Program availability:* Part-time, evening/weekend. *Degree requirements:* For master's, thesis. *Entrance requirements:* For master's, official

undergraduate transcripts, letters of reference, essay, interview. Electronic applications accepted. *Faculty research:* Health disparities and the African-American Church, Christian community development, teaching for social change, technology and theological education, best practices in historically black theological schools.

**Shepherds Theological Seminary,** Graduate Programs, Cary, NC 27518. Offers Biblical literature and languages (MA); church ministry (MA); ministry (MTS); New Testament (M Div); Old Testament (M Div); theology (M Div). *Degree requirements:* For master's, thesis. Application fee: $40. *Expenses: Tuition:* Full-time $5400; part-time $300 per credit hour. Tuition and fees vary according to program. *Application contact:* Lucy Burggraff, Registrar, 919-573-1572, Fax: 919-573-1438, E-mail: lburggraff@shepherds.edu.
Website: https://shepherds.edu/academic-programs/

**Shepherd University,** School of Theology, Los Angeles, CA 90065. Offers M Div, D Min. *Accreditation:* ATS.

**Shiloh University,** Graduate Programs, Kalona, IA 52247. Offers Christian ministries (M Div); leadership of church and spiritual formation (D Min); theological studies (MA). *Program availability:* Part-time, evening/weekend, online only, 100% online. *Faculty:* 2 full-time (0 women), 12 part-time/adjunct (2 women). *Students:* 7 full-time (3 women), 29 part-time (10 women); includes 8 minority (4 Black or African American, non-Hispanic/Latino; 3 Hispanic/Latino; 1 Native Hawaiian or other Pacific Islander, non-Hispanic/Latino), 1 international. Average age 50. 29 applicants, 86% accepted, 17 enrolled. In 2016, 2 master's awarded. *Degree requirements:* For master's, variable foreign language requirement, thesis optional; for doctorate, comprehensive exam, thesis/dissertation. *Entrance requirements:* For master's, bachelor's degree or educational equivalent from accredited school with minimum GPA of 2.5 on undergraduate work; for doctorate, M Div or equivalent with minimum GPA of 2.5 on graduate work; three years of ministry experience. Additional exam requirements/recommendations for international students: Recommended—TOEFL (minimum score 540 paper-based; 76 iBT), IELTS (minimum score 6.5). *Application deadline:* For fall admission, 7/3 priority date for domestic and international students; for spring admission, 11/6 priority date for domestic and international students; for summer admission, 3/4 priority date for domestic and international students. Applications are processed on a rolling basis. Application fee: $0. Electronic applications accepted. *Expenses:* $167 per credit hour; certain international applicants receive discounted rate depending on country of residence. *Financial support:* In 2016–17, 2 students received support. Scholarships/grants available. Financial award applicants required to submit FAFSA. *Faculty research:* New testament theology, Pauline literature, relational theology. *Unit head:* Christopher Reeves, President, 319-656-2447, Fax: 319-656-2448, E-mail: chris.reeves@shilouniversity.edu. *Application contact:* Andrew Thompson, Admissions Coordinator, 319-656-2447, Fax: 319-656-2448, E-mail: admissions@shilouniversity.edu.
Website: http://www.shilohuniversity.edu/academics/

**Sh'or Yoshuv Rabbinical College,** Graduate Programs, Far Rockaway, NY 11691-4002. *Accreditation:* AARTS.

**Sioux Falls Seminary,** Graduate and Professional Programs, Master of Divinity Program, Sioux Falls, SD 57105-1599. Offers marriage and family therapy (M Div); pastoral care and counseling (M Div). Program also offered in Omaha, NE. *Accreditation:* ACIPE. *Program availability:* Part-time, online learning. *Application deadline:* For fall admission, 8/1 priority date for domestic students; for spring admission, 1/1 priority date for domestic students. Applications are processed on a rolling basis. Application fee: $25. *Financial support:* Career-related internships or fieldwork and scholarships/grants available. Support available to part-time students. *Unit head:* Larry Caldwell, Chief Academic Officer/Dean, 605-336-6588, Fax: 605-335-9090, E-mail: lcaldwell@sfseminary.edu. *Application contact:* Dustin Brouwer, Director of Enrollment Management, 605-336-6588, Fax: 605-335-9090, E-mail: dbrouwer@sfseminary.edu.
Website: http://sfseminary.edu/prospective-students/programs/master-of-divinity/

**Sioux Falls Seminary,** Graduate and Professional Programs, Program in Bible and Theology, Sioux Falls, SD 57105-1599. Offers MA. *Accreditation:* ACIPE; ATS. *Program availability:* Part-time, online learning. *Degree requirements:* For master's, 2 foreign languages, thesis or alternative. *Entrance requirements:* For master's, minimum GPA of 2.5. *Application deadline:* For fall admission, 8/1 priority date for domestic students; for spring admission, 1/1 priority date for domestic students. Applications are processed on a rolling basis. Application fee: $25. *Financial support:* Scholarships/grants available. *Unit head:* Larry Caldwell, Chief Academic Officer/Dean, 605-336-6588, Fax: 605-335-9090, E-mail: lcaldwell@sfseminary.edu. *Application contact:* Dustin Brouwer, Director of Enrollment Management, 605-336-6588, Fax: 605-335-9090, E-mail: dbrouwer@sfseminary.edu.
Website: http://sfseminary.edu/prospective-students/programs/ma-bible-theology/

**Sioux Falls Seminary,** Graduate and Professional Programs, Program in Ministry, Sioux Falls, SD 57105-1599. Offers D Min. *Accreditation:* ACIPE. *Program availability:* Part-time. *Degree requirements:* For doctorate, thesis/dissertation. *Entrance requirements:* For doctorate, M Div, 3 years of ministry. *Application deadline:* Applications are processed on a rolling basis. Application fee: $25. *Financial support:* Career-related internships or fieldwork and scholarships/grants available. Support available to part-time students. *Unit head:* Dr. Gary Strickland, Director, 605-336-6588, Fax: 605-335-9090, E-mail: gstrickland@sfseminary.edu. *Application contact:* Dustin Brouwer, Director of Enrollment Management, 605-336-6588, Fax: 605-335-9090, E-mail: dbrouwer@sfseminary.edu.
Website: http://sfseminary.edu/prospective-students/programs/doctor-of-ministry/

**Sioux Falls Seminary,** Graduate and Professional Programs, Program in Theological Studies, Sioux Falls, SD 57105-1599. Offers Certificate. *Application deadline:* For fall admission, 8/1 priority date for domestic students; for spring admission, 1/1 priority date for domestic students. Applications are processed on a rolling basis. Application fee: $25. *Unit head:* Larry Caldwell, Chief Academic Officer/Dean, 605-336-6588, Fax: 605-335-9090, E-mail: lcaldwell@sfseminary.edu. *Application contact:* Dustin Brouwer, Director of Enrollment Management, 605-336-6588, Fax: 605-335-9090, E-mail: dbrouwer@sfseminary.edu.

**Southeastern Baptist Theological Seminary,** Graduate and Professional Programs, Wake Forest, NC 27588-1889. Offers advanced biblical studies (M Div); Christian education (M Div, MACE); Christian ethics (PhD); Christian ministry (M Div); Christian planting (M Div); church music (MACM); counseling (MACO); evangelism (PhD); language (M Div); ministry (D Min); New Testament (PhD); Old Testament (PhD); philosophy (PhD); theology (Th M, PhD); women's studies (M Div). *Accreditation:* ACIPE; ATS (one or more programs are accredited). *Degree requirements:* For master's, thesis (for some programs), oral exam; for doctorate, thesis/dissertation, fieldwork. *Entrance requirements:* For master's, Cooperative English Test, minimum GPA of 2.0, M Div or equivalent (Th M); for doctorate, GRE General Test or MAT, Cooperative English Test, M Div or equivalent, 3 years of professional experience.

**Southeastern University,** Barnett College of Ministry and Theology, Lakeland, FL 33801-6099. Offers ministerial leadership (MA, D Min); theological studies (MA); theology (M Div). *Program availability:* Evening/weekend, online learning. *Degree*

*requirements:* For master's, thesis/project. *Expenses: Tuition:* Full-time $9450; part-time $6300 per credit. *Required fees:* $500; $250 per semester. One-time fee: $150. Tuition and fees vary according to degree level, campus/location and program. *Unit head:* Dean, 863-667-5000.
Website: http://www.seu.edu/ministry/

**Southern Adventist University,** School of Religion, Collegedale, TN 37315-0370. Offers Biblical and theological studies (MA); church leadership and management (M Min); church ministry and homiletics (M Min); evangelism and world mission (M Min); religious studies (MA). *Program availability:* Part-time. *Degree requirements:* For master's, comprehensive exam, thesis (for some programs). *Entrance requirements:* For master's, GRE. Additional exam requirements/recommendations for international students: Required—TOEFL (minimum score 600 paper-based). *Faculty research:* Biblical archaeology.

**The Southern Baptist Theological Seminary,** Billy Graham School of Missions, Evangelism and Ministry, Louisville, KY 40280-0004. Offers ministry (D Min); missiology (MA, D Miss); missions and evangelism (M Div, Th M, PhD); theological studies (MA). *Accreditation:* ATS. *Program availability:* Part-time, evening/weekend, online learning. *Degree requirements:* For master's, 2 foreign languages; for doctorate, 4 foreign languages, thesis/dissertation. *Entrance requirements:* For doctorate, GRE General Test, MAT, M Div. Additional exam requirements/recommendations for international students: Required—TOEFL, TWE. *Faculty research:* Assimilation of church congregants, effective methodologies of evangelism, expectations of church members, spiritual warfare literature, formative church discipline.

**The Southern Baptist Theological Seminary,** School of Theology, Louisville, KY 40280-0004. Offers applied theology (D Min); biblical and theological studies (M Div); biblical counseling (M Div, MA, D Min); biblical spirituality (D Min); Christian ministry (M Div); expository preaching (D Min); pastoral studies (M Div); theological studies (MA); theology (Th M, PhD); worldview and apologetics (M Div). *Program availability:* Part-time, evening/weekend, online learning. *Degree requirements:* For master's, 2 foreign languages, thesis; for doctorate, 4 foreign languages, thesis/dissertation. *Entrance requirements:* For master's, GRE General Test, MAT, M Div; for doctorate, GRE General Test, MAT, interview, M Div, field essay. Additional exam requirements/ recommendations for international students: Required—TOEFL, TWE. *Faculty research:* Biblical studies, contemporary theology, church history, pastoral care, ministry/missions studies.

**Southern California Seminary,** Graduate and Professional Programs, El Cajon, CA 92019. Offers Biblical studies (MABS); counseling psychology (MACP); marriage and family therapy (MAMFT); psychology (Psy D); religious studies (MRS); theology (M Div). *Program availability:* Part-time, evening/weekend, online learning. *Degree requirements:* For master's, thesis (for some programs); for doctorate, thesis/dissertation. *Entrance requirements:* For doctorate, master's degree in psychology. Additional exam requirements/recommendations for international students: Required—TOEFL (minimum score 550 paper-based). Electronic applications accepted.

**Southern Evangelical Seminary,** Graduate Programs, Matthews, NC 28105. Offers apologetics (MA, D Min, Certificate); Christian education (MA); church ministry (MA, Certificate); divinity (Certificate), including apologetics (M Div, Certificate); Islamic studies (MA, Certificate); Jewish studies (MA); philosophy (MA); philosophy of religion (PhD); religion (MA); theology (M Div), including apologetics (M Div, Certificate), Biblical studies; youth ministry (MA). *Program availability:* Part-time, evening/weekend, online learning. *Degree requirements:* For master's, thesis (for some programs); for doctorate, 2 foreign languages, comprehensive exam (for some programs), thesis/dissertation. *Entrance requirements:* Additional exam requirements/recommendations for international students: Required—TOEFL (minimum score 600 paper-based).

**Southern Methodist University,** Dedman College of Humanities and Sciences, Graduate Program in Religious Studies, Dallas, TX 75275-0133. Offers Hebrew Bible/ Old Testament (PhD); history of the Christian tradition (PhD); New Testament (PhD); religion and culture (PhD); religious ethics (PhD); religious studies (MA); systematics theology (PhD). Terminal master's awarded for partial completion of doctoral program. *Degree requirements:* For master's, one foreign language, thesis, oral and written exams; for doctorate, variable foreign language requirement, thesis/dissertation, oral and written exams. *Entrance requirements:* For master's and doctorate, GRE General Test, minimum GPA of 3.0, course work in religion. Additional exam requirements/ recommendations for international students: Required—TOEFL (minimum score 550 paper-based; 79 iBT). Electronic applications accepted. *Faculty research:* Theology, religious ethics, Biblical studies, history of Christianity, religion and culture.

**Southern Methodist University,** Perkins School of Theology, Dallas, TX 75275. Offers CMM, M Div, MSM, MTS, D Min. *Accreditation:* ACIPE. *Program availability:* Part-time. *Degree requirements:* For master's, thesis (for some programs), internship; for doctorate, internship, oral exam, professional project. *Entrance requirements:* For master's, minimum GPA of 2.75; for doctorate, minimum graduate GPA of 3.0, M Div or equivalent, 3 years of ministry experience. Additional exam requirements/ recommendations for international students: Required—TOEFL (minimum score 600 paper-based; 100 iBT), TWE. *Expenses:* Contact institution.

**South Florida Bible College and Theological Seminary,** Graduate Programs, Deerfield Beach, FL 33441. Offers biblical studies (MA); theology (M Div). *Degree requirements:* For master's, thesis.

**Southwestern Assemblies of God University,** Thomas F. Harrison School of Graduate Studies, Program in Theological Studies, Waxahachie, TX 75165-5735. Offers Bible and theology (MS); Biblical studies (M Div); counseling (M Div); cross cultural missions (M Div); practical theology (M Div); theological studies (M Div). *Program availability:* Online learning. *Degree requirements:* For master's, comprehensive written and oral exams. *Entrance requirements:* For master's, GRE General Test, minimum GPA of 2.5. Electronic applications accepted.

**Southwestern Baptist Theological Seminary,** Roy Fish School of Evangelism and Missions, Fort Worth, TX 76122-0000. Offers cross-cultural missions (MTS); evangelism (M Div); evangelism and missions (D Min); international church planting (M Div); Islamic studies (M Div, MA Islamic); missiology (MA Miss); missions (M Div); North American church planting (M Div); North American evangelism and international missions (D Min); theology (Th M); world Christian studies (PhD).

**Southwestern Baptist Theological Seminary,** School of Theology, Fort Worth, TX 76122-0000. Offers ministry (D Min); theology (PhD). *Accreditation:* ACIPE; ATS (one or more programs are accredited). *Program availability:* Part-time, evening/weekend. Terminal master's awarded for partial completion of doctoral program. *Degree requirements:* For master's, 2 foreign languages, thesis (for some programs); for doctorate, 2 foreign languages, comprehensive exam, thesis/dissertation, oral exams. *Entrance requirements:* For doctorate, GRE, M Div or equivalent. Additional exam requirements/recommendations for international students: Required—TOEFL. Electronic applications accepted.

**Spring Arbor University,** School of Arts and Sciences, Spring Arbor, MI 49283-9799. Offers communication (MA); spiritual formation and leadership (MA). *Program availability:* Part-time, online learning. *Degree requirements:* For master's, thesis (for

some programs). *Entrance requirements:* For master's, GRE (minimum score of 40th percentile and taken within last 5 years), bachelor's degree from regionally-accredited college or university, minimum GPA of 3.0 for at least the last two years of the bachelor's degree, at least two recommendations from professional/academic individuals. Additional exam requirements/recommendations for international students: Required— TOEFL (minimum score 600 paper-based). *Expenses:* Contact institution.

**Spring Hill College,** Graduate Programs, Program in Theology, Mobile, AL 36608-1791. Offers faith companioning (Postbaccalaureate Certificate); pastoral ministry (Postbaccalaureate Certificate); pastoral studies (MPS); spiritual direction (Postbaccalaureate Certificate); theological studies (MTS); theology (MA). *Program availability:* Part-time, evening/weekend. *Faculty:* 6 full-time (0 women), 2 part-time/ adjunct (both women). *Students:* 1 full-time (0 women), 37 part-time (18 women); includes 7 minority (2 Black or African American, non-Hispanic/Latino; 1 American Indian or Alaska Native, non-Hispanic/Latino; 2 Asian, non-Hispanic/Latino; 2 Hispanic/ Latino), 2 international. Average age 46. In 2016, 6 master's, 11 other advanced degrees awarded. *Degree requirements:* For master's, variable foreign language requirement, comprehensive exam, thesis (for some programs), completion of program within 6 calendar years of initial enrollment (MTS, MPS); completion of program within 4 1/2 calendar years of formal acceptance (MA). *Entrance requirements:* For master's, bachelor's degree with minimum undergraduate GPA of 3.0; six hours of undergraduate theology, religious studies, or unquestioned equivalency. Additional exam requirements/ recommendations for international students: Required—TOEFL (minimum score 550 paper-based; 80 iBT), IELTS (minimum score 6.5), CPE or CAE (minimum score C), Michigan English Language Assessment Battery (minimum score 90). *Application deadline:* For fall admission, 8/1 priority date for domestic and international students; for spring admission, 12/1 priority date for domestic and international students. Applications are processed on a rolling basis. Application fee: $25 ($35 for international students). Electronic applications accepted. *Expenses: Tuition:* Full-time $8200; part-time $490 per credit hour. Tuition and fees vary according to program. *Financial support:* Applicants required to submit FAFSA. *Unit head:* Dr. Timothy R. Carmody, Director, 251-380-4665, Fax: 251-460-2194, E-mail: carmody@shc.edu. *Application contact:* Robert Stewart, Vice President of Enrollment, 251-380-3030, Fax: 251-460-2186, E-mail: rstewart@shc.edu.
Website: http://ug.shc.edu/graduate-degrees/master-arts-theological-studies/

**Starr King School for the Ministry,** Professional Program, Berkeley, CA 94709-1209. Offers M Div. *Accreditation:* ACIPE; ATS.

**SUM Bible College & Theological Seminary,** Graduate Programs, Oakland, CA 94603. Offers biblical studies (MA); Christian leadership (MA); theology (M Div). *Entrance requirements:* For master's, minimum GPA of 2.5, currently active in ministry.

**Talmudic University,** Program in Talmudic Law, Miami Beach, FL 33140. Offers MRE. *Accreditation:* AARTS. *Degree requirements:* For master's, 2 foreign languages. *Entrance requirements:* For master's, oral exam, undergraduate Judaic studies degree.

**Taylor College and Seminary,** Graduate and Professional Programs, Edmonton, AB T6J 4T3, Canada. Offers Christian studies (Diploma); intercultural studies (MA, Diploma), including intercultural studies (Diploma), TESOL; theology (M Div, MTS). *Accreditation:* ATS. *Program availability:* Part-time, online learning. *Degree requirements:* For master's, thesis optional. *Entrance requirements:* Additional exam requirements/recommendations for international students: Required—TOEFL (minimum score 550 paper-based; 80 iBT), IELTS (minimum score 6.5). *Faculty research:* Biblical studies, administration and organization, world religions, ethics, missiology.

**Toronto School of Theology,** Graduate Programs, Toronto, ON M5S 2C3, Canada. Offers M Div, MA, MAMS, MPS, MRE, MSM, MTS, Th M, D Min, PhD, Th D. *Program availability:* Online learning. Terminal master's awarded for partial completion of doctoral program. *Degree requirements:* For master's, 2 foreign languages, thesis; for doctorate, 3 foreign languages, comprehensive exam, thesis/dissertation. *Entrance requirements:* For master's, language exams, minimum B+ average in undergraduate course work; for doctorate, language exams, first-class standing in master's program. Additional exam requirements/recommendations for international students: Required—TOEFL, IELTS. Electronic applications accepted.

**Trinity Bible College and Graduate School,** Graduate School, Ellendale, ND 58436. Offers global theology (MA); missional leadership (MA).

**Trinity College,** Faculty of Divinity, Toronto, ON M5S 1H8, Canada. Offers ministry (Diploma); ministry for church musicians (Diploma); theology (M Div, MA, MTS, Th M, D Min, PhD, Th D, Diploma, L Th); M Div/MA. *Accreditation:* ATS. *Program availability:* Part-time. *Degree requirements:* For master's, 2 foreign languages, thesis (for some programs); for doctorate, 3 foreign languages, comprehensive exam, thesis/dissertation; for other advanced degree, thesis (for some programs). *Entrance requirements:* For master's, 1 language (modern or ancient), interview; for doctorate, 2 languages (modern and ancient). Additional exam requirements/recommendations for international students: Required—TOEFL, TWE. *Faculty research:* Interreligious dialogue, feminist theology, systematic theology, philosophy of religion, pastoral theology.

**Trinity International University,** Trinity Evangelical Divinity School, Deerfield, IL 60015-1284. Offers academic ministry (M Div); Biblical and Near Eastern archaeology and languages (MA); chaplaincy and ministry care (MA); Christian studies (Certificate); church and parachurch ministry (M Div); church history (MA, Th M); counseling (Th M); educational ministries (MA); educational ministry (Th M); educational studies (PhD); intercultural studies (MA, PhD); leadership and management (D Min); mental health counseling (MA); military chaplaincy (D Min); ministry (MA); missions (Th M); missions and evangelism (D Min); New Testament (MA, Th M); Old Testament (Th M); Old Testament and Semitic languages (MA); pastoral ministry and care (D Min); pastoral theology (Th M); preaching and teaching (D Min); spiritual formation and education (D Min); systematic theology (MA, Th M); theological studies (MA, PhD); urban ministry (MA). *Program availability:* Part-time, online learning. *Students:* 578 full-time (141 women), 711 part-time (202 women). *Degree requirements:* For master's, comprehensive exam, thesis, fieldwork; for doctorate, comprehensive exam (for some programs), thesis/dissertation; for Certificate, comprehensive exam, integrative papers. *Entrance requirements:* For master's, GRE, MAT, minimum cumulative undergraduate GPA of 3.0; for doctorate, GRE, minimum cumulative graduate GPA of 3.2; for Certificate, GRE, MAT, minimum undergraduate GPA of 2.5. Additional exam requirements/recommendations for international students: Required—TOEFL (minimum score 580 paper-based), TWE (minimum score 4). *Application deadline:* For fall admission, 7/15 priority date for domestic and international students. Applications are processed on a rolling basis. Application fee: $25. Electronic applications accepted. *Expenses: Tuition, area resident:* Full-time $19,898. *Required fees:* $200. *Financial support:* Fellowships with partial tuition reimbursements, teaching assistantships with partial tuition reimbursements, career-related internships or fieldwork, Federal Work-Study, scholarships/grants, and tuition waivers (partial) available. Financial award application deadline: 4/1; financial award applicants required to submit FAFSA. *Unit head:* Dr. Tite Tienou, Academic Dean, 847-317-8086, Fax: 847-317-8014, E-mail: ttienou@teds.edu. *Application contact:* Ron Campbell, Director of Admissions, 800-345-8337, Fax: 847-317-8097, E-mail: rcampbel@tiu.edu.
Website: https://divinity.tiu.edu/

*Theology*

**Trinity Lutheran Seminary,** Graduate and Professional Programs, Columbus, OH 43209-2334. Offers African American studies (MTS); Biblical studies (MTS, STM); Christian education (MA); Christian spirituality (STM); church in the world (MTS); church music (MA); divinity (M Div); general theological studies (MTS); mission and evangelism (STM); pastoral leadership and practice (STM); youth and family ministry (MA); MSN/MTS; MTS/JD. *Accreditation:* ACIPE; ATS. *Program availability:* Part-time. *Degree requirements:* For master's, variable foreign language requirement, comprehensive exam (for some programs), thesis (for some programs), field experience (for some programs). *Entrance requirements:* For master's, BA or equivalent (for MA, M Div, MTS); M Div, MTS, or equivalent (for STM); audition (for MACM). Additional exam requirements/recommendations for international students: Required—TOEFL. Electronic applications accepted. *Expenses:* Contact institution.

**Trinity School for Ministry,** Graduate Programs, Ambridge, PA 15003-2397. Offers Anglican studies (Diploma); basic Christian studies (Diploma); divinity (M Div); ministry (D Min); mission and evangelism (MAME, Diploma); religion (MAR); youth ministry (Diploma). *Program availability:* Part-time. *Degree requirements:* For master's, thesis optional; for doctorate, thesis/dissertation. *Entrance requirements:* Additional exam requirements/recommendations for international students: Required—TOEFL. *Faculty research:* Pauline Epistles, contemporary theology, history of Anglican liturgy, book of Ruth, biblical theology.

**Trinity Western University,** ACTS Seminaries, Langley, BC V2Y 1Y1, Canada. Offers Christian studies (MA); cross cultural ministry (MA); theology (M Div, M Th, MAMFT, MLE, MTS, D Min). *Program availability:* Part-time. *Degree requirements:* For master's, thesis (for some programs), internship. *Entrance requirements:* For doctorate, M Div or equivalent. Additional exam requirements/recommendations for international students: Required—TOEFL. *Expenses:* Contact institution. *Faculty research:* Theology of leadership.

**Trinity Western University,** School of Graduate Studies, Program in Biblical Studies, Langley, BC V2Y 1Y1, Canada. Offers MA. *Accreditation:* ATS. *Program availability:* Part-time. *Degree requirements:* For master's, 2 foreign languages, thesis, 2 years Greek, 2 years Hebrew. *Entrance requirements:* For master's, minimum GPA of 3.0, degree in biblical studies, master of divinity or 42 hours Biblical Study credit. Additional exam requirements/recommendations for international students: Required—TOEFL (minimum score 600 paper-based). Electronic applications accepted. *Faculty research:* Intertestamental literature, Dead Sea Scrolls, Biblical literature, history of Jesus, ancient languages.

**Tri-State Bible College,** Graduate Program, South Point, OH 45680-8402. Offers MA. *Entrance requirements:* For master's, bachelor's degree, minimum undergraduate GPA of 2.75, autobiographical statement, two letters of recommendation. Electronic applications accepted.

**Truett McConnell University,** Balthasar Hubmaier School of Theology and Missions, Cleveland, GA 30528. Offers theology (MA). *Program availability:* Part-time, 100% online. In 2016, 1 master's awarded. *Application deadline:* Applications are processed on a rolling basis. Electronic applications accepted. *Expenses: Tuition:* Full-time $2925; part-time $325 per semester hour. *Required fees:* $660 per semester hour. Tuition and fees vary according to course load. *Financial support:* Application deadline: 8/1; applicants required to submit FAFSA. *Unit head:* Dr. Jason Graffagnino, Dean, 706-865-2134 Ext. 3002, E-mail: jgraffagnino@truett.edu. *Application contact:* Morgan Graffagnino, Administrative Assistant, 706-865-2134 Ext. 3002, E-mail: mgraffagnino@truett.edu.

**Tyndale University College & Seminary,** Graduate Programs, Toronto, ON M2M 3S4, Canada. Offers Biblical studies (M Div); Christian foundations (M Div); Christian studies (Diploma); counseling (M Div); educational ministry (M Div); missions (M Div, Diploma); pastoral and Chinese ministry (M Div); pastoral ministry (M Div); Pentecostal studies (MTS); spiritual formation (M Div, Diploma); theological studies (M Div); theology (Th M); worship and liturgy (M Div, MTS); youth and family ministry (M Div). *Accreditation:* ATS. *Program availability:* Part-time, online learning. *Entrance requirements:* For master's and Diploma, minimum C+ average in undergraduate course work. Additional exam requirements/recommendations for international students: Required—TOEFL (minimum score 570 paper-based), TWE (minimum score 5). Electronic applications accepted. *Faculty research:* Canadian church history, Chinese church history, Old Testament, counseling ministries (narrative therapy), world religions.

**Unification Theological Seminary,** Graduate Program, Main Campus, Barrytown, NY 12507. Offers divinity (M Div); ministry (D Min); religious education (MRE), including interfaith peacebuilding (MA, MRE); religious studies (MA), including interfaith peacebuilding (MA, MRE); non-profit leadership, theological studies, unification studies. *Program availability:* Part-time, evening/weekend. *Faculty:* 3 full-time (1 woman), 3 part-time/adjunct (0 women). *Students:* 27 full-time (8 women); includes 15 minority (11 Black or African American, non-Hispanic/Latino; 2 Asian, non-Hispanic/Latino; 1 Hispanic/Latino; 1 Two or more races, non-Hispanic/Latino), 6 international. Average age 50. In 2016, 12 master's, 5 doctorates awarded. *Degree requirements:* For master's, variable foreign language requirement, thesis (for some programs); for doctorate, thesis/dissertation. *Entrance requirements:* For master's, bachelor's degree; for doctorate, M Div or equivalency. Additional exam requirements/recommendations for international students: Required—TOEFL (minimum score 450 paper-based; 45 iBT). *Application deadline:* For fall admission, 3/15 priority date for domestic and international students; for spring admission, 9/15 priority date for domestic and international students. Applications are processed on a rolling basis. Application fee: $30. Electronic applications accepted. *Expenses:* Contact institution. *Financial support:* In 2016–17, 2 students received support. Scholarships/grants available. Financial award application deadline: 6/15; financial award applicants required to submit FAFSA. *Faculty research:* Church leadership, church history, world religions, ecumenism, interfaith peace building, service-learning. *Unit head:* Dr. Kathy Winings, Vice-President for Academic Affairs, 845-752-3000 Ext. 228, Fax: 845-752-3014, E-mail: academics@uts.edu. *Application contact:* Henry Christopher, Director of Admissions, 212-563-6647 Ext. 105, Fax: 845-752-3014, E-mail: h.christopher@uts.edu. Website: http://www.uts.edu

**Unification Theological Seminary,** Graduate Program, Maryland Satellite Center, Clinton, MD 20735. Offers M Div, MA, MRE. *Program availability:* Part-time, evening/weekend. *Faculty:* 1 full-time (1 woman) part-time/adjunct. *Students:* 25 part-time (14 women); all minorities (all Black or African American, non-Hispanic/Latino). Average age 41. *Degree requirements:* For master's, variable foreign language requirement, thesis (for some programs). *Entrance requirements:* For master's, bachelor's degree. Additional exam requirements/recommendations for international students: Required—TOEFL (minimum score 450 paper-based; 45 iBT). *Application deadline:* For fall admission, 3/15 priority date for domestic and international students; for spring admission, 9/15 priority date for domestic and international students. Applications are processed on a rolling basis. Application fee: $30. Electronic applications accepted. *Expenses: Tuition:* Full-time $11,760; part-time $490 per credit. *Required fees:* $320; $250 per credit. $125 per semester. Tuition and fees vary according to degree level. *Financial support:* In 2016–17, 25 students received support. Scholarships/grants available. Financial award application deadline: 6/15; financial award applicants required

to submit FAFSA. *Unit head:* John Paul James, Director, 240-384-7860. *Application contact:* Henry Christopher, Director of Admissions and Financial Aid, 212-563-6647 Ext. 105, E-mail: admissions@uts.edu.

**Unification Theological Seminary,** New York Extension Center, New York, NY 10036. Offers divinity (M Div); religious education (MRE), including interfaith peacebuilding (MA, MRE); religious studies (MA), including interfaith peacebuilding (MA, MRE), non-profit leadership, theological studies, unification studies. *Program availability:* Part-time, evening/weekend. *Faculty:* 4 full-time (0 women), 7 part-time/adjunct (1 woman). *Students:* 25 full-time (9 women), 23 part-time (6 women); includes 24 minority (8 Black or African American, non-Hispanic/Latino; 9 Asian, non-Hispanic/Latino; 3 Hispanic/Latino; 4 Two or more races, non-Hispanic/Latino), 14 international. Average age 43. *Degree requirements:* For master's, variable foreign language requirement, thesis (for some programs). *Entrance requirements:* For master's, bachelor's degree. Additional exam requirements/recommendations for international students: Required—TOEFL (minimum score 450 paper-based; 45 iBT). *Application deadline:* For fall admission, 8/15 for domestic students, 3/15 priority date for international students; for spring admission, 1/15 for domestic students, 9/15 priority date for international students. Applications are processed on a rolling basis. Application fee: $30. Electronic applications accepted. *Expenses: Tuition:* Full-time $11,760; part-time $490 per credit. *Required fees:* $320; $250 per credit. $125 per semester. Tuition and fees vary according to degree level. *Financial support:* In 2016–17, 48 students received support. Career-related internships or fieldwork, scholarships/grants, tuition waivers (partial), and on-campus employment (for international students) available. Support available to part-time students. Financial award application deadline: 6/15; financial award applicants required to submit FAFSA. *Faculty research:* Church history, world religions, ecumenism, interfaith peace building, service-learning. *Unit head:* Dr. Kathy Winings, Vice-President for Academic Affairs, 212-563-6647 Ext. 101, Fax: 212-563-6431, E-mail: academics@uts.edu. *Application contact:* Joy Theriot, Recruiter, 212-563-6647 Ext. 110, Fax: 212-563-6431, E-mail: j.theriot@uts.edu.
Website: http://www.uts.edu

**Union Theological Seminary in the City of New York,** Graduate and Professional Programs, New York, NY 10027-5710. Offers M Div, MA, STM, Ed D, PhD, M Div/MSSW. Ed D offered jointly with Teachers College, Columbia University; M Div/MSSW with Columbia University. *Accreditation:* ACIPE; ATS (one or more programs are accredited). *Program availability:* Part-time. *Degree requirements:* For master's, one foreign language, thesis; for doctorate, 2 foreign languages, thesis/dissertation. *Entrance requirements:* For doctorate, GRE General Test, sample of written work. *Faculty research:* American religious history, psychiatry and religion, Christian ethics, New Testament.

**United Talmudical Seminary,** Graduate Programs, Brooklyn, NY 11211. *Accreditation:* AARTS.

**United Theological Seminary,** Graduate and Professional Programs, Dayton, OH 45426. Offers Christian ministries (MA); ministry (M Div, D Min); theological studies (MTS). *Accreditation:* ATS. *Program availability:* Part-time, evening/weekend, online learning. *Degree requirements:* For master's, thesis (for some programs); for doctorate, thesis/dissertation, final exam. *Entrance requirements:* For master's, minimum GPA of 2.5, interview, 5 letters of recommendation; for doctorate, minimum GPA of 3.0, 2 letters of recommendation, interview. Additional exam requirements/recommendations for international students: Required—TOEFL (minimum score 550 paper-based). *Application deadline:* For fall admission, 8/1 for domestic students, 1/15 for international students; for spring admission, 1/1 for domestic students. Applications are processed on a rolling basis. Application fee: $60. Electronic applications accepted. *Expenses: Tuition:* Full-time $13,630; part-time $6815 per semester. Tuition and fees vary according to program. *Financial support:* Career-related internships or fieldwork, Federal Work-Study, and scholarships/grants available. Financial award application deadline: 4/1; financial award applicants required to submit CSS PROFILE or FAFSA. *Unit head:* Dr. David Watson, Academic Dean/Vice President for Academic Affairs, 937-529-2257, E-mail: dwatson@united.edu. *Application contact:* Kathleen Boston, Admissions Associate, 937-529-2225 Ext. 4237, E-mail: utsadmis@united.edu.

**United Theological Seminary of the Twin Cities,** Graduate Programs, New Brighton, MN 55112-2598. Offers advanced theological studies (Diploma); justice and peace studies (M Div, MA); leadership toward racial justice (M Div, MA, Certificate); Methodist studies (M Div, MA, Certificate); ministry (D Min); ministry renewal and professional development (Certificate); pastoral care and counseling (M Div, MA, MARL); religion and theology (MA); theological and religious studies (Certificate); theology and the arts (M Div, MA); urban ministry (M Div, MA, MARL); women's studies: religion, theology and ministry (M Div, MA). *Accreditation:* ACIPE; ATS. *Program availability:* Part-time, evening/weekend. *Degree requirements:* For master's, thesis; for doctorate, comprehensive exam, thesis/dissertation. *Entrance requirements:* For master's, minimum GPA of 2.75; strong analytical, reflective thinking and writing skills; vocational and academic goals compatible with those of Seminary; for doctorate, M Div or equivalent, minimum GPA of 3.0, 3 years experience in professional ministry; for other advanced degree, BA or equivalent life experience; strong analytical, reflective thinking and writing skills (Certificate); proficiency in English language, previous study of theology at a theological school, recommendation of student's denomination (Diploma). Additional exam requirements/recommendations for international students: Required—TOEFL (minimum score 550 paper-based).

**Université de Montréal,** Faculty of Theology and Sciences of Religions, Montréal, QC H3C 3J7, Canada. Offers health, spirituality and bioethics (DESS); practical theology (MA, PhD); religious sciences (MA, PhD); theology (MA, D Th, PhD, L Th); theology-Biblical studies (PhD). *Degree requirements:* For master's, one foreign language; for doctorate, 2 foreign languages, thesis/dissertation, general exam. Electronic applications accepted.

**Université de Sherbrooke,** Faculty of Theology and Religious Studies, Sherbrooke, QC J1K 2R1, Canada. Offers applied ethics (Diploma); human science of religions (MA); intercultural training (Diploma); philosophy (MA, PhD); spiritual anthropology (Diploma); theology (MA, PhD, Diploma). *Program availability:* Part-time, evening/weekend, online learning. Terminal master's awarded for partial completion of doctoral program. *Entrance requirements:* For master's, bachelor's degree in related discipline; for doctorate, master's degree in related discipline. *Faculty research:* Faith and culture interrelation.

**Université du Québec à Chicoutimi,** Graduate Programs, Program in Theology (Pastoral Studies), Chicoutimi, QC G7H 2B1, Canada. Offers MA, PhD. Programs offered jointly with Université de Montréal. *Program availability:* Part-time. *Degree requirements:* For doctorate, thesis/dissertation. *Entrance requirements:* For master's, appropriate bachelor's degree, proficiency in French; for doctorate, appropriate master's degree, proficiency in French.

**Université Laval,** Faculty of Theology and Religious Sciences, Program in Practical Theology, Québec, QC G1K 7P4, Canada. Offers D Th P. *Program availability:* Part-time. *Degree requirements:* For doctorate, comprehensive exam, thesis/dissertation. *Entrance requirements:* For doctorate, knowledge of French and English. Electronic applications accepted.

**Université Laval,** Faculty of Theology and Religious Sciences, Programs in Theology, Québec, QC G1K 7P4, Canada. Offers MA, PhD. Terminal master's awarded for partial completion of doctoral program. *Degree requirements:* For master's, thesis (for some programs); for doctorate, comprehensive exam, thesis/dissertation. *Entrance requirements:* For master's and doctorate, knowledge of French, comprehension of written English. Electronic applications accepted.

**University of Chicago,** Divinity School, PhD Program, Chicago, IL 60637. Offers anthropology and sociology of religions (PhD); Bible (PhD); history of Christianity (PhD); history of Judaism (PhD); history of religions (PhD); Islamic studies (PhD); philosophy of religions (PhD); religion, literature, and visual culture (PhD); religions in America (PhD); religious ethics (PhD); theology (PhD). *Students:* 161 full-time (47 women), 1 (woman) part-time; includes 22 minority (6 Black or African American, non-Hispanic/Latino; 10 Asian, non-Hispanic/Latino; 2 Hispanic/Latino; 4 Two or more races, non-Hispanic/Latino), 26 international. 171 applicants, 16% accepted, 15 enrolled. *Degree requirements:* For doctorate, 2 foreign languages, comprehensive exam, thesis/dissertation. *Entrance requirements:* For doctorate, GRE General Test. Additional exam requirements/recommendations for international students: Required—TOEFL (minimum score 600 paper-based; 104 iBT), IELTS (minimum score 7). *Application deadline:* For fall admission, 12/15 for domestic and international students. Application fee: $75. Electronic applications accepted. *Financial support:* In 2016–17, 20 fellowships with full tuition reimbursements (averaging $24,000 per year) were awarded; Federal Work-Study, institutionally sponsored loans, scholarships/grants, and health care benefits also available. Financial award application deadline: 12/15; financial award applicants required to submit FAFSA. *Faculty research:* Constructive studies (philosophy of religion, religious ethics, and theology); historical studies (Bible, history of Christianity, and history of Judaism); religion and the human sciences (anthropology and sociology of religion, history of religions, and religion, literature, and visual culture); Islamic studies; religions in America. *Unit head:* Dr. Richard A. Rosengarten, Dean/Associate Professor of Religion and Literature, 773-702-8200. *Application contact:* John W. Howell, Coordinator for Recruiting and Admissions, 773-702-8249, Fax: 773-834-4581, E-mail: divinityadmissions@uchicago.edu.
Website: http://divinity.uchicago.edu/doctoral-program-phd

**University of Dallas,** Braniff Graduate School of Liberal Arts, Department of Theology, Irving, TX 75062-4736. Offers M Th, MA. *Program availability:* Part-time. *Degree requirements:* For master's, one foreign language, comprehensive exam, thesis (for some programs). *Entrance requirements:* For master's, GRE General Test. *Faculty research:* Patristics, justice in the Old and New Testament, Pauline literature, Christology, theology of the Trinity.

**University of Dayton,** Department of Religious Studies, Dayton, OH 45469. Offers pastoral ministry (MA); theological studies (MA); theology (PhD). *Program availability:* Part-time. *Faculty:* 19 full-time (7 women), 6 part-time/adjunct (2 women). *Students:* 48 full-time (17 women), 8 part-time (4 women); includes 6 minority (1 Black or African American, non-Hispanic/Latino; 3 Asian, non-Hispanic/Latino; 2 Hispanic/Latino), 1 international. Average age 33. 62 applicants, 48% accepted. In 2016, 15 master's, 5 doctorates awarded. *Degree requirements:* For master's, thesis or alternative; for doctorate, one foreign language, comprehensive exam, thesis/dissertation, ecclesiastical Latin. *Entrance requirements:* For master's, minimum undergraduate GPA of 3.0, 3 letters of recommendation, personal statement, official transcript(s); for doctorate, GRE General Test (minimum score 600 verbal previous scale, 160 current scale), minimum GPA of 3.5, academic writing sample, 3 letters of recommendation, official transcript(s). Additional exam requirements/recommendations for international students: Required—TOEFL (minimum score 550 paper-based; 80 iBT). *Application deadline:* For fall admission, 2/2 priority date for domestic and international students. Applications are processed on a rolling basis. Application fee: $0 ($50 for international students). Electronic applications accepted. *Expenses:* $603 per fall/spring credit hour, $420 per summer credit hour (for MA); $722 per credit hour (for PhD); $25 per term registration fee. *Financial support:* In 2016–17, 36 students received support, including 4 fellowships with full tuition reimbursements available (averaging $17,600 per year), 7 research assistantships with full tuition reimbursements available (averaging $11,000 per year), 16 teaching assistantships with full tuition reimbursements available (averaging $17,952 per year); scholarships/grants, health care benefits, and unspecified assistantships also available. Support available to part-time students. Financial award application deadline: 2/2; financial award applicants required to submit FAFSA. *Faculty research:* Practical/constructive theology, theological ethics, U.S. Catholic/Christian life and thought, methodologies in Biblical studies, religion and science. *Unit head:* Dr. Daniel Thompson, Chair, 937-229-4321, Fax: 937-229-4330. *Application contact:* Amy Doorley, Graduate Program Coordinator, 937-229-4321, Fax: 937-229-4330, E-mail: adoorley1@udayton.edu.
Website: http://www.udayton.edu/artssciences/academics/religiousstudies/welcome/index.php

**University of Dubuque,** University of Dubuque Theological Seminary, Dubuque, IA 52001. Offers M Div, D Min. *Accreditation:* ACIPE; ATS. *Program availability:* Part-time, 100% online, blended/hybrid learning. *Faculty:* 10 full-time (4 women), 11 part-time/adjunct (5 women). *Students:* 92 full-time (52 women); includes 8 minority (7 Black or African American, non-Hispanic/Latino; 1 Asian, non-Hispanic/Latino). Average age 38. 72 applicants, 76% accepted, 38 enrolled. In 2016, 20 master's, 7 doctorates awarded. *Degree requirements:* For doctorate, thesis/dissertation. *Entrance requirements:* Additional exam requirements/recommendations for international students: Recommended—TOEFL (minimum score 550 paper-based; 80 iBT). *Application deadline:* For fall admission, 4/15 priority date for domestic students, 12/1 priority date for international students; for spring admission, 11/1 priority date for domestic students. Applications are processed on a rolling basis. Application fee: $30. Electronic applications accepted. *Financial support:* In 2016–17, 69 students received support. Career-related internships or fieldwork, Federal Work-Study, institutionally sponsored loans, scholarships/grants, and tuition waivers (full and partial) available. Support available to part-time students. Financial award application deadline: 6/1; financial award applicants required to submit FAFSA. *Faculty research:* Biblical studies, reformed history and theology, pastoral theology, homiletics. *Unit head:* Dr. Annette Huizenga, Associate Dean, 563-589-3858, Fax: 563-589-3110, E-mail: ahuizenga@dbq.edu. *Application contact:* Kimberly S. Burnett-Hackbarth, Director, Seminary Admissions, 563-589-3405, Fax: 563-589-3490, E-mail: khackbarth@dbq.edu.
Website: http://udts.dbq.edu/

**The University of Manchester,** School of Arts, Histories and Cultures, Manchester, United Kingdom. Offers anthropology, media and performance (PhD); applied theatre professional (PhD); archaeology (PhD); art history and visual studies (PhD); arts management and cultural policy (PhD); classics and ancient history (PhD); composition (PhD); creative writing (PhD); drama (PhD); economic and social history (PhD); electroacoustic composition (PhD); English and American studies (PhD); history (PhD); humanitarianism and conflict response (PhD); museology (PhD); music (PhD); musicology (PhD); religions and theology (PhD).

**University of Northwestern–St. Paul,** Master of Arts in Theological Studies Program, St. Paul, MN 55113-1598. Offers MATS. *Program availability:* Part-time, evening/weekend, online learning. *Application deadline:* Applications are processed on a rolling basis. Electronic applications accepted. *Application contact:* College of Adult and Graduate Studies Admissions, 651-631-5200, E-mail: gradstudies@unwsp.edu.
Website: https://www.unwsp.edu/web/graduate-studies/master-of-arts-in-theological-studies

**University of Northwestern–St. Paul,** Master of Divinity Program, St. Paul, MN 55113-1598. Offers M Div. *Program availability:* Part-time, evening/weekend, online learning. *Application deadline:* Applications are processed on a rolling basis. Electronic applications accepted. *Application contact:* College of Adult and Graduate Studies Admissions, 651-631-5200, E-mail: gradstudies@unwsp.edu.
Website: https://www.unwsp.edu/web/graduate-studies/master-of-divinity

**University of Notre Dame,** Graduate School, College of Arts and Letters, Division of Humanities, Department of Theology, Notre Dame, IN 46556. Offers M Div, MA, MSM, MTS, PhD. *Accreditation:* ACIPE; ATS. Terminal master's awarded for partial completion of doctoral program. *Degree requirements:* For master's, one foreign language, comprehensive exam, thesis or alternative; for doctorate, 3 foreign languages, comprehensive exam, thesis/dissertation, candidacy exam. *Entrance requirements:* For master's and doctorate, GRE General Test. Additional exam requirements/recommendations for international students: Required—TOEFL (minimum score 600 paper-based; 80 iBT). Electronic applications accepted. *Faculty research:* Liturgy, ethics, historical studies, Biblical studies, systematic theology.

**University of Notre Dame,** Graduate School, College of Arts and Letters, Division of Humanities, Program in History and Philosophy of Science, Notre Dame, IN 46556. Offers history and philosophy of science (MA, PhD); theology and science (PhD). *Degree requirements:* For doctorate, 2 foreign languages, comprehensive exam, thesis/dissertation, candidacy exam. *Entrance requirements:* For doctorate, GRE General Test. Additional exam requirements/recommendations for international students: Required—TOEFL (minimum score 600 paper-based; 80 iBT). Electronic applications accepted. *Faculty research:* Philosophy of physics, science and ethics, history and philosophy of biology, history of medicine and technology, history and philosophy of economics.

**University of Philosophical Research,** Master's in Consciousness Studies Program, Los Angeles, CA 90027. Offers MA. *Degree requirements:* For master's, thesis. Electronic applications accepted.

**University of Philosophical Research,** Master's in Transformational Psychology Program, Los Angeles, CA 90027. Offers MA. *Degree requirements:* For master's, thesis. Electronic applications accepted.

**University of Saint Mary of the Lake–Mundelein Seminary,** Graduate and Professional Programs, Mundelein, IL 60060. Offers liturgical studies (MA); ministry (D Min); pastoral studies (MA); theology (M Div). *Accreditation:* ATS (one or more programs are accredited). *Faculty:* 60 full-time (6 women), 21 part-time/adjunct (9 women). *Students:* 266 full-time (8 women); includes 10 minority (2 Black or African American, non-Hispanic/Latino; 3 Asian, non-Hispanic/Latino; 5 Hispanic/Latino), 78 international. 99 applicants, 81% accepted, 80 enrolled. In 2016, 34 master's awarded. *Degree requirements:* For doctorate, 2 foreign languages, comprehensive exam, thesis/dissertation. *Entrance requirements:* For master's and doctorate, bachelor's degree. Additional exam requirements/recommendations for international students: Required—TOEFL (minimum score 550 paper-based). *Application deadline:* For fall admission, 8/1 for domestic and international students. Applications are processed on a rolling basis. Application fee: $0. Electronic applications accepted. *Expenses: Tuition:* Full-time $25,366. *Required fees:* $300. Full-time tuition and fees vary according to program. *Financial support:* Career-related internships or fieldwork available. *Unit head:* Very Rev. Thomas A. Baima, Dean of the Graduate School, 847-566-6401. *Application contact:* Very Rev. John Kartje, Rector-President, 847-566-6401, Fax: 847-932-3305.

**University of St. Michael's College,** Faculty of Theology, Toronto, ON M5S 1J4, Canada. Offers Catholic leadership (MA); eastern Christian studies (Diploma); religious education (Diploma); theological studies (Diploma); theology (M Div, MA, MRE, MTS, D Min, PhD, Th D); theology and Jewish studies (MA). Th D offered jointly with University of Toronto. *Accreditation:* ATS (one or more programs are accredited). *Program availability:* Part-time. *Degree requirements:* For master's, thesis (for some programs), 1 foreign language (MA), 2 foreign languages (Th M); for doctorate, 3 foreign languages, comprehensive exam, thesis/dissertation; for other advanced degree, thesis optional. *Entrance requirements:* For master's, M Div or BA, course work in an ancient or modern language, minimum GPA of 3.3; for doctorate, MA in theology, Th M, or M Div with thesis, minimum GPA of 3.7; for other advanced degree, minimum GPA of 2.7. Additional exam requirements/recommendations for international students: Required—TOEFL (minimum score 600 paper-based). Electronic applications accepted. *Expenses:* Contact institution. *Faculty research:* Patristics, eastern Christianity, ecology and theology, ecumenism, Jewish Christian studies.

**University of St. Thomas,** Graduate Studies, The Saint Paul Seminary School of Divinity, St. Paul, MN 55105. Offers pastoral ministry (MAPM); religious education (MARE); theology (MA). *Accreditation:* ACIPE; ATS. *Program availability:* Part-time, evening/weekend. *Degree requirements:* For master's, one foreign language, comprehensive exam (for some programs), thesis (for some programs). *Entrance requirements:* For master's, GRE, 3 letters of recommendation, interview. Additional exam requirements/recommendations for international students: Required—TOEFL (minimum score 550 paper-based). *Application deadline:* For fall admission, 6/1 priority date for domestic students. Applications are processed on a rolling basis. Application fee: $40. Electronic applications accepted. *Expenses:* Contact institution. *Financial support:* Fellowships, research assistantships, institutionally sponsored loans, and scholarships/grants available. Support available to part-time students. Financial award application deadline: 4/1; financial award applicants required to submit FAFSA. *Faculty research:* Theological education. *Unit head:* Rev. Msgr. Aloysius R. Callaghan, Rector/Vice President, 651-962-5052, Fax: 651-962-5790, E-mail: arcallaghan@stthomas.edu. *Application contact:* Rev. Peter Williams, Vice Rector for Formation, 651-962-5775, Fax: 651-962-5790, E-mail: will2750@stthomas.edu.
Website: http://www.stthomas.edu/spssod/

**University of St. Thomas,** School of Theology, Houston, TX 77024. Offers divinity (M Div); pastoral studies (MAPS); theological studies (MA). *Accreditation:* ATS. *Program availability:* Part-time. *Faculty:* 8 full-time (2 women), 5 part-time/adjunct (0 women). *Students:* 89 full-time (1 woman), 70 part-time (24 women); includes 62 minority (5 Black or African American, non-Hispanic/Latino; 22 Asian, non-Hispanic/Latino; 33 Hispanic/Latino; 2 Two or more races, non-Hispanic/Latino), 20 international. Average age 37. 50 applicants, 100% accepted, 37 enrolled. In 2016, 32 master's awarded. *Degree requirements:* For master's, variable foreign language requirement, comprehensive exam. *Entrance requirements:* For master's, BA, BS or equivalent; personal essay (for some programs); undergraduate philosophy or theology courses; 2 letters of recommendation. Additional exam requirements/recommendations for international students: Required—TOEFL (minimum score 550 paper-based; 79 iBT), IELTS (minimum score 6.5), PTE (minimum score 53). *Application deadline:* Applications are processed on a rolling basis. Application fee: $10. Electronic applications accepted. *Expenses:* Contact institution. *Financial support:* In 2016–17, 4 students received support. Scholarships/grants available. Support available to part-time students. Financial award application deadline: 4/15; financial award applicants required to submit FAFSA. *Unit head:* Dr. Sandra C. Magie, Dean, 713-686-4345 Ext. 242, Fax: 713-683-8673, E-mail: smagie@stthom.edu. *Application contact:* Connie M. Henry, Office Manager, 713-686-4345 Ext. 231, Fax: 713-683-8673, E-mail: sms@stthom.edu. Website: http://www.stthom.edu/Academics/School_of_Theology_at_St_Marys_Seminary/Index.aqf

**The University of Scranton,** College of Arts and Sciences, Program in Theology, Scranton, PA 18510. Offers MA. *Program availability:* Part-time, evening/weekend. *Degree requirements:* For master's, comprehensive exam (for some programs), thesis (for some programs), capstone experience. *Entrance requirements:* For master's, minimum GPA of 3.0, three letters of reference. Additional exam requirements/recommendations for international students: Required—TOEFL (minimum score 500 paper-based; 80 iBT), IELTS (minimum score 6.5). Electronic applications accepted.

**University of South Africa,** College of Human Sciences, Pretoria, South Africa. Offers adult education (M Ed); African languages (MA, PhD); African politics (MA, PhD); Afrikaans (MA, PhD); ancient history (MA, PhD); ancient Near Eastern studies (MA, PhD); anthropology (MA, PhD); applied linguistics (MA); Arabic (MA, PhD); archaeology (MA); art history (MA); Biblical archaeology (MA); Biblical studies (M Th, D Th, PhD); Christian spirituality (M Th, D Th); church history (M Th, D Th); classical studies (MA, PhD); clinical psychology (MA); communication (MA, PhD); comparative education (M Ed, Ed D); consulting psychology (D Admin, D Com, PhD); curriculum studies (M Ed, Ed D); development studies (M Admin, MA, D Admin, PhD); didactics (M Ed, Ed D); education (M Tech); education management (M Ed, Ed D); educational psychology (M Ed); English (MA); environmental education (M Ed); French (MA, PhD); German (MA, PhD); Greek (MA); guidance and counseling (M Ed); health studies (MA, PhD), including health sciences education (MA), health services management (MA), medical and surgical nursing science (critical care general) (MA), midwifery and neonatal nursing science (MA), trauma and emergency care (MA); history (MA, PhD); history of education (Ed D); inclusive education (M Ed, Ed D); information and communications technology policy and regulation (MA); information science (MA, MIS, PhD); international politics (MA, PhD); Islamic studies (MA, PhD); Italian (MA, PhD); Judaica (MA, PhD); linguistics (MA, PhD); mathematical education (M Ed); mathematics education (MA); missiology (M Th, D Th); modern Hebrew (MA, PhD); musicology (MA, MMus, D Mus, PhD); natural science education (M Ed); New Testament (M Th, D Th); Old Testament (D Th); pastoral therapy (M Th, D Th); philosophy (MA); philosophy of education (M Ed, Ed D); politics (MA, PhD); Portuguese (MA, PhD); practical theology (M Th, D Th); psychology (MA, MS, PhD); psychology of education (M Ed, Ed D); public health (MA); religious studies (MA, D Th, PhD); Romance languages (MA); Russian (MA, PhD); Semitic languages (MA, PhD); social behavior studies in HIV/AIDS (MA); social science (mental health) (MA); social science in development studies (MA); social science in psychology (MA); social science in social work (MA); social science in sociology (MA); social work (MSW, DSW, PhD); socio-education (M Ed, Ed D); sociolinguistics (MA); sociology (MA, PhD); Spanish (MA, PhD); systematic theology (M Th, D Th); TESOL (teaching English to speakers of other languages) (MA); theological ethics (M Th, D Th); theory of literature (MA, PhD); urban ministries (D Th); urban ministry (M Th).

**University of the West,** Program in Buddhist Chaplaincy, Rosemead, CA 91770. Offers M Div. *Entrance requirements:* Additional exam requirements/recommendations for international students: Required—TOEFL (minimum score 550 paper-based; 79 iBT); Recommended—IELTS. *Application deadline:* For fall admission, 3/15 for domestic and international students; for spring admission, 11/15 for domestic and international students. Applications are processed on a rolling basis. Application fee: $50. *Expenses: Tuition:* Full-time $9324; part-time $4662 per year. *Required fees:* $900; $640 per unit. $320 per semester. Tuition and fees vary according to program. *Unit head:* Dr. Victor Gabriel, Coordinator, 626-571-8811 Ext. 359, E-mail: victorg@uwest.edu. *Application contact:* Rica Toribio, Director of Enrollment Services, 626-571-8811 Ext. 311, Fax: 626-571-1413, E-mail: ricat@uwest.edu.

**University of Valley Forge,** Program in Theology, Phoenixville, PA 19460. Offers MA. *Degree requirements:* For master's, project.

**The University of Winnipeg,** Faculty of Theology, Winnipeg, MB R3B 2E9, Canada. Offers marriage and family therapy (MMFT, Certificate); sacred theology (STM); theology (M Div). *Accreditation:* AAMFT/COAMFTE; ATS. *Program availability:* Part-time.

**Urshan Graduate School of Theology,** Graduate Programs, Florissant, MO 63031. Offers M Div, MACM, MTS. *Accreditation:* ATS. *Program availability:* Online learning. *Degree requirements:* For master's, capstone project (for MACM and MTS); portfolio (for M Div).

**Ursuline College,** School of Graduate Studies, Theological and Pastoral Studies Program, Pepper Pike, OH 44124-4398. Offers MA. *Program availability:* Part-time. *Faculty:* 3 full-time (all women). *Students:* 1 (woman) full-time, 5 part-time (4 women); includes 5 minority (all Black or African American, non-Hispanic/Latino). Average age 55. 3 applicants, 67% accepted, 1 enrolled. *Degree requirements:* For master's, thesis. *Entrance requirements:* For master's, GRE when GPA under 3.0, minimum undergraduate GPA of 3.0, interview. Additional exam requirements/recommendations for international students: Required—TOEFL (minimum score 550 paper-based; 80 iBT). *Application deadline:* For fall admission, 8/1 priority date for domestic students. Applications are processed on a rolling basis. Application fee: $25. Electronic applications accepted. *Expenses:* $1,052 per credit hour. *Financial support:* In 2016–17, 6 students received support. Scholarships/grants available. Financial award application deadline: 3/1; financial award applicants required to submit FAFSA. *Faculty research:* Household codes of Ephesians, cosmology of Ephesians, early Christian families, the use of theological reflection in integrative education for ministry, premillennial dispensationalism and the politics of the religious right in the United States. *Unit head:* Dr. Linda Martin, Director, 440-646-8191, Fax: 440-684-6088, E-mail: lmartin@ursuline.edu. *Application contact:* Melanie Steele, Director, Graduate Admissions, 440-646-8146, Fax: 440-684-6138, E-mail: graduateadmissions@ursuline.edu.

**Valparaiso University,** Graduate School and Continuing Education, Programs in Liberal Studies, Concentration in Theology, Valparaiso, IN 46383. Offers MALS, Post-Master's Certificate, JD/MALS. *Program availability:* Part-time, evening/weekend. *Entrance requirements:* For master's, minimum GPA of 3.0. Additional exam requirements/recommendations for international students: Required—TOEFL (minimum score 550 paper-based; 80 iBT), IELTS (minimum score 6). Electronic applications accepted. *Expenses: Tuition:* Full-time $11,070; part-time $615 per credit hour. *Required fees:* $116 per semester. Tuition and fees vary according to course load, degree level and program.

**Valparaiso University,** Graduate School and Continuing Education, Programs in Liberal Studies, Concentration in Theology and Ministry, Valparaiso, IN 46383. Offers MALS, Post-Master's Certificate. *Program availability:* Part-time, evening/weekend. *Entrance requirements:* For master's, minimum GPA of 3.0. Additional exam requirements/recommendations for international students: Required—TOEFL (minimum score 550 paper-based; 80 iBT), IELTS (minimum score 6). Electronic applications

accepted. *Expenses: Tuition:* Full-time $11,070; part-time $615 per credit hour. *Required fees:* $116 per semester. Tuition and fees vary according to course load, degree level and program.

**Vancouver School of Theology,** Graduate and Professional Programs, Vancouver, BC V6T 1L4, Canada. Offers public and pastoral leadership (MA); public and pastoral leadership in spiritual care (MA); theological studies (MATS, Diploma); theology (M Div, Th M). *Accreditation:* ATS. *Program availability:* Part-time, online learning. *Degree requirements:* For master's, comprehensive exam (for some programs), thesis (for some programs); for Diploma, one foreign language, thesis. *Entrance requirements:* Additional exam requirements/recommendations for international students: Required—TOEFL (minimum score 80 iBT); Recommended—IELTS (minimum score 6.5). *Application deadline:* Applications are processed on a rolling basis. Application fee: $75 Canadian dollars. Electronic applications accepted. *Expenses: Tuition:* Part-time $281 per credit hour. Part-time tuition and fees vary according to degree level, campus/location and program. *Financial support:* Fellowships, research assistantships with partial tuition reimbursements, teaching assistantships with partial tuition reimbursements, career-related internships or fieldwork, scholarships/grants, and tuition waivers (partial) available. Support available to part-time students. Financial award application deadline: 3/30. *Faculty research:* Old Testament studies, pastoral theology, New Testament studies, field education, church history, systematic theology, spirituality. *Unit head:* Rev. Dr. Richard Topping, Principal, 604-822-9808, Fax: 604-822-9212. *Application contact:* Anita Fast, Registrar, 604-822-9563, Fax: 604-822-9212, E-mail: afast@vst.edu. Website: http://vst.edu/ccl/about/degree-programs/graduate-degrees

**Vanderbilt University,** Divinity School, Nashville, TN 37240. Offers M Div, MTS, JD/M Div, JD/MTS, M Div/M Ed, MBA/M Div, MBA/MTS, MD/M Div, MD/MTS, MSN/M Div, MSN/MTS. *Accreditation:* ACIPE; ATS. *Program availability:* Part-time. *Entrance requirements:* Additional exam requirements/recommendations for international students: Required—TOEFL (minimum score 600 paper-based; 95 iBT), IELTS (minimum score 7). Electronic applications accepted. *Expenses: Tuition:* Part-time $1854 per credit hour.

**Vanguard University of Southern California,** Graduate Programs in Religion, Costa Mesa, CA 92626-9601. Offers leadership studies (MA); theological studies (MTS). *Program availability:* Part-time, evening/weekend. *Degree requirements:* For master's, comprehensive exam (for some programs), thesis (for some programs). *Entrance requirements:* For master's, minimum GPA of 3.0 (MA), 2.5 (MTS). Additional exam requirements/recommendations for international students: Required—TOEFL (minimum score 550 paper-based; 79 iBT). Electronic applications accepted. *Expenses:* Contact institution. *Faculty research:* Narrative theology, ecumenism and Pentecost, leadership studies.

**Victoria University,** Emmanuel College, Toronto, ON M5S 1K7, Canada. Offers M Div, MA, MPS, MRE, MSMus, MTS, Th M, D Min, PhD, Th D, Certificate, Diploma, L Th, M Div/MA, M Div/MPS, M Div/MRE. M Div, MRE, Th M, Th D, M Div/MA, M Div/MRE, M Div/MPS offered jointly with University of Toronto; MA, Th D with University of St. Michael's College. Terminal master's awarded for partial completion of doctoral program. *Degree requirements:* For master's, variable foreign language requirement, thesis (for some programs); for doctorate, 2 foreign languages, thesis/dissertation. *Entrance requirements:* For master's and other advanced degree, BA, BSc; for doctorate, M Div, MA, MTS, Th M. Additional exam requirements/recommendations for international students: Required—TOEFL (minimum score 600 paper-based; 100 iBT), IELTS (minimum score 7), TWE (minimum score 5). Electronic applications accepted. *Faculty research:* New Testament and Old Testament hermeneutics, religious symbolism, Reformation, liberation theology, Canadian church history.

**Villanova University,** Graduate School of Liberal Arts and Sciences, Department of Theology, Villanova, PA 19085-1699. Offers MA, PhD. *Program availability:* Part-time, evening/weekend. *Faculty:* 11. *Students:* 28 full-time (14 women), 6 part-time (1 woman); includes 2 minority (1 Black or African American, non-Hispanic/Latino; 1 Two or more races, non-Hispanic/Latino), 4 international. Average age 34. 40 applicants, 50% accepted, 17 enrolled. In 2016, 17 master's awarded. *Degree requirements:* For master's, variable foreign language requirement, comprehensive exam (for some programs), thesis optional; for doctorate, variable foreign language requirement, comprehensive exam (for some programs), thesis/dissertation. *Entrance requirements:* For master's, minimum GPA of 3.0, statement of goals, 3 recommendation letters; for doctorate, transcripts, 3 recommendation letters, essay, curriculum vitae or resume. Additional exam requirements/recommendations for international students: Required—TOEFL. *Application deadline:* For fall admission, 3/1 for domestic students, 5/1 priority date for international students; for spring admission, 11/15 for domestic students, 10/15 for international students; for summer admission, 5/1 for domestic students. Applications are processed on a rolling basis. Application fee: $50. Electronic applications accepted. *Financial support:* Research assistantships, teaching assistantships, scholarships/grants, and unspecified assistantships available. Financial award applicants required to submit FAFSA. *Unit head:* Dr. Edward Hastings, Program Director, 610-519-6476. Website: http://www1.villanova.edu/villanova/artsci/theology/graduate.html

**Virginia Baptist College,** Graduate Programs, Fredericksburg, VA 22407. Offers MBS, MCE, MM.

**Virginia Beach Theological Seminary,** Graduate Programs, Virginia Beach, VA 23464. Offers Biblical studies (MBS, Th M); chaplaincy (MBS); ministry (M Div). *Program availability:* Online learning. *Faculty:* 5 full-time (0 women), 2 part-time/adjunct (0 women). *Students:* 7 full-time (0 women), 29 part-time (3 women). *Entrance requirements:* For master's, GRE, interview, minimum cumulative GPA of 2.4, church endorsement, 3 recommendations. Electronic applications accepted. *Expenses: Tuition:* Full-time $7920; part-time $330 per credit hour. *Required fees:* $265 per semester. *Financial support:* Scholarships/grants available. *Application contact:* Edward Estes, Director of Admissions, 757-479-3706, E-mail: eestes@vbts.edu. Website: http://www.vbts.edu/academics/

**Virginia Theological Seminary,** Graduate and Professional Programs, Alexandria, VA 22304. Offers Christian spirituality (D Min); educational leadership (D Ed Min, D Min); ministry development (D Min); theology (M Div, MA). *Accreditation:* ATS. *Program availability:* Part-time. *Faculty:* 26 full-time (11 women), 29 part-time/adjunct (11 women). *Students:* 220. *Degree requirements:* For master's, 2 foreign languages, thesis; for doctorate, thesis/dissertation. *Entrance requirements:* For master's and doctorate, GRE General Test. *Application deadline:* For fall admission, 5/1 for domestic students. Application fee: $0. *Expenses: Tuition:* Full-time $13,800; part-time $636 per credit hour. *Required fees:* $140. *Financial support:* Career-related internships or fieldwork, Federal Work-Study, and institutionally sponsored loans available. *Application contact:* Rachel Holm, Associate Director for Admissions, Financial Aid and Housing, 703-370-6600.

**Virginia Union University,** Samuel DeWitt Proctor School of Theology, Richmond, VA 23220-1170. Offers M Div, D Min. *Accreditation:* ACIPE. *Program availability:* Part-time, evening/weekend. *Entrance requirements:* Additional exam requirements/recommendations for international students: Required—TOEFL.

**Walsh University,** Graduate Programs, Master of Arts in Theology Program, North Canton, OH 44720-3396. Offers parish administration (MA); pastoral ministry (MA);

religious education (MA). *Program availability:* Part-time, evening/weekend. *Faculty:* 4 full-time (0 women). *Students:* 5 full-time (2 women), 10 part-time (3 women); includes 1 minority (Black or African American, non-Hispanic/Latino), 1 international. Average age 41. 6 applicants, 67% accepted, 4 enrolled. In 2016, 7 master's awarded. *Degree requirements:* For master's, thesis or alternative, culminating assignment. *Entrance requirements:* For master's, MAT or GRE (minimum scores: Verbal 145, Quantitative 146, Combined 291, Writing 3.0), minimum GPA of 3.0. Additional exam requirements/ recommendations for international students: Required—TOEFL. *Application deadline:* For fall admission, 7/15 for domestic students. Applications are processed on a rolling basis. Application fee: $25. Electronic applications accepted. Application fee is waived when completed online. *Expenses:* $332 per credit hour tuition. *Financial support:* Research assistantships available. Financial award application deadline: 12/31; financial award applicants required to submit FAFSA. *Faculty research:* Cardinal Newman, phenomenological method, Flavius Josephus, post-conciliar moral teaching. *Unit head:* Dr. Bradley Beach, Chair, 330-244-4732, Fax: 330-244-4955, E-mail: bbeach@walsh.edu. *Application contact:* Audra Dice, Graduate Admissions Counselor, 330-490-7181, Fax: 330-244-4925, E-mail: adice@walsh.edu.

**Wartburg Theological Seminary,** Graduate and Professional Programs, Dubuque, IA 52004-5004. Offers diaconal ministry (MA); ministry (M Div); theology (MA). *Accreditation:* ACIPE; ATS. *Program availability:* Online learning. *Degree requirements:* For master's, thesis (for some programs). *Entrance requirements:* For master's, minimum GPA of 3.0 (STM). Additional exam requirements/recommendations for international students: Required—TOEFL (minimum score 500 paper-based; 80 iBT). Electronic applications accepted.

**Wayland Baptist University,** Graduate Programs, Programs in Religion, Plainview, TX 79072-6998. Offers Christian ministry (MCM); divinity (M Div); religion (MA). *Program availability:* Part-time, evening/weekend, online learning. *Degree requirements:* For master's, comprehensive exam. *Entrance requirements:* For master's, GRE or MAT, minimum GPA of 3.0; letter of endorsement from Christian congregation, one academic and one personal letter of recommendation (for M Div). Additional exam requirements/ recommendations for international students: Required—TOEFL (minimum score 500 paper-based; 61 iBT). Electronic applications accepted.

**Wesley Biblical Seminary,** Graduate Programs, Jackson, MS 39206. Offers apologetics (MA); Biblical languages (M Div); Biblical literature (MA); Christian studies (MA); context and mission (M Div); honors research (M Div); interpretation (M Div); ministry (M Div); spiritual formation (M Div); teaching (M Div); theology (MA). *Accreditation:* ATS. *Program availability:* Part-time. *Degree requirements:* For master's, thesis. *Entrance requirements:* Additional exam requirements/recommendations for international students: Required—TOEFL. Electronic applications accepted. *Faculty research:* Patristics, missiology, culture, hermeneutics.

**Wesley Theological Seminary,** Graduate and Professional Programs, Washington, DC 20016-5690. Offers M Div, MA, MTS, D Min, M Div/MA, M Div/MTS. *Accreditation:* ACIPE; ATS. *Program availability:* Part-time. *Degree requirements:* For master's, thesis; for doctorate, thesis/dissertation. *Entrance requirements:* For master's, minimum GPA of 2.7; for doctorate, minimum GPA of 3.0.

**Western Seminary,** Graduate Programs, Master of Divinity Program, Portland, OR 97215-3367. Offers M Div. *Entrance requirements:* Additional exam requirements/ recommendations for international students: Required—TOEFL.

**Western Seminary,** Graduate Programs, Program in Biblical and Theological Studies, Portland, OR 97215-3367. Offers biblical and theological studies (MA, G Dip); biblical studies (Certificate); theology (Th M). *Accreditation:* ATS. *Program availability:* Part-time, evening/weekend. *Degree requirements:* For master's, thesis or alternative, practicum. *Entrance requirements:* Additional exam requirements/recommendations for international students: Required—TOEFL.

**Western Seminary–Sacramento Campus,** Graduate Certificate Programs, Sacramento, CA 95821. Offers Bible (Graduate Certificate); coaching (Graduate Certificate); pastoral care to women (Graduate Certificate); theology (Graduate Certificate); youth and family (Graduate Certificate). *Program availability:* Online learning. *Entrance requirements:* For degree, essays, undergraduate transcripts, 4 recommendations. Additional exam requirements/recommendations for international students: Required—TOEFL.

**Western Seminary–Sacramento Campus,** Graduate Diploma Programs, Sacramento, CA 95821. Offers Bible and theology (Graduate Diploma); ministry (Graduate Diploma); pastoral care to women (Graduate Diploma). *Entrance requirements:* For degree, essays, undergraduate transcripts, 4 recommendations. Additional exam requirements/ recommendations for international students: Required—TOEFL.

**Western Seminary–Sacramento Campus,** Master of Divinity Program, Sacramento, CA 95821. Offers M Div. *Entrance requirements:* Additional exam requirements/ recommendations for international students: Required—TOEFL.

**Western Seminary–Sacramento Campus,** Program in Biblical and Theological Studies, Sacramento, CA 95821. Offers MA. *Entrance requirements:* For master's, essays, undergraduate transcripts, 4 recommendations. Additional exam requirements/ recommendations for international students: Required—TOEFL.

**Western Seminary–San Jose Campus,** Graduate Programs, Los Gatos, CA 95032-4520. Offers Bible and theology (Graduate Diploma); Bible, camp and conference ministry (CGS); Biblical and theological studies (MA), including exegetical track, theological track; coaching (CGS); expositional ministry (M Div); marital and family therapy (MA); ministry (Graduate Diploma); ministry and leadership (MA), including camp and conference ministry, coaching, pastoral care to women, youth ministry; pastoral care to women (CGS, Graduate Diploma); pastoral ministry (M Div); theology (CGS); youth and family (CGS). *Program availability:* Part-time, evening/weekend, online learning. *Entrance requirements:* For master's, minimum GPA of 3.0. Electronic applications accepted.

**Western Theological Seminary,** Graduate and Professional Programs, Holland, MI 49423-3622. Offers divinity (M Div); ministry (D Min); theology (M Th, MA); urban pastoral ministry (Graduate Certificate); M Div/MSW. *Accreditation:* ACIPE; ATS. *Program availability:* Part-time, 100% online, blended/hybrid learning. *Degree requirements:* For doctorate, thesis/dissertation. *Entrance requirements:* Additional exam requirements/recommendations for international students: Required—TOEFL. Electronic applications accepted.

**Westminster Seminary California,** Programs in Theology, Escondido, CA 92027-4128. Offers Biblical studies (MA); historical theology (MA); theological studies (M Div, MA). *Accreditation:* ATS. *Program availability:* Part-time, evening/weekend. *Degree requirements:* For master's, 2 foreign languages, thesis (for some programs). *Entrance requirements:* For master's, 2 letters of reference. Additional exam requirements/ recommendations for international students: Required—TOEFL (minimum score 570 paper-based; 89 iBT), TWE (minimum score 4.5). *Faculty research:* Neo-paganism, New Testament background, eschatology, Protestant scholasticism, Ezekiel.

**Westminster Theological Seminary,** Graduate and Professional Programs, Philadelphia, PA 19118. Offers apologetics (Th M); Biblical and urban studies (Certificate); Biblical counseling (MA); biblical studies (MAR); Christian studies (Certificate); church history (Th M); counseling (M Div); general studies (M Div, MAR); hermeneutics and Bible interpretations (PhD); historical and theological studies (PhD); historical theology (Th M); New Testament (Th M); Old Testament (Th M); pastoral counseling (D Min); pastoral ministry (M Div, D Min); systematic theology (Th M); theological studies (MAR); urban missions (M Div, MA, MAR, D Min). *Accreditation:* ATS. *Program availability:* Part-time. Terminal master's awarded for partial completion of doctoral program. *Degree requirements:* For master's, thesis (for some programs); for doctorate, 4 foreign languages, comprehensive exam (for some programs), thesis/ dissertation. *Entrance requirements:* For doctorate, GRE General Test. Additional exam requirements/recommendations for international students: Required—TOEFL, TWE.

**Wheaton College,** Graduate School, Department of Biblical and Theological Studies, Wheaton, IL 60187-5593. Offers Biblical and theological studies (PhD); Biblical archaeology (MA); Biblical exegesis (MA); Biblical studies (MA); general theological studies (MA); historical and systematic theology (MA), including biblical and theological studies; history of Christianity (MA), including Biblical and theological studies. *Program availability:* Part-time. *Faculty:* 8 full-time (1 woman), 1 part-time/adjunct (0 women). *Students:* 53 full-time (12 women), 48 part-time (20 women); includes 14 minority (3 Black or African American, non-Hispanic/Latino; 5 Asian, non-Hispanic/Latino; 3 Hispanic/Latino; 3 Two or more races, non-Hispanic/Latino), 18 international. Average age 34. 116 applicants, 63% accepted, 35 enrolled. In 2016, 32 master's, 2 doctorates awarded. *Degree requirements:* For doctorate, thesis/dissertation. *Entrance requirements:* For master's, GRE General Test. Additional exam requirements/ recommendations for international students: Required—TOEFL (minimum score 550 paper-based; 80 iBT), IELTS (minimum score 6.5), TOEFL (minimum score 600 paper-based; 90 iBT) or IELTS (minimum score 7.5) for PhD. *Application deadline:* For fall admission, 1/1 priority date for domestic students, 1/1 for international students; for spring admission, 11/1 for domestic students. Applications are processed on a rolling basis. Application fee: $30. Electronic applications accepted. *Expenses: Tuition:* Full-time $19,080; part-time $795 per credit hour. Tuition and fees vary according to degree level and program. *Financial support:* Scholarships/grants and unspecified assistantships available. Financial award application deadline: 3/1; financial award applicants required to submit FAFSA. *Unit head:* Dr. Lynn Cohick, Interim Associate Dean, 630-752-5054. *Application contact:* Dusty Di Santo, Director of Graduate Admissions, 630-752-5195, Fax: 630-752-7047, E-mail: graduate.admissions@wheaton.edu.
Website: http://www.wheaton.edu/academics/departments/theology

**Wheaton College,** Graduate School, Department of Evangelism, Wheaton, IL 60187-5593. Offers evangelism and leadership (MA); missional church movements (MA). *Program availability:* Part-time. *Faculty:* 1 full-time (0 women). *Students:* 2 full-time (0 women), 5 part-time (1 woman); includes 1 minority (Hispanic/Latino). Average age 34. 5 applicants, 100% accepted, 4 enrolled. In 2016, 13 master's awarded. *Degree requirements:* For master's, thesis or alternative. *Entrance requirements:* For master's, GRE or MAT. Additional exam requirements/recommendations for international students: Required—TOEFL (minimum score 550 paper-based; 80 iBT), IELTS (minimum score 6.5). *Application deadline:* For fall admission, 3/1 priority date for domestic students, 1/1 for international students; for spring admission, 11/1 for domestic students. Applications are processed on a rolling basis. Application fee: $30. Electronic applications accepted. *Expenses: Tuition:* Full-time $19,080; part-time $795 per credit hour. Tuition and fees vary according to degree level and program. *Financial support:* Career-related internships or fieldwork, Federal Work-Study, scholarships/grants, and unspecified assistantships available. Financial award application deadline: 3/1; financial award applicants required to submit FAFSA. *Unit head:* Dr. Ed Stetzer, Chair, 630-752-5806, E-mail: evangelism.leadership@wheaton.edu. *Application contact:* Dusty Di Santo, Director of Graduate Admissions, 630-752-5195, Fax: 630-752-7047, E-mail: graduate.admissions@wheaton.edu.
Website: http://www.wheaton.edu/graduate-school/degrees/evangelism-and-leadership

**Whitworth University,** Master of Arts in Theology Program, Spokane, WA 99251-0001. Offers MA. *Program availability:* Part-time, evening/weekend.

**Wilfrid Laurier University,** Waterloo Lutheran Seminary, Waterloo, ON N2L 3C5, Canada. Offers divinity (M Div); multifaith spiritual care and counseling (Diploma); pastoral leadership (D Min); spiritual care and counseling (D Min); theology (M Th, MTS); M Div/MTS/MSW. *Accreditation:* ATS. *Program availability:* Part-time. *Degree requirements:* For master's, one foreign language, thesis (for some programs); for doctorate, thesis/dissertation. *Entrance requirements:* For master's, two letters of reference; for doctorate, M Div, two letters of reference. Additional exam requirements/ recommendations for international students: Required—TOEFL (minimum score 573 paper-based; 89 iBT), IELTS (minimum score 7). Electronic applications accepted. *Expenses:* Contact institution. *Faculty research:* Biblical study, church history, systematic theology.

**Winebrenner Theological Seminary,** Graduate Programs, Findlay, OH 45840. Offers clinical counseling (MA); family ministry (MA); practical theology (MA); theological and ministerial studies (M Div, D Min); theological studies (MA). *Accreditation:* ATS (one or more programs are accredited). *Program availability:* Part-time, 100% online, blended/ hybrid learning. *Faculty:* 7 full-time (2 women), 22 part-time/adjunct (8 women). *Students:* 16 full-time (10 women), 50 part-time (23 women); includes 12 minority (8 Black or African American, non-Hispanic/Latino; 2 Asian, non-Hispanic/Latino; 2 Two or more races, non-Hispanic/Latino), 2 international. Average age 41. 25 applicants, 76% accepted, 12 enrolled. In 2016, 8 master's, 2 doctorates awarded. *Degree requirements:* For master's, variable foreign language requirement, thesis (for some programs); for doctorate, thesis/dissertation. *Entrance requirements:* For doctorate, 3 years of post-M Div full-time ministry. Additional exam requirements/recommendations for international students: Required—TOEFL (minimum score 550 paper-based; 80 iBT). *Application deadline:* For fall admission, 8/15 priority date for domestic students, 7/15 priority date for international students; for winter admission, 12/15 priority date for domestic students, 11/15 priority date for international students; for spring admission, 4/15 priority date for domestic students, 3/15 priority date for international students. Applications are processed on a rolling basis. Application fee: $30. Electronic applications accepted. *Expenses: Tuition:* Full-time $14,175; part-time $525 per credit hour. *Required fees:* $450; $150 per trimester. Tuition and fees vary according to degree level. *Financial support:* In 2016–17, 32 students received support, including 3 teaching assistantships with partial tuition reimbursements available (averaging $1,575 per year); research assistantships, institutionally sponsored loans, scholarships/grants, unspecified assistantships, and denominational discounts, spousal discounts also available. Financial award application deadline: 7/1; financial award applicants required to submit FAFSA. *Faculty research:* Inductive biblical language grammar; review of Tobias Hagerland's "Jesus and the Scriptures"; Teleios profile of student wholeness; Puritanism; theological aesthetics. *Unit head:* Dr. Joel W. Cocklin, Academic Dean, 419-434-4250, Fax: 419-434-4267, E-mail: jcocklin@winebrenner.edu. *Application contact:* Jim Smarkel, Director of Enrollment Management, 419-434-4220, Fax: 419-434-4267, E-mail: admissions@winebrenner.edu.
Website: http://www.winebrenner.edu

*Theology*

**Wycliffe College,** Division of Advanced Degree Studies, Toronto, ON M5S 1H7, Canada. Offers MA, Th M, D Min, PhD, Th D. PhD, D Min, MA offered jointly with Toronto School of Theology; Th D, Th M with University of Toronto. *Accreditation:* ATS (one or more programs are accredited). *Program availability:* Part-time. Terminal master's awarded for partial completion of doctoral program. *Degree requirements:* For master's, 2 foreign languages, thesis (for some programs); for doctorate, 3 foreign languages, thesis/dissertation. *Entrance requirements:* Additional exam requirements/ recommendations for international students: Required—TOEFL (minimum score 600 paper-based). *Expenses:* Contact institution. *Faculty research:* Old and New Testament, doctrine, ethics, philosophy, history.

**Wycliffe College,** Division of Basic Degree Studies, Toronto, ON M5S 1H7, Canada. Offers Christian Studies (Diploma); theology (M Div, M Rel, MTS). M Div, M Rel, MTS offered jointly with University of Toronto. *Accreditation:* ATS. *Program availability:* Part-time. *Degree requirements:* For master's, one foreign language, thesis. *Entrance requirements:* Additional exam requirements/recommendations for international students: Required—TOEFL (minimum score 580 paper-based).

**Xavier University,** College of Arts and Sciences, Department of Theology, Cincinnati, OH 45207. Offers health care mission integration (MA); theology (MA), including religious education, social and pastoral ministry, theology. *Program availability:* Part-time, evening/weekend. *Degree requirements:* For master's, final paper (or thesis) and defense or comprehension exam. *Entrance requirements:* For master's, MAT or GRE, 2 letters of recommendation; statement of reasons and goals for enrolling in program (1,000-2,000 words); resume; transcript. Additional exam requirements/ recommendations for international students: Required—TOEFL (minimum score 550 paper-based; 79 iBT). Electronic applications accepted. Application fee is waived when completed online. *Expenses:* Contact institution. *Faculty research:* Scripture, ethics, constructive theology, historical theology.

**Xavier University of Louisiana,** Graduate School, Institute for Black Catholic Studies, New Orleans, LA 70125. Offers pastoral theology (Th M). *Program availability:* Part-time. *Degree requirements:* For master's, comprehensive exam, practicum. *Entrance requirements:* For master's, GRE General Test, MAT, minimum GPA of 2.5. Additional exam requirements/recommendations for international students: Required—TOEFL.

**Yale University,** Yale Divinity School, New Haven, CT 06511. Offers M Div, MAR, STM, JD/M Div, JD/MAR, M Div/MBA, M Div/MF, M Div/MSN, M Div/MSW, MAR/MSN, MAR/ MSW, MD/M Div, MD/MAR. *Accreditation:* ACIPE; ATS. *Program availability:* Part-time. *Entrance requirements:* Additional exam requirements/recommendations for international students: Required—IELTS (minimum score 7). Electronic applications accepted. *Expenses:* Contact institution.

**Yeshiva Beth Moshe,** Graduate Programs, Scranton, PA 18505-2124. Offers Second Talmudical Degree, Talmudic Fellow Degree. *Accreditation:* AARTS.

**Yeshiva Karlin Stolin Rabbinical Institute,** Graduate Programs, Brooklyn, NY 11204. Offers Advanced Rabbinical Degree. *Accreditation:* AARTS.

**Yeshiva of Nitra Rabbinical College,** Graduate Programs, Mount Kisco, NY 10549. *Accreditation:* AARTS.

**Yeshiva Shaar Hatorah Talmudic Research Institute,** Graduate Programs, Kew Gardens, NY 11418-1469. *Accreditation:* AARTS.

**Yeshivath Zichron Moshe,** Graduate Programs, South Fallsburg, NY 12779. Offers Advanced Talmudic Degree, Talmudic Scholar Degree. *Accreditation:* AARTS. *Program availability:* Part-time.

# Section 13
# Writing

This section contains a directory of institutions offering graduate work in writing, Additional information about programs listed in the directory but not augmented by an in-depth entry may be obtained by writing directly to the dean of a graduate school or chair of a department at the address given in the directory.

For programs offering related work, see also in this book *Communication and Media* and *Language and Literature.*

## CONTENTS

# Technical Writing

**Carnegie Mellon University,** Dietrich College of Humanities and Social Sciences, Department of English, Program in Professional Writing, Pittsburgh, PA 15213-3891. Offers editing and publishing (MAPW); policy and non-profit communication (MAPW); public and media relations/corporate communications (MAPW); science or healthcare communication (MAPW); technical writing (MAPW); writing for new media (MAPW); writing for print media (MAPW). *Program availability:* Part-time. *Entrance requirements:* For master's, GRE General Test. Additional exam requirements/recommendations for international students: Required—TOEFL, TWE.

**Drexel University,** College of Arts and Sciences, Department of Communication, Culture and Media, Philadelphia, PA 19104-2875. Offers communication (MS), including public communication, science communication, technical communication. *Program availability:* Part-time, evening/weekend. *Faculty:* 19 full-time (6 women), 12 part-time/adjunct (6 women). *Students:* 5 full-time (4 women), 35 part-time (25 women); includes 9 minority (3 Black or African American, non-Hispanic/Latino; 3 Asian, non-Hispanic/Latino; 3 Hispanic/Latino), 7 international. Average age 30. In 2016, 12 master's awarded. *Degree requirements:* For master's, internship, professional portfolio. *Entrance requirements:* Additional exam requirements/recommendations for international students: Required—TOEFL. *Application deadline:* For fall admission, 8/21 for domestic students. Applications are processed on a rolling basis. Application fee: $50. Electronic applications accepted. *Expenses: Tuition:* Full-time $32,184; part-time $1192 per credit hour. *Required fees:* $280. Tuition and fees vary according to campus/location and program. *Financial support:* Research assistantships, teaching assistantships, career-related internships or fieldwork, Federal Work-Study, institutionally sponsored loans, tuition waivers (partial), and unspecified assistantships available. Financial award application deadline: 2/1. *Faculty research:* Science information and attitudes, science influence on literature, process of technical writing, document design, software documentation. *Unit head:* Dr. Douglas Porpora, Head, 215-895-2446, Fax: 215-895-1071. *Application contact:* Director of Graduate Admissions, 215-895-6700, Fax: 215-895-5939, E-mail: enroll@drexel.edu.

**Illinois Institute of Technology,** Graduate College, Lewis College of Human Sciences, Department of Humanities, Chicago, IL 60616. Offers information architecture (MS); technical communication (PhD); technical communication and information design (MS). *Program availability:* Part-time. *Degree requirements:* For master's, comprehensive exam, thesis or alternative; for doctorate, comprehensive exam, thesis/dissertation. *Entrance requirements:* For master's, GRE General Test (minimum score 144 Quantitative, 153 Verbal, and 4.0 Analytical Writing), minimum undergraduate GPA of 3.0; 2 letters of recommendation from faculty or supervisors; professional statement discussing academic goals; for doctorate, GRE General Test (minimum score 144 Quantitative, 153 Verbal, and 4.0 Analytical Writing), bachelor's or master's degree in a field that, in combination with the 27-credit hour technical core, would provide a solid basis for advanced academic work leading to original research in the field; 3 letters of recommendation from faculty or supervisors; professional statement discussing academic goals. Additional exam requirements/recommendations for international students: Required—TOEFL (minimum score 95 iBT); Recommended—IELTS (minimum score 7). Electronic applications accepted. *Faculty research:* Linguistics, punishment theory, political communication, gender and technology, philosophical and ethical issues in neuroscience.

**James Madison University,** The Graduate School, College of Arts and Letters, Program in Writing, Rhetoric, and Technical Communication, Harrisonburg, VA 22802. Offers MA, MS. *Program availability:* Part-time. *Faculty:* 20 full-time (11 women), 1 (woman) part-time/adjunct. *Students:* 10 full-time (9 women), 3 part-time (2 women); includes 3 minority (1 Asian, non-Hispanic/Latino; 1 Hispanic/Latino; 1 Two or more races, non-Hispanic/Latino), 1 international. Average age 30. 12 applicants, 83% accepted, 8 enrolled. In 2016, 6 master's awarded. Application fee: $55. Electronic applications accepted. *Financial support:* In 2016–17, 15 students received support, including 3 teaching assistantships with full tuition reimbursements available (averaging $9,284 per year); fellowships, career-related internships or fieldwork, Federal Work-Study, and 7 assistantships (averaging $7911) also available. Financial award application deadline: 3/1; financial award applicants required to submit FAFSA. *Unit head:* Dr. Traci A. Zimmerman, Director of the School of Writing, Rhetoric and Technical Communication, 540-568-2334, E-mail: zimmerta@jmu.edu. *Application contact:* Lynette D. Michael, Director of Graduate Admissions, 540-568-6131 Ext. 6395, Fax: 540-568-7860, E-mail: michaeld@jmu.edu. Website: http://www.jmu.edu/wrtc/

**Johns Hopkins University,** Zanvyl Krieger School of Arts and Sciences, Advanced Academic Programs, Program in Writing, Washington, DC 20036. Offers science writing (MA, Certificate); writing (MA). *Program availability:* Part-time, evening/weekend. *Degree requirements:* For master's, thesis. *Entrance requirements:* For master's, minimum GPA of 3.0, writing samples. Additional exam requirements/recommendations for international students: Required—TOEFL (minimum score 600 paper-based; 100 iBT). Electronic applications accepted.

**Laurentian University,** School of Graduate Studies and Research, Programme in Science Communication, Sudbury, ON P3E 2C6, Canada. Offers G Dip.

**Louisiana Tech University,** Graduate School, College of Liberal Arts, Department of English, Ruston, LA 71272. Offers English (MA); technical writing (Graduate Certificate). *Program availability:* Part-time. *Degree requirements:* For master's, thesis or alternative. *Entrance requirements:* For master's, GRE General Test. *Application deadline:* For fall admission, 7/29 for domestic students; for spring admission, 2/3 for domestic students. Applications are processed on a rolling basis. Application fee: $40. *Financial support:* Fellowships, research assistantships, teaching assistantships, and career-related internships or fieldwork available. Financial award application deadline: 2/1. *Unit head:* Dr. Susan Roach, Director, School of Literature and Language, 318-257-2718, Fax: 318-257-2719, E-mail: msroach@latech.edu. *Application contact:* Marilyn J. Robinson, Assistant to the Dean of the Graduate School, 318-257-2924, Fax: 318-257-4487. Website: http://liberalarts.latech.edu/literature_language/english/

**Massachusetts Institute of Technology,** School of Humanities, Arts, and Social Sciences, Program in Comparative Media Studies/Writing, Graduate Program in Science Writing, Cambridge, MA 02139. Offers SM. *Faculty:* 6 full-time (1 woman). *Students:* 8 full-time (6 women); includes 1 minority (Hispanic/Latino), 1 international. Average age 26. 43 applicants, 23% accepted, 8 enrolled. In 2016, 7 master's awarded. *Degree requirements:* For master's, thesis. *Entrance requirements:* For master's, GRE General Test. Additional exam requirements/recommendations for international students: Required—TOEFL, IELTS. *Application deadline:* For fall admission, 1/15 for domestic and international students. Application fee: $75. Electronic applications accepted. *Expenses: Tuition:* Full-time $46,400; part-time $725 per credit. One-time fee: $312 full-time. Full-time tuition and fees vary according to course load and program.

*Financial support:* In 2016–17, 8 students received support, including 3 fellowships (averaging $10,700 per year), 3 research assistantships (averaging $14,900 per year); teaching assistantships, Federal Work-Study, institutionally sponsored loans, scholarships/grants, traineeships, health care benefits, unspecified assistantships, and resident tutors also available. Support available to part-time students. Financial award application deadline: 5/1; financial award applicants required to submit FAFSA. *Faculty research:* Communicating science to the public; digital media; investigative journalism; documentary film. *Total annual research expenditures:* $7,000. *Unit head:* Prof. Thomas Levenson, Program Head, 617-253-6668, Fax: 617-253-6910, E-mail: sciwrite-www@mit.edu. *Application contact:* 617-253-5036, E-mail: sciwrite-www@mit.edu. Website: http://sciwrite.mit.edu/

**Metropolitan State University,** College of Arts and Sciences, St. Paul, MN 55106-5000. Offers computer science (MS); liberal studies (MA); technical communication (MS). *Program availability:* Part-time, evening/weekend. *Entrance requirements:* For master's, minimum GPA of 2.75, resume. Additional exam requirements/recommendations for international students: Required—TOEFL (minimum score 550 paper-based). Electronic applications accepted.

**Texas Tech University,** Graduate School, College of Arts and Sciences, Department of English, Lubbock, TX 79409-3091. Offers English (MA, PhD); technical communication (MA); technical communication and rhetoric (PhD). *Program availability:* Part-time, 100% online, blended/hybrid learning. *Faculty:* 60 full-time (37 women), 22 part-time/adjunct (11 women). *Students:* 93 full-time (59 women), 86 part-time (58 women); includes 24 minority (8 Black or African American, non-Hispanic/Latino; 1 American Indian or Alaska Native, non-Hispanic/Latino; 3 Asian, non-Hispanic/Latino; 8 Hispanic/Latino; 4 Two or more races, non-Hispanic/Latino), 11 international. Average age 33. 173 applicants, 30% accepted, 36 enrolled. In 2016, 15 master's, 17 doctorates awarded. Terminal master's awarded for partial completion of doctoral program. *Degree requirements:* For master's, variable foreign language requirement, comprehensive exam, thesis optional; for doctorate, variable foreign language requirement, comprehensive exam, thesis/dissertation. *Entrance requirements:* For master's and doctorate, GRE General Test. Additional exam requirements/recommendations for international students: Required—TOEFL (minimum score 550 paper-based; 79 iBT), IELTS (minimum score 6.5). *Application deadline:* For fall admission, 6/1 priority date for domestic students, 1/15 for international students; for spring admission, 9/1 priority date for domestic students, 6/15 priority date for international students. Applications are processed on a rolling basis. Application fee: $75. Electronic applications accepted. *Expenses:* $300 per credit hour full-time resident tuition; $708 per credit hour full-time non-resident tuition; $50.50 per credit hour fee plus $608 per term fee. *Financial support:* In 2016–17, 116 students received support, including 102 fellowships (averaging $3,457 per year), 6 research assistantships (averaging $13,381 per year), 78 teaching assistantships (averaging $15,273 per year); career-related internships or fieldwork, Federal Work-Study, scholarships/grants, and unspecified assistantships also available. Financial award application deadline: 12/15; financial award applicants required to submit FAFSA. *Faculty research:* American, British, and comparative literature; creative writing; linguistics; film; technical communication and rhetoric. *Total annual research expenditures:* $65,992. *Unit head:* Dr. Bruce Clarke, Professor, 806-834-7652, Fax: 806-742-0989, E-mail: bruce.clarke@ttu.edu. *Application contact:* Dr. Kanika Batra, Director of Graduate Studies, 806-834-1246, Fax: 806-742-0989, E-mail: english.gradadvisor@ttu.edu. Website: http://www.english.ttu.edu/

**The University of Alabama in Huntsville,** School of Graduate Studies, College of Arts, Humanities, and Social Sciences, Department of English, Huntsville, AL 35899. Offers education (MA); English (MA); technical writing (Certificate); TESOL (Certificate). *Program availability:* Part-time, evening/weekend. *Degree requirements:* For master's, one foreign language, comprehensive exam, thesis or alternative, oral and written exams. *Entrance requirements:* For master's and Certificate, GRE General Test, minimum GPA of 3.0. Additional exam requirements/recommendations for international students: Required—TOEFL (minimum score 500 paper-based; 80 iBT), IELTS (minimum score 6.5). Electronic applications accepted. *Expenses:* Tuition, state resident: full-time $9834; part-time $600 per credit hour. Tuition, nonresident: full-time $21,830; part-time $1325 per credit hour. *Faculty research:* Fiction and identity, Shakespeare, science fiction, eighteenth-century literature, technical writing.

**University of Arkansas at Little Rock,** Graduate School, College of Social Sciences and Communication, Department of Rhetoric and Writing, Little Rock, AR 72204-1099. Offers professional and technical writing (MA). *Program availability:* Part-time, evening/weekend. *Degree requirements:* For master's, thesis or alternative, oral defense of final project. *Entrance requirements:* For master's, GRE, minimum GPA of 3.0, writing portfolio. *Faculty research:* Writing for industry, science, business, and government; composition and rhetorical theory; writing nonfiction; teaching of writing.

**The University of North Carolina at Charlotte,** College of Liberal Arts and Sciences, Department of English, Charlotte, NC 28223-0001. Offers applied linguistics (Graduate Certificate); English (MA); technical and professional writing (Graduate Certificate). *Program availability:* Part-time, evening/weekend. *Faculty:* 30 full-time (16 women), 2 part-time/adjunct (1 woman). *Students:* 28 full-time (22 women), 30 part-time (19 women); includes 13 minority (4 Black or African American, non-Hispanic/Latino; 1 Asian, non-Hispanic/Latino; 8 Hispanic/Latino), 4 international. Average age 30. 33 applicants, 91% accepted, 20 enrolled. In 2016, 30 master's, 1 other advanced degree awarded. *Degree requirements:* For master's, comprehensive exam (for some programs), thesis, comprehensive exam, or project. *Entrance requirements:* For master's, GRE, MAT, minimum undergraduate GPA of 3.0, statement of purpose, recommendation letters; for Graduate Certificate, statement of purpose, three letters of recommendation, writing sample, minimum GPA of 2.75. Additional exam requirements/recommendations for international students: Required—TOEFL (minimum score 523 paper-based, 70 iBT) or IELTS (6.5). *Application deadline:* For fall admission, 3/1 priority date for domestic and international students; for spring admission, 10/1 priority date for domestic and international students; for summer admission, 4/1 priority date for domestic and international students. Applications are processed on a rolling basis. Application fee: $75. Electronic applications accepted. *Expenses:* Tuition, state resident: full-time $4252. Tuition, nonresident: full-time $17,423. *Required fees:* $3026. Tuition and fees vary according to course load and program. *Financial support:* In 2016–17, 17 students received support, including 1 research assistantship (averaging $8,000 per year), 16 teaching assistantships (averaging $8,562 per year); career-related internships or fieldwork, institutionally sponsored loans, scholarships/grants, and unspecified assistantships also available. Support available to part-time students. Financial award application deadline: 3/1; financial award applicants required to submit FAFSA. *Total annual research expenditures:* $61,484. *Unit head:* Dr. Mark West, Chair, 704-687-0618, E-mail: miwest@uncc.edu. *Application contact:* Kathy B. Giddings,

Director of Graduate Admissions, 704-687-5503, Fax: 704-687-1668, E-mail: gradadm@uncc.edu. Website: http://english.uncc.edu/

**The University of North Carolina at Greensboro,** Graduate School, College of Arts and Sciences, Department of English, Greensboro, NC 27412-5001. Offers creative writing (MFA); English (M Ed, MA, PhD, Certificate), including American literature (PhD), English (M Ed, MA), English literature (PhD), rhetoric and composition (PhD), technical writing (Certificate), women's studies (Certificate). *Degree requirements:* For master's, comprehensive exam; for doctorate, variable foreign language requirement, thesis/dissertation, preliminary exam. *Entrance requirements:* For master's, GRE General Test, minimum GPA of 3.0; for doctorate, GRE General Test, GRE Subject Test, critical writing sample, minimum GPA of 3.0. Additional exam requirements/recommendations for international students: Required—TOEFL. Electronic applications accepted.

**University of the Sciences,** Program in Biomedical Writing, Philadelphia, PA 19104-4495. Offers biomedical writing (MS); medical marketing writing (Certificate); regulatory affairs writing (Certificate). *Program availability:* Part-time, evening/weekend, online learning. *Entrance requirements:* For master's, GRE General Test. Additional exam requirements/recommendations for international students: Required—TOEFL, TWE. *Expenses:* Contact institution.

**University of Waterloo,** Graduate Studies, Faculty of Arts, Department of English Language and Literature, Waterloo, ON N2L 3G1, Canada. Offers English language and literature (PhD); literary studies (MA); rhetoric and communication design (MA). *Program availability:* Part-time. *Degree requirements:* For master's, one foreign language, thesis optional; for doctorate, 2 foreign languages, thesis/dissertation. *Entrance requirements:* For master's, honors degree, minimum B+ average; for doctorate, master's degree, minimum A- average. Additional exam requirements/recommendations for international students: Required—TOEFL, IELTS, PTE. Electronic applications accepted. *Faculty research:* Shakespeare, American literature, rhetoric, Romantics, moderns.

# Writing

**Abilene Christian University,** Graduate Programs, College of Arts and Sciences, Department of English, Abilene, TX 79699. Offers composition/rhetoric (MA); creative writing (MA); literature (MA). *Program availability:* Part-time. *Faculty:* 16 part-time/adjunct (6 women). *Students:* 8 full-time (6 women), 3 part-time (1 woman). 17 applicants, 53% accepted, 4 enrolled. In 2016, 6 master's awarded. *Degree requirements:* For master's, one foreign language, comprehensive exam (for some programs), thesis (for some programs). *Entrance requirements:* For master's, GRE General Test. Additional exam requirements/recommendations for international students: Required—TOEFL (minimum score 80 iBT), IELTS (minimum score 6), PTE. *Application deadline:* For fall admission, 8/11 for domestic students; for spring admission, 11/1 for domestic students. Applications are processed on a rolling basis. Application fee: $50. Electronic applications accepted. *Expenses: Tuition:* Full-time $19,890; part-time $1105 per credit hour. Tuition and fees vary according to course load and program. *Financial support:* In 2016–17, 11 students received support, including 6 teaching assistantships with partial tuition reimbursements available (averaging $5,800 per year); Federal Work-Study and scholarships/grants also available. Support available to part-time students. Financial award application deadline: 4/1; financial award applicants required to submit FAFSA. *Faculty research:* Feminism, Shakespearean dimensions of new literature, poetic consciousness, deconstruction myths. *Unit head:* Dr. William Carroll, Graduate Director, 325-674-2083, Fax: 325-674-2408, E-mail: william.carroll@acu.edu. *Application contact:* Corey Patterson, Director of Graduate Admission and Recruiting, 325-674-6566, Fax: 325-674-6717, E-mail: gradinfo@acu.edu. Website: http://www.acu.edu/graduate/academics/english.html

**Academy of Art University,** Graduate Programs, School of Writing for Film, Television and Digital Media, San Francisco, CA 94105-3410. Offers MFA. *Program availability:* Part-time, 100% online. *Faculty:* 2 full-time (1 woman), 9 part-time/adjunct (2 women). *Students:* 11 full-time (7 women), 17 part-time (8 women); includes 10 minority (5 Black or African American, non-Hispanic/Latino; 1 American Indian or Alaska Native, non-Hispanic/Latino; 2 Hispanic/Latino; 2 Two or more races, non-Hispanic/Latino), 4 international. Average age 35. 4 applicants, 100% accepted, 3 enrolled. *Degree requirements:* For master's, final review. *Entrance requirements:* For master's, statement of intent; resume; portfolio/reel; official college transcripts. *Application deadline:* Applications are processed on a rolling basis. Application fee: $50. Electronic applications accepted. *Expenses: Tuition:* Part-time $982 per unit. *Financial support:* Career-related internships or fieldwork, Federal Work-Study, and scholarships/grants available. Financial award application deadline: 8/10; financial award applicants required to submit FAFSA. *Unit head:* 800-544-ARTS, E-mail: info@academyart.edu. *Application contact:* 800-544-ARTS, E-mail: info@academyart.edu. Website: http://www.academyart.edu/academics/writing-film-television-digital-media

**Adelphi University,** College of Arts and Sciences, Program in Creative Writing, Garden City, NY 11530-0701. Offers MFA. *Program availability:* Part-time, evening/weekend. *Students:* 9 full-time (6 women), 7 part-time (3 women); includes 50 minority (6 Black or African American, non-Hispanic/Latino; 19 Asian, non-Hispanic/Latino; 19 Hispanic/Latino; 6 Two or more races, non-Hispanic/Latino), 6 international. Average age 28. 53 applicants, 57% accepted, 9 enrolled. In 2016, 6 master's awarded. *Degree requirements:* For master's, thesis. *Entrance requirements:* For master's, 2 letters of reference, manuscript in chosen genre (poetry, fiction, playwriting), personal statement essay, college transcript. Additional exam requirements/recommendations for international students: Required—TOEFL (minimum score 550 paper-based; 80 iBT), IELTS (minimum score 6.5). *Application deadline:* For fall admission, 5/1 priority date for international students; for spring admission, 11/1 priority date for international students. Applications are processed on a rolling basis. Application fee: $50. Electronic applications accepted. *Expenses:* Contact institution. *Financial support:* Research assistantships, teaching assistantships, career-related internships or fieldwork, institutionally sponsored loans, scholarships/grants, traineeships, and unspecified assistantships available. Support available to part-time students. *Unit head:* Judith Baumel, Director, 516-877-4031, E-mail: baumel@adelphi.edu. *Application contact:* Christine Murphy, Director of Admissions, 516-877-3050, Fax: 516-877-3039, E-mail: graduateadmissions@adelphi.edu. Website: http://academics.adelphi.edu/artsci/creativewriting/

**Albertus Magnus College,** Master of Fine Arts in Creative Writing Program, New Haven, CT 06511-1189. Offers MFA. *Program availability:* Part-time, evening/weekend, blended/hybrid learning. *Faculty:* 5 full-time (1 woman), 1 part-time/adjunct (0 women). *Students:* 5 full-time (3 women), 1 (woman) part-time; includes 3 minority (1 Black or African American, non-Hispanic/Latino; 2 Hispanic/Latino). Average age 35. In 2016, 5 master's awarded. *Degree requirements:* For master's, thesis, project, minimum cumulative GPA of 3.0, completion of all requirements within seven years of matriculation. *Entrance requirements:* Additional exam requirements/recommendations for international students: Recommended—TOEFL (minimum score 550 paper-based; 80 iBT). *Application deadline:* For fall admission, 8/15 for domestic students; for spring admission, 1/15 for domestic students. Applications are processed on a rolling basis. Application fee: $50. Electronic applications accepted. *Expenses:* Contact institution. *Financial support:* Federal Work-Study and unspecified assistantships available. Support available to part-time students. Financial award applicants required to submit FAFSA. *Unit head:* Charles Rafferty, Co-Director, 203-773-6901, Fax: 203-777-3701, E-mail: crafferty@albertus.edu. *Application contact:* Prof. Sarah Harris Wallman, Co-Director, 203-777-4473, Fax: 203-777-3701, E-mail: swallman@albertus.edu. Website: http://www.albertus.edu/fine-arts/mfa/

**American University,** College of Arts and Sciences, Department of Literature, Washington, DC 20016-8047. Offers creative writing (MFA); literature (MA). *Program availability:* Part-time, evening/weekend. *Faculty:* 47 full-time (29 women), 24 part-time/adjunct (15 women). *Students:* 37 full-time (24 women), 20 part-time (11 women); includes 20 minority (9 Black or African American, non-Hispanic/Latino; 1 Asian, non-Hispanic/Latino; 8 Hispanic/Latino; 2 Two or more races, non-Hispanic/Latino), 3 international. Average age 33. 121 applicants, 67% accepted, 20 enrolled. In 2016, 21 master's awarded. *Degree requirements:* For master's, comprehensive exam. *Entrance requirements:* For master's, GRE, writing sample, statement of purpose, transcripts, 2 letters of recommendation, resume. Additional exam requirements/recommendations for international students: Required—TOEFL (minimum score 100 iBT), IELTS (minimum score 7), PTE (minimum score 68). *Application deadline:* For fall admission, 2/1 for domestic students; for spring admission, 11/1 for domestic students. Application fee: $55. *Expenses:* $1,579 per credit tuition; $690 mandatory fees. *Financial support:* Institutionally sponsored loans and unspecified assistantships available. Financial award application deadline: 2/1; financial award applicants required to submit FAFSA. *Unit head:* Dr. David Pike, Department Chair, 202-885-2996, E-mail: dpike@american.edu. *Application contact:* Kathleen Clowery, Associate Director of Graduate Admissions, 202-885-3620, Fax: 202-885-1344, E-mail: clowery@american.edu. Website: http://www.american.edu/cas/literature/

**Antioch University Los Angeles,** Graduate Programs, Program in Creative Writing, Culver City, CA 90230. Offers creative writing (MFA); pedagogy of creative writing (Certificate). *Program availability:* Online learning. *Degree requirements:* For master's, thesis. *Entrance requirements:* For master's, sample of written work. Additional exam requirements/recommendations for international students: Required—TOEFL. *Faculty research:* Creative nonfiction, fiction, poetry.

**Antioch University Santa Barbara,** Program in Writing and Contemporary Media, Santa Barbara, CA 93101-1581. Offers MFA. *Program availability:* Part-time. *Degree requirements:* For master's, thesis project.

**Arcadia University,** College of Arts and Sciences, Department of English, Program in Creative Writing, Glenside, PA 19038-3295. Offers MFA. *Faculty:* 3 full-time (1 woman), 5 part-time/adjunct (2 women). *Students:* 4 full-time (all women), 31 part-time (23 women); includes 7 minority (3 Black or African American, non-Hispanic/Latino; 1 Hispanic/Latino; 3 Two or more races, non-Hispanic/Latino), 2 international. In 2016, 12 master's awarded. *Expenses:* Contact institution. *Unit head:* Joshua Isard, Director, 267-620-4886, E-mail: isardj@arcadia.edu. *Application contact:* 215-572-2925, Fax: 215-572-2126, E-mail: grad@arcadia.edu.

**Arizona State University at the Tempe campus,** College of Liberal Arts and Sciences, Department of English, Interdisciplinary Program in Creative Writing, Tempe, AZ 85287-0302. Offers MFA. *Degree requirements:* For master's, thesis, practicum (9 hours). *Entrance requirements:* For master's, undergraduate major in English or creative writing (preferred), minimum GPA of 3.0, 3 letters of recommendation, resume or curriculum vitae, personal statement, official transcripts, 3 copies of manuscript sample (20 pages of poetry, 30 pages of prose, or both). Additional exam requirements/recommendations for international students: Required—TOEFL, IELTS, or PTE. Electronic applications accepted.

**Arizona State University at the Tempe campus,** Herberger Institute for Design and the Arts, School of Film, Dance and Theatre, Tempe, AZ 85287-2002. Offers dance (MFA), including dance, interdisciplinary digital media and performance; theatre (MA, MFA, PhD), including arts entrepreneurship and management (MFA), directing (MFA), dramatic writing (MFA), interdisciplinary digital media and performance (MFA), performance (MFA), performance design (MFA), theatre (MFA), theatre and performance of the Americas (PhD), theatre for youth (MFA, PhD). Terminal master's awarded for partial completion of doctoral program. *Degree requirements:* For master's, comprehensive exam (for some programs), thesis (for some programs), applied project (for some programs); interactive Program of Study (iPOS) submitted before completing 50 percent of required credit hours; for doctorate, comprehensive exam, thesis/dissertation, interactive Program of Study (iPOS) submitted before completing 50 percent of required credit hours. *Entrance requirements:* For master's, GRE or MAT, minimum GPA of 3.0 in last 2 years of work leading to bachelor's degree (depending on program); for doctorate, GRE, minimum GPA of 3.0 or equivalent in last 2 years of work leading to bachelor's degree, 3 letters of recommendation, resume, scholarly writing sample, statement of purpose. Additional exam requirements/recommendations for international students: Required—TOEFL, IELTS, or PTE. Electronic applications accepted.

**Armstrong State University,** School of Graduate Studies, Program in Professional Communication and Leadership, Savannah, GA 31419-1997. Offers MA, Certificate. *Program availability:* Part-time, evening/weekend. *Faculty:* 3 full-time (2 women), 1 (woman) part-time/adjunct. *Students:* 26 full-time (17 women), 44 part-time (32 women); includes 43 minority (36 Black or African American, non-Hispanic/Latino; 1 Asian, non-Hispanic/Latino; 3 Hispanic/Latino; 3 Two or more races, non-Hispanic/Latino), 2 international. Average age 25. 50 applicants, 54% accepted, 19 enrolled. In 2016, 27 master's awarded. *Degree requirements:* For master's, comprehensive exam, project. *Entrance requirements:* For master's, minimum GPA of 2.5, letters of recommendation, letter of intent, resume. Additional exam requirements/recommendations for

## Writing

international students: Required—TOEFL (minimum score 523 paper-based; 70 iBT). *Application deadline:* For fall admission, 6/1 priority date for domestic students, 5/1 priority date for international students; for spring admission, 11/15 priority date for domestic students, 9/15 priority date for international students; for summer admission, 4/15 for domestic students, 9/15 priority date for international students. Applications are processed on a rolling basis. Application fee: $30. *Expenses:* Tuition, state resident: full-time $1781; part-time $161.93 per credit hour. Tuition, nonresident: full-time $6482; part-time $589.27 per credit hour. *Required fees:* $1224 per unit. $612 per semester. Tuition and fees vary according to course load, campus/location and program. *Financial support:* In 2016–17, research assistantships with full tuition reimbursements (averaging $5,000 per year) were awarded; scholarships/grants and unspecified assistantships also available. Financial award application deadline: 3/15; financial award applicants required to submit FAFSA. *Faculty research:* Organizational communication, conflict resolution and mediation, rhetoric and language identity, brand identity and marketing, communication theory. *Unit head:* Dr. Robert Terry, 912-344-3606, E-mail: robert.terry@armstrong.edu. *Application contact:* McKenzie Peterman, Assistant Director of Graduate Admissions, 912-344-2503, Fax: 912-344-3417, E-mail: graduate@armstrong.edu.
Website: http://www.armstrong.edu/Majors/degree/master_professional_communication_leadership

**Asbury University,** School of Graduate and Professional Studies, Wilmore, KY 40390-1198. Offers biology: alternative certificate (MA Ed); chemistry: alternative certificate (MA Ed); English (MA Ed); English as a second language (MA Ed); ESL (MA Ed); French (MA Ed); Latin: alternative certificate (MA Ed); mathematics: alternative certificate (MA Ed); reading/writing endorsement (MA Ed); social studies (MA Ed); social work (MSW), including child and family services; Spanish (MA Ed); special education (MA Ed); special education: alternative certificate (MA Ed); teacher as leader endorsement (MA Ed). *Accreditation:* NCATE. *Program availability:* Part-time. *Degree requirements:* For master's, action research project, portfolio. *Entrance requirements:* For master's, PRAXIS/NTE, minimum GPA of 2.75, letters of recommendation. Additional exam requirements/recommendations for international students: Required—TOEFL (minimum score 550 paper-based). Electronic applications accepted.

**Ashland University,** College of Arts and Sciences, Program in Creative Writing, Ashland, OH 44805-3702. Offers MFA. *Program availability:* Online learning. *Degree requirements:* For master's, thesis. *Entrance requirements:* For master's, writing sample, minimum GPA of 2.75. *Application deadline:* For fall admission, 2/1 priority date for domestic students; for winter admission, 9/1 priority date for domestic students. Applications are processed on a rolling basis. Application fee: $30. Electronic applications accepted. *Expenses:* Contact institution. *Financial support:* Career-related internships or fieldwork, Federal Work-Study, and institutionally sponsored loans available. Financial award application deadline: 4/15; financial award applicants required to submit FAFSA. *Unit head:* Dr. Stephen Haven, Director, MFA Program, 419-289-5979, Fax: 419-289-5255, E-mail: shaven@ashland.edu. *Application contact:* Sarah Marie Wells, Administrative Director, MFA Program, 419-289-5957, Fax: 419-289-5255, E-mail: swells@ashland.edu.

**Auburn University at Montgomery,** College of Arts and Sciences, Department of English and Philosophy, Montgomery, AL 36124-4023. Offers teaching of writing (MA).

**Ball State University,** Graduate School, College of Sciences and Humanities, Department of English, Muncie, IN 47306. Offers English (MA, PhD), including composition (MA), creative writing (MA), literature, rhetoric and composition; linguistics (MA), including linguistics, teaching English to speakers of other languages (TESOL) and linguistics. *Program availability:* Part-time. *Degree requirements:* For doctorate, variable foreign language requirement, thesis/dissertation. *Entrance requirements:* For master's, GRE General Test, minimum baccalaureate GPA of 2.75 or 3.0 in latter half of baccalaureate, statement of purpose, writing sample, three letters of recommendation; for doctorate, GRE General Test, GRE Subject Test, minimum graduate GPA of 3.2, statement of purpose, writing sample, three letters of recommendation. Additional exam requirements/recommendations for international students: Required—TOEFL (minimum score 550 paper-based; 79 iBT), IELTS (minimum score 6.5). Electronic applications accepted. *Faculty research:* American literature; literary editing; medieval, Renaissance, and eighteenth-century British literature; rhetoric.

**Bay Path University,** Program in Creative Nonfiction, Longmeadow, MA 01106-2292. Offers MFA. *Program availability:* Part-time, evening/weekend, online only, 100% online. *Students:* 13 full-time (11 women), 37 part-time (35 women); includes 7 minority (5 Black or African American, non-Hispanic/Latino; 2 Hispanic/Latino). Average age 47. 28 applicants, 75% accepted, 18 enrolled. In 2016, 7 master's awarded. *Entrance requirements:* For master's, minimum GPA of 3.0 or minimum B grades in English and/or writing classes. *Application deadline:* Applications are processed on a rolling basis. Application fee: $45. Electronic applications accepted. Application fee is waived when completed online. *Expenses:* $19,440. *Financial support:* Applicants required to submit FAFSA. *Unit head:* Leanne James Blackwell, Director, 413-565-1232, E-mail: ljblackwell@baypath.edu. *Application contact:* Diane Ranaldi, Dean of Graduate Admissions, 413-565-1332, Fax: 413-565-1250, E-mail: dranaldi@baypath.edu.
Website: http://graduate.baypath.edu/graduate-programs/programs-online/mfa-program/creative-nonfiction

**Bennington College,** Graduate Programs, MFA Program in Writing, Bennington, VT 05201. Offers MFA. *Program availability:* Online learning. *Degree requirements:* For master's, thesis, collection of essays or poems, or collection of short stories and/or a novel. *Entrance requirements:* For master's, manuscript. *Expenses:* Contact institution.

**Binghamton University, State University of New York,** Graduate School, Harpur College of Arts and Sciences, Department of English, Binghamton, NY 13902-6000. Offers creative writing (MA); English (PhD); English/American literature (MA). *Program availability:* Part-time. *Faculty:* 29 full-time (18 women), 19 part-time/adjunct (9 women). *Students:* 39 full-time (24 women), 49 part-time (28 women); includes 11 minority (3 Black or African American, non-Hispanic/Latino; 1 American Indian or Alaska Native, non-Hispanic/Latino; 5 Asian, non-Hispanic/Latino; 2 Hispanic/Latino), 18 international. Average age 33. 97 applicants, 51% accepted, 20 enrolled. In 2016, 11 master's, 13 doctorates awarded. Terminal master's awarded for partial completion of doctoral program. *Degree requirements:* For master's, one foreign language, thesis; for doctorate, one foreign language, comprehensive exam, thesis/dissertation. *Entrance requirements:* For master's and doctorate, GRE General Test, writing sample. Additional exam requirements/recommendations for international students: Required—TOEFL (minimum score 550 paper-based; 80 iBT). *Application deadline:* For fall admission, 2/15 priority date for domestic and international students; for spring admission, 11/15 priority date for domestic and international students. Application fee: $75. Electronic applications accepted. *Financial support:* In 2016–17, 36 students received support, including 1 fellowship with full tuition reimbursement available (averaging $15,000 per year), 1 research assistantship (averaging $9,000 per year), 30 teaching assistantships with full tuition reimbursements available (averaging $15,000 per year); career-related internships or fieldwork, Federal Work-Study, institutionally sponsored loans, scholarships/grants, health care benefits, tuition waivers (full and partial), and unspecified assistantships also available. Financial award applicants required to submit FAFSA. *Unit head:* Praseeda Gopinath, Graduate Director, 607-777-2033, Fax: 607-777-2408, E-mail: gopinath@binghamton.edu. *Application contact:* Ben Balkaya, Assistant Dean and Director, 607-777-2151, Fax: 607-777-2501, E-mail: balkaya@binghamton.edu.
Website: http://www2.binghamton.edu/english/

**Boise State University,** College of Arts and Sciences, Department of English, Boise, ID 83725-1525. Offers creative writing (MFA); English (MA); rhetoric and composition (MA); teaching English language (MA); technical communication (MA). *Program availability:* Part-time. *Faculty:* 26. *Students:* 44 full-time (28 women), 38 part-time (29 women); includes 6 minority (2 American Indian or Alaska Native, non-Hispanic/Latino; 2 Asian, non-Hispanic/Latino; 1 Hispanic/Latino; 1 Two or more races, non-Hispanic/Latino), 3 international. Average age 33. 242 applicants, 15% accepted, 28 enrolled. In 2016, 29 master's awarded. *Degree requirements:* For master's, thesis (for some programs). *Entrance requirements:* For master's, GRE General Test, minimum GPA of 3.0. Additional exam requirements/recommendations for international students: Required—TOEFL (minimum score 550 paper-based; 80 iBT), IELTS (minimum score 6). *Application deadline:* For fall admission, 4/15 for domestic and international students; for spring admission, 10/15 for domestic and international students. Application fee: $65 ($95 for international students). Electronic applications accepted. *Expenses:* Tuition, state resident: full-time $6058; part-time $358 per credit hour. Tuition, nonresident: full-time $20,108; part-time $608 per credit hour. *Required fees:* $2108. Tuition and fees vary according to program. *Financial support:* In 2016–17, 10 students received support, including 32 teaching assistantships (averaging $8,109 per year); scholarships/grants and unspecified assistantships also available. Financial award application deadline: 1/15; financial award applicants required to submit FAFSA. *Unit head:* Dr. Michelle Payne, Chair, 208-426-3426, Fax: 208-426-4373, E-mail: mpayne@boisestate.edu. *Application contact:* Dr. Tom Hillard, Director of English, 208-426-2991, E-mail: thomashillard@boisestate.edu.
Website: http://english.boisestate.edu/graduate-programs/

**Boston University,** Graduate School of Arts and Sciences, Creative Writing Program, Boston, MA 02215. Offers MFA. *Students:* 25 full-time (15 women), 13 part-time (10 women); includes 7 minority (2 Black or African American, non-Hispanic/Latino; 4 Asian, non-Hispanic/Latino; 1 Two or more races, non-Hispanic/Latino), 8 international. Average age 32. 700 applicants, 4% accepted, 18 enrolled. In 2016, 17 master's awarded. *Degree requirements:* For master's, one foreign language, thesis. *Entrance requirements:* Additional exam requirements/recommendations for international students: Required—TOEFL (minimum score 550 paper-based; 84 iBT). *Application deadline:* For fall admission, 2/1 for domestic and international students. Application fee: $95. Electronic applications accepted. *Financial support:* In 2016–17, 18 students received support, including teaching assistantships with full tuition reimbursements available (averaging $13,250 per year); Federal Work-Study, scholarships/grants, health care benefits, and unspecified assistantships also available. Financial award application deadline: 2/1. *Unit head:* Ha Jin, Director, 617-353-2510, Fax: 617-353-3653, E-mail: xjin@bu.edu. *Application contact:* Catherine Con, Administrative Coordinator, 617-353-2510, Fax: 617-353-3653, E-mail: crwr@bu.edu.
Website: http://www.bu.edu/creativewriting

**Boston University,** Graduate School of Arts and Sciences, Editorial Institute, Boston, MA 02215. Offers MA. *Students:* 16 full-time (10 women), 5 part-time (3 women); includes 5 minority (4 Hispanic/Latino; 1 Two or more races, non-Hispanic/Latino), 1 international. Average age 35. 1 applicant. *Degree requirements:* For master's, thesis. *Entrance requirements:* For master's, GRE General Test, thesis proposal, 3 letters of recommendation, transcripts, personal statement. Additional exam requirements/recommendations for international students: Required—TOEFL (minimum score 550 paper-based; 84 iBT). *Application deadline:* For fall admission, 4/15 for domestic and international students. Application fee: $95. Electronic applications accepted. *Financial support:* In 2016–17, 16 students received support, including fellowships with full tuition reimbursements available (averaging $21,500 per year), 5 research assistantships with full tuition reimbursements available (averaging $21,500 per year), 3 teaching assistantships with full tuition reimbursements available (averaging $21,500 per year); Federal Work-Study, scholarships/grants, and health care benefits also available. Financial award application deadline: 1/15. *Unit head:* Archie Burnett, Director, 617-353-6631, E-mail: burnetta@bu.edu. *Application contact:* Ellen Wrigley, Administrative Assistant, 617-353-6631, Fax: 617-353-6917, E-mail: ellen@bu.edu.
Website: http://www.bu.edu/editinst/

**Boston University,** Graduate School of Arts and Sciences, Playwriting Program, Boston, MA 02215. Offers MFA. Program offered jointly with College of Fine Arts; program admits students in even-numbered years. *Students:* 11 full-time (7 women); includes 2 minority (1 Asian, non-Hispanic/Latino; 1 Hispanic/Latino), 2 international. Average age 27. 28 applicants, 29% accepted, 5 enrolled. *Degree requirements:* For master's, one foreign language. *Entrance requirements:* For master's, GRE, 3 letters of recommendation, one original full-length play or two one-act plays, transcripts, personal statement, curriculum vitae, ability to read or speak a foreign language. Additional exam requirements/recommendations for international students: Required—TOEFL (minimum score 550 paper-based; 84 iBT). *Application deadline:* For fall admission, 2/15 for domestic and international students. Application fee: $95. Electronic applications accepted. *Financial support:* In 2016–17, 10 students received support, including 2 teaching assistantships with full tuition reimbursements available (averaging $10,750 per year); Federal Work-Study, scholarships/grants, health care benefits, and unspecified assistantships also available. Financial award application deadline: 2/15. *Unit head:* Katherine Snodgrass, Artistic Director, 617-353-5104, Fax: 617-353-6196, E-mail: ksnodgra@bu.edu. *Application contact:* Martin Gastmann, Assistant Director of Admissions and Financial Aid, 617-353-2696, Fax: 617-358-5492, E-mail: grs@bu.edu.
Website: http://www.bu.edu/playwriting

**Bowling Green State University,** Graduate College, College of Arts and Sciences, Department of English, Program in Creative Writing, Bowling Green, OH 43403. Offers fiction (MFA); poetry (MFA). *Program availability:* Part-time. *Degree requirements:* For master's, thesis or alternative. *Entrance requirements:* For master's, GRE General Test. Additional exam requirements/recommendations for international students: Required—TOEFL. *Application deadline:* For fall admission, 2/15 priority date for domestic students. Applications are processed on a rolling basis. Application fee: $30. Electronic applications accepted. *Financial support:* Research assistantships with full tuition reimbursements, teaching assistantships with full tuition reimbursements, Federal Work-Study, and unspecified assistantships available. Financial award applicants required to submit FAFSA. *Faculty research:* Poetry, criticism, novels, translation, travel writing. *Unit head:* Dr. Lawrence Coates, Director, 419-372-7543, E-mail: coatesl@bgsu.edu. *Application contact:* Dr. Piya Lapinski, Graduate Coordinator, 419-372-6864.

**Bowling Green State University,** Graduate College, College of Arts and Sciences, Department of English, Program in English, Bowling Green, OH 43403. Offers English (MA, PhD); literature (MA); rhetoric and writing (PhD); scientific and technical communication (MA). *Program availability:* Part-time. *Degree requirements:* For master's, thesis or alternative; for doctorate, comprehensive exam, thesis/dissertation, foreign language or proficiency in Old English. *Entrance requirements:* For master's and doctorate, GRE General Test. Additional exam requirements/recommendations for international students: Required—TOEFL. *Application deadline:* For fall admission, 2/15 priority date for domestic students. Applications are processed on a rolling basis. Application fee: $30. Electronic applications accepted. *Financial support:* Fellowships with full tuition reimbursements, research assistantships with full tuition reimbursements, teaching assistantships with full tuition reimbursements, Federal Work-Study, and unspecified assistantships available. Financial award applicants required to submit FAFSA. *Faculty research:* Postmodern literary theory, rhetorical theory, ethnic American literature, literature and culture, composition pedagogy. *Unit head:* Dr. Lawrence Coates, Chair, 419-372-7543, E-mail: coatesl@bgsu.edu. *Application contact:* Dr. Piya Lapinski, Graduate Coordinator, 419-372-6864.

**Brigham Young University,** Graduate Studies, College of Humanities, Department of English, Provo, UT 84602-1001. Offers creative writing (MFA); literature (MA); rhetoric/composition (MA). *Faculty:* 54 full-time (16 women). *Students:* 75 full-time (52 women), 4 part-time (all women); includes 3 minority (1 Asian, non-Hispanic/Latino; 2 Hispanic/Latino). Average age 25. 44 applicants, 64% accepted, 24 enrolled. In 2016, 21 master's awarded. *Degree requirements:* For master's, variable foreign language requirement, comprehensive exam, thesis. *Entrance requirements:* For master's, GRE General Test, creative portfolio (for MFA). *Application deadline:* For fall admission, 1/15 for domestic and international students. Application fee: $50. Electronic applications accepted. *Expenses: Tuition:* Full-time $6680; part-time $393 per credit. Tuition and fees vary according to course load, program and student's religious affiliation. *Financial support:* In 2016–17, 22 students received support, including 10 research assistantships (averaging $4,000 per year), 62 teaching assistantships (averaging $6,000 per year); career-related internships or fieldwork, institutionally sponsored loans, scholarships/grants, and tuition waivers (partial) also available. Support available to part-time students. Financial award application deadline: 3/15. *Faculty research:* English literature, American literature, rhetoric, creative writing. *Unit head:* Prof. Phillip Snyder, Head, 801-422-2487, Fax: 801-422-0221, E-mail: phillip_snyder@byu.edu. *Application contact:* Danielle N. Steed, Graduate Secretary and English Program Manager, 801-422-8673, Fax: 801-422-0221, E-mail: danielle-steed@byu.edu.
Website: http://english.byu.edu/

**Brooklyn College of the City University of New York,** School of Humanities and Social Sciences, Department of English, Brooklyn, NY 11210-2889. Offers creative writing (MFA), including fiction, playwriting, poetry; English (MA). *Program availability:* Part-time, evening/weekend. *Degree requirements:* For master's, one foreign language, comprehensive exam (for some programs), thesis (for some programs). *Entrance requirements:* For master's, advanced undergraduate courses in English, 2 letters of recommendation, writing sample, statement of purpose. Additional exam requirements/recommendations for international students: Required—TOEFL. Electronic applications accepted. *Faculty research:* Cultural studies, medieval literature, Virginia Woolf.

**Brown University,** Graduate School, Department of English, Providence, RI 02912. Offers English (PhD); literary arts (MFA). *Degree requirements:* For doctorate, thesis/dissertation. *Entrance requirements:* For master's and doctorate, GRE General Test, GRE Subject Test.

**Butler University,** College of Liberal Arts and Sciences, Department of English, Indianapolis, IN 46208-3485. Offers creative writing (MFA); English (MA). *Program availability:* Part-time, evening/weekend. *Faculty:* 10 full-time (4 women), 4 part-time/adjunct (2 women). *Students:* 8 full-time (3 women), 48 part-time (28 women); includes 7 minority (4 Black or African American, non-Hispanic/Latino; 1 Hispanic/Latino; 2 Two or more races, non-Hispanic/Latino), 1 international. Average age 33. 44 applicants, 59% accepted, 11 enrolled. In 2016, 9 master's awarded. *Degree requirements:* For master's, thesis (for some programs). *Entrance requirements:* For master's, minimum GPA of 3.0, 350-word statement of purpose, and 7-12 page sample essay (for MA); writing sample in intended genre (12 pages of poetry or 30 pages of prose), statement of interest (1-2 pages), two letters of recommendation, and transcripts from all undergraduate and graduate institutions attended (for MFA). *Application deadline:* For fall admission, 2/15 for domestic and international students; for spring admission, 9/15 for domestic and international students. Applications are processed on a rolling basis. Application fee: $0. Electronic applications accepted. *Financial support:* In 2016–17, 15 students received support. Scholarships/grants, tuition waivers (full and partial), and unspecified assistantships available. Financial award application deadline: 7/15; financial award applicants required to submit FAFSA. *Faculty research:* Novel, poetry, screenplay and creative nonfiction writing; literary and cultural theory; American literature and culture; British and Postcolonial literature. *Unit head:* Dr. Lee Garver, Director of Graduate Studies, Department of English Language and Literature, 317-940-9859, E-mail: lgarver@butler.edu. *Application contact:* Diane Dubord, Graduate Student Services Specialist, 317-940-8107, Fax: 317-940-8250, E-mail: ddubord@butler.edu.
Website: https://www.butler.edu/english/graduate-studies/ma-english

**California College of the Arts,** Graduate Programs, MFA in Writing Program, San Francisco, CA 94107. Offers creative non-fiction (MFA); fiction (MFA); poetry (MFA). *Faculty:* 5 full-time (3 women), 11 part-time/adjunct (7 women). *Students:* 33 full-time (21 women); includes 15 minority (5 Black or African American, non-Hispanic/Latino; 1 Asian, non-Hispanic/Latino; 9 Hispanic/Latino). Average age 30. In 2016, 17 master's awarded. *Degree requirements:* For master's, thesis. *Entrance requirements:* For master's, appropriate bachelor's degree, portfolio, transcripts, letters of recommendation. Additional exam requirements/recommendations for international students: Required—TOEFL, IELTS, or PTE. *Application deadline:* For fall admission, 1/10 for domestic and international students. Applications are processed on a rolling basis. Application fee: $70. Electronic applications accepted. *Expenses:* $1,641 per unit, $39,384 per year tuition; $490 fees. *Financial support:* In 2016–17, fellowships (averaging $22,000 per year), teaching assistantships (averaging $2,000 per year) were awarded; career-related internships or fieldwork, Federal Work-Study, scholarships/grants, health care benefits, and unspecified assistantships also available. Financial award application deadline: 7/31; financial award applicants required to submit FAFSA. *Unit head:* Gloria Frym, Chair, 415-551-9285, E-mail: gfrym@cca.edu. *Application contact:* Wes Fanelli, Assistant Director of Graduate Admissions, 415-703-9533, Fax: 415-703-9539, E-mail: wfanelli@cca.edu.

**California Institute of Integral Studies,** School of Consciousness and Transformation, San Francisco, CA 94103. Offers anthropology and social change (MA, PhD); Asian philosophies and cultures (MA); creative inquiry/interdisciplinary arts (MFA); East-West psychology (MA, PhD); integral and transpersonal psychology (PhD); philosophy and religion (PhD), including ecology, spirituality, and religion, philosophy, cosmology, and consciousness, women's spirituality; theater and performance making (MFA); transformative leadership (MA); transformative studies (PhD); women, gender, spirituality and social justice (MA); writing and consciousness (MFA). *Program availability:* Part-time, evening/weekend, 100% online, blended/hybrid learning. *Students:* 390 full-time (256 women), 121 part-time (84 women); includes 135 minority (39 Black or African American, non-Hispanic/Latino; 2 American Indian or Alaska Native, non-Hispanic/Latino; 22 Asian, non-Hispanic/Latino; 40 Hispanic/Latino; 2 Native Hawaiian or other Pacific Islander, non-Hispanic/Latino; 30 Two or more races, non-Hispanic/Latino), 51 international. Average age 38. 195 applicants, 92% accepted, 124 enrolled. In 2016, 35 master's, 41 doctorates awarded. Terminal master's awarded for partial completion of doctoral program. *Degree requirements:* For master's, thesis optional; for doctorate, comprehensive exam, thesis/dissertation, 1 foreign language (for

Asian philosophies and cultures). *Entrance requirements:* For master's, minimum GPA of 3.0, letters of recommendation, writing sample; for doctorate, master's degree, minimum GPA of 3.0, letters of recommendation, writing sample. Additional exam requirements/recommendations for international students: Required—TOEFL. *Application deadline:* For fall admission, 2/1 priority date for domestic and international students; for spring admission, 10/15 priority date for domestic and international students. Applications are processed on a rolling basis. Application fee: $65. Electronic applications accepted. *Expenses: Tuition:* Full-time $19,728; part-time $1098 per semester hour. *Required fees:* $320; $320 per semester hour. *Financial support:* Research assistantships, teaching assistantships, career-related internships or fieldwork, Federal Work-Study, and scholarships/grants available. Support available to part-time students. Financial award application deadline: 4/15; financial award applicants required to submit FAFSA. *Faculty research:* Ecology and sustainability, philosophy and religion, East-West psychology, integrative health, social and cultural anthropology, transformative leadership. *Application contact:* Ellen Durst, Director of Admissions, 415-575-6100, Fax: 415-575-1268, E-mail: admissions@ciis.edu.
Website: http://www.ciis.edu/

**California Institute of the Arts,** School of Critical Studies, Valencia, CA 91355-2340. Offers writing (MFA, Adv C). *Entrance requirements:* For master's, portfolio. Additional exam requirements/recommendations for international students: Required—TOEFL.

**California State University, East Bay,** Office of Graduate Studies, College of Letters, Arts, and Social Sciences, Department of English, Hayward, CA 94542-3000. Offers creative writing (MA); literary studies (MA); teaching English to speakers of other languages (MA). *Program availability:* Part-time. *Students:* 10 full-time (8 women), 35 part-time (24 women); includes 19 minority (4 Black or African American, non-Hispanic/Latino; 3 Asian, non-Hispanic/Latino; 7 Hispanic/Latino; 5 Two or more races, non-Hispanic/Latino), 8 international. Average age 36. 35 applicants, 63% accepted, 13 enrolled. In 2016, 25 master's awarded. *Degree requirements:* For master's, one foreign language, comprehensive exam, thesis optional. *Entrance requirements:* For master's, minimum GPA of 3.0 in field; 2 letters of recommendation; academic or professional writing sample; teaching experience and some degree of bilingualism (preferred for TESOL). Additional exam requirements/recommendations for international students: Required—TOEFL (minimum score 550 paper-based); Recommended—IELTS (minimum score 6.5). *Application deadline:* For fall admission, 6/30 for domestic and international students. Applications are processed on a rolling basis. Application fee: $55. Electronic applications accepted. *Financial support:* Fellowships, teaching assistantships, career-related internships or fieldwork, Federal Work-Study, institutionally sponsored loans, and scholarships/grants available. Support available to part-time students. Financial award application deadline: 3/2; financial award applicants required to submit FAFSA. *Unit head:* Dr. Sarah Nielsen, Acting Chair, 510-885-3151, Fax: 510-885-4797. *Application contact:* Dr. Donna Wiley, Interim Associate Vice President for Academic Programs and Graduate Studies, 510-885-3716, Fax: 510-885-4777, E-mail: donna.wiley@csueastbay.edu.
Website: http://www20.csueastbay.edu/class/departments/english/index.html

**California State University, Fresno,** Division of Research and Graduate Studies, College of Arts and Humanities, Department of English, Fresno, CA 93740-8027. Offers creative writing (MFA); literature (MA); rhetoric and writing studies (MA). *Program availability:* Part-time, evening/weekend. *Degree requirements:* For master's, one foreign language, thesis. *Entrance requirements:* For master's, GRE General Test, minimum GPA of 3.0, writing sample. Additional exam requirements/recommendations for international students: Required—TOEFL. *Application deadline:* For fall admission, 5/1 for domestic and international students; for spring admission, 10/1 for domestic and international students. Applications are processed on a rolling basis. Application fee: $55. Electronic applications accepted. *Financial support:* Teaching assistantships, career-related internships or fieldwork, Federal Work-Study, and scholarships/grants available. Support available to part-time students. Financial award application deadline: 3/1; financial award applicants required to submit FAFSA. *Faculty research:* American literature, Renaissance literature, foreign literature. *Unit head:* Dr. Lisa Weston, Chair, 559-278-2553, Fax: 559-278-7143, E-mail: lisaw@csufresno.edu.
Website: http://www.fresnostate.edu/artshum/english/

**California State University, Long Beach,** Graduate Studies, College of Liberal Arts, Department of English, Long Beach, CA 90840. Offers creative writing (MFA); English (MA). *Program availability:* Part-time. *Degree requirements:* For master's, one foreign language, comprehensive exam or thesis. *Entrance requirements:* For master's, GRE Subject Test, minimum GPA of 3.0 in English. *Application deadline:* For fall admission, 5/1 for domestic students. Applications are processed on a rolling basis. Application fee: $55. Electronic applications accepted. *Financial support:* Federal Work-Study, institutionally sponsored loans, and scholarships/grants available. Financial award application deadline: 3/2. *Faculty research:* English and American literature, literary theory, linguistics, rhetoric and composition. *Unit head:* Dr. Eileen S. Klink, Chair, 562-985-4223, Fax: 562-985-2369, E-mail: eklink@csulb.edu. *Application contact:* Dr. Beth Lau, Graduate Adviser, 562-985-4252, Fax: 562-985-4223, E-mail: blau@csulb.edu.

**California State University, Northridge,** Graduate Studies, College of Humanities, Department of English, Northridge, CA 91330. Offers creative writing (MA); literature (MA); rhetoric and composition theory (MA). *Program availability:* Part-time, evening/weekend. *Faculty:* 31 full-time (15 women), 104 part-time/adjunct (34 women). *Students:* 34 full-time (18 women), 60 part-time (34 women); includes 35 minority (4 Black or African American, non-Hispanic/Latino; 4 American Indian or Alaska Native, non-Hispanic/Latino; 2 Asian, non-Hispanic/Latino; 21 Hispanic/Latino; 4 Two or more races, non-Hispanic/Latino), 1 international. Average age 33. 49 applicants, 71% accepted, 22 enrolled. *Degree requirements:* For master's, thesis or alternative. *Entrance requirements:* For master's, writing proficiency test, GRE General Test or minimum GPA of 3.0. Additional exam requirements/recommendations for international students: Required—TOEFL. *Application deadline:* For fall admission, 11/30 for domestic students. Application fee: $55. *Expenses:* Tuition, state resident: full-time $4152. *Financial support:* Teaching assistantships available. Financial award application deadline: 3/1. *Faculty research:* Reading improvement, professional writing, Dickens, Shaw, English as a second language. *Unit head:* Kent Baxter, Chair, 818-677-3431.
Website: http://www.csun.edu/english/index.php

**California State University, Sacramento,** Office of Graduate Studies, College of Arts and Letters, Department of English, Sacramento, CA 95819. Offers composition (MA); creative writing (MA); literature (MA); teaching English to speakers of other languages (MA). *Program availability:* Part-time. *Students:* 36 full-time (26 women), 47 part-time (35 women); includes 22 minority (5 Black or African American, non-Hispanic/Latino; 1 American Indian or Alaska Native, non-Hispanic/Latino; 8 Asian, non-Hispanic/Latino; 8 Hispanic/Latino). Average age 30. 54 applicants, 69% accepted, 26 enrolled. In 2016, 29 master's awarded. *Degree requirements:* For master's, thesis, project, or comprehensive exam; TESOL exam; writing proficiency exam. *Entrance requirements:* For master's, portfolio (creative writing); minimum GPA of 3.0 in English and overall during previous 2 years. Additional exam requirements/recommendations for international students: Required—TOEFL (minimum score 600 paper-based; 100 iBT). *Application deadline:* For fall admission, 2/15 for domestic students, 3/1 for international students; for spring admission, 9/30 for international students. Applications are

## Writing

processed on a rolling basis. Application fee: $55. Electronic applications accepted. *Expenses:* $4,302 full-time tuition and fees per semester, $2,796 part-time. *Financial support:* Research assistantships, teaching assistantships, career-related internships or fieldwork, and Federal Work-Study available. Support available to part-time students. Financial award application deadline: 3/1; financial award applicants required to submit FAFSA. *Faculty research:* Teaching composition, remedial writing. *Unit head:* Dr. David Toise, Chair, 916-278-6586, E-mail: dwtoise@csus.edu. *Application contact:* Jose Martinez, Graduate Admissions Supervisor, 916-278-7871, E-mail: martinj@skymail.csus.edu. Website: http://www.csus.edu/engl

**California State University, San Bernardino,** Graduate Studies, College of Arts and Letters, Program in English, San Bernardino, CA 92407. Offers creative writing (MFA), including fiction; English composition (MA), including composition. *Program availability:* Part-time, evening/weekend. *Faculty:* 8 full-time (all women). *Students:* 16 full-time (11 women), 56 part-time (39 women); includes 38 minority (6 Black or African American, non-Hispanic/Latino; 1 Asian, non-Hispanic/Latino; 29 Hispanic/Latino; 2 Two or more races, non-Hispanic/Latino). 32 applicants, 66% accepted, 21 enrolled. In 2016, 26 master's awarded. *Degree requirements:* For master's, one foreign language, thesis. *Entrance requirements:* Additional exam requirements/recommendations for international students: Required—TOEFL. *Application deadline:* For fall admission, 7/16 for domestic students. Application fee: $55. *Expenses:* Tuition, state resident: full-time $7843; part-time $5011.20 per year. Tuition and fees vary according to course load, degree level, program and reciprocity agreements. *Financial support:* Application deadline: 3/1. *Unit head:* Dr. Sunny Hyon, Chair, 909-537-5834, Fax: 909-537-7086, E-mail: shyon@csusb.edu. *Application contact:* Dr. Francisca Beer, Dean of Graduate Studies, 909-537-5058, Fax: 909-537-5078, E-mail: fbeer@csusb.edu.

**California State University, San Marcos,** College of Humanities, Arts, Behavioral and Social Sciences, Program in Literature and Writing Studies, San Marcos, CA 92096-0001. Offers MA. *Program availability:* Part-time, evening/weekend. *Degree requirements:* For master's, one foreign language, thesis. *Entrance requirements:* For master's, GRE General Test, minimum GPA of 3.0, writing sample. *Expenses:* Tuition, state resident: full-time $6738. Tuition, nonresident: full-time $13,434. *Required fees:* $1906. Tuition and fees vary according to campus/location and program. *Faculty research:* Postcolonialism, feminism rhetoric, cultural studies, creative writing, critical theory.

**California State University, Stanislaus,** College of Humanities and Social Sciences, Program in English (MA), Turlock, CA 95382. Offers literature (Certificate); rhetoric and teaching writing (MA); teaching English to speakers of other languages (MA). *Program availability:* Part-time. *Degree requirements:* For master's, comprehensive exam, thesis or alternative. *Entrance requirements:* For master's, GRE, minimum GPA of 3.0, 2 letters of reference, personal statement. Additional exam requirements/recommendations for international students: Required—TOEFL (minimum score 575 paper-based), TWE (minimum score 4). Electronic applications accepted. *Faculty research:* Transnational literacies, Renaissance and medieval literature, abolition writings and slave narratives, qualitative writing.

**Carlow University,** College of Learning and Innovation, Program in Creative Writing, Pittsburgh, PA 15213-3165. Offers fiction (MFA); non-fiction (MFA); poetry (MFA). *Program availability:* Part-time, evening/weekend, low-residency. *Students:* 22 part-time (17 women); includes 3 minority (1 American Indian or Alaska Native, non-Hispanic/Latino; 1 Hispanic/Latino; 1 Two or more races, non-Hispanic/Latino). Average age 37. 2 applicants, 50% accepted. In 2016, 4 master's awarded. *Degree requirements:* For master's, manuscript. *Entrance requirements:* For master's, two essays, sample of writing, two letters of recommendation, resume/curriculum vitae. Additional exam requirements/recommendations for international students: Required—TOEFL (minimum score 550 paper-based). *Application deadline:* Applications are processed on a rolling basis. Electronic applications accepted. *Expenses:* Contact institution. *Financial support:* Application deadline: 4/1; applicants required to submit FAFSA. *Unit head:* Dr. Kevin Haworth, Program Director, MFA in Creative Writing, 412-578-6597, Fax: 412-578-8722, E-mail: khaworth@carlow.edu. Website: http://www.carlow.edu/Master_of_Fine_Arts_in_Creative_Writing.aspx

**Carnegie Mellon University,** Dietrich College of Humanities and Social Sciences, Department of English, Program in Professional Writing, Pittsburgh, PA 15213-3891. Offers editing and publishing (MAPW); policy and non-profit communication (MAPW); public and media relations/corporate communications (MAPW); science or healthcare communication (MAPW); technical writing (MAPW); writing for new media (MAPW); writing for print media (MAPW). *Program availability:* Part-time. *Entrance requirements:* For master's, GRE General Test. Additional exam requirements/recommendations for international students: Required—TOEFL, TWE.

**Cedar Crest College,** Program in Creative Writing, Allentown, PA 18104-6196. Offers MFA. *Program availability:* Part-time, evening/weekend, blended/hybrid learning. *Faculty:* 5 part-time/adjunct (2 women). *Students:* 14 part-time (11 women). Average age 38. In 2016, 10 master's awarded. *Degree requirements:* For master's, final book-length creative thesis. *Application deadline:* Applications are processed on a rolling basis. Electronic applications accepted. *Expenses:* $721 per credit. *Unit head:* Allison Wellford, Director of Writing Program, 610-606-4666 Ext. 3474, E-mail: acwellfo@cedarcrest.edu. *Application contact:* Mary Ellen Hickes, Director of School of Adult and Graduate Education, 610-437-4471, E-mail: sage@cedarcrest.edu. Website: http://sage.cedarcrest.edu/graduate/mfa

**Central Michigan University,** College of Graduate Studies, College of Humanities and Social and Behavioral Sciences, Department of English Language and Literature, Mount Pleasant, MI 48859. Offers English composition and communication (MA); English language and literature (MA), including children's and young adult literature, creative writing, English language and literature; TESOL: teaching English to speakers of other languages (MA). *Program availability:* Part-time, evening/weekend. *Degree requirements:* For master's, thesis or alternative. Electronic applications accepted. *Faculty research:* Composition theory, science fiction history and bibliography, children's and young adult literature, nineteenth century American literature, applied linguistics.

**Chapman University,** Wilkinson College of Arts, Humanities, and Social Sciences, Department of English, Orange, CA 92866. Offers creative writing (MFA); English (MA). *Program availability:* Part-time, evening/weekend. *Faculty:* 18 full-time (10 women), 17 part-time/adjunct (12 women). *Students:* 39 full-time (24 women), 20 part-time (16 women); includes 50 minority (33 Black or African American, non-Hispanic/Latino; 4 Asian, non-Hispanic/Latino; 10 Hispanic/Latino; 3 Two or more races, non-Hispanic/Latino), 3 international. Average age 29. 88 applicants, 90% accepted, 23 enrolled. In 2016, 31 master's awarded. *Degree requirements:* For master's, thesis. *Entrance requirements:* For master's, GRE (if undergraduate GPA less than 3.0), minimum undergraduate GPA of 2.5. Additional exam requirements/recommendations for international students: Required—TOEFL (minimum score 550 paper-based, 80 iBT), IELTS (6.5), PTE Academic (53), or CAE. *Application deadline:* For fall admission, 2/1 for domestic students. Applications are processed on a rolling basis. Application fee: $60. Electronic applications accepted. *Expenses:* Contact institution. *Financial support:* Fellowships, teaching assistantships, Federal Work-Study, and scholarships/grants available. Financial award applicants required to submit FAFSA. *Unit head:* Mark Axelrod, Director, 714-997-6586, E-mail: axelrod@chapman.edu. *Application contact:* Shannon McCance, Graduate Admission Counselor, 714-997-6711, E-mail: smccance@chapman.edu. Website: http://www.chapman.edu/wilkinson/english/

**Chatham University,** Program in Writing, Pittsburgh, PA 15232-2826. Offers children's writing (MFA); fiction (MFA); non-fiction (MFA); poetry (MFA); professional writing (MPW); screenwriting (MFA). *Program availability:* Part-time, evening/weekend, online learning. *Entrance requirements:* For master's, minimum GPA of 3.0, writing sample, recommendation letters. Additional exam requirements/recommendations for international students: Required—TOEFL (minimum score 600 paper-based; 100 iBT), IELTS (minimum score 7), TWE. Electronic applications accepted. Application fee is waived when completed online. *Expenses: Tuition:* Full-time $16,254; part-time $903 per credit hour. *Required fees:* $468; $26 per credit hour. *Faculty research:* Ecopoetics; environment and culture; wilderness and literature; literature of exploration, exile, and home.

**Chicago State University,** School of Graduate and Professional Studies, College of Arts and Sciences, Department of English, Foreign Languages and Literatures, Chicago, IL 60628. Offers creative writing (MFA); English (MA). *Degree requirements:* For master's, comprehensive exam (for some programs), thesis (for some programs). *Entrance requirements:* For master's, minimum GPA of 3.0.

**City College of the City University of New York,** Graduate School, Division of Humanities and the Arts, Department of English, Program in Creative Writing, New York, NY 10031-9198. Offers MFA. *Degree requirements:* For master's, one foreign language, comprehensive exam, thesis. *Entrance requirements:* For master's, minimum GPA of 3.0, 10-15 poems or 30-50 pages of fiction (short stories or novel excerpt). Additional exam requirements/recommendations for international students: Required—TOEFL (minimum score 600 paper-based; 100 iBT). Electronic applications accepted. Tuition and fees vary according to course load, degree level and program.

**Claremont Graduate University,** Graduate Programs, School of Arts and Humanities, Department of English, Claremont, CA 91711-6160. Offers American studies (MA, PhD); critical theory (MA, PhD); early modern studies (MA, PhD); English (M Phil, MA, PhD); literary theory (PhD); literature (MA, PhD); literature and creative writing (MA); literature and film (MA); MBA/MA; MBA/PhD. *Program availability:* Part-time. *Faculty:* 3 full-time (1 woman), 1 part-time/adjunct (0 women). *Students:* 61 full-time (46 women), 20 part-time (14 women); includes 23 minority (4 Black or African American, non-Hispanic/Latino; 1 American Indian or Alaska Native, non-Hispanic/Latino; 9 Asian, non-Hispanic/Latino; 4 Hispanic/Latino; 5 Two or more races, non-Hispanic/Latino), 6 international. Average age 37. In 2016, 10 master's, 8 doctorates awarded. *Entrance requirements:* For master's and doctorate, GRE General Test. Additional exam requirements/recommendations for international students: Required—TOEFL (minimum score 75 iBT). *Application deadline:* For fall admission, 2/1 priority date for domestic and international students. Applications are processed on a rolling basis. Application fee: $80. Electronic applications accepted. *Expenses: Tuition:* Full-time $44,328; part-time $1847 per unit. *Required fees:* $600; $300 per semester. Tuition and fees vary according to course load and program. *Financial support:* Fellowships, Federal Work-Study, institutionally sponsored loans, and scholarships/grants available. Support available to part-time students. Financial award application deadline: 2/15; financial award applicants required to submit FAFSA. *Faculty research:* American, comparative, and English Renaissance literature; modernism; feminist literature and theory. *Unit head:* Lori Anne Ferrell, Chair, 909-607-2652, E-mail: lorianne.ferrell@cgu.edu. *Application contact:* Amy Sandefur, Assistant Director of Admissions, 909-607-9101, E-mail: amy.sandefur@cgu.edu. Website: https://www.cgu.edu/departments/english/

**Clemson University,** Graduate School, College of Architecture, Arts, and Humanities, Department of English, Program in Professional Communication, Clemson, SC 29634. Offers MA. *Program availability:* Part-time. *Faculty:* 66 full-time (34 women), 3 part-time/adjunct (2 women). *Students:* 22 full-time (18 women), 2 part-time (both women); includes 4 minority (3 Black or African American, non-Hispanic/Latino; 1 Hispanic/Latino), 2 international. Average age 26. 18 applicants, 56% accepted, 10 enrolled. In 2016, 13 master's awarded. *Degree requirements:* For master's, comprehensive exam, thesis or alternative. *Entrance requirements:* For master's, GRE General Test, unofficial transcripts, resume, writing sample, letters of recommendation. Additional exam requirements/recommendations for international students: Required—TOEFL (minimum score 80 iBT), IELTS (minimum score 6.5). *Application deadline:* For fall admission, 2/1 priority date for domestic and international students. Application fee: $80 ($90 for international students). Electronic applications accepted. *Expenses:* $4,264 per semester full-time resident, $8,485 per semester full-time non-resident, $471 per credit hour part-time resident, $942 per credit hour part-time non-resident. *Financial support:* In 2016–17, 25 students received support, including 1 research assistantship with partial tuition reimbursement available (averaging $11,374 per year), 8 teaching assistantships with partial tuition reimbursements available (averaging $13,009 per year); career-related internships or fieldwork and unspecified assistantships also available. Financial award application deadline: 2/1. *Faculty research:* Usability and user experience design, rhetoric, intercultural communication, digital publishing, social media authoring, technical writing. *Unit head:* Dr. Lee Morrissey, Department Chair, 864-656-3151, E-mail: lmorris@clemson.edu. *Application contact:* Dr. William Stockton, Graduate Program Coordinator, 864-656-6689, Fax: 864-656-1345, E-mail: wstockt@clemson.edu. Website: http://aahsites.clemson.edu/mapc/

**Cleveland State University,** College of Graduate Studies, College of Liberal Arts and Social Sciences, Department of English, Cleveland, OH 44115. Offers creative writing (MFA), including fiction, non-fiction, playwriting, poetry. *Program availability:* Part-time, evening/weekend. *Faculty:* 14 full-time (8 women), 14 part-time/adjunct (4 women). *Students:* 28 full-time (17 women), 35 part-time (23 women); includes 5 minority (5 Black or African American, non-Hispanic/Latino; 1 Asian, non-Hispanic/Latino; 1 Two or more races, non-Hispanic/Latino), 2 international. Average age 33. 38 applicants, 68% accepted, 9 enrolled. In 2016, 15 master's awarded. *Degree requirements:* For master's, thesis. *Entrance requirements:* For master's, minimum GPA of 2.75, undergraduate concentration in English, writing sample, portfolio. Additional exam requirements/recommendations for international students: Required—TOEFL (minimum score 550 paper-based; 78 iBT). *Application deadline:* For fall admission, 7/15 priority date for domestic students, 5/15 for international students; for spring admission, 12/15 for domestic students, 11/1 for international students; for summer admission, 4/1 for domestic students, 3/15 for international students. Applications are processed on a rolling basis. Application fee: $40. Electronic applications accepted. *Expenses:* Tuition, state resident: full-time $9565. Tuition, nonresident: full-time $17,980. Tuition and fees vary according to program. *Financial support:* In 2016–17, 20 students received support, including 12 teaching assistantships with full tuition reimbursements available (averaging $7,000 per year); tuition waivers (full and partial) and unspecified assistantships also available. Financial award application deadline: 2/1; financial award applicants required to submit FAFSA. *Faculty research:* Literary history and criticism, literature, creative writing. *Total annual research expenditures:* $5,000. *Application contact:* Dr. James J. Marino, Associate Professor/Director of Graduate Studies, 216-687-6874, Fax: 216-687-6943, E-mail: j.marino22@csuohio.edu. Website: http://www.csuohio.edu/class/english/english

**Coastal Carolina University,** Thomas W. and Robin W. Edwards College of Humanities and Fine Arts, Conway, SC 29528-6054. Offers liberal studies (MA); writing (MA). *Program availability:* Part-time, evening/weekend. *Faculty:* 16 full-time (7 women), 1 (woman) part-time/adjunct. *Students:* 23 full-time (15 women), 14 part-time (11 women); includes 7 minority (4 Black or African American, non-Hispanic/Latino; 1 American Indian or Alaska Native, non-Hispanic/Latino; 2 Hispanic/Latino). Average age 34. 24 applicants, 83% accepted, 13 enrolled. In 2016, 13 master's awarded. *Entrance requirements:* For master's, GRE, official transcripts, 3 letters of recommendation, writing sample, minimum GPA of 3.3 in 18 hours of coursework in English or related discipline. Additional exam requirements/recommendations for international students: Required—TOEFL (minimum score 550 paper-based; 79 iBT), IELTS (minimum score 6.5). *Application deadline:* For fall admission, 5/15 priority date for domestic and international students; for spring admission, 11/15 priority date for domestic and international students. Applications are processed on a rolling basis. Application fee: $45. Electronic applications accepted. *Expenses:* Tuition, state resident: full-time $9990; part-time $555 per credit hour. Tuition, nonresident: full-time $18,108; part-time $1006 per credit hour. *Required fees:* $90; $5 per credit hour. *Financial support:* Fellowships, research assistantships, and unspecified assistantships available. Support available to part-time students. Financial award application deadline: 3/1; financial award applicants required to submit FAFSA. *Unit head:* Joseph R. Oestreich, Associate Professor/Coordinator of Graduate Study, 843-349-2433, E-mail: joeo@coastal.edu. *Application contact:* Dr. James O. Luken, Associate Provost/Vice-Dean of the Coastal Environment, 843-349-2235, Fax: 843-349-6444, E-mail: joluken@coastal.edu. Website: http://www.coastal.edu/humanities/

**The College at Brockport, State University of New York,** School of Arts and Sciences, Department of English, Brockport, NY 14420-2997. Offers creative writing (AGC); English (MA), including creative writing, literature. *Program availability:* Part-time. *Faculty:* 8 full-time (3 women). *Students:* 19 full-time (13 women), 15 part-time (9 women); includes 2 minority (1 Black or African American, non-Hispanic/Latino; 1 Hispanic/Latino), 1 international. 24 applicants, 88% accepted, 16 enrolled. In 2016, 11 master's, 2 other advanced degrees awarded. *Degree requirements:* For master's, thesis. *Entrance requirements:* For master's, minimum GPA of 3.0, letters of recommendation, writing sample. Additional exam requirements/recommendations for international students: Required—TOEFL (minimum score 550 paper-based; 79 iBT), IELTS (minimum score 6.5). *Application deadline:* For fall admission, 4/15 priority date for domestic and international students; for spring admission, 11/15 priority date for domestic and international students; for summer admission, 4/15 priority date for domestic and international students. Application fee: $50. Electronic applications accepted. *Expenses:* Contact institution. *Financial support:* In 2016–17, 3 teaching assistantships with full tuition reimbursements (averaging $6,000 per year) were awarded; Federal Work-Study, scholarships/grants, and unspecified assistantships also available. Support available to part-time students. Financial award application deadline: 3/15; financial award applicants required to submit FAFSA. *Faculty research:* British and American literature, creative writing, film studies, children's literature, ancient and modern world literature. *Unit head:* Dr. Jennifer Haytock, Chairperson, 585-395-5832, Fax: 585-395-2391, E-mail: jhaytock@brockport.edu. *Application contact:* Dr. Gregory Garvey, Graduate Program Director, 585-395-5712, Fax: 585-395-5487, E-mail: tgarvey@brockport.edu. Website: http://www.brockport.edu/english/graduate/

**College of Charleston,** Graduate School, School of Humanities and Social Sciences, Program in Creative Writing, Charleston, SC 29424-0001. Offers MFA. *Unit head:* Bret Lott, Director, 843-953-3180, E-mail: lottb@cofc.edu. *Application contact:* Susan Hallatt, Director of Graduate Admissions, 843-953-5614, Fax: 843-953-1434, E-mail: hallatts@cofc.edu.

**Colorado State University,** College of Liberal Arts, Department of English, Fort Collins, CO 80523-1773. Offers creative nonfiction (MA); creative writing (MFA); literature (MA); rhetoric and composition (MA); TESL/TEFL (MA). *Program availability:* Part-time. *Faculty:* 31 full-time (21 women), 25 part-time/adjunct (23 women). *Students:* 71 full-time (54 women), 30 part-time (21 women); includes 7 minority (1 Black or African American, non-Hispanic/Latino; 2 Asian, non-Hispanic/Latino; 2 Hispanic/Latino; 2 Two or more races, non-Hispanic/Latino), 13 international. Average age 29. 177 applicants, 42% accepted, 39 enrolled. In 2016, 33 master's awarded. *Degree requirements:* For master's, thesis (for some programs). *Entrance requirements:* For master's, BA/BS or equivalent with minimum cumulative undergraduate GPA of 3.0, transcripts, writing sample, statement of purpose, 3 letters of recommendation. Additional exam requirements/recommendations for international students: Recommended—TOEFL (minimum score 550 paper-based; 80 iBT), IELTS (minimum score 6.5). *Application deadline:* For spring admission, 9/15 for domestic and international students. Electronic applications accepted. *Expenses:* Tuition, state resident: full-time $9628. Tuition, nonresident: full-time $23,603. *Required fees:* $2253; $528.14 per credit hour. $264.07 per semester. Tuition and fees vary according to course load and program. *Financial support:* In 2016–17, 39 students received support, including 38 teaching assistantships with full and partial tuition reimbursements available (averaging $14,005 per year); scholarships/grants, health care benefits, and unspecified assistantships also available. Financial award application deadline: 1/1. *Faculty research:* Literary texts in historical and cultural contexts; creation and criticism of fiction, poetry, creative nonfiction and hybrid genres; critical literacies, multimodalities, and technologies including pedagogical theory and practice; linguistics, second language acquisition and TEFL/TESOL; rhetoric and social change. *Total annual research expenditures:* $154,039. *Unit head:* Louann Reid, Professor, 970-491-6428, E-mail: louann.reid@colostate.edu. *Application contact:* Marnie Leonard, Administrative Assistant, 970-491-2403, E-mail: marnie.leonard@colostate.edu. Website: http://english.colostate.edu/

**Columbia College Chicago,** Graduate School, Department of Creative Writing, Chicago, IL 60605-1996. Offers fiction (MFA); nonfiction (MFA); poetry (MFA). *Program availability:* Part-time. *Degree requirements:* For master's, thesis. *Entrance requirements:* For master's, self-assessment essay, work samples, letters of recommendation. Additional exam requirements/recommendations for international students: Required—TOEFL (minimum score 600 paper-based; 100 iBT). Electronic applications accepted.

**Columbia University,** School of the Arts, Writing Program, New York, NY 10027. Offers fiction (MFA); nonfiction (MFA); poetry (MFA). *Degree requirements:* For master's, thesis. *Entrance requirements:* For master's, 3 letters of recommendation, writing sample. Additional exam requirements/recommendations for international students: Required—TOEFL (minimum score 600 paper-based). Electronic applications accepted.

See Display on page 147 and Close-Up on page 201.

**Concordia University,** School of Graduate Studies, Faculty of Arts and Science, Department of English, Program in Creative Writing, Montréal, QC H3G 1M8, Canada.

Offers MA. *Degree requirements:* For master's, one foreign language, thesis. *Entrance requirements:* For master's, honors degree in English, minimum GPA of 3.3 in English literature, portfolio. *Faculty research:* Fiction, poetry, prose, drama.

**Cornell University,** Graduate School, Graduate Fields of Arts and Sciences, Field of English Language and Literature, Ithaca, NY 14853. Offers African-American literature (PhD); American literature after 1865 (PhD); American literature to 1865 (PhD); American studies (PhD); colonial and postcolonial literatures (PhD); creative writing (MFA); cultural studies (PhD); dramatic literature (PhD); English poetry (PhD); English Renaissance to 1660 (PhD); lesbian, bisexual, and gay literary studies (PhD); literary criticism and theory (PhD); Old and Middle English (PhD); prose fiction (PhD); Restoration and the eighteenth-century (PhD); the nineteenth century (PhD); the twentieth century (PhD); women's literature (PhD); MFA/PhD. Terminal master's awarded for partial completion of doctoral program. *Degree requirements:* For master's, one foreign language, thesis; for doctorate, one foreign language, comprehensive exam, thesis/dissertation, teaching experience. *Entrance requirements:* For master's, GRE General Test, 3 letters of recommendation, creative writing sample; for doctorate, GRE General Test, GRE Subject Test (English), 3 letters of recommendation, writing sample. Additional exam requirements/recommendations for international students: Required—TOEFL (minimum score 600 paper-based; 77 iBT). Electronic applications accepted. *Faculty research:* English and American literature, women's writing, ethnic and post-colonial literature, critical theory, medievalism.

**Creighton University,** Graduate School, College of Arts and Sciences, Department of English, Omaha, NE 68178-0001. Offers creative writing (MA, MFA). *Program availability:* Part-time. *Faculty:* 15 full-time (8 women), 1 part-time/adjunct (0 women). *Students:* 6 full-time (5 women), 1 (woman) part-time, 1 international. Average age 27. 31 applicants, 87% accepted, 6 enrolled. In 2016, 5 master's awarded. *Degree requirements:* For master's, thesis optional. *Entrance requirements:* For master's, 10-15 page writing sample, 3 letters of recommendation. Additional exam requirements/recommendations for international students: Required—TOEFL (minimum score 90 iBT). *Application deadline:* For fall admission, 3/15 priority date for domestic and international students. Application fee: $50. Electronic applications accepted. *Expenses: Tuition:* Full-time $14,400; part-time $800 per credit hour. *Required fees:* $158 per semester. Tuition and fees vary according to course load, campus/location, program, reciprocity agreements and student's religious affiliation. *Financial support:* In 2016–17, 5 fellowships with tuition reimbursements (averaging $11,465 per year) were awarded; scholarships/grants, tuition waivers (full and partial), and unspecified assistantships also available. Financial award applicants required to submit FAFSA. *Faculty research:* Henry James letters. *Unit head:* Dr. Robert Whipple, Director, 402-280-2520, E-mail: whippl@creighton.edu. *Application contact:* Lindsay Johnson, Director of Graduate and Adult Recruitment, 402-280-2703, Fax: 402-280-2423, E-mail: gradschool@creighton.edu.

**DePaul University,** College of Liberal Arts and Social Sciences, Chicago, IL 60614. Offers Arabic (MA); Chinese (MA); English (MA); French (MA); German (MA); history (MA); interdisciplinary studies (MA, MS); international public service (MS); international studies (MA); Italian (MA); Japanese (MA); leadership and policy studies (MA); liberal studies (MA); new media studies (MA); nonprofit management (MNM); public administration (MPA); public health (MPH); public service management (MS); social work (MSW); sociology (MA); Spanish (MA); sustainable urban development (MA); women and gender studies (MA); writing and publishing (MA); writing, rhetoric, and discourse (MA); MA/PhD. *Program availability:* Part-time, evening/weekend, online learning. Terminal master's awarded for partial completion of doctoral program. *Degree requirements:* For master's, variable foreign language requirement, comprehensive exam (for some programs), thesis (for some programs). Electronic applications accepted.

**Dominican University of California,** School of Arts, Humanities and Social Sciences, Humanities Program, San Rafael, CA 94901-2298. Offers applied music (MA); art history (MA); creative writing (MA); gender studies (MA); history (MA); literature (MA); philosophy (MA); political theory (MA); religion (MA). *Program availability:* Part-time. *Degree requirements:* For master's, thesis or alternative. *Entrance requirements:* For master's, minimum GPA of 3.0, interview. Additional exam requirements/recommendations for international students: Required—TOEFL (minimum score 550 paper-based; 80 iBT), IELTS (minimum score 6.5). Electronic applications accepted. Application fee is waived when completed online. *Expenses:* Contact institution.

**Drew University,** Caspersen School of Graduate Studies, Madison, NJ 07940-1493. Offers conflict resolution and leadership (Certificate), including community leadership, moderation, peace building; history and culture (MA, PhD), including American history, book history, British history, European history, Holocaust and genocide (M Litt, MA, D Litt, PhD), intellectual history, Irish history, print culture, public history; K-12 education (MAT), including art, biology, chemistry, elementary education, English, French, Italian, math, secondary education, special education, teacher of students with disabilities; liberal studies (M Litt, D Litt), including history, Holocaust and genocide (M Litt, MA, D Litt, PhD), Irish/Irish-American studies, literature (M Litt, MMH, D Litt, DMH, CMH), religion, spirituality, teaching in the two-year college, writing; medical humanities (MMH, DMH, CMH), including arts, health, healthcare, literature (M Litt, MMH, D Litt, DMH, CMH), scientific research; poetry (MFA). *Program availability:* Part-time, evening/weekend. *Faculty:* 4 full-time (2 women), 31 part-time/adjunct (16 women). *Students:* 62 full-time (41 women), 199 part-time (130 women); includes 38 minority (17 Black or African American, non-Hispanic/Latino; 3 Asian, non-Hispanic/Latino; 17 Hispanic/Latino; 1 Two or more races, non-Hispanic/Latino), 3 international. Average age 27. 93 applicants, 81% accepted, 46 enrolled. In 2016, 39 master's, 27 doctorates, 26 other advanced degrees awarded. Terminal master's awarded for partial completion of doctoral program. *Degree requirements:* For master's and other advanced degree, thesis (for some programs); for doctorate, one foreign language, comprehensive exam (for some programs), thesis/dissertation. *Entrance requirements:* For master's, PRAXIS Core and Subject Area tests (for MAT), resume, transcripts, writing sample, personal statement, letters of recommendation; for doctorate, GRE (PhD in history and culture), resume, transcripts, writing sample, personal statement, letters of recommendation. Additional exam requirements/recommendations for international students: Required—TOEFL (minimum score 587 paper-based; 94 iBT), IELTS (minimum score 7), TWE (minimum score 4). *Application deadline:* For fall admission, 8/1 for domestic students, 6/1 for spring admission, 12/1 for domestic students, 10/1 for international students. Applications are processed on a rolling basis. Application fee: $35. Electronic applications accepted. Tuition and fees vary according to program. *Financial support:* Fellowships, research assistantships, teaching assistantships, career-related internships or fieldwork, Federal Work-Study, scholarships/grants, and unspecified assistantships available. Support available to part-time students. Financial award applicants required to submit FAFSA. *Application contact:* Leanne Horinko, Director of Caspersen Admissions, 973-408-3280, E-mail: gradm@drew.edu. Website: http://www.drew.edu/caspersen

**East Carolina University,** Graduate School, Thomas Harriot College of Arts and Sciences, Department of English, Greenville, NC 27858-4353. Offers creative writing (MA); English studies (MA); linguistics (MA); literature (MA); multicultural and transnational literatures (MA, Certificate); rhetoric and composition (MA); rhetoric,

# Writing

writing, and professional communication (PhD); teaching English in the two-year college (Certificate); teaching English to speakers of other languages (MA, Certificate); technical and professional communication (MA). *Program availability:* Part-time, evening/weekend. *Students:* 54 full-time (36 women), 95 part-time (77 women); includes 32 minority (19 Black or African American, non-Hispanic/Latino; 3 Asian, non-Hispanic/Latino; 6 Hispanic/Latino; 4 Two or more races, non-Hispanic/Latino), 1 international. Average age 35. 78 applicants, 96% accepted, 50 enrolled. In 2016, 34 master's, 1 doctorate awarded. *Degree requirements:* For master's, one foreign language, comprehensive exam, thesis optional. *Entrance requirements:* For master's, GRE General Test, MAT (for MA Ed). Additional exam requirements/recommendations for international students: Required—TOEFL. *Application deadline:* For fall admission, 6/1 priority date for domestic students; for spring admission, 10/15 for domestic students. Applications are processed on a rolling basis. Application fee: $50. *Financial support:* Research assistantships with partial tuition reimbursements, teaching assistantships with partial tuition reimbursements, and Federal Work-Study available. Support available to part-time students. Financial award application deadline: 6/1. *Unit head:* Dr. Jeffrey Johnson, Chair, 252-328-6041, E-mail: johnsonj@ecu.edu. *Application contact:* Dean of Graduate School, 252-328-6012, Fax: 252-328-6071, E-mail: gradschool@ecu.edu. Website: http://www.ecu.edu/cs-cas/engl/graduate/

**Eastern Kentucky University,** The Graduate School, College of Arts and Sciences, Department of English and Theatre, Richmond, KY 40475-3102. Offers creative writing (MFA); English (MA). *Program availability:* Part-time, evening/weekend. *Degree requirements:* For master's, thesis optional. *Entrance requirements:* For master's, GRE General Test, minimum GPA of 2.5, minor in English with 3.0 GPA. *Faculty research:* Old English, Victorian studies, women's studies, rhetoric, popular culture, novel studies.

**Eastern Michigan University,** Graduate School, College of Arts and Sciences, Department of English Language and Literature, Program in Creative Writing, Ypsilanti, MI 48197. Offers MA. *Program availability:* Part-time, evening/weekend, online learning. *Students:* 3 full-time (1 woman), 7 part-time (4 women); includes 1 minority (Black or African American, non-Hispanic/Latino). Average age 27. 17 applicants, 53% accepted, 4 enrolled. In 2016, 2 master's awarded. *Entrance requirements:* Additional exam requirements/recommendations for international students: Required—TOEFL. *Application deadline:* Applications are processed on a rolling basis. Application fee: $45. *Financial support:* Fellowships, research assistantships with full tuition reimbursements, teaching assistantships with full tuition reimbursements, career-related internships or fieldwork, Federal Work-Study, institutionally sponsored loans, scholarships/grants, tuition waivers (partial), and unspecified assistantships available. Support available to part-time students. Financial award applicants required to submit FAFSA. *Application contact:* Dr. Carla Harryman, Graduate Coordinator, 734-487-3173, Fax: 734-483-9744, E-mail: charryma@emich.edu.

**Eastern Michigan University,** Graduate School, College of Arts and Sciences, Department of English Language and Literature, Programs in Written Communication, Ypsilanti, MI 48197. Offers technical communication (Graduate Certificate); written communication (MA). *Program availability:* Part-time, evening/weekend, online learning. *Students:* 7 full-time (6 women), 14 part-time (10 women); includes 2 minority (both Black or African American, non-Hispanic/Latino). Average age 31. 13 applicants, 85% accepted, 8 enrolled. In 2016, 5 master's, 2 other advanced degrees awarded. *Entrance requirements:* Additional exam requirements/recommendations for international students: Required—TOEFL. *Application deadline:* Applications are processed on a rolling basis. Application fee: $45. *Financial support:* Fellowships, research assistantships with full tuition reimbursements, teaching assistantships with full tuition reimbursements, career-related internships or fieldwork, Federal Work-Study, institutionally sponsored loans, scholarships/grants, tuition waivers (partial), and unspecified assistantships available. Support available to part-time students. Financial award applicants required to submit FAFSA. *Application contact:* Dr. Steve Benninghoff, Program Coordinator, 734-487-2075, Fax: 734-483-9744, E-mail: steve.benninghoff@emich.edu.

**Eastern Oregon University,** MFA in Creative Writing Program, La Grande, OR 97850-2899. Offers MFA. *Faculty:* 2 full-time (1 woman), 4 part-time/adjunct (2 women). *Students:* 10 full-time (6 women), 3 part-time (2 women); includes 2 minority (1 Black or African American, non-Hispanic/Latino; 1 American Indian or Alaska Native, non-Hispanic/Latino). Average age 49. *Degree requirements:* For master's, thesis. *Entrance requirements:* For master's, minimum GPA of 3.0 on last 60 quarter hours completed of undergraduate upper-division coursework or 15 quarter hours of approved graduate-level coursework; two reference letters; creative portfolio; essays. *Application deadline:* Applications are processed on a rolling basis. Application fee: $50 ($90 for international students). *Expenses:* $404.50 per credit; $84 summer term residency and building/incidental fees. *Financial support:* In 2016–17, 3 students received support. Federal Work-Study, scholarships/grants, and tuition waivers (full and partial) available. Support available to part-time students. *Unit head:* Dr. Regina Braker, Interim Dean, College of Arts and Sciences, 541-962 3555, Fax: 541-962 3701, E-mail: rbraker@eou.edu. *Application contact:* Kerry Bullard, Administrative Program Assistant, 541-962 3555, Fax: 541-962-3701, E-mail: kbullard@eou.edu. Website: http://www.eou.edu/mfa/

**Eastern Washington University,** Graduate Studies, College of Arts, Letters and Education, Inland Northwest Center for Writers, Cheney, WA 99004-2431. Offers MFA. *Faculty:* 5 full-time (2 women), 4 part-time/adjunct (2 women). *Students:* 39 full-time (24 women), 2 part-time (both women); includes 6 minority (1 American Indian or Alaska Native, non-Hispanic/Latino; 3 Asian, non-Hispanic/Latino; 2 Hispanic/Latino), 1 international. Average age 30. 48 applicants, 58% accepted, 15 enrolled. In 2016, 21 master's awarded. *Degree requirements:* For master's, comprehensive exam, thesis. *Entrance requirements:* For master's, GRE General Test, minimum GPA of 3.0, sample of written work. Additional exam requirements/recommendations for international students: Required—PTE (minimum score 63), TOEFL (minimum score 580 paper-based, 92 iBT) or IELTS (7). *Application deadline:* For fall admission, 4/1 priority date for domestic students; for spring admission, 1/15 for domestic students. Applications are processed on a rolling basis. Application fee: $75. Electronic applications accepted. *Expenses:* Tuition, state resident: full-time $11,000; part-time $5500 per credit. Tuition, nonresident: full-time $24,000; part-time $12,000 per credit. *Required fees:* $1300. One-time fee: $50 full-time. Part-time tuition and fees vary according to course load, campus/location and program. *Financial support:* In 2016–17, 7 students received support, including 7 teaching assistantships with partial tuition reimbursements available (averaging $10,000 per year); career-related internships or fieldwork, Federal Work-Study, institutionally sponsored loans, scholarships/grants, health care benefits, tuition waivers (partial), and unspecified assistantships also available. Support available to part-time students. Financial award application deadline: 2/1; financial award applicants required to submit FAFSA. *Unit head:* Prof. Greg Spatz, Director, 509-359-4956, Fax: 509-623-4238. *Application contact:* Pamela Russell, Program Coordinator, 509-828-1434, E-mail: prussell@ewu.edu. Website: http://sites.ewu.edu/mfa/

**Emerson College,** Graduate Studies, School of the Arts, Department of Visual and Media Arts, Program in Writing for Film and Television, Boston, MA 02116-4624. Offers MFA. *Faculty:* 85 full-time (48 women), 6 part-time/adjunct (3 women). *Students:* 13 full-

time (7 women). Average age 34. 37 applicants, 65% accepted, 12 enrolled. *Entrance requirements:* Additional exam requirements/recommendations for international students: Required—TOEFL (minimum score 577 paper-based), IELTS (minimum score 7). *Application deadline:* Applications are processed on a rolling basis. Application fee: $60 ($75 for international students). Electronic applications accepted. *Financial support:* In 2016–17, 11 students received support, including 11 fellowships (averaging $5,700 per year). *Application contact:* Leanda Ferland, Director of Graduate Admission, 617-824-8610, Fax: 617-824-8614, E-mail: gradapp@emerson.edu. Website: http://www.emerson.edu/visual-and-media-arts/low-residency-mfa

**Emerson College,** Graduate Studies, School of the Arts, Department of Writing, Literature and Publishing, Program in Creative Writing, Boston, MA 02116-4624. Offers MFA. *Program availability:* Part-time, evening/weekend. *Faculty:* 43 full-time (20 women), 6 part-time/adjunct (3 women). *Students:* 95 full-time (58 women), 10 part-time (7 women); includes 22 minority (7 Black or African American, non-Hispanic/Latino; 4 Asian, non-Hispanic/Latino; 8 Hispanic/Latino; 3 Two or more races, non-Hispanic/Latino), 3 international. Average age 27. 189 applicants, 72% accepted, 39 enrolled. In 2016, 37 master's awarded. *Entrance requirements:* For master's, GRE General Test, 15-page writing sample. Additional exam requirements/recommendations for international students: Required—TOEFL (minimum score 550 paper-based; 80 iBT), IELTS (minimum score 6.5). *Application deadline:* For fall admission, 2/15 for domestic and international students. Applications are processed on a rolling basis. Application fee: $60 ($75 for international students). Electronic applications accepted. *Financial support:* In 2016–17, 34 students received support, including 34 fellowships with tuition reimbursements available (averaging $20,698 per year); research assistantships with partial tuition reimbursements available, Federal Work-Study, scholarships/grants, and unspecified assistantships also available. Financial award application deadline: 2/15; financial award applicants required to submit FAFSA. *Application contact:* Leanda Ferland, Director of Graduate Admission, 617-824-8610, Fax: 617-824-8614, E-mail: gradapp@emerson.edu. Website: http://www.emerson.edu/graduate_admission

**Emerson College,** Graduate Studies, School of the Arts, Department of Writing, Literature and Publishing, Program in Popular Fiction Writing and Publishing, Boston, MA 02116-4624. Offers MFA. *Program availability:* Online only, 100% online. *Faculty:* 43 full-time (20 women), 6 part-time/adjunct (3 women). *Students:* 11 full-time (7 women), 1 part-time (0 women); includes 6 minority (3 Hispanic/Latino; 3 Two or more races, non-Hispanic/Latino). Average age 27. 31 applicants, 55% accepted, 11 enrolled. *Entrance requirements:* Additional exam requirements/recommendations for international students: Required—TOEFL (minimum score 577 paper-based; 90 iBT), IELTS (minimum score 7). *Application deadline:* Applications are processed on a rolling basis. Application fee: $60 ($75 for international students). Electronic applications accepted. *Financial support:* In 2016–17, 12 students received support. Scholarships/grants available. Financial award applicants required to submit FAFSA. *Application contact:* Leanda Ferland, Office of Graduate Admission, 617-824-8610, Fax: 617-824-8614, E-mail: gradapp@emerson.edu. Website: http://www.emerson.edu/writing-literature-publishing/mfa-popular-fiction-writing-publishing

**Emerson College,** Graduate Studies, School of the Arts, Department of Writing, Literature and Publishing, Program in Publishing and Writing, Boston, MA 02116-4624. Offers MA. *Program availability:* Part-time, evening/weekend. *Faculty:* 43 full-time (20 women), 6 part-time/adjunct (3 women). *Students:* 84 full-time (77 women), 10 part-time (9 women); includes 18 minority (3 Black or African American, non-Hispanic/Latino; 2 Asian, non-Hispanic/Latino; 12 Hispanic/Latino; 1 Two or more races, non-Hispanic/Latino), 3 international. Average age 25. 100 applicants, 88% accepted, 36 enrolled. In 2016, 45 master's awarded. *Degree requirements:* For master's, thesis or alternative. *Entrance requirements:* For master's, GRE General Test, 15-page writing sample. Additional exam requirements/recommendations for international students: Required—TOEFL (minimum score 550 paper-based; 80 iBT), IELTS (minimum score 6.5). *Application deadline:* For fall admission, 3/1 priority date for domestic and international students. Applications are processed on a rolling basis. Application fee: $60 ($75 for international students). Electronic applications accepted. *Financial support:* In 2016–17, 43 students received support, including 43 fellowships with partial tuition reimbursements available (averaging $5,741 per year); research assistantships with partial tuition reimbursements available, Federal Work-Study, scholarships/grants, and unspecified assistantships also available. Financial award application deadline: 3/1; financial award applicants required to submit FAFSA. *Faculty research:* Publishing. *Application contact:* Leanda Ferland, Director of Graduate Admission, 617-824-8610, Fax: 617-824-8614, E-mail: gradapp@emerson.edu. Website: http://www.emerson.edu/graduate_admission

**Fairfield University,** College of Arts and Sciences, Fairfield, CT 06824. Offers American studies (MA); communication (MA); creative writing (MFA); mathematics (MS); public administration (MPA). *Program availability:* Part-time, evening/weekend, online learning. *Faculty:* 17 full-time (9 women), 12 part-time/adjunct (6 women). *Students:* 60 full-time (40 women), 51 part-time (28 women); includes 24 minority (9 Black or African American, non-Hispanic/Latino; 1 Asian, non-Hispanic/Latino; 11 Hispanic/Latino; 3 Two or more races, non-Hispanic/Latino), 8 international. Average age 34. 84 applicants, 74% accepted, 38 enrolled. In 2016, 68 master's awarded. *Degree requirements:* For master's, capstone research course. *Entrance requirements:* For master's, minimum GPA of 3.0, 2 letters of recommendation, resume, personal statement. Additional exam requirements/recommendations for international students: Required—TOEFL (minimum score 550 paper-based; 80 iBT) or IELTS (minimum score 6.5). *Application deadline:* For fall admission, 5/15 for international students; for spring admission, 10/15 for international students. Applications are processed on a rolling basis. Application fee: $60. Electronic applications accepted. *Expenses:* Contact institution. *Financial support:* In 2016–17, 17 students received support. Scholarships/grants and unspecified assistantships available. Financial award applicants required to submit FAFSA. *Faculty research:* Ethical theory, media industries, community-based teaching and learning, non commutative algebra and partial differential equations, cancer research in biology and physics. *Unit head:* Dr. Yohuru Williams, Dean, 203-254-4000 Ext. 2221, Fax: 203-254-4119, E-mail: ywilliams@fairfield.edu. *Application contact:* Marianne Gumpper, Director of Graduate Admission, 203-254-4184, Fax: 203-254-4073, E-mail: gradadmis@fairfield.edu. Website: http://www.fairfield.edu/cas

**Fairleigh Dickinson University, College at Florham,** Maxwell Becton College of Arts and Sciences, Department of English, Communication and Philosophy, Program in Creative Writing, Madison, NJ 07940-1099. Offers creative nonfiction (MFA); fiction (MFA); literary translation (MFA); poetry (MFA); writing for young adults (MFA).

**Fairleigh Dickinson University, College at Florham,** Maxwell Becton College of Arts and Sciences, Department of English, Communication and Philosophy, Program in Creative Writing and Literature for Educators, Madison, NJ 07940-1099. Offers MA.

**Florida International University,** College of Arts, Sciences, and Education, Department of English, Miami, FL 33199. Offers creative writing (MFA); English (MA), including literature; linguistics (MA). *Program availability:* Part-time, evening/weekend. *Faculty:* 55 full-time (29 women), 47 part-time/adjunct (29 women). *Students:* 47 full-

(30 women), 35 part-time (19 women); includes 43 minority (6 Black or African American, non-Hispanic/Latino; 36 Hispanic/Latino; 1 Two or more races, non-Hispanic/Latino), 8 international. Average age 31. 59 applicants, 39% accepted, 16 enrolled. In 2016, 27 master's awarded. *Degree requirements:* For master's, thesis. *Entrance requirements:* For master's, GRE General Test, minimum undergraduate GPA of 3.0 (upper-level coursework), letter of intent, two letters of recommendation. Additional exam requirements/recommendations for international students: Required—TOEFL (minimum score 550 paper-based; 80 iBT). *Application deadline:* For fall admission, 2/1 for domestic and international students; for spring admission, 10/1 for domestic students, 9/1 for international students. Applications are processed on a rolling basis. Application fee: $30. Electronic applications accepted. *Expenses:* Tuition, state resident: full-time $8912; part-time $446 per credit hour. Tuition, nonresident: full-time $21,393; part-time $992 per credit hour. *Required fees:* $2185; $195 per semester. Tuition and fees vary according to program. *Financial support:* Institutionally sponsored loans and scholarships/grants available. Financial award application deadline: 3/1; financial award applicants required to submit FAFSA. *Unit head:* Dr. Heather Russell, Chair, 305-348-3369, Fax: 305-348-3878, E-mail: heather.russell@fiu.edu. *Application contact:* Nanett Rojas, Assistant Director, Graduate Admissions, 305-348-7464, Fax: 305-348-7441, E-mail: gradadm@fiu.edu.

**Florida State University,** The Graduate School, College of Arts and Sciences, Department of English, Tallahassee, FL 32312. Offers creative writing (MFA); English (PhD), including creative writing, literature, rhetoric and composition; literature (MA); rhetoric and composition (MA). *Program availability:* Part-time. *Faculty:* 47 full-time (24 women), 2 part-time/adjunct (1 woman). *Students:* 142 full-time (80 women), 31 part-time (23 women); includes 44 minority (17 Black or African American, non-Hispanic/Latino; 1 American Indian or Alaska Native, non-Hispanic/Latino; 12 Asian, non-Hispanic/Latino; 5 Hispanic/Latino; 9 Two or more races, non-Hispanic/Latino), 9 international. Average age 30. 307 applicants, 20% accepted, 38 enrolled. In 2016, 21 master's, 24 doctorates awarded. *Degree requirements:* For master's, one foreign language, 33 hours of coursework including capstone essay, thesis or portfolio (MA); 45 hours of coursework including 9-12 thesis hours (MFA); for doctorate, one foreign language, comprehensive exam, thesis/dissertation, 27 hours of coursework, 24 hours of dissertation work. *Entrance requirements:* For master's and doctorate, GRE General Test, sample of written work, 3 letters of recommendation, resume. Additional exam requirements/recommendations for international students: Required—TOEFL. *Application deadline:* For fall admission, 1/1 priority date for domestic and international students. Application fee: $30. Electronic applications accepted. *Expenses:* Tuition, state resident: full-time $7263; part-time $403.51 per credit hour. Tuition, nonresident: full-time $18,087; part-time $1004.85 per credit hour. *Required fees:* $1365; $75.81 per credit hour. $20 per semester. Tuition and fees vary according to campus/location. *Financial support:* In 2016–17, 132 students received support, including 5 fellowships with tuition reimbursements available, teaching assistantships with tuition reimbursements available (averaging $13,250 per year); career-related internships or fieldwork, Federal Work-Study, and institutionally sponsored loans also available. Financial award application deadline: 8/1; financial award applicants required to submit FAFSA. *Faculty research:* British and Irish literature, American literature, creative writing, rhetoric and composition, multiethnic transnational literature, history of text technologies. *Unit head:* Dr. Gary Taylor, Chair, 850-644-4230, Fax: 850-644-0811, E-mail: ewalker@fsu.edu. *Application contact:* Ginger Martin, Senior Graduate Academic Coordinator, 850-644-1081, Fax: 850-644-9656, E-mail: vmartin@fsu.edu.
Website: http://english.fsu.edu/

**Florida State University,** The Graduate School, College of Motion Picture Arts, Tallahassee, FL 32306-2350. Offers film production (MFA); screenwriting (MFA). *Faculty:* 24 full-time (7 women), 3 part-time/adjunct (1 woman). *Students:* 59 full-time (25 women); includes 29 minority (9 Black or African American, non-Hispanic/Latino; 13 Asian, non-Hispanic/Latino; 4 Hispanic/Latino; 3 Two or more races, non-Hispanic/Latino). Average age 25. 187 applicants, 16% accepted, 30 enrolled. In 2016, 30 master's awarded. *Degree requirements:* For master's, thesis, thesis film project. *Entrance requirements:* For master's, GRE (for MFA in writing), minimum GPA of 3.0, resume, statement of purpose, writing sample, 3 letters of recommendation, creative portfolio. Additional exam requirements/recommendations for international students: Required—TOEFL (minimum score 550 paper-based; 80 iBT). *Application deadline:* For fall admission, 12/1 for domestic and international students. Application fee: $30. Electronic applications accepted. *Expenses:* $44,639 in-state (for production degree); $30,739 in-state (for writing degree). *Financial support:* In 2016–17, 20 students received support, including 20 teaching assistantships with partial tuition reimbursements available (averaging $5,500 per year); institutionally sponsored loans and unspecified assistantships also available. Financial award application deadline: 12/1; financial award applicants required to submit FAFSA. *Faculty research:* Producing, screenwriting, directing, cinematography, editing. *Unit head:* Reb Braddock, Interim Dean, 850-644-0453, Fax: 850-644-2626. *Application contact:* Gloria McElroy, Staff Director of Admissions and Recruitment, 850-644-8524, Fax: 850-644-2626, E-mail: gmcelroy@fsu.edu.
Website: http://film.fsu.edu/

**See Display on page 216 and Close-Up on page 225.**

**Full Sail University,** Creative Writing Master of Fine Arts Program - Online, Winter Park, FL 32792-7437. Offers MFA. *Program availability:* Online learning.

**George Mason University,** College of Humanities and Social Sciences, Department of English, Program in Creative Writing, Fairfax, VA 22030. Offers MFA. *Faculty:* 13 full-time (7 women), 1 (woman) part-time/adjunct. *Students:* 63 full-time (40 women), 24 part-time (19 women); includes 10 minority (1 Black or African American, non-Hispanic/Latino; 3 Asian, non-Hispanic/Latino; 3 Hispanic/Latino; 3 Two or more races, non-Hispanic/Latino). Average age 30. 80 applicants, 78% accepted, 21 enrolled. In 2016, 22 master's awarded. *Degree requirements:* For master's, one foreign language, thesis, exam or project. *Entrance requirements:* For master's, expanded goals statement; 2 letters of recommendation; portfolio; official transcripts. Additional exam requirements/recommendations for international students: Required—TOEFL (minimum score 575 paper-based; 88 iBT), IELTS (minimum score 6.5), PTE (minimum score 59). *Application deadline:* For fall admission, 1/2 priority date for domestic students. Application fee: $75 ($80 for international students). Electronic applications accepted. *Expenses:* Tuition, state resident: full-time $10,628; part-time $443 per credit. Tuition, nonresident: full-time $29,306; part-time $1221 per credit. *Required fees:* $3096; $129 per credit. Tuition and fees vary according to program. *Financial support:* In 2016–17, 53 students received support, including 1 fellowship (averaging $7,895 per year), 3 research assistantships with tuition reimbursements available (averaging $13,575 per year), 50 teaching assistantships with tuition reimbursements available (averaging $13,353 per year); career-related internships or fieldwork, Federal Work-Study, scholarships/grants, unspecified assistantships, and health care benefits (for full-time research or teaching assistantship recipients) also available. Support available to part-time students. Financial award application deadline: 3/1; financial award applicants required to submit FAFSA. *Faculty research:* British Romantic poetry and literary celebrity, Arab feminist novelists in the West, masculinity and African-American culture, public rhetoric and the South African Truth Commission, the origins of children's

literature in eighteenth and nineteenth century Britain. *Unit head:* William Miller, Director, 703-993-2763, Fax: 703-993-1161, E-mail: wmiller@gmu.edu. *Application contact:* Jay Patel, Graduate Coordinator, 703-993-1180, Fax: 703-993-1161, E-mail: jpatel2@gmu.edu.
Website: http://creativewriting.gmu.edu/

**Georgia College & State University,** Graduate School, College of Arts and Sciences, Department of English and Rhetoric, Program in Creative Writing, Milledgeville, GA 31061. Offers MFA. *Program availability:* Part-time, evening/weekend. *Students:* 12 full-time (9 women), 16 part-time (10 women); includes 6 minority (2 Black or African American, non-Hispanic/Latino; 1 Asian, non-Hispanic/Latino; 2 Hispanic/Latino; 1 Two or more races, non-Hispanic/Latino). Average age 32. 49 applicants, 55% accepted, 11 enrolled. In 2016, 9 master's awarded. *Degree requirements:* For master's, thesis, complete program in no more than 4 years. *Entrance requirements:* For master's, writing portfolio, letters of recommendation, statement of purpose, transcript. *Application deadline:* For fall admission, 1/21 priority date for domestic students. Applications are processed on a rolling basis. Application fee: $40. Electronic applications accepted. *Expenses:* $288 per credit hour in-state, $1,027 per credit hour out-of-state; $1,990 per year full-time fees. *Financial support:* In 2016–17, 24 students received support. Unspecified assistantships available. Support available to part-time students. Financial award application deadline: 3/1; financial award applicants required to submit FAFSA. *Unit head:* Dr. Allen Gee, Coordinator, 478-445-3509, E-mail: mfa@gcsu.edu. *Application contact:* Kate Marshall, Graduate Admissions Coordinator, 478-445-1184, Fax: 478-445-1336, E-mail: grad-admit@gcsu.edu.
Website: http://catalog.gcsu.edu/en/2015-2016/Graduate-Catalog/College-of-Arts-and-Sciences/Master-of-Fine-Arts-in-Creative-Writing

**Georgia State University,** College of Arts and Sciences, Department of English, Program in Creative Writing, Atlanta, GA 30302-3083. Offers creative writing (PhD); fiction (MA, MFA); poetry (MA, MFA). *Program availability:* Part-time. *Degree requirements:* For master's, one foreign language, comprehensive exam, thesis, 27 hours of coursework plus 6 hours of thesis credit; for doctorate, one foreign language, comprehensive exam, thesis/dissertation, 30-39 hours of coursework plus 20 hours of thesis credit. *Entrance requirements:* For master's and doctorate, GRE. Additional exam requirements/recommendations for international students: Required—TOEFL (minimum score 550 paper-based; 80 iBT). *Application deadline:* For fall admission, 1/15 for domestic and international students. Application fee: $50. Electronic applications accepted. *Expenses:* Tuition, state resident: full-time $6876; part-time $382 per credit hour. Tuition, nonresident: full-time $22,374; part-time $1243 per credit hour. *Required fees:* $2128; $1064 per term. Part-time tuition and fees vary according to course load and program. *Financial support:* In 2016–17, research assistantships with full tuition reimbursements (averaging $6,000 per year), teaching assistantships with full tuition reimbursements (averaging $15,000 per year) were awarded; unspecified assistantships also available. *Faculty research:* Poetry writing, fiction writing, contemporary poetry, contemporary fiction, form and theory of fiction and poetry. *Unit head:* Dr. Josh Russell, Co-Director of the Creative Writing Program, 404-413-5800, Fax: 404-413-5830, E-mail: josh@gsu.edu.
Website: http://www.english.gsu.edu

**Goddard College,** Graduate Division, Master of Fine Arts in Creative Writing Program, Plainfield, VT 05667-9432. Offers MFA. Program residency available in Plainfield, VT or Port Townsend, WA. *Program availability:* Online learning. *Degree requirements:* For master's, thesis, completed full-length manuscript, teaching practicum, 3 critical papers, annotations of 45 to 60 literary works. *Entrance requirements:* For master's, statement of purpose, preliminary bibliography, creative portfolio, three letters of recommendation. Electronic applications accepted. *Expenses:* Contact institution.

**Goucher College,** MA and MFA Programs, Baltimore, MD 21204-2794. Offers arts administration (MA); creative nonfiction (MFA); cultural sustainability (MA); digital arts (MA, MFA); environmental studies (MA); historic preservation (MA); management (MA). *Program availability:* Part-time, evening/weekend, blended/hybrid learning. *Faculty:* 6 full-time (4 women), 100 part-time/adjunct (56 women). *Students:* 70 full-time (50 women), 69 part-time (52 women); includes 15 minority (7 Black or African American, non-Hispanic/Latino; 1 American Indian or Alaska Native, non-Hispanic/Latino; 1 Asian, non-Hispanic/Latino; 4 Hispanic/Latino; 2 Two or more races, non-Hispanic/Latino), 2 international. 74 applicants, 88% accepted, 42 enrolled. In 2016, 83 master's awarded. *Degree requirements:* For master's, thesis, e-portfolio. *Entrance requirements:* For master's, digital portfolio (for MA, MFA in digital arts); writing sample (for MFA in creative nonfiction). Additional exam requirements/recommendations for international students: Required—TOEFL (minimum score 550 paper-based; 80 iBT). *Application deadline:* Applications are processed on a rolling basis. Application fee: $75. Electronic applications accepted. *Expenses:* Contact institution. *Financial support:* Scholarships/grants and unspecified assistantships available. Financial award application deadline: 4/15; financial award applicants required to submit FAFSA. *Unit head:* Leslie Rubinkowski, Assistant Provost, 410-337-6200, E-mail: leslie.rubinkowski@goucher.edu. *Application contact:* Shelby Hillers, Admissions Coordinator, 410-337-6200, Fax: 410-337-6200, E-mail: shelby.hillers@goucher.edu.
Website: http://www.goucher.edu/grad

**Hamline University,** College of Liberal Arts, St. Paul, MN 55104-1284. Offers creative writing (MFA); creative writing for children and young adults (MFA). *Program availability:* Part-time, evening/weekend. *Faculty:* 9 full-time (8 women), 6 part-time/adjunct (5 women). *Students:* 89 full-time (65 women), 75 part-time (52 women); includes 14 minority (1 Black or African American, non-Hispanic/Latino; 1 American Indian or Alaska Native, non-Hispanic/Latino; 4 Asian, non-Hispanic/Latino; 3 Hispanic/Latino; 5 Two or more races, non-Hispanic/Latino), 2 international. Average age 37. 51 applicants, 55% accepted, 12 enrolled. In 2016, 46 master's awarded. *Degree requirements:* For master's, thesis. *Entrance requirements:* For master's, letters of recommendation, official transcripts, personal statement, resume. Additional exam requirements/recommendations for international students: Required—TOEFL (minimum score 550 paper-based; 80 iBT), IELTS (minimum score 6.5). *Application deadline:* For fall admission, 6/1 for domestic and international students; for spring admission, 11/1 for domestic students, 10/1 for international students; for summer admission, 3/1 for domestic students, 2/1 for international students. Applications are processed on a rolling basis. Application fee: $0 ($100 for international students). Electronic applications accepted. *Expenses:* Contact institution. *Financial support:* Federal Work-Study and scholarships/grants available. Support available to part-time students. Financial award applicants required to submit FAFSA. *Unit head:* Dr. Marcela Kostihova, Interim Dean, 651-523-2206, Fax: 651-523-3055, E-mail: cladean@hamline.edu. *Application contact:* Shawn Skoog, Director of Graduate Admission and Recruitment, 651-523-2900, Fax: 651-523-3058, E-mail: gradprog@hamline.edu.
Website: http://www.hamline.edu/cla

**Hofstra University,** College of Liberal Arts and Sciences, Programs in Creative Writing and English Literature, Hempstead, NY 11549. Offers MFA. *Program availability:* Part-time. *Students:* 13 full-time (7 women), 11 part-time (8 women); includes 4 minority (2 Asian, non-Hispanic/Latino; 2 Hispanic/Latino), 1 international. Average age 31. 26 applicants, 81% accepted, 6 enrolled. In 2016, 16 master's awarded. *Degree requirements:* For master's, thesis optional, minimum GPA of 3.0. *Entrance requirements*

## Writing

*requirements:* For master's, writing sample, essay, minimum GPA of 3.0 in literature courses. Additional exam requirements/recommendations for international students: Required—TOEFL (minimum score 550 paper-based; 80 iBT). *Application deadline:* Applications are processed on a rolling basis. Application fee: $75. Electronic applications accepted. *Expenses: Tuition:* Full-time $1240. *Required fees:* $970. Tuition and fees vary according to program. *Financial support:* In 2016–17, 13 students received support, including 12 fellowships with full and partial tuition reimbursements available (averaging $4,182 per year), 1 research assistantship with full and partial tuition reimbursement available (averaging $10,463 per year); career-related internships or fieldwork, Federal Work-Study, institutionally sponsored loans, scholarships/grants, tuition waivers (full and partial), and unspecified assistantships also available. Support available to part-time students. Financial award applicants required to submit FAFSA. *Faculty research:* English lyric poetry; Victorian poets and poetics; creative nonfiction; historical research and current politics through the lens of fiction; medieval and monastic studies. *Unit head:* Dr. Stephen Russell, Program Director, 516-463-6284, Fax: 516-463-6395, E-mail: stephen.russell@hofstra.edu. *Application contact:* Sunil Samuel, Assistant Vice President of Admissions, 516-463-4723, Fax: 516-463-4664, E-mail: graduateadmission@hofstra.edu.
Website: http://www.hofstra.edu/hclas

**Hollins University,** Graduate Programs, Program in Children's Literature, Roanoke, VA 24020. Offers children's book writing and illustrating (MFA); children's literature (MA, MFA). Program offered during summer only. *Program availability:* Part-time. *Faculty:* 2 full-time (both women), 8 part-time/adjunct (7 women). *Students:* 40 full-time (38 women), 6 part-time (5 women); includes 6 minority (1 Black or African American, non-Hispanic/Latino; 1 Asian, non-Hispanic/Latino; 3 Hispanic/Latino; 1 Two or more races, non-Hispanic/Latino). Average age 35. 24 applicants, 96% accepted, 10 enrolled. In 2016, 11 master's awarded. *Degree requirements:* For master's, one foreign language, comprehensive exam, thesis. *Entrance requirements:* For master's, transcripts, letters of recommendation, portfolio, personal statement of educational objectives. Additional exam requirements/recommendations for international students: Required—TOEFL (minimum score 550 paper-based; 79 iBT), IELTS (minimum score 6.5). *Application deadline:* For summer admission, 2/15 for domestic and international students. Application fee: $40. Electronic applications accepted. *Expenses:* Contact institution. *Financial support:* Fellowships, Federal Work-Study, and scholarships/grants available. Support available to part-time students. Financial award application deadline: 2/15; financial award applicants required to submit FAFSA. *Faculty research:* Fantasy, children's film, young adult fiction, gender studies, mythology and folk tales, children's poetry, picture books. *Unit head:* Amanda Cockrell, Director, 540-362-6024, Fax: 540-362-6642, E-mail: acockrell@hollins.edu. *Application contact:* Cathy S. Koon, Manager of Graduate Services, 540-362-6326, Fax: 540-362-6288, E-mail: ckoon@hollins.edu.

**Hollins University,** Graduate Programs, Program in Creative Writing, Roanoke, VA 24020. Offers MFA. *Faculty:* 7 full-time (4 women). *Students:* 23 full-time (19 women); includes 5 minority (1 Black or African American, non-Hispanic/Latino; 1 Asian, non-Hispanic/Latino; 3 Hispanic/Latino). Average age 28. 87 applicants, 24% accepted, 11 enrolled. In 2016, 12 master's awarded. *Degree requirements:* For master's, comprehensive exam, thesis. *Entrance requirements:* For master's, portfolio of original work, 3 letters of recommendation, undergraduate transcript, statement of educational objectives. Additional exam requirements/recommendations for international students: Required—TOEFL (minimum score 550 paper-based; 80 iBT), IELTS (minimum score 6.5). *Application deadline:* For fall admission, 1/6 for domestic and international students. Application fee: $40. Electronic applications accepted. *Expenses:* Contact institution. *Financial support:* In 2016–17, 23 students received support, including 6 teaching assistantships; fellowships with tuition reimbursements available, scholarships/grants, tuition waivers (full), and unspecified assistantships also available. Support available to part-time students. Financial award application deadline: 1/6; financial award applicants required to submit FAFSA. *Faculty research:* Poetry, fiction, creative nonfiction, literary criticism, literary theory. *Unit head:* Thorpe Moeckel, Director, 540-362-6427, Fax: 540-362-6097, E-mail: tmoeckel@hollins.edu. *Application contact:* Cathy S. Koon, Manager of Graduate Programs, 540-362-6326, Fax: 540-362-6288, E-mail: ckoon@hollins.edu.
Website: http://www.hollins.edu/academics/graduate-degrees/creative-writing-mfa/

**Hollins University,** Graduate Programs, Program in Playwriting, Roanoke, VA 24020. Offers new play directing (Certificate); new play performance (Certificate); playwriting (MFA). *Program availability:* Part-time. *Degree requirements:* For master's, comprehensive exam, thesis. *Entrance requirements:* For master's, letters of recommendation, bachelor's degree, undergraduate transcripts, manuscript. Additional exam requirements/recommendations for international students: Required—TOEFL (minimum score 550 paper-based; 80 iBT), IELTS (minimum score 6.5). *Application deadline:* For summer admission, 2/15 priority date for domestic and international students. Application fee: $40. *Expenses:* $830 per credit hour. *Financial support:* Fellowships and scholarships/grants available. Financial award application deadline: 2/15. *Unit head:* Todd Ristau, Director, 540-362-6386, E-mail: tristau@hollins.edu. *Application contact:* Cathy S. Koon, Manager of Graduate Programs, 540-362-6326, Fax: 540-362-6288, E-mail: ckoon@hollins.edu.
Website: http://www.hollins.edu/academics/graduate-degrees/playwriting/

**Hollins University,** Graduate Programs, Program in Screenwriting and Film Studies, Roanoke, VA 24020. Offers screenwriting (MFA); screenwriting and film studies (MA). Program offered during summer only. *Program availability:* Part-time. *Degree requirements:* For master's, one foreign language, comprehensive exam, thesis. *Entrance requirements:* For master's, letters of recommendation, portfolio. Additional exam requirements/recommendations for international students: Required—TOEFL (minimum score 550 paper-based; 80 iBT), IELTS (minimum score 6.5). *Application deadline:* For summer admission, 2/15 for domestic and international students. Application fee: $40. Electronic applications accepted. *Expenses:* $830 per credit hour. *Financial support:* Fellowships, Federal Work-Study, institutionally sponsored loans, and scholarships/grants available. Support available to part-time students. Financial award application deadline: 2/15; financial award applicants required to submit FAFSA. *Faculty research:* Censorship, minorities in film, writing for television, new media. *Unit head:* Dr. Tim Albaugh, Director, 540-362-6575, E-mail: hugrad@hollins.edu. *Application contact:* Cathy S. Koon, Manager of Graduate Programs, 540-362-6326, Fax: 540-362-6288, E-mail: ckoon@hollins.edu.
Website: https://www.hollins.edu/academics/graduate-degrees/mfa-screenwriting-film-studies/

**Holy Names University,** Graduate Division, Master of Arts in English: The Writer's Craft Program, Oakland, CA 94619-1699. Offers MA. *Students:* 3 full-time (2 women), 2 part-time (1 woman); includes 4 minority (2 Black or African American, non-Hispanic/Latino; 2 Asian, non-Hispanic/Latino). Average age 35. 3 applicants, 33% accepted. *Entrance requirements:* For master's, two recommendations, writing sample. Additional exam requirements/recommendations for international students: Required—TOEFL (minimum score 550 paper-based; 79 iBT). *Application deadline:* For fall admission, 8/1 priority date for domestic students, 7/15 for international students; for spring admission, 12/1 priority date for domestic students, 12/1 for international students; for summer admission, 5/5 for international students. Applications are processed on a rolling basis.

Application fee: $65. Electronic applications accepted. Application fee is waived when completed online. *Expenses: Tuition:* Full-time $17,532; part-time $974 per credit hour. *Required fees:* $500; $250 per credit hour. *Financial support:* Career-related internships or fieldwork, Federal Work-Study, scholarships/grants, and unspecified assistantships available. Financial award application deadline: 3/2; financial award applicants required to submit FAFSA. *Unit head:* Dr. Anne F. Walker, Director of The Writer's Craft, 510-436-1507, E-mail: awalker@hnu.edu. *Application contact:* Graduate Admissions Office, 800-430-1321, Fax: 510-436-1325, E-mail: graduateadmissions@hnu.edu.
Website: http://www.hnu.edu/academics/graduatePrograms/english.html

**Hunter College of the City University of New York,** Graduate School, School of Arts and Sciences, Department of English, Program in Creative Writing, New York, NY 10065-5085. Offers fiction (MFA); memoir (MFA); poetry (MFA). *Program availability:* Part-time, evening/weekend. *Students:* 37 part-time (25 women); includes 6 minority (2 Black or African American, non-Hispanic/Latino; 2 Asian, non-Hispanic/Latino; 2 Hispanic/Latino), 1 international. Average age 32. 447 applicants, 4% accepted, 19 enrolled. In 2016, 10 master's awarded. *Degree requirements:* For master's, thesis. *Entrance requirements:* For master's, creative writing manuscript (up to 10 pages of poetry or 25-30 pages of fiction or nonfiction), nonfiction proposal (for nonfiction applicants only), statement of purpose. *Application deadline:* For fall admission, 2/1 for domestic and international students. Electronic applications accepted. *Financial support:* Fellowships, Federal Work-Study, and tuition waivers (partial) available. Support available to part-time students. Financial award application deadline: 4/15. *Unit head:* Peter Carey, Executive Director, 212-772-5074, E-mail: pcarey@hunter.cuny.edu. *Application contact:* Elena Georgiou, Coordinator, 212-772-5164, Fax: 212-772-5076, E-mail: egeorgio@hunter.cuny.edu.
Website: http://www.hunter.cuny.edu/creativewriting

**Hunter College of the City University of New York,** Graduate School, School of Arts and Sciences, Department of Theatre, Program in Playwriting, New York, NY 10065-5085. Offers MFA. *Students:* 10 part-time (6 women); includes 1 minority (Black or African American, non-Hispanic/Latino), 1 international. Average age 30. 24 applicants, 21% accepted, 5 enrolled. In 2016, 2 master's awarded. *Entrance requirements:* For master's, GRE, bachelor's degree, two letters of recommendation, full-length or one-act play of at least 40 pages (both hard copy and PDF attachment). Additional exam requirements/recommendations for international students: Required—TOEFL (minimum score 550 paper-based; 60 iBT). *Application deadline:* For fall admission, 4/1 for domestic students. *Unit head:* Brighde Mullins, Director, 212-362-0219, E-mail: bm1882@hunter.cuny.edu. *Application contact:* Milena Solo, Graduate Admissions Director, 212-772-4480, E-mail: admissions@hunter.cuny.edu.
Website: http://www.hunter.cuny.edu/theatre/graduate-program/m.f.a.-in-playwriting

**Illinois State University,** Graduate School, College of Arts and Sciences, Department of English, Program in Writing, Normal, IL 61790-2200. Offers Postbaccalaureate Certificate.

**Indiana State University,** College of Graduate and Professional Studies, College of Arts and Sciences, Department of English, Terre Haute, IN 47809. Offers British and American literature (MA); English (MA); writing (MA). *Program availability:* Part-time, evening/weekend. *Degree requirements:* For master's, one foreign language, thesis optional. *Entrance requirements:* For master's, minimum GPA of 2.75 in all English courses above freshman level. Additional exam requirements/recommendations for international students: Required—TOEFL (minimum score 550 paper-based). Electronic applications accepted.

**Indiana University Bloomington,** University Graduate School, College of Arts and Sciences, Department of English, Bloomington, IN 47405. Offers creative writing (MA, MFA), including fiction (MFA), poetry (MFA); literature (PhD); rhetoric (PhD). *Faculty:* 51 full-time (23 women). *Students:* 132 full-time (87 women), 2 part-time (1 woman); includes 24 minority (4 Black or African American, non-Hispanic/Latino; 11 Asian, non-Hispanic/Latino; 3 Hispanic/Latino; 6 Two or more races, non-Hispanic/Latino), 8 international. Average age 30. 273 applicants, 18% accepted, 21 enrolled. In 2016, 16 master's, 16 doctorates awarded. *Degree requirements:* For master's, 30-36 credit hours plus one language proficiency (for MA); 60 credit hours plus thesis (for MFA); for doctorate, thesis/dissertation, qualifying exam; 90 credit hours; 2nd language proficiency or one language only if acquired at in-depth level. *Entrance requirements:* For master's, GRE General Test, GRE Subject Test (for all but MFA and MA in creative writing), minimum GPA of 3.5; for doctorate, GRE General Test, GRE Subject Test, minimum GPA of 3.7. Additional exam requirements/recommendations for international students: Required—TOEFL (minimum score 550 paper-based; 79 iBT), IELTS (minimum score 6.5). *Application deadline:* For fall admission, 1/2 priority date for domestic students, 12/1 for international students. Application fee: $55 ($65 for international students). Electronic applications accepted. *Financial support:* In 2016–17, 8 students received support, including 8 fellowships with full and partial tuition reimbursements available (averaging $18,000 per year), 98 teaching assistantships with full tuition reimbursements available (averaging $15,750 per year); health care benefits also available. Financial award application deadline: 2/1. *Unit head:* Dr. Patricia Ingham, Chair, 812-855-0521, Fax: 812-855-9535, E-mail: pingham@indiana.edu. *Application contact:* Rae Greiner, Director of Graduate Studies, 812-855-9536, Fax: 812-855-9535, E-mail: drgreine@indiana.edu.
Website: http://www.indiana.edu/~engweb/

**Indiana University–Purdue University Indianapolis,** School of Liberal Arts, Department of English, Indianapolis, IN 46202. Offers English (MA); teaching English to speakers of other languages (TESOL) (Certificate); teaching writing (Certificate). *Entrance requirements:* For master's, GRE. Additional exam requirements/recommendations for international students: Required—TOEFL.

**Indiana University South Bend,** College of Liberal Arts and Sciences, South Bend, IN 46634-7111. Offers advanced computer programming (Graduate Certificate); applied informatics (Graduate Certificate); applied mathematics and computer science (MS); behavior modification (Graduate Certificate); computer applications (Graduate Certificate); computer programming (Graduate Certificate); correctional management and supervision (Graduate Certificate); English (MA); health systems management (Graduate Certificate); international studies (Graduate Certificate); liberal studies (MLS); nonprofit management (Graduate Certificate); paralegal studies (Graduate Certificate); professional writing (Graduate Certificate); public affairs (MPA); public management (Graduate Certificate); social and cultural diversity (Graduate Certificate); strategic sustainability leadership (Graduate Certificate); technology for administration (Graduate Certificate). *Program availability:* Part-time, evening/weekend. *Faculty:* 79 full-time (33 women). *Students:* 31 full-time (11 women), 92 part-time (53 women); includes 28 minority (9 Black or African American, non-Hispanic/Latino; 8 Asian, non-Hispanic/Latino; 5 Hispanic/Latino; 6 Two or more races, non-Hispanic/Latino), 19 international. Average age 38. 51 applicants, 84% accepted, 31 enrolled. In 2016, 30 master's, 6 other advanced degrees awarded. *Degree requirements:* For master's, variable foreign language requirement, thesis (for some programs). *Entrance requirements:* For master's, minimum GPA of 3.0. Additional exam requirements/recommendations for international students: Required—TOEFL (minimum score 550 paper-based; 80 iBT). *Application deadline:* For fall admission, 7/31 priority date for domestic students, 7/1 priority date for international students; for spring admission, 3/31 priority date for

domestic students, 11/1 priority date for international students. Applications are processed on a rolling basis. Application fee: $40 ($60 for international students). *Expenses:* $276.98 per credit hour in-state; $652.54 per credit hour out-of-state. *Financial support:* In 2016–17, 5 teaching assistantships were awarded; Federal Work-Study also available. Support available to part-time students. Financial award application deadline: 3/10. *Faculty research:* Artificial intelligence, bioinformatics, English language and literature, creative writing, computer networks. *Total annual research expenditures:* $127,000. *Unit head:* Dr. Elizabeth E. Dunn, Dean, 574-520-4290, E-mail: elizdunn@iusb.edu. *Application contact:* Admissions Counselor, 574-520-4839, Fax: 574-520-4834, E-mail: graduate@iusb.edu.
Website: https://www.iusb.edu/clas/

**Institute of American Indian Arts,** Low Residency MFA in Creative Writing Program, Santa Fe, NM 87508. Offers MFA. *Program availability:* Low-residency. *Students:* 58 full-time (34 women), 2 part-time (both women); includes 38 minority (1 Black or African American, non-Hispanic/Latino; 27 American Indian or Alaska Native, non-Hispanic/Latino; 7 Hispanic/Latino; 3 Two or more races, non-Hispanic/Latino). In 2016, 26 master's awarded. *Entrance requirements:* For master's, sample of creative work, essay, sample craft or scholarly essay, two letters of recommendation, all official college transcripts. *Application deadline:* For fall admission, 1/31 for domestic and international students. Application fee: $25. Electronic applications accepted. *Expenses:* Tuition, state resident: full-time $10,680; part-time $445 per semester hour. Tuition, nonresident: full-time $10,680; part-time $445 per semester hour. *Required fees:* $720; $360 per semester. *Financial support:* Scholarships/grants available. Financial award application deadline: 1/31; financial award applicants required to submit FAFSA. *Unit head:* Jon Davis, Director, Low Residency MFA in Creative Writing, 505-424-2365, Fax: 505-424-3030, E-mail: mfa@iaia.edu.
Website: https://iaia.edu/academics/degree-programs/creative-writing-mfa/

**Iowa State University of Science and Technology,** Department of English, Ames, IA 50011. Offers creative writing (MFA); English (MA); rhetoric and professional communication (PhD). *Degree requirements:* For master's, thesis or alternative; for doctorate, thesis/dissertation. *Entrance requirements:* For master's, GRE General Test, sample of written work, resume, portfolio in creative writing; for doctorate, GRE General Test, sample of written work, resume. Additional exam requirements/recommendations for international students: Required—TOEFL (minimum score 600 paper-based; 100 iBT), IELTS (minimum score 7). *Application deadline:* For fall admission, 1/5 priority date for domestic and international students). Application fee: $60 ($90 for international students). Electronic applications accepted. *Faculty research:* Creative writing, literature, rhetoric, composition and professional communication, teaching English as a second language, applied linguistics. *Application contact:* Teresa Smiley, Application Contact, 515-294-2477, Fax: 515-294-6814, E-mail: englgrad@iastate.edu.
Website: http://www.engl.iastate.edu/resources/graduate-studies/

**Iowa State University of Science and Technology,** Program in Creative Writing and Environment, Ames, IA 50011. Offers MFA. *Entrance requirements:* For master's, GRE, official academic transcripts, resume, three letters of recommendation, statement of personal goals, writing samples. Additional exam requirements/recommendations for international students: Required—TOEFL (minimum score 600 paper-based; 100 iBT), IELTS (minimum score 7). *Application deadline:* For fall admission, 1/5 for domestic students. Application fee: $60 ($90 for international students). Electronic applications accepted. *Application contact:* Teresa Smiley, Application Contact, 515-294-2477, Fax: 515-294-6814, E-mail: englgrad@iastate.edu.
Website: http://engl.iastate.edu/resources/graduate-studies/

**Ithaca College,** Roy H. Park School of Communications, Program in Image Text, Ithaca, NY 14850. Offers MFA. *Program availability:* Part-time-only. *Faculty:* 3 full-time (1 woman). *Students:* 8 part-time (3 women); includes 1 minority (Hispanic/Latino). Average age 28. 15 applicants, 87% accepted, 8 enrolled. *Degree requirements:* For master's, thesis optional. *Entrance requirements:* Additional exam requirements/recommendations for international students: Required—TOEFL (minimum score 550 paper-based; 80 iBT). *Application deadline:* For fall admission, 3/15 for domestic and international students; for spring admission, 12/1 for domestic and international students. Applications are processed on a rolling basis. Application fee: $40. Electronic applications accepted. *Expenses:* Contact institution. *Financial support:* In 2016–17, 7 students received support, including 7 fellowships (averaging $5,089 per year); career-related internships or fieldwork, Federal Work-Study, and scholarships/grants also available. Support available to part-time students. Financial award application deadline: 3/1; financial award applicants required to submit CSS PROFILE or FAFSA. *Unit head:* Nicholas Muellner, Co-Director, 607- 274-1984, E-mail: nmuellner@ithaca.edu. *Application contact:* Nicole Eversley Bradwell, Director, Office of Admission, 607-274-3124, Fax: 607-274-1263, E-mail: admission@ithaca.edu.
Website: http://www.ithaca.edu/gradprograms/image-text

**James Madison University,** The Graduate School, College of Arts and Letters, Program in Writing, Rhetoric, and Technical Communication, Harrisonburg, VA 22802. Offers MA, MS. *Program availability:* Part-time. *Faculty:* 20 full-time (11 women), 1 (woman) part-time/adjunct. *Students:* 10 full-time (9 women), 3 part-time (2 women); includes 3 minority (1 Asian, non-Hispanic/Latino; 1 Hispanic/Latino; 1 Two or more races, non-Hispanic/Latino), 1 international. Average age 30. 12 applicants, 83% accepted, 8 enrolled. In 2016, 6 master's awarded. Application fee: $55. Electronic applications accepted. *Financial support:* In 2016–17, 15 students received support, including 3 teaching assistantships with full tuition reimbursements available (averaging $9,284 per year); fellowships, career-related internships or fieldwork, Federal Work-Study, and 7 assistantships (averaging $7911) also available. Financial award application deadline: 3/1; financial award applicants required to submit FAFSA. *Unit head:* Dr. Traci A. Zimmerman, Director of the School of Writing, Rhetoric and Technical Communication, 540-568-2334, E-mail: zimmerta@jmu.edu. *Application contact:* Lynette D. Michael, Director of Graduate Admissions, 540-568-6131 Ext. 6395, Fax: 540-568-7860, E-mail: michaeld@jmu.edu.
Website: http://www.jmu.edu/wrtc/

**Johns Hopkins University,** Zanvyl Krieger School of Arts and Sciences, Advanced Academic Programs, Program in Writing, Washington, DC 20036. Offers science writing (MA, Certificate); writing (MA). *Program availability:* Part-time, evening/weekend. *Degree requirements:* For master's, thesis. *Entrance requirements:* For master's, minimum GPA of 3.0, writing samples. Additional exam requirements/recommendations for international students: Required—TOEFL (minimum score 600 paper-based; 100 iBT). Electronic applications accepted.

**Johns Hopkins University,** Zanvyl Krieger School of Arts and Sciences, The Writing Seminars, Baltimore, MD 21218. Offers fiction writing (MFA); poetry (MFA). *Degree requirements:* For master's, one foreign language, thesis, foreign language exam (MFA). *Entrance requirements:* For master's, GRE General Test, GRE Subject Test (recommended), foreign language exam, sample of written work, 3 letters of recommendation, transcripts of all college/university course work. Additional exam requirements/recommendations for international students: Required—TOEFL (minimum score 600 paper-based; 100 iBT). Electronic applications accepted. *Faculty research:* Contemporary fiction and poetry, film history, literary criticism, psychoanalysis.

**Kean University,** College of Liberal Arts, Program in English Writing Studies, Union, NJ 07083. Offers MA. *Program availability:* Part-time. *Faculty:* 11 full-time (6 women). *Students:* 6 full-time (all women), 13 part-time (10 women); includes 8 minority (5 Black or African American, non-Hispanic/Latino; 3 Hispanic/Latino). Average age 33. 10 applicants, 80% accepted, 6 enrolled. In 2016, 8 master's awarded. *Degree requirements:* For master's, thesis. *Entrance requirements:* For master's, GRE General Test, minimum GPA of 3.0, official transcripts from all institutions attended, two letters of recommendation, personal statement, professional resume/curriculum vitae. Additional exam requirements/recommendations for international students: Required—TOEFL (minimum score 550 paper-based; 79 iBT), IELTS (minimum score 6.5). *Application deadline:* For fall admission, 6/1 for domestic and international students; for spring admission, 12/8 for domestic and international students. Applications are processed on a rolling basis. Application fee: $75. Electronic applications accepted. *Expenses:* Tuition, state resident: full-time $13,156; part-time $640 per credit. Tuition, nonresident: full-time $17,831; part-time $785 per credit. *Required fees:* $3316; $151 per credit. Tuition and fees vary according to course level, course load, degree level and program. *Financial support:* Scholarships/grants and unspecified assistantships available. Financial award applicants required to submit FAFSA. *Unit head:* Dr. Mia Zamora, Program Coordinator, 908-737-0385, E-mail: schandler@kean.edu. *Application contact:* Amy Clark, Program Assistant, 908-737-7100, E-mail: grad-adm@kean.edu.
Website: http://grad.kean.edu/masters-programs/english-writing-studies

**Kennesaw State University,** College of Humanities and Social Sciences, Program in Professional Writing, Kennesaw, GA 30144. Offers MAPW. *Program availability:* Part-time, evening/weekend. *Degree requirements:* For master's, thesis optional. *Entrance requirements:* For master's, GRE General Test, minimum GPA of 2.5, writing sample. Additional exam requirements/recommendations for international students: Required—TOEFL (minimum score 550 paper-based; 80 iBT), IELTS (minimum score 6.5). Electronic applications accepted.

**Kent State University,** College of Arts and Sciences, Department of English, Kent, OH 44242-0001. Offers creative writing (MFA); English (MA, PhD); English for teachers (MA); literature and writing (MA); rhetoric and composition (PhD); teaching English as a second language (MA). MFA program offered jointly with Cleveland State University, The University of Akron, and Youngstown State University. *Program availability:* Part-time. *Faculty:* 45 full-time (29 women). *Students:* 111 full-time (75 women), 19 part-time (13 women); includes 8 minority (3 Black or African American, non-Hispanic/Latino; 1 Asian, non-Hispanic/Latino; 2 Hispanic/Latino; 2 Two or more races, non-Hispanic/Latino), 27 international. Average age 30. 98 applicants, 61% accepted, 19 enrolled. In 2016, 30 master's, 8 doctorates awarded. *Degree requirements:* For master's, one foreign language, thesis (for some programs), final portfolio, final exam, or thesis (for MA in teaching English as a second language); for doctorate, one foreign language, comprehensive exam, thesis/dissertation. *Entrance requirements:* For master's and doctorate, GRE General Test, statement of purpose, 3 letters of recommendation, writing sample or undergraduate/graduate paper, transcripts. Additional exam requirements/recommendations for international students: Required—TOEFL (minimum score of 600 paper-based, 100 iBT), IELTS (minimum score of 7.0), Michigan English Language Assessment Battery (minimum score of 85), or PTE (minimum score of 68). *Application deadline:* For fall admission, 1/15 for domestic and international students. Applications are processed on a rolling basis. Application fee: $45 ($70 for international students). Electronic applications accepted. *Expenses:* Tuition, state resident: full-time $10,864; part-time $495 per credit hour. Tuition, nonresident: full-time $18,380; part-time $837 per credit hour. *Financial support:* Fellowships with full tuition reimbursements, teaching assistantships with full tuition reimbursements, and unspecified assistantships available. Financial award application deadline: 1/15. *Unit head:* Dr. Robert Trogdon, Chair, 330-672-2676, E-mail: rtrogdon@kent.edu. *Application contact:* Kevin Floyd, Professor and Graduate Coordinator, 330-672-1708, E-mail: kfloyd@kent.edu.
Website: http://www.kent.edu/english/

**Lake Forest College,** Graduate Program in Liberal Studies, Lake Forest, IL 60045. Offers American studies (MLS); environmental studies (MLS); history (MLS); Medieval and Renaissance art (MLS); philosophy (MLS); Spanish (MLS); writing (MLS). *Program availability:* Part-time, evening/weekend. *Faculty:* 9 full-time (3 women), 1 part-time/adjunct (0 women). *Students:* 1 full-time (0 women), 38 part-time (20 women); includes 5 minority (1 Black or African American, non-Hispanic/Latino; 2 Asian, non-Hispanic/Latino; 2 Hispanic/Latino). Average age 38. 19 applicants, 53% accepted, 7 enrolled. In 2016, 4 master's awarded. *Degree requirements:* For master's, thesis optional, 8 courses, including at least 3 interdisciplinary seminars. *Entrance requirements:* For master's, transcript, essay, interview. Additional exam requirements/recommendations for international students: Required—TOEFL (minimum score 550 paper-based; 83 iBT); Recommended—IELTS (minimum score 6.5). *Application deadline:* For fall admission, 7/15 priority date for domestic students, 6/1 priority date for international students; for spring admission, 12/1 priority date for domestic students, 10/1 priority date for international students. Applications are processed on a rolling basis. Application fee: $30. *Expenses:* $2,600 per course. *Financial support:* In 2016–17, 2 students received support. Partial tuition grants for full-time teachers available. *Faculty research:* Realigning of the international order; Renaissance women artists; literature of Latin Americans in the U.S.; modern Chinese history; environmental biology. *Unit head:* Prof. D. L. LeMahieu, Director, 847-735-5133, Fax: 847-735-6291, E-mail: lemahieu@lakeforest.edu. *Application contact:* Prof. Carol Gayle, Associate Director, 847-735-5083, Fax: 847-735-6291, E-mail: gayle@lakeforest.edu.
Website: http://www.lakeforest.edu/academics/programs/mls/

**La Sierra University,** College of Arts and Sciences, Department of English and Communication, Riverside, CA 92515. Offers communication (MA), including public relations/advertising, theory emphasis; English (MA), including literary emphasis, writing emphasis. *Program availability:* Part-time. *Degree requirements:* For master's, one foreign language. *Entrance requirements:* For master's, GRE General Test.

**Lenoir-Rhyne University,** Graduate Programs, School of Arts and Letters, Program in Writing, Hickory, NC 28601. Offers MA. *Entrance requirements:* For master's, GRE General Test or MAT, essay; resume; minimum GPA of 2.7 undergraduate, 3.0 graduate. Additional exam requirements/recommendations for international students: Required—TOEFL (minimum score 600 paper-based). Electronic applications accepted. *Expenses:* Contact institution.

**Lesley University,** Graduate School of Arts and Social Sciences, Cambridge, MA 02138-2790. Offers clinical mental health counseling (MA), including holistic counseling, school and community counseling, trauma studies; counseling psychology (MA, CAGS), including professional counseling (MA), school counseling (MA); creative writing (MFA); expressive therapies (MA, PhD, CAGS), including art (MA), clinical mental health counseling (MA), dance (MA), expressive therapies (MA), music (MA); independent studies (CAGS); independent study (MA); intercultural relations (MA, CAGS); interdisciplinary studies (MA), including individualized studies, integrative holistic health, mindfulness studies, peace and conflict transformation, trauma sensitive assessment, intervention, and consultation, women's studies; urban environmental leadership (MA). *Program availability:* Part-time, online learning. *Degree requirements:* For master's, internship, practicum, thesis (for expressive therapies); for doctorate, thesis/dissertation,

---

# Writing

arts apprenticeship, field placement; for CAGS, thesis, internship (for counseling psychology, expressive therapies). *Entrance requirements:* For master's, MAT (counseling psychology), interview, writing samples, art portfolio; for doctorate, GRE or MAT, interview, master's degree; for CAGS, interview, master's degree. Additional exam requirements/recommendations for international students: Required—TOEFL (minimum score 550 paper-based; 80 iBT). Electronic applications accepted. *Faculty research:* Psychotherapy and culture; psychotherapy and psychological trauma; women's issues in art, teaching and psychotherapy; community-based art, psycho-spiritual inquiry.

**Lindenwood University,** Graduate Programs, School of Accelerated Degree Programs, St. Charles, MO 63301-1695. Offers administration (MSA), including management, marketing, project management; business administration (MBA); communications (MA), including digital and multimedia, media management, promotions, training and development; criminal justice and administration (MS); healthcare administration (MS); human resource management (MS); information technology (Certificate); managing information security (MS); managing information technology (MS); managing virtualization and cloud computing (MS); writing (MFA). *Program availability:* Part-time, evening/weekend, 100% online. *Faculty:* 16 full-time (7 women), 75 part-time/adjunct (27 women). *Students:* 609 full-time (386 women), 179 part-time (121 women); includes 257 minority (202 Black or African American, non-Hispanic/Latino; 4 American Indian or Alaska Native, non-Hispanic/Latino; 5 Asian, non-Hispanic/Latino; 28 Hispanic/Latino; 1 Native Hawaiian or other Pacific Islander, non-Hispanic/Latino; 17 Two or more races, non-Hispanic/Latino), 28 international. Average age 36. 332 applicants, 70% accepted, 205 enrolled. In 2016, 479 master's awarded. *Degree requirements:* For master's, thesis (for some programs), minimum cumulative GPA of 3.0; for Certificate, minimum cumulative GPA of 3.0. *Entrance requirements:* For master's, resume, personal statement, official undergraduate transcript, minimum undergraduate cumulative GPA of 3.0. Additional exam requirements/recommendations for international students: Required—TOEFL (minimum score 550 paper-based; 80 iBT); Recommended—IELTS (minimum score 6.5). *Application deadline:* For fall admission, 9/26 priority date for domestic and international students; for winter admission, 1/3 priority date for domestic and international students; for spring admission, 3/31 priority date for domestic and international students; for summer admission, 7/3 priority date for domestic and international students. Applications are processed on a rolling basis. Application fee: $30 ($100 for international students). Electronic applications accepted. *Expenses:* Tuition: Full-time $15,672; part-time $453 per credit hour. *Required fees:* $205 per semester. Tuition and fees vary according to course level, course load and degree level. *Financial support:* In 2016–17, 467 students received support. Career-related internships or fieldwork, institutionally sponsored loans, scholarships/grants, tuition waivers (partial), and unspecified assistantships available. Financial award application deadline: 6/30; financial award applicants required to submit FAFSA. *Unit head:* Dr. Gina Ganahl, Dean, Accelerated Degree Programs, 636-949-4501, Fax: 636-949-4505, E-mail: gganahl@lindenwood.edu. *Application contact:* Tyler Kostich, Director, Evening and Graduate Admissions, 636-949-4138, Fax: 636-949-4109, E-mail: adultadmissions@lindenwood.edu.
Website: http://www.lindenwood.edu/academics/academic-schools/school-of-accelerated-degree-programs/

**Lipscomb University,** Program in Film and Creative Media, Nashville, TN 37204-3951. Offers writer/director (MFA); MFA/MBA. *Program availability:* Part-time, evening/weekend. *Faculty:* 5 full-time (1 woman), 4 part-time/adjunct (1 woman). *Students:* 21 full-time (14 women), 6 part-time (5 women); includes 12 minority (10 Black or African American, non-Hispanic/Latino; 1 Hispanic/Latino; 1 Two or more races, non-Hispanic/Latino), 1 international. Average age 30. 21 applicants, 48% accepted, 8 enrolled. In 2016, 7 master's awarded. *Degree requirements:* For master's, professional practicum, portfolio. *Entrance requirements:* For master's, GRE or MAT, 2 references, resume, video portfolio. Additional exam requirements/recommendations for international students: Required—TOEFL (minimum score 570 paper-based; 80 iBT). *Application deadline:* Applications are processed on a rolling basis. Application fee: $50 ($75 for international students). Electronic applications accepted. *Expenses:* $966 per hour. *Financial support:* Unspecified assistantships available. Financial award applicants required to submit FAFSA. *Unit head:* David DeBorde, Director, 615-966-7111, E-mail: david.deborde@lipscomb.edu. *Application contact:* Josh Link, Recruiting and Marketing Coordinator, 615-966-6005, E-mail: josh.link@lipscomb.edu.
Website: http://www.lipscomb.edu/cinematicarts/graduate-programs

**London Metropolitan University,** Graduate Programs, London, United Kingdom. Offers applied psychology (M Sc); architecture (MA); biomedical science (M Sc); blood science (M Sc); cancer pharmacology (M Sc); computer networking and cyber security (M Sc); computing and information systems (M Sc); conference interpreting (MA); counter-terrorism studies (M Sc); creative, digital and professional writing (MA); crime, violence and prevention (M Sc); criminology (M Sc); curating contemporary art (MA); data analytics (M Sc); digital media (MA); early childhood studies (MA); education (MA, Ed D); financial services law, regulation and compliance (LL M); food science (M Sc); forensic psychology (M Sc); health and social care management and policy (M Sc); human nutrition (M Sc); human resource management (MA); human rights and international conflict (MA); information technology (M Sc); intelligence and security studies (M Sc); international oil, gas and energy law (LL M); international relations (MA); interpreting (MA); learning and teaching in higher education (MA); legal practice (LL M); media and entertainment law (LL M); organizational and consumer psychology (M Sc); psychological therapy (M Sc); psychology of mental health (M Sc); public health (M Sc); public policy and management (MPA); security studies (M Sc); social work (M Sc); spatial planning and urban design (MA); sports therapy (M Sc); supporting older children and young people with dyslexia (MA); teaching languages (MA), including Arabic, English; translation (MA); woman and child abuse (MA).

**Long Island University–LIU Brooklyn,** Richard L. Conolly College of Liberal Arts and Sciences, Brooklyn, NY 11201-8423. Offers biology (MS); chemistry (MS); clinical psychology (PhD); communication sciences and disorders (MS); creative writing (MFA); English (MA); media arts (MA, MFA); political science (MA); psychology (MA); social science (MS); sociology (MA); speech-language pathology (MS); United Nations (Advanced Certificate); urban studies (MA); writing and production for television (MFA). *Program availability:* Part-time, evening/weekend. *Faculty:* 90 full-time (35 women), 125 part-time/adjunct (67 women). *Students:* 355 full-time (276 women), 220 part-time (161 women); includes 245 minority (119 Black or African American, non-Hispanic/Latino; 32 Asian, non-Hispanic/Latino; 80 Hispanic/Latino; 1 Native Hawaiian or other Pacific Islander, non-Hispanic/Latino; 13 Two or more races, non-Hispanic/Latino), 85 international. 792 applicants, 41% accepted, 141 enrolled. In 2016, 154 master's, 18 doctorates, 4 other advanced degrees awarded. *Degree requirements:* For master's, comprehensive exam (for some programs), thesis (for some programs); for doctorate, comprehensive exam (for some programs), thesis/dissertation (for some programs). *Entrance requirements:* For master's and doctorate, GRE. Additional exam requirements/recommendations for international students: Recommended—TOEFL (minimum score 550 paper-based; 79 iBT). *Application deadline:* Applications are processed on a rolling basis. Application fee: $50. Electronic applications accepted. *Expenses:* Tuition: Full-time $28,272; part-time $1178 per credit. *Required fees:* $451 per term. Tuition and fees vary according to degree level, program and student level. *Financial support:* In 2016–17, 120 fellowships with full and partial tuition reimbursements (averaging $915 per year), 5 research assistantships with full and partial tuition reimbursements (averaging $2,300 per year), 136 teaching assistantships with full and partial tuition reimbursements (averaging $2,300 per year) were awarded; career-related internships or fieldwork, Federal Work-Study, institutionally sponsored loans, scholarships/grants, tuition waivers (full and partial), and unspecified assistantships also available. Support available to part-time students. Financial award application deadline: 2/15; financial award applicants required to submit FAFSA. *Faculty research:* Nanocrystal polymerization of cellulose using electron microscopy. *Unit head:* Dr. Kevin Lauth, Acting Dean, 718-488-1347, E-mail: kevin.lauth@liu.edu. *Application contact:* Gabrielle Gannon, Director of Graduate Admissions, 718-488-1011, Fax: 718-780-6110, E-mail: bkln-admissions@liu.edu.

**Louisiana State University and Agricultural & Mechanical College,** Graduate School, College of Humanities and Social Sciences, Department of English, Baton Rouge, LA 70803. Offers creative writing (MFA); English (MA, PhD).

**Loyola Marymount University,** School of Film and Television, Department of Screenwriting, Writing for the Screen Program, Los Angeles, CA 90045-8347. Offers MFA. *Students:* 38 full-time (18 women); includes 17 minority (8 Black or African American, non-Hispanic/Latino; 1 Asian, non-Hispanic/Latino; 5 Hispanic/Latino; 3 Two or more races, non-Hispanic/Latino), 2 international. Average age 27. 60 applicants, 57% accepted, 16 enrolled. In 2016, 9 master's awarded. *Degree requirements:* For master's, thesis, project or script. *Entrance requirements:* For master's, GRE, writing sample, 2 letters of recommendation, personal statement. Additional exam requirements/recommendations for international students: Required—TOEFL (minimum score 600 paper-based; 100 iBT). *Application deadline:* For fall admission, 1/10 for domestic students. Application fee: $50. Electronic applications accepted. *Financial support:* In 2016–17, 22 students received support, including 1 teaching assistantship; career-related internships or fieldwork and scholarships/grants also available. Support available to part-time students. Financial award application deadline: 6/30; financial award applicants required to submit FAFSA. *Unit head:* Karol Hoeffner, Graduate Director, 310-338-3033, E-mail: khoeffne@lmu.edu. *Application contact:* Chake H. Kouyoumjian, Associate Dean of Graduate Studies, 310-338-2721, E-mail: ckouyoum@lmu.edu.
Website: http://sftv.lmu.edu/academics/graduateprograms/writingforthescreen/

**Maharishi University of Management,** Graduate Studies, Program in Screenwriting, Fairfield, IA 52557. Offers MFA.

**Manhattanville College,** Master of Fine Arts in Creative Writing Program, Purchase, NY 10577-2132. Offers MFA. *Program availability:* Part-time. *Faculty:* 3 full-time (1 woman), 5 part-time/adjunct (4 women). *Students:* 11 full-time (7 women), 7 part-time (3 women). Average age 29. 21 applicants, 76% accepted, 5 enrolled. *Degree requirements:* For master's, thesis. *Entrance requirements:* For master's, 2 letters of recommendation, 2-3 page autobiographical essay, 10-12 page writing sample, official transcripts. *Application deadline:* Applications are processed on a rolling basis. Application fee: $0. Electronic applications accepted. *Expenses:* Contact institution. *Financial support:* Fellowships, Federal Work-Study, scholarships/grants, tuition waivers (partial), and unspecified assistantships available. Financial award application deadline: 7/15; financial award applicants required to submit FAFSA. *Faculty research:* Fiction, non-fiction, poetry, cross-genre writing, social justice. *Unit head:* Lori Soderlind, Program Director, 914-323-5239, E-mail: mfa@mville.edu. *Application contact:* Jeanine Pardey-Levine, Director of Graduate Enrollment Management, 914-323-3208, E-mail: jeanine.pardey@mville.edu.
Website: http://mvillemfa.com

**Massachusetts Institute of Technology,** School of Humanities, Arts, and Social Sciences, Program in Comparative Media Studies/Writing, Graduate Program in Science Writing, Cambridge, MA 02139. Offers SM. *Faculty:* 6 full-time (1 woman). *Students:* 8 full-time (6 women); includes 1 minority (Hispanic/Latino), 1 international. Average age 26. 43 applicants, 23% accepted, 8 enrolled. In 2016, 7 master's awarded. *Degree requirements:* For master's, thesis. *Entrance requirements:* For master's, GRE General Test. Additional exam requirements/recommendations for international students: Required—TOEFL, IELTS. *Application deadline:* For fall admission, 1/15 for domestic and international students. Application fee: $75. Electronic applications accepted. *Expenses:* Tuition: Full-time $46,400; part-time $725 per credit. One-time fee: $312 full-time. Full-time tuition and fees vary according to course load and program. *Financial support:* In 2016–17, 8 students received support, including 3 fellowships (averaging $10,700 per year), 3 research assistantships (averaging $14,900 per year); teaching assistantships, Federal Work-Study, institutionally sponsored loans, scholarships/grants, traineeships, health care benefits, unspecified assistantships, and resident tutors also available. Support available to part-time students. Financial award application deadline: 5/1; financial award applicants required to submit FAFSA. *Faculty research:* Communicating science to the public; digital media; investigative journalism; documentary film. *Total annual research expenditures:* $7,000. *Unit head:* Prof. Thomas Levenson, Program Head, 617-253-6668, Fax: 617-253-6910, E-mail: sciwrite-www@mit.edu. *Application contact:* 617-253-5036, E-mail: sciwrite-www@mit.edu.
Website: http://sciwrite.mit.edu/

**McDaniel College,** Graduate and Professional Studies, Program in Liberal Arts, Westminster, MD 21157-4390. Offers liberal arts (MLA); writing for children and young adults (Postbaccalaureate Certificate). *Program availability:* Part-time, evening/weekend, 100% online. *Faculty:* 2 full-time (both women), 6 part-time/adjunct (4 women). *Students:* 2 full-time (both women), 26 part-time (22 women); includes 3 minority (2 Black or African American, non-Hispanic/Latino; 1 Asian, non-Hispanic/Latino). Average age 41. 22 applicants, 100% accepted. In 2016, 8 master's, 2 other advanced degrees awarded. *Degree requirements:* For master's, final project. *Entrance requirements:* For master's, 3 recommendations. Additional exam requirements/recommendations for international students: Required—TOEFL (minimum score 79 iBT), IELTS (minimum score 6). *Application deadline:* For fall admission, 6/1 priority date for domestic students; for spring admission, 11/1 priority date for domestic students; for summer admission, 3/1 priority date for domestic students. Applications are processed on a rolling basis. Application fee: $75. Electronic applications accepted. *Expenses:* Tuition: Full-time $8370; part-time $465 per credit. *Required fees:* $75 per semester. Tuition and fees vary according to course load, program and reciprocity agreements. *Financial support:* Application deadline: 3/1; applicants required to submit FAFSA. *Unit head:* E-mail: gradadms@mcdaniel.edu. *Application contact:* Crystal L. Perry, Assistant Director, Graduate Enrollment Management, 410-857-2516, Fax: 410-857-2515, E-mail: cperry@mcdaniel.edu.

**McNeese State University,** Doré School of Graduate Studies, College of Liberal Arts, Department of English and Foreign Languages, Program in Creative Writing, Lake Charles, LA 70609. Offers MFA. *Program availability:* Evening/weekend. *Degree requirements:* For master's, thesis, public reading. *Entrance requirements:* For master's, GRE, writing sample.

**Michigan State University,** The Graduate School, College of Arts and Letters, Program in Rhetoric and Writing, East Lansing, MI 48824. Offers critical studies in literacy and pedagogy (MA); digital rhetoric and professional writing (MA); rhetoric and writing (PhD). *Entrance requirements:* Additional exam requirements/recommendations for international students: Required—TOEFL. Electronic applications accepted. *Faculty* *research:* Rhetoric, writing and communication studies; media studies; technical communication, writing for digital environments.

**Millersville University of Pennsylvania,** College of Graduate Studies and Adult Learning, College of Arts, Humanities and Social Sciences, Department of English, Millersville, PA 17551-0302. Offers English (M Ed, MA); writing (Postbaccalaureate Certificate). *Program availability:* Part-time, evening/weekend. *Faculty:* 17 full-time (10 women), 1 (woman) part-time/adjunct. *Students:* 7 full-time (5 women), 18 part-time (14 women); includes 6 minority (2 Black or African American, non-Hispanic/Latino; 4 Asian, non-Hispanic/Latino; 1 international. Average age 34. 7 applicants, 100% accepted, 5 enrolled. In 2016, 9 master's awarded. *Degree requirements:* For master's, one foreign language, thesis optional. *Entrance requirements:* For master's, GRE or MAT. Additional exam requirements/recommendations for international students: Required—TOEFL (minimum score 600 paper-based), IELTS (minimum score 6). *Application deadline:* Applications are processed on a rolling basis. Application fee: $40. Electronic applications accepted. *Expenses:* $483 per credit resident tuition; $725 per credit non-resident tuition. *Financial support:* In 2016–17, 3 students received support. Unspecified assistantships available. Financial award application deadline: 3/15; financial award applicants required to submit FAFSA. *Faculty research:* Film studies; critical theory; narrative studies; literacy narratives; multicultural issues surrounding literacy; African American literature and rhetorical traditions; writing pedagogy; public and civic discourse; civic engagement; academic, workplace, and community literacy; grounded theory; critical discourse analysis; rhetorical theory; composition theory; science writing; technical writing; environmental rhetoric; rhetoric of place; public sphere theory. *Unit head:* Dr. Jill R. Craven, Chair, 717-871-7385, Fax: 717-871-7933, E-mail: jill.craven@millersville.edu. *Application contact:* Dr. Victor S. DeSantis, Dean of College of Graduate Studies and Adult Learning/Associate Provost for Civic and Community Engagement, 717-871-7619, Fax: 717-871-7954,
E-mail: victor.desantis@millersville.edu.
Website: http://www.millersville.edu/english/

**Mills College,** Graduate Studies, Department of English, Oakland, CA 94613-1000. Offers book art and creative writing (MFA); literature (MA); poetry (MFA); prose (MFA); Spanish creative writing (Certificate); translation (MFA). *Program availability:* Part-time. *Faculty:* 4 full-time (3 women), 4 part-time/adjunct (3 women). *Students:* 47 full-time (38 women), 2 part-time (both women); includes 28 minority (8 Black or African American, non-Hispanic/Latino; 3 Asian, non-Hispanic/Latino; 9 Hispanic/Latino; 8 Two or more races, non-Hispanic/Latino). Average age 32. 78 applicants, 95% accepted, 27 enrolled. In 2016, 29 master's awarded. *Degree requirements:* For master's, comprehensive exam, thesis. *Entrance requirements:* For master's, 15-20 page writing sample. Additional exam requirements/recommendations for international students: Required—TOEFL (minimum score 600 paper-based; 100 iBT), IELTS (minimum score 7). *Application deadline:* For fall admission, 12/15 priority date for domestic students, 12/15 for international students. Applications are processed on a rolling basis. Application fee: $50. Electronic applications accepted. *Expenses: Tuition:* Full-time $31,620. *Required fees:* $1118. Tuition and fees vary according to course load, degree level and program. *Financial support:* In 2016–17, 40 students received support, including 22 fellowships with partial tuition reimbursements available (averaging $9,099 per year), 18 teaching assistantships with tuition reimbursements available (averaging $4,798 per year); research assistantships and scholarships/grants also available. Support available to part-time students. Financial award application deadline: 2/1; financial award applicants required to submit FAFSA. *Faculty research:* Creative writing, African-American literature, Victorian women writers, theories of sexuality, Shakespeare. *Unit head:* Dr. Ajuan Mance, Chair of the English Department, 510-430-2218, E-mail: dcady@mills.edu. *Application contact:* Robynne Lofton, Director of Admissions, 510-430-3295, Fax: 510-430-2159, E-mail: grad-admission@mills.edu.
Website: http://www.mills.edu/english/

**Mills College,** Graduate Studies, Program in Book Art and Creative Writing, Oakland, CA 94613-1000. Offers MFA. *Program availability:* Part-time. *Faculty:* 5 full-time (4 women), 8 part-time/adjunct (7 women). *Students:* 4 full-time (all women), 3 part-time (2 women); includes 1 minority (Hispanic/Latino). Average age 28. 12 applicants, 100% accepted, 2 enrolled. In 2016, 3 master's awarded. *Degree requirements:* For master's, thesis project. *Entrance requirements:* For master's, visual portfolio of 15-25 images, written portfolio sample (for creative writing program). Additional exam requirements/recommendations for international students: Required—TOEFL (minimum score 600 paper-based; 100 iBT), IELTS (minimum score 7). *Application deadline:* For fall admission, 12/15 priority date for domestic students, 12/15 for international students. Application fee: $50. Electronic applications accepted. *Expenses: Tuition:* Full-time $31,620. *Required fees:* $1118. Tuition and fees vary according to course load, degree level and program. *Financial support:* In 2016–17, 15 students received support, including 9 fellowships with tuition reimbursements available (averaging $9,719 per year), 6 teaching assistantships with tuition reimbursements available (averaging $6,302 per year). Financial award application deadline: 2/1; financial award applicants required to submit FAFSA. *Unit head:* Kathleen Walkup, Professor of Book Arts, 510-430-2001, Fax: 510-430-2159, E-mail: kwalk@mills.edu. *Application contact:* Robynne Lofton, Director of Admissions, 510-430-3295, Fax: 510-430-2159, E-mail: grad-admission@mills.edu.
Website: http://www.mills.edu/academics/graduate/eng/programs/MFA_in_bookart.php

**Minnesota State University Mankato,** College of Graduate Studies and Research, College of Arts and Humanities, Department of English, Mankato, MN 56001. Offers communication and composition (MA); creative writing (MFA); English studies (MA); teaching English as a second language (MA, Certificate); technical communication (MA, Certificate). *Program availability:* Part-time. *Students:* 59 full-time (44 women), 106 part-time (67 women). *Degree requirements:* For master's, one foreign language, comprehensive exam, thesis or alternative. *Entrance requirements:* For master's, minimum GPA of 3.0 during previous 2 years, writing sample (MFA). Additional exam requirements/recommendations for international students: Required—TOEFL (minimum score 500 paper-based; 61 iBT). *Application deadline:* For fall admission, 7/1 for domestic students, 5/1 for international students. Applications are processed on a rolling basis. Application fee: $40. Electronic applications accepted. *Financial support:* Research assistantships with full tuition reimbursements, teaching assistantships with full tuition reimbursements, career-related internships or fieldwork, Federal Work-Study, and unspecified assistantships available. Financial award application deadline: 3/15; financial award applicants required to submit FAFSA. *Unit head:* Matthew Sewell, Chair, 507-389-2117, E-mail: matthew.sewell@mnsu.edu.
Website: http://english.mnsu.edu/

**Missouri State University,** Graduate College, College of Arts and Letters, Department of English, Springfield, MO 65897. Offers applied second language acquisition (MASLA); English (MA); English education (MS Ed); teaching English to speakers of other languages (Certificate); writing (MA). MASLA offered with the Department of Modern and Classical Languages. *Program availability:* Part-time, evening/weekend. *Faculty:* 25 full-time (18 women), 5 part-time/adjunct (2 women). *Students:* 47 full-time (34 women), 44 part-time (32 women); includes 4 minority (1 Asian, non-Hispanic/Latino; 3 Two or more races, non-Hispanic/Latino), 17 international. Average age 29. 79 applicants, 63% accepted, 27 enrolled. In 2016, 49 master's awarded. *Degree*

*requirements:* For master's, one foreign language, comprehensive exam, thesis or alternative. *Entrance requirements:* For master's, GRE (for MA), 9-12 teacher certification (MS Ed); minimum GPA of 3.0 (MA); personal statement (200- to 250-word description of reasons and goals behind interest in English graduate studies); at least two letters of recommendation from individuals able to speak of the applicant's academic achievements and potential; writing sample. Additional exam requirements/recommendations for international students: Required—TOEFL (minimum score 550 paper-based; 79 iBT), IELTS (minimum score 6). *Application deadline:* For fall admission, 3/1 priority date for domestic students, 3/1 for international students; for spring admission, 10/1 priority date for domestic students, 10/1 for international students. Applications are processed on a rolling basis. Application fee: $35 ($50 for international students). Electronic applications accepted. *Expenses:* Tuition, state resident: full-time $5830. Tuition, nonresident: full-time $10,708. *Required fees:* $1130. Tuition and fees vary according to class time, course level, course load and program. *Financial support:* In 2016–17, 2 teaching assistantships with full tuition reimbursements (averaging $8,772 per year) were awarded; Federal Work-Study, institutionally sponsored loans, scholarships/grants, and unspecified assistantships also available. Financial award application deadline: 3/31; financial award applicants required to submit FAFSA. *Faculty research:* History of rhetoric, modern poetry, African-American literature, digital writing, teaching English to speakers of other languages. *Unit head:* Dr. W. D. Blackmon, Department Head, 417-836-5107, Fax: 417-836-6940, E-mail: english@missouristate.edu. *Application contact:* Michael Edwards, Coordinator of Graduate Admissions, 417-836-5330, Fax: 417-836-6200, E-mail: michaeledwards@missouristate.edu.
Website: http://english.missouristate.edu/

**Missouri Western State University,** Program in Written Communication, St. Joseph, MO 64507-2294. Offers teaching of writing (Graduate Certificate); technical communication (MAA); writing studies (MAA). *Program availability:* Part-time. *Students:* 1 full-time (0 women), 8 part-time (7 women). Average age 33. In 2016, 7 master's, 1 other advanced degree awarded. *Entrance requirements:* For master's, minimum undergraduate GPA of 3.0, portfolio, 3 letters of reference. Additional exam requirements/recommendations for international students: Recommended—TOEFL (minimum score 79 iBT), IELTS (minimum score 6). *Application deadline:* For fall admission, 7/15 for domestic and international students; for spring admission, 10/1 for domestic and international students; for summer admission, 3/15 for domestic students. Applications are processed on a rolling basis. Application fee: $50. Electronic applications accepted. *Expenses:* Tuition, state resident: full-time $6548; part-time $327.39 per credit hour. Tuition, nonresident: full-time $11,848; part-time $592.39 per credit hour. *Required fees:* $542; $99 per credit hour. $176 per semester. One-time fee: $50. Tuition and fees vary according to course load and program. *Financial support:* Scholarships/grants and unspecified assistantships available. Support available to part-time students. *Unit head:* Dr. Cynthia Jeney, Associate Professor/Interim Director of Graduate Studies, 816-271-4447, E-mail: jeney@missouriwestern.edu. *Application contact:* Dr. Benjamin D. Caldwell, Dean of the Graduate School, 816-271-4394, Fax: 816-271-4525, E-mail: graduate@missouriwestern.edu.
Website: https://www.missouriwestern.edu/eml/maawc/

**Monmouth University,** Graduate Studies, Department of English, West Long Branch, NJ 07764-1898. Offers creative writing (MA); literature (MA); rhetoric and writing (MA). *Program availability:* Part-time, evening/weekend. *Degree requirements:* For master's, comprehensive exam (for some programs), thesis. *Entrance requirements:* For master's, minimum overall GPA of 2.75, fifteen or more credits in literature or related field, essay of 1000 words describing interest and goals, two letters of recommendation, creative writing sample. Additional exam requirements/recommendations for international students: Required—TOEFL (minimum 550 paper-based, 79 internet-based test), IELTS (minimum score 6), Michigan English Language Assessment Battery (minimum score 77) or CAE (minimum score of B2). Electronic applications accepted. *Faculty research:* Renaissance and medieval literature, nineteenth-century American literature, eighteenth-century British literature and women's studies, Old and Middle English, African diaspora and African post-colonial literature.

**Montclair State University,** The Graduate School, College of Humanities and Social Sciences, Teaching Writing Certificate Program, Montclair, NJ 07043-1624. Offers Certificate. *Program availability:* Part-time, evening/weekend. *Entrance requirements:* For degree, 2 letters of recommendation, essay. Additional exam requirements/recommendations for international students: Required—TOEFL (minimum score 83 iBT), IELTS (minimum score 6.5). Electronic applications accepted. *Expenses:* Tuition, state resident: part-time $553 per credit. Tuition, nonresident: part-time $854 per credit. *Required fees:* $91 per credit. Tuition and fees vary according to program. *Faculty research:* Pedagogy in writing.

**Mount Mary University,** Graduate Programs, Program in English, Milwaukee, WI 53222-4597. Offers creative writing (MA); professional and new media writing (MA). *Program availability:* Part-time, evening/weekend. *Faculty:* 4 full-time (all women), 2 part-time/adjunct (1 woman). *Students:* 8 full-time (6 women), 16 part-time (13 women); includes 10 minority (5 Black or African American, non-Hispanic/Latino; 1 American Indian or Alaska Native, non-Hispanic/Latino; 1 Hispanic/Latino; 3 Two or more races, non-Hispanic/Latino). Average age 42. 4 applicants, 50% accepted, 2 enrolled. In 2016, 5 master's awarded. *Degree requirements:* For master's, comprehensive exam, thesis or alternative. *Entrance requirements:* For master's, minimum GPA of 2.75. Additional exam requirements/recommendations for international students: Required—TOEFL (minimum score 550 paper-based; 80 iBT); Recommended—IELTS (minimum score 6.5). *Application deadline:* For fall admission, 8/1 for domestic and international students; for spring admission, 12/1 for domestic and international students; for summer admission, 5/1 for domestic and international students. Applications are processed on a rolling basis. Application fee: $45. Electronic applications accepted. *Expenses:* Contact institution. *Financial support:* Career-related internships or fieldwork and Federal Work-Study available. Support available to part-time students. Financial award application deadline: 5/1; financial award applicants required to submit FAFSA. *Unit head:* Ann Angel, Graduate Program Chair, 414-930-3109, E-mail: angela@mtmary.edu. *Application contact:* Kirk Heller de Messer, Director, Graduate Admissions, 414-930-3221, E-mail: hellerk@mtmary.edu.
Website: http://www.mtmary.edu/majors-programs/graduate/english/index.html

**Mount Saint Mary's University,** Graduate Division, Los Angeles, CA 90049. Offers business administration (MBA); counseling psychology (MS); creative writing (MFA); education (MS, Certificate); film and television (MFA); health policy and management (MS); humanities (MA); nursing (MSN, Certificate); physical therapy (DPT); religious studies (MA). *Program availability:* Part-time, evening/weekend. *Faculty:* 50 full-time (35 women), 116 part-time/adjunct (81 women). *Students:* 670 full-time (518 women), 147 part-time (116 women); includes 414 minority (73 Black or African American, non-Hispanic/Latino; 4 American Indian or Alaska Native, non-Hispanic/Latino; 60 Asian, non-Hispanic/Latino; 259 Hispanic/Latino; 7 Native Hawaiian or other Pacific Islander, non-Hispanic/Latino; 11 Two or more races, non-Hispanic/Latino), 4 international. Average age 32. 1,398 applicants, 21% accepted, 242 enrolled. In 2016, 170 master's, 28 doctorates, 35 other advanced degrees awarded. *Entrance requirements:* Additional exam requirements/recommendations for international students: Required—TOEFL.

# Writing

*Application deadline:* For fall admission, 6/30 priority date for domestic and international students; for spring admission, 10/30 priority date for domestic and international students; for summer admission, 3/30 priority date for domestic and international students. Applications are processed on a rolling basis. Application fee: $50. Electronic applications accepted. *Expenses: Tuition:* Full-time $9983; part-time $829 per unit. One-time fee: $135. Tuition and fees vary according to degree level and program. *Financial support:* Career-related internships or fieldwork, Federal Work-Study, institutionally sponsored loans, and tuition waivers (full and partial) available. Support available to part-time students. Financial award application deadline: 3/15; financial award applicants required to submit FAFSA. *Unit head:* Albert Ramos, Director of Graduate Admissions, 213-477-2800, E-mail: gradprograms@msmu.edu. *Application contact:* Shawn Peters, Graduate Admission Counselor, 213-477-2676, E-mail: gradprograms@msmu.edu.
Website: http://www.msmu.edu/graduate-programs/

**Murray State University,** College of Humanities and Fine Arts, Department of English and Philosophy, Program in Creative Writing, Murray, KY 42071. Offers MFA.

**Naropa University,** Graduate Programs, Program in Creative Writing, Boulder, CO 80302-6697. Offers MFA. *Program availability:* Part-time, blended/hybrid learning. *Faculty:* 4 full-time (3 women), 2 part-time/adjunct (1 woman). *Students:* 9 part-time (6 women); includes 1 minority (Asian, non-Hispanic/Latino). Average age 42. 10 applicants, 80% accepted, 5 enrolled. In 2016, 1 master's awarded. *Degree requirements:* For master's, thesis. *Entrance requirements:* For master's, creative writing sample; resume/curriculum vitae with pertinent academic, employment and volunteer activities; transcripts; 2 letters of recommendation; letter of interest. Additional exam requirements/recommendations for international students: Required—TOEFL (minimum score 550 paper-based; 80 iBT). *Application deadline:* For fall admission, 1/13 priority date for domestic students, 1/15 priority date for international students; for spring admission, 10/15 for domestic students, 10/15 priority date for international students. Applications are processed on a rolling basis. Application fee: $60. Electronic applications accepted. *Expenses:* $20,520 for first year of program. *Financial support:* In 2016–17, 2 students received support. Career-related internships or fieldwork, Federal Work-Study, scholarships/grants, tuition waivers (partial), and unspecified assistantships available. Support available to part-time students. Financial award application deadline: 3/1; financial award applicants required to submit FAFSA. *Unit head:* Sue Hammond West, Dean, School of the Arts and Jack Kerouac School, 303-546-3583, E-mail: suewest@naropa.edu. *Application contact:* Office of Admissions, 303-546-3572, Fax: 303-546-3583, E-mail: admissions@naropa.edu.
Website: http://www.naropa.edu/academics/masters/creative-writing-low-residency/index.php

**Naropa University,** Graduate Programs, Program in Creative Writing and Poetics, Boulder, CO 80302-6697. Offers MFA. *Faculty:* 6 full-time (3 women), 6 part-time/adjunct (4 women). *Students:* 31 full-time (19 women), 2 part-time (1 woman); includes 4 minority (3 Hispanic/Latino; 1 Two or more races, non-Hispanic/Latino), 1 international. Average age 29. 31 applicants, 97% accepted, 11 enrolled. In 2016, 18 master's awarded. *Degree requirements:* For master's, thesis. *Entrance requirements:* For master's, resume/curriculum vitae with pertinent academic, employment and volunteer activity; 2 letters of recommendation; transcripts; statement of interest; 10-15 page creative writing sample; phone interview. Additional exam requirements/recommendations for international students: Required—TOEFL (minimum score 550 paper-based; 80 iBT). *Application deadline:* For fall admission, 1/15 priority date for domestic and international students; for spring admission, 10/15 priority date for domestic and international students. Applications are processed on a rolling basis. Application fee: $60. Electronic applications accepted. *Expenses:* $24,730 for first year. *Financial support:* In 2016–17, 20 students received support, including 4 fellowships with full tuition reimbursements available (averaging $3,000 per year), 3 teaching assistantships with partial tuition reimbursements available (averaging $1,500 per year); research assistantships, career-related internships or fieldwork, scholarships/grants, tuition waivers (partial), and unspecified assistantships also available. Support available to part-time students. Financial award application deadline: 3/1; financial award applicants required to submit FAFSA. *Unit head:* Sue Hammond West, Dean of the Arts and Jack Kerouac School, 303-546-3583, E-mail: suewest@naropa.edu. *Application contact:* Office of Admissions, 303-546-3572, Fax: 303-546-3583, E-mail: admissions@naropa.edu.
Website: http://www.naropa.edu/academics/masters/creative-writing-poetics/index.php

**National Louis University,** College of Arts and Sciences, Chicago, IL 60603. Offers adult education (Ed D); counseling and human services (MS); language and academic development (M Ed, Certificate); psychology (MA, PhD, Certificate); public policy (MA); written communication (MS, Certificate). *Program availability:* Part-time, evening/weekend, online learning. *Degree requirements:* For master's and Certificate, comprehensive exam (for some programs), thesis (for some programs); for doctorate, thesis/dissertation. *Entrance requirements:* For master's, MAT or GRE, 3 professional or academic references, interview, minimum GPA of 3.0; for doctorate, GRE General Test, MAT, or Watson-Glaser Critical Thinking Appraisal, three professional or academic references, statement of academic and professional goals, 3 years of experience in field, interview, master's degree, resume, writing sample; for Certificate, GRE, MAT, or Watson-Glaser Critical Thinking Appraisal, three professional or academic references, statement of academic and professional goals, interview, minimum GPA of 3.0. Additional exam requirements/recommendations for international students: Required—Department of Language Studies Assessment or TOEFL (minimum score 550 paper-based; 79 iBT). Electronic applications accepted.

**National University,** Academic Affairs, College of Letters and Sciences, La Jolla, CA 92037-1011. Offers biology (MS); counseling psychology (MA), including licensed professional clinical counseling; creative writing (MFA). *Program availability:* Part-time, evening/weekend, 100% online, blended/hybrid learning. *Faculty:* 68 full-time (33 women), 70 part-time/adjunct (34 women). *Students:* 566 full-time (408 women), 287 part-time (197 women); includes 394 minority (101 Black or African American, non-Hispanic/Latino; 3 American Indian or Alaska Native, non-Hispanic/Latino; 47 Asian, non-Hispanic/Latino; 185 Hispanic/Latino; 8 Native Hawaiian or other Pacific Islander, non-Hispanic/Latino; 50 Two or more races, non-Hispanic/Latino), 3 international. Average age 34. In 2016, 450 master's awarded. *Degree requirements:* For master's, thesis (for some programs). *Entrance requirements:* For master's, interview, minimum GPA of 2.5. Additional exam requirements/recommendations for international students: Required—TOEFL (minimum score 550 paper-based; 79 iBT), IELTS (minimum score 6). *Application deadline:* Applications are processed on a rolling basis. Application fee: $60 ($65 for international students). Electronic applications accepted. *Financial support:* Career-related internships or fieldwork, institutionally sponsored loans, scholarships/grants, and tuition waivers (partial) available. Support available to part-time students. Financial award application deadline: 6/30; financial award applicants required to submit FAFSA. *Unit head:* College of Letters and Sciences, 800-628-8648, E-mail: cols@nu.edu. *Application contact:* Brandon Jouganatos, Interim Vice President for Enrollment Services, 800-628-8648, E-mail: advisor@nu.edu.
Website: http://www.nu.edu/OurPrograms/CollegeOfLettersAndSciences.html

**New England College,** Programs in Writing, Henniker, NH 03242-3293. Offers poetry (MFA); professional writing (MA). *Program availability:* Part-time, evening/weekend. Electronic applications accepted. *Faculty research:* Poetry collections.

**New Hampshire Institute of Art,** Graduate Studies, Manchester, NH 03104. Offers art education (MA); creative writing (MFA); photography (MFA); teaching visual arts (MAT); visual arts (MFA); writing for stage and screen (MFA). *Accreditation:* NASAD. *Faculty:* 31 part-time/adjunct (14 women). *Students:* 59 full-time (42 women), 6 part-time (3 women); includes 2 minority (1 Asian, non-Hispanic/Latino; 1 Hispanic/Latino). Average age 43. 36 applicants, 58% accepted. In 2016, 2 master's awarded. *Degree requirements:* For master's, thesis, corresponding exhibition and artist talk. *Entrance requirements:* For master's, writing sample or visual art portfolio; curriculum vitae; transcripts; letters of recommendation. Additional exam requirements/recommendations for international students: Required—TOEFL (minimum score 530 paper-based; 71 iBT). *Application deadline:* For fall admission, 5/1 priority date for domestic students; for spring admission, 11/1 priority date for domestic students. Applications are processed on a rolling basis. Application fee: $75. Electronic applications accepted. *Expenses:* $9,745 tuition per semester/residency plus $745 residency fee. *Financial support:* In 2016–17, 2 teaching assistantships (averaging $1,200 per year) were awarded; scholarships/grants and unspecified assistantships also available. Support available to part-time students. Financial award application deadline: 6/1; financial award applicants required to submit FAFSA. *Faculty research:* Fine arts - visual arts, photography, creative writing, writing for stage and screen; art education. *Unit head:* Lucinda Bliss, Dean of Graduate Studies, 603-836 2522, E-mail: lucindabliss@nhia.edu. *Application contact:* Moriah Billups, Graduate Admissions Coordinator, 603-836 2588, E-mail: gradadmissions@nhia.edu.
Website: http://www.nhia.edu/graduate-studies

**New Mexico Highlands University,** Graduate Studies, College of Arts and Sciences, Department of English, Las Vegas, NM 87701. Offers English (MA), including creative writing, language, rhetoric and composition, literature. *Degree requirements:* For master's, comprehensive exam, thesis. *Entrance requirements:* For master's, minimum undergraduate GPA of 3.0. Additional exam requirements/recommendations for international students: Required—TOEFL (minimum score 540 paper-based). *Faculty research:* Twentieth-century literature, life path writing in homeless shelters, native American philosophy, medieval intellectual and cultural history, creating pedagogical tools for teaching law.

**New Mexico State University,** College of Arts and Sciences, Department of English, Las Cruces, NM 88003. Offers creative writing (MFA); English (MA), including creative writing, English studies for teachers, literature, rhetoric and professional communication; rhetoric and professional communication (PhD). *Program availability:* Part-time. *Faculty:* 19 full-time (9 women), 1 (woman) part-time/adjunct. *Students:* 48 full-time (33 women), 24 part-time (14 women); includes 19 minority (2 Asian, non-Hispanic/Latino; 15 Hispanic/Latino; 2 Two or more races, non-Hispanic/Latino), 6 international. Average age 34. 90 applicants, 32% accepted, 19 enrolled. In 2016, 21 master's, 5 doctorates awarded. *Degree requirements:* For master's, one foreign language, thesis (for some programs); for doctorate, comprehensive exam, thesis/dissertation, internship. *Entrance requirements:* For master's and doctorate, sample of written work. Additional exam requirements/recommendations for international students: Required—TOEFL (minimum score 550 paper-based; 79 iBT), IELTS (minimum score 6.5). *Application deadline:* For fall admission, 2/1 for domestic and international students. Application fee: $40 ($50 for international students). Electronic applications accepted. *Expenses:* Tuition, state resident: full-time $4086. Tuition, nonresident: full-time $14,254. *Required fees:* $853. Tuition and fees vary according to course load. *Financial support:* In 2016–17, 47 students received support, including 42 teaching assistantships (averaging $17,394 per year); career-related internships or fieldwork, Federal Work-Study, scholarships/grants, traineeships, health care benefits, and unspecified assistantships also available. Support available to part-time students. Financial award application deadline: 3/1. *Faculty research:* Composition research, history and theory of rhetoric, technical/professional communication, creative writing, English and American literature. *Total annual research expenditures:* $10,316. *Unit head:* Dr. Barry L. Thatcher, Department Head, 575-646-3931, Fax: 575-646-7725, E-mail: bathatch@nmsu.edu. *Application contact:* Dr. Tracey Eileen Miller-Tomlinson, Director of Graduate Studies, 575-646-2213, Fax: 575-646-7725, E-mail: tomlin@nmsu.edu.
Website: http://english.nmsu.edu

**The New School,** Schools of Public Engagement, Creative Writing Program, New York, NY 10011. Offers MFA. *Program availability:* Part-time. *Faculty:* 5 full-time (2 women), 25 part-time/adjunct (17 women). *Students:* 168 full-time (109 women), 1 (woman) part-time; includes 45 minority (8 Black or African American, non-Hispanic/Latino; 14 Asian, non-Hispanic/Latino; 19 Hispanic/Latino; 4 Two or more races, non-Hispanic/Latino), 22 international. Average age 29. 365 applicants, 76% accepted, 81 enrolled. In 2016, 79 master's awarded. *Degree requirements:* For master's, thesis. *Entrance requirements:* For master's, transcripts, recommendation letters, statement of purpose, writing portfolio, resume. Additional exam requirements/recommendations for international students: Required—TOEFL (minimum score 100 iBT), IELTS (minimum score 7), PTE (minimum score 68). *Application deadline:* For fall admission, 1/15 priority date for domestic and international students. Applications are processed on a rolling basis. Application fee: $50. Electronic applications accepted. *Expenses:* Contact institution. *Financial support:* Fellowships, research assistantships, teaching assistantships, career-related internships or fieldwork, scholarships/grants, and unspecified assistantships available. Financial award application deadline: 2/1; financial award applicants required to submit FAFSA. *Faculty research:* Fiction, poetry, writing for children/young adults, non-fiction, multi-genre. *Unit head:* Luis Jaramillo, Chair, 212-229-5611 Ext. 2346, E-mail: jaramillo@newschool.edu. *Application contact:* Merida Gasbarro, Director, 212-229-5600 Ext. 1108, E-mail: escandom@newschool.edu.
Website: http://www.newschool.edu/

**New York University,** Graduate School of Arts and Science, Program in Creative Writing, New York, NY 10012-1019. Offers MA, MFA. *Program availability:* Part-time, evening/weekend. *Degree requirements:* For master's, one foreign language, thesis or alternative. *Entrance requirements:* For master's, GRE General Test, sample of written work. Additional exam requirements/recommendations for international students: Required—TOEFL. *Faculty research:* Fiction, poetry.

**New York University,** School of Continuing and Professional Studies, Division of Humanities, Arts, and Writing, New York, NY 10012-1019. Offers professional writing (MS). *Program availability:* Part-time, evening/weekend, online learning. *Degree requirements:* For master's, thesis. *Entrance requirements:* For master's, GRE or GMAT (only upon request), bachelor's degree, resume with relevant professional work, internship or volunteer experience, two letters of recommendation, statement of purpose. Additional exam requirements/recommendations for international students: Required—TOEFL (minimum score 600 paper-based; 100 iBT), IELTS (minimum score 7). Electronic applications accepted.

**New York University,** Tisch School of the Arts, Rita and Burton Goldberg Department of Dramatic Writing, New York, NY 10012-1019. Offers MFA. *Degree requirements:* For master's, thesis, play or screenplay, internship. *Entrance requirements:* For master's, writing sample. Additional exam requirements/recommendations for international students: Required—TOEFL or IELTS. Electronic applications accepted. *Faculty research:* Craft of screenwriting film story analysis, production elements in film and theatre.

**North Carolina State University,** Graduate School, College of Humanities and Social Sciences, Department of English, Program in Creative Writing, Raleigh, NC 27695. Offers MFA. *Degree requirements:* For master's, thesis optional. *Entrance requirements:* For master's, GRE. Electronic applications accepted. *Faculty research:* Science fiction, Asian poetry, translation, Southern writers, satiric fiction.

**North Dakota State University,** College of Graduate and Interdisciplinary Studies, College of Arts, Humanities and Social Sciences, Department of English, Fargo, ND 58102. Offers composition (MA); literature (MA); rhetoric, writing and culture (PhD). *Program availability:* Part-time. *Degree requirements:* For master's, one foreign language, thesis. *Entrance requirements:* Additional exam requirements/recommendations for international students: Required—TOEFL (minimum score 600 paper-based; 100 iBT), IELTS (minimum score 7). Electronic applications accepted. *Faculty research:* American and English literature, women's studies, language attitudes, composition practices, computers and composition.

**See Display on page 756 and Close-Up on page 767.**

**Northeastern Illinois University,** College of Graduate Studies and Research, College of Arts and Sciences, Programs in English, Chicago, IL 60625-4699. Offers composition/writing (MA); literature (MA). *Program availability:* Part-time, evening/weekend. *Degree requirements:* For master's, comprehensive exam, thesis optional. *Entrance requirements:* For master's, 30 hours of undergraduate course work in literature and composition (literature), BA in English or approval (composition/writing), minimum GPA of 2.75. Additional exam requirements/recommendations for international students: Required—TOEFL (minimum score 550 paper-based; 79 iBT). Electronic applications accepted. *Faculty research:* Arthurian literature, Southern American literature, rhetoric and theories of authorship.

**Northern Arizona University,** Graduate College, College of Arts and Letters, Department of English, Flagstaff, AZ 86011. Offers applied linguistics (PhD); creative writing (MFA), including creative writing; English (MA), including English education, literature, professional writing, rhetoric, writing, and digital media studies; professional writing (Certificate); teaching English as a second language (MA, Certificate). *Program availability:* Part-time. *Degree requirements:* For master's, comprehensive exam (for some programs), thesis (for some programs), departmental qualifying exam; for doctorate, comprehensive exam, thesis/dissertation, departmental qualifying exam. *Entrance requirements:* For master's, minimum GPA of 3.0 or GRE; for doctorate, GRE General Test. Additional exam requirements/recommendations for international students: Required—TOEFL (minimum score 550 paper-based; 80 iBT), IELTS (minimum score 7), TOEFL (minimum score 600 paper-based; 100 iBT) for PhD; TOEFL (minimum score 570 paper-based; 89 iBT) for MA. Electronic applications accepted. *Expenses:* Tuition, state resident: full-time $8971; part-time $444 per credit hour. Tuition, nonresident: full-time $20,958; part-time $1164 per credit hour. *Required fees:* $1018; $644 per credit hour. Tuition and fees vary according to course load, campus/location and program.

**Northern Kentucky University,** Office of Graduate Programs, College of Arts and Sciences, Program in English, Highland Heights, KY 41099. Offers composition and rhetoric (Certificate); creative writing (Certificate); cultural studies and discourses (Certificate); English (MA); professional writing (Certificate). *Program availability:* Part-time, evening/weekend. *Degree requirements:* For master's, comprehensive exam (for some programs), capstone (thesis, portfolio, project, or exams); 30 hours of credit; for Certificate, 18 hours of credit. *Entrance requirements:* For master's, bachelor's degree in English or related field from regionally-accredited institution with minimum GPA of 3.0 in major or cognate area coursework; official transcripts for all undergraduate and graduate work; two letters of reference; for Certificate, official transcripts for all undergraduate and graduate work; bachelor's degree from regionally-accredited institution; minimum undergraduate GPA of 2.5. Additional exam requirements/recommendations for international students: Required—TOEFL (minimum score 79 iBT); Recommended—IELTS (minimum score 6.5). Electronic applications accepted.

**Northern Michigan University,** Office of Graduate Education and Research, College of Arts and Sciences, Department of English, Marquette, MI 49855-5301. Offers creative writing (MFA); literature (MA); pedagogy (MA); teaching English to speakers of other languages (Graduate Certificate); theater (MA); writing (MA). *Program availability:* Part-time, evening/weekend. Terminal master's awarded for partial completion of doctoral program. *Degree requirements:* For master's, capstone project; thesis, practicum or portfolio (for MA); thesis (for MFA); for Graduate Certificate, one foreign language. *Entrance requirements:* For master's, minimum GPA of 3.0; bachelor's degree in English or minimum of 30 credit hours in undergraduate English; statement of purpose; resume; critical essay; 3 letters of recommendation; for Graduate Certificate, bachelor's degree. Additional exam requirements/recommendations for international students: Required—TOEFL (minimum score 550 paper-based; 79 iBT), IELTS (minimum score 6.5). Electronic applications accepted. *Faculty research:* Modern Arabic literature, British literature (medieval to contemporary), postcolonial literature, Native and African-American literature, creative writing, critical theory, pedagogy.

**Northwestern University,** Medill School of Journalism, Media, and Integrated Marketing Communications, Evanston, IL 60208. Offers integrated marketing communications (MSIMC), including brand strategy, content marketing, direct and interactive marketing, marketing analytics, strategic communications; interactive publishing (MSJ); magazine writing/editing (MSJ); reporting (MSJ); video/broadcast (MSJ). *Accreditation:* ACEJMC (one or more programs are accredited). *Entrance requirements:* For master's, GRE General Test, GMAT or LSAT (for MSJ). Additional exam requirements/recommendations for international students: Required—TOEFL. Electronic applications accepted. *Expenses:* Contact institution. *Faculty research:* Web business journalism, cultural stereotypes, voter apathy, digital television.

**Northwestern University,** School of Professional Studies, Program in Creative Writing, Evanston, IL 60208. Offers MA, MFA.

**Oklahoma City University,** Petree College of Arts and Sciences, Oklahoma City, OK 73106-1402. Offers applied behavioral studies (M Ed); applied sociology: nonprofit leadership (MA); creative writing (MFA); criminology (MS); early childhood education (M Ed); elementary education (M Ed); general studies (MLA); leadership/management (MLA); moving image arts (MFA); professional counseling (M Ed); teaching (MA); teaching English to speakers of other languages (MA). *Program availability:* Part-time, evening/weekend. *Faculty:* 11 full-time (5 women), 15 part-time/adjunct (6 women). *Students:* 77 full-time (55 women), 46 part-time (30 women); includes 32 minority (13 Black or African American, non-Hispanic/Latino; 1 American Indian or Alaska Native, non-Hispanic/Latino; 2 Asian, non-Hispanic/Latino; 12 Hispanic/Latino; 4 Two or more races, non-Hispanic/Latino), 37 international. Average age 34. 92 applicants, 74% accepted, 46 enrolled. In 2016, 72 master's awarded. *Degree requirements:* For master's, capstone/practicum. *Entrance requirements:* For master's, bachelor's degree from accredited institution with minimum GPA of 3.0, essay, recommendation letters. Additional exam requirements/recommendations for international students: Required—TOEFL (minimum score 550 paper-based; 80 iBT). *Application deadline:* Applications are processed on a rolling basis. Application fee: $50. Electronic applications accepted. *Expenses:* Contact institution. *Financial support:* In 2016–17, 16 students received support. Federal Work-Study, institutionally sponsored loans, scholarships/grants, and tuition waivers (full and partial) available. Support available to part-time students. Financial award application deadline: 6/1; financial award applicants required to submit FAFSA. *Unit head:* Dr. Amy Cataldi, Dean, 405-208-5446, Fax: 405-208-5447, E-mail: acataldi@okcu.edu. *Application contact:* Michael Harrington, Director of Graduate Admissions, 800-633-7242, Fax: 405-208-5356, E-mail: gadmissions@okcu.edu. Website: http://www.okcu.edu/petree/

**Oklahoma State University,** College of Arts and Sciences, Department of English, Stillwater, OK 74078. Offers creative writing (MFA); English (MA, PhD). *Faculty:* 62 full-time (34 women), 3 part-time/adjunct (1 woman). *Students:* 6 full-time (4 women), 118 part-time (60 women); includes 17 minority (3 Black or African American, non-Hispanic/Latino; 5 American Indian or Alaska Native, non-Hispanic/Latino; 1 Asian, non-Hispanic/Latino; 3 Hispanic/Latino; 5 Two or more races, non-Hispanic/Latino), 20 international. Average age 32. 121 applicants, 34% accepted, 33 enrolled. In 2016, 19 master's, 12 doctorates awarded. *Degree requirements:* For master's, comprehensive exam, thesis; for doctorate, comprehensive exam, thesis/dissertation. *Entrance requirements:* For master's, GRE General Test, minimum GPA of 3.0, writing sample; for doctorate, GRE General Test, minimum GPA of 3.5, writing sample. Additional exam requirements/recommendations for international students: Required—TOEFL (minimum score 550 paper-based; 79 iBT). *Application deadline:* For fall admission, 3/1 priority date for international students; for spring admission, 8/1 priority date for international students. Applications are processed on a rolling basis. Application fee: $40 ($75 for international students). Electronic applications accepted. *Expenses:* Tuition, state resident: full-time $3775; part-time $209.70 per credit hour. Tuition, nonresident: full-time $14,851; part-time $825.05 per credit hour. *Required fees:* $2027; $112.60 per credit hour. Tuition and fees vary according to campus/location. *Financial support:* In 2016–17, 1 research assistantship (averaging $3,106 per year), 106 teaching assistantships (averaging $15,887 per year) were awarded; career-related internships or fieldwork, Federal Work-Study, scholarships/grants, health care benefits, tuition waivers (partial), and unspecified assistantships also available. Support available to part-time students. Financial award application deadline: 3/1; financial award applicants required to submit FAFSA. *Faculty research:* American and British novels, poetry, and autobiography; Native American languages and literature; institutional history of American film, history, and adaptations; rhetoric and theories of human communication; learning strategies of second language learners. *Unit head:* Dr. Richard Frohock, Department Head, 405-744-9474, Fax: 405-744-6326, E-mail: richard.frohock@okstate.edu. Website: http://english.okstate.edu/

**Old Dominion University,** College of Arts and Letters, MFA Program in Creative Writing, Norfolk, VA 23529. Offers MFA. *Program availability:* Part-time. *Faculty:* 7 full-time (3 women), 5 part-time/adjunct (all women). *Students:* 26 full-time (13 women), 5 part-time (3 women); includes 5 minority (2 Black or African American, non-Hispanic/Latino; 1 Asian, non-Hispanic/Latino; 2 Hispanic/Latino). Average age 32. 60 applicants, 30% accepted, 12 enrolled. In 2016, 9 master's awarded. *Degree requirements:* For master's, comprehensive exam, thesis. *Entrance requirements:* For master's, GRE General Test, 24 hours of previous course work in English, sample of written work. Additional exam requirements/recommendations for international students: Required—TOEFL. *Application deadline:* For fall admission, 2/1 for domestic students. Application fee: $50. Electronic applications accepted. *Expenses:* Tuition, state resident: full-time $8604; part-time $478 per credit hour. Tuition, nonresident: full-time $21,510; part-time $1195 per credit hour. *Required fees:* $66 per semester. Tuition and fees vary according to campus/location, program and reciprocity agreements. *Financial support:* In 2016–17, 17 students received support, including 2 fellowships with full tuition reimbursements available (averaging $11,000 per year), 3 research assistantships with full tuition reimbursements available (averaging $10,000 per year), 6 teaching assistantships with full tuition reimbursements available (averaging $10,000 per year); scholarships/grants and unspecified assistantships also available. Financial award application deadline: 2/1. *Faculty research:* Literary fiction, nonfiction, poetry. *Total annual research expenditures:* $35,000. *Unit head:* Dr. Luisa Igloria, Graduate Program Director, 757-683-3929, Fax: 757-683-3241, E-mail: ligloria@odu.edu. *Application contact:* Dr. David C. Earnest, Associate Dean, 757-683-6077, Fax: 757-683-5746, E-mail: dearnest@odu.edu. Website: http://al.odu.edu/english/mfacw/

**Oregon State University,** College of Liberal Arts, Program in Creative Writing, Corvallis, OR 97331. Offers fiction (MFA); nonfiction writing (MFA); poetry (MFA). *Program availability:* Part-time. *Faculty:* 26 full-time (10 women), 8 part-time/adjunct (7 women). *Students:* 47 full-time (33 women), 1 part-time (0 women); includes 4 minority (1 Asian, non-Hispanic/Latino; 3 Two or more races, non-Hispanic/Latino), 3 international. Average age 32. 428 applicants, 9% accepted, 22 enrolled. In 2016, 25 master's awarded. *Entrance requirements:* Additional exam requirements/recommendations for international students: Required—TOEFL (minimum score 80 iBT), IELTS (minimum score 6.5). *Application deadline:* For fall admission, 1/3 for domestic and international students. Application fee: $75 ($85 for international students). *Expenses:* Tuition, state resident: full-time $12,150; part-time $450 per credit. Tuition, nonresident: full-time $21,789; part-time $807 per credit. *Required fees:* $1651; $1507 per credit. One-time fee: $350. Tuition and fees vary according to course load, campus/location and program. *Financial support:* Fellowships and teaching assistantships available. Financial award application deadline: 1/4. *Unit head:* Susan Rodgers, MFA Director, Creative Writing, 541-737-1658, E-mail: susan.rodgers@oregonstate.edu. Website: http://liberalarts.oregonstate.edu/wlf/mfa

**Otis College of Art and Design,** Program in Writing, Los Angeles, CA 90045-9785. Offers MFA. *Degree requirements:* For master's, thesis. *Entrance requirements:* For master's, writing sample. Electronic applications accepted.

**Our Lady of the Lake University,** College of Arts and Sciences, Programs in English, San Antonio, TX 78207-4689. Offers literature, creative writing, and social justice (MA); MA/MFA. Program offered jointly with University of the Incarnate Word and St. Mary's University. *Program availability:* Part-time, evening/weekend. *Faculty:* 6 full-time (4 women), 1 (woman) part-time/adjunct. *Students:* 10 full-time (7 women), 10 part-time (all women); includes 17 minority (1 Black or African American, non-Hispanic/Latino; 16 Hispanic/Latino). Average age 35. 10 applicants, 60% accepted, 5 enrolled. In 2016, 1 master's awarded. *Degree requirements:* For master's, comprehensive exam, thesis optional. *Entrance requirements:* For master's, GRE General Test or MAT taken within the last 5 years, bachelor's degree with at least 18 hours of advanced course work in English and/or communication arts with minimum cumulative GPA of 2.5; 2 letters of recommendation; samples of creative and scholarly writing (25 pages total); personal statement. Additional exam requirements/recommendations for international students: Required—TOEFL. *Application deadline:* For fall admission, 6/15 for domestic and international students; for spring admission, 11/15 for domestic and international students; for summer admission, 4/15 for domestic and international students. Applications are processed on a rolling basis. Application fee: $40 ($50 for international students). Electronic applications accepted. Application fee is waived when completed

## Writing

online. *Expenses: Tuition:* Full-time $14,796. Tuition and fees vary according to course load, degree level, campus/location and program. *Financial support:* In 2016–17, 8 students received support. Federal Work-Study, scholarships/grants, unspecified assistantships, and tuition discounts available. Support available to part-time students. Financial award application deadline: 5/1; financial award applicants required to submit FAFSA. *Unit head:* Leah Larson, Chair of the English, Mass Communications and Drama Department, 210-431-6503, E-mail: llarson@ollusa.edu. *Application contact:* Office of Graduate Admissions, 210-431-3995, Fax: 210-431-3945, E-mail: gradadm@ollusa.edu.
Website: http://www.ollusa.edu/s/1190/hybrid/default-hybrid-ollu.aspx?sid-1190&gid-1&pgid-7884

**Pacific Lutheran University,** Division of Humanities, Tacoma, WA 98447. Offers creative writing (MFA). *Program availability:* Part-time, blended/hybrid learning. *Degree requirements:* For master's, thesis, final residency including teaching class. *Entrance requirements:* For master's, portfolio, book review. Additional exam requirements/ recommendations for international students: Required—TOEFL. Electronic applications accepted. *Expenses:* Contact institution.

**Pacific University,** Program in Writing, Forest Grove, OR 97116-1797. Offers MFA. *Program availability:* Part-time.

**Park University,** School of Graduate and Professional Studies, Kansas City, MO 54105. Offers adult education (M Ed); business and government leadership (Graduate Certificate); business, government, and global society (MPA); communication and leadership (MA); creative and life writing (Graduate Certificate); disaster and emergency management (MPA, Graduate Certificate); educational leadership (M Ed); finance (MBA, Graduate Certificate); general business (MBA); global business (Graduate Certificate); healthcare administration (MHA); healthcare services management and leadership (Graduate Certificate); international business (MBA); language and literacy (M Ed), including English for speakers of other languages, special reading teacher/ literacy coach; leadership of international healthcare organizations (Graduate Certificate); management information systems (MBA, Graduate Certificate); music performance (ADP, Graduate Certificate), including cello (MM, ADP), piano (MM, ADP), viola (MM, ADP), violin (MM, ADP); nonprofit and community services management (MPA); nonprofit leadership (Graduate Certificate); performance (MM), including cello (MM, ADP), piano (MM, ADP), viola (MM, ADP), violin (MM, ADP); public management (MPA); social work (MSW); teacher leadership (M Ed), including curriculum and assessment, instructional leader. *Program availability:* Part-time, evening/weekend, online learning. *Degree requirements:* For master's, comprehensive exam (for some programs), thesis (for some programs), internship (for some programs); exam (for some programs). *Entrance requirements:* For master's, GRE or GMAT (for some programs), teacher certification (for some M Ed programs), letters of recommendation, essay, resume (for some programs). Additional exam requirements/recommendations for international students: Required—TOEFL (minimum score 550 paper-based; 79 iBT), IELTS (minimum score 6). Electronic applications accepted.

**Penn State Harrisburg,** Graduate School, School of Humanities, Middletown, PA 17057. Offers American studies (MA, PhD); communications (MA); heritage and museum practice (Certificate); humanities (MA); writing instruction specialist (Certificate). *Program availability:* Evening/weekend. *Unit head:* Dr. Mukund S. Kulkarni, Chancellor, 717-948-6105, Fax: 717-948-6452. *Application contact:* Robert W. Coffman, Jr., Director of Enrollment Management, Admissions, 717-948-6250, Fax: 717-948-6325, E-mail: hbgadmit@psu.edu.
Website: https://harrisburg.psu.edu/humanities

**Pepperdine University,** Seaver College, Division of Humanities, Malibu, CA 90263. Offers American studies (MA); writing for screen and television (MFA). *Program availability:* Part-time. *Students:* 9 full-time (7 women), 41 part-time (23 women); includes 12 minority (3 Black or African American, non-Hispanic/Latino; 2 Asian, non-Hispanic/Latino; 5 Hispanic/Latino; 2 Two or more races, non-Hispanic/Latino), 3 international. Average age 31. In 2016, 15 master's awarded. *Degree requirements:* For master's, oral and written exams. *Entrance requirements:* For master's, GRE General Test, writing sample, letters of recommendation. Additional exam requirements/ recommendations for international students: Required—TOEFL. *Application deadline:* For fall admission, 2/1 priority date for domestic students. Applications are processed on a rolling basis. Application fee: $65. *Financial support:* Applicants required to submit FAFSA. *Unit head:* Dr. Michael G. Ditmore, Chair/Professor of English, 310-506-4182, Fax: 310-506-7307, E-mail: michael.ditmore@pepperdine.edu. *Application contact:* Hayley Wolf, Director of Admission, 310-506-4392,
E-mail: hayley.wolf@pepperdine.edu.
Website: http://seaver.pepperdine.edu/humanities/default.htm

**Pittsburg State University,** Graduate School, College of Arts and Sciences, Department of English and Modern Languages, Pittsburg, KS 66762. Offers English (MA), including creative writing, literature. *Program availability:* Part-time. *Students:* 18 (12 women); includes 1 minority (Asian, non-Hispanic/Latino). In 2016, 9 master's awarded. *Degree requirements:* For master's, thesis or alternative. *Entrance requirements:* Additional exam requirements/recommendations for international students: Required—TOEFL (minimum score 550 paper-based; 79 iBT), IELTS (minimum score 6.5), PTE (minimum score 53). *Application deadline:* For fall admission, 7/15 for domestic students, 6/1 for international students; for spring admission, 12/15 for domestic students, 10/15 for international students; for summer admission, 5/15 for domestic students, 4/1 for international students. Applications are processed on a rolling basis. Application fee: $35 ($60 for international students). Electronic applications accepted. *Expenses:* Contact institution. *Financial support:* In 2016–17, 10 teaching assistantships with full tuition reimbursements (averaging $8,000 per year) were awarded; career-related internships or fieldwork, Federal Work-Study, and unspecified assistantships also available. Financial award application deadline: 2/1; financial award applicants required to submit FAFSA. *Faculty research:* American fiction, American poetry, British fiction, British poetry, composition theory, creative writing. *Unit head:* Dr. Celia Patterson, Chairperson, 620-235-4689, E-mail: cpatterson@pittstate.edu. *Application contact:* Lisa Allen, Assistant Director of Graduate and Continuing Studies, 620-235-4223, Fax: 620-235-4219, E-mail: lallen@pittstate.edu.

**Pratt Institute,** School of Liberal Arts and Sciences, Program in Writing, Brooklyn, NY 11205-3899. Offers MFA. *Students:* 22 full-time (15 women); includes 17 minority (8 Black or African American, non-Hispanic/Latino; 1 Asian, non-Hispanic/Latino; 5 Hispanic/Latino; 3 Two or more races, non-Hispanic/Latino). Average age 28. 70 applicants, 51% accepted, 11 enrolled. In 2016, 10 master's awarded. *Degree requirements:* For master's, thesis. *Entrance requirements:* For master's, writing sample. Additional exam requirements/recommendations for international students: Required—TOEFL (minimum score 600 paper-based; 100 iBT). *Application deadline:* For fall admission, 1/5 for domestic and international students; for spring admission, 10/1 for domestic and international students. Application fee: $50 ($90 for international students). Electronic applications accepted. *Expenses:* $29,646 full-time tuition, $1,938 fees. *Financial support:* Career-related internships or fieldwork, Federal Work-Study, institutionally sponsored loans, scholarships/grants, health care benefits, and unspecified assistantships available. Support available to part-time students. Financial award application deadline: 2/1; financial award applicants required to submit FAFSA.

*Unit head:* Christian Hawkey, Chairperson, 718-636-3790, E-mail: chawkey@pratt.edu. *Application contact:* Natalie Capannelli, Director of Graduate Admissions, 718-636-3551, Fax: 718-399-4242, E-mail: ncapanne@pratt.edu.
Website: https://www.pratt.edu/academics/liberal-arts-and-sciences/graduate-writing/
**See Display on page 746 and Close-Up on page 769.**

**Purdue University,** Graduate School, College of Liberal Arts, Department of English, West Lafayette, IN 47907. Offers creative writing (MFA); literature (MA, PhD), including linguistics, literature and philosophy (PhD); rhetoric and composition, theory and cultural studies (PhD). *Program availability:* Part-time. *Faculty:* 57 full-time (26 women), 3 part-time/adjunct (all women). *Students:* 130 full-time (82 women), 50 part-time (28 women); includes 21 minority (6 Black or African American, non-Hispanic/Latino; 5 Asian, non-Hispanic/Latino; 7 Hispanic/Latino; 3 Two or more races, non-Hispanic/Latino), 31 international. Average age 31. 299 applicants, 14% accepted, 29 enrolled. In 2016, 19 master's, 26 doctorates awarded. *Degree requirements:* For master's, one foreign language, comprehensive exam (for some programs), thesis (for some programs); for doctorate, one foreign language, comprehensive exam, thesis/dissertation. *Entrance requirements:* For master's, GRE General Test; GRE Subject Test in English literature (recommended for students applying to literary studies), minimum undergraduate GPA of 3.0 or equivalent; for doctorate, GRE General Test; GRE Subject Test in English literature (recommended for students applying to literary studies), master's degree. Additional exam requirements/recommendations for international students: Required—TOEFL (minimum score 620 paper-based; 77 iBT). *Application deadline:* For fall admission, 1/15 for domestic and international students. Applications are processed on a rolling basis. Application fee: $60 ($75 for international students). Electronic applications accepted. *Financial support:* Fellowships with tuition reimbursements and teaching assistantships with tuition reimbursements available. Support available to part-time students. Financial award application deadline: 1/15; financial award applicants required to submit FAFSA. *Faculty research:* Cultural studies, postmodern narrative, contemporary women writers, composition theory, slave narratives. *Unit head:* Krista L. Ratcliffe, Head, 765-494-6478, E-mail: ratcliffe@purdue.edu. *Application contact:* Jill M. Quirk, Graduate Contact, 765-494-3748, Fax: 765-494-1700, E-mail: griff@purdue.edu.
Website: https://www.cla.purdue.edu/english/

**Queens College of the City University of New York,** Arts and Humanities Division, Department of English, Queens, NY 11367-1597. Offers creative writing and literary translation (MFA); early childhood birth-2nd grade (Advanced Certificate); English (MA). *Program availability:* Part-time. *Faculty:* 51 full-time (26 women), 74 part-time/adjunct (47 women). *Students:* 66 part-time (39 women); includes 29 minority (8 Black or African American, non-Hispanic/Latino; 4 Asian, non-Hispanic/Latino; 14 Hispanic/Latino; 3 Two or more races, non-Hispanic/Latino), 2 international. Average age 31. 88 applicants, 55% accepted, 21 enrolled. In 2016, 29 master's awarded. *Degree requirements:* For master's, thesis, oral exam (English language and literature). *Entrance requirements:* For master's, manuscript (creative writing), minimum GPA of 3.0. Additional exam requirements/recommendations for international students: Required—TOEFL (minimum score 100 iBT), IELTS (minimum score 7). *Application deadline:* For fall admission, 4/1 for domestic students; for spring admission, 11/1 for domestic students. Applications are processed on a rolling basis. Application fee: $125. Electronic applications accepted. *Expenses:* Tuition, state resident: full-time $5065; part-time $425 per credit. Tuition, nonresident: part-time $780 per credit. *Required fees:* $522; $397 per credit. Part-time tuition and fees vary according to course load and program. *Financial support:* Career-related internships or fieldwork available. Financial award application deadline: 4/1; financial award applicants required to submit FAFSA. *Unit head:* Prof. Glenn Burger, Chairperson, 718-997-4600, E-mail: glenn.burger@qc.cuny.edu.

**Queens University of Charlotte,** College of Arts and Sciences, Charlotte, NC 28274-0002. Offers creative writing (MFA); interior design (MA). *Program availability:* Part-time, online learning. Electronic applications accepted.

**Regent University,** Graduate School, School of Communication and the Arts, Virginia Beach, VA 23464-9800. Offers communication (MA, PhD), including media and arts management and promotion (MA), political communication (MA), strategic communication (MA); directing for cinema/television (MFA); film and TV (MA), including producing, production, script writing; journalism (MA); producing for cinema/television (MFA); script and screenwriting (MFA); theatre (MA). *Program availability:* Part-time, 100% online, blended/hybrid learning. *Faculty:* 19 full-time (3 women), 51 part-time/ adjunct (17 women). *Students:* 92 full-time (52 women), 344 part-time (225 women); includes 163 minority (116 Black or African American, non-Hispanic/Latino; 6 American Indian or Alaska Native, non-Hispanic/Latino; 7 Asian, non-Hispanic/Latino; 25 Hispanic/ Latino; 1 Native Hawaiian or other Pacific Islander, non-Hispanic/Latino; 8 Two or more races, non-Hispanic/Latino), 8 international. Average age 37. 368 applicants, 52% accepted, 124 enrolled. In 2016, 91 master's, 7 doctorates awarded. *Degree requirements:* For master's, thesis or alternative; for doctorate, thesis/dissertation. *Entrance requirements:* For master's, transcripts, writing sample, resume, audition (for MFA programs); for doctorate, GRE General Test, resume, writing sample, recommendations, interview, transcripts, personal goals statement. Additional exam requirements/recommendations for international students: Required—TOEFL (minimum score 577 paper-based). *Application deadline:* For fall admission, 3/1 priority date for domestic students; for spring admission, 10/1 priority date for domestic students. Applications are processed on a rolling basis. Application fee: $50. Electronic applications accepted. *Expenses:* $685 per credit (for MA); $895 per credit (for MFA in acting); $885 per credit (for PhD); $250 per semester technology fee. *Financial support:* In 2016–17, 178 students received support, including 2 fellowships (averaging $10,000 per year); career-related internships or fieldwork, scholarships/grants, and unspecified assistantships also available. Support available to part-time students. *Faculty research:* Screenwriting, digital media production, communication, acting, directing. *Unit head:* Dr. Mitch Land, Dean, 757-352-4916, Fax: 757-352-4291, E-mail: mland@regent.edu. *Application contact:* Heidi Cece, Assistant Vice President of Enrollment Management, 800-373-5504, Fax: 757-352-4381, E-mail: admissions@regent.edu.
Website: http://www.regent.edu/sca/

**Regis University,** College of Contemporary Liberal Studies, Denver, CO 80221-1099. Offers creative writing (MFA); criminology (M Sc); curriculum, instruction and assessment (M Ed); education - teacher leadership (M Ed); educational leadership (M Ed); elementary education (M Ed); literacy (Certificate); reading (M Ed); secondary education (M Ed); special education (M Ed); teacher academic leadership (Certificate); teacher leadership (MA); teacher/educational leadership (M Ed); teaching the linguistically diverse (M Ed). *Program availability:* Part-time, evening/weekend, 100% online, blended/hybrid learning. *Faculty:* 18 full-time (12 women), 42 part-time/adjunct (26 women). *Students:* 302 full-time (234 women), 270 part-time (218 women); includes 148 minority (33 Black or African American, non-Hispanic/Latino; 3 American Indian or Alaska Native, non-Hispanic/Latino; 13 Asian, non-Hispanic/Latino; 83 Hispanic/Latino; 16 Two or more races, non-Hispanic/Latino), 3 international. Average age 36. 431 applicants, 90% accepted, 110 enrolled. In 2016, 308 master's awarded. *Degree requirements:* For master's, thesis (for some programs). *Entrance requirements:* For master's, official transcript reflecting baccalaureate degree awarded from regionally-accredited college or university, work experience, resume, letters of recommendation. Additional exam requirements/recommendations for international students: Required—

TOEFL (minimum score 550 paper-based; 82 iBT). *Application deadline:* For fall admission, 8/15 priority date for domestic students, 7/13 for international students; for winter admission, 10/10 priority date for domestic students, 9/8 for international students; for spring admission, 1/10 priority date for domestic students, 11/17 for international students; for summer admission, 5/1 priority date for domestic students. Applications are processed on a rolling basis. Application fee: $75. Electronic applications accepted. *Expenses:* $485 per credit hour. *Financial support:* Scholarships/grants available. Financial award application deadline: 4/15; financial award applicants required to submit FAFSA. *Unit head:* Dr. Elisa Robyn, Academic Dean. *Application contact:* Cate Clark, Director of Admissions, 303-458-4900, Fax: 303-964-5534, E-mail: ruadmissions@regis.edu.
Website: http://www.regis.edu/CCLS.aspx

**Rhode Island College,** School of Graduate Studies, Faculty of Arts and Sciences, Department of English, Providence, RI 02908-1991. Offers creative writing (MA, CGS); English (MA); literature (CGS). *Program availability:* Part-time, evening/weekend. *Faculty:* 6 full-time (2 women). *Students:* 5 full-time (2 women), 6 part-time (3 women). Average age 30. In 2016, 4 master's awarded. *Degree requirements:* For master's, thesis (for some programs). *Entrance requirements:* For master's, GRE General Test, 3 letters of recommendation, interview. Additional exam requirements/recommendations for international students: Recommended—TOEFL (minimum score 550 paper-based; 79 iBT). *Application deadline:* For fall admission, 3/1 for domestic students; for spring admission, 11/1 for domestic students. Applications are processed on a rolling basis. Application fee: $50. *Expenses:* Tuition, state resident: full-time $8928; part-time $372 per credit. Tuition, nonresident: full-time $17,376; part-time $724 per credit. *Required fees:* $604; $22 per credit. One-time fee: $74. *Financial support:* In 2016–17, 1 teaching assistantship with full tuition reimbursement (averaging $3,000 per year) was awarded; career-related internships or fieldwork, Federal Work-Study, scholarships/grants, health care benefits, and unspecified assistantships also available. Support available to part-time students. Financial award application deadline: 5/15; financial award applicants required to submit FAFSA. *Unit head:* Dr. Daniel Scott, III, Chair, 401-456-8028. *Application contact:* Graduate Studies, 401-456-8700.
Website: http://www.ric.edu/english/index.php

**Rivier University,** School of Graduate Studies, Department of English, Nashua, NH 03060. Offers English (MAT); writing and literature (MA). *Program availability:* Part-time, evening/weekend. *Degree requirements:* For master's, comprehensive exam (for some programs). *Entrance requirements:* For master's, GRE Subject Test.

**Roosevelt University,** Graduate Division, College of Arts and Sciences, Department of Literature and Languages, Program in Creative Writing, Chicago, IL 60605. Offers MFA. *Program availability:* Part-time, evening/weekend. *Faculty research:* Poetry, fiction, nonfiction, script writing.

**Rosemont College,** Schools of Graduate and Professional Studies, Creative Writing Program, Rosemont, PA 19010-1699. Offers MFA. *Program availability:* Part-time, evening/weekend. *Degree requirements:* For master's, comprehensive exam, thesis. *Entrance requirements:* For master's, 3 letters of recommendation, baccalaureate degree with minimum GPA of 3.0, writing sample. Additional exam requirements/recommendations for international students: Required—TOEFL. Electronic applications accepted. Application fee is waived when completed online.

**Rowan University,** Graduate School, College of Communication and Creative Arts, Program in Writing, Glassboro, NJ 08028-1701. Offers MA. *Program availability:* Part-time, evening/weekend. *Degree requirements:* For master's, thesis. *Entrance requirements:* For master's, GRE General Test. Additional exam requirements/recommendations for international students: Required—TOEFL. Electronic applications accepted.

**Rowan University,** Graduate School, College of Communication and Creative Arts, Writing, Composition, and Rhetoric Certificate of Graduate Study Program, Glassboro, NJ 08028-1701. Offers CGS.

**Rutgers University–Camden,** Graduate School of Arts and Sciences, Program in Creative Writing, Camden, NJ 08102. Offers MFA. *Program availability:* Part-time, evening/weekend. *Degree requirements:* For master's, thesis, 42 credits. *Entrance requirements:* For master's, GRE (for assistantships), 2 letters of recommendation, writing sample, statement of personal, professional, and academic goals. Additional exam requirements/recommendations for international students: Required—TOEFL, IELTS. Electronic applications accepted. *Faculty research:* Poetry, fiction, nonfiction.

**Rutgers University–Newark,** Graduate School, Program in Creative Writing, Newark, NJ 07102. Offers MFA. *Entrance requirements:* For master's, GRE, minimum undergraduate B average.

**Rutgers University–New Brunswick,** Mason Gross School of the Arts, Theater Department, New Brunswick, NJ 08901. Offers acting (MFA); design (MFA); playwriting (MFA); stage management (MFA); technical direction (MFA). *Degree requirements:* For master's, thesis (for some programs), performance project. *Entrance requirements:* For master's, audition, interview, portfolio. Additional exam requirements/recommendations for international students: Required—TOEFL (minimum score 550 paper-based), IELTS (minimum score 7). Electronic applications accepted. *Faculty research:* Faculty of working professional.

**St. Joseph's College, New York,** Program in Creative Writing, Brooklyn, NY 11205-3688. Offers MFA. *Program availability:* Part-time, evening/weekend. *Faculty:* 4 part-time/adjunct (1 woman). *Students:* 34 full-time (25 women); includes 12 minority (4 Black or African American, non-Hispanic/Latino; 3 Asian, non-Hispanic/Latino; 4 Hispanic/Latino; 1 Two or more races, non-Hispanic/Latino). Average age 35. 34 applicants, 82% accepted, 19 enrolled. In 2016, 11 master's awarded. *Entrance requirements:* For master's, official transcripts, 3 letters of references, manuscript, personal statement, resume. Additional exam requirements/recommendations for international students: Required—TOEFL (minimum score 80 iBT). *Application deadline:* Applications are processed on a rolling basis. Electronic applications accepted. *Expenses:* Contact institution. *Financial support:* In 2016–17, 27 students received support. *Unit head:* Ted Hamm, Associate Professor/Chair, 718-940-5307, E-mail: thamm@sjcny.edu.

**Saint Joseph's University,** College of Arts and Sciences, Program in Writing Studies, Philadelphia, PA 19131-1395. Offers MA. *Program availability:* Part-time, evening/weekend. *Faculty:* 8 full-time (6 women), 1 (woman) part-time/adjunct. *Students:* 9 full-time (6 women), 19 part-time (12 women); includes 4 minority (3 Black or African American, non-Hispanic/Latino; 1 Hispanic/Latino). Average age 33. 15 applicants, 93% accepted, 6 enrolled. In 2016, 13 master's awarded. *Entrance requirements:* For master's, 2 letters of recommendation, resume, 2 writing samples. Additional exam requirements/recommendations for international students: Required—TOEFL (minimum score 550 paper-based; 80 iBT). *Application deadline:* For fall admission, 7/15 for international students; for spring admission, 11/1 for international students. Applications are processed on a rolling basis. Application fee: $35. Electronic applications accepted. *Expenses:* $852 per credit. *Financial support:* In 2016–17, 4 students received support. Unspecified assistantships available. Financial award application deadline: 5/1; financial award applicants required to submit FAFSA. *Unit head:* Dr. Tenaya Darlington, Director,

610-660-3131, E-mail: gradcas@sju.edu. *Application contact:* Graduate Admissions, College of Arts and Sciences, 610-660-3131, E-mail: gradcas@sju.edu.
Website: https://www.sju.edu/majors-programs/graduate-arts-sciences/masters/writing-studies-ma

**Saint Leo University,** Graduate Studies in Creative Writing, Saint Leo, FL 33574-6665. Offers creative writing (MA); war literature and writing for veterans (MA). *Program availability:* Part-time. *Faculty:* 2 full-time (0 women). *Students:* 15 part-time (8 women); includes 2 minority (both Black or African American, non-Hispanic/Latino). Average age 40. 23 applicants, 87% accepted, 13 enrolled. *Entrance requirements:* For master's, official transcripts, 2 professional recommendations, personal statement, bachelor's degree from regionally-accredited university with minimum GPA of 3.25, writing sample. *Application deadline:* For fall admission, 7/1 priority date for domestic and international students; for spring admission, 11/1 priority date for domestic and international students. Applications are processed on a rolling basis. Application fee: $80. Electronic applications accepted. Application fee is waived when completed online. *Expenses:* $615 per semester hour. *Financial support:* Scholarships/grants and health care benefits available. *Faculty research:* Writing fiction, writing poetry, writing by veterans, war literature, writing creative nonfiction. *Unit head:* Dr. Steve Kistulentz, Director, 352-588-7218, Fax: 352-588-8300, E-mail: steven.kistulentz@saintleo.edu. *Application contact:* Jennifer Shelley, Senior Associate Director of Graduate Admissions, 800-707-8846, Fax: 352-588-7873, E-mail: grad.admissions@saintleo.edu.
Website: http://www.saintleo.edu/academics/graduate/creative-writing.aspx

**Saint Mary's College of California,** School of Liberal Arts, MFA Program in Creative Writing, Moraga, CA 94575. Offers MFA. *Degree requirements:* For master's, thesis. *Entrance requirements:* For master's, sample of written work. Electronic applications accepted. *Faculty research:* Poetry, fiction, nonfiction.

**Salisbury University,** Department of English, Salisbury, MD 21801-6837. Offers English (MA), including creative writing, film, literature, secondary education, TESOL, writing and rhetoric. *Program availability:* Part-time. *Faculty:* 11 full-time (5 women), 1 (woman) part-time/adjunct. *Students:* 11 full-time (9 women), 24 part-time (19 women); includes 1 minority (Black or African American, non-Hispanic/Latino), 4 international. Average age 33. 18 applicants, 67% accepted, 9 enrolled. In 2016, 17 master's awarded. *Degree requirements:* For master's, comprehensive exam, thesis optional. *Entrance requirements:* Additional exam requirements/recommendations for international students: Required—TOEFL (minimum score 550 paper-based, 79 iBT) or IELTS (6.5). *Application deadline:* For fall admission, 8/1 for domestic and international students; for spring admission, 1/1 for domestic and international students. Application fee: $65. Electronic applications accepted. *Expenses:* $381 per credit hour resident tuition, $670 per credit hour non-resident tuition; $84 per credit hour fees. *Financial support:* In 2016–17, 2 students received support, including 11 teaching assistantships with full tuition reimbursements available (averaging $9,395 per year); career-related internships or fieldwork and scholarships/grants also available. Support available to part-time students. Financial award application deadline: 3/1; financial award applicants required to submit FAFSA. *Faculty research:* Literature; linguistics; film studies; rhetoric and composition; TESOL. *Unit head:* Dr. Christopher Vilmar, Graduate Program Director, English, 410-677-6511, E-mail: csvilmar@salisbury.edu.
Website: http://www.salisbury.edu/gsr/gradstudies/ENGpage.html

**Sam Houston State University,** College of Humanities and Social Sciences, Department of English, Huntsville, TX 77341. Offers creative writing, editing, and publishing (MFA); English (MA). *Program availability:* Part-time. *Degree requirements:* For master's, comprehensive exam, thesis optional. *Entrance requirements:* For master's, GRE General Test, creative writing sample, letters of recommendation. Additional exam requirements/recommendations for international students: Required—TOEFL (minimum score 550 paper-based; 79 iBT), IELTS (minimum score 6.5). Electronic applications accepted.

**San Diego State University,** Graduate and Research Affairs, College of Arts and Letters, Department of English and Comparative Literature, San Diego, CA 92182. Offers creative writing (MFA); English (MA). *Degree requirements:* For master's, one foreign language, comprehensive exam (for some programs), thesis (for some programs). *Entrance requirements:* For master's, GRE General Test, minimum GPA of 2.85, writing sample, 3 letters of recommendation. Additional exam requirements/recommendations for international students: Required—TOEFL. Electronic applications accepted.

**San Diego State University,** Graduate and Research Affairs, College of Arts and Letters, Department of Rhetoric and Writing Studies, San Diego, CA 92182. Offers MA. *Program availability:* Part-time. *Degree requirements:* For master's, thesis. *Entrance requirements:* For master's, GRE General Test, writing sample, 3 letters of reference. Additional exam requirements/recommendations for international students: Required—TOEFL. Electronic applications accepted.

**San Francisco State University,** Division of Graduate Studies, College of Liberal and Creative Arts, Department of Creative Writing, San Francisco, CA 94132-1722. Offers MA, MFA. *Program availability:* Part-time. *Degree requirements:* For master's, thesis. *Expenses:* Tuition, state resident: full-time $6738. Tuition, nonresident: full-time $15,666. *Required fees:* $1012. Tuition and fees vary according to degree level and program. *Financial support:* Career-related internships or fieldwork and Federal Work-Study available. *Unit head:* Paul Hoover, Acting Chair, 415-338-1891, Fax: 415-338-6159, E-mail: viridian@sfsu.edu. *Application contact:* Barbara Eaton, Academic Office Coordinator, 415-338-1810, Fax: 415-338-6159, E-mail: cwriting@sfsu.edu.
Website: http://creativewriting.sfsu.edu/

**San Jose State University,** Graduate Studies and Research, College of Humanities and the Arts, San Jose, CA 95192-0001. Offers art (MA, MFA), including art history and visual culture (MA), digital media art (MFA), photography (MFA), pictorial art (MFA), spatial art (MFA); computational linguistics (Certificate); English (MA, MFA), including creative writing (MFA); French (MA); humanities and arts (Certificate); linguistics (MA); music (MA); philosophy (MA); professional and technical communication (Certificate); Spanish (MA); teaching English to speakers of other languages (MA); TESOL (Certificate); theatre arts (MA). Electronic applications accepted.

**Sarah Lawrence College,** Graduate Studies, Program in Writing, Bronxville, NY 10708-5999. Offers creative non-fiction (MFA); fiction (MFA); poetry (MFA). *Program availability:* Part-time. *Degree requirements:* For master's, thesis. *Entrance requirements:* For master's, sample of creative writing, minimum B average in undergraduate course work. Additional exam requirements/recommendations for international students: Required—TOEFL (minimum score 600 paper-based).

**Savannah College of Art and Design,** Graduate School, Program in Dramatic Writing, Savannah, GA 31402-3146. Offers MFA. *Program availability:* Part-time. *Faculty:* 4 full-time (1 woman), 1 (woman) part-time/adjunct. *Students:* 17 full-time (12 women), 5 part-time (2 women); includes 11 minority (all Black or African American, non-Hispanic/Latino), 4 international. Average age 28. 26 applicants, 58% accepted, 8 enrolled. In 2016, 3 master's awarded. *Degree requirements:* For master's, thesis. *Entrance requirements:* For master's, GRE (recommended), portfolio (submitted in digital format), audition or writing submission, resume, statement of purpose, two letters of recommendation. Additional exam requirements/recommendations for international students: Required—TOEFL (minimum score 550 paper-based, 85 iBT), IELTS (minimum score 6.5), or ACTFL. *Application deadline:* For fall admission, 4/1 for domestic and international students. Applications are processed on a rolling basis. Application fee: $40. Electronic applications accepted. *Expenses: Tuition:* Full-time $36,045. Tuition and fees vary according to course load. *Financial support:* Career-related internships or fieldwork, Federal Work-Study, and scholarships/grants available. Financial award application deadline: 4/1; financial award applicants required to submit FAFSA. *Unit head:* Averie Storck, Academic Program Coordinator. *Application contact:* Jenny Jaquillard, Executive Director of Admissions, Recruitment and Events, 912-525-5100, Fax: 912-525-5985, E-mail: admission@scad.edu. Website: http://www.scad.edu/academics/programs/dramatic-writing

**Savannah College of Art and Design,** Graduate School, Program in Writing, Savannah, GA 31402-3146. Offers MFA. *Program availability:* Part-time, 100% online. *Faculty:* 6 full-time (2 women), 1 (woman) part-time/adjunct. *Students:* 29 full-time (24 women), 25 part-time (18 women); includes 22 minority (18 Black or African American, non-Hispanic/Latino; 2 Asian, non-Hispanic/Latino; 2 Hispanic/Latino), 1 international. Average age 31. 63 applicants, 41% accepted, 12 enrolled. In 2016, 12 master's awarded. *Degree requirements:* For master's, thesis. *Entrance requirements:* For master's, GRE (recommended), portfolio (submitted in digital format), audition or writing submission, resume, statement of purpose, two letters of recommendation. Additional exam requirements/recommendations for international students: Required—TOEFL (minimum score 550 paper-based, 85 iBT), IELTS (minimum score 6.5), or ACTFL. *Application deadline:* For fall admission, 4/1 for domestic and international students. Applications are processed on a rolling basis. Application fee: $40. Electronic applications accepted. *Expenses: Tuition:* Full-time $36,045. Tuition and fees vary according to course load. *Financial support:* Career-related internships or fieldwork, Federal Work-Study, and scholarships/grants available. Financial award application deadline: 4/1; financial award applicants required to submit FAFSA. *Unit head:* Dr. Beth Concepcion, Dean, School of Liberal Arts. *Application contact:* Jenny Jaquillard, Executive Director of Admissions, Recruitment and Events, 912-525-5100, Fax: 912-525-5985, E-mail: admission@scad.edu. Website: http://www.scad.edu/academics/programs/writing

**School of the Art Institute of Chicago,** Graduate Division, Program in Writing, Chicago, IL 60603-3103. Offers MFA, Certificate. *Entrance requirements:* Additional exam requirements/recommendations for international students: Required—TOEFL.

**School of Visual Arts,** Graduate Programs, Program in Visual Narrative, New York, NY 10010-3994. Offers MFA. Summer admission only. *Degree requirements:* For master's, thesis, 60 credits, including all required courses. *Entrance requirements:* For master's, portfolio, statement of purpose; unique and complete short story/visual narrative (minimum 2-5 pages/images, or 2-5 minutes for video or animation submissions). Additional exam requirements/recommendations for international students: Required—TOEFL (minimum score 550 paper-based; 79 iBT). Electronic applications accepted. *Faculty research:* Storytelling, animation, design, illustration, art history, painting, printmaking, writing, graphic novels.

**Seattle Pacific University,** Master of Fine Arts in Creative Writing Program, Seattle, WA 98119-1997. Offers MFA. *Program availability:* Part-time. *Degree requirements:* For master's, thesis. *Entrance requirements:* For master's, 10 pages of poetry or 25 to 30 double-spaced pages of prose, whether of fiction or creative nonfiction, in the student's chosen genre; three- to four-page (double-spaced) personal essay describing development as writer and as person of faith; three recommendations; bachelor's degree; official transcripts from previous schools attended. Electronic applications accepted.

**Seton Hill University,** Program in Writing Popular Fiction, Greensburg, PA 15601. Offers MFA, Certificate. *Program availability:* Part-time. *Entrance requirements:* For master's, 10-page writing sample, 3 letters of recommendation, resume, letter of intent, official transcripts. Additional exam requirements/recommendations for international students: Required—TOEFL (minimum score 650 paper-based; 114 iBT), IELTS (minimum score 7). Application fee is waived when completed online.

**Sewanee: The University of the South,** Sewanee School of Letters, Sewanee, TN 37383-1000. Offers American and English literature (MA); creative writing (MFA). *Program availability:* Part-time. *Faculty:* 1 full-time (0 women), 10 part-time/adjunct (7 women). *Students:* 54 part-time (31 women); includes 4 minority (1 Black or African American, non-Hispanic/Latino; 3 Two or more races, non-Hispanic/Latino), 1 international. Average age 41. In 2016, 10 master's awarded. *Degree requirements:* For master's, thesis (for some programs). *Entrance requirements:* For master's, writing sample, two letters of recommendation, official transcripts. *Application deadline:* Applications are processed on a rolling basis. Application fee: $40. Electronic applications accepted. *Expenses:* $5,707 tuition and fees for 2 courses (full-time), or $2,941 for one course. *Financial support:* Institutionally sponsored loans and scholarships/grants available. Financial award applicants required to submit FAFSA. *Unit head:* Dr. John M. Grammer, Director, 931-598-1483, Fax: 931-598-3303, E-mail: jgrammer@sewanee.edu. *Application contact:* April R. Alvarez, Coordinator, 931-598-1636, Fax: 931-598-3303. Website: http://letters.sewanee.edu/

**Simmons College,** School of Library and Information Science, Boston, MA 02115. Offers children's literature (MA); library and information science (MS, PhD, Certificate), including archives management (MS), cultural heritage (MS), information science and technology (MS), school library teacher (MS); writing for children (MFA); MA/MA; MA/MAT; MA/MFA; MS/MA. *Accreditation:* ALA (one or more programs are accredited). *Program availability:* Part-time, evening/weekend, 100% online, blended/hybrid learning. *Faculty:* 23 full-time (17 women), 23 part-time/adjunct (16 women). *Students:* 313 full-time (262 women), 511 part-time (420 women); includes 88 minority (13 Black or African American, non-Hispanic/Latino; 10 Asian, non-Hispanic/Latino; 41 Hispanic/Latino; 24 Two or more races, non-Hispanic/Latino), 19 international. Average age 30. 568 applicants, 98% accepted, 319 enrolled. In 2016, 245 master's, 3 doctorates, 4 other advanced degrees awarded. *Degree requirements:* For master's, thesis optional, capstone project experience; for doctorate, comprehensive exam, thesis/dissertation, 36 credit hours. *Entrance requirements:* For doctorate, GRE, transcripts, personal statement, resume, recommendations, master's degree. Additional exam requirements/recommendations for international students: Required—TOEFL (minimum score 550 paper-based; 79 iBT), IELTS (minimum score 7). *Application deadline:* For fall admission, 3/1 for domestic and international students; for spring admission, 9/1 for domestic and international students; for summer admission, 2/1 for domestic and international students. Applications are processed on a rolling basis. Application fee: $65. Electronic applications accepted. *Expenses:* $1,210 per credit, $3,630 per course, $52 activity fee per semester. *Financial support:* In 2016–17, 10 fellowships with partial tuition reimbursements were awarded; scholarships/grants, tuition waivers, and unspecified assistantships also available. Support available to part-time students. Financial award application deadline: 2/1; financial award applicants required to submit FAFSA. *Faculty research:* Archives and social justice, information-seeking behavior, information retrieval, organization of information, cultural heritage informatics. *Unit head:* Dr. Eileen G. Abels, Dean, 617-521-2869. *Application contact:* Sarah Petrakos, Assistant Dean for Admission and Recruitment, 617-521-2868, Fax: 617-521-3192,

E-mail: gslisadm@simmons.edu.
Website: http://www.simmons.edu/slis/

**Sonoma State University,** Department of English, Rohnert Park, CA 94928. Offers American literature (MA); creative writing (MA); English literature (MA); world literature (MA). *Program availability:* Part-time, evening/weekend. *Degree requirements:* For master's, one foreign language, thesis or alternative. *Entrance requirements:* For master's, minimum GPA of 2.5. Additional exam requirements/recommendations for international students: Required—TOEFL (minimum score 500 paper-based). *Application deadline:* For fall admission, 11/30 priority date for domestic students. Application fee: $55. *Expenses:* Tuition, state resident: full-time $6738; part-time $3906 per unit. *Required fees:* $1916; $1916 per year. Tuition and fees vary according to course load, degree level and program. *Financial support:* Fellowships, teaching assistantships, career-related internships or fieldwork, and Federal Work-Study available. Financial award application deadline: 3/2; financial award applicants required to submit FAFSA. *Unit head:* Brantley L. Bryant, Chair, 707-664-2164, E-mail: brantley.bryant@sonoma.edu. *Application contact:* Dr. Anne Goldman, Chair of Graduate Studies, 707-664-2651, Fax: 707-664-6040, E-mail: goldmana@sonoma.edu. Website: http://www.sonoma.edu/english/programs/ma-program.html

**Southeastern Louisiana University,** College of Arts, Humanities and Social Sciences, Department of English, Hammond, LA 70402. Offers creative writing (MA); language and theory (MA); professional writing (MA); publishing studies (MA). *Program availability:* Part-time. *Faculty:* 12 full-time (4 women), 1 part-time/adjunct (0 women). *Students:* 12 full-time (9 women), 15 part-time (10 women); includes 4 minority (1 Black or African American, non-Hispanic/Latino; 2 Hispanic/Latino; 1 Two or more races, non-Hispanic/Latino). Average age 28. 10 applicants, 60% accepted, 4 enrolled. In 2016, 15 master's awarded. *Degree requirements:* For master's, comprehensive exam, thesis optional. *Entrance requirements:* Additional exam requirements/recommendations for international students: Required—TOEFL (minimum score 500 paper-based; 61 iBT), IELTS (minimum score 5.5). *Application deadline:* For fall admission, 7/15 priority date for domestic students, 6/1 priority date for international students; for spring admission, 12/1 priority date for domestic students, 10/1 priority date for international students. Applications are processed on a rolling basis. Application fee: $20 ($30 for international students). Electronic applications accepted. *Expenses:* Tuition, state resident: full-time $6540; part-time $465 per credit hour. Tuition, nonresident: full-time $19,017; part-time $1158 per credit hour. *Required fees:* $1829. *Financial support:* In 2016–17, 16 students received support, including 8 research assistantships (averaging $9,688 per year), 2 teaching assistantships (averaging $9,900 per year); institutionally sponsored loans, scholarships/grants, and unspecified assistantships also available. Support available to part-time students. Financial award application deadline: 5/1; financial award applicants required to submit FAFSA. *Faculty research:* John Ruskin, animal studies, linguistics, film studies. *Unit head:* Dr. David Hanson, Department Head, 985-549-2100, Fax: 985-549-5021, E-mail: dhanson@southeastern.edu. *Application contact:* Amanda Harper, Graduate Admissions Analyst, 985-549-5620, Fax: 985-549-5632, E-mail: admissions@southeastern.edu.
Website: http://www.southeastern.edu/acad_research/depts/engl

**Southern Illinois University Carbondale,** Graduate School, College of Liberal Arts, Department of English, Program in Creative Writing, Carbondale, IL 62901-4701. Offers MFA. *Degree requirements:* For master's, one foreign language, thesis. *Entrance requirements:* For master's, GRE General Test, GRE Subject Test, minimum GPA of 2.7. Additional exam requirements/recommendations for international students: Required—TOEFL.

**Southern Illinois University Edwardsville,** Graduate School, College of Arts and Sciences, Department of English Language and Literature, Program in Creative Writing, Edwardsville, IL 62026-0001. Offers MA. *Program availability:* Part-time. *Degree requirements:* For master's, one foreign language, thesis. *Entrance requirements:* Additional exam requirements/recommendations for international students: Required—TOEFL (minimum score 550 paper-based, 79 iBT), IELTS (minimum score 6.5), Michigan Test of English Language Proficiency or PTE. Electronic applications accepted.

**Southern New Hampshire University,** School of Arts and Sciences, Manchester, NH 03106-1045. Offers community mental health (Graduate Certificate); community mental health and mental health counseling (MS); fiction and nonfiction (MFA); teaching English as a foreign language (MS). *Program availability:* Part-time, evening/weekend. *Degree requirements:* For master's, one foreign language, thesis. *Entrance requirements:* For master's, minimum GPA of 2.75 (for MS in teaching English as a foreign language), 3.0 (for MFA). Additional exam requirements/recommendations for international students: Required—TOEFL (minimum score 550 paper-based; 79 iBT), IELTS (minimum score 6.5), TWE (minimum score 5). Electronic applications accepted. *Expenses:* Contact institution. *Faculty research:* Action research, state of the art practice in behavioral health services, wraparound approaches to working with youth, learning styles.

**Spalding University,** Graduate Studies, College of Social Sciences and Humanities, Master of Fine Arts in Writing Program, Louisville, KY 40203-2188. Offers MFA. *Program availability:* Online learning. *Faculty:* 1 (woman) full-time, 4 part-time/adjunct (all women). *Students:* 112 full-time (88 women), 31 part-time (21 women); includes 23 minority (13 Black or African American, non-Hispanic/Latino; 2 American Indian or Alaska Native, non-Hispanic/Latino; 4 Asian, non-Hispanic/Latino; 1 Native Hawaiian or other Pacific Islander, non-Hispanic/Latino; 3 Two or more races, non-Hispanic/Latino), 1 international. Average age 44. 50 applicants, 80% accepted, 39 enrolled. In 2016, 40 master's awarded. *Degree requirements:* For master's, thesis. *Entrance requirements:* For master's, writing sample, letters of recommendation, personal essays. Additional exam requirements/recommendations for international students: Required—TOEFL (minimum score 535 paper-based). *Application deadline:* For fall admission, 8/1 priority date for domestic students, 7/1 for international students; for spring admission, 2/1 priority date for domestic students, 1/15 for international students. Applications are processed on a rolling basis. Application fee: $30. Electronic applications accepted. *Expenses: Tuition:* Full-time $15,300. *Financial support:* Scholarships/grants and unspecified assistantships available. Financial award applicants required to submit FAFSA. *Faculty research:* Fiction, creative nonfiction, poetry, writing for children, playwriting/screenwriting. *Unit head:* Dr. Sena Jeter Naslund, Director, 502-873-4401, E-mail: snaslund@spalding.edu. *Application contact:* Karen J. Mann, Administrative Director, 502-873-4399, E-mail: kmann@spalding.edu. Website: http://www.spalding.edu/mfa

**Stephens College,** Division of Graduate and Continuing Studies, Columbia, MO 65215-0002. Offers counseling (M Ed), including addictions counseling, clinical mental health counseling, school counseling; health information administration (Postbaccalaureate Certificate); physician assistant studies (MPAS); TV and screenwriting (MFA). *Program availability:* Part-time, evening/weekend, online learning. *Faculty:* 14 full-time (9 women), 30 part-time/adjunct (19 women). *Students:* 117 full-time (101 women), 107 part-time (96 women); includes 25 minority (2 Black or African American, non-Hispanic/Latino; 2 American Indian or Alaska Native, non-Hispanic/Latino; 1 Asian, non-Hispanic/Latino; 2 Hispanic/Latino; 1 Native Hawaiian or other Pacific Islander, non-Hispanic/Latino; 17 Two or more races, non-Hispanic/Latino), 1 international. Average age 35. 226 applicants, 43% accepted, 87 enrolled. In 2016, 44 master's awarded. *Entrance* *requirements:* For master's, minimum GPA of 3.0 in last 60 hours. Additional exam requirements/recommendations for international students: Required—TOEFL (minimum score 79 iBT). *Application deadline:* For fall admission, 8/15 priority date for domestic and international students; for winter admission, 1/9 priority date for domestic and international students; for spring admission, 6/5 priority date for domestic and international students. Applications are processed on a rolling basis. Application fee: $50. Electronic applications accepted. *Expenses: Tuition:* Full-time $3564; part-time $396 per credit hour. *Required fees:* $45 per credit hour. *Financial support:* In 2016–17, 5 fellowships with full tuition reimbursements (averaging $7,673 per year) were awarded; unspecified assistantships also available. Financial award applicants required to submit FAFSA. *Faculty research:* Educational psychology, outcomes assessment. *Unit head:* Dr. Brian Sajko, Vice President of Strategic Enrollment Management, 800-388-7579, Fax: 573-876-7237, E-mail: online@stephens.edu. *Application contact:* Lindsey Boudinot, Director of Graduate and Online Admissions, 800-388-7579, E-mail: online@stephens.edu.

**Stetson University,** College of Arts and Sciences, Department of English, DeLand, FL 32723. Offers MFA. *Program availability:* Blended/hybrid learning. *Degree requirements:* For master's, book-length project. *Entrance requirements:* For master's, GRE General Test, writing sample. Additional exam requirements/recommendations for international students: Required—TOEFL (minimum score 90 iBT), IELTS (minimum score 7). Electronic applications accepted. *Expenses:* Contact institution.

**Stony Brook University, State University of New York,** Graduate School, College of Arts and Sciences, Program in Writing and Rhetoric, Stony Brook, NY 11794. Offers teaching writing (Graduate Certificate). *Faculty:* 26 full-time (12 women), 17 part-time/adjunct (12 women). *Students:* 2 part-time (both women). In 2016, 3 Graduate Certificates awarded. *Degree requirements:* For Graduate Certificate, practicum. *Entrance requirements:* For degree, two letters of recommendation, statement of purpose. *Application deadline:* For fall admission, 1/15 for domestic students. *Expenses:* Contact institution. *Financial support:* Teaching assistantships available. *Faculty research:* Composition, creative writing, fiction, rhetoric, writing. *Unit head:* Dr. Eugene Hammond, Director, 631-632-9277, E-mail: eugene.hammond@stonybrook.edu. *Application contact:* Adam Schultheiss, Coordinator, 631-632-7390, E-mail: adam.schultheiss@stonybrook.edu.
Website: http://www.stonybrook.edu/commcms/writrhet//

**Stony Brook University, State University of New York,** Stony Brook Southampton, Program in Creative Writing and Literature, Stony Brook, NY 11794. Offers fiction (MFA); poetry (MFA); scientific writing (MFA), including environmental, medical, technological; scriptwriting (MFA). *Faculty:* 5 full-time (3 women), 36 part-time/adjunct (19 women). *Students:* 29 full-time (20 women), 52 part-time (38 women); includes 7 minority (1 Black or African American, non-Hispanic/Latino; 2 Asian, non-Hispanic/Latino; 4 Hispanic/Latino), 1 international. 67 applicants, 60% accepted, 13 enrolled. In 2016, 28 master's awarded. *Entrance requirements:* Additional exam requirements/recommendations for international students: Required—TOEFL. *Application deadline:* For fall admission, 1/15 for domestic students; for spring admission, 10/1 for domestic students. Application fee: $100. *Expenses:* Contact institution. *Financial support:* In 2016–17, 7 teaching assistantships were awarded. *Unit head:* Dr. Julie Sheehan, Director, 631-632-5032, Fax: 631-632-2576, E-mail: julie.sheehan@stonybrook.edu. *Application contact:* Margaret S. Grigonis, Coordinator, 631-632-5028, Fax: 631-632-2576, E-mail: margaret.grigonis@stonybrook.edu.
Website: http://www.stonybrook.edu/southampton/mfa/cwl/index.html

**Syracuse University,** College of Arts and Sciences, MFA Program in Creative Writing, Syracuse, NY 13244. Offers MFA. *Students:* Average age 29. *Degree requirements:* For master's, thesis. *Entrance requirements:* For master's, statement of purpose, transcript(s) from undergraduate/graduate institution, three letters of recommendation. Additional exam requirements/recommendations for international students: Required—TOEFL (minimum score 100 iBT). *Application deadline:* For fall admission, 12/15 priority date for domestic and international students. Application fee: $75. Electronic applications accepted. *Expenses: Tuition:* Full-time $25,974; part-time $1443 per credit hour. *Required fees:* $802; $50 per course. Tuition and fees vary according to course load and program. *Financial support:* Fellowships with full tuition reimbursements, teaching assistantships with tuition reimbursements, and scholarships/grants available. Financial award application deadline: 1/1. *Faculty research:* Literary process, the craft and quality of literary writing, creative writing. *Unit head:* Christopher Kennedy, Associate Professor, English/Director, MFA Program in Creative Writing, 315-443-3755, E-mail: ckennedy@syr.edu. *Application contact:* Terri Zollo, Graduate Coordinator, 315-443-2174, E-mail: tazollo@syr.edu.
Website: http://english.syr.edu/creative_writing/index.html

**Syracuse University,** College of Arts and Sciences, PhD Program in Composition and Cultural Rhetoric, Syracuse, NY 13244. Offers PhD. *Degree requirements:* For doctorate, comprehensive exam, thesis/dissertation. *Entrance requirements:* For doctorate, GRE, three letters of recommendation, essay on intellectual history and academic interests, statement about teaching interests and practical experience, resume, transcripts. Additional exam requirements/recommendations for international students: Required—TOEFL (minimum score 100 iBT). *Application deadline:* For fall admission, 1/15 priority date for domestic and international students. Application fee: $75. Electronic applications accepted. *Expenses: Tuition:* Full-time $25,974; part-time $1443 per credit hour. *Required fees:* $802; $50 per course. Tuition and fees vary according to course load and program. *Financial support:* Fellowships with tuition reimbursements, teaching assistantships with tuition reimbursements, and scholarships/grants available. Financial award application deadline: 1/15; financial award applicants required to submit FAFSA. *Faculty research:* American ethnic rhetorics, authorship studies, composition studies and pedagogies, studies of gender and sexuality, transnational rhetorics and globalization. *Unit head:* Prof. Eileen Schell, Associate Professor, Writing and Rhetoric/Director of Graduate Studies, 315-443-1067, E-mail: eeschell@syr.edu. *Application contact:* Kristen Krause, Graduate Program Coordinator, 315-443-5146, E-mail: ccr@syr.edu.
Website: http://ccr.syr.edu/

**Temple University,** Center for the Performing and Cinematic Arts, Division of Theater, Film and Media Arts, Department of Theater, Philadelphia, PA 19122. Offers acting (MFA); design (MFA); directing (MFA); musical theater collaboration (MFA); musical theater studies (MA); playwriting (MFA). *Accreditation:* NAST. *Program availability:* Part-time. *Degree requirements:* For master's, thesis (for some programs). *Entrance requirements:* For master's, minimum GPA of 3.0; audition/interview, portfolio, or samples of written work. Additional exam requirements/recommendations for international students: Required—TOEFL (minimum score 550 paper-based; 79 iBT). Electronic applications accepted. *Expenses:* Contact institution. *Faculty research:* Acting/voice/speech/movement, theatrical design and production, musical theater, directing, playwriting.

**Temple University,** College of Liberal Arts, Department of English, Philadelphia, PA 19122-6096. Offers creative writing (MFA); English (MA, PhD). *Program availability:* Part-time. *Degree requirements:* For doctorate, 2 foreign languages, thesis/dissertation. *Entrance requirements:* For master's and doctorate, GRE General Test, minimum GPA of 3.0; 3 letters of recommendation. Additional exam requirements/recommendations for

international students: Required—TOEFL (minimum score 620 paper-based; 105 iBT). Electronic applications accepted. *Faculty research:* Early modern British literature, American literature, modernism, critical theory, rhetoric, composition.

**Texas A&M University–Commerce,** College of Humanities, Social Sciences and Arts, Commerce, TX 75429-3011. Offers applied criminology (MS); applied linguistics (MA, MS); art (MA, MFA); Christianity in history (Graduate Certificate); computational linguistics (Graduate Certificate); creative writing (Graduate Certificate); English (MA, MS, PhD); film studies (Graduate Certificate); history (MA, MS); music (MM); political science (MA, MS); public history (Graduate Certificate); sociology (MS); Spanish (MA); studies in children's and adolescent literature and culture (Graduate Certificate); teaching English to speakers of other languages (Graduate Certificate); theater (MA, MS). *Program availability:* Part-time. *Faculty:* 53 full-time (26 women), 7 part-time/adjunct (2 women). *Students:* 87 full-time (55 women), 528 part-time (362 women); includes 198 minority (86 Black or African American, non-Hispanic/Latino; 2 American Indian or Alaska Native, non-Hispanic/Latino; 8 Asian, non-Hispanic/Latino; 84 Hispanic/Latino; 18 Two or more races, non-Hispanic/Latino), 27 international. Average age 37. 333 applicants, 56% accepted, 149 enrolled. In 2016, 66 master's, 8 doctorates awarded. *Degree requirements:* For master's, one foreign language, comprehensive exam, thesis (for some programs); for doctorate, one foreign language, comprehensive exam, thesis/dissertation, departmental qualifying exam. *Entrance requirements:* For master's and doctorate, GRE General Test. Additional exam requirements/recommendations for international students: Required—TOEFL (minimum score 550 paper-based; 79 iBT), IELTS (minimum score 6). *Application deadline:* Applications are processed on a rolling basis. Application fee: $50. Electronic applications accepted. *Expenses:* Contact institution. *Financial support:* In 2016–17, 255 students received support, including 9 research assistantships with partial tuition reimbursements available (averaging $9,000 per year), 68 teaching assistantships with partial tuition reimbursements available (averaging $9,000 per year); Federal Work-Study, institutionally sponsored loans, scholarships/grants, health care benefits, and unspecified assistantships also available. Financial award application deadline: 5/1; financial award applicants required to submit FAFSA. *Unit head:* Dr. Salvatore Attardo, Dean, 903-886-5166, Fax: 903-886-5774, E-mail: salvatore.attardo@tamuc.edu. *Application contact:* Shelby Miller, Graduate Recruiter, 903-468-8123, Fax: 903-886-5774, E-mail: shelby.miller@tamuc.edu.
Website: http://www.tamuc.edu/academics/graduateSchool/programs/humanitiesSocialScienceArts/default.aspx

**Texas State University,** The Graduate College, College of Fine Arts and Communication, Program in Theatre Arts, San Marcos, TX 78666. Offers design (MFA); directing (MFA); dramatic writing (MFA); theatre history, dramatic criticism and dramaturgy (MA). *Program availability:* Part-time, evening/weekend. *Faculty:* 17 full-time (9 women), 2 part-time/adjunct. *Students:* 18 full-time (8 women), 1 (woman) part-time; includes 3 minority (2 Black or African American, non-Hispanic/Latino; 1 Two or more races, non-Hispanic/Latino). Average age 33. 25 applicants, 44% accepted, 8 enrolled. In 2016, 11 master's awarded. *Degree requirements:* For master's, comprehensive exam, thesis (for some programs). *Entrance requirements:* For master's, GRE General Test (minimum preferred score of 300), baccalaureate degree from regionally-accredited institution with minimum GPA of 2.75 in last 60 hours of undergraduate course work, 2 letters of recommendation, statement of purpose, curriculum vitae/resume; writing sample (for playwriting applicants only); interview (for directing applicants only). Additional exam requirements/recommendations for international students: Required—TOEFL (minimum score 550 paper-based; 78 iBT), IELTS (minimum score 6.5). *Application deadline:* For fall admission, 3/15 for domestic and international students. Applications are processed on a rolling basis. Application fee: $40 ($90 for international students). Electronic applications accepted. *Expenses:* $4,851 per semester. *Financial support:* In 2016–17, 18 teaching assistantships (averaging $13,246 per year) were awarded; research assistantships, Federal Work-Study, institutionally sponsored loans, scholarships/grants, and unspecified assistantships also available. Support available to part-time students. Financial award application deadline: 3/1; financial award applicants required to submit FAFSA. *Unit head:* Dr. Sandra Mayo, Graduate Advisor, 512-245-7889, Fax: 512-245-8440, E-mail: th_gradadvisor@txstate.edu. *Application contact:* Dr. Andrea Golato, Dean of Graduate School, 512-245-2581, Fax: 512-245-8365, E-mail: gradcollege@txstate.edu.
Website: http://www.theatreanddance.txstate.edu/

**Texas State University,** The Graduate College, College of Liberal Arts, Program in Creative Writing, San Marcos, TX 78666. Offers MFA. *Program availability:* Part-time, evening/weekend. *Faculty:* 7 full-time (3 women). *Students:* 40 full-time (21 women), 15 part-time (7 women); includes 12 minority (2 Asian, non-Hispanic/Latino; 10 Hispanic/Latino). Average age 30. 117 applicants, 44% accepted, 14 enrolled. In 2016, 21 master's awarded. *Degree requirements:* For master's, comprehensive exam, thesis. *Entrance requirements:* For master's, baccalaureate degree from regionally-accredited university with minimum GPA of 2.75 on last 60 undergraduate semester hours, portfolio, 2-3 short stories or up to 25 pages of novel (for fiction); 12 to 15 poems (for poetry). Additional exam requirements/recommendations for international students: Required—TOEFL (minimum score 550 paper-based; 78 iBT), IELTS (minimum score 6.5). *Application deadline:* For fall admission, 1/15 for domestic and international students; for spring admission, 11/1 for domestic and international students. Applications are processed on a rolling basis. Application fee: $40 ($90 for international students). Electronic applications accepted. *Expenses:* $4,851 per semester. *Financial support:* In 2016–17, 36 students received support, including 2 research assistantships (averaging $16,965 per year), 33 teaching assistantships (averaging $16,493 per year); Federal Work-Study, institutionally sponsored loans, and scholarships/grants also available. Support available to part-time students. Financial award application deadline: 3/1; financial award applicants required to submit FAFSA. *Unit head:* Doug Dorst, Graduate Adviser, 512-245-7681, Fax: 512-245-8546, E-mail: dd35@txstate.edu. *Application contact:* Dr. Andrea Golato, Dean of Graduate School, 512-245-2581, Fax: 512-245-8365, E-mail: gradcollege@txstate.edu.
Website: http://www.english.txstate.edu/

**Tiffin University,** Program in Humanities, Tiffin, OH 44883-2161. Offers art and visual media (MH); communication (MH); creative writing (MH); English (MH); film studies (MH); humanities (MH); individualized studies (MH). *Program availability:* Part-time, evening/weekend, online only, 100% online, blended/hybrid learning. *Students:* 17 full-time (15 women), 116 part-time (75 women); includes 25 minority (15 Black or African American, non-Hispanic/Latino; 2 Asian, non-Hispanic/Latino; 6 Hispanic/Latino; 2 Two or more races, non-Hispanic/Latino). Average age 36. 84 applicants, 80% accepted, 43 enrolled. In 2016, 42 master's awarded. *Entrance requirements:* For master's, work experience. Additional exam requirements/recommendations for international students: Required—TOEFL (minimum score 550 paper-based; 79 iBT). *Application deadline:* For fall admission, 9/1 for domestic students; for spring admission, 1/9 for domestic students. Applications are processed on a rolling basis. Application fee: $50. Electronic applications accepted. Application fee is waived when completed online. *Expenses:* Contact institution. *Financial support:* Unspecified assistantships available. Financial award applicants required to submit FAFSA. *Unit head:* Dr. Jason Slone, Program Chair, 419-448-5851, Fax: 419-443-5002, E-mail: slonedj@tiffin.edu. *Application contact:* Nikki

## Writing

Hintze, Director of Graduate and Distance Education Academic Advising, 800-968-6446 Ext. 3596, Fax: 419-443-5002, E-mail: hintzenm@tiffin.edu.

**Towson University,** Program in Professional Writing, Towson, MD 21252-0001. Offers MS. *Program availability:* Part-time, evening/weekend. *Students:* 18 full-time (10 women), 49 part-time (41 women); includes 17 minority (11 Black or African American, non-Hispanic/Latino; 1 Asian, non-Hispanic/Latino; 3 Hispanic/Latino; 2 Two or more races, non-Hispanic/Latino). *Degree requirements:* For master's, thesis optional. *Entrance requirements:* For master's, sample of written work, minimum GPA of 3.0, 2 letters of recommendation, essay. *Application deadline:* For fall admission, 3/1 for domestic students; for spring admission, 10/1 for domestic students. Applications are processed on a rolling basis. Application fee: $45. Electronic applications accepted. *Expenses:* Tuition, state resident: full-time $7580; part-time $379 per unit. Tuition, nonresident: full-time $15,700; part-time $785 per unit. *Required fees:* $2480. *Financial support:* Application deadline: 4/1. *Unit head:* Prof. Goeffrey Becker, Graduate Program Director, 410-704-5196, E-mail: gbecker@towson.edu. *Application contact:* Coverley Beidleman, Assistant Director of Graduate Admissions, 410-704-2113, Fax: 410-704-3030, E-mail: grads@towson.edu.
Website: http://www.towson.edu/cla/departments/english/gradwriting/

**Trinity College,** Graduate Programs, Program in English, Hartford, CT 06106-3100. Offers literary studies (MA); writing, rhetoric, and media arts (MA). *Program availability:* Part-time, evening/weekend. *Degree requirements:* For master's, thesis (for some programs). *Entrance requirements:* For master's, minimum GPA of 3.0.

**Union Institute & University,** Master of Arts Program, Cincinnati, OH 45206-1925. Offers creativity studies (MA); health and wellness (MA); history and culture (MA); leadership, public policy, and social issues (MA); literature and writing (MA). *Program availability:* Part-time, online only, 100% online. *Faculty:* 2 full-time (both women), 9 part-time/adjunct (7 women). *Students:* 9 full-time (7 women), 70 part-time (56 women); includes 33 minority (22 Black or African American, non-Hispanic/Latino; 1 American Indian or Alaska Native, non-Hispanic/Latino; 6 Hispanic/Latino; 4 Two or more races, non-Hispanic/Latino). Average age 40. In 2016, 45 master's awarded. *Degree requirements:* For master's, thesis. *Entrance requirements:* For master's, transcript, essay, 3 letters of recommendation, resume. Additional exam requirements/recommendations for international students: Recommended—TOEFL. *Application deadline:* For spring admission, 3/13 for domestic students. Applications are processed on a rolling basis. Application fee: $50. Electronic applications accepted. *Expenses:* Contact institution. *Financial support:* Career-related internships or fieldwork and tuition waivers available. Financial award applicants required to submit FAFSA. *Unit head:* Elden Golden, Director, 513-487-1153, E-mail: elden.golden@myunion.edu. *Application contact:* Director of Admissions, 800-861-6400.

**The University of Akron,** Graduate School, Buchtel College of Arts and Sciences, Department of English, Northeast Ohio MFA Program in Creative Writing, Akron, OH 44325. Offers MFA. Program offered jointly with Cleveland State University, Kent State University, and Youngstown State University. *Expenses:* Tuition, state resident: full-time $8618; part-time $359 per credit hour. Tuition, nonresident: full-time $17,149; part-time $715 per credit hour. *Required fees:* $1652. *Financial support:* Unspecified assistantships available. *Unit head:* David Giffels, Campus Coordinator, 330-972-6604, E-mail: dg36@uakron.edu. *Application contact:* Dr. Joseph Ceccio, Director of Graduate Studies, 330-972-7603, E-mail: jceccio@uakron.edu.
Website: http://neomfa.org

**The University of Akron,** Graduate School, Buchtel College of Arts and Sciences, Department of English, Program in Composition, Akron, OH 44325. Offers MA. *Degree requirements:* For master's, one foreign language, thesis optional. *Entrance requirements:* For master's, BA in English, minimum GPA of 2.75. *Application deadline:* For fall admission, 8/28 for domestic students. Applications are processed on a rolling basis. Application fee: $25 ($50 for international students). *Expenses:* Tuition, state resident: full-time $8618; part-time $359 per credit hour. Tuition, nonresident: full-time $17,149; part-time $715 per credit hour. *Required fees:* $1652. *Financial support:* Application deadline: 3/1. *Unit head:* Dr. Martin McKoski, Director, 330-972-7472. *Application contact:* Dr. Tom Dukes, Director of Graduate Studies, 330-972-7969, E-mail: jdukes@uakron.edu.

**The University of Alabama,** Graduate School, College of Arts and Sciences, Department of English, Tuscaloosa, AL 35487. Offers composition and rhetoric (PhD); creative writing (MFA), including fiction, poetry; literature (MA, PhD); rhetoric and composition (MA); teaching English as a second language (MATESOL). *Faculty:* 38 full-time (20 women). *Students:* 129 full-time (69 women), 6 part-time (5 women); includes 23 minority (12 Black or African American, non-Hispanic/Latino; 1 Asian, non-Hispanic/Latino; 7 Hispanic/Latino; 3 Two or more races, non-Hispanic/Latino), 3 international. Average age 29. 406 applicants, 13% accepted, 35 enrolled. In 2016, 31 master's, 4 doctorates awarded. *Degree requirements:* For master's, one foreign language, comprehensive exam, thesis optional; for doctorate, 2 foreign languages, comprehensive exam, thesis/dissertation. *Entrance requirements:* For master's, GRE (minimum score of 300, except for MFA), minimum GPA of 3.0, critical writing sample; for doctorate, GRE (minimum score of 300), minimum GPA of 3.5 on master's or equivalent graduate work, critical writing sample. Additional exam requirements/recommendations for international students: Required—TOEFL (minimum score 550 paper-based; 79 iBT). *Application deadline:* For fall admission, 12/31 priority date for domestic and international students. Application fee: $50 ($60 for international students). Electronic applications accepted. *Expenses:* Tuition, state resident: full-time $10,470. Tuition, nonresident: full-time $26,950. *Financial support:* In 2016–17, 128 students received support, including 11 fellowships with full tuition reimbursements available (averaging $15,000 per year), 13 research assistantships with full tuition reimbursements available (averaging $13,500 per year), 100 teaching assistantships with full tuition reimbursements available (averaging $13,500 per year); career-related internships or fieldwork, scholarships/grants, health care benefits, and unspecified assistantships also available. Financial award application deadline: 12/31. *Faculty research:* American literature, British literature, composition/rhetoric, applied linguistics, creative writing. *Unit head:* Prof. Joel Brouwer, Department Chair, 205-348-5065, Fax: 205-348-1388, E-mail: joel.brouwer@ua.edu. *Application contact:* Jennifer Fuqua, Graduate Coordinator, 205-348-0766, Fax: 205-348-1388, E-mail: jfuqua@ua.edu.

**The University of Alabama at Birmingham,** College of Arts and Sciences, Program in English, Birmingham, AL 35294. Offers creative writing (MA); literature (MA); rhetoric and composition (MA). *Program availability:* Part-time. *Degree requirements:* For master's, one foreign language, comprehensive exam, thesis or alternative. *Entrance requirements:* For master's, GRE General Test or MAT, minimum GPA of 2.75. Electronic applications accepted. Full-time tuition and fees vary according to course load and program.

**University of Alaska Anchorage,** College of Arts and Sciences, Program in Creative Writing and Literary Arts, Anchorage, AK 99508. Offers MFA. *Program availability:* Part-time. *Degree requirements:* For master's, comprehensive exam, thesis or alternative. *Entrance requirements:* For master's, portfolio, minimum GPA of 3.0. Additional exam requirements/recommendations for international students: Required—TOEFL (minimum score 550 paper-based). *Faculty research:* Alaska Quarterly Review publications, feminist studies, ecocriticism and native writing, poetry.

**University of Alaska Fairbanks,** College of Liberal Arts, Department of English, Fairbanks, AK 99775-5720. Offers creative writing (MFA); literature (MA); MA/MFA. *Program availability:* Part-time. *Faculty:* 13 full-time (5 women). *Students:* 23 full-time (16 women), 10 part-time (7 women); includes 6 minority (1 Asian, non-Hispanic/Latino; 2 Hispanic/Latino; 3 Two or more races, non-Hispanic/Latino). Average age 31. 52 applicants, 35% accepted, 9 enrolled. In 2016, 7 master's awarded. *Degree requirements:* For master's, comprehensive exam, oral defense of project or thesis. *Entrance requirements:* For master's, GRE General Test, bachelor's degree from accredited institution with minimum cumulative undergraduate and major GPA of 3.0, academic writing sample. Additional exam requirements/recommendations for international students: Required—TOEFL (minimum score 550 paper-based; 79 iBT), IELTS (minimum score 6.5). *Application deadline:* For fall admission, 6/1 for domestic students, 3/1 for international students; for spring admission, 10/15 for domestic students, 9/1 for international students. Applications are processed on a rolling basis. Application fee: $60. Electronic applications accepted. *Expenses:* Tuition, state resident: full-time $7992; part-time $444 per credit. Tuition, nonresident: full-time $16,326; part-time $907 per credit. *Required fees:* $39 per credit. $322 per semester. Tuition and fees vary according to course level, course load, campus/location, program and reciprocity agreements. *Financial support:* In 2016–17, 20 teaching assistantships with full tuition reimbursements (averaging $5,867 per year) were awarded; fellowships with full tuition reimbursements, research assistantships with full tuition reimbursements, Federal Work-Study, scholarships/grants, health care benefits, and unspecified assistantships also available. Support available to part-time students. Financial award application deadline: 7/1; financial award applicants required to submit FAFSA. *Unit head:* Richard Carr, Department Chair, 907-474-7193, Fax: 907-474-5247, E-mail: uaf-english-dept@alaska.edu. *Application contact:* Mary Kreta, Director of Admissions, 907-474-7500, Fax: 907-474-7097, E-mail: admissions@uaf.edu.
Website: http://www.uaf.edu/english

**The University of Arizona,** College of Humanities, Department of English, Program in Creative Writing, Tucson, AZ 85721. Offers MFA. *Entrance requirements:* Additional exam requirements/recommendations for international students: Required—TOEFL (minimum score 550 paper-based; 79 iBT). Electronic applications accepted.

**University of Arkansas,** Graduate School, J. William Fulbright College of Arts and Sciences, Department of English, Program in Creative Writing, Fayetteville, AR 72701. Offers MFA. In 2016, 8 master's awarded. *Degree requirements:* For master's, thesis. *Application deadline:* For fall admission, 4/1 for international students; for spring admission, 10/1 for international students. Applications are processed on a rolling basis. Application fee: $40 ($50 for international students). Electronic applications accepted. *Financial support:* In 2016–17, 1 research assistantship, 29 teaching assistantships were awarded; fellowships with tuition reimbursements, career-related internships or fieldwork, and Federal Work-Study also available. Support available to part-time students. Financial award application deadline: 4/1; financial award applicants required to submit FAFSA. *Unit head:* Dr. Davis McCombs, Director, 479-575-4301, Fax: 479-575-5919, E-mail: dmccomb@uark.edu. *Application contact:* Dr. Davis McCombs, Graduate Coordinator, 479-575-4301, Fax: 479-575-5919, E-mail: dmccomb@uark.edu.
Website: http://mfa.uark.edu/

**University of Arkansas at Little Rock,** Graduate School, College of Social Sciences and Communication, Department of Rhetoric and Writing, Little Rock, AR 72204-1099. Offers professional and technical writing (MA). *Program availability:* Part-time, evening/weekend. *Degree requirements:* For master's, thesis or alternative, oral defense of final project. *Entrance requirements:* For master's, GRE, minimum GPA of 3.0, writing portfolio. *Faculty research:* Writing for industry, science, business, and government; composition and rhetorical theory; writing nonfiction; teaching of writing.

**University of Baltimore,** Graduate School, Yale Gordon College of Arts and Sciences, Program in Creative Writing and Publishing Arts, Baltimore, MD 21201-5779. Offers MFA. *Program availability:* Part-time, evening/weekend. *Entrance requirements:* Additional exam requirements/recommendations for international students: Required—TOEFL.

**University of Baltimore,** Graduate School, Yale Gordon College of Arts and Sciences, Program in Publications Design, Baltimore, MD 21201-5779. Offers MA. *Program availability:* Part-time, evening/weekend. *Degree requirements:* For master's, seminar project. *Entrance requirements:* For master's, minimum GPA of 3.0, portfolio, interview. Additional exam requirements/recommendations for international students: Required—TOEFL (minimum score 550 paper-based). Electronic applications accepted. *Faculty research:* Communication theory, graphic design, media technology.

**The University of British Columbia,** Faculty of Arts, Creative Writing Program, Vancouver, BC V6T 1Z1, Canada. Offers creative writing (MFA); creative writing and theatre (MFA); film production and creative writing (MFA). *Program availability:* Part-time, online learning. *Degree requirements:* For master's, thesis. *Entrance requirements:* For master's, sample of written work. Additional exam requirements/recommendations for international students: Required—TOEFL. Application fee: $100 Canadian dollars ($162 Canadian dollars for international students). Electronic applications accepted. *Expenses:* $4,802 per year tuition and fees, $8,436 per year international; $592 per credit, $996 per credit international (online). *Financial support:* Fellowships, teaching assistantships, Federal Work-Study, institutionally sponsored loans, and unspecified assistantships available. *Faculty research:* Writing of fiction; poetry, creative nonfiction, plays for stage, screen, television, radio, writing for children and translation, song lyrics and libretto, new media and graphic novel. *Application contact:* Heather Miller, Graduate Program Staff, 604-822-0699, E-mail: crwr.grad@ubc.ca.
Website: http://creativewriting.ubc.ca/

**The University of British Columbia,** Faculty of Arts and Faculty of Graduate Studies, Department of Theatre and Film, Vancouver, BC V6T 1Z2, Canada. Offers film (MA, MFA), including creative writing and film production (MFA), film production (MFA), film studies (MA); theatre (MA, MFA, PhD), including theatre (MA, PhD), theatre design (MFA), theatre directing (MFA). Terminal master's awarded for partial completion of doctoral program. *Degree requirements:* For master's, variable foreign language requirement, comprehensive exam, thesis; for doctorate, one foreign language, comprehensive exam, thesis/dissertation. *Entrance requirements:* For master's, BA or equivalent; portfolio (for MFA). Additional exam requirements/recommendations for international students: Required—TOEFL. Application fee: $100 Canadian dollars ($162 Canadian dollars for international students). *Expenses:* $4,802 per year tuition and fees, $8,436 per year international. *Financial support:* Fellowships, research assistantships, teaching assistantships, career-related internships or fieldwork, Federal Work-Study, institutionally sponsored loans, scholarships/grants, health care benefits, and unspecified assistantships available. Support available to part-time students. *Faculty research:* Dramatic literature, theatrical history, criticism, playwriting, directing, film studies and production, film theory and violence, American and European cinema, cult cinema, Irish cinema. *Application contact:* Karen Tong, Graduate Program Staff, 604-

822-6342, Fax: 604-822-5985, E-mail: thtr.sec@ubc.ca. Website: http://theatrefilm.ubc.ca/

**University of California, Berkeley,** UC Berkeley Extension, Certificate Programs in Writing, Editing and Technical Communication, Berkeley, CA 94720-1500. Offers writing (Postbaccalaureate Certificate). *Program availability:* Online learning.

**University of California, Davis,** Graduate Studies, Program in English, Davis, CA 95616. Offers creative writing (MA); English (MA, PhD). Terminal master's awarded for partial completion of doctoral program. *Degree requirements:* For master's, one foreign language, thesis optional; for doctorate, 2 foreign languages, thesis/dissertation. *Entrance requirements:* For master's and doctorate, GRE General Test, GRE Subject Test, minimum GPA of 3.0, writing sample. Additional exam requirements/recommendations for international students: Required—TOEFL (minimum score 550 paper-based). Electronic applications accepted. *Faculty research:* Feminist theory, ethnic literature, literary theory, history of literature, literature of nature.

**University of California, Irvine,** School of Humanities, Department of English, Program in Writing, Irvine, CA 92697. Offers creative writing (MFA), including fiction, poetry. *Students:* 35 full-time (17 women); includes 10 minority (1 Black or African American, non-Hispanic/Latino; 3 Asian, non-Hispanic/Latino; 3 Hispanic/Latino; 3 Two or more races, non-Hispanic/Latino). Average age 31. 464 applicants, 3% accepted, 12 enrolled. In 2016, 12 master's awarded. *Degree requirements:* For master's, thesis. *Entrance requirements:* For master's, minimum GPA of 3.0, sample of written work. *Application deadline:* For fall admission, 1/15 for domestic and international students. Application fee: $105 ($125 for international students). Electronic applications accepted. *Financial support:* Fellowships with tuition reimbursements, research assistantships, teaching assistantships with partial tuition reimbursements, institutionally sponsored loans, and tuition waivers (full and partial) available. Financial award application deadline: 3/1; financial award applicants required to submit FAFSA. *Unit head:* Michael Ryan, Director, 949-824-8773, Fax: 949-824-2916, E-mail: mryan@uci.edu. *Application contact:* Sandy Mueller, Graduate Administrator, 949-824-6718, Fax: 949-824-2916, E-mail: slmuelle@uci.edu.

**University of California, Riverside,** Graduate Division, Program in Creative Writing and Writing for the Performing Arts, Riverside, CA 92211. Offers MFA. Program also offered at Palm Desert Graduate Center. *Degree requirements:* For master's, thesis. *Entrance requirements:* For master's, writing sample. Additional exam requirements/recommendations for international students: Required—TOEFL (minimum score 550 paper-based; 80 iBT). Electronic applications accepted. *Expenses:* Tuition, state resident: full-time $16,666. Tuition, nonresident: full-time $31,768. *Required fees:* $11,055.54 per quarter. $3685.18 per quarter. Tuition and fees vary according to campus/location and program. *Faculty research:* Non-fiction, playwriting, screenwriting, poetry, fiction.

**University of California, San Diego,** Graduate Division, Department of Literature, La Jolla, CA 92093. Offers literature (PhD); writing (MFA). *Students:* 64 full-time (46 women), 2 part-time (1 woman). 223 applicants, 16% accepted, 14 enrolled. In 2016, 7 master's, 10 doctorates awarded. *Degree requirements:* For master's, thesis, for doctorate, one foreign language, comprehensive exam, thesis/dissertation, 3 quarters of teaching assistantship. *Entrance requirements:* For master's, writing sample; for doctorate, GRE General Test, writing sample. Additional exam requirements/recommendations for international students: Required—TOEFL (minimum score 550 paper-based; 80 iBT), IELTS (minimum score 7); Recommended—TSE. *Application deadline:* For fall admission, 11/30 for domestic students. Application fee: $105 ($125 for international students). Electronic applications accepted. *Expenses:* Tuition, state resident: full-time $11,220. Tuition, nonresident: full-time $26,322. *Required fees:* $1864. *Financial support:* Fellowships, research assistantships, teaching assistantships, scholarships/grants, and readerships available. Financial award applicants required to submit FAFSA. *Faculty research:* Chicano/a-Latino/a studies, European studies, film studies and visual culture, Latin American literary and cultural studies, medieval/early modern studies, transnational Africa/African diaspora studies, transnational Asia/Asian diaspora studies. *Unit head:* Yingjin Zhang, Chair, 858-534-5991, Fax: 858-534-7395, E-mail: litchair@ucsd.edu. *Application contact:* Graduate Coordinator, 858-534-3217, E-mail: litgrad@ucsd.edu.
Website: http://literature.ucsd.edu

**University of California, Santa Barbara,** Graduate Division, College of Letters and Sciences, Division of Humanities and Fine Arts, Department of English, Santa Barbara, CA 93106-3170. Offers English (PhD), including environment and society, European medieval studies, feminist studies, global studies, technology and society, translation studies, writing studies; MA/PhD. Terminal master's awarded for partial completion of doctoral program. *Degree requirements:* For doctorate, one foreign language, comprehensive exam, thesis/dissertation. *Entrance requirements:* For doctorate, GRE General Test, GRE Subject Test (English literature). Additional exam requirements/recommendations for international students: Required—TOEFL (minimum score 550 paper-based; 80 iBT), IELTS (minimum score 7). Electronic applications accepted. *Faculty research:* Medieval, Romantic and Victorian studies; gender studies and feminist theory; literature and the mind; American literature; literature and new media/information culture.

**University of California, Santa Cruz,** Division of Graduate Studies, Division of Social Sciences, Program in Social Documentation, Santa Cruz, CA 95064. Offers MA. *Entrance requirements:* For master's, resume or curriculum vitae, sample of documentary production work. Additional exam requirements/recommendations for international students: Required—TOEFL (minimum score 550 paper-based; 83 iBT); Recommended—IELTS (minimum score 8). Electronic applications accepted. *Faculty research:* Documentation of underrepresented areas of community life.

**University of Central Arkansas,** Graduate School, College of Fine Arts and Communication, Program in Creative Writing, Conway, AR 72035-0001. Offers MFA. *Degree requirements:* For master's, thesis project. *Entrance requirements:* For master's, GRE. Electronic applications accepted.

**University of Central Florida,** College of Arts and Humanities, Department of English, Orlando, FL 32816. Offers creative writing (MFA); English (MA, Certificate); texts and technology (PhD). *Program availability:* Part-time, evening/weekend. *Faculty:* 41 full-time (21 women), 12 part-time/adjunct (9 women). *Students:* 76 full-time (53 women), 72 part-time (54 women); includes 23 minority (4 Black or African American, non-Hispanic/Latino; 3 Asian, non-Hispanic/Latino; 14 Hispanic/Latino; 2 Two or more races, non-Hispanic/Latino), 5 international. Average age 33. 142 applicants, 62% accepted, 49 enrolled. In 2016, 31 master's, 7 doctorates, 8 other advanced degrees awarded. *Degree requirements:* For master's, one foreign language, thesis or alternative. *Entrance requirements:* For master's, GRE General Test, minimum GPA of 3.0 in last 60 hours of course work. Additional exam requirements/recommendations for international students: Required—TOEFL. *Application deadline:* For fall admission, 3/30 for domestic students; for spring admission, 11/1 for domestic students. Application fee: $30. Electronic applications accepted. *Expenses:* Tuition, state resident: part-time $288.16 per credit hour. Tuition, nonresident: part-time $1071.31 per credit hour. *Financial support:* In 2016–17, 49 students received support, including 19 fellowships with partial tuition reimbursements available (averaging $5,874 per year), 12 research

assistantships with partial tuition reimbursements available (averaging $8,630 per year), 34 teaching assistantships with partial tuition reimbursements available (averaging $9,949 per year); career-related internships or fieldwork, Federal Work-Study, institutionally sponsored loans, tuition waivers (partial), and unspecified assistantships also available. Financial award application deadline: 3/1; financial award applicants required to submit FAFSA. *Unit head:* Dr. Trey Philpotts, Chair, 407-823-1159, E-mail: trey.philpotts@ucf.edu. *Application contact:* Assistant Director, Graduate Admissions, 407-823-2766, Fax: 407-823-6442, E-mail: gradadmissions@ucf.edu.
Website: http://www.english.cah.ucf.edu/

**University of Central Oklahoma,** The Jackson College of Graduate Studies, College of Liberal Arts, Department of English, Edmond, OK 73034-5209. Offers creative writing (MA, MFA); traditional studies (MA). *Program availability:* Part-time. *Degree requirements:* For master's, variable foreign language requirement, comprehensive exam (for some programs), thesis (for some programs), portfolio. *Entrance requirements:* For master's, GRE, 18-24 hours of course work in English language and literature; writing sample; essay. Additional exam requirements/recommendations for international students: Required—TOEFL (minimum score 550 paper-based; 79 iBT), IELTS (minimum score 6.5). Electronic applications accepted. *Faculty research:* John Milton, Harriet Beecher Stowe.

**University of Chicago,** Division of the Humanities, Master of Arts Program in the Humanities, Chicago, IL 60637. Offers art history (MA); cinema and media studies (MA); classic languages (MA); comparative literature (MA); creative writing (MA); cultural policy studies (MA); digital humanities (MA); East Asian languages and civilizations (MA); English language and literature (MA); gender and sexuality studies (MA); Germanic studies (MA); linguistics (MA); music (MA); near Eastern languages and civilizations (MA); philosophy (MA); poetics (MA); race, politics and culture (MA); Romance languages and literatures (MA); Slavic languages and literatures (MA); South Asian languages and civilizations (MA); theater and performance studies (MA). *Students:* 80 full-time (43 women), 7 part-time (3 women); includes 20 minority (5 Black or African American, non-Hispanic/Latino; 1 American Indian or Alaska Native, non-Hispanic/Latino; 6 Asian, non-Hispanic/Latino; 5 Hispanic/Latino; 3 Two or more races, non-Hispanic/Latino), 11 international. Average age 26. 706 applicants, 15% accepted, 42 enrolled. In 2016, 92 master's awarded. *Degree requirements:* For master's, thesis. *Entrance requirements:* For master's, GRE General Test. Additional exam requirements/recommendations for international students: Required—TOEFL (minimum score 104 iBT), IELTS (minimum score 7). *Application deadline:* For fall admission, 1/3 for domestic and international students. Application fee: $90. Electronic applications accepted. *Financial support:* In 2016–17, 8 fellowships with partial tuition reimbursements (averaging $12,000 per year) were awarded; Federal Work-Study, institutionally sponsored loans, scholarships/grants, and tuition waivers (partial) also available. Financial award application deadline: 12/15; financial award applicants required to submit FAFSA. *Unit head:* Malynne Sternstein, Co-Director, 773-834-1201, Fax: 773-834-7526. *Application contact:* Program Coordinator, 773-834-1201, Fax: 773-834-7526, E-mail: ma-humanities@uchicago.edu.
Website: http://maph.uchicago.edu/

**University of Colorado Boulder,** Graduate School, College of Arts and Sciences, Department of English, Boulder, CO 80309. Offers literature (MA, PhD), including creative writing (MA). *Faculty:* 47 full-time (28 women). *Students:* 95 full-time (58 women), 4 part-time (3 women); includes 21 minority (5 Black or African American, non-Hispanic/Latino; 2 American Indian or Alaska Native, non-Hispanic/Latino; 3 Asian, non-Hispanic/Latino; 9 Hispanic/Latino; 2 Two or more races, non-Hispanic/Latino), 1 international. Average age 30. 406 applicants, 25% accepted, 28 enrolled. In 2016, 26 master's, 4 doctorates awarded. Terminal master's awarded for partial completion of doctoral program. *Degree requirements:* For master's, one foreign language, comprehensive exam, thesis or alternative; for doctorate, 2 foreign languages, comprehensive exam, thesis/dissertation. *Entrance requirements:* For master's, GRE General Test, GRE Subject Test, minimum undergraduate GPA of 3.0; for doctorate, GRE General Test, GRE Subject Test. *Application deadline:* For fall admission, 2/1 for domestic students, 12/1 for international students. Application fee: $60 ($80 for international students). Electronic applications accepted. Application fee is waived when completed online. *Financial support:* In 2016–17, 207 students received support, including 49 fellowships (averaging $2,399 per year), 5 research assistantships with full and partial tuition reimbursements available (averaging $25,901 per year), 62 teaching assistantships with full and partial tuition reimbursements available (averaging $30,862 per year); institutionally sponsored loans, scholarships/grants, health care benefits, and unspecified assistantships also available. Financial award application deadline: 1/1; financial award applicants required to submit FAFSA. *Faculty research:* Literary criticism, English language/literature, literary history, arts/humanities/cultural activities, fiction. *Total annual research expenditures:* $4.3 million. *Application contact:* E-mail: gsengl@colorado.edu.
Website: http://english.colorado.edu/

**University of Colorado Denver,** School of Education and Human Development, Teacher Education Programs, Denver, CO 80217. Offers elementary linguistically diverse education (MA); elementary math and science education (MA); elementary math education (MA); elementary reading and writing (MA); elementary science education (MA); secondary English education (MA); secondary linguistically diverse education (MA); secondary math education (MA); secondary reading and writing (MA); secondary science education (MA); special education (MA). *Accreditation:* NCATE. *Program availability:* Part-time, evening/weekend. *Students:* 142 full-time (117 women), 184 part-time (159 women); includes 56 minority (6 Black or African American, non-Hispanic/Latino; 1 American Indian or Alaska Native, non-Hispanic/Latino; 4 Asian, non-Hispanic/Latino; 38 Hispanic/Latino; 1 Native Hawaiian or other Pacific Islander, non-Hispanic/Latino; 6 Two or more races, non-Hispanic/Latino), 1 international. Average age 30. 18 applicants, 67% accepted, 9 enrolled. In 2016, 134 master's awarded. *Degree requirements:* For master's, comprehensive exam. *Entrance requirements:* For master's, GRE or MAT (for those with GPA below 2.75), transcripts, resume, letters of recommendation. Additional exam requirements/recommendations for international students: Required—TOEFL (minimum score 537 paper-based; 75 iBT); Recommended—IELTS (minimum score 6.5). *Application deadline:* For fall admission, 4/15 for domestic students, 4/1 for international students; for spring admission, 9/15 for domestic students, 9/1 for international students; for summer admission, 2/15 for domestic students, 2/1 for international students. Applications are processed on a rolling basis. Application fee: $50 ($75 for international students). Electronic applications accepted. *Expenses:* Contact institution. *Financial support:* In 2016–17, 26 students received support. Fellowships, research assistantships, teaching assistantships, Federal Work-Study, institutionally sponsored loans, scholarships/grants, and traineeships available. Financial award application deadline: 4/1; financial award applicants required to submit FAFSA. *Faculty research:* Linguistically diverse education/ESL, elementary reading and writing, elementary teacher education, secondary teacher education, special education. *Unit head:* Cindy Gutierrez, Director, 303-315-4982, E-mail: cindy.gutierrez@ucdenver.edu. *Application contact:* 303-315-6300, E-mail: education@ucdenver.edu.
Website: http://www.ucdenver.edu/academics/colleges/SchoolOfEducation/Academics/MASTERS/Pages/default.aspx

# Writing

**University of Dayton,** Department of English, Dayton, OH 45469. Offers literary and cultural studies (MA); teaching English to speakers of other languages (TESOL) (MA); writing and rhetoric (MA). *Program availability:* Part-time. *Faculty:* 22 full-time (11 women). *Students:* 15 full-time (10 women), 2 part-time (1 woman); includes 1 minority (Black or African American, non-Hispanic/Latino), 7 international. Average age 27. 55 applicants, 29% accepted. In 2016, 8 master's awarded. *Degree requirements:* For master's, thesis. *Entrance requirements:* For master's, 24 undergraduate-level semester hours in literature and/or writing; minimum GPA of 3.0; transcripts; personal statement; 8-10 page writing sample; three professional letters of recommendation. Additional exam requirements/recommendations for international students: Required—TOEFL (minimum score 550 paper-based, 80 iBT) or IELTS. *Application deadline:* For fall admission, 6/15 priority date for domestic and international students; for spring admission, 12/15 priority date for domestic and international students. Applications are processed on a rolling basis. Application fee: $0 ($50 for international students). Electronic applications accepted. *Expenses:* $890 per credit hour, $25 registration fee. *Financial support:* In 2016–17, 9 teaching assistantships with full tuition reimbursements (averaging $11,000 per year) were awarded; institutionally sponsored loans and health care benefits also available. Financial award application deadline: 12/15; financial award applicants required to submit FAFSA. *Faculty research:* Gender and Victorian periodicals; literature and human rights; Paul Lawrence Dunbar, the archetype of the Indian princess; Amish country. *Total annual research expenditures:* $35,000. *Unit head:* Dr. Andrew Slade, Chair, 937-229-3434, Fax: 937-229-3563, E-mail: aslade1@udayton.edu. *Application contact:* Dr. Tereza Szeghi, Director of Graduate Studies, 937-229-3443, E-mail: tszeghi1@udayton.edu.
Website: https://www.udayton.edu/artssciences/academics/english/welcome/index.php

**University of Denver,** Division of Arts, Humanities and Social Sciences, Department of English, Denver, CO 80208. Offers creative writing (PhD); literary studies (MA, PhD). *Program availability:* Part-time. *Faculty:* 19 full-time (8 women), 1 (woman) part-time/adjunct. *Students:* 30 full-time (22 women), 4 part-time (3 women); includes 10 minority (1 Black or African American, non-Hispanic/Latino; 2 Asian, non-Hispanic/Latino; 4 Hispanic/Latino; 3 Two or more races, non-Hispanic/Latino), 1 international. Average age 33. 165 applicants, 13% accepted, 10 enrolled. In 2016, 3 master's, 9 doctorates awarded. *Degree requirements:* For master's, one foreign language, comprehensive exam, thesis; for doctorate, 2 foreign languages, comprehensive exam, thesis/dissertation. *Entrance requirements:* For master's, GRE General Test, GRE Subject Test (advanced literature), bachelor's degree, transcripts, academic essay, statement of intent, three letters of recommendation; for doctorate, GRE General Test, GRE Subject Test (advanced literature), master's degree, transcripts, academic essay, statement of intent, three letters of recommendation, and a writing sample (creative writing program only). Additional exam requirements/recommendations for international students: Required—TOEFL (minimum score 570 paper-based; 88 iBT). *Application deadline:* For fall admission, 1/1 priority date for domestic and international students. Applications are processed on a rolling basis. Application fee: $65. Electronic applications accepted. *Expenses:* $29,022 per year full-time. *Financial support:* In 2016–17, 34 students received support, including 21 teaching assistantships with tuition reimbursements available (averaging $17,500 per year); Federal Work-Study, institutionally sponsored loans, scholarships/grants, and unspecified assistantships also available. Support available to part-time students. Financial award application deadline: 2/15; financial award applicants required to submit FAFSA. *Faculty research:* African diaspora semiotics, Susan Howe's poetics, Renaissance drama and emblematic culture, New England Colonial literature, postmodern literature. *Unit head:* Dr. Clark Davis, Professor and Chair, 303-871-2900, Fax: 303-871-2853, E-mail: cldavis@du.edu. *Application contact:* Dr. Adam Rovner, Associate Professor and Director of Graduate Studies, 303-871-2861, Fax: 303-871-2853, E-mail: adam.rovner@du.edu.
Website: http://www.du.edu/ahss/english

**University of Denver,** University College, Denver, CO 80208. Offers arts and culture (MA, Certificate); communication management (MS, Certificate), including translation studies (Certificate), world history and culture (Certificate); environmental policy and management (MS); geographic information systems (MS); global affairs (MA, Certificate), including human capital in organizations (Certificate), philanthropic leadership (Certificate), project management (Certificate), strategic innovation and change (Certificate); healthcare leadership (MS); information communications and technology (MS); leadership and organizations (MS); professional creative writing (MA, Certificate), including emergency planning and response (Certificate), organizational security (Certificate); security management (MS, Certificate); strategic human resources (Certificate). *Program availability:* Part-time, evening/weekend, online learning. *Faculty:* 118 part-time/adjunct (62 women). *Students:* 59 full-time (22 women), 1,285 part-time (750 women); includes 316 minority (111 Black or African American, non-Hispanic/Latino; 8 American Indian or Alaska Native, non-Hispanic/Latino; 39 Asian, non-Hispanic/Latino; 123 Hispanic/Latino; 3 Native Hawaiian or other Pacific Islander, non-Hispanic/Latino; 32 Two or more races, non-Hispanic/Latino), 85 international. Average age 35. 703 applicants, 89% accepted, 390 enrolled. In 2016, 428 master's, 138 other advanced degrees awarded. *Degree requirements:* For master's, capstone project. *Entrance requirements:* For master's, transcripts, two letters of recommendation, personal statement, resume. Additional exam requirements/recommendations for international students: Required—TOEFL (minimum score 550 paper-based; 80 iBT). *Application deadline:* For fall admission, 6/21 priority date for domestic students, 5/1 priority date for international students; for winter admission, 9/14 priority date for domestic students, 9/19 priority date for international students; for spring admission, 1/11 priority date for domestic students, 12/12 priority date for international students; for summer admission, 3/29 priority date for domestic students, 3/6 priority date for international students. Applications are processed on a rolling basis. Application fee: $75. Electronic applications accepted. *Expenses:* $7,236 per year full-time. *Financial support:* In 2016–17, 27 students received support, including 1 teaching assistantship (averaging $1,489 per year). Financial award applicants required to submit FAFSA. *Unit head:* Dr. Michael McGuire, Dean, 303-871-3518, Fax: 303-871-3303, E-mail: mmcguire@du.edu. *Application contact:* Information Contact, 303-871-2291, E-mail: ucoladm@du.edu.
Website: http://universitycollege.du.edu/

**The University of Findlay,** Office of Graduate Admissions, Findlay, OH 45840-3653. Offers applied security and analytics (MSAS); athletic training (MAT); business (MBA), including certified management accountant, certified public accountant, health care management, hospitality management; education (MA Ed, Ed D), including children's literature (MA Ed), curriculum and teaching (MA Ed), education (MA Ed), educational administration (MA Ed), human resource development (MA Ed), reading (MA Ed), science education (MA Ed), superintendent (Ed D), teaching (Ed D), technology (MA Ed); environmental, safety and health management (MSEM); health informatics (MS); occupational therapy (MOT); pharmacy (Pharm D); physical therapy (DPT); physician assistant (MPA); rhetoric and writing (MA); teaching English to speakers of other languages (TESOL) and bilingual education (MA). *Program availability:* Part-time, evening/weekend, 100% online, blended/hybrid learning. *Faculty:* 114 full-time (63 women), 44 part-time/adjunct (18 women). *Students:* 751 full-time (452 women), 573 part-time (323 women); includes 164 minority (82 Black or African American, non-Hispanic/Latino; 1 American Indian or Alaska Native, non-Hispanic/Latino; 27 Asian,

non-Hispanic/Latino; 37 Hispanic/Latino; 17 Two or more races, non-Hispanic/Latino), 280 international. Average age 28. 661 applicants, 52% accepted, 288 enrolled. In 2016, 366 master's, 137 doctorates awarded. *Degree requirements:* For master's, comprehensive exam (for some programs), thesis, cumulative project, capstone project; for doctorate, thesis/dissertation. *Entrance requirements:* For master's, GRE (for some programs), bachelor's degree from accredited institution, minimum undergraduate GPA of 3.0 in last 64 hours of course work; for doctorate, MAT, minimum cumulative GPA of 3.0, master's degree. Additional exam requirements/recommendations for international students: Recommended—TOEFL (minimum score 79 iBT), IELTS (minimum score 7). *Application deadline:* For fall admission, 6/15 for international students; for spring admission, 12/1 for international students; for summer admission, 4/1 for international students. Applications are processed on a rolling basis. Electronic applications accepted. *Expenses:* Contact institution. *Financial support:* In 2016–17, 139 students received support, including 15 research assistantships with partial tuition reimbursements available (averaging $7,200 per year), 25 teaching assistantships with partial tuition reimbursements available (averaging $7,200 per year); Federal Work-Study, institutionally sponsored loans, and unspecified assistantships also available. Financial award application deadline: 4/1; financial award applicants required to submit FAFSA. *Unit head:* Christopher M. Harris, Director of Admissions, 419-434-4347, E-mail: harrisc1@findlay.edu. *Application contact:* Madeline Fauser Brennan, Graduate Admissions Counselor, 419-434-4636, Fax: 419-434-4898, E-mail: fauserbrennan@findlay.edu.
Website: http://www.findlay.edu/admissions/graduate/Pages/default.aspx

**University of Florida,** Graduate School, College of Liberal Arts and Sciences, Department of English, Gainesville, FL 32611. Offers creative writing (MFA); English (MA, PhD). *Degree requirements:* For master's, one foreign language, comprehensive exam, thesis or alternative; for doctorate, one foreign language, comprehensive exam, thesis/dissertation. *Entrance requirements:* For master's and doctorate, GRE General Test, minimum GPA of 3.0. Additional exam requirements/recommendations for international students: Required—TOEFL (minimum score 550 paper-based; 80 iBT), IELTS (minimum score 6). Electronic applications accepted. *Faculty research:* Modern global literatures in English, film and media studies, cultural studies and critical theory, American literature, English literature.

**University of Houston,** College of Liberal Arts and Social Sciences, Department of English, Houston, TX 77204. Offers applied English linguistics (MA); creative writing (MFA); creative writing and literature (MA, PhD); English (MA, PhD). *Degree requirements:* For master's, one foreign language, comprehensive exam (for some programs), thesis (MFA); for doctorate, 2 foreign languages, comprehensive exam, thesis/dissertation. *Entrance requirements:* For master's, GRE General Test, minimum GPA of 3.0 in last 60 hours of course work; for doctorate, GRE General Test, GRE Subject Test (literature), writing sample. Additional exam requirements/recommendations for international students: Required—TOEFL (minimum score 550 paper-based; 79 iBT). Electronic applications accepted.

**University of Houston–Victoria,** School of Arts and Sciences, Program in Creative Writing, Victoria, TX 77901-4450. Offers MFA. *Degree requirements:* For master's, thesis. *Entrance requirements:* For master's, GRE, two letters of recommendation, twenty- to thirty-page creative writing sample.

**University of Idaho,** College of Graduate Studies, College of Letters, Arts and Social Sciences, Department of English, Moscow, ID 83844. Offers creative writing (MFA); English (MA, MAT); teaching English as a second language (MA). *Faculty:* 14 full-time (7 women). *Students:* 53 full-time, 10 part-time. Average age 31. In 2016, 40 master's awarded. *Entrance requirements:* For master's, minimum GPA of 3.0. Additional exam requirements/recommendations for international students: Required—TOEFL. *Application deadline:* For fall admission, 8/1 for domestic students; for spring admission, 12/15 for domestic students. Applications are processed on a rolling basis. Application fee: $60. Electronic applications accepted. *Expenses:* Tuition, state resident: full-time $6460; part-time $414 per credit hour. Tuition, nonresident: full-time $21,268; part-time $1237 per credit hour. *Required fees:* $2070; $60 per credit hour. Full-time tuition and fees vary according to course load and reciprocity agreements. *Financial support:* Research assistantships and teaching assistantships available. Financial award applicants required to submit FAFSA. *Unit head:* Dr. Scott Slovic, Chair, 208-885-6156, E-mail: englishdept@uidaho.edu. *Application contact:* Sean Scoggin, Graduate Recruitment Coordinator, 208-885-4723, Fax: 208-885-4406, E-mail: graduateadmissions@uidaho.edu.
Website: https://www.uidaho.edu/class/english

**University of Illinois at Urbana–Champaign,** Graduate College, College of Liberal Arts and Sciences, Department of English, Champaign, IL 61820. Offers creative writing (MFA); English (MA, PhD).

**The University of Iowa,** Graduate College, College of Liberal Arts and Sciences, Department of English, Iowa City, IA 52242-1316. Offers English (PhD); literary studies (MA); nonfiction writing (MFA). *Degree requirements:* For master's, thesis (for some programs), exam; for doctorate, comprehensive exam, thesis/dissertation. *Entrance requirements:* For master's and doctorate, GRE General Test, minimum GPA of 3.0. Additional exam requirements/recommendations for international students: Required—TOEFL (minimum score 640 paper-based; 111 iBT). Electronic applications accepted.

**The University of Iowa,** Graduate College, College of Liberal Arts and Sciences, Department of Spanish and Portuguese, Iowa City, IA 52242-1316. Offers Spanish (MA, PhD); Spanish creative writing (MFA). *Degree requirements:* For master's, thesis optional, exam; for doctorate, comprehensive exam, thesis/dissertation. *Entrance requirements:* For master's and doctorate, GRE General Test, minimum GPA of 3.0. Additional exam requirements/recommendations for international students: Required—TOEFL (minimum score 600 paper-based; 100 iBT). Electronic applications accepted.

**The University of Kansas,** Graduate Studies, College of Liberal Arts and Sciences, Department of English, Lawrence, KS 66045. Offers creative writing (MFA), including fine arts/creative writing; English (MA, PhD). *Program availability:* Part-time. *Students:* 93 full-time (57 women), 3 part-time (1 woman); includes 14 minority (7 Black or African American, non-Hispanic/Latino; 1 Asian, non-Hispanic/Latino; 3 Hispanic/Latino; 3 Two or more races, non-Hispanic/Latino), 8 international. Average age 30. 143 applicants, 29% accepted, 28 enrolled. In 2016, 9 master's, 3 doctorates awarded. *Entrance requirements:* For master's and doctorate, GRE General Test, two examples of academic writing; resume; statement of approximately 500 words describing interests, training, experience (including teaching experience), academic ability, and goals; three letters of recommendation; official transcripts. Additional exam requirements/recommendations for international students: Required—TOEFL or IELTS. *Application deadline:* For fall admission, 12/31 for domestic and international students. Application fee: $65 ($85 for international students). Electronic applications accepted. *Financial support:* Fellowships, research assistantships, teaching assistantships, and unspecified assistantships available. *Faculty research:* Ecocriticism and science/science fiction writing; gender and sexuality studies; U.S. ethnic literatures, race, and diaspora studies; composition, rhetoric, and language studies; creative writing. *Unit head:* Anna Neill, Chair, 785-864-2521, E-mail: aneill@ku.edu. *Application contact:* Lydia Ash, Graduate

Secretary, 785-864-2518, E-mail: lash@ku.edu.
Website: http://www.english.ku.edu

**University of King's College,** Graduate and Advanced Programs, Halifax, NS B3H 2A1, Canada. Offers creative nonfiction (MFA); journalism (MJ).

**University of Louisiana at Lafayette,** College of Liberal Arts, Department of English, Lafayette, LA 70504. Offers British and American literature (MA), including creative writing, folklore, rhetoric; creative writing (PhD); literature (PhD); rhetoric (PhD). *Program availability:* Part-time. Terminal master's awarded for partial completion of doctoral program. *Degree requirements:* For master's, one foreign language, thesis or alternative; for doctorate, 2 foreign languages, comprehensive exam, thesis/dissertation. *Entrance requirements:* For master's, GRE General Test, minimum GPA of 2.75; for doctorate, GRE General Test, minimum GPA of 3.0. Additional exam requirements/recommendations for international students: Required—TOEFL (minimum score 550 paper-based). Electronic applications accepted. *Faculty research:* Composition theory, Southern literature, medieval literature.

**University of Louisville,** Graduate School, College of Arts and Sciences, Department of English, Louisville, KY 40292. Offers English (MA), including creative writing, literature, rhetoric and composition (MA, PhD); English rhetoric and composition (PhD), including rhetoric and composition (MA, PhD). *Program availability:* Part-time, evening/weekend. *Faculty:* 36 full-time (19 women), 6 part-time/adjunct (3 women). *Students:* 54 full-time (39 women), 17 part-time (12 women); includes 9 minority (3 Black or African American, non-Hispanic/Latino; 1 Asian, non-Hispanic/Latino; 3 Hispanic/Latino; 2 Two or more races, non-Hispanic/Latino), 1 international. Average age 30. 87 applicants, 53% accepted, 20 enrolled. In 2016, 16 master's, 2 doctorates awarded. *Degree requirements:* For master's, one foreign language, thesis optional, culminating project of 25-30 pages; for doctorate, one foreign language, comprehensive exam, thesis/dissertation. *Entrance requirements:* For master's and doctorate, GRE General Test. Additional exam requirements/recommendations for international students: Required—TOEFL (minimum score 600 paper-based) or IELTS (6.5). *Application deadline:* Applications are processed on a rolling basis. Application fee: $60. Electronic applications accepted. *Expenses:* $12,448. *Financial support:* In 2016–17, 3 fellowships with full tuition reimbursements (averaging $20,000 per year), 2 research assistantships (averaging $17,750 per year), 34 teaching assistantships with full tuition reimbursements (averaging $17,750 per year) were awarded; health care benefits and unspecified assistantships also available. Financial award application deadline: 1/5. *Faculty research:* Rhetoric and composition, creative writing, eighteenth- and nineteenth-century British literature, nineteenth-century American literature, critical theory. *Total annual research expenditures:* $124,449. *Unit head:* Dr. Glynis Ridley, Chair, 502-852-6803, E-mail: glynis.ridley@louisville.edu. *Application contact:* Annelise Gray, Senior Program Assistant, 502-852-0505, E-mail: annelise.gray@louisville.edu. Website: http://www.louisville.edu/english/graduate

**The University of Manchester,** School of Arts, Histories and Cultures, Manchester, United Kingdom. Offers anthropology, media and performance (PhD); applied theatre professional (PhD); archaeology (PhD); art history and visual studies (PhD); arts management and cultural policy (PhD); classics and ancient history (PhD); composition (PhD); creative writing (PhD); drama (PhD); economic and social history (PhD); electroacoustic composition (PhD); English and American studies (PhD); history (PhD); humanitarianism and conflict response (PhD); museology (PhD); music (PhD); musicology (PhD); religions and theology (PhD).

**University of Maryland, College Park,** Academic Affairs, College of Arts and Humanities, Department of English, Creative Writing Program, College Park, MD 20742. Offers MA, MFA, PhD. *Degree requirements:* For master's, thesis optional, written exam; for doctorate, one foreign language, oral and written exams. *Entrance requirements:* For master's, GRE General Test, writing sample, 3 letters of recommendation. Additional exam requirements/recommendations for international students: Required—TOEFL. Electronic applications accepted. *Faculty research:* Early British literature, American literature.

**University of Massachusetts Amherst,** Graduate School, College of Humanities and Fine Arts, Department of English, Amherst, MA 01003. Offers American studies (PhD); composition and rhetoric (PhD); creative writing (MFA); English and American literature (MA, PhD). *Program availability:* Part-time. Terminal master's awarded for partial completion of doctoral program. *Degree requirements:* For master's, one foreign language, thesis optional; for doctorate, one foreign language, comprehensive exam, thesis/dissertation. *Entrance requirements:* For master's, manuscript; for doctorate, GRE General Test, manuscript. Additional exam requirements/recommendations for international students: Required—TOEFL (minimum score 550 paper-based; 80 iBT), IELTS (minimum score 6.5). Electronic applications accepted.

**University of Massachusetts Boston,** College of Liberal Arts, Program in Creative Writing, Boston, MA 02125-3393. Offers MFA. *Students:* 18 full-time (11 women), 8 part-time (6 women); includes 4 minority (1 Black or African American, non-Hispanic/Latino; 1 Asian, non-Hispanic/Latino; 2 Two or more races, non-Hispanic/Latino), 1 international. Average age 28. 99 applicants, 21% accepted, 11 enrolled. In 2016, 5 master's awarded. *Degree requirements:* For master's, thesis. *Application deadline:* For fall admission, 1/15 for domestic students. *Expenses:* Tuition, state resident: full-time $16,863. Tuition, nonresident: full-time $32,913. *Required fees:* $177. *Unit head:* Jill McDonough, Director, 617-287-6700, E-mail: jill.mcdonough@umb.edu. *Application contact:* Peggy Roldan Patel, Graduate Admissions Coordinator, 617-287-6400, Fax: 617-287-6236, E-mail: bos.gadm@dpc.umassp.edu.
Website: http://www.umb.edu/academics/cla/english/grad/mfa

**University of Massachusetts Dartmouth,** Graduate School, College of Arts and Sciences, Program in Professional Writing, North Dartmouth, MA 02747-2300. Offers MA, Postbaccalaureate Certificate. *Program availability:* Part-time. *Faculty:* 35 full-time (21 women), 15 part-time/adjunct (11 women). *Students:* 7 full-time (6 women), 7 part-time (4 women); includes 1 minority (Two or more races, non-Hispanic/Latino). Average age 35. 9 applicants, 78% accepted, 3 enrolled. In 2016, 5 master's awarded. *Degree requirements:* For master's, thesis or portfolio. *Entrance requirements:* For master's, MAT or GRE, statement of purpose (minimum of 300 words), resume, 3 letters of recommendation, official transcripts, writing samples (minimum of 10 pages); for Postbaccalaureate Certificate, statement of purpose (minimum of 3 pages in length), resume, official transcripts. Additional exam requirements/recommendations for international students: Required—TOEFL (minimum score 533 paper-based; 72 iBT). *Application deadline:* Applications are processed on a rolling basis. Application fee: $60. Electronic applications accepted. *Expenses:* Tuition, state resident: full-time $14,994; part-time $624.75 per credit. Tuition, nonresident: full-time $27,068; part-time $1127.83 per credit. *Required fees:* $405; $25.88 per credit. Tuition and fees vary according to course load and reciprocity agreements. *Financial support:* In 2016–17, 7 fellowships (averaging $7,000 per year) were awarded; career-related internships or fieldwork, institutionally sponsored loans, scholarships/grants, and unspecified assistantships also available. Support available to part-time students. Financial award application deadline: 3/1; financial award applicants required to submit FAFSA. *Faculty research:* Rhetoric/communication studies, ethnic literature, women writers, pedagogy, journalism and related nonfiction, public relations, emerging media; technical, professional and political

communication; discourse analysis. *Total annual research expenditures:* $354,000. *Unit head:* Jerry Blitefield, Graduate Program Director, Professional Writing, 508-999-8270, E-mail: jblitefield@umassd.edu. *Application contact:* Steven Briggs, Director of Marketing and Recruitment for Graduate Studies, 508-999-8604, Fax: 508-999-8183, E-mail: graduate@umassd.edu.
Website: http://www.umassd.edu/cas/english/graduateprograms/mainprofessionalwriting

**University of Memphis,** Graduate School, College of Arts and Sciences, Department of English, Memphis, TN 38152. Offers African-American literature (Graduate Certificate); applied linguistics (PhD); composition studies (PhD); creative writing (MFA); English as a second language (MA); linguistics (MA); literary and cultural studies (PhD), including African-American literature; literature (MA); professional writing (MA, PhD); teaching English as a second/foreign language (Graduate Certificate). *Program availability:* Part-time, evening/weekend, 100% online. *Faculty:* 31 full-time (14 women), 1 (woman) part-time/adjunct. *Students:* 86 full-time (44 women), 78 part-time (51 women); includes 36 minority (19 Black or African American, non-Hispanic/Latino; 3 Asian, non-Hispanic/Latino; 10 Hispanic/Latino; 4 Two or more races, non-Hispanic/Latino), 32 international. Average age 35. 68 applicants, 87% accepted, 33 enrolled. In 2016, 39 master's, 17 doctorates, 16 other advanced degrees awarded. Terminal master's awarded for partial completion of doctoral program. *Degree requirements:* For master's, one foreign language, comprehensive exam, thesis optional; for doctorate, 2 foreign languages, comprehensive exam, thesis/dissertation, qualifying exam. *Entrance requirements:* For master's, GRE, minimum undergraduate GPA of 3.0, statement of purpose, two letters of recommendation; for doctorate, GRE, minimum undergraduate and graduate GPA of 3.25, statement of purpose, writing sample, three letters of recommendation. Additional exam requirements/recommendations for international students: Required—TOEFL. *Application deadline:* For fall admission, 1/15 for domestic students; for spring admission, 10/15 for domestic students. Applications are processed on a rolling basis. Application fee: $35 ($60 for international students). Electronic applications accepted. *Expenses:* $5,231.50 per semester full-time in-state, $9,623.50 full-time out-of-state. *Financial support:* In 2016–17, 123 students received support, including 11 research assistantships with full tuition reimbursements available (averaging $17,064 per year), 25 teaching assistantships with full tuition reimbursements available (averaging $17,340 per year); Federal Work-Study, scholarships/grants, and unspecified assistantships also available. Financial award application deadline: 2/1; financial award applicants required to submit FAFSA. *Faculty research:* Applied linguistics, British and American literature, professional writing, composition studies. *Unit head:* Dr. Joshua Phillips, Chair, 901-678-2651, Fax: 901-678-2226, E-mail: jsphllps@memphis.edu. *Application contact:* Dr. Jeffrey Scraba, Coordinator of Graduate Studies, 901-678-4768, Fax: 901-678-2226, E-mail: jscraba@memphis.edu.
Website: http://www.memphis.edu/english

**University of Miami,** Graduate School, College of Arts and Sciences, Department of English, Coral Gables, FL 33124. Offers creative writing (MFA); English (MA, PhD). *Program availability:* Part-time. Terminal master's awarded for partial completion of doctoral program. *Degree requirements:* For master's, one foreign language, thesis optional; for doctorate, one foreign language, thesis/dissertation. *Entrance requirements:* For master's and doctorate, GRE General Test. Electronic applications accepted. *Faculty research:* Anglo-Irish literature, feminist criticism and theory, Caribbean literature, early modern literature and culture, postcolonial and ethnic studies.

**University of Michigan,** Rackham Graduate School, College of Literature, Science, and the Arts, Department of English Language and Literature, Helen Zell Writer's Program, Ann Arbor, MI 48109. Offers MFA. *Faculty:* 9 full-time (4 women). *Students:* 40 full-time (24 women); includes 11 minority (3 Black or African American, non-Hispanic/Latino; 1 American Indian or Alaska Native, non-Hispanic/Latino; 4 Asian, non-Hispanic/Latino; 1 Hispanic/Latino; 2 Two or more races, non-Hispanic/Latino), 3 international. Average age 29. 931 applicants, 4% accepted, 18 enrolled. In 2016, 22 master's awarded. *Degree requirements:* For master's, comprehensive exam, thesis. *Entrance requirements:* For master's, writing sample. Additional exam requirements/recommendations for international students: Required—TOEFL (minimum score 620 paper-based; 106 iBT). *Application deadline:* For fall admission, 1/1 for domestic and international students. Application fee: $75 ($90 for international students). Electronic applications accepted. *Expenses:* Tuition, state resident: full-time $21,466; part-time $1152 per credit hour. Tuition, nonresident: full-time $43,346; part-time $2367 per credit hour. Part-time tuition and fees vary according to course load, degree level and program. *Financial support:* Fellowships with tuition reimbursements, teaching assistantships with tuition reimbursements, and health care benefits available. Financial award application deadline: 1/1. *Faculty research:* Prose, poetry. *Application contact:* Graduate Admissions Office, 734-763-4139, Fax: 734-763-3128, E-mail: grad.eng.admis@um.cc.umich.edu.
Website: http://www.lsa.umich.edu/writers

**University of Michigan–Flint,** College of Arts and Sciences, Program in English Language and Literature, Flint, MI 48502-1950. Offers literature (MA); writing and rhetoric (MA). *Program availability:* Part-time. *Faculty:* 26 full-time (17 women), 1 (woman) part-time/adjunct. *Students:* 2 full-time (1 woman), 17 part-time (14 women); includes 5 minority (1 Black or African American, non-Hispanic/Latino; 2 Hispanic/Latino; 2 Two or more races, non-Hispanic/Latino), 1 international. Average age 34. 12 applicants, 83% accepted, 7 enrolled. In 2016, 14 master's awarded. *Degree requirements:* For master's, thesis optional. *Entrance requirements:* For master's, bachelor's degree with major or significant coursework in English or related fields from regionally-accredited institution; minimum overall undergraduate GPA of 3.0. Additional exam requirements/recommendations for international students: Required—TOEFL (minimum score 84 iBT), IELTS (minimum score 6.5). *Application deadline:* For fall admission, 8/1 for domestic students, 5/1 for international students; for winter admission, 11/15 for domestic students, 9/1 for international students; for spring admission, 3/15 for domestic students, 1/1 for international students; for summer admission, 5/15 for domestic students. Applications are processed on a rolling basis. Application fee: $55. Electronic applications accepted. *Expenses:* Contact institution. *Financial support:* Federal Work-Study, scholarships/grants, and unspecified assistantships available. Support available to part-time students. Financial award application deadline: 3/1; financial award applicants required to submit FAFSA. *Unit head:* Dr. Suzanne Knight, Director, 810-762-0145, E-mail: suknight@umflint.edu. *Application contact:* Bradley T. Maki, Director of Graduate Admissions, 810-762-3171, Fax: 810-766-6789, E-mail: bmaki@umflint.edu.
Website: http://www.umflint.edu/graduateprograms/english-language-and-literature-ma

**University of Missouri–St. Louis,** College of Arts and Sciences, Department of English, St. Louis, MO 63121. Offers creative writing (MFA); English (MA). *Program availability:* Part-time, evening/weekend. *Faculty:* 17 full-time (6 women), 6 part-time/adjunct (4 women). *Students:* 21 full-time (13 women), 40 part-time (26 women); includes 9 minority (3 Black or African American, non-Hispanic/Latino; 2 Asian, non-Hispanic/Latino; 2 Hispanic/Latino; 2 Two or more races, non-Hispanic/Latino), 3 international. 29 applicants, 90% accepted, 17 enrolled. *Degree requirements:* For master's, thesis optional. *Entrance requirements:* For master's, two letters of recommendation; writing sample (MFA). Additional exam requirements/

# Writing

recommendations for international students: Required—TOEFL (minimum score 550 paper-based; 79 iBT), IELTS (minimum score 6.5). *Application deadline:* For fall admission, 7/1 priority date for domestic and international students; for spring admission, 12/1 priority date for domestic and international students. Applications are processed on a rolling basis. Application fee: $50 ($40 for international students). Electronic applications accepted. *Financial support:* Teaching assistantships with tuition reimbursements available. Financial award applicants required to submit FAFSA. *Faculty research:* Victorian literature, Shakespeare and Renaissance literature, eighteenth-century literature, composition theory. *Unit head:* Dr. Frank Grady, Chair, 314-516-5510, Fax: 314-516-5781, E-mail: fgrady@umsl.edu. *Application contact:* 314-516-5458, Fax: 314-516-5310, E-mail: gradadm@umsl.edu. Website: http://www.umsl.edu/divisions/artscience/english/

**University of Montana,** Graduate School, College of Humanities and Sciences, Department of English, Program in Creative Writing, Missoula, MT 59812-0002. Offers fiction (MFA); non-fiction (MFA); poetry (MFA). *Degree requirements:* For master's, final creative paper. *Entrance requirements:* For master's, GRE General Test, sample of written work. Additional exam requirements/recommendations for international students: Required—TOEFL. *Faculty research:* Fiction, poetry, nonfiction.

**University of Nebraska at Kearney,** College of Fine Arts and Humanities, Department of English, Kearney, NE 68849-0001. Offers creative writing (MA); literature (MA); writing (MA). *Program availability:* Part-time, evening/weekend, online learning. *Faculty:* 13 full-time (8 women). *Students:* 2 full-time (1 woman), 10 part-time (9 women); includes 2 minority (1 Black or African American, non-Hispanic/Latino; 1 Hispanic/Latino). Average age 41. 4 applicants, 100% accepted, 3 enrolled. In 2016, 3 master's awarded. *Degree requirements:* For master's, comprehensive exam (for some programs), thesis optional, thesis or exam (for literature option). *Entrance requirements:* For master's, writing sample, three letters of recommendation, letter of interest. Additional exam requirements/recommendations for international students: Recommended—TOEFL (minimum score 550 paper-based; 79 iBT), IELTS (minimum score 6.5). *Application deadline:* For fall admission, 6/15 for domestic and international students; for spring admission, 10/15 for domestic and international students; for summer admission, 3/15 for domestic and international students. Application fee: $45. Electronic applications accepted. *Expenses:* Tuition, state resident: full-time $4064; part-time $225.75 per credit hour. Tuition, nonresident: full-time $8915; part-time $495.25 per credit hour. *Required fees:* $772; $23 per credit hour. Part-time tuition and fees vary according to course load, campus/location, program and reciprocity agreements. *Financial support:* In 2016–17, 2 students received support, including 2 teaching assistantships with full tuition reimbursements available (averaging $11,500 per year); research assistantships, career-related internships or fieldwork, scholarships/grants, and unspecified assistantships also available. Support available to part-time students. Financial award application deadline: 2/28; financial award applicants required to submit FAFSA. *Faculty research:* Narrative theory, popular culture, western and plains literature, women's studies, media studies, children's literature, poetry, speculative fiction, creative writing, comics, composition and rhetoric, renaissance drama, film studies, ecocriticism. *Unit head:* Dr. Martha Kruse, Committee Chair, 308-865-8415, E-mail: krusem@unk.edu. *Application contact:* Linda Johnson, Director, Graduate Admissions and Programs, 308-717-7881, E-mail: gradstudies@unk.edu. Website: http://www.unk.edu/academics/english/graduate_program.php

**University of Nebraska at Omaha,** Graduate Studies, College of Arts and Sciences, Department of English, Omaha, NE 68182. Offers advanced writing (Certificate); English (MA); teaching English to speakers of other languages (Certificate); technical communication (Certificate). *Program availability:* Part-time, evening/weekend. *Faculty:* 10 full-time (6 women). *Students:* 9 full-time (7 women), 43 part-time (24 women); includes 1 minority (Two or more races, non-Hispanic/Latino), 3 international. Average age 32. 39 applicants, 46% accepted, 14 enrolled. In 2016, 21 master's, 12 other advanced degrees awarded. *Degree requirements:* For master's, comprehensive exam, thesis (for some programs). *Entrance requirements:* For master's, GRE or MAT, minimum GPA of 3.0, transcripts, 3 letters of recommendation, statement of purpose, writing sample; for Certificate, minimum GPA of 3.0, transcripts, statement of purpose. Additional exam requirements/recommendations for international students: Required—TOEFL, IELTS, PTE. *Application deadline:* Applications are processed on a rolling basis. Application fee: $45. Electronic applications accepted. *Financial support:* In 2016–17, 15 students received support, including 15 teaching assistantships with tuition reimbursements available; fellowships, research assistantships, Federal Work-Study, institutionally sponsored loans, scholarships/grants, health care benefits, tuition waivers (partial), and unspecified assistantships also available. Support available to part-time students. Financial award application deadline: 3/1; financial award applicants required to submit FAFSA. *Unit head:* Dr. Tracy Bridgeford, Chairperson, 402-554-2341, E-mail: graduate@unomaha.edu. *Application contact:* Dr. Ramon Guerra, Graduate Program Chair, 402-554-2341, E-mail: graduate@unomaha.edu.

**University of Nebraska at Omaha,** Graduate Studies, College of Communication, Fine Arts and Media, Writer's Workshop, Omaha, NE 68182. Offers MFA. *Program availability:* Online learning. *Students:* 25 full-time (16 women); includes 1 minority (Hispanic/Latino). Average age 38. 24 applicants, 50% accepted, 10 enrolled. In 2016, 12 master's awarded. *Entrance requirements:* For master's, 3 letters of recommendation, statement of purpose, writing sample, minimum GPA of 3.0, official transcripts. Additional exam requirements/recommendations for international students: Required—TOEFL, IELTS, PTE. *Application deadline:* For fall admission, 5/1 priority date for domestic and international students; for spring admission, 10/1 priority date for domestic students, 9/1 priority date for international students. Applications are processed on a rolling basis. Application fee: $45. Electronic applications accepted. *Financial support:* Scholarships/grants, health care benefits, and tuition waivers (partial) available. Financial award application deadline: 3/1; financial award applicants required to submit FAFSA. *Unit head:* Miles Waggener, Coordinator, 402-554-2341, E-mail: graduate@unomaha.edu. *Application contact:* Dr. Peter Madsen, Graduate Program Chair, 402-554-2341, E-mail: graduate@unomaha.edu.

**University of Nebraska–Lincoln,** Graduate College, College of Arts and Sciences, Department of English, Lincoln, NE 68588-0333. Offers composition and rhetoric (MA, PhD); creative writing (MA, PhD); literature studies (MA, PhD). *Degree requirements:* For master's, thesis optional; for doctorate, one foreign language, comprehensive exam, thesis/dissertation. *Entrance requirements:* For master's, writing sample; for doctorate, GRE General Test, writing sample. Additional exam requirements/recommendations for international students: Required—TOEFL (minimum score 600 paper-based). Electronic applications accepted. *Faculty research:* Creative writing, composition and rhetoric, women's studies, North American literature, medieval/Renaissance studies.

**University of Nevada, Las Vegas,** Graduate College, College of Fine Arts, Department of Film, Las Vegas, NV 89154-5015. Offers film/writing for dramatic media (MFA); writing for dramatic media (Certificate). *Program availability:* Part-time. *Faculty:* 2 full-time (0 women). *Students:* 8 full-time (6 women); includes 1 minority (Black or African American, non-Hispanic/Latino), 3 international. Average age 33. 17 applicants, 18% accepted, 2 enrolled. In 2016, 2 master's awarded. *Degree requirements:* For master's, thesis, creative project and defense; for Certificate, creative project and defense. *Entrance requirements:* For master's, writing sample. Additional exam requirements/

recommendations for international students: Required—TOEFL (minimum score 550 paper-based; 80 iBT), IELTS (minimum score 7). *Application deadline:* For fall admission, 1/15 for domestic students. Application fee: $60 ($95 for international students). Electronic applications accepted. *Expenses:* $269.25 per credit, $792 per 3-credit course; $9,634 per year resident; $23,274 per year non-resident; $7,094 fees non-resident (7 credits or more); $1,307 annual health insurance fee. *Financial support:* In 2016–17, 8 teaching assistantships with partial tuition reimbursements (averaging $15,250 per year) were awarded; institutionally sponsored loans, scholarships/grants, health care benefits, and unspecified assistantships also available. Financial award application deadline: 3/15. *Faculty research:* Screenplay, stage play, television series, Web entertainment content, production. *Unit head:* Dr. Heather Addison, Chair/Professor, 702-895-3547, Fax: 702-895-4395, E-mail: heather.addison@unlv.edu. *Application contact:* Dr. Sean Clark, Graduate Coordinator, 702-895-2442, Fax: 702-895-4395, E-mail: sean.clark@unlv.edu. Website: http://film.unlv.edu/

**University of Nevada, Las Vegas,** Graduate College, College of Liberal Arts, Department of English, Las Vegas, NV 89154-5011. Offers creative writing (MFA); English (MA, PhD). *Program availability:* Part-time. *Faculty:* 22 full-time (13 women), 1 (woman) part-time/adjunct. *Students:* 61 full-time (28 women), 16 part-time (7 women); includes 20 minority (1 Black or African American, non-Hispanic/Latino; 7 Asian, non-Hispanic/Latino; 7 Hispanic/Latino; 2 Native Hawaiian or other Pacific Islander, non-Hispanic/Latino; 3 Two or more races, non-Hispanic/Latino), 2 international. Average age 33. 144 applicants, 17% accepted, 17 enrolled. In 2016, 19 master's, 4 doctorates awarded. *Degree requirements:* For master's, one foreign language, comprehensive exam (for some programs), thesis, creative thesis; for doctorate, one foreign language, comprehensive exam, thesis/dissertation. *Entrance requirements:* For master's, GRE General Test, GRE Subject Test, writing sample; statement of purpose; 2 letters of recommendation; transcripts from all colleges; for doctorate, GRE General Test, GRE Subject Test, MA in English with minimum GPA 3.5; writing sample; 3 letters of recommendation; statement of purpose. Additional exam requirements/recommendations for international students: Required—TOEFL (minimum score 550 paper-based; 80 iBT), IELTS (minimum score 7). *Application deadline:* For fall admission, 1/15 for domestic students; for spring admission, 11/1 for domestic students. Application fee: $60 ($95 for international students). Electronic applications accepted. *Expenses:* $269.25 per credit, $792 per 3-credit course; $9,634 per year resident; $23,274 per year non-resident; $7,094 fees non-resident (7 credits or more); $1,307 annual health insurance fee. *Financial support:* In 2016–17, 58 teaching assistantships with partial tuition reimbursements (averaging $15,388 per year) were awarded; institutionally sponsored loans, scholarships/grants, health care benefits, and unspecified assistantships also available. Financial award application deadline: 3/15. *Faculty research:* Creative writing, poetry, fiction. *Unit head:* Dr. Gary Totten, Chair/Professor, 702-895-1258, Fax: 702-895-4801, E-mail: gary.totten@unlv.edu. *Application contact:* Christopher Decker, Graduate Coordinator, 702-895-3088, Fax: 702-895-4180, E-mail: christopher.decker@unlv.edu. Website: http://english.unlv.edu/

**University of New Hampshire,** Graduate School, College of Liberal Arts, Department of English, Durham, NH 03824. Offers composition (PhD); English education (MST); language and linguistics (MA); literature (MA, PhD); writing (MFA). *Program availability:* Part-time. *Degree requirements:* For master's, one foreign language; for doctorate, 2 foreign languages, thesis/dissertation. *Entrance requirements:* For master's, GRE General Test, sample of written work; for doctorate, GRE General Test, GRE Subject Test, sample of written work. Additional exam requirements/recommendations for international students: Required—TOEFL (minimum score 550 paper-based; 80 iBT). Electronic applications accepted.

**University of New Mexico,** Graduate Studies, College of Arts and Sciences, Program in Creative Writing, Albuquerque, NM 87131. Offers MFA. *Faculty:* 8 full-time (3 women). *Students:* 13 full-time (7 women), 6 part-time (4 women); includes 7 minority (1 Black or African American, non-Hispanic/Latino; 1 American Indian or Alaska Native, non-Hispanic/Latino; 3 Hispanic/Latino; 2 Two or more races, non-Hispanic/Latino), 2 international. Average age 36. 87 applicants, 7% accepted, 6 enrolled. In 2016, 3 master's awarded. *Degree requirements:* For master's, comprehensive exam, thesis. *Entrance requirements:* For master's, writing sample. *Application deadline:* For fall admission, 1/15 for domestic and international students. Application fee: $50. Electronic applications accepted. *Financial support:* Teaching assistantships with tuition reimbursements, health care benefits, and unspecified assistantships available. Financial award application deadline: 1/15. *Faculty research:* Creative writing, fiction, creative non-fiction, poetry. *Unit head:* Dr. Gail Turley Houston, Chair, 505-277-6347, Fax: 505-277-0021, E-mail: ghouston@unm.edu. *Application contact:* N. Ezra Meier, Graduate Advisor, 505-277-4437, Fax: 505-277-0021, E-mail: nezra@unm.edu. Website: http://english.unm.edu/graduate/master-of-fine-arts/index.html

**University of New Mexico,** Graduate Studies, College of Fine Arts, Department of Theatre and Dance, Albuquerque, NM 87131-2039. Offers dance (MFA); dance history (MA); dramatic writing (MFA); theatre education and outreach (MA). *Accreditation:* NASD; NAST. *Faculty:* 6 full-time (3 women), 2 part-time/adjunct (both women). *Students:* 13 full-time (7 women), 3 part-time (all women); includes 13 minority (1 Black or African American, non-Hispanic/Latino; 1 American Indian or Alaska Native, non-Hispanic/Latino; 9 Hispanic/Latino; 2 Two or more races, non-Hispanic/Latino). Average age 36. 15 applicants, 53% accepted, 7 enrolled. In 2016, 4 master's awarded. *Degree requirements:* For master's, comprehensive exam (for some programs), thesis (for some programs). *Entrance requirements:* For master's, minimum GPA of 3.0; undergraduate major in theatre, dance or closely-related field; 3 letters of recommendation; letter of intent; BA, BFA, BS, or MA in dance movement science or related field, or equivalent experience (for MFA in dance). *Application deadline:* For fall admission, 4/15 for domestic students; for spring admission, 11/10 for domestic students. Application fee: $50. Electronic applications accepted. *Financial support:* Fellowships, research assistantships with partial tuition reimbursements, teaching assistantships with partial tuition reimbursements, Federal Work-Study, health care benefits, tuition waivers (partial), and unspecified assistantships available. Financial award application deadline: 3/1; financial award applicants required to submit FAFSA. *Faculty research:* Theater education and outreach, choreography, dramatic writing, dance history/criticism. *Unit head:* Bill Liotta, Chair, 505-277-4332, Fax: 505-277-8921, E-mail: wliotta@unm.edu. *Application contact:* Christina Squire, Administrator II, 505-277-7362, Fax: 505-277-8921, E-mail: csquire@unm.edu. Website: http://theatredance.unm.edu

**The University of North Carolina at Charlotte,** College of Liberal Arts and Sciences, Department of English, Charlotte, NC 28223-0001. Offers applied linguistics (Graduate Certificate); English (MA); technical and professional writing (Graduate Certificate). *Program availability:* Part-time, evening/weekend. *Faculty:* 30 full-time (16 women), 2 part-time/adjunct (1 woman). *Students:* 28 full-time (22 women), 30 part-time (19 women); includes 13 minority (4 Black or African American, non-Hispanic/Latino; 1 Asian, non-Hispanic/Latino; 8 Hispanic/Latino), 4 international. Average age 30. 33 applicants, 91% accepted, 20 enrolled. In 2016, 30 master's, 1 other advanced degree awarded. *Degree requirements:* For master's, comprehensive exam (for some

programs), thesis, comprehensive exam, or project. *Entrance requirements:* For master's, GRE, MAT, minimum undergraduate GPA of 3.0, statement of purpose, recommendation letters; for Graduate Certificate, statement of purpose, three letters of recommendation, writing sample, minimum GPA of 2.75. Additional exam requirements/recommendations for international students: Required—TOEFL (minimum score 523 paper-based, 70 iBT) or IELTS (6.5). *Application deadline:* For fall admission, 3/1 priority date for domestic and international students; for spring admission, 10/1 priority date for domestic and international students; for summer admission, 4/1 priority date for domestic and international students. Applications are processed on a rolling basis. Application fee: $75. Electronic applications accepted. *Expenses:* Tuition, state resident: full-time $4252. Tuition, nonresident: full-time $17,423. *Required fees:* $3026. Tuition and fees vary according to course load and program. *Financial support:* In 2016–17, 17 students received support, including 1 research assistantship (averaging $8,000 per year), 16 teaching assistantships (averaging $8,562 per year); career-related internships or fieldwork, institutionally sponsored loans, scholarships/grants, and unspecified assistantships also available. Support available to part-time students. Financial award application deadline: 3/1; financial award applicants required to submit FAFSA. *Total annual research expenditures:* $61,484. *Unit head:* Dr. Mark West, Chair, 704-687-0618, E-mail: miwest@uncc.edu. *Application contact:* Kathy B. Giddings, Director of Graduate Admissions, 704-687-5503, Fax: 704-687-1668, E-mail: gradadm@uncc.edu.
Website: http://english.uncc.edu/

**The University of North Carolina at Greensboro,** Graduate School, College of Arts and Sciences, Department of English, Program in Creative Writing, Greensboro, NC 27412-5001. Offers MFA. *Degree requirements:* For master's, comprehensive exam, thesis. *Entrance requirements:* For master's, GRE General Test, minimum GPA of 3.0, writing sample. Additional exam requirements/recommendations for international students: Required—TOEFL. Electronic applications accepted. *Faculty research:* Fiction, poetry, science fiction, film studies.

**The University of North Carolina Wilmington,** College of Arts and Sciences, Department of Creative Writing, Wilmington, NC 28403-3297. Offers MFA. *Program availability:* Part-time. *Faculty:* 15 full-time (8 women). *Students:* 44 full-time (27 women), 19 part-time (12 women); includes 6 minority (2 Black or African American, non-Hispanic/Latino; 2 Asian, non-Hispanic/Latino; 2 Hispanic/Latino), 1 international. Average age 29. 177 applicants, 35% accepted, 23 enrolled. In 2016, 24 master's awarded. *Degree requirements:* For master's, comprehensive exam, thesis. *Entrance requirements:* For master's, writing sample, 3 letters of recommendation, statement of interest. Additional exam requirements/recommendations for international students: Required—TOEFL (minimum score 79 iBT), IELTS (minimum score 6.5). *Application deadline:* For fall admission, 1/5 for domestic students. Applications are processed on a rolling basis. Application fee: $60. Electronic applications accepted. *Expenses:* Contact institution. *Financial support:* Scholarships/grants and unspecified assistantships available. Support available to part-time students. Financial award application deadline: 3/15; financial award applicants required to submit FAFSA. *Unit head:* Dr. David Gessner, Chair, 910-962-7489, Fax: 910-962-7461, E-mail: gessnerdm@uncw.edu. *Application contact:* Melissa Crowe, MFA Coordinator, 910-962-3436, Fax: 910-962-7461, E-mail: crowem@uncw.edu.
Website: http://uncw.edu/writers/mfa/index.html

**University of Northern Iowa,** Graduate College, College of Humanities, Arts and Sciences, Department of Languages and Literatures, MA Program in English, Cedar Falls, IA 50614. Offers creative writing (MA); English (MA); literature (MA). *Program availability:* Part-time, evening/weekend. *Degree requirements:* For master's, one foreign language, comprehensive exam, thesis or alternative, portfolio. *Entrance requirements:* Additional exam requirements/recommendations for international students: Required—TOEFL (minimum score 600 paper-based; 100 iBT). Electronic applications accepted.

**University of North Florida,** College of Arts and Sciences, Department of English, Jacksonville, FL 32224. Offers MA. *Program availability:* Part-time, evening/weekend. *Faculty:* 14 full-time (7 women). *Students:* 18 full-time (10 women), 25 part-time (20 women); includes 5 minority (1 Asian, non-Hispanic/Latino; 2 Hispanic/Latino; 2 Two or more races, non-Hispanic/Latino). Average age 31. 34 applicants, 82% accepted, 19 enrolled. In 2016, 15 master's awarded. *Degree requirements:* For master's, comprehensive exam, thesis optional. *Entrance requirements:* For master's, GRE General Test, minimum GPA of 3.0 in last 60 hours, writing sample. Additional exam requirements/recommendations for international students: Required—TOEFL (minimum score 500 paper-based; 61 iBT). *Application deadline:* For fall admission, 8/1 priority date for domestic students, 5/1 for international students; for spring admission, 12/1 priority date for domestic students, 10/1 for international students; for summer admission, 3/15 priority date for domestic students, 2/1 for international students. Application fee: $30. Electronic applications accepted. Tuition and fees vary according to course load, campus/location and program. *Financial support:* In 2016–17, 10 students received support. Research assistantships, teaching assistantships, Federal Work-Study, and scholarships/grants available. Financial award application deadline: 4/1; financial award applicants required to submit FAFSA. *Unit head:* Dr. Brian A. Striar, Chair, 904-620-1245, Fax: 904-620-3940, E-mail: bstriar@unf.edu. *Application contact:* Dr. Amanda Pascale, Director, The Graduate School, 904-620-1360, Fax: 904-620-1362, E-mail: graduateschool@unf.edu.
Website: http://www.unf.edu/coas/english/

**University of North Texas,** Robert B. Toulouse School of Graduate Studies, Denton, TX 76203-5459. Offers accounting (MS); applied anthropology (MA, MS); applied behavior analysis (Certificate); applied geography (MA); applied technology and performance improvement (M Ed, MS); art education (MA); art history (MA); art museum education (Certificate); arts leadership (Certificate); audiology (Au D); behavior analysis (MS); behavioral science (PhD); biochemistry and molecular biology (MS); biology (MA, MS); biomedical engineering (MS); business analysis (MS); chemistry (MS); clinical health psychology (PhD); communication studies (MA, MS); computer engineering (MS); computer science (MS); counseling (M Ed, MS), including clinical mental health counseling (MS), college and university counseling, elementary school counseling, secondary school counseling; creative writing (MA); criminal justice (MS); curriculum and instruction (M Ed); decision sciences (MBA); design (MA, MFA), including fashion design (MFA), innovation studies, interior design (MFA); early childhood studies (MS); economics (MS); educational leadership (M Ed, Ed D); educational psychology (MS, PhD), including family studies (MS), gifted and talented (MS), human development (MS), learning and cognition (MS), research measurement and evaluation (MS); electrical engineering (MS); emergency management (MPA); engineering technology (MS); English (MA); English as a second language (MA); environmental science (MS); finance (MBA, MS); financial management (MPA); French (MA); health services management (MBA); higher education (M Ed, Ed D); history (MA, MS); hospitality management (MS); human resources management (MPA); information science (MS); information systems (PhD); information technologies (MBA); interdisciplinary studies (MA, MS); international studies (MA); international sustainable tourism (MS); jazz studies (MM); journalism (MA, MJ, Graduate Certificate), including interactive and virtual digital communication (Graduate Certificate), narrative journalism (Graduate Certificate), public relations (Graduate Certificate); kinesiology (MS); linguistics (MA); local government management (MPA); logistics (PhD); logistics and supply chain management (MBA); long-term care, senior housing, and aging services (MA); management (PhD); marketing (MBA); mathematics (MA, MS); mechanical and energy engineering (MS, PhD); music (MA), including ethnomusicology, music theory, musicology, performance; music composition (PhD); music education (MM Ed, PhD); nonprofit management (MPA); operations and supply chain management (MBA); performance (MM, DMA); philosophy (MA); political science (MA); professional and technical communication (MA); radio, television and film (MA, MFA); rehabilitation counseling (Certificate); sociology (MA); Spanish (MA); special education (M Ed); speech-language pathology (MA); strategic management (MBA); studio art (MFA); teaching (M Ed); MBA/MS. *Program availability:* Part-time, evening/weekend, online learning. Terminal master's awarded for partial completion of doctoral program. *Degree requirements:* For master's, variable foreign language requirement, comprehensive exam (for some programs), thesis (for some programs); for doctorate, variable foreign language requirement, comprehensive exam (for some programs), thesis/dissertation; for other advanced degree, variable foreign language requirement, comprehensive exam (for some programs). *Entrance requirements:* For master's and doctorate, GRE, GMAT. Additional exam requirements/recommendations for international students: Required—TOEFL (minimum score 550 paper-based; 79 iBT). Electronic applications accepted.

**University of Notre Dame,** Graduate School, College of Arts and Letters, Division of Humanities, Department of English, Creative Writing Program, Notre Dame, IN 46556. Offers MFA. *Degree requirements:* For master's, thesis. *Entrance requirements:* For master's, GRE General Test, minimum GPA of 3.0. Additional exam requirements/recommendations for international students: Required—TOEFL (minimum score 600 paper-based; 80 iBT). Electronic applications accepted. *Faculty research:* Novels, stories, poetry.

**University of Oklahoma,** Gaylord College of Journalism and Mass Communication, Program in Professional Writing, Norman, OK 73019. Offers MPW. *Program availability:* Part-time. *Students:* 8 full-time (3 women), 5 part-time (2 women); includes 3 minority (1 Black or African American, non-Hispanic/Latino; 1 American Indian or Alaska Native, non-Hispanic/Latino; 1 Two or more races, non-Hispanic/Latino). Average age 28. 6 applicants, 83% accepted, 5 enrolled. In 2016, 6 master's awarded. *Degree requirements:* For master's, project. *Entrance requirements:* For master's, GRE, 50-page writing sample, 2 letters of recommendation, resume, personal statement, minimum GPA of 3.2. Additional exam requirements/recommendations for international students: Required—TOEFL (minimum score 79 iBT) or IELTS (minimum score 6.5). *Application deadline:* For fall admission, 7/1 for domestic students, 3/1 for international students; for spring admission, 11/1 for domestic students, 9/1 for international students. Application fee: $50 ($100 for international students). Electronic applications accepted. *Expenses:* Tuition, state resident: full-time $4886; part-time $203.60 per credit hour. Tuition, nonresident: full-time $18,989; part-time $791.20 per credit hour. *Required fees:* $3283; $126.25 per credit hour. $126.50 per semester. *Financial support:* In 2016–17, 8 students received support. Career-related internships or fieldwork, institutionally sponsored loans, scholarships/grants, health care benefits, unspecified assistantships, and McNair fellowships available. Support available to part-time students. Financial award application deadline: 6/1; financial award applicants required to submit FAFSA. *Faculty research:* General fiction, novel writing, non-fiction, screenwriting. *Unit head:* Dr. Katerina Tsetsura, Director of Graduate Studies, 405-325-6195, Fax: 405-325-7565, E-mail: tsetsura@ou.edu. *Application contact:* Larry Laneer, Graduate Advisor, 405-325-2722, Fax: 405-325-7565, E-mail: llaneer@ou.edu.
Website: http://www.ou.edu/content/gaylord/graduate.html

**University of Oregon,** Graduate School, College of Arts and Sciences, Department of Creative Writing, Eugene, OR 97403. Offers MFA. *Degree requirements:* For master's, thesis, exam. *Entrance requirements:* For master's, minimum GPA of 3.0. Additional exam requirements/recommendations for international students: Required—TOEFL. *Faculty research:* Poetry, fiction, literary nonfiction.

**University of Pittsburgh,** Dietrich School of Arts and Sciences, Department of English, Pittsburgh, PA 15260. Offers English (MA, PhD); writing (MFA). *Program availability:* Part-time. *Faculty:* 56 full-time (26 women), 3 part-time/adjunct (1 woman). *Students:* 126 full-time (87 women); includes 41 minority (13 Black or African American, non-Hispanic/Latino; 1 American Indian or Alaska Native, non-Hispanic/Latino; 16 Asian, non-Hispanic/Latino; 11 Hispanic/Latino), 1 international. Average age 30. 333 applicants, 20% accepted, 22 enrolled. In 2016, 13 master's, 7 doctorates awarded. Terminal master's awarded for partial completion of doctoral program. *Degree requirements:* For master's, variable foreign language requirement, thesis; for doctorate, variable foreign language requirement, comprehensive exam, thesis/dissertation. *Entrance requirements:* For master's and doctorate, GRE General Test, writing sample. Additional exam requirements/recommendations for international students: Required—TOEFL (minimum score 550 paper-based; 90 iBT). *Application deadline:* For fall admission, 12/10 for domestic and international students. Application fee: $50. Electronic applications accepted. Tuition and fees vary according to program. *Financial support:* In 2016–17, 18 fellowships with full tuition reimbursements (averaging $22,042 per year), 15 research assistantships with full and partial tuition reimbursements (averaging $14,620 per year), 56 teaching assistantships with full tuition reimbursements (averaging $18,620 per year) were awarded; Federal Work-Study, institutionally sponsored loans, scholarships/grants, health care benefits, tuition waivers (full and partial), and unspecified assistantships also available. Support available to part-time students. Financial award application deadline: 12/10. *Faculty research:* Cultural studies, literary history and theory, film, composition. *Unit head:* Dr. Don Bialostosky, Chair, 412-624-6509, Fax: 412-624-6639, E-mail: dhb2@pitt.edu. *Application contact:* Jesse Daugherty, Graduate Administrator, 412-624-6549, Fax: 412-624-6639, E-mail: engrad@pitt.edu.
Website: http://www.english.pitt.edu

**University of Regina,** Faculty of Graduate Studies and Research, Faculty of Arts, Department of English, Regina, SK S4S 0A2, Canada. Offers creative writing (MA); English (MA, PhD). PhD program is a special case provision. *Program availability:* Part-time. *Faculty:* 21 full-time (9 women), 1 part-time/adjunct (0 women). *Students:* 8 full-time (5 women), 5 part-time (4 women). 12 applicants, 50% accepted. In 2016, 2 master's awarded. *Degree requirements:* For master's, thesis (for some programs); for doctorate, thesis/dissertation. *Entrance requirements:* For master's, writing sample and portfolio of creative material (for creative writing). Additional exam requirements/recommendations for international students: Required—TOEFL (minimum score 600 paper-based; 100 iBT), IELTS (minimum score 7.5), PTE (minimum score 59). *Application deadline:* For fall admission, 4/15 for domestic and international students; for winter admission, 10/15 for domestic and international students; for spring admission, 2/15 for domestic and international students. Application fee: $100. Electronic applications accepted. *Financial support:* In 2016–17, 2 fellowships (averaging $6,000 per year), 1 teaching assistantship (averaging $2,501 per year) were awarded; scholarships/grants also available. Financial award application deadline: 6/15. *Faculty research:* British, American, and Canadian literature; sixteenth-, eighteenth-, nineteenth-, and twentieth-century literature; literary theory. *Unit head:* Dr. Troni Grande, Department Head, 306-585-4570, Fax: 306-585-5429, E-mail: troni.grande@uregina.ca. *Application contact:* Dr.

## Writing

Susan Johnston, Graduate Chair, 306-585-4672, Fax: 306-585-5429, E-mail: susan.johnston@uregina.ca. Website: http://www.uregina.ca/arts/english

**University of San Francisco,** College of Arts and Sciences, Program in Writing, San Francisco, CA 94117-1080. Offers MFA. *Program availability:* Part-time, evening/weekend. *Faculty:* 5 full-time (2 women), 9 part-time/adjunct (4 women). *Students:* 82 full-time (48 women), 3 part-time (2 women); includes 27 minority (3 Black or African American, non-Hispanic/Latino; 6 Asian, non-Hispanic/Latino; 14 Hispanic/Latino; 4 Two or more races, non-Hispanic/Latino), 3 international. Average age 31. 163 applicants, 72% accepted, 34 enrolled. In 2016, 30 master's awarded. *Degree requirements:* For master's, thesis. *Entrance requirements:* For master's, minimum overall GPA of 2.7, writing sample, 2 letters of recommendation, resume, interview. Additional exam requirements/recommendations for international students: Required—TOEFL (minimum score 550 paper-based; 79 iBT), IELTS, PTE. *Application deadline:* For fall admission, 1/15 for domestic and international students. Applications are processed on a rolling basis. Application fee: $55 ($65 for international students). Electronic applications accepted. *Expenses:* Tuition: Full-time $23,310; part-time $1295 per credit. Tuition and fees vary according to course load, degree level, campus/location and program. *Financial support:* In 2016–17, 28 students received support. Fellowships and institutionally sponsored loans available. Support available to part-time students. Financial award application deadline: 3/2; financial award applicants required to submit FAFSA. *Faculty research:* Techniques of teaching the novel to writers, oral history. *Unit head:* Dr. Micah Ballard, Director of Administration, 415-422-6066, Fax: 415-422-6996, E-mail: mfaw@usfca.edu. *Application contact:* Mark Landerghini, Information Contact, 415-422-5101, Fax: 415-422-2217, E-mail: asgraduate@usfca.edu. Website: https://www.usfca.edu/arts-sciences/graduate-programs/writing

**University of South Alabama,** College of Arts and Sciences, Department of English, Mobile, AL 36688. Offers creative writing (MA); literature (MA). *Program availability:* Part-time, evening/weekend. *Faculty:* 10 full-time (3 women). *Students:* 17 full-time (9 women), 13 part-time (12 women); includes 6 minority (3 Black or African American, non-Hispanic/Latino; 1 Hispanic/Latino; 2 Two or more races, non-Hispanic/Latino). Average age 31. 12 applicants, 58% accepted, 7 enrolled. In 2016, 3 master's awarded. *Degree requirements:* For master's, one foreign language, comprehensive exam, thesis optional. *Entrance requirements:* For master's, GRE General Test, BA in English or 30 hours of course work in English, minimum GPA of 3.0. Additional exam requirements/recommendations for international students: Required—TOEFL (minimum score 535 paper-based; 79 iBT). *Application deadline:* For fall admission, 7/15 priority date for domestic students, 5/15 priority date for international students; for spring admission, 12/1 priority date for domestic students, 11/1 priority date for international students; for summer admission, 5/1 for domestic students. Applications are processed on a rolling basis. Application fee: $35. Electronic applications accepted. *Expenses:* Tuition, state resident: full-time $9768; part-time $407 per credit hour. Tuition, nonresident: full-time $19,536; part-time $814 per credit hour. *Financial support:* Fellowships, research assistantships, teaching assistantships, career-related internships or fieldwork, Federal Work-Study, institutionally sponsored loans, scholarships/grants, and unspecified assistantships available. Support available to part-time students. Financial award application deadline: 4/21; financial award applicants required to submit FAFSA. *Unit head:* Dr. Steven Trout, Chair, English, 251-460-6439, E-mail: strout@southalabama.edu. *Application contact:* Dr. Ellen B. Harrington, Graduate Coordinator, English, 251-460-7326, E-mail: eharrington@southalabama.edu. Website: http://www.southalabama.edu/colleges/artsandsci/english/

**University of South Carolina,** The Graduate School, College of Arts and Sciences, Department of English Language and Literature, Columbia, SC 29208. Offers creative writing (MFA); English (MA, PhD); English education (MAT); MLIS/MA. MAT offered in cooperation with the College of Education. *Program availability:* Part-time. *Degree requirements:* For master's, one foreign language, comprehensive exam, thesis; for doctorate, 2 foreign languages, comprehensive exam, thesis/dissertation. *Entrance requirements:* For master's, GRE General Test (MFA), GRE Subject Test (MA, MAT), sample of written work; for doctorate, GRE General Test, GRE Subject Test, sample of written work. Additional exam requirements/recommendations for international students: Required—TOEFL. Electronic applications accepted. *Faculty research:* American literature, British literature, composition and rhetoric, linguistics, speech communication.

**University of Southern California,** Graduate School, Dana and David Dornsife College of Letters, Arts and Sciences, Department of English, Los Angeles, CA 90089. Offers English (MA, PhD); literature and creative writing (PhD). Terminal master's awarded for partial completion of doctoral program. *Degree requirements:* For doctorate, one foreign language, comprehensive exam, thesis/dissertation. *Entrance requirements:* For doctorate, GRE General Test, GRE Subject Test (English literature). Additional exam requirements/recommendations for international students: Required—TOEFL. Electronic applications accepted. *Faculty research:* Creative writing and literature; early modern studies; gender and sexuality; narrative studies; poetry and poetics; media, film, and popular culture; studies in race and minority literature.

**University of Southern California,** Graduate School, Dana and David Dornsife College of Letters, Arts and Sciences, Master of Professional Writing Program, Los Angeles, CA 90089. Offers MPW. *Program availability:* Part-time, evening/weekend. *Degree requirements:* For master's, thesis. *Entrance requirements:* For master's, GRE. Additional exam requirements/recommendations for international students: Required—TOEFL. Electronic applications accepted. *Faculty research:* Creative writing including fiction, creative nonfiction, screenwriting, television writing, playwriting, poetry, Internet writing; publishing in electronic media; book and film reviewing; teaching.

**University of Southern Maine,** College of Arts, Humanities, and Social Sciences, Program in Creative Writing, Portland, ME 04104. Offers MFA.

**University of Southern Mississippi,** Graduate School, College of Arts and Letters, Department of English, Hattiesburg, MS 39406-0001. Offers creative writing (MA, PhD); English education (MA); literature (MA, PhD). *Degree requirements:* For master's, one foreign language, comprehensive exam, thesis; for doctorate, 2 foreign languages, comprehensive exam, thesis/dissertation. *Entrance requirements:* For master's, GRE General Test, minimum GPA of 3.0 in field of study, 2.75 in last 2 years; for doctorate, GRE General Test, minimum GPA of 3.5. Additional exam requirements/recommendations for international students: Required—TOEFL, IELTS. *Application deadline:* For fall admission, 3/15 priority date for domestic students, 3/15 for international students. Application fee: $60. Electronic applications accepted. *Expenses: Tuition, area resident:* Full-time $15,708; part-time $437 per credit hour. *Financial support:* Fellowships, research assistantships with full tuition reimbursements, teaching assistantships with full tuition reimbursements, Federal Work-Study, institutionally sponsored loans, scholarships/grants, and unspecified assistantships available. Financial award application deadline: 3/15; financial award applicants required to submit FAFSA. *Faculty research:* English and American literature, critical theory and cultural studies, creative writing. *Unit head:* Dr. Luis Iglesias, Chair, 601-266-4060, Fax: 601-266-5757, E-mail: luis.iglesias@usm.edu. *Application contact:* Dr. Monika Gehlawat, Director, Graduate Studies, 601-266-4070, Fax: 601-266-5757, E-mail: monika.gehlawat@usm.edu. Website: https://www.usm.edu/english

**University of South Florida,** College of Arts and Sciences, Department of English, Tampa, FL 33620-9951. Offers creative writing (MFA), including fiction, poetry; English (MA, PhD), including literature, rhetoric and composition. *Program availability:* Part-time, evening/weekend. *Faculty:* 26 full-time (14 women). *Students:* 73 full-time (50 women), 28 part-time (21 women); includes 17 minority (3 Black or African American, non-Hispanic/Latino; 3 Asian, non-Hispanic/Latino; 9 Hispanic/Latino; 2 Two or more races, non-Hispanic/Latino), 2 international. Average age 33. 114 applicants, 55% accepted, 27 enrolled. In 2016, 12 master's, 10 doctorates awarded. *Degree requirements:* For master's, comprehensive exam, thesis (for MFA); thesis or portfolio (for MA); for doctorate, one foreign language, comprehensive exam, thesis/dissertation. *Entrance requirements:* For master's, GRE General Test, minimum undergraduate GPA of 3.5 (for MA), 3.2 (for MFA); three letters of recommendation; personal statement; writing sample from 10 to 20 pages (depending on genre); for doctorate, GRE General Test, minimum graduate GPA of 3.7; three letters of recommendation; 2-3 page personal statement; 2500-word writing sample from English coursework. Additional exam requirements/recommendations for international students: Required—TOEFL (minimum score 550 paper-based; 79 iBT) or IELTS (minimum score 6.5) for MA and PhD; TOEFL (minimum score 600 paper-based) for MFA. *Application deadline:* For fall admission, 1/1 for domestic and international students. Applications are processed on a rolling basis. Application fee: $30. Electronic applications accepted. *Expenses:* Tuition, state resident: full-time $7766; part-time $431.43 per credit hour. Tuition, nonresident: full-time $15,789; part-time $877.17 per credit hour. *Required fees:* $37 per term. *Financial support:* In 2016–17, 20 students received support, including 2 research assistantships (averaging $17,221 per year), 79 teaching assistantships with tuition reimbursements available (averaging $11,576 per year); unspecified assistantships also available. Financial award application deadline: 6/30; financial award applicants required to submit FAFSA. *Faculty research:* British and American literature, rhetoric and composition, world and comparative literatures, creative writing, gender and sexuality studies, women's literature, film and genre studies, literary theory, popular and visual culture, textual and translation studies. *Total annual research expenditures:* $44,400. *Unit head:* Dr. Hunt Hawkins, Professor and Chairperson, 813-974-9492, Fax: 813-974-2270, E-mail: hhawkins@usf.edu. *Application contact:* Dr. Marty Gould, Associate Professor and Graduate Director, 813-974-9474, Fax: 813-974-2270, E-mail: mgould@usf.edu. Website: http://english.usf.edu/

**University of South Florida,** Innovative Education, Tampa, FL 33620-9951. Offers adult, career and higher education (Graduate Certificate), including college teaching, leadership in developing human resources, leadership in higher education; Africana studies (Graduate Certificate), including diasporas and health disparities, genocide and human rights; aging studies (Graduate Certificate), including gerontology; art research (Graduate Certificate), including museum studies; business foundations (Graduate Certificate); chemical and biomedical engineering (Graduate Certificate), including materials science and engineering, water, health and sustainability; child and family studies (Graduate Certificate), including positive behavior support; civil and industrial engineering (Graduate Certificate), including transportation systems analysis; community and family health (Graduate Certificate), including maternal and child health, social marketing and public health, violence and injury: prevention and intervention, women's health; criminology (Graduate Certificate), including criminal justice administration; educational measurement and research (Graduate Certificate), including evaluation; English (Graduate Certificate), including comparative literary studies, creative writing, professional and technical communication; entrepreneurship (Graduate Certificate); environmental health (Graduate Certificate), including safety management; epidemiology and biostatistics (Graduate Certificate), including applied biostatistics, biostatistics, concepts and tools of epidemiology, epidemiology, epidemiology of infectious diseases; geography, environment and planning (Graduate Certificate), including community development, environmental policy and management, geographical information systems; geology (Graduate Certificate), including hydrogeology; global health (Graduate Certificate), including disaster management, global health and Latin American and Caribbean studies, global health practice, humanitarian assistance, infection control; government and international affairs (Graduate Certificate), including Cuban studies, globalization studies; health policy and management (Graduate Certificate), including health management and leadership, public health policy and programs; hearing specialist: early intervention (Graduate Certificate); industrial and management systems engineering (Graduate Certificate), including systems engineering, technology management; information studies (Graduate Certificate), including school library media specialist; information systems/decision sciences (Graduate Certificate), including analytics and business intelligence; instructional technology (Graduate Certificate), including distance education, Florida digital/virtual educator, instructional design, multimedia design, Web design; internal medicine, bioethics and medical humanities (Graduate Certificate), including biomedical ethics; Latin American and Caribbean studies (Graduate Certificate); mass communications (Graduate Certificate), including multimedia journalism; mathematics and statistics (Graduate Certificate), including mathematics; medicine (Graduate Certificate), including aging and neuroscience, bioinformatics, biotechnology, brain fitness and memory management, clinical investigation, health informatics, health sciences, integrative weight management, intellectual property, medicine and gender, metabolic and nutritional medicine, metabolic cardiology, pharmacy sciences; national and competitive intelligence (Graduate Certificate); psychological and social foundations (Graduate Certificate), including career counseling, college teaching, diversity in education, mental health counseling, school counseling; public affairs (Graduate Certificate), including nonprofit management, public management, research administration; public health (Graduate Certificate), including environmental health, health equity, public health generalist, translational research in adolescent behavioral health; public health practices (Graduate Certificate), including planning for healthy communities; rehabilitation and mental health counseling (Graduate Certificate), including integrative mental health care, marriage and family therapy, rehabilitation technology; secondary education (Graduate Certificate), including ESOL, foreign language education: culture and content, foreign language education: professional; social work (Graduate Certificate), including geriatric social work/clinical gerontology; special education (Graduate Certificate), including autism spectrum disorder, disabilities education: severe/profound; world languages (Graduate Certificate), including teaching English as a second language (TESL) or foreign language. *Expenses:* Tuition, state resident: full-time $7766; part-time $431.43 per credit hour. Tuition, nonresident: full-time $15,789; part-time $877.17 per credit hour. *Required fees:* $37 per term. *Unit head:* Kathy Barnes, Interdisciplinary Programs Coordinator, 813-974-8031, Fax: 813-974-7061, E-mail: barnesk@usf.edu. *Application contact:* Karen Tylinski, Metro Initiatives, 813-974-9943, Fax: 813-974-7061, E-mail: ktylinsk@usf.edu. Website: http://www.usf.edu/innovative-education/

**The University of Tampa,** Program in Creative Writing, Tampa, FL 33606-1490. Offers MFA. *Program availability:* Part-time. *Faculty:* 3 full-time (1 woman), 11 part-time/adjunct (3 women). *Students:* 56 full-time (34 women); includes 13 minority (3 Black or African American, non-Hispanic/Latino; 1 Asian, non-Hispanic/Latino; 7 Hispanic/Latino; 2 Two or more races, non-Hispanic/Latino). Average age 39. 51 applicants, 55% accepted, 14 enrolled. In 2016, 30 master's awarded. *Degree requirements:* For master's, capstone. *Entrance requirements:* For master's, official transcripts from all colleges and/or universities previously attended, resume, personal statement, letters of recommendation, creative writing sample in genre. Additional exam requirements/recommendations for international students: Required—TOEFL (minimum score 577 paper-based; 90 iBT), IELTS (minimum score 7.5). *Application deadline:* Applications are processed on a rolling basis. Application fee: $40. Electronic applications accepted. *Expenses:* $7,917 per term tuition and fees, $1,500 residency fee for the culminating residency. *Financial support:* In 2016–17, 11 students received support. Career-related internships or fieldwork, scholarships/grants, and unspecified assistantships available. Financial award applicants required to submit FAFSA. *Unit head:* Dr. Erica Dawson, Director, 813-257-6311, E-mail: edawson@ut.edu. *Application contact:* Chanelle Cox, Staff Assistant, Graduate and Continuing Studies, 813-253-6249, E-mail: ccox@ut.edu. Website: http://www.ut.edu/mfacw/

**The University of Tennessee at Chattanooga,** Program in English, Chattanooga, TN 37403. Offers creative writing (MA); literary study (MA); rhetoric and writing (MA). *Program availability:* Part-time. *Faculty:* 22 full-time (11 women), 1 (woman) part-time/adjunct. *Students:* 16 full-time (11 women), 21 part-time (16 women); includes 3 minority (1 Asian, non-Hispanic/Latino; 1 Hispanic/Latino; 1 Two or more races, non-Hispanic/Latino). Average age 28. 20 applicants, 100% accepted, 17 enrolled. In 2016, 8 master's awarded. *Degree requirements:* For master's, comprehensive exam, thesis. *Entrance requirements:* For master's, minimum GPA of 3.0 in English, two letters of recommendation. Additional exam requirements/recommendations for international students: Required—TOEFL (minimum score 550 paper-based; 79 iBT), IELTS (minimum score 6). *Application deadline:* For fall admission, 6/15 priority date for domestic students, 7/1 for international students; for spring admission, 11/1 priority date for domestic students, 11/1 for international students. Applications are processed on a rolling basis. Application fee: $35 ($40 for international students). Electronic applications accepted. *Expenses:* $9,876 full-time in-state; $25,994 full-time out-of-state; $450 per credit part-time in-state; $1,345 per credit part-time out-of-state. *Financial support:* In 2016–17, 4 teaching assistantships were awarded; research assistantships, career-related internships or fieldwork, scholarships/grants, health care benefits, and unspecified assistantships also available. Support available to part-time students. Financial award application deadline: 7/1; financial award applicants required to submit FAFSA. *Faculty research:* Technical writing, African-American literature, Milton, creative writing and poetry, American modernism and gender theory. *Total annual research expenditures:* $6,000. *Unit head:* Dr. Christopher Stuart, Department Head, 423-425-2140, Fax: 423-425-2282, E-mail: chris-stuart@utc.edu. *Application contact:* Dr. Joanne Romagni, Dean of the Graduate School, 423-425-4478, Fax: 423-425-5223, E-mail: joanne-romagni@utc.edu.
Website: http://www.utc.edu/english/

**The University of Texas at Austin,** Graduate School, College of Liberal Arts, Department of English, Austin, TX 78712-1111. Offers creative writing (MFA); English (MA, PhD). *Program availability:* Part-time. Terminal master's awarded for partial completion of doctoral program. *Degree requirements:* For master's, 2 foreign languages; for doctorate, variable foreign language requirement. *Entrance requirements:* For master's and doctorate, GRE General Test. Electronic applications accepted.

**The University of Texas at Austin,** Graduate School, Michener Center for Writers, Austin, TX 78712-1111. Offers fiction (MFA); playwriting (MFA); poetry (MFA); screenwriting (MFA). Electronic applications accepted.

**The University of Texas at El Paso,** Graduate School, College of Liberal Arts, Department of Creative Writing, El Paso, TX 79968-0001. Offers creative writing (MFA); creative writing of the Americas (MFA). *Program availability:* Part-time, evening/weekend, online learning. *Degree requirements:* For master's, thesis. *Entrance requirements:* For master's, minimum GPA of 3.0, letters of recommendation, writing sample. Additional exam requirements/recommendations for international students: Recommended—TOEFL, IELTS. Electronic applications accepted.

**The University of Texas at El Paso,** Graduate School, College of Liberal Arts, Department of English, El Paso, TX 79968-0001. Offers bilingual professional writing (Certificate); English and American literature (MA); rhetoric and composition (PhD); rhetoric and writing studies (MA); teaching English (MAT). *Program availability:* Part-time, evening/weekend. *Degree requirements:* For master's, thesis optional. *Entrance requirements:* For master's, GRE General Test, minimum GPA of 3.0. Additional exam requirements/recommendations for international students: Required—TOEFL. Electronic applications accepted. *Faculty research:* Literature, creative writing, literary theory.

**The University of Texas Rio Grande Valley,** College of Fine Arts, Program in Creative Writing, Edinburg, TX 78539. Offers MFA. *Program availability:* Part-time. Tuition and fees vary according to course load and program. *Unit head:* Dr. Dahlia Guerra, Interim Dean. *Application contact:* Stephanie Ozuna, Graduate Student Recruiter, 956-665-3558, E-mail: stephanie.ozuna@utrgv.edu.

**University of the Sacred Heart,** Graduate Programs, Department of Communication, San Juan, PR 00914-0383. Offers contemporary culture and media (MA); digital journalism (MA, Certificate); editing for media (MA, Certificate); public relations (MA, Certificate); publicity (MA, Certificate); scriptwriting (MA, Certificate). *Program availability:* Part-time, evening/weekend. *Degree requirements:* For master's, thesis.

**University of the Sacred Heart,** Graduate Programs, Program in Creative Writing, San Juan, PR 00914-0383. Offers MFA, Certificate.

**The University of Toledo,** College of Graduate Studies, College of Languages, Literature and Social Sciences, Department of English Language and Literature, Toledo, OH 43606-3390. Offers English as a second language (MA); teaching of writing (Certificate). *Program availability:* Part-time. *Degree requirements:* For master's, thesis. *Entrance requirements:* For master's, GRE if GPA is less than 3.0, minimum cumulative point-hour ratio of 2.7 for all previous academic work, three letters of recommendation, transcripts from all prior institutions attended, critical essay; for Certificate, statement of purpose, transcripts from all prior institutions attended, 2 letters of recommendation. Additional exam requirements/recommendations for international students: Required—TOEFL (minimum score 550 paper-based; 80 iBT). Electronic applications accepted. *Faculty research:* Literary criticism, linguistics, creative writing, folklore and cultural studies.

**University of Toronto,** School of Graduate Studies, Faculty of Arts and Science, Department of English, Toronto, ON M5S 1A1, Canada. Offers creative writing (MA); English (MA, PhD); JD/MA. *Program availability:* Part-time. *Degree requirements:* For master's, thesis optional; for doctorate, 2 foreign languages, thesis/dissertation. *Entrance requirements:* For master's, minimum B+ average, 2 letters of reference, portfolio (creative writing program); for doctorate, minimum A- average, 2 letters of reference, writing sample. Additional exam requirements/recommendations for international students: Required—TOEFL (minimum score 580 paper-based; 93 iBT), TWE (minimum score 5). Electronic applications accepted.

**University of Utah,** Graduate School, College of Humanities, Department of English, Salt Lake City, UT 84112. Offers English (MA, MFA, PhD), including creative writing (MFA, PhD), literature and cultural studies (MA, PhD), rhetoric and composition (MA,

PhD). *Faculty:* 28 full-time (11 women), 1 part-time/adjunct (0 women). *Students:* 43 full-time (23 women), 23 part-time (14 women); includes 12 minority (1 Black or African American, non-Hispanic/Latino; 4 Asian, non-Hispanic/Latino; 3 Hispanic/Latino; 4 Two or more races, non-Hispanic/Latino), 3 international. Average age 35. 225 applicants, 17% accepted, 14 enrolled. In 2016, 5 master's, 4 doctorates awarded. Terminal master's awarded for partial completion of doctoral program. *Degree requirements:* For master's, 1 standard-level language; exam (for MA); thesis (for MFA); for doctorate, comprehensive exam, thesis/dissertation, 2 standard-level languages/1 advanced-level language. *Entrance requirements:* For master's and doctorate, GRE General Test, minimum GPA of 3.2. Additional exam requirements/recommendations for international students: Required—TOEFL (minimum score 650 paper-based; 115 iBT); Recommended—IELTS (minimum score 9), TSE. *Application deadline:* For fall admission, 12/15 for domestic and international students. Application fee: $55 ($65 for international students). Electronic applications accepted. *Expenses:* Tuition, state resident: full-time $7011; part-time $3918.24 per credit hour. Tuition, nonresident: full-time $22,154; part-time $11,665.42 per credit hour. *Financial support:* In 2016–17, 39 students received support, including 10 fellowships (averaging $18,000 per year), 29 teaching assistantships with full tuition reimbursements available (averaging $16,500 per year); health care benefits also available. Financial award application deadline: 12/15; financial award applicants required to submit FAFSA. *Faculty research:* Creative writing including poetics and modern poetry, fiction, and experimental forms; nineteenth- and twentieth-century British and American literature; American Studies, the American west, and environmental studies; critical theory and practice; race and gender studies. *Total annual research expenditures:* $126,500. *Unit head:* Prof. Barry L. Weller, Department Chair, 801-581-6168, Fax: 801-585-5167, E-mail: barry.weller@utah.edu. *Application contact:* Prof. Andrew Franta, Director of Graduate Studies, 801-581-7850, Fax: 801-585-5167, E-mail: a.franta@utah.edu.
Website: http://english.utah.edu/

**University of Victoria,** Faculty of Graduate Studies, Faculty of Fine Arts, Department of Writing, Victoria, BC V8W 2Y2, Canada. Offers MFA. *Entrance requirements:* For master's, portfolio, 2 letters of reference.

**University of Virginia,** College and Graduate School of Arts and Sciences, Department of English Language and Literature, Program in Creative Writing, Charlottesville, VA 22903. Offers MFA. *Faculty:* 5 full-time (4 women). *Students:* 24 full-time (13 women); includes 1 minority (Black or African American, non-Hispanic/Latino), 1 international. Average age 28. 603 applicants, 3% accepted, 10 enrolled. In 2016, 11 master's awarded. *Degree requirements:* For master's, comprehensive exam, thesis. *Entrance requirements:* For master's, GRE General Test, writing sample. Additional exam requirements/recommendations for international students: Required—TOEFL (minimum score 600 paper-based; 90 iBT), IELTS (minimum score 7). *Application deadline:* For fall admission, 1/1 for domestic students, 1/4 for international students. Application fee: $60. Electronic applications accepted. *Expenses:* Tuition, state resident: full-time $15,026; part-time $834 per credit hour. Tuition, nonresident: full-time $25,168; part-time $1378 per credit hour. *Required fees:* $2654. *Financial support:* Fellowships and teaching assistantships available. Financial award application deadline: 1/4; financial award applicants required to submit FAFSA. *Unit head:* Jane Alison, Director, 434-924-8607, Fax: 434-924-1478, E-mail: ct2a@virginia.edu.
Website: http://www.engl.virginia.edu/creativewriting/

**University of Washington,** Graduate School, College of Arts and Sciences, Department of English, Program in Creative Writing, Seattle, WA 98195. Offers MFA. *Entrance requirements:* For master's, GRE, GMAT. Additional exam requirements/recommendations for international students: Required—TOEFL (minimum score 550 paper-based). Electronic applications accepted.

**University of Washington, Bothell,** Program in Creative Writing and Poetics, Bothell, WA 98011. Offers MFA.

**University of West Florida,** College of Arts, Social Sciences, and Humanities, Department of English, Pensacola, FL 32514-5750. Offers creative writing (MA); literature (MA). *Program availability:* Part-time, evening/weekend. *Degree requirements:* For master's, thesis. *Entrance requirements:* For master's, GRE (minimum score: verbal 500, writing 4.5) or MAT (minimum score 413), official transcripts; two-page statement of purpose; writing sample (2,500 words of literary analysis for literature track or 2,500 words of fiction/non-fiction prose or 10 poems for creative writing track); three letters of recommendation from instructors; 20 hours upper-division undergraduate coursework in English. Additional exam requirements/recommendations for international students: Required—TOEFL (minimum score 550 paper-based). *Application deadline:* For fall admission, 6/1 for domestic and international students; for spring admission, 10/1 for domestic and international students. Applications are processed on a rolling basis. Application fee: $30. *Expenses:* Tuition, state resident: full-time $5316.12. Tuition, nonresident: full-time $11,308. *Required fees:* $583.92. Tuition and fees vary according to course load and program. *Financial support:* Fellowships with partial tuition reimbursements, research assistantships with partial tuition reimbursements, teaching assistantships with partial tuition reimbursements, and unspecified assistantships available. Financial award application deadline: 4/15; financial award applicants required to submit FAFSA. *Faculty research:* Faulkner, Shakespeare, American humor, women's studies, poetry. *Unit head:* Dr. Bob Yeager, Chairperson, 850-474-2923. *Application contact:* Terry McCray, Assistant Director of Graduate Admissions, 850-473-7718, Fax: 850-473-7714, E-mail: gradadmissions@uwf.edu.
Website: http://uwf.edu/cassh/departments/english/

**University of Windsor,** Faculty of Graduate Studies, Faculty of Arts and Social Sciences, Department of English Language, Literature and Creative Writing, Windsor, ON N9B 3P4, Canada. Offers English: creative writing and language and literature (MA); English: language and literature (MA). *Program availability:* Part-time. *Degree requirements:* For master's, thesis. *Entrance requirements:* For master's, minimum B average, portfolio. Additional exam requirements/recommendations for international students: Required—TOEFL (minimum score 600 paper-based). Electronic applications accepted. *Faculty research:* Use of gender-related terms in popular culture; international and Aboriginal literatures: expression of cultural identity; critical analysis of authors: Pope, Munroe, Lady Morgan, Orwell, Thomas; the "feminine" voice in literature and contemporary culture.

**University of Wisconsin–Eau Claire,** College of Arts and Sciences, Program in English, Eau Claire, WI 54702-4004. Offers literature and textual interpretation (MA); writing (MA). *Program availability:* Part-time. *Degree requirements:* For master's, oral defense with thesis. *Entrance requirements:* For master's, minimum GPA of 3.25 in English, 3.0 overall; bachelor's degree with minimum of 24 credits in English. Additional exam requirements/recommendations for international students: Required—TOEFL (minimum score 79 iBT).

**University of Wisconsin–Madison,** Graduate School, College of Letters and Science, Department of English, Madison, WI 53706-1380. Offers applied English linguistics (MA); composition and rhetoric (PhD); creative writing (MFA); English language and linguistics (PhD); literary studies (MA, PhD). *Degree requirements:* For doctorate, thesis/dissertation.

## Writing

**University of Wisconsin–Milwaukee,** Graduate School, College of Letters and Science, Department of English, Milwaukee, WI 53201-0413. Offers English (MA, PhD), including creative writing, literature and cultural theory, media, cinema and digital studies, professional writing, rhetoric and composition. *Students:* 87 full-time (47 women), 50 part-time (27 women); includes 14 minority (4 Asian, non-Hispanic/Latino; 1 Hispanic/Latino; 9 Two or more races, non-Hispanic/Latino), 7 international. Average age 33. 189 applicants, 48% accepted, 31 enrolled. In 2016, 15 master's, 13 doctorates awarded. *Degree requirements:* For master's, thesis or alternative; for doctorate, one foreign language, thesis/dissertation. *Entrance requirements:* For master's, GRE General Test, GRE Subject Test; for doctorate, GRE. Additional exam requirements/recommendations for international students: Required—TOEFL (minimum score 550 paper-based; 79 iBT), IELTS (minimum score 6.5). *Application deadline:* For fall admission, 1/1 priority date for domestic students; for spring admission, 9/1 for domestic students. Applications are processed on a rolling basis. Application fee: $56 ($96 for international students). Electronic applications accepted. *Financial support:* In 2016–17, 4 fellowships, 1 research assistantship, 84 teaching assistantships were awarded; career-related internships or fieldwork, unspecified assistantships, and project assistantships also available. Support available to part-time students. Financial award application deadline: 4/15; financial award applicants required to submit FAFSA. *Unit head:* Mark Netzloff, Department Chair, 414-229-4511, E-mail: netzloff@uwm.edu. *Application contact:* General Information Contact, 414-229-4982, Fax: 414-229-6967, E-mail: gradschool@uwm.edu.
Website: https://uwm.edu/english/

**University of Wyoming,** College of Arts and Sciences, Department of English, Laramie, WY 82071. Offers creative writing (MFA); English (MA). *Program availability:* Part-time. *Degree requirements:* For master's, thesis or alternative, internship. *Entrance requirements:* For master's, GRE General Test, minimum GPA of 3.0. Electronic applications accepted. *Faculty research:* Literature and theory, creative writing, English as a second language, ethnic and women's studies, composition.

**Utah State University,** School of Graduate Studies, College of Humanities, Arts and Social Sciences, Department of English, Logan, UT 84322. Offers American studies (MA, MS), including folklore, western American literature and culture; English (MA, MS), including literature and writing, technical writing. *Program availability:* Part-time, evening/weekend. *Degree requirements:* For master's, thesis or alternative. *Entrance requirements:* For master's, GRE General Test or MAT, minimum GPA of 3.0, recommendation letters, writing samples. Additional exam requirements/recommendations for international students: Required—TOEFL. *Faculty research:* Scottish enlightenment, material culture, composition theory, creative nonfiction, literary criticism.

**Vanderbilt University,** Program in Creative Writing, Nashville, TN 37240-1001. Offers MFA. *Faculty:* 32 full-time (22 women). *Students:* 15 full-time (10 women); includes 5 minority (1 Black or African American, non-Hispanic/Latino; 1 Asian, non-Hispanic/Latino; 1 Hispanic/Latino; 2 Two or more races, non-Hispanic/Latino), 1 international. Average age 27. 519 applicants, 2% accepted, 7 enrolled. In 2016, 6 master's awarded. *Degree requirements:* For master's, comprehensive exam, thesis. *Entrance requirements:* For master's, GRE General Test, sample of written work. Additional exam requirements/recommendations for international students: Required—TOEFL (minimum score 570 paper-based; 88 iBT). *Application deadline:* For fall admission, 1/15 for domestic and international students. Electronic applications accepted. *Expenses: Tuition:* Part-time $1854 per credit hour. *Financial support:* Fellowships with tuition reimbursements, teaching assistantships with tuition reimbursements, Federal Work-Study, institutionally sponsored loans, and health care benefits available. Financial award application deadline: 1/15; financial award applicants required to submit CSS PROFILE or FAFSA. *Unit head:* Dr. Dana Nelson, Chair, 615-322-2541, E-mail: dana.d.nelson@vanderbilt.edu. *Application contact:* Katherine Daniels, Director of Graduate Studies, 615-322-2541, E-mail: kate.daniels@vanderbilt.edu.
Website: http://www.vanderbilt.edu/creativewriting/

**Vermont College of Fine Arts,** MFA in Writing and Publishing Program, Montpelier, VT 05602. Offers MFA. *Faculty:* 5 full-time (3 women). *Students:* 18 full-time (13 women); includes 2 minority (1 American Indian or Alaska Native, non-Hispanic/Latino; 1 Two or more races, non-Hispanic/Latino), 1 international. Average age 32. *Degree requirements:* For master's, thesis. *Expenses:* Contact institution. *Financial support:* Fellowships and scholarships/grants available. *Unit head:* Miciah Gault, Director. *Application contact:* David Markow, Director of Enrollment Management, 802-828-8535, E-mail: admissions@vcfa.edu.
Website: http://vcfa.edu/writing-publishing

**Vermont College of Fine Arts,** MFA in Writing for Children and Young Adults Program, Montpelier, VT 05602. Offers MFA. *Faculty:* 25 part-time/adjunct (18 women). *Students:* 96 full-time (87 women); includes 12 minority (1 Black or African American, non-Hispanic/Latino; 2 Asian, non-Hispanic/Latino; 4 Hispanic/Latino; 5 Two or more races, non-Hispanic/Latino), 7 international. Average age 43. 47 applicants, 68% accepted, 28 enrolled. In 2016, 39 master's awarded. *Degree requirements:* For master's, thesis. *Entrance requirements:* For master's, original work, bachelor's degree. *Application deadline:* For fall admission, 3/1 for domestic and international students; for spring admission, 9/1 for domestic and international students. Applications are processed on a rolling basis. Application fee: $75. Electronic applications accepted. *Expenses:* Contact institution. *Financial support:* Scholarships/grants available. Financial award applicants required to submit FAFSA. *Unit head:* Melissa Fisher, Program Director, 802-828-8696, E-mail: melissa.fisher@vcfa.edu. *Application contact:* Jennifer Skinder, Assistant Director of Admissions, 802-828-8829, E-mail: jennifer.skinder@vcfa.edu.
Website: http://vcfa.edu/wcya

**Vermont College of Fine Arts,** MFA in Writing Program, Montpelier, VT 05602. Offers MFA. *Faculty:* 36 part-time/adjunct (17 women). *Students:* 114 full-time (86 women); includes 7 minority (2 Black or African American, non-Hispanic/Latino; 1 Asian, non-Hispanic/Latino; 2 Hispanic/Latino; 2 Two or more races, non-Hispanic/Latino), 4 international. Average age 42. 123 applicants, 63% accepted, 36 enrolled. In 2016, 66 master's awarded. *Degree requirements:* For master's, thesis. *Entrance requirements:* For master's, original work, bachelor's degree; evidence of exceptional academic, literary and/or publishing background. *Application deadline:* For fall admission, 3/20 for domestic and international students; for spring admission, 8/15 for domestic and international students. Application fee: $75. *Expenses:* Contact institution. *Financial support:* Scholarships/grants available. Financial award applicants required to submit FAFSA. *Unit head:* Melissa Hammerle, Program Director, 802-828-8840, E-mail: melissa.hammerle@vcfa.edu. *Application contact:* Ann Cardinal, Director of Student Recruitment, 802-828-8589, E-mail: ann.cardinal@vcfa.edu.
Website: http://www.vcfa.edu/writing

**Virginia Commonwealth University,** Graduate School, College of Humanities and Sciences, Department of English, Program in Creative Writing, Richmond, VA 23284-9005. Offers dual genre (MFA); fiction (MFA); poetry (MFA). *Program availability:* Part-time. *Entrance requirements:* For master's, GRE General Test, portfolio. Additional exam requirements/recommendations for international students: Required—TOEFL (minimum score 600 paper-based; 100 iBT) or IELTS (minimum score 6.5). *Application deadline:* For fall admission, 2/1 priority date for domestic students. Applications are processed on a rolling basis. Application fee: $50. Electronic applications accepted. *Financial support:* Federal Work-Study, institutionally sponsored loans, and tuition waivers (full and partial) available. Support available to part-time students. Financial award applicants required to submit FAFSA. *Faculty research:* Poetry, fiction. *Unit head:* Clint McCown, Director, 804-828-1331, E-mail: jcmccown@vcu.edu. *Application contact:* Thom Didato, Graduate Programs Advisor, 804-828-1329, E-mail: tndidato@vcu.edu.

**Virginia Polytechnic Institute and State University,** Graduate School, College of Liberal Arts and Human Sciences, Blacksburg, VA 24061. Offers career and technical education (MS Ed, Ed D, PhD, Ed S); communication (MA); counselor education (MA Ed, Ed D, PhD, Ed S); creative writing (MFA); curriculum and instruction (MA Ed, Ed D, PhD, Ed S); educational leadership and policy studies (MA Ed, Ed D, PhD, Ed S); educational research and evaluation (PhD); English (MA); foreign languages, cultures, and literatures (MA); higher education (PhD); higher education and student affairs (MA Ed); history (MA); human development (MS, PhD); material culture and public humanities (MA); philosophy (MA); political science (MA); rhetoric and writing (PhD); science and technology studies (MS, PhD); social, political, ethical, and cultural thought (PhD); sociology (MS, PhD); theater arts (MFA). *Faculty:* 408 full-time (204 women), 3 part-time/adjunct (2 women). *Students:* 657 full-time (446 women), 457 part-time (292 women); includes 213 minority (114 Black or African American, non-Hispanic/Latino; 3 American Indian or Alaska Native, non-Hispanic/Latino; 29 Asian, non-Hispanic/Latino; 44 Hispanic/Latino; 23 Two or more races, non-Hispanic/Latino), 93 international. Average age 33. 805 applicants, 55% accepted, 328 enrolled. In 2016, 270 master's, 91 doctorates awarded. *Degree requirements:* For master's, comprehensive exam (for some programs), thesis (for some programs); for doctorate, comprehensive exam (for some programs), thesis/dissertation (for some programs). *Entrance requirements:* For master's and doctorate, GRE/GMAT. Additional exam requirements/recommendations for international students: Required—TOEFL (minimum score 80 iBT). *Application deadline:* For fall admission, 8/1 for domestic students, 4/1 for international students; for spring admission, 1/1 for domestic students, 9/1 for international students. Applications are processed on a rolling basis. Application fee: $75. Electronic applications accepted. *Expenses: Tuition,* state resident: full-time $12,467; part-time $692.50 per credit hour. Tuition, nonresident: full-time $25,095; part-time $1394.25 per credit hour. *Required fees:* $2669; $491.50 per semester. Tuition and fees vary according to course load, campus/location and program. *Financial support:* In 2016–17, 21 research assistantships with full tuition reimbursements (averaging $19,817 per year), 237 teaching assistantships with full tuition reimbursements (averaging $15,497 per year) were awarded. Financial award application deadline: 3/1; financial award applicants required to submit FAFSA. *Total annual research expenditures:* $6.6 million. *Unit head:* Rosemary Blieszner, Interim Dean, 540-231-6779, Fax: 540-231-7157, E-mail: liberalartsdean@vt.edu. *Application contact:* Chelsea Blanchet, Executive Assistant, 540-231-6779, Fax: 540-231-7157, E-mail: bchels1@vt.edu.
Website: http://www.liberalarts.vt.edu/

**Warren Wilson College,** MFA Program for Writers, Asheville, NC 28815-9000. Offers MFA. *Program availability:* Online learning. *Degree requirements:* For master's, thesis, public reading, critical essay in 3rd semester. *Entrance requirements:* For master's, manuscript of creative work; personal essay; critical essay. Electronic applications accepted. *Expenses:* Contact institution. *Faculty research:* Poetry and fiction writing, analytic writing, creative and analytic study of literature, literary craft instruction.

**Washington & Jefferson College,** Graduate and Continuing Studies, Washington, PA 15301. Offers applied health care economics and outcomes management (MS); professional accounting (MAC); professional writing (Graduate Certificate); thanatology (Graduate Certificate).

**Washington University in St. Louis,** The Graduate School, Department of English, Writing Program, St. Louis, MO 63130-4899. Offers MFA. *Degree requirements:* For master's, thesis or written exam. *Entrance requirements:* For master's, GRE General Test, sample of written work. Additional exam requirements/recommendations for international students: Required—TOEFL. Electronic applications accepted. *Faculty research:* Fiction, nonfiction, poetry writing.

**Wayne State University,** College of Liberal Arts and Sciences, Department of English, Detroit, MI 48202. Offers English (MA); film and media studies (PhD); literary and cultural studies (PhD); rhetoric and composition studies (PhD). *Faculty:* 30. *Students:* 78 full-time (48 women), 23 part-time (10 women); includes 22 minority (10 Black or African American, non-Hispanic/Latino; 3 Asian, non-Hispanic/Latino; 6 Hispanic/Latino; 3 Two or more races, non-Hispanic/Latino), 7 international. Average age 35. 114 applicants, 33% accepted, 18 enrolled. In 2016, 15 master's, 5 doctorates awarded. Terminal master's awarded for partial completion of doctoral program. *Degree requirements:* For master's, variable foreign language requirement, essay, thesis, or portfolio of work approved by Director of Graduate Studies; for doctorate, one foreign language, comprehensive exam, thesis/dissertation. *Entrance requirements:* For master's, statement of purpose; two academic letters of reference; sample essay from previous English course; for doctorate, GRE General Test, statement of purpose; two academic letters of reference; sample of scholarly or critical writing. Additional exam requirements/recommendations for international students: Required—TOEFL (minimum score 550 paper-based; 79 iBT), TWE (minimum score 5.5), Michigan English Language Assessment Battery (minimum score 85); Recommended—IELTS (minimum score 6.5). *Application deadline:* For fall admission, 1/15 for domestic students. Applications are processed on a rolling basis. Application fee: $50. Electronic applications accepted. *Expenses:* $16,503 per year resident tuition and fees, $33,697 per year non-resident tuition and fees. *Financial support:* In 2016–17, 63 students received support, including 5 fellowships with tuition reimbursements available (averaging $15,800 per year), 30 teaching assistantships with tuition reimbursements available (averaging $17,994 per year); research assistantships with tuition reimbursements available, scholarships/grants, and unspecified assistantships also available. Financial award applicants required to submit FAFSA. *Faculty research:* Literary and cultural studies, film and new media studies, rhetoric and composition studies, linguistics, and creative writing. *Unit head:* Dr. Kenneth Jackson, Chair and Professor, 313-577-7692, E-mail: ai4054@wayne.edu. *Application contact:* Dr. Carolin Maun, Director of Graduate Studies, 313-577-7694, E-mail: caroline.maun@wayne.edu.
Website: http://clas.wayne.edu/english/

**Wesleyan University,** Graduate Liberal Studies Program, Middletown, CT 06459. Offers liberal arts (M Phil); liberal studies (MALS); writing (Graduate Certificate). *Program availability:* Part-time, evening/weekend. *Degree requirements:* For master's, thesis optional; for Graduate Certificate, thesis. *Entrance requirements:* For master's, essay, undergraduate transcripts, two letters of recommendation. Additional exam requirements/recommendations for international students: Required—TOEFL (minimum score 100 iBT), IELTS (minimum score 7). *Application deadline:* For fall admission, 7/10 for domestic students; for spring admission, 11/6 for domestic students; for summer admission, 4/16 for domestic students. Applications are processed on a rolling basis. Application fee: $100. *Expenses:* Contact institution. *Financial support:* Scholarships/grants available. Support available to part-time students. *Faculty research:* Interdisciplinary studies. *Unit head:* Jennifer Curran, Director, 860-685-3338, Fax: 860-685-2901, E-mail: jcurran@wesleyan.edu. *Application contact:* Sarah-Jane Ripa,

Associate Director, Student Services and Outreach, 860-685-3345, Fax: 860-685-2901, E-mail: sripa@wesleyan.edu.
Website: http://www.wesleyan.edu/masters/

**West Chester University of Pennsylvania,** College of Arts and Humanities, Department of English, West Chester, PA 19383. Offers English (MA), including creative writing, literature, writing, teaching, and criticism; publishing (Certificate); secondary English (Teaching Certificate). *Program availability:* Part-time, evening/weekend, blended/hybrid learning. *Faculty:* 12 full-time (8 women). *Students:* 21 full-time (14 women), 38 part-time (25 women); includes 3 minority (1 Black or African American, non-Hispanic/Latino; 2 Two or more races, non-Hispanic/Latino). Average age 28. 30 applicants, 97% accepted, 18 enrolled. In 2016, 13 master's, 2 other advanced degrees awarded. *Degree requirements:* For master's, thesis optional; for other advanced degree, capstone internship and e-portfolio (for Certificate). *Entrance requirements:* For master's, minimum GPA of 2.8, two letters of recommendation, writing sample, goals statement, official transcripts; for other advanced degree, undergraduate degree, statement of goals, and two letters of recommendation (for Certificate). Additional exam requirements/recommendations for international students: Required—TOEFL or IELTS. *Application deadline:* For fall admission, 5/15 for international students; for spring admission, 10/15 for international students. Applications are processed on a rolling basis. Application fee: $50. Electronic applications accepted. *Expenses:* Tuition, state resident: full-time $8694; part-time $483 per credit. Tuition, nonresident: full-time $13,050; part-time $725 per credit. *Required fees:* $2399; $119.05 per credit. Tuition and fees vary according to campus/location and program. *Financial support:* Scholarships/grants and unspecified assistantships available. Financial award application deadline: 2/15; financial award applicants required to submit FAFSA. *Faculty research:* Critical theory, cultural studies, literature, rhetoric and composition, creative writing. *Unit head:* Dr. Rodney Mader, Chair, 610-436-2822, Fax: 610-738-0516, E-mail: rmader@wcupa.edu. *Application contact:* Dr. Eleanor Shevlin, Graduate Coordinator for English, 610-436-2745, Fax: 610-738-0516, E-mail: eshevlin@wcupa.edu.
Website: http://www.wcupa.edu/arts-humanities/english/

**Western Connecticut State University,** Division of Graduate Studies, Maricostas School of Arts and Sciences, Department of Writing, Linguistics, and Creative Process, Danbury, CT 06810-6885. Offers creative and professional writing (MFA). *Program availability:* Part-time. *Degree requirements:* For master's, thesis, completion of program within 4 years, enrichment project that compliments course of study. *Entrance requirements:* For master's, 2 writing samples: a 20-50 page portfolio of previous writing and a brief essay. Additional exam requirements/recommendations for international students: Recommended—TOEFL (minimum score 550 paper-based; 79 iBT), IELTS (minimum score 6). *Expenses:* Contact institution. *Faculty research:* Creativity, chaos.

**Western Illinois University,** School of Graduate Studies, College of Arts and Sciences, Department of English and Journalism, Macomb, IL 61455-1390. Offers English (MA); literary studies (Certificate); professional writing (Certificate); teaching writing (Certificate). *Program availability:* Part-time. *Students:* 9 full-time (7 women), 28 part-time (14 women); includes 1 minority (Hispanic/Latino), 1 international. Average age 31. 16 applicants, 94% accepted, 11 enrolled. In 2016, 11 master's, 2 other advanced degrees awarded. *Degree requirements:* For master's, thesis or alternative. *Entrance requirements:* Additional exam requirements/recommendations for international students: Required—TOEFL (minimum score 575 paper-based; 88 iBT). *Application deadline:* Applications are processed on a rolling basis. Application fee: $30. Electronic applications accepted. *Financial support:* In 2016–17, 17 students received support, including 5 teaching assistantships with full tuition reimbursements available (averaging $8,688 per year). Financial award applicants required to submit FAFSA. *Unit head:* Dr. Mark Mossman, Chairperson, 309-298-1103. *Application contact:* Dr. Nancy Parsons, Associate Provost and Director of Graduate Studies, 309-298-1806, Fax: 309-298-2345, E-mail: grad-office@wiu.edu.
Website: http://wiu.edu/English

**Western Kentucky University,** Graduate Studies, Potter College of Arts and Letters, Department of English, Bowling Green, KY 42101. Offers education (MA); English (MA Ed); literature (MA), including American literature, British literature, literary theory, women writers, world literature; teaching English as a second language (MA); writing (MA). *Program availability:* Part-time, evening/weekend. *Degree requirements:* For master's, comprehensive exam, thesis optional, final exam. *Entrance requirements:* For master's, GRE General Test, minimum GPA of 2.75. Additional exam requirements/recommendations for international students: Required—TOEFL (minimum score 555 paper-based; 79 iBT). *Faculty research:* Improving writing, linking teacher knowledge and performance, Victorian women writers, Kentucky women writers, Kentucky poets.

**Western Michigan University,** Graduate College, College of Arts and Sciences, Department of English, Kalamazoo, MI 49008. Offers creative writing (MFA, PhD); English (MA, PhD); English teaching (MA). *Degree requirements:* For doctorate, one foreign language, thesis/dissertation.

**Western New England University,** College of Arts and Sciences, Program in Creative Writing, Springfield, MA 01119. Offers MFA. *Program availability:* Part-time, evening/weekend. *Faculty:* 15 full-time (9 women). *Students:* 8 part-time (4 women); includes 1 minority (Asian, non-Hispanic/Latino). Average age 39. *Entrance requirements:* For master's, official transcripts, two letters of recommendation, writing sample, personal narrative, resume. Additional exam requirements/recommendations for international students: Required—TOEFL (minimum score 79 iBT). *Application deadline:* Applications are processed on a rolling basis. Application fee: $30. Electronic applications accepted. *Expenses:* Contact institution. *Financial support:* Application deadline: 4/15; applicants required to submit FAFSA. *Unit head:* Pearl Abraham, Director, 413-782-1338, E-mail: pearl.abraham@wne.edu. *Application contact:* Matthew Fox, Director of Admissions for Graduate Students and Adult Learners, 413-782-1410, Fax: 413-782-1777, E-mail: study@wne.edu.
Website: http://www1.wne.edu/academics/graduate/mfa.cfm

**Western State Colorado University,** Program in Creative Writing, Gunnison, CO 81231. Offers mainstream genre fiction (MFA); poetry (MFA); screenwriting (MFA). *Program availability:* Online learning. *Degree requirements:* For master's, thesis.

**Westminster College,** Program in Professional Communication, Salt Lake City, UT 84105-3697. Offers MPC, MSC. *Program availability:* Part-time, evening/weekend. *Faculty:* 4 full-time (2 women), 3 part-time/adjunct (1 woman). *Students:* 24 full-time (14 women), 9 part-time (6 women); includes 5 minority (1 American Indian or Alaska Native, non-Hispanic/Latino; 1 Asian, non-Hispanic/Latino; 2 Hispanic/Latino; 1 Native Hawaiian or other Pacific Islander, non-Hispanic/Latino), 2 international. Average age

35. 4 applicants, 50% accepted, 1 enrolled. In 2016, 24 master's awarded. *Degree requirements:* For master's, capstone project. *Entrance requirements:* For master's, GRE, resume, personal statement of intent, official transcripts, two letters of recommendation, writing sample. Additional exam requirements/recommendations for international students: Required—TOEFL (minimum score 600 paper-based; 100 iBT), IELTS (minimum score 7.5). *Application deadline:* For fall admission, 4/1 priority date for domestic and international students; for spring admission, 10/16 priority date for domestic and international students. Applications are processed on a rolling basis. Application fee: $50. Electronic applications accepted. Application fee is waived when completed online. *Expenses:* Contact institution. *Financial support:* Career-related internships or fieldwork, scholarships/grants, unspecified assistantships, and tuition reimbursements, tuition remission available. Support available to part-time students. Financial award applicants required to submit FAFSA. *Faculty research:* Diversity in higher education, communication pedagogy, mass media law and ethics, impact of new technologies on society, rhetorical theory, feminism and popular culture, critical communication pedagogy. *Unit head:* Dr. Helen Hodgson, Director, 801-832-2821, Fax: 801-832-3102, E-mail: hhodgson@westminstercollege.edu. *Application contact:* Ashley Williams, Director of Graduate Admissions, 801-832-2213, Fax: 801-832-3101, E-mail: awilliams@westminstercollege.edu.
Website: http://www.westminstercollege.edu/mpc

**West Virginia University,** Eberly College of Arts and Sciences, Department of English, Program in Creative Writing, Morgantown, WV 26506. Offers MFA. *Program availability:* Part-time, evening/weekend.

**West Virginia Wesleyan College,** Program in Creative Writing, Buckhannon, WV 26201. Offers MFA.

**Wichita State University,** Graduate School, Fairmount College of Liberal Arts and Sciences, Department of English, Wichita, KS 67260. Offers creative writing (MFA); English (MA). *Program availability:* Part-time, evening/weekend. *Entrance requirements:* For master's, writing sample (MFA). *Unit head:* Dr. Mary Waters, Chair, 316-978-3130, Fax: 316-978-3548, E-mail: mary.waters@wichita.edu. *Application contact:* Jordan Oleson, Admissions Coordinator, 316-978-3095, Fax: 316-978-3253, E-mail: jordan.oleson@wichita.edu.
Website: http://www.wichita.edu/english

**Wilkes University,** College of Graduate and Professional Studies, Program in Creative Writing, Wilkes-Barre, PA 18766-0002. Offers MA, MFA. *Program availability:* Part-time, blended/hybrid learning. *Students:* 64 full-time (39 women), 10 part-time (6 women); includes 9 minority (6 Black or African American, non-Hispanic/Latino; 1 Asian, non-Hispanic/Latino; 2 Two or more races, non-Hispanic/Latino). Average age 40. In 2016, 38 master's awarded. *Entrance requirements:* Additional exam requirements/recommendations for international students: Required—TOEFL (minimum score 550 paper-based; 79 iBT). *Application deadline:* Applications are processed on a rolling basis. Application fee: $35. Electronic applications accepted. *Expenses:* Contact institution. *Financial support:* Unspecified assistantships available. Financial award application deadline: 3/1; financial award applicants required to submit FAFSA. *Unit head:* Dr. Bonnie Culver, Director, 570-408-4527, Fax: 570-408-7846, E-mail: bonnie.culver@wilkes.edu. *Application contact:* Director of Graduate Education, 570-408-4234, Fax: 570-408-7846.
Website: http://www.wilkes.edu/academics/graduate-programs/masters-programs/creative-writing-ma-mfa/index.aspx

**William Paterson University of New Jersey,** College of Humanities and Social Sciences, Wayne, NJ 07470-8420. Offers applied sociology (MA); clinical and counseling psychology (MA); clinical psychology (Psy D); creative and professional writing (MFA); English (MA); history (MA); political science and public policy (MA); public policy and international affairs (MA). *Program availability:* Part-time, evening/weekend. *Faculty:* 35 full-time (19 women), 8 part-time/adjunct (5 women). *Students:* 58 full-time (38 women), 62 part-time (46 women); includes 40 minority (9 Black or African American, non-Hispanic/Latino; 6 Asian, non-Hispanic/Latino; 21 Hispanic/Latino; 4 Two or more races, non-Hispanic/Latino), 4 international. Average age 32. 160 applicants, 55% accepted, 50 enrolled. In 2016, 56 master's awarded. *Degree requirements:* For master's, thesis (for some programs), internship (for some programs). *Entrance requirements:* For master's, GRE/MAT, minimum GPA of 3.0; 2 letters of recommendation; writing sample/personal statement. Additional exam requirements/recommendations for international students: Required—TOEFL (minimum score 550 paper-based; 79 iBT), IELTS (minimum score 6). *Application deadline:* For fall admission, 8/1 for domestic students, 4/1 for international students; for spring admission, 12/1 for domestic students, 11/1 for international students; for summer admission, 5/1 for domestic students, 2/1 for international students. Applications are processed on a rolling basis. Application fee: $50. Electronic applications accepted. *Expenses:* Tuition, state resident: full-time $12,480; part-time $611 per credit. Tuition, nonresident: full-time $20,263; part-time $992 per credit. *Required fees:* $1573; $77 per credit. Tuition and fees vary according to course load, degree level and program. *Financial support:* Career-related internships or fieldwork, Federal Work-Study, scholarships/grants, and unspecified assistantships available. Support available to part-time students. Financial award applicants required to submit FAFSA. *Faculty research:* Relationship violence among adolescents; autism in young children; game theory; gender, governance and empowerment in India; Chinese development policies concerning Africa. *Total annual research expenditures:* $162,900. *Unit head:* Dr. Kara Rabbitt, Dean, 973-720-2180, Fax: 973-720-2955, E-mail: rabbittk@wpunj.edu. *Application contact:* Tinu Adeniran, Associate Director, Graduate Admissions, 973-720-2764, Fax: 973-720-2035, E-mail: adenirant@wpunj.edu.
Website: http://www.wpunj.edu/cohss

**Yale University,** School of Drama, New Haven, CT 06520. Offers acting (MFA, Certificate); design (MFA, Certificate), including costume design, lighting design, projection design, set design; directing (MFA, Certificate); dramaturgy and dramatic criticism (MFA, DFA); playwriting (MFA, Certificate); sound design (MFA, Certificate); stage management (MFA, Certificate); technical design and production (MFA, Certificate); theater management (MFA); MFA/MBA. *Degree requirements:* For master's, comprehensive exam (for some programs), thesis (for some programs); for doctorate, thesis/dissertation, oral and written comprehensive exams. *Entrance requirements:* For master's, GRE (verbal, quantitative, and analytical), in-person audition (for acting); portfolio review (for design). Additional exam requirements/recommendations for international students: Required—TOEFL. Electronic applications accepted.

# ACADEMIC AND PROFESSIONAL PROGRAMS IN INTERDISCIPLINARY STUDIES

# Section 14
# Interdisciplinary Studies

This section contains a directory of institutions offering graduate work in interdisciplinary studies. Additional information about programs listed in the directory may be obtained by writing directly to the dean of a graduate school or chair of a department at the address given in the directory.

For programs offering related work, see also in this book *Comparative and Interdisciplinary Arts, Humanities,* and *Social Sciences.*

## CONTENTS

# Interdisciplinary Studies

**Alaska Pacific University,** Graduate Programs, Liberal Studies Department, Self-Designed Programs, Anchorage, AK 99508-4672. Offers MA. *Program availability:* Part-time, evening/weekend. *Degree requirements:* For master's, thesis or project. *Entrance requirements:* For master's, MAT (preferred), GRE General Test or GMAT. *Expenses:* Contact institution.

**Amberton University,** Graduate School, Program in Professional Development, Garland, TX 75041-5595. Offers MA. *Program availability:* Part-time, evening/weekend, online learning. *Entrance requirements:* For master's, minimum GPA of 3.0.

**Antioch University Midwest,** Graduate Programs, Individualized Interdisciplinary Studies and Social Sciences Program, Yellow Springs, OH 45387-1609. Offers applied psychology (MA); conflict studies (MA); health and human development (MA); integral studies (MA); peace studies (MA); systems and organizations (MA). *Program availability:* Part-time, evening/weekend, online learning. *Degree requirements:* For master's, thesis or alternative. *Entrance requirements:* For master's, resume, goal statement, interview. *Application deadline:* For fall admission, 8/1 for domestic students; for winter admission, 12/1 for domestic students; for spring admission, 3/10 for domestic students. Applications are processed on a rolling basis. Application fee: $50. Electronic applications accepted. *Expenses:* $799 per credit hour. *Financial support:* Federal Work-Study available. Financial award applicants required to submit FAFSA. *Application contact:* Deena Kent-Hummel, Director of Admissions, 937-769-1800, Fax: 937-769-1804, E-mail: dkent@antioch.edu.
Website: https://www.antioch.edu/midwest/degrees-programs/business-management-leadership/individualized-master-of-arts-ma/interdisciplinary-studies-and-social-

**Antioch University New England,** Graduate School, Department of Environmental Studies, Self-Designed Studies Program, Keene, NH 03431-3552. Offers MS. *Degree requirements:* For master's, practicum, seminar, thesis or project. *Entrance requirements:* For master's, detailed proposal. Additional exam requirements/recommendations for international students: Required—TOEFL (minimum score 550 paper-based).

**Arizona State University at the Tempe campus,** New College of Interdisciplinary Arts and Sciences, Program in Interdisciplinary Studies, Phoenix, AZ 85069-7100. Offers MA. *Program availability:* Part-time, evening/weekend. *Degree requirements:* For master's, thesis or alternative, research paper or applied project; interactive Program of Study (iPOS) submitted before completing 50 percent of required credit hours. *Entrance requirements:* For master's, GRE (if GPA less than 3.0 in last 60 hours of undergraduate study), minimum GPA of 3.0 or equivalent in last 2 years of work leading to bachelor's degree, 3 letters of recommendation, official transcripts, personal statement, writing sample of scholarly work or example of professional activities. Additional exam requirements/recommendations for international students: Required—TOEFL, IELTS, or PTE. Electronic applications accepted. *Faculty research:* Comparative politics, foreign policy, world religions, African and African-American folklore, British modernism, English Renaissance drama, physiological psychology, sociology of health and illness, gender/race/class/sexuality, applied ethics, borderland theories.

**Athabasca University,** Centre for Interdisciplinary Studies, Athabasca, AB T9S 3A3, Canada. Offers adult education (MA); community studies (MA); cultural studies (MA); educational studies (MA); global change (MA); heritage resource management (Postbaccalaureate Certificate); legislative drafting (Postbaccalaureate Certificate); work, organization, and leadership (MA). *Program availability:* Part-time, evening/weekend, online learning. *Degree requirements:* For master's, project. *Entrance requirements:* Additional exam requirements/recommendations for international students: Required—TOEFL (minimum score 560 paper-based). Electronic applications accepted. *Faculty research:* Women's history, literature and culture studies, sustainable development, labor and education.

**Baylor University,** Graduate School, College of Arts and Sciences, The Institute of Ecological, Earth and Environmental Sciences, Waco, TX 76798. Offers PhD. *Faculty:* 24 full-time (4 women). *Students:* 4 full-time (0 women), 1 part-time (0 women); includes 2 minority (1 Asian, non-Hispanic/Latino; 1 Hispanic/Latino), 1 international. 8 applicants, 25% accepted, 2 enrolled. In 2016, 1 doctorate awarded. *Degree requirements:* For doctorate, variable foreign language requirement, comprehensive exam, thesis/dissertation. *Entrance requirements:* For doctorate, GRE. Additional exam requirements/recommendations for international students: Required—TOEFL (minimum score 550 paper-based; 80 iBT); Recommended—IELTS (minimum score 6.5). *Application deadline:* For fall admission, 2/15 priority date for domestic and international students; for spring admission, 11/15 for domestic and international students. Application fee: $40. Electronic applications accepted. *Expenses:* $1,650 tuition per semester hour. *Financial support:* In 2016–17, 5 students received support, including 5 research assistantships with full and partial tuition reimbursements available (averaging $22,000 per year), 5 teaching assistantships with full and partial tuition reimbursements available (averaging $22,000 per year); scholarships/grants, health care benefits, tuition waivers (partial), and unspecified assistantships also available. Financial award application deadline: 2/15. *Faculty research:* Ecosystem processes, environmental toxicology and risk assessment, biogeochemical cycling, chemical fate and transport, conservation management. *Unit head:* Dr. Joe C. Yelderman, Jr., Director, 254-710-2224, E-mail: joe_yelderman@baylor.edu. *Application contact:* Shannon Koehler, Office Manager, 254-710-2224, Fax: 254-710-2298, E-mail: shannon_koehler@baylor.edu.
Website: http://www.baylor.edu/TIEEES/

**Boise State University,** College of Arts and Sciences, Program in Interdisciplinary Studies, Boise, ID 83725-1500. Offers MA, MS. *Program availability:* Part-time. *Students:* 4 full-time (3 women), 10 part-time (7 women); includes 1 minority (Hispanic/Latino). Average age 37. 7 applicants, 71% accepted, 3 enrolled. In 2016, 2 master's awarded. *Degree requirements:* For master's, thesis or alternative. *Entrance requirements:* For master's, minimum GPA of 3.0. Additional exam requirements/recommendations for international students: Required—TOEFL (minimum score 500 paper-based; 80 iBT), IELTS (minimum score 6). *Application deadline:* For fall admission, 3/1 for domestic students; for spring admission, 10/1 for domestic students. Application fee: $65 ($95 for international students). Electronic applications accepted. *Expenses:* Tuition, state resident: full-time $6058; part-time $358 per credit hour. Tuition, nonresident: full-time $20,108; part-time $608 per credit hour. *Required fees:* $2108. Tuition and fees vary according to program. *Financial support:* Scholarships/grants and unspecified assistantships available. Financial award applicants required to submit FAFSA. *Unit head:* Dr. Daryl Jones, Director, 208-426-1414, Fax: 208-426-3006, E-mail: aprjones@boisestate.edu.
Website: http://coas.boisestate.edu/interdisciplinary-studies-program/

**Bowling Green State University,** Graduate College, Interdisciplinary Studies, Bowling Green, OH 43403. Offers M Ed, MA, MS, PhD. *Program availability:* Part-time. *Degree requirements:* For master's, thesis or alternative; for doctorate, comprehensive exam, thesis/dissertation. *Entrance requirements:* For master's and doctorate, GRE General Test. Additional exam requirements/recommendations for international students: Required—TOEFL. Application fee: $30. Electronic applications accepted. *Financial support:* Fellowships with full tuition reimbursements, research assistantships with full tuition reimbursements, teaching assistantships with full tuition reimbursements, Federal Work-Study, and unspecified assistantships available. Financial award applicants required to submit FAFSA. *Unit head:* Dr. Deanne Snavely, Acting Vice Provost for Research/Dean, 419-372-7714, Fax: 419-372-8569, E-mail: snavely@bgsu.edu. *Application contact:* Dr. Terry L. Lawrence, Assistant Dean for Graduate Admissions and Studies, 419-372-7713, Fax: 419-372-8569, E-mail: tlawren@bgnet.bgsu.edu.

**Buffalo State College, State University of New York,** The Graduate School, Program in Multidisciplinary Studies, Buffalo, NY 14222-1095. Offers MA, MS. *Program availability:* Part-time, evening/weekend. *Degree requirements:* For master's, thesis or project. *Entrance requirements:* For master's, minimum GPA of 2.5. Additional exam requirements/recommendations for international students: Required—TOEFL (minimum score 550 paper-based).

**California College of the Arts,** Graduate Programs, Fine Arts Programs, San Francisco, CA 94107. Offers ceramics (MFA); film/video/performance (MFA); glass (MFA); interdisciplinary studies (MFA); jewelry/metal arts (MFA); media studies (MFA); painting/drawing (MFA); photography (MFA); printmaking (MFA); sculpture (MFA); textiles (MFA); wood/furniture (MFA). *Accreditation:* NASAD. *Faculty:* 23 full-time (14 women), 17 part-time/adjunct (12 women). *Students:* 75 full-time (55 women); includes 20 minority (7 Black or African American, non-Hispanic/Latino; 2 American Indian or Alaska Native, non-Hispanic/Latino; 6 Asian, non-Hispanic/Latino; 5 Hispanic/Latino), 15 international. Average age 29. 224 applicants, 54% accepted, 43 enrolled. In 2016, 27 master's awarded. *Degree requirements:* For master's, thesis, exhibit. *Entrance requirements:* For master's, appropriate bachelor's degree, portfolio, resume, 2 letters of recommendation, transcript. Additional exam requirements/recommendations for international students: Required—TOEFL, IELTS, or PTE. *Application deadline:* For fall admission, 1/10 for domestic and international students. Applications are processed on a rolling basis. Application fee: $70. Electronic applications accepted. *Expenses:* $1,641 per unit, $49,230 per year tuition; $490 fees. *Financial support:* In 2016–17, fellowships (averaging $42,000 per year), teaching assistantships (averaging $2,000 per year) were awarded; career-related internships or fieldwork, Federal Work-Study, scholarships/grants, health care benefits, and unspecified assistantships also available. Financial award application deadline: 7/31; financial award applicants required to submit FAFSA. *Unit head:* James Gobel, Chair, 415-551-9214, Fax: 415-703-9539, E-mail: jgobel@cca.edu. *Application contact:* Wes Fanelli, Assistant Director of Graduate Admissions, 415-703-9533, Fax: 415-703-9539, E-mail: wfanelli@cca.edu.

**California Institute of Integral Studies,** School of Consciousness and Transformation, San Francisco, CA 94103. Offers anthropology and social change (MA, PhD); Asian philosophies and cultures (MA); creative inquiry/interdisciplinary arts (MFA); East-West psychology (MA, PhD); integral and transpersonal psychology (PhD); philosophy and religion (PhD), including ecology, spirituality, and religion, philosophy, cosmology, and consciousness, women's spirituality; theater and performance making (MFA); transformative leadership (MA); transformative studies (PhD); women, gender, spirituality and social justice (MA); writing and consciousness (MFA). *Program availability:* Part-time, evening/weekend, 100% online, blended/hybrid learning. *Students:* 390 full-time (256 women), 121 part-time (84 women); includes 135 minority (39 Black or African American, non-Hispanic/Latino; 2 American Indian or Alaska Native, non-Hispanic/Latino; 22 Asian, non-Hispanic/Latino; 40 Hispanic/Latino; 2 Native Hawaiian or other Pacific Islander, non-Hispanic/Latino; 30 Two or more races, non-Hispanic/Latino), 51 international. Average age 38. 195 applicants, 92% accepted, 124 enrolled. In 2016, 35 master's, 41 doctorates awarded. Terminal master's awarded for partial completion of doctoral program. *Degree requirements:* For master's, thesis optional; for doctorate, comprehensive exam, thesis/dissertation, 1 foreign language (for Asian philosophies and cultures). *Entrance requirements:* For master's, minimum GPA of 3.0, letters of recommendation, writing sample; for doctorate, master's degree, minimum GPA of 3.0, letters of recommendation, writing sample. Additional exam requirements/recommendations for international students: Required—TOEFL. *Application deadline:* For fall admission, 2/1 priority date for domestic and international students; for spring admission, 10/15 priority date for domestic and international students. Applications are processed on a rolling basis. Application fee: $65. Electronic applications accepted. *Expenses: Tuition:* Full-time $19,728; part-time $1098 per semester hour. *Required fees:* $320; $320 per semester hour. *Financial support:* Research assistantships, teaching assistantships, career-related internships or fieldwork, Federal Work-Study, and scholarships/grants available. Support available to part-time students. Financial award application deadline: 4/15; financial award applicants required to submit FAFSA. *Faculty research:* Ecology and sustainability, philosophy and religion, East-West psychology, integrative health, social and cultural anthropology, transformative leadership. *Application contact:* Ellen Durst, Director of Admissions, 415-575-6100, Fax: 415-575-1268, E-mail: admissions@ciis.edu.
Website: http://www.ciis.edu/

**California State University, Bakersfield,** Division of Graduate Studies, Program in Interdisciplinary Studies, Bakersfield, CA 93311. Offers MA. *Degree requirements:* For master's, thesis or project. *Entrance requirements:* For master's, minimum GPA of 3.0 in last 90 quarter units, baccalaureate degree. Additional exam requirements/recommendations for international students: Required—TOEFL (minimum score 550 paper-based). Application fee: $55. Electronic applications accepted. *Expenses:* Tuition, state resident: full-time $2246; part-time $1302 per semester. *Faculty research:* Ethics, physical education and health. *Unit head:* Dr. Vandana Kohli, Director, Graduate Student Center, 661-654-2786, Fax: 661-654-2791, E-mail: vkohli@csub.edu. *Application contact:* Debbie Blowers, Assistant Director of Admissions and Evaluations, 661-664-3381, Fax: 661-654-3389, E-mail: dblowers@csub.edu.
Website: http://www.csub.edu/interdisciplinary/index.html

**California State University, East Bay,** Office of Graduate Studies, Interdisciplinary Programs, Hayward, CA 94542-3000. Offers MA, MS. *Program availability:* Part-time. *Students:* 1 part-time (0 women); minority (Black or African American, non-Hispanic/Latino). Average age 27. 5 applicants. *Degree requirements:* For master's, comprehensive exam, project or thesis. *Entrance requirements:* For master's, thesis. Additional exam requirements/recommendations for international students: Required—TOEFL (minimum score 550 paper-based). *Application deadline:* For fall admission, 6/30 for domestic and international students. Applications are processed on a rolling basis. Application fee: $55. Electronic applications accepted. *Financial support:* Fellowships, teaching assistantships, Federal Work-Study, institutionally sponsored loans, and scholarships/grants available. Support available to part-time students. Financial award application deadline: 3/2; financial award applicants required to submit FAFSA. *Unit head:* Jennifer

Eagan, Coordinator, 510-885-3716, Fax: 510-885-4777, E-mail: jennifer.eagan@csueastbay.edu. *Application contact:* Dr. Donna Wiley, Interim Associate Vice President for Academic Programs and Graduate Studies, 510-885-3716, Fax: 510-885-4777, E-mail: donna.wiley@csueastbay.edu.
Website: http://www.csueastbay.edu/gradprograms/

**California State University, San Bernardino,** Graduate Studies, Interdisciplinary Programs, San Bernardino, CA 92407. Offers integrative studies (MA). *Program availability:* Part-time, evening/weekend. *Students:* 4 full-time (2 women), 5 part-time (3 women); includes 4 minority (2 Black or African American, non-Hispanic/Latino; 2 Hispanic/Latino). 2 applicants, 50% accepted, 1 enrolled. In 2016, 2 master's awarded. *Degree requirements:* For master's, thesis or alternative. *Entrance requirements:* Additional exam requirements/recommendations for international students: Required—TOEFL. *Application deadline:* For fall admission, 7/16 for domestic students; for winter admission, 10/16 for domestic students; for spring admission, 1/22 for domestic students. Application fee: $55. *Expenses:* Tuition, state resident: full-time $7843; part-time $5011.20 per year. Tuition and fees vary according to course load, degree level, program and reciprocity agreements. *Financial support:* Application deadline: 3/1. *Unit head:* Dr. Francisca Beer, Dean of Graduate Studies, 909-537-5058, Fax: 909-537-7034, E-mail: fbeer@csusb.edu. *Application contact:* Olivia Rosas, Associate Vice President for Enrollment Services, 909-537-7577, Fax: 909-537-7034, E-mail: orosas@csusb.edu.

**California State University, Stanislaus,** College of Humanities and Social Sciences, Programs in Interdisciplinary Studies (MA/MS), Turlock, CA 95382. Offers MA, MS. *Program availability:* Part-time, evening/weekend. *Degree requirements:* For master's, thesis. *Entrance requirements:* For master's, GRE, minimum GPA of 3.0, personal statement. Additional exam requirements/recommendations for international students: Required—TOEFL (minimum score 550 paper-based). Electronic applications accepted.

**Cambridge College,** School of Education, Cambridge, MA 02138-5304. Offers autism specialist (M Ed); autism/behavior analyst (M Ed); behavior analyst (Post-Master's Certificate); behavioral management (M Ed); early childhood teacher (M Ed); education specialist in curriculum and instruction (CAGS); educational leadership (Ed D); elementary teacher (M Ed); English as a second language (M Ed, Certificate); general science (M Ed); health education (Post-Master's Certificate); health/family and consumer sciences (M Ed); history (M Ed); individualized (M Ed); information technology literacy (M Ed); instructional technology (M Ed); interdisciplinary studies (M Ed); library teacher (M Ed); literacy education (M Ed); mathematics (M Ed); mathematics specialist (Certificate); middle school mathematics and science (M Ed); school administration (M Ed, CAGS); school guidance counselor (M Ed); school nurse education (M Ed); school social worker/school adjustment counselor (M Ed); special education administrator (CAGS); special education/moderate disabilities (M Ed); teaching skills and methodologies (M Ed). *Program availability:* Part-time, evening/weekend, online learning. *Degree requirements:* For master's, thesis, internship/practicum (licensure program only); for doctorate, thesis/dissertation; for other advanced degree, thesis. *Entrance requirements:* For master's, interview, resume, documentation of licensure, 2 professional references; for doctorate, official transcripts, interview, resume, documentation of licensure (if any), written personal statement/essay, portfolio of scholarly and professional work, qualifying assessment, 2 professional references, health insurance, immunizations form; for other advanced degree, official transcripts, interview, resume, documentation of licensure (if any), written personal statement/essay, 2 professional references, health insurance, immunizations form. Additional exam requirements/recommendations for international students: Required—TOEFL (minimum score 550 paper-based; 79 iBT), Michigan English Language Assessment Battery (minimum score 85); Recommended—IELTS (minimum score 6). Electronic applications accepted. *Expenses:* Contact institution. *Faculty research:* Adult education, accelerated learning, mathematics education, brain compatible learning, special education and law.

**Campbell University,** Graduate and Professional Programs, School of Education, Buies Creek, NC 27506. Offers elementary education (M Ed); interdisciplinary studies (M Ed); middle grades education (M Ed); physical education (M Ed); school administration (MSA); school counseling (M Ed); secondary education (M Ed). *Accreditation:* NCATE. *Program availability:* Part-time, evening/weekend. *Degree requirements:* For master's, comprehensive exam. *Entrance requirements:* For master's, GRE General Test, minimum GPA 2.7. *Faculty research:* Spiritual values and wellness issues in counseling, stress and professional burnout among counselors, thinking strategies, leadership, adaptive technology.

**Central Washington University,** Graduate Studies and Research, Individual Studies Program, Ellensburg, WA 98926. Offers M Ed, MA, MS. *Program availability:* Part-time. *Degree requirements:* For master's, thesis. *Entrance requirements:* For master's, GRE General Test, minimum GPA of 3.0. Additional exam requirements/recommendations for international students: Required—TOEFL (minimum score 550 paper-based; 79 iBT). Electronic applications accepted.

**The Citadel, The Military College of South Carolina,** Citadel Graduate College, Zucker Family School of Education, Charleston, SC 29409. Offers elementary/secondary school administration and supervision (M Ed); elementary/secondary school counseling (M Ed); interdisciplinary STEM education (M Ed); literacy education (M Ed, Graduate Certificate); middle grades (MAT), including English, mathematics, science, social studies; physical education (grades K-12) (MAT); school superintendency (Ed S); secondary education (MAT), including biology, English, mathematics, social studies; student affairs (Graduate Certificate); student affairs and college counseling (M Ed). *Accreditation:* NCATE. *Program availability:* Part-time, evening/weekend, 100% online, blended/hybrid learning. *Faculty:* 9 full-time (4 women), 9 part-time/adjunct (5 women). *Students:* 70 full-time (58 women), 249 part-time (200 women); includes 87 minority (70 Black or African American, non-Hispanic/Latino; 1 Asian, non-Hispanic/Latino; 9 Hispanic/Latino; 7 Two or more races, non-Hispanic/Latino), 2 international. 146 applicants, 98% accepted, 105 enrolled. In 2016, 85 master's, 7 other advanced degrees awarded. *Degree requirements:* For master's, comprehensive exam (for some programs). *Entrance requirements:* For master's, GRE (minimum combined verbal and quantitative score of 290) or MAT (minimum score 396). Additional exam requirements/recommendations for international students: Required—TOEFL (minimum score 550 paper-based; 79 iBT). *Application deadline:* Applications are processed on a rolling basis. Application fee: $40. Electronic applications accepted. *Expenses:* Tuition, state resident: full-time $5121; part-time $569 per credit hour. Tuition, nonresident: full-time $8613; part-time $957 per credit hour. *Required fees:* $90 per term. *Financial support:* Fellowships and unspecified assistantships available. Support available to part-time students. Financial award application deadline: 7/1; financial award applicants required to submit FAFSA. *Unit head:* Dr. Larry G. Daniel, Dean, 843-953-5097, E-mail: ldaniel@citadel.edu. *Application contact:* Dr. Tammy J. Graham, Associate Professor, 843-953-6854, E-mail: tammy.graham@citadel.edu.
Website: http://www.citadel.edu/root/education-graduate-programs

**Clarkson University,** Wallace H. Coulter School of Engineering, Program in Interdisciplinary Engineering Science, Potsdam, NY 13699. Offers MS, PhD. *Students:* 7 full-time (1 woman), 1 international. 2 applicants, 100% accepted, 2 enrolled. *Degree requirements:* For master's, thesis; for doctorate, comprehensive exam, thesis/

dissertation. *Entrance requirements:* For master's and doctorate, GRE. Additional exam requirements/recommendations for international students: Required—TOEFL (minimum score 550 paper-based, 80 iBT) or IELTS (6.5). *Application deadline:* Applications are processed on a rolling basis. Application fee: $50. Electronic applications accepted. *Expenses: Tuition:* Full-time $23,400; part-time $1300 per credit hour. Tuition and fees vary according to campus/location and program. *Financial support:* Scholarships/grants and unspecified assistantships available. *Unit head:* Dr. William Jemison, Dean of Engineering, 315-268-6446, E-mail: wjemison@clarkson.edu. *Application contact:* Dan Capogna, Graduate Admissions Contact, 518-631-9910, E-mail: graduate@clarkson.edu.
Website: http://graduate.clarkson.edu

**Concordia University,** School of Graduate Studies, Special Individualized Programs, Montréal, QC H3G 1M8, Canada. Offers M Sc, MA, PhD. *Degree requirements:* For master's, comprehensive exam, thesis; for doctorate, one foreign language, comprehensive exam, thesis/dissertation.

**Dalhousie University,** Faculty of Graduate Studies, Interdisciplinary PhD Program, Halifax, NS B3H 4H6, Canada. Offers PhD. *Degree requirements:* For doctorate, thesis/dissertation. *Entrance requirements:* Additional exam requirements/recommendations for international students: Required—TOEFL, IELTS, CANTEST, CAEL, or Michigan English Language Assessment Battery. Electronic applications accepted. *Expenses:* Contact institution.

**Dallas Baptist University,** Gary Cook School of Leadership, Program in Higher Education, Dallas, TX 75211-9299. Offers administration (M Ed), including community college leadership, distance learning, interdisciplinary studies, student affairs leadership; instructional (M Ed). *Program availability:* Part-time, evening/weekend, 100% online, blended/hybrid learning. *Application deadline:* Applications are processed on a rolling basis. Application fee: $25. Electronic applications accepted. Application fee is waived when completed online. *Expenses: Tuition:* Full-time $15,408; part-time $856 per credit hour. *Required fees:* $400 per semester. Tuition and fees vary according to course load and degree level. *Faculty research:* Enrollment management, portfolio assessment, servant leadership. *Unit head:* Mamo Ishida, Director, 214-333-5812, E-mail: mamo@dbu.edu. *Application contact:* Bobby Soto, Director of Admissions, 214-333-5242, E-mail: graduate@dbu.edu.
Website: http://www3.dbu.edu/leadership/hied/

**Dallas Baptist University,** Professional Development Program, Dallas, TX 75211-9299. Offers accounting (MA); church leadership (MA); communication (MA); counseling (MA); criminal justice (MA); English as a second language (MA); finance (MA); higher education (MA); leadership studies (MA); management (MA); management information systems (MA); marketing (MA); missions (MA); professional life coaching (MA); training and development (MA). *Program availability:* Part-time, evening/weekend, 100% online, blended/hybrid learning. *Application deadline:* Applications are processed on a rolling basis. Application fee: $25. Electronic applications accepted. Application fee is waived when completed online. *Expenses: Tuition:* Full-time $15,408; part-time $856 per credit hour. *Required fees:* $400 per semester. Tuition and fees vary according to course load and degree level. *Unit head:* Jared Ingram, Director, 214-333-5584, E-mail: jaredi@dbu.edu. *Application contact:* Bobby Soto, Director of Admissions, 214-333-5242, E-mail: graduate@dbu.edu.
Website: http://www3.dbu.edu/graduate/mapd.asp

**DePaul University,** College of Liberal Arts and Social Sciences, Chicago, IL 60614. Offers Arabic (MA); Chinese (MA); English (MA); French (MA); German (MA); history (MA); interdisciplinary studies (MA, MS); international public service (MS); international studies (MA); Italian (MA); Japanese (MA); leadership and policy studies (MS); liberal studies (MA); new media studies (MA); nonprofit management (MNM); public administration (MPA); public health (MPH); public service management (MS); social work (MSW); sociology (MA); Spanish (MA); sustainable urban development (MA); women and gender studies (MA); writing and publishing (MA); writing, rhetoric, and discourse (MA); MA/PhD. *Program availability:* Part-time, evening/weekend, online learning. Terminal master's awarded for partial completion of doctoral program. *Degree requirements:* For master's, variable foreign language requirement, comprehensive exam (for some programs), thesis (for some programs). Electronic applications accepted.

**Eastern Washington University,** Graduate Studies, Interdisciplinary Studies, Cheney, WA 99004-2431. Offers MA, MS. *Students:* 10 full-time (3 women), 6 part-time (3 women); includes 3 minority (1 American Indian or Alaska Native, non-Hispanic/Latino; 1 Asian, non-Hispanic/Latino; 1 Hispanic/Latino). Average age 37. 7 applicants, 86% accepted, 5 enrolled. In 2016, 4 master's awarded. *Degree requirements:* For master's, comprehensive exam, thesis or alternative. *Entrance requirements:* For master's, minimum GPA of 3.0. Additional exam requirements/recommendations for international students: Required—TOEFL (minimum score 580 paper-based; 90 iBT), IELTS (minimum score 7), PTE (minimum score 63). *Application deadline:* For fall admission, 4/1 priority date for domestic students; for spring admission, 1/15 for domestic students. Applications are processed on a rolling basis. Application fee: $75. Electronic applications accepted. *Expenses:* Tuition, state resident: full-time $11,000; part-time $5500 per credit. Tuition, nonresident: full-time $24,000; part-time $12,000 per credit. *Required fees:* $1300. One-time fee: $50 full-time. Part-time tuition and fees vary according to course load, campus/location and program. *Financial support:* In 2016–17, 2 teaching assistantships with partial tuition reimbursements (averaging $10,000 per year) were awarded; career-related internships or fieldwork, Federal Work-Study, institutionally sponsored loans, scholarships/grants, health care benefits, tuition waivers (partial), and unspecified assistantships also available. Support available to part-time students. Financial award application deadline: 2/1; financial award applicants required to submit FAFSA. *Application contact:* Kathy White, Advisor/Recruiter for Graduate Studies, 509-359-6297, Fax: 509-359-6044, E-mail: gradprograms@ewu.edu.

**Emory University,** Laney Graduate School, Graduate Institute of the Liberal Arts, Atlanta, GA 30322-1100. Offers PhD. *Degree requirements:* For doctorate, one foreign language, comprehensive exam, thesis/dissertation. *Entrance requirements:* For doctorate, GRE General Test. Additional exam requirements/recommendations for international students: Recommended—TOEFL. Electronic applications accepted. *Faculty research:* American cultural criticism, intellectual history, psychoanalysis, history of science, popular culture.

**Fitchburg State University,** Division of Graduate and Continuing Education, Program in Interdisciplinary Studies, Fitchburg, MA 01420-2697. Offers applied communications (CAGS); counseling/psychology (CAGS); individualized track (CAGS); reading specialist (CAGS). *Program availability:* Part-time, evening/weekend. *Entrance requirements:* Additional exam requirements/recommendations for international students: Required—TOEFL (minimum score 550 paper-based; 79 iBT). Electronic applications accepted. *Expenses:* Tuition, state resident: full-time $2871; part-time $1914 per year. Tuition, nonresident: full-time $2871; part-time $1914 per year. *Required fees:* $3828. Tuition and fees vary according to program.

**Florida Gulf Coast University,** College of Health Professions and Social Work, Program in Health Science, Fort Myers, FL 33965-6565. Offers MS. *Program availability:* Part-time, evening/weekend, online learning. *Faculty:* 66 full-time (45

## Interdisciplinary Studies

women), 42 part-time/adjunct (21 women). *Students:* 8 full-time (7 women), 32 part-time (21 women); includes 10 minority (7 Black or African American, non-Hispanic/Latino; 3 Hispanic/Latino). Average age 31. 22 applicants, 64% accepted, 9 enrolled. In 2016, 10 master's awarded. *Degree requirements:* For master's, final project or thesis. *Entrance requirements:* For master's, GRE General Test or MAT, minimum GPA of 3.0. Additional exam requirements/recommendations for international students: Required—TOEFL (minimum score 550 paper-based). *Application deadline:* For fall admission, 7/1 priority date for domestic students; for spring admission, 11/15 for domestic students. Applications are processed on a rolling basis. Application fee: $30. Electronic applications accepted. *Expenses:* Tuition, state resident: full-time $6721. Tuition, nonresident: full-time $28,170. *Required fees:* $1987. Tuition and fees vary according to course load and degree level. *Financial support:* In 2016–17, 6 students received support. Career-related internships or fieldwork available. Financial award application deadline: 3/1; financial award applicants required to submit FAFSA. *Faculty research:* Health services administration, gerontology, therapeutic recreation, health professions education, exercise physiology. *Unit head:* Dr. Joan Glacken, Chair, 239-590-7498, Fax: 239-590-7474, E-mail: jglacken@fgcu.edu. *Application contact:* Lynn O'Hare, Administrative Assistant, 239-590-7451, Fax: 239-590-7474, E-mail: lohare@fgcu.edu. Website: http://www.fgcu.edu/chpsw/hs/

**Florida Institute of Technology,** College of Science, Program in Interdisciplinary Science, Melbourne, FL 32901-6975. Offers MS. *Students:* 1 full-time (0 women), 3 part-time (1 woman). Average age 26. 3 applicants, 67% accepted, 2 enrolled. *Degree requirements:* For master's, comprehensive exam (for some programs), thesis optional, minimum of 31 credit hours. *Entrance requirements:* For master's, STEM undergraduate degree, 2 letters of recommendations, resume, statement of objectives. Additional exam requirements/recommendations for international students: Required—TOEFL (minimum score 550 paper-based; 79 iBT). *Application deadline:* Applications are processed on a rolling basis. Electronic applications accepted. *Expenses: Tuition:* Full-time $22,338; part-time $1241 per credit hour. *Required fees:* $250. Tuition and fees vary according to degree level, campus/location and program. *Financial support:* Applicants required to submit FAFSA. *Unit head:* Dr. Ken Lindeman, Professor, 321-674-7370, Fax: 321-674-7598, E-mail: lindeman@fit.edu. *Application contact:* Cheryl A. Brown, Associate Director of Graduate Admissions, 321-674-7581, Fax: 321-723-9468, E-mail: cbrown@fit.edu. Website: http://cos.fit.edu/education/

**Fresno Pacific University,** Graduate Programs, Individualized Study Program, Fresno, CA 93702-4709. Offers MA. *Program availability:* Part-time, evening/weekend. *Degree requirements:* For master's, thesis. *Entrance requirements:* For master's, GMAT, GRE General Test, or MAT, interview. Additional exam requirements/recommendations for international students: Required—TOEFL (minimum score 550 paper-based). Electronic applications accepted. *Expenses:* Contact institution.

**Frostburg State University,** Graduate School, College of Education, Department of Educational Professions, Program in Interdisciplinary Education, Frostburg, MD 21532-1099. Offers M Ed. *Program availability:* Part-time, evening/weekend. *Degree requirements:* For master's, thesis or alternative. *Entrance requirements:* Additional exam requirements/recommendations for international students: Required—TOEFL. Electronic applications accepted.

**George Mason University,** College of Humanities and Social Sciences, Interdisciplinary Studies Program, Fairfax, VA 22030. Offers community college teaching (MAIS); computational social science (MAIS); energy and sustainability (MAIS); folklore studies (MAIS); individualized studies (MAIS); neuroethics (MAIS); religion, culture, and values (MAIS); social entrepreneurship (MAIS); social justice and human rights (MAIS); war and the military in society (MAIS); women and gender studies (MAIS). *Faculty:* 10 full-time (3 women), 9 part-time/adjunct (4 women). *Students:* 25 full-time (21 women), 70 part-time (48 women); includes 31 minority (15 Black or African American, non-Hispanic/Latino; 5 Asian, non-Hispanic/Latino; 7 Hispanic/Latino; 4 Two or more races, non-Hispanic/Latino), 3 international. Average age 33. 52 applicants, 92% accepted, 23 enrolled. In 2016, 40 master's awarded. *Degree requirements:* For master's, project or thesis. *Entrance requirements:* For master's, 3 letters of recommendation; writing sample; official transcript; resume. Additional exam requirements/recommendations for international students: Required—TOEFL (minimum score 575 paper-based; 88 iBT), IELTS (minimum score 6.5), PTE (minimum score 59). *Application deadline:* For fall admission, 3/1 for domestic students. Application fee: $75 ($80 for international students). Electronic applications accepted. *Expenses:* Tuition, state resident: full-time $10,628; part-time $443 per credit. Tuition, nonresident: full-time $29,306; part-time $1221 per credit. *Required fees:* $3096; $129 per credit. Tuition and fees vary according to program. *Financial support:* In 2016–17, 8 students received support, including 3 research assistantships with tuition reimbursements available (averaging $9,629 per year), 5 teaching assistantships with tuition reimbursements available (averaging $12,814 per year); career-related internships or fieldwork, Federal Work-Study, scholarships/grants, unspecified assistantships, and health care benefits (for full-time research or teaching assistantship recipients) also available. Support available to part-time students. Financial award application deadline: 3/1; financial award applicants required to submit FAFSA. *Faculty research:* Combined English and folklore, religious and cultural studies (Christianity and Muslim society). *Unit head:* Meredith H. Lair, Director, 703-993-2159, Fax: 703-993-1251, E-mail: mlair@gmu.edu. *Application contact:* Morgan Fisher, Graduate Coordinator, 703-993-8762, E-mail: mfisherb@gmu.edu. Website: http://mais.gmu.edu

**George Mason University,** College of Humanities and Social Sciences, Program in Global Affairs, Fairfax, VA 22030. Offers MA. *Faculty:* 18 full-time (8 women), 5 part-time/adjunct (3 women). *Students:* 23 full-time (13 women), 20 part-time (13 women); includes 16 minority (6 Black or African American, non-Hispanic/Latino; 1 Asian, non-Hispanic/Latino; 8 Hispanic/Latino; 1 Two or more races, non-Hispanic/Latino), 4 international. Average age 29. 42 applicants, 93% accepted, 17 enrolled. In 2016, 33 master's awarded. *Degree requirements:* For master's, capstone seminar. *Entrance requirements:* For master's, GRE, expanded goals statement, 2 letters of recommendation, evidence of professional competency in a second language tested through Language Testing International or other means approved by the department. Additional exam requirements/recommendations for international students: Required—TOEFL (minimum score 575 paper-based; 88 iBT), IELTS (minimum score 6.5), PTE (minimum score 59). *Application deadline:* For fall admission, 3/15 for domestic students. Application fee: $75 ($80 for international students). Electronic applications accepted. *Expenses:* Tuition, state resident: full-time $10,628; part-time $443 per credit. Tuition, nonresident: full-time $29,306; part-time $1221 per credit. *Required fees:* $3096; $129 per credit. Tuition and fees vary according to program. *Financial support:* Career-related internships or fieldwork, Federal Work-Study, and scholarships/grants available. Financial award application deadline: 3/1; financial award applicants required to submit FAFSA. *Faculty research:* Social movements, globalization, law and economics, comparative politics, global environmentalism and governance, international business and economic development. *Unit head:* Lisa Breglia, Director, 703-993-9184, Fax: 703-993-1244, E-mail: lbreglia@gmu.edu. *Application contact:* Stephanie Lister,

Graduate Coordinator, 703-993-5056, Fax: 703-993-1244, E-mail: slister1@gmu.edu. Website: http://globalaffairs.gmu.edu

**Georgetown University,** Graduate School of Arts and Sciences, School of Continuing Studies, Washington, DC 20057. Offers American studies (MALS); Catholic studies (MALS); classical civilizations (MALS); emergency and disaster management (MPS); ethics and the professions (MALS); global strategic communications (MPS); hospitality management (MPS); human resources management (MPS); humanities (MALS); individualized study (MALS); integrated marketing communications (MPS); international affairs (MALS); Islam and Muslim-Christian relations (MALS); journalism (MPS); liberal studies (DLS); literature and society (MALS); medieval and early modern European studies (MALS); public relations and corporate communications (MPS); real estate (MPS); religious studies (MALS); social and public policy (MALS); sports industry management (MPS); systems engineering management (MPS); technology management (MPS); the theory and practice of American democracy (MALS); urban and regional planning (MPS); visual culture (MALS). MPS in systems engineering management offered jointly with Stevens Institute of Technology. *Entrance requirements:* Additional exam requirements/recommendations for international students: Required—TOEFL.

**Goddard College,** Graduate Division, Individualized Master of Arts Program, Plainfield, VT 05667-9432. Offers consciousness studies (MA); transformative language arts (MA). *Program availability:* Part-time. *Degree requirements:* For master's, thesis. *Entrance requirements:* For master's, 3 letters of recommendation, interview. Electronic applications accepted. *Expenses:* Contact institution.

**The Graduate Center, City University of New York,** Graduate Studies, Interdisciplinary Studies, New York, NY 10016-4039. Offers language in social context (PhD); medieval studies (PhD); public policy (MA, PhD); urban studies (MA, PhD); women's studies (MA, PhD). Terminal master's awarded for partial completion of doctoral program. *Degree requirements:* For master's, thesis; for doctorate, comprehensive exam, thesis/dissertation. *Entrance requirements:* For master's and doctorate, GRE General Test.

**Harrison Middleton University,** Graduate Program, Tempe, AZ 85282. Offers education (MA, Ed D); humanities (MA); imaginative literature (MA); interdisciplinary studies (DA); jurisprudence (MA); natural science (MA); philosophy and religion (MA); social science (MA). *Program availability:* Part-time, evening/weekend, online learning. *Degree requirements:* For master's and doctorate, capstone project. *Entrance requirements:* For master's, interview; for doctorate, 2 academic letters of reference, interview, essay. Additional exam requirements/recommendations for international students: Required—TOEFL (minimum score 550 paper-based; 80 iBT). Electronic applications accepted. *Faculty research:* Japanese animation, educational leadership, war art, John Muir's wilderness.

**Hiram College,** Graduate Studies, Hiram, OH 44234. Offers MAIS. *Program availability:* Part-time, evening/weekend. *Degree requirements:* For master's, two seminars, capstone research project. *Entrance requirements:* For master's, bachelor's degree from an accredited institution, 2 letters of recommendation, writing sample, interview.

**Hollins University,** Graduate Programs, Program in Liberal Studies, Roanoke, VA 24020. Offers humanities (MALS); interdisciplinary studies (MALS); leadership (MALS); social sciences (MALS); visual and performing arts (MALS). *Program availability:* Part-time, evening/weekend. *Degree requirements:* For master's, thesis. *Entrance requirements:* For master's, three letters of recommendation, interview, bachelor's degree, undergraduate transcripts, statement of educational objectives. Additional exam requirements/recommendations for international students: Required—TOEFL (minimum score 550 paper-based; 80 iBT), IELTS (minimum score 6.5). *Application deadline:* Applications are processed on a rolling basis. Application fee: $40. Electronic applications accepted. *Expenses:* $395 per credit hour. *Financial support:* Fellowships and scholarships/grants available. Support available to part-time students. Financial award application deadline: 7/15; financial award applicants required to submit FAFSA. *Faculty research:* Diversity, gender and women's studies, political science, leadership. *Unit head:* Director, 540-362-6576, Fax: 540-362-6288, E-mail: hugrad@hollins.edu. *Application contact:* Cathy S. Koon, Manager of Graduate Programs, 540-362-6326, Fax: 540-362-6288, E-mail: ckoon@hollins.edu. Website: http://www.hollins.edu/academics/graduate-degrees/liberal-studies/

**Idaho State University,** Office of Graduate Studies, Department of Interdisciplinary Studies, Pocatello, ID 83209. Offers general interdisciplinary (M Ed, MA, MNS); waste management and environmental science (MS). *Program availability:* Part-time. *Degree requirements:* For master's, comprehensive exam, thesis optional. *Entrance requirements:* For master's, GRE General Test or MAT, minimum GPA of 3.0. Additional exam requirements/recommendations for international students: Required—TOEFL (minimum score 550 paper-based; 80 iBT).

**Indiana University Southeast,** Master of Interdisciplinary Studies Program, New Albany, IN 47150-6405. Offers MIS, Graduate Certificate. *Program availability:* Part-time. *Students:* 1 full-time (0 women), 25 part-time (20 women); includes 5 minority (4 Black or African American, non-Hispanic/Latino; 1 American Indian or Alaska Native, non-Hispanic/Latino). Average age 40. 12 applicants, 83% accepted, 10 enrolled. In 2016, 2 master's, 3 other advanced degrees awarded. *Degree requirements:* For master's, thesis or alternative. *Entrance requirements:* For master's, GRE, 3 letters of recommendation, interview. *Application deadline:* For fall admission, 8/10 for domestic and international students; for spring admission, 1/2 for domestic and international students; for summer admission, 4/15 for domestic and international students. Application fee: $40. Electronic applications accepted. *Expenses:* $276.98 per credit hour in-state; $652.54 per credit hour out-of-state. *Financial support:* Fellowships and scholarships/grants available. Financial award applicants required to submit FAFSA. *Unit head:* Dr. Deborah Finkel, MLS Director, 812-941-2668, E-mail: dfinkel@ius.edu. Website: http://www.ius.edu/mis/

**Iowa State University of Science and Technology,** Program in Interdisciplinary Graduate Studies, Ames, IA 50011. Offers MA, MS. *Entrance requirements:* For master's, GRE. Additional exam requirements/recommendations for international students: Recommended—TOEFL (minimum score 550 paper-based; 79 iBT), IELTS (minimum score 6.5). *Application deadline:* For fall admission, 7/15 for domestic students; for spring admission, 11/15 for domestic students. Application fee: $60 ($90 for international students). Electronic applications accepted. *Application contact:* Melissa Stolt, Application Contact, 515-294-1170, Fax: 515-294-3003, E-mail: mstolt@iastate.edu. Website: http://www.grad-college.iastate.edu/igs/admission.html

**Kansas State University,** Graduate School, School of Applied and Interdisciplinary Studies, Olathe, KS 66061. Offers applied science and technology (PSM); professional interdisciplinary sciences (Graduate Certificate); professional skills for STEM practitioners (Graduate Certificate). *Program availability:* Part-time, 100% online, blended/hybrid learning. *Faculty:* 22 full-time (16 women), 2 part-time/adjunct (1 woman). *Students:* 8 part-time (2 women); includes 1 minority (Black or African American, non-Hispanic/Latino). Average age 35. 9 applicants, 100% accepted, 8 enrolled. *Degree requirements:* For master's, capstone experience and/or internship. *Entrance requirements:* Additional exam requirements/recommendations for

international students: Required—TOEFL (minimum score 550 paper-based; 79 iBT), IELTS (minimum score 6.5), PTE (minimum score 58). *Application deadline:* Applications are processed on a rolling basis. Application fee: $65 ($75 for international students). Electronic applications accepted. *Expenses:* Tuition, state resident: full-time $9670. Tuition, nonresident: full-time $21,828. *Required fees:* $862. *Financial support:* In 2016–17, 8 students received support. Scholarships/grants available. *Faculty research:* Applied and interdisciplinary science, food science, diagnostic medicine and pathobiology, adult education and leadership dynamics, horticulture and urban food systems. *Unit head:* Dr. Ralph Richardson, Dean and CEO, 913-541-1220, Fax: 913-541-1488, E-mail: olatheinfo@ksu.edu. *Application contact:* Dr. Janice Barrow, Associate Dean for Academic Affairs and Executive Education, 913-541-1220, E-mail: jbarrow@k-state.edu.
Website: http://olathe.k-state.edu/

**Lehigh University,** P.C. Rossin College of Engineering and Applied Science and College of Arts and Sciences, Center for Polymer Science and Engineering, Bethlehem, PA 18015. Offers M Eng, MS, PhD. *Program availability:* Part-time, evening/weekend, 100% online, blended/hybrid learning. *Faculty:* 24 full-time (4 women). *Students:* 5 full-time (4 women), 22 part-time (5 women); includes 8 minority (1 Black or African American, non-Hispanic/Latino; 6 Asian, non-Hispanic/Latino; 1 Native Hawaiian or other Pacific Islander, non-Hispanic/Latino), 4 international. Average age 31. 48 applicants, 21% accepted, 6 enrolled. In 2016, 4 master's awarded. Terminal master's awarded for partial completion of doctoral program. *Degree requirements:* For master's, thesis (for some programs); for doctorate, thesis/dissertation. *Entrance requirements:* For master's and doctorate, GRE General Test. Additional exam requirements/recommendations for international students: Required—TOEFL (minimum score 487 paper-based; 85 iBT), IELTS (minimum score 6.5). *Application deadline:* For fall admission, 7/15 for domestic students, 1/15 for international students; for spring admission, 12/1 for domestic and international students. Applications are processed on a rolling basis. Application fee: $75. Electronic applications accepted. *Expenses:* $1,420 per credit. *Financial support:* In 2016–17, 1 student received support, including 1 research assistantship (averaging $27,106 per year); teaching assistantships, scholarships/grants, and health care benefits also available. Financial award application deadline: 1/15. *Faculty research:* Polymer colloids, polymer coatings, blends and composites, polymer interfaces, emulsion polymer. *Unit head:* Dr. Raymond A. Pearson, Director, 610-758-3857, Fax: 610-758-3526, E-mail: rp02@lehigh.edu. *Application contact:* James E. Roberts, Chair, Polymer Education Committee, 610-758-4841, Fax: 610-758-6536, E-mail: jer1@lehigh.edu.
Website: http://www.lehigh.edu/~inpcreng/academics/graduate/polymerscieng.html

**Lesley University,** Graduate School of Arts and Social Sciences, Cambridge, MA 02138-2790. Offers clinical mental health counseling (MA), including holistic counseling, school and community counseling, trauma studies; counseling psychology (MA, CAGS), including professional counseling (MA), school counseling (MA); creative writing (MFA); expressive therapies (MA, PhD, CAGS), including art (MA), clinical mental health counseling (MA), dance (MA), expressive therapies (MA), music (MA); independent studies (CAGS); independent study (MA); intercultural relations (MA, CAGS); interdisciplinary studies (MA), including individualized studies, integrative holistic health, mindfulness studies, peace and conflict studies, trauma sensitive assessment, intervention, and consultation, women's studies; urban environmental leadership (MA). *Program availability:* Part-time, online learning. *Degree requirements:* For master's, internship, practicum, thesis (for expressive therapies); for doctorate, thesis/dissertation, arts apprenticeship, field placement; for CAGS, thesis, internship (for counseling psychology, expressive therapies). *Entrance requirements:* For master's, MAT (counseling psychology), interview, writing samples, art portfolio; for doctorate, GRE or MAT, interview, master's degree; for CAGS, interview, master's degree. Additional exam requirements/recommendations for international students: Required—TOEFL (minimum score 550 paper-based; 80 iBT). Electronic applications accepted. *Faculty research:* Psychotherapy and culture; psychotherapy and psychological trauma; women's issues in art, teaching and psychotherapy; community-based art, psycho-spiritual inquiry.

**Long Island University–LIU Post,** College of Education, Information and Technology, Brookville, NY 11548-1300. Offers adolescence education (MS); adolescence education 7-12 (MS); archives and records management (AC); art education (MS); childhood education (MS); childhood teaching literacy B-6 (MS); childhood/special education (MS); clinical mental health counseling (MS, AC); early childhood education (MS); early childhood education/childhood education (MS); educational leadership (AC); educational technology (MS); information studies (PhD); interdisciplinary educational studies (Ed D); middle childhood education (MS); music education (MS); school counselor (MS); special education (MS Ed); speech-language pathology (MA); students with disabilities, 7-12 generalist (AC); TESOL (MA). *Accreditation:* TEAC. *Program availability:* Part-time, 100% online, blended/hybrid learning. *Faculty:* 55 full-time (35 women), 104 part-time/adjunct (57 women). *Students:* 464 full-time (390 women), 740 part-time (580 women); includes 265 minority (99 Black or African American, non-Hispanic/Latino; 45 Asian, non-Hispanic/Latino; 113 Hispanic/Latino; 1 Native Hawaiian or other Pacific Islander, non-Hispanic/Latino; 7 Two or more races, non-Hispanic/Latino), 33 international. 928 applicants, 76% accepted, 406 enrolled. In 2016, 334 master's, 10 doctorates, 137 other advanced degrees awarded. Terminal master's awarded for partial completion of doctoral program. *Degree requirements:* For master's, variable foreign language requirement, comprehensive exam (for some programs), thesis optional; for doctorate, comprehensive exam, thesis/dissertation. *Entrance requirements:* For master's and AC, GRE. Additional exam requirements/recommendations for international students: Required—PTE, TOEFL (minimum score 550 paper-based, 75 iBT) or IELTS. *Application deadline:* Applications are processed on a rolling basis. Application fee: $50. Electronic applications accepted. *Expenses: Tuition:* Full-time $28,272; part-time $1178 per credit. *Required fees:* $451 per term. Tuition and fees vary according to degree level and program. *Financial support:* Career-related internships or fieldwork, Federal Work-Study, institutionally sponsored loans, scholarships/grants, tuition waivers (partial), and unspecified assistantships available. Support available to part-time students. Financial award application deadline: 2/15; financial award applicants required to submit FAFSA. *Faculty research:* English language learners, early childhood literacy development through play, sleep, social justice through education, using a structured protocol for discussing bad news. *Total annual research expenditures:* $575,000. *Unit head:* Dr. Albert Inserra, Dean, 516-299-2210, E-mail: albert.inserra@liu.edu. *Application contact:* Carol Zerah, Director of Graduate Admissions, 516-299-2900, Fax: 516-299-2137, E-mail: post-enroll@liu.edu.
Website: http://liu.edu/CWPost/Academics/College-of-Education-Information-and-Technology

**Long Island University–LIU Post,** College of Liberal Arts and Sciences, Brookville, NY 11548-1300. Offers applied mathematics (MS); behavior analysis (MA); biology (MS); criminal justice (MS); earth science (MS); English (MA); environmental sustainability (MS); genetic counseling (MS); history (MA); interdisciplinary studies (MA, MS); mathematics for secondary school teachers (MS); mobile GIS application development (Advanced Certificate); political science (MS); psychology (MA). *Program availability:* Part-time, evening/weekend, blended/hybrid learning. *Faculty:* 68 full-time (30 women), 20 part-time/adjunct (13 women). *Students:* 155 full-time (117 women), 125 part-time (82 women); includes 65 minority (17 Black or African American, non-Hispanic/Latino;

14 Asian, non-Hispanic/Latino; 27 Hispanic/Latino; 7 Two or more races, non-Hispanic/Latino), 19 international. 485 applicants, 36% accepted, 77 enrolled. In 2016, 91 master's, 15 other advanced degrees awarded. *Degree requirements:* For master's, comprehensive exam (for some programs), thesis (for some programs). *Entrance requirements:* Additional exam requirements/recommendations for international students: Required—PTE, TOEFL (minimum score 550 paper-based, 75 iBT) or IELTS (6.5). *Application deadline:* Applications are processed on a rolling basis. Application fee: $50. Electronic applications accepted. *Expenses: Tuition:* Full-time $28,272; part-time $1178 per credit. *Required fees:* $451 per term. Tuition and fees vary according to degree level and program. *Financial support:* In 2016–17, 24 teaching assistantships with partial tuition reimbursements (averaging $410 per year) were awarded; fellowships, research assistantships, career-related internships or fieldwork, Federal Work-Study, institutionally sponsored loans, scholarships/grants, tuition waivers (partial), and unspecified assistantships also available. Support available to part-time students. Financial award application deadline: 2/15; financial award applicants required to submit FAFSA. *Faculty research:* Biology, criminal justice, environmental sustainability, mathematics, psychology. *Total annual research expenditures:* $218,000. *Unit head:* Dr. Jeffrey Belnap, Acting Dean, 516-299-2233, Fax: 516-299-4140, E-mail: jeffrey.belnap@liu.edu. *Application contact:* Carol Zerah, Director of Graduate Admissions, 516-299-2900, Fax: 516-299-2137, E-mail: post-enroll@liu.edu.
Website: http://liu.edu/CWPost/Academics/Schools/CLAS

**Marquette University,** Graduate School, Interdisciplinary PhD Program, Milwaukee, WI 53201-1881. Offers PhD. *Program availability:* Part-time. *Students:* 1 full-time (0 women). Average age 44. In 2016, 1 doctorate awarded. *Degree requirements:* For doctorate, thesis/dissertation. *Entrance requirements:* For doctorate, GRE General Test. Additional exam requirements/recommendations for international students: Required—TOEFL (minimum score 630 paper-based). *Application deadline:* Applications are processed on a rolling basis. Application fee: $50. Electronic applications accepted. *Financial support:* Institutionally sponsored loans and scholarships/grants available. Financial award application deadline: 2/15. *Unit head:* Dr. Douglas Woods. *Application contact:* Carl Wainscott.
Website: http://www.marquette.edu/grad/programs_interdis.shtml

**Marylhurst University,** Department of Interdisciplinary Studies, Marylhurst, OR 97036-0261. Offers MA. *Program availability:* Part-time, evening/weekend. *Students:* 15 (13 women); includes 4 minority (1 Hispanic/Latino; 2 Native Hawaiian or other Pacific Islander, non-Hispanic/Latino; 1 Two or more races, non-Hispanic/Latino). Average age 50. In 2016, 23 master's awarded. *Degree requirements:* For master's, thesis. *Entrance requirements:* For master's, official transcripts from institution where degree was earned, personal statement, recommendations, writing sample, interview. Additional exam requirements/recommendations for international students: Required—PTE, TOEFL (minimum score 79 iBT) or IELTS (minimum score 6.5). *Application deadline:* Applications are processed on a rolling basis. Application fee: $0. Electronic applications accepted. *Expenses:* $618 per credit. *Financial support:* Scholarships/grants available. Support available to part-time students. Financial award applicants required to submit FAFSA. *Faculty research:* World religions, spirituality and literature, philosophy, humanities. *Unit head:* Dr. Sean Gillon, Chair, Department of Interdisciplinary and Applied Liberal Arts, 503-534-4037, E-mail: sgillon@marylhurst.edu. *Application contact:* Maruska Lynch, Graduate Admissions Counselor, 800-699-6322, E-mail: admissions@marylhurst.edu.
Website: http://www.marylhurst.edu

**Marywood University,** Academic Affairs, Center for Interdisciplinary Studies, Scranton, PA 18509-1598. Offers human development (PhD), including educational administration, health promotion, higher education administration, instructional leadership, social work. *Program availability:* Part-time. Electronic applications accepted. *Expenses:* Contact institution.

**Massachusetts College of Art and Design,** Graduate Programs, MFA Program, Boston, MA 02115-5882. Offers 2D fine arts (MFA), including painting, printmaking; 3D fine arts (MFA), including ceramics, fibers, glass, jewelry and metalsmithing, sculpture; design (MFA, Postbaccalaureate Certificate), including dynamic media; fine arts (MFA), including interdisciplinary; media arts (MFA, Postbaccalaureate Certificate), including film/video (MFA), photography. *Accreditation:* NASAD. *Faculty:* 40 full-time (19 women), 55 part-time/adjunct (23 women). *Students:* 58 full-time (39 women), 16 part-time (12 women); includes 10 minority (1 Black or African American, non-Hispanic/Latino; 4 Asian, non-Hispanic/Latino; 4 Hispanic/Latino; 1 Native Hawaiian or other Pacific Islander, non-Hispanic/Latino), 28 international. 247 applicants, 52% accepted, 47 enrolled. In 2016, 34 master's, 3 other advanced degrees awarded. *Degree requirements:* For master's, thesis, thesis exhibition (for fine arts programs); thesis project and document (for design/dynamic media program). *Entrance requirements:* For master's, portfolio, college transcripts, resume, statement of purpose, letters of reference, interview, 6 credits of art history taken prior to or during MFA program; for Postbaccalaureate Certificate, portfolio, college transcripts, resume, statement of purpose, letters of reference, interview. Additional exam requirements/recommendations for international students: Required—TOEFL (minimum score 550 paper-based; 85 iBT); Recommended—IELTS (minimum score 6.5). *Application deadline:* For fall admission, 1/4 priority date for domestic and international students; for summer admission, 1/4 priority date for domestic and international students. Application fee: $90. Electronic applications accepted. *Expenses:* $780 per credit tuition. *Financial support:* In 2016–17, 57 students received support, including 33 teaching assistantships (averaging $2,160 per year); fellowships, research assistantships, career-related internships or fieldwork, scholarships/grants, tuition waivers (partial), unspecified assistantships, and 6-8 one-term adjunct co-teaching positions; 27 full-year general assistantships also available. Support available to part-time students. Financial award application deadline: 1/4; financial award applicants required to submit FAFSA. *Faculty research:* Painting and printmaking, sculpture, photography, film and video, dynamic media design. *Unit head:* Paul Paturzo, Dean of Graduate Studies, 617-879-7166, E-mail: pjpaturzo@massart.edu. *Application contact:* Lauren O'Neill, Assistant Director of Graduate Admissions, 617-879-7222, E-mail: gradadmissions@massart.edu.
Website: http://www.massart.edu/Admissions/Graduate_Programs.html

**Michigan Technological University,** Graduate School, Interdisciplinary Programs, Houghton, MI 49931. Offers atmospheric sciences (PhD); biochemistry and molecular biology (PhD); computational science and engineering (PhD); data science (MS, Graduate Certificate); engineering (M Eng); environmental engineering (PhD); international profile (Graduate Certificate); nanotechnology (Graduate Certificate); sustainability (Graduate Certificate); sustainable water resources systems (Graduate Certificate). *Program availability:* Part-time. *Faculty:* 122 full-time (26 women), 13 part-time/adjunct. *Students:* 58 full-time (18 women), 17 part-time (5 women); includes 1 minority (Black or African American, non-Hispanic/Latino), 56 international. Average age 28. 395 applicants, 20% accepted, 22 enrolled. In 2016, 3 master's, 7 doctorates, 8 other advanced degrees awarded. Terminal master's awarded for partial completion of doctoral program. *Degree requirements:* For master's, comprehensive exam (for some programs), thesis (for some programs); for doctorate, comprehensive exam, thesis/dissertation. *Entrance requirements:* For master's, doctorate, and Graduate Certificate, GRE, statement of purpose, personal statement, official transcripts, 2-3 letters of

# Interdisciplinary Studies

recommendation. Additional exam requirements/recommendations for international students: Required—TOEFL or IELTS. *Application deadline:* Applications are processed on a rolling basis. Electronic applications accepted. *Expenses:* Tuition, state resident: full-time $16,290; part-time $905 per credit. Tuition, nonresident: full-time $16,290; part-time $905 per credit. *Required fees:* $248; $124 per term. Tuition and fees vary according to course load and program. *Financial support:* In 2016–17, 54 students received support, including 7 fellowships with tuition reimbursements available (averaging $15,242 per year), 19 research assistantships with tuition reimbursements available (averaging $15,242 per year), 5 teaching assistantships with tuition reimbursements available (averaging $15,242 per year); career-related internships or fieldwork, Federal Work-Study, scholarships/grants, health care benefits, unspecified assistantships, and cooperative program also available. Financial award applicants required to submit FAFSA. *Faculty research:* Big data, atmospheric sciences, bioinformatics and systems biology, molecular dynamics, environmental studies. *Unit head:* Dr. Pushpalathata Murthy, Dean of the Graduate School/Associate Provost for Graduate Education, 906-487-3007, Fax: 906-487-2284, E-mail: ppmurthy@mtu.edu. *Application contact:* Carol T. Wingerson, Administrative Aide, 906-487-2328, Fax: 906-487-2284, E-mail: gradadms@mtu.edu.

**Mills College,** Graduate Studies, Program in Computer Science, Oakland, CA 94613-1000. Offers computer science (Certificate); interdisciplinary computer science (MA). *Program availability:* Part-time. *Faculty:* 1 (woman) full-time, 1 part-time/adjunct (0 women). *Students:* 20 full-time (6 women), 2 part-time (1 woman); includes 10 minority (5 Asian, non-Hispanic/Latino; 3 Hispanic/Latino; 2 Two or more races, non-Hispanic/Latino). Average age 27. 21 applicants, 90% accepted, 14 enrolled. In 2016, 2 master's awarded. *Degree requirements:* For master's, thesis. *Entrance requirements:* For master's, three letters of recommendation. Additional exam requirements/recommendations for international students: Required—TOEFL (minimum score 600 paper-based; 100 iBT) or IELTS (minimum score 7). *Application deadline:* For fall admission, 2/1 priority date for domestic students, 12/15 for international students; for spring admission, 11/1 priority date for domestic students, 10/1 for international students. Applications are processed on a rolling basis. Application fee: $50. Electronic applications accepted. *Expenses:* Tuition: Full-time $31,620. *Required fees:* $1118. Tuition and fees vary according to course load, degree level and program. *Financial support:* In 2016–17, 30 students received support, including 15 fellowships with tuition reimbursements available (averaging $4,626 per year), 15 teaching assistantships with tuition reimbursements available (averaging $4,626 per year); career-related internships or fieldwork, institutionally sponsored loans, and scholarships/grants also available. Support available to part-time students. Financial award application deadline: 2/1; financial award applicants required to submit FAFSA. *Faculty research:* Dynamical systems, linear programming, theory of computer viruses, interface design, intelligent tutoring systems. *Total annual research expenditures:* $7,483. *Unit head:* Susan S. Wang, Department Head, 510-430-2138, E-mail: wang@mills.edu. *Application contact:* Robynne Lofton, Director of Admissions, 510-430-3295, Fax: 510-430-2159, E-mail: grad-admission@mills.edu.
Website: http://www.mills.edu/ics

**Minnesota State University Mankato,** College of Graduate Studies and Research, Program in Cross-disciplinary Studies, Mankato, MN 56001. Offers MS. *Program availability:* Part-time, evening/weekend. *Students:* 1 (woman) full-time. *Degree requirements:* For master's, comprehensive exam, thesis or alternative. *Entrance requirements:* For master's, GRE General Test, minimum GPA of 3.0 during previous 2 years. Additional exam requirements/recommendations for international students: Required—TOEFL. *Application deadline:* For fall admission, 7/1 priority date for domestic students; for spring admission, 11/1 for domestic students. Applications are processed on a rolling basis. Application fee: $40. Electronic applications accepted. *Financial support:* Research assistantships with full tuition reimbursements, teaching assistantships with full tuition reimbursements, career-related internships or fieldwork, Federal Work-Study, and unspecified assistantships available. Support available to part-time students. Financial award application deadline: 3/15; financial award applicants required to submit FAFSA.

**Montana State University Billings,** College of Education, Department of Educational Theory and Practice, Option in Interdisciplinary Studies, Billings, MT 59101. Offers M Ed. *Program availability:* Part-time, 100% online, blended/hybrid learning. *Faculty:* 15 full-time (10 women), 1 (woman) part-time/adjunct. *Students:* 1. *Degree requirements:* For master's, thesis or alternative. *Entrance requirements:* For master's, GRE General Test or MAT, minimum GPA of 3.0. Additional exam requirements/recommendations for international students: Required—TOEFL (minimum score 79 iBT), IELTS (minimum score 6.5). *Application deadline:* For fall admission, 7/15 for domestic students; for spring admission, 12/1 for domestic students. Applications are processed on a rolling basis. Application fee: $40. Electronic applications accepted. *Expenses:* Tuition, state resident: full-time $5265; part-time $3436 per year. Tuition, nonresident: full-time $14,030; part-time $9280 per year. *International tuition:* $19,295 full-time. Tuition and fees vary according to degree level, campus/location and program. *Financial support:* Teaching assistantships with partial tuition reimbursements, career-related internships or fieldwork, Federal Work-Study, institutionally sponsored loans, scholarships/grants, tuition waivers (partial), and unspecified assistantships available. Support available to part-time students. Financial award application deadline: 5/1; financial award applicants required to submit FAFSA. *Unit head:* Dr. Ken Miller, Chair, 406-657-2034, Fax: 406-657-2807, E-mail: kmiller@msubillings.edu. *Application contact:* David M. Sullivan, Graduate Studies Counselor, 406-657-2053, Fax: 406-657-2299, E-mail: dsullivan@msubillings.edu.

**Montana Tech of The University of Montana,** Interdisciplinary Program, Butte, MT 59701-8997. Offers MS. *Program availability:* Part-time. *Faculty:* 7 full-time (4 women), 4 part-time/adjunct (2 women). *Students:* 8 full-time (3 women), 2 part-time (1 woman); includes 3 minority (2 Black or African American, non-Hispanic/Latino; 1 Hispanic/Latino). 3 applicants, 67% accepted, 2 enrolled. In 2016, 3 master's awarded. *Degree requirements:* For master's, comprehensive exam (for some programs), thesis optional. *Entrance requirements:* For master's, GRE General Test, minimum GPA of 3.0. Additional exam requirements/recommendations for international students: Required—TOEFL (minimum score 545 paper-based; 78 iBT), IELTS (minimum score 6.5). *Application deadline:* For fall admission, 4/1 for domestic students, 3/1 priority date for international students; for spring admission, 10/1 for domestic students, 6/1 priority date for international students. Application fee: $50. *Expenses:* Tuition, state resident: full-time $2901; part-time $1450.68 per degree program. Tuition, nonresident: full-time $8432; part-time $4215.84 per degree program. *Required fees:* $668; $354 per degree program. Tuition and fees vary according to course load and program. *Financial support:* In 2016–17, 3 students received support. Research assistantships, teaching assistantships, career-related internships or fieldwork, tuition waivers (full and partial), and unspecified assistantships available. *Unit head:* Dr. Beverly Hartline, Vice Chancellor of Research/Dean of the Graduate School, 406-496-4456, E-mail: graduatedean@mtech.edu. *Application contact:* Daniel Stirling, Administrator, Graduate School, 406-496-4304, Fax: 406-496-4710, E-mail: gradschool@mtech.edu.
Website: http://www.mtech.edu/academics/gradschool/degreeprograms/degrees-interdisciplinary-ms.htm

**New Mexico State University,** Graduate School, Interdisciplinary Program, Las Cruces, NM 88003. Offers MA, MS, PhD. *Program availability:* Part-time, blended/hybrid learning. *Students:* 8 full-time (6 women), 18 part-time (7 women); includes 9 minority (2 Black or African American, non-Hispanic/Latino; 7 Hispanic/Latino), 4 international. Average age 43. 1 applicant, 100% accepted, 1 enrolled. In 2016, 5 master's, 2 doctorates awarded. *Degree requirements:* For master's, comprehensive exam, thesis; for doctorate, comprehensive exam, thesis/dissertation. *Entrance requirements:* For master's, GRE General Test, minimum GPA of 2.5; for doctorate, GRE General Test, minimum GPA of 3.0. Additional exam requirements/recommendations for international students: Required—TOEFL (minimum score 550 paper-based; 79 iBT), IELTS (minimum score 6.5). *Application deadline:* Applications are processed on a rolling basis. Application fee: $40 ($50 for international students). Electronic applications accepted. *Expenses:* Tuition, state resident: full-time $4086. Tuition, nonresident: full-time $14,254. *Required fees:* $853. Tuition and fees vary according to course load. *Financial support:* In 2016–17, 10 students received support. Career-related internships or fieldwork, Federal Work-Study, scholarships/grants, traineeships, health care benefits, and unspecified assistantships available. Support available to part-time students. Financial award application deadline: 3/1. *Unit head:* Dr. Loui Reyes, Dean of Graduate School, 575-646-5746, Fax: 575-646-7758, E-mail: gradinfo@nmsu.edu. *Application contact:* Graduate Admissions, 575-646-3121, E-mail: admissions@nmsu.edu.
Website: http://idsas.nmsu.edu

**New York Institute of Technology,** School of Interdisciplinary Studies and Education, Old Westbury, NY 11568-8000. Offers MA, MS, Advanced Certificate, Advanced Diploma. *Accreditation:* NCATE. *Program availability:* Part-time, evening/weekend, 100% online, blended/hybrid learning. *Faculty:* 12 full-time (7 women), 19 part-time/adjunct (11 women). *Students:* 58 full-time (48 women), 284 part-time (210 women); includes 95 minority (33 Black or African American, non-Hispanic/Latino; 1 American Indian or Alaska Native, non-Hispanic/Latino; 13 Asian, non-Hispanic/Latino; 42 Hispanic/Latino; 6 Two or more races, non-Hispanic/Latino), 4 international. Average age 33. 247 applicants, 74% accepted, 135 enrolled. In 2016, 76 master's, 13 other advanced degrees awarded. *Entrance requirements:* Additional exam requirements/recommendations for international students: Required—TOEFL (minimum score 79 iBT), IELTS (minimum score 6). *Application deadline:* Applications are processed on a rolling basis. Application fee: $50. Electronic applications accepted. *Expenses:* $1,215 per credit. *Financial support:* Career-related internships or fieldwork, Federal Work-Study, scholarships/grants, tuition waivers (full and partial), and unspecified assistantships available. Support available to part-time students. Financial award application deadline: 3/1; financial award applicants required to submit FAFSA. *Unit head:* Dr. Jess Boronico, Interim Dean, 516-686-7403, E-mail: soeinfo@nyit.edu. *Application contact:* Alice Dolitsky, Director, Graduate Admissions, 516-686-7520, Fax: 516-686-1116, E-mail: nyitgrad@nyit.edu.
Website: http://www.nyit.edu/interdisciplinary

**New York University,** Gallatin School of Individualized Study, New York, NY 10003. Offers MA. *Program availability:* Part-time, evening/weekend. *Degree requirements:* For master's, thesis. *Entrance requirements:* Additional exam requirements/recommendations for international students: Required—TOEFL. Electronic applications accepted. *Expenses:* Contact institution. *Faculty research:* Arts and performance studies, media studies, political and social thought, literary and cultural studies, environmental and global studies, gender studies.

**Niagara University,** Graduate Division of Arts and Sciences, Program in Interdisciplinary Studies, Niagara University, NY 14109. Offers MA. *Program availability:* Part-time. *Students:* 5 full-time (1 woman), 6 part-time (5 women); includes 3 minority (1 Black or African American, non-Hispanic/Latino; 1 Hispanic/Latino; 1 Two or more races, non-Hispanic/Latino), 4 international. Average age 32. In 2016, 2 master's awarded. *Entrance requirements:* Additional exam requirements/recommendations for international students: Required—TOEFL (minimum score 550 paper-based; 79 iBT), IELTS (minimum score 6). *Application deadline:* For fall admission, 8/1 for domestic students. Applications are processed on a rolling basis. Electronic applications accepted. *Expenses:* $735 per credit hour. *Financial support:* Research assistantships with tuition reimbursements, teaching assistantships with tuition reimbursements, career-related internships or fieldwork, Federal Work-Study, scholarships/grants, and unspecified assistantships available. Financial award application deadline: 4/15; financial award applicants required to submit FAFSA. *Unit head:* Dr. Mustafa Gokcek, Director, 716-286-8195, E-mail: gokcek@niagara.edu. *Application contact:* Evan Pierce, Associate Director of Graduate Recruitment, 716-286-8769, Fax: 716-286-8710, E-mail: epierce@niagara.edu.
Website: http://www.niagara.edu/mais

**Northeastern University,** Bouvé College of Health Sciences, Boston, MA 02115-5096. Offers applied behavior analysis (MS); audiology (Au D); counseling psychology (MS, PhD, CAGS); exercise science (MS); nursing (MS, PhD, CAGS), including administration (MS), adult-gerontology acute care nurse practitioner (MS, CAGS), adult-gerontology primary care nurse practitioner (MS, CAGS), anesthesia (MS), family nurse practitioner (MS, CAGS), neonatal nurse practitioner (MS, CAGS), pediatric nurse practitioner (MS, CAGS), psychiatric mental health nurse practitioner (MS, CAGS); nursing practice (DNP); pharmaceutical sciences (MS, PhD), including interdisciplinary concentration, pharmaceutics and drug delivery systems; pharmacology (MS); pharmacy (Pharm D); school psychology (PhD); urban health (MPH); MS/MBA. *Accreditation:* ACPE (one or more programs are accredited). *Program availability:* Part-time, evening/weekend, online learning. *Faculty:* 192 full-time (119 women), 194 part-time/adjunct (156 women). *Students:* 1,371 full-time (1,009 women), 262 part-time (219 women). In 2016, 352 master's, 312 doctorates, 25 other advanced degrees awarded. *Degree requirements:* For doctorate, thesis/dissertation (for some programs); for CAGS, comprehensive exam. Application fee: $75. Electronic applications accepted. *Expenses:* Contact institution. *Financial support:* Fellowships, research assistantships, teaching assistantships, career-related internships or fieldwork, scholarships/grants, health care benefits, tuition waivers, and unspecified assistantships available. Support available to part-time students. Financial award applicants required to submit FAFSA. *Unit head:* Susan L. Parish, Dean, Bouve College of Health Sciences, 617-373-3323, Fax: 617-373-3030. *Application contact:* E-mail: bouvegrad@northeastern.edu.
Website: http://www.northeastern.edu/bouve/

**Northeastern University,** College of Engineering, Boston, MA 02115-5096. Offers bioengineering (MS, PhD); chemical engineering (MS, PhD); civil engineering (MS, PhD); computer engineering (PhD); computer systems engineering (MS); electrical and computer engineering (MS); electrical and computer engineering leadership (MS); electrical engineering (PhD); energy systems (MS); engineering and public policy (MS); engineering management (MS, Certificate); environmental engineering (MS); industrial engineering (MS, PhD); information assurance (PhD); information systems (MS); interdisciplinary engineering (PhD); mechanical engineering (PhD); operations research (MS); telecommunication systems management (MS). *Program availability:* Part-time, online learning. *Faculty:* 202 full-time (59 women), 53 part-time/adjunct (9 women). *Students:* 2,982 full-time (954 women), 192 part-time (38 women). In 2016, 851 master's, 74 doctorates awarded. Application fee: $75. Electronic applications accepted.

*Expenses:* $1,471 per credit. *Financial support:* Fellowships, research assistantships, teaching assistantships, career-related internships or fieldwork, scholarships/grants, health care benefits, tuition waivers, and unspecified assistantships available. Support available to part-time students. Financial award applicants required to submit FAFSA. *Unit head:* Dr. Nadine Aubry, Dean, College of Engineering. *Application contact:* Jeffery Hengel, Director of Graduate Admissions, 617-373-2711, E-mail: j.hengel@northeastern.edu.
Website: http://www.coe.neu.edu/academics/graduate-school-engineering

**Nova Southeastern University,** College of Arts, Humanities, and Social Sciences, Fort Lauderdale, FL 33314-7796. Offers advanced conflict resolution practice (Graduate Certificate); college student affairs (MS); conflict analysis and resolution (MS, PhD); cross-disciplinary studies (Graduate Certificate); family studies (Graduate Certificate); family systems health care (Graduate Certificate); family therapy (MS, PhD); marriage and family therapy (DMFT); peace studies (Graduate Certificate); qualitative research (Graduate Certificate); solution focused coaching (Graduate Certificate). *Accreditation:* AAMFT/COAMFTE (one or more programs are accredited). *Program availability:* Part-time, evening/weekend, 100% online, blended/hybrid learning. *Faculty:* 29 full-time (18 women), 27 part-time/adjunct (21 women). *Students:* 306 full-time (242 women), 889 part-time (683 women); includes 677 minority (403 Black or African American, non-Hispanic/Latino; 2 American Indian or Alaska Native, non-Hispanic/Latino; 20 Asian, non-Hispanic/Latino; 224 Hispanic/Latino; 1 Native Hawaiian or other Pacific Islander, non-Hispanic/Latino; 27 Two or more races, non-Hispanic/Latino; 53 international. Average age 37. 624 applicants, 61% accepted, 285 enrolled. In 2016, 303 master's, 71 doctorates, 34 other advanced degrees awarded. *Degree requirements:* For master's, thesis optional, comprehensive exams, portfolios (for some programs), table-top exams (for some programs); for doctorate, comprehensive exam, thesis/dissertation, qualifying exams, portfolios (for some programs). *Entrance requirements:* For master's, interview, minimum GPA of 3.0, writing sample; for doctorate, interview, minimum GPA of 3.5, master's degree in related field, writing sample; for Graduate Certificate, minimum GPA of 3.0. Additional exam requirements/recommendations for international students: Required—TOEFL. *Application deadline:* For fall admission, 5/17 priority date for domestic and international students; for winter admission, 12/1 priority date for domestic and international students; for spring admission, 4/1 priority date for domestic and international students. Applications are processed on a rolling basis. Application fee: $50. Electronic applications accepted. *Expenses:* $1,005. *Financial support:* In 2016–17, 170 students received support. Career-related internships or fieldwork, Federal Work-Study, scholarships/grants, and unspecified assistantships available. Financial award application deadline: 4/1; financial award applicants required to submit CSS PROFILE. *Faculty research:* Conflict resolution, family therapy, peace research, international conflict, multi-disciplinary studies, college student affairs, national security affairs, health care conflict resolution, family systems health care, advanced family systems, qualitative research, solution-focused coaching. *Unit head:* Dr. Honggang Yang, Dean, 954-262-3016, Fax: 954-262-3968, E-mail: yangh@nova.edu. *Application contact:* Marcia Arango, Student Recruitment Coordinator, 954-262-3006, Fax: 954-262-3968, E-mail: marango@nsu.nova.edu.
Website: http://cahss.nova.edu/

**The Ohio State University,** Graduate School, College of Arts and Sciences, Division of Arts and Humanities, Department of Comparative Studies, Columbus, OH 43210. Offers MA, PhD. *Faculty:* 17. *Students:* 24 full-time (14 women), 2 part-time (1 woman). Average age 31. In 2016, 2 master's, 2 doctorates awarded. Terminal master's awarded for partial completion of doctoral program. *Degree requirements:* For doctorate, thesis/dissertation. *Entrance requirements:* For master's and doctorate, GRE General Test. Additional exam requirements/recommendations for international students: Required—TOEFL (minimum score 550 paper-based; 79 iBT), Michigan English Language Assessment Battery (minimum score 82); Recommended—IELTS (minimum score 7). *Application deadline:* For fall admission, 11/30 priority date for domestic and international students; for spring admission, 3/1 for domestic students, 2/1 for international students. Applications are processed on a rolling basis. Application fee: $60 ($70 for international students). Electronic applications accepted. *Financial support:* Fellowships with tuition reimbursements, research assistantships with tuition reimbursements, teaching assistantships with tuition reimbursements, Federal Work-Study, institutionally sponsored loans, and unspecified assistantships available. Support available to part-time students. *Unit head:* Barry Shank, Chair, 614-688-2559, E-mail: shank.46@osu.edu. *Application contact:* Graduate and Professional Admissions, 614-292-9444, Fax: 614-292-3895, E-mail: gpadmissions@osu.edu.
Website: http://comparativestudies.osu.edu/

**Oregon State University,** Interdisciplinary/Institutional Programs, Program in Interdisciplinary Studies, Corvallis, OR 97331. Offers MAIS. Program focuses on three areas of study and must include at least one area of study in liberal arts. *Program availability:* Part-time. *Students:* 34 full-time (17 women), 11 part-time (7 women); includes 12 minority (2 Black or African American, non-Hispanic/Latino; 2 Asian, non-Hispanic/Latino; 7 Hispanic/Latino; 1 Two or more races, non-Hispanic/Latino), 3 international. Average age 31. 25 applicants, 76% accepted, 12 enrolled. In 2016, 13 master's awarded. *Degree requirements:* For master's, thesis optional. *Entrance requirements:* Additional exam requirements/recommendations for international students: Required—TOEFL (minimum score 80 iBT), IELTS (minimum score 6.5). *Application deadline:* For fall admission, 3/1 for domestic and international students. Application fee: $75 ($85 for international students). *Expenses:* Tuition, state resident: full-time $12,150; part-time $450 per credit. Tuition, nonresident: full-time $21,789; part-time $807 per credit. *Required fees:* $1651; $1507 per credit. One-time fee: $350. Tuition and fees vary according to course load, campus/location and program. *Financial support:* Fellowships, research assistantships, and teaching assistantships available. *Unit head:* Dr. David Bernell, Program Director, 541-737-6281, E-mail: david.bernell@oregonstate.edu.
Website: http://oregonstate.edu/dept/grad_school/mais.html

**Regent University,** Graduate School, School of Business and Leadership, Virginia Beach, VA 23464-9800. Offers business administration (MBA), including accounting, entrepreneurship, finance and investing, general management, healthcare management (MA, MBA), human resource management, innovation management; leadership (Certificate); organizational leadership (MA, PhD), including ecclesial leadership (PhD), entrepreneurial leadership (PhD), future studies (MA), healthcare management (MA, MBA), human resource development (PhD), interdisciplinary studies (MA), international organizations (MA), leadership coaching and mentoring (MA), not-for-profit management (MA), organizational communication (MA), organizational development consulting (MA); strategic leadership (DSL), including global consulting, leadership coaching, strategic foresight. *Program availability:* Part-time, evening/weekend, 100% online, blended/hybrid learning. *Faculty:* 9 full-time (2 women), 28 part-time/adjunct (10 women). *Students:* 100 full-time (56 women), 1,008 part-time (528 women); includes 562 minority (453 Black or African American, non-Hispanic/Latino; 7 American Indian or Alaska Native, non-Hispanic/Latino; 30 Asian, non-Hispanic/Latino; 51 Hispanic/Latino; 1 Native Hawaiian or other Pacific Islander, non-Hispanic/Latino; 20 Two or more races, non-Hispanic/Latino), 76 international. Average age 40. 1,240 applicants, 45% accepted, 352 enrolled. In 2016, 95 master's, 71 doctorates awarded. *Degree requirements:* For master's, thesis or alternative, 3-credit hour culminating experience;

for doctorate, thesis/dissertation. *Entrance requirements:* For master's, college transcripts, resume, essay; for doctorate, college transcripts, resume, essay, writing sample; for Certificate, writing sample, resume, transcripts. Additional exam requirements/recommendations for international students: Required—TOEFL (minimum score 577 paper-based). *Application deadline:* For fall admission, 5/1 priority date for domestic students; for spring admission, 10/1 priority date for domestic students. Applications are processed on a rolling basis. Application fee: $50. Electronic applications accepted. *Expenses:* Contact institution. *Financial support:* In 2016–17, 631 students received support. Career-related internships or fieldwork, scholarships/grants, and unspecified assistantships available. Support available to part-time students. *Faculty research:* Servant leadership, global business, team effectiveness, technology utilization, leadership development. *Unit head:* Dr. Doris Gomez, Dean, 757-352-4686, Fax: 757-352-4634, E-mail: dorigom@regent.edu. *Application contact:* Heidi Cece, Assistant Vice President of Enrollment Management, 800-373-5504, Fax: 757-352-4381, E-mail: admissions@regent.edu.
Website: http://www.regent.edu/sbl/

**Regent University,** Graduate School, School of Divinity, Virginia Beach, VA 23464-9800. Offers divinity (M Div), including Biblical studies (M Div, MTS, PhD), chaplain ministry, Christian theology (M Div, MTS, PhD), church and ministry (M Div, MA), history of Christianity (M Div, MTS, PhD), inter-cultural studies (M Div, MA), interdisciplinary studies (M Div, MA, MTS), marketplace ministry, worship and media (M Div, MA); leadership and renewal (D Min), including Christian leadership and renewal, clinical pastoral education, community transformation, military ministry, ministry leadership coaching; practical theology (MA), including church and ministry (M Div, MA), inter-cultural studies (M Div, MA), interdisciplinary studies (M Div, MA, MTS), worship and media (M Div, MA); theological studies (MTS, PhD), including Biblical studies (M Div, MTS, PhD), Christian theology (M Div, MTS, PhD), history of Christianity (M Div, MTS, PhD), interdisciplinary studies (M Div, MA, MTS). *Accreditation:* ACIPE; ATS. *Program availability:* Part-time, evening/weekend, 100% online, blended/hybrid learning. *Faculty:* 15 full-time (3 women), 51 part-time/adjunct (6 women). *Students:* 148 full-time (60 women), 787 part-time (321 women); includes 506 minority (416 Black or African American, non-Hispanic/Latino; 1 American Indian or Alaska Native, non-Hispanic/Latino; 23 Asian, non-Hispanic/Latino; 54 Hispanic/Latino; 1 Native Hawaiian or other Pacific Islander, non-Hispanic/Latino; 11 Two or more races, non-Hispanic/Latino), 31 international. Average age 43. 1,020 applicants, 42% accepted, 276 enrolled. In 2016, 127 master's, 25 doctorates awarded. *Degree requirements:* For master's, comprehensive exam, thesis or alternative, internship; for doctorate, thesis/dissertation or alternative. *Entrance requirements:* For master's, minimum undergraduate GPA of 2.75, writing sample, personal goal statement, college transcripts; for doctorate, GRE, minimum graduate GPA of 3.5 (PhD), 3.0 (D Min); clergy recommendations; writing sample; transcripts; resume; interview. Additional exam requirements/recommendations for international students: Required—TOEFL (minimum score 577 paper-based). *Application deadline:* For fall admission, 5/1 priority date for domestic students. Applications are processed on a rolling basis. Application fee: $50. Electronic applications accepted. *Expenses:* Contact institution. *Financial support:* In 2016–17, 602 students received support. Career-related internships or fieldwork, scholarships/grants, and unspecified assistantships available. Support available to part-time students. *Faculty research:* Greek and Hebrew, theology, spiritual formation, global missions and world Christianity, women in ministry leadership. *Unit head:* Dr. Cornelius Bekker, Dean, 757-352-4401, Fax: 757-352-4597, E-mail: clbekker@regent.edu. *Application contact:* Heidi Cece, Assistant Vice President of Enrollment Management, 800-373-5504, Fax: 757-352-4381, E-mail: admissions@regent.edu.
Website: http://www.regent.edu/sod/

**Rensselaer Polytechnic Institute,** Graduate School, School of Science, Program in Multi-Disciplinary Science, Troy, NY 12180-3590. Offers MS, PhD. Terminal master's awarded for partial completion of doctoral program. *Degree requirements:* For master's, comprehensive exam (for some programs), thesis optional; for doctorate, comprehensive exam, thesis/dissertation. *Entrance requirements:* For master's and doctorate, GRE. Additional exam requirements/recommendations for international students: Required—TOEFL (minimum score 600 paper-based; 100 iBT), IELTS (minimum score 7), PTE (minimum score 68). Electronic applications accepted. *Expenses: Tuition:* Full-time $49,520; part-time $2060 per credit hour. *Required fees:* $2617.

**Rochester Institute of Technology,** Graduate Enrollment Services, School of Individualized Study, Graduate Programs Department, MS Program in Professional Studies, Rochester, NY 14623. Offers MS. *Program availability:* Part-time, evening/weekend, 100% online, blended/hybrid learning. *Students:* 37 full-time (18 women), 34 part-time (16 women); includes 8 minority (5 Black or African American, non-Hispanic/Latino; 1 American Indian or Alaska Native, non-Hispanic/Latino; 2 Hispanic/Latino), 21 international. Average age 35. 40 applicants, 58% accepted, 13 enrolled. In 2016, 28 master's awarded. *Degree requirements:* For master's, thesis or alternative. *Entrance requirements:* For master's, minimum GPA of 3.0. Additional exam requirements/recommendations for international students: Required—TOEFL (minimum score 550 paper-based; 79 iBT), IELTS (minimum score 6.5), PTE (minimum score 58). *Application deadline:* Applications are processed on a rolling basis. Application fee: $60. Electronic applications accepted. *Expenses:* $1,742 per credit hour (classroom), $993 per credit hour (online). *Financial support:* In 2016–17, 6 students received support. Career-related internships or fieldwork, scholarships/grants, and unspecified assistantships available. Support available to part-time students. Financial award applicants required to submit FAFSA. *Faculty research:* Interdisciplinary entrepreneurship; non-profit management; educational innovation; technology and work in the 21st century; professional development and leadership. *Unit head:* Peter Boyd, Graduate Program Director, 585-475-6320, Fax: 585-475-6292, E-mail: sois@rit.edu. *Application contact:* Diane Ellison, Associate Vice President, Graduate Enrollment Services, 585-475-2229, Fax: 585-475-7164, E-mail: gradinfo@rit.edu.
Website: http://www.rit.edu/academicaffairs/sois/getting-started/graduate/graduate-degrees-programs

**Rosalind Franklin University of Medicine and Science,** College of Health Professions, Department of Interprofessional Healthcare Studies, Interprofessional Studies Program, North Chicago, IL 60064-3095. Offers interprofessional studies (D Sc). *Program availability:* Part-time, online learning. *Degree requirements:* For doctorate, comprehensive exam, thesis/dissertation. *Entrance requirements:* For doctorate, GRE. Additional exam requirements/recommendations for international students: Required—TOEFL. *Faculty research:* Interprofessional education.

**Rutgers University–New Brunswick,** Graduate School-New Brunswick, BioMaPS Institute for Quantitative Biology, Piscataway, NJ 08854-8097. Offers computational biology and molecular biophysics (PhD). *Degree requirements:* For doctorate, comprehensive exam, thesis/dissertation. *Entrance requirements:* For doctorate, GRE. Additional exam requirements/recommendations for international students: Required—TOEFL. Electronic applications accepted. *Faculty research:* Structural biology, systems biology, bioinformatics, translational medicine, genomics.

**San Diego State University,** Graduate and Research Affairs, Interdisciplinary Studies, San Diego, CA 92182. Offers MA, MS. *Program availability:* Part-time. *Degree*

## Interdisciplinary Studies

*requirements:* For master's, thesis. *Entrance requirements:* For master's, GRE General Test. Additional exam requirements/recommendations for international students: Required—TOEFL. Electronic applications accepted.

**Sonoma State University,** School of Science and Technology, Department of Kinesiology, Rohnert Park, CA 94928. Offers adapted physical education (MA); interdisciplinary (MA); interdisciplinary pre-occupational therapy (MA); lifetime physical activity (MA), including coach education, fitness and wellness; physical education (MA); pre-physical therapy (MA). *Program availability:* Part-time. *Degree requirements:* For master's, thesis, oral exam. *Entrance requirements:* For master's, minimum GPA of 2.8. Additional exam requirements/recommendations for international students: Required—TOEFL (minimum score 500 paper-based). *Application deadline:* For fall admission, 11/30 for domestic students; for spring admission, 9/1 for domestic students. Applications are processed on a rolling basis. Application fee: $55. *Expenses:* Tuition, state resident: full-time $6738; part-time $3906 per unit. *Required fees:* $1916; $1916 per year. Tuition and fees vary according to course load, degree level and program. *Financial support:* Career-related internships or fieldwork available. Financial award application deadline: 3/2; financial award applicants required to submit FAFSA. *Unit head:* Dr. Steven Winter, Chair, 707-664-2188, E-mail: steven.winter@sonoma.edu. *Application contact:* Dr. Bulent Sokmen, Graduate Coordinator, 707-664-2789, E-mail: sokmen@sonoma.edu. Website: http://www.sonoma.edu/kinesiology/

**Southern Illinois University Edwardsville,** Graduate School, Program in Integrative Studies, Edwardsville, IL 62026. Offers cultural heritage and resources management (MA, MS); diversity training (MA, MS); organizational design thinking (MS); sustainability (MS). *Program availability:* Part-time, evening/weekend. *Degree requirements:* For master's, variable foreign language requirement, comprehensive exam (for some programs), thesis (for some programs). *Entrance requirements:* Additional exam requirements/recommendations for international students: Required—TOEFL (minimum score 550 paper-based; 79 iBT), IELTS (minimum score 6.5). Electronic applications accepted.

**Southern Oregon University,** Graduate Studies, Program in Interdisciplinary Studies, Ashland, OR 97520. Offers MIS. *Program availability:* Part-time, online learning. *Faculty:* 150 full-time (64 women), 85 part-time/adjunct (52 women). *Students:* 8 full-time (4 women), 3 part-time (2 women); includes 3 minority (1 American Indian or Alaska Native, non-Hispanic/Latino; 1 Hispanic/Latino; 1 Two or more races, non-Hispanic/Latino). Average age 43. 8 applicants, 75% accepted, 3 enrolled. In 2016, 3 master's awarded. *Degree requirements:* For master's, thesis (for some programs). *Entrance requirements:* For master's, GRE General Test, minimum cumulative GPA of 3.0 in the last 90 quarter credits (60 semester credits) of undergraduate coursework. Additional exam requirements/recommendations for international students: Required—TOEFL (minimum score 540 paper-based; 76 iBT), IELTS (minimum score 6), ELPT (minimum score 964) or ELS (minimum score 112). *Application deadline:* For fall admission, 7/31 priority date for domestic and international students; for winter admission, 11/15 priority date for domestic students, 11/14 priority date for international students; for spring admission, 1/7 priority date for domestic and international students. Applications are processed on a rolling basis. Application fee: $60. Electronic applications accepted. *Expenses:* Tuition, state resident: full-time $10,719; part-time $397 per credit. Tuition, nonresident: full-time $13,419; part-time $497 per credit. *Required fees:* $548. *Financial support:* Career-related internships or fieldwork, institutionally sponsored loans, scholarships/grants, and unspecified assistantships available. *Unit head:* Dr. Garth Pittman, Graduate Program Coordinator, 541-552-6671, E-mail: pittman@sou.edu. *Application contact:* Kelly Moutsatson, Director of Admissions, 541-552-6411, Fax: 541-552-8403, E-mail: admissions@sou.edu. Website: http://www.sou.edu/miis/index.html

**State University of New York at Fredonia,** College of Liberal Arts and Sciences, Fredonia, NY 14063. Offers biology (MS); interdisciplinary studies (MS); speech pathology (MS); MA/MS. *Program availability:* Part-time, evening/weekend. *Faculty:* 58 full-time (28 women), 24 part-time/adjunct (16 women). *Students:* 73 full-time (62 women), 9 part-time (6 women); includes 7 minority (1 Black or African American, non-Hispanic/Latino; 1 Asian, non-Hispanic/Latino; 2 Hispanic/Latino; 1 Native Hawaiian or other Pacific Islander, non-Hispanic/Latino; 2 Two or more races, non-Hispanic/Latino). Average age 24. 200 applicants, 25% accepted, 43 enrolled. In 2016, 41 master's awarded. *Degree requirements:* For master's, comprehensive exam (for some programs), thesis (for some programs). *Entrance requirements:* For master's, GRE. Additional exam requirements/recommendations for international students: Required—TOEFL (minimum score 79 iBT), IELTS (minimum score 6.5), Cambridge English Advanced (minimum score: 52) recommended. *Application deadline:* For fall admission, 4/1 priority date for domestic and international students; for spring admission, 11/1 priority date for domestic students, 11/1 for international students. Applications are processed on a rolling basis. Application fee: $75. Electronic applications accepted. *Expenses:* Tuition, state resident: full-time $10,370; part-time $453 per credit. Tuition, nonresident: full-time $20,190; part-time $925 per credit. *Required fees:* $1619; $67.30 per credit hour. $403.80 per semester. *Financial support:* In 2016–17, 5 students received support, including 14 teaching assistantships with full and partial tuition reimbursements available (averaging $5,957 per year); tuition waivers (full and partial) and unspecified assistantships also available. *Faculty research:* Immunology/microbiology, applied human physiology, ecology and evolution, invertebrate biology, molecular biology, biochemistry, physiology, animal behavior, science education, vertebrate physiology, cell biology, plant biology, developmental biology, aquatic ecology, bilingual language acquisition, bilingual language acquisition and disorders, augmentative and alternate communication with ALS, World War I, Zweig, environmental literature, editing, adolescent literature, pedagogy. *Unit head:* Dr. John L. Kijinski, Dean, 716-673-3173, E-mail: kijinski@fredonia.edu. *Application contact:* Wendy S. Dunst, Interim Graduate Recruitment and Admissions Associate, 716-673-3808, Fax: 716-673-3712, E-mail: wendy.dunst@fredonia.edu. Website: http://www.fredonia.edu/clas

**Stephen F. Austin State University,** Graduate School, College of Applied Arts and Science, Program in Interdisciplinary Studies, Nacogdoches, TX 75962. Offers MIS. *Program availability:* Part-time. *Degree requirements:* For master's, comprehensive exam, thesis optional. *Entrance requirements:* For master's, GRE General Test. Additional exam requirements/recommendations for international students: Required—TOEFL (minimum score 550 paper-based).

**Teachers College, Columbia University,** Interdisciplinary Programs, New York, NY 10027-6696. Offers Ed M, MA, ME, Ed D. *Program availability:* Part-time. *Students:* 16 full-time (11 women), 21 part-time (13 women); includes 11 minority (6 Black or African American, non-Hispanic/Latino; 3 Asian, non-Hispanic/Latino; 1 Hispanic/Latino; 1 Two or more races, non-Hispanic/Latino), 12 international. 27 applicants, 85% accepted, 15 enrolled. Terminal master's awarded for partial completion of doctoral program. *Degree requirements:* For doctorate, thesis/dissertation. *Expenses:* Tuition: Full-time $36,288; part-time $1512 per credit. *Required fees:* $438 per semester. One-time fee: $510 full-time. Full-time tuition and fees vary according to course load. *Application contact:* David Estrella, Director of Admissions, 212-678-3305, E-mail: estrella@tc.columbia.edu.

**Texas A&M University–Texarkana,** Graduate Studies and Research, College of Education and Liberal Arts, Texarkana, TX 75505-5518. Offers adult education (MS);

curriculum and instruction (M Ed); education (MS); educational administration (M Ed); English (MA); instructional technology (MS); interdisciplinary studies (MA, MS); special education (MS). *Program availability:* Part-time, evening/weekend. *Degree requirements:* For master's, comprehensive exam (for some programs), thesis optional. *Entrance requirements:* For master's, minimum GPA of 2.5 on last 60 hours of bachelor's degree. Additional exam requirements/recommendations for international students: Required—TOEFL. Electronic applications accepted.

**Texas State University,** The Graduate College, College of Applied Arts, Interdisciplinary Studies Program in Occupational Education, San Marcos, TX 78666. Offers MAIS, MSIS. *Program availability:* Part-time. *Faculty:* 5 full-time (3 women), 1 part-time/adjunct (0 women). *Students:* 28 full-time (14 women), 34 part-time (20 women); includes 34 minority (15 Black or African American, non-Hispanic/Latino; 2 Asian, non-Hispanic/Latino; 16 Hispanic/Latino; 1 Two or more races, non-Hispanic/Latino), 1 international. Average age 38. 34 applicants, 91% accepted, 20 enrolled. In 2016, 21 master's awarded. *Degree requirements:* For master's, comprehensive exam, thesis optional. *Entrance requirements:* For master's, minimum GPA of 2.75 for last 60 hours of undergraduate work, statement of personal goals. Additional exam requirements/recommendations for international students: Required—TOEFL (minimum score 550 paper-based; 78 iBT). *Application deadline:* For fall admission, 2/15 priority date for domestic and international students; for spring admission, 10/15 priority date for domestic students, 10/1 for international students. Applications are processed on a rolling basis. Application fee: $40 ($90 for international students). Electronic applications accepted. *Expenses:* $9,702 per year. *Financial support:* In 2016–17, 39 students received support, including 1 research assistantship (averaging $15,000 per year); teaching assistantships, Federal Work-Study, institutionally sponsored loans, scholarships/grants, health care benefits, and unspecified assistantships also available. Support available to part-time students. Financial award application deadline: 4/1; financial award applicants required to submit FAFSA. *Unit head:* Dr. Matthew Eichler, Director, 512-245-2115, E-mail: me21@txstate.edu. *Application contact:* Dr. Andrea Golato, Dean of Graduate School, 512-245-2581, Fax: 512-245-8365, E-mail: gradcollege@txstate.edu. Website: http://www.OCED.txstate.edu/

**Texas Tech University,** Graduate School, Interdisciplinary Programs, Lubbock, TX 79409. Offers arid land studies (MS); biotechnology (MS); interdisciplinary studies (MA, MS); museum science (MA); wind science and engineering (PhD); JD/MS. *Program availability:* Part-time. *Faculty:* 10 full-time (4 women). *Students:* 122 full-time (56 women), 83 part-time (46 women); includes 78 minority (25 Black or African American, non-Hispanic/Latino; 1 American Indian or Alaska Native, non-Hispanic/Latino; 2 Asian, non-Hispanic/Latino; 41 Hispanic/Latino; 1 Native Hawaiian or other Pacific Islander, non-Hispanic/Latino; 8 Two or more races, non-Hispanic/Latino), 32 international. Average age 29. 114 applicants, 71% accepted, 60 enrolled. In 2016, 55 master's, 1 doctorate awarded. Terminal master's awarded for partial completion of doctoral program. *Degree requirements:* For master's, comprehensive exam (for some programs), thesis (for some programs); for doctorate, comprehensive exam, thesis/dissertation (for some programs). *Entrance requirements:* Additional exam requirements/recommendations for international students: Required—TOEFL (minimum score 550 paper-based; 79 iBT), IELTS (minimum score 6.5), PTE (minimum score 60), Cambridge Advanced (B), Cambridge Proficiency (C), ELS English for Academic Purposes (Level 112). *Application deadline:* For fall admission, 6/1 priority date for domestic students, 1/15 priority date for international students; for spring admission, 9/1 priority date for domestic students, 6/15 priority date for international students. Applications are processed on a rolling basis. Application fee: $75. Electronic applications accepted. *Expenses:* Tuition, state resident: full-time $7200; part-time $300 per credit hour. Tuition, nonresident: full-time $16,992; part-time $708 per credit hour. *Required fees:* $2428; $50.50 per credit hour. $608 per semester. Tuition and fees vary according to program. *Financial support:* In 2016–17, 116 students received support, including 107 fellowships (averaging $4,360 per year), 10 research assistantships (averaging $10,619 per year), 7 teaching assistantships (averaging $9,152 per year); scholarships/grants and unspecified assistantships also available. Financial award application deadline: 4/15; financial award applicants required to submit FAFSA. *Total annual research expenditures:* $2 million. *Unit head:* Dr. Mark Sheridan, Vice Provost for Graduate and Postdoctoral Affairs/Dean of the Graduate School, 806-742-2787, Fax: 806-742-1746, E-mail: mark.sheridan@ttu.edu. *Application contact:* Amanda Wysinger, Academic Advisor, 806-834-0822, Fax: 806-742-4038, E-mail: amanda.wysinger@ttu.edu. Website: http://www.depts.ttu.edu/gradschool/about/INDS/index.php

**Trinity Western University,** School of Graduate Studies, Program in Interdisciplinary Humanities, Langley, BC V2Y 1Y1, Canada. Offers general humanities (MAIH); specialized (MAIH), including English, history, philosophy. *Program availability:* Part-time. *Degree requirements:* For master's, thesis or alternative, 36 semester hours. *Entrance requirements:* For master's, strong undergraduate degree in humanities or English, history or philosophy. Additional exam requirements/recommendations for international students: Recommended—TOEFL. Electronic applications accepted. *Faculty research:* Literary theory, gender, medieval and early modern literature, philosophy of religion, Thomas Merton's poetics.

**Tufts University,** Graduate School of Arts and Sciences, Interdisciplinary Doctoral Program, Medford, MA 02155. Offers PhD. *Students:* 3 full-time (2 women), all international. Average age 41. 4 applicants. *Degree requirements:* For doctorate, thesis/dissertation. *Entrance requirements:* Additional exam requirements/recommendations for international students: Required—TOEFL (minimum score 550 paper-based; 80 iBT), IELTS (minimum score 6.5). *Application deadline:* For fall admission, 1/15 for domestic and international students. Application fee: $85. Electronic applications accepted. *Expenses:* $29,936 full-time tuition (for PhD). *Financial support:* In 2016–17, 3 students received support. Research assistantships, teaching assistantships, Federal Work-Study, scholarships/grants, health care benefits, tuition waivers (full and partial), and unspecified assistantships available. Financial award application deadline: 1/15. *Unit head:* Dr. Susan Ernst, Director, 617-627-3541, E-mail: sernst@tufts.edu. *Application contact:* Office of Graduate Admissions, 617-627-3395, E-mail: gradadmissions@tufts.edu. Website: http://gsas.tufts.edu/academics/interdisciplinary.htm

**Tulane University,** School of Science and Engineering, Interdisciplinary PhD Program, New Orleans, LA 70118-5669. Offers PhD. *Expenses:* Tuition: Full-time $50,920; part-time $2829 per credit hour. *Required fees:* $2040; $44.50 per credit hour. $580 per term. Tuition and fees vary according to course load, degree level and program.

**Union Institute & University,** Master of Arts Program, Cincinnati, OH 45206-1925. Offers creativity studies (MA); health and wellness (MA); history and culture (MA); leadership, public policy, and social issues (MA); literature and writing (MA). *Program availability:* Part-time, online only, 100% online. *Faculty:* 2 full-time (both women), 9 part-time/adjunct (7 women). *Students:* 9 full-time (7 women), 70 part-time (56 women); includes 33 minority (22 Black or African American, non-Hispanic/Latino; 1 American Indian or Alaska Native, non-Hispanic/Latino; 6 Hispanic/Latino; 4 Two or more races, non-Hispanic/Latino). Average age 40. In 2016, 45 master's awarded. *Degree requirements:* For master's, thesis. *Entrance requirements:* For master's, transcript, essay, 3 letters of recommendation, resume. Additional exam requirements/recommendations for international students: Recommended—TOEFL. *Application deadline:* For spring admission, 3/13 for domestic students. Applications are processed on a rolling basis. Application fee: $50. Electronic applications accepted. *Expenses:* Contact institution. *Financial support:* Career-related internships or fieldwork and tuition waivers available. Financial award applicants required to submit FAFSA. *Unit head:* Elden Golden, Director, 513-487-1153, E-mail: elden.golden@myunion.edu. *Application contact:* Director of Admissions, 800-861-6400.

**Union Institute & University,** PhD Program in Interdisciplinary Studies, Cincinnati, OH 45206-1925. Offers education studies (PhD), including Martin Luther King studies. Program requires participation in brief on-campus residencies twice each year (January and July). *Program availability:* Part-time, online only, blended/hybrid learning. *Faculty:* 9 full-time (5 women), 16 part-time/adjunct (7 women). *Students:* 122 full-time (76 women), 19 part-time (14 women); includes 76 minority (58 Black or African American, non-Hispanic/Latino; 4 American Indian or Alaska Native, non-Hispanic/Latino; 2 Asian, non-Hispanic/Latino; 8 Hispanic/Latino; 3 Native Hawaiian or other Pacific Islander, non-Hispanic/Latino; 1 Two or more races, non-Hispanic/Latino). Average age 46. In 2016, 22 doctorates awarded. *Degree requirements:* For doctorate, comprehensive exam, thesis/dissertation. *Entrance requirements:* For doctorate, master's degree, three letters of recommendation, statement of purpose. Additional exam requirements/recommendations for international students: Required—TOEFL. *Application deadline:* Applications are processed on a rolling basis. Application fee: $50. Electronic applications accepted. *Expenses:* Contact institution. *Financial support:* Federal Work-Study and scholarships/grants available. Financial award application deadline: 5/1; financial award applicants required to submit FAFSA. *Faculty research:* Social responsibility, ethical leadership, Martin Luther King studies. *Unit head:* Dr. Michael Raffanti, Dean, 513-861-6400, E-mail: michael.raffanti@myunion.edu. *Application contact:* Admissions Counselor, 800-486-3116.
Website: https://myunion.edu/academics/doctoral/

**University at Buffalo, the State University of New York,** Graduate School, College of Arts and Sciences, Program in Interdisciplinary Studies, Buffalo, NY 14260. Offers humanities (MA); natural sciences (MS); social sciences (MS). *Program availability:* Part-time. *Entrance requirements:* Additional exam requirements/recommendations for international students: Required—TOEFL (minimum score 550 paper-based; 79 iBT). *Application deadline:* For fall admission, 2/1 priority date for domestic students, 1/1 priority date for international students; for spring admission, 11/1 priority date for domestic students, 10/1 priority date for international students. Applications are processed on a rolling basis. Electronic applications accepted. *Expenses:* Contact institution. *Financial support:* Fellowships, research assistantships, and teaching assistantships available. *Unit head:* Danielle Lewis, Graduate Interdisciplinary Program Coordinator, 716-645-1457, E-mail: dvegas@buffalo.edu.
Website: http://gradidp.buffalo.edu/

**The University of Alabama,** Interdisciplinary Programs, Tuscaloosa, AL 35487. Offers PhD. *Program availability:* Part-time, evening/weekend. *Students:* 6 full-time (4 women), 8 part-time (5 women); includes 2 minority (both Black or African American, non-Hispanic/Latino). Average age 41. 2 applicants, 100% accepted, 2 enrolled. In 2016, 2 doctorates awarded. *Degree requirements:* For doctorate, comprehensive exam, thesis/dissertation. *Entrance requirements:* For doctorate, GRE (minimum score of 300), MAT (above 50th percentile), GMAT (minimum score 500). Additional exam requirements/recommendations for international students: Required—TOEFL (minimum score 79 iBT), IELTS (minimum score 6.5). *Application deadline:* For fall admission, 5/1 for international students; for winter admission, 9/15 for international students. Applications are processed on a rolling basis. Electronic applications accepted. *Expenses:* Tuition, state resident: full-time $10,470. Tuition, nonresident: full-time $26,950. *Unit head:* Dr. Andrew Mark Goodliffe, Assistant Dean of the Graduate School, 205-348-8283, Fax: 205-348-0400, E-mail: amg@ua.edu. *Application contact:* Patrick D. Fuller, Senior Graduate Admissions Counselor, 205-348-5923, Fax: 205-348-0400, E-mail: patrick.d.fuller@ua.edu.
Website: http://graduate.ua.edu

**The University of Alabama at Birmingham,** School of Engineering, Program in Interdisciplinary Engineering, Birmingham, AL 35294. Offers computational engineering (PhD). *Students:* 12 full-time (0 women), 28 part-time (5 women); includes 14 minority (4 Black or African American, non-Hispanic/Latino; 9 Asian, non-Hispanic/Latino; 1 Two or more races, non-Hispanic/Latino). Average age 38. In 2016, 7 doctorates awarded. *Degree requirements:* For doctorate, comprehensive exam, thesis/dissertation. *Entrance requirements:* For doctorate, GRE (minimum rank 50% in both Quantitative Reasoning and Verbal Reasoning sections), undergraduate degree in a supporting field, official transcripts, minimum undergraduate GPA of 3.0. Additional exam requirements/recommendations for international students: Required—TOEFL (minimum score 100 iBT); Recommended—IELTS (minimum score 6.5). *Application deadline:* For fall admission, 7/1 for domestic students; for spring admission, 11/1 for domestic students; for summer admission, 4/1 for domestic students. Applications are processed on a rolling basis. Application fee: $50 ($60 for international students). Electronic applications accepted. *Expenses:* $396 per hour resident tuition; $935 per hour non-resident tuition; $150 per course online course fee. *Unit head:* Dr. Timothy Wick, Associate Dean of Graduate Programs, 205-934-8400, E-mail: tmwick@uab.edu. *Application contact:* Holly Hebard, Director of Graduate School Operations, 205-934-8227, Fax: 205-934-8413, E-mail: gradschool@uab.edu.
Website: http://www.uab.edu/engineering/home/degrees-cert/phd?id-189:phd-in-interdisciplinary-engineering&catid-3

**University of Alaska Anchorage,** College of Arts and Sciences, Program in Interdisciplinary Studies, Anchorage, AK 99508. Offers MA, MS. *Program availability:* Part-time. *Entrance requirements:* For master's, GRE General Test, GRE Subject Test, minimum GPA of 3.0. Additional exam requirements/recommendations for international students: Required—TOEFL (minimum score 550 paper-based).

**University of Alaska Fairbanks,** Graduate School for Interdisciplinary Studies, Fairbanks, AK 99775-7560. Offers indigenous studies (PhD); interdisciplinary studies (MA, MS, PhD). *Program availability:* Part-time. *Faculty:* 4 full-time (all women). *Students:* 6 full-time (all women), 21 part-time (17 women); includes 11 minority (7 American Indian or Alaska Native, non-Hispanic/Latino; 1 Hispanic/Latino; 1 Native Hawaiian or other Pacific Islander, non-Hispanic/Latino; 2 Two or more races, non-Hispanic/Latino), 1 international. Average age 49. 30 applicants, 3% accepted, 1 enrolled. In 2016, 2 master's, 3 doctorates awarded. *Degree requirements:* For master's, comprehensive exam (for some programs), oral defense of project or thesis; for doctorate, one foreign language, comprehensive exam, thesis/dissertation, oral defense of dissertation. *Entrance requirements:* For master's, GRE General Test, bachelor's degree from accredited institution with minimum cumulative undergraduate and major GPA of 3.0; for doctorate, GRE General Test, minimum cumulative GPA of 3.0. Additional exam requirements/recommendations for international students: Required—TOEFL (minimum score 550 paper-based; 80 iBT). *Application deadline:* For fall admission, 3/1 for domestic and international students; for spring admission, 10/1 for domestic students, 9/1 for international students. Applications are processed on a rolling basis. Application fee: $60. Electronic applications accepted. *Expenses:* Tuition, state

resident: full-time $7992; part-time $444 per credit. Tuition, nonresident: full-time $16,326; part-time $907 per credit. *Required fees:* $39 per credit. $322 per semester. Tuition and fees vary according to course level, course load, campus/location, program and reciprocity agreements. *Financial support:* In 2016–17, 1 research assistantship with full tuition reimbursement (averaging $1,416 per year), 1 teaching assistantship with full tuition reimbursement (averaging $4,798 per year) were awarded; fellowships with full tuition reimbursements, career-related internships or fieldwork, Federal Work-Study, scholarships/grants, health care benefits, and unspecified assistantships also available. Support available to part-time students. Financial award application deadline: 2/15; financial award applicants required to submit FAFSA. *Total annual research expenditures:* $10,000. *Unit head:* John Eichelberger, Dean, 907-474-7716, Fax: 907-474-1984, E-mail: fyinds@uaf.edu. *Application contact:* Mary Kreta, Director of Admissions, 907-474-7500, Fax: 907-474-7097, E-mail: admissions@uaf.edu.
Website: http://www.uaf.edu/gradsch/

**The University of Arizona,** Graduate Interdisciplinary Programs, Tucson, AZ 85721. Offers American Indian studies (MA, PhD); applied mathematics (MS, PMS, PhD), including applied mathematics (MS, PhD), mathematical sciences (PMS); biomedical engineering (MS, PhD); cancer biology (PhD); entomology (MA); entomology and insect science (MS, PhD); genetics (MS, PhD); neuroscience (PhD); physiological sciences (MS, PhD); second language acquisition and teaching (PhD); statistics (MS, PhD). *Program availability:* Part-time. *Entrance requirements:* Additional exam requirements/recommendations for international students: Required—TOEFL (minimum score 550 paper-based; 79 iBT).

**University of Arkansas,** Graduate School, Interdisciplinary Program in Comparative Literature and Cultural Studies, Fayetteville, AR 72701. Offers MA, PhD. *Degree requirements:* For doctorate, 2 foreign languages, comprehensive exam, thesis/dissertation optional. *Entrance requirements:* For doctorate, GRE General Test, official transcripts of all undergraduate and graduate work, three letters of recommendation, writing sample, statement of purpose. Additional exam requirements/recommendations for international students: Required—TOEFL (minimum score 550 paper-based; 80 iBT) or IELTS (minimum score 6.5). Application fee: $40 ($50 for international students). *Financial support:* In 2016–17, 1 research assistantship, 13 teaching assistantships were awarded; fellowships, Federal Work-Study, and institutionally sponsored loans also available. *Faculty research:* Literary and cultural theory, cultural studies, postcolonial theory, gender studies, world literature. *Unit head:* Prof. Luis Restrepo, Director, 479-575-7580, Fax: 479-575-6795, E-mail: lrestr@uark.edu. *Application contact:* Graduate Admissions, 479-575-6246, Fax: 479-575-5908, E-mail: gradinfo@uark.edu.
Website: http://fulbright.uark.edu/programs/comparative-literature-cultural-studies/index.php/

**University of Arkansas,** Graduate School, Interdisciplinary Program in Environmental Dynamics, Fayetteville, AR 72701. Offers PhD. In 2016, 3 doctorates awarded. *Degree requirements:* For doctorate, thesis/dissertation. *Application deadline:* For fall admission, 4/1 for international students; for spring admission, 10/1 for international students. Applications are processed on a rolling basis. Application fee: $40 ($50 for international students). Electronic applications accepted. *Financial support:* In 2016–17, 5 research assistantships, 9 teaching assistantships were awarded; fellowships with tuition reimbursements also available. Financial award application deadline: 4/1. *Unit head:* Dr. Peter Ungar, Head, 479-575-6603, Fax: 479-575-6361, E-mail: pungar@uark.edu. *Application contact:* Graduate Admissions, 479-575-6246, Fax: 479-575-5908, E-mail: gradinfo@uark.edu.
Website: http://endy.uark.edu/

**University of Arkansas at Little Rock,** Graduate School, College of Arts, Letters, and Sciences, Department of Philosophy and Interdisciplinary Studies, Little Rock, AR 72204-1099. Offers MA. *Entrance requirements:* For master's, GRE.

**University of California, Santa Barbara,** Graduate Division, College of Letters and Sciences, Division of Social Sciences, Department of Sociology, Santa Barbara, CA 93106-9430. Offers interdisciplinary emphasis: Black studies (PhD); interdisciplinary emphasis: environment and society (PhD); interdisciplinary emphasis: feminist studies (PhD); interdisciplinary emphasis: global studies (PhD); interdisciplinary emphasis: language, interaction and social organization (PhD); interdisciplinary emphasis: quantitative methods in the social sciences (PhD); interdisciplinary emphasis: technology and society (PhD); sociology (PhD); MA/PhD. Terminal master's awarded for partial completion of doctoral program. *Degree requirements:* For doctorate, comprehensive exam, thesis/dissertation. *Entrance requirements:* For doctorate, GRE General Test. Additional exam requirements/recommendations for international students: Required—TOEFL (minimum score 550 paper-based; 80 iBT), IELTS (minimum score 7). Electronic applications accepted. *Faculty research:* Gender and sexualities, race/ethnicity, social movements, conversation analysis, global sociology.

**University of California, Santa Cruz,** Division of Graduate Studies, Division of the Arts, Department of Music, Santa Cruz, CA 95064. Offers ethnomusicology (MA); music (PhD), including cross-cultural and interdisciplinary studies; music composition (MA, DMA), including world music composition (DMA); music composition (DMA), including computer-assisted (algorithmic) composition; performance practice (MA). *Degree requirements:* For master's, one foreign language, thesis, recital; for doctorate, one foreign language, thesis/dissertation, qualifying and final examinations. *Entrance requirements:* For master's, GRE General Test, 3 letters of recommendation, writing or composition sample, 10-20 minute unedited recording; for doctorate, GRE General Test, 3 letters of recommendation, writing sample. Additional exam requirements/recommendations for international students: Required—TOEFL (minimum score 550 paper-based; 83 iBT); Recommended—IELTS (minimum score 8). Electronic applications accepted. *Faculty research:* Western music history, new music, composition, ethnomusicology, musicology.

**University of Central Florida,** College of Graduate Studies, Program in Interdisciplinary Studies, Orlando, FL 32816. Offers geographic information systems (Certificate); interdisciplinary studies (MA, MS). *Students:* 7 full-time (4 women), 25 part-time (17 women); includes 9 minority (3 Black or African American, non-Hispanic/Latino; 1 Asian, non-Hispanic/Latino; 4 Hispanic/Latino; 1 Two or more races, non-Hispanic/Latino). Average age 32. 38 applicants, 82% accepted, 27 enrolled. In 2016, 7 master's awarded. *Degree requirements:* For master's, thesis or alternative. *Entrance requirements:* For master's, GRE General Test, minimum GPA of 3.0 in last 60 hours. Additional exam requirements/recommendations for international students: Required—TOEFL. *Application deadline:* For fall admission, 7/15 for domestic students; for spring admission, 12/1 for domestic students. Application fee: $30. Electronic applications accepted. *Expenses:* Tuition, state resident: part-time $288.16 per credit hour. Tuition, nonresident: part-time $1071.31 per credit hour. *Financial support:* Teaching assistantships available. Financial award application deadline: 3/1; financial award applicants required to submit FAFSA. *Unit head:* Dr. John Weishampel, Associate Dean, 407-823-6634, E-mail: john.weishampel@ucf.edu. *Application contact:* Assistant Director, Graduate Admissions, 407-823-2766, Fax: 407-823-6442, E-mail: gradadmissions@ucf.edu.
Website: https://www.graduate.ucf.edu/IDS/

## Interdisciplinary Studies

**University of Central Oklahoma,** The Jackson College of Graduate Studies, College of Education and Professional Studies, Department of Adult Education and Safety Science, Edmond, OK 73034-5209. Offers adult and higher education (M Ed), including adult and higher education, interdisciplinary studies, student personnel, training. *Program availability:* Part-time. *Degree requirements:* For master's, comprehensive exam (for some programs), thesis (for some programs). *Entrance requirements:* For master's, GRE General Test. Additional exam requirements/recommendations for international students: Required—TOEFL (minimum score 550 paper-based; 79 iBT), IELTS (minimum score 6.5). Electronic applications accepted. *Faculty research:* Violence in the workplace/schools, aging issues, trade and industrial education.

**University of Cincinnati,** Graduate School, McMicken College of Arts and Sciences, Interdisciplinary Studies Program, Cincinnati, OH 45221. Offers PhD. *Entrance requirements:* For doctorate, GRE General Test. Electronic applications accepted. *Expenses: Tuition, area resident:* Full-time $12,790; part-time $389 per credit hour. Tuition, state resident: full-time $13,290; part-time $419 per credit hour. Tuition, nonresident: full-time $24,532; part-time $976 per credit hour. *International tuition:* $24,832 full-time. *Required fees:* $3958; $140 per credit hour. Tuition and fees vary according to course load, degree level, program and reciprocity agreements.

**University of Colorado Colorado Springs,** College of Letters, Arts and Sciences, Master of Sciences Program, Colorado Springs, CO 80918. Offers interdisciplinary sciences (M Sc). *Program availability:* Part-time. *Students:* 59 full-time (40 women), 36 part-time (22 women); includes 15 minority (3 Asian, non-Hispanic/Latino; 9 Hispanic/Latino; 3 Two or more races, non-Hispanic/Latino), 6 international. Average age 27. 105 applicants, 44% accepted, 41 enrolled. In 2016, 45 master's awarded. *Degree requirements:* For master's, thesis or alternative. *Entrance requirements:* For master's, minimum GPA of 2.75. Additional exam requirements/recommendations for international students: Required—TOEFL (minimum score 525 paper-based; 80 iBT); Recommended—IELTS (minimum score 6.5). *Application deadline:* For fall admission, 3/1 priority date for domestic and international students; for spring admission, 6/1 priority date for domestic and international students. Applications are processed on a rolling basis. Application fee: $60 ($100 for international students). Electronic applications accepted. *Expenses:* Tuition, state resident: full-time $9983. Tuition, nonresident: full-time $20,153. Tuition and fees vary according to course load, degree level, program and reciprocity agreements. *Financial support:* In 2016–17, 62 students received support. Career-related internships or fieldwork, Federal Work-Study, scholarships/grants, and unspecified assistantships available. Support available to part-time students. Financial award application deadline: 3/1; financial award applicants required to submit FAFSA. *Faculty research:* Molecular and cellular biology, exercise science, ecology and evolution, analytical chemistry, biochemistry, inorganic chemistry, organic chemistry, physical chemistry, health promotion, athletic training and strength and conditioning, athlete development, sport nutrition. *Unit head:* Dr. Kelli Klebe, Dean, 719-255-3779, E-mail: kklebe@uccs.edu. *Application contact:* KrisAnn McBroom, Academic Services Specialist, 719-255-3567, E-mail: kmcbroom@uccs.edu.

**University of Florida,** Graduate School, College of Public Health and Health Professions, Department of Environmental and Global Health, Gainesville, FL 32611. Offers environmental health (PhD); one health (MHS, PhD). *Entrance requirements:* For master's and doctorate, GRE, minimum GPA of 3.0. Additional exam requirements/recommendations for international students: Required—TOEFL (minimum score 550 paper-based; 80 iBT), IELTS (minimum score 6).

**University of Houston–Victoria,** School of Arts and Sciences, Program in Interdisciplinary Studies, Victoria, TX 77901-4450. Offers MAIS. *Program availability:* Part-time, evening/weekend, online learning. *Degree requirements:* For master's, comprehensive exam or thesis. *Entrance requirements:* For master's, GRE General Test, official transcript, essay. Additional exam requirements/recommendations for international students: Required—TOEFL (minimum score 550 paper-based). Electronic applications accepted.

**University of Idaho,** College of Graduate Studies, College of Art and Architecture, Program in Bioregional Planning and Community Design, Moscow, ID 83844. Offers MS. *Faculty:* 2 full-time. *Students:* 3 full-time, 2 part-time. Average age 28. In 2016, 2 master's awarded. *Entrance requirements:* For master's, GRE, minimum GPA of 3.0. Additional exam requirements/recommendations for international students: Required—TOEFL. *Application deadline:* Applications are processed on a rolling basis. Application fee: $60. Electronic applications accepted. *Expenses:* Tuition, state resident: full-time $6460; part-time $414 per credit hour. Tuition, nonresident: full-time $21,268; part-time $1237 per credit hour. *Required fees:* $2070; $60 per credit hour. Full-time tuition and fees vary according to course load and reciprocity agreements. *Financial support:* Applicants required to submit FAFSA. *Faculty research:* Environment and behavior interaction, geographic trade, design development, economic development, natural resource policy. *Unit head:* Dr. Shauna Corry, Interim Dean, 208-885-4409, E-mail: bioregionalplanning@uidaho.edu. *Application contact:* Sean Scoggin, Graduate Recruitment Coordinator, 208-885-4001, Fax: 208-805-4406, E-mail: graduateadmissions@uidaho.edu.
Website: http://www.uidaho.edu/caa/programs/biop

**University of Idaho,** College of Graduate Studies, Program in Interdisciplinary Studies, Moscow, ID 83844. Offers MA, MS. *Faculty:* 3 full-time. *Students:* 2 full-time. In 2016, 1 master's awarded. *Entrance requirements:* For master's, GRE, minimum GPA of 3.0. Additional exam requirements/recommendations for international students: Required—TOEFL. *Application deadline:* For fall admission, 8/1 for domestic students; for spring admission, 12/15 for domestic students. Applications are processed on a rolling basis. Application fee: $60. Electronic applications accepted. *Expenses:* Tuition, state resident: full-time $6460; part-time $414 per credit hour. Tuition, nonresident: full-time $21,268; part-time $1237 per credit hour. *Required fees:* $2070; $60 per credit hour. Full-time tuition and fees vary according to course load and reciprocity agreements. *Financial support:* Applicants required to submit FAFSA. *Unit head:* Dr. Jerry McMurtry, Dean of Graduate Studies, 208-885-6243, E-mail: uigrad@uidaho.edu. *Application contact:* Sean Scoggin, Graduate Recruitment Coordinator, 208-885-4723, Fax: 208-885-4406, E-mail: gadms@uidaho.edu.
Website: https://www.uidaho.edu/cogs/programs-offered/interdisciplinary-studies

**University of Illinois at Chicago,** Program in Learning Sciences, Chicago, IL 60607-7128. Offers PhD.

**University of Illinois at Springfield,** Graduate Programs, College of Liberal Arts and Sciences, Department of Liberal and Integrative Studies, Springfield, IL 62703-5407. Offers MA. *Program availability:* Part-time, evening/weekend, 100% online, blended/hybrid learning. *Faculty:* 4 full-time (2 women). *Students:* 1 (woman) full-time, 26 part-time (14 women); includes 12 minority (9 Black or African American, non-Hispanic/Latino; 1 Hispanic/Latino; 2 Two or more races, non-Hispanic/Latino). Average age 43. 22 applicants, 41% accepted, 8 enrolled. In 2016, 11 master's awarded. *Degree requirements:* For master's, project or thesis. *Entrance requirements:* For master's, 2 letters of reference; interview; two- to three-page statement of educational goals, background, and reasons for requesting admission to the program; minimum GPA of 2.5 (for campus-based students), 3.0 (for online students). Additional exam requirements/recommendations for international students: Required—TOEFL (minimum score 500

paper-based; 61 iBT). *Application deadline:* Applications are processed on a rolling basis. Application fee: $60 ($75 for international students). Electronic applications accepted. *Expenses:* Tuition, state resident: part-time $329 per credit hour. Tuition, nonresident: part-time $675 per credit hour. *Financial support:* In 2016–17, fellowships with full tuition reimbursements (averaging $9,900 per year), research assistantships with full tuition reimbursements (averaging $9,991 per year), teaching assistantships with full tuition reimbursements (averaging $10,059 per year) were awarded; career-related internships or fieldwork, Federal Work-Study, scholarships/grants, health care benefits, and unspecified assistantships also available. Support available to part-time students. Financial award application deadline: 11/15; financial award applicants required to submit FAFSA. *Unit head:* Dr. Eric Hadley-Ives, Program Administrator, 217-206-6962, Fax: 217-206-6217, E-mail: hadleyiv@uis.edu. *Application contact:* Dr. Cecelia Cornell, Associate Vice Chancellor for Graduate Education, 217-206-7230, E-mail: ccorn1@uis.edu.
Website: http://www.uis.edu/ino/

**University of Illinois at Urbana–Champaign,** Graduate College, College of Liberal Arts and Sciences, School of Literatures, Cultures and Linguistics, Program in Romance Linguistics, Champaign, IL 61820. Offers PhD.

**The University of Kansas,** University of Kansas Medical Center, School of Medicine, Interdisciplinary Graduate Program in Biomedical Sciences (IGPBS), Kansas City, KS 66160. Offers PhD, MD/PhD. *Students:* 15 full-time (10 women); includes 1 minority (Two or more races, non-Hispanic/Latino), 1 international. Average age 25. 115 applicants, 13% accepted, 15 enrolled. Terminal master's awarded for partial completion of doctoral program. *Degree requirements:* For doctorate, comprehensive exam, thesis/dissertation. *Entrance requirements:* For doctorate, GRE. Additional exam requirements/recommendations for international students: Required—TOEFL. *Application deadline:* For fall admission, 12/1 priority date for domestic and international students. Applications are processed on a rolling basis. Application fee: $60. Electronic applications accepted. *Financial support:* In 2016–17, 3 research assistantships with full tuition reimbursements (averaging $24,000 per year), 18 teaching assistantships with full tuition reimbursements (averaging $24,000 per year) were awarded; scholarships/grants and unspecified assistantships also available. Financial award application deadline: 3/1; financial award applicants required to submit FAFSA. *Faculty research:* Cardiovascular biology, neurosciences, signal transduction and cancer biology, molecular biology and genetics, developmental biology. *Unit head:* Dr. Michael J. Werle, Director, 913-588-7491, Fax: 913-588-2710, E-mail: mwerle@kumc.edu. *Application contact:* Martin J. Graham, Coordinator, 913-588-2719, Fax: 913-588-5242, E-mail: mgraham4@kumc.edu.
Website: http://www.kumc.edu/igpbs.html

**University of Louisville,** School of Interdisciplinary and Graduate Studies, Louisville, KY 40292. Offers interdisciplinary (MA, MS, PhD), including bioethics and medical humanities (MA), bioinformatics (PhD), sustainability (MA, MS), translational bioengineering (PhD), translational neuroscience (PhD). *Program availability:* Part-time. *Students:* 24 full-time (16 women), 8 part-time (4 women); includes 4 minority (1 Asian, non-Hispanic/Latino; 1 Hispanic/Latino; 2 Two or more races, non-Hispanic/Latino), 7 international. Average age 31. 35 applicants, 51% accepted, 12 enrolled. *Degree requirements:* For master's, variable foreign language requirement, comprehensive exam (for some programs), thesis (for some programs); for doctorate, variable foreign language requirement, comprehensive exam, thesis/dissertation. *Entrance requirements:* For master's and doctorate, GRE General Test, 3 letters of recommendation, transcripts from previous post-secondary educational institutions. Additional exam requirements/recommendations for international students: Required—TOEFL (minimum score 550 paper-based; 79 iBT), IELTS (minimum score 6.5). *Application deadline:* For fall admission, 12/1 priority date for domestic and international students; for winter admission, 11/1 for domestic students, 6/1 for international students; for spring admission, 11/1 for domestic students, 6/1 for international students; for summer admission, 4/1 for domestic students, 1/1 for international students. Applications are processed on a rolling basis. Application fee: $65. Electronic applications accepted. *Expenses:* Tuition, state resident: full-time $12,246; part-time $681 per credit hour. Tuition, nonresident: full-time $25,486; part-time $1417 per credit hour. *Required fees:* $196. Tuition and fees vary according to program and reciprocity agreements. *Financial support:* In 2016–17, 120 fellowships with full tuition reimbursements (averaging $20,000 per year) were awarded. Financial award application deadline: 1/15. *Unit head:* Dr. Beth A. Boehm, Dean and Vice Provost for Graduate Affairs, 502-852-6495, E-mail: beth.boehm@louisville.edu. *Application contact:* Dr. Paul DeMarco, Associate Dean, 502-852-6490, E-mail: gradadm@louisville.edu.
Website: http://www.graduate.louisville.edu

**University of Maine,** Graduate School, Interdisciplinary Doctoral Program, Orono, ME 04469. Offers PhD. *Program availability:* Part-time, evening/weekend. *Students:* 8 full-time (6 women), 12 part-time (8 women); includes 2 minority (both American Indian or Alaska Native, non-Hispanic/Latino), 1 international. Average age 46. 4 applicants, 25% accepted. In 2016, 5 doctorates awarded. *Degree requirements:* For doctorate, comprehensive exam, thesis/dissertation. *Entrance requirements:* For doctorate, GRE General Test, master's degree. Additional exam requirements/recommendations for international students: Required—TOEFL. *Application deadline:* For fall admission, 4/1 for domestic students; for spring admission, 11/1 for domestic students. Applications are processed on a rolling basis. Application fee: $65. Electronic applications accepted. *Expenses:* Tuition, state resident: full-time $7524; part-time $2508 per credit. Tuition, nonresident: full-time $24,498; part-time $8166 per credit. *Required fees:* $1148; $571 per credit. *Financial support:* In 2016–17, 4 students received support, including 2 research assistantships (averaging $14,600 per year); unspecified assistantships also available. Financial award application deadline: 3/1. *Unit head:* Scott G. Delcourt, Assistant Vice President for Graduate Studies/Senior Associate Dean, 207-581-3291, Fax: 207-581-3232, E-mail: graduate@maine.edu.
Website: http://umaine.edu/graduate/

**University of Maine,** Graduate School, Master of Arts in Interdisciplinary Studies Program, Orono, ME 04469. Offers MA. *Program availability:* Part-time, evening/weekend. *Students:* 6 full-time (all women), 13 part-time (7 women); includes 3 minority (1 American Indian or Alaska Native, non-Hispanic/Latino; 2 Hispanic/Latino). Average age 43. 15 applicants, 93% accepted, 7 enrolled. In 2016, 3 master's awarded. *Degree requirements:* For master's, thesis or alternative, project. *Entrance requirements:* Additional exam requirements/recommendations for international students: Required—TOEFL. *Application deadline:* For fall admission, 4/1 for domestic students; for spring admission, 11/1 for domestic students. Applications are processed on a rolling basis. Application fee: $65. Electronic applications accepted. *Expenses:* Tuition, state resident: full-time $7524; part-time $2508 per credit. Tuition, nonresident: full-time $24,498; part-time $8166 per credit. *Required fees:* $1148; $571 per credit. *Financial support:* In 2016–17, 1 student received support. Federal Work-Study and institutionally sponsored loans available. Financial award application deadline: 3/1. *Application contact:* Scott G. Delcourt, Assistant Vice President for Graduate Studies and Senior Associate Dean, 207-581-3291, Fax: 207-581-3232, E-mail: graduate@maine.edu.
Website: http://umaine.edu/graduate/

**University of Manitoba,** Faculty of Graduate Studies, Interdisciplinary Programs, Individual Interdisciplinary Programs, Winnipeg, MB R3T 2N2, Canada. Offers M Sc, MA, PhD.

**University of Massachusetts Medical School,** Graduate School of Biomedical Sciences, Worcester, MA 01655-0115. Offers biomedical sciences (PhD), including biochemistry and molecular pharmacology, bioinformatics and computational biology, cancer biology, cell biology, immunology and microbiology, interdisciplinary, neuroscience, translational science; biomedical sciences (millennium program) (PhD); clinical and population health research (PhD); clinical investigation (MS). *Faculty:* 1,354 full-time (540 women), 311 part-time/adjunct (192 women). *Students:* 341 full-time (176 women); includes 57 minority (12 Black or African American, non-Hispanic/Latino; 1 American Indian or Alaska Native, non-Hispanic/Latino; 31 Asian, non-Hispanic/Latino; 13 Hispanic/Latino), 129 international. Average age 29. 617 applicants, 29% accepted, 51 enrolled. In 2016, 4 master's, 55 doctorates awarded. Terminal master's awarded for partial completion of doctoral program. *Degree requirements:* For master's, comprehensive exam, thesis; for doctorate, comprehensive exam, thesis/dissertation. *Entrance requirements:* For master's, MD, PhD, DVM, or PharmD; for doctorate, GRE General Test, bachelor's degree. Additional exam requirements/recommendations for international students: Required—TOEFL (minimum score 90 iBT) or IELTS (minimum score 7.0). *Application deadline:* For fall admission, 12/15 for domestic and international students; for spring admission, 5/15 for domestic students. Application fee: $80. Electronic applications accepted. *Expenses:* $7,356 in-state tuition and fees per year, $14,572 out-of-state. *Financial support:* In 2016–17, 7 fellowships (averaging $34,000 per year), 391 research assistantships with full tuition reimbursements (averaging $31,000 per year) were awarded; scholarships/grants also available. Support available to part-time students. Financial award application deadline: 5/15. *Faculty research:* RNA biology, molecular/cell/developmental/metabolic biology, bioinformatics and computational biology, clinical/translational research, infectious disease and immunology. *Total annual research expenditures:* $253 million. *Unit head:* Dr. Anthony Carruthers, Dean, 508-856-4135, E-mail: anthony.carruthers@umassmed.edu. *Application contact:* Dr. Kendall Knight, Assistant Vice Provost for Admissions, 508-856-5628, Fax: 508-856-3659, E-mail: kendall.knight@umassmed.edu. Website: http://www.umassmed.edu/gsbs/

**University of Memphis,** Graduate School, College of Arts and Sciences, Department of Earth Sciences, Memphis, TN 38152. Offers earth sciences (MA, MS, PhD), including archaeology (MS), geography (MS), geology (MS), geophysics (MS), interdisciplinary studies (MS); geographic information systems (Graduate Certificate), including geographic information systems, GIS educator, GIS planning, GIS professional. *Program availability:* Part-time, evening/weekend. *Faculty:* 17 full-time (3 women), 5 part-time/adjunct (0 women). *Students:* 37 full-time (10 women), 25 part-time (6 women); includes 3 minority (2 Black or African American, non-Hispanic/Latino; 1 Two or more races, non-Hispanic/Latino), 22 international. Average age 33. 30 applicants, 60% accepted, 12 enrolled. In 2016, 21 master's, 5 doctorates, 6 other advanced degrees awarded. Terminal master's awarded for partial completion of doctoral program. *Degree requirements:* For master's, comprehensive exam, thesis, seminar presentation; for doctorate, comprehensive exam, thesis/dissertation, qualifying exam, submission of two manuscripts for publication in peer-reviewed journal or books. *Entrance requirements:* For master's, GRE General Test, 3 letters of recommendation, statement of research interests; for doctorate, GRE General Test, 2 letters of recommendation, resume, personal statement. Additional exam requirements/recommendations for international students: Required—TOEFL (minimum score 550 paper-based; 79 iBT). *Application deadline:* For fall admission, 1/15 for domestic students; for spring admission, 11/1 for domestic students. Applications are processed on a rolling basis. Application fee: $35 ($60 for international students). Electronic applications accepted. *Expenses:* $5,231.50 per semester full-time in-state, $9,623.50 full-time out-of-state. *Financial support:* In 2016–17, 18 students received support, including 4 research assistantships with full tuition reimbursements available (averaging $13,960 per year), 11 teaching assistantships with full tuition reimbursements available (averaging $18,864 per year); fellowships with full tuition reimbursements available, Federal Work-Study, scholarships/grants, and unspecified assistantships also available. Financial award application deadline: 2/1; financial award applicants required to submit FAFSA. *Faculty research:* Hazards, active tectonics, geophysics, hydrology and water resources, spatial analysis. *Unit head:* Dr. Daniel Larsen, Chair, 901-678-4538, Fax: 901-678-2178, E-mail: dlarsen@memphis.edu. *Application contact:* Dr. Randel T. Cox, Graduate Coordinator, 901-678-4361, Fax: 901-678-2178, E-mail: randycox@memphis.edu. Website: http://www.memphis.edu/earthsciences/

**University of Minnesota, Twin Cities Campus,** Graduate School, College of Liberal Arts, Department of Cultural Studies and Comparative Literature, Program in Comparative Studies in Discourse and Society, Minneapolis, MN 55455-0213. Offers PhD. *Degree requirements:* For doctorate, 2 foreign languages, thesis/dissertation. *Entrance requirements:* For doctorate, GRE General Test, sample of written work. Additional exam requirements/recommendations for international students: Required— TOEFL. *Faculty research:* Cultural theory; music; architecture, space, and urbanism; body and gender; film and popular culture.

**University of Missouri–Kansas City,** School of Graduate Studies, Kansas City, MO 64110-2499. Offers interdisciplinary studies (PhD), including art history, cell biology and biophysics, chemistry, computer and electrical engineering, computer science and informatics, economics, education, engineering, English, entrepreneurship and innovation, geosciences, history, mathematics and statistics, molecular biology and biochemistry, music education, oral and craniofacial sciences, pharmaceutical sciences, pharmacology, physics, political science, public affairs and administration, religious studies, social science, telecommunications and computer networking; PMBA/MHA. *Students:* 74 full-time (23 women), 314 part-time (120 women); includes 52 minority (24 Black or African American, non-Hispanic/Latino; 1 American Indian or Alaska Native, non-Hispanic/Latino; 10 Asian, non-Hispanic/Latino; 14 Hispanic/Latino; 3 Two or more races, non-Hispanic/Latino), 155 international. Average age 35. 252 applicants, 33% accepted, 73 enrolled. In 2016, 48 doctorates awarded. *Degree requirements:* For doctorate, comprehensive exam, thesis/dissertation, residency. *Entrance requirements:* For doctorate, GRE General Test, minimum GPA of 2.75 (undergraduate), 3.0 (graduate). Additional exam requirements/recommendations for international students: Required—TOEFL (minimum score 550 paper-based; 80 iBT), TWE (minimum score 4). *Application deadline:* For fall admission, 1/15 priority date for domestic and international students. Applications are processed on a rolling basis. Application fee: $45 ($50 for international students). Electronic applications accepted. *Financial support:* Career-related internships or fieldwork, Federal Work-Study, tuition waivers (partial), and unspecified assistantships available. Support available to part-time students. Financial award application deadline: 3/1; financial award applicants required to submit FAFSA. *Unit head:* Dr. Denis M. Medeiros, Dean, 816-235-1301, Fax: 816-235-1310, E-mail: medeirosd@umkc.edu. *Application contact:* Quincy Bennett Johnson, Coordinator of Admissions and Recruitment, Interdisciplinary PhD Program, 816-235-1559, Fax: 816-235-1310, E-mail: bennettq@umkc.edu. Website: http://sgs.umkc.edu/

**University of Montana,** Graduate School, College of Humanities and Sciences, Division of Biological Sciences, Interdisciplinary Program in Systems Ecology, Missoula, MT 59812-0002. Offers MS, PhD.

**University of Montana,** Graduate School, Program in Interdisciplinary Studies, Missoula, MT 59812-0002. Offers individualized interdisciplinary studies (PhD); interdisciplinary studies (MIS). *Degree requirements:* For doctorate, thesis/dissertation. *Entrance requirements:* For master's, GRE General Test. Additional exam requirements/recommendations for international students: Required—TOEFL.

**University of New Brunswick Fredericton,** School of Graduate Studies, Interdisciplinary Studies Program, Fredericton, NB E3B 5A3, Canada. Offers M IDST, PhD. *Degree requirements:* For master's, thesis; for doctorate, comprehensive exam, thesis/dissertation. *Entrance requirements:* For master's, BA honors degree, minimum GPA of 3.3; for doctorate, master's degree with thesis; minimum A- average. Additional exam requirements/recommendations for international students: Required—TOEFL (minimum score 600 paper-based; 100 iBT), IELTS (minimum score 7), TWE (minimum score 5.5). Electronic applications accepted.

**University of North Alabama,** College of Arts and Sciences, Department of Interdisciplinary and Professional Studies, Florence, AL 35632-0001. Offers professional studies (MPS), including community development, information technology, security and safety leadership. *Program availability:* Part-time. *Faculty:* 1 full-time (0 women), 1 part-time/adjunct (0 women). *Students:* 12 full-time (8 women), 40 part-time (29 women); includes 6 minority (5 Black or African American, non-Hispanic/Latino; 1 Asian, non-Hispanic/Latino), 8 international. Average age 35. 25 applicants, 76% accepted, 15 enrolled. In 2016, 11 master's awarded. *Degree requirements:* For master's, thesis optional. *Entrance requirements:* For master's, ETS PPI, baccalaureate degree from accredited institution; minimum cumulative GPA of 2.75 or 3.0 in last 60 hours of undergraduate study; personal statement. Additional exam requirements/recommendations for international students: Required—TOEFL (minimum score 79 iBT), IELTS (minimum score 6), PTE (minimum score 54). *Application deadline:* Applications are processed on a rolling basis. Application fee: $50 ($100 for international students). Electronic applications accepted. *Expenses:* Tuition, state resident: full-time $2799; part-time $1866 per semester. Tuition, nonresident: full-time $5598; part-time $3732 per semester. *Required fees:* $915; $642 per semester. Tuition and fees vary according to course load. *Financial support:* In 2016–17, 9 students received support. Scholarships/grants and unspecified assistantships available. Financial award application deadline: 12/1; financial award applicants required to submit FAFSA. *Unit head:* Dr. Craig T. Robertson, Director, 256-765-5003, E-mail: ctrobertson@una.edu. *Application contact:* Hillary N. Coats, Graduate Admissions Coordinator, 256-765-4447, E-mail: graduate@una.edu. Website: https://www.una.edu/interdisciplinary-studies/

**The University of North Carolina at Charlotte,** College of Liberal Arts and Sciences, Interdisciplinary Liberal Arts and Sciences Programs, Charlotte, NC 28223-0001. Offers gender, sexuality, and women's studies (Graduate Certificate); gerontology (MA, Graduate Certificate); Latin American studies (MA); liberal studies (MA); organizational science (PhD); public policy (PhD). *Program availability:* Part-time, evening/weekend. *Faculty:* 1 (woman) part-time/adjunct. *Students:* 65 full-time (49 women), 61 part-time (50 women); includes 31 minority (11 Black or African American, non-Hispanic/Latino; 1 American Indian or Alaska Native, non-Hispanic/Latino; 2 Asian, non-Hispanic/Latino; 16 Hispanic/Latino; 1 Two or more races, non-Hispanic/Latino), 15 international. Average age 32. 128 applicants, 41% accepted, 40 enrolled. In 2016, 15 master's, 12 doctorates, 7 other advanced degrees awarded. *Degree requirements:* For master's, comprehensive exam (for some programs), thesis (for some programs), practicum, project; for doctorate, comprehensive exam, thesis/dissertation; for Graduate Certificate, practicum (for gerontology). *Entrance requirements:* For master's, GRE General Test or MAT, bachelor's degree from accredited college or university; official transcripts of all previous academic work attempted beyond high school; minimum overall GPA of 3.0 on applicant's previous work beyond high school; statement of purpose; recommendation letters; for doctorate, GRE or GMAT, statement of purpose discussing interest in program and objectives for pursuing degree, current resume or curriculum vitae, unofficial transcripts; for Graduate Certificate, bachelor's degree from accredited university and either be enrolled in and in good standing in a graduate degree program at UNC Charlotte or have a minimum undergraduate GPA of 3.0. Additional exam requirements/recommendations for international students: Required—TOEFL (minimum score 523 paper-based, 70 iBT) or IELTS (6.5). *Application deadline:* For fall admission, 2/15 for domestic and international students; for spring admission, 10/1 for domestic and international students; for summer admission, 4/1 for domestic and international students. Applications are processed on a rolling basis. Application fee: $75. Electronic applications accepted. *Expenses:* Tuition, state resident: full-time $4252. Tuition, nonresident: full-time $17,423. *Required fees:* $3026. Tuition and fees vary according to course load and program. *Financial support:* In 2016–17, 26 students received support, including 17 research assistantships (averaging $12,840 per year), 7 teaching assistantships (averaging $14,442 per year); career-related internships or fieldwork, institutionally sponsored loans, scholarships/grants, unspecified assistantships, and administrative assistantships also available. Support available to part-time students. Financial award application deadline: 3/1; financial award applicants required to submit FAFSA. *Unit head:* Dr. Nancy A. Gutierrez, Dean, 704-687-0081, E-mail: ngutierr@uncc.edu. *Application contact:* Kathy B. Giddings, Director of Graduate Admissions, 704-687-5503, Fax: 704-687-3279, E-mail: gradadm@uncc.edu. Website: http://clas.uncc.edu/academics

**University of Northern British Columbia,** Office of Graduate Studies, Prince George, BC V2N 4Z9, Canada. Offers business administration (Diploma); community health science (M Sc); disability management (MA); education (M Ed); first nations studies (MA); gender studies (MA); history (MA); interdisciplinary studies (MA); international studies (MA); mathematical, computer and physical sciences (M Sc); natural resources and environmental studies (M Sc, MA, MNRES, PhD); political science (MA); psychology (M Sc, PhD); social work (MSW). *Program availability:* Part-time, evening/weekend, online learning. *Degree requirements:* For master's, thesis; for doctorate, thesis/dissertation. *Entrance requirements:* For master's, GRE, minimum B average in undergraduate course work; for doctorate, candidacy exam, minimum A average in graduate course work.

**University of North Texas,** Robert B. Toulouse School of Graduate Studies, Denton, TX 76203-5459. Offers accounting (MS); applied anthropology (MA, MS); applied behavior analysis (Certificate); applied geography (MA); applied technology and performance improvement (M Ed, MS); art education (MA); art history (MA); art museum education (Certificate); arts leadership (Certificate); audiology (Au D); behavior analysis (MS); behavioral science (PhD); biochemistry and molecular biology (MS); biology (MA, MS); biomedical engineering (MS); business analysis (MS); chemistry (MS); clinical health psychology (PhD); communication studies (MA, MS); computer engineering (MS); computer science (MS); counseling (M Ed, MS), including clinical mental health counseling (MS), college and university counseling, elementary school counseling, secondary school counseling; creative writing (MA); criminal justice (MS); curriculum and instruction (M Ed); decision sciences (MBA); design (MA, MFA), including fashion design (MFA), innovation studies, interior design (MFA); early childhood studies (MS);

*Interdisciplinary Studies*

economics (MS); educational leadership (M Ed, Ed D); educational psychology (MS, PhD), including family studies (MS), gifted and talented (MS), human development (MS), learning and cognition (MS), research, measurement and evaluation (MS); electrical engineering (MS); emergency management (MPA); engineering technology (MS); English (MA); English as a second language (MA); environmental science (MS); finance (MBA, MS); financial management (MPA); French (MA); health services management (MBA); higher education (M Ed, Ed D); history (MA, MS); hospitality management (MS); human resources management (MPA); information science (MS); information systems (PhD); information technologies (MBA); interdisciplinary studies (MA, MS); international studies (MA); international sustainable tourism (MS); jazz studies (MM); journalism (MA, MJ, Graduate Certificate), including interactive and virtual digital communication (Graduate Certificate), narrative journalism (Graduate Certificate), public relations (Graduate Certificate); kinesiology (MS); linguistics (MA); local government management (MPA); logistics (PhD); logistics and supply chain management (MBA); long-term care, senior housing, and aging services (MA); management (PhD); marketing (MBA); mathematics (MA, MS); mechanical and energy engineering (MS, PhD); music (MA), including ethnomusicology, music theory, musicology, performance; music composition (PhD); music education (MM Ed, PhD); nonprofit management (MPA); operations and supply chain management (MBA); performance (MM, DMA); philosophy (MA); political science (MA); professional and technical communication (MA); radio, television and film (MA, MFA); rehabilitation counseling (Certificate); sociology (MA); Spanish (MA); special education (M Ed); speech-language pathology (MA); strategic management (MBA); studio art (MFA); teaching (M Ed); MBA/MS. *Program availability:* Part-time, evening/weekend, online learning. Terminal master's awarded for partial completion of doctoral program. *Degree requirements:* For master's, variable foreign language requirement, comprehensive exam (for some programs), thesis (for some programs); for doctorate, variable foreign language requirement, comprehensive exam (for some programs), thesis/dissertation; for other advanced degree, variable foreign language requirement, comprehensive exam (for some programs). *Entrance requirements:* For master's and doctorate, GRE, GMAT. Additional exam requirements/recommendations for international students: Required—TOEFL (minimum score 550 paper-based; 79 iBT). Electronic applications accepted.

**University of Oklahoma,** Graduate College, Program in Interdisciplinary Studies, Norman, OK 73019-0390. Offers MA, MS, PhD. *Program availability:* Part-time, evening/weekend. *Students:* 13 full-time (5 women), 128 part-time (44 women); includes 35 minority (8 Black or African American, non-Hispanic/Latino; 3 American Indian or Alaska Native, non-Hispanic/Latino; 8 Asian, non-Hispanic/Latino; 12 Hispanic/Latino; 4 Two or more races, non-Hispanic/Latino), 4 international. Average age 37. 23 applicants, 52% accepted. In 2016, 89 master's, 7 doctorates awarded. *Entrance requirements:* Additional exam requirements/recommendations for international students: Required—TOEFL (minimum score 79 iBT) or IELTS (minimum score 6.5). *Application deadline:* For fall admission, 4/1 for international students; for spring admission, 9/1 for international students; for summer admission, 2/1 for international students. Applications are processed on a rolling basis. Application fee: $50 ($100 for international students). Electronic applications accepted. *Expenses:* Tuition, state resident: full-time $4886; part-time $203.60 per credit hour. Tuition, nonresident: full-time $18,989; part-time $791.20 per credit hour. *Required fees:* $3283; $126.25 per credit hour. $126.50 per semester. *Financial support:* In 2016–17, 7 students received support. Research assistantships, teaching assistantships, and unspecified assistantships available. Financial award applicants required to submit FAFSA. *Unit head:* Dr. Randall S. Hewes, Interim Dean and Professor, 405-325-3811, Fax: 405-325-5343, E-mail: hewes@ou.edu. *Application contact:* Amy Shaw, Director, Office of Graduate Admissions, 405-325-6765, Fax: 405-325-5345, E-mail: ashaw@ou.edu.

**University of Oregon,** Graduate School, Interdisciplinary Program in Applied Information Management, Eugene, OR 97403. Offers MS. *Program availability:* Part-time, online learning. *Degree requirements:* For master's, project. *Entrance requirements:* Additional exam requirements/recommendations for international students: Required—TOEFL. Electronic applications accepted. *Expenses:* Contact institution. *Faculty research:* Business management, information design.

**University of Ottawa,** Faculty of Graduate and Postdoctoral Studies, Interdisciplinary Programs, Ottawa, ON K1N 6N5, Canada. Offers e-business (Certificate); e-commerce (Certificate); finance (Certificate); health services and policies research (Diploma); population health (PhD); population health risk assessment and management (Certificate); public management and governance (Certificate); systems science (Certificate).

**University of Pittsburgh,** School of Medicine, Graduate Programs in Medicine, Interdisciplinary Biomedical Graduate Program, Pittsburgh, PA 15260. Offers PhD. *Faculty:* 277 full-time (72 women). *Students:* 26 full-time (14 women); includes 3 minority (all Asian, non-Hispanic/Latino), 4 international. Average age 26. 383 applicants, 20% accepted, 26 enrolled. *Degree requirements:* For doctorate, comprehensive exam, thesis/dissertation. *Entrance requirements:* For doctorate, GRE General Test, minimum GPA of 3.2, 3 letters of recommendation, official transcripts, baccalaureate degree. Additional exam requirements/recommendations for international students: Required—TOEFL (minimum score 100 iBT), IELTS (minimum score 7). *Application deadline:* For fall admission, 12/1 priority date for domestic and international students. Application fee: $50. Tuition and fees vary according to program. *Financial support:* In 2016–17, 26 students received support, including 26 fellowships with full tuition reimbursements available (averaging $28,500 per year); traineeships also available. *Faculty research:* Cell biology and molecular physiology, cellular and molecular pathology, immunology, molecular genetics and developmental biology, molecular pharmacology, molecular virology and microbiology. *Unit head:* Dr. John Horn, Director, 412-648-8957, Fax: 412-648-1077, E-mail: gradstudies@medschool.pitt.edu. *Application contact:* Carol Williams, Admissions and Recruiting Manager, 412-648-8957, Fax: 412-648-1077, E-mail: gradstudies@medschool.pitt.edu.
Website: http://www.gradbiomed.pitt.edu/

**University of Regina,** Faculty of Graduate Studies and Research, Faculty of Media, Art, and Performance, Department of Visual Arts, Regina, SK S4S 0A2, Canada. Offers ceramics (MFA); drawing (MFA); interdisciplinary studies (MA, MFA); intermedia (MFA); painting (MFA); sculpture (MFA). *Faculty:* 9 full-time (5 women), 3 part-time/adjunct (1 woman). *Students:* 7 full-time (5 women). 6 applicants, 50% accepted. In 2016, 3 master's awarded. *Degree requirements:* For master's, exhibition, support paper, oral defense. *Entrance requirements:* For master's, documentation of recent work. Additional exam requirements/recommendations for international students: Required—TOEFL (minimum score 580 paper-based; 80 iBT), IELTS (minimum score 6.5), PTE (minimum score 59). *Application deadline:* For fall admission, 1/15 for domestic and international students. Application fee: $100. Electronic applications accepted. *Financial support:* In 2016–17, 5 fellowships (averaging $6,000 per year), 3 teaching assistantships (averaging $2,501 per year) were awarded; scholarships/grants also available. Financial award application deadline: 6/15. *Faculty research:* Contemporary visual art theory and practice; art history; curatorial practice; print media; drawing/painting, sculpture, and ceramics. *Unit head:* Leesa Streifler, Department Head, 306-585-5529, Fax: 306-585-5526, E-mail: leesa.steifler@uregina.ca. *Application contact:* Dr. Robert Truszkowski,

Graduate Coordinator, Visual Arts, 306-585-5574, Fax: 306-585-5526, E-mail: robert.truszkowski@uregina.ca.

**University of South Alabama,** Graduate School, Mobile, AL 36688. Offers clinical and counseling psychology (PhD); environmental toxicology (MS). *Program availability:* Part-time, evening/weekend. *Faculty:* 8 full-time (4 women). *Students:* 36 full-time (22 women), 7 part-time (5 women); includes 7 minority (5 Black or African American, non-Hispanic/Latino; 1 American Indian or Alaska Native, non-Hispanic/Latino; 1 Two or more races, non-Hispanic/Latino). Average age 27. 123 applicants, 15% accepted, 16 enrolled. In 2016, 9 master's, 5 doctorates awarded. *Degree requirements:* For master's, comprehensive exam, research project or thesis; for doctorate, thesis/dissertation. *Entrance requirements:* For master's, GRE, BA/BS in related discipline, minimum undergraduate GPA of 3.0; for doctorate, GRE, three letters of recommendation, statement of purpose, curriculum vitae. Additional exam requirements/recommendations for international students: Required—TOEFL (minimum score 525 paper-based; 71 iBT). *Application deadline:* For fall admission, 7/1 priority date for domestic students, 6/1 priority date for international students; for spring admission, 12/1 priority date for domestic students, 11/1 priority date for international students. Applications are processed on a rolling basis. Application fee: $35. Electronic applications accepted. *Expenses:* Tuition, state resident: full-time $9768; part-time $407 per credit hour. Tuition, nonresident: full-time $19,536; part-time $814 per credit hour. *Financial support:* Fellowships, research assistantships, teaching assistantships, career-related internships or fieldwork, Federal Work-Study, institutionally sponsored loans, scholarships/grants, and unspecified assistantships available. Support available to part-time students. Financial award application deadline: 5/31; financial award applicants required to submit FAFSA. *Unit head:* Dr. Julio Turrens, Interim Dean of the Graduate School, 251-460-6310, E-mail: jturrens@southalabama.edu. *Application contact:* Deanna Cobb, Graduate School Services Specialist, 251-460-6310, E-mail: dcobb@southalabama.edu.
Website: http://www.southalabama.edu/graduatemajors/graduateschool/

**The University of South Dakota,** Graduate School, Interdisciplinary Studies Program, Vermillion, SD 57069. Offers MA. *Program availability:* Part-time, online learning. *Degree requirements:* For master's, thesis or alternative. *Entrance requirements:* For master's, minimum GPA of 2.7. Additional exam requirements/recommendations for international students: Required—TOEFL (minimum score 550 paper-based; 79 iBT). Electronic applications accepted.

**University of South Florida,** Morsani College of Medicine and College of Graduate Studies, Graduate Programs in Medical Sciences, Tampa, FL 33620-9951. Offers advanced athletic training (MS); athletic training (MS); bioinformatics and computational biology (MSBCB); biotechnology (MSB); health informatics (MSHI); medical sciences (MSMS, PhD), including aging and neuroscience (MSMS), allergy, immunology and infectious disease (PhD), anatomy, biochemistry and molecular biology, clinical and translational research, health science (MSMS), interdisciplinary medical sciences (MSMS), medical microbiology and immunology (MSMS), metabolic and nutritional medicine (MSMS), microbiology and immunology (PhD), molecular medicine, molecular pharmacology and physiology (PhD), neuroscience (PhD), pathology and cell biology (PhD), women's health (MSMS). *Students:* 454 full-time (239 women), 273 part-time (173 women); includes 347 minority (110 Black or African American, non-Hispanic/Latino; 1 American Indian or Alaska Native, non-Hispanic/Latino; 99 Asian, non-Hispanic/Latino; 113 Hispanic/Latino; 1 Native Hawaiian or other Pacific Islander, non-Hispanic/Latino; 23 Two or more races, non-Hispanic/Latino), 61 international. Average age 27. 7,242 applicants, 8% accepted, 395 enrolled. In 2016, 374 master's, 13 doctorates awarded. Terminal master's awarded for partial completion of doctoral program. *Degree requirements:* For master's, comprehensive exam, thesis; for doctorate, comprehensive exam, thesis/dissertation. *Entrance requirements:* For master's, GRE General Test or GMAT, bachelor's degree or equivalent from regionally-accredited university with minimum GPA of 3.0 in upper-division sciences coursework; prerequisites in general biology, general chemistry, general physics, organic chemistry, quantitative analysis, and integral and differential calculus; for doctorate, GRE General Test, bachelor's degree from regionally-accredited university with minimum GPA of 3.0 in upper-division sciences coursework; 3 letters of recommendation; personal interview; 1-2 page personal statement; prerequisites in biology, chemistry, physics, organic chemistry, quantitative analysis, and integral/differential calculus. Additional exam requirements/recommendations for international students: Required—TOEFL (minimum score 550 paper-based; 79 iBT) or IELTS (minimum score 6.5). *Application deadline:* For fall admission, 2/1 for domestic and international students. Application fee: $30. Electronic applications accepted. *Financial support:* In 2016–17, 116 students received support. *Faculty research:* Anatomy, biochemistry, cancer biology, cardiovascular disease, cell biology, immunology, microbiology, molecular biology, neuroscience, pharmacology, physiology. *Total annual research expenditures:* $42.3 million. *Unit head:* Dr. Michael Barber, Professor/Associate Dean for Graduate and Postdoctoral Affairs, 813-974-9908, Fax: 813-974-4317, E-mail: mbarber@health.usf.edu. *Application contact:* Dr. Eric Bennett, Graduate Director, PhD Program in Medical Sciences, 813-974-1545, Fax: 813-974-4317, E-mail: esbennet@health.usf.edu.
Website: http://health.usf.edu/nocms/medicine/graduatestudies/

**The University of Tennessee at Martin,** Graduate Programs, College of Education, Health and Behavioral Sciences, Program in Teaching, Martin, TN 38238. Offers curriculum and instruction (MS Ed), including 7-12, K-6; initial licensure (MS Ed), including elementary education, secondary education; initial licensure K-12 (MS Ed), including physical education, special education; interdisciplinary (MS Ed). *Students:* 21 full-time (14 women), 125 part-time (87 women); includes 22 minority (18 Black or African American, non-Hispanic/Latino; 3 Hispanic/Latino; 1 Two or more races, non-Hispanic/Latino). 115 applicants, 81% accepted, 51 enrolled. In 2016, 26 master's awarded. *Expenses:* Tuition, state resident: full-time $8254; part-time $459 per credit hour. Tuition, nonresident: full-time $22,198; part-time $1234 per credit hour. *Required fees:* $79 per credit hour. Part-time tuition and fees vary according to course load and campus/location. *Faculty research:* Special education, science/math/technology, school reform, reading. *Unit head:* Cynthia West, Dean, 731-881-7125, Fax: 731-881-7975, E-mail: cwest@utm.edu. *Application contact:* Jolene L. Cunningham, Student Services Specialist, 731-881-7012, Fax: 731-881-7499, E-mail: jcunningham@utm.edu.

**The University of Texas at Dallas,** School of Interdisciplinary Studies, Richardson, TX 75080. Offers MA. *Program availability:* Part-time, evening/weekend. *Faculty:* 3 full-time (2 women). *Students:* 10 full-time (6 women), 15 part-time (11 women); includes 12 minority (2 Black or African American, non-Hispanic/Latino; 1 Asian, non-Hispanic/Latino; 7 Hispanic/Latino; 2 Two or more races, non-Hispanic/Latino), 2 international. Average age 38. 48 applicants, 83% accepted, 9 enrolled. In 2016, 4 master's awarded. *Degree requirements:* For master's, research project, seminar. *Entrance requirements:* For master's, GRE General Test, minimum GPA of 3.0. Additional exam requirements/recommendations for international students: Required—TOEFL (minimum score 550 paper-based). *Application deadline:* For fall admission, 7/15 for domestic students, 5/1 priority date for international students; for spring admission, 11/15 for domestic students, 9/1 priority date for international students. Applications are processed on a rolling basis. Application fee: $50 ($100 for international students). Electronic applications accepted.

*Expenses:* Tuition, state resident: full-time $12,418; part-time $690 per semester hour. Tuition, nonresident: full-time $24,150; part-time $1342 per semester hour. Tuition and fees vary according to course load. *Financial support:* In 2016–17, 14 students received support. Research assistantships with partial tuition reimbursements available, teaching assistantships with partial tuition reimbursements available, career-related internships or fieldwork, Federal Work-Study, institutionally sponsored loans, and scholarships/grants available. Support available to part-time students. Financial award application deadline: 4/30; financial award applicants required to submit FAFSA. *Faculty research:* Education of homeless children and youths. *Total annual research expenditures:* $351. *Unit head:* Dr. George Fair, Dean, 972-883-2350, Fax: 972-883-2440, E-mail: gwfair@utdallas.edu. *Application contact:* Becky Wiser, 972-883-2354, Fax: 972-883-2440, E-mail: rwiser@utdallas.edu.
Website: http://www.utdallas.edu/is

**The University of Texas at El Paso,** Graduate School, College of Liberal Arts, Master of Arts in Interdisciplinary Studies Program, El Paso, TX 79968-0001. Offers MAIS. *Program availability:* Part-time, evening/weekend. *Entrance requirements:* For master's, GRE, minimum GPA of 3.0, letters of recommendation. Additional exam requirements/recommendations for international students: Required—TOEFL; Recommended—IELTS. Electronic applications accepted.

**The University of Texas at San Antonio,** College of Education and Human Development, Department of Interdisciplinary Learning and Teaching, San Antonio, TX 78249-0617. Offers education (MA), including curriculum and instruction, early childhood and elementary education, instructional technology, reading and literacy, special education; interdisciplinary learning and teaching (PhD). *Program availability:* Part-time, evening/weekend. *Faculty:* 25 full-time (18 women), 4 part-time/adjunct (2 women). *Students:* 70 full-time (53 women), 256 part-time (222 women); includes 185 minority (22 Black or African American, non-Hispanic/Latino; 10 Asian, non-Hispanic/Latino; 148 Hispanic/Latino; 1 Native Hawaiian or other Pacific Islander, non-Hispanic/Latino; 4 Two or more races, non-Hispanic/Latino), 4 international. Average age 34. 145 applicants, 88% accepted, 100 enrolled. In 2016, 90 master's, 4 doctorates awarded. *Degree requirements:* For master's, comprehensive exam, thesis optional, 36 hours of course work without thesis (33 with thesis); for doctorate, comprehensive exam, thesis/dissertation, minimum of 60 semester credit hours. *Entrance requirements:* For master's, bachelor's degree with minimum GPA of 3.0 in last 60 hours of coursework; 18 hours of undergraduate coursework in education or related field; for doctorate, GRE, transcripts from all colleges and universities attended, professional vitae demonstrating experience in work environment where education was primary professional emphasis, 3 letters of recommendation, statement of purpose, minimum GPA of 3.5. Additional exam requirements/recommendations for international students: Required—TOEFL (minimum score 550 paper-based; 79 iBT), IELTS (minimum score 6.5). *Application deadline:* For fall admission, 7/1 for domestic students, 4/1 for international students; for spring admission, 11/1 for domestic students, 9/1 for international students. Applications are processed on a rolling basis. Application fee: $45 ($80 for international students). Electronic applications accepted. *Financial support:* Career-related internships or fieldwork, Federal Work-Study, and scholarships/grants available. Support available to part-time students. *Faculty research:* Explorations of science, learning and teaching, family involvement in early childhood, culturally-responsive literacy instruction in diverse settings, STEM education, autism spectrum disorder. *Total annual research expenditures:* $766,662. *Unit head:* Dr. Maria R. Cortez, Department Chair, 210-458-4413, Fax: 210-458-7281, E-mail: mari.cortez@utsa.edu. *Application contact:* Elizabeth Narvaes, Student Development Specialist, 210-458-7443, Fax: 210-458-7281, E-mail: elizabeth.narvaez@utsa.edu.
Website: http://education.utsa.edu/interdisciplinary_learning_and_teaching/

**The University of Texas at Tyler,** College of Arts and Sciences, Department of Art and Art History, Tyler, TX 75799-0001. Offers art history (MA); interdisciplinary (MAIS); studio art (MFA). *Degree requirements:* For master's, thesis, graduate committee review. *Entrance requirements:* For master's, minimum GPA of 3.0. Additional exam requirements/recommendations for international students: Required—TOEFL. *Faculty research:* Classical myths in contemporary art, social issues in contemporary art, casting methods, Renaissance art.

**The University of Texas at Tyler,** College of Arts and Sciences, Department of Biology, Tyler, TX 75799-0001. Offers biology (MS); interdisciplinary studies (MSIS). *Degree requirements:* For master's, comprehensive exam, thesis, oral qualifying exam, thesis defense. *Entrance requirements:* For master's, GRE General Test, GRE Subject Test, bachelor's degree in biology or equivalent. Additional exam requirements/recommendations for international students: Required—TOEFL. Electronic applications accepted. *Faculty research:* Phenotypic plasticity and heritability of life history traits, invertebrate ecology and genetics, systematics and phylogenetics of reptiles, hibernation physiology in turtles, landscape ecology, host-microbe interaction, outer membrane proteins in bacteria.

**The University of Texas at Tyler,** College of Arts and Sciences, Department of Literature and Languages, Tyler, TX 75799-0001. Offers English (MA); interdisciplinary studies (MAIS). *Program availability:* Part-time, evening/weekend. *Degree requirements:* For master's, one foreign language, comprehensive exam, thesis optional. *Entrance requirements:* For master's, GRE General Test, minimum GPA of 3.0; four semesters or the equivalent of one foreign language. Additional exam requirements/recommendations for international students: Required—TOEFL. Electronic applications accepted. *Faculty research:* Medieval and Tudor drama, Shakespeare, British Romanticism, British and Irish modernism, American realism, Greek drama, nineteenth-century American literature.

**The University of Texas at Tyler,** College of Education and Psychology, Department of Psychology and Counseling, Tyler, TX 75799-0001. Offers clinical psychology (MS), including neuropsychology, school psychology; counseling psychology (MA), including general, marriage and family; interdisciplinary studies (MSIS); school counseling (MA). *Program availability:* Part-time, evening/weekend. *Degree requirements:* For master's, comprehensive exam, thesis optional. *Entrance requirements:* For master's, GRE General Test, minimum GPA of 3.0. Additional exam requirements/recommendations for international students: Required—TOEFL. Electronic applications accepted. *Faculty research:* Neuropsychology, child abuse, psychometric properties of psychological instruments, maternal behavior, clinical practice issues, victimization of women, post-traumatic stress disorder.

**The University of Texas Health Science Center at San Antonio,** Graduate School of Biomedical Sciences, Integrated Biomedical Sciences Program, San Antonio, TX 78229-3900. Offers PhD. *Degree requirements:* For doctorate, comprehensive exam, thesis/dissertation.

**The University of Texas Rio Grande Valley,** College of Liberal Arts, Program in Interdisciplinary Studies, Edinburg, TX 78539. Offers MAIS, MSIS. *Program availability:* Part-time, evening/weekend. *Degree requirements:* For master's, comprehensive exam, thesis or alternative. *Entrance requirements:* For master's, GRE General Test, minimum GPA of 3.0. Tuition and fees vary according to course load and program.

**University of Vermont,** Graduate College, College of Education and Social Services, Department of Leadership and Developmental Sciences, Interdisciplinary Major,

Burlington, VT 05405. Offers M Ed. *Degree requirements:* For master's, thesis or alternative. *Entrance requirements:* Additional exam requirements/recommendations for international students: Required—TOEFL (minimum score 550 paper-based; 80 iBT). Electronic applications accepted. *Expenses:* Tuition, state resident: full-time $5814. Tuition, nonresident: full-time $14,670.

**University of Virginia,** College and Graduate School of Arts and Sciences, Program in Art and Architectural History, Charlottesville, VA 22903. Offers MA, PhD. *Faculty:* 24 full-time (13 women), 2 part-time/adjunct (1 woman). *Students:* 30 full-time (18 women); includes 5 minority (1 Black or African American, non-Hispanic/Latino; 2 Asian, non-Hispanic/Latino; 1 Hispanic/Latino; 1 Two or more races, non-Hispanic/Latino), 2 international. Average age 31. 64 applicants, 14% accepted, 5 enrolled. In 2016, 9 doctorates awarded. *Degree requirements:* For master's, one foreign language, comprehensive exam, thesis; for doctorate, 2 foreign languages, thesis/dissertation, oral exam. *Entrance requirements:* For master's and doctorate, GRE, 2 letters of recommendation. *Application deadline:* For fall admission, 12/7 for domestic and international students. Applications are processed on a rolling basis. Application fee: $60. Electronic applications accepted. *Expenses:* Tuition, state resident: full-time $15,026; part-time $834 per credit hour. Tuition, nonresident: full-time $25,168; part-time $1378 per credit hour. *Required fees:* $2654. *Financial support:* Application deadline: 12/7. *Unit head:* Larry Goedde, Chair, 434-924-3541, Fax: 434-924-3647, E-mail: artdept@virginia.edu. *Application contact:* Sheila Crane, Director of Graduate Studies, 434-243-2342, Fax: 434-924-3647, E-mail: artdept@virginia.edu.
Website: http://www.virginia.edu/art/phd-program/

**University of Washington, Tacoma,** Graduate Programs, Interdisciplinary Studies Program, Tacoma, WA 98402-3100. Offers MA. *Program availability:* Part-time, evening/weekend. *Degree requirements:* For master's, thesis or project. *Entrance requirements:* For master's, GRE, statement of intended area of focus, two official transcripts from every college attended, copy of current resume, three recommendations. Additional exam requirements/recommendations for international students: Required—TOEFL. Electronic applications accepted. *Faculty research:* American history, political and social theory, political economy of labor, human rights; African-American, labor, and ethnic studies; South Asian art, aesthetics, semiotics, and modes of creative practice; social movements.

**The University of Western Ontario,** Faculty of Graduate Studies, Center for the Study of Theory and Criticism, London, ON N6A 5B8, Canada. Offers MA, PhD. *Degree requirements:* For master's, one foreign language, thesis; for doctorate, one foreign language, comprehensive exam, thesis/dissertation. *Entrance requirements:* For master's, honors degree or equivalent, minimum B+ average, 2 samples of written work; for doctorate, MA in humanities or social sciences.

**Virginia Commonwealth University,** Graduate School, Program in Interdisciplinary Studies, Richmond, VA 23284-9005. Offers MIS. *Program availability:* Part-time. *Degree requirements:* For master's, thesis optional. *Entrance requirements:* For master's, GRE General Test, minimum GPA of 3.0. Additional exam requirements/recommendations for international students: Required—TOEFL (minimum score 600 paper-based; 100 iBT); Recommended—IELTS (minimum score 6.5). *Application deadline:* For fall admission, 5/1 for domestic students; for spring admission, 10/1 for domestic students. Applications are processed on a rolling basis. Application fee: $50. Electronic applications accepted. *Financial support:* Federal Work-Study and institutionally sponsored loans available. Support available to part-time students. *Unit head:* Dr. Angelina E. Overvold, Graduate Program Director, 804-827-3416, E-mail: aovervol@vcu.edu. *Application contact:* K. Stone, Education Support Specialist, 804-827-4546, Fax: 804-827-6949, E-mail: stoneke@vcu.edu.
Website: http://www.vcu.edu/gradweb/

**Virginia Polytechnic Institute and State University,** Graduate School, Intercollege, Blacksburg, VA 24061. Offers genetics, bioinformatics and computational biology (PhD); information technology (MIT); macromolecular science and engineering (MS, PhD); translational biology, medicine, and health (PhD). *Students:* 175 full-time (82 women), 763 part-time (279 women); includes 217 minority (71 Black or African American, non-Hispanic/Latino; 1 American Indian or Alaska Native, non-Hispanic/Latino; 77 Asian, non-Hispanic/Latino; 43 Hispanic/Latino; 1 Native Hawaiian or other Pacific Islander, non-Hispanic/Latino; 24 Two or more races, non-Hispanic/Latino), 83 international. Average age 33. 626 applicants, 74% accepted, 373 enrolled. In 2016, 91 master's, 18 doctorates awarded. *Degree requirements:* For master's, comprehensive exam (for some programs), thesis (for some programs); for doctorate, comprehensive exam (for some programs), thesis/dissertation (for some programs). *Entrance requirements:* For master's and doctorate, GRE/GMAT. Additional exam requirements/recommendations for international students: Required—TOEFL (minimum score 80 iBT). *Application deadline:* For fall admission, 8/1 for domestic students, 4/1 for international students; for spring admission, 1/1 for domestic students, 9/1 for international students. Applications are processed on a rolling basis. Application fee: $75. Electronic applications accepted. *Expenses:* Tuition, state resident: full-time $12,467; part-time $692.50 per credit hour. Tuition, nonresident: full-time $25,095; part-time $1394.25 per credit hour. *Required fees:* $2669; $491.50 per semester. Tuition and fees vary according to course load, campus/location and program. *Financial support:* In 2016–17, 100 research assistantships with full tuition reimbursements (averaging $23,321 per year), 10 teaching assistantships with full tuition reimbursements (averaging $20,748 per year) were awarded. Financial award application deadline: 3/1; financial award applicants required to submit FAFSA. *Unit head:* Dr. Karen P. DePauw, Vice President and Dean for Graduate Education, 540-231-7581, Fax: 540-231-1670, E-mail: kpdepauw@vt.edu.
Website: http://www.graduateschool.vt.edu/graduate_catalog/colleges.htm

**Virginia State University,** College of Graduate Studies, Program in Interdisciplinary Studies, Petersburg, VA 23806-0001. Offers MIS. Program offered jointly with Virginia Commonwealth University. *Degree requirements:* For master's, thesis optional.

**Walden University,** Graduate Programs, School of Nursing, Minneapolis, MN 55401. Offers adult-gerontology acute care nurse practitioner (MSN); adult-gerontology nurse practitioner (MSN); education (MSN); family nurse practitioner (MSN); informatics (MSN); leadership and management (MSN); nursing (PhD, Post-Master's Certificate), including education (PhD), healthcare administration (PhD), interdisciplinary health (PhD), leadership (PhD), nursing education (Post-Master's Certificate), nursing informatics (Post-Master's Certificate), nursing leadership and management (Post-Master's Certificate), public health policy (PhD); nursing practice (DNP); psychiatric mental health (MSN). *Accreditation:* AACN. *Program availability:* Part-time, evening/weekend, online only, 100% online. *Degree requirements:* For doctorate, thesis/dissertation (for some programs), residency (for some programs), field experience (for some programs). *Entrance requirements:* For master's, bachelor's degree or equivalent in related field or RN; minimum GPA of 2.5; official transcripts; goal statement (for some programs); access to computer and Internet; for doctorate, master's degree or higher; RN; three years of related professional or academic experience; goal statement; access to computer and Internet; for Post-Master's Certificate, relevant work experience; access to computer and Internet. Additional exam requirements/recommendations for international students: Required—TOEFL (minimum score 550 paper-based, 79 iBT), IELTS (minimum score 6.5), Michigan English Language Assessment Battery (minimum score 82), or PTE (minimum score 53). Electronic applications accepted.

## Interdisciplinary Studies

**Washington State University,** College of Agricultural, Human, and Natural Resource Sciences, Department of Human Development, Pullman, WA 99164-4852. Offers prevention science (PhD). Program also offered at the Spokane campus. *Program availability:* Part-time. *Degree requirements:* For doctorate, comprehensive exam, thesis/dissertation. *Entrance requirements:* For doctorate, GRE General Test, bachelor's or master's degree in prevention science related field (e.g., communication, educational psychology, human development, nursing, psychology, sociology); written statement specifying qualifications, educational goals, and career objectives; official copies of all college transcripts; three letters of reference. Additional exam requirements/recommendations for international students: Required—TOEFL, IELTS. Electronic applications accepted. *Faculty research:* Prevention science, program implementation and dissemination, drug and alcohol prevention, health communication, equine assisted interventions, obesity prevention, health promotion in emerging adulthood, family processes, disenfranchised youth, rural poverty, adolescent sexuality, cultural competency, community collaborations, parent-child relationships, healthy aging.

**Wayland Baptist University,** Graduate Programs, Program in Multidisciplinary Science, Plainview, TX 79072-6998. Offers MS. *Program availability:* Part-time, evening/weekend. *Degree requirements:* For master's, comprehensive exam. *Entrance requirements:* For master's, GRE or MAT. Additional exam requirements/recommendations for international students: Required—TOEFL (minimum score 500 paper-based; 61 iBT). Electronic applications accepted.

**Western Kentucky University,** Graduate Studies, College of Education and Behavioral Sciences, School of Teacher Education, Bowling Green, KY 42101. Offers elementary education (MAE, Ed S); exceptional education: learning and behavioral disorders (MAE); exceptional education: moderate and severe disabilities (MAE); instructional design (MS); interdisciplinary early childhood education (MAE); library media education (MS); literacy education (MAE); middle grades education (MAE); secondary education (MAE, Ed S). *Program availability:* Part-time, evening/weekend, online learning. *Degree requirements:* For master's, comprehensive exam. *Entrance requirements:* For master's, GRE General Test. Additional exam requirements/recommendations for international students: Required—TOEFL (minimum score 555 paper-based; 79 iBT). *Faculty research:* Teacher preparation in moderate/severe disabilities.

**Western New Mexico University,** Graduate Division, Interdisciplinary Studies, Silver City, NM 88062-0680. Offers MA. *Program availability:* Part-time, online learning. *Degree requirements:* For master's, comprehensive exam (for some programs), thesis optional. *Entrance requirements:* For master's, GRE General Test, GRE Subject Test, minimum GPA of 3.2 in last 64 hours of undergraduate study. Additional exam requirements/recommendations for international students: Required—TOEFL (minimum score 550 paper-based).

**West Texas A&M University,** Program in Interdisciplinary Studies, Canyon, TX 79016-0001. Offers MA, MS. *Program availability:* Part-time, evening/weekend. *Degree requirements:* For master's, comprehensive exam, thesis or alternative. *Entrance requirements:* Additional exam requirements/recommendations for international students: Required—TOEFL. *Application deadline:* For fall admission, 8/1 for domestic students, 6/1 for international students; for spring admission, 12/1 for domestic students, 11/1 for international students; for summer admission, 5/1 for domestic students. Applications are processed on a rolling basis. Application fee: $40 ($75 for international students). Electronic applications accepted. *Financial support:* Application deadline: 2/

1; applicants required to submit FAFSA. *Application contact:* Dr. Rex Pjesky, Associate Dean of Graduate School and Research, 806-651-2737.

**Worcester Polytechnic Institute,** Graduate Studies and Research, Department of Social Science and Policy Studies, Worcester, MA 01609-2280. Offers interdisciplinary social science (PhD); system dynamics (MS, Graduate Certificate). *Program availability:* Part-time, evening/weekend, 100% online. *Faculty:* 3 full-time (1 woman), 4 part-time/adjunct (1 woman). *Students:* 2 full-time (1 woman), 7 part-time (0 women), 2 international. 5 applicants, 100% accepted, 2 enrolled. In 2016, 2 master's awarded. *Entrance requirements:* For master's and doctorate, GRE General Test, 3 letters of recommendation, statement of purpose. Additional exam requirements/recommendations for international students: Required—TOEFL (minimum score 563 paper-based; 84 iBT), IELTS (minimum score 7). *Application deadline:* For fall admission, 1/1 priority date for domestic students, 1/1 for international students; for spring admission, 10/1 priority date for domestic students, 10/1 for international students. Applications are processed on a rolling basis. Application fee: $70. Electronic applications accepted. *Financial support:* Research assistantships, teaching assistantships, career-related internships or fieldwork, institutionally sponsored loans, scholarships/grants, and unspecified assistantships available. Financial award application deadline: 1/1; financial award applicants required to submit FAFSA. *Unit head:* Dr. James K. Doyle, Head, 508-831-5296, Fax: 508-831-5896, E-mail: doyle@wpi.edu. *Application contact:* Dr. Khalid Saeed, Graduate Coordinator, 508-831-5296, Fax: 508-831-5896, E-mail: saeed@wpi.edu.
Website: http://www.wpi.edu/academics/ssps

**Worcester Polytechnic Institute,** Graduate Studies and Research, Programs in Interdisciplinary Studies, Worcester, MA 01609-2280. Offers bioscience administration (MS); impact engineering (MS); manufacturing engineering management (MS); power systems management (MS); social science (PhD); systems modeling (MS). *Program availability:* Part-time, evening/weekend. *Faculty:* 1 part-time/adjunct (0 women). *Students:* 5 full-time (2 women), 54 part-time (21 women); includes 14 minority (3 Black or African American, non-Hispanic/Latino; 5 Asian, non-Hispanic/Latino; 5 Hispanic/Latino; 1 Two or more races, non-Hispanic/Latino), 4 international. 18 applicants, 89% accepted, 8 enrolled. *Degree requirements:* For master's, thesis; for doctorate, comprehensive exam, thesis/dissertation. *Entrance requirements:* For master's and doctorate, 3 letters of recommendation. Additional exam requirements/recommendations for international students: Required—TOEFL (minimum score 563 paper-based; 84 iBT), IELTS (minimum score 7). *Application deadline:* For fall admission, 1/1 priority date for domestic students, 1/1 for international students; for spring admission, 10/1 priority date for domestic students, 10/1 for international students. Applications are processed on a rolling basis. Application fee: $70. Electronic applications accepted. *Financial support:* Institutionally sponsored loans, scholarships/grants, and unspecified assistantships available. Financial award application deadline: 1/1; financial award applicants required to submit FAFSA. *Unit head:* Dr. Fred J. Looft, Head, 508-831-5231, Fax: 508-831-5491, E-mail: fjlooft@wpi.edu. *Application contact:* Lynne Dougherty, Administrative Assistant, 508-831-5301, Fax: 508-831-5717, E-mail: grad@wpi.edu.

**York University,** Faculty of Graduate Studies, Program in Interdisciplinary Studies, Toronto, ON M3J 1P3, Canada. Offers MA. *Program availability:* Part-time. *Degree requirements:* For master's, thesis or alternative. Electronic applications accepted.

# ACADEMIC AND PROFESSIONAL PROGRAMS IN THE SOCIAL SCIENCES

# Section 15
# Area and Cultural Studies

This section contains a directory of institutions offering graduate work in area and cultural studies. Additional information about programs listed in the directory may be obtained by writing directly to the dean of a graduate school or chair of a department at the address given in the directory.

For programs offering related work, see also in this book *Geography, History, Language and Literature, Political Science and International Affairs,* and *Sociology, Anthropology, and Archaeology.*

## CONTENTS

# African-American Studies

**Boston University,** Graduate School of Arts and Sciences, Program in African American Studies, Boston, MA 02215. Offers MA. *Students:* 2 full-time (1 woman); both minorities (both Black or African American, non-Hispanic/Latino). Average age 23. 3 applicants, 67% accepted. In 2016, 2 master's awarded. *Degree requirements:* For master's, one foreign language, comprehensive exam, two major research papers. *Entrance requirements:* For master's, GRE General Test, 3 letters of recommendation, transcripts, personal statement, curriculum vitae, writing sample. Additional exam requirements/recommendations for international students: Required—TOEFL (minimum score 550 paper-based; 84 iBT). *Application deadline:* For fall admission, 1/31 for domestic and international students. Application fee: $95. Electronic applications accepted. *Financial support:* Federal Work-Study available. Financial award application deadline: 1/31. *Unit head:* John Thornton, Director, 617-358-1423, Fax: 617-353-0455, E-mail: jkthorn@bu.edu. *Application contact:* Deirdre James, Program Administrator, 617-358-1421, Fax: 617-353-0455, E-mail: dejames@bu.edu. Website: http://www.bu.edu/afam/

**Carnegie Mellon University,** Dietrich College of Humanities and Social Sciences, Department of History, Pittsburgh, PA 15213-3891. Offers African and African-American diaspora (PhD); culture and power (PhD); labor, politics and social movements (PhD); technology, environment, science and health (PhD); women, gender and the family (PhD). *Program availability:* Part-time. *Degree requirements:* For doctorate, oral and written comprehensive exams, dissertation defense. *Entrance requirements:* For doctorate, GRE General Test. Additional exam requirements/recommendations for international students: Required—TOEFL. Electronic applications accepted. *Faculty research:* Anthropology and history, African-American history, technology/environment, cultural history analysis.

**Clark Atlanta University,** School of Arts and Sciences, Department of African-American Studies, Atlanta, GA 30314. Offers MA, DAH. *Program availability:* Part-time. *Faculty:* 2 full-time (0 women). *Students:* 18 full-time (11 women), 14 part-time (8 women); includes 29 minority (all Black or African American, non-Hispanic/Latino). Average age 36. 18 applicants, 78% accepted, 9 enrolled. In 2016, 5 master's awarded. *Degree requirements:* For master's, one foreign language, comprehensive exam, thesis optional; for doctorate, one foreign language, comprehensive exam, thesis/dissertation. *Entrance requirements:* For master's, GRE General Test, minimum GPA of 2.5. Additional exam requirements/recommendations for international students: Required—TOEFL (minimum score 500 paper-based; 61 iBT). *Application deadline:* For fall admission, 4/1 for domestic and international students; for spring admission, 11/1 for domestic and international students. Applications are processed on a rolling basis. Application fee: $40 ($55 for international students). Electronic applications accepted. *Expenses: Tuition:* Full-time $15,498; part-time $861 per credit hour. *Required fees:* $1326; $1326 per credit hour. Tuition and fees vary according to course load. *Financial support:* Scholarships/grants available. Financial award application deadline: 4/30; financial award applicants required to submit FAFSA. *Unit head:* Dr. Stephanie Evans, Chairperson, 404-880-6352, E-mail: sevans@cau.edu. *Application contact:* Graduate Program Admissions, 404-880-8483, E-mail: cauadmissions@cau.edu.

**Clark Atlanta University,** School of Arts and Sciences, Department of Africana Women's Studies, Atlanta, GA 30314. Offers MA, DAH. *Program availability:* Part-time. *Faculty:* 2 full-time (both women). *Students:* 6 full-time (5 women), 11 part-time (all women); all minorities (all Black or African American, non-Hispanic/Latino). Average age 33. 3 applicants, 100% accepted, 2 enrolled. In 2016, 1 master's awarded. *Degree requirements:* For master's, one foreign language, comprehensive exam, thesis optional; for doctorate, one foreign language, comprehensive exam, thesis/dissertation. *Entrance requirements:* For master's, GRE General Test, minimum GPA of 2.5; for doctorate, GRE General Test, minimum graduate GPA of 3.0. Additional exam requirements/recommendations for international students: Required—TOEFL (minimum score 500 paper-based; 61 iBT). *Application deadline:* For fall admission, 4/1 for domestic and international students; for spring admission, 11/1 for domestic and international students. Applications are processed on a rolling basis. Application fee: $40 ($55 for international students). Electronic applications accepted. *Expenses: Tuition:* Full-time $15,498; part-time $861 per credit hour. *Required fees:* $1326; $1326 per credit hour. Tuition and fees vary according to course load. *Financial support:* Scholarships/grants available. Financial award application deadline: 4/30; financial award applicants required to submit FAFSA. *Faculty research:* Concerns of women of African descent globally. *Unit head:* Dr. Stephanie Evans, Chairperson, 404-880-6352, E-mail: sevans@cau.edu. *Application contact:* Graduate Program Admissions, 404-880-8483, E-mail: graduateadmissions@cau.edu.

**Columbia University,** Graduate School of Arts and Sciences, New York, NY 10027. Offers African-American studies (MA); American studies (MA); anthropology (MA, PhD); art history and archaeology (MA, PhD); astronomy (PhD); biological sciences (PhD); biotechnology (MA); chemical physics (PhD); chemistry (PhD); classical studies (MA, PhD); classics (MA, PhD); climate and society (MA); conservation biology (MA); earth and environmental sciences (PhD); East Asia: regional studies (MA); East Asian languages and cultures (MA, PhD); ecology, evolution and environmental biology (MA), including conservation biology; ecology, evolution, and environmental biology (PhD), including ecology and evolutionary biology, evolutionary primatology; economics (MA, PhD); English and comparative literature (MA, PhD); French and Romance philology (MA, PhD); Germanic languages (MA, PhD); global French studies (MA); global thought (MA); Hispanic cultural studies (MA); history (PhD); history and literature (MA); human rights studies (MA); Islamic studies (MA); Italian (MA, PhD); Japanese pedagogy (MA); Jewish studies (MA); Latin America and the Caribbean: regional studies (MA); Latin American and Iberian cultures (PhD); mathematics (MA, PhD), including finance (MA); medieval and Renaissance studies (MA); Middle Eastern, South Asian, and African studies (MA, PhD); modern art: critical and curatorial studies (MA); modern European studies (MA); museum anthropology (MA); music (DMA, PhD); oral history (MA); philosophical foundations of physics (MA); philosophy (MA, PhD); physics (PhD); political science (MA, PhD); psychology (PhD); quantitative methods in the social sciences (MA); religion (MA, PhD); Russia, Eurasia and East Europe: regional studies (MA); Russian translation (MA); Slavic cultures (MA); Slavic languages (MA, PhD); sociology (MA, PhD); South Asian studies (MA); statistics (MA, PhD); theatre (PhD). Dual-degree programs require admission to both Graduate School of Arts and Sciences and another Columbia school. *Program availability:* Part-time. Terminal master's awarded for partial completion of doctoral program. *Degree requirements:* For master's, variable foreign language requirement, comprehensive exam (for some programs), thesis (for some programs); for doctorate, variable foreign language requirement, comprehensive exam (for some programs), thesis/dissertation. *Entrance requirements:* For master's and doctorate, GRE General Test, GRE Subject Test (for some programs). Additional exam requirements/recommendations for international students: Required—TOEFL, IELTS. Electronic applications accepted.

**Cornell University,** Graduate School, Graduate Fields of Arts and Sciences, Field of African and African-American Studies, Ithaca, NY 14853. Offers African studies (MPS); African-American studies (MPS); Africana studies (PhD). *Degree requirements:* For master's, thesis. *Entrance requirements:* For master's, GRE General Test (recommended), 3 letters of recommendation; for doctorate, GRE General Test (recommended), 3 letters of recommendation, personal statement, writing sample. Additional exam requirements/recommendations for international students: Required—TOEFL (minimum score 550 paper-based; 77 iBT). Electronic applications accepted. *Faculty research:* African-American literature, art, cinema and theater; African-American politics and public policy; African history, politics and art; Caribbean politics and Africana diaspora.

**Cornell University,** Graduate School, Graduate Fields of Arts and Sciences, Field of English Language and Literature, Ithaca, NY 14853. Offers African-American literature (PhD); American literature after 1865 (PhD); American literature to 1865 (PhD); American studies (PhD); colonial and postcolonial literatures (PhD); creative writing (MFA); cultural studies (PhD); dramatic literature (PhD); English poetry (PhD); English Renaissance to 1660 (PhD); lesbian, bisexual, and gay literary studies (PhD); literary criticism and theory (PhD); Old and Middle English (PhD); prose fiction (PhD); Restoration and the eighteenth-century (PhD); the nineteenth century (PhD); the twentieth century (PhD); women's literature (PhD); MFA/PhD. Terminal master's awarded for partial completion of doctoral program. *Degree requirements:* For master's, one foreign language, thesis; for doctorate, one foreign language, comprehensive exam, thesis/dissertation, teaching experience. *Entrance requirements:* For master's, GRE General Test, 3 letters of recommendation, creative writing sample; for doctorate, GRE General Test, GRE Subject Test (English), 3 letters of recommendation, writing sample. Additional exam requirements/recommendations for international students: Required—TOEFL (minimum score 600 paper-based; 77 iBT). Electronic applications accepted. *Faculty research:* English and American literature, women's writing, ethnic and post-colonial literature, critical theory, medievalism.

**Eastern Michigan University,** Graduate School, College of Arts and Sciences, Department of Africology and African-American Studies, Ypsilanti, MI 48197. Offers Graduate Certificate. *Faculty:* 3 full-time (2 women). *Students:* 1 full-time (0 women), 1 (woman) part-time; both minorities (both Black or African American, non-Hispanic/Latino). Average age 56. 4 applicants, 50% accepted, 2 enrolled. In 2016, 1 Graduate Certificate awarded. *Entrance requirements:* For degree, bachelor's degree with minimum GPA of 2.7, two letters of reference. *Application deadline:* Applications are processed on a rolling basis. Application fee: $45. *Unit head:* Dr. Victor Okafor, Department Head, 734-487-3460, Fax: 734-487-6891, E-mail: victor.okafor@emich.edu. Website: http://www.emich.edu/aas/

**Georgia State University,** College of Arts and Sciences, Department of African-American Studies, Atlanta, GA 30302-3083. Offers MA. *Program availability:* Part-time. *Faculty:* 7 full-time (4 women). *Students:* 26 full-time (17 women), 6 part-time (5 women); includes 29 minority (27 Black or African American, non-Hispanic/Latino; 2 Two or more races, non-Hispanic/Latino), 1 international. Average age 29. 31 applicants, 68% accepted, 18 enrolled. In 2016, 7 master's awarded. *Degree requirements:* For master's, thesis. *Entrance requirements:* For master's, GRE. Additional exam requirements/recommendations for international students: Required—TOEFL (minimum score 550 paper-based; 80 iBT). *Application deadline:* For fall admission, 4/15 for domestic and international students. Application fee: $50. Electronic applications accepted. *Expenses:* Tuition, state resident: full-time $6876; part-time $382 per credit hour. Tuition, nonresident: full-time $22,374; part-time $1243 per credit hour. *Required fees:* $2128; $1064 per term. Part-time tuition and fees vary according to course load and program. *Financial support:* In 2016–17, research assistantships with tuition reimbursements (averaging $4,200 per year), teaching assistantships with tuition reimbursements (averaging $4,000 per year) were awarded; health care benefits and unspecified assistantships also available. Financial award applicants required to submit FAFSA. *Faculty research:* HIV prevention education and culturally relevant praxis; African-American women's activism and social movements; narrative therapy and family counseling; African women's history; African-American social movements, civil rights, and Black power movements. *Unit head:* Dr. Akinyele Umoja, Chair, Department of African-American Studies, 404-413-5137, Fax: 404-413-5140, E-mail: aadaku@gsu.edu. *Application contact:* Dr. Sarita Kaya Davis, Graduate Program Director, 404-413-5134, Fax: 404-413-5140, E-mail: saritadavis@gsu.edu. Website: http://www2.gsu.edu/~wwwaad/

**Harvard University,** Graduate School of Arts and Sciences, Department of African and African American Studies, Cambridge, MA 02138. Offers PhD.

**Indiana University Bloomington,** University Graduate School, College of Arts and Sciences, Department of African American and African Diaspora Studies, Bloomington, IN 47405-7000. Offers MA, PhD. *Faculty:* 4 full-time (3 women). *Students:* 15 full-time (11 women), 1 (woman) part-time; includes 13 minority (all Black or African American, non-Hispanic/Latino), 1 international. Average age 29. 17 applicants, 29% accepted, 2 enrolled. In 2016, 1 master's, 1 doctorate awarded. *Entrance requirements:* For master's and doctorate, GRE, minimum GPA of 3.0. Additional exam requirements/recommendations for international students: Required—TOEFL. *Application deadline:* For fall admission, 1/15 priority date for domestic students, 12/15 for international students; for spring admission, 9/1 for domestic and international students. Application fee: $55 ($65 for international students). Electronic applications accepted. *Expenses:* $15,750. *Financial support:* In 2016–17, 1 fellowship with full tuition reimbursement (averaging $18,000 per year), 1 research assistantship with full tuition reimbursement (averaging $15,750 per year), 2 teaching assistantships with full tuition reimbursements (averaging $15,750 per year) were awarded; scholarships/grants, health care benefits, and unspecified assistantships also available. *Unit head:* Dr. Carolyn Calloway-Thomas, Chair, 812-855-0524, E-mail: calloway@indiana.edu. *Application contact:* Dr. Valerie Grim, Director of Graduate Studies, 812-855-4726, E-mail: vgrim@indiana.edu. Website: http://www.indiana.edu/~afroamer/

**Michigan State University,** The Graduate School, College of Arts and Letters, Program in African American and African Studies, East Lansing, MI 48824. Offers MA, PhD. *Entrance requirements:* Additional exam requirements/recommendations for international students: Required—TOEFL. Electronic applications accepted. *Faculty research:* Black American and diasporic studies, comparative communities of color.

**Morgan State University,** School of Graduate Studies, College of Liberal Arts, Department of History and Geography, Baltimore, MD 21251. Offers African-American studies (MA); history (MA, PhD); museum studies and historic preservation (MA). *Program availability:* Part-time, evening/weekend. *Degree requirements:* For master's, comprehensive exam, thesis; for doctorate, comprehensive exam, thesis/dissertation. *Entrance requirements:* For master's, minimum GPA of 2.5; for doctorate, GRE or MAT.

Additional exam requirements/recommendations for international students: Required—TOEFL (minimum score 550 paper-based). *Faculty research:* Women's history, African diaspora history, urban history.

**North Carolina Agricultural and Technical State University,** School of Graduate Studies, College of Arts and Sciences, Department of English, Program in English and African-American Literature, Greensboro, NC 27411. Offers MA. *Program availability:* Part-time, evening/weekend. *Degree requirements:* For master's, comprehensive exam, qualifying exam. *Entrance requirements:* For master's, GRE General Test, minimum GPA of 3.0.

**Northwestern University,** The Graduate School, Judd A. and Marjorie Weinberg College of Arts and Sciences, Department of African American Studies, Evanston, IL 60208. Offers PhD.

**Oblate School of Theology,** Graduate and Professional Programs, San Antonio, TX 78216-6693. Offers African-American pastoral leadership (D Min); divinity (M Div); pastoral leadership (D Min); pastoral ministry (MAP Min); pastoral studies (Certificate); spiritual formation in the local community (D Min); spirituality (MA Sp, PhD); spirituality and ministry (D Min); theology (MA Th); U.S. Hispanic/Latino ministry (D Min); M Div/MA Th. *Accreditation:* ACIPE; ATS (one or more programs are accredited). *Program availability:* Part-time, online learning. *Faculty:* 24 full-time (8 women), 4 part-time/adjunct (0 women). *Students:* 76 full-time (10 women), 51 part-time (32 women); includes 56 minority (8 Black or African American, non-Hispanic/Latino; 9 Asian, non-Hispanic/Latino; 39 Hispanic/Latino), 41 international. Average age 40. In 2016, 31 master's, 3 doctorates awarded. *Degree requirements:* For master's, comprehensive exam (for some programs), thesis (for some programs), practicum; for doctorate, one foreign language, comprehensive exam, thesis/dissertation, paper, practicum. *Entrance requirements:* For master's, MAT, interview, course work in theology or religious studies, minimum GPA of 2.5; for doctorate, M Div, MA Th, or MA Sp. Additional exam requirements/recommendations for international students: Required—TOEFL (minimum score 71 iBT). *Application deadline:* For fall admission, 6/15 priority date for domestic and international students; for winter admission, 11/30 for domestic and international students; for spring admission, 11/30 for domestic and international students; for summer admission, 4/1 for domestic and international students. Applications are processed on a rolling basis. Application fee: $65. *Expenses:* Contact institution. *Financial support:* In 2016–17, 25 students received support. Scholarships/grants available. Support available to part-time students. Financial award application deadline: 8/1; financial award applicants required to submit FAFSA. *Unit head:* Dr. R. Scott Woodward, Academic Dean, 210-341-1366, Fax: 210-341-4519, E-mail: rsw@ost.edu. *Application contact:* Mario A. Porter, Registrar, 210-341-1366 Ext. 226, Fax: 210-341-4519, E-mail: registrar@ost.edu.

**The Ohio State University,** Graduate School, College of Arts and Sciences, Division of Arts and Humanities, Department of African-American and African Studies, Columbus, OH 43210. Offers MA, PhD. *Faculty:* 13. *Students:* 10 full-time (6 women), 1 (woman) part-time. Average age 28. In 2016, 4 master's awarded. *Degree requirements:* For master's, comprehensive exam (for some programs), thesis (for some programs), thesis or comprehensive written examination; for doctorate, thesis/dissertation. *Entrance requirements:* For master's and doctorate, GRE General Test. Additional exam requirements/recommendations for international students: Required—TOEFL (minimum score 550 paper-based, 79 iBT), Michigan English Language Assessment Battery (minimum score 82); Recommended—IELTS (minimum score 7). *Application deadline:* For fall admission, 12/1 priority date for domestic students, 11/30 priority date for international students; for spring admission, 3/1 for domestic students, 2/1 for international students. Applications are processed on a rolling basis. Application fee: $60 ($70 for international students). Electronic applications accepted. *Financial support:* Fellowships with tuition reimbursements, research assistantships with tuition reimbursements, teaching assistantships with tuition reimbursements, Federal Work-Study, institutionally sponsored loans, and unspecified assistantships available. Support available to part-time students. *Unit head:* Valerie Lee, Acting Chair, 614-292-0116, E-mail: lee.89@osu.edu. *Application contact:* Graduate and Professional Admissions, 614-292-9444, Fax: 614-292-3895, E-mail: gpadmissions@osu.edu. Website: http://aaas.osu.edu/

**Rutgers University–New Brunswick,** Graduate School-New Brunswick, Program in History, Piscataway, NJ 08854-8097. Offers African-American history (PhD); early American history (PhD); early modern European history (PhD); east Asian history (PhD); global and comparative history (PhD); history (PhD); history of diplomacy and foreign relations (PhD); history of technology, environment and health (PhD); history of the Atlantic cultures and African diaspora (PhD); Latin American history (PhD); medieval history (PhD); modern European history (PhD); nineteenth and twentieth century American history (PhD); women's and gender history (PhD). *Degree requirements:* For doctorate, thesis/dissertation. *Entrance requirements:* For doctorate, GRE General Test, sample of written work. Electronic applications accepted. *Faculty research:* American history, European history, Afro-American history, women's history, Latin American history.

**Syracuse University,** College of Arts and Sciences, MA Program in Pan-African Studies, Syracuse, NY 13244. Offers MA. *Students:* Average age 30. *Degree requirements:* For master's, thesis. *Entrance requirements:* For master's, GRE General Test (recommended), personal statement, resume, three letters of recommendation, writing sample (10-12 pages), transcripts. Additional exam requirements/recommendations for international students: Required—TOEFL (minimum score 100 iBT). *Application deadline:* For fall admission, 1/10 priority date for domestic and international students. Application fee: $75. Electronic applications accepted. *Expenses:* Tuition: Full-time $25,974; part-time $1443 per credit hour. *Required fees:* $802; $54 per course. Tuition and fees vary according to course load and program. *Financial support:* Fellowships with tuition reimbursements, teaching assistantships with tuition reimbursements, and scholarships/grants available. Financial award application deadline: 1/1. *Faculty research:* African American studies, African American history, Francophone African/Caribbean literatures, African archaeology. *Unit head:* Dr. Joan Bryant, Chair, 315-443-4399, E-mail: jobryant@syr.edu. *Application contact:* Ajajielle Brown, Administrative Assistant, 315-443-5599, E-mail: aabrow02@syr.edu. Website: http://aas.syr.edu/graduate/index.html

**Temple University,** College of Liberal Arts, Department of African American Studies, Philadelphia, PA 19122-6096. Offers MA, PhD. Terminal master's awarded for partial completion of doctoral program. *Degree requirements:* For master's, comprehensive exam; for doctorate, one foreign language, thesis/dissertation, oral and written qualifying exams. *Entrance requirements:* For master's, GRE, 3 letters of recommendation; minimum GPA of 3.0; for doctorate, GRE, MA in African American studies; 3 letters of recommendation; minimum GPA of 3.0. Additional exam requirements/recommendations for international students: Required—TOEFL (minimum score 550 paper-based, 79 iBT). Electronic applications accepted. *Faculty research:* African history and civilization, contemporary political and cultural developments, identity, African diaspora history and culture.

**Trinity Lutheran Seminary,** Graduate and Professional Programs, Columbus, OH 43209-2334. Offers African American studies (MTS); Biblical studies (MTS, STM);

Christian education (MA); Christian spirituality (STM); church in the world (MTS); church music (MA); divinity (M Div); general theological studies (MTS); mission and evangelism (STM); pastoral leadership and practice (STM); youth and family ministry (MA); MSN/MTS; MTS/JD. *Accreditation:* ACIPE; ATS. *Program availability:* Part-time. *Degree requirements:* For master's, variable foreign language requirement, comprehensive exam (for some programs), thesis (for some programs), field experience (for some programs). *Entrance requirements:* For master's, BA or equivalent (for MA, M Div, MTS); M Div, MTS, or equivalent (for STM); audition (for MACM). Additional exam requirements/recommendations for international students: Required—TOEFL. Electronic applications accepted. *Expenses:* Contact institution.

**University at Albany, State University of New York,** College of Arts and Sciences, Department of Africana Studies, Albany, NY 12222-0001. Offers African studies (MA); Afro-American studies (MA). *Program availability:* Part-time, evening/weekend. *Faculty:* 4 full-time (2 women), 1 part-time/adjunct (0 women). *Students:* 9 full-time (7 women), 4 part-time (3 women); all minorities (10 Black or African American, non-Hispanic/Latino; 1 Hispanic/Latino; 2 Two or more races, non-Hispanic/Latino). Average age 29. 13 applicants, 92% accepted, 8 enrolled. In 2016, 5 master's awarded. *Entrance requirements:* Additional exam requirements/recommendations for international students: Required—TOEFL (minimum score 550 paper-based). *Application deadline:* For fall admission, 5/15 for international students; for spring admission, 11/1 for international students. Applications are processed on a rolling basis. Application fee: $75. Electronic applications accepted. *Expenses:* Tuition, state resident: full-time $10,870; part-time $453 per credit hour. Tuition, nonresident: full-time $22,210; part-time $925 per credit hour. *International tuition:* $21,550 full-time. *Required fees:* $1864; $96 per credit hour. *Financial support:* Fellowships, teaching assistantships, and Federal Work-Study available. Financial award application deadline: 5/1. *Faculty research:* The black family, Afro-centricity in poetry, black women in U.S. literature, African economic development, African American history. *Unit head:* Oscar Williams, Chair, 518-442-4730, Fax: 518-442-2569, E-mail: owilliams@albany.edu. *Application contact:* Michael DeRensis, Director, Graduate Admissions, 518-442-3980, Fax: 518-442-3922, E-mail: graduate@albany.edu. Website: http://www.albany.edu/africana/

**University of California, Berkeley,** Graduate Division, College of Letters and Science, Department of African American Studies, Berkeley, CA 94720-1500. Offers PhD. *Faculty:* 4 full-time. *Students:* 26 full-time (17 women); includes 22 minority (21 Black or African American, non-Hispanic/Latino; 1 Asian, non-Hispanic/Latino), 1 international. Average age 30. 97 applicants, 2 enrolled. In 2016, 3 doctorates awarded. *Degree requirements:* For doctorate, one foreign language, thesis/dissertation. *Entrance requirements:* For doctorate, minimum GPA of 3.0, 3 letters of recommendation. Additional exam requirements/recommendations for international students: Required—TOEFL (minimum score 570 paper-based, 90 iBT) or IELTS (minimum score 7). *Application deadline:* For fall admission, 12/15 for domestic students. Application fee: $105 ($125 for international students). Electronic applications accepted. *Financial support:* Fellowships with full tuition reimbursements, research assistantships with partial tuition reimbursements, teaching assistantships with partial tuition reimbursements, health care benefits, and unspecified assistantships available. Financial award applicants required to submit FAFSA. *Faculty research:* Black influence on U. S. foreign policy, black intellectuals, ethnic space in urban society, representation in museums of African-Americans and British Americans during slavery. *Unit head:* E-mail: afamchair@berkeley.edu. *Application contact:* Lindsey Herbert, Graduate Advisor, 510-642-3419, E-mail: africam@berkeley.edu. Website: http://africam.berkeley.edu/

**University of California, Los Angeles,** Graduate Division, College of Letters and Science, Interdepartmental Program in Afro-American Studies, Los Angeles, CA 90095. Offers MA, MA/JD. *Degree requirements:* For master's, one foreign language, comprehensive exam or thesis. *Entrance requirements:* For master's, GRE General Test, bachelor's degree; minimum undergraduate GPA of 3.0 (or its equivalent if letter grade system not used); writing sample. Additional exam requirements/recommendations for international students: Required—TOEFL. Electronic applications accepted.

**University of California, Santa Barbara,** Graduate Division, College of Letters and Sciences, Division of Social Sciences, Department of Sociology, Santa Barbara, CA 93106-9430. Offers interdisciplinary emphasis: Black studies (PhD); interdisciplinary emphasis: environment and society (PhD); interdisciplinary emphasis: feminist studies (PhD); interdisciplinary emphasis: global studies (PhD); interdisciplinary emphasis: language, interaction and social organization (PhD); interdisciplinary emphasis: quantitative methods in the social sciences (PhD); interdisciplinary emphasis: technology and society (PhD); sociology (PhD); MA/PhD. Terminal master's awarded for partial completion of doctoral program. *Degree requirements:* For doctorate, comprehensive exam, thesis/dissertation. *Entrance requirements:* For doctorate, GRE General Test. Additional exam requirements/recommendations for international students: Required—TOEFL (minimum score 550 paper-based; 80 iBT), IELTS (minimum score 7). Electronic applications accepted. *Faculty research:* Gender and sexualities, race/ethnicity, social movements, conversation analysis, global sociology.

**The University of Kansas,** Graduate Studies, College of Liberal Arts and Sciences, Department of African and African-American Studies, Lawrence, KS 66045. Offers African and African-American studies (MA); African studies (Graduate Certificate). *Program availability:* Part-time. *Students:* 10 full-time (6 women); includes 5 minority (3 Black or African American, non-Hispanic/Latino; 2 Two or more races, non-Hispanic/Latino). Average age 28. 5 applicants, 80% accepted, 4 enrolled. In 2016, 1 master's awarded. *Entrance requirements:* For master's, GRE, all academic transcripts, 3 letters of recommendation, personal statement of purpose, writing sample. Additional exam requirements/recommendations for international students: Required—TOEFL, IELTS. *Application deadline:* For fall admission, 5/1 for domestic and international students; for spring admission, 10/1 for domestic and international students. Application fee: $65 ($85 for international students). Electronic applications accepted. *Financial support:* Application deadline: 4/15. *Faculty research:* African theatre, YaKuur culture, interracial communication, African development and urban planning, African literature, Muslim women in West Africa, identity formation in African and Diasporan settings, African-American history, North African and Arab societies, civil rights, black urban communities. *Unit head:* Dr. Lang Clarence, Chairperson, 785-864-3054, E-mail: celang@ku.edu. *Application contact:* Shawn Alexander, Director of Graduate Studies, 785-864-3054, E-mail: slalexan@ku.edu. Website: http://www.afs.ku.edu

**University of Louisville,** Graduate School, College of Arts and Sciences, Department of Pan-African Studies, Louisville, KY 40292. Offers African and Diaspora studies (MA); African-American studies (MA); MSSW/MA. *Program availability:* Part-time. *Faculty:* 10 full-time (5 women), 3 part-time/adjunct (2 women). *Students:* 15 full-time (10 women), 8 part-time (5 women); all minorities (21 Black or African American, non-Hispanic/Latino; 2 Two or more races, non-Hispanic/Latino). Average age 32. 18 applicants, 83% accepted, 9 enrolled. In 2016, 2 master's awarded. *Degree requirements:* For master's, comprehensive exam, thesis optional. *Entrance requirements:* For master's, GRE General Test. Additional exam requirements/recommendations for international

*African-American Studies*

students: Required—TOEFL (minimum score 550 paper-based; 79 iBT). *Application deadline:* For fall admission, 3/15 for domestic students, 5/1 priority date for international students; for spring admission, 10/15 for domestic students, 11/1 priority date for international students; for summer admission, 4/1 priority date for international students. Applications are processed on a rolling basis. Application fee: $60. Electronic applications accepted. *Expenses:* Tuition, state resident: full-time $12,246; part-time $681 per credit hour. Tuition, nonresident: full-time $25,486; part-time $1417 per credit hour. *Required fees:* $196. Tuition and fees vary according to program and reciprocity agreements. *Financial support:* Teaching assistantships available. Financial award application deadline: 3/3; financial award applicants required to submit FAFSA. *Faculty research:* African popular culture, black male identity development, education and retention, contemporary politics in Nigeria, poverty in the Caribbean. *Total annual research expenditures:* $72,938. *Unit head:* Dr. Ricky L. Jones, Chair, 502-852-0027, E-mail: ricky.jones@louisville.edu. *Application contact:* Libby Leggett, Director, Graduate Admissions, 502-852-3101, E-mail: gradadm@louisville.edu.
Website: http://www.louisville.edu/panafricanstudies

**University of Massachusetts Amherst,** Graduate School, College of Humanities and Fine Arts, Department of Afro-American Studies, Amherst, MA 01003. Offers MA, PhD. *Program availability:* Part-time. Terminal master's awarded for partial completion of doctoral program. *Degree requirements:* For master's, thesis or alternative; for doctorate, comprehensive exam, thesis/dissertation. *Entrance requirements:* For master's and doctorate, writing sample, 3 letters of recommendation. Additional exam requirements/recommendations for international students: Required—TOEFL (minimum score 550 paper-based; 80 iBT), IELTS (minimum score 6.5). Electronic applications accepted.

**University of Memphis,** Graduate School, College of Arts and Sciences, Department of English, Memphis, TN 38152. Offers African-American literature (Graduate Certificate); applied linguistics (PhD); composition studies (PhD); creative writing (MFA); English as a second language (MA); linguistics (MA); literary and cultural studies (PhD), including African-American literature; literature (MA); professional writing (MA, PhD); teaching English as a second/foreign language (Graduate Certificate). *Program availability:* Part-time, evening/weekend, 100% online. *Faculty:* 31 full-time (14 women), 1 (woman) part-time/adjunct. *Students:* 86 full-time (44 women), 78 part-time (51 women); includes 36 minority (19 Black or African American, non-Hispanic/Latino; 3 Asian, non-Hispanic/Latino; 10 Hispanic/Latino; 4 Two or more races, non-Hispanic/Latino), 32 international. Average age 35. 68 applicants, 87% accepted, 33 enrolled. In 2016, 39 master's, 17 doctorates, 16 other advanced degrees awarded. Terminal master's awarded for partial completion of doctoral program. *Degree requirements:* For master's, one foreign language, comprehensive exam, thesis optional; for doctorate, 2 foreign languages, comprehensive exam, thesis/dissertation, qualifying exam. *Entrance requirements:* For master's, GRE, minimum undergraduate GPA of 3.0, statement of purpose, two letters of recommendation; for doctorate, GRE, minimum undergraduate and graduate GPA of 3.25, statement of purpose, writing sample, three letters of recommendation. Additional exam requirements/recommendations for international students: Required—TOEFL. *Application deadline:* For fall admission, 1/15 for domestic students; for spring admission, 10/15 for domestic students. Applications are processed on a rolling basis. Application fee: $35 ($60 for international students). Electronic applications accepted. *Expenses:* $5,231.50 per semester full-time in-state, $9,623.50 full-time out-of-state. *Financial support:* In 2016–17, 123 students received support, including 11 research assistantships with full tuition reimbursements available (averaging $17,064 per year), 25 teaching assistantships with full tuition reimbursements available (averaging $17,340 per year); Federal Work-Study, scholarships/grants, and unspecified assistantships also available. Financial award application deadline: 2/1; financial award applicants required to submit FAFSA. *Faculty research:* Applied linguistics, British and American literature, professional writing, composition studies. *Unit head:* Dr. Joshua Phillips, Chair, 901-678-2651, Fax: 901-678-2226, E-mail: jsphllps@memphis.edu. *Application contact:* Dr. Jeffrey Scraba, Coordinator of Graduate Studies, 901-678-4768, Fax: 901-678-2226, E-mail: jscraba@memphis.edu.
Website: http://www.memphis.edu/english

**University of Wisconsin–Madison,** Graduate School, College of Letters and Science, Department of Afro-American Studies, Madison, WI 53706-1380. Offers MA. *Degree requirements:* For master's, thesis or alternative. *Entrance requirements:* For master's, bachelor's degree in related field, minimum GPA of 3.0. Additional exam requirements/recommendations for international students: Required—TOEFL. Electronic applications accepted. *Faculty research:* Afro American art, history, music, literature, and culture.

**West Virginia University,** Eberly College of Arts and Sciences, Department of History, Morgantown, WV 26506. Offers African history (MA, PhD); African-American history (MA, PhD); American history (MA, PhD); Appalachian/regional history (MA, PhD); East Asian history (MA, PhD); European history (MA, PhD); history of science and technology (MA, PhD); Latin American history (MA). *Program availability:* Part-time. *Degree requirements:* For master's, one foreign language, thesis (for some programs), oral exam, thesis defense; for doctorate, one foreign language, comprehensive exam, thesis/dissertation, dissertation defense. *Entrance requirements:* For master's, GRE General Test, minimum GPA of 3.0; for doctorate, GRE General Test. Additional exam requirements/recommendations for international students: Required—TOEFL (minimum score 550 paper-based), IELTS (minimum score 6.5). Electronic applications accepted. *Faculty research:* United States, Appalachia, modern Europe, Africa, colonial and post-colonial societies.

**Yale University,** Graduate School of Arts and Sciences, Interdisciplinary Program in African-American Studies, New Haven, CT 06520. Offers PhD. *Entrance requirements:* For doctorate, GRE General Test.

# African Studies

**Arizona State University at the Tempe campus,** College of Liberal Arts and Sciences, School of Social Transformation, Tempe, AZ 85287-4902. Offers African studies (Graduate Certificate); gender studies (PhD, Graduate Certificate); justice studies (MS, PhD); social and cultural pedagogy (MA); socio-economic justice (Graduate Certificate); PhD/JD. *Program availability:* Part-time. Terminal master's awarded for partial completion of doctoral program. *Degree requirements:* For master's, thesis or alternative, interactive Program of Study (iPOS) submitted before completing 50 percent of required credit hours; for doctorate, comprehensive exam, thesis/dissertation, interactive Program of Study (iPOS) submitted before completing 50 percent of required credit hours. *Entrance requirements:* For master's, GRE or LSAT, minimum GPA of 3.0 or equivalent in last 2 years of work leading to bachelor's degree; for doctorate, GRE or LSAT (for justice studies program), minimum GPA of 3.0 or equivalent in last 2 years of work leading to bachelor's degree. Additional exam requirements/recommendations for international students: Required—TOEFL, IELTS, or PTE. Electronic applications accepted.

**California State University, Long Beach,** Graduate Studies, College of Liberal Arts, Department of History, Long Beach, CA 90840. Offers Africa and the Middle East (MA). *Program availability:* Part-time, evening/weekend. *Degree requirements:* For master's, one foreign language, comprehensive exam or thesis. *Application deadline:* For fall admission, 3/1 for domestic students. Applications are processed on a rolling basis. Application fee: $55. Electronic applications accepted. *Financial support:* Research assistantships, Federal Work-Study, institutionally sponsored loans, and scholarships/grants available. Financial award application deadline: 3/2. *Faculty research:* All periods of European and American history, recent Asian and African history. *Unit head:* David A. Shefer, Chair, 562-985-4431, Fax: 562-985-5431. *Application contact:* Dr. Houri Berberian, Graduate Advisor, 562-985-4524, Fax: 562-985-4431, E-mail: hberber@csulb.edu.
Website: http://www.csulb.edu/colleges/cla/departments/history/

**Carnegie Mellon University,** Dietrich College of Humanities and Social Sciences, Department of History, Pittsburgh, PA 15213-3891. Offers African and African-American diaspora (PhD); culture and power (PhD); labor, politics and social movements (PhD); technology, environment, science and health (PhD); women, gender and the family (PhD). *Program availability:* Part-time. *Degree requirements:* For doctorate, oral and written comprehensive exams, dissertation defense. *Entrance requirements:* For doctorate, GRE General Test. Additional exam requirements/recommendations for international students: Required—TOEFL. Electronic applications accepted. *Faculty research:* Anthropology and history, African-American history, technology/environment, cultural history analysis.

**Claremont Graduate University,** Graduate Programs, School of Arts and Humanities, Department of History, Claremont, CA 91711-6160. Offers Africana history (Certificate); American studies and U.S. history (MA, PhD); archival studies (MA); early modern studies (MA, PhD); European studies (MA, PhD); oral history (MA, PhD); MBA/MA; MBA/PhD. *Faculty:* 5 full-time (3 women), 2 part-time/adjunct (0 women). *Students:* 45 full-time (23 women), 24 part-time (14 women); includes 21 minority (2 Black or African American, non-Hispanic/Latino; 1 American Indian or Alaska Native, non-Hispanic/Latino; 5 Asian, non-Hispanic/Latino; 6 Hispanic/Latino; 1 Native Hawaiian or other Pacific Islander, non-Hispanic/Latino; 6 Two or more races, non-Hispanic/Latino). Average age 38. In 2016, 5 master's, 2 doctorates awarded. Terminal master's awarded for partial completion of doctoral program. *Entrance requirements:* For master's and doctorate, GRE General Test. Additional exam requirements/recommendations for international students: Required—TOEFL (minimum score 75 iBT). *Application deadline:* For fall admission, 2/1 priority date for domestic and international students. Applications are processed on a rolling basis. Application fee: $80. Electronic applications accepted. *Expenses: Tuition:* Full-time $44,328; part-time $1847 per unit. *Required fees:* $600; $300 per semester. Tuition and fees vary according to course load and program. *Financial support:* Fellowships, research assistantships, Federal Work-Study, institutionally sponsored loans, and scholarships/grants available. Support available to part-time students. Financial award application deadline: 2/15; financial award applicants required to submit FAFSA. *Faculty research:* Intellectual and social history, cultural studies, gender studies, Western history, Chicano history. *Unit head:* Joshua Goode, Chair, 909-607-7430, E-mail: joshua.goode@cgu.edu. *Application contact:* Amy Sandefur, Assistant Director of Admissions, 909-607-9101, E-mail: amy.sandefur@cgu.edu.
Website: https://www.cgu.edu/departments/history/

**Claremont Graduate University,** Graduate Programs, School of Educational Studies, Claremont, CA 91711-6160. Offers Africana education (Certificate); education and policy (MA, PhD); higher education/student affairs (MA, PhD); human development (MA, PhD); public school administration (MA, PhD); quantitative evaluation (MA, PhD); special education (MA, PhD); teacher education (MA); teaching and learning (MA, PhD); urban leadership (PhD); MBA/PhD. PhD program offered jointly with San Diego State University. *Program availability:* Part-time. *Faculty:* 14 full-time (9 women), 1 part-time/adjunct (0 women). *Students:* 195 full-time (143 women), 196 part-time (137 women); includes 217 minority (43 Black or African American, non-Hispanic/Latino; 4 American Indian or Alaska Native, non-Hispanic/Latino; 32 Asian, non-Hispanic/Latino; 117 Hispanic/Latino; 2 Native Hawaiian or other Pacific Islander, non-Hispanic/Latino; 19 Two or more races, non-Hispanic/Latino), 14 international. Average age 38. In 2016, 48 master's, 39 doctorates, 7 other advanced degrees awarded. Terminal master's awarded for partial completion of doctoral program. *Entrance requirements:* For master's and doctorate, GRE General Test. Additional exam requirements/recommendations for international students: Required—TOEFL (minimum score 75 iBT). *Application deadline:* For fall admission, 3/1 priority date for domestic and international students. Applications are processed on a rolling basis. Application fee: $80. Electronic applications accepted. *Expenses: Tuition:* Full-time $44,328; part-time $1847 per unit. *Required fees:* $600; $300 per semester. Tuition and fees vary according to course load and program. *Financial support:* Fellowships, research assistantships, Federal Work-Study, institutionally sponsored loans, and scholarships/grants available. Support available to part-time students. Financial award application deadline: 2/15; financial award applicants required to submit FAFSA. *Faculty research:* Education administration, K-12 and higher education, multicultural education, education policy, diversity in higher education, faculty issues. *Unit head:* Allen Omoto, Dean, 909-607-3786, E-mail: allen.omoto@cgu.edu. *Application contact:* Rachel Camacho, Senior Assistant Director of Admission, 909-607-9418, E-mail: camacho@cgu.edu.
Website: https://www.cgu.edu/school/school-of-educational-studies/

**College of Staten Island of the City University of New York,** Graduate Programs, Division of Humanities and Social Sciences, Program in History, Staten Island, NY 10314-6600. Offers history of Africa and the Middle East (MA); history of Asia (MA); history of Europe (MA); history of Latin America and the Caribbean (MA); history of the United States (MA). *Program availability:* Part-time, evening/weekend. *Faculty:* 2 full-time. *Students:* 11 part-time. Average age 36. 8 applicants, 25% accepted, 2 enrolled. In 2016, 5 master's awarded. *Degree requirements:* For master's, comprehensive exam (for some programs), 32 credits (total of eight courses); thesis or portfolio. *Entrance requirements:* For master's, bachelor's degree with minimum GPA of 3.0 overall and in undergraduate history courses, two letters of recommendation, letter of interest, research-based writing sample. Additional exam requirements/recommendations for

international students: Required—TOEFL (minimum score 550 paper-based; 79 iBT), IELTS (minimum score 6.5). *Application deadline:* For fall admission, 5/10 priority date for domestic and international students; for spring admission, 12/2 priority date for domestic and international students. Applications are processed on a rolling basis. Application fee: $125. Electronic applications accepted. *Expenses:* Tuition, state resident: full-time $10,130; part-time $425 per credit. Tuition, nonresident: full-time $18,720; part-time $780 per credit. *Required fees:* $181.10 per semester. Tuition and fees vary according to program. *Faculty research:* African and African diaspora history, South Asian history, Middle Eastern history, U.S. history, environmental history. *Unit head:* John Dixon, Graduate Program Coordinator, 718-982-3307, E-mail: john.dixon@csi.cuny.edu. *Application contact:* Sasha Spence, Associate Director for Graduate Admissions, 718-982-2019, Fax: 718-982-2500, E-mail: sasha.spence@csi.cuny.edu.
Website: http://www.csi.cuny.edu/catalog/graduate/master-of-arts-in-history-ma.htm

**Columbia University,** Graduate School of Arts and Sciences, New York, NY 10027. Offers African-American studies (MA); American studies (MA); anthropology (MA, PhD); art history and archaeology (MA, PhD); astronomy (PhD); biological sciences (PhD); biotechnology (MA); chemical physics (PhD); chemistry (PhD); classical studies (MA, PhD); classics (MA, PhD); climate and society (MA); conservation biology (MA); earth and environmental sciences (PhD); East Asia: regional studies (MA); East Asian languages and cultures (MA, PhD); ecology, evolution and environmental biology (MA), including conservation biology; ecology, evolution, and environmental biology (PhD), including ecology and evolutionary biology, evolutionary primatology; economics (MA, PhD); English and comparative literature (MA, PhD); French and Romance philology (MA, PhD); Germanic languages (MA, PhD); global French studies (MA); global thought (MA); Hispanic cultural studies (MA); history (PhD); history and literature (MA); human rights studies (MA); Islamic studies (MA); Italian (MA, PhD); Japanese pedagogy (MA); Jewish studies (MA); Latin America and the Caribbean: regional studies (MA); Latin American and Iberian cultures (PhD); mathematics (MA, PhD), including finance (MA); medieval and Renaissance studies (MA); Middle Eastern, South Asian, and African studies (MA, PhD); modern art: critical and curatorial studies (MA); modern European studies (MA); museum anthropology (MA); music (DMA, PhD); oral history (MA); philosophical foundations of physics (MA); philosophy (MA, PhD); physics (PhD); political science (MA, PhD); psychology (PhD); quantitative methods in the social sciences (MA); religion (MA, PhD); Russia, Eurasia and East Europe: regional studies (MA); Russian translation (MA); Slavic cultures (MA); Slavic languages (MA, PhD); sociology (MA, PhD); South Asian studies (MA); statistics (MA, PhD); theatre (PhD). Dual-degree programs require admission to both Graduate School of Arts and Sciences and another Columbia school. *Program availability:* Part-time. Terminal master's awarded for partial completion of doctoral program. *Degree requirements:* For master's, variable foreign language requirement, comprehensive exam (for some programs), thesis (for some programs); for doctorate, variable foreign language requirement, comprehensive exam (for some programs), thesis/dissertation. *Entrance requirements:* For master's and doctorate, GRE General Test, GRE Subject Test (for some programs). Additional exam requirements/recommendations for international students: Required—TOEFL, IELTS. Electronic applications accepted.

**Cornell University,** Graduate School, Graduate Fields of Arts and Sciences, Field of African and African-American Studies, Ithaca, NY 14853. Offers African studies (MPS); African-American studies (MPS); Africana studies (PhD). *Degree requirements:* For master's, thesis. *Entrance requirements:* For master's, GRE General Test (recommended), 3 letters of recommendation; for doctorate, GRE General Test (recommended), 3 letters of recommendation, personal statement, writing sample. Additional exam requirements/recommendations for international students: Required—TOEFL (minimum score 550 paper-based; 77 iBT). Electronic applications accepted. *Faculty research:* African-American literature, art, cinema and theater; African-American politics and public policy; African history, politics and art; Caribbean politics and Africana diaspora.

**Cornell University,** Graduate School, Graduate Fields of Arts and Sciences, Field of History, Ithaca, NY 14853. Offers African history (MA, PhD); American history (MA, PhD); ancient Greek history (PhD); ancient history (MA, PhD); ancient Roman history (PhD); early modern European history (MA, PhD); English history (MA, PhD); French history (MA, PhD); German history (MA, PhD); history of science (MA, PhD); Korean history (PhD); Latin American history (MA, PhD); medieval Chinese history (MA, PhD); medieval history (MA, PhD); modern Chinese history (MA, PhD); modern European history (MA, PhD); modern Japanese history (MA, PhD); modern Middle Eastern history (PhD); premodern Islamic history (MA, PhD); premodern Japanese history (MA, PhD); Renaissance history (MA, PhD); Russian history (MA, PhD); South Asian history (PhD); Southeast Asian history (MA, PhD). Terminal master's awarded for partial completion of doctoral program. *Degree requirements:* For master's, thesis; for doctorate, 2 foreign languages, comprehensive exam, thesis/dissertation, 1 year of teaching experience. *Entrance requirements:* For master's and doctorate, GRE General Test, writing sample, 3 letters of recommendation. Additional exam requirements/recommendations for international students: Required—TOEFL (minimum score 550 paper-based; 77 iBT). Electronic applications accepted.

**Florida International University,** Steven J. Green School of International and Public Affairs, Program in African and African Diaspora Studies, Miami, FL 33199. Offers MA, MA/PhD. *Program availability:* Part-time, evening/weekend. *Faculty:* 2 part-time/adjunct (both women). *Students:* 2 full-time (1 woman); both minorities (both Black or African American, non-Hispanic/Latino). Average age 28. 8 applicants, 50% accepted, 1 enrolled. In 2016, 4 master's awarded. Terminal master's awarded for partial completion of doctoral program. *Degree requirements:* For master's, one foreign language, thesis optional, minimum GPA of 3.0. *Entrance requirements:* For master's, GRE General Test, BA with minimum GPA of 3.0, 2 letters of recommendation, examples of written work. Additional exam requirements/recommendations for international students: Required—TOEFL (minimum score 80 iBT). *Application deadline:* For fall admission, 2/1 for domestic and international students; for spring admission, 10/1 for domestic students, 9/1 for international students. Application fee: $30. Electronic applications accepted. *Expenses:* Tuition, state resident: full-time $8912; part-time $446 per credit hour. Tuition, nonresident: full-time $21,393; part-time $992 per credit hour. *Required fees:* $2185; $195 per semester. Tuition and fees vary according to program. *Financial support:* Institutionally sponsored loans, scholarships/grants, and unspecified assistantships available. Financial award application deadline: 3/1; financial award applicants required to submit FAFSA. *Faculty research:* African diaspora in Latin America, Haitian Creole phonology and culture, racial/ethnic minority sexual health, African-American labor and southern history, gendered perspective of the development of racial science. *Unit head:* Dr. Jean Muteba Rahier, Director, 305-348-2246, Fax: 305-348-3270, E-mail: jrahier@fiu.edu. *Application contact:* Nanett Rojas, Manager, Admissions Operations, 305-348-7464, Fax: 305-348-7441, E-mail: gradadm@fiu.edu.

**Harvard University,** Graduate School of Arts and Sciences, Department of African and African American Studies, Cambridge, MA 02138. Offers PhD.

**Howard University,** Graduate School, Department of African Studies, Washington, DC 20059-0002. Offers MA, PhD. *Program availability:* Part-time. *Degree requirements:* For master's, one foreign language, comprehensive exam, thesis, internship; for doctorate,

2 foreign languages, comprehensive exam, thesis/dissertation, field research for some. *Entrance requirements:* For master's, GRE General Test, minimum GPA of 3.0; for doctorate, GRE General Test, minimum GPA of 3.5. Electronic applications accepted. *Faculty research:* African literature and film, economics of Africa, international relations, public policy analysis, gender.

**Indiana University Bloomington,** University Graduate School, College of Arts and Sciences, School of Global and International Studies, African Studies Program, Bloomington, IN 47408. Offers MA. *Students:* 2 full-time (both women), 1 international. Average age 32. 4 applicants, 75% accepted, 1 enrolled. In 2016, 2 master's awarded. *Entrance requirements:* Additional exam requirements/recommendations for international students: Required—TOEFL. *Application deadline:* For fall admission, 1/15 for domestic students, 12/1 for international students. Application fee: $55 ($65 for international students). Electronic applications accepted. *Unit head:* Dr. John Hanson, Director, 812-855-8284, E-mail: jhhanson@indiana.edu. *Application contact:* Wayne Parkinson, Student Services Assistant, 812-855-8284, Fax: 812-855-6734, E-mail: wparkins@indiana.edu.
Website: http://www.indiana.edu/~afrist/

**Michigan State University,** The Graduate School, College of Arts and Letters, Program in African American and African Studies, East Lansing, MI 48824. Offers MA, PhD. *Entrance requirements:* Additional exam requirements/recommendations for international students: Required—TOEFL. Electronic applications accepted. *Faculty research:* Black American and diasporic studies, comparative communities of color.

**New York University,** Graduate School of Arts and Science, Department of History, New York, NY 10012-1019. Offers African diaspora (PhD); African history (PhD); archival management (Advanced Certificate); Atlantic history (PhD); French studies/history (PhD); Hebrew and Judaic studies/history (PhD); history (MA, PhD), including Europe (PhD), Latin America and the Caribbean (PhD), United States (PhD), women's history (MA); Middle Eastern history (MA); Middle Eastern studies/history (PhD); public history (Advanced Certificate); world history (PhD); JD/MA; MA/Advanced Certificate. *Program availability:* Part-time. Terminal master's awarded for partial completion of doctoral program. *Degree requirements:* For master's, seminar paper; for doctorate, one foreign language, thesis/dissertation, oral and written exams; for Advanced Certificate, internship. *Entrance requirements:* For master's, GRE General Test, minimum GPA of 3.0, writing sample; for doctorate, GRE. Additional exam requirements/recommendations for international students: Required—TOEFL. *Faculty research:* African, East Asian, medieval, early modern, and modern European history; U.S. history; African and African diaspora; Latin American history; Atlantic world.

**New York University,** Graduate School of Arts and Science, Program in Africana Studies, New York, NY 10012-1019. Offers MA. *Degree requirements:* For master's, thesis or alternative. *Entrance requirements:* For master's, GRE, sample of written work. Additional exam requirements/recommendations for international students: Required—TOEFL. *Faculty research:* Pan-Africanism, black urban studies, film and literature of black Diaspora, cultural politics and theory, politics of identity.

**New York University,** Graduate School of Arts and Science, Program in Museum Studies, New York, NY 10012-1019. Offers museum studies (MA, Advanced Certificate), including Africana studies (MA), Hebrew and Judaic studies (MA), Latin American and Caribbean studies (MA), Near Eastern studies (MA). *Program availability:* Part-time, evening/weekend. *Entrance requirements:* For master's, GRE General Test; for Advanced Certificate, master's degree or PhD. Additional exam requirements/recommendations for international students: Required—TOEFL. *Faculty research:* Modern and contemporary art, history of museums and exhibitions, conservation of cultural materials, museum anthropology, ethnography.

**Northwestern University,** The Graduate School, Judd A. and Marjorie Weinberg College of Arts and Sciences, Program of African Studies, Evanston, IL 60208. Offers Graduate Certificate. *Degree requirements:* For Graduate Certificate, one foreign language. *Faculty research:* Collapsing states in Africa, HIV/AIDS in Africa, Islam in Africa, African philosophy.

**The Ohio State University,** Graduate School, College of Arts and Sciences, Division of Arts and Humanities, Department of African-American and African Studies, Columbus, OH 43210. Offers MA, PhD. *Faculty:* 13. *Students:* 10 full-time (6 women), 1 (woman) part-time. Average age 28. In 2016, 4 master's awarded. *Degree requirements:* For master's, comprehensive exam (for some programs), thesis (for some programs), thesis or comprehensive written examination; for doctorate, thesis/dissertation. *Entrance requirements:* For master's and doctorate, GRE General Test. Additional exam requirements/recommendations for international students: Required—TOEFL (minimum score 550 paper-based; 79 iBT), Michigan English Language Assessment Battery (minimum score 82); Recommended—IELTS (minimum score 7). *Application deadline:* For fall admission, 12/1 priority date for domestic students, 11/30 priority date for international students; for spring admission, 3/1 for domestic students, 2/1 for international students. Applications are processed on a rolling basis. Application fee: $60 ($70 for international students). Electronic applications accepted. *Financial support:* Fellowships with tuition reimbursements, research assistantships with tuition reimbursements, teaching assistantships with tuition reimbursements, Federal Work-Study, institutionally sponsored loans, and unspecified assistantships available. Support available to part-time students. *Unit head:* Valerie Lee, Acting Chair, 614-292-0116, E-mail: lee.89@osu.edu. *Application contact:* Graduate and Professional Admissions, 614-292-9444, Fax: 614-292-3895, E-mail: gpadmissions@osu.edu.
Website: http://aaas.osu.edu/

**Ohio University,** Graduate College, Center for International Studies, Program in African Studies, Athens, OH 45701. Offers MA. *Program availability:* Part-time. *Degree requirements:* For master's, one foreign language, thesis optional. *Entrance requirements:* For master's, minimum GPA of 3.0. Additional exam requirements/recommendations for international students: Required—TOEFL (minimum score 550 paper-based; 80 iBT), IELTS (minimum score 6.5). *Application deadline:* For fall admission, 1/1 for domestic and international students. Application fee: $50 ($55 for international students). *Financial support:* Fellowships with full tuition reimbursements, research assistantships with full tuition reimbursements, teaching assistantships with full tuition reimbursements, Federal Work-Study, institutionally sponsored loans, scholarships/grants, tuition waivers (partial), and unspecified assistantships available. Financial award application deadline: 1/1. *Faculty research:* African social sciences and the humanities. *Unit head:* Dr. W. Stephen Howard, Director, 740-593-1840, E-mail: showard1@ohio.edu. *Application contact:* Patti Malloy, Administrative Assistant, 740-593-1836, Fax: 740-593-1837, E-mail: malloyp@ohio.edu.
Website: http://www.ohio.edu/african/

**Rice University,** Graduate Programs, School of Humanities, Department of Religious Studies, Houston, TX 77251-1892. Offers African religions (PhD); African-American religions (PhD); contemplative studies (PhD); ghosticism, esotericism, mysticism (PhD); Islam (PhD); Jewish thought and philosophy (PhD); modern Christianity in thought and popular culture (PhD); psychology of religion (PhD); the Bible and beyond (PhD). *Degree requirements:* For doctorate, 2 foreign languages, comprehensive exam, thesis/dissertation. *Entrance requirements:* For doctorate, GRE, letters of recommendation, writing sample. Additional exam requirements/recommendations for international

## African Studies

students: Required—TOEFL (minimum score 600 paper-based; 90 iBT). Electronic applications accepted. *Faculty research:* Origins and historical development of Islam, history of Christianity, the study of comparative religion, African-American religion, religion and culture.

**Rutgers University–New Brunswick,** Graduate School-New Brunswick, Program in History, Piscataway, NJ 08854-8097. Offers African-American history (PhD); early American history (PhD); early modern European history (PhD); east Asian history (PhD); global and comparative history (PhD); history (PhD); history of diplomacy and foreign relations (PhD); history of technology, environment and health (PhD); history of the Atlantic cultures and African diaspora (PhD); Latin American history (PhD); medieval history (PhD); modern European history (PhD); nineteenth and twentieth century American history (PhD); women's and gender history (PhD). *Degree requirements:* For doctorate, thesis/dissertation. *Entrance requirements:* For doctorate, GRE General Test, sample of written work. Electronic applications accepted. *Faculty research:* American history, European history, Afro-American history, women's history, Latin American history.

**Stony Brook University, State University of New York,** Graduate School, College of Arts and Sciences, Department of Africana Studies, Stony Brook, NY 11794. Offers MA, Certificate. *Faculty:* 7 full-time (3 women), 3 part-time/adjunct (all women). *Students:* 2 full-time (1 woman), 2 part-time (both women); includes 2 minority (both Black or African American, non-Hispanic/Latino). Average age 30. 4 applicants, 75% accepted, 2 enrolled. In 2016, 1 master's awarded. *Degree requirements:* For master's, research thesis project, research seminar. *Entrance requirements:* For master's, GRE General Test, minimum GPA of 3.0, 3 letters of recommendation, bachelor's degree with minimum GPA of 3.0 in all social science and humanities courses. Additional exam requirements/recommendations for international students: Required—TOEFL (minimum score 85 iBT). *Application deadline:* For fall admission, 1/15 for domestic students; for spring admission, 10/1 for domestic students. Application fee: $100. *Expenses:* Contact institution. *Financial support:* Teaching assistantships available. *Faculty research:* Ethnic studies, humanities, African studies, African-American studies, African-Americans. *Unit head:* Dr. Tracey L. Walters, Chair, 631-632-7470, E-mail: tracey.walters@stonybrook.edu. *Application contact:* Ann Berrios, Coordinator, 631-632-7470, Fax: 631-632-7794, E-mail: ann.berrios@stonybrook.edu.
Website: http://www.stonybrook.edu/commcms/africana-studies//

**Syracuse University,** College of Arts and Sciences, MA Program in Pan-African Studies, Syracuse, NY 13244. Offers MA. *Students:* Average age 30. *Degree requirements:* For master's, thesis. *Entrance requirements:* For master's, GRE General Test (recommended), personal statement, resume, three letters of recommendation, writing sample (10-12 pages), transcripts. Additional exam requirements/recommendations for international students: Required—TOEFL (minimum score 100 iBT). *Application deadline:* For fall admission, 1/10 priority date for domestic and international students. Application fee: $75. Electronic applications accepted. *Expenses:* Tuition: Full-time $25,974; part-time $1443 per credit hour. *Required fees:* $802; $50 per course. Tuition and fees vary according to course load and program. *Financial support:* Fellowships with tuition reimbursements, teaching assistantships with tuition reimbursements, and scholarships/grants available. Financial award application deadline: 1/1. *Faculty research:* African American studies, African American history, Francophone African/Caribbean literatures, African archaeology. *Unit head:* Dr. Joan Bryant, Chair, 315-443-4399, E-mail: jobryant@syr.edu. *Application contact:* Ajajielle Brown, Administrative Assistant, 315-443-5599, E-mail: aabrow02@syr.edu.
Website: http://aas.syr.edu/graduate/index.html

**University at Albany, State University of New York,** College of Arts and Sciences, Department of Africana Studies, Albany, NY 12222-0001. Offers African studies (MA); Afro-American studies (MA). *Program availability:* Part-time, evening/weekend. *Faculty:* 4 full-time (2 women), 1 part-time/adjunct (0 women). *Students:* 9 full-time (7 women), 4 part-time (3 women); all minorities (10 Black or African American, non-Hispanic/Latino; 1 Hispanic/Latino; 2 Two or more races, non-Hispanic/Latino). Average age 29. 13 applicants, 92% accepted, 8 enrolled. In 2016, 5 master's awarded. *Entrance requirements:* Additional exam requirements/recommendations for international students: Required—TOEFL (minimum score 550 paper-based). *Application deadline:* For fall admission, 5/15 for international students; for spring admission, 11/1 for international students. Applications are processed on a rolling basis. Application fee: $75. Electronic applications accepted. *Expenses:* Tuition, state resident: full-time $10,870; part-time $453 per credit hour. Tuition, nonresident: full-time $22,210; part-time $925 per credit hour. *International tuition:* $21,550 full-time. *Required fees:* $1864; $96 per credit hour. *Financial support:* Fellowships, teaching assistantships, and Federal Work-Study available. Financial award application deadline: 5/1. *Faculty research:* The black family, Afro-centricity in poetry, black women in U.S. literature, African economic development, African American history. *Unit head:* Oscar Williams, Chair, 518-442-4730, Fax: 518-442-2569, E-mail: owilliams@albany.edu. *Application contact:* Michael DeRensis, Director, Graduate Admissions, 518-442-3980, Fax: 518-442-3922, E-mail: graduate@albany.edu.
Website: http://www.albany.edu/africana/

**The University of Arizona,** College of Social and Behavioral Sciences, School of Middle Eastern and North African Studies, Tucson, AZ 85721. Offers MA, PhD, Graduate Certificate. *Program availability:* Part-time, evening/weekend. Terminal master's awarded for partial completion of doctoral program. *Degree requirements:* For master's, one foreign language; for doctorate, 3 foreign languages, thesis/dissertation. *Entrance requirements:* For master's, GRE General Test, 3 letters of recommendation, statement of purpose, curriculum vitae, writing sample; for doctorate, GRE General Test, 3 letters of recommendation, curriculum vitae, writing sample. Additional exam requirements/recommendations for international students: Required—TOEFL (minimum score 550 paper-based; 79 iBT). Electronic applications accepted.

**University of California, Los Angeles,** Graduate Division, International Institute, Interdepartmental Program in African Studies, Los Angeles, CA 90095. Offers MA, MPH/MA. *Degree requirements:* For master's, one foreign language, comprehensive exam or thesis. *Entrance requirements:* For master's, GRE General Test, bachelor's degree; minimum undergraduate GPA of 3.0 (or its equivalent if letter grade system not used); writing sample. Additional exam requirements/recommendations for international students: Required—TOEFL. Electronic applications accepted.

**University of Illinois at Urbana–Champaign,** Graduate College, College of Liberal Arts and Sciences, Center for African Studies, Champaign, IL 61820. Offers MA, MA/MS.

**The University of Kansas,** Graduate Studies, College of Liberal Arts and Sciences, Department of African and African-American Studies, Lawrence, KS 66045. Offers African and African-American studies (MA); African studies (Graduate Certificate). *Program availability:* Part-time. *Students:* 10 full-time (6 women); includes 5 minority (3 Black or African American, non-Hispanic/Latino; 2 Two or more races, non-Hispanic/Latino). Average age 28. 5 applicants, 80% accepted, 4 enrolled. In 2016, 1 master's awarded. *Entrance requirements:* For master's, GRE, all academic transcripts, 3 letters of recommendation, personal statement of purpose, writing sample. Additional exam requirements/recommendations for international students: Required—TOEFL, IELTS.

*Application deadline:* For fall admission, 5/1 for domestic and international students; for spring admission, 10/1 for domestic and international students. Application fee: $65 ($85 for international students). Electronic applications accepted. *Financial support:* Application deadline: 4/15. *Faculty research:* African theatre, YaKuur culture, interracial communication, African development and urban planning, African literature, Muslim women in West Africa, identity formation in African and Diasporan settings, African-American history, North African and Arab societies, civil rights, black urban communities. *Unit head:* Dr. Lang Clarence, Chairperson, 785-864-3054, E-mail: celang@ku.edu. *Application contact:* Shawn Alexander, Director of Graduate Studies, 785-864-3054, E-mail: slalexan@ku.edu.
Website: http://www.afs.ku.edu

**University of Louisville,** Graduate School, College of Arts and Sciences, Department of Pan-African Studies, Louisville, KY 40292. Offers African and Diaspora studies (MA); African-American studies (MA); MSSW/MA. *Program availability:* Part-time. *Faculty:* 10 full-time (5 women), 3 part-time/adjunct (2 women). *Students:* 15 full-time (10 women), 8 part-time (5 women); all minorities (21 Black or African American, non-Hispanic/Latino; 2 Two or more races, non-Hispanic/Latino). Average age 32. 18 applicants, 83% accepted, 9 enrolled. In 2016, 2 master's awarded. *Degree requirements:* For master's, comprehensive exam, thesis optional. *Entrance requirements:* For master's, GRE General Test. Additional exam requirements/recommendations for international students: Required—TOEFL (minimum score 550 paper-based; 79 iBT). *Application deadline:* For fall admission, 3/15 for domestic students, 5/1 priority date for international students; for spring admission, 10/15 for domestic students, 11/1 priority date for international students; for summer admission, 4/1 priority date for international students. Applications are processed on a rolling basis. Application fee: $60. Electronic applications accepted. *Expenses:* Tuition, state resident: full-time $12,246; part-time $681 per credit hour. Tuition, nonresident: full-time $25,486; part-time $1417 per credit hour. *Required fees:* $196. Tuition and fees vary according to program and reciprocity agreements. *Financial support:* Teaching assistantships available. Financial award application deadline: 3/3; financial award applicants required to submit FAFSA. *Faculty research:* African popular culture, black male identity development, education and retention, contemporary politics in Nigeria, poverty in the Caribbean. *Total annual research expenditures:* $72,938. *Unit head:* Dr. Ricky L. Jones, Chair, 502-852-0027, E-mail: ricky.jones@louisville.edu. *Application contact:* Libby Leggett, Director, Graduate Admissions, 502-852-3101, E-mail: gradadm@louisville.edu.
Website: http://www.louisville.edu/panafricanstudies

**The University of North Carolina at Charlotte,** College of Liberal Arts and Sciences, Department of Africana Studies, Charlotte, NC 28223-0001. Offers Graduate Certificate. *Program availability:* Part-time. *Faculty:* 5 full-time (2 women), 1 part-time/adjunct (0 women). *Students:* 3 part-time (all women); all minorities (all Black or African American, non-Hispanic/Latino). Average age 34. 2 applicants, 100% accepted, 1 enrolled. In 2016, 3 Graduate Certificates awarded. *Entrance requirements:* For degree, bachelor's degree from accredited university with minimum cumulative GPA of 3.0 or be enrolled and in good standing in a graduate degree program at UNC Charlotte; official transcripts; two-page statement of purpose explaining applicant's educational and work background, interests, and plans. Additional exam requirements/recommendations for international students: Required—TOEFL (minimum score 523 paper-based, 70 iBT) or IELTS (6.5). *Application deadline:* For fall admission, 3/1 priority date for domestic and international students; for spring admission, 10/1 priority date for domestic and international students; for summer admission, 4/1 priority date for domestic and international students. Applications are processed on a rolling basis. Application fee: $75. Electronic applications accepted. *Expenses:* Tuition, state resident: full-time $4252. Tuition, nonresident: full-time $17,423. *Required fees:* $3026. Tuition and fees vary according to course load and program. *Financial support:* Institutionally sponsored loans, scholarships/grants, and unspecified assistantships available. Support available to part-time students. Financial award application deadline: 3/1; financial award applicants required to submit FAFSA. *Total annual research expenditures:* $54,634. *Unit head:* Dr. Akin Ogundiran, Chair, 704-687-5162, E-mail: ogundiran@uncc.edu. *Application contact:* Kathy B. Giddings, Director of Graduate Admissions, 704-687-5503, Fax: 704-687-1668, E-mail: gradadm@uncc.edu.
Website: http://africana.uncc.edu/

**University of Pennsylvania,** School of Arts and Sciences, Program in Africana Studies, Philadelphia, PA 19104. Offers MA, PhD. *Faculty:* 15 full-time (10 women), 1 (woman) part-time/adjunct. *Students:* 18 full-time (14 women); includes 13 minority (10 Black or African American, non-Hispanic/Latino; 1 Asian, non-Hispanic/Latino; 1 Hispanic/Latino; 1 Two or more races, non-Hispanic/Latino), 3 international. Average age 30. 47 applicants, 13% accepted, 3 enrolled. In 2016, 15 master's, 2 doctorates awarded. *Expenses:* Tuition: Full-time $31,068; part-time $5762 per course. *Required fees:* $3200; $336 per course. Full-time tuition and fees vary according to degree level, program and student level. Part-time tuition and fees vary according to course load, degree level and program.
Website: https://africana.sas.upenn.edu/

**University of Pittsburgh,** University Center for International Studies, Pittsburgh, PA 15260. Offers African studies (Certificate); Asian studies (Certificate); European Union studies (Certificate); global studies (Certificate); Latin American studies (Certificate); Russian and East European studies (Certificate); West European studies (Certificate). *Program availability:* Part-time, evening/weekend, online learning. *Students:* 175 full-time (105 women), 14 part-time (10 women); includes 78 minority (5 Black or African American, non-Hispanic/Latino; 30 Asian, non-Hispanic/Latino; 42 Hispanic/Latino; 1 Two or more races, non-Hispanic/Latino). Average age 29. *Degree requirements:* For Certificate, one foreign language, comprehensive exam (for some programs), thesis (for some programs). *Entrance requirements:* Additional exam requirements/recommendations for international students: Required—TOEFL. *Expenses:* Contact institution. *Financial support:* In 2016–17, 22 fellowships with full tuition reimbursements (averaging $17,878 per year) were awarded; scholarships/grants, traineeships, health care benefits, tuition waivers, and unspecified assistantships also available. *Unit head:* Dr. Ariel Armony, Director, 412-648-7374, Fax: 412-624-4672, E-mail: armony@pitt.edu.
Website: http://www.ucis.pitt.edu

**University of South Florida,** College of Arts and Sciences, Department of Humanities and Cultural Studies, Tampa, FL 33620-9951. Offers liberal arts (MA), including Africana studies, American studies, film studies, humanities, social and political thought. *Program availability:* Part-time, evening/weekend. *Faculty:* 6 full-time (1 woman). *Students:* 17 full-time (10 women), 9 part-time (3 women); includes 3 minority (all Black or African American, non-Hispanic/Latino), 2 international. Average age 33. 23 applicants, 83% accepted, 14 enrolled. In 2016, 6 master's awarded. *Degree requirements:* For master's, comprehensive exam, thesis, language (for humanities subconcentration). *Entrance requirements:* For master's, GRE General Test, minimum GPA of 3.0 in upper-division courses, personal statement, writing sample. Additional exam requirements/recommendations for international students: Required—TOEFL (minimum score 550 paper-based; 79 iBT) or IELTS (minimum score 6.5). *Application deadline:* For fall admission, 2/15 priority date for domestic students, 2/15 for international students; for spring admission, 10/15 priority date for domestic students, 9/15 for international students; for summer admission, 2/15 for domestic students, 1/15 for international

students. Application fee: $30. Electronic applications accepted. *Expenses:* Tuition, state resident: full-time $7766; part-time $431.43 per credit hour. Tuition, nonresident: full-time $15,789; part-time $877.17 per credit hour. *Required fees:* $37 per term. *Financial support:* In 2016–17, 5 students received support, including 15 teaching assistantships with tuition reimbursements available (averaging $12,437 per year); scholarships/grants also available. Financial award application deadline: 4/1. *Faculty research:* American South, American autobiography, material culture, critical theory, cultural studies, film studies. *Unit head:* Dr. William Cummings, Professor and Chair, 813-974-9380, Fax: 813-974-9409, E-mail: wcummings@usf.edu. *Application contact:* Dr. Brook Sadler, Associate Professor and Graduate Program Director, 813-974-8841, Fax: 813-974-9409, E-mail: brooksadler@usf.edu.
Website: http://humanities.usf.edu/

**University of South Florida,** Innovative Education, Tampa, FL 33620-9951. Offers adult, career and higher education (Graduate Certificate), including college teaching, leadership in developing human resources, leadership in higher education; Africana studies (Graduate Certificate), including diasporas and health disparities, genocide and human rights; aging studies (Graduate Certificate), including gerontology; art research (Graduate Certificate), including museum studies; business foundations (Graduate Certificate); chemical and biomedical engineering (Graduate Certificate), including materials science and engineering, water, health and sustainability; child and family studies (Graduate Certificate), including positive behavior support; civil and industrial engineering (Graduate Certificate), including transportation systems analysis; community and family health (Graduate Certificate), including maternal and child health, social marketing and public health, violence and injury: prevention and intervention, women's health; criminology (Graduate Certificate), including criminal justice administration; educational measurement and research (Graduate Certificate), including evaluation; English (Graduate Certificate), including comparative literary studies, creative writing, professional and technical communication; entrepreneurship (Graduate Certificate); environmental health (Graduate Certificate), including safety management; epidemiology and biostatistics (Graduate Certificate), including applied biostatistics, biostatistics, concepts and tools of epidemiology, epidemiology, epidemiology of infectious diseases; geography, environment and planning (Graduate Certificate), including community development, environmental policy and management, geographical information systems; geology (Graduate Certificate), including hydrogeology; global health (Graduate Certificate), including disaster management, global health and Latin American and Caribbean studies, global health practice, humanitarian assistance, infection control; government and international affairs (Graduate Certificate), including Cuban studies, globalization studies; health policy and management (Graduate Certificate), including health management and leadership, public health policy and programs; hearing specialist: early intervention (Graduate Certificate); industrial and management systems engineering (Graduate Certificate), including systems engineering, technology management; information studies (Graduate Certificate), including school library media specialist; information systems/decision sciences (Graduate Certificate), including analytics and business intelligence; instructional technology (Graduate Certificate), including distance education, Florida digital/virtual educator, instructional design, multimedia design, Web design; internal medicine, bioethics and medical humanities (Graduate Certificate), including biomedical ethics; Latin American and Caribbean studies (Graduate Certificate); mass communications (Graduate Certificate), including multimedia journalism; mathematics and statistics (Graduate Certificate), including mathematics; medicine (Graduate Certificate), including aging and neuroscience, bioinformatics, biotechnology, brain fitness and memory management, clinical investigation, health informatics, health sciences, integrative weight management, intellectual property, medicine and gender, metabolic and nutritional medicine, metabolic cardiology, pharmacy sciences; national and competitive intelligence (Graduate Certificate); psychological and social foundations (Graduate Certificate), including career counseling, college teaching, diversity in education, mental health counseling, school counseling; public affairs (Graduate Certificate), including nonprofit management, public management, research administration; public health (Graduate Certificate), including environmental health, health equity, public health generalist, translational research in adolescent behavioral health; public health practices (Graduate Certificate), including planning for healthy communities; rehabilitation and mental health counseling (Graduate Certificate), including integrative mental health care, marriage and family therapy, rehabilitation technology; secondary education (Graduate Certificate), including ESOL, foreign language education: culture and content, foreign language education: professional; social work (Graduate Certificate), including geriatric social work/clinical gerontology; special education (Graduate Certificate), including autism spectrum disorder, disabilities education: severe/profound; world languages (Graduate Certificate), including teaching English as a second language (TESL) or foreign language. *Expenses:* Tuition, state resident: full-time $7766; part-time $431.43 per credit hour. Tuition, nonresident: full-time $15,789; part-time $877.17 per credit hour. *Required fees:* $37 per term. *Unit head:* Kathy Barnes, Interdisciplinary Programs Coordinator, 813-974-8031, Fax: 813-974-7061, E-mail: barnesk@usf.edu. *Application contact:* Karen Tylinski, Metro Initiatives, 813-974-9943, Fax: 813-974-7061, E-mail: ktylinsk@usf.edu.
Website: http://www.usf.edu/innovative-education/

**The University of Texas at Austin,** Graduate School, College of Liberal Arts, John L. Warfield Center for African and African American Studies, Austin, TX 78712-1111. Offers African Diaspora studies (MA, PhD). *Program availability:* Part-time. *Degree requirements:* For master's, one foreign language, thesis. *Entrance requirements:* For master's, GRE General Test. Electronic applications accepted.

**University of Wisconsin–Madison,** Graduate School, College of Letters and Science, Department of African Languages and Literature, Madison, WI 53706-1380. Offers MA, PhD. *Program availability:* Part-time. *Degree requirements:* For master's, one foreign language, thesis; for doctorate, 2 foreign languages, comprehensive exam, thesis/dissertation. *Entrance requirements:* For master's, BA in African language and literature; for doctorate, MA in African language and literature. Electronic applications accepted. *Faculty research:* Oral traditions, language pedagogy, stylistics, sociolinguistics, literary criticism.

**University of Wisconsin–Madison,** Graduate School, College of Letters and Science, Department of History, Madison, WI 53706-1380. Offers African history (MA, PhD); Central Asian history (MA, PhD); comparative world history (MA, PhD); East Asian history (MA, PhD); European history (MA, PhD); gender and women's history (MA, PhD); Latin American and Caribbean history (MA, PhD); Middle Eastern history (MA, PhD); South Asian history (MA, PhD); Southeast Asian history (MA, PhD); United States history (MA, PhD). Terminal master's awarded for partial completion of doctoral program. *Degree requirements:* For master's, thesis (for some programs); for doctorate, variable foreign language requirement, thesis/dissertation. *Entrance requirements:* For master's and doctorate, GRE General Test. Additional exam requirements/recommendations for international students: Required—Michigan English Language Assessment Battery or TOEFL. Electronic applications accepted. *Faculty research:* American, African, European, Asian, Latin American, and Middle Eastern history.

**University of Wisconsin–Milwaukee,** Graduate School, College of Letters and Science, Department of Africology, Milwaukee, WI 53201-0413. Offers Africology (PhD), including culture and society: Africa and the African diaspora, political economy and public policy. *Students:* 6 full-time (5 women), 3 part-time (2 women); all minorities (all Black or African American, non-Hispanic/Latino). Average age 35. 5 applicants. *Degree requirements:* For doctorate, comprehensive exam. *Entrance requirements:* For doctorate, GRE General Test. Additional exam requirements/recommendations for international students: Required—TOEFL (minimum score 550 paper-based; 79 iBT), IELTS (minimum score 6.5). *Application deadline:* Applications are processed on a rolling basis. Application fee: $56 ($96 for international students). Electronic applications accepted. *Financial support:* In 2016–17, 1 fellowship, 5 teaching assistantships were awarded; research assistantships and unspecified assistantships also available. *Unit head:* Erin N. Winkler, Department Chair, 414-229-5080, E-mail: winklere@uwm.edu. *Application contact:* General Information Contact, 414-229-4982, Fax: 414-229-6967, E-mail: gradschool@uwm.edu.
Website: https://uwm.edu/letters-science/programs/?discipline-Africology

**Wayne State University,** College of Liberal Arts and Sciences, Department of History, Detroit, MI 48202. Offers Africa (PhD); America (PhD); Asia (PhD); Europe (PhD); gender (PhD); history (MA); labor (PhD); public history (MA); science and technology (PhD); world history (PhD, Graduate Certificate); JD/MA; M Ed/MA; MLIS/MA. Doctoral program admits for fall only. *Program availability:* Evening/weekend. *Faculty:* 18. *Students:* 23 full-time (8 women), 21 part-time (5 women); includes 8 minority (3 Black or African American, non-Hispanic/Latino; 2 Hispanic/Latino; 3 Two or more races, non-Hispanic/Latino). Average age 40. 55 applicants, 38% accepted, 15 enrolled. In 2016, 6 master's, 5 doctorates awarded. *Degree requirements:* For master's, comprehensive exam, thesis (for some programs), final oral exam on thesis or essay and seminar; internship and project (for public history); for doctorate, variable foreign language requirement, comprehensive exam, thesis/dissertation, qualifying exam in 4 fields of history. *Entrance requirements:* For master's, GRE General Test, minimum undergraduate GPA of 3.25 in history, 3.0 overall; at least 18 credits in history and related subjects at the advanced undergraduate level; foreign language; letter of intent; research paper; at least two letters of recommendation from former instructors; for doctorate, GRE General Test, minimum GPA of 3.0, 3.25 in minimum of 18 semester credits in history and related subjects; letter of intent; research paper; at least three letters of recommendation from former professors; for Graduate Certificate, baccalaureate degree from accredited college or university; minimum GPA of 3.0, 3.25 in a minimum of eighteen semester credits in history and related subjects at the advanced undergraduate level. Additional exam requirements/recommendations for international students: Required—TOEFL (minimum score 550 paper-based; 79 iBT), TWE (minimum score 5.5), Michigan English Language Assessment Battery (minimum score 85); Recommended—IELTS (minimum score 6.5). *Application deadline:* For fall admission, 2/1 priority date for domestic and international students; for winter admission, 11/1 for domestic students, 10/1 priority date for international students; for spring admission, 2/1 for domestic students, 1/1 priority date for international students. Application fee: $50. Electronic applications accepted. *Expenses:* $16,503 per year resident tuition and fees, $33,697 per year non-resident tuition and fees. *Financial support:* In 2016–17, 16 students received support, including 2 fellowships with tuition reimbursements available (averaging $18,796 per year), 1 research assistantship with tuition reimbursement available (averaging $21,593 per year), 6 teaching assistantships with tuition reimbursements available (averaging $17,994 per year); scholarships/grants, health care benefits, and unspecified assistantships also available. Financial award applicants required to submit FAFSA. *Faculty research:* African, American, Asian, European, gender, German, labor, science and technology, urban/labor, violence, world. *Unit head:* Dr. Elizabeth V. Faue, Professor/Chair, 313-577-2525, E-mail: evfaue@wayne.edu. *Application contact:* Dr. Eric Ash, Associate Professor and Director of Graduate Studies, 313-577-2525, E-mail: ericash@wayne.edu.
Website: http://clas.wayne.edu/history/

**West Virginia University,** Eberly College of Arts and Sciences, Department of History, Morgantown, WV 26506. Offers African history (MA, PhD); African-American history (MA, PhD); American history (MA, PhD); Appalachian/regional history (MA, PhD); East Asian history (MA, PhD); European history (MA, PhD); history of science and technology (MA, PhD); Latin American history (MA). *Program availability:* Part-time. *Degree requirements:* For master's, one foreign language, thesis (for some programs), oral exam, thesis defense; for doctorate, one foreign language, comprehensive exam, thesis/dissertation, dissertation defense. *Entrance requirements:* For master's, GRE General Test, minimum GPA of 3.0; for doctorate, GRE General Test. Additional exam requirements/recommendations for international students: Required—TOEFL (minimum score 550 paper-based), IELTS (minimum score 6.5). Electronic applications accepted. *Faculty research:* United States, Appalachia, modern Europe, Africa, colonial and post-colonial societies.

**Yale University,** Graduate School of Arts and Sciences, Interdisciplinary Program in African Studies, New Haven, CT 06520. Offers MA. *Degree requirements:* For master's, one foreign language, thesis. *Entrance requirements:* For master's, GRE General Test.

# American Indian/Native American Studies

**Central Michigan University,** College of Graduate Studies, College of Humanities and Social and Behavioral Sciences, Program in Humanities, Mount Pleasant, MI 48859. Offers humanities (MA), including contemporary issues in the humanities: race, class, and gender, images and ideas of self, Native American issues in modern culture, popular culture studies, the rise of industrial society. *Program availability:* Part-time, evening/weekend. *Degree requirements:* For master's, thesis or alternative. Electronic applications accepted. *Faculty research:* Rise of industrial society; images and ideas of self; contemporary issues of race, class, and gender; popular culture; Native American issues in modern culture.

**Montana State University,** The Graduate School, College of Letters and Science, Department of Native American Studies, Bozeman, MT 59717. Offers MA. *Program*

## American Indian/Native American Studies

*availability:* Part-time, online learning. *Degree requirements:* For master's, comprehensive exam. *Entrance requirements:* For master's, minimum GPA of 3.0; 3 letters of recommendation; 2 academic writing samples; statement of purpose. Additional exam requirements/recommendations for international students: Required—TOEFL (minimum score 550 paper-based). Electronic applications accepted. *Faculty research:* Federal Indian law and policy, contemporary Native film and literature, tribal colleges and Native Americans in higher education, Native veterans, native land rights.

**Navajo Technical University,** Program in Dine Studies, Crownpoint, NM 87313. Offers MA. *Entrance requirements:* For master's, bachelor's degree, Certificate of Indian Blood (CIB) for tribal eligibility, three letters of recommendation, 500-word essay.

**Northeastern State University,** College of Liberal Arts, Department of Cherokee and Indigenous Studies, Tahlequah, OK 74464-2399. Offers American studies (MA). *Program availability:* Part-time, evening/weekend. *Faculty:* 2 full-time (both women). *Students:* 7 full-time (5 women), 14 part-time (10 women); includes 13 minority (6 American Indian or Alaska Native, non-Hispanic/Latino; 3 Hispanic/Latino; 4 Two or more races, non-Hispanic/Latino). Average age 40. In 2016, 3 master's awarded. *Degree requirements:* For master's, thesis, written and oral examinations. *Entrance requirements:* For master's, GRE, minimum GPA of 2.5. Additional exam requirements/recommendations for international students: Required—TOEFL. *Application deadline:* For fall admission, 6/1 priority date for domestic students. Applications are processed on a rolling basis. Application fee: $25. Electronic applications accepted. *Expenses:* Tuition, state resident: full-time $2816; part-time $216.60 per credit hour. Tuition, nonresident: full-time $6365; part-time $489.60 per credit hour. *Required fees:* $37.40 per credit hour. *Financial support:* Teaching assistantships and Federal Work-Study available. Financial award application deadline: 3/1. *Unit head:* Dr. Cari Keller, Program Coordinator, 918-444-3514, E-mail: kellerc@nsuok.edu. *Application contact:* Josh McCollum, Graduate Coordinator, 918-444-2093, E-mail: mccolluj@nsuok.edu. Website: http://catalog.nsuok.edu/preview_program.php?catoid-12&amp;poid-947&amp;returnto-333

**Trent University,** Graduate Studies, The Frost Centre for Canadian Studies and Indigenous Studies, Peterborough, ON K9J 7B8, Canada. Offers Canadian studies (PhD); Canadian studies and indigenous studies (MA). *Program availability:* Part-time. *Degree requirements:* For master's, thesis. *Entrance requirements:* For master's, honors degree. *Faculty research:* Native community-based socioeconomic development, environmental and social impact inventory, regional studies.

**Trent University,** Graduate Studies, Program in Indigenous Studies, Peterborough, ON K9J 7B8, Canada. Offers PhD. *Program availability:* Part-time. *Degree requirements:* For doctorate, thesis/dissertation. *Entrance requirements:* For doctorate, master's degree.

**The University of Arizona,** Graduate Interdisciplinary Programs, Graduate Interdisciplinary Program in American Indian Studies, Tucson, AZ 85721. Offers MA, PhD. *Program availability:* Part-time. *Degree requirements:* For master's, thesis; for doctorate, one foreign language, comprehensive exam, thesis/dissertation. *Entrance requirements:* For master's, 3 letters of recommendation, 2 writing samples, resume; for doctorate, statement of purpose, 3 letters of recommendation, 2 writing samples, resume. Additional exam requirements/recommendations for international students: Required—TOEFL (minimum score 550 paper-based; 79 iBT). Electronic applications accepted. *Faculty research:* Indian law and policy, Indian societies, Indian language and literature, Indian education.

**University of California, Davis,** Graduate Studies, Program in Native American Studies, Davis, CA 95616. Offers MA, PhD. Terminal master's awarded for partial completion of doctoral program. *Degree requirements:* For master's, comprehensive exam (for some programs), thesis (for some programs); for doctorate, thesis/dissertation. *Entrance requirements:* For doctorate, GRE. Additional exam requirements/recommendations for international students: Required—TOEFL (minimum score 550 paper-based).

**University of California, Los Angeles,** Graduate Division, College of Letters and Science, Interdepartmental Program in American Indian Studies, Los Angeles, CA 90095. Offers MA, JD/MA. *Degree requirements:* For master's, comprehensive exam or thesis. *Entrance requirements:* For master's, GRE General Test (recommended), bachelor's degree; minimum undergraduate GPA of 3.0 (or its equivalent if letter grade system not used). Additional exam requirements/recommendations for international students: Required—TOEFL. Electronic applications accepted.

**University of Idaho,** College of Law, Moscow, ID 83844-2321. Offers business law and entrepreneurship (JD); law (JD); litigation and alternative dispute resolution (JD); Native American law (JD); natural resources and environmental law (JD). *Accreditation:* ABA. *Faculty:* 32 full-time, 11 part-time/adjunct. *Students:* Average age 28. *Entrance requirements:* For doctorate, LSAT, Law School Admission Council Credential Assembly Service (CAS) Report. Additional exam requirements/recommendations for international students: Required—TOEFL. *Application deadline:* For fall admission, 3/15 priority date for domestic students. Applications are processed on a rolling basis. Application fee: $50 ($60 for international students). Electronic applications accepted. *Expenses:* Contact institution. *Financial support:* Career-related internships or fieldwork, Federal Work-Study, and institutionally sponsored loans available. Financial award applicants required to submit FAFSA. *Faculty research:* Transboundary river governance, tribal protection and stewardship, regional water issues, environmental law. *Unit head:* Mark Adams, Dean, 208-885-4977, E-mail: uilaw@uidaho.edu. *Application contact:* Carole Wells, Director of Admissions, 208-885-2300, Fax: 208-885-2252, E-mail: lawadmit@uidaho.edu.
Website: http://www.uidaho.edu/law/

**The University of Kansas,** Graduate Studies, College of Liberal Arts and Sciences, Indigenous Studies Program, Lawrence, KS 66045-7515. Offers MA, Graduate Certificate. *Program availability:* Part-time. *Students:* 4 full-time (3 women), 1 part-time (0 women); includes 3 minority (2 American Indian or Alaska Native, non-Hispanic/Latino; 1 Two or more races, non-Hispanic/Latino). Average age 35. 4 applicants, 100% accepted, 2 enrolled. In 2016, 1 master's awarded. *Entrance requirements:* For master's, GRE, resume, writing sample, minimum GPA of 3.0 (preferred), 3 recommendations, original transcript, 2-page personal statement. Additional exam requirements/recommendations for international students: Required—TOEFL or IELTS. *Application deadline:* For fall admission, 4/1 priority date for domestic and international students; for spring admission, 10/1 priority date for domestic and international students. Application fee: $65 ($85 for international students). Electronic applications accepted. *Financial support:* Fellowships, research assistantships, teaching assistantships, Federal Work-Study, institutionally sponsored loans, and scholarships/grants available. Support available to part-time students. Financial award application deadline: 4/1; financial award applicants required to submit FAFSA. *Unit head:* Dr. Stephanie Fitzgerald, Director, 785-864-2586, E-mail: sfitzger@ku.edu. *Application contact:* Graduate Admission Contact, 785-864-2660, E-mail: indigenous@ku.edu.
Website: http://www.indigenous.ku.edu

**University of Lethbridge,** School of Graduate Studies, Lethbridge, AB T1K 3M4, Canada. Offers addictions counseling (M Sc); agricultural biotechnology (M Sc); agricultural studies (M Sc, MA); anthropology (MA); archaeology (M Sc, MA); art (MA,

MFA); biochemistry (M Sc); biological sciences (M Sc); biomolecular science (PhD); biosystems and biodiversity (PhD); Canadian studies (MA); chemistry (M Sc); computer science (M Sc); computer science and geographical information science (M Sc); counseling (MC); counseling psychology (M Ed); dramatic arts (MA); earth, space, and physical science (PhD); economics (MA); education (MA, PhD); educational leadership (M Ed); English (MA); environmental science (M Sc); evolution and behavior (PhD); exercise science (M Sc); French (MA); French/German (MA); French/Spanish (MA); general education (M Ed); geography (M Sc, MA); German (MA); health sciences (M Sc); individualized multidisciplinary (M Sc, MA); kinesiology (M Sc, MA); management (M Sc), including accounting, finance, human resource management and labor relations, information systems, international management, marketing, policy and strategy; mathematics (M Sc); music (M Mus, MA); Native American studies (MA); neuroscience (M Sc, PhD); new media (MA, MFA); nursing (M Sc, MN); philosophy (MA); physics (M Sc); political science (MA); psychology (M Sc, MA); religious studies (MA); sociology (MA); theatre and dramatic arts (MFA); theoretical and computational science (PhD); urban and regional studies (MA); women and gender studies (MA). *Program availability:* Part-time, evening/weekend. *Degree requirements:* For master's, thesis (for some programs); for doctorate, comprehensive exam, thesis/dissertation. *Entrance requirements:* For master's, GMAT (for M Sc in management), bachelor's degree in related field, minimum GPA of 3.0 during previous 20 graded semester courses, 2 years' teaching or related experience (M Ed); for doctorate, master's degree, minimum graduate GPA of 3.5. Additional exam requirements/recommendations for international students: Required—TOEFL (minimum score 580 paper-based; 93 iBT). Electronic applications accepted. *Faculty research:* Movement and brain plasticity, gibberellin physiology, photosynthesis, carbon cycling, molecular properties of main-group ring components.

**University of Manitoba,** Faculty of Graduate Studies, Faculty of Arts, Department of Native Studies, Winnipeg, MB R3T 2N2, Canada. Offers MA.

**University of New Mexico,** Graduate Studies, College of Education, Program in Language, Literacy and Sociocultural Studies, Albuquerque, NM 87131. Offers American Indian education (MA); bilingual education (MA, PhD); educational linguistics (PhD); educational thought and sociocultural studies (MA, PhD); literacy/language arts (MA, PhD); social studies (MA); TESOL (MA, PhD). *Faculty:* 17 full-time (10 women), 4 part-time/adjunct (3 women). *Students:* 57 full-time (38 women), 129 part-time (105 women); includes 102 minority (8 Black or African American, non-Hispanic/Latino; 16 American Indian or Alaska Native, non-Hispanic/Latino; 6 Asian, non-Hispanic/Latino; 67 Hispanic/Latino; 5 Two or more races, non-Hispanic/Latino), 32 international. Average age 39. 50 applicants, 60% accepted, 23 enrolled. In 2016, 36 master's, 4 doctorates awarded. *Degree requirements:* For master's, comprehensive exam, thesis optional; for doctorate, comprehensive exam, thesis/dissertation, research skills. *Entrance requirements:* For master's, letter of intent, 3 letters of recommendation, resume, BA/BS, department demographic form, transcripts; for doctorate, writing sample, letter of intent, 3 letters of recommendation, resume, BA/BS, MA, department demographic form, transcripts. Additional exam requirements/recommendations for international students: Required—TOEFL. *Application deadline:* For fall admission, 12/1 for domestic and international students; for spring admission, 9/15 for domestic and international students. Application fee: $50. Electronic applications accepted. *Financial support:* Fellowships, research assistantships, teaching assistantships with tuition reimbursements, career-related internships or fieldwork, institutionally sponsored loans, scholarships/grants, and unspecified assistantships available. Support available to part-time students. Financial award application deadline: 3/1; financial award applicants required to submit FAFSA. *Faculty research:* School reform, professional development, history of education, Native American education, politics of education, feminism and issues of sexual identity, critical race theory, bilingualism, literacy reading, adolescent literature, second language acquisition, critical theory and schooling, indigenous languages. *Unit head:* Dr. Lois M. Meyer, Chair, 505-277-7244, Fax: 505-277-8362, E-mail: lsmeyer@unm.edu. *Application contact:* Debra Schaffer, Administrative Assistant, 505-277-0437, Fax: 505-277-8362, E-mail: schaffer@unm.edu.
Website: http://coe.unm.edu/departments-programs/llss/index.html

**University of Oklahoma,** College of Arts and Sciences, Department of Native American Studies, Norman, OK 73019. Offers MA, JD/MA. *Program availability:* Part-time. *Faculty:* 21 full-time (8 women). *Students:* 10 full-time (3 women), 3 part-time (2 women); all minorities (10 American Indian or Alaska Native, non-Hispanic/Latino; 2 Hispanic/Latino; 2 Two or more races, non-Hispanic/Latino). Average age 32. 5 applicants, 80% accepted, 4 enrolled. In 2016, 3 master's awarded. *Degree requirements:* For master's, one foreign language, thesis or exam. *Entrance requirements:* For master's, BA or BS in related area. Additional exam requirements/recommendations for international students: Required—TOEFL (minimum score 79 iBT) or IELTS (minimum score 6.5). *Application deadline:* Applications are processed on a rolling basis. Application fee: $50 ($100 for international students). Electronic applications accepted. *Expenses:* Tuition, state resident: full-time $4886; part-time $203.60 per credit hour. Tuition, nonresident: full-time $18,989; part-time $791.20 per credit hour. *Required fees:* $3283; $126.25 per credit hour. $126.50 per semester. *Financial support:* In 2016–17, 9 students received support, including 1 research assistantship (averaging $10,966 per year), 6 teaching assistantships with full tuition reimbursements available (averaging $10,400 per year); health care benefits also available. Financial award application deadline: 6/1; financial award applicants required to submit FAFSA. *Faculty research:* Tribal governance and policy; indigenous media and arts; language, cultural knowledge, and history. *Unit head:* Dr. Amanda Cobb-Greethan, Chair, 405-325-2312, Fax: 405-325-0842, E-mail: nas@ou.edu.
Website: http://nas.ou.edu

**The University of Tulsa,** College of Law, Tulsa, OK 74104. Offers American Indian and indigenous law (LL M); American law for foreign lawyers (LL M); energy and natural resources law (LL M); energy law (MJ); health law (Certificate); Indian law (MJ); law (JD); Native American law (Certificate); natural resources, energy, and environmental law (Certificate); JD/MA; JD/MBA; JD/MS. *Accreditation:* ABA. *Program availability:* Part-time, 100% online. *Faculty:* 23 full-time (13 women), 12 part-time/adjunct (4 women). *Students:* 233 full-time (103 women), 30 part-time (17 women); includes 70 minority (10 Black or African American, non-Hispanic/Latino; 16 American Indian or Alaska Native, non-Hispanic/Latino; 2 Asian, non-Hispanic/Latino; 12 Hispanic/Latino; 30 Two or more races, non-Hispanic/Latino), 5 international. Average age 27. 602 applicants, 40% accepted, 92 enrolled. In 2016, 5 master's, 81 doctorates awarded. *Degree requirements:* For master's, thesis optional. *Entrance requirements:* For master's, JD from an ABA-approved U.S. law school or a JD equivalent from non-U.S. university; for doctorate, LSAT, BS or BA from 4-year regionally-accredited college/university; for Certificate, BS or BA from 4-year regionally-accredited college/university. Additional exam requirements/recommendations for international students: Required—TOEFL (minimum score 570 paper-based; 90 iBT), IELTS (minimum score 6.5). *Application deadline:* For fall admission, 7/31 priority date for domestic and international students; for spring admission, 12/5 priority date for domestic students, 12/5 for international students; for summer admission, 4/13 for domestic and international students. Applications are processed on a rolling basis. Application fee: $30. Electronic applications accepted. *Expenses:* $37,960 per year tuition; $654 fees. *Financial support:* In 2016–17, 255 students received support. Scholarships/grants available. Support available to part-time students. Financial award application deadline: 8/1; financial award applicants required to submit FAFSA. *Faculty research:* Native American law, criminal law, commercial speech, copyright law, international law. *Unit head:* Prof. Lyn Suzanne Entzeroth, Dean, 918-631-2400, Fax: 918-631-3126, E-mail: lyn-entzeroth@utulsa.edu. *Application contact:* April M. Fox, Associate Dean of Admissions and Financial Aid, 918-631-2406, Fax: 918-631-3630, E-mail: april-fox@utulsa.edu. Website: http://www.utulsa.edu/law/

# American Studies

**American Public University System,** AMU/APU Graduate Programs, Charles Town, WV 25414. Offers accounting (MBA, MS); applied business analytics (MBA, MS); criminal justice (MA), including business administration, emergency and disaster management, general (MA, MS); educational leadership (M Ed); emergency and disaster management (MA); entrepreneurship (MBA); environmental policy and management (MS), including environmental planning, environmental sustainability, fish and wildlife management, general (MA, MS), global environmental management; finance (MBA); general (MBA); government contracting and acquisition (MBA); health care administration (MBA); health information management (MS); history (MA), including American history, ancient and classical history, European history, global history, public history; homeland security (MA), including business administration, counterterrorism studies, criminal justice, cyber, emergency management and public health, intelligence studies, transportation security; homeland security resource allocation (MBA); humanities (MA); information technology (MS), including digital forensics, enterprise software development, information assurance and security, IT project management; information technology management (MBA); intelligence studies (MA), including criminal intelligence, cyber, general (MA, MS), homeland security, intelligence analysis, intelligence collection, intelligence management, intelligence operations, terrorism studies; international relations and conflict resolution (MA), including comparative and security issues, conflict resolution, international and transnational security issues, peacekeeping; legal studies (MA); management (MA), including strategic consulting; marketing (MBA); military history (MA), including American military history, American Revolution, civil war, war since 1945, World War II; military studies (MA), including joint warfare, strategic leadership; national security studies (MA), including cyber, general (MA, MS), homeland security, regional security studies, security and intelligence analysis, terrorism studies; nonprofit management (MBA); political science (MA), including American politics and government, comparative government and development, general (MA, MS), international relations, public policy; psychology (MA); public administration (MPA), including disaster management, environmental policy, health policy, human resources, national security, organizational management, security management; public health (MPH); reverse logistics management (MA); security management (MA); space studies (MS), including aerospace science, general (MA, MS), planetary science; sports and health sciences (MS); sports management (MBA); teaching (M Ed), including autism spectrum disorder, curriculum and instruction for elementary teachers, elementary reading, English language learners, instructional leadership, online learning, special education, STEAM (STEM plus the arts); transportation and logistics management (MA). *Program availability:* Part-time, evening/weekend, online only, 100% online. *Faculty:* 401 full-time (228 women), 1,678 part-time/adjunct (781 women). *Students:* 378 full-time (184 women), 8,455 part-time (3,484 women); includes 2,972 minority (1,552 Black or African American, non-Hispanic/Latino; 52 American Indian or Alaska Native, non-Hispanic/Latino; 211 Asian, non-Hispanic/Latino; 791 Hispanic/Latino; 70 Native Hawaiian or other Pacific Islander, non-Hispanic/Latino; 296 Two or more races, non-Hispanic/Latino), 109 international. Average age 37. In 2016, 3,185 master's awarded. *Degree requirements:* For master's, comprehensive exam or practicum. *Entrance requirements:* For master's, official transcript showing earned bachelor's degree from institution accredited by recognized accrediting body. Additional exam requirements/recommendations for international students: Required—TOEFL (minimum score 550 paper-based), IELTS (minimum score 6.5). *Application deadline:* Applications are processed on a rolling basis. Application fee: $0. Electronic applications accepted. *Expenses: Tuition:* Part-time $350 per credit hour. *Required fees:* $50 per course. *Financial support:* Scholarships/grants available. Financial award applicants required to submit FAFSA. *Unit head:* Dr. Karan Powell, President, 877-468-6268, Fax: 304-724-3780. *Application contact:* Terry Grant, Vice President of Enrollment Management, 877-468-6268, Fax: 304-724-3780, E-mail: info@apus.edu. Website: http://www.apus.edu

**American University,** School of International Service, Washington, DC 20016-8071. Offers comparative and regional studies (Certificate); cross-cultural communication (Certificate); development management (MS); ethics, peace, and global affairs (MA); European studies (Certificate); global environmental policy (MA, Certificate); global information technology (Certificate); international affairs (MA), including comparative and international disability policy, comparative and regional studies, international economic relations, international politics, natural resources and sustainable development, U.S. foreign policy; international arts management (Certificate); international communication (MA, Certificate); international development (MA); international economic policy (Certificate); international economic relations (Certificate); international economics (MA); international media (MA); international peace and conflict resolution (MA, Certificate); international politics (Certificate); international relations (MA, PhD); international service (MIS); peacebuilding (Certificate); social enterprise (MA); the Americas (Certificate); United States foreign policy (Certificate); JD/MA. *Program availability:* Part-time, evening/weekend, 100% online. *Faculty:* 116 full-time (53 women), 57 part-time/adjunct (19 women). *Students:* 575 full-time (360 women), 491 part-time (277 women); includes 287 minority (100 Black or African American, non-Hispanic/Latino; 6 American Indian or Alaska Native, non-Hispanic/Latino; 58 Asian, non-Hispanic/Latino; 92 Hispanic/Latino; 1 Native Hawaiian or other Pacific Islander, non-Hispanic/Latino; 30 Two or more races, non-Hispanic/Latino), 151 international. Average age 29. 1,504 applicants, 84% accepted, 403 enrolled. In 2016, 374 master's, 3 doctorates, 1 other advanced degree awarded. Terminal master's awarded for partial completion of doctoral program. *Degree requirements:* For master's, one foreign language, comprehensive exam, thesis or alternative; for doctorate, one foreign language, comprehensive exam, thesis/dissertation. *Entrance requirements:* For master's, GRE; GMAT or GRE (for MA in social enterprise), transcripts, resume, 2 letters of recommendation, statement of purpose; for doctorate, GRE, transcripts, resume, 3 letters of recommendation, statement of purpose. Additional exam requirements/recommendations for international students: Required—TOEFL (minimum score 600 paper-based, 100 iBT), IELTS (minimum score 7 ), or PTE (minimum score of 68). *Application fee:* $55. Electronic applications accepted. *Expenses:* $1,579 per credit tuition; $1,930 mandatory fees. *Financial support:* Research assistantships, teaching assistantships, institutionally sponsored loans, scholarships/grants, and unspecified assistantships available. Financial award application deadline: 1/15; financial award applicants required to submit FAFSA. *Unit head:* Dr. James Goldgeier, Dean, 202-885-

1603, Fax: 202-885-2494, E-mail: goldgeier@american.edu. *Application contact:* Jia Jiang, Associate Director, Graduate Education Enrollment, 202-885-1689, Fax: 202-885-1109, E-mail: jiang@american.edu. Website: http://www.american.edu/sis/

**American University of Beirut,** Graduate Programs, Faculty of Arts and Sciences, Beirut, Lebanon. Offers anthropology (MA); Arab and Middle Eastern history (PhD); Arabic language and literature (MA, PhD); archaeology (MA); art history and curating (MA); biology (MS); cell and molecular biology (PhD); chemistry (MS); clinical psychology (MA); computational sciences (MS); computer science (MS); economics (MA); education (MA); English language (MA); English literature (MA); environmental policy planning (MA); financial economics (MAFE); geology (MS); Islamic studies (MA); mathematics (MS); media studies (MA); Middle Eastern studies (MA); physics (MS); political studies (MA); psychology (MA); public administration (MA); public policy and international affairs (MA); sociology (MA); statistics (MA, MS); theoretical physics (PhD); transnational American studies (MA). *Program availability:* Part-time. *Faculty:* 133 full-time (42 women), 6 part-time/adjunct (2 women). *Students:* 240 full-time (172 women), 227 part-time (166 women). Average age 27. 286 applicants, 67% accepted, 108 enrolled. In 2016, 60 master's, 3 doctorates awarded. Terminal master's awarded for partial completion of doctoral program. *Degree requirements:* For master's, one foreign language, comprehensive exam, thesis (for some programs); for doctorate, one foreign language, comprehensive exam, thesis/dissertation. *Entrance requirements:* For master's, GRE (for some MA, MS programs), letters of recommendation; for doctorate, GRE, letters of recommendation. Additional exam requirements/recommendations for international students: Required—TOEFL (minimum score 600 paper-based; 97 iBT), IELTS (minimum score 7). *Application deadline:* For fall admission, 4/3 for domestic students; for winter admission, 11/3 for domestic students. Application fee: $50. Electronic applications accepted. *Expenses:* Contact institution. *Financial support:* In 2016–17, 4 fellowships (averaging $11,200 per year), 18 research assistantships (averaging $5,400 per year) were awarded; teaching assistantships, career-related internships or fieldwork, Federal Work-Study, institutionally sponsored loans, scholarships/grants, traineeships, health care benefits, tuition waivers (full), and unspecified assistantships also available. Support available to part-time students. *Faculty research:* Development economics, spatial econometrics, health economics, labor economics, energy economics, hydrogeology, geophysics, petrophysics, structural geology, mineralogy, petrology, geochemistry, multilingualism, comparative/world literature, translation studies, book histories/ cultures, biocatalysis, molecular recognition, photocatalysis, photophysical and biophysical chemistry, probe chemistry, machine learning, data science. *Unit head:* Dr. Nadia Maria El Cheikh, Dean, Faculty of Arts and Sciences, 961-1374374 Ext. 3800, Fax: 961-1744461, E-mail: nmcheikh@aub.edu.lb. *Application contact:* Dr. Salim Kanaan, Director, Admissions Office, 961-1350000 Ext. 2590, Fax: 961-1750775, E-mail: sk00@aub.edu.lb. Website: http://www.aub.edu.lb/fas/

**Appalachian State University,** Cratis D. Williams Graduate School, Center for Appalachian Studies, Boone, NC 28608. Offers culture (MA). *Program availability:* Part-time. *Degree requirements:* For master's, one foreign language, comprehensive exam, thesis optional. *Entrance requirements:* For master's, GRE General Test, 3 letters of recommendation. Additional exam requirements/recommendations for international students: Required—TOEFL (minimum score 570 paper-based; 79 iBT), IELTS (minimum score 6.5). *Application deadline:* For fall admission, 3/15 priority date for domestic students, 2/1 for international students; for spring admission, 11/1 for domestic students, 7/1 for international students. Applications are processed on a rolling basis. Application fee: $55. Electronic applications accepted. *Expenses:* Tuition, state resident: full-time $4744. Tuition, nonresident: full-time $17,913. Full-time tuition and fees vary according to program. *Financial support:* Fellowships, research assistantships, teaching assistantships, career-related internships or fieldwork, Federal Work-Study, scholarships/grants, and unspecified assistantships available. Financial award application deadline: 4/1; financial award applicants required to submit FAFSA. *Faculty research:* Appalachian culture, sustainable development, Appalachian music. *Unit head:* Dr. Pat Beaver, Director, 828-262-2550, E-mail: beaverpd@appstate.edu. *Application contact:* Dr. Dave Wood, Graduate Program Director, 828-262-7199, E-mail: wooddh@appstate.edu. Website: http://www.appstudies.appstate.edu

**Armstrong State University,** School of Graduate Studies, Program in History, Savannah, GA 31419-1997. Offers American and European history (MA); public history (MA). *Program availability:* Part-time, evening/weekend. *Faculty:* 6 full-time (1 woman), 1 (woman) part-time/adjunct. *Students:* 5 full-time (3 women), 11 part-time (4 women); includes 2 minority (1 Black or African American, non-Hispanic/Latino; 1 Hispanic/Latino). Average age 37. 17 applicants, 71% accepted, 8 enrolled. In 2016, 3 master's awarded. *Degree requirements:* For master's, one foreign language, comprehensive exam (for some programs), thesis (for some programs), thesis, internship, or advanced fieldwork. *Entrance requirements:* For master's, GRE General Test, minimum GPA of 3.0, letters of recommendation, BA in history or equivalent. Additional exam requirements/recommendations for international students: Required—TOEFL (minimum score 523 paper-based; 70 iBT). *Application deadline:* For fall admission, 6/30 priority date for domestic students, 5/1 priority date for international students; for spring admission, 11/15 priority date for domestic students, 9/15 priority date for international students; for summer admission, 4/15 priority date for domestic students, 9/15 for international students. Applications are processed on a rolling basis. Application fee: $30. Electronic applications accepted. *Expenses:* Tuition, state resident: full-time $1781; part-time $161.93 per credit hour. Tuition, nonresident: full-time $6482; part-time $589.27 per credit hour. *Required fees:* $1224 per unit. $612 per semester. Tuition and fees vary according to course load, campus/location and program. *Financial support:* In 2016–17, research assistantships with full tuition reimbursements (averaging $5,000 per year) were awarded; career-related internships or fieldwork, Federal Work-Study, and unspecified assistantships also available. Support available to part-time students. Financial award application deadline: 3/15; financial award applicants required to submit FAFSA. *Faculty research:* Public history; European, Latin American, African, and United States history. *Unit head:* Dr. Christopher Hendricks, Interim Department Head, 912-344-2725, Fax: 912-344-3451, E-mail: chris.hendricks@armstrong.edu. *Application contact:* McKenzie Peterman, Assistant Director of Graduate Admissions, 912-344-

## American Studies

2503, Fax: 912-344-3417, E-mail: graduate@armstrong.edu. Website: http://www.armstrong.edu/Liberal_Arts/history/history_graduate_program

**Baylor University,** Graduate School, College of Arts and Sciences, Program in American Studies, Waco, TX 76798. Offers MA. *Students:* 2 full-time (0 women), 1 part-time (0 women); includes 1 minority (Two or more races, non-Hispanic/Latino). In 2016, 2 master's awarded. *Degree requirements:* For master's, thesis, final oral exam. *Entrance requirements:* For master's, GRE General Test, 24 semester hours of course work in subjects with American content. *Application deadline:* For fall admission, 8/1 for domestic students. Applications are processed on a rolling basis. Application fee: $25. *Expenses: Tuition:* Full-time $28,494; part-time $1583 per credit hour. *Required fees:* $167 per credit hour. Tuition and fees vary according to course load and program. *Financial support:* Fellowships, Federal Work-Study, and institutionally sponsored loans available. Financial award application deadline: 4/15. *Unit head:* Dr. Mia N. Moody-Ramirez, Graduate Program Director, 254-710-7247, Fax: 254-710-7247, E-mail: mia_moody@baylor.edu. *Application contact:* Margaret Kramer, Administrative Assistant, 254-710-4350, Fax: 254-710-3870, E-mail: margaret_kramer@baylor.edu. Website: http://www.baylor.edu/American_Studies/

**Boston University,** Graduate School of Arts and Sciences, Program in American and New England Studies, Boston, MA 02215. Offers PhD. *Students:* 38 full-time (21 women), 6 part-time (5 women); includes 5 minority (4 Black or African American, non-Hispanic/Latino; 1 Two or more races, non-Hispanic/Latino), 1 international. Average age 31. 43 applicants, 30% accepted, 5 enrolled. In 2016, 2 doctorates awarded. *Degree requirements:* For doctorate, one foreign language, comprehensive exam, thesis/dissertation. *Entrance requirements:* For doctorate, GRE General Test, scholarly writing sample, 3 letters of recommendation, transcripts, personal statement, curriculum vitae. Additional exam requirements/recommendations for international students: Required—TOEFL (minimum score 550 paper-based; 84 iBT). *Application deadline:* For fall admission, 1/5 for domestic and international students. Application fee: $95. Electronic applications accepted. *Financial support:* In 2016–17, 41 students received support, including 15 fellowships with full tuition reimbursements available (averaging $21,500 per year), 1 research assistantship with full tuition reimbursement available (averaging $21,500 per year), 15 teaching assistantships with full tuition reimbursements available (averaging $21,500 per year); career-related internships or fieldwork, Federal Work-Study, scholarships/grants, health care benefits, and unspecified assistantships also available. Financial award application deadline: 1/5. *Unit head:* William Moore, Director, 617-353-9912, Fax: 617-353-2556, E-mail: moorewd@bu.edu. *Application contact:* Julia Kline, Senior Program Coordinator, 617-353-2948, Fax: 617-353-2556, E-mail: jgawle@bu.edu. Website: http://www.bu.edu/AMNESP/

**Bowling Green State University,** Graduate College, College of Arts and Sciences, American Culture Studies Program, Bowling Green, OH 43403. Offers MA, PhD. *Program availability:* Part-time. *Degree requirements:* For master's, thesis or alternative; for doctorate, comprehensive exam, thesis/dissertation. *Entrance requirements:* For master's and doctorate, GRE General Test. Additional exam requirements/recommendations for international students: Required—TOEFL. *Application deadline:* For fall admission, 2/1 for domestic students. Application fee: $30. Electronic applications accepted. *Financial support:* Fellowships with full tuition reimbursements, research assistantships with full tuition reimbursements, teaching assistantships with full tuition reimbursements, Federal Work-Study, and unspecified assistantships available. Financial award applicants required to submit FAFSA. *Faculty research:* Race and ethnicity, gender, popular culture. *Unit head:* Dr. Don McQuarie, Chair, 419-372-0586. *Application contact:* Dr. Terry L. Lawrence, Assistant Dean for Graduate Admissions and Studies, 419-372-7713, Fax: 419-372-8569, E-mail: tlawren@bgnet.bgsu.edu.

**Bowling Green State University,** Graduate College, College of Arts and Sciences, Department of Popular Culture, Bowling Green, OH 43403. Offers MA. *Program availability:* Part-time. *Degree requirements:* For master's, thesis or alternative. *Entrance requirements:* For master's, GRE General Test. Additional exam requirements/recommendations for international students: Required—TOEFL. *Application deadline:* For fall admission, 2/15 priority date for domestic students. Application fee: $30. Electronic applications accepted. *Financial support:* Research assistantships with full tuition reimbursements, teaching assistantships with full tuition reimbursements, career-related internships or fieldwork, Federal Work-Study, institutionally sponsored loans, and unspecified assistantships available. Financial award applicants required to submit FAFSA. *Faculty research:* Mass media (popular film, TV, and music); folklore/folk life; ritual, festival, celebration, and holidays; global, international, and popular culture; nineteenth century everyday life. *Unit head:* Dr. Angela Nelson, Chair, 419-372-0284. *Application contact:* Dr. Jeffrey Brown, Graduate Coordinator, 419-372-2982.

**Brown University,** Graduate School, Department of American Studies, Providence, RI 02912. Offers American studies (PhD); American studies for international students (MA); public humanities (MA). *Degree requirements:* For doctorate, thesis/dissertation, preliminary exam.

**California State University, Fullerton,** Graduate Studies, College of Humanities and Social Sciences, Department of American Studies, Fullerton, CA 92834-9480. Offers MA. *Program availability:* Part-time. *Degree requirements:* For master's, comprehensive exam or thesis. *Entrance requirements:* For master's, minimum GPA of 3.0 in major, 2.5 in last 60 hours. Application fee: $55. *Expenses: Tuition:* state resident: full-time $3369; part-time $1953 per unit. Tuition, nonresident: full-time $3915; part-time $2499 per unit. Tuition and fees vary according to course load, degree level and program. *Financial support:* Federal Work-Study, institutionally sponsored loans, and scholarships/grants available. Support available to part-time students. Financial award application deadline: 3/1; financial award applicants required to submit FAFSA. *Unit head:* Leila Zenderland, Chair, 657-278-3800, E-mail: lzenderland@fullerton.edu. *Application contact:* Admissions/Applications, 657-278-2371.

**The Catholic University of America,** School of Arts and Sciences, Department of History, Washington, DC 20064. Offers history (MA, PhD), including early modern Europe, Latin America (MA), Medieval, modern Europe, U.S.; religion and society in the late medieval and early modern world (MA); MA/JD; MSLS/MA. *Program availability:* Part-time. *Faculty:* 14 full-time (6 women), 3 part-time/adjunct (2 women). *Students:* 7 full-time (2 women), 20 part-time (6 women); includes 3 minority (all Two or more races, non-Hispanic/Latino), 2 international. Average age 30. 22 applicants, 45% accepted, 4 enrolled. In 2016, 4 master's, 5 doctorates awarded. Terminal master's awarded for partial completion of doctoral program. *Degree requirements:* For master's, one foreign language, comprehensive exam, thesis optional, 2 languages (for medievalists), one of which must be Latin; for doctorate, 2 foreign languages, comprehensive exam, thesis/dissertation, 3 languages (for medievalists), one of which must be Latin. *Entrance requirements:* For master's and doctorate, GRE General Test, statement of purpose, official copies of academic transcripts, three letters of recommendation, writing sample. Additional exam requirements/recommendations for international students: Required—TOEFL (minimum score 550 paper-based; 80 iBT). *Application deadline:* For fall admission, 7/15 priority date for domestic students, 7/1 for international students; for spring admission, 11/15 priority date for domestic students, 11/1 for international students. Applications are processed on a rolling basis. Application fee: $55. Electronic applications accepted. *Expenses:* $42,850 per year; $1,170 per credit; $200 per semester part-time fees. *Financial support:* Fellowships, research assistantships, teaching assistantships, Federal Work-Study, scholarships/grants, tuition waivers (full and partial), and unspecified assistantships available. Financial award application deadline: 2/1; financial award applicants required to submit FAFSA. *Faculty research:* Medieval history, including the Islamic Middle East, with particular expertise in later medieval religious, social, and economic history and early medieval and late antique history; European and American intellectual history; renaissance, reformation, catholic reformation; US catholic history; history of immigration. *Total annual research expenditures:* $42,594. *Unit head:* Dr. Katherine Jansen, Chair, 202-319-5484, Fax: 202-319-5569, E-mail: jansen@cua.edu. *Application contact:* Director of Graduate Admissions, 202-319-5057, Fax: 202-319-6533, E-mail: cua-admissions@cua.edu. Website: http://history.cua.edu/

**Central Michigan University,** College of Graduate Studies, College of Humanities and Social and Behavioral Sciences, Department of History, Mount Pleasant, MI 48859. Offers European history (Graduate Certificate); history (MA); modern history (Graduate Certificate); United States history (Graduate Certificate); MA/PhD. *Program availability:* Part-time. *Degree requirements:* For master's, thesis or alternative. Electronic applications accepted. *Faculty research:* Colonial and revolutionary United States history, modern European history, Latin American and transatlantic history, transnational and comparative history, United States social history.

**Claremont Graduate University,** Graduate Programs, School of Arts and Humanities, Department of English, Claremont, CA 91711-6160. Offers American studies (MA, PhD); critical theory (MA, PhD); early modern studies (MA, PhD); English (M Phil, MA, PhD); literary theory (PhD); literature (MA, PhD); literature and creative writing (MA); literature and film (MA); MBA/MA; MBA/PhD. *Program availability:* Part-time. *Faculty:* 3 full-time (1 woman), 1 part-time/adjunct (0 women). *Students:* 61 full-time (46 women), 20 part-time (14 women); includes 23 minority (4 Black or African American, non-Hispanic/Latino; 1 American Indian or Alaska Native, non-Hispanic/Latino; 9 Asian, non-Hispanic/Latino; 4 Hispanic/Latino; 5 Two or more races, non-Hispanic/Latino), 6 international. Average age 37. In 2016, 10 master's, 8 doctorates awarded. *Entrance requirements:* For master's and doctorate, GRE General Test. Additional exam requirements/recommendations for international students: Required—TOEFL (minimum score 75 iBT). *Application deadline:* For fall admission, 2/1 priority date for domestic and international students. Applications are processed on a rolling basis. Application fee: $80. Electronic applications accepted. *Expenses: Tuition:* Full-time $44,328; part-time $1847 per unit. *Required fees:* $600; $300 per semester. Tuition and fees vary according to course load and program. *Financial support:* Fellowships, Federal Work-Study, institutionally sponsored loans, and scholarships/grants available. Support available to part-time students. Financial award application deadline: 2/15; financial award applicants required to submit FAFSA. *Faculty research:* American, comparative, and English Renaissance literature; modernism; feminist literature and theory. *Unit head:* Lori Anne Ferrell, Chair, 909-607-2652, E-mail: lorianne.ferrell@cgu.edu. *Application contact:* Amy Sandefur, Assistant Director of Admissions, 909-607-9101, E-mail: amy.sandefur@cgu.edu. Website: https://www.cgu.edu/departments/english/

**Claremont Graduate University,** Graduate Programs, School of Arts and Humanities, Department of History, Claremont, CA 91711-6160. Offers Africana history (Certificate); American studies and U.S. history (MA, PhD); archival studies (MA); early modern studies (MA, PhD); European studies (MA, PhD); oral history (MA, PhD); MBA/MA; MBA/PhD. *Faculty:* 5 full-time (3 women), 2 part-time/adjunct (0 women). *Students:* 45 full-time (23 women), 24 part-time (14 women); includes 21 minority (2 Black or African American, non-Hispanic/Latino; 1 American Indian or Alaska Native, non-Hispanic/Latino; 5 Asian, non-Hispanic/Latino; 6 Hispanic/Latino; 1 Native Hawaiian or other Pacific Islander, non-Hispanic/Latino; 6 Two or more races, non-Hispanic/Latino). Average age 38. In 2016, 5 master's, 2 doctorates awarded. Terminal master's awarded for partial completion of doctoral program. *Entrance requirements:* For master's and doctorate, GRE General Test. Additional exam requirements/recommendations for international students: Required—TOEFL (minimum score 75 iBT). *Application deadline:* For fall admission, 2/1 priority date for domestic and international students. Applications are processed on a rolling basis. Application fee: $80. Electronic applications accepted. *Expenses: Tuition:* Full-time $44,328; part-time $1847 per unit. *Required fees:* $600; $300 per semester. Tuition and fees vary according to course load and program. *Financial support:* Fellowships, research assistantships, Federal Work-Study, institutionally sponsored loans, and scholarships/grants available. Support available to part-time students. Financial award application deadline: 2/15; financial award applicants required to submit FAFSA. *Faculty research:* Intellectual and social history, cultural studies, gender studies, Western history, Chicano history. *Unit head:* Joshua Goode, Chair, 909-607-7430, E-mail: joshua.goode@cgu.edu. *Application contact:* Amy Sandefur, Assistant Director of Admissions, 909-607-9101, E-mail: amy.sandefur@cgu.edu. Website: https://www.cgu.edu/departments/history/

**Clark University,** Graduate School, Department of History, Program in United States and Atlantic History, Worcester, MA 01610-1477. Offers history of the Atlantic world (PhD); history of the United States (PhD). *Students:* 9 full-time (3 women), 7 part-time (3 women), 1 international. Average age 59. 14 applicants, 43% accepted, 6 enrolled. In 2016, 1 doctorate awarded. *Application deadline:* For fall admission, 1/15 for domestic students. Application fee: $75. *Expenses: Tuition:* Full-time $44,050. *Required fees:* $80. Tuition and fees vary according to course load and program. *Financial support:* In 2016–17, fellowships with tuition reimbursements (averaging $17,000 per year), research assistantships with tuition reimbursements (averaging $17,000 per year), teaching assistantships with tuition reimbursements (averaging $17,000 per year) were awarded. *Faculty research:* American political history, comparative history, American family history. *Unit head:* Dr. Willem Klooster, Professor, 508-421-3768. *Application contact:* Diane Fenner, Department Assistant, 508-793-7288, Fax: 508-793-8816, E-mail: dfenner@clarku.edu.

**The College at Brockport, State University of New York,** School of Arts and Sciences, Department of History, Brockport, NY 14420-2997. Offers history (MA), including American and world history, American history, American public history, world history. *Program availability:* Part-time, evening/weekend. *Faculty:* 9 full-time (5 women). *Students:* 8 full-time (5 women), 17 part-time (9 women); includes 1 minority (Black or African American, non-Hispanic/Latino). 17 applicants, 82% accepted, 11 enrolled. In 2016, 15 master's awarded. *Degree requirements:* For master's, thesis or alternative. *Entrance requirements:* For master's, minimum GPA of 3.0, writing sample, letters of recommendation, statement of objectives. Additional exam requirements/recommendations for international students: Required—TOEFL (minimum score 550 paper-based; 79 iBT), IELTS (minimum score 6.5). *Application deadline:* For fall admission, 7/1 priority date for domestic and international students; for spring admission, 11/15 priority date for domestic and international students; for summer admission, 4/15 for domestic and international students. Application fee: $50. Electronic applications accepted. *Expenses:* Contact institution. *Financial support:* In 2016–17, 1 fellowship with tuition reimbursement (averaging $3,750 per year), 2 teaching assistantships with full tuition reimbursements (averaging $6,000 per year) were awarded; Federal Work-Study, scholarships/grants, and unspecified assistantships also available. Support available to part-time students. Financial award application deadline: 3/15; financial award applicants required to submit FAFSA. *Faculty research:* American history, women's history, European history, world history, cultural history. *Unit head:* Dr. Owen Steve Ireland, Chairperson, 585-395-5627, Fax: 585-395-2620, E-mail: oireland@brockport.edu. *Application contact:* Dr. Morag Martin, Graduate Director, 585-395-5690, Fax: 585-395-2620, E-mail: mmartin@brockport.edu. Website: http://www.brockport.edu/history/grad/

**College of Staten Island of the City University of New York,** Graduate Programs, Division of Humanities and Social Sciences, Program in History, Staten Island, NY 10314-6600. Offers history of Africa and the Middle East (MA); history of Asia (MA); history of Europe (MA); history of Latin America and the Caribbean (MA); history of the United States (MA). *Program availability:* Part-time, evening/weekend. *Faculty:* 2 full-time. *Students:* 11 part-time. Average age 36. 8 applicants, 25% accepted, 2 enrolled. In 2016, 5 master's awarded. *Degree requirements:* For master's, comprehensive exam (for some programs), 32 credits (total of eight courses); thesis or portfolio. *Entrance requirements:* For master's, bachelor's degree with minimum GPA of 3.0 overall and in undergraduate history courses, two letters of recommendation, letter of interest, research-based writing sample. Additional exam requirements/recommendations for international students: Required—TOEFL (minimum score 550 paper-based; 79 iBT), IELTS (minimum score 6.5). *Application deadline:* For fall admission, 5/10 priority date for domestic and international students; for spring admission, 12/2 priority date for domestic and international students. Applications are processed on a rolling basis. Application fee: $125. Electronic applications accepted. *Expenses:* Tuition, state resident: full-time $10,130; part-time $425 per credit. Tuition, nonresident: full-time $18,720; part-time $780 per credit. *Required fees:* $181.10 per semester. Tuition and fees vary according to program. *Faculty research:* African and African diaspora history, South Asian history, Middle Eastern history, U.S. history, environmental history. *Unit head:* John Dixon, Graduate Program Coordinator, 718-982-3307, E-mail: john.dixon@csi.cuny.edu. *Application contact:* Sasha Spence, Associate Director for Graduate Admissions, 718-982-2019, Fax: 718-982-2500, E-mail: sasha.spence@csi.cuny.edu. Website: http://www.csi.cuny.edu/catalog/graduate/master-of-arts-in-history-ma.htm

**The College of William and Mary,** Faculty of Arts and Sciences, American Studies Program, Williamsburg, VA 23187-8795. Offers MA, PhD, JD/MA. *Program availability:* Part-time. *Faculty:* 13 full-time (6 women), 1 (woman) part-time/adjunct. *Students:* 33 full-time (21 women), 2 part-time (both women); includes 15 minority (4 Black or African American, non-Hispanic/Latino; 5 Asian, non-Hispanic/Latino; 2 Hispanic/Latino; 4 Two or more races, non-Hispanic/Latino), 2 international. Average age 29. 43 applicants, 35% accepted, 8 enrolled. In 2016, 3 master's, 5 doctorates awarded. Terminal master's awarded for partial completion of doctoral program. *Degree requirements:* For master's, thesis; for doctorate, one foreign language, comprehensive exam, thesis/dissertation. *Entrance requirements:* For master's, GRE; for doctorate, GRE, MA. Additional exam requirements/recommendations for international students: Required—TOEFL. *Application deadline:* For fall admission, 1/1 for domestic and international students. Application fee: $45. Electronic applications accepted. *Expenses:* Tuition, state resident: full-time $9000; part-time $500 per credit hour. Tuition, nonresident: full-time $24,686; part-time $1200 per credit hour. *Required fees:* $5258. One-time fee: $400 full-time. *Financial support:* In 2016–17, 24 students received support, including 20 fellowships with full tuition reimbursements available (averaging $20,400 per year); career-related internships or fieldwork and unspecified assistantships also available. Financial award application deadline: 1/1. *Faculty research:* Nineteenth- and twentieth-century U.S. cultural history; nineteenth- and twentieth-century American literature; material culture, visual culture, and art historical studies; African-American studies; Native American studies; mass and popular culture studies. *Unit head:* Dr. Charles McGovern, Director, 757-221-1296, Fax: 757-221-1287, E-mail: cfmcgo@wm.edu. *Application contact:* Jean Brown, Program Administrator, 757-221-1275, Fax: 757-221-1287, E-mail: jxbrow@wm.edu. Website: http://www.wm.edu/americanstudies/

**The Colorado College,** Education Department, Experienced Teacher Program, Colorado Springs, CO 80903-3294. Offers arts and humanities (MAT); integrated natural sciences (MAT); liberal arts (MAT); Southwest studies (MAT). Programs offered during summer only. *Program availability:* Part-time. *Degree requirements:* For master's, thesis, oral exam, 50-page paper. *Expenses:* Contact institution.

**Columbia University,** Graduate School of Arts and Sciences, New York, NY 10027. Offers African-American studies (MA); American studies (MA); anthropology (MA, PhD); art history and archaeology (MA, PhD); astronomy (PhD); biological sciences (PhD); biotechnology (MA); chemical physics (PhD); chemistry (PhD); classical studies (MA, PhD); classics (MA, PhD); climate and society (MA); conservation biology (MA); earth and environmental sciences (PhD); East Asia: regional studies (MA); East Asian languages and cultures (MA, PhD); ecology, evolution and environmental biology (MA), including conservation biology; ecology, evolution, and environmental biology (PhD), including ecology and evolutionary biology, evolutionary primatology; economics (MA, PhD); English and comparative literature (MA, PhD); French and Romance philology (MA, PhD); Germanic languages (MA, PhD); global French studies (MA); global thought (MA); Hispanic cultural studies (MA); history (PhD); history and literature (MA); human rights studies (MA); Islamic studies (MA); Italian (MA, PhD); Japanese pedagogy (MA); Jewish studies (MA); Latin America and the Caribbean: regional studies (MA); Latin American and Iberian cultures (PhD); mathematics (MA, PhD), including finance (MA); medieval and Renaissance studies (MA); Middle Eastern, South Asian, and African studies (MA, PhD); modern art: critical and curatorial studies (MA); modern European studies (MA); museum anthropology (MA); music (DMA, PhD); oral history (MA); philosophical foundations of physics (MA); philosophy (MA, PhD); physics (PhD); political science (MA, PhD); psychology (PhD); quantitative methods in the social sciences (MA); religion (MA, PhD); Russia, Eurasia and East Europe: regional studies (MA); Russian translation (MA); Slavic cultures (MA); Slavic languages (MA, PhD); sociology (MA, PhD); South Asian studies (MA); statistics (MA, PhD); theatre (PhD). Dual-degree programs require admission to both Graduate School of Arts and Sciences and another Columbia school. *Program availability:* Part-time. Terminal master's awarded for partial completion of doctoral program. *Degree requirements:* For master's, variable foreign language requirement, comprehensive exam (for some programs), thesis (for some programs); for doctorate, variable foreign language requirement, comprehensive exam (for some programs), thesis/dissertation. *Entrance requirements:* For master's and doctorate, GRE General Test, GRE Subject Test (for some programs). Additional exam requirements/recommendations for international students: Required—TOEFL, IELTS. Electronic applications accepted.

**Cornell University,** Graduate School, Graduate Fields of Arts and Sciences, Field of English Language and Literature, Ithaca, NY 14853. Offers African-American literature (PhD); American literature after 1865 (PhD); American literature to 1865 (PhD); American studies (PhD); colonial and postcolonial literatures (PhD); creative writing (MFA); cultural studies (PhD); dramatic literature (PhD); English poetry (PhD); English Renaissance to 1660 (PhD); lesbian, bisexual, and gay literary studies (PhD); literary criticism and theory (PhD); Old and Middle English (PhD); prose fiction (PhD); Restoration and the eighteenth-century (PhD); the nineteenth century (PhD); the

twentieth century (PhD); women's literature (PhD); MFA/PhD. Terminal master's awarded for partial completion of doctoral program. *Degree requirements:* For master's, one foreign language, thesis; for doctorate, one foreign language, comprehensive exam, thesis/dissertation, teaching experience. *Entrance requirements:* For master's, GRE General Test, 3 letters of recommendation, creative writing sample; for doctorate, GRE General Test, GRE Subject Test (English), 3 letters of recommendation, writing sample. Additional exam requirements/recommendations for international students: Required—TOEFL (minimum score 600 paper-based; 77 iBT). Electronic applications accepted. *Faculty research:* English and American literature, women's writing, ethnic and post-colonial literature, critical theory, medievalism.

**Cornell University,** Graduate School, Graduate Fields of Arts and Sciences, Field of History, Ithaca, NY 14853. Offers African history (MA, PhD); American history (MA, PhD); ancient Greek history (PhD); ancient history (MA, PhD); ancient Roman history (PhD); early modern European history (MA, PhD); English history (MA, PhD); French history (MA, PhD); German history (MA, PhD); history of science (MA, PhD); Korean history (PhD); Latin American history (MA, PhD); medieval Chinese history (MA, PhD); medieval history (MA, PhD); modern Chinese history (MA, PhD); modern European history (MA, PhD); modern Japanese history (MA, PhD); modern Middle Eastern history (PhD); premodern Islamic history (MA, PhD); premodern Japanese history (MA, PhD); Renaissance history (MA, PhD); Russian history (MA, PhD); South Asian history (PhD); Southeast Asian history (MA, PhD). Terminal master's awarded for partial completion of doctoral program. *Degree requirements:* For master's, thesis; for doctorate, 2 foreign languages, comprehensive exam, thesis/dissertation, 1 year of teaching experience. *Entrance requirements:* For master's and doctorate, GRE General Test, writing sample, 3 letters of recommendation. Additional exam requirements/recommendations for international students: Required—TOEFL (minimum score 550 paper-based; 77 iBT). Electronic applications accepted.

**Cornell University,** Graduate School, Graduate Fields of Arts and Sciences, Field of History of Art, Archaeology and Visual Studies, Ithaca, NY 14853. Offers 19th century art (PhD); African, African American and African diaspora (PhD); American art (PhD); ancient art and archaeology (PhD); Asian American art (PhD); Baroque art (PhD); comparative modernities (PhD); digital art (PhD); East Asian art (PhD); history of photography (PhD); Islamic art (PhD); Latin American art (PhD); medieval art (PhD); modern art (PhD); Renaissance art (PhD); Southeast Asian art (PhD); theory and criticism (PhD); visual studies (PhD). *Degree requirements:* For doctorate, one foreign language, comprehensive exam, thesis/dissertation, general exams in 3 areas. *Entrance requirements:* For doctorate, GRE General Test, sample of written work, 3 letters of recommendation. Additional exam requirements/recommendations for international students: Required—TOEFL (minimum score 550 paper-based; 77 iBT). Electronic applications accepted.

**Drew University,** Caspersen School of Graduate Studies, Madison, NJ 07940-1493. Offers conflict resolution and leadership (Certificate), including community leadership, moderation, peace building; history and culture (MA, PhD), including American history, book history, British history, European history, Holocaust and genocide (M Litt, MA, D Litt, PhD), intellectual history, Irish history, print culture, public history; K-12 education (MAT), including art, biology, chemistry, elementary education, English, French, Italian, math, secondary education, special education, teacher of students with disabilities; liberal studies (M Litt, D Litt), including history, Holocaust and genocide (M Litt, MA, D Litt, PhD), Irish/Irish-American studies, literature (M Litt, MMH, D Litt, DMH, CMH), religion, spirituality, teaching in the two-year college, writing; medical humanities (MMH, DMH, CMH), including arts, health, healthcare, literature (M Litt, MMH, D Litt, DMH, CMH), scientific research; poetry (MFA). *Program availability:* Part-time, evening/weekend. *Faculty:* 4 full-time (2 women), 31 part-time/adjunct (16 women). *Students:* 62 full-time (41 women), 199 part-time (130 women); includes 38 minority (17 Black or African American, non-Hispanic/Latino; 3 Asian, non-Hispanic/Latino; 17 Hispanic/Latino; 1 Two or more races, non-Hispanic/Latino), 3 international. Average age 27. 93 applicants, 81% accepted, 46 enrolled. In 2016, 39 master's, 27 doctorates, 26 other advanced degrees awarded. Terminal master's awarded for partial completion of doctoral program. *Degree requirements:* For master's and other advanced degree, thesis (for some programs); for doctorate, one foreign language, comprehensive exam (for some programs), thesis/dissertation. *Entrance requirements:* For master's, PRAXIS Core and Subject Area tests (for MAT), resume, transcripts, writing sample, personal statement, letters of recommendation; for doctorate, GRE (PhD in history and culture), resume, transcripts, writing sample, personal statement, letters of recommendation. Additional exam requirements/recommendations for international students: Required—TOEFL (minimum score 587 paper-based; 94 iBT), IELTS (minimum score 7), TWE (minimum score 4). *Application deadline:* For fall admission, 8/1 for domestic students, 6/1 for international students; for spring admission, 12/1 for domestic students, 10/1 for international students. Applications are processed on a rolling basis. Application fee: $35. Electronic applications accepted. Tuition and fees vary according to program. *Financial support:* Fellowships, research assistantships, teaching assistantships, career-related internships or fieldwork, Federal Work-Study, scholarships/grants, and unspecified assistantships available. Support available to part-time students. Financial award applicants required to submit FAFSA. *Application contact:* Leanne Horinko, Director of Caspersen Admissions, 973-408-3280, E-mail: gradm@drew.edu. Website: http://www.drew.edu/caspersen

**East Carolina University,** Graduate School, Thomas Harriot College of Arts and Sciences, Department of History, Greenville, NC 27858-4353. Offers American history (MA); Atlantic world (MA); European history (MA); history education (MA Ed); maritime studies (MA); military history (MA); public history (MA). *Program availability:* Part-time, evening/weekend. *Students:* 44 full-time (21 women), 48 part-time (27 women); includes 8 minority (1 Black or African American, non-Hispanic/Latino; 5 Hispanic/Latino; 2 Two or more races, non-Hispanic/Latino), 2 international. Average age 29. 46 applicants, 80% accepted, 23 enrolled. In 2016, 24 master's awarded. *Degree requirements:* For master's, one foreign language, comprehensive exam, thesis. *Entrance requirements:* For master's, GRE General Test, GRE Subject Test. Additional exam requirements/recommendations for international students: Required—TOEFL. *Application deadline:* For fall admission, 6/1 priority date for domestic students; for spring admission, 10/15 for domestic students. Applications are processed on a rolling basis. Application fee: $50. *Financial support:* Fellowships, research assistantships with partial tuition reimbursements, teaching assistantships with partial tuition reimbursements, and Federal Work-Study available. Support available to part-time students. Financial award application deadline: 6/1. *Unit head:* Dr. Gerry Prokopowicz, Chair, 252-328-6587, E-mail: prokopowiczg@ecu.edu. Website: http://www.ecu.edu/cs-cas/history/graduatedegrees.cfm

**Emory & Henry College,** Graduate Programs, Emory, VA 24327-0947. Offers American history (MA Ed); organizational leadership (MCOL); professional studies (M Ed); reading specialist (MA Ed). *Program availability:* Part-time, evening/weekend. *Entrance requirements:* For master's, GRE or PRAXIS I, recommendations, writing sample. Additional exam requirements/recommendations for international students: Recommended—TOEFL.

**Fairfield University,** College of Arts and Sciences, Fairfield, CT 06824. Offers American studies (MA); communication (MA); creative writing (MFA); mathematics (MS);

## American Studies

public administration (MPA). *Program availability:* Part-time, evening/weekend, online learning. *Faculty:* 17 full-time (9 women), 12 part-time/adjunct (6 women). *Students:* 60 full-time (40 women), 51 part-time (28 women); includes 24 minority (9 Black or African American, non-Hispanic/Latino; 1 Asian, non-Hispanic/Latino; 11 Hispanic/Latino; 3 Two or more races, non-Hispanic/Latino), 8 international. Average age 34. 84 applicants, 74% accepted, 38 enrolled. In 2016, 68 master's awarded. *Degree requirements:* For master's, capstone research course. *Entrance requirements:* For master's, minimum GPA of 3.0, 2 letters of recommendation, resume, personal statement. Additional exam requirements/recommendations for international students: Required—TOEFL (minimum score 550 paper-based; 80 iBT) or IELTS (minimum score 6.5). *Application deadline:* For fall admission, 5/15 for international students; for spring admission, 10/15 for international students. Applications are processed on a rolling basis. Application fee: $60. Electronic applications accepted. *Expenses:* Contact institution. *Financial support:* In 2016–17, 17 students received support. Scholarships/grants and unspecified assistantships available. Financial award applicants required to submit FAFSA. *Faculty research:* Ethical theory, media industries, community-based teaching and learning, non commutative algebra and partial differential equations, cancer research in biology and physics. *Unit head:* Dr. Yohuru Williams, Dean, 203-254-4000 Ext. 2221, Fax: 203-254-4119, E-mail: ywilliams@fairfield.edu. *Application contact:* Marianne Gumpper, Director of Graduate Admission, 203-254-4184, Fax: 203-254-4073, E-mail: gradadmis@fairfield.edu.
Website: http://www.fairfield.edu/cas

**Florida State University,** The Graduate School, College of Fine Arts, School of Dance, Tallahassee, FL 32306-2120. Offers American dance studies (MA); dance (MFA); studio and related studies (MA). *Accreditation:* NASD. *Faculty:* 20 full-time (13 women), 1 (woman) part-time/adjunct. *Students:* 25 full-time (19 women); includes 9 minority (6 Black or African American, non-Hispanic/Latino; 1 Asian, non-Hispanic/Latino; 2 Hispanic/Latino). Average age 28. 18 applicants, 72% accepted, 9 enrolled. In 2016, 14 master's awarded. *Degree requirements:* For master's, comprehensive exam (for some programs), thesis (for some programs), 1 foreign language (for MA in American dance studies). *Entrance requirements:* For master's, GRE General Test or minimum GPA of 3.0 (for MA in American dance studies), writing sample, audition and interview (for MFA, MA in studio and related studies). Additional exam requirements/recommendations for international students: Required—TOEFL (minimum score 550 paper-based, 80 iBT), IELTS (minimum score 6.5) or Michigan English Language Assessment Battery (minimum score 77). *Application deadline:* For fall admission, 2/1 priority date for domestic and international students; for spring admission, 11/1 priority date for domestic and international students. Applications are processed on a rolling basis. Application fee: $30. Electronic applications accepted. *Expenses:* Contact institution. *Financial support:* In 2016–17, 23 students received support, including 3 fellowships with full tuition reimbursements available (averaging $16,666 per year), 10 research assistantships with full tuition reimbursements available (averaging $5,000 per year), 13 teaching assistantships with full tuition reimbursements available (averaging $5,000 per year); scholarships/grants, health care benefits, tuition waivers (full), and unspecified assistantships also available. Financial award application deadline: 6/30; financial award applicants required to submit FAFSA. *Faculty research:* Choreography, performance, dance and cultural significance, American dance history, dance technology, critical dance theory. *Unit head:* Prof. Josephine Garibaldi, Associate Professor and Chair, 850-644-1024, Fax: 850-644-1277, E-mail: jgaribaldi@fsu.edu. *Application contact:* Stephanie Mills, Academic Coordinator, 850-644-1023, Fax: 850-644-1277, E-mail: smmills@fsu.edu.
Website: http://dance.fsu.edu/

**Florida State University,** The Graduate School, College of Social Sciences and Public Policy, Department of Political Science, Tallahassee, FL 32306-2230. Offers applied American politics and policy (MA, MS); political science (PhD). *Program availability:* Part-time. *Faculty:* 22 full-time (5 women), 1 part-time/adjunct (0 women). *Students:* 58 full-time (26 women), 26 part-time (11 women); includes 20 minority (4 Black or African American, non-Hispanic/Latino; 2 Asian, non-Hispanic/Latino; 4 Hispanic/Latino; 10 Two or more races, non-Hispanic/Latino). Average age 25. 77 applicants, 58% accepted, 29 enrolled. In 2016, 24 master's, 5 doctorates awarded. Terminal master's awarded for partial completion of doctoral program. *Degree requirements:* For master's, thesis optional; for doctorate, comprehensive exam, thesis/dissertation. *Entrance requirements:* For master's, GRE General Test, minimum undergraduate GPA of 3.0; for doctorate, GRE General Test, minimum graduate GPA of 3.5, undergraduate 3.0. Additional exam requirements/recommendations for international students: Required—TOEFL (minimum score 600 paper-based; 100 iBT). *Application deadline:* For fall admission, 1/15 priority date for domestic and international students. Applications are processed on a rolling basis. Application fee: $30. Electronic applications accepted. *Expenses:* Tuition, state resident: full-time $7263; part-time $403.51 per credit hour. Tuition, nonresident: full-time $18,087; part-time $1004.85 per credit hour. *Required fees:* $1365; $75.81 per credit hour. $20 per semester. Tuition and fees vary according to campus/location. *Financial support:* In 2016–17, 38 students received support, including 2 fellowships with full tuition reimbursements available (averaging $20,000 per year), 32 research assistantships with full tuition reimbursements available (averaging $17,000 per year), 4 teaching assistantships with full tuition reimbursements available (averaging $17,000 per year); Federal Work-Study, institutionally sponsored loans, scholarships/grants, and unspecified assistantships also available. Financial award application deadline: 1/15; financial award applicants required to submit FAFSA. *Faculty research:* American government, international relations, comparative government, public policy. *Total annual research expenditures:* $130,000. *Unit head:* Dr. Mark Souva, Director of Graduate Studies, 850-644-7315, Fax: 850-644-1367, E-mail: msouva@fsu.edu. *Application contact:* Jeremiah J. Fisher, Academic Coordinator, 850-644-7305, Fax: 850-644-1367, E-mail: jeremiah.fisher@fsu.edu.
Website: http://coss.fsu.edu/polisci

**Georgetown University,** Graduate School of Arts and Sciences, School of Continuing Studies, Washington, DC 20057. Offers American studies (MALS); Catholic studies (MALS); classical civilizations (MALS); emergency and disaster management (MPS); ethics and the professions (MALS); global strategic communications (MPS); hospitality management (MPS); human resources management (MPS); humanities (MALS); individualized study (MALS); integrated marketing communications (MPS); international affairs (MALS); Islam and Muslim-Christian relations (MALS); journalism (MPS); liberal studies (DLS); literature and society (MALS); medieval and early modern European studies (MALS); public relations and corporate communications (MPS); real estate (MPS); religious studies (MALS); social and public policy (MALS); sports industry management (MPS); systems engineering management (MPS); technology management (MPS); the theory and practice of American democracy (MALS); urban and regional planning (MPS); visual culture (MALS). MPS in systems engineering management offered jointly with Stevens Institute of Technology. *Entrance requirements:* Additional exam requirements/recommendations for international students: Required—TOEFL.

**The George Washington University,** Columbian College of Arts and Sciences, Department of American Studies, Washington, DC 20052. Offers American studies (PhD); folk life (MA); historic preservation (MA); material culture (MA). *Program availability:* Part-time, evening/weekend. *Faculty:* 18 full-time (14 women), 15 part-time/adjunct (10 women). *Students:* 18 full-time (14 women), 15 part-time (10 women); includes 9 minority (5 Black or African American, non-Hispanic/Latino; 3 Asian, non-Hispanic/Latino; 1 Hispanic/Latino). Average age 29. 87 applicants, 29% accepted, 10 enrolled. In 2016, 7 master's, 13 doctorates awarded. Terminal master's awarded for partial completion of doctoral program. *Degree requirements:* For master's, comprehensive exam; for doctorate, one foreign language, thesis/dissertation, general exam. *Entrance requirements:* For master's and doctorate, GRE General Test, minimum GPA of 3.0. Additional exam requirements/recommendations for international students: Required—TOEFL (minimum score 550 paper-based; 80 iBT). *Application deadline:* For fall admission, 1/15 priority date for domestic and international students; for spring admission, 10/1 for domestic students. Application fee: $75. *Financial support:* In 2016–17, 22 students received support. Fellowships, research assistantships, teaching assistantships, career-related internships or fieldwork, Federal Work-Study, institutionally sponsored loans, and tuition waivers available. Financial award application deadline: 1/15. *Unit head:* Melanie McAlister, Chair, 202-994-7244, E-mail: jam@gwu.edu. *Application contact:* Information Contact, 202-994-6070, Fax: 202-994-8651, E-mail: amst@gwu.edu.
Website: http://departments.columbian.gwu.edu/americanstudies/

**Harvard University,** Graduate School of Arts and Sciences, Committee on History of American Civilization, Cambridge, MA 02138. Offers PhD. *Degree requirements:* For doctorate, 2 foreign languages, thesis/dissertation. *Entrance requirements:* For doctorate, GRE General Test, GRE Subject Test (recommended). Additional exam requirements/recommendations for international students: Required—TOEFL. *Faculty research:* American history, literature, and religion in the Colonial era; twentieth-century American history, literature, and law; Southern literature, history, and sociology.

**Inter American University of Puerto Rico, Metropolitan Campus,** Graduate Programs, Program in History, San Juan, PR 00919-1293. Offers American history (PhD); history (MA, PhD).

**James Madison University,** The Graduate School, College of Arts and Letters, Program in History, Harrisonburg, VA 22807. Offers local/regional/public history (MA); United States history (MA); world history (MA). *Program availability:* Part-time. *Faculty:* 31 full-time (9 women). *Students:* 19 full-time (6 women), 9 part-time (2 women). Average age 30. 32 applicants, 84% accepted, 13 enrolled. In 2016, 13 master's awarded. *Degree requirements:* For master's, one foreign language, comprehensive exam, thesis. Application fee: $55. Electronic applications accepted. *Financial support:* In 2016–17, 3 teaching assistantships with full tuition reimbursements (averaging $9,284 per year) were awarded; fellowships, Federal Work-Study, and 7 assistantships (averaging $7911) also available. Financial award application deadline: 3/1; financial award applicants required to submit FAFSA. *Unit head:* Dr. Gabrielle Lanier, Department Head, 540-568-6132, E-mail: laniergm@jmu.edu. *Application contact:* Lynette D. Michael, Director of Graduate Admissions, 540-568-6131 Ext. 6395, Fax: 540-568-7860, E-mail: michaeld@jmu.edu.
Website: http://www.jmu.edu/history

**Kennesaw State University,** College of Humanities and Social Sciences, Master of Arts in American Studies Program, Kennesaw, GA 30144. Offers MA. *Program availability:* Part-time, evening/weekend. *Degree requirements:* For master's, one foreign language, thesis optional. *Entrance requirements:* For master's, GRE. Additional exam requirements/recommendations for international students: Required—TOEFL (minimum score 550 paper-based; 80 iBT), IELTS (minimum score 6.5). Electronic applications accepted.

**Lake Forest College,** Graduate Program in Liberal Studies, Lake Forest, IL 60045. Offers American studies (MLS); environmental studies (MLS); history (MLS); Medieval and Renaissance art (MLS); philosophy (MLS); Spanish (MLS); writing (MLS). *Program availability:* Part-time, evening/weekend. *Faculty:* 9 full-time (3 women), 1 part-time/adjunct (0 women). *Students:* 1 full-time (0 women), 38 part-time (20 women); includes 5 minority (1 Black or African American, non-Hispanic/Latino; 2 Asian, non-Hispanic/Latino; 2 Hispanic/Latino). Average age 38. 19 applicants, 53% accepted, 7 enrolled. In 2016, 4 master's awarded. *Degree requirements:* For master's, thesis optional, 8 courses, including at least 3 interdisciplinary seminars. *Entrance requirements:* For master's, transcript, essay, interview. Additional exam requirements/recommendations for international students: Required—TOEFL (minimum score 550 paper-based; 80 iBT); Recommended—IELTS (minimum score 6.5). *Application deadline:* For fall admission, 7/15 priority date for domestic students, 6/1 priority date for international students; for spring admission, 12/1 priority date for domestic students, 10/1 priority date for international students. Applications are processed on a rolling basis. Application fee: $30. *Expenses:* $2,600 per course. *Financial support:* In 2016–17, 2 students received support. Partial tuition grants for full-time teachers available. *Faculty research:* Realigning of the international order; Renaissance women artists; literature of Latin Americans in the U.S.; modern Chinese history; environmental biology. *Unit head:* Prof. D. L. LeMahieu, Director, 847-735-5133, Fax: 847-735-6291, E-mail: lemahieu@lakeforest.edu. *Application contact:* Prof. Carol Gayle, Associate Director, 847-735-5083, Fax: 847-735-6291, E-mail: gayle@lakeforest.edu.
Website: http://www.lakeforest.edu/academics/programs/mls/

**La Salle University,** School of Arts and Sciences, Program in History, Philadelphia, PA 19141-1199. Offers American history (Certificate); European history (Certificate); history (MA); history for educators (MA); public history (MA); teaching advanced placement history (Certificate); world history (Certificate). *Program availability:* Part-time. *Faculty:* 4 full-time (1 woman), 1 (woman) part-time/adjunct. *Students:* 4 full-time (1 woman), 16 part-time (7 women); includes 2 minority (1 Hispanic/Latino; 1 Two or more races, non-Hispanic/Latino). Average age 33. 8 applicants, 75% accepted, 3 enrolled. In 2016, 11 master's awarded. *Degree requirements:* For master's, thesis or comprehensive exam. *Entrance requirements:* For master's, GRE or MAT, 18 hours of undergraduate coursework in history or a related discipline with minimum GPA of 3.0; two letters of recommendation; brief personal statement (250 to 500 words); writing sample (preferably from an undergraduate research paper). Additional exam requirements/recommendations for international students: Required—TOEFL. *Application deadline:* For fall admission, 8/15 priority date for domestic students, 7/15 for international students; for spring admission, 12/15 priority date for domestic students, 11/15 for international students; for summer admission, 4/15 priority date for domestic students, 3/15 for international students. Applications are processed on a rolling basis. Application fee: $35. Electronic applications accepted. Application fee is waived when completed online. *Expenses:* Contact institution. *Financial support:* In 2016–17, 1 student received support. Scholarships/grants available. Support available to part-time students. Financial award application deadline: 8/31; financial award applicants required to submit FAFSA. *Unit head:* Dr. George B. Stow, Director, 215-951-1097, E-mail: grahis@lasalle.edu. *Application contact:* Elizabeth Heenan, Director, Graduate and Adult Enrollment, 215-951-1100, Fax: 215-951-1462, E-mail: heenan@lasalle.edu.
Website: http://www.lasalle.edu/master-history/

**Lehigh University,** College of Arts and Sciences, Department of History, Bethlehem, PA 18015. Offers Atlantic world (PhD); British history (PhD); history (MA); industrial and modern America (PhD); public history (MA). *Program availability:* Part-time. *Faculty:* 14 full-time (7 women). *Students:* 18 full-time (7 women), 19 part-time (5 women); includes 2 minority (1 Black or African American, non-Hispanic/Latino; 1 Two or more races, non-

Hispanic/Latino), 2 international. Average age 34. 10 applicants, 50% accepted, 3 enrolled. In 2016, 6 master's, 3 doctorates awarded. Terminal master's awarded for partial completion of doctoral program. *Degree requirements:* For master's, comprehensive exam (for some programs), thesis (for some programs), comprehensive exam or thesis; for doctorate, comprehensive exam, thesis/dissertation. *Entrance requirements:* For master's, GRE General Test, recommendations, writing sample; for doctorate, GRE General Test, recommendations, writing samples. Additional exam requirements/recommendations for international students: Required—TOEFL. *Application deadline:* For fall admission, 2/15 priority date for domestic and international students. Applications are processed on a rolling basis. Application fee: $75. Electronic applications accepted. *Expenses:* Contact institution. *Financial support:* In 2016–17, 2 fellowships with full tuition reimbursements (averaging $22,500 per year), 10 teaching assistantships with full tuition reimbursements (averaging $10,000 per year) were awarded; research assistantships, institutionally sponsored loans, scholarships/grants, tuition waivers (full and partial), and unspecified assistantships also available. Financial award application deadline: 1/15. *Faculty research:* Colonial America, modern America, history of technology, Atlantic world, French Atlantic, Spanish Atlantic, British empire, gender, intellectual history, African diaspora history. *Unit head:* Prof. John Pettegrew, Chairman, 610-758-3360, Fax: 610-758-6554, E-mail: jcp5@lehigh.edu. *Application contact:* Dr. John Savage, Graduate Coordinator, 610-758-3363, Fax: 610-758-6554, E-mail: jms8@lehigh.edu.
Website: http://history.cas2.lehigh.edu/

**Lehigh University,** College of Arts and Sciences, Program in American Studies, Bethlehem, PA 18015. Offers American studies (MA); documentary film (Graduate Certificate). *Program availability:* Part-time. *Students:* 2 full-time (both women), 6 part-time (2 women); includes 1 minority (Black or African American, non-Hispanic/Latino). Average age 30. 5 applicants, 80% accepted, 1 enrolled. In 2016, 1 master's awarded. *Degree requirements:* For master's, thesis. *Entrance requirements:* For master's, GRE, writing sample, essay, minimum GPA of 2.75, 2 letters of recommendation. Additional exam requirements/recommendations for international students: Required—TOEFL (minimum score 85 iBT). *Application deadline:* For fall admission, 1/1 for domestic students, 7/15 for international students; for spring admission, 12/1 for domestic and international students. Application fee: $75. *Expenses:* $1,420 per credit. *Financial support:* Application deadline: 1/1. *Faculty research:* War; media and video games; social movements; community identity and narrative; traditional eighteenth-, nineteenth-, and twentieth-century literature and history; gender and popular culture. *Unit head:* Prof. Jacqueline Krasas, Interim Director, 610-758-5823, Fax: 610-758-2131, E-mail: amstdgrad@lehigh.edu. *Application contact:* Cassandra L. Petroski, Graduate Coordinator, 610-758-4281, Fax: 610-758-6554, E-mail: amstdgrad@lehigh.edu.
Website: http://american.cas2.lehigh.edu/

**Michigan State University,** The Graduate School, College of Arts and Letters, Program in American Studies, East Lansing, MI 48824. Offers MA, PhD. *Entrance requirements:* Additional exam requirements/recommendations for international students: Required—TOEFL. Electronic applications accepted.

**Mississippi State University,** College of Arts and Sciences, Department of History, Mississippi State, MS 39762. Offers U.S. and European history (MA). *Program availability:* Part-time. *Faculty:* 22 full-time (5 women). *Students:* 43 full-time (14 women), 12 part-time (3 women); includes 10 minority (7 Black or African American, non-Hispanic/Latino; 3 Two or more races, non-Hispanic/Latino), 2 international. Average age 30. 27 applicants, 89% accepted, 19 enrolled. In 2016, 10 master's, 3 doctorates awarded. *Degree requirements:* For master's, one foreign language, comprehensive exam, thesis optional; for doctorate, 2 foreign languages, thesis/dissertation, comprehensive oral and written exam. *Entrance requirements:* For master's, minimum GPA of 3.0 on last two years of undergraduate courses; for doctorate, GRE, writing sample, minimum graduate GPA of 3.0. Additional exam requirements/recommendations for international students: Required—TOEFL (minimum score 550 paper-based). *Application deadline:* For fall admission, 4/1 for domestic students, 5/1 for international students; for spring admission, 11/1 for domestic students, 9/1 for international students. Applications are processed on a rolling basis. Application fee: $60. Electronic applications accepted. *Expenses:* Tuition, state resident: full-time $7670; part-time $852.50 per credit hour. Tuition, nonresident: full-time $20,790; part-time $2310.50 per credit hour. Part-time tuition and fees vary according to course load. *Financial support:* In 2016–17, 1 research assistantship with full tuition reimbursement (averaging $15,269 per year), 36 teaching assistantships with full tuition reimbursements (averaging $11,977 per year) were awarded; Federal Work-Study, institutionally sponsored loans, scholarships/grants, and unspecified assistantships also available. Financial award application deadline: 4/1; financial award applicants required to submit FAFSA. *Faculty research:* U.S. political, diplomatic, military, social, and cultural history; modern Europe; Latin America; Asian history; African history. *Unit head:* Dr. Alan I. Marcus, Department Head, 662-325-7075, Fax: 662-325-1139, E-mail: aimarcus@history.msstate.edu. *Application contact:* Linda Bonner, Senior Admissions Assistant, 662-325-3363, E-mail: lbonner@grad.msstate.edu.
Website: http://www.history.msstate.edu

**Monmouth University,** Graduate Studies, Department of History, West Long Branch, NJ 07764-1898. Offers European history (MA); history of the U.S. (MA); world history (MA). *Program availability:* Part-time, evening/weekend. *Degree requirements:* For master's, comprehensive exam (for some programs), thesis (for some programs). *Entrance requirements:* For master's, minimum GPA of 3.0 in major, 2.5 overall; two letters of recommendation; statement describing historical areas of interest and how graduate study will contribute to professional and academic goals. Additional exam requirements/recommendations for international students: Required—TOEFL (minimum score 550 paper-based; 79 iBT), IELTS (minimum score 6) or Michigan English Language Assessment Battery (minimum score 77). Electronic applications accepted. *Faculty research:* British, German, and French Revolutions; Soviet Union; Africa; English history; U.S. military; women's history.

**New Mexico Highlands University,** Graduate Studies, College of Arts and Sciences, Department of Social and Behavioral Sciences, Las Vegas, NM 87701. Offers psychology (MS), including clinical psychology/counseling, general psychology; public affairs (MA), including applied sociology; Southwest studies (MA), including anthropology. *Program availability:* Part-time. *Degree requirements:* For master's, comprehensive exam, thesis or alternative. *Entrance requirements:* For master's, minimum undergraduate GPA of 3.0. Additional exam requirements/recommendations for international students: Required—TOEFL (minimum score 540 paper-based). *Faculty research:* Southwest Native American resettlement development, community-level interventions, neurochemistry of personality, comparative criminal justice, social theory and activism.

**New York University,** Graduate School of Arts and Science, Program in American Studies, New York, NY 10012-1019. Offers MA, PhD. *Program availability:* Part-time. *Degree requirements:* For master's, one foreign language, thesis; for doctorate, 2 foreign languages, thesis/dissertation. *Entrance requirements:* For master's and doctorate, GRE General Test, writing sample. Additional exam requirements/recommendations for international students: Required—TOEFL. *Faculty research:*

Cultural politics; race, gender, and sexuality studies; nationalism and transnationalism; science and technology; urban and suburban studies.

**New York University,** Graduate School of Arts and Science, Program in Irish and Irish American Studies, New York, NY 10012-1019. Offers MA. *Program availability:* Part-time. *Degree requirements:* For master's, one foreign language. *Entrance requirements:* For master's, GRE General Test. Additional exam requirements/recommendations for international students: Required—TOEFL.

**Northwestern Oklahoma State University,** Program in American Studies, Alva, OK 73717. Offers MA. *Program availability:* Part-time. *Degree requirements:* For master's, comprehensive exam, thesis optional. *Entrance requirements:* For master's, GRE or MAT, at least 12 upper-level undergraduate hours in history and/or literature. *Faculty research:* Literary history of Oklahoma, Oklahoma Poets Laureate, American naturalism, Lincoln studies, public service and policy studies.

**Northwestern University,** School of Professional Studies, Program in Liberal Studies, Evanston, IL 60208. Offers American studies (MA); history (MA); religious and ethical studies (MA).

**Penn State Harrisburg,** Graduate School, School of Humanities, Middletown, PA 17057. Offers American studies (MA, PhD); communications (MA); heritage and museum practice (Certificate); humanities (MA); writing instruction specialist (Certificate). *Program availability:* Evening/weekend. *Unit head:* Dr. Mukund S. Kulkarni, Chancellor, 717-948-6105, Fax: 717-948-6452. *Application contact:* Robert W. Coffman, Jr., Director of Enrollment Management, Admissions, 717-948-6250, Fax: 717-948-6325, E-mail: hbgadmit@psu.edu.
Website: https://harrisburg.psu.edu/humanities

**Pepperdine University,** Seaver College, Division of Humanities, Malibu, CA 90263. Offers American studies (MA); writing for screen and television (MFA). *Program availability:* Part-time. *Students:* 9 full-time (7 women), 41 part-time (23 women); includes 12 minority (3 Black or African American, non-Hispanic/Latino; 2 Asian, non-Hispanic/Latino; 5 Hispanic/Latino; 2 Two or more races, non-Hispanic/Latino), 3 international. Average age 31. In 2016, 15 master's awarded. *Degree requirements:* For master's, oral and written exams. *Entrance requirements:* For master's, GRE General Test, writing sample, letters of recommendation. Additional exam requirements/recommendations for international students: Required—TOEFL. *Application deadline:* For fall admission, 2/1 priority date for domestic students. Applications are processed on a rolling basis. Application fee: $65. *Financial support:* Applicants required to submit FAFSA. *Unit head:* Dr. Michael G. Ditmore, Chair/Professor of English, 310-506-4182, Fax: 310-506-7307, E-mail: michael.ditmore@pepperdine.edu. *Application contact:* Hayley Wolf, Director of Admission, 310-506-4392, E-mail: hayley.wolf@pepperdine.edu.
Website: http://seaver.pepperdine.edu/humanities/default.htm

**Providence College,** Department of History, Providence, RI 02918. Offers American history (MA); modern European history (MA). *Program availability:* Part-time, evening/weekend. *Faculty:* 6 full-time (1 woman), 4 part-time/adjunct (0 women). *Students:* 13 full-time (6 women), 19 part-time (2 women); includes 1 minority (Two or more races, non-Hispanic/Latino). Average age 33. 14 applicants, 100% accepted, 11 enrolled. In 2016, 20 master's awarded. *Degree requirements:* For master's, comprehensive exam, thesis optional. *Entrance requirements:* Additional exam requirements/recommendations for international students: Required—TOEFL (minimum score 577 paper-based; 90 iBT). *Application deadline:* For fall admission, 7/15 priority date for domestic and international students; for spring admission, 11/15 priority date for domestic and international students; for summer admission, 3/15 priority date for domestic students, 3/15 for international students. Application fee: $55. *Expenses:* Contact institution. *Financial support:* Career-related internships or fieldwork, institutionally sponsored loans, and unspecified assistantships available. Support available to part-time students. Financial award application deadline: 8/1; financial award applicants required to submit FAFSA. *Faculty research:* American history, modern European history, Medieval history, Native American history, religion, slavery, western civilization, labor movements, Japanese and Asian history, early modern Europe.
Website: http://www.providence.edu/academics/Pages/master-arts-history.aspx

**Purdue University,** Graduate School, College of Liberal Arts, Program in American Studies, West Lafayette, IN 47907. Offers MA, PhD. *Students:* 30 full-time (22 women), 9 part-time (5 women); includes 18 minority (11 Black or African American, non-Hispanic/Latino; 3 Asian, non-Hispanic/Latino; 3 Hispanic/Latino; 1 Two or more races, non-Hispanic/Latino), 7 international. Average age 33. 35 applicants, 29% accepted, 4 enrolled. In 2016, 3 master's, 2 doctorates awarded. *Degree requirements:* For master's, essay; for doctorate, one foreign language, thesis/dissertation. *Entrance requirements:* For master's, GRE General Test, minimum undergraduate GPA of 3.0 or equivalent; writing sample; for doctorate, GRE General Test, minimum undergraduate GPA of 3.0 or equivalent; writing sample; master's degree with minimum GPA of 3.0 or equivalent. Additional exam requirements/recommendations for international students: Required—TOEFL (minimum score 550 paper-based; 77 iBT), TWE. *Application deadline:* For fall admission, 1/15 priority date for domestic students, 1/15 for international students. Applications are processed on a rolling basis. Application fee: $60 ($75 for international students). Electronic applications accepted. *Financial support:* In 2016–17, 34 students received support, including teaching assistantships with tuition reimbursements available (averaging $14,150 per year); fellowships also available. Support available to part-time students. Financial award application deadline: 1/15; financial award applicants required to submit FAFSA. *Faculty research:* African American studies; critical race theory; women, gender and sexuality studies; popular culture; transnational studies; U.S. social movements; ecocriticism. *Unit head:* Dr. Rayvon D. Fouche, Director, 765-494-7161, E-mail: rfouche@purdue.edu. *Application contact:* Elsa Schirmer, Graduate Contact, 765-496-9629, E-mail: eschirme@purdue.edu.
Website: http://www.cla.purdue.edu/american-studies/

**Regent University,** Graduate School, Robertson School of Government, Virginia Beach, VA 23464-9800. Offers government (MA), including American government, healthcare policy and ethics (MA, MPA), international relations, law and public policy, national security studies, political communication, political theory, religion and politics; public administration (MPA), including emergency management and homeland security, federal government, general public administration, healthcare policy and ethics (MA, MPA), law, nonprofit administration and faith-based organizations, public leadership and management, servant leadership. *Program availability:* Part-time, evening/weekend, 100% online, blended/hybrid learning. *Faculty:* 8 full-time (1 woman), 19 part-time/adjunct (3 women). *Students:* 40 full-time (27 women), 119 part-time (69 women); includes 73 minority (47 Black or African American, non-Hispanic/Latino; 3 Asian, non-Hispanic/Latino; 15 Hispanic/Latino; 8 Two or more races, non-Hispanic/Latino), 6 international. Average age 35. 253 applicants, 41% accepted, 70 enrolled. In 2016, 34 master's awarded. *Degree requirements:* For master's, thesis optional, internship. *Entrance requirements:* For master's, GRE General Test or LSAT, personal essay, writing sample, resume, college transcripts. Additional exam requirements/recommendations for international students: Required—TOEFL (minimum score 577 paper-based). *Application deadline:* For fall admission, 5/1 priority date for domestic

students; for spring admission, 11/1 priority date for domestic students. Applications are processed on a rolling basis. Application fee: $50. Electronic applications accepted. *Expenses:* $650 per credit (MA/MPA); $250 per semester technology fee. *Financial support:* In 2016–17, 78 students received support. Career-related internships or fieldwork, scholarships/grants, and unspecified assistantships available. Support available to part-time students. *Faculty research:* International relations and politics, public administration, leadership and ethics, Biblical law, Constitutional law and Supreme Court. *Unit head:* Dr. Eric Patterson, Dean, 757-352-4616, Fax: 757-352-4735, E-mail: epatterson@regent.edu. *Application contact:* Heidi Cece, Assistant Vice President of Enrollment Management, 800-373-5504, Fax: 757-352-4381, E-mail: admissions@regent.edu.
Website: http://www.regent.edu/rsg/

**Rice University,** Graduate Programs, School of Humanities, Department of Religious Studies, Houston, TX 77251-1892. Offers African religions (PhD); African-American religions (PhD); contemplative studies (PhD); ghosticism, esotericism, mysticism (PhD); Islam (PhD); Jewish thought and philosophy (PhD); modern Christianity in thought and popular culture (PhD); psychology of religion (PhD); the Bible and beyond (PhD). *Degree requirements:* For doctorate, 2 foreign languages, comprehensive exam, thesis/dissertation. *Entrance requirements:* For doctorate, GRE, letters of recommendation, writing sample. Additional exam requirements/recommendations for international students: Required—TOEFL (minimum score 600 paper-based; 90 iBT). Electronic applications accepted. *Faculty research:* Origins and historical development of Islam, history of Christianity, the study of comparative religion, African-American religion, religion and culture.

**Rutgers University–Newark,** Graduate School, Program in American Studies, Newark, NJ 07102. Offers MA, PhD. *Entrance requirements:* For master's and doctorate, GRE, minimum undergraduate B average.

**Saint Louis University,** Graduate Education, College of Arts and Sciences and Graduate Education, Department of American Studies, St. Louis, MO 63103. Offers MA, MA-R, PhD. *Program availability:* Part-time. *Degree requirements:* For master's, thesis optional, comprehensive written and oral exams; for doctorate, one foreign language, comprehensive exam, thesis/dissertation, preliminary exams. *Entrance requirements:* For master's, GRE General Test, letters of recommendation, resume; for doctorate, GRE General Test, letters of recommendation, resumé, goal statement, transcripts. Additional exam requirements/recommendations for international students: Required—TOEFL (minimum score 525 paper-based). Electronic applications accepted. *Faculty research:* Urban studies, American religion, intellectual history, southern culture, African-American literature.

**Salisbury University,** Department of History, Salisbury, MD 21801-6837. Offers history (MA), including colonial and revolutionary American history, history of the Chesapeake Bay region, United States history in the 19th and 20th centuries, world history. *Program availability:* Part-time, evening/weekend. *Faculty:* 8 full-time (2 women). *Students:* 4 full-time (2 women), 9 part-time (2 women); includes 1 minority (Black or African American, non-Hispanic/Latino). Average age 27. 4 applicants, 100% accepted, 2 enrolled. In 2016, 3 master's awarded. *Degree requirements:* For master's, comprehensive exam, thesis optional. *Entrance requirements:* Additional exam requirements/recommendations for international students: Required—TOEFL (minimum score 550 paper-based, 79 iBT) or IELTS (6.5). *Application deadline:* For fall admission, 4/15 priority date for domestic and international students; for spring admission, 10/15 priority date for domestic and international students. Applications are processed on a rolling basis. Application fee: $65. Electronic applications accepted. *Expenses:* $381 per credit hour resident tuition, $670 per credit hour non-resident tuition; $84 per credit hour fees. *Financial support:* In 2016–17, 2 teaching assistantships with full tuition reimbursements (averaging $8,000 per year) were awarded; career-related internships or fieldwork and scholarships/grants also available. Support available to part-time students. Financial award application deadline: 3/1; financial award applicants required to submit FAFSA. *Faculty research:* Chesapeake studies (regional focus), 20th century U.S. history, African American history, Native American history (minorities/ethnic focus), Afro-Asia (transitional topic). *Unit head:* Dr. Celine Carayon, Graduate Program Director, 410-677-3251, E-mail: cxcarayon@salisbury.edu.
Website: http://www.salisbury.edu/gsr/gradstudies/HISTpage.html

**Stockton University,** Office of Graduate Studies, Program in American Studies, Galloway, NJ 08205-9441. Offers MA, Certificate. *Program availability:* Part-time. *Faculty:* 2 full-time (1 woman), 2 part-time/adjunct (1 woman). *Students:* 2 full-time (1 woman), 11 part-time (9 women); includes 1 minority (Hispanic/Latino). Average age 36. 8 applicants, 75% accepted, 6 enrolled. In 2016, 7 master's awarded. *Application deadline:* For fall admission, 7/1 for domestic and international students; for winter admission, 11/1 for international students; for spring admission, 12/1 for domestic students. Applications are processed on a rolling basis. Application fee: $50. Electronic applications accepted. *Expenses:* $772 per credit in-state. *Financial support:* Fellowships, research assistantships, scholarships/grants, and unspecified assistantships available. *Unit head:* Dr. Kristin Jacobson, Program Director, 609-626-5581, E-mail: gradschool@stockton.edu. *Application contact:* Tara Williams, Assistant Director of Enrollment Management, 609-626-3640, Fax: 609-626-6050, E-mail: gradschool@stockton.edu.

**Texas Christian University,** AddRan College of Liberal Arts, Department of History, Fort Worth, TX 76129. Offers Latin America (MA, PhD); United States (MA, PhD). *Faculty:* 16 full-time (4 women). *Students:* 49 full-time (22 women); includes 6 minority (1 Black or African American, non-Hispanic/Latino; 4 Hispanic/Latino; 1 Two or more races, non-Hispanic/Latino). Average age 34. 24 applicants, 33% accepted, 5 enrolled. In 2016, 6 master's, 4 doctorates awarded. Terminal master's awarded for partial completion of doctoral program. *Degree requirements:* For master's, comprehensive exam, thesis or alternative; for doctorate, one foreign language, comprehensive exam, thesis/dissertation. *Entrance requirements:* For master's and doctorate, GRE General Test. Additional exam requirements/recommendations for international students: Recommended—TOEFL. *Application deadline:* 2/1 for domestic and international students; for summer admission, 2/1 for domestic and international students. Applications are processed on a rolling basis. Application fee: $60. Electronic applications accepted. *Expenses: Tuition:* Full-time $26,640; part-time $1480 per credit hour. *Required fees:* $48. Tuition and fees vary according to program. *Financial support:* In 2016–17, 50 students received support, including 3 fellowships with full tuition reimbursements available (averaging $20,000 per year), 15 research assistantships with full tuition reimbursements available (averaging $17,500 per year), 5 teaching assistantships with full tuition reimbursements available (averaging $17,500 per year); tuition waivers (full) also available. Financial award application deadline: 2/1. *Faculty research:* U.S. South, Latin American history, Atlantic World history, American West. *Total annual research expenditures:* $140,000. *Unit head:* Dr. Jodi Campbell, Associate Professor, 817-257-5882, Fax: 817-257-5650, E-mail: j.campbell@tcu.edu. *Application contact:* Heather Confessore, Administrative Assistant, 817-257-7288, Fax: 817-257-5650, E-mail: h.confessore@tcu.edu.
Website: http://www.his.tcu.edu/graduate.asp

**Trinity College,** Graduate Programs, Program in American Studies, Hartford, CT 06106-3100. Offers American culture studies (MA); museums and communities (MA).

*Program availability:* Part-time, evening/weekend. *Degree requirements:* For master's, thesis or alternative. *Entrance requirements:* For master's, minimum GPA of 3.0.

**Universidad de las Américas Puebla,** Division of Graduate Studies, School of Social Sciences, Program in American Studies, Puebla, Mexico. Offers MA. *Program availability:* Part-time, evening/weekend. *Degree requirements:* For master's, one foreign language, thesis. *Faculty research:* NAFTA, technology, culture, politics and economics in NAFTA region.

**University at Buffalo, the State University of New York,** Graduate School, College of Arts and Sciences, Department of Transnational Studies, Buffalo, NY 14260. Offers American studies (MA); Canadian studies (MA, Advanced Certificate); global gender studies (MA, PhD). *Program availability:* Part-time. *Faculty:* 17 full-time (9 women), 4 part-time/adjunct (1 woman). *Students:* 78 full-time (46 women); includes 29 minority (11 Black or African American, non-Hispanic/Latino; 6 American Indian or Alaska Native, non-Hispanic/Latino; 10 Asian, non-Hispanic/Latino; 2 Hispanic/Latino). Average age 34. 53 applicants, 94% accepted, 21 enrolled. In 2016, 4 master's, 7 doctorates awarded. *Degree requirements:* For master's and Advanced Certificate, comprehensive exam (for some programs), thesis optional; for doctorate, comprehensive exam, thesis/dissertation. *Entrance requirements:* For master's, minimum GPA of 3.0; for doctorate, GRE, minimum GPA of 3.0. Additional exam requirements/recommendations for international students: Required—TOEFL (minimum score 550 paper-based; 79 iBT), IELTS. *Application deadline:* For fall admission, 8/28 priority date for domestic students, 6/15 priority date for international students; for winter admission, 2/1 for domestic and international students; for spring admission, 1/28 priority date for domestic students, 11/15 priority date for international students. Applications are processed on a rolling basis. Application fee: $75. Electronic applications accepted. *Expenses:* Contact institution. *Financial support:* In 2016–17, 20 students received support, including 4 fellowships with full tuition reimbursements available (averaging $13,060 per year), 16 teaching assistantships with full tuition reimbursements available (averaging $13,060 per year); research assistantships, career-related internships or fieldwork, institutionally sponsored loans, scholarships/grants, and unspecified assistantships also available. Financial award application deadline: 1/1. *Faculty research:* Native American, intercultural and indigenous people's studies, border theory, cultural studies, American pop culture, feminist theory, construction of gender in society. *Unit head:* Dr. Cecil Foster, Chair, 716-645-0786, Fax: 716-645-5976, E-mail: cecilfos@buffalo.edu. *Application contact:* Karen M. Reinard, Graduate Coordinator, 716-645-0797, Fax: 716-645-5976, E-mail: kreinard@buffalo.edu.
Website: http://transnationalstudies.buffalo.edu/

**The University of Alabama,** Graduate School, College of Arts and Sciences, Department of American Studies, Tuscaloosa, AL 35487. Offers MA. *Program availability:* Part-time. *Faculty:* 11 full-time (5 women). *Students:* 10 full-time (4 women), 1 part-time (0 women); includes 2 minority (1 Black or African American, non-Hispanic/Latino; 1 Hispanic/Latino), 1 international. Average age 28. 13 applicants, 62% accepted, 5 enrolled. In 2016, 8 master's awarded. *Degree requirements:* For master's, comprehensive exam, thesis optional. *Entrance requirements:* For master's, GRE or MAT. Additional exam requirements/recommendations for international students: Required—TOEFL. *Application deadline:* For fall admission, 1/15 priority date for domestic and international students; for spring admission, 11/30 priority date for domestic and international students; for summer admission, 1/15 for domestic and international students. Applications are processed on a rolling basis. Application fee: $50 ($60 for international students). Electronic applications accepted. *Expenses:* Tuition, state resident: full-time $10,470. Tuition, nonresident: full-time $26,950. *Financial support:* In 2016–17, 8 teaching assistantships with full tuition reimbursements (averaging $14,181 per year) were awarded; career-related internships or fieldwork, health care benefits, and unspecified assistantships also available. Financial award application deadline: 1/10; financial award applicants required to submit FAFSA. *Faculty research:* Social and cultural history, popular music and popular culture, African-American arts and education, the culture and environment of the South, gender and sexuality, Asian-American studies, sports, Latino Studies. *Unit head:* Dr. Lynne M. Adrian, Chair and Associate Professor, 205-348-5940, Fax: 205-348-9766, E-mail: ladrian@ua.edu. *Application contact:* Patrick D. Fuller, Senior Graduate Admissions Counselor, 205-348-5923, Fax: 205-348-0400, E-mail: patrick.d.fuller@ua.edu.
Website: http://ams.ua.edu/

**University of Colorado Denver,** College of Liberal Arts and Sciences, Department of History, Denver, CO 80217. Offers European history (MA); global history (MA); public history (MA); U.S. history (MA). *Program availability:* Part-time, evening/weekend. *Faculty:* 12 full-time (4 women), 2 part-time/adjunct (0 women). *Students:* 24 full-time (15 women), 16 part-time (10 women); includes 10 minority (1 Asian, non-Hispanic/Latino; 6 Hispanic/Latino; 3 Two or more races, non-Hispanic/Latino). Average age 35. 23 applicants, 70% accepted, 7 enrolled. In 2016, 15 master's awarded. *Degree requirements:* For master's, comprehensive exam, thesis optional, 36 semester hours (12 courses). *Entrance requirements:* For master's, GRE General Test, writing sample, minimum undergraduate GPA of 3.25, three letters of recommendation, statement of purpose addressing any weaknesses in academic record. Additional exam requirements/recommendations for international students: Required—TOEFL (minimum score 537 paper-based; 75 iBT); Recommended—IELTS (minimum score 6.5). *Application deadline:* For fall admission, 1/20 for domestic and international students; for spring admission, 10/1 for domestic and international students. Application fee: $50 ($75 for international students). Electronic applications accepted. *Expenses:* Tuition, state resident: full-time $11,006; part-time $474 per credit. Tuition, nonresident: full-time $28,212; part-time $1264 per credit hour. *Required fees:* $256 per semester. One-time fee: $94.32. Tuition and fees vary according to campus/location and program. *Financial support:* In 2016–17, 8 students received support. Fellowships, research assistantships, teaching assistantships, Federal Work-Study, institutionally sponsored loans, scholarships/grants, and traineeships available. Financial award application deadline: 4/1; financial award applicants required to submit FAFSA. *Faculty research:* Uses of pre-modern Islamic heritage in modern India; relationship between liberal understandings of democracy, crime, and police discretion; relationships between gender, class, health, and welfare in nineteenth and early twentieth century England; U.S. business cultures and their influences on marketing and personnel practices; intersection of business and political ideologies; social and environmental history of the Rocky Mountain West. *Unit head:* Dr. Kariann Akemi Yokota, Associate Chair, 303-315-1784, E-mail: kariann.yokota@ucdenver.edu. *Application contact:* Tabitha Fitzpatrick, Program Assistant, 303-315-1776, E-mail: tabitha.fitzpatrick@ucdenver.edu.
Website: http://www.ucdenver.edu/academics/colleges/CLAS/Departments/history/Programs/Masters/Pages/MasterofArts.aspx

**University of Dallas,** Braniff Graduate School of Liberal Arts, Program in American Studies, Irving, TX 75062-4736. Offers MAS. *Program availability:* Part-time. *Degree requirements:* For master's, comprehensive exam. *Entrance requirements:* For master's, GRE General Test. *Faculty research:* Shakespeare, Milton, Melville, Hawthorne, liberty and American literature.

**University of Delaware,** College of Arts and Sciences, Winterthur Program in American Material Culture, Newark, DE 19716. Offers MA. *Degree requirements:* For master's, thesis. *Entrance requirements:* For master's, GRE General Test, minimum GPA of 3.0. Electronic applications accepted. *Faculty research:* American material culture, American studies, decorative arts.

**University of Hawaii at Manoa,** Graduate Division, College of Arts and Humanities, Department of American Studies, Honolulu, HI 96822. Offers American studies (MA, PhD); historic preservation (Graduate Certificate); museum studies (Graduate Certificate). *Program availability:* Part-time. *Degree requirements:* For master's, comprehensive exam (for some programs), thesis (for some programs); for doctorate, comprehensive exam, thesis/dissertation. *Entrance requirements:* For master's and doctorate, GRE General Test. Additional exam requirements/recommendations for international students: Required—TOEFL (minimum score 600 paper-based; 100 iBT), IELTS (minimum score 7). *Faculty research:* Ethnicity and race, popular culture, historic preservation, arts and culture, international relations.

**The University of Iowa,** Graduate College, College of Liberal Arts and Sciences, Department of American Studies, Iowa City, IA 52242-1316. Offers MA, PhD. *Degree requirements:* For master's, thesis optional, exam; for doctorate, comprehensive exam, thesis/dissertation. *Entrance requirements:* For master's and doctorate, GRE General Test, minimum GPA of 3.0. Additional exam requirements/recommendations for international students: Required—TOEFL (minimum score 550 paper-based; 81 iBT). Electronic applications accepted.

**The University of Kansas,** Graduate Studies, College of Liberal Arts and Sciences, Department of American Studies, Lawrence, KS 66045. Offers MA, PhD, MUP/MA. *Program availability:* Part-time. *Students:* 33 full-time (24 women), 2 part-time (1 woman); includes 6 minority (4 Black or African American, non-Hispanic/Latino; 1 Hispanic/Latino; 1 Two or more races, non-Hispanic/Latino), 4 international. Average age 34. 20 applicants, 70% accepted, 8 enrolled. In 2016, 1 master's, 2 doctorates awarded. Terminal master's awarded for partial completion of doctoral program. *Entrance requirements:* For master's and doctorate, GRE General Test, resume, statement of purpose, three letters of recommendation, official transcripts of all undergraduate and graduate study completed, writing sample. *Application deadline:* For fall admission, 12/1 priority date for domestic and international students. Applications are processed on a rolling basis. Application fee: $65 ($85 for international students). Electronic applications accepted. *Financial support:* Fellowships, research assistantships, teaching assistantships, Federal Work-Study, scholarships/grants, health care benefits, and unspecified assistantships available. Financial award application deadline: 12/1. *Unit head:* Margaret Kelley, Director of Graduate Studies, 785-864-6927, E-mail: mskelley@ku.edu. *Application contact:* Kay Isbell, Graduate Admissions Contact, 785-864-2957, E-mail: kisbell@ku.edu.
Website: http://americanstudies.ku.edu

**University of Louisiana at Lafayette,** College of Liberal Arts, Department of Modern Languages, Program in Francophone Studies, Lafayette, LA 70504. Offers PhD. *Degree requirements:* For doctorate, 2 foreign languages, comprehensive exam, thesis/dissertation. *Entrance requirements:* For doctorate, GRE General Test, minimum GPA of 2.75. Additional exam requirements/recommendations for international students: Required—TOEFL (minimum score 550 paper-based). Electronic applications accepted. *Faculty research:* Louisiana folklore, eighteenth-century French literature, contemporary criticism.

**University of Maryland, College Park,** Academic Affairs, College of Arts and Humanities, Department of American Studies, College Park, MD 20742. Offers MA, PhD. *Degree requirements:* For master's, thesis or scholarly paper and exam; for doctorate, thesis/dissertation, 3 comprehensive exams. *Entrance requirements:* For master's, GRE General Test, minimum GPA of 3.0, writing sample, 3 letters of recommendation; for doctorate, GRE General Test. Additional exam requirements/recommendations for international students: Required—TOEFL. Electronic applications accepted. *Faculty research:* Material culture, modes of culture, cultural movements, popular culture, ethnography.

**University of Massachusetts Amherst,** Graduate School, College of Humanities and Fine Arts, Department of English, Amherst, MA 01003. Offers American studies (PhD); composition and rhetoric (PhD); creative writing (MFA); English and American literature (MA, PhD). *Program availability:* Part-time. Terminal master's awarded for partial completion of doctoral program. *Degree requirements:* For master's, one foreign language, thesis optional; for doctorate, one foreign language, comprehensive exam, thesis/dissertation. *Entrance requirements:* For master's, manuscript; for doctorate, GRE General Test, manuscript. Additional exam requirements/recommendations for international students: Required—TOEFL (minimum score 550 paper-based; 80 iBT), IELTS (minimum score 6.5). Electronic applications accepted.

**University of Massachusetts Boston,** College of Liberal Arts, Program in American Studies, Boston, MA 02125-3393. Offers MA. *Program availability:* Part-time, evening/weekend. *Faculty:* 8 full-time (5 women), 10 part-time/adjunct (5 women). *Students:* 6 full-time (4 women), 14 part-time (8 women); includes 5 minority (2 Black or African American, non-Hispanic/Latino; 2 Hispanic/Latino; 1 Two or more races, non-Hispanic/Latino). Average age 34. 7 applicants, 86% accepted, 4 enrolled. In 2016, 4 master's awarded. *Degree requirements:* For master's, thesis or capstone project. *Entrance requirements:* For master's, minimum GPA of 2.75. *Application deadline:* For fall admission, 3/1 for domestic students; for spring admission, 11/1 for domestic students. *Expenses:* Tuition, state resident: full-time $16,863. Tuition, nonresident: full-time $32,913. *Required fees:* $177. *Financial support:* Research assistantships with full tuition reimbursements, teaching assistantships with full tuition reimbursements, career-related internships or fieldwork, Federal Work-Study, and unspecified assistantships available. Support available to part-time students. Financial award application deadline: 3/1; financial award applicants required to submit FAFSA. *Faculty research:* War in American culture, immigration history, Latin Americans, history of race and popular music, education and Asian Americans. *Unit head:* Dr. Judy Smith, Director, 617-287-6770, E-mail: amsty@umbsky.cc.umb.edu. *Application contact:* Peggy Roldan Patel, Graduate Admissions Coordinator, 617-287-6400, Fax: 617-287-6236, E-mail: bos.gadm@dpc.umassp.edu.

**University of Michigan,** Rackham Graduate School, College of Literature, Science, and the Arts, Department of American Culture, Ann Arbor, MI 48109-1045. Offers AM, PhD. *Faculty:* 41 full-time (22 women), 4 part-time/adjunct (1 woman). *Students:* 37 full-time (27 women); includes 24 minority (6 Black or African American, non-Hispanic/Latino; 2 American Indian or Alaska Native, non-Hispanic/Latino; 9 Asian, non-Hispanic/Latino; 7 Hispanic/Latino), 2 international. 92 applicants, 11% accepted, 8 enrolled. In 2016, 9 doctorates awarded. Terminal master's awarded for partial completion of doctoral program. *Degree requirements:* For doctorate, comprehensive exam, thesis/dissertation, preliminary exams, field exams, oral defense of dissertation. *Entrance requirements:* For doctorate, sample of written work. Additional exam requirements/recommendations for international students: Required—TOEFL. *Application deadline:* For fall admission, 12/1 for domestic and international students. Application fee: $89. Electronic applications accepted. *Expenses:* Tuition, state resident: full-time $21,466; part-time $1152 per credit hour. Tuition, nonresident: full-time $43,346; part-time $2367 per credit hour. Part-time tuition and fees vary according to course load, degree level and program. *Financial support:* In 2016–17, 37 students received support, including 27

fellowships with full tuition reimbursements available (averaging $28,000 per year), 10 teaching assistantships with full tuition reimbursements available (averaging $28,000 per year); research assistantships and health care benefits also available. *Faculty research:* Cultural studies, ethnic studies, American culture methodology, literature, history. *Unit head:* Alexandra Stern, Chair, 734-763-1460, Fax: 734-936-1967, E-mail: ac.inq@umich.edu. *Application contact:* Marlene Moore, Graduate Student Coordinator, 734-647-9533, Fax: 734-936-1967, E-mail: ac.inq@umich.edu.
Website: http://www.lsa.umich.edu/ac/

**University of Michigan–Flint,** College of Arts and Sciences, Program in Social Sciences, Flint, MI 48502-1950. Offers gender studies (MA); global studies (MA); U.S. history and politics (MA). *Program availability:* Part-time. *Faculty:* 9 full-time (1 woman), 1 (woman) part-time/adjunct. *Students:* 4 full-time (1 woman), 21 part-time (14 women); includes 12 minority (9 Black or African American, non-Hispanic/Latino; 2 Hispanic/Latino; 1 Two or more races, non-Hispanic/Latino). Average age 39. 17 applicants, 82% accepted, 7 enrolled. In 2016, 7 master's awarded. *Entrance requirements:* For master's, bachelor's degree from regionally-accredited institution, minimum overall undergraduate GPA of 3.0. Additional exam requirements/recommendations for international students: Required—TOEFL (minimum score 84 iBT), IELTS (minimum score 6.5). *Application deadline:* For fall admission, 8/1 for domestic students, 5/1 for international students; for winter admission, 11/15 for domestic students, 9/1 for international students; for spring admission, 3/15 for domestic students, 1/1 for international students; for summer admission, 5/15 for domestic students. Applications are processed on a rolling basis. Application fee: $55. Electronic applications accepted. *Financial support:* Federal Work-Study, scholarships/grants, and unspecified assistantships available. Support available to part-time students. Financial award application deadline: 3/1; financial award applicants required to submit FAFSA. *Unit head:* Dr. Adam Lutzker, Director, 810-762-3470, Fax: 810-762-3281, E-mail: alutzker@umflint.edu. *Application contact:* Bradley T. Maki, Director of Graduate Admissions, 810-762-3171, Fax: 810-766-6789, E-mail: bmaki@umflint.edu.
Website: http://www.umflint.edu/graduateprograms/social-sciences-ma

**University of Michigan–Flint,** Graduate Programs, Program in Liberal Studies, Flint, MI 48502. Offers MA, MLS. *Program availability:* Part-time, evening/weekend, 100% online. *Faculty:* 5 full-time (4 women), 2 part-time/adjunct (0 women). *Students:* 1 full-time (0 women), 20 part-time (9 women); includes 6 minority (2 Black or African American, non-Hispanic/Latino; 2 American Indian or Alaska Native, non-Hispanic/Latino; 1 Asian, non-Hispanic/Latino; 1 Two or more races, non-Hispanic/Latino). Average age 46. 13 applicants, 85% accepted, 9 enrolled. In 2016, 9 master's awarded. *Degree requirements:* For master's, thesis. *Entrance requirements:* For master's, bachelor's degree from accredited institution; minimum overall undergraduate GPA of 3.0; undergraduate course work totaling 24 credit hours, primarily in the humanities and social sciences. Additional exam requirements/recommendations for international students: Required—TOEFL (minimum score 84 iBT), IELTS (minimum score 6.5). *Application deadline:* For fall admission, 8/1 for domestic students, 5/1 for international students; for winter admission, 11/15 for domestic students, 9/1 for international students; for spring admission, 3/15 for domestic students, 1/1 for international students; for summer admission, 5/15 for domestic students. Applications are processed on a rolling basis. Application fee: $55. Electronic applications accepted. *Expenses:* Contact institution. *Financial support:* Federal Work-Study, scholarships/grants, and unspecified assistantships available. Support available to part-time students. Financial award application deadline: 3/1; financial award applicants required to submit FAFSA. *Unit head:* Dr. Jan Furman, Director, 810-762-3285, E-mail: jfurman@umflint.edu. *Application contact:* Bradley T. Maki, Director of Graduate Admissions, 810-762-3171, Fax: 810-766-6789, E-mail: bmaki@umflint.edu.
Website: https://www.umflint.edu/graduateprograms/liberal-studies-american-culture-ma

**University of Minnesota, Twin Cities Campus,** Graduate School, College of Liberal Arts, Department of American Studies, Minneapolis, MN 55455. Offers PhD. *Degree requirements:* For doctorate, one foreign language, comprehensive exam, thesis/dissertation. *Entrance requirements:* For doctorate, GRE General Test, sample of written work, 3 letters of recommendation. Additional exam requirements/recommendations for international students: Required—TOEFL (minimum score 550 paper-based). *Faculty research:* American Indian history, nationalism/transnationalism, gender and sexuality, race and ethnicity.

**University of Missouri–St. Louis,** College of Arts and Sciences, Department of Political Science, St. Louis, MO 63121. Offers American politics (MA); comparative politics (MA); international politics (MA); political process and behavior (MA); political science (PhD); public administration and public policy (MA); urban and regional politics (MA). *Program availability:* Part-time, evening/weekend. *Faculty:* 17 full-time (5 women), 8 part-time/adjunct (4 women). *Students:* 28 full-time (8 women), 30 part-time (12 women); includes 8 minority (7 Black or African American, non-Hispanic/Latino; 1 Two or more races, non-Hispanic/Latino), 5 international. 17 applicants, 82% accepted, 9 enrolled. Terminal master's awarded for partial completion of doctoral program. *Degree requirements:* For master's, thesis optional; for doctorate, thesis/dissertation. *Entrance requirements:* For master's, GRE General Test, 2 letters of recommendation, statement of purpose; for doctorate, GRE General Test, 3 letters of recommendation, statement of purpose. Additional exam requirements/recommendations for international students: Required—TOEFL (minimum score 550 paper-based; 79 iBT), IELTS (minimum score 6.5). *Application deadline:* For fall admission, 2/15 priority date for domestic and international students; for winter admission, 10/15 for domestic and international students; for spring admission, 10/15 priority date for domestic and international students. Applications are processed on a rolling basis. Application fee: $50 ($40 for international students). Electronic applications accepted. *Financial support:* Fellowships, research assistantships with tuition reimbursements, teaching assistantships with tuition reimbursements, and career-related internships or fieldwork available. Support available to part-time students. Financial award application deadline: 3/15; financial award applicants required to submit FAFSA. *Faculty research:* Public policy, urban politics and administration, American government. *Unit head:* Dave Robertson, Chair, 314-516-5521, Fax: 314-516-7236. *Application contact:* 314-516-5458, Fax: 314-516-6996, E-mail: gradadm@umsl.edu.
Website: http://www.umsl.edu/~polisci/

**University of New Mexico,** Graduate Studies, College of Arts and Sciences, Program in American Studies, Albuquerque, NM 87131. Offers MA, PhD. *Program availability:* Part-time. *Faculty:* 14 full-time (7 women). *Students:* 16 full-time (7 women), 36 part-time (26 women); includes 31 minority (5 American Indian or Alaska Native, non-Hispanic/Latino; 21 Hispanic/Latino; 1 Native Hawaiian or other Pacific Islander, non-Hispanic/Latino; 4 Two or more races, non-Hispanic/Latino), 2 international. Average age 38. 32 applicants, 41% accepted, 6 enrolled. In 2016, 5 master's, 2 doctorates awarded. *Degree requirements:* For master's, comprehensive exam (for some programs), thesis (for some programs); for doctorate, one foreign language, comprehensive exam, thesis/dissertation. *Entrance requirements:* For master's, BA in related field; for doctorate, MA in related field, complete dossier. Additional exam requirements/recommendations for international students: Required—TOEFL. *Application deadline:* For fall admission, 1/15 for domestic and international students. Application fee: $50. Electronic applications

## American Studies

accepted. *Financial support:* Research assistantships with partial tuition reimbursements, teaching assistantships with partial tuition reimbursements, Federal Work-Study, health care benefits, tuition waivers (partial), and unspecified assistantships available. Support available to part-time students. Financial award application deadline: 2/20; financial award applicants required to submit FAFSA. *Faculty research:* Cultural studies, environment/science/technology, gender, race/class/ethnicity, popular culture, Southwest studies. *Unit head:* Dr. Alex Lubin, Chair, 505-277-3929, Fax: 505-277-1208, E-mail: alubin@unm.edu. *Application contact:* Sandy Rodrigue, Department Administrator, 505-277-3929, Fax: 505-277-1208, E-mail: amstudy@unm.edu.
Website: http://www.unm.edu/~amstudy/

**University of New Mexico,** Graduate Studies, College of Fine Arts, Program in Art History, Albuquerque, NM 87131. Offers art history (MA); art of the Americas (MA); history of architecture (PhD); history of graphic arts (PhD); history of photography (PhD); modern Latin American art (PhD); Native American art (PhD); Pre-Columbian art and architecture (PhD); Spanish colonial art (PhD). *Program availability:* Part-time. *Faculty:* 4 full-time (2 women). *Students:* 8 full-time (all women), 22 part-time (19 women); includes 9 minority (3 American Indian or Alaska Native, non-Hispanic/Latino; 5 Hispanic/Latino; 1 Two or more races, non-Hispanic/Latino), 3 international. Average age 40. 19 applicants, 42% accepted, 4 enrolled. In 2016, 5 master's, 1 doctorate awarded. *Degree requirements:* For master's, one foreign language, comprehensive exam (for some programs), thesis, symposium; for doctorate, 2 foreign languages, comprehensive exam, thesis/dissertation, symposium. *Entrance requirements:* Additional exam requirements/recommendations for international students: Required—TOEFL (minimum score 550 paper-based), IELTS (minimum score 6). *Application deadline:* For fall admission, 1/15 for domestic students; for spring admission, 1/15 for domestic students. Application fee: $50. Electronic applications accepted. *Financial support:* Fellowships, research assistantships with tuition reimbursements, teaching assistantships with partial tuition reimbursements, Federal Work-Study, institutionally sponsored loans, scholarships/grants, health care benefits, and unspecified assistantships available. Support available to part-time students. Financial award application deadline: 3/1; financial award applicants required to submit FAFSA. *Faculty research:* Native American, modern Latin American, pre-Columbian, architectural, American, medieval, Spanish Colonial, and Latin American art; history of photography. *Unit head:* Prof. Mary Tsiongas, Chair, 505-277-5861, Fax: 505-277-5955, E-mail: tsiongas@unm.edu. *Application contact:* Kat Heatherington, Graduate Advisor, 505-277-6672, Fax: 505-277-5955, E-mail: art255@unm.edu.
Website: http://art.unm.edu/

**University of Rochester,** School of Arts and Sciences, Department of History, Rochester, NY 14627. Offers American history (MA, PhD); European history (MA, PhD); global history (MA, PhD). *Faculty:* 19 full-time (4 women). *Students:* 28 full-time (12 women); includes 2 minority (1 Asian, non-Hispanic/Latino; 1 Two or more races, non-Hispanic/Latino), 2 international. Average age 31. 32 applicants, 28% accepted, 5 enrolled. In 2016, 5 master's, 4 doctorates awarded. Terminal master's awarded for partial completion of doctoral program. *Degree requirements:* For master's, one foreign language, thesis or alternative; for doctorate, 2 foreign languages, thesis/dissertation, comprehensive oral exam, qualifying exam. *Entrance requirements:* For master's and doctorate, GRE General Test, sample of written work. Additional exam requirements/recommendations for international students: Required—TOEFL. *Application deadline:* For fall admission, 1/15 for domestic and international students. Application fee: $60. Electronic applications accepted. *Expenses:* $1,538 per credit. *Financial support:* In 2016–17, 24 students received support, including 7 fellowships (averaging $20,000 per year); tuition waivers (full and partial) also available. Financial award application deadline: 1/15. *Unit head:* Matthew Lenoe, Chair, 585-275-9355, E-mail: matthew.lenoe@rochester.edu. *Application contact:* Alissa Clark, Secretary, 585-275-2053.
Website: http://www.rochester.edu/College/HIS/

**University of Southern California,** Graduate School, Dana and David Dornsife College of Letters, Arts and Sciences, Department of American Studies and Ethnicity, Los Angeles, CA 90089. Offers PhD. *Degree requirements:* For doctorate, one foreign language, thesis/dissertation, qualifying exam. *Entrance requirements:* For doctorate, GRE. Additional exam requirements/recommendations for international students: Recommended—TOEFL. Electronic applications accepted. *Faculty research:* Interdisciplinary study of race and ethnicity, regional focus on Los Angeles and the American West, multidisciplinary exploration of culture, interdisciplinary study of gender and sexuality.

**University of Southern Maine,** College of Arts, Humanities, and Social Sciences, Program in American and New England Studies, Portland, ME 04103. Offers MA, CGS. *Program availability:* Part-time, evening/weekend. *Degree requirements:* For master's, thesis optional. *Entrance requirements:* For master's, GRE General Test or MAT. Additional exam requirements/recommendations for international students: Required—TOEFL. *Faculty research:* Social history, regional culture, landscape of literature, material culture, art and architecture.

**University of South Florida,** College of Arts and Sciences, Department of History, Tampa, FL 33620-9951. Offers history (MA, PhD), including American history (MA), ancient history (MA), European history (MA), Latin American history (MA), Medieval history (MA). *Program availability:* Part-time, evening/weekend. *Faculty:* 17 full-time (8 women). *Students:* 39 full-time (9 women), 14 part-time (8 women); includes 7 minority (1 Black or African American, non-Hispanic/Latino; 1 American Indian or Alaska Native, non-Hispanic/Latino; 1 Asian, non-Hispanic/Latino; 4 Hispanic/Latino), 1 international. Average age 35. 34 applicants, 68% accepted, 15 enrolled. In 2016, 8 master's, 2 doctorates awarded. *Degree requirements:* For master's, one foreign language, comprehensive exam, thesis optional; for doctorate, one foreign language, comprehensive exam, thesis/dissertation. *Entrance requirements:* For master's, GRE General Test, minimum GPA of 3.0, two letters of recommendation, 2-page statement of purpose, writing sample; for doctorate, GRE General Test, minimum GPA of 3.5 in master's degree coursework, three letters of recommendation, statement of purpose, writing sample, foreign language proficiency in the field of study. Additional exam requirements/recommendations for international students: Required—TOEFL (minimum score 550 paper-based; 79 iBT) or IELTS (minimum score 6.5). *Application deadline:* For fall admission, 12/1 priority date for domestic students, 12/1 for international students. Applications are processed on a rolling basis. Application fee: $30. Electronic applications accepted. *Expenses:* Tuition, state resident: full-time $7766; part-time $431.43 per credit hour. Tuition, nonresident: full-time $15,789; part-time $877.17 per credit hour. *Required fees:* $37 per term. *Financial support:* In 2016–17, 20 students received support, including 17 teaching assistantships with tuition reimbursements available (averaging $12,750 per year); unspecified assistantships also available. Financial award application deadline: 1/15. *Faculty research:* North American and U.S. history, European history, nineteenth- and twentieth-centuries/modern world, early modern world, ancient history, history of gender/sexuality, Latin American history, history of science and medicine. *Total annual research expenditures:* $195,413. *Unit head:* Dr. Fraser Ottanelli, Professor and Chair, 813-974-6209, Fax: 813-974-6228, E-mail: ottanelli@usf.edu. *Application contact:* Dr. Brian Connolly, Associate Professor and Graduate Program Director, 813-974-1087, Fax: 813-974-6228, E-mail: bconnelly@usf.edu.
Website: http://history.usf.edu

**University of South Florida,** College of Arts and Sciences, Department of Humanities and Cultural Studies, Tampa, FL 33620-9951. Offers liberal arts (MA), including Africana studies, American studies, film studies, humanities, social and political thought. *Program availability:* Part-time, evening/weekend. *Faculty:* 6 full-time (1 woman). *Students:* 17 full-time (10 women), 9 part-time (3 women); includes 3 minority (all Black or African American, non-Hispanic/Latino), 2 international. Average age 33. 23 applicants, 83% accepted, 14 enrolled. In 2016, 6 master's awarded. *Degree requirements:* For master's, comprehensive exam, thesis, language (for humanities subconcentration). *Entrance requirements:* For master's, GRE General Test, minimum GPA of 3.0 in upper-division courses, personal statement, writing sample. Additional exam requirements/recommendations for international students: Required—TOEFL (minimum score 550 paper-based; 79 iBT) or IELTS (minimum score 6.5). *Application deadline:* For fall admission, 2/15 priority date for domestic students, 2/15 for international students; for spring admission, 10/15 priority date for domestic students, 9/15 for international students; for summer admission, 2/15 for domestic students, 1/15 for international students. Application fee: $30. Electronic applications accepted. *Expenses:* Tuition, state resident: full-time $7766; part-time $431.43 per credit hour. Tuition, nonresident: full-time $15,789; part-time $877.17 per credit hour. *Required fees:* $37 per term. *Financial support:* In 2016–17, 5 students received support, including 15 teaching assistantships with tuition reimbursements available (averaging $12,437 per year); scholarships/grants also available. Financial award application deadline: 4/1. *Faculty research:* American South, American autobiography, material culture, critical theory, cultural studies, film studies. *Unit head:* Dr. William Cummings, Professor and Chair, 813-974-9380, Fax: 813-974-9409, E-mail: wcummings@usf.edu. *Application contact:* Dr. Brook Sadler, Associate Professor and Graduate Program Director, 813-974-8841, Fax: 813-974-9409, E-mail: brooksadler@usf.edu.
Website: http://humanities.usf.edu/

**The University of Texas at Austin,** Graduate School, College of Liberal Arts, Department of American Studies, Austin, TX 78712-1111. Offers MA, PhD. *Program availability:* Part-time. *Degree requirements:* For master's, thesis; for doctorate, one foreign language, thesis/dissertation, qualifying oral exam. *Entrance requirements:* For master's and doctorate, GRE General Test, minimum GPA of 3.5. Electronic applications accepted. *Faculty research:* Race, gender, and ethnicity; history of the American West; American design and archaeology; literary cultural history; religion and psychology in American culture.

**University of Utah,** Graduate School, College of Social and Behavioral Science, Department of Political Science, Program in Political Science, Salt Lake City, UT 84112. Offers American politics (MA, MS, PhD); comparative politics (MA, MS, PhD); international relations (MA, MS, PhD); political theory (MA, MS, PhD); public administration (MA, MS, PhD). *Faculty:* 31 full-time (8 women), 10 part-time/adjunct (3 women). *Students:* 45 full-time (16 women), 19 part-time (9 women); includes 6 minority (2 Asian, non-Hispanic/Latino; 2 Hispanic/Latino; 2 Two or more races, non-Hispanic/Latino), 4 international. Average age 35. 37 applicants, 49% accepted, 7 enrolled. In 2016, 2 master's, 4 doctorates awarded. Terminal master's awarded for partial completion of doctoral program. *Degree requirements:* For master's, variable foreign language requirement, thesis or research paper; for doctorate, comprehensive exam, thesis/dissertation. *Entrance requirements:* For master's and doctorate, GRE General Test, minimum GPA of 3.2. Additional exam requirements/recommendations for international students: Required—TOEFL (minimum score 580 paper-based; 61 iBT), IELTS (minimum score 6). *Application deadline:* For fall admission, 1/15 priority date for domestic and international students. Electronic applications accepted. *Expenses:* Contact institution. *Financial support:* In 2016–17, 10 students received support, including 5 fellowships with full tuition reimbursements available (averaging $15,250 per year), 13 teaching assistantships with full tuition reimbursements available (averaging $15,000 per year); career-related internships or fieldwork, scholarships/grants, health care benefits, and unspecified assistantships also available. Financial award application deadline: 1/15; financial award applicants required to submit FAFSA. *Faculty research:* International politics, comparative politics, political theory, American politics, public administration. *Total annual research expenditures:* $15,000. *Unit head:* Mark Button, Chair, 801-585-7987, Fax: 801-585-6492, E-mail: mark.button@poli-sci.utah.edu. *Application contact:* Sandy Hiskey, Graduate Academic Advisor, 801-581-8608, Fax: 801-585-6492, E-mail: sandy.hiskey@utah.edu.
Website: http://www.poli-sci.utah.edu/

**University of West Florida,** College of Arts, Social Sciences, and Humanities, Department of History, Pensacola, FL 32514-5750. Offers early American studies (MA); public history (MA); traditional history (MA). *Program availability:* Part-time, evening/weekend. *Degree requirements:* For master's, thesis or alternative. *Entrance requirements:* For master's, GRE (minimum score: verbal 500, writing 3.5) or MAT (minimum score 415), minimum GPA of 3.0, minimum 15 hours of upper-level history courses; official transcripts; letter of intent; writing sample (undergraduate research paper preferred). Additional exam requirements/recommendations for international students: Required—TOEFL (minimum score 550 paper-based). *Application deadline:* For fall admission, 6/1 for domestic and international students; for spring admission, 10/1 for domestic and international students. Applications are processed on a rolling basis. Application fee: $30. *Expenses:* Tuition, state resident: full-time $5316.12. Tuition, nonresident: full-time $11,308. *Required fees:* $583.92. Tuition and fees vary according to course load and program. *Financial support:* Fellowships with partial tuition reimbursements, research assistantships with partial tuition reimbursements, teaching assistantships with partial tuition reimbursements, and unspecified assistantships available. Financial award application deadline: 4/15; financial award applicants required to submit FAFSA. *Unit head:* Dr. Erin Stone, Program Director, 850-474-2685, Fax: 850-857-6015, E-mail: estone@uwf.edu. *Application contact:* Terry McCray, Assistant Director of Graduate Admissions, 850-473-7718, Fax: 850-473-7714, E-mail: gradadmissions@uwf.edu.
Website: http://uwf.edu/history/

**University of Wisconsin–Madison,** Graduate School, College of Letters and Science, Department of History, Madison, WI 53706-1380. Offers African history (MA, PhD); Central Asian history (MA, PhD); comparative world history (MA, PhD); East Asian history (MA, PhD); European history (MA, PhD); gender and women's history (MA, PhD); Latin American and Caribbean history (MA, PhD); Middle Eastern history (MA, PhD); South Asian history (MA, PhD); Southeast Asian history (MA, PhD); United States history (MA, PhD). Terminal master's awarded for partial completion of doctoral program. *Degree requirements:* For master's, thesis (for some programs); for doctorate, variable foreign language requirement, thesis/dissertation. *Entrance requirements:* For master's and doctorate, GRE General Test. Additional exam requirements/recommendations for international students: Required—Michigan English Language Assessment Battery or TOEFL. Electronic applications accepted. *Faculty research:* American, African, European, Asian, Latin American, and Middle Eastern history.

**University of Wyoming,** College of Arts and Sciences, American Studies Program, Laramie, WY 82071. Offers MA. *Program availability:* Part-time. *Degree requirements:* For master's, thesis optional. *Entrance requirements:* For master's, GRE General Test, minimum GPA of 3.0. *Faculty research:* Material culture, American culture, ethnicity, cultural environments, public culture.

**Utah State University,** School of Graduate Studies, College of Humanities, Arts and Social Sciences, Department of English and Department of History, Program in American Studies, Logan, UT 84322. Offers folklore (MA, MS); western American literature and culture (MA, MS). *Program availability:* Part-time, evening/weekend. *Degree requirements:* For master's, thesis or alternative. *Entrance requirements:* For master's, GRE General Test or MAT, minimum GPA of 3.0, 3 letters of recommendation, writing sample. Additional exam requirements/recommendations for international students: Required—TOEFL. *Faculty research:* Folklore and folklife, American culture, regional studies, material culture, Jewish folklore, Native American folklore.

**Washington State University,** College of Arts and Sciences, Program in American Studies, Pullman, WA 99164-4010. Offers MA, PhD. Program applications must be made through the Pullman campus. *Program availability:* Part-time. *Degree requirements:* For master's, one foreign language, comprehensive exam, thesis optional, oral exam; for doctorate, one foreign language, comprehensive exam, thesis/dissertation, oral exam. *Entrance requirements:* For master's and doctorate, official college transcripts sent directly from each institution attended, 3-5 page statement of purpose describing areas of interest, minimum GPA of 3.0, writing sample, 3 letters of recommendation. Additional exam requirements/recommendations for international students: Required—TOEFL.

**Wayne State University,** College of Liberal Arts and Sciences, Department of History, Detroit, MI 48202. Offers Africa (PhD); America (PhD); Asia (PhD); Europe (PhD); gender (PhD); history (MA); labor (PhD); public history (MA); science and technology (PhD); world history (PhD, Graduate Certificate); JD/MA; M Ed/MA; MLIS/MA. Doctoral program admits for fall only. *Program availability:* Evening/weekend. *Faculty:* 18. *Students:* 23 full-time (8 women), 21 part-time (5 women); includes 8 minority (3 Black or African American, non-Hispanic/Latino; 2 Hispanic/Latino; 3 Two or more races, non-Hispanic/Latino). Average age 40. 55 applicants, 38% accepted, 15 enrolled. In 2016, 6 master's, 5 doctorates awarded. *Degree requirements:* For master's, comprehensive exam, thesis (for some programs), final oral exam on thesis or essay and seminar; internship and project (for public history); for doctorate, variable foreign language requirement, comprehensive exam, thesis/dissertation, qualifying exam in 4 fields of history. *Entrance requirements:* For master's, GRE General Test, minimum undergraduate GPA of 3.25 in history, 3.0 overall; at least 18 credits in history and related subjects at the advanced undergraduate level; foreign language; letter of intent; research paper; at least two letters of recommendation from former instructors; for doctorate, GRE General Test, minimum GPA of 3.0, 3.25 in minimum of 18 semester credits in history and related subjects; letter of intent; research paper; at least three letters of recommendation from former professors; for Graduate Certificate, baccalaureate degree from accredited college or university; minimum GPA of 3.0, 3.25 in a minimum of eighteen semester credits in history and related subjects at the advanced undergraduate level. Additional exam requirements/recommendations for international students: Required—TOEFL (minimum score 550 paper-based; 79 iBT), TWE (minimum score 5.5), Michigan English Language Assessment Battery (minimum score 85); Recommended—IELTS (minimum score 6.5). *Application deadline:* For fall admission, 2/1 priority date for domestic and international students; for winter admission, 11/1 for domestic students, 10/1 priority date for international students; for spring admission, 2/1 for domestic students, 1/1 priority date for international students. Application fee: $50. Electronic applications accepted. *Expenses:* $16,503 per year resident tuition and fees, $33,697 per year non-resident tuition and fees. *Financial support:* In 2016–17, 16 students received support, including 2 fellowships with tuition reimbursements available (averaging $18,796 per year), 1 research assistantship with tuition reimbursement available (averaging $21,593 per year), 6 teaching assistantships with tuition reimbursements available (averaging $17,994 per year); scholarships/grants, health care benefits, and unspecified assistantships also available. Financial award applicants required to submit FAFSA. *Faculty research:* African, American, Asian, European, gender, German, labor, science and technology, urban/labor, violence, world. *Unit head:* Dr. Elizabeth V. Faue, Professor/Chair, 313-577-2525, E-mail: evfaue@wayne.edu. *Application contact:* Dr. Eric Ash, Associate Professor and Director of Graduate Studies, 313-577-2525, E-mail: ericash@wayne.edu.
Website: http://clas.wayne.edu/history/

**West Virginia University,** Eberly College of Arts and Sciences, Department of History, Morgantown, WV 26506. Offers African history (MA, PhD); African-American history (MA, PhD); American history (MA, PhD); Appalachian/regional history (MA, PhD); East Asian history (MA, PhD); European history (MA, PhD); history of science and technology (MA, PhD); Latin American history (MA). *Program availability:* Part-time. *Degree requirements:* For master's, one foreign language, thesis (for some programs), oral exam, thesis defense; for doctorate, one foreign language, comprehensive exam, thesis/dissertation, dissertation defense. *Entrance requirements:* For master's, GRE General Test, minimum GPA of 3.0; for doctorate, GRE General Test. Additional exam requirements/recommendations for international students: Required—TOEFL (minimum score 550 paper-based), IELTS (minimum score 6.5). Electronic applications accepted. *Faculty research:* United States, Appalachia, modern Europe, Africa, colonial and post-colonial societies.

**Wilfrid Laurier University,** Faculty of Graduate and Postdoctoral Studies, Faculty of Arts, Department of Religion and Culture, Waterloo, ON N2L 3C5, Canada. Offers religion and culture (MA); religious diversity of North America (PhD). *Program availability:* Part-time. *Degree requirements:* For master's, thesis optional; for doctorate, thesis/dissertation. *Entrance requirements:* For master's, honors BA or the equivalent in religious studies or other interdisciplinary social science or humanities program, minimum B average in overall undergraduate course work, B+ average in the undergraduate major; for doctorate, MA in religious studies, minimum A- average. Additional exam requirements/recommendations for international students: Required—TOEFL (minimum score 89 iBT). Electronic applications accepted. *Faculty research:* Religious diversity in North America.

**Yale University,** Graduate School of Arts and Sciences, Interdisciplinary Program in American Studies, New Haven, CT 06520. Offers PhD. *Degree requirements:* For doctorate, one foreign language, thesis/dissertation. *Entrance requirements:* For doctorate, GRE General Test.

# Asian-American Studies

**Binghamton University, State University of New York,** Graduate School, Harpur College of Arts and Sciences, Department of Asian and Asian American Studies, Binghamton, NY 13902-6000. Offers MA, Certificate. *Program availability:* Part-time. *Faculty:* 19 full-time (10 women), 11 part-time/adjunct (8 women). *Students:* 8 full-time (5 women), 2 part-time (both women); includes 2 minority (1 Asian, non-Hispanic/Latino; 1 Two or more races, non-Hispanic/Latino), 7 international. Average age 28. 14 applicants, 86% accepted, 3 enrolled. In 2016, 8 master's awarded. *Degree requirements:* For master's, variable foreign language requirement, comprehensive exam (for some programs), thesis (for some programs). *Entrance requirements:* For master's, GRE General Test, writing sample. Additional exam requirements/recommendations for international students: Required—TOEFL (minimum score 80 iBT). *Application deadline:* For fall admission, 1/15 priority date for domestic and international students. Application fee: $75. Electronic applications accepted. *Financial support:* Applicants required to submit FAFSA. *Unit head:* Prof. Robert Ji Song Ku, Chair, 607-777-4517, E-mail: jku@binghamton.edu. *Application contact:* Ben Balkaya, Assistant Dean and Director, 607-777-2151, Fax: 607-777-2501, E-mail: balkaya@binghamton.edu.
Website: http://www.binghamton.edu/aaas/

**California State University, Long Beach,** Graduate Studies, College of Liberal Arts, Department of Asian and Asian American Studies, Long Beach, CA 90840. Offers Asian studies (MA). *Program availability:* Part-time. *Degree requirements:* For master's, one foreign language, comprehensive exam or thesis. *Application deadline:* For fall admission, 5/1 for domestic students. Applications are processed on a rolling basis. Application fee: $55. Electronic applications accepted. *Financial support:* Federal Work-Study, institutionally sponsored loans, and scholarships/grants available. Financial award application deadline: 3/2. *Faculty research:* South Asia, China, Japan, Southeast Asia, Asian-Americans in the U.S. *Unit head:* Teri Yamada, Chair, 562-985-4645, Fax: 562-985-1535.

**San Francisco State University,** Division of Graduate Studies, College of Ethnic Studies, Program in Asian American Studies, San Francisco, CA 94132-1722. Offers MA. *Expenses:* Tuition, state resident: full-time $6738. Tuition, nonresident: full-time $15,666. *Required fees:* $1012. Tuition and fees vary according to degree level and program. *Unit head:* Dr. Grace J. Yoo, Chair, 415-338-2698, Fax: 415-338-0500, E-mail: aas@sfsu.edu. *Application contact:* Dr. Russell Mark Jeung, MA Coordinator, 415-338-7586, Fax: 415-338-0500, E-mail: rjeung@sfsu.edu.
Website: http://aas.sfsu.edu/

**Stony Brook University, State University of New York,** Graduate School, College of Arts and Sciences, Department of Asian and Asian American Studies, Stony Brook, NY 11794-5343. Offers contemporary Asian and Asian American studies (MA). *Faculty:* 15 full-time (10 women), 8 part-time/adjunct (all women). *Students:* 4 full-time (all women); includes 2 minority (1 Black or African American, non-Hispanic/Latino; 1 Asian, non-Hispanic/Latino). Average age 27. 7 applicants, 86% accepted, 4 enrolled. *Degree requirements:* For master's, thesis or final project. *Entrance requirements:* For master's, GRE, undergraduate transcript, statement of purpose, three letters of recommendation. Additional exam requirements/recommendations for international students: Required—TOEFL. *Application deadline:* For fall admission, 1/15 for domestic students; for spring admission, 10/1 for domestic students. Application fee: $100. Electronic applications accepted. *Expenses:* Tuition, state resident: full-time $10,870; part-time $453 per credit hour. Tuition, nonresident: full-time $22,210; part-time $925 per credit hour. *Financial support:* Applicants required to submit FAFSA. *Faculty research:* Asian studies, English as a second language, humanities, sociolinguistics. *Total annual research expenditures:* $14,322. *Unit head:* Dr. Agnes He, Chair, 631-632-4041, Fax: 631-632-4098, E-mail: agnes.he@stonybrook.edu. *Application contact:* Melissa Jordan, Assistant Dean for Records and Admission, 631-632-9712, Fax: 631-632-7243, E-mail: melissa.jordan@stonybrook.edu.
Website: http://www.stonybrook.edu/commcms/asianamerican/

**University of California, Los Angeles,** Graduate Division, College of Letters and Science, Program in Asian-American Studies, Los Angeles, CA 90095. Offers MA, MA/MPH, MA/MSW. *Degree requirements:* For master's, one foreign language, comprehensive exam or thesis. *Entrance requirements:* For master's, bachelor's degree; minimum undergraduate GPA of 3.0 (or its equivalent if letter grade system not used); paper or article preferably on Asian Americans. Additional exam requirements/recommendations for international students: Required—TOEFL. Electronic applications accepted.

# Asian Studies

**American University,** College of Arts and Sciences, Critical Race, Gender, and Culture Studies Collaborative, Washington, DC 20016-8001. Offers Asian studies (Graduate Certificate); women's, gender, and sexuality studies (Graduate Certificate). *Expenses:* Tuition: Full-time $28,422; part-time $1579 per credit hour. *Required fees:* $690; $200 per term. Tuition and fees vary according to course load, degree level and program.

## Asian Studies

**Binghamton University, State University of New York,** Graduate School, Harpur College of Arts and Sciences, Department of Asian and Asian American Studies, Binghamton, NY 13902-6000. Offers MA, Certificate. *Program availability:* Part-time. *Faculty:* 19 full-time (10 women), 11 part-time/adjunct (8 women). *Students:* 8 full-time (5 women), 2 part-time (both women); includes 2 minority (1 Asian, non-Hispanic/Latino; 1 Two or more races, non-Hispanic/Latino), 7 international. Average age 28. 14 applicants, 86% accepted, 3 enrolled. In 2016, 8 master's awarded. *Degree requirements:* For master's, variable foreign language requirement, comprehensive exam (for some programs), thesis (for some programs). *Entrance requirements:* For master's, GRE General Test, writing sample. Additional exam requirements/recommendations for international students: Required—TOEFL (minimum score 80 iBT). *Application deadline:* For fall admission, 1/15 priority date for domestic and international students. Application fee: $75. Electronic applications accepted. *Financial support:* Applicants required to submit FAFSA. *Unit head:* Prof. Robert Ji Song Ku, Chair, 607-777-4517, E-mail: jku@binghamton.edu. *Application contact:* Ben Balkaya, Assistant Dean and Director, 607-777-2151, Fax: 607-777-2501, E-mail: balkaya@binghamton.edu.
Website: http://www.binghamton.edu/aaas/

**Brown University,** Graduate School, Department of Egyptology and Ancient Western Asian Studies, Providence, RI 02912. Offers ancient western Asian studies (PhD); Egyptology (PhD); history of the exact sciences in antiquity (PhD). *Degree requirements:* For doctorate, 2 foreign languages, comprehensive exam, thesis/dissertation. *Entrance requirements:* For doctorate, GRE General Test.

**Brown University,** Graduate School, Department of Religious Studies, Providence, RI 02912. Offers Asian religious traditions (PhD); religion and critical thought (PhD); religions of the ancient Mediterranean (PhD). *Degree requirements:* For doctorate, 2 foreign languages, thesis/dissertation. *Entrance requirements:* For doctorate, GRE General Test.

**California Institute of Integral Studies,** School of Consciousness and Transformation, San Francisco, CA 94103. Offers anthropology and social change (MA, PhD); Asian philosophies and cultures (MA); creative inquiry/interdisciplinary arts (MFA); East-West psychology (MA, PhD); integral and transpersonal psychology (PhD); philosophy and religion (PhD), including ecology, spirituality, and religion, philosophy, cosmology, and consciousness, women's spirituality; theater and performance making (MFA); transformative leadership (MA); transformative studies (PhD); women, gender, spirituality and social justice (MA); writing and consciousness (MFA). *Program availability:* Part-time, evening/weekend, 100% online, blended/hybrid learning. *Students:* 390 full-time (256 women), 121 part-time (84 women); includes 135 minority (39 Black or African American, non-Hispanic/Latino; 2 American Indian or Alaska Native, non-Hispanic/Latino; 22 Asian, non-Hispanic/Latino; 40 Hispanic/Latino; 2 Native Hawaiian or other Pacific Islander, non-Hispanic/Latino; 30 Two or more races, non-Hispanic/Latino), 51 international. Average age 38. 195 applicants, 92% accepted, 124 enrolled. In 2016, 35 master's, 41 doctorates awarded. Terminal master's awarded for partial completion of doctoral program. *Degree requirements:* For master's, thesis optional; for doctorate, comprehensive exam, thesis/dissertation, 1 foreign language (for Asian philosophies and cultures). *Entrance requirements:* For master's, minimum GPA of 3.0, letters of recommendation, writing sample; for doctorate, master's degree, minimum GPA of 3.0, letters of recommendation, writing sample. Additional exam requirements/recommendations for international students: Required—TOEFL. *Application deadline:* For fall admission, 2/1 priority date for domestic and international students; for spring admission, 10/15 priority date for domestic and international students. Applications are processed on a rolling basis. Application fee: $65. Electronic applications accepted. *Expenses:* Tuition: Full-time $19,728; part-time $1098 per semester hour. *Required fees:* $320; $320 per semester hour. *Financial support:* Research assistantships, teaching assistantships, career-related internships or fieldwork, Federal Work-Study, and scholarships/grants available. Support available to part-time students. Financial award application deadline: 4/15; financial award applicants required to submit FAFSA. *Faculty research:* Ecology and sustainability, philosophy and religion, East-West psychology, integrative health, social and cultural anthropology, transformative leadership. *Application contact:* Ellen Durst, Director of Admissions, 415-575-6100, Fax: 415-575-1268, E-mail: admissions@ciis.edu.
Website: http://www.ciis.edu/

**California State University, Long Beach,** Graduate Studies, College of Liberal Arts, Department of Asian and Asian American Studies, Long Beach, CA 90840. Offers Asian studies (MA). *Program availability:* Part-time. *Degree requirements:* For master's, one foreign language, comprehensive exam or thesis. *Application deadline:* For fall admission, 5/1 for domestic students. Applications are processed on a rolling basis. Application fee: $55. Electronic applications accepted. *Financial support:* Federal Work-Study, institutionally sponsored loans, and scholarships/grants available. Financial award application deadline: 3/2. *Faculty research:* South Asia, China, Japan, Southeast Asia, Asian-Americans in the U.S. *Unit head:* Teri Yamada, Chair, 562-985-4645, Fax: 562-985-1535.

**Columbia University,** Graduate School of Arts and Sciences, New York, NY 10027. Offers African-American studies (MA); American studies (MA); anthropology (MA, PhD); art history and archaeology (MA, PhD); astronomy (PhD); biological sciences (PhD); biotechnology (MA); chemical physics (PhD); chemistry (PhD); classical studies (MA, PhD); classics (MA, PhD); climate and society (MA); conservation biology (MA); earth and environmental sciences (PhD); East Asia: regional studies (MA); East Asian languages and cultures (MA, PhD); ecology, evolution and environmental biology (MA), including conservation biology; ecology, evolution, and environmental biology (PhD), including ecology and evolutionary biology, evolutionary primatology; economics (MA, PhD); English and comparative literature (MA, PhD); French and Romance philology (MA, PhD); Germanic languages (MA, PhD); global French studies (MA); global thought (MA); Hispanic cultural studies (MA); history (MA); history and literature (MA); human rights studies (MA); Islamic studies (MA); Italian (MA, PhD); Japanese pedagogy (MA); Jewish studies (MA); Latin America and the Caribbean: regional studies (MA); Latin American and Iberian cultures (PhD); mathematics (MA, PhD), including finance (MA); medieval and Renaissance studies (MA); Middle Eastern, South Asian, and African studies (MA, PhD); modern art: critical and curatorial studies (MA); modern European studies (MA); museum anthropology (MA); music (DMA, PhD); oral history (MA); philosophical foundations of physics (MA); philosophy (MA, PhD); physics (PhD); political science (MA, PhD); psychology (PhD); quantitative methods in the social sciences (MA); religion (MA, PhD); Russia, Eurasia and East Europe: regional studies (MA); Russian translation (MA); Slavic cultures (MA); Slavic languages (MA, PhD); sociology (MA, PhD); South Asian studies (MA); statistics (MA, PhD); theatre (PhD). Dual-degree programs require admission to both Graduate School of Arts and Sciences and another Columbia school. *Program availability:* Part-time. Terminal master's awarded for partial completion of doctoral program. *Degree requirements:* For master's, variable foreign language requirement, comprehensive exam (for some programs), thesis (for some programs); for doctorate, variable foreign language requirement, comprehensive exam (for some programs), thesis/dissertation. *Entrance requirements:* For master's and doctorate, GRE General Test, GRE Subject Test (for some programs).

Additional exam requirements/recommendations for international students: Required—TOEFL, IELTS. Electronic applications accepted.

**Columbia University,** South Asia Institute, New York, NY 10027. Offers MA, Certificate. Students must be enrolled in a separate graduate degree program at Columbia University. Electronic applications accepted.

**Cornell University,** Graduate School, Graduate Fields of Arts and Sciences, Field of Asian Literature, Religion and Culture, Ithaca, NY 14853. Offers Asian religions (MA, PhD); Chinese philosophy (PhD); classical Chinese literature (PhD); classical Japanese literature (PhD); East Asian literature and culture (PhD); Korean literature (PhD); modern Chinese literature (PhD); modern Japanese literature (PhD); South Asian literature and culture (PhD); Southeast Asian literature and culture (PhD). *Degree requirements:* For doctorate, comprehensive exam, thesis/dissertation. *Entrance requirements:* For doctorate, GRE General Test, academic writing sample, 3 letters of recommendation. Additional exam requirements/recommendations for international students: Required—TOEFL (minimum score 600 paper-based; 77 iBT). Electronic applications accepted.

**Cornell University,** Graduate School, Graduate Fields of Arts and Sciences, Field of Asian Studies, Ithaca, NY 14853. Offers East Asian studies (MA); East Asian studies (MA); South Asian linguistics (MA); South Asian studies (MA); Southeast Asian linguistics (MA); Southeast Asian studies (MA). *Degree requirements:* For master's, one foreign language, thesis. *Entrance requirements:* For master's, GRE General Test, 3 letters of recommendation. Additional exam requirements/recommendations for international students: Required—TOEFL (minimum score 550 paper-based; 77 iBT). Electronic applications accepted. *Faculty research:* East Asian studies, South Asian studies, Southeast Asian studies.

**Cornell University,** Graduate School, Graduate Fields of Arts and Sciences, Field of History, Ithaca, NY 14853. Offers African history (MA, PhD); American history (MA, PhD); ancient Greek history (PhD); ancient history (MA, PhD); ancient Roman history (PhD); early modern European history (MA, PhD); English history (MA, PhD); French history (MA, PhD); German history (MA, PhD); history of science (MA, PhD); Korean history (PhD); Latin American history (MA, PhD); medieval Chinese history (MA, PhD); medieval history (MA, PhD); modern Chinese history (MA, PhD); modern European history (MA, PhD); modern Japanese history (MA, PhD); modern Middle Eastern history (PhD); premodern Islamic history (MA, PhD); premodern Japanese history (MA, PhD); Renaissance history (MA, PhD); Russian history (MA, PhD); South Asian history (PhD); Southeast Asian history (MA, PhD). Terminal master's awarded for partial completion of doctoral program. *Degree requirements:* For master's, thesis; for doctorate, 2 foreign languages, comprehensive exam, thesis/dissertation, 1 year of teaching experience. *Entrance requirements:* For master's and doctorate, GRE General Test, writing sample, 3 letters of recommendation. Additional exam requirements/recommendations for international students: Required—TOEFL (minimum score 550 paper-based; 77 iBT). Electronic applications accepted.

**Cornell University,** Graduate School, Graduate Fields of Arts and Sciences, Field of History of Art, Archaeology and Visual Studies, Ithaca, NY 14853. Offers 19th century art (PhD); African, African American and African diaspora (PhD); American art (PhD); ancient art and archaeology (PhD); Asian American art (PhD); Baroque art (PhD); comparative modernities (PhD); digital art (PhD); East Asian art (PhD); history of photography (PhD); Islamic art (PhD); Latin American art (PhD); medieval art (PhD); modern art (PhD); Renaissance art (PhD); Southeast Asian art (PhD); theory and criticism (PhD); visual studies (PhD). *Degree requirements:* For doctorate, one foreign language, comprehensive exam, thesis/dissertation, general exams in 3 areas. *Entrance requirements:* For doctorate, GRE General Test, sample of written work, 3 letters of recommendation. Additional exam requirements/recommendations for international students: Required—TOEFL (minimum score 550 paper-based; 77 iBT). Electronic applications accepted.

**Cornell University,** Graduate School, Graduate Fields of Arts and Sciences, Field of Linguistics, Ithaca, NY 14853. Offers applied linguistics (MA, PhD); East Asian linguistics (MA, PhD); English linguistics (MA, PhD); general linguistics (MA, PhD); Germanic linguistics (MA, PhD); Indo-European linguistics (MA, PhD); phonetics (MA, PhD); phonological theory (MA, PhD); Romance linguistics (MA, PhD); second language acquisition (MA, PhD); semantics (MA, PhD); Slavic linguistics (MA, PhD); sociolinguistics (MA, PhD); South Asian linguistics (MA, PhD); Southeast Asian linguistics (MA, PhD); syntactic theory (MA, PhD). Terminal master's awarded for partial completion of doctoral program. *Degree requirements:* For master's, one foreign language, thesis; for doctorate, one foreign language, comprehensive exam, thesis/dissertation. *Entrance requirements:* For master's and doctorate, GRE General Test, 2 letters of recommendation. Additional exam requirements/recommendations for international students: Required—TOEFL (minimum score 600 paper-based; 77 iBT). Electronic applications accepted. *Faculty research:* Phonology and phonetics, syntax and semantics, historical linguistics, philosophy of language, language acquisition.

**Creighton University,** Graduate School, College of Arts and Sciences, Program in East-West Studies, Omaha, NE 68178-0001. Offers MA. *Program availability:* Part-time. *Faculty:* 6 full-time (2 women). *Students:* 2 full-time (0 women), 3 part-time (1 woman); includes 1 minority (Hispanic/Latino), 2 international. Average age 37. 2 applicants, 50% accepted. In 2016, 3 master's awarded. *Degree requirements:* For master's, one foreign language. *Entrance requirements:* For master's, 3 recommendations; personal essay; interview. Additional exam requirements/recommendations for international students: Required—TOEFL (minimum score 90 iBT). *Application deadline:* For fall admission, 7/1 for domestic and international students; for summer admission, 5/1 for domestic and international students. Application fee: $50. Electronic applications accepted. *Expenses:* Contact institution. *Financial support:* Scholarships/grants available. Financial award application deadline: 5/1; financial award applicants required to submit FAFSA. *Unit head:* Dr. Jinmei Yuan, Associate Professor, 402-280-3309, E-mail: jinmeiyuan@creighton.edu. *Application contact:* Lindsay Johnson, Director of Graduate and Adult Recruitment, 402-280-2703, Fax: 402-280-2423, E-mail: gradschool@creighton.edu.

**Dallas Baptist University,** Gary Cook School of Leadership, Program in International Studies, Dallas, TX 75211-9299. Offers East Asian studies (MA); European studies (MA); general international studies (MA); global business (MA); international immersion (MA); international ministry (MA); international relations (MA). *Program availability:* Part-time, evening/weekend. *Application deadline:* Applications are processed on a rolling basis. Application fee: $25. Electronic applications accepted. Application fee is waived when completed online. *Expenses:* Tuition: Full-time $15,408; part-time $856 per credit hour. *Required fees:* $400 per semester. Tuition and fees vary according to course load and degree level. *Unit head:* Dr. Brent A. Thomason, Director, 214-333-5236, E-mail: brentt@dbu.edu. *Application contact:* Bobby Soto, Director of Admissions, 214-333-5242, E-mail: graduate@dbu.edu.
Website: http://www4.dbu.edu/leadership/maimternational

**Dallas Baptist University,** Graduate School of Ministry, Program in Global Leadership, Dallas, TX 75211-9299. Offers church planting (MA); East Asian Studies (MA); English as a second language (MA); general studies (MA); global communication (MA); global studies (MA); international business (MA); leading the nonprofit organization (MA);

missions (MA); small group ministry (MA); urban ministry (MA). *Program availability:* Part-time, evening/weekend. *Application deadline:* Applications are processed on a rolling basis. Application fee: $25. Electronic applications accepted. Application fee is waived when completed online. *Expenses: Tuition:* Full-time $15,408; part-time $856 per credit hour. *Required fees:* $400 per semester. Tuition and fees vary according to course load and degree level. *Unit head:* Dr. Bob Garrett, Director, 214-333-5508, E-mail: bobg@dbu.edu. *Application contact:* Bobby Soto, Director of Admissions, 214-333-5242, E-mail: graduate@dbu.edu.
Website: http://www3.dbu.edu/gsom/global-leadership/

**Dallas Baptist University,** Liberal Arts Program, Dallas, TX 75211-9299. Offers art (MLA); Christian studies (MLA); commercial art (MLA); East Asian studies (MLA); English (MLA); English as a second language (MLA); fine arts (MLA); history (MLA); missions (MLA); political science (MLA). *Program availability:* Part-time, evening/weekend, 100% online, blended/hybrid learning. *Application deadline:* Applications are processed on a rolling basis. Application fee: $25. Electronic applications accepted. Application fee is waived when completed online. *Expenses: Tuition:* Full-time $15,408; part-time $856 per credit hour. *Required fees:* $400 per semester. Tuition and fees vary according to course load and degree level. *Faculty research:* Milton and seventeenth-century Puritans, inter-Biblical years, nineteenth-century literature, Latin American and Texas history. *Unit head:* Jared Ingram, Director, 214-333-5584, E-mail: jaredi@dbu.edu. *Application contact:* Bobby Soto, Director of Admissions, 214-333-5242, E-mail: graduate@dbu.edu.
Website: http://www3.dbu.edu/graduate/mla.asp

**Duke University,** Graduate School, Department of East Asian Studies, Durham, NC 27708. Offers AM, Certificate. *Program availability:* Part-time. *Entrance requirements:* For master's, GRE General Test. Additional exam requirements/recommendations for international students: Required—TOEFL (minimum score 577 paper-based; 90 iBT) or IELTS (minimum score 7). Electronic applications accepted.

**Florida International University,** Steven J. Green School of International and Public Affairs, Program in Asian Studies, Miami, FL 33199. Offers MA, MA/PhD. *Program availability:* Part-time, evening/weekend. *Faculty:* 4 part-time/adjunct (1 woman). *Students:* 10 full-time (6 women), 3 part-time (2 women); includes 8 minority (6 Hispanic/Latino; 2 Two or more races, non-Hispanic/Latino), 1 international. Average age 26. 14 applicants, 100% accepted, 7 enrolled. In 2016, 14 master's awarded. *Degree requirements:* For master's, thesis. *Entrance requirements:* For master's, minimum GPA of 3.0, letter of intent, letter of recommendation. Additional exam requirements/recommendations for international students: Required—TOEFL (minimum score 550 paper-based; 80 iBT). *Application deadline:* For fall admission, 6/1 for domestic students, 4/1 for international students; for spring admission, 10/1 for domestic students, 9/1 for international students. Applications are processed on a rolling basis. Application fee: $30. Electronic applications accepted. *Expenses:* Tuition, state resident: full-time $8912; part-time $446 per credit hour. Tuition, nonresident: full-time $21,393; part-time $992 per credit hour. *Required fees:* $2185; $195 per semester. Tuition and fees vary according to program. *Financial support:* Institutionally sponsored loans, scholarships/grants, and tuition waivers available. Financial award application deadline: 3/1; financial award applicants required to submit FAFSA. *Unit head:* Dr. Steven Heine, Program Director, 305-348-1788, Fax: 305-348-6586, E-mail: asian@fiu.edu. *Application contact:* Nanett Rojas, Manager, Admissions Operations, 305-348-7464, Fax: 305-348-7441, E-mail: gradadm@fiu.edu.

**Florida State University,** The Graduate School, College of Social Sciences and Public Policy, Program in Asian Studies, Tallahassee, FL 32306. Offers MA, MS. *Program availability:* Part-time. *Faculty:* 4 full-time (all women), 4 part-time/adjunct (0 women). *Students:* 4 full-time (3 women), 1 part-time (0 women); includes 2 minority (1 Black or African American, non-Hispanic/Latino; 1 Asian, non-Hispanic/Latino), 1 international. Average age 27. 10 applicants, 50% accepted, 2 enrolled. In 2016, 6 master's awarded. *Degree requirements:* For master's, one foreign language, comprehensive exam, thesis optional. *Entrance requirements:* For master's, GRE General Test, minimum GPA of 3.0. Additional exam requirements/recommendations for international students: Required—TOEFL (minimum score 550 paper-based, 80 iBT) or IELTS (6.5). *Application deadline:* For fall admission, 7/1 for domestic and international students; for spring admission, 11/1 for domestic and international students; for summer admission, 3/1 for domestic and international students. Applications are processed on a rolling basis. Application fee: $30. Electronic applications accepted. *Expenses:* Contact institution. *Financial support:* In 2016–17, 1 student received support, including 1 research assistantship with full tuition reimbursement available (averaging $5,000 per year); teaching assistantships, Federal Work-Study, institutionally sponsored loans, and unspecified assistantships also available. Financial award application deadline: 2/1; financial award applicants required to submit FAFSA. *Faculty research:* Art history of the Orient, Asian history and politics, deception in World War II. *Unit head:* Dr. Lee K. Metcalf, Director, 850-644-4418, Fax: 850-645-4981, E-mail: lmetcalf@fsu.edu. *Application contact:* Sam Bandak, Program Specialist, 850-644-4418, Fax: 850-644-4981, E-mail: sbandak@fsu.edu.
Website: http://coss.fsu.edu/inaprog/programs/graduate/g-asian

**Georgetown University,** Graduate School of Arts and Sciences, Walsh School of Foreign Service, Program in Asian Studies, Washington, DC 20057. Offers MA. *Degree requirements:* For master's, comprehensive exam, research project. *Entrance requirements:* Additional exam requirements/recommendations for international students: Required—TOEFL.

**The George Washington University,** Elliott School of International Affairs, Program in Asian Studies, Washington, DC 20052. Offers MA. *Program availability:* Part-time. *Students:* 25 full-time (15 women), 8 part-time (6 women); includes 14 minority (7 Asian, non-Hispanic/Latino; 3 Hispanic/Latino; 1 Two or more races, non-Hispanic/Latino), 11 international. Average age 26. 63 applicants, 70% accepted, 12 enrolled. In 2016, 10 master's awarded. *Degree requirements:* For master's, one foreign language, capstone project. *Entrance requirements:* For master's, GRE General Test, 2 years (or the equivalent) of an approved Asian language. Additional exam requirements/recommendations for international students: Required—TOEFL (minimum score 100 iBT), IELTS (minimum score 7). *Application deadline:* For fall admission, 1/15 priority date for domestic students; for spring admission, 10/1 for domestic students. Application fee: $75. Electronic applications accepted. *Financial support:* In 2016–17, 7 students received support. Fellowships with partial tuition reimbursements available and Federal Work-Study available. Financial award application deadline: 1/15; financial award applicants required to submit FAFSA. *Faculty research:* Sino-Soviet studies, Japanese-U.S. relations, Chinese foreign policy, economic development in China. *Unit head:* Prof. Daqing Yang, Director, 202-994-5886, Fax: 202-994-2484, E-mail: asia@gwu.edu. *Application contact:* Nicole A. Campbell, Director of Graduate Admissions, 202-994-7050, Fax: 202-994-9537, E-mail: esiagrad@gwu.edu.
Website: http://www.gwu.edu/graduate-programs/asian-studies

**Harvard University,** Graduate School of Arts and Sciences, Committee on Inner Asian and Altaic Studies, Cambridge, MA 02138. Offers PhD. *Degree requirements:* For doctorate, 2 foreign languages, thesis/dissertation, oral general exam. *Entrance requirements:* For doctorate, GRE General Test, proficiency in a related foreign language. Additional exam requirements/recommendations for international students: Required—TOEFL.

**Harvard University,** Graduate School of Arts and Sciences, Committee on Regional Studies–East Asia, Cambridge, MA 02138. Offers Chinese studies (AM); Japanese studies (AM); Korean studies (AM); Mongolian studies (AM); Vietnamese studies (AM). *Degree requirements:* For master's, one foreign language, seminar paper. *Entrance requirements:* For master's, GRE General Test. Additional exam requirements/recommendations for international students: Required—TOEFL.

**Harvard University,** Graduate School of Arts and Sciences, Department of Sanskrit and Indian Studies, Cambridge, MA 02138. Offers Indian philosophy (AM, PhD); Pali (AM, PhD); Sanskrit (AM, PhD); Tibetan (AM, PhD); Urdu (AM, PhD). Terminal master's awarded for partial completion of doctoral program. *Degree requirements:* For master's, 3 foreign languages; for doctorate, 3 foreign languages, thesis/dissertation. *Entrance requirements:* For master's, GRE General Test; for doctorate, GRE General Test, proficiency in French and German. Additional exam requirements/recommendations for international students: Required—TOEFL.

**Indiana University Bloomington,** University Graduate School, College of Arts and Sciences, School of Global and International Studies, Department of Central Eurasian Studies, Bloomington, IN 47405-7000. Offers MA, PhD. Terminal master's awarded for partial completion of doctoral program. *Degree requirements:* For master's, one foreign language, thesis; for doctorate, 2 foreign languages, thesis/dissertation, qualifying exams. *Entrance requirements:* For master's, minimum GPA of 3.0, 2 years of a foreign language; for doctorate, minimum GPA of 3.5, 1 research language. Additional exam requirements/recommendations for international students: Required—TOEFL. Electronic applications accepted. *Faculty research:* Central Asia, Hungarian civilization, Tibetan civilization, Turkish studies, Mongolian philology.

**Indiana University Bloomington,** University Graduate School, College of Arts and Sciences, School of Global and International Studies, Department of East Asian Languages and Cultures, Bloomington, IN 47408. Offers Chinese (MA, PhD); Chinese language pedagogy (MA); East Asian studies (MA); Japanese (MA, PhD); Japanese language pedagogy (MA). *Program availability:* Part-time. *Degree requirements:* For master's, one foreign language, thesis; for doctorate, 2 foreign languages, comprehensive exam, thesis/dissertation. *Entrance requirements:* Additional exam requirements/recommendations for international students: Required—TOEFL (minimum score 93 iBT). Electronic applications accepted. *Faculty research:* Modern East Asian history; politics and society; traditional Chinese thought and society; medieval and premodern Japanese history, literature and society; modern Chinese and Japanese film and literature; Chinese, Japanese, Korean language and linguistics.

**Johns Hopkins University,** School of Advanced International Studies, Washington, DC 20036. Offers global risk (MA); international development (MA, Certificate), including international economics (MA); international economics and finance (MA); international public policy (MIPP); international relations (PhD); international studies (Certificate); Japan studies (MA), including international economics; Korea studies (MA), including international economics; South Asia studies (MA), including international economics; Southeast Asia studies (MA), including international economics; JD/MA; MBA/MA; MHS/MA. Terminal master's awarded for partial completion of doctoral program. *Degree requirements:* For master's, 4-6 international economics courses, 5-6 functional or regional concentration courses, 2 core examinations, proficiency in language other than native language, capstone project; for doctorate, 2 foreign languages, thesis/dissertation, 3 comprehensive exams, economics, quantitative and qualitative course, dissertation prospectus and defense. *Entrance requirements:* For master's, GMAT or GRE General Test, previous course work in economics, foreign language, undergraduate degree; for doctorate, GRE General Test, master's degree. Additional exam requirements/recommendations for international students: Required—TOEFL (minimum score 600 paper-based; 100 iBT) or IELTS (minimum score 7). Electronic applications accepted. *Expenses:* Contact institution. *Faculty research:* Regional studies, international relations, international economics, energy and environment, international development.

**Maharishi University of Management,** Graduate Studies, Program in Maharishi Vedic Science, Fairfield, IA 52557. Offers MA, PhD. *Program availability:* Evening/weekend. *Degree requirements:* For master's, thesis; for doctorate, thesis/dissertation. *Entrance requirements:* For master's, minimum GPA of 3.0; for doctorate, GRE, minimum GPA of 3.0. Additional exam requirements/recommendations for international students: Required—TOEFL. *Faculty research:* Modern science and Vedic science, unification of knowledge, philosophy of science, Sanskrit.

**McGill University,** Faculty of Graduate and Postdoctoral Studies, Faculty of Arts, Department of East Asian Studies, Montréal, QC H3A 2T5, Canada. Offers MA, PhD.

**New York University,** Graduate School of Arts and Science, Department of East Asian Studies, New York, NY 10012-1019. Offers MA, PhD. *Program availability:* Part-time. *Degree requirements:* For master's and doctorate, one foreign language. *Entrance requirements:* Additional exam requirements/recommendations for international students: Required—TOEFL. Electronic applications accepted.

**The Ohio State University,** Graduate School, East Asian Studies Center, Columbus, OH 43210. Offers MA. *Students:* 12 full-time (7 women). Average age 27. In 2016, 2 master's awarded. *Degree requirements:* For master's, thesis optional. *Entrance requirements:* For master's, GRE General Test. Additional exam requirements/recommendations for international students: Required—TOEFL (minimum score 550 paper-based; 79 iBT), IELTS (minimum score 7). *Application deadline:* For fall admission, 12/13 priority date for domestic students, 11/30 priority date for international students; for spring admission, 12/1 for domestic students, 11/1 for international students; for summer admission, 4/10 for domestic students, 3/13 for international students. Applications are processed on a rolling basis. Application fee: $60 ($70 for international students). Electronic applications accepted. *Unit head:* Dr. Etsuyo Yuasa, Associate Professor, 614-292-5816, E-mail: yuasa.1@osu.edu. *Application contact:* Graduate and Professional Admissions, 614-292-9444, Fax: 614-292-3895, E-mail: gpadmissions@osu.edu.
Website: http://www.easc.osu.edu/

**Ohio University,** Graduate College, Center for International Studies, Program in Asian Studies, Athens, OH 45701-2979. Offers MA. *Program availability:* Part-time. *Degree requirements:* For master's, one foreign language, thesis optional. *Entrance requirements:* For master's, minimum GPA of 3.0. Additional exam requirements/recommendations for international students: Required—TOEFL (minimum score 550 paper-based; 80 iBT); Recommended—IELTS (minimum score 6.5). *Application deadline:* For fall admission, 1/1 for domestic and international students. Application fee: $50 ($55 for international students). Electronic applications accepted. *Financial support:* Research assistantships with full tuition reimbursements, teaching assistantships with full tuition reimbursements, career-related internships or fieldwork, Federal Work-Study, institutionally sponsored loans, scholarships/grants, tuition waivers (partial), and unspecified assistantships available. Financial award application deadline: 1/1. *Faculty research:* Indonesian and Malaysian political, history, literature, media, Islam, and environmental problems. *Unit head:* Dr. Takaaki Suzuki, Director, 740-593-9781, E-mail: suzuki@ohio.edu. *Application contact:* Patti Malloy, Administrative Assistant, 740-593-1836, Fax: 740-593-1837, E-mail: malloyp@ohio.edu.
Website: http://www.ohiou.edu/seas/

## Asian Studies

**Princeton University,** Graduate School, Department of East Asian Studies, Princeton, NJ 08544-1019. Offers PhD. *Degree requirements:* For doctorate, 2 foreign languages, thesis/dissertation. *Entrance requirements:* For doctorate, GRE General Test, fluency in Japanese and/or Chinese. Additional exam requirements/recommendations for international students: Required—TOEFL (minimum score 600 paper-based). Electronic applications accepted. *Faculty research:* Modern and classical Japanese literature, premodern Chinese and Japanese history, Chinese narrative and poetry.

**Rutgers University–New Brunswick,** Graduate School-New Brunswick, Program in East Asian Languages and Cultures, Piscataway, NJ 08854-8097. Offers MA. *Degree requirements:* For master's, one foreign language, final exam. *Entrance requirements:* For master's, GRE, official transcripts, two letters of recommendation, personal statement, writing sample. Additional exam requirements/recommendations for international students: Required—TOEFL or IELTS.

**Rutgers University–New Brunswick,** Graduate School-New Brunswick, Program in History, Piscataway, NJ 08854-8097. Offers African-American history (PhD); early American history (PhD); early modern European history (PhD); east Asian history (PhD); global and comparative history (PhD); history (PhD); history of diplomacy and foreign relations (PhD); history of technology, environment and health (PhD); history of the Atlantic cultures and African diaspora (PhD); Latin American history (PhD); medieval history (PhD); modern European history (PhD); nineteenth and twentieth century American history (PhD); women's and gender history (PhD). *Degree requirements:* For doctorate, thesis/dissertation. *Entrance requirements:* For doctorate, GRE General Test, sample of written work. Electronic applications accepted. *Faculty research:* American history, European history, Afro-American history, women's history, Latin American history.

**St. John's College,** Graduate Institute in Liberal Education, Program in Eastern Classics, Santa Fe, NM 87505. Offers MA. *Program availability:* Part-time, evening/weekend. *Entrance requirements:* For master's, 2 letters of recommendation. Additional exam requirements/recommendations for international students: Required—TOEFL, TWE. *Expenses:* Contact institution.

**St. John's University,** St. John's College of Liberal Arts and Sciences, Institute of Asian Studies, Queens, NY 11439. Offers Asian studies (Adv C); Chinese studies (MA, Adv C); East Asian culture studies (Adv C); East Asian studies (MA). *Program availability:* Part-time, evening/weekend. *Degree requirements:* For master's, one foreign language, comprehensive exam, thesis optional. *Entrance requirements:* For master's, 6 semester hours of course work in the field, minimum GPA of 3.0. Additional exam requirements/recommendations for international students: Required—TOEFL (minimum score 600 paper-based; 100 iBT), IELTS (minimum score 7). Electronic applications accepted. *Faculty research:* East Asian philosophy and religions; government and politics of East Asia; business and economy of East Asia; legal systems and trade relations of East Asian countries; Chinese, Japanese, and Korean languages and civilization; modern China, Japan, and Korea; Chinese, Japanese, and Korean art and history.

**San Diego State University,** Graduate and Research Affairs, College of Arts and Letters, Center for Asian Studies, San Diego, CA 92182. Offers MA. *Degree requirements:* For master's, one foreign language, thesis. *Entrance requirements:* For master's, GRE General Test, 3 letters of reference, writing sample. Additional exam requirements/recommendations for international students: Required—TOEFL. Electronic applications accepted. *Faculty research:* Language acquisition process, social organization of Asia, economic development.

**Seton Hall University,** College of Arts and Sciences, Department of Languages, Literatures and Cultures, South Orange, NJ 07079-2697. Offers Asian studies (MA). *Program availability:* Part-time, evening/weekend. *Degree requirements:* For master's, thesis optional. *Entrance requirements:* For master's, strong background in Asian studies or related discipline. Additional exam requirements/recommendations for international students: Required—TOEFL. Electronic applications accepted. *Faculty research:* Modern Chinese history, contemporary Chinese politics, ancient Chinese history, Hinduism, Asian business, Japanese history.

**Stanford University,** School of Humanities and Sciences, Center for East Asian Studies, Stanford, CA 94305-2004. Offers MA. *Degree requirements:* For master's, one foreign language, thesis. *Entrance requirements:* For master's, GRE General Test. Additional exam requirements/recommendations for international students: Required—TOEFL. Electronic applications accepted. *Expenses: Tuition:* Full-time $47,331. *Required fees:* $609.

**Stony Brook University, State University of New York,** Graduate School, College of Arts and Sciences, Department of Asian and Asian American Studies, Stony Brook, NY 11794-5343. Offers contemporary Asian and Asian American studies (MA). *Faculty:* 15 full-time (10 women), 8 part-time/adjunct (all women). *Students:* 4 full-time (all women); includes 2 minority (1 Black or African American, non-Hispanic/Latino; 1 Asian, non-Hispanic/Latino). Average age 27. 7 applicants, 86% accepted, 4 enrolled. *Degree requirements:* For master's, thesis or final project. *Entrance requirements:* For master's, GRE, undergraduate transcript, statement of purpose, three letters of recommendation. Additional exam requirements/recommendations for international students: Required—TOEFL. *Application deadline:* For fall admission, 1/15 for domestic students; for spring admission, 10/1 for domestic students. Application fee: $100. Electronic applications accepted. *Expenses:* Tuition, state resident: full-time $10,870; part-time $453 per credit hour. Tuition, nonresident: full-time $22,210; part-time $925 per credit hour. *Financial support:* Applicants required to submit FAFSA. *Faculty research:* Asian studies, English as a second language, humanities, sociolinguistics. *Total annual research expenditures:* $14,322. *Unit head:* Dr. Agnes He, Chair, 631-632-4041, Fax: 631-632-4098, E-mail: agnes.he@stonybrook.edu. *Application contact:* Melissa Jordan, Assistant Dean for Records and Admission, 631-632-9712, Fax: 631-632-7243, E-mail: melissa.jordan@stonybrook.edu.
Website: http://www.stonybrook.edu/commcms/asianamerican/

**United Theological Seminary of the Twin Cities,** Graduate Programs, New Brighton, MN 55112-2598. Offers advanced theological studies (Diploma); justice and peace studies (M Div, MA); leadership toward racial justice (M Div, MA, Certificate); Methodist studies (M Div, MA, Certificate); ministry (D Min); ministry renewal and professional development (Certificate); pastoral care and counseling (M Div, MA, MARL); religion and theology (MA); theological and religious studies (Certificate); theology and the arts (M Div, MA); urban ministry (M Div, MA, MARL); women's studies: religion, theology and ministry (M Div, MA). *Accreditation:* ACIPE; ATS. *Program availability:* Part-time, evening/weekend. *Degree requirements:* For master's, thesis; for doctorate, comprehensive exam, thesis/dissertation. *Entrance requirements:* For master's, minimum GPA of 2.75; strong analytical, reflective thinking and writing skills; vocational and academic goals compatible with those of Seminary; for doctorate, M Div or equivalent, minimum GPA of 3.0, 3 years experience in professional ministry; for other advanced degree, BA or equivalent life experience; strong analytical, reflective thinking and writing skills (Certificate); proficiency in English language, previous study of theology at a theological school, recommendation of student's denomination (Diploma). Additional exam requirements/recommendations for international students: Required—TOEFL (minimum score 550 paper-based).

**University of Alberta,** Faculty of Graduate Studies and Research, Department of East Asian Studies, Edmonton, AB T6G 2E1, Canada. Offers Chinese literature (MA); East Asian interdisciplinary studies (MA); Japanese literature (MA). *Program availability:* Part-time. *Degree requirements:* For master's, one foreign language, thesis. *Entrance requirements:* Additional exam requirements/recommendations for international students: Required—TOEFL. Electronic applications accepted. *Faculty research:* Classical Chinese poetry and poetics, Chinese philosophy, modern/contemporary Chinese literature, modern Japanese literature and culture, Japanese women's writing.

**The University of Arizona,** College of Humanities, Department of East Asian Studies, Tucson, AZ 85721. Offers MA, PhD. *Program availability:* Part-time. Terminal master's awarded for partial completion of doctoral program. *Degree requirements:* For master's, one foreign language; for doctorate, 2 foreign languages. *Entrance requirements:* For master's, GRE General Test, 2 letters of recommendation; for doctorate, GRE General Test, 2 letters of recommendation, statement of purpose, writing sample. Additional exam requirements/recommendations for international students: Required—TOEFL (minimum score 550 paper-based; 79 iBT). Electronic applications accepted. *Faculty research:* Chinese history; Chinese/Japanese linguistics, literature and religion.

**University of Bridgeport,** College of Public and International Affairs, Bridgeport, CT 06604. Offers East Asian and Pacific Rim studies (MA); global development and peace (MA); global media and communication studies (MA). *Program availability:* Part-time, evening/weekend. *Degree requirements:* For master's, thesis. *Entrance requirements:* Additional exam requirements/recommendations for international students: Recommended—TOEFL (minimum score 550 paper-based; 80 iBT), IELTS (minimum score 6.5).

**The University of British Columbia,** Faculty of Arts, Department of Asian Studies, Vancouver, BC V6T 1Z2, Canada. Offers MA, PhD. *Degree requirements:* For master's, one foreign language, thesis; for doctorate, 2 foreign languages, thesis/dissertation. *Entrance requirements:* For master's, BA; for doctorate, master's degree in Asian studies or equivalent. Additional exam requirements/recommendations for international students: Required—TOEFL. *Application deadline:* Applications are processed on a rolling basis. Application fee: $100 Canadian dollars ($162 Canadian dollars for international students). Electronic applications accepted. *Expenses:* $4,802 per year tuition and fees, $8,436 per year international. *Financial support:* Fellowships, research assistantships, and teaching assistantships available. *Faculty research:* Language; linguistics; literature; religion and philosophy; premodern history of China, Japan, Korea, South and South East Asia. *Application contact:* Jasmina Miodragovic, Graduate Program Staff, 604-822-5728, Fax: 604-822-8937, E-mail: asiagrad@mail.ubc.ca.
Website: http://www.asia.ubc.ca/

**The University of British Columbia,** Institute of Asian Research, Vancouver, BC V6T 1Z2, Canada. Offers Asia Pacific policy studies (MAAPPS); public policy and global affairs (MPPGA). *Degree requirements:* For master's, thesis optional. *Entrance requirements:* Additional exam requirements/recommendations for international students: Required—TOEFL. Application fee: $100 ($162 for international students). Electronic applications accepted. *Expenses:* $26,842 per year tuition and fees, $42,648 per year international. *Financial support:* Fellowships with tuition reimbursements, research assistantships, career-related internships or fieldwork, institutionally sponsored loans, scholarships/grants, and tuition waivers (partial) available. *Faculty research:* Social cohesion, globalization, social safety nets, policy research, research and development alliances, knowledge-based workshops on Asia-Pacific studies. *Application contact:* Kerry Ross, Graduate Program Staff, 604-822-4571, E-mail: mppga.program@ubc.ca.
Website: http://iar.ubc.ca/

**University of California, Berkeley,** Graduate Division, College of Letters and Science, Department of South and Southeast Asian Studies, Berkeley, CA 94720-1500. Offers Hindi (MA, PhD); Indonesian (MA, PhD); Sanskrit (MA, PhD); Tamil (MA, PhD). *Faculty:* 6 full-time, 14 part-time/adjunct. *Students:* 25 full-time (16 women); includes 6 minority (5 Asian, non-Hispanic/Latino; 1 Hispanic/Latino), 3 international. Average age 34. 31 applicants, 3 enrolled. In 2016, 4 master's, 4 doctorates awarded. Terminal master's awarded for partial completion of doctoral program. *Degree requirements:* For master's, 2 foreign languages, thesis; for doctorate, 2 foreign languages, thesis/dissertation, oral qualifying exam. *Entrance requirements:* For master's and doctorate, GRE General Test, minimum GPA of 3.0, 3 letters of recommendation. *Application deadline:* For fall admission, 12/9 for domestic students. Application fee: $105 ($125 for international students). Electronic applications accepted. *Financial support:* Fellowships, research assistantships, teaching assistantships, institutionally sponsored loans, health care benefits, and unspecified assistantships available. *Unit head:* Prof. Jacob Dalton, Chair, 510-642-4564. *Application contact:* Cassandra Dunn, 510-642-3672, E-mail: cassandrajj@berkeley.edu.
Website: http://sseas.berkeley.edu

**University of California, Berkeley,** Graduate Division, College of Letters and Science, Group in Buddhist Studies, Berkeley, CA 94720-1500. Offers PhD. *Faculty:* 9 full-time. *Students:* 8 full-time (4 women), 1 international. Average age 31. 15 applicants, 1 enrolled. In 2016, 1 doctorate awarded. *Degree requirements:* For doctorate, 4 foreign languages, thesis/dissertation, dissertation defense, qualifying exam. *Entrance requirements:* For doctorate, GRE General Test, MA in Japanese, Chinese, or Sanskrit; minimum GPA of 3.0; 3 letters of recommendation. *Application deadline:* For fall admission, 12/5 for domestic students. Application fee: $105 ($125 for international students). Electronic applications accepted. *Financial support:* Fellowships, research assistantships, teaching assistantships, institutionally sponsored loans, health care benefits, and unspecified assistantships available. *Unit head:* Prof. Robert Sharf, Chair, 510-642-3480, E-mail: gbs@berkeley.edu. *Application contact:* Information Contact, 510-642-3480, E-mail: gbs@berkeley.edu.
Website: http://buddhiststudies.berkeley.edu/

**University of California, Berkeley,** Graduate Division, Group in Asian Studies, Berkeley, CA 94720-1500. Offers East Asian studies (MA); Northeast Asian studies (MA); South Asian studies (MA); Southeast Asian studies (MA); JD/MA; MBA/MA; MJ/MA. *Students:* 13 full-time (2 women); includes 4 minority (all Asian, non-Hispanic/Latino), 2 international. Average age 30. 105 applicants, 6 enrolled. In 2016, 6 master's awarded. *Degree requirements:* For master's, one foreign language, comprehensive exam or thesis. *Entrance requirements:* For master's, GRE General Test, minimum GPA of 3.0, 3 letters of recommendation. *Application deadline:* For fall admission, 12/1 for domestic students. Application fee: $105 ($125 for international students). Electronic applications accepted. *Financial support:* Fellowships, research assistantships, teaching assistantships, Federal Work-Study, and unspecified assistantships available. Financial award applicants required to submit FAFSA. *Unit head:* Prof. Aihwa Ong, Chair, 510-642-0333, E-mail: asianst@berkeley.edu. *Application contact:* Dreux Montgomery, Student Affairs Officer, 510-642-3873, E-mail: asianst@berkeley.edu.
Website: http://ieas.berkeley.edu/gas/

**University of California, Los Angeles,** Graduate Division, College of Letters and Science, Department of Asian Languages and Cultures, Los Angeles, CA 90095. Offers MA, PhD. Terminal master's awarded for partial completion of doctoral program. *Degree requirements:* For master's, one foreign language, comprehensive exam or thesis; for doctorate, 2 foreign languages, thesis/dissertation, oral and written qualifying exams. *Entrance requirements:* For master's, GRE General Test, bachelor's degree; minimum undergraduate GPA of 3.0 (or its equivalent if letter grade system not used); writing sample; for doctorate, GRE General Test, master's degree; minimum undergraduate GPA of 3.0 (or its equivalent if letter grade system not used); writing sample. Additional exam requirements/recommendations for international students: Required—TOEFL. Electronic applications accepted.

**University of California, Los Angeles,** Graduate Division, International Institute, Interdepartmental Program in East Asian Studies, Los Angeles, CA 90095. Offers MA. *Degree requirements:* For master's, one foreign language, comprehensive exam. *Entrance requirements:* For master's, GRE General Test, bachelor's degree; minimum undergraduate GPA of 3.0 (or its equivalent if letter grade system not used). Additional exam requirements/recommendations for international students: Required—TOEFL. Electronic applications accepted.

**University of California, Riverside,** Graduate Division, Program in Southeast Asian Studies, Riverside, CA 92521. Offers MA. *Degree requirements:* For master's, one foreign language, thesis or comprehensive exam. *Entrance requirements:* For master's, GRE, statement of purpose to indicate serious interest in Southeast Asian Studies (or specific country or area in this region), writing sample. Additional exam requirements/recommendations for international students: Required—TOEFL; Recommended—IELTS (minimum score 7). Electronic applications accepted. *Expenses:* Tuition, state resident: full-time $16,666. Tuition, nonresident: full-time $31,768. *Required fees:* $11,055.54 per quarter. $3685.18 per quarter. Tuition and fees vary according to campus/location and program. *Faculty research:* Southeast Asian texts, rituals and performance, music and technoculture, dance ethnography, ethnomusicology.

**University of California, Santa Barbara,** Graduate Division, College of Letters and Sciences, Division of Humanities and Fine Arts, Department of East Asian Languages and Cultural Studies, Santa Barbara, CA 93106-7075. Offers applied linguistics (PhD); East Asian languages and cultural studies (MA); translation studies (PhD). *Degree requirements:* For master's, one foreign language, comprehensive exam (for some programs), thesis (for some programs); for doctorate, 2 foreign languages, thesis/ dissertation, methodology. *Entrance requirements:* For master's and doctorate, GRE General Test. Additional exam requirements/recommendations for international students: Required—TOEFL (minimum score 550 paper-based; 80 iBT), IELTS (minimum score 7). Electronic applications accepted. *Faculty research:* Chinese literature, Chinese film, Japanese society, Japanese literature, East Asian cultural studies.

**University of Chicago,** Division of the Humanities, Department of East Asian Languages and Civilizations, Chicago, IL 60637. Offers PhD. *Students:* 32 full-time (18 women); includes 3 minority (all Asian, non-Hispanic/Latino), 16 international. 63 applicants, 13% accepted, 3 enrolled. In 2016, 2 doctorates awarded. Terminal master's awarded for partial completion of doctoral program. *Degree requirements:* For doctorate, 2 foreign languages, comprehensive exam, thesis/dissertation, qualifying exam. *Entrance requirements:* For doctorate, GRE General Test. Additional exam requirements/recommendations for international students: Required—TOEFL (minimum score 104 iBT), IELTS (minimum score 7). *Application deadline:* For fall admission, 12/15 for domestic and international students. Application fee: $90. Electronic applications accepted. *Financial support:* Fellowships with full tuition reimbursements, teaching assistantships with tuition reimbursements, Federal Work-Study, institutionally sponsored loans, scholarships/grants, traineeships, and health care benefits available. Financial award application deadline: 12/15; financial award applicants required to submit FAFSA. *Faculty research:* East Asian literature, material culture, religious and intellectual history, paleography of early China, performance studies. *Unit head:* Dr. Jacob Eyferth, Chair, 773-834-1677, E-mail: eyferth@uchicago.edu. *Application contact:* Michael Beetley, Assistant Dean of Students, Admissions and Fellowships, 773-702-1552, Fax: 773-834-9148, E-mail: humanitiesadmissions@uchicago.edu. Website: http://ealc.uchicago.edu/

**University of Chicago,** Division of the Humanities, Department of South Asian Languages and Civilizations, Chicago, IL 60637. Offers South Asian languages and civilizations (PhD), including Bengali, Hindi, Sanskrit, Tamil, Urdu. *Students:* 29 full-time (17 women); includes 4 minority (1 Black or African American, non-Hispanic/Latino; 1 Asian, non-Hispanic/Latino; 2 Two or more races, non-Hispanic/Latino), 15 international. 39 applicants, 15% accepted, 6 enrolled. In 2016, 2 doctorates awarded. Terminal master's awarded for partial completion of doctoral program. *Degree requirements:* For doctorate, 3 foreign languages, comprehensive exam, thesis/dissertation. *Entrance requirements:* For doctorate, GRE General Test. Additional exam requirements/ recommendations for international students: Required—TOEFL (minimum score 104 iBT), IELTS (minimum score 7). *Application deadline:* For fall admission, 12/15 for domestic and international students. Application fee: $90. Electronic applications accepted. *Financial support:* Fellowships with full tuition reimbursements, teaching assistantships with full tuition reimbursements, Federal Work-Study, institutionally sponsored loans, scholarships/grants, and health care benefits available. Financial award application deadline: 12/15; financial award applicants required to submit FAFSA. *Unit head:* Gary Tubb, Chair, 773-834-2825, E-mail: tubb@uchicago.edu. *Application contact:* Michael Beetley, Assistant Dean of Students, Admissions and Fellowships, 773-702-1552, Fax: 773-834-9148, E-mail: humanitiesadmissions@uchicago.edu. Website: http://salc.uchicago.edu

**University of Chicago,** Division of the Humanities, Master of Arts Program in the Humanities, Chicago, IL 60637. Offers art history (MA); cinema and media studies (MA); classic languages (MA); comparative literature (MA); creative writing (MA); cultural policy studies (MA); digital humanities (MA); East Asian languages and civilizations (MA); English language and literature (MA); gender and sexuality studies (MA); Germanic studies (MA); linguistics (MA); music (MA); near Eastern languages and civilizations (MA); philosophy (MA); poetics (MA); race, politics and culture (MA); Romance languages and literatures (MA); Slavic languages and literatures (MA); South Asian languages and civilizations (MA); theater and performance studies (MA). *Students:* 80 full-time (43 women), 7 part-time (3 women); includes 20 minority (5 Black or African American, non-Hispanic/Latino; 1 American Indian or Alaska Native, non-Hispanic/Latino; 6 Asian, non-Hispanic/Latino; 5 Hispanic/Latino; 3 Two or more races, non-Hispanic/Latino), 11 international. Average age 26. 706 applicants, 15% accepted, 42 enrolled. In 2016, 92 master's awarded. *Degree requirements:* For master's, thesis. *Entrance requirements:* For master's, GRE General Test. Additional exam requirements/ recommendations for international students: Required—TOEFL (minimum score 104 iBT), IELTS (minimum score 7). *Application deadline:* For fall admission, 1/3 for domestic and international students. Application fee: $90. Electronic applications accepted. *Financial support:* In 2016–17, 8 fellowships with partial tuition reimbursements (averaging $12,000 per year) were awarded; Federal Work-Study, institutionally sponsored loans, scholarships/grants, and tuition waivers (partial) also available. Financial award application deadline: 12/15; financial award applicants required to submit FAFSA. *Unit head:* Malynne Sternstein, Co-Director, 773-834-1201, Fax: 773-834-7526. *Application contact:* Program Coordinator, 773-834-1201, Fax: 773-834-7526, E-mail: ma-humanities@uchicago.edu. Website: http://maph.uchicago.edu/

**University of Colorado Boulder,** Graduate School, College of Arts and Sciences, Department of Asian Languages and Civilizations, Boulder, CO 80309. Offers MA, PhD. *Faculty:* 13 full-time (5 women). *Students:* 22 full-time (16 women); includes 6 minority (2 Asian, non-Hispanic/Latino; 2 Hispanic/Latino; 2 Two or more races, non-Hispanic/ Latino), 8 international. Average age 29. 33 applicants, 42% accepted, 6 enrolled. In 2016, 11 master's awarded. Terminal master's awarded for partial completion of doctoral program. *Degree requirements:* For master's, comprehensive exam. *Entrance requirements:* For master's, BA in Chinese or Japanese, minimum undergraduate GPA of 3.0. Additional exam requirements/recommendations for international students: Required—TOEFL. *Application deadline:* For fall admission, 1/1 for domestic students, 12/1 for international students; for spring admission, 10/1 for domestic students, 9/1 for international students. Applications are processed on a rolling basis. Application fee: $60 ($80 for international students). Electronic applications accepted. Application fee is waived when completed online. *Financial support:* In 2016–17, 86 students received support, including 39 fellowships (averaging $1,598 per year), 20 teaching assistantships with full and partial tuition reimbursements available (averaging $29,447 per year); institutionally sponsored loans, scholarships/grants, health care benefits, and unspecified assistantships also available. Financial award application deadline: 2/1; financial award applicants required to submit FAFSA. *Faculty research:* Asian languages/literature, Chinese language/literature, literary criticism, religious literature, literary history. *Total annual research expenditures:* $209,262. *Application contact:* E-mail: dalc@colorado.edu. Website: http://alc.colorado.edu/

**University of Hawaii at Manoa,** Graduate Division, School of Pacific and Asian Studies, Program in Asian Studies, Concentration in Korean Studies, Honolulu, HI 96822. Offers Graduate Certificate. *Program availability:* Part-time. *Degree requirements:* For Graduate Certificate, one foreign language. *Entrance requirements:* For degree, GRE. Additional exam requirements/recommendations for international students: Required—TOEFL (minimum score 560 paper-based; 83 iBT), IELTS (minimum score 5).

**University of Hawaii at Manoa,** Graduate Division, School of Pacific and Asian Studies, Program in Asian Studies, Concentration in Southeast Asian Studies, Honolulu, HI 96822. Offers Graduate Certificate. *Program availability:* Part-time. *Degree requirements:* For Graduate Certificate, one foreign language. *Entrance requirements:* For degree, GRE. Additional exam requirements/recommendations for international students: Required—TOEFL (minimum score 560 paper-based; 83 iBT), IELTS (minimum score 5).

**University of Illinois at Urbana–Champaign,** Graduate College, College of Liberal Arts and Sciences, Center for South Asian and Middle Eastern Studies, Champaign, IL 61820. Offers MA. *Degree requirements:* For master's, one foreign language, comprehensive exam, thesis or alternative.

**University of Illinois at Urbana–Champaign,** Graduate College, College of Liberal Arts and Sciences, School of Literatures, Cultures and Linguistics, Department of East Asian Languages and Cultures, Champaign, IL 61820. Offers East Asian languages and cultures (PhD); East Asian studies (MA).

**The University of Iowa,** Graduate College, College of Liberal Arts and Sciences, Program in Asian Civilizations, Iowa City, IA 52242-1316. Offers Chinese (MA); Hindi (MA); Sanskrit (MA); South Asian studies (MA). *Degree requirements:* For master's, thesis optional, exam. *Entrance requirements:* For master's, GRE General Test, minimum GPA of 3.0. Additional exam requirements/recommendations for international students: Required—TOEFL (minimum score 590 paper-based; 96 iBT). Electronic applications accepted.

**The University of Kansas,** Graduate Studies, College of Liberal Arts and Sciences, Department of East Asian Languages and Cultures, Lawrence, KS 66045. Offers MA, Graduate Certificate. *Program availability:* Part-time. *Students:* 5 full-time (2 women), 3 part-time (1 woman); includes 1 minority (Two or more races, non-Hispanic/Latino), 3 international. Average age 28. 5 applicants, 40% accepted, 1 enrolled. In 2016, 1 master's awarded. *Entrance requirements:* For master's, GRE, current curriculum vitae, statement of purpose explaining academic objectives, writing sample that demonstrates writing skills and basic research capacity, three letters of recommendation, transcripts. Additional exam requirements/recommendations for international students: Required— TOEFL. *Application deadline:* For fall admission, 2/1 priority date for domestic and international students. Application fee: $65 ($85 for international students). Electronic applications accepted. *Financial support:* Fellowships, teaching assistantships, and unspecified assistantships available. *Faculty research:* Gender relations in literature, ancient Chinese law, visual culture of modern Japan, Japanese language pedagogy, Chinese paleography, Korean shamanism, folklore, traditional Chinese and Japanese literature, Chinese linguistics and language pedagogy. *Unit head:* Dr. Maggie Childs, Chair, 785-864-9128, E-mail: mgchilds@ku.edu. *Application contact:* Cari Ann Kreienhop, Graduate Programs and Admissions Contact, 785-864-3665, E-mail: ckreienhop@ku.edu. Website: http://ealc.ku.edu/

**The University of Manchester,** School of Languages, Linguistics and Cultures, Manchester, United Kingdom. Offers Arab world studies (PhD); Chinese studies (M Phil, PhD); East Asian studies (M Phil, PhD); English language (PhD); French studies (M Phil, PhD); German studies (M Phil, PhD); interpreting studies (PhD); Italian studies (M Phil, PhD); Japanese studies (M Phil, PhD); Latin American cultural studies (M Phil, PhD); linguistics (M Phil, PhD); Middle Eastern studies (M Phil, PhD); Polish studies (M Phil, PhD); Portuguese studies (M Phil, PhD); Russian studies (M Phil, PhD); Spanish studies (M Phil, PhD); translation and intercultural studies (M Phil, PhD).

**University of Michigan,** Rackham Graduate School, College of Literature, Science, and the Arts, Center for Japanese Studies, Ann Arbor, MI 48109-1042. Offers AM, JD/AM, MBA/AM. *Program availability:* Part-time. *Faculty:* 45 full-time (19 women), 14 part-time/adjunct (4 women). *Students:* 18 full-time (11 women); includes 5 minority (1 Asian, non-Hispanic/Latino; 2 Hispanic/Latino; 2 Two or more races, non-Hispanic/Latino), 4 international. 22 applicants, 68% accepted, 7 enrolled. In 2016, 3 master's awarded. *Degree requirements:* For master's, one foreign language, thesis optional, 24 credits; 6th-term proficiency (3 years) in Japanese language; seminars with independent research/writing component. *Entrance requirements:* For master's, GRE General Test, academic statement of purpose; curriculum vitae; official transcripts of postsecondary education; 3 letters of recommendation. Additional exam requirements/ recommendations for international students: Required—TOEFL (minimum score 560 paper-based; 84 iBT); Recommended—IELTS (minimum score 6.5). *Application deadline:* For fall admission, 12/15 for domestic and international students. Application fee: $75 ($90 for international students). Electronic applications accepted. *Expenses:* Tuition, state resident: full-time $21,466; part-time $1152 per credit hour. Tuition, nonresident: full-time $43,346; part-time $2367 per credit hour. Part-time tuition and fees vary according to course load, degree level and program. *Financial support:* In 2016–17, 11 students received support, including 9 fellowships with full tuition reimbursements available (averaging $15,000 per year); research assistantships with tuition reimbursements available, teaching assistantships with tuition reimbursements available, career-related internships or fieldwork, Federal Work-Study, scholarships/

*Asian Studies*

grants, health care benefits, and unspecified assistantships also available. Support available to part-time students. Financial award application deadline: 1/15; financial award applicants required to submit FAFSA. *Faculty research:* Japanese literature; Japanese history (premodern and modern); Japanese linguistics and language pedagogy; modern Japanese society and culture; gender and sexuality in Japan; Japanese art, art history and visual culture; Japanese film; Buddhism and religion in Japan; Japanese law; Japanese health care (medicine, nursing, psychiatry and social work). *Unit head:* Dr. Kiyoteru Tsutsui, Director, 734-764-6307, Fax: 734-936-2948, E-mail: umcjs@umich.edu. *Application contact:* Azumi Ann Takata, Graduate Academic Services Coordinator, 734-763-4528, Fax: 734-615-9058, E-mail: ii-gradadvising@umich.edu.
Website: http://www.ii.umich.edu/cjs/

**University of Michigan,** Rackham Graduate School, College of Literature, Science, and the Arts, Center for South Asian Studies, Ann Arbor, MI 48109. Offers MA, Certificate, MBA/MA. *Program availability:* Part-time. *Faculty:* 42 full-time (14 women), 2 part-time/adjunct (both women). *Students:* 3 full-time (1 woman); includes 1 minority (Asian, non-Hispanic/Latino). 7 applicants, 43% accepted, 2 enrolled. In 2016, 1 master's awarded. *Degree requirements:* For master's, one foreign language, thesis, 24 credits; for Certificate, one foreign language. *Entrance requirements:* For master's, GRE General Test, academic statement of purpose; curriculum vitae; writing sample; official transcripts of postsecondary education; 3 letters of recommendation; for Certificate, GRE General Test, academic statement of purpose; official transcripts; letter of recommendation from academic advisor. Additional exam requirements/recommendations for international students: Required—TOEFL (minimum score 560 paper-based; 84 iBT); Recommended—IELTS (minimum score 6.5). *Application deadline:* For fall admission, 12/15 for domestic and international students. Application fee: $75 ($90 for international students). Electronic applications accepted. *Expenses:* Tuition, state resident: full-time $21,466; part-time $1152 per credit hour. Tuition, nonresident: full-time $43,346; part-time $2367 per credit hour. Part-time tuition and fees vary according to course load, degree level and program. *Financial support:* In 2016–17, 2 students received support, including 2 fellowships with full tuition reimbursements available (averaging $15,000 per year); research assistantships, teaching assistantships, career-related internships or fieldwork, Federal Work-Study, institutionally sponsored loans, scholarships/grants, health care benefits, and unspecified assistantships also available. Support available to part-time students. Financial award application deadline: 1/15; financial award applicants required to submit FAFSA. *Faculty research:* History of Islam in South Asia; British colonialism and the postcolonial predicament; ethnicity and nationalism; global and transnational feminism; South Asian architecture and urbanism. *Unit head:* Dr. Farina Mir, Director. *Application contact:* Julie E. Burnett, Graduate Academic Services Coordinator, 734-763-4528, Fax: 734-615-9058, E-mail: ii-gradadvising@umich.edu.
Website: http://www.ii.umich.edu/csas/

**University of Michigan,** Rackham Graduate School, College of Literature, Science, and the Arts, Center for Southeast Asian Studies, Ann Arbor, MI 48109-1042. Offers MA, Graduate Certificate, MBA/MA, MPP/MA. *Program availability:* Part-time. *Faculty:* 33 full-time (18 women). *Students:* 7 full-time (4 women); includes 3 minority (1 Black or African American, non-Hispanic/Latino; 1 Asian, non-Hispanic/Latino; 1 Two or more races, non-Hispanic/Latino). 10 applicants, 70% accepted, 2 enrolled. In 2016, 2 master's awarded. *Degree requirements:* For master's, one foreign language, thesis, 25 credits; for Graduate Certificate, one foreign language. *Entrance requirements:* For master's, GRE General Test, academic statement of purpose; curriculum vitae; writing sample; official transcript of postsecondary education; 3 letters of recommendation; for Graduate Certificate, GRE General Test, academic statement of purpose; official transcripts; letter of recommendation from academic advisor. Additional exam requirements/recommendations for international students: Required—TOEFL (minimum score 560 paper-based; 84 iBT); Recommended—IELTS (minimum score 6.5). *Application deadline:* For fall admission, 1/15 for domestic and international students. Application fee: $75 ($90 for international students). Electronic applications accepted. *Expenses:* Tuition, state resident: full-time $21,466; part-time $1152 per credit hour. Tuition, nonresident: full-time $43,346; part-time $2367 per credit hour. Part-time tuition and fees vary according to course load, degree level and program. *Financial support:* In 2016–17, 2 students received support, including 2 fellowships with full tuition reimbursements available (averaging $15,000 per year); research assistantships, teaching assistantships, career-related internships or fieldwork, Federal Work-Study, institutionally sponsored loans, scholarships/grants, health care benefits, and unspecified assistantships also available. Support available to part-time students. Financial award application deadline: 1/15; financial award applicants required to submit FAFSA. *Faculty research:* Politics, political parties, civil society, the law and human rights in Southeast Asia; nationalism and modernity in late colonial Southeast Asia; Islam, religion, language and media; urbanization, globalization and business; pre-modern Southeast Asia in a global/Eurasian context. *Unit head:* Prof. Christi-Anne Castro, Director. *Application contact:* Azumi Ann Takata, Graduate Academic Services Coordinator, 734-763-4528, Fax: 734-615-9058, E-mail: ii-gradadvising@umich.edu.
Website: http://www.ii.umich.edu/cseas/

**University of Michigan,** Rackham Graduate School, College of Literature, Science, and the Arts, Department of Asian Languages and Cultures, Ann Arbor, MI 48104. Offers PhD. *Faculty:* 24 full-time (10 women). *Students:* 20 full-time (11 women); includes 5 minority (4 Asian, non-Hispanic/Latino; 1 Two or more races, non-Hispanic/Latino), 7 international. Average age 32. 60 applicants, 13% accepted, 5 enrolled. In 2016, 2 doctorates awarded. Terminal master's awarded for partial completion of doctoral program. *Degree requirements:* For doctorate, 2 foreign languages, thesis/dissertation, preliminary exams, oral defense of dissertation. *Entrance requirements:* Additional exam requirements/recommendations for international students: Required—TOEFL (minimum score 560 paper-based; 84 iBT), IELTS (minimum score 6.5). *Application deadline:* For fall admission, 12/1 for domestic and international students. Application fee: $75 ($90 for international students). Electronic applications accepted. *Expenses:* Tuition, state resident: full-time $21,466; part-time $1152 per credit hour. Tuition, nonresident: full-time $43,346; part-time $2367 per credit hour. Part-time tuition and fees vary according to course load, degree level and program. *Financial support:* In 2016–17, 20 students received support. Fellowships with full tuition reimbursements available, teaching assistantships with full tuition reimbursements available, scholarships/grants, health care benefits, and spring/summer stipends available. Financial award application deadline: 12/1. *Faculty research:* Literature, religion, visual culture, history, modern culture. *Unit head:* Prof. Donald S. Lopez, Jr., Chair, 734-615-6571, Fax: 734-647-0157, E-mail: um-alc@umich.edu. *Application contact:* ALC Student Services, 734-734-8286, Fax: 734-647-0157, E-mail: alc-gradservices@umich.edu.
Website: http://www.lsa.umich.edu/asian/

**University of Michigan,** Rackham Graduate School, College of Literature, Science, and the Arts, Kenneth G. Lieberthal and Richard H. Rogel Center for Chinese Studies, Ann Arbor, MI 48109-1042. Offers MA, Graduate Certificate, JD/AM, MBA/AM, MPP/AM. *Program availability:* Part-time. *Faculty:* 41 full-time. *Students:* 10 full-time (5 women); includes 3 minority (1 Asian, non-Hispanic/Latino; 1 Hispanic/Latino; 1 Two or more races, non-Hispanic/Latino), 3 international. 60 applicants, 35% accepted, 4 enrolled. In 2016, 6 master's awarded. *Degree requirements:* For master's, one foreign

language, thesis or alternative, 24 credits; 6th term proficiency in Chinese language; for Graduate Certificate, one foreign language. *Entrance requirements:* For master's, GRE General Test, academic statement of purpose; curriculum vitae; official transcript of postsecondary education; 3 letters of recommendation. Additional exam requirements/recommendations for international students: Required—TOEFL (minimum score 560 paper-based; 84 iBT); Recommended—IELTS (minimum score 6.5). *Application deadline:* For fall admission, 12/15 for domestic and international students. Application fee: $75 ($90 for international students). Electronic applications accepted. *Expenses:* Tuition, state resident: full-time $21,466; part-time $1152 per credit hour. Tuition, nonresident: full-time $43,346; part-time $2367 per credit hour. Part-time tuition and fees vary according to course load, degree level and program. *Financial support:* In 2016–17, 9 students received support, including 2 fellowships with full tuition reimbursements available (averaging $15,000 per year); research assistantships, teaching assistantships, Federal Work-Study, scholarships/grants, health care benefits, and unspecified assistantships also available. Support available to part-time students. Financial award application deadline: 1/15; financial award applicants required to submit FAFSA. *Faculty research:* Political and economic reform in China, Chinese religion, history of late Imperial China, Chinese foreign policy, Chinese music and music history. *Unit head:* Mary Gallagher, PhD, Director, 734-764-6308, Fax: 734-764-5540, E-mail: chinese.studies@umich.edu. *Application contact:* Azumi Ann Takata, Graduate Academic Services Coordinator, 734-763-4528, Fax: 734-615-9058, E-mail: ii-gradadvising@umich.edu.
Website: http://www.ii.umich.edu/lrccs

**University of Minnesota, Twin Cities Campus,** Graduate School, College of Liberal Arts, Department of Asian Languages and Literatures, Minneapolis, MN 55455-0213. Offers Asian literatures, cultures, and media (PhD). *Degree requirements:* For doctorate, comprehensive exam, thesis/dissertation. *Entrance requirements:* For doctorate, GRE, 3 letters of recommendation. Additional exam requirements/recommendations for international students: Required—TOEFL (minimum score 550 paper-based), IELTS (minimum score 6.5). Electronic applications accepted. *Faculty research:* Gender studies, post-colonial theory, poetics and poetic theory, film studies, post modernist thought.

**University of Oregon,** Graduate School, College of Arts and Sciences, Program in Asian Studies, Eugene, OR 97403. Offers MA. *Program availability:* Part-time. *Degree requirements:* For master's, one foreign language, thesis or alternative. *Entrance requirements:* For master's, GRE General Test. Additional exam requirements/recommendations for international students: Required—TOEFL. *Faculty research:* East and Southeast Asia, Pacific Islands.

**University of Pennsylvania,** School of Arts and Sciences, Graduate Group in East Asian Languages and Civilizations, Philadelphia, PA 19104. Offers AM, PhD. *Faculty:* 19 full-time (6 women), 3 part-time/adjunct (0 women). *Students:* 48 full-time (35 women), 6 part-time (5 women); includes 3 minority (all Asian, non-Hispanic/Latino), 40 international. Average age 28. 142 applicants, 35% accepted, 23 enrolled. In 2016, 10 master's, 7 doctorates awarded. *Expenses: Tuition:* Full-time $31,068; part-time $5762 per course. *Required fees:* $3200; $336 per course. Full-time tuition and fees vary according to degree level, program and student level. Part-time tuition and fees vary according to course load, degree level and program.
Website: http://www.sas.upenn.edu/ealc/graduate-program

**University of Pennsylvania,** School of Arts and Sciences, Graduate Group in South Asian Regional Studies, Philadelphia, PA 19104. Offers AM, PhD. *Faculty:* 15 full-time (5 women), 9 part-time/adjunct (2 women). *Students:* 19 full-time (9 women), 1 part-time (0 women); includes 5 minority (all Asian, non-Hispanic/Latino), 10 international. Average age 31. 33 applicants, 36% accepted, 5 enrolled. In 2016, 7 master's, 3 doctorates awarded. Terminal master's awarded for partial completion of doctoral program. Application fee: $70. *Expenses: Tuition:* Full-time $31,068; part-time $5762 per course. *Required fees:* $3200; $336 per course. Full-time tuition and fees vary according to degree level, program and student level. Part-time tuition and fees vary according to course load, degree level and program.
Website: http://www.southasia.upenn.edu/graduate-programs

**University of Pittsburgh,** Dietrich School of Arts and Sciences, Department of East Asian Languages and Literatures, Pittsburgh, PA 15260. Offers Chinese (MA); Japanese (MA). *Program availability:* Part-time. *Faculty:* 18 full-time (11 women), 11 part-time/adjunct (all women). *Students:* 5 full-time (4 women); includes 3 minority (all Asian, non-Hispanic/Latino). Average age 26. 18 applicants, 22% accepted, 1 enrolled. In 2016, 2 master's awarded. *Degree requirements:* For master's, one foreign language, thesis, oral comprehensive exam. *Entrance requirements:* For master's, GRE General Test, 2 years of college-level Chinese or Japanese, minimum QPA of 3.0. Additional exam requirements/recommendations for international students: Required—TOEFL (minimum score 600 paper-based; 90 iBT). *Application deadline:* For fall admission, 1/15 for domestic and international students. Application fee: $50. Electronic applications accepted. Tuition and fees vary according to program. *Financial support:* In 2016–17, 5 students received support, including 5 fellowships with full tuition reimbursements available (averaging $21,812 per year); research assistantships, teaching assistantships, Federal Work-Study, scholarships/grants, tuition waivers (full and partial), and unspecified assistantships also available. Financial award application deadline: 1/15. *Faculty research:* Chinese literature, film, and poetry; Japanese literature, film, and theater; Chinese society and culture; East Asian foreign policy, security studies, and economic history; Japanese performing arts and fine arts translation studies; cultural studies; intellectual history; language and linguistics; second language acquisition; Japanese government; Japanese and Chinese history; ethnomusicology; religious studies. *Unit head:* Dr. Hiroshi Nara, Chair, 412-624-5579, Fax: 412-624-3458, E-mail: hnara@pitt.edu. *Application contact:* Keanna Cash, Graduate Administrator, 412-624-5906, Fax: 412-624-6263, E-mail: kec176@pitt.edu.
Website: http://www.deall.pitt.edu/

**University of Pittsburgh,** University Center for International Studies, Pittsburgh, PA 15260. Offers African studies (Certificate); Asian studies (Certificate); European Union studies (Certificate); global studies (Certificate); Latin American studies (Certificate); Russian and East European studies (Certificate); West European studies (Certificate). *Program availability:* Part-time, evening/weekend, online learning. *Students:* 175 full-time (105 women), 14 part-time (10 women); includes 78 minority (5 Black or African American, non-Hispanic/Latino; 30 Asian, non-Hispanic/Latino; 42 Hispanic/Latino; 1 Two or more races, non-Hispanic/Latino). Average age 29. *Degree requirements:* For Certificate, one foreign language, comprehensive exam (for some programs), thesis (for some programs). *Entrance requirements:* Additional exam requirements/recommendations for international students: Required—TOEFL. *Expenses:* Contact institution. *Financial support:* In 2016–17, 22 fellowships with full tuition reimbursements (averaging $17,878 per year) were awarded; scholarships/grants, traineeships, health care benefits, tuition waivers, and unspecified assistantships also available. *Unit head:* Dr. Ariel Armony, Director, 412-648-7374, Fax: 412-624-4672, E-mail: armony@pitt.edu.
Website: http://www.ucis.pitt.edu

**University of San Francisco,** College of Arts and Sciences, Program in Asia Pacific Studies, San Francisco, CA 94117-1080. Offers MA, MA/MBA. *Program availability:* Part-time, evening/weekend. *Faculty:* 3 full-time (all women), 9 part-time/adjunct (5

women). *Students:* 45 full-time (21 women), 2 part-time (both women); includes 16 minority (9 Asian, non-Hispanic/Latino; 4 Hispanic/Latino; 3 Two or more races, non-Hispanic/Latino), 18 international. Average age 28. 45 applicants, 87% accepted, 28 enrolled. In 2016, 19 master's awarded. *Degree requirements:* For master's, one foreign language, thesis. *Entrance requirements:* For master's, minimum GPA of 3.0. Additional exam requirements/recommendations for international students: Required—TOEFL, IELTS, PTE. *Application deadline:* For fall admission, 4/1 for domestic and international students. Applications are processed on a rolling basis. Application fee: $55 ($65 for international students). Electronic applications accepted. *Expenses: Tuition:* Full-time $23,310; part-time $1295 per credit. Tuition and fees vary according to course load, degree level, campus/location and program. *Financial support:* In 2016–17, 31 students received support. Career-related internships or fieldwork, Federal Work-Study, and institutionally sponsored loans available. Financial award application deadline: 3/2; financial award applicants required to submit FAFSA. *Faculty research:* History of Christianity in China, U.S.-China policy, East Asian economies and political systems, sociolinguistic aspects of Japanese. *Unit head:* Dr. Brian Komei Dempster, Director, 415-422-6357, Fax: 415-422-5933. *Application contact:* Mark Landerghini, Information Contact, 415-422-5101, Fax: 415-422-2217, E-mail: asgraduate@usfca.edu.
Website: https://www.usfca.edu/arts-sciences/graduate-programs/asia-pacific-studies

**University of Southern California,** Graduate School, Dana and David Dornsife College of Letters, Arts and Sciences, Department of East Asian Languages and Cultures, Los Angeles, CA 90089. Offers classical Chinese literature (MA, PhD); classical Japanese literature (MA, PhD); linguistics (MA, PhD); modern Chinese literature (MA, PhD); modern Japanese literature (MA, PhD); modern Korean literature (MA, PhD). *Degree requirements:* For master's, thesis; for doctorate, 2 foreign languages, comprehensive exam, thesis/dissertation. *Entrance requirements:* For master's and doctorate, GRE, BA in relevant field. Additional exam requirements/recommendations for international students: Required—TOEFL. Electronic applications accepted. *Faculty research:* Gender, visual studies, multimedia, ecocriticism, second language acquisition.

**University of Southern California,** Graduate School, Dana and David Dornsife College of Letters, Arts and Sciences, East Asian Studies Center, Los Angeles, CA 90089. Offers MA, MA/MBA. *Program availability:* Part-time. *Degree requirements:* For master's, one foreign language, thesis, language proficiency in an East Asian language (equivalent to 3 years of study). *Entrance requirements:* For master's, GRE (minimum score 1000). Additional exam requirements/recommendations for international students: Required—TOEFL (minimum score 600 paper-based; 100 iBT). Electronic applications accepted. *Faculty research:* East Asian visual cultures (Chinese, Japanese, and Korean film, culture and art); East Asian politics, society and history; East Asian literature and culture.

**The University of Texas at Austin,** Graduate School, College of Liberal Arts, Department of Asian Studies, Austin, TX 78712-1111. Offers Asian cultures and languages (MA, PhD); Asian studies (MA). *Program availability:* Part-time. *Degree requirements:* For master's, thesis; for doctorate, 3 foreign languages, thesis/dissertation. *Entrance requirements:* For master's and doctorate, GRE General Test. Electronic applications accepted. *Faculty research:* Modern Taiwanese fiction, modern Japanese literature, religious studies in South Asia during classical period.

**University of Toronto,** School of Graduate Studies, Faculty of Arts and Science, Department of East Asian Studies, Toronto, ON M5S 1A1, Canada. Offers MA, PhD. *Program availability:* Part-time. *Degree requirements:* For master's, thesis optional; for doctorate, 2 foreign languages, comprehensive exam, thesis/dissertation. *Entrance requirements:* For master's, writing sample, 2 letters of recommendation, BA in a specialist or East Asian studies program, minimum B+ average in final year; for doctorate, writing sample, 3 letters of recommendation, MA in East Asian studies. Additional exam requirements/recommendations for international students: Required—TOEFL (minimum score 600 paper-based), TWE (minimum score 5). Electronic applications accepted.

**University of Utah,** Graduate School, College of Humanities, Asian Studies Program, Salt Lake City, UT 84112. Offers MA. *Program availability:* Part-time, evening/weekend. *Students:* 1 full-time (0 women); minority (Asian, non-Hispanic/Latino). Average age 25. 12 applicants, 33% accepted, 1 enrolled. In 2016, 1 master's awarded. *Degree requirements:* For master's, one foreign language, thesis, 3rd-year proficiency in one Asian language. *Entrance requirements:* For master's, GRE. Additional exam requirements/recommendations for international students: Required—TOEFL (minimum score 580 paper-based). *Application deadline:* For fall admission, 2/1 for domestic and international students; for spring admission, 9/15 for domestic students. Application fee: $55 ($65 for international students). Electronic applications accepted. *Expenses:* Tuition, state resident: full-time $7011; part-time $3918.24 per credit hour. Tuition, nonresident: full-time $22,154; part-time $11,665.42 per credit hour. *Financial support:* In 2016–17, 6 students received support, including 6 fellowships with full tuition reimbursements available (averaging $15,000 per year). Financial award application deadline: 2/1; financial award applicants required to submit FAFSA. *Faculty research:* Asian health studies, history, literature, culture, politics, economics. *Unit head:* Dr. Kim Korinek, Director, 801-581-6101, Fax: 801-581-6105, E-mail: kim.korinek@soc.utah.edu. *Application contact:* Ashley Glenn, Academic Advisor, 801-581-6101, Fax: 801-581-6105, E-mail: ea.glenn@utah.edu.
Website: http://asia-center.utah.edu/

**University of Victoria,** Faculty of Graduate Studies, Faculty of Humanities, Department of Pacific and Asian Studies, Victoria, BC V8W 2Y2, Canada. Offers MA. *Degree requirements:* For master's, thesis. *Entrance requirements:* For master's, minimum B+ average, writing sample. Additional exam requirements/recommendations for international students: Required—TOEFL (minimum score 575 paper-based), IELTS (minimum score 7). Electronic applications accepted. *Faculty research:* Culture, ethnicity and identity; economy and society; gender studies; languages and linguistics; literature.

**University of Virginia,** College and Graduate School of Arts and Sciences, Department of East Asian Languages, Literatures, and Cultures, Charlottesville, VA 22903. Offers East Asian studies (MA); MBA/MA. *Faculty:* 16 full-time (11 women). *Students:* 2 full-time (0 women), 1 (woman) part-time. Average age 26. 13 applicants, 23% accepted. In 2016, 2 master's awarded. *Degree requirements:* For master's, one foreign language, comprehensive exam, thesis. *Entrance requirements:* For master's, GRE General Test, 2 letters of recommendation. Additional exam requirements/recommendations for international students: Required—TOEFL, IELTS. *Application deadline:* For fall admission, 1/15 for domestic and international students; for winter admission, 9/15 for domestic and international students. Applications are processed on a rolling basis. Application fee: $60. Electronic applications accepted. *Expenses:* Tuition, state resident: full-time $15,026; part-time $834 per credit hour. Tuition, nonresident: full-time $25,168; part-time $1378 per credit hour. *Required fees:* $2654. *Financial support:* Applicants required to submit FAFSA. *Unit head:* Charles Laughlin, Chair, 434-924-8950, Fax: 434-243-1528, E-mail: cal5m@virginia.edu.
Website: http://eastasian.virginia.edu/

**University of Virginia,** College and Graduate School of Arts and Sciences, Department of Middle Eastern and South Asian Languages and Cultures, Charlottesville, VA 22903. Offers Middle Eastern and South Asian studies (MA). *Faculty:* 16 full-time (8 women).

*Students:* 11 full-time (6 women), 2 part-time (0 women); includes 1 minority (Hispanic/Latino), 1 international. Average age 31. 19 applicants, 89% accepted, 6 enrolled. In 2016, 3 master's awarded. Application fee: $60. *Expenses:* Tuition, state resident: full-time $15,026; part-time $834 per credit hour. Tuition, nonresident: full-time $25,168; part-time $1378 per credit hour. *Required fees:* $2654. *Unit head:* Farzaneh Milani, Chair, 434-243-4930, Fax: 434-243-1528, E-mail: fmm2z@virginia.edu. *Application contact:* Robert Hueckstedt, Director of Graduate Studies, 434-243-8228, Fax: 434-243-1528, E-mail: rah2k@virginia.edu.
Website: http://mesalc.virginia.edu/

**University of Washington,** Graduate School, College of Arts and Sciences, Department of Asian Languages and Literature, Seattle, WA 98195. Offers Buddhist studies (MA, PhD); Chinese language and literature (MA, PhD); Japanese language and literature (MA, PhD); Korean language and literature (MA, PhD); South Asian language and literature (MA, PhD). *Degree requirements:* For master's, 2 foreign languages, general exam, thesis or 2 research papers; for doctorate, 3 foreign languages, thesis/dissertation, general exam. *Entrance requirements:* For master's, GRE, minimum GPA of 3.0; for doctorate, GRE, master's degree in related field, minimum GPA of 3.0. Additional exam requirements/recommendations for international students: Required—TOEFL. Electronic applications accepted. *Faculty research:* Textual, linguistic, philological, and literary study of languages and literatures of Asia.

**University of Washington,** Graduate School, College of Arts and Sciences, Henry M. Jackson School of International Studies, China Studies Program, Seattle, WA 98195. Offers MAIS. *Degree requirements:* For master's, one foreign language, thesis optional. *Entrance requirements:* For master's, GRE General Test, minimum GPA of 3.0 in last 2 years. Additional exam requirements/recommendations for international students: Required—TOEFL (minimum score 500 paper-based; 92 iBT), IELTS (minimum score 7). Electronic applications accepted.

**University of Washington,** Graduate School, College of Arts and Sciences, Henry M. Jackson School of International Studies, Japan Studies Program, Seattle, WA 98195. Offers MAIS. *Degree requirements:* For master's, one foreign language. *Entrance requirements:* For master's, GRE General Test, minimum GPA of 3.0 in last two years. Additional exam requirements/recommendations for international students: Required—TOEFL (minimum score 500 paper-based; 92 iBT), IELTS (minimum score 7). Electronic applications accepted.

**University of Washington,** Graduate School, College of Arts and Sciences, Henry M. Jackson School of International Studies, Korea Studies Program, Seattle, WA 98195. Offers MAIS. *Degree requirements:* For master's, one foreign language. *Entrance requirements:* For master's, GRE General Test, minimum GPA of 3.0 in last two years. Additional exam requirements/recommendations for international students: Required—TOEFL (minimum score 500 paper-based; 92 iBT), IELTS (minimum score 7). Electronic applications accepted.

**University of Washington,** Graduate School, College of Arts and Sciences, Henry M. Jackson School of International Studies, Russian, East European and Central Asian Studies Program, Seattle, WA 98195. Offers Central Asian studies (MAIS); East European studies (MAIS); Russian studies (MAIS). *Degree requirements:* For master's, one foreign language, thesis. *Entrance requirements:* For master's, GRE General Test, 2 years of relevant language, minimum GPA of 3.0 in last two years. Additional exam requirements/recommendations for international students: Required—TOEFL (minimum score 500 paper-based; 92 iBT), IELTS (minimum score 7). Electronic applications accepted.

**University of Washington,** Graduate School, College of Arts and Sciences, Henry M. Jackson School of International Studies, South Asian Studies Program, Seattle, WA 98195. Offers MAIS. *Degree requirements:* For master's, one foreign language, thesis optional. *Entrance requirements:* For master's, GRE General Test, minimum GPA of 3.0 in last two years. Additional exam requirements/recommendations for international students: Required—TOEFL (minimum score 500 paper-based; 92 iBT), IELTS (minimum score 7). Electronic applications accepted.

**University of Washington,** Graduate School, College of Arts and Sciences, Henry M. Jackson School of International Studies, Southeast Asian Studies Program, Seattle, WA 98195. Offers MAIS. *Degree requirements:* For master's, one foreign language, thesis optional. *Entrance requirements:* For master's, GRE General Test, minimum GPA of 3.0 in last two years. Additional exam requirements/recommendations for international students: Required—TOEFL (minimum score 500 paper-based; 92 iBT), IELTS (minimum score 7). Electronic applications accepted.

**University of Wisconsin–Madison,** Graduate School, College of Letters and Science, Center for Southeast Asian Studies, Madison, WI 53706. Offers MA. *Program availability:* Part-time. *Degree requirements:* For master's, one foreign language, oral defense of seminar paper. Electronic applications accepted. *Faculty research:* Economic development, censorship, political change, pedagogical developments in Indonesia, Philippine historical demography, environment photography.

**University of Wisconsin–Madison,** Graduate School, College of Letters and Science, Department of East Asian Languages and Literature, Madison, WI 53706-1380. Offers Chinese literature (MA, PhD); Chinese thought (MA, PhD); Japanese linguistics (MA, PhD); Japanese literature (MA, PhD). *Program availability:* Part-time. Terminal master's awarded for partial completion of doctoral program. *Degree requirements:* For master's, one foreign language, seminars, written exam; for doctorate, 3 foreign languages, thesis/dissertation, seminars, preliminary exams, oral exams. *Entrance requirements:* For master's, GRE General Test, BA or equivalent in major field; for doctorate, GRE General Test, MA or equivalent in major field. Electronic applications accepted. *Faculty research:* Modern and historical linguistics, literature, literary and cultural history.

**University of Wisconsin–Madison,** Graduate School, College of Letters and Science, Department of History, Madison, WI 53706-1380. Offers African history (MA, PhD); Central Asian history (MA, PhD); comparative world history (MA, PhD); East Asian history (MA, PhD); European history (MA, PhD); gender and women's history (MA, PhD); Latin American and Caribbean history (MA, PhD); Middle Eastern history (MA, PhD); South Asian history (MA, PhD); Southeast Asian history (MA, PhD); United States history (MA, PhD). Terminal master's awarded for partial completion of doctoral program. *Degree requirements:* For master's, thesis (for some programs); for doctorate, variable foreign language requirement, thesis/dissertation. *Entrance requirements:* For master's and doctorate, GRE General Test. Additional exam requirements/recommendations for international students: Required—Michigan English Language Assessment Battery or TOEFL. Electronic applications accepted. *Faculty research:* American, African, European, Asian, Latin American, and Middle Eastern history.

**University of Wisconsin–Madison,** Graduate School, College of Letters and Science, Department of Languages and Cultures of Asia, Madison, WI 53706-1380. Offers civilizations and cultures (PhD); languages and cultures of Asia (MA); languages and literatures (PhD); religions of Asia (PhD). *Program availability:* Part-time. Terminal master's awarded for partial completion of doctoral program. *Degree requirements:* For master's, one foreign language, thesis or alternative; for doctorate, 2 foreign languages, thesis/dissertation. *Entrance requirements:* For master's, minimum GPA of 3.0; for doctorate, minimum GPA of 3.25, master's degree. Electronic applications accepted. *Faculty research:* Literature, folklore, religion.

**Washington University in St. Louis,** The Graduate School, Department of East Asian Languages and Cultures, St. Louis, MO 63130-4899. Offers Chinese (MA); Chinese and comparative literature (PhD); Chinese language and literature (PhD); East Asian studies (MA); Japanese (MA); Japanese and comparative literature (PhD); Japanese language and literature (PhD). Terminal master's awarded for partial completion of doctoral program. *Degree requirements:* For master's, thesis optional; for doctorate, thesis/dissertation. *Entrance requirements:* For master's and doctorate, GRE General Test. Additional exam requirements/recommendations for international students: Required—TOEFL. Electronic applications accepted. *Faculty research:* Chinese; Japanese; Chinese fiction, theater, poetry, modern literature; Japanese modern and classical fiction, translation theory.

**Wayne State University,** College of Liberal Arts and Sciences, Department of History, Detroit, MI 48202. Offers Africa (PhD); America (PhD); Asia (PhD); Europe (PhD); gender (PhD); history (MA); labor (PhD); public history (MA); science and technology (PhD); world history (PhD, Graduate Certificate); JD/MA; M Ed/MA; MLIS/MA. Doctoral program admits for fall only. *Program availability:* Evening/weekend. *Faculty:* 18. *Students:* 23 full-time (8 women), 21 part-time (5 women); includes 8 minority (3 Black or African American, non-Hispanic/Latino; 2 Hispanic/Latino; 3 Two or more races, non-Hispanic/Latino). Average age 40. 55 applicants, 38% accepted, 15 enrolled. In 2016, 6 master's, 5 doctorates awarded. *Degree requirements:* For master's, comprehensive exam, thesis (for some programs), final oral exam on thesis or essay and seminar; internship and project (for public history); for doctorate, variable foreign language requirement, comprehensive exam, thesis/dissertation, qualifying exam in 4 fields of history. *Entrance requirements:* For master's, GRE General Test, minimum undergraduate GPA of 3.25 in history, 3.0 overall; at least 18 credits in history and related subjects at the advanced undergraduate level; foreign language; letter of intent; research paper; at least two letters of recommendation from former instructors; for doctorate, GRE General Test, minimum GPA of 3.0, 3.25 in minimum of 18 semester credits in history and related subjects; letter of intent; research paper; at least three letters of recommendation from former professors; for Graduate Certificate, baccalaureate degree from accredited college or university; minimum GPA of 3.0, 3.25 in a minimum of eighteen semester credits in history and related subjects at the advanced undergraduate level. Additional exam requirements/recommendations for international students: Required—TOEFL (minimum score 550 paper-based; 79 iBT), TWE (minimum score 5.5), Michigan English Language Assessment Battery (minimum score 85); Recommended—IELTS (minimum score 6.5). *Application deadline:* For fall admission, 2/1 priority date for domestic and international students; for winter admission, 11/1 for domestic students, 10/1 priority date for international students; for spring admission, 2/1 for domestic students, 1/1 priority date for international students. Application fee: $50. Electronic applications accepted. *Expenses:* $16,503 per year resident tuition and fees, $33,697 per year non-resident tuition and fees. *Financial support:* In 2016–17, 16 students received support, including 2 fellowships with tuition reimbursements available (averaging $18,796 per year), 1 research assistantship with tuition reimbursement available (averaging $21,593 per year), 6 teaching assistantships with tuition reimbursements available (averaging $17,994 per year); scholarships/grants, health care benefits, and unspecified assistantships also available. Financial award applicants required to submit FAFSA. *Faculty research:* African, American, Asian, European, gender, German, labor, science and technology, urban/labor, violence, world. *Unit head:* Dr. Elizabeth V. Faue, Professor/Chair, 313-577-2525, E-mail: evfaue@wayne.edu. *Application contact:* Dr. Eric Ash, Associate Professor and Director of Graduate Studies, 313-577-2525, E-mail: ericash@wayne.edu. Website: http://clas.wayne.edu/history/

**West Virginia University,** Eberly College of Arts and Sciences, Department of History, Morgantown, WV 26506. Offers African history (MA, PhD); African-American history (MA, PhD); American history (MA, PhD); Appalachian/regional history (MA, PhD); East Asian history (MA, PhD); European history (MA, PhD); history of science and technology (MA, PhD); Latin American history (MA). *Program availability:* Part-time. *Degree requirements:* For master's, one foreign language, thesis (for some programs), oral exam, thesis defense; for doctorate, one foreign language, comprehensive exam, thesis/dissertation, dissertation defense. *Entrance requirements:* For master's, GRE General Test, minimum GPA of 3.0; for doctorate, GRE General Test. Additional exam requirements/recommendations for international students: Required—TOEFL (minimum score 550 paper-based), IELTS (minimum score 6.5). Electronic applications accepted. *Faculty research:* United States, Appalachia, modern Europe, Africa, colonial and post-colonial societies.

**Yale University,** Graduate School of Arts and Sciences, Program in East Asian Studies, New Haven, CT 06520. Offers MA. *Degree requirements:* For master's, one foreign language. *Entrance requirements:* For master's, GRE General Test.

# Canadian Studies

**Carleton University,** Faculty of Graduate Studies, Faculty of Arts and Social Sciences, School of Canadian Studies, Ottawa, ON K1S 5B6, Canada. Offers MA, PhD. PhD program offered jointly with Trent University. *Degree requirements:* For master's, one foreign language, thesis optional; for doctorate, one foreign language, thesis/dissertation. *Entrance requirements:* For master's, honors degree. Additional exam requirements/recommendations for international students: Required—TOEFL. Electronic applications accepted. *Faculty research:* Modern Canada, cultural studies, women's studies, aboriginal studies and the north, heritage conservation.

**Queen's University at Kingston,** School of Graduate Studies, Faculty of Arts and Sciences, Department of Political Studies, Kingston, ON K7L 3N6, Canada. Offers Canadian politics (PhD); comparative politics (PhD); gender and politics (PhD); international relations (PhD); political theory (PhD). *Degree requirements:* For master's, thesis or alternative; for doctorate, one foreign language, thesis/dissertation, qualifying exams. *Entrance requirements:* Additional exam requirements/recommendations for international students: Required—TOEFL (minimum score 600 paper-based). *Faculty research:* Canadian politics, comparative politics, political thought, international politics, women and politics.

**Saint Mary's University,** Faculty of Arts, Program in Atlantic Canada Studies, Halifax, NS B3H 3C3, Canada. Offers MA, Certificate. *Program availability:* Part-time, evening/weekend. *Degree requirements:* For master's, thesis. *Entrance requirements:* For master's, honors degree. Electronic applications accepted. *Expenses:* Contact institution.

**Trent University,** Graduate Studies, The Frost Centre for Canadian Studies and Indigenous Studies, Peterborough, ON K9J 7B8, Canada. Offers Canadian studies (PhD); Canadian studies and indigenous studies (MA). *Program availability:* Part-time. *Degree requirements:* For master's, thesis. *Entrance requirements:* For master's, honors degree. *Faculty research:* Native community-based socioeconomic development, environmental and social impact inventory, regional studies.

**Université de Saint-Boniface,** Program in Canadian Studies, Saint-Boniface, MB R2H 0H7, Canada. Offers MA.

**Université de Sherbrooke,** Faculty of Letters and Human Sciences, Department of Letters and Communications, Sherbrooke, QC J1K 2R1, Canada. Offers comparative Canadian literature (MA, PhD); French literature (MA, PhD); linguistics (MA); theatre (MA). *Degree requirements:* For master's, thesis or alternative; for doctorate, thesis/dissertation. *Entrance requirements:* For master's, minimum GPA of 2.8; for doctorate, minimum GPA of 3.0.

**Université du Québec à Chicoutimi,** Graduate Programs, Program in Regional Studies, Chicoutimi, QC G7H 2B1, Canada. Offers MA. *Program availability:* Part-time. *Degree requirements:* For master's, thesis. *Entrance requirements:* For master's, appropriate bachelor's degree, proficiency in French.

**University at Buffalo, the State University of New York,** Graduate School, College of Arts and Sciences, Department of Transnational Studies, Buffalo, NY 14260. Offers American studies (MA, PhD); Canadian studies (MA, Advanced Certificate); global gender studies (MA, PhD). *Program availability:* Part-time. *Faculty:* 17 full-time (9 women), 4 part-time/adjunct (1 woman). *Students:* 78 full-time (46 women); includes 29 minority (11 Black or African American, non-Hispanic/Latino; 6 American Indian or Alaska Native, non-Hispanic/Latino; 10 Asian, non-Hispanic/Latino; 2 Hispanic/Latino). Average age 34. 53 applicants, 94% accepted, 21 enrolled. In 2016, 4 master's, 7 doctorates awarded. *Degree requirements:* For master's and Advanced Certificate, comprehensive exam (for some programs), thesis optional; for doctorate, comprehensive exam, thesis/dissertation. *Entrance requirements:* For master's, minimum GPA of 3.0; for doctorate, GRE, minimum GPA of 3.0. Additional exam requirements/recommendations for international students: Required—TOEFL (minimum score 550 paper-based; 79 iBT), IELTS. *Application deadline:* For fall admission, 8/28 priority date for domestic students, 6/15 priority date for international students; for winter admission, 2/1 for domestic and international students; for spring admission, 1/28 priority date for domestic students, 11/15 priority date for international students. Applications are processed on a rolling basis. Application fee: $75. Electronic applications accepted. *Expenses:* Contact institution. *Financial support:* In 2016–17, 20 students received support, including 4 fellowships with full tuition reimbursements available (averaging $13,060 per year), 16 teaching assistantships with full tuition reimbursements available (averaging $13,060 per year); research assistantships, career-related internships or fieldwork, institutionally sponsored loans, scholarships/grants, and unspecified assistantships also available. Financial award application deadline: 1/1. *Faculty research:* Native American, intercultural and indigenous people's studies, border theory, cultural studies, American pop culture, feminist theory, construction of gender in society. *Unit head:* Dr. Cecil Foster, Chair, 716-645-0786, Fax: 716-645-5976, E-mail: cecilfos@buffalo.edu. *Application contact:* Karen M. Reinard, Graduate Coordinator, 716-645-0797, Fax: 716-645-5976, E-mail: kreinard@buffalo.edu. Website: http://transnationalstudies.buffalo.edu/

**University of Lethbridge,** School of Graduate Studies, Lethbridge, AB T1K 3M4, Canada. Offers addictions counseling (M Sc); agricultural biotechnology (M Sc); agricultural studies (M Sc, MA); anthropology (MA); archaeology (M Sc, MA); art (MA, MFA); biochemistry (M Sc); biological sciences (M Sc); biomolecular science (M Sc); biosystems and biodiversity (PhD); Canadian studies (MA); chemistry (M Sc); computer science (M Sc); computer science and geographical information science (M Sc); counseling (MC); counseling psychology (M Ed); dramatic arts (MA); earth, space, and physical science (PhD); economics (MA); education (MA, PhD); educational leadership (M Ed); English (MA); environmental science (M Sc); evolution and behavior (PhD); exercise science (M Sc); French (MA); French/German (MA); French/Spanish (MA); general education (M Ed); geography (M Sc, MA); German (MA); health sciences (M Sc); individualized multidisciplinary (M Sc, MA); kinesiology (M Sc, MA); management (M Sc), including accounting, finance, human resource management and labor relations, information systems, international management, marketing, policy and strategy; mathematics (M Sc); music (M Mus, MA); Native American studies (MA); neuroscience (M Sc, PhD); new media (MA, MFA); nursing (M Sc, MN); philosophy (MA); physics (M Sc); political science (MA); psychology (M Sc, MA); religious studies (MA); sociology (MA); theatre and dramatic arts (MFA); theoretical and computational science (PhD); urban and regional studies (MA); women and gender studies (MA). *Program availability:* Part-time, evening/weekend. *Degree requirements:* For master's, thesis (for some programs); for doctorate, comprehensive exam, thesis/dissertation. *Entrance requirements:* For master's, GMAT (for M Sc in management), bachelor's degree in related field, minimum GPA of 3.0 during previous 20 graded semester courses, 2 years' teaching or related experience (M Ed); for doctorate, master's degree, minimum graduate GPA of 3.5. Additional exam requirements/recommendations for international students: Required—TOEFL (minimum score 580 paper-based; 93 iBT). Electronic applications accepted. *Faculty research:* Movement and brain plasticity, gibberellin physiology, photosynthesis, carbon cycling, molecular properties of main-group ring components.

**University of Manitoba,** Faculty of Graduate Studies, College Universitaire de Saint Boniface, Program in Canadian Studies, Winnipeg, MB R3T 2N2, Canada. Offers MA.

**University of Ottawa,** Faculty of Graduate and Postdoctoral Studies, Faculty of Arts, Institute of Canadian Studies, Ottawa, ON K1N 6N5, Canada. Offers economics (PhD); English (PhD); geography (PhD); history (PhD); lettres Franlfcaises (PhD); linguistics (PhD); philosophy (PhD); political science (PhD); psychology (PhD); religious studies (PhD); translation studies (PhD). *Degree requirements:* For doctorate, comprehensive exam, thesis/dissertation.

**University of Regina,** Faculty of Graduate Studies and Research, Faculty of Arts, Canadian Plains Studies Program, Regina, SK S4S 0A2, Canada. Offers MA, PhD. Offered as a special case program. *Program availability:* Part-time. *Students:* 2 full-time (1 woman). *Degree requirements:* For master's, thesis; for doctorate, thesis/dissertation. *Entrance requirements:* Additional exam requirements/recommendations for international students: Required—TOEFL (minimum score 580 paper-based; 80 iBT), IELTS (minimum score 6.5), PTE (minimum score 59). *Application deadline:*

Applications are processed on a rolling basis. Application fee: $100. Electronic applications accepted. *Financial support:* Fellowships, teaching assistantships, and scholarships/grants available. Financial award application deadline: 6/15. *Unit head:* Dr. Nilgun Onder, Associate Dean of Arts, Research and Graduate Studies, 306-585-4336, Fax: 306-585-5368, E-mail: arts-assocdean-rg@uregina.ca.

**University of Saskatchewan,** College of Graduate Studies and Research, College of Arts and Science, Department of Native Studies, Saskatoon, SK S7N 5A2, Canada. Offers MA, PhD. *Degree requirements:* For master's, thesis; for doctorate, comprehensive exam (for some programs), thesis/dissertation. *Entrance requirements:* Additional exam requirements/recommendations for international students: Required— TOEFL (minimum score 80 iBT); Recommended—IELTS (minimum score 6.5). Electronic applications accepted.

**Wilfrid Laurier University,** Faculty of Graduate and Postdoctoral Studies, Faculty of Arts, Department of Political Science, Waterloo, ON N2L 3C5, Canada. Offers Canadian political studies (MA); comparative politics/international relations (MA). *Program availability:* Part-time. *Degree requirements:* For master's, thesis optional. *Entrance requirements:* For master's, honors bachelor's degree or the equivalent in political science, minimum B average in undergraduate course work. Additional exam requirements/recommendations for international students: Required—TOEFL (minimum score 89 iBT). Electronic applications accepted. *Faculty research:* Political behavior/political psychology, Canadian political studies, comparative, politics/relations, public opinion and electoral studies, international.

**Wilfrid Laurier University,** Faculty of Graduate and Postdoctoral Studies, Lyle S. Hallman Faculty of Social Work, Waterloo, ON N2L 3C5, Canada. Offers Aboriginal studies (MSW); community, policy, planning and organizations (MSW); critical social policy and organizational studies (PhD); individuals, families and groups (MSW); social work practice (individuals, families, groups and communities) (PhD); social work practice: individuals, families, groups and communities (PhD). *Program availability:* Part-time. *Degree requirements:* For master's, thesis optional; for doctorate, thesis/dissertation. *Entrance requirements:* For master's, course work in social science, research methodology, and statistics; honors BA with a minimum B average; for doctorate, master's degree in social work, minimum A- average. Additional exam requirements/recommendations for international students: Required—TOEFL (minimum score 89 iBT). Electronic applications accepted. *Expenses:* Contact institution.

# Cultural Studies

**American University,** College of Arts and Sciences, Critical Race, Gender, and Culture Studies Collaborative, Washington, DC 20016-8001. Offers Asian studies (Graduate Certificate); women's, gender, and sexuality studies (Graduate Certificate). *Expenses: Tuition:* Full-time $28,422; part-time $1579 per credit hour. *Required fees:* $690; $200 per term. Tuition and fees vary according to course load, degree level and program.

**American University,** School of International Service, Washington, DC 20016-8071. Offers comparative and regional studies (Certificate); cross-cultural communication (Certificate); development management (MS); ethics, peace, and global affairs (MA); European studies (Certificate); global environmental policy (MA, Certificate); global information technology (Certificate); international affairs (MA), including comparative and international disability policy, comparative and regional studies, international economic relations, international politics, natural resources and sustainable development, U.S. foreign policy; international arts management (Certificate); international communication (MA, Certificate); international development (MA); international economic policy (Certificate); international economic relations (Certificate); international economics (MA); international media (MA); international peace and conflict resolution (MA, Certificate); international politics (Certificate); international relations (MA, PhD); international service (MIS); peacebuilding (Certificate); social enterprise (MA); the Americas (Certificate); United States foreign policy (Certificate); JD/MA. *Program availability:* Part-time, evening/weekend, 100% online. *Faculty:* 116 full-time (53 women), 57 part-time/adjunct (19 women). *Students:* 575 full-time (360 women), 491 part-time (277 women); includes 287 minority (100 Black or African American, non-Hispanic/Latino; 6 American Indian or Alaska Native, non-Hispanic/Latino; 58 Asian, non-Hispanic/Latino; 92 Hispanic/Latino; 1 Native Hawaiian or other Pacific Islander, non-Hispanic/Latino; 30 Two or more races, non-Hispanic/Latino), 151 international. Average age 29. 1,504 applicants, 84% accepted, 403 enrolled. In 2016, 374 master's, 3 doctorates, 1 other advanced degree awarded. Terminal master's awarded for partial completion of doctoral program. *Degree requirements:* For master's, one foreign language, comprehensive exam, thesis or alternative; for doctorate, one foreign language, comprehensive exam, thesis/dissertation. *Entrance requirements:* For master's, GRE; GMAT or GRE (for MA in social enterprise), transcripts, resume, 2 letters of recommendation, statement of purpose; for doctorate, GRE, transcripts, resume, 3 letters of recommendation, statement of purpose. Additional exam requirements/recommendations for international students: Required—TOEFL (minimum score 600 paper-based, 100 iBT), IELTS (minimum score 7 ), or PTE (minimum score of 68). Application fee: $55. Electronic applications accepted. *Expenses:* $1,579 per credit tuition; $1,930 mandatory fees. *Financial support:* Research assistantships, teaching assistantships, institutionally sponsored loans, scholarships/grants, and unspecified assistantships available. Financial award application deadline: 1/15; financial award applicants required to submit FAFSA. *Unit head:* Dr. James Goldgeier, Dean, 202-885-1603, Fax: 202-885-2494, E-mail: goldgeier@american.edu. *Application contact:* Jia Jiang, Associate Director, Graduate Education Enrollment, 202-885-1689, Fax: 202-885-1109, E-mail: jiang@american.edu.
Website: http://www.american.edu/sis/

**The American University of Paris,** Graduate Programs, Paris, France. Offers cross-cultural and sustainable business management (MA); cultural translation (MA); global communications (MA); global communications and civil society (MA); international affairs (MA); international affairs, conflict resolution and civil society development (MA); Middle East and Islamic studies (MA); Middle East and Islamic studies and international affairs (MA); public policy and international affairs (MA); public policy and international law (MA). *Degree requirements:* For master's, thesis (for some programs) *Entrance requirements:* For master's, minimum undergraduate GPA of 3.0. Additional exam requirements/recommendations for international students: Recommended—TOEFL, IELTS. Electronic applications accepted.

**Appalachian State University,** Cratis D. Williams Graduate School, Center for Appalachian Studies, Boone, NC 28608. Offers culture (MA). *Program availability:* Part-time. *Degree requirements:* For master's, one foreign language, comprehensive exam, thesis optional. *Entrance requirements:* For master's, GRE General Test, 3 letters of recommendation. Additional exam requirements/recommendations for international students: Required—TOEFL (minimum score 570 paper-based; 79 iBT), IELTS (minimum score 6.5). *Application deadline:* For fall admission, 3/15 priority date for domestic students, 2/1 for international students; for spring admission, 11/1 for domestic students, 7/1 for international students. Applications are processed on a rolling basis. Application fee: $55. Electronic applications accepted. *Expenses:* Tuition, state resident: full-time $4744. Tuition, nonresident: full-time $17,913. Full-time tuition and fees vary according to program. *Financial support:* Fellowships, research assistantships, teaching assistantships, career-related internships or fieldwork, Federal Work-Study, scholarships/grants, and unspecified assistantships available. Financial award application deadline: 4/1; financial award applicants required to submit FAFSA. *Faculty research:* Appalachian culture, sustainable development, Appalachian music. *Unit head:* Dr. Pat Beaver, Director, 828-262-2550, E-mail: beaverpd@appstate.edu. *Application contact:* Dr. Dave Wood, Graduate Program Director, 828-262-7199, E-mail: wooddh@appstate.edu.
Website: http://www.appstudies.appstate.edu

**Arizona State University at the Tempe campus,** College of Liberal Arts and Sciences, Department of English, Program in Film and Media Studies, Tempe, AZ 85287-0402.

Offers American media and popular culture (MAS). *Program availability:* Part-time, evening/weekend, online learning. *Degree requirements:* For master's, integrated project. *Entrance requirements:* For master's, minimum GPA of 3.0 or equivalent in last 2 years of work leading to bachelor's degree. Additional exam requirements/recommendations for international students: Required—TOEFL, IELTS, or PTE. Electronic applications accepted. *Expenses:* Contact institution.

**Arizona State University at the Tempe campus,** College of Liberal Arts and Sciences, School of International Letters and Cultures, Program in Spanish, Tempe, AZ 85287-0202. Offers cultural studies (PhD); linguistics (MA), including second language acquisition/applied linguistics, sociolinguistics; literature (PhD); literature and culture (MA). *Program availability:* Part-time. Terminal master's awarded for partial completion of doctoral program. *Degree requirements:* For master's, thesis, oral defense; written comprehensive exam (literature and culture); portfolio review (linguistics); interactive Program of Study (iPOS) submitted before completing 50 percent of required credit hours; for doctorate, comprehensive exam, thesis/dissertation, interactive Program of Study (iPOS) submitted before completing 50 percent of required credit hours. *Entrance requirements:* For master's, GRE (recommended), BA in Spanish or close equivalent from accredited institution with minimum GPA of 3.5, 3 letters of recommendation, personal statement, academic writing sample; for doctorate, GRE (recommended), MA in Spanish or equivalent from accredited institution with minimum GPA of 3.75, 3 letters of recommendation, personal statement, academic writing sample. Additional exam requirements/recommendations for international students: Required— TOEFL (minimum score 550 paper-based; 83 iBT), IELTS (minimum score 6.5). Electronic applications accepted.

**Assemblies of God Theological Seminary,** Graduate and Professional Programs, Springfield, MO 65802. Offers Biblical interpretation and theology (PhD); Christian ministries (MA); divinity (M Div); intercultural studies (MA, PhD); ministry (D Min); missiology (DAIS); pastoral studies (MPL); theological studies (MA, Th M). *Accreditation:* ATS. *Program availability:* Part-time, evening/weekend, 100% online. *Degree requirements:* For master's, variable foreign language requirement; for doctorate, thesis/dissertation. *Entrance requirements:* For master's, minimum GPA of 2.5; for doctorate, GRE (for PhD in Bible theology), minimum GPA of 3.0. Additional exam requirements/recommendations for international students: Required—TOEFL (minimum score 550 paper-based; 80 iBT). Electronic applications accepted.

**Athabasca University,** Centre for Interdisciplinary Studies, Athabasca, AB T9S 3A3, Canada. Offers adult education (MA); community studies (MA); cultural studies (MA); educational studies (MA); global change (MA); heritage resource management (Postbaccalaureate Certificate); legislative drafting (Postbaccalaureate Certificate); work, organization, and leadership (MA). *Program availability:* Part-time, evening/weekend, online learning. *Degree requirements:* For master's, project. *Entrance requirements:* Additional exam requirements/recommendations for international students: Required—TOEFL (minimum score 560 paper-based). Electronic applications accepted. *Faculty research:* Women's history, literature and culture studies, sustainable development, labor and education.

**Baptist Bible College,** Graduate School of Theology, Springfield, MO 65803-3498. Offers biblical counseling (MA); biblical studies (MA); church ministry (MA); intercultural studies (MA); theology (M Div). *Program availability:* Part-time. *Entrance requirements:* Additional exam requirements/recommendations for international students: Required— TOEFL. Electronic applications accepted.

**Binghamton University, State University of New York,** Graduate School, Harpur College of Arts and Sciences, Philosophy, Interpretation and Culture Program, Binghamton, NY 13902-6000. Offers MA, PhD. *Program availability:* Part-time. *Students:* 12 part-time (8 women); includes 3 minority (1 Black or African American, non-Hispanic/Latino; 1 Asian, non-Hispanic/Latino; 1 Hispanic/Latino), 5 international. Average age 44. In 2016, 2 doctorates awarded. *Degree requirements:* For doctorate, thesis/dissertation. *Entrance requirements:* Additional exam requirements/recommendations for international students: Required—TOEFL. Application fee: $75. *Financial support:* In 2016–17, 5 students received support. Fellowships, career-related internships or fieldwork, Federal Work-Study, institutionally sponsored loans, scholarships/grants, health care benefits, and unspecified assistantships available. Financial award applicants required to submit FAFSA. *Unit head:* Dr. Nkiru Nzegwu, Graduate Coordinator, 607-777-3082, E-mail: panap@binghamton.edu. *Application contact:* Ben Balkaya, Assistant Dean and Director, 607-777-2151, Fax: 607-777-2501, E-mail: balkaya@binghamton.edu.

**Biola University,** Cook School of Intercultural Studies, La Mirada, CA 90639-0001. Offers anthropology (MA); applied linguistics (MA); intercultural education (PhD); intercultural studies (MA, PhD); linguistics (Certificate; linguistics and Biblical languages (MA); missiology (D Miss); missions (MA); teaching English to speakers of other languages (MA, Certificate); teaching English to speakers of other languages (online) (MA). *Program availability:* Part-time, 100% online. *Entrance requirements:* For master's, minimum undergraduate GPA of 3.0; for doctorate, master's degree or equivalent, 3 years of cross-cultural experience, minimum graduate GPA of 3.3. Additional exam requirements/recommendations for international students: Required— TOEFL. Electronic applications accepted. *Faculty research:* Linguistics, anthropology, intercultural studies, teaching English to speakers of other languages, missions, missiology.

## Cultural Studies

**Biola University,** Talbot School of Theology, La Mirada, CA 90639-0001. Offers adult/family ministry (MACE); Bible exposition (MA, Th M); Biblical and theological studies (Certificate); biblical and theological studies/diversified (MA); children's ministry (MACE); Christian education (M Div); cross-cultural education ministry (MACE); educational studies (Ed D, PhD); evangelism and discipleship (M Div); general Christian education (MACE); Messianic Jewish studies (M Div, Certificate); missions and intercultural studies (M Div); New Testament (MA, Th M); Old Testament (MA); Old Testament and Semitics (Th M); pastoral and general ministry (M Div); pastoral care and counseling (M Div, MACML); philosophy (MA); preaching and pastoral ministry (MACML); spiritual formation (M Div, Certificate); spiritual formation and soul care (MA); sports ministry (MACML); theology (MA, Th M, D Min, Certificate); youth ministry (MACE). *Accreditation:* ATS. *Program availability:* Part-time, evening/weekend. *Entrance requirements:* For master's, bachelor's degree from accredited college or university; minimum GPA of 2.6 (for M Div), 3.0 (for MA); for doctorate, M Div or MA. Additional exam requirements/recommendations for international students: Required—TOEFL (minimum score 600 paper-based; 88 iBT). Electronic applications accepted. *Faculty research:* New Testament, Old Testament, spiritual formation, Christian education, theological studies, Christian ministry, preaching and pastoral ministry, language and literature, bible exposition, Christian leadership.

**Boston University,** Metropolitan College, Program in Gastronomy, Boston, MA 02215. Offers communications (MLA); history and culture (MLA). *Program availability:* Part-time, evening/weekend. *Faculty:* 3 full-time (2 women), 14 part-time/adjunct (8 women). *Students:* 7 full-time (all women), 88 part-time (74 women); includes 16 minority (4 Black or African American, non-Hispanic/Latino; 3 Asian, non-Hispanic/Latino; 6 Hispanic/Latino; 3 Two or more races, non-Hispanic/Latino), 10 international. Average age 30. 58 applicants, 76% accepted, 27 enrolled. In 2016, 36 master's awarded. *Degree requirements:* For master's, thesis optional. *Entrance requirements:* Additional exam requirements/recommendations for international students: Required—TOEFL. *Application deadline:* Applications are processed on a rolling basis. Application fee: $85. Electronic applications accepted. *Expenses:* Contact institution. *Financial support:* In 2016–17, 4 research assistantships (averaging $4,200 per year) were awarded; career-related internships or fieldwork, scholarships/grants, and unspecified assistantships also available. Support available to part-time students. Financial award applicants required to submit FAFSA. *Faculty research:* Food studies. *Unit head:* Faculty Coordinator, 617-353-6916, Fax: 617-353-4130, E-mail: gastrmla@bu.edu. *Application contact:* Barbara Rotger, Program Manager, 617-353-6916; Fax: 617-353-4130, E-mail: brotger@bu.edu. Website: http://www.bu.edu/met/gastronomy

**Brock University,** Faculty of Graduate Studies, Faculty of Social Sciences, Program in Popular Culture, St. Catharines, ON L2S 3A1, Canada. Offers MA. *Program availability:* Part-time. *Degree requirements:* For master's, thesis optional. *Entrance requirements:* For master's, honors BA. Additional exam requirements/recommendations for international students: Required—TOEFL (minimum score 550 paper-based; 80 iBT), IELTS (minimum score 6.5), TWE (minimum score 4). Electronic applications accepted. *Faculty research:* Film and television studies, popular music, historical aspects of popular culture, popular literature.

**Carnegie Mellon University,** Dietrich College of Humanities and Social Sciences, Department of History, Pittsburgh, PA 15213-3891. Offers African and African-American diaspora (PhD); culture and power (PhD); labor, politics and social movements (PhD); technology, environment, science and health (PhD); women, gender and the family (PhD). *Program availability:* Part-time. *Degree requirements:* For doctorate, oral and written comprehensive exams, dissertation defense. *Entrance requirements:* For doctorate, GRE General Test. Additional exam requirements/recommendations for international students: Required—TOEFL. Electronic applications accepted. *Faculty research:* Anthropology and history, African-American history, technology/environment, cultural history analysis.

**Central Michigan University,** College of Graduate Studies, College of Humanities and Social and Behavioral Sciences, Program in Humanities, Mount Pleasant, MI 48859. Offers humanities (MA), including contemporary issues in the humanities: race, class, and gender, images and ideas of self, Native American issues in modern culture, popular culture studies, the rise of industrial society. *Program availability:* Part-time, evening/weekend. *Degree requirements:* For master's, thesis or alternative. Electronic applications accepted. *Faculty research:* Rise of industrial society; images and ideas of self; contemporary issues of race, class, and gender; popular culture; Native American issues in modern culture.

**Chapman University,** College of Educational Studies, Orange, CA 92866. Offers counseling (MA), including school counseling (MA, Credential); education (PhD), including cultural and curricular studies, disability studies, leadership studies, school psychology (PhD, Credential); educational psychology (MA); leadership development (MA); multiple subjects (Credential), including Spanish/English bilingual; pupil personnel services (Credential), including school counseling (MA, Credential), school psychology (PhD, Credential); school psychology (Ed S); single subject (Credential); special education (MA, Credential), including mild/moderate (Credential), moderate/severe (Credential); teaching (MA), including elementary education, secondary education, secondary music education. *Accreditation:* TEAC. *Program availability:* Part-time, evening/weekend. *Faculty:* 29 full-time (14 women), 36 part-time/adjunct (28 women). *Students:* 186 full-time (148 women), 186 part-time (134 women); includes 144 minority (9 Black or African American, non-Hispanic/Latino; 39 Asian, non-Hispanic/Latino; 78 Hispanic/Latino; 2 Native Hawaiian or other Pacific Islander, non-Hispanic/Latino; 16 Two or more races, non-Hispanic/Latino), 8 international. Average age 29. 143 applicants, 63% accepted, 64 enrolled. In 2016, 111 master's, 24 doctorates awarded. *Degree requirements:* For doctorate, thesis/dissertation. *Entrance requirements:* Additional exam requirements/recommendations for international students: Required—TOEFL (minimum score 550 paper-based, 80 iBT), IELTS (6.5), PTE Academic (53), or CAE. *Application deadline:* Applications are processed on a rolling basis. Application fee: $60. Electronic applications accepted. *Expenses:* Contact institution. *Financial support:* Fellowships and scholarships/grants available. Financial award application deadline: 3/2; financial award applicants required to submit FAFSA. *Unit head:* Dr. Margaret Grogan, Dean, 714-516-5968, E-mail: grogan@chapman.edu. *Application contact:* Sara Simon, Graduate Admission Counselor, 714-997-6770, E-mail: simon@chapman.edu.
Website: http://www.chapman.edu/CES/

**Charlotte Christian College and Theological Seminary,** Graduate Program, Charlotte, NC 28205. Offers urban Christian ministry (MA), including church planting, multi-cultural studies, sacred music, youth ministry. *Program availability:* Part-time, evening/weekend. *Degree requirements:* For master's, thesis. *Entrance requirements:* For master's, MAT, writing sample/essay. Additional exam requirements/recommendations for international students: Required—TOEFL, IELTS. Electronic applications accepted. *Expenses:* Contact institution.

**Claremont Graduate University,** Graduate Programs, School of Arts and Humanities, Department of Cultural Studies, Claremont, CA 91711-6160. Offers Africana studies (Certificate); cultural studies (MA, PhD); media studies (MA, PhD); museum studies (MA). *Program availability:* Part-time. *Faculty:* 5 full-time (1 woman). *Students:* 47 full-time (35 women), 84 part-time (8 women); includes 28 minority (5 Black or African American, non-Hispanic/Latino; 1 American Indian or Alaska Native, non-Hispanic/Latino; 7 Asian, non-Hispanic/Latino; 12 Hispanic/Latino; 3 Two or more races, non-Hispanic/Latino), 5 international. Average age 35. In 2016, 4 master's, 2 doctorates, 1 other advanced degree awarded. *Entrance requirements:* For master's and doctorate, GRE General Test. Additional exam requirements/recommendations for international students: Required—TOEFL (minimum score 75 iBT). *Application deadline:* For fall admission, 2/1 priority date for domestic and international students. Applications are processed on a rolling basis. Application fee: $80. Electronic applications accepted. *Expenses: Tuition:* Full-time $44,328; part-time $1847 per unit. *Required fees:* $600; $300 per semester. Tuition and fees vary according to course load and program. *Financial support:* Fellowships, research assistantships, Federal Work-Study, institutionally sponsored loans, and scholarships/grants available. Support available to part-time students. Financial award application deadline: 2/15; financial award applicants required to submit FAFSA. *Unit head:* David Luis-Brown, Chair, 909-607-3337, E-mail: david.luis-brown@cgu.edu. *Application contact:* Amy Sandefur, Assistant Director of Admissions, 909-607-9101, E-mail: amy.sandefur@cgu.edu.
Website: https://www.cgu.edu/departments/cultural-studies/

**Clarks Summit University,** Graduate Studies, South Abington Township, PA 18411. Offers Bible (MA); counseling (MA, MS); curriculum and instruction (M Ed); educational administration (M Ed); intercultural studies (MA); literature (MA); missions (MA); organizational leadership (MA); reading specialist (M Ed); secondary English/communications (M Ed); social entrepreneurship (MA); worldview studies (MA). MA in missions program available only for Association of Baptists for World Evangelism missionary personnel. *Program availability:* Part-time, evening/weekend, online learning. *Entrance requirements:* Additional exam requirements/recommendations for international students: Required—TOEFL (minimum score 500 paper-based).

**Columbia International University,** Seminary and School of Ministry, Columbia, SC 29230-3122. Offers academic ministries (M Div); Bible and theology (Certificate); bible exposition (M Div, MABE); Biblical ministry (Certificate); chaplaincy (M Div); intercultural studies (MAIS); leadership (D Min); member care (D Min); missions (D Min); preaching (D Min); theological studies (MA). *Accreditation:* ATS (one or more programs are accredited). *Program availability:* Part-time, evening/weekend. *Degree requirements:* For doctorate, comprehensive exam, thesis/dissertation. *Entrance requirements:* For doctorate, 3 years of ministerial experience, M Div. Additional exam requirements/recommendations for international students: Required—TOEFL. Electronic applications accepted.

**Concordia University Irvine,** School of Theology, Irvine, CA 92612-3299. Offers Christian leadership (MA); research in theology (MA); theology and culture (MA). *Program availability:* Part-time, evening/weekend. *Degree requirements:* For master's, project/thesis or vicarage. *Entrance requirements:* For master's, official college transcript(s), statement of intent, 2 references, interview. Additional exam requirements/recommendations for international students: Required—TOEFL. Electronic applications accepted. *Expenses:* Contact institution.

**Cornell University,** Graduate School, Graduate Fields of Arts and Sciences, Field of English Language and Literature, Ithaca, NY 14853. Offers African-American literature (PhD); American literature after 1865 (PhD); American literature to 1865 (PhD); American studies (PhD); colonial and postcolonial literatures (PhD); creative writing (MFA); cultural studies (PhD); dramatic literature (PhD); English poetry (PhD); English Renaissance to 1660 (PhD); lesbian, bisexual, and gay literary studies (PhD); literary criticism and theory (PhD); Old and Middle English (PhD); prose fiction (PhD); Restoration and the eighteenth-century (PhD); the nineteenth century (PhD); the twentieth century (PhD); women's literature (PhD); MFA/PhD. Terminal master's awarded for partial completion of doctoral program. *Degree requirements:* For master's, one foreign language, thesis; for doctorate, one foreign language, comprehensive exam, thesis/dissertation, teaching experience. *Entrance requirements:* For master's, GRE General Test, 3 letters of recommendation, creative writing sample; for doctorate, GRE General Test, GRE Subject Test (English), 3 letters of recommendation, writing sample. Additional exam requirements/recommendations for international students: Required—TOEFL (minimum score 600 paper-based; 77 iBT). Electronic applications accepted. *Faculty research:* English and American literature, women's writing, ethnic and post-colonial literature, critical theory, medievalism.

**Drew University,** Caspersen School of Graduate Studies, Madison, NJ 07940-1493. Offers conflict resolution and leadership (Certificate), including community leadership, moderation, peace building; history and culture (MA, PhD), including American history, book history, British history, European history, Holocaust and genocide (M Litt, MA, D Litt, PhD), intellectual history, Irish history, print culture, public history; K-12 education (MAT), including art, biology, chemistry, elementary education, English, French, Italian, math, secondary education, special education, teacher of students with disabilities; liberal studies (M Litt, D Litt), including history, Holocaust and genocide (M Litt, MA, D Litt, PhD), Irish/Irish-American studies, literature (M Litt, MMH, D Litt, DMH, CMH), religion, spirituality, teaching in the two-year college, writing; medical humanities (MMH, DMH, CMH), including arts, health, healthcare, literature (M Litt, MMH, D Litt, DMH, CMH), scientific research; poetry (MFA). *Program availability:* Part-time, evening/weekend. *Faculty:* 4 full-time (2 women), 31 part-time/adjunct (16 women). *Students:* 62 full-time (41 women), 199 part-time (130 women); includes 38 minority (17 Black or African American, non-Hispanic/Latino; 3 Asian, non-Hispanic/Latino; 17 Hispanic/Latino; 1 Two or more races, non-Hispanic/Latino), 3 international. Average age 27. 93 applicants, 81% accepted, 46 enrolled. In 2016, 39 master's, 27 doctorates, 26 other advanced degrees awarded. Terminal master's awarded for partial completion of doctoral program. *Degree requirements:* For master's and other advanced degree, thesis (for some programs); for doctorate, one foreign language, comprehensive exam (for some programs), thesis/dissertation. *Entrance requirements:* For master's, PRAXIS Core and Subject Area tests (for MAT), resume, transcripts, writing sample, personal statement, letters of recommendation; for doctorate, GRE (PhD in history and culture), resume, transcripts, writing sample, personal statement, letters of recommendation. Additional exam requirements/recommendations for international students: Required—TOEFL (minimum score 587 paper-based; 94 iBT), IELTS (minimum score 7), TWE (minimum score 4). *Application deadline:* For fall admission, 8/1 for domestic students, 6/1 for international students; for spring admission, 12/1 for domestic students, 10/1 for international students. Applications are processed on a rolling basis. Application fee: $35. Electronic applications accepted. Tuition and fees vary according to program. *Financial support:* Fellowships, research assistantships, teaching assistantships, career-related internships or fieldwork, Federal Work-Study, scholarships/grants, and unspecified assistantships available. Support available to part-time students. Financial award applicants required to submit FAFSA. *Application contact:* Leanne Horinko, Director of Caspersen Admissions, 973-408-3280, E-mail: gradm@drew.edu.
Website: http://www.drew.edu/caspersen

**Eastern Michigan University,** Graduate School, College of Arts and Sciences, Department of Sociology, Anthropology and Criminology, Program in Cultural Museum Studies, Ypsilanti, MI 48197. Offers Graduate Certificate. *Program availability:* Part-time, evening/weekend, online learning. *Students:* 1 applicant, 0% accepted. In 2016, 5 Graduate Certificates awarded. *Entrance requirements:* Additional exam requirements/recommendations for international students: Required—TOEFL. *Application deadline:*

Applications are processed on a rolling basis. Application fee: $45. *Financial support:* Fellowships, research assistantships with full tuition reimbursements, teaching assistantships with full tuition reimbursements, career-related internships or fieldwork, Federal Work-Study, institutionally sponsored loans, scholarships/grants, tuition waivers (partial), and unspecified assistantships available. Support available to part-time students. Financial award applicants required to submit FAFSA. *Application contact:* Dr. Liza Cerroni-Long, Advisor, 734-487-0012, Fax: 734-487-9666, E-mail: liza.cerroni-long@emich.edu.

**Florida State University,** The Graduate School, College of Fine Arts, Department of Art History, Tallahassee, FL 32306. Offers art history (MA, PhD); museum and cultural heritage studies (MA). *Accreditation:* NASAD. *Program availability:* Part-time. *Faculty:* 11 full-time (4 women), 9 part-time/adjunct (5 women). *Students:* 48 full-time (43 women), 6 part-time (5 women); includes 10 minority (1 Black or African American, non-Hispanic/Latino; 2 Asian, non-Hispanic/Latino; 6 Hispanic/Latino; 1 Two or more races, non-Hispanic/Latino). Average age 32. 35 applicants, 91% accepted, 21 enrolled. In 2016, 14 master's, 1 doctorate awarded. Terminal master's awarded for partial completion of doctoral program. *Degree requirements:* For master's, one foreign language, thesis (for some programs), capstone project (for some programs); for doctorate, 2 foreign languages, comprehensive exam, thesis/dissertation. *Entrance requirements:* For master's, GRE General Test, minimum GPA of 3.0; for doctorate, GRE General Test, minimum GPA of 3.5. Additional exam requirements/recommendations for international students: Required—TOEFL (minimum score 550 paper-based; 80 iBT), IELTS (minimum score 6.5). *Application deadline:* For fall admission, 4/1 for domestic and international students. Applications are processed on a rolling basis. Application fee: $35. Electronic applications accepted. *Expenses:* $479.32 per credit hour in-state, $1,110.72 per credit hour out-of-state. *Financial support:* In 2016–17, 34 students received support, including 7 fellowships with full tuition reimbursements available (averaging $10,900 per year), 19 research assistantships with full tuition reimbursements available (averaging $5,395 per year), 8 teaching assistantships with full tuition reimbursements available (averaging $6,609 per year); career-related internships or fieldwork, Federal Work-Study, institutionally sponsored loans, and unspecified assistantships also available. Financial award application deadline: 1/1; financial award applicants required to submit FAFSA. *Faculty research:* Modern art and critical theory, medieval, Renaissance and Baroque, Pre-Columbian and Spanish Colonial, visual arts of the Americas. *Unit head:* Dr. Adam Jolles, Associate Professor of Art History/Department Chair, 850-644-7066, E-mail: ajolles@fsu.edu. *Application contact:* Juan Barcelo-Gonzalez, Academic Program Specialist/Graduate Student Advisor, 850-644-8207, E-mail: juan.barcelo@fsu.edu.
Website: http://arthistory.fsu.edu/

**Gardner-Webb University,** School of Divinity, Boiling Springs, NC 28017. Offers biblical studies (M Div); Christian education and formation (M Div); intercultural studies (M Div); ministry (D Min); missiology (M Div); pastoral care and counseling (M Div); pastoral care and counseling/member care for missionaries (D Min); pastoral studies (M Div); M Div/MA; M Div/MBA. *Accreditation:* ACIPE. *Program availability:* Part-time. *Faculty:* 12 full-time (2 women), 3 part-time/adjunct (1 woman). *Students:* 115 full-time (59 women), 68 part-time (27 women); includes 86 minority (80 Black or African American, non-Hispanic/Latino; 5 Asian, non-Hispanic/Latino; 1 Hispanic/Latino). Average age 40. 86 applicants, 44% accepted, 16 enrolled. In 2016, 40 master's, 3 doctorates awarded. *Entrance requirements:* For master's, minimum GPA of 2.6; for doctorate, minimum GPA of 2.75. Additional exam requirements/recommendations for international students: Required—TOEFL (minimum score 500 paper-based; 61 iBT). *Application deadline:* Applications are processed on a rolling basis. Electronic applications accepted. *Expenses:* Contact institution. *Financial support:* Fellowships, institutionally sponsored loans, and unspecified assistantships available. Support available to part-time students. Financial award application deadline: 5/15. *Faculty research:* Jewish-Christian dialogue, Islam. *Unit head:* Dr. Robert W. Canoy, Sr., Dean, 704-406-4400, Fax: 704-406-3935, E-mail: rcanoy@gardner-webb.edu. *Application contact:* Kheresa Harmon, Director of Admissions, 704-406-3205, Fax: 704-406-3895, E-mail: kharmon@gardner-webb.edu.
Website: http://gardner-webb.edu/academic-programs-and-resources/colleges-and-schools/divinity/index

**George Fox University,** Portland Seminary, Portland, OR 97223. Offers Biblical studies (M Div, MA); chaplaincy (M Div); Christian history and theology (M Div, MA); creation care (M Div, MA); intercultural studies (M Div, MA); leadership (M Div, MA); leadership and global perspectives (D Min); leadership and spiritual formation (D Min); semiotics and future studies (D Min); spiritual direction (MA, Certificate); spiritual direction supervision (M Div, MA, Certificate); spiritual formation and discipleship (M Div, MA, Certificate). *Accreditation:* ACIPE; ATS. *Program availability:* Part-time, evening/weekend, online learning. *Entrance requirements:* For master's, resume, three references (one pastoral, one academic or professional, one personal), one official transcript from each college or university attended; for doctorate, resume, 3 references (1 professional, 1 academic, 1 personal), one official transcript from each college or university attended. Additional exam requirements/recommendations for international students: Required—TOEFL (minimum score 577 paper-based; 90 iBT). Electronic applications accepted. *Expenses:* Contact institution.

**George Mason University,** College of Humanities and Social Sciences, Program in Cultural Studies, Fairfax, VA 22030. Offers PhD. *Faculty:* 11 full-time (5 women). *Students:* 27 full-time (17 women), 24 part-time (17 women); includes 11 minority (2 Black or African American, non-Hispanic/Latino; 1 American Indian or Alaska Native, non-Hispanic/Latino; 3 Asian, non-Hispanic/Latino; 2 Hispanic/Latino; 3 Two or more races, non-Hispanic/Latino), 2 international. Average age 33. 24 applicants, 58% accepted, 6 enrolled. In 2016, 16 doctorates awarded. *Degree requirements:* For doctorate, one foreign language, comprehensive exam, thesis/dissertation, foreign language exams. *Entrance requirements:* For doctorate, GRE, expanded goals statement; 3 letters of recommendation from academic sources; writing sample; master's degree in relevant field; official transcripts. Additional exam requirements/recommendations for international students: Required—TOEFL (minimum score 575 paper-based; 88 iBT), IELTS (minimum score 6.5), PTE (minimum score 59). Application fee: $75 ($80 for international students). Electronic applications accepted. *Expenses:* Tuition, state resident: full-time $10,628; part-time $443 per credit. Tuition, nonresident: full-time $29,306; part-time $1221 per credit. *Required fees:* $3096; $129 per credit. Tuition and fees vary according to program. *Financial support:* In 2016–17, 25 students received support, including 1 fellowship (averaging $10,000 per year), 2 research assistantships with tuition reimbursements available (averaging $22,000 per year), 23 teaching assistantships with tuition reimbursements available (averaging $19,526 per year); career-related internships or fieldwork, Federal Work-Study, scholarships/grants, unspecified assistantships, and health care benefits (for full-time research or teaching assistantship recipients) also available. Support available to part-time students. Financial award application deadline: 3/15; financial award applicants required to submit FAFSA. *Faculty research:* Early modern cultural studies, Shakespeare and film, feminism, Michel Foucault, science and technology studies. *Unit head:* Denise Albanese, Director, 703-993-2869, Fax: 703-993-2852, E-mail: dalbanes@gmu.edu.
Website: http://culturalstudies.gmu.edu

**Georgia State University,** College of Arts and Sciences, Department of World Languages and Cultures, Atlanta, GA 30302-3083. Offers French (MA), including applied linguistics and pedagogy, French studies, literature and culture; Latin American studies (Certificate); Spanish (MA); translation and interpretation (Certificate), including interpretation, translation. *Program availability:* Part-time. *Faculty:* 36 full-time (20 women). *Students:* 17 full-time (12 women), 4 part-time (2 women); includes 18 minority (7 Black or African American, non-Hispanic/Latino; 6 Asian, non-Hispanic/Latino; 5 Hispanic/Latino), 5 international. Average age 38. 18 applicants, 83% accepted, 11 enrolled. In 2016, 3 other advanced degrees awarded. *Degree requirements:* For master's, 2 foreign languages, comprehensive exam, thesis or alternative, Graduate Foreign Language Reading Exam. *Entrance requirements:* For master's, GRE, statement of purpose, writing sample in the target language, 2 letters of recommendation, official transcripts; for Certificate, entrance examination involving translating one passage from English to the target language and one passage from the target language to English, 3 letters of recommendation, resume/curriculum vitae, official transcripts. Additional exam requirements/recommendations for international students: Required—TOEFL (minimum score 79 iBT). *Application deadline:* For fall admission, 3/15 priority date for domestic and international students; for spring admission, 11/15 priority date for domestic and international students. Application fee: $50. Electronic applications accepted. *Expenses:* Tuition, state resident: full-time $6876; part-time $382 per credit hour. Tuition, nonresident: full-time $22,374; part-time $1243 per credit hour. *Required fees:* $2128; $1064 per term. Part-time tuition and fees vary according to course load and program. *Financial support:* Applicants required to submit FAFSA. *Faculty research:* French literature and culture, Francophone literature and culture, Latin American literature and culture, Spanish literature and culture, Hispanic linguistics. *Unit head:* Dr. Fernando Reati, Department Chair, 404-413-5984, Fax: 404-413-5982, E-mail: freati@gsu.edu. *Application contact:* Amber Amari, Director, Graduate and Scheduling Services, 404-413-5037, E-mail: aamari@gsu.edu.
Website: http://wlc.gsu.edu/

**Goucher College,** MA and MFA Programs, Baltimore, MD 21204-2794. Offers arts administration (MA); creative nonfiction (MFA); cultural sustainability (MA); digital arts (MA, MFA); environmental studies (MA); historic preservation (MA); management (MA). *Program availability:* Part-time, evening/weekend, blended/hybrid learning. *Faculty:* 6 full-time (4 women), 100 part-time/adjunct (56 women). *Students:* 70 full-time (50 women), 69 part-time (52 women); includes 15 minority (7 Black or African American, non-Hispanic/Latino; 1 American Indian or Alaska Native, non-Hispanic/Latino; 1 Asian, non-Hispanic/Latino; 4 Hispanic/Latino; 2 Two or more races, non-Hispanic/Latino), 2 international. 74 applicants, 88% accepted, 42 enrolled. In 2016, 83 master's awarded. *Degree requirements:* For master's, thesis, e-portfolio. *Entrance requirements:* For master's, digital portfolio (for MA, MFA in digital arts); writing sample (for MFA in creative nonfiction). Additional exam requirements/recommendations for international students: Required—TOEFL (minimum score 550 paper-based; 80 iBT). *Application deadline:* Applications are processed on a rolling basis. Application fee: $75. Electronic applications accepted. *Expenses:* Contact institution. *Financial support:* Scholarships/grants and unspecified assistantships available. Financial award application deadline: 4/15; financial award applicants required to submit FAFSA. *Unit head:* Leslie Rubinkowski, Assistant Provost, 410-337-6200, E-mail: leslie.rubinkowski@goucher.edu. *Application contact:* Shelby Hillers, Admissions Coordinator, 410-337-6200, Fax: 410-337-6200, E-mail: shelby.hillers@goucher.edu.
Website: http://www.goucher.edu/grad

**Grace Theological Seminary,** Graduate and Professional Programs, Winona Lake, IN 46590-9907. Offers biblical studies (Certificate); chaplaincy (M Div); exegetical studies (M Div); intercultural studies (M Div, MA, D Min); local church ministry (MA), including camp administration, women's leadership; pastoral counseling (M Div); pastoral studies (M Div, D Min); theology (Diploma). *Accreditation:* ATS. *Program availability:* Part-time, online learning. *Degree requirements:* For master's, thesis optional; for doctorate, 2 foreign languages, thesis/dissertation. *Entrance requirements:* For master's, MAT, minimum GPA of 2.5. Electronic applications accepted. *Faculty research:* Biblical theology, language, and church ministries.

**Graduate Theological Union,** Graduate Programs, Berkeley, CA 94709-1212. Offers art and religion (MA, PhD, Th D); biblical languages (MA); biblical studies (MA); Biblical studies (PhD, Th D); Buddhist studies (MA); Christian spirituality (MA, PhD, Th D); cultural and historical studies of religions (MA, PhD, Th D); ethics and social theory (PhD, Th D); history (MA, PhD, Th D); homiletics (MA, PhD, Th D); interdisciplinary studies (PhD, Th D); Jewish studies (MA, PhD, Th D, Certificate); liturgical studies (MA, PhD, Th D); Near Eastern religions (PhD, Th D); Orthodox Christian studies (MA); religion and psychology (MA, PhD, Th D); religion and society/ethics and social theory (MA); systematic and philosophical theology (MA, PhD, Th D). PhD programs in Jewish studies and Near Eastern religions offered jointly with University of California, Berkeley. *Accreditation:* ATS. Terminal master's awarded for partial completion of doctoral program. *Degree requirements:* For master's, one foreign language, thesis; for doctorate, one foreign language, comprehensive exam, thesis/dissertation. *Entrance requirements:* For master's, GRE General Test; for doctorate, GRE General Test, MA or M Div. Additional exam requirements/recommendations for international students: Required—TOEFL. Electronic applications accepted.

**Johnson University,** Graduate and Professional Programs, Knoxville, TN 37998-1001. Offers biblical interpretation (Graduate Certificate); business administration (MBA); Christian ministries (Graduate Certificate); clinical mental health counseling (MA); educational technology (MA); intercultural studies (MA); leadership (MBA); leadership studies (PhD); New Testament (MA); nonprofit management (MBA); school counseling (MA); spiritual formation and leadership (Graduate Certificate); strategic ministry (MA); teacher education (MA). *Program availability:* Part-time, evening/weekend, 100% online, blended/hybrid learning. *Faculty:* 26 full-time (10 women), 32 part-time/adjunct (9 women). *Students:* 126 full-time (46 women), 170 part-time (65 women); includes 33 minority (13 Black or African American, non-Hispanic/Latino; 1 American Indian or Alaska Native, non-Hispanic/Latino; 4 Asian, non-Hispanic/Latino; 8 Hispanic/Latino; 7 Two or more races, non-Hispanic/Latino), 21 international. Average age 35. In 2016, 106 master's, 3 doctorates awarded. *Degree requirements:* For master's, variable foreign language requirement, comprehensive exam, thesis (for some programs), internships; for doctorate, variable foreign language requirement, comprehensive exam, thesis/dissertation, internships. *Entrance requirements:* For master's, PRAXIS (for MA in teacher education); MAT (for counseling); GRE or GMAT (for MBA), interview, 3 references, transcripts, essay, minimum GPA of 2.5 or 3.0 (depending on program); for doctorate, GRE or MAT (taken not less than 5 years prior), interview, 3 references, transcripts, essay, minimum GPA of 3.0; for Graduate Certificate, interview, 3 references, transcripts, essay, minimum GPA of 3.0. Additional exam requirements/recommendations for international students: Required—TOEFL (minimum score 527 paper-based; 71 iBT). *Application deadline:* For fall admission, 7/1 for domestic students; for spring admission, 11/1 for domestic students; for summer admission, 4/1 for domestic students. Application fee: $50. Electronic applications accepted. *Expenses:* Contact institution. *Financial support:* Scholarships/grants available. Financial award application deadline: 4/15; financial award applicants required to submit FAFSA. *Unit head:* Richard Clark, Vice President for External Relations, 865-251-2327, E-mail:

rclark@johnsonu.edu. *Application contact:* Lisa Tarwater, Director of Graduate Admissions, 865-251-3400, E-mail: ltarwater@johnsonu.edu.

**Lincoln Christian University,** Graduate Programs, Lincoln, IL 62656-2167. Offers Biblical studies (MA); church history/historical theology (MA); intercultural studies (MA); ministry (MA); organizational leadership (MA); philosophy and apologetics (MA); spiritual formation (MA); theology (MA). MA in spiritual formation offered in Normal, IL. *Program availability:* Online learning. *Faculty:* 22 full-time (6 women), 27 part-time/adjunct (9 women). *Students:* 89 full-time (45 women), 225 part-time (91 women). Average age 39. *Entrance requirements:* For master's, minimum cumulative GPA of 2.5 in undergraduate degree studies. Additional exam requirements/recommendations for international students: Required—TOEFL (minimum score 550 paper-based); Recommended—IELTS (minimum score 6). *Application deadline:* For fall admission, 8/1 for domestic students, 3/1 for international students; for spring admission, 11/15 for domestic students, 11/1 for international students. *Application fee:* $25 ($50 for international students). Application fee is waived when completed online. *Expenses: Tuition:* Full-time $7812; part-time $5208 per credit hour. *Required fees:* $1000; $1000 per credit hour. One-time fee: $150. Full-time tuition and fees vary according to campus/location and program. *Financial support:* Applicants required to submit FAFSA. *Application contact:* Lindsey Clark, Associate Director of Graduate and Seminary Enrollment, 217-732-3168 Ext. 2398, E-mail: lclark@lincolnchristian.edu.
Website: https://lincolnchristian.edu/academics/programs/masters/

**Maranatha Baptist University,** Master of Arts in Intercultural Studies Program, Watertown, WI 53094. Offers MA. *Program availability:* Part-time. *Entrance requirements:* For master's, BA or BS. Additional exam requirements/recommendations for international students: Required—TOEFL. *Application deadline:* Applications are processed on a rolling basis. *Application fee:* $50. *Expenses: Tuition:* Full-time $6300; part-time $3150 per credit. *Required fees:* $210; $35 per course. Tuition and fees vary according to course load and degree level. *Financial support:* Scholarships/grants and tuition waivers (full and partial) available. Support available to part-time students. *Unit head:* Dr. Larry Oats, Dean of Maranatha Baptist Seminary, 920-206-2324, Fax: 920-261-9109, E-mail: larry.oats@mbu.edu. *Application contact:* Dr. Jim Harrison, Director of Admissions, 920-206-2327, Fax: 920-261-9109, E-mail: admissions@mbu.edu.
Website: http://www.mbu.edu/seminary/academics/programs/inter-cultural-studies/

**McMaster University,** School of Graduate Studies, Faculty of Humanities, Department of English and Cultural Studies, Hamilton, ON L8S 4M2, Canada. Offers cultural studies and critical theory (MA); English (MA, PhD). *Program availability:* Part-time. *Degree requirements:* For master's, one foreign language, thesis; for doctorate, one foreign language, comprehensive exam, thesis/dissertation. *Entrance requirements:* For master's, honors degree, minimum B+ average in at least 6 full courses of English beyond year 1; for doctorate, MA; minimum A- average in two of three courses. Additional exam requirements/recommendations for international students: Required—TOEFL (minimum score 580 paper-based). *Faculty research:* Literary theory, feminist theory, literature of migration, Bakhting globalization.

**Michigan Technological University,** Graduate School, College of Sciences and Arts, Department of Humanities, Houghton, MI 49931. Offers rhetoric, theory and culture (MS, PhD). *Program availability:* Part-time. *Faculty:* 35 full-time (22 women), 6 part-time/adjunct (3 women). *Students:* 32 full-time (20 women), 12 part-time (8 women); includes 3 minority (all Two or more races, non-Hispanic/Latino), 14 international. Average age 34. 77 applicants, 31% accepted, 17 enrolled. In 2016, 5 master's, 7 doctorates awarded. Terminal master's awarded for partial completion of doctoral program. *Degree requirements:* For master's, comprehensive exam (for some programs), thesis (for some programs); for doctorate, one foreign language, comprehensive exam, thesis/dissertation. *Entrance requirements:* For master's, GRE, statement of purpose, personal statement, official transcripts, 3 letters of recommendation, resume/curriculum vitae, writing sample (10-15 pages); for doctorate, GRE, statement of purpose, personal statement, official transcripts, 3 letters of recommendation, resume/curriculum vitae, writing sample (10-15 pages), master's degree. Additional exam requirements/recommendations for international students: Required—TOEFL (recommended minimum score 100 iBT) or IELTS. *Application deadline:* For fall admission, 1/15 priority date for domestic and international students. Applications are processed on a rolling basis. Electronic applications accepted. *Expenses:* Tuition, state resident: full-time $16,290; part-time $905 per credit. Tuition, nonresident: full-time $16,290; part-time $905 per credit. *Required fees:* $248; $124 per term. Tuition and fees vary according to course load and program. *Financial support:* In 2016–17, 33 students received support, including 2 fellowships (averaging $15,242 per year), 27 teaching assistantships with tuition reimbursements available (averaging $15,242 per year); career-related internships or fieldwork, Federal Work-Study, scholarships/grants, health care benefits, unspecified assistantships, and cooperative program also available. Financial award applicants required to submit FAFSA. *Faculty research:* Rhetoric and composition; communication and cultural studies; studies of science, technology, and society; technical communication and digital media. *Total annual research expenditures:* $6,920. *Unit head:* Dr. Ronald L. Strickland, Chair, 906-487-2376, Fax: 906-487-3559, E-mail: rlstrick@mtu.edu. *Application contact:* Alex Renshaw, Administrative Aide, 906-487-2540, Fax: 906-487-3559, E-mail: ajrensha@mtu.edu.
Website: http://www.mtu.edu/humanities/

**Nazarene Theological Seminary,** Graduate and Professional Programs, Kansas City, MO 64131-1263. Offers Christian formation and discipleship (MA); intercultural studies (MA); theological studies (MA); theology (M Div, D Min). *Accreditation:* ACIPE; ATS. *Program availability:* Part-time. *Faculty:* 11 full-time (2 women), 26 part-time/adjunct (4 women). *Students:* 105 full-time (33 women), 155 part-time (45 women); includes 22 minority (7 Black or African American, non-Hispanic/Latino; 1 American Indian or Alaska Native, non-Hispanic/Latino; 1 Asian, non-Hispanic/Latino; 9 Hispanic/Latino; 4 Two or more races, non-Hispanic/Latino), 29 international. *Degree requirements:* For master's, comprehensive exam (for some programs), thesis (for some programs); for doctorate, thesis/dissertation. *Entrance requirements:* For master's, three references; for doctorate, three references, interview. Additional exam requirements/recommendations for international students: Required—TOEFL (minimum score 550 paper-based; 80 iBT). *Application deadline:* For fall admission, 3/1 for domestic and international students; for spring admission, 11/1 for domestic and international students. Applications are processed on a rolling basis. *Application fee:* $50. Electronic applications accepted. *Expenses:* $525 per credit hour. *Financial support:* Teaching assistantships, institutionally sponsored loans, and scholarships/grants available. Support available to part-time students. Financial award application deadline: 3/1; financial award applicants required to submit FAFSA. *Unit head:* Dr. Josh Sweeden, Dean of the Faculty, 816-268-5412, Fax: 816-268-5500, E-mail: jsweeden@nts.edu. *Application contact:* Pamala J. Asher, Registrar/Director of Admissions, 816-268-5442, Fax: 816-268-5500, E-mail: pjasher@nts.edu.

**New Mexico State University,** College of Education, Department of Curriculum and Instruction, Las Cruces, NM 88003. Offers bilingual education (MA); curriculum and instruction (Ed D); early childhood education (MA); educational diagnostics (Ed S); language, literacy and culture (MA); learning design and technologies (MA); teaching (MAT), including Spanish; teaching English to speakers of other languages (MA). *Accreditation:* NCATE. *Program availability:* Part-time, evening/weekend, 100% online.

*Faculty:* 23 full-time (17 women), 7 part-time/adjunct (5 women). *Students:* 114 full-time (81 women), 219 part-time (159 women); includes 190 minority (16 Black or African American, non-Hispanic/Latino; 2 American Indian or Alaska Native, non-Hispanic/Latino; 5 Asian, non-Hispanic/Latino; 160 Hispanic/Latino; 7 Two or more races, non-Hispanic/Latino), 33 international. Average age 37. 126 applicants, 75% accepted, 65 enrolled. In 2016, 92 master's, 19 doctorates awarded. *Degree requirements:* For master's, comprehensive exam, thesis optional; for doctorate, comprehensive exam, thesis/dissertation. *Entrance requirements:* For master's, minimum cumulative GPA of 3.0; for doctorate, portfolio, minimum cumulative GPA of 3.0. Additional exam requirements/recommendations for international students: Required—TOEFL (minimum score 550 paper-based; 79 iBT), IELTS (minimum score 6.5). *Application deadline:* For fall admission, 12/15 priority date for domestic and international students; for spring admission, 11/1 for domestic students. Applications are processed on a rolling basis. *Application fee:* $40 ($50 for international students). Electronic applications accepted. *Expenses:* Tuition, state resident: full-time $4086. Tuition, nonresident: full-time $14,254. *Required fees:* $853. Tuition and fees vary according to course load. *Financial support:* In 2016–17, 102 students received support, including 2 fellowships (averaging $4,076 per year), 2 research assistantships (averaging $18,070 per year), 16 teaching assistantships (averaging $16,454 per year); career-related internships or fieldwork, Federal Work-Study, scholarships/grants, traineeships, health care benefits, and unspecified assistantships also available. Support available to part-time students. Financial award application deadline: 3/1. *Faculty research:* STEM education, bilingual and English as a second language education, critical pedagogy/multicultural education, learning design and technology, early childhood education. *Total annual research expenditures:* $29,926. *Unit head:* Dr. David Rutledge, Department Head, 575-646-5411, Fax: 575-646-5436, E-mail: rutledge@nmsu.edu. *Application contact:* Dr. David Rutledge, Associate Department Head for Graduate Programs, 575-646-5411, Fax: 575-646-5436, E-mail: rutledge@nmsu.edu.
Website: http://ci.education.nmsu.edu

**New York University,** Steinhardt School of Culture, Education, and Human Development, New York, NY 10003. Offers MA, MFA, MM, MPH, MS, DPS, DPT, Ed D, PhD, Advanced Certificate, Post Master's Certificate, Postbaccalaureate Certificate, Advanced Certificate/MPH, MA/Advanced Certificate, MA/MA, MA/MS, MLIS/MA. *Accreditation:* TEAC. *Program availability:* Part-time. *Degree requirements:* For master's, thesis (for some programs); for doctorate, comprehensive exam (for some programs), thesis/dissertation. *Entrance requirements:* For doctorate, GRE General Test, interview. Additional exam requirements/recommendations for international students: Required—TOEFL (minimum score 100 iBT). Electronic applications accepted. *Expenses:* Contact institution. *Faculty research:* Equity, urban adolescents, arts in education, globalization, multivariate analysis, psychometrics.

**North Central College,** School of Graduate and Professional Studies, Program in Liberal Studies, Naperville, IL 60566-7063. Offers culture and society (MALS). *Program availability:* Part-time, evening/weekend. *Faculty:* 8 full-time (5 women), 8 part-time/adjunct (4 women). *Students:* 6 full-time (1 woman), 13 part-time (9 women); includes 5 minority (1 Black or African American, non-Hispanic/Latino; 1 Asian, non-Hispanic/Latino; 3 Hispanic/Latino). Average age 29. 20 applicants, 60% accepted, 8 enrolled. In 2016, 10 master's awarded. *Degree requirements:* For master's, thesis optional, project. *Entrance requirements:* For master's, interview. Additional exam requirements/recommendations for international students: Required—TOEFL (minimum score 550 paper-based; 80 iBT), IELTS (minimum score 6.5). *Application deadline:* For fall admission, 8/15 for domestic students, 7/15 for international students; for winter admission, 12/1 for domestic students, 11/1 for international students; for spring admission, 2/1 for domestic students, 12/1 for international students. Applications are processed on a rolling basis. *Application fee:* $25. Electronic applications accepted. Application fee is waived when completed online. *Expenses:* Contact institution. *Financial support:* Scholarships/grants available. Support available to part-time students. Financial award applicants required to submit FAFSA. *Unit head:* Dr. Pamela Monaco, Dean of Graduate and Professional Studies, 630-637-5384, E-mail: pjmonaco@noctrl.edu. *Application contact:* Wendy Kulpinski, Director of Graduate and Professional Studies Admission, 630-637-5808, Fax: 630-637-5844, E-mail: wekulpinski@noctrl.edu.
Website: http://northcentralcollege.edu/admission/liberal-studies

**Northern Kentucky University,** Office of Graduate Programs, College of Arts and Sciences, Program in English, Highland Heights, KY 41099. Offers composition and rhetoric (Certificate); creative writing (Certificate); cultural studies and discourses (Certificate); English (MA); professional writing (Certificate). *Program availability:* Part-time, evening/weekend. *Degree requirements:* For master's, comprehensive exam (for some programs), capstone (thesis, portfolio, project, or exams); 30 hours of credit; for Certificate, 18 hours of credit. *Entrance requirements:* For master's, bachelor's degree in English or related field from regionally-accredited institution with minimum GPA of 3.0 in major or cognate area coursework; official transcripts for all undergraduate and graduate work; two letters of reference; for Certificate, official transcripts for all undergraduate and graduate work; bachelor's degree from regionally-accredited institution; minimum undergraduate GPA of 2.5. Additional exam requirements/recommendations for international students: Required—TOEFL (minimum score 79 iBT); Recommended—IELTS (minimum score 6.5). Electronic applications accepted.

**Northwest University,** College of Ministry, Kirkland, WA 98033. Offers ministry (MIM); missional leadership (MA); theology and culture (MA). *Program availability:* Part-time, evening/weekend, online learning. *Degree requirements:* For master's, comprehensive exam (for some programs), thesis (for some programs). *Entrance requirements:* Additional exam requirements/recommendations for international students: Required—TOEFL (minimum score 550 paper-based; 75 iBT). Electronic applications accepted.

**Old Dominion University,** College of Arts and Letters, Graduate Program in International Studies, Norfolk, VA 23529. Offers conflict and cooperation (MA, PhD); interdependence and transnationalism (MA, PhD); international cultural studies (MA, PhD); international political economy and development (MA, PhD); modeling and simulation (MA, PhD); U.S. foreign policy and international relations (MA, PhD). *Program availability:* Part-time. *Faculty:* 18 full-time (4 women). *Students:* 35 full-time (13 women), 38 part-time (20 women); includes 14 minority (9 Black or African American, non-Hispanic/Latino; 2 Asian, non-Hispanic/Latino; 1 Hispanic/Latino; 2 Two or more races, non-Hispanic/Latino), 19 international. Average age 37. 99 applicants, 54% accepted, 34 enrolled. In 2016, 24 master's, 11 doctorates awarded. Terminal master's awarded for partial completion of doctoral program. *Degree requirements:* For master's, one foreign language, comprehensive exam, thesis optional; for doctorate, one foreign language, comprehensive exam, thesis/dissertation. *Entrance requirements:* For master's, GRE General Test, sample of written work, 2 letters of recommendation; for doctorate, GRE General Test, sample of written work, 3 letters of recommendation. Additional exam requirements/recommendations for international students: Required—TOEFL (minimum score 570 paper-based). *Application deadline:* For fall admission, 1/15 for domestic and international students; for spring admission, 10/15 for domestic and international students. *Application fee:* $50. Electronic applications accepted. *Expenses:* Contact institution. *Financial support:* In 2016–17, 12 students received support, including 1 fellowship (averaging $15,000 per year), 5 research assistantships with

tuition reimbursements available (averaging $15,000 per year), 4 teaching assistantships with tuition reimbursements available (averaging $15,000 per year); career-related internships or fieldwork, institutionally sponsored loans, and unspecified assistantships also available. Financial award application deadline: 1/15; financial award applicants required to submit FAFSA. *Faculty research:* U.S. foreign policy, international security, Transatlantic and Transpacific relations, transnational issues, international political economy and development. *Total annual research expenditures:* $330,391. *Unit head:* Dr. Regina Karp, Graduate Program Director, 757-683-5700, Fax: 757-683-5701, E-mail: rkarp@odu.edu. *Application contact:* Dr. David C. Earnest, Associate Dean, 757-683-6077, Fax: 757-683-5746, E-mail: dearnest@odu.edu.
Website: http://www.odu.edu/gpis

**Pacific Northwest College of Art,** Program in Critical Theory and Creative Research, Portland, OR 97209. Offers MA, MA/MFA.

**Plymouth State University,** College of Graduate Studies, Graduate Studies in Education, Program in Integrated Arts, Plymouth, NH 03264-1595. Offers M Ed. *Degree requirements:* For master's, practicum.

**Regent University,** Graduate School, School of Divinity, Virginia Beach, VA 23464-9800. Offers divinity (M Div), including Biblical studies (M Div, MTS, PhD), chaplain ministry, Christian theology (M Div, MTS, PhD), church and ministry (M Div, MA), history of Christianity (M Div, MTS, PhD), inter-cultural studies (M Div, MA), interdisciplinary studies (M Div, MA, MTS), marketplace ministry, worship and media (M Div, MA); leadership and renewal (D Min), including Christian leadership and renewal, clinical pastoral education, community transformation, military ministry, ministry leadership coaching; practical theology (MA), including church and ministry (M Div, MA), inter-cultural studies (M Div, MA), interdisciplinary studies (M Div, MA, MTS), worship and media (M Div, MA); theological studies (MTS, PhD), including Biblical studies (M Div, MTS, PhD), Christian theology (M Div, MTS, PhD), history of Christianity (M Div, MTS, PhD), interdisciplinary studies (M Div, MA, MTS). *Accreditation:* ACIPE; ATS. *Program availability:* Part-time, evening/weekend, 100% online, blended/hybrid learning. *Faculty:* 15 full-time (3 women), 51 part-time/adjunct (6 women). *Students:* 148 full-time (60 women), 787 part-time (321 women); includes 506 minority (416 Black or African American, non-Hispanic/Latino; 1 American Indian or Alaska Native, non-Hispanic/Latino; 23 Asian, non-Hispanic/Latino; 54 Hispanic/Latino; 1 Native Hawaiian or other Pacific Islander, non-Hispanic/Latino; 11 Two or more races, non-Hispanic/Latino), 31 international. Average age 43. 1,020 applicants, 42% accepted, 276 enrolled. In 2016, 127 master's, 25 doctorates awarded. *Degree requirements:* For master's, comprehensive exam, thesis or alternative, internship; for doctorate, thesis/dissertation or alternative. *Entrance requirements:* For master's, minimum undergraduate GPA of 2.75, writing sample, personal goal statement, college transcripts; for doctorate, GRE, minimum graduate GPA of 3.5 (PhD), 3.0 (D Min); clergy recommendations; writing sample; transcripts; resume; interview. Additional exam requirements/recommendations for international students: Required—TOEFL (minimum score 577 paper-based). *Application deadline:* For fall admission, 5/1 priority date for domestic students. Applications are processed on a rolling basis. Application fee: $50. Electronic applications accepted. *Expenses:* Contact institution. *Financial support:* In 2016–17, 602 students received support. Career-related internships or fieldwork, scholarships/grants, and unspecified assistantships available. Support available to part-time students. *Faculty research:* Greek and Hebrew, theology, spiritual formation, global missions and world Christianity, women in ministry leadership. *Unit head:* Dr. Cornelius Bekker, Dean, 757-352-4401, Fax: 757-352-4597, E-mail: clbekker@regent.edu. *Application contact:* Heidi Cece, Assistant Vice President of Enrollment Management, 800-373-5504, Fax: 757-352-4381, E-mail: admissions@regent.edu.
Website: http://www.regent.edu/sod

**Regis College,** Program in Heritage Studies for a Global Society, Weston, MA 02493. Offers heritage studies for a global society (MA). *Program availability:* Part-time, blended/hybrid learning. *Degree requirements:* For master's, capstone. *Entrance requirements:* Additional exam requirements/recommendations for international students: Required—TOEFL; Recommended—IELTS. *Application deadline:* Applications are processed on a rolling basis. Application fee: $65. Electronic applications accepted. *Financial support:* Federal Work-Study and unspecified assistantships available. Financial award applicants required to submit FAFSA. *Unit head:* Kathryn Edney, Director, 781-768-7196.

**St. Francis Xavier University,** Graduate Studies, Department of Celtic Studies, Antigonish, NS B2G 2W5, Canada. Offers MA. *Degree requirements:* For master's, thesis. *Entrance requirements:* Additional exam requirements/recommendations for international students: Required—TOEFL (minimum score 580 paper-based). Application fee: $40. *Expenses: Tuition:* Full-time $9060 Canadian dollars; part-time $725 Canadian dollars per credit. *Required fees:* $789 Canadian dollars; $78.84 Canadian dollars per credit. Tuition and fees vary according to course load, degree level and program. *Faculty research:* Scottish Gaelic in Nova Scotia. *Unit head:* Dr. Michael Linkletter, Head, 902-867-3632, Fax: 902-867-5395, E-mail: mlinklet@stfx.ca. *Application contact:* Dr. Michael Linkletter, Head, 902-867-3632, Fax: 902-867-5395, E-mail: mlinklet@stfx.ca.
Website: http://sites.stfx.ca/celtic_studies/

**San Francisco State University,** Division of Graduate Studies, College of Health and Social Sciences, Human Sexuality Studies Program, San Francisco, CA 94132-1722. Offers MA. *Expenses:* Tuition, state resident: full-time $6738. Tuition, nonresident: full-time $15,666. *Required fees:* $1012. Tuition and fees vary according to degree level and program. *Unit head:* Dr. Andreana Clay, Chair, 415-338-1090, Fax: 415-338-2653, E-mail: andreana@sfsu.edu. *Application contact:* Dr. Jessica Fields, Graduate Coordinator, 415-405-0589, Fax: 415-338-2653, E-mail: jfields@sfsu.edu.
Website: http://sxs.sfsu.edu/

**School of Visual Arts,** Graduate Programs, Critical Theory and the Arts Department, New York, NY 10010-3994. Offers MA. *Degree requirements:* For master's, thesis, 36 credits with minimum cumulative GPA of 3.0. *Entrance requirements:* For master's, writing statement of approximately 1,000 words explaining the development of interest in pursuing an MA; transcripts for previous colleges /universities attended; three letters of recommendation; current resume/curriculum vitae. Additional exam requirements/recommendations for international students: Required—TOEFL (minimum score 600 paper-based; 100 iBT). Electronic applications accepted. *Expenses:* Contact institution.

**Simmons College,** College of Arts and Sciences, Boston, MA 02115. Offers elementary education (MAT); English (MA); gender/cultural studies (MA); history (MA); public health (MPH); public policy (MPP). *Program availability:* Part-time. *Faculty:* 19 full-time (12 women), 1 (woman) part-time/adjunct. *Students:* 6 full-time (all women), 38 part-time (27 women); includes 10 minority (4 Black or African American, non-Hispanic/Latino; 1 Asian, non-Hispanic/Latino; 2 Hispanic/Latino; 3 Two or more races, non-Hispanic/Latino), 1 international. Average age 26. 50 applicants, 88% accepted, 17 enrolled. In 2016, 19 master's awarded. Terminal master's awarded for partial completion of doctoral program. *Degree requirements:* For master's, thesis (for some programs). *Entrance requirements:* For master's, GRE. Additional exam requirements/ recommendations for international students: Required—TOEFL (minimum score 600 paper-based; 100 iBT). *Application deadline:* For fall admission, 8/1 for domestic and

international students; for spring admission, 12/15 for domestic and international students; for summer admission, 5/1 for domestic and international students. Applications are processed on a rolling basis. Application fee: $35. Electronic applications accepted. *Expenses:* $1,050 per credit, $4,200 per course, $52 activity fee per semester. *Financial support:* In 2016–17, 4 fellowships with partial tuition reimbursements, 22 teaching assistantships with partial tuition reimbursements were awarded; scholarships/grants and unspecified assistantships also available. Support available to part-time students. Financial award applicants required to submit FAFSA. *Unit head:* Dr. Renee White, Dean, 617-521-2079. *Application contact:* Patricia Flaherty, Director, Graduate Studies Admission, 617-521-3902, Fax: 617-521-3058, E-mail: gsa@simmons.edu.
Website: http://www.simmons.edu/gradstudies/

**Simon Fraser University,** Office of Graduate Studies and Postdoctoral Fellows, Faculty of Education, Program in Languages, Cultures, and Literacies, Burnaby, BC V5A 1S6, Canada. Offers PhD. *Unit head:* Dr. Shawn Bullock, Associate Dean, Graduate Studies in Education, 778-782-4102, Fax: 778-782-4320, E-mail: mesbit@sfu.ca. *Application contact:* Administrative Assistant, 778-782-9488, Fax: 778-782-4320, E-mail: gse-sec@sfu.ca.

**Southern Illinois University Carbondale,** Graduate School, College of Liberal Arts, Department of Foreign Languages and Literatures, Carbondale, IL 62901-4701. Offers MA. *Program availability:* Part-time. *Degree requirements:* For master's, one foreign language, thesis. *Entrance requirements:* For master's, minimum GPA of 2.7. Additional exam requirements/recommendations for international students: Required—TOEFL. *Faculty research:* Bibliography, historical linguistics, language pedagogy, philology, commercial facets.

**Stanford University,** School of Humanities and Sciences, Department of Anthropology, Stanford, CA 94305-2004. Offers anthropology (MA); archaeology (PhD); culture and society (PhD); ecology and environment (PhD). Terminal master's awarded for partial completion of doctoral program. *Degree requirements:* For master's, thesis; for doctorate, one foreign language, thesis/dissertation. *Entrance requirements:* For master's and doctorate, GRE General Test. Additional exam requirements/ recommendations for international students: Required—TOEFL. Electronic applications accepted. *Expenses: Tuition:* Full-time $47,331. *Required fees:* $609.

**Stony Brook University, State University of New York,** Graduate School, College of Arts and Sciences, Department of Cultural Studies and Comparative Literature, Stony Brook, NY 11794. Offers comparative literature (MA, PhD); cultural studies (PhD, Certificate). *Program availability:* Evening/weekend. *Faculty:* 12 full-time (4 women). *Students:* 57 full-time (40 women), 4 part-time (all women); includes 7 minority (2 Black or African American, non-Hispanic/Latino; 4 Asian, non-Hispanic/Latino; 1 Hispanic/Latino), 24 international. Average age 34. 58 applicants, 48% accepted, 14 enrolled. In 2016, 3 master's, 1 doctorate, 3 other advanced degrees awarded. Terminal master's awarded for partial completion of doctoral program. *Degree requirements:* For master's, 2 foreign languages, exam; for doctorate, 3 foreign languages, comprehensive exam, thesis/dissertation. *Entrance requirements:* For master's and doctorate, GRE General Test, minimum GPA of 3.5 in major, 3.0 overall. Additional exam requirements/ recommendations for international students: Required—TOEFL. *Application deadline:* For fall admission, 1/15 for domestic students; for spring admission, 10/1 for domestic students. Application fee: $100. Electronic applications accepted. *Expenses:* Contact institution. *Financial support:* In 2016–17, 1 research assistantship, 30 teaching assistantships were awarded; fellowships also available. *Faculty research:* Humanities, women's studies, literary criticism, gender studies, philosophy. *Unit head:* Dr. Robert Harvey, Chair, 631-632-7464, E-mail: robert.harvey@stonybrook.edu. *Application contact:* Mary Moran-Luba, Coordinator, 631-632-7460, Fax: 631-632-5707, E-mail: mary.moran-luba@stonybrook.edu.
Website: http://www.stonybrook.edu/commcms/cat/index.html

**Taylor College and Seminary,** Graduate and Professional Programs, Edmonton, AB T6J 4T3, Canada. Offers Christian studies (Diploma); intercultural studies (MA, Diploma), including intercultural studies (Diploma), TESOL; theology (M Div, MTS). *Accreditation:* ATS. *Program availability:* Part-time, online learning. *Degree requirements:* For master's, thesis optional. *Entrance requirements:* Additional exam requirements/recommendations for international students: Required—TOEFL (minimum score 550 paper-based; 80 iBT), IELTS (minimum score 6.5). *Faculty research:* Biblical studies, administration and organization, world religions, ethics, missiology.

**Texas A&M University,** College of Liberal Arts, Department of Performance Studies, College Station, TX 77843. Offers MA. *Faculty:* 12. *Students:* 1 (woman) full-time; minority (Black or African American, non-Hispanic/Latino). Average age 25. 6 applicants, 83% accepted. In 2016, 8 master's awarded. *Degree requirements:* For master's, comprehensive exam (for some programs), thesis or alternative. *Entrance requirements:* For master's, GRE General Test. Additional exam requirements/ recommendations for international students: Required—TOEFL (minimum score 550 paper-based; 80 iBT), IELTS (minimum score 6), PTE (minimum score 53). *Application deadline:* For fall admission, 12/1 for domestic students; for spring admission, 10/15 for domestic students. Applications are processed on a rolling basis. Application fee: $50 ($90 for international students). Electronic applications accepted. *Expenses:* Contact institution. *Financial support:* Unspecified assistantships available. Financial award application deadline: 3/15; financial award applicants required to submit FAFSA. *Unit head:* Dr. Donnlee Dox, Department Head, 979-458-1870, E-mail: dox@tamu.edu. *Application contact:* Dr. Kirsten Pullen, Director of Graduate Studies, 979-845-2899, Fax: 979-845-5164, E-mail: kpullen@tamu.edu.
Website: http://performancestudies.tamu.edu/

**Texas A&M University–Kingsville,** College of Graduate Studies, College of Arts and Sciences, Department of Language and Literature, Program in Cultural Studies, Kingsville, TX 78363. Offers MA. *Entrance requirements:* Additional exam requirements/recommendations for international students: Required—TOEFL (minimum score 550 paper-based; 79 iBT); Recommended—IELTS. Electronic applications accepted.

**Texas Tech University,** Graduate School, College of Arts and Sciences, Department of Classical and Modern Languages and Literatures, Lubbock, TX 79409. Offers applied linguistics (MA); classics (MA); German (MA); languages and cultures (MA); Romance languages (MA); Spanish (PhD); MBA/MA. *Program availability:* Part-time. *Faculty:* 56 full-time (37 women), 4 part-time/adjunct (2 women). *Students:* 80 full-time (39 women), 13 part-time (9 women); includes 20 minority (19 Hispanic/Latino; 1 Two or more races, non-Hispanic/Latino), 49 international. Average age 32. 68 applicants, 68% accepted, 31 enrolled. In 2016, 30 master's, 4 doctorates awarded. *Degree requirements:* For master's, comprehensive exam, thesis or alternative; for doctorate, comprehensive exam, thesis/dissertation. *Entrance requirements:* Additional exam requirements/ recommendations for international students: Required—TOEFL (minimum score 550 paper-based; 79 iBT). *Application deadline:* For fall admission, 6/1 priority date for domestic students, 1/15 priority date for international students; for spring admission, 9/1 priority date for domestic students, 6/15 priority date for international students. Applications are processed on a rolling basis. Application fee: $75. Electronic applications accepted. *Expenses:* $300 per credit hour full-time resident tuition, $708 per

credit hour full-time non-resident tuition; $50.50 per credit hour fee plus $608 per term fee. *Financial support:* In 2016–17, 78 students received support, including 60 fellowships (averaging $2,488 per year), 76 teaching assistantships (averaging $13,011 per year); research assistantships, Federal Work-Study, scholarships/grants, and unspecified assistantships also available. Financial award application deadline: 4/15; financial award applicants required to submit FAFSA. *Faculty research:* Literature, comparative literature, linguistics, culture, applied linguistics. *Total annual research expenditures:* $36,152. *Unit head:* Dr. Erin Collopy, Chair and Associate Professor, 806-834-8497, Fax: 806-742-3306, E-mail: erin.collopy@ttu.edu. *Application contact:* Carla Burrus, Senior Advisor, 806-834-3282, Fax: 806-742-3306, E-mail: carla.burrus@ttu.edu.
Website: http://www.depts.ttu.edu/classic_modern/

**Trent University,** Graduate Studies, Program in Cultural Studies, Peterborough, ON K9J 7B8, Canada. Offers PhD.

**Trinity College,** Graduate Programs, Program in American Studies, Hartford, CT 06106-3100. Offers American culture studies (MA); museums and communities (MA). *Program availability:* Part-time, evening/weekend. *Degree requirements:* For master's, thesis or alternative. *Entrance requirements:* For master's, minimum GPA of 3.0.

**Union Institute & University,** Master of Arts Program, Cincinnati, OH 45206-1925. Offers creativity studies (MA); health and wellness (MA); history and culture (MA); leadership, public policy, and social issues (MA); literature and writing (MA). *Program availability:* Part-time, online only, 100% online. *Faculty:* 2 full-time (both women), 9 part-time/adjunct (7 women). *Students:* 9 full-time (7 women), 70 part-time (56 women); includes 33 minority (22 Black or African American, non-Hispanic/Latino; 1 American Indian or Alaska Native, non-Hispanic/Latino; 6 Hispanic/Latino; 4 Two or more races, non-Hispanic/Latino). Average age 40. In 2016, 45 master's awarded. *Degree requirements:* For master's, thesis. *Entrance requirements:* For master's, transcript, essay, 3 letters of recommendation, resume. Additional exam requirements/recommendations for international students: Recommended—TOEFL. *Application deadline:* For spring admission, 3/13 for domestic students. Applications are processed on a rolling basis. Application fee: $50. Electronic applications accepted. *Expenses:* Contact institution. *Financial support:* Career-related internships or fieldwork and tuition waivers available. Financial award applicants required to submit FAFSA. *Unit head:* Elden Golden, Director, 513-487-1153, E-mail: elden.golden@myunion.edu. *Application contact:* Director of Admissions, 800-861-6400.

**Union University,** Institute for International and Intercultural Studies, Jackson, TN 38305-3697. Offers MAIS. *Program availability:* Part-time, evening/weekend. *Degree requirements:* For master's, capstone course. *Entrance requirements:* For master's, GRE, minimum undergraduate GPA of 3.0, 3 letters of reference. Additional exam requirements/recommendations for international students: Required—TOEFL (minimum score 560 paper-based). Electronic applications accepted. *Expenses: Tuition:* Full-time $10,300. *Required fees:* $20. *Faculty research:* International education, ethnographic field research, intercultural training for professionals and students, language and culture.

**University of Alaska Fairbanks,** College of Liberal Arts, Department of Cross-Cultural Studies, Fairbanks, AK 99775-6300. Offers MA. *Program availability:* Part-time. *Faculty:* 4 full-time (2 women). *Students:* 1 (woman) full-time, 4 part-time (all women); includes 6 minority (3 American Indian or Alaska Native, non-Hispanic/Latino; 2 Hispanic/Latino; 1 Native Hawaiian or other Pacific Islander, non-Hispanic/Latino). Average age 44. 1 applicant, 100% accepted, 1 enrolled. *Degree requirements:* For master's, comprehensive exam, project, oral defense of project. *Entrance requirements:* For master's, bachelor's degree from accredited institution with minimum cumulative undergraduate and major GPA of 3.0. Additional exam requirements/recommendations for international students: Required—TOEFL (minimum score 550 paper-based; 79 iBT), IELTS (minimum score 8.5). *Application deadline:* For fall admission, 6/1 for domestic students, 3/1 for international students; for spring admission, 10/15 for domestic students, 9/1 for international students. Applications are processed on a rolling basis. Application fee: $60. Electronic applications accepted. *Expenses:* Tuition, state resident: full-time $7992; part-time $444 per credit. Tuition, nonresident: full-time $16,326; part-time $907 per credit. *Required fees:* $39 per credit. $322 per semester. Tuition and fees vary according to course level, course load, campus/location, program and reciprocity agreements. *Financial support:* Fellowships with full tuition reimbursements, research assistantships with full tuition reimbursements, teaching assistantships with full tuition reimbursements, Federal Work-Study, scholarships/grants, health care benefits, and unspecified assistantships available. Support available to part-time students. Financial award application deadline: 7/1; financial award applicants required to submit FAFSA. *Faculty research:* Alaska native literature, oral traditions, history, law and policy, cultures, art; Native American religion and philosophy. *Total annual research expenditures:* $10,000. *Unit head:* Lawrence Kaplan, Acting Director of the Center for Cross-Cultural Studies, 907-474-1902, Fax: 907-474-1957, E-mail: fycxcs@uaf.edu. *Application contact:* Mary Kreta, Director of Admissions, 907-474-7500, Fax: 907-474-7097, E-mail: admissions@uaf.edu.
Website: http://www.uaf.edu/cxcs

**University of California, Davis,** Graduate Studies, Graduate Group in Cultural Studies, Davis, CA 95616. Offers MA, PhD. *Degree requirements:* For master's, thesis; for doctorate, thesis/dissertation. *Entrance requirements:* For doctorate, GRE. Additional exam requirements/recommendations for international students: Required—TOEFL (minimum score 550 paper-based). Electronic applications accepted.

**University of California, Irvine,** School of Humanities, Program in Culture and Theory, Irvine, CA 92697. Offers PhD. *Students:* 14 full-time (10 women); includes 8 minority (2 Black or African American, non-Hispanic/Latino; 3 Asian, non-Hispanic/Latino; 2 Hispanic/Latino; 1 Two or more races, non-Hispanic/Latino). Average age 31. In 2016, 4 doctorates awarded. Application fee: $105 ($125 for international students). *Unit head:* Nasrin Rahimieh, Interim Director, 949-824-0406, E-mail: nasrin.rahimieh@uci.edu. *Application contact:* Arielle Hinojosa, Graduate Counselor, 949-824-6441, Fax: 949-824-7006, E-mail: hinojosa@uci.edu.
Website: http://www.humanities.uci.edu/cultureandtheory/

**University of California, Riverside,** Graduate Division, Department of Ethnic Studies, Riverside, CA 92521. Offers cultural politics and production (PhD). Terminal master's awarded for partial completion of doctoral program. *Degree requirements:* For doctorate, variable foreign language requirement, comprehensive exam, thesis/dissertation. *Entrance requirements:* For doctorate, GRE, writing sample, statement of purpose, personal history statement, 3 letters of recommendation. Additional exam requirements/recommendations for international students: Required—TOEFL (minimum score 550 paper-based; 80 iBT); Recommended—IELTS (minimum score 7.0). Electronic applications accepted. *Expenses:* Tuition, state resident: full-time $16,666. Tuition, nonresident: full-time $31,768. *Required fees:* $11,055.54 per quarter. $3685.18 per quarter. Tuition and fees vary according to campus/location and program. *Faculty research:* The political economy of race, class, gender, sexuality, cultural production, the state, law, criminal justice and grass roots responses.

**University of California, Santa Barbara,** Graduate Division, College of Letters and Sciences, Division of Social Sciences, Department of Global Studies, Santa Barbara, CA 93106-7065. Offers global culture, ideology, and religion (MA, PhD); global

government, human rights, and civil society (MA, PhD); political economy, sustainable development, and the environment (MA, PhD). *Degree requirements:* For master's, one foreign language, thesis, 2 years of a second language; for doctorate, one foreign language, thesis/dissertation, reading proficiency in at least one language other than English. *Entrance requirements:* For master's, GRE, 2 years of a second language with minimum B grade in the final term, statement of purpose, resume or curriculum vitae, 3 letters of recommendation, transcripts (from all post-secondary institutions attended), writing sample (15-20 pages); for doctorate, GRE, statement of purpose, personal achievements/contributions statement, resume or curriculum vitae, 3 letters of recommendation, transcripts from all post-secondary institutions attended, writing sample (15-20 pages). Additional exam requirements/recommendations for international students: Required—TOEFL (minimum score 600 paper-based; 94 iBT), IELTS (minimum score 7). Electronic applications accepted.

**University of Dayton,** Department of English, Dayton, OH 45469. Offers literary and cultural studies (MA); teaching English to speakers of other languages (TESOL) (MA); writing and rhetoric (MA). *Program availability:* Part-time. *Faculty:* 22 full-time (11 women). *Students:* 15 full-time (10 women), 2 part-time (1 woman); includes 1 minority (Black or African American, non-Hispanic/Latino), 7 international. Average age 27. 55 applicants, 29% accepted. In 2016, 8 master's awarded. *Degree requirements:* For master's, thesis. *Entrance requirements:* For master's, 24 undergraduate-level semester hours in literature and/or writing; minimum GPA of 3.0; transcripts; personal statement; 8-10 page writing sample; three professional letters of recommendation. Additional exam requirements/recommendations for international students: Required—TOEFL (minimum score 550 paper-based, 80 iBT) or IELTS. *Application deadline:* For fall admission, 6/15 priority date for domestic and international students; for spring admission, 12/15 priority date for domestic and international students. Applications are processed on a rolling basis. Application fee: $0 ($50 for international students). Electronic applications accepted. *Expenses:* $890 per credit hour, $25 registration fee. *Financial support:* In 2016–17, 9 teaching assistantships with full tuition reimbursements (averaging $11,000 per year) were awarded; institutionally sponsored loans and health care benefits also available. Financial award application deadline: 12/15; financial award applicants required to submit FAFSA. *Faculty research:* Gender and Victorian periodicals; literature and human rights; Paul Lawrence Dunbar; the archetype of the Indian princess; Amish country. *Total annual research expenditures:* $35,000. *Unit head:* Dr. Andrew Slade, Chair, 937-229-3434, Fax: 937-229-3563, E-mail: aslade1@udayton.edu. *Application contact:* Dr. Tereza Szeghi, Director of Graduate Studies, 937-229-3443, E-mail: tszeghi1@udayton.edu.
Website: https://www.udayton.edu/artssciences/academics/english/welcome/index.php

**University of Denver,** Division of Arts, Humanities and Social Sciences, Department of Media, Film and Journalism Studies, Denver, CO 80208. Offers international and intercultural communication (MA); media and globalization (MA). *Program availability:* Part-time. *Faculty:* 16 full-time (10 women), 5 part-time/adjunct (4 women). *Students:* 8 full-time (7 women), 18 part-time (14 women); includes 8 minority (1 Black or African American, non-Hispanic/Latino; 2 Asian, non-Hispanic/Latino; 5 Hispanic/Latino), 1 international. Average age 27. 54 applicants, 78% accepted, 14 enrolled. In 2016, 21 master's awarded. *Degree requirements:* For master's, thesis (for some programs). *Entrance requirements:* For master's, GRE General Test, bachelor's degree, transcripts, personal statement, three letters of recommendation. Additional exam requirements/recommendations for international students: Required—TOEFL (minimum score 620 paper-based; 105 iBT). *Application deadline:* For fall admission, 2/15 priority date for domestic students, 1/1 priority date for international students. Applications are processed on a rolling basis. Application fee: $65. Electronic applications accepted. *Expenses:* $29,022 per year full-time. *Financial support:* In 2016–17, 16 students received support, including 2 teaching assistantships with tuition reimbursements available (averaging $12,500 per year); career-related internships or fieldwork, Federal Work-Study, institutionally sponsored loans, scholarships/grants, and unspecified assistantships also available. Support available to part-time students. Financial award application deadline: 2/15; financial award applicants required to submit FAFSA. *Faculty research:* Branding; public relations; health communication; social media; international communication. *Unit head:* Dr. Lynn Schofield Clark, Professor and Chair, 303-871-3984, Fax: 303-871-4949, E-mail: lynn.clark@du.edu. *Application contact:* Information Contact, 303-871-2166, E-mail: mfjs@du.edu.
Website: http://www.du.edu/ahss/mfjs

**University of Denver,** University College, Denver, CO 80208. Offers arts and culture (MA, Certificate); communication management (MS, Certificate), including translation studies (Certificate); world history and culture (Certificate); environmental policy and management (MS); geographic information systems (MS); global affairs (MA, Certificate), including human capital in organizations (Certificate), philanthropic leadership (Certificate), project management (Certificate), strategic innovation and change (Certificate); healthcare leadership (MS); information communications and technology (MS); leadership and organizations (MS); professional creative writing (MA, Certificate), including emergency planning and response (Certificate), organizational security (Certificate); security management (MS, Certificate); strategic human resources (Certificate). *Program availability:* Part-time, evening/weekend, online learning. *Faculty:* 118 part-time/adjunct (62 women). *Students:* 59 full-time (22 women), 1,285 part-time (750 women); includes 316 minority (111 Black or African American, non-Hispanic/Latino; 8 American Indian or Alaska Native, non-Hispanic/Latino; 39 Asian, non-Hispanic/Latino; 123 Hispanic/Latino; 3 Native Hawaiian or other Pacific Islander, non-Hispanic/Latino; 32 Two or more races, non-Hispanic/Latino), 85 international. Average age 35. 703 applicants, 89% accepted, 390 enrolled. In 2016, 428 master's, 138 other advanced degrees awarded. *Degree requirements:* For master's, capstone project. *Entrance requirements:* For master's, transcripts, two letters of recommendation, personal statement, resume. Additional exam requirements/recommendations for international students: Required—TOEFL (minimum score 550 paper-based; 80 iBT). *Application deadline:* For fall admission, 6/21 priority date for domestic students, 5/1 priority date for international students; for winter admission, 9/14 priority date for domestic students, 9/19 priority date for international students; for spring admission, 1/11 priority date for domestic students, 12/12 priority date for international students; for summer admission, 3/29 priority date for domestic students, 3/6 priority date for international students. Applications are processed on a rolling basis. Application fee: $75. Electronic applications accepted. *Expenses:* $7,236 per year full-time. *Financial support:* In 2016–17, 27 students received support, including 1 teaching assistantship (averaging $1,489 per year). Financial award applicants required to submit FAFSA. *Unit head:* Dr. Michael McGuire, Dean, 303-871-3518, Fax: 303-871-3303, E-mail: mmcguire@du.edu. *Application contact:* Information Contact, 303-871-2291, E-mail: ucoladm@du.edu.
Website: http://universitycollege.du.edu/

**University of Hawaii at Hilo,** Program in Hawaiian and Indigenous Language and Culture Revitalization, Hilo, HI 96720-4091. Offers PhD. *Entrance requirements:* Additional exam requirements/recommendations for international students: Required—TOEFL, IELTS. Electronic applications accepted.

**University of Hawaii at Hilo,** Program in Indigenous Language and Culture Education, Hilo, HI 96720-4091. Offers MA. *Entrance requirements:* Additional exam requirements/

recommendations for international students: Required—TOEFL, IELTS. Electronic applications accepted.

**University of Hawaii at Manoa,** Graduate Division, International Cultural Studies Graduate Certificate Program, Honolulu, HI 96822. Offers Graduate Certificate. *Program availability:* Part-time. *Entrance requirements:* For degree, GRE General Test. Additional exam requirements/recommendations for international students: Required—TOEFL (minimum score 540 paper-based; 76 iBT), IELTS (minimum score 5).

**University of Houston,** College of Liberal Arts and Social Sciences, Department of Modern and Classical Languages, Houston, TX 77204. Offers world cultures and literatures (MA). *Degree requirements:* For master's, one foreign language, thesis optional. *Entrance requirements:* For master's, GRE General Test, minimum GPA of 3.0 in last 60 hours of course work. Additional exam requirements/recommendations for international students: Required—TOEFL (minimum score 500 paper-based). Electronic applications accepted.

**University of Houston–Clear Lake,** School of Human Sciences and Humanities, Programs in Human Sciences, Houston, TX 77058-1002. Offers behavioral sciences (MA), including criminology, cross cultural studies, general psychology, sociology; clinical psychology (MA); criminology (MA); cross cultural studies (MA); family therapy (MA); fitness and human performance (MA); school psychology (MA). *Accreditation:* AAMFT/COAMFTE. *Program availability:* Part-time, evening/weekend, online learning. *Degree requirements:* For master's, thesis or alternative. *Entrance requirements:* For master's, GRE General Test. Additional exam requirements/recommendations for international students: Required—TOEFL (minimum score 550 paper-based). Electronic applications accepted. *Faculty research:* Smoking cessation, adolescent sexuality, white collar crime, serial murder, human factors/human computer interaction.

**The University of Kansas,** Graduate Studies, School of Education, Department of Educational Leadership and Policy Studies, Education Leadership and Policy Program, Lawrence, KS 66045-3101. Offers policy studies (PhD); social and cultural studies (MSE, PhD). *Program availability:* Part-time, evening/weekend. *Students:* 123 full-time (66 women), 35 part-time (17 women); includes 31 minority (12 Black or African American, non-Hispanic/Latino; 2 American Indian or Alaska Native, non-Hispanic/Latino; 3 Asian, non-Hispanic/Latino; 7 Hispanic/Latino; 7 Two or more races, non-Hispanic/Latino; 24 international. Average age 38. 36 applicants, 72% accepted, 16 enrolled. In 2016, 26 doctorates awarded. *Entrance requirements:* For master's, minimum GPA of 3.0, resume or curriculum vitae, statement of purpose, official academic transcripts, three letters of recommendation; for doctorate, GRE General Test, minimum graduate GPA of 3.5, resume or curriculum vitae, statement of purpose, official academic transcripts, three letters of recommendation, writing sample. Additional exam requirements/recommendations for international students: Required—TOEFL or IELTS. *Application deadline:* For fall admission, 7/1 for domestic and international students; for spring admission, 11/1 for domestic and international students; for summer admission, 4/1 for domestic and international students. Application fee: $65 ($85 for international students). Electronic applications accepted. *Financial support:* Fellowships, research assistantships, teaching assistantships, scholarships/grants, and unspecified assistantships available. Financial award application deadline: 3/15. *Faculty research:* Historical and philosophical issues in education, education policy and leadership, higher education faculty, research on college students, education technology. *Unit head:* Dr. Susan B. Twombly, Chair, 785-864-9721, E-mail: stwombly@ku.edu. *Application contact:* Denise Brubaker, Admissions Coordinator, 785-864-7973, E-mail: brubaker@ku.edu.
Website: http://elps.soe.ku.edu/

**University of Louisville,** Graduate School, College of Arts and Sciences, Department of Comparative Humanities, Louisville, KY 40292-0001. Offers civic leadership (MA); culture, criticism, and contemporary thought (PhD); linguistics (MA); public arts and letters (PhD); traditional humanities (MA); MA/JD; MA/MBA. *Program availability:* Part-time. *Faculty:* 15 full-time (6 women), 2 part-time/adjunct (both women). *Students:* 49 full-time (32 women), 21 part-time (12 women); includes 11 minority (3 Black or African American, non-Hispanic/Latino; 2 Asian, non-Hispanic/Latino; 1 Hispanic/Latino; 5 Two or more races, non-Hispanic/Latino), 4 international. Average age 38. 21 applicants, 71% accepted, 10 enrolled. In 2016, 3 master's, 2 doctorates awarded. *Degree requirements:* For master's, one foreign language, thesis or alternative, directed study culminating project; for doctorate, 2 foreign languages, comprehensive exam, thesis/dissertation, internship. *Entrance requirements:* For master's, GRE General Test, two letters of recommendation, transcripts from all institutions attended; for doctorate, GRE General Test, three letters of recommendation, statement of intent, scholarly writing sample, transcripts from all institutions attended. Additional exam requirements/recommendations for international students: Recommended—TOEFL. *Application deadline:* For fall admission, 1/15 for domestic and international students. Application fee: $60. Electronic applications accepted. *Expenses:* Contact institution. *Financial support:* In 2016–17, 1 fellowship with full tuition reimbursement (averaging $18,000 per year), 10 teaching assistantships with full tuition reimbursements (averaging $18,000 per year) were awarded. Financial award application deadline: 1/15. *Faculty research:* Literary studies, medieval studies;, religious studies, linguistics, translation studies. *Total annual research expenditures:* $7,733. *Unit head:* Dr. Ann Hall, Chair, 502-852-6805, Fax: 502-852-0078, E-mail: ann.hall@louisville.edu. *Application contact:* Libby Leggett, Director, Graduate Admissions, 502-852-3101, Fax: 502-852-6536, E-mail: gradadm@louisville.edu.
Website: http://louisville.edu/humanities/

**The University of Manchester,** School of Arts, Histories and Cultures, Manchester, United Kingdom. Offers anthropology, media and performance (PhD); applied theatre professional (PhD); archaeology (PhD); art history and visual studies (PhD); arts management and cultural policy (PhD); classics and ancient history (PhD); composition (PhD); creative writing (PhD); drama (PhD); economic and social history (PhD); electroacoustic composition (PhD); English and American studies (PhD); history (PhD); humanitarianism and conflict response (PhD); museology (PhD); music (PhD); musicology (PhD); religions and theology (PhD).

**The University of Manchester,** School of Languages, Linguistics and Cultures, Manchester, United Kingdom. Offers Arab world studies (PhD); Chinese studies (M Phil, PhD); East Asian studies (M Phil); English language (PhD); French studies (M Phil, PhD); German studies (M Phil, PhD); interpreting studies (PhD); Italian studies (M Phil, PhD); Japanese studies (M Phil, PhD); Latin American cultural studies (M Phil, PhD); linguistics (M Phil, PhD); Middle Eastern studies (M Phil, PhD); Polish studies (M Phil, PhD); Portuguese studies (M Phil, PhD); Russian studies (M Phil, PhD); Spanish studies (M Phil, PhD); translation and intercultural studies (M Phil, PhD).

**The University of Manchester,** School of Social Sciences, Manchester, United Kingdom. Offers ethnographic documentary (M Phil); interdisciplinary study of culture (PhD); philosophy (PhD); politics (PhD); social anthropology (PhD); social anthropology with visual media (PhD); social change (PhD); social statistics (PhD); sociology (PhD); visual anthropology (M Phil).

**University of Massachusetts Boston,** College of Liberal Arts, Program in Transnational, Cultural, and Community Studies, Boston, MA 02125-3393. Offers MS. *Students:* 10 full-time (8 women), 3 part-time (all women); includes 11 minority (2 Black

or African American, non-Hispanic/Latino; 4 Asian, non-Hispanic/Latino; 4 Hispanic/Latino; 1 Two or more races, non-Hispanic/Latino), 1 international. Average age 33. 8 applicants, 100% accepted, 6 enrolled. *Expenses:* Tuition, state resident: full-time $16,863. Tuition, nonresident: full-time $32,913. *Required fees:* $177. *Unit head:* Dr. Karen L. Suyemoto, Director, 617-287-6370, E-mail: tccs.program@umb.edu. *Application contact:* Peggy Roldan Patel, Graduate Admissions Coordinator, 617-287-6400, Fax: 617-287-6236, E-mail: bos.gadm@dpc.umassp.edu.

**University of Minnesota, Twin Cities Campus,** Graduate School, College of Liberal Arts, Department of Cultural Studies and Comparative Literature, Program in Comparative Studies in Discourse and Society, Minneapolis, MN 55455-0213. Offers PhD. *Degree requirements:* For doctorate, 2 foreign languages, thesis/dissertation. *Entrance requirements:* For doctorate, GRE General Test, sample of written work. Additional exam requirements/recommendations for international students: Required—TOEFL. *Faculty research:* Cultural theory; music; architecture, space, and urbanism; body and gender; film and popular culture.

**University of Montana,** Graduate School, Phyllis J. Washington College of Education and Human Sciences, Department of Counselor Education, Missoula, MT 59812-0002. Offers clinical mental health counseling (MA); counseling and supervision (Ed D); counselor education (Ed S); intercultural youth and family development (MA); school counseling (MA). *Accreditation:* ACA. *Degree requirements:* For doctorate, thesis/dissertation. *Entrance requirements:* For master's, doctorate, and Ed S, GRE General Test. Additional exam requirements/recommendations for international students: Required—TOEFL.

**University of New Mexico,** Graduate Studies, College of Education, Program in Language, Literacy and Sociocultural Studies, Albuquerque, NM 87131. Offers American Indian education (MA); bilingual education (MA, PhD); educational linguistics (PhD); educational thought and sociocultural studies (MA, PhD); literacy/language arts (MA, PhD); social studies (MA); TESOL (MA, PhD). *Faculty:* 17 full-time (10 women), 4 part-time/adjunct (3 women). *Students:* 57 full-time (38 women), 129 part-time (105 women); includes 102 minority (8 Black or African American, non-Hispanic/Latino; 16 American Indian or Alaska Native, non-Hispanic/Latino; 6 Asian, non-Hispanic/Latino; 67 Hispanic/Latino; 5 Two or more races, non-Hispanic/Latino), 32 international. Average age 39. 50 applicants, 60% accepted, 23 enrolled. In 2016, 36 master's, 4 doctorates awarded. *Degree requirements:* For master's, comprehensive exam, thesis optional; for doctorate, comprehensive exam, thesis/dissertation, research skills. *Entrance requirements:* For master's, letter of intent, 3 letters of recommendation, resume, BA/BS, department demographic form, transcripts; for doctorate, writing sample, letter of intent, 3 letters of recommendation, resume, BA/BS, MA, department demographic form, transcripts. Additional exam requirements/recommendations for international students: Required—TOEFL. *Application deadline:* For fall admission, 12/1 for domestic and international students; for spring admission, 9/15 for domestic and international students. Application fee: $50. Electronic applications accepted. *Financial support:* Fellowships, research assistantships, teaching assistantships with tuition reimbursements, career-related internships or fieldwork, institutionally sponsored loans, scholarships/grants, and unspecified assistantships available. Support available to part-time students. Financial award application deadline: 3/1; financial award applicants required to submit FAFSA. *Faculty research:* School reform, professional development, history of education, Native American education, politics of education, feminism and issues of sexual identity, critical race theory, bilingualism, literacy reading, adolescent literature, second language acquisition, critical theory and schooling, indigenous languages. *Unit head:* Dr. Lois M. Meyer, Chair, 505-277-7244, Fax: 505-277-8362, E-mail: lsmeyer@unm.edu. *Application contact:* Debra Schaffer, Administrative Assistant, 505-277-0437, Fax: 505-277-8362, E-mail: schaffer@unm.edu.
Website: http://coe.unm.edu/departments-programs/llss/index.html

**University of North Carolina at Asheville,** Master of Liberal Arts and Sciences Program, Asheville, NC 28804-3299. Offers climate change and society (Graduate Certificate); environmental and cultural sustainability (Graduate Certificate). *Program availability:* Part-time, evening/weekend. *Faculty:* 5 full-time (1 woman), 4 part-time/adjunct (0 women). *Students:* 2 full-time (1 woman), 19 part-time (9 women); includes 2 minority (1 Black or African American, non-Hispanic/Latino; 1 Asian, non-Hispanic/Latino). Average age 43. 18 applicants, 83% accepted, 8 enrolled. In 2016, 19 master's awarded. *Degree requirements:* For master's, thesis. *Entrance requirements:* For master's and Graduate Certificate, essay, 3 letters of recommendation, official transcripts. Additional exam requirements/recommendations for international students: Required—TOEFL (minimum score 85 iBT) or IELTS (6.5). *Application deadline:* For fall admission, 4/15 for domestic students; for spring admission, 11/15 for domestic students. Applications are processed on a rolling basis. Application fee: $75. Electronic applications accepted. *Expenses:* Tuition, state resident: full-time $4818. Tuition, nonresident: full-time $20,820. *Required fees:* $2936. Part-time tuition and fees vary according to course load. *Financial support:* Health care benefits available. Financial award application deadline: 5/1; financial award applicants required to submit FAFSA. *Unit head:* Gerard Voos, Director, Master of Liberal Arts and Sciences Program and the Asheville Graduate Center, 828-232-5040, E-mail: gvoos@unca.edu. *Application contact:* Jordan Dolfi, Program Associate, Master of Liberal Arts and Sciences Program and the Asheville Graduate Center, 828-251-6099, E-mail: jdolfi@unca.edu.
Website: https://mlas.unca.edu/

**The University of North Carolina at Charlotte,** College of Liberal Arts and Sciences, Department of Languages and Culture Studies, Charlotte, NC 28223-0001. Offers languages and culture studies: translating (MA); translating (Graduate Certificate). *Program availability:* Part-time, evening/weekend. *Faculty:* 14 full-time (8 women). *Students:* 1 (woman) full-time, 8 part-time (6 women); includes 3 minority (all Hispanic/Latino). Average age 39. 3 applicants, 67% accepted, 1 enrolled. In 2016, 4 master's, 3 other advanced degrees awarded. *Degree requirements:* For master's, comprehensive exam, thesis, internship; for Graduate Certificate, internship. *Entrance requirements:* For master's, GRE, baccalaureate degree in Spanish or related field with minimum overall GPA of 2.75; essay that addresses the applicant's motivation for enrolling in program, to include particular areas of research interests and career or professional goals; three letters of reference; oral interview; for Graduate Certificate, GRE or MAT, essay in English that addresses applicant's motivation for seeking enrollment in program; three letters of recommendation; portfolio of best writing samples in both English and Spanish or of translations into each language; oral interview. Additional exam requirements/recommendations for international students: Required—TOEFL (minimum score 523 paper-based, 70 iBT) or IELTS (6.5). *Application deadline:* For fall admission, 3/1 priority date for domestic and international students; for spring admission, 10/1 priority date for domestic and international students. Applications are processed on a rolling basis. Application fee: $75. Electronic applications accepted. *Expenses:* Tuition, state resident: full-time $4252. Tuition, nonresident: full-time $17,423. *Required fees:* $3026. Tuition and fees vary according to course load and program. *Financial support:* In 2016–17, 3 students received support, including 2 research assistantships (averaging $5,000 per year), 1 teaching assistantship (averaging $8,000 per year); career-related internships or fieldwork, institutionally sponsored loans, scholarships/grants, and unspecified assistantships also available. Support available to part-time students. Financial award application deadline: 3/1; financial award applicants required to submit

## Cultural Studies

FAFSA. *Total annual research expenditures:* $12,433. *Unit head:* Ann Gonzalez, Chair, 704-687-8761, E-mail: abgonzal@uncc.edu. *Application contact:* Kathy B. Giddings, Director of Graduate Admissions, 704-687-5503, Fax: 704-687-1668, E-mail: gradadm@uncc.edu.
Website: https://languages.uncc.edu/

**University of Oklahoma,** College of Arts and Sciences, Department of English, Norman, OK 73019. Offers composition and rhetoric (MA, PhD); literary and cultural studies (MA, PhD). *Program availability:* Part-time. *Faculty:* 31 full-time (15 women). *Students:* 26 full-time (16 women), 18 part-time (9 women); includes 9 minority (2 American Indian or Alaska Native, non-Hispanic/Latino; 2 Asian, non-Hispanic/Latino; 3 Hispanic/Latino; 2 Two or more races, non-Hispanic/Latino), 1 international. Average age 32. 38 applicants, 34% accepted, 3 enrolled. In 2016, 7 master's, 7 doctorates awarded. *Degree requirements:* For master's, one foreign language, comprehensive exam (for some programs), thesis (for some programs), exam or thesis; for doctorate, one foreign language, comprehensive exam, thesis/dissertation. *Entrance requirements:* For master's, BA in English or related field; for doctorate, MA in English or related field. Additional exam requirements/recommendations for international students: Required—TOEFL (minimum score 79 iBT) or IELTS (minimum score 6.5). *Application deadline:* For fall admission, 1/5 priority date for domestic and international students. Application fee: $50 ($100 for international students). Electronic applications accepted. *Expenses:* Tuition, state resident: full-time $4886; part-time $203.60 per credit hour. Tuition, nonresident: full-time $18,989; part-time $791.20 per credit hour. *Required fees:* $3283; $126.25 per credit hour. $126.50 per semester. *Financial support:* In 2016–17, 40 students received support, including 5 research assistantships (averaging $13,011 per year), 32 teaching assistantships (averaging $12,550 per year); fellowships, scholarships/grants, health care benefits, and unspecified assistantships also available. Financial award application deadline: 6/1; financial award applicants required to submit FAFSA. *Faculty research:* American Indian literature and culture; composition and rhetoric; American literature; British literature; postcolonial literature and culture. *Unit head:* Dr. Daniela Garofalo, Professor and Chair, 405-325-4661, Fax: 405-325-0831, E-mail: dg@ou.edu. *Application contact:* Sara Day, Graduate Assistant, 405-325-0489, Fax: 405-325-0831, E-mail: redpanda@ou.edu.
Website: http://cas.ou.edu/english

**University of Pittsburgh,** Dietrich School of Arts and Sciences, Graduate Program for Cultural Studies, Pittsburgh, PA 15260. Offers Certificate. *Faculty:* 183 full-time (85 women). *Students:* 77 full-time (44 women); includes 23 minority (4 Black or African American, non-Hispanic/Latino; 1 American Indian or Alaska Native, non-Hispanic/Latino; 8 Asian, non-Hispanic/Latino; 8 Hispanic/Latino; 1 Native Hawaiian or other Pacific Islander, non-Hispanic/Latino; 1 Two or more races, non-Hispanic/Latino). Average age 33. 15 applicants, 100% accepted, 15 enrolled. In 2016, 4 degrees awarded. *Degree requirements:* For Certificate, one foreign language. *Entrance requirements:* For degree, good academic standing in a University of Pittsburgh graduate degree-granting department or school. Additional exam requirements/ recommendations for international students: Required—TOEFL. *Application deadline:* Applications are processed on a rolling basis. Application fee: $0. Electronic applications accepted. Tuition and fees vary according to program. *Financial support:* In 2016–17, 77 students received support, including 2 fellowships with full tuition reimbursements available (averaging $18,000 per year). Financial award application deadline: 1/15. *Faculty research:* Diachronic and synchronic cultural critique; cultural politics and critical theory; interdisciplinary approaches to arts, literatures, media, and ethnographies in international cultural contexts. *Unit head:* Dr. Ronald J. Zboray, Director, 412-624-6969, Fax: 412-624-6492, E-mail: zboray@pitt.edu. *Application contact:* Kathryn Briar Somerville, Administrator, 412-624-6564, Fax: 412-383-6999, E-mail: kbs47@pitt.edu.
Website: http://www.culturalstudies.pitt.edu

**University of Southern California,** Graduate School, Dana and David Dornsife College of Letters, Arts and Sciences, Comparative Studies in Literature and Culture Doctoral Program, Los Angeles, CA 90089. Offers comparative literature (PhD); comparative media and culture (PhD); Spanish and Latin American studies (PhD). *Degree requirements:* For doctorate, 2 foreign languages, comprehensive exam, thesis/ dissertation. *Entrance requirements:* For doctorate, GRE, competence in language other than English (highly recommended). Additional exam requirements/recommendations for international students: Required—TOEFL. Electronic applications accepted. *Faculty research:* Literary theory, Japanese film and contemporary fiction, Francophone literature and cinema, Latin American and Caribbean literature, Spanish literature and film, nineteenth and twentieth century British and American literature.

**University of Southern Indiana,** Graduate Studies, College of Liberal Arts, Program in Second Language Acquisition, Policy, and Culture, Evansville, IN 47712-3590. Offers MA. *Program availability:* Part-time. *Students:* 16 full-time (11 women), 2 part-time (both women); includes 4 minority (1 Black or African American, non-Hispanic/Latino; 1 American Indian or Alaska Native, non-Hispanic/Latino; 1 Asian, non-Hispanic/Latino; 1 Hispanic/Latino), 4 international. Average age 38. *Entrance requirements:* For master's, minimum GPA of 3.0, letter of intent, 3 letters of recommendation. Additional exam requirements/recommendations for international students: Required—TOEFL (minimum score 550 paper-based; 79 iBT), IELTS (minimum score 6). *Expenses:* Tuition, state resident: full-time $8497. Tuition, nonresident: full-time $16,691. *Required fees:* $500. *Financial support:* In 2016–17, 3 students received support. Federal Work-Study, scholarships/grants, tuition waivers (full and partial), and unspecified assistantships available. Financial award application deadline: 3/1; financial award applicants required to submit FAFSA. *Unit head:* Dr. Silvia Rode, Chair, 812-465-7026, E-mail: sarode@usi.edu. *Application contact:* Dr. Mayola Rowser, Director, Graduate Studies, 812-465-7015, E-mail: mrowser@usi.edu.
Website: http://www.usi.edu/liberal-arts/ma-language/

**University of Southern Maine,** College of Management and Human Service, School of Education and Human Development, Program in Counselor Education, Portland, ME 04103. Offers clinical mental health counseling (MS); counseling (CAS); culturally responsive practices in education and human development (CGS); mental health rehabilitation technician/community (CGS); rehabilitation counseling (MS); school counseling (MS); substance abuse counseling (CGS). *Accreditation:* ACA (one or more programs are accredited); CORE; TEAC. *Program availability:* Part-time, evening/ weekend. *Degree requirements:* For master's, comprehensive exam, thesis or alternative; for other advanced degree, thesis or alternative. *Entrance requirements:* For master's, GRE General Test or MAT, interview; for other advanced degree, master's degree. Additional exam requirements/recommendations for international students: Required—TOEFL (minimum score 550 paper-based; 79 iBT). Electronic applications accepted. *Faculty research:* Counselor licensure, group dynamics, counseling theories, healthy adaptation, counselor educator well-being.

**The University of Texas at Austin,** Graduate School, College of Education, Department of Curriculum and Instruction, Austin, TX 78712-1111. Offers bilingual/ bicultural education (M Ed, MA, PhD); cultural studies in education (M Ed, MA, PhD); early childhood education (M Ed, MA, PhD); language and literacy studies (M Ed, PhD); learning technologies (M Ed, MA, PhD); physical education (M Ed, MA, PhD). Terminal master's awarded for partial completion of doctoral program. *Degree requirements:* For

doctorate, thesis/dissertation. *Entrance requirements:* For master's and doctorate, GRE General Test. Electronic applications accepted.

**The University of Texas at Austin,** Graduate School, College of Liberal Arts, Department of Anthropology, Program in Cultural Forms, Austin, TX 78712-1111. Offers MA, PhD. *Program availability:* Part-time. Terminal master's awarded for partial completion of doctoral program. *Degree requirements:* For master's, one foreign language, thesis, report; for doctorate, one foreign language, thesis/dissertation. *Entrance requirements:* For master's and doctorate, GRE General Test. Electronic applications accepted. *Faculty research:* Expressive culture, gender, genre, folklore and culture of British Isles, ethnography of speaking.

**The University of Texas at Austin,** Graduate School, College of Liberal Arts, Department of Slavic and Eurasian Studies, Austin, TX 78712-1111. Offers applied linguistics/pedagogy (PhD); literature and culture (PhD); Slavic languages (MA); Slavic linguistics (PhD). *Degree requirements:* For master's, 2 foreign languages, thesis; for doctorate, 3 foreign languages, thesis/dissertation. *Entrance requirements:* For master's and doctorate, GRE General Test. Electronic applications accepted. *Faculty research:* Slavic linguistics; applied linguistics; Russian, Czech, and Slavic literature and culture.

**The University of Texas at Austin,** Graduate School, College of Liberal Arts, Teresa Lozano Long Institute of Latin American Studies, Austin, TX 78712-1111. Offers cultural politics of Afro-Latin and indigenous peoples (MA); development studies (MA); environmental studies (MA); human rights (MA); Latin American and international law (LL M); JD/MA; MA/MA; MBA/MA; MP Aff/MA; MSCRP/MA. LL M offered jointly with The University of Texas School of Law. *Entrance requirements:* For master's, GRE General Test.

**The University of Texas at San Antonio,** College of Education and Human Development, Department of Bicultural and Bilingual Studies, San Antonio, TX 78249-0617. Offers bicultural and bilingual studies (MA), including bicultural and bilingual education, bicultural studies; culture, literacy, and language (PhD); teaching English as a second language (MA). *Program availability:* Part-time, evening/weekend. *Faculty:* 19 full-time (13 women), 2 part-time/adjunct (1 woman). *Students:* 32 full-time (21 women), 109 part-time (86 women); includes 80 minority (3 Black or African American, non-Hispanic/Latino; 4 Asian, non-Hispanic/Latino; 72 Hispanic/Latino; 1 Two or more races, non-Hispanic/Latino), 11 international. Average age 37. 70 applicants, 77% accepted, 36 enrolled. In 2016, 28 master's, 10 doctorates awarded. *Degree requirements:* For master's, one foreign language, comprehensive exam, thesis optional; for doctorate, one foreign language, comprehensive exam, thesis/dissertation. *Entrance requirements:* For master's, bachelor's degree with 18 credit hours in field of study or in another appropriate field of study; for doctorate, GRE General Test, resume or curriculum vitae, 3 letters of recommendation, statement of purpose, master's degree. Additional exam requirements/recommendations for international students: Required—TOEFL (minimum score 550 paper-based; 79 iBT), IELTS (minimum score 6.5). *Application deadline:* For fall admission, 7/1 for domestic students, 4/1 for international students; for spring admission, 11/1 for domestic students, 9/1 for international students. Applications are processed on a rolling basis. Application fee: $45 ($80 for international students). Electronic applications accepted. *Expenses:* Contact institution. *Financial support:* In 2016–17, 18 students received support, including 18 fellowships (averaging $28,000 per year), 2 research assistantships (averaging $12,468 per year), 16 teaching assistantships (averaging $11,000 per year); scholarships/grants and unspecified assistantships also available. Financial award application deadline: 4/15. *Faculty research:* Bilingual and ESL teacher preparation; transnational communities; applied linguistics; cultural studies; bilingualism, biliteracy and second language acquisition. *Total annual research expenditures:* $300,234. *Unit head:* Dr. Belinda Flores, Chair, 210-458-5570, Fax: 210-458-5962, E-mail: belinda.flores@utsa.edu. *Application contact:* Rahnuma Islam, Student Development Specialist, 210-458-6619, Fax: 210-458-5576, E-mail: rahnuma.islam@utsa.edu.
Website: http://education.utsa.edu/bicultural-bilingual_studies

**University of the Sacred Heart,** Graduate Programs, Department of Communication, Program in Contemporary Culture and Media, San Juan, PR 00914-0383. Offers MA. *Degree requirements:* For master's, thesis.

**University of Washington, Bothell,** Master of Arts in Cultural Studies Program, Bothell, WA 98011. Offers MA. *Program availability:* Evening/weekend. *Degree requirements:* For master's, thesis. *Entrance requirements:* Additional exam requirements/recommendations for international students: Required—TOEFL. Electronic applications accepted.

**Washington State University,** College of Education, Department of Teaching and Learning, Pullman, WA 99164-2132. Offers cultural studies and social thought in education (PhD); curriculum and instruction (Ed M, MA); English language learners (Ed M, MA); language, literacy and technology (PhD); literacy education (Ed M, MA); mathematics education (PhD); special education (Ed M, MA, PhD); teacher leadership (Ed D); teaching (MIT), including elementary education, secondary education. Programs offered at the Pullman, Spokane, Tri-cities, Vancouver and Global (online) campuses. *Program availability:* Part-time, online learning. *Degree requirements:* For master's, comprehensive exam, thesis, oral or written exam; for doctorate, comprehensive exam, thesis/dissertation, oral and written exam. *Entrance requirements:* For master's, GRE General Test, minimum GPA of 3.0, 3 letters of recommendation, letter of intent, transcripts, resume/curriculum vitae; for doctorate, GRE General Test, minimum GPA of 3.0, 3 letters of recommendation, letter of intent, transcripts, writing sample, resume/ curriculum vitae. Additional exam requirements/recommendations for international students: Required—TOEFL (minimum score 550 paper-based; 80 iBT). Electronic applications accepted. *Faculty research:* Intersection of gender, youth cultures and schooling; examination of ideology of power in children's literature; early childhood special education; analyzing pre-service and in-service teacher development; second language acquisition.

**West Chester University of Pennsylvania,** College of Arts and Humanities, Department of Languages and Cultures, West Chester, PA 19383. Offers French (Teaching Certificate); German (Teaching Certificate); languages and cultures (MA), including French, German, Spanish; Spanish (Teaching Certificate). *Program availability:* Part-time, evening/weekend, minimal on-campus study. *Faculty:* 12 full-time (9 women). *Students:* 7 full-time (6 women), 26 part-time (23 women); includes 7 minority (all Hispanic/Latino). Average age 31. 14 applicants, 100% accepted, 11 enrolled. In 2016, 8 master's, 2 other advanced degrees awarded. *Degree requirements:* For master's, one foreign language, comprehensive exam, portfolio, exit exam, capstone project; for Teaching Certificate, one foreign language. *Entrance requirements:* For master's and Teaching Certificate, ACTFL OPI and WPT, undergraduate major or equivalent. Additional exam requirements/recommendations for international students: Required—TOEFL or IELTS. *Application deadline:* For fall admission, 5/15 for international students; for spring admission, 10/15 for international students. Applications are processed on a rolling basis. Application fee: $45. Electronic applications accepted. *Expenses:* Tuition, state resident: full-time $8694; part-time $483 per credit. Tuition, nonresident: full-time $13,050; part-time $725 per credit. *Required fees:* $2399; $119.05 per credit. Tuition and fees vary according to campus/location and program. *Financial support:* Scholarships/grants and unspecified assistantships

available. Financial award application deadline: 2/15; financial award applicants required to submit FAFSA. *Faculty research:* Language structure, literature, film, culture, pedagogy, technology. *Unit head:* Dr. Jerome Williams, Interim Chair, 610-436-2700, Fax: 610-436-3048, E-mail: isanchez@wcupa.edu. *Application contact:* Dr. Rebecca Pauly, Graduate Coordinator, 610-436-4746, Fax: 610-436-3048, E-mail: mvanliew@wcupa.edu.
Website: http://www.wcupa.edu/arts-humanities/languagesCultures/

**Wheaton College,** Graduate School, Department of Intercultural Studies, Wheaton, IL 60187-5593. Offers intercultural studies (MA); intercultural studies/teaching English as a second language (MA); missions (MA); teaching English as a second language (Certificate). *Program availability:* Part-time. *Faculty:* 5 full-time (2 women), 2 part-time/adjunct (both women). *Students:* 25 full-time (20 women), 15 part-time (9 women); includes 8 minority (1 Black or African American, non-Hispanic/Latino; 6 Asian, non-Hispanic/Latino; 1 Hispanic/Latino), 8 international. Average age 32. 35 applicants, 94% accepted, 20 enrolled. In 2016, 23 master's awarded. *Degree requirements:* For master's, thesis or alternative. *Entrance requirements:* For master's, GRE General Test, MAT. Additional exam requirements/recommendations for international students: Required—TOEFL (minimum score 550 paper-based; 80 iBT), IELTS (minimum score 6.5), TOEFL (minimum score 600 paper-based; 90 iBT) or IELTS (minimum score 7.5) for MA in TESOL. *Application deadline:* For fall admission, 5/1 for domestic students, 1/1 for international students; for spring admission, 11/1 for domestic students. Applications are processed on a rolling basis. Application fee: $30. Electronic applications accepted. *Expenses:* Tuition: Full-time $19,080; part-time $795 per credit hour. Tuition and fees vary according to degree level and program. *Financial support:* Career-related internships or fieldwork, scholarships/grants, and unspecified assistantships available. Financial award application deadline: 3/1; financial award applicants required to submit FAFSA. *Unit head:* Dr. Robert Gallagher, Chair, 630-752-5593, E-mail: intercultural.studies@wheaton.edu. *Application contact:* Dusty Di Santo, Director of Graduate Admissions, 630-752-5195, Fax: 630-752-5047, E-mail: graduate.admissions@wheaton.edu.
Website: http://www.wheaton.edu/academics/departments/intr

**Wilfrid Laurier University,** Faculty of Graduate and Postdoctoral Studies, Faculty of Arts, Cultural Analysis and Social Theory Program, Waterloo, ON N2L 3C5, Canada. Offers body politics (MA); cultural representation and social theory (MA); gender, sexuality and embodiment (MA); globalization, identity and social movements (MA). *Program availability:* Part-time. *Entrance requirements:* For master's, honours BA in humanities, social science or interdisciplinary program with social theory, minimum B+ in final year of full-time study. Additional exam requirements/recommendations for international students: Required—TOEFL (minimum score 89 iBT). Electronic applications accepted. *Faculty research:* Globalization; identity and social movements; body politics: gender, sexuality and embodiment; cultural representation and social theory.

**Wilfrid Laurier University,** Faculty of Graduate and Postdoctoral Studies, Faculty of Arts, Department of Communication Studies, Waterloo, ON N2L 3C5, Canada. Offers media, technology and culture (MA); visual communication and culture (MA). *Degree requirements:* For master's, thesis optional. *Entrance requirements:* For master's, honours BA in communication studies or a cognate discipline from an approved university with a minimum B+ overall in last two years of study and in undergraduate major. Additional exam requirements/recommendations for international students: Required—TOEFL (minimum score 89 iBT). Electronic applications accepted. *Faculty research:* Visual communication and culture, media, technology and culture.

**Wilson College,** Graduate Programs, Chambersburg, PA 17201-1285. Offers accounting (M Acc); choreography and visual art (MFA); education (M Ed); healthcare management for sustainability (MHM); humanities (MA), including art and culture, critical/cultural theory, English language and literature, women's studies; management (MSM); nursing (MSN), including nursing education, nursing leadership and management. *Program availability:* Evening/weekend. *Degree requirements:* For master's, project. *Entrance requirements:* For master's, PRAXIS, minimum undergraduate cumulative GPA of 3.0, 2 letters of recommendation, current certification for eligibility to teach in grades K-12, resume, personal interview. Electronic applications accepted.

# East European and Russian Studies

**Boston College,** Graduate School of Arts and Sciences, Department of Slavic and Eastern Languages and Literatures, Program in Slavic Studies, Chestnut Hill, MA 02467-3800. Offers MA, MA/JD, MBA/MA. *Faculty:* 6 full-time. *Students:* 2 full-time (1 woman), 1 international. 2 applicants, 100% accepted, 1 enrolled. *Degree requirements:* For master's, 3 foreign languages, comprehensive exam, thesis or alternative. *Entrance requirements:* Additional exam requirements/recommendations for international students: Required—TOEFL (minimum score 600 paper-based; 100 iBT), IELTS (minimum score 8). *Application deadline:* For fall admission, 2/2 for domestic and international students. Application fee: $75. Electronic applications accepted. Tuition and fees vary according to program. *Financial support:* In 2016–17, fellowships with full tuition reimbursements (averaging $9,200 per year), teaching assistantships with full tuition reimbursements (averaging $9,200 per year) were awarded; tuition waivers (full and partial) and unspecified assistantships also available. Financial award application deadline: 3/1. *Unit head:* Dr. Michael Connolly, Chairperson, 617-552-3912.
Website: http://www.bc.edu/sl

**Brown University,** Graduate School, Department of Slavic Languages, Providence, RI 02912. Offers Russian language and literature (AM); Slavic linguistics (AM); Slavic studies (PhD). *Degree requirements:* For master's, one foreign language; for doctorate, 2 foreign languages, thesis/dissertation, preliminary exam.

**Carleton University,** Faculty of Graduate Studies, Faculty of Public Affairs and Management, Institute of European and Russian Studies, Ottawa, ON K1S 5B6, Canada. Offers European and European Union studies (MA); European integration studies (Diploma); Russian, Eurasian and transition studies (MA). *Degree requirements:* For master's, one foreign language, thesis optional. *Entrance requirements:* For master's, honors degree or equivalent; 2 years of Russian, German or other central east European language. Additional exam requirements/recommendations for international students: Required—TOEFL. *Faculty research:* East-West relations, minority rights in Russia and Eastern Europe.

**Columbia University,** Graduate School of Arts and Sciences, New York, NY 10027. Offers African-American studies (MA); American studies (MA); anthropology (MA, PhD); art history and archaeology (MA, PhD); astronomy (PhD); biological sciences (PhD); biotechnology (MA); chemical physics (PhD); chemistry (PhD); classical studies (MA, PhD); classics (MA, PhD); climate and society (MA); conservation biology (MA); earth and environmental sciences (PhD); East Asia: regional studies (MA); East Asian languages and cultures (MA, PhD); ecology, evolution and environmental biology (MA), including conservation biology; ecology, evolution, and environmental biology (PhD), including ecology and evolutionary biology, evolutionary primatology; economics (MA, PhD); English and comparative literature (MA, PhD); French and Romance philology (MA, PhD); Germanic languages (MA, PhD); global French studies (MA); global thought (MA); Hispanic cultural studies (MA); history (PhD); history and literature (MA); human rights studies (MA); Islamic studies (MA); Italian (MA, PhD); Japanese pedagogy (MA); Jewish studies (MA); Latin America and the Caribbean: regional studies (MA); Latin American and Iberian cultures (PhD); mathematics (MA, PhD), including finance (MA); medieval and Renaissance studies (MA); Middle Eastern, South Asian, and African studies (MA, PhD); modern art: critical and curatorial studies (MA); modern European studies (MA); museum anthropology (MA); music (DMA, PhD); oral history (MA); philosophical foundations of physics (MA); philosophy (MA, PhD); physics (PhD); political science (MA, PhD); psychology (PhD); quantitative methods in the social sciences (MA); religion (MA, PhD); Russia, Eurasia and East Europe: regional studies (MA); Russian translation (MA); Slavic cultures (MA); Slavic languages (MA, PhD); sociology (MA, PhD); South Asian studies (MA); statistics (MA, PhD); theatre (PhD). Dual-degree programs require admission to both Graduate School of Arts and Sciences and another Columbia school. *Program availability:* Part-time. Terminal master's awarded for partial completion of doctoral program. *Degree requirements:* For master's, variable foreign language requirement, comprehensive exam (for some programs), thesis (for some programs); for doctorate, variable foreign language requirement, comprehensive exam (for some programs), thesis/dissertation. *Entrance requirements:* For master's and doctorate, GRE General Test, GRE Subject Test (for some programs). Additional exam requirements/recommendations for international students: Required—TOEFL, IELTS. Electronic applications accepted.

**Cornell University,** Graduate School, Graduate Fields of Arts and Sciences, Field of History, Ithaca, NY 14853. Offers African history (MA, PhD); American history (MA, PhD); ancient Greek history (PhD); ancient history (MA, PhD); ancient Roman history (PhD); early modern European history (MA, PhD); English history (MA, PhD); French history (MA, PhD); German history (MA, PhD); history of science (MA, PhD); Korean history (PhD); Latin American history (MA, PhD); medieval Chinese history (MA, PhD); medieval history (MA, PhD); modern Chinese history (MA, PhD); modern European history (MA, PhD); modern Japanese history (MA, PhD); modern Middle Eastern history (PhD); premodern Islamic history (MA, PhD); premodern Japanese history (MA, PhD); Renaissance history (MA, PhD); Russian history (MA, PhD); South Asian history (PhD); Southeast Asian history (MA, PhD). Terminal master's awarded for partial completion of doctoral program. *Degree requirements:* For master's, thesis; for doctorate, 2 foreign languages, comprehensive exam, thesis/dissertation, 1 year of teaching experience. *Entrance requirements:* For master's and doctorate, GRE General Test, writing sample, 3 letters of recommendation. Additional exam requirements/recommendations for international students: Required—TOEFL (minimum score 550 paper-based; 77 iBT). Electronic applications accepted.

**Florida State University,** The Graduate School, College of Social Sciences and Public Policy, Program in Russian and East European Studies, Tallahassee, FL 32306. Offers Russian and east European studies (MA, MS). *Program availability:* Part-time. *Faculty:* 4 full-time (all women), 4 part-time/adjunct. *Students:* 1 full-time (0 women), 2 part-time (1 woman); includes 1 minority (Two or more races, non-Hispanic/Latino). Average age 26. 2 applicants, 100% accepted, 1 enrolled. In 2016, 4 master's awarded. *Degree requirements:* For master's, one foreign language, comprehensive exam, thesis optional. *Entrance requirements:* For master's, GRE General Test, minimum GPA of 3.0. Additional exam requirements/recommendations for international students: Required—TOEFL (minimum score 550 paper-based, 80 iBT) or IELTS (6.5). *Application deadline:* For fall admission, 7/1 for domestic and international students; for spring admission, 11/1 for domestic and international students; for summer admission, 3/1 for domestic and international students. Applications are processed on a rolling basis. Application fee: $30. Electronic applications accepted. *Expenses:* Contact institution. *Financial support:* Fellowships, research assistantships, teaching assistantships, career-related internships or fieldwork, Federal Work-Study, institutionally sponsored loans, and unspecified assistantships available. Financial award application deadline: 2/1; financial award applicants required to submit FAFSA. *Faculty research:* Deception in World War II. *Unit head:* Dr. Lee K. Metcalf, Director, 850-644-4418, Fax: 850-645-4981, E-mail: lmetcalf@fsu.edu. *Application contact:* Sam Bandak, Academic Program Specialist, 850-644-4418, Fax: 850-645-4981, E-mail: sbandak@fsu.edu.
Website: http://coss.fsu.edu/inaprog/programs/graduate/g-european

**Georgetown University,** Graduate School of Arts and Sciences, Walsh School of Foreign Service, Center for Eurasian, Russian and East European Studies, Washington, DC 20057. Offers MA, MA/JD, MA/PhD. *Degree requirements:* For master's, one foreign language, comprehensive exam, thesis optional. *Entrance requirements:* For master's, GRE General Test. Additional exam requirements/recommendations for international students: Required—TOEFL. *Faculty research:* East-West trade.

**The George Washington University,** Elliott School of International Affairs, Program in European and Eurasian Studies, Washington, DC 20052. Offers MA. *Program availability:* Part-time. *Students:* 16 full-time (7 women), 11 part-time (7 women); includes 2 minority (1 Hispanic/Latino; 1 Two or more races, non-Hispanic/Latino), 2 international. Average age 27. 45 applicants, 89% accepted, 10 enrolled. In 2016, 9 master's awarded. *Degree requirements:* For master's, one foreign language, capstone project. *Entrance requirements:* For master's, GRE General Test, 2 years (or the equivalent) of a modern European language or Russian, 2 semesters of introductory economics (macro or micro). Additional exam requirements/recommendations for international students: Required—TOEFL (minimum score 100 iBT), IELTS (minimum score 7). *Application deadline:* For fall admission, 1/15 priority date for domestic and international students; for spring admission, 10/1 for domestic students. Application fee: $75. Electronic applications accepted. *Financial support:* In 2016–17, 3 students received support. Fellowships with partial tuition reimbursements available and Federal Work-Study available. Financial award application deadline: 1/15; financial award applicants required to submit FAFSA. *Faculty research:* NATO, European economics, European history, European Union. *Unit head:* Peter Rollberg, Director, 202-994-6340, E-mail: rgpeter@gwu.edu. *Application contact:* Nicole A. Campbell, Director of Graduate

## East European and Russian Studies

Admissions, 202-994-7050, Fax: 202-994-9537, E-mail: esiagrad@gwu.edu. Website: http://elliott.gwu.edu/academics/grad/ees/index.cfm

**Harvard University,** Graduate School of Arts and Sciences, Committee on Regional Studies-Russia, Eastern Europe, and Central Asia, Cambridge, MA 02138. Offers AM. *Degree requirements:* For master's, one foreign language. *Entrance requirements:* For master's, GRE General Test. Additional exam requirements/recommendations for international students: Required—TOEFL. *Faculty research:* Strategic policy, ethnography and demography of U.S.S.R., non-Russian nationality language training.

**Indiana University Bloomington,** University Graduate School, College of Arts and Sciences, School of Global and International Studies, Russian and East European Institute, Bloomington, IN 47405. Offers MA, Certificate, JD/MA, MA/MA, MBA/MA, MIS/MA, MLS/MA, MPA/MA, MPH/MA, MSSI/MA. *Faculty:* 1 part-time/adjunct (0 women). *Students:* 10 full-time (5 women); includes 3 minority (1 Asian, non-Hispanic/Latino; 1 Hispanic/Latino; 1 Two or more races, non-Hispanic/Latino), 1 international. Average age 26. 28 applicants, 82% accepted, 9 enrolled. In 2016, 9 master's awarded. *Degree requirements:* For master's, one foreign language, essay, written exams; for Certificate, one foreign language, oral and proficiency exams. *Entrance requirements:* For master's, GRE General Test, minimum 2 years of college Russian (for Russian area studies); for Certificate, GRE General Test. Additional exam requirements/recommendations for international students: Recommended—TOEFL (minimum score 550 paper-based). *Application deadline:* For fall admission, 1/15 for domestic students, 12/1 for international students; for spring admission, 9/15 for domestic students, 8/15 for international students. Application fee: $55 ($65 for international students). *Expenses:* $362.30 per credit hour in-state; $1,184.15 per credit hour out-of-state; $650 mandatory fees. *Financial support:* In 2016–17, 5 students received support, including 2 fellowships with tuition reimbursements available (averaging $15,000 per year), teaching assistantships with tuition reimbursements available (averaging $15,750 per year); health care benefits and unspecified assistantships also available. Financial award application deadline: 2/1; financial award applicants required to submit FAFSA. *Faculty research:* Political and economic transition of former Soviet Union and eastern Europe, Russian and Soviet history, Slavic literature and linguistics, education and mass media of former Soviet Union and Eastern Europe. *Unit head:* Prof. Sarah Phillips, Director, 812-855-7309. *Application contact:* Mary Belding, Administrative Secretary, 812-855-3869, Fax: 812-855-6411, E-mail: mebeldin@indiana.edu. Website: http://www.indiana.edu/~reeiweb/

**The Ohio State University,** Graduate School, Center for Slavic and East European Studies, Columbus, OH 43210. Offers MA. *Students:* 10 full-time (2 women). Average age 25. In 2016, 5 master's awarded. *Degree requirements:* For master's, exam or thesis. *Entrance requirements:* For master's, GRE General Test. Additional exam requirements/recommendations for international students: Required—TOEFL (minimum score 550 paper-based; 79 iBT), Michigan English Language Assessment Battery (minimum score 82); Recommended—IELTS (minimum score 7). *Application deadline:* For fall admission, 12/13 priority date for domestic students, 11/30 priority date for international students; for spring admission, 11/10 for domestic and international students; for summer admission, 3/13 for domestic and international students. Applications are processed on a rolling basis. Application fee: $60 ($70 for international students). Electronic applications accepted. *Financial support:* Fellowships, Federal Work-Study, and institutionally sponsored loans available. Support available to part-time students. *Unit head:* Dr. Yana Hashamova, Director, E-mail: hashamova.1@osu.edu. *Application contact:* Graduate and Professional Admissions, 614-292-9444, Fax: 614-292-3895, E-mail: gpadmissions@osu.edu. Website: http://slaviccenter.osu.edu

**The Ohio State University,** Graduate School, College of Arts and Sciences, Division of Arts and Humanities, Department of Slavic and East European Languages and Cultures, Columbus, OH 43210. Offers Slavic linguistics (MA, PhD); Slavic literature, film, and cultural studies (MA, PhD). *Faculty:* 11. *Students:* 14 full-time (10 women), 1 (woman) part-time. Average age 30. In 2016, 2 master's, 2 doctorates awarded. Terminal master's awarded for partial completion of doctoral program. *Degree requirements:* For master's, variable foreign language requirement, thesis optional; for doctorate, variable foreign language requirement, thesis/dissertation. *Entrance requirements:* For master's and doctorate, GRE General Test, at least 3 years of Russian language study or equivalent. Additional exam requirements/recommendations for international students: Required—TOEFL (minimum score 550 paper-based; 79 iBT), Michigan English Language Assessment Battery (minimum score 82); Recommended—IELTS (minimum score 7). *Application deadline:* For fall admission, 12/12 priority date for domestic students, 11/30 priority date for international students; for spring admission, 3/1 for domestic students, 2/1 for international students. Applications are processed on a rolling basis. Application fee: $60 ($70 for international students). Electronic applications accepted. *Financial support:* Fellowships with tuition reimbursements, teaching assistantships with tuition reimbursements, Federal Work-Study, and institutionally sponsored loans available. Support available to part-time students. *Faculty research:* Polish literature. *Unit head:* Dr. Yana Hashamova, Chair and Professor, 614-292-6733, E-mail: hashamova.1@osu.edu. *Application contact:* Graduate and Professional Admissions, 614-292-9444, Fax: 614-292-3895, E-mail: gpadmissions@osu.edu. Website: http://slavic.osu.edu/

**Stanford University,** School of Humanities and Sciences, Center for Russian, East European and Eurasian Studies, Stanford, CA 94305-2004. Offers MA. *Degree requirements:* For master's, one foreign language. *Entrance requirements:* For master's, GRE General Test. Additional exam requirements/recommendations for international students: Required—TOEFL. Electronic applications accepted. *Expenses:* Tuition: Full-time $47,331. *Required fees:* $609.

**University of Alberta,** Faculty of Graduate Studies and Research, Department of Modern Languages and Cultural Studies, Edmonton, AB T6G 2E1, Canada. Offers applied linguistics (Germanic, Romance, Slavic) (MA); French language, literatures and linguistics (PhD); French language, literatures, and linguistics (MA); Germanic languages, literatures and linguistics (PhD); Germanic languages, literatures, and linguistics (MA); Italian studies (MA); Slavic languages and literatures (Russian, Ukrainian) (MA, PhD); Slavic linguistics (Russian, Ukrainian) (MA, PhD); Spanish and Latin American studies (MA, PhD); Ukrainian folklore (MA, PhD). *Program availability:* Part-time. *Degree requirements:* For master's, one foreign language, thesis; for doctorate, 2 foreign languages, comprehensive exam, thesis/dissertation. *Entrance requirements:* For master's and doctorate, 1 language other than English. Additional exam requirements/recommendations for international students: Required—Michigan English Language Assessment Battery or TOEFL (minimum score 550 paper-based). Electronic applications accepted. *Faculty research:* Russian/Ukrainian studies; German studies; contemporary Latin American, French and Francophone studies; Italian studies.

**The University of British Columbia,** Faculty of Arts and Faculty of Graduate Studies, Department of Central, Eastern and Northern European Studies, Vancouver, BC V6T 1Z1, Canada. Offers Germanic studies (MA, PhD). *Program availability:* Part-time. *Degree requirements:* For master's, one foreign language, thesis optional, exam; for doctorate, one foreign language, comprehensive exam, thesis/dissertation. *Entrance requirements:* For master's, BA in German; for doctorate, MA in German. Additional exam requirements/recommendations for international students: Required—TOEFL.

*Application deadline:* Applications are processed on a rolling basis. Application fee: $100 Canadian dollars ($162 Canadian dollars for international students). Electronic applications accepted. *Expenses:* $4,802 per year tuition and fees, $8,436 per year international. *Financial support:* Fellowships, research assistantships, teaching assistantships, career-related internships or fieldwork, scholarships/grants, tuition waivers (full and partial), and unspecified assistantships available. Support available to part-time students. Financial award application deadline: 1/1. *Faculty research:* Second language acquisition, media theory, performance theory, gender studies, cultural studies. *Application contact:* Kate Wilczak, Graduate Program Assistant, 604-827-3500, Fax: 604-822-9344, E-mail: cenes.dept@ubc.ca. Website: http://cenes.ubc.ca/

**University of Illinois at Chicago,** College of Liberal Arts and Sciences, School of Literatures, Cultural Studies and Linguistics, Department of Slavic and Baltic Languages and Literatures, Chicago, IL 60607-7128. Offers Slavic studies (MA, PhD). *Program availability:* Evening/weekend. Terminal master's awarded for partial completion of doctoral program. *Degree requirements:* For doctorate, one foreign language, thesis/dissertation. *Entrance requirements:* For master's and doctorate, GRE General Test, minimum GPA of 3.0. Additional exam requirements/recommendations for international students: Required—TOEFL. Electronic applications accepted. *Faculty research:* Twentieth-century Polish literature and culture, Russian and Polish modernisms, nineteenth- and twentieth-century Russian literature, Lithuanian language, Polish-Jewish culture and history, Yiddish literature and language.

**University of Illinois at Urbana–Champaign,** Graduate College, College of Liberal Arts and Sciences, Russian, East European, and Eurasian Center, Champaign, IL 61820. Offers MA.

**The University of Kansas,** Graduate Studies, College of Liberal Arts and Sciences, Center for Russian, East European and Eurasian Studies, Lawrence, KS 66045. Offers foreign area officer (MA); Russian, East European and Eurasian studies (MA, Graduate Certificate); JD/MA. *Program availability:* Part-time. *Students:* 10 full-time (4 women), 1 international. Average age 27. 12 applicants, 67% accepted, 3 enrolled. In 2016, 1 other advanced degree awarded. *Entrance requirements:* For master's, GRE General Test, two-page statement of educational and professional objectives, three letters of recommendation, official transcripts. Additional exam requirements/recommendations for international students: Required—TOEFL. Application fee: $65 ($85 for international students). Electronic applications accepted. *Financial support:* Fellowships, research assistantships, and scholarships/grants available. Financial award application deadline: 1/1; financial award applicants required to submit FAFSA. *Faculty research:* Russian and East Central European history and culture; Ukrainian, Russian, and Central Asian domestic politics and international security; Slavic languages, linguistics, and literatures. *Unit head:* Vitaly Chernetsky, Acting Director, 785-864-4236, E-mail: vchernetsky@ku.edu. *Application contact:* Alyssa McDonald, Graduate Admissions Contact, 785-864-4236, E-mail: crees@ku.edu. Website: http://www.crees.ku.edu/

**University of Michigan,** Rackham Graduate School, College of Literature, Science, and the Arts, Center for Russian, East European, and Eurasian Studies, Ann Arbor, MI 48109-1106. Offers AM, Certificate, JD/AM, MBA/AM, MPP/AM. *Program availability:* Part-time. *Faculty:* 71 full-time (48 women), 4 part-time/adjunct (2 women). *Students:* 17 full-time (7 women); includes 3 minority (all Hispanic/Latino). 22 applicants, 86% accepted, 5 enrolled. In 2016, 4 master's awarded. *Degree requirements:* For master's and Certificate, one foreign language, thesis. *Entrance requirements:* For master's, GRE General Test. Additional exam requirements/recommendations for international students: Required—TOEFL (minimum score 560 paper-based; 84 iBT). *Application deadline:* For fall admission, 12/15 for domestic and international students. Application fee: $75 ($90 for international students). Electronic applications accepted. *Expenses:* Tuition, state resident: full-time $21,466; part-time $1152 per credit hour. Tuition, nonresident: full-time $43,346; part-time $2367 per credit hour. Part-time tuition and fees vary according to course load, degree level and program. *Financial support:* In 2016–17, 4 students received support, including 3 fellowships with full tuition reimbursements available (averaging $15,000 per year), 2 teaching assistantships with full tuition reimbursements available (averaging $8,000 per year); career-related internships or fieldwork, scholarships/grants, and health care benefits also available. Financial award application deadline: 1/15; financial award applicants required to submit FAFSA. *Faculty research:* Russia, East Europe, Eurasia, Central Asia, Caucasus. *Unit head:* Dr. Genevieve Zubrzycki, Director, 734-764-7501, E-mail: ii-gradadvising@umich.edu. *Application contact:* Julie E. Burnett, Academic Services Coordinator, 734-936-1842, Fax: 734-615-9158, E-mail: ii-gradadvising@umich.edu. Website: http://www.ii.umich.edu/crees

**The University of North Carolina at Chapel Hill,** Graduate School, College of Arts and Sciences, Curriculum in Russian and East European Studies, Chapel Hill, NC 27599. Offers MA. *Program availability:* Part-time. *Degree requirements:* For master's, one foreign language, thesis. *Entrance requirements:* For master's, GRE General Test. Additional exam requirements/recommendations for international students: Required—TOEFL. Electronic applications accepted. *Faculty research:* Language, area studies, social sciences, sciences, professional schools.

**University of Pittsburgh,** University Center for International Studies, Pittsburgh, PA 15260. Offers African studies (Certificate); Asian studies (Certificate); European Union studies (Certificate); global studies (Certificate); Latin American studies (Certificate); Russian and East European studies (Certificate); West European studies (Certificate). *Program availability:* Part-time, evening/weekend, online learning. *Students:* 175 full-time (105 women), 14 part-time (10 women); includes 78 minority (5 Black or African American, non-Hispanic/Latino; 30 Asian, non-Hispanic/Latino; 42 Hispanic/Latino; 1 Two or more races, non-Hispanic/Latino). Average age 29. *Degree requirements:* For Certificate, one foreign language, comprehensive exam (for some programs), thesis (for some programs). *Entrance requirements:* Additional exam requirements/recommendations for international students: Required—TOEFL. *Expenses:* Contact institution. *Financial support:* In 2016–17, 22 fellowships with full tuition reimbursements (averaging $17,878 per year) were awarded; scholarships/grants, traineeships, health care benefits, tuition waivers, and unspecified assistantships also available. *Unit head:* Dr. Ariel Armony, Director, 412-648-7374, Fax: 412-624-4672, E-mail: armony@pitt.edu. Website: http://www.ucis.pitt.edu

**University of Saskatchewan,** College of Graduate Studies and Research, College of Arts and Science, Department of Languages and Linguistics, Saskatoon, SK S7N 5A2, Canada. Offers MA. *Degree requirements:* For master's, 2 foreign languages, thesis. *Entrance requirements:* Additional exam requirements/recommendations for international students: Required—TOEFL (minimum score 80 iBT); Recommended—IELTS (minimum score 6.5). Electronic applications accepted.

**The University of Texas at Austin,** Graduate School, College of Liberal Arts, Center for Russian, East European, and Eurasian Studies, Austin, TX 78712-1111. Offers MA, JD/MA, MA/MA, MBA/MA, MGPS/MA, MP Aff/MA. *Program availability:* Part-time. *Degree requirements:* For master's, one foreign language, report or thesis. *Entrance requirements:* For master's, GRE General Test, 3 years of formal language training or equivalent, minimum GPA of 3.0. Electronic applications accepted. *Faculty research:*

East European gypsies, elite transformation and democracy in Eastern Europe, elite partisanship as an intervening variable in Russian politics, post-Soviet youth in Russia.

**University of Toronto,** School of Graduate Studies, Munk School of Global Affairs, Centre for European, Russian and Eurasian Studies, Toronto, ON M5S 1A1, Canada. Offers MA, JD/MA. *Degree requirements:* For master's, one foreign language, language proficiency test. *Entrance requirements:* For master's, minimum B+ average in final year, coursework in Russian/East European subjects, 2 years of study in a relevant language. Additional exam requirements/recommendations for international students: Required—TOEFL (minimum score 580 paper-based; 93 iBT), TWE (minimum score 5). Electronic applications accepted.

**University of Washington,** Graduate School, College of Arts and Sciences, Henry M. Jackson School of International Studies, Russian, East European and Central Asian Studies Program, Seattle, WA 98195. Offers Central Asian studies (MAIS); East European studies (MAIS); Russian studies (MAIS). *Degree requirements:* For master's,

one foreign language, thesis. *Entrance requirements:* For master's, GRE General Test, 2 years of relevant language, minimum GPA of 3.0 in last two years. Additional exam requirements/recommendations for international students: Required—TOEFL (minimum score 500 paper-based; 92 iBT), IELTS (minimum score 7). Electronic applications accepted.

**Yale University,** Graduate School of Arts and Sciences, Department of Slavic Languages and Literatures, New Haven, CT 06520. Offers medieval Slavic literature and philology (PhD); Polish literature (PhD); Russian literature (PhD); Slavic languages and literatures and film studies (PhD). *Degree requirements:* For doctorate, 3 foreign languages, thesis/dissertation. *Entrance requirements:* For doctorate, GRE General Test.

**Yale University,** Graduate School of Arts and Sciences, Program in Russian and East European Studies, New Haven, CT 06520. Offers MA. *Degree requirements:* For master's, 2 foreign languages. *Entrance requirements:* For master's, GRE General Test.

# Ethnic Studies

**Colorado State University,** College of Liberal Arts, Department of Ethnic Studies, Fort Collins, CO 80523. Offers MA. *Program availability:* Part-time. *Faculty:* 7 full-time (3 women), 1 (woman) part-time/adjunct. *Students:* 6 full-time (5 women), 9 part-time (4 women); includes 7 minority (2 Black or African American, non-Hispanic/Latino; 2 Asian, non-Hispanic/Latino; 2 Hispanic/Latino; 1 Two or more races, non-Hispanic/Latino), 2 international. Average age 33. 7 applicants, 86% accepted, 5 enrolled. In 2016, 5 master's awarded. *Degree requirements:* For master's, thesis (for some programs), professional paper. *Entrance requirements:* For master's, personal statement, resume/ curriculum vitae, official transcripts, 3 letters of recommendation, minimum GPA of 3.0. Additional exam requirements/recommendations for international students: Required— TOEFL (minimum score 550 paper-based; 80 iBT). *Application deadline:* For fall admission, 2/15 priority date for domestic and international students. Applications are processed on a rolling basis. Application fee: $60 ($70 for international students). Electronic applications accepted. *Expenses:* Tuition, state resident: full-time $9628. Tuition, nonresident: full-time $23,603. *Required fees:* $2253; $528.14 per credit hour. $264.07 per semester. Tuition and fees vary according to course load and program. *Financial support:* In 2016–17, 5 students received support, including 5 teaching assistantships with full and partial tuition reimbursements available (averaging $13,932 per year); scholarships/grants also available. Financial award application deadline: 2/15; financial award applicants required to submit FAFSA. *Faculty research:* Athletics and racial disparities, health disparities, migrant/immigration labor, gender, queer studies and the relationship to ethnicity and race. *Unit head:* Joon K. Kim, Professor/Department Chair, 970-491-6732, Fax: 970-491-2717, E-mail: joon.kim@colostate.edu. *Application contact:* Abby Marweg, Administrative Assistant, 970-491-2418, Fax: 970-491-2717, E-mail: abby.marweg@colostate.edu.
Website: http://ethnicstudies.colostate.edu/

**Cornell University,** Graduate School, Graduate Fields of Arts and Sciences, Field of Sociology, Ithaca, NY 14853. Offers economy and society (MA, PhD); gender and life course (MA, PhD); methodology (MA, PhD); organizations (MA, PhD); policy analysis (MA, PhD); political sociology/social movements (MA, PhD); racial and ethnic relations (MA, PhD); social networks (MA, PhD); social psychology (MA, PhD); social stratification (MA, PhD). Terminal master's awarded for partial completion of doctoral program. *Degree requirements:* For master's, thesis; for doctorate, thesis/dissertation, 1 year of teaching experience. *Entrance requirements:* For master's and doctorate, GRE General Test, 2 letters of recommendation, writing sample. Additional exam requirements/ recommendations for international students: Required—TOEFL (minimum score 550 paper-based; 77 iBT). Electronic applications accepted. *Faculty research:* Comparative societal analysis, work and family, simulations, social class and mobility, racial segregation and inequality.

**Minnesota State University Mankato,** College of Graduate Studies and Research, College of Social and Behavioral Sciences, Department of Ethnic Studies, Mankato, MN 56001. Offers MS. *Students:* 6 full-time (all women), 5 part-time (3 women). *Degree requirements:* For master's, thesis optional. *Entrance requirements:* For master's, minimum undergraduate GPA of 3.0, baccalaureate degree, at least 9 undergraduate credits in ethnic and cross-cultural areas, knowledge of or skills in two languages, statement of purpose. *Application deadline:* For fall admission, 7/1 for domestic students, 5/1 for international students; for winter admission, 11/1 for domestic students; for spring admission, 10/1 for international students. Applications are processed on a rolling basis. Electronic applications accepted. *Unit head:* Kebba Darboe, Chair, 507-389-5014, E-mail: kebba.darboe@mnsu.edu. *Application contact:* Hanh Huy Phan, Director of Graduate Studies, 507-389-5276, E-mail: hanh-huy.phan@mnsu.edu.
Website: http://sbs.mnsu.edu/ethnic/

**Northern Arizona University,** Graduate College, College of Social and Behavioral Sciences, Ethnic Studies Program, Flagstaff, AZ 86011. Offers Graduate Certificate. *Program availability:* Part-time. *Entrance requirements:* For degree, bachelor's degree with minimum GPA of 2.5. Additional exam requirements/recommendations for international students: Required—TOEFL (minimum score 550 paper-based; 80 iBT), IELTS (minimum score 7). Electronic applications accepted. *Expenses:* Tuition, state resident: full-time $8971; part-time $444 per credit hour. Tuition, nonresident: full-time $20,958; part-time $1164 per credit hour. *Required fees:* $1018; $644 per credit hour. Tuition and fees vary according to course load, campus/location and program.

**San Francisco State University,** Division of Graduate Studies, College of Ethnic Studies, Program in Ethnic Studies, San Francisco, CA 94132-1722. Offers MA. *Expenses:* Tuition, state resident: full-time $6738. Tuition, nonresident: full-time $15,666. *Required fees:* $1012. Tuition and fees vary according to degree level and program. *Unit head:* Dr. Kenneth P. Monteiro, Dean, 415-338-1693, Fax: 415-338-1739, E-mail: ethnicst@sfsu.edu. *Application contact:* Dr. Katynka Z. Martinez, Graduate Coordinator, 415-338-3182, Fax: 415-338-1739, E-mail: katynka@sfsu.edu.
Website: http://ethnicstudies.sfsu.edu/

**United Theological Seminary of the Twin Cities,** Graduate Programs, New Brighton, MN 55112-2598. Offers advanced theological studies (Diploma); justice and peace studies (M Div, MA); leadership toward racial justice (M Div, MA, Certificate); Methodist studies (M Div, MA, Certificate); ministry (D Min); ministry renewal and professional development (Certificate); pastoral care and counseling (M Div, MA, MARL); religion and theology (MA); theological and religious studies (Certificate); theology and the arts (M Div, MA); urban ministry (M Div, MA, MARL); women's studies: religion, theology and ministry (M Div, MA). *Accreditation:* ACIPE; ATS. *Program availability:* Part-time, evening/weekend. *Degree requirements:* For master's, thesis; for doctorate,

comprehensive exam, thesis/dissertation. *Entrance requirements:* For master's, minimum GPA of 2.75; strong analytical, reflective thinking and writing skills; vocational and academic goals compatible with those of Seminary; for doctorate, M Div or equivalent, minimum GPA of 3.0, 3 years experience in professional ministry; for other advanced degree, BA or equivalent life experience; strong analytical, reflective thinking and writing skills (Certificate); proficiency in English language, previous study of theology at a theological school, recommendation of student's denomination (Diploma). Additional exam requirements/recommendations for international students: Required— TOEFL (minimum score 550 paper-based).

**Université Laval,** Faculty of Letters, Department of History, Programs in Ethnology of French-Speaking People in North America, Québec, QC G1K 7P4, Canada. Offers MA, PhD. Terminal master's awarded for partial completion of doctoral program. *Degree requirements:* For master's, thesis; for doctorate, comprehensive exam, thesis/ dissertation. *Entrance requirements:* For master's and doctorate, English exam (comprehension of written English), knowledge of French. Electronic applications accepted.

**The University of British Columbia,** Faculty of Arts, Department of Classical, Near Eastern and Religious Studies, Vancouver, BC V6T 1Z1, Canada. Offers ancient culture, religion, and ethnicity (MA); classical and Near eastern archaeology (MA); classics (MA, PhD), including classics; religious studies (MA). *Program availability:* Part-time. *Degree requirements:* For master's, 2 foreign languages, comprehensive exam, thesis optional; for doctorate, 2 foreign languages, comprehensive exam, thesis/ dissertation. *Entrance requirements:* For master's, BA; for doctorate, MA. Additional exam requirements/recommendations for international students: Required—TOEFL, IELTS. *Application deadline:* Applications are processed on a rolling basis. Application fee: $100 Canadian dollars ($162 Canadian dollars for international students). Electronic applications accepted. *Expenses:* $4,802 per year tuition and fees, $8,436 per year international. *Financial support:* Fellowships, teaching assistantships, scholarships/ grants, and health care benefits available. *Faculty research:* Classical literature, ancient history, Biblical studies, archaeology, classical languages, Judaic studies. *Application contact:* Odessa Cadieux-Rey, Graduate Program Staff, 604-822-2515, Fax: 604-822-9431, E-mail: cners.gradsec@ubc.ca.
Website: http://cnrs.ubc.ca/

**University of California, Berkeley,** Graduate Division, College of Letters and Science, Department of Ethnic Studies, Berkeley, CA 94720-1500. Offers PhD. *Faculty:* 17 full-time. *Students:* 32 full-time (22 women); includes 28 minority (6 American Indian or Alaska Native, non-Hispanic/Latino; 10 Asian, non-Hispanic/Latino; 12 Hispanic/Latino), 3 international. Average age 34. 98 applicants. In 2016, 6 doctorates awarded. *Degree requirements:* For doctorate, one foreign language, thesis/dissertation, qualifying exam. *Entrance requirements:* For doctorate, minimum GPA of 3.0, 3 letters of recommendation. *Application deadline:* For fall admission, 12/1 for domestic students. Application fee: $105 ($125 for international students). Electronic applications accepted. *Financial support:* Fellowships with full tuition reimbursements, research assistantships with partial tuition reimbursements, teaching assistantships with partial tuition reimbursements, institutionally sponsored loans, health care benefits, and unspecified assistantships available. *Faculty research:* Gender and race, Asian American visual art, racial theory and politics, Chicana/o literature and visual arts, history of Native North Americans. *Unit head:* Prof. Shari Huhndorf, Chair, 510-643-0796, E-mail: ethnicst@berkeley.edu. *Application contact:* Information Contact, 510-642-6643, Fax: 510-642-6456, E-mail: ethnicst@berkeley.edu.
Website: http://ethnicstudies.berkeley.edu/

**University of California, Riverside,** Graduate Division, Department of Ethnic Studies, Riverside, CA 92521. Offers cultural politics and production (PhD). Terminal master's awarded for partial completion of doctoral program. *Degree requirements:* For doctorate, variable foreign language requirement, comprehensive exam, thesis/dissertation. *Entrance requirements:* For doctorate, GRE, writing sample, statement of purpose, personal history statement, 3 letters of recommendation. Additional exam requirements/ recommendations for international students: Required—TOEFL (minimum score 550 paper-based; 80 iBT); Recommended—IELTS (minimum score 7). Electronic applications accepted. *Expenses:* Tuition, state resident: full-time $16,666. Tuition, nonresident: full-time $31,768. *Required fees:* $11,055.54 per quarter. $3685.18 per quarter. Tuition and fees vary according to campus/location and program. *Faculty research:* The political economy of race, class, gender, sexuality, cultural production, the state, law, criminal justice and grass roots responses.

**University of California, San Diego,** Graduate Division, Department of Ethnic Studies, La Jolla, CA 92093. Offers PhD. *Students:* 41 full-time (31 women). 83 applicants, 13% accepted, 5 enrolled. In 2016, 6 doctorates awarded. *Degree requirements:* For doctorate, one foreign language, comprehensive exam, thesis/dissertation. *Entrance requirements:* For doctorate, GRE General Test, writing sample. Additional exam requirements/recommendations for international students: Required—TOEFL (minimum score 550 paper-based; 80 iBT), IELTS (minimum score 7). *Application deadline:* For fall admission, 1/4 for domestic students. Application fee: $105 ($125 for international students). Electronic applications accepted. *Expenses:* Tuition, state resident: full-time $11,220. Tuition, nonresident: full-time $26,322. *Required fees:* $1864. *Financial support:* Fellowships, teaching assistantships, and scholarships/grants available. Financial award applicants required to submit FAFSA. *Faculty research:* Cultural studies, gender studies, refugee studies, Native American history and culture, theories of performance. *Unit head:* Ross Frank, Chair, 858-534-6646, E-mail: rfrank@ucsd.edu.

*Ethnic Studies*

*Application contact:* Christa Ludeking, Graduate Coordinator, 858-534-6040, E-mail: ethnicstudiesphd@ucsd.edu.
Website: http://ethnicstudies.ucsd.edu

**University of Colorado Boulder,** Graduate School, College of Arts and Sciences, Department of Ethnic Studies, Boulder, CO 80309. Offers PhD. *Faculty:* 10 full-time (5 women). *Students:* 5 full-time (2 women); all minorities (1 Black or African American, non-Hispanic/Latino; 3 Hispanic/Latino; 1 Two or more races, non-Hispanic/Latino). Average age 35. 16 applicants, 38% accepted. *Application deadline:* For fall admission, 12/1 for domestic and international students. Application fee: $60 ($80 for international students). Electronic applications accepted. Application fee is waived when completed online. *Financial support:* In 2016–17, 10 students received support, including 5 teaching assistantships with full and partial tuition reimbursements available (averaging $38,466 per year); institutionally sponsored loans, scholarships/grants, health care benefits, and unspecified assistantships also available. Financial award applicants required to submit FAFSA. *Faculty research:* American history, history, social history, ethnic studies, racism/race relations. *Total annual research expenditures:* $72,259. *Application contact:* E-mail: grad.ethnst@colorado.edu.
Website: http://ethnicstudies.colorado.edu/

**University of New Mexico,** Graduate Studies, College of Arts and Sciences, Program in Anthropology, Albuquerque, NM 87131-2039. Offers archaeology (MA, MS, PhD); ethnology (MA, MS, PhD); evolutionary anthropology (PhD); public archaeology (MA, MS, PhD). *Faculty:* 24 full-time (13 women). *Students:* 38 full-time (29 women), 68 part-time (39 women); includes 24 minority (3 American Indian or Alaska Native, non-Hispanic/Latino; 2 Asian, non-Hispanic/Latino; 14 Hispanic/Latino; 5 Two or more races, non-Hispanic/Latino), 9 international. Average age 33. 67 applicants, 46% accepted, 18 enrolled. In 2016, 18 master's, 14 doctorates awarded. Terminal master's awarded for partial completion of doctoral program. *Degree requirements:* For master's, comprehensive exam (for some programs), thesis or alternative, 1-2 exams; for doctorate, one foreign language, comprehensive exam, thesis/dissertation, exam, proposal, oral defense, skill and/or second language. *Entrance requirements:* For master's and doctorate, GRE General Test, 3 letters of recommendation, letter of interest, transcripts. Additional exam requirements/recommendations for international students: Required—TOEFL (minimum score 550 paper-based), IELTS (minimum score 7). *Application deadline:* For fall admission, 1/4 for domestic and international students. Application fee: $50. Electronic applications accepted. *Financial support:* Fellowships, research assistantships with partial tuition reimbursements, teaching assistantships with partial tuition reimbursements, career-related internships or fieldwork, Federal Work-Study, institutionally sponsored loans, scholarships/grants, traineeships, health care benefits, tuition waivers (partial), and unspecified assistantships available. Support available to part-time students. Financial award application deadline: 3/1; financial award applicants required to submit FAFSA. *Faculty research:* Ethnology, archaeology, evolutionary anthropology, environment, water and land use, gender and social frameworks, Greater Southwest, Latin America, political economy, public anthropology. *Total annual research expenditures:* $875,790. *Unit head:* Michael W. Graves, Chair, 505-277-4524, Fax: 505-277-0874, E-mail: mwgraves@unm.edu. *Application contact:* Erika E. Gerety, Program Advisement Coordinator, 505-277-2732, Fax: 505-277-0874, E-mail: erika@unm.edu.
Website: http://www.unm.edu/~anthro/

# Folklore

**The George Washington University,** Columbian College of Arts and Sciences, Department of American Studies, Washington, DC 20052. Offers American studies (PhD); folk life (MA); historic preservation (MA); material culture (MA). *Program availability:* Part-time, evening/weekend. *Faculty:* 18 full-time (14 women), 15 part-time/adjunct (10 women). *Students:* 18 full-time (14 women), 15 part-time (10 women); includes 9 minority (5 Black or African American, non-Hispanic/Latino; 3 Asian, non-Hispanic/Latino; 1 Hispanic/Latino). Average age 29. 87 applicants, 29% accepted, 10 enrolled. In 2016, 7 master's, 13 doctorates awarded. Terminal master's awarded for partial completion of doctoral program. *Degree requirements:* For master's, comprehensive exam; for doctorate, one foreign language, thesis/dissertation, general exam. *Entrance requirements:* For master's and doctorate, GRE General Test, minimum GPA of 3.0. Additional exam requirements/recommendations for international students: Required—TOEFL (minimum score 550 paper-based; 80 iBT). *Application deadline:* For fall admission, 1/15 priority date for domestic and international students; for spring admission, 10/1 for domestic students. Application fee: $75. *Financial support:* In 2016–17, 22 students received support. Fellowships, research assistantships, teaching assistantships, career-related internships or fieldwork, Federal Work-Study, institutionally sponsored loans, and tuition waivers available. Financial award application deadline: 1/15. *Unit head:* Melanie McAlister, Chair, 202-994-7244, E-mail: jam@gwu.edu. *Application contact:* Information Contact, 202-994-6070, Fax: 202-994-8651, E-mail: amst@gwu.edu.
Website: http://departments.columbian.gwu.edu/americanstudies/

**Indiana University Bloomington,** University Graduate School, College of Arts and Sciences, Department of Folklore and Ethnomusicology, Bloomington, IN 47405. Offers ethnomusicology (MA, PhD), including folklore. *Faculty:* 15 full-time (5 women), 1 (woman) part-time/adjunct. *Students:* 71 full-time (46 women), 2 part-time (1 woman); includes 15 minority (5 Black or African American, non-Hispanic/Latino; 4 Asian, non-Hispanic/Latino; 4 Hispanic/Latino; 2 Two or more races, non-Hispanic/Latino), 13 international. Average age 32. 40 applicants, 53% accepted, 9 enrolled. In 2016, 7 master's, 6 doctorates awarded. Terminal master's awarded for partial completion of doctoral program. *Degree requirements:* For master's, one foreign language, comprehensive exam, project, thesis, or exam; for doctorate, 2 foreign languages, comprehensive exam, thesis/dissertation. *Entrance requirements:* For master's, GRE General Test (minimum scores: 151 for Verbal, 150 for Quantitative, 4.5 for Analytical), minimum GPA of 3.0, writing sample, curriculum vitae, 3 letters of recommendation, personal statement; for doctorate, GRE General Test (minimum scores: 151 for Verbal, 150 for Quantitative, 4.5 for Analytical), minimum GPA of 3.0, writing sample, curriculum vitae, 3 letters of recommendation, personal statement, MA. Additional exam requirements/recommendations for international students: Required—TOEFL (minimum score 550 paper-based; 79 iBT). *Application deadline:* For fall admission, 12/1 for domestic and international students. Application fee: $55 ($65 for international students). Electronic applications accepted. *Expenses:* $36,500 per year. *Financial support:* In 2016–17, 34 students received support, including 3 fellowships with full tuition reimbursements available (averaging $18,000 per year), 15 research assistantships with full tuition reimbursements available (averaging $15,750 per year), 20 teaching assistantships with full tuition reimbursements available (averaging $15,750 per year); Federal Work-Study, scholarships/grants, health care benefits, tuition waivers, and unspecified assistantships also available. Financial award application deadline: 3/1; financial award applicants required to submit FAFSA. *Faculty research:* Narrative, performance studies, material culture, popular culture, music, public practice. *Unit head:* Dr. John McDowell, Chair, 812-855-0390, Fax: 812-855-4008, E-mail: mcdowell@indiana.edu. *Application contact:* Michelle Melhouse, Graduate Recorder, 812-855-0389, Fax: 812-855-4008, E-mail: mmelhous@indiana.edu.
Website: http://www.indiana.edu/~folklore/

**Memorial University of Newfoundland,** School of Graduate Studies, Department of Folklore, St. John's, NL A1C 5S7, Canada. Offers MA, PhD. *Program availability:* Part-time. *Degree requirements:* For master's, thesis optional; for doctorate, one foreign language, comprehensive exam, thesis/dissertation, oral thesis defense. *Entrance requirements:* For master's, 36 credit hours of course work in folklore, humanities, or social studies; honors degree; for doctorate, MA in folklore or related field. Electronic applications accepted. *Faculty research:* Narrative, folk life, belief theory, methodology, popular culture.

**Penn State Harrisburg,** Graduate School, School of Behavioral Sciences and Education, Middletown, PA 17057. Offers adult education in the health and medical professions (Certificate); applied behavior analysis (MA); applied clinical psychology (MA); applied psychological research (MA); community psychology and social change (MA); English as a second language (ESL) program specialist and leadership (Certificate); folklore and ethnography (Certificate); health education (M Ed); lifelong learning and adult education (M Ed, D Ed); literacy education (M Ed); literacy leadership (Certificate); psychology: applications in clinical psychology (Certificate); psychology: health psychology (Certificate); teaching and curriculum (M Ed); training and development (M Ed, Certificate). *Program availability:* Part-time, evening/weekend. *Unit head:* Dr. Mukund S. Kulkarni, Chancellor, 717-948-6105, Fax: 717-948-6452. *Application contact:* Robert W. Coffman, Jr., Director of Enrollment Management, Recruitment and Admissions, 717-948-6250, Fax: 717-948-6325, E-mail: hbgadmit@psu.edu.
Website: https://harrisburg.psu.edu/behavioral-sciences-and-education/

**University of Alberta,** Faculty of Graduate Studies and Research, Department of Modern Languages and Cultural Studies, Edmonton, AB T6G 2E1, Canada. Offers applied linguistics (Germanic, Romance, Slavic) (MA); French language, literatures and linguistics (PhD); French language, literatures, and linguistics (MA); Germanic languages, literatures and linguistics (PhD); Germanic languages, literatures, and linguistics (MA); Italian studies (MA); Slavic languages and literatures (Russian, Ukrainian) (MA, PhD); Slavic linguistics (Russian, Ukrainian) (MA, PhD); Spanish and Latin American studies (MA, PhD); Ukrainian folklore (MA, PhD). *Program availability:* Part-time. *Degree requirements:* For master's, one foreign language, thesis; for doctorate, 2 foreign languages, comprehensive exam, thesis/dissertation. *Entrance requirements:* For master's and doctorate, 1 language other than English. Additional exam requirements/recommendations for international students: Required—Michigan English Language Assessment Battery or TOEFL (minimum score 550 paper-based). Electronic applications accepted. *Faculty research:* Russian/Ukrainian studies; German studies; contemporary Latin American, French and Francophone studies; Italian studies.

**University of California, Berkeley,** Graduate Division, College of Letters and Science, Department of Anthropology, Group in Folklore, Berkeley, CA 94720-1500. Offers MA. *Students:* 8 full-time (4 women), 1 international. Average age 29. 21 applicants, 3 enrolled. In 2016, 5 master's awarded. *Entrance requirements:* For master's, GRE General Test, minimum GPA of 3.0, 3 letters of recommendation. Additional exam requirements/recommendations for international students: Recommended—TOEFL (minimum score 570 paper-based; 90 iBT). *Application deadline:* For fall admission, 12/15 for domestic students. Application fee: $105 ($125 for international students). Electronic applications accepted. *Financial support:* Fellowships, research assistantships, teaching assistantships, institutionally sponsored loans, health care benefits, and unspecified assistantships available. *Unit head:* Prof. Charles Briggs, Chair, 510-643-7934, E-mail: ucbfolklore@berkeley.edu. *Application contact:* Information Contact, 510-643-7934, E-mail: ucbfolklore@berkeley.edu.
Website: http://folklore.berkeley.edu/

**University of Louisiana at Lafayette,** College of Liberal Arts, Department of English, Lafayette, LA 70504. Offers British and American literature (MA), including creative writing, folklore, rhetoric; creative writing (PhD); literature (PhD); rhetoric (PhD). *Program availability:* Part-time. Terminal master's awarded for partial completion of doctoral program. *Degree requirements:* For master's, one foreign language, thesis or alternative; for doctorate, 2 foreign languages, comprehensive exam, thesis/dissertation. *Entrance requirements:* For master's, GRE General Test, minimum GPA of 2.75; for doctorate, GRE General Test, minimum GPA of 3.0. Additional exam requirements/recommendations for international students: Required—TOEFL (minimum score 550 paper-based). Electronic applications accepted. *Faculty research:* Composition theory, Southern literature, medieval literature.

**The University of North Carolina at Chapel Hill,** Graduate School, College of Arts and Sciences, Curriculum in Folklore, Chapel Hill, NC 27599. Offers MA. *Degree requirements:* For master's, one foreign language, comprehensive exam, thesis. *Entrance requirements:* For master's, GRE General Test, minimum GPA of 3.0, writing sample. Electronic applications accepted. *Faculty research:* Public folklore, politics of culture, folklore and feminist theory, belief and health systems, Southern culture.

**University of Oregon,** Graduate School, College of Arts and Sciences, Folklore Program, Eugene, OR 97403. Offers independent study: folklore (MA, MS). *Program availability:* Part-time. *Degree requirements:* For master's, one foreign language, project or thesis. *Entrance requirements:* For master's, GRE General Test, minimum GPA of 3.0. Additional exam requirements/recommendations for international students: Required—TOEFL. *Faculty research:* American folklore, East European folklore, film and folklore, folk religion and belief, ballad.

**The University of Texas at Austin,** Graduate School, College of Liberal Arts, Department of Anthropology, Program in Cultural Forms, Austin, TX 78712-1111. Offers MA, PhD. *Program availability:* Part-time. Terminal master's awarded for partial completion of doctoral program. *Degree requirements:* For master's, one foreign language, thesis, report; for doctorate, one foreign language, thesis/dissertation. *Entrance requirements:* For master's and doctorate, GRE General Test. Electronic applications accepted. *Faculty research:* Expressive culture, gender, genre, folklore and culture of British Isles, ethnography of speaking.

**University of Wisconsin–Madison,** Graduate School, College of Letters and Science, Department of Scandinavian Studies, Madison, WI 53706-1380. Offers area studies (MA); folklore (PhD); literature (MA, PhD); philology (PhD). *Program availability:* Part-time. *Degree requirements:* For master's, 2 foreign languages; exam; for doctorate, thesis/dissertation, exam. *Entrance requirements:* For master's, minimum GPA of 3.25; for doctorate, minimum GPA of 3.5. Electronic applications accepted. *Faculty research:* Historical fiction, Icelandic poetry, nineteenth-century literature, theater, gender studies, folklore.

**Utah State University,** School of Graduate Studies, College of Humanities, Arts and Social Sciences, Department of English and Department of History, Program in American Studies, Logan, UT 84322. Offers folklore (MA, MS); western American literature and culture (MA, MS). *Program availability:* Part-time, evening/weekend. *Degree requirements:* For master's, thesis or alternative. *Entrance requirements:* For master's, GRE General Test or MAT, minimum GPA of 3.0, 3 letters of recommendation, writing sample. Additional exam requirements/recommendations for international students: Required—TOEFL. *Faculty research:* Folklore and folklife, American culture, regional studies, material culture, Jewish folklore, Native American folklore.

# Gender Studies

**American University,** College of Arts and Sciences, Critical Race, Gender, and Culture Studies Collaborative, Washington, DC 20016-8001. Offers Asian studies (Graduate Certificate); women's, gender, and sexuality studies (Graduate Certificate). *Expenses: Tuition:* Full-time $28,422; part-time $1579 per credit hour. *Required fees:* $690; $200 per term. Tuition and fees vary according to course load, degree level and program.

**American University,** College of Arts and Sciences, Department of Economics, Washington, DC 20016-8029. Offers applied microeconomics (Certificate); economics (MA, PhD); gender analysis in economics (Certificate); international economic relations (Certificate); international economics (MA). *Program availability:* Part-time, evening/weekend, 100% online. *Faculty:* 29 full-time (8 women), 10 part-time/adjunct (3 women). *Students:* 110 full-time (55 women), 71 part-time (32 women); includes 26 minority (8 Black or African American, non-Hispanic/Latino; 6 Asian, non-Hispanic/Latino; 7 Hispanic/Latino; 4 Two or more races, non-Hispanic/Latino), 64 international. Average age 31. 241 applicants, 78% accepted, 48 enrolled. In 2016, 34 master's, 13 doctorates, 5 other advanced degrees awarded. Terminal master's awarded for partial completion of doctoral program. *Degree requirements:* For master's, comprehensive exam, thesis or alternative; for doctorate, comprehensive exam, thesis/dissertation. *Entrance requirements:* For master's and doctorate, GRE, statement of purpose, transcripts, 2 letters of recommendation, resume; for Certificate, bachelor's degree, statement of purpose, transcripts, resume. Additional exam requirements/recommendations for international students: Required—TOEFL (minimum score 100 iBT), IELTS (minimum score 7), PTE (minimum score 68). *Application deadline:* For fall admission, 3/1 for domestic students; for spring admission, 11/1 for domestic students. Applications are processed on a rolling basis. Application fee: $55. Electronic applications accepted. *Expenses:* $1,579 per credit tuition; $690 mandatory fees. *Financial support:* Research assistantships, teaching assistantships, institutionally sponsored loans, and unspecified assistantships available. Financial award application deadline: 2/1; financial award applicants required to submit FAFSA. *Faculty research:* Political economy, development, labor, gender. *Unit head:* Dr. Thomas Husted, Department Chair, 202-885-3773, Fax: 202-885-3790, E-mail: husted@american.edu. *Application contact:* Kathleen Clowery, Associate Director of Graduate Admissions, 202-885-3620, Fax: 202-885-1344, E-mail: clowery@american.edu.
Website: http://www.american.edu/cas/economics/

**The American University in Cairo,** School of Global Affairs and Public Policy, Cairo, Egypt. Offers gender and women's studies (MA); global affairs (MGA); international and comparative law (LL M); international human rights law (MA); journalism and mass communication (MA); Middle East studies (MA); migration and refugee studies (MA, Diploma); public administration (MPA); public policy (MPP); television and digital journalism (MA). *Program availability:* Part-time, evening/weekend. *Faculty:* 27 full-time (13 women), 5 part-time/adjunct (3 women). *Students:* 69 full-time (40 women), 194 part-time (134 women), 33 international. Average age 29. 322 applicants, 51% accepted, 86 enrolled. In 2016, 112 master's awarded. *Degree requirements:* For master's, comprehensive exam (for some programs), thesis (for some programs). *Entrance requirements:* Additional exam requirements/recommendations for international students: Required—TOEFL (minimum score 450 paper-based; 45 iBT), IELTS (minimum score 5). *Application deadline:* For fall admission, 2/1 for domestic and international students; for spring admission, 10/15 for domestic and international students. Applications are processed on a rolling basis. Application fee: $80. Electronic applications accepted. *Expenses:* Contact institution. *Financial support:* Fellowships with partial tuition reimbursements, scholarships/grants, and unspecified assistantships available. Financial award application deadline: 3/10. *Faculty research:* Law, media and journalism; public policy and public administration, gender studies, Middle East Studies, global affairs, refugees studies. *Unit head:* Dr. Nabil Fahmy, Dean, 20-2-2615-2671, E-mail: nfahmy@aucegypt.edu. *Application contact:* Maha Hegazi, Director for Graduate Admissions, 20-2-2615-1462, E-mail: mahahegazi@aucegypt.edu.
Website: http://www.aucegypt.edu/GAPP/Pages/default.aspx

**Arizona State University at the Tempe campus,** College of Liberal Arts and Sciences, School of Social Transformation, Tempe, AZ 85287-4902. Offers African studies (Graduate Certificate); gender studies (PhD, Graduate Certificate); justice studies (MS, PhD); social and cultural pedagogy (MA); socio-economic justice (Graduate Certificate); PhD/JD. *Program availability:* Part-time. Terminal master's awarded for partial completion of doctoral program. *Degree requirements:* For master's, thesis or alternative, interactive Program of Study (iPOS) submitted before completing 50 percent of required credit hours; for doctorate, comprehensive exam, thesis/dissertation, interactive Program of Study (iPOS) submitted before completing 50 percent of required credit hours. *Entrance requirements:* For master's, GRE or LSAT, minimum GPA of 3.0 or equivalent in last 2 years of work leading to bachelor's degree; for doctorate, GRE or LSAT (for justice studies program), minimum GPA of 3.0 or equivalent in last 2 years of work leading to bachelor's degree. Additional exam requirements/recommendations for international students: Required—TOEFL, IELTS, or PTE. Electronic applications accepted.

**Brandeis University,** Graduate School of Arts and Sciences, Department of Anthropology, Waltham, MA 02454. Offers anthropology (MA, PhD); anthropology/women's, gender, and sexuality studies (MA). *Program availability:* Part-time. *Faculty:* 9 full-time (5 women), 4 part-time/adjunct (1 woman). *Students:* 38 full-time (25 women), 1 part-time (0 women); includes 7 minority (2 Black or African American, non-Hispanic/Latino; 3 Hispanic/Latino; 2 Two or more races, non-Hispanic/Latino), 6 international. 62 applicants, 48% accepted, 15 enrolled. In 2016, 14 master's, 2 doctorates awarded. *Degree requirements:* For master's, thesis or alternative; for doctorate, one foreign language, comprehensive exam, thesis/dissertation. *Entrance requirements:* For master's and doctorate, GRE General Test, sample of written work, resume, letters of recommendation. Additional exam requirements/recommendations for international students: Required—TOEFL (minimum score 600 paper-based; 100 iBT);

Recommended—IELTS (minimum score 7), TSE (minimum score 68). *Application deadline:* For fall admission, 1/15 for domestic students. Application fee: $75. Electronic applications accepted. *Financial support:* In 2016–17, 39 students received support, including 11 fellowships with full tuition reimbursements available (averaging $24,000 per year), 20 teaching assistantships with partial tuition reimbursements available (averaging $3,200 per year); scholarships/grants, health care benefits, and tuition waivers (partial) also available. Support available to part-time students. Financial award application deadline: 4/15; financial award applicants required to submit FAFSA. *Faculty research:* Sociocultural anthropology, archaeology, gender and sexuality, linguistic anthropology, physical anthropology. *Unit head:* Dr. Sarah Lamb, Director of Graduate Studies, 781-736-2210, Fax: 781-736-2232, E-mail: lamb@brandeis.edu. *Application contact:* Laurel Carpenter, Academic Administrator, 781-736-2210, Fax: 781-736-2232, E-mail: lcarpenter@brandeis.edu.
Website: http://www.brandeis.edu/gsas

**Brandeis University,** Graduate School of Arts and Sciences, Department of English, Waltham, MA 02454-9110. Offers English (MA, PhD); English and women's, gender, and sexuality studies (MA). *Program availability:* Part-time. *Faculty:* 18 full-time (9 women), 12 part-time/adjunct (6 women). *Students:* 42 full-time (24 women), 1 part-time (0 women); includes 7 minority (2 Black or African American, non-Hispanic/Latino; 1 Asian, non-Hispanic/Latino; 3 Hispanic/Latino; 1 Two or more races, non-Hispanic/Latino), 8 international. 126 applicants, 28% accepted, 9 enrolled. In 2016, 3 master's, 3 doctorates awarded. Terminal master's awarded for partial completion of doctoral program. *Degree requirements:* For master's, one foreign language, thesis or alternative; for doctorate, 2 foreign languages, thesis/dissertation, field exam, symposium presentation, prospectus defense. *Entrance requirements:* For master's, GRE, resume, sample of work, 2 letters of recommendation, statement of purpose, transcript(s); for doctorate, GRE General Test; GRE Subject Test, resume, sample of work, 2 letters of recommendation, statement of purpose, transcript(s). Additional exam requirements/recommendations for international students: Required—TOEFL (minimum score 600 paper-based; 100 iBT); Recommended—IELTS (minimum score 7), TSE (minimum score 68). *Application deadline:* For fall admission, 1/5 for domestic and international students. Application fee: $75. Electronic applications accepted. *Financial support:* In 2016–17, 23 fellowships with full tuition reimbursements (averaging $24,000 per year), 11 teaching assistantships with partial tuition reimbursements (averaging $3,200 per year) were awarded; Federal Work-Study, scholarships/grants, health care benefits, and tuition waivers (partial) also available. Support available to part-time students. Financial award application deadline: 4/15; financial award applicants required to submit FAFSA. *Faculty research:* Feminist and gender theory, American literature and post-Colonial theory, early modern (Renaissance) English literature, modernism, literature and science, literary theory and philosophy, contemporary poetry. *Unit head:* Dr. John Plotz, Director of Graduate Studies, 781-736-2130, Fax: 781-736-2179, E-mail: chaucer@brandeis.edu. *Application contact:* Lisa Pannella, Department Academic Administrator, 781-736-2130, Fax: 781-736-2179, E-mail: pannella@brandeis.edu.
Website: http://www.brandeis.edu/gsas

**Brandeis University,** Graduate School of Arts and Sciences, Department of Near Eastern and Judaic Studies, Waltham, MA 02454-9110. Offers Near Eastern and Judaic studies (MA, PhD); Near Eastern and Judaic studies and women's, gender, and sexuality studies (MA); teaching of Hebrew (MAT). *Program availability:* Part-time. *Faculty:* 24 full-time (10 women), 6 part-time/adjunct (3 women). *Students:* 44 full-time (18 women), 2 part-time (0 women); includes 7 minority (2 Black or African American, non-Hispanic/Latino; 1 Asian, non-Hispanic/Latino; 4 Hispanic/Latino), 9 international. 67 applicants, 45% accepted, 12 enrolled. In 2016, 9 master's, 3 doctorates awarded. Terminal master's awarded for partial completion of doctoral program. *Degree requirements:* For master's, one foreign language, thesis or alternative, proseminar, capstone; for doctorate, variable foreign language requirement, comprehensive exam, thesis/dissertation. *Entrance requirements:* For master's, GRE (recommended), 2 letters of recommendation, transcript(s), statement of purpose, writing sample, resume; for doctorate, GRE (recommended), 3 letters of recommendation, transcript(s), statement of purpose, writing sample, resume. Additional exam requirements/recommendations for international students: Required—TOEFL (minimum score 600 paper-based; 100 iBT); Recommended—IELTS (minimum score 7), TSE (minimum score 68). *Application deadline:* For fall admission, 1/15 priority date for domestic and international students. Application fee: $75. Electronic applications accepted. *Financial support:* In 2016–17, 28 students received support, including 16 fellowships with full tuition reimbursements available (averaging $24,000 per year), 2 teaching assistantships with partial tuition reimbursements available (averaging $3,200 per year); Federal Work-Study, scholarships/grants, health care benefits, and tuition waivers (full and partial) also available. Support available to part-time students. Financial award application deadline: 4/15; financial award applicants required to submit FAFSA. *Faculty research:* Bible and ancient Near East, Judaic Studies, Israel Studies, modern Middle East, Arabic and Islamic civilizations. *Unit head:* Dr. Jonathan Decter, Department Chair, 781-736-2950, Fax: 781-736-2070, E-mail: decter@brandeis.edu. *Application contact:* Joanne Arnish, Department Administrator, 781-736-2950, Fax: 781-736-2070, E-mail: arnish@brandeis.edu.
Website: http://www.brandeis.edu/gsas

**Brandeis University,** Graduate School of Arts and Sciences, Joint Master's Programs in Women's, Gender, and Sexuality Studies, Waltham, MA 02454-9110. Offers anthropology and women's, gender, and sexuality studies (MA); English and women's, gender, and sexuality studies (MA); near Eastern and Judaic studies and women's, gender, and sexuality studies (MA); public policy and women's, gender, and sexuality studies (MA); sociology and women's, gender, and sexuality studies (MA); sustainable international development and women's, gender, and sexuality studies (MA). *Degree requirements:* For master's, thesis. *Entrance requirements:* For master's, GRE, sample

of written work, resume, statement of purpose, transcript(s), two letters of recommendation. Additional exam requirements/recommendations for international students: Required—TOEFL (minimum score 600 paper-based; 100 iBT), PTE (minimum score 68). Recommended—IELTS (minimum score 7). *Application deadline:* For fall admission, 1/15 for domestic students. Application fee: $75. Electronic applications accepted. *Financial support:* Fellowships with full tuition reimbursements and teaching assistantships with partial tuition reimbursements available. Financial award application deadline: 4/15; financial award applicants required to submit FAFSA. *Faculty research:* Anthropology, English, history, music, Near Eastern and Judaic studies, public policy, psychology, sociology, and sustainable international development. *Unit head:* Elizabeth Brainerd, Director of Graduate Study, 781-736-4816, E-mail: ebrainer@brandeis.edu. *Application contact:* Shannon Hunt, Program Administrator, 781-736-3045, Fax: 781-736-3044, E-mail: shunt@brandeis.edu.
Website: http://www.brandeis.edu/gsas

**Brandeis University,** Graduate School of Arts and Sciences, MA Program in Women's and Gender Studies, Waltham, MA 02454-9110. Offers MA. *Faculty:* 20 full-time (19 women), 3 part-time/adjunct (all women). *Students:* 15 full-time (all women); includes 3 minority (2 Black or African American, non-Hispanic/Latino; 1 Two or more races, non-Hispanic/Latino), 2 international. 19 applicants, 47% accepted, 4 enrolled. In 2016, 3 master's awarded. *Degree requirements:* For master's, thesis, proseminar. *Entrance requirements:* For master's, GRE, three letters of recommendation, curriculum vitae or resume, statement of purpose, critical writing sample, transcript(s). Additional exam requirements/recommendations for international students: Required—TOEFL (minimum score 600 paper-based; 100 iBT); Recommended—IELTS (minimum score 7), TSE (minimum score 68). *Application deadline:* For fall admission, 1/15 for domestic and international students. Application fee: $75. Electronic applications accepted. *Financial support:* In 2016–17, 15 students received support, including 4 fellowships with partial tuition reimbursements available, 6 teaching assistantships with partial tuition reimbursements available (averaging $3,200 per year); Federal Work-Study, scholarships/grants, and tuition waivers (partial) also available. Financial award application deadline: 4/15; financial award applicants required to submit FAFSA. *Faculty research:* Gender and legal studies, sexuality studies, social and public policy, comparative literature and culture, anthropology, English, music, near eastern and Judaic studies, public policy, sociology, sustainable international development, history, psychology. *Unit head:* Elizabeth Brainerd, Director of Graduate Study, 781-736-3045, Fax: 781-736-3045, E-mail: wgstudies@brandeis.edu. *Application contact:* Shannon Hunt, Academic Administrator, 781-736-3045, Fax: 781-736-3044, E-mail: shunt@brandeis.edu.
Website: http://www.brandeis.edu/programs/wgs/graduate/index.html

**Carnegie Mellon University,** Dietrich College of Humanities and Social Sciences, Department of History, Pittsburgh, PA 15213-3891. Offers African and African-American diaspora (PhD); culture and power (PhD); labor, politics and social movements (PhD); technology, environment, science and health (PhD); women, gender and the family (PhD). *Program availability:* Part-time. *Degree requirements:* For doctorate, oral and written comprehensive exams, dissertation defense. *Entrance requirements:* For doctorate, GRE General Test. Additional exam requirements/recommendations for international students: Required—TOEFL. Electronic applications accepted. *Faculty research:* Anthropology and history, African-American history, technology/environment, cultural history analysis.

**Central European University,** Department of Gender Studies, Budapest, Hungary. Offers MA, PhD. *Faculty:* 10 full-time (9 women), 1 (woman) part-time/adjunct. *Students:* 85 full-time (74 women). Average age 29. 436 applicants, 11% accepted, 38 enrolled. In 2016, 38 master's, 4 doctorates awarded. *Degree requirements:* For master's, one foreign language, thesis; for doctorate, one foreign language, comprehensive exam, thesis/dissertation. *Entrance requirements:* For master's and doctorate, essay, interview, statement of purpose. Additional exam requirements/recommendations for international students: Required—TOEFL (minimum score 570 paper-based); Recommended—IELTS (minimum score 6.5). *Application deadline:* For fall admission, 2/4 for domestic and international students. Application fee: $30. Electronic applications accepted. *Expenses: Tuition:* Full-time 13,500 euros. Tuition and fees vary according to degree level, program and student level. *Financial support:* Fellowships, career-related internships or fieldwork, scholarships/grants, health care benefits, and tuition waivers (full and partial) available. Financial award application deadline: 2/4. *Faculty research:* Theories of gender, gendering theory; science and gender; activism, social movements and policy; gender dimensions of post-state socialism; gendered borders, nationalism, and transnational flows; political violence, war and gender; raced and sexed identities; cultural studies; feminist knowledge production. *Unit head:* Elissa Helms, Head of Department, 36 1 327-3034, Fax: 36-1-327-3296, E-mail: gender@ceu.edu. *Application contact:* Zsuzsanna Jaszberenyi, Admissions Officer, 361-324-3009, Fax: 367-327-3211, E-mail: admissions@ceu.edu.
Website: http://gender.ceu.edu/

**Central Michigan University,** College of Graduate Studies, College of Humanities and Social and Behavioral Sciences, Program in Humanities, Mount Pleasant, MI 48859. Offers humanities (MA), including contemporary issues in the humanities: race, class, and gender, images and ideas of self, Native American issues in modern culture, popular culture studies, the rise of industrial society. *Program availability:* Part-time, evening/weekend. *Degree requirements:* For master's, thesis or alternative. Electronic applications accepted. *Faculty research:* Rise of industrial society; images and ideas of self; contemporary issues of race, class, and gender; popular culture; Native American issues in modern culture.

**The College of New Jersey,** Office of Graduate and Advancing Education, School of Humanities and Social Sciences, Department of Women's and Gender Studies, Ewing, NJ 08628. Offers gender studies (Certificate). *Program availability:* Part-time. *Entrance requirements:* For degree, two letters of recommendation, official transcripts, essay. Additional exam requirements/recommendations for international students: Required—TOEFL. Electronic applications accepted.

**Cornell University,** Graduate School, Graduate Fields of Arts and Sciences, Field of Sociology, Ithaca, NY 14853. Offers economy and society (MA, PhD); gender and life course (MA, PhD); methodology (MA, PhD); organizations (MA, PhD); policy analysis (MA, PhD); political sociology/social movements (MA, PhD); racial and ethnic relations (MA, PhD); social networks (MA, PhD); social psychology (MA, PhD); social stratification (MA, PhD). Terminal master's awarded for partial completion of doctoral program. *Degree requirements:* For master's, thesis; for doctorate, thesis/dissertation, 1 year of teaching experience. *Entrance requirements:* For master's and doctorate, GRE General Test, 2 letters of recommendation, writing sample. Additional exam requirements/recommendations for international students: Required—TOEFL (minimum score 550 paper-based; 77 iBT). Electronic applications accepted. *Faculty research:* Comparative societal analysis, work and family, simulations, social class and mobility, racial segregation and inequality.

**Delta State University,** Graduate Programs, College of Arts and Sciences, Program in Liberal Studies, Cleveland, MS 38733-0001. Offers evolving human voices (MALS); gender and diversity studies (MALS); globalization studies (MALS); Mississippi Delta

studies (MALS); philosophy (MALS); religious studies (MALS). *Degree requirements:* For master's, oral and/or written comprehensive exam.

**Dominican University of California,** School of Arts, Humanities and Social Sciences, Humanities Program, San Rafael, CA 94901-2298. Offers applied music (MA); art history (MA); creative writing (MA); gender studies (MA); history (MA); literature (MA); philosophy (MA); political theory (MA); religion (MA). *Program availability:* Part-time. *Degree requirements:* For master's, thesis or alternative. *Entrance requirements:* For master's, minimum GPA of 3.0, interview. Additional exam requirements/recommendations for international students: Required—TOEFL (minimum score 550 paper-based; 80 iBT), IELTS (minimum score 6.5). Electronic applications accepted. Application fee is waived when completed online. *Expenses:* Contact institution.

**Eastern Michigan University,** Graduate School, College of Arts and Sciences, Department of Women's and Gender Studies, Ypsilanti, MI 48197. Offers MA, Graduate Certificate. *Program availability:* Part-time, evening/weekend. *Faculty:* 2 full-time (both women). *Students:* 9 full-time (all women), 8 part-time (all women); includes 4 minority (3 Black or African American, non-Hispanic/Latino; 1 Hispanic/Latino), 1 international. Average age 34. 16 applicants, 94% accepted, 5 enrolled. In 2016, 5 master's, 1 other advanced degree awarded. *Degree requirements:* For master's, thesis, research project, or practicum. *Entrance requirements:* Additional exam requirements/recommendations for international students: Required—TOEFL. *Application deadline:* For fall admission, 6/15 for domestic and international students; for winter admission, 9/15 for domestic and international students; for spring admission, 3/1 for domestic and international students. Applications are processed on a rolling basis. Application fee: $45. *Financial support:* Fellowships, research assistantships with full tuition reimbursements, teaching assistantships with full tuition reimbursements, career-related internships or fieldwork, Federal Work-Study, institutionally sponsored loans, scholarships/grants, tuition waivers (partial), and unspecified assistantships available. Support available to part-time students. Financial award applicants required to submit FAFSA. *Unit head:* Dr. Jacqueline Goodman, Department Head, 734-487-1177, Fax: 734-487-5029, E-mail: jgoodma9@emich.edu. *Application contact:* Dr. Suzanne Gray, Program Advisor, 734-487-1177, Fax: 734-487-5029, E-mail: sgray17@emich.edu.
Website: http://www.emich.edu/wgstudies/

**George Mason University,** College of Humanities and Social Sciences, Interdisciplinary Studies Program, Fairfax, VA 22030. Offers community college teaching (MAIS); computational social science (MAIS); energy and sustainability (MAIS); folklore studies (MAIS); individualized studies (MAIS); neuroethics (MAIS); religion, culture, and values (MAIS); social entrepreneurship (MAIS); social justice and human rights (MAIS); war and the military in society (MAIS); women and gender studies (MAIS). *Faculty:* 10 full-time (3 women), 9 part-time/adjunct (4 women). *Students:* 25 full-time (21 women), 70 part-time (48 women); includes 31 minority (15 Black or African American, non-Hispanic/Latino; 5 Asian, non-Hispanic/Latino; 7 Hispanic/Latino; 4 Two or more races, non-Hispanic/Latino), 3 international. Average age 33. 52 applicants, 92% accepted, 23 enrolled. In 2016, 40 master's awarded. *Degree requirements:* For master's, project or thesis. *Entrance requirements:* For master's, 3 letters of recommendation; writing sample; official transcript; resume. Additional exam requirements/recommendations for international students: Required—TOEFL (minimum score 575 paper-based; 88 iBT), IELTS (minimum score 6.5), PTE (minimum score 59). *Application deadline:* For fall admission, 3/1 for domestic students. Application fee: $75 ($80 for international students). Electronic applications accepted. *Expenses:* Tuition, state resident: full-time $10,628; part-time $443 per credit. Tuition, nonresident: full-time $29,306; part-time $1221 per credit. *Required fees:* $3096; $129 per credit. Tuition and fees vary according to program. *Financial support:* In 2016–17, 8 students received support, including 3 research assistantships with tuition reimbursements available (averaging $9,629 per year), 5 teaching assistantships with tuition reimbursements available (averaging $12,814 per year); career-related internships or fieldwork, Federal Work-Study, scholarships/grants, unspecified assistantships, and health care benefits (for full-time research or teaching assistantship recipients) also available. Support available to part-time students. Financial award application deadline: 3/1; financial award applicants required to submit FAFSA. *Faculty research:* Combined English and folklore, religious and cultural studies (Christianity and Muslim society). *Unit head:* Meredith H. Lair, Director, 703-993-2159, Fax: 703-993-1251, E-mail: mlair@gmu.edu. *Application contact:* Morgan Fisher, Graduate Coordinator, 703-993-8762, E-mail: mfisherb@gmu.edu.
Website: http://mais.gmu.edu

**The George Washington University,** Elliott School of International Affairs, Program in Global Gender Policy, Washington, DC 20052. Offers Graduate Certificate. *Students:* Average age 24. 2 applicants, 100% accepted. In 2016, 1 Graduate Certificate awarded. *Unit head:* Michael Brown, Dean, 202-994-6240, Fax: 202-994-0335, E-mail: elliott@gwu.edu. *Application contact:* Nicole A. Campbell, Director of Graduate Admissions, 202-994-7050, Fax: 202-994-9537, E-mail: esiagrad@gwu.edu.

**Indiana University Bloomington,** University Graduate School, College of Arts and Sciences, Department of Gender Studies, Bloomington, IN 47405. Offers PhD. *Faculty:* 14 full-time (11 women). *Students:* 21 full-time (17 women); includes 6 minority (3 Black or African American, non-Hispanic/Latino; 1 Asian, non-Hispanic/Latino; 2 Two or more races, non-Hispanic/Latino), 4 international. Average age 29. 48 applicants, 15% accepted, 3 enrolled. In 2016, 4 doctorates awarded. Terminal master's awarded for partial completion of doctoral program. *Degree requirements:* For doctorate, comprehensive exam. *Entrance requirements:* Additional exam requirements/recommendations for international students: Required—TOEFL (minimum score 550 paper-based; 79 iBT) or IELTS. *Application deadline:* For fall admission, 12/1 priority date for domestic and international students. Application fee: $55 ($65 for international students). Electronic applications accepted. *Financial support:* In 2016–17, 19 students received support, including 4 fellowships with tuition reimbursements available (averaging $18,000 per year), 2 research assistantships with tuition reimbursements available (averaging $15,750 per year), 15 teaching assistantships with tuition reimbursements available (averaging $15,750 per year); scholarships/grants, health care benefits, and unspecified assistantships also available. Financial award application deadline: 12/1. *Unit head:* Colin R. Johnson, Director of Graduate Studies, 812-855-6702, E-mail: crj2@indiana.edu. *Application contact:* Nina Taylor, Graduate Program Coordinator, 812-856-1906, E-mail: njtaylor@indiana.edu.
Website: http://www.indiana.edu/~gender

**Indiana University Northwest,** College of Arts and Sciences, Gary, IN 46408. Offers clinical counseling (MS), including drug and alcohol counseling; community development/urban studies (Graduate Certificate); computer information systems (Graduate Certificate); liberal studies (MLS); race-ethnic studies (Graduate Certificate); women's and gender studies (Graduate Certificate). *Program availability:* Part-time, evening/weekend. *Students:* 4 full-time (all women), 18 part-time (10 women); includes 10 minority (9 Black or African American, non-Hispanic/Latino; 1 Hispanic/Latino). Average age 39. 22 applicants, 77% accepted, 13 enrolled. In 2016, 6 master's awarded. *Entrance requirements:* For master's, GRE (recommended for MS), minimum undergraduate GPA of 3.0, bachelor's degree from accredited university (for MS). *Application deadline:* For fall admission, 7/1 priority date for domestic and international students; for spring admission, 12/1 priority date for domestic and international students.

Application fee: $40 ($60 for international students). Electronic applications accepted. *Expenses:* $276.98 per credit hour in-state; $652.54 per credit hour out-of-state. *Financial support:* Applicants required to submit FAFSA. *Unit head:* Mark Hoyert, Dean, E-mail: mhoyert@iun.edu.
Website: http://www.iun.edu/coas/

**Indiana University–Purdue University Indianapolis,** School of Liberal Arts, Department of Sociology, Indianapolis, IN 46202. Offers family/gender studies (MA); medical sociology (MA); work/occupations (MA).

**Instituto Tecnologico de Santo Domingo,** Graduate School, Area of Humanities and Social Sciences, Santo Domingo, Dominican Republic. Offers accounting (Certificate); adult education (Certificate); applied linguistics (MA); economics (MA); education (M Ed); educational psychology (MA, Certificate); gender and development (MA, Certificate); humanistic studies (MA); international marketing management (Certificate); international relations in the Caribbean basin (Certificate); intervention systems in family therapy (MA); linguistic and literary communication (Certificate); pedagogical support (MA); social science education (M Ed); sustainable human development (MA); terminal illness and death psychology (Certificate); youth and adult education (M Ed).

**Kansas State University,** Graduate School, College of Arts and Sciences, Department of Gender, Women and Sexuality Studies, Manhattan, KS 66506. Offers Graduate Certificate. *Faculty:* 5 full-time (4 women), 45 part-time/adjunct (39 women). *Students:* 13 full-time (11 women), 1 (woman) part-time; includes 6 minority (1 Black or African American, non-Hispanic/Latino; 4 Hispanic/Latino; 1 Two or more races, non-Hispanic/Latino). Average age 27. In 2016, 5 Graduate Certificates awarded. *Entrance requirements:* For degree, minimum GPA of 3.0, letters of recommendation. Additional exam requirements/recommendations for international students: Required—TOEFL, TWE, or IELTS. *Expenses:* Tuition, state resident: full-time $9670. Tuition, nonresident: full-time $21,828. *Required fees:* $862. *Financial support:* In 2016–17, 2 teaching assistantships with partial tuition reimbursements (averaging $6,000 per year) were awarded. Financial award application deadline: 3/5. *Faculty research:* Gender and violence, queer and transgender studies, girls' studies, ecofeminism, animal studies. *Unit head:* Angela E. Hubler, Head, 785-532-5738, Fax: 785-532-3299, E-mail: ahubler@ksu.edu. *Application contact:* Valerie Padilla Carroll, Coordinator, 785-532-5738, Fax: 785-532-3299, E-mail: padillacarroll@ksu.edu.
Website: http://www.k-state.edu/womst/

**Memorial University of Newfoundland,** School of Graduate Studies, Department of Sociology, St. John's, NL A1C 5S7, Canada. Offers gender (PhD); maritime sociology (PhD); sociology (M Phil, MA); work and development (PhD). *Program availability:* Part-time. *Degree requirements:* For master's, comprehensive exam, thesis optional, program journal (M Phil); for doctorate, one foreign language, comprehensive exam, thesis/dissertation, oral defense of thesis. *Entrance requirements:* For master's, 2nd class degree from university of recognized standing in area of study; for doctorate, MA, M Phil, or equivalent. Electronic applications accepted. *Faculty research:* Work and development, gender, maritime sociology.

**Memorial University of Newfoundland,** School of Graduate Studies, Interdisciplinary Program in Gender Studies, St. John's, NL A1C 5S7, Canada. Offers MGS. *Program availability:* Part-time. Electronic applications accepted.

**Middle Tennessee State University,** College of Graduate Studies, College of Liberal Arts, Program in Women's and Gender Studies, Murfreesboro, TN 37132. Offers Graduate Certificate. *Program availability:* Part-time, evening/weekend, online learning. Electronic applications accepted.

**Minnesota State University Mankato,** College of Graduate Studies and Research, College of Social and Behavioral Sciences, Department of Gender and Women's Studies, Mankato, MN 56001. Offers MS. *Program availability:* Part-time. *Students:* 5 full-time (4 women), 6 part-time (5 women). *Degree requirements:* For master's, comprehensive exam, thesis or alternative. *Entrance requirements:* For master's, minimum GPA of 3.0, essay. Additional exam requirements/recommendations for international students: Required—TOEFL. *Application deadline:* For fall admission, 3/30 priority date for domestic students. Applications are processed on a rolling basis. Application fee: $40. *Financial support:* Research assistantships, teaching assistantships with full tuition reimbursements, career-related internships or fieldwork, Federal Work-Study, institutionally sponsored loans, and unspecified assistantships available. Support available to part-time students. Financial award application deadline: 3/15; financial award applicants required to submit FAFSA. *Unit head:* Shannon Miller, Chair, 507-389-5024, E-mail: shannon.miller@mnsu.edu.
Website: http://sbs.mnsu.edu/women/

**Northern Arizona University,** Graduate College, College of Social and Behavioral Sciences, Women's and Gender Studies Program, Flagstaff, AZ 86011. Offers Graduate Certificate. *Program availability:* Part-time. *Entrance requirements:* Additional exam requirements/recommendations for international students: Required—TOEFL (minimum score 550 paper-based; 80 iBT). Electronic applications accepted. *Expenses:* Tuition, state resident: full-time $8971; part-time $444 per credit hour. Tuition, nonresident: full-time $20,958; part-time $1164 per credit hour. *Required fees:* $1018; $644 per credit hour. Tuition and fees vary according to course load, campus/location and program.

**Northwestern University,** The Graduate School, Program in Gender and Sexuality Studies, Evanston, IL 60208. Offers Graduate Certificate. *Faculty research:* Anthropology, gender in Victorian period, autobiography, performance ethnographies, Slavic literature, women in the law.

**The Ohio State University,** Graduate School, College of Arts and Sciences, Division of Arts and Humanities, Department of Women's, Gender and Sexuality Studies, Columbus, OH 43210. Offers MA, PhD. *Faculty:* 14. *Students:* 26 full-time (24 women), 6 international. Average age 28. In 2016, 1 master's, 4 doctorates awarded. Terminal master's awarded for partial completion of doctoral program. *Degree requirements:* For master's, thesis optional; for doctorate, thesis/dissertation. *Entrance requirements:* For master's and doctorate, GRE (if GPA is less than 3.0 for all work), scholarly writing sample. Additional exam requirements/recommendations for international students: Required—TOEFL (minimum score 550 paper-based; 79 iBT), Michigan English Language Assessment Battery (minimum score 82); Recommended—IELTS (minimum score 7). *Application deadline:* For fall admission, 12/1 priority date for domestic students, 11/15 priority date for international students; for spring admission, 3/1 for domestic students, 2/1 for international students. Applications are processed on a rolling basis. Application fee: $60 ($70 for international students). Electronic applications accepted. *Financial support:* Fellowships with tuition reimbursements, research assistantships with tuition reimbursements, teaching assistantships with tuition reimbursements, career-related internships or fieldwork, Federal Work-Study, institutionally sponsored loans, and unspecified assistantships available. Support available to part-time students. *Unit head:* Dr. Shannon Winnubst, Chair and Professor, 614-292-3915, E-mail: winnubst.1@osu.edu. *Application contact:* Graduate and Professional Admissions, 614-292-9444, Fax: 614-292-3895, E-mail: gpadmissions@osu.edu.
Website: http://wgss.osu.edu/

**Oregon State University,** College of Liberal Arts, Program in Women, Gender, and Sexuality Studies, Corvallis, OR 97331. Offers feminist leadership (PhD); gender, rhetoric, and representation (PhD); health and gender justice (PhD); social justice theory and practice (PhD). *Program availability:* Part-time. *Faculty:* 12 full-time (7 women), 1 (woman) part-time/adjunct. *Students:* 20 full-time (19 women), 5 part-time (all women); includes 4 minority (1 American Indian or Alaska Native, non-Hispanic/Latino; 2 Hispanic/Latino; 1 Two or more races, non-Hispanic/Latino), 8 international. Average age 30. 66 applicants, 30% accepted, 10 enrolled. In 2016, 4 master's awarded. *Degree requirements:* For master's, one foreign language; for doctorate, thesis/dissertation. *Entrance requirements:* Additional exam requirements/recommendations for international students: Required—TOEFL (minimum score 80 iBT), IELTS (minimum score 6.5). *Application deadline:* For fall admission, 12/1 for domestic and international students. Application fee: $75 ($85 for international students). *Expenses:* Tuition, state resident: full-time $12,150; part-time $450 per credit. Tuition, nonresident: full-time $21,789; part-time $807 per credit. *Required fees:* $1651; $1507 per credit. One-time fee: $350. Tuition and fees vary according to course load, campus/location and program. *Financial support:* Application deadline: 4/1. *Unit head:* Dr. Larry Roper, Professor and Director of the School of Language, Culture, and Society. *Application contact:* Dr. Qwo-Li Driskill, Director of Graduate Studies, 541-737-1114, E-mail: quo-li.driskill@oregonstate.edu.
Website: http://liberalarts.oregonstate.edu/slcs/wgss/

**Queen's University at Kingston,** School of Graduate Studies, Faculty of Arts and Sciences, Department of Political Studies, Kingston, ON K7L 3N6, Canada. Offers Canadian politics (PhD); comparative politics (PhD); gender and politics (PhD); international relations (PhD); political theory (PhD). *Degree requirements:* For master's, thesis or alternative; for doctorate, one foreign language, thesis/dissertation, qualifying exams. *Entrance requirements:* Additional exam requirements/recommendations for international students: Required—TOEFL (minimum score 600 paper-based). *Faculty research:* Canadian politics, comparative politics, political thought, international politics, women and politics.

**Roosevelt University,** Graduate Division, College of Arts and Sciences, Department of Literature and Languages, Program in Women's and Gender Studies, Chicago, IL 60605. Offers MA, Certificate. *Program availability:* Part-time, evening/weekend. *Degree requirements:* For master's, thesis. *Entrance requirements:* For master's, minimum GPA of 2.7. *Faculty research:* Feminist economics; philosophy of feminism; race, class, and gender; women and art; women's history.

**Rutgers University–New Brunswick,** Graduate School-New Brunswick, Program in Women's and Gender Studies, Piscataway, NJ 08854-8097. Offers MA, PhD. *Program availability:* Part-time. *Degree requirements:* For master's, thesis or alternative; for doctorate, comprehensive exam, thesis/dissertation. *Entrance requirements:* For master's and doctorate, GRE General Test, writing sample, 3 letters of recommendation. Additional exam requirements/recommendations for international students: Required—TOEFL. *Faculty research:* Feminist theory, gender and sexuality, global and cultural studies, women in history, literature, and politics, feminist politics.

**Saint Mary's University,** Faculty of Arts, Program in Women and Gender Studies, Halifax, NS B3H 3C3, Canada. Offers MA. Program offered jointly with Mount Saint Vincent University. *Program availability:* Part-time. *Degree requirements:* For master's, thesis. *Entrance requirements:* For master's, honors degree.

**San Diego State University,** Graduate and Research Affairs, College of Arts and Letters, Program in Lesbian, Gay, Bisexual and Transgender Studies, San Diego, CA 92182. Offers Graduate Certificate.

**Simmons College,** College of Arts and Sciences, Boston, MA 02115. Offers elementary education (MAT); English (MA); gender/cultural studies (MA); history (MA); public health (MPH); public policy (MPP). *Program availability:* Part-time. *Faculty:* 19 full-time (12 women), 1 (woman) part-time/adjunct. *Students:* 6 full-time (all women), 38 part-time (27 women); includes 10 minority (4 Black or African American, non-Hispanic/Latino; 1 Asian, non-Hispanic/Latino; 2 Hispanic/Latino; 3 Two or more races, non-Hispanic/Latino), 1 international. Average age 26. 50 applicants, 88% accepted, 17 enrolled. In 2016, 19 master's awarded. Terminal master's awarded for partial completion of doctoral program. *Degree requirements:* For master's, thesis (for some programs). *Entrance requirements:* For master's, GRE. Additional exam requirements/recommendations for international students: Required—TOEFL (minimum score 600 paper-based; 100 iBT). *Application deadline:* For fall admission, 8/1 for domestic and international students; for spring admission, 12/15 for domestic and international students; for summer admission, 5/1 for domestic and international students. Applications are processed on a rolling basis. Application fee: $35. Electronic applications accepted. *Expenses:* $1,050 per credit, $4,200 per course, $52 activity fee per semester. *Financial support:* In 2016–17, 4 fellowships with partial tuition reimbursements, 22 teaching assistantships with partial tuition reimbursements were awarded; scholarships/grants and unspecified assistantships also available. Support available to part-time students. Financial award applicants required to submit FAFSA. *Unit head:* Dr. Renee White, Dean, 617-521-2079. *Application contact:* Patricia Flaherty, Director, Graduate Studies Admission, 617-521-3902, Fax: 617-521-3058, E-mail: gsa@simmons.edu.
Website: http://www.simmons.edu/gradstudies/

**Simon Fraser University,** Office of Graduate Studies and Postdoctoral Fellows, Faculty of Arts and Social Sciences, Department of Gender, Sexuality and Women's Studies, Burnaby, BC V5A 1S6, Canada. Offers MA, PhD. *Faculty:* 6 full-time (all women). *Students:* 21 full-time (16 women). 40 applicants, 40% accepted, 8 enrolled. In 2016, 1 master's, 1 doctorate awarded. *Degree requirements:* For master's, thesis or alternative; for doctorate, comprehensive exam, thesis/dissertation. *Entrance requirements:* For master's, minimum GPA of 3.0 (on scale of 4.33) or 3.33 based on last 60 credits of undergraduate courses; for doctorate, minimum GPA of 3.5 (on scale of 4.33). Additional exam requirements/recommendations for international students: Recommended—TOEFL (minimum score 580 paper-based; 93 iBT), IELTS (minimum score 7), TWE (minimum score 5). *Application deadline:* For spring admission, 3/1 for domestic students. Applications are processed on a rolling basis. Application fee: $90 ($125 for international students). Electronic applications accepted. *Financial support:* In 2016–17, 8 students received support, including 6 fellowships (averaging $6,500 per year), teaching assistantships (averaging $5,608 per year); research assistantships and scholarships/grants also available. *Faculty research:* Gender history, feminist labor studies/economics, queer theory, women and media, feminist research methods. *Unit head:* Dr. Jen Marchbank, Graduate Chair, 778-782-3333, Fax: 778-782-5518, E-mail: gsws-grad-chair@sfu.ca. *Application contact:* Kathryn Hunter, Graduate Secretary, 778-782-3333, Fax: 778-782-5518, E-mail: gswssec@sfu.ca.
Website: http://www.sfu.ca/gsws.html

**Stony Brook University, State University of New York,** Graduate School, College of Arts and Sciences, Program in Women's, Gender, and Sexuality Studies, Stony Brook, NY 11794. Offers Certificate. In 2016, 7 Certificates awarded. *Degree requirements:* For Certificate, interdisciplinary research colloquium. *Entrance requirements:* For degree, GRE, minimum GPA of 2.75, 3 letters of recommendation. Additional exam requirements/recommendations for international students: Required—TOEFL.

## Gender Studies

*Expenses:* Contact institution. *Faculty research:* Exercise, gender studies, humanities, literary criticism, women's studies. *Unit head:* Prof. Mary Jo Bona, Chair, 631-632-6355, E-mail: maryjo.bona@stonybrook.edu. *Application contact:* Graduate Program Director, 631-632-7461.
Website: http://www.stonybrook.edu/commcms/wgss/

**Texas Woman's University,** Graduate School, College of Arts and Sciences, Department of Multicultural Women's and Gender Studies, Denton, TX 76201. Offers MA, PhD. *Program availability:* Part-time. *Students:* 5 full-time (4 women), 37 part-time (35 women); includes 20 minority (9 Black or African American, non-Hispanic/Latino; 1 American Indian or Alaska Native, non-Hispanic/Latino; 3 Asian, non-Hispanic/Latino; 5 Hispanic/Latino; 2 Two or more races, non-Hispanic/Latino), 1 international. Average age 36. In 2016, 9 master's awarded. Terminal master's awarded for partial completion of doctoral program. *Degree requirements:* For master's, comprehensive exam, thesis (for some programs); for doctorate, comprehensive exam, thesis/dissertation. *Entrance requirements:* For master's, 2 letters of reference, personal essay; for doctorate, personal essay, writing sample, curriculum vitae, 2 reference letters. Additional exam requirements/recommendations for international students: Required—TOEFL (minimum score 550 paper-based; 79 iBT). *Application deadline:* For fall admission, 2/1 for domestic and international students; for spring admission, 12/1 priority date for domestic students, 7/1 for international students. Applications are processed on a rolling basis. Application fee: $50 ($75 for international students). Electronic applications accepted. *Expenses:* Tuition, state resident: full-time $9046; part-time $251 per credit hour. Tuition, nonresident: full-time $22,922; part-time $614 per credit hour. *International tuition:* $23,046 full-time. *Required fees:* $2690; $1285 per credit hour. One-time fee: $50. Tuition and fees vary according to course level, course load, program and reciprocity agreements. *Financial support:* Research assistantships, teaching assistantships, career-related internships or fieldwork, Federal Work-Study, institutionally sponsored loans, scholarships/grants, traineeships, health care benefits, and unspecified assistantships available. Support available to part-time students. Financial award application deadline: 3/1; financial award applicants required to submit FAFSA. *Faculty research:* Feminist/womanist theories and epistemologies, history of U.S. feminism, U.S. women of color, feminism and religion/spirituality, critical race theories. *Unit head:* Dr. Ana Louise Keating, Interim Chair, 940-898-2129, Fax: 940-898-2101, E-mail: akeating@mail.twu.edu. *Application contact:* Dr. Samuel Wheeler, Assistant Director of Admissions, 940-898-3188, Fax: 940-898-3081, E-mail: wheelersr@twu.edu.
Website: http://www.twu.edu/ws/

**University at Buffalo, the State University of New York,** Graduate School, College of Arts and Sciences, Department of Transnational Studies, Buffalo, NY 14260. Offers American studies (MA, PhD); Canadian studies (MA, Advanced Certificate); global gender studies (MA, PhD). *Program availability:* Part-time. *Faculty:* 17 full-time (9 women), 4 part-time/adjunct (1 woman). *Students:* 78 full-time (46 women); includes 29 minority (11 Black or African American, non-Hispanic/Latino; 6 American Indian or Alaska Native, non-Hispanic/Latino; 10 Asian, non-Hispanic/Latino; 2 Hispanic/Latino). Average age 34. 53 applicants, 94% accepted, 21 enrolled. In 2016, 4 master's, 7 doctorates awarded. *Degree requirements:* For master's and Advanced Certificate, comprehensive exam (for some programs), thesis optional; for doctorate, comprehensive exam, thesis/dissertation. *Entrance requirements:* For master's, minimum GPA of 3.0; for doctorate, GRE, minimum GPA of 3.0. Additional exam requirements/recommendations for international students: Required—TOEFL (minimum score 550 paper-based; 79 iBT), IELTS. *Application deadline:* For fall admission, 8/28 priority date for domestic students, 6/15 priority date for international students; for winter admission, 2/1 for domestic and international students; for spring admission, 1/28 priority date for domestic students, 11/15 priority date for international students. Applications are processed on a rolling basis. Application fee: $75. Electronic applications accepted. *Expenses:* Contact institution. *Financial support:* In 2016–17, 20 students received support, including 4 fellowships with full tuition reimbursements available (averaging $13,060 per year), 16 teaching assistantships with full tuition reimbursements available (averaging $13,060 per year); research assistantships, career-related internships or fieldwork, institutionally sponsored loans, scholarships/grants, and unspecified assistantships also available. Financial award application deadline: 1/1. *Faculty research:* Native American, intercultural and indigenous people's studies, border theory, cultural studies, American pop culture, feminist theory, construction of gender in society. *Unit head:* Dr. Cecil Foster, Chair, 716-645-0786, Fax: 716-645-5976, E-mail: cecilfos@buffalo.edu. *Application contact:* Karen M. Reinard, Graduate Coordinator, 716-645-0797, Fax: 716-645-5976, E-mail: kreinard@buffalo.edu.
Website: http://transnationalstudies.buffalo.edu/

**The University of Arizona,** College of Social and Behavioral Sciences, Department of Gender and Women's Studies, Tucson, AZ 85721. Offers MA, PhD, Certificate. *Program availability:* Part-time. *Degree requirements:* For master's, thesis/project. *Entrance requirements:* For master's and doctorate, GRE (minimum score: 500 verbal, 500 quantitative, 4.5 analytical), 3 letters of recommendation. Additional exam requirements/recommendations for international students: Required—TOEFL (minimum score 600 paper-based; 100 iBT). Electronic applications accepted. *Faculty research:* Gender, race and border studies; sexuality and the body; gender health and science; cultural representation and theory; public policy and social movements.

**The University of British Columbia,** Faculty of Arts, Institute for Gender, Race, Sexuality, and Social Justice, Vancouver, BC V6T 1Z2, Canada. Offers MA, PhD. Application fee: $100 ($162 for international students). *Expenses:* $4,802 per year tuition and fees, $8,436 per year international. *Application contact:* Wynn Archibald, Graduate Program Staff, 604-822-9171, Fax: 604-822-9169, E-mail: wynn.archibald@ubc.ca.
Website: http://grsj.arts.ubc.ca/

**University of California, Los Angeles,** Graduate Division, College of Letters and Science, Program in Gender Studies, Los Angeles, CA 90095. Offers MA, PhD. Terminal master's awarded for partial completion of doctoral program. *Degree requirements:* For master's, comprehensive exam, thesis; for doctorate, one foreign language, thesis/dissertation, written and oral qualifying exams. *Entrance requirements:* For doctorate, GRE General Test, bachelor's degree; minimum undergraduate GPA of 3.0 (or its equivalent if letter grade system not used); writing sample. Additional exam requirements/recommendations for international students: Required—TOEFL. Electronic applications accepted.

**University of Chicago,** Division of the Humanities, Master of Arts Program in the Humanities, Chicago, IL 60637. Offers art history (MA); cinema and media studies (MA); classic languages (MA); comparative literature (MA); creative writing (MA); cultural policy studies (MA); digital humanities (MA); East Asian languages and civilizations (MA); English language and literature (MA); gender and sexuality studies (MA); Germanic studies (MA); linguistics (MA); music (MA); near Eastern languages and civilizations (MA); philosophy (MA); poetics (MA); race, politics and culture (MA); Romance languages and literatures (MA); Slavic languages and literatures (MA); South Asian languages and civilizations (MA); theater and performance studies (MA). *Students:* 80 full-time (43 women), 7 part-time (3 women); includes 20 minority (5 Black

or African American, non-Hispanic/Latino; 1 American Indian or Alaska Native, non-Hispanic/Latino; 6 Asian, non-Hispanic/Latino; 5 Hispanic/Latino; 3 Two or more races, non-Hispanic/Latino), 11 international. Average age 26. 706 applicants, 15% accepted, 42 enrolled. In 2016, 92 master's awarded. *Degree requirements:* For master's, thesis. *Entrance requirements:* For master's, GRE General Test. Additional exam requirements/recommendations for international students: Required—TOEFL (minimum score 104 iBT), IELTS (minimum score 7). *Application deadline:* For fall admission, 1/3 for domestic and international students. Application fee: $90. Electronic applications accepted. *Financial support:* In 2016–17, 8 fellowships with partial tuition reimbursements (averaging $12,000 per year) were awarded; Federal Work-Study, institutionally sponsored loans, scholarships/grants, and tuition waivers (partial) also available. Financial award application deadline: 12/15; financial award applicants required to submit FAFSA. *Unit head:* Malynne Sternstein, Co-Director, 773-834-1201, Fax: 773-834-7526. *Application contact:* Program Coordinator, 773-834-1201, Fax: 773-834-7526, E-mail: ma-humanities@uchicago.edu.
Website: http://maph.uchicago.edu/

**University of Colorado Denver,** College of Liberal Arts and Sciences, Program in Humanities, Denver, CO 80217. Offers community health science (MSS); humanities (MH); international studies (MSS); philosophy and theory (MH); social justice (MSS); society and the environment (MSS); visual studies (MH); women's and gender studies (MSS). *Program availability:* Part-time, evening/weekend. *Faculty:* 3 full-time (1 woman). *Students:* 12 full-time (6 women), 15 part-time (7 women); includes 6 minority (1 American Indian or Alaska Native, non-Hispanic/Latino; 3 Hispanic/Latino; 2 Two or more races, non-Hispanic/Latino). Average age 41. 4 applicants, 100% accepted, 4 enrolled. In 2016, 5 master's awarded. *Degree requirements:* For master's, 36 credit hours, project or thesis. *Entrance requirements:* For master's, writing sample, statement of purpose/letter of intent, three letters of recommendation. Additional exam requirements/recommendations for international students: Required—TOEFL (minimum score 537 paper-based; 75 iBT); Recommended—IELTS (minimum score 6.5). *Application deadline:* For fall admission, 5/15 for domestic students, 5/15 priority date for international students; for spring admission, 10/15 for domestic students, 10/15 priority date for international students; for summer admission, 3/15 for domestic and international students. Application fee: $50 ($75 for international students). Electronic applications accepted. *Expenses:* Tuition, state resident: full-time $11,006; part-time $474 per credit. Tuition, nonresident: full-time $28,212; part-time $1264 per credit hour. *Required fees:* $256 per semester. One-time fee: $94.32. Tuition and fees vary according to campus/location and program. *Financial support:* In 2016–17, 2 students received support. Fellowships, research assistantships, teaching assistantships, Federal Work-Study, institutionally sponsored loans, scholarships/grants, and traineeships available. Financial award application deadline: 4/1; financial award applicants required to submit FAFSA. *Faculty research:* Women and gender in the classical Mediterranean, communication theory and democracy, relationship between psychology and philosophy. *Unit head:* Margaret Woodhull, Director of Humanities, 303-315-3568, E-mail: margaret.woodhull@ucdenver.edu. *Application contact:* Angela Beale, Program Assistant, 303-315-3565, E-mail: mastershs@ucdenver.edu.
Website: http://www.ucdenver.edu/academics/colleges/CLAS/Programs/HumanitiesSocialSciences/Programs/Pages/MasterofHumanities.aspx

**University of Florida,** Graduate School, College of Liberal Arts and Sciences, Center for Women's Studies and Gender Research, Gainesville, FL 32611. Offers gender and development (Graduate Certificate); women's studies (MA, Graduate Certificate); MA/JD; MA/MA. Terminal master's awarded for partial completion of doctoral program. *Degree requirements:* For master's, thesis or project. *Entrance requirements:* For master's, GRE General Test (minimum score 1000), minimum GPA of 3.2. Additional exam requirements/recommendations for international students: Required—TOEFL (minimum score 550 paper-based; 80 iBT), IELTS (minimum score 6). Electronic applications accepted. *Faculty research:* Prejudice, discrimination, intersections, resistance, history.

**University of Lethbridge,** School of Graduate Studies, Lethbridge, AB T1K 3M4, Canada. Offers addictions counseling (M Sc); agricultural biotechnology (M Sc); agricultural studies (M Sc, MA); anthropology (MA); archaeology (M Sc, MA); art (MA, MFA); biochemistry (M Sc); biological sciences (M Sc); biomolecular science (PhD); biosystems and biodiversity (PhD); Canadian studies (MA); chemistry (M Sc); computer science (M Sc); computer science and geographical information science (M Sc); counseling (MC); counseling psychology (M Ed); dramatic arts (MA); earth, space, and physical science (PhD); economics (MA); education (MA, PhD); educational leadership (M Ed); English (MA); environmental science (M Sc); evolution and behavior (PhD); exercise science (M Sc); French (MA); French/German (MA); French/Spanish (MA); general education (M Ed); geography (M Sc, MA); German (MA); health sciences (M Sc); individualized multidisciplinary (M Sc, MA); kinesiology (M Sc, MA); management (M Sc), including accounting, finance, human resource management and labor relations, information systems, international management, marketing, policy and strategy; mathematics (M Sc); music (M Mus, MA); Native American studies (MA); neuroscience (M Sc, PhD); new media (MA, MFA); nursing (M Sc, MN); philosophy (MA); physics (M Sc); political science (MA); psychology (M Sc, MA); religious studies (MA); sociology (MA); theatre and dramatic arts (MFA); theoretical and computational science (PhD); urban and regional studies (MA); women and gender studies (MA). *Program availability:* Part-time, evening/weekend. *Degree requirements:* For master's, thesis (for some programs); for doctorate, comprehensive exam, thesis/dissertation. *Entrance requirements:* For master's, GMAT (for M Sc in management), bachelor's degree in related field, minimum GPA of 3.0 during previous 20 graded semester courses, 2 years' teaching or related experience (M Ed); for doctorate, master's degree, minimum graduate GPA of 3.5. Additional exam requirements/recommendations for international students: Required—TOEFL (minimum score 580 paper-based; 93 iBT). Electronic applications accepted. *Faculty research:* Movement and brain plasticity, gibberellin physiology, photosynthesis, carbon cycling, molecular properties of main-group ring components.

**University of Memphis,** Graduate School, College of Arts and Sciences, Program in Interdisciplinary Studies, Memphis, TN 38152. Offers museum studies (Graduate Certificate); women's and gender studies (Graduate Certificate). *Faculty:* 2 full-time (1 woman). *Students:* 6 full-time (2 women), 7 part-time (3 women); includes 3 minority (1 Black or African American, non-Hispanic/Latino; 1 Hispanic/Latino; 1 Two or more races, non-Hispanic/Latino), 6 international. Average age 30. 19 applicants, 79% accepted, 6 enrolled. In 2016, 6 Graduate Certificates awarded. *Degree requirements:* For Graduate Certificate, minimum GPA of 3.0. *Entrance requirements:* For degree, GRE, letter of interest, undergraduate transcript. Additional exam requirements/recommendations for international students: Required—TOEFL (minimum score 550 paper-based). *Application deadline:* For fall admission, 4/3 for domestic students. Application fee: $35 ($60 for international students). *Expenses:* Contact institution. *Financial support:* In 2016–17, 11 students received support, including 8 research assistantships with full tuition reimbursements available (averaging $11,736 per year); teaching assistantships with full tuition reimbursements available, Federal Work-Study, scholarships/grants, and unspecified assistantships also available. Financial award application deadline: 2/1; financial award applicants required to submit FAFSA. *Unit head:* Dr. Henry A. Kurtz, Dean, 901-678-2251, Fax: 901-678-4831, E-mail: hkurtz@memphis.edu. *Application* *contact:* Dr. Kathy Schultz, Director of Women's and Gender Studies, 901-678-2651, E-mail: klschltz@memphis.edu. Website: http://www.memphis.edu/isc/

**University of Michigan–Flint,** College of Arts and Sciences, Program in Social Sciences, Flint, MI 48502-1950. Offers gender studies (MA); global studies (MA); U.S. history and politics (MA). *Program availability:* Part-time. *Faculty:* 9 full-time (1 woman), 1 (woman) part-time/adjunct. *Students:* 4 full-time (1 woman), 21 part-time (14 women); includes 12 minority (9 Black or African American, non-Hispanic/Latino; 2 Hispanic/Latino; 1 Two or more races, non-Hispanic/Latino). Average age 39. 17 applicants, 82% accepted, 7 enrolled. In 2016, 7 master's awarded. *Entrance requirements:* For master's, bachelor's degree from regionally-accredited institution, minimum overall undergraduate GPA of 3.0. Additional exam requirements/recommendations for international students: Required—TOEFL (minimum score 84 iBT), IELTS (minimum score 6.5). *Application deadline:* For fall admission, 8/1 for domestic students, 5/1 for international students; for winter admission, 11/15 for domestic students, 9/1 for international students; for spring admission, 3/15 for domestic students, 1/1 for international students; for summer admission, 5/15 for domestic students. Applications are processed on a rolling basis. Application fee: $55. Electronic applications accepted. *Financial support:* Federal Work-Study, scholarships/grants, and unspecified assistantships available. Support available to part-time students. Financial award application deadline: 3/1; financial award applicants required to submit FAFSA. *Unit head:* Dr. Adam Lutzker, Director, 810-762-3470, Fax: 810-762-3281, E-mail: alutzker@umflint.edu. *Application contact:* Bradley T. Maki, Director of Graduate Admissions, 810-762-3171, Fax: 810-766-6789, E-mail: bmaki@umflint.edu. Website: http://www.umflint.edu/graduateprograms/social-sciences-ma

**The University of North Carolina at Charlotte,** College of Liberal Arts and Sciences, Interdisciplinary Liberal Arts and Sciences Programs, Charlotte, NC 28223-0001. Offers gender, sexuality, and women's studies (Graduate Certificate); gerontology (MA, Graduate Certificate); Latin American studies (MA); liberal studies (MA); organizational science (PhD); public policy (PhD). *Program availability:* Part-time, evening/weekend. *Faculty:* 1 (woman) part-time/adjunct. *Students:* 65 full-time (49 women), 61 part-time (50 women); includes 31 minority (11 Black or African American, non-Hispanic/Latino; 1 American Indian or Alaska Native, non-Hispanic/Latino; 2 Asian, non-Hispanic/Latino; 16 Hispanic/Latino; 1 Two or more races, non-Hispanic/Latino), 15 international. Average age 32. 128 applicants, 41% accepted, 40 enrolled. In 2016, 15 master's, 12 doctorates, 7 other advanced degrees awarded. *Degree requirements:* For master's, comprehensive exam (for some programs), thesis (for some programs), practicum, project; for doctorate, comprehensive exam, thesis/dissertation; for Graduate Certificate, practicum (for gerontology). *Entrance requirements:* For master's, GRE General Test or MAT, bachelor's degree from accredited college or university; official transcripts of all previous academic work attempted beyond high school; minimum overall GPA of 3.0 on applicant's previous work beyond high school; statement of purpose; recommendation letters; for doctorate, GRE or GMAT, statement of purpose discussing interest in program and objectives for pursuing degree, current resume or curriculum vitae, unofficial transcripts; for Graduate Certificate, bachelor's degree from accredited university and either be enrolled in and in good standing in a graduate degree program at UNC Charlotte or have a minimum undergraduate GPA of 3.0. Additional exam requirements/recommendations for international students: Required—TOEFL (minimum score 523 paper-based, 70 iBT) or IELTS (6.5). *Application deadline:* For fall admission, 2/15 for domestic and international students; for spring admission, 10/1 for domestic and international students; for summer admission, 4/1 for domestic and international students. Applications are processed on a rolling basis. Application fee: $75. Electronic applications accepted. *Expenses:* Tuition, state resident: full-time $4252. Tuition, nonresident: full-time $17,423. *Required fees:* $3026. Tuition and fees vary according to course load and program. *Financial support:* In 2016–17, 26 students received support, including 17 research assistantships (averaging $12,840 per year), 7 teaching assistantships (averaging $14,442 per year); career-related internships or fieldwork, institutionally sponsored loans, scholarships/grants, unspecified assistantships, and administrative assistantships also available. Support available to part-time students. Financial award application deadline: 3/1; financial award applicants required to submit FAFSA. *Unit head:* Dr. Nancy A. Gutierrez, Dean, 704-687-0081, E-mail: ngutierr@uncc.edu. *Application contact:* Kathy B. Giddings, Director of Graduate Admissions, 704-687-5503, Fax: 704-687-3279, E-mail: gradadm@uncc.edu. Website: http://clas.uncc.edu/academics

**The University of North Carolina at Greensboro,** Graduate School, College of Arts and Sciences, Program in Women's and Gender Studies, Greensboro, NC 27412-5001. Offers MA, Certificate. Electronic applications accepted.

**University of Northern British Columbia,** Office of Graduate Studies, Prince George, BC V2N 4Z9, Canada. Offers business administration (Diploma); community health science (M Sc); disability management (MA); education (M Ed); first nations studies (MA); gender studies (MA); history (MA); interdisciplinary studies (MA); international studies (MA); mathematical, computer and physical sciences (M Sc); natural resources and environmental studies (M Sc, MA, MNRES, PhD); political science (MA); psychology (M Sc, PhD); social work (MSW). *Program availability:* Part-time, evening/weekend, online learning. *Degree requirements:* For master's, thesis; for doctorate, thesis/dissertation. *Entrance requirements:* For master's, GRE, minimum B average in undergraduate course work; for doctorate, candidacy exam, minimum A average in graduate course work.

**University of Northern Iowa,** Graduate College, MA Program in Women's and Gender Studies, Cedar Falls, IA 50614. Offers MA. *Degree requirements:* For master's, comprehensive exam (for some programs), thesis or alternative. *Entrance requirements:* For master's, minimum GPA of 3.0. Additional exam requirements/recommendations for international students: Required—TOEFL (minimum score 500 paper-based; 61 iBT). Electronic applications accepted.

**University of Oklahoma,** College of Arts and Sciences, Women's and Gender Studies Program, Norman, OK 73019. Offers Graduate Certificate. *Program availability:* Part-time, evening/weekend. *Faculty:* 1 (woman) full-time. *Students:* 9 full-time (6 women), 12 part-time (11 women); includes 7 minority (2 Black or African American, non-Hispanic/Latino; 2 American Indian or Alaska Native, non-Hispanic/Latino; 2 Hispanic/Latino; 1 Two or more races, non-Hispanic/Latino), 1 international. Average age 39. 1 applicant, 100% accepted, 1 enrolled. In 2016, 7 Graduate Certificates awarded. *Entrance requirements:* Additional exam requirements/recommendations for international students: Required—TOEFL (minimum score 79 iBT) or IELTS (minimum score 6.5). *Application deadline:* For fall admission, 3/15 for domestic and international students; for spring admission, 11/15 for domestic and international students. Applications are processed on a rolling basis. Application fee: $50 ($100 for international students). Electronic applications accepted. *Expenses:* Tuition, state resident: full-time $4886; part-time $203.60 per credit hour. Tuition, nonresident: full-time $18,989; part-time $791.20 per credit hour. *Required fees:* $3283; $126.25 per credit hour. $126.50 per semester. *Financial support:* In 2016–17, 1 teaching assistantship with partial tuition reimbursement (averaging $10,372 per year) was awarded; research assistantships with partial tuition reimbursements and unspecified assistantships also available. Financial award application deadline: 6/1; financial award applicants required to submit FAFSA.

*Faculty research:* Black feminism, terrorism, popular culture, indigenous, reproductive justice. *Total annual research expenditures:* $29,546. *Unit head:* Dr. Maria Lupe Davidson, Director, 405-325-3481, Fax: 405-325-3573, E-mail: mdavidson@ou.edu. Website: http://wgs.ou.edu

**University of Rhode Island,** Graduate School, College of Arts and Sciences, Department of English, Kingston, RI 02881. Offers American and British literature and culture (PhD); creative writing (PhD); English (MA); film (PhD); gender studies (PhD); MLIS/MA. *Program availability:* Part-time. *Faculty:* 18 full-time (11 women). *Students:* 40 full-time (31 women), 13 part-time (9 women); includes 4 minority (2 Black or African American, non-Hispanic/Latino; 1 Asian, non-Hispanic/Latino; 1 Hispanic/Latino), 4 international. In 2016, 2 master's, 9 doctorates awarded. *Degree requirements:* For master's, comprehensive exam (for some programs), thesis optional; for doctorate, comprehensive exam, thesis/dissertation. *Entrance requirements:* For doctorate, GRE General Test, 3 letters of recommendation, writing sample, curriculum vitae. Additional exam requirements/recommendations for international students: Required—TOEFL (minimum score 91 iBT). *Application deadline:* For fall admission, 1/15 for domestic and international students. Application fee: $65. Electronic applications accepted. *Expenses:* Tuition, state resident: full-time $11,796; part-time $655 per credit. Tuition, nonresident: full-time $24,206; part-time $1345 per credit. *Required fees:* $1546; $44 per credit. One-time fee: $155 full-time; $35 part-time. *Financial support:* In 2016–17, 30 teaching assistantships with tuition reimbursements (averaging $17,264 per year) were awarded. Financial award application deadline: 1/15; financial award applicants required to submit FAFSA. *Unit head:* Dr. Travis Williams, Chair, 401-874-9501, E-mail: tdwilliams@uri.edu. *Application contact:* Dr. David Faflik, Director of Graduate Studies, 401-874-4670, E-mail: faflik@uri.edu. Website: http://www.uri.edu/artsci/eng/

**University of Rhode Island,** Graduate School, College of Arts and Sciences, Program in Gender and Women's Studies, Kingston, RI 02881. Offers Graduate Certificate. *Faculty:* 2 full-time (both women). *Students:* 3 full-time (all women). In 2016, 3 Graduate Certificates awarded. *Entrance requirements:* For degree, personal statement, college transcript(s). Application fee: $65. Electronic applications accepted. *Expenses:* Tuition, state resident: full-time $11,796; part-time $655 per credit. Tuition, nonresident: full-time $24,206; part-time $1345 per credit. *Required fees:* $1546; $44 per credit. One-time fee: $155 full-time; $35 part-time. *Financial support:* In 2016–17, 1 teaching assistantship (averaging $9,148 per year) was awarded. *Unit head:* Dr. Rosaria Pisa, Director, 401-874-2482, E-mail: rpisa@uri.edu. *Application contact:* Graduate Admissions, 401-874-2872, E-mail: gradadm@etal.uri.edu. Website: http://web.uri.edu/gws/graduate-certificate-program/

**University of Saskatchewan,** College of Graduate Studies and Research, College of Arts and Science, Department of Women's and Gender Studies, Saskatoon, SK S7N 5A2, Canada. Offers MA, PhD. *Degree requirements:* For master's, thesis; for doctorate, comprehensive exam (for some programs), thesis/dissertation. *Entrance requirements:* Additional exam requirements/recommendations for international students: Required—TOEFL (minimum score 80 iBT); Recommended—IELTS (minimum score 6.5). Electronic applications accepted.

**University of South Florida,** College of Arts and Sciences, Department of Women's Studies, Tampa, FL 33620-9951. Offers women's and gender studies (MA). *Program availability:* Part-time. *Faculty:* 6 full-time (4 women). *Students:* 11 full-time (all women), 3 part-time (all women); includes 2 minority (1 Black or African American, non-Hispanic/Latino; 1 Hispanic/Latino), 1 international. Average age 25. 7 applicants, 100% accepted, 6 enrolled. In 2016, 7 master's awarded. *Degree requirements:* For master's, comprehensive exam, thesis (for some programs), thesis or internship. *Entrance requirements:* For master's, GRE General Test, minimum GPA of 3.0, three letters of recommendation, personal narrative statement of purpose, scholarly writing sample (examples include term paper or research paper); undergraduate major or minor in women's studies (recommended). Additional exam requirements/recommendations for international students: Required—TOEFL (minimum score 550 paper-based; 79 iBT) or IELTS (minimum score 6.5). *Application deadline:* For fall admission, 2/15 for domestic and international students; for spring admission, 10/15 for domestic students, 9/15 for international students; for summer admission, 2/15 for domestic students, 1/15 for international students. Applications are processed on a rolling basis. Application fee: $30. Electronic applications accepted. *Expenses:* Tuition, state resident: full-time $7766; part-time $431.43 per credit hour. Tuition, nonresident: full-time $15,789; part-time $877.17 per credit hour. *Required fees:* $37 per term. *Financial support:* In 2016–17, 6 students received support. Teaching assistantships with tuition reimbursements available available. Financial award application deadline: 3/1. *Faculty research:* Performance studies, feminist theory and pedagogy; constructions of gender in public discourse, including education, mass media, and popular culture; women's health, reproductive justice, and sexuality; bodies and cultural representations; feminist theory as it relates to learning disabilities, critical race theory, postmodernist and queer theory; hiring practices in higher education, mothering; women of color feminisms. *Unit head:* Dr. Diane Price Herndl, Professor and Chairperson, 813-974-0987, Fax: 813-974-0336, E-mail: priceherndl@usf.edu. *Application contact:* Dr. Kim Golombisky, Associate Professor and Graduate Director, 813-974-0986, Fax: 813-974-0336, E-mail: kgolombi@usf.edu. Website: http://wgs.usf.edu/

**University of South Florida,** Innovative Education, Tampa, FL 33620-9951. Offers adult, career and higher education (Graduate Certificate), including college teaching, leadership in developing human resources, leadership in higher education; Africana studies (Graduate Certificate), including diasporas and health disparities, genocide and human rights; aging studies (Graduate Certificate), including gerontology; art research (Graduate Certificate), including museum studies; business foundations (Graduate Certificate); chemical and biomedical engineering (Graduate Certificate), including materials science and engineering, water, health and sustainability; child and family studies (Graduate Certificate), including positive behavior support; civil and industrial engineering (Graduate Certificate), including transportation systems analysis; community and family health (Graduate Certificate), including maternal and child health, social marketing and public health, violence and injury: prevention and intervention, women's health; criminology (Graduate Certificate), including criminal justice administration; educational measurement and research (Graduate Certificate), including evaluation; English (Graduate Certificate), including comparative literary studies, creative writing, professional and technical communication; entrepreneurship (Graduate Certificate); environmental health (Graduate Certificate), including safety management; epidemiology and biostatistics (Graduate Certificate), including applied biostatistics, biostatistics, concepts and tools of epidemiology, epidemiology, epidemiology of infectious diseases; geography, environment and planning (Graduate Certificate), including community development, environmental policy and management, geographical information systems; geology (Graduate Certificate), including hydrogeology; global health (Graduate Certificate), including disaster management, global health and Latin American and Caribbean studies, global health practice, humanitarian assistance, infection control; government and international affairs (Graduate Certificate), including Cuban studies, globalization studies; health policy and management (Graduate Certificate), including health management and leadership,

*Gender Studies*

public health policy and programs; hearing specialist: early intervention (Graduate Certificate); industrial and management systems engineering (Graduate Certificate), including systems engineering, technology management; information studies (Graduate Certificate), including school library media specialist; information systems/decision sciences (Graduate Certificate), including analytics and business intelligence; instructional technology (Graduate Certificate), including distance education, Florida digital/virtual educator, instructional design, multimedia design, Web design; internal medicine, bioethics and medical humanities (Graduate Certificate), including biomedical ethics; Latin American and Caribbean studies (Graduate Certificate); mass communications (Graduate Certificate), including multimedia journalism; mathematics and statistics (Graduate Certificate), including mathematics; medicine (Graduate Certificate), including aging and neuroscience, bioinformatics, biotechnology, brain fitness and memory management, clinical investigation, health informatics, health sciences, integrative weight management, intellectual property, medicine and gender, metabolic and nutritional medicine, metabolic cardiology, pharmacy sciences; national and competitive intelligence (Graduate Certificate); psychological and social foundations (Graduate Certificate), including career counseling, college teaching, diversity in education, mental health counseling, school counseling; public affairs (Graduate Certificate), including nonprofit management, public management, research administration; public health (Graduate Certificate), including environmental health, health equity, public health generalist, translational research in adolescent behavioral health; public health practices (Graduate Certificate), including planning for healthy communities; rehabilitation and mental health counseling (Graduate Certificate), including integrative mental health care, marriage and family therapy, rehabilitation technology; secondary education (Graduate Certificate), including ESOL, foreign language education: culture and content, foreign language education: professional; social work (Graduate Certificate), including geriatric social work/clinical gerontology; special education (Graduate Certificate), including autism spectrum disorder, disabilities education: severe/profound; world languages (Graduate Certificate), including teaching English as a second language (TESL) or foreign language. *Expenses:* Tuition, state resident: full-time $7766; part-time $431.43 per credit hour. Tuition, nonresident: full-time $15,789; part-time $877.17 per credit hour. *Required fees:* $37 per term. *Unit head:* Kathy Barnes, Interdisciplinary Programs Coordinator, 813-974-8031, Fax: 813-974-7061, E-mail: barnesk@usf.edu. *Application contact:* Karen Tylinski, Metro Initiatives, 813-974-9943, Fax: 813-974-7061, E-mail: ktylinsk@usf.edu. Website: http://www.usf.edu/innovative-education/

**The University of Toledo,** College of Graduate Studies, College of Languages, Literature and Social Sciences, Department of Women's and Gender Studies, Toledo, OH 43606-3390. Offers Certificate. *Program availability:* Part-time.

**University of Toronto,** School of Graduate Studies, Faculty of Arts and Science, Women and Gender Studies Institute, Toronto, ON M5S 1A1, Canada. Offers MA, PhD. *Entrance requirements:* For master's, minimum B+ in final year of undergraduate study. Additional exam requirements/recommendations for international students: Required—TOEFL (minimum score 580 paper-based; 93 iBT), TWE (minimum score 5). Electronic applications accepted.

**University of Wisconsin–Milwaukee,** Graduate School, College of Letters and Science, Department of Women's and Gender Studies, Milwaukee, WI 53201-0413. Offers MA, Graduate Certificate. *Program availability:* Part-time. *Students:* 4 full-time (all women), 2 part-time (both women); includes 2 minority (1 Black or African American, non-Hispanic/Latino; 1 Two or more races, non-Hispanic/Latino). Average age 42. 11 applicants, 55% accepted, 4 enrolled. In 2016, 1 master's awarded. *Entrance requirements:* For master's, three letters of recommendation, sample of written work, letter of intent. *Application deadline:* Applications are processed on a rolling basis. Application fee: $56 ($96 for international students). Electronic applications accepted. *Financial support:* In 2016–17, 2 teaching assistantships with full tuition reimbursements were awarded; fellowships, research assistantships, health care benefits, and unspecified assistantships also available. Financial award applicants required to submit FAFSA. *Unit head:* Dr. Gwynne Kennedy, Director, 414-229-5918, E-mail: gkennedy@uwm.edu. *Application contact:* General Information Contact, 414-229-4982, Fax: 414-229-6967, E-mail: gradschool@uwm.edu. Website: http://uwm.edu/womens-gender-studies/

**Wayne State University,** College of Liberal Arts and Sciences, Department of History, Detroit, MI 48202. Offers Africa (PhD); America (PhD); Asia (PhD); Europe (PhD); gender (PhD); history (MA); labor (PhD); public history (MA); science and technology (PhD); world history (PhD, Graduate Certificate); JD/MA; M Ed/MA; MLIS/MA. Doctoral program admits for fall only. *Program availability:* Evening/weekend. *Faculty:* 18. *Students:* 23 full-time (8 women), 21 part-time (5 women); includes 8 minority (3 Black or African American, non-Hispanic/Latino; 2 Hispanic/Latino; 3 Two or more races, non-Hispanic/Latino). Average age 40. 55 applicants, 38% accepted, 15 enrolled. In 2016, 6 master's, 5 doctorates awarded. *Degree requirements:* For master's, comprehensive exam, thesis (for some programs), final oral exam on thesis or essay and seminar; internship and project (for public history); for doctorate, variable foreign language requirement, comprehensive exam, thesis/dissertation, qualifying exam in 4 fields of history. *Entrance requirements:* For master's, GRE General Test, minimum undergraduate GPA of 3.25 in history, 3.0 overall; at least 18 credits in history and related subjects at the advanced undergraduate level; foreign language; letter of intent; research paper; at least two letters of recommendation from former instructors; for doctorate, GRE General Test, minimum GPA of 3.0, 3.25 in minimum of 18 semester credits in history and related subjects; letter of intent; research paper; at least three letters of recommendation from former professors; for Graduate Certificate, baccalaureate degree from accredited college or university; minimum GPA of 3.0, 3.25 in a minimum of eighteen semester credits in history and related subjects at the advanced undergraduate level. Additional exam requirements/recommendations for international students: Required—TOEFL (minimum score 500 paper-based; 79 iBT), TWE (minimum score 5.5), Michigan English Language Assessment Battery (minimum score 85); Recommended—IELTS (minimum score 6.5). *Application deadline:* For fall admission, 2/1 priority date for domestic and international students; for winter admission, 11/1 for domestic students, 10/1 priority date for international students; for spring admission, 2/1 for domestic students, 1/1 priority date for international students. Application fee: $50. Electronic applications accepted. *Expenses:* $16,503 per year resident tuition and fees, $33,697 per year non-resident tuition and fees. *Financial support:* In 2016–17, 16 students received support, including 2 fellowships with tuition reimbursements available (averaging $18,796 per year), 1 research assistantship with tuition reimbursement available (averaging $21,593 per year), 6 teaching assistantships with tuition reimbursements available (averaging $17,994 per year); scholarships/grants, health care benefits, and unspecified assistantships also available. Financial award applicants required to submit FAFSA. *Faculty research:* African, American, Asian, European, gender, German, labor, science and technology, urban/labor, violence, world. *Unit head:* Dr. Elizabeth V. Faue, Professor/Chair, 313-577-2525, E-mail: evfaue@wayne.edu. *Application contact:* Dr. Eric Ash, Associate Professor and Director of Graduate Studies, 313-577-2525, E-mail: ericash@wayne.edu. Website: http://clas.wayne.edu/history/

**Wilfrid Laurier University,** Faculty of Graduate and Postdoctoral Studies, Faculty of Arts, Cultural Analysis and Social Theory Program, Waterloo, ON N2L 3C5, Canada. Offers body politics (MA); cultural representation and social theory (MA); gender, sexuality and embodiment (MA); globalization, identity and social movements (MA). *Program availability:* Part-time. *Entrance requirements:* For master's, honours BA in humanities, social science or interdisciplinary program with social theory, minimum B+ in final year of full-time study. Additional exam requirements/recommendations for international students: Required—TOEFL (minimum score 89 iBT). Electronic applications accepted. *Faculty research:* Globalization; identity and social movements; body politics: gender, sexuality and embodiment; cultural representation and social theory.

**York University,** Faculty of Graduate Studies, Faculty of Liberal Arts and Professional Studies, Program in Gender, Feminist and Women's Studies, Toronto, ON M3J 1P3, Canada. Offers MA, PhD. *Degree requirements:* For master's, thesis or alternative; for doctorate, comprehensive exam, thesis/dissertation. Electronic applications accepted.

# Hispanic Studies

**Brown University,** Graduate School, Department of Hispanic Studies, Providence, RI 02912. Offers PhD. *Degree requirements:* For doctorate, 2 foreign languages, thesis/dissertation, preliminary exam.

**California State University, Los Angeles,** Graduate Studies, College of Natural and Social Sciences, Department of Chicano Studies, Los Angeles, CA 90032-8530. Offers Mexican-American studies (MA). *Program availability:* Part-time, evening/weekend. *Degree requirements:* For master's, one foreign language, comprehensive exam or thesis. *Entrance requirements:* For master's, undergraduate major in Mexican-American studies or related area, 20 upper-division units in Chicano studies, minimum GPA of 2.75 in last 90 quarter units. Additional exam requirements/recommendations for international students: Required—TOEFL (minimum score 500 paper-based). Electronic applications accepted. *Faculty research:* U.S.-Mexican relations, Chicano literature, community organization among Chicanos and Hispanics, Spanish language in the American Southwest.

**California State University, Northridge,** Graduate Studies, College of Humanities, Department of Chicana and Chicano Studies, Northridge, CA 91330. Offers MA. *Faculty:* 24 full-time (7 women), 32 part-time/adjunct (23 women). *Students:* 8 full-time (6 women), 23 part-time (18 women); includes 30 minority (all Hispanic/Latino). Average age 28. 21 applicants, 86% accepted, 12 enrolled. *Degree requirements:* For master's, thesis, project. *Entrance requirements:* Additional exam requirements/recommendations for international students: Required—TOEFL. *Application deadline:* For fall admission, 11/30 for domestic students. Application fee: $55. *Expenses:* Tuition, state resident: full-time $4152. *Financial support:* Application deadline: 3/1. *Unit head:* Dr. Gabriel Gutierrez, Chair, 818-677-2734. Website: http://www.csun.edu/chicanostudies/

**California State University, San Marcos,** College of Humanities, Arts, Behavioral and Social Sciences, Program in Spanish, San Marcos, CA 92096-0001. Offers Hispanic cultures and society (MA); Hispanic language and linguistics (MA); Hispanic literatures and literary theory (MA). *Program availability:* Part-time, evening/weekend. *Degree requirements:* For master's, 2 foreign languages, exam. *Entrance requirements:* For master's, GRE General Test, minimum GPA of 3.0 overall and in upper-division Spanish courses, official transcripts, three letters of recommendation, 750-word statement of purpose (in English), academic writing sample (in Spanish). Additional exam requirements/recommendations for international students: Required—TOEFL (minimum score 500 paper-based), TWE (minimum score 4.5). Electronic applications accepted. *Expenses:* Tuition, state resident: full-time $6738. Tuition, nonresident: full-time $13,434. *Required fees:* $1906. Tuition and fees vary according to campus/location and program. *Faculty research:* Applied linguistics, Golden Age Spanish literature, Latin American literature, poetry, Chicano studies.

**The Catholic University of America,** School of Arts and Sciences, Department of Modern Languages and Literatures, Washington, DC 20064. Offers Hispanic studies (MA, PhD). *Program availability:* Part-time. *Faculty:* 24 full-time (18 women), 3 part-time/adjunct (all women). *Students:* 4 full-time (2 women), 3 part-time (2 women); includes 2 minority (both Hispanic/Latino), 5 international. Average age 37. 4 applicants, 25% accepted. In 2016, 2 master's awarded. *Degree requirements:* For master's, comprehensive exam; for doctorate, one foreign language, comprehensive exam, thesis/dissertation, annotated bibliography; oral defense of the proposal; oral defense of the dissertation. *Entrance requirements:* For master's, GRE General Test, statement of purpose, official copies of academic transcripts, two letters of recommendation, sample of academic writing; for doctorate, GRE General Test, statement of purpose, official copies of academic transcripts, three letters of recommendation, sample of academic writing (20-25-pages long). Additional exam requirements/recommendations for international students: Required—TOEFL (minimum score 550 paper-based; 80 iBT). *Application deadline:* For fall admission, 7/15 priority date for domestic students, 7/1 for international students; for spring admission, 11/15 priority date for domestic students, 11/1 for international students. Applications are processed on a rolling basis. Application fee: $55. Electronic applications accepted. *Expenses:* $42,850 per year; $1,170 per credit; $200 per semester part-time fees. *Financial support:* Fellowships, research assistantships, teaching assistantships, Federal Work-Study, scholarships/grants, tuition waivers (full and partial), and unspecified assistantships available. Financial award application deadline: 2/1; financial award applicants required to submit FAFSA. *Faculty research:* Golden age Spain; 18th-21st-century Spain; colonial/postcolonial Latin American and transatlantic studies; modern and contemporary Latin America; theory, criticism, and language teaching methodology. *Total annual research expenditures:* $1,440. *Unit head:* Dr. Margaret Kassen, Chair, 202-319-5240, Fax: 202-319-6077, E-mail: kassen@cua.edu. *Application contact:* Director of Graduate Admissions, 202-319-5057, Fax: 202-319-6533, E-mail: cua-admissions@cua.edu. Website: http://modernlanguages.cua.edu/

**The Citadel, The Military College of South Carolina,** Citadel Graduate College, School of Humanities and Social Sciences, Department of Modern Languages, Literatures and Cultures, Charleston, SC 29409. Offers Hispanic studies (Graduate Certificate). *Entrance requirements:* Additional exam requirements/recommendations for international students: Required—TOEFL (minimum score 550 paper-based; 79 iBT). *Application deadline:* Applications are processed on a rolling basis. Application fee: $40. Electronic applications accepted. *Expenses:* Tuition, state resident: full-time $5121; part-time $569 per credit hour. Tuition, nonresident: full-time $8613; part-time $957 per credit hour. *Required fees:* $90 per term. *Financial support:* Application deadline: 7/1; applicants required to submit FAFSA. *Unit head:* Dr. Guy D. Toubiana, Department Head, 843-953-6804, E-mail: guy.toubiana@citadel.edu. *Application contact:* Dr. Sara Fernandez-Medina, Associate Professor, 843-953-5065, E-mail: fernandezs@citadel.edu.
Website: http://www.citadel.edu/root/mlng

**Columbia University,** Graduate School of Arts and Sciences, New York, NY 10027. Offers African-American studies (MA); American studies (MA); anthropology (MA, PhD); art history and archaeology (MA, PhD); astronomy (PhD); biological sciences (PhD); biotechnology (MA); chemical physics (PhD); chemistry (PhD); classical studies (MA, PhD); classics (MA, PhD); climate and society (MA); conservation biology (MA); earth and environmental sciences (PhD); East Asia: regional studies (MA); East Asian languages and cultures (MA, PhD); ecology, evolution and environmental biology (MA), including conservation biology; ecology, evolution, and environmental biology (PhD), including ecology and evolutionary biology, evolutionary primatology; economics (MA, PhD); English and comparative literature (MA, PhD); French and Romance philology (MA, PhD); Germanic languages (MA, PhD); global French studies (PhD); global thought (MA); Hispanic cultural studies (MA); history (PhD); history and literature (MA); human rights studies (MA); Islamic studies (MA); Italian (MA, PhD); Japanese pedagogy (MA); Jewish studies (MA); Latin America and the Caribbean: regional studies (MA); Latin American and Iberian cultures (PhD); mathematics (MA, PhD), including finance (MA); medieval and Renaissance studies (MA); Middle Eastern, South Asian, and African studies (MA, PhD); modern art: critical and curatorial studies (MA); modern European studies (MA); museum anthropology (MA); music (DMA, PhD); oral history (MA); philosophical foundations of physics (MA); philosophy (MA, PhD); physics (PhD); political science (MA, PhD); psychology (PhD); quantitative methods in the social sciences (MA); religion (MA, PhD); Russia, Eurasia and East Europe: regional studies (MA); Russian translation (MA); Slavic cultures (MA); Slavic languages (MA, PhD); sociology (MA, PhD); South Asian studies (MA); statistics (MA, PhD); theatre (PhD). Dual-degree programs require admission to both Graduate School of Arts and Sciences and another Columbia school. *Program availability:* Part-time. Terminal master's awarded for partial completion of doctoral program. *Degree requirements:* For master's, variable foreign language requirement, comprehensive exam (for some programs), thesis (for some programs); for doctorate, variable foreign language requirement, comprehensive exam (for some programs), thesis/dissertation. *Entrance requirements:* For master's and doctorate, GRE General Test, GRE Subject Test (for some programs). Additional exam requirements/recommendations for international students: Required—TOEFL, IELTS. Electronic applications accepted.

**La Salle University,** School of Arts and Sciences, Hispanic Institute, Philadelphia, PA 19141-1199. Offers bilingual/bicultural studies (MA); ESL program specialist (Certificate); interpretation: English/Spanish-Spanish/English (Certificate); teaching English to speakers of other languages (MA); translation and interpretation (MA); translation: English/Spanish-Spanish/English (Certificate). *Program availability:* Part-time, evening/weekend. *Faculty:* 2 full-time (1 woman), 6 part-time/adjunct (3 women). *Students:* 1 (woman) full-time, 26 part-time (18 women); includes 15 minority (5 Black or African American, non-Hispanic/Latino; 10 Hispanic/Latino), 1 international. Average age 37. 17 applicants, 76% accepted, 7 enrolled. In 2016, 7 master's, 4 other advanced degrees awarded. *Degree requirements:* For master's, one foreign language, project or thesis. *Entrance requirements:* For master's, GRE, MAT, or GMAT, professional resume; two letters of recommendation; for Certificate, GRE, MAT, or GMAT, professional resume; two letters of recommendation; evidence of an advanced level in Spanish. Additional exam requirements/recommendations for international students: Required—TOEFL. *Application deadline:* For fall admission, 8/15 priority date for domestic students, 7/15 for international students; for spring admission, 12/15 priority date for domestic students, 11/15 for international students; for summer admission, 4/15 priority date for domestic students, 3/15 for international students. Applications are processed on a rolling basis. Application fee: $35. Electronic applications accepted. Application fee is waived when completed online. *Expenses:* Contact institution. *Financial support:* In 2016–17, 3 students received support. Scholarships/grants available. Support available to part-time students. Financial award application deadline: 8/31; financial award applicants required to submit FAFSA. *Faculty research:* Puerto Rican literature, cross-cultural communication, English as a second language methodology, Spanish language. *Unit head:* Guadalupe Da Costa Montesinos, Director, 215-951-1209, Fax: 215-991-3506, E-mail: montesin@lasalle.edu. *Application contact:* Elizabeth Heenan, Director, Graduate and Adult Enrollment, 215-951-1100, Fax: 215-951-1462, E-mail: heenan@lasalle.edu.
Website: http://www.lasalle.edu/hispanic-institute/

**Louisiana State University and Agricultural & Mechanical College,** Graduate School, College of Humanities and Social Sciences, Department of Foreign Languages and Literatures, Baton Rouge, LA 70803. Offers Hispanic studies (MA).

**McGill University,** Faculty of Graduate and Postdoctoral Studies, Faculty of Arts, Department of Hispanic Studies, Montréal, QC H3A 2T5, Canada. Offers MA, PhD.

**Michigan State University,** The Graduate School, College of Arts and Letters, Department of Spanish and Portuguese, East Lansing, MI 48824. Offers applied Spanish linguistics (MA); Hispanic cultural studies (PhD); Hispanic literatures (MA). *Entrance requirements:* Additional exam requirements/recommendations for international students: Required—TOEFL. Electronic applications accepted.

**Oregon State University,** College of Liberal Arts, Program in Contemporary Hispanic Studies, Corvallis, OR 97331. Offers MA. *Faculty:* 4 full-time (1 woman), 1 (woman) part-time/adjunct. In 2016, 2 master's awarded. *Entrance requirements:* For master's, ACTFL OPI (Oral Proficiency Interview). Application fee: $75 ($85 for international students). *Expenses:* Tuition, state resident: full-time $12,150; part-time $450 per credit. Tuition, nonresident: full-time $21,789; part-time $807 per credit. *Required fees:* $1651; $1507 per credit. One-time fee: $350. Tuition and fees vary according to course load, campus/location and program. *Unit head:* Dr. Juan Trujillo, Assistant Professor, 541-737-3956, E-mail: jtrujillo@oregonstate.edu.
Website: http://liberalarts.oregonstate.edu/slcs

**Pontifical Catholic University of Puerto Rico,** College of Arts and Humanities, Department of Hispanic Studies, Ponce, PR 00717-0777. Offers grammar and writing (Professional Certificate); Hispanic studies (MA). *Program availability:* Part-time, evening/weekend. *Degree requirements:* For master's, variable foreign language requirement, comprehensive exam, thesis or alternative. *Entrance requirements:* For master's, GRE General Test, 2 letters of recommendation, interview, minimum GPA of 2.75. Electronic applications accepted.

**Queen's University at Kingston,** School of Graduate Studies, Faculty of Arts and Sciences, Department of Spanish and Italian, Kingston, ON K7L 3N6, Canada. Offers Spanish language and literature (MA). *Program availability:* Part-time. *Degree requirements:* For master's, one foreign language, thesis. *Entrance requirements:* Additional exam requirements/recommendations for international students: Required—TOEFL. Electronic applications accepted. *Faculty research:* Golden Age, nineteenth- and twentieth-century Peninsular novel, literary theory, colonial Latin America, nineteenth-and-twentieth century Latin America.

**St. Thomas University,** School of Leadership Studies, Program in Hispanic Media, Miami Gardens, FL 33054-6459. Offers MA, Certificate. *Program availability:* Part-time, evening/weekend. *Degree requirements:* For master's, comprehensive exam. *Entrance requirements:* Additional exam requirements/recommendations for international students: Required—TOEFL (minimum score 550 paper-based; 79 iBT). Electronic applications accepted.

**San Jose State University,** Graduate Studies and Research, College of Social Sciences, San Jose, CA 95192-0001. Offers applications of technology in planning (Certificate); applied anthropology (MA); communication studies (MS); community design and development (Certificate); economics (MA), including applied economics, social sciences; environmental planning (Certificate); geographic information science (Certificate); geography (MA); global citizenship (Certificate); history (MA), including history education, social sciences; Mexican American studies (MA); psychology (MA, MS), including clinical psychology (MS), industrial/organizational psychology (MS); research and experimental psychology (MA); public administration (MA); real estate development (Certificate); social sciences (MPA, MS); sociology (MA); transportation and land use planning (Certificate). *Program availability:* Part-time, evening/weekend. *Entrance requirements:* For master's, minimum GPA of 3.0. Electronic applications accepted.

**Texas A&M International University,** Office of Graduate Studies and Research, College of Arts and Sciences, Department of Humanities, Laredo, TX 78041-1900. Offers English (MA); Hispanic studies (PhD); history and political thought (MA); language, literature and translation (MA). *Degree requirements:* For master's, comprehensive exam (for some programs), thesis (for some programs). *Entrance requirements:* For master's, GRE General Test. Additional exam requirements/recommendations for international students: Required—TOEFL (minimum score 550 paper-based; 79 iBT).

**Texas A&M University–Kingsville,** College of Graduate Studies, College of Arts and Sciences, Department of Language and Literature, Interdisciplinary Program in Hispanic Culture, Kingsville, TX 78363. Offers PhD. *Degree requirements:* For doctorate, variable foreign language requirement, comprehensive exam, thesis/dissertation. *Entrance requirements:* For doctorate, GRE, MAT, GMAT, minimum GPA of 3.2, at least three letters of recommendation, demonstrated oral and written proficiency in Spanish. Additional exam requirements/recommendations for international students: Required—TOEFL (minimum score 550 paper-based; 79 iBT). Electronic applications accepted.

**University of Alberta,** Faculty of Graduate Studies and Research, Department of Modern Languages and Cultural Studies, Edmonton, AB T6G 2E1, Canada. Offers applied linguistics (Germanic, Romance, Slavic) (MA); French language, literatures and linguistics (PhD); French language, literatures, and linguistics (MA); Germanic languages, literatures and linguistics (PhD); Germanic languages, literatures, and linguistics (MA); Italian studies (MA); Slavic languages and literatures (Russian, Ukrainian) (MA, PhD); Slavic linguistics (Russian, Ukrainian) (MA, PhD); Spanish and Latin American studies (MA, PhD); Ukrainian folklore (MA, PhD). *Program availability:* Part-time. *Degree requirements:* For master's, one foreign language, thesis; for doctorate, 2 foreign languages, comprehensive exam, thesis/dissertation. *Entrance requirements:* For master's and doctorate, 1 language other than English. Additional exam requirements/recommendations for international students: Required—Michigan English Language Assessment Battery or TOEFL (minimum score 550 paper-based). Electronic applications accepted. *Faculty research:* Russian/Ukrainian studies; German studies; contemporary Latin American, French and Francophone studies; Italian studies.

**The University of British Columbia,** Faculty of Arts and Faculty of Graduate Studies, Department of French, Hispanic and Italian Studies, Vancouver, BC V6T 1Z1, Canada. Offers French (MA, PhD); Hispanic studies (MA, PhD). *Program availability:* Part-time. *Degree requirements:* For master's, thesis optional; for doctorate, 2 foreign languages, comprehensive exam, thesis/dissertation. *Entrance requirements:* For doctorate, MA. Additional exam requirements/recommendations for international students: Required—TOEFL. *Application deadline:* Applications are processed on a rolling basis. Application fee: $100 Canadian dollars ($162 Canadian dollars for international students). Electronic applications accepted. *Expenses:* $4,802 per year tuition and fees, $8,436 per year international. *Financial support:* Fellowships with tuition reimbursements, research assistantships, teaching assistantships, Federal Work-Study, and tuition waivers (partial) available. Financial award application deadline: 2/1. *Faculty research:* Medieval and Renaissance literature, modern literature, romance philology and linguistics, cultural studies, women's literature. *Application contact:* Carole Schoenfeld, Graduate Program Staff, 604-822-0016, Fax: 604-822-6675, E-mail: fhis.grad@ubc.ca.
Website: http://fhis.ubc.ca/

**University of California, Riverside,** Graduate Division, Department of Hispanic Studies, Riverside, CA 92521-0102. Offers Spanish (MA, PhD). Terminal master's awarded for partial completion of doctoral program. *Degree requirements:* For master's, one foreign language, comprehensive exam; for doctorate, one foreign language, thesis/dissertation, qualifying exams, 1 quarter of teaching experience. *Entrance requirements:* For master's and doctorate, GRE General Test, minimum GPA of 3.0. Additional exam requirements/recommendations for international students: Required—TOEFL (minimum score 550 paper-based; 80 iBT). Electronic applications accepted. *Expenses:* Tuition, state resident: full-time $16,666. Tuition, nonresident: full-time $31,768. *Required fees:* $11,055.54 per quarter. $3685.18 per quarter. Tuition and fees vary according to campus/location and program. *Faculty research:* Spanish literature of the sixteenth-, seventeenth- and twentieth-century; pre-Columbian and colonial Latin American literature; nineteenth- and twentieth-century Latin American literature.

**University of California, Santa Barbara,** Graduate Division, College of Letters and Sciences, Division of Humanities and Fine Arts, Department of Spanish and Portuguese, Santa Barbara, CA 93106-4150. Offers Hispanic languages and literatures (PhD), including European medieval studies, feminist studies, Hispanic linguistics, Hispanic literature, Luso-Brazilian literature; Hispanic linguistics (MA); Luso-Brazilian literature (MA); Spanish or Spanish-American literature (MA); MA/PhD. Terminal master's awarded for partial completion of doctoral program. *Degree requirements:* For master's, 2 foreign languages, comprehensive exam (for some programs), thesis optional; for doctorate, 3 foreign languages, comprehensive exam, thesis/dissertation. *Entrance requirements:* For master's and doctorate, GRE. Additional exam requirements/recommendations for international students: Required—TOEFL (minimum score 550 paper-based; 80 iBT), IELTS (minimum score 7). Electronic applications accepted. *Faculty research:* Nineteenth-century Spanish and Portuguese literature, Spanish and Spanish-American literature, nineteenth- and twentieth-century Portuguese and Brazilian literatures, Hispanic linguistics, Catalan language and culture.

*Hispanic Studies*

**University of California, Santa Barbara,** Graduate Division, College of Letters and Sciences, Division of Social Sciences, Department of Chicana and Chicano Studies, Santa Barbara, CA 93106-4120. Offers MA/PhD. *Entrance requirements:* Additional exam requirements/recommendations for international students: Required—TOEFL (minimum score 550 paper-based; 80 iBT), IELTS (minimum score 7). Electronic applications accepted. *Faculty research:* History and narrative, cultural production, social processes, gender and sexuality studies.

**University of Houston,** College of Liberal Arts and Social Sciences, Department of Hispanic Studies, Houston, TX 77204. Offers Spanish (MA, PhD). *Program availability:* Part-time. *Degree requirements:* For master's, comprehensive exam, thesis optional; for doctorate, 2 foreign languages, comprehensive exam, thesis/dissertation. *Entrance requirements:* For master's and doctorate, GRE. Additional exam requirements/recommendations for international students: Required—TOEFL (minimum score 550 paper-based; 79 iBT); Recommended—IELTS (minimum score 6.5). Electronic applications accepted.

**University of Illinois at Chicago,** College of Liberal Arts and Sciences, School of Literatures, Cultural Studies and Linguistics, Department of Hispanic and Italian Studies, Chicago, IL 60607-7128. Offers Hispanic linguistics (PhD). *Program availability:* Part-time. Terminal master's awarded for partial completion of doctoral program. *Degree requirements:* For master's, one foreign language, departmental qualifying exam. *Entrance requirements:* For master's, GRE General Test, minimum GPA of 2.75, undergraduate major in Spanish. Additional exam requirements/recommendations for international students: Required—TOEFL. Electronic applications accepted. *Faculty research:* Linguistic competence of bilingual speakers as a window to understanding the human faculty of language, neurocognitive processing of language among different speakers and learners, how languages are used within their social contexts.

**University of Kentucky,** Graduate School, College of Arts and Sciences, Program in Hispanic Studies, Lexington, KY 40506-0032. Offers MA, PhD. *Degree requirements:* For master's, one foreign language, comprehensive exam, thesis optional; for doctorate, 2 foreign languages, comprehensive exam, thesis/dissertation. *Entrance requirements:* For master's, GRE General Test, minimum undergraduate GPA of 2.75; for doctorate, GRE General Test, minimum graduate GPA of 3.0. Additional exam requirements/recommendations for international students: Required—TOEFL (minimum score 550 paper-based). Electronic applications accepted. *Faculty research:* Hispanic linguistics, medieval Spanish literature and civilization, Renaissance and Golden Age literature and civilization, Spanish American literature and civilization.

**The University of Manchester,** School of Languages, Linguistics and Cultures, Manchester, United Kingdom. Offers Arab world studies (PhD); Chinese studies (M Phil, PhD); East Asian studies (M Phil, PhD); English language (PhD); French studies (M Phil, PhD); German studies (M Phil, PhD); interpreting studies (PhD); Italian studies (M Phil, PhD); Japanese studies (M Phil, PhD); Latin American cultural studies (M Phil, PhD); linguistics (M Phil, PhD); Middle Eastern studies (M Phil, PhD); Polish studies (M Phil, PhD); Portuguese studies (M Phil, PhD); Russian studies (M Phil, PhD); Spanish studies (M Phil, PhD); translation and intercultural studies (M Phil, PhD).

**University of Nevada, Las Vegas,** Graduate College, College of Liberal Arts, Department of World Languages and Cultures, Las Vegas, NV 89154-5047. Offers Hispanic studies (MA). *Program availability:* Part-time. *Faculty:* 4 full-time (all women), 1 (woman) part-time/adjunct. *Students:* 4 full-time (all women), 8 part-time (4 women); includes 6 minority (all Hispanic/Latino), 2 international. Average age 37. 7 applicants, 57% accepted, 3 enrolled. *Degree requirements:* For master's, one foreign language, comprehensive exam, final research project. *Entrance requirements:* For master's, minimum GPA of 3.0; 2 letters of recommendation. Additional exam requirements/recommendations for international students: Required—TOEFL (minimum score 550 paper-based; 80 iBT), IELTS (minimum score 7). *Application deadline:* For fall admission, 5/1 for domestic students; for spring admission, 11/15 for domestic students. Application fee: $60 ($95 for international students). Electronic applications accepted. *Expenses:* $269.25 per credit, $792 per 3-credit course; $9,634 per year resident; $23,274 per year non-resident; $7,094 fees non-resident (7 credits or more); $1,307 annual health insurance fee. *Financial support:* In 2016–17, 5 teaching assistantships with partial tuition reimbursements (averaging $10,000 per year) were awarded; institutionally sponsored loans, scholarships/grants, health care benefits, and unspecified assistantships also available. Financial award application deadline: 3/15. *Faculty research:* Spanish Golden Age poetry, prose and theater; Miguel de Cervantes; history of ideas in creative letters; historical linguistics (French/Spanish); Spanish sociolinguistics; second language acquisition; women narrators of Mexico and Spain; translation studies; Mexican film and culture. *Unit head:* Dr. Susan Byrne, Chair, 702-895-3464, Fax: 702-895-1226, E-mail: susan.byrne@unlv.edu. *Application contact:* Dr. Margarita Jara, Graduate Coordinator, 702-895-1690, Fax: 702-895-1226, E-mail:

margarita.jara@unlv.edu. Website: http://liberalarts.unlv.edu/Foreign_Languages/graduates.html

**The University of North Carolina at Greensboro,** Graduate School, College of Arts and Sciences, Department of Languages, Literatures, and Cultures, Program in Spanish, Greensboro, NC 27412-5001. Offers advanced Spanish language and Hispanic cultural studies (Certificate); Spanish (MA). *Degree requirements:* For master's, one foreign language, comprehensive exam, thesis or alternative. *Entrance requirements:* For master's, GRE General Test, 3-5 minute tape demonstrating foreign language proficiency, composition in Spanish, sample paper in English. Additional exam requirements/recommendations for international students: Required—TOEFL. Electronic applications accepted.

**University of Puerto Rico, Mayagüez Campus,** Graduate Studies, College of Arts and Sciences, Department of Hispanic Studies, Mayagüez, PR 00681-9000. Offers MA. *Program availability:* Part-time. *Faculty:* 23 full-time (14 women), 3 part-time/adjunct (all women). *Students:* 11 full-time (7 women), 3 part-time (all women); includes 13 minority (all Hispanic/Latino), 1 international. Average age 25. 4 applicants, 75% accepted, 2 enrolled. In 2016, 3 master's awarded. *Degree requirements:* For master's, comprehensive exam, thesis. *Entrance requirements:* For master's, minimum GPA of 2.75, BA in Hispanic studies or its equivalent. *Application deadline:* For fall admission, 2/15 for domestic and international students; for spring admission, 9/15 for domestic and international students. Applications are processed on a rolling basis. Application fee: $25. Electronic applications accepted. *Expenses: Tuition, area resident:* Full-time $2466. *International tuition:* $7166 full-time. *Required fees:* $210. One-time fee: $5 full-time. Tuition and fees vary according to course level, campus/location, program and student level. *Financial support:* In 2016–17, 3 students received support, including 3 teaching assistantships (averaging $3,621 per year); unspecified assistantships also available. *Faculty research:* Spanish literature, Hispanic-American literature, Puerto Rican literature, stylistics, linguistics. *Unit head:* Hilton Alers, PhD, Interim Director, 787-265-3843, Fax: 787-265-3843, E-mail: hilton.alers@upr.edu. *Application contact:* Jeannette Altiery, Administrative Assistant IV, 787-832-4040 Ext. 3843, Fax: 787-265-3843, E-mail: jeannette.altiery@upr.edu. Website: http://www.uprm.edu/hispanicos/

**University of Puerto Rico, Río Piedras Campus,** College of Humanities, Department of Hispanic Studies, San Juan, PR 00931-3300. Offers Hispanic linguistics (PhD); Hispanic studies (MA); Latin American literature (PhD); Puerto Rican literature (PhD); Spanish literature (PhD). *Program availability:* Part-time. *Degree requirements:* For master's, one foreign language, comprehensive exam, thesis; for doctorate, one foreign language, comprehensive exam, thesis/dissertation. *Entrance requirements:* For master's, PAEG or GRE, interview, minimum GPA of 3.0, letter of recommendation (2); for doctorate, PAEG or GRE, interview, master's degree, minimum GPA of 3.0, letter of recommendation (2). *Faculty research:* Poetry of Luis Palés Matos, short stories in Puerto Rico, language in the social process, "Decima Popular", Anglicism.

**The University of Texas at Austin,** Graduate School, College of Liberal Arts, Center for Mexican American Studies, Austin, TX 78712-1111. Offers MA.

**University of Victoria,** Faculty of Graduate Studies, Faculty of Humanities, Department of Hispanic and Italian Studies, Victoria, BC V8W 2Y2, Canada. Offers Hispanic and Italian studies (MA); Hispanic studies (MA). *Degree requirements:* For master's, one foreign language, comprehensive exam, thesis (for some programs). *Entrance requirements:* For master's, undergraduate major in Hispanic studies, minimum B+ average. Additional exam requirements/recommendations for international students: Required—TOEFL (minimum score 575 paper-based), IELTS (minimum score 7). Electronic applications accepted. *Faculty research:* Medieval/Renaissance Spanish and Italian literature, Golden Age literature, Latin American literature.

**Villanova University,** Graduate School of Liberal Arts and Sciences, Department of Romance Languages and Literatures, Villanova, PA 19085-1699. Offers Hispanic studies (MA). *Program availability:* Part-time, evening/weekend. *Faculty:* 3. *Students:* 10 applicants, 100% accepted, 5 enrolled. In 2016, 7 master's awarded. *Degree requirements:* For master's, one foreign language, comprehensive exam. *Entrance requirements:* For master's, minimum GPA of 3.0, writing sample in Spanish. Additional exam requirements/recommendations for international students: Required—TOEFL. *Application deadline:* For fall admission, 3/1 for domestic students, 5/1 for international students; for spring admission, 11/15 for domestic students, 10/15 for international students; for summer admission, 5/1 for domestic students. Applications are processed on a rolling basis. Application fee: $50. Electronic applications accepted. *Financial support:* Teaching assistantships with tuition reimbursements, scholarships/grants, and unspecified assistantships available. Financial award applicants required to submit FAFSA. Website: http://www1.villanova.edu/villanova/artsci/romancelanglit/academics/graduateprograminhispanicstudies.html

# Holocaust and Genocide Studies

**Chapman University,** Wilkinson College of Arts, Humanities, and Social Sciences, War and Society Program, Orange, CA 92866. Offers MA. *Program availability:* Part-time, evening/weekend. *Faculty:* 4 full-time (3 women), 5 part-time/adjunct (3 women). *Students:* 6 full-time (3 women), 4 part-time (1 woman); includes 4 minority (all Hispanic/Latino). Average age 32. 8 applicants, 88% accepted, 5 enrolled. In 2016, 1 master's awarded. *Degree requirements:* For master's, thesis. *Entrance requirements:* For master's, GRE (if undergraduate GPA less than 3.0). Additional exam requirements/recommendations for international students: Required—TOEFL (minimum score 550 paper-based, 80 iBT), IELTS (6.5), PTE Academic (53), or CAE. *Application deadline:* Applications are processed on a rolling basis. Application fee: $60. Electronic applications accepted. *Expenses:* Contact institution. *Financial support:* Fellowships, teaching assistantships, Federal Work-Study, scholarships/grants, and unspecified assistantships available. *Unit head:* Dr. Gregory A. Daddis, Director, 714-997-6834, E-mail: daddis@chapman.edu. *Application contact:* Jon Hernandez, Graduate Admission Counselor, 714-997-6770, E-mail: jonherna@chapman.edu. Website: http://www.chapman.edu/wilkinson/graduate-studies/ma-warsociety.aspx

**Clark University,** Graduate School, Department of History, Program in Holocaust History and Genocide Studies, Worcester, MA 01610-1477. Offers genocide studies (PhD); history of the Holocaust (PhD). *Students:* 20 full-time (12 women), 1 (woman) part-time, 10 international. Average age 45. 31 applicants, 13% accepted, 3 enrolled. In 2016, 2 doctorates awarded. *Degree requirements:* For doctorate, thesis/dissertation. *Entrance requirements:* Additional exam requirements/recommendations for international students: Required—TOEFL. *Application deadline:* For fall admission, 1/15

for domestic students. Application fee: $75. *Expenses: Tuition:* Full-time $44,050. *Required fees:* $80. Tuition and fees vary according to course load and program. *Financial support:* In 2016–17, fellowships with tuition reimbursements (averaging $17,000 per year), research assistantships with tuition reimbursements (averaging $17,000 per year), teaching assistantships with tuition reimbursements (averaging $17,000 per year) were awarded; tuition waivers (partial) also available. *Faculty research:* Jewish persecution, children and survivors, Germany's role in the Holocaust. *Unit head:* Deborah Dwork, Professor, 508-793-7450. *Application contact:* Mary Jane Rein, Executive Director, 508-793-8897, Fax: 508-793-8827, E-mail: mrein@clarku.edu.

**Gratz College,** Graduate Programs, Programs in Holocaust and Genocide Studies, Melrose Park, PA 19027. Offers MA, PhD. *Program availability:* Online learning. *Unit head:* Michael Steinlauf, Director, 215-635-7300 Ext. 154, E-mail: msteinlauf@gratz.edu. *Application contact:* Joanna Boeing Bratton, Director of Admissions, 215-635-7300 Ext. 140, Fax: 215-635-7399, E-mail: admissions@gratz.edu.

**Kean University,** College of Liberal Arts, Program in Holocaust and Genocide Studies, Union, NJ 07083. Offers MA. *Program availability:* Part-time. *Faculty:* 12 full-time (5 women). *Students:* 4 full-time (3 women), 9 part-time (4 women); includes 1 minority (Black or African American, non-Hispanic/Latino). Average age 32. 7 applicants, 14% accepted, 1 enrolled. In 2016, 7 master's awarded. *Degree requirements:* For master's, thesis. *Entrance requirements:* For master's, minimum cumulative GPA of 3.0, official transcripts from all institutions attended, two letters of recommendation from professional associates, personal statement, professional resume/curriculum vitae.

SECTION 15: AREA AND CULTURAL STUDIES

Jewish Studies

Additional exam requirements/recommendations for international students: Required—TOEFL (minimum score 550 paper-based; 79 iBT), IELTS (minimum score 6.5). *Application deadline:* For fall admission, 6/1 for domestic and international students; for spring admission, 12/1 for domestic and international students. Applications are processed on a rolling basis. Application fee: $75. Electronic applications accepted. *Expenses:* Tuition, state resident: full-time $13,156; part-time $640 per credit. Tuition, nonresident: full-time $17,831; part-time $785 per credit. *Required fees:* $3316; $151 per credit. Tuition and fees vary according to course level, course load, degree level and program. *Financial support:* Scholarships/grants and unspecified assistantships available. Financial award applicants required to submit FAFSA. *Unit head:* Dr. Dennis Klein, Program Coordinator, 908-737-0256, E-mail: dklein@kean.edu. *Application contact:* Amy Clark, Program Assistant, 908-737-7100, E-mail: grad-adm@kean.edu. Website: http://grad.kean.edu/mahgs

**Seton Hill University,** Program in Genocide and Holocaust Studies, Greensburg, PA 15601. Offers Certificate. *Program availability:* Part-time, evening/weekend, online learning. *Entrance requirements:* For degree, letter of recommendation, resume, personal statements. Additional exam requirements/recommendations for international students: Required—TOEFL (minimum score 600 paper-based; 100 iBT), IELTS (minimum score 6.5). Electronic applications accepted.

**Stockton University,** Office of Graduate Studies, Program in Holocaust and Genocide Studies, Galloway, NJ 08205-9441. Offers MA. *Program availability:* Part-time, evening/weekend, online only, 100% online. *Faculty:* 4 full-time (2 women), 1 part-time/adjunct (0 women). *Students:* 4 full-time (all women), 21 part-time (15 women); includes 6 minority (1 Black or African American, non-Hispanic/Latino; 4 Hispanic/Latino; 1 Two or more races, non-Hispanic/Latino). Average age 39. 17 applicants, 88% accepted, 8 enrolled. In 2016, 6 master's awarded. *Degree requirements:* For master's, thesis optional. *Entrance requirements:* Additional exam requirements/recommendations for international students: Required—TOEFL. *Application deadline:* For fall admission, 7/1 for domestic and international students; for spring admission, 12/1 for domestic students, 11/1 for international students. Applications are processed on a rolling basis. Application fee: $50. Electronic applications accepted. *Expenses:* $772 per credit in-state. *Financial support:* Fellowships, research assistantships, career-related internships or fieldwork, Federal Work-Study, scholarships/grants, and unspecified assistantships available. Financial award application deadline: 3/1; financial award applicants required to submit FAFSA. *Faculty research:* Women and the Holocaust, survivor perspectives, liberty and persecution. *Unit head:* Dr. Elisa Forgey, Program Director, 609-626-3640, Fax: 609-626-6050, E-mail: mahg@stockton.edu. *Application contact:* Tara Williams, Assistant Director of Graduate Enrollment Management, 609-626-3640, Fax: 609-626-6050, E-mail: gradschool@stockton.edu.

**West Chester University of Pennsylvania,** College of Arts and Humanities, Program in Holocaust and Genocide Studies, West Chester, PA 19383. Offers Holocaust and genocide studies (MA). *Program availability:* Part-time, evening/weekend. *Students:* 3 full-time (all women), 8 part-time (6 women); includes 1 minority (Two or more races, non-Hispanic/Latino). Average age 28. 11 applicants, 91% accepted, 4 enrolled. In 2016, 7 master's awarded. *Degree requirements:* For master's, thesis optional; for Certificate, 18 hours of coursework. *Entrance requirements:* For master's and Certificate, statement of professional goals, two letters of recommendation, minimum GPA of 2.8. Additional exam requirements/recommendations for international students: Required—TOEFL or IELTS. *Application deadline:* For fall admission, 5/15 for international students; for spring admission, 10/15 for international students. Applications are processed on a rolling basis. Application fee: $50. Electronic applications accepted. *Expenses:* Tuition, state resident: full-time $8694; part-time $483 per credit. Tuition, nonresident: full-time $13,050; part-time $725 per credit. *Required fees:* $2399; $119.05 per credit. Tuition and fees vary according to campus/location and program. *Financial support:* Scholarships/grants and unspecified assistantships available. Financial award application deadline: 3/15; financial award applicants required to submit FAFSA. *Faculty research:* Holocaust, genocide history, German history, human rights studies, Jewish history. *Unit head:* Dr. Jonathan Friedman, Director and Graduate Coordinator, 610-436-2972, Fax: 610-436-3150, E-mail: jfriedman@wcupa.edu. *Application contact:* Office of Graduate Studies and Extended Education, 610-436-2943, Fax: 610-436-2763, E-mail: gradstudy@wcupa.edu. Website: http://www.wcupa.edu/arts-humanities/holocaust/

# Jewish Studies

**American Jewish University,** Graduate School of Nonprofit Management, Program in Jewish Communal Studies, Bel Air, CA 90077-1599. Offers MAJCS. *Degree requirements:* For master's, thesis. *Entrance requirements:* For master's, GMAT or GRE General Test, interview.

**Biola University,** Talbot School of Theology, La Mirada, CA 90639-0001. Offers adult/family ministry (MACE); Bible exposition (MA, Th M); Biblical and theological studies (Certificate); biblical and theological studies/diversified (MA); children's ministry (MACE); Christian education (M Div); cross-cultural education ministry (MACE); educational studies (Ed D, PhD); evangelism and discipleship (M Div); general Christian education (MACE); Messianic Jewish studies (M Div, Certificate); missions and intercultural studies (M Div); New Testament (MA, Th M); Old Testament (MA); Old Testament and Semitics (Th M); pastoral and general ministry (M Div); pastoral care and counseling (M Div, MACML); philosophy (MA); preaching and pastoral ministry (MACML); spiritual formation (M Div, Certificate); spiritual formation and soul care (MA); sports ministry (MACML); theology (MA, Th M, D Min, Certificate); youth ministry (MACE). *Accreditation:* ATS. *Program availability:* Part-time, evening/weekend. *Entrance requirements:* For master's, bachelor's degree from accredited college or university; minimum GPA of 2.6 (for M Div), 3.0 (for MA); for doctorate, M Div or MA. Additional exam requirements/recommendations for international students: Required—TOEFL (minimum score 600 paper-based; 88 iBT). Electronic applications accepted. *Faculty research:* New Testament, Old Testament, spiritual formation, Christian education, theological studies, Christian ministry, preaching and pastoral ministry, language and literature, bible exposition, Christian leadership.

**Brandeis University,** Graduate School of Arts and Sciences, Department of Near Eastern and Judaic Studies, Waltham, MA 02454-9110. Offers Near Eastern and Judaic studies (MA, PhD); Near Eastern and Judaic studies and women's, gender, and sexuality studies (MA); teaching of Hebrew (MAT). *Program availability:* Part-time. *Faculty:* 24 full-time (10 women), 6 part-time/adjunct (3 women). *Students:* 44 full-time (18 women), 2 part-time (0 women); includes 7 minority (2 Black or African American, non-Hispanic/Latino; 1 Asian, non-Hispanic/Latino; 4 Hispanic/Latino), 9 international. 67 applicants, 45% accepted, 12 enrolled. In 2016, 9 master's, 3 doctorates awarded. Terminal master's awarded for partial completion of doctoral program. *Degree requirements:* For master's, one foreign language, thesis or alternative, proseminar, capstone; for doctorate, variable foreign language requirement, comprehensive exam, thesis/dissertation. *Entrance requirements:* For master's, GRE (recommended), 2 letters of recommendation, transcript(s), statement of purpose, writing sample, resume; for doctorate, GRE (recommended), 3 letters of recommendation, transcript(s), statement of purpose, writing sample, resume. Additional exam requirements/recommendations for international students: Required—TOEFL (minimum score 600 paper-based; 100 iBT); Recommended—IELTS (minimum score 7), TSE (minimum score 68). *Application deadline:* For fall admission, 1/15 priority date for domestic and international students. Application fee: $75. Electronic applications accepted. *Financial support:* In 2016–17, 28 students received support, including 16 fellowships with full tuition reimbursements available (averaging $24,000 per year), 2 teaching assistantships with partial tuition reimbursements available (averaging $3,200 per year); Federal Work-Study, scholarships/grants, health care benefits, and tuition waivers (full and partial) also available. Support available to part-time students. Financial award application deadline: 4/15; financial award applicants required to submit FAFSA. *Faculty research:* Bible and ancient Near East, Judaic Studies, Israel Studies, modern Middle East, Arabic and Islamic civilizations. *Unit head:* Dr. Jonathan Decter, Department Chair, 781-736-2950, Fax: 781-736-2070, E-mail: decter@brandeis.edu. *Application contact:* Joanne Arnish, Department Administrator, 781-736-2950, Fax: 781-736-2070, E-mail: arnish@brandeis.edu. Website: http://www.brandeis.edu/gsas

**Brandeis University,** Graduate School of Arts and Sciences, Hornstein Jewish Professional Leadership Program, Waltham, MA 02454-9110. Offers MA/MA, MBA/MA, MPP/MA. *Faculty:* 3 full-time (1 woman), 2 part-time/adjunct (0 women). *Students:* 20 full-time (13 women), 1 part-time (0 women), 8 international. 15 applicants, 73% accepted, 9 enrolled. *Entrance requirements:* Additional exam requirements/recommendations for international students: Required—TOEFL (minimum score 600 paper-based; 100 iBT); Recommended—IELTS (minimum score 7), TSE (minimum score 68). *Application deadline:* For fall admission, 1/15 priority date for domestic and international students. Applications are processed on a rolling basis. Application fee: $75. Electronic applications accepted. *Financial support:* In 2016–17, 24 students received support. Fellowships with partial tuition reimbursements available, Federal Work-Study, scholarships/grants, and tuition waivers (partial) available. Financial award application deadline: 4/15; financial award applicants required to submit FAFSA. *Faculty research:* Leadership, Jewish professional leadership, business administration, nonprofit management, public policy, Near Eastern and Judaic studies, Israel-Diaspora relations. *Unit head:* Dr. Jonathan Sarna, Program Chair, 781-736-2990, Fax: 781-736-2070, E-mail: hornstein@brandeis.edu. *Application contact:* Carol Hengerle, Program Administrator, 781-736-2990, Fax: 781-736-2070, E-mail: hornstein@brandeis.edu. Website: http://www.brandeis.edu/hornstein

**Brandeis University,** Graduate School of Arts and Sciences, Joint Master's Programs in Women's, Gender, and Sexuality Studies, Waltham, MA 02454-9110. Offers anthropology and women's, gender, and sexuality studies (MA); English and women's, gender, and sexuality studies (MA); near Eastern and Judaic studies and women's, gender, and sexuality studies (MA); public policy and women's, gender, and sexuality studies (MA); sociology and women's, gender, and sexuality studies (MA); sustainable international development and women's, gender, and sexuality studies (MA). *Degree requirements:* For master's, thesis. *Entrance requirements:* For master's, GRE, sample of written work, resume, statement of purpose, transcript(s), two letters of recommendation. Additional exam requirements/recommendations for international students: Required—TOEFL (minimum score 600 paper-based; 100 iBT), PTE (minimum score 68); Recommended—IELTS (minimum score 7). *Application deadline:* For fall admission, 1/15 for domestic students. Application fee: $75. Electronic applications accepted. *Financial support:* Fellowships with full tuition reimbursements and teaching assistantships with partial tuition reimbursements available. Financial award application deadline: 4/15; financial award applicants required to submit FAFSA. *Faculty research:* Anthropology, English, history, music, Near Eastern and Judaic studies, public policy, psychology, sociology, and sustainable international development. *Unit head:* Elizabeth Brainerd, Director of Graduate Study, 781-736-4816, E-mail: ebrainer@brandeis.edu. *Application contact:* Shannon Hunt, Program Administrator, 781-736-3045, Fax: 781-736-3044, E-mail: shunt@brandeis.edu. Website: http://www.brandeis.edu/gsas

**Brooklyn College of the City University of New York,** School of Humanities and Social Sciences, Department of Judaic Studies, Brooklyn, NY 11210-2889. Offers MA. *Program availability:* Part-time, evening/weekend. *Degree requirements:* For master's, 2 foreign languages, comprehensive exam or thesis. *Entrance requirements:* For master's, 18 upper-level credits in Judaic studies, interview, 2 letters of recommendation. Additional exam requirements/recommendations for international students: Required—TOEFL (minimum score 525 paper-based; 70 iBT). Electronic applications accepted. *Faculty research:* Biblical studies, Talmud and Midrash, modern Jewish history and thought.

**Central Yeshiva Tomchei Tmimim-Lubavitch,** Graduate Programs, Brooklyn, NY 11230. Offers Jewish/Judaic studies (MA); Talmudic studies (MA). *Accreditation:* AARTS.

**Columbia University,** Graduate School of Arts and Sciences, New York, NY 10027. Offers African-American studies (MA); American studies (MA); anthropology (MA, PhD); art history and archaeology (MA, PhD); astronomy (PhD); biological sciences (PhD); biotechnology (MA); chemical physics (PhD); chemistry (PhD); classical studies (MA, PhD); classics (MA, PhD); climate and society (MA); conservation biology (MA); earth and environmental sciences (PhD); East Asia: regional studies (MA); East Asian languages and cultures (MA, PhD); ecology, evolution and environmental biology (MA), including conservation biology; ecology, evolution, and environmental biology (PhD), including ecology and evolutionary biology, evolutionary primatology; economics (MA, PhD); English and comparative literature (MA, PhD); French and Romance philology (MA, PhD); Germanic languages (MA, PhD); global French studies (MA); global thought (MA); Hispanic cultural studies (MA); history (PhD); history and literature (MA); human rights studies (MA); Islamic studies (MA); Italian (MA, PhD); Japanese pedagogy (MA); Jewish studies (MA); Latin America and the Caribbean: regional studies (MA); Latin American and Iberian cultures (PhD); mathematics (MA, PhD), including finance (MA); medieval and Renaissance studies (MA); Middle Eastern, South Asian, and African studies (MA, PhD); modern art: critical and curatorial studies (MA); modern European

## Jewish Studies

studies (MA); museum anthropology (MA); music (DMA, PhD); oral history (MA); philosophical foundations of physics (MA); philosophy (MA, PhD); physics (PhD); political science (MA, PhD); psychology (PhD); quantitative methods in the social sciences (MA); religion (MA, PhD); Russia, Eurasia and East Europe: regional studies (MA); Russian translation (MA); Slavic cultures (MA); Slavic languages (MA, PhD); sociology (MA, PhD); South Asian studies (MA); statistics (MA, PhD); theatre (PhD). Dual-degree programs require admission to both Graduate School of Arts and Sciences and another Columbia school. *Program availability:* Part-time. Terminal master's awarded for partial completion of doctoral program. *Degree requirements:* For master's, variable foreign language requirement, comprehensive exam (for some programs), thesis (for some programs); for doctorate, variable foreign language requirement, comprehensive exam (for some programs), thesis/dissertation. *Entrance requirements:* For master's and doctorate, GRE General Test, GRE Subject Test (for some programs). Additional exam requirements/recommendations for international students: Required—TOEFL, IELTS. Electronic applications accepted.

**Concordia University,** School of Graduate Studies, Faculty of Arts and Science, Department of Religion, Program in Judaic Studies, Montréal, QC H3G 1M8, Canada. Offers MA. *Degree requirements:* For master's, one foreign language, comprehensive exam, thesis optional. *Entrance requirements:* For master's, Hebrew exam, honors degree in Judaic studies or equivalent. Additional exam requirements/recommendations for international students: Required—TOEFL. *Faculty research:* Jewish religious reflections and modern philosophy of religion, Judaism and modernity, Judaism in late antiquity.

**Cornell University,** Graduate School, Graduate Fields of Arts and Sciences, Field of Near Eastern Studies, Ithaca, NY 14853. Offers ancient Near Eastern studies (MA, PhD); Arabic and Islamic studies (MA, PhD); biblical studies (MA, PhD); Hebrew and Judaic studies (MA, PhD). Terminal master's awarded for partial completion of doctoral program. *Degree requirements:* For master's, one foreign language, thesis; for doctorate, 2 foreign languages, comprehensive exam, thesis/dissertation. *Entrance requirements:* For master's and doctorate, GRE General Test, 2 years of 1 Near Eastern language, 3 letters of recommendation, writing sample. Additional exam requirements/recommendations for international students: Required—TOEFL (minimum score 550 paper-based; 77 iBT). Electronic applications accepted. *Faculty research:* Ancient Near East (including archeology), Hebrew and Judaic studies (including Bible), early Christianity, Arabic and Islamic studies, modern Middle East.

**Criswell College,** Graduate School of the Bible, Dallas, TX 75246-1537. Offers biblical studies (M Div); Christian leadership (MA); counseling (MA); Jewish studies (MA); ministry (MA); theological and biblical studies (MA). *Program availability:* Part-time. *Degree requirements:* For master's, 2 foreign languages, thesis optional. *Entrance requirements:* For master's, GRE General Test, minimum GPA of 2.5. Electronic applications accepted. *Faculty research:* Emphasis on biblical languages (Hebrew and Greek), expository preaching and evangelism in the local church.

**Dallas Theological Seminary,** Graduate Programs, Dallas, TX 75204-6499. Offers adult education (Th M); apologetics (Th M); Bible backgrounds (Th M); Bible translation (Th M); Biblical and theological studies (Certificate); biblical counseling (MA); biblical exegesis and linguistics (MA); biblical exposition (PhD); biblical studies (MA); Biblical theology (Th M); children's education (Th M); Christian education (MA, D Min); Christian leadership (MA); cross-cultural ministries (MA); educational administration (Th M); educational leadership (Th M); evangelism and discipleship (Th M); exposition of Biblical books (Th M); family life education (Th M); general studies (Th M); Hebrew and cognate studies (Th M); hermeneutics (Th M); historical theology (Th M); homiletics (Th M); intercultural ministries (Th M); Jesus studies (Th M); leadership studies (Th M); media and communication (MA); media arts (Th M); ministry (D Min); ministry with women (Th M); New Testament studies (Th M, PhD); Old Testament studies (Th M, PhD); parachurch ministries (Th M); pastoral care and counseling (Th M); pastoral theology and practice (Th M); philosophy (Th M); sacred theology (STM); spiritual formation (Th M); systematic theology (Th M); teaching in Christian institutions (Th M); theological studies (PhD); urban ministries (Th M); worship studies (Th M); youth education (Th M). *Program availability:* Part-time, online learning. *Degree requirements:* For master's, variable foreign language requirement, thesis (for some programs); for doctorate, 2 foreign languages, thesis/dissertation. *Entrance requirements:* For master's, GRE or MAT (if minimum undergraduate cumulative GPA is below 2.5 or undergraduate degree is unaccredited). Additional exam requirements/recommendations for international students: Required—TOEFL (minimum score 575 paper-based; 85 iBT), TWE. Electronic applications accepted.

**Graduate Theological Union,** Graduate Programs, Berkeley, CA 94709-1212. Offers art and religion (MA, PhD, Th D); biblical languages (MA); biblical studies (MA); Biblical studies (PhD, Th D); Buddhist studies (MA); Christian spirituality (MA, PhD, Th D); cultural and historical studies of religions (MA, PhD, Th D); ethics and social theory (PhD, Th D); history (MA, PhD, Th D); homiletics (MA, PhD, Th D); interdisciplinary studies (PhD, Th D); Jewish studies (MA, PhD, Th D, Certificate); liturgical studies (MA, PhD, Th D); Near Eastern religions (PhD, Th D); Orthodox Christian studies (MA); religion and psychology (MA, PhD, Th D); religion and society/ethics and social theory (MA); systematic and philosophical theology (MA, PhD, Th D). PhD programs in Jewish studies and Near Eastern religions offered jointly with University of California, Berkeley. *Accreditation:* ATS. Terminal master's awarded for partial completion of doctoral program. *Degree requirements:* For master's, one foreign language, thesis; for doctorate, one foreign language, comprehensive exam, thesis/dissertation. *Entrance requirements:* For master's, GRE General Test; for doctorate, GRE General Test, MA or M Div. Additional exam requirements/recommendations for international students: Required—TOEFL. Electronic applications accepted.

**Gratz College,** Graduate Programs, Program in Jewish Christian Studies, Melrose Park, PA 19027. Offers Graduate Certificate. *Program availability:* Online learning. *Unit head:* Dr. Ruth Sandberg, Director, 215-635-7300 Ext. 168, Fax: 215-635-7320, E-mail: rsandberg@gratz.edu. *Application contact:* Joanna Boeing Bratton, Director of Admissions, 215-635-7300 Ext. 140, Fax: 215-635-7399, E-mail: admissions@gratz.edu.
Website: https://www.gratz.edu/academics/jewish-christian-studies

**Gratz College,** Graduate Programs, Program in Jewish Studies, Melrose Park, PA 19027. Offers MA. *Program availability:* Part-time, online learning. *Degree requirements:* For master's, one foreign language, comprehensive exam, thesis optional. *Application deadline:* Applications are processed on a rolling basis. Application fee: $50. *Financial support:* Fellowships, Federal Work-Study, and unspecified assistantships available. Support available to part-time students. Financial award application deadline: 4/15; financial award applicants required to submit FAFSA. *Unit head:* Dr. Ruth Sandberg, Director, 215-635-7300 Ext. 168, Fax: 215-635-7320, E-mail: rsandberg@gratz.edu. *Application contact:* Joanna Boeing Bratton, Director of Admissions, 215-635-7300 Ext. 140, Fax: 215-635-7399, E-mail: admissions@gratz.edu.

**Harvard University,** Graduate School of Arts and Sciences, Department of Near Eastern Languages and Civilizations, Cambridge, MA 02138. Offers Akkadian (AM, PhD); Arabic (AM, PhD); Armenian (AM, PhD); biblical history (AM, PhD); Hebrew (AM, PhD); Indo-Muslim culture (AM, PhD); Iranian (AM, PhD); Jewish

history and literature (AM, PhD); Persian (AM, PhD); Semitic philology (AM, PhD); Syro-Palestinian archaeology (AM, PhD); Turkish (AM, PhD). *Degree requirements:* For doctorate, variable foreign language requirement, thesis/dissertation, general exams. *Entrance requirements:* For master's, GRE General Test; for doctorate, GRE General Test, proficiency in a Near Eastern language. Additional exam requirements/recommendations for international students: Required—TOEFL.

**Hebrew College,** Cantor Educator Program, Newton Centre, MA 02459. Offers MJ Ed. *Entrance requirements:* For master's, GRE, interview. Additional exam requirements/recommendations for international students: Required—TOEFL.

**Hebrew College,** Program in Jewish Studies, Newton Centre, MA 02459. Offers Jewish liturgical music (Certificate); Jewish music education (Certificate); Jewish studies (MA). *Program availability:* Part-time, evening/weekend, online learning. *Degree requirements:* For master's, one foreign language. *Entrance requirements:* For master's, GRE, interview. Additional exam requirements/recommendations for international students: Required—TOEFL.

**Hebrew Union College–Jewish Institute of Religion,** School of Graduate Studies, Program in Judaic Studies, New York, NY 10012-1186. Offers MAJS. *Program availability:* Part-time. *Degree requirements:* For master's, one foreign language, thesis. *Entrance requirements:* For master's, GRE, minimum 2 years of college-level Hebrew. *Faculty research:* Philosophy and theology, Bible, Hebrew, history and Rabbinics.

**Indiana University Bloomington,** University Graduate School, College of Arts and Sciences, Robert A. and Sandra S. Borns Jewish Studies Program, Bloomington, IN 47405. Offers Jewish studies (MA), including nonprofit management; Jewish studies and history (MA). *Faculty:* 24 full-time (9 women). *Students:* 7 full-time (3 women), 1 part-time (0 women); includes 1 minority (Hispanic/Latino). Average age 33. 11 applicants, 64% accepted, 6 enrolled. *Degree requirements:* For master's, one foreign language, thesis. *Entrance requirements:* Additional exam requirements/recommendations for international students: Required—TOEFL. *Application deadline:* For fall admission, 1/1 for domestic students, 12/1 for international students. Application fee: $55 ($65 for international students). Electronic applications accepted. *Financial support:* In 2016–17, 16 students received support, including 16 fellowships with full and partial tuition reimbursements available (averaging $17,800 per year); teaching assistantships, scholarships/grants, health care benefits, and grants-in-aid also available. Financial award application deadline: 1/15. *Faculty research:* Jewish studies, religious studies, history, Holocaust study. *Unit head:* Mark Roseman, Director, 812-855-0453, Fax: 812-855-4314, E-mail: marrosem@indiana.edu. *Application contact:* Carolyn Lipson-Walker, Assistant Director, 812-855-0453, Fax: 812-855-4314, E-mail: clipsonw@indiana.edu. Website: http://www.indiana.edu/~jsp/index.shtml

**The Jewish Theological Seminary,** The Graduate School, New York, NY 10027-4649. Offers ancient Judaism (MA, DHL, PhD); Bible and ancient Semitic languages (MA, DHL, PhD); interdepartmental studies (MA); Jewish art and visual culture (MA); Jewish gender and women's studies (MA); Jewish history (MA, DHL, PhD); Jewish literature (MA, DHL, PhD); Jewish philosophy (DHL); Jewish thought (MA, PhD); liturgy (MA, DHL, PhD); medieval Jewish studies (MA, DHL, PhD); Midrash (DHL); Midrash and scriptural interpretation (MA, PhD); modern Jewish studies (MA, DHL, PhD); Talmud and rabbinics (MA, DHL, PhD); MA/MSW. MA/MSW offered jointly with Columbia University. *Accreditation:* ACIPE. *Program availability:* Part-time. Terminal master's awarded for partial completion of doctoral program. *Degree requirements:* For master's, one foreign language, comprehensive exam (for some programs), thesis (for some programs); for doctorate, 3 foreign languages, comprehensive exam (for some programs), thesis/dissertation. *Entrance requirements:* For master's, GRE or MAT, 3 letters of recommendation, writing sample; for doctorate, GRE or MAT, 3 letters of recommendation, writing research sample. Additional exam requirements/recommendations for international students: Required—TOEFL.

**The Jewish Theological Seminary,** William Davidson Graduate School of Jewish Education, New York, NY 10027-4649. Offers MA, Ed D. Offered in conjunction with The Rabbinical School; H. L. Miller Cantorial School and College of Jewish Music; Teacher's College, Columbia University; and Union Theological Seminary. *Program availability:* Part-time, online learning. *Degree requirements:* For master's, one foreign language, thesis optional; for doctorate, one foreign language, comprehensive exam, thesis/dissertation. *Entrance requirements:* For master's, GRE or MAT, 3 letters of recommendation; for doctorate, GRE or MAT, writing sample, 3 letters of recommendation. Additional exam requirements/recommendations for international students: Recommended—TOEFL.

**McGill University,** Faculty of Graduate and Postdoctoral Studies, Faculty of Arts, Department of Jewish Studies, Montréal, QC H3A 2T5, Canada. Offers MA.

**New York University,** Graduate School of Arts and Science, Program in Museum Studies, New York, NY 10012-1019. Offers museum studies (MA, Advanced Certificate), including Africana studies (MA), Hebrew and Judaic studies (MA), Latin American and Caribbean studies (MA), Near Eastern studies (MA). *Program availability:* Part-time, evening/weekend. *Entrance requirements:* For master's, GRE General Test; for Advanced Certificate, master's degree or PhD. Additional exam requirements/recommendations for international students: Required—TOEFL. *Faculty research:* Modern and contemporary art, history of museums and exhibitions, conservation of cultural materials, museum anthropology, ethnography.

**New York University,** Graduate School of Arts and Science, Skirball Department of Hebrew and Judaic Studies, New York, NY 10012-1019. Offers Hebrew and Judaic studies (MA, PhD); Hebrew and Judaic studies/museum studies (MA). *Program availability:* Part-time. Terminal master's awarded for partial completion of doctoral program. *Degree requirements:* For master's, 2 foreign languages, comprehensive exam, thesis optional; for doctorate, 4 foreign languages, comprehensive exam, thesis/dissertation. *Entrance requirements:* For master's and doctorate, GRE General Test. Additional exam requirements/recommendations for international students: Required—TOEFL. *Faculty research:* Post-Biblical and Talmudic literature and history, mysticism, Bible and ancient Near East, medieval and modern Jewish history, medieval and modern Jewish philosophy.

**New York University,** Steinhardt School of Culture, Education, and Human Development, Department of Humanities and Social Sciences in the Professions, Program in Education and Jewish Studies, New York, NY 10012-1019. Offers MA, PhD, MA/MA. *Program availability:* Part-time. *Degree requirements:* For doctorate, thesis/dissertation. *Entrance requirements:* For doctorate, GRE General Test, interview. Additional exam requirements/recommendations for international students: Required—TOEFL (minimum score 100 iBT). Electronic applications accepted. *Faculty research:* Jewish education, educational history, Judaic studies.

**Reconstructionist Rabbinical College,** Graduate Programs, Wyncote, PA 19095-1898. Offers Jewish studies (MAJS); rabbinics (MAHL, DHL); women's studies (Certificate). Certificate offered jointly with Temple University. *Program availability:* Part-time. *Degree requirements:* For master's, one foreign language, thesis (MAJS), completion of rabbinical program (MAHL); for doctorate, one foreign language. *Entrance requirements:* For master's, GRE General Test; placement examinations in Hebrew and

Judaism (MAHL); for doctorate, GRE General Test, placement examinations in Hebrew and Judaism. *Faculty research:* Bible, Hebrew Semitic texts, contemporary Judaism.

**Rice University,** Graduate Programs, School of Humanities, Department of Religious Studies, Houston, TX 77251-1892. Offers African religions (PhD); African-American religions (PhD); contemplative studies (PhD); ghosticism, esotericism, mysticism (PhD); Islam (PhD); Jewish thought and philosophy (PhD); modern Christianity in thought and popular culture (PhD); psychology of religion (PhD); the Bible and beyond (PhD). *Degree requirements:* For doctorate, 2 foreign languages, comprehensive exam, thesis/dissertation. *Entrance requirements:* For doctorate, GRE, letters of recommendation, writing sample. Additional exam requirements/recommendations for international students: Required—TOEFL (minimum score 600 paper-based; 90 iBT). Electronic applications accepted. *Faculty research:* Origins and historical development of Islam, history of Christianity, the study of comparative religion, African-American religion, religion and culture.

**Rutgers University–New Brunswick,** Graduate School-New Brunswick, Department of Jewish Studies, New Brunswick, NJ 08901. Offers MA, Certificate. *Program availability:* Part-time.

**Seton Hall University,** College of Arts and Sciences, Department of Religion, South Orange, NJ 07079-2697. Offers Jewish-Christian studies (MA). *Program availability:* Part-time, evening/weekend. *Degree requirements:* For master's, thesis optional. *Entrance requirements:* For master's, interview or suitable correspondence with department chair. Additional exam requirements/recommendations for international students: Required—TOEFL. Electronic applications accepted. *Faculty research:* Jewish-Christian issues, Biblical studies, Holocaust studies.

**Southern Evangelical Seminary,** Graduate Programs, Matthews, NC 28105. Offers apologetics (MA, D Min, Certificate); Christian education (MA); church ministry (MA, Certificate); divinity (Certificate), including apologetics (M Div, Certificate); Islamic studies (MA, Certificate); Jewish studies (MA); philosophy (MA); philosophy of religion (PhD); religion (MA); theology (M Div), including apologetics (M Div, Certificate), Biblical studies; youth ministry (MA). *Program availability:* Part-time, evening/weekend, online learning. *Degree requirements:* For master's, thesis (for some programs); for doctorate, 2 foreign languages, comprehensive exam (for some programs), thesis/dissertation. *Entrance requirements:* Additional exam requirements/recommendations for international students: Required—TOEFL (minimum score 600 paper-based).

**Spertus Institute for Jewish Learning and Leadership,** Program in Jewish Studies, Chicago, IL 60605-1901. Offers MAJPS, MAJS, DJS, DSJS. *Program availability:* Part-time, evening/weekend, online learning. *Degree requirements:* For master's, one foreign language, thesis (for some programs); for doctorate, one foreign language, thesis/dissertation. *Entrance requirements:* For master's, interview, BAJS (for MAJS); for doctorate, MAJS.

**Telshe Yeshiva–Chicago,** Graduate Program, Chicago, IL 60625-5598. Offers Second Talmudic Degree. *Accreditation:* AARTS.

**Touro College,** Graduate School of Jewish Studies, New York, NY 10010. Offers MA. *Program availability:* Part-time. *Faculty:* 4 full-time (2 women), 5 part-time/adjunct (2 women). *Students:* 5 full-time (2 women), 29 part-time (16 women), 1 international. Average age 38. *Degree requirements:* For master's, one foreign language, thesis. *Entrance requirements:* For master's, previous course work in Jewish studies, proficiency in Hebrew. Application fee: $50. *Financial support:* Tuition waivers (full and partial) available. Support available to part-time students. *Faculty research:* Medieval and modern Jewish history, Jewish philosophy, Holocaust studies, Jewish education. *Unit head:* Dr. Michael Shmidman, Dean, 212-213-2230. *Application contact:* Karen Rubin, Executive Assistant to the Dean, 212-463-0400 Ext. 5581, E-mail: karen.rubin@touro.edu.

**Towson University,** Baltimore Hebrew Institute, Towson, MD 21252-0001. Offers Jewish communal service (MAJCS, Postbaccalaureate Certificate); Jewish education (Postbaccalaureate Certificate); Jewish studies (MAJS). *Students:* 6 full-time (5 women), 11 part-time (6 women); includes 2 minority (1 Black or African American, non-Hispanic/Latino; 1 Hispanic/Latino), 1 international. *Entrance requirements:* For master's, bachelor's degree, minimum GPA of 3.0, letters of recommendation, statement of intent, sample of work, interview, resume; for Postbaccalaureate Certificate, bachelor's degree, minimum GPA of 3.0, statement of intent, sample of work, interview, 2 letters of recommendation, resume. Additional exam requirements/recommendations for international students: Required—TOEFL. *Application deadline:* Applications are processed on a rolling basis. Application fee: $45. Electronic applications accepted. *Expenses:* Tuition, state resident: full-time $7580; part-time $379 per unit. Tuition, nonresident: full-time $15,700; part-time $785 per unit. *Required fees:* $2480. *Unit head:* Jill Max, Director, 410-704-7120, E-mail: jmax@towson.edu. *Application contact:* Coverley Beidleman, Assistant Director of Graduate Admissions, 410-704-2113, Fax: 410-704-3030, E-mail: grads@towson.edu.
Website: http://www.towson.edu/cla/centers/baltimorehebrewinstitute

**University of California, San Diego,** Graduate Division, Department of History, La Jolla, CA 92093. Offers history (MA, PhD); Judaic studies (MA). *Students:* 93 full-time (38 women), 2 part-time (1 woman). 119 applicants, 19% accepted, 12 enrolled. In 2016, 7 master's, 7 doctorates awarded. *Degree requirements:* For master's, one foreign language, comprehensive exam; for doctorate, one foreign language, comprehensive exam, thesis/dissertation. *Entrance requirements:* For master's, GRE General Test, minimum GPA of 3.0; for doctorate, GRE General Test, writing sample (7-15 pages long), preferably in a history course. Additional exam requirements/recommendations for international students: Required—TOEFL (minimum score 550 paper-based; 80 iBT), IELTS (minimum score 7). *Application deadline:* For fall admission, 1/9 for domestic students. Application fee: $105 ($125 for international students). Electronic applications accepted. *Expenses:* Tuition, state resident: full-time $11,220. Tuition, nonresident: full-time $26,322. *Required fees:* $1864. *Financial support:* Fellowships, research assistantships, teaching assistantships, career-related internships or fieldwork, scholarships/grants, and readerships available. Financial award applicants required to submit FAFSA. *Faculty research:* Ancient history, east Asian history, history of science, Jewish studies, global transnational studies. *Unit head:* Pamela Radcliff, Chair, 858-534-8919, E-mail: pradcliff@ucsd.edu. *Application contact:* Amber Rieder, Graduate Coordinator, 858-822-0664, E-mail: arieder@ucsd.edu.
Website: http://history.ucsd.edu

**University of Connecticut,** Graduate School, College of Liberal Arts and Sciences, Field of International Studies, Program in Judaic Studies, Storrs, CT 06269. Offers MA. *Entrance requirements:* Additional exam requirements/recommendations for international students: Required—TOEFL (minimum score 550 paper-based). Electronic applications accepted.

**University of Florida,** Graduate School, College of Liberal Arts and Sciences, Department of History, Gainesville, FL 32611. Offers historic preservation (MA, PhD); history (MA, PhD); Jewish studies (MA); women's and gender studies (PhD); JD/MA; JD/PhD. *Program availability:* Part-time. Terminal master's awarded for partial completion of doctoral program. *Degree requirements:* For master's, variable foreign language requirement, thesis optional, 30 credit hours; for doctorate, variable foreign

language requirement, comprehensive exam, thesis/dissertation, 90 credit hours. *Entrance requirements:* For master's and doctorate, GRE General Test, minimum GPA of 3.0. Additional exam requirements/recommendations for international students: Required—TOEFL (minimum score 550 paper-based; 80 iBT), IELTS (minimum score 6). Electronic applications accepted. *Faculty research:* Latin American and Caribbean history, nineteenth century U.S. history, medieval European history, African history and Atlantic world history.

**University of Florida,** Graduate School, College of Liberal Arts and Sciences, Department of Religion, Gainesville, FL 32611. Offers Jewish studies (MA); religion (MA, PhD); tropical conservation and development (MA, PhD); women's and gender studies (MA, PhD). *Program availability:* Part-time. *Degree requirements:* For master's, one foreign language, thesis optional; for doctorate, one foreign language, comprehensive exam, thesis/dissertation. *Entrance requirements:* For master's, GRE General Test, minimum GPA of 3.0. Additional exam requirements/recommendations for international students: Required—TOEFL (minimum score 550 paper-based; 80 iBT), IELTS (minimum score 6). Electronic applications accepted. *Faculty research:* Religion in America, Christian thought, Islam, religions of India, comparative religion.

**University of Maryland, College Park,** Academic Affairs, College of Arts and Humanities, Meyerhoff Center for Jewish Studies, College Park, MD 20742. Offers MA. *Degree requirements:* For master's, thesis or 2 major research papers. *Entrance requirements:* For master's, GRE General Test, 3 letters of recommendation, writing sample. Additional exam requirements/recommendations for international students: Required—TOEFL.

**University of Michigan,** Rackham Graduate School, College of Literature, Science, and the Arts, Department of Near Eastern Studies, Ann Arbor, MI 48109. Offers ancient Near Eastern studies (AM, PhD); Arabic for professional purposes (AM); Arabic language and literature (AM, PhD); Armenian studies (AM, PhD); Christianity in late antiquity (AM, PhD); Egyptology (AM, PhD); Hebrew Bible and ancient Israel (AM, PhD); Hebrew literature (AM, PhD); Islamic studies (AM, PhD); Jewish cultural studies (AM, PhD); Jewish mysticism (AM, PhD); Persian and Iranian studies (AM, PhD); Rabbinic literature (AM, PhD); Second Temple Judaism (AM, PhD); teaching Arabic as a foreign language (AM); Turkish studies (AM, PhD). *Faculty:* 27 full-time (8 women). *Students:* 28 full-time (12 women); includes 2 minority (1 Black or African American, non-Hispanic/Latino; 1 Asian, non-Hispanic/Latino), 10 international. Average age 32. 85 applicants, 8% accepted, 3 enrolled. In 2016, 4 master's, 3 doctorates awarded. Terminal master's awarded for partial completion of doctoral program. *Degree requirements:* For master's, 2 foreign languages; for doctorate, 4 foreign languages, comprehensive exam, thesis/dissertation, preliminary exams, oral defense of dissertation. *Entrance requirements:* Additional exam requirements/recommendations for international students: Required—TOEFL (minimum score 560 paper-based; 84 iBT), IELTS (minimum score 6.5). *Application deadline:* For fall admission, 12/1 for domestic and international students. Application fee: $75 ($90 for international students). Electronic applications accepted. *Expenses:* Tuition, state resident: full-time $21,466; part-time $1152 per credit hour. Tuition, nonresident: full-time $43,346; part-time $2367 per credit hour. Part-time tuition and fees vary according to course load, degree level and program. *Financial support:* In 2016–17, 28 students received support. Fellowships with full tuition reimbursements available, teaching assistantships with full tuition reimbursements available, scholarships/grants, health care benefits, unspecified assistantships, and spring/summer stipends available. Financial award application deadline: 12/1. *Faculty research:* Middle and Near Eastern literatures, languages, cultures from ancient times to the present. *Unit head:* Prof. Gottfried Hagen, Chair, 734-764-0314, E-mail: nes-chair@umich.edu. *Application contact:* Student Services, 734-764-0315, E-mail: nes-gradservices@umich.edu.
Website: http://www.lsa.umich.edu/neareast/

**University of Michigan,** Rackham Graduate School, College of Literature, Science, and the Arts, Jean and Samuel Frankel Center for Judaic Studies, Ann Arbor, MI 48104. Offers MA, Graduate Certificate. *Program availability:* Part-time. *Degree requirements:* For master's, one foreign language, thesis, fourth-term proficiency in either Hebrew or Yiddish; for Graduate Certificate, one foreign language, capstone course (including public lecture), reading knowledge of 1 Jewish language. *Entrance requirements:* For master's, GRE General Test; for Graduate Certificate, currently enrolled in a PhD or professional degree program at the University of Michigan. Additional exam requirements/recommendations for international students: Required—TOEFL (minimum score 560 paper-based). Electronic applications accepted. *Expenses:* Tuition, state resident: full-time $21,466; part-time $1152 per credit hour. Tuition, nonresident: full-time $43,346; part-time $2367 per credit hour. Part-time tuition and fees vary according to course load, degree level and program. *Faculty research:* Jewish culture and history; Jews in modern Europe; Jewish languages; Bible and ancient Judaism; Mediterranean and Sephardic.

**University of St. Michael's College,** Faculty of Theology, Toronto, ON M5S 1J4, Canada. Offers Catholic leadership (MA); eastern Christian studies (Diploma); religious education (Diploma); theological studies (Diploma); theology (M Div, MA, MRE, MTS, D Min, PhD, Th D); theology and Jewish studies (MA). Th D offered jointly with University of Toronto. *Accreditation:* ATS (one or more programs are accredited). *Program availability:* Part-time. *Degree requirements:* For master's, thesis (for some programs), 1 foreign language (MA), 2 foreign languages (Th M); for doctorate, 3 foreign languages, comprehensive exam, thesis/dissertation; for other advanced degree, thesis optional. *Entrance requirements:* For master's, M Div or BA, course work in an ancient or modern language, minimum GPA of 3.3; for doctorate, MA in theology, Th M, or M Div with thesis, minimum GPA of 3.7; for other advanced degree, minimum GPA of 2.7. Additional exam requirements/recommendations for international students: Required—TOEFL (minimum score 600 paper-based). Electronic applications accepted. *Expenses:* Contact institution. *Faculty research:* Patristics, eastern Christianity, ecology and theology, ecumenism, Jewish Christian studies.

**University of Wisconsin–Madison,** Graduate School, College of Letters and Science, Department of Hebrew and Semitic Studies, Madison, WI 53706-1380. Offers MA, PhD. Terminal master's awarded for partial completion of doctoral program. *Degree requirements:* For master's, 2 foreign languages; for doctorate, thesis/dissertation. *Entrance requirements:* For master's and doctorate, GRE. Electronic applications accepted. *Faculty research:* Biblical language and literature, Northwest Semitic languages.

**Washington University in St. Louis,** The Graduate School, Department of Jewish, Islamic, and Near Eastern Languages and Cultures, St. Louis, MO 63130-4899. Offers Islamic and Near Eastern studies (MA); Jewish studies (MA). *Degree requirements:* For master's, one foreign language, thesis (for some programs). *Entrance requirements:* For master's, GRE General Test. Additional exam requirements/recommendations for international students: Required—TOEFL. Electronic applications accepted. *Faculty research:* Islamic and Near Eastern studies (Islamic history; Arabic language and literature, modern Middle East history); Jewish studies (Hebrew Bible, Rabbinic literature, Jewish history, modern Hebrew literature).

**Yeshiva University,** Bernard Revel Graduate School of Jewish Studies, New York, NY 10033-3201. Offers MA, PhD. *Program availability:* Part-time. Terminal master's awarded for partial completion of doctoral program. *Degree requirements:* For master's, comprehensive exam; for doctorate, 2 foreign languages, comprehensive exam, thesis/dissertation. *Entrance requirements:* For master's and doctorate, GRE General Test

(recommended), reading knowledge of Hebrew, minimum GPA of 3.0. *Faculty research:* Bible, Jewish history, Jewish philosophy and mysticism, Talmud, Semitic languages.

# Latin American Studies

**American University,** College of Arts and Sciences, Department of World Languages and Cultures, Washington, DC 20016-8045. Offers Spanish: Latin American studies (MA); teaching English as a foreign language (MA); teaching English to speakers of other languages (MA, Certificate); translation: French (Certificate); translation: Russian (Certificate); translation: Spanish (Certificate). *Program availability:* Part-time, evening/weekend. *Faculty:* 42 full-time (31 women), 27 part-time/adjunct (18 women). *Students:* 41 full-time (31 women), 31 part-time (23 women); includes 14 minority (3 Black or African American, non-Hispanic/Latino; 2 Asian, non-Hispanic/Latino; 7 Hispanic/Latino; 2 Two or more races, non-Hispanic/Latino), 9 international. Average age 32. 73 applicants, 92% accepted, 20 enrolled. In 2016, 24 master's, 6 other advanced degrees awarded. *Degree requirements:* For master's, one foreign language, comprehensive exam, thesis or alternative. *Entrance requirements:* For master's, GRE, writing sample, statement of purpose, transcripts, 2 letters of recommendation, resume; for Certificate, bachelor's degree, statement of purpose, transcripts, resume. Additional exam requirements/recommendations for international students: Required—TOEFL (minimum score 100 iBT), IELTS (minimum score 7), PTE (minimum score 68). *Application deadline:* For fall admission, 2/1 for domestic students; for spring admission, 11/1 for domestic students. Application fee: $55. *Expenses:* $1,579 per credit tuition; $690 mandatory fees. *Financial support:* Institutionally sponsored loans, scholarships/grants, and unspecified assistantships available. Financial award application deadline: 2/1; financial award applicants required to submit FAFSA. *Unit head:* Henry Gerfen, Chair, 202-885-2385, Fax: 202-885-1076, E-mail: gerfen@american.edu. *Application contact:* Kathleen Clowery, Director of Graduate Admissions, 202-885-3620, Fax: 202-885-1344, E-mail: clowery@american.edu.
Website: http://www.american.edu/cas/wlc/

**Boricua College,** Program in Latin American and Caribbean Studies, New York, NY 10032-1560. Offers MA. Program offered in Brooklyn and Manhattan. *Program availability:* Evening/weekend. *Degree requirements:* For master's, thesis. *Entrance requirements:* For master's, interview by the faculty. *Application deadline:* Applications are processed on a rolling basis. Application fee: $100. *Expenses: Tuition:* Full-time $13,000. *Required fees:* $100. *Financial support:* Career-related internships or fieldwork and Federal Work-Study available. Financial award applicants required to submit FAFSA. *Unit head:* Dr. Maria Montes, Senior Vice President, 718-782-2200 Ext. 222. *Application contact:* Miriam Pfeffer, Director of Admissions, 718-782-2200 Ext. 210, E-mail: mpfeffer@boricuacollege.edu.

**Brown University,** Graduate School, Department of Portuguese and Brazilian Studies, Providence, RI 02912. Offers Brazilian studies (AM); English as a second language and cross-cultural studies (AM); Portuguese and Brazilian studies (AM, PhD); Portuguese bilingual education and cross-cultural studies (AM). *Degree requirements:* For doctorate, thesis/dissertation.

**California State University, Los Angeles,** Graduate Studies, College of Natural and Social Sciences, Department of Latin American Studies, Los Angeles, CA 90032-8530. Offers MA. *Program availability:* Part-time, evening/weekend. *Degree requirements:* For master's, one foreign language, comprehensive exam, thesis. *Entrance requirements:* For master's, minimum GPA of 2.5. Additional exam requirements/recommendations for international students: Required—TOEFL (minimum score 500 paper-based). Electronic applications accepted. *Faculty research:* Central America, Cuba, Third World development, labor history, redemocratization.

**The Catholic University of America,** School of Arts and Sciences, Department of History, Washington, DC 20064. Offers history (MA, PhD), including early modern Europe, Latin America (MA), Medieval, modern Europe, U.S.; religion and society in the late medieval and early modern world (MA); MA/JD; MSLS/MA. *Program availability:* Part-time. *Faculty:* 14 full-time (6 women), 3 part-time/adjunct (2 women). *Students:* 7 full-time (2 women), 20 part-time (6 women); includes 3 minority (all Two or more races, non-Hispanic/Latino), 2 international. Average age 30. 22 applicants, 45% accepted, 4 enrolled. In 2016, 4 master's, 5 doctorates awarded. Terminal master's awarded for partial completion of doctoral program. *Degree requirements:* For master's, one foreign language, comprehensive exam, thesis optional, 2 languages (for medievalists), one of which must be Latin; for doctorate, 2 foreign languages, comprehensive exam, thesis/dissertation, 3 languages (for medievalists), one of which must be Latin. *Entrance requirements:* For master's and doctorate, GRE General Test, statement of purpose, official copies of academic transcripts, three letters of recommendation, writing sample. Additional exam requirements/recommendations for international students: Required—TOEFL (minimum score 550 paper-based; 80 iBT). *Application deadline:* For fall admission, 7/15 priority date for domestic students, 7/1 for international students; for spring admission, 11/15 priority date for domestic students, 11/1 for international students. Applications are processed on a rolling basis. Application fee: $55. Electronic applications accepted. *Expenses:* $42,850 per year; $1,170 per credit; $200 per semester part-time fees. *Financial support:* Fellowships, research assistantships, teaching assistantships, Federal Work-Study, scholarships/grants, tuition waivers (full and partial), and unspecified assistantships available. Financial award application deadline: 2/1; financial award applicants required to submit FAFSA. *Faculty research:* Medieval history, including the Islamic Middle East, with particular expertise in later medieval religious, social, and economic history and early medieval and late antique history; European and American intellectual history; renaissance, reformation, catholic reformation; US catholic history; history of immigration. *Total annual research expenditures:* $42,594. *Unit head:* Dr. Katherine Jansen, Chair, 202-319-5484, Fax: 202-319-5569, E-mail: jansen@cua.edu. *Application contact:* Director of Graduate Admissions, 202-319-5057, Fax: 202-319-6533, E-mail: cua-admissions@cua.edu.
Website: http://history.cua.edu/

**Centro de Estudios Avanzados de Puerto Rico y el Caribe,** Graduate Program in Puerto Rican and Caribbean Studies, Old San Juan, PR 00902-3970. Offers Puerto Rican and Caribbean history (MA, PhD); Puerto Rican and Caribbean literature (MA, PhD); Puerto Rican studies (MA). *Program availability:* Part-time, evening/weekend. *Degree requirements:* For master's, comprehensive exam, thesis; for doctorate, 2 foreign languages, comprehensive exam, thesis/dissertation. *Entrance requirements:* For master's and doctorate, interview. *Faculty research:* Literature, history, art, folklore, and culture of Puerto Rico and Caribbean countries.

**College of Staten Island of the City University of New York,** Graduate Programs, Division of Humanities and Social Sciences, Program in History, Staten Island, NY

10314-6600. Offers history of Africa and the Middle East (MA); history of Asia (MA); history of Europe (MA); history of Latin America and the Caribbean (MA); history of the United States (MA). *Program availability:* Part-time, evening/weekend. *Faculty:* 2 full-time. *Students:* 11 part-time. Average age 36. 8 applicants, 25% accepted, 2 enrolled. In 2016, 5 master's awarded. *Degree requirements:* For master's, comprehensive exam (for some programs), 32 credits (total of eight courses); thesis or portfolio. *Entrance requirements:* For master's, bachelor's degree with minimum GPA of 3.0 overall and in undergraduate history courses, two letters of recommendation, letter of interest, research-based writing sample. Additional exam requirements/recommendations for international students: Required—TOEFL (minimum score 550 paper-based; 79 iBT), IELTS (minimum score 6.5). *Application deadline:* For fall admission, 5/10 priority date for domestic and international students; for spring admission, 12/2 priority date for domestic and international students. Applications are processed on a rolling basis. Application fee: $125. Electronic applications accepted. *Expenses:* Tuition, state resident: full-time $10,130; part-time $425 per credit. Tuition, nonresident: full-time $18,720; part-time $780 per credit. *Required fees:* $181.10 per semester. Tuition and fees vary according to program. *Faculty research:* African and African diaspora history, South Asian history, Middle Eastern history, U.S. history, environmental history. *Unit head:* John Dixon, Graduate Program Coordinator, 718-982-3307, E-mail: john.dixon@csi.cuny.edu. *Application contact:* Sasha Spence, Associate Director for Graduate Admissions, 718-982-2019, Fax: 718-982-2500, E-mail: sasha.spence@csi.cuny.edu.
Website: http://www.csi.cuny.edu/catalog/graduate/master-of-arts-in-history-ma.htm

**Columbia University,** Graduate School of Arts and Sciences, New York, NY 10027. Offers African-American studies (MA); American studies (MA); anthropology (MA, PhD); art history and archaeology (MA, PhD); astronomy (PhD); biological sciences (PhD); biotechnology (MA); chemical physics (PhD); chemistry (PhD); classical studies (MA, PhD); classics (MA, PhD); climate and society (MA); conservation biology (MA); earth and environmental sciences (PhD); East Asia: regional studies (MA); East Asian languages and cultures (MA, PhD); ecology, evolution and environmental biology (MA), including conservation biology; ecology, evolution, and environmental biology (PhD), including ecology and evolutionary biology, evolutionary primatology; economics (MA, PhD); English and comparative literature (MA, PhD); French and Romance philology (MA, PhD); Germanic languages (MA, PhD); global French studies (MA); global thought (MA); Hispanic cultural studies (MA); history (PhD); history and literature (MA); human rights studies (MA); Islamic studies (MA); Italian (MA, PhD); Japanese pedagogy (MA); Jewish studies (MA); Latin America and the Caribbean: regional studies (MA); Latin American and Iberian cultures (PhD); mathematics (MA, PhD), including finance (MA); medieval and Renaissance studies (MA); Middle Eastern, South Asian, and African studies (MA, PhD); modern art: critical and curatorial studies (MA); modern European studies (MA); museum anthropology (MA); music (DMA, PhD); oral history (MA); philosophical foundations of physics (MA); philosophy (MA, PhD); physics (PhD); political science (MA, PhD); psychology (PhD); quantitative methods in the social sciences (MA); religion (MA, PhD); Russia, Eurasia and East Europe: regional studies (MA); Russian translation (MA); Slavic cultures (MA); Slavic languages (MA, PhD); sociology (MA, PhD); South Asian studies (MA); statistics (MA, PhD); theatre (PhD). Dual-degree programs require admission to both Graduate School of Arts and Sciences and another Columbia school. *Program availability:* Part-time. Terminal master's awarded for partial completion of doctoral program. *Degree requirements:* For master's, variable foreign language requirement, comprehensive exam (for some programs), thesis (for some programs); for doctorate, variable foreign language requirement, comprehensive exam (for some programs), thesis/dissertation. *Entrance requirements:* For master's and doctorate, GRE General Test, GRE Subject Test (for some programs). Additional exam requirements/recommendations for international students: Required—TOEFL, IELTS. Electronic applications accepted.

**Cornell University,** Graduate School, Graduate Fields of Arts and Sciences, Field of Archaeology, Ithaca, NY 14853. Offers environmental archaeology (MA); historical archaeology (MA); Latin American archaeology (MA); medieval archaeology (MA); Mediterranean and Near Eastern archaeology (MA); Stone Age archaeology (MA). *Degree requirements:* For master's, one foreign language, thesis. *Entrance requirements:* For master's, GRE General Test, 3 letters of recommendation, sample of written work. Additional exam requirements/recommendations for international students: Required—TOEFL (minimum score 550 paper-based; 77 iBT). Electronic applications accepted. *Faculty research:* Anatolia, Lydia, Sardis, classical and Hellenistic Greece, science in archaeology, North American Indians, Stone Age Africa, Mayan trade.

**Cornell University,** Graduate School, Graduate Fields of Arts and Sciences, Field of History, Ithaca, NY 14853. Offers African history (MA, PhD); American history (MA, PhD); ancient Greek history (PhD); ancient history (MA, PhD); ancient Roman history (PhD); early modern European history (MA, PhD); English history (MA, PhD); French history (MA, PhD); German history (MA, PhD); history of science (MA, PhD); Korean history (PhD); Latin American history (MA, PhD); medieval Chinese history (MA, PhD); medieval history (MA, PhD); modern Chinese history (MA, PhD); modern European history (MA, PhD); modern Japanese history (MA, PhD); modern Middle Eastern history (PhD); premodern Islamic history (MA, PhD); premodern Japanese history (MA, PhD); Renaissance history (MA, PhD); Russian history (MA, PhD); South Asian history (PhD); Southeast Asian history (MA, PhD). Terminal master's awarded for partial completion of doctoral program. *Degree requirements:* For master's, thesis; for doctorate, 2 foreign languages, comprehensive exam, thesis/dissertation, 1 year of teaching experience. *Entrance requirements:* For master's and doctorate, GRE General Test, writing sample, 3 letters of recommendation. Additional exam requirements/recommendations for international students: Required—TOEFL (minimum score 550 paper-based; 77 iBT). Electronic applications accepted.

**Cornell University,** Graduate School, Graduate Fields of Arts and Sciences, Field of History of Art, Archaeology and Visual Studies, Ithaca, NY 14853. Offers 19th century art (PhD); African, African American and African diaspora (PhD); American art (PhD); ancient art and archaeology (PhD); Asian American art (PhD); Baroque art (PhD); comparative modernities (PhD); digital art (PhD); East Asian art (PhD); history of photography (PhD); Islamic art (PhD); Latin American art (PhD); medieval art (PhD); modern art (PhD); Renaissance art (PhD); Southeast Asian art (PhD); theory and criticism (PhD); visual studies (PhD). *Degree requirements:* For doctorate, one foreign language, comprehensive exam, thesis/dissertation, general exams in 3 areas. *Entrance requirements:* For doctorate, GRE General Test, sample of written work, 3 letters of recommendation. Additional exam requirements/recommendations for international students: Required—TOEFL (minimum score 550 paper-based; 77 iBT). Electronic applications accepted.

**Duke University,** Graduate School, Department of History, Durham, NC 27708. Offers history (AM, PhD); Latin American studies (PhD); JD/AM. *Degree requirements:* For doctorate, 2 foreign languages, thesis/dissertation. *Entrance requirements:* For doctorate, GRE General Test. Additional exam requirements/recommendations for international students: Required—TOEFL (minimum score 577 paper-based; 90 iBT) or IELTS (minimum score 7). Electronic applications accepted.

**Florida International University,** Steven J. Green School of International and Public Affairs, Program in Latin American and Caribbean Studies, Miami, FL 33199. Offers MA. *Program availability:* Part-time, evening/weekend. *Faculty:* 2 full-time (0 women), 1 part-time/adjunct (0 women). *Students:* 3 full-time (2 women), 6 part-time (2 women); includes 5 minority (all Hispanic/Latino), 3 international. Average age 34. 10 applicants, 60% accepted, 1 enrolled. In 2016, 6 master's awarded. *Degree requirements:* For master's, one foreign language, thesis or alternative. *Entrance requirements:* For master's, GRE General Test (minimum score 1000); GMAT, LSAT, or EXADEP (minimum 62nd percentile), minimum GPA of 3.0, 3 letters of recommendation, letter of intent. Additional exam requirements/recommendations for international students: Required—TOEFL (minimum score 550 paper-based; 80 iBT). *Application deadline:* For fall admission, 2/1 for domestic and international students; for spring admission, 10/1 for domestic students, 9/1 for international students. Applications are processed on a rolling basis. Application fee: $30. Electronic applications accepted. *Expenses:* Tuition, state resident: full-time $8912; part-time $446 per credit hour. Tuition, nonresident: full-time $21,393; part-time $992 per credit hour. *Required fees:* $2185; $195 per semester. Tuition and fees vary according to program. *Financial support:* Institutionally sponsored loans and scholarships/grants available. Financial award application deadline: 3/1; financial award applicants required to submit FAFSA. *Unit head:* Dr. Jose Cruz, Director, 305-348-2894, Fax: 305-348-3593, E-mail: jose.cruz6@fiu.edu. *Application contact:* Nanett Rojas, Manager, Admissions Operations, 305-348-7464, Fax: 305-348-7441, E-mail: gradadm@fiu.edu.

**Georgetown University,** Graduate School of Arts and Sciences, Walsh School of Foreign Service, Center for Latin American Studies, Washington, DC 20057-1026. Offers MA, MA/JD, MA/PhD. *Program availability:* Part-time, evening/weekend. *Degree requirements:* For master's, one foreign language, comprehensive exam, thesis optional. *Entrance requirements:* For master's, GRE General Test, minimum B average. Additional exam requirements/recommendations for international students: Required—TOEFL. Electronic applications accepted.

**The George Washington University,** Elliott School of International Affairs, Program in Latin American and Hemispheric Studies, Washington, DC 20052. Offers MA. *Program availability:* Part-time. *Students:* 9 full-time (6 women), 4 part-time (all women); includes 6 minority (1 Asian, non-Hispanic/Latino; 5 Hispanic/Latino). Average age 27. 18 applicants, 100% accepted, 8 enrolled. In 2016, 8 master's awarded. *Degree requirements:* For master's, one foreign language, capstone project. *Entrance requirements:* For master's, GRE General Test, 2 years (or the equivalent) of Spanish or Portuguese. Additional exam requirements/recommendations for international students: Required—TOEFL (minimum score 100 iBT), IELTS (minimum score 7). *Application deadline:* For fall admission, 1/15 priority date for domestic and international students; for spring admission, 10/1 for domestic students. Application fee: $75. Electronic applications accepted. *Financial support:* In 2016–17, 4 students received support. Fellowships with partial tuition reimbursements available, Federal Work-Study, and scholarships/grants available. Financial award application deadline: 1/15; financial award applicants required to submit FAFSA. *Faculty research:* Democracy and change in Andean nations, rural economic development, peasant cooperatives and political change. *Unit head:* Robert Maguire, Director, 202-994-4060, E-mail: lasp@gwu.edu. *Application contact:* Nicole A. Campbell, Director of Graduate Admissions, 202-994-7050, Fax: 202-994-9537, E-mail: esiagrad@gwu.edu. Website: http://elliott.gwu.edu/latin-american-studies

**Georgia State University,** College of Arts and Sciences, Department of World Languages and Cultures, Atlanta, GA 30302-3083. Offers French (MA), including applied linguistics and pedagogy, French studies, literature and culture; Latin American studies (Certificate); Spanish (MA); translation and interpretation (Certificate), including interpretation, translation. *Program availability:* Part-time. *Faculty:* 36 full-time (20 women). *Students:* 17 full-time (12 women), 4 part-time (2 women); includes 18 minority (7 Black or African American, non-Hispanic/Latino; 6 Asian, non-Hispanic/Latino; 5 Hispanic/Latino), 5 international. Average age 38. 18 applicants, 83% accepted, 11 enrolled. In 2016, 3 other advanced degrees awarded. *Degree requirements:* For master's, 2 foreign languages, comprehensive exam, thesis or alternative, Graduate Foreign Language Reading Exam. *Entrance requirements:* For master's, GRE, statement of purpose, writing sample in the target language, 2 letters of recommendation, official transcripts; for Certificate, entrance examination involving translating one passage from English to the target language and one passage from the target language to English, 3 letters of recommendation, resume/curriculum vitae, official transcripts. Additional exam requirements/recommendations for international students: Required—TOEFL (minimum score 79 iBT). *Application deadline:* For fall admission, 3/15 priority date for domestic and international students; for spring admission, 11/15 priority date for domestic and international students. Application fee: $50. Electronic applications accepted. *Expenses:* Tuition, state resident: full-time $6876; part-time $382 per credit hour. Tuition, nonresident: full-time $22,374; part-time $1243 per credit hour. *Required fees:* $2128; $1064 per term. Part-time tuition and fees vary according to course load and program. *Financial support:* Applicants required to submit FAFSA. *Faculty research:* French literature and culture, Francophone literature and culture, Latin American literature and culture, Spanish literature and culture, Hispanic linguistics. *Unit head:* Dr. Fernando Reati, Department Chair, 404-413-5984, Fax: 404-413-5982, E-mail: freati@gsu.edu. *Application contact:* Amber Amari, Director, Graduate and Scheduling Services, 404-413-5037, E-mail: aamari@gsu.edu. Website: http://wlc.gsu.edu/

**Indiana University Bloomington,** University Graduate School, College of Arts and Sciences, School of Global and International Studies, Center for Latin American and Caribbean Studies, Bloomington, IN 47405. Offers MA, MBA/MA, MIS/MA, MLS/MA, MPA/MA, MPH/MA. *Program availability:* Part-time. *Degree requirements:* For master's, one foreign language, oral and written exam. *Entrance requirements:* For master's, GRE General Test. Additional exam requirements/recommendations for international students: Required—TOEFL. Electronic applications accepted.

**La Salle University,** School of Arts and Sciences, Hispanic Institute, Philadelphia, PA 19141-1199. Offers bilingual/bicultural studies (MA); ESL program specialist (Certificate); interpretation: English/Spanish-Spanish/English (Certificate); teaching English to speakers of other languages (MA); translation and interpretation (MA); translation: English/Spanish-Spanish/English (Certificate). *Program availability:* Part-time, evening/weekend. *Faculty:* 2 full-time (1 woman), 6 part-time/adjunct (3 women). *Students:* 1 (woman) full-time, 26 part-time (18 women); includes 15 minority (5 Black or

African American, non-Hispanic/Latino; 10 Hispanic/Latino), 1 international. Average age 37. 17 applicants, 76% accepted, 7 enrolled. In 2016, 7 master's, 4 other advanced degrees awarded. *Degree requirements:* For master's, one foreign language, project or thesis. *Entrance requirements:* For master's, GRE, MAT, or GMAT, professional resume; two letters of recommendation; for Certificate, GRE, MAT, or GMAT, professional resume; two letters of recommendation; evidence of an advanced level in Spanish. Additional exam requirements/recommendations for international students: Required—TOEFL. *Application deadline:* For fall admission, 8/15 priority date for domestic students, 7/15 for international students; for spring admission, 12/15 priority date for domestic students, 11/15 for international students; for summer admission, 4/15 priority date for domestic students, 3/15 for international students. Applications are processed on a rolling basis. Application fee: $35. Electronic applications accepted. Application fee is waived when completed online. *Expenses:* Contact institution. *Financial support:* In 2016–17, 3 students received support. Scholarships/grants available. Support available to part-time students. Financial award application deadline: 8/31; financial award applicants required to submit FAFSA. *Faculty research:* Puerto Rican literature, cross-cultural communication, English as a second language methodology, Spanish language. *Unit head:* Guadalupe Da Costa Montesinos, Director, 215-951-1209, Fax: 215-991-3506, E-mail: montesin@lasalle.edu. *Application contact:* Elizabeth Heenan, Director, Graduate and Adult Enrollment, 215-951-1100, Fax: 215-951-1462, E-mail: heenan@lasalle.edu. Website: http://www.lasalle.edu/hispanic-institute/

**Michigan State University,** The Graduate School, College of Social Science, Program in Chicano/Latino Studies, East Lansing, MI 48824. Offers PhD. *Entrance requirements:* Additional exam requirements/recommendations for international students: Required—TOEFL. Electronic applications accepted.

**New York University,** Graduate School of Arts and Science, Center for Latin American and Caribbean Studies, New York, NY 10012-1019. Offers MA, JD/MA. *Program availability:* Part-time. *Degree requirements:* For master's, one foreign language, thesis or alternative, major project. *Entrance requirements:* For master's, GRE General Test, knowledge of Portuguese or Spanish. Additional exam requirements/recommendations for international students: Required—TOEFL. *Faculty research:* Latin American politics, Caribbean societies, Andean history, political economy of cultural policies.

**New York University,** Graduate School of Arts and Science, Program in Museum Studies, New York, NY 10012-1019. Offers museum studies (MA, Advanced Certificate), including Africana studies (MA), Hebrew and Judaic studies (MA), Latin American and Caribbean studies (MA), Near Eastern studies (MA). *Program availability:* Part-time, evening/weekend. *Entrance requirements:* For master's, GRE General Test; for Advanced Certificate, master's degree or PhD. Additional exam requirements/recommendations for international students: Required—TOEFL. *Faculty research:* Modern and contemporary art, history of museums and exhibitions, conservation of cultural materials, museum anthropology, ethnography.

**Northeastern Illinois University,** College of Graduate Studies and Research, College of Arts and Sciences, Program in Latin American Literatures and Cultures, Chicago, IL 60625-4699. Offers MA.

**The Ohio State University,** Graduate School, Center for Latin American Studies, Columbus, OH 43210. Offers MA. *Students:* 1 full-time. In 2016, 1 master's awarded. *Entrance requirements:* For master's, GRE General Test. Additional exam requirements/recommendations for international students: Required—TOEFL (minimum score 550 paper-based; 79 iBT), IELTS (minimum score 7). *Application deadline:* For fall admission, 12/13 priority date for domestic students, 11/30 priority date for international students; for spring admission, 12/12 for domestic students, 11/10 for international students; for summer admission, 4/10 for domestic students, 3/13 for international students. Applications are processed on a rolling basis. Application fee: $60 ($70 for international students). Electronic applications accepted. *Financial support:* Fellowships with tuition reimbursements available. *Unit head:* Dr. Abril Trigo, Director, 614-292-8695, E-mail: trigo.1@osu.edu. *Application contact:* Graduate and Professional Admissions, 614-292-9444, Fax: 614-292-3895, E-mail: gpadmissions@osu.edu. Website: http://clas.osu.edu

**Ohio University,** Graduate College, Center for International Studies, Program in Latin American Studies, Athens, OH 45701-2979. Offers MA. *Program availability:* Part-time. *Degree requirements:* For master's, one foreign language, thesis optional. *Entrance requirements:* For master's, minimum GPA of 3.0. Additional exam requirements/recommendations for international students: Required—TOEFL (minimum score 550 paper-based; 80 iBT), IELTS (minimum score 6.5). *Application deadline:* For fall admission, 1/1 priority date for domestic and international students. Applications are processed on a rolling basis. Application fee: $50 ($55 for international students). Electronic applications accepted. *Financial support:* Research assistantships with full tuition reimbursements, career-related internships or fieldwork, Federal Work-Study, institutionally sponsored loans, scholarships/grants, tuition waivers (partial), and unspecified assistantships available. Financial award application deadline: 1/1. *Faculty research:* Central America, Ecuador, Brazil, transnational migration, microfinance. *Unit head:* Marina Peterson, Director, E-mail: petersm2@ohio.edu. *Application contact:* Patti Malloy, Administrative Assistant, 740-593-1836, Fax: 740-593-1837, E-mail: malloyp@ohio.edu. Website: http://www.ohio.edu/latinamerican/

**San Diego State University,** Graduate and Research Affairs, College of Arts and Letters, Center for Latin American Studies, San Diego, CA 92182. Offers MA, MBA/MA. *Degree requirements:* For master's, 2 foreign languages, thesis or alternative. *Entrance requirements:* For master's, GRE General Test, 3 letters of reference. Additional exam requirements/recommendations for international students: Required—TOEFL. Electronic applications accepted. *Faculty research:* Latin American politics and economics.

**Simon Fraser University,** Office of Graduate Studies and Postdoctoral Fellows, Faculty of Arts and Social Sciences, Latin American Studies Program, Vancouver, BC V6B 5K3, Canada. Offers MA, Graduate Certificate. *Faculty:* 10 part-time/adjunct (5 women). *Students:* 2 full-time (both women). In 2016, 3 master's, 1 other advanced degree awarded. *Degree requirements:* For master's, one foreign language, thesis; for Graduate Certificate, one foreign language, Spanish or Portuguese language exam. *Entrance requirements:* For master's, minimum GPA of 3.0 (on scale of 4.33) or 3.33 based on last 60 credits of undergraduate courses; for Graduate Certificate, current enrollment in a master's or doctoral program. Additional exam requirements/recommendations for international students: Recommended—TOEFL (minimum score 580 paper-based; 93 iBT), IELTS (minimum score 7), TWE (minimum score 5). *Application deadline:* For fall admission, 1/3 for domestic and international students; for winter admission, 2/1 for domestic students. Application fee: $90 ($125 for international students). Electronic applications accepted. *Financial support:* In 2016–17, teaching assistantships (averaging $5,608 per year) were awarded; fellowships, research assistantships, and scholarships/grants also available. Financial award application deadline: 3/15. *Faculty research:* Theories and strategies of development, political economy, globalization, political sociology, health communications and promotion. *Unit head:* Gerardo Otero, Director, 778-782-4508, Fax: 778-782-7837, E-mail: las-grad-

## Latin American Studies

chair@sfu.ca. *Application contact:* Joel Blok, Graduate Secretary, 778-782-7148, Fax: 778-782-7837, E-mail: intst@sfu.ca.
Website: http://www.las.sfu.ca/

**Texas Christian University,** AddRan College of Liberal Arts, Department of History, Fort Worth, TX 76129. Offers Latin America (MA, PhD); United States (MA, PhD). *Faculty:* 16 full-time (4 women). *Students:* 49 full-time (22 women); includes 6 minority (1 Black or African American, non-Hispanic/Latino; 4 Hispanic/Latino; 1 Two or more races, non-Hispanic/Latino). Average age 34. 24 applicants, 33% accepted, 5 enrolled. In 2016, 6 master's, 4 doctorates awarded. Terminal master's awarded for partial completion of doctoral program. *Degree requirements:* For master's, comprehensive exam, thesis or alternative; for doctorate, one foreign language, comprehensive exam, thesis/dissertation. *Entrance requirements:* For master's and doctorate, GRE General Test. Additional exam requirements/recommendations for international students: Recommended—TOEFL. *Application deadline:* 2/1 for domestic and international students; for summer admission, 2/1 for domestic and international students. Applications are processed on a rolling basis. Application fee: $60. Electronic applications accepted. *Expenses: Tuition:* Full-time $26,640; part-time $1480 per credit hour. *Required fees:* $48. Tuition and fees vary according to program. *Financial support:* In 2016–17, 50 students received support, including 3 fellowships with full tuition reimbursements available (averaging $20,000 per year), 15 research assistantships with full tuition reimbursements available (averaging $17,500 per year), 5 teaching assistantships with full tuition reimbursements available (averaging $17,500 per year); tuition waivers (full) also available. Financial award application deadline: 2/1. *Faculty research:* U.S. South, Latin American history, Atlantic World history, American West. Total annual research expenditures: $140,000. *Unit head:* Dr. Jodi Campbell, Associate Professor, 817-257-5882, Fax: 817-257-5650, E-mail: j.campbell@tcu.edu. *Application contact:* Heather Confessore, Administrative Assistant, 817-257-7288, Fax: 817-257-5650, E-mail: h.confessore@tcu.edu.
Website: http://www.his.tcu.edu/graduate.asp

**Tulane University,** School of Liberal Arts, Roger Thayer Stone Center for Latin American Studies, New Orleans, LA 70118-5669. Offers MA, PhD, MBA/MA, MCL/MA. Terminal master's awarded for partial completion of doctoral program. *Degree requirements:* For master's, one foreign language, thesis optional; for doctorate, 2 foreign languages, thesis/dissertation. *Entrance requirements:* For master's, GRE General Test, minimum B average in undergraduate course work; for doctorate, GRE General Test. Additional exam requirements/recommendations for international students: Required—TOEFL. Electronic applications accepted. *Expenses: Tuition:* Full-time $50,920; part-time $2829 per credit hour. *Required fees:* $2040; $44.50 per credit hour. $580 per term. Tuition and fees vary according to course load, degree level and program.

**University at Albany, State University of New York,** College of Arts and Sciences, Department of Latin American, Caribbean, and U.S. Latino Studies, Albany, NY 12222-0001. Offers MA, PhD, Certificate. *Program availability:* Part-time. *Students:* 7 full-time (5 women), 24 part-time (18 women); includes 24 minority (1 Black or African American, non-Hispanic/Latino; 22 Hispanic/Latino; 1 Two or more races, non-Hispanic/Latino). 12 applicants, 92% accepted, 4 enrolled. In 2016, 5 master's, 1 doctorate, 1 other advanced degree awarded. *Degree requirements:* For master's, thesis. *Entrance requirements:* For master's, ability to read and write Spanish. Additional exam requirements/recommendations for international students: Required—TOEFL (minimum score 550 paper-based). *Application deadline:* For fall admission, 3/15 for domestic students, 5/1 for international students; for spring admission, 11/1 for international students. Applications are processed on a rolling basis. Application fee: $75. Electronic applications accepted. *Expenses:* Tuition, state resident: full-time $10,870; part-time $453 per credit hour. Tuition, nonresident: full-time $22,210; part-time $925 per credit hour. *International tuition:* $21,550 full-time. *Required fees:* $1864; $96 per credit hour. *Financial support:* Fellowships, research assistantships, and teaching assistantships available. Financial award application deadline: 3/15. *Faculty research:* Meso-American anthropology, Latin American women's studies, Latinos in the U.S. *Unit head:* Pedro Caban, Chair, 518-442-4890, Fax: 518-442-4790, E-mail: pcaban@albany.edu. *Application contact:* Michael DeRensis, Director, Graduate Admissions, 518-442-3980, Fax: 518-442-3922, E-mail: graduate@albany.edu.
Website: http://www.albany.edu/lacs/

**The University of Arizona,** College of Social and Behavioral Sciences, Center for Latin American Studies, Tucson, AZ 85721. Offers MA. *Program availability:* Part-time. *Degree requirements:* For master's, 2 foreign languages, comprehensive exam, thesis optional. *Entrance requirements:* For master's, GRE, 2 letters of recommendation, resume. Additional exam requirements/recommendations for international students: Required—TOEFL (minimum score 550 paper-based; 79 iBT). Electronic applications accepted. *Faculty research:* Comparative analyses of national identities and of democratization across Latin America, environmental problems and management along the U.S.-Mexican border, integration efforts along the Peru/Ecuador border, social justice issues in Guatemala.

**University of California, Los Angeles,** Graduate Division, International Institute, Interdepartmental Program in Latin American Studies, Los Angeles, CA 90095. Offers MA, M Ed/MA, MA/MA, MBA/MA, MLIS/MA, MPH/MA. *Degree requirements:* For master's, 2 foreign languages, comprehensive exam or thesis. *Entrance requirements:* For master's, GRE General Test, bachelor's degree; minimum undergraduate GPA of 3.0 (or its equivalent if letter grade system not used); language requirement. Additional exam requirements/recommendations for international students: Required—TOEFL. Electronic applications accepted.

**University of California, San Diego,** Graduate Division, Latin American Studies Program, La Jolla, CA 92093. Offers MA. *Students:* 11 full-time (6 women). 18 applicants, 61% accepted, 4 enrolled. In 2016, 5 master's awarded. *Degree requirements:* For master's, one foreign language, thesis. *Entrance requirements:* For master's, GRE General Test, minimum GPA of 3.0; writing sample. Additional exam requirements/recommendations for international students: Required—TOEFL (minimum score 550 paper-based; 80 iBT), IELTS (minimum score 7). Application fee: $105 ($125 for international students). Electronic applications accepted. *Expenses:* Tuition, state resident: full-time $11,220. Tuition, nonresident: full-time $26,322. *Required fees:* $1864. *Financial support:* Fellowships, research assistantships, teaching assistantships, scholarships/grants, unspecified assistantships, and readerships available. Financial award applicants required to submit FAFSA. *Faculty research:* Cultural studies, gender studies, history, international migration, sociology. *Unit head:* Scott Desposato, Director, E-mail: las-director@ucsd.edu. *Application contact:* Jessica Cassidy, Graduate Coordinator, 858-534-7967, E-mail: las@ucsd.edu.

**University of California, Santa Barbara,** Graduate Division, College of Letters and Sciences, Division of Humanities and Fine Arts, Program in Latin American and Iberian Studies, Santa Barbara, CA 93106-4150. Offers MA. *Degree requirements:* For master's, one foreign language, comprehensive exam (for some programs), thesis. *Entrance requirements:* For master's, GRE. Additional exam requirements/recommendations for international students: Required—TOEFL (minimum score 550 paper-based; 80 iBT), IELTS (minimum score 7). Electronic applications accepted. *Faculty research:* Political science, anthropology, history, sociology, Portuguese.

**University of Chicago,** Division of the Social Sciences and Division of the Humanities, Center for Latin American Studies, Chicago, IL 60637. Offers MA. *Students:* 6 full-time (4 women); includes 1 minority (Hispanic/Latino). Average age 25. 16 applicants, 50% accepted, 3 enrolled. In 2016, 3 master's awarded. *Degree requirements:* For master's, one foreign language, thesis. *Entrance requirements:* For master's, GRE General Test. Additional exam requirements/recommendations for international students: Required—TOEFL (minimum score 104 iBT), IELTS (minimum score 7). *Application deadline:* For fall admission, 1/5 priority date for domestic and international students. Application fee: $90. Electronic applications accepted. *Financial support:* In 2016–17, 6 students received support. Federal Work-Study, institutionally sponsored loans, and scholarships/grants available. Financial award application deadline: 1/5. *Unit head:* Prof. Brodwyn Fischer, Director, 773-834-4608, Fax: 773-702-7550, E-mail: clas@uchicago.edu. *Application contact:* Office of the Dean of Students, 773-702-8415, E-mail: admissions@ssd.uchicago.edu.
Website: http://clas.uchicago.edu

**University of Connecticut,** Graduate School, College of Liberal Arts and Sciences, Field of International Studies, Program in International Studies, Storrs, CT 06269. Offers European studies (MA); Italian history and culture (MA); Latin and Latin American studies (MA). *Degree requirements:* For master's, comprehensive exam. *Entrance requirements:* For master's, GRE General Test. Additional exam requirements/recommendations for international students: Required—TOEFL (minimum score 550 paper-based). Electronic applications accepted.

**University of Florida,** Graduate School, College of Liberal Arts and Sciences, Center for Latin American Studies, Gainesville, FL 32611. Offers Latin American studies (MA, Certificate); sustainable development practice (MDP); tropical conservation and development (MA); JD/MA. *Program availability:* Part-time. *Degree requirements:* For master's, thesis. *Entrance requirements:* For master's, GRE General Test, minimum GPA of 3.0. Additional exam requirements/recommendations for international students: Required—TOEFL (minimum score 550 paper-based; 80 iBT), IELTS (minimum score 6). Electronic applications accepted. *Faculty research:* Tropical conservation and development; ethnicity in the Americas, Brazil, and Cuba; North American Free Trade Agreement (NAFTA).

**University of Illinois at Chicago,** College of Liberal Arts and Sciences, Latin American and Latino Studies Program, Chicago, IL 60607-7128. Offers MA. *Faculty research:* Representation of nation, race, gender and labor in film; Colonial political discourse and social resistance; social structures and religious rituals among the Maya; rural development and ecology in Mexico; Latina reproductive rights; youth activism; transnational Cuban migration; globalization and labor strategies of women in Brazil; Mexican hometown associations; local, national and global immigrant rights struggles.

**University of Illinois at Urbana–Champaign,** Graduate College, College of Liberal Arts and Sciences, Center for Latin American and Caribbean Studies, Champaign, IL 61820. Offers Latin American studies (MA).

**The University of Kansas,** Graduate Studies, College of Liberal Arts and Sciences, Latin American and Caribbean Studies Program, Lawrence, KS 66045. Offers Brazilian studies (Graduate Certificate); Central American and Mexican studies (Graduate Certificate); Latin American and Caribbean studies (Graduate Certificate); Latin American studies (MA). *Program availability:* Part-time. *Students:* 2 full-time (0 women), 3 part-time (all women); includes 1 minority (Two or more races, non-Hispanic/Latino), 1 international. Average age 29. 4 applicants, 100% accepted, 3 enrolled. *Entrance requirements:* For master's, GRE, minimum GPA of 3.0; three letters of recommendation; 10-page writing sample, preferably in one of the social sciences or humanities; resume; language proficiency in either Spanish or Portuguese. Additional exam requirements/recommendations for international students: Required—TOEFL. Application fee: $65 ($85 for international students). Electronic applications accepted. *Financial support:* Fellowships, research assistantships, teaching assistantships, scholarships/grants, and unspecified assistantships available. *Faculty research:* New migration studies; analysis and implementation of sustainable rural water projects in the developing world; develop research collaborations involving institutions in Campinas, São Paulo in Brazil…. *Unit head:* Marta Caminero-Santangelo, Interim Director, Center for Latin American and Caribbean Studies, E-mail: camsan@ku.edu. *Application contact:* Alyssa McDonald, Graduate Admissions Contact, 785-864-9814, E-mail: mcdonalda@ku.edu.
Website: https://latamst.ku.edu/

**The University of Manchester,** School of Languages, Linguistics and Cultures, Manchester, United Kingdom. Offers Arab world studies (PhD); Chinese studies (M Phil, PhD); East Asian studies (M Phil, PhD); English language (PhD); French studies (M Phil, PhD); German studies (M Phil, PhD); interpreting studies (PhD); Italian studies (M Phil, PhD); Japanese studies (M Phil, PhD); Latin American cultural studies (M Phil, PhD); linguistics (M Phil, PhD); Middle Eastern studies (M Phil, PhD); Polish studies (M Phil, PhD); Portuguese studies (M Phil, PhD); Russian studies (M Phil, PhD); Spanish studies (M Phil, PhD); translation and intercultural studies (M Phil, PhD).

**University of Massachusetts Dartmouth,** Graduate School, College of Arts and Sciences, Department of Portuguese, North Dartmouth, MA 02747-2300. Offers Luso-Afro Brazilian studies and theory (PhD); Portuguese (MA). *Program availability:* Part-time. *Faculty:* 5 full-time (2 women), 1 part-time/adjunct (0 women). *Students:* 7 full-time (5 women), 7 part-time (6 women); includes 7 minority (1 Black or African American, non-Hispanic/Latino; 1 Asian, non-Hispanic/Latino; 4 Hispanic/Latino; 1 Two or more races, non-Hispanic/Latino), 3 international. Average age 37. 7 applicants, 43% accepted, 1 enrolled. In 2016, 2 master's, 1 doctorate awarded. Terminal master's awarded for partial completion of doctoral program. *Degree requirements:* For master's, comprehensive exam or project; for doctorate, comprehensive exam, thesis/dissertation. *Entrance requirements:* For master's, GRE (recommended), statement of purpose (minimum of 300 words), resume, 3 letters of recommendation, official transcripts, writing samples in Portuguese (minimum of 10 pages); for doctorate, GRE (recommended), statement of purpose (minimum of 300 words), resume, 3 letters of recommendation, official transcripts, scholarly writing sample (minimum of 10 pages). Additional exam requirements/recommendations for international students: Required—TOEFL (minimum score 533 paper-based; 72 iBT). *Application deadline:* For fall admission, 2/1 priority date for domestic students, 1/1 priority date for international students; for spring admission, 12/1 priority date for domestic students, 11/1 priority date for international students. Application fee: $60. Electronic applications accepted. *Expenses:* Tuition, state resident: full-time $14,994; part-time $624.75 per credit. Tuition, nonresident: full-time $27,068; part-time $1127.83 per credit. *Required fees:* $405; $25.88 per credit. Tuition and fees vary according to course load and reciprocity agreements. *Financial support:* In 2016–17, 9 fellowships (averaging $19,333 per year) were awarded; institutionally sponsored loans and scholarships/grants also available. Support available to part-time students. Financial award application deadline: 3/1; financial award applicants required to submit FAFSA. *Faculty research:* Literature in Luso-Afro-Brazilian studies, literary and cultural theory, studies in ethnicity and migration, bi- and multi-lingualism, gender studies, translation studies. Total annual research expenditures: $354,000. *Unit head:* Victor Mendes, Director of Graduate Studies, Department of Portuguese, 508-999-8338, Fax: 508-910-9272, E-mail: vmendes@umassd.edu. *Application contact:* Steven Briggs, Director of Marketing and

Recruitment for Graduate Studies, 508-999-8604, Fax: 508-999-8183, E-mail: graduate@umassd.edu.
Website: http://www.umassd.edu/portgrad/

**University of Miami,** Graduate School, College of Arts and Sciences, Department of Latin American and Caribbean Studies, Coral Gables, FL 33124. Offers Latin American studies (MA). *Program availability:* Part-time. *Degree requirements:* For master's, comprehensive exam (for some programs), thesis, linguistic competency in Spanish or Portuguese, reading competency in a second Latin American language. *Entrance requirements:* For master's, GRE, 3 letters of recommendation. Additional exam requirements/recommendations for international students: Required—TOEFL. Electronic applications accepted. *Faculty research:* Literary, media, religious, visual and cultural studies; environment and tourism studies; US-Latin American Relations and drug trafficking; migration, globalization, and social movements; democratization, regime transitions, and citizenship.

**University of New Mexico,** Graduate School, College of Arts and Sciences, Program in Latin American Studies, Albuquerque, NM 87131. Offers MA, PhD, JD/MA, MA/MA, MA/MPH, MBA/MA, MCRP/MA. *Program availability:* Part-time. *Faculty:* 7 full-time (5 women). *Students:* 17 full-time (14 women), 3 part-time (1 woman); includes 3 minority (all Hispanic/Latino), 10 international. Average age 35. 17 applicants, 59% accepted, 5 enrolled. In 2016, 9 master's awarded. *Degree requirements:* For master's, one foreign language, comprehensive exam (for some programs), thesis (for some programs); for doctorate, 2 foreign languages, comprehensive exam, thesis/dissertation. *Entrance requirements:* For master's, GRE General Test, intermediate competence in Spanish, Portuguese or indigenous Latin American language; for doctorate, GRE General Test, master's degree in related field, one Latin American language. Additional exam requirements/recommendations for international students: Required—TOEFL. *Application deadline:* For fall admission, 2/1 priority date for domestic and international students; for spring admission, 11/1 for domestic and international students. Application fee: $50. Electronic applications accepted. *Financial support:* Fellowships with full tuition reimbursements, research assistantships with full tuition reimbursements, teaching assistantships with full tuition reimbursements, Federal Work-Study, scholarships/grants, health care benefits, tuition waivers (full), and unspecified assistantships available. Financial award application deadline: 2/1; financial award applicants required to submit FAFSA. *Unit head:* Dr. Susan Tiano, Director, 505-277-2961, Fax: 505-277-5989, E-mail: stiano@unm.edu. *Application contact:* Matias Fontenla, Associate Director for Academic Programs, 505-277-2961, Fax: 505-277-5989, E-mail: fontenla@unm.edu.
Website: http://laii.unm.edu

**University of New Mexico,** Graduate Studies, College of Fine Arts, Program in Art History, Albuquerque, NM 87131. Offers art history (MA); art of the Americas (MA); history of architecture (PhD); history of graphic arts (PhD); history of photography (PhD); modern Latin American art (PhD); Native American art (PhD); Pre-Columbian art and architecture (PhD); Spanish colonial art (PhD). *Program availability:* Part-time. *Faculty:* 4 full-time (2 women). *Students:* 8 full-time (all women), 22 part-time (19 women); includes 9 minority (3 American Indian or Alaska Native, non-Hispanic/Latino; 5 Hispanic/Latino; 1 Two or more races, non-Hispanic/Latino), 3 international. Average age 40. 19 applicants, 42% accepted, 4 enrolled. In 2016, 5 master's, 1 doctorate awarded. *Degree requirements:* For master's, one foreign language, comprehensive exam (for some programs), thesis, symposium; for doctorate, 2 foreign languages, comprehensive exam, thesis/dissertation, symposium. *Entrance requirements:* Additional exam requirements/recommendations for international students: Required—TOEFL (minimum score 550 paper-based), IELTS (minimum score 6). *Application deadline:* For fall admission, 1/15 for domestic students; for spring admission, 1/15 for domestic students. Application fee: $50. Electronic applications accepted. *Financial support:* Fellowships, research assistantships with tuition reimbursements, teaching assistantships with partial tuition reimbursements, Federal Work-Study, institutionally sponsored loans, scholarships/grants, health care benefits, and unspecified assistantships available. Support available to part-time students. Financial award application deadline: 3/1; financial award applicants required to submit FAFSA. *Faculty research:* Native American, modern Latin American, pre-Columbian, architectural, American, medieval, Spanish Colonial, and Latin American art; history of photography. *Unit head:* Prof. Mary Tsiongas, Chair, 505-277-5861, Fax: 505-277-5955, E-mail: tsiongas@unm.edu. *Application contact:* Kat Heatherington, Graduate Advisor, 505-277-6672, Fax: 505-277-5955, E-mail: art255@unm.edu.
Website: http://art.unm.edu/

**The University of North Carolina at Chapel Hill,** Graduate School, College of Arts and Sciences, Department of Political Science, Chapel Hill, NC 27599. Offers Latin American studies (Certificate); political science (MA, PhD); trans-Atlantic studies (MA). *Degree requirements:* For master's, comprehensive exam; for doctorate, one foreign language, comprehensive exam, thesis/dissertation. *Entrance requirements:* For master's and doctorate, GRE General Test, minimum GPA of 3.0 recommended. Electronic applications accepted.

**The University of North Carolina at Charlotte,** College of Liberal Arts and Sciences, Interdisciplinary Liberal Arts and Sciences Programs, Charlotte, NC 28223-0001. Offers gender, sexuality, and women's studies (Graduate Certificate); gerontology (MA, Graduate Certificate); Latin American studies (MA); liberal studies (MA); organizational science (PhD); public policy (PhD). *Program availability:* Part-time, evening/weekend. *Faculty:* 1 (woman) part-time/adjunct. *Students:* 65 full-time (49 women), 61 part-time (50 women); includes 31 minority (11 Black or African American, non-Hispanic/Latino; 1 American Indian or Alaska Native, non-Hispanic/Latino; 2 Asian, non-Hispanic/Latino; 16 Hispanic/Latino; 1 Two or more races, non-Hispanic/Latino), 15 international. Average age 32. 128 applicants, 41% accepted, 40 enrolled. In 2016, 15 master's, 12 doctorates, 7 other advanced degrees awarded. *Degree requirements:* For master's, comprehensive exam (for some programs), thesis (for some programs), practicum, project; for doctorate, comprehensive exam, thesis/dissertation; for Graduate Certificate, practicum (for gerontology). *Entrance requirements:* For master's, GRE General Test or MAT, bachelor's degree from accredited college or university; official transcripts of all previous academic work attempted beyond high school; minimum overall GPA of 3.0 on applicant's previous work beyond high school; statement of purpose; recommendation letters; for doctorate, GRE or GMAT, statement of purpose discussing interest in program and objectives for pursuing degree, current resume or curriculum vitae, unofficial transcripts; for Graduate Certificate, bachelor's degree from accredited university and either be enrolled in and in good standing in a graduate degree program at UNC Charlotte or have a minimum undergraduate GPA of 3.0. Additional exam requirements/recommendations for international students: Required—TOEFL (minimum score 523 paper-based, 70 iBT) or IELTS (6.5). *Application deadline:* For fall admission, 2/15 for domestic and international students; for spring admission, 10/1 for domestic and international students; for summer admission, 4/1 for domestic and international students. Applications are processed on a rolling basis. Application fee: $75. Electronic applications accepted. *Expenses:* Tuition, state resident: full-time $4252. Tuition, nonresident: full-time $17,423. *Required fees:* $3026. Tuition and fees vary according to course load and program. *Financial support:* In 2016–17, 26 students received support, including 17 research assistantships (averaging $12,840 per year), 7 teaching

assistantships (averaging $14,442 per year); career-related internships or fieldwork, institutionally sponsored loans, scholarships/grants, unspecified assistantships, and administrative assistantships also available. Support available to part-time students. Financial award application deadline: 3/1; financial award applicants required to submit FAFSA. *Unit head:* Dr. Nancy A. Gutierrez, Dean, 704-687-0081, E-mail: ngutierr@uncc.edu. *Application contact:* Kathy B. Giddings, Director of Graduate Admissions, 704-687-5503, Fax: 704-687-3279, E-mail: gradadm@uncc.edu.
Website: http://clas.uncc.edu/academics

**University of Notre Dame,** Graduate School, College of Arts and Letters, Division of Humanities, Department of Romance Languages and Literatures, Notre Dame, IN 46556. Offers French and Francophone studies (MA); Iberian and Latin American studies (MA); Italian studies (MA); Romance literatures (MA). *Degree requirements:* For master's, 2 foreign languages, comprehensive exam, thesis optional. *Entrance requirements:* For master's, GRE General Test, BA in target language. Additional exam requirements/recommendations for international students: Required—TOEFL (minimum score 600 paper-based; 80 iBT). Electronic applications accepted. *Faculty research:* Literature of discovery and exploration, modern literature, literary criticism, medieval literature, feminist critical theory.

**University of Pittsburgh,** University Center for International Studies, Pittsburgh, PA 15260. Offers African studies (Certificate); Asian studies (Certificate); European Union studies (Certificate); global studies (Certificate); Latin American studies (Certificate); Russian and East European studies (Certificate); West European studies (Certificate). *Program availability:* Part-time, evening/weekend, online learning. *Students:* 175 full-time (105 women), 14 part-time (10 women); includes 78 minority (5 Black or African American, non-Hispanic/Latino; 30 Asian, non-Hispanic/Latino; 42 Hispanic/Latino; 1 Two or more races, non-Hispanic/Latino). Average age 29. *Degree requirements:* For Certificate, one foreign language, comprehensive exam (for some programs), thesis (for some programs). *Entrance requirements:* Additional exam requirements/recommendations for international students: Required—TOEFL. *Expenses:* Contact institution. *Financial support:* In 2016–17, 22 fellowships with full tuition reimbursements (averaging $17,878 per year) were awarded; scholarships/grants, traineeships, health care benefits, tuition waivers, and unspecified assistantships also available. *Unit head:* Dr. Ariel Armony, Director, 412-648-7374, Fax: 412-624-4672, E-mail: armony@pitt.edu.
Website: http://www.ucis.pitt.edu

**University of Southern California,** Graduate School, Dana and David Dornsife College of Letters, Arts and Sciences, Comparative Studies in Literature and Culture Doctoral Program, Los Angeles, CA 90089. Offers comparative literature (PhD); comparative media and culture (PhD); Spanish and Latin American studies (PhD). *Degree requirements:* For doctorate, 2 foreign languages, comprehensive exam, thesis/dissertation. *Entrance requirements:* For doctorate, GRE, competence in language other than English (highly recommended). Additional exam requirements/recommendations for international students: Required—TOEFL. Electronic applications accepted. *Faculty research:* Literary theory, Japanese film and contemporary fiction, Francophone literature and cinema, Latin American and Caribbean literature, Spanish literature and film, nineteenth and twentieth century British and American literature.

**University of South Florida,** College of Arts and Sciences, Department of Government and International Affairs, Tampa, FL 33620-9951. Offers government (PhD); Latin American, Caribbean and Latino studies (MA); political science (MA), including comparative government and politics; public administration (MPA). *Program availability:* Part-time, evening/weekend. *Faculty:* 15 full-time (3 women). *Students:* 47 full-time (26 women), 40 part-time (22 women); includes 15 minority (6 Black or African American, non-Hispanic/Latino; 1 Asian, non-Hispanic/Latino; 7 Hispanic/Latino; 1 Two or more races, non-Hispanic/Latino), 15 international. Average age 32. 59 applicants, 58% accepted, 21 enrolled. In 2016, 30 master's, 3 doctorates awarded. *Degree requirements:* For master's, comprehensive exam, thesis; for doctorate, comprehensive exam, thesis/dissertation. *Entrance requirements:* For master's, GRE General Test, minimum GPA of 3.0 in upper-division undergraduate course work; letters of recommendation (2 for MPA, 3 for MS); 500-word personal statement and undergraduate background in political science or related fields (for MS); one-page career statement (for MPA); for doctorate, GRE General Test, 500-word personal statement, three letters of recommendation, transcripts of MA/BA coursework, writing sample. Additional exam requirements/recommendations for international students: Required—TOEFL (minimum score 550 paper-based; 79 iBT) or IELTS (minimum score 6.5). *Application deadline:* For fall admission, 1/5 for domestic and international students; for spring admission, 10/15 for domestic students, 9/15 for international students. Applications are processed on a rolling basis. Application fee: $30. Electronic applications accepted. *Expenses:* Tuition, state resident: full-time $7766; part-time $431.43 per credit hour. Tuition, nonresident: full-time $15,789; part-time $877.17 per credit hour. *Required fees:* $37 per term. *Financial support:* In 2016–17, 1 student received support, including 18 teaching assistantships with tuition reimbursements available (averaging $12,390 per year); unspecified assistantships also available. Financial award application deadline: 4/1. *Faculty research:* Citizenship and identity, social movements, global governance, American politics, public policy. Total annual research expenditures: $222,648. *Unit head:* Dr. Steven Tauber, Associate Professor/Interim Chair, 813-974-2278, Fax: 813-974-0832, E-mail: stauber@usf.edu. *Application contact:* Dr. Bernd Reiter, Associate Professor and Director of Graduate Studies, 813-974-3583, Fax: 813-974-0832, E-mail: breiter@usf.edu.
Website: http://gia.usf.edu/

**University of South Florida,** College of Arts and Sciences, Department of History, Tampa, FL 33620-9951. Offers history (MA, PhD), including American history (MA), ancient history (MA), European history (MA), Latin American history (MA), Medieval history (MA). *Program availability:* Part-time, evening/weekend. *Faculty:* 17 full-time (8 women). *Students:* 39 full-time (9 women), 14 part-time (8 women); includes 7 minority (1 Black or African American, non-Hispanic/Latino; 1 American Indian or Alaska Native, non-Hispanic/Latino; 1 Asian, non-Hispanic/Latino; 4 Hispanic/Latino), 1 international. Average age 35. 34 applicants, 68% accepted, 15 enrolled. In 2016, 8 master's, 2 doctorates awarded. *Degree requirements:* For master's, one foreign language, comprehensive exam, thesis optional; for doctorate, one foreign language, comprehensive exam, thesis/dissertation. *Entrance requirements:* For master's, GRE General Test, minimum GPA of 3.0, two letters of recommendation, 2-page statement of purpose, writing sample; for doctorate, GRE General Test, minimum GPA of 3.5 in master's degree coursework, three letters of recommendation, statement of purpose, writing sample, foreign language proficiency in the field of study. Additional exam requirements/recommendations for international students: Required—TOEFL (minimum score 550 paper-based; 79 iBT) or IELTS (minimum score 6.5). *Application deadline:* For fall admission, 12/1 priority date for domestic students, 12/1 for international students. Applications are processed on a rolling basis. Application fee: $30. Electronic applications accepted. *Expenses:* Tuition, state resident: full-time $7766; part-time $431.43 per credit hour. Tuition, nonresident: full-time $15,789; part-time $877.17 per credit hour. *Required fees:* $37 per term. *Financial support:* In 2016–17, 20 students received support, including 17 teaching assistantships with tuition reimbursements available (averaging $12,750 per year); unspecified assistantships also available. Financial award application deadline: 1/15. *Faculty research:* North American and U.S.

history, European history, nineteenth- and twentieth-centuries/modern world, early modern world, ancient history, history of gender/sexuality, Latin American history, history of science and medicine. *Total annual research expenditures:* $195,413. *Unit head:* Dr. Fraser Ottanelli, Professor and Chair, 813-974-6209, Fax: 813-974-6228, E-mail: ottanelli@usf.edu. *Application contact:* Dr. Brian Connolly, Associate Professor and Graduate Program Director, 813-974-1087, Fax: 813-974-6228, E-mail: bconnelly@usf.edu.
Website: http://history.usf.edu

**University of South Florida,** Innovative Education, Tampa, FL 33620-9951. Offers adult, career and higher education (Graduate Certificate), including college teaching, leadership in developing human resources, leadership in higher education; Africana studies (Graduate Certificate), including diasporas and health disparities, genocide and human rights; aging studies (Graduate Certificate), including gerontology; art research (Graduate Certificate), including museum studies; business foundations (Graduate Certificate); chemical and biomedical engineering (Graduate Certificate), including materials science and engineering, water, health and sustainability; child and family studies (Graduate Certificate), including positive behavior support; civil and industrial engineering (Graduate Certificate), including transportation systems analysis; community and family health (Graduate Certificate), including maternal and child health, social marketing and public health, violence and injury: prevention and intervention, women's health; criminology (Graduate Certificate), including criminal justice administration; educational measurement and research (Graduate Certificate), including evaluation; English (Graduate Certificate), including comparative literary studies, creative writing, professional and technical communication; entrepreneurship (Graduate Certificate); environmental health (Graduate Certificate), including safety management; epidemiology and biostatistics (Graduate Certificate), including applied biostatistics, biostatistics, concepts and tools of epidemiology, epidemiology, epidemiology of infectious diseases; geography, environment and planning (Graduate Certificate), including community development, environmental policy and management, geographical information systems; geology (Graduate Certificate), including hydrogeology; global health (Graduate Certificate), including disaster management, global health and Latin American and Caribbean studies, global health practice, humanitarian assistance, infection control; government and international affairs (Graduate Certificate), including Cuban studies, globalization studies; health policy and management (Graduate Certificate), including health management and leadership, public health policy and programs; hearing specialist: early intervention (Graduate Certificate); industrial and management systems engineering (Graduate Certificate), including systems engineering, technology management; information studies (Graduate Certificate), including school library media specialist; information systems/decision sciences (Graduate Certificate), including analytics and business intelligence; instructional technology (Graduate Certificate), including distance education, Florida digital/virtual educator, instructional design, multimedia design, Web design; internal medicine, bioethics and medical humanities (Graduate Certificate), including biomedical ethics; Latin American and Caribbean studies (Graduate Certificate); mass communications (Graduate Certificate), including multimedia journalism; mathematics and statistics (Graduate Certificate), including mathematics; medicine (Graduate Certificate), including aging and neuroscience, bioinformatics, biotechnology, brain fitness and memory management, clinical investigation, health informatics, health sciences, integrative weight management, intellectual property, medicine and gender, metabolic and nutritional medicine, metabolic cardiology, pharmacy sciences; national and competitive intelligence (Graduate Certificate); psychological and social foundations (Graduate Certificate), including career counseling, college teaching, diversity in education, mental health counseling, school counseling; public affairs (Graduate Certificate), including nonprofit management, public management, research administration; public health (Graduate Certificate), including environmental health, health equity, public health generalist, translational research in adolescent behavioral health; public health practices (Graduate Certificate), including planning for healthy communities; rehabilitation and mental health counseling (Graduate Certificate), including integrative mental health care, marriage and family therapy, rehabilitation technology; secondary education (Graduate Certificate), including ESOL, foreign language education: culture and content, foreign language education: professional; social work (Graduate Certificate), including geriatric social work/clinical gerontology; special education (Graduate Certificate), including autism spectrum disorder, disabilities education: severe/profound; world languages (Graduate Certificate), including teaching English as a second language (TESL) or foreign language. *Expenses:* Tuition, state resident: full-time $7766; part-time $431.43 per credit hour. Tuition, nonresident: full-time $15,789; part-time $877.17 per credit hour. *Required fees:* $37 per term. *Unit head:* Kathy Barnes, Interdisciplinary Programs Coordinator, 813-974-8031, Fax: 813-974-7061, E-mail: barnesk@usf.edu. *Application contact:* Karen Tylinski, Metro Initiatives, 813-974-9943, Fax: 813-974-7061, E-mail: ktylinsk@usf.edu.
Website: http://www.usf.edu/innovative-education/

**The University of Texas at Austin,** Graduate School, College of Liberal Arts, Teresa Lozano Long Institute of Latin American Studies, Austin, TX 78712-1111. Offers cultural politics of Afro-Latin and indigenous peoples (MA); development studies (MA); environmental studies (MA); human rights (MA); Latin American and international law (LL M); JD/MA; MA/MA; MBA/MA; MP Aff/MA; MSCRP/MA. LL M offered jointly with The University of Texas School of Law. *Entrance requirements:* For master's, GRE General Test.

**The University of Texas at Dallas,** School of Arts and Humanities, Richardson, TX 75080. Offers history (MA); humanities (MA, PhD), including aesthetic studies, history of ideas, studies in literature (PhD), studies of literature (MA); Latin American studies (MA). *Program availability:* Part-time, evening/weekend. *Faculty:* 46 full-time (15 women), 5 part-time/adjunct (1 woman). *Students:* 129 full-time (78 women), 127 part-time (81 women); includes 63 minority (12 Black or African American, non-Hispanic/Latino; 4 American Indian or Alaska Native, non-Hispanic/Latino; 13 Asian, non-Hispanic/Latino; 23 Hispanic/Latino; 11 Two or more races, non-Hispanic/Latino), 27 international. Average age 41. 113 applicants, 58% accepted, 38 enrolled. In 2016, 39 master's, 16 doctorates awarded. *Degree requirements:* For master's, one foreign language, portfolio; for doctorate, one foreign language, thesis/dissertation. *Entrance requirements:* For master's and doctorate, minimum GPA of 3.0 in undergraduate course work in field. Additional exam requirements/recommendations for international students: Required—TOEFL (minimum score 550 paper-based). *Application deadline:* For fall admission, 7/15 for domestic students, 5/1 priority date for international students; for spring admission, 11/15 for domestic students, 9/1 priority date for international

students. Applications are processed on a rolling basis. Application fee: $50 ($100 for international students). Electronic applications accepted. *Expenses:* Tuition, state resident: full-time $12,418; part-time $690 per semester hour. Tuition, nonresident: full-time $24,150; part-time $1342 per semester hour. Tuition and fees vary according to course load. *Financial support:* In 2016–17, 135 students received support, including 1 fellowship (averaging $2,000 per year), 12 research assistantships with partial tuition reimbursements available (averaging $23,948 per year), 69 teaching assistantships with partial tuition reimbursements available (averaging $15,001 per year); Federal Work-Study, institutionally sponsored loans, scholarships/grants, and unspecified assistantships also available. Support available to part-time students. Financial award application deadline: 4/30; financial award applicants required to submit FAFSA. *Faculty research:* Science and the arts and humanities, intellectual and philosophical history, cultural studies, translation studies. *Total annual research expenditures:* $177,908. *Unit head:* Dr. Dennis M. Kratz, Dean, 972-883-2984, Fax: 972-883-2989, E-mail: dkratz@utdallas.edu. *Application contact:* Dr. John Gooch, Associate Dean of Graduate Studies, 972-883-2756, Fax: 972-883-2989, E-mail: john.gooch@utdallas.edu.
Website: http://www.utdallas.edu/ah/

**University of Utah,** Graduate School, College of Humanities, Latin American Studies Program, Salt Lake City, UT 84112. Offers MA. *Program availability:* Part-time, evening/weekend. *Students:* 1 full-time (0 women), 2 part-time (1 woman); includes 1 minority (Hispanic/Latino). 1 applicant, 100% accepted, 1 enrolled. In 2016, 2 master's awarded. *Degree requirements:* For master's, 2 foreign languages, thesis, third-year proficiency in one of the two major Latin American languages, first-year proficiency in the other (Spanish or Portuguese). *Entrance requirements:* For master's, GRE, minimum undergraduate GPA of 3.0, graduate 3.4. Additional exam requirements/recommendations for international students: Required—TOEFL (minimum score 580 paper-based). *Application deadline:* For fall admission, 2/1 priority date for domestic and international students. Application fee: $55 ($65 for international students). Electronic applications accepted. *Expenses:* Tuition, state resident: full-time $7011; part-time $3918.24 per credit hour. Tuition, nonresident: full-time $22,154; part-time $11,665.42 per credit hour. *Financial support:* Application deadline: 4/15. *Faculty research:* Latin American health studies, history, literature, culture, politics, economics. *Unit head:* Dr. Claudio Holzner, Director, 801-581-6101, E-mail: claudio.holzner@poli-sci.utah.edu. *Application contact:* Ashley Glenn, Academic Coordinator, 801-584-6101, Fax: 801-581-6105, E-mail: ea.glenn@utah.edu.
Website: http://latin-american-studies.utah.edu/

**University of Wisconsin–Madison,** Graduate School, College of Letters and Science, Department of History, Madison, WI 53706-1380. Offers African history (MA, PhD); Central Asian history (MA, PhD); comparative world history (MA, PhD); East Asian history (MA, PhD); European history (MA, PhD); gender and women's history (MA, PhD); Latin American and Caribbean history (MA, PhD); Middle Eastern history (MA, PhD); South Asian history (MA, PhD); Southeast Asian history (MA, PhD); United States history (MA, PhD). Terminal master's awarded for partial completion of doctoral program. *Degree requirements:* For master's, thesis (for some programs); for doctorate, variable foreign language requirement, thesis/dissertation. *Entrance requirements:* For master's and doctorate, GRE General Test. Additional exam requirements/recommendations for international students: Required—Michigan English Language Assessment Battery or TOEFL. Electronic applications accepted. *Faculty research:* American, African, European, Asian, Latin American, and Middle Eastern history.

**University of Wisconsin–Madison,** Graduate School, College of Letters and Science, Latin American, Caribbean and Iberian Studies Program, Madison, WI 53706-1380. Offers MA, MA/JD. *Degree requirements:* For master's, 2 foreign languages, thesis. *Entrance requirements:* For master's, minimum GPA of 3.0. Electronic applications accepted. *Faculty research:* Development, gender, social movements, cultural studies, history.

**Vanderbilt University,** Program in Latin American Studies, Nashville, TN 37240-1001. Offers MA, LL M/MA, MBA/MA. *Faculty:* 63 full-time (22 women). *Students:* 8 full-time (5 women); includes 1 minority (Hispanic/Latino), 1 international. Average age 26. 19 applicants, 37% accepted, 3 enrolled. In 2016, 5 master's awarded. *Degree requirements:* For master's, 2 foreign languages, thesis or alternative. *Entrance requirements:* For master's, GRE General Test. Additional exam requirements/recommendations for international students: Required—TOEFL (minimum score 570 paper-based; 88 iBT). *Application deadline:* For fall admission, 1/15 for domestic and international students. Application fee: $0. Electronic applications accepted. *Expenses:* Tuition: Part-time $1854 per credit hour. *Financial support:* Teaching assistantships with full tuition reimbursements, Federal Work-Study, institutionally sponsored loans, and health care benefits available. Financial award application deadline: 1/15; financial award applicants required to submit CSS PROFILE or FAFSA. *Faculty research:* Latin American and Iberian studies, anthropology, history, Spanish and Portuguese, social and political science. *Unit head:* Dr. Edward Fischer, Director, 615-322-2527, Fax: 615-343-6002, E-mail: edward.f.fischer@vanderbilt.edu. *Application contact:* Nicolette M. Kostiw, Assistant Director/Director of Graduate Studies, 615-322-2527, Fax: 615-343-6002, E-mail: nicolette.m.wilhide@vanderbilt.edu.
Website: http://www.vanderbilt.edu/clas/graduate-programs/

**West Virginia University,** Eberly College of Arts and Sciences, Department of History, Morgantown, WV 26506. Offers African history (MA, PhD); African-American history (MA, PhD); American history (MA, PhD); Appalachian/regional history (MA, PhD); East Asian history (MA, PhD); European history (MA, PhD); history of science and technology (MA, PhD); Latin American history (MA). *Program availability:* Part-time. *Degree requirements:* For master's, one foreign language, thesis (for some programs), oral exam, thesis defense; for doctorate, one foreign language, comprehensive exam, thesis/dissertation, dissertation defense. *Entrance requirements:* For master's, GRE General Test, minimum GPA of 3.0; for doctorate, GRE General Test. Additional exam requirements/recommendations for international students: Required—TOEFL (minimum score 550 paper-based), IELTS (minimum score 6.5). Electronic applications accepted. *Faculty research:* United States, Appalachia, modern Europe, Africa, colonial and post-colonial societies.

**Yale University,** Graduate School of Arts and Sciences, Department of Spanish and Portuguese, New Haven, CT 06520. Offers Latin American literature (PhD); Luso-Brazilian and Spanish/Spanish American literatures (PhD); Spanish peninsular literature (PhD). Terminal master's awarded for partial completion of doctoral program. *Degree requirements:* For doctorate, 3 foreign languages, thesis/dissertation. *Entrance requirements:* For doctorate, GRE General Test.

# Near and Middle Eastern Studies

**The American University in Cairo,** School of Humanities and Social Sciences, Cairo, Egypt. Offers Arab and Islamic civilizations (Graduate Diploma); Arabic studies (MA); comparative literary studies (Graduate Diploma); Egyptology and Coptology (MA); English and comparative literature (MA); humanities and social sciences (Graduate Diploma); philosophy (MA); psychology (MA); sociology and anthropology (MA); teaching Arabic as a foreign language (MA); teaching English to speakers of other languages (MA). *Program availability:* Part-time, evening/weekend. *Faculty:* 51 full-time (29 women), 4 part-time/adjunct (2 women). *Students:* 65 full-time (47 women), 179 part-time (138 women), 32 international. Average age 30. 221 applicants, 45% accepted, 54 enrolled. In 2016, 95 master's awarded. *Degree requirements:* For master's, comprehensive exam (for some programs), thesis (for some programs). *Entrance requirements:* Additional exam requirements/recommendations for international students: Required—TOEFL (minimum score 450 paper-based; 45 iBT), IELTS (minimum score 5). *Application deadline:* For fall admission, 2/1 priority date for domestic and international students; for spring admission, 10/15 priority date for domestic and international students. Applications are processed on a rolling basis. Application fee: $80. Electronic applications accepted. *Expenses:* Contact institution. *Financial support:* Fellowships with partial tuition reimbursements, scholarships/grants, tuition waivers (partial), and unspecified assistantships available. Financial award application deadline: 3/10. *Faculty research:* English literature, political science, psychology, sociology, anthropology and Egyptology, teaching English for non-speakers, teaching Arabic as a foreign language, philosophy, Arabic studies. *Unit head:* Dr. Nathaniel Bowditch, Dean, 20-2-2615-1788, E-mail: nbowditch@aucegypt.edu. *Application contact:* Maha Hegazi, Director for Graduate Admissions, 20-2-2615-1462, E-mail: mahahegazi@aucegypt.edu.
Website: http://www.aucegypt.edu/huss/Pages/default.aspx

**American University of Beirut,** Graduate Programs, Faculty of Arts and Sciences, Beirut, Lebanon. Offers anthropology (MA); Arab and Middle Eastern history (PhD); Arabic language and literature (MA, PhD); archaeology (MA); art history and curating (MA); biology (MS); cell and molecular biology (PhD); chemistry (MS); clinical psychology (MA); computational sciences (MS); computer science (MS); economics (MA); education (MA); English language (MA); English literature (MA); environmental policy planning (MA); financial economics (MAFE) (MA); geology (MS); history (MA); Islamic studies (MA); mathematics (MS); media studies (MA); Middle Eastern studies (MA); physics (MS); political studies (MA); psychology (MA); public administration (MA); public policy and international affairs (MA); sociology (MA); statistics (MA, MS); theoretical physics (PhD); transnational American studies (MA). *Program availability:* Part-time. *Faculty:* 133 full-time (42 women), 6 part-time/adjunct (2 women). *Students:* 240 full-time (172 women), 227 part-time (166 women). Average age 27. 286 applicants, 67% accepted, 108 enrolled. In 2016, 60 master's, 3 doctorates awarded. Terminal master's awarded for partial completion of doctoral program. *Degree requirements:* For master's, one foreign language, comprehensive exam, thesis (for some programs); for doctorate, one foreign language, comprehensive exam, thesis/dissertation. *Entrance requirements:* For master's, GRE (for some MA, MS programs), letters of recommendation; for doctorate, GRE, letters of recommendation. Additional exam requirements/recommendations for international students: Required—TOEFL (minimum score 600 paper-based; 97 iBT), IELTS (minimum score 7). *Application deadline:* For fall admission, 4/3 for domestic students; for winter admission, 11/3 for domestic students. Application fee: $50. Electronic applications accepted. *Expenses:* Contact institution. *Financial support:* In 2016–17, 4 fellowships (averaging $11,200 per year), 18 research assistantships (averaging $5,400 per year) were awarded; teaching assistantships, career-related internships or fieldwork, Federal Work-Study, institutionally sponsored loans, scholarships/grants, traineeships, health care benefits, tuition waivers (full), and unspecified assistantships also available. Support available to part-time students. *Faculty research:* Development economics, spatial econometrics, health economics, labor economics, energy economics, hydrogeology, geophysics, petrophysics, structural geology, mineralogy, petrology, geochemistry, multilingualism, comparative/world literature, translation studies, book histories/ cultures, biocatalysis, molecular recognition, photocatalysis, photophysical and biophysical chemistry, probe chemistry, machine learning, data science. *Unit head:* Dr. Nadia Maria El Cheikh, Dean, Faculty of Arts and Sciences, 961-1374374 Ext. 3800, Fax: 961-1744461, E-mail: nmcheikh@aub.edu.lb. *Application contact:* Dr. Salim Kanaan, Director, Admissions Office, 961-1350000 Ext. 2590, Fax: 961-1750775, E-mail: sk00@aub.edu.lb.
Website: http://www.aub.edu.lb/fas/

**The American University of Paris,** Graduate Programs, Paris, France. Offers cross-cultural and sustainable business management (MA); cultural translation (MA); global communications (MA); global communications and civil society (MA); international affairs (MA); international affairs, conflict resolution and civil society development (MA); Middle East and Islamic studies (MA); Middle East and Islamic studies and international affairs (MA); public policy and international affairs (MA); public policy and international law (MA). *Degree requirements:* For master's, thesis (for some programs). *Entrance requirements:* For master's, minimum undergraduate GPA of 3.0. Additional exam requirements/recommendations for international students: Recommended—TOEFL, IELTS. Electronic applications accepted.

**Brandeis University,** Graduate School of Arts and Sciences, Department of Near Eastern and Judaic Studies, Waltham, MA 02454-9110. Offers Near Eastern and Judaic studies (MA, PhD); Near Eastern and Judaic studies and women's, gender, and sexuality studies (MA); teaching of Hebrew (MAT). *Program availability:* Part-time. *Faculty:* 24 full-time (10 women), 6 part-time/adjunct (3 women). *Students:* 44 full-time (18 women), 2 part-time (0 women); includes 7 minority (4 Black or African American, non-Hispanic/Latino; 1 Asian, non-Hispanic/Latino; 4 Hispanic/Latino), 9 international. 67 applicants, 45% accepted, 12 enrolled. In 2016, 9 master's, 3 doctorates awarded. Terminal master's awarded for partial completion of doctoral program. *Degree requirements:* For master's, one foreign language, thesis or alternative, proseminar, capstone; for doctorate, variable foreign language requirement, comprehensive exam, thesis/dissertation. *Entrance requirements:* For master's, GRE (recommended), 2 letters of recommendation, transcript(s), statement of purpose, writing sample, resume; for doctorate, GRE (recommended), 3 letters of recommendation, transcript(s), statement of purpose, writing sample, resume. Additional exam requirements/recommendations for international students: Required—TOEFL (minimum score 600 paper-based; 100 iBT); Recommended—IELTS (minimum score 7), TSE (minimum score 68). *Application deadline:* For fall admission, 1/15 priority date for domestic and international students. Application fee: $75. Electronic applications accepted. *Financial support:* In 2016–17, 28 students received support, including 16 fellowships with full tuition reimbursements available (averaging $24,000 per year), 2 teaching assistantships with partial tuition reimbursements available (averaging $3,200 per year); Federal Work-Study, scholarships/grants, health care benefits, and tuition waivers (full and partial) also available. Support available to part-time students. Financial award application deadline: 4/15; financial award applicants required to submit FAFSA. *Faculty research:* Bible and ancient Near East, Judaic Studies, Israel Studies, modern Middle East, Arabic and Islamic civilizations. *Unit head:* Dr. Jonathan Decter, Department Chair, 781-736-2950, Fax: 781-736-2070, E-mail: decter@brandeis.edu. *Application contact:* Joanne Arnish, Department Administrator, 781-736-2950, Fax: 781-736-2070, E-mail: arnish@brandeis.edu.
Website: http://www.brandeis.edu/gsas

**Brown University,** Graduate School, Department of Egyptology and Ancient Western Asian Studies, Providence, RI 02912. Offers ancient western Asian studies (PhD); Egyptology (PhD); history of the exact sciences in antiquity (PhD). *Degree requirements:* For doctorate, 2 foreign languages, comprehensive exam, thesis/dissertation. *Entrance requirements:* For doctorate, GRE General Test.

**California State University, Long Beach,** Graduate Studies, College of Liberal Arts, Department of History, Long Beach, CA 90840. Offers Africa and the Middle East (MA). *Program availability:* Part-time, evening/weekend. *Degree requirements:* For master's, one foreign language, comprehensive exam or thesis. *Application deadline:* For fall admission, 3/1 for domestic students. Applications are processed on a rolling basis. Application fee: $55. Electronic applications accepted. *Financial support:* Research assistantships, Federal Work-Study, institutionally sponsored loans, and scholarships/grants available. Financial award application deadline: 3/2. *Faculty research:* All periods of European and American history, recent Asian and African history. *Unit head:* David A. Shefer, Chair, 562-985-4431, Fax: 562-985-5431. *Application contact:* Dr. Houri Berberian, Graduate Advisor, 562-985-4524, Fax: 562-985-4431, E-mail: hberber@csulb.edu.
Website: http://www.csulb.edu/colleges/cla/departments/history/

**The Catholic University of America,** School of Arts and Sciences, Department of Semitic and Egyptian Languages and Literatures, Washington, DC 20064. Offers ancient Near East (Biblical Hebrew/Aramaic) (MA, PhD); Arabic (PhD); Christian Near East (Biblical Hebrew/Aramaic) (MA); Coptic (MA, PhD); Syriac (MA, PhD). *Program availability:* Part-time. *Faculty:* 3 full-time (0 women), 2 part-time/adjunct (1 woman). *Students:* 18 full-time (2 women), 14 part-time (4 women); includes 4 minority (1 Asian, non-Hispanic/Latino; 1 Hispanic/Latino; 2 Two or more races, non-Hispanic/Latino), 4 international. Average age 36. 11 applicants, 82% accepted, 7 enrolled. In 2016, 3 master's, 2 doctorates awarded. Terminal master's awarded for partial completion of doctoral program. *Degree requirements:* For master's, one foreign language, comprehensive exam; for doctorate, 2 foreign languages, comprehensive exam, thesis/dissertation. *Entrance requirements:* For master's, GRE General Test, statement of purpose, official copies of academic transcripts, three letters of recommendation; for doctorate, GRE General Test, statement of purpose, official copies of academic transcripts, three letters of recommendation, successful completion of MA field. Additional exam requirements/recommendations for international students: Required—TOEFL (minimum score 550 paper-based; 80 iBT). *Application deadline:* For fall admission, 7/15 priority date for domestic students, 7/1 for international students; for spring admission, 11/15 priority date for domestic students, 11/1 for international students. Applications are processed on a rolling basis. Application fee: $55. Electronic applications accepted. *Expenses:* $42,850 per year; $1,170 per credit; $200 per semester part-time fees. *Financial support:* Fellowships, research assistantships, teaching assistantships, Federal Work-Study, scholarships/grants, tuition waivers (full and partial), and unspecified assistantships available. Financial award application deadline: 2/1; financial award applicants required to submit FAFSA. *Faculty research:* Christian history and literature of the Near East, Biblical Hebrew, Arabic Christianity, Coptic, Syriac. *Unit head:* Dr. Andrew D. Gross, Chair, 202-319-5083, Fax: 202-319-4735, E-mail: grossa@cua.edu. *Application contact:* Director of Graduate Admissions, 202-319-5057, Fax: 202-319-6533, E-mail: cua-admissions@cua.edu.
Website: http://semitics.cua.edu/

**The Catholic University of America,** School of Arts and Sciences, Program in Medieval and Byzantine Studies, Washington, DC 20064. Offers Byzantine and Orthodox studies (MA); Medieval and Byzantine studies (PhD, Certificate); the Islamic world (MA); the Medieval West (MA). *Program availability:* Part-time. *Students:* 6 full-time (2 women), 5 part-time (2 women). Average age 31. 13 applicants, 54% accepted, 3 enrolled. In 2016, 2 master's awarded. *Degree requirements:* For master's, one foreign language, comprehensive exam, thesis or alternative; for doctorate, 2 foreign languages, comprehensive exam, thesis/dissertation. *Entrance requirements:* For master's and doctorate, GRE General Test, statement of purpose, official copies of academic transcripts, three letters of recommendation, writing sample; for Certificate, bachelor's degree. Additional exam requirements/recommendations for international students: Required—TOEFL (minimum score 550 paper-based; 80 iBT). *Application deadline:* For fall admission, 7/15 priority date for domestic students, 7/1 for international students; for spring admission, 11/15 priority date for domestic students, 11/1 for international students. Applications are processed on a rolling basis. Application fee: $55. Electronic applications accepted. *Expenses:* $42,850 per year; $1,170 per credit; $200 per semester part-time fees. *Financial support:* Fellowships, research assistantships, teaching assistantships, Federal Work-Study, scholarships/grants, tuition waivers (full and partial), and unspecified assistantships available. Financial award application deadline: 2/1; financial award applicants required to submit FAFSA. *Faculty research:* Scholasticism and medieval theology; early and late medieval history; medieval philosophy; liturgical studies; medieval English literature. *Unit head:* Dr. Lilla Kopar, Director, 202-319-5794, Fax: 202-319-6609, E-mail: kopar@cua.edu. *Application contact:* Director of Graduate Admissions, 202-319-5057, Fax: 202-319-6533, E-mail: cua-admissions@cua.edu.
Website: http://mbs.cua.edu/

**College of Staten Island of the City University of New York,** Graduate Programs, Division of Humanities and Social Sciences, Program in History, Staten Island, NY 10314-6600. Offers history of Africa and the Middle East (MA); history of Asia (MA); history of Europe (MA); history of Latin America and the Caribbean (MA); history of the United States (MA). *Program availability:* Part-time, evening/weekend. *Faculty:* 2 full-time. *Students:* 11 part-time. Average age 36. 8 applicants, 25% accepted, 2 enrolled. In 2016, 5 master's awarded. *Degree requirements:* For master's, comprehensive exam (for some programs), 32 credits (total of eight courses); thesis or portfolio. *Entrance requirements:* For master's, bachelor's degree with minimum GPA of 3.0 overall and in undergraduate history courses, two letters of recommendation, letter of interest, research-based writing sample. Additional exam requirements/recommendations for international students: Required—TOEFL (minimum score 550 paper-based; 79 iBT), IELTS (minimum score 6.5). *Application deadline:* For fall admission, 5/10 priority date for domestic and international students; for spring admission, 12/2 priority date for domestic and international students. Applications are processed on a rolling basis.

## Near and Middle Eastern Studies

Application fee: $125. Electronic applications accepted. *Expenses:* Tuition, state resident: full-time $10,130; part-time $425 per credit. Tuition, nonresident: full-time $18,720; part-time $780 per credit. *Required fees:* $181.10 per semester. Tuition and fees vary according to program. *Faculty research:* African and African diaspora history, South Asian history, Middle Eastern history, U.S. history, environmental history. *Unit head:* John Dixon, Graduate Program Coordinator, 718-982-3307, E-mail: john.dixon@csi.cuny.edu. *Application contact:* Sasha Spence, Associate Director for Graduate Admissions, 718-982-2019, Fax: 718-982-2500, E-mail: sasha.spence@csi.cuny.edu.
Website: http://www.csi.cuny.edu/catalog/graduate/master-of-arts-in-history-ma.htm

**Columbia University,** Graduate School of Arts and Sciences, New York, NY 10027. Offers African-American studies (MA); American studies (MA); anthropology (MA, PhD); art history and archaeology (MA, PhD); astronomy (PhD); biological sciences (PhD); biotechnology (MA); chemical physics (PhD); chemistry (PhD); classical studies (MA, PhD); classics (MA, PhD); climate and society (MA); conservation biology (MA); earth and environmental sciences (PhD); East Asia: regional studies (MA); East Asian languages and cultures (MA, PhD); ecology, evolution and environmental biology (MA), including conservation biology; ecology, evolution, and environmental biology (PhD), including ecology and evolutionary biology, evolutionary primatology; economics (MA, PhD); English and comparative literature (MA, PhD); French and Romance philology (MA, PhD); Germanic languages (MA, PhD); global French studies (MA); global thought (MA); Hispanic cultural studies (MA); history (PhD); history and literature (MA); human rights studies (MA); Islamic studies (MA); Italian (MA, PhD); Japanese pedagogy (MA); Jewish studies (MA); Latin America and the Caribbean: regional studies (MA); Latin American and Iberian cultures (PhD); mathematics (MA, PhD), including finance (MA); medieval and Renaissance studies (MA); Middle Eastern, South Asian, and African studies (MA, PhD); modern art: critical and curatorial studies (MA); modern European studies (MA); museum anthropology (MA); music (DMA, PhD); oral history (MA); philosophical foundations of physics (MA); philosophy (MA, PhD); physics (PhD); political science (MA, PhD); psychology (PhD); quantitative methods in the social sciences (MA); religion (MA, PhD); Russia, Eurasia and East Europe: regional studies (MA); Russian translation (MA); Slavic cultures (MA); Slavic languages (MA, PhD); sociology (MA, PhD); South Asian studies (MA); statistics (MA, PhD); theatre (PhD). Dual-degree programs require admission to both Graduate School of Arts and Sciences and another Columbia school. *Program availability:* Part-time. Terminal master's awarded for partial completion of doctoral program. *Degree requirements:* For master's, variable foreign language requirement, comprehensive exam (for some programs), thesis (for some programs); for doctorate, variable foreign language requirement, comprehensive exam (for some programs), thesis/dissertation. *Entrance requirements:* For master's and doctorate, GRE General Test, GRE Subject Test (for some programs). Additional exam requirements/recommendations for international students: Required—TOEFL, IELTS. Electronic applications accepted.

**Cornell University,** Graduate School, Graduate Fields of Arts and Sciences, Field of Archaeology, Ithaca, NY 14853. Offers environmental archaeology (MA); historical archaeology (MA); Latin American archaeology (MA); medieval archaeology (MA); Mediterranean and Near Eastern archaeology (MA); Stone Age archaeology (MA). *Degree requirements:* For master's, one foreign language, thesis. *Entrance requirements:* For master's, GRE General Test, 3 letters of recommendation, sample of written work. Additional exam requirements/recommendations for international students: Required—TOEFL (minimum score 550 paper-based; 77 iBT). Electronic applications accepted. *Faculty research:* Anatolia, Lydia, Sardis, classical and Hellenistic Greece, science in archaeology, North American Indians, Stone Age Africa, Mayan trade.

**Cornell University,** Graduate School, Graduate Fields of Arts and Sciences, Field of History, Ithaca, NY 14853. Offers African history (MA, PhD); American history (MA, PhD); ancient Greek history (PhD); ancient history (MA, PhD); ancient Roman history (PhD); early modern European history (MA, PhD); English history (PhD); French history (MA, PhD); German history (MA, PhD); history of science (MA, PhD); Korean history (PhD); Latin American history (MA, PhD); medieval Chinese history (MA, PhD); medieval history (MA, PhD); modern Chinese history (MA, PhD); modern European history (MA, PhD); modern Japanese history (MA, PhD); modern Middle Eastern history (PhD); premodern Islamic history (MA, PhD); premodern Japanese history (MA, PhD); Renaissance history (MA, PhD); Russian history (MA, PhD); South Asian history (PhD); Southeast Asian history (MA, PhD). Terminal master's awarded for partial completion of doctoral program. *Degree requirements:* For master's, thesis; for doctorate, 2 foreign languages, comprehensive exam, thesis/dissertation, 1 year of teaching experience. *Entrance requirements:* For master's and doctorate, GRE General Test, writing sample, 3 letters of recommendation. Additional exam requirements/recommendations for international students: Required—TOEFL (minimum score 550 paper-based; 77 iBT). Electronic applications accepted.

**Cornell University,** Graduate School, Graduate Fields of Arts and Sciences, Field of History of Art, Archaeology and Visual Studies, Ithaca, NY 14853. Offers 19th century art (PhD); African, African American and African diaspora (PhD); American art (PhD); ancient art and archaeology (PhD); Asian American art (PhD); Baroque art (PhD); comparative modernities (PhD); digital art (PhD); East Asian art (PhD); history of photography (PhD); Islamic art (PhD); Latin American art (PhD); medieval art (PhD); modern art (PhD); Renaissance art (PhD); Southeast Asian art (PhD); theory and criticism (PhD); visual studies (PhD). *Degree requirements:* For doctorate, one foreign language, comprehensive exam, thesis/dissertation, general exams in 3 areas. *Entrance requirements:* For doctorate, GRE General Test, sample of written work, 3 letters of recommendation. Additional exam requirements/recommendations for international students: Required—TOEFL (minimum score 550 paper-based; 77 iBT). Electronic applications accepted.

**Cornell University,** Graduate School, Graduate Fields of Arts and Sciences, Field of Near Eastern Studies, Ithaca, NY 14853. Offers ancient Near Eastern studies (MA, PhD); Arabic and Islamic studies (MA, PhD); biblical studies (MA, PhD); Hebrew and Judaic studies (MA, PhD). Terminal master's awarded for partial completion of doctoral program. *Degree requirements:* For master's, one foreign language, thesis; for doctorate, 2 foreign languages, comprehensive exam, thesis/dissertation. *Entrance requirements:* For master's and doctorate, GRE General Test, 2 years of 1 Near Eastern language, 3 letters of recommendation, writing sample. Additional exam requirements/recommendations for international students: Required—TOEFL (minimum score 550 paper-based; 77 iBT). Electronic applications accepted. *Faculty research:* Ancient Near East (including archeology), Hebrew and Judaic studies (including Bible), early Christianity, Arabic and Islamic studies, modern Middle East.

**George Mason University,** College of Humanities and Social Sciences, Program in Middle East and Islamic Studies, Fairfax, VA 22030. Offers MA, Certificate. *Faculty:* 14 full-time (4 women), 1 (woman) part-time/adjunct. *Students:* 4 full-time (2 women), 13 part-time (8 women); includes 3 minority (1 Black or African American, non-Hispanic/Latino; 1 Asian, non-Hispanic/Latino; 1 Hispanic/Latino), 1 international. Average age 29. 24 applicants, 96% accepted, 7 enrolled. In 2016, 4 master's awarded. *Entrance requirements:* For master's, GRE, resume, 3 letters of recommendation, goals statement, writing sample, official transcripts. Additional exam requirements/recommendations for international students: Required—TOEFL (minimum score 575

paper-based; 88 iBT), IELTS (minimum score 6.5), PTE (minimum score 59). *Application deadline:* For fall admission, 2/15 for domestic students. Application fee: $75 ($80 for international students). Electronic applications accepted. *Expenses:* Tuition, state resident: full-time $10,628; part-time $443 per credit. Tuition, nonresident: full-time $29,306; part-time $1221 per credit. *Required fees:* $3096; $129 per credit. Tuition and fees vary according to program. *Financial support:* In 2016–17, 2 students received support, including 2 research assistantships with tuition reimbursements available (averaging $4,000 per year); career-related internships or fieldwork, Federal Work-Study, institutionally sponsored loans, scholarships/grants, unspecified assistantships, and health care benefits (for full-time research or teaching assistantship recipients) also available. *Total annual research expenditures:* $498,784. *Unit head:* Bassam S. Haddad, Middle East Studies Program Director, 703-993-2962, Fax: 703-993-1399, E-mail: bhaddad@gmu.edu.
Website: http://meis.gmu.edu

**Georgetown University,** Graduate School of Arts and Sciences, Walsh School of Foreign Service, The Center for Contemporary Arab Studies, Washington, DC 20057. Offers MA, Certificate, MA/JD, MA/PhD. *Degree requirements:* For master's, one foreign language, comprehensive exam, thesis or alternative, proficiency in Arabic. *Entrance requirements:* For master's, GRE, minimum GPA of 3.0. Additional exam requirements/recommendations for international students: Required—TOEFL (minimum score 600 paper-based; 100 iBT). Electronic applications accepted. *Faculty research:* Contemporary Arab world.

**The George Washington University,** Columbian College of Arts and Sciences, Department of Religion, Washington, DC 20052. Offers Islam (MA), including Hinduism and Islam. *Program availability:* Part-time, evening/weekend. *Faculty:* 8 full-time (3 women). *Students:* 9 full-time (6 women), 4 part-time (2 women); includes 3 minority (1 Black or African American, non-Hispanic/Latino; 2 Asian, non-Hispanic/Latino), 6 international. Average age 31. 22 applicants, 68% accepted, 7 enrolled. In 2016, 5 master's awarded. *Degree requirements:* For master's, one foreign language, comprehensive exam, thesis. *Entrance requirements:* For master's, GRE General Test, interview, minimum GPA of 3.0. Additional exam requirements/recommendations for international students: Required—TOEFL (minimum score 550 paper-based; 80 iBT). *Application deadline:* For fall admission, 4/1 priority date for domestic students, 1/15 priority date for international students; for spring admission, 10/1 priority date for domestic students, 9/1 priority date for international students. Applications are processed on a rolling basis. Application fee: $75. Electronic applications accepted. *Financial support:* In 2016–17, 1 student received support. Federal Work-Study and tuition waivers available. *Unit head:* Dr. Robert Eisen, Chair, 202-994-4780, Fax: 202-994-9379, E-mail: eisen@gwu.edu. *Application contact:* Information Contact, 202-994-6325, Fax: 202-994-9379, E-mail: religion@gwu.edu.
Website: http://religion.columbian.gwu.edu/

**The George Washington University,** Elliott School of International Affairs, Program in Middle East Studies, Washington, DC 20052. Offers MA. *Program availability:* Part-time. *Students:* 26 full-time (15 women), 15 part-time (8 women); includes 9 minority (2 Black or African American, non-Hispanic/Latino; 1 Asian, non-Hispanic/Latino; 3 Hispanic/Latino; 3 Two or more races, non-Hispanic/Latino). Average age 26. 64 applicants, 86% accepted, 16 enrolled. In 2016, 15 master's awarded. *Degree requirements:* For master's, one foreign language, capstone project. *Entrance requirements:* For master's, GRE General Test, 2 years (or equivalent) of an approved regional language. Additional exam requirements/recommendations for international students: Required—TOEFL (minimum score 100 iBT), IELTS (minimum score 7). *Application deadline:* For fall admission, 1/15 priority date for domestic and international students; for spring admission, 10/1 for domestic students. Application fee: $75. Electronic applications accepted. *Financial support:* In 2016–17, 7 students received support. Fellowships with partial tuition reimbursements available, Federal Work-Study, and scholarships/grants available. Financial award application deadline: 1/15; financial award applicants required to submit FAFSA. *Unit head:* Prof. Marc Lynch, Director, 202-994-9249, E-mail: mesp@gwu.edu. *Application contact:* Nicole A. Campbell, Director of Graduate Admissions, 202-994-7050, Fax: 202-994-9537, E-mail: esiagrad@gwu.edu.
Website: http://elliott.gwu.edu/middle-east-studies

**Harvard University,** Graduate School of Arts and Sciences, Committee on Middle Eastern Studies, Cambridge, MA 02138. Offers anthropology and Middle Eastern studies (PhD); economics and Middle Eastern studies (PhD); fine arts and Middle Eastern studies (PhD); history and Middle Eastern studies (PhD); regional studies–Middle East (AM). Terminal master's awarded for partial completion of doctoral program. *Degree requirements:* For master's, one foreign language; for doctorate, 2 foreign languages, thesis/dissertation. *Entrance requirements:* For master's, GRE General Test; for doctorate, GRE General Test, 1 year of course work in Middle Eastern regional studies, proficiency in a related language. Additional exam requirements/recommendations for international students: Required—TOEFL.

**Harvard University,** Graduate School of Arts and Sciences, Department of Near Eastern Languages and Civilizations, Cambridge, MA 02138. Offers Akkadian and Sumerian (AM, PhD); Arabic (AM, PhD); Armenian (AM, PhD); biblical history (AM, PhD); Hebrew (AM, PhD); Indo-Muslim culture (AM, PhD); Iranian (AM, PhD); Jewish history and literature (AM, PhD); Persian (AM, PhD); Semitic philology (AM, PhD); Syro-Palestinian archaeology (AM, PhD); Turkish (AM, PhD). *Degree requirements:* For doctorate, variable foreign language requirement, thesis/dissertation, general exams. *Entrance requirements:* For master's, GRE General Test; for doctorate, GRE General Test, proficiency in a Near Eastern language. Additional exam requirements/recommendations for international students: Required—TOEFL.

**Johns Hopkins University,** Zanvyl Krieger School of Arts and Sciences, Department of Near Eastern Studies, Baltimore, MD 21218. Offers archaeology (PhD); Assyriology (PhD); Egyptology (PhD); Hebrew Bible/Northwest Semitics (PhD). *Degree requirements:* For doctorate, 2 foreign languages, comprehensive exam, thesis/dissertation. *Entrance requirements:* For doctorate, GRE. Additional exam requirements/recommendations for international students: Required—TOEFL (minimum score 600 paper-based; 100 iBT); Recommended—IELTS. Electronic applications accepted. *Faculty research:* Egyptology, Assyriology, Hebrew Bible/Northwest Semitic languages, Demotic Egyptian, archaeology.

**McGill University,** Faculty of Graduate and Postdoctoral Studies, Faculty of Arts, Institute of Islamic Studies, Montréal, QC H3A 2T5, Canada. Offers MA, PhD, Diploma.

**New York University,** Graduate School of Arts and Science, Hagop Kevorkian Center for Near Eastern Studies, Department of Middle Eastern and Islamic Studies, New York, NY 10012-1019. Offers Middle Eastern and Islamic studies (MA); Middle Eastern and Islamic studies/history (PhD). *Program availability:* Part-time. Terminal master's awarded for partial completion of doctoral program. *Degree requirements:* For master's, 2 foreign languages, thesis; for doctorate, 4 foreign languages, comprehensive exam, thesis/dissertation. *Entrance requirements:* For doctorate, GRE General Test. Additional exam requirements/recommendations for international students: Required—TOEFL. *Faculty research:* Middle Eastern history, Arabic/Persian/Turkish language and literature, cultures and societies of Middle East, Islamic studies.

**New York University,** Graduate School of Arts and Science, Hagop Kevorkian Center for Near Eastern Studies, Program in Near Eastern Studies, New York, NY 10012-1019. Offers Near Eastern studies (MA); Near Eastern studies/journalism (MA); Near Eastern studies/museum studies (MA). *Program availability:* Part-time. *Degree requirements:* For master's, one foreign language, thesis. *Entrance requirements:* For master's, GRE General Test. Additional exam requirements/recommendations for international students: Required—TOEFL. *Faculty research:* Politics, political economy, anthropology, history and culture of the Middle East.

**New York University,** Graduate School of Arts and Science, Program in Museum Studies, New York, NY 10012-1019. Offers museum studies (MA, Advanced Certificate), including Africana studies (MA), Hebrew and Judaic studies (MA), Latin American and Caribbean studies (MA), Near Eastern studies (MA). *Program availability:* Part-time, evening/weekend. *Entrance requirements:* For master's, GRE General Test; for Advanced Certificate, master's degree or PhD. Additional exam requirements/recommendations for international students: Required—TOEFL. *Faculty research:* Modern and contemporary art, history of museums and exhibitions, conservation of cultural materials, museum anthropology, ethnography.

**Princeton University,** Graduate School, Department of Near Eastern Studies, Princeton, NJ 08544-1019. Offers MA, PhD. *Degree requirements:* For master's, one foreign language, thesis; for doctorate, 2 foreign languages, thesis/dissertation. *Entrance requirements:* For master's and doctorate, GRE General Test. Additional exam requirements/recommendations for international students: Required—TOEFL. Electronic applications accepted.

**Rice University,** Graduate Programs, School of Humanities, Department of Religious Studies, Houston, TX 77251-1892. Offers African religions (PhD); African-American religions (PhD); contemplative studies (PhD); ghosticism, esotericism, mysticism (PhD); Islam (PhD); Jewish thought and philosophy (PhD); modern Christianity in thought and popular culture (PhD); psychology of religion (PhD); the Bible and beyond (PhD). *Degree requirements:* For doctorate, 2 foreign languages, comprehensive exam, thesis/dissertation. *Entrance requirements:* For doctorate, GRE, letters of recommendation, writing sample. Additional exam requirements/recommendations for international students: Required—TOEFL (minimum score 600 paper-based; 90 iBT). Electronic applications accepted. *Faculty research:* Origins and historical development of Islam, history of Christianity, the study of comparative religion, African-American religion, religion and culture.

**Southern Evangelical Seminary,** Graduate Programs, Matthews, NC 28105. Offers apologetics (MA, D Min, Certificate); Christian education (MA); church ministry (MA, Certificate); divinity (Certificate), including apologetics (M Div, Certificate); Islamic studies (MA, Certificate); Jewish studies (MA); philosophy (MA); philosophy of religion (PhD); religion (MA); theology (MA), including apologetics (M Div, Certificate), Biblical studies; youth ministry (MA). *Program availability:* Part-time, evening/weekend, online learning. *Degree requirements:* For master's, thesis (for some programs); for doctorate, 2 foreign languages, comprehensive exam (for some programs), thesis/dissertation. *Entrance requirements:* Additional exam requirements/recommendations for international students: Required—TOEFL (minimum score 600 paper-based).

**Southwestern Baptist Theological Seminary,** Roy Fish School of Evangelism and Missions, Fort Worth, TX 76122-0000. Offers cross-cultural missions (MTS); evangelism (M Div); evangelism and missions (D Min); international church planting (M Div); Islamic (M Div, MA Islamic); missiology (MA Miss); missions (M Div); North American church planting (M Div); North American evangelism and international missions (D Min); theology (Th M); world Christian studies (PhD).

**The University of Arizona,** College of Social and Behavioral Sciences, School of Middle Eastern and North African Studies, Tucson, AZ 85721. Offers MA, PhD, Graduate Certificate. *Program availability:* Part-time, evening/weekend. Terminal master's awarded for partial completion of doctoral program. *Degree requirements:* For master's, one foreign language; for doctorate, 3 foreign languages, thesis/dissertation. *Entrance requirements:* For master's, GRE General Test, 3 letters of recommendation, statement of purpose, curriculum vitae, writing sample; for doctorate, GRE General Test, 3 letters of recommendation, curriculum vitae, writing sample. Additional exam requirements/recommendations for international students: Required—TOEFL (minimum score 550 paper-based; 79 iBT). Electronic applications accepted.

**University of California, Berkeley,** Graduate Division, College of Letters and Science, Department of Near Eastern Studies, Berkeley, CA 94720-1500. Offers Near Eastern studies (MA, PhD). *Students:* 27 full-time (16 women); includes 1 minority (Asian, non-Hispanic/Latino), 3 international. 84 applicants, 3 enrolled. In 2016, 2 master's, 5 doctorates awarded. *Degree requirements:* For doctorate, 2 foreign languages, thesis/dissertation, qualifying exam. *Entrance requirements:* For master's and doctorate, GRE General Test, minimum GPA of 3.0, 3 letters of recommendation. *Application deadline:* For fall admission, 12/15 for domestic students. Application fee: $105 ($125 for international students). Electronic applications accepted. *Financial support:* Fellowships, research assistantships, teaching assistantships, institutionally sponsored loans, health care benefits, and unspecified assistantships available. *Unit head:* Dr. Carol Redmount, Chair, 510-642-3757, E-mail: nes@berkeley.edu. *Application contact:* 510-642-6162, Fax: 510-643-8430, E-mail: nes@berkeley.edu.
Website: http://neareastern.berkeley.edu/

**University of California, Los Angeles,** Graduate Division, College of Letters and Science, Department of Near Eastern Languages and Cultures, Los Angeles, CA 90034. Offers MA, PhD. *Degree requirements:* For master's, one foreign language, comprehensive exam; for doctorate, 2 foreign languages, thesis/dissertation, oral and written qualifying exams. *Entrance requirements:* For master's, GRE General Test, bachelor's degree; minimum undergraduate GPA of 3.25 (or its equivalent if letter grade system not used); for doctorate, GRE General Test, master's degree; minimum undergraduate GPA of 3.25 (or its equivalent if letter grade system not used). Additional exam requirements/recommendations for international students: Required—TOEFL. Electronic applications accepted.

**University of California, Los Angeles,** Graduate Division, College of Letters and Science, Interdepartmental Program in Indo-European Studies, Los Angeles, CA 90095. Offers PhD. *Degree requirements:* For doctorate, 2 foreign languages, thesis/dissertation, oral and written qualifying exams. *Entrance requirements:* For doctorate, bachelor's degree; minimum undergraduate GPA of 3.0 (or its equivalent if letter grade system not used); writing sample; competence in Latin. Additional exam requirements/recommendations for international students: Required—TOEFL. Electronic applications accepted.

**University of California, Los Angeles,** Graduate Division, International Institute, Interdepartmental Program in Islamic Studies, Los Angeles, CA 90095. Offers MA, PhD, MPH/MA. *Degree requirements:* For master's, one foreign language, comprehensive exam; for doctorate, one foreign language, thesis/dissertation, oral and written qualifying exams. *Entrance requirements:* For master's, GRE General Test, bachelor's degree; minimum undergraduate GPA of 3.0 (or its equivalent if letter grade system not used); language requirement; for doctorate, GRE General Test, master's degree; minimum undergraduate GPA of 3.0 (or its equivalent if letter grade system not used); proficiency

in Arabic. Additional exam requirements/recommendations for international students: Required—TOEFL. Electronic applications accepted.

**University of Chicago,** Divinity School, PhD Program, Chicago, IL 60637. Offers anthropology and sociology of religions (PhD); Bible (PhD); history of Christianity (PhD); history of Judaism (PhD); history of religions (PhD); Islamic studies (PhD); philosophy of religions (PhD); religion, literature, and visual culture (PhD); religions in America (PhD); religious ethics (PhD); theology (PhD). *Students:* 161 full-time (47 women), 1 (woman) part-time; includes 22 minority (6 Black or African American, non-Hispanic/Latino; 10 Asian, non-Hispanic/Latino; 2 Hispanic/Latino; 4 Two or more races, non-Hispanic/Latino), 26 international. 171 applicants, 16% accepted, 15 enrolled. *Degree requirements:* For doctorate, 2 foreign languages, comprehensive exam, thesis/dissertation. *Entrance requirements:* For doctorate, GRE General Test. Additional exam requirements/recommendations for international students: Required—TOEFL (minimum score 600 paper-based; 104 iBT), IELTS (minimum score 7). *Application deadline:* For fall admission, 12/15 for domestic and international students. Application fee: $75. Electronic applications accepted. *Financial support:* In 2016–17, 20 fellowships with full tuition reimbursements (averaging $24,000 per year) were awarded; Federal Work-Study, institutionally sponsored loans, scholarships/grants, and health care benefits also available. Financial award application deadline: 12/15; financial award applicants required to submit FAFSA. *Faculty research:* Constructive studies (philosophy of religion, religious ethics, and theology); historical studies (Bible, history of Christianity, and history of Judaism); religion and the human sciences (anthropology and sociology of religion, history of religions, and religion, literature, and visual culture); Islamic studies; religions in America. *Unit head:* Dr. Richard A. Rosengarten, Dean/Associate Professor of Religion and Literature, 773-702-8200. *Application contact:* John W. Howell, Coordinator for Recruiting and Admissions, 773-702-8249, Fax: 773-834-4581, E-mail: divinityadmissions@uchicago.edu.
Website: http://divinity.uchicago.edu/doctoral-program-phd

**University of Chicago,** Division of the Humanities, Department of Near Eastern Languages and Civilizations, Chicago, IL 60637. Offers PhD. *Students:* 119 full-time (43 women); includes 11 minority (3 Asian, non-Hispanic/Latino; 5 Hispanic/Latino; 3 Two or more races, non-Hispanic/Latino), 28 international. 120 applicants, 18% accepted, 15 enrolled. In 2016, 10 doctorates awarded. Terminal master's awarded for partial completion of doctoral program. *Degree requirements:* For doctorate, 2 foreign languages, comprehensive exam, thesis/dissertation. *Entrance requirements:* For doctorate, GRE General Test. Additional exam requirements/recommendations for international students: Required—TOEFL (minimum score 104 iBT), IELTS (minimum score 7). *Application deadline:* For fall admission, 12/15 for domestic and international students. Application fee: $90. Electronic applications accepted. *Financial support:* Fellowships with full tuition reimbursements, teaching assistantships with full tuition reimbursements, Federal Work-Study, institutionally sponsored loans, scholarships/grants, and health care benefits available. Financial award application deadline: 12/15; financial award applicants required to submit FAFSA. *Faculty research:* Archaeology and history of the ancient near East, Middle Eastern history and civilization, Semitic language and literature, Middle Eastern languages and literatures. *Unit head:* Dr. Frank Lewis, Chair, E-mail: flewis@uchicago.edu. *Application contact:* Michael Beetley, Assistant Dean of Students, Admissions and Fellowships, 773-702-1552, Fax: 773-834-9148, E-mail: humanitiesadmissions@uchicago.edu.
Website: http://nelc.uchicago.edu/

**University of Chicago,** Division of the Social Sciences and Division of the Humanities, Center for Middle Eastern Studies, Chicago, IL 60637. Offers MA. *Students:* 23 full-time (15 women); includes 2 minority (1 Asian, non-Hispanic/Latino; 1 Hispanic/Latino), 7 international. 35 applicants, 86% accepted. In 2016, 11 master's awarded. *Degree requirements:* For master's, one foreign language, thesis. *Entrance requirements:* For master's, GRE General Test. Additional exam requirements/recommendations for international students: Required—TOEFL (minimum score 104 iBT), IELTS (minimum score 7). *Application deadline:* For fall admission, 1/5 for domestic and international students. Application fee: $90. Electronic applications accepted. *Financial support:* In 2016–17, 8 students received support. Federal Work-Study, institutionally sponsored loans, and scholarships/grants available. Financial award application deadline: 1/5. *Unit head:* Prof. Hakan Karateke, Director, 773-702-5375, E-mail: karateke@uchicago.edu. *Application contact:* Office of the Dean of Students, 773-702-8415, E-mail: admissions@ssd.uchicago.edu.
Website: http://cmes.uchicago.edu

**University of Illinois at Urbana–Champaign,** Graduate College, College of Liberal Arts and Sciences, Center for South Asian and Middle Eastern Studies, Champaign, IL 61820. Offers MA. *Degree requirements:* For master's, one foreign language, comprehensive exam, thesis or alternative.

**The University of Kansas,** Graduate Studies, College of Liberal Arts and Sciences, Center for Russian, East European and Eurasian Studies, Lawrence, KS 66045. Offers foreign area officer (MA); Russian, East European and Eurasian studies (MA, Graduate Certificate); JD/MA. *Program availability:* Part-time. *Students:* 10 full-time (4 women), 1 international. Average age 27. 12 applicants, 67% accepted, 3 enrolled. In 2016, 1 other advanced degree awarded. *Entrance requirements:* For master's, GRE General Test, two-page statement of educational and professional objectives, three letters of recommendation, official transcripts. Additional exam requirements/recommendations for international students: Required—TOEFL. Application fee: $65 ($85 for international students). Electronic applications accepted. *Financial support:* Fellowships, research assistantships, and scholarships/grants available. Financial award application deadline: 1/1; financial award applicants required to submit FAFSA. *Faculty research:* Russian and East Central European history and culture; Ukrainian, Russian, and Central Asian domestic politics and international security; Slavic languages, linguistics, and literatures. *Unit head:* Vitaly Chernetsky, Acting Director, 785-864-4236, E-mail: vchernetsky@ku.edu. *Application contact:* Alyssa McDonald, Graduate Admissions Contact, 785-864-4236, E-mail: crees@ku.edu.
Website: http://www.crees.ku.edu/

**The University of Manchester,** Faculty of Life Sciences, Manchester, United Kingdom. Offers adaptive organismal biology (M Phil, PhD); animal biology (M Phil, PhD); biochemistry (M Phil, PhD); bioinformatics (M Phil, PhD); biomolecular sciences (M Phil, PhD); biotechnology (M Phil, PhD); cell biology (M Phil, PhD); cell matrix research (M Phil, PhD); channels and transporters (M Phil, PhD); developmental biology (M Phil, PhD); Egyptology (M Phil, PhD); environmental biology (M Phil, PhD); evolutionary biology (M Phil, PhD); gene expression (M Phil, PhD); genetics (M Phil, PhD); history of science, technology and medicine (M Phil, PhD); immunology (M Phil, PhD); integrative neurobiology and behavior (M Phil, PhD); membrane trafficking (M Phil, PhD); microbiology (M Phil, PhD); molecular and cellular neuroscience (M Phil, PhD); molecular biology (M Phil, PhD); molecular cancer studies (M Phil, PhD); neuroscience (M Phil, PhD); ophthalmology (M Phil, PhD); optometry (M Phil, PhD); organelle function (M Phil, PhD); pharmacology (M Phil, PhD); physiology (M Phil, PhD); plant sciences (M Phil, PhD); stem cell research (M Phil, PhD); structural biology (M Phil, PhD); systems neuroscience (M Phil, PhD); toxicology (M Phil, PhD).

**The University of Manchester,** School of Languages, Linguistics and Cultures, Manchester, United Kingdom. Offers Arab world studies (PhD); Chinese studies (M Phil,

## Near and Middle Eastern Studies

PhD); East Asian studies (M Phil, PhD); English language (PhD); French studies (M Phil, PhD); German studies (M Phil, PhD); interpreting studies (PhD); Italian studies (M Phil, PhD); Japanese studies (M Phil, PhD); Latin American cultural studies (M Phil, PhD); linguistics (M Phil, PhD); Middle Eastern studies (M Phil, PhD); Polish studies (M Phil, PhD); Portuguese studies (M Phil, PhD); Russian studies (M Phil, PhD); Spanish studies (M Phil, PhD); translation and intercultural studies (M Phil, PhD).

**University of Memphis,** Graduate School, College of Arts and Sciences, Department of History, Memphis, TN 38152. Offers ancient Egyptian history (MA, PhD). *Program availability:* 100% online. *Faculty:* 20 full-time (8 women), 3 part-time/adjunct (2 women). *Students:* 30 full-time (20 women), 37 part-time (20 women); includes 14 minority (11 Black or African American, non-Hispanic/Latino; 1 Hispanic/Latino; 2 Two or more races, non-Hispanic/Latino), 1 international. Average age 35. 40 applicants, 65% accepted, 17 enrolled. In 2016, 20 master's, 10 doctorates awarded. *Degree requirements:* For master's, comprehensive exam, thesis optional; for doctorate, one foreign language, comprehensive exam, thesis/dissertation, 60 credits plus 12 dissertation credits, 2 research seminars. *Entrance requirements:* For master's, GRE General Test or MAT, 18 undergraduate hours of course work in history with minimum GPA of 3.0, 2 letters of recommendation, writing sample, statement of research interest; for doctorate, GRE General Test, GRE Subject Test, MA in history or related field, three letters of recommendation, writing sample, statement of purpose. Additional exam requirements/recommendations for international students: Required—TOEFL (minimum score 550 paper-based; 79 iBT). *Application deadline:* For fall admission, 1/15 for domestic students; for spring admission, 9/15 for domestic students. Applications are processed on a rolling basis. Application fee: $35 ($60 for international students). Electronic applications accepted. *Expenses:* $5,231.50 per semester full-time in-state, $9,623.50 full-time out-of-state. *Financial support:* In 2016–17, 54 students received support, including 1 research assistantship with full tuition reimbursement available (averaging $12,000 per year), 20 teaching assistantships with full tuition reimbursements available (averaging $17,350 per year); career-related internships or fieldwork, Federal Work-Study, scholarships/grants, and unspecified assistantships also available. Financial award application deadline: 2/1; financial award applicants required to submit FAFSA. *Faculty research:* African/African-American history; U.S. history; ancient Egyptian history; modern European history; women, gender, and family studies. *Unit head:* Dr. Aram Goudsouzian, Chair, 901-678-2516, Fax: 901-678-2720, E-mail: agoudszn@memphis.edu. *Application contact:* Dr. Daniel Unowsky, Coordinator of Graduate Studies, 901-678-3385, Fax: 901-678-2720, E-mail: dunowsky@memphis.edu.
Website: http://history.memphis.edu/

**University of Michigan,** Rackham Graduate School, College of Literature, Science, and the Arts, Center for Middle Eastern and North African Studies, Ann Arbor, MI 48109. Offers AM, JD/AM, MBA/AM. *Program availability:* Part-time. *Faculty:* 78 full-time (24 women), 1 (woman) part-time/adjunct. *Students:* 7 full-time (4 women), 1 part-time (0 women); includes 1 minority (Black or African American, non-Hispanic/Latino). 27 applicants, 48% accepted, 3 enrolled. In 2016, 3 master's awarded. *Degree requirements:* For master's, one foreign language, thesis or alternative. *Entrance requirements:* For master's, GRE General Test. Additional exam requirements/recommendations for international students: Required—TOEFL (minimum score 560 paper-based; 84 iBT). *Application deadline:* For fall admission, 12/15 for domestic and international students. Application fee: $75 ($90 for international students). Electronic applications accepted. *Expenses:* Tuition, state resident: full-time $21,466; part-time $1152 per credit hour. Tuition, nonresident: full-time $43,346; part-time $2367 per credit hour. Part-time tuition and fees vary according to course load, degree level and program. *Financial support:* In 2016–17, 3 students received support, including 3 fellowships with tuition reimbursements available (averaging $15,000 per year); teaching assistantships, career-related internships or fieldwork, Federal Work-Study, scholarships/grants, health care benefits, and Richard P. Mitchell Memorial Prize also available. Support available to part-time students. Financial award application deadline: 1/15; financial award applicants required to submit FAFSA. *Faculty research:* Middle East and North Africa. *Unit head:* Dr. Juan R. Cole, Director, 734-763-1599, E-mail: ii-gradadvising@umich.edu. *Application contact:* Julie E. Burnett, Graduate Academic Services Coordinator, 734-936-1842, Fax: 734-615-9158, E-mail: ii-gradadvising@umich.edu.
Website: http://www.ii.umich.edu/cmenas/

**University of Michigan,** Rackham Graduate School, College of Literature, Science, and the Arts, Department of Near Eastern Studies, Ann Arbor, MI 48109. Offers ancient Near Eastern studies (AM, PhD); Arabic for professional purposes (AM); Arabic language and literature (AM, PhD); Armenian studies (AM, PhD); Christianity in late antiquity (AM, PhD); Egyptology (AM, PhD); Hebrew Bible and ancient Israel (AM, PhD); Hebrew literature (AM, PhD); Islamic studies (AM, PhD); Jewish cultural studies (AM, PhD); Jewish mysticism (AM, PhD); Persian and Iranian studies (AM, PhD); Rabbinic literature (AM, PhD); Second Temple Judaism (AM, PhD); teaching Arabic as a foreign language (AM); Turkish studies (AM, PhD). *Faculty:* 27 full-time (8 women). *Students:* 28 full-time (12 women); includes 2 minority (1 Black or African American, non-Hispanic/Latino; 1 Asian, non-Hispanic/Latino), 10 international. Average age 32. 85 applicants, 8% accepted, 3 enrolled. In 2016, 4 master's, 3 doctorates awarded. Terminal master's awarded for partial completion of doctoral program. *Degree requirements:* For master's, 2 foreign languages; for doctorate, 4 foreign languages, comprehensive exam, thesis/dissertation, preliminary exams, oral defense of dissertation. *Entrance requirements:* Additional exam requirements/recommendations for international students: Required—TOEFL (minimum score 560 paper-based; 84 iBT), IELTS (minimum score 6.5). *Application deadline:* For fall admission, 12/1 for domestic and international students. Application fee: $75 ($90 for international students). Electronic applications accepted. *Expenses:* Tuition, state resident: full-time $21,466; part-time $1152 per credit hour. Tuition, nonresident: full-time $43,346; part-time $2367 per credit hour. Part-time tuition and fees vary according to course load, degree level and program. *Financial support:* In 2016–17, 28 students received support. Fellowships with full tuition reimbursements available, teaching assistantships with full tuition reimbursements available, scholarships/grants, health care benefits, unspecified assistantships, and spring/summer stipends available. Financial award application deadline: 12/1. *Faculty research:* Middle and Near Eastern literatures, languages, cultures from ancient times to the present. *Unit head:* Prof. Gottfried Hagen, Chair, 734-764-0314, E-mail: nes-chair@umich.edu. *Application contact:* Student Services, 734-764-0315, E-mail: nes-gradservices@umich.edu. Website: http://www.lsa.umich.edu/neareast/

**University of Pennsylvania,** School of Arts and Sciences, Graduate Group in Near Eastern Languages and Civilizations, Philadelphia, PA 19104. Offers AM, PhD. *Faculty:* 23 full-time (10 women), 6 part-time/adjunct (0 women). *Students:* 20 full-time (11 women), 3 part-time (1 woman); includes 2 minority (1 Hispanic/Latino; 1 Two or more races, non-Hispanic/Latino), 7 international. Average age 33. 67 applicants, 3% accepted, 1 enrolled. In 2016, 3 master's, 5 doctorates awarded. Application fee: $70. *Expenses: Tuition:* full-time $31,068; part-time $5762 per course. *Required fees:* $3200; $336 per course. Full-time tuition and fees vary according to degree level, program and student level. Part-time tuition and fees vary according to course load, degree level and program.
Website: http://www.sas.upenn.edu/nelc/grad_programs/grad_programs.html

**University of South Africa,** College of Human Sciences, Pretoria, South Africa. Offers adult education (M Ed); African languages (MA, PhD); African politics (MA, PhD); Afrikaans (MA, PhD); ancient history (MA, PhD); ancient Near Eastern studies (MA, PhD); anthropology (MA, PhD); applied linguistics (MA); Arabic (MA, PhD); archaeology (MA); art history (MA); Biblical archaeology (MA); Biblical studies (M Th, D Th, PhD); Christian spirituality (M Th, D Th); church history (M Th, D Th); classical studies (MA, PhD); clinical psychology (MA); communication (MA, PhD); comparative education (M Ed, Ed D); consulting psychology (D Admin, D Com, PhD); curriculum studies (M Ed, Ed D); development studies (M Admin, MA, D Admin, PhD); didactics (M Ed, Ed D); education (M Tech); education management (M Ed, Ed D); educational psychology (M Ed); English (MA); environmental education (M Ed); French (MA, PhD); German (MA, PhD); Greek (MA); guidance and counseling (M Ed); health studies (MA, PhD), including health sciences education (MA), health services management (MA), medical and surgical nursing science (critical care general) (MA), midwifery and neonatal nursing science (MA), trauma and emergency care (MA); history (MA, PhD); history of education (Ed D); inclusive education (M Ed, Ed D); information and communications technology policy and regulation (MA); information science (MA, MIS, PhD); international politics (MA, PhD); Islamic studies (MA, PhD); Italian (MA, PhD); Judaica (MA, PhD); linguistics (MA, PhD); mathematical education (M Ed); mathematics education (MA); missiology (M Th, D Th); modern Hebrew (MA, PhD); musicology (MA, MMus, D Mus, PhD); natural science education (M Ed); New Testament (M Th, D Th); Old Testament (D Th); pastoral therapy (M Th, D Th); philosophy (MA); philosophy of education (M Ed, Ed D); politics (MA, PhD); Portuguese (MA, PhD); practical theology (M Th, D Th); psychology (MA, MS, PhD); psychology of education (M Ed, Ed D); public health (MA); religious studies (MA, D Th, PhD); Romance languages (MA); Russian (MA, PhD); Semitic languages (MA, PhD); social behavior studies in HIV/AIDS (MA); social science (mental health) (MA); social science in development studies (MA); social science in psychology (MA); social science in social work (MA); social science in sociology (MA); social work (MSW, DSW, PhD); socio-education (M Ed, Ed D); sociolinguistics (MA); sociology (MA, PhD); Spanish (MA, PhD); systematic theology (M Th, D Th); TESOL (teaching English to speakers of other languages) (MA); theological ethics (M Th, D Th); theory of literature (MA, PhD); urban ministries (D Th); urban ministry (M Th).

**The University of Texas at Austin,** Graduate School, College of Liberal Arts, Department of Middle Eastern Studies, Austin, TX 78712-1111. Offers Middle Eastern languages and cultures (MA, PhD); Middle Eastern studies (MA); JD/MA; MA/M Sc; MA/MA; MBA/MA; MPA/MA. *Degree requirements:* For master's, one foreign language, comprehensive exam, thesis; for doctorate, 2 foreign languages, comprehensive exam, thesis/dissertation. *Entrance requirements:* For master's and doctorate, GRE General Test. Additional exam requirements/recommendations for international students: Required—TOEFL. Electronic applications accepted. *Faculty research:* Islamic studies, Persian language and literature, Hebrew language, Jewish studies, Arabic literature and language.

**University of Toronto,** School of Graduate Studies, Faculty of Arts and Science, Department of Near and Middle Eastern Civilizations, Toronto, ON M5S 1A1, Canada. Offers MA, PhD. *Program availability:* Part-time. *Degree requirements:* For master's, thesis optional; for doctorate, 2 foreign languages, thesis/dissertation, language proficiency exams. *Entrance requirements:* For master's, BA in relevant area, minimum B+ average in final year, prior coursework in ancient Near Eastern or Islamic civilizations, 2 letters of reference; for doctorate, MA in relevant area with a minimum A-average, 2 letters of reference. Additional exam requirements/recommendations for international students: Required—TOEFL (minimum score 580 paper-based; 93 iBT), TWE (minimum score 5). Electronic applications accepted.

**University of Utah,** Graduate School, College of Humanities, Program in Middle East Studies, Salt Lake City, UT 84112. Offers Arabic (MA, PhD); Hebrew (MA); history (MA, PhD); Persian (MA, PhD); political science (MA, PhD). *Students:* 3 part-time (2 women); includes 1 minority (Asian, non-Hispanic/Latino), 1 international. In 2016, 2 master's awarded. Terminal master's awarded for partial completion of doctoral program. *Degree requirements:* For master's, 2 foreign languages, comprehensive exam, thesis optional; for doctorate, 3 foreign languages, comprehensive exam, thesis/dissertation. *Entrance requirements:* For master's, GRE General Test, minimum GPA of 3.2; for doctorate, GRE General Test, MA in Middle East studies or equivalent, minimum GPA of 3.2. Additional exam requirements/recommendations for international students: Required—TOEFL (minimum score 580 paper-based; 92 iBT); Recommended—IELTS (minimum score 7). *Application deadline:* For fall admission, 1/15 priority date for domestic and international students. Application fee: $55 ($65 for international students). Electronic applications accepted. *Expenses:* Tuition, state resident: full-time $7011; part-time $3918.24 per credit hour. Tuition, nonresident: full-time $22,154; part-time $11,665.42 per credit hour. *Financial support:* In 2016–17, 5 students received support, including 2 teaching assistantships with full tuition reimbursements available (averaging $13,500 per year); fellowships and unspecified assistantships also available. Financial award application deadline: 1/15. *Faculty research:* Islamic studies; Middle Eastern history; political science; Judaic studies; anthropology; Arabic, Persian, Hebrew, and Turkish language and literature. *Unit head:* Johanna Watzinger-Tharp, Director, 801-581-7148, Fax: 801-581-6105, E-mail: j.tharp@utah.edu. *Application contact:* Kellie Hubbard, Academic Advisor, 801-581-5362, Fax: 801-581-6105, E-mail: kellie.hubbard@utah.edu.
Website: http://www.mec.utah.edu

**University of Virginia,** College and Graduate School of Arts and Sciences, Department of Middle Eastern and South Asian Languages and Cultures, Charlottesville, VA 22903. Offers Middle Eastern and South Asian studies (MA). *Faculty:* 16 full-time (8 women). *Students:* 11 full-time (6 women), 2 part-time (0 women); includes 1 minority (Hispanic/Latino), 1 international. Average age 31. 19 applicants, 89% accepted, 6 enrolled. In 2016, 3 master's awarded. Application fee: $60. *Expenses:* Tuition, state resident: full-time $15,026; part-time $834 per credit hour. Tuition, nonresident: full-time $25,168; part-time $1378 per credit hour. *Required fees:* $2654. *Unit head:* Farzaneh Milani, Chair, 434-243-4930, Fax: 434-243-1528, E-mail: fmm2z@virginia.edu. *Application contact:* Robert Hueckstedt, Director of Graduate Studies, 434-243-8228, Fax: 434-243-1528, E-mail: rah2k@virginia.edu. Website: http://mesalc.virginia.edu/

**University of Washington,** Graduate School, College of Arts and Sciences, Department of Near Eastern Languages and Civilization, Seattle, WA 98195. Offers MA. *Degree requirements:* For master's, 2 foreign languages, exams. *Entrance requirements:* For master's, GRE, minimum GPA of 3.0. Additional exam requirements/recommendations for international students: Required—TOEFL. Electronic applications accepted. *Faculty research:* Arabic, Hebrew, Persian, and Turkish literature; Islamic civilization and religion; Central Asian Turkic language and literature; Hebrew Bible and ancient Near East; ancient Christianity.

**University of Washington,** Graduate School, College of Arts and Sciences, Henry M. Jackson School of International Studies, Middle East Studies Program, Seattle, WA 98195. Offers MAIS. *Degree requirements:* For master's, one foreign language, thesis optional. *Entrance requirements:* For master's, GRE General Test, minimum GPA of 3.0 in last two years. Additional exam requirements/recommendations for international students: Required—TOEFL (minimum score 500 paper-based; 92 iBT), IELTS (minimum score 7). Electronic applications accepted.

**University of Washington,** Graduate School, Interdisciplinary Program in Near and Middle Eastern Studies, Seattle, WA 98195. Offers PhD. *Degree requirements:* For doctorate, 3 foreign languages, thesis/dissertation. *Entrance requirements:* For doctorate, GRE General Test, minimum GPA of 3.0. Additional exam requirements/recommendations for international students: Required—TOEFL. Electronic applications accepted.

**University of Waterloo,** Graduate Studies, Faculty of Arts, Department of Classical Studies, Waterloo, ON N2L 3G1, Canada. Offers ancient Mediterranean cultures (MA). *Degree requirements:* For master's, one foreign language. *Faculty research:* Ancient history, philosophy, anthropology, religion, culture.

**University of Wisconsin–Madison,** Graduate School, College of Letters and Science, Department of History, Madison, WI 53706-1380. Offers African history (MA, PhD); Central Asian history (MA, PhD); comparative world history (MA, PhD); East Asian history (MA, PhD); European history (MA, PhD); gender and women's history (MA, PhD); Latin American and Caribbean history (MA, PhD); Middle Eastern history (MA, PhD); South Asian history (MA, PhD); Southeast Asian history (MA, PhD); United States history (MA, PhD). Terminal master's awarded for partial completion of doctoral program. *Degree requirements:* For master's, thesis (for some programs); for doctorate, variable foreign language requirement, thesis/dissertation. *Entrance requirements:* For master's and doctorate, GRE General Test. Additional exam requirements/recommendations for international students: Required—Michigan English Language Assessment Battery or TOEFL. Electronic applications accepted. *Faculty research:* American, African, European, Asian, Latin American, and Middle Eastern history.

**Washington University in St. Louis,** The Graduate School, Department of Jewish, Islamic, and Near Eastern Languages and Cultures, St. Louis, MO 63130-4899. Offers Islamic and Near Eastern studies (MA); Jewish studies (MA). *Degree requirements:* For master's, one foreign language, thesis (for some programs). *Entrance requirements:* For master's, GRE General Test. Additional exam requirements/recommendations for international students: Required—TOEFL. Electronic applications accepted. *Faculty research:* Islamic and Near Eastern studies (Islamic history; Arabic language and literature, modern Middle East history); Jewish studies (Hebrew Bible, Rabbinic literature, Jewish history, modern Hebrew literature).

**Wayne State University,** College of Liberal Arts and Sciences, Department of Classical and Modern Languages, Literatures, and Cultures, Detroit, MI 48202. Offers classics (MA), including ancient Greek and Latin, ancient studies, classics, Latin; German (MA); language learning (MALL), including Arabic (MA, MALL), French (MA, MALL, PhD), German (MALL, PhD), Italian (MA, MALL), Spanish (MA, MALL, PhD); modern languages (PhD), including French (MA, MALL, PhD), German (MALL, PhD), Spanish (MA, MALL, PhD); Near Eastern languages (MA), including Arabic (MA, MALL), Hebrew; Romance languages (MA), including French (MA, MALL, PhD), Italian (MA, MALL), Spanish (MA, MALL, PhD). *Faculty:* 26. *Students:* 25 full-time (20 women), 14 part-time (8 women); includes 7 minority (2 Black or African American, non-Hispanic/Latino; 1 American Indian or Alaska Native, non-Hispanic/Latino; 1 Asian, non-Hispanic/Latino; 2 Hispanic/Latino; 1 Two or more races, non-Hispanic/Latino), 3 international. Average age 35. 29 applicants, 31% accepted, 5 enrolled. In 2016, 15 master's, 5 doctorates awarded. *Degree requirements:* For master's, variable foreign language requirement, comprehensive exam (for some programs), thesis (for some programs); for doctorate, one foreign language, comprehensive exam, thesis/dissertation. *Entrance requirements:* For master's, GRE (for some programs); for doctorate, GRE. Additional exam requirements/recommendations for international students: Required—TOEFL (minimum score 550 paper-based; 79 iBT), TWE (minimum score 5.5), Michigan English Language Assessment Battery (minimum score 85); Recommended—IELTS (minimum score 6.5). Application fee: $50. Electronic applications accepted. *Expenses:* $16,503 per year resident tuition and fees, $33,697 per year non-resident tuition and fees. *Financial support:* In 2016–17, 22 students received support, including 4 fellowships with tuition reimbursements available (averaging $13,500 per year), 17 teaching assistantships with tuition reimbursements available (averaging $17,994 per year); research assistantships, scholarships/grants, and unspecified assistantships also available. Financial award applicants required to submit FAFSA. *Faculty research:* Classical and modern literature and culture (Greek, Latin, Arabic, Chinese, French, German, Russian, Spanish) including colonial studies and exile and Holocaust studies; critical theory (French, German, Slavic, Spanish); theoretical and applied linguistics (Arabic, Chinese, French, Spanish); area studies (Arabic, Near Eastern, classical, Islamic, and Judaic studies). *Unit head:* Dr. Anne Duggan, Department Chair, 313-577-6244, Fax: 313-577-6243, E-mail: a.duggan@wayne.edu. Website: http://clas.wayne.edu/languages/

**Yale University,** Graduate School of Arts and Sciences, Department of Near Eastern Languages and Civilizations, New Haven, CT 06520. Offers Arabic and Islamic studies (MA, PhD); archaeology of the ancient Near East (MA, PhD); Assyriology (MA, PhD); Egyptology (MA, PhD); Graeco-Arabic studies (MA, PhD); Northwest Semitic, Bible, comparative Semitics (MA, PhD). *Degree requirements:* For doctorate, 2 foreign languages, thesis/dissertation. *Entrance requirements:* For doctorate, GRE General Test.

# Northern Studies

**University of Alaska Fairbanks,** College of Liberal Arts, Department of Arctic and Northern Studies, Fairbanks, AK 99775-6460. Offers Arctic policy (MA); environmental politics and policy (MA); Northern history (MA). *Program availability:* Part-time. *Students:* 13 full-time (9 women), 15 part-time (11 women); includes 2 minority (1 American Indian or Alaska Native, non-Hispanic/Latino; 1 Two or more races, non-Hispanic/Latino), 5 international. Average age 35. 7 applicants, 43% accepted, 1 enrolled. In 2016, 8 master's awarded. *Degree requirements:* For master's, comprehensive exam, oral defense of project or thesis. *Entrance requirements:* For master's, bachelor's degree from accredited institution with minimum cumulative undergraduate and major GPA of 3.0. Additional exam requirements/recommendations for international students: Required—TOEFL (minimum score 550 paper-based; 79 iBT), IELTS (minimum score 6.5). *Application deadline:* For fall admission, 6/1 for domestic students, 3/1 for international students; for spring admission, 10/15 for domestic students, 9/1 for international students. Applications are processed on a rolling basis. Application fee: $60. Electronic applications accepted. *Expenses:* Tuition, state resident: full-time $7992; part-time $444 per credit. Tuition, nonresident: full-time $16,326; part-time $907 per credit. *Required fees:* $39 per credit. $322 per semester. Tuition and fees vary according to course level, course load, campus/location, program and reciprocity agreements. *Financial support:* In 2016–17, 1 research assistantship with full tuition reimbursement (averaging $7,574 per year), 9 teaching assistantships with full tuition reimbursements (averaging $5,653 per year) were awarded; fellowships with full tuition reimbursements, career-related internships or fieldwork, Federal Work-Study, scholarships/grants, health care benefits, and unspecified assistantships also available. Support available to part-time students. Financial award application deadline: 1/1; financial award applicants required to submit FAFSA. *Total annual research expenditures:* $64,000. *Unit head:* Mary Ehrlander, Director, 907-474-7126, Fax: 907-474-5817, E-mail: fynors@uaf.edu. *Application contact:* Mary Kreta, Director of Admissions, 907-474-7500, Fax: 907-474-7097, E-mail: admissions@uaf.edu. Website: http://www.uaf.edu/northern/

**University of Manitoba,** Faculty of Graduate Studies, Faculty of Arts, Department of Icelandic Language and Literature, Winnipeg, MB R3T 2N2, Canada. Offers MA.

# Pacific Area/Pacific Rim Studies

**The University of British Columbia,** Institute of Asian Research, Vancouver, BC V6T 1Z2, Canada. Offers Asia Pacific policy studies (MAAPPS); public policy and global affairs (MPPGA). *Degree requirements:* For master's, thesis optional. *Entrance requirements:* Additional exam requirements/recommendations for international students: Required—TOEFL. Application fee: $100 ($162 for international students). Electronic applications accepted. *Expenses:* $26,842 per year tuition and fees, $42,648 per year international. *Financial support:* Fellowships with tuition reimbursements, research assistantships, career-related internships or fieldwork, institutionally sponsored loans, scholarships/grants, and tuition waivers (partial) available. *Faculty research:* Social cohesion, globalization, social safety nets, policy research, research and development alliances, knowledge-based workshops on Asia-Pacific studies. *Application contact:* Kerry Ross, Graduate Program Staff, 604-822-4571, E-mail: mppga.program@ubc.ca. Website: http://iar.ubc.ca/

**University of Guam,** Office of Graduate Studies, College of Liberal Arts and Social Sciences, Micronesian Studies Program, Mangilao, GU 96923. Offers MA. *Degree requirements:* For master's, thesis. *Entrance requirements:* For master's, GRE General Test. Additional exam requirements/recommendations for international students: Required—TOEFL. *Faculty research:* Adolescent suicide in Micronesia, history of Micronesia, traditional agriculture in the Pacific, Micronesian languages, health and cultural practices.

**University of Hawaii at Manoa,** Graduate Division, School of Pacific and Asian Studies, Program in Pacific Island Studies, Honolulu, HI 96822. Offers MA, Graduate Certificate. *Program availability:* Part-time. *Degree requirements:* For master's, thesis optional. *Entrance requirements:* Additional exam requirements/recommendations for international students: Required—TOEFL (minimum score 580 paper-based; 92 iBT), IELTS (minimum score 5).

**University of San Francisco,** College of Arts and Sciences, Program in Asia Pacific Studies, San Francisco, CA 94117-1080. Offers MA, MA/MBA. *Program availability:* Part-time, evening/weekend. *Faculty:* 3 full-time (all women), 9 part-time/adjunct (5 women). *Students:* 45 full-time (21 women), 2 part-time (both women); includes 16 minority (9 Asian, non-Hispanic/Latino; 4 Hispanic/Latino; 3 Two or more races, non-Hispanic/Latino), 18 international. Average age 28. 45 applicants, 87% accepted, 28 enrolled. In 2016, 19 master's awarded. *Degree requirements:* For master's, one foreign language, thesis. *Entrance requirements:* For master's, minimum GPA of 3.0. Additional exam requirements/recommendations for international students: Required—TOEFL, IELTS, PTE. *Application deadline:* For fall admission, 4/1 for domestic and international students. Applications are processed on a rolling basis. Application fee: $55 ($65 for international students). Electronic applications accepted. *Expenses: Tuition:* Full-time $23,310; part-time $1295 per credit. Tuition and fees vary according to course load, degree level, campus/location and program. *Financial support:* In 2016–17, 31 students received support. Career-related internships or fieldwork, Federal Work-Study, and institutionally sponsored loans available. Financial award application deadline: 3/2; financial award applicants required to submit FAFSA. *Faculty research:* History of Christianity in China, U.S.-China policy, East Asian economies and political systems, sociolinguistic aspects of Japanese. *Unit head:* Dr. Brian Komei Dempster, Director, 415-422-6357, Fax: 415-422-5933. *Application contact:* Mark Landerghini, Information Contact, 415-422-5101, Fax: 415-422-2217, E-mail: asgraduate@usfca.edu. Website: https://www.usfca.edu/arts-sciences/graduate-programs/asia-pacific-studies

**University of Victoria,** Faculty of Graduate Studies, Faculty of Humanities, Department of Pacific and Asian Studies, Victoria, BC V8W 2Y2, Canada. Offers MA. *Degree requirements:* For master's, thesis. *Entrance requirements:* For master's, minimum B+ average, writing sample. Additional exam requirements/recommendations for international students: Required—TOEFL (minimum score 575 paper-based), IELTS (minimum score 7). Electronic applications accepted. *Faculty research:* Culture, ethnicity and identity; economy and society; gender studies; languages and linguistics; literature.

# Western European Studies

**American Public University System,** AMU/APU Graduate Programs, Charles Town, WV 25414. Offers accounting (MBA, MS); applied business analytics (MBA, MS); criminal justice (MA), including business administration, emergency and disaster management, general (MA, MS); educational leadership (M Ed); emergency and disaster management (MA); entrepreneurship (MBA); environmental policy and management (MS), including environmental planning, environmental sustainability, fish and wildlife management, general (MA, MS), global environmental management; finance (MBA); general (MBA); government contracting and acquisition (MBA); health care administration (MBA); health information management (MS); history (MA), including American history, ancient and classical history, European history, global history, public history; homeland security (MA), including business administration, counterterrorism studies, criminal justice, cyber, emergency management and public health, intelligence studies, transportation security; homeland security resource allocation (MBA); humanities (MA); information technology (MS), including digital forensics, enterprise software development, information assurance and security, IT project management; information technology management (MBA); intelligence studies (MA), including criminal intelligence, cyber, general (MA, MS), homeland security, intelligence analysis, intelligence collection, intelligence management, intelligence operations, terrorism studies; international relations and conflict resolution (MA), including comparative and security issues, conflict resolution, international and transnational security issues, peacekeeping; legal studies (MA); management (MA), including strategic consulting; marketing (MBA); military history (MA), including American military history, American Revolution, civil war, war since 1945, World War II; military studies (MA), including joint warfare, strategic leadership; national security studies (MA), including cyber, general (MA, MS), homeland security, regional security studies, security and intelligence analysis, terrorism studies; nonprofit management (MBA); political science (MA), including American politics and government, comparative government and development, general (MA, MS), international relations, public policy; psychology (MA); public administration (MPA), including disaster management, environmental policy, health policy, human resources, national security, organizational management, security management; public health (MPH); reverse logistics management (MA); security management (MA); space studies (MS), including aerospace science, general (MA, MS), planetary science; sports and health sciences (MS); sports management (MBA); teaching (M Ed), including autism spectrum disorder, curriculum and instruction for elementary teachers, elementary reading, English language learners, instructional leadership, online learning, special education, STEAM (STEM plus the arts); transportation and logistics management (MA). *Program availability:* Part-time, evening/weekend, online only, 100% online. *Faculty:* 401 full-time (228 women), 1,678 part-time/adjunct (781 women). *Students:* 378 full-time (184 women), 8,455 part-time (3,484 women); includes 2,972 minority (1,552 Black or African American, non-Hispanic/Latino; 52 American Indian or Alaska Native, non-Hispanic/Latino; 211 Asian, non-Hispanic/Latino; 791 Hispanic/Latino; 70 Native Hawaiian or other Pacific Islander, non-Hispanic/Latino; 296 Two or more races, non-Hispanic/Latino), 109 international. Average age 37. In 2016, 3,185 master's awarded. *Degree requirements:* For master's, comprehensive exam or practicum. *Entrance requirements:* For master's, official transcript showing earned bachelor's degree from institution accredited by recognized accrediting body. Additional exam requirements/recommendations for international students: Required—TOEFL (minimum score 550 paper-based), IELTS (minimum score 6.5). *Application deadline:* Applications are processed on a rolling basis. Application fee: $0. Electronic applications accepted. *Expenses: Tuition:* Part-time $350 per credit hour. *Required fees:* $50 per course. *Financial support:* Scholarships/grants available. Financial award applicants required to submit FAFSA. *Unit head:* Dr. Karan Powell, President, 877-468-6268, Fax: 304-724-3780. *Application contact:* Terry Grant, Vice President of Enrollment Management, 877-468-6268, Fax: 304-724-3780, E-mail: info@apus.edu.
Website: http://www.apus.edu

**American University,** School of International Service, Washington, DC 20016-8071. Offers comparative and regional studies (Certificate); cross-cultural communication (Certificate); development management (MS); ethics, peace, and global affairs (MA); European studies (Certificate); global environmental policy (MA, Certificate); global information technology (Certificate); international affairs (MA), including comparative and international disability policy, comparative and regional studies, international economic relations, international politics, natural resources and sustainable development, U.S. foreign policy; international arts management (Certificate); international communication (MA, Certificate); international development (MA); international economic policy (Certificate); international economic relations (Certificate); international economics (MA); international media (MA); international peace and conflict resolution (MA, Certificate); international politics (Certificate); international relations (MA, PhD); international service (MIS); peacebuilding (Certificate); social enterprise (MA); the Americas (Certificate); United States foreign policy (Certificate); JD/MA. *Program availability:* Part-time, evening/weekend, 100% online. *Faculty:* 116 full-time (53 women), 57 part-time/adjunct (19 women). *Students:* 575 full-time (360 women), 491 part-time (277 women); includes 287 minority (100 Black or African American, non-Hispanic/Latino; 6 American Indian or Alaska Native, non-Hispanic/Latino; 58 Asian, non-Hispanic/Latino; 92 Hispanic/Latino; 1 Native Hawaiian or other Pacific Islander, non-Hispanic/Latino; 30 Two or more races, non-Hispanic/Latino), 151 international. Average age 29. 1,504 applicants, 84% accepted, 403 enrolled. In 2016, 374 master's, 3 doctorates, 1 other advanced degree awarded. Terminal master's awarded for partial completion of doctoral program. *Degree requirements:* For master's, one foreign language, comprehensive exam, thesis or alternative; for doctorate, one foreign language, comprehensive exam, thesis/dissertation. *Entrance requirements:* For master's, GRE; GMAT or GRE (for MA in social enterprise), transcripts, resume, 2 letters of recommendation, statement of purpose; for doctorate, GRE, transcripts, resume, 3 letters of recommendation, statement of purpose. Additional exam requirements/recommendations for international students: Required—TOEFL (minimum score 600 paper-based, 100 iBT), IELTS (minimum score 7 ), or PTE (minimum score of 68). Application fee: $55. Electronic applications accepted. *Expenses:* $1,579 per credit tuition; $1,930 mandatory fees. *Financial support:* Research assistantships, teaching assistantships, institutionally sponsored loans, scholarships/grants, and unspecified assistantships available. Financial award application deadline: 1/15; financial award applicants required to submit FAFSA. *Unit head:* Dr. James Goldgeier, Dean, 202-885-1603, Fax: 202-885-2494, E-mail: goldgeier@american.edu. *Application contact:* Jia Jiang, Associate Director, Graduate Education Enrollment, 202-885-1689, Fax: 202-885-1109, E-mail: jiang@american.edu.
Website: http://www.american.edu/sis/

**Armstrong State University,** School of Graduate Studies, Program in History, Savannah, GA 31419-1997. Offers American and European history (MA); public history (MA). *Program availability:* Part-time, evening/weekend. *Faculty:* 6 full-time (1 woman), 1 (woman) part-time/adjunct. *Students:* 5 full-time (3 women), 11 part-time (4 women);

includes 2 minority (1 Black or African American, non-Hispanic/Latino; 1 Hispanic/Latino). Average age 37. 17 applicants, 71% accepted, 8 enrolled. In 2016, 3 master's awarded. *Degree requirements:* For master's, one foreign language, comprehensive exam (for some programs), thesis (for some programs), thesis, internship, or advanced fieldwork. *Entrance requirements:* For master's, GRE General Test, minimum GPA of 3.0, letters of recommendation, BA in history or equivalent. Additional exam requirements/recommendations for international students: Required—TOEFL (minimum score 523 paper-based; 70 iBT). *Application deadline:* For fall admission, 6/30 priority date for domestic students, 5/1 priority date for international students; for spring admission, 11/15 priority date for domestic students, 9/15 priority date for international students; for summer admission, 4/15 priority date for domestic students, 9/15 for international students. Applications are processed on a rolling basis. Application fee: $30. Electronic applications accepted. *Expenses:* Tuition, state resident: full-time $1781; part-time $161.93 per credit hour. Tuition, nonresident: full-time $6482; part-time $589.27 per credit hour. *Required fees:* $1224 per unit. $612 per semester. Tuition and fees vary according to course load, campus/location and program. *Financial support:* In 2016–17, research assistantships with full tuition reimbursements (averaging $5,000 per year) were awarded; career-related internships or fieldwork, Federal Work-Study, and unspecified assistantships also available. Support available to part-time students. Financial award application deadline: 3/15; financial award applicants required to submit FAFSA. *Faculty research:* Public history; European, Latin American, African, and United States history. *Unit head:* Dr. Christopher Hendricks, Interim Department Head, 912-344-2725, Fax: 912-344-3451, E-mail: chris.hendricks@armstrong.edu. *Application contact:* McKenzie Peterman, Assistant Director of Graduate Admissions, 912-344-2503, Fax: 912-344-3417, E-mail: graduate@armstrong.edu.
Website: http://www.armstrong.edu/Liberal_Arts/history/history_graduate_program

**Boston College,** Graduate School of Arts and Sciences, Department of History, Chestnut Hill, MA 02467-3800. Offers European national studies (MA); history (MA, PhD); medieval studies (MA). *Faculty:* 44 full-time. *Students:* 56 full-time (24 women); includes 6 minority (1 Black or African American, non-Hispanic/Latino; 3 Hispanic/Latino; 2 Two or more races, non-Hispanic/Latino), 3 international. 162 applicants, 34% accepted, 16 enrolled. In 2016, 12 master's, 6 doctorates awarded. Terminal master's awarded for partial completion of doctoral program. *Degree requirements:* For master's, one foreign language, comprehensive exam, thesis optional; for doctorate, 2 foreign languages, comprehensive exam, thesis/dissertation. *Entrance requirements:* For master's and doctorate, GRE General Test, writing sample. Additional exam requirements/recommendations for international students: Required—TOEFL (minimum score 600 paper-based; 100 iBT), IELTS (minimum score 8). *Application deadline:* For fall admission, 1/2 for domestic and international students. Application fee: $75. Electronic applications accepted. Tuition and fees vary according to program. *Financial support:* In 2016–17, fellowships with full tuition reimbursements (averaging $21,400 per year), teaching assistantships with full tuition reimbursements (averaging $21,400 per year) were awarded; Federal Work-Study, scholarships/grants, health care benefits, and unspecified assistantships also available. Support available to part-time students. Financial award application deadline: 3/1; financial award applicants required to submit FAFSA. *Faculty research:* U.S. history, medieval history, early modern European history, modern European history, British and Irish history, Latin American history, Asian history, Middle eastern history, international and global history, transnational history. *Unit head:* Dr. Kevin Kenny, Chairperson, 617-552-1196, E-mail: kevin.kenny@bc.edu. *Application contact:* Dr. Prasannan Pathasarathi, Director of Graduate Studies, 617-552-3781, E-mail: pathasa@bc.edu.
Website: http://www.bc.edu/history

**Brown University,** Graduate School, Department of Portuguese and Brazilian Studies, Providence, RI 02912. Offers Brazilian studies (AM); English as a second language and cross-cultural studies (AM); Portuguese and Brazilian studies (AM, PhD); Portuguese bilingual education and cross-cultural studies (AM). *Degree requirements:* For doctorate, thesis/dissertation.

**Carleton University,** Faculty of Graduate Studies, Faculty of Public Affairs and Management, Institute of European and Russian Studies, Ottawa, ON K1S 5B6, Canada. Offers European and European Union studies (MA); European integration studies (Diploma); Russian, Eurasian and transition studies (MA). *Degree requirements:* For master's, one foreign language, thesis optional. *Entrance requirements:* For master's, honors degree or equivalent; 2 years of Russian, German or other central east European language. Additional exam requirements/recommendations for international students: Required—TOEFL. *Faculty research:* East-West relations, minority rights in Russia and Eastern Europe.

**The Catholic University of America,** School of Arts and Sciences, Department of History, Washington, DC 20064. Offers history (MA, PhD), including early modern Europe, Latin America (MA), Medieval, modern Europe, U.S.; religion and society in the late medieval and early modern world (MA); MA/JD; MSLS/MA. *Program availability:* Part-time. *Faculty:* 14 full-time (6 women), 3 part-time/adjunct (2 women). *Students:* 7 full-time (2 women), 20 part-time (6 women); includes 3 minority (all Two or more races, non-Hispanic/Latino), 2 international. Average age 30. 22 applicants, 45% accepted, 4 enrolled. In 2016, 4 master's, 5 doctorates awarded. Terminal master's awarded for partial completion of doctoral program. *Degree requirements:* For master's, one foreign language, comprehensive exam, thesis optional, 2 languages (for medievalists), one of which must be Latin; for doctorate, 2 foreign languages, comprehensive exam, thesis/dissertation, 3 languages (for medievalists), one of which must be Latin. *Entrance requirements:* For master's and doctorate, GRE General Test, statement of purpose, official copies of academic transcripts, three letters of recommendation, writing sample. Additional exam requirements/recommendations for international students: Required—TOEFL (minimum score 550 paper-based; 80 iBT). *Application deadline:* For fall admission, 7/15 priority date for domestic students, 7/1 for international students; for spring admission, 11/15 priority date for domestic students, 11/1 for international students. Applications are processed on a rolling basis. Application fee: $55. Electronic applications accepted. *Expenses:* $42,850 per year; $1,170 per credit; $200 per semester part-time fees. *Financial support:* Fellowships, research assistantships, teaching assistantships, Federal Work-Study, scholarships/grants, tuition waivers (full and partial), and unspecified assistantships available. Financial award application deadline: 2/1; financial award applicants required to submit FAFSA. *Faculty research:* Medieval history, including the Islamic Middle East, with particular expertise in later medieval religious, social, and economic history and early medieval and late antique history; European and American intellectual history; renaissance, reformation, catholic reformation; US catholic history; history of immigration. *Total annual research expenditures:* $42,594. *Unit head:* Dr. Katherine Jansen, Chair, 202-319-5484, Fax: 202-319-5569, E-mail: jansen@cua.edu. *Application contact:* Director of Graduate

Admissions, 202-319-5057, Fax: 202-319-6533, E-mail: cua-admissions@cua.edu. Website: http://history.cua.edu/

**Central Michigan University,** College of Graduate Studies, College of Humanities and Social and Behavioral Sciences, Department of History, Mount Pleasant, MI 48859. Offers European history (Graduate Certificate); history (MA); modern history (Graduate Certificate); United States history (Graduate Certificate); MA/PhD. *Program availability:* Part-time. *Degree requirements:* For master's, thesis or alternative. Electronic applications accepted. *Faculty research:* Colonial and revolutionary United States history, modern European history, Latin American and transatlantic history, transnational and comparative history, United States social history.

**Claremont Graduate University,** Graduate Programs, School of Arts and Humanities, Department of History, Claremont, CA 91711-6160. Offers Africana history (Certificate); American studies and U.S. history (MA, PhD); archival studies (MA); early modern studies (MA, PhD); European studies (MA, PhD); oral history (MA, PhD); MBA/MA; MBA/PhD. *Faculty:* 5 full-time (3 women), 2 part-time/adjunct (0 women). *Students:* 45 full-time (23 women), 24 part-time (14 women); includes 21 minority (2 Black or African American, non-Hispanic/Latino; 1 American Indian or Alaska Native, non-Hispanic/Latino; 5 Asian, non-Hispanic/Latino; 6 Hispanic/Latino; 1 Native Hawaiian or other Pacific Islander, non-Hispanic/Latino; 6 Two or more races, non-Hispanic/Latino). Average age 38. In 2016, 5 master's, 2 doctorates awarded. Terminal master's awarded for partial completion of doctoral program. *Entrance requirements:* For master's and doctorate, GRE General Test. Additional exam requirements/recommendations for international students: Required—TOEFL (minimum score 75 iBT). *Application deadline:* For fall admission, 2/1 priority date for domestic and international students. Applications are processed on a rolling basis. Application fee: $80. Electronic applications accepted. *Expenses: Tuition:* Full-time $44,328; part-time $1847 per unit. *Required fees:* $600; $300 per semester. Tuition and fees vary according to course load and program. *Financial support:* Fellowships, research assistantships, Federal Work-Study, institutionally sponsored loans, and scholarships/grants available. Support available to part-time students. Financial award application deadline: 2/15; financial award applicants required to submit FAFSA. *Faculty research:* Intellectual and social history, cultural studies, gender studies, Western history, Chicano history. *Unit head:* Joshua Goode, Chair, 909-607-7430, E-mail: joshua.goode@cgu.edu. *Application contact:* Amy Sandefur, Assistant Director of Admissions, 909-607-9101, E-mail: amy.sandefur@cgu.edu.
Website: https://www.cgu.edu/departments/history/

**College of Staten Island of the City University of New York,** Graduate Programs, Division of Humanities and Social Sciences, Program in History, Staten Island, NY 10314-6600. Offers history of Africa and the Middle East (MA); history of Asia (MA); history of Europe (MA); history of Latin America and the Caribbean (MA); history of the United States (MA). *Program availability:* Part-time, evening/weekend. *Faculty:* 2 full-time. *Students:* 11 part-time. Average age 36. 8 applicants, 25% accepted, 2 enrolled. In 2016, 5 master's awarded. *Degree requirements:* For master's, comprehensive exam (for some programs), 32 credits (total of eight courses); thesis or portfolio. *Entrance requirements:* For master's, bachelor's degree with minimum GPA of 3.0 overall and in undergraduate history courses, two letters of recommendation, letter of interest, research-based writing sample. Additional exam requirements/recommendations for international students: Required—TOEFL (minimum score 550 paper-based; 79 iBT), IELTS (minimum score 6.5). *Application deadline:* For fall admission, 5/10 priority date for domestic and international students; for spring admission, 12/2 priority date for domestic and international students. Applications are processed on a rolling basis. Application fee: $125. Electronic applications accepted. *Expenses:* Tuition, state resident: full-time $10,130; part-time $425 per credit. Tuition, nonresident: full-time $18,720; part-time $780 per credit. *Required fees:* $181.10 per semester. Tuition and fees vary according to program. *Faculty research:* African and African diaspora history, South Asian history, Middle Eastern history, U.S. history, environmental history. *Unit head:* John Dixon, Graduate Program Coordinator, 718-982-3307, E-mail: john.dixon@csi.cuny.edu. *Application contact:* Sasha Spence, Associate Director for Graduate Admissions, 718-982-2019, Fax: 718-982-2500, E-mail: sasha.spence@csi.cuny.edu.
Website: http://www.csi.cuny.edu/catalog/graduate/master-of-arts-in-history-ma.htm

**Columbia University,** Graduate School of Arts and Sciences, New York, NY 10027. Offers African-American studies (MA); American studies (MA); anthropology (MA, PhD); art history and archaeology (MA, PhD); astronomy (PhD); biological sciences (PhD); biotechnology (MA); chemical physics (PhD); chemistry (PhD); classical studies (MA, PhD); classics (MA, PhD); climate and society (MA); conservation biology (MA); earth and environmental sciences (PhD); East Asia: regional studies (MA); East Asian languages and cultures (MA, PhD); ecology, evolution and environmental biology (MA), including conservation biology; ecology, evolution, and environmental biology (PhD), including ecology and evolutionary biology, evolutionary primatology; economics (MA, PhD); English and comparative literature (MA, PhD); French and Romance philology (MA, PhD); Germanic languages (MA, PhD); global French studies (MA); global thought (MA); Hispanic cultural studies (MA); history (PhD); history and literature (MA); human rights studies (MA); Islamic studies (MA); Italian (MA, PhD); Japanese pedagogy (MA); Jewish studies (MA); Latin America and the Caribbean: regional studies (MA); Latin American and Iberian cultures (PhD); mathematics (MA, PhD), including finance (MA); medieval and Renaissance studies (MA); Middle Eastern, South Asian, and African studies (MA, PhD); modern art: critical and curatorial studies (MA); modern European studies (MA); museum anthropology (MA); music (DMA, PhD); oral history (MA); philosophical foundations of physics (MA); philosophy (MA, PhD); physics (PhD); political science (MA, PhD); psychology (PhD); quantitative methods in the social sciences (MA); religion (MA, PhD); Russia, Eurasia and East Europe: regional studies (MA); Russian translation (MA); Slavic cultures (MA); Slavic languages (MA, PhD); sociology (MA, PhD); South Asian studies (MA); statistics (MA, PhD); theatre (PhD). Dual-degree programs require admission to both Graduate School of Arts and Sciences and another Columbia school. *Program availability:* Part-time. Terminal master's awarded for partial completion of doctoral program. *Degree requirements:* For master's, variable foreign language requirement, comprehensive exam (for some programs), thesis (for some programs); for doctorate, variable foreign language requirement, comprehensive exam (for some programs), thesis/dissertation. *Entrance requirements:* For master's and doctorate, GRE General Test, GRE Subject Test (for some programs). Additional exam requirements/recommendations for international students: Required—TOEFL, IELTS. Electronic applications accepted.

**Cornell University,** Graduate School, Graduate Fields of Arts and Sciences, Field of History, Ithaca, NY 14853. Offers African history (MA, PhD); American history (MA, PhD); ancient Greek history (PhD); ancient history (MA, PhD); ancient Roman history (PhD); early modern European history (MA, PhD); English history (PhD); French history (MA, PhD); German history (MA, PhD); history of science (MA, PhD); Korean history (PhD); Latin American history (MA, PhD); medieval Chinese history (MA, PhD); medieval history (MA, PhD); modern Chinese history (MA, PhD); modern European history (MA, PhD); modern Japanese history (MA, PhD); modern Middle Eastern history (PhD); premodern Islamic history (MA, PhD); premodern Japanese history (MA, PhD); Renaissance history (MA, PhD); Russian history (MA, PhD); South Asian history (PhD);

Southeast Asian history (MA, PhD). Terminal master's awarded for partial completion of doctoral program. *Degree requirements:* For master's, thesis; for doctorate, 2 foreign languages, comprehensive exam, thesis/dissertation, 1 year of teaching experience. *Entrance requirements:* For master's and doctorate, GRE General Test, writing sample, 3 letters of recommendation. Additional exam requirements/recommendations for international students: Required—TOEFL (minimum score 550 paper-based; 77 iBT). Electronic applications accepted.

**Creighton University,** Graduate School, College of Arts and Sciences, Program in East-West Studies, Omaha, NE 68178-0001. Offers MA. *Program availability:* Part-time. *Faculty:* 6 full-time (2 women). *Students:* 2 full-time (0 women), 3 part-time (1 woman); includes 1 minority (Hispanic/Latino), 2 international. Average age 37. 2 applicants, 50% accepted. In 2016, 3 master's awarded. *Degree requirements:* For master's, no foreign language. *Entrance requirements:* For master's, 3 recommendations; personal essay; interview. Additional exam requirements/recommendations for international students: Required—TOEFL (minimum score 90 iBT). *Application deadline:* For fall admission, 7/1 for domestic and international students; for summer admission, 5/1 for domestic and international students. Application fee: $50. Electronic applications accepted. *Expenses:* Contact institution. *Financial support:* Scholarships/grants available. Financial award application deadline: 5/1; financial award applicants required to submit FAFSA. *Unit head:* Dr. Jinmei Yuan, Associate Professor, 402-280-3309, E-mail: jinmeiyuan@creighton.edu. *Application contact:* Lindsay Johnson, Director of Graduate and Adult Recruitment, 402-280-2703, Fax: 402-280-2423, E-mail: gradschool@creighton.edu.

**Dallas Baptist University,** Gary Cook School of Leadership, Program in International Studies, Dallas, TX 75211-9299. Offers East Asian studies (MA); European studies (MA); general international studies (MA); global business (MA); international immersion (MA); international ministry (MA); international relations (MA). *Program availability:* Part-time, evening/weekend. *Application deadline:* Applications are processed on a rolling basis. Application fee: $25. Electronic applications accepted. Application fee is waived when completed online. *Expenses: Tuition:* Full-time $15,408; part-time $856 per credit hour. *Required fees:* $400 per semester. Tuition and fees vary according to course load and degree level. *Unit head:* Dr. Brent A. Thomason, Director, 214-333-5236, E-mail: brentt@dbu.edu. *Application contact:* Bobby Soto, Director of Admissions, 214-333-5242, E-mail: graduate@dbu.edu.
Website: http://www4.dbu.edu/leadership/mainternational

**Drew University,** Caspersen School of Graduate Studies, Madison, NJ 07940-1493. Offers conflict resolution and leadership (Certificate), including community leadership, moderation, peace building; history and culture (MA, PhD), including American history, book history, British history, European history, Holocaust and genocide (M Litt, MA, D Litt, PhD), intellectual history, Irish history, print culture, public history; K-12 education (MAT), including art, biology, chemistry, elementary education, English, French, Italian, math, secondary education, special education, teacher of students with disabilities; liberal studies (M Litt, D Litt), including history, Holocaust and genocide (M Litt, MA, D Litt, PhD), Irish/Irish-American studies, literature (M Litt, MMH, D Litt, DMH, CMH); religion, spirituality, teaching in the two-year college, writing; medical humanities (MMH, DMH, CMH), including arts, health, healthcare, literature (M Litt, MMH, D Litt, DMH, CMH), scientific research; poetry (MFA). *Program availability:* Part-time, evening/weekend. *Faculty:* 4 full-time (2 women), 31 part-time/adjunct (16 women). *Students:* 62 full-time (41 women), 199 part-time (130 women); includes 38 minority (17 Black or African American, non-Hispanic/Latino; 3 Asian, non-Hispanic/Latino; 17 Hispanic/Latino; 1 Two or more races, non-Hispanic/Latino), 3 international. Average age 27. 93 applicants, 81% accepted, 46 enrolled. In 2016, 39 master's, 27 doctorates, 26 other advanced degrees awarded. Terminal master's awarded for partial completion of doctoral program. *Degree requirements:* For master's and other advanced degree, thesis (for some programs); for doctorate, one foreign language, comprehensive exam (for some programs), thesis/dissertation. *Entrance requirements:* For master's, PRAXIS Core and Subject Area tests (for MAT), resume, transcripts, writing sample, personal statement, letters of recommendation; for doctorate, GRE (PhD in history and culture), resume, transcripts, writing sample, personal statement, letters of recommendation. Additional exam requirements/recommendations for international students: Required—TOEFL (minimum score 587 paper-based; 94 iBT), IELTS (minimum score 7), TWE (minimum score 4). *Application deadline:* For fall admission, 8/1 for domestic students, 6/1 for international students; for spring admission, 12/1 for domestic students, 10/1 for international students. Applications are processed on a rolling basis. Application fee: $35. Electronic applications accepted. Tuition and fees vary according to program. *Financial support:* Fellowships, research assistantships, teaching assistantships, career-related internships or fieldwork, Federal Work-Study, scholarships/grants, and unspecified assistantships available. Support available to part-time students. Financial award applicants required to submit FAFSA. *Application contact:* Leanne Horinko, Director of Caspersen Admissions, 973-408-3280, E-mail: gradm@drew.edu.
Website: http://www.drew.edu/caspersen

**East Carolina University,** Graduate School, Thomas Harriot College of Arts and Sciences, Department of History, Greenville, NC 27858-4353. Offers American history (MA); Atlantic world (MA); European history (MA); history education (MA Ed); maritime studies (MA); military history (MA); public history (MA). *Program availability:* Part-time, evening/weekend. *Students:* 44 full-time (21 women), 48 part-time (27 women); includes 8 minority (1 Black or African American, non-Hispanic/Latino; 5 Hispanic/Latino; 2 Two or more races, non-Hispanic/Latino), 2 international. Average age 29. 46 applicants, 80% accepted, 23 enrolled. In 2016, 24 master's awarded. *Degree requirements:* For master's, one foreign language, comprehensive exam, thesis. *Entrance requirements:* For master's, GRE General Test, GRE Subject Test. Additional exam requirements/recommendations for international students: Required—TOEFL. *Application deadline:* For fall admission, 6/1 priority date for domestic students; for spring admission, 10/15 for domestic students. Applications are processed on a rolling basis. Application fee: $50. *Financial support:* Fellowships, research assistantships with partial tuition reimbursements, teaching assistantships with partial tuition reimbursements, and Federal Work-Study available. Support available to part-time students. Financial award application deadline: 6/1. *Unit head:* Dr. Gerry Prokopowicz, Chair, 252-328-6587, E-mail: prokopowiczg@ecu.edu.
Website: http://www.ecu.edu/cs-cas/history/graduatedegrees.cfm

**Georgetown University,** Graduate School of Arts and Sciences, Walsh School of Foreign Service, BMW Center for German and European Studies, Washington, DC 20057. Offers MA, MA/JD, MA/PhD. *Degree requirements:* For master's, 2 foreign languages, comprehensive exam. *Entrance requirements:* For master's, GRE General Test. Additional exam requirements/recommendations for international students: Required—TOEFL. Electronic applications accepted. *Faculty research:* Transatlantic relations, European Union, German and European Studies.

**The George Washington University,** Elliott School of International Affairs, Program in European and Eurasian Studies, Washington, DC 20052. Offers MA. *Program availability:* Part-time. *Students:* 16 full-time (7 women), 11 part-time (7 women); includes 2 minority (1 Hispanic/Latino; 1 Two or more races, non-Hispanic/Latino), 2 international. Average age 27. 45 applicants, 89% accepted, 10 enrolled. In 2016, 9 master's awarded. *Degree requirements:* For master's, one foreign language, capstone

*Western European Studies*

project. *Entrance requirements:* For master's, GRE General Test, 2 years (or the equivalent) of a modern European language or Russian, 2 semesters of introductory economics (macro or micro). Additional exam requirements/recommendations for international students: Required—TOEFL (minimum score 100 iBT), IELTS (minimum score 7). *Application deadline:* For fall admission, 1/15 priority date for domestic and international students; for spring admission, 10/1 for domestic students. Application fee: $75. Electronic applications accepted. *Financial support:* In 2016–17, 3 students received support. Fellowships with partial tuition reimbursements available and Federal Work-Study available. Financial award application deadline: 1/15; financial award applicants required to submit FAFSA. *Faculty research:* NATO, European economics, European history, European Union. *Unit head:* Peter Rollberg, Director, 202-994-6340, E-mail: rgpeter@gwu.edu. *Application contact:* Nicole A. Campbell, Director of Graduate Admissions, 202-994-7050, Fax: 202-994-9537, E-mail: esiagrad@gwu.edu. Website: http://elliott.gwu.edu/academics/grad/ees/index.cfm

**Indiana University Bloomington,** University Graduate School, College of Arts and Sciences, School of Global and International Studies, Institute for European Studies, Bloomington, IN 47405. Offers MA, MA/MBA, MPA/MA. *Program availability:* Part-time. *Degree requirements:* For master's, one foreign language, thesis. *Entrance requirements:* For master's, GRE General Test. Additional exam requirements/recommendations for international students: Required—TOEFL. Electronic applications accepted. *Faculty research:* European integration, economics of Europe, European Union, European culture and identity, expansion of European Union.

**La Salle University,** School of Arts and Sciences, Program in History, Philadelphia, PA 19141-1199. Offers American history (Certificate); European history (Certificate); history (MA); history for educators (MA); public history (MA); teaching advanced placement history (Certificate); world history (Certificate). *Program availability:* Part-time. *Faculty:* 4 full-time (1 woman), 1 (woman) part-time/adjunct. *Students:* 4 full-time (1 woman), 16 part-time (7 women); includes 2 minority (1 Hispanic/Latino; 1 Two or more races, non-Hispanic/Latino). Average age 33. 8 applicants, 75% accepted, 3 enrolled. In 2016, 11 master's awarded. *Degree requirements:* For master's, thesis or comprehensive exam. *Entrance requirements:* For master's, GRE or MAT, 18 hours of undergraduate coursework in history or a related discipline with minimum GPA of 3.0; two letters of recommendation; brief personal statement (250 to 500 words); writing sample (preferably from an undergraduate research paper). Additional exam requirements/recommendations for international students: Required—TOEFL. *Application deadline:* For fall admission, 8/15 priority date for domestic students, 7/15 for international students; for spring admission, 12/15 priority date for domestic students, 11/15 for international students; for summer admission, 4/15 priority date for domestic students, 3/15 for international students. Applications are processed on a rolling basis. Application fee: $35. Electronic applications accepted. Application fee is waived when completed online. *Expenses:* Contact institution. *Financial support:* In 2016–17, 1 student received support. Scholarships/grants available. Support available to part-time students. Financial award application deadline: 8/31; financial award applicants required to submit FAFSA. *Unit head:* Dr. George B. Stow, Director, 215-951-1097, E-mail: grahis@lasalle.edu. *Application contact:* Elizabeth Heenan, Director, Graduate and Adult Enrollment, 215-951-1100, Fax: 215-951-1462, E-mail: heenan@lasalle.edu. Website: http://www.lasalle.edu/master-history/

**Mississippi State University,** College of Arts and Sciences, Department of History, Mississippi State, MS 39762. Offers U.S. and European history (MA). *Program availability:* Part-time. *Faculty:* 22 full-time (5 women). *Students:* 43 full-time (14 women), 12 part-time (3 women); includes 10 minority (7 Black or African American, non-Hispanic/Latino; 3 Two or more races, non-Hispanic/Latino), 2 international. Average age 30. 27 applicants, 89% accepted, 19 enrolled. In 2016, 10 master's, 3 doctorates awarded. *Degree requirements:* For master's, one foreign language, comprehensive exam, thesis optional; for doctorate, 2 foreign languages, thesis/dissertation, comprehensive oral and written exam. *Entrance requirements:* For master's, minimum GPA of 3.0 on last two years of undergraduate courses; for doctorate, GRE, writing sample, minimum graduate GPA of 3.0. Additional exam requirements/recommendations for international students: Required—TOEFL (minimum score 550 paper-based). *Application deadline:* For fall admission, 4/1 for domestic students, 5/1 for international students; for spring admission, 11/1 for domestic students, 9/1 for international students. Applications are processed on a rolling basis. Application fee: $60. Electronic applications accepted. *Expenses:* Tuition, state resident: full-time $7670; part-time $852.50 per credit hour. Tuition, nonresident: full-time $20,790; part-time $2310.50 per credit hour. Part-time tuition and fees vary according to course load. *Financial support:* In 2016–17, 1 research assistantship with full tuition reimbursement (averaging $15,269 per year), 36 teaching assistantships with full tuition reimbursements (averaging $11,977 per year) were awarded; Federal Work-Study, institutionally sponsored loans, scholarships/grants, and unspecified assistantships also available. Financial award application deadline: 4/1; financial award applicants required to submit FAFSA. *Faculty research:* U.S. political, diplomatic, military, social, and cultural history; modern Europe; Latin America; Asian history; African history. *Unit head:* Dr. Alan I. Marcus, Department Head, 662-325-7075, Fax: 662-325-1139, E-mail: aimarcus@history.msstate.edu. *Application contact:* Linda Bonner, Senior Admissions Assistant, 662-325-3363, E-mail: lbonner@grad.msstate.edu. Website: http://www.history.msstate.edu

**Monmouth University,** Graduate Studies, Department of History, West Long Branch, NJ 07764-1898. Offers European history (MA); history of the U.S. (MA); world history (MA). *Program availability:* Part-time, evening/weekend. *Degree requirements:* For master's, comprehensive exam (for some programs), thesis (for some programs). *Entrance requirements:* For master's, minimum GPA of 3.0 in major, 2.5 overall; two letters of recommendation; statement describing historical areas of interest and how graduate study will contribute to professional and academic goals. Additional exam requirements/recommendations for international students: Required—TOEFL (minimum score 550 paper-based; 79 iBT), IELTS (minimum score 6) or Michigan English Language Assessment Battery (minimum score 77). Electronic applications accepted. *Faculty research:* British, German, and French Revolutions; Soviet Union; Africa; English history; U.S. military; women's history.

**New York University,** Graduate School of Arts and Science, Center for European Studies, New York, NY 10012-1019. Offers MA. *Entrance requirements:* For master's, GRE General Test. Additional exam requirements/recommendations for international students: Required—TOEFL. Electronic applications accepted. *Faculty research:* Xenophobia, migration, and identity politics in Europe; European Union and political economy; Central Eastern Europe.

**San Diego State University,** Graduate and Research Affairs, College of Arts and Letters, Department of European Studies, San Diego, CA 92182. Offers MA. *Degree requirements:* For master's, one foreign language. *Entrance requirements:* For master's, GRE General Test. Additional exam requirements/recommendations for international students: Required—TOEFL. Electronic applications accepted.

**University of Colorado Denver,** College of Liberal Arts and Sciences, Department of History, Denver, CO 80217. Offers European history (MA); global history (MA); public history (MA); U.S. history (MA). *Program availability:* Part-time, evening/weekend. *Faculty:* 12 full-time (4 women), 2 part-time/adjunct (0 women). *Students:* 24 full-time

(15 women), 16 part-time (10 women); includes 10 minority (1 Asian, non-Hispanic/Latino; 6 Hispanic/Latino; 3 Two or more races, non-Hispanic/Latino). Average age 35. 23 applicants, 70% accepted, 7 enrolled. In 2016, 15 master's awarded. *Degree requirements:* For master's, comprehensive exam, thesis optional, 36 semester hours (12 courses). *Entrance requirements:* For master's, GRE General Test, writing sample, minimum undergraduate GPA of 3.25, three letters of recommendation, statement of purpose addressing any weaknesses in academic record. Additional exam requirements/recommendations for international students: Required—TOEFL (minimum score 537 paper-based; 75 iBT); Recommended—IELTS (minimum score 6.5). *Application deadline:* For fall admission, 1/20 for domestic and international students; for spring admission, 10/1 for domestic and international students. Application fee: $50 ($75 for international students). Electronic applications accepted. *Expenses:* Tuition, state resident: full-time $11,006; part-time $474 per credit. Tuition, nonresident: full-time $28,212; part-time $1264 per credit hour. *Required fees:* $256 per semester. One-time fee: $94.32. Tuition and fees vary according to campus/location and program. *Financial support:* In 2016–17, 8 students received support. Fellowships, research assistantships, teaching assistantships, Federal Work-Study, institutionally sponsored loans, scholarships/grants, and traineeships available. Financial award application deadline: 4/1; financial award applicants required to submit FAFSA. *Faculty research:* Uses of pre-modern Islamic heritage in modern India; relationship between liberal understandings of democracy, crime, and police discretion; relationships between gender, class, health, and welfare in nineteenth and early twentieth century England; U.S. business cultures and their influences on marketing and personnel practices; intersection of business and political ideologies; social and environmental history of the Rocky Mountain West. *Unit head:* Dr. Kariann Akemi Yokota, Associate Chair, 303-315-1784, E-mail: kariann.yokota@ucdenver.edu. *Application contact:* Tabitha Fitzpatrick, Program Assistant, 303-315-1776, E-mail: tabitha.fitzpatrick@ucdenver.edu. Website: http://www.ucdenver.edu/academics/colleges/CLAS/Departments/history/Programs/Masters/Pages/MasterofArts.aspx

**University of Connecticut,** Graduate School, College of Liberal Arts and Sciences, Field of International Studies, Program in International Studies, Storrs, CT 06269. Offers European studies (MA); Italian history and culture (MA); Latino and Latin American studies (MA). *Degree requirements:* For master's, comprehensive exam. *Entrance requirements:* For master's, GRE General Test. Additional exam requirements/recommendations for international students: Required—TOEFL (minimum score 550 paper-based). Electronic applications accepted.

**University of Guelph,** Graduate Studies, College of Arts, School of Languages and Literatures, Program in European Studies, Guelph, ON N1G 2W1, Canada. Offers MA. *Degree requirements:* For master's, research paper. *Entrance requirements:* For master's, curriculum vitae, writing sample, 2 letters of recommendation.

**University of Illinois at Urbana–Champaign,** Graduate College, College of Liberal Arts and Sciences, European Union Center, Champaign, IL 61820. Offers MA. *Degree requirements:* For master's, one foreign language.

**University of Nevada, Reno,** Graduate School, Interdisciplinary Program in Basque Studies, Reno, NV 89557. Offers PhD. *Degree requirements:* For doctorate, thesis/dissertation. *Entrance requirements:* For doctorate, GRE General Test, master's degree in related field, minimum GPA of 3.0. Additional exam requirements/recommendations for international students: Required—TOEFL (minimum score 500 paper-based; 61 iBT), IELTS (minimum score 6). Electronic applications accepted. *Faculty research:* Ethnic groups, Basque society, migration studies, symbolic anthropology, terrorism.

**University of Pittsburgh,** University Center for International Studies, Pittsburgh, PA 15260. Offers African studies (Certificate); Asian studies (Certificate); European Union studies (Certificate); global studies (Certificate); Latin American studies (Certificate); Russian and East European studies (Certificate); West European studies (Certificate). *Program availability:* Part-time, evening/weekend, online learning. *Students:* 175 full-time (105 women), 14 part-time (10 women); includes 78 minority (5 Black or African American, non-Hispanic/Latino; 30 Asian, non-Hispanic/Latino; 42 Hispanic/Latino; 1 Two or more races, non-Hispanic/Latino). Average age 29. *Degree requirements:* For Certificate, one foreign language, comprehensive exam (for some programs), thesis (for some programs). *Entrance requirements:* Additional exam requirements/recommendations for international students: Required—TOEFL. *Expenses:* Contact institution. *Financial support:* In 2016–17, 22 fellowships with full tuition reimbursements (averaging $17,878 per year) were awarded; scholarships/grants, traineeships, health care benefits, tuition waivers, and unspecified assistantships also available. *Unit head:* Dr. Ariel Armony, Director, 412-648-7374, Fax: 412-624-4672, E-mail: armony@pitt.edu. Website: http://www.ucis.pitt.edu

**University of Rochester,** School of Arts and Sciences, Department of History, Rochester, NY 14627. Offers American history (MA, PhD); European history (MA, PhD); global history (MA, PhD). *Faculty:* 19 full-time (4 women). *Students:* 28 full-time (12 women); includes 2 minority (1 Asian, non-Hispanic/Latino; 1 Two or more races, non-Hispanic/Latino), 2 international. Average age 31. 32 applicants, 28% accepted, 5 enrolled. In 2016, 5 master's, 4 doctorates awarded. Terminal master's awarded for partial completion of doctoral program. *Degree requirements:* For master's, one foreign language, thesis or alternative; for doctorate, 2 foreign languages, thesis/dissertation, comprehensive oral exam, qualifying exam. *Entrance requirements:* For master's and doctorate, GRE General Test, sample of written work. Additional exam requirements/recommendations for international students: Required—TOEFL. *Application deadline:* For fall admission, 1/15 for domestic and international students. Application fee: $60. Electronic applications accepted. *Expenses:* $1,538 per credit. *Financial support:* In 2016–17, 24 students received support, including 7 fellowships (averaging $20,000 per year); tuition waivers (full and partial) also available. Financial award application deadline: 1/15. *Unit head:* Matthew Lenoe, Chair, 585-275-9355, E-mail: matthew.lenoe@rochester.edu. *Application contact:* Alissa Clark, Secretary, 585-275-2053. Website: http://www.rochester.edu/College/HIS/

**University of South Florida,** College of Arts and Sciences, Department of History, Tampa, FL 33620-9951. Offers history (MA, PhD), including American history (MA), ancient history (MA), European history (MA), Latin American history (MA), Medieval history (MA). *Program availability:* Part-time, evening/weekend. *Faculty:* 17 full-time (8 women). *Students:* 39 full-time (9 women), 14 part-time (8 women); includes 7 minority (1 Black or African American, non-Hispanic/Latino; 1 American Indian or Alaska Native, non-Hispanic/Latino; 1 Asian, non-Hispanic/Latino; 4 Hispanic/Latino), 1 international. Average age 35. 34 applicants, 68% accepted, 15 enrolled. In 2016, 8 master's, 2 doctorates awarded. *Degree requirements:* For master's, one foreign language, comprehensive exam, thesis optional; for doctorate, one foreign language, comprehensive exam, thesis/dissertation. *Entrance requirements:* For master's, GRE General Test, minimum GPA of 3.0, two letters of recommendation, 2-page statement of purpose, writing sample; for doctorate, GRE General Test, minimum GPA of 3.5 in master's degree coursework, three letters of recommendation, statement of purpose, writing sample, foreign language proficiency in the field of study. Additional exam requirements/recommendations for international students: Required—TOEFL (minimum score 550 paper-based; 79 iBT) or IELTS (minimum score 6.5). *Application deadline:* For fall admission, 12/1 priority date for domestic students, 12/1 for international

students. Applications are processed on a rolling basis. Application fee: $30. Electronic applications accepted. *Expenses:* Tuition, state resident: full-time $7766; part-time $431.43 per credit hour. Tuition, nonresident: full-time $15,789; part-time $877.17 per credit hour. *Required fees:* $37 per term. *Financial support:* In 2016–17, 20 students received support, including 17 teaching assistantships with tuition reimbursements available (averaging $12,750 per year); unspecified assistantships also available. Financial award application deadline: 1/15. *Faculty research:* North American and U.S. history, European history, nineteenth- and twentieth-centuries/modern world, early modern world, ancient history, history of gender/sexuality, Latin American history, history of science and medicine. *Total annual research expenditures:* $195,413. *Unit head:* Dr. Fraser Ottanelli, Professor and Chair, 813-974-6209, Fax: 813-974-6228, E-mail: ottanelli@usf.edu. *Application contact:* Dr. Brian Connolly, Associate Professor and Graduate Program Director, 813-974-1087, Fax: 813-974-6228, E-mail: bconnolly@usf.edu.
Website: http://history.usf.edu

**Wayne State University,** College of Liberal Arts and Sciences, Department of History, Detroit, MI 48202. Offers Africa (PhD); America (PhD); Asia (PhD); Europe (PhD); gender (PhD); history (MA); labor (PhD); public history (MA); science and technology (PhD); world history (PhD, Graduate Certificate); JD/MA; M Ed/MA; MLIS/MA. Doctoral program admits for fall only. *Program availability:* Evening/weekend. *Faculty:* 18. *Students:* 23 full-time (8 women), 21 part-time (5 women); includes 8 minority (3 Black or African American, non-Hispanic/Latino; 2 Hispanic/Latino; 3 Two or more races, non-Hispanic/Latino). Average age 40. 55 applicants, 38% accepted, 15 enrolled. In 2016, 6 master's, 5 doctorates awarded. *Degree requirements:* For master's, comprehensive exam, thesis (for some programs), final oral exam on thesis or essay and seminar; internship and project (for public history); for doctorate, variable foreign language requirement, comprehensive exam, thesis/dissertation, qualifying exam in 4 fields of history. *Entrance requirements:* For master's, GRE General Test, minimum

undergraduate GPA of 3.25 in history, 3.0 overall; at least 18 credits in history and related subjects at the advanced undergraduate level; foreign language; letter of intent; research paper; at least two letters of recommendation from former instructors; for doctorate, GRE General Test, minimum GPA of 3.0, 3.25 in minimum of 18 semester credits in history and related subjects; letter of intent; research paper; at least three letters of recommendation from former professors; for Graduate Certificate, baccalaureate degree from accredited college or university; minimum GPA of 3.0, 3.25 in a minimum of eighteen semester credits in history and related subjects at the advanced undergraduate level. Additional exam requirements/recommendations for international students: Required—TOEFL (minimum score 550 paper-based; 79 iBT), TWE (minimum score 5.5), Michigan English Language Assessment Battery (minimum score 85); Recommended—IELTS (minimum score 6.5). *Application deadline:* For fall admission, 2/1 priority date for domestic and international students; for winter admission, 11/1 for domestic students, 10/1 priority date for international students; for spring admission, 2/1 for domestic students, 1/1 priority date for international students. Application fee: $50. Electronic applications accepted. *Expenses:* $16,503 per year resident tuition and fees, $33,697 per year non-resident tuition and fees. *Financial support:* In 2016–17, 16 students received support, including 2 fellowships with tuition reimbursements available (averaging $18,796 per year), 1 research assistantship with tuition reimbursement available (averaging $21,593 per year), 6 teaching assistantships with tuition reimbursements available (averaging $17,994 per year); scholarships/grants, health care benefits, and unspecified assistantships also available. Financial award applicants required to submit FAFSA. *Faculty research:* African, American, Asian, European, gender, German, labor, science and technology, urban/labor, violence, world. *Unit head:* Dr. Elizabeth V. Faue, Professor/Chair, 313-577-2525, E-mail: evfaue@wayne.edu. *Application contact:* Dr. Eric Ash, Associate Professor and Director of Graduate Studies, 313-577-2525, E-mail: ericash@wayne.edu.
Website: http://clas.wayne.edu/history/

# Women's Studies

**American University,** College of Arts and Sciences, Critical Race, Gender, and Culture Studies Collaborative, Washington, DC 20016-8001. Offers Asian studies (Graduate Certificate); women's, gender, and sexuality studies (Graduate Certificate). *Expenses: Tuition:* Full-time $28,422; part-time $1579 per credit hour. *Required fees:* $690; $200 per term. Tuition and fees vary according to course load, degree level and program.

**The American University in Cairo,** School of Global Affairs and Public Policy, Cairo, Egypt. Offers gender and women's studies (MA); global affairs (MGA); international and comparative law (LL M); international human rights law (MA); journalism and mass communication (MA); Middle East studies (MA); migration and refugee studies (MA, Diploma); public administration (MPA); public policy (MPP); television and digital journalism (MA). *Program availability:* Part-time, evening/weekend. *Faculty:* 27 full-time (13 women), 5 part-time/adjunct (3 women). *Students:* 69 full-time (40 women), 194 part-time (134 women), 33 international. Average age 29. 322 applicants, 51% accepted, 86 enrolled. In 2016, 112 master's awarded. *Degree requirements:* For master's, comprehensive exam (for some programs), thesis (for some programs). *Entrance requirements:* Additional exam requirements/recommendations for international students: Required—TOEFL (minimum score 450 paper-based; 45 iBT), IELTS (minimum score 5). *Application deadline:* For fall admission, 2/1 for domestic and international students; for spring admission, 10/15 for domestic and international students. Applications are processed on a rolling basis. Application fee: $80. Electronic applications accepted. *Expenses:* Contact institution. *Financial support:* Fellowships with partial tuition reimbursements, scholarships/grants, and unspecified assistantships available. Financial award application deadline: 3/10. *Faculty research:* Law, media and journalism; public policy and public administration, gender studies, Middle East Studies, global affairs, refugees studies. *Unit head:* Dr. Nabil Fahmy, Dean, 20-2-2615-2671, E-mail: nfahmy@aucegypt.edu. *Application contact:* Maha Hegazi, Director for Graduate Admissions, 20-2-2615-1462, E-mail: mahahegazi@aucegypt.edu.
Website: http://www.aucegypt.edu/GAPP/Pages/default.aspx

**Benedictine University,** Graduate Programs, Program in Leadership, Lisle, IL 60532. Offers MS. *Students:* 10 applicants, 100% accepted, 9 enrolled. *Degree requirements:* For master's, capstone. *Expenses: Tuition:* Full-time $15,600; part-time $650 per hour. *Required fees:* $300. One-time fee: $125 part-time. Tuition and fees vary according to class time, course load, campus/location and program. *Unit head:* Dr. Theresa Sak, Associate Dean of Adult and Professional Programs, 630-829-6114, E-mail: tsak@ben.edu. *Application contact:* Kari Gibbons, Associate Vice President, Enrollment Center, 630-829-6200, Fax: 630-829-6584, E-mail: kgibbons@ben.edu.

**Brandeis University,** Graduate School of Arts and Sciences, Department of Anthropology, Waltham, MA 02454. Offers anthropology (MA, PhD); anthropology/women's, gender, and sexuality studies (MA). *Program availability:* Part-time. *Faculty:* 9 full-time (5 women), 4 part-time/adjunct (1 woman). *Students:* 38 full-time (25 women), 1 part-time (0 women); includes 7 minority (2 Black or African American, non-Hispanic/Latino; 3 Hispanic/Latino; 2 Two or more races, non-Hispanic/Latino), 6 international. 62 applicants, 48% accepted, 15 enrolled. In 2016, 14 master's, 2 doctorates awarded. *Degree requirements:* For master's, thesis or alternative; for doctorate, one foreign language, comprehensive exam, thesis/dissertation. *Entrance requirements:* For master's and doctorate, GRE General Test, sample of written work, resume, letters of recommendation. Additional exam requirements/recommendations for international students: Required—TOEFL (minimum score 600 paper-based; 100 iBT); Recommended—IELTS (minimum score 7), TSE (minimum score 68). *Application deadline:* For fall admission, 1/15 for domestic students. Application fee: $75. Electronic applications accepted. *Financial support:* In 2016–17, 39 students received support, including 11 fellowships with full tuition reimbursements available (averaging $24,000 per year), 20 teaching assistantships with partial tuition reimbursements available (averaging $3,200 per year); scholarships/grants, health care benefits, and tuition waivers (partial) also available. Support available to part-time students. Financial award application deadline: 4/15; financial award applicants required to submit FAFSA. *Faculty research:* Sociocultural anthropology, archaeology, gender and sexuality, linguistic anthropology, physical anthropology. *Unit head:* Dr. Sarah Lamb, Director of Graduate Studies, 781-736-2210, Fax: 781-736-2232, E-mail: lamb@brandeis.edu. *Application contact:* Laurel Carpenter, Academic Administrator, 781-736-2210, Fax: 781-736-2232, E-mail: lcarpenter@brandeis.edu.
Website: http://www.brandeis.edu/gsas

**Brandeis University,** Graduate School of Arts and Sciences, Department of English, Waltham, MA 02454-9110. Offers English (MA, PhD); English and women's, gender, and sexuality studies (MA). *Program availability:* Part-time. *Faculty:* 18 full-time (9

women), 12 part-time/adjunct (6 women). *Students:* 42 full-time (24 women), 1 part-time (0 women); includes 7 minority (2 Black or African American, non-Hispanic/Latino; 1 Asian, non-Hispanic/Latino; 3 Hispanic/Latino; 1 Two or more races, non-Hispanic/Latino), 8 international. 126 applicants, 28% accepted, 9 enrolled. In 2016, 3 master's, 3 doctorates awarded. Terminal master's awarded for partial completion of doctoral program. *Degree requirements:* For master's, one foreign language, thesis or alternative; for doctorate, 2 foreign languages, thesis/dissertation, field exam, symposium presentation, prospectus defense. *Entrance requirements:* For master's, GRE, resume, sample of work, 2 letters of recommendation, statement of purpose, transcript(s); for doctorate, GRE General Test; GRE Subject Test, resume, sample of work, 2 letters of recommendation, statement of purpose, transcript(s). Additional exam requirements/recommendations for international students: Required—TOEFL (minimum score 600 paper-based; 100 iBT); Recommended—IELTS (minimum score 7), TSE (minimum score 68). *Application deadline:* For fall admission, 1/5 for domestic and international students. Application fee: $75. Electronic applications accepted. *Financial support:* In 2016–17, 23 fellowships with full tuition reimbursements (averaging $24,000 per year), 11 teaching assistantships with partial tuition reimbursements (averaging $3,200 per year) were awarded; Federal Work-Study, scholarships/grants, health care benefits, and tuition waivers (partial) also available. Support available to part-time students. Financial award application deadline: 4/15; financial award applicants required to submit FAFSA. *Faculty research:* Feminist and gender theory, American literature and post-Colonial theory, early modern (Renaissance) English literature, modernism, literature and science, literary theory and philosophy, contemporary poetry. *Unit head:* Dr. John Plotz, Director of Graduate Studies, 781-736-2130, Fax: 781-736-2179, E-mail: chaucer@brandeis.edu. *Application contact:* Lisa Pannella, Department Academic Administrator, 781-736-2130, Fax: 781-736-2179, E-mail: pannella@brandeis.edu.
Website: http://www.brandeis.edu/gsas

**Brandeis University,** Graduate School of Arts and Sciences, Department of Near Eastern and Judaic Studies, Waltham, MA 02454-9110. Offers Near Eastern and Judaic studies (MA, PhD); Near Eastern and Judaic studies and women's, gender, and sexuality studies (MA); teaching of Hebrew (MAT). *Program availability:* Part-time. *Faculty:* 24 full-time (10 women), 6 part-time/adjunct (3 women). *Students:* 44 full-time (18 women), 2 part-time (0 women); includes 7 minority (2 Black or African American, non-Hispanic/Latino; 1 Asian, non-Hispanic/Latino; 4 Hispanic/Latino), 9 international. 67 applicants, 45% accepted, 12 enrolled. In 2016, 9 master's, 3 doctorates awarded. Terminal master's awarded for partial completion of doctoral program. *Degree requirements:* For master's, one foreign language, thesis or alternative, proseminar, capstone; for doctorate, variable foreign language requirement, comprehensive exam, thesis/dissertation. *Entrance requirements:* For master's, GRE (recommended), 2 letters of recommendation, transcript(s), statement of purpose, writing sample, resume; for doctorate, GRE (recommended), 3 letters of recommendation, transcript(s), statement of purpose, writing sample, resume. Additional exam requirements/recommendations for international students: Required—TOEFL (minimum score 600 paper-based; 100 iBT); Recommended—IELTS (minimum score 7), TSE (minimum score 68). *Application deadline:* For fall admission, 1/15 priority date for domestic and international students. Application fee: $75. Electronic applications accepted. *Financial support:* In 2016–17, 28 students received support, including 16 fellowships with full tuition reimbursements available (averaging $24,000 per year), 2 teaching assistantships with partial tuition reimbursements available (averaging $3,200 per year); Federal Work-Study, scholarships/grants, health care benefits, and tuition waivers (full and partial) also available. Support available to part-time students. Financial award application deadline: 4/15; financial award applicants required to submit FAFSA. *Faculty research:* Bible and ancient Near East, Judaic Studies, Israel Studies, modern Middle East, Arabic and Islamic civilizations. *Unit head:* Dr. Jonathan Decter, Department Chair, 781-736-2950, Fax: 781-736-2070, E-mail: decter@brandeis.edu. *Application contact:* Joanne Arnish, Department Administrator, 781-736-2950, Fax: 781-736-2070, E-mail: arnish@brandeis.edu.
Website: http://www.brandeis.edu/gsas

**Brandeis University,** Graduate School of Arts and Sciences, Joint Master's Programs in Women's, Gender, and Sexuality Studies, Waltham, MA 02454-9110. Offers anthropology and women's, gender, and sexuality studies (MA); English and women's, gender, and sexuality studies (MA); near Eastern and Judaic studies and women's, gender, and sexuality studies (MA); public policy and women's, gender, and sexuality studies (MA); sociology and women's, gender, and sexuality studies (MA); sustainable international development and women's, gender, and sexuality studies (MA). *Degree requirements:* For master's, thesis. *Entrance requirements:* For master's, GRE, sample of written work, resume, statement of purpose, transcript(s), two letters of recommendation. Additional exam requirements/recommendations for international students: Required—TOEFL (minimum score 600 paper-based; 100 iBT), PTE (minimum score 68); Recommended—IELTS (minimum score 7). *Application deadline:* For fall admission, 1/15 for domestic students. Application fee: $75. Electronic applications accepted. *Financial support:* Fellowships with full tuition reimbursements and teaching assistantships with partial tuition reimbursements available. Financial award application deadline: 4/15; financial award applicants required to submit FAFSA. *Faculty research:* Anthropology, English, history, music, Near Eastern and Judaic studies, public policy, psychology, sociology, and sustainable international development. *Unit head:* Elizabeth Brainerd, Director of Graduate Study, 781-736-4816, E-mail: ebrainer@brandeis.edu. *Application contact:* Shannon Hunt, Program Administrator, 781-736-3045, Fax: 781-736-3044, E-mail: shunt@brandeis.edu. Website: http://www.brandeis.edu/gsas

**Brandeis University,** Graduate School of Arts and Sciences, MA Program in Women's and Gender Studies, Waltham, MA 02454-9110. Offers MA. *Faculty:* 20 full-time (19 women), 3 part-time/adjunct (all women). *Students:* 15 full-time (all women); includes 3 minority (2 Black or African American, non-Hispanic/Latino; 1 Two or more races, non-Hispanic/Latino), 2 international. 19 applicants, 47% accepted, 4 enrolled. In 2016, 3 master's awarded. *Degree requirements:* For master's, thesis, proseminar. *Entrance requirements:* For master's, GRE, three letters of recommendation, curriculum vitae or resume, statement of purpose, critical writing sample, transcript(s). Additional exam requirements/recommendations for international students: Required—TOEFL (minimum score 600 paper-based; 100 iBT); Recommended—IELTS (minimum score 7), TSE (minimum score 68). *Application deadline:* For fall admission, 1/15 for domestic and international students. Application fee: $75. Electronic applications accepted. *Financial support:* In 2016–17, 15 students received support, including 4 fellowships with partial tuition reimbursements available, 6 teaching assistantships with partial tuition reimbursements available (averaging $3,200 per year); Federal Work-Study, scholarships/grants, and tuition waivers (partial) also available. Financial award application deadline: 4/15; financial award applicants required to submit FAFSA. *Faculty research:* Gender and legal studies, sexuality studies, social and public policy, comparative literature and culture, anthropology, English, music, near eastern and Judaic studies, public policy, sociology, sustainable international development, history, psychology. *Unit head:* Elizabeth Brainerd, Director of Graduate Study, 781-736-3045, Fax: 781-736-3045, E-mail: wgstudies@brandeis.edu. *Application contact:* Shannon Hunt, Academic Administrator, 781-736-3045, Fax: 781-736-3044, E-mail: shunt@brandeis.edu. Website: http://www.brandeis.edu/programs/wgs/graduate/index.html

**California Institute of Integral Studies,** School of Consciousness and Transformation, San Francisco, CA 94103. Offers anthropology and social change (MA, PhD); Asian philosophies and cultures (MA); creative inquiry/interdisciplinary arts (MFA); East-West psychology (MA, PhD); integral and transpersonal psychology (PhD); philosophy and religion (PhD), including ecology, spirituality, and religion, philosophy, cosmology, and consciousness, women's spirituality; theater and performance making (MFA); transformative leadership (MA); transformative studies (PhD); women, gender, spirituality and social justice (MA); writing and consciousness (MFA). *Program availability:* Part-time, evening/weekend, 100% online, blended/hybrid learning. *Students:* 390 full-time (256 women), 121 part-time (84 women); includes 135 minority (39 Black or African American, non-Hispanic/Latino; 2 American Indian or Alaska Native, non-Hispanic/Latino; 22 Asian, non-Hispanic/Latino; 40 Hispanic/Latino; 2 Native Hawaiian or other Pacific Islander, non-Hispanic/Latino; 30 Two or more races, non-Hispanic/Latino), 51 international. Average age 38. 195 applicants, 92% accepted, 124 enrolled. In 2016, 35 master's, 41 doctorates awarded. Terminal master's awarded for partial completion of doctoral program. *Degree requirements:* For master's, thesis optional; for doctorate, comprehensive exam, thesis/dissertation, 1 foreign language (for Asian philosophies and cultures). *Entrance requirements:* For master's, minimum GPA of 3.0, letters of recommendation, writing sample; for doctorate, master's degree, minimum GPA of 3.0, letters of recommendation, writing sample. Additional exam requirements/recommendations for international students: Required—TOEFL. *Application deadline:* For fall admission, 2/1 priority date for domestic and international students; for spring admission, 10/15 priority date for domestic and international students. Applications are processed on a rolling basis. Application fee: $65. Electronic applications accepted. *Expenses: Tuition:* Full-time $19,728; part-time $1098 per semester hour. *Required fees:* $320; $320 per semester hour. *Financial support:* Research assistantships, teaching assistantships, career-related internships or fieldwork, Federal Work-Study, and scholarships/grants available. Support available to part-time students. Financial award application deadline: 4/15; financial award applicants required to submit FAFSA. *Faculty research:* Ecology and sustainability, philosophy and religion, East-West psychology, integrative health, social and cultural anthropology, transformative leadership. *Application contact:* Ellen Durst, Director of Admissions, 415-575-6100, Fax: 415-575-1268, E-mail: admissions@ciis.edu. Website: http://www.ciis.edu/

**Carnegie Mellon University,** Dietrich College of Humanities and Social Sciences, Department of History, Pittsburgh, PA 15213-3891. Offers African and African-American diaspora (PhD); culture and power (PhD); labor, politics and social movements (PhD); technology, environment, science and health (PhD); women, gender and the family (PhD). *Program availability:* Part-time. *Degree requirements:* For doctorate, oral and written comprehensive exams, dissertation defense. *Entrance requirements:* For doctorate, GRE General Test. Additional exam requirements/recommendations for international students: Required—TOEFL. Electronic applications accepted. *Faculty research:* Anthropology and history, African-American history, technology/environment, cultural history analysis.

**Chatham University,** Program in Business Administration, Pittsburgh, PA 15232-2826. Offers business administration (MBA); healthcare management (MBA); sustainability (MBA); women's leadership (MBA). *Program availability:* Part-time, evening/weekend. *Entrance requirements:* For master's, minimum GPA of 3.0, letters of recommendation. Additional exam requirements/recommendations for international students: Required—TOEFL (minimum score 600 paper-based; 100 iBT), IELTS (minimum score 7), TWE. Electronic applications accepted. Application fee is waived when completed online. *Expenses: Tuition:* Full-time $16,254; part-time $903 per credit hour. *Required fees:* $468; $26 per credit hour.

**Claremont Graduate University,** Graduate Programs, School of Arts and Humanities, Department of Religion, Claremont, CA 91711-6160. Offers Hebrew Bible (MA, PhD); history of Christianity and religions of North America (MA, PhD); New Testament (MA, PhD); philosophy of religion and theology (MA, PhD); theology, ethics and culture (MA, PhD); women's studies in religion (MA, PhD); MA/PhD; MPhil/PhD. *Program availability:* Part-time. *Faculty:* 7 full-time (4 women), 2 part-time/adjunct (0 women). *Students:* 121 full-time (46 women), 13 part-time (6 women); includes 28 minority (10 Black or African American, non-Hispanic/Latino; 1 American Indian or Alaska Native, non-Hispanic/Latino; 6 Asian, non-Hispanic/Latino; 7 Hispanic/Latino; 1 Native Hawaiian or other Pacific Islander, non-Hispanic/Latino; 3 Two or more races, non-Hispanic/Latino), 19 international. Average age 39. In 2016, 11 master's, 21 doctorates awarded. Terminal

master's awarded for partial completion of doctoral program. *Entrance requirements:* For master's and doctorate, GRE General Test. Additional exam requirements/recommendations for international students: Required—TOEFL (minimum score 75 iBT). *Application deadline:* For fall admission, 2/1 priority date for domestic and international students. Applications are processed on a rolling basis. Application fee: $80. Electronic applications accepted. *Expenses: Tuition:* Full-time $44,328; part-time $1847 per unit. *Required fees:* $600; $300 per semester. Tuition and fees vary according to course load and program. *Financial support:* Fellowships, research assistantships, teaching assistantships, Federal Work-Study, institutionally sponsored loans, and scholarships/grants available. Support available to part-time students. Financial award application deadline: 2/15; financial award applicants required to submit FAFSA. *Unit head:* Ruqayya Kahn, Chair, 909-607-0488, E-mail: ruqayya.kahn@cgu.edu. *Application contact:* Amy Sandefur, Assistant Director of Admissions, 909-607-9101, E-mail: amy.sandefur@cgu.edu. Website: https://www.cgu.edu/departments/religion/

**Claremont Graduate University,** Graduate Programs, School of Arts and Humanities, Program in Applied Women's Studies, Claremont, CA 91711-6160. Offers MA. *Faculty:* 2 full-time (both women). *Students:* 6 full-time (all women), 3 part-time (all women); includes 6 minority (2 Black or African American, non-Hispanic/Latino; 4 Hispanic/Latino). Average age 27. In 2016, 5 master's awarded. *Entrance requirements:* For master's, GRE General Test. Additional exam requirements/recommendations for international students: Required—TOEFL (minimum score 75 iBT). *Application deadline:* For fall admission, 2/1 priority date for domestic and international students. Applications are processed on a rolling basis. Application fee: $80. Electronic applications accepted. *Expenses: Tuition:* Full-time $44,328; part-time $1847 per unit. *Required fees:* $600; $300 per semester. Tuition and fees vary according to course load and program. *Financial support:* Fellowships, research assistantships, teaching assistantships, Federal Work-Study, institutionally sponsored loans, and scholarships/grants available. Support available to part-time students. Financial award application deadline: 2/15; financial award applicants required to submit FAFSA. *Unit head:* Linda Perkins, Director, 909-621-8696, E-mail: linda.perkins@cgu.edu. *Application contact:* Amy Sandefur, Assistant Director of Admissions, 909-607-9101, E-mail: amy.sandefur@cgu.edu. Website: https://www.cgu.edu/departments/applied-womens-studies/

**Clark Atlanta University,** School of Arts and Sciences, Department of Africana Women's Studies, Atlanta, GA 30314. Offers MA, DAH. *Program availability:* Part-time. *Faculty:* 2 full-time (both women). *Students:* 6 full-time (5 women), 11 part-time (all women); all minorities (all Black or African American, non-Hispanic/Latino). Average age 33. 3 applicants, 100% accepted, 2 enrolled. In 2016, 1 master's awarded. *Degree requirements:* For master's, one foreign language, comprehensive exam, thesis optional; for doctorate, one foreign language, comprehensive exam, thesis/dissertation. *Entrance requirements:* For master's, GRE General Test, minimum GPA of 2.5; for doctorate, GRE General Test, minimum graduate GPA of 3.0. Additional exam requirements/recommendations for international students: Required—TOEFL (minimum score 500 paper-based; 61 iBT). *Application deadline:* For fall admission, 4/1 for domestic and international students; for spring admission, 11/1 for domestic and international students. Applications are processed on a rolling basis. Application fee: $40 ($55 for international students). Electronic applications accepted. *Expenses: Tuition:* Full-time $15,498; part-time $861 per credit hour. *Required fees:* $1326; $1326 per credit hour. Tuition and fees vary according to course load. *Financial support:* Scholarships/grants available. Financial award application deadline: 4/30; financial award applicants required to submit FAFSA. *Faculty research:* Concerns of women of African descent globally. *Unit head:* Dr. Stephanie Evans, Chairperson, 404-880-6352, E-mail: sevans@cau.edu. *Application contact:* Graduate Program Admissions, 404-880-8483, E-mail: graduateadmissions@cau.edu.

**Cornell University,** Graduate School, Graduate Fields of Arts and Sciences, Field of English Language and Literature, Ithaca, NY 14853. Offers African-American literature (PhD); American literature after 1865 (PhD); American literature to 1865 (PhD); American studies (PhD); colonial and postcolonial literatures (PhD); creative writing (MFA); cultural studies (PhD); dramatic literature (PhD); English poetry (PhD); English Renaissance to 1660 (PhD); lesbian, bisexual, and gay literary studies (PhD); literary criticism and theory (PhD); Old and Middle English (PhD); prose fiction (PhD); Restoration and the eighteenth-century (PhD); the nineteenth century (PhD); the twentieth century (PhD); women's literature (PhD); MFA/PhD. Terminal master's awarded for partial completion of doctoral program. *Degree requirements:* For master's, one foreign language, thesis; for doctorate, one foreign language, comprehensive exam, thesis/dissertation, teaching experience. *Entrance requirements:* For master's, GRE General Test, 3 letters of recommendation, creative writing sample; for doctorate, GRE General Test, GRE Subject Test (English), 3 letters of recommendation, writing sample. Additional exam requirements/recommendations for international students: Required—TOEFL (minimum score 600 paper-based; 77 iBT). Electronic applications accepted. *Faculty research:* English and American literature, women's writing, ethnic and post-colonial literature, critical theory, medievalism.

**DePaul University,** College of Liberal Arts and Social Sciences, Chicago, IL 60614. Offers Arabic (MA); Chinese (MA); English (MA); French (MA); German (MA); history (MA); interdisciplinary studies (MA, MS); international public service (MS); international studies (MA); Italian (MA); Japanese (MA); leadership and policy studies (MS); liberal studies (MA); new media studies (MA); nonprofit management (MNM); public administration (MPA); public health (MPH); public service management (MS); social work (MSW); sociology (MA); Spanish (MA); sustainable urban development (MA); women and gender studies (MA); writing and publishing (MA); writing, rhetoric, and discourse (MA); MA/PhD. *Program availability:* Part-time, evening/weekend, online learning. Terminal master's awarded for partial completion of doctoral program. *Degree requirements:* For master's, variable foreign language requirement, comprehensive exam (for some programs), thesis (for some programs). Electronic applications accepted.

**Eastern Michigan University,** Graduate School, College of Arts and Sciences, Department of Women's and Gender Studies, Ypsilanti, MI 48197. Offers MA, Graduate Certificate. *Program availability:* Part-time, evening/weekend. *Faculty:* 2 full-time (both women). *Students:* 9 full-time (all women), 8 part-time (all women); includes 4 minority (3 Black or African American, non-Hispanic/Latino; 1 Hispanic/Latino), 1 international. Average age 34. 16 applicants, 94% accepted, 5 enrolled. In 2016, 5 master's, 1 other advanced degree awarded. *Degree requirements:* For master's, thesis, research project, or practicum. *Entrance requirements:* Additional exam requirements/recommendations for international students: Required—TOEFL. *Application deadline:* For fall admission, 6/15 for domestic and international students; for winter admission, 9/15 for domestic and international students; for spring admission, 3/1 for domestic and international students. Applications are processed on a rolling basis. Application fee: $45. *Financial support:* Fellowships, research assistantships with full tuition reimbursements, teaching assistantships with full tuition reimbursements, career-related internships or fieldwork, Federal Work-Study, institutionally sponsored loans, scholarships/grants, tuition waivers (partial), and unspecified assistantships available. Support available to part-time students. Financial award applicants required to submit FAFSA. *Unit head:* Dr. Jacqueline Goodman, Department Head, 734-487-1177, Fax: 734-487-5029, E-mail:

jgoodma9@emich.edu. *Application contact:* Dr. Suzanne Gray, Program Advisor, 734-487-1177, Fax: 734-487-5029, E-mail: sgray17@emich.edu.
Website: http://www.emich.edu/wgstudies/

**Emory University,** Laney Graduate School, Department of Comparative Literature, Atlanta, GA 30322-1100. Offers comparative literature (PhD); philosophy (Certificate); psychoanalytic studies (PhD); women's studies (Certificate). *Degree requirements:* For doctorate, 2 foreign languages, comprehensive exam, thesis/dissertation. *Entrance requirements:* For doctorate, GRE General Test, minimum GPA of 3.0. Additional exam requirements/recommendations for international students: Required—TOEFL. Electronic applications accepted. *Faculty research:* Literary theory, psychoanalysis trauma and testimony, literature and religion, literature and technology, literature and philosophy, politics and global culture, literature and aesthetics.

**Emory University,** Laney Graduate School, Department of Spanish and Portuguese, Atlanta, GA 30322-1100. Offers comparative literature (Certificate); film studies (Certificate); Spanish (PhD); women's studies (Certificate). *Degree requirements:* For doctorate, 2 foreign languages, comprehensive exam, thesis/dissertation. *Entrance requirements:* For doctorate, GRE General Test. Additional exam requirements/recommendations for international students: Required—TOEFL. Electronic applications accepted. *Faculty research:* Spanish literature, Spanish American literature, literary theory, criticism, cultural studies.

**Emory University,** Laney Graduate School, Department of Women's, Gender, and Sexuality Studies, Atlanta, GA 30322-1100. Offers PhD. *Degree requirements:* For doctorate, comprehensive exam, thesis/dissertation. *Entrance requirements:* For doctorate, GRE General Test, writing sample. Additional exam requirements/recommendations for international students: Required—TOEFL. Electronic applications accepted. *Faculty research:* Feminist theory, women's literature, African-American literature, gender in cross-cultural perspective, public policy and globalization.

**Florida Atlantic University,** Dorothy F. Schmidt College of Arts and Letters, Center for Women, Gender and Sexuality Studies, Boca Raton, FL 33431-0991. Offers MA. *Program availability:* Part-time. *Students:* 6 full-time (5 women), 5 part-time (all women); includes 5 minority (3 Hispanic/Latino; 2 Two or more races, non-Hispanic/Latino). Average age 27. 5 applicants, 60% accepted, 2 enrolled. In 2016, 4 master's awarded. *Degree requirements:* For master's, comprehensive exam, thesis or alternative. *Entrance requirements:* For master's, GRE General Test, minimum GPA of 3.0. Additional exam requirements/recommendations for international students: Required—TOEFL (minimum score 500 paper-based; 61 iBT), IELTS (minimum score 6). *Application deadline:* For fall admission, 7/1 for domestic students, 2/15 for international students; for spring admission, 11/1 for domestic students, 7/15 for international students. Applications are processed on a rolling basis. Application fee: $30. Electronic applications accepted. *Expenses:* Tuition, state resident: full-time $7392; part-time $369.82 per credit hour. Tuition, nonresident: full-time $19,432; part-time $1024.81 per credit hour. *Financial support:* Fellowships with tuition reimbursements, teaching assistantships with tuition reimbursements, career-related internships or fieldwork, Federal Work-Study, institutionally sponsored loans, scholarships/grants, and unspecified assistantships available. Support available to part-time students. Financial award applicants required to submit FAFSA. *Faculty research:* Women and science/technology, feminist theory, violence against women, women and international development, feminist medical anthropology. *Unit head:* Regina Gloncalves, Senior Secretary, 561-297-3865, E-mail: rgoncal@fau.edu.
Website: http://www.fau.edu/WomensStudies/

**George Mason University,** College of Humanities and Social Sciences, Interdisciplinary Studies Program, Fairfax, VA 22030. Offers community college teaching (MAIS); computational social science (MAIS); energy and sustainability (MAIS); folklore studies (MAIS); individualized studies (MAIS); neuroethics (MAIS); religion, culture, and values (MAIS); social entrepreneurship (MAIS); social justice and human rights (MAIS); war and the military in society (MAIS); women and gender studies (MAIS). *Faculty:* 10 full-time (3 women), 9 part-time/adjunct (4 women). *Students:* 25 full-time (21 women), 70 part-time (48 women); includes 31 minority (15 Black or African American, non-Hispanic/Latino; 5 Asian, non-Hispanic/Latino; 4 Two or more races, non-Hispanic/Latino), 3 international. Average age 33. 52 applicants, 92% accepted, 23 enrolled. In 2016, 40 master's awarded. *Degree requirements:* For master's, project or thesis. *Entrance requirements:* For master's, 3 letters of recommendation; writing sample; official transcript; resume. Additional exam requirements/recommendations for international students: Required—TOEFL (minimum score 575 paper-based; 88 iBT), IELTS (minimum score 6.5), PTE (minimum score 59). *Application deadline:* For fall admission, 3/1 for domestic students. Application fee: $75 ($80 for international students). Electronic applications accepted. *Expenses:* Tuition, state resident: full-time $10,628; part-time $443 per credit. Tuition, nonresident: full-time $29,306; part-time $1221 per credit. *Required fees:* $3096; $129 per credit. Tuition and fees vary according to program. *Financial support:* In 2016–17, 8 students received support, including 3 research assistantships with tuition reimbursements available (averaging $9,629 per year), 5 teaching assistantships with tuition reimbursements available (averaging $12,814 per year); career-related internships or fieldwork, Federal Work-Study, scholarships/grants, unspecified assistantships, and health care benefits (for full-time research or teaching assistantship recipients) also available. Support available to part-time students. Financial award application deadline: 3/1; financial award applicants required to submit FAFSA. *Faculty research:* Combined English and folklore, religious and cultural studies (Christianity and Muslim society). *Unit head:* Meredith H. Lair, Director, 703-993-2159, Fax: 703-993-1251, E-mail: mlair@gmu.edu. *Application contact:* Morgan Fisher, Graduate Coordinator, 703-993-8762, E-mail: mfisherb@gmu.edu.
Website: http://mais.gmu.edu

**The George Washington University,** Columbian College of Arts and Sciences, Department of Women's Studies, Washington, DC 20052. Offers MA, Certificate. *Program availability:* Part-time, evening/weekend. *Faculty:* 3 full-time (all women), 3 part-time/adjunct (all women). *Students:* 15 full-time (12 women), 9 part-time (all women); includes 7 minority (1 Black or African American, non-Hispanic/Latino; 6 Hispanic/Latino), 2 international. Average age 30. 35 applicants, 83% accepted, 9 enrolled. In 2016, 1 master's awarded. *Degree requirements:* For master's, comprehensive exam, thesis or alternative. *Entrance requirements:* For master's, GRE General Test, minimum GPA of 3.0. Additional exam requirements/recommendations for international students: Required—TOEFL (minimum score 550 paper-based; 80 iBT). *Application deadline:* For fall admission, 4/1 priority date for domestic students, 1/15 priority date for international students; for spring admission, 10/1 priority date for domestic students, 9/1 priority date for international students. Applications are processed on a rolling basis. Application fee: $75. Electronic applications accepted. *Financial support:* In 2016–17, 2 students received support. Fellowships with tuition reimbursements available, teaching assistantships with tuition reimbursements available, Federal Work-Study, institutionally sponsored loans, and tuition waivers available. Financial award application deadline: 1/15. *Unit head:* Dr. Daniel Moshenberg, Director, 202-994-9086, Fax: 202-994-7249. *Application contact:* Information Contact, 202-994-6942, Fax: 202-994-2249, E-mail: wstu@gwu.edu.
Website: http://womensstudies.columbian.gwu.edu/

**Georgia State University,** College of Arts and Sciences, Institute for Women's, Gender, and Sexuality Studies, Atlanta, GA 30302-3083. Offers MA, Graduate Certificate. *Program availability:* Part-time. *Faculty:* 5 full-time (5 women). *Students:* 12 full-time (all women), 2 part-time (both women); includes 9 minority (5 Black or African American, non-Hispanic/Latino; 2 Asian, non-Hispanic/Latino; 2 Two or more races, non-Hispanic/Latino), 1 international. Average age 32. 18 applicants, 89% accepted, 7 enrolled. In 2016, 8 master's, 2 other advanced degrees awarded. *Degree requirements:* For master's, comprehensive exam, thesis or alternative. *Entrance requirements:* For master's and Graduate Certificate, GRE, two official transcripts from each college or university attended, three letters of recommendation addressing student's ability to undertake graduate study, 750-1000 word statement of purpose, academic writing sample. Additional exam requirements/recommendations for international students: Required—TOEFL (minimum score 550 paper-based; 80 iBT). *Application deadline:* For fall admission, 2/15 for domestic and international students. Application fee: $50. Electronic applications accepted. *Expenses:* Tuition, state resident: full-time $6876; part-time $382 per credit hour. Tuition, nonresident: full-time $22,374; part-time $1243 per credit hour. *Required fees:* $2128; $1064 per term. Part-time tuition and fees vary according to course load and program. *Financial support:* In 2016–17, research assistantships with full tuition reimbursements (averaging $7,000 per year), teaching assistantships with full tuition reimbursements (averaging $7,500 per year) were awarded; career-related internships or fieldwork, health care benefits, and unspecified assistantships also available. Financial award application deadline: 2/15. *Faculty research:* Gender, sexuality, and youth studies; gender and neoliberalism; transnational feminisms; cultural studies; queer theories. *Unit head:* Dr. Susan Talburt, Director, 404-413-6581, Fax: 404-413-6585, E-mail: stalburt@gsu.edu. *Application contact:* Dr. Amira Jarmakani, Director of Graduate Studies, 404-413-6583, Fax: 404-413-6585, E-mail: amira@gsu.edu.
Website: http://www2.gsu.edu/~wwwwsi/

**Grace Theological Seminary,** Graduate and Professional Programs, Winona Lake, IN 46590-9907. Offers biblical studies (Certificate); chaplaincy (M Div); exegetical studies (M Div); intercultural studies (M Div, MA, D Min); local church ministry (MA), including camp administration, women's leadership; pastoral counseling (M Div); pastoral studies (M Div, D Min); theology (Diploma). *Accreditation:* ATS. *Program availability:* Part-time, online learning. *Degree requirements:* For master's, thesis optional; for doctorate, 2 foreign languages, thesis/dissertation. *Entrance requirements:* For master's, MAT, minimum GPA of 2.5. Electronic applications accepted. *Faculty research:* Biblical theology, language, and church ministries.

**The Graduate Center, City University of New York,** Graduate Studies, Interdisciplinary Studies, New York, NY 10016-4039. Offers language in social context (PhD); medieval studies (PhD); public policy (MA, PhD); urban studies (MA, PhD); women's studies (MA, PhD). Terminal master's awarded for partial completion of doctoral program. *Degree requirements:* For master's, thesis; for doctorate, comprehensive exam, thesis/dissertation. *Entrance requirements:* For master's and doctorate, GRE General Test.

**Inter American University of Puerto Rico, Metropolitan Campus,** Graduate Programs, Program in Women's and Gender Studies, San Juan, PR 00919-1293. Offers MA.

**The Jewish Theological Seminary,** The Graduate School, New York, NY 10027-4649. Offers ancient Judaism (MA, DHL, PhD); Bible and ancient Semitic languages (MA, DHL, PhD); interdepartmental studies (MA); Jewish art and visual culture (MA); Jewish gender and women's studies (MA); Jewish history (MA, DHL, PhD); Jewish literature (MA, DHL, PhD); Jewish philosophy (DHL); Jewish thought (MA, PhD); liturgy (MA, DHL, PhD); medieval Jewish studies (MA, DHL, PhD); Midrash (DHL); Midrash and scriptural interpretation (MA, PhD); modern Jewish studies (MA, DHL, PhD); Talmud and rabbinics (MA, DHL, PhD); MA/MSW. MA/MSW offered jointly with Columbia University. *Accreditation:* ACIPE. *Program availability:* Part-time. Terminal master's awarded for partial completion of doctoral program. *Degree requirements:* For master's, one foreign language, comprehensive exam (for some programs), thesis (for some programs); for doctorate, 3 foreign languages, comprehensive exam (for some programs), thesis/dissertation. *Entrance requirements:* For master's, GRE or MAT, 3 letters of recommendation, writing sample; for doctorate, GRE or MAT, 3 letters of recommendation, writing research sample. Additional exam requirements/recommendations for international students: Required—TOEFL.

**Kansas State University,** Graduate School, College of Arts and Sciences, Department of Gender, Women and Sexuality Studies, Manhattan, KS 66506. Offers Graduate Certificate. *Faculty:* 5 full-time (4 women), 45 part-time/adjunct (39 women). *Students:* 13 full-time (11 women), 1 (woman) part-time; includes 6 minority (1 Black or African American, non-Hispanic/Latino; 4 Hispanic/Latino; 1 Two or more races, non-Hispanic/Latino). Average age 27. In 2016, 5 Graduate Certificates awarded. *Entrance requirements:* For degree, minimum GPA of 3.0, letters of recommendation. Additional exam requirements/recommendations for international students: Required—TOEFL, TWE, or IELTS. *Expenses:* Tuition, state resident: full-time $9670. Tuition, nonresident: full-time $21,828. *Required fees:* $862. *Financial support:* In 2016–17, 2 teaching assistantships with partial tuition reimbursements (averaging $6,000 per year) were awarded. Financial award application deadline: 3/5. *Faculty research:* Gender and violence, queer and transgender studies, girls' studies, ecofeminism, animal studies. *Unit head:* Angela E. Hubler, Head, 785-532-5738, Fax: 785-532-3299, E-mail: ahubler@ksu.edu. *Application contact:* Valerie Padilla Carroll, Coordinator, 785-532-5738, Fax: 785-532-3299, E-mail: padillacarroll@ksu.edu.
Website: http://www.k-state.edu/womst/

**Lakehead University,** Graduate Studies, Department of History, Thunder Bay, ON P7B 5E1, Canada. Offers gerontology (MA); history (MA); women's studies (MA). *Program availability:* Part-time. *Degree requirements:* For master's, one foreign language, thesis. *Entrance requirements:* For master's, minimum B average. Additional exam requirements/recommendations for international students: Required—TOEFL. *Faculty research:* Canadian history, British history, Russian/German history, women's studies.

**Lakehead University,** Graduate Studies, Faculty of Education, Thunder Bay, ON P7B 5E1, Canada. Offers educational studies (M Ed); gerontology (M Ed); women's studies (M Ed). *Program availability:* Part-time, evening/weekend. *Degree requirements:* For master's, project or thesis. *Entrance requirements:* For master's, minimum B average. Additional exam requirements/recommendations for international students: Required—TOEFL. *Faculty research:* Art education, AIDS education, language arts education, gerontology, women's studies.

**Lakehead University,** Graduate Studies, Faculty of Social Sciences and Humanities, Department of English, Thunder Bay, ON P7B 5E1, Canada. Offers English (MA); women's studies (MA). *Program availability:* Part-time, evening/weekend. *Degree requirements:* For master's, one foreign language, thesis optional. *Entrance requirements:* For master's, minimum B average. Additional exam requirements/recommendations for international students: Required—TOEFL. *Faculty research:* Rhetoric and literary studies, children's literature, nineteenth- and twentieth-century American literature, modern literature, women's studies.

## Women's Studies

**Lakehead University,** Graduate Studies, Faculty of Social Sciences and Humanities, Department of Sociology, Thunder Bay, ON P7B 5E1, Canada. Offers gerontology (MA); health services and policy research (MA); sociology (MA); women's studies (MA). *Program availability:* Part-time, evening/weekend. *Degree requirements:* For master's, research project or thesis. *Entrance requirements:* For master's, minimum B average. Additional exam requirements/recommendations for international students: Required—TOEFL. *Faculty research:* Sociology of medicine, cultural and social change, health human resources, gerontology, women's studies.

**Lakehead University,** Graduate Studies, School of Social Work, Thunder Bay, ON P7B 5E1, Canada. Offers gerontology (MSW); social work (MSW); women's studies (MSW). *Program availability:* Part-time. *Degree requirements:* For master's, thesis or project. *Entrance requirements:* For master's, minimum B average. Additional exam requirements/recommendations for international students: Required—TOEFL. *Faculty research:* Clinical psychology, social work and practice theory, long-term care, health care for frail elderly, women's studies.

**Lakehead University,** Graduate Studies, Women's Studies Collaborative Program, Thunder Bay, ON P7B 5E1, Canada. Offers M Ed, MA, MSW. *Program availability:* Part-time. *Degree requirements:* For master's, thesis (for some programs). *Entrance requirements:* Additional exam requirements/recommendations for international students: Required—TOEFL. *Faculty research:* Feminist thought, feminist pedagogy, women of literature, Canadian women's history, well-being of women.

**Lesley University,** Graduate School of Arts and Social Sciences, Cambridge, MA 02138-2790. Offers clinical mental health counseling (MA), including holistic counseling, school and community counseling, trauma studies; counseling psychology (MA, CAGS), including professional counseling (MA), school counseling (MA); creative writing (MFA); expressive therapies (MA, PhD, CAGS), including art (MA), clinical mental health counseling (MA), dance (MA), expressive therapies (MA), music (MA); independent studies (CAGS); independent study (MA); intercultural relations (MA, CAGS); interdisciplinary studies (MA), including individualized studies, integrative holistic health, mindfulness studies, peace and conflict transformation, trauma sensitive assessment, intervention, and consultation, women's studies; urban environmental leadership (MA). *Program availability:* Part-time, online learning. *Degree requirements:* For master's, internship, practicum, thesis (for expressive therapies); for doctorate, thesis/dissertation, arts apprenticeship, field placement; for CAGS, thesis, internship (for counseling psychology, expressive therapies). *Entrance requirements:* For master's, MAT (counseling psychology), interview, writing samples, art portfolio; for doctorate, GRE or MAT, interview, master's degree; for CAGS, interview, master's degree. Additional exam requirements/recommendations for international students: Required—TOEFL (minimum score 550 paper-based; 80 iBT). Electronic applications accepted. *Faculty research:* Psychotherapy and culture; psychotherapy and psychological trauma; women's issues in art, teaching and psychotherapy; community-based art, psycho-spiritual inquiry.

**London Metropolitan University,** Graduate Programs, London, United Kingdom. Offers applied psychology (M Sc); architecture (MA); biomedical science (M Sc); blood science (M Sc); cancer pharmacology (M Sc); computer networking and cyber security (M Sc); computing and information systems (M Sc); conference interpreting (MA); counter-terrorism studies (M Sc); creative, digital and professional writing (MA); crime, violence and prevention (M Sc); criminology (M Sc); curating contemporary art (MA); data analytics (M Sc); digital media (MA); early childhood studies (MA); education (MA, Ed D); financial services law, regulation and compliance (LL M); food science (M Sc); forensic psychology (M Sc); health and social care management and policy (M Sc); human nutrition (M Sc); human resource management (MA); human rights and international conflict (MA); information technology (M Sc); intelligence and security studies (M Sc); international oil, gas and energy law (LL M); international relations (MA); interpreting (MA); learning and teaching in higher education (MA); legal practice (LL M); media and entertainment law (LL M); organizational and consumer psychology (M Sc); psychological therapy (M Sc); psychology of mental health (M Sc); public health (M Sc); public policy and management (MPA); security studies (M Sc); social work (M Sc); spatial planning and urban design (MA); sports therapy (M Sc); supporting older children and young people with dyslexia (MA); teaching languages (MA), including Arabic, English; translation (MA); woman and child abuse (MA).

**Middle Tennessee State University,** College of Graduate Studies, College of Liberal Arts, Program in Women's and Gender Studies, Murfreesboro, TN 37132. Offers Graduate Certificate. *Program availability:* Part-time, evening/weekend, online learning. Electronic applications accepted.

**Minnesota State University Mankato,** College of Graduate Studies and Research, College of Social and Behavioral Sciences, Department of Gender and Women's Studies, Mankato, MN 56001. Offers MS. *Program availability:* Part-time. *Students:* 5 full-time (4 women), 6 part-time (5 women). *Degree requirements:* For master's, comprehensive exam, thesis or alternative. *Entrance requirements:* For master's, minimum GPA of 3.0, essay. Additional exam requirements/recommendations for international students: Required—TOEFL. *Application deadline:* For fall admission, 3/30 priority date for domestic students. Applications are processed on a rolling basis. Application fee: $40. *Financial support:* Research assistantships, teaching assistantships with full tuition reimbursements, career-related internships or fieldwork, Federal Work-Study, institutionally sponsored loans, and unspecified assistantships available. Support available to part-time students. Financial award application deadline: 3/15; financial award applicants required to submit FAFSA. *Unit head:* Shannon Miller, Chair, 507-389-5024, E-mail: shannon.miller@mnsu.edu.
Website: http://sbs.mnsu.edu/women/

**Mount Saint Vincent University,** Graduate Programs, Department of Women's Studies, Halifax, NS B3M 2J6, Canada. Offers MA. Program offered jointly with Dalhousie University, Saint Mary's University. *Program availability:* Part-time. *Degree requirements:* For master's, thesis. Electronic applications accepted.

**Northern Arizona University,** Graduate College, College of Social and Behavioral Sciences, Women's and Gender Studies Program, Flagstaff, AZ 86011. Offers Graduate Certificate. *Program availability:* Part-time. *Entrance requirements:* Additional exam requirements/recommendations for international students: Required—TOEFL (minimum score 550 paper-based; 80 iBT). Electronic applications accepted. *Expenses:* Tuition, state resident: full-time $8971; part-time $444 per credit hour. Tuition, nonresident: full-time $20,958; part-time $1164 per credit hour. *Required fees:* $1018; $644 per credit hour. Tuition and fees vary according to course load, campus/location and program.

**The Ohio State University,** Graduate School, College of Arts and Sciences, Division of Arts and Humanities, Department of Women's, Gender and Sexuality Studies, Columbus, OH 43210. Offers MA, PhD. *Faculty:* 14. *Students:* 26 full-time (24 women), 6 international. Average age 28. In 2016, 1 master's, 4 doctorates awarded. Terminal master's awarded for partial completion of doctoral program. *Degree requirements:* For master's, thesis optional; for doctorate, thesis/dissertation. *Entrance requirements:* For master's and doctorate, GRE (if GPA is less than 3.0 for all work), scholarly writing sample. Additional exam requirements/recommendations for international students: Required—TOEFL (minimum score 550 paper-based; 79 iBT), Michigan English Language Assessment Battery (minimum score 82); Recommended—IELTS (minimum score 7). *Application deadline:* For fall admission, 12/1 priority date for domestic

students, 11/15 priority date for international students; for spring admission, 3/1 for domestic students, 2/1 for international students. Applications are processed on a rolling basis. Application fee: $60 ($70 for international students). Electronic applications accepted. *Financial support:* Fellowships with tuition reimbursements, research assistantships with tuition reimbursements, teaching assistantships with tuition reimbursements, career-related internships or fieldwork, Federal Work-Study, institutionally sponsored loans, and unspecified assistantships available. Support available to part-time students. *Unit head:* Dr. Shannon Winnubst, Chair and Professor, 614-292-3915, E-mail: winnubst.1@osu.edu. *Application contact:* Graduate and Professional Admissions, 614-292-9444, Fax: 614-292-3895, E-mail: gpadmissions@osu.edu.
Website: http://wgss.osu.edu/

**Old Dominion University,** College of Arts and Letters, Program in Applied Sociology, Norfolk, VA 23529. Offers criminal justice (MA); general sociology (MA); women's studies (MA). *Program availability:* Part-time, evening/weekend. *Faculty:* 19 full-time (11 women). *Students:* 11 full-time (8 women), 2 part-time (1 woman); includes 6 minority (3 Black or African American, non-Hispanic/Latino; 3 Two or more races, non-Hispanic/Latino). Average age 23. 26 applicants, 65% accepted, 12 enrolled. In 2016, 4 master's awarded. *Degree requirements:* For master's, thesis. *Entrance requirements:* For master's, GRE General Test, minimum GPA of 3.0; 12 credits in criminal justice, sociology, or women's studies. Additional exam requirements/recommendations for international students: Required—TOEFL. *Application deadline:* For fall admission, 3/1 for domestic and international students. Application fee: $50. Electronic applications accepted. *Expenses:* Contact institution. *Financial support:* In 2016–17, 8 students received support, including 2 research assistantships (averaging $10,000 per year), 6 teaching assistantships (averaging $10,000 per year); career-related internships or fieldwork, scholarships/grants, and unspecified assistantships also available. Financial award application deadline: 2/15. *Faculty research:* Quantitative methodology, theory, family, gender/class/race, crime. *Total annual research expenditures:* $350,000. *Unit head:* Dr. Ingrid Whitaker, Graduate Program Director, 757-683-3811, Fax: 757-683-5634, E-mail: iwhitake@odu.edu. *Application contact:* Dr. David C. Earnest, Associate Dean, 757-683-6077, Fax: 757-683-5746, E-mail: dearnest@odu.edu.
Website: http://al.odu.edu/sociology/gradprogram/graduatehome.shtml

**Oregon State University,** College of Liberal Arts, Program in Women, Gender, and Sexuality Studies, Corvallis, OR 97331. Offers feminist leadership (PhD); gender, rhetoric, and representation (PhD); health and gender justice (PhD); social justice theory and practice (PhD). *Program availability:* Part-time. *Faculty:* 12 full-time (7 women), 1 (woman) part-time/adjunct. *Students:* 20 full-time (19 women), 5 part-time (all women); includes 4 minority (1 American Indian or Alaska Native, non-Hispanic/Latino; 2 Hispanic/Latino; 1 Two or more races, non-Hispanic/Latino), 8 international. Average age 30. 66 applicants, 30% accepted, 10 enrolled. In 2016, 4 master's awarded. *Degree requirements:* For master's, one foreign language; for doctorate, thesis/dissertation. *Entrance requirements:* Additional exam requirements/recommendations for international students: Required—TOEFL (minimum score 80 iBT), IELTS (minimum score 6.5). *Application deadline:* For fall admission, 12/1 for domestic and international students. Application fee: $75 ($85 for international students). *Expenses:* Tuition, state resident: full-time $12,150; part-time $450 per credit. Tuition, nonresident: full-time $21,789; part-time $807 per credit. *Required fees:* $1651; $1507 per credit. One-time fee: $350. Tuition and fees vary according to course load, campus/location and program. *Financial support:* Application deadline: 4/1. *Unit head:* Dr. Larry Roper, Professor and Director of the School of Language, Culture, and Society. *Application contact:* Dr. Qwo-Li Driskill, Director of Graduate Studies, 541-737-1114, E-mail: quo-li.driskill@oregonstate.edu.
Website: http://liberalarts.oregonstate.edu/slcs/wgss/

**Queen's University at Kingston,** School of Graduate Studies, Faculty of Arts and Sciences, Department of Sociology, Kingston, ON K7L 3N6, Canada. Offers communication and Information technology (MA, PhD); feminist sociology (MA, PhD); socio-legal studies (MA, PhD); sociological theory (MA, PhD). *Program availability:* Part-time. *Degree requirements:* For master's, thesis; for doctorate, comprehensive exam, thesis/dissertation. *Entrance requirements:* For master's, honors bachelors degree in sociology; for doctorate, honors bachelors degree, masters degree in sociology. Additional exam requirements/recommendations for international students: Required—TOEFL. *Faculty research:* Social change and modernization, social control, deviance and criminology, surveillance.

**Reconstructionist Rabbinical College,** Graduate Programs, Wyncote, PA 19095-1898. Offers Jewish studies (MAJS); rabbinics (MAHL, DHL); women's studies (Certificate). Certificate offered jointly with Temple University. *Program availability:* Part-time. *Degree requirements:* For master's, one foreign language, thesis (MAJS), completion of rabbinical program (MAHL); for doctorate, one foreign language. *Entrance requirements:* For master's, GRE General Test; placement examinations in Hebrew and Judaism (MAHL); for doctorate, GRE General Test, placement examinations in Hebrew and Judaism. *Faculty research:* Bible, Hebrew Semitic texts, contemporary Judaism.

**Roosevelt University,** Graduate Division, College of Arts and Sciences, Department of Literature and Languages, Program in Women's and Gender Studies, Chicago, IL 60605. Offers MA, Certificate. *Program availability:* Part-time, evening/weekend. *Degree requirements:* For master's, thesis. *Entrance requirements:* For master's, minimum GPA of 2.7. *Faculty research:* Feminist economics; philosophy of feminism; race, class, and gender; women and art; women's history.

**Rutgers University–New Brunswick,** Graduate School-New Brunswick, Department of Political Science, Piscataway, NJ 08854-8097. Offers American politics (PhD); comparative politics (PhD); international relations (PhD); political theory (PhD); public law (PhD); United Nations and global policy studies (MA); women and politics (PhD). *Degree requirements:* For doctorate, one foreign language, comprehensive exam, thesis/dissertation. *Entrance requirements:* For master's, bachelor's degree from accredited U.S. college or university or a comparable institution in another country; for doctorate, GRE General Test. Additional exam requirements/recommendations for international students: Required—TOEFL.

**Rutgers University–New Brunswick,** Graduate School-New Brunswick, Program in Women's and Gender Studies, Piscataway, NJ 08854-8097. Offers MA, PhD. *Program availability:* Part-time. *Degree requirements:* For master's, thesis or alternative; for doctorate, comprehensive exam, thesis/dissertation. *Entrance requirements:* For master's and doctorate, GRE General Test, writing sample, 3 letters of recommendation. Additional exam requirements/recommendations for international students: Required—TOEFL. *Faculty research:* Feminist theory, gender and sexuality, global and cultural studies, women in history, literature, and politics, feminist politics.

**Saint Mary's University,** Faculty of Arts, Program in Women and Gender Studies, Halifax, NS B3H 3C3, Canada. Offers MA. Program offered jointly with Mount Saint Vincent University. *Program availability:* Part-time. *Degree requirements:* For master's, thesis. *Entrance requirements:* For master's, honors degree.

**San Diego State University,** Graduate and Research Affairs, College of Arts and Letters, Department of Women's Studies, San Diego, CA 92182. Offers MA. *Entrance requirements:* For master's, GRE General Test, 2 letters of reference. Additional exam requirements/recommendations for international students: Required—TOEFL. Electronic applications accepted.

**San Francisco State University,** Division of Graduate Studies, College of Liberal and Creative Arts, Department of Women and Gender Studies, San Francisco, CA 94132-1722. Offers MA. *Program availability:* Part-time, evening/weekend. *Expenses:* Tuition, state resident: full-time $6738. Tuition, nonresident: full-time $15,666. *Required fees:* $1012. Tuition and fees vary according to degree level and program. *Unit head:* Dr. Julietta Hua, Chair, 415-338-3065, Fax: 415-338-6159, E-mail: jyhua@sfsu.edu. *Application contact:* Dr. Deborah Cohler, Graduate Coordinator, 415-338-3150, Fax: 415-338-6159, E-mail: dcohler@sfsu.edu.
Website: http://wgsdept.sfsu.edu/

**Sarah Lawrence College,** Graduate Studies, Program in Women's History, Bronxville, NY 10708-5999. Offers MA. *Program availability:* Part-time. *Degree requirements:* For master's, thesis. *Entrance requirements:* For master's, previous course work in history, minimum B average in undergraduate course work. Additional exam requirements/recommendations for international students: Required—TOEFL (minimum score 600 paper-based). Electronic applications accepted.

**Simon Fraser University,** Office of Graduate Studies and Postdoctoral Fellows, Faculty of Arts and Social Sciences, Department of Gender, Sexuality and Women's Studies, Burnaby, BC V5A 1S6, Canada. Offers MA, PhD. *Faculty:* 6 full-time (all women). *Students:* 21 full-time (16 women). 40 applicants, 40% accepted, 8 enrolled. In 2016, 1 master's, 1 doctorate awarded. *Degree requirements:* For master's, thesis or alternative; for doctorate, comprehensive exam, thesis/dissertation. *Entrance requirements:* For master's, minimum GPA of 3.0 (on scale of 4.33) or 3.33 based on last 60 credits of undergraduate courses; for doctorate, minimum GPA of 3.5 (on scale of 4.33). Additional exam requirements/recommendations for international students: Recommended—TOEFL (minimum score 580 paper-based; 93 iBT), IELTS (minimum score 7), TWE (minimum score 5). *Application deadline:* For spring admission, 3/1 for domestic students. Applications are processed on a rolling basis. Application fee: $90 ($125 for international students). Electronic applications accepted. *Financial support:* In 2016–17, 8 students received support, including 6 fellowships (averaging $6,500 per year), teaching assistantships (averaging $5,608 per year); research assistantships and scholarships/grants also available. *Faculty research:* Gender history, feminist labor studies/economics, queer theory, women and media, feminist research methods. *Unit head:* Dr. Jen Marchbank, Graduate Chair, 778-782-3333, Fax: 778-782-5518, E-mail: gsws-grad-chair@sfu.ca. *Application contact:* Kathryn Hunter, Graduate Secretary, 778-782-3333, Fax: 778-782-5518, E-mail: gswssec@sfu.ca.
Website: http://www.sfu.ca/gsws.html

**Smith College,** Graduate and Special Programs, Center for Women in Mathematics Post-Baccalaureate Program, Northampton, MA 01063. Offers Postbaccalaureate Certificate. *Students:* 12 full-time (all women); includes 5 minority (3 Black or African American, non-Hispanic/Latino; 2 Asian, non-Hispanic/Latino). Average age 25. 33 applicants, 48% accepted, 12 enrolled. In 2016, 12 Postbaccalaureate Certificates awarded. *Entrance requirements:* Additional exam requirements/recommendations for international students: Required—TOEFL (minimum score 595 paper-based; 97 iBT), IELTS (minimum score 7.5). *Application deadline:* For fall admission, 3/15 for domestic students; for spring admission, 10/15 for domestic students. Application fee: $60. *Expenses: Tuition:* Full-time $34,560; part-time $1440 per credit. Tuition and fees vary according to course load and program. *Financial support:* In 2016–17, 12 students received support. Scholarships/grants and tuition waivers (full) available. Financial award application deadline: 3/15. *Unit head:* Ruth Haas, Director, 413-585-3872, E-mail: rhaas@smith.edu. *Application contact:* Ruth Morgan, Program Assistant, 413-585-3050, Fax: 413-585-3054, E-mail: rmorgan@smith.edu.

**Southeastern Baptist Theological Seminary,** Graduate and Professional Programs, Wake Forest, NC 27588-1889. Offers advanced biblical studies (M Div); Christian education (M Div, MACE); Christian ethics (PhD); Christian ministry (M Div); Christian planting (M Div); church music (MACM); counseling (MACO); evangelism (PhD); language (M Div); ministry (D Min); New Testament (PhD); Old Testament (PhD); philosophy (PhD); theology (Th M, PhD); women's studies (M Div). *Accreditation:* ACIPE; ATS (one or more programs are accredited). *Degree requirements:* For master's, thesis (for some programs), oral exam; for doctorate, thesis/dissertation, fieldwork. *Entrance requirements:* For master's, Cooperative English Test, minimum GPA of 2.0, M Div or equivalent (Th M); for doctorate, GRE General Test or MAT, Cooperative English Test, M Div or equivalent, 3 years of professional experience.

**Southern Connecticut State University,** School of Graduate Studies, School of Arts and Sciences, Program in Women's Studies, New Haven, CT 06515-1355. Offers MA. *Program availability:* Part-time, evening/weekend. *Faculty:* 1 (woman) part-time/adjunct. *Students:* 5 full-time (all women), 6 part-time (all women); includes 3 minority (1 Black or African American, non-Hispanic/Latino; 2 Two or more races, non-Hispanic/Latino). Average age 32. 6 applicants, 17% accepted. In 2016, 11 master's awarded. *Degree requirements:* For master's, thesis or alternative. *Entrance requirements:* For master's, interview. *Application deadline:* Applications are processed on a rolling basis. Application fee: $50. Electronic applications accepted. *Expenses:* Tuition, state resident: full-time $6497; part-time $519 per credit hour. Tuition, nonresident: full-time $18,102; part-time $535 per credit hour. *Required fees:* $4722; $55 per semester. Tuition and fees vary according to program. *Financial support:* Career-related internships or fieldwork, scholarships/grants, and unspecified assistantships available. Financial award application deadline: 4/15; financial award applicants required to submit FAFSA. *Unit head:* Dr. Tricia Lin, Director, 203-392-6832, Fax: 203-392-5670, E-mail: liny4@southernct.edu. *Application contact:* Lisa Galvin, Director of Graduate Admissions, 203-392-5240, Fax: 203-392-5235, E-mail: galvinl1@southernct.edu.

**Stony Brook University, State University of New York,** Graduate School, College of Arts and Sciences, Program in Women's, Gender, and Sexuality Studies, Stony Brook, NY 11794. Offers Certificate. In 2016, 7 Certificates awarded. *Degree requirements:* For Certificate, interdisciplinary research colloquium. *Entrance requirements:* For degree, GRE, minimum GPA of 2.75, 3 letters of recommendation. Additional exam requirements/recommendations for international students: Required—TOEFL. *Expenses:* Contact institution. *Faculty research:* Exercise, gender studies, humanities, literary criticism, women's studies. *Unit head:* Prof. Mary Jo Bona, Chair, 631-632-6355, E-mail: maryjo.bona@stonybrook.edu. *Application contact:* Graduate Program Director, 631-632-7461.
Website: http://www.stonybrook.edu/commcms/wgss/

**Texas Woman's University,** Graduate School, College of Arts and Sciences, Department of Multicultural Women's and Gender Studies, Denton, TX 76201. Offers MA, PhD. *Program availability:* Part-time. *Students:* 5 full-time (4 women), 37 part-time (35 women); includes 20 minority (9 Black or African American, non-Hispanic/Latino; 1 American Indian or Alaska Native, non-Hispanic/Latino; 3 Asian, non-Hispanic/Latino; 5 Hispanic/Latino; 2 Two or more races, non-Hispanic/Latino), 1 international. Average age 36. In 2016, 9 master's awarded. Terminal master's awarded for partial completion of doctoral program. *Degree requirements:* For master's, comprehensive exam, thesis (for some programs); for doctorate, comprehensive exam, thesis/dissertation. *Entrance requirements:* For master's, 2 letters of reference, personal essay; for doctorate,

personal essay, writing sample, curriculum vitae, 2 reference letters. Additional exam requirements/recommendations for international students: Required—TOEFL (minimum score 550 paper-based; 79 iBT). *Application deadline:* For fall admission, 2/1 for domestic and international students; for spring admission, 12/1 priority date for domestic students, 7/1 for international students. Applications are processed on a rolling basis. Application fee: $50 ($75 for international students). Electronic applications accepted. *Expenses:* Tuition, state resident: full-time $9046; part-time $251 per credit hour. Tuition, nonresident: full-time $22,922; part-time $614 per credit hour. *International tuition:* $23,046 full-time. *Required fees:* $2690; $1285 per credit hour. One-time fee: $50. Tuition and fees vary according to course level, course load, program and reciprocity agreements. *Financial support:* Research assistantships, teaching assistantships, career-related internships or fieldwork, Federal Work-Study, institutionally sponsored loans, scholarships/grants, traineeships, health care benefits, and unspecified assistantships available. Support available to part-time students. Financial award application deadline: 3/1; financial award applicants required to submit FAFSA. *Faculty research:* Feminist/womanist theories and epistemologies, history of U.S. feminism, U.S. women of color, feminism and religion/spirituality, critical race theories. *Unit head:* Dr. Ana Louise Keating, Interim Chair, 940-898-2129, Fax: 940-898-2101, E-mail: akeating@mail.twu.edu. *Application contact:* Dr. Samuel Wheeler, Assistant Director of Admissions, 940-898-3188, Fax: 940-898-3081, E-mail: wheelersr@twu.edu.
Website: http://www.twu.edu/ws/

**Towson University,** Program in Women's Studies, Towson, MD 21252-0001. Offers MS, Postbaccalaureate Certificate. *Students:* 6 full-time (5 women), 5 part-time (all women); includes 2 minority (both Black or African American, non-Hispanic/Latino), 3 international. *Degree requirements:* For master's, thesis optional. *Entrance requirements:* For master's, bachelor's degree with minimum GPA of 3.0, 9 credits of course work in women's studies and/or the social sciences, essay, 2 letters of recommendation; for Postbaccalaureate Certificate, bachelor's degree, 9 units in women's studies and/or the social sciences, 2 letters of recommendation, essay. *Application deadline:* Applications are processed on a rolling basis. Application fee: $45. Electronic applications accepted. *Expenses:* Tuition, state resident: full-time $7580; part-time $379 per unit. Tuition, nonresident: full-time $15,700; part-time $785 per unit. *Required fees:* $2480. *Financial support:* Application deadline: 4/1. *Unit head:* Dr. Esther Wangari, Graduate Program Director, 410-704-2580, E-mail: ewangari@towson.edu. *Application contact:* Coverley Beidleman, Assistant Director of Graduate Admissions, 410-704-2113, Fax: 410-704-3030, E-mail: grads@towson.edu.
Website: http://www.towson.edu/cla/departments/womengender/grad/womengender/

**United Theological Seminary of the Twin Cities,** Graduate Programs, New Brighton, MN 55112-2598. Offers advanced theological studies (Diploma); justice and peace studies (M Div, MA); leadership toward racial justice (M Div, MA, Certificate); Methodist studies (M Div, MA, Certificate); ministry (D Min); ministry renewal and professional development (Certificate); pastoral care and counseling (M Div, MA, MARL); religion and theology (MA); theological and religious studies (Certificate); theology and the arts (M Div, MA); urban ministry (M Div, MA, MARL); women's studies: religion, theology and ministry (M Div, MA). *Accreditation:* ACIPE; ATS. *Program availability:* Part-time, evening/weekend. *Degree requirements:* For master's, thesis; for doctorate, comprehensive exam, thesis/dissertation. *Entrance requirements:* For master's, minimum GPA of 2.75; strong analytical, reflective thinking and writing skills; vocational and academic goals compatible with those of Seminary; for doctorate, M Div or equivalent, minimum GPA of 3.0, 3 years experience in professional ministry; for other advanced degree, BA or equivalent life experience; strong analytical, reflective thinking and writing skills (Certificate); proficiency in English language, previous study of theology at a theological school, recommendation of student's denomination (Diploma). Additional requirements/recommendations for international students: Required—TOEFL (minimum score 550 paper-based).

**Université Laval,** Faculty of Social Sciences, Program in Feminist Studies, Québec, QC G1K 7P4, Canada. Offers Diploma. *Program availability:* Part-time. *Entrance requirements:* For degree, knowledge of French, comprehension of written English. Electronic applications accepted.

**University at Albany, State University of New York,** College of Arts and Sciences, Department of Women's, Gender and Sexuality Studies, Albany, NY 12222-0001. Offers MA. *Faculty:* 3 full-time (all women). *Students:* 12 full-time (all women), 3 part-time (2 women); includes 2 minority (1 Hispanic/Latino; 1 Two or more races, non-Hispanic/Latino), 4 international. 21 applicants, 86% accepted, 8 enrolled. In 2016, 6 master's awarded. *Entrance requirements:* Additional exam requirements/recommendations for international students: Required—TOEFL (minimum score 550 paper-based). *Application deadline:* For fall admission, 8/1 for domestic students, 5/1 for international students. Applications are processed on a rolling basis. Application fee: $75. Electronic applications accepted. *Expenses:* Tuition, state resident: full-time $10,870; part-time $453 per credit hour. Tuition, nonresident: full-time $22,210; part-time $925 per credit hour. *International tuition:* $21,550 full-time. *Required fees:* $1864; $96 per credit hour. *Faculty research:* Feminist pedagogy, lesbian and gay studies, women in the African diaspora, women's health policy, literature of feminism. *Unit head:* Vivian Ng, Chair, 518-442-4220, Fax: 518-442-4419, E-mail: vng@albany.edu. *Application contact:* Michael DeRensis, Director, Graduate Admissions, 518-442-3980, Fax: 518-442-3922, E-mail: graduate@albany.edu.
Website: http://www.albany.edu/ws/

**The University of Alabama,** Graduate School, College of Arts and Sciences, Department of Gender and Race Studies, Tuscaloosa, AL 35487. Offers women's studies (MA). *Program availability:* Part-time. *Faculty:* 6 full-time (4 women). *Students:* 11 full-time (8 women), 7 part-time (all women); includes 10 minority (9 Black or African American, non-Hispanic/Latino; 1 Hispanic/Latino). Average age 25. 13 applicants, 85% accepted, 6 enrolled. In 2016, 16 master's awarded. *Degree requirements:* For master's, comprehensive exam, thesis optional. *Entrance requirements:* For master's, MAT or GRE. Additional exam requirements/recommendations for international students: Required—TOEFL. *Application deadline:* For fall admission, 3/7 priority date for domestic students, 3/7 for international students. Applications are processed on a rolling basis. Application fee: $50 ($60 for international students). Electronic applications accepted. *Expenses:* Tuition, state resident: full-time $10,470. Tuition, nonresident: full-time $26,950. *Financial support:* In 2016–17, 6 students received support, including 3 research assistantships with tuition reimbursements available (averaging $10,908 per year), 3 teaching assistantships with tuition reimbursements available (averaging $10,908 per year); health care benefits and unspecified assistantships also available. Financial award application deadline: 4/1. *Faculty research:* Black feminist theory, African-American women's discursive practices, black women's leadership, feminist theory, queer theory. *Unit head:* Dr. Utz McKnight, Chair, 205-348-5528, E-mail: umcknigh@bama.ua.edu. *Application contact:* Patrick D. Fuller, Senior Graduate Admissions Counselor, 205-348-5923, Fax: 205-348-0400, E-mail: patrick.d.fuller@ua.edu.
Website: http://www.as.ua.edu/grs/

**The University of Arizona,** College of Social and Behavioral Sciences, Department of Gender and Women's Studies, Tucson, AZ 85721. Offers MA, PhD, Certificate. *Program*

## Women's Studies

*availability:* Part-time. *Degree requirements:* For master's, thesis/project. *Entrance requirements:* For master's and doctorate, GRE (minimum score: 500 verbal, 500 quantitative, 4.5 analytical), 3 letters of recommendation. Additional exam requirements/recommendations for international students: Required—TOEFL (minimum score 600 paper-based; 100 iBT). Electronic applications accepted. *Faculty research:* Gender, race and border studies; sexuality and the body; gender health and science; cultural representation and theory; public policy and social movements.

**University of California, Santa Barbara,** Graduate Division, College of Letters and Sciences, Division of Humanities and Fine Arts, Department of English, Santa Barbara, CA 93106-3170. Offers English (PhD), including environment and society, European medieval studies, feminist studies, global studies, technology and society, translation studies, writing studies; MA/PhD. Terminal master's awarded for partial completion of doctoral program. *Degree requirements:* For doctorate, one foreign language, comprehensive exam, thesis/dissertation. *Entrance requirements:* For doctorate, GRE General Test, GRE Subject Test (English literature). Additional exam requirements/recommendations for international students: Required—TOEFL (minimum score 550 paper-based; 80 iBT), IELTS (minimum score 7). Electronic applications accepted. *Faculty research:* Medieval, Romantic and Victorian studies; gender studies and feminist theory; literature and the mind; American literature; literature and new media/information culture.

**University of California, Santa Barbara,** Graduate Division, College of Letters and Sciences, Division of Humanities and Fine Arts, Department of History, Santa Barbara, CA 93106-9410. Offers European medieval studies (PhD); global studies (PhD); public historical studies (PhD); technology and society (PhD); women's studies (PhD); MA/PhD. *Degree requirements:* For doctorate, variable foreign language requirement, comprehensive exam, thesis/dissertation. *Entrance requirements:* For doctorate, GRE. Additional exam requirements/recommendations for international students: Required—TOEFL (minimum score 550 paper-based; 80 iBT), IELTS (minimum score 7). Electronic applications accepted. *Faculty research:* Europe, United States, Latin America, Africa, Middle East, East Asia.

**University of California, Santa Barbara,** Graduate Division, College of Letters and Sciences, Division of Humanities and Fine Arts, Department of History of Art and Architecture, Santa Barbara, CA 93106-2014. Offers art history (PhD), including art history, European medieval studies, feminist studies; MA/PhD. Terminal master's awarded for partial completion of doctoral program. *Degree requirements:* For doctorate, 2 foreign languages, comprehensive exam, thesis/dissertation. *Entrance requirements:* For doctorate, GRE. Additional exam requirements/recommendations for international students: Required—TOEFL (minimum score 550 paper-based; 80 iBT), IELTS (minimum score 7). Electronic applications accepted. *Faculty research:* History of architecture, Renaissance-Italian, Baroque, American, Chinese, Japanese, contemporary, Northern Renaissance.

**University of California, Santa Barbara,** Graduate Division, College of Letters and Sciences, Division of Humanities and Fine Arts, Department of Religious Studies, Santa Barbara, CA 93106-3130. Offers ancient Mediterranean studies (PhD); cognitive science (PhD); European medieval studies (PhD); feminist studies (PhD); global studies (PhD); religious studies (MA, PhD); translation studies (PhD); MA/PhD. Terminal master's awarded for partial completion of doctoral program. *Degree requirements:* For master's, one foreign language, comprehensive exam (for some programs), thesis (for some programs); for doctorate, 2 foreign languages, thesis/dissertation, methodology. *Entrance requirements:* For master's and doctorate, GRE General Test. Additional exam requirements/recommendations for international students: Required—TOEFL (minimum score 550 paper-based; 80 iBT), IELTS (minimum score 7). Electronic applications accepted. *Faculty research:* Area studies; religious traditions; theory and method in the study of religion; religion, culture, and politics; spirituality and religious experience.

**University of California, Santa Barbara,** Graduate Division, College of Letters and Sciences, Division of Humanities and Fine Arts, Department of Spanish and Portuguese, Santa Barbara, CA 93106-4150. Offers Hispanic languages and literatures (PhD), including European medieval studies, feminist studies, Hispanic linguistics, Hispanic literature, Luso-Brazilian literature; Hispanic linguistics (MA); Luso-Brazilian literature (MA); Spanish or Spanish-American literature (MA); MA/PhD. Terminal master's awarded for partial completion of doctoral program. *Degree requirements:* For master's, 2 foreign languages, comprehensive exam (for some programs), thesis optional; for doctorate, 3 foreign languages, comprehensive exam, thesis/dissertation. *Entrance requirements:* For master's and doctorate, GRE. Additional exam requirements/recommendations for international students: Required—TOEFL (minimum score 550 paper-based; 80 iBT), IELTS (minimum score 7). Electronic applications accepted. *Faculty research:* Nineteenth-century Spanish and Portuguese literature, Spanish and Spanish-American literature, nineteenth- and twentieth-century Portuguese and Brazilian literatures, Hispanic linguistics, Catalan language and culture.

**University of California, Santa Barbara,** Graduate Division, College of Letters and Sciences, Division of Humanities and Fine Arts, Department of Theater and Dance, Santa Barbara, CA 93106-7060. Offers theater studies (MA, PhD), including European medieval studies (PhD), feminist studies (PhD), theatre studies (PhD); MA/PhD. Terminal master's awarded for partial completion of doctoral program. *Degree requirements:* For master's, comprehensive exam, thesis; for doctorate, one foreign language, comprehensive exam, thesis/dissertation. *Entrance requirements:* For master's and doctorate, GRE. Additional exam requirements/recommendations for international students: Required—TOEFL (minimum score 550 paper-based; 80 iBT), IELTS (minimum score 7). Electronic applications accepted. *Faculty research:* English and American theater and Ancient Greek; Spanish, Latin American and Caribbean performance; Renaissance and Baroque drama and intercultural theory; East Asian performance, gender and nationalism; Korean cultural studies, Russian literature, and Slavic folklore; history of German theater, Shakespeare, and European opera; postcolonialism, performance-based ethnography, globalism and national identity formation in Africa.

**University of California, Santa Barbara,** Graduate Division, College of Letters and Sciences, Division of Humanities and Fine Arts, Program in Comparative Literature, Santa Barbara, CA 93106-4130. Offers comparative literature (PhD); East Asian literatures (PhD); feminist studies (PhD); French (PhD); global studies (PhD); translation studies (PhD); MA/PhD. *Degree requirements:* For doctorate, 2 foreign languages, comprehensive exam, thesis/dissertation. *Entrance requirements:* For doctorate, GRE. Additional exam requirements/recommendations for international students: Required—TOEFL (minimum score 550 paper-based; 80 iBT), IELTS (minimum score 7). Electronic applications accepted. *Faculty research:* Comparative literary studies in global context, critical theory, translation studies, media technological studies, trauma studies.

**University of California, Santa Barbara,** Graduate Division, College of Letters and Sciences, Division of Social Sciences, Department of Communication, Santa Barbara, CA 93106-4020. Offers cognitive science (PhD); communication (PhD); feminist studies (PhD); language, interaction and social organization (PhD); quantitative methods in the social sciences (PhD); society and technology (PhD); MA/PhD. Terminal master's awarded for partial completion of doctoral program. *Degree requirements:* For doctorate, comprehensive exam, thesis/dissertation. *Entrance requirements:* For doctorate, GRE.

Additional exam requirements/recommendations for international students: Required—TOEFL (minimum score 80 iBT), IELTS (minimum score 7). Electronic applications accepted. *Faculty research:* Interpersonal, intergroup, intercultural, organizational, health, media.

**University of California, Santa Barbara,** Graduate Division, College of Letters and Sciences, Division of Social Sciences, Department of Feminist Studies, Santa Barbara, CA 93106-7110. Offers MA, PhD, MA/PhD. Terminal master's awarded for partial completion of doctoral program. *Degree requirements:* For master's, thesis (for some programs); for doctorate, one foreign language, comprehensive exam, thesis/dissertation. *Entrance requirements:* For master's and doctorate, GRE. Additional exam requirements/recommendations for international students: Required—TOEFL (minimum score 550 paper-based; 80 iBT), IELTS (minimum score 7). Electronic applications accepted. *Faculty research:* Genders and sexualities, productive and reproductive labors, race and nation, discourse and theory, media and new technologies.

**University of California, Santa Barbara,** Graduate Division, College of Letters and Sciences, Division of Social Sciences, Department of Sociology, Santa Barbara, CA 93106-9430. Offers interdisciplinary emphasis: Black studies (PhD); interdisciplinary emphasis: environment and society (PhD); interdisciplinary emphasis: feminist studies (PhD); interdisciplinary emphasis: global studies (PhD); interdisciplinary emphasis: language, interaction and social organization (PhD); interdisciplinary emphasis: quantitative methods in the social sciences (PhD); interdisciplinary emphasis: technology and society (PhD); sociology (PhD); MA/PhD. Terminal master's awarded for partial completion of doctoral program. *Degree requirements:* For doctorate, comprehensive exam, thesis/dissertation. *Entrance requirements:* For doctorate, GRE General Test. Additional exam requirements/recommendations for international students: Required—TOEFL (minimum score 550 paper-based; 80 iBT), IELTS (minimum score 7). Electronic applications accepted. *Faculty research:* Gender and sexualities, race/ethnicity, social movements, conversation analysis, global sociology.

**University of Cincinnati,** Graduate School, McMicken College of Arts and Sciences, Department of Women's, Gender, and Sexuality Studies, Cincinnati, OH 45221-0164. Offers MA, Certificate, MA/JD. *Program availability:* Part-time. Terminal master's awarded for partial completion of doctoral program. *Degree requirements:* For master's, comprehensive exam, final paper/project. *Entrance requirements:* For master's, GRE General Test, 3 letters of recommendation. Additional exam requirements/recommendations for international students: Required—TOEFL (minimum score 600 paper-based), IELTS (minimum score 6.5). Electronic applications accepted. *Expenses: Tuition, area resident:* Full-time $12,790; part-time $389 per credit hour. Tuition, state resident: full-time $13,290; part-time $419 per credit hour. Tuition, nonresident: full-time $24,532; part-time $976 per credit hour. *International tuition:* $24,832 full-time. *Required fees:* $3958; $140 per credit hour. Tuition and fees vary according to course load, degree level, program and reciprocity agreements. *Faculty research:* Feminist legal issues, sexuality, international political economy, Latin America, cultural/literary and environmental studies.

**University of Colorado Denver,** College of Liberal Arts and Sciences, Program in Humanities, Denver, CO 80217. Offers community health science (MSS); humanities (MH); international studies (MSS); philosophy and theory (MH); social justice (MSS); society and the environment (MSS); visual studies (MH); women's and gender studies (MSS). *Program availability:* Part-time, evening/weekend. *Faculty:* 3 full-time (1 woman). *Students:* 12 full-time (6 women), 15 part-time (7 women); includes 6 minority (1 American Indian or Alaska Native, non-Hispanic/Latino; 3 Hispanic/Latino; 2 Two or more races, non-Hispanic/Latino). Average age 41. 4 applicants, 100% accepted, 4 enrolled. In 2016, 5 master's awarded. *Degree requirements:* For master's, 36 credit hours, project or thesis. *Entrance requirements:* For master's, writing sample, statement of purpose/letter of intent, three letters of recommendation. Additional exam requirements/recommendations for international students: Required—TOEFL (minimum score 537 paper-based; 75 iBT); Recommended—IELTS (minimum score 6.5). *Application deadline:* For fall admission, 5/15 for domestic students, 5/15 priority date for international students; for spring admission, 10/15 for domestic students, 10/15 priority date for international students; for summer admission, 3/15 for domestic and international students. Application fee: $50 ($75 for international students). Electronic applications accepted. *Expenses:* Tuition, state resident: full-time $11,006; part-time $474 per credit. Tuition, nonresident: full-time $28,212; part-time $1264 per credit hour. *Required fees:* $256 per semester. One-time fee: $94.32. Tuition and fees vary according to campus/location and program. *Financial support:* In 2016–17, 2 students received support. Fellowships, research assistantships, teaching assistantships, Federal Work-Study, institutionally sponsored loans, scholarships/grants, and traineeships available. Financial award application deadline: 4/1; financial award applicants required to submit FAFSA. *Faculty research:* Women and gender in the classical Mediterranean, communication theory and democracy, relationship between psychology and philosophy. *Unit head:* Margaret Woodhull, Director of Humanities, 303-315-3568, E-mail: margaret.woodhull@ucdenver.edu. *Application contact:* Angela Beale, Program Assistant, 303-315-3565, E-mail: mastershs@ucdenver.edu.
Website: http://www.ucdenver.edu/academics/colleges/CLAS/Programs/HumanitiesSocialSciences/Programs/Pages/MasterofHumanities.aspx

**University of Florida,** Graduate School, College of Liberal Arts and Sciences, Center for Women's Studies and Gender Research, Gainesville, FL 32611. Offers gender and development (Graduate Certificate); women's studies (MA, Graduate Certificate); MA/JD; MA/MA. Terminal master's awarded for partial completion of doctoral program. *Degree requirements:* For master's, thesis or project. *Entrance requirements:* For master's, GRE General Test (minimum score 1000), minimum GPA of 3.2. Additional exam requirements/recommendations for international students: Required—TOEFL (minimum score 550 paper-based; 80 iBT), IELTS (minimum score 6). Electronic applications accepted. *Faculty research:* Prejudice, discrimination, intersections, resistance, history.

**University of Georgia,** Franklin College of Arts and Sciences, Institute for Women's Studies, Athens, GA 30602. Offers Certificate. *Unit head:* Dr. Juanita Johnson-Bailey, Director, 706-542-2846, E-mail: jjb@uga.edu. *Application contact:* Dr. Patricia L. Richards, Assistant Director, 706-542-3235, Fax: 706-542-0049, E-mail: plr333@uga.edu.

**University of Hawaii at Manoa,** Graduate Division, College of Social Sciences, Advanced Women's Studies Program, Honolulu, HI 96822. Offers Graduate Certificate. *Program availability:* Part-time. *Entrance requirements:* Additional exam requirements/recommendations for international students: Required—TOEFL (minimum score 500 paper-based; 61 iBT), IELTS (minimum score 5).

**The University of Iowa,** Graduate College, College of Liberal Arts and Sciences, Department of Gender, Women's and Sexuality Studies, Iowa City, IA 52242-1316. Offers Certificate. *Entrance requirements:* Additional exam requirements/recommendations for international students: Required—TOEFL (minimum score 550 paper-based; 81 iBT).

**University of Lethbridge,** School of Graduate Studies, Lethbridge, AB T1K 3M4, Canada. Offers addictions counseling (M Sc); agricultural biotechnology (M Sc); agricultural studies (M Sc, MA); anthropology (MA); archaeology (M Sc, MA); art (MA,

MFA); biochemistry (M Sc); biological sciences (M Sc); biomolecular science (PhD); biosystems and biodiversity (PhD); Canadian studies (MA); chemistry (M Sc); computer science (M Sc); computer science and geographical information science (M Sc); counseling (MC); counseling psychology (M Ed); dramatic arts (MA); earth, space, and physical science (PhD); economics (MA); education (MA, PhD); educational leadership (M Ed); English (MA); environmental science (M Sc); evolution and behavior (PhD); exercise science (M Sc); French (MA); French/German (MA); French/Spanish (MA); general education (M Ed); geography (M Sc, MA); German (MA); health sciences (M Sc); individualized multidisciplinary (M Sc, MA); kinesiology (M Sc, MA); management (M Sc), including accounting, finance, human resource management and labor relations, information systems, international management, marketing, policy and strategy; mathematics (M Sc); music (M Mus, MA); Native American studies (MA); neuroscience (M Sc, PhD); new media (MA, MFA); nursing (M Sc, MN); philosophy (MA); physics (M Sc); political science (MA); psychology (M Sc, MA); religious studies (MA); sociology (MA); theatre and dramatic arts (MFA); theoretical and computational science (PhD); urban and regional studies (MA); women and gender studies (MA). *Program availability:* Part-time, evening/weekend. *Degree requirements:* For master's, thesis (for some programs); for doctorate, comprehensive exam, thesis/dissertation. *Entrance requirements:* For master's, GMAT (for M Sc in management), bachelor's degree in related field, minimum GPA of 3.0 during previous 20 graded semester courses, 2 years' teaching or related experience (M Ed); for doctorate, master's degree, minimum graduate GPA of 3.5. Additional exam requirements/recommendations for international students: Required—TOEFL (minimum score 580 paper-based; 93 iBT). Electronic applications accepted. *Faculty research:* Movement and brain plasticity, gibberellin physiology, photosynthesis, carbon cycling, molecular properties of main-group ring components.

**University of Louisville,** Graduate School, College of Arts and Sciences, Department of Women's and Gender Studies, Louisville, KY 40292. Offers MA, Certificate, MSSW/MA. *Program availability:* Part-time. *Faculty:* 7 full-time (all women), 7 part-time/adjunct (6 women). *Students:* 17 full-time (15 women), 4 part-time (3 women); includes 4 minority (3 Black or African American, non-Hispanic/Latino; 1 Two or more races, non-Hispanic/Latino). Average age 29. 10 applicants, 100% accepted, 7 enrolled. In 2016, 3 master's, 1 other advanced degree awarded. *Degree requirements:* For master's, thesis or alternative. *Entrance requirements:* For master's, undergraduate degree; two letters of recommendation; writing sample; letter of intent. Additional exam requirements/recommendations for international students: Required—TOEFL. *Application deadline:* For fall admission, 7/15 for domestic students, 7/16 priority date for international students; for spring admission, 12/5 for domestic students, 11/5 priority date for international students; for summer admission, 4/1 for domestic students, 4/1 priority date for international students. Applications are processed on a rolling basis. Application fee: $60. *Expenses:* Tuition, state resident: full-time $12,246; part-time $681 per credit hour. Tuition, nonresident: full-time $25,486; part-time $1417 per credit hour. *Required fees:* $196. Tuition and fees vary according to program and reciprocity agreements. *Financial support:* In 2016–17, 1 teaching assistantship with full tuition reimbursement (averaging $12,000 per year) was awarded; scholarships/grants, health care benefits, and tuition waivers (full) also available. Support available to part-time students. Financial award application deadline: 3/15; financial award applicants required to submit FAFSA. *Faculty research:* History of gender/sexualities/social justice, gender in popular culture/media/literature/music, black feminisms/black lesbian studies/queer studies, girl cultures, feminism and art. Total annual research expenditures: $67,720. *Unit head:* Dr. Nancy M. Theriot, Chairperson, 502-852-8160, Fax: 502-852-4421, E-mail: nancy.theriot@louisville.edu. *Application contact:* Libby Leggett, Director, Graduate Admissions, 502-852-3101, Fax: 502-852-6536, E-mail: gradadm@louisville.edu. Website: http://louisville.edu/wgs/

**University of Maryland, College Park,** Academic Affairs, College of Arts and Humanities, Department of Women's Studies, College Park, MD 20742. Offers MA, PhD. *Degree requirements:* For master's, thesis or alternative; for doctorate, one foreign language, thesis/dissertation or alternative. *Entrance requirements:* For master's, GRE General Test, writing sample, 3 letters of recommendation. Additional exam requirements/recommendations for international students: Required—TOEFL. *Faculty research:* Gender roles, national and global diversity, sexuality.

**University of Michigan,** Rackham Graduate School, College of Literature, Science, and the Arts, Department of Women's Studies, Ann Arbor, MI 48109. Offers English and women's studies (PhD); history and women's studies (PhD); LGBTQ studies (Certificate); psychology and women's studies (PhD); women's studies (Certificate). *Degree requirements:* For doctorate, variable foreign language requirement, comprehensive exam (for some programs), thesis/dissertation. *Entrance requirements:* For doctorate, GRE General Test, previous undergraduate coursework in women's studies. Electronic applications accepted. *Expenses:* Tuition, state resident: full-time $21,466; part-time $1152 per credit hour. Tuition, nonresident: full-time $43,346; part-time $2367 per credit hour. Part-time tuition and fees vary according to course load, degree level and program. *Faculty research:* LGBTQ studies, sexuality studies, feminist science studies, global feminism, health studies, international studies, cultural studies.

**University of Minnesota, Twin Cities Campus,** Graduate School, College of Liberal Arts, Department of Gender, Women, and Sexuality Studies, Minneapolis, MN 55455-0213. Offers feminist studies (PhD). *Degree requirements:* For doctorate, comprehensive exam, thesis/dissertation. *Entrance requirements:* For doctorate, GRE. Additional exam requirements/recommendations for international students: Required—TOEFL (minimum score 550 paper-based). Electronic applications accepted. *Faculty research:* Transnational feminist theories, critical development theory, feminist postcolonialisms, feminist science studies and studying of health, literature, Asian diasporas, sexuality and queer theory.

**The University of North Carolina at Charlotte,** College of Liberal Arts and Sciences, Interdisciplinary Liberal Arts and Sciences Programs, Charlotte, NC 28223-0001. Offers gender, sexuality, and women's studies (Graduate Certificate); gerontology (MA, Graduate Certificate); Latin American studies (MA); liberal studies (MA); organizational science (PhD); public policy (PhD). *Program availability:* Part-time, evening/weekend. *Faculty:* 1 (woman) part-time/adjunct. *Students:* 65 full-time (49 women), 61 part-time (50 women); includes 31 minority (11 Black or African American, non-Hispanic/Latino; 1 American Indian or Alaska Native, non-Hispanic/Latino; 2 Asian, non-Hispanic/Latino; 16 Hispanic/Latino; 1 Two or more races, non-Hispanic/Latino), 15 international. Average age 32. 128 applicants, 41% accepted, 40 enrolled. In 2016, 15 master's, 12 doctorates, 7 other advanced degrees awarded. *Degree requirements:* For master's, comprehensive exam (for some programs), thesis (for some programs), practicum, project; for doctorate, comprehensive exam, thesis/dissertation; for Graduate Certificate, practicum (for gerontology). *Entrance requirements:* For master's, GRE General Test or MAT, bachelor's degree from accredited college or university; official transcripts of all previous academic work attempted beyond high school; minimum overall GPA of 3.0 on applicant's previous work beyond high school; statement of purpose; recommendation letters; for doctorate, GRE or GMAT, statement of purpose discussing interest in program and objectives for pursuing degree, current resume or curriculum vitae, unofficial transcripts; for Graduate Certificate, bachelor's degree from accredited university and either be enrolled in and in good standing in a graduate degree program

at UNC Charlotte or have a minimum undergraduate GPA of 3.0. Additional exam requirements/recommendations for international students: Required—TOEFL (minimum score 523 paper-based, 70 iBT) or IELTS (6.5). *Application deadline:* For fall admission, 2/15 for domestic and international students; for spring admission, 10/1 for domestic and international students; for summer admission, 4/1 for domestic and international students. Applications are processed on a rolling basis. Application fee: $75. Electronic applications accepted. *Expenses:* Tuition, state resident: full-time $4252. Tuition, nonresident: full-time $17,423. *Required fees:* $3026. Tuition and fees vary according to course load and program. *Financial support:* In 2016–17, 26 students received support, including 17 research assistantships (averaging $12,840 per year), 7 teaching assistantships (averaging $14,442 per year); career-related internships or fieldwork, institutionally sponsored loans, scholarships/grants, unspecified assistantships, and administrative assistantships also available. Support available to part-time students. Financial award application deadline: 3/1; financial award applicants required to submit FAFSA. *Unit head:* Dr. Nancy A. Gutierrez, Dean, 704-687-0081, E-mail: ngutierr@uncc.edu. *Application contact:* Kathy B. Giddings, Director of Graduate Admissions, 704-687-5503, Fax: 704-687-3279, E-mail: gradadm@uncc.edu. Website: http://clas.uncc.edu/academics

**The University of North Carolina at Greensboro,** Graduate School, College of Arts and Sciences, Department of English, Greensboro, NC 27412-5001. Offers creative writing (MFA); English (M Ed, MA, PhD, Certificate), including American literature (PhD), English (M Ed, MA), English literature (PhD), rhetoric and composition (PhD), technical writing (Certificate), women's studies (Certificate). *Degree requirements:* For master's, comprehensive exam; for doctorate, variable foreign language requirement, thesis/dissertation, preliminary exam. *Entrance requirements:* For master's, GRE General Test, minimum GPA of 3.0; for doctorate, GRE General Test, GRE Subject Test, critical writing sample, minimum GPA of 3.0. Additional exam requirements/recommendations for international students: Required—TOEFL. Electronic applications accepted.

**The University of North Carolina at Greensboro,** Graduate School, College of Arts and Sciences, Program in Women's and Gender Studies, Greensboro, NC 27412-5001. Offers MA, Certificate. Electronic applications accepted.

**University of Northern Iowa,** Graduate College, MA Program in Women's and Gender Studies, Cedar Falls, IA 50614. Offers MA. *Degree requirements:* For master's, comprehensive exam (for some programs), thesis or alternative. *Entrance requirements:* For master's, minimum GPA of 3.0. Additional exam requirements/recommendations for international students: Required—TOEFL (minimum score 500 paper-based; 61 iBT). Electronic applications accepted.

**University of Oklahoma,** College of Arts and Sciences, Women's and Gender Studies Program, Norman, OK 73019. Offers Graduate Certificate. *Program availability:* Part-time, evening/weekend. *Faculty:* 1 (woman) full-time. *Students:* 9 full-time (6 women), 12 part-time (11 women); includes 7 minority (2 Black or African American, non-Hispanic/Latino; 2 American Indian or Alaska Native, non-Hispanic/Latino; 2 Hispanic/Latino; 1 Two or more races, non-Hispanic/Latino), 1 international. Average age 39. 1 applicant, 100% accepted, 1 enrolled. In 2016, 7 Graduate Certificates awarded. *Entrance requirements:* Additional exam requirements/recommendations for international students: Required—TOEFL (minimum score 79 iBT) or IELTS (minimum score 6.5). *Application deadline:* For fall admission, 3/15 for domestic and international students; for spring admission, 11/15 for domestic and international students. Applications are processed on a rolling basis. Application fee: $50 ($100 for international students). Electronic applications accepted. *Expenses:* Tuition, state resident: full-time $4886; part-time $203.60 per credit hour. Tuition, nonresident: full-time $18,989; part-time $791.20 per credit hour. *Required fees:* $3283; $126.25 per credit hour. $126.50 per semester. *Financial support:* In 2016–17, 1 teaching assistantship with partial tuition reimbursement (averaging $10,372 per year) was awarded; research assistantships with partial tuition reimbursements and unspecified assistantships also available. Financial award application deadline: 6/1; financial award applicants required to submit FAFSA. *Faculty research:* Black feminism, terrorism, popular culture, indigenous, reproductive justice. Total annual research expenditures: $29,546. *Unit head:* Dr. Maria Lupe Davidson, Director, 405-325-3481, Fax: 405-325-3573, E-mail: mdavidson@ou.edu. Website: http://wgs.ou.edu

**University of Ottawa,** Faculty of Graduate and Postdoctoral Studies, Faculty of Social Sciences, Institute of Women's Studies, Ottawa, ON K1N 6N5, Canada. Offers criminology (MA, MCA); education (MA); English (MA); history (MA); human kinetics (MA); law (LL M); lettres Franlfcaises (MA); nursing (M Sc); pastoral studies (MA); political science (MA); religious studies (MA); sociology (MA). *Degree requirements:* For master's, thesis or alternative.

**University of Pittsburgh,** Dietrich School of Arts and Sciences, Gender, Sexuality, and Women's Studies Program, Pittsburgh, PA 15260. Offers Doctoral Certificate, Master's Certificate. *Program availability:* Part-time. *Faculty:* 103 full-time (77 women), 5 part-time/adjunct (4 women). *Students:* 56 full-time (39 women); includes 18 minority (4 Black or African American, non-Hispanic/Latino; 4 Asian, non-Hispanic/Latino; 7 Hispanic/Latino; 3 Two or more races, non-Hispanic/Latino). Average age 30. *Entrance requirements:* For degree, good academic standing in a University of Pittsburgh graduate degree-granting department. Additional exam requirements/recommendations for international students: Required—TOEFL. *Application deadline:* Applications are processed on a rolling basis. Application fee: $0. Electronic applications accepted. Tuition and fees vary according to program. *Financial support:* Application deadline: 2/9. *Faculty research:* Global feminisms; intersectionality; anthropology of gender; masculinities. *Unit head:* Dr. Todd Reeser, Director, 412-624-6486, Fax: 412-624-6492. Website: http://www.gsws.pitt.edu/

**University of Regina,** Faculty of Graduate Studies and Research, Faculty of Arts, Department of Women's and Gender Studies, Regina, SK S4S 0A2, Canada. Offers MA. Offered as a special case program. *Program availability:* Part-time. *Faculty:* 3 full-time (all women), 2 part-time/adjunct (0 women). *Students:* 1 (woman) full-time. 1 applicant, 100% accepted. *Degree requirements:* For master's, thesis. *Entrance requirements:* Additional exam requirements/recommendations for international students: Required—TOEFL (minimum score 580 paper-based; 80 iBT), IELTS (minimum score 6.5), PTE (minimum score 59). *Application deadline:* Applications are processed on a rolling basis. Application fee: $100. Electronic applications accepted. *Financial support:* Fellowships, teaching assistantships, and scholarships/grants available. Financial award application deadline: 6/15. *Faculty research:* Feminist theory; mapping sexualities; mapping gender; women, feminism, and globalization. *Unit head:* Dr. Darlene Juschka, Department Head, 306-585-5280, E-mail: darlene.juschka@uregina.ca. *Application contact:* Cordelia McDonald, Administrative Assistant, 306-585-4972, E-mail: cordelia.mcdonald@uregina.ca. Website: http://www.uregina.ca/arts/womens-gender-studies

**University of Rhode Island,** Graduate School, College of Arts and Sciences, Program in Gender and Women's Studies, Kingston, RI 02881. Offers Graduate Certificate. *Faculty:* 2 full-time (both women). *Students:* 3 full-time (all women). In 2016, 3 Graduate Certificates awarded. *Entrance requirements:* For degree, personal statement, college transcript(s). Application fee: $65. Electronic applications accepted. *Expenses:* Tuition, state resident: full-time $11,796; part-time $655 per credit. Tuition, nonresident: full-time

$24,206; part-time $1345 per credit. *Required fees:* $1546; $44 per credit. One-time fee: $155 full-time; $35 part-time. *Financial support:* In 2016–17, 1 teaching assistantship (averaging $9,148 per year) was awarded. *Unit head:* Dr. Rosaria Pisa, Director, 401-874-2482, E-mail: rpisa@uri.edu. *Application contact:* Graduate Admissions, 401-874-2872, E-mail: gradadm@etal.uri.edu.
Website: http://web.uri.edu/gws/graduate-certificate-program/

**University of Saskatchewan,** College of Graduate Studies and Research, College of Arts and Science, Department of Women's and Gender Studies, Saskatoon, SK S7N 5A2, Canada. Offers MA, PhD. *Degree requirements:* For master's, thesis; for doctorate, comprehensive exam (for some programs), thesis/dissertation. *Entrance requirements:* Additional exam requirements/recommendations for international students: Required—TOEFL (minimum score 80 iBT); Recommended—IELTS (minimum score 6.5). Electronic applications accepted.

**University of South Carolina,** The Graduate School, College of Arts and Sciences, Program in Women's Studies, Columbia, SC 29208. Offers Certificate. *Program availability:* Part-time. *Entrance requirements:* For degree, GRE General Test or MAT. Additional exam requirements/recommendations for international students: Required—TOEFL. Electronic applications accepted. *Faculty research:* Health; pedagogy; intersection of race, class, gender; public policy; politics of culture and representations; feminist political economics.

**University of South Florida,** College of Arts and Sciences, Department of Women's Studies, Tampa, FL 33620-9951. Offers women's and gender studies (MA). *Program availability:* Part-time. *Faculty:* 6 full-time (4 women). *Students:* 11 full-time (all women), 3 part-time (all women); includes 2 minority (1 Black or African American, non-Hispanic/Latino; 1 Hispanic/Latino), 1 international. Average age 25. 7 applicants, 100% accepted, 6 enrolled. In 2016, 7 master's awarded. *Degree requirements:* For master's, comprehensive exam, thesis (for some programs), thesis or internship. *Entrance requirements:* For master's, GRE General Test, minimum GPA of 3.0, three letters of recommendation, personal narrative statement of purpose, scholarly writing sample (examples include term paper or research paper); undergraduate major or minor in women's studies (recommended). Additional exam requirements/recommendations for international students: Required—TOEFL (minimum score 550 paper-based; 79 iBT) or IELTS (minimum score 6.5). *Application deadline:* For fall admission, 2/15 for domestic and international students; for spring admission, 10/15 for domestic students, 9/15 for international students; for summer admission, 2/15 for domestic students, 1/15 for international students. Applications are processed on a rolling basis. Application fee: $30. Electronic applications accepted. *Expenses:* Tuition, state resident: full-time $7766; part-time $431.43 per credit hour. Tuition, nonresident: full-time $15,789; part-time $877.17 per credit hour. *Required fees:* $37 per term. *Financial support:* In 2016–17, 6 students received support. Teaching assistantships with tuition reimbursements available available. Financial award application deadline: 3/1. *Faculty research:* Performance studies, feminist theory and pedagogy; constructions of gender in public discourse, including education, mass media, and popular culture; women's health, reproductive justice, and sexuality; bodies and cultural representations; feminist theory as it relates to learning disabilities, critical race theory, postmodernist and queer theory; hiring practices in higher education, mothering; women of color feminisms. *Unit head:* Dr. Diane Price Herndl, Professor and Chairperson, 813-974-0987, Fax: 813-974-0336, E-mail: priceherndl@usf.edu. *Application contact:* Dr. Kim Golombisky, Associate Professor and Graduate Director, 813-974-0986, Fax: 813-974-0336, E-mail: kgolombi@usf.edu.
Website: http://wgs.usf.edu/

**The University of Toledo,** College of Graduate Studies, College of Languages, Literature and Social Sciences, Department of Women's and Gender Studies, Toledo, OH 43606-3390. Offers Certificate. *Program availability:* Part-time.

**University of Toronto,** School of Graduate Studies, Faculty of Arts and Science, Women and Gender Studies Institute, Toronto, ON M5S 1A1, Canada. Offers MA, PhD. *Entrance requirements:* For master's, minimum B+ in final year of undergraduate study. Additional exam requirements/recommendations for international students: Required—TOEFL (minimum score 580 paper-based; 93 iBT), TWE (minimum score 5). Electronic applications accepted.

**University of Washington,** Graduate School, College of Arts and Sciences, Department of Gender, Women and Sexuality Studies, Seattle, WA 98195. Offers PhD. Terminal master's awarded for partial completion of doctoral program. *Degree requirements:* For doctorate, one foreign language, thesis/dissertation, exam. *Entrance requirements:* For doctorate, GRE General Test. Additional exam requirements/recommendations for international students: Required—TOEFL. Electronic applications accepted. *Faculty research:* Women's history in U.S. and China; Native American ethnography and identity; women, science, and technology; political economy of development, feminism and nationalism.

**University of Wisconsin–Madison,** Graduate School, College of Letters and Science, Department of History, Madison, WI 53706-1380. Offers African history (MA, PhD); Central Asian history (MA, PhD); comparative world history (MA, PhD); East Asian history (MA, PhD); European history (MA, PhD); gender and women's history (MA, PhD); Latin American and Caribbean history (MA, PhD); Middle Eastern history (MA, PhD); South Asian history (MA, PhD); Southeast Asian history (MA, PhD); United States history (MA, PhD). Terminal master's awarded for partial completion of doctoral program. *Degree requirements:* For master's, thesis (for some programs); for doctorate, variable foreign language requirement, thesis/dissertation. *Entrance requirements:* For master's and doctorate, GRE General Test. Additional exam requirements/recommendations for international students: Required—Michigan English Language Assessment Battery or TOEFL. Electronic applications accepted. *Faculty research:* American, African, European, Asian, Latin American, and Middle Eastern history.

**University of Wisconsin–Milwaukee,** Graduate School, College of Letters and Science, Department of Women's and Gender Studies, Milwaukee, WI 53201-0413. Offers MA, Graduate Certificate. *Program availability:* Part-time. *Students:* 4 full-time (all women), 2 part-time (both women); includes 2 minority (1 Black or African American, non-Hispanic/Latino; 1 Two or more races, non-Hispanic/Latino). Average age 42. 11 applicants, 55% accepted, 4 enrolled. In 2016, 1 master's awarded. *Entrance requirements:* For master's, three letters of recommendation, sample of written work, letter of intent. *Application deadline:* Applications are processed on a rolling basis. Application fee: $56 ($96 for international students). Electronic applications accepted. *Financial support:* In 2016–17, 2 teaching assistantships with full tuition reimbursements were awarded; fellowships, research assistantships, health care benefits, and unspecified assistantships also available. Financial award applicants required to submit FAFSA. *Unit head:* Dr. Gwynne Kennedy, Director, 414-229-5918, E-mail: gkennedy@uwm.edu. *Application contact:* General Information Contact, 414-229-4982, Fax: 414-229-6967, E-mail: gradschool@uwm.edu.
Website: http://uwm.edu/womens-gender-studies/

**Western Seminary,** Graduate Programs, Program in Ministry and Leadership, Portland, OR 97215-3367. Offers chaplaincy (MA); coaching (MA); Jewish ministry (MA); pastoral care to women (MA); youth ministry (MA). *Degree requirements:* For master's, practicum. *Entrance requirements:* Additional exam requirements/recommendations for international students: Required—TOEFL.

**Western Seminary–Sacramento Campus,** Graduate Certificate Programs, Sacramento, CA 95821. Offers Bible (Graduate Certificate); coaching (Graduate Certificate); pastoral care to women (Graduate Certificate); theology (Graduate Certificate); youth and family (Graduate Certificate). *Program availability:* Online learning. *Entrance requirements:* For degree, essays, undergraduate transcripts, 4 recommendations. Additional exam requirements/recommendations for international students: Required—TOEFL.

**Western Seminary–Sacramento Campus,** Graduate Diploma Programs, Sacramento, CA 95821. Offers Bible and theology (Graduate Diploma); ministry (Graduate Diploma); pastoral care to women (Graduate Diploma). *Entrance requirements:* For degree, essays, undergraduate transcripts, 4 recommendations. Additional exam requirements/recommendations for international students: Required—TOEFL.

**Western Seminary–San Jose Campus,** Graduate Programs, Los Gatos, CA 95032-4520. Offers Bible and theology (Graduate Diploma); Bible, camp and conference ministry (CGS); Biblical and theological studies (MA), including exegetical track, theological track; coaching (CGS); expositional ministry (M Div); marital and family therapy (MA); ministry (Graduate Diploma); ministry and leadership (MA), including camp and conference ministry, coaching, pastoral care to women, youth ministry; pastoral care to women (CGS, Graduate Diploma); pastoral ministry (M Div); theology (CGS); youth and family (CGS). *Program availability:* Part-time, evening/weekend, online learning. *Entrance requirements:* For master's, minimum GPA of 3.0. Electronic applications accepted.

**Wilson College,** Graduate Programs, Chambersburg, PA 17201-1285. Offers accounting (M Acc); choreography and visual art (MFA); education (M Ed); healthcare management for sustainability (MHM); humanities (MA), including art and culture, critical/cultural theory, English language and literature, women's studies; management (MSM); nursing (MSN), including nursing education, nursing leadership and management. *Program availability:* Evening/weekend. *Degree requirements:* For master's, project. *Entrance requirements:* For master's, PRAXIS, minimum undergraduate cumulative GPA of 3.0, 2 letters of recommendation, current certification for eligibility to teach in grades K-12, resume, personal interview. Electronic applications accepted.

**York University,** Faculty of Graduate Studies, Faculty of Liberal Arts and Professional Studies, Program in Gender, Feminist and Women's Studies, Toronto, ON M3J 1P3, Canada. Offers MA, PhD. *Degree requirements:* For master's, thesis or alternative; for doctorate, comprehensive exam, thesis/dissertation. Electronic applications accepted.

# Section 16
# Communication and Media

This section contains a directory of institutions offering graduate work in communication and media, followed by an in-depth entries submitted by institutions that chose to prepare detailed program descriptions. Additional information about programs listed in the directory but not augmented by an in-depth entry may be obtained by writing directly to the dean of a graduate school or chair of a department at the address given in the directory.

For programs offering related work, see also in this book *Film, Television, and Video; Language and Literature;* and *Psychology and Counseling.* In the other guides in this series:

**Graduate Programs in Engineering & Applied Sciences**

See *Computer Science and Information Technology* and *Telecommunications*

**Graduate Programs in Business, Education, Information Studies, Law & Social Work**

See *Advertising and Public Relations*

## CONTENTS

# Communication—General

**Abilene Christian University,** Graduate Programs, College of Arts and Sciences, Department of Communication, Program in Communication, Abilene, TX 79699. Offers MA. *Program availability:* Part-time. *Faculty:* 9 part-time/adjunct (4 women). *Students:* 11 full-time (9 women), 1 (woman) part-time; includes 4 minority (3 Hispanic/Latino; 1 Two or more races, non-Hispanic/Latino), 1 international. 14 applicants, 50% accepted, 5 enrolled. In 2016, 6 master's awarded. *Degree requirements:* For master's, comprehensive exam, thesis optional. *Entrance requirements:* For master's, GRE General Test. Additional exam requirements/recommendations for international students: Required—TOEFL (minimum score 80 iBT), IELTS (minimum score 6), PTE. *Application deadline:* For fall admission, 8/11 for domestic students; for spring admission, 11/1 for domestic students. Applications are processed on a rolling basis. Application fee: $50. Electronic applications accepted. *Expenses: Tuition:* Full-time $19,890; part-time $1105 per credit hour. Tuition and fees vary according to course load and program. *Financial support:* In 2016–17, 11 students received support. Federal Work-Study, scholarships/grants, and unspecified assistantships available. Support available to part-time students. Financial award application deadline: 4/1; financial award applicants required to submit FAFSA. *Faculty research:* Intercultural communication, family communication, forensics, organizational communication. *Unit head:* Dr. Lauren Lemley, Graduate Director, 325-674-2136, Fax: 325-674-6966, E-mail: lauren.lemly@acu.edu. *Application contact:* Corey Patterson, Director of Graduate Admission and Recruiting, 325-674-6566, Fax: 325-674-6717, E-mail: gradinfo@acu.edu.
Website: http://www.acu.edu/graduate/degree-programs/communication/index.html

**American University,** School of Communication, Washington, DC 20016-8001. Offers MA, MFA, PhD. *Accreditation:* ACEJMC (one or more programs are accredited). *Program availability:* Part-time, evening/weekend, 100% online. *Faculty:* 39 full-time (20 women). *Students:* 170 full-time (115 women), 290 part-time (194 women); includes 160 minority (98 Black or African American, non-Hispanic/Latino; 2 American Indian or Alaska Native, non-Hispanic/Latino; 13 Asian, non-Hispanic/Latino; 36 Hispanic/Latino; 11 Two or more races, non-Hispanic/Latino), 45 international. 709 applicants, 33% accepted, 190 enrolled. In 2016, 137 master's, 2 doctorates awarded. *Degree requirements:* For master's, comprehensive exam, thesis or alternative; for doctorate, comprehensive exam, thesis/dissertation. *Entrance requirements:* For doctorate, GRE General Test. Additional exam requirements/recommendations for international students: Required—TOEFL (minimum score 600 paper-based; 100 iBT), IELTS (minimum score 7). *Application deadline:* For fall admission, 2/1 priority date for domestic and international students; for spring admission, 11/1 for domestic and international students. Applications are processed on a rolling basis. Application fee: $55. Electronic applications accepted. *Expenses: Tuition:* Full-time $28,422; part-time $1579 per credit hour. *Required fees:* $690; $200 per term. Tuition and fees vary according to course load, degree level and program. *Financial support:* In 2016–17, 210 students received support, including 3 fellowships with partial tuition reimbursements available (averaging $20,000 per year), 30 research assistantships with partial tuition reimbursements available (averaging $15,000 per year), 30 teaching assistantships with partial tuition reimbursements available (averaging $15,000 per year); career-related internships or fieldwork, Federal Work-Study, institutionally sponsored loans, scholarships/grants, tuition waivers (partial), and unspecified assistantships also available. Support available to part-time students. Financial award application deadline: 2/1; financial award applicants required to submit FAFSA. *Faculty research:* New communication technology; documentaries and public broadcasting; litigation and public relations; dissident media; race, gender, and the media; international journalism and human rights; social media. *Unit head:* Dr. Jeffrey Rutenbeck, Dean, 202-885-2058, Fax: 202-885-2099, E-mail: jeff@american.edu. *Application contact:* Christine Rials, Assistant Director for Graduate Admissions, 202-885-2040, Fax: 202-885-2019, E-mail: gradcomm@american.edu.
Website: http://www.soc.american.edu/

**The American University in Cairo,** School of Sciences and Engineering, Cairo, Egypt. Offers biotechnology (MS); chemistry (MS); computer science (MS); computing (M Comp); construction engineering (M Eng, MS); electronics and communications engineering (M Eng); environmental engineering (MS); environmental system design (M Eng); mechanical engineering (M Eng, MS); nanotechnology (MS); physics (MS); robotics, control and smart systems (MS); sciences and engineering (PhD); sustainable development (MS, Graduate Diploma). *Program availability:* Part-time, evening/weekend. *Faculty:* 43 full-time (4 women), 12 part-time/adjunct (1 woman). *Students:* 50 full-time (21 women), 262 part-time (128 women), 13 international. Average age 28. 193 applicants, 46% accepted, 55 enrolled. In 2016, 71 master's, 5 doctorates awarded. *Degree requirements:* For master's, comprehensive exam (for some programs), thesis (for some programs); for doctorate, comprehensive exam (for some programs), thesis/dissertation. *Entrance requirements:* Additional exam requirements/recommendations for international students: Required—TOEFL (minimum score 450 paper-based; 45 iBT), IELTS (minimum score 5). *Application deadline:* For fall admission, 2/1 priority date for domestic and international students; for spring admission, 10/15 priority date for domestic and international students. Applications are processed on a rolling basis. Application fee: $80. Electronic applications accepted. *Expenses:* Contact institution. *Financial support:* Fellowships with partial tuition reimbursements, scholarships/grants, and unspecified assistantships available. Financial award application deadline: 3/10. *Faculty research:* Construction, mechanical and electronics engineering, physics, computer science, biotechnology and nanotechnology. *Unit head:* Dr. Hassan El Fawal, Dean, 20-2-2615-2926, E-mail: hassan.elfawal@aucegypt.edu. *Application contact:* Maha Hegazi, Director for Graduate Admissions, 20-2-2615-1462, E-mail: mahahegazi@aucegypt.edu.
Website: http://www.aucegypt.edu/sse/Pages/default.aspx

**The American University of Paris,** Graduate Programs, Paris, France. Offers cross-cultural and sustainable business management (MA); cultural translation (MA); global communications (MA); global communications and civil society (MA); international affairs (MA); international affairs, conflict resolution and civil society development (MA); Middle East and Islamic studies (MA); Middle East and Islamic studies and international affairs (MA); public policy and international affairs (MA); public policy and international law (MA). *Degree requirements:* For master's, thesis (for some programs). *Entrance requirements:* For master's, minimum undergraduate GPA of 3.0. Additional exam requirements/recommendations for international students: Recommended—TOEFL, IELTS. Electronic applications accepted.

**Andrews University,** School of Graduate Studies, College of Arts and Sciences, Interdisciplinary Studies in Communication Program, Berrien Springs, MI 49104. Offers MA. *Faculty:* 3 full-time (all women). *Students:* 5 full-time (4 women), 5 part-time (4 women); includes 5 minority (4 Black or African American, non-Hispanic/Latino; 1 Native Hawaiian or other Pacific Islander, non-Hispanic/Latino), 3 international. Average age 34. In 2016, 8 master's awarded. *Application deadline:* Applications are processed on a rolling basis. Application fee: $40. *Unit head:* Steve Hanson, Chair, 269-471-3126. *Application contact:* Justina Clayburn, Supervisor of Graduate Admission, 800-253-2874, Fax: 269-471-3228, E-mail: graduate@andrews.edu.
Website: https://www.andrews.edu/wp/comm/graduate-degrees/program-information.html

**Angelo State University,** College of Graduate Studies and Research, College of Arts and Humanities, Department of Communication and Mass Media, San Angelo, TX 76909. Offers communication (MA). *Program availability:* Part-time, evening/weekend. *Students:* 10 full-time (4 women), 5 part-time (4 women); includes 5 minority (2 Black or African American, non-Hispanic/Latino; 3 Hispanic/Latino), 2 international. Average age 28. *Degree requirements:* For master's, comprehensive exam, thesis optional. *Entrance requirements:* Additional exam requirements/recommendations for international students: Required—TOEFL or IELTS. *Application deadline:* For fall admission, 7/15 priority date for domestic students, 6/10 for international students; for spring admission, 12/1 priority date for domestic students, 11/1 for international students. Applications are processed on a rolling basis. Application fee: $40 ($50 for international students). Electronic applications accepted. *Expenses:* Tuition, state resident: full-time $3726; part-time $2484 per year. Tuition, nonresident: full-time $10,746; part-time $7164 per year. *Required fees:* $2538; $1702 per unit. *Financial support:* Teaching assistantships, career-related internships or fieldwork, Federal Work-Study, scholarships/grants, and unspecified assistantships available. Support available to part-time students. Financial award application deadline: 3/1; financial award applicants required to submit FAFSA. *Unit head:* Dr. Herman Otis Howard, Chair, 325-942-2031, Fax: 325-942-2551, E-mail: herman.howard@angelo.edu. *Application contact:* Dr. June H. Smith, Graduate Advisor, 325-486-6088, Fax: 325-942-2551, E-mail: june.smith@angelo.edu.
Website: http://www.angelo.edu/dept/communication-mass-media/

**Arizona State University at the Tempe campus,** College of Liberal Arts and Sciences, Hugh Downs School of Human Communication, Tempe, AZ 85287. Offers communication (PhD). *Program availability:* Evening/weekend. *Degree requirements:* For doctorate, comprehensive exam, thesis/dissertation, interactive Program of Study (iPOS) submitted before completing 50 percent of required credit hours. *Entrance requirements:* For doctorate, GRE, minimum GPA of 3.0 or equivalent in last 2 years of work leading to bachelor's degree. Additional exam requirements/recommendations for international students: Required—TOEFL, IELTS, or PTE. Electronic applications accepted.

**Arizona State University at the Tempe campus,** New College of Interdisciplinary Arts and Sciences, Program in Communication Studies, Phoenix, AZ 85069-7100. Offers MA. *Program availability:* Part-time, evening/weekend. *Degree requirements:* For master's, thesis, applied project or written comprehensive exam; interactive Program of Study (iPOS) submitted before completing 50 percent of required credit hours. *Entrance requirements:* For master's, GRE (if GPA less than 3.0 in last 60 hours of undergraduate study), minimum GPA of 3.0 or equivalent in last 2 years of work leading to bachelor's degree, 3 letters of recommendation, official transcripts, writing sample of scholarly work or example of professional activities. Additional exam requirements/recommendations for international students: Required—TOEFL, IELTS, or PTE. Electronic applications accepted. *Faculty research:* Organizational, applied, and environmental communication; intergenerational family communication and its connectedness to wellness; communication in personal and work relationships; popular culture; technology and culture; cultural dimensions of new mobile communication and computing technologies.

**Arkansas State University,** Graduate School, College of Media and Communication, Department of Communication, State University, AR 72467. Offers communication studies (MA, SCCT); health communications (Graduate Certificate). *Program availability:* Part-time. *Degree requirements:* For master's, one foreign language, comprehensive exam, thesis or alternative; for other advanced degree, comprehensive exam. *Entrance requirements:* For master's, GRE General Test or MAT, appropriate bachelor's degree, writing sample, letter of recommendation, official transcripts, immunization records; for other advanced degree, GRE or MAT, appropriate master's degree, interview, official transcript, immunization records. Additional exam requirements/recommendations for international students: Required—TOEFL (minimum score 550 paper-based; 79 iBT), IELTS (minimum score 6), PTE (minimum score 56). Electronic applications accepted.

**Auburn University,** Graduate School, College of Liberal Arts, Department of Communication and Journalism, Auburn University, AL 36849. Offers MA, Graduate Certificate. *Program availability:* Part-time. *Faculty:* 31 full-time (17 women), 6 part-time/adjunct (4 women). *Students:* 20 full-time (13 women), 2 part-time (1 woman); includes 5 minority (1 Black or African American, non-Hispanic/Latino; 1 Asian, non-Hispanic/Latino; 1 Hispanic/Latino; 2 Two or more races, non-Hispanic/Latino), 2 international. Average age 26. 37 applicants, 35% accepted, 10 enrolled. In 2016, 6 master's awarded. *Degree requirements:* For master's, thesis (for some programs). *Entrance requirements:* For master's, GRE General Test. *Application deadline:* Applications are processed on a rolling basis. Application fee: $50 ($60 for international students). Electronic applications accepted. *Expenses:* Tuition, state resident: full-time $9072; part-time $504 per credit hour. Tuition, nonresident: full-time $27,216; part-time $1512 per credit hour. *Required fees:* $812 per semester. Tuition and fees vary according to degree level and program. *Financial support:* Teaching assistantships and Federal Work-Study available. Support available to part-time students. Financial award application deadline: 3/15; financial award applicants required to submit FAFSA. *Unit head:* Dr. Jennifer Adams, Director, 334-844-2727. *Application contact:* Dr. George Flowers, Dean of the Graduate School, 334-844-2125.
Website: http://www.cla.auburn.edu/cmjn/

**Austin Peay State University,** College of Graduate Studies, College of Arts and Letters, Department of Communication, Clarksville, TN 37044. Offers communication arts (MA). *Program availability:* Part-time, evening/weekend, online learning. *Faculty:* 8 full-time (4 women), 2 part-time/adjunct (both women). *Students:* 1 full-time (0 women), 61 part-time (41 women); includes 24 minority (16 Black or African American, non-Hispanic/Latino; 1 Asian, non-Hispanic/Latino; 4 Hispanic/Latino; 3 Two or more races, non-Hispanic/Latino). Average age 31. 31 applicants, 87% accepted, 24 enrolled. In 2016, 25 master's awarded. *Degree requirements:* For master's, comprehensive exam, thesis (for some programs). *Entrance requirements:* For master's, GRE General Test, minimum GPA of 2.5. Additional exam requirements/recommendations for international students: Required—TOEFL (minimum score 500 paper-based). *Application deadline:* For fall admission, 8/9 priority date for domestic students. Applications are processed on a rolling basis. Application fee: $45 ($50 for international students). Electronic applications accepted. *Expenses:* Tuition, state resident: full-time $8300; part-time $415 per credit hour. Tuition, nonresident: full-time $22,280; part-time $1114 per credit hour.

*Required fees:* $1473; $73.65 per credit hour. *Financial support:* Research assistantships with full tuition reimbursements, career-related internships or fieldwork, Federal Work-Study, institutionally sponsored loans, scholarships/grants, and unspecified assistantships available. Support available to part-time students. Financial award application deadline: 4/1; financial award applicants required to submit FAFSA. *Unit head:* Dr. Pam Gray, Interim Chair, 931-221-7378, Fax: 931-221-7265, E-mail: grayp@apsu.edu. *Application contact:* Brad Averitt, Coordinator of Graduate Admissions, 800-859-4723, Fax: 931-221-7641, E-mail: gradadmissions@apsu.edu. Website: http://www.apsu.edu/communication

**Ball State University,** Graduate School, College of Communication, Information, and Media, Muncie, IN 47306. Offers MA, MS, Certificate. *Program availability:* Part-time, 100% online, blended/hybrid learning. *Degree requirements:* For master's, comprehensive exam (for some programs), thesis (for some programs). *Entrance requirements:* For master's, GRE (for some programs), minimum baccalaureate GPA of 2.75 or 3.0 in latter half of baccalauareate. Additional exam requirements/recommendations for international students: Required—TOEFL (minimum score 550 paper-based; 79 iBT), IELTS (minimum score 6.5). Electronic applications accepted.

**Barry University,** College of Arts and Sciences, Department of Communication, Miami Shores, FL 33161-6695. Offers broadcasting (Certificate); communication (MA), including broadcast communication, public relations and corporate communications; organizational communication (MS). *Program availability:* Part-time, evening/weekend. *Degree requirements:* For master's, thesis (for some programs). *Entrance requirements:* For master's, GRE General Test, MAT, minimum GPA of 3.0. Electronic applications accepted. *Faculty research:* Organizational communication, broadcast communication, intercultural communication, advertising, leadership.

**Baylor University,** Graduate School, College of Arts and Sciences, Department of Communication, Waco, TX 76798. Offers MA. *Program availability:* Part-time. *Faculty:* 17 full-time (3 women). *Students:* 16 full-time (5 women), 5 part-time (1 woman); includes 3 minority (1 Asian, non-Hispanic/Latino; 1 Hispanic/Latino; 1 Two or more races, non-Hispanic/Latino), 1 international. Average age 24. 42 applicants, 48% accepted, 18 enrolled. In 2016, 15 master's awarded. *Degree requirements:* For master's, thesis optional. *Entrance requirements:* For master's, GRE General Test, transcripts; 3 letters of recommendation; personal statement of intent; scholarly writing sample. Additional exam requirements/recommendations for international students: Required—TOEFL, IELTS, PTE. *Application deadline:* For fall admission, 11/1 priority date for domestic and international students; for spring admission, 2/1 priority date for domestic and international students; for summer admission, 7/1 for domestic and international students. Applications are processed on a rolling basis. Application fee: $50. Electronic applications accepted. *Expenses: Tuition:* Full-time $28,494; part-time $1583 per credit hour. *Required fees:* $167 per credit hour. Tuition and fees vary according to course load and program. *Financial support:* In 2016–17, 14 students received support, including 1 research assistantship with full tuition reimbursement available (averaging $14,200 per year), 13 teaching assistantships with full tuition reimbursements available (averaging $14,200 per year); career-related internships or fieldwork, Federal Work-Study, institutionally sponsored loans, scholarships/grants, and tuition waivers (full and partial) also available. Financial award application deadline: 2/1; financial award applicants required to submit CSS PROFILE. *Faculty research:* Rhetoric, interpersonal and family communication, organizational communication, film and digital media, new technology. *Unit head:* Dr. Mark T. Morman, Graduate Program Director, 254-710-1621, Fax: 254-710-1563, E-mail: mark_morman@baylor.edu. *Application contact:* Marilyn Spivey, Office Manager, 254-710-1621, Fax: 254-710-1563, E-mail: marilyn_spivey@baylor.edu. Website: http://www.baylor.edu/comm_studies/

**Bellarmine University,** School of Communication, Louisville, KY 40205. Offers MA, MSDM. *Program availability:* Part-time, evening/weekend. *Faculty:* 6 full-time (3 women). *Students:* 3 full-time (all women), 25 part-time (16 women); includes 6 minority (5 Black or African American, non-Hispanic/Latino; 1 Hispanic/Latino), 3 international. Average age 29. In 2016, 15 master's awarded. *Degree requirements:* For master's, thesis optional. *Entrance requirements:* For master's, GRE, GMAT or LSAT. Additional exam requirements/recommendations for international students: Required—TOEFL (minimum score 550 paper-based; 80 iBT). *Application deadline:* Applications are processed on a rolling basis. Application fee: $40. Electronic applications accepted. Tuition and fees vary according to program. *Financial support:* Applicants required to submit FAFSA. *Unit head:* Dr. Lara Needham, Dean, 502-272-7965, E-mail: lneedham@bellarmine.edu. *Application contact:* Dr. Sara Pettingill, Dean of Graduate Admission, 502-272-8401, Fax: 502-272-8002, E-mail: spettingill@bellarmine.edu. Website: http://www.bellarmine.edu/admissions/graduate/majorsandprograms/mactop.aspx

**Boise State University,** College of Arts and Sciences, Department of Communication, Boise, ID 83725-1920. Offers MA. *Program availability:* Part-time. *Faculty:* 8. *Students:* 10 full-time (5 women), 11 part-time (8 women); includes 5 minority (1 Asian, non-Hispanic/Latino; 3 Hispanic/Latino; 1 Two or more races, non-Hispanic/Latino). Average age 34. 20 applicants, 45% accepted, 6 enrolled. In 2016, 3 master's awarded. *Degree requirements:* For master's, thesis. *Entrance requirements:* For master's, GRE General Test, minimum GPA of 3.0, writing sample. Additional exam requirements/recommendations for international students: Required—TOEFL (minimum score 550 paper-based; 80 iBT), IELTS (minimum score 6). *Application deadline:* For fall admission, 2/15 for domestic and international students. Application fee: $65 ($95 for international students). Electronic applications accepted. *Expenses:* Tuition, state resident: full-time $6058; part-time $358 per credit hour. Tuition, nonresident: full-time $20,108; part-time $608 per credit hour. *Required fees:* $2108. Tuition and fees vary according to program. *Financial support:* In 2016–17, 3 students received support, including 1 research assistantship (averaging $4,083 per year), 5 teaching assistantships (averaging $3,696 per year); unspecified assistantships also available. Financial award application deadline: 2/15; financial award applicants required to submit FAFSA. *Unit head:* Todd Norton, Department Chair, 208-426-1922, E-mail: toddnorton@boisestate.edu. *Application contact:* Dr. John McClellan, Director of Graduate Studies, 208-426-2450, E-mail: johnmcclellan@boisestate.edu. Website: http://communication.boisestate.edu/

**Boston University,** College of Communication, Boston, MA 02215. Offers MA, MFA, MS, PhD, JD/MS. *Program availability:* Part-time. *Faculty:* 67 full-time, 73 part-time/adjunct. *Students:* 333 full-time (256 women), 16 part-time (12 women); includes 46 minority (7 Black or African American, non-Hispanic/Latino; 8 Asian, non-Hispanic/Latino; 24 Hispanic/Latino; 7 Two or more races, non-Hispanic/Latino), 149 international. Average age 24. 975 applicants, 61% accepted, 222 enrolled. In 2016, 169 master's awarded. *Degree requirements:* For master's, comprehensive exam (for some programs), thesis (for some programs); for doctorate, comprehensive exam, thesis/dissertation. *Entrance requirements:* For master's, GRE General Test, transcripts, essays, 3 letters of recommendation, resume; for doctorate, GRE General Test, transcripts, essays, 3 letters of recommendation, resume, writing sample. Additional exam requirements/recommendations for international students: Required—TOEFL (minimum score 600 paper-based; 100 iBT), IELTS. *Application deadline:* For fall admission, 5/1 for domestic and international students. Applications are processed on a

rolling basis. Application fee: $95. Electronic applications accepted. *Financial support:* In 2016–17, 125 students received support, including 5 research assistantships (averaging $10,000 per year), 50 teaching assistantships (averaging $8,000 per year); career-related internships or fieldwork, Federal Work-Study, institutionally sponsored loans, scholarships/grants, health care benefits, and unspecified assistantships also available. Support available to part-time students. Financial award application deadline: 5/1; financial award applicants required to submit FAFSA. *Unit head:* Thomas Fiedler, Dean, 617-353-3450, Fax: 617-358-0399, E-mail: comdean@bu.edu. *Application contact:* Manny Dotel, Assistant Director, Graduate Affairs, 617-353-3481, E-mail: comgrad@bu.edu. Website: http://www.bu.edu/com/grad/

**Bowling Green State University,** Graduate College, College of Arts and Sciences, School of Media and Communication, Bowling Green, OH 43403. Offers media and communication (MA, PhD); strategic communication (MA). *Program availability:* Part-time. Terminal master's awarded for partial completion of doctoral program. *Degree requirements:* For master's, thesis or alternative; for doctorate, comprehensive exam, thesis/dissertation. *Entrance requirements:* For master's and doctorate, GRE General Test. Additional exam requirements/recommendations for international students: Required—TOEFL. *Application deadline:* For fall admission, 1/1 priority date for domestic students. Application fee: $30. Electronic applications accepted. *Financial support:* Fellowships with full tuition reimbursements, research assistantships with full tuition reimbursements, teaching assistantships with full tuition reimbursements, career-related internships or fieldwork, Federal Work-Study, and unspecified assistantships available. Financial award applicants required to submit FAFSA. *Unit head:* Dr. Oliver Boyd-Barrett, Director, 419-372-6018. *Application contact:* Dr. Radhika Gajjala, Assistant Professor, 419-372-0528. Website: http://www.bgsu.edu/arts-and-sciences/media-and-communication.html

**Brigham Young University,** Graduate Studies, College of Fine Arts and Communications, School of Communications, Provo, UT 84602. Offers mass communications (MA). *Faculty:* 16 full-time (1 woman). *Students:* 19 full-time (14 women), 21 part-time (10 women); includes 7 minority (2 Asian, non-Hispanic/Latino; 5 Hispanic/Latino), 6 international. Average age 31. 19 applicants, 63% accepted, 12 enrolled. In 2016, 13 master's awarded. *Degree requirements:* For master's, comprehensive exam, thesis. *Entrance requirements:* For master's, GRE, minimum GPA of 3.0 in last 60 hours of course work. Additional exam requirements/recommendations for international students: Required—TOEFL (minimum score 580 paper-based; 85 iBT). *Application deadline:* For fall admission, 3/31 priority date for domestic and international students. Applications are processed on a rolling basis. Application fee: $50. Electronic applications accepted. *Expenses: Tuition:* Full-time $6680; part-time $393 per credit. Tuition and fees vary according to course load, program and student's religious affiliation. *Financial support:* In 2016–17, 21 students received support, including 26 research assistantships with full and partial tuition reimbursements available (averaging $3,373 per year), 2 teaching assistantships with partial tuition reimbursements available (averaging $2,824 per year); career-related internships or fieldwork, institutionally sponsored loans, scholarships/grants, unspecified assistantships, and supplementary awards also available. Financial award application deadline: 4/30; financial award applicants required to submit FAFSA. *Faculty research:* Ethics, international, magazine, newspaper, media effects, social media. *Unit head:* Edward Carter, Director, 801-422-2997, Fax: 801-422-0160, E-mail: comms_secretary@byu.edu. *Application contact:* Debby Jackson, Graduate Program Manager, 801-422-2632, Fax: 801-422-0160, E-mail: debby_jackson@byu.edu. Website: http://cfac.byu.edu/departments/communications

**Bryant University,** College of Arts and Sciences, Smithfield, RI 02917. Offers communication (MA, Graduate Certificate), including general communication (MA), managerial communication (Graduate Certificate), professional communication (Graduate Certificate), public communication (Graduate Certificate); global environmental studies (MS); health care communication (MA); organizational communication (MA); sustainability practices (Graduate Certificate). *Program availability:* Part-time, evening/weekend. *Faculty:* 2 full-time (0 women), 2 part-time/adjunct (1 woman). *Students:* 4 full-time (all women), 10 part-time (8 women); includes 2 minority (1 Black or African American, non-Hispanic/Latino; 1 Two or more races, non-Hispanic/Latino), 1 international. Average age 32. 29 applicants, 31% accepted, 6 enrolled. In 2016, 6 master's, 2 other advanced degrees awarded. *Degree requirements:* For master's, thesis. *Entrance requirements:* For master's, GRE. Additional exam requirements/recommendations for international students: Required—TOEFL (minimum score 550 paper-based; 80 iBT). *Application deadline:* For fall admission, 8/15 for domestic and international students; for spring admission, 1/15 for domestic and international students; for summer admission, 5/15 for domestic and international students. Applications are processed on a rolling basis. Application fee: $80. Electronic applications accepted. *Expenses:* $932 per credit hour. *Financial support:* Fellowships and research assistantships available. Financial award applicants required to submit FAFSA. *Faculty research:* Mass media and social construction of reality; development and improvement of media literacy skills; sociocultural influences on cognition and learning in K-12 populations, oil pollution impacts on marine and estuarine microbial communities; wetlands ecology. *Unit head:* Bradford Martin, Associate Dean, College of Arts and Sciences, 401-232-6929, E-mail: bmartin@bryant.edu. *Application contact:* Terri Rogers, Admission Assistant, Graduate School, 401-232-6230, E-mail: graduateprograms@bryant.edu. Website: http://gradschool.bryant.edu/arts-and-sciences/

**California Baptist University,** Program in Communication, Riverside, CA 92503. Offers MA. *Program availability:* Part-time, evening/weekend, online only, 100% online. *Faculty:* 5 full-time (2 women). *Students:* 13 full-time (8 women), 7 part-time (3 women); includes 11 minority (2 Black or African American, non-Hispanic/Latino; 8 Hispanic/Latino; 1 Two or more races, non-Hispanic/Latino). Average age 29. 14 applicants, 71% accepted, 6 enrolled. In 2016, 9 master's awarded. *Degree requirements:* For master's, thesis or alternative, comprehensive project, defended paper. *Entrance requirements:* For master's, bachelor's degree, official transcripts, 2 recommendations, current resume, 500-word essay, minimum GPA of 2.5. Additional exam requirements/recommendations for international students: Required—TOEFL (minimum score 80 iBT). *Application deadline:* For fall admission, 8/1 priority date for domestic students, 7/1 priority date for international students; for spring admission, 12/1 priority date for domestic students, 11/1 priority date for international students. Applications are processed on a rolling basis. Application fee: $45. Electronic applications accepted. *Expenses:* Contact institution. *Financial support:* In 2016–17, 2 students received support. Federal Work-Study and scholarships/grants available. Financial award applicants required to submit CSS PROFILE or FAFSA. *Faculty research:* Millennials, social media, new media, convergent media. *Unit head:* Dr. David Poole, Vice President of Online and Professional Studies, 951-343-3901, E-mail: dpoole@calbaptist.edu. *Application contact:* Dr. MaryAnn Pearson, Program Director of MA in Communication, 951-343-3967, E-mail: mpearson@calbaptist.edu. Website: https://www.cbuonline.edu/degrees/master-of-arts-in-communication

**California State University, Chico,** Office of Graduate Studies, College of Communication and Education, Department of Communication Arts and Sciences,

## Communication—General

Program in Communication Studies, Chico, CA 95929-0722. Offers MA. *Students:* 5 full-time (all women), 9 part-time (6 women); includes 3 minority (2 Hispanic/Latino; 1 Two or more races, non-Hispanic/Latino). 12 applicants, 75% accepted, 7 enrolled. *Degree requirements:* For master's, thesis or project. *Entrance requirements:* For master's, GRE, three letters of recommendation, example of writing, one-page statement of purpose, minimum GPA of 3.0. Additional exam requirements/recommendations for international students: Required—TOEFL (minimum score 550 paper-based; 80 iBT), IELTS (minimum score 6.5), PTE (minimum score 59). *Application deadline:* For fall admission, 3/1 priority date for domestic students, 3/1 for international students; for spring admission, 9/15 priority date for domestic students, 9/15 for international students. Application fee: $55. Electronic applications accepted. *Financial support:* Teaching assistantships, career-related internships or fieldwork, scholarships/grants, traineeships, and unspecified assistantships available. Financial award application deadline: 3/1; financial award applicants required to submit FAFSA. *Unit head:* Dr. Susan Avanzino, Department Chair, 530-898-5751, Fax: 530-898-4096, E-mail: cmst@csuchico.edu. *Application contact:* Judy L. Morris, Graduate Coordinator, 530-898-5751, Fax: 530-898-3342, E-mail: jlmorris@csuchico.edu.
Website: http://www.csuchico.edu/cmst/

**California State University, East Bay,** Office of Graduate Studies, College of Letters, Arts, and Social Sciences, Department of Communication, Hayward, CA 94542-3000. Offers MA. *Program availability:* Part-time. *Students:* 4 full-time (2 women), 18 part-time (12 women); includes 13 minority (2 Black or African American, non-Hispanic/Latino; 4 Asian, non-Hispanic/Latino; 4 Hispanic/Latino; 3 Two or more races, non-Hispanic/Latino), 5 international. Average age 33. 22 applicants, 32% accepted, 4 enrolled. In 2016, 10 master's awarded. *Degree requirements:* For master's, comprehensive exam, project, thesis, or exam. *Entrance requirements:* For master's, GRE, minimum GPA of 3.0 in field; 3 letters of recommendation; sample of scholarly writing. Additional exam requirements/recommendations for international students: Required—TOEFL (minimum score 550 paper-based). *Application deadline:* For fall admission, 6/30 for domestic and international students. Applications are processed on a rolling basis. Application fee: $55. Electronic applications accepted. *Financial support:* Fellowships, teaching assistantships, career-related internships or fieldwork, Federal Work-Study, institutionally sponsored loans, scholarships/grants, and unspecified assistantships available. Support available to part-time students. Financial award application deadline: 3/2; financial award applicants required to submit FAFSA. *Unit head:* Dr. Mary Cardaras, Chair, 510-885-3925, Fax: 510-885-4099, E-mail: mary.cardaras@csueastbay.edu. *Application contact:* Dr. Donna Wiley, Interim Associate Vice President for Academic Programs and Graduate Studies, 510-885-3716, Fax: 510-885-4777, E-mail: donna.wiley@csueastbay.edu.
Website: http://www20.csueastbay.edu/class/departments/communication/

**California State University, Fresno,** Division of Research and Graduate Studies, College of Arts and Humanities, Department of Communication, Fresno, CA 93740-8027. Offers MA. *Program availability:* Part-time, evening/weekend. *Degree requirements:* For master's, thesis or alternative. *Entrance requirements:* For master's, GRE General Test, minimum GPA of 3.1. Additional exam requirements/recommendations for international students: Required—TOEFL. *Application deadline:* For fall admission, 5/1 for domestic and international students; for spring admission, 10/1 for domestic and international students. Applications are processed on a rolling basis. Application fee: $55. Electronic applications accepted. *Financial support:* Teaching assistantships, career-related internships or fieldwork, Federal Work-Study, and scholarships/grants available. Support available to part-time students. Financial award application deadline: 3/1; financial award applicants required to submit FAFSA. *Faculty research:* Learning styles, education, critical thinking. *Unit head:* Dr. Douglas Fraleigh, Chair, 559-278-2826, Fax: 559-278-4113, E-mail: douglasf@csufresno.edu. *Application contact:* Dr. Kevin J. Ayotte, Graduate Program Coordinator, 559-278-4086, Fax: 559-278-4113, E-mail: kjayotte@csufresno.edu.
Website: http://www.fresnostate.edu/artshum/communication/

**California State University, Fullerton,** Graduate Studies, Department of Communications, Fullerton, CA 92834-9480. Offers communications in tourism and entertainment (MA); mass communications research and theory (MA); professional communications (MA). *Program availability:* Part-time. *Degree requirements:* For master's, project or thesis. *Entrance requirements:* For master's, GRE General Test. Application fee: $55. *Expenses:* Tuition, state resident: full-time $3369; part-time $1953 per unit. Tuition, nonresident: full-time $3915; part-time $2499 per unit. Tuition and fees vary according to course load, degree level and program. *Financial support:* Teaching assistantships, career-related internships or fieldwork, Federal Work-Study, institutionally sponsored loans, and scholarships/grants available. Support available to part-time students. Financial award application deadline: 3/1; financial award applicants required to submit FAFSA. *Unit head:* Jason Shepard, Chair, 657-278-5301, E-mail: jshepard@fullerton.edu. *Application contact:* Coordinator, 657-278-3832.

**California State University, Fullerton,** Graduate Studies, College of Communications, Department of Human Communication Studies, Fullerton, CA 92834-9480. Offers communication studies (MA); communicative disorders (MA). *Accreditation:* ASHA. *Program availability:* Part-time. *Degree requirements:* For master's, comprehensive exam, thesis or alternative. *Entrance requirements:* For master's, minimum GPA of 3.0 in major. Application fee: $55. *Expenses:* Tuition, state resident: full-time $3369; part-time $1953 per unit. Tuition, nonresident: full-time $3915; part-time $2499 per unit. Tuition and fees vary according to course load, degree level and program. *Financial support:* Teaching assistantships, career-related internships or fieldwork, Federal Work-Study, institutionally sponsored loans, and scholarships/grants available. Support available to part-time students. Financial award application deadline: 3/1; financial award applicants required to submit FAFSA. *Faculty research:* Speech therapy. *Unit head:* Gary Ruud, Chair, 657-278-4198, E-mail: gruud@fullerton.edu. *Application contact:* Admissions/Applications, 657-278-2371.
Website: http://communications.fullerton.edu/hcom/

**California State University, Long Beach,** Graduate Studies, College of Liberal Arts, Department of Communication Studies, Long Beach, CA 90840. Offers MA. *Program availability:* Part-time. *Degree requirements:* For master's, comprehensive exam or thesis. *Entrance requirements:* For master's, GRE. *Application deadline:* For fall admission, 2/25 for domestic students. Applications are processed on a rolling basis. Application fee: $55. Electronic applications accepted. *Financial support:* Federal Work-Study, institutionally sponsored loans, and scholarships/grants available. Financial award application deadline: 3/2. *Faculty research:* Rhetoric, public address, communication theory, interpersonal communication, intercultural communication. *Unit head:* Dr. Ann Johnson, Chair, 562-985-4301.

**California State University, Los Angeles,** Graduate Studies, College of Arts and Letters, Department of Communication Studies, Los Angeles, CA 90032-8530. Offers MA, MFA. *Program availability:* Part-time, evening/weekend. *Degree requirements:* For master's, comprehensive exam or thesis. *Entrance requirements:* For master's, minimum GPA of 2.75 in last 90 units of course work. Additional exam requirements/recommendations for international students: Required—TOEFL (minimum score 500 paper-based). Electronic applications accepted. *Faculty research:* Organizational, interpersonal, intercultural, and instructional communication; rhetorical theories.

**California State University, Northridge,** Graduate Studies, College of Arts, Media, and Communication, Northridge, CA 91330. Offers MA, MFA, MM. *Program availability:* Part-time, evening/weekend. *Faculty:* 102 full-time (47 women), 275 part-time/adjunct (128 women). *Students:* 128 full-time (74 women), 91 part-time (52 women); includes 74 minority (7 Black or African American, non-Hispanic/Latino; 2 American Indian or Alaska Native, non-Hispanic/Latino; 10 Asian, non-Hispanic/Latino; 38 Hispanic/Latino; 2 Native Hawaiian or other Pacific Islander, non-Hispanic/Latino; 15 Two or more races, non-Hispanic/Latino), 42 international. Average age 31. 365 applicants, 41% accepted, 81 enrolled. *Entrance requirements:* Additional exam requirements/recommendations for international students: Required—TOEFL. *Application deadline:* For fall admission, 11/30 for domestic students. Application fee: $55. *Expenses:* Tuition, state resident: full-time $4152. *Financial support:* Teaching assistantships, career-related internships or fieldwork, Federal Work-Study, and unspecified assistantships available. Support available to part-time students. Financial award application deadline: 3/1. *Unit head:* Dan Hosken, Interim Dean, 818-677-2246, E-mail: dan.hosken@csun.edu.
Website: http://www.csun.edu/mike-curb-arts-media-communication

**California State University, Sacramento,** Office of Graduate Studies, College of Arts and Letters, Department of Communication Studies, Sacramento, CA 95819. Offers MA. *Program availability:* Part-time. *Students:* 2 full-time (1 woman), 21 part-time (13 women); includes 8 minority (3 Black or African American, non-Hispanic/Latino; 2 Asian, non-Hispanic/Latino; 3 Hispanic/Latino). Average age 30. 21 applicants, 52% accepted, 6 enrolled. In 2016, 17 master's awarded. *Degree requirements:* For master's, thesis or project; writing proficiency exam. *Entrance requirements:* For master's, GRE, minimum GPA of 3.25 during previous 2 years. Additional exam requirements/recommendations for international students: Required—TOEFL (minimum score 550 paper-based; 80 iBT). *Application deadline:* For fall admission, 1/3 for domestic students, 3/1 for international students; for spring admission, 9/30 for international students. Applications are processed on a rolling basis. Application fee: $55. Electronic applications accepted. *Expenses:* $4,302 full-time tuition and fees per semester, $2,796 part-time. *Financial support:* Research assistantships, teaching assistantships, career-related internships or fieldwork, and Federal Work-Study available. Support available to part-time students. Financial award application deadline: 3/1; financial award applicants required to submit FAFSA. *Faculty research:* Hypermedia development; information literacy in higher education; representations of race and ethnicity; the definition of "newsworthy" as it relates to front-page newspaper coverage; journalism ethics. *Unit head:* Dr. Gerri Smith, Chair, 916-278-6688, E-mail: smithg@csus.edu. *Application contact:* Jose Martinez, Outreach and Graduate Diversity Coordinator, 916-278-6470, Fax: 916-278-5669, E-mail: martinj@skymail.csus.edu.
Website: http://www.al.csus.edu/coms

**California State University, San Bernardino,** Graduate Studies, College of Arts and Letters, Program in Communication Studies, San Bernardino, CA 92407. Offers communication studies (MA); integrated marketing communication (MA). *Faculty:* 5 full-time (3 women). *Students:* 10 full-time (8 women), 27 part-time (20 women); includes 19 minority (4 Black or African American, non-Hispanic/Latino; 2 Asian, non-Hispanic/Latino; 12 Hispanic/Latino; 1 Two or more races, non-Hispanic/Latino), 3 international. 35 applicants, 60% accepted, 17 enrolled. In 2016, 5 master's awarded. *Degree requirements:* For master's, comprehensive exam. *Entrance requirements:* Additional exam requirements/recommendations for international students: Required—TOEFL. *Application deadline:* For fall admission, 5/15 for domestic students. Application fee: $55. *Expenses:* Tuition, state resident: full-time $7843; part-time $5011.20 per year. Tuition and fees vary according to course load, degree level, program and reciprocity agreements. *Unit head:* Dr. Michael Salvador, Chair, 909-537-5820, Fax: 909-537-7009, E-mail: salvador@csusb.edu. *Application contact:* Dr. Francisca Beer, Dean of Graduate Studies, 909-537-5058, Fax: 909-537-7034, E-mail: fbeer@csusb.edu.

**Carleton University,** Faculty of Graduate Studies, Faculty of Public Affairs and Management, School of Journalism and Communication, Program in Communication, Ottawa, ON K1S 5B6, Canada. Offers MA, PhD. *Degree requirements:* For master's, thesis optional; for doctorate, comprehensive exam, thesis/dissertation. *Entrance requirements:* For master's, honors degree. Additional exam requirements/recommendations for international students: Required—TOEFL. *Faculty research:* History of communication and media systems, communication/information technologies and society, communication and social relations, communication policy and political economy.

**Carnegie Mellon University,** Dietrich College of Humanities and Social Sciences, Department of English, Pittsburgh, PA 15213-3891. Offers communication planning and design (M Des); literary and cultural studies (MA, PhD); professional writing (MAPW), including editing and publishing, policy and non-profit communication, public and media relations / corporate communications, science or healthcare communication, technical writing, writing for new media, writing for print media; rhetoric (MA, PhD). *Program availability:* Part-time. Terminal master's awarded for partial completion of doctoral program. *Degree requirements:* For doctorate, 2 foreign languages, comprehensive exam, thesis/dissertation. *Entrance requirements:* For master's and doctorate, GRE General Test. Additional exam requirements/recommendations for international students: Required—TOEFL, TWE. *Faculty research:* Cognitive processes in discourse with emphasis on writing, testing, and evaluation.

**Central Connecticut State University,** School of Graduate Studies, College of Liberal Arts and Social Sciences, Department of Communication, New Britain, CT 06050-4010. Offers MS, Certificate. *Program availability:* Part-time, evening/weekend. *Faculty:* 7 full-time (1 woman). *Students:* 7 full-time (4 women), 27 part-time (21 women); includes 12 minority (2 Black or African American, non-Hispanic/Latino; 8 Hispanic/Latino; 2 Two or more races, non-Hispanic/Latino), 1 international. Average age 28. 23 applicants, 74% accepted, 12 enrolled. In 2016, 7 master's awarded. *Degree requirements:* For master's, comprehensive exam, thesis and alternative, special project; for Certificate, qualifying exam. *Entrance requirements:* For master's, minimum undergraduate GPA of 3.0, resume, references, essay. Additional exam requirements/recommendations for international students: Required—TOEFL (minimum score 550 paper-based; 79 iBT). *Application deadline:* For fall admission, 6/1 for domestic students, 5/1 for international students; for spring admission, 11/1 for domestic and international students. Applications are processed on a rolling basis. Application fee: $50. Electronic applications accepted. *Expenses: Tuition, area resident:* Full-time $6497; part-time $606 per credit. Tuition, state resident: full-time $9748; part-time $622 per credit. Tuition, nonresident: full-time $18,102; part-time $622 per credit. *Required fees:* $4459; $246 per credit. *Financial support:* In 2016–17, 1 student received support. Career-related internships or fieldwork, Federal Work-Study, scholarships/grants, and unspecified assistantships available. Support available to part-time students. Financial award application deadline: 3/1; financial award applicants required to submit FAFSA. *Faculty research:* Organizational communication, mass communication, intercultural communication, political communication, information management. *Unit head:* Dr. Christopher Pudlinski, Chair, 860-832-2690, E-mail: pudlinskic@ccsu.edu. *Application contact:* Patricia Gardner, Associate Director of Graduate Studies, 860-832-2350, Fax: 860-832-2362.
Website: http://comm.ccsu.edu/

**Central Michigan University,** College of Graduate Studies, College of Communication and Fine Arts, Department of Communication and Dramatic Arts, Mount Pleasant, MI 48859. Offers communication (MA), including communication and dramatic arts. *Program availability:* Part-time. *Degree requirements:* For master's, thesis. *Entrance requirements:* Additional exam requirements/recommendations for international students: Recommended—TOEFL (minimum score 100 iBT), IELTS. Electronic applications accepted. *Faculty research:* Communication theory, interpersonal/nonverbal communication, organizational communication, family and interpersonal communication, political communication.

**Chatham University,** Program in Communication, Pittsburgh, PA 15232-2826. Offers environmental communication (M Comm); health communication (M Comm); strategic communication (M Comm). *Program availability:* Online learning. *Expenses: Tuition:* Full-time $16,254; part-time $903 per credit hour. *Required fees:* $468; $26 per credit hour.

**Clarion University of Pennsylvania,** Office of Transfer, Adult and Graduate Admissions, Online Master of Science Programs, Clarion, PA 16214. Offers accounting (MS); applied data analytics (MS); clinical mental health counseling (MS); library science (MSLS); mass media arts and journalism (MS). *Program availability:* Part-time, 100% online. *Faculty:* 15 full-time (7 women), 3 part-time/adjunct (2 women). *Students:* 84 full-time (69 women), 304 part-time (246 women); includes 36 minority (19 Black or African American, non-Hispanic/Latino; 3 Asian, non-Hispanic/Latino; 10 Hispanic/Latino; 4 Two or more races, non-Hispanic/Latino; 1 international. Average age 34. 179 applicants, 93% accepted, 131 enrolled. In 2016, 146 master's awarded. *Degree requirements:* For master's, comprehensive exam, thesis or alternative. *Entrance requirements:* For master's, minimum QPA of 3.0. Additional exam requirements/recommendations for international students: Required—TOEFL (minimum score 600 paper-based; 100 iBT), IELTS (minimum score 7.5). *Application deadline:* For fall admission, 8/1 priority date for domestic students, 4/15 priority date for international students; for spring admission, 12/1 priority date for domestic students, 9/15 priority date for international students. Applications are processed on a rolling basis. Application fee: $40. Electronic applications accepted. *Expenses:* $632.35 per credit. *Financial support:* Career-related internships or fieldwork, Federal Work-Study, scholarships/grants, and unspecified assistantships available. Support available to part-time students. Financial award application deadline: 3/1. *Application contact:* Dana Bearer, Associate Director, Transfer, Adult, and Graduate Programs, 814-393-2337, Fax: 814-393-2772, E-mail: gradstudies@clarion.edu.
Website: http://www.clarion.edu/admissions/graduate/index.html

**Clarks Summit University,** Baptist Bible Seminary, South Abington Township, PA 18411. Offers Biblical apologetics (MA); church education (M Div, M Min); church planting (M Div, M Min); global ministry (M Div, M Min); leadership in communication (D Min); leadership in counseling and spiritual development (D Min); leadership in global ministry (D Min); leadership in pastoral ministry (D Min); leadership in theological studies (D Min); military chaplaincy (M Div); ministry (PhD); organizational leadership (M Min); outreach pastor (M Div, M Min); pastoral counseling (M Div, M Min); pastoral leadership (M Div, M Min); theology (Th M); worship ministries leadership (M Div, M Min); youth pastor (M Div, M Min). *Program availability:* Part-time, evening/weekend, online learning. Terminal master's awarded for partial completion of doctoral program. *Degree requirements:* For master's, 2 foreign languages, thesis, oral exam (for M Div); for doctorate, 2 foreign languages, comprehensive exam (for some programs), thesis/dissertation, oral exam. *Entrance requirements:* For doctorate, Greek and Hebrew entrance exams (for PhD). Electronic applications accepted.

**Clarks Summit University,** Graduate Studies, South Abington Township, PA 18411. Offers Bible (MA); counseling (MA, MS); curriculum and instruction (M Ed); educational administration (M Ed); intercultural studies (MA); literature (MA); missions (MA); organizational leadership (MA); reading specialist (M Ed); secondary English/communications (M Ed); social entrepreneurship (MA); worldview studies (MA). MA in missions program available only for Association of Baptists for World Evangelism missionary personnel. *Program availability:* Part-time, evening/weekend, online learning. *Entrance requirements:* Additional exam requirements/recommendations for international students: Required—TOEFL (minimum score 500 paper-based).

**Clark University,** Graduate School, School of Professional Studies, Program in Professional Communication, Worcester, MA 01610-1477. Offers MSPC. *Students:* 40 full-time (31 women), 22 part-time (20 women); includes 3 minority (1 Black or African American, non-Hispanic/Latino; 2 Hispanic/Latino), 38 international. Average age 27. 98 applicants, 88% accepted, 36 enrolled. In 2016, 22 master's awarded. *Degree requirements:* For master's, thesis optional. *Entrance requirements:* Additional exam requirements/recommendations for international students: Required—TOEFL. *Application deadline:* Applications are processed on a rolling basis. Application fee: $75. Electronic applications accepted. *Expenses: Tuition:* Full-time $44,050. *Required fees:* $80. Tuition and fees vary according to course load and program. *Application contact:* Dr. John Chetro-Szivos, Associate Dean of Professional Studies and Online Education, 508-793-7623, E-mail: jchetroszivos@clarku.edu.
Website: http://www.clarku.edu/programs/masters-professional-communication

**Clemson University,** Graduate School, College of Architecture, Arts, and Humanities, Department of English, Program in Professional Communication, Clemson, SC 29634. Offers MA. *Program availability:* Part-time. *Faculty:* 66 full-time (34 women), 3 part-time/adjunct (2 women). *Students:* 22 full-time (18 women), 2 part-time (both women); includes 4 minority (3 Black or African American, non-Hispanic/Latino; 1 Hispanic/Latino), 2 international. Average age 26. 18 applicants, 56% accepted, 10 enrolled. In 2016, 13 master's awarded. *Degree requirements:* For master's, comprehensive exam, thesis or alternative. *Entrance requirements:* For master's, GRE General Test, unofficial transcripts, resume, writing sample, letters of recommendation. Additional exam requirements/recommendations for international students: Required—TOEFL (minimum score 80 iBT), IELTS (minimum score 6.5). *Application deadline:* For fall admission, 2/1 priority date for domestic and international students. Application fee: $80 ($90 for international students). Electronic applications accepted. *Expenses:* $4,264 per semester full-time resident, $8,485 per semester full-time non-resident, $471 per credit hour part-time resident, $942 per credit hour part-time non-resident. *Financial support:* In 2016–17, 25 students received support, including 1 research assistantship with partial tuition reimbursement available (averaging $11,374 per year), 8 teaching assistantships with partial tuition reimbursements available (averaging $13,009 per year); career-related internships or fieldwork and unspecified assistantships also available. Financial award application deadline: 2/1. *Faculty research:* Usability and user experience design, rhetoric, intercultural communication, digital publishing, social media authoring, technical writing. *Unit head:* Dr. Lee Morrissey, Department Chair, 864-656-3151, E-mail: lmorris@clemson.edu. *Application contact:* Dr. William Stockton, Graduate Program Coordinator, 864-656-6689, Fax: 864-656-1345, E-mail: wstockt@clemson.edu.
Website: http://aahsites.clemson.edu/mapc/

**Clemson University,** Graduate School, College of Architecture, Arts, and Humanities, Program in Rhetorics, Communication, and Information Design, Clemson, SC 29634. Offers PhD. *Faculty:* 6 full-time (3 women). *Students:* 25 full-time (12 women), 9 part-time (7 women); includes 4 minority (2 Black or African American, non-Hispanic/Latino;

2 Hispanic/Latino), 5 international. Average age 34. 25 applicants, 56% accepted, 12 enrolled. In 2016, 5 doctorates awarded. *Degree requirements:* For doctorate, thesis/dissertation. *Entrance requirements:* For doctorate, GRE General Test, unofficial transcripts, letters of recommendation. Additional exam requirements/recommendations for international students: Required—TOEFL (minimum score 80 iBT), IELTS (minimum score 6.5). *Application deadline:* For fall admission, 2/1 priority date for domestic and international students. Applications are processed on a rolling basis. Application fee: $80 ($90 for international students). Electronic applications accepted. *Expenses:* $4,264 per semester full-time resident, $8,485 per semester full-time non-resident, $471 per credit hour part-time resident, $942 per credit hour part-time non-resident. *Financial support:* In 2016–17, 34 students received support, including 1 fellowship with partial tuition reimbursement available (averaging $5,000 per year), 2 research assistantships with partial tuition reimbursements available (averaging $17,500 per year), 38 teaching assistantships with partial tuition reimbursements available (averaging $18,800 per year); career-related internships or fieldwork and unspecified assistantships also available. Financial award application deadline: 2/1. *Faculty research:* Historiography and philology, multimodal writing, health communication, future of the book, readability studies. *Unit head:* Dr. Victor Vitanza, Director, 864-656-6411, E-mail: sophist@clemson.edu.
Website: https://rcid.sites.clemson.edu/

**Clemson University,** Graduate School, College of Behavioral, Social and Health Sciences, Department of Communication, Clemson, SC 29634. Offers communication, technology and society (MA). *Program availability:* Part-time. *Faculty:* 25 full-time (14 women), 3 part-time/adjunct (1 woman). *Students:* 15 full-time (13 women), 1 (woman) part-time; includes 3 minority (2 Black or African American, non-Hispanic/Latino; 1 Hispanic/Latino), 2 international. Average age 24. 30 applicants, 27% accepted, 8 enrolled. In 2016, 9 master's awarded. *Degree requirements:* For master's, comprehensive exam (for some programs), thesis (for some programs). *Entrance requirements:* For master's, GRE General Test, resume, unofficial transcripts, letters of recommendation. Additional exam requirements/recommendations for international students: Required—TOEFL (minimum score 80 iBT), IELTS (minimum score 6.5), PTE. *Application deadline:* For fall admission, 2/1 priority date for domestic and international students; for spring admission, 9/1 priority date for domestic and international students. Applications are processed on a rolling basis. Application fee: $80 ($90 for international students). Electronic applications accepted. *Expenses:* $4,264 per semester full-time resident, $8,485 per semester full-time non-resident, $471 per credit hour part-time resident, $942 per credit hour part-time non-resident. *Financial support:* In 2016–17, 15 students received support, including 14 teaching assistantships with partial tuition reimbursements available (averaging $12,000 per year); unspecified assistantships also available. Financial award application deadline: 2/1. *Total annual research expenditures:* $23,955. *Unit head:* Dr. Bryan Denham, Acting Department Chair, 864-656-1567, E-mail: bdenham@clemson.edu. *Application contact:* Dr. D. Travers Scott, Director of Graduate Studies, 864-656-1567, E-mail: dscott3@clemson.edu.
Website: http://www.clemson.edu/cbshs/departments/communication/index.html

**Clemson University,** Graduate School, College of Business, Department of Graphic Communications, Clemson, SC 29634. Offers MS. *Program availability:* Part-time. *Faculty:* 13 full-time (5 women), 1 part-time/adjunct (0 women). *Students:* 5 full-time (2 women). Average age 23. 4 applicants, 50% accepted, 2 enrolled. In 2016, 4 master's awarded. *Degree requirements:* For master's, thesis optional. *Entrance requirements:* For master's, GRE General Test, unofficial transcripts, letters of recommendation, personal statement, resume. Additional exam requirements/recommendations for international students: Required—TOEFL (minimum score 80 iBT), IELTS (minimum score 6.5). *Application deadline:* For fall admission, 5/15 for domestic and international students; for spring admission, 10/15 for domestic and international students. Applications are processed on a rolling basis. Application fee: $80 ($90 for international students). Electronic applications accepted. *Expenses:* $4,264 per semester full-time resident, $8,485 per semester full-time non-resident, $471 per credit hour part-time resident, $942 per credit hour part-time non-resident. *Financial support:* In 2016–17, 4 students received support, including 1 research assistantship with partial tuition reimbursement available (averaging $14,784 per year); career-related internships or fieldwork and unspecified assistantships also available. Financial award application deadline: 5/15. *Total annual research expenditures:* $54,125. *Unit head:* Dr. Chip Tonkin, Department Chair, 864-656-3447, E-mail: tonkin@clemson.edu. *Application contact:* Dr. Nona Woolbright, Graduate Coordinator, 864-656-0105, E-mail: nwoolbr@clemson.edu.
Website: https://www.clemson.edu/business/departments/graphics/

**Cleveland State University,** College of Graduate Studies, College of Liberal Arts and Social Sciences, School of Communication, Cleveland, OH 44115. Offers applied communication theory and methodology (MA). *Program availability:* Part-time, evening/weekend. *Faculty:* 10 full-time (5 women), 1 part-time/adjunct (0 women). *Students:* 10 full-time (8 women), 7 part-time (4 women); includes 5 minority (3 Black or African American, non-Hispanic/Latino; 2 Two or more races, non-Hispanic/Latino), 4 international. Average age 27. 16 applicants, 81% accepted, 7 enrolled. In 2016, 10 master's awarded. *Degree requirements:* For master's, comprehensive exam (for some programs), thesis, project, comprehensive exam, or collaborative project. *Entrance requirements:* For master's, GRE or MAT, minimum undergraduate GPA of 2.75, 2 letters of recommendation, statement of interest. Additional exam requirements/recommendations for international students: Required—TOEFL (minimum score 550 paper-based; 78 iBT). *Application deadline:* For fall admission, 7/1 priority date for domestic students, 5/15 priority date for international students; for spring admission, 11/15 priority date for domestic students, 11/1 priority date for international students; for summer admission, 4/1 for domestic students, 3/15 for international students. Applications are processed on a rolling basis. Application fee: $40. Electronic applications accepted. *Expenses:* Contact institution. *Financial support:* In 2016–17, 14 students received support, including 9 teaching assistantships with partial tuition reimbursements available (averaging $13,218 per year); tuition waivers (partial) also available. Financial award application deadline: 8/1. *Faculty research:* Interpersonal, organizational, and mass communication; health communication. *Unit head:* Dr. Cheryl Bracken, Professor and Graduate Program Director, 216-687-4512, Fax: 216-687-5435, E-mail: c.bracken@csuohio.edu. *Application contact:* Sandra M. Thorp, Administrative Secretary, 216-687-2116, Fax: 216-687-5435, E-mail: s.m.thorp@csuohio.edu.
Website: http://www.csuohio.edu/class/communication/communication

**Cleveland State University,** College of Graduate Studies, Maxine Goodman Levin College of Urban Affairs, Program in Urban Studies and Public Affairs, Cleveland, OH 44115. Offers communication (PhD); public administration (PhD); urban policy and development (PhD). *Program availability:* Part-time, evening/weekend. *Faculty:* 16 full-time (8 women), 13 part-time/adjunct (5 women). *Students:* 8 full-time (6 women), 17 part-time (8 women); includes 5 minority (3 Black or African American, non-Hispanic/Latino; 1 Hispanic/Latino; 1 Two or more races, non-Hispanic/Latino), 6 international. Average age 43. 32 applicants, 34% accepted, 2 enrolled. In 2016, 4 doctorates awarded. *Degree requirements:* For doctorate, comprehensive exam, thesis/dissertation. *Entrance requirements:* For doctorate, GRE General Test (minimum score: verbal and quantitative 50th percentile, analytical writing 4.0), minimum GPA of 3.5. Additional exam requirements/recommendations for international students: Required—

## Communication—General

TOEFL (minimum score 550 paper-based; 78 iBT), IELTS (6.0), or International Test of English Proficiency (iTEP). *Application deadline:* For fall admission, 1/31 for domestic and international students. Application fee: $40. Electronic applications accepted. *Expenses:* Contact institution. *Financial support:* In 2016–17, 15 students received support, including 5 research assistantships with full tuition reimbursements available (averaging $11,800 per year), 1 teaching assistantship with full tuition reimbursement available (averaging $11,800 per year); scholarships/grants, tuition waivers (full and partial), and unspecified assistantships also available. Support available to part-time students. Financial award application deadline: 3/1; financial award applicants required to submit FAFSA. *Faculty research:* Urban and public policy, public affairs. *Unit head:* Dr. Bill Bowen, Professor/PhD Program Director, 216-687-9226, E-mail: w.bowen@csuohio.edu. *Application contact:* David Arrighi, Graduate Academic Advisor, 216-523-7522, Fax: 216-687-5398, E-mail: d.arrighi@csuohio.edu. Website: http://urban.csuohio.edu/academics/graduate/phd/

**The College at Brockport, State University of New York,** School of Arts and Sciences, Department of Communication, Brockport, NY 14420-2997. Offers MA. *Program availability:* Part-time, evening/weekend. *Faculty:* 6 full-time (3 women). *Students:* 13 full-time (8 women), 14 part-time (9 women); includes 6 minority (3 Black or African American, non-Hispanic/Latino; 1 American Indian or Alaska Native, non-Hispanic/Latino; 1 Hispanic/Latino; 1 Two or more races, non-Hispanic/Latino), 2 international. 24 applicants, 75% accepted, 14 enrolled. In 2016, 3 master's awarded. *Degree requirements:* For master's, thesis or alternative, research project. *Entrance requirements:* For master's, minimum GPA of 3.0, letters of recommendation. Additional exam requirements/recommendations for international students: Required—TOEFL (minimum score 550 paper-based; 79 iBT), IELTS (minimum score 6.5). *Application deadline:* For fall admission, 7/15 priority date for domestic and international students; for spring admission, 11/15 priority date for domestic and international students; for summer admission, 4/1 priority date for domestic and international students. Application fee: $50. Electronic applications accepted. *Expenses:* Contact institution. *Financial support:* In 2016–17, 1 fellowship with full tuition reimbursement (averaging $7,500 per year), 2 teaching assistantships with full tuition reimbursements (averaging $6,000 per year) were awarded; Federal Work-Study, scholarships/grants, and unspecified assistantships also available. Support available to part-time students. Financial award application deadline: 3/15; financial award applicants required to submit FAFSA. *Faculty research:* Organizational communication, rhetorical theory and criticism, media theory and criticism, interpersonal communication, communication theory. *Unit head:* Dr. Monica Brasted, Chairperson, 585-395-2511, Fax: 585-395-5771, E-mail: mbrasted@brockport.edu. *Application contact:* Dr. Alex Lyon, Graduate Director, 585-395-5772, Fax: 585-395-5771, E-mail: alyon@brockport.edu. Website: http://www.brockport.edu/cmc/grad/

**The College of New Rochelle,** Graduate School, Division of Art and Communication Studies, Program in Communication Studies, New Rochelle, NY 10805-2308. Offers MS, Certificate. *Program availability:* Part-time, evening/weekend. *Degree requirements:* For master's, thesis or alternative, thesis or comprehensive exam. *Entrance requirements:* For master's, GRE General Test, interview, minimum GPA of 3.0. Additional exam requirements/recommendations for international students: Required—TOEFL.

**Columbia University,** Graduate School of Business, Doctoral Program in Business, New York, NY 10027. Offers business (PhD), including accounting, decision, risk, and operations, finance and economics, management, marketing. *Accreditation:* AACSB. *Degree requirements:* For doctorate, comprehensive exam, thesis/dissertation, major field exam, research paper, thesis proposal. *Entrance requirements:* For doctorate, GMAT or GRE (finance), 2 letters of reference, resume. Additional exam requirements/recommendations for international students: Required—TOEFL. Electronic applications accepted. *Expenses:* Contact institution. *Faculty research:* Human decision making and behavioral research; real estate market and mortgage defaults; financial crisis and corporate governance; international business; security analysis and accounting.

**Columbia University,** Graduate School of Business, MBA Program, New York, NY 10027. Offers accounting (MBA); decision, risk, and operations (MBA); entrepreneurship (MBA); finance and economics (MBA); healthcare and pharmaceutical management (MBA); human resource management (MBA); international business (MBA); leadership and ethics (MBA); management (MBA); marketing (MBA); media (MBA); private equity (MBA); real estate (MBA); social enterprise (MBA); value investing (MBA); DDS/MBA; JD/MBA; MBA/MIA; MBA/MPH; MBA/MS; MD/MBA. *Entrance requirements:* For master's, GMAT, 2 letters of recommendation. Additional exam requirements/recommendations for international students: Required—TOEFL. Electronic applications accepted. *Expenses:* Contact institution. *Faculty research:* Human decision making and behavioral research; real estate market and mortgage defaults; financial crisis and corporate governance; international business; security analysis and accounting.

**Columbia University,** School of Continuing Education, Program in Communications Practice, New York, NY 10027. Offers MS. Electronic applications accepted.

**Concordia University,** School of Graduate Studies, Faculty of Arts and Science, Department of Communication Studies, Montréal, QC H3G 1M8, Canada. Offers communication (PhD); communication studies (Diploma); media studies (MA). PhD program offered jointly with Universityé de Montréal and Universityé du Quebec à Montréal. *Degree requirements:* For master's, thesis optional; for doctorate, one foreign language, comprehensive exam, thesis/dissertation, research practicum, seminar. *Entrance requirements:* For master's, bachelor's degree in communications, 2 years of media-related experience; for doctorate, MA in communications. *Faculty research:* Communication and development, organizational communication, cultural studies, rhetoric, future studies.

**Cornell University,** Graduate School, Graduate Fields of Agriculture and Life Sciences, Field of Communication, Ithaca, NY 14853. Offers communication (MS, PhD); human-computer interaction (MS, PhD); language and communication (MS, PhD); media communication and society (MS, PhD); organizational communication (MS, PhD); science, environment and health communication (MS, PhD); social psychology of communication (MS, PhD). *Degree requirements:* For master's, thesis (MS); for doctorate, comprehensive exam, thesis/dissertation. *Entrance requirements:* For master's and doctorate, GRE General Test, 3 letters of recommendation. Additional exam requirements/recommendations for international students: Required—TOEFL (minimum score 600 paper-based; 100 iBT). Electronic applications accepted. *Faculty research:* Mass communication, communication technologies, science and environmental communication.

**Dallas Baptist University,** College of Fine Arts, Dallas, TX 75211-9299. Offers communication (MA), including communication for ministry, communication leadership, communication studies, marketing communication, organizational communication management, worship studies. *Program availability:* Part-time, evening/weekend. *Application deadline:* Applications are processed on a rolling basis. Application fee: $25. Electronic applications accepted. Application fee is waived when completed online. *Expenses: Tuition:* Full-time $15,408; part-time $856 per credit hour. *Required fees:* $400 per semester. Tuition and fees vary according to course load and degree level. *Unit head:* Ronald E. Bowles, Dean, 214-333-5316, E-mail: ronb@dbu.edu. *Application*

*contact:* Dr. Joanne Morgan, Program Director, 214-333-6854, E-mail: joannem@dbu.edu. Website: http://www3.dbu.edu/graduate/macoma.asp

**Dallas Baptist University,** Graduate School of Ministry, Program in Global Leadership, Dallas, TX 75211-9299. Offers church planting (MA); East Asian Studies (MA); English as a second language (MA); general studies (MA); global communication (MA); global studies (MA); international business (MA); leading the nonprofit organization (MA); missions (MA); small group ministry (MA); urban ministry (MA). *Program availability:* Part-time, evening/weekend. *Application deadline:* Applications are processed on a rolling basis. Application fee: $25. Electronic applications accepted. Application fee is waived when completed online. *Expenses: Tuition:* Full-time $15,408; part-time $856 per credit hour. *Required fees:* $400 per semester. Tuition and fees vary according to course load and degree level. *Unit head:* Dr. Bob Garrett, Director, 214-333-5508, E-mail: bobg@dbu.edu. *Application contact:* Bobby Soto, Director of Admissions, 214-333-5242, E-mail: graduate@dbu.edu. Website: http://www3.dbu.edu/gsom/global-leadership/

**Dallas Baptist University,** Professional Development Program, Dallas, TX 75211-9299. Offers accounting (MA); church leadership (MA); communication (MA); counseling (MA); criminal justice (MA); English as a second language (MA); finance (MA); higher education (MA); leadership studies (MA); management (MA); management information systems (MA); marketing (MA); missions (MA); professional life coaching (MA); training and development (MA). *Program availability:* Part-time, evening/weekend, 100% online, blended/hybrid learning. *Application deadline:* Applications are processed on a rolling basis. Application fee: $25. Electronic applications accepted. Application fee is waived when completed online. *Expenses: Tuition:* Full-time $15,408; part-time $856 per credit hour. *Required fees:* $400 per semester. Tuition and fees vary according to course load and degree level. *Unit head:* Jared Ingram, Director, 214-333-5584, E-mail: jaredi@dbu.edu. *Application contact:* Bobby Soto, Director of Admissions, 214-333-5242, E-mail: graduate@dbu.edu. Website: http://www3.dbu.edu/graduate/mapd.asp

**DePaul University,** College of Communication, Chicago, IL 60614. Offers digital communication and media arts (MA); health communication (MA); journalism (MA); media and cinema studies (MA); organizational and multicultural communication (MA); public relations and advertising (MA); relational communication (MA). *Program availability:* Part-time, evening/weekend. *Entrance requirements:* Additional exam requirements/recommendations for international students: Required—TOEFL (minimum score 590 paper-based; 96 iBT), IELTS (minimum score 7.5) or PTE. Electronic applications accepted.

**DEREE - The American College of Greece,** Graduate Programs, Athens, Greece. Offers applied psychology (MS); communication (MA); leadership (MS); marketing (MS).

**Drake University,** School of Journalism and Mass Communication, Des Moines, IA 50311-4516. Offers MCL. *Program availability:* Part-time, evening/weekend. *Faculty:* 4 full-time (3 women). *Students:* 19 part-time (14 women); includes 2 minority (1 Black or African American, non-Hispanic/Latino; 1 Hispanic/Latino). Average age 33. 5 applicants, 100% accepted, 5 enrolled. In 2016, 8 master's awarded. *Expenses: Tuition:* Full-time $38,244; part-time $555 per credit hour. *Required fees:* $146; $73 per semester. Tuition and fees vary according to course load, program and student level. *Unit head:* Dr. Kathleen Richardson, Dean, 515-271-2295, Fax: 515-271-4518, E-mail: kathleen.richardson@drake.edu.

**Drexel University,** College of Arts and Sciences, Department of Communication, Culture and Media, Philadelphia, PA 19104-2875. Offers communication (MS), including public communication, science communication, technical communication. *Program availability:* Part-time, evening/weekend. *Faculty:* 19 full-time (6 women), 12 part-time/adjunct (6 women). *Students:* 5 full-time (4 women), 35 part-time (25 women); includes 9 minority (3 Black or African American, non-Hispanic/Latino; 3 Asian, non-Hispanic/Latino; 3 Hispanic/Latino), 7 international. Average age 30. In 2016, 12 master's awarded. *Degree requirements:* For master's, internship, professional portfolio. *Entrance requirements:* Additional exam requirements/recommendations for international students: Required—TOEFL. *Application deadline:* For fall admission, 8/21 for domestic students. Applications are processed on a rolling basis. Application fee: $50. Electronic applications accepted. *Expenses: Tuition:* Full-time $32,184; part-time $1192 per credit hour. *Required fees:* $280. Tuition and fees vary according to campus/location and program. *Financial support:* Research assistantships, teaching assistantships, career-related internships or fieldwork, Federal Work-Study, institutionally sponsored loans, tuition waivers (partial), and unspecified assistantships available. Financial award application deadline: 2/1. *Faculty research:* Science information and attitudes, science influence on literature, process of technical writing, document design, software documentation. *Unit head:* Dr. Douglas Porpora, Head, 215-895-2446, Fax: 215-895-1071. *Application contact:* Director of Graduate Admissions, 215-895-6700, Fax: 215-895-5939, E-mail: enroll@drexel.edu.

**Drury University,** Master of Arts in Communication Program, Springfield, MO 65802. Offers integrated marketing communications (MA); organizational leadership and change (MA). *Program availability:* Part-time, evening/weekend. *Faculty:* 3 full-time (1 woman), 2 part-time/adjunct (0 women). *Students:* 39 full-time (32 women); includes 4 minority (1 Black or African American, non-Hispanic/Latino; 2 Hispanic/Latino; 1 Two or more races, non-Hispanic/Latino), 2 international. Average age 27. 8 applicants, 88% accepted, 7 enrolled. In 2016, 8 master's awarded. *Entrance requirements:* For master's, GRE. Additional exam requirements/recommendations for international students: Required—TOEFL (minimum score 80 iBT); Recommended—IELTS (minimum score 6.5). *Application deadline:* For fall admission, 8/4 priority date for domestic and international students; for spring admission, 1/5 priority date for domestic and international students; for summer admission, 5/26 priority date for domestic and international students. Applications are processed on a rolling basis. Application fee: $25 ($50 for international students). Electronic applications accepted. *Expenses:* $453 per credit hour, $7 technology fee, $100 graduation fee. *Financial support:* Career-related internships or fieldwork, scholarships/grants, and unspecified assistantships available. Financial award application deadline: 6/30; financial award applicants required to submit FAFSA. *Faculty research:* Nonprofit leadership, organizational change, leadership accountability, digital media, health communication. *Unit head:* Charles Taylor, Director, Master of Arts in Communication, 417-873-7391, E-mail: ctaylor@drury.edu. Website: http://www.drury.edu/communication-masters

**Duquesne University,** Graduate School of Liberal Arts, Department of Communication and Rhetorical Studies, Pittsburgh, PA 15282-0001. Offers communication (MA); rhetoric (PhD). *Program availability:* Part-time, evening/weekend, 100% online. *Faculty:* 10 full-time (4 women), 5 part-time/adjunct (3 women). *Students:* 100 full-time (63 women), 7 part-time (all women); includes 9 minority (6 Black or African American, non-Hispanic/Latino; 1 Hispanic/Latino; 2 Two or more races, non-Hispanic/Latino), 22 international. Average age 34. 62 applicants, 90% accepted, 28 enrolled. In 2016, 13 master's, 8 doctorates awarded. Terminal master's awarded for partial completion of doctoral program. *Degree requirements:* For master's, thesis optional, practicum; for doctorate, 2 foreign languages, comprehensive exam, thesis/dissertation. *Entrance*

*requirements:* For master's and doctorate, GRE General Test. Additional exam requirements/recommendations for international students: Required—TOEFL. *Application deadline:* For fall admission, 2/1 priority date for domestic and international students; for spring admission, 11/1 priority date for domestic and international students. Applications are processed on a rolling basis. Application fee: $0. Electronic applications accepted. *Expenses: Tuition:* Full-time $22,212; part-time $1234 per credit. Tuition and fees vary according to program. *Financial support:* In 2016–17, 24 students received support, including 7 research assistantships with full tuition reimbursements available (averaging $8,000 per year), 14 teaching assistantships with full tuition reimbursements available (averaging $17,000 per year); career-related internships or fieldwork, Federal Work-Study, institutionally sponsored loans, scholarships/grants, tuition waivers (full and partial), and unspecified assistantships also available. Financial award application deadline: 5/1. *Unit head:* Dr. Ronald Arnett, Chair, 412-396-5076, E-mail: arnett@duq.edu. *Application contact:* Linda Rendulic, Assistant to the Dean, 412-396-6400, Fax: 412-396-5265, E-mail: rendulic@duq.edu.
Website: http://www.duq.edu/academics/schools/liberal-arts/graduate-school/programs/communication-

**Eastern Michigan University,** Graduate School, College of Arts and Sciences, School of Communication, Media and Theatre Arts, Program in Communication, Ypsilanti, MI 48197. Offers MA. *Program availability:* Part-time, evening/weekend, online learning. *Students:* 6 full-time (4 women), 33 part-time (22 women); includes 15 minority (14 Black or African American, non-Hispanic/Latino; 1 Hispanic/Latino), 3 international. Average age 30. 26 applicants, 73% accepted, 11 enrolled. In 2016, 12 master's awarded. *Degree requirements:* For master's, thesis or alternative. *Entrance requirements:* Additional exam requirements/recommendations for international students: Required—TOEFL. *Application deadline:* Applications are processed on a rolling basis. Application fee: $45. *Financial support:* Fellowships, research assistantships with full tuition reimbursements, teaching assistantships with full tuition reimbursements, career-related internships or fieldwork, Federal Work-Study, institutionally sponsored loans, scholarships/grants, tuition waivers (partial), and unspecified assistantships available. Support available to part-time students. Financial award applicants required to submit FAFSA. *Application contact:* Dr. Donald Ritzenhein, Coordinator, 734-487-3130, Fax: 734-487-3443, E-mail: dritzenh@emich.edu.

**Eastern New Mexico University,** Graduate School, College of Fine Arts, Portales, NM 88130. Offers communicative arts and sciences (MA). *Program availability:* Part-time, online learning. *Degree requirements:* For master's, comprehensive exam, thesis optional. *Entrance requirements:* For master's, minimum GPA of 3.0, submission of writing sample. Additional exam requirements/recommendations for international students: Required—TOEFL (minimum score 550 paper-based; 79 iBT), IELTS (minimum score 6). Electronic applications accepted.

**Eastern University,** Loeb School of Education, St. Davids, PA 19087-3696. Offers ESL program specialist (K-12) (Certificate); general supervisor (PreK-12) (Certificate); health and physical education (K-12) (Certificate; middle level (4-8) (Certificate); multicultural education (M Ed); organizational leadership with education (PhD); Pre K-4 (Certificate); Pre K-4 with special education (Certificate); reading (M Ed); reading specialist (K-12) (Certificate); reading supervisor (K-12) (Certificate); school health supervisor (Certificate); school nurse (K-12) (Certificate); secondary biology education (7-12) (Certificate); secondary chemistry education (7-12) (Certificate); secondary communication education (7-12) (Certificate); secondary education (7-12) (Certificate); secondary English education (7-12) (Certificate); secondary math education (7-12) (Certificate); secondary social studies education (7-12) (Certificate); special education (M Ed); special education (7-12) (Certificate); special education (Pre K-8) (Certificate); special education supervisor (N-12) (Certificate); TESOL (M Ed); world language (Certificate), including French, Spanish. *Program availability:* Part-time, evening/weekend, online learning. *Students:* 41 full-time (32 women), 89 part-time (68 women); includes 54 minority (38 Black or African American, non-Hispanic/Latino; 3 Asian, non-Hispanic/Latino; 11 Hispanic/Latino; 2 Two or more races, non-Hispanic/Latino), 2 international. Average age 37. In 2016, 64 master's awarded. *Entrance requirements:* Additional exam requirements/recommendations for international students: Required—TOEFL. *Application deadline:* Applications are processed on a rolling basis. Application fee: $35. Electronic applications accepted. Application fee is waived when completed online. *Expenses:* $690 per credit. *Unit head:* Michael Dziedziak, Executive Director of Enrollment, 800-452-0996, E-mail: gpsadmissions@eastern.edu.
Website: http://www.eastern.edu/academics/programs/loeb-school-education-0

**Eastern Washington University,** Graduate Studies, College of Social Sciences, Department of Communication Studies, Cheney, WA 99004-2431. Offers MSC. *Program availability:* Part-time, evening/weekend. *Faculty:* 7 full-time (4 women). *Students:* 24 full-time (11 women), 4 part-time (all women); includes 8 minority (5 Black or African American, non-Hispanic/Latino; 2 American Indian or Alaska Native, non-Hispanic/Latino; 1 Hispanic/Latino), 1 international. Average age 35. 17 applicants, 35% accepted, 5 enrolled. In 2016, 11 master's awarded. *Degree requirements:* For master's, comprehensive exam, thesis or alternative. *Entrance requirements:* For master's, GRE General Test, minimum GPA of 3.0. Additional exam requirements/recommendations for international students: Required—TOEFL (minimum score 580 paper-based; 92 iBT), IELTS (minimum score 7), TWE, PTE (minimum score 63). *Application deadline:* For fall admission, 4/1 priority date for domestic students; for spring admission, 1/15 for domestic students. Applications are processed on a rolling basis. Application fee: $75. Electronic applications accepted. *Expenses:* Tuition, state resident: full-time $11,000; part-time $5500 per credit. Tuition, nonresident: full-time $24,000; part-time $12,000 per credit. *Required fees:* $1300. One-time fee: $50 full-time. Part-time tuition and fees vary according to course load, campus/location and program. *Financial support:* In 2016–17, 7 teaching assistantships with partial tuition reimbursements (averaging $10,000 per year) were awarded; career-related internships or fieldwork, Federal Work-Study, institutionally sponsored loans, scholarships/grants, health care benefits, tuition waivers (partial), and unspecified assistantships also available. Support available to part-time students. Financial award application deadline: 2/1; financial award applicants required to submit FAFSA. *Unit head:* Dr. Jeffrey Stafford, Professor/Chair of the Department of Communication, 509-359-7929. *Application contact:* Kathy White, Advisor/Recruiter for Graduate Studies, 509-359-6297, Fax: 509-359-6044, E-mail: gradprograms@ewu.edu.

**East Tennessee State University,** School of Graduate Studies, College of Arts and Sciences, Department of Communication and Performance, Johnson City, TN 37614. Offers professional communication (MA), including communication studies, storytelling and theatre, strategic communication. Program offered with Department of Mass Communications. *Program availability:* Part-time. *Degree requirements:* For master's, comprehensive exam, thesis optional. *Entrance requirements:* For master's, GRE General Test, minimum GPA of 3.0; three letters of recommendation. Additional exam requirements/recommendations for international students: Required—TOEFL (minimum score 550 paper-based; 79 iBT). Electronic applications accepted. *Faculty research:* Political communications, visual communication, depictions of gender and ethnicity in print and online media and online corporate media, presidential rhetoric and newspaper coverage of presidential speeches.

**Edinboro University of Pennsylvania,** Department of Communication Studies, Edinboro, PA 16444. Offers MA. *Program availability:* Part-time, evening/weekend.

*Degree requirements:* For master's, thesis or alternative, competency exam. *Entrance requirements:* For master's, GRE or MAT, minimum QPA of 2.5. Electronic applications accepted.

**Emerson College,** Graduate Studies, School of Communication, Department of Communication Studies, Boston, MA 02116-4624. Offers communication management (MA). *Program availability:* Part-time, evening/weekend. *Faculty:* 19 full-time (8 women). *Students:* 32 full-time (23 women), 6 part-time (5 women), 11 international. Average age 27. 49 applicants, 84% accepted, 18 enrolled. In 2016, 15 master's awarded. *Entrance requirements:* For master's, GMAT or GRE General Test. Additional exam requirements/recommendations for international students: Required—TOEFL (minimum score 550 paper-based; 80 iBT), IELTS (minimum score 6.5). *Application deadline:* For fall admission, 3/1 priority date for domestic and international students; for spring admission, 11/1 for domestic and international students. Applications are processed on a rolling basis. Application fee: $60 ($75 for international students). Electronic applications accepted. *Financial support:* In 2016–17, 8 students received support, including 8 fellowships (averaging $5,318 per year); research assistantships, Federal Work-Study, scholarships/grants, and unspecified assistantships also available. Financial award application deadline: 3/1; financial award applicants required to submit FAFSA. *Application contact:* Leanda Ferland, Director of Graduate Admission, 617-824-8610, Fax: 617-824-8614, E-mail: gradapp@emerson.edu.
Website: http://www.emerson.edu/graduate_admission

**Fairfield University,** College of Arts and Sciences, Fairfield, CT 06824. Offers American studies (MA); communication (MA); creative writing (MFA); mathematics (MS); public administration (MPA). *Program availability:* Part-time, evening/weekend, online learning. *Faculty:* 17 full-time (9 women), 12 part-time/adjunct (6 women). *Students:* 60 full-time (40 women), 51 part-time (28 women); includes 24 minority (9 Black or African American, non-Hispanic/Latino; 1 Asian, non-Hispanic/Latino; 11 Hispanic/Latino; 3 Two or more races, non-Hispanic/Latino), 8 international. Average age 34. 84 applicants, 74% accepted, 38 enrolled. In 2016, 68 master's awarded. *Degree requirements:* For master's, capstone research course. *Entrance requirements:* For master's, minimum GPA of 3.0, 2 letters of recommendation, resume, personal statement. Additional exam requirements/recommendations for international students: Required—TOEFL (minimum score 550 paper-based; 80 iBT) or IELTS (minimum score 6.5). *Application deadline:* For fall admission, 5/15 for international students; for spring admission, 10/15 for international students. Applications are processed on a rolling basis. Application fee: $60. Electronic applications accepted. *Expenses:* Contact institution. *Financial support:* In 2016–17, 17 students received support. Scholarships/grants and unspecified assistantships available. Financial award applicants required to submit FAFSA. *Faculty research:* Ethical theory, media industries, community-based teaching and learning, non commutative algebra and partial differential equations, cancer research in biology and physics. *Unit head:* Dr. Yohuru Williams, Dean, 203-254-4000 Ext. 2221, Fax: 203-254-4119, E-mail: ywilliams@fairfield.edu. *Application contact:* Marianne Gumpper, Director of Graduate Admission, 203-254-4184, Fax: 203-254-4073, E-mail: gradadmis@fairfield.edu.
Website: http://www.fairfield.edu/cas

**Fairleigh Dickinson University, Metropolitan Campus,** University College: Arts, Sciences, and Professional Studies, School of Art and Media Studies, Program in Media and Communications, Teaneck, NJ 07666-1914. Offers MA.

**Fitchburg State University,** Division of Graduate and Continuing Education, Program in Applied Communications, Fitchburg, MA 01420-2697. Offers MS. *Program availability:* Part-time, evening/weekend. *Faculty:* 4 full-time (1 woman), 1 part-time/adjunct (0 women). *Students:* 1 (woman) full-time, 18 part-time (11 women); includes 5 minority (2 Black or African American, non-Hispanic/Latino; 1 Asian, non-Hispanic/Latino; 1 Hispanic/Latino; 1 Two or more races, non-Hispanic/Latino). Average age 37. 2 applicants, 100% accepted, 2 enrolled. In 2016, 6 master's awarded. *Entrance requirements:* Additional exam requirements/recommendations for international students: Required—TOEFL (minimum score 550 paper-based; 79 iBT). *Application deadline:* For fall admission, 7/15 for international students; for spring admission, 12/1 for international students. Applications are processed on a rolling basis. Application fee: $50. Electronic applications accepted. *Expenses:* $319 per credit. *Financial support:* In 2016–17, research assistantships with partial tuition reimbursements (averaging $5,500 per year) were awarded; Federal Work-Study, scholarships/grants, and unspecified assistantships also available. Support available to part-time students. Financial award application deadline: 3/1; financial award applicants required to submit FAFSA. *Unit head:* Dr. Viera Lorencova, Chair, 978-665-4856, Fax: 978-665-3658, E-mail: gce@fitchburgstate.edu. *Application contact:* Ganas Sean, Director of Admissions, 978-665-3144, Fax: 978-665-4540, E-mail: admissions@fsc.edu.

**Fitchburg State University,** Division of Graduate and Continuing Education, Program in Interdisciplinary Studies, Fitchburg, MA 01420-2697. Offers applied communications (CAGS); counseling/psychology (CAGS); individualized track (CAGS); reading specialist (CAGS). *Program availability:* Part-time, evening/weekend. *Entrance requirements:* Additional exam requirements/recommendations for international students: Required—TOEFL (minimum score 550 paper-based; 79 iBT). Electronic applications accepted. *Expenses:* Tuition, state resident: full-time $2871; part-time $1914 per year. Tuition, nonresident: full-time $2871; part-time $1914 per year. *Required fees:* $3828. Tuition and fees vary according to program.

**Florida Atlantic University,** Dorothy F. Schmidt College of Arts and Letters, School of Communication and Multimedia Studies, Boca Raton, FL 33431-0991. Offers communication studies (MA); film and video (Certificate); media, technology and entertainment (MFA). *Program availability:* Part-time. *Faculty:* 25 full-time (8 women). *Students:* 21 full-time (15 women), 17 part-time (9 women); includes 16 minority (6 Black or African American, non-Hispanic/Latino; 1 Asian, non-Hispanic/Latino; 9 Hispanic/Latino), 3 international. Average age 33. 39 applicants, 72% accepted, 14 enrolled. In 2016, 8 master's awarded. *Degree requirements:* For master's, one foreign language, comprehensive exam (for some programs), thesis (for some programs). *Entrance requirements:* For master's, GRE General Test, minimum GPA of 3.0, essay, letters of recommendation. *Application deadline:* For fall admission, 7/1 priority date for domestic students, 4/1 for international students; for spring admission, 11/1 for domestic students, 10/1 for international students. Applications are processed on a rolling basis. Application fee: $30. Electronic applications accepted. *Expenses:* Tuition, state resident: full-time $7392; part-time $369.82 per credit hour. Tuition, nonresident: full-time $19,432; part-time $1024.81 per credit hour. *Financial support:* Teaching assistantships with partial tuition reimbursements, Federal Work-Study, institutionally sponsored loans, scholarships/grants, and unspecified assistantships available. Support available to part-time students. Financial award application deadline: 3/1; financial award applicants required to submit FAFSA. *Faculty research:* Cultural studies, gender studies, film, communication theory, journalism, new media. *Unit head:* Dr. David Williams, Director, 561-297-0045, Fax: 561-297-2615, E-mail: dcwill@fau.edu. *Application contact:* Dr. Eric M. Freedman, Graduate Coordinator, 561-297-2534, Fax: 561-297-2615, E-mail: efreedma@fau.edu.
Website: http://www.fau.edu/scms/

**Florida Institute of Technology,** College of Psychology and Liberal Arts, Program in Global Strategic Communication, Melbourne, FL 32901-6975. Offers MS. *Program*

## Communication—General

availability: Part-time. *Students:* 12 full-time (9 women), 5 part-time (all women); includes 3 minority (all Hispanic/Latino), 6 international. Average age 27. 27 applicants, 59% accepted, 3 enrolled. In 2016, 6 master's awarded. *Degree requirements:* For master's, comprehensive exam, thesis optional, minimum of 36 credit hours. *Entrance requirements:* For master's, GRE General Test (recommended), 2 letters of recommendation, statement of objectives, previous work experience. Additional exam requirements/recommendations for international students: Required—TOEFL (minimum score 550 paper-based; 79 iBT). *Application deadline:* Applications are processed on a rolling basis. Electronic applications accepted. *Expenses: Tuition:* Full-time $22,338; part-time $1241 per credit hour. *Required fees:* $250. Tuition and fees vary according to degree level, campus/location and program. *Financial support:* Applicants required to submit FAFSA. *Unit head:* Dr. Judith B. Strother, Professor/Chair, MS in Global Strategic Communication, 321-674-7358, Fax: 321-674-8109, E-mail: strother@fit.edu. *Application contact:* Cheryl A. Brown, Associate Director of Graduate Admissions, 321-674-7581, Fax: 321-723-9468, E-mail: cbrown@fit.edu.
Website: http://cpla.fit.edu/sac/global-strategic-communication/

**Florida International University,** College of Communication, Architecture and The Arts, School of Communication and Journalism, Miami, FL 33199. Offers mass communication (MS), including global strategic communications, Spanish language journalism. *Program availability:* Part-time, evening/weekend. *Faculty:* 12 full-time (6 women), 8 part-time/adjunct (4 women). *Students:* 94 full-time (72 women), 51 part-time (33 women); includes 110 minority (25 Black or African American, non-Hispanic/Latino; 81 Hispanic/Latino; 4 Two or more races, non-Hispanic/Latino), 19 international. Average age 29. 127 applicants, 62% accepted, 59 enrolled. In 2016, 53 master's awarded. *Degree requirements:* For master's, thesis optional. *Entrance requirements:* For master's, 2 letters of recommendation; minimum GPA of 3.0 during last 60 hours of upper-level work; resume. Additional exam requirements/recommendations for international students: Required—TOEFL (minimum score 550 paper-based; 80 iBT). *Application deadline:* For fall admission, 6/1 for domestic students, 4/1 for international students; for spring admission, 10/1 for domestic students, 9/1 for international students. Applications are processed on a rolling basis. Application fee: $30. Electronic applications accepted. *Expenses:* Tuition, state resident: full-time $8912; part-time $446 per credit hour. Tuition, nonresident: full-time $21,393; part-time $992 per credit hour. *Required fees:* $2185; $195 per semester. Tuition and fees vary according to program. *Financial support:* Institutionally sponsored loans and scholarships/grants available. Financial award application deadline: 3/1; financial award applicants required to submit FAFSA. *Unit head:* Dr. Maria Elena Villar, Chair, 305-919-5795, Fax: 305-919-5215, E-mail: mariaelena.villar@fiu.edu. *Application contact:* Nanett Rojas, Assistant Director, Graduate Admissions, 305-348-7442, Fax: 305-348-7441, E-mail: gradadm@fiu.edu.
Website: https://scj.fiu.edu/

**Florida State University,** The Graduate School, College of Communication and Information, School of Communication, Tallahassee, FL 32306-2664. Offers communication theory and research (PhD); integrated marketing communication (MA, MS); media and communication studies (MA, MS); public interest media and communication (MA, MS). *Program availability:* Part-time. *Faculty:* 22 full-time (11 women), 2 part-time/adjunct (1 woman). *Students:* 71 full-time (53 women), 72 part-time (46 women); includes 77 minority (20 Black or African American, non-Hispanic/Latino; 36 Asian, non-Hispanic/Latino; 19 Hispanic/Latino; 2 Two or more races, non-Hispanic/Latino). Average age 24. 140 applicants, 57% accepted, 46 enrolled. In 2016, 83 master's, 5 doctorates awarded. *Degree requirements:* For master's, thesis (for some programs); for doctorate, comprehensive exam, thesis/dissertation. *Entrance requirements:* For master's, GRE General Test, minimum GPA of 3.0; for doctorate, GRE General Test, minimum GPA of 3.3 in graduate course work. Additional exam requirements/recommendations for international students: Required—TOEFL (minimum score 600 paper-based; 100 iBT), IELTS (minimum score 7). *Application deadline:* For fall admission, 7/1 priority date for domestic students, 5/1 priority date for international students; for spring admission, 11/1 priority date for domestic and international students; for summer admission, 3/1 priority date for domestic and international students. Applications are processed on a rolling basis. Application fee: $30. Electronic applications accepted. *Expenses:* $479.32 per credit hour in-state, $1,110.72 per credit hour out-of-state. *Financial support:* In 2016–17, 87 students received support, including 17 research assistantships with full tuition reimbursements available (averaging $16,192 per year), 46 teaching assistantships with full tuition reimbursements available (averaging $16,192 per year); fellowships, career-related internships or fieldwork, Federal Work-Study, institutionally sponsored loans, scholarships/grants, health care benefits, tuition waivers (full and partial), and unspecified assistantships also available. Support available to part-time students. Financial award application deadline: 12/15; financial award applicants required to submit FAFSA. *Faculty research:* Communication in the public interest; strategic communication; media and technology; multicultural, intercultural, and international communication. *Total annual research expenditures:* $52,979. *Unit head:* Dr. Gary Heald, Director, 850-644-5034, Fax: 850-644-8642, E-mail: gheald@fsu.edu. *Application contact:* Natashia Hinson-Turner, Graduate Coordinator, 850-644-5034, Fax: 850-644-8642, E-mail: comgradadvising@cci.fsu.edu.
Website: http://www.cci.fsu.edu

**Fordham University,** Gabelli School of Business, New York, NY 10023. Offers accounting (MBA, MS); applied statistics and decision-making (MS); business administration (EMBA); business analytics (MS); communications and media management (MBA); electronic business (MBA); entrepreneurship (MBA); finance (MBA); global finance (MS); global sustainability (MBA); healthcare management (MBA); information systems (MBA, MS); investor relations (MS); management (MBA, MS); marketing (MBA); marketing intelligence (MS); media management (MS); nonprofit leadership (MS); quantitative finance (MS); taxation (MS); JD/MBA; MS/MBA. *Accreditation:* AACSB. *Program availability:* Part-time, evening/weekend. *Faculty:* 132 full-time (44 women), 51 part-time/adjunct (7 women). *Students:* 1,117 full-time (668 women), 553 part-time (282 women); includes 207 minority (44 Black or African American, non-Hispanic/Latino; 92 Asian, non-Hispanic/Latino; 69 Hispanic/Latino; 2 Native Hawaiian or other Pacific Islander, non-Hispanic/Latino), 1,088 international. Average age 27. 4,745 applicants, 46% accepted, 752 enrolled. In 2016, 996 master's awarded. Terminal master's awarded for partial completion of doctoral program. *Degree requirements:* For master's, internships (required for MS in quantitative finance, recommended for MBA). *Entrance requirements:* For master's, GMAT/GRE, 2 letters of recommendation, resume, 2 essays, transcripts. Additional exam requirements/recommendations for international students: Required—TOEFL (minimum score 100 iBT), IELTS (minimum score 7). *Application deadline:* For fall admission, 11/15 priority date for domestic and international students; for winter admission, 1/15 priority date for domestic students, 1/1 priority date for international students; for spring admission, 3/1 for domestic and international students; for summer admission, 6/1 for domestic students. Application fee: $130. Electronic applications accepted. *Expenses:* $1,397 per credit. *Financial support:* In 2016–17, 78 students received support. Career-related internships or fieldwork, institutionally sponsored loans, scholarships/grants, and unspecified assistantships available. Support available to part-time students. Financial award application deadline: 6/30; financial award applicants required to submit FAFSA. *Unit head:* Dr. Donna Rapaccioli, Dean, 212-636-6165, Fax: 212-307-1779, E-mail: rapaccioli@fordham.edu. *Application contact:* Lawrence Murray, Senior Assistant Dean of Graduate Admissions and Advising, 212-636-6200, Fax: 212-636-7076, E-mail: admissionsgb@fordham.edu.
Website: http://www.fordham.edu/gabelli

**Fort Hays State University,** Graduate School, College of Arts and Sciences, Department of Communication Studies, Hays, KS 67601-4099. Offers communication (MS). *Program availability:* Part-time. *Degree requirements:* For master's, comprehensive exam, thesis optional. *Entrance requirements:* Additional exam requirements/recommendations for international students: Required—TOEFL (minimum score 550 paper-based). Electronic applications accepted. *Faculty research:* Listening skills development, oral sensory motor skills, speech, reading, articulation in preschool children.

**George Mason University,** College of Humanities and Social Sciences, Department of Communication, Fairfax, VA 22030. Offers MA, PhD, Certificate. *Faculty:* 38 full-time (13 women), 23 part-time/adjunct (14 women). *Students:* 43 full-time (26 women), 30 part-time (22 women); includes 18 minority (7 Black or African American, non-Hispanic/Latino; 1 American Indian or Alaska Native, non-Hispanic/Latino; 4 Asian, non-Hispanic/Latino; 2 Hispanic/Latino; 1 Native Hawaiian or other Pacific Islander, non-Hispanic/Latino; 3 Two or more races, non-Hispanic/Latino), 5 international. Average age 31. 79 applicants, 59% accepted, 23 enrolled. In 2016, 20 master's, 5 doctorates awarded. *Degree requirements:* For master's, comprehensive exam, thesis or project; for doctorate, comprehensive exam, thesis/dissertation. *Entrance requirements:* For master's, GRE, expanded goals statement; 3 letters of recommendation; resume; official transcripts; for doctorate, GRE, 3 letters of recommendation; expanded goals statement; resume; official transcript; writing sample; for Certificate, GRE, expanded goals statement, resume, 2 letters of recommendation, official transcripts. Additional exam requirements/recommendations for international students: Required—TOEFL (minimum score 570 paper-based; 88 iBT), IELTS (minimum score 6.5), PTE (minimum score 59). Application fee: $75 ($80 for international students). Electronic applications accepted. *Expenses:* Tuition, state resident: full-time $10,628; part-time $443 per credit. Tuition, nonresident: full-time $29,306; part-time $1221 per credit. *Required fees:* $3096; $129 per credit. Tuition and fees vary according to program. *Financial support:* In 2016–17, 31 students received support, including 1 fellowship (averaging $1,000 per year), 4 research assistantships with tuition reimbursements available (averaging $16,038 per year), 29 teaching assistantships with tuition reimbursements available (averaging $3,547 per year); career-related internships or fieldwork, Federal Work-Study, scholarships/grants, unspecified assistantships, and health care benefits (for full-time research or teaching assistantship recipients) also available. Support available to part-time students. Financial award application deadline: 3/1; financial award applicants required to submit FAFSA. *Faculty research:* Theoretical and multi-methodological promotion, disease prevention, quality of care, risk assessment, crisis management, consumer/provider relationships, health campaigns, communication policy. *Total annual research expenditures:* $2 million. *Unit head:* Dr. Anne M. Nicotera, Chair, 703-993-8296, Fax: 703-993-1096, E-mail: anicoter@gmu.edu. *Application contact:* Brittany Sanders, Graduate Programs Coordinator, 703-993-1090, Fax: 703-993-1096, E-mail: bsander7@gmu.edu.
Website: http://communication.gmu.edu

**Georgetown University,** Graduate School of Arts and Sciences, Program in Communication, Culture, and Technology, Washington, DC 20057. Offers MA. *Program availability:* Part-time, evening/weekend. *Degree requirements:* For master's, thesis (for some programs). *Entrance requirements:* For master's, GRE General Test, 3 letters of recommendation, writing sample. Additional exam requirements/recommendations for international students: Required—TOEFL (minimum score 600 paper-based). Electronic applications accepted.

**The George Washington University,** Elliott School of International Affairs, Program in Global Communication, Washington, DC 20052. Offers MA. *Program availability:* Part-time. *Students:* 25 full-time (21 women), 19 part-time (17 women); includes 10 minority (3 Black or African American, non-Hispanic/Latino; 3 Asian, non-Hispanic/Latino; 4 Hispanic/Latino), 9 international. Average age 27. 84 applicants, 75% accepted, 15 enrolled. In 2016, 27 master's awarded. *Degree requirements:* For master's, one foreign language, capstone project. *Entrance requirements:* For master's, GRE General Test, 2 years (or equivalent) of a modern, spoken foreign language; introductory microeconomics/macroeconomics. Additional exam requirements/recommendations for international students: Required—TOEFL (minimum score 100 iBT), IELTS (minimum score 7). *Application deadline:* For fall admission, 1/15 priority date for domestic and international students; for spring admission, 10/1 for domestic students. Electronic applications accepted. *Financial support:* Fellowships, Federal Work-Study, and scholarships/grants available. Financial award application deadline: 1/15; financial award applicants required to submit FAFSA. *Unit head:* Prof. Sean Aday, 202-994-8137, E-mail: ipdgc@gwu.edu. *Application contact:* Nicole A. Campbell, Director of Graduate Admissions, 202-994-7050, Fax: 202-994-9537, E-mail: esiagrad@gwu.edu.
Website: http://www.gwu.edu/~elliott/academics/grad/gc/

**Georgia State University,** College of Arts and Sciences, Department of Communication, Atlanta, GA 30302-3083. Offers film, video, and digital imaging (MA), including critical studies, production, screenwriting; human communication and social influence (MA); mass communication (MA); media and society (PhD); moving image studies (PhD); public communication (PhD); rhetoric and politics (PhD). *Program availability:* Part-time. *Faculty:* 57 full-time (34 women). *Students:* 113 full-time (69 women), 56 part-time (33 women); includes 59 minority (37 Black or African American, non-Hispanic/Latino; 1 American Indian or Alaska Native, non-Hispanic/Latino; 2 Asian, non-Hispanic/Latino; 9 Hispanic/Latino; 10 Two or more races, non-Hispanic/Latino), 18 international. Average age 32. 134 applicants, 58% accepted, 47 enrolled. In 2016, 22 master's, 11 doctorates awarded. *Degree requirements:* For master's, variable foreign language requirement, thesis (for some programs); for doctorate, comprehensive exam, thesis/dissertation. *Entrance requirements:* For master's and doctorate, GRE. Additional exam requirements/recommendations for international students: Required—TOEFL (minimum score 550 paper-based; 80 iBT), IELTS (minimum score 6.5). *Application deadline:* For fall admission, 2/10 for domestic and international students; for spring admission, 10/15 for domestic and international students. Application fee: $50. Electronic applications accepted. *Expenses:* Tuition, state resident: full-time $6876; part-time $382 per credit hour. Tuition, nonresident: full-time $22,374; part-time $1243 per credit hour. *Required fees:* $2128; $1064 per term. Part-time tuition and fees vary according to course load and program. *Financial support:* In 2016–17, fellowships with tuition reimbursements (averaging $15,000 per year), teaching assistantships with tuition reimbursements (averaging $15,000 per year) were awarded; career-related internships or fieldwork and unspecified assistantships also available. Financial award applicants required to submit FAFSA. *Faculty research:* New media, mass media and journalism, rhetoric, film and media studies, film production. *Unit head:* Dr. Greg Lisby, Chair, 404-413-5639, Fax: 404-413-5634, E-mail: glisby@gsu.edu.
Website: http://communication.gsu.edu

**Governors State University,** College of Arts and Sciences, Program in Communication and Training, University Park, IL 60484. Offers communication studies (MA); media communication (MA). *Program availability:* Part-time. *Faculty:* 91 full-time (43 women),

125 part-time/adjunct (64 women). *Students:* 9 full-time (7 women), 62 part-time (52 women); includes 58 minority (55 Black or African American, non-Hispanic/Latino; 1 Asian, non-Hispanic/Latino; 1 Hispanic/Latino; 1 Two or more races, non-Hispanic/Latino), 1 international. Average age 43. 66 applicants, 48% accepted, 25 enrolled. In 2016, 36 master's awarded. *Entrance requirements:* Additional exam requirements/recommendations for international students: Required—TOEFL (minimum score 550 paper-based; 80 iBT), IELTS. *Application deadline:* For fall admission, 4/1 for domestic students. Application fee: $50. Electronic applications accepted. *Expenses:* $307 per credit hour; $38 per term or $76 per credit hour fees. *Financial support:* Application deadline: 5/1; applicants required to submit FAFSA. *Unit head:* Lori Montalbano, Chair of Division of Communication, Visual and Performing Arts, 708-235-2802, E-mail: lmontalbano@govst.edu. *Application contact:* Yakeea Daniels, Assistant Vice President for Enrollment Services/Director of Admission, 708-534-4510, E-mail: ydaniels@govst.edu.

**Grand Valley State University,** College of Liberal Arts and Sciences, School of Communications, Allendale, MI 49401-9403. Offers MS. *Program availability:* Part-time, evening/weekend. *Faculty:* 8 full-time (2 women), 2 part-time/adjunct (0 women). *Students:* 11 full-time (8 women), 39 part-time (28 women); includes 10 minority (4 Black or African American, non-Hispanic/Latino; 4 Hispanic/Latino; 2 Two or more races, non-Hispanic/Latino), 5 international. Average age 30. 36 applicants, 94% accepted, 15 enrolled. In 2016, 16 master's awarded. *Degree requirements:* For master's, project or thesis. *Entrance requirements:* For master's, minimum GPA of 3.0 in last 60 hours, 2 letters of recommendation, interview, essay or personal statement. Additional exam requirements/recommendations for international students: Required—TOEFL (minimum score 550 paper-based, 80 iBT), IELTS (6.5), or Michigan English Language Assessment Battery. *Application deadline:* For fall admission, 8/15 priority date for domestic students; for winter admission, 12/15 priority date for domestic students; for spring admission, 4/15 priority date for domestic students. Applications are processed on a rolling basis. Application fee: $30. Electronic applications accepted. *Expenses:* $604 per credit hour. *Financial support:* In 2016–17, 11 students received support, including 7 fellowships, 4 research assistantships with full and partial tuition reimbursements available (averaging $8,000 per year); career-related internships or fieldwork, Federal Work-Study, and institutionally sponsored loans also available. Support available to part-time students. Financial award application deadline: 4/15. *Faculty research:* Communication technology, databases, organizational communication, systems theory, public relations and advertising. *Unit head:* Dr. Vandana Pednekar Magal, Director, 616-331-3606, Fax: 616-895-2700, E-mail: thompsoa@gvsu.edu. *Application contact:* Dr. Alex Nesterenko, Graduate Program Director, 616-331-3668, Fax: 616-331-2700, E-mail: nesterea@gvsu.edu.

**Harvard University,** Extension School, Cambridge, MA 02138-3722. Offers applied sciences (CAS); biotechnology (ALM); educational technologies (ALM); educational technology (CET); English for graduate and professional studies (DGP); environmental management (ALM, CEM); information technology (ALM); journalism (ALM); liberal arts (ALM); management (ALM, CM); mathematics for teaching (ALM); museum studies (ALM); premedical studies (Diploma); publication and communication (CPC). *Program availability:* Part-time, evening/weekend. *Degree requirements:* For master's, thesis. *Entrance requirements:* For master's, 3 completed graduate courses with grade of B or higher. Additional exam requirements/recommendations for international students: Required—TOEFL (minimum score 600 paper-based), TWE (minimum score 5). *Expenses:* Contact institution.

**Hawai`i Pacific University,** College of Liberal Arts, Program in Communication, Honolulu, HI 96813. Offers MA. *Program availability:* Part-time, evening/weekend. *Faculty:* 5 full-time (1 woman), 2 part-time/adjunct (1 woman). *Students:* 23 full-time (14 women), 15 part-time (10 women); includes 20 minority (1 Black or African American, non-Hispanic/Latino; 2 Asian, non-Hispanic/Latino; 8 Hispanic/Latino; 9 Two or more races, non-Hispanic/Latino), 11 international. Average age 30. 28 applicants, 82% accepted, 11 enrolled. In 2016, 23 master's awarded. *Entrance requirements:* Additional exam requirements/recommendations for international students: Recommended—TOEFL (minimum score 550 paper-based; 80 iBT), IELTS (minimum score 6), TWE (minimum score 5). *Application deadline:* For fall admission, 2/15 priority date for domestic students; for spring admission, 10/15 priority date for domestic students. Applications are processed on a rolling basis. Application fee: $50. Electronic applications accepted. *Expenses: Tuition:* Full-time $17,190; part-time $955 per credit. *Required fees:* $150; $26 per credit. Tuition and fees vary according to course load and program. *Financial support:* In 2016–17, 12 students received support. Career-related internships or fieldwork, Federal Work-Study, scholarships/grants, tuition waivers, and unspecified assistantships available. Financial award application deadline: 3/1; financial award applicants required to submit FAFSA. *Unit head:* Dr. John Hart, Department Chair, 808-544-0805, E-mail: jhart@hpu.edu. *Application contact:* Danny Lam, Assistant Director of Graduate Admissions, 808-544-1135, E-mail: graduate@hpu.edu. Website: http://www.hpu.edu/CHSS/Communication/MA_COM/index.html

**Howard University,** School of Communications, Washington, DC 20059-0002. Offers MA, MFA, MS, PhD. *Program availability:* Part-time, evening/weekend. Terminal master's awarded for partial completion of doctoral program. *Degree requirements:* For master's, comprehensive exam (for some programs), thesis optional; for doctorate, one foreign language, comprehensive exam, thesis/dissertation. *Entrance requirements:* For master's, GRE General Test, minimum GPA of 3.0; for doctorate, GRE General Test, minimum GPA of 3.2. Additional exam requirements/recommendations for international students: Required—TOEFL. Electronic applications accepted. *Expenses:* Contact institution. *Faculty research:* Communication disorders, intercultural communication, communication skills, race and media.

**Illinois Institute of Technology,** Graduate College, Lewis College of Human Sciences, Department of Humanities, Chicago, IL 60616. Offers information architecture (MS); technical communication (PhD); technical communication and information design (MS). *Program availability:* Part-time. *Degree requirements:* For master's, comprehensive exam, thesis or alternative; for doctorate, comprehensive exam, thesis/dissertation. *Entrance requirements:* For master's, GRE General Test (minimum score 144 Quantitative, 153 Verbal, and 4.0 Analytical Writing), minimum undergraduate GPA of 3.0; 2 letters of recommendation from faculty or supervisors; professional statement discussing academic goals; for doctorate, GRE General Test (minimum score 144 Quantitative, 153 Verbal, and 4.0 Analytical Writing), bachelor's or master's degree in a field that, in combination with the 27-credit hour technical core, would provide a solid basis for advanced academic work leading to original research in the field; 3 letters of recommendation from faculty or supervisors; professional statement discussing academic goals. Additional exam requirements/recommendations for international students: Required—TOEFL (minimum score 95 iBT); Recommended—IELTS (minimum score 7). Electronic applications accepted. *Faculty research:* Linguistics, punishment theory, political communication, gender and technology, philosophical and ethical issues in neuroscience.

**Illinois State University,** Graduate School, College of Arts and Sciences, School of Communication, Normal, IL 61790-2200. Offers MA, MS. *Degree requirements:* For master's, thesis or alternative. *Entrance requirements:* For master's, GRE General Test,

minimum GPA of 2.8 in last 60 hours of course work. Additional exam requirements/recommendations for international students: Required—TOEFL.

**Indiana State University,** College of Graduate and Professional Studies, College of Arts and Sciences, Department of Communication, Terre Haute, IN 47809. Offers communication studies (MA); radio, television and film (MA). *Program availability:* Part-time. *Degree requirements:* For master's, thesis (for some programs), oral and written exam. *Entrance requirements:* For master's, GRE General Test. Additional exam requirements/recommendations for international students: Required—TOEFL. *Faculty research:* Women in media, communication apprehension, media history.

**Indiana University of Pennsylvania,** School of Graduate Studies and Research, College of Education and Educational Technology, Department of Communications Media, Indiana, PA 15705. Offers communications media and instructional technology (PhD). *Program availability:* Part-time, evening/weekend. *Faculty:* 10 full-time (4 women). *Students:* 13 full-time (3 women), 37 part-time (15 women); includes 4 minority (3 Black or African American, non-Hispanic/Latino; 1 Two or more races, non-Hispanic/Latino), 5 international. Average age 38. 65 applicants, 26% accepted, 6 enrolled. In 2016, 10 doctorates awarded. Terminal master's awarded for partial completion of doctoral program. *Degree requirements:* For doctorate, comprehensive exam, thesis/dissertation. *Entrance requirements:* For doctorate, GRE, goal statement, resume, writing sample, two letters of recommendation. Additional exam requirements/recommendations for international students: Required—TOEFL (minimum score 540 paper-based). *Application deadline:* Applications are processed on a rolling basis. Application fee: $50. Electronic applications accepted. *Expenses:* Tuition, state resident: full-time $8694; part-time $483 per credit. Tuition, nonresident: full-time $13,050; part-time $725 per credit. *Required fees:* $157 per credit. $50 per term. Tuition and fees vary according to course load and program. *Financial support:* In 2016–17, 2 fellowships with full tuition reimbursements (averaging $2,296 per year), 7 research assistantships with tuition reimbursements (averaging $5,769 per year), 3 teaching assistantships with partial tuition reimbursements (averaging $23,305 per year) were awarded; career-related internships or fieldwork, Federal Work-Study, scholarships/grants, tuition waivers (full), and unspecified assistantships also available. Support available to part-time students. Financial award application deadline: 4/15; financial award applicants required to submit FAFSA. *Unit head:* Dr. Gail Wilson, Chairperson, 724-357-2492, Fax: 724-357-5503, E-mail: bgwilson@iup.edu. *Application contact:* Dr. Zachary Stiegler, Graduate Coordinator, 724-357-3219, E-mail: zachary.stiegler@iup.edu.
Website: http://www.iup.edu/commmedia/

**Indiana University–Purdue University Fort Wayne,** College of Arts and Sciences, Department of Communication, Fort Wayne, IN 46805-1499. Offers professional communication (MA, MS). *Program availability:* Part-time. *Entrance requirements:* For master's, minimum GPA of 3.0. Additional exam requirements/recommendations for international students: Required—TOEFL (minimum score 550 paper-based; 79 iBT); Recommended—TWE. Electronic applications accepted. *Faculty research:* Cosmetic surgery and Chinese women, First Amendment and online information.

**Indiana University–Purdue University Indianapolis,** School of Liberal Arts, Department of Communication Studies, Indianapolis, IN 46225. Offers applied communication (MA); health communication (PhD). *Program availability:* Part-time. *Degree requirements:* For master's, comprehensive exam, thesis; for doctorate, thesis/dissertation. *Entrance requirements:* For doctorate, master's degree. Additional exam requirements/recommendations for international students: Required—TOEFL; Recommended—IELTS. Electronic applications accepted.

**Indiana University South Bend,** Ernestine M. Raclin School of the Arts, South Bend, IN 46634-7111. Offers communication studies (MA); music (MM), including composition, performance; music performance (AD). *Accreditation:* NASM. *Program availability:* Part-time. *Faculty:* 1 full-time (0 women). *Students:* 2 full-time (1 woman), 11 part-time (3 women); includes 2 minority (1 Black or African American, non-Hispanic/Latino; 1 Hispanic/Latino), 3 international. Average age 32. 23 applicants, 65% accepted, 6 enrolled. In 2016, 4 master's awarded. *Entrance requirements:* For master's, performance audition. Additional exam requirements/recommendations for international students: Required—TOEFL (minimum score 600 paper-based; 90 iBT). *Application deadline:* For fall admission, 7/1 priority date for domestic students; for spring admission, 11/1 for domestic students. Applications are processed on a rolling basis. Application fee: $40 ($60 for international students). Electronic applications accepted. *Expenses:* $276.98 per credit hour in-state; $652.54 per credit hour out-of-state. *Financial support:* Fellowships, teaching assistantships, and Federal Work-Study available. Support available to part-time students. Financial award application deadline: 3/1; financial award applicants required to submit FAFSA. *Faculty research:* Orchestral conducting. *Unit head:* Dr. Marvin V. Curtis, Dean, 574-520-4170, E-mail: mvcurtis@iusb.edu. *Application contact:* Admissions Counselor, 574-520-4839, Fax: 574-520-4834, E-mail: graduate@iusb.edu.
Website: https://www.iusb.edu/arts/

**Instituto Tecnologico de Santo Domingo,** Graduate School, Area of Humanities and Social Sciences, Santo Domingo, Dominican Republic. Offers accounting (Certificate); adult education (Certificate); applied linguistics (MA); economics (MA); education (M Ed); educational psychology (MA, Certificate); gender and development (MA, Certificate); humanistic studies (MA); international marketing management (Certificate); international relations in the Caribbean basin (Certificate); intervention systems in family therapy (MA); linguistic and literary communication (Certificate); pedagogical support (MA); social science education (M Ed); sustainable human development (MA); terminal illness and death psychology (Certificate); youth and adult education (M Ed).

**Instituto Tecnológico y de Estudios Superiores de Monterrey, Campus Ciudad Obregón,** Programs in Education, Program in Communications, Ciudad Obregón, Mexico. Offers ME.

**Instituto Tecnológico y de Estudios Superiores de Monterrey, Campus Monterrey,** Graduate and Research Division, Program in Natural and Social Sciences, Monterrey, Mexico. Offers biotechnology (MS); chemistry (MS, PhD); communications (MS); education (MA). *Program availability:* Part-time. *Degree requirements:* For master's, one foreign language, thesis; for doctorate, one foreign language, thesis/dissertation. *Entrance requirements:* For master's, EXADEP; for doctorate, EXADEP, master's degree in related field. Additional exam requirements/recommendations for international students: Required—TOEFL. *Faculty research:* Cultural industries, mineral substances, bioremediation, food processing, CQ in industrial chemical processing.

**International University in Geneva,** Leadership Programs, Geneva, Switzerland. Offers international relations and diplomacy (MIRD); media and communication (MA); public administration (DPA). *Degree requirements:* For master's, comprehensive exam. *Entrance requirements:* Additional exam requirements/recommendations for international students: Required—TOEFL. Electronic applications accepted.

**James Madison University,** The Graduate School, College of Arts and Letters, Program in Communication and Advocacy, Harrisonburg, VA 22807. Offers environmental communication (MA); health communication (MA); strategic communication (MA). *Program availability:* Part-time, evening/weekend. *Faculty:* 22 full-time (13 women), 1 (woman) part-time/adjunct. *Students:* 20 full-time (15 women);

*Communication—General*

includes 5 minority (3 Black or African American, non-Hispanic/Latino; 1 Asian, non-Hispanic/Latino; 1 Two or more races, non-Hispanic/Latino), 1 international. Average age 30. 18 applicants, 100% accepted, 9 enrolled. In 2016, 9 master's awarded. Application fee: $55. Electronic applications accepted. *Financial support:* In 2016–17, 16 students received support, including 6 teaching assistantships with full tuition reimbursements available (averaging $9,284 per year); fellowships, Federal Work-Study, and 10 assistantships (averaging $7911) also available. Financial award application deadline: 3/1; financial award applicants required to submit FAFSA. *Unit head:* Dr. Eric M. Fife, Director of the School of Communication Studies, 540-568-6449, E-mail: fifeem@jmu.edu. *Application contact:* Lynette D. Michael, Director of Graduate Admissions, 540-568-6131 Ext. 6395, Fax: 540-568-7860, E-mail: michaeld@jmu.edu. Website: http://www.jmu.edu/commstudies/

**Johns Hopkins University,** Engineering Program for Professionals, Part-time Program in Computer Science, Baltimore, MD 21218. Offers communications and networking (MS); computer science (Post-Master's Certificate). *Program availability:* Part-time, evening/weekend, 100% online, blended/hybrid learning. *Faculty:* 48 part-time/adjunct (7 women). *Students:* 15 full-time (3 women), 437 part-time (75 women); includes 79 minority (14 Black or African American, non-Hispanic/Latino; 31 Asian, non-Hispanic/Latino; 28 Hispanic/Latino; 1 Native Hawaiian or other Pacific Islander, non-Hispanic/Latino; 5 Two or more races, non-Hispanic/Latino), 17 international. Average age 29. 290 applicants, 34% accepted, 76 enrolled. In 2016, 131 master's awarded. *Entrance requirements:* Additional exam requirements/recommendations for international students: Required—TOEFL (minimum score 600 paper-based; 100 iBT). *Application deadline:* Applications are processed on a rolling basis. Application fee: $0. Electronic applications accepted. *Unit head:* Dr. Thomas A. Longstaff, Program Chair, 443-778-9389, E-mail: thomas.longstaff@jhuapl.edu. *Application contact:* Doug Schiller, Admissions Director, 410-516-2300, Fax: 410-579-8049, E-mail: schiller@jhu.edu. Website: http://www.ep.jhu.edu/

**Johns Hopkins University,** Engineering Program for Professionals, Part-time Program in Electrical and Computer Engineering, Baltimore, MD 21218. Offers communications and networking (MS); electrical and computer engineering (Graduate Certificate, Post-Master's Certificate); photonics (MS). *Program availability:* Part-time, evening/weekend, 100% online, blended/hybrid learning. *Faculty:* 48 part-time/adjunct (2 women). *Students:* 5 full-time (0 women), 303 part-time (52 women); includes 63 minority (11 Black or African American, non-Hispanic/Latino; 24 Asian, non-Hispanic/Latino; 24 Hispanic/Latino; 4 Two or more races, non-Hispanic/Latino). Average age 28. 108 applicants, 68% accepted, 53 enrolled. In 2016, 78 master's, 2 other advanced degrees awarded. *Degree requirements:* For master's and other advanced degree, thesis optional. *Entrance requirements:* Additional exam requirements/recommendations for international students: Required—TOEFL (minimum score 600 paper-based; 100 iBT). *Application deadline:* Applications are processed on a rolling basis. Application fee: $0. Electronic applications accepted. *Unit head:* Dr. Brian Jennison, Program Chair, 443-778-6421, E-mail: brian.jennison@jhuapl.edu. *Application contact:* Doug Schiller, Admissions Director, 410-516-2300, Fax: 410-579-8049, E-mail: schiller@jhu.edu. Website: http://www.ep.jhu.edu/

**Johns Hopkins University,** Zanvyl Krieger School of Arts and Sciences, Advanced Academic Programs, Program in Communication, Washington, DC 20036. Offers MA, MA/MBA. *Program availability:* Part-time, evening/weekend, online learning. *Degree requirements:* For master's, thesis. *Entrance requirements:* For master's, minimum GPA of 3.0, strong writing skills. Additional exam requirements/recommendations for international students: Required—TOEFL (minimum score 100 iBT). Electronic applications accepted.

**Kansas State University,** Graduate School, College of Arts and Sciences, A.Q. Miller School of Journalism and Mass Communications, Manhattan, KS 66506. Offers advertising (MS); community journalism (MS); global communication (MS); health communication (MS); media management (MS); public relations (MS). *Program availability:* Part-time, evening/weekend. *Faculty:* 13 full-time (6 women), 1 (woman) part-time/adjunct. *Students:* 13 full-time (10 women), 6 part-time (4 women); includes 1 minority (Hispanic/Latino), 8 international. Average age 29. 7 applicants, 71% accepted, 3 enrolled. In 2016, 7 master's awarded. *Degree requirements:* For master's, comprehensive exam, thesis. *Entrance requirements:* For master's, GRE General Test, minimum GPA of 3.0. Additional exam requirements/recommendations for international students: Required—TOEFL (minimum score 79 iBT). *Application deadline:* For fall admission, 2/1 priority date for domestic and international students; for spring admission, 8/1 priority date for domestic and international students. Applications are processed on a rolling basis. Application fee: $50 ($75 for international students). Electronic applications accepted. *Expenses:* Tuition, state resident: full-time $9670. Tuition, nonresident: full-time $21,828. *Required fees:* $862. *Financial support:* In 2016–17, 2 research assistantships with full tuition reimbursements (averaging $11,180 per year), 7 teaching assistantships with full tuition reimbursements (averaging $7,729 per year) were awarded; scholarships/grants, health care benefits, and unspecified assistantships also available. Financial award application deadline: 2/1; financial award applicants required to submit FAFSA. *Faculty research:* Health communication, risk communication, strategic communications, community journalism, global communication. *Total annual research expenditures:* $219,641. *Unit head:* Dr. Jean Folkerts, Director, 785-532-6890, Fax: 785-532-5484, E-mail: jeanfolk@ksu.edu. *Application contact:* Dr. Barbara DeSanto, Associate Director of Graduate Studies, 785-532-3890, Fax: 785-532-5484, E-mail: desantoi@ksu.edu. Website: http://jmc.ksu.edu/

**Kansas State University,** Graduate School, College of Arts and Sciences, Department of Communication Studies, Manhattan, KS 66505. Offers MA. *Faculty:* 8 full-time (3 women). *Students:* 17 full-time (9 women), 11 part-time (5 women); includes 4 minority (3 Black or African American, non-Hispanic/Latino; 1 Hispanic/Latino), 2 international. Average age 26. 19 applicants, 79% accepted, 9 enrolled. In 2016, 1 master's awarded. *Degree requirements:* For master's, thesis or alternative. *Entrance requirements:* For master's, GRE General Test (recommended), minimum GPA of 3.0. Additional exam requirements/recommendations for international students: Required—TOEFL. *Application deadline:* For fall admission, 2/15 priority date for domestic students, 2/1 priority date for international students; for spring admission, 8/1 for domestic and international students. Applications are processed on a rolling basis. Application fee: $50 ($75 for international students). Electronic applications accepted. *Expenses:* Tuition, state resident: full-time $9670. Tuition, nonresident: full-time $21,828. *Required fees:* $862. *Financial support:* Career-related internships or fieldwork, institutionally sponsored loans, and scholarships/grants available. Support available to part-time students. Financial award application deadline: 3/1; financial award applicants required to submit FAFSA. *Faculty research:* Conflict, public deliberation, political communication, intercultural communication, relational communication. *Unit head:* Dr. Colene Lind, Graduate Director, 785-532-6818, Fax: 785-532-3714, E-mail: colenejlind@ksu.edu. Website: http://commstudies.k-state.edu

**Kansas State University,** Graduate School, College of Arts and Sciences, Department of English, Manhattan, KS 66506. Offers English (MA); technical writing and professional communication (Graduate Certificate). *Program availability:* Part-time.

*Faculty:* 39 full-time (24 women). *Students:* 42 full-time (26 women), 12 part-time (10 women); includes 7 minority (1 Asian, non-Hispanic/Latino; 5 Hispanic/Latino; 1 Two or more races, non-Hispanic/Latino), 1 international. Average age 26. 38 applicants, 76% accepted, 22 enrolled. In 2016, 24 master's awarded. *Degree requirements:* For master's, one foreign language, thesis optional. *Entrance requirements:* For master's, GRE, minimum B average in English. Additional exam requirements/recommendations for international students: Required—TOEFL. *Application deadline:* For fall admission, 2/1 priority date for domestic and international students; for spring admission, 8/1 priority date for domestic and international students. Applications are processed on a rolling basis. Application fee: $50 ($75 for international students). Electronic applications accepted. *Expenses:* Tuition, state resident: full-time $9670. Tuition, nonresident: full-time $21,828. *Required fees:* $862. *Financial support:* In 2016–17, 40 teaching assistantships with full tuition reimbursements (averaging $12,000 per year) were awarded; career-related internships or fieldwork, Federal Work-Study, institutionally sponsored loans, scholarships/grants, and tuition waivers (full) also available. Support available to part-time students. Financial award application deadline: 3/1; financial award applicants required to submit FAFSA. *Faculty research:* Cultural studies, children's literature, American literature, rhetorical and composition theory, British literature. *Unit head:* Karin Westman, Head, 785-532-2190, Fax: 785-532-2192, E-mail: westmank@ksu.edu. *Application contact:* Anne Longmuir, Director of Graduate Studies, 785-532-2169, Fax: 785-532-2192, E-mail: longmuir@ksu.edu. Website: http://www.k-state.edu/english/

**Kansas State University,** Graduate School, College of Engineering, Department of Electrical and Computer Engineering, Manhattan, KS 66506. Offers electrical engineering (MS), including bioengineering, communication systems, design of computer systems, electrical engineering, energy and power systems, integrated circuits and devices, real time embedded systems, renewable energy, signal processing. *Program availability:* Part-time, evening/weekend, online learning. *Faculty:* 21 full-time (4 women), 1 (woman) part-time/adjunct. *Students:* 47 full-time (11 women), 51 part-time (5 women); includes 13 minority (6 Black or African American, non-Hispanic/Latino; 6 Asian, non-Hispanic/Latino; 1 Two or more races, non-Hispanic/Latino), 40 international. Average age 31. 146 applicants, 29% accepted, 17 enrolled. In 2016, 16 master's, 5 doctorates awarded. *Degree requirements:* For master's, thesis or alternative, final exam; for doctorate, thesis/dissertation, final exam, preliminary exams. *Entrance requirements:* For master's, GRE General Test, bachelor's degree in electrical engineering or computer science, minimum GPA of 3.0; for doctorate, GRE General Test. Additional exam requirements/recommendations for international students: Required—TOEFL (minimum score 600 paper-based; 85 iBT). *Application deadline:* For fall admission, 1/1 priority date for domestic and international students; for spring admission, 8/1 priority date for domestic and international students. Applications are processed on a rolling basis. Application fee: $50 ($75 for international students). Electronic applications accepted. *Expenses:* Tuition, state resident: full-time $9670. Tuition, nonresident: full-time $21,828. *Required fees:* $862. *Financial support:* In 2016–17, 40 students received support, including 22 research assistantships with tuition reimbursements available (averaging $12,100 per year), 18 teaching assistantships with full tuition reimbursements available (averaging $12,220 per year); career-related internships or fieldwork, institutionally sponsored loans, and scholarships/grants also available. Support available to part-time students. Financial award application deadline: 3/1; financial award applicants required to submit FAFSA. *Faculty research:* Energy systems and renewable energy, computer systems and real time embedded systems, communication systems and signal processing, integrated circuits and devices, bioengineering. *Total annual research expenditures:* $1.3 million. *Unit head:* Dr. Don Gruenbacher, Head, 785-532-5600, Fax: 785-532-1188, E-mail: grue@k-state.edu. *Application contact:* Dr. Andrew Rys, Graduate Program Director, 785-532-4665, Fax: 785-532-1188, E-mail: andrys@k-state.edu. Website: http://www.ece.k-state.edu/

**Kean University,** College of Liberal Arts, Program in Communication Studies, Union, NJ 07083. Offers MA. *Program availability:* Part-time. *Faculty:* 14 full-time (6 women). *Students:* 11 full-time (8 women), 14 part-time (11 women); includes 14 minority (9 Black or African American, non-Hispanic/Latino; 1 Asian, non-Hispanic/Latino; 3 Hispanic/Latino; 1 Two or more races, non-Hispanic/Latino). Average age 35. 21 applicants, 38% accepted, 6 enrolled. In 2016, 16 master's awarded. *Degree requirements:* For master's, comprehensive exam, thesis optional. *Entrance requirements:* For master's, GRE General Test, minimum cumulative GPA of 3.0, official transcripts from all institutions attended, three letters of recommendation, professional resume/curriculum vitae, personal statement. Additional exam requirements/recommendations for international students: Required—TOEFL (minimum score 550 paper-based; 79 iBT), IELTS (minimum score 6.5). *Application deadline:* For fall admission, 6/1 for domestic and international students; for spring admission, 12/1 for domestic and international students. Applications are processed on a rolling basis. Application fee: $75. Electronic applications accepted. *Expenses:* Tuition, state resident: full-time $13,156; part-time $640 per credit. Tuition, nonresident: full-time $17,831; part-time $785 per credit. *Required fees:* $3316; $151 per credit. Tuition and fees vary according to course level, course load, degree level and program. *Financial support:* Scholarships/grants and unspecified assistantships available. Financial award applicants required to submit FAFSA. *Unit head:* Dr. Wenli Yuan, Program Coordinator, 908-737-0471, E-mail: wyuan@kean.edu. *Application contact:* Amy Clark, Program Assistant, 908-737-7100, E-mail: grad-adm@kean.edu. Website: http://grad.kean.edu/masters-programs/communication-studies

**Kennesaw State University,** College of Humanities and Social Sciences, Program in Integrated Global Communication, Kennesaw, GA 30144. Offers MA. *Entrance requirements:* For master's, GRE, BA or BS in communication or related field from accredited college or university; official transcripts; two-page resume; 500-word personal statement; three letters of recommendation. Additional exam requirements/recommendations for international students: Required—TOEFL (minimum score 550 paper-based; 80 iBT), IELTS (minimum score 6.5). Electronic applications accepted.

**Kent State University,** College of Communication and Information, School of Communication Studies, Kent, OH 44242-0001. Offers communication studies (MA); MBA/MA. *Program availability:* Part-time. *Faculty:* 16 full-time (9 women). *Students:* 30 full-time (24 women), 10 part-time (9 women); includes 4 minority (3 Asian, non-Hispanic/Latino; 1 Hispanic/Latino), 12 international. Average age 30. 44 applicants, 55% accepted, 14 enrolled. In 2016, 10 master's awarded. *Degree requirements:* For master's, thesis, coursework, project, or internship. *Entrance requirements:* For master's, GRE General Test, minimum GPA of 3.0, goal statement, undergraduate major/minor in communication, writing sample, 3 letters of recommendation, curriculum vitae/resume. Additional exam requirements/recommendations for international students: Required—TOEFL (minimum score 580 paper-based; 92 iBT), IELTS (minimum score of 6.5), Michigan English Language Assessment Battery (minimum score of 81), or PTE (minimum score of 62). *Application deadline:* For fall admission, 1/15 for domestic students, 12/25 for international students; for spring admission, 11/15 for domestic students, 10/25 for international students. Applications are processed on a rolling basis. Application fee: $45 ($70 for international students). Electronic applications accepted. *Expenses:* Tuition, state resident: full-time $10,864; part-time $495 per credit hour. Tuition, nonresident: full-time $18,380; part-time $837 per credit hour. *Financial*

*support:* Research assistantships with full tuition reimbursements, teaching assistantships with full tuition reimbursements, career-related internships or fieldwork, health care benefits, and unspecified assistantships available. Financial award application deadline: 1/15. *Unit head:* Dr. Elizabeth E. Graham, Director, 330-672-3087, E-mail: egraha18@kent.edu. *Application contact:* Dr. Nichole Egbert, Professor and Graduate Coordinator, 330-672-3314, E-mail: negbert@kent.edu.
Website: http://www.kent.edu/comm/

**La Salle University,** School of Arts and Sciences, Program in Strategic Communication, Philadelphia, PA 19141-1199. Offers communication consulting and development (MA); communication management (MA); general professional communication (MA); professional and business communication (Certificate); public relations (MA); social and new media (Certificate). *Program availability:* Part-time, evening/weekend, online learning. *Faculty:* 4 full-time (all women), 1 (woman) part-time/adjunct. *Students:* 11 full-time (7 women), 39 part-time (29 women); includes 18 minority (15 Black or African American, non-Hispanic/Latino; 2 Hispanic/Latino; 1 Two or more races, non-Hispanic/Latino), 2 international. Average age 27. 13 applicants, 92% accepted, 6 enrolled. In 2016, 41 master's, 4 other advanced degrees awarded. *Degree requirements:* For master's, practicum. *Entrance requirements:* For master's, writing assessment, professional resume; minimum overall B average; two letters of recommendation (if GPA below 3.25); brief personal statement (about 500 words); interview; for Certificate, writing assessment, minimum GPA of 2.75 in undergraduate studies; brief personal statement (about 500 words); interview. Additional exam requirements/recommendations for international students: Required—TOEFL. *Application deadline:* For fall admission, 8/15 priority date for domestic students, 7/15 for international students; for spring admission, 12/15 priority date for domestic students, 11/15 for international students; for summer admission, 4/15 priority date for domestic students, 3/15 for international students. Applications are processed on a rolling basis. Application fee: $35. Electronic applications accepted. Application fee is waived when completed online. *Expenses:* Contact institution. *Financial support:* In 2016–17, 7 students received support. Scholarships/grants available. Support available to part-time students. Financial award application deadline: 8/31; financial award applicants required to submit FAFSA. *Unit head:* Dr. Pamela Lannutti, Director, 215-951-1935, Fax: 215-951-5043, E-mail: annutti95@lasalle.edu. *Application contact:* Elizabeth Heenan, Director, Graduate and Adult Enrollment, 215-951-1100, Fax: 214-951-1462, E-mail: heenan@lasalle.edu.
Website: http://www.lasalle.edu/strategic-communication/

**Lasell College,** Graduate and Professional Studies in Communication, Newton, MA 02466. Offers health communication (MSC, Graduate Certificate); integrated marketing communication (MSC, Graduate Certificate); public relations (MSC, Graduate Certificate). *Program availability:* Part-time, evening/weekend, 100% online, blended/hybrid learning. *Faculty:* 4 full-time (2 women), 5 part-time/adjunct (2 women). *Students:* 12 full-time (9 women), 38 part-time (28 women); includes 11 minority (8 Black or African American, non-Hispanic/Latino; 1 Asian, non-Hispanic/Latino; 2 Hispanic/Latino), 8 international. Average age 31. 60 applicants, 43% accepted, 13 enrolled. In 2016, 71 master's, 3 other advanced degrees awarded. *Degree requirements:* For master's, comprehensive exam, thesis or alternative, minimum GPA of 3.0; special project or internship. *Entrance requirements:* For master's, one-page personal statement, 2 letters of recommendation, resume, bachelor's degree transcript; for Graduate Certificate, bachelor's degree transcript, 2 letters of recommendation, 1-page personal statement, resume. Additional exam requirements/recommendations for international students: Required—TOEFL (minimum score 550 paper-based, 79 iBT) or IELTS (minimum score 6). *Application deadline:* For fall admission, 8/31 priority date for domestic students, 6/30 priority date for international students; for spring admission, 12/31 priority date for domestic students, 10/31 priority date for international students. Applications are processed on a rolling basis. *Expenses:* $600 per credit. *Financial support:* In 2016–17, 6 students received support. Federal Work-Study, scholarships/grants, and tuition discounts available. Support available to part-time students. Financial award application deadline: 8/31; financial award applicants required to submit FAFSA. *Faculty research:* Terrorists' use of the internet; refugees' use of cell phones as means of communication in Jordan and Germany; political communication, analysis of the media coverage of the conflict and peace process in northern Ireland; interpersonal communication, strategies to address bullying in online communities, in schools and in the workplace. *Unit head:* Dr. Joan Dolamore, Dean of Graduate and Professional Studies, 617-243-2485, Fax: 617-243-2450, E-mail: gradinfo@lasell.edu. *Application contact:* Adrienne Franciosi, Director of Graduate Enrollment, 617-243-2214, Fax: 617-243-2450, E-mail: gradinfo@lasell.edu.
Website: http://www.lasell.edu/academics/graduate-and-professional-studies/programs-of-study/master-of-science-in-communication.html

**La Sierra University,** College of Arts and Sciences, Department of English and Communication, Riverside, CA 92515. Offers communication (MA), including public relations/advertising, theory emphasis; English (MA), including literary emphasis, writing emphasis. *Program availability:* Part-time. *Degree requirements:* For master's, one foreign language. *Entrance requirements:* For master's, GRE General Test.

**Lawrence Technological University,** College of Arts and Sciences, Southfield, MI 48075-1058. Offers bioinformatics (Graduate Certificate); computer science (MS), including data science, big data, and data mining, intelligent systems; instructional design, communication, and presentation (Graduate Certificate); instructional technology (Graduate Certificate); premedical studies (Graduate Certificate); technical and professional communication (MS, Graduate Certificate); writing for the digital age (Graduate Certificate). *Program availability:* Part-time, evening/weekend. *Faculty:* 6 full-time (2 women), 10 part-time/adjunct (5 women). *Students:* 37 part-time (18 women); includes 4 minority (1 Black or African American, non-Hispanic/Latino; 1 Asian, non-Hispanic/Latino; 2 Hispanic/Latino), 8 international. Average age 33. 301 applicants, 23% accepted, 9 enrolled. In 2016, 22 master's, 2 other advanced degrees awarded. *Degree requirements:* For master's, thesis (for some programs). *Entrance requirements:* Additional exam requirements/recommendations for international students: Required—TOEFL (minimum score 550 paper-based; 79 iBT), IELTS (minimum score 6.5). *Application deadline:* For fall admission, 5/22 for international students; for spring admission, 10/11 for international students; for summer admission, 2/16 for international students. Applications are processed on a rolling basis. Application fee: $50. Electronic applications accepted. *Expenses: Tuition:* Full-time $14,868; part-time $1062 per credit. *Required fees:* $75 per semester. Tuition and fees vary according to campus/location. *Financial support:* In 2016–17, 9 students received support. Scholarships/grants and tuition reduction available. Financial award application deadline: 4/1; financial award applicants required to submit FAFSA. *Faculty research:* Computer analysis of visual art, psychology of numbers games, neural basis of moral judgement, synthesis of glycosylated warfarin analogs for potential use as antiviral drugs, observation of chemotaxis behavior in c. elegans. *Total annual research expenditures:* $530,625. *Unit head:* Dr. Hsiao-Ping Moore, Dean, 248-204-3500, Fax: 248-204-3518, E-mail: scidean@ltu.edu. *Application contact:* Jane Rohrback, Director of Admissions, 248-204-3160, Fax: 248-204-2228, E-mail: admissions@ltu.edu.

**Liberty University,** School of Communication and Creative Arts, Lynchburg, VA 24515. Offers strategic communication (MA); studio and digital arts (MFA). *Program availability:* Part-time. *Students:* 120 full-time (82 women), 142 part-time (90 women); includes 56 minority (45 Black or African American, non-Hispanic/Latino; 1 Asian, non-Hispanic/Latino; 1 Hispanic/Latino; 9 Two or more races, non-Hispanic/Latino), 12 international. Average age 32. 384 applicants, 33% accepted, 66 enrolled. In 2016, 58 master's awarded. *Degree requirements:* For master's, thesis (for some programs). *Entrance requirements:* For master's, minimum undergraduate GPA of 3.0, faculty recommendation, written statement of purpose, writing sample. Additional exam requirements/recommendations for international students: Required—TOEFL (minimum score 600 paper-based; 100 iBT). *Application deadline:* For fall admission, 6/1 for domestic students; for spring admission, 11/1 for domestic students. Applications are processed on a rolling basis. Application fee: $50. Electronic applications accepted. *Financial support:* Federal Work-Study and unspecified assistantships available. Financial award applicants required to submit FAFSA. *Unit head:* Dr. Norman Mintle, Dean, 434-582-2077, E-mail: cvkramer@liberty.edu. *Application contact:* Dr. Terry Elam, Director of Graduate Admissions, 434-582-2111, Fax: 434-582-7836, E-mail: gradadmissions@liberty.edu.

**Lindenwood University,** Graduate Programs, School of Accelerated Degree Programs, St. Charles, MO 63301-1695. Offers administration (MSA), including management, marketing, project management; business administration (MBA); communications (MA), including digital and multimedia, media management, promotions, training and development; criminal justice and administration (MS); healthcare administration (MS); human resource management (MS); information technology (Certificate); managing information security (MS); managing information technology (MS); managing virtualization and cloud computing (MS); writing (MFA). *Program availability:* Part-time, evening/weekend, 100% online. *Faculty:* 16 full-time (7 women), 75 part-time/adjunct (27 women). *Students:* 609 full-time (386 women), 179 part-time (121 women); includes 257 minority (202 Black or African American, non-Hispanic/Latino; 4 American Indian or Alaska Native, non-Hispanic/Latino; 5 Asian, non-Hispanic/Latino; 28 Hispanic/Latino; 1 Native Hawaiian or other Pacific Islander, non-Hispanic/Latino; 17 Two or more races, non-Hispanic/Latino), 28 international. Average age 36. 332 applicants, 70% accepted, 205 enrolled. In 2016, 479 master's awarded. *Degree requirements:* For master's, thesis (for some programs), minimum cumulative GPA of 3.0; for Certificate, minimum cumulative GPA of 3.0. *Entrance requirements:* For master's, resume, personal statement, official undergraduate transcript, minimum undergraduate cumulative GPA of 3.0. Additional exam requirements/recommendations for international students: Required—TOEFL (minimum score 550 paper-based; 80 iBT); Recommended—IELTS (minimum score 6.5). *Application deadline:* For fall admission, 9/26 priority date for domestic and international students; for winter admission, 1/3 priority date for domestic and international students; for spring admission, 3/31 priority date for domestic and international students; for summer admission, 7/3 priority date for domestic and international students. Applications are processed on a rolling basis. Application fee: $30 ($100 for international students). Electronic applications accepted. *Expenses: Tuition:* Full-time $15,672; part-time $453 per credit hour. *Required fees:* $205 per semester. Tuition and fees vary according to course level, course load and degree level. *Financial support:* In 2016–17, 467 students received support. Career-related internships or fieldwork, institutionally sponsored loans, scholarships/grants, tuition waivers (partial), and unspecified assistantships available. Financial award application deadline: 6/30; financial award applicants required to submit FAFSA. *Unit head:* Dr. Gina Ganahl, Dean, Accelerated Degree Programs, 636-949-4501, Fax: 636-949-4505, E-mail: gganahl@lindenwood.edu. *Application contact:* Tyler Kostich, Director, Evening and Graduate Admissions, 636-949-4138, Fax: 636-949-4109, E-mail: adultadmissions@lindenwood.edu.
Website: http://www.lindenwood.edu/academics/academic-schools/school-of-accelerated-degree-programs/

**Lindenwood University–Belleville,** Graduate Programs, Belleville, IL 62226. Offers business administration (MBA); communications (MA), including digital and multimedia, media management, promotions, training and development; counseling (MA); criminal justice administration (MS); education (MA); healthcare administration (MS); human resource management (MS); school administration (MA); teaching (MAT).

**Louisiana State University and Agricultural & Mechanical College,** Graduate School, College of Humanities and Social Sciences, Department of Communication Studies, Baton Rouge, LA 70803. Offers MA, PhD.

**Loyola University Chicago,** Graduate School, School of Communication, Chicago, IL 60660. Offers digital storytelling (MC); global strategic communication (MS). *Students:* 39 full-time (26 women), 15 part-time (10 women); includes 24 minority (17 Black or African American, non-Hispanic/Latino; 1 American Indian or Alaska Native, non-Hispanic/Latino; 6 Hispanic/Latino), 7 international. Average age 29. 96 applicants, 45% accepted, 25 enrolled. In 2016, 17 master's awarded. *Expenses: Tuition:* Full-time $18,594. *Required fees:* $848. Part-time tuition and fees vary according to course load, degree level and program. *Unit head:* Dr. Don Heider, Dean, 312-915-6548, E-mail: dheider@luc.edu. *Application contact:* Ron Martin, Associate Director of Enrollment Management, 312-915-8950, Fax: 312-915-8905, E-mail: gradapp@luc.edu.
Website: http://www.luc.edu/soc/

**Lynn University,** Eugene M. and Christine E. Lynn College of International Communication, Boca Raton, FL 33431-5598. Offers communication and media (MS), including digital media, media studies and practice; digital media (Certificate). *Program availability:* Part-time, evening/weekend. *Faculty:* 15 full-time (8 women), 6 part-time/adjunct (3 women). *Students:* 24 full-time (20 women), 15 part-time (14 women); includes 11 minority (7 Black or African American, non-Hispanic/Latino; 2 Asian, non-Hispanic/Latino; 2 Hispanic/Latino), 14 international. Average age 27. 38 applicants, 87% accepted, 17 enrolled. In 2016, 18 master's, 1 other advanced degree awarded. *Degree requirements:* For master's, project or thesis. *Entrance requirements:* For master's, resume, letter of recommendation, official transcripts, bachelor's degree from accredited institution, personal statement. Additional exam requirements/recommendations for international students: Required—TOEFL (minimum score 550 paper-based; 80 iBT), IELTS (minimum score 6.5). *Application deadline:* For fall admission, 8/18 for domestic students, 8/4 for international students; for spring admission, 12/15 for domestic students, 12/1 for international students; for summer admission, 4/17 for domestic students, 4/3 for international students. Applications are processed on a rolling basis. Application fee: $45. Electronic applications accepted. *Expenses:* $725 per credit hour. *Financial support:* In 2016–17, 7 students received support. Career-related internships or fieldwork, Federal Work-Study, institutionally sponsored loans, scholarships/grants, tuition waivers (partial), and unspecified assistantships available. Support available to part-time students. Financial award application deadline: 8/1; financial award applicants required to submit FAFSA. *Unit head:* Dr. David L. Jaffe, Dean, 561-237-7099, Fax: 561-237-7097, E-mail: djaffe@lynn.edu. *Application contact:* Steven Pruitt, Director of Graduate Admission, 561-237-7834, Fax: 561-237-7100, E-mail: admission@lynn.edu.
Website: http://www.lynn.edu/academics/colleges/international-communication

**Marist College,** Graduate Programs, School of Communication and the Arts, Poughkeepsie, NY 12601-1387. Offers communication (MA); integrated marketing communication (MA); museum studies (MA). *Program availability:* Part-time, online learning. *Degree requirements:* For master's, thesis or comprehensive exam. *Entrance* *requirements:* For master's, GRE, minimum undergraduate GPA of 3.0, resume, 3 letters of recommendation. Additional exam requirements/recommendations for international students: Required—TOEFL (minimum score 550 paper-based; 80 iBT); Recommended—IELTS (minimum score 6.5). Electronic applications accepted.

**Marquette University,** Graduate School, College of Communication, Milwaukee, WI 53201-1881. Offers advertising and public relations (MA); communication studies (MA); digital storytelling (Certificate); journalism (MA); mass communication (MA); science, health and environmental communication (MA). *Accreditation:* ACEJMC (one or more programs are accredited). *Program availability:* Part-time, evening/weekend. *Faculty:* 36 full-time (18 women), 45 part-time/adjunct (20 women). *Students:* 25 full-time (22 women), 23 part-time (16 women); includes 9 minority (3 Black or African American, non-Hispanic/Latino; 1 American Indian or Alaska Native, non-Hispanic/Latino; 4 Hispanic/Latino; 1 Two or more races, non-Hispanic/Latino), 4 international. Average age 28. 55 applicants, 62% accepted, 21 enrolled. In 2016, 10 master's, 1 other advanced degree awarded. *Degree requirements:* For master's, comprehensive exam, thesis or alternative. *Entrance requirements:* For master's, GRE, official transcripts from all current and previous colleges/universities except Marquette, three letters of recommendation, statement of academic and professional goals. Additional exam requirements/recommendations for international students: Required—TOEFL (minimum score 530 paper-based). *Application deadline:* Applications are processed on a rolling basis. Electronic applications accepted. *Financial support:* Fellowships, research assistantships, teaching assistantships, career-related internships or fieldwork, scholarships/grants, health care benefits, tuition waivers (full and partial), and unspecified assistantships available. Support available to part-time students. Financial award application deadline: 2/15. *Faculty research:* Urban journalism, gender and communication, intercultural communication, religious communication. *Total annual research expenditures:* $7,941. *Unit head:* Dr. Sarah Feldner, Associate Dean. *Application contact:* Dr. Sarah Bonewits Feldner.
Website: http://diederich.marquette.edu/

**Marshall University,** Academic Affairs Division, College of Liberal Arts, Department of Communication Studies, Huntington, WV 25755. Offers MA. *Degree requirements:* For master's, thesis optional. *Entrance requirements:* For master's, GRE General Test.

**Marywood University,** Academic Affairs, Insalaco College of Creative and Performing Arts, Department of Communication Arts, Scranton, PA 18509-1598. Offers MA. *Program availability:* Part-time. Electronic applications accepted.

**McGill University,** Faculty of Graduate and Postdoctoral Studies, Faculty of Arts, Department of Art History and Communication Studies, Montréal, QC H3A 2T5, Canada. Offers MA, PhD.

**Michigan State University,** The Graduate School, College of Communication Arts and Sciences, Department of Communication, East Lansing, MI 48824. Offers MA, PhD. *Entrance requirements:* Additional exam requirements/recommendations for international students: Required—TOEFL (minimum score 580 paper-based). Electronic applications accepted.

**Minnesota State University Mankato,** College of Graduate Studies and Research, College of Arts and Humanities, Department of Communication Studies, Mankato, MN 56001. Offers communication education (Certificate); communication studies (MA, MS); forensics (MFA); professional communication (Certificate). *Students:* 16 full-time (9 women), 48 part-time (31 women). *Degree requirements:* For master's, one foreign language, comprehensive exam, thesis. *Entrance requirements:* For master's, minimum GPA of 3.0 during previous 2 years, writing sample. *Application deadline:* For fall admission, 7/1 priority date for domestic students, 5/1 for international students; for spring admission, 11/1 for domestic students, 10/1 for international students. Applications are processed on a rolling basis. Application fee: $40. Electronic applications accepted. *Financial support:* Research assistantships, teaching assistantships with full tuition reimbursements, career-related internships or fieldwork, Federal Work-Study, and institutionally sponsored loans available. Support available to part-time students. Financial award application deadline: 3/15; financial award applicants required to submit FAFSA.
Website: http://www.mnsu.edu/cmst/

**Minnesota State University Mankato,** College of Graduate Studies and Research, College of Arts and Humanities, Department of English, Mankato, MN 56001. Offers communication and composition (MA); creative writing (MFA); English studies (MA); teaching English as a second language (MA, Certificate); technical communication (MA, Certificate). *Program availability:* Part-time. *Students:* 59 full-time (44 women), 106 part-time (67 women). *Degree requirements:* For master's, one foreign language, comprehensive exam, thesis or alternative. *Entrance requirements:* For master's, minimum GPA of 3.0 during previous 2 years, writing sample (MFA). Additional exam requirements/recommendations for international students: Required—TOEFL (minimum score 500 paper-based; 61 iBT). *Application deadline:* For fall admission, 7/1 for domestic students, 5/1 for international students. Applications are processed on a rolling basis. Application fee: $40. Electronic applications accepted. *Financial support:* Research assistantships with full tuition reimbursements, teaching assistantships with full tuition reimbursements, career-related internships or fieldwork, Federal Work-Study, and unspecified assistantships available. Financial award application deadline: 3/15; financial award applicants required to submit FAFSA. *Unit head:* Matthew Sewell, Chair, 507-389-2117, E-mail: matthew.sewell@mnsu.edu.
Website: http://english.mnsu.edu/

**Mississippi College,** Graduate School, College of Arts and Sciences, School of Christian Studies and the Arts, Department of Communication, Clinton, MS 39058. Offers applied communication (MSC); public relations and corporate communication (MSC). *Program availability:* Part-time. *Degree requirements:* For master's, comprehensive exam, thesis optional. *Entrance requirements:* For master's, GRE or NTE, minimum GPA of 2.5. Additional exam requirements/recommendations for international students: Recommended—TOEFL, IELTS. Electronic applications accepted.

**Missouri State University,** Graduate College, College of Arts and Letters, Department of Communication and Mass Media, Springfield, MO 65897. Offers MA. *Program availability:* Part-time, 100% online, blended/hybrid learning. *Faculty:* 13 full-time (8 women). *Students:* 14 full-time (12 women), 35 part-time (24 women); includes 4 minority (1 Black or African American, non-Hispanic/Latino; 1 Native Hawaiian or other Pacific Islander, non-Hispanic/Latino; 2 Two or more races, non-Hispanic/Latino), 5 international. Average age 30. 43 applicants, 67% accepted, 16 enrolled. In 2016, 6 master's awarded. *Degree requirements:* For master's, comprehensive exam, thesis or alternative. *Entrance requirements:* For master's, GRE General Test or MAT, minimum GPA of 3.0 for last 60 credit hours of academic work. Additional exam requirements/recommendations for international students: Required—TOEFL (minimum score 550 paper-based; 79 iBT), IELTS (minimum score 6). *Application deadline:* For fall admission, 6/1 priority date for domestic students, 5/1 for international students; for spring admission, 11/1 priority date for domestic students, 9/1 for international students. Applications are processed on a rolling basis. Application fee: $35 ($50 for international students). Electronic applications accepted. *Expenses:* Tuition, state resident: full-time $5830. Tuition, nonresident: full-time $10,708. *Required fees:* $1130. Tuition and fees vary according to class time, course level, course load and program. *Financial support:* In 2016–17, 10 teaching assistantships with full tuition reimbursements (averaging $8,772 per year) were awarded; career-related internships or fieldwork, Federal Work-Study, institutionally sponsored loans, scholarships/grants, and unspecified assistantships also available. Support available to part-time students. Financial award application deadline: 3/31; financial award applicants required to submit FAFSA. *Faculty research:* Conflict resolution, media analysis, intercultural communication, political communication, communication theory and organizational praxis. *Unit head:* Dr. Shawn Wahl, Department Head, 417-836-4423, Fax: 417-836-4774, E-mail: communication@missouristate.edu. *Application contact:* Michael Edwards, Coordinator of Graduate Admissions, 417-836-5330, Fax: 417-836-6200, E-mail: michaeledwards@missouristate.edu.
Website: http://communication.missouristate.edu/

**Missouri State University,** Graduate College, Interdisciplinary Program in Professional Studies, Springfield, MO 65897. Offers administrative studies (Certificate); applied communication (MS); criminal justice (MS); environmental management (MS); homeland security (MS); individualized (MS); screenwriting and producing (MS); sports management (MS). *Program availability:* Part-time, evening/weekend, 100% online, blended/hybrid learning. *Students:* 60 full-time (34 women), 66 part-time (29 women); includes 17 minority (7 Black or African American, non-Hispanic/Latino; 1 Asian, non-Hispanic/Latino; 5 Hispanic/Latino; 4 Two or more races, non-Hispanic/Latino), 43 international. Average age 33. 76 applicants, 58% accepted, 38 enrolled. In 2016, 48 master's awarded. *Degree requirements:* For master's, comprehensive exam, thesis or alternative. *Entrance requirements:* For master's, GRE, GMAT (if GPA less than 3.0). Additional exam requirements/recommendations for international students: Required—TOEFL (minimum score 550 paper-based; 79 iBT), IELTS (minimum score 6). *Application deadline:* For fall admission, 7/15 priority date for domestic students; for spring admission, 12/1 priority date for domestic students; for summer admission, 5/1 for domestic students. Applications are processed on a rolling basis. Application fee: $35 ($50 for international students). Electronic applications accepted. *Expenses:* Tuition, state resident: full-time $5830. Tuition, nonresident: full-time $10,708. *Required fees:* $1130. Tuition and fees vary according to class time, course level, course load and program. *Financial support:* Career-related internships or fieldwork, Federal Work-Study, institutionally sponsored loans, scholarships/grants, and unspecified assistantships available. Support available to part-time students. Financial award application deadline: 3/31; financial award applicants required to submit FAFSA. *Unit head:* Dr. Gerald Masterson, Program Director, 417-836-5251, Fax: 417-836-6888, E-mail: mps@missouristate.edu. *Application contact:* Michael Edwards, Coordinator of Graduate Admissions, 417-836-5330, Fax: 417-836-6200, E-mail: michaeledwards@missouristate.edu.
Website: http://mps.missouristate.edu

**Monmouth University,** Graduate Studies, Department of Corporate and Public Communication, West Long Branch, NJ 07764-1898. Offers corporate and public communication (MA); human resources management and communication (Certificate); public service communication specialist (Certificate); strategic public relations and new media (Certificate). *Program availability:* Part-time, evening/weekend. *Degree requirements:* For master's, comprehensive exam (for some programs), thesis (for some programs), project. *Entrance requirements:* For master's, GRE, baccalaureate degree with minimum GPA of 3.0 in major, 2.75 overall; two letters of recommendation; personal essay (750 words or less describing preparation for study and personal objectives); digital or hard copy portfolio of select samples of work including a writing sample; resume. Additional exam requirements/recommendations for international students: Required—TOEFL (minimum score 550 paper-based; 79 iBT), IELTS (minimum score 6), Michigan English Language Assessment Battery (minimum score 77). Electronic applications accepted. *Faculty research:* Service-learning, history of television, feminism and the media, executive communication, public relations pedagogy.

**Montana State University Billings,** College of Arts and Sciences, Department of Communication and Theater, Billings, MT 59101. Offers public relations (MS). *Program availability:* Part-time, 100% online, blended/hybrid learning. *Faculty:* 4 full-time (1 woman). *Students:* 11. *Degree requirements:* For master's, comprehensive exam, thesis optional. *Entrance requirements:* For master's, GRE General Test, minimum undergraduate GPA of 3.0, letters of recommendation, letter of intent, resume. Additional exam requirements/recommendations for international students: Required—TOEFL (minimum score 79 iBT), IELTS (minimum score 6.5). *Application deadline:* For fall admission, 3/15 for domestic students, 7/15 for international students; for spring admission, 10/15 for domestic students, 12/1 for international students. Applications are processed on a rolling basis. Application fee: $40. Electronic applications accepted. *Expenses:* Tuition, state resident: full-time $5265; part-time $3436 per year. Tuition, nonresident: full-time $14,030; part-time $9280 per year. International tuition: $19,295 full-time. Tuition and fees vary according to degree level, campus/location and program. *Financial support:* Research assistantships with partial tuition reimbursements, teaching assistantships with partial tuition reimbursements, career-related internships or fieldwork, Federal Work-Study, institutionally sponsored loans, scholarships/grants, and unspecified assistantships available. Support available to part-time students. Financial award application deadline: 5/1; financial award applicants required to submit FAFSA. *Unit head:* Dr. Sarah Keller, Chair, 406-896-5824, E-mail: skeller@msubillings.edu. *Application contact:* David M. Sullivan, Graduate Studies Counselor, 406-657-2053, Fax: 406-657-2299, E-mail: dsullivan@msubillings.edu.

**Moore College of Art & Design,** Program in Social Engagement, Philadelphia, PA 19103. Offers MA. *Program availability:* Part-time. *Degree requirements:* For master's, thesis.

**Morehead State University,** Graduate Programs, Caudill College of Arts, Humanities and Social Sciences, Department of Communication, Media and Leadership Studies, Morehead, KY 40351. Offers communication (MA). *Program availability:* Part-time, evening/weekend. *Degree requirements:* For master's, comprehensive exam, exit assessment, written examination, oral interview. *Entrance requirements:* For master's, GRE General Test, bachelor's degree in communications or closely related field. Additional exam requirements/recommendations for international students: Required—TOEFL (minimum score 500 paper-based). Electronic applications accepted. *Faculty research:* Mass media effects, organizational communications, advertising/public relations.

**New Mexico State University,** College of Arts and Sciences, Department of Communication Studies, Las Cruces, NM 88003. Offers MA. *Program availability:* Part-time. *Faculty:* 6 full-time (3 women). *Students:* 14 full-time (6 women), 2 part-time (both women); includes 8 minority (7 Hispanic/Latino; 1 Two or more races, non-Hispanic/Latino), 2 international. Average age 35. 15 applicants, 73% accepted, 5 enrolled. In 2016, 7 master's awarded. *Degree requirements:* For master's, comprehensive exam (for some programs), thesis optional. *Entrance requirements:* For master's, minimum GPA of 3.25. Additional exam requirements/recommendations for international students: Required—TOEFL (minimum score 550 paper-based; 79 iBT), IELTS (minimum score 6.5). *Application deadline:* For fall admission, 2/15 priority date for domestic students; for spring admission, 11/15 priority date for domestic students. Applications are processed on a rolling basis. Application fee: $40 ($50 for international students). Electronic applications accepted. *Expenses:* Tuition, state resident: full-time $4086. Tuition, nonresident: full-time $14,254. *Required fees:* $853. Tuition and fees vary according to course load. *Financial support:* In 2016–17, 11 students received support, including 1 fellowship (averaging $1,000 per year), 2 research assistantships (averaging $13,821 per year), 10 teaching assistantships (averaging $17,234 per year); career-related internships or fieldwork, Federal Work-Study, scholarships/grants, traineeships, health care benefits, and unspecified assistantships also available. Support available to part-time students. Financial award application deadline: 3/1. *Faculty research:* Interpersonal, organizational, intercultural, political, and health communication. *Total annual research expenditures:* $10,145. *Unit head:* Dr. Kenneth Hacker, Department Head, 575-646-4937, Fax: 575-646-4642, E-mail: comstudy@nmsu.edu. *Application contact:* 575-646-2801, Fax: 575-646-4642, E-mail: comstudy@nmsu.edu. Website: http://commstudies.nmsu.edu

**New York Institute of Technology,** College of Arts and Sciences, Department of Communication Arts, Old Westbury, NY 11568-8000. Offers MA. *Program availability:* Part-time, evening/weekend. *Faculty:* 9 full-time (4 women), 17 part-time/adjunct (7 women). *Students:* 114 full-time (69 women), 51 part-time (29 women); includes 16 minority (9 Black or African American, non-Hispanic/Latino; 1 Asian, non-Hispanic/Latino; 6 Hispanic/Latino), 118 international. Average age 25. 131 applicants, 79% accepted, 45 enrolled. In 2016, 71 master's awarded. *Degree requirements:* For master's, thesis or alternative. *Entrance requirements:* For master's, minimum undergraduate GPA of 2.85. Additional exam requirements/recommendations for international students: Required—TOEFL (minimum score 79 iBT), IELTS (minimum score 6). *Application deadline:* Applications are processed on a rolling basis. Application fee: $50. Electronic applications accepted. *Expenses:* $1,215 per credit. *Financial support:* Career-related internships or fieldwork, Federal Work-Study, scholarships/grants, tuition waivers (full and partial), and unspecified assistantships available. Support available to part-time students. Financial award application deadline: 3/1; financial award applicants required to submit FAFSA. *Faculty research:* Effects of new media, interactive technology for promoting healthy behavior, video games and virtual reality, social media, health communications. *Unit head:* Don Fizzinoglia, Department Chair, 516-686-1468, E-mail: dfizzino@nyit.edu. *Application contact:* Alice Dolitsky, Director, Graduate Admissions, 516-686-7520, Fax: 516-686-1116, E-mail: nyitgrad@nyit.edu. Website: http://www.nyit.edu/degrees/communication_arts_ma

**New York University,** Steinhardt School of Culture, Education, and Human Development, Department of Media, Culture and Communication, New York, NY 10010. Offers media, culture and communication (MA, PhD); MLIS/MA. *Program availability:* Part-time. Terminal master's awarded for partial completion of doctoral program. *Degree requirements:* For master's, thesis (for some programs); for doctorate, thesis/dissertation. *Entrance requirements:* For master's, GRE General Test; for doctorate, GRE General Test, interview. Additional exam requirements/recommendations for international students: Required—TOEFL (minimum score 100 iBT). Electronic applications accepted. *Faculty research:* Digital media and new technologies, media criticism, flow of media and culture transnationally and transculturally.

**Norfolk State University,** School of Graduate Studies, School of Liberal Arts, Department of Media and Communication, Norfolk, VA 23504. Offers MA. *Program availability:* Part-time. *Degree requirements:* For master's, thesis. *Entrance requirements:* For master's, GRE, minimum GPA of 2.5, letters of recommendation. Additional exam requirements/recommendations for international students: Required—TOEFL.

**North Carolina State University,** Graduate School, College of Humanities and Social Sciences, Department of Communication, Raleigh, NC 27695. Offers MS. *Program availability:* Part-time. *Degree requirements:* For master's, thesis optional. *Entrance requirements:* For master's, GRE, minimum undergraduate GPA of 3.0 during last 60 hours. Electronic applications accepted. *Faculty research:* Instructional communication, political communication, organizational conflict management, intercultural communication, communication technology.

**North Dakota State University,** College of Graduate and Interdisciplinary Studies, College of Arts, Humanities and Social Sciences, Department of Communication, Fargo, ND 58102. Offers communication (PhD); mass communication (MA, MS); speech communication (MA, MS). *Program availability:* Part-time, online learning. Terminal master's awarded for partial completion of doctoral program. *Degree requirements:* For master's, thesis (for some programs); for doctorate, comprehensive exam, thesis/dissertation, 2-3 publications. *Entrance requirements:* For master's, GRE, minimum undergraduate GPA of 3.25; for doctorate, GRE, minimum undergraduate GPA of 3.5. Additional exam requirements/recommendations for international students: Required—TOEFL (minimum score 600 paper-based; 100 iBT), IELTS (minimum score 7). Electronic applications accepted. *Faculty research:* Communication and rhetorical theory, organizational communication, broadcast and print journalism, international communication, public relations and advertising.

**Northeastern State University,** College of Liberal Arts, Department of Communication, Art and Theatre, Tahlequah, OK 74464-2399. Offers communication (MA). *Program availability:* Part-time, evening/weekend. *Faculty:* 2 full-time (1 woman). *Students:* 2 full-time (0 women), 13 part-time (11 women); includes 4 minority (1 Black or African American, non-Hispanic/Latino; 2 American Indian or Alaska Native, non-Hispanic/Latino; 1 Hispanic/Latino). Average age 30. In 2016, 6 master's awarded. *Degree requirements:* For master's, comprehensive exam. *Entrance requirements:* For master's, GRE, MAT, minimum GPA of 2.5. Additional exam requirements/recommendations for international students: Required—TOEFL. *Application deadline:* For fall admission, 6/1 priority date for domestic students. Applications are processed on a rolling basis. Application fee: $25. Electronic applications accepted. *Expenses:* Tuition, state resident: full-time $2816; part-time $216.60 per credit hour. Tuition, nonresident: full-time $6365; part-time $489.60 per credit hour. *Required fees:* $37.40 per credit hour. *Financial support:* Teaching assistantships and Federal Work-Study available. Financial award application deadline: 3/1. *Unit head:* Dr. Dana Eversole, Department Chair, 918-444-2891, E-mail: eversole@nsuok.edu. *Application contact:* Josh McCollum, Graduate Coordinator, 918-444-2093, E-mail: mccolluj@nsuok.edu. Website: http://academics.nsuok.edu/communicationstudies/MasterofArts.aspx

**Northern Arizona University,** Graduate College, College of Social and Behavioral Sciences, School of Communication, Flagstaff, AZ 86011. Offers MA. *Program availability:* Part-time. *Degree requirements:* For master's, thesis or project. *Entrance requirements:* For master's, GRE General Test. Additional exam requirements/recommendations for international students: Required—TOEFL (minimum score 550 paper-based; 80 iBT), IELTS (minimum score 7). Electronic applications accepted. *Expenses:* Tuition, state resident: full-time $8971; part-time $444 per credit hour. Tuition, nonresident: full-time $20,958; part-time $1164 per credit hour. *Required fees:* $1018; $644 per credit hour. Tuition and fees vary according to course load, campus/location and program.

**Northern Illinois University,** Graduate School, College of Liberal Arts and Sciences, Department of Communication, De Kalb, IL 60115-2854. Offers communication studies (MA). *Program availability:* Part-time. *Faculty:* 24 full-time (11 women), 1 part-time/

adjunct (0 women). *Students:* 23 full-time (13 women), 5 part-time (3 women); includes 3 minority (1 Black or African American, non-Hispanic/Latino; 1 Asian, non-Hispanic/Latino; 1 Two or more races, non-Hispanic/Latino), 1 international. Average age 27. 29 applicants, 59% accepted, 11 enrolled. In 2016, 14 master's awarded. *Degree requirements:* For master's, comprehensive exam, thesis optional. *Entrance requirements:* For master's, GRE General Test, minimum GPA of 2.75. Additional exam requirements/recommendations for international students: Required—TOEFL (minimum score 550 paper-based). *Application deadline:* For fall admission, 6/1 for domestic students, 5/1 for international students; for spring admission, 11/1 for domestic students, 10/1 for international students. Applications are processed on a rolling basis. Application fee: $40. Electronic applications accepted. *Financial support:* In 2016–17, 25 teaching assistantships with full tuition reimbursements were awarded; fellowships with full tuition reimbursements, research assistantships with full tuition reimbursements, career-related internships or fieldwork, Federal Work-Study, scholarships/grants, tuition waivers (full), and unspecified assistantships also available. Support available to part-time students. Financial award applicants required to submit FAFSA. *Faculty research:* Journalism, history film studies, rhetoric or criticism, globalization, mass media law. *Unit head:* Dr. Gary Burns, Chair, 815-753-7028, Fax: 815-753-7109, E-mail: gburns@niu.edu. *Application contact:* Dr. Kathleen Valde, Director, Graduate Studies, 815-753-7005, E-mail: kvalde@niu.edu. Website: http://www.comm.niu.edu/

**Northern Kentucky University,** Office of Graduate Programs, College of Informatics, Program in Communication, Highland Heights, KY 41099. Offers communication (MA); communication teaching (Certificate); documentary studies (Certificate); public relations (Certificate); relationships (Certificate). *Program availability:* Part-time, evening/weekend. Terminal master's awarded for partial completion of doctoral program. *Degree requirements:* For master's, comprehensive exams, thesis or applied capstone project. *Entrance requirements:* For master's, GRE, minimum GPA of 3.0, 3 letters of recommendation, letter of intent. Additional exam requirements/recommendations for international students: Required—TOEFL (minimum score 79 iBT); Recommended—IELTS (minimum score 6.5). Electronic applications accepted. *Faculty research:* Mediating effect of health communication, organizational communication, quantitative and qualitative research methods, family and interpersonal communication.

**Northwestern University,** The Graduate School, School of Communication, Department of Communication Studies, Evanston, IL 60208. Offers communication studies (PhD), including interaction and social influence, rhetoric and public culture; managerial communication (MSC); media, technology and society (PhD); technology and social behavior (PhD). PhD admissions and degree offered through The Graduate School. Terminal master's awarded for partial completion of doctoral program. *Degree requirements:* For doctorate, thesis/dissertation. *Entrance requirements:* For master's and doctorate, GRE General Test. Additional exam requirements/recommendations for international students: Required—TOEFL. Electronic applications accepted.

**Notre Dame of Maryland University,** Graduate Studies, Program in Contemporary Communication, Baltimore, MD 21210-2476. Offers MA. *Program availability:* Part-time, evening/weekend. *Degree requirements:* For master's, thesis optional. *Entrance requirements:* For master's, minimum GPA of 3.0. Additional exam requirements/recommendations for international students: Required—TOEFL (minimum score 500 paper-based; 61 iBT). Electronic applications accepted.

**The Ohio State University,** Graduate School, College of Arts and Sciences, Division of Social and Behavioral Sciences, School of Communication, Columbus, OH 43210. Offers MA, PhD. *Faculty:* 29. *Students:* 57 full-time (36 women), 12 international. Average age 28. In 2016, 5 master's, 19 doctorates awarded. *Degree requirements:* For doctorate, thesis/dissertation. *Entrance requirements:* For master's and doctorate, GRE. Additional exam requirements/recommendations for international students: Required—TOEFL (minimum score 640 paper-based; 111 iBT); Recommended—IELTS (minimum score 8.5). *Application deadline:* For fall admission, 12/1 for domestic and international students. Applications are processed on a rolling basis. Application fee: $60 ($70 for international students). Electronic applications accepted. *Financial support:* Fellowships with tuition reimbursements, research assistantships with tuition reimbursements, and teaching assistantships with tuition reimbursements available. *Unit head:* Dr. Daniel McDonald, Professor and Director, 614-292-0451, E-mail: mcdonald.221@osu.edu. *Application contact:* Graduate and Professional Admissions, 614-292-9444, Fax: 614-292-3895, E-mail: gpadmissions@osu.edu. Website: http://www.comm.osu.edu/

**Ohio University,** Graduate College, Scripps College of Communication, Athens, OH 45701-2979. Offers MA, MCTP, MS, PhD. *Program availability:* Part-time. *Degree requirements:* For master's, comprehensive exam (for some programs), thesis or alternative; for doctorate, comprehensive exam, thesis/dissertation. *Entrance requirements:* For master's and doctorate, GRE General Test. Additional exam requirements/recommendations for international students: Required—TOEFL or IELTS. Application fee: $50 ($55 for international students). Electronic applications accepted. *Expenses:* Contact institution. *Financial support:* Fellowships with tuition reimbursements, research assistantships with full and partial tuition reimbursements, teaching assistantships with full tuition reimbursements, career-related internships or fieldwork, Federal Work-Study, institutionally sponsored loans, tuition waivers (full and partial), and unspecified assistantships available. Financial award applicants required to submit FAFSA. *Unit head:* Dr. Scott Titsworth, Interim Dean, 740-593-4882, Fax: 740-593-0459, E-mail: titswort@ohio.edu. *Application contact:* Dr. Eric Rothenbuhler, Associate Dean, 740-593-4885, Fax: 740-593-0459. Website: http://www.scrippscollege.ohio.edu

**Penn State Harrisburg,** Graduate School, School of Humanities, Middletown, PA 17057. Offers American studies (MA, PhD); communications (MA); heritage and museum practice (Certificate); humanities (MA); writing instruction specialist (Certificate). *Program availability:* Evening/weekend. *Unit head:* Dr. Mukund S. Kulkarni, Chancellor, 717-948-6105, Fax: 717-948-6452. *Application contact:* Robert W. Coffman, Jr., Director of Enrollment Management, Admissions, 717-948-6250, Fax: 717-948-6325, E-mail: hbgadmit@psu.edu. Website: https://harrisburg.psu.edu/humanities

**Penn State University Park,** Graduate School, College of the Liberal Arts, Department of Communication Arts and Sciences, University Park, PA 16802. Offers MA, PhD. *Unit head:* Dr. Susan Welch, Dean, 814-865-7691, Fax: 814-863-2085. *Application contact:* Lori Hawn, Director, Graduate Student Services, 814-865-1795, Fax: 814-863-4627, E-mail: l-gswww@lists.psu.edu. Website: http://cas.la.psu.edu/

**Pepperdine University,** Seaver College, Division of Communication, Malibu, CA 90263. Offers cinematic media production (MFA); strategic communication (MA). *Program availability:* Part-time. *Students:* 7 full-time (3 women), 26 part-time (16 women); includes 11 minority (4 Black or African American, non-Hispanic/Latino; 1 American Indian or Alaska Native, non-Hispanic/Latino; 3 Asian, non-Hispanic/Latino; 2 Hispanic/Latino; 1 Native Hawaiian or other Pacific Islander, non-Hispanic/Latino), 4 international. Average age 27. In 2016, 8 master's awarded. *Entrance requirements:* For master's, GRE General Test, letters of recommendation, writing sample. Additional exam requirements/recommendations for international students: Required—TOEFL. *Application deadline:* For fall admission, 2/1 priority date for domestic students, 2/1 for international students. Applications are processed on a rolling basis. Application fee: $65. Electronic applications accepted. *Financial support:* Research assistantships, teaching assistantships, career-related internships or fieldwork, and scholarships/grants available. Support available to part-time students. Financial award applicants required to submit FAFSA. *Unit head:* Dr. Kenneth E. Waters, Divisional Dean/Professor of Journalism, 310-506-4245, E-mail: ken.waters@pepperdine.edu. *Application contact:* Hayley Wolf, Director of Admission, 310-506-4392, E-mail: hayley.wolf@pepperdine.edu.

**Pittsburg State University,** Graduate School, College of Arts and Sciences, Department of Communication, Pittsburg, KS 66762. Offers MA. *Program availability:* Part-time. *Students:* 26 (19 women); includes 3 minority (1 Black or African American, non-Hispanic/Latino; 1 Hispanic/Latino; 1 Two or more races, non-Hispanic/Latino), 1 international. In 2016, 13 master's awarded. *Degree requirements:* For master's, thesis or alternative. *Entrance requirements:* Additional exam requirements/recommendations for international students: Required—TOEFL (minimum score 550 paper-based; 79 iBT), IELTS (minimum score 6.5), PTE (minimum score 53). *Application deadline:* For fall admission, 7/15 for domestic students, 6/1 for international students; for spring admission, 12/15 for domestic students, 10/15 for international students; for summer admission, 5/15 for domestic students, 4/1 for international students. Applications are processed on a rolling basis. Application fee: $35 ($60 for international students). Electronic applications accepted. *Expenses:* Contact institution. *Financial support:* In 2016–17, 9 teaching assistantships with full tuition reimbursements (averaging $5,500 per year) were awarded; career-related internships or fieldwork, Federal Work-Study, and unspecified assistantships also available. Financial award application deadline: 2/1; financial award applicants required to submit FAFSA. *Unit head:* Dr. Cynthia Allan, Chairperson, 620-235-4724, E-mail: callan@pittstate.edu. *Application contact:* Lisa Allen, Assistant Director of Graduate and Continuing Studies, 620-235-4223, Fax: 620-235-4219, E-mail: lallen@pittstate.edu.

**Point Park University,** School of Communication, Pittsburgh, PA 15222-1984. Offers MA. *Program availability:* Part-time, evening/weekend. *Degree requirements:* For master's, comprehensive exam (for some programs), thesis or alternative. *Entrance requirements:* For master's, GRE (if GPA less than 2.75), minimum GPA of 2.75, 2 letters of recommendation, statement of intent. Additional exam requirements/recommendations for international students: Required—TOEFL (minimum score 570 paper-based; 88 iBT), IELTS (minimum score 6.5); Recommended—TWE (minimum score 5). Electronic applications accepted.

**Purdue University,** Graduate School, College of Liberal Arts, Department of Communication, West Lafayette, IN 47907. Offers MA, MS, PhD. *Faculty:* 28 full-time (12 women). *Students:* 54 full-time (40 women), 430 part-time (312 women); includes 123 minority (52 Black or African American, non-Hispanic/Latino; 1 American Indian or Alaska Native, non-Hispanic/Latino; 11 Asian, non-Hispanic/Latino; 43 Hispanic/Latino; 2 Native Hawaiian or other Pacific Islander, non-Hispanic/Latino; 14 Two or more races, non-Hispanic/Latino), 21 international. Average age 34. 320 applicants, 58% accepted, 166 enrolled. In 2016, 75 master's, 10 doctorates awarded. *Degree requirements:* For master's, comprehensive exams or thesis; for doctorate, thesis/dissertation. *Entrance requirements:* For master's and doctorate, GRE General Test, minimum undergraduate GPA of 3.0 or equivalent. Additional exam requirements/recommendations for international students: Required—TOEFL (minimum score 600 paper-based; 77 iBT). *Application deadline:* For fall admission, 1/1 priority date for domestic students, 1/1 for international students; for spring admission, 8/1 for domestic and international students. Applications are processed on a rolling basis. Application fee: $60 ($75 for international students). Electronic applications accepted. *Financial support:* In 2016–17, 70 students received support. Fellowships, research assistantships, teaching assistantships, and scholarships/grants available. Financial award application deadline: 1/1; financial award applicants required to submit FAFSA. *Faculty research:* Interpersonal communication, mass communication, organizational communication, public affairs and issue management, rhetorical studies. *Unit head:* Dr. Marifran Mattson, Head, 765-494-7596, E-mail: mmattson@purdue.edu. *Application contact:* Deanna Bush, Graduate Contact, 765-496-9629, E-mail: bushd@purdue.edu.
Website: http://www.cla.purdue.edu/communication/

**Purdue University Northwest,** Graduate Studies Office, School of Liberal Arts and Social Sciences, Department of Communication and Creative Arts, Hammond, IN 46323-2094. Offers communication (MA). *Program availability:* Part-time, evening/weekend. *Degree requirements:* For master's, comprehensive exam, thesis or extended course work. *Entrance requirements:* For master's, minimum GPA of 3.0. Additional exam requirements/recommendations for international students: Required—TOEFL. Electronic applications accepted. *Faculty research:* International communication, gender studies, political rhetoric, media effects, media accountability.

**Queen's University at Kingston,** School of Graduate Studies, Faculty of Arts and Sciences, Department of Sociology, Kingston, ON K7L 3N6, Canada. Offers communication and Information technology (MA, PhD); feminist sociology (MA, PhD); socio-legal studies (MA, PhD); sociological theory (MA, PhD). *Program availability:* Part-time. *Degree requirements:* For master's, thesis; for doctorate, comprehensive exam, thesis/dissertation. *Entrance requirements:* For master's, honors bachelors degree in sociology; for doctorate, honors bachelors degree, masters degree in sociology. Additional exam requirements/recommendations for international students: Required—TOEFL. *Faculty research:* Social change and modernization, social control, deviance and criminology, surveillance.

**Queens University of Charlotte,** Knight School of Communication, Charlotte, NC 28274-0002. Offers organizational and strategic communication (MA). *Program availability:* Part-time, evening/weekend, online learning. *Degree requirements:* For master's, capstone course. *Entrance requirements:* Additional exam requirements/recommendations for international students: Required—TOEFL. *Expenses:* Contact institution.

**Quincy University,** Master of Arts in Communication Program, Quincy, IL 62301-2699. Offers MA. *Program availability:* Part-time, evening/weekend, online learning. *Degree requirements:* For master's, capstone project: thesis, internship, or creative project. *Entrance requirements:* For master's, official transcripts, two recommendations, minimum cumulative undergraduate GPA of 3.0, resume. Additional exam requirements/recommendations for international students: Required—TOEFL (minimum score 550 paper-based; 79 iBT). Electronic applications accepted.

**Quinnipiac University,** School of Communications, Hamden, CT 06518-1940. Offers MS. *Program availability:* Part-time, evening/weekend, online learning. *Faculty:* 13 full-time (7 women), 32 part-time/adjunct (8 women). *Students:* 34 full-time (15 women), 99 part-time (61 women); includes 40 minority (20 Black or African American, non-Hispanic/Latino; 2 Asian, non-Hispanic/Latino; 14 Hispanic/Latino; 4 Two or more races, non-Hispanic/Latino), 3 international. 112 applicants, 84% accepted, 65 enrolled. In 2016, 69 master's awarded. *Entrance requirements:* Additional exam requirements/recommendations for international students: Required—TOEFL (minimum score 575 paper-based; 90 iBT), IELTS (minimum score 6.5). *Application deadline:* For fall

admission, 7/30 priority date for domestic students, 4/30 priority date for international students; for spring admission, 12/15 priority date for domestic students, 9/30 priority date for international students. Applications are processed on a rolling basis. Application fee: $45. Electronic applications accepted. *Expenses: Tuition:* Part-time $985 per credit. *Required fees:* $40 per credit. $150 per semester. Tuition and fees vary according to program. *Financial support:* Career-related internships or fieldwork, Federal Work-Study, scholarships/grants, and unspecified assistantships available. Financial award application deadline: 6/1; financial award applicants required to submit FAFSA. *Unit head:* Phillip Simon, Program Director.
Website: http://www.qu.edu/gradprograms

**Regent University,** Graduate School, School of Communication and the Arts, Virginia Beach, VA 23464-9800. Offers communication (MA, PhD), including media and arts management and promotion (MA), political communication (MA), strategic communication (MA); directing for cinema/television (MFA); film and TV (MA), including producing, production, script writing; journalism (MA); producing for cinema/television (MFA); script and screenwriting (MFA); theatre (MA). *Program availability:* Part-time, 100% online, blended/hybrid learning. *Faculty:* 19 full-time (9 women), 51 part-time/adjunct (17 women). *Students:* 92 full-time (52 women), 344 part-time (225 women); includes 163 minority (116 Black or African American, non-Hispanic/Latino; 6 American Indian or Alaska Native, non-Hispanic/Latino; 7 Asian, non-Hispanic/Latino; 25 Hispanic/Latino; 1 Native Hawaiian or other Pacific Islander, non-Hispanic/Latino; 8 Two or more races, non-Hispanic/Latino), 8 international. Average age 37. 368 applicants, 52% accepted, 124 enrolled. In 2016, 91 master's, 7 doctorates awarded. *Degree requirements:* For master's, thesis or alternative; for doctorate, thesis/dissertation. *Entrance requirements:* For master's, transcripts, writing sample, resume, audition (for MFA programs); for doctorate, GRE General Test, resume, writing sample, recommendations, interview, transcripts, personal goals statement. Additional exam requirements/recommendations for international students: Required—TOEFL (minimum score 577 paper-based). *Application deadline:* For fall admission, 3/1 priority date for domestic students; for spring admission, 10/1 priority date for domestic students. Applications are processed on a rolling basis. Application fee: $50. Electronic applications accepted. *Expenses:* $685 per credit (for MA); $895 per credit (for MFA in acting); $885 per credit (for PhD); $250 per semester technology fee. *Financial support:* In 2016–17, 178 students received support, including 2 fellowships (averaging $10,000 per year); career-related internships or fieldwork, scholarships/grants, and unspecified assistantships also available. Support available to part-time students. *Faculty research:* Screenwriting, digital media production, communication, acting, directing. *Unit head:* Dr. Mitch Land, Dean, 757-352-4916, Fax: 757-352-4291, E-mail: mland@regent.edu. *Application contact:* Heidi Cece, Assistant Vice President of Enrollment Management, 800-373-5504, Fax: 757-352-4381, E-mail: admissions@regent.edu.
Website: http://www.regent.edu/sca/

**Rochester Institute of Technology,** Graduate Enrollment Services, College of Imaging Arts and Sciences, School of Media Sciences, Rochester, NY 14623-5603. Offers MS. *Program availability:* Part-time. *Students:* 14 full-time (7 women), 5 part-time (4 women), 16 international. Average age 25. 11 applicants, 73% accepted, 3 enrolled. In 2016, 1 master's awarded. *Degree requirements:* For master's, thesis. *Entrance requirements:* For master's, GRE, minimum GPA of 3.0 (recommended). Additional exam requirements/recommendations for international students: Required—PTE (minimum score 58), TOEFL (minimum score 550 paper-based, 79 iBT) or IELTS (minimum score 6.5). *Application deadline:* For fall admission, 2/15 priority date for domestic and international students; for spring admission, 12/15 for domestic and international students. Applications are processed on a rolling basis. Application fee: $60. Electronic applications accepted. *Expenses:* $1,742 per credit hour. *Financial support:* In 2016–17, 12 students received support. Research assistantships with partial tuition reimbursements available, teaching assistantships with partial tuition reimbursements available, career-related internships or fieldwork, scholarships/grants, and unspecified assistantships available. Support available to part-time students. Financial award applicants required to submit FAFSA. *Faculty research:* Digital publishing and digital content management; media distribution and media business transformation; 3D, functional, and packaging print processes; color management; cross-media publishing; digital printing. *Unit head:* Dr. Gregory D'Amico, Graduate Program Director, 585-475-5992, E-mail: mxcppr@rit.edu. *Application contact:* Diane Ellison, Associate Vice President, Graduate Enrollment Services, 585-475-2229, Fax: 585-475-7164, E-mail: gradinfo@rit.edu.
Website: http://cias.rit.edu/schools/media-sciences

**Rochester Institute of Technology,** Graduate Enrollment Services, College of Liberal Arts, School of Communication, MS Program in Communication and Media Technologies, Rochester, NY 14623. Offers MS. *Program availability:* Part-time. *Students:* 13 full-time (9 women), 9 part-time (5 women); includes 2 minority (1 Black or African American, non-Hispanic/Latino; 1 American Indian or Alaska Native, non-Hispanic/Latino), 10 international. Average age 28. 27 applicants, 48% accepted, 7 enrolled. In 2016, 11 master's awarded. *Degree requirements:* For master's, thesis. *Entrance requirements:* For master's, minimum GPA of 3.0 (recommended), writing sample. Additional exam requirements/recommendations for international students: Required—TOEFL (minimum score 570 paper-based; 88 iBT), IELTS (minimum score 6.5), PTE (minimum score 61). *Application deadline:* For fall admission, 2/15 priority date for domestic and international students; for spring admission, 12/15 priority date for domestic and international students. Applications are processed on a rolling basis. Application fee: $60. Electronic applications accepted. *Expenses:* $1,742 per credit hour. *Financial support:* In 2016–17, 13 students received support. Research assistantships with partial tuition reimbursements available, teaching assistantships with partial tuition reimbursements available, career-related internships or fieldwork, scholarships/grants, and unspecified assistantships available. Support available to part-time students. Financial award applicants required to submit FAFSA. *Faculty research:* Media and culture, visual communication, mass media, technology and media. *Unit head:* Dr. Grant Cos, Graduate Program Director, 585-475-6646, Fax: 585-475-7732, E-mail: communication@rit.edu. *Application contact:* Diane Ellison, Associate Vice President, Graduate Enrollment Services, 585-475-2229, Fax: 585-475-7164, E-mail: gradinfo@rit.edu.
Website: http://www.rit.edu/cla/communication/graduate-programs/ms-communication-media-technologies/overview

**Roosevelt University,** Graduate Division, College of Arts and Sciences, Department of Communication, Chicago, IL 60605. Offers integrated marketing communications (MSIMC); journalism (MSJ). *Program availability:* Part-time, evening/weekend.

**Rutgers University–New Brunswick,** School of Communication and Information, Program in Communication, Information and Library Studies, Piscataway, NJ 08854-8097. Offers PhD. *Program availability:* Part-time. *Degree requirements:* For doctorate, comprehensive exam, thesis/dissertation, qualifying exams. *Entrance requirements:* For doctorate, GRE General Test, proficiency in statistics. Additional exam requirements/recommendations for international students: Required—TOEFL (minimum score 600 paper-based). Electronic applications accepted. *Faculty research:* Information science, media studies.

**Sacred Heart University,** Graduate Programs, College of Arts and Sciences, School of Communication and Media Arts, Fairfield, CT 06825. Offers corporate communications and public relations (MA Comm); digital multimedia journalism (MA Comm); digital multimedia production (MA Comm); film and television production (MA); media literacy and digital culture (MA), including children, health and media, media and social justice, political action and media production; sports communication and media (MA), including athletic communications and promotions, sports broadcasting. *Program availability:* Part-time, evening/weekend. *Faculty:* 9 full-time (1 woman), 3 part-time/adjunct (2 women). *Students:* 60 full-time (34 women), 44 part-time (23 women); includes 23 minority (14 Black or African American, non-Hispanic/Latino; 7 Hispanic/Latino; 2 Two or more races, non-Hispanic/Latino), 18 international. Average age 26. 135 applicants, 93% accepted, 72 enrolled. In 2016, 69 master's awarded. *Degree requirements:* For master's, thesis or alternative. *Entrance requirements:* For master's, bachelor's degree. Additional exam requirements/recommendations for international students: Required—TOEFL (minimum score 570 paper-based, 80 iBT), TWE, or IELTS (6.5); Recommended—TSE. *Application deadline:* Applications are processed on a rolling basis. Application fee: $75. Electronic applications accepted. *Expenses:* $935 per credit. *Financial support:* Unspecified assistantships available. Financial award applicants required to submit FAFSA. *Unit head:* Dr. Andrew Miller, Chair, 203-396-8087, E-mail: millera@sacredheart.edu. *Application contact:* William Sweeney, Director of Graduate Admissions Operations, 203-365-7619, Fax: 203-365-4732, E-mail: graduatestudies@sacredheart.edu.
Website: http://www.sacredheart.edu/academics/collegeofartssciences/academicdepartments/communicationmediastudies/

**Saginaw Valley State University,** College of Arts and Behavioral Sciences, Program in Communication and Media Administration, University Center, MI 48710. Offers MA. *Program availability:* Part-time, evening/weekend. *Students:* 27 full-time (15 women), 8 part-time (6 women); includes 2 minority (1 Black or African American, non-Hispanic/Latino; 1 Asian, non-Hispanic/Latino), 24 international. Average age 27. 24 applicants, 46% accepted, 7 enrolled. In 2016, 13 master's awarded. *Degree requirements:* For master's, thesis. *Entrance requirements:* For master's, minimum GPA of 3.0. Additional exam requirements/recommendations for international students: Required—TOEFL (minimum score 540 paper-based; 76 iBT). *Application deadline:* For fall admission, 7/15 for international students; for winter admission, 11/15 for international students; for spring admission, 4/15 for international students. Applications are processed on a rolling basis. Application fee: $30 ($90 for international students). Electronic applications accepted. *Expenses:* Tuition, state resident: full-time $9652; part-time $536 per credit hour. Tuition, nonresident: full-time $12,259; part-time $1022 per credit hour. *Required fees:* $263; $14.60 per credit hour. Tuition and fees vary according to degree level. *Financial support:* Federal Work-Study and scholarships/grants available. Support available to part-time students. Financial award application deadline: 4/1; financial award applicants required to submit FAFSA. *Unit head:* Dr. Robert Drew, Professor of Communication, 989-964-7495, E-mail: rdrew@svsu.edu. *Application contact:* Jenna Briggs, Director, Graduate and International Admissions, 989-964-6096, Fax: 989-964-2788, E-mail: gradadm@svsu.edu.

**Saint Louis University,** Graduate Education, College of Arts and Sciences and Graduate Education, Department of Communication, St. Louis, MO 63103. Offers MA, MA-R. *Program availability:* Part-time. *Degree requirements:* For master's, thesis (for some programs), comprehensive oral and written exams. *Entrance requirements:* For master's, GRE General Test, letters of recommendation, resume, interview. Additional exam requirements/recommendations for international students: Required—TOEFL (minimum score 525 paper-based). Electronic applications accepted. *Faculty research:* Media studies, organizational communication, dialogue, intercultural communication, qualitative research methods.

**St. Mary's University,** Graduate Studies, Program in Communication Studies, San Antonio, TX 78228-8507. Offers communication studies (MA); public communication, public policy and public leadership (Certificate); JD/MA. *Program availability:* Part-time, evening/weekend, online learning. *Faculty:* 7 full-time (3 women), 3 part-time/adjunct (2 women). *Students:* 15 full-time (9 women); includes 13 minority (4 Black or African American, non-Hispanic/Latino; 9 Hispanic/Latino), 2 international. Average age 30. 14 applicants, 43% accepted, 2 enrolled. In 2016, 5 master's awarded. *Degree requirements:* For master's, thesis (for some programs). *Entrance requirements:* For master's, GRE General Test, MAT, minimum GPA of 3.1; professional experience. Additional exam requirements/recommendations for international students: Required—TOEFL (minimum score 550 paper-based; 80 iBT), IELTS (minimum score 6). *Application deadline:* For fall admission, 7/1 priority date for domestic students; for spring admission, 11/15 for domestic students; for summer admission, 4/1 for domestic students. Applications are processed on a rolling basis. Application fee: $0. Electronic applications accepted. *Expenses:* Tuition: Full-time $15,600; part-time $865 per credit hour. *Required fees:* $148 per semester. *Financial support:* Research assistantships, career-related internships or fieldwork, Federal Work-Study, institutionally sponsored loans, scholarships/grants, and health care benefits available. Financial award application deadline: 3/31; financial award applicants required to submit FAFSA. *Faculty research:* Interpersonal communication, rhetorical communication. *Unit head:* Dr. William Israel, Graduate Program Director, 210-436-3650, E-mail: bisrael@stmarytx.edu. *Application contact:* Kim Thornton, Director, Graduate and Adult Enrollment Services, 210-436-3101, E-mail: kthornton@stmarytx.edu.
Website: https://www.stmarytx.edu/academics/graduate/masters/communication/

**St. Thomas University,** School of Leadership Studies, Miami Gardens, FL 33054-6459. Offers MA, MPS, MS, Ed D, Certificate. *Program availability:* Part-time, evening/weekend. *Entrance requirements:* Additional exam requirements/recommendations for international students: Required—TOEFL (minimum score 550 paper-based; 79 iBT).

**Sam Houston State University,** College of Humanities and Social Sciences, Department of Communication Studies, Huntsville, TX 77341. Offers MA. *Program availability:* Part-time, evening/weekend, online learning. *Degree requirements:* For master's, comprehensive exam, thesis optional. *Entrance requirements:* For master's, GRE General Test, three letters of recommendation. Additional exam requirements/recommendations for international students: Required—TOEFL (minimum score 550 paper-based; 79 iBT), IELTS (minimum score 6.5). Electronic applications accepted.

**San Diego State University,** Graduate and Research Affairs, College of Professional Studies and Fine Arts, School of Communication, San Diego, CA 92182. Offers advertising and public relations (MA); critical-cultural studies (MA); interaction studies (MA); intercultural and international studies (MA); new media studies (MA); news and information studies (MA); telecommunications and media management (MA). *Degree requirements:* For master's, thesis. *Entrance requirements:* For master's, GRE General Test, 3 letters of recommendation. Additional exam requirements/recommendations for international students: Required—TOEFL. Electronic applications accepted.

**San Jose State University,** Graduate Studies and Research, College of Humanities and the Arts, San Jose, CA 95192-0001. Offers art (MA, MFA), including art history and visual culture (MA), digital media art (MFA), photography (MFA), pictorial art (MFA), spatial art (MFA); computational linguistics (Certificate); English (MA, MFA), including creative writing (MFA); French (MA); humanities and arts (Certificate); linguistics (MA); music (MA); philosophy (MA); professional and technical communication (Certificate); Spanish (MA); teaching English to speakers of other languages (MA); TESOL (Certificate); theatre arts (MA). Electronic applications accepted.

**San Jose State University,** Graduate Studies and Research, College of Social Sciences, San Jose, CA 95192-0001. Offers applications of technology in planning (Certificate); applied anthropology (MA); communication studies (MS); community design and development (Certificate); economics (MA), including applied economics, social sciences; environmental planning (Certificate); geographic information science (Certificate); geography (MA); global citizenship (Certificate); history (MA), including history education, social sciences; Mexican American studies (MA); psychology (MA, MS), including clinical psychology (MS), industrial/organizational psychology (MS), research and experimental psychology (MA); public administration (MA); real estate development (Certificate); social sciences (MPA, MS); sociology (MA); transportation and land use planning (Certificate). *Program availability:* Part-time, evening/weekend. *Entrance requirements:* For master's, minimum GPA of 3.0. Electronic applications accepted.

**Seton Hall University,** College of Communication and the Arts, South Orange, NJ 07079-2697. Offers museum professions (MA), including exhibition development, museum education, museum management, museum registration; public relations (MA); strategic communication (MA). *Program availability:* Part-time, evening/weekend, online learning. *Degree requirements:* For master's, thesis. *Entrance requirements:* Additional exam requirements/recommendations for international students: Required—TOEFL. Electronic applications accepted. *Faculty research:* Managerial communication, communication consulting, communication and development.

**Shippensburg University of Pennsylvania,** School of Graduate Studies, College of Arts and Sciences, Department of Communication/Journalism, Shippensburg, PA 17257-2299. Offers communication studies (MS). *Program availability:* Part-time, evening/weekend. *Faculty:* 5 full-time (3 women), 2 part-time/adjunct (both women). *Students:* 18 full-time (9 women), 7 part-time (5 women); includes 1 minority (Black or African American, non-Hispanic/Latino), 8 international. Average age 26. 38 applicants, 45% accepted, 12 enrolled. In 2016, 9 master's awarded. *Degree requirements:* For master's, 6-credit thesis or 3-credit professional project, candidacy. *Entrance requirements:* For master's, GRE or MAT (if GPA less than 2.75), 3 professional references, resume, essay, 500-word statement of purpose. Additional exam requirements/recommendations for international students: Required—TOEFL (minimum score 550 paper-based, 68 iBT) or IELTS (minimum score 6). *Application deadline:* For fall admission, 4/30 for international students; for spring admission, 9/30 for international students. Applications are processed on a rolling basis. Application fee: $45. Electronic applications accepted. *Expenses:* Tuition, state resident: part-time $483 per credit. Tuition, nonresident: part-time $725 per credit. *Required fees:* $141 per credit. *Financial support:* In 2016–17, 6 students received support. Career-related internships or fieldwork, scholarships/grants, unspecified assistantships, and resident hall director and student payroll positions available. Support available to part-time students. Financial award application deadline: 3/1; financial award applicants required to submit FAFSA. *Unit head:* Dr. Kimberly D. Garris, Chair and Program Coordinator, 717-477-1521, Fax: 717-477-4013, E-mail: kdgarr@ship.edu. *Application contact:* Megan N. Luft, Assistant Dean of Graduate Admissions, 717-477-1231, Fax: 717-477-4016, E-mail: mnluft@ship.edu.
Website: http://www.ship.edu/communication-journalism/

**Simmons College,** School of Management, Boston, MA 02115. Offers business administration (MBA); health care (MBA); management (MS, MSM), including communications management (MS), non-profit management (MS); MBA/MSW; MS/MA. *Accreditation:* AACSB. *Program availability:* Part-time, evening/weekend. *Faculty:* 14 full-time (10 women), 5 part-time/adjunct (3 women). *Students:* 23 full-time (20 women), 141 part-time (126 women); includes 41 minority (20 Black or African American, non-Hispanic/Latino; 7 Asian, non-Hispanic/Latino; 13 Hispanic/Latino; 1 Two or more races, non-Hispanic/Latino), 7 international. Average age 32. 62 applicants, 74% accepted, 32 enrolled. In 2016, 58 master's awarded. *Entrance requirements:* For master's, GMAT or GRE. Additional exam requirements/recommendations for international students: Required—TOEFL. *Application deadline:* For fall admission, 7/18 priority date for domestic students; for summer admission, 4/24 priority date for domestic students. Applications are processed on a rolling basis. Application fee: $75. Electronic applications accepted. *Expenses:* $1,374 per credit, $4,122 per course, $102 activity fee per semester. *Financial support:* Scholarships/grants and unspecified assistantships available. Financial award applicants required to submit FAFSA. *Faculty research:* Gender and organizations, leadership, health care management. *Unit head:* Patricia Deyton, Associate Dean for Graduate Programs, 617-521-3876.
Website: http://www.simmons.edu/som

**Simon Fraser University,** Office of Graduate Studies and Postdoctoral Fellows, Faculty of Communication, Art and Technology, School of Communication, Burnaby, BC V5A 1S6, Canada. Offers MA, PhD, MA/MA. MA/MA program in global communication offered jointly with the Communication University of China. *Faculty:* 28 full-time (9 women). *Students:* 112 full-time (77 women). 141 applicants, 24% accepted, 28 enrolled. In 2016, 22 master's, 5 doctorates awarded. *Degree requirements:* For master's, thesis or alternative, annual formal review; for doctorate, comprehensive exam, thesis/dissertation, annual formal review. *Entrance requirements:* For master's, minimum GPA of 3.0 (on scale of 4.33) or 3.33 based on last 60 credits of undergraduate courses; for doctorate, minimum GPA of 3.5 (on scale of 4.33). Additional exam requirements/recommendations for international students: Recommended—TOEFL (minimum score 580 paper-based; 93 iBT), IELTS (minimum score 7), TWE (minimum score 5). *Application deadline:* For fall admission, 12/15 for domestic students, 12/5 for international students; for spring admission, 1/15 for domestic students. Application fee: $90 ($125 for international students). Electronic applications accepted. *Financial support:* In 2016–17, 57 students received support, including 24 fellowships (averaging $6,365 per year), teaching assistantships (averaging $5,608 per year); research assistantships and scholarships/grants also available. *Faculty research:* Cultural policy and politics; globalization, social change, and social justice; history and theory of communication; media and cultural studies; technology and society. *Unit head:* Dr. Kirsten McAllister, Graduate Chair, 778-782-3238, Fax: 778-782-4024, E-mail: cmns-grad-chair@sfu.edu. *Application contact:* Jason Congdon, Graduate Coordinator, 778-782-3595, Fax: 778-782-4024, E-mail: gradcmns@sfu.ca.
Website: http://www.sfu.ca/communication.html

**South Dakota State University,** Graduate School, College of Arts and Science, Department of Journalism and Mass Communication, Brookings, SD 57007. Offers communication studies and journalism (MS). *Accreditation:* ACEJMC. *Program availability:* Part-time, evening/weekend. *Degree requirements:* For master's, thesis, oral exam. *Entrance requirements:* Additional exam requirements/recommendations for international students: Required—TOEFL (minimum score 550 paper-based; 79 iBT). *Faculty research:* Mass communication applications.

**Southeastern Louisiana University,** College of Arts, Humanities and Social Sciences, Department of Languages and Communication, Hammond, LA 70402. Offers organizational communication (MA). *Program availability:* Part-time, evening/weekend. *Faculty:* 6 full-time (4 women). *Students:* 8 full-time (3 women), 13 part-time (7 women); includes 7 minority (6 Black or African American, non-Hispanic/Latino; 1 Two or more

races, non-Hispanic/Latino). Average age 28. 16 applicants, 81% accepted, 7 enrolled. In 2016, 9 master's awarded. *Degree requirements:* For master's, comprehensive exam. *Entrance requirements:* Additional exam requirements/recommendations for international students: Required—TOEFL (minimum score 500 paper-based; 61 iBT). *Application deadline:* For fall admission, 7/15 priority date for domestic students, 6/1 priority date for international students; for spring admission, 12/1 priority date for domestic students, 10/1 priority date for international students. Applications are processed on a rolling basis. Application fee: $20 ($30 for international students). Electronic applications accepted. *Expenses:* Tuition, state resident: full-time $6540; part-time $465 per credit hour. Tuition, nonresident: full-time $19,017; part-time $1158 per credit hour. *Required fees:* $1829. *Financial support:* In 2016–17, 6 students received support, including 4 research assistantships (averaging $10,100 per year); Federal Work-Study, institutionally sponsored loans, scholarships/grants, traineeships, and unspecified assistantships also available. Financial award application deadline: 5/1; financial award applicants required to submit FAFSA. *Faculty research:* Communicate with the millennial generation to enhance organizational effectiveness, conflict resolution and mediation among nations, journalism history, media law, media writing, media convergence, external compliances accreditation and strategic planning. *Unit head:* Dr. Lucia Guzzi Harrison, Department Head, 985-549-2105, Fax: 985-549-5014, E-mail: lharrison@southeastern.edu. *Application contact:* Amanda Harper, Graduate Admissions Analyst, 985-549-5620, Fax: 985-549-5632, E-mail: admissions@southeastern.edu.
Website: http://www.southeastern.edu/acad_research/depts/lang_comm/index.html

**Southern Illinois University Carbondale,** Graduate School, College of Mass Communication and Media Arts, Carbondale, IL 62901-4701. Offers MA, MFA, MS, PhD, MBA/MA. *Program availability:* Part-time. *Degree requirements:* For doctorate, thesis/dissertation. *Entrance requirements:* For doctorate, GRE General Test, minimum GPA of 3.25. Additional exam requirements/recommendations for international students: Required—TOEFL.

**Southern Utah University,** Program in Communication, Cedar City, UT 84720-2498. Offers MA. *Program availability:* Part-time, online learning. *Faculty:* 7 full-time (1 woman). *Students:* 15 full-time (11 women), 42 part-time (24 women); includes 7 minority (1 Black or African American, non-Hispanic/Latino; 1 Asian, non-Hispanic/Latino; 4 Hispanic/Latino; 1 Native Hawaiian or other Pacific Islander, non-Hispanic/Latino). Average age 30. 32 applicants, 63% accepted, 17 enrolled. In 2016, 17 master's awarded. *Entrance requirements:* For master's, GRE. Additional exam requirements/recommendations for international students: Required—TOEFL (minimum score 550 paper-based, 79 iBT) or IELTS (minimum score 6). *Application deadline:* For fall admission, 6/15 for domestic and international students; for spring admission, 10/15 for domestic and international students. Applications are processed on a rolling basis. Application fee: $60 ($65 for international students). Electronic applications accepted. *Expenses:* $6,792 per year residents or online full-time; $20,420 per year on-campus non-resident full-time. *Financial support:* Teaching assistantships with tuition reimbursements and unspecified assistantships available. Financial award application deadline: 3/15. *Unit head:* Dr. Arthur Challis, Department Chair, 435-586-7861, Fax: 435-865-8352, E-mail: challis@suu.edu. *Application contact:* Dr. Matthew Barton, Graduate Coordinator, 435-586-7970, Fax: 435-865-8352, E-mail: bartonm@suu.edu. Website: https://www.suu.edu/hss/comm/masters/

**Spring Arbor University,** School of Arts and Sciences, Spring Arbor, MI 49283-9799. Offers communication (MA); spiritual formation and leadership (MA). *Program availability:* Part-time, online learning. *Degree requirements:* For master's, thesis (for some programs). *Entrance requirements:* For master's, GRE (minimum score of 40th percentile and taken within last 5 years), bachelor's degree from regionally-accredited college or university, minimum GPA of 3.0 for at least the last two years of the bachelor's degree, at least two recommendations from professional/academic individuals. Additional exam requirements/recommendations for international students: Required—TOEFL (minimum score 600 paper-based). *Expenses:* Contact institution.

**Stanford University,** School of Humanities and Sciences, Department of Communication, Stanford, CA 94305-2050. Offers MA, PhD. *Faculty:* 11 full-time (2 women), 4 part-time/adjunct (3 women). *Students:* 71 full-time (43 women). Average age 29. 148 applicants, 14% accepted, 15 enrolled. In 2016, 20 master's, 3 doctorates awarded. Terminal master's awarded for partial completion of doctoral program. *Degree requirements:* For master's, thesis, project; for doctorate, thesis/dissertation, qualifying examination, area examination, 2 projects. *Entrance requirements:* For master's and doctorate, GRE General Test. Additional exam requirements/recommendations for international students: Required—TOEFL (minimum score 650 paper-based; 115 iBT). *Application deadline:* For fall admission, 12/6 for domestic and international students. Application fee: $125. Electronic applications accepted. *Expenses: Tuition:* Full-time $47,331. *Required fees:* $609. *Financial support:* Fellowships, research assistantships, and teaching assistantships available. *Faculty research:* Virtual reality, deliberative democracy, computational journalism, technology and deception, journalism ethics, political campaigns, survey methodology, censorship in authoritarian regimes, media psychology, social impact of digital media. *Unit head:* Fred Turner, Chair, 650-723-0706, E-mail: fturner@stanford.edu. *Application contact:* Katrin Wheeler, Student Services Manager, 650-724-8920, Fax: 650-725-2472, E-mail: comm-studentservices@stanford.edu.
Website: http://communication.stanford.edu/

**State University of New York at Oswego,** Graduate Studies, School of Communication, Media and the Arts, Oswego, NY 13126. Offers strategic communication (MA), including health communication, integrated media and social networks, organizational communication. *Entrance requirements:* For master's, GRE, official transcript, statement of purpose, resume, two letters of recommendation.

**State University of New York College at Potsdam,** School of Arts and Sciences, Department of English and Communication, Potsdam, NY 13676. Offers MA. *Program availability:* Part-time, evening/weekend. *Degree requirements:* For master's, one foreign language, thesis or alternative. *Entrance requirements:* For master's, minimum GPA of 3.0 in last 60 hours of undergraduate course work. Additional exam requirements/recommendations for international students: Required—TOEFL (minimum score 550 paper-based; 80 iBT), IELTS (minimum score 6). Electronic applications accepted.

**Stephen F. Austin State University,** Graduate School, College of Applied Arts and Science, Department of Communication, Nacogdoches, TX 75962. Offers communication (MA); mass communication (MA). *Program availability:* Part-time. *Degree requirements:* For master's, comprehensive exam, thesis optional. *Entrance requirements:* For master's, GRE General Test. Additional exam requirements/recommendations for international students: Required—TOEFL (minimum score 550 paper-based).

**Stevens Institute of Technology,** Graduate School, Charles V. Schaefer Jr. School of Engineering and Science, Department of Electrical and Computer Engineering, Program in Electrical Engineering, Hoboken, NJ 07030. Offers autonomous robotics (Certificate); electrical engineering (M Eng, PhD, Certificate), including computer architecture and digital systems (M Eng), microelectronics and photonics science and technology (M Eng), signal processing for communications (M Eng), telecommunications systems engineering (M Eng), wireless communications (M Eng, Certificate). *Program availability:* Part-time, evening/weekend. *Students:* 190 full-time (47 women), 31 part-time (5 women); includes 14 minority (6 Black or African American, non-Hispanic/Latino; 8 Asian, non-Hispanic/Latino), 181 international. Average age 25. 851 applicants, 59% accepted, 93 enrolled. In 2016, 152 master's, 6 doctorates awarded. *Degree requirements:* For master's, thesis optional, minimum B average in major field and overall; for doctorate, comprehensive exam (for some programs), thesis/dissertation; for Certificate, minimum B average. *Entrance requirements:* Additional exam requirements/recommendations for international students: Required—TOEFL (minimum score 74 iBT), IELTS (minimum score 6). *Application deadline:* For fall admission, 6/1 for domestic students, 4/15 for international students; for spring admission, 11/30 for domestic students, 11/1 for international students. Applications are processed on a rolling basis. Application fee: $65. Electronic applications accepted. *Expenses:* Contact institution. *Financial support:* Fellowships, research assistantships, teaching assistantships, career-related internships or fieldwork, Federal Work-Study, scholarships/grants, and unspecified assistantships available. Financial award application deadline: 2/15; financial award applicants required to submit FAFSA. *Unit head:* Cristina Comaniciu, Program Director, 201-216-5606, Fax: 201-216-8246, E-mail: ccomanic@stevens.edu. *Application contact:* Graduate Admissions, 888-783-8367, Fax: 888-511-1306, E-mail: graduate@stevens.edu.

**Stevenson University,** Program in Communication Studies, Stevenson, MD 21153. Offers MS. *Program availability:* Part-time, online only, 100% online, blended/hybrid learning. *Faculty:* 6 part-time/adjunct (4 women). *Students:* 10 full-time (6 women), 22 part-time (15 women); includes 13 minority (9 Black or African American, non-Hispanic/Latino; 1 Asian, non-Hispanic/Latino; 3 Hispanic/Latino). Average age 27. 27 applicants, 85% accepted, 13 enrolled. *Degree requirements:* For master's, project or thesis. *Entrance requirements:* For master's, bachelor's degree from regionally-accredited institution; official college transcripts from all previous academic work; minimum cumulative GPA of 3.0 in past academic work; 250-350 word personal statement. *Application deadline:* Applications are processed on a rolling basis. Electronic applications accepted. *Expenses:* $670 per credit hour. *Financial support:* Unspecified assistantships available. Financial award applicants required to submit FAFSA. *Unit head:* Dr. Nadene Vevea, Associate Dean, Communications Studies, 443-394-9498, E-mail: nvevea@stevenson.edu. *Application contact:* Amanda Courter, Senior Enrollment Counselor, 443-352-4243, Fax: 443-352-4440, E-mail: acourter@stevenson.edu.
Website: http://www.stevenson.edu/graduate-professional-studies/graduate-programs/communication-studies/index.html

**Syracuse University,** College of Visual and Performing Arts, MA Program in Communication and Rhetorical Studies, Syracuse, NY 13244. Offers MA. *Program availability:* Part-time. *Degree requirements:* For master's, comprehensive exam (for some programs), thesis (for some programs). *Entrance requirements:* For master's, GRE General Test, three letters of recommendation, writing sample, transcripts, personal statement, resume. Additional exam requirements/recommendations for international students: Required—TOEFL (minimum score 100 iBT). *Application deadline:* For fall admission, 2/1 priority date for domestic and international students. Application fee: $75. Electronic applications accepted. *Expenses: Tuition:* Full-time $25,974; part-time $1443 per credit hour. *Required fees:* $802; $50 per course. Tuition and fees vary according to course load and program. *Financial support:* In 2016–17, 9 students received support. Fellowships with full tuition reimbursements available, teaching assistantships with tuition reimbursements available, and tuition waivers available. Financial award application deadline: 1/1; financial award applicants required to submit FAFSA. *Faculty research:* Language and social interaction, communication and critical/cultural studies, rhetorical theory and criticism. *Unit head:* Dr. Dana Cloud, Chair, 315-443-5140, E-mail: dlcloud@syr.edu. *Application contact:* Therese West, Information Contact, 315-443-0137, E-mail: admissg@syr.edu.
Website: http://vpa.syr.edu/

**Syracuse University,** S. I. Newhouse School of Public Communications, Syracuse, NY 13244. Offers MA, MS, PhD, JD/MA, JD/MS, MS/MA. *Accreditation:* ACEJMC (one or more programs are accredited). *Program availability:* Online learning. *Faculty:* 73 full-time (29 women), 63 part-time/adjunct (32 women). *Students:* 234 full-time (170 women), 243 part-time (193 women); includes 155 minority (82 Black or African American, non-Hispanic/Latino; 3 American Indian or Alaska Native, non-Hispanic/Latino; 14 Asian, non-Hispanic/Latino; 41 Hispanic/Latino; 1 Native Hawaiian or other Pacific Islander, non-Hispanic/Latino; 14 Two or more races, non-Hispanic/Latino), 115 international. Average age 28. 805 applicants, 65% accepted, 240 enrolled. In 2016, 213 master's, 3 doctorates awarded. *Degree requirements:* For master's, comprehensive exam (for some programs); for doctorate, thesis/dissertation, qualifying exams. *Entrance requirements:* For master's and doctorate, GRE General Test, resume, official transcripts, personal statement, three letters of recommendation. Additional exam requirements/recommendations for international students: Required—TOEFL (minimum score 100 iBT), IELTS (minimum score 7). *Application deadline:* For fall admission, 1/15 priority date for domestic and international students; for summer admission, 1/15 priority date for domestic and international students. Application fee: $45. Electronic applications accepted. *Expenses: Tuition:* Full-time $25,974; part-time $1443 per credit hour. *Required fees:* $802; $50 per course. Tuition and fees vary according to course load and program. *Financial support:* Fellowships with full tuition reimbursements, research assistantships with partial tuition reimbursements, scholarships/grants, and instructional associate positions with partial tuition reimbursements available. Financial award application deadline: 2/1. *Faculty research:* Media convergence, political reporting, interactive multimedia, popular television, advertising effectiveness. *Unit head:* Lorraine Branham, Dean, 315-443-3372, E-mail: lbranham@syr.edu. *Application contact:* Martha Coria, Graduate Records Office, 315-443-4039, Fax: 315-443-1834, E-mail: pcgrad@syr.edu.
Website: http://newhouse.syr.edu/

**Tarleton State University,** College of Graduate Studies, College of Liberal and Fine Arts, Department of Communication Studies, Stephenville, TX 76402. Offers MA. *Program availability:* Part-time. *Faculty:* 2 part-time/adjunct (both women). *Students:* 1 (woman) full-time, 20 part-time (16 women); includes 7 minority (2 Black or African American, non-Hispanic/Latino; 5 Hispanic/Latino). 13 applicants, 100% accepted, 10 enrolled. *Degree requirements:* For master's, comprehensive exam. *Entrance requirements:* Additional exam requirements/recommendations for international students: Required—TOEFL (minimum score 550 paper-based; 80 iBT). *Application deadline:* Applications are processed on a rolling basis. Application fee: $45 ($145 for international students). Electronic applications accepted. *Expenses:* $3,672 tuition; $2,437 fees. *Financial support:* Applicants required to submit FAFSA. *Unit head:* Dr. Charles Howard, Department Head, 254-968-9640, E-mail: choward@tarleton.edu. *Application contact:* Information Contact, 254-968-9104, Fax: 254-968-9670, E-mail: gradoffice@tarleton.edu.
Website: http://www.tarleton.edu/degrees/masters/ma-communication-studies/index.html

**Teachers College, Columbia University,** Department of Mathematics, Science and Technology, New York, NY 10027-6696. Offers biology 7-12 (MA); chemistry 7-12 (MA); communication and education (MA, Ed D); computing in education (MA); earth science 7-12 (MA); instructional technology and media (Ed M, MA, Ed D); mathematics education (Ed M, MA, Ed D, Ed DCT, PhD); physics 7-12 (MA); science and dental education (MA); science education (Ed M, MS, Ed DCT, PhD); supervisor/teacher of science education (MA); technology specialist (MA). *Program availability:* Part-time, evening/weekend, online learning. *Students:* Full-time (133 women), 222 part-time (139 women); includes 152 minority (44 Black or African American, non-Hispanic/Latino; 66 Asian, non-Hispanic/Latino; 32 Hispanic/Latino; 10 Two or more races, non-Hispanic/Latino), 106 international. 368 applicants, 65% accepted, 123 enrolled. Terminal master's awarded for partial completion of doctoral program. *Degree requirements:* For doctorate, thesis/dissertation. *Expenses:* Tuition: Full-time $36,288; part-time $1512 per credit. *Required fees:* $438 per semester. One-time fee: $510 full-time. Full-time tuition and fees vary according to course load. *Unit head:* Dr. O. Roger Anderson, Chair, 212-678-3405, Fax: 212-678-8129, E-mail: ora@ldeo.columbia.edu. *Application contact:* David Estrella, Director of Admission, 212-678-3305, E-mail: estrella@tc.columbia.edu. Website: http://www.tc.columbia.edu/mathematics-science-and-technology/

**Temple University,** School of Media and Communication, Philadelphia, PA 19122-6096. Offers MA, MJ, MS, PhD. *Program availability:* Part-time, evening/weekend. *Degree requirements:* For master's, comprehensive exam (for some programs); for doctorate, one foreign language, comprehensive exam, thesis/dissertation. *Entrance requirements:* For master's and doctorate, GRE General Test, minimum GPA of 3.0. Additional exam requirements/recommendations for international students: Required—TOEFL. Electronic applications accepted.

**Texas A&M University,** College of Liberal Arts, Department of Communication, College Station, TX 77843. Offers MA, PhD. *Faculty:* 24. *Students:* 41 full-time (24 women), 3 part-time (2 women); includes 5 minority (1 Black or African American, non-Hispanic/Latino; 3 Hispanic/Latino; 1 Two or more races, non-Hispanic/Latino), 11 international. Average age 30. 53 applicants, 25% accepted, 6 enrolled. In 2016, 3 master's, 10 doctorates awarded. *Degree requirements:* For master's, thesis or alternative; for doctorate, thesis/dissertation. *Entrance requirements:* For master's, GRE General Test. Additional exam requirements/recommendations for international students: Required—TOEFL (minimum score 550 paper-based; 80 iBT), IELTS (minimum score 6), PTE (minimum score 53). *Application deadline:* For fall admission, 12/15 for domestic students. Applications are processed on a rolling basis. Application fee: $50 ($90 for international students). Electronic applications accepted. *Expenses:* Contact institution. *Financial support:* In 2016–17, 43 students received support, including 7 fellowships with tuition reimbursements available (averaging $13,557 per year), 7 research assistantships with tuition reimbursements available (averaging $6,961 per year), 34 teaching assistantships with tuition reimbursements available (averaging $12,684 per year); career-related internships or fieldwork, institutionally sponsored loans, scholarships/grants, traineeships, health care benefits, tuition waivers (full and partial), and unspecified assistantships also available. Support available to part-time students. Financial award application deadline: 3/15; financial award applicants required to submit FAFSA. *Faculty research:* Rhetoric and public affairs, communication and health, communication and organizations. *Unit head:* Dr. J. Kevin Barge, Head, 979-845-5514, E-mail: kbarge@tamu.edu. *Application contact:* Kristan Poirot, Graduate Program Director, 979-845-2842, E-mail: poirot@tamu.edu. Website: http://comm.tamu.edu/

**Texas A&M University–Corpus Christi,** College of Graduate Studies, College of Liberal Arts, Corpus Christi, TX 78412-5503. Offers communication (MA); English (MA); history (MA); psychology (MA), including clinical psychology, general psychology; public administration (MPA); studio art (MFA). *Program availability:* Part-time, evening/weekend. *Faculty:* 76 full-time (39 women), 9 part-time/adjunct (4 women). *Students:* 81 full-time (49 women), 102 part-time (71 women); includes 90 minority (8 Black or African American, non-Hispanic/Latino; 2 Asian, non-Hispanic/Latino; 76 Hispanic/Latino; 4 Two or more races, non-Hispanic/Latino), 13 international. Average age 32. 134 applicants, 56% accepted, 57 enrolled. In 2016, 48 master's awarded. *Degree requirements:* For master's, comprehensive exam (for some programs), thesis (for some programs). *Entrance requirements:* For master's, portfolio. Additional exam requirements/recommendations for international students: Required—TOEFL (minimum score 550 paper-based; 79 iBT), IELTS (minimum score 6.5). *Application deadline:* For fall admission, 7/15 for domestic students, 5/1 for international students; for spring admission, 11/15 priority date for domestic students, 9/1 priority date for international students. Applications are processed on a rolling basis. Application fee: $50 ($70 for international students). Electronic applications accepted. *Financial support:* Research assistantships, teaching assistantships, career-related internships or fieldwork, Federal Work-Study, institutionally sponsored loans, scholarships/grants, health care benefits, and unspecified assistantships available. Support available to part-time students. Financial award application deadline: 3/15; financial award applicants required to submit FAFSA. *Unit head:* Dr. Mark Hartlaub, Interim Dean, 361-825-2659, Fax: 361-825-5844, E-mail: mark.hartlaub@tamucc.edu. *Application contact:* Graduate Admissions Coordinator, 361-825-2177, Fax: 361-825-2755, E-mail: gradweb@tamucc.edu. Website: http://cla.tamucc.edu/

**Texas Christian University,** Bob Schieffer College of Communication, Fort Worth, TX 76129. Offers communication studies (MS); strategic communication (MS). *Program availability:* Part-time. *Faculty:* 26 full-time (12 women). *Students:* 28 full-time (23 women), 1 part-time; includes 6 minority (1 Black or African American, non-Hispanic/Latino; 2 Asian, non-Hispanic/Latino; 1 Hispanic/Latino; 2 Two or more races, non-Hispanic/Latino), 1 international. Average age 26. 35 applicants, 46% accepted, 9 enrolled. In 2016, 11 master's awarded. *Degree requirements:* For master's, comprehensive exam (for some programs), thesis (for some programs). *Entrance requirements:* For master's, GRE General Test. Additional exam requirements/recommendations for international students: Required—TOEFL (minimum score 550 paper-based; 80 iBT). *Application deadline:* For fall admission, 2/15 for domestic and international students; for spring admission, 10/15 for domestic and international students. Application fee: $60. Electronic applications accepted. *Expenses:* Contact institution. *Financial support:* In 2016–17, 25 students received support, including 18 teaching assistantships with full tuition reimbursements available (averaging $10,000 per year); research assistantships, health care benefits, tuition waivers (full and partial), and unspecified assistantships also available. Financial award application deadline: 2/15. *Faculty research:* Interpersonal communication, family communication, social networking, media history, media studies, media law, media ethics, mobile communications. *Unit head:* Dr. Daxton Stewart, Associate Dean, 817-257-5911, Fax: 817-257-5921, E-mail: d.stewart@tcu.edu. *Application contact:* Alicia E. Craff, Academic Program Specialist, 817-257-5917, Fax: 817-257-5921, E-mail: a.e.craff@tcu.edu. Website: http://www.schieffercollege.tcu.edu/

**Texas Southern University,** Tavis Smiley School of Communication, Houston, TX 77004-4584. Offers MA. *Program availability:* Part-time. *Degree requirements:* For master's, comprehensive exam, thesis. *Entrance requirements:* For master's, GRE General Test, minimum GPA of 2.5. Additional exam requirements/recommendations for international students: Required—TOEFL. Electronic applications accepted.

**Texas State University,** The Graduate College, College of Fine Arts and Communication, Program in Communication Studies, San Marcos, TX 78666. Offers MA. *Program availability:* Part-time, evening/weekend. *Faculty:* 11 full-time (9 women). *Students:* 46 full-time (27 women), 11 part-time (8 women); includes 24 minority (6 Black or African American, non-Hispanic/Latino; 16 Hispanic/Latino; 2 Two or more races, non-Hispanic/Latino), 2 international. Average age 27. 44 applicants, 77% accepted, 24 enrolled. In 2016, 18 master's awarded. *Degree requirements:* For master's, comprehensive exam, thesis optional. *Entrance requirements:* For master's, baccalaureate degree from regionally-accredited institution with minimum GPA of 3.2 in last 60 hours of undergraduate course work, 3 letters of recommendation, statement of purpose. Additional exam requirements/recommendations for international students: Required—TOEFL (minimum score 550 paper-based; 78 iBT), IELTS (minimum score 6.5). *Application deadline:* For fall admission, 3/1 priority date for domestic and international students; for spring admission, 10/15 priority date for domestic students, 10/1 priority date for international students; for summer admission, 3/1 for domestic and international students. Applications are processed on a rolling basis. Application fee: $40 ($90 for international students). Electronic applications accepted. *Expenses:* $4,851 per semester. *Financial support:* In 2016–17, 33 students received support, including 36 teaching assistantships (averaging $15,778 per year); research assistantships, career-related internships or fieldwork, Federal Work-Study, institutionally sponsored loans, scholarships/grants, and unspecified assistantships also available. Support available to part-time students. Financial award application deadline: 3/1; financial award applicants required to submit FAFSA. *Faculty research:* Risk perception, sense making and performance: sounds of wildland firefighting action; sexual health assessment and risk education; parent-child processes affecting long term post-disaster psycho-social adjustments. *Total annual research expenditures:* $438,615. *Unit head:* Dr. Maureen Keeley, Graduate Adviser, 512-245-3133, Fax: 512-245-3138, E-mail: mk09@txstate.edu. *Application contact:* Dr. Andrea Golato, Dean of Graduate School, 512-245-2581, Fax: 512-245-8365, E-mail: gradcollege@txstate.edu. Website: http://www.finearts.txstate.edu/commstudies

**Texas Tech University,** Graduate School, College of Media and Communication, Department of Communication Studies, Lubbock, TX 79409. Offers MA. *Program availability:* Part-time. *Faculty:* 7 full-time (5 women), 7 part-time/adjunct (4 women). *Students:* 13 full-time (8 women), 3 part-time (1 woman); includes 5 minority (1 Black or African American, non-Hispanic/Latino; 4 Hispanic/Latino). Average age 27. 33 applicants, 39% accepted, 3 enrolled. In 2016, 5 master's awarded. *Degree requirements:* For master's, comprehensive exam (for some programs), thesis or alternative, 33 hours. *Entrance requirements:* For master's, GRE (only if GPA is under 3.0), minimum undergraduate GPA of 3.0. Additional exam requirements/recommendations for international students: Required—TOEFL (minimum score 550 paper-based; 79 iBT). *Application deadline:* For fall admission, 6/1 priority date for domestic students, 1/15 priority date for international students; for spring admission, 9/1 priority date for domestic students, 6/15 priority date for international students. Applications are processed on a rolling basis. Application fee: $75. Electronic applications accepted. *Expenses:* $315 per credit hour full-time resident tuition, $723 per credit hour full-time non-resident tuition; $50.50 per credit hour fee plus $608 per term fee. *Financial support:* In 2016–17, 7 students received support, including 7 fellowships (averaging $3,668 per year); teaching assistantships and unspecified assistantships also available. Financial award application deadline: 4/15; financial award applicants required to submit FAFSA. *Faculty research:* Organizational communication, interpersonal communication, instructional communication, intercultural communication, rhetoric and public affairs, media studies. *Unit head:* Dr. Brian L. Ott, Professor/Chair, 806-834-2928, E-mail: brian.ott@ttu.edu. *Application contact:* Dr. Mark A. Gring, Associate Professor/Assistant Graduate Director for the College of Media and Communication, 806-843-3913, E-mail: mark.gring@ttu.edu. Website: http://www.depts.ttu.edu/comc/programs/commstudies/

**Tiffin University,** Program in Humanities, Tiffin, OH 44883-2161. Offers art and visual media (MH); communication (MH); creative writing (MH); English (MH); film studies (MH); humanities (MH); individualized studies (MH). *Program availability:* Part-time, evening/weekend, online only, 100% online, blended/hybrid learning. *Students:* 17 full-time (15 women), 116 part-time (75 women); includes 25 minority (15 Black or African American, non-Hispanic/Latino; 2 Asian, non-Hispanic/Latino; 6 Hispanic/Latino; 2 Two or more races, non-Hispanic/Latino). Average age 36. 84 applicants, 80% accepted, 43 enrolled. In 2016, 42 master's awarded. *Entrance requirements:* For master's, work experience. Additional exam requirements/recommendations for international students: Required—TOEFL (minimum score 550 paper-based; 79 iBT). *Application deadline:* For fall admission, 9/1 for domestic students; for spring admission, 1/9 for domestic students. Applications are processed on a rolling basis. Application fee: $50. Electronic applications accepted. Application fee is waived when completed online. *Expenses:* Contact institution. *Financial support:* Unspecified assistantships available. Financial award applicants required to submit FAFSA. *Unit head:* Dr. Jason Slone, Program Chair, 419-448-5851, Fax: 419-443-5002, E-mail: slonedj@tiffin.edu. *Application contact:* Nikki Hintze, Director of Graduate and Distance Education Academic Advising, 800-968-6446 Ext. 3596, Fax: 419-443-5002, E-mail: hintzenm@tiffin.edu.

**Towson University,** Program in Communications Management, Towson, MD 21252-0001. Offers MS. *Students:* 3 full-time (2 women), 18 part-time (14 women); includes 6 minority (all Black or African American, non-Hispanic/Latino). *Degree requirements:* For master's, thesis. *Entrance requirements:* For master's, bachelor's degree with 24 credits in mass communications, public relations, advertising or communication studies; advanced writing and basic statistics courses; professional experience; minimum GPA of 3.0; letter of recommendation; resume. Additional exam requirements/recommendations for international students: Required—TOEFL. *Application deadline:* For fall admission, 1/15 for domestic students. Application fee: $45. Electronic applications accepted. *Expenses:* Tuition, state resident: full-time $7580; part-time $379 per unit. Tuition, nonresident: full-time $15,700; part-time $785 per unit. *Required fees:* $2480. *Financial support:* Application deadline: 4/1. *Unit head:* Dr. Beth Haller, Graduate Program Director, 410-704-2442, E-mail: bhaller@towson.edu. *Application contact:* Coverley Beidleman, Assistant Director of Graduate Admissions, 410-704-2113, Fax: 410-704-3030, E-mail: grads@towson.edu. Website: http://www.towson.edu/cofac/departments/communication/gradcommunicationmgmt/

**Trinity Washington University,** School of Business and Graduate Studies, Washington, DC 20017-1094. Offers business administration (MBA); communication (MA); international security studies (MA); organizational management (MSA), including federal program management, human resource management, nonprofit management, organizational development, public and community health. *Program availability:* Part-time, evening/weekend. *Degree requirements:* For master's, thesis (for some programs), capstone project (MSA). *Entrance requirements:* For master's, minimum GPA of 2.5. Additional exam requirements/recommendations for international students: Required—TOEFL (minimum score 550 paper-based).

**Troy University,** Graduate School, College of Communication and Fine Arts, Troy, AL 36082. Offers strategic communication (MS). *Program availability:* Part-time, evening/weekend. *Faculty:* 6 full-time (3 women). *Students:* 35 full-time (24 women), 58 part-time

## Communication—General

(42 women); includes 68 minority (30 Black or African American, non-Hispanic/Latino; 2 Hispanic/Latino; 1 Native Hawaiian or other Pacific Islander, non-Hispanic/Latino; 35 Two or more races, non-Hispanic/Latino). Average age 29. 52 applicants, 100% accepted, 24 enrolled. In 2016, 58 master's awarded. *Degree requirements:* For master's, comprehensive exam, thesis optional, minimum GPA of 3.0, admission to candidacy. *Entrance requirements:* For master's, GRE (minimum score of 850 on old exam or 290 on new exam), MAT (minimum score of 385) or GMAT (minimum score of 380), bachelor's degree; minimum undergraduate GPA of 2.5 or 3.0 on last 30 semester hours. Additional exam requirements/recommendations for international students: Required—TOEFL (minimum score 523 paper-based; 70 iBT), IELTS (minimum score 6). *Application deadline:* For fall admission, 6/1 for international students; for spring admission, 10/15 for international students. Applications are processed on a rolling basis. Application fee: $50. Electronic applications accepted. *Expenses:* Tuition, state resident: full-time $7146; part-time $397 per credit hour. Tuition, nonresident: full-time $14,292; part-time $794 per credit hour. *Required fees:* $802; $50 per semester. Tuition and fees vary according to campus/location and program. *Financial support:* Fellowships, career-related internships or fieldwork, and scholarships/grants available. Support available to part-time students. Financial award applicants required to submit FAFSA. *Unit head:* Dr. Larry Blocher, Dean, 334-670-3869, Fax: 334-670-3547, E-mail: lblocher@troy.edu. *Application contact:* Jessica A. Kimbro, Director of Graduate Admissions, 334-670-3178, E-mail: jacord@troy.edu.

**Université de Montréal,** Faculty of Arts and Sciences, Department of Communication, Montréal, QC H3C 3J7, Canada. Offers communication (PhD); communication sciences (M Sc). *Degree requirements:* For master's, thesis; for doctorate, one foreign language, thesis/dissertation, general exam. *Entrance requirements:* For doctorate, proficiency in French. Electronic applications accepted. *Faculty research:* Mass media/new communication technologies, organizational communication.

**Université du Québec à Montréal,** Graduate Programs, Program in Communications, Montréal, QC H3C 3P8, Canada. Offers MA, PhD. PhD offered jointly with Concordia University and Université de Montréal. *Program availability:* Part-time. *Degree requirements:* For master's, thesis; for doctorate, thesis/dissertation. *Entrance requirements:* For master's, appropriate bachelor's degree or equivalent, proficiency in French; for doctorate, appropriate master's degree or equivalent, proficiency in French.

**Université du Québec à Trois-Rivières,** Graduate Programs, Program in Social Communication, Trois-Rivières, QC G9A 5H7, Canada. Offers MA, DESS.

**University at Albany, State University of New York,** College of Arts and Sciences, Department of Communication, Albany, NY 12222-0001. Offers communication (MA); sociology and communication (PhD). *Program availability:* Part-time. *Faculty:* 15 full-time (6 women), 26 part-time/adjunct (16 women). *Students:* 25 full-time (19 women), 33 part-time (21 women); includes 13 minority (8 Black or African American, non-Hispanic/Latino; 2 Asian, non-Hispanic/Latino; 2 Hispanic/Latino; 1 Two or more races, non-Hispanic/Latino), 12 international. 70 applicants, 56% accepted, 16 enrolled. In 2016, 21 master's awarded. *Degree requirements:* For master's, comprehensive exam, thesis or alternative; for doctorate, comprehensive exam, thesis/dissertation. *Entrance requirements:* For master's, minimum GPA of 3.0; for doctorate, GRE, minimum GPA of 3.0. Additional exam requirements/recommendations for international students: Required—TOEFL (minimum score 550 paper-based). *Application deadline:* For fall admission, 2/20 priority date for domestic students, 5/1 for international students. Applications are processed on a rolling basis. Application fee: $75. Electronic applications accepted. *Expenses:* Tuition, state resident: full-time $10,870; part-time $453 per credit hour. Tuition, nonresident: full-time $22,210; part-time $925 per credit hour. *International tuition:* $21,550 full-time. *Required fees:* $1864; $96 per credit hour. *Financial support:* Fellowships, teaching assistantships, career-related internships or fieldwork, and institutionally sponsored loans available. Financial award application deadline: 3/1. *Faculty research:* Language and social interaction, campaign communication, media agenda-setting, high-speed management, organizational boundary-spanning. *Total annual research expenditures:* $25,868. *Unit head:* Annis Golden, Chair, 518-442-4871, Fax: 518-442-3884, E-mail: agolden@albany.edu. *Application contact:* Michael DeRensis, Director, Graduate Admissions, 518-442-3980, Fax: 518-442-3922, E-mail: graduate@albany.edu. Website: http://www.albany.edu/communication/

**University at Buffalo, the State University of New York,** Graduate School, College of Arts and Sciences, Department of Communication, Buffalo, NY 14260. Offers MA, PhD. Terminal master's awarded for partial completion of doctoral program. *Degree requirements:* For master's, thesis; for doctorate, comprehensive exam, thesis/dissertation. *Entrance requirements:* For master's and doctorate, GRE General Test, minimum GPA of 3.0. Additional exam requirements/recommendations for international students: Required—TOEFL (minimum score 600 paper-based; 100 iBT); Recommended—TWE. Electronic applications accepted. *Faculty research:* Technology, health.

**The University of Akron,** Graduate School, Buchtel College of Arts and Sciences, School of Communication, Akron, OH 44325. Offers MA. *Program availability:* Part-time, evening/weekend. *Faculty:* 12 full-time (6 women). *Students:* 11 full-time (8 women), 3 part-time (2 women); includes 2 minority (both Black or African American, non-Hispanic/Latino), 3 international. Average age 27. 8 applicants, 100% accepted, 7 enrolled. In 2016, 13 master's awarded. *Degree requirements:* For master's, thesis, project or written comprehensive exam. *Entrance requirements:* For master's, baccalaureate degree in communication, journalism, or a related field; three letters of recommendation; statement of purpose; resume. Additional exam requirements/recommendations for international students: Required—TOEFL (minimum score 550 paper-based; 79 iBT), IELTS (minimum score 6.5). *Application deadline:* For fall admission, 5/1 for domestic and international students. Application fee: $45 ($70 for international students). Electronic applications accepted. *Expenses:* Tuition, state resident: full-time $8618; part-time $359 per credit hour. Tuition, nonresident: full-time $17,149; part-time $715 per credit hour. *Required fees:* $1652. *Financial support:* In 2016–17, 6 teaching assistantships with full tuition reimbursements were awarded; instructional support assistantships also available. *Faculty research:* Communications theory, business and organization communications, criticism of communications, film and video studies, interpersonal and intercultural communications. *Total annual research expenditures:* $41,020. *Unit head:* Dr. Theodore Avtgis, Director, 330-972-7600, E-mail: tavtgis@uakron.edu. *Application contact:* Dr. Tang Tang, Graduate Director, 330-972-7606, E-mail: tang@uakron.edu. Website: http://www.uakron.edu/schlcomm/

**The University of Alabama,** Graduate School, College of Communication and Information Sciences, Tuscaloosa, AL 35487-0172. Offers MA, MFA, MLIS, PhD. *Accreditation:* ACEJMC (one or more programs are accredited at the [master's] level). *Faculty:* 61 full-time (28 women), 1 (woman) part-time/adjunct. *Students:* 131 full-time (83 women), 194 part-time (150 women); includes 49 minority (24 Black or African American, non-Hispanic/Latino; 1 American Indian or Alaska Native, non-Hispanic/Latino; 3 Asian, non-Hispanic/Latino; 12 Hispanic/Latino; 9 Two or more races, non-Hispanic/Latino), 31 international. Average age 32. 277 applicants, 61% accepted, 132 enrolled. In 2016, 139 master's, 8 doctorates awarded. *Degree requirements:* For master's, comprehensive exam, thesis or alternative; for doctorate, comprehensive

exam, thesis/dissertation. *Entrance requirements:* For master's, GRE; for doctorate, GRE, minimum graduate GPA of 3.0, master's degree. Additional exam requirements/recommendations for international students: Required—TOEFL (minimum score 600 paper-based; 100 iBT). *Application deadline:* For fall admission, 2/15 priority date for domestic and international students; for winter admission, 11/1 priority date for international students; for spring admission, 11/1 priority date for domestic students. Applications are processed on a rolling basis. Application fee: $50 ($60 for international students). Electronic applications accepted. *Expenses:* Tuition, state resident: full-time $10,470. Tuition, nonresident: full-time $26,950. *Financial support:* Fellowships with tuition reimbursements, research assistantships with tuition reimbursements, teaching assistantships with tuition reimbursements, institutionally sponsored loans, health care benefits, and unspecified assistantships available. Financial award application deadline: 2/15. *Faculty research:* Mass media research; media effects; information studies; cultural, critical, and rhetorical studies; electronic media; law and policy. *Total annual research expenditures:* $19,729. *Unit head:* Dr. Mark Nelson, Dean, 205-348-4787, E-mail: mnelson@ua.edu. *Application contact:* Marylou Cox, Information Contact, 205-348-8593, Fax: 205-348-6774, E-mail: mcox@ua.edu. Website: http://www.cis.ua.edu

**The University of Alabama at Birmingham,** College of Arts and Sciences, Program in Communication Management, Birmingham, AL 35294. Offers MA. *Program availability:* Part-time, evening/weekend. Terminal master's awarded for partial completion of doctoral program. *Degree requirements:* For master's, comprehensive exam, thesis or alternative. *Entrance requirements:* For master's, GRE (recommended) or MAT, minimum undergraduate GPA of 3.0, letters of reference. Additional exam requirements/recommendations for international students: Required—TOEFL (minimum score 550 paper-based; 80 iBT), IELTS (minimum score 6.5). Electronic applications accepted. Full-time tuition and fees vary according to course load and program. *Faculty research:* Deception, political communication, nonverbal communication, virtual world, game theory.

**University of Alaska Fairbanks,** College of Liberal Arts, Department of Communications, Fairbanks, AK 99775-5680. Offers professional communication (MA). *Program availability:* Part-time. *Faculty:* 7 full-time (2 women). *Students:* 8 full-time (6 women), 6 part-time (2 women); includes 5 minority (2 Black or African American, non-Hispanic/Latino; 1 Hispanic/Latino; 2 Two or more races, non-Hispanic/Latino), 2 international. Average age 33. 8 applicants, 50% accepted, 4 enrolled. In 2016, 2 master's awarded. *Degree requirements:* For master's, comprehensive exam, thesis, oral defense of thesis. *Entrance requirements:* For master's, bachelor's degree from accredited institution with minimum cumulative undergraduate and major GPA of 3.0, academic writing sample. Additional exam requirements/recommendations for international students: Required—TOEFL (minimum score 550 paper-based; 79 iBT), IELTS (minimum score 6.5). *Application deadline:* For fall admission, 6/1 for domestic students, 3/1 for international students; for spring admission, 10/15 for domestic students, 9/1 for international students. Applications are processed on a rolling basis. Application fee: $60. Electronic applications accepted. *Expenses:* Tuition, state resident: full-time $7992; part-time $444 per credit. Tuition, nonresident: full-time $16,326; part-time $907 per credit. *Required fees:* $39 per credit. $322 per semester. Tuition and fees vary according to course level, course load, campus/location, program and reciprocity agreements. *Financial support:* In 2016–17, 7 teaching assistantships with full tuition reimbursements (averaging $6,542 per year) were awarded; fellowships with full tuition reimbursements, Federal Work-Study, scholarships/grants, tuition waivers, and unspecified assistantships also available. Support available to part-time students. Financial award application deadline: 7/1; financial award applicants required to submit FAFSA. *Faculty research:* Interpersonal communications, health communications, intercultural communications, politeness and face management in conversation, gender communication. *Unit head:* Dr. Peter DeCaro, Department Chair, 907-474-6591, Fax: 907-474-5858, E-mail: fycomm@uaf.edu. *Application contact:* Mary Kreta, Director of Admissions, 907-474-7500, Fax: 907-474-7097, E-mail: admissions@uaf.edu. Website: http://www.uaf.edu/comm/

**University of Alberta,** Faculty of Extension, Edmonton, AB T6G 2E1, Canada. Offers communications and technology (MA).

**University of Alberta,** Faculty of Graduate Studies and Research, Program in Communications and Technology, Edmonton, AB T6G 2E1, Canada. Offers MACT.

**The University of Arizona,** College of Social and Behavioral Sciences, Department of Communication, Tucson, AZ 85721. Offers MA, PhD. *Program availability:* Part-time. Terminal master's awarded for partial completion of doctoral program. *Degree requirements:* For master's, thesis optional; for doctorate, comprehensive exam, thesis/dissertation. *Entrance requirements:* For master's, GRE General Test, minimum GPA of 3.25, writing sample, 3 letters of recommendation; for doctorate, GRE General Test, minimum GPA of 3.5, writing sample, 3 letters of recommendation, statement of purpose. Additional exam requirements/recommendations for international students: Required—TOEFL (minimum score 600 paper-based; 90 iBT). Electronic applications accepted. *Faculty research:* Health communication, new communication technologies.

**University of Arkansas,** Graduate School, J. William Fulbright College of Arts and Sciences, Department of Communication, Fayetteville, AR 72701. Offers MA. *Program availability:* Part-time. In 2016, 12 master's awarded. *Degree requirements:* For master's, thesis. *Entrance requirements:* For master's, GRE General Test. *Application deadline:* For fall admission, 4/1 for international students; for spring admission, 10/1 for international students. Applications are processed on a rolling basis. Application fee: $40 ($50 for international students). Electronic applications accepted. *Financial support:* In 2016–17, 21 teaching assistantships were awarded; fellowships, research assistantships, career-related internships or fieldwork, and Federal Work-Study also available. Support available to part-time students. Financial award application deadline: 4/1; financial award applicants required to submit FAFSA. *Unit head:* Dr. Robert Brady, Department Chairperson, 479-575-3046, Fax: 479-575-6734, E-mail: rbrady@uark.edu. *Application contact:* Dr. Myria Allen, Graduate Coordinator, 479-575-5952, E-mail: myria@uark.edu. Website: http://www.uark.edu/depts/comm/

**University of Bridgeport,** College of Public and International Affairs, Bridgeport, CT 06604. Offers East Asian and Pacific Rim studies (MA); global development and peace (MA); global media and communication studies (MA). *Program availability:* Part-time, evening/weekend. *Degree requirements:* For master's, thesis. *Entrance requirements:* Additional exam requirements/recommendations for international students: Recommended—TOEFL (minimum score 550 paper-based; 80 iBT), IELTS (minimum score 6.5).

**University of Calgary,** Faculty of Graduate Studies, Faculty of Arts, Department of Communication and Culture, Calgary, AB T2N 1N4, Canada. Offers MA, MCS, PhD. *Program availability:* Part-time, evening/weekend. *Degree requirements:* For master's, project (MCS), thesis (MA); for doctorate, thesis/dissertation. *Entrance requirements:* For master's, minimum GPA of 3.0; for doctorate, master's degree, minimum GPA of 3.0, BA degree, min GPA of 3.0. Additional exam requirements/recommendations for international students: Required—TOEFL (minimum score 600 paper-based);

Recommended—IELTS (minimum score 8). Electronic applications accepted. *Faculty research:* Science communications, structuration theory, organizational communication, communication theory, media law.

**University of California, Davis,** Graduate Studies, Program in Communication, Davis, CA 95616. Offers MA. *Degree requirements:* For master's, comprehensive exam (for some programs), thesis (for some programs). *Entrance requirements:* For master's, GRE. Additional exam requirements/recommendations for international students: Required—TOEFL (minimum score 550 paper-based).

**University of California, San Diego,** Graduate Division, Department of Communication, La Jolla, CA 92093. Offers PhD. *Students:* 41 full-time (27 women). 96 applicants, 13% accepted, 6 enrolled. In 2016, 11 doctorates awarded. *Degree requirements:* For doctorate, one foreign language, comprehensive exam, thesis/dissertation, 3 quarters of teaching assistantship. *Entrance requirements:* For doctorate, GRE General Test, demonstrated competence in a natural language other than English, writing samples, letters of recommendation. Additional exam requirements/recommendations for international students: Required—TOEFL (minimum score 550 paper-based; 80 iBT), IELTS (minimum score 7), PTE. *Application deadline:* For fall admission, 1/12 for domestic students. Application fee: $105 ($125 for international students). Electronic applications accepted. *Expenses:* Tuition, state resident: full-time $11,220. Tuition, nonresident: full-time $26,322. *Required fees:* $1864. *Financial support:* Fellowships, research assistantships, teaching assistantships, and scholarships/grants available. Financial award applicants required to submit FAFSA. *Faculty research:* Communication and culture, communication as a social force, communication and the person, communications and science and technology studies, digital media, political communication and journalism studies, language, cognition, media systems. *Unit head:* Valerie Hartouni, Chair, 858-534-2366, E-mail: vhartouni@ucsd.edu. *Application contact:* Graduate Coordinator, 858-534-2379, E-mail: comm-gradadmit@ucsd.edu.
Website: http://communication.ucsd.edu

**University of California, Santa Barbara,** Graduate Division, College of Letters and Sciences, Division of Social Sciences, Department of Communication, Santa Barbara, CA 93106-4020. Offers cognitive science (PhD); communication (PhD); feminist studies (PhD); language, interaction and social organization (PhD); quantitative methods in the social sciences (PhD); society and technology (PhD); MA/PhD. Terminal master's awarded for partial completion of doctoral program. *Degree requirements:* For doctorate, comprehensive exam, thesis/dissertation. *Entrance requirements:* For doctorate, GRE. Additional exam requirements/recommendations for international students: Required—TOEFL (minimum score 80 iBT), IELTS (minimum score 7). Electronic applications accepted. *Faculty research:* Interpersonal, intergroup, intercultural, organizational, health, media.

**University of California, Santa Cruz,** Division of Graduate Studies, Division of Physical and Biological Sciences, Program in Science Communication, Santa Cruz, CA 95064. Offers Certificate. *Entrance requirements:* For degree, GRE General Test, GRE Subject Test, bachelor's degree in science. Additional exam requirements/recommendations for international students: Required—TOEFL (minimum score 550 paper-based; 83 iBT); Recommended—IELTS (minimum score 8). Electronic applications accepted. *Faculty research:* Science writing.

**University of Central Florida,** College of Sciences, Nicholson School of Communication, Orlando, FL 32816. Offers communication (MA); corporate communication (Certificate). *Program availability:* Part-time, evening/weekend. *Faculty:* 46 full-time (21 women), 17 part-time/adjunct (11 women). *Students:* 34 full-time (24 women), 21 part-time (16 women); includes 19 minority (7 Black or African American, non-Hispanic/Latino; 10 Hispanic/Latino; 2 Two or more races, non-Hispanic/Latino), 11 international. Average age 27. 41 applicants, 83% accepted, 22 enrolled. In 2016, 26 master's, 12 other advanced degrees awarded. *Degree requirements:* For master's, thesis or alternative. *Entrance requirements:* For master's, GRE General Test, minimum GPA of 3.0 in last 60 hours of course work. Additional exam requirements/recommendations for international students: Required—TOEFL. *Application deadline:* For fall admission, 6/1 for domestic students; for spring admission, 11/1 for domestic students. Application fee: $30. Electronic applications accepted. *Expenses:* Tuition, state resident: part-time $288.16 per credit hour. Tuition, nonresident: part-time $1071.31 per credit hour. *Financial support:* In 2016–17, 20 students received support, including 1 fellowship with partial tuition reimbursement available (averaging $4,000 per year), 5 research assistantships with partial tuition reimbursements available (averaging $6,742 per year), 15 teaching assistantships with partial tuition reimbursements available (averaging $9,141 per year); career-related internships or fieldwork, Federal Work-Study, institutionally sponsored loans, tuition waivers (partial), and unspecified assistantships also available. Financial award application deadline: 3/1; financial award applicants required to submit FAFSA. *Faculty research:* Persuasion, interpersonal communication, nonverbal communication, conflict resolution. *Unit head:* Dr. Arlen Chase, Acting Director, 407-823-2316, E-mail: arlen.chase@ucf.edu. *Application contact:* Assistant Director, Graduate Admissions, 407-823-2766, Fax: 407-823-6442, E-mail: gradadmissions@ucf.edu.
Website: http://communication.cos.ucf.edu/

**University of Central Missouri,** The Graduate School, Warrensburg, MO 64093. Offers accountancy (MA); accounting (MBA); applied mathematics (MS); aviation safety (MA); biology (MS); business administration (MBA); career and technical education leadership (MS); college student personnel administration (MS); communication (MA); computer science (MS); counseling (MS); criminal justice (MS); educational leadership (Ed D); educational technology (MS); elementary and early childhood education (MSE); English (MA); environmental studies (MA); finance (MBA); history (MA); human services/educational technology (Ed S); human services/learning resources (Ed S); human services/professional counseling (Ed S); industrial hygiene (MS); industrial management (MS); information systems (MBA); information technology (MS); kinesiology (MS); library science and information services (MS); literacy education (MSE); marketing (MBA); mathematics (MS); music (MA); occupational safety management (MS); psychology (MS); rural family nursing (MS); school administration (MSE); social gerontology (MS); sociology (MA); special education (MSE); speech language pathology (MS); superintendency (Ed S); teaching (MAT); teaching English as a second language (MA); technology (MS); technology management (PhD); theatre (MA). *Program availability:* Part-time, 100% online, blended/hybrid learning. *Degree requirements:* For master's and Ed S, comprehensive exam (for some programs), thesis (for some programs). *Entrance requirements:* Additional exam requirements/recommendations for international students: Required—TOEFL (minimum score 550 paper-based; 79 iBT). Electronic applications accepted.

**University of Cincinnati,** Graduate School, McMicken College of Arts and Sciences, Department of Communication, Cincinnati, OH 45221. Offers MA. *Program availability:* Part-time. *Degree requirements:* For master's, comprehensive exam, thesis or alternative. *Entrance requirements:* For master's, GRE General Test, undergraduate course work in communication. Additional exam requirements/recommendations for international students: Required—TOEFL. Electronic applications accepted. *Expenses:* Tuition, area resident: Full-time $12,790; part-time $389 per credit hour. Tuition, state resident: full-time $13,290; part-time $419 per credit hour. Tuition, nonresident: full-time

$24,532; part-time $976 per credit hour. *International tuition:* $24,832 full-time. *Required fees:* $3958; $140 per credit hour. Tuition and fees vary according to course load, degree level, program and reciprocity agreements. *Faculty research:* Political communication, health communication, organizational communication, interpersonal communication.

**University of Colorado Boulder,** Graduate School, College of Media, Communication and Information, Program in Communication, Boulder, CO 80309. Offers MA, PhD. *Faculty:* 18 full-time (10 women). *Students:* 54 full-time (33 women), 3 part-time (2 women); includes 4 minority (1 Black or African American, non-Hispanic/Latino; 3 Hispanic/Latino), 4 international. Average age 30. 69 applicants, 23% accepted, 13 enrolled. In 2016, 12 master's, 12 doctorates awarded. Terminal master's awarded for partial completion of doctoral program. *Degree requirements:* For master's, comprehensive exam, thesis optional; for doctorate, comprehensive exam, thesis/dissertation. *Entrance requirements:* For master's and doctorate, GRE General Test, minimum undergraduate GPA of 3.2. *Application deadline:* For fall admission, 12/10 for domestic students, 12/1 for international students; for spring admission, 9/15 for domestic students, 8/15 for international students. Applications are processed on a rolling basis. Application fee: $60 ($80 for international students). Electronic applications accepted. Application fee is waived when completed online. *Financial support:* In 2016–17, 184 students received support, including 47 fellowships (averaging $1,150 per year), 21 research assistantships with full and partial tuition reimbursements available (averaging $25,515 per year), 44 teaching assistantships with full and partial tuition reimbursements available (averaging $36,083 per year); institutionally sponsored loans, scholarships/grants, health care benefits, and unspecified assistantships also available. Financial award application deadline: 12/15; financial award applicants required to submit FAFSA. *Faculty research:* Communications, organizational theory and behavior, culture, ethnography, democracy. *Total annual research expenditures:* $66,373. *Application contact:* E-mail: larry.frey@colorado.edu.
Website: http://www.colorado.edu/communication/

**University of Colorado Colorado Springs,** College of Letters, Arts and Sciences, Department of Communication, Colorado Springs, CO 80918. Offers MA. *Program availability:* Part-time, blended/hybrid learning. *Faculty:* 7 full-time (5 women), 5 part-time/adjunct (4 women). *Students:* 6 full-time (5 women), 19 part-time (10 women); includes 5 minority (2 Hispanic/Latino; 3 Two or more races, non-Hispanic/Latino). Average age 35. 15 applicants, 73% accepted, 8 enrolled. In 2016, 13 master's awarded. *Degree requirements:* For master's, thesis optional. *Entrance requirements:* For master's, GRE. Additional exam requirements/recommendations for international students: Recommended—TOEFL (minimum score 550 paper-based; 80 iBT), IELTS (minimum score 6.5). *Application deadline:* Applications are processed on a rolling basis. Application fee: $60 ($100 for international students). Electronic applications accepted. *Expenses:* Tuition, state resident: full-time $9983. Tuition, nonresident: full-time $20,153. Tuition and fees vary according to course load, degree level, program and reciprocity agreements. *Financial support:* In 2016–17, 11 students received support. Career-related internships or fieldwork, Federal Work-Study, scholarships/grants, and unspecified assistantships available. Support available to part-time students. Financial award application deadline: 3/1; financial award applicants required to submit FAFSA. *Faculty research:* Instructional communication, popular culture, strategic communication efforts in public relations, the impact of gender and culture on leadership behavior, leadership succession, organizational trust, intercultural communication, psychological and social effects of media, organizational communication. *Unit head:* Dr. Chris Bell, Director of Graduate Studies, 719-255-8193, Fax: 719-255-4030, E-mail: cbell3@uccs.edu. *Application contact:* Debbie MacDonald, Program Assistant, 719-255-4114, Fax: 719-255-4030, E-mail: debbie.macdonald@uccs.edu.
Website: http://www.uccs.edu/comm/

**University of Colorado Denver,** College of Liberal Arts and Sciences, Department of Communication, Denver, CO 80217. Offers MA. *Program availability:* Part-time, evening/weekend. *Faculty:* 10 full-time (6 women). *Students:* 16 full-time (all women), 7 part-time (4 women); includes 6 minority (2 Black or African American, non-Hispanic/Latino; 1 Hispanic/Latino; 3 Two or more races, non-Hispanic/Latino). Average age 30. 18 applicants, 83% accepted, 7 enrolled. In 2016, 8 master's awarded. *Degree requirements:* For master's, comprehensive exam, 33 credits; thesis or substantial writing project. *Entrance requirements:* For master's, GRE General Test (minimum score of 153) or LSAT (minimum score of 150), minimum undergraduate GPA of 3.25, three letters of recommendation, two official transcripts, resume, academic writing sample. Additional exam requirements/recommendations for international students: Required—TOEFL (minimum score 80 iBT); Recommended—IELTS (minimum score 6.5). *Application deadline:* For fall admission, 2/1 for domestic students, 1/1 priority date for international students; for spring admission, 10/1 for domestic students, 9/1 priority date for international students. Application fee: $50 ($75 for international students). Electronic applications accepted. *Expenses:* Tuition, state resident: full-time $11,006; part-time $474 per credit. Tuition, nonresident: full-time $28,212; part-time $1264 per credit hour. *Required fees:* $256 per semester. One-time fee: $94.32. Tuition and fees vary according to campus/location and program. *Financial support:* In 2016–17, 8 students received support. Fellowships, research assistantships, teaching assistantships, Federal Work-Study, institutionally sponsored loans, scholarships/grants, and traineeships available. Financial award application deadline: 4/1; financial award applicants required to submit FAFSA. *Faculty research:* Diversity, difference, and intercultural communication; health communication/medical rhetoric; organizational communication; rhetoric and public affairs; social justice and civic engagement. *Unit head:* Dr. Stephen Hartnett, Professor and Department Chair, 303-315-1914, E-mail: stephen.hartnett@ucdenver.edu. *Application contact:* Michelle Medal, Program Assistant, 303-315-1919, E-mail: michelle.medal@ucdenver.edu.
Website: http://www.ucdenver.edu/academics/colleges/CLAS/Departments/communication/Programs/Masters/Pages/Overview.aspx

**University of Connecticut,** Graduate School, College of Liberal Arts and Sciences, Department of Communication Sciences, Program in Communication Processes, Storrs, CT 06269. Offers MA. *Degree requirements:* For master's, comprehensive exam. *Entrance requirements:* For master's, GRE General Test. Additional exam requirements/recommendations for international students: Required—TOEFL (minimum score 550 paper-based). Electronic applications accepted.

**University of Dayton,** Department of Communication, Dayton, OH 45469. Offers communication (MA); interdisciplinary communication (MA). *Program availability:* Part-time, evening/weekend. *Faculty:* 11 full-time (5 women). *Students:* 15 full-time (13 women), 3 part-time (2 women); includes 1 minority (Black or African American, non-Hispanic/Latino), 3 international. Average age 33. 58 applicants, 33% accepted, 10 enrolled. In 2016, 22 master's awarded. *Degree requirements:* For master's, comprehensive exam, thesis optional, 36 credit hours of course work. *Entrance requirements:* For master's, GRE, minimum undergraduate GPA of 3.0, 3 letters of recommendation, personal statement, curriculum vitae/resume, transcripts, writing samples (if applying for a graduate assistantship). Additional exam requirements/recommendations for international students: Required—TOEFL (minimum score 550 paper-based; 80 iBT). *Application deadline:* Applications are processed on a rolling basis. Application fee: $0 ($50 for international students). Electronic applications

## Communication—General

accepted. *Expenses:* $15,750. *Financial support:* In 2016–17, 7 students received support, including 1 research assistantship with full tuition reimbursement available (averaging $10,914 per year), 8 teaching assistantships with full tuition reimbursements available (averaging $10,914 per year); institutionally sponsored loans, health care benefits, and unspecified assistantships also available. Financial award application deadline: 3/9; financial award applicants required to submit FAFSA. *Faculty research:* Public relations and international public relations; tourism public relations, hospitality and tourism management; social influence theory; media effects; media use; health communication; media portrayals; gender and communication; rhetoric, religious communication; political communication, pedagogy; interactive technologies; media policy; family communication. *Unit head:* Dr. Jon A. Hess, Chair, 937-229-2028, E-mail: jhess1@udayton.edu. *Application contact:* Dr. JeeHee Han, Graduate Program Director, 937-229-2486, E-mail: jhan01@udayton.edu.
Website: https://www.udayton.edu/artssciences/academics/communication/welcome/index.php

**University of Delaware,** College of Arts and Sciences, Department of Communication, Newark, DE 19716. Offers MA. *Program availability:* Part-time, evening/weekend. *Degree requirements:* For master's, comprehensive exam (for some programs), thesis (for some programs). *Entrance requirements:* For master's, GRE General Test, minimum GPA of 3.0. Additional exam requirements/recommendations for international students: Required—TOEFL (minimum score 600 paper-based). Electronic applications accepted. *Faculty research:* Politics and the media, online social interaction technologies, mass communication law, media and the perceptions of reality, the role of communication in public opinion processes, small group research, communication during resource dilemmas.

**University of Denver,** Division of Arts, Humanities and Social Sciences, Department of Communication Studies, Denver, CO 80208. Offers culture and communication (MA, PhD); interpersonal and family communication (MA, PhD); rhetoric and communication ethics (MA, PhD). *Program availability:* Part-time. *Faculty:* 11 full-time (7 women), 1 (woman) part-time/adjunct. *Students:* 19 full-time (13 women), 11 part-time (9 women); includes 10 minority (2 Black or African American, non-Hispanic/Latino; 1 Asian, non-Hispanic/Latino; 6 Hispanic/Latino; 1 Two or more races, non-Hispanic/Latino), 4 international. Average age 33. 62 applicants, 37% accepted, 7 enrolled. In 2016, 2 master's, 3 doctorates awarded. *Degree requirements:* For master's, comprehensive exam (for some programs), thesis (for some programs), comprehensive exam or thesis; for doctorate, one foreign language, thesis/dissertation. *Entrance requirements:* For master's, GRE General Test, bachelor's degree in communication or a related field, transcripts, essay, resume or curriculum vitae, three letters of recommendation; for doctorate, GRE General Test, bachelor's or master's degree in communication or related field, transcripts, essay, resume or curriculum vitae, three letters of recommendation. Additional exam requirements/recommendations for international students: Required—TOEFL (minimum score 570 paper-based; 88 iBT). *Application deadline:* For fall admission, 12/15 priority date for domestic and international students; for winter admission, 3/15 priority date for domestic and international students; for spring admission, 6/15 priority date for domestic and international students. Applications are processed on a rolling basis. Application fee: $65. Electronic applications accepted. *Expenses:* $29,022 per year full-time. *Financial support:* In 2016–17, 25 received support, including 8 teaching assistantships with tuition reimbursements available (averaging $17,500 per year); career-related internships or fieldwork, Federal Work-Study, institutionally sponsored loans, scholarships/grants, and unspecified assistantships also available. Support available to part-time students. Financial award application deadline: 2/15; financial award applicants required to submit FAFSA. *Faculty research:* Successful community collaborative efforts, long-term marriages, cross-ethnic friendships, public dialogue about environmental risk, women's international cooperation. *Unit head:* Dr. Christina R. Foust, Associate Professor and Chair, 303-871-4330, Fax: 303-871-4316, E-mail: cfoust@du.edu. *Application contact:* Dr. Mary Claire Morr Serweicz, Associate Professor and Director of Graduate Studies, 303-871-4332, Fax: 303-871-4316, E-mail: mserewic@du.edu.
Website: http://www.du.edu/ahss/comn

**University of Denver,** University College, Denver, CO 80208. Offers arts and culture (MA, Certificate); communication management (MS, Certificate), including translation studies (Certificate), world history and culture (Certificate); environmental policy and management (MS); geographic information systems (MS); global affairs (MA, Certificate), including human capital in organizations (Certificate), philanthropic leadership (Certificate), project management (Certificate), strategic innovation and change (Certificate); healthcare leadership (MS); information communications and technology (MS); leadership and organizations (MS); professional creative writing (MA, Certificate), including emergency planning and response (Certificate), organizational security (Certificate); security management (MS, Certificate); strategic human resources (Certificate). *Program availability:* Part-time, evening/weekend, online learning. *Faculty:* 118 part-time/adjunct (62 women). *Students:* 59 full-time (22 women), 1,285 part-time (750 women); includes 316 minority (111 Black or African American, non-Hispanic/Latino; 8 American Indian or Alaska Native, non-Hispanic/Latino; 39 Asian, non-Hispanic/Latino; 123 Hispanic/Latino; 3 Native Hawaiian or other Pacific Islander, non-Hispanic/Latino; 32 Two or more races, non-Hispanic/Latino), 85 international. Average age 35. 703 applicants, 89% accepted, 390 enrolled. In 2016, 428 master's, 138 other advanced degrees awarded. *Degree requirements:* For master's, capstone project. *Entrance requirements:* For master's, transcripts, two letters of recommendation, personal statement, resume. Additional exam requirements/recommendations for international students: Required—TOEFL (minimum score 550 paper-based; 80 iBT). *Application deadline:* For fall admission, 6/21 priority date for domestic students, 5/1 priority date for international students; for winter admission, 9/14 priority date for domestic students, 9/19 priority date for international students; for spring admission, 1/11 priority date for domestic students, 12/12 priority date for international students; for summer admission, 3/29 priority date for domestic students, 3/6 priority date for international students. Applications are processed on a rolling basis. Application fee: $75. Electronic applications accepted. *Expenses:* $7,236 per year full-time. *Financial support:* In 2016–17, 27 students received support, including 1 teaching assistantship (averaging $1,489 per year). Financial award applicants required to submit FAFSA. *Unit head:* Dr. Michael McGuire, Dean, 303-871-3518, Fax: 303-871-3303, E-mail: mmcguire@du.edu. *Application contact:* Information Contact, 303-871-2291, E-mail: ucoladm@du.edu.
Website: http://universitycollege.du.edu/

**University of Dubuque,** Program in Communication, Dubuque, IA 52001-5099. Offers information technologies communication (MAC); leadership and management (MAC); strategic and corporate communication (MAC). *Program availability:* Part-time, evening/weekend. *Degree requirements:* For master's, thesis optional. *Entrance requirements:* For master's, GRE, minimum GPA of 2.5, 3 recommendations. Additional exam requirements/recommendations for international students: Required—TOEFL (minimum score 550 paper-based). Electronic applications accepted. *Faculty research:* Intercultural communication, management communication.

**University of Florida,** Graduate School, College of Journalism and Communications, Gainesville, FL 32611. Offers advertising (M Adv); mass communication (MAMC, PhD),

including international/intercultural communication (MAMC), journalism (MAMC), mass communication, public relations (MAMC), science/health communication (MAMC), telecommunication (MAMC); JD/MAMC; JD/PhD. *Accreditation:* ACEJMC (one or more programs are accredited). *Program availability:* Part-time, online learning. *Degree requirements:* For master's, comprehensive exam (for some programs), thesis; for doctorate, comprehensive exam (for some programs), thesis/dissertation. *Entrance requirements:* For master's and doctorate, GRE General Test (minimum scores: 156 Verbal, 146 Quantitative), minimum GPA of 3.0, resume, statement of goals, 3 letters of recommendation. Additional exam requirements/recommendations for international students: Required—TOEFL (minimum score 550 paper-based; 80 iBT), IELTS (minimum score 6). Electronic applications accepted. *Faculty research:* Translational communication in science, technology, engineering, medicine, and health; international and intercultural communication; audience analysis and media effects; social interest communication, grassroots activism, and civic engagement; corporate social responsibility.

**University of Georgia,** Grady College of Journalism and Mass Communication, Athens, GA 30602. Offers journalism and mass communication (MA); mass communication (PhD). *Degree requirements:* For master's, comprehensive exam, thesis (MA); for doctorate, comprehensive exam, thesis/dissertation. *Entrance requirements:* For master's and doctorate, GRE General Test. Additional exam requirements/recommendations for international students: Required—TOEFL, TWE for PhD. *Application deadline:* For spring admission, 2/15 for domestic students. Application fee: $50. Electronic applications accepted. *Financial support:* Research assistantships, teaching assistantships, tuition waivers (full), and unspecified assistantships available. *Unit head:* Dr. E. Culpepper Clark, Dean, 706-542-1704, Fax: 706-542-2183, E-mail: cully@uga.edu. *Application contact:* Dr. Jeffrey K. Springston, Associate Dean, 706-542-7833, Fax: 706-542-2183, E-mail: jspring@grady.uga.edu.
Website: http://www.grady.uga.edu/

**University of Hartford,** College of Arts and Sciences, Program in Communication, West Hartford, CT 06117-1599. Offers MA. *Program availability:* Part-time, evening/weekend. *Degree requirements:* For master's, comprehensive exam, thesis optional. *Entrance requirements:* For master's, GRE, 3 letters of recommendation. Additional exam requirements/recommendations for international students: Required—TOEFL (minimum score 550 paper-based). Electronic applications accepted. *Expenses:* Contact institution. *Faculty research:* Communication reticence, relational communication, media literacy, journalism history, media audience attitude and behavior.

**University of Hawaii at Manoa,** Graduate Division, College of Social Sciences, School of Communications, Honolulu, HI 96822. Offers communication (MA); telecommunication and information resource management (Graduate Certificate). *Program availability:* Part-time. *Degree requirements:* For master's, thesis optional. *Entrance requirements:* Additional exam requirements/recommendations for international students: Required—TOEFL (minimum score 600 paper-based; 100 iBT), IELTS (minimum score 7). *Faculty research:* Communication technology policy and development, intercultural communication, organizational communication.

**University of Houston,** College of Liberal Arts and Social Sciences, Jack J. Valenti School of Communication, Houston, TX 77204. Offers health communication (MA); mass communication studies (MA); public relations studies (MA); speech communication (MA). *Program availability:* Part-time. *Degree requirements:* For master's, comprehensive exam (for some programs), thesis (for some programs), 30-33 hours. *Entrance requirements:* For master's, GRE. Additional exam requirements/recommendations for international students: Required—TOEFL. Electronic applications accepted.

**University of Illinois at Chicago,** College of Liberal Arts and Sciences, Department of Communication, Chicago, IL 60607-7128. Offers MA, PhD. *Program availability:* Evening/weekend. *Degree requirements:* For master's, thesis. *Entrance requirements:* For master's, GRE General Test, minimum GPA of 3.0 in last 90 hours. Additional exam requirements/recommendations for international students: Required—TOEFL. Electronic applications accepted. *Faculty research:* Organizational, political, and interpersonal communication; public relations.

**University of Illinois at Springfield,** Graduate Programs, College of Liberal Arts and Sciences, Program in Communication, Springfield, IL 62703-5407. Offers MA. *Program availability:* Part-time, evening/weekend. *Faculty:* 4 full-time (3 women). *Students:* 4 full-time (3 women), 13 part-time (12 women); includes 4 minority (3 Black or African American, non-Hispanic/Latino; 1 Two or more races, non-Hispanic/Latino). Average age 28. 20 applicants, 45% accepted, 4 enrolled. In 2016, 7 master's awarded. *Degree requirements:* For master's, comprehensive exam, thesis, or project. *Entrance requirements:* For master's, in-house writing exam, departmental writing proficiency exam, minimum undergraduate GPA of 3.0; two letters of recommendation, including one from an academic source; one- to two-page personal statement of purpose. Additional exam requirements/recommendations for international students: Required—TOEFL (minimum score 580 paper-based). *Application deadline:* Applications are processed on a rolling basis. Application fee: $60 ($75 for international students). Electronic applications accepted. *Expenses:* Tuition, state resident: part-time $329 per credit hour. Tuition, nonresident: part-time $675 per credit hour. *Financial support:* In 2016–17, fellowships with full tuition reimbursements (averaging $9,900 per year), research assistantships with full tuition reimbursements (averaging $9,991 per year), teaching assistantships with full tuition reimbursements (averaging $10,059 per year) were awarded; career-related internships or fieldwork, Federal Work-Study, scholarships/grants, health care benefits, and unspecified assistantships also available. Support available to part-time students. Financial award application deadline: 11/15; financial award applicants required to submit FAFSA. *Unit head:* Dr. Amie Kincaid, Program Administrator, 217-206-8415, Fax: 217-206-6217, E-mail: akinc2@uis.edu. *Application contact:* Dr. Cecelia Cornell, Associate Vice Chancellor for Graduate Education, 217-206-7230, E-mail: ccorn1@uis.edu.

**University of Illinois at Urbana–Champaign,** Graduate College, College of Liberal Arts and Sciences, Department of Communication, Champaign, IL 61820. Offers MA, PhD. *Program availability:* Part-time, evening/weekend, online learning. Terminal master's awarded for partial completion of doctoral program.

**University of Illinois at Urbana–Champaign,** Graduate College, College of Media, Institute of Communications Research, Champaign, IL 61820. Offers communications and media (PhD). *Faculty research:* Feminist cultural studies, media technology, international communications, Latino studies, economics of media.

**The University of Iowa,** Graduate College, College of Liberal Arts and Sciences, Department of Communication Studies, Iowa City, IA 52242-1316. Offers interpersonal communication and relationships (MA, PhD); media studies (MA, PhD); rhetoric and public advocacy (MA, PhD). *Degree requirements:* For master's, thesis optional, exam; for doctorate, comprehensive exam, thesis/dissertation. *Entrance requirements:* For master's and doctorate, GRE General Test, minimum GPA of 3.0. Additional exam requirements/recommendations for international students: Required—TOEFL (minimum score 550 paper-based; 81 iBT). Electronic applications accepted.

**The University of Kansas,** Graduate Studies, College of Liberal Arts and Sciences, Department of Communication Studies, Lawrence, KS 66045-7574. Offers communication studies (MA, PhD); professional workplace communication (Graduate Certificate). *Program availability:* Part-time, evening/weekend. *Students:* 55 full-time (27 women), 10 part-time (8 women); includes 7 minority (4 Black or African American, non-Hispanic/Latino; 1 Asian, non-Hispanic/Latino; 1 Hispanic/Latino; 1 Two or more races, non-Hispanic/Latino), 6 international. Average age 31. 56 applicants, 64% accepted, 16 enrolled. In 2016, 9 master's, 8 doctorates awarded. *Entrance requirements:* For master's and doctorate, GRE General Test, official transcript, three letters of recommendation, two- to three-page statement of purpose, resume, research writing sample. Additional exam requirements/recommendations for international students: Required—TOEFL. *Application deadline:* For fall admission, 5/5 for domestic and international students; for spring admission, 11/15 for domestic and international students; for summer admission, 4/15 for domestic and international students. Application fee: $65 ($85 for international students). Electronic applications accepted. *Financial support:* Fellowships, research assistantships, teaching assistantships, and unspecified assistantships available. Financial award application deadline: 1/15; financial award applicants required to submit FAFSA. *Faculty research:* Rhetoric, interpersonal communication, organizational communication, intercultural communication, legal communication. *Unit head:* Tom D. Beisecker, Chair, 785-864-9882, E-mail: south40@ku.edu. *Application contact:* Michelle Reames, Graduate Admission Contact/Senior Graduate Academic Advisor, E-mail: michelle.reames@ku.edu.
Website: http://www.coms.ku.edu

**University of Kentucky,** Graduate School, College of Communication and Information, Program in Communication, Lexington, KY 40506-0032. Offers MA, PhD. *Degree requirements:* For master's, comprehensive exam, thesis optional; for doctorate, comprehensive exam, thesis/dissertation. *Entrance requirements:* For master's, GRE General Test, minimum undergraduate GPA of 2.75; for doctorate, GRE General Test, minimum graduate GPA of 3.0, undergraduate 2.75. Additional exam requirements/recommendations for international students: Required—TOEFL (minimum score 550 paper-based). Electronic applications accepted. *Faculty research:* Public service campaigns, health communication, mass media law and public policy, political communication, international and intercultural communication.

**University of Louisiana at Lafayette,** College of Liberal Arts, Department of Communication, Lafayette, LA 70504. Offers mass communications (MS). *Program availability:* Part-time. *Degree requirements:* For master's, thesis optional. *Entrance requirements:* For master's, GRE General Test, minimum GPA of 2.75. Additional exam requirements/recommendations for international students: Required—TOEFL (minimum score 550 paper-based). Electronic applications accepted. *Faculty research:* Mass media problems, issues and ethics, mass communication, historical studies, conflict of interest and law and ethics in journalism, contemporary issues and trends in publications.

**University of Louisiana at Monroe,** Graduate School, College of Arts, Education, and Sciences, Department of Communication, Monroe, LA 71209-0001. Offers MA. *Faculty:* 3 full-time (2 women). *Students:* 8 full-time (5 women), 3 part-time (1 woman); includes 2 minority (both Black or African American, non-Hispanic/Latino), 6 international. Average age 29. 19 applicants, 32% accepted, 3 enrolled. In 2016, 2 master's awarded. *Degree requirements:* For master's, thesis. *Entrance requirements:* For master's, GRE (minimum verbal and quantitative score: 900). Additional exam requirements/recommendations for international students: Required—TOEFL (minimum score 500 paper-based; 61 iBT). *Application deadline:* For fall admission, 8/24 priority date for domestic students, 7/1 for international students; for winter admission, 12/14 priority date for domestic students; for spring admission, 1/19 priority date for domestic students, 11/1 for international students. Applications are processed on a rolling basis. Application fee: $20 ($30 for international students). Electronic applications accepted. *Expenses:* Tuition, state resident: full-time $6489. Tuition, nonresident: full-time $18,589. *Required fees:* $8984. Tuition and fees vary according to course level, course load, degree level and program. *Financial support:* Career-related internships or fieldwork, Federal Work-Study, and unspecified assistantships available. Financial award application deadline: 4/1; financial award applicants required to submit FAFSA. *Faculty research:* Interactive media, rhetoric progress, interpersonal, journalism history, gender/multicultural issues, forensics. *Unit head:* Dr. Carl L. Thameling, Head, 318-342-3184, Fax: 318-342-1422, E-mail: thameling@ulm.edu. *Application contact:* Dr. Leslie Pace, Graduate Coordinator, 318-342-1165, Fax: 318-342-1422, E-mail: pace@ulm.edu.
Website: http://www.ulm.edu/communication

**University of Louisville,** Graduate School, College of Arts and Sciences, Department of Communication, Louisville, KY 40292-0001. Offers MA. *Program availability:* Part-time, evening/weekend, online learning. *Faculty:* 24 full-time (14 women), 26 part-time/adjunct (15 women). *Students:* 10 full-time (7 women), 9 part-time (all women); includes 5 minority (4 Black or African American, non-Hispanic/Latino; 1 Asian, non-Hispanic/Latino). Average age 29. 19 applicants, 68% accepted, 8 enrolled. In 2016, 8 master's awarded. *Degree requirements:* For master's, comprehensive exam (for some programs), thesis or alternative. *Entrance requirements:* For master's, GRE General Test. Additional exam requirements/recommendations for international students: Required—TOEFL (minimum score 550 paper-based; 79 iBT). *Application deadline:* For fall admission, 7/1 for domestic students, 5/1 priority date for international students; for spring admission, 11/1 for domestic students, 11/1 priority date for international students; for summer admission, 4/1 priority date for international students. Applications are processed on a rolling basis. Application fee: $60. Electronic applications accepted. *Expenses:* Tuition, state resident: full-time $12,246; part-time $681 per credit hour. Tuition, nonresident: full-time $25,486; part-time $1417 per credit hour. *Required fees:* $196. Tuition and fees vary according to program and reciprocity agreements. *Financial support:* Research assistantships with full tuition reimbursements, teaching assistantships with tuition reimbursements, scholarships/grants, tuition waivers (partial), and unspecified assistantships available. Support available to part-time students. Financial award applicants required to submit FAFSA. *Faculty research:* Health communication, interpersonal communication, computer-mediated communication, strategic communication, mass communication. *Total annual research expenditures:* $744. *Unit head:* Dr. Al Futrell, Chair, 502-852-6976, E-mail: al@louisville.edu. *Application contact:* Libby Leggett, Director, Graduate Admissions, 502-852-3101, Fax: 502-852-6536, E-mail: gradadm@louisville.edu.
Website: http://louisville.edu/communication

**University of Maine,** Graduate School, College of Liberal Arts and Sciences, Department of Communication and Journalism, Orono, ME 04469. Offers MA, PhD. *Program availability:* Part-time. *Faculty:* 8 full-time (3 women), 7 part-time/adjunct (3 women). *Students:* 16 full-time (7 women), 2 part-time (1 woman); includes 2 minority (1 Hispanic/Latino; 1 Two or more races, non-Hispanic/Latino), 2 international. Average age 27. 19 applicants, 53% accepted, 7 enrolled. In 2016, 7 master's, 1 doctorate awarded. *Degree requirements:* For master's, thesis (for some programs); for doctorate, comprehensive exam, thesis/dissertation. *Entrance requirements:* For master's, GRE General Test. Additional exam requirements/recommendations for international

students: Required—TOEFL. *Application deadline:* For fall admission, 2/1 priority date for domestic students. Applications are processed on a rolling basis. Application fee: $65. Electronic applications accepted. *Expenses:* Tuition, state resident: full-time $7524; part-time $2508 per credit. Tuition, nonresident: full-time $24,498; part-time $8166 per credit. *Required fees:* $1148; $571 per credit. *Financial support:* In 2016–17, 14 students received support, including 2 research assistantships (averaging $14,600 per year), 12 teaching assistantships with full tuition reimbursements available (averaging $14,600 per year); career-related internships or fieldwork, Federal Work-Study, institutionally sponsored loans, and tuition waivers (full and partial) also available. Support available to part-time students. Financial award application deadline: 3/1. *Faculty research:* Rhetorical theory, semiotics, discourse analysis, gender and communication, children's talk/communication disorders. *Total annual research expenditures:* $104,293. *Unit head:* Dr. Nathan Stormer, Chair, 207-581-1938, Fax: 207-581-1286, E-mail: nathan@maine.edu. *Application contact:* Scott G. Delcourt, Assistant Vice President for Graduate Studies and Senior Associate Dean, 207-581-3291, Fax: 207-581-3232, E-mail: graduate@maine.edu.
Website: http://cmj.umaine.edu/graduate-program/

**University of Maryland, Baltimore County,** The Graduate School, College of Arts, Humanities and Social Sciences, Department of Modern Languages and Linguistics, Program in Intercultural Communication, Baltimore, MD 21250. Offers MA. *Program availability:* Part-time, evening/weekend. *Faculty:* 16 full-time (9 women). *Students:* 12 full-time (5 women), 2 part-time (both women); includes 2 minority (1 Black or African American, non-Hispanic/Latino; 1 Hispanic/Latino), 6 international. Average age 27. 15 applicants, 80% accepted, 8 enrolled. In 2016, 8 master's awarded. *Degree requirements:* For master's, one foreign language, comprehensive exam (for some programs), thesis (for some programs). *Entrance requirements:* For master's, GRE General Test, minimum GPA of 3.0, 3 letters of recommendation, self-evaluation and statement of support, resume, writing sample in modern language. Additional exam requirements/recommendations for international students: Required—TOEFL (minimum score 550 paper-based, 80 iBT) or IELTS. *Application deadline:* For fall admission, 1/31 for domestic and international students. Application fee: $50. Electronic applications accepted. *Expenses:* Tuition, state resident: full-time $13,294. Tuition, nonresident: full-time $20,286. *Financial support:* In 2016–17, 7 students received support, including 5 teaching assistantships with full tuition reimbursements available (averaging $12,560 per year); Federal Work-Study, scholarships/grants, health care benefits, and tuition waivers (full) also available. Financial award application deadline: 1/31; financial award applicants required to submit FAFSA. *Faculty research:* Comparative television research-cross-cultural; cultural studies; social developments in Latin America; intercultural communication; French civilization and cultural studies; language, gender and sexuality; sociolinguistics; African linguistics; immigrants in U.S. and Latin American societies. *Unit head:* Dr. Edward Larkey, Interim Director, 410-455-2104, Fax: 410-455-1025, E-mail: larkey@umbc.edu.
Website: http://www.umbc.edu/mll/incc/

**University of Maryland, College Park,** Academic Affairs, College of Arts and Humanities, Department of Communication, College Park, MD 20742. Offers MA, PhD. *Degree requirements:* For master's, thesis optional; for doctorate, comprehensive exam, thesis/dissertation. *Entrance requirements:* For master's, GRE General Test, minimum GPA of 3.0, sample of scholarly writing, 3 letters of recommendation, statement of goals and experiences; for doctorate, GRE General Test. Additional exam requirements/recommendations for international students: Required—TOEFL. Electronic applications accepted. *Faculty research:* Health communication, interpersonal communication, persuasion, intercultural communication, contemporary rhetoric theory.

**University of Massachusetts Amherst,** Graduate School, College of Social and Behavioral Sciences, Department of Communication, Amherst, MA 01003. Offers MA, PhD. *Program availability:* Part-time. Terminal master's awarded for partial completion of doctoral program. *Degree requirements:* For master's, thesis or alternative; for doctorate, comprehensive exam, thesis/dissertation. *Entrance requirements:* For master's and doctorate, GRE General Test, 3 letters of recommendation. Additional exam requirements/recommendations for international students: Required—TOEFL (minimum score 550 paper-based; 80 iBT), IELTS (minimum score 6.5). Electronic applications accepted.

**University of Memphis,** Graduate School, College of Communication and Fine Arts, Department of Communication, Memphis, TN 38152. Offers communication (MA); communication arts (PhD); film and video production (MA). *Program availability:* Part-time. *Faculty:* 13 full-time (6 women). *Students:* 20 full-time (8 women), 23 part-time (12 women); includes 14 minority (7 Black or African American, non-Hispanic/Latino; 2 Asian, non-Hispanic/Latino; 2 Hispanic/Latino; 3 Two or more races, non-Hispanic/Latino), 2 international. Average age 35. 38 applicants, 68% accepted, 17 enrolled. In 2016, 13 master's, 1 doctorate awarded. *Degree requirements:* For master's, comprehensive exam, thesis or alternative, culminating project; for doctorate, comprehensive exam, thesis/dissertation. *Entrance requirements:* For master's and doctorate, GRE General Test, personal goal statement, letters of recommendation, writing sample. Additional exam requirements/recommendations for international students: Required—TOEFL (minimum score 600 paper-based). *Application deadline:* For fall admission, 1/13 priority date for domestic students. Applications are processed on a rolling basis. Application fee: $35 ($60 for international students). *Expenses:* $5,231.50 per semester full-time in-state, $9,623.50 full-time out-of-state. *Financial support:* In 2016–17, 27 students received support, including 6 research assistantships with full tuition reimbursements available (averaging $12,000 per year), 12 teaching assistantships with full tuition reimbursements available (averaging $22,042 per year); Federal Work-Study, scholarships/grants, and unspecified assistantships also available. Financial award application deadline: 2/1; financial award applicants required to submit FAFSA. *Faculty research:* Rhetoric, media studies, applied communication (health communication). *Unit head:* Dr. Sandra Sarkela, Interim Department Chair, 901-678-2565, Fax: 901-678-4331, E-mail: ssarkela@memphis.edu. *Application contact:* Dr. Antonio de Velasco, Coordinator of Graduate Studies, 901-678-3185, Fax: 901-678-4331, E-mail: adevelsc@memphis.edu.
Website: http://www.memphis.edu/ccfa/index.php

**University of Miami,** Graduate School, School of Communication, Coral Gables, FL 33124. Offers communication (PhD); communication studies (MA); film studies (MA, PhD); motion pictures (MFA), including production, producing, and screenwriting; print journalism (MA); public relations (MA); Spanish language journalism (MA); television broadcast journalism (MA). *Program availability:* Part-time. *Degree requirements:* For master's, comprehensive exam (for some programs), thesis (for some programs); for doctorate, comprehensive exam, thesis/dissertation. *Entrance requirements:* For master's, GRE General Test; for doctorate, GRE General Test, master's thesis or scholarly research. Additional exam requirements/recommendations for international students: Required—TOEFL (minimum score 600 paper-based; 100 iBT). Electronic applications accepted. *Faculty research:* Communication studies, mass communication, international/interpersonal communication, film studies, journalism.

**University of Michigan,** Rackham Graduate School, College of Literature, Science, and the Arts, Department of Communication Studies, Ann Arbor, MI 48109-1285. Offers PhD. *Faculty:* 24 full-time (11 women). *Students:* 31 full-time (21 women); includes 8

## Communication—General

minority (5 Black or African American, non-Hispanic/Latino; 1 Hispanic/Latino; 2 Two or more races, non-Hispanic/Latino), 10 international. Average age 29. 84 applicants, 12% accepted, 6 enrolled. In 2016, 6 doctorates awarded. *Degree requirements:* For doctorate, comprehensive exam, thesis/dissertation, first-year research project, 2 terms in student instructor position, publications, presentations. *Entrance requirements:* For doctorate, GRE, U.S. bachelor's degree or its equivalent from accredited institution. Additional exam requirements/recommendations for international students: Required—TOEFL (minimum score 600 paper-based; 102 iBT). *Application deadline:* 12/1 for domestic and international students. Application fee: $75 ($90 for international students). Electronic applications accepted. *Expenses:* Tuition, state resident: full-time $21,466; part-time $1152 per credit hour. Tuition, nonresident: full-time $43,346; part-time $2367 per credit hour. Part-time tuition and fees vary according to course load, degree level and program. *Financial support:* In 2016–17, 31 students received support, including 24 fellowships with full tuition reimbursements available (averaging $19,800 per year), 3 research assistantships with full tuition reimbursements available (averaging $19,737 per year), 28 teaching assistantships with full tuition reimbursements available (averaging $19,900 per year); scholarships/grants, traineeships, and health care benefits also available. Financial award application deadline: 4/30; financial award applicants required to submit FAFSA. *Faculty research:* Media psychology; political communication; global and comparative media; media, technology, and society; critical media studies. *Unit head:* Prof. Nojin Kwak, Professor and Chair, 734-764-0420, Fax: 734-764-3288, E-mail: commchair@umich.edu. *Application contact:* Amy B. Eaton, Graduate Program Coordinator, 734-615-8974, Fax: 734-764-3288, E-mail: lsa-commphd@umich.edu.
Website: http://www.lsa.umich.edu/comm/

**University of Michigan–Flint,** College of Arts and Sciences, Program in Applied Communication, Flint, MI 48502-1950. Offers MA. *Program availability:* Part-time, evening/weekend, 100% online. *Faculty:* 21 full-time (11 women), 9 part-time/adjunct (5 women). *Students:* 1 full-time (0 women), 30 part-time (21 women); includes 7 minority (5 Black or African American, non-Hispanic/Latino; 1 Asian, non-Hispanic/Latino; 1 Two or more races, non-Hispanic/Latino). Average age 38. 29 applicants, 79% accepted, 17 enrolled. *Entrance requirements:* For master's, bachelor's degree from accredited institution, minimum overall undergraduate GPA of 3.0. Additional exam requirements/recommendations for international students: Required—TOEFL (minimum score 84 iBT), IELTS (minimum score 6.5). *Application deadline:* For fall admission, 6/1 for domestic students, 3/1 for international students; for winter admission, 11/15 for domestic students, 9/1 for international students; for spring admission, 3/15 for domestic students, 1/1 for international students; for summer admission, 5/15 for domestic students. Applications are processed on a rolling basis. Application fee: $55. Electronic applications accepted. *Expenses:* Contact institution. *Financial support:* Federal Work-Study, scholarships/grants, and unspecified assistantships available. Support available to part-time students. Financial award application deadline: 3/1; financial award applicants required to submit FAFSA. *Unit head:* Dr. Dan Lair, Director, 810-424-5348, E-mail: danlair@umflint.edu. *Application contact:* Bradley T. Maki, Director of Graduate Admissions, 810-762-3171, Fax: 810-766-6789, E-mail: bmaki@umflint.edu.

**University of Minnesota, Twin Cities Campus,** Graduate School, College of Design, Department of Design, Housing, and Apparel, Minneapolis, MN 55455-0213. Offers apparel (MA, MS, PhD); design communication (MA, MS, PhD); housing studies (MA, MS, PhD, Postbaccalaureate Certificate); interactive design (MFA); interior design (MA, MS, PhD). *Program availability:* Part-time. *Degree requirements:* For master's and Postbaccalaureate Certificate, comprehensive exam, thesis (for some programs); for doctorate, comprehensive exam, thesis/dissertation. *Entrance requirements:* For master's, GRE General Test, minimum GPA of 3.0 (preferred), portfolio, 3 letters of recommendation; for doctorate, GRE General Test, minimum GPA of 3.0 (preferred), portfolio, 3 letters of recommendation, writing sample; for Postbaccalaureate Certificate, GRE General Test, minimum GPA of 3.0 (preferred). Additional exam requirements/recommendations for international students: Required—TOEFL (minimum score 550 paper-based; 79 iBT). Electronic applications accepted. *Faculty research:* Housing policy and community development; consumer behavior; interactive design; design history; social, cultural, and behavioral issues related to designed environments.

**University of Minnesota, Twin Cities Campus,** Graduate School, College of Liberal Arts, Department of Communication Studies, Minneapolis, MN 55455-0213. Offers MA, PhD. *Degree requirements:* For master's, thesis or alternative; for doctorate, thesis/dissertation. *Entrance requirements:* For master's, GRE General Test, minimum GPA of 3.0; for doctorate, GRE General Test, minimum graduate GPA of 3.5. Additional exam requirements/recommendations for international students: Required—TOEFL. Electronic applications accepted. *Faculty research:* Rhetorical studies, communication theory, media studies, gender and communication, public address.

**University of Missouri,** Office of Research and Graduate Studies, College of Arts and Science, Department of Communication, Columbia, MO 65211. Offers MA, PhD. *Faculty:* 13 full-time (6 women). *Students:* 26 full-time (17 women), 10 part-time (5 women). Terminal master's awarded for partial completion of doctoral program. *Degree requirements:* For doctorate, comprehensive exam, thesis/dissertation. *Entrance requirements:* For master's and doctorate, GRE General Test (minimum score 500 verbal, 500 quantitative, 4.0 analytical preferred), minimum GPA of 3.0. Additional exam requirements/recommendations for international students: Required—TOEFL (minimum score 600 paper-based; 100 iBT). *Application deadline:* For fall admission, 1/15 priority date for domestic students, 1/15 for international students. Applications are processed on a rolling basis. Application fee: $75 ($90 for international students). Electronic applications accepted. *Expenses:* Tuition, state resident: full-time $6347; part-time $352.60 per credit hour. Tuition, nonresident: full-time $17,379; part-time $965.50 per credit hour. *Required fees:* $1035. Tuition and fees vary according to course load, campus/location and program. *Financial support:* Fellowships with full tuition reimbursements, research assistantships with full tuition reimbursements, teaching assistantships with full tuition reimbursements, institutionally sponsored loans, health care benefits, and unspecified assistantships available. *Faculty research:* Interpersonal, mass media, organizational, and political communication.
Website: https://communication.missouri.edu/?q-grad/about

**University of Missouri–St. Louis,** College of Arts and Sciences, Department of Communication and Media, St. Louis, MO 63121. Offers communication (MA). *Program availability:* Part-time, evening/weekend. *Faculty:* 7 full-time (6 women), 1 (woman) part-time/adjunct. *Students:* 4 full-time (all women), 10 part-time (5 women); includes 1 minority (Black or African American, non-Hispanic/Latino), 4 international. Average age 29. 16 applicants, 69% accepted, 6 enrolled. *Degree requirements:* For master's, thesis optional. *Entrance requirements:* For master's, 3 letters of recommendation, minimum GPA of 3.25, BA in communication or related discipline. Additional exam requirements/recommendations for international students: Required—TOEFL (minimum score 600 paper-based). *Application deadline:* For fall admission, 7/1 for domestic students, 5/1 for international students; for spring admission, 12/1 for domestic students, 10/1 for international students. Application fee: $50 ($40 for international students). Electronic applications accepted. *Financial support:* Teaching assistantships available. Financial award application deadline: 4/1; financial award applicants required to submit FAFSA. *Faculty research:* Theory and methodology: intercultural, interpersonal, and mass organizational. *Unit head:* Dr. Alice Hall, Chair, 314-516-6662, Fax: 314-516-5816, E-mail: halla@umsl.edu. *Application contact:* 314-516-5458, Fax: 314-516-6996, E-mail: gradadm@umsl.edu.
Website: http://www.umsl.edu/~comm/

**University of Montana,** Graduate School, College of Humanities and Sciences, Department of Communication Studies, Missoula, MT 59812-0002. Offers MA. *Degree requirements:* For master's, thesis (for some programs). *Entrance requirements:* For master's, GRE General Test. Additional exam requirements/recommendations for international students: Required—TOEFL (minimum score 525 paper-based). *Faculty research:* Conflict management, organizational communication, language, personal relationships, rhetoric.

**University of Nebraska at Omaha,** Graduate Studies, College of Communication, Fine Arts and Media, School of Communication, Omaha, NE 68182. Offers communication (MA); human resources and training (Certificate); technical communication (Certificate). *Program availability:* Part-time, evening/weekend. *Faculty:* 7 full-time (4 women). *Students:* 6 full-time (4 women), 33 part-time (20 women); includes 9 minority (2 Black or African American, non-Hispanic/Latino; 2 Asian, non-Hispanic/Latino; 2 Hispanic/Latino; 3 Two or more races, non-Hispanic/Latino), 2 international. Average age 31. 14 applicants, 57% accepted, 6 enrolled. In 2016, 11 master's, 5 other advanced degrees awarded. *Degree requirements:* For master's, comprehensive exam, thesis (for some programs). *Entrance requirements:* For master's, minimum GPA of 3.0, 15 undergraduate communication courses, resume, statement of purpose, 3 letters of recommendation. Additional exam requirements/recommendations for international students: Required—TOEFL, IELTS, PTE. *Application deadline:* For fall admission, 3/1 priority date for domestic and international students; for spring admission, 10/1 priority date for domestic and international students. Applications are processed on a rolling basis. Application fee: $45. Electronic applications accepted. *Financial support:* In 2016–17, 13 students received support, including 13 teaching assistantships with tuition reimbursements available; fellowships, research assistantships with tuition reimbursements available, Federal Work-Study, institutionally sponsored loans, scholarships/grants, health care benefits, tuition waivers (partial), and unspecified assistantships also available. Support available to part-time students. Financial award application deadline: 3/1; financial award applicants required to submit FAFSA. *Unit head:* Dr. Hugh Reilly, Director, 402-554-2341, E-mail: graduate@unomaha.edu. *Application contact:* Dr. Adam Tyma, Graduate Program Chair, 402-554-2341, E-mail: graduate@unomaha.edu.

**University of Nebraska–Lincoln,** Graduate College, College of Arts and Sciences, Department of Communication Studies, Lincoln, NE 68588. Offers instructional communication (MA, PhD); interpersonal communication (MA, PhD); marketing, communication studies, and advertising (MA, PhD); organizational communication (MA, PhD); rhetoric and culture (MA, PhD). *Degree requirements:* For master's, thesis optional; for doctorate, comprehensive exam, thesis/dissertation. *Entrance requirements:* For master's and doctorate, GRE General Test, writing sample. Additional exam requirements/recommendations for international students: Required—TOEFL (minimum score 600 paper-based). Electronic applications accepted. *Faculty research:* Message strategies, gender communication, political communication, organizational communication, instructional communication.

**University of Nevada, Las Vegas,** Graduate College, Greenspun College of Urban Affairs, Department of Communication Studies, Las Vegas, NV 89154-4052. Offers MA. *Program availability:* Part-time. *Faculty:* 5 full-time (3 women), 2 part-time/adjunct (1 woman). *Students:* 20 full-time (12 women), 2 part-time (1 woman); includes 6 minority (1 Black or African American, non-Hispanic/Latino; 3 Hispanic/Latino; 2 Two or more races, non-Hispanic/Latino), 3 international. Average age 26. 25 applicants, 72% accepted, 10 enrolled. In 2016, 5 master's awarded. *Degree requirements:* For master's, comprehensive exam (for some programs), thesis optional. *Entrance requirements:* For master's, GRE General Test, writing sample; 3 letters of recommendation; statement of purpose. Additional exam requirements/recommendations for international students: Required—TOEFL (minimum score 550 paper-based; 80 iBT), IELTS (minimum score 7). *Application deadline:* For fall admission, 1/15 for domestic students. Application fee: $60 ($95 for international students). Electronic applications accepted. *Expenses:* $269.25 per credit, $792 per 3-credit course; $9,634 per year resident; $23,274 per year non-resident; $7,094 fees non-resident (7 credits or more); $1,307 annual health insurance fee. *Financial support:* In 2016–17, 3 research assistantships with partial tuition reimbursements (averaging $10,367 per year), 16 teaching assistantships with partial tuition reimbursements (averaging $10,000 per year) were awarded; institutionally sponsored loans, scholarships/grants, health care benefits, and unspecified assistantships also available. Financial award application deadline: 3/15. *Faculty research:* Rhetoric/public address and persuasion, argumentation, debate; interpersonal, family and health communication, conflict resolution; media and political communication; sex and gender, inter-cultural communication; cultural studies, memory studies, food studies. *Unit head:* Dr. David Henry, Chair/Professor, 702-895-3030, Fax: 702-895-4805, E-mail: david.henry@unlv.edu. *Application contact:* Dr. Donovan Conley, Graduate Coordinator, 702-895-5137, Fax: 702-895-4805, E-mail: donovan.conley@unlv.edu.
Website: http://communicationstudies.unlv.edu/

**University of New Mexico,** Graduate Studies, College of Arts and Sciences, Program in Communication, Albuquerque, NM 87131-2039. Offers MA, PhD. *Program availability:* Part-time. *Faculty:* 16 full-time (12 women). *Students:* 31 full-time (20 women), 23 part-time (19 women); includes 19 minority (1 Black or African American, non-Hispanic/Latino; 1 American Indian or Alaska Native, non-Hispanic/Latino; 1 Asian, non-Hispanic/Latino; 13 Hispanic/Latino; 3 Two or more races, non-Hispanic/Latino), 12 international. Average age 35. 37 applicants, 51% accepted, 12 enrolled. In 2016, 9 master's, 7 doctorates awarded. *Degree requirements:* For master's, 30 hours of class work and 6-hour thesis or project, or 36 hours of class work and comprehensive exam; for doctorate, 2 foreign languages, comprehensive exam, thesis/dissertation. *Entrance requirements:* For master's, GRE General Test, letters of recommendation, letter of intent, curriculum vitae, transcripts; for doctorate, GRE General Test, letters of recommendation, writing sample, letter of intent, curriculum vitae, transcripts. Additional exam requirements/recommendations for international students: Required—TOEFL (minimum score 550 paper-based). *Application deadline:* For fall admission, 1/15 for domestic and international students. Application fee: $50. Electronic applications accepted. *Financial support:* Fellowships with tuition reimbursements, research assistantships, teaching assistantships with tuition reimbursements, career-related internships or fieldwork, scholarships/grants, health care benefits, and unspecified assistantships available. Financial award application deadline: 3/1; financial award applicants required to submit FAFSA. *Faculty research:* Health communication, intercultural communication, interpersonal/organizational communication, mass communication. *Total annual research expenditures:* $82,797. *Unit head:* Dr. Karen Foss, Chair, 505-277-5305, Fax: 505-277-2068, E-mail: kfoss@unm.edu. *Application contact:* Gregoria Arienda Cavazos, Student Advisement Coordinator, 505-277-5305, Fax: 505-277-2068, E-mail: cjadvise@unm.edu.
Website: http://www.unm.edu/~cjdept/

*deadline:* For fall admission, 8/1 for domestic students, 4/1 for international students; for spring admission, 1/1 for domestic students, 9/1 for international students. Applications are processed on a rolling basis. Application fee: $75. Electronic applications accepted. *Expenses:* Tuition, state resident: full-time $12,467; part-time $692.50 per credit hour. Tuition, nonresident: full-time $25,095; part-time $1394.25 per credit hour. *Required fees:* $2669; $491.50 per semester. Tuition and fees vary according to course load, campus/location and program. *Financial support:* In 2016–17, 21 research assistantships with full tuition reimbursements (averaging $19,817 per year), 237 teaching assistantships with full tuition reimbursements (averaging $15,497 per year) were awarded. Financial award application deadline: 3/1; financial award applicants required to submit FAFSA. *Total annual research expenditures:* $6.6 million. *Unit head:* Rosemary Blieszner, Interim Dean, 540-231-6779, Fax: 540-231-7157, E-mail: liberalartsdean@vt.edu. *Application contact:* Chelsea Blanchet, Executive Assistant, 540-231-6779, Fax: 540-231-7157, E-mail: bchels1@vt.edu. Website: http://www.liberalarts.vt.edu/

**Wake Forest University,** Graduate School of Arts and Sciences, Department of Communication, Winston-Salem, NC 27106. Offers speech communication (MA). *Program availability:* Part-time. *Degree requirements:* For master's, one foreign language, thesis. *Entrance requirements:* For master's, GRE General Test, writing sample. Additional exam requirements/recommendations for international students: Required—TOEFL (minimum score 79 iBT). Electronic applications accepted.

**Walden University,** Graduate Programs, School of Management, Minneapolis, MN 55401. Offers accounting (MBA, MS, DBA), including accounting for the professional (MS), accounting with CPA emphasis (MS), self-designed (MS); advanced project management (Graduate Certificate); applied project management (Graduate Certificate); auditing (Graduate Certificate); bridge to business administration (Post-Doctoral Certificate); bridge to management (Post-Doctoral Certificate); business management (Graduate Certificate); communication (MBA); corporate finance (MBA); digital marketing (Graduate Certificate); entrepreneurship (DBA); entrepreneurship and small business (MBA); finance (MS, DBA), including finance for the professional (MS), finance with CFA/investment (MS), finance with CPA emphasis (MS); global supply chain management (DBA); healthcare management (MBA, DBA); human resource management (MBA, MS, Graduate Certificate), including functional human resource management (MS), general program (MS); integrating functional and strategic human resource management (MS), organizational strategy (MS); human resources management (DBA); information systems management (DBA); international business (MBA, DBA); leadership (MBA, MS, DBA, Graduate Certificate), including general program (MS), human resource leadership (MS), leader development (MS), self-designed (MS); management (MS, PhD), including communications (MS), finance (PhD), general program (MS), healthcare management (MS), human resource management (MS), human resources management (PhD), information systems management (PhD), international business (MS), leadership (MS), leadership and organizational change (PhD), marketing (MS), project management (MS), strategy and operations (MS); managerial accounting (Graduate Certificate); marketing (MBA, MS, DBA); project management (MBA, MS, DBA); self-designed (MBA, DBA); social impact management (DBA); technology entrepreneurship (DBA). *Accreditation:* ACBSP. *Program availability:* Part-time, evening/weekend, online only, 100% online. *Degree requirements:* For master's, thesis (for some programs), residency (for EMBA); for doctorate, thesis/dissertation (for some programs), residency. *Entrance requirements:* For master's, bachelor's degree or higher; minimum GPA of 2.5; official transcripts; goal statement (for some programs); access to computer and Internet; for doctorate, master's degree or higher; three years of related professional or academic experience (preferred); minimum GPA of 3.0; goal statement and current resume (for select programs); official transcripts; access to computer and Internet; for other advanced degree, relevant work experience; access to computer and Internet. Additional exam requirements/recommendations for international students: Required—TOEFL (minimum score 550 paper-based, 79 iBT), IELTS (minimum score 6.5), Michigan English Language Assessment Battery (minimum score 82), or PTE (minimum score 53). Electronic applications accepted.

**Washington State University,** The Edward R. Murrow College of Communication, Pullman, WA 99164-2520. Offers communication (MA, PhD); strategic communication (MA). MA in strategic communication offered at the Global (online) campus. *Degree requirements:* For master's, comprehensive exam (for some programs), thesis optional, oral exam; for doctorate, comprehensive exam, thesis/dissertation. *Entrance requirements:* For master's, GRE General Test, minimum GPA of 3.25, 3 letters of recommendation; for doctorate, GRE General Test, minimum undergraduate GPA of 3.25, graduate 3.5; MA in communication; 3 letters of recommendation. Additional exam requirements/recommendations for international students: Required—TOEFL (minimum score 580 paper-based). Electronic applications accepted. *Faculty research:* Communication technology, health communication, science communication, political communication, intercultural communication.

**Wayne State College,** School of Education and Counseling, Department of Educational Foundations and Leadership, Program in Curriculum and Instruction, Wayne, NE 68787. Offers alternative education (MSE); business and information technology education (MSE); communication arts education (MSE); early childhood education (MSE); elementary education (MSE); English as a second language (MSE); English education (MSE); family and consumer sciences education (MSE); industrial technology and vocational education (MSE); learning communities (MSE); mathematics education (MSE); music education (MSE); science education (MSE); social science education (MSE). *Accreditation:* NCATE. *Program availability:* Part-time, evening/weekend. *Degree requirements:* For master's, comprehensive exam, thesis optional. *Entrance requirements:* For master's, GRE General Test. Additional exam requirements/recommendations for international students: Required—TOEFL (minimum score 550 paper-based).

**Wayne State University,** College of Fine, Performing and Communication Arts, Department of Communication, Detroit, MI 48202. Offers communication (PhD), including democratic participation and culture, identity and representation, media, society and culture, risk, crisis and conflict, wellness, work life and relationships; communication and new media (Graduate Certificate); communication studies (MA); dispute resolution (MADR, Graduate Certificate); health communication (Graduate Certificate); journalism (MA); media arts (MA); media studies (MA); public relations and organizational communication (MA); JD/MADR. Doctoral program admits for fall only. *Faculty:* 20. *Students:* 59 full-time (32 women), 113 part-time (75 women); includes 69 minority (54 Black or African American, non-Hispanic/Latino; 2 Asian, non-Hispanic/Latino; 7 Hispanic/Latino; 6 Two or more races, non-Hispanic/Latino), 12 international. Average age 34. 154 applicants, 39% accepted, 41 enrolled. In 2016, 31 master's, 10 doctorates, 4 other advanced degrees awarded. *Degree requirements:* For master's, thesis (for some programs), thesis or essay; for doctorate, thesis/dissertation. *Entrance requirements:* For master's, GRE (if undergraduate GPA less than 3.2), personal statement; BA or BS in communication or related field with minimum upper-division GPA of 3.2 and minimum upper-division undergraduate GPA of 3.0, personal statement, and sample of academic writing (for MA); 3 letters of recommendation (for MADR); for doctorate, GRE, MA in communication or related field with minimum GPA of 3.5; three

letters of recommendation; personal statement; sample of written scholarship. Additional exam requirements/recommendations for international students: Required—TOEFL (minimum score 600 paper-based; 100 iBT), IELTS, TWE. Application fee: $50. Electronic applications accepted. *Expenses:* $17,240 per year resident tuition and fees, $34,434 per year non-resident tuition and fees. *Financial support:* In 2016–17, 61 students received support, including 4 fellowships with tuition reimbursements available (averaging $16,000 per year), 2 research assistantships with tuition reimbursements available (averaging $19,570 per year), 21 teaching assistantships with tuition reimbursements available (averaging $17,994 per year); scholarships/grants and unspecified assistantships also available. Financial award applicants required to submit FAFSA. *Faculty research:* Rhetorical theory and criticism; mass media theory and research; argumentation; organizational communication; risk and crisis communication; interpersonal, family, and health communication. *Unit head:* Dr. Lillian Black, Professor and Chair, 313-577-2943, E-mail: eh8899@wayne.edu. *Application contact:* E-mail: communication@wayne.edu. Website: http://comm.wayne.edu/

**Weber State University,** Telitha E. Lindquist College of Arts and Humanities, Department of Communication, Ogden, UT 84408-1001. Offers MPC. *Program availability:* Part-time, evening/weekend. *Faculty:* 9 full-time (8 women), 2 part-time/adjunct (1 woman). *Students:* 7 full-time (6 women), 36 part-time (23 women); includes 6 minority (1 Black or African American, non-Hispanic/Latino; 1 Asian, non-Hispanic/Latino; 3 Hispanic/Latino; 1 Two or more races, non-Hispanic/Latino), 1 international. Average age 35. In 2016, 19 master's awarded. *Entrance requirements:* For master's, GRE. Additional exam requirements/recommendations for international students: Required—TOEFL (minimum score 550 paper-based; 85 iBT). *Application deadline:* For fall admission, 4/1 for domestic students. Application fee: $60 ($90 for international students). Electronic applications accepted. *Expenses:* Contact institution. *Financial support:* In 2016–17, 4 students received support. Scholarships/grants and tuition waivers (full and partial) available. Financial award application deadline: 4/1; financial award applicants required to submit FAFSA. *Unit head:* Dr. Sarah Steimel, Program Director, 801-626-6535, Fax: 801-626-7760, E-mail: sarahsteimel@weber.edu. *Application contact:* Shari Love, Office Specialist, 801-626-7499, Fax: 801-626-7975, E-mail: slove@weber.edu. Website: http://www.weber.edu/mpc

**Webster University,** School of Communications, St. Louis, MO 63119-3194. Offers MA. *Program availability:* Part-time, evening/weekend, online learning. *Degree requirements:* For master's, thesis (for some programs). *Entrance requirements:* For master's, 36 hours of graduate course work. Additional exam requirements/recommendations for international students: Required—TOEFL. *Application deadline:* Applications are processed on a rolling basis. Application fee: $35 ($50 for international students). *Expenses: Tuition:* Full-time $21,900; part-time $730 per credit hour. Tuition and fees vary according to campus/location and program. *Financial support:* Career-related internships or fieldwork and Federal Work-Study available. Support available to part-time students. Financial award application deadline: 4/1; financial award applicants required to submit FAFSA. *Unit head:* Brenda Fyfe, Dean, 314-968-6913.

**Webster University,** School of Education, Department of Multidisciplinary Studies, St. Louis, MO 63119-3194. Offers applied educational psychology (MA, Ed S); communication arts (MA); early childhood education (MA, MAT); education and innovation (MA); educational technology (MET); elementary education (MAT); mathematics for educators (MA); middle school education (MAT); multidisciplinary studies (MAT); multimodal literacy for global impact (MA); reading (MA); secondary school education (MAT); special education (MA, MAT); teaching English as a second language (MA); transformative learning in the global community (Ed S). *Program availability:* Part-time. *Entrance requirements:* For master's, minimum GPA of 2.5. Additional exam requirements/recommendations for international students: Required—TOEFL. *Application deadline:* Applications are processed on a rolling basis. Application fee: $35 ($50 for international students). *Expenses: Tuition:* Full-time $21,900; part-time $730 per credit hour. Tuition and fees vary according to campus/location and program. *Financial support:* Federal Work-Study available. Support available to part-time students. Financial award application deadline: 4/1; financial award applicants required to submit FAFSA. *Unit head:* Dr. Deborah Stiles, Chair, 314-968-7056, Fax: 314-968-7118, E-mail: stilesda@webster.edu.

**West Chester University of Pennsylvania,** College of Arts and Humanities, Department of Communication Studies, West Chester, PA 19383. Offers MA. *Program availability:* Part-time, evening/weekend. *Faculty:* 8 full-time (2 women), 1 (woman) part-time/adjunct. *Students:* 12 full-time (10 women), 16 part-time (12 women); includes 7 minority (6 Black or African American, non-Hispanic/Latino; 1 Hispanic/Latino). Average age 29. 25 applicants, 84% accepted, 14 enrolled. In 2016, 8 master's awarded. *Degree requirements:* For master's, comprehensive exam, thesis optional. *Entrance requirements:* For master's, GRE (minimum 50th percentile in two of the three tested areas) or minimum GPA of 3.5, minimum GPA of 2.8 overall, 3.0 in major; writing sample; two letters of reference; courses or experience that indicate skill in public speaking, communication theory, and communication (or related) research. Additional exam requirements/recommendations for international students: Required—TOEFL or IELTS. *Application deadline:* For fall admission, 5/15 for international students; for spring admission, 10/1 for international students. Applications are processed on a rolling basis. Application fee: $50. Electronic applications accepted. *Expenses:* Tuition, state resident: full-time $8694; part-time $483 per credit. Tuition, nonresident: full-time $13,050; part-time $725 per credit. *Required fees:* $2399; $119.05 per credit. Tuition and fees vary according to campus/location and program. *Financial support:* Scholarships/grants and unspecified assistantships available. Financial award application deadline: 2/15; financial award applicants required to submit FAFSA. *Faculty research:* Rhetorical communication, media/social media, intercultural communication, interpersonal and group communication, conflict management. *Unit head:* Dr. Timothy Brown, Chair, 610-436-2500, Fax: 610-436-2500, E-mail: tbrown@wcupa.edu. *Application contact:* Dr. Elizabeth Munz, Graduate Coordinator, 610-436-2180, E-mail: emunz@wcupa.edu. Website: http://communicationstudies.org/

**Western Illinois University,** School of Graduate Studies, College of Fine Arts and Communication, Department of Communication, Macomb, IL 61455-1390. Offers MA. *Program availability:* Part-time. *Students:* 12 full-time (8 women), 5 part-time (3 women); includes 7 minority (all Black or African American, non-Hispanic/Latino), 1 international. Average age 25. 17 applicants, 100% accepted, 9 enrolled. In 2016, 12 master's awarded. *Degree requirements:* For master's, comprehensive exam (for some programs), thesis or alternative. *Entrance requirements:* Additional exam requirements/recommendations for international students: Required—TOEFL (minimum score 580 paper-based; 92 iBT). *Application deadline:* Applications are processed on a rolling basis. Application fee: $30. Electronic applications accepted. *Financial support:* In 2016–17, 12 students received support, including 1 research assistantship with full tuition reimbursement available (averaging $7,544 per year), 4 teaching assistantships with full tuition reimbursements available (averaging $8,688 per year); unspecified assistantships also available. Financial award applicants required to submit FAFSA. *Unit head:* Dr. Pete Jorgensen, Chairperson, 309-298-1507. *Application contact:* Dr. Nancy

## Communication—General

Parsons, Associate Provost and Director of Graduate Studies, 309-298-1806, Fax: 309-298-2345, E-mail: grad-office@wiu.edu.
Website: http://www.wiu.edu/comm

**Western Kentucky University,** Graduate Studies, Potter College of Arts and Letters, Department of Communication, Bowling Green, KY 42101. Offers communication (MA); organizational communication (Graduate Certificate). *Program availability:* Part-time, evening/weekend. *Degree requirements:* For master's, comprehensive exam, thesis optional, final exam. *Entrance requirements:* For master's, GRE General Test, minimum GPA of 2.75. Additional exam requirements/recommendations for international students: Required—TOEFL (minimum score 555 paper-based; 79 iBT). *Faculty research:* Public rhetoric and public address organization communication, teamwork in communication, intercultural crisis communication.

**Western Michigan University,** Graduate College, College of Arts and Sciences, School of Communication, Kalamazoo, MI 49008. Offers MA.

**Western New England University,** College of Arts and Sciences, Program in Communication, Springfield, MA 01119. Offers public relations (MA). *Program availability:* Part-time, evening/weekend. *Faculty:* 6 full-time (5 women). *Students:* 17 part-time (11 women); includes 4 minority (2 Black or African American, non-Hispanic/Latino; 1 Asian, non-Hispanic/Latino; 1 Hispanic/Latino). Average age 32. 8 applicants, 88% accepted, 5 enrolled. In 2016, 8 master's awarded. *Degree requirements:* For master's, independent study or thesis. *Entrance requirements:* For master's, official transcript, personal statement, resume, three letters of recommendation. Additional exam requirements/recommendations for international students: Required—TOEFL (minimum score 79 iBT). *Application deadline:* Applications are processed on a rolling basis. Application fee: $30. Electronic applications accepted. *Expenses:* Contact institution. *Financial support:* Application deadline: 4/15; applicants required to submit FAFSA. *Unit head:* Dr. Saeed Ghahramani, Dean, 413-782-1218, Fax: 413-796-2118, E-mail: sghahram@wne.edu. *Application contact:* Matthew Fox, Director of Graduate Admissions, Enrollment Management Group, 413-782-1410, Fax: 413-782-1777, E-mail: study@wne.edu.
Website: http://www1.wne.edu/academics/graduate/ma-communication.cfm

**Westminster College,** Program in Professional Communication, Salt Lake City, UT 84105-3697. Offers MPC, MSC. *Program availability:* Part-time, evening/weekend. *Faculty:* 4 full-time (2 women), 3 part-time/adjunct (1 woman). *Students:* 24 full-time (14 women), 9 part-time (6 women); includes 5 minority (1 American Indian or Alaska Native, non-Hispanic/Latino; 1 Asian, non-Hispanic/Latino; 2 Hispanic/Latino; 1 Native Hawaiian or other Pacific Islander, non-Hispanic/Latino), 2 international. Average age 35. 4 applicants, 50% accepted, 1 enrolled. In 2016, 24 master's awarded. *Degree requirements:* For master's, capstone project. *Entrance requirements:* For master's, GRE, resume, personal statement of intent, official transcripts, two letters of recommendation, writing sample. Additional exam requirements/recommendations for international students: Required—TOEFL (minimum score 600 paper-based; 100 iBT), IELTS (minimum score 7.5). *Application deadline:* For fall admission, 4/1 priority date for domestic and international students; for spring admission, 10/16 priority date for domestic and international students. Applications are processed on a rolling basis. Application fee: $50. Electronic applications accepted. Application fee is waived when completed online. *Expenses:* Contact institution. *Financial support:* Career-related internships or fieldwork, scholarships/grants, unspecified assistantships, and tuition reimbursements, tuition remission available. Support available to part-time students. Financial award applicants required to submit FAFSA. *Faculty research:* Diversity in higher education, communication pedagogy, mass media law and ethics, impact of new technologies on society, rhetorical theory, feminism and popular culture, critical communication pedagogy. *Unit head:* Dr. Helen Hodgson, Director, 801-832-2821, Fax: 801-832-3102, E-mail: hhodgson@westminstercollege.edu. *Application contact:* Ashley Williams, Director of Graduate Admissions, 801-832-2213, Fax: 801-832-3101, E-mail:

awilliams@westminstercollege.edu.
Website: http://www.westminstercollege.edu/mpc

**West Texas A&M University,** College of Fine Arts and Humanities, Department of Communication, Canyon, TX 79016-0001. Offers MA. *Program availability:* Part-time. *Entrance requirements:* For master's, comprehensive exam, thesis optional. *Entrance requirements:* For master's, GRE General Test, 24 hours of undergraduate communications courses, letter of recommendation, interview with communication advisor. Additional exam requirements/recommendations for international students: Required—TOEFL (minimum score 550 paper-based). *Application deadline:* For fall admission, 8/1 for domestic students, 5/1 for international students; for spring admission, 12/1 for domestic students, 10/30 for international students; for summer admission, 5/1 for domestic students. Applications are processed on a rolling basis. Application fee: $40 ($75 for international students). Electronic applications accepted. *Financial support:* Research assistantships, teaching assistantships with partial tuition reimbursements, Federal Work-Study, institutionally sponsored loans, and tuition waivers (partial) available. Support available to part-time students. Financial award applicants required to submit CSS PROFILE or FAFSA. *Faculty research:* Comparison student learning in basic public speaking in traditional versus online format, impact of supervisor immediacy and power on organizational outcomes, storytelling, gender, nonverbal. *Unit head:* Dr. Trudy L. Hanson, Head, E-mail: thanson@wtamu.edu. *Application contact:* Dr. Enyonam Osei-Hwere, Associate Professor of Mass Communication, 806-651-2411, E-mail: eosei-hwere@wtamu.edu.
Website: http://www.wtamu.edu/academics/communication.aspx

**West Virginia University,** Eberly College of Arts and Sciences, Department of Communication Studies, Morgantown, WV 26506. Offers communication in instruction (MA); communication studies (PhD); communication theory and research (MA); corporate and organizational communication (MA). *Program availability:* Part-time. *Degree requirements:* For master's, comprehensive exam (for some programs), thesis (for some programs); for doctorate, comprehensive exam, thesis/dissertation. *Entrance requirements:* For master's and doctorate, minimum GPA of 3.0. Additional exam requirements/recommendations for international students: Required—TOEFL. Electronic applications accepted. *Faculty research:* Instructional communication, interpersonal communication, health communication, influence, instructional communication, social influence.

**Wichita State University,** Graduate School, Fairmount College of Liberal Arts and Sciences, Elliott School of Communication, Wichita, KS 67260. Offers MA. *Program availability:* Part-time. *Unit head:* Dr. Jeffrey Jarman, Interim Director, 316-978-3185, Fax: 316-978-3006, E-mail: jeffrey.jarman@wichita.edu. *Application contact:* Jordan Oleson, Admissions Coordinator, 316-978-3095, E-mail: jordan.oleson@wichita.edu.
Website: http://www.wichita.edu/esc

**Wilfrid Laurier University,** Faculty of Graduate and Postdoctoral Studies, Faculty of Arts, Department of Communication Studies, Waterloo, ON N2L 3C5, Canada. Offers media, technology and culture (MA); visual communication and culture (MA). *Degree requirements:* For master's, thesis optional. *Entrance requirements:* For master's, honours BA in communication studies or a cognate discipline from an approved university with a minimum B+ overall in last two years of study and in undergraduate major. Additional exam requirements/recommendations for international students: Required—TOEFL (minimum score 89 iBT). Electronic applications accepted. *Faculty research:* Visual communication and culture, media, technology and culture.

**York University,** Faculty of Graduate Studies, Program in Communication and Culture, Toronto, ON M3J 1P3, Canada. Offers MA, PhD. Program offered jointly with Ryerson University. *Degree requirements:* For master's, thesis or alternative; for doctorate, comprehensive exam, thesis/dissertation. Electronic applications accepted.

# Arts Journalism

**Academy of Art University,** Graduate Programs, Program in Fashion Journalism, San Francisco, CA 94105-3410. Offers MA. *Program availability:* Part-time, evening/weekend, 100% online. *Faculty:* 23 full-time (14 women), 70 part-time/adjunct (54 women). *Students:* 25 full-time (23 women), 19 part-time (16 women); includes 16 minority (10 Black or African American, non-Hispanic/Latino; 1 American Indian or Alaska Native, non-Hispanic/Latino; 2 Asian, non-Hispanic/Latino; 2 Hispanic/Latino; 1 Two or more races, non-Hispanic/Latino), 17 international. Average age 27. 23 applicants, 100% accepted, 15 enrolled. In 2016, 12 master's awarded. *Degree requirements:* For master's, final review. *Entrance requirements:* For master's, statement of intent; resume; portfolio/reel; official college transcripts. *Application deadline:* Applications are processed on a rolling basis. Application fee: $100. Electronic applications accepted. *Expenses: Tuition:* Part-time $982 per unit. *Financial support:* Career-related internships or fieldwork, Federal Work-Study, and scholarships/grants available. Financial award application deadline: 8/10; financial award applicants required to submit FAFSA. *Application contact:* 800-544-ARTS, E-mail: info@academyart.edu. Website: http://www.academyart.edu/academics/fashion/graduate-degrees

**School of the Art Institute of Chicago,** Graduate Division, Program in New Arts Journalism, Chicago, IL 60603-3103. Offers MA. *Entrance requirements:* Additional exam requirements/recommendations for international students: Required—TOEFL, IELTS.

**Syracuse University,** S. I. Newhouse School of Public Communications, MA Program in Arts Journalism, Syracuse, NY 13244. Offers MA. *Accreditation:* ACEJMC. *Students:* Average age 24. *Degree requirements:* For master's, capstone project. *Entrance requirements:* For master's, GRE General Test, resume, official transcripts, personal statement, three letters of recommendation. Additional exam requirements/recommendations for international students: Required—TOEFL (minimum score 600 paper-based; 100 iBT). *Application deadline:* For summer admission, 1/15 for domestic students, 1/15 priority date for international students. Application fee: $45. Electronic applications accepted. *Expenses: Tuition:* Full-time $25,974; part-time $1443 per credit hour. *Required fees:* $802; $50 per course. Tuition and fees vary according to course load and program. *Financial support:* Fellowships with full tuition reimbursements, research assistantships with partial tuition reimbursements, and teaching assistantships with partial tuition reimbursements available. Financial award application deadline: 2/1. *Faculty research:* Arts journalism, communications, online journalism, television, radio, film. *Unit head:* Eric Grode, Director, 315-443-2305, E-mail: ejgrode@syr.edu. *Application contact:* Martha Coria, Graduate Records Office, 315-443-4039, Fax: 315-443-1834, E-mail: pcgrad@syr.edu.
Website: http://newhouse.syr.edu/

# Broadcast Journalism

**The American University in Cairo,** School of Global Affairs and Public Policy, Cairo, Egypt. Offers gender and women's studies (MA); global affairs (MGA); international and comparative law (LL M); international human rights law (MA); journalism and mass communication (MA); Middle East studies (MA); migration and refugee studies (MA, Diploma); public administration (MPA); public policy (MPP); television and digital journalism (MA). *Program availability:* Part-time, evening/weekend. *Faculty:* 27 full-time (13 women), 5 part-time/adjunct (3 women). *Students:* 69 full-time (40 women), 194 part-time (134 women), 33 international. Average age 29. 322 applicants, 51%

accepted, 86 enrolled. In 2016, 112 master's awarded. *Degree requirements:* For master's, comprehensive exam (for some programs), thesis (for some programs). *Entrance requirements:* Additional exam requirements/recommendations for international students: Required—TOEFL (minimum score 450 paper-based; 45 iBT), IELTS (minimum score 5). *Application deadline:* For fall admission, 2/1 for domestic and international students; for spring admission, 10/15 for domestic and international students. Applications are processed on a rolling basis. Application fee: $80. Electronic applications accepted. *Expenses:* Contact institution. *Financial support:* Fellowships

with partial tuition reimbursements, scholarships/grants, and unspecified assistantships available. Financial award application deadline: 3/10. *Faculty research:* Law, media and journalism; public policy and public administration, gender studies, Middle East Studies, global affairs, refugees studies. *Unit head:* Dr. Nabil Fahmy, Dean, 20-2-2615-2671, E-mail: nfahmy@aucegypt.edu. *Application contact:* Maha Hegazi, Director for Graduate Admissions, 20-2-2615-1462, E-mail: mahahegazi@aucegypt.edu.
Website: http://www.aucegypt.edu/GAPP/Pages/default.aspx

**Emerson College,** Graduate Studies, School of Communication, Department of Journalism, Boston, MA 02116-4624. Offers journalism (MA), including broadcast journalism. *Faculty:* 14 full-time (6 women), 4 part-time/adjunct (1 woman). *Students:* 20 full-time (16 women); includes 10 minority (5 Black or African American, non-Hispanic/Latino; 5 Hispanic/Latino), 6 international. Average age 26. 70 applicants, 67% accepted, 12 enrolled. In 2016, 13 master's awarded. *Entrance requirements:* For master's, GRE General Test. Additional exam requirements/recommendations for international students: Required—TOEFL (minimum score 550 paper-based; 80 iBT), IELTS (minimum score 7). *Application deadline:* For summer admission, 3/1 priority date for domestic and international students. Applications are processed on a rolling basis. Application fee: $60 ($75 for international students). Electronic applications accepted. *Financial support:* In 2016–17, 13 students received support, including 13 fellowships with partial tuition reimbursements available (averaging $9,625 per year); research assistantships with partial tuition reimbursements available, Federal Work-Study, scholarships/grants, and unspecified assistantships also available. Financial award application deadline: 3/1; financial award applicants required to submit FAFSA. *Faculty research:* Journalism. *Application contact:* Leanda Ferland, Office of Graduate Admission, 617-824-8610, Fax: 617-824-8614, E-mail: gradapp@emerson.edu.
Website: http://www.emerson.edu/graduate_admission

**Northwestern University,** Medill School of Journalism, Media, and Integrated Marketing Communications, Evanston, IL 60208. Offers integrated marketing communications (MSIMC), including brand strategy, content marketing, direct and interactive marketing, marketing analytics, strategic communications; interactive publishing (MSJ); magazine writing/editing (MSJ); reporting (MSJ); video/broadcast (MSJ). *Accreditation:* ACEJMC (one or more programs are accredited). *Entrance requirements:* For master's, GRE General Test, GMAT or LSAT (for MSJ). Additional exam requirements/recommendations for international students: Required—TOEFL. Electronic applications accepted. *Expenses:* Contact institution. *Faculty research:* Web business journalism, cultural stereotypes, voter apathy, digital television.

**Quinnipiac University,** School of Communications, Program in Journalism, Hamden, CT 06518-1940. Offers journalism (MS), including broadcast/multimedia, writing; sports journalism (MS), including broadcast/multimedia. *Program availability:* Part-time, evening/weekend. *Faculty:* 3 full-time (1 woman), 10 part-time/adjunct (1 woman). *Students:* 10 full-time (5 women), 5 part-time (3 women); includes 6 minority (2 Black or African American, non-Hispanic/Latino; 3 Hispanic/Latino; 1 Two or more races, non-Hispanic/Latino), 3 international. 9 applicants, 56% accepted, 2 enrolled. In 2016, 4 master's awarded. *Degree requirements:* For master's, project. *Entrance requirements:* For master's, minimum GPA of 3.0, portfolio or writing sample. Additional exam requirements/recommendations for international students: Required—TOEFL (minimum score 575 paper-based; 90 iBT), IELTS (minimum score 6.5). *Application deadline:* For fall admission, 7/30 priority date for domestic students, 4/15 priority date for international students. Applications are processed on a rolling basis. Application fee: $45. Electronic applications accepted. *Expenses: Tuition:* Part-time $985 per credit. *Required fees:* $40 per credit. $150 per semester. Tuition and fees vary according to program. *Financial support:* Federal Work-Study, scholarships/grants, and unspecified assistantships available. Financial award application deadline: 6/1; financial award applicants required to submit FAFSA. *Faculty research:* Journalism history, federal law enforcement and journalism, social media and journalism, online journalism, sports journalism, American football history and media, journalism and film, McCarthyism and journalism. *Unit head:* Phillip Simon, Program Director, 203-582-8672, E-mail: graduate@qu.edu. *Application contact:* Office of Graduate Admissions, 800-462-1944, Fax: 203-582-3443, E-mail: graduate@qu.edu.
Website: http://www.qu.edu/gradjournalism

**Quinnipiac University,** School of Communications, Program in Sports Journalism, Hamden, CT 06518-1940. Offers MS. *Program availability:* Part-time, evening/weekend. *Faculty:* 3 full-time (1 woman), 10 part-time/adjunct (1 woman). *Students:* 12 full-time (3 women), 11 part-time (2 women); includes 8 minority (3 Black or African American, non-Hispanic/Latino; 5 Hispanic/Latino). 31 applicants, 87% accepted, 16 enrolled. In 2016, 9 master's awarded. *Entrance requirements:* For master's, minimum GPA of 3.0, portfolio or writing sample. Additional exam requirements/recommendations for international students: Required—TOEFL (minimum score 575 paper-based; 90 iBT), IELTS (minimum score 6.5). *Application deadline:* For fall admission, 7/30 priority date for domestic students, 4/30 priority date for international students. Applications are processed on a rolling basis. Application fee: $45. Electronic applications accepted. *Expenses: Tuition:* Part-time $985 per credit. *Required fees:* $40 per credit. $150 per semester. Tuition and fees vary according to program. *Financial support:* Federal Work-Study, scholarships/grants, and unspecified assistantships available. Financial award application deadline: 6/1; financial award applicants required to submit FAFSA. *Unit head:* Phillip Simon, Director of Graduate Programs, School of Education, 203-582-8672, E-mail: graduate@qu.edu. *Application contact:* Office of Graduate Admissions, 203-582-8672, Fax: 203-582-3443, E-mail: graduate@qu.edu.
Website: http://www.qu.edu/gradsportsjournalism

**Syracuse University,** S. I. Newhouse School of Public Communications, MS Program in Broadcast and Digital Journalism, Syracuse, NY 13244. Offers MS. *Accreditation:* ACEJMC. *Degree requirements:* For master's, capstone course. *Entrance requirements:* For master's, GRE General Test, resume, official transcripts, personal statement, three letters of recommendation. Additional exam requirements/recommendations for international students: Required—TOEFL (minimum score 100 iBT). *Application deadline:* For summer admission, 1/15 for domestic and international students. Application fee: $45. Electronic applications accepted. *Expenses: Tuition:* Full-time $25,974; part-time $1443 per credit hour. *Required fees:* $802; $50 per course. Tuition and fees vary according to course load and program. *Financial support:* Fellowships with full tuition reimbursements, research assistantships with partial tuition reimbursements, and teaching assistantships with partial tuition reimbursements available. Financial award application deadline: 2/1. *Faculty research:* Electronic journalism, broadcast and digital journalism, anchoring in traditional and new platforms, producing. *Unit head:* Prof. Hub Brown, Associate Dean for Research, Creativity, International Initiatives and Diversity/Associate Professor, 315-443-4177, E-mail: hwbrown@syr.edu. *Application contact:* Martha Coria, Graduate Records Office, 315-443-5749, Fax: 315-443-1834, E-mail: pcgrad@syr.edu.
Website: http://newhouse.syr.edu/

**University of Maryland, College Park,** Academic Affairs, Phillip Merrill College of Journalism, College Park, MD 20742. Offers broadcast journalism (MA); journalism (MA); journalism and media studies (PhD); online news (MA); public affairs reporting (MA). *Accreditation:* ACEJMC (one or more programs are accredited). *Program availability:* Part-time, evening/weekend. *Degree requirements:* For doctorate, thesis/dissertation, preliminary written and oral comprehensive exams. *Entrance requirements:* For master's and doctorate, GRE General Test, minimum GPA of 3.0, 3 letters of recommendation. Additional exam requirements/recommendations for international students: Required—TOEFL. Electronic applications accepted. *Faculty research:* Mass communication theory, specialized journalism, new telecommunication technologies, press integration.

**University of Miami,** Graduate School, School of Communication, Coral Gables, FL 33124. Offers communication (PhD); communication studies (MA); film studies (MA, PhD); motion pictures (MFA), including production, producing, and screenwriting; print journalism (MA); public relations (MA); Spanish language journalism (MA); television broadcast journalism (MA). *Program availability:* Part-time. *Degree requirements:* For master's, comprehensive exam (for some programs), thesis (for some programs); for doctorate, comprehensive exam, thesis/dissertation. *Entrance requirements:* For master's, GRE General Test; for doctorate, GRE General Test, master's thesis or scholarly research. Additional exam requirements/recommendations for international students: Required—TOEFL (minimum score 600 paper-based; 100 iBT). Electronic applications accepted. *Faculty research:* Communication studies, mass communication, international/interpersonal communication, film studies, journalism.

**University of the Sacred Heart,** Graduate Programs, Department of Communication, San Juan, PR 00914-0383. Offers contemporary culture and media (MA); digital journalism (MA, Certificate); editing for media (MA, Certificate); public relations (MA, Certificate); publicity (MA, Certificate); scriptwriting (MA, Certificate). *Program availability:* Part-time, evening/weekend. *Degree requirements:* For master's, thesis.

# Corporate and Organizational Communication

**Argosy University, Schaumburg,** Graduate School of Business and Management, Schaumburg, IL 60173-5403. Offers accounting (DBA, Adv C); customized professional concentration (MBA, DBA); finance (MBA, Certificate); fraud examination (MBA); healthcare administration (MBA, Certificate); human resource management (MS); information systems (Adv C, Certificate); information systems management (MBA); international business (MBA, DBA, Adv C, Certificate); management (MBA, MSM, DBA, Adv C, Certificate); marketing (MBA, DBA, Adv C, Certificate); organizational leadership (MS, Ed D); public administration (MBA); sustainable management (MBA).

**Armstrong State University,** School of Graduate Studies, Program in Professional Communication and Leadership, Savannah, GA 31419-1997. Offers MA, Certificate. *Program availability:* Part-time, evening/weekend. *Faculty:* 3 full-time (2 women), 1 (woman) part-time/adjunct. *Students:* 26 full-time (17 women), 44 part-time (32 women); includes 43 minority (36 Black or African American, non-Hispanic/Latino; 1 Asian, non-Hispanic/Latino; 3 Hispanic/Latino; 3 Two or more races, non-Hispanic/Latino), 2 international. Average age 25. 50 applicants, 54% accepted, 19 enrolled. In 2016, 27 master's awarded. *Degree requirements:* For master's, comprehensive exam, project. *Entrance requirements:* For master's, minimum GPA of 2.5, letters of recommendation, letter of intent, resume. Additional exam requirements/recommendations for international students: Required—TOEFL (minimum score 523 paper-based; 70 iBT). *Application deadline:* For fall admission, 6/1 priority date for domestic students, 5/1 priority date for international students; for spring admission, 11/15 priority date for domestic students, 9/15 priority date for international students; for summer admission, 4/15 for domestic students, 9/15 priority date for international students. Applications are processed on a rolling basis. Application fee: $30. Electronic applications accepted. *Expenses:* Tuition, state resident: full-time $1781; part-time $161.93 per credit hour. Tuition, nonresident: full-time $6482; part-time $589.27 per credit hour. *Required fees:* $1224 per unit. $612 per semester. Tuition and fees vary according to course load, campus/location and program. *Financial support:* In 2016–17, research assistantships with full tuition reimbursements (averaging $5,000 per year) were awarded; scholarships/grants and unspecified assistantships also available. Financial award application deadline: 3/15; financial award applicants required to submit FAFSA. *Faculty research:* Organizational communication, conflict resolution and mediation, rhetoric and language identity, brand identity and marketing, communication theory. *Unit head:* Dr. Robert Terry, 912-344-3606, E-mail: robert.terry@armstrong.edu. *Application contact:* McKenzie Peterman, Assistant Director of Graduate Admissions, 912-344-2503, Fax: 912-344-3417, E-mail: graduate@armstrong.edu.
Website: http://www.armstrong.edu/Majors/degree/master_professional_communication_leadership

**Ashland University,** College of Arts and Sciences, Program in Corporate and Strategic Communication, Ashland, OH 44805-3702. Offers MA. *Program availability:* Online learning. *Unit head:* Dr. Theodore Avtgis, Director, 419-289-5593, E-mail: tavtgis@ashland.edu. *Application contact:* Dr. W. Gregory Gerrick, Dean, Graduate School, 419-289-5750, Fax: 419-289-5949, E-mail: ggerrick@ashland.edu.

**Barry University,** College of Arts and Sciences, Department of Communication, Miami Shores, FL 33161-6695. Offers broadcasting (Certificate); communication (MA), including broadcast communication, public relations and corporate communications; organizational communication (MS). *Program availability:* Part-time, evening/weekend. *Degree requirements:* For master's, thesis (for some programs). *Entrance requirements:* For master's, GRE General Test, MAT, minimum GPA of 3.0. Electronic applications accepted. *Faculty research:* Organizational communication, broadcast communication, intercultural communication, advertising, leadership.

**Baruch College of the City University of New York,** Weissman School of Arts and Sciences, Program in Corporate Communication, New York, NY 10010-5585. Offers MA. *Program availability:* Part-time, evening/weekend. *Faculty:* 7 full-time (3 women), 5 part-time/adjunct (0 women). *Students:* 66. 37 applicants, 73% accepted, 17 enrolled. In 2016, 24 master's awarded. *Degree requirements:* For master's, thesis or alternative. *Entrance requirements:* For master's, GRE/GMAT, 3 letters of recommendation; personal essay; resume; official transcripts. Additional exam requirements/recommendations for international students: Required—TOEFL. *Application deadline:*

### Corporate and Organizational Communication

For fall admission, 5/15 for domestic students, 5/15 priority date for international students; for spring admission, 12/1 for domestic students, 12/1 priority date for international students. Applications are processed on a rolling basis. Application fee: $125. Electronic applications accepted. *Financial support:* Career-related internships or fieldwork, Federal Work-Study, and unspecified assistantships available. Financial award applicants required to submit FAFSA. *Faculty research:* Media history; cultural studies; film studies; social implications of contemporary digital media; improving public argument; intercultural and international aspects of communication; intercultural friendship formation; use of technology in communication education; strategic corporate communication; immersive spectatorship; global corporate communication; communications strategy development; public and media relations; crisis management; work and life balance. *Unit head:* Prof. Michael Goodman, Director, 646-312-3723, Fax: 646-312-3721, E-mail: michael.goodman@baruch.cuny.edu. *Application contact:* Cathy Levkulic, Assistant Director, Graduate Studies, 646-312-4493, Fax: 646-312-3871, E-mail: wsas.graduate.studies@baruch.cuny.edu.
Website: http://www.baruch.cuny.edu/wsas/academics/corporate_communication/index.htm

**Bellevue University,** Graduate School, College of Arts and Sciences, Bellevue, NE 68005-3098. Offers clinical counseling (MS); healthcare administration (MHA); human services (MA); international security and intelligence studies (MS); managerial communication (MA). *Program availability:* Online learning.

**Boston University,** Metropolitan College, Program in Gastronomy, Boston, MA 02215. Offers communications (MLA); history and culture (MLA). *Program availability:* Part-time, evening/weekend. *Faculty:* 3 full-time (2 women), 14 part-time/adjunct (8 women). *Students:* 7 full-time (all women), 88 part-time (74 women); includes 16 minority (4 Black or African American, non-Hispanic/Latino; 3 Asian, non-Hispanic/Latino; 6 Hispanic/Latino; 3 Two or more races, non-Hispanic/Latino), 10 international. Average age 30. 58 applicants, 76% accepted, 27 enrolled. In 2016, 36 master's awarded. *Degree requirements:* For master's, thesis optional. *Entrance requirements:* Additional exam requirements/recommendations for international students: Required—TOEFL. *Application deadline:* Applications are processed on a rolling basis. Application fee: $85. Electronic applications accepted. *Expenses:* Contact institution. *Financial support:* In 2016–17, 4 research assistantships (averaging $4,200 per year) were awarded; career-related internships or fieldwork, scholarships/grants, and unspecified assistantships also available. Support available to part-time students. Financial award applicants required to submit FAFSA. *Faculty research:* Food studies. *Unit head:* Faculty Coordinator, 617-353-6916, Fax: 617-353-4130, E-mail: gastrmla@bu.edu. *Application contact:* Barbara Rotger, Program Manager, 617-353-6916, Fax: 617-353-4130, E-mail: brotger@bu.edu. Website: http://www.bu.edu/met/gastronomy

**Bowie State University,** Graduate Programs, Program in Organizational Communication, Bowie, MD 20715-9465. Offers MA, Certificate. *Program availability:* Part-time, evening/weekend. *Degree requirements:* For master's, comprehensive exam, thesis optional, research paper. *Entrance requirements:* For master's, minimum GPA of 2.5. Electronic applications accepted. *Faculty research:* International telecommunications, developmental communications.

**Bryant University,** College of Arts and Sciences, Smithfield, RI 02917. Offers communication (MA, Graduate Certificate), including general communication (MA), managerial communication (Graduate Certificate), professional communication (Graduate Certificate), public communication (Graduate Certificate); global environmental studies (MS); health care communication (MA); organizational communication (MA); sustainability practices (Graduate Certificate). *Program availability:* Part-time, evening/weekend. *Faculty:* 2 full-time (0 women), 2 part-time/adjunct (1 woman). *Students:* 4 full-time (all women), 10 part-time (8 women); includes 2 minority (1 Black or African American, non-Hispanic/Latino; 1 Two or more races, non-Hispanic/Latino), 1 international. Average age 32. 29 applicants, 31% accepted, 6 enrolled. In 2016, 6 master's, 2 other advanced degrees awarded. *Degree requirements:* For master's, thesis. *Entrance requirements:* For master's, GRE. Additional exam requirements/recommendations for international students: Required—TOEFL (minimum score 550 paper-based; 80 iBT). *Application deadline:* For fall admission, 8/15 for domestic and international students; for spring admission, 1/15 for domestic and international students; for summer admission, 5/15 for domestic and international students. Applications are processed on a rolling basis. Application fee: $80. Electronic applications accepted. *Expenses:* $932 per credit hour. *Financial support:* Fellowships and research assistantships available. Financial award applicants required to submit FAFSA. *Faculty research:* Mass media and social construction of reality; development and improvement of media literacy skills; sociocultural influences on cognition and learning in K-12 populations, oil pollution impacts on marine and estuarine microbial communities; wetlands ecology. *Unit head:* Bradford Martin, Associate Dean, College of Arts and Sciences, 401-232-6929, E-mail: bmartin@bryant.edu. *Application contact:* Terri Rogers, Admission Assistant, Graduate School, 401-232-6230, E-mail: graduateprograms@bryant.edu.
Website: http://gradschool.bryant.edu/arts-and-sciences/

**California State University, San Bernardino,** Graduate Studies, College of Arts and Letters, Program in Communication Studies, San Bernardino, CA 92407. Offers communication studies (MA); integrated marketing communication (MA). *Faculty:* 5 full-time (3 women). *Students:* 10 full-time (8 women), 27 part-time (20 women); includes 19 minority (4 Black or African American, non-Hispanic/Latino; 2 Asian, non-Hispanic/Latino; 12 Hispanic/Latino; 1 Two or more races, non-Hispanic/Latino), 3 international. 35 applicants, 60% accepted, 17 enrolled. In 2016, 5 master's awarded. *Degree requirements:* For master's, comprehensive exam. *Entrance requirements:* Additional exam requirements/recommendations for international students: Required—TOEFL. *Application deadline:* For fall admission, 5/15 for domestic students. Application fee: $55. *Expenses:* Tuition, state resident: full-time $7843; part-time $5011.20 per year. Tuition and fees vary according to course load, degree level, program and reciprocity agreements. *Unit head:* Dr. Michael Salvador, Chair, 909-537-5820, Fax: 909-537-7009, E-mail: salvador@csusb.edu. *Application contact:* Dr. Francisca Beer, Dean of Graduate Studies, 909-537-5058, Fax: 909-537-7034, E-mail: fbeer@csusb.edu.

**Canisius College,** Graduate Division, College of Arts and Sciences, Department of Communication Studies, Buffalo, NY 14208-1098. Offers communication and leadership (MS). *Program availability:* Part-time, evening/weekend. *Faculty:* 2 full-time (both women), 1 (woman) part-time/adjunct. *Students:* 5 full-time (4 women), 15 part-time (12 women); includes 3 minority (2 Black or African American, non-Hispanic/Latino; 1 Hispanic/Latino). Average age 26. 21 applicants, 38% accepted, 4 enrolled. *Degree requirements:* For master's, thesis. *Entrance requirements:* For master's, GRE (recommended), BA, minimum GPA of 3.0, official transcript of all college work, 2 letters of recommendation. Additional exam requirements/recommendations for international students: Required—TOEFL (minimum score 550 paper-based, 80 iBT), IELTS (minimum score 6.5), or CAEL (minimum score 70). *Application deadline:* For fall admission, 7/15 priority date for domestic students; for spring admission, 4/15 priority date for domestic students. Applications are processed on a rolling basis. Application fee: $25. Electronic applications accepted. Application fee is waived when completed online. *Expenses:* Tuition: Full-time $14,742. *Required fees:* $724. *Financial support:* Career-related internships or fieldwork, Federal Work-Study, scholarships/grants, tuition

waivers (partial), and unspecified assistantships available. Support available to part-time students. Financial award application deadline: 4/30; financial award applicants required to submit FAFSA. *Faculty research:* Conflict and communication, health and communication, leadership. *Unit head:* Dr. Rosanne L. Hartman, Graduate Program Director/Professor, Communication and Leadership, 716-888-2589, Fax: 716-888-3118, E-mail: hartmanr@canisius.edu. *Application contact:* Kathleen B. Davis, Vice President of Enrollment Management, 716-888-2500, Fax: 716-888-3195, E-mail: daviskb@canisius.edu.
Website: http://www.canisius.edu/graduate/

**Carnegie Mellon University,** Dietrich College of Humanities and Social Sciences, Department of English, Program in Professional Writing, Pittsburgh, PA 15213-3891. Offers editing and publishing (MAPW); policy and non-profit communication (MAPW); public and media relations/corporate communications (MAPW); science or healthcare communication (MAPW); technical writing (MAPW); writing for new media (MAPW); writing for print media (MAPW). *Program availability:* Part-time. *Entrance requirements:* For master's, GRE General Test. Additional exam requirements/recommendations for international students: Required—TOEFL, TWE.

**City College of the City University of New York,** Graduate School, Division of Humanities and the Arts, Department of Media and Communication Arts, Program in Branding and Integrated Communications, New York, NY 10031. Offers MPS. *Entrance requirements:* Additional exam requirements/recommendations for international students: Required—TOEFL (minimum score 90 iBT). Tuition and fees vary according to course load, degree level and program.

**Columbia University,** Graduate School of Business, MBA Program, New York, NY 10027. Offers accounting (MBA); decision, risk, and operations (MBA); entrepreneurship (MBA); finance and economics (MBA); healthcare and pharmaceutical management (MBA); human resource management (MBA); international business (MBA); leadership and ethics (MBA); management (MBA); marketing (MBA); media (MBA); private equity (MBA); real estate (MBA); social enterprise (MBA); value investing (MBA); DDS/MBA; JD/MBA; MBA/MIA; MBA/MPH; MBA/MS; MD/MBA. *Entrance requirements:* For master's, GMAT, 2 letters of recommendation. Additional exam requirements/recommendations for international students: Required—TOEFL. Electronic applications accepted. *Expenses:* Contact institution. *Faculty research:* Human decision making and behavioral research; real estate market and mortgage defaults; financial crisis and corporate governance; international business; security analysis and accounting.

**Columbia University,** School of Continuing Education, Program in Strategic Communications, New York, NY 10027. Offers MS. *Program availability:* Part-time, evening/weekend. *Entrance requirements:* For master's, minimum undergraduate GPA of 3.0. Additional exam requirements/recommendations for international students: Required—American Language Program placement test. Electronic applications accepted. *Faculty research:* Marketing communications, public relations, crisis management.

**Concordia University, St. Paul,** College of Business, St. Paul, MN 55104-5494. Offers business administration (MBA), including cyber-security leadership; business and organizational leadership (MBA); health care management (MBA); human resource management (MA); leadership and management (MA); strategic communication management (MA). *Accreditation:* ACBSP. *Program availability:* Part-time, evening/weekend, 100% online, blended/hybrid learning. *Faculty:* 12 full-time (4 women), 36 part-time/adjunct (15 women). *Students:* 462 full-time (288 women), 25 part-time (16 women); includes 123 minority (59 Black or African American, non-Hispanic/Latino; 1 American Indian or Alaska Native, non-Hispanic/Latino; 36 Asian, non-Hispanic/Latino; 10 Hispanic/Latino; 1 Native Hawaiian or other Pacific Islander, non-Hispanic/Latino; 16 Two or more races, non-Hispanic/Latino), 28 international. Average age 34. 269 applicants, 73% accepted, 137 enrolled. In 2016, 192 master's awarded. *Degree requirements:* For master's, thesis (for some programs). *Entrance requirements:* For master's, official transcripts from regionally-accredited institution stating the conferral of a bachelor's degree with minimum cumulative GPA of 3.0; personal statement; professional resume. Additional exam requirements/recommendations for international students: Recommended—TOEFL (minimum score 547 paper-based; 78 iBT), IELTS (minimum score 6). *Application deadline:* For fall admission, 8/1 for domestic and international students; for spring admission, 12/1 for domestic and international students; for summer admission, 5/1 for domestic and international students. Applications are processed on a rolling basis. Application fee: $50. Electronic applications accepted. *Expenses:* Contact institution. *Financial support:* In 2016–17, 259 students received support. Scholarships/grants and unspecified assistantships available. Financial award applicants required to submit FAFSA. *Faculty research:* Alternative dispute resolution, franchising, entrepreneurship, applied business ethics, strategic leadership development. *Unit head:* Dr. Kevin Hall, Dean, 651-603-6165, Fax: 651-641-8807, E-mail: khall@csp.edu. *Application contact:* Kimberly Craig, Associate Vice President, Cohort Enrollment Management, 651-603-6223, Fax: 651-603-6320, E-mail: craig@csp.edu.

**Concordia University Wisconsin,** Graduate Programs, School of Business Administration, MBA Program, Mequon, WI 53097-2402. Offers finance (MBA); health care administration (MBA); human resource management (MBA); international business (MBA); international business-bilingual English/Chinese (MBA); management (MBA); management information systems (MBA); managerial communications (MBA); marketing (MBA); public administration (MBA); risk management (MBA). *Program availability:* Online learning. *Degree requirements:* For master's, comprehensive exam, thesis or alternative. *Entrance requirements:* Additional exam requirements/recommendations for international students: Required—TOEFL. *Application deadline:* For fall admission, 8/1 priority date for domestic students; for spring admission, 1/15 for domestic students. Applications are processed on a rolling basis. Application fee: $50. *Expenses:* Contact institution. *Financial support:* Application deadline: 8/1. *Unit head:* Dr. David Borst, Director, 262-243-4298, Fax: 262-243-4428, E-mail: david.borst@cuw.edu. *Application contact:* Mary Eberhardt, Graduate Admissions, 262-243-4551, Fax: 262-243-4428, E-mail: mary.eberhardt@cuw.edu.

**Cornell University,** Graduate School, Graduate Fields of Agriculture and Life Sciences, Field of Communication, Ithaca, NY 14853. Offers communication (MS, PhD); human-computer interaction (MS, PhD); language and communication (MS, PhD); media communication and society (MS, PhD); organizational communication (MS, PhD); science, environment and health communication (MS, PhD); social psychology of communication (MS, PhD). *Degree requirements:* For master's, thesis (MS); for doctorate, comprehensive exam, thesis/dissertation. *Entrance requirements:* For master's and doctorate, GRE General Test, 3 letters of recommendation. Additional exam requirements/recommendations for international students: Required—TOEFL (minimum score 600 paper-based; 100 iBT). Electronic applications accepted. *Faculty research:* Mass communication, communication technologies, science and environmental communication.

**Dallas Baptist University,** College of Business, Business Administration Program, Dallas, TX 75211-9299. Offers accounting (MBA); business communication (MBA); conflict resolution management (MBA); entrepreneurship (MBA); finance (MBA); health care management (MBA); international business (MBA); leading the non-profit

organization (MBA); management (MBA); management information systems (MBA); marketing (MBA); project management (MBA); technology and engineering management (MBA). *Accreditation:* ACBSP. *Program availability:* Part-time, evening/weekend, 100% online, blended/hybrid learning. *Application deadline:* Applications are processed on a rolling basis. Application fee: $25. Electronic applications accepted. Application fee is waived when completed online. *Expenses:* Tuition: Full-time $15,408; part-time $856 per credit hour. *Required fees:* $400 per semester. Tuition and fees vary according to course load and degree level. *Unit head:* Dr. Sandra Reid, Chair of Graduate Business Programs, 214-333-5280, E-mail: sandra@dbu.edu. *Application contact:* Bobby Soto, Director of Admissions, 214-333-5242, E-mail: graduate@dbu.edu.
Website: http://www3.dbu.edu/graduate/mba.asp

**Dallas Baptist University,** College of Business, Management Program, Dallas, TX 75211-9299. Offers conflict resolution management (MA); general management (MA, MS); health care management (MA); human resource management (MA); organizational communication (MA); performance management (MA); professional sales and management optimization (MA). *Program availability:* Part-time, evening/weekend, 100% online, blended/hybrid learning. *Application deadline:* Applications are processed on a rolling basis. Application fee: $25. Electronic applications accepted. Application fee is waived when completed online. *Expenses:* Tuition: Full-time $15,408; part-time $856 per credit hour. *Required fees:* $400 per semester. Tuition and fees vary according to course load and degree level. *Unit head:* Richard Nassar, Director, 214-333-5280, E-mail: richardn@dbu.edu. *Application contact:* Bobby Soto, Director of Admissions, 214-333-5242, E-mail: graduate@dbu.edu.
Website: http://www.dbu.edu/gsb/ma-in-management

**DePaul University,** College of Communication, Chicago, IL 60614. Offers digital communication and media arts (MA); health communication (MA); journalism (MA); media and cinema studies (MA); organizational and multicultural communication (MA); public relations and advertising (MA); relational communication (MA). *Program availability:* Part-time, evening/weekend. *Entrance requirements:* Additional exam requirements/recommendations for international students: Required—TOEFL (minimum score 590 paper-based; 96 iBT), IELTS (minimum score 7.5) or PTE. Electronic applications accepted.

**Drexel University,** College of Arts and Sciences, Department of Communication, Culture and Media, Program in Communication, Philadelphia, PA 19104-2875. Offers public communication (MS); science communication (MS); technical communication (MS). *Program availability:* Part-time, evening/weekend. *Faculty:* 12 full-time (6 women), 14 part-time/adjunct (8 women). *Students:* 12 full-time (6 women), 27 part-time (21 women); includes 5 minority (2 Black or African American, non-Hispanic/Latino; 1 American Indian or Alaska Native, non-Hispanic/Latino; 1 Asian, non-Hispanic/Latino; 1 Native Hawaiian or other Pacific Islander, non-Hispanic/Latino), 4 international. Average age 30. In 2016, 25 master's awarded. *Degree requirements:* For master's, internship, professional portfolio. *Entrance requirements:* For master's, GRE or minimum GPA of 3.0. Additional exam requirements/recommendations for international students: Required—TOEFL. *Application deadline:* For fall admission, 8/21 for domestic students. Applications are processed on a rolling basis. Application fee: $50. Electronic applications accepted. *Expenses:* Tuition: Full-time $32,184; part-time $1192 per credit hour. *Required fees:* $280. Tuition and fees vary according to campus/location and program. *Financial support:* Research assistantships, teaching assistantships, career-related internships or fieldwork, Federal Work-Study, institutionally sponsored loans, tuition waivers (partial), and unspecified assistantships available. Financial award application deadline: 2/1. *Unit head:* Dr. Douglas Porpora, Head, 215-895-2446, Fax: 215-895-1071. *Application contact:* Director of Graduate Admissions, 215-895-6700, Fax: 215-895-5939, E-mail: enroll@drexel.edu.

**Eastern Michigan University,** Graduate School, Academic and Student Affairs Division, Ypsilanti, MI 48197. Offers individualized studies (MA, MS); integrated marketing communications (MS). *Students:* 2 full-time (both women), 50 part-time (33 women); includes 8 minority (3 Black or African American, non-Hispanic/Latino; 4 Asian, non-Hispanic/Latino; 1 Two or more races, non-Hispanic/Latino), 1 international. 84 applicants, 83% accepted, 31 enrolled. *Entrance requirements:* Additional exam requirements/recommendations for international students: Required—TOEFL. Application fee: $45. *Unit head:* Dr. Wade Tornquist, Interim Dean, 734-487-0042, Fax: 734-487-0050, E-mail: wade.tornquist@emich.edu. *Application contact:* Graduate Admissions, 734-487-2400, Fax: 734-487-6559, E-mail: graduate.admissions@emich.edu.

**Eastern Michigan University,** Graduate School, College of Business, Department of Marketing, Program in Integrated Marketing Communications, Ypsilanti, MI 48197. Offers MS, Postbaccalaureate Certificate. *Students:* 15 full-time (11 women), 40 part-time (33 women); includes 14 minority (10 Black or African American, non-Hispanic/Latino; 4 Two or more races, non-Hispanic/Latino). Average age 32. 29 applicants, 72% accepted, 15 enrolled. In 2016, 23 master's, 1 other advanced degree awarded. Application fee: $45. *Application contact:* K. Michelle Henry, Director, Graduate Business Programs, 734-487-4444, Fax: 734-478-1316, E-mail: cob.graduate@emich.edu.

**East Tennessee State University,** School of Graduate Studies, College of Arts and Sciences, Department of Communication and Performance, Johnson City, TN 37614. Offers professional communication (MA), including communication studies, storytelling and theatre, strategic communication. Program offered with Department of Mass Communications. *Program availability:* Part-time. *Degree requirements:* For master's, comprehensive exam, thesis optional. *Entrance requirements:* For master's, GRE General Test, minimum GPA of 3.0; three letters of recommendation. Additional exam requirements/recommendations for international students: Required—TOEFL (minimum score 550 paper-based; 79 iBT). Electronic applications accepted. *Faculty research:* Political communications, visual communication, depictions of gender and ethnicity in print and online media and online corporate media, presidential rhetoric and newspaper coverage of presidential speeches.

**Emerson College,** Graduate Studies, School of Communication, Department of Communication Studies, Program in Communication Management, Boston, MA 02116-4624. Offers MA. *Program availability:* Part-time, evening/weekend. *Faculty:* 19 full-time (8 women). *Students:* 32 full-time (23 women), 6 part-time (5 women), 11 international. Average age 25. 49 applicants, 84% accepted, 18 enrolled. In 2016, 15 master's awarded. *Entrance requirements:* For master's, GMAT or GRE General Test. Additional exam requirements/recommendations for international students: Required—TOEFL (minimum score 550 paper-based; 80 iBT), IELTS (minimum score 6.5). *Application deadline:* For fall admission, 3/1 priority date for domestic and international students; for spring admission, 11/1 for domestic and international students. Applications are processed on a rolling basis. Application fee: $60 ($75 for international students). Electronic applications accepted. *Financial support:* In 2016–17, 6 students received support, including 16 fellowships with partial tuition reimbursements available (averaging $5,344 per year); research assistantships with partial tuition reimbursements available, Federal Work-Study, scholarships/grants, and unspecified assistantships also available. Financial award application deadline: 3/1; financial award applicants required to submit FAFSA. *Faculty research:* Organizational management, corporate and organizational communication. *Application contact:* Leanda Ferland, Director of Graduate Admission, 617-824-8610, Fax: 617-824-8614, E-mail: gradapp@emerson.edu.
Website: http://www.emerson.edu/graduate_admission

**Emerson College,** Graduate Studies, School of Communication, Department of Marketing Communication, Program in Integrated Marketing Communication, Boston, MA 02116-4624. Offers MA. *Program availability:* Part-time, evening/weekend. *Faculty:* 16 full-time (6 women), 5 part-time/adjunct (1 woman). *Students:* 85 full-time (71 women), 8 part-time (all women); includes 8 minority (4 Black or African American, non-Hispanic/Latino; 1 Asian, non-Hispanic/Latino; 1 Hispanic/Latino; 2 Two or more races, non-Hispanic/Latino), 55 international. Average age 26. 164 applicants, 84% accepted, 43 enrolled. In 2016, 61 master's awarded. *Entrance requirements:* For master's, GMAT or GRE General Test. Additional exam requirements/recommendations for international students: Required—TOEFL (minimum score 550 paper-based; 80 iBT), IELTS (minimum score 6.5). *Application deadline:* For fall admission, 6/1 priority date for domestic students, 5/1 priority date for international students; for spring admission, 11/1 priority date for domestic students. Applications are processed on a rolling basis. Application fee: $60 ($75 for international students). Electronic applications accepted. *Financial support:* In 2016–17, 29 students received support, including 36 fellowships with partial tuition reimbursements available (averaging $8,306 per year); research assistantships with partial tuition reimbursements available, Federal Work-Study, scholarships/grants, and unspecified assistantships also available. Financial award application deadline: 3/1; financial award applicants required to submit FAFSA. *Faculty research:* Marketing, international business. *Application contact:* Leanda Ferland, Director of Graduate Admission, 617-824-8610, Fax: 617-824-8614, E-mail: gradapp@emerson.edu.
Website: http://www.emerson.edu/graduate_admission

**Fairleigh Dickinson University, College at Florham,** Maxwell Becton College of Arts and Sciences, Department of English, Communication and Philosophy, Program in Corporate and Organizational Communication, Madison, NJ 07940-1099. Offers MA, MA/MBA. *Entrance requirements:* For master's, GRE General Test.

**Florida State University,** The Graduate School, College of Communication and Information, School of Communication, Tallahassee, FL 32306-2664. Offers communication theory and research (PhD); integrated marketing communication (MA, MS); media and communication studies (MA, MS); public interest media and communication (MA, MS). *Program availability:* Part-time. *Faculty:* 22 full-time (11 women), 2 part-time/adjunct (1 woman). *Students:* 71 full-time (53 women), 72 part-time (46 women); includes 77 minority (20 Black or African American, non-Hispanic/Latino; 36 Asian, non-Hispanic/Latino; 19 Hispanic/Latino; 2 Two or more races, non-Hispanic/Latino). Average age 24. 140 applicants, 57% accepted, 46 enrolled. In 2016, 83 master's, 5 doctorates awarded. *Degree requirements:* For master's, thesis (for some programs); for doctorate, comprehensive exam, thesis/dissertation. *Entrance requirements:* For master's, GRE General Test, minimum GPA of 3.0; for doctorate, GRE General Test, minimum GPA of 3.3 in graduate course work. Additional exam requirements/recommendations for international students: Required—TOEFL (minimum score 600 paper-based; 100 iBT), IELTS (minimum score 7). *Application deadline:* For fall admission, 7/1 priority date for domestic students, 5/1 priority date for international students; for spring admission, 11/1 priority date for domestic and international students; for summer admission, 3/1 priority date for domestic and international students. Applications are processed on a rolling basis. Application fee: $30. Electronic applications accepted. *Expenses:* $479.32 per credit hour in-state, $1,110.72 per credit hour out-of-state. *Financial support:* In 2016–17, 87 students received support, including 17 research assistantships with full tuition reimbursements available (averaging $16,192 per year), 46 teaching assistantships with full tuition reimbursements available (averaging $16,192 per year); fellowships, career-related internships or fieldwork, Federal Work-Study, institutionally sponsored loans, scholarships/grants, health care benefits, tuition waivers (full and partial), and unspecified assistantships also available. Support available to part-time students. Financial award application deadline: 12/15; financial award applicants required to submit FAFSA. *Faculty research:* Communication in the public interest; strategic communication; media and technology; multicultural, intercultural, and international communication. *Total annual research expenditures:* $52,979. *Unit head:* Dr. Gary Heald, Director, 850-644-5034, Fax: 850-644-8642, E-mail: gheald@fsu.edu. *Application contact:* Natashia Hinson-Turner, Graduate Coordinator, 850-644-5034, Fax: 850-644-8642, E-mail: comgradadvising@cci.fsu.edu.
Website: http://www.cci.fsu.edu

**Franklin University,** Marketing and Communication Program, Columbus, OH 43215-5399. Offers MS. *Program availability:* Part-time, evening/weekend. *Entrance requirements:* For master's, minimum undergraduate GPA of 2.75. Additional exam requirements/recommendations for international students: Required—TOEFL (minimum score 550 paper-based). Electronic applications accepted.

**Golden Gate University,** Ageno School of Business, San Francisco, CA 94105-2968. Offers accounting (MBA); business administration (EMBA, MBA, PMBA, DBA); business analytics (MS); finance (MBA, MS, Certificate); financial planning (MS, Certificate); healthcare information systems (Certificate); human resource management (MBA, MS); human resources management (Certificate); information systems (MS); information technology (MBA); information technology management (Certificate); integrated marketing and communications (MS, Certificate); international business (MBA); management (MBA); marketing (MBA, MS, Certificate); operations supply chain management (Certificate); psychology (MA, Certificate); public administration (EMPA); public relations (MS, Certificate); technical market analysis (Certificate); JD/MBA. *Program availability:* Part-time, evening/weekend. *Faculty:* 18 full-time (3 women), 117 part-time/adjunct (44 women). *Students:* 458 full-time (254 women), 664 part-time (331 women); includes 346 minority (75 Black or African American, non-Hispanic/Latino; 2 American Indian or Alaska Native, non-Hispanic/Latino; 132 Asian, non-Hispanic/Latino; 105 Hispanic/Latino; 9 Native Hawaiian or other Pacific Islander, non-Hispanic/Latino; 23 Two or more races, non-Hispanic/Latino), 354 international. Average age 34. 905 applicants, 83% accepted, 165 enrolled. In 2016, 350 master's, 2 doctorates awarded. *Degree requirements:* For doctorate, thesis/dissertation, qualifying examination. *Entrance requirements:* For master's, GMAT (for MBA), minimum GPA of 2.5 (MS). Additional exam requirements/recommendations for international students: Required—TOEFL (minimum score 550 paper-based; 79 iBT). *Application deadline:* For fall admission, 5/15 for domestic and international students; for winter admission, 1/15 for domestic and international students; for spring admission, 9/15 for domestic and international students. Applications are processed on a rolling basis. Application fee: $70 ($110 for international students). Electronic applications accepted. *Expenses:* Contact institution. *Financial support:* In 2016–17, 372 students received support. Career-related internships or fieldwork, Federal Work-Study, institutionally sponsored loans, and scholarships/grants available. Support available to part-time students. Financial award applicants required to submit FAFSA. *Unit head:* Dr. Gordon Swartz, Dean, 415-442-7027, Fax: 415-442-6579, E-mail: gswartz@ggu.edu. *Application contact:* Angela Melero, Enrollment Services, 415-442-7800, Fax: 415-442-7807, E-mail: info@ggu.edu.
Website: http://www.ggu.edu/programs/business-and-management

## Corporate and Organizational Communication

**HEC Montreal,** School of Business Administration, Graduate Diploma Programs in Administration, Program in Marketing Communication, Montréal, QC H3T 2A7, Canada. Offers Graduate Diploma. All courses are given in English. *Students:* 91 part-time (71 women). 76 applicants, 51% accepted, 32 enrolled. In 2016, 26 Graduate Diplomas awarded. *Degree requirements:* For Graduate Diploma, one foreign language. *Entrance requirements:* For degree, bachelor's degree in administration (for marketing option), two years of work experience. *Application deadline:* For fall admission, 4/15 for domestic and international students. Application fee: $86 Canadian dollars. Electronic applications accepted. *Expenses: Tuition, area resident:* Part-time $77.80 Canadian dollars per credit. Tuition, state resident: full-time $2797 Canadian dollars; part-time $240.92 Canadian dollars per credit. Tuition, nonresident: full-time $8673 Canadian dollars; part-time $531.43 Canadian dollars per credit. *International tuition:* $19,131 Canadian dollars full-time. *Required fees:* $1699 Canadian dollars; $40.58 Canadian dollars per credit. $67.32 Canadian dollars per term. Tuition and fees vary according to degree level and program. *Financial support:* In 2016–17, 814 students received support. Research assistantships, teaching assistantships, and scholarships/grants available. Financial award application deadline: 9/2. *Unit head:* Renaud Lachance, Director, 514-340-7165, E-mail: renaud.lachance@hec.ca. *Application contact:* Anny Caron, Administrative Director, 514-340-3598, Fax: 514-340-6411, E-mail: anny.caron@hec.ca.
Website: http://www.hec.ca/programmes/dess/dess-gestion-communication-marketing/index.html

**High Point University,** Norcross Graduate School, High Point, NC 27268. Offers business administration (MBA); educational leadership (M Ed); elementary education (M Ed); history (MA); nonprofit management (MA); secondary math (M Ed); special education (M Ed); strategic communication (MA); teaching elementary education k-6 (MAT); teaching secondary mathematics 9-12 (MAT). *Accreditation:* NCATE. *Program availability:* Part-time, evening/weekend. *Degree requirements:* For master's, comprehensive exam (for some programs), thesis (for some programs). *Entrance requirements:* For master's, GMAT (MBA), GRE, MAT, minimum GPA of 3.0. Additional exam requirements/recommendations for international students: Required—TOEFL (minimum score 550 paper-based). Electronic applications accepted.

**Howard University,** School of Communications, Department of Communication and Culture, Washington, DC 20059-0002. Offers intercultural communication (MA, PhD); organizational communication (MA, PhD). Offered through the Graduate School of Arts and Sciences. *Program availability:* Part-time. Terminal master's awarded for partial completion of doctoral program. *Degree requirements:* For master's, comprehensive exam or thesis; for doctorate, one foreign language, comprehensive exam, thesis/dissertation. *Entrance requirements:* For master's, English proficiency exam, GRE General Test, minimum GPA of 3.0; for doctorate, English proficiency exam, GRE General Test, master's degree in related field, minimum GPA of 3.5. Additional exam requirements/recommendations for international students: Required—TOEFL. *Faculty research:* Media effects, black discourse, development communication, African-American organizations.

**Illinois Institute of Technology,** Stuart School of Business, Program in Marketing Analytics and Communication, Chicago, IL 60661. Offers MS, MBA/MS. *Program availability:* Part-time, evening/weekend. *Entrance requirements:* For master's, GRE (minimum score 1000) or GMAT (500). Additional exam requirements/recommendations for international students: Required—TOEFL (minimum score 600 paper-based; 85 iBT); Recommended—IELTS (minimum score 7). Electronic applications accepted. *Expenses:* Contact institution.

**Iowa State University of Science and Technology,** Department of English, Ames, IA 50011. Offers creative writing (MFA); English (MA); rhetoric and professional communication (PhD). *Degree requirements:* For master's, thesis or alternative; for doctorate, thesis/dissertation. *Entrance requirements:* For master's, GRE General Test, sample of written work, resume, portfolio in creative writing; for doctorate, GRE General Test, sample of written work, resume. Additional exam requirements/recommendations for international students: Required—TOEFL (minimum score 600 paper-based; 100 iBT), IELTS (minimum score 7). *Application deadline:* For fall admission, 1/5 priority date for domestic and international students. Application fee: $60 ($90 for international students). Electronic applications accepted. *Faculty research:* Creative writing, literature, rhetoric, composition and professional communication, teaching English as a second language, applied linguistics. *Application contact:* Teresa Smiley, Application Contact, 515-294-2477, Fax: 515-294-6814, E-mail: englgrad@iastate.edu.
Website: http://www.engl.iastate.edu/resources/graduate-studies/

**Iowa State University of Science and Technology,** Program in Rhetoric and Professional Communication, Ames, IA 50011. Offers PhD. *Entrance requirements:* For doctorate, GRE, official academic transcripts, resume, three letters of recommendation, writing sample. Additional exam requirements/recommendations for international students: Required—TOEFL (minimum score 640 paper-based; 111 iBT), IELTS (minimum score 7.5). *Application deadline:* For fall admission, 1/5 for domestic students. Application fee: $60 ($90 for international students). Electronic applications accepted. *Application contact:* Teresa Smiley, Application Contact, 515-294-2477, Fax: 515-294-6814, E-mail: englgrad@iastate.edu.
Website: http://engl.iastate.edu/resources/graduate-studies/

**Iowa State University of Science and Technology,** Program in Rhetoric, Composition, and Professional Communication, Ames, IA 50011. Offers MA. *Entrance requirements:* For master's, GRE, official academic transcripts, resume, three letters of recommendation, writing sample. Additional exam requirements/recommendations for international students: Required—TOEFL (minimum score 600 paper-based; 100 iBT), IELTS (minimum score 7). *Application deadline:* For fall admission, 1/5 for domestic students. Application fee: $60 ($90 for international students). Electronic applications accepted. *Application contact:* Teresa Smiley, Application Contact, 515-294-2477, Fax: 515-294-6814, E-mail: englgrad@iastate.edu.
Website: http://engl.iastate.edu/resources/graduate-studies/

**La Salle University,** School of Arts and Sciences, Program in Strategic Communication, Philadelphia, PA 19141-1199. Offers communication consulting and development (MA); communication management (MA); general professional communication (MA); professional and business communication (Certificate); public relations (MA); social and new media (Certificate). *Program availability:* Part-time, evening/weekend, online learning. *Faculty:* 4 full-time (all women), 1 (woman) part-time/adjunct. *Students:* 11 full-time (7 women), 39 part-time (29 women); includes 18 minority (15 Black or African American, non-Hispanic/Latino; 2 Hispanic/Latino; 1 Two or more races, non-Hispanic/Latino), 2 international. Average age 27. 13 applicants, 92% accepted, 6 enrolled. In 2016, 41 master's, 4 other advanced degrees awarded. *Degree requirements:* For master's, practicum. *Entrance requirements:* For master's, writing assessment, professional resume; minimum overall B average; two letters of recommendation (if GPA below 3.25); brief personal statement (about 500 words); interview; for Certificate, writing assessment, minimum GPA of 2.75 in undergraduate studies; brief personal statement (about 500 words); interview. Additional exam requirements/recommendations for international students: Required—TOEFL. *Application deadline:* For fall admission, 8/15 priority date for domestic students, 7/15 for international students; for spring admission, 12/15 priority date for domestic students, 11/15 for international students; for summer admission, 4/15 priority date for domestic students, 3/

15 for international students. Applications are processed on a rolling basis. Application fee: $35. Electronic applications accepted. Application fee is waived when completed online. *Expenses:* Contact institution. *Financial support:* In 2016–17, 7 students received support. Scholarships/grants available. Support available to part-time students. Financial award application deadline: 8/31; financial award applicants required to submit FAFSA. *Unit head:* Dr. Pamela Lannutti, Director, 215-951-1935, Fax: 215-951-5043, E-mail: annutti95@lasalle.edu. *Application contact:* Elizabeth Heenan, Director, Graduate and Adult Enrollment, 215-951-1100, Fax: 214-951-1462, E-mail: heenan@lasalle.edu.
Website: http://www.lasalle.edu/strategic-communication/

**Lasell College,** Graduate and Professional Studies in Communication, Newton, MA 02466. Offers health communication (MSC, Graduate Certificate); integrated marketing communication (MSC, Graduate Certificate); public relations (MSC, Graduate Certificate). *Program availability:* Part-time, evening/weekend, 100% online, blended/hybrid learning. *Faculty:* 4 full-time (2 women), 5 part-time/adjunct (2 women). *Students:* 12 full-time (9 women), 38 part-time (28 women); includes 11 minority (8 Black or African American, non-Hispanic/Latino; 1 Asian, non-Hispanic/Latino; 2 Hispanic/Latino), 8 international. Average age 31. 60 applicants, 43% accepted, 13 enrolled. In 2016, 71 master's, 3 other advanced degrees awarded. *Degree requirements:* For master's, comprehensive exam, thesis or alternative, minimum GPA 3.0; special project or internship. *Entrance requirements:* For master's, one-page personal statement, 2 letters of recommendation, resume, bachelor's degree transcript; for Graduate Certificate, bachelor's degree transcript, 2 letters of recommendation, 1-page personal statement, resume. Additional exam requirements/recommendations for international students: Required—TOEFL (minimum score 550 paper-based, 79 iBT) or IELTS (minimum score 6). *Application deadline:* For fall admission, 8/31 priority date for domestic students, 6/30 priority date for international students; for spring admission, 12/31 priority date for domestic students, 10/31 priority date for international students. Applications are processed on a rolling basis. Electronic applications accepted. *Expenses:* $600 per credit. *Financial support:* In 2016–17, 6 students received support. Federal Work-Study, scholarships/grants, and tuition discounts available. Support available to part-time students. Financial award application deadline: 8/31; financial award applicants required to submit FAFSA. *Faculty research:* Terrorists' use of the internet; refugees' use of cell phones as means of communication in Jordan and Germany; political communication, analysis of the media coverage of the conflict and peace process in northern Ireland; interpersonal communication, strategies to address bullying in online communities, in schools and in the workplace. *Unit head:* Dr. Joan Dolamore, Dean of Graduate and Professional Studies, 617-243-2485, Fax: 617-243-2450, E-mail: gradinfo@lasell.edu. *Application contact:* Adrienne Franciosi, Director of Graduate Enrollment, 617-243-2214, Fax: 617-243-2450, E-mail: gradinfo@lasell.edu.
Website: http://www.lasell.edu/academics/graduate-and-professional-studies/programs-of-study/master-of-science-in-communication.html

**Loyola University Chicago,** Quinlan School of Business, Master of Science in Integrated Marketing Communications Program, Chicago, IL 60611. Offers MSIMC, MSIMC/MBA. *Program availability:* Part-time, evening/weekend. *Faculty:* 10 full-time (8 women), 6 part-time/adjunct (1 woman). *Students:* 30 full-time (22 women), 3 part-time (all women); includes 2 minority (1 Black or African American, non-Hispanic/Latino; 1 Hispanic/Latino), 24 international. Average age 26. 108 applicants, 60% accepted, 16 enrolled. In 2016, 30 master's awarded. *Entrance requirements:* For master's, GMAT or GRE, official transcripts, two letters of recommendation, statement of purpose, resume. Additional exam requirements/recommendations for international students: Required—TOEFL (minimum score 90 iBT) or IELTS (minimum score 6.5). *Application deadline:* For fall admission, 7/15 for domestic and international students; for winter admission, 10/1 for domestic and international students; for spring admission, 1/15 for domestic and international students; for summer admission, 4/1 for domestic and international students. Applications are processed on a rolling basis. Application fee: $50. Electronic applications accepted. Application fee is waived when completed online. *Expenses:* Contact institution. *Financial support:* In 2016–17, 6 students received support. Federal Work-Study, scholarships/grants, health care benefits, and unspecified assistantships available. Support available to part-time students. *Faculty research:* Brand strategy, consumer behavior, digital/interactive marketing, international marketing. *Unit head:* Dr. Mary Ann McGrath, Chair, 312-915-6136, E-mail: mmcgrat@luc.edu. *Application contact:* Lauren Griffin, Enrollment Advisor, Quinlan School of Business Graduate Programs, 312-915-6124, Fax: 312-915-7207, E-mail: lgriffin3@luc.edu.
Website: http://luc.edu/quinlan/mba/masters-in-marketing/

**Manhattanville College,** School of Business, Master of Science in International Management Program, Purchase, NY 10577-2132. Offers business leadership (MS); finance (MS); human resource management (MS); marketing communication management (MS). *Program availability:* Part-time, evening/weekend. *Students:* 10 (9 women); includes 6 minority (2 Black or African American, non-Hispanic/Latino; 3 Hispanic/Latino; 1 Two or more races, non-Hispanic/Latino). Average age 30. 17 applicants, 35% accepted, 3 enrolled. In 2016, 1 master's awarded. *Degree requirements:* For master's, thesis (for some programs), final project. *Entrance requirements:* For master's, transcripts, 2 letters of recommendation, resume. Additional exam requirements/recommendations for international students: Required—TOEFL (minimum score 563 paper-based; 85 iBT). *Application deadline:* Applications are processed on a rolling basis. Application fee: $75. Electronic applications accepted. *Expenses: Tuition:* Full-time $16,470; part-time $915 per credit. *Required fees:* $60 per semester. Part-time tuition and fees vary according to course load and program. *Financial support:* Federal Work-Study, institutionally sponsored loans, scholarships/grants, and unspecified assistantships available. Financial award applicants required to submit FAFSA. *Faculty research:* Market entry in Cuba, linking strategy and customer satisfaction. *Unit head:* Laura Persky, Graduate Program Director, 914-323-5188, E-mail: laura.persky@mville.edu. *Application contact:* Monika Pottgen, Assistant Director, Recruitment and Admissions, 914-323-5150, E-mail: business@mville.edu.
Website: https://www.mville.edu/programs/ms-international-management

**Manhattanville College,** School of Business, Master of Science in Marketing Communication Management Program, Purchase, NY 10577-2132. Offers MS. *Program availability:* Part-time, evening/weekend. *Students:* 21 (15 women); includes 9 minority (3 Black or African American, non-Hispanic/Latino; 1 Asian, non-Hispanic/Latino; 5 Hispanic/Latino). Average age 29. 28 applicants, 25% accepted, 4 enrolled. In 2016, 5 master's awarded. *Degree requirements:* For master's, thesis (for some programs), final project. *Entrance requirements:* For master's, transcripts, 2 letters of recommendation, resume. Additional exam requirements/recommendations for international students: Required—TOEFL (minimum score 563 paper-based; 85 iBT). *Application deadline:* Applications are processed on a rolling basis. Application fee: $75. Electronic applications accepted. *Expenses: Tuition:* Full-time $16,470; part-time $915 per credit. *Required fees:* $60 per semester. Part-time tuition and fees vary according to course load and program. *Financial support:* Federal Work-Study, institutionally sponsored loans, scholarships/grants, and unspecified assistantships available. Financial award applicants required to submit FAFSA. *Faculty research:* Crisis communications, public relations. *Unit head:* Laura Persky, Graduate Program Director, 914-323-5188, E-mail: laura.persky@mville.edu. *Application contact:* Monika Pottgen, Assistant Director,

Recruitment and Admissions, 914-323-5150, E-mail: business@mville.edu. Website: https://www.mville.edu/programs/ms-marketing-communication-management

**Marist College,** Graduate Programs, School of Communication and the Arts, Program in Integrated Marketing Communication, Poughkeepsie, NY 12601-1387. Offers MA. *Entrance requirements:* For master's, GRE or GMAT, official undergraduate/graduate transcripts from all institutions attended; current resume; completed recommendation forms for three references; personal statement.

**Minnesota State University Mankato,** College of Graduate Studies and Research, College of Arts and Humanities, Department of Communication Studies, Mankato, MN 56001. Offers communication education (Certificate); communication studies (MA, MS); forensics (MFA); professional communication (Certificate). *Students:* 16 full-time (9 women), 48 part-time (31 women). *Degree requirements:* For master's, one foreign language, comprehensive exam, thesis. *Entrance requirements:* For master's, minimum GPA of 3.0 during previous 2 years, writing sample. *Application deadline:* For fall admission, 7/1 priority date for domestic students, 5/1 for international students; for spring admission, 11/1 for domestic students, 10/1 for international students. Applications are processed on a rolling basis. Application fee: $40. Electronic applications accepted. *Financial support:* Research assistantships, teaching assistantships with full tuition reimbursements, career-related internships or fieldwork, Federal Work-Study, and institutionally sponsored loans available. Support available to part-time students. Financial award application deadline: 3/15; financial award applicants required to submit FAFSA.
Website: http://www.mnsu.edu/cmst/

**Mississippi College,** Graduate School, College of Arts and Sciences, School of Christian Studies and the Arts, Department of Communication, Clinton, MS 39058. Offers applied communication (MSC); public relations and corporate communication (MSC). *Program availability:* Part-time. *Degree requirements:* For master's, comprehensive exam, thesis optional. *Entrance requirements:* For master's, GRE or NTE, minimum GPA of 2.5. Additional exam requirements/recommendations for international students: Recommended—TOEFL, IELTS. Electronic applications accepted.

**Monmouth University,** Graduate Studies, Department of Corporate and Public Communication, West Long Branch, NJ 07764-1898. Offers corporate and public communication (MA); human resources management and communication (Certificate); public service communication specialist (Certificate); strategic public relations and new media (Certificate). *Program availability:* Part-time, evening/weekend. *Degree requirements:* For master's, comprehensive exam (for some programs), thesis (for some programs), project. *Entrance requirements:* For master's, GRE, baccalaureate degree with minimum GPA of 3.0 in major, 2.75 overall; two letters of recommendation; personal essay (750 words or less describing preparation for study and personal objectives); digital or hard copy portfolio of select samples of work including a writing sample; resume. Additional exam requirements/recommendations for international students: Required—TOEFL (minimum score 550 paper-based; 79 iBT), IELTS (minimum score 6), Michigan English Language Assessment Battery (minimum score 77). Electronic applications accepted. *Faculty research:* Service-learning, history of television, feminism and the media, executive communication, public relations pedagogy.

**Montclair State University,** The Graduate School, College of the Arts, MA Program in Public and Organizational Relations, Montclair, NJ 07043-1624. Offers MA. *Program availability:* Part-time, evening/weekend. *Degree requirements:* For master's, comprehensive exam. *Entrance requirements:* For master's, GRE General Test, 2 letters of recommendation. Additional exam requirements/recommendations for international students: Required—TOEFL (minimum score 83 iBT) or IELTS (minimum score 6.5). Electronic applications accepted. *Expenses:* Tuition, state resident: part-time $553 per credit. Tuition, nonresident: part-time $854 per credit. *Required fees:* $91 per credit. Tuition and fees vary according to program. *Faculty research:* Organizational problem solving and innovation, social media, health communication, globalization, organizational change management.

**Murray State University,** College of Business and Public Affairs, Program in Organizational Communication, Murray, KY 42071. Offers MA, MS. *Program availability:* Part-time. *Degree requirements:* For master's, thesis (for some programs). *Entrance requirements:* For master's, minimum GPA of 2.5 for conditional admittance, 3.0 for unconditional admittance. Additional exam requirements/recommendations for international students: Required—TOEFL (minimum score 550 paper-based). *Faculty research:* Organizational learning, organizational culture, leadership, health communication, personality.

**New Mexico State University,** College of Arts and Sciences, Department of English, Las Cruces, NM 88003. Offers creative writing (MFA); English (MA), including creative writing, English studies for teachers, literature, rhetoric and professional communication; rhetoric and professional communication (PhD). *Program availability:* Part-time. *Faculty:* 19 full-time (9 women), 1 (woman) part-time/adjunct. *Students:* 48 full-time (33 women), 24 part-time (14 women); includes 19 minority (2 Asian, non-Hispanic/Latino; 15 Hispanic/Latino; 2 Two or more races, non-Hispanic/Latino), 6 international. Average age 34. 90 applicants, 32% accepted, 19 enrolled. In 2016, 21 master's, 5 doctorates awarded. *Degree requirements:* For master's, one foreign language, thesis (for some programs); for doctorate, comprehensive exam, thesis/dissertation, internship. *Entrance requirements:* For master's and doctorate, sample of written work. Additional exam requirements/recommendations for international students: Required—TOEFL (minimum score 550 paper-based; 79 iBT), IELTS (minimum score 6.5). *Application deadline:* For fall admission, 2/1 for domestic and international students. Application fee: $40 ($50 for international students). Electronic applications accepted. *Expenses:* Tuition, state resident: full-time $4086. Tuition, nonresident: full-time $14,254. *Required fees:* $853. Tuition and fees vary according to course load. *Financial support:* In 2016–17, 47 students received support, including 42 teaching assistantships (averaging $17,394 per year); career-related internships or fieldwork, Federal Work-Study, scholarships/grants, traineeships, health care benefits, and unspecified assistantships also available. Support available to part-time students. Financial award application deadline: 3/1. *Faculty research:* Composition research, history and theory of rhetoric, technical/professional communication, creative writing, English and American literature. *Total annual research expenditures:* $10,316. *Unit head:* Dr. Barry L. Thatcher, Department Head, 575-646-3931, Fax: 575-646-7725, E-mail: bathatch@nmsu.edu. *Application contact:* Dr. Tracey Eileen Miller-Tomlinson, Director of Graduate Studies, 575-646-2213, Fax: 575-646-7725, E-mail: tomlin@nmsu.edu.
Website: http://english.nmsu.edu

**New York University,** School of Continuing and Professional Studies, Division of Programs in Business, Program in Integrated Marketing, New York, NY 10012-1019. Offers brand management (MS); digital marketing (MS); marketing analytics (MS). *Program availability:* Part-time, evening/weekend. *Degree requirements:* For master's, comprehensive exam, thesis, capstone; writing of complete business plan. *Entrance requirements:* For master's, GRE or GMAT (only upon request), bachelor's degree, resume with relevant professional work, internship or volunteer experience, two letters of recommendation, statement of purpose. Additional exam requirements/recommendations for international students: Required—TOEFL (minimum score 600 paper-based; 100 iBT), IELTS (minimum score 7). Electronic applications accepted. *Faculty research:* Branding, digital marketing, Web analytics, consumer behavior, customer loyalty, campaign planning and management.

**New York University,** School of Continuing and Professional Studies, Division of Programs in Business, Programs in Marketing and Public Relations, New York, NY 10012-1019. Offers corporate and organizational communication (MS); public relations management (MS). *Program availability:* Part-time, evening/weekend. *Degree requirements:* For master's, thesis. *Entrance requirements:* For master's, GRE or GMAT (only upon request), bachelor's degree, resume with relevant professional work, internship or volunteer experience, two letters of recommendation, statement of purpose. Additional exam requirements/recommendations for international students: Required—TOEFL (minimum score 600 paper-based; 100 iBT), IELTS (minimum score 7). Electronic applications accepted.

**Northeastern University,** College of Professional Studies, Boston, MA 02115-5096. Offers applied nutrition (MS); college athletics administration (MSL); commerce and economic development (MS); corporate and organizational communication (MS); criminal justice (MS); digital media (MPS); elearning and instructional design (M Ed); elementary education (MAT); geographic information technology (MPS); global studies and international relations (MS); higher education administration (M Ed); homeland security (MA); human services (MS); informatics (MPS); leadership (MS); learning analytics (M Ed); learning and instruction (M Ed); nonprofit management (MS); professional sports administration (MSL); project management (MS); regulatory affairs for drugs, biologics, and medical devices (MS); respiratory care leadership (MS); special education (M Ed); technical communication (MS). *Program availability:* Part-time, evening/weekend, 100% online, blended/hybrid learning. *Faculty:* 82 full-time (51 women), 853 part-time/adjunct (366 women). *Students:* 4,947 part-time (3,076 women). In 2016, 1,456 master's awarded. *Application deadline:* Applications are processed on a rolling basis. Application fee: $0. Electronic applications accepted. *Expenses:* Contact institution. *Financial support:* Applicants required to submit FAFSA. *Unit head:* Dr. Mary Loeffelholz, Interim Dean of the College of Professional Studies.
Website: http://www.cps.neu.edu/

**Northwestern University,** The Graduate School, School of Communication, Department of Communication Studies, Evanston, IL 60208. Offers communication studies (PhD), including interaction and social influence, rhetoric and public culture; managerial communication (MSC); media, technology and society (PhD); technology and social behavior (PhD). PhD admissions and degree offered through The Graduate School. Terminal master's awarded for partial completion of doctoral program. *Degree requirements:* For doctorate, thesis/dissertation. *Entrance requirements:* For master's and doctorate, GRE General Test. Additional exam requirements/recommendations for international students: Required—TOEFL. Electronic applications accepted.

**Northwestern University,** Medill School of Journalism, Media, and Integrated Marketing Communications, Integrated Marketing Communications Program, Evanston, IL 60208. Offers brand strategy (MSIMC); content marketing (MSIMC); direct and interactive marketing (MSIMC); marketing analytics (MSIMC); strategic communications (MSIMC). *Program availability:* Part-time. *Entrance requirements:* For master's, GRE General Test or GMAT, full-time work experience (preferred). Additional exam requirements/recommendations for international students: Required—TOEFL. Electronic applications accepted. *Faculty research:* Data mining, business to business marketing, values in advertising, political advertising.

**Ohio University,** Graduate College, Scripps College of Communication, School of Communication Studies, Athens, OH 45701-2979. Offers health communication (PhD); organizational communication (MA); relating and organizing (PhD); rhetoric and public culture (PhD). *Program availability:* Part-time, online learning. Terminal master's awarded for partial completion of doctoral program. *Degree requirements:* For master's, capstone; for doctorate, comprehensive exam, thesis/dissertation. *Entrance requirements:* For master's, GRE; for doctorate, GRE General Test, minimum GPA of 3.0. Additional exam requirements/recommendations for international students: Required—TOEFL (minimum score 550 paper-based; 80 iBT) or IELTS (minimum score 6.5). *Application deadline:* For fall admission, 1/15 priority date for domestic and international students. Application fee: $50 ($55 for international students). Electronic applications accepted. *Financial support:* In 2016–17, 12 students received support. Fellowships with full tuition reimbursements available, research assistantships with full tuition reimbursements available, teaching assistantships with full tuition reimbursements available, career-related internships or fieldwork, Federal Work-Study, and institutionally sponsored loans available. Financial award application deadline: 1/15. *Faculty research:* Rhetoric and public culture, relating and organizing, health communication. *Unit head:* Dr. Claudia Hale, Interim Director, 740-593-4825, E-mail: hale@ohio.edu. *Application contact:* Dr. Benjamin Bates, Associate Director for Graduate Studies, 740-593-9163, Fax: 740-593-4810, E-mail: batesb@ohio.edu.
Website: http://www.coms.ohiou.edu/

**Radford University,** College of Graduate Studies and Research, Program in Corporate and Professional Communication, Radford, VA 24142. Offers MS. *Program availability:* Part-time, evening/weekend. *Faculty:* 7 full-time (2 women). *Students:* 18 full-time (14 women), 2 part-time (1 woman); includes 3 minority (all Black or African American, non-Hispanic/Latino), 1 international. Average age 26. 18 applicants, 94% accepted, 13 enrolled. In 2016, 8 master's awarded. *Degree requirements:* For master's, comprehensive exam, thesis optional. *Entrance requirements:* For master's, GRE, minimum GPA of 2.75, short essay, 3 letters of reference, resume, official transcripts. Additional exam requirements/recommendations for international students: Required—TOEFL (minimum score 550 paper-based; 79 iBT), IELTS (minimum score 6.5). *Application deadline:* For fall admission, 2/15 priority date for domestic students, 12/1 for international students; for spring admission, 7/1 for international students. Applications are processed on a rolling basis. Application fee: $50. Electronic applications accepted. *Expenses:* Tuition, state resident: full-time $7868; part-time $328 per credit hour. Tuition, nonresident: full-time $16,394; part-time $683 per credit hour. *Required fees:* $3090; $130 per credit hour. Tuition and fees vary according to course load and program. *Financial support:* In 2016–17, 15 students received support, including 4 research assistantships (averaging $10,000 per year), 8 teaching assistantships (averaging $10,500 per year); career-related internships or fieldwork, scholarships/grants, and unspecified assistantships also available. Support available to part-time students. Financial award application deadline: 3/1; financial award applicants required to submit FAFSA. *Faculty research:* Rhetoric and persuasion in organizations, media relations, organizational legitimacy, issues management, social capital. *Unit head:* Dr. John Brummette, Coordinator, 540-831-6553, Fax: 540-831-5883, E-mail: comm@radford.edu.
Website: http://www.radford.edu/content/chbs/home/comm.html

**Regent University,** Graduate School, School of Business and Leadership, Virginia Beach, VA 23464-9800. Offers business administration (MBA), including accounting, entrepreneurship, finance and investing, general management, healthcare management (MA, MBA), human resource management, innovation management; leadership (Certificate); organizational leadership (MA, PhD), including ecclesial leadership (PhD), entrepreneurial leadership (PhD), future studies (MA), healthcare management (MA, MBA), human resource development (PhD), interdisciplinary studies (MA), international

## Corporate and Organizational Communication

organizations (MA), leadership coaching and mentoring (MA), not-for-profit management (MA), organizational communication (MA), organizational development consulting (MA); strategic leadership (DSL), including global consulting, leadership coaching, strategic foresight. *Program availability:* Part-time, evening/weekend, 100% online, blended/hybrid learning. *Faculty:* 9 full-time (2 women), 28 part-time/adjunct (10 women). *Students:* 100 full-time (56 women), 1,008 part-time (528 women); includes 562 minority (453 Black or African American, non-Hispanic/Latino; 7 American Indian or Alaska Native, non-Hispanic/Latino; 30 Asian, non-Hispanic/Latino; 51 Hispanic/Latino; 1 Native Hawaiian or other Pacific Islander, non-Hispanic/Latino; 20 Two or more races, non-Hispanic/Latino), 76 international. Average age 40. 1,240 applicants, 45% accepted, 352 enrolled. In 2016, 95 master's, 71 doctorates awarded. *Degree requirements:* For master's, thesis or alternative, 3-credit hour culminating experience; for doctorate, thesis/dissertation. *Entrance requirements:* For master's, college transcripts, resume, essay; for doctorate, college transcripts, resume, essay, writing sample; for Certificate, writing sample, resume, transcripts. Additional exam requirements/recommendations for international students: Required—TOEFL (minimum score 577 paper-based). *Application deadline:* For fall admission, 5/1 priority date for domestic students; for spring admission, 10/1 priority date for domestic students. Applications are processed on a rolling basis. Application fee: $50. Electronic applications accepted. *Expenses:* Contact institution. *Financial support:* In 2016–17, 631 students received support. Career-related internships or fieldwork, scholarships/grants, and unspecified assistantships available. Support available to part-time students. *Faculty research:* Servant leadership, global business, team effectiveness, technology utilization, leadership development. *Unit head:* Dr. Doris Gomez, Dean, 757-352-4686, Fax: 757-352-4634, E-mail: dorigom@regent.edu. *Application contact:* Heidi Cece, Assistant Vice President of Enrollment Management, 800-373-5504, Fax: 757-352-4381, E-mail: admissions@regent.edu.
Website: http://www.regent.edu/sbl/

**Regent University,** Graduate School, School of Communication and the Arts, Virginia Beach, VA 23464-9800. Offers communication (MA, PhD), including media and arts management and promotion (MA), political communication (MA), strategic communication (MA); directing for cinema/television (MFA); film and TV (MA), including producing, production, script writing; journalism (MA); producing for cinema/television (MFA); script and screenwriting (MFA); theatre (MA). *Program availability:* Part-time, 100% online, blended/hybrid learning. *Faculty:* 19 full-time (3 women), 51 part-time/adjunct (17 women). *Students:* 92 full-time (52 women), 344 part-time (225 women); includes 163 minority (116 Black or African American, non-Hispanic/Latino; 6 American Indian or Alaska Native, non-Hispanic/Latino; 7 Asian, non-Hispanic/Latino; 25 Hispanic/Latino; 1 Native Hawaiian or other Pacific Islander, non-Hispanic/Latino; 8 Two or more races, non-Hispanic/Latino), 8 international. Average age 37. 368 applicants, 52% accepted, 124 enrolled. In 2016, 91 master's, 7 doctorates awarded. *Degree requirements:* For master's, thesis or alternative; for doctorate, thesis/dissertation. *Entrance requirements:* For master's, transcripts, writing sample, resume, audition (for MFA programs); for doctorate, GRE General Test, resume, writing sample, recommendations, interview, transcripts, personal goals statement. Additional exam requirements/recommendations for international students: Required—TOEFL (minimum score 577 paper-based). *Application deadline:* For fall admission, 3/1 priority date for domestic students; for spring admission, 10/1 priority date for domestic students. Applications are processed on a rolling basis. Application fee: $50. Electronic applications accepted. *Expenses:* $685 per credit (for MA); $895 per credit (for MFA in acting); $885 per credit (for PhD); $250 per semester technology fee. *Financial support:* In 2016–17, 178 students received support, including 2 fellowships (averaging $10,000 per year); career-related internships or fieldwork, scholarships/grants, and unspecified assistantships also available. Support available to part-time students. *Faculty research:* Screenwriting, digital media production, communication, acting, directing. *Unit head:* Dr. Mitch Land, Dean, 757-352-4916, Fax: 757-352-4291, E-mail: mland@regent.edu. *Application contact:* Heidi Cece, Assistant Vice President of Enrollment Management, 800-373-5504, Fax: 757-352-4381, E-mail: admissions@regent.edu.
Website: http://www.regent.edu/sca/

**Regis College,** Program in Organizational and Professional Communication, Weston, MA 02493. Offers MS. *Program availability:* Part-time, evening/weekend, blended/hybrid learning. *Degree requirements:* For master's, thesis. *Entrance requirements:* For master's, GRE or MAT. Additional exam requirements/recommendations for international students: Required—TOEFL; Recommended—IELTS. *Application deadline:* Applications are processed on a rolling basis. Application fee: $65. Electronic applications accepted. *Financial support:* Federal Work-Study and unspecified assistantships available. Financial award applicants required to submit FAFSA. *Unit head:* Colleen Malachowski, Director, 781-768-7373, E-mail: colleen.malachowski@regiscollege.edu.

**Rider University,** College of Liberal Arts, Education, and Sciences, Lawrenceville, NJ 08648-3001. Offers applied psychology (MA); business communication (MA). *Program availability:* Part-time, evening/weekend. *Entrance requirements:* For master's, official transcripts, current resume, two professional letters of recommendation, statement of aims and objectives, personal interview by invitation of faculty. Additional exam requirements/recommendations for international students: Required—TOEFL (minimum score 550 paper-based). Electronic applications accepted.

**Roosevelt University,** Graduate Division, College of Arts and Sciences, Department of Communication, Program in Integrated Marketing Communications, Chicago, IL 60605. Offers MSIMC. *Program availability:* Part-time, evening/weekend. *Faculty research:* Print journalism, urban high school journalism.

**Rowan University,** Graduate School, College of Communication and Creative Arts, Integrated Marketing Communication and New Media Certificate of Graduate Study Program, Glassboro, NJ 08028-1701. Offers CGS. Electronic applications accepted.

**St. Bonaventure University,** School of Graduate Studies, Jandoli School of Communication, Program in Integrated Marketing Communications, St. Bonaventure, NY 14778-2284. Offers MA. *Program availability:* Part-time, evening/weekend, 100% online. *Faculty:* 4 full-time (1 woman), 7 part-time/adjunct (6 women). *Students:* 29 full-time (17 women), 20 part-time (16 women); includes 10 minority (4 Black or African American, non-Hispanic/Latino; 5 Hispanic/Latino; 1 Two or more races, non-Hispanic/Latino), 3 international. Average age 28. 60 applicants, 75% accepted, 28 enrolled. In 2016, 24 master's awarded. *Degree requirements:* For master's, campaign project. *Entrance requirements:* For master's, transcripts, essay describing desire to pursue the IMC program. Additional exam requirements/recommendations for international students: Required—TOEFL (minimum score 550 paper-based; 79 iBT). *Application deadline:* For fall admission, 6/5 for domestic students, 2/1 for international students; for spring admission, 10/15 for domestic students, 7/1 for international students. Applications are processed on a rolling basis. Application fee: $0. Electronic applications accepted. *Expenses:* $733 per credit, $100 graduation fee. *Financial support:* Federal Work-Study, scholarships/grants, health care benefits, and unspecified assistantships available. Support available to part-time students. Financial award application deadline: 4/15; financial award applicants required to submit FAFSA. *Faculty research:* Network analysis of internal and external communication networks in organizations, organizational behavior, student engagement in active learning. *Unit head:* Dr. Richard

Lee, Director, 716-375-2563, Fax: 716-375-2588, E-mail: rlee@sbu.edu. *Application contact:* Bruce Campbell, Director of Graduate Admissions, 716-375-2429, Fax: 716-375-4015, E-mail: gradsch@sbu.edu.
Website: http://www.sbu.edu/academics/schools/journalism-and-mass-communications/graduate-degrees/ma-integrated-marketing-communications

**St. Bonaventure University,** School of Graduate Studies, Jandoli School of Communication, Program in Strategic Leadership, St. Bonaventure, NY 14778-2284. Offers MA. *Program availability:* Part-time, online only, 100% online. *Faculty:* 1 (woman) full-time, 2 part-time/adjunct (both women). *Students:* 4 full-time (1 woman), 24 part-time (14 women); includes 6 minority (2 Black or African American, non-Hispanic/Latino; 1 Asian, non-Hispanic/Latino; 2 Hispanic/Latino; 1 Two or more races, non-Hispanic/Latino), 1 international. Average age 36. 28 applicants, 86% accepted, 14 enrolled. In 2016, 13 master's awarded. *Degree requirements:* For master's, portfolio, project. *Entrance requirements:* For master's, bachelor's degree, transcripts, three years of work experience, current resume, short essay (500 words) on candidate's goals for engaging in such a learning experience. Additional exam requirements/recommendations for international students: Required—TOEFL (minimum score 550 paper-based; 79 iBT). *Application deadline:* For fall admission, 6/15 for domestic students, 2/1 for international students; for spring admission, 10/15 for domestic students, 7/1 for international students. Applications are processed on a rolling basis. Application fee: $0. Electronic applications accepted. *Expenses:* $733 per credit, $100 graduation fee. *Financial support:* Federal Work-Study, scholarships/grants, and health care benefits available. Support available to part-time students. Financial award application deadline: 4/15; financial award applicants required to submit FAFSA. *Faculty research:* Internet addiction. *Unit head:* Dr. Kimberly Young, Director, 716-375-2076, Fax: 716-375-2588, E-mail: kyoung@sbu.edu. *Application contact:* Bruce Campbell, Director of Graduate Admissions, 716-375-2429, Fax: 716-375-4015, E-mail: gradsch@sbu.edu.
Website: http://www.sbu.edu/academics/schools/journalism-and-mass-communications/graduate-degrees/ms-strategic-leadership/(online)

**Seton Hall University,** College of Communication and the Arts, South Orange, NJ 07079-2697. Offers museum professions (MA), including exhibition development, museum education, museum management, museum registration; public relations (MA); strategic communication (MA). *Program availability:* Part-time, evening/weekend, online learning. *Degree requirements:* For master's, thesis. *Entrance requirements:* Additional exam requirements/recommendations for international students: Required—TOEFL. Electronic applications accepted. *Faculty research:* Managerial communication, communication consulting, communication and development.

**Southern Illinois University Edwardsville,** Graduate School, College of Arts and Sciences, Department of Applied Communication Studies, Program in Corporate and Organizational Communication, Edwardsville, IL 62026. Offers MA. *Program availability:* Part-time, evening/weekend. *Degree requirements:* For master's, comprehensive exam (for some programs), thesis (for some programs). *Entrance requirements:* Additional exam requirements/recommendations for international students: Required—TOEFL (minimum score 550 paper-based, 79 iBT), IELTS (minimum score 6.5), Michigan Test of English Language Proficiency or PTE. Electronic applications accepted.

**Spalding University,** Graduate Studies, College of Social Sciences and Humanities, Program in Business and Communication, Louisville, KY 40203-2188. Offers MS. *Program availability:* Part-time, evening/weekend. *Faculty:* 13 full-time (5 women), 7 part-time/adjunct (2 women). *Students:* 32 full-time (19 women), 33 part-time (18 women); includes 25 minority (21 Black or African American, non-Hispanic/Latino; 1 Asian, non-Hispanic/Latino; 1 Hispanic/Latino; 2 Two or more races, non-Hispanic/Latino). Average age 38. 33 applicants, 85% accepted, 28 enrolled. In 2016, 34 master's awarded. *Degree requirements:* For master's, project. *Entrance requirements:* For master's, GRE or GMAT, personal essay, interview, letters of recommendation, transcripts, resume. Additional exam requirements/recommendations for international students: Required—TOEFL (minimum score 535 paper-based). *Application deadline:* Applications are processed on a rolling basis. Application fee: $30. *Expenses: Tuition:* Full-time $15,300. *Financial support:* In 2016–17, 2 research assistantships (averaging $10,148 per year) were awarded; scholarships/grants and unspecified assistantships also available. Financial award applicants required to submit FAFSA. *Faculty research:* Curriculum development, consumer behavior, interdisciplinary pedagogy. *Unit head:* Dr. Robin Hinkle, Director, 502-873-4244, E-mail: rhinkle@spalding.edu. *Application contact:* Lorraine Carner, Administrative Assistant, 502-585-7120, E-mail: lcarner@spalding.edu.

**State University of New York at Oswego,** Graduate Studies, School of Communication, Media and the Arts, Oswego, NY 13126. Offers strategic communication (MA), including health communication, integrated media and social networks, organizational communication. *Entrance requirements:* For master's, GRE, official transcript, statement of purpose, resume, two letters of recommendation.

**Stevens Institute of Technology,** Graduate School, School of Business, Program in Professional Communications, Hoboken, NJ 07030. Offers Certificate. *Program availability:* Part-time, evening/weekend. *Degree requirements:* For Certificate, minimum B average. *Entrance requirements:* Additional exam requirements/recommendations for international students: Required—TOEFL (minimum score 74 iBT), IELTS (minimum score 6). *Application deadline:* For fall admission, 6/1 for domestic students, 4/15 for international students; for spring admission, 11/30 for domestic students, 11/1 for international students. Applications are processed on a rolling basis. Application fee: $65. Electronic applications accepted. *Expenses:* Contact institution. *Financial support:* Fellowships, research assistantships, teaching assistantships, career-related internships or fieldwork, Federal Work-Study, scholarships/grants, and unspecified assistantships available. Financial award application deadline: 2/15; financial award applicants required to submit FAFSA. *Unit head:* Deborah Sinnreich-Levi, Director, 201-216-5403. *Application contact:* Graduate Admissions, 800-496-4935, Fax: 201-216-8044, E-mail: gradadmissions@stevens.edu.

**Suffolk University,** College of Arts and Sciences, Advertising and Public Relations Department, Boston, MA 02108-2770. Offers communication studies (MAC); integrated marketing communication (MAC); public relations and advertising (MAC). *Program availability:* Part-time, evening/weekend. *Faculty:* 5 full-time (3 women). *Students:* 14 full-time (9 women), 17 part-time (14 women); includes 5 minority (2 Black or African American, non-Hispanic/Latino; 3 Hispanic/Latino), 12 international. Average age 27. 64 applicants, 66% accepted, 15 enrolled. In 2016, 18 master's awarded. *Degree requirements:* For master's, thesis optional. *Entrance requirements:* For master's, GRE General Test, MAT, or GMAT, 2 letters of recommendation, resume. Additional exam requirements/recommendations for international students: Required—TOEFL (minimum score 550 paper-based; 80 iBT). *Application deadline:* For fall admission, 3/15 priority date for domestic and international students; for spring admission, 10/15 priority date for domestic and international students. Applications are processed on a rolling basis. Application fee: $50. Electronic applications accepted. *Expenses:* $27,456 per year full-time tuition, $1,144 per credit hour part-time tuition, $52 per year student activity fee. *Financial support:* In 2016–17, 22 students received support, including 18 fellowships (averaging $9,186 per year); career-related internships or fieldwork, Federal Work-Study, institutionally sponsored loans, and scholarships/grants also available. Support available to part-time students. Financial award application deadline: 4/1; financial

award applicants required to submit FAFSA. *Faculty research:* Branding law and management, health care communication, gender roles and violence in video games, new media, political communication. *Unit head:* Robert Rosenthal, Chair, 617-573-8502, E-mail: rrosenthal@suffolk.edu. *Application contact:* Mara Marzocchi, Associate Director of Graduate Admissions, 617-573-8302, Fax: 617-305-1733, E-mail: grad.admission@suffolk.edu.
Website: http://www.suffolk.edu/college/graduate/69298.php

**Temple University,** School of Media and Communication, Department of Strategic Communication, Philadelphia, PA 19122-6096. Offers communication management (MS). *Program availability:* Part-time, evening/weekend. *Degree requirements:* For master's, capstone. *Entrance requirements:* For master's, GRE General Test. Additional exam requirements/recommendations for international students: Required—TOEFL (minimum score 620 paper-based; 105 iBT). Electronic applications accepted. *Expenses:* Contact institution.

**Texas Christian University,** Bob Schieffer College of Communication, Fort Worth, TX 76129. Offers communication studies (MS); strategic communication (MS). *Program availability:* Part-time. *Faculty:* 26 full-time (12 women). *Students:* 28 full-time (23 women), 1 part-time; includes 6 minority (1 Black or African American, non-Hispanic/Latino; 2 Asian, non-Hispanic/Latino; 1 Hispanic/Latino; 2 Two or more races, non-Hispanic/Latino), 1 international. Average age 26. 35 applicants, 46% accepted, 9 enrolled. In 2016, 11 master's awarded. *Degree requirements:* For master's, comprehensive exam (for some programs), thesis (for some programs). *Entrance requirements:* For master's, GRE General Test. Additional exam requirements/recommendations for international students: Required—TOEFL (minimum score 550 paper-based; 80 iBT). *Application deadline:* For fall admission, 2/15 for domestic and international students; for spring admission, 10/15 for domestic and international students. Application fee: $60. Electronic applications accepted. *Expenses:* Contact institution. *Financial support:* In 2016-17, 25 students received support, including 18 teaching assistantships with full tuition reimbursements available (averaging $10,000 per year); research assistantships, health care benefits, tuition waivers (full and partial), and unspecified assistantships also available. Financial award application deadline: 2/15. *Faculty research:* Interpersonal communication, family communication, social networking, media history, media studies, media law, media ethics, mobile communications. *Unit head:* Dr. Daxton Stewart, Associate Dean, 817-257-5911, Fax: 817-257-5921, E-mail: d.stewart@tcu.edu. *Application contact:* Alicia E. Craff, Academic Program Specialist, 817-257-5917, Fax: 817-257-5921, E-mail: a.e.craff@tcu.edu.
Website: http://www.schieffercollege.tcu.edu/

**Towson University,** Program in Communications Management, Towson, MD 21252-0001. Offers MS. *Students:* 3 full-time (2 women), 18 part-time (14 women); includes 6 minority (all Black or African American, non-Hispanic/Latino). *Degree requirements:* For master's, thesis. *Entrance requirements:* For master's, bachelor's degree with 24 credits in mass communications, public relations, advertising or communication studies; advanced writing and basic statistics courses; professional experience; minimum GPA of 3.0; letter of recommendation; resume. Additional exam requirements/recommendations for international students: Required—TOEFL. *Application deadline:* For fall admission, 1/15 for domestic students. Application fee: $45. Electronic applications accepted. *Expenses:* Tuition, state resident: full-time $7580; part-time $379 per unit. Tuition, nonresident: full-time $15,700; part-time $785 per unit. *Required fees:* $2480. *Financial support:* Application deadline: 4/1. *Unit head:* Dr. Beth Haller, Graduate Program Director, 410-704-2442, E-mail: bhaller@towson.edu. *Application contact:* Coverley Beidleman, Assistant Director of Graduate Admissions, 410-704-2113, Fax: 410-704-3030, E-mail: grads@towson.edu.
Website: http://www.towson.edu/cofac/departments/communication/gradcommunicationmgmt/

**Troy University,** Graduate School, College of Communication and Fine Arts, Troy, AL 36082. Offers strategic communication (MS). *Program availability:* Part-time, evening/weekend. *Faculty:* 6 full-time (3 women). *Students:* 35 full-time (24 women), 58 part-time (42 women); includes 68 minority (30 Black or African American, non-Hispanic/Latino; 2 Hispanic/Latino; 1 Native Hawaiian or other Pacific Islander, non-Hispanic/Latino; 35 Two or more races, non-Hispanic/Latino). Average age 29. 52 applicants, 100% accepted, 24 enrolled. In 2016, 58 master's awarded. *Degree requirements:* For master's, comprehensive exam, thesis optional, minimum GPA of 3.0, admission to candidacy. *Entrance requirements:* For master's, GRE (minimum score of 850 on old exam or 290 on new exam), MAT (minimum score of 385) or GMAT (minimum score of 380), bachelor's degree; minimum undergraduate GPA of 2.5 or 3.0 on last 30 semester hours. Additional exam requirements/recommendations for international students: Required—TOEFL (minimum score 523 paper-based; 70 iBT), IELTS (minimum score 6). *Application deadline:* For fall admission, 6/1 for international students; for spring admission, 10/15 for international students. Applications are processed on a rolling basis. Application fee: $50. Electronic applications accepted. *Expenses:* Tuition, state resident: full-time $7146; part-time $397 per credit hour. Tuition, nonresident: full-time $14,292; part-time $794 per credit hour. *Required fees:* $802; $50 per semester. Tuition and fees vary according to campus/location and program. *Financial support:* Fellowships, career-related internships or fieldwork, and scholarships/grants available. Support available to part-time students. Financial award applicants required to submit FAFSA. *Unit head:* Dr. Larry Blocher, Dean, 334-670-3869, Fax: 334-670-3547, E-mail: lblocher@troy.edu. *Application contact:* Jessica A. Kimbro, Director of Graduate Admissions, 334-670-3178, E-mail: jacord@troy.edu.

**Universidad Autonoma de Guadalajara,** Graduate Programs, Guadalajara, Mexico. Offers administrative law and justice (LL M); advertising and corporate communications (MA); architecture (M Arch); business (MBA); computational science (MCC); education (Ed M, Ed D); English-Spanish translation (MA); entrepreneurship and management (MBA); integrated management of digital animation (MA); international business (MIB); international corporate law (LL M); internet technologies (MS); manufacturing systems (MMS); occupational health (MS); philosophy (MA, PhD); power electronics (MS); quality systems (MQS); renewable energy (MS); social evaluation of projects (MBA); strategic market research (MBA); tax law (MA); teaching mathematics (MA).

**Universidad Iberoamericana,** Graduate School, Santo Domingo D.N., Dominican Republic. Offers business administration (MBA, PMBA); constitutional law (LL M); dentistry (DMD); educational management (MA); integrated marketing communication (MA); psychopedagogical intervention (M Ed); real estate law (LL M); strategic management of human talent (MM).

**Université de Sherbrooke,** Faculty of Administration, Program in Marketing Communications, Sherbrooke, QC J1K 2R1, Canada. Offers M Adm. *Degree requirements:* For master's, one foreign language, thesis. *Entrance requirements:* For master's, bachelor's degree in related field, minimum GPA of 3.0 (on 4.3 scale). Electronic applications accepted.

**University of Alaska Fairbanks,** College of Liberal Arts, Department of Communications, Fairbanks, AK 99775-5680. Offers professional communication (MA). *Program availability:* Part-time. *Faculty:* 7 full-time (2 women). *Students:* 8 full-time (6 women), 6 part-time (2 women); includes 5 minority (2 Black or African American, non-Hispanic/Latino; 1 Hispanic/Latino; 2 Two or more races, non-Hispanic/Latino), 2

international. Average age 33. 8 applicants, 50% accepted, 4 enrolled. In 2016, 2 master's awarded. *Degree requirements:* For master's, comprehensive exam, thesis, oral defense of thesis. *Entrance requirements:* For master's, bachelor's degree from accredited institution with minimum cumulative undergraduate and major GPA of 3.0, academic writing sample. Additional exam requirements/recommendations for international students: Required—TOEFL (minimum score 550 paper-based; 79 iBT), IELTS (minimum score 6.5). *Application deadline:* For fall admission, 6/1 for domestic students, 3/1 for international students; for spring admission, 10/15 for domestic students, 9/1 for international students. Applications are processed on a rolling basis. Application fee: $60. Electronic applications accepted. *Expenses:* Tuition, state resident: full-time $7992; part-time $444 per credit. Tuition, nonresident: full-time $16,326; part-time $907 per credit. *Required fees:* $39 per credit. $322 per semester. Tuition and fees vary according to course level, course load, campus/location, program and reciprocity agreements. *Financial support:* In 2016-17, 7 teaching assistantships with full tuition reimbursements (averaging $6,542 per year) were awarded; fellowships with full tuition reimbursements, Federal Work-Study, scholarships/grants, tuition waivers, and unspecified assistantships also available. Support available to part-time students. Financial award application deadline: 7/1; financial award applicants required to submit FAFSA. *Faculty research:* Interpersonal communications, health communications, intercultural communications, politeness and face management in conversation, gender communication. *Unit head:* Dr. Peter DeCaro, Department Chair, 907-474-6591, Fax: 907-474-5858, E-mail: fycomm@uaf.edu. *Application contact:* Mary Kreta, Director of Admissions, 907-474-7500, Fax: 907-474-7097, E-mail: admissions@uaf.edu.
Website: http://www.uaf.edu/comm/

**University of Central Florida,** College of Sciences, Nicholson School of Communication, Orlando, FL 32816. Offers communication (MA); corporate communication (Certificate). *Program availability:* Part-time, evening/weekend. *Faculty:* 46 full-time (21 women), 17 part-time/adjunct (11 women). *Students:* 34 full-time (24 women), 21 part-time (16 women); includes 19 minority (7 Black or African American, non-Hispanic/Latino; 10 Hispanic/Latino; 2 Two or more races, non-Hispanic/Latino), 11 international. Average age 27. 41 applicants, 83% accepted, 22 enrolled. In 2016, 26 master's, 12 other advanced degrees awarded. *Degree requirements:* For master's, thesis or alternative. *Entrance requirements:* For master's, GRE General Test, minimum GPA of 3.0 in last 60 hours of course work. Additional exam requirements/recommendations for international students: Required—TOEFL. *Application deadline:* For fall admission, 6/1 for domestic students; for spring admission, 11/1 for domestic students. Application fee: $30. Electronic applications accepted. *Expenses:* Tuition, state resident: part-time $288.16 per credit hour. Tuition, nonresident: part-time $1071.31 per credit hour. *Financial support:* In 2016-17, 20 students received support, including 1 fellowship with partial tuition reimbursement available (averaging $4,000 per year), 5 research assistantships with partial tuition reimbursements available (averaging $6,742 per year), 15 teaching assistantships with partial tuition reimbursements available (averaging $9,141 per year); career-related internships or fieldwork, Federal Work-Study, institutionally sponsored loans, tuition waivers (partial), and unspecified assistantships also available. Financial award application deadline: 3/1; financial award applicants required to submit FAFSA. *Faculty research:* Persuasion, interpersonal communication, nonverbal communication, conflict resolution. *Unit head:* Dr. Arlen Chase, Acting Director, 407-823-2316, E-mail: arlen.chase@ucf.edu. *Application contact:* Assistant Director, Graduate Admissions, 407-823-2766, Fax: 407-823-6442, E-mail: gradadmissions@ucf.edu.
Website: http://communication.cos.ucf.edu/

**University of Colorado Denver,** Business School, Program in Marketing, Denver, CO 80217. Offers brand management and marketing communication (MS); global marketing (MS); high-tech and entrepreneurial marketing (MS); marketing for sustainability (MS); marketing research (MS); sports and entertainment marketing (MS). *Program availability:* Part-time, evening/weekend. *Students:* 30 full-time (19 women), 7 part-time (5 women); includes 5 minority (2 Black or African American, non-Hispanic/Latino; 1 Asian, non-Hispanic/Latino; 2 Hispanic/Latino), 12 international. Average age 28. 47 applicants, 62% accepted, 13 enrolled. In 2016, 23 master's awarded. *Degree requirements:* For master's, 30 semester hours (21 of marketing core courses, 9 of marketing electives). *Entrance requirements:* For master's, GMAT, resume, essay, two letters of recommendation, financial statements (for international applicants). Additional exam requirements/recommendations for international students: Required—TOEFL (minimum score 525 paper-based; 71 iBT); Recommended—IELTS (minimum score 6.5). *Application deadline:* For fall admission, 4/15 priority date for domestic students, 3/15 priority date for international students; for spring admission, 10/15 priority date for domestic students, 9/15 priority date for international students; for summer admission, 2/15 priority date for domestic students, 1/15 priority date for international students. Applications are processed on a rolling basis. Application fee: $50 ($75 for international students). Electronic applications accepted. *Expenses:* Contact institution. *Financial support:* In 2016-17, 7 students received support. Fellowships, research assistantships, teaching assistantships, Federal Work-Study, institutionally sponsored loans, scholarships/grants, and traineeships available. Financial award application deadline: 4/1; financial award applicants required to submit FAFSA. *Faculty research:* Marketing issues in the Chinese environment, impact of individual difference and contextual factors on the risk-taking behaviors of managers making new-business creation decisions, attribution theory perspective of conflict between marketers and engineers, organizational identity and identification, international market entry strategies. *Unit head:* Vicki Lane, Director of Marketing Program, 303-315-8468, E-mail: vicki.lane@ucdenver.edu. *Application contact:* 303-315-8200, E-mail: bschool.admissions@ucdenver.edu.
Website: http://www.ucdenver.edu/academics/colleges/business/degrees/ms/marketing/Pages/Marketing.aspx

**University of Nebraska–Lincoln,** Graduate College, College of Arts and Sciences, Department of Communication Studies, Lincoln, NE 68588. Offers instructional communication (MA, PhD); interpersonal communication (MA, PhD); marketing, communication studies, and advertising (MA, PhD); organizational communication (MA, PhD); rhetoric and culture (MA, PhD). *Degree requirements:* For master's, thesis optional; for doctorate, comprehensive exam, thesis/dissertation. *Entrance requirements:* For master's and doctorate, GRE General Test, writing sample. Additional exam requirements/recommendations for international students: Required—TOEFL (minimum score 600 paper-based). Electronic applications accepted. *Faculty research:* Message strategies, gender communication, political communication, organizational communication, instructional communication.

**University of Oklahoma,** College of Arts and Sciences, Department of Communication, Norman, OK 73019. Offers communication (MA); communication technology (PhD); health communication (PhD); intercultural/international communication (PhD); interpersonal communication/social influence (PhD); organizational communication (PhD); political/mass communication (PhD). *Program availability:* Part-time. *Faculty:* 19 full-time (9 women). *Students:* 28 full-time (17 women), 40 part-time (19 women); includes 19 minority (6 Black or African American, non-Hispanic/Latino; 2 American Indian or Alaska Native, non-Hispanic/Latino; 9 Hispanic/Latino; 2 Two or more races, non-Hispanic/Latino), 9 international. Average age 36. 35 applicants, 60% accepted, 10

## Corporate and Organizational Communication

enrolled. In 2016, 14 master's, 8 doctorates awarded. *Degree requirements:* For master's, comprehensive exam (for some programs), thesis (for some programs), comprehensive exams or thesis; for doctorate, comprehensive exam, thesis/dissertation. *Entrance requirements:* For master's, GRE (for assistantship), statement of purpose, transcripts, writing sample, letters of recommendation; for doctorate, GRE, statement of purpose, transcripts, writing sample, letters of recommendation. Additional exam requirements/recommendations for international students: Required—TOEFL (minimum score 79 iBT) or IELTS (minimum score 6.5). *Application deadline:* For fall admission, 1/15 priority date for domestic students, 1/15 for international students; for spring admission, 10/15 for domestic and international students. Application fee: $50 ($100 for international students). Electronic applications accepted. *Expenses:* Tuition, state resident: full-time $4886; part-time $203.60 per credit hour. Tuition, nonresident: full-time $18,989; part-time $791.20 per credit hour. *Required fees:* $3283; $126.25 per credit hour. $126.50 per semester. *Financial support:* In 2016–17, 31 students received support, including 1 research assistantship with full tuition reimbursement available (averaging $10,373 per year), 26 teaching assistantships with full tuition reimbursements available (averaging $16,515 per year); health care benefits also available. Financial award application deadline: 6/1; financial award applicants required to submit FAFSA. *Faculty research:* Interpersonal/social influence, organizational, political/mass communication, health communication, intercultural/international. *Total annual research expenditures:* $12,383. *Unit head:* Dr. Michael W. Kramer, Chair and Professor, 405-325-9503, Fax: 405-325-7625, E-mail: mkramer@ou.edu. *Application contact:* Shay Glover, Academic Advisor, 405-325-7710, Fax: 405-325-7625, E-mail: shay.glover@ou.edu.
Website: http://cas.ou.edu/comm

**University of Portland,** Department of Communication Studies, Portland, OR 97203-5798. Offers communication (MA); management communication (MS). *Program availability:* Part-time, evening/weekend. *Degree requirements:* For master's, thesis optional. *Entrance requirements:* For master's, GRE General Test, minimum GPA of 3.25, 3 letters of recommendation, resume, statement of goals, official transcripts. Additional exam requirements/recommendations for international students: Required—TOEFL (minimum score 600 paper-based; 100 iBT), IELTS (minimum score 7.5).

**University of Southern California,** Graduate School, Annenberg School for Communication and Journalism, School of Communication, Program in Communication Management, Los Angeles, CA 90089. Offers MCM, JD/MCM, MCM/MAJCS. *Program availability:* Part-time, evening/weekend, online learning. *Students:* 153 full-time, 76 part-time; includes 104 minority (31 Black or African American, non-Hispanic/Latino; 29 Asian, non-Hispanic/Latino; 39 Hispanic/Latino; 1 Native Hawaiian or other Pacific Islander, non-Hispanic/Latino; 4 Two or more races, non-Hispanic/Latino), 64 international. Average age 25. 576 applicants, 44% accepted, 161 enrolled. In 2016, 151 master's awarded. *Degree requirements:* For master's, professional project. *Entrance requirements:* For master's, GRE General Test or GMAT, resume, writing samples, recommendation letters, statement of purpose. Additional exam requirements/recommendations for international students: Required—TOEFL (minimum score 114 iBT), IELTS (minimum score 8). *Application deadline:* For fall admission, 6/5 priority date for domestic students, 1/1 priority date for international students. Applications are processed on a rolling basis. Application fee: $90. Electronic applications accepted. *Financial support:* Career-related internships or fieldwork, Federal Work-Study, and scholarships/grants available. Support available to part-time students. Financial award application deadline: 1/1; financial award applicants required to submit FAFSA. *Faculty research:* Global communication, communication law and policy, entertainment management, marketing communication, strategic and corporate communication management. *Unit head:* Dr. Rebecca Weintraub, Director, 213-821-0764, Fax: 213-740-8036, E-mail: weintrau@usc.edu. *Application contact:* Allyson Hill, Associate Dean for Admissions, 213-821-0770, Fax: 213-740-1933, E-mail: ascadm@usc.edu.
Website: http://www.annenberg.usc.edu

**University of South Florida,** College of Arts and Sciences, School of Mass Communications, Tampa, FL 33620-9951. Offers mass communications (MA), including media studies, multimedia journalism, strategic communication management. *Program availability:* Part-time, evening/weekend. *Faculty:* 11 full-time (6 women). *Students:* 27 full-time (23 women), 18 part-time (10 women); includes 5 minority (2 Black or African American, non-Hispanic/Latino; 2 Hispanic/Latino; 1 Native Hawaiian or other Pacific Islander, non-Hispanic/Latino), 25 international. Average age 27. 39 applicants, 82% accepted, 21 enrolled. In 2016, 16 master's awarded. *Degree requirements:* For master's, comprehensive exam, thesis optional. *Entrance requirements:* For master's, GRE General Test, minimum GPA of 3.0 in last 60 hours of course work, three letters of recommendation, letter of intent, resume/curriculum vitae. Additional exam requirements/recommendations for international students: Required—TOEFL (minimum score 550 paper-based; 79 iBT) or IELTS (minimum score 6.5). *Application deadline:* For fall admission, 2/15 for domestic and international students. Application fee: $30. Electronic applications accepted. *Expenses:* Tuition, state resident: full-time $7766; part-time $431.43 per credit hour. Tuition, nonresident: full-time $15,789; part-time $877.17 per credit hour. *Required fees:* $37 per term. *Financial support:* In 2016–17, 5 students received support, including 9 teaching assistantships with tuition reimbursements available (averaging $10,513 per year); unspecified assistantships also available. Financial award application deadline: 2/28. *Faculty research:* First Amendment analysis, civic journalism, public opinion, media ethics, media effects research in sports public relations, public relations management, advertisement, telecommunications. *Total annual research expenditures:* $88,114. *Unit head:* Dr. Jim Andrews, Interim Director/Associate Professor, 813-974-2108, Fax: 813-974-2592, E-mail: jimandrews@usf.edu. *Application contact:* Dr. Michael Mitrook, Assistant Professor, 813-974-8890, Fax: 813-974-2592, E-mail: mmitrook@usf.edu.
Website: http://masscom.usf.edu/grad/

**University of South Florida,** Innovative Education, Tampa, FL 33620-9951. Offers adult, career and higher education (Graduate Certificate), including college teaching, leadership in developing human resources, leadership in higher education; Africana studies (Graduate Certificate), including diasporas and health disparities, genocide and human rights; aging studies (Graduate Certificate), including gerontology; art research (Graduate Certificate), including museum studies; business foundations (Graduate Certificate); chemical and biomedical engineering (Graduate Certificate), including materials science and engineering, water, health and sustainability; child and family studies (Graduate Certificate), including positive behavior support; civil and industrial engineering (Graduate Certificate), including transportation systems analysis; community and family health (Graduate Certificate), including maternal and child health, social marketing and public health, violence and injury: prevention and intervention, women's health; criminology (Graduate Certificate), including criminal justice administration; educational measurement and research (Graduate Certificate), including evaluation; English (Graduate Certificate), including comparative literary studies, creative writing, professional and technical communication; entrepreneurship (Graduate Certificate); environmental health (Graduate Certificate), including safety management; epidemiology and biostatistics (Graduate Certificate), including applied biostatistics, biostatistics, concepts and tools of epidemiology, epidemiology, epidemiology of infectious diseases; geography, environment and planning (Graduate Certificate), including community development, environmental policy and management,

geographical information systems; geology (Graduate Certificate), including hydrogeology; global health (Graduate Certificate), including disaster management, global health and Latin American and Caribbean studies, global health practice, humanitarian assistance, infection control; government and international affairs (Graduate Certificate), including Cuban studies, globalization studies; health policy and management (Graduate Certificate), including health management and leadership, public health policy and programs; hearing specialist: early intervention (Graduate Certificate); industrial and management systems engineering (Graduate Certificate), including systems engineering, technology management; information studies (Graduate Certificate), including school library media specialist; information systems/decision sciences (Graduate Certificate), including analytics and business intelligence; instructional technology (Graduate Certificate), including distance education, Florida digital/virtual educator, instructional design, multimedia design, Web design; internal medicine, bioethics and medical humanities (Graduate Certificate), including biomedical ethics; Latin American and Caribbean studies (Graduate Certificate); mass communications (Graduate Certificate), including multimedia journalism; mathematics and statistics (Graduate Certificate), including mathematics; medicine (Graduate Certificate), including aging and neuroscience, bioinformatics, biotechnology, brain fitness and memory management, clinical investigation, health informatics, health sciences, integrative weight management, intellectual property, medicine and gender, metabolic and nutritional medicine, metabolic cardiology, pharmacy sciences; national and competitive intelligence (Graduate Certificate); psychological and social foundations (Graduate Certificate), including career counseling, college teaching, diversity in education, mental health counseling, school counseling; public affairs (Graduate Certificate), including nonprofit management, public management, research administration; public health (Graduate Certificate), including environmental health, health equity, public health generalist, translational research in adolescent behavioral health; public health practices (Graduate Certificate), including planning for healthy communities; rehabilitation and mental health counseling (Graduate Certificate), including integrative mental health care, marriage and family therapy, rehabilitation technology; secondary education (Graduate Certificate), including ESOL, foreign language education: culture and content, foreign language education: professional; social work (Graduate Certificate), including geriatric social work/clinical gerontology; special education (Graduate Certificate), including autism spectrum disorder, disabilities education: severe/profound; world languages (Graduate Certificate), including teaching English as a second language (TESL) or foreign language. *Expenses:* Tuition, state resident: full-time $7766; part-time $431.43 per credit hour. Tuition, nonresident: full-time $15,789; part-time $877.17 per credit hour. *Required fees:* $37 per term. *Unit head:* Kathy Barnes, Interdisciplinary Programs Coordinator, 813-974-8031, Fax: 813-974-7061, E-mail: barnesk@usf.edu. *Application contact:* Karen Tylinski, Metro Initiatives, 813-974-9943, Fax: 813-974-7061, E-mail: ktylinsk@usf.edu.
Website: http://www.usf.edu/innovative-education/

**University of Wisconsin–Milwaukee,** Graduate School, College of Letters and Science, Department of Communication, Milwaukee, WI 53201-0413. Offers communication (MA, PhD), including interpersonal communication (MA), organizational communication (MA), rhetoric and public communication (MA), rhetorical leadership; rhetorical leadership (Graduate Certificate). *Program availability:* Part-time. *Faculty:* 18 full-time (11 women). *Students:* 24 full-time (14 women), 15 part-time (11 women); includes 5 minority (1 Black or African American, non-Hispanic/Latino; 1 Asian, non-Hispanic/Latino; 1 Hispanic/Latino; 2 Two or more races, non-Hispanic/Latino), 4 international. Average age 34. 44 applicants, 52% accepted, 9 enrolled. In 2016, 2 master's, 8 doctorates awarded. *Degree requirements:* For master's, thesis or alternative; for doctorate, comprehensive exam. *Entrance requirements:* For master's, GRE General Test, minimum GPA of 3.0. Additional exam requirements/recommendations for international students: Required—TOEFL (minimum score 550 paper-based; 79 iBT), IELTS (minimum score 6). *Application deadline:* For fall admission, 1/1 priority date for domestic students; for spring admission, 9/1 for domestic students. Applications are processed on a rolling basis. Application fee: $56. Electronic applications accepted. *Financial support:* In 2016–17, 3 fellowships, 34 teaching assistantships were awarded; research assistantships, career-related internships or fieldwork, unspecified assistantships, and project assistantships also available. Support available to part-time students. Financial award application deadline: 4/15; financial award applicants required to submit FAFSA. *Unit head:* Mike Allen, Department Chair, 414-229-4510, E-mail: mikealle@uwm.edu. *Application contact:* General Information Contact, 414-229-4982, Fax: 414-229-6967, E-mail: gradschool@uwm.edu.
Website: https://uwm.edu/communication/

**University of Wisconsin–Stevens Point,** College of Fine Arts and Communication, Division of Communication, Stevens Point, WI 54481-3897. Offers interpersonal communication (MA); media studies (MA); organizational communication (MA); public relations (MA). *Program availability:* Part-time. *Degree requirements:* For master's, thesis or alternative. *Entrance requirements:* For master's, GRE. Additional exam requirements/recommendations for international students: Required—TOEFL (minimum score 575 paper-based). *Faculty research:* Communication theory and research, film history.

**University of Wisconsin–Whitewater,** School of Graduate Studies, College of Arts and Communications, Department of Communication, Whitewater, WI 53190-1790. Offers corporate communication (MS); mass communication (MS). *Program availability:* Part-time, evening/weekend, online learning. *Degree requirements:* For master's, thesis or alternative. *Entrance requirements:* For master's, 2 letters of recommendation, goal statement. Additional exam requirements/recommendations for international students: Required—TOEFL (minimum score 550 paper-based; 80 iBT), IELTS (minimum score 6). Electronic applications accepted.

**Washington State University,** The Edward R. Murrow College of Communication, Pullman, WA 99164-2520. Offers communication (MA, PhD); strategic communication (MA). MA in strategic communication offered at the Global (online) campus. *Degree requirements:* For master's, comprehensive exam (for some programs), thesis optional, oral exam; for doctorate, comprehensive exam, thesis/dissertation. *Entrance requirements:* For master's, GRE General Test, minimum GPA of 3.25, 3 letters of recommendation; for doctorate, GRE General Test, minimum undergraduate GPA of 3.25, graduate 3.5; MA in communication; 3 letters of recommendation. Additional exam requirements/recommendations for international students: Required—TOEFL (minimum score 580 paper-based). Electronic applications accepted. *Faculty research:* Communication technology, health communication, science communication, political communication, intercultural communication.

**Webster University,** School of Communications, Program in Communications Management, St. Louis, MO 63119-3194. Offers MA. *Expenses:* Tuition: Full-time $21,900; part-time $730 per credit hour. Tuition and fees vary according to campus/location and program.

**Western Kentucky University,** Graduate Studies, Potter College of Arts and Letters, Department of Communication, Bowling Green, KY 42101. Offers communication (MA); organizational communication (Graduate Certificate). *Program availability:* Part-time, evening/weekend. *Degree requirements:* For master's, comprehensive exam, thesis optional, final exam. *Entrance requirements:* For master's, GRE General Test, minimum

GPA of 2.75. Additional exam requirements/recommendations for international students: Required—TOEFL (minimum score 555 paper-based; 79 iBT). *Faculty research:* Public rhetoric and public address organization communication, teamwork in communication, intercultural crisis communication.

**West Virginia University,** Eberly College of Arts and Sciences, Department of Communication Studies, Morgantown, WV 26506. Offers communication in instruction (MA); communication studies (PhD); communication theory and research (MA); corporate and organizational communication (MA). *Program availability:* Part-time. *Degree requirements:* For master's, comprehensive exam (for some programs), thesis (for some programs); for doctorate, comprehensive exam, thesis/dissertation. *Entrance requirements:* For master's and doctorate, minimum GPA of 3.0. Additional exam requirements/recommendations for international students: Required—TOEFL. Electronic applications accepted. *Faculty research:* Instructional communication, interpersonal communication, health communication, influence, instructional communication, social influence.

**West Virginia University,** Reed College of Media, Program in Digital Marketing Communications, Morgantown, WV 26506. Offers Graduate Certificate. *Program availability:* Online learning. *Entrance requirements:* For degree, resume. Electronic applications accepted.

**West Virginia University,** Reed College of Media, Program in Integrated Marketing Communications, Morgantown, WV 26501. Offers MS, Graduate Certificate. *Program availability:* Part-time, online learning. *Entrance requirements:* For master's, GRE or GMAT (waived with minimum undergraduate GPA of 3.3 or at least 6 years of related professional experience), undergraduate transcript, resume; letters of recommendation (strongly recommended). Additional exam requirements/recommendations for international students: Required—TOEFL.

# Health Communication

**Arkansas State University,** Graduate School, College of Media and Communication, Department of Communication, State University, AR 72467. Offers communication studies (MA, SCCT); health communications (Graduate Certificate). *Program availability:* Part-time. *Degree requirements:* For master's, one foreign language, comprehensive exam, thesis or alternative; for other advanced degree, comprehensive exam. *Entrance requirements:* For master's, GRE General Test or MAT, appropriate bachelor's degree, writing sample, letter of recommendation, official transcripts, immunization records; for other advanced degree, GRE or MAT, appropriate master's degree, interview, official transcript, immunization records. Additional exam requirements/recommendations for international students: Required—TOEFL (minimum score 550 paper-based; 79 iBT), IELTS (minimum score 6), PTE (minimum score 56). Electronic applications accepted.

**Boston University,** Metropolitan College, Program in Health Communication, Boston, MA 02215. Offers MS. *Program availability:* Part-time, online learning. *Faculty:* 1 full-time (0 women), 9 part-time/adjunct (5 women). *Students:* 106 part-time (99 women); includes 36 minority (19 Black or African American, non-Hispanic/Latino; 6 Asian, non-Hispanic/Latino; 10 Hispanic/Latino; 1 Two or more races, non-Hispanic/Latino), 1 international. Average age 36. 30 applicants, 93% accepted, 28 enrolled. In 2016, 26 master's awarded. *Entrance requirements:* For master's, bachelor's degree, minimum GPA of 3.0, professional experience. Additional exam requirements/recommendations for international students: Required—TOEFL (minimum score 100 iBT). *Application deadline:* For fall admission, 7/13 for domestic students; for spring admission, 11/21 for domestic students; for summer admission, 3/28 for domestic students. Applications are processed on a rolling basis. Application fee: $85. Electronic applications accepted. *Expenses:* Contact institution. *Financial support:* Unspecified assistantships available. Support available to part-time students. Financial award applicants required to submit FAFSA. *Faculty research:* Public relations and health communication. *Unit head:* Leigh Curtin-Wilding, Director.
Website: http://www.bu.edu/online/online_programs/graduate_degree/master_health_communication/

**Chapman University,** Wilkinson College of Arts, Humanities, and Social Sciences, Health and Strategic Communication Program, Orange, CA 92866. Offers MS. *Program availability:* Evening/weekend. *Faculty:* 19 full-time (11 women), 6 part-time/adjunct (3 women). *Students:* 5 full-time (3 women), 3 part-time (2 women); includes 4 minority (1 Black or African American, non-Hispanic/Latino; 2 Hispanic/Latino; 1 Native Hawaiian or other Pacific Islander, non-Hispanic/Latino), 1 international. Average age 23. 10 applicants, 100% accepted, 7 enrolled. In 2016, 9 master's awarded. *Degree requirements:* For master's, capstone research project. *Entrance requirements:* For master's, GRE, minimum undergraduate GPA of 3.0. Additional exam requirements/recommendations for international students: Required—TOEFL (minimum score 550 paper-based, 80 iBT), IELTS (6.5), PTE Academic (53), or CAE. *Application deadline:* Applications are processed on a rolling basis. Application fee: $60. Electronic applications accepted. *Expenses:* Contact institution. *Financial support:* Fellowships, research assistantships, Federal Work-Study, scholarships/grants, and unspecified assistantships available. Financial award applicants required to submit FAFSA. *Unit head:* Dr. Jennifer Bevan, Graduate Director, 714-532-7768, E-mail: bevan@chapman.edu. *Application contact:* Shannon McCance, Admission Counselor, 714-997-6711, E-mail: smccance@chapman.edu.
Website: http://www.chapman.edu/communication/academic-programs/health-strategic-communication.aspx

**Chatham University,** Program in Communication, Pittsburgh, PA 15232-2826. Offers environmental communication (M Comm); health communication (M Comm); strategic communication (M Comm). *Program availability:* Online learning. *Expenses:* Tuition: Full-time $16,254; part-time $903 per credit hour. *Required fees:* $468; $26 per credit hour.

**Cornell University,** Graduate School, Graduate Fields of Agriculture and Life Sciences, Field of Communication, Ithaca, NY 14853. Offers communication (MS, PhD); human-computer interaction (MS, PhD); language and communication (MS, PhD); media communication and society (MS, PhD); organizational communication (MS, PhD); science, environment and health communication (MS, PhD); social psychology of communication (MS, PhD). *Degree requirements:* For master's, thesis (MS); for doctorate, comprehensive exam, thesis/dissertation. *Entrance requirements:* For master's and doctorate, GRE General Test, 3 letters of recommendation. Additional exam requirements/recommendations for international students: Required—TOEFL (minimum score 600 paper-based; 100 iBT). Electronic applications accepted. *Faculty research:* Mass communication, communication technologies, science and environmental communication.

**DePaul University,** College of Communication, Chicago, IL 60614. Offers digital communication and media arts (MA); health communication (MA); journalism (MA); media and cinema studies (MA); organizational and multicultural communication (MA); public relations and advertising (MA); relational communication (MA). *Program availability:* Part-time, evening/weekend. *Entrance requirements:* Additional exam requirements/recommendations for international students: Required—TOEFL (minimum score 590 paper-based; 96 iBT), IELTS (minimum score 7.5) or PTE. Electronic applications accepted.

**East Carolina University,** Graduate School, College of Fine Arts and Communication, School of Communication, Greenville, NC 27858-4353. Offers health communication (MA). *Students:* 13 full-time (10 women), 33 part-time (26 women); includes 14 minority (10 Black or African American, non-Hispanic/Latino; 1 Hispanic/Latino; 3 Two or more races, non-Hispanic/Latino). Average age 31. 26 applicants, 88% accepted, 19 enrolled. In 2016, 14 master's awarded. *Entrance requirements:* For master's, GRE. *Financial support:* Teaching assistantships available. *Unit head:* Dr. Linda Kean, Director, 252-328-4227, E-mail: keanl@ecu.edu. *Application contact:* Dean of Graduate School, 252-328-6012, Fax: 252-328-6071, E-mail: gradschool@ecu.edu.
Website: http://www.ecu.edu/cs-cfac/comm/graduate/index.cfm

**Fontbonne University,** Graduate Programs, St. Louis, MO 63105-3098. Offers accounting (MBA, MS); art (MA); art (K-12) (MAT); business (MBA); computer science (MS); deaf education (MA); early intervention in deaf education (MA); education (MA), including autism spectrum disorders, curriculum and instruction, diverse learners, early childhood education, reading, special education; elementary education (MAT); family and consumer sciences (MA), including multidisciplinary health communication studies; fine arts (MFA); instructional design and technology (MS); management and leadership (MM); middle school education (MAT); secondary education (MAT); special education (MAT); speech-language pathology (MS); supply chain management (MS); theatre (MA). *Program availability:* Part-time, evening/weekend, online learning. *Faculty:* 32 full-time (24 women), 43 part-time/adjunct (26 women). *Students:* 456 full-time (313 women), 102 part-time (77 women); includes 138 minority (118 Black or African American, non-Hispanic/Latino; 1 American Indian or Alaska Native, non-Hispanic/Latino; 7 Asian, non-Hispanic/Latino; 9 Hispanic/Latino; 3 Two or more races, non-Hispanic/Latino), 37 international. *Degree requirements:* For master's, comprehensive exam (for some programs), thesis (for some programs). *Entrance requirements:* Additional exam requirements/recommendations for international students: Required—TOEFL (minimum score 500 paper-based; 65 iBT). *Application deadline:* For fall admission, 8/1 for international students; for spring admission, 12/1 for international students. Applications are processed on a rolling basis. Application fee: $25 ($30 for international students). Electronic applications accepted. *Expenses:* Tuition: Full-time $8436; part-time $703 per credit hour. *Required fees:* $18 per credit hour. Tuition and fees vary according to course load. *Financial support:* Teaching assistantships with partial tuition reimbursements and scholarships/grants available. Support available to part-time students. Financial award application deadline: 4/1; financial award applicants required to submit FAFSA. *Unit head:* Dr. Carey Adams, Vice President for Academic Affairs, 314-719-3609, E-mail: cadams@fontbonne.edu. *Application contact:* Lauryn Filip, Coordinator, Graduate Admission and Professional Studies, 314-889-4650, E-mail: admissions@fontbonne.edu.
Website: https://www.fontbonne.edu/academics/graduate-programs/

**Gannon University,** School of Graduate Studies, College of Humanities, Education, and Social Sciences, School of Humanities, Program in Health Communication, Erie, PA 16541-0001. Offers MA. *Students:* 4 full-time (3 women), 3 part-time (all women), 1 international. Average age 31. 11 applicants, 55% accepted. *Entrance requirements:* For master's, bachelor's degree from accredited college or university, transcripts, 3 professional letters of recommendation, statement of professional and career goals. Additional exam requirements/recommendations for international students: Required—TOEFL (minimum score 79 iBT). *Application deadline:* Applications are processed on a rolling basis. Application fee: $25. Electronic applications accepted. Application fee is waived when completed online. *Expenses:* Tuition: Full-time $17,370. *Required fees:* $550. Tuition and fees vary according to course load and program. *Financial support:* Federal Work-Study and unspecified assistantships available. Financial award application deadline: 7/1; financial award applicants required to submit FAFSA. *Unit head:* Dr. Jennifer Allen Catellier, Director, 814-871-5626, E-mail: allenca001@gannon.edu. *Application contact:* Bridget Philip, Director of Graduate Admissions, 814-871-7412, E-mail: graduate@gannon.edu.

**The George Washington University,** Milken Institute School of Public Health, Department of Global Health, Washington, DC 20052. Offers global health (Dr PH); global health communication (MPH). *Accreditation:* CEPH. *Faculty:* 16 full-time (9 women). *Students:* 3 full-time (2 women), 9 part-time (4 women); includes 3 minority (2 Black or African American, non-Hispanic/Latino; 1 Asian, non-Hispanic/Latino), 2 international. Average age 35. 46 applicants, 20% accepted, 3 enrolled. In 2016, 6 master's, 6 doctorates awarded. *Degree requirements:* For master's, case study or special project. *Entrance requirements:* For master's, GMAT, GRE General Test, or MCAT. Additional exam requirements/recommendations for international students: Required—TOEFL. *Application deadline:* For fall admission, 4/15 priority date for domestic students, 4/15 for international students; for spring admission, 11/1 for domestic and international students. Applications are processed on a rolling basis. Application fee: $75. *Financial support:* In 2016–17, 24 students received support. Tuition waivers available. Financial award application deadline: 2/15. *Unit head:* Prof. James Tielsch, Chair, 202-994-4124, Fax: 202-994-1955, E-mail: jtielsch@gwu.edu. *Application contact:* Jane Smith, Director of Admissions, 202-994-0248, Fax: 202-994-1860, E-mail: sphhsinfo@gwumc.edu.

**Indiana University–Purdue University Indianapolis,** School of Liberal Arts, Department of Communication Studies, Indianapolis, IN 46225. Offers applied communication (MA); health communication (PhD). *Program availability:* Part-time. *Degree requirements:* For master's, comprehensive exam, thesis; for doctorate, thesis/dissertation. *Entrance requirements:* For doctorate, master's degree. Additional exam requirements/recommendations for international students: Required—TOEFL; Recommended—IELTS. Electronic applications accepted.

**Johns Hopkins University,** Bloomberg School of Public Health, Department of Health, Behavior and Society, Baltimore, MD 21218. Offers genetic counseling (Sc M); health education and health communication (MSPH); social and behavioral sciences (Dr PH,

PhD); social factors in health (MHS). *Degree requirements:* For master's, comprehensive exam (for some programs), thesis (for some programs); for doctorate, comprehensive exam, thesis/dissertation. *Entrance requirements:* For master's, GRE, curriculum vitae, 3 letters of recommendation; for doctorate, GRE, transcripts, curriculum vitae, 3 recommendation letters. Additional exam requirements/recommendations for international students: Required—TOEFL (minimum score 600 paper-based; 100 iBT). Electronic applications accepted. *Faculty research:* Social determinants of health and structural and community-level inventions to improve health, communication and health education, behavioral and social aspects of genetic counseling.

**Kansas State University,** Graduate School, College of Arts and Sciences, A.Q. Miller School of Journalism and Mass Communications, Manhattan, KS 66506. Offers advertising (MS); community journalism (MS); global communication (MS); health communication (MS); media management (MS); public relations (MS). *Program availability:* Part-time, evening/weekend. *Faculty:* 13 full-time (6 women), 1 (woman) part-time/adjunct. *Students:* 13 full-time (10 women), 6 part-time (4 women); includes 1 minority (Hispanic/Latino), 8 international. Average age 29. 7 applicants, 71% accepted, 3 enrolled. In 2016, 7 master's awarded. *Degree requirements:* For master's, comprehensive exam, thesis. *Entrance requirements:* For master's, GRE General Test, minimum GPA of 3.0. Additional exam requirements/recommendations for international students: Required—TOEFL (minimum score 79 iBT). *Application deadline:* For fall admission, 2/1 priority date for domestic and international students; for spring admission, 8/1 priority date for domestic and international students. Applications are processed on a rolling basis. Application fee: $50 ($75 for international students). Electronic applications accepted. *Expenses:* Tuition, state resident: full-time $9670. Tuition, nonresident: full-time $21,828. *Required fees:* $862. *Financial support:* In 2016–17, 2 research assistantships with full tuition reimbursements (averaging $11,180 per year), 7 teaching assistantships with full tuition reimbursements (averaging $7,729 per year) were awarded; scholarships/grants, health care benefits, and unspecified assistantships also available. Financial award application deadline: 2/1; financial award applicants required to submit FAFSA. *Faculty research:* Health communication, risk communication, strategic communications, community journalism, global communication. *Total annual research expenditures:* $219,641. *Unit head:* Dr. Jean Folkerts, Director, 785-532-6890, Fax: 785-532-5484, E-mail: jeanfolk@ksu.edu. *Application contact:* Dr. Barbara DeSanto, Associate Director of Graduate Studies, 785-532-3890, Fax: 785-532-5484, E-mail: desantoi@ksu.edu. Website: http://jmc.ksu.edu/

**Lasell College,** Graduate and Professional Studies in Communication, Newton, MA 02466. Offers health communication (MSC, Graduate Certificate); integrated marketing communication (MSC, Graduate Certificate); public relations (MSC, Graduate Certificate). *Program availability:* Part-time, evening/weekend, 100% online, blended/hybrid learning. *Faculty:* 4 full-time (2 women), 5 part-time/adjunct (2 women). *Students:* 12 full-time (9 women), 38 part-time (28 women); includes 11 minority (8 Black or African American, non-Hispanic/Latino; 1 Asian, non-Hispanic/Latino; 2 Hispanic/Latino), 8 international. Average age 31. 60 applicants, 43% accepted, 13 enrolled. In 2016, 71 master's, 3 other advanced degrees awarded. *Degree requirements:* For master's, comprehensive exam, thesis or alternative, minimum GPA of 3.0; special project or internship. *Entrance requirements:* For master's, one-page personal statement, 2 letters of recommendation, resume, bachelor's degree transcript; for Graduate Certificate, bachelor's degree transcript, 2 letters of recommendation, 1-page personal statement, resume. Additional exam requirements/recommendations for international students: Required—TOEFL (minimum score 550 paper-based, 79 iBT) or IELTS (minimum score 6). *Application deadline:* For fall admission, 8/31 priority date for domestic students, 6/30 priority date for international students; for spring admission, 12/31 priority date for domestic students, 10/31 priority date for international students. Applications are processed on a rolling basis. Electronic applications accepted. *Expenses:* $600 per credit. *Financial support:* In 2016–17, 6 students received support. Federal Work-Study, scholarships/grants, and tuition discounts available. Support available to part-time students. Financial award application deadline: 8/31; financial award applicants required to submit FAFSA. *Faculty research:* Terrorists' use of the internet; refugees' use of cell phones as means of communication in Jordan and Germany; political communication, analysis of the media coverage of the conflict and peace process in northern Ireland; interpersonal communication, strategies to address bullying in online communities, in schools and in the workplace. *Unit head:* Dr. Joan Dolamore, Dean of Graduate and Professional Studies, 617-243-2485, Fax: 617-243-2450, E-mail: gradinfo@lasell.edu. *Application contact:* Adrienne Franciosi, Director of Graduate Enrollment, 617-243-2214, Fax: 617-243-2450, E-mail: gradinfo@lasell.edu. Website: http://www.lasell.edu/academics/graduate-and-professional-studies/programs-of-study/master-of-science-in-communication.html

**Marquette University,** Graduate School, College of Communication, Milwaukee, WI 53201-1881. Offers advertising and public relations (MA); communication studies (MA); digital storytelling (Certificate); journalism (MA); mass communication (MA); science, health and environmental communication (MA). *Accreditation:* ACEJMC (one or more programs are accredited). *Program availability:* Part-time, evening/weekend. *Faculty:* 36 full-time (18 women), 45 part-time/adjunct (20 women). *Students:* 25 full-time (22 women), 23 part-time (16 women); includes 9 minority (3 Black or African American, non-Hispanic/Latino; 1 American Indian or Alaska Native, non-Hispanic/Latino; 4 Hispanic/Latino; 1 Two or more races, non-Hispanic/Latino), 4 international. Average age 28. 55 applicants, 62% accepted, 21 enrolled. In 2016, 10 master's, 1 other advanced degree awarded. *Degree requirements:* For master's, comprehensive exam, thesis or alternative. *Entrance requirements:* For master's, GRE, official transcripts from all current and previous colleges/universities except Marquette, three letters of recommendation, statement of academic and professional goals. Additional exam requirements/recommendations for international students: Required—TOEFL (minimum score 530 paper-based). *Application deadline:* Applications are processed on a rolling basis. Electronic applications accepted. *Financial support:* Fellowships, research assistantships, teaching assistantships, career-related internships or fieldwork, scholarships/grants, health care benefits, tuition waivers (full and partial), and unspecified assistantships available. Support available to part-time students. Financial award application deadline: 2/15. *Faculty research:* Urban journalism, gender and communication, intercultural communication, religious communication. *Total annual research expenditures:* $7,941. *Unit head:* Dr. Sarah Feldner, Associate Dean. *Application contact:* Dr. Sarah Bonewits Feldner. Website: http://diederich.marquette.edu/

**Michigan State University,** The Graduate School, College of Communication Arts and Sciences, Program in Health Communication, East Lansing, MI 48824. Offers MA. *Entrance requirements:* Additional exam requirements/recommendations for international students: Required—TOEFL. Electronic applications accepted. *Faculty research:* Mass communication and public health, health communication for diverse populations, descriptive and analytical epidemiology.

**Ohio University,** Graduate College, Scripps College of Communication, School of Communication Studies, Athens, OH 45701-2979. Offers health communication (PhD); organizational communication (MA); relating and organizing (PhD); rhetoric and public culture (PhD). *Program availability:* Part-time, online learning. Terminal master's awarded for partial completion of doctoral program. *Degree requirements:* For master's, capstone; for doctorate, comprehensive exam, thesis/dissertation. *Entrance requirements:* For master's, GRE; for doctorate, GRE General Test, minimum GPA of 3.0. Additional exam requirements/recommendations for international students: Required—TOEFL (minimum score 550 paper-based; 80 iBT) or IELTS (minimum score 6.5). *Application deadline:* For fall admission, 1/15 priority date for domestic and international students. Application fee: $50 ($55 for international students). Electronic applications accepted. *Financial support:* In 2016–17, 12 students received support. Fellowships with full tuition reimbursements available, research assistantships with full tuition reimbursements available, teaching assistantships with full tuition reimbursements available, career-related internships or fieldwork, Federal Work-Study, and institutionally sponsored loans available. Financial award application deadline: 1/15. *Faculty research:* Rhetoric and public culture, relating and organizing, health communication. *Unit head:* Dr. Claudia Hale, Interim Director, 740-593-4825, E-mail: hale@ohio.edu. *Application contact:* Dr. Benjamin Bates, Associate Director for Graduate Studies, 740-593-9163, Fax: 740-593-4810, E-mail: batesb@ohio.edu. Website: http://www.coms.ohiou.edu/

**Southern Illinois University Edwardsville,** Graduate School, College of Arts and Sciences, Department of Applied Communication Studies, Program in Health Communication, Edwardsville, IL 62026. Offers MA. *Program availability:* Part-time, evening/weekend. *Degree requirements:* For master's, comprehensive exam (for some programs), thesis (for some programs). *Entrance requirements:* Additional exam requirements/recommendations for international students: Required—TOEFL (minimum score 550 paper-based, 79 iBT), IELTS (minimum score 6.5), Michigan Test of English Language Proficiency or PTE. Electronic applications accepted.

**State University of New York at Oswego,** Graduate Studies, School of Communication, Media and the Arts, Oswego, NY 13126. Offers strategic communication (MA), including health communication, integrated media and social networks, organizational communication. *Entrance requirements:* For master's, GRE, official transcript, statement of purpose, resume, two letters of recommendation.

**Stony Brook University, State University of New York,** School of Journalism, Stony Brook, NY 11794. Offers health communication (Certificate); journalism (MS). *Faculty:* 9 full-time (2 women), 22 part-time/adjunct (7 women). *Students:* 3 full-time (2 women), 3 part-time (2 women); includes 1 minority (Hispanic/Latino), 1 international. Average age 29. In 2016, 4 master's awarded. *Entrance requirements:* For master's, GRE, MCAT, DAT, or GMAT, bachelor's degree with minimum GPA of 3.0. Additional exam requirements/recommendations for international students: Required—TOEFL (minimum score 600 paper-based; 100 iBT). *Application deadline:* For fall admission, 4/30 for domestic students; for spring admission, 10/1 for domestic students. Application fee: $100. *Expenses:* Contact institution. *Financial support:* In 2016–17, 1 teaching assistantship was awarded. *Faculty research:* Journalism, newspaper journalism, non-fiction, children's literature, Constitutional law. *Total annual research expenditures:* $408,274. *Unit head:* Prof. Howard Schneider, Dean, 631-632-7403, E-mail: howard.schneider@stonybrook.edu. *Application contact:* Maureen Robinson, Coordinator, 631-632-7403, Fax: 631-632-7550, E-mail: maureen.robinson@stonybrook.edu. Website: https://journalism.cc.stonybrook.edu/

**Stony Brook University, State University of New York,** Stony Brook Medicine, School of Medicine, Program in Public Health, Stony Brook, NY 11794. Offers community health (MPH); evaluation sciences (MPH); family violence (MPH); health communication (Certificate); health economics (MPH); population health (MPH); substance abuse (MPH). *Accreditation:* CEPH. *Program availability:* Part-time, evening/weekend. *Students:* 32 full-time (28 women), 19 part-time (16 women); includes 20 minority (7 Black or African American, non-Hispanic/Latino; 7 Asian, non-Hispanic/Latino; 5 Hispanic/Latino; 1 Two or more races, non-Hispanic/Latino), 2 international. Average age 29. 148 applicants, 68% accepted, 37 enrolled. In 2016, 25 master's, 2 other advanced degrees awarded. *Entrance requirements:* For master's, GRE, 3 references, bachelor's degree from accredited college or university with minimum GPA of 3.0, essays, interview. Additional exam requirements/recommendations for international students: Required—TOEFL (minimum score 90 iBT). *Application deadline:* For fall admission, 6/1 for domestic students, 3/15 for international students. Application fee: $100. Electronic applications accepted. *Expenses:* Contact institution. *Financial support:* Fellowships available. *Faculty research:* Abnormal psychology, academic achievement, broadcast media, communications, communications systems, public health. *Total annual research expenditures:* $252,529. *Unit head:* Dr. Lisa A. Benz Scott, Director, 631-444-8811, E-mail: lisa.benzscott@stonybrook.edu. *Application contact:* Joanie Maniaci, Senior Academic Coordinator, 631-444-2074, Fax: 631-444-6035, E-mail: joanmarie.maniaci@stonybrook.edu. Website: http://publichealth.stonybrookmedicine.edu/

**Tufts University,** School of Medicine, Public Health and Professional Degree Programs, Boston, MA 02111. Offers biomedical sciences (MS); health communication (MS, Certificate); pain research, education and policy (MS, Certificate); physician assistant (MS); public health (MPH, Dr PH), including behavioral science (MPH), biostatistics (MPH), epidemiology (MPH), health communication (MPH), health services (MPH), management and policy (MPH), nutrition (MPH); DMD/MPH; DVM/MPH; JD/MPH; MD/MPH; MMS/MPH; MS/MBA; MS/MPH. MS programs offered jointly with Emerson College. *Accreditation:* CEPH (one or more programs are accredited). *Program availability:* Part-time, evening/weekend. *Degree requirements:* For master's, thesis (for some programs); for doctorate, thesis/dissertation. *Entrance requirements:* For master's, GRE General Test, MCAT, or GMAT; for doctorate, GRE General Test or MCAT. Additional exam requirements/recommendations for international students: Required—TOEFL (minimum score 100 iBT). Electronic applications accepted. *Expenses:* Contact institution. *Faculty research:* Environmental and occupational health, nutrition, epidemiology, health communication, biostatics, obesity/chronic disease, health policy and health care delivery, global health, health inequality and social determinants of health.

**University of Florida,** Graduate School, College of Health and Human Performance, Department of Health Education and Behavior, Gainesville, FL 32611. Offers health and human performance (PhD), including health behavior; health communication (Graduate Certificate); health education and behavior (MS). *Accreditation:* NCATE (one or more programs are accredited). *Program availability:* Part-time. Terminal master's awarded for partial completion of doctoral program. *Degree requirements:* For master's, comprehensive exam, thesis (for some programs); for doctorate, comprehensive exam, thesis/dissertation. *Entrance requirements:* For master's and doctorate, GRE General Test (minimum score 293), minimum GPA of 3.0. Additional exam requirements/recommendations for international students: Required—TOEFL (minimum score 550 paper-based; 80 iBT), IELTS (minimum score 6). Electronic applications accepted. *Faculty research:* Community-based participatory research; health disparities issues; health; cancer prevention and control; obesity-related issues; community capacity building; training community health workers; use of community based research principles to design, implement, an evaluate community health worker interventions;

obesity; weight management; health literacy; health disparities (ethnic, gender, age, urban/rural); tailored health messages; entertainment education; COPD.

**University of Florida,** Graduate School, College of Journalism and Communications, Program in Mass Communication, Gainesville, FL 32611. Offers international/intercultural communication (MAMC); journalism (MAMC); mass communication (MAMC, PhD), including clinical translational science (MAMC); public relations (MAMC); science/health communication (MAMC); telecommunication (MAMC). *Accreditation:* ACEJMC. *Entrance requirements:* For master's and doctorate, GRE General Test, minimum GPA of 3.0.

**University of Houston,** College of Liberal Arts and Social Sciences, Jack J. Valenti School of Communication, Houston, TX 77204. Offers health communication (MA); mass communication studies (MA); public relations studies (MA); speech communication (MA). *Program availability:* Part-time. *Degree requirements:* For master's, comprehensive exam (for some programs), thesis (for some programs), 30-33 hours. *Entrance requirements:* For master's, GRE. Additional exam requirements/recommendations for international students: Required—TOEFL. Electronic applications accepted.

**University of Missouri,** Office of Research and Graduate Studies, School of Journalism, Columbia, MO 65211. Offers health communications (MA); journalism (PhD). *Accreditation:* ACEJMC (one or more programs are accredited). *Program availability:* Part-time. *Faculty:* 72 full-time (34 women), 3 part-time/adjunct (0 women). *Students:* 134 full-time (97 women), 76 part-time (50 women); includes 29 minority (6 Black or African American, non-Hispanic/Latino; 5 Asian, non-Hispanic/Latino; 12 Hispanic/Latino; 6 Two or more races, non-Hispanic/Latino), 50 international. Average age 29. Terminal master's awarded for partial completion of doctoral program. *Degree requirements:* For master's, thesis (for some programs); for doctorate, 2 foreign languages, thesis/dissertation. *Entrance requirements:* For master's and doctorate, GRE General Test, minimum GPA of 3.0. Additional exam requirements/recommendations for international students: Required—TOEFL (minimum score 600 paper-based; 100 iBT), IELTS (minimum score 7). *Application deadline:* For fall admission, 12/15 priority date for domestic and international students; for winter admission, 9/1 priority date for domestic and international students. Applications are processed on a rolling basis. Application fee: $75 ($90 for international students). Electronic applications accepted. *Expenses:* Tuition, state resident: full-time $6347; part-time $352.60 per credit hour. Tuition, nonresident: full-time $17,379; part-time $965.50 per credit hour. *Required fees:* $1035. Tuition and fees vary according to course load, campus/location and program. *Financial support:* Fellowships with tuition reimbursements, research assistantships with tuition reimbursements, teaching assistantships with tuition reimbursements, career-related internships or fieldwork, institutionally sponsored loans, scholarships/grants, health care benefits, and unspecified assistantships available. Support available to part-time students. Website: http://www.journalism.missouri.edu/graduate/

**University of Oklahoma,** College of Arts and Sciences, Department of Communication, Norman, OK 73019. Offers communication (MA); communication technology (PhD); health communication (PhD); intercultural/international communication (PhD); interpersonal communication/social influence (PhD); organizational communication (PhD); political/mass communication (PhD). *Program availability:* Part-time. *Faculty:* 19 full-time (9 women). *Students:* 28 full-time (17 women), 40 part-time (19 women); includes 19 minority (6 Black or African American, non-Hispanic/Latino; 2 American Indian or Alaska Native, non-Hispanic/Latino; 9 Hispanic/Latino; 2 Two or more races, non-Hispanic/Latino), 9 international. Average age 36. 35 applicants, 60% accepted, 10 enrolled. In 2016, 14 master's, 8 doctorates awarded. *Degree requirements:* For master's, comprehensive exam (for some programs), thesis (for some programs), comprehensive exams or thesis; for doctorate, comprehensive exam, thesis/dissertation. *Entrance requirements:* For master's, GRE (for assistantship), statement of purpose, transcripts, writing sample, letters of recommendation; for doctorate, GRE, statement of purpose, transcripts, writing sample, letters of recommendation. Additional exam requirements/recommendations for international students: Required—TOEFL (minimum score 79 iBT) or IELTS (minimum score 6.5). *Application deadline:* For fall admission, 1/15 priority date for domestic students, 1/15 for international students; for spring admission, 10/15 for domestic and international students. Application fee: $50 ($100 for international students). Electronic applications accepted. *Expenses:* Tuition, state resident: full-time $4886; part-time $203.60 per credit hour. Tuition, nonresident: full-time $18,989; part-time $791.20 per credit hour. *Required fees:* $3283; $126.25 per credit hour. $126.50 per semester. *Financial support:* In 2016–17, 31 students received support, including 1 research assistantship with full tuition reimbursement available (averaging $10,373 per year), 26 teaching assistantships with full tuition reimbursements available (averaging $16,515 per year); health care benefits also available. Financial award application deadline: 6/1; financial award applicants required to submit FAFSA. *Faculty research:* Interpersonal/social influence, organizational, political/mass communication, health communication, intercultural/international. *Total annual research expenditures:* $12,383. *Unit head:* Dr. Michael W. Kramer, Chair and Professor, 405-325-9503, Fax: 405-325-7625, E-mail: mkramer@ou.edu. *Application contact:* Shay Glover, Academic Advisor, 405-325-7710, Fax: 405-325-7625, E-mail: shay.glover@ou.edu. Website: http://cas.ou.edu/comm

**University of Southern California,** Graduate School, Annenberg School for Communication and Journalism, School of Communication, Program in Communication, Los Angeles, CA 90089. Offers culture and community (PhD); global and transnational communication (PhD); groups, organizations and networks (PhD); health communication and social dynamics (PhD); information, political economy and entertainment (PhD); new media and technology (PhD); rhetoric, politics and public media (PhD). *Students:* 95 full-time (71 women); includes 22 minority (5 Black or African American, non-Hispanic/Latino; 6 Asian, non-Hispanic/Latino; 6 Hispanic/Latino; 5 Two or more races, non-Hispanic/Latino), 36 international. Average age 27. 144 applicants, 15% accepted, 16 enrolled. In 2016, 21 doctorates awarded. *Degree requirements:* For doctorate, thesis/dissertation. *Entrance requirements:* For doctorate, GRE General Test, resume or curriculum vitae, scholarly writing, 3 letters of recommendation, statement of purpose. Additional exam requirements/recommendations for international students: Required—TOEFL (minimum score 114 iBT), IELTS (minimum score 8); Recommended—TWE. *Application deadline:* For fall admission, 12/1 for domestic and international students. Application fee: $90. Electronic applications accepted. *Financial support:* In 2016–17, 16 students received support, including 16 fellowships with full tuition reimbursements available (averaging $5,796 per year); research assistantships, health care benefits, and unspecified assistantships also available. Financial award application deadline: 12/1; financial award applicants required to submit FAFSA. *Faculty research:* Computer-mediated communication, public health campaigns, communication democracy and the public sphere, new communication technologies in organizations, communication and community. *Unit head:* Dr. Peter Monge, Director of the PhD Program, 213-740-0921, E-mail: monge@usc.edu. *Application contact:* Allyson Hill, Associate Dean for Admissions, 213-821-0770, Fax: 213-740-1933, E-mail: ascadm@usc.edu.
Website: http://www.annenberg.usc.edu

**University of Southern California,** Keck School of Medicine and Graduate School, Graduate Programs in Medicine, Department of Preventive Medicine, Master of Public Health Program, Los Angeles, CA 90032-3628. Offers biostatistics and epidemiology (MPH); child and family health (MPH); environmental health (MPH); global health leadership (MPH); health communication (MPH); health education and promotion (MPH); public health policy (MPH). *Accreditation:* CEPH. *Program availability:* Part-time, evening/weekend. *Faculty:* 22 full-time (12 women), 3 part-time/adjunct (0 women). *Students:* 168 full-time (124 women), 30 part-time (22 women); includes 104 minority (14 Black or African American, non-Hispanic/Latino; 64 Asian, non-Hispanic/Latino; 26 Hispanic/Latino), 37 international. Average age 24. 246 applicants, 67% accepted, 76 enrolled. In 2016, 89 master's awarded. *Degree requirements:* For master's, practicum, final report, oral presentation. *Entrance requirements:* For master's, GRE General Test, MCAT, GMAT, minimum GPA of 3.0. Additional exam requirements/recommendations for international students: Required—TOEFL (minimum score 600 paper-based; 90 iBT). *Application deadline:* For fall admission, 12/1 priority date for domestic students, 5/1 priority date for international students; for spring admission, 9/1 priority date for domestic and international students; for summer admission, 3/1 for domestic and international students. Applications are processed on a rolling basis. Application fee: $90. Electronic applications accepted. *Expenses:* Contact institution. *Financial support:* Career-related internships or fieldwork, Federal Work-Study, institutionally sponsored loans, and scholarships/grants available. Support available to part-time students. Financial award application deadline: 5/4; financial award applicants required to submit CSS PROFILE or FAFSA. *Faculty research:* Substance abuse prevention, cancer and heart disease prevention, mass media and health communication research, health promotion, treatment compliance. *Unit head:* Dr. Louise A. Rohrbach, Director, 323-442-8237, Fax: 323-442-8297, E-mail: rohrbac@usc.edu. *Application contact:* Valerie Burris, Admissions Counselor, 323-442-7257, Fax: 323-442-8297, E-mail: valeriem@usc.edu. Website: http://mph.usc.edu/

**Wayne State University,** College of Fine, Performing and Communication Arts, Department of Communication, Detroit, MI 48202. Offers communication (PhD), including democratic participation and culture, identity and representation, media, society and culture, risk, crisis and conflict, wellness, work life and relationships; communication and new media (Graduate Certificate); communication studies (MA); dispute resolution (MADR, Graduate Certificate); health communication (Graduate Certificate); journalism (MA); media arts (MA); media studies (MA); public relations and organizational communication (MA); JD/MADR. Doctoral program admits for fall only. *Faculty:* 20. *Students:* 59 full-time (32 women), 113 part-time (75 women); includes 69 minority (54 Black or African American, non-Hispanic/Latino; 2 Asian, non-Hispanic/Latino; 7 Hispanic/Latino; 6 Two or more races, non-Hispanic/Latino), 12 international. Average age 34. 154 applicants, 39% accepted, 41 enrolled. In 2016, 31 master's, 10 doctorates, 4 other advanced degrees awarded. *Degree requirements:* For master's, thesis (for some programs), thesis or essay; for doctorate, thesis/dissertation. *Entrance requirements:* For master's, GRE (if undergraduate GPA less than 3.2), personal statement; BA or BS in communication or related field with minimum upper-division GPA of 3.2 and minimum upper-division undergraduate GPA of 3.0, personal statement, and sample of academic writing (for MA); 3 letters of recommendation (for MADR); for doctorate, GRE, MA in communication or related field with minimum GPA of 3.5; three letters of recommendation; personal statement; sample of written scholarship. Additional exam requirements/recommendations for international students: Required—TOEFL (minimum score 600 paper-based; 100 iBT), IELTS, TWE. Application fee: $50. Electronic applications accepted. *Expenses:* $17,240 per year resident tuition and fees, $34,434 per year non-resident tuition and fees. *Financial support:* In 2016–17, 61 students received support, including 4 fellowships with tuition reimbursements available (averaging $16,000 per year), 2 research assistantships with tuition reimbursements available (averaging $19,570 per year), 21 teaching assistantships with tuition reimbursements available (averaging $17,994 per year); scholarships/grants and unspecified assistantships also available. Financial award applicants required to submit FAFSA. *Faculty research:* Rhetorical theory and criticism; mass media theory and research; argumentation; organizational communication; risk and crisis communication; interpersonal, family, and health communication. *Unit head:* Dr. Lillian Black, Professor and Chair, 313-577-2943, E-mail: eh8899@wayne.edu. *Application contact:* E-mail: communication@wayne.edu.
Website: http://comm.wayne.edu/

# Internet and Interactive Multimedia

**Academy of Art University,** Graduate Programs, School of Communications and Media Technologies, San Francisco, CA 94105-3410. Offers communications and media technologies (MA). *Program availability:* Part-time, 100% online. *Faculty:* 3 full-time (0 women), 11 part-time/adjunct (3 women). *Students:* 60 full-time (40 women), 23 part-time (14 women); includes 7 minority (3 Black or African American, non-Hispanic/Latino; 4 Hispanic/Latino), 60 international. Average age 28. 31 applicants, 100% accepted, 19 enrolled. In 2016, 59 master's awarded. *Degree requirements:* For master's, final review. *Entrance requirements:* For master's, statement of intent; resume; portfolio/reel; official college transcripts. *Application deadline:* Applications are processed on a rolling basis. Application fee: $50. Electronic applications accepted.

*Expenses: Tuition:* Part-time $982 per unit. *Financial support:* Career-related internships or fieldwork, Federal Work-Study, and scholarships/grants available. Financial award application deadline: 8/10; financial award applicants required to submit FAFSA. *Unit head:* 800-544-ARTS, E-mail: info@academyart.edu. *Application contact:* 800-544-ARTS, E-mail: info@academyart.edu.
Website: http://www.academyart.edu/multimedia-communications-school/

**Alfred University,** Graduate School, College of Ceramics, School of Art and Design, Alfred, NY 14802. Offers ceramic art (MFA); electronic integrated arts (MFA); painting (MFA); sculpture/dimensional studies (MFA). *Accreditation:* NASAD. *Faculty:* 19 full-time (11 women), 14 part-time/adjunct (9 women). *Students:* 34 full-time (18 women);

includes 2 minority (1 Asian, non-Hispanic/Latino; 1 Hispanic/Latino), 10 international. Average age 28. 32 applicants, 66% accepted, 19 enrolled. In 2016, 15 master's awarded. *Degree requirements:* For master's, thesis, exhibit. *Entrance requirements:* For master's, portfolio. Additional exam requirements/recommendations for international students: Required—TOEFL (minimum score 550 paper-based; 80 iBT), IELTS (minimum score 6). *Application deadline:* For fall admission, 1/15 for domestic and international students. Application fee: $60. Electronic applications accepted. *Expenses:* Contact institution. *Financial support:* In 2016–17, 34 students received support. Teaching assistantships with full tuition reimbursements available and tuition waivers (full) available. Financial award application deadline: 8/1; financial award applicants required to submit FAFSA. *Faculty research:* Ceramic art, sculpture, glass art, new media, time-based media. *Unit head:* Gerar Edizel, Interim Dean, 607-871-2412, E-mail: fedizel@alfred.edu. *Application contact:* Sara Love, Coordinator of Graduate Admissions, 607-871-2115, Fax: 607-871-2198, E-mail: gradinquiry@alfred.edu. Website: http://art.alfred.edu/graduate/

**Ball State University,** Graduate School, College of Communication, Information, and Media, Department of Journalism, Program in Emerging Media Design and Development, Muncie, IN 47306. Offers MA. *Program availability:* Part-time, evening/weekend. *Entrance requirements:* For master's, GRE General Test (minimum score 150 verbal), minimum baccalaureate GPA of 2.75 or 3.0 in latter half of baccalauareate, transcripts of all prior course work, three letters of recommendation, current resume, statement of purpose, writing sample, portfolio. Additional exam requirements/recommendations for international students: Required—TOEFL (minimum score 550 paper-based; 79 iBT), IELTS (minimum score 6.5). Electronic applications accepted.

**Boston University,** Metropolitan College, Department of Computer Science, Boston, MA 02215. Offers computer information systems (MS), including computer networks, data analytics, database management and business intelligence, health informatics, IT project management, security, Web application development; computer networks (Certificate); computer science (MS); data analytics (Certificate); digital forensics (Certificate); health informatics (Certificate); information technology project management (Certificate); software development (MS); software engineering in health care systems (Certificate); telecommunications (MS), including security. *Program availability:* Part-time, evening/weekend, online learning. *Faculty:* 13 full-time (3 women), 43 part-time/adjunct (3 women). *Students:* 108 full-time (36 women), 1,294 part-time (364 women); includes 428 minority (115 Black or African American, non-Hispanic/Latino; 2 American Indian or Alaska Native, non-Hispanic/Latino; 187 Asian, non-Hispanic/Latino; 98 Hispanic/Latino; 2 Native Hawaiian or other Pacific Islander, non-Hispanic/Latino; 24 Two or more races, non-Hispanic/Latino), 314 international. Average age 33. 463 applicants, 79% accepted, 248 enrolled. In 2016, 311 master's awarded. *Degree requirements:* For master's, thesis optional. *Entrance requirements:* For master's and Certificate, official transcripts from regionally-accredited bachelor's degree program, 3 letters of recommendation, professional resume, personal statement. Additional exam requirements/recommendations for international students: Required—TOEFL (minimum score 84 iBT), IELTS. *Application deadline:* For fall admission, 6/1 priority date for international students; for spring admission, 10/1 priority date for international students. Applications are processed on a rolling basis. Application fee: $85. Electronic applications accepted. *Expenses:* Contact institution. *Financial support:* In 2016–17, 11 research assistantships (averaging $8,400 per year) were awarded; unspecified assistantships also available. Support available to part-time students. Financial award applicants required to submit FAFSA. *Faculty research:* Medical informatics, Web technologies, telecom and networks, security and forensics, software engineering, programming languages, multimedia and artificial intelligence (AI), information systems and IT project management. *Unit head:* Dr. Anatoly Temkin, Chair, 617-353-2566, Fax: 617-353-2367, E-mail: csinfo@bu.edu. *Application contact:* Lesley Moreau, Academic Program Coordinator, 617-353-2566, Fax: 617-353-2367, E-mail: metcs@bu.edu. Website: http://www.bu.edu/csmet/

**Brandeis University,** Rabb School of Continuing Studies, Division of Graduate Professional Studies, Master of Science in Digital Marketing and Design Program, Waltham, MA 02454-9110. Offers MS. *Program availability:* Part-time-only. *Faculty:* 45 part-time/adjunct (16 women). *Students:* 12 part-time (10 women); includes 1 minority (Black or African American, non-Hispanic/Latino). Average age 37. 4 applicants, 100% accepted, 4 enrolled. *Entrance requirements:* For master's, undergraduate degree with at least 2 marketing courses and/or 2 years of relevant work experience; four-year bachelor's degree from U.S. accredited institution or equivalent; statement of goals; resume or curriculum vitae; letter of recommendation. Additional exam requirements/recommendations for international students: Required—TWE (minimum score 4.5), TOEFL (minimum scores: 600 paper-based, 100 iBT), IELTS (7), or PTE (68). *Application deadline:* For fall admission, 6/21 priority date for domestic and international students; for winter admission, 9/13 priority date for domestic and international students; for spring admission, 12/20 priority date for domestic and international students; for summer admission, 3/14 for domestic students, 3/14 priority date for international students. Applications are processed on a rolling basis. Application fee: $50. Electronic applications accepted. *Expenses:* $3,400 per course, $100 graduation fee. *Financial support:* Applicants required to submit FAFSA. *Unit head:* Steven Dupree, Chair, 781-736-8787, E-mail: sdupree@brandeis.edu. *Application contact:* Frances Stearns, Director of Admissions and Recruitment, 781-736-8785, E-mail: fstearns@brandeis.edu.

**Brooklyn College of the City University of New York,** School of Visual, Media and Performing Arts, Program in Performance and Interactive Media Arts, Brooklyn, NY 11210-2889. Offers MFA. *Entrance requirements:* For master's, 2 letters of recommendation, resume, portfolio, interview. Additional exam requirements/recommendations for international students: Required—TOEFL (minimum score 550 paper-based; 61 iBT). Electronic applications accepted.

**California State University, East Bay,** Office of Graduate Studies, College of Letters, Arts, and Social Sciences, Multimedia Graduate Program, Hayward, CA 94542-3000. Offers MA. *Program availability:* Part-time. *Students:* 11 full-time (7 women), 6 part-time (3 women); includes 7 minority (2 Black or African American, non-Hispanic/Latino; 3 Asian, non-Hispanic/Latino; 2 Hispanic/Latino), 4 international. Average age 32. 22 applicants, 77% accepted, 9 enrolled. In 2016, 1 master's awarded. *Degree requirements:* For master's, multimedia project or thesis. *Entrance requirements:* For master's, minimum GPA of 2.5; resume; 2 letters of recommendation; multimedia portfolio; statement of purpose. Additional exam requirements/recommendations for international students: Required—TOEFL (minimum score 550 paper-based). *Application deadline:* For fall admission, 6/15 for domestic and international students. Application fee: $55. Electronic applications accepted. *Expenses:* Contact institution. *Financial support:* Fellowships, teaching assistantships, Federal Work-Study, institutionally sponsored loans, and scholarships/grants available. Support available to part-time students. Financial award application deadline: 3/1; financial award applicants required to submit FAFSA. *Unit head:* Ian Pollock, Director, 510-885-2427, E-mail: ian.pollock@csueastbay.edu. Website: http://multimedia.csueastbay.edu

**Champlain College,** Graduate Studies, Burlington, VT 05402-0670. Offers business (MBA); digital forensic science (MS); early childhood education (M Ed); emergent media (MFA, MS); executive leadership (MS); health care administration (MS); information

security operations (MS); law (MS); mediation and applied conflict studies (MS). MS in emergent media program held in Shanghai. *Program availability:* Part-time, online learning. *Degree requirements:* For master's, capstone project. *Entrance requirements:* Additional exam requirements/recommendations for international students: Required—TOEFL (minimum score 550 paper-based; 80 iBT). Electronic applications accepted.

**Concordia University,** School of Graduate Studies, Faculty of Engineering and Computer Science, Concordia Institute for Information Systems Engineering (CIISE), Montréal, QC H3G 1M8, Canada. Offers 3D graphics and game development (Certificate); information and systems engineering (PhD); information systems security (M Eng, MA Sc); quality systems engineering (M Eng, MA Sc); service engineering and network management (Certificate).

**DePaul University,** College of Computing and Digital Media, Chicago, IL 60604. Offers animation (MA, MFA); business information technology (MS); cinema (MFA); cinema production (MS); computational finance (MS); computer and information sciences (PhD); computer game development (MS); computer information and network security (MS); computer science (MS); e-commerce technology (MS); health informatics (MS); human-computer interaction (MS); information systems (MS); information technology project management (MS); network engineering and management (MS); predictive analytics (MS); screenwriting (MFA); software engineering (MS); JD/MS. *Program availability:* Part-time, evening/weekend, online learning. *Degree requirements:* For master's, thesis (for some programs); for doctorate, comprehensive exam, thesis/dissertation. *Entrance requirements:* For master's, GRE or GMAT (for MS in computational finance only), bachelor's degree, resume (MS in predictive analytics only), IT experience (MS in information technology project management only), portfolio review (all MFA programs and MA in animation); for doctorate, GRE, master's degree in computer science. Additional exam requirements/recommendations for international students: Required—TOEFL (minimum score 590 paper-based; 80 iBT), IELTS (minimum score 6.5), PTE (minimum score 53). Electronic applications accepted. *Expenses:* Contact institution. *Faculty research:* Data mining, computer science, human-computer interaction, security, animation and film.

**Elon University,** Program in Interactive Media, Elon, NC 27244-2010. Offers MA. *Faculty:* 12 full-time (3 women). *Students:* 26 full-time (20 women); includes 7 minority (3 Black or African American, non-Hispanic/Latino; 1 American Indian or Alaska Native, non-Hispanic/Latino; 2 Hispanic/Latino; 1 Two or more races, non-Hispanic/Latino). Average age 33. 48 applicants, 81% accepted, 27 enrolled. In 2016, 36 master's awarded. *Degree requirements:* For master's, 6-hour capstone. *Entrance requirements:* For master's, GRE. Additional exam requirements/recommendations for international students: Required—TOEFL (minimum score 550 paper-based; 79 iBT). *Application deadline:* For fall admission, 5/1 priority date for domestic students. Applications are processed on a rolling basis. Application fee: $50. Electronic applications accepted. *Financial support:* Federal Work-Study and scholarships/grants available. Support available to part-time students. Financial award application deadline: 3/15; financial award applicants required to submit FAFSA. *Faculty research:* Effects of service-learning (local and international) on the quality of learning for interactive media students, pedagogy for visual communication, impact of reviewer comments on consumer product and news perceptions, visual communication, social media in pedagogy. *Unit head:* Dr. Paul Parsons, Dean of the School of Communications, 336-278-5724, E-mail: pparsons@elon.edu. *Application contact:* Art Fadde, Director of Graduate Admissions, 800-334-8448 Ext. 3, Fax: 336-278-7699, E-mail: afadde@elon.edu. Website: http://www.elon.edu/imedia

**Excelsior College,** School of Business and Technology, Albany, NY 12203-5159. Offers business administration (MBA); cybersecurity management (MBA, Graduate Certificate); general business management (MS); health care management (MBA); human performance technology (MBA); human resource management (MS); human resources management (MBA); leadership (MBA, MS); mediation and arbitration (MBA, MS); social media management (MBA); technology management (MBA). *Program availability:* Part-time, evening/weekend, online learning. *Faculty:* 25 part-time/adjunct (9 women). *Students:* 1,801 part-time (487 women); includes 775 minority (424 Black or African American, non-Hispanic/Latino; 5 American Indian or Alaska Native, non-Hispanic/Latino; 58 Asian, non-Hispanic/Latino; 209 Hispanic/Latino; 15 Native Hawaiian or other Pacific Islander, non-Hispanic/Latino; 64 Two or more races, non-Hispanic/Latino), 11 international. Average age 39. In 2016, 288 master's awarded. *Application deadline:* Applications are processed on a rolling basis. Application fee: $50. Electronic applications accepted. *Expenses:* Tuition: Part-time $645 per credit. *Required fees:* $265 per credit. *Financial support:* Scholarships/grants available. *Unit head:* Dr. Lifang Shih, Dean, 888-647-2388. *Application contact:* Admissions, 888-647-2388 Ext. 133, Fax: 518-464-8777, E-mail: admissions@excelsior.edu.

**Fairfield University,** School of Engineering, Fairfield, CT 06824. Offers database management (CAS); electrical and computer engineering (MS); information security (CAS); management of technology (MS); mechanical engineering (MS); network technology (CAS); software engineering (MS); Web application development (CAS). *Program availability:* Part-time, evening/weekend. *Faculty:* 7 full-time (1 woman), 5 part-time/adjunct (2 women). *Students:* 104 full-time (31 women), 56 part-time (15 women); includes 17 minority (8 Black or African American, non-Hispanic/Latino; 5 Asian, non-Hispanic/Latino; 4 Hispanic/Latino), 108 international. Average age 28. 193 applicants, 63% accepted, 20 enrolled. In 2016, 173 master's awarded. *Degree requirements:* For master's, capstone course. *Entrance requirements:* For master's, resume, 2 recommendations. Additional exam requirements/recommendations for international students: Required—TOEFL (minimum score 550 paper-based; 80 iBT) or IELTS (minimum score 6.5). *Application deadline:* For fall admission, 5/15 for international students; for spring admission, 10/15 for international students. Applications are processed on a rolling basis. Application fee: $60. Electronic applications accepted. *Expenses:* $800 per credit hour. *Financial support:* In 2016–17, 27 students received support. Scholarships/grants and unspecified assistantships available. Financial award applicants required to submit FAFSA. *Faculty research:* Artificial intelligence and information visualization, natural language processing, thermofluids, microwaves and electromagnetics, micro-/nano-manufacturing. *Unit head:* Dr. Bruce Berdanier, Dean, 203-254-4147, Fax: 203-254-4013, E-mail: bberdanier@fairfield.edu. *Application contact:* Marianne Gumpper, Director of Graduate and Continuing Studies Admission, 203-254-4184, Fax: 203-254-4073, E-mail: gradadmis@fairfield.edu. Website: http://www.fairfield.edu/soe

**Full Sail University,** Education Media Design and Technology Master of Science Program - Online, Winter Park, FL 32792-7437. Offers MS. *Program availability:* Online learning. *Entrance requirements:* Additional exam requirements/recommendations for international students: Required—TOEFL (minimum score 550 paper-based; 79 iBT).

**Full Sail University,** Game Design Master of Science Program - Campus, Winter Park, FL 32792-7437. Offers MS.

**Full Sail University,** Internet Marketing Master of Science Program - Online, Winter Park, FL 32792-7437. Offers MS. *Program availability:* Online learning.

**Georgetown University,** Graduate School of Arts and Sciences, Program in Communication, Culture, and Technology, Washington, DC 20057. Offers MA. *Program*

*availability:* Part-time, evening/weekend. *Degree requirements:* For master's, thesis (for some programs). *Entrance requirements:* For master's, GRE General Test, 3 letters of recommendation, writing sample. Additional exam requirements/recommendations for international students: Required—TOEFL (minimum score 600 paper-based). Electronic applications accepted.

**Georgia Institute of Technology,** Graduate Studies, Ivan Allen College of Liberal Arts, School of Literature, Media, and Communication, Atlanta, GA 30332-0001. Offers digital media (MS, PhD). *Program availability:* Part-time. Terminal master's awarded for partial completion of doctoral program. *Degree requirements:* For master's, thesis optional, project studio, paid internship, responsible conduct of research training; for doctorate, comprehensive exam, thesis/dissertation, portfolio review, responsible conduct of research training. *Entrance requirements:* For master's and doctorate, GRE, three letters of recommendation, transcripts from each college/university attended, design portfolio, statement of purpose. Additional exam requirements/recommendations for international students: Required—TOEFL (minimum score 650 paper-based; 114 iBT). Electronic applications accepted. *Faculty research:* New media studies.

**Indiana University–Purdue University Indianapolis,** School of Informatics and Computing, Indianapolis, IN 46202. Offers MLS, MS, PhD. *Program availability:* Part-time, evening/weekend. *Degree requirements:* For master's, thesis optional; for doctorate, thesis/dissertation. *Entrance requirements:* For master's, minimum undergraduate GPA of 3.0, graduate 3.2. Additional exam requirements/ recommendations for international students: Required—TOEFL. Electronic applications accepted.

**Ithaca College,** Roy H. Park School of Communications, Executive Master's in Communications Innovation Program, Ithaca, NY 14850. Offers MS. *Program availability:* Part-time-only, blended/hybrid learning. *Faculty:* 3 full-time (1 woman). *Students:* 10 part-time (5 women), 1 international. Average age 38. 10 applicants, 80% accepted, 5 enrolled. In 2016, 6 master's awarded. *Degree requirements:* For master's, thesis optional, project. *Entrance requirements:* Additional exam requirements/ recommendations for international students: Required—TOEFL (minimum score 550 paper-based; 80 iBT). *Application deadline:* For fall admission, 3/15 for domestic and international students; for spring admission, 12/1 for domestic and international students. Applications are processed on a rolling basis. Application fee: $40. Electronic applications accepted. *Expenses:* Contact institution. *Financial support:* In 2016–17, 6 students received support, including 4 fellowships (averaging $7,500 per year); career-related internships or fieldwork, Federal Work-Study, and scholarships/grants also available. Support available to part-time students. Financial award application deadline: 2/1; financial award applicants required to submit CSS PROFILE or FAFSA. *Unit head:* Bob Regan, Director, 607-274-1081, E-mail: rregan@ithaca.edu. *Application contact:* Nicole Eversley Bradwell, Director, Office of Admission, 607-274-3124, Fax: 607-274-1263, E-mail: admission@ithaca.edu.
Website: http://www.ithaca.edu/gradprograms/innovation/

**Kutztown University of Pennsylvania,** College of Visual and Performing Arts, Program in Communication Design, Kutztown, PA 19530-0730. Offers MFA. *Program availability:* Part-time. *Faculty:* 8 full-time (6 women), 1 (woman) part-time/adjunct. *Students:* 8 full-time (7 women), 3 part-time (2 women), 2 international. Average age 33. 8 applicants, 100% accepted, 3 enrolled. In 2016, 2 master's awarded. *Degree requirements:* For master's, thesis optional. *Entrance requirements:* For master's, resume documenting a minimum of 3 years professional experience in the field, artist's statement, porfolio. Additional exam requirements/recommendations for international students: Required—TOEFL (minimum score 550 paper-based, 79 iBT) or IELTS (minimum score 6.5). *Application deadline:* For fall admission, 3/1 priority date for domestic and international students. Application fee: $35. Electronic applications accepted. *Expenses:* Tuition, state resident: full-time $4347; part-time $483 per credit. Tuition, nonresident: full-time $6525; part-time $725 per credit. *Required fees:* $88 per credit. One-time fee: $50 full-time. *Financial support:* Career-related internships or fieldwork, Federal Work-Study, scholarships/grants, and unspecified assistantships available. Financial award application deadline: 3/1; financial award applicants required to submit FAFSA. *Unit head:* Todd McFeely, Chairperson, 610-683-4531, Fax: 610-683-4619, E-mail: mcfeely@kutztown.edu.
Website: http://kucd.kutztown.edu/mfa

**Lindenwood University–Belleville,** Graduate Programs, Belleville, IL 62226. Offers business administration (MBA); communications (MA), including digital and multimedia, media management, promotions, training and development; counseling (MA); criminal justice administration (MS); education (MA); healthcare administration (MS); human resource management (MS); school administration (MA); teaching (MAT).

**Lindsey Wilson College,** Louisville Center for Design, Columbia, KY 42728. Offers interactive design (MA). *Program availability:* Online learning.

**London Metropolitan University,** Graduate Programs, London, United Kingdom. Offers applied psychology (MA); architecture (MA); biomedical science (M Sc); blood science (M Sc); cancer pharmacology (M Sc); computer networking and cyber security (M Sc); computing and information systems (M Sc); conference interpreting (MA); counter-terrorism studies (M Sc); creative, digital and professional writing (MA); crime, violence and prevention (M Sc); criminology (M Sc); curating contemporary art (MA); data analytics (M Sc); digital media (MA); early childhood studies (MA); education (MA, Ed D); financial services law, regulation and compliance (LL M); food science (M Sc); forensic psychology (M Sc); health and social care management and policy (M Sc); human nutrition (M Sc); human resource management (MA); human rights and international conflict (MA); information technology (M Sc); intelligence and security studies (M Sc); international oil, gas and energy law (LL M); international relations (MA); interpreting (MA); learning and teaching in higher education (MA); legal practice (LL M); media and entertainment law (LL M); organizational and consumer psychology (M Sc); psychological therapy (M Sc); psychology of mental health (M Sc); public health (M Sc); public policy and management (MPA); security studies (M Sc); social work (M Sc); spatial planning and urban design (MA); sports therapy (M Sc); supporting older children and young people with dyslexia (MA); teaching languages (MA), including Arabic, English; translation (MA); woman and child abuse (MA).

**Long Island University–LIU Post,** College of Arts, Communications and Design, Brookville, NY 11548-1300. Offers art (MA); clinical art therapy (MA); clinical art therapy and counseling (MA); digital game design and development (MA); fine arts and design (MFA); interactive multimedia arts (MA); music (MA); theater (MA); theatre (MFA). *Faculty:* 36 full-time (19 women), 144 part-time/adjunct (74 women). *Students:* 123 full-time (91 women), 21 part-time (18 women); includes 25 minority (6 Black or African American, non-Hispanic/Latino; 1 American Indian or Alaska Native, non-Hispanic/Latino; 6 Asian, non-Hispanic/Latino; 11 Hispanic/Latino; 1 Two or more races, non-Hispanic/Latino), 32 international. 175 applicants, 73% accepted, 46 enrolled. In 2016, 68 master's awarded. *Degree requirements:* For master's, variable foreign language requirement, comprehensive exam (for some programs), thesis (for some programs). *Entrance requirements:* For master's, performance audition or portfolio. Additional exam requirements/recommendations for international students: Required—TOEFL (minimum score 550 paper-based; 79 iBT). *Application deadline:* Applications are processed on a rolling basis. Application fee: $50. Electronic applications accepted. *Expenses:* Tuition:

Full-time $28,272; part-time $1178 per credit. *Required fees:* $451 per term. Tuition and fees vary according to degree level and program. *Financial support:* In 2016–17, 6 research assistantships with partial tuition reimbursements (averaging $1,020 per year), 14 teaching assistantships with partial tuition reimbursements (averaging $670 per year) were awarded; career-related internships or fieldwork, Federal Work-Study, institutionally sponsored loans, scholarships/grants, tuition waivers (full and partial), and unspecified assistantships also available. Support available to part-time students. Financial award application deadline: 2/15; financial award applicants required to submit FAFSA. *Faculty research:* Game design, new plays, musical theatre, compositions for wind symphony, jazz ensemble, jazz combo and vocal jazz. *Unit head:* Dr. Christine Kerr, Acting Dean, 516-299-2309, E-mail: christine.kerr@liu.edu. *Application contact:* Carol Zerah, Director of Graduate Admissions, 516-299-2900, Fax: 516-299-2137, E-mail: post-enroll@liu.edu.
Website: http://www.liu.edu/CWPost/Academics/School-of-Visual-Arts-Communications-and-Digital-Technologies

**Louisiana State University and Agricultural & Mechanical College,** Graduate School, College of Art and Design, Program in Digital Media Arts and Engineering, Baton Rouge, LA 70803. Offers M Sc. *Entrance requirements:* For master's, GRE, digital portfolio.

**Lynn University,** Eugene M. and Christine E. Lynn College of International Communication, Boca Raton, FL 33431-5598. Offers communication and media (MS), including digital media, media studies and practice; digital media (Certificate). *Program availability:* Part-time, evening/weekend. *Faculty:* 15 full-time (8 women), 6 part-time/ adjunct (3 women). *Students:* 24 full-time (20 women), 15 part-time (14 women); includes 11 minority (7 Black or African American, non-Hispanic/Latino; 2 Asian, non-Hispanic/Latino; 2 Hispanic/Latino), 14 international. Average age 27. 38 applicants, 87% accepted, 17 enrolled. In 2016, 18 master's, 1 other advanced degree awarded. *Degree requirements:* For master's, project or thesis. *Entrance requirements:* For master's, resume, letter of recommendation, official transcripts, bachelor's degree from accredited institution, personal statement. Additional exam requirements/ recommendations for international students: Required—TOEFL (minimum score 550 paper-based; 80 iBT), IELTS (minimum score 6.5). *Application deadline:* For fall admission, 8/18 for domestic students, 8/4 for international students; for spring admission, 12/15 for domestic students, 12/1 for international students; for summer admission, 4/17 for domestic students, 4/3 for international students. Applications are processed on a rolling basis. Application fee: $45. Electronic applications accepted. *Expenses:* $725 per credit hour. *Financial support:* In 2016–17, 7 students received support. Career-related internships or fieldwork, Federal Work-Study, institutionally sponsored loans, scholarships/grants, tuition waivers (partial), and unspecified assistantships available. Support available to part-time students. Financial award application deadline: 8/1; financial award applicants required to submit FAFSA. *Unit head:* Dr. David L. Jaffe, Dean, 561-237-7099, Fax: 561-237-7097, E-mail: djaffe@lynn.edu. *Application contact:* Steven Pruitt, Director of Graduate Admission, 561-237-7834, Fax: 561-237-7100, E-mail: admission@lynn.edu.
Website: http://www.lynn.edu/academics/colleges/international-communication

**Marlboro College,** Graduate and Professional Studies, Program in Teaching with Technology, Marlboro, VT 05344. Offers educational technology (Certificate); teaching with technology (MAT). *Program availability:* Part-time, evening/weekend, blended/ hybrid learning. *Faculty:* 1 full-time (0 women), 8 part-time/adjunct (5 women). *Students:* 6 full-time (3 women), 13 part-time (5 women); includes 3 minority (1 Black or African American, non-Hispanic/Latino; 2 Two or more races, non-Hispanic/Latino). Average age 44. 8 applicants, 88% accepted, 7 enrolled. In 2016, 5 master's awarded. *Degree requirements:* For master's, 36 credits including capstone project. *Entrance requirements:* For master's, statement of intent, 2 letters of recommendation, transcripts. *Application deadline:* For fall admission, 7/1 priority date for domestic students; for winter admission, 11/1 priority date for domestic students; for spring admission, 3/1 priority date for domestic students. Applications are processed on a rolling basis. Application fee: $0. Electronic applications accepted. *Expenses:* $765 per credit. *Financial support:* In 2016–17, 2 students received support. Scholarships/grants available. Financial award application deadline: 8/5; financial award applicants required to submit FAFSA. *Unit head:* Caleb Clark, Degree Chair, 802-258-9207, Fax: 802-258-9201, E-mail: cclark@gradschool.marlboro.edu. *Application contact:* Don Parker, Admissions Assistant, 802-451-7505, Fax: 802-258-9201, E-mail: graduateadmissions@marlboro.edu.
Website: https://www.marlboro.edu/academics/graduate/mat

**Mississippi State University,** College of Education, Department of Instructional Systems and Workforce Development, Mississippi State, MS 39762. Offers distance education (MSIT); instructional design (MSIT); instructional systems and workforce development (MST, PhD); multimedia (MSIT); technology (Ed S). *Faculty:* 12 full-time (8 women). *Students:* 14 full-time (10 women), 53 part-time (44 women); includes 41 minority (39 Black or African American, non-Hispanic/Latino; 1 American Indian or Alaska Native, non-Hispanic/Latino; 1 Two or more races, non-Hispanic/Latino). Average age 38. 17 applicants, 47% accepted, 8 enrolled. In 2016, 6 master's, 3 doctorates, 5 other advanced degrees awarded. *Degree requirements:* For master's, thesis optional, comprehensive oral or written exam; for doctorate, thesis/dissertation, comprehensive oral and written exam; for Ed S, thesis, comprehensive written exam. *Entrance requirements:* For master's, GRE, minimum GPA of 2.75 on undergraduate work, 3.0 graduate; for doctorate, GRE, minimum GPA of 3.4 on graduate work; for Ed S, GRE, minimum GPA of 3.2, master's degree. Additional exam requirements/ recommendations for international students: Required—TOEFL (minimum score 550 paper-based; 79 iBT); Recommended—IELTS (minimum score 6.5). *Application deadline:* For fall admission, 7/1 for domestic students, 5/1 for international students; for spring admission, 11/1 for domestic students, 9/1 for international students. Applications are processed on a rolling basis. Application fee: $60. Electronic applications accepted. *Expenses:* Tuition, state resident: full-time $7670; part-time $852.50 per credit hour. Tuition, nonresident: full-time $20,790; part-time $2310.50 per credit hour. Part-time tuition and fees vary according to course load. *Financial support:* In 2016–17, 2 research assistantships with full tuition reimbursements (averaging $13,755 per year), 2 teaching assistantships with full tuition reimbursements (averaging $10,800 per year) were awarded; Federal Work-Study, institutionally sponsored loans, scholarships/ grants, and unspecified assistantships also available. Financial award application deadline: 4/1; financial award applicants required to submit FAFSA. *Faculty research:* Computer technology, nontraditional students, interactive video, instructional technology, educational leadership. *Unit head:* Dr. Connie Forde, Professor and Department Head, 662-325-2281, Fax: 662-325-7599, E-mail: cforde@colled.msstate.edu. *Application contact:* Linda Bonner, Senior Admissions Assistant, 662-325-3363, E-mail: lbonner@grad.msstate.edu.
Website: http://www.iswd.msstate.edu

**Mount Mary University,** Graduate Programs, Program in English, Milwaukee, WI 53222-4597. Offers creative writing (MA); professional and new media writing (MA). *Program availability:* Part-time, evening/weekend. *Faculty:* 4 full-time (all women), 2 part-time/adjunct (1 woman). *Students:* 8 full-time (6 women), 16 part-time (13 women); includes 10 minority (5 Black or African American, non-Hispanic/Latino; 1 American

Indian or Alaska Native, non-Hispanic/Latino; 1 Hispanic/Latino; 3 Two or more races, non-Hispanic/Latino). Average age 42. 4 applicants, 50% accepted, 2 enrolled. In 2016, 5 master's awarded. *Degree requirements:* For master's, comprehensive exam, thesis or alternative. *Entrance requirements:* For master's, minimum GPA of 2.75. Additional exam requirements/recommendations for international students: Required—TOEFL (minimum score 550 paper-based; 80 iBT); Recommended—IELTS (minimum score 6.5). *Application deadline:* For fall admission, 8/1 for domestic and international students; for spring admission, 12/1 for domestic and international students; for summer admission, 5/1 for domestic and international students. Applications are processed on a rolling basis. Application fee: $45. Electronic applications accepted. *Expenses:* Contact institution. *Financial support:* Career-related internships or fieldwork and Federal Work-Study available. Support available to part-time students. Financial award application deadline: 5/1; financial award applicants required to submit FAFSA. *Unit head:* Ann Angel, Graduate Program Chair, 414-930-3109, E-mail: angela@mtmary.edu. *Application contact:* Kirk Heller de Messer, Director, Graduate Admissions, 414-930-3221, E-mail: hellerk@mtmary.edu.
Website: http://www.mtmary.edu/majors-programs/graduate/english/index.html

**National University,** Academic Affairs, School of Professional Studies, La Jolla, CA 92037-1011. Offers criminal justice (MCJ); digital cinema (MFA); digital journalism (MA); juvenile justice (MS); public administration (MPA), including human resource management. *Program availability:* Part-time, evening/weekend, 100% online, blended/hybrid learning. *Faculty:* 21 full-time (8 women), 35 part-time/adjunct (9 women). *Students:* 280 full-time (155 women), 100 part-time (54 women); includes 226 minority (76 Black or African American, non-Hispanic/Latino; 1 American Indian or Alaska Native, non-Hispanic/Latino; 27 Asian, non-Hispanic/Latino; 102 Hispanic/Latino; 3 Native Hawaiian or other Pacific Islander, non-Hispanic/Latino; 17 Two or more races, non-Hispanic/Latino), 3 international. Average age 37. In 2016, 21 master's awarded. *Degree requirements:* For master's, thesis (for some programs). *Entrance requirements:* For master's, interview, minimum GPA of 2.5. Additional exam requirements/recommendations for international students: Required—TOEFL (minimum score 550 paper-based; 79 iBT), IELTS (minimum score 6). *Application deadline:* Applications are processed on a rolling basis. Application fee: $60 ($65 for international students). Electronic applications accepted. *Financial support:* Career-related internships or fieldwork, institutionally sponsored loans, scholarships/grants, and tuition waivers (partial) available. Support available to part-time students. Financial award application deadline: 6/30; financial award applicants required to submit FAFSA. *Unit head:* School of Professional Studies, 800-628-8648, E-mail: sops@nu.edu. *Application contact:* Brandon Jouganatos, Vice President for Enrollment Services, 800-628-8648, E-mail: advisor@nu.edu.
Website: http://www.nu.edu/OurPrograms/School-of-Professional-Studies.html

**New Mexico Highlands University,** Graduate Studies, College of Arts and Sciences, Department of Computer Sciences, Las Vegas, NM 87701. Offers media arts and computer science (MS), including computer science. *Degree requirements:* For master's, comprehensive exam, thesis. *Entrance requirements:* For master's, minimum undergraduate GPA of 3.0. Additional exam requirements/recommendations for international students: Required—TOEFL (minimum score 540 paper-based). *Faculty research:* Advanced digital compositing, photographic installations and exhibition design, pattern recognition, parallel and distributed computing, computer security education.

**New York University,** Polytechnic School of Engineering, Department of Technology, Culture and Society, New York, NY 10012-1019. Offers integrated digital media (MS, Graduate Certificate). *Program availability:* Part-time, evening/weekend. *Degree requirements:* For master's, comprehensive exam (for some programs), thesis (for some programs). *Entrance requirements:* Additional exam requirements/recommendations for international students: Required—TOEFL (minimum score 550 paper-based; 80 iBT); Recommended—IELTS (minimum score 6.5). Electronic applications accepted. *Faculty research:* Trade magazine journalism, technical writing, financial reporting, medical and science reporting, industrial advertising and public relations.

**New York University,** Polytechnic School of Engineering, Major in Integrated Digital Media, New York, NY 10012-1019. Offers MS, Graduate Certificate. *Program availability:* Part-time. *Entrance requirements:* Additional exam requirements/recommendations for international students: Required—TOEFL (minimum score 550 paper-based; 80 iBT); Recommended—IELTS (minimum score 6.5). Electronic applications accepted.

**New York University,** Tisch School of the Arts, Interactive Telecommunications Program, New York, NY 10012-1019. Offers MPS. *Degree requirements:* For master's, thesis. *Entrance requirements:* Additional exam requirements/recommendations for international students: Required—TOEFL (minimum score 600 paper-based; 100 iBT) or IELTS (minimum score 6). Electronic applications accepted. *Faculty research:* Interactive narrative/storytelling, interactive media, Web technology, physical computing, ubiquitous computing.

**Northeastern University,** College of Professional Studies, Boston, MA 02115-5096. Offers applied nutrition (MS); college athletics administration (MSL); commerce and economic development (MS); corporate and organizational communication (MS); criminal justice (MS); digital media (MPS); elearning and instructional design (M Ed); elementary education (MAT); geographic information technology (MPS); global studies and international relations (MS); higher education administration (M Ed); homeland security (MA); human services (MS); informatics (MPS); leadership (MS); learning analytics (M Ed); learning and instruction (M Ed); nonprofit management (MS); professional sports administration (MSL); project management (MS); regulatory affairs for drugs, biologics, and medical devices (MS); respiratory care leadership (MS); special education (M Ed); technical communication (MS). *Program availability:* Part-time, evening/weekend, 100% online, blended/hybrid learning. *Faculty:* 82 full-time (51 women), 853 part-time/adjunct (366 women). *Students:* 4,947 part-time (3,076 women). In 2016, 1,456 master's awarded. *Application deadline:* Applications are processed on a rolling basis. Application fee: $0. Electronic applications accepted. *Expenses:* Contact institution. *Financial support:* Applicants required to submit FAFSA. *Unit head:* Dr. Mary Loeffelholz, Interim Dean of the College of Professional Studies.
Website: http://www.cps.neu.edu/

**Northwestern University,** School of Professional Studies, Program in Information Systems, Evanston, IL 60208. Offers analytics and business intelligence (MS); database and Internet technologies (MS); information systems (MS); information systems management (MS); information systems security (MS); medical informatics (MS); software project management and development (MS).

**The Ohio State University,** Graduate School, College of Arts and Sciences, Division of Arts and Humanities, Department of Design, Columbus, OH 43210. Offers design (MA); design research and development (MFA); digital animation and interactive media (MFA). *Accreditation:* NASAD. *Program availability:* Part-time. *Faculty:* 15. *Students:* 23 full-time (12 women), 7 international. Average age 29. In 2016, 8 master's awarded. *Degree requirements:* For master's, project or thesis. *Entrance requirements:* For master's, GRE General Test (for all applicants with cumulative GPA below 3.0), portfolio. Additional exam requirements/recommendations for international students: Recommended—

TOEFL (minimum score 550 paper-based; 79 iBT). *Application deadline:* For fall admission, 12/13 priority date for domestic students, 11/30 priority date for international students; for spring admission, 3/1 for domestic students, 2/1 for international students. Applications are processed on a rolling basis. Application fee: $60 ($70 for international students). Electronic applications accepted. *Financial support:* Fellowships with tuition reimbursements, research assistantships with tuition reimbursements, teaching assistantships with tuition reimbursements, career-related internships or fieldwork, Federal Work-Study, institutionally sponsored loans, and unspecified assistantships available. Support available to part-time students. Financial award application deadline: 5/1. *Unit head:* Dr. Mary Anne Beecher, Chair, 614-688-6746, E-mail: beecher.17@osu.edu. *Application contact:* Graduate and Professional Admissions, 614-292-9444, Fax: 614-292-3895, E-mail: gpadmissions@osu.edu.
Website: http://design.osu.edu/

**Pace University,** Lubin School of Business, Marketing Program, New York, NY 10038. Offers analytics and customer intelligence (MS); marketing management (MBA); social media and mobile marketing (MS). *Program availability:* Evening/weekend. *Students:* 31 full-time (21 women), 19 part-time (11 women); includes 7 minority (1 Black or African American, non-Hispanic/Latino; 2 Asian, non-Hispanic/Latino; 2 Hispanic/Latino; 2 Two or more races, non-Hispanic/Latino), 31 international. Average age 26. 126 applicants, 56% accepted, 26 enrolled. In 2016, 23 master's awarded. *Entrance requirements:* For master's, GMAT, GRE, undergraduate degree, transcripts from all accredited colleges/universities attended, two letters of recommendation, resume, personal statement. Additional exam requirements/recommendations for international students: Required—TOEFL (minimum score 90 iBT), IELTS (minimum score 7) or PTE (minimum score 61). *Application deadline:* For fall admission, 8/1 priority date for domestic students, 6/1 for international students; for spring admission, 12/1 for domestic students, 10/1 for international students. Applications are processed on a rolling basis. Application fee: $70. Electronic applications accepted. *Expenses: Tuition:* Part-time $1195 per credit. *Required fees:* $260 per semester. Tuition and fees vary according to degree level, campus/location and program. *Financial support:* Research assistantships, career-related internships or fieldwork, and Federal Work-Study available. Support available to part-time students. Financial award application deadline: 2/15; financial award applicants required to submit FAFSA. *Unit head:* Dr. Ipshita Ray, Chairperson, 212-618-6505, E-mail: iray@pace.edu. *Application contact:* Susan Ford-Goldschein, Director of Graduate Admissions, 212-346-1531, Fax: 212-346-1585, E-mail: graduateadmission@pace.edu.
Website: http://www.pace.edu/lubin/mba-in-marketing-management

**Pace University,** Seidenberg School of Computer Science and Information Systems, New York, NY 10038. Offers chief information security officer (APC); computer science (MS, PhD); enterprise analytics (MS); information and communication technology strategy and innovation (APC); information systems (MS, APC); Internet technology (MS); professional studies in computing (DPS); secure software and information engineering (APC); security and information assurance (Certificate); software development and engineering (MS, Certificate); telecommunications systems and networks (MS, Certificate). *Program availability:* Part-time, evening/weekend, online only, 100% online, blended/hybrid learning. *Faculty:* 26 full-time (7 women), 7 part-time/adjunct (2 women). *Students:* 537 full-time (175 women), 303 part-time (85 women); includes 192 minority (79 Black or African American, non-Hispanic/Latino; 3 American Indian or Alaska Native, non-Hispanic/Latino; 53 Asian, non-Hispanic/Latino; 49 Hispanic/Latino; 8 Two or more races, non-Hispanic/Latino), 486 international. Average age 32. 599 applicants, 89% accepted, 248 enrolled. In 2016, 180 master's, 19 doctorates, 1 other advanced degree awarded. *Degree requirements:* For master's, thesis or alternative, capstone course; for doctorate, comprehensive exam (for some programs), thesis/dissertation. *Entrance requirements:* For master's, GRE General Test. Additional exam requirements/recommendations for international students: Required—TOEFL (minimum score 78 iBT), IELTS (minimum score 6.5) or PTE (minimum score 52). *Application deadline:* For fall admission, 8/1 priority date for domestic students, 6/1 for international students; for spring admission, 12/1 for domestic students, 10/1 for international students. Applications are processed on a rolling basis. Application fee: $70. Electronic applications accepted. *Expenses:* Contact institution. *Financial support:* In 2016–17, 45 students received support. Research assistantships, career-related internships or fieldwork, scholarships/grants, and unspecified assistantships available. Support available to part-time students. Financial award application deadline: 2/15; financial award applicants required to submit FAFSA. *Faculty research:* Cyber security/digital forensics; mobile app development; big data/enterprise analytics; artificial intelligence; software development. *Total annual research expenditures:* $314,545. *Unit head:* Dr. Jonathan Hill, Dean, Seidenberg School of Computer Science and Information Systems, 212-346-1864, E-mail: jhill@pace.edu. *Application contact:* Susan Ford-Goldschein, Director of Graduate Admissions, 914-422-4283, Fax: 212-346-1585, E-mail: graduateadmission@pace.edu.
Website: http://www.pace.edu/seidenberg

**Philadelphia University,** School of Design and Engineering, Program in Interactive Design and Media, Philadelphia, PA 19144. Offers MS. *Entrance requirements:* For master's, portfolio. Additional exam requirements/recommendations for international students: Required—TOEFL (minimum score 550 paper-based; 79 iBT). Electronic applications accepted.

**Pratt Institute,** School of Art, Program in Digital Arts, Brooklyn, NY 11205-3899. Offers MFA, MS/MFA. *Accreditation:* NASAD. *Faculty:* 5 full-time (1 woman), 27 part-time/adjunct (8 women). *Students:* 64 full-time (50 women), 4 part-time (3 women); includes 8 minority (1 Black or African American, non-Hispanic/Latino; 4 Asian, non-Hispanic/Latino; 3 Hispanic/Latino), 51 international. Average age 26. 210 applicants, 33% accepted, 25 enrolled. In 2016, 29 master's awarded. *Degree requirements:* For master's, thesis, exhibit. *Entrance requirements:* For master's, portfolio or video, letters of recommendation. Additional exam requirements/recommendations for international students: Required—TOEFL (minimum score 550 paper-based; 79 iBT). *Application deadline:* For fall admission, 1/5 for domestic and international students; for spring admission, 10/1 for domestic and international students. Application fee: $50 ($90 for international students). Electronic applications accepted. *Expenses:* $29,646 full-time tuition, $1,938 fees. *Financial support:* Career-related internships or fieldwork, Federal Work-Study, institutionally sponsored loans, scholarships/grants, health care benefits, and unspecified assistantships available. Support available to part-time students. Financial award application deadline: 2/1; financial award applicants required to submit FAFSA. *Unit head:* Peter Patchen, Chair, 718-636-3693, Fax: 718-399-4494, E-mail: ppatchen@pratt.edu. *Application contact:* Natalie Capannelli, Director of Graduate Admissions, 718-636-3551, Fax: 718-399-4242, E-mail: ncapanne@pratt.edu.
Website: https://www.pratt.edu/academics/school-of-art/graduate-school-of-art/digital-arts-grad/

**See Display on page 156 and Close-Up on page 209.**

**Quinnipiac University,** School of Communications, Program in Interactive Media, Hamden, CT 06518-1940. Offers interactive media (MS); media design (MS); social media (MS); UX design (MS). *Program availability:* Part-time, evening/weekend, online only, 100% online. *Faculty:* 2 full-time (1 woman), 10 part-time/adjunct (5 women). *Students:* 5 full-time (3 women), 74 part-time (51 women); includes 23 minority (13 Black or African American, non-Hispanic/Latino; 2 Asian, non-Hispanic/Latino; 6 Hispanic/Latino; 2 Two or more races, non-Hispanic/Latino). 50 applicants, 86% accepted, 38 enrolled. In 2016, 48 master's awarded. *Entrance requirements:* For master's, minimum GPA of 3.0, portfolio or writing sample. Additional exam requirements/recommendations for international students: Required—TOEFL (minimum score 575 paper-based; 90 iBT), IELTS (minimum score 6.5). *Application deadline:* For fall admission, 7/30 priority date for domestic students, 4/30 priority date for international students; for spring admission, 12/30 priority date for domestic students, 9/30 priority date for international students. Applications are processed on a rolling basis. Application fee: $45. Electronic applications accepted. *Expenses:* Contact institution. *Financial support:* Federal Work-Study and unspecified assistantships available. Financial award application deadline: 6/1; financial award applicants required to submit FAFSA. *Faculty research:* User experience, social media, semiotics and communication, online distribution of news, Web-based interventions for research. *Unit head:* Phillip Simon, Director, 203-582-8274, E-mail: phillip.simon@qu.edu. *Application contact:* Quinnipiac University Online Admissions Office, 800-462-1944, E-mail: quonlineadmissions@qu.edu. Website: https://quonline.quinnipiac.edu/online-programs/online-graduate-programs/ms-in-interactive-media/

**Robert Morris University,** School of Communications and Information Systems, Moon Township, PA 15108-1189. Offers communication and information systems (MS); cyber security (MS); data analytics (MS); information security and assurance (MS); information systems and communications (D Sc); information systems management (MS); information technology project management (MS); Internet information systems (MS); organizational leadership (MS). *Program availability:* Part-time, evening/weekend, online learning. *Faculty:* 28 full-time (11 women), 6 part-time/adjunct (0 women). *Students:* 269 part-time (110 women); includes 49 minority (29 Black or African American, non-Hispanic/Latino; 10 Asian, non-Hispanic/Latino; 5 Hispanic/Latino; 5 Two or more races, non-Hispanic/Latino), 49 international. Average age 34. 239 applicants, 46% accepted, 83 enrolled. In 2016, 110 master's, 15 doctorates awarded. *Degree requirements:* For doctorate, thesis/dissertation. *Entrance requirements:* For doctorate, employer letter of endorsement, interview. Additional exam requirements/recommendations for international students: Required—TOEFL (minimum score 550 paper-based; 79 iBT). *Application deadline:* For fall admission, 7/1 priority date for domestic and international students; for spring admission, 11/1 priority date for domestic and international students. Applications are processed on a rolling basis. Application fee: $35. Electronic applications accepted. Application fee is waived when completed online. *Expenses:* $870 per credit (for master's degree). *Financial support:* Institutionally sponsored loans available. Support available to part-time students. Financial award application deadline: 5/1. *Unit head:* Ann Marie M. Le Blanc, Dean, 412-397-6433, Fax: 412-397-6469, E-mail: leblanc@rmu.edu. *Application contact:* Kellie L. Laurenzi, Associate Vice President, 412-397-5200, Fax: 412-397-5915, E-mail: graduateadmissions@rmu.edu. Website: http://www.rmu.edu/web/cms/schools/scis/Pages/default.aspx

**Rochester Institute of Technology,** Graduate Enrollment Services, College of Imaging Arts and Sciences, School of Design, Advanced Certificate Program in User Experience Design and Development, Rochester, NY 14623-5603. Offers Advanced Certificate. *Program availability:* Part-time, evening/weekend, online only, 100% online. *Students:* 3 part-time (all women). 7 applicants, 57% accepted. In 2016, 7 Advanced Certificates awarded. *Entrance requirements:* Additional exam requirements/recommendations for international students: Required—TOEFL (minimum score 550 paper-based; 79 iBT), IELTS (minimum score 6.5), PTE (minimum score 58). *Application deadline:* Applications are processed on a rolling basis. Application fee: $60. Electronic applications accepted. *Expenses:* $993 per credit hour (for online study). *Financial support:* Available to part-time students. Applicants required to submit FAFSA. *Faculty research:* User experience planning and process, visual design for interactive design, interaction modeling and prototyping. *Unit head:* Adam Smith, Graduate Director, 585-475-4552, E-mail: aesfaa@rit.edu. *Application contact:* Diane Ellison, Associate Vice President, Graduate Enrollment Services, 585-475-2229, Fax: 585-475-7164, E-mail: gradinfo@rit.edu.
Website: https://www.rit.edu/ritonline/program/UXDE-ACT

**Rochester Institute of Technology,** Graduate Enrollment Services, College of Liberal Arts, School of Communication, Advanced Certificate Program in Communication and Digital Media, Rochester, NY 14623-5603. Offers Advanced Certificate. *Program availability:* Part-time, evening/weekend, online only, 100% online. *Students:* 5 applicants. *Entrance requirements:* Additional exam requirements/recommendations for international students: Required—TOEFL (minimum score 570 paper-based; 88 iBT), IELTS (minimum score 6.5), PTE (minimum score 61). *Application deadline:* Applications are processed on a rolling basis. Application fee: $60. Electronic applications accepted. *Expenses:* $993 per credit hour (for online study). *Financial support:* Available to part-time students. Applicants required to submit FAFSA. *Unit head:* Dr. Grant Cos, Director of Graduate Programs, 585-475-6646, E-mail: gccgpt@rit.edu. *Application contact:* Diane Ellison, Associate Vice President, Graduate Enrollment Services, 585-475-2229, Fax: 585-475-7164, E-mail: gradinfo@rit.edu.
Website: https://www.rit.edu/ritonline/program/COMTCH-ACT

**Rochester Institute of Technology,** Graduate Enrollment Services, Golisano College of Computing and Information Sciences, Information Science and Technologies Department, Advanced Certificate Program in Web Development, Rochester, NY 14623. Offers Advanced Certificate. *Program availability:* Part-time, evening/weekend. *Students:* 2 part-time (1 woman). 3 applicants. *Entrance requirements:* For degree, minimum GPA of 3.0. Additional exam requirements/recommendations for international students: Required—TOEFL (minimum score 570 paper-based; 88 iBT), IELTS (minimum score 6.5), PTE (minimum score 61). *Application deadline:* Applications are processed on a rolling basis. Application fee: $60. Electronic applications accepted. *Expenses:* $1,742 per credit hour. *Financial support:* In 2016–17, 1 student received support. Available to part-time students. Applicants required to submit FAFSA. *Faculty research:* Web development, mobile computing, service computing, advanced software development, health informatics. *Unit head:* Qi Yu, Graduate Program Director, 585-475-2700, Fax: 585-475-6584, E-mail: informaticsgrad@rit.edu. *Application contact:* Diane Ellison, Associate Vice President, Graduate Enrollment Services, 585-475-2229, Fax: 585-475-7164, E-mail: gradinfo@rit.edu.
Website: http://www.ist.rit.edu/degrees/graduate/advanced-cert.php

**Rocky Mountain College of Art + Design,** Program in Education, Leadership + Emerging Technologies, Lakewood, CO 80214. Offers MA. *Accreditation:* NASAD. *Program availability:* Online learning.

**Sam Houston State University,** College of Fine Arts and Mass Communication, Department of Mass Communication, Huntsville, TX 77341. Offers digital media (MA). *Program availability:* Part-time. *Degree requirements:* For master's, comprehensive exam (for some programs), thesis optional. *Entrance requirements:* For master's, GRE General Test, personal statement, digital media portfolio. Electronic applications accepted.

**San Diego State University,** Graduate and Research Affairs, College of Professional Studies and Fine Arts, School of Communication, San Diego, CA 92182. Offers advertising and public relations (MA); critical-cultural studies (MA); interaction studies (MA); intercultural and international studies (MA); new media studies (MA); news and

information studies (MA); telecommunications and media management (MA). *Degree requirements:* For master's, thesis. *Entrance requirements:* For master's, GRE General Test, 3 letters of recommendation. Additional exam requirements/recommendations for international students: Required—TOEFL. Electronic applications accepted.

**Savannah College of Art and Design,** Graduate School, Program in Interactive Design and Game Development, Savannah, GA 31402-3146. Offers MA, MFA. *Program availability:* Part-time, 100% online. *Faculty:* 14 full-time (4 women), 5 part-time/adjunct (0 women). *Students:* 66 full-time (29 women), 34 part-time (8 women); includes 10 minority (2 Black or African American, non-Hispanic/Latino; 6 Asian, non-Hispanic/Latino; 2 Hispanic/Latino), 56 international. Average age 28. 124 applicants, 40% accepted, 22 enrolled. In 2016, 27 master's awarded. *Degree requirements:* For master's, final project (for MA); thesis (for MFA). *Entrance requirements:* For master's, GRE (recommended), portfolio (submitted in digital format), audition or writing submission, resume, statement of purpose, two letters of recommendation. Additional exam requirements/recommendations for international students: Required—TOEFL (minimum score 550 paper-based, 85 iBT), IELTS (minimum score 6.5), or ACTFL. *Application deadline:* For fall admission, 4/1 for domestic and international students. Applications are processed on a rolling basis. Application fee: $40. Electronic applications accepted. *Expenses: Tuition:* Full-time $36,045. Tuition and fees vary according to course load. *Financial support:* Career-related internships or fieldwork, Federal Work-Study, and scholarships/grants available. Financial award application deadline: 4/1; financial award applicants required to submit FAFSA. *Unit head:* SuAnne Fu, Chair, Interactive Design and Game Development. *Application contact:* Jenny Jaquillard, Executive Director of Admissions, Recruitment and Events, 912-525-5100, Fax: 912-525-5985, E-mail: admission@scad.edu.
Website: http://www.scad.edu/academics/programs/interactive-design-and-game-development

**School of Visual Arts,** Graduate Programs, Interaction Design Department, New York, NY 10010-3994. Offers MFA. *Degree requirements:* For master's, thesis, 60 credits, residency of two academic years, thesis project. *Entrance requirements:* For master's, portfolio, statement of purpose, resume. Additional exam requirements/recommendations for international students: Required—TOEFL (minimum score 550 paper-based; 79 iBT). Electronic applications accepted. *Faculty research:* Data analysis and visualization, service design, interaction design.

**School of Visual Arts,** Graduate Programs, Program in Photography, Video and Related Media, New York, NY 10010-3994. Offers MFA. *Accreditation:* NASAD. *Degree requirements:* For master's, thesis, 60 credits and all course requirements; minimum GPA of 3.3; thesis project. *Entrance requirements:* For master's, portfolio (still images and/or videos) through SlideRoom. Additional exam requirements/recommendations for international students: Required—TOEFL (minimum score 550 paper-based; 79 iBT). Electronic applications accepted. *Faculty research:* Contemporary and responsible creative initiatives, including experimental, narrative or documentary video, installation and conceptual art, tableau and real-world-witness photography.

**Southern New Hampshire University,** School of Business, Manchester, NH 03106-1045. Offers accounting (MBA, MS, Graduate Certificate); accounting finance (MS); accounting/auditing (MS); accounting/forensic accounting (MS); accounting/taxation (MS); athletic administration (MBA, Graduate Certificate); business administration (IMBA, MBA, Certificate, Graduate Certificate), including accounting (Certificate), business administration (MBA), business information systems (Graduate Certificate), human resource management (Certificate); corporate social responsibility (MBA); entrepreneurship (MBA); finance (MBA, MS, Graduate Certificate); finance/corporate finance (MS); finance/investments and securities (MS); forensic accounting (MBA); healthcare informatics (MBA); healthcare management (MBA); human resource management (Graduate Certificate); information technology (MS, Graduate Certificate); information technology management (MBA); international business (Graduate Certificate); international business and information technology (Graduate Certificate); international finance (Graduate Certificate); international sport management (Graduate Certificate); justice studies (MBA); leadership of nonprofit organizations (Graduate Certificate); management (MS); marketing (MBA, MS, Graduate Certificate); operations and project management (MS); operations and supply chain management (MBA, Graduate Certificate); organizational leadership (MS); project management (MBA, Graduate Certificate); Six Sigma (MBA); Six Sigma quality (Graduate Certificate); social media marketing (MBA); sport management (MBA, MS, Graduate Certificate); sustainability and environmental compliance (MBA); workplace conflict management (MBA); MBA/Certificate. *Accreditation:* ACBSP. *Program availability:* Part-time, evening/weekend, online learning. Terminal master's awarded for partial completion of doctoral program. *Degree requirements:* For master's, one foreign language, comprehensive exam (for some programs), thesis or alternative. *Entrance requirements:* For master's, minimum GPA of 2.5. Additional exam requirements/recommendations for international students: Required—TOEFL (minimum score 500 paper-based). Electronic applications accepted.

**State University of New York at Oswego,** Graduate Studies, Department of Art, Oswego, NY 13126. Offers art (MA); graphic design and digital media (MA). *Accreditation:* NASAD. *Program availability:* Part-time. *Degree requirements:* For master's, exhibit, final presentation. *Entrance requirements:* For master's, slides of previous work. Additional exam requirements/recommendations for international students: Required—TOEFL (minimum score 560 paper-based). *Faculty research:* Ancient and primitive art, nineteenth century art, medieval art, Renaissance art.

**Stevens Institute of Technology,** Graduate School, Charles V. Schaefer Jr. School of Engineering and Science, Department of Computer Science, Hoboken, NJ 07030. Offers computer graphics (Certificate), including computer graphics; computer science (MS, PhD); computer systems (Certificate), including computer systems; cybersecurity (MS); database management systems (Certificate), including databases; distributed systems (Certificate), including distributed systems; elements of computer science (Certificate), including cybersecurity; enterprise and cloud computing (MS); enterprise computing (Certificate), including enterprise and cloud computing; enterprise security and information assurance (Certificate), including enterprise security and information assurance; health informatics (Certificate), including health informatics; multimedia experience and management (Certificate), including multimedia experience and management; networks and systems administration (Certificate), including cloud computing; service oriented computing (Certificate), including service oriented computing. *Program availability:* Part-time, evening/weekend. *Faculty:* 21 full-time (4 women), 13 part-time/adjunct (2 women). *Students:* 436 full-time (124 women), 72 part-time (12 women); includes 27 minority (4 Black or African American, non-Hispanic/Latino; 21 Asian, non-Hispanic/Latino; 1 Hispanic/Latino; 1 Two or more races, non-Hispanic/Latino), 423 international. Average age 25. 1,183 applicants, 54% accepted, 184 enrolled. In 2016, 225 master's, 4 doctorates, 18 other advanced degrees awarded. Terminal master's awarded for partial completion of doctoral program. *Degree requirements:* For master's, thesis optional, minimum B average in major field and overall; for doctorate, comprehensive exam (for some programs), thesis/dissertation; for Certificate, minimum B average. *Entrance requirements:* Additional exam requirements/recommendations for international students: Required—TOEFL (minimum score 74 iBT), IELTS (minimum score 6). *Application deadline:* For fall admission, 6/1 for

*Internet and Interactive Multimedia*

domestic students, 4/15 for international students; for spring admission, 11/30 for domestic students, 11/1 for international students. Applications are processed on a rolling basis. Application fee: $65. Electronic applications accepted. *Expenses:* Contact institution. *Financial support:* Fellowships, research assistantships, teaching assistantships, career-related internships or fieldwork, Federal Work-Study, scholarships/grants, and unspecified assistantships available. Financial award application deadline: 2/15; financial award applicants required to submit FAFSA. *Faculty research:* Computer security, computer vision, dynamic scene analysis, privacy-preserving data mining, visualization. *Unit head:* Giuseppe Ateniese, Director, 201-216-3741, E-mail: gatenies@stevens.edu. *Application contact:* Graduate Admissions, 888-783-8367, Fax: 888-511-1306, E-mail: graduate@stevens.edu.
Website: https://www.stevens.edu/schaefer-school-engineering-science/departments/computer-science

**Tennessee Technological University,** College of Graduate Studies, College of Engineering, Department of Computer Science, Cookeville, TN 38505. Offers computer software and scientific applications (MS); Internet-based computing (MS). *Program availability:* Part-time. *Students:* 11 full-time (4 women), 9 part-time (0 women); includes 1 minority (Black or African American, non-Hispanic/Latino), 10 international. 99 applicants, 44% accepted, 8 enrolled. In 2016, 5 master's awarded. *Degree requirements:* For master's, thesis or alternative. *Entrance requirements:* For master's, GRE. Additional exam requirements/recommendations for international students: Required—TOEFL (minimum score 550 paper-based; 79 iBT), IELTS (minimum score 5.5), PTE (minimum score 53), or TOEIC (Test of English as an International Communication). *Application deadline:* For fall admission, 8/1 for domestic students, 5/1 for international students; for spring admission, 12/1 for domestic students, 10/1 for international students; for summer admission, 5/1 for domestic students, 2/1 for international students. Applications are processed on a rolling basis. Application fee: $35 ($40 for international students). Electronic applications accepted. *Expenses:* Tuition, state resident: full-time $9375; part-time $534 per credit hour. Tuition, nonresident: full-time $22,443; part-time $1260 per credit hour. *Financial support:* In 2016–17, 6 research assistantships (averaging $7,500 per year), 8 teaching assistantships (averaging $7,500 per year) were awarded. Financial award application deadline: 4/1. *Unit head:* Dr. Jerry Gannod, Chairperson, 931-372-3691, Fax: 931-372-3686, E-mail: jgannod@tntech.edu. *Application contact:* Shelia K. Kendrick, Coordinator of Graduate Studies, 931-372-3808, Fax: 931-372-3497, E-mail: skendrick@tntech.edu.

**Touro College,** Graduate School of Technology, New York, NY 10010. Offers information systems (MS); instructional technology (MS); Web and multimedia design (MA). *Faculty:* 18 part-time/adjunct (6 women). *Students:* 100 full-time (37 women), 122 part-time (59 women); includes 78 minority (31 Black or African American, non-Hispanic/Latino; 1 American Indian or Alaska Native, non-Hispanic/Latino; 25 Asian, non-Hispanic/Latino; 18 Hispanic/Latino; 3 Two or more races, non-Hispanic/Latino), 83 international. Average age 34. *Entrance requirements:* Additional exam requirements/recommendations for international students: Required—TOEFL (minimum score 83 iBT), IELTS (minimum score 6.5), PTE (minimum score 58). *Unit head:* Dr. Issac Herskowitz, Dean of the Graduate School of Technology, 202-463-0400 Ext. 5231, E-mail: issac.herskowitz@touro.edu. *Application contact:* Jack Romano, Program Director, 212-463-0400 Ext. 5462.
Website: http://www.touro.edu/gst/

**Towson University,** Program in Applied Information Technology, Towson, MD 21252-0001. Offers applied information technology (MS, D Sc); database management systems (Postbaccalaureate Certificate); information security and assurance (Postbaccalaureate Certificate); information systems management (Postbaccalaureate Certificate); Internet applications development (Postbaccalaureate Certificate); networking technologies (Postbaccalaureate Certificate); software engineering (Postbaccalaureate Certificate). *Students:* 135 full-time (50 women), 154 part-time (50 women); includes 119 minority (81 Black or African American, non-Hispanic/Latino; 26 Asian, non-Hispanic/Latino; 4 Hispanic/Latino; 8 Two or more races, non-Hispanic/Latino), 82 international. *Entrance requirements:* For master's and Postbaccalaureate Certificate, bachelor's degree, minimum GPA of 3.0; for doctorate, master's degree in computer science, information systems, information technology, or closely-related area; minimum GPA of 3.0; 2 letters of recommendation; resume. Additional exam requirements/recommendations for international students: Required—TOEFL. *Application deadline:* Applications are processed on a rolling basis. Application fee: $45. Electronic applications accepted. *Expenses:* Tuition, state resident: full-time $7580; part-time $379 per unit. Tuition, nonresident: full-time $15,700; part-time $785 per unit. *Required fees:* $2480. *Unit head:* Dr. Jinjuan Feng, Graduate Program Director, 410-704-3463, E-mail: ait@towson.edu. *Application contact:* Coverley Beidleman, Assistant Director of Graduate Admissions, 410-704-2113, Fax: 410-704-3030, E-mail: grads@towson.edu.
Website: https://www.towson.edu/fcsm/departments/emergingtech/

**Towson University,** Program in Interactive Media Design, Towson, MD 21252-0001. Offers Postbaccalaureate Certificate. *Program availability:* Online learning. *Students:* 9 part-time (4 women); includes 1 minority (Black or African American, non-Hispanic/Latino). *Entrance requirements:* For degree, minimum GPA of 3.0; resume; letter of intent; bachelor's degree in art or art education, or a bachelor's degree in another discipline with a minimum of 9 credits of course work in studio art and/or professional experience working in the field of art education or graphic design. *Application deadline:* Applications are processed on a rolling basis. Application fee: $45. Electronic applications accepted. *Expenses:* Tuition, state resident: full-time $7580; part-time $379 per unit. Tuition, nonresident: full-time $15,700; part-time $785 per unit. *Required fees:* $2480. *Unit head:* Prof. Bridget Sullivan, Graduate Program Director, 410-704-2802, E-mail: bsullivan@towson.edu. *Application contact:* Coverley Beidleman, Assistant Director of Graduate Admissions, 410-704-2113, Fax: 410-704-3030, E-mail: grads@towson.edu.
Website: http://www.towson.edu/cofac/departments/art/grad/interactivemediadesign/index.html

**Universidad Autonoma de Guadalajara,** Graduate Programs, Guadalajara, Mexico. Offers administrative law and justice (LL M); advertising and corporate communications (MA); architecture (M Arch); business (MBA); computational science (MCC); education (Ed M, Ed D); English-Spanish translation (MA); entrepreneurship and management (MBA); integrated management of digital animation (MA); international business (MIB); international corporate law (LL M); internet technologies (MS); manufacturing systems (MMS); occupational health (MS); philosophy (MA, PhD); power electronics (MS); quality systems (MQS); renewable energy (MS); social evaluation of projects (MBA); strategic market research (MBA); tax law (MA); teaching mathematics (MA).

**University of Advancing Technology,** Master of Science Program in Technology, Tempe, AZ 85283-1042. Offers advancing computer science (MS); emerging technologies (MS); game production and management (MS); information assurance (MS); technology leadership (MS). *Degree requirements:* For master's, project or thesis. *Entrance requirements:* Additional exam requirements/recommendations for international students: Required—TOEFL (minimum score 550 paper-based). Electronic applications accepted. *Faculty research:* Artificial intelligence, fractals, organizational management.

**University of Colorado Boulder,** Graduate School, College of Media, Communication and Information, Program in Intermedia Art, Writing and Performance, Boulder, CO 80309. Offers PhD. *Students:* 5 full-time (2 women), 1 part-time (0 women); includes 1 minority (Hispanic/Latino). Average age 34. 14 applicants, 21% accepted, 1 enrolled. *Application deadline:* For fall admission, 1/15 for domestic students, 12/1 for international students. Application fee: $60 ($80 for international students). Electronic applications accepted. Application fee is waived when completed online. *Financial support:* In 2016–17, 14 students received support, including 1 fellowship (averaging $2,000 per year), 4 research assistantships with full and partial tuition reimbursements available (averaging $33,006 per year), 3 teaching assistantships with full and partial tuition reimbursements available (averaging $34,779 per year); institutionally sponsored loans, scholarships/grants, health care benefits, and unspecified assistantships also available. Financial award application deadline: 2/1; financial award applicants required to submit FAFSA. *Application contact:* E-mail: cmci.iawp@colorado.edu.
Website: http://www.colorado.edu/cmci/academics/phd-intermedia-art-writing-and-

**University of Massachusetts Dartmouth,** Graduate School, College of Visual and Performing Arts, Department of Design, North Dartmouth, MA 02747-2300. Offers digital media (MFA); digital multi-media (MFA); graphic design (MFA); illustration (MFA); photography (MFA); typography (MFA). *Accreditation:* NASAD. *Program availability:* Part-time. *Faculty:* 16 full-time (7 women), 3 part-time/adjunct (1 woman). *Students:* 1 (woman) full-time, 10 part-time (7 women), 6 international. Average age 28. 30 applicants, 43% accepted, 4 enrolled. In 2016, 1 degree awarded. *Degree requirements:* For master's, visual thesis, written thesis. *Entrance requirements:* For master's, statement of purpose (minimum of 300 words), resume, 2 letters of recommendation, official transcripts, portfolio (20 images representing applicant's art work, process of thinking, implementation of concepts and studio production). Additional exam requirements/recommendations for international students: Required—TOEFL (minimum score 533 paper-based; 72 iBT). *Application deadline:* For fall admission, 1/11 priority date for domestic students, 12/9 priority date for international students; for spring admission, 10/15 priority date for domestic students, 9/15 priority date for international students. Applications are processed on a rolling basis. Application fee: $60. Electronic applications accepted. *Expenses:* Tuition, state resident: full-time $14,994; part-time $624.75 per credit. Tuition, nonresident: full-time $27,068; part-time $1127.83 per credit. *Required fees:* $405; $25.88 per credit. Tuition and fees vary according to course load and reciprocity agreements. *Financial support:* In 2016–17, 2 fellowships (averaging $2,600 per year) were awarded; teaching assistantships, scholarships/grants, unspecified assistantships, and studio assistantships also available. Support available to part-time students. Financial award application deadline: 3/1; financial award applicants required to submit FAFSA. *Faculty research:* Web design, multimedia design, broadcast design, product design, typography, illustration, photography and design for arts. *Total annual research expenditures:* $113,333. *Unit head:* Ziddi Msagni, Graduate Program Director, Visual Design, 508-999-9291, E-mail: zmsagni@umassd.edu. *Application contact:* Steven Briggs, Director of Marketing and Recruitment for Graduate Studies, 508-999-8604, Fax: 508-999-8183, E-mail: graduate@umassd.edu.
Website: http://www.umassd.edu/cvpa/graduate/visualdesign/

**University of Miami,** Graduate School, College of Arts and Sciences, Department of Art and Art History, Coral Gables, FL 33124. Offers art history (MA); ceramics/glass (MFA); graphic design/multimedia (MFA); painting (MFA); photography/digital imaging (MFA); printmaking (MFA); sculpture (MFA). *Program availability:* Part-time. *Degree requirements:* For master's, variable foreign language requirement, thesis, exhibit (MFA), comprehensive exam (MA). *Entrance requirements:* For master's, GRE General Test (MA), research paper (MA), slide portfolio (MFA). Additional exam requirements/recommendations for international students: Required—TOEFL. Electronic applications accepted. *Faculty research:* Installation art, public art.

**University of Montana,** Graduate School, College of Visual and Performing Arts, School of Media Arts, Missoula, MT 59812-0002. Offers digital filmmaking (MFA); integrated digital media (MFA).

**University of North Texas,** Robert B. Toulouse School of Graduate Studies, Denton, TX 76203-5459. Offers accounting (MS); applied anthropology (MA, MS); applied behavior analysis (Certificate); applied geography (MA); applied technology and performance improvement (M Ed, MS); art education (MA); art history (MA); art museum education (Certificate); arts leadership (Certificate); audiology (Au D); behavior analysis (MS); behavioral science (PhD); biochemistry and molecular biology (MS); biology (MA, MS); biomedical engineering (MS); business analysis (MS); chemistry (MS); clinical health psychology (PhD); communication studies (MA, MS); computer engineering (MS); computer science (MS); counseling (M Ed, MS), including clinical mental health counseling (MS), college and university counseling, elementary school counseling, secondary school counseling; creative writing (MA); criminal justice (MS); curriculum and instruction (M Ed); decision sciences (MBA); design (MA, MFA), including fashion design (MFA), innovation studies, interior design (MFA); early childhood studies (MS); economics (MS); educational leadership (M Ed, Ed D); educational psychology (MS, PhD), including family studies (MS), gifted and talented (MS), human development (MS), learning and cognition (MS), research, measurement and evaluation (MS); electrical engineering (MS); emergency management (MPA); engineering technology (MS); English (MA); English as a second language (MA); environmental science (MS); finance (MBA, MS); financial management (MPA); French (MA); health services management (MBA); higher education (M Ed, Ed D); history (MA, MS); hospitality management (MS); human resources management (MPA); information science (MS); information systems (PhD); information technologies (MBA); interdisciplinary studies (MA, MS); international studies (MA); international sustainable tourism (MS); jazz studies (MM); journalism (MA, MJ, Graduate Certificate), including interactive and virtual digital communication (Graduate Certificate), narrative journalism (Graduate Certificate), public relations (Graduate Certificate); kinesiology (MS); linguistics (MA); local government management (MPA); logistics (PhD); logistics and supply chain management (MBA); long-term care, senior housing, and aging services (MS); management (PhD); marketing (MBA); mathematics (MA, MS); mechanical and energy engineering (MS, PhD); music (MA), including ethnomusicology, music theory, musicology, performance; music composition (PhD); music education (MM Ed, PhD); nonprofit management (MPA); operations and supply chain management (MBA); performance (MM, DMA); philosophy (MA); political science (MA); professional and technical communication (MA); radio, television and film (MA, MFA); rehabilitation counseling (Certificate); sociology (MA); Spanish (MA); special education (M Ed); speech-language pathology (MA); strategic management (MBA); studio art (MFA); teaching (M Ed); MBA/MS. *Program availability:* Part-time, evening/weekend, online learning. Terminal master's awarded for partial completion of doctoral program. *Degree requirements:* For master's, variable foreign language requirement, comprehensive exam (for some programs), thesis (for some programs); for doctorate, variable foreign language requirement, comprehensive exam (for some programs), thesis/dissertation; for other advanced degree, variable foreign language requirement, comprehensive exam (for some programs). *Entrance requirements:* For master's and doctorate, GRE, GMAT. Additional exam requirements/recommendations for international students: Required—TOEFL (minimum score 550 paper-based; 79 iBT). Electronic applications accepted.

**University of Pennsylvania,** School of Design, Department of Fine Arts, Philadelphia, PA 19104. Offers emerging design and research (Certificate); fine arts (MFA); time-based and interactive media (Certificate). *Faculty:* 7 full-time (3 women), 1 part-time/adjunct (0 women). *Students:* 34 full-time (23 women), 1 part-time (0 women); includes 10 minority (1 Black or African American, non-Hispanic/Latino; 2 Asian, non-Hispanic/Latino; 5 Hispanic/Latino; 2 Two or more races, non-Hispanic/Latino), 4 international. Average age 28. 131 applicants, 39% accepted, 18 enrolled. In 2016, 20 master's awarded. *Degree requirements:* For master's, thesis. *Application deadline:* Applications are processed on a rolling basis. Electronic applications accepted. *Expenses: Tuition:* Full-time $31,068; part-time $5762 per course. *Required fees:* $3200; $336 per course. Full-time tuition and fees vary according to degree level, program and student level. Part-time tuition and fees vary according to course load, degree level and program. *Financial support:* In 2016–17, 30 students received support, including teaching assistantships (averaging $6,000 per year); fellowships with full tuition reimbursements available, research assistantships, Federal Work-Study, scholarships/grants, health care benefits, and unspecified assistantships also available. Financial award applicants required to submit FAFSA. *Faculty research:* Performance art, photography and video, drawing and painting, sculpture, animation and creative research. *Unit head:* Joshua Mosley, Professor/Chair/Director of Graduate Program, 215-898-8374, E-mail: jmosley@design.upenn.edu. *Application contact:* Leighann Bogner, Administrative Assistant, 215-898-8374, Fax: 215-573-2459, E-mail: mfa@pobox.upenn.edu. Website: http://www.design.upenn.edu/mfa

**University of Southern California,** Graduate School, School of Cinematic Arts, Interactive Media Division, Los Angeles, CA 90089. Offers interactive media (MFA); media arts and practice (PhD). *Degree requirements:* For master's, thesis, thesis project. *Entrance requirements:* Additional exam requirements/recommendations for international students: Required—TOEFL (minimum score 600 paper-based; 100 iBT). Electronic applications accepted. *Expenses:* Contact institution. *Faculty research:* Immersive media, mobile media, stereoscopic, game design and development, serious games and games for health and learning, experiments in game play.

**University of Southern California,** Graduate School, Viterbi School of Engineering, Department of Computer Science, Los Angeles, CA 90089. Offers computer networks (MS); computer science (MS, PhD); computer security (MS); game development (MS); high performance computing and simulations (MS); human language technology (MS); intelligent robotics (MS); multimedia and creative technologies (MS); software engineering (MS). *Program availability:* Part-time, evening/weekend, online learning. *Entrance requirements:* For master's and doctorate, GRE General Test. Additional exam requirements/recommendations for international students: Required—TOEFL. Electronic applications accepted. *Faculty research:* Databases, computer graphics and computer vision, software engineering, networks and security, robotics, multimedia and virtual reality.

**University of Southern California,** Graduate School, Viterbi School of Engineering, Ming Hsieh Department of Electrical Engineering, Los Angeles, CA 90089. Offers computer engineering (MS, PhD); electric power (MS); electrical engineering (MS, PhD, Engr); engineering technology commercialization (Graduate Certificate); multimedia and creative technologies (MS); telecommunications (MS); VLSI design (MS); wireless health technology (MS). *Program availability:* Part-time, online learning. Terminal master's awarded for partial completion of doctoral program. *Degree requirements:* For master's, thesis optional; for doctorate, thesis/dissertation. *Entrance requirements:* For master's and doctorate, GRE General Test. Additional exam requirements/recommendations for international students: Recommended—TOEFL. Electronic applications accepted. *Faculty research:* Communications, computer engineering and networks, control systems, integrated circuits and systems, electromagnetics and energy conversion, micro electro-mechanical systems and nanotechnology, photonics and quantum electronics, plasma research, signal and image processing.

**University of South Florida,** College of Arts and Sciences, School of Mass Communications, Tampa, FL 33620-9951. Offers mass communications (MA), including media studies, multimedia journalism, strategic communication management. *Program availability:* Part-time, evening/weekend. *Faculty:* 11 full-time (6 women). *Students:* 27 full-time (23 women), 18 part-time (10 women); includes 5 minority (2 Black or African American, non-Hispanic/Latino; 2 Hispanic/Latino; 1 Native Hawaiian or other Pacific Islander, non-Hispanic/Latino), 25 international. Average age 27. 39 applicants, 82% accepted, 21 enrolled. In 2016, 16 master's awarded. *Degree requirements:* For master's, comprehensive exam, thesis optional. *Entrance requirements:* For master's, GRE General Test, minimum GPA of 3.0 in last 60 hours of course work, three letters of recommendation, letter of intent, resume/curriculum vitae. Additional exam requirements/recommendations for international students: Required—TOEFL (minimum score 550 paper-based; 79 iBT) or IELTS (minimum score 6.5). *Application deadline:* For fall admission, 2/15 for domestic and international students. Application fee: $30. Electronic applications accepted. *Expenses:* Tuition, state resident: full-time $7766; part-time $431.43 per credit hour. Tuition, nonresident: full-time $15,789; part-time $877.17 per credit hour. *Required fees:* $37 per term. *Financial support:* In 2016–17, 5 students received support, including 9 teaching assistantships with tuition reimbursements available (averaging $10,513 per year); unspecified assistantships also available. Financial award application deadline: 2/28. *Faculty research:* First Amendment analysis, civic journalism, public opinion, media ethics, media effects research in sports public relations, public relations management, advertisement, telecommunications. *Total annual research expenditures:* $88,114. *Unit head:* Dr. Jim Andrews, Interim Director/Associate Professor, 813-974-2108, Fax: 813-974-2592, E-mail: jimandrews@usf.edu. *Application contact:* Dr. Michael Mitrook, Assistant Professor, 813-974-8890, Fax: 813-974-2592, E-mail: mmitrook@usf.edu. Website: http://masscom.usf.edu/grad/

**University of South Florida,** Innovative Education, Tampa, FL 33620-9951. Offers adult, career and higher education (Graduate Certificate), including college teaching, leadership in developing human resources, leadership in higher education; Africana studies (Graduate Certificate), including diasporas and health disparities, genocide and human rights; aging studies (Graduate Certificate), including gerontology; art research (Graduate Certificate), including museum studies; business foundations (Graduate Certificate); chemical and biomedical engineering (Graduate Certificate), including materials science and engineering, water, health and sustainability; child and family studies (Graduate Certificate), including positive behavior support; civil and industrial engineering (Graduate Certificate), including transportation systems analysis; community and family health (Graduate Certificate), including maternal and child health, social marketing and public health, violence and injury: prevention and intervention, women's health; criminology (Graduate Certificate), including criminal justice administration; educational measurement and research (Graduate Certificate), including evaluation; English (Graduate Certificate), including comparative literary studies, creative writing, professional and technical communication; entrepreneurship (Graduate Certificate); environmental health (Graduate Certificate), including safety management; epidemiology and biostatistics (Graduate Certificate), including applied biostatistics, biostatistics, concepts and tools of epidemiology, epidemiology, epidemiology of infectious diseases; geography, environment and planning (Graduate Certificate), including community development, environmental policy and management,

geographical information systems; geology (Graduate Certificate), including hydrogeology; global health (Graduate Certificate), including disaster management, global health and Latin American and Caribbean studies, global health practice, humanitarian assistance, infection control; government and international affairs (Graduate Certificate), including Cuban studies, globalization studies; health policy and management (Graduate Certificate), including health management and leadership, public health policy and programs; hearing specialist: early intervention (Graduate Certificate); industrial and management systems engineering (Graduate Certificate), including systems engineering, technology management; information studies (Graduate Certificate), including school library media specialist; information systems/decision sciences (Graduate Certificate), including analytics and business intelligence; instructional technology (Graduate Certificate), including distance education, Florida digital/virtual educator, instructional design, multimedia design, Web design; internal medicine, bioethics and medical humanities (Graduate Certificate), including biomedical ethics; Latin American and Caribbean studies (Graduate Certificate); mass communications (Graduate Certificate), including multimedia journalism; mathematics and statistics (Graduate Certificate), including mathematics; medicine (Graduate Certificate), including aging and neuroscience, bioinformatics, biotechnology, brain fitness and memory management, clinical investigation, health informatics, health sciences, integrative weight management, intellectual property, medicine and gender, metabolic and nutritional medicine, metabolic cardiology, pharmacy sciences; national and competitive intelligence (Graduate Certificate); psychological and social foundations (Graduate Certificate), including career counseling, college teaching, diversity in education, mental health counseling, school counseling; public affairs (Graduate Certificate), including nonprofit management, public management, research administration; public health (Graduate Certificate), including environmental health, health equity, public health generalist, translational research in adolescent behavioral health; public health practices (Graduate Certificate), including planning for healthy communities; rehabilitation and mental health counseling (Graduate Certificate), including integrative mental health care, marriage and family therapy, rehabilitation technology; secondary education (Graduate Certificate), including ESOL, foreign language education: culture and content, foreign language education: professional; social work (Graduate Certificate), including geriatric social work/clinical gerontology; special education (Graduate Certificate), including autism spectrum disorder, disabilities education: severe/profound; world languages (Graduate Certificate), including teaching English as a second language (TESL) or foreign language. *Expenses:* Tuition, state resident: full-time $7766; part-time $431.43 per credit hour. Tuition, nonresident: full-time $15,789; part-time $877.17 per credit hour. *Required fees:* $37 per term. *Unit head:* Kathy Barnes, Interdisciplinary Programs Coordinator, 813-974-8031, Fax: 813-974-7061, E-mail: barnesk@usf.edu. *Application contact:* Karen Tylinski, Metro Initiatives, 813-974-9943, Fax: 813-974-7061, E-mail: ktylinsk@usf.edu. Website: http://www.usf.edu/innovative-education/

**The University of Texas at Dallas,** School of Arts, Technology, and Emerging Communication, Richardson, TX 75080. Offers arts and technology (MA, MFA, PhD); emerging media and communication (MA). *Faculty:* 23 full-time (9 women), 3 part-time/adjunct (0 women). *Students:* 73 full-time (34 women), 55 part-time (27 women); includes 38 minority (11 Black or African American, non-Hispanic/Latino; 9 Asian, non-Hispanic/Latino; 16 Hispanic/Latino; 2 Two or more races, non-Hispanic/Latino), 23 international. Average age 33. 127 applicants, 34% accepted, 29 enrolled. In 2016, 47 master's, 3 doctorates awarded. *Degree requirements:* For master's and doctorate, portfolio, thesis, or capstone project. *Entrance requirements:* For master's and doctorate, minimum GPA of 3.3 in upper-level coursework in field. Additional exam requirements/recommendations for international students: Required—TOEFL (minimum score 550 paper-based). *Application deadline:* For fall admission, 7/15 for domestic students, 5/1 priority date for international students; for spring admission, 11/15 for domestic students, 9/1 priority date for international students. Applications are processed on a rolling basis. Application fee: $50 ($100 for international students). Electronic applications accepted. *Expenses:* Tuition, state resident: full-time $12,418; part-time $690 per semester hour. Tuition, nonresident: full-time $24,150; part-time $1342 per semester hour. Tuition and fees vary according to course load. *Financial support:* In 2016–17, 82 students received support, including 11 research assistantships with partial tuition reimbursements available (averaging $23,709 per year), 24 teaching assistantships with partial tuition reimbursements available (averaging $14,306 per year); career-related internships or fieldwork, Federal Work-Study, institutionally sponsored loans, scholarships/grants, and unspecified assistantships also available. Support available to part-time students. Financial award application deadline: 4/30; financial award applicants required to submit FAFSA. *Faculty research:* Motion capture, conversational/interactive robotics, simulations as modern teaching tools. *Total annual research expenditures:* $1.1 million. *Unit head:* Dr. Anne Balsamo, Dean, 972-883-4376, E-mail: atecdean@utdallas.edu. *Application contact:* Dr. Monica Evans, Associate Dean for Graduate Studies, 972-883-4332, E-mail: mevans@utdallas.edu. Website: http://www.utdallas.edu/atec/

**University of the Sacred Heart,** Graduate Programs, Department of Communication, San Juan, PR 00914-0383. Offers contemporary culture and media (MA); digital journalism (MA, Certificate); editing for media (MA, Certificate); public relations (MA, Certificate); publicity (MA, Certificate); scriptwriting (MA, Certificate). *Program availability:* Part-time, evening/weekend. *Degree requirements:* For master's, thesis.

**University of the Sacred Heart,** Graduate Programs, Department of Education, San Juan, PR 00914-0383. Offers early childhood education (M Ed); information technology and multimedia (Certificate); instruction systems and education technology (M Ed), including English, information technology and multimedia, instructional design, mathematics, Spanish. *Program availability:* Part-time, evening/weekend. *Degree requirements:* For master's, thesis. *Entrance requirements:* For master's, EXADEP, minimum undergraduate GPA of 2.75, interview.

**University of Utah,** Graduate School, College of Engineering, Program in Entertainment Arts and Engineering, Salt Lake City, UT 84112. Offers game art (MEAE); game engineering (MEAE); game production (MEAE); technical art (MEAE). *Program availability:* Part-time. *Faculty:* 7 full-time (0 women). *Students:* 120 full-time (21 women), 1 part-time (0 women); includes 19 minority (1 Black or African American, non-Hispanic/Latino; 9 Asian, non-Hispanic/Latino; 5 Hispanic/Latino; 1 Native Hawaiian or other Pacific Islander, non-Hispanic/Latino; 3 Two or more races, non-Hispanic/Latino), 55 international. Average age 25. 160 applicants, 50% accepted, 60 enrolled. In 2016, 53 master's awarded. *Entrance requirements:* For master's, GRE (recommended for game engineering and game production track applicants). Additional exam requirements/recommendations for international students: Required—TOEFL (minimum score 550 paper-based; 80 iBT), IELTS (minimum score 6.5). *Application deadline:* For fall admission, 2/28 for domestic and international students. Application fee: $65. Electronic applications accepted. *Expenses:* Contact institution. *Financial support:* In 2016–17, 50 research assistantships with partial tuition reimbursements (averaging $7,000 per year), 53 teaching assistantships with partial tuition reimbursements (averaging $7,000 per year) were awarded; career-related internships or fieldwork, scholarships/grants, health care benefits, and unspecified assistantships also available. Financial award application deadline: 2/28; financial award applicants required to submit

*Internet and Interactive Multimedia*

FAFSA. *Faculty research:* Games for health, simulation. *Unit head:* Corrinne Lewis, Academic Program Manager, 801-585-6491, E-mail: corrinne.lewis@utah.edu. *Application contact:* Hallie Huber, Program Coordinator/Academic Advisor, 801-581-5460, E-mail: hallie.huber@utah.edu.
Website: http://eae.utah.edu/

**Virginia Polytechnic Institute and State University,** Graduate School, College of Architecture and Urban Studies, Blacksburg, VA 24061. Offers architecture (MS Arch); architecture and design research (PhD); building/construction science and management (MS); creative technologies (MFA); environmental design and planning (PhD); landscape architecture (MLA); planning, governance, and globalization (PhD); public administration (MPA); public administration/public affairs (PhD, Certificate); public and international affairs (MPIA); urban and regional planning (MURP). *Accreditation:* ASLA (one or more programs are accredited). *Faculty:* 136 full-time (53 women). *Students:* 371 full-time (185 women), 210 part-time (104 women); includes 118 minority (49 Black or African American, non-Hispanic/Latino; 1 American Indian or Alaska Native, non-Hispanic/Latino; 30 Asian, non-Hispanic/Latino; 32 Hispanic/Latino; 6 Two or more races, non-Hispanic/Latino), 137 international. Average age 31. 566 applicants, 55% accepted, 160 enrolled. In 2016, 137 master's, 24 doctorates awarded. *Degree requirements:* For master's, comprehensive exam (for some programs), thesis (for some programs); for doctorate, comprehensive exam (for some programs), thesis/dissertation (for some programs). *Entrance requirements:* For master's and doctorate, GRE/GMAT. Additional exam requirements/recommendations for international students: Required—TOEFL (minimum score 80 iBT). *Application deadline:* For fall admission, 8/1 for domestic students, 4/1 for international students; for spring admission, 1/1 for domestic students, 9/1 for international students. Applications are processed on a rolling basis. Application fee: $75. Electronic applications accepted. *Expenses:* Tuition, state resident: full-time $12,467; part-time $692.50 per credit hour. Tuition, nonresident: full-time $25,095; part-time $1394.25 per credit hour. *Required fees:* $2669; $491.50 per semester. Tuition and fees vary according to course load, campus/location and program. *Financial support:* In 2016–17, 11 research assistantships with full tuition reimbursements (averaging $19,474 per year), 45 teaching assistantships with full tuition reimbursements (averaging $16,014 per year) were awarded. Financial award application deadline: 3/1; financial award applicants required to submit FAFSA. *Total annual research expenditures:* $3.6 million. *Unit head:* Dr. A. J. Davis, Dean, 540-231-6416, Fax: 540-231-6332, E-mail: davisa@vt.edu. *Application contact:* Christine Mattsson-Coon, Executive Assistant, 540-231-6416, Fax: 540-231-6332, E-mail: cmattsso@vt.edu.
Website: http://www.caus.vt.edu/

**Webster University,** School of Communications, Program in New Media Production, St. Louis, MO 63119-3194. Offers MA. *Expenses: Tuition:* Full-time $21,900; part-time $730 per credit hour. Tuition and fees vary according to campus/location and program. *Unit head:* Eric Rothenbuhler, Dean, 314-968-7154. *Application contact:* Sarah Nandor, Director, Graduate and Transfer Admissions, 314-968-7109, E-mail: gadmit@webster.edu.

**Wilmington University,** College of Technology, New Castle, DE 19720-6491. Offers geographic information systems (MS); information assurance (MS); information systems technologies (MS); Internet/Web design (MS); management and management information systems (MS). *Program availability:* Part-time, evening/weekend. *Faculty:* 5 full-time (1 woman), 114 part-time/adjunct (31 women). *Students:* 1,316 full-time (321 women), 263 part-time (79 women); includes 71 minority (53 Black or African American, non-Hispanic/Latino; 5 American Indian or Alaska Native, non-Hispanic/Latino; 8 Asian, non-Hispanic/Latino; 4 Hispanic/Latino; 1 Two or more races, non-Hispanic/Latino), 1,437 international. Average age 26. 856 applicants, 100% accepted, 332 enrolled. In 2016, 756 master's awarded. *Entrance requirements:* Additional exam requirements/recommendations for international students: Required—TOEFL (minimum score 500 paper-based). *Application deadline:* Applications are processed on a rolling basis. Application fee: $35. Electronic applications accepted. *Expenses: Tuition:* Full-time $8388; part-time $466 per credit. *Required fees:* $25 per semester. Tuition and fees vary according to degree level. *Unit head:* Dr. Mary Ann K. Westerfield, Dean. *Application contact:* Laura Morris, Director of Admissions, 877-967-5464, E-mail: infocenter@wilmu.edu.
Website: http://www.wilmu.edu/technology/

**Worcester Polytechnic Institute,** Graduate Studies and Research, Program in Interactive Media and Game Development, Worcester, MA 01609-2280. Offers MS. *Program availability:* Part-time, evening/weekend. *Students:* 15 full-time (2 women), 9 international. 57 applicants, 67% accepted, 11 enrolled. In 2016, 7 master's awarded. *Entrance requirements:* For master's, GRE (recommended), 3 letters of recommendation, statement of purpose, portfolio (recommended). Additional exam requirements/recommendations for international students: Required—TOEFL (minimum score 563 paper-based; 84 iBT), IELTS (minimum score 7). *Application deadline:* For fall admission, 1/1 for domestic and international students; for spring admission, 10/1 for domestic and international students. Applications are processed on a rolling basis. Application fee: $70. Electronic applications accepted. *Financial support:* Research assistantships, teaching assistantships, and health care benefits available. Financial award application deadline: 1/1; financial award applicants required to submit FAFSA. *Unit head:* Jennifer DeWinter, Graduate Coordinator, 508-831-4977, Fax: 508-831-5776, E-mail: jdewinter@wpi.edu. *Application contact:* Alison Darling, Administrative Assistant, 508-831-4977, E-mail: ajdarling@wpi.edu.
Website: http://www.wpi.edu/academics/imgd

# Journalism

**American University,** School of Communication, Program in Journalism and Public Affairs, Washington, DC 20016-8001. Offers broadcast journalism (MA); international journalism (MA); investigative journalism (MA). *Accreditation:* ACEJMC. *Faculty:* 13 full-time (5 women), 4 part-time/adjunct (all women). *Students:* 28 full-time (20 women); includes 13 minority (7 Black or African American, non-Hispanic/Latino; 1 Asian, non-Hispanic/Latino; 4 Hispanic/Latino; 1 Two or more races, non-Hispanic/Latino), 4 international. 110 applicants, 73% accepted, 28 enrolled. In 2016, 28 master's awarded. *Degree requirements:* For master's, comprehensive exam, thesis or alternative. *Entrance requirements:* Additional exam requirements/recommendations for international students: Required—TOEFL (minimum score 600 paper-based; 100 iBT), IELTS (minimum score 7). *Application deadline:* For fall admission, 2/1 priority date for domestic and international students. Applications are processed on a rolling basis. Application fee: $55. Electronic applications accepted. *Expenses: Tuition:* Full-time $28,422; part-time $1579 per credit hour. *Required fees:* $690; $200 per term. Tuition and fees vary according to course load, degree level and program. *Financial support:* In 2016–17, 3 fellowships with tuition reimbursements (averaging $27,000 per year), 14 research assistantships with partial tuition reimbursements (averaging $7,000 per year), 3 teaching assistantships with partial tuition reimbursements (averaging $7,000 per year) were awarded; career-related internships or fieldwork, Federal Work-Study, institutionally sponsored loans, scholarships/grants, tuition waivers (partial), and unspecified assistantships also available. Financial award application deadline: 2/1; financial award applicants required to submit FAFSA. *Faculty research:* Government and media effects of journalistic practices and policies; race, gender, and the media; investigative reporting; computer-assisted reporting; data driven journalism. *Unit head:* Prof. John Watson, Division Director, 202-885-2083, Fax: 202-885-2099, E-mail: jwatson@american.edu. *Application contact:* Christine Rials, Assistant Director for Graduate Admissions, 202-885-2040, Fax: 202-885-2019, E-mail: crials@american.edu.
Website: http://www.american.edu/soc/journalism/index.cfm

**American University,** School of Communication, Weekend Programs in Communication, Washington, DC 20016-8001. Offers journalism and digital storytelling (MA); producing film, TV and video (MA). *Accreditation:* ACEJMC. *Program availability:* Part-time, evening/weekend. *Students:* 66 part-time (41 women); includes 45 minority (31 Black or African American, non-Hispanic/Latino; 4 Asian, non-Hispanic/Latino; 7 Hispanic/Latino; 3 Two or more races, non-Hispanic/Latino), 1 international. 111 applicants, 31% accepted, 19 enrolled. *Degree requirements:* For master's, comprehensive exam, thesis or alternative. *Entrance requirements:* Additional exam requirements/recommendations for international students: Required—TOEFL (minimum score 600 paper-based; 100 iBT). *Application deadline:* For fall admission, 8/1 for domestic students. Applications are processed on a rolling basis. Application fee: $55. Electronic applications accepted. *Expenses: Tuition:* Full-time $28,422; part-time $1579 per credit hour. *Required fees:* $690; $200 per term. Tuition and fees vary according to course load, degree level and program. *Financial support:* Institutionally sponsored loans and tuition waivers available. Financial award applicants required to submit FAFSA. *Unit head:* Christine Rials, Assistant Director for Graduate Admissions, 202-885-2040, E-mail: crials@american.edu. *Application contact:* Christine Rials, Assistant Director for Graduate Admissions, 202-885-2040, E-mail: crials@american.edu.
Website: http://american.edu/soc/admissions/weekend.cfm

**The American University in Cairo,** School of Global Affairs and Public Policy, Cairo, Egypt. Offers gender and women's studies (MA); global affairs (MGA); international and comparative law (LL M); international human rights law (MA); journalism and mass communication (MA); Middle East studies (MA); migration and refugee studies (MA, Diploma); public administration (MPA); public policy (MPP); television and digital journalism (MA). *Program availability:* Part-time, evening/weekend. *Faculty:* 27 full-time (13 women), 5 part-time/adjunct (3 women). *Students:* 69 full-time (40 women), 194 part-time (134 women), 33 international. Average age 29. 322 applicants, 51% accepted, 86 enrolled. In 2016, 112 master's awarded. *Degree requirements:* For master's, comprehensive exam (for some programs), thesis (for some programs). *Entrance requirements:* Additional exam requirements/recommendations for international students: Required—TOEFL (minimum score 450 paper-based; 45 iBT), IELTS (minimum score 5). *Application deadline:* For fall admission, 2/1 for domestic and international students; for spring admission, 10/15 for domestic and international students. Applications are processed on a rolling basis. Application fee: $80. Electronic applications accepted. *Expenses:* Contact institution. *Financial support:* Fellowships with partial tuition reimbursements, scholarships/grants, and unspecified assistantships available. Financial award application deadline: 3/10. *Faculty research:* Law, media and journalism; public policy and public administration, gender studies, Middle East Studies, global affairs, refugees studies. *Unit head:* Dr. Nabil Fahmy, Dean, 20-2-2615-2671, E-mail: nfahmy@aucegypt.edu. *Application contact:* Maha Hegazi, Director for Graduate Admissions, 20-2-2615-1462, E-mail: mahahegazi@aucegypt.edu.
Website: http://www.aucegypt.edu/GAPP/Pages/default.aspx

**Arizona State University at the Tempe campus,** Walter Cronkite School of Journalism and Mass Communication, Phoenix, AZ 85004. Offers journalism and mass communication (PhD); mass communication (MMC). *Accreditation:* ACEJMC. Terminal master's awarded for partial completion of doctoral program. *Degree requirements:* For master's, 9-hour professional capstone experience; interactive Program of Study (iPOS) submitted before completing 50 percent of required credit hours; for doctorate, comprehensive exam, thesis/dissertation, interactive Program of Study (iPOS) submitted before completing 50 percent of required credit hours. *Entrance requirements:* For master's and doctorate, GRE, minimum GPA of 3.0 or equivalent in last 2 years of work leading to bachelor's degree. Additional exam requirements/recommendations for international students: Required—TOEFL, IELTS, or PTE. Electronic applications accepted. *Expenses:* Contact institution.

**Arkansas State University,** Graduate School, College of Media and Communication, Department of Media, State University, AR 72467. Offers mass communications (MSMC). *Program availability:* Part-time. *Degree requirements:* For master's, comprehensive exam, thesis or alternative. *Entrance requirements:* For master's, GRE General Test or MAT, appropriate bachelor's degree, letters of reference, educational experience, professional experience, official transcripts, immunization records. Additional exam requirements/recommendations for international students: Required—TOEFL (minimum score 550 paper-based; 79 iBT), IELTS (minimum score 6), PTE (minimum score 56). Electronic applications accepted.

**Arkansas Tech University,** College of Arts and Humanities, Russellville, AR 72801. Offers applied sociology (MS); English (M Ed, MA); history (MA); liberal arts (MLA); multi-media journalism (MA); psychology (MS); teaching English as a second language (MA). *Program availability:* Part-time. *Students:* 56 full-time (42 women), 121 part-time (85 women); includes 23 minority (7 Black or African American, non-Hispanic/Latino; 1 Asian, non-Hispanic/Latino; 11 Hispanic/Latino; 4 Two or more races, non-Hispanic/Latino), 34 international. Average age 32. In 2016, 90 master's awarded. *Degree requirements:* For master's, comprehensive exam (for some programs), thesis (for some programs), project. *Entrance requirements:* For master's, GRE General Test or GMAT. Additional exam requirements/recommendations for international students: Required—TOEFL (minimum score 550 paper-based; 79 iBT), IELTS (minimum score 6). *Application deadline:* For fall admission, 3/1 priority date for domestic students, 5/1 priority date for international students; for spring admission, 10/1 priority date for domestic and international students. Applications are processed on a rolling basis. Application fee: $25 ($75 for international students). Electronic applications accepted.

*Expenses:* Tuition, state resident: full-time $4932; part-time $274 per credit hour. Tuition, nonresident: full-time $9864; part-time $548 per credit hour. *Required fees:* $513 per semester. Tuition and fees vary according to course load. *Financial support:* In 2016–17, research assistantships with full tuition reimbursements (averaging $4,800 per year), teaching assistantships with full tuition reimbursements (averaging $4,800 per year) were awarded; career-related internships or fieldwork, Federal Work-Study, scholarships/grants, health care benefits, and unspecified assistantships also available. Support available to part-time students. Financial award application deadline: 4/15; financial award applicants required to submit FAFSA. *Unit head:* Dr. Jeffrey Woods, Dean, 479-968-0274, Fax: 479-964-0812, E-mail: jwoods@atu.edu. *Application contact:* Dr. Mary B. Gunter, Dean of Graduate College, 479-968-0398, Fax: 479-964-0542, E-mail: gradcollege@atu.edu.
Website: http://www.atu.edu/humanities/

**Ball State University,** Graduate School, College of Communication, Information, and Media, Department of Journalism, Program in Journalism, Muncie, IN 47306. Offers MA. *Program availability:* Online only, 100% online. *Entrance requirements:* For master's, GRE General Test (minimum score 150 verbal), minimum baccalaureate GPA of 2.75 or 3.0 in latter half of baccalauareate, transcripts of all prior course work, current resume or curriculum vitae, 1000-word statement of purpose, writing sample. Additional exam requirements/recommendations for international students: Required—TOEFL (minimum score 550 paper-based; 79 iBT), IELTS (minimum score 6.5). Electronic applications accepted.

**Baylor University,** Graduate School, College of Arts and Sciences, Department of Journalism, Public Relations and New Media, Waco, TX 76798. Offers international journalism (MIJ); journalism (MA). *Students:* 6 full-time (4 women), 4 part-time (all women); includes 2 minority (1 Hispanic/Latino; 1 Two or more races, non-Hispanic/Latino). Average age 24. In 2016, 3 master's awarded. *Degree requirements:* For master's, proficiency in 1 foreign language (for MIJ). *Entrance requirements:* For master's, GRE General Test. *Application deadline:* Applications are processed on a rolling basis. Application fee: $25. *Expenses: Tuition:* Full-time $28,494; part-time $1583 per credit hour. *Required fees:* $167 per credit hour. Tuition and fees vary according to course load and program. *Financial support:* Research assistantships, teaching assistantships, career-related internships or fieldwork, Federal Work-Study, and institutionally sponsored loans available. Support available to part-time students. *Faculty research:* International politics, mass media and society, journalism history, editing practices. *Unit head:* Dr. Mia N. Moody-Ramirez, Graduate Program Director, 254-710-7247, Fax: 254-710-7347, E-mail: mia_moody@baylor.edu. *Application contact:* Jan Loosier, Administrative Assistant, 254-710-3261, Fax: 254-710-3870, E-mail: jan_loosier@baylor.edu.
Website: http://www.baylor.edu/journalism/

**Bob Jones University,** Graduate Programs, Greenville, SC 29614. Offers accountancy (MS); Bible (MA); Bible translation (MA); Biblical studies (Certificate); broadcast management (MS); business administration (MBA); church history (MA, PhD); church ministries (MA); church music (MM); cinema and video production (MA); counseling (MS); curriculum and instruction (Ed D); divinity (M Div); dramatic production (MA); educational leadership (MS, Ed D, Ed S); elementary education (M Ed, MAT); English (M Ed, MA, MAT); fine arts (MA); graphic design (MA); history (M Ed, MA); illustration (MA); interpretative speech (MA); mathematics (M Ed, MAT); medical missions (Certificate); ministry (MM, D Min); multi-categorical special education (M Ed, MAT); music (M Ed); New Testament interpretation (PhD); Old Testament interpretation (PhD); orchestral instrument performance (MM); organ performance (MM); pastoral studies (MA); personnel services (MS, Ed S); piano pedagogy (MM); piano performance (MM); platform arts (MA); radio and television broadcasting (MS); rhetoric and public address (MA); secondary education (M Ed); studio art (MA); teaching Bible (MA); theology (MA, PhD); voice performance (MM); youth ministries (MA); M Div/MM.

**Boston University,** College of Communication, Department of Journalism, Boston, MA 02215. Offers MS. *Program availability:* Part-time. *Faculty:* 24 full-time, 15 part-time/adjunct. *Students:* 71 full-time (52 women), 3 part-time (2 women); includes 9 minority (2 Black or African American, non-Hispanic/Latino; 1 Asian, non-Hispanic/Latino; 5 Hispanic/Latino; 1 Two or more races, non-Hispanic/Latino), 21 international. Average age 25. 210 applicants, 72% accepted, 42 enrolled. In 2016, 68 master's awarded. *Degree requirements:* For master's, thesis. *Entrance requirements:* For master's, GRE General Test, resume, writing samples, letters of recommendation. Additional exam requirements/recommendations for international students: Required—TOEFL (minimum score 600 paper-based; 100 iBT), IELTS. *Application deadline:* For fall admission, 5/1 for domestic and international students. Applications are processed on a rolling basis. Application fee: $80. Electronic applications accepted. *Financial support:* Teaching assistantships with partial tuition reimbursements, career-related internships or fieldwork, Federal Work-Study, institutionally sponsored loans, scholarships/grants, and unspecified assistantships available. Support available to part-time students. Financial award application deadline: 5/1; financial award applicants required to submit FAFSA. *Unit head:* William McKeen, Chairman, 617-353-3484, Fax: 617-353-1086, E-mail: wmckeen@bu.edu. *Application contact:* Haley Nielsen, Administrator of Admission and Financial Aid, 617-353-3481, E-mail: comgrad@bu.edu.
Website: http://www.bu.edu/com/academics/journalism/

**California State University, Northridge,** Graduate Studies, College of Arts, Media, and Communication, Department of Journalism, Northridge, CA 91330. Offers mass communication (MA). *Program availability:* Part-time, evening/weekend. *Faculty:* 15 full-time (9 women), 16 part-time/adjunct (7 women). *Students:* 12 full-time (9 women), 17 part-time (9 women); includes 9 minority (2 Black or African American, non-Hispanic/Latino; 1 American Indian or Alaska Native, non-Hispanic/Latino; 1 Asian, non-Hispanic/Latino; 4 Hispanic/Latino; 1 Two or more races, non-Hispanic/Latino), 8 international. Average age 30. 44 applicants, 41% accepted, 9 enrolled. *Degree requirements:* For master's, thesis. *Entrance requirements:* For master's, GRE General Test. Additional exam requirements/recommendations for international students: Required—TOEFL. *Application deadline:* For fall admission, 11/30 for domestic students. Application fee: $55. *Expenses:* Tuition, state resident: full-time $4152. *Financial support:* Career-related internships or fieldwork and Federal Work-Study available. Financial award application deadline: 3/1. *Unit head:* Linda Bowen, Chair, 818-677-3135.
Website: http://www.csun.edu/journalism/

**Carleton University,** Faculty of Graduate Studies, Faculty of Public Affairs and Management, School of Journalism and Communication, Ottawa, ON K1S 5B6, Canada. Offers communication (MA, PhD); journalism (MJ). *Degree requirements:* For master's, thesis optional; for doctorate, comprehensive exam, thesis/dissertation. *Entrance requirements:* For master's, honors degree. Additional exam requirements/recommendations for international students: Required—TOEFL. *Faculty research:* Specialized print reporting, broadcast journalism, journalism studies.

**Columbia College Chicago,** Graduate School, Department of Journalism, Chicago, IL 60605-1996. Offers MA. *Degree requirements:* For master's, thesis. *Entrance requirements:* For master's, self-assessment essay, work sample, interview, letters of recommendation. Additional exam requirements/recommendations for international students: Required—TOEFL (minimum score 600 paper-based; 100 iBT). Electronic applications accepted. *Expenses:* Contact institution.

**Columbia University,** Fu Foundation School of Engineering and Applied Science, Department of Computer Science, New York, NY 10027. Offers computer science (MS, Eng Sc D, PhD); computer science and journalism (MS). PhD offered through the Graduate School of Arts and Sciences. *Program availability:* Part-time, online learning. Terminal master's awarded for partial completion of doctoral program. *Degree requirements:* For master's, thesis optional; for doctorate, comprehensive exam, thesis/dissertation, candidacy exam. *Entrance requirements:* For master's and doctorate, GRE General Test. Additional exam requirements/recommendations for international students: Required—TOEFL, IELTS, PTE. Electronic applications accepted. *Faculty research:* Natural language processing, machine learning, software systems, network systems, computer security, computational biology, foundations of computer science, vision and graphics.

**Columbia University,** Graduate School of Journalism, New York, NY 10027. Offers MA, MS, PhD, JD/MS, MIA/MS, MS/MBA. *Accreditation:* ACEJMC. *Program availability:* Part-time. *Degree requirements:* For master's, thesis; for doctorate, thesis/dissertation. *Entrance requirements:* For master's, writing test, 2-3 samples of journalistic work, minimum typing speed of 50 words per minute; for doctorate, GRE. Additional exam requirements/recommendations for international students: Required—TOEFL. *Expenses:* Contact institution. *Faculty research:* International communication, communication technologies, ethics in journalism, journalism history.

**Concordia University,** School of Graduate Studies, Faculty of Arts and Science, Department of Journalism, Montréal, QC H3G 1M8, Canada. Offers journalism (Graduate Diploma); journalism studies (MA); visual journalism (Diploma). *Degree requirements:* For other advanced degree, one foreign language. *Entrance requirements:* Additional exam requirements/recommendations for international students: Required—departmental English test or TOEFL.

**CUNY Graduate School of Journalism,** Graduate Program, New York, NY 10018. Offers entrepreneurial journalism (MA); journalism (MA); social journalism (MA). *Accreditation:* ACEJMC. *Faculty:* 9 full-time (3 women), 68 part-time/adjunct (29 women). *Students:* 120 full-time (78 women). *Degree requirements:* For master's, internship, final or capstone project. *Entrance requirements:* For master's, 3 letters of recommendation, personal statement, resume, interview, 3 writing samples. Additional exam requirements/recommendations for international students: Required—TOEFL (minimum score 105 iBT). *Application deadline:* For fall admission, 1/9 for domestic and international students. Application fee: $125. Electronic applications accepted. *Expenses:* Tuition, state resident: full-time $17,510. Tuition, nonresident: full-time $30,780. International tuition: $37,780 full-time. *Financial support:* Career-related internships or fieldwork, Federal Work-Study, institutionally sponsored loans, and scholarships/grants available. Financial award application deadline: 3/1; financial award applicants required to submit FAFSA. *Application contact:* Colleen Leigh, Director of Admissions, 646-758-7852, Fax: 646-758-7709, E-mail: colleen.leigh@journalism.cuny.edu.
Website: http://www.journalism.cuny.edu/

**DePaul University,** College of Communication, Chicago, IL 60614. Offers digital communication and media arts (MA); health communication (MA); journalism (MA); media and cinema studies (MA); organizational and multicultural communication (MA); public relations and advertising (MA); relational communication (MA). *Program availability:* Part-time, evening/weekend. *Entrance requirements:* Additional exam requirements/recommendations for international students: Required—TOEFL (minimum score 590 paper-based; 96 iBT), IELTS (minimum score 7.5) or PTE. Electronic applications accepted.

**Emerson College,** Graduate Studies, School of Communication, Department of Journalism, Boston, MA 02116-4624. Offers journalism (MA), including broadcast journalism. *Faculty:* 14 full-time (6 women), 4 part-time/adjunct (1 woman). *Students:* 20 full-time (16 women); includes 10 minority (5 Black or African American, non-Hispanic/Latino; 5 Hispanic/Latino), 6 international. Average age 26. 70 applicants, 67% accepted, 12 enrolled. In 2016, 13 master's awarded. *Entrance requirements:* For master's, GRE General Test. Additional exam requirements/recommendations for international students: Required—TOEFL (minimum score 550 paper-based; 80 iBT), IELTS (minimum score 7). *Application deadline:* For summer admission, 3/1 priority date for domestic and international students. Applications are processed on a rolling basis. Application fee: $60 ($75 for international students). Electronic applications accepted. *Financial support:* In 2016–17, 13 students received support, including 13 fellowships with partial tuition reimbursements available (averaging $9,625 per year); research assistantships with partial tuition reimbursements available, Federal Work-Study, scholarships/grants, and unspecified assistantships also available. Financial award application deadline: 3/1; financial award applicants required to submit FAFSA. *Faculty research:* Journalism. *Application contact:* Leanda Ferland, Office of Graduate Admission, 617-824-8610, Fax: 617-824-8614, E-mail: gradapp@emerson.edu.
Website: http://www.emerson.edu/graduate_admission

**Florida Agricultural and Mechanical University,** Division of Graduate Studies, Research, and Continuing Education, School of Journalism and Graphic Communication, Tallahassee, FL 32307-3200. Offers journalism (MS). *Degree requirements:* For master's, comprehensive exam, thesis (for some programs). *Entrance requirements:* For master's, GRE General Test, minimum GPA of 3.0. Additional exam requirements/recommendations for international students: Required—TOEFL.

**Florida International University,** College of Communication, Architecture and The Arts, School of Communication and Journalism, Miami, FL 33199. Offers mass communication (MS), including global strategic communications, Spanish language journalism. *Program availability:* Part-time, evening/weekend. *Faculty:* 12 full-time (6 women), 8 part-time/adjunct (4 women). *Students:* 94 full-time (72 women), 51 part-time (33 women); includes 110 minority (25 Black or African American, non-Hispanic/Latino; 81 Hispanic/Latino; 4 Two or more races, non-Hispanic/Latino), 19 international. Average age 29. 127 applicants, 62% accepted, 59 enrolled. In 2016, 53 master's awarded. *Degree requirements:* For master's, thesis optional. *Entrance requirements:* For master's, 2 letters of recommendation; minimum GPA of 3.0 during last 60 hours of upper-level work; resume. Additional exam requirements/recommendations for international students: Required—TOEFL (minimum score 550 paper-based; 80 iBT). *Application deadline:* For fall admission, 6/1 for domestic students, 4/1 for international students; for spring admission, 10/1 for domestic students, 9/1 for international students. Applications are processed on a rolling basis. Application fee: $30. Electronic applications accepted. *Expenses:* Tuition, state resident: full-time $8912; part-time $446 per credit hour. Tuition, nonresident: full-time $21,393; part-time $992 per credit hour. *Required fees:* $2185; $195 per semester. Tuition and fees vary according to program. *Financial support:* Institutionally sponsored loans and scholarships/grants available. Financial award application deadline: 3/1; financial award applicants required to submit FAFSA. *Unit head:* Dr. Maria Elena Villar, Chair, 305-919-5795, Fax: 305-919-5215, E-mail: mariaelena.villar@fiu.edu. *Application contact:* Nanett Rojas, Assistant Director, Graduate Admissions, 305-348-7442, Fax: 305-348-7441, E-mail: gradadm@fiu.edu.
Website: https://scj.fiu.edu/

**Full Sail University,** New Media Journalism Master of Arts Program - Online, Winter Park, FL 32792-7437. Offers MA.

## Journalism

**Georgetown University,** Graduate School of Arts and Sciences, School of Continuing Studies, Washington, DC 20057. Offers American studies (MALS); Catholic studies (MALS); classical civilizations (MALS); emergency and disaster management (MPS); ethics and the professions (MALS); global strategic communications (MPS); hospitality management (MPS); human resources management (MPS); humanities (MALS); individualized study (MALS); integrated marketing communications (MPS); international affairs (MALS); Islam and Muslim-Christian relations (MALS); journalism (MPS); liberal studies (DLS); literature and society (MALS); medieval and early modern European studies (MALS); public relations and corporate communications (MPS); real estate (MPS); religious studies (MALS); social and public policy (MALS); sports industry management (MPS); systems engineering management (MPS); technology management (MPS); the theory and practice of American democracy (MALS); urban and regional planning (MPS); visual culture (MALS). MPS in systems engineering management offered jointly with Stevens Institute of Technology. *Entrance requirements:* Additional exam requirements/recommendations for international students: Required—TOEFL.

**Harvard University,** Extension School, Cambridge, MA 02138-3722. Offers applied sciences (CAS); biotechnology (ALM); educational technologies (ALM); educational technology (CET); English for graduate and professional studies (DGP); environmental management (ALM, CEM); information technology (ALM); journalism (ALM); liberal arts (ALM); management (ALM, CM); mathematics for teaching (ALM); museum studies (ALM); premedical studies (Diploma); publication and communication (CPC). *Program availability:* Part-time, evening/weekend. *Degree requirements:* For master's, thesis. *Entrance requirements:* For master's, 3 completed graduate courses with grade of B or higher. Additional exam requirements/recommendations for international students: Required—TOEFL (minimum score 600 paper-based), TWE (minimum score 5). *Expenses:* Contact institution.

**Hofstra University,** Lawrence Herbert School of Communication, Programs in Journalism and Public Relations, Hempstead, NY 11549. Offers journalism (MA); public relations (MA). *Program availability:* Part-time, evening/weekend. *Students:* 58 full-time (43 women), 22 part-time (16 women); includes 38 minority (19 Black or African American, non-Hispanic/Latino; 3 Asian, non-Hispanic/Latino; 13 Hispanic/Latino; 3 Two or more races, non-Hispanic/Latino), 8 international. Average age 25. 89 applicants, 73% accepted, 33 enrolled. In 2016, 30 master's awarded. *Degree requirements:* For master's, thesis. *Entrance requirements:* For master's, minimum GPA of 2.75; bachelor's degree. Additional exam requirements/recommendations for international students: Required—TOEFL (minimum score 550 paper-based; 95 iBT). *Application deadline:* Applications are processed on a rolling basis. Application fee: $75. Electronic applications accepted. *Expenses:* Tuition: Full-time $1240. *Required fees:* $970. Tuition and fees vary according to program. *Financial support:* In 2016–17, 43 students received support, including 10 fellowships with full and partial tuition reimbursements available (averaging $3,045 per year), 3 research assistantships with full and partial tuition reimbursements available (averaging $7,125 per year); career-related internships or fieldwork, Federal Work-Study, institutionally sponsored loans, scholarships/grants, tuition waivers (full and partial), and unspecified assistantships also available. Support available to part-time students. Financial award applicants required to submit FAFSA. *Faculty research:* Hybrid media theory, particularly as it relates to journalism and politics; political communication, public relations and international communication; impact of convergence and interactive-based technologies and the impact of immigration and globalization on health information campaigns; mediated message design, rational and emotional appeals in strategic messaging, crisis communications, public relations, persuasion; the crossroads of popular culture, politics, new media, and civic engagement. *Unit head:* Dr. Gregory S. Smith, Chairperson, 516-463-4270, Fax: 516-463-4866, E-mail: gregory.s.smith@hofstra.edu. *Application contact:* Sunil Samuel, Assistant Vice President of Admissions, 516-463-4723, Fax: 516-463-4664, E-mail: graduateadmission@hofstra.edu.
Website: http://www.hofstra.edu/academics/colleges/soc/

**Iowa State University of Science and Technology,** Greenlee School of Journalism and Mass Communication, Ames, IA 50011. Offers MS. *Entrance requirements:* For master's, GRE General Test. Additional exam requirements/recommendations for international students: Required—TOEFL (minimum score 570 paper-based; 88 iBT), IELTS (minimum score 6.5). *Application deadline:* For fall admission, 3/1 priority date for international students; for spring admission, 10/1 priority date for international students. Applications are processed on a rolling basis. Application fee: $60 ($90 for international students). Electronic applications accepted. *Application contact:* Daniela Dimitrova, Application Contact, 515-294-5951, Fax: 515-294-5108, E-mail: danielad@iastate.edu. Website: http://www.jlmc.iastate.edu/graduate/

**Kansas State University,** Graduate School, College of Arts and Sciences, A.Q. Miller School of Journalism and Mass Communications, Manhattan, KS 66506. Offers advertising (MS); community journalism (MS); global communication (MS); health communication (MS); media management (MS); public relations (MS). *Program availability:* Part-time, evening/weekend. *Faculty:* 13 full-time (6 women), 1 (woman) part-time/adjunct. *Students:* 13 full-time (10 women), 6 part-time (4 women); includes 1 minority (Hispanic/Latino), 8 international. Average age 29. 7 applicants, 71% accepted, 3 enrolled. In 2016, 7 master's awarded. *Degree requirements:* For master's, comprehensive exam, thesis. *Entrance requirements:* For master's, GRE General Test, minimum GPA of 3.0. Additional exam requirements/recommendations for international students: Required—TOEFL (minimum score 79 iBT). *Application deadline:* For fall admission, 2/1 priority date for domestic and international students; for spring admission, 8/1 priority date for domestic and international students. Applications are processed on a rolling basis. Application fee: $50 ($75 for international students). Electronic applications accepted. *Expenses:* Tuition, state resident: full-time $9670. Tuition, nonresident: full-time $21,828. *Required fees:* $862. *Financial support:* In 2016–17, 2 research assistantships with full tuition reimbursements (averaging $11,180 per year), 7 teaching assistantships with full tuition reimbursements (averaging $7,729 per year) were awarded; scholarships/grants, health care benefits, and unspecified assistantships also available. Financial award application deadline: 2/1; financial award applicants required to submit FAFSA. *Faculty research:* Health communication, risk communication, strategic communications, community journalism, global communication. *Total annual research expenditures:* $219,641. *Unit head:* Dr. Jean Folkerts, Director, 785-532-6890, Fax: 785-532-5484, E-mail: jeanfolk@ksu.edu. *Application contact:* Dr. Barbara DeSanto, Associate Director of Graduate Studies, 785-532-3890, Fax: 785-532-5484, E-mail: desantoi@ksu.edu.
Website: http://jmc.ksu.edu/

**Kent State University,** College of Communication and Information, School of Journalism and Mass Communication, Kent, OH 44242-0001. Offers journalism and mass communication (MA), including media management, public relations, reporting and editing-broadcast, reporting and editing-convergence, reporting and editing-journalism educators, reporting and editing-magazine, reporting and editing-newspaper. *Program availability:* Part-time, online learning. *Faculty:* 25 full-time (13 women). *Students:* 12 full-time (7 women), 102 part-time (68 women); includes 19 minority (14 Black or African American, non-Hispanic/Latino; 3 Hispanic/Latino; 2 Two or more races, non-Hispanic/Latino), 5 international. Average age 30. 46 applicants, 67% accepted, 20

enrolled. In 2016, 79 master's awarded. *Degree requirements:* For master's, thesis or project. *Entrance requirements:* For master's, GRE, minimum GPA of 3.0, statement of purpose, 3 online recommendations, resume. Additional exam requirements/recommendations for international students: Required—TOEFL (minimum score of 600 paper-based, 100 iBT), IELTS (minimum score of 7.0), Michigan English Language Assessment Battery (minimum score of 85), or PTE (minimum score of 68). *Application deadline:* For fall admission, 7/1 for domestic and international students. Applications are processed on a rolling basis. Application fee: $45 ($70 for international students). Electronic applications accepted. *Expenses:* Tuition, state resident: full-time $10,864; part-time $495 per credit hour. Tuition, nonresident: full-time $18,380; part-time $837 per credit hour. *Financial support:* Research assistantships with full tuition reimbursements, teaching assistantships with full tuition reimbursements, scholarships/grants, and unspecified assistantships available. Financial award application deadline: 3/1. *Unit head:* Thor Wasbotten, Director and Professor, 330-672-4066, E-mail: thor@kent.edu. *Application contact:* Mark Goodman, Graduate Coordinator/Professor, 330-672-6239, E-mail: mgoodm10@kent.edu.
Website: http://www.kent.edu/jmc

**Marquette University,** Graduate School, College of Communication, Milwaukee, WI 53201-1881. Offers advertising and public relations (MA); communication studies (MA); digital storytelling (Certificate); journalism (MA); mass communication (MA); science, health and environmental communication (MA). *Accreditation:* ACEJMC (one or more programs are accredited). *Program availability:* Part-time, evening/weekend. *Faculty:* 36 full-time (18 women), 45 part-time/adjunct (20 women). *Students:* 25 full-time (22 women), 23 part-time (16 women); includes 9 minority (3 Black or African American, non-Hispanic/Latino; 1 American Indian or Alaska Native, non-Hispanic/Latino; 4 Hispanic/Latino; 1 Two or more races, non-Hispanic/Latino), 4 international. Average age 28. 55 applicants, 62% accepted, 21 enrolled. In 2016, 10 master's, 1 other advanced degree awarded. *Degree requirements:* For master's, comprehensive exam, thesis or alternative. *Entrance requirements:* For master's, GRE, official transcripts from all current and previous colleges/universities except Marquette, three letters of recommendation, statement of academic and professional goals. Additional exam requirements/recommendations for international students: Required—TOEFL (minimum score 530 paper-based). *Application deadline:* Applications are processed on a rolling basis. Electronic applications accepted. *Financial support:* Fellowships, research assistantships, teaching assistantships, career-related internships or fieldwork, scholarships/grants, health care benefits, tuition waivers (full and partial), and unspecified assistantships available. Support available to part-time students. Financial award application deadline: 2/15. *Faculty research:* Urban journalism, gender and communication, intercultural communication, religious communication. *Total annual research expenditures:* $7,941. *Unit head:* Dr. Sarah Feldner, Associate Dean. *Application contact:* Dr. Sarah Bonewits Feldner.
Website: http://diederich.marquette.edu/

**Marshall University,** Academic Affairs Division, College of Arts and Media, Program in Journalism, Huntington, WV 25755. Offers journalism (MAJ), including health care public relations. *Degree requirements:* For master's, thesis optional. *Entrance requirements:* For master's, GRE General Test.

**Michigan State University,** The Graduate School, College of Communication Arts and Sciences, School of Journalism, East Lansing, MI 48824. Offers MA. *Entrance requirements:* Additional exam requirements/recommendations for international students: Required—TOEFL. Electronic applications accepted.

**National University,** Academic Affairs, School of Professional Studies, La Jolla, CA 92037-1011. Offers criminal justice (MCJ); digital cinema (MFA); digital journalism (MA); juvenile justice (MS); public administration (MPA), including human resource management. *Program availability:* Part-time, evening/weekend, 100% online, blended/hybrid learning. *Faculty:* 21 full-time (8 women), 35 part-time/adjunct (9 women). *Students:* 280 full-time (155 women), 100 part-time (54 women); includes 226 minority (76 Black or African American, non-Hispanic/Latino; 1 American Indian or Alaska Native, non-Hispanic/Latino; 27 Asian, non-Hispanic/Latino; 102 Hispanic/Latino; 3 Native Hawaiian or other Pacific Islander, non-Hispanic/Latino; 17 Two or more races, non-Hispanic/Latino), 3 international. Average age 37. In 2016, 21 master's awarded. *Degree requirements:* For master's, thesis (for some programs). *Entrance requirements:* For master's, interview, minimum GPA of 2.5. Additional exam requirements/recommendations for international students: Required—TOEFL (minimum score 550 paper-based; 79 iBT), IELTS (minimum score 6). *Application deadline:* Applications are processed on a rolling basis. Application fee: $60 ($65 for international students). Electronic applications accepted. *Financial support:* Career-related internships or fieldwork, institutionally sponsored loans, scholarships/grants, and tuition waivers (partial) available. Support available to part-time students. Financial award application deadline: 6/30; financial award applicants required to submit FAFSA. *Unit head:* School of Professional Studies, 800-628-8648, E-mail: sops@nu.edu. *Application contact:* Brandon Jouganatos, Vice President for Enrollment Services, 800-628-8648, E-mail: advisor@nu.edu.
Website: http://www.nu.edu/OurPrograms/School-of-Professional-Studies.html

**New York University,** Graduate School of Arts and Science, Department of Biology, New York, NY 10012-1019. Offers biology (PhD); biomedical journalism (MS); cancer and molecular biology (PhD); computational biology (PhD); computers in biological research (MS); developmental genetics (PhD); general biology (MS); immunology and microbiology (PhD); molecular genetics (PhD); neurobiology (PhD); oral biology (MS); plant biology (PhD); recombinant DNA technology (MS); MS/MBA. *Program availability:* Part-time. Terminal master's awarded for partial completion of doctoral program. *Degree requirements:* For master's, thesis or alternative, qualifying paper; for doctorate, comprehensive exam, thesis/dissertation. *Entrance requirements:* For master's and doctorate, GRE General Test. Additional exam requirements/recommendations for international students: Required—TOEFL. *Faculty research:* Genomics, molecular and cell biology, development and molecular genetics, molecular evolution of plants and animals.

**New York University,** Graduate School of Arts and Science, Department of Journalism, New York, NY 10012-1019. Offers biomedical journalism (MS); cultural reporting and criticism (MA); French studies/journalism (MA); journalism (MA); Latin American and Caribbean studies/journalism (MA); Near Eastern studies/journalism (MA); science and environmental reporting (Advanced Certificate); MA/Advanced Certificate. *Accreditation:* ACEJMC. *Program availability:* Part-time. *Degree requirements:* For master's, written projects. *Entrance requirements:* For master's, GRE General Test, sample of written work. Additional exam requirements/recommendations for international students: Required—TOEFL. *Faculty research:* Newspaper, magazine, and broadcast journalism; business and financial reporting; media studies.

**Northeastern University,** College of Arts, Media and Design, Boston, MA 02115-5096. Offers architecture (M Arch); game science and design (MS); information design and visualization (MFA); interdisciplinary arts (MFA); journalism (MA); music industry leadership (MS); studio art (MFA); sustainable building systems (MS); sustainable urban environments (M Des). *Faculty:* 142 full-time (55 women), 80 part-time/adjunct (34 women). *Students:* 239 full-time (147 women), 16 part-time (12 women). In 2016, 83 master's awarded. Application fee: $75. Electronic applications accepted. *Expenses:*

$1,365 per credit. *Financial support:* Applicants required to submit FAFSA. *Unit head:* Dr. Elizabeth Hudson, Dean. *Application contact:* Jane Amidon, Associate Dean for Graduate Programs and Research, 617-373-4614, E-mail: gscamd@northeastern.edu. Website: http://www.northeastern.edu/camd/

**Northwestern University,** Medill School of Journalism, Media, and Integrated Marketing Communications, Evanston, IL 60208. Offers integrated marketing communications (MSIMC), including brand strategy, content marketing, direct and interactive marketing, marketing analytics, strategic communications; interactive publishing (MSJ); magazine writing/editing (MSJ); reporting (MSJ); video/broadcast (MSJ). *Accreditation:* ACEJMC (one or more programs are accredited). *Entrance requirements:* For master's, GRE General Test, GMAT or LSAT (for MSJ). Additional exam requirements/recommendations for international students: Required—TOEFL. Electronic applications accepted. *Expenses:* Contact institution. *Faculty research:* Web business journalism, cultural stereotypes, voter apathy, digital television.

**Ohio University,** Graduate College, Scripps College of Communication, E.W. Scripps School of Journalism, Athens, OH 45701-2979. Offers MS, PhD. *Program availability:* Part-time. *Degree requirements:* For master's, thesis or alternative; for doctorate, comprehensive exam, thesis/dissertation. *Entrance requirements:* For master's and doctorate, GRE General Test, minimum GPA of 3.0. Additional exam requirements/recommendations for international students: Required—TOEFL (minimum score 550 paper-based; 80 iBT) or IELTS (minimum score 6.5). *Application deadline:* For fall admission, 2/1 for domestic and international students. Application fee: $50 ($55 for international students). Electronic applications accepted. *Financial support:* Fellowships, research assistantships with full tuition reimbursements, teaching assistantships with full tuition reimbursements, career-related internships or fieldwork, Federal Work-Study, institutionally sponsored loans, and unspecified assistantships available. Financial award application deadline: 2/1. *Faculty research:* Newspaper, magazine, broadcasting, public relations, advertising. *Unit head:* Thomas Hodson, Director, 740-593-2550, Fax: 740-593-2592, E-mail: hodson@ohio.edu. *Application contact:* Dr. Michael Sweeney, Associate Director, 740-593-2589 Ext. 740, Fax: 740-593-2592, E-mail: sweenem3@ohio.edu. Website: http://scrippsjschool.org/

**Point Park University,** School of Communication, Pittsburgh, PA 15222-1984. Offers MA. *Program availability:* Part-time, evening/weekend. *Degree requirements:* For master's, comprehensive exam (for some programs), thesis or alternative. *Entrance requirements:* For master's, GRE (if GPA less than 2.75), minimum GPA of 2.75, 2 letters of recommendation, statement of intent. Additional exam requirements/recommendations for international students: Required—TOEFL (minimum score 570 paper-based; 88 iBT), IELTS (minimum score 6.5); Recommended—TWE (minimum score 5). Electronic applications accepted.

**Quinnipiac University,** School of Communications, Program in Journalism, Hamden, CT 06518-1940. Offers journalism (MS), including broadcast/multimedia, writing; sports journalism (MS), including broadcast/multimedia. *Program availability:* Part-time, evening/weekend. *Faculty:* 3 full-time (1 woman), 10 part-time/adjunct (1 woman). *Students:* 10 full-time (5 women), 5 part-time (3 women); includes 6 minority (2 Black or African American, non-Hispanic/Latino; 3 Hispanic/Latino; 1 Two or more races, non-Hispanic/Latino), 3 international. 9 applicants, 56% accepted, 2 enrolled. In 2016, 4 master's awarded. *Degree requirements:* For master's, project. *Entrance requirements:* For master's, minimum GPA of 3.0, portfolio or writing sample. Additional exam requirements/recommendations for international students: Required—TOEFL (minimum score 575 paper-based; 90 iBT), IELTS (minimum score 6.5). *Application deadline:* For fall admission, 7/30 priority date for domestic students, 4/15 priority date for international students. Applications are processed on a rolling basis. Application fee: $45. Electronic applications accepted. *Expenses:* Tuition: Part-time $985 per credit. *Required fees:* $40 per credit. $150 per semester. Tuition and fees vary according to program. *Financial support:* Federal Work-Study, scholarships/grants, and unspecified assistantships available. Financial award application deadline: 6/1; financial award applicants required to submit FAFSA. *Faculty research:* Journalism history, federal law enforcement and journalism, social media and journalism, online journalism, sports journalism, American football history and media, journalism and film, McCarthyism and journalism. *Unit head:* Phillip Simon, Program Director, 203-582-8672, E-mail: graduate@qu.edu. *Application contact:* Office of Graduate Admissions, 800-462-1944, Fax: 203-582-3443, E-mail: graduate@qu.edu. Website: http://www.qu.edu/gradjournalism

**Regent University,** Graduate School, School of Communication and the Arts, Virginia Beach, VA 23464-9800. Offers communication (MA, PhD), including media and arts management and promotion (MA), political communication (MA), strategic communication (MA); directing for cinema/television (MFA); film and TV (MA), including producing, production, script writing; journalism (MA); producing for cinema/television (MFA); script and screenwriting (MFA); theatre (MA). *Program availability:* Part-time, 100% online, blended/hybrid learning. *Faculty:* 19 full-time (3 women), 51 part-time/adjunct (17 women). *Students:* 92 full-time (52 women), 344 part-time (225 women); includes 163 minority (116 Black or African American, non-Hispanic/Latino; 6 American Indian or Alaska Native, non-Hispanic/Latino; 7 Asian, non-Hispanic/Latino; 25 Hispanic/Latino; 1 Native Hawaiian or other Pacific Islander, non-Hispanic/Latino; 8 Two or more races, non-Hispanic/Latino), 8 international. Average age 37. 368 applicants, 52% accepted, 124 enrolled. In 2016, 91 master's, 7 doctorates awarded. *Degree requirements:* For master's, thesis or alternative; for doctorate, thesis/dissertation. *Entrance requirements:* For master's, transcripts, writing sample, resume, audition (for MFA programs); for doctorate, GRE General Test, resume, writing sample, recommendations, interview, transcripts, personal goals statement. Additional exam requirements/recommendations for international students: Required—TOEFL (minimum score 577 paper-based). *Application deadline:* For fall admission, 3/1 priority date for domestic students; for spring admission, 10/1 priority date for domestic students. Applications are processed on a rolling basis. Application fee: $50. Electronic applications accepted. *Expenses:* $685 per credit (for MA); $895 per credit (for MFA in acting); $885 per credit (for PhD); $250 per semester technology fee. *Financial support:* In 2016–17, 178 students received support, including 2 fellowships (averaging $10,000 per year); career-related internships or fieldwork, scholarships/grants, and unspecified assistantships also available. Support available to part-time students. *Faculty research:* Screenwriting, digital media production, communication, acting, directing. *Unit head:* Dr. Mitch Land, Dean, 757-352-4916, Fax: 757-352-4291, E-mail: mland@regent.edu. *Application contact:* Heidi Cece, Assistant Vice President of Enrollment Management, 800-373-5504, Fax: 757-352-4381, E-mail: admissions@regent.edu. Website: http://www.regent.edu/sca/

**Roosevelt University,** Graduate Division, College of Arts and Sciences, Department of Communication, Program in Journalism, Chicago, IL 60605. Offers MSJ. *Program availability:* Part-time, evening/weekend.

**Sacred Heart University,** Graduate Programs, College of Arts and Sciences, School of Communication and Media Arts, Fairfield, CT 06825. Offers corporate communications and public relations (MA Comm); digital multimedia journalism (MA Comm); digital multimedia production (MA Comm); film and television production (MA); media literacy and digital culture (MA), including children, health and media, media and social justice,

political action and media production; sports communication and media (MA), including athletic communications and promotions, sports broadcasting. *Program availability:* Part-time, evening/weekend. *Faculty:* 9 full-time (1 woman), 3 part-time/adjunct (2 women). *Students:* 60 full-time (34 women), 44 part-time (23 women); includes 23 minority (14 Black or African American, non-Hispanic/Latino; 7 Hispanic/Latino; 2 Two or more races, non-Hispanic/Latino), 18 international. Average age 26. 135 applicants, 93% accepted, 72 enrolled. In 2016, 69 master's awarded. *Degree requirements:* For master's, thesis or alternative. *Entrance requirements:* For master's, bachelor's degree. Additional exam requirements/recommendations for international students: Required—TOEFL (minimum score 570 paper-based, 80 iBT), TWE, or IELTS (6.5); Recommended—TSE. *Application deadline:* Applications are processed on a rolling basis. Application fee: $75. Electronic applications accepted. *Expenses:* $935 per credit. *Financial support:* Unspecified assistantships available. Financial award applicants required to submit FAFSA. *Unit head:* Dr. Andrew Miller, Chair, 203-396-8087, E-mail: millera@sacredheart.edu. *Application contact:* William Sweeney, Director of Graduate Admissions Operations, 203-365-7619, Fax: 203-365-4732, E-mail: graduatestudies@sacredheart.edu. Website: http://www.sacredheart.edu/academics/collegeofartssciences/academicdepartments/communicationmediastudies/

**School of the Art Institute of Chicago,** Graduate Division, Program in New Arts Journalism, Chicago, IL 60603-3103. Offers MA. *Entrance requirements:* Additional exam requirements/recommendations for international students: Required—TOEFL, IELTS.

**South Dakota State University,** Graduate School, College of Arts and Science, Department of Journalism and Mass Communication, Brookings, SD 57007. Offers communication studies and journalism (MS). *Accreditation:* ACEJMC. *Program availability:* Part-time, evening/weekend. *Degree requirements:* For master's, thesis, oral exam. *Entrance requirements:* Additional exam requirements/recommendations for international students: Required—TOEFL (minimum score 550 paper-based; 79 iBT). *Faculty research:* Mass communication applications.

**Stony Brook University, State University of New York,** School of Journalism, Stony Brook, NY 11794. Offers health communication (Certificate); journalism (MS). *Faculty:* 9 full-time (2 women), 22 part-time/adjunct (7 women). *Students:* 3 full-time (2 women), 3 part-time (2 women); includes 1 minority (Hispanic/Latino), 1 international. Average age 29. In 2016, 4 master's awarded. *Entrance requirements:* For master's, GRE, MCAT, DAT, or GMAT, bachelor's degree with minimum GPA of 3.0. Additional exam requirements/recommendations for international students: Required—TOEFL (minimum score 600 paper-based; 100 iBT). *Application deadline:* For fall admission, 4/30 for domestic students; for spring admission, 10/1 for domestic students. Application fee: $100. *Expenses:* Contact institution. *Financial support:* In 2016–17, 1 teaching assistantship was awarded. *Faculty research:* Journalism, newspaper journalism, non-fiction, children's literature, Constitutional law. Total annual research expenditures: $408,274. *Unit head:* Prof. Howard Schneider, Dean, 631-632-7403, E-mail: howard.schneider@stonybrook.edu. *Application contact:* Maureen Robinson, Coordinator, 631-632-7403, Fax: 631-632-7550, E-mail: maureen.robinson@stonybrook.edu. Website: https://journalism.cc.stonybrook.edu/

**Syracuse University,** S. I. Newhouse School of Public Communications, MA Program in Magazine, Newspaper and Online Journalism, Syracuse, NY 13244. Offers MA. *Accreditation:* ACEJMC. *Students:* Average age 24. *Degree requirements:* For master's, capstone course. *Entrance requirements:* For master's, GRE General Test, resume, official transcripts, personal statement, three letters of recommendation. Additional exam requirements/recommendations for international students: Required—TOEFL (minimum score 600 paper-based; 100 iBT). *Application deadline:* For summer admission, 1/15 priority date for domestic and international students. Application fee: $45. Electronic applications accepted. *Expenses:* Tuition: Full-time $25,974; part-time $1443 per credit hour. *Required fees:* $802; $50 per course. Tuition and fees vary according to course load and program. *Financial support:* Fellowships with full tuition reimbursements, research assistantships with partial tuition reimbursements, and teaching assistantships with partial tuition reimbursements available. Financial award application deadline: 2/1; financial award applicants required to submit FAFSA. *Faculty research:* Media law, content management, reporting and writing, magazine and newspaper editing. *Unit head:* Melissa Chessher, Director, 315-443-4004, Fax: 315-443-3946, E-mail: pcgrad@syr.edu. *Application contact:* Graduate Records Office, 315-443-4039, Fax: 315-443-1834, E-mail: pcgrad@syr.edu. Website: http://newhouse.syr.edu/

**Syracuse University,** S. I. Newhouse School of Public Communications, MS Program in Broadcast and Digital Journalism, Syracuse, NY 13244. Offers MS. *Accreditation:* ACEJMC. *Degree requirements:* For master's, capstone course. *Entrance requirements:* For master's, GRE General Test, resume, official transcripts, personal statement, three letters of recommendation. Additional exam requirements/recommendations for international students: Required—TOEFL (minimum score 100 iBT). *Application deadline:* For summer admission, 1/15 for domestic and international students. Application fee: $45. Electronic applications accepted. *Expenses:* Tuition: Full-time $25,974; part-time $1443 per credit hour. *Required fees:* $802; $50 per course. Tuition and fees vary according to course load and program. *Financial support:* Fellowships with full tuition reimbursements, research assistantships with partial tuition reimbursements, and teaching assistantships with partial tuition reimbursements available. Financial award application deadline: 2/1. *Faculty research:* Electronic journalism, broadcast and digital journalism, anchoring in traditional and new platforms, producing. *Unit head:* Prof. Hub Brown, Associate Dean for Research, Creativity, International Initiatives and Diversity/Associate Professor, 315-443-4177, E-mail: hwbrown@syr.edu. *Application contact:* Martha Coria, Graduate Records Office, 315-443-5749, Fax: 315-443-1834, E-mail: pcgrad@syr.edu. Website: http://newhouse.syr.edu/

**Syracuse University,** S. I. Newhouse School of Public Communications, MS Program in Computational Journalism, Syracuse, NY 13244. Offers MS. *Entrance requirements:* For master's, GRE, resume, official transcripts, personal statement, three letters of recommendation. Additional exam requirements/recommendations for international students: Required—TOEFL (minimum score 100 iBT). *Application deadline:* For summer admission, 1/15 priority date for domestic and international students. Application fee: $45. Electronic applications accepted. Application fee is waived when completed online. *Expenses:* Tuition: Full-time $25,974; part-time $1443 per credit hour. *Required fees:* $802; $50 per course. Tuition and fees vary according to course load and program. *Financial support:* Fellowships, research assistantships, and teaching assistantships available. Financial award application deadline: 1/15. *Faculty research:* Media law, visual communication theory and practice, news writing and reporting, web journalism and innovation, applied research in content management. *Unit head:* Prof. Stephen Masiclat, Co-Director, 315-443-9243. *Application contact:* Martha Coria, Graduate Programs Office, 315-443-4039, Fax: 315-443-1834, E-mail: pcgrad@syr.edu. Website: http://newhouse.syr.edu/

**Temple University,** School of Media and Communication, Department of Journalism, Philadelphia, PA 19122-6096. Offers MJ. *Program availability:* Part-time, evening/

weekend. *Degree requirements:* For master's, comprehensive exam, written exam. *Entrance requirements:* For master's, GRE General Test, minimum GPA of 3.0. Additional exam requirements/recommendations for international students: Required—TOEFL (minimum score 620 paper-based; 105 iBT). Electronic applications accepted. *Expenses:* Contact institution. *Faculty research:* Journalism history, advertising research, media law, media institutions.

**Université Laval,** Faculty of Letters, Department of Information and Communication, Program in International Journalism, Québec, QC G1K 7P4, Canada. Offers Diploma. Offered jointly with École Supérieure De Journalisme De Lille (France). *Entrance requirements:* For degree, English exam, French exam, test on international current events, interview, knowledge of French, knowledge of English. Electronic applications accepted.

**The University of Alabama,** Graduate School, College of Communication and Information Sciences, Department of Journalism and Creative Media, Tuscaloosa, AL 35487-0172. Offers journalism and creative media (MA). *Program availability:* Part-time, evening/weekend, 100% online. *Faculty:* 6 full-time (2 women). *Students:* 16 full-time (9 women), 4 part-time (1 woman); includes 2 minority (both Black or African American, non-Hispanic/Latino), 1 international. Average age 27. 25 applicants, 56% accepted, 11 enrolled. In 2016, 10 master's awarded. Terminal master's awarded for partial completion of doctoral program. *Degree requirements:* For master's, comprehensive exam (for some programs), thesis (for some programs). *Entrance requirements:* For master's, GRE (minimum score of 300, minimum Writing score of 4.5), minimum GPA of 3.0. Additional exam requirements/recommendations for international students: Required—TOEFL (minimum score 550 paper-based; 79 iBT). *Application deadline:* For fall admission, 3/31 priority date for domestic students, 1/15 priority date for international students; for spring admission, 11/1 priority date for domestic students, 9/15 priority date for international students. Applications are processed on a rolling basis. Application fee: $50 ($60 for international students). Electronic applications accepted. *Expenses:* Tuition, state resident: full-time $10,470. Tuition, nonresident: full-time $26,950. *Financial support:* Application deadline: 3/15; applicants required to submit FAFSA. *Faculty research:* Journalistic processes, practices and ethics, media effects, media sociology, history, law. *Unit head:* Dr. Cory Armstrong, Department Chair, 205-348-9684, Fax: 205-348-9684, E-mail: cory.i.armstrong@ua.edu. *Application contact:* Dr. Chris Roberts, Graduate Coordinator, 205-348-8619, Fax: 205-348-9684, E-mail: croberts@ua.edu.
Website: http://www.jcm.ua.edu/

**The University of Arizona,** College of Social and Behavioral Sciences, School of Journalism, Tucson, AZ 85721. Offers international journalism studies (MA); professional journalism (MA). *Program availability:* Part-time. *Degree requirements:* For master's, project. *Entrance requirements:* For master's, GRE, minimum GPA of 3.0. Additional exam requirements/recommendations for international students: Required—TOEFL. Electronic applications accepted. *Faculty research:* Press law, military censorship, Latin American press, media and minorities, reporting public affairs.

**University of Arkansas,** Graduate School, J. William Fulbright College of Arts and Sciences, Department of Journalism, Fayetteville, AR 72701. Offers MA. In 2016, 4 master's awarded. Application fee: $40 ($50 for international students). *Financial support:* In 2016–17, 4 research assistantships, 3 teaching assistantships were awarded; fellowships with tuition reimbursements, career-related internships or fieldwork, and Federal Work-Study also available. Support available to part-time students. Financial award application deadline: 4/1; financial award applicants required to submit FAFSA. *Unit head:* Dr. Larry Foley, Departmental Chairperson, 479-575-3601, Fax: 479-575-4314, E-mail: lfoley@uark.edu. *Application contact:* Dr. Patsy Watkins, Graduate Coordinator, 479-575-5964, Fax: 479-575-4314, E-mail: pwatkins@uark.edu. Website: http://journalism.uark.edu/index.php

**The University of British Columbia,** Faculty of Arts and Faculty of Graduate Studies, School of Journalism, Vancouver, BC V6T 1Z2, Canada. Offers MJ. *Degree requirements:* For master's, thesis, 3-month internship. *Entrance requirements:* For master's, portfolio, resume, letters of reference. Additional exam requirements/recommendations for international students: Required—TOEFL, IELTS. Application fee: $100 Canadian dollars ($162 Canadian dollars for international students). Electronic applications accepted. *Expenses:* $7,032 per year tuition and fees, $22,669 per year international. *Financial support:* Fellowships, research assistantships, and teaching assistantships available. *Faculty research:* New media, media coverage, journalistic ethics, international journalism, multimedia. *Application contact:* Andrea Yan, Graduate Program Staff, 604-822-6688, Fax: 604-822-6707, E-mail: jrnl.journal@ubc.ca. Website: http://www.journalism.ubc.ca/

**University of California, Berkeley,** Graduate Division, Graduate School of Journalism, Berkeley, CA 94720-1500. Offers MJ, JD/MJ, MJ/MA. *Students:* 105 full-time (69 women); includes 32 minority (9 Black or African American, non-Hispanic/Latino; 4 American Indian or Alaska Native, non-Hispanic/Latino; 9 Asian, non-Hispanic/Latino; 10 Hispanic/Latino), 14 international. Average age 29. 315 applicants, 53 enrolled. In 2016, 68 master's awarded. *Degree requirements:* For master's, project. *Entrance requirements:* For master's, GRE General Test, 3 work samples, minimum GPA of 3.0, 3 letters of recommendation. Additional exam requirements/recommendations for international students: Required—TOEFL (minimum score 600 paper-based). *Application deadline:* For fall admission, 12/1 for domestic students. Application fee: $105 ($125 for international students). Electronic applications accepted. *Financial support:* Fellowships, research assistantships, career-related internships or fieldwork, Federal Work-Study, institutionally sponsored loans, scholarships/grants, tuition waivers (full and partial), and unspecified assistantships available. Financial award applicants required to submit FAFSA. *Faculty research:* Documentary, new media, print (newspaper and magazine), broadcast (television and radio), photography. *Unit head:* Edward Wasserman, Dean, 510-642-3383. *Application contact:* Information Contact, 510-642-7928, E-mail: applysoj@journalism.berkeley.edu. Website: http://www.journalism.berkeley.edu/

**University of Colorado Boulder,** Graduate School, College of Media, Communication and Information, Program in Journalism, Boulder, CO 80309. Offers journalism (MA); media research and practice (PhD). *Accreditation:* ACEJMC. *Faculty:* 9 full-time (4 women). *Students:* 27 full-time (19 women), 3 part-time (2 women); includes 4 minority (2 Asian, non-Hispanic/Latino; 2 Hispanic/Latino), 1 international. Average age 31. 42 applicants, 93% accepted, 15 enrolled. In 2016, 13 master's awarded. *Application deadline:* For fall admission, 1/1 for domestic students, 12/1 for international students. Application fee: $60 ($80 for international students). Electronic applications accepted. Application fee is waived when completed online. *Financial support:* In 2016–17, 50 students received support, including 10 fellowships (averaging $1,646 per year), 7 research assistantships with full and partial tuition reimbursements available (averaging $19,640 per year), 14 teaching assistantships with full and partial tuition reimbursements available (averaging $18,937 per year); institutionally sponsored loans, scholarships/grants, health care benefits, and unspecified assistantships also available. Financial award application deadline: 2/1; financial award applicants required to submit FAFSA. *Faculty research:* Journalism, mass communication/media, print media, American history, media arts. *Application contact:* E-mail: paul.voakes@colorado.edu. Website: http://www.colorado.edu/cmci/academics/journalism

**University of Florida,** Graduate School, College of Journalism and Communications, Program in Mass Communication, Gainesville, FL 32611. Offers international/intercultural communication (MAMC); journalism (MAMC); mass communication (MAMC, PhD), including clinical translational science (MAMC); public relations (MAMC); science/health communication (MAMC); telecommunication (MAMC). *Accreditation:* ACEJMC. *Entrance requirements:* For master's and doctorate, GRE General Test, minimum GPA of 3.0.

**University of Georgia,** Grady College of Journalism and Mass Communication, Athens, GA 30602. Offers journalism and mass communication (MA); mass communication (PhD). *Degree requirements:* For master's, comprehensive exam, thesis (MA); for doctorate, comprehensive exam, thesis/dissertation. *Entrance requirements:* For master's and doctorate, GRE General Test. Additional exam requirements/recommendations for international students: Required—TOEFL, TWE for PhD. *Application deadline:* For spring admission, 2/15 for domestic students. Application fee: $50. Electronic applications accepted. *Financial support:* Research assistantships, teaching assistantships, tuition waivers (full), and unspecified assistantships available. *Unit head:* Dr. E. Culpepper Clark, Dean, 706-542-1704, Fax: 706-542-2183, E-mail: cully@uga.edu. *Application contact:* Dr. Jeffrey K. Springston, Associate Dean, 706-542-7833, Fax: 706-542-2183, E-mail: jspring@grady.uga.edu. Website: http://www.grady.uga.edu/

**University of Illinois at Springfield,** Graduate Programs, College of Public Affairs and Administration, Public Affairs Reporting Program, Springfield, IL 62703-5407. Offers MA. *Program availability:* Part-time, evening/weekend. *Faculty:* 1 full-time (0 women). *Students:* 12 full-time (8 women); includes 7 minority (2 Black or African American, non-Hispanic/Latino; 5 Hispanic/Latino). Average age 25. 21 applicants, 62% accepted, 12 enrolled. In 2016, 14 master's awarded. *Degree requirements:* For master's, internship, professional portfolio. *Entrance requirements:* For master's, literacy/competency writing test, interview, written work sample, narrative statement on qualifications and interest in program, 3 letters of reference. Additional exam requirements/recommendations for international students: Required—TOEFL (minimum score 500 paper-based; 61 iBT). *Application deadline:* Applications are processed on a rolling basis. Application fee: $60 ($75 for international students). Electronic applications accepted. *Expenses:* Tuition, state resident: part-time $329 per credit hour. Tuition, nonresident: part-time $675 per credit hour. *Financial support:* In 2016–17, fellowships with full tuition reimbursements (averaging $9,900 per year), research assistantships with full tuition reimbursements (averaging $9,991 per year), teaching assistantships with full tuition reimbursements (averaging $10,059 per year) were awarded; career-related internships or fieldwork, Federal Work-Study, scholarships/grants, health care benefits, and unspecified assistantships also available. Support available to part-time students. Financial award application deadline: 11/15; financial award applicants required to submit FAFSA. *Unit head:* Dr. Charles Wheeler, Director, 217-206-6535, Fax: 217-206-7807, E-mail: cwhee1@uis.edu. *Application contact:* Dr. Cecelia Cornell, Associate Vice Chancellor for Graduate Education, 217-206-7230, E-mail: ccorn1@uis.edu. Website: http://www.uis.edu/publicaffairsreporting/

**University of Illinois at Urbana–Champaign,** Graduate College, College of Media, Department of Journalism, Champaign, IL 61820. Offers MS, MS/JD, MS/MBA.

**The University of Iowa,** Graduate College, College of Liberal Arts and Sciences, School of Journalism and Mass Communication, Iowa City, IA 52242-1316. Offers journalism and media communication (MA); mass communication (PhD); strategic communication (MA); JD/MA; JD/PhD. *Degree requirements:* For master's, thesis optional, exam; for doctorate, comprehensive exam, thesis/dissertation. *Entrance requirements:* For master's and doctorate, GRE General Test, minimum GPA of 3.0. Additional exam requirements/recommendations for international students: Required—TOEFL (minimum score 637 paper-based; 110 iBT). Electronic applications accepted. *Faculty research:* Verbal and visual aspects of historical, legal, social, and cross-cultural communication.

**The University of Kansas,** Graduate Studies, William Allen White School of Journalism and Mass Communications, Lawrence, KS 66045. Offers journalism (MS); journalism and mass communications (PhD); JD/MS. *Accreditation:* ACEJMC. *Program availability:* Part-time. *Students:* 29 full-time (21 women), 55 part-time (43 women); includes 17 minority (6 Black or African American, non-Hispanic/Latino; 1 American Indian or Alaska Native, non-Hispanic/Latino; 2 Asian, non-Hispanic/Latino; 1 Hispanic/Latino; 1 Native Hawaiian or other Pacific Islander, non-Hispanic/Latino; 6 Two or more races, non-Hispanic/Latino), 7 international. Average age 33. 74 applicants, 81% accepted, 46 enrolled. In 2016, 16 master's, 1 doctorate awarded. Terminal master's awarded for partial completion of doctoral program. *Entrance requirements:* For master's and doctorate, GRE, minimum GPA of 3.0; official transcript; current resume; two writing samples, preferably academic, or samples of professional work that reflect years of experience; statement of academic interests and professional goals; three letters of reference. Additional exam requirements/recommendations for international students: Required—TOEFL or IELTS. *Application deadline:* For fall admission, 1/1 priority date for domestic and international students; for spring admission, 11/1 for domestic and international students. Application fee: $65 ($85 for international students). Electronic applications accepted. *Financial support:* Fellowships, research assistantships, teaching assistantships, career-related internships or fieldwork, scholarships/grants, and unspecified assistantships available. Support available to part-time students. Financial award application deadline: 2/1; financial award applicants required to submit FAFSA. *Faculty research:* Advertising, creativity, public relations, integrated marketing communication; media economics, online journalism; new media, visual communication; health communication, sports communication; political journalism, press law. *Unit head:* Ann Brill, Dean, 785-864-4755, E-mail: abrill@ku.edu. *Application contact:* Jammie A. Johnson, Graduate Advisor/Administrative Assistant, 785-864-7649, E-mail: jamjohn@ku.edu.
Website: http://www.journalism.ku.edu/

**University of King's College,** Graduate and Advanced Programs, Halifax, NS B3H 2A1, Canada. Offers creative nonfiction (MFA); journalism (MJ).

**University of Maryland, College Park,** Academic Affairs, Phillip Merrill College of Journalism, College Park, MD 20742. Offers broadcast journalism (MA); journalism (MA); journalism and media studies (PhD); online news (MA); public affairs reporting (MA). *Accreditation:* ACEJMC (one or more programs are accredited). *Program availability:* Part-time, evening/weekend. *Degree requirements:* For doctorate, thesis/dissertation, preliminary written and oral comprehensive exams. *Entrance requirements:* For master's and doctorate, GRE General Test, minimum GPA of 3.0, 3 letters of recommendation. Additional exam requirements/recommendations for international students: Required—TOEFL. Electronic applications accepted. *Faculty research:* Mass communication theory, specialized journalism, new telecommunication technologies, press integration.

**University of Memphis,** Graduate School, College of Communication and Fine Arts, Department of Journalism and Strategic Media, Memphis, TN 38152. Offers entrepreneurial journalism (Graduate Certificate); journalism and strategic media (MA). *Program availability:* Part-time, evening/weekend, online learning. *Faculty:* 8 full-time (4 women), 1 (woman) part-time/adjunct. *Students:* 13 full-time (8 women), 18 part-time (10

women); includes 12 minority (8 Black or African American, non-Hispanic/Latino; 1 Hispanic/Latino; 3 Two or more races, non-Hispanic/Latino). Average age 33. 21 applicants, 86% accepted, 9 enrolled. In 2016, 19 master's, 2 other advanced degrees awarded. *Degree requirements:* For master's, comprehensive exam, thesis (for some programs), culminating experience: project, thesis, or referred paper. *Entrance requirements:* For master's, GRE General Test, MAT, transcripts, resume, goal statement. Additional exam requirements/recommendations for international students: Required—TOEFL (minimum score 600 paper-based). *Application deadline:* For fall admission, 6/1 for domestic and international students; for spring admission, 10/1 for domestic and international students; for summer admission, 2/1 for domestic and international students. Applications are processed on a rolling basis. Application fee: $35 ($60 for international students). Electronic applications accepted. *Expenses:* $5,231.50 per semester full-time in-state, $9,623.50 full-time out-of-state. *Financial support:* In 2016–17, 25 students received support, including 7 research assistantships with full tuition reimbursements available (averaging $12,400 per year); Federal Work-Study, scholarships/grants, and unspecified assistantships also available. Support available to part-time students. Financial award application deadline: 2/1; financial award applicants required to submit FAFSA. *Faculty research:* Spirit of libel law, statistical software packages, college yearbooks, computer-assisted grammar project, newspaper in education. *Unit head:* Dr. David Arant, Chair, 901-678-2401, Fax: 901-678-4287, E-mail: darant@memphis.edu. *Application contact:* Dr. Thomas Hrach, Coordinator of Graduate Studies, 901-678-4779, Fax: 901-678-4287, E-mail: thrach@memphis.edu.
Website: http://www.memphis.edu/jrsm/

**University of Miami,** Graduate School, School of Communication, Coral Gables, FL 33124. Offers communication (PhD); communication studies (MA); film studies (MA, PhD); motion pictures (MFA), including production, producing, and screenwriting; print journalism (MA); public relations (MA); Spanish language journalism (MA); television broadcast journalism (MA). *Program availability:* Part-time. *Degree requirements:* For master's, comprehensive exam (for some programs), thesis (for some programs); for doctorate, comprehensive exam, thesis/dissertation. *Entrance requirements:* For master's, GRE General Test; for doctorate, GRE General Test, master's thesis or scholarly research. Additional exam requirements/recommendations for international students: Required—TOEFL (minimum score 600 paper-based; 100 iBT). Electronic applications accepted. *Faculty research:* Communication studies, mass communication, international/interpersonal communication, film studies, journalism.

**University of Mississippi,** Graduate School, Meek School of Journalism and New Media, University, MS 38677. Offers journalism (MA). *Faculty:* 28 full-time (14 women), 21 part-time/adjunct (13 women). *Students:* 47 full-time (21 women), 15 part-time (4 women); includes 16 minority (10 Black or African American, non-Hispanic/Latino; 1 Asian, non-Hispanic/Latino; 2 Hispanic/Latino; 1 Native Hawaiian or other Pacific Islander, non-Hispanic/Latino; 2 Two or more races, non-Hispanic/Latino), 6 international. Average age 24. In 2016, 11 master's awarded. *Degree requirements:* For master's, thesis. Application fee: $40. *Unit head:* Dr. Will Norton, Jr., Dean, 662-915-7146, Fax: 662-915-7765, E-mail: meekschool@olemiss.edu. *Application contact:* Dr. Christy M. Wyandt, Associate Dean, 662-915-7474, Fax: 662-915-7577, E-mail: cwyandt@olemiss.edu.
Website: http://meek.olemiss.edu/

**University of Missouri,** Office of Research and Graduate Studies, School of Journalism, Columbia, MO 65211. Offers health communications (MA); journalism (PhD). *Accreditation:* ACEJMC (one or more programs are accredited). *Program availability:* Part-time. *Faculty:* 72 full-time (34 women), 3 part-time/adjunct (0 women). *Students:* 134 full-time (97 women), 76 part-time (50 women); includes 29 minority (6 Black or African American, non-Hispanic/Latino; 5 Asian, non-Hispanic/Latino; 12 Hispanic/Latino; 6 Two or more races, non-Hispanic/Latino), 50 international. Average age 29. Terminal master's awarded for partial completion of doctoral program. *Degree requirements:* For master's, thesis (for some programs); for doctorate, 2 foreign languages, thesis/dissertation. *Entrance requirements:* For master's and doctorate, GRE General Test, minimum GPA of 3.0. Additional exam requirements/recommendations for international students: Required—TOEFL (minimum score 600 paper-based; 100 iBT), IELTS (minimum score 7). *Application deadline:* For fall admission, 12/15 priority date for domestic and international students; for winter admission, 9/1 priority date for domestic and international students. Applications are processed on a rolling basis. Application fee: $75 ($90 for international students). Electronic applications accepted. *Expenses:* Tuition, state resident: full-time $6347; part-time $352.60 per credit hour. Tuition, nonresident: full-time $17,379; part-time $965.50 per credit hour. *Required fees:* $1035. Tuition and fees vary according to course load, campus/location and program. *Financial support:* Fellowships with tuition reimbursements, research assistantships with tuition reimbursements, teaching assistantships with tuition reimbursements, career-related internships or fieldwork, institutionally sponsored loans, scholarships/grants, health care benefits, and unspecified assistantships available. Support available to part-time students.
Website: http://www.journalism.missouri.edu/graduate/

**University of Montana,** Graduate School, School of Journalism, Missoula, MT 59812-0002. Offers MA. *Degree requirements:* For master's, thesis or alternative, professional project. *Entrance requirements:* For master's, GRE. Additional exam requirements/recommendations for international students: Required—TOEFL (minimum score 580 paper-based). Electronic applications accepted. *Faculty research:* Native American issues, natural resources, public affairs, economy, photojournalism, multimedia, media law.

**University of Nebraska–Lincoln,** Graduate College, College of Journalism and Mass Communications, Lincoln, NE 68588. Offers marketing, communication and advertising (MA); professional journalism (MA). *Program availability:* Online learning. *Degree requirements:* For master's, thesis. *Entrance requirements:* For master's, samples of work. Additional exam requirements/recommendations for international students: Required—TOEFL (minimum score 600 paper-based). Electronic applications accepted. *Faculty research:* Interactive media and the Internet, community newspapers, children's radio, advertising involvement, telecommunications policy.

**University of Nevada, Las Vegas,** Graduate College, Greenspun College of Urban Affairs, Hank Greenspun School of Journalism and Media Studies, Las Vegas, NV 89154-5007. Offers MA. *Program availability:* Part-time. *Faculty:* 5 full-time (0 women). *Students:* 6 full-time (5 women), 2 part-time (1 woman); includes 4 minority (2 Black or African American, non-Hispanic/Latino; 1 Hispanic/Latino; 1 Two or more races, non-Hispanic/Latino), 2 international. Average age 28. 10 applicants, 70% accepted, 4 enrolled. In 2016, 6 master's awarded. *Degree requirements:* For master's, comprehensive exam, thesis optional, oral exam. *Entrance requirements:* For master's, GRE General Test, bachelor's degree with minimum GPA 3.0; 3 letters of recommendation; statement of purpose; writing sample. Additional exam requirements/recommendations for international students: Required—TOEFL (minimum score 550 paper-based; 80 iBT), IELTS (minimum score 7). *Application deadline:* For fall admission, 3/15 for domestic students. Application fee: $60 ($95 for international students). Electronic applications accepted. *Expenses:* $269.25 per credit, $792 per 3-credit course; $9,634 per year resident; $23,274 per year non-resident; $7,094 fees non-

resident (7 credits or more); $1,307 annual health insurance fee. *Financial support:* In 2016–17, 6 teaching assistantships with partial tuition reimbursements (averaging $10,000 per year) were awarded; institutionally sponsored loans, scholarships/grants, health care benefits, and unspecified assistantships also available. Financial award application deadline: 3/15. *Faculty research:* Journalism, mass communication and media history; media law, First Amendment theory, First Amendment law, privacy, obscenity, libel; visual literacy, aesthetics and rhetoric, social psychology of visually-mediated world; global media, audience reception theory and research, video criticism, and advertising; intersection of society and media technologies, emerging technology. *Unit head:* Dr. Joel Lieberman, Interim Director/Professor, 702-895-0249, Fax: 702-895-0252, E-mail: joel.lieberman@unlv.edu. *Application contact:* Dr. Julian Kilker, Graduate Coordinator, 702-895-3729, Fax: 702-895-5189, E-mail: julian.kilker@unlv.edu.
Website: http://journalism.unlv.edu/

**University of Nevada, Reno,** Graduate School, Donald W. Reynolds School of Journalism, Reno, NV 89557. Offers MA. *Degree requirements:* For master's, thesis. *Entrance requirements:* For master's, GRE General Test, minimum GPA of 2.75. Additional exam requirements/recommendations for international students: Required—TOEFL (minimum score 500 paper-based; 61 iBT), IELTS (minimum score 6). Electronic applications accepted. *Faculty research:* Interactive environmental journalism.

**University of North Texas,** Robert B. Toulouse School of Graduate Studies, Denton, TX 76203-5459. Offers accounting (MS); applied anthropology (MA, MS); applied behavior analysis (Certificate); applied geography (MA); applied technology and performance improvement (M Ed, MS); art education (MA); art history (MA); art museum education (Certificate); arts leadership (Certificate); audiology (Au D); behavior analysis (MS); behavioral science (PhD); biochemistry and molecular biology (MS); biology (MA, MS); biomedical engineering (MS); business analysis (MS); chemistry (MS); clinical health psychology (PhD); communication studies (MA, MS); computer engineering (MS); computer science (MS); counseling (M Ed, MS), including clinical mental health counseling (MS), college and university counseling, elementary school counseling, secondary school counseling; creative writing (MA); criminal justice (MS); curriculum and instruction (M Ed); decision sciences (MBA); design (MA, MFA), including fashion design (MFA), innovation studies, interior design (MFA); early childhood studies (MS); economics (MS); educational leadership (M Ed, Ed D); educational psychology (MS, PhD), including family studies (MS), gifted and talented (MS), human development (MS), learning and cognition (MS), research, measurement and evaluation (MS); electrical engineering (MS); emergency management (MPA); engineering technology (MS); English (MA); English as a second language (MA); environmental science (MS); finance (MBA, MS); financial management (MPA); French (MA); health services management (MBA); higher education (M Ed, Ed D); history (MA, MS); hospitality management (MS); human resources management (MPA); information science (MS); information systems (PhD); information technologies (MBA); interdisciplinary studies (MA, MS); international studies (MA); international sustainable tourism (MS); jazz studies (MM); journalism (MA, MJ, Graduate Certificate), including interactive and virtual digital communication (Graduate Certificate), narrative journalism (Graduate Certificate), public relations (Graduate Certificate); kinesiology (MS); linguistics (MA); local government management (MPA); logistics (PhD); logistics and supply chain management (MBA); long-term care, senior housing, and aging services (MA); management (PhD); marketing (MBA); mathematics (MA, MS); mechanical and energy engineering (MS, PhD); music (MA), including ethnomusicology, music theory, musicology, performance; music composition (PhD); music education (MM Ed, PhD); nonprofit management (MPA); operations and supply chain management (MBA); performance (MM, DMA); philosophy (MA); political science (MA); professional and technical communication (MA); radio, television and film (MA, MFA); rehabilitation counseling (Certificate); sociology (MA); Spanish (MA); special education (M Ed); speech-language pathology (MS); strategic management (MBA); studio art (MFA); teaching (M Ed); MBA/MS. *Program availability:* Part-time, evening/weekend, online learning. Terminal master's awarded for partial completion of doctoral program. *Degree requirements:* For master's, variable foreign language requirement, comprehensive exam (for some programs), thesis (for some programs); for doctorate, variable foreign language requirement, comprehensive exam (for some programs), thesis/dissertation; for other advanced degree, variable foreign language requirement, comprehensive exam (for some programs). *Entrance requirements:* For master's and doctorate, GRE, GMAT. Additional exam requirements/recommendations for international students: Required—TOEFL (minimum score 550 paper-based; 79 iBT). Electronic applications accepted.

**University of Oklahoma,** Gaylord College of Journalism and Mass Communication, Program in Journalism and Mass Communication, Norman, OK 73019. Offers MA, PhD. *Program availability:* Part-time. *Students:* 32 full-time (19 women), 15 part-time (7 women); includes 7 minority (2 Black or African American, non-Hispanic/Latino; 1 Asian, non-Hispanic/Latino; 2 Hispanic/Latino; 2 Two or more races, non-Hispanic/Latino), 21 international. Average age 33. 20 applicants, 50% accepted, 9 enrolled. In 2016, 8 master's, 2 doctorates awarded. *Degree requirements:* For master's, comprehensive exam (for some programs), thesis (for some programs); for doctorate, comprehensive exam, thesis/dissertation. *Entrance requirements:* For master's, GRE, resume, statement of purpose, two letters of recommendation, official transcript; for doctorate, GRE, resume, statement of purpose, three letters of recommendation, official transcript. Additional exam requirements/recommendations for international students: Required—TOEFL (minimum score 79 iBT) or IELTS (minimum score 6.5). *Application deadline:* For fall admission, 5/1 for domestic students, 3/1 for international students; for spring admission, 11/1 for domestic students, 10/1 for international students; for summer admission, 3/1 for domestic students. Applications are processed on a rolling basis. Application fee: $50 ($100 for international students). Electronic applications accepted. *Expenses:* Tuition, state resident: full-time $4886; part-time $203.60 per credit hour. Tuition, nonresident: full-time $18,989; part-time $791.20 per credit hour. *Required fees:* $3283; $126.25 per credit hour. $126.50 per semester. *Financial support:* In 2016–17, 33 students received support. Fellowships, research assistantships with full tuition reimbursements available, teaching assistantships with full tuition reimbursements available, career-related internships or fieldwork, scholarships/grants, health care benefits, unspecified assistantships, and research and research travel awards available. Financial award application deadline: 6/1; financial award applicants required to submit FAFSA. *Faculty research:* Strategic communication: global public relations, corporate and nonprofit public relations, interactive advertising, message testing; creative media production: documentary, entertainment TV, commercial production; journalism: multimedia journalism, broadcasting, online; media management. *Unit head:* Dr. Katerina Tsetsura, Director of Graduate Studies/Professor of Strategic Communication, 405-325-2722, Fax: 405-325-7565, E-mail: gaylordgrad@ou.edu. *Application contact:* Larry Laneer, Graduate Advisor, 405-325-2722, Fax: 405-325-7565,
E-mail: llaneer@ou.edu. Website: http://www.ou.edu/content/gaylord/graduate.html

**University of Oregon,** Graduate School, School of Journalism and Communication, Eugene, OR 97403. Offers journalism (MA, MS); media studies (MA, MS, PhD); multimedia journalism (MA, MS); strategic communication (MA, MS). *Accreditation:* ASHA. *Program availability:* Part-time. *Degree requirements:* For master's, thesis or alternative. *Entrance requirements:* For master's, GRE General Test; for doctorate, master's degree. *Faculty research:* Impact of mass communication, media technology, media accountability, craft attitudes, media economics.

## Journalism

**University of Puerto Rico, Río Piedras Campus,** School of Communication, Program in Journalism, San Juan, PR 00931-3300. Offers MA.

**University of Regina,** Faculty of Graduate Studies and Research, Faculty of Arts, School of Journalism, Regina, SK S4S 0A2, Canada. Offers MJ. *Program availability:* Part-time. *Faculty:* 5 full-time (2 women). *Students:* 7 full-time (6 women), 1 (woman) part-time. 19 applicants, 26% accepted. In 2016, 4 master's awarded. *Degree requirements:* For master's, project. *Entrance requirements:* For master's, written project concept; statement of interest; statement of ability. Additional exam requirements/recommendations for international students: Required—TOEFL (minimum score 580 paper-based; 80 iBT), IELTS (minimum score 6.5), PTE (minimum score 59). *Application deadline:* For fall admission, 1/15 for domestic and international students. Application fee: $100. Electronic applications accepted. Financial support: In 2016–17, 2 fellowships (averaging $6,000 per year), 2 teaching assistantships (averaging $2,501 per year) were awarded; scholarships/grants also available. Financial award application deadline: 6/15. *Unit head:* Dr. Gennadiy Chernov, Department Head, 306-585-4090, Fax: 306-585-4867, E-mail: gennadiy.chernov@uregina.ca. *Application contact:* Patricia Elliot, Graduate Program Coordinator, 306-585-4449, Fax: 306-585-4867, E-mail: patricia.elliott@uregina.ca.
Website: http://www.uregina.ca/arts/journalism/

**University of South Carolina,** The Graduate School, College of Mass Communications and Information Studies, School of Journalism and Mass Communications, Columbia, SC 29208. Offers MA, MMC, PhD. *Accreditation:* ACEJMC. *Program availability:* Part-time. *Degree requirements:* For master's, comprehensive exam, thesis (for some programs); for doctorate, one foreign language, comprehensive exam, thesis/dissertation. *Entrance requirements:* For master's and doctorate, GRE General Test, minimum GPA of 3.0. Additional exam requirements/recommendations for international students: Required—TOEFL (minimum score 600 paper-based; 75 iBT). Electronic applications accepted. *Faculty research:* Ethics, communications law, international communications, science/health/environmental/risk communications, convergent media.

**University of Southern California,** Graduate School, Annenberg School for Communication and Journalism, School of Journalism, Program in Journalism, Los Angeles, CA 90089. Offers MS. Program enrolls new students to Summer term only. *Accreditation:* ACEJMC. *Program availability:* Part-time. *Students:* 33 full-time (27 women); includes 9 minority (3 Black or African American, non-Hispanic/Latino; 2 Asian, non-Hispanic/Latino; 4 Hispanic/Latino), 6 international. Average age 25. 127 applicants, 61% accepted, 34 enrolled. In 2016, 36 master's awarded. *Degree requirements:* For master's, professional project. *Entrance requirements:* For master's, GRE General Test, resume, writing samples, letters of recommendation, statement of purpose. Additional exam requirements/recommendations for international students: Required—TOEFL (minimum score 114 iBT), IELTS (minimum score 8). *Application deadline:* For summer admission, 1/1 priority date for domestic and international students. Application fee: $90. Electronic applications accepted. *Financial support:* In 2016–17, 25 fellowships with full and partial tuition reimbursements (averaging $30,000 per year), 4 teaching assistantships with full and partial tuition reimbursements (averaging $20,000 per year) were awarded; career-related internships or fieldwork, Federal Work-Study, institutionally sponsored loans, scholarships/grants, health care benefits, and unspecified assistantships also available. Support available to part-time students. Financial award application deadline: 1/1; financial award applicants required to submit FAFSA. *Unit head:* Willow Bay, Director, 213-740-3914, Fax: 213-740-8624, E-mail: jourbks@usc.edu. *Application contact:* Allyson Hill, Associate Dean for Admissions, 213-821-0770, Fax: 213-740-1933, E-mail: ascadm@usc.edu.
Website: http://www.annenberg.usc.edu

**University of Southern California,** Graduate School, Annenberg School for Communication and Journalism, School of Journalism, Program in Specialized Journalism, Los Angeles, CA 90089. Offers specialized journalism (MA); specialized journalism (the arts) (MA). Program enrolls new students to Summer term only. *Accreditation:* ACEJMC. *Program availability:* Part-time. *Students:* 35 full-time (28 women); includes 15 minority (4 Black or African American, non-Hispanic/Latino; 3 Asian, non-Hispanic/Latino; 5 Hispanic/Latino; 3 Two or more races, non-Hispanic/Latino), 8 international. Average age 35. 65 applicants, 75% accepted, 21 enrolled. In 2016, 24 master's awarded. *Degree requirements:* For master's, thesis or alternative, professional project. *Entrance requirements:* For master's, GRE General Test, resume, portfolio of professional work, letters of recommendation, statement of purpose. Additional exam requirements/recommendations for international students: Required—TOEFL (minimum score 114 iBT), IELTS (minimum score 8). *Application deadline:* For summer admission, 1/31 priority date for domestic and international students. Applications are processed on a rolling basis. Application fee: $90. Electronic applications accepted. *Financial support:* In 2016–17, 4 fellowships with full and partial tuition reimbursements (averaging $60,000 per year) were awarded; research assistantships, Federal Work-Study, scholarships/grants, and health care benefits also available. Support available to part-time students. Financial award application deadline: 1/1; financial award applicants required to submit FAFSA. *Unit head:* Willow Bay, Director, 213-743-5324. *Application contact:* Allyson Hill, Associate Dean for Admissions, 213-821-0770, Fax: 213-740-1933, E-mail: ascadm@usc.edu.

**University of South Florida,** College of Arts and Sciences, School of Mass Communications, Tampa, FL 33620-9951. Offers mass communications (MA), including media studies, multimedia journalism, strategic communication management. *Program availability:* Part-time, evening/weekend. *Faculty:* 11 full-time (6 women). *Students:* 27 full-time (23 women), 18 part-time (10 women); includes 5 minority (2 Black or African American, non-Hispanic/Latino; 2 Hispanic/Latino; 1 Native Hawaiian or other Pacific Islander, non-Hispanic/Latino), 25 international. Average age 27. 39 applicants, 82% accepted, 21 enrolled. In 2016, 16 master's awarded. *Degree requirements:* For master's, comprehensive exam, thesis optional. *Entrance requirements:* For master's, GRE General Test, minimum GPA of 3.0 in last 60 hours of course work, three letters of recommendation, letter of intent, resume/curriculum vitae. Additional exam requirements/recommendations for international students: Required—TOEFL (minimum score 550 paper-based; 79 iBT) or IELTS (minimum score 6.5). *Application deadline:* For fall admission, 2/15 for domestic and international students. Application fee: $30. Electronic applications accepted. *Expenses:* Tuition, state resident: full-time $7766; part-time $431.43 per credit hour. Tuition, nonresident: full-time $15,789; part-time $877.17 per credit hour. *Required fees:* $37 per term. *Financial support:* In 2016–17, 5 students received support, including 9 teaching assistantships with tuition reimbursements available (averaging $10,513 per year); unspecified assistantships also available. Financial award application deadline: 2/28. *Faculty research:* First Amendment analysis, civic journalism, public opinion, media ethics, media effects research in sports public relations, public relations management, advertisement, telecommunications. *Total annual research expenditures:* $88,114. *Unit head:* Dr. Jim Andrews, Interim Director/Associate Professor, 813-974-2108, Fax: 813-974-2592, E-mail: jimandrews@usf.edu. *Application contact:* Dr. Michael Mitrook, Assistant Professor, 813-974-8890, Fax: 813-974-2592, E-mail: mmitrook@usf.edu.
Website: http://masscom.usf.edu/grad/

**University of South Florida,** Innovative Education, Tampa, FL 33620-9951. Offers adult, career and higher education (Graduate Certificate), including college teaching, leadership in developing human resources, leadership in higher education; Africana studies (Graduate Certificate), including diasporas and health disparities, genocide and human rights; aging studies (Graduate Certificate), including gerontology; art research (Graduate Certificate), including museum studies; business foundations (Graduate Certificate); chemical and biomedical engineering (Graduate Certificate), including materials science and engineering, water, health and sustainability; child and family studies (Graduate Certificate), including positive behavior support; civil and industrial engineering (Graduate Certificate), including transportation systems analysis; community and family health (Graduate Certificate), including maternal and child health, social marketing and public health, violence and injury: prevention and intervention, women's health; criminology (Graduate Certificate), including criminal justice administration; educational measurement and research (Graduate Certificate), including evaluation; English (Graduate Certificate), including comparative literary studies, creative writing, professional and technical communication; entrepreneurship (Graduate Certificate); environmental health (Graduate Certificate), including safety management; epidemiology and biostatistics (Graduate Certificate), including applied biostatistics, biostatistics, concepts and tools of epidemiology, epidemiology, epidemiology of infectious diseases; geography, environment and planning (Graduate Certificate), including community development, environmental policy and management, geographical information systems; geology (Graduate Certificate), including hydrogeology; global health (Graduate Certificate), including disaster management, global health and Latin American and Caribbean studies, global health practice, humanitarian assistance, infection control; government and international affairs (Graduate Certificate), including Cuban studies, globalization studies; health policy and management (Graduate Certificate), including health management and leadership, public health policy and programs; hearing specialist: early intervention (Graduate Certificate); industrial and management systems engineering (Graduate Certificate), including systems engineering, technology management; information studies (Graduate Certificate), including school library media specialist; information systems/decision sciences (Graduate Certificate), including analytics and business intelligence; instructional technology (Graduate Certificate), including distance education, Florida digital/virtual educator, instructional design, multimedia design, Web design; internal medicine, bioethics and medical humanities (Graduate Certificate), including biomedical ethics; Latin American and Caribbean studies (Graduate Certificate); mass communications (Graduate Certificate), including multimedia journalism; mathematics and statistics (Graduate Certificate), including mathematics; medicine (Graduate Certificate), including aging and neuroscience, bioinformatics, biotechnology, brain fitness and memory management, clinical investigation, health informatics, health sciences, integrative weight management, intellectual property, medicine and gender, metabolic and nutritional medicine, metabolic cardiology, pharmacy sciences; national and competitive intelligence (Graduate Certificate); psychological and social foundations (Graduate Certificate), including career counseling, college teaching, diversity in education, mental health counseling, school counseling; public affairs (Graduate Certificate), including nonprofit management, public management, research administration; public health (Graduate Certificate), including environmental health, health equity, public health generalist, translational research in adolescent behavioral health; public health practices (Graduate Certificate), including planning for healthy communities; rehabilitation and mental health counseling (Graduate Certificate), including integrative mental health care, marriage and family therapy, rehabilitation technology; secondary education (Graduate Certificate), including ESOL, foreign language education: culture and content, foreign language education: professional; social work (Graduate Certificate), including geriatric social work/clinical gerontology; special education (Graduate Certificate), including autism spectrum disorder, disabilities education: severe/profound; world languages (Graduate Certificate), including teaching English as a second language (TESL) or foreign language. *Expenses:* Tuition, state resident: full-time $7766; part-time $431.43 per credit hour. Tuition, nonresident: full-time $15,789; part-time $877.17 per credit hour. *Required fees:* $37 per term. *Unit head:* Kathy Barnes, Interdisciplinary Programs Coordinator, 813-974-8031, Fax: 813-974-7061, E-mail: barnesk@usf.edu. *Application contact:* Karen Tylinski, Metro Initiatives, 813-974-9943, Fax: 813-974-7061, E-mail: ktylinsk@usf.edu.
Website: http://www.usf.edu/innovative-education/

**University of South Florida, St. Petersburg,** College of Arts and Sciences, St. Petersburg, FL 33701. Offers digital journalism and design (MA); environmental science and policy (MA, MS); Florida studies (MLA); journalism and media studies (MA); liberal studies (MLA); psychology (MA). *Program availability:* Part-time, online learning. *Degree requirements:* For master's, comprehensive exam, thesis or project. *Entrance requirements:* For master's, GRE, LSAT, MCAT (varies by program), letter of intent, 3 letters of recommendation, writing samples, bachelor's degree from regionally-accredited institution with minimum GPA of 3.0 overall or in upper two years. Additional exam requirements/recommendations for international students: Required—TOEFL (minimum score 550 paper-based; 79 iBT); Recommended—IELTS. Electronic applications accepted.

**The University of Tennessee,** Graduate School, College of Communication and Information, Knoxville, TN 37996. Offers advertising (MS, PhD); broadcasting (MS, PhD); communications (MS, PhD); information sciences (MS, PhD); journalism (MS, PhD); public relations (MS, PhD); speech communication (MS, PhD). *Program availability:* Part-time, evening/weekend, online learning. *Degree requirements:* For master's, thesis or alternative; for doctorate, thesis/dissertation. *Entrance requirements:* For master's and doctorate, GRE General Test, minimum GPA of 2.7. Additional exam requirements/recommendations for international students: Required—TOEFL. Electronic applications accepted.

**The University of Texas at Austin,** Graduate School, College of Communication, School of Journalism, Austin, TX 78712-1111. Offers MA, PhD, MA/MA, MBA/MA, MP Aff/MA. *Program availability:* Part-time. *Degree requirements:* For master's, thesis; for doctorate, one foreign language, thesis/dissertation. *Entrance requirements:* For master's and doctorate, GRE General Test. Electronic applications accepted. *Faculty research:* Politics of race, gender, and sexuality; visual ethics; media law and ethics; national television violence study; agenda setting and public opinion.

**The University of Western Ontario,** Faculty of Graduate Studies, Faculty of Information and Media Studies, Program in Journalism, London, ON N6A 5B8, Canada. Offers MA. *Degree requirements:* For master's, internship. *Entrance requirements:* For master's, honors degree, minimum B average during previous 2 years of course work. Additional exam requirements/recommendations for international students: Required—TOEFL (minimum score 640 paper-based), TWE (minimum score 5). Electronic applications accepted.

**University of Wisconsin–Madison,** Graduate School, College of Agricultural and Life Sciences, Department of Life Sciences Communication, Madison, WI 53706-1380. Offers life sciences communication (MPS, MS); mass communications (PhD). *Program availability:* Part-time. Terminal master's awarded for partial completion of doctoral program. *Degree requirements:* For master's, thesis (for some programs); for doctorate, thesis/dissertation. *Entrance requirements:* For master's, GRE; for doctorate, GRE, master's degree in a communication field or related area of study. Additional exam requirements/recommendations for international students: Required—TOEFL.

Electronic applications accepted. *Faculty research:* Science and risk communication, new communication technologies, health communication, mass communication, political communication, history of communication, indigenous communication.

**University of Wisconsin–Madison,** Graduate School, College of Letters and Science, School of Journalism and Mass Communication, Program in Journalism and Mass Communication, Madison, WI 53706-1380. Offers MA.

**Virginia Commonwealth University,** Graduate School, College of Humanities and Sciences, School of Mass Communications, Program in Mass Communications, Richmond, VA 23284-9005. Offers multimedia journalism (MS); strategic public relations (MS). *Degree requirements:* For master's, comprehensive exam, thesis optional. *Entrance requirements:* For master's, GRE General Test. Additional exam requirements/recommendations for international students: Required—TOEFL (minimum score 600 paper-based; 100 iBT); Recommended—IELTS (minimum score 6.5). *Application deadline:* For fall admission, 3/15 for domestic students. Applications are processed on a rolling basis. Application fee: $50. Electronic applications accepted. *Financial support:* Teaching assistantships, career-related internships or fieldwork, Federal Work-Study, institutionally sponsored loans, and tuition waivers (full and partial) available. Support available to part-time students. Financial award applicants required to submit FAFSA. *Faculty research:* Multimedia journalism, strategic public relations. *Unit head:* Dr. Terry Oggel, Interim Director, School of Mass Communications, 804-828-2660, Fax: 804-828-9175, E-mail: masscomm@vcu.edu. *Application contact:* June O. Nicholson, Director of Graduate Studies, 804-827-0251, Fax: 804-828-9175, E-mail: jonichol@vcu.edu. Website: http://www.has.vcu.edu/mac/

**Wayne State University,** College of Fine, Performing and Communication Arts, Department of Communication, Detroit, MI 48202. Offers communication (PhD), including democratic participation and culture, identity and representation, media, society and culture, risk, crisis and conflict, wellness, work life and relationships; communication and new media (Graduate Certificate); communication studies (MA); dispute resolution (MADR, Graduate Certificate); health communication (Graduate Certificate); journalism (MA); media arts (MA); media studies (MA); public relations and organizational communication (MA); JD/MADR. Doctoral program admits for fall only. *Faculty:* 20. *Students:* 59 full-time (32 women), 113 part-time (75 women); includes 69 minority (54 Black or African American, non-Hispanic/Latino; 2 Asian, non-Hispanic/ Latino; 7 Hispanic/Latino; 6 Two or more races, non-Hispanic/Latino), 12 international. Average age 34. 154 applicants, 39% accepted, 41 enrolled. In 2016, 31 master's, 10 doctorates, 4 other advanced degrees awarded. *Degree requirements:* For master's, thesis (for some programs), thesis or essay; for doctorate, thesis/dissertation. *Entrance requirements:* For master's, GRE (if undergraduate GPA less than 3.2), personal statement; BA or BS in communication or related field with minimum upper-division GPA of 3.2 and minimum upper-division undergraduate GPA of 3.0, personal statement, and sample of academic writing (for MA); 3 letters of recommendation (for MADR); for doctorate, GRE, MA in communication or related field with minimum GPA of 3.5; three letters of recommendation; personal statement; sample of written scholarship. Additional exam requirements/recommendations for international students: Required—TOEFL (minimum score 600 paper-based; 100 iBT), IELTS, TWE. Application fee: $50. Electronic applications accepted. *Expenses:* $17,240 per year resident tuition and fees, $34,434 per year non-resident tuition and fees. *Financial support:* In 2016–17, 61 students received support, including 4 fellowships with tuition reimbursements available (averaging $16,000 per year), 2 research assistantships with tuition reimbursements available (averaging $19,570 per year), 21 teaching assistantships with tuition reimbursements available (averaging $17,994 per year); scholarships/grants and unspecified assistantships also available. Financial award applicants required to submit FAFSA. *Faculty research:* Rhetorical theory and criticism; mass media theory and research; argumentation; organizational communication; risk and crisis communication; interpersonal, family, and health communication. *Unit head:* Dr. Lillian Black, Professor and Chair, 313-577-2943, E-mail: eh8899@wayne.edu. *Application contact:* E-mail: communication@wayne.edu.
Website: http://comm.wayne.edu/

**West Virginia University,** Reed College of Media, Morgantown, WV 26506-6010. Offers integrated marketing communications (MS, Graduate Certificate); journalism (MSJ). *Program availability:* Part-time, online learning. *Degree requirements:* For master's, thesis or alternative. *Entrance requirements:* For master's, GRE General Test, minimum GPA of 3.0, writing samples. Additional exam requirements/recommendations for international students: Required—TOEFL (minimum score 550 paper-based). Electronic applications accepted. *Faculty research:* History, law, and women in media; press management; public opinion; advertising effectiveness; international advertising.

# Mass Communication

**American University,** School of Communication, Program in Global Media, Washington, DC 20016-8001. Offers MA. *Program availability:* Part-time. *Students:* 15 full-time (13 women), 5 part-time (4 women); includes 5 minority (2 Black or African American, non-Hispanic/Latino; 1 Asian, non-Hispanic/Latino; 1 Hispanic/Latino; 1 Two or more races, non-Hispanic/Latino), 6 international. *Degree requirements:* For master's, one foreign language, comprehensive exam, thesis or alternative. *Entrance requirements:* For master's, GRE General Test, bachelor's degree with minimum cumulative GPA of 3.3, 2 letters of reference. Additional exam requirements/recommendations for international students: Required—TOEFL (minimum score 600 paper-based; 100 iBT), IELTS (minimum score 7). *Application deadline:* For fall admission, 2/1 priority date for domestic and international students. Applications are processed on a rolling basis. Application fee: $55. Electronic applications accepted. *Expenses:* Tuition: Full-time $28,422; part-time $1579 per credit hour. *Required fees:* $690; $200 per term. Tuition and fees vary according to course load, degree level and program. *Financial support:* In 2016–17, 6 research assistantships with partial tuition reimbursements (averaging $8,000 per year) were awarded; career-related internships or fieldwork, Federal Work-Study, scholarships/grants, and unspecified assistantships also available. Financial award application deadline: 2/1; financial award applicants required to submit FAFSA. *Unit head:* Rhonda Zaharna, Program Director, 202-885-3995, Fax: 202-885-2019, E-mail: zaharna@american.edu. *Application contact:* Leila Hernandez, Assistant Director for Graduate Admissions, 202-885-2040, Fax: 202-885-2019, E-mail: crials@american.edu.

**American University,** School of Communication, Program in Strategic Communication, Washington, DC 20016-8001. Offers MA. *Accreditation:* ACEJMC. *Program availability:* Part-time, evening/weekend. *Students:* 28 full-time (25 women), 25 part-time (17 women); includes 23 minority (17 Black or African American, non-Hispanic/Latino; 2 Asian, non-Hispanic/Latino; 3 Hispanic/Latino; 1 Two or more races, non-Hispanic/Latino), 6 international. *Degree requirements:* For master's, comprehensive exam, thesis or alternative. *Entrance requirements:* Additional exam requirements/recommendations for international students: Required—TOEFL (minimum score 600 paper-based; 100 iBT), IELTS (minimum score 7). *Application deadline:* For fall admission, 2/1 priority date for domestic students, 4/1 priority date for international students. Applications are processed on a rolling basis. Application fee: $50. Electronic applications accepted. *Expenses:* Tuition: Full-time $28,422; part-time $1579 per credit hour. *Required fees:* $690; $200 per term. Tuition and fees vary according to course load, degree level and program. *Financial support:* Research assistantships with partial tuition reimbursements, teaching assistantships with partial tuition reimbursements, career-related internships or fieldwork, Federal Work-Study, institutionally sponsored loans, scholarships/grants, tuition waivers (partial), and unspecified assistantships available. Financial award application deadline: 2/1; financial award applicants required to submit FAFSA. *Faculty research:* Litigation and public relations, cross-cultural and intercultural communication, statistical public relations, African-Americans and women in public communication, international public relations. *Unit head:* Pallavi Kumar, Public Communication Division Director, 202-885-2047, E-mail: kumar@american.edu. *Application contact:* Christine Rials, Assistant Director of Graduate Admissions, 202-885-2040, Fax: 202-885-2019, E-mail: gradcomm@american.edu.
Website: http://www.american.edu/soc/communication/degrees/MA-SCOM.cfm

**American University,** School of International Service, Washington, DC 20016-8071. Offers comparative and regional studies (Certificate); cross-cultural communication (Certificate); development management (MS); ethics, peace, and global affairs (MA); European studies (Certificate); global environmental policy (MA, Certificate); global information technology (Certificate); international affairs (MA), including comparative and international disability policy, comparative and regional studies, international economic relations, international politics, natural resources and sustainable development, U.S. foreign policy; international arts management (Certificate); international communication (MA, Certificate); international development (MA); international economic policy (Certificate); international economic relations (Certificate); international economics (MA); international media (MA); international peace and conflict resolution (MA, Certificate); international politics (Certificate); international relations (MA, PhD); international service (MIS); peacebuilding (Certificate); social enterprise (MA); the Americas (Certificate); United States foreign policy (Certificate); JD/MA. *Program availability:* Part-time, evening/weekend, 100% online. *Faculty:* 116 full-time (53 women), 57 part-time/adjunct (19 women). *Students:* 575 full-time (360 women), 491 part-time (277 women); includes 287 minority (100 Black or African American, non-Hispanic/Latino; 6 American Indian or Alaska Native, non-Hispanic/Latino; 58 Asian, non-Hispanic/Latino; 92 Hispanic/Latino; 1 Native Hawaiian or other Pacific Islander, non-Hispanic/Latino; 30 Two or more races, non-Hispanic/Latino), 151 international. Average age 29. 1,504 applicants, 84% accepted, 403 enrolled. In 2016, 374 master's, 3 doctorates, 1 other advanced degree awarded. Terminal master's awarded for partial completion of doctoral program. *Degree requirements:* For master's, one foreign language, comprehensive exam, thesis or alternative; for doctorate, one foreign language, comprehensive exam, thesis/dissertation. *Entrance requirements:* For master's, GRE, GMAT or GRE (for MA in social enterprise), transcripts, resume, 2 letters of recommendation, statement of purpose; for doctorate, GRE, transcripts, resume, 3 letters of recommendation, statement of purpose. Additional exam requirements/recommendations for international students: Required—TOEFL (minimum score 600 paper-based, 100 iBT), IELTS (minimum score 7 ), or PTE (minimum score of 68). Application fee: $55. Electronic applications accepted. *Expenses:* $1,579 per credit tuition; $1,930 mandatory fees. *Financial support:* Research assistantships, teaching assistantships, institutionally sponsored loans, scholarships/grants, and unspecified assistantships available. Financial award application deadline: 1/15; financial award applicants required to submit FAFSA. *Unit head:* Dr. James Goldgeier, Dean, 202-885-1603, Fax: 202-885-2494, E-mail: goldgeier@american.edu. *Application contact:* Jia Jiang, Associate Director, Graduate Education Enrollment, 202-885-1689, Fax: 202-885-1109, E-mail: jiang@american.edu.
Website: http://www.american.edu/sis/

**The American University in Cairo,** School of Global Affairs and Public Policy, Cairo, Egypt. Offers gender and women's studies (MA); global affairs (MGA); international and comparative law (LL M); international human rights law (MA); journalism and mass communication (MA); Middle East studies (MA); migration and refugee studies (MA, Diploma); public administration (MPA); public policy (MPP); television and digital journalism (MA). *Program availability:* Part-time, evening/weekend. *Faculty:* 27 full-time (13 women), 5 part-time/adjunct (3 women). *Students:* 69 full-time (40 women), 194 part-time (134 women), 33 international. Average age 29. 322 applicants, 51% accepted, 86 enrolled. In 2016, 112 master's awarded. *Degree requirements:* For master's, comprehensive exam (for some programs), thesis (for some programs). *Entrance requirements:* Additional exam requirements/recommendations for international students: Required—TOEFL (minimum score 450 paper-based; 45 iBT), IELTS (minimum score 5). *Application deadline:* For fall admission, 2/1 for domestic and international students; for spring admission, 10/15 for domestic and international students. Applications are processed on a rolling basis. Application fee: $80. Electronic applications accepted. *Expenses:* Contact institution. *Financial support:* Fellowships with partial tuition reimbursements, scholarships/grants, and unspecified assistantships available. Financial award application deadline: 3/10. *Faculty research:* Law, media and journalism; public policy and public administration, gender studies, Middle East Studies, global affairs, refugees studies. *Unit head:* Dr. Nabil Fahmy, Dean, 20-2-2615-2671, E-mail: nfahmy@aucegypt.edu. *Application contact:* Maha Hegazi, Director for Graduate Admissions, 20-2-2615-1462, E-mail: mahahegazi@aucegypt.edu.
Website: http://www.aucegypt.edu/GAPP/Pages/default.aspx

**Arizona State University at the Tempe campus,** Walter Cronkite School of Journalism and Mass Communication, Phoenix, AZ 85004. Offers journalism and mass communication (PhD); mass communication (MMC). *Accreditation:* ACEJMC. Terminal master's awarded for partial completion of doctoral program. *Degree requirements:* For master's, 9-hour professional capstone experience; interactive Program of Study (iPOS) submitted before completing 50 percent of required credit hours; for doctorate, comprehensive exam, thesis/dissertation, interactive Program of Study (iPOS) submitted before completing 50 percent of required credit hours. *Entrance requirements:* For master's and doctorate, GRE, minimum GPA of 3.0 or equivalent in last 2 years of work leading to bachelor's degree. Additional exam requirements/recommendations for international students: Required—TOEFL, IELTS, or PTE. Electronic applications accepted. *Expenses:* Contact institution.

**Arkansas State University,** Graduate School, College of Media and Communication, Department of Media, State University, AR 72467. Offers mass communications (MSMC). *Program availability:* Part-time. *Degree requirements:* For master's, comprehensive exam, thesis or alternative. *Entrance requirements:* For master's, GRE General Test or MAT, appropriate bachelor's degree, letters of reference, educational experience, professional experience, official transcripts, immunization records. Additional exam requirements/recommendations for international students: Required—TOEFL (minimum score 550 paper-based; 79 iBT), IELTS (minimum score 6), PTE (minimum score 56). Electronic applications accepted.

**Boston University,** College of Communication, Department of Mass Communication, Advertising, and Public Relations, Boston, MA 02215. Offers advertising (MS); JD/MS. *Program availability:* Part-time. *Faculty:* 26 full-time, 33 part-time/adjunct. *Students:* 269 full-time (214 women), 11 part-time (10 women); includes 37 minority (6 Black or African American, non-Hispanic/Latino; 7 Asian, non-Hispanic/Latino; 19 Hispanic/Latino; 5 Two or more races, non-Hispanic/Latino), 173 international. Average age 24. 429 applicants, 48% accepted, 81 enrolled. In 2016, 51 master's awarded. *Degree requirements:* For master's, comprehensive exam (for some programs), thesis (for some programs). *Entrance requirements:* For master's, GRE General Test, resume, letters of recommendation. Additional exam requirements/recommendations for international students: Required—TOEFL (minimum score 600 paper-based; 100 iBT), IELTS. *Application deadline:* For fall admission, 5/1 for domestic and international students. Applications are processed on a rolling basis. Application fee: $80. Electronic applications accepted. *Financial support:* Research assistantships, teaching assistantships with partial tuition reimbursements, career-related internships or fieldwork, Federal Work-Study, institutionally sponsored loans, scholarships/grants, and unspecified assistantships available. Support available to part-time students. Financial award application deadline: 5/1; financial award applicants required to submit FAFSA. *Unit head:* Tobe Berkovitz, Interim Chairman, 617-353-3482, E-mail: tobetv@bu.edu. *Application contact:* Haley Nielsen, Administrator of Admission and Financial Aid, 617-353-3481, E-mail: comgrad@bu.edu.
Website: http://www.bu.edu/com/academics/masscomm-ad-pr/

**Brigham Young University,** Graduate Studies, College of Fine Arts and Communications, School of Communications, Provo, UT 84602. Offers mass communications (MA). *Faculty:* 16 full-time (1 woman). *Students:* 19 full-time (14 women), 21 part-time (10 women); includes 7 minority (2 Asian, non-Hispanic/Latino; 5 Hispanic/Latino), 6 international. Average age 31. 19 applicants, 63% accepted, 12 enrolled. In 2016, 13 master's awarded. *Degree requirements:* For master's, comprehensive exam, thesis. *Entrance requirements:* For master's, GRE, minimum GPA of 3.0 in last 60 hours of course work. Additional exam requirements/recommendations for international students: Required—TOEFL (minimum score 580 paper-based; 85 iBT). *Application deadline:* For fall admission, 3/31 priority date for domestic and international students. Applications are processed on a rolling basis. Application fee: $50. Electronic applications accepted. *Expenses: Tuition:* Full-time $6680; part-time $393 per credit. Tuition and fees vary according to course load, program and student's religious affiliation. *Financial support:* In 2016–17, 21 students received support, including 26 research assistantships with full and partial tuition reimbursements available (averaging $3,373 per year), 2 teaching assistantships with partial tuition reimbursements available (averaging $2,824 per year); career-related internships or fieldwork, institutionally sponsored loans, scholarships/grants, unspecified assistantships, and supplementary awards also available. Financial award application deadline: 4/30; financial award applicants required to submit FAFSA. *Faculty research:* Ethics, international, magazine, newspaper, media effects, social media. *Unit head:* Edward Carter, Director, 801-422-2997, Fax: 801-422-0160, E-mail: comms_secretary@byu.edu. *Application contact:* Debby Jackson, Graduate Program Manager, 801-422-2632, Fax: 801-422-0160, E-mail: debby_jackson@byu.edu.
Website: http://cfac.byu.edu/departments/communications

**Bryant University,** College of Arts and Sciences, Smithfield, RI 02917. Offers communication (MA, Graduate Certificate), including general communication (MA), managerial communication (Graduate Certificate), professional communication (Graduate Certificate), public communication (Graduate Certificate); global environmental studies (MS); health care communication (MA); organizational communication (MA); sustainability practices (Graduate Certificate). *Program availability:* Part-time, evening/weekend. *Faculty:* 2 full-time (0 women), 2 part-time/adjunct (1 woman). *Students:* 4 full-time (all women), 10 part-time (8 women); includes 2 minority (1 Black or African American, non-Hispanic/Latino; 1 Two or more races, non-Hispanic/Latino), 1 international. Average age 32. 29 applicants, 31% accepted, 6 enrolled. In 2016, 6 master's, 2 other advanced degrees awarded. *Degree requirements:* For master's, thesis. *Entrance requirements:* For master's, GRE. Additional exam requirements/recommendations for international students: Required—TOEFL (minimum score 550 paper-based; 80 iBT). *Application deadline:* For fall admission, 8/15 for domestic and international students; for spring admission, 1/15 for domestic and international students; for summer admission, 5/15 for domestic and international students. Applications are processed on a rolling basis. Application fee: $80. Electronic applications accepted. *Expenses:* $932 per credit hour. *Financial support:* Fellowships and research assistantships available. Financial award applicants required to submit FAFSA. *Faculty research:* Mass media and social construction of reality; development and improvement of media literacy skills; sociocultural influences on cognition and learning in K-12 populations, oil pollution impacts on marine and estuarine microbial communities; wetlands ecology. *Unit head:* Bradford Martin, Associate Dean, College of Arts and Sciences, 401-232-6929, E-mail: bmartin@bryant.edu. *Application contact:* Terri Rogers, Admission Assistant, Graduate School, 401-232-6230, E-mail: graduateprograms@bryant.edu.
Website: http://gradschool.bryant.edu/arts-and-sciences/

**California State University, Fullerton,** Graduate Studies, College of Communications, Department of Communications, Fullerton, CA 92834-9480. Offers communications in tourism and entertainment (MA); mass communications research and theory (MA); professional communications (MA). *Program availability:* Part-time. *Degree requirements:* For master's, project or thesis. *Entrance requirements:* For master's, GRE General Test. Application fee: $55. *Expenses:* Tuition, state resident: full-time $3369; part-time $1953 per unit. Tuition, nonresident: full-time $3915; part-time $2499 per unit. Tuition and fees vary according to course load, degree level and program. *Financial support:* Teaching assistantships, career-related internships or fieldwork, Federal Work-Study, institutionally sponsored loans, and scholarships/grants available. Support available to part-time students. Financial award application deadline: 3/1; financial award applicants required to submit FAFSA. *Unit head:* Jason Shepard, Chair, 657-278-5301, E-mail: jshepard@fullerton.edu. *Application contact:* Coordinator, 657-278-3832.

**California State University, Northridge,** Graduate Studies, College of Arts, Media, and Communication, Department of Journalism, Northridge, CA 91330. Offers mass communication (MA). *Program availability:* Part-time, evening/weekend. *Faculty:* 15 full-time (9 women), 16 part-time/adjunct (7 women). *Students:* 12 full-time (9 women), 17 part-time (9 women); includes 9 minority (2 Black or African American, non-Hispanic/

Latino; 1 American Indian or Alaska Native, non-Hispanic/Latino; 1 Asian, non-Hispanic/Latino; 4 Hispanic/Latino; 1 Two or more races, non-Hispanic/Latino), 8 international. Average age 30. 44 applicants, 41% accepted, 9 enrolled. *Degree requirements:* For master's, thesis. *Entrance requirements:* For master's, GRE General Test. Additional exam requirements/recommendations for international students: Required—TOEFL. *Application deadline:* For fall admission, 11/30 for domestic students. Application fee: $55. *Expenses:* Tuition, state resident: full-time $4152. *Financial support:* Career-related internships or fieldwork and Federal Work-Study available. Financial award application deadline: 3/1. *Unit head:* Linda Bowen, Chair, 818-677-3135.
Website: http://www.csun.edu/journalism/

**Drexel University,** College of Arts and Sciences, Department of Communication, Culture and Media, Program in Communication, Philadelphia, PA 19104-2875. Offers public communication (MS); science communication (MS); technical communication (MS). *Program availability:* Part-time, evening/weekend. *Faculty:* 12 full-time (6 women), 14 part-time/adjunct (8 women). *Students:* 12 full-time (6 women), 27 part-time (21 women); includes 5 minority (2 Black or African American, non-Hispanic/Latino; 1 American Indian or Alaska Native, non-Hispanic/Latino; 1 Asian, non-Hispanic/Latino; 1 Native Hawaiian or other Pacific Islander, non-Hispanic/Latino), 4 international. Average age 30. In 2016, 25 master's awarded. *Degree requirements:* For master's, internship, professional portfolio. *Entrance requirements:* For master's, GRE or minimum GPA of 3.0. Additional exam requirements/recommendations for international students: Required—TOEFL. *Application deadline:* For fall admission, 8/21 for domestic students. Applications are processed on a rolling basis. Application fee: $50. Electronic applications accepted. *Expenses: Tuition:* Full-time $32,184; part-time $1192 per credit hour. *Required fees:* $280. Tuition and fees vary according to campus/location and program. *Financial support:* Research assistantships, teaching assistantships, career-related internships or fieldwork, Federal Work-Study, institutionally sponsored loans, tuition waivers (partial), and unspecified assistantships available. Financial award application deadline: 2/1. *Unit head:* Dr. Douglas Porpora, Head, 215-895-2446, Fax: 215-895-1071. *Application contact:* Director of Graduate Admissions, 215-895-6700, Fax: 215-895-5939, E-mail: enroll@drexel.edu.

**Florida International University,** College of Communication, Architecture and The Arts, School of Communication and Journalism, Miami, FL 33199. Offers mass communication (MS), including global strategic communications, Spanish language journalism. *Program availability:* Part-time, evening/weekend. *Faculty:* 12 full-time (6 women), 8 part-time/adjunct (4 women). *Students:* 94 full-time (72 women), 51 part-time (33 women); includes 110 minority (25 Black or African American, non-Hispanic/Latino; 81 Hispanic/Latino; 4 Two or more races, non-Hispanic/Latino), 19 international. Average age 29. 127 applicants, 62% accepted, 59 enrolled. In 2016, 53 master's awarded. *Degree requirements:* For master's, thesis optional. *Entrance requirements:* For master's, 2 letters of recommendation; minimum GPA of 3.0 during last 60 hours of upper-level work; resume. Additional exam requirements/recommendations for international students: Required—TOEFL (minimum score 550 paper-based; 80 iBT). *Application deadline:* For fall admission, 6/1 for domestic students, 4/1 for international students; for spring admission, 10/1 for domestic students, 9/1 for international students. Applications are processed on a rolling basis. Application fee: $30. Electronic applications accepted. *Expenses:* Tuition, state resident: full-time $8912; part-time $446 per credit hour. Tuition, nonresident: full-time $21,393; part-time $992 per credit hour. *Required fees:* $2185; $195 per semester. Tuition and fees vary according to program. *Financial support:* Institutionally sponsored loans and scholarships/grants available. Financial award application deadline: 3/1; financial award applicants required to submit FAFSA. *Unit head:* Dr. Maria Elena Villar, Chair, 305-919-5795, Fax: 305-919-5215, E-mail: mariaelena.villar@fiu.edu. *Application contact:* Nanett Rojas, Assistant Director, Graduate Admissions, 305-348-7442, Fax: 305-348-7441, E-mail: gradadm@fiu.edu.
Website: https://scj.fiu.edu/

**The George Washington University,** Columbian College of Arts and Sciences, School of Media and Public Affairs, Washington, DC 20052. Offers MA, Graduate Certificate. *Faculty:* 22 full-time (10 women). *Students:* 31 full-time (20 women), 19 part-time (15 women); includes 10 minority (7 Black or African American, non-Hispanic/Latino; 1 Asian, non-Hispanic/Latino; 1 Hispanic/Latino; 1 Native Hawaiian or other Pacific Islander, non-Hispanic/Latino), 9 international. Average age 27. 86 applicants, 59% accepted, 24 enrolled. In 2016, 22 master's, 13 other advanced degrees awarded. *Degree requirements:* For master's, thesis optional. *Entrance requirements:* For master's, GRE General Test. Additional exam requirements/recommendations for international students: Required—TOEFL (minimum score 550 paper-based; 80 iBT). *Application deadline:* For fall admission, 4/1 priority date for domestic students, 1/15 priority date for international students; for spring admission, 10/1 priority date for domestic students, 9/1 priority date for international students. Applications are processed on a rolling basis. Application fee: $75. Electronic applications accepted. *Financial support:* In 2016–17, fellowships with tuition reimbursements (averaging $10,000 per year), teaching assistantships with tuition reimbursements (averaging $5,000 per year) were awarded. Financial award application deadline: 1/15. *Unit head:* Frank Sesno, Director, 202-994-9553, E-mail: sesno@gwu.edu. *Application contact:* Information Contact, 202-994-6227, Fax: 202-994-5806, E-mail: smpa@gwu.edu.
Website: http://smpa.gwu.edu/

**Georgia State University,** College of Arts and Sciences, Department of Communication, Atlanta, GA 30302-3083. Offers film, video, and digital imaging (MA), including critical studies, production, screenwriting; human communication and social influence (MA); mass communication (MA); media and society (PhD); moving image studies (PhD); public communication (PhD); rhetoric and politics (PhD). *Program availability:* Part-time. *Faculty:* 57 full-time (34 women). *Students:* 113 full-time (69 women), 56 part-time (33 women); includes 59 minority (37 Black or African American, non-Hispanic/Latino; 1 American Indian or Alaska Native, non-Hispanic/Latino; 2 Asian, non-Hispanic/Latino; 9 Hispanic/Latino; 10 Two or more races, non-Hispanic/Latino), 18 international. Average age 32. 134 applicants, 58% accepted, 47 enrolled. In 2016, 22 master's, 11 doctorates awarded. *Degree requirements:* For master's, variable foreign language requirement, thesis (for some programs); for doctorate, comprehensive exam, thesis/dissertation. *Entrance requirements:* For master's and doctorate, GRE. Additional exam requirements/recommendations for international students: Required—TOEFL (minimum score 550 paper-based; 80 iBT), IELTS (minimum score 6.5). *Application deadline:* For fall admission, 2/10 for domestic and international students; for spring admission, 10/15 for domestic and international students. Application fee: $50. Electronic applications accepted. *Expenses:* Tuition, state resident: full-time $6876; part-time $382 per credit hour. Tuition, nonresident: full-time $22,374; part-time $1243 per credit hour. *Required fees:* $2128; $1064 per term. Part-time tuition and fees vary according to course load and program. *Financial support:* In 2016–17, fellowships with tuition reimbursements (averaging $15,000 per year), teaching assistantships with tuition reimbursements (averaging $15,000 per year) were awarded; career-related internships or fieldwork and unspecified assistantships also available. Financial award applicants required to submit FAFSA. *Faculty research:* New media, mass media and journalism, rhetoric, film and media studies, film production. *Unit head:* Dr. Greg Lisby, Chair, 404-413-5639, Fax: 404-413-5634, E-mail: glisby@gsu.edu.
Website: http://communication.gsu.edu

**Grambling State University,** School of Graduate Studies and Research, College of Professional Studies, Department of Mass Communication, Grambling, LA 71245. Offers MA. *Program availability:* Part-time. *Degree requirements:* For master's, comprehensive exam, thesis optional. *Entrance requirements:* For master's, GRE, minimum GPA of 2.5 on last degree. Additional exam requirements/recommendations for international students: Required—TOEFL (minimum score 500 paper-based; 62 iBT). Electronic applications accepted.

**Howard University,** School of Communications, Division of Mass Communication and Media Studies, Washington, DC 20059-0002. Offers mass communication (MA, PhD); media studies (MA, PhD). *Program availability:* Part-time, evening/weekend. *Degree requirements:* For master's, comprehensive exam (for some programs), thesis optional; for doctorate, one foreign language, comprehensive exam, thesis/dissertation. *Entrance requirements:* For master's, GRE, minimum GPA of 3.0; for doctorate, GRE, minimum graduate GPA of 3.5. Additional exam requirements/recommendations for international students: Required—TOEFL. Electronic applications accepted. *Faculty research:* Advertising, public relations, journalism new media.

**Iona College,** School of Arts and Science, Department of Mass Communication, New Rochelle, NY 10801-1890. Offers non-profit public relations (Certificate); public relations (MA); sports communication and media (MA). *Accreditation:* ACEJMC (one or more programs are accredited). *Program availability:* Part-time, evening/weekend. *Faculty:* 3 full-time (1 woman), 8 part-time/adjunct (4 women). *Students:* 10 full-time (4 women), 28 part-time (22 women); includes 17 minority (10 Black or African American, non-Hispanic/Latino; 7 Hispanic/Latino), 3 international. Average age 27. 19 applicants, 95% accepted, 11 enrolled. In 2016, 19 master's, 6 other advanced degrees awarded. *Degree requirements:* For master's, comprehensive exam (for some programs), thesis or alternative. *Entrance requirements:* For master's, GRE General Test if undergraduate GPA is below 3.0. Additional exam requirements/recommendations for international students: Required—TOEFL (minimum score 550 paper-based; 80 iBT), IELTS (minimum score 6). *Application deadline:* For fall admission, 8/1 for domestic students, 5/1 for international students; for spring admission, 1/1 for domestic students, 9/1 for international students. Applications are processed on a rolling basis. Application fee: $50. Electronic applications accepted. *Expenses:* Contact institution. *Financial support:* In 2016–17, 15 students received support. Scholarships/grants, tuition waivers (partial), and unspecified assistantships available. Support available to part-time students. Financial award application deadline: 4/15; financial award applicants required to submit FAFSA. *Faculty research:* Media ecology, new media, corporate communication, media images, organizational learning in public relations, media law, medicine ethics. *Unit head:* Anthony Kelso, PhD, Chair, 914-633-7795, E-mail: akelso@iona.edu. *Application contact:* Katelyn Brunck, Assistant Director of Graduate Admissions, 914-633-2492, Fax: 914-633-2277, E-mail: kbrunck@iona.edu.
Website: http://www.iona.edu/Academics/School-of-Arts-Science/Departments/Mass-Communication/Graduate-Programs.aspx

**Iowa State University of Science and Technology,** Greenlee School of Journalism and Mass Communication, Ames, IA 50011. Offers MS. *Entrance requirements:* For master's, GRE General Test. Additional exam requirements/recommendations for international students: Required—TOEFL (minimum score 570 paper-based; 88 iBT), IELTS (minimum score 6.5). *Application deadline:* For fall admission, 3/1 priority date for international students; for spring admission, 10/1 priority date for international students. Applications are processed on a rolling basis. Application fee: $60 ($90 for international students). Electronic applications accepted. *Application contact:* Daniela Dimitrova, Application Contact, 515-294-5951, Fax: 515-294-5108, E-mail: danielad@iastate.edu.
Website: http://www.jlmc.iastate.edu/graduate/

**Kansas State University,** Graduate School, College of Arts and Sciences, A.Q. Miller School of Journalism and Mass Communications, Manhattan, KS 66506. Offers advertising (MS); community journalism (MS); global communication (MS); health communication (MS); media management (MS); public relations (MS). *Program availability:* Part-time, evening/weekend. *Faculty:* 13 full-time (6 women), 1 (woman) part-time/adjunct. *Students:* 13 full-time (10 women), 6 part-time (4 women); includes 1 minority (Hispanic/Latino), 8 international. Average age 29. 7 applicants, 71% accepted, 3 enrolled. In 2016, 7 master's awarded. *Degree requirements:* For master's, comprehensive exam, thesis. *Entrance requirements:* For master's, GRE General Test, minimum GPA of 3.0. Additional exam requirements/recommendations for international students: Required—TOEFL (minimum score 79 iBT). *Application deadline:* For fall admission, 2/1 priority date for domestic and international students; for spring admission, 8/1 priority date for domestic and international students. Applications are processed on a rolling basis. Application fee: $50 ($75 for international students). Electronic applications accepted. *Expenses:* Tuition, state resident: full-time $9670. Tuition, nonresident: full-time $21,828. *Required fees:* $862. *Financial support:* In 2016–17, 2 research assistantships with full tuition reimbursements (averaging $11,180 per year), 7 teaching assistantships with full tuition reimbursements (averaging $7,729 per year) were awarded; scholarships/grants, health care benefits, and unspecified assistantships also available. Financial award application deadline: 2/1; financial award applicants required to submit FAFSA. *Faculty research:* Health communication, risk communication, strategic communications, community journalism, global communication. *Total annual research expenditures:* $219,641. *Unit head:* Dr. Jean Folkerts, Director, 785-532-6890, Fax: 785-532-5484, E-mail: jeanfolk@ksu.edu. *Application contact:* Dr. Barbara DeSanto, Associate Director of Graduate Studies, 785-532-3890, Fax: 785-532-5484, E-mail: desantoi@ksu.edu.
Website: http://jmc.ksu.edu/

**Kent State University,** College of Communication and Information, School of Journalism and Mass Communication, Kent, OH 44242-0001. Offers journalism and mass communication (MA), including media management, public relations, reporting and editing-broadcast, reporting and editing-convergence, reporting and editing-journalism educators, reporting and editing-magazine, reporting and editing-newspaper. *Program availability:* Part-time, online learning. *Faculty:* 25 full-time (13 women). *Students:* 12 full-time (7 women), 102 part-time (68 women); includes 19 minority (14 Black or African American, non-Hispanic/Latino; 3 Hispanic/Latino; 2 Two or more races, non-Hispanic/Latino), 5 international. Average age 30. 46 applicants, 67% accepted, 20 enrolled. In 2016, 79 master's awarded. *Degree requirements:* For master's, thesis or project. *Entrance requirements:* For master's, GRE, minimum GPA of 3.0, statement of purpose, 3 online recommendations, resume. Additional exam requirements/recommendations for international students: Required—TOEFL (minimum score of 600 paper-based, 100 iBT), IELTS (minimum score of 7.0), Michigan English Language Assessment Battery (minimum score of 85), or PTE (minimum score of 68). *Application deadline:* For fall admission, 7/1 for domestic and international students. Applications are processed on a rolling basis. Application fee: $45 ($70 for international students). Electronic applications accepted. *Expenses:* Tuition, state resident: full-time $10,864; part-time $495 per credit hour. Tuition, nonresident: full-time $18,380; part-time $837 per credit hour. *Financial support:* Research assistantships with full tuition reimbursements, teaching assistantships with full tuition reimbursements, scholarships/grants, and unspecified assistantships available. Financial award application deadline: 3/1. *Unit head:* Thor Wasbotten, Director and Professor, 330-672-4066, E-mail: thor@kent.edu. *Application contact:* Mark Goodman, Graduate Coordinator/Professor,

330-672-6239, E-mail: mgoodm10@kent.edu.
Website: http://www.kent.edu/jmc

**Louisiana State University and Agricultural & Mechanical College,** Graduate School, Manship School of Mass Communication, Baton Rouge, LA 70803. Offers MMC, PhD, JD/MMC. *Accreditation:* ACEJMC.

**Lynn University,** Eugene M. and Christine E. Lynn College of International Communication, Boca Raton, FL 33431-5598. Offers communication and media (MS), including digital media, media studies and practice; digital media (Certificate). *Program availability:* Part-time, evening/weekend. *Faculty:* 15 full-time (8 women), 6 part-time/adjunct (3 women). *Students:* 24 full-time (20 women), 15 part-time (14 women); includes 11 minority (7 Black or African American, non-Hispanic/Latino; 2 Asian, non-Hispanic/Latino; 2 Hispanic/Latino), 14 international. Average age 27. 38 applicants, 87% accepted, 17 enrolled. In 2016, 18 master's, 1 other advanced degree awarded. *Degree requirements:* For master's, project or thesis. *Entrance requirements:* For master's, resume, letter of recommendation, official transcripts, bachelor's degree from accredited institution, personal statement. Additional exam requirements/recommendations for international students: Required—TOEFL (minimum score 550 paper-based; 80 iBT), IELTS (minimum score 6.5). *Application deadline:* For fall admission, 8/18 for domestic students, 8/4 for international students; for spring admission, 12/15 for domestic students, 12/1 for international students; for summer admission, 4/17 for domestic students, 4/3 for international students. Applications are processed on a rolling basis. Application fee: $45. Electronic applications accepted. *Expenses:* $725 per credit hour. *Financial support:* In 2016–17, 7 students received support. Career-related internships or fieldwork, Federal Work-Study, institutionally sponsored loans, scholarships/grants, tuition waivers (partial), and unspecified assistantships available. Support available to part-time students. Financial award application deadline: 8/1; financial award applicants required to submit FAFSA. *Unit head:* Dr. David L. Jaffe, Dean, 561-237-7099, Fax: 561-237-7097, E-mail: djaffe@lynn.edu. *Application contact:* Steven Pruitt, Director of Graduate Admission, 561-237-7834, Fax: 561-237-7100, E-mail: admission@lynn.edu.
Website: http://www.lynn.edu/academics/colleges/international-communication

**Marquette University,** Graduate School, College of Communication, Milwaukee, WI 53201-1881. Offers advertising and public relations (MA); communication studies (MA); digital storytelling (Certificate); journalism (MA); mass communication (MA); science, health and environmental communication (MA). *Accreditation:* ACEJMC (one or more programs are accredited). *Program availability:* Part-time, evening/weekend. *Faculty:* 36 full-time (18 women), 45 part-time/adjunct (20 women). *Students:* 25 full-time (22 women), 23 part-time (16 women); includes 9 minority (3 Black or African American, non-Hispanic/Latino; 1 American Indian or Alaska Native, non-Hispanic/Latino; 4 Hispanic/Latino; 1 Two or more races, non-Hispanic/Latino), 4 international. Average age 28. 55 applicants, 62% accepted, 21 enrolled. In 2016, 10 master's, 1 other advanced degree awarded. *Degree requirements:* For master's, comprehensive exam, thesis or alternative. *Entrance requirements:* For master's, GRE, official transcripts from all current and previous colleges/universities except Marquette, three letters of recommendation, statement of academic and professional goals. Additional exam requirements/recommendations for international students: Required—TOEFL (minimum score 530 paper-based). *Application deadline:* Applications are processed on a rolling basis. Electronic applications accepted. *Financial support:* Fellowships, research assistantships, teaching assistantships, career-related internships or fieldwork, scholarships/grants, health care benefits, tuition waivers (full and partial), and unspecified assistantships available. Support available to part-time students. Financial award application deadline: 2/15. *Faculty research:* Urban journalism, gender and communication, intercultural communication, religious communication. *Total annual research expenditures:* $7,941. *Unit head:* Dr. Sarah Feldner, Associate Dean. *Application contact:* Dr. Sarah Bonewits Feldner.
Website: http://diederich.marquette.edu/

**Middle Tennessee State University,** College of Graduate Studies, College of Mass Communication, Program in Mass Communication, Murfreesboro, TN 37132. Offers MS. *Program availability:* Part-time, evening/weekend, online learning. *Degree requirements:* For master's, comprehensive exam, thesis optional. *Entrance requirements:* For master's, GRE. Additional exam requirements/recommendations for international students: Required—TOEFL (minimum score 525 paper-based; 71 iBT) or IELTS (minimum score 6).

**Murray State University,** College of Business and Public Affairs, Program in Mass Communications, Murray, KY 42071. Offers MA, MS. *Program availability:* Part-time. *Entrance requirements:* Additional exam requirements/recommendations for international students: Required—TOEFL (minimum score 550 paper-based). *Faculty research:* AH media on the Internet, visual communication and learning, persuasion, media framing, history of radio and wireless technology.

**North Dakota State University,** College of Graduate and Interdisciplinary Studies, College of Arts, Humanities and Social Sciences, Department of Communication, Fargo, ND 58102. Offers communication (PhD); mass communication (MA, MS); speech communication (MA, MS). *Program availability:* Part-time, online learning. Terminal master's awarded for partial completion of doctoral program. *Degree requirements:* For master's, thesis (for some programs); for doctorate, comprehensive exam, thesis/dissertation, 2-3 publications. *Entrance requirements:* For master's, GRE, minimum undergraduate GPA of 3.25; for doctorate, GRE, minimum undergraduate GPA of 3.5. Additional exam requirements/recommendations for international students: Required—TOEFL (minimum score 600 paper-based; 100 iBT), IELTS (minimum score 7). Electronic applications accepted. *Faculty research:* Communication and rhetorical theory, organizational communication, broadcast and print journalism, international communication, public relations and advertising.

**Oklahoma State University,** College of Arts and Sciences, School of Media and Strategic Communications, Stillwater, OK 74078. Offers mass communication (MS). *Faculty:* 17 full-time (4 women), 5 part-time/adjunct (2 women). *Students:* 10 full-time (7 women), 27 part-time (17 women); includes 10 minority (6 Black or African American, non-Hispanic/Latino; 2 American Indian or Alaska Native, non-Hispanic/Latino; 1 Hispanic/Latino; 1 Two or more races, non-Hispanic/Latino), 1 international. Average age 27. 23 applicants, 65% accepted, 13 enrolled. In 2016, 7 master's awarded. *Degree requirements:* For master's, thesis, project/creative component. *Entrance requirements:* For master's, GRE, minimum GPA of 3.0. Additional exam requirements/recommendations for international students: Required—TOEFL (minimum score 550 paper-based; 79 iBT). *Application deadline:* For fall admission, 3/1 priority date for international students; for spring admission, 8/1 priority date for international students. Applications are processed on a rolling basis. Application fee: $40 ($75 for international students). Electronic applications accepted. *Expenses:* Tuition, state resident: full-time $3775; part-time $209.70 per credit hour. Tuition, nonresident: full-time $14,851; part-time $825.05 per credit hour. *Required fees:* $2027; $112.60 per credit hour. Tuition and fees vary according to campus/location. *Financial support:* In 2016–17, 2 research assistantships (averaging $14,489 per year), 7 teaching assistantships (averaging $15,033 per year) were awarded; career-related internships or fieldwork, Federal Work-Study, scholarships/grants, health care benefits, tuition waivers (partial), and unspecified assistantships also available. Support available to part-time students.

## Mass Communication

Financial award application deadline: 3/1; financial award applicants required to submit FAFSA. *Unit head:* Dr. Craig Freem, Director, 405-744-7676, Fax: 405-744-7104, E-mail: freemanc@okstate.edu.
Website: http://media.okstate.edu

**Penn State University Park,** Graduate School, College of Communications, Department of Communications, University Park, PA 16802. Offers mass communications (PhD); media studies (MA). *Unit head:* Dr. Marie C. Hardin, Dean, 814-863-1484, Fax: 814-863-8044. *Application contact:* Lori Hawn, Director, Graduate Student Services, 814-865-1795, Fax: 814-863-4627, E-mail: l-gswww@lists.psu.edu.
Website: http://comm.psu.edu/

**Point Park University,** School of Communication, Pittsburgh, PA 15222-1984. Offers MA. *Program availability:* Part-time, evening/weekend. *Degree requirements:* For master's, comprehensive exam (for some programs), thesis or alternative. *Entrance requirements:* For master's, GRE (if GPA less than 2.75), minimum GPA of 2.75, 2 letters of recommendation, statement of intent. Additional exam requirements/recommendations for international students: Required—TOEFL (minimum score 570 paper-based; 88 iBT), IELTS (minimum score 6.5); Recommended—TWE (minimum score 5). Electronic applications accepted.

**St. Cloud State University,** School of Graduate Studies, College of Liberal Arts, Department of Mass Communications, St. Cloud, MN 56301-4498. Offers MS. *Degree requirements:* For master's, thesis or alternative. *Entrance requirements:* For master's, minimum GPA of 2.75. Additional exam requirements/recommendations for international students: Required—Michigan English Language Assessment Battery; Recommended—TOEFL (minimum score 600 paper-based), IELTS (minimum score 6.5). Electronic applications accepted.

**San Jose State University,** Graduate Studies and Research, College of Applied Sciences and Arts, San Jose, CA 95192-0001. Offers big data (Certificate); California library media teacher services (Credential); collaborative response to family violence (Certificate); justice studies (MS); kinesiology (MA), including applied sciences and arts (MA, MS), athletic training, exercise physiology, sport management, sport studies; library and information science (MLIS, Certificate); mass communication (MA); nutritional science (MS); occupational therapy (MS); public health (MPH); pupil personnel services (Credential); recreation (MS), including applied sciences and arts (MA, MS), international tourism; social work (MSW); Spanish language counseling (Certificate); strategic management of digital assets and services (Certificate). *Program availability:* Part-time, evening/weekend. Electronic applications accepted.

**Southern Illinois University Carbondale,** Graduate School, College of Mass Communication and Media Arts, Department of Mass Communication and Media Arts, Carbondale, IL 62901-4701. Offers MFA, PhD. *Degree requirements:* For doctorate, thesis/dissertation. *Entrance requirements:* For master's, minimum GPA of 2.7; for doctorate, GRE, minimum GPA of 3.25. Additional exam requirements/recommendations for international students: Required—TOEFL (minimum score 100 iBT).

**Southern Illinois University Edwardsville,** Graduate School, Department of Arts and Sciences, Department of Mass Communications, Program in Mass Communications, Edwardsville, IL 62026. Offers MS. *Program availability:* Part-time, evening/weekend. *Degree requirements:* For master's, comprehensive exam (for some programs), thesis (for some programs). *Entrance requirements:* Additional exam requirements/recommendations for international students: Required—TOEFL (minimum score 550 paper-based; 79 iBT), IELTS (minimum score 6.5). Electronic applications accepted.

**Southern University and Agricultural and Mechanical College,** Graduate School, College of Arts and Humanities, Department of Mass Communication, Baton Rouge, LA 70813. Offers MA. *Degree requirements:* For master's, comprehensive exam, thesis. *Entrance requirements:* For master's, GRE General Test. Additional exam requirements/recommendations for international students: Required—TOEFL (minimum score 525 paper-based). *Faculty research:* Photojournalism, textbook on broadcast.

**Stephen F. Austin State University,** Graduate School, College of Applied Arts and Science, Department of Communication, Nacogdoches, TX 75962. Offers communication (MA); mass communication (MA). *Program availability:* Part-time. *Degree requirements:* For master's, comprehensive exam, thesis optional. *Entrance requirements:* For master's, GRE General Test. Additional exam requirements/recommendations for international students: Required—TOEFL (minimum score 550 paper-based).

**Syracuse University,** S. I. Newhouse School of Public Communications, MS Program in Communications Management, Syracuse, NY 13244. Offers MS. *Accreditation:* ACEJMC. *Program availability:* Part-time, evening/weekend, online learning. *Students:* Average age 43. In 2016, 22 master's awarded. *Degree requirements:* For master's, comprehensive exam, internship. *Entrance requirements:* For master's, GRE General Test, minimum 5 years of experience in public relations or related field; portfolio; 3 letters of recommendation including 1 from current employer, client, or business partner; resume. Additional exam requirements/recommendations for international students: Required—TOEFL (minimum score 100 iBT). *Application deadline:* For fall admission, 1/15 priority date for domestic and international students. Application fee: $45. Electronic applications accepted. *Expenses: Tuition:* Full-time $25,974; part-time $1443 per credit hour. *Required fees:* $802; $50 per course. Tuition and fees vary according to course load and program. *Financial support:* Fellowships, research assistantships, and teaching assistantships available. Financial award application deadline: 1/1; financial award applicants required to submit FAFSA. *Faculty research:* Public relations theory, public opinion research, communications law, public relations management, measurement and evaluation in communication. *Unit head:* Anthony D'Angelo, Professor of Practice/Director, 315-443-3858, E-mail: dangeloa@syr.edu. *Application contact:* Martha Coria, Graduate Records Office, 315-443-5749, E-mail: pcgrad@syr.edu.
Website: http://newhouse.syr.edu/

**Syracuse University,** S. I. Newhouse School of Public Communications, PhD Program in Mass Communications, Syracuse, NY 13244. Offers PhD. *Students:* Average age 33. In 2016, 4 doctorates awarded. *Degree requirements:* For doctorate, comprehensive exam, thesis/dissertation, qualifying exams. *Entrance requirements:* For doctorate, GRE General Test, resume, personal statement, official transcript, three letters of recommendation, writing sample. Additional exam requirements/recommendations for international students: Required—TOEFL (minimum score 100 iBT). *Application deadline:* For fall admission, 12/1 priority date for domestic and international students. Application fee: $45. Electronic applications accepted. *Expenses: Tuition:* Full-time $25,974; part-time $1443 per credit hour. *Required fees:* $802; $50 per course. Tuition and fees vary according to course load and program. *Financial support:* Fellowships with full tuition reimbursements, research assistantships with partial tuition reimbursements, teaching assistantships with partial tuition reimbursements, career-related internships or fieldwork, and tuition waivers (partial) available. Financial award application deadline: 12/10. *Faculty research:* Communications theory, social effects of television, theories of media content, quantitative methods for mass communications research. *Unit head:* Dr. Dennis Kinsey, Director of Doctoral Studies, 315-443-3372, Fax: 315-443-3946, E-mail: masscomm@syr.edu. *Application contact:* Amy Arends,

Doctoral Office, 315-443-3372, E-mail: masscomm@syr.edu.
Website: http://newhouse.syr.edu/

**Texas Christian University,** Bob Schieffer College of Communication, Department of Strategic Communication, Fort Worth, TX 76129. Offers MS. *Program availability:* Part-time. *Faculty:* 8 full-time (6 women). *Students:* 17 full-time (13 women), 1 part-time (0 women); includes 5 minority (1 Black or African American, non-Hispanic/Latino; 1 Asian, non-Hispanic/Latino; 1 Hispanic/Latino; 2 Two or more races, non-Hispanic/Latino), 1 international. Average age 27. 22 applicants, 36% accepted, 4 enrolled. In 2016, 5 master's awarded. *Entrance requirements:* For master's, GRE General Test, 15 semester hours (five courses) in undergraduate journalism, advertising or public relations, or substantial professional experience in a communication discipline as determined by the graduate faculty. Additional exam requirements/recommendations for international students: Required—TOEFL (minimum score 100 iBT). *Application deadline:* For fall admission, 6/1 for domestic and international students; for spring admission, 10/15 for domestic and international students. Applications are processed on a rolling basis. Application fee: $60. Electronic applications accepted. *Expenses:* Contact institution. *Financial support:* In 2016–17, 14 students received support, including 9 teaching assistantships with full tuition reimbursements available (averaging $9,000 per year); tuition waivers (full) also available. Financial award application deadline: 2/15; financial award applicants required to submit FAFSA. *Faculty research:* Social and digital media, advertising and public relations, health communication, crisis communication, ethics. *Unit head:* Dr. Jacque Lambiase, Department Chair, 817-257-6552, Fax: 817-257-7322, E-mail: j.lambiase@tcu.edu. *Application contact:* Dr. Julie O'Neil, Graduate Director, 817-257-6966, Fax: 817-257-7322, E-mail: j.oneil@tcu.edu.
Website: http://stco.tcu.edu/

**Texas State University,** The Graduate College, College of Fine Arts and Communication, Program in Mass Communication, San Marcos, TX 78666. Offers MA. *Program availability:* Part-time. *Faculty:* 12 full-time (8 women), 1 (woman) part-time/adjunct. *Students:* 31 full-time (25 women), 14 part-time (8 women); includes 21 minority (4 Black or African American, non-Hispanic/Latino; 1 American Indian or Alaska Native, non-Hispanic/Latino; 14 Hispanic/Latino; 2 Two or more races, non-Hispanic/Latino), 2 international. Average age 27. 28 applicants, 68% accepted, 11 enrolled. In 2016, 18 master's awarded. *Degree requirements:* For master's, comprehensive exam, thesis optional. *Entrance requirements:* For master's, GRE General Test (minimum preferred score of 303 with no less than 153 on the verbal section, 150 on the quantitative section, and 4.5 on the analytical writing section), baccalaureate degree from regionally-accredited institution with minimum GPA of 3.0 in last 60 hours of course work, statement of purpose, 2 letters of recommendation, current resume. Additional exam requirements/recommendations for international students: Required—TOEFL (minimum score 100 iBT), IELTS (minimum score 7). *Application deadline:* For fall admission, 2/1 for domestic and international students; for spring admission, 10/15 priority date for domestic students, 10/1 for international students; for summer admission, 2/1 for domestic and international students. Applications are processed on a rolling basis. Application fee: $40 ($90 for international students). Electronic applications accepted. *Expenses:* $4,851 per semester. *Financial support:* In 2016–17, 28 students received support, including 15 teaching assistantships (averaging $13,735 per year); research assistantships, career-related internships or fieldwork, Federal Work-Study, and institutionally sponsored loans also available. Support available to part-time students. Financial award application deadline: 3/1; financial award applicants required to submit FAFSA. *Faculty research:* Medicare improvements for patients, telling stories about music in central Texas communities with data. *Total annual research expenditures:* $208,361. *Unit head:* Dr. Judith Oskam, Graduate Advisor, 512-245-2656, Fax: 512-245-7649, E-mail: jo18@txstate.edu. *Application contact:* Dr. Andrea Golato, Dean of the Graduate College, 512-245-2581, Fax: 512-245-8365, E-mail: gradcollege@txstate.edu.
Website: http://www.masscomm.txstate.edu/

**Texas Tech University,** Graduate School, College of Media and Communication, Department of Media and Communication, Lubbock, TX 79409. Offers mass communications (MA, PhD); strategic communication and innovation (MA). *Program availability:* Part-time, evening/weekend, 100% online. *Faculty:* 49 full-time (16 women), 6 part-time/adjunct (3 women). *Students:* 70 full-time (45 women), 100 part-time (72 women); includes 50 minority (11 Black or African American, non-Hispanic/Latino; 2 Asian, non-Hispanic/Latino; 32 Hispanic/Latino; 5 Two or more races, non-Hispanic/Latino), 13 international. Average age 29. 130 applicants, 61% accepted, 65 enrolled. In 2016, 53 master's, 7 doctorates awarded. *Degree requirements:* For master's, thesis optional; for doctorate, comprehensive exam, thesis/dissertation. *Entrance requirements:* For doctorate, GRE. Additional exam requirements/recommendations for international students: Required—TOEFL (minimum score 550 paper-based; 79 iBT), GRE. *Application deadline:* For fall admission, 6/1 priority date for domestic students, 1/15 priority date for international students; for spring admission, 9/1 priority date for domestic students, 6/15 priority date for international students. Applications are processed on a rolling basis. Application fee: $75. Electronic applications accepted. *Expenses:* $315 per credit hour full-time resident tuition, $723 per credit hour full-time non-resident tuition; $50.50 per credit hour fee plus $608 per term fee. *Financial support:* In 2016–17, 82 students received support, including 82 fellowships (averaging $3,876 per year); research assistantships, teaching assistantships, career-related internships or fieldwork, scholarships/grants, and unspecified assistantships also available. Support available to part-time students. Financial award application deadline: 4/15; financial award applicants required to submit FAFSA. *Faculty research:* Media effects, political communication, health communication, critical/cultural/rhetorical, Hispanic and international communication. *Total annual research expenditures:* $183,606. *Unit head:* Dr. Coy Callison, Graduate Director, 806-834-5344, E-mail: coy.callison@ttu.edu. *Application contact:* Bridget Christopherson, Administrative Assistant, 806-834-1619, E-mail: bridget.christopherson@ttu.edu.

**Université Laval,** Faculty of Letters, Department of Information and Communication, Program in Public Communication, Québec, QC G1K 7P4, Canada. Offers MA, PhD. *Program availability:* Part-time. *Degree requirements:* For master's, thesis (for some programs). *Entrance requirements:* For master's, knowledge of French, knowledge of English. Electronic applications accepted.

**The University of Alabama,** Graduate School, College of Communication and Information Sciences, Communication and Information Sciences Program, Tuscaloosa, AL 35487-0172. Offers PhD. *Faculty:* 11 full-time (2 women). *Students:* 37 full-time (21 women), 12 part-time (7 women); includes 4 minority (1 American Indian or Alaska Native, non-Hispanic/Latino; 1 Asian, non-Hispanic/Latino; 2 Two or more races, non-Hispanic/Latino), 23 international. Average age 33. 22 applicants, 55% accepted, 8 enrolled. In 2016, 8 doctorates awarded. *Degree requirements:* For doctorate, comprehensive exam, thesis/dissertation. *Entrance requirements:* For doctorate, GRE, master's degree, minimum undergraduate and graduate GPA of 3.0. Additional exam requirements/recommendations for international students: Required—TOEFL (minimum score 100 iBT). *Application deadline:* For fall admission, 2/15 priority date for domestic students, 2/15 for international students; for winter admission, 11/1 priority date for domestic students, 11/1 for international students. Applications are processed on a rolling basis. Application fee: $50 ($60 for international students). Electronic applications

accepted. *Expenses:* Tuition, state resident: full-time $10,470. Tuition, nonresident: full-time $26,950. *Financial support:* In 2016–17, 28 students received support, including 4 fellowships with full tuition reimbursements available (averaging $15,000 per year), 14 research assistantships with full tuition reimbursements available (averaging $13,045 per year), 10 teaching assistantships with full tuition reimbursements available (averaging $13,045 per year); institutionally sponsored loans, health care benefits, and unspecified assistantships also available. Financial award application deadline: 3/1. *Faculty research:* Mass media; mass media effects; information studies; cultural, critical and rhetorical studies; policy and law; electronic media. *Unit head:* Dr. William Evans, Associate Dean for Graduate Studies, 205-348-3176, Fax: 205-348-6774, E-mail: wevans@ua.edu. *Application contact:* Marylou Cox, Program Assistant, 205-348-8593, E-mail: mcox@ua.edu.
Website: http://www.cis.ua.edu/graduate

**University of Arkansas at Little Rock,** Graduate School, College of Social Sciences and Communication, School of Mass Communication, Little Rock, AR 72204-1099. Offers MA. *Program availability:* Part-time, evening/weekend. *Degree requirements:* For master's, comprehensive exam, thesis optional. *Entrance requirements:* For master's, GRE General Test, minimum GPA of 2.7. *Faculty research:* Theory and practice of mass communication, social role of the mass media.

**University of Colorado Boulder,** Graduate School, College of Media, Communication and Information, Boulder, CO 80309. Offers MA, MFA, PhD. *Faculty:* 55 full-time (26 women). *Students:* 136 full-time (81 women), 8 part-time (5 women); includes 14 minority (1 Black or African American, non-Hispanic/Latino; 4 Asian, non-Hispanic/Latino; 9 Hispanic/Latino), 11 international. Average age 30. 226 applicants, 50% accepted, 63 enrolled. In 2016, 25 master's, 12 doctorates awarded. Terminal master's awarded for partial completion of doctoral program. *Degree requirements:* For master's, comprehensive exam, thesis or alternative; for doctorate, comprehensive exam, thesis/dissertation. *Entrance requirements:* For master's, GRE General Test, minimum undergraduate GPA of 2.75; for doctorate, GRE General Test, minimum undergraduate GPA of 3.2, graduate 3.5. *Application deadline:* For fall admission, 2/1 for domestic students, 12/1 for international students. Applications are processed on a rolling basis. Application fee: $60 ($80 for international students). Electronic applications accepted. Application fee is waived when completed online. *Financial support:* In 2016–17, 366 students received support, including 99 fellowships (averaging $3,721 per year), 52 research assistantships with full and partial tuition reimbursements available (averaging $27,137 per year), 82 teaching assistantships with full and partial tuition reimbursements available (averaging $30,022 per year); institutionally sponsored loans, scholarships/grants, health care benefits, and unspecified assistantships also available. Financial award application deadline: 3/1; financial award applicants required to submit FAFSA. *Faculty research:* Mass communication/media, journalism, electronic media, culture, communications. *Total annual research expenditures:* $139,346. *Application contact:* E-mail: cmcigrad@colorado.edu.
Website: http://www.colorado.edu/cmci/

**University of Denver,** Division of Arts, Humanities and Social Sciences, Department of Media, Film and Journalism Studies, Denver, CO 80208. Offers international and intercultural communication (MA); media and globalization (MA). *Program availability:* Part-time. *Faculty:* 16 full-time (10 women), 5 part-time/adjunct (4 women). *Students:* 8 full-time (7 women), 18 part-time (14 women); includes 8 minority (1 Black or African American, non-Hispanic/Latino; 2 Asian, non-Hispanic/Latino; 5 Hispanic/Latino), 1 international. Average age 27. 54 applicants, 78% accepted, 14 enrolled. In 2016, 21 master's awarded. *Degree requirements:* For master's, thesis (for some programs). *Entrance requirements:* For master's, GRE General Test, bachelor's degree, transcripts, personal statement, three letters of recommendation. Additional exam requirements/recommendations for international students: Required—TOEFL (minimum score 620 paper-based; 105 iBT). *Application deadline:* For fall admission, 2/15 priority date for domestic students, 1/1 priority date for international students. Applications are processed on a rolling basis. Application fee: $65. Electronic applications accepted. *Expenses:* $29,022 per year full-time. *Financial support:* In 2016–17, 16 students received support, including 2 teaching assistantships with tuition reimbursements available (averaging $12,500 per year); career-related internships or fieldwork, Federal Work-Study, institutionally sponsored loans, scholarships/grants, and unspecified assistantships also available. Support available to part-time students. Financial award application deadline: 2/15; financial award applicants required to submit FAFSA. *Faculty research:* Branding; public relations; health communication; social media; international communication. *Unit head:* Dr. Lynn Schofield Clark, Professor and Chair, 303-871-3984, Fax: 303-871-4949, E-mail: lynn.clark@du.edu. *Application contact:* Information Contact, 303-871-2166, E-mail: mfjs@du.edu.
Website: http://www.du.edu/ahss/mfjs

**University of Florida,** Graduate School, College of Journalism and Communications, Program in Mass Communication, Gainesville, FL 32611. Offers international/intercultural communication (MAMC); journalism (MAMC); mass communication (MAMC, PhD), including clinical translational science (MAMC); public relations (MAMC); science/health communication (MAMC); telecommunication (MAMC). *Accreditation:* ACEJMC. *Entrance requirements:* For master's and doctorate, GRE General Test, minimum GPA of 3.0.

**University of Georgia,** Grady College of Journalism and Mass Communication, Athens, GA 30602. Offers journalism and mass communication (MA); mass communication (PhD). *Degree requirements:* For master's, comprehensive exam, thesis (MA); for doctorate, comprehensive exam, thesis/dissertation. *Entrance requirements:* For master's and doctorate, GRE General Test. Additional exam requirements/recommendations for international students: Required—TOEFL, TWE for PhD. *Application deadline:* For spring admission, 2/15 for domestic students. Application fee: $50. Electronic applications accepted. *Financial support:* Research assistantships, teaching assistantships, tuition waivers (full), and unspecified assistantships available. *Unit head:* Dr. E. Culpepper Clark, Dean, 706-542-1704, Fax: 706-542-2183, E-mail: cully@uga.edu. *Application contact:* Dr. Jeffrey K. Springston, Associate Dean, 706-542-7833, Fax: 706-542-2183, E-mail: jspring@grady.uga.edu.
Website: http://www.grady.uga.edu/

**University of Houston,** College of Liberal Arts and Social Sciences, Jack J. Valenti School of Communication, Houston, TX 77204. Offers health communication (MA); mass communication studies (MA); public relations studies (MA); speech communication (MA). *Program availability:* Part-time. *Degree requirements:* For master's, comprehensive exam (for some programs), thesis (for some programs), 30-33 hours. *Entrance requirements:* For master's, GRE. Additional exam requirements/recommendations for international students: Required—TOEFL. Electronic applications accepted.

**The University of Iowa,** Graduate College, College of Liberal Arts and Sciences, School of Journalism and Mass Communication, Iowa City, IA 52242-1316. Offers journalism and media communication (MA); mass communication (PhD); strategic communication (MA); JD/MA; JD/PhD. *Degree requirements:* For master's, thesis optional, exam; for doctorate, comprehensive exam, thesis/dissertation. *Entrance requirements:* For master's and doctorate, GRE General Test, minimum GPA of 3.0. Additional exam requirements/recommendations for international students: Required—

TOEFL (minimum score 637 paper-based; 110 iBT). Electronic applications accepted. *Faculty research:* Verbal and visual aspects of historical, legal, social, and cross-cultural communication.

**University of Louisiana at Lafayette,** College of Liberal Arts, Department of Communication, Lafayette, LA 70504. Offers mass communications (MS). *Program availability:* Part-time. *Degree requirements:* For master's, thesis optional. *Entrance requirements:* For master's, GRE General Test, minimum GPA of 2.75. Additional exam requirements/recommendations for international students: Required—TOEFL (minimum score 550 paper-based). Electronic applications accepted. *Faculty research:* Mass media problems, issues and ethics, mass communication, historical studies, conflict of interest and law and ethics in journalism, contemporary issues and trends in publications.

**University of Michigan,** Rackham Graduate School, College of Literature, Science, and the Arts, Department of Communication Studies, Ann Arbor, MI 48109-1285. Offers PhD. *Faculty:* 24 full-time (11 women). *Students:* 31 full-time (21 women); includes 6 minority (5 Black or African American, non-Hispanic/Latino; 1 Hispanic/Latino; 2 Two or more races, non-Hispanic/Latino), 10 international. Average age 29. 84 applicants, 12% accepted, 6 enrolled. In 2016, 6 doctorates awarded. *Degree requirements:* For doctorate, comprehensive exam, thesis/dissertation, first-year research project, 2 terms in student instructor position, publications, presentations. *Entrance requirements:* For doctorate, GRE, U.S. bachelor's degree or its equivalent from accredited institution. Additional exam requirements/recommendations for international students: Required—TOEFL (minimum score 600 paper-based; 102 iBT). *Application deadline:* For fall admission, 12/1 for domestic and international students. Application fee: $75 ($90 for international students). Electronic applications accepted. *Expenses:* Tuition, state resident: full-time $21,466; part-time $1152 per credit hour. Tuition, nonresident: full-time $43,346; part-time $2367 per credit hour. Part-time tuition and fees vary according to course load, degree level and program. *Financial support:* In 2016–17, 31 students received support, including 24 fellowships with full tuition reimbursements available (averaging $19,800 per year), 3 research assistantships with full tuition reimbursements available (averaging $19,737 per year), 28 teaching assistantships with full tuition reimbursements available (averaging $19,900 per year); scholarships/grants, traineeships, and health care benefits also available. Financial award application deadline: 4/30; financial award applicants required to submit FAFSA. *Faculty research:* Media psychology; political communication; global and comparative media; media, technology, and society; critical media studies. *Unit head:* Prof. Nojin Kwak, Professor and Chair, 734-764-0420, Fax: 734-764-3288, E-mail: commchair@umich.edu. *Application contact:* Amy B. Eaton, Graduate Program Coordinator, 734-615-8974, Fax: 734-764-3288, E-mail: lsa-commphd@umich.edu.
Website: http://www.lsa.umich.edu/comm/

**University of Minnesota, Twin Cities Campus,** Graduate School, College of Liberal Arts, School of Journalism and Mass Communication, Minneapolis, MN 55455-0213. Offers mass communication (MA, PhD); strategic communication (professional program) (MA). *Degree requirements:* For master's, thesis; for doctorate, comprehensive exam, thesis/dissertation. *Entrance requirements:* For master's, GRE; GMAT (for strategic communications program), letters of recommendation, minimum undergraduate GPA of 3.0, writing sample; two years professional experience (for strategic communications program); for doctorate, GRE, letters of recommendation, minimum undergraduate GPA of 3.0, writing sample. Additional exam requirements/recommendations for international students: Required—TOEFL (minimum score 79 iBT). Electronic applications accepted. *Faculty research:* Communication law, regulation, and ethics; history; mass media effects; new media, health communication.

**University of Nebraska–Lincoln,** Graduate College, College of Journalism and Mass Communications, Lincoln, NE 68588. Offers marketing, communication and advertising (MA); professional journalism (MA). *Program availability:* Online learning. *Degree requirements:* For master's, thesis. *Entrance requirements:* For master's, samples of work. Additional exam requirements/recommendations for international students: Required—TOEFL (minimum score 600 paper-based). Electronic applications accepted. *Faculty research:* Interactive media and the Internet, community newspapers, children's radio, advertising involvement, telecommunications policy.

**The University of North Carolina at Chapel Hill,** Graduate School, School of Media and Journalism, Chapel Hill, NC 27599. Offers mass communication (MA, PhD); technology and communication (MA, Certificate); JD/PhD; MA/JD. MA/JD and JD/PhD offered jointly with School of Law. *Accreditation:* ACEJMC (one or more programs are accredited). *Program availability:* Part-time, online learning. *Faculty:* 47 full-time (21 women), 4 part-time/adjunct (2 women). *Students:* 68 full-time (51 women), 59 part-time (42 women); includes 35 minority (10 Black or African American, non-Hispanic/Latino; 4 Asian, non-Hispanic/Latino; 4 Hispanic/Latino; 1 Native Hawaiian or other Pacific Islander, non-Hispanic/Latino; 16 Two or more races, non-Hispanic/Latino), 8 international. Average age 33. 179 applicants, 28% accepted, 42 enrolled. In 2016, 11 master's, 10 doctorates awarded. *Degree requirements:* For master's, comprehensive exam, thesis; for doctorate, comprehensive exam, thesis/dissertation. *Entrance requirements:* For master's and doctorate, GRE General Test, minimum GPA of 3.0. Additional exam requirements/recommendations for international students: Required—TOEFL (minimum score 620 paper-based, 105 iBT) or IELTS (7.5). Application fee: $85. Electronic applications accepted. *Expenses:* $7,094.58 per semester in-state, $15,120.58 per semester out-of-state; $625.42 per credit hour in-state (online), $1,412.42 per credit hour out-of-state (online). *Financial support:* In 2016–17, 55 students received support, including 47 fellowships with full tuition reimbursements available (averaging $17,319 per year), 3 research assistantships with full tuition reimbursements available (averaging $14,000 per year); scholarships/grants and health care benefits also available. Financial award application deadline: 12/5; financial award applicants required to submit FAFSA. *Faculty research:* Media processes and production; legal and regulatory issues in communication; media uses and effects; health communication; political, social, and strategic communication. *Total annual research expenditures:* $1 million. *Unit head:* Susan King, Dean, 919-962-1204, Fax: 919-962-0620, E-mail: susanking@unc.edu. *Application contact:* Casey Hart, Marketing and Instructional Design Coordinator, 919-843-9471, Fax: 919-962-0620, E-mail: mjgrad@unc.edu.
Website: http://mj.unc.edu/

**University of Oklahoma,** College of Arts and Sciences, Department of Communication, Norman, OK 73019. Offers communication (MA); communication technology (PhD); health communication (PhD); intercultural/international communication (PhD); interpersonal communication/social influence (PhD); organizational communication (PhD); political/mass communication (PhD). *Program availability:* Part-time. *Faculty:* 19 full-time (9 women). *Students:* 28 full-time (17 women), 40 part-time (19 women); includes 19 minority (6 Black or African American, non-Hispanic/Latino; 2 American Indian or Alaska Native, non-Hispanic/Latino; 9 Hispanic/Latino; 2 Two or more races, non-Hispanic/Latino), 9 international. Average age 36. 35 applicants, 60% accepted, 10 enrolled. In 2016, 14 master's, 8 doctorates awarded. *Degree requirements:* For master's, comprehensive exam (for some programs), thesis (for some programs), comprehensive exams or thesis; for doctorate, comprehensive exam, thesis/dissertation. *Entrance requirements:* For master's, GRE (for assistantship), statement of

purpose, transcripts, writing sample, letters of recommendation; for doctorate, GRE, statement of purpose, transcripts, writing sample, letters of recommendation. Additional exam requirements/recommendations for international students: Required—TOEFL (minimum score 79 iBT) or IELTS (minimum score 6.5). *Application deadline:* For fall admission, 1/15 priority date for domestic students, 1/15 for international students; for spring admission, 10/15 for domestic and international students. Application fee: $50 ($100 for international students). Electronic applications accepted. *Expenses:* Tuition, state resident: full-time $4886; part-time $203.60 per credit hour. Tuition, nonresident: full-time $18,989; part-time $791.20 per credit hour. *Required fees:* $3283; $126.25 per credit hour. $126.50 per semester. *Financial support:* In 2016–17, 31 students received support, including 1 research assistantship with full tuition reimbursement available (averaging $10,373 per year), 26 teaching assistantships with full tuition reimbursements available (averaging $16,515 per year); health care benefits also available. Financial award application deadline: 6/1; financial award applicants required to submit FAFSA. *Faculty research:* Interpersonal/social influence, organizational, political/mass communication, health communication, intercultural/international. *Total annual research expenditures:* $12,383. *Unit head:* Dr. Michael W. Kramer, Chair and Professor, 405-325-9503, Fax: 405-325-7625, E-mail: mkramer@ou.edu. *Application contact:* Shay Glover, Academic Advisor, 405-325-7710, Fax: 405-325-7625, E-mail: shay.glover@ou.edu.
Website: http://cas.ou.edu/comm

**University of Oklahoma,** Gaylord College of Journalism and Mass Communication, Program in Journalism and Mass Communication, Norman, OK 73019. Offers MA, PhD. *Program availability:* Part-time. *Students:* 32 full-time (19 women), 15 part-time (7 women); includes 7 minority (2 Black or African American, non-Hispanic/Latino; 1 Asian, non-Hispanic/Latino; 2 Hispanic/Latino; 2 Two or more races, non-Hispanic/Latino), 21 international. Average age 33. 20 applicants, 50% accepted, 9 enrolled. In 2016, 8 master's, 2 doctorates awarded. *Degree requirements:* For master's, comprehensive exam (for some programs), thesis (for some programs); for doctorate, comprehensive exam, thesis/dissertation. *Entrance requirements:* For master's, GRE, resume, statement of purpose, two letters of recommendation, official transcript; for doctorate, GRE, resume, statement of purpose, three letters of recommendation, official transcript. Additional exam requirements/recommendations for international students: Required—TOEFL (minimum score 79 iBT) or IELTS (minimum score 6.5). *Application deadline:* For fall admission, 5/1 for domestic students, 3/1 for international students; for spring admission, 11/1 for domestic students, 10/1 for international students; for summer admission, 3/1 for domestic students. Applications are processed on a rolling basis. Application fee: $50 ($100 for international students). Electronic applications accepted. *Expenses:* Tuition, state resident: full-time $4886; part-time $203.60 per credit hour. Tuition, nonresident: full-time $18,989; part-time $791.20 per credit hour. *Required fees:* $3283; $126.25 per credit hour. $126.50 per semester. *Financial support:* In 2016–17, 33 students received support. Fellowships, research assistantships with full tuition reimbursements available, teaching assistantships with full tuition reimbursements available, career-related internships or fieldwork, scholarships/grants, health care benefits, unspecified assistantships, and research and research travel awards available. Financial award application deadline: 6/1; financial award applicants required to submit FAFSA. *Faculty research:* Strategic communication: global public relations, corporate and nonprofit public relations, interactive advertising, message testing; creative media production: documentary, entertainment TV, commercial production; journalism: multimedia journalism, broadcasting, online; media management. *Unit head:* Dr. Katerina Tsetsura, Director of Graduate Studies/Professor of Strategic Communication, 405-325-2722, Fax: 405-325-7565, E-mail: gaylordgrad@ou.edu. *Application contact:* Larry Laneer, Graduate Advisor, 405-325-2722, Fax: 405-325-7565, E-mail: llaneer@ou.edu.
Website: http://www.ou.edu/content/gaylord/graduate.html

**University of Puerto Rico, Río Piedras Campus,** School of Communication, San Juan, PR 00931-3300. Offers MA. *Program availability:* Part-time. *Degree requirements:* For master's, comprehensive exam, thesis. *Entrance requirements:* For master's, GRE, PAEG, minimum GPA of 3.0, 2 letters of recommendation, interview.

**University of Southern Mississippi,** Graduate School, College of Arts and Letters, School of Mass Communication and Journalism, Hattiesburg, MS 39406. Offers mass communication (MA, MS, PhD); public relations (MA, MS). *Program availability:* Part-time. *Degree requirements:* For master's, comprehensive exam, thesis optional; for doctorate, comprehensive exam, thesis/dissertation. *Entrance requirements:* For master's, GRE General Test, minimum GPA of 3.0 in field of study, 2.75 in last 2 years; for doctorate, GRE General Test, minimum GPA of 3.5. Additional exam requirements/recommendations for international students: Required—TOEFL, IELTS. *Application deadline:* For fall admission, 3/1 priority date for domestic students, 3/1 for international students; for spring admission, 1/10 priority date for domestic and international students. Applications are processed on a rolling basis. Application fee: $60. *Expenses:* Tuition, area resident: Full-time $15,708; part-time $437 per credit hour. *Financial support:* Fellowships with full tuition reimbursements, research assistantships with full tuition reimbursements, teaching assistantships with full tuition reimbursements, career-related internships or fieldwork, Federal Work-Study, institutionally sponsored loans, scholarships/grants, health care benefits, and unspecified assistantships available. Financial award application deadline: 3/15; financial award applicants required to submit FAFSA. *Unit head:* Dr. David R. Davies, Director, 601-266-4258, Fax: 601-266-4263, E-mail: dave.davies@usm.edu. *Application contact:* Dr. Cheryl Jenkins, Graduate Coordinator, 601-266-6241, Fax: 601-266-6473, E-mail: cheryl.jenkins@usm.edu.
Website: https://www.usm.edu/school-of-journalism-and-media-studies

**University of South Florida,** College of Arts and Sciences, School of Mass Communications, Tampa, FL 33620-9951. Offers mass communications (MA), including media studies, multimedia journalism, strategic communication management. *Program availability:* Part-time, evening/weekend. *Faculty:* 11 full-time (6 women). *Students:* 27 full-time (23 women), 18 part-time (10 women); includes 5 minority (2 Black or African American, non-Hispanic/Latino; 2 Hispanic/Latino; 1 Native Hawaiian or other Pacific Islander, non-Hispanic/Latino), 25 international. Average age 27. 39 applicants, 82% accepted, 21 enrolled. In 2016, 16 master's awarded. *Degree requirements:* For master's, comprehensive exam, thesis optional. *Entrance requirements:* For master's, GRE General Test, minimum GPA of 3.0 in last 60 hours of course work, three letters of recommendation, letter of intent, resume/curriculum vitae. Additional exam requirements/recommendations for international students: Required—TOEFL (minimum score 550 paper-based; 79 iBT) or IELTS (minimum score 6.5). *Application deadline:* For fall admission, 2/15 for domestic and international students. Application fee: $30. Electronic applications accepted. *Expenses:* Tuition, state resident: full-time $7766; part-time $431.43 per credit hour. Tuition, nonresident: full-time $15,789; part-time $877.17 per credit hour. *Required fees:* $37 per term. *Financial support:* In 2016–17, 5 students received support, including 9 teaching assistantships with tuition reimbursements available (averaging $10,513 per year); unspecified assistantships also available. Financial award application deadline: 2/28. *Faculty research:* First Amendment analysis, civic journalism, public opinion, media ethics, media effects research in sports public relations, public relations management, advertisement, telecommunications. *Total annual research expenditures:* $88,114. *Unit head:* Dr. Jim Andrews, Interim Director/Associate Professor, 813-974-2108, Fax: 813-974-2592, E-mail: jimandrews@usf.edu. *Application contact:* Dr. Michael Mitrook, Assistant Professor, 813-974-8890, Fax: 813-974-2592, E-mail: mmitrook@usf.edu.
Website: http://masscom.usf.edu/grad/

**University of South Florida,** Innovative Education, Tampa, FL 33620-9951. Offers adult, career and higher education (Graduate Certificate), including college teaching, leadership in developing human resources, leadership in higher education; Africana studies (Graduate Certificate), including diasporas and health disparities, genocide and human rights; aging studies (Graduate Certificate), including gerontology; art research (Graduate Certificate), including museum studies; business foundations (Graduate Certificate); chemical and biomedical engineering (Graduate Certificate), including materials science and engineering, water, health and sustainability; child and family studies (Graduate Certificate), including positive behavior support; civil and industrial engineering (Graduate Certificate), including transportation systems analysis; community and family health (Graduate Certificate), including maternal and child health, social marketing and public health, violence and injury: prevention and intervention, women's health; criminology (Graduate Certificate), including criminal justice administration; educational measurement and research (Graduate Certificate), including evaluation; English (Graduate Certificate), including comparative literary studies, creative writing, professional and technical communication; entrepreneurship (Graduate Certificate); environmental health (Graduate Certificate), including safety management; epidemiology and biostatistics (Graduate Certificate), including applied biostatistics, biostatistics, concepts and tools of epidemiology, epidemiology, epidemiology of infectious diseases; geography, environment and planning (Graduate Certificate), including community development, environmental policy and management, geographical information systems; geology (Graduate Certificate), including hydrogeology; global health (Graduate Certificate), including disaster management, global health and Latin American and Caribbean studies, global health practice, humanitarian assistance, infection control; government and international affairs (Graduate Certificate), including Cuban studies, globalization studies; health policy and management (Graduate Certificate), including health management and leadership, public health policy and programs; hearing specialist: early intervention (Graduate Certificate); industrial and management systems engineering (Graduate Certificate), including systems engineering, technology management; information studies (Graduate Certificate), including school library media specialist; information systems/decision sciences (Graduate Certificate), including analytics and business intelligence; instructional technology (Graduate Certificate), including distance education, Florida digital/virtual educator, instructional design, multimedia design, Web design; internal medicine, bioethics and medical humanities (Graduate Certificate), including biomedical ethics; Latin American and Caribbean studies (Graduate Certificate); mass communications (Graduate Certificate), including multimedia journalism; mathematics and statistics (Graduate Certificate), including mathematics; medicine (Graduate Certificate), including aging and neuroscience, bioinformatics, biotechnology, brain fitness and memory management, clinical investigation, health informatics, health sciences, integrative weight management, intellectual property, medicine and gender, metabolic and nutritional medicine, metabolic cardiology, pharmacy sciences; national and competitive intelligence (Graduate Certificate); psychological and social foundations (Graduate Certificate), including career counseling, college teaching, diversity in education, mental health counseling, school counseling; public affairs (Graduate Certificate), including nonprofit management, public management, research administration; public health (Graduate Certificate), including environmental health, health equity, public health generalist, translational research in adolescent behavioral health; public health practices (Graduate Certificate), including planning for healthy communities; rehabilitation and mental health counseling (Graduate Certificate), including integrative mental health care, marriage and family therapy, rehabilitation technology; secondary education (Graduate Certificate), including ESOL, foreign language education: culture and content, foreign language education: professional; social work (Graduate Certificate), including geriatric social work/clinical gerontology; special education (Graduate Certificate), including autism spectrum disorder, disabilities education: severe/profound; world languages (Graduate Certificate), including teaching English as a second language (TESL) or foreign language. *Expenses:* Tuition, state resident: full-time $7766; part-time $431.43 per credit hour. Tuition, nonresident: full-time $15,789; part-time $877.17 per credit hour. *Required fees:* $37 per term. *Unit head:* Kathy Barnes, Interdisciplinary Programs Coordinator, 813-974-8031, Fax: 813-974-7061, E-mail: barnesk@usf.edu. *Application contact:* Karen Tylinski, Metro Initiatives, 813-974-9943, Fax: 813-974-7061, E-mail: ktylinsk@usf.edu.
Website: http://www.usf.edu/innovative-education/

**University of Wisconsin–Madison,** Graduate School, College of Letters and Science, School of Journalism and Mass Communication, Program in Journalism and Mass Communication, Madison, WI 53706-1380. Offers MA.

**University of Wisconsin–Madison,** Graduate School, College of Letters and Science, School of Journalism and Mass Communication, Program in Mass Communication, Madison, WI 53706-1380. Offers PhD. *Degree requirements:* For doctorate, thesis/dissertation.

**University of Wisconsin–Milwaukee,** Graduate School, College of Letters and Science, Department of Communication, Milwaukee, WI 53201-0413. Offers communication (MA, PhD), including interpersonal communication (MA), organizational communication (MA), rhetoric and public communication (MA), rhetorical leadership; rhetorical leadership (Graduate Certificate). *Program availability:* Part-time. *Faculty:* 18 full-time (11 women). *Students:* 24 full-time (14 women), 15 part-time (11 women); includes 5 minority (1 Black or African American, non-Hispanic/Latino; 1 Asian, non-Hispanic/Latino; 1 Hispanic/Latino; 2 Two or more races, non-Hispanic/Latino), 4 international. Average age 34. 44 applicants, 52% accepted, 9 enrolled. In 2016, 2 master's, 8 doctorates awarded. *Degree requirements:* For master's, thesis or alternative; for doctorate, comprehensive exam. *Entrance requirements:* For master's, GRE General Test, minimum GPA of 3.0. Additional exam requirements/recommendations for international students: Required—TOEFL (minimum score 550 paper-based; 79 iBT), IELTS (minimum score 6). *Application deadline:* For fall admission, 1/1 priority date for domestic students; for spring admission, 9/1 for domestic students. Applications are processed on a rolling basis. Application fee: $56. Electronic applications accepted. *Financial support:* In 2016–17, 3 fellowships, 34 teaching assistantships were awarded; research assistantships, career-related internships or fieldwork, unspecified assistantships, and project assistantships also available. Support available to part-time students. Financial award application deadline: 4/15; financial award applicants required to submit FAFSA. *Unit head:* Mike Allen, Department Chair, 414-229-4510, E-mail: mikealle@uwm.edu. *Application contact:* General Information Contact, 414-229-4982, Fax: 414-229-6967, E-mail: gradschool@uwm.edu.
Website: https://uwm.edu/communication/

**University of Wisconsin–Superior,** Graduate Division, Department of Communicating Arts, Superior, WI 54880-4500. Offers mass communication (MA); speech communication (MA); theater (MA). *Program availability:* Part-time. *Degree requirements:* For master's, comprehensive exam, thesis or alternative, position paper or project. *Entrance requirements:* For master's, minimum GPA of 2.75. Electronic

applications accepted. *Faculty research:* Multimedia technology, ethics in journalism, diversity, electronic portfolio assessment.

**University of Wisconsin–Whitewater,** School of Graduate Studies, College of Arts and Communications, Department of Communication, Whitewater, WI 53190-1790. Offers corporate communication (MS); mass communication (MS). *Program availability:* Part-time, evening/weekend, online learning. *Degree requirements:* For master's, thesis or alternative. *Entrance requirements:* For master's, 2 letters of recommendation, goal statement. Additional exam requirements/recommendations for international students: Required—TOEFL (minimum score 550 paper-based; 80 iBT), IELTS (minimum score 6). Electronic applications accepted.

**Virginia Commonwealth University,** Graduate School, College of Humanities and Sciences, School of Mass Communications, Program in Mass Communications, Richmond, VA 23284-9005. Offers multimedia journalism (MS); strategic public relations (MS). *Degree requirements:* For master's, comprehensive exam, thesis optional.

*Entrance requirements:* For master's, GRE General Test. Additional exam requirements/recommendations for international students: Required—TOEFL (minimum score 600 paper-based; 100 iBT); Recommended—IELTS (minimum score 6.5). *Application deadline:* For fall admission, 3/15 for domestic students. Applications are processed on a rolling basis. Application fee: $50. Electronic applications accepted. *Financial support:* Teaching assistantships, career-related internships or fieldwork, Federal Work-Study, institutionally sponsored loans, and tuition waivers (full and partial) available. Support available to part-time students. Financial award applicants required to submit FAFSA. *Faculty research:* Multimedia journalism, strategic public relations. *Unit head:* Dr. Terry Oggel, Interim Director, School of Mass Communications, 804-828-2660, Fax: 804-828-9175, E-mail: masscomm@vcu.edu. *Application contact:* June O. Nicholson, Director of Graduate Studies, 804-827-0251, Fax: 804-828-9175, E-mail: jonichol@vcu.edu. Website: http://www.has.vcu.edu/mac/

# Media Studies

**American University,** School of Communication, Film and Electronic Media Program, Washington, DC 20016-8001. Offers MFA. *Students:* 13 full-time (9 women), 4 part-time (0 women); includes 8 minority (4 Black or African American, non-Hispanic/Latino; 3 Hispanic/Latino; 1 Two or more races, non-Hispanic/Latino), 1 international. *Degree requirements:* For master's, comprehensive exam, thesis or alternative. *Entrance requirements:* For master's, GRE General Test. Additional exam requirements/recommendations for international students: Required—TOEFL (minimum score 600 paper-based; 100 iBT), IELTS. *Application deadline:* For fall admission, 2/1 priority date for domestic and international students. Applications are processed on a rolling basis. Application fee: $50. Electronic applications accepted. *Expenses: Tuition:* Full-time $28,422; part-time $1579 per credit hour. *Required fees:* $690; $200 per term. Tuition and fees vary according to course load, degree level and program. *Financial support:* Fellowships with partial tuition reimbursements, research assistantships with partial tuition reimbursements, teaching assistantships with partial tuition reimbursements, career-related internships or fieldwork, Federal Work-Study, institutionally sponsored loans, scholarships/grants, tuition waivers (partial), and unspecified assistantships available. Financial award application deadline: 2/1; financial award applicants required to submit FAFSA. *Faculty research:* Documentary film production, social media, media and public policy, visual literacy, new technology. *Unit head:* Prof. Brigid Maher, Director, Film and Media Arts Division, 202-885-2664, Fax: 202-885-2019, E-mail: bmaher@american.edu. *Application contact:* Leila Hernandez, Program Coordinator, Student Services, 202-885-2040, Fax: 202-885-2019, E-mail: leila@american.edu. Website: http://www.american.edu/soc/film/degrees/MFA-FLEM.cfm

**American University,** School of Communication, PhD Program in Communication, Washington, DC 20016-8001. Offers media industries and institutions (PhD); media, public issues, and engagement (PhD); media, technology, and culture (PhD). *Faculty:* 10 full-time (4 women). *Students:* 20 full-time (14 women); includes 4 minority (2 Black or African American, non-Hispanic/Latino; 2 Hispanic/Latino), 9 international. 48 applicants, 17% accepted, 5 enrolled. In 2016, 5 doctorates awarded. *Degree requirements:* For doctorate, comprehensive exam, thesis/dissertation. *Entrance requirements:* For doctorate, GRE General Test. Additional exam requirements/recommendations for international students: Required—TOEFL (minimum score 600 paper-based; 100 iBT), IELTS (minimum score 7). *Application deadline:* For fall admission, 12/15 priority date for domestic and international students. Applications are processed on a rolling basis. Application fee: $55. Electronic applications accepted. *Expenses: Tuition:* Full-time $28,422; part-time $1579 per credit hour. *Required fees:* $690; $200 per term. Tuition and fees vary according to course load, degree level and program. *Financial support:* In 2016–17, 5 students received support, including 20 research assistantships with full tuition reimbursements available (averaging $42,000 per year); Federal Work-Study, scholarships/grants, and unspecified assistantships also available. Financial award application deadline: 12/15; financial award applicants required to submit FAFSA. *Faculty research:* Public policy advocacy; social impact of mass media and communication policies; science, health, and environmental communication; intercultural and international strategic communication. *Unit head:* Prof. Kathryn Montgomery, Director, 202-885-2680, Fax: 202-885-2099, E-mail: kcm@american.edu. *Application contact:* Leila Hernandez, Program Coordinator, Student Services, 202-885-2040, Fax: 202-885-2019, E-mail: leila@american.edu. Website: http://www.american.edu/soc/communication-studies/degrees/phd-in-communication.cfm

**American University of Beirut,** Graduate Programs, Faculty of Arts and Sciences, Beirut, Lebanon. Offers anthropology (MA); Arab and Middle Eastern history (PhD); Arabic language and literature (MA, PhD); archaeology (MA); art history and curating (MA); biology (MS); cell and molecular biology (PhD); chemistry (MS); clinical psychology (MA); computational sciences (MS); computer science (MS); economics (MA); education (MA); English language (MA); English literature (MA); environmental policy planning (MS); financial economics (MAFE); geology (MS); history (MA); Islamic studies (MA); mathematics (MS); media studies (MA); Middle Eastern studies (MA); physics (MS); political studies (MA); psychology (MA); public administration (MA); public policy and international affairs (MA); sociology (MA); statistics (MA, MS); theoretical physics (PhD); transnational American studies (MA). *Program availability:* Part-time. *Faculty:* 133 full-time (42 women), 6 part-time/adjunct (2 women). *Students:* 240 full-time (172 women), 227 part-time (166 women). Average age 27. 286 applicants, 67% accepted, 108 enrolled. In 2016, 60 master's, 3 doctorates awarded. Terminal master's awarded for partial completion of doctoral program. *Degree requirements:* For master's, one foreign language, comprehensive exam, thesis (for some programs); for doctorate, one foreign language, comprehensive exam, thesis/dissertation. *Entrance requirements:* For master's, GRE (for some MA, MS programs), letters of recommendation; for doctorate, GRE, letters of recommendation. Additional exam requirements/recommendations for international students: Required—TOEFL (minimum score 600 paper-based; 97 iBT), IELTS (minimum score 7). *Application deadline:* For fall admission, 4/3 for domestic students; for winter admission, 11/3 for domestic students. Application fee: $50. Electronic applications accepted. *Expenses:* Contact institution. *Financial support:* In 2016–17, 4 fellowships (averaging $11,200 per year), 18 research assistantships (averaging $5,400 per year) were awarded; teaching assistantships, career-related internships or fieldwork, Federal Work-Study, institutionally sponsored loans, scholarships/grants, traineeships, health care benefits, tuition waivers (full), and unspecified assistantships also available. Support available to part-time students. *Faculty research:* Development economics, spatial econometrics, health economics, labor economics, energy economics, hydrogeology, geophysics, petrophysics, structural

geology, mineralogy, petrology, geochemistry, multilingualism, comparative/world literature, translation studies, book histories/ cultures, biocatalysis, molecular recognition, photocatalysis, photophysical and biophysical chemistry, probe chemistry, machine learning, data science. *Unit head:* Dr. Nadia Maria El Cheikh, Dean, Faculty of Arts and Sciences, 961-1374374 Ext. 3800, Fax: 961-1744461, E-mail: nmcheikh@aub.edu.lb. *Application contact:* Dr. Salim Kanaan, Director, Admissions Office, 961-1350000 Ext. 2590, Fax: 961-1750775, E-mail: sk00@aub.edu.lb. Website: http://www.aub.edu.lb/fas/

**Angelo State University,** College of Graduate Studies and Research, College of Arts and Humanities, Department of Communication and Mass Media, San Angelo, TX 76909. Offers communication (MA). *Program availability:* Part-time, evening/weekend. *Students:* 10 full-time (2 women), 5 part-time (4 women); includes 5 minority (2 Black or African American, non-Hispanic/Latino; 3 Hispanic/Latino), 2 international. Average age 28. *Degree requirements:* For master's, comprehensive exam, thesis optional. *Entrance requirements:* Additional exam requirements/recommendations for international students: Required—TOEFL or IELTS. *Application deadline:* For fall admission, 7/15 priority date for domestic students, 6/10 for international students; for spring admission, 12/1 priority date for domestic students, 11/1 for international students. Applications are processed on a rolling basis. Application fee: $40 ($50 for international students). Electronic applications accepted. *Expenses:* Tuition, state resident: full-time $3726; part-time $2484 per year. Tuition, nonresident: full-time $10,746; part-time $7164 per year. *Required fees:* $2538; $1702 per unit. *Financial support:* Teaching assistantships, career-related internships or fieldwork, Federal Work-Study, scholarships/grants, and unspecified assistantships available. Support available to part-time students. Financial award application deadline: 3/1; financial award applicants required to submit FAFSA. *Unit head:* Dr. Herman Otis Howard, Chair, 325-942-2031, Fax: 325-942-2551, E-mail: herman.howard@angelo.edu. *Application contact:* Dr. June H. Smith, Graduate Advisor, 325-486-6088, Fax: 325-942-2551, E-mail: june.smith@angelo.edu. Website: http://www.angelo.edu/dept/communication-mass-media/

**Arizona State University at the Tempe campus,** College of Liberal Arts and Sciences, Department of English, Program in Film and Media Studies, Tempe, AZ 85287-0402. Offers American media and popular culture (MAS). *Program availability:* Part-time, evening/weekend, online learning. *Degree requirements:* For master's, integrated project. *Entrance requirements:* For master's, minimum GPA of 3.0 or equivalent in last 2 years of work leading to bachelor's degree. Additional exam requirements/recommendations for international students: Required—TOEFL, IELTS, or PTE. Electronic applications accepted. *Expenses:* Contact institution.

**Arizona State University at the Tempe campus,** Herberger Institute for Design and the Arts, School of Arts, Media and Engineering, Tempe, AZ 85287-8709. Offers media arts and sciences (PhD). *Degree requirements:* For doctorate, comprehensive exam, thesis/dissertation, interactive Program of Study (iPOS) submitted before completing 50 percent of required credit hours. *Entrance requirements:* For doctorate, GRE, minimum GPA of 3.25 in last 2 years of work leading to bachelor's degree, portfolio of supporting material, statement of educational/career goals, 3 letters of recommendation, resume/curriculum vitae. Additional exam requirements/recommendations for international students: Required—TOEFL, IELTS, or PTE. Electronic applications accepted.

**Arkansas State University,** Graduate School, College of Media and Communication, Department of Media, State University, AR 72467. Offers mass communications (MSMC). *Program availability:* Part-time. *Degree requirements:* For master's, comprehensive exam, thesis or alternative. *Entrance requirements:* For master's, GRE General Test or MAT, appropriate bachelor's degree, letters of reference, educational experience, professional experience, official transcripts, immunization records. Additional exam requirements/recommendations for international students: Required—TOEFL (minimum score 550 paper-based; 79 iBT), IELTS (minimum score 6), PTE (minimum score 56). Electronic applications accepted.

**Bob Jones University,** Graduate Programs, Greenville, SC 29614. Offers accountancy (MS); Bible (MA); Bible translation (MA); Biblical studies (Certificate); broadcast management (MS); business administration (MBA); church history (MA, PhD); church ministries (MA); church music (MM); cinema and video production (MA); counseling (MS); curriculum and instruction (Ed D); divinity (M Div); dramatic production (MA); educational leadership (MS, Ed D, Ed S); elementary education (M Ed, MAT); English (M Ed, MA, MAT); fine arts (MA); graphic design (MA); history (M Ed, MA); illustration (MA); interpretative speech (MA); mathematics (M Ed, MAT); medical missions (Certificate); ministry (MM, D Min); multi-categorical special education (M Ed, MAT); music (M Ed); New Testament interpretation (PhD); Old Testament interpretation (PhD); orchestral instrument performance (MM); organ performance (MM); pastoral studies (MA); personnel services (MS, Ed S); piano pedagogy (MM); piano performance (MM); platform arts (MA); radio and television broadcasting (MS); rhetoric and public address (MA); secondary education (M Ed); studio art (MA); teaching Bible (MA); theology (MA, PhD); voice performance (MM); youth ministries (MA); M Div/MM.

**Boston University,** College of Communication, Department of Film and Television, Boston, MA 02215. Offers MFA, MS. *Program availability:* Part-time. *Faculty:* 17 full-time, 25 part-time/adjunct. *Students:* 86 full-time (47 women), 13 part-time (8 women); includes 27 minority (7 Black or African American, non-Hispanic/Latino; 2 American Indian or Alaska Native, non-Hispanic/Latino; 5 Asian, non-Hispanic/Latino; 9 Hispanic/Latino; 4 Two or more races, non-Hispanic/Latino), 16 international. Average age 26. 352 applicants, 41% accepted, 67 enrolled. In 2016, 31 master's awarded. *Degree requirements:* For master's, thesis. *Entrance requirements:* For master's, GRE General

*Media Studies*

Test, resume, writing and creative samples, letters of recommendation. Additional exam requirements/recommendations for international students: Required—TOEFL (minimum score 600 paper-based; 100 iBT), IELTS (minimum score 7). *Application deadline:* For fall admission, 5/1 for domestic and international students. Applications are processed on a rolling basis. Application fee: $95. Electronic applications accepted. *Financial support:* Research assistantships, teaching assistantships with partial tuition reimbursements, career-related internships or fieldwork, Federal Work-Study, institutionally sponsored loans, scholarships/grants, and unspecified assistantships available. Support available to part-time students. Financial award application deadline: 5/1; financial award applicants required to submit FAFSA. *Unit head:* Paul Schneider, Chairman, 617-353-3483, Fax: 617-353-1084, E-mail: ftvchair@bu.edu. *Application contact:* Haley Nielsen, Administrator of Admission and Financial Aid, 617-353-3481, E-mail: comgrad@bu.edu.
Website: http://www.bu.edu/com/academics/film-tv/

**Boston University,** College of Communication, Division of Emerging Media Studies, Boston, MA 02215. Offers MA, PhD. *Program availability:* Part-time. *Faculty:* 4 full-time (1 woman). *Students:* 46 full-time (37 women), 5 part-time (3 women); includes 7 minority (3 Black or African American, non-Hispanic/Latino; 2 Asian, non-Hispanic/Latino; 1 Hispanic/Latino; 1 Two or more races, non-Hispanic/Latino), 24 international. Average age 24. 72 applicants, 44% accepted, 15 enrolled. In 2016, 18 master's awarded. *Degree requirements:* For master's, thesis; for doctorate, comprehensive exam, thesis/dissertation. *Entrance requirements:* For master's and doctorate, GRE, resume, writing samples, letters of recommendation. Additional exam requirements/recommendations for international students: Required—TOEFL (minimum score 600 paper-based; 100 iBT), IELTS. *Application deadline:* For fall admission, 5/1 for domestic and international students. Applications are processed on a rolling basis. Application fee: $95. Electronic applications accepted. *Financial support:* Fellowships, research assistantships, teaching assistantships, career-related internships or fieldwork, Federal Work-Study, institutionally sponsored loans, scholarships/grants, health care benefits, and unspecified assistantships available. Financial award application deadline: 5/1; financial award applicants required to submit FAFSA. *Unit head:* Dr. James Katz, Professor of Emerging Media/Chair of the Division of Emerging Media Studies, 617-353-7733, E-mail: katz2020@bu.edu. *Application contact:* Haley Nielsen, Administrator of Admission and Financial Aid, 617-353-3481, E-mail: comgrad@bu.edu.
Website: http://www.bu.edu/com/academics/emerging-media/

**Bowling Green State University,** Graduate College, College of Arts and Sciences, School of Media and Communication, Bowling Green, OH 43403. Offers media and communication (MA, PhD); strategic communication (MA). *Program availability:* Part-time. Terminal master's awarded for partial completion of doctoral program. *Degree requirements:* For master's, thesis or alternative; for doctorate, comprehensive exam, thesis/dissertation. *Entrance requirements:* For master's and doctorate, GRE General Test. Additional exam requirements/recommendations for international students: Required—TOEFL. *Application deadline:* For fall admission, 1/1 priority date for domestic students. Application fee: $30. Electronic applications accepted. *Financial support:* Fellowships with full tuition reimbursements, research assistantships with full tuition reimbursements, teaching assistantships with full tuition reimbursements, career-related internships or fieldwork, Federal Work-Study, and unspecified assistantships available. Financial award applicants required to submit FAFSA. *Unit head:* Dr. Oliver Boyd-Barrett, Director, 419-372-6018. *Application contact:* Dr. Radhika Gajjala, Assistant Professor, 419-372-0528.
Website: http://www.bgsu.edu/arts-and-sciences/media-and-communication.html

**Brooklyn College of the City University of New York,** School of Visual, Media and Performing Arts, Department of Television and Radio, Brooklyn, NY 11210-2889. Offers media studies (MS); television production (MFA). *Program availability:* Part-time, evening/weekend. *Degree requirements:* For master's, comprehensive exam. *Entrance requirements:* For master's, GRE General Test or MAT, 12 credits in television/radio with a minimum B average, 2 letters of recommendation. Additional exam requirements/recommendations for international students: Required—TOEFL (minimum score 580 paper-based; 92 iBT). Electronic applications accepted. *Faculty research:* Criticism, research methods, audience behavior, policy and regulation, program history, international television and radio.

**California College of the Arts,** Graduate Programs, Fine Arts Programs, San Francisco, CA 94107. Offers ceramics (MFA); film/video/performance (MFA); glass (MFA); interdisciplinary studies (MFA); jewelry/metal arts (MFA); media studies (MFA); painting/drawing (MFA); photography (MFA); printmaking (MFA); sculpture (MFA); textiles (MFA); wood/furniture (MFA). *Accreditation:* NASAD. *Faculty:* 23 full-time (14 women), 17 part-time/adjunct (12 women). *Students:* 75 full-time (55 women); includes 20 minority (7 Black or African American, non-Hispanic/Latino; 2 American Indian or Alaska Native, non-Hispanic/Latino; 6 Asian, non-Hispanic/Latino; 5 Hispanic/Latino), 15 international. Average age 29. 224 applicants, 54% accepted, 43 enrolled. In 2016, 27 master's awarded. *Degree requirements:* For master's, thesis, exhibit. *Entrance requirements:* For master's, appropriate bachelor's degree, portfolio, resume, 2 letters of recommendation, transcript. Additional exam requirements/recommendations for international students: Required—TOEFL, IELTS, or PTE. *Application deadline:* For fall admission, 1/10 for domestic and international students. Applications are processed on a rolling basis. Application fee: $70. Electronic applications accepted. *Expenses:* $1,641 per unit, $49,230 per year tuition; $490 fees. *Financial support:* In 2016–17, fellowships (averaging $42,000 per year), teaching assistantships (averaging $2,000 per year) were awarded; career-related internships or fieldwork, Federal Work-Study, scholarships/grants, health care benefits, and unspecified assistantships also available. Financial award application deadline: 7/31; financial award applicants required to submit FAFSA. *Unit head:* James Gobel, Chair, 415-551-9214, Fax: 415-703-9539, E-mail: jgobel@cca.edu. *Application contact:* Wes Fanelli, Assistant Director of Graduate Admissions, 415-703-9533, Fax: 415-703-9539, E-mail: wfanelli@cca.edu.

**Carnegie Mellon University,** School of Computer Science and College of Fine Arts, Program in Entertainment Technology, Pittsburgh, PA 15213-3891. Offers MET.

**Central Michigan University,** College of Graduate Studies, College of Communication and Fine Arts, School of Broadcasting and Cinematic Arts, Mount Pleasant, MI 48859. Offers electronic media management (MA); electronic media production (MA); electronic media studies (MA); film theory and criticism (MA). *Program availability:* Part-time. *Degree requirements:* For master's, thesis or alternative. *Entrance requirements:* For master's, undergraduate degree in broadcasting, film studies, or an associated discipline with minimum GPA of 2.7. Electronic applications accepted. *Faculty research:* Multimedia production, film history and criticism, writing and promotions, international broadcasting and media systems, history of American broadcasting.

**Champlain College,** Graduate Studies, Burlington, VT 05402-0670. Offers business (MBA); digital forensic science (MS); early childhood education (M Ed); emergent media (MFA, MS); executive leadership (MS); health care administration (MS); information security operations (MS); law (MS); mediation and applied conflict studies (MS). MS in emergent media program held in Shanghai. *Program availability:* Part-time, online learning. *Degree requirements:* For master's, capstone project. *Entrance requirements:* Additional exam requirements/recommendations for international students: Required—TOEFL (minimum score 550 paper-based; 80 iBT). Electronic applications accepted.

**City College of the City University of New York,** Graduate School, Division of Humanities and the Arts, Department of Media and Communication Arts, Program in Film, New York, NY 10031-9198. Offers MFA. *Entrance requirements:* For master's, BA or BFA with minimum GPA of 3.0, undergraduate training in film and video or equivalent work/industry experience, online video portfolio, 2 letters of recommendation, official transcripts, resume. Additional exam requirements/recommendations for international students: Required—TOEFL (minimum score 575 paper-based; 91 iBT), IELTS (minimum score 6.5). Electronic applications accepted. Tuition and fees vary according to course load, degree level and program.

**Claremont Graduate University,** Graduate Programs, School of Arts and Humanities, Department of Cultural Studies, Claremont, CA 91711-6160. Offers Africana studies (Certificate); cultural studies (MA, PhD); media studies (MA, PhD); museum studies (MA). *Program availability:* Part-time. *Faculty:* 5 full-time (1 woman). *Students:* 47 full-time (35 women), 84 part-time (8 women); includes 28 minority (5 Black or African American, non-Hispanic/Latino; 1 American Indian or Alaska Native, non-Hispanic/Latino; 7 Asian, non-Hispanic/Latino; 12 Hispanic/Latino; 3 Two or more races, non-Hispanic/Latino), 5 international. Average age 35. In 2016, 4 master's, 2 doctorates, 1 other advanced degree awarded. *Entrance requirements:* For master's and doctorate, GRE General Test. Additional exam requirements/recommendations for international students: Required—TOEFL (minimum score 75 iBT). *Application deadline:* For fall admission, 2/1 priority date for domestic and international students. Applications are processed on a rolling basis. Application fee: $80. Electronic applications accepted. *Expenses: Tuition:* Full-time $44,328; part-time $1847 per unit. *Required fees:* $600; $300 per semester. Tuition and fees vary according to course load and program. *Financial support:* Fellowships, research assistantships, Federal Work-Study, institutionally sponsored loans, and scholarships/grants available. Support available to part-time students. Financial award application deadline: 2/15; financial award applicants required to submit FAFSA. *Unit head:* David Luis-Brown, Chair, 909-607-3337, E-mail: david.luis-brown@cgu.edu. *Application contact:* Amy Sandefur, Assistant Director of Admissions, 909-607-9101, E-mail: amy.sandefur@cgu.edu.
Website: https://www.cgu.edu/departments/cultural-studies/

**College of Staten Island of the City University of New York,** Graduate Programs, Division of Humanities and Social Sciences, Program in Cinema and Media Studies, Staten Island, NY 10314-6600. Offers MA. *Program availability:* Part-time, evening/weekend. *Faculty:* 4 full-time, 1 part-time/adjunct. *Students:* 10 part-time. Average age 31. 12 applicants, 58% accepted, 4 enrolled. In 2016, 1 master's awarded. *Degree requirements:* For master's, comprehensive exam (for some programs), 36 credits in cinema and media studies courses; written thesis, production thesis, or examination. *Entrance requirements:* For master's, bachelor's degree with minimum B average in undergraduate cinema studies or communications courses; 10-12 page writing sample; three letters of recommendation; 1-2 page statement of intent detailing interest in field, background in film and media studies, and/or research interests. Additional exam requirements/recommendations for international students: Required—TOEFL (minimum score 550 paper-based; 79 iBT), IELTS (minimum score 6.5). *Application deadline:* For fall admission, 6/15 priority date for domestic and international students; for spring admission, 11/25 priority date for domestic and international students. Applications are processed on a rolling basis. Application fee: $125. Electronic applications accepted. *Expenses:* Tuition, state resident: full-time $10,130; part-time $425 per credit. Tuition, nonresident: full-time $18,720; part-time $780 per credit. *Required fees:* $181.10 per semester. Tuition and fees vary according to program. *Faculty research:* Political communication, Latino/a media and audience, gender and sexuality, representation of race and ethnicity, video surveillance. *Unit head:* Jillian Baez, Graduate Program Coordinator, 718-982-2143, E-mail: cinemamasters@csi.cuny.edu. *Application contact:* Sasha Spence, Associate Director of Graduate Admissions, 718-982-2019, Fax: 718-982-2500, E-mail: sasha.spence@csi.cuny.edu.
Website: http://csivc.csi.cuny.edu/mediaculture/files

**Colorado State University,** College of Liberal Arts, Department of Journalism and Media Communication, Fort Collins, CO 80523-1785. Offers communications and media management (MCMM); public communication and technology (MS, PhD). *Program availability:* Part-time. *Faculty:* 13 full-time (6 women). *Students:* 26 full-time (18 women), 40 part-time (29 women); includes 11 minority (1 Black or African American, non-Hispanic/Latino; 2 American Indian or Alaska Native, non-Hispanic/Latino; 4 Hispanic/Latino; 4 Two or more races, non-Hispanic/Latino), 9 international. Average age 32. 28 applicants, 71% accepted, 14 enrolled. In 2016, 9 master's, 4 doctorates awarded. Terminal master's awarded for partial completion of doctoral program. *Degree requirements:* For master's, thesis (for some programs), research project; for doctorate, comprehensive exam, thesis/dissertation. *Entrance requirements:* For master's and doctorate, GRE General Test, minimum GPA of 3.0. Additional exam requirements/recommendations for international students: Required—TOEFL (minimum score 550 paper-based; 80 iBT); Recommended—IELTS (minimum score 6.5). Application fee: $60 ($70 for international students). Electronic applications accepted. *Expenses:* Tuition, state resident: full-time $9628. Tuition, nonresident: full-time $23,603. *Required fees:* $2253; $528.14 per credit hour. $264.07 per semester. Tuition and fees vary according to course load and program. *Financial support:* In 2016–17, 20 students received support, including 1 research assistantship with full and partial tuition reimbursement available (averaging $18,663 per year), 32 teaching assistantships with full and partial tuition reimbursements available (averaging $14,987 per year); fellowships with full and partial tuition reimbursements available, scholarships/grants, and health care benefits also available. Financial award application deadline: 1/15; financial award applicants required to submit FAFSA. *Faculty research:* Media and human behavior; strategic communication; risk, science and health communication; media ethics and policy; news and information. *Total annual research expenditures:* $558,539. *Unit head:* Greg Luft, Professor and Department Chair, 970-491-1979, Fax: 970-491-2908, E-mail: greg.luft@colostate.edu. *Application contact:* Linda Kidder, Graduate Program Administrator, 970-491-5132, Fax: 970-491-2908, E-mail: linda.kidder@colostate.edu.
Website: http://journalism.colostate.edu/

**Concordia University,** School of Graduate Studies, Faculty of Arts and Science, Department of Communication Studies, Montréal, QC H3G 1M8, Canada. Offers communication (PhD); communication studies (Diploma); media studies (MA). PhD program offered jointly with Universityé de Montréal and Universityé du Quebec à Montréal. *Degree requirements:* For master's, thesis optional; for doctorate, one foreign language, comprehensive exam, thesis/dissertation, research practicum, seminar. *Entrance requirements:* For master's, bachelor's degree in communications, 2 years of media-related experience; for doctorate, MA in communications. *Faculty research:* Communication and development, organizational communication, cultural studies, rhetoric, future studies.

**Concordia University,** School of Graduate Studies, Faculty of Fine Arts, Department of Studio Arts, Montréal, QC H3G 1M8, Canada. Offers studio arts (MFA), including fibers and material practices, film production, intermedia, painting and drawing, photography, print media, sculpture. *Degree requirements:* For master's, thesis or alternative. *Entrance requirements:* For master's, portfolio.

**Cornell University,** Graduate School, Graduate Fields of Agriculture and Life Sciences, Field of Communication, Ithaca, NY 14853. Offers communication (MS, PhD); human-computer interaction (MS, PhD); language and communication (MS, PhD); media communication and society (MS, PhD); organizational communication (MS, PhD); science, environment and health communication (MS, PhD); social psychology of communication (MS, PhD). *Degree requirements:* For master's, thesis (MS); for doctorate, comprehensive exam, thesis/dissertation. *Entrance requirements:* For master's and doctorate, GRE General Test, 3 letters of recommendation. Additional exam requirements/recommendations for international students: Required—TOEFL (minimum score 600 paper-based; 100 iBT). Electronic applications accepted. *Faculty research:* Mass communication, communication technologies, science and environmental communication.

**Dallas Theological Seminary,** Graduate Programs, Dallas, TX 75204-6499. Offers adult education (Th M); apologetics (Th M); Bible backgrounds (Th M); Bible translation (Th M); Biblical and theological studies (Certificate); biblical counseling (MA); biblical exegesis and linguistics (MA); biblical exposition (PhD); biblical studies (MA); Biblical theology (Th M); children's education (Th M); Christian education (MA, D Min); Christian leadership (MA); cross-cultural ministries (MA); educational administration (Th M); educational leadership (Th M); evangelism and discipleship (Th M); exposition of Biblical books (Th M); family life education (Th M); general studies (Th M); Hebrew and cognate studies (Th M); hermeneutics (Th M); historical theology (Th M); homiletics (Th M); intercultural ministries (Th M); Jesus studies (Th M); leadership studies (Th M); media and communication (MA); media arts (Th M); ministry (D Min); ministry with women (Th M); New Testament studies (Th M, PhD); Old Testament studies (Th M, PhD); parachurch ministries (Th M); pastoral care and counseling (Th M); pastoral theology and practice (Th M); philosophy (Th M); sacred theology (STM); spiritual formation (Th M); systematic theology (Th M); teaching in Christian institutions (Th M); theological studies (PhD); urban ministries (Th M); worship (Th M); youth education (Th M). *Program availability:* Part-time, online learning. *Degree requirements:* For master's, variable foreign language requirement, thesis (for some programs); for doctorate, 2 foreign languages, thesis/dissertation. *Entrance requirements:* For master's, GRE or MAT (if minimum undergraduate cumulative GPA is below 2.5 or undergraduate degree is unaccredited). Additional exam requirements/recommendations for international students: Required—TOEFL (minimum score 575 paper-based; 85 iBT), TWE. Electronic applications accepted.

**DePaul University,** College of Communication, Chicago, IL 60614. Offers digital communication and media arts (MA); health communication (MA); journalism (MA); media and cinema studies (MA); organizational and multicultural communication (MA); public relations and advertising (MA); relational communication (MA). *Program availability:* Part-time, evening/weekend. *Entrance requirements:* Additional exam requirements/recommendations for international students: Required—TOEFL (minimum score 590 paper-based; 96 iBT), IELTS (minimum score 7.5) or PTE. Electronic applications accepted.

**DePaul University,** College of Liberal Arts and Social Sciences, Chicago, IL 60614. Offers Arabic (MA); Chinese (MA); English (MA); French (MA); German (MA); history (MA); interdisciplinary studies (MA, MS); international public service (MS); international studies (MA); Italian (MA); Japanese (MA); leadership and policy studies (MS); liberal studies (MA); new media studies (MA); nonprofit management (MNM); public administration (MPA); public health (MPH); public service management (MS); social work (MSW); sociology (MA); Spanish (MA); sustainable urban development (MA); women and gender studies (MA); writing and publishing (MA); writing, rhetoric, and discourse (MA); MA/PhD. *Program availability:* Part-time, evening/weekend, online learning. Terminal master's awarded for partial completion of doctoral program. *Degree requirements:* For master's, variable foreign language requirement, comprehensive exam (for some programs), thesis (for some programs). Electronic applications accepted.

**Digital Media Arts College,** Graduate Programs, Boca Raton, FL 33487. Offers graphic design (MFA); special FX animation (MFA).

**Drexel University,** College of Arts and Sciences, Department of Communication, Culture and Media, Philadelphia, PA 19104-2875. Offers communication (MS), including public communication, science communication, technical communication. *Program availability:* Part-time, evening/weekend. *Faculty:* 19 full-time (6 women), 12 part-time/adjunct (6 women). *Students:* 5 full-time (4 women) 35 part-time (25 women); includes 9 minority (3 Black or African American, non-Hispanic/Latino; 3 Asian, non-Hispanic/Latino; 3 Hispanic/Latino), 7 international. Average age 30. In 2016, 12 master's awarded. *Degree requirements:* For master's, internship, professional portfolio. *Entrance requirements:* Additional exam requirements/recommendations for international students: Required—TOEFL. *Application deadline:* For fall admission, 8/21 for domestic students. Applications are processed on a rolling basis. Application fee: $50. Electronic applications accepted. *Expenses:* Tuition: Full-time $32,184; part-time $1192 per credit hour. *Required fees:* $280. Tuition and fees vary according to campus/location and program. *Financial support:* Research assistantships, teaching assistantships, career-related internships or fieldwork, Federal Work-Study, institutionally sponsored loans, tuition waivers (partial), and unspecified assistantships available. Financial award application deadline: 2/1. *Faculty research:* Science information and attitudes, science influence on literature, process of technical writing, document design, software documentation. *Unit head:* Dr. Douglas Porpora, Head, 215-895-2446, Fax: 215-895-1071. *Application contact:* Director of Graduate Admissions, 215-895-6700, Fax: 215-895-5939, E-mail: enroll@drexel.edu.

**Duke University,** Graduate School, Master of Fine Arts in Experimental and Documentary Arts Program, Durham, NC 27708. Offers MFA. *Degree requirements:* For master's, thesis, final project. *Entrance requirements:* For master's, portfolio. Additional exam requirements/recommendations for international students: Required—TOEFL (minimum score 577 paper-based; 90 iBT) or IELTS (minimum score 7). Electronic applications accepted.

**Emerson College,** Graduate Studies, School of Communication, Program in Civic Media: Art and Practice, Boston, MA 02116-4624. Offers MA. *Faculty:* 5 full-time (3 women). *Students:* 9 full-time (7 women); includes 2 minority (both Black or African American, non-Hispanic/Latino). Average age 26. 14 applicants, 93% accepted, 8 enrolled. *Entrance requirements:* Additional exam requirements/recommendations for international students: Required—TOEFL (minimum score 577 paper-based; 90 iBT), IELTS (minimum score 7). *Application deadline:* For fall admission, 7/14 for domestic students. Applications are processed on a rolling basis. Application fee: $65 ($70 for international students). *Financial support:* In 2016–17, 9 students received support. Applicants required to submit FAFSA. *Application contact:* Leanda Ferland, Director of Graduate Admission, 617-824-8610, Fax: 617-824-8614, E-mail: gradapp@emerson.edu. Website: http://www.emerson.edu/academics/civic-media-art-practice-ma

**Emerson College,** Graduate Studies, School of the Arts, Department of Visual and Media Arts, Program in Media Art, Boston, MA 02116-4624. Offers MFA. *Faculty:* 57 full-time (19 women), 6 part-time/adjunct (3 women). *Students:* 72 full-time (41 women), 14 part-time (6 women); includes 15 minority (4 Black or African American, non-Hispanic/Latino; 7 Hispanic/Latino; 1 Native Hawaiian or other Pacific Islander, non-Hispanic/Latino; 3 Two or more races, non-Hispanic/Latino), 44 international. Average age 27. 126 applicants, 54% accepted, 28 enrolled. In 2016, 22 master's awarded. *Entrance requirements:* For master's, creative portfolio. Additional exam requirements/recommendations for international students: Required—TOEFL (minimum score 550 paper-based; 80 iBT), IELTS (minimum score 6.5). *Application deadline:* For fall admission, 2/15 for domestic and international students. Applications are processed on a rolling basis. Application fee: $60 ($75 for international students). Electronic applications accepted. *Financial support:* In 2016–17, 18 students received support, including 31 fellowships with tuition reimbursements available (averaging $13,178 per year); research assistantships with partial tuition reimbursements available, Federal Work-Study, scholarships/grants, and unspecified assistantships also available. Financial award application deadline: 1/15; financial award applicants required to submit FAFSA. *Faculty research:* Media studies. *Unit head:* E-mail: l_marc_fields@emerson.edu. *Application contact:* Leanda Ferland, Director of Graduate Admission, 617-824-8610, Fax: 617-824-8614, E-mail: gradapp@emerson.edu. Website: http://www.emerson.edu/graduate_admission

**Fairleigh Dickinson University, Metropolitan Campus,** University College: Arts, Sciences, and Professional Studies, School of Art and Media Studies, Program in Media and Communications, Teaneck, NJ 07666-1914. Offers MA.

**Fielding Graduate University,** Graduate Programs, School of Psychology, Programs in Media Psychology, Santa Barbara, CA 93105-3814. Offers MA, PhD, Certificate. *Program availability:* Part-time, 100% online, blended/hybrid learning. *Faculty:* 4 full-time (3 women), 19 part-time/adjunct (10 women). *Students:* 77 full-time (51 women), 37 part-time (27 women); includes 35 minority (16 Black or African American, non-Hispanic/Latino; 1 Asian, non-Hispanic/Latino; 10 Hispanic/Latino; 8 Two or more races, non-Hispanic/Latino). Average age 42. 30 applicants, 100% accepted, 18 enrolled. In 2016, 6 master's, 10 doctorates, 21 other advanced degrees awarded. *Degree requirements:* For doctorate, thesis/dissertation. *Entrance requirements:* For master's, bachelor's degree from regionally-accredited U.S. institution or equivalent, resume, statement of purpose, official transcript; for doctorate, bachelor's or master's degree from regionally-accredited U.S. institution or equivalent, curriculum vitae, statement of purpose, critical thinking writing sample, 2 letters of recommendation, official transcript; for Certificate, bachelor's degree from regionally-accredited U.S. institution or equivalent. *Application deadline:* For fall admission, 7/16 for domestic and international students; for spring admission, 11/1 for domestic and international students; for summer admission, 3/1 for domestic and international students. Application fee: $75. Electronic applications accepted. *Expenses:* $9,060 per term (for PhD); $3,500 per term (for MA); $570 per credit (for Graduate Certificate). *Financial support:* In 2016–17, 4 students received support, including 1 research assistantship (averaging $1,530 per year), 1 teaching assistantship (averaging $468 per year); scholarships/grants also available. Financial award applicants required to submit FAFSA. *Unit head:* Dr. Jerri Lynn Hogg, E-mail: jhogg@fielding.edu. *Application contact:* Enrollment Coordinator, 800-340-1099 Ext. 4098, Fax: 805-687-9793, E-mail: psyadmission@fielding.edu. Website: http://www.fielding.edu/our-programs/school-of-psychology/

**Florida Atlantic University,** Dorothy F. Schmidt College of Arts and Letters, School of Communication and Multimedia Studies, Boca Raton, FL 33431-0991. Offers communication studies (MA); film and video (Certificate); media, technology and entertainment (MFA). *Program availability:* Part-time. *Faculty:* 25 full-time (8 women). *Students:* 21 full-time (15 women), 17 part-time (9 women); includes 16 minority (6 Black or African American, non-Hispanic/Latino; 1 Asian, non-Hispanic/Latino; 9 Hispanic/Latino), 3 international. Average age 33. 39 applicants, 72% accepted, 14 enrolled. In 2016, 8 master's awarded. *Degree requirements:* For master's, one foreign language, comprehensive exam (for some programs), thesis (for some programs). *Entrance requirements:* For master's, GRE General Test, minimum GPA of 3.0, essay, letters of recommendation. *Application deadline:* For fall admission, 7/1 priority date for domestic students, 4/1 for international students; for spring admission, 11/1 for domestic students, 10/1 for international students. Applications are processed on a rolling basis. Application fee: $30. Electronic applications accepted. *Expenses:* Tuition, state resident: full-time $7392; part-time $369.82 per credit hour. Tuition, nonresident: full-time $19,432; part-time $1024.81 per credit hour. *Financial support:* Teaching assistantships with partial tuition reimbursements, Federal Work-Study, institutionally sponsored loans, scholarships/grants, and unspecified assistantships available. Support available to part-time students. Financial award application deadline: 3/1; financial award applicants required to submit FAFSA. *Faculty research:* Cultural studies, gender studies, film, communication theory, journalism, new media. *Unit head:* Dr. David Williams, Director, 561-297-0045, Fax: 561-297-2615, E-mail: dcwill@fau.edu. *Application contact:* Dr. Eric M. Freedman, Graduate Coordinator, 561-297-2534, Fax: 561-297-2615, E-mail: efreedma@fau.edu. Website: http://www.fau.edu/scms/

**Florida State University,** The Graduate School, College of Communication and Information, School of Communication, Tallahassee, FL 32306-2664. Offers communication theory and research (PhD); integrated marketing communication (MA, MS); media and communication studies (MA, MS); public interest media and communication (MA, MS). *Program availability:* Part-time. *Faculty:* 22 full-time (11 women), 2 part-time/adjunct (1 woman). *Students:* 71 full-time (53 women), 72 part-time (46 women); includes 77 minority (20 Black or African American, non-Hispanic/Latino; 36 Asian, non-Hispanic/Latino; 19 Hispanic/Latino; 2 Two or more races, non-Hispanic/Latino). Average age 24. 140 applicants, 57% accepted, 46 enrolled. In 2016, 83 master's, 5 doctorates awarded. *Degree requirements:* For master's, thesis (for some programs); for doctorate, comprehensive exam, thesis/dissertation. *Entrance requirements:* For master's, GRE General Test, minimum GPA of 3.0; for doctorate, GRE General Test, minimum GPA of 3.3 in graduate course work. Additional exam requirements/recommendations for international students: Required—TOEFL (minimum score 600 paper-based; 100 iBT), IELTS (minimum score 7). *Application deadline:* For fall admission, 7/1 priority date for domestic students, 5/1 priority date for international students; for spring admission, 11/1 priority date for domestic and international students; for summer admission, 3/1 priority date for domestic and international students. Applications are processed on a rolling basis. Application fee: $30. Electronic applications accepted. *Expenses:* $479.32 per credit hour in-state, $1,110.72 per credit hour out-of-state. *Financial support:* In 2016–17, 87 students received support, including 17 research assistantships with full tuition reimbursements available (averaging $16,192 per year), 46 teaching assistantships with full tuition reimbursements available (averaging $16,192 per year); fellowships, career-related internships or fieldwork, Federal Work-Study, institutionally sponsored loans, scholarships/grants, health care benefits, tuition waivers (full and partial), and unspecified assistantships also available. Support available to part-time students. Financial award application deadline: 12/15; financial award applicants required to submit FAFSA. *Faculty research:* Communication in the public interest; strategic communication; media and technology; multicultural, intercultural, and international communication. *Total annual research expenditures:* $52,979. *Unit head:* Dr. Gary Heald, Director, 850-644-5034, Fax: 850-644-8642, E-mail: gheald@fsu.edu. *Application contact:* Natashia Hinson-Turner, Graduate Coordinator, 850-644-5034,

*Media Studies*

Fax: 850-644-8642, E-mail: comgradadvising@cci.fsu.edu.
Website: http://www.cci.fsu.edu

**Fordham University,** Gabelli School of Business, New York, NY 10023. Offers accounting (MBA, MS); applied statistics and decision-making (MS); business administration (EMBA); business analytics (MS); communications and media management (MBA); electronic business (MBA); entrepreneurship (MBA); finance (MBA); global finance (MS); global sustainability (MBA); healthcare management (MBA); information systems (MBA, MS); investor relations (MS); management (MBA, MS); marketing (MBA); marketing intelligence (MS); media management (MS); nonprofit leadership (MS); quantitative finance (MS); taxation (MS); JD/MBA; MS/MBA. *Accreditation:* AACSB. *Program availability:* Part-time, evening/weekend. *Faculty:* 132 full-time (44 women), 51 part-time/adjunct (7 women). *Students:* 1,117 full-time (668 women), 553 part-time (282 women); includes 207 minority (44 Black or African American, non-Hispanic/Latino; 92 Asian, non-Hispanic/Latino; 69 Hispanic/Latino; 2 Native Hawaiian or other Pacific Islander, non-Hispanic/Latino), 1,088 international. Average age 27. 4,745 applicants, 46% accepted, 752 enrolled. In 2016, 996 master's awarded. Terminal master's awarded for partial completion of doctoral program. *Degree requirements:* For master's, internships (required for MS in quantitative finance, recommended for MBA). *Entrance requirements:* For master's, GMAT/GRE, 2 letters of recommendation, resume, 2 essays, transcripts. Additional exam requirements/recommendations for international students: Required—TOEFL (minimum score 100 iBT), IELTS (minimum score 7). *Application deadline:* For fall admission, 11/15 priority date for domestic and international students; for winter admission, 1/15 priority date for domestic students, 1/1 priority date for international students; for spring admission, 3/1 for domestic and international students; for summer admission, 6/1 for domestic students. Application fee: $130. Electronic applications accepted. *Expenses:* $1,397 per credit. *Financial support:* In 2016–17, 78 students received support. Career-related internships or fieldwork, institutionally sponsored loans, scholarships/grants, and unspecified assistantships available. Support available to part-time students. Financial award application deadline: 6/30; financial award applicants required to submit FAFSA. *Unit head:* Dr. Donna Rapaccioli, Dean, 212-636-6165, Fax: 212-307-1779, E-mail: rapaccioli@fordham.edu. *Application contact:* Lawrence Murray, Senior Assistant Dean of Graduate Admissions and Advising, 212-636-6200, Fax: 212-636-7076, E-mail: admissionsgb@fordham.edu.
Website: http://www.fordham.edu/gabelli

**Full Sail University,** Media Design Master of Fine Arts Program - Online, Winter Park, FL 32792-7437. Offers MFA. *Program availability:* Online learning.

**Georgetown University,** Graduate School of Arts and Sciences, School of Continuing Studies, Washington, DC 20057. Offers American studies (MALS); Catholic studies (MALS); classical civilizations (MALS); emergency and disaster management (MPS); ethics and the professions (MALS); global strategic communications (MPS); hospitality management (MPS); human resources management (MPS); humanities (MALS); individualized study (MALS); integrated marketing communications (MPS); international affairs (MALS); Islam and Muslim-Christian relations (MALS); journalism (MPS); liberal studies (DLS); literature and society (MALS); medieval and early modern European studies (MALS); public relations and corporate communications (MPS); real estate (MPS); religious studies (MALS); social and public policy (MALS); sports industry management (MPS); systems engineering management (MPS); technology management (MPS); the theory and practice of American democracy (MALS); urban and regional planning (MPS); visual culture (MALS). MPS in systems engineering management offered jointly with Stevens Institute of Technology. *Entrance requirements:* Additional exam requirements/recommendations for international students: Required—TOEFL.

**Georgia State University,** College of Arts and Sciences, Department of Communication, Atlanta, GA 30302-3083. Offers film, video, and digital imaging (MA), including critical studies, production, screenwriting; human communication and social influence (MA); mass communication (MA); media and society (PhD); moving image studies (PhD); public communication (PhD); rhetoric and politics (PhD). *Program availability:* Part-time. *Faculty:* 57 full-time (34 women). *Students:* 113 full-time (69 women), 56 part-time (33 women); includes 59 minority (37 Black or African American, non-Hispanic/Latino; 1 American Indian or Alaska Native, non-Hispanic/Latino; 2 Asian, non-Hispanic/Latino; 9 Hispanic/Latino; 10 Two or more races, non-Hispanic/Latino), 18 international. Average age 32. 134 applicants, 58% accepted, 47 enrolled. In 2016, 22 master's, 11 doctorates awarded. *Degree requirements:* For master's, variable foreign language requirement, thesis (for some programs); for doctorate, comprehensive exam, thesis/dissertation. *Entrance requirements:* For master's and doctorate, GRE. Additional exam requirements/recommendations for international students: Required—TOEFL (minimum score 550 paper-based; 80 iBT), IELTS (minimum score 6.5). *Application deadline:* For fall admission, 2/10 for domestic and international students; for spring admission, 10/15 for domestic and international students. Application fee: $50. Electronic applications accepted. *Expenses:* Tuition, state resident: full-time $6876; part-time $382 per credit hour. Tuition, nonresident: full-time $22,374; part-time $1243 per credit hour. *Required fees:* $2128; $1064 per term. Part-time tuition and fees vary according to course load and program. *Financial support:* In 2016–17, fellowships with tuition reimbursements (averaging $15,000 per year), teaching assistantships with tuition reimbursements (averaging $15,000 per year) were awarded; career-related internships or fieldwork and unspecified assistantships also available. Financial award applicants required to submit FAFSA. *Faculty research:* New media, mass media and journalism, rhetoric, film and media studies, film production. *Unit head:* Dr. Greg Lisby, Chair, 404-413-5639, Fax: 404-413-5634, E-mail: glisby@gsu.edu.
Website: http://communication.gsu.edu

**Governors State University,** College of Arts and Sciences, Program in Communication and Training, University Park, IL 60484. Offers communication studies (MA); media communication (MA). *Program availability:* Part-time. *Faculty:* 91 full-time (43 women), 125 part-time/adjunct (64 women). *Students:* 9 full-time (7 women), 62 part-time (52 women); includes 58 minority (55 Black or African American, non-Hispanic/Latino; 1 Asian, non-Hispanic/Latino; 1 Hispanic/Latino; 1 Two or more races, non-Hispanic/Latino), 1 international. Average age 43. 66 applicants, 48% accepted, 25 enrolled. In 2016, 36 master's awarded. *Entrance requirements:* Additional exam requirements/recommendations for international students: Required—TOEFL (minimum score 550 paper-based; 80 iBT), IELTS. *Application deadline:* For fall admission, 4/1 for domestic students. Application fee: $50. Electronic applications accepted. *Expenses:* $307 per credit hour; $38 per term or $76 per credit hour fees. *Financial support:* Application deadline: 5/1; applicants required to submit FAFSA. *Unit head:* Lori Montalbano, Chair of Division of Communication, Visual and Performing Arts, 708-235-2802, E-mail: lmontalbano@govst.edu. *Application contact:* Yakeea Daniels, Assistant Vice President for Enrollment Services/Director of Admission, 708-534-4510, E-mail: ydaniels@govst.edu.

**Howard University,** School of Communications, Division of Mass Communication and Media Studies, Washington, DC 20059-0002. Offers mass communication (MA, PhD); media studies (MA, PhD). *Program availability:* Part-time, evening/weekend. *Degree requirements:* For master's, comprehensive exam (for some programs), thesis optional; for doctorate, one foreign language, comprehensive exam, thesis/dissertation. *Entrance*

*requirements:* For master's, GRE, minimum GPA of 3.0; for doctorate, GRE, minimum graduate GPA of 3.5. Additional exam requirements/recommendations for international students: Required—TOEFL. Electronic applications accepted. *Faculty research:* Advertising, public relations, journalism new media.

**Hunter College of the City University of New York,** Graduate School, School of Arts and Sciences, Department of Film and Media Studies, Program in Integrated Media Arts, New York, NY 10065-5085. Offers MFA. *Program availability:* Part-time, evening/weekend. *Students:* 2 full-time (1 woman), 51 part-time (35 women); includes 18 minority (6 Black or African American, non-Hispanic/Latino; 7 Asian, non-Hispanic/Latino; 5 Hispanic/Latino), 6 international. Average age 35. 27 applicants, 78% accepted, 13 enrolled. In 2016, 7 master's awarded. *Entrance requirements:* For master's, GRE General Test, 3 letters of recommendation, portfolio of media works, minimum GPA of 3.0. Additional exam requirements/recommendations for international students: Required—TOEFL, TWE. *Application deadline:* For fall admission, 2/1 for domestic students. *Financial support:* Federal Work-Study and tuition waivers (partial) available. Support available to part-time students. *Faculty research:* Nonfiction production, Internet as medium, public interest journalism, social and historical roots of media arts. *Unit head:* Kelly Anderson, Deputy Chair, 212-772-6008. *Application contact:* Mary Flanagan, New Media Advisor, 212-650-3219, E-mail: maryflanagan@hunter.cuny.edu.
Website: http://fm.hunter.cuny.edu/

**Indiana State University,** College of Graduate and Professional Studies, College of Arts and Sciences, Department of Communication, Terre Haute, IN 47809. Offers communication studies (MA); radio, television and film (MA). *Program availability:* Part-time. *Degree requirements:* For master's, thesis (for some programs), oral and written exam. *Entrance requirements:* For master's, GRE General Test. Additional exam requirements/recommendations for international students: Required—TOEFL. *Faculty research:* Women in media, communication apprehension, media history.

**Indiana University Bloomington,** University Graduate School, College of Arts and Sciences, The Media School, Bloomington, IN 47405-7000. Offers media (MS); media arts and sciences (MA, PhD). *Faculty:* 61 full-time (25 women). *Students:* 128 full-time (68 women), 7 part-time (4 women); includes 18 minority (6 Black or African American, non-Hispanic/Latino; 1 American Indian or Alaska Native, non-Hispanic/Latino; 4 Asian, non-Hispanic/Latino; 5 Hispanic/Latino; 2 Two or more races, non-Hispanic/Latino), 34 international. Average age 33. 91 applicants, 34% accepted, 16 enrolled. In 2016, 15 master's, 10 doctorates awarded. *Degree requirements:* For master's, comprehensive exam (for some programs), thesis (for some programs); for doctorate, comprehensive exam, thesis/dissertation. *Entrance requirements:* Additional exam requirements/recommendations for international students: Required—TOEFL. Application fee: $55 ($65 for international students). Electronic applications accepted. *Financial support:* In 2016–17, 47 students received support. Fellowships, research assistantships, teaching assistantships, health care benefits, and unspecified assistantships available. Financial award application deadline: 1/15. *Faculty research:* Film and cinema studies, communication science, journalism, media design and production. *Unit head:* Dr. Andrew Weaver, Director of Graduate Studies, 812-856-2552, E-mail: weaveraj@indiana.edu. *Application contact:* Kathy Teige, Graduate Studies Administrative Associate, 812-855-0570, E-mail: kteige@indiana.edu.
Website: http://mediaschool.indiana.edu/

**Indiana University of Pennsylvania,** School of Graduate Studies and Research, College of Education and Educational Technology, Department of Communications Media, Program in Communications Media and Instructional Technology, Indiana, PA 15705. Offers PhD. *Faculty:* 10 full-time (4 women). *Students:* 13 full-time (3 women), 37 part-time (15 women); includes 4 minority (3 Black or African American, non-Hispanic/Latino; 1 Two or more races, non-Hispanic/Latino), 5 international. Average age 38. 65 applicants, 26% accepted, 6 enrolled. In 2016, 10 doctorates awarded. Application fee: $50. *Expenses:* Contact institution. *Financial support:* In 2016–17, 2 fellowships with full tuition reimbursements (averaging $2,296 per year), 7 research assistantships with tuition reimbursements (averaging $5,769 per year), 3 teaching assistantships with partial tuition reimbursements (averaging $23,305 per year) were awarded. *Unit head:* Dr. Zachary Stiegler, Coordinator, 724-357-3219, E-mail: zachary.stiegler@iup.edu.
Website: http://www.iup.edu/commmedia/programs/phdcmit/

**International University in Geneva,** Leadership Programs, Geneva, Switzerland. Offers international relations and diplomacy (MIRD); media and communication (MA); public administration (DPA). *Degree requirements:* For master's, comprehensive exam. *Entrance requirements:* Additional exam requirements/recommendations for international students: Required—TOEFL. Electronic applications accepted.

**Johns Hopkins University,** Zanvyl Krieger School of Arts and Sciences, Advanced Academic Programs, Program in Film and Media, Baltimore, MD 21218. Offers MA. Students choose two concentrations from business, sound, and writing. *Program availability:* Part-time.

**Kent State University,** College of Communication and Information, School of Journalism and Mass Communication, Kent, OH 44242-0001. Offers journalism and mass communication (MA), including media management, public relations, reporting and editing-broadcast, reporting and editing-convergence, reporting and editing-journalism educators, reporting and editing-magazine, reporting and editing-newspaper. *Program availability:* Part-time, online learning. *Faculty:* 25 full-time (13 women). *Students:* 12 full-time (7 women), 102 part-time (68 women); includes 19 minority (14 Black or African American, non-Hispanic/Latino; 3 Hispanic/Latino; 2 Two or more races, non-Hispanic/Latino), 5 international. Average age 30. 46 applicants, 67% accepted, 20 enrolled. In 2016, 79 master's awarded. *Degree requirements:* For master's, thesis or project. *Entrance requirements:* For master's, GRE, minimum GPA of 3.0, statement of purpose, 3 online recommendations, resume. Additional exam requirements/recommendations for international students: Required—TOEFL (minimum score of 600 paper-based, 100 iBT), IELTS (minimum score of 7.0), Michigan English Language Assessment Battery (minimum score of 85), or PTE (minimum score of 68). *Application deadline:* For fall admission, 7/1 for domestic and international students. Applications are processed on a rolling basis. Application fee: $45 ($70 for international students). Electronic applications accepted. *Expenses:* Tuition, state resident: full-time $10,864; part-time $495 per credit hour. Tuition, nonresident: full-time $18,380; part-time $837 per credit hour. *Financial support:* Research assistantships with full tuition reimbursements, teaching assistantships with full tuition reimbursements, scholarships/grants, and unspecified assistantships available. Financial award application deadline: 3/1. *Unit head:* Thor Wasbotten, Director and Professor, 330-672-4066, E-mail: thor@kent.edu. *Application contact:* Mark Goodman, Graduate Coordinator/Professor, 330-672-6239, E-mail: mgoodm10@kent.edu.
Website: http://www.kent.edu/jmc

**La Salle University,** School of Arts and Sciences, Program in Strategic Communication, Philadelphia, PA 19141-1199. Offers communication consulting and development (MA); communication management (MA); general professional communication (MA); professional and business communication (Certificate); public relations (MA); social and new media (Certificate). *Program availability:* Part-time, evening/weekend, online learning. *Faculty:* 4 full-time (all women), 1 (woman) part-time/adjunct. *Students:* 11 full-

time (7 women), 39 part-time (29 women); includes 18 minority (15 Black or African American, non-Hispanic/Latino; 2 Hispanic/Latino; 1 Two or more races, non-Hispanic/Latino), 2 international. Average age 27. 13 applicants, 92% accepted, 6 enrolled. In 2016, 41 master's, 4 other advanced degrees awarded. *Degree requirements:* For master's, practicum. *Entrance requirements:* For master's, writing assessment, professional resume; minimum overall B average; two letters of recommendation (if GPA below 3.25); brief personal statement (about 500 words); interview; for Certificate, writing assessment, minimum GPA of 2.75 in undergraduate studies; brief personal statement (about 500 words); interview. Additional exam requirements/recommendations for international students: Required—TOEFL. *Application deadline:* For fall admission, 8/15 priority date for domestic students, 7/15 for international students; for spring admission, 12/15 priority date for domestic students, 11/15 for international students; for summer admission, 4/15 priority date for domestic students, 3/15 for international students. Applications are processed on a rolling basis. Application fee: $35. Electronic applications accepted. Application fee is waived when completed online. *Expenses:* Contact institution. *Financial support:* In 2016–17, 7 students received support. Scholarships/grants available. Support available to part-time students. Financial award application deadline: 8/31; financial award applicants required to submit FAFSA. *Unit head:* Dr. Pamela Lannutti, Director, 215-951-1935, Fax: 215-951-5043, E-mail: annutti95@lasalle.edu. *Application contact:* Elizabeth Heenan, Director, Graduate and Adult Enrollment, 215-951-1100, Fax: 214-951-1462, E-mail: heenan@lasalle.edu.
Website: http://www.lasalle.edu/strategic-communication/

**Lindenwood University,** Graduate Programs, School of Accelerated Degree Programs, St. Charles, MO 63301-1695. Offers administration (MSA), including management, marketing, project management; business administration (MBA); communications (MA), including digital and multimedia, media management, promotions, training and development; criminal justice and administration (MS); healthcare administration (MS); human resource management (MS); information technology (Certificate); managing information security (MS); managing information technology (MS); managing virtualization and cloud computing (MS); writing (MFA). *Program availability:* Part-time, evening/weekend, 100% online. *Faculty:* 16 full-time (7 women), 75 part-time/adjunct (27 women). *Students:* 609 full-time (386 women), 179 part-time (121 women); includes 257 minority (202 Black or African American, non-Hispanic/Latino; 4 American Indian or Alaska Native, non-Hispanic/Latino; 5 Asian, non-Hispanic/Latino; 28 Hispanic/Latino; 1 Native Hawaiian or other Pacific Islander, non-Hispanic/Latino; 17 Two or more races, non-Hispanic/Latino), 28 international. Average age 36. 332 applicants, 70% accepted, 205 enrolled. In 2016, 479 master's awarded. *Degree requirements:* For master's, thesis (for some programs), minimum cumulative GPA of 3.0; for Certificate, minimum cumulative GPA of 3.0. *Entrance requirements:* For master's, resume, personal statement, official undergraduate transcript, minimum undergraduate cumulative GPA of 3.0. Additional exam requirements/recommendations for international students: Required—TOEFL (minimum score 550 paper-based; 80 iBT); Recommended—IELTS (minimum score 6.5). *Application deadline:* For fall admission, 9/26 priority date for domestic and international students; for winter admission, 1/3 priority date for domestic and international students; for spring admission, 3/31 priority date for domestic and international students; for summer admission, 7/3 priority date for domestic and international students. Applications are processed on a rolling basis. Application fee: $30 ($100 for international students). Electronic applications accepted. *Expenses: Tuition:* Full-time $15,672; part-time $453 per credit hour. *Required fees:* $205 per semester. Tuition and fees vary according to course level, course load and degree level. *Financial support:* In 2016–17, 467 students received support. Career-related internships or fieldwork, institutionally sponsored loans, scholarships/grants, tuition waivers (partial), and unspecified assistantships available. Financial award application deadline: 6/30; financial award applicants required to submit FAFSA. *Unit head:* Dr. Gina Ganahl, Dean, Accelerated Degree Programs, 636-949-4501, Fax: 636-949-4505, E-mail: gganahl@lindenwood.edu. *Application contact:* Tyler Kostich, Director, Evening and Graduate Admissions, 636-949-4138, Fax: 636-949-4109, E-mail: adultadmissions@lindenwood.edu.
Website: http://www.lindenwood.edu/academics/academic-schools/school-of-accelerated-degree-programs/

**Lindenwood University,** Graduate Programs, School of Arts, Media, and Communications, St. Charles, MO 63301-1695. Offers cinema and media arts (MFA). *Program availability:* Part-time. *Faculty:* 17 full-time (6 women), 6 part-time/adjunct (5 women). *Students:* 15 full-time (8 women), 5 part-time (3 women); includes 4 minority (2 Black or African American, non-Hispanic/Latino; 1 Hispanic/Latino; 1 Two or more races, non-Hispanic/Latino), 3 international. Average age 30. 16 applicants, 56% accepted, 6 enrolled. In 2016, 8 master's awarded. *Degree requirements:* For master's, thesis (for some programs), minimum cumulative GPA of 3.0. *Entrance requirements:* For master's, audition or interview, minimum GPA of 3.0, portfolio, letter of recommendation. Additional exam requirements/recommendations for international students: Required—TOEFL (minimum score 550 paper-based; 80 iBT); Recommended—IELTS (minimum score 6.5). *Application deadline:* For fall admission, 8/28 priority date for domestic and international students; for spring admission, 1/8 for domestic students, 1/8 priority date for international students; for summer admission, 6/5 priority date for domestic and international students. Applications are processed on a rolling basis. Application fee: $30 ($100 for international students). Electronic applications accepted. *Expenses: Tuition:* Full-time $15,672; part-time $453 per credit hour. *Required fees:* $205 per semester. Tuition and fees vary according to course level, course load and degree level. *Financial support:* In 2016–17, 12 students received support. Career-related internships or fieldwork, institutionally sponsored loans, scholarships/grants, tuition waivers (partial), and unspecified assistantships available. Financial award application deadline: 6/30; financial award applicants required to submit FAFSA. *Unit head:* Dr. Joseph Alsobrook, Dean, School of Arts, Media, and Communications, 636-949-4164, Fax: 636-949-4910, E-mail: jalsobrook@lindenwood.edu. *Application contact:* Tyler Kostich, Director, Evening and Graduate Admissions, 636-949-4138, Fax: 636-949-4109, E-mail: adultadmissions@lindenwood.edu.
Website: http://www.lindenwood.edu/academics/academic-schools/school-of-arts-media-and-communications/

**Lindenwood University–Belleville,** Graduate Programs, Belleville, IL 62226. Offers business administration (MBA); communications (MA), including digital and multimedia, media management, promotions, training and development; counseling (MA); criminal justice administration (MS); education (MA); healthcare administration (MS); human resource management (MS); school administration (MA); teaching (MAT).

**Long Island University–LIU Brooklyn,** Richard L. Conolly College of Liberal Arts and Sciences, Brooklyn, NY 11201-8423. Offers biology (MS); chemistry (MS); clinical psychology (PhD); communication sciences and disorders (MA); creative writing (MFA); English (MA); media arts (MA, MFA); political science (MA); psychology (MA); social science (MS); sociology (MA); speech-language pathology (MS); United Nations (Advanced Certificate); urban studies (MA); writing and production for television (MFA). *Program availability:* Part-time, evening/weekend. *Faculty:* 90 full-time (35 women), 125 part-time/adjunct (67 women). *Students:* 355 full-time (276 women), 220 part-time (161 women); includes 245 minority (119 Black or African American, non-Hispanic/Latino; 32 Asian, non-Hispanic/Latino; 80 Hispanic/Latino; 1 Native Hawaiian or other Pacific

Islander, non-Hispanic/Latino; 13 Two or more races, non-Hispanic/Latino), 85 international. 792 applicants, 41% accepted, 141 enrolled. In 2016, 154 master's, 18 doctorates, 4 other advanced degrees awarded. *Degree requirements:* For master's, comprehensive exam (for some programs), thesis (for some programs); for doctorate, comprehensive exam (for some programs), thesis/dissertation (for some programs). *Entrance requirements:* For master's and doctorate, GRE. Additional exam requirements/recommendations for international students: Recommended—TOEFL (minimum score 550 paper-based; 79 iBT). *Application deadline:* Applications are processed on a rolling basis. Application fee: $50. Electronic applications accepted. *Expenses: Tuition:* Full-time $28,272; part-time $1178 per credit. *Required fees:* $451 per term. Tuition and fees vary according to degree level, program and student level. *Financial support:* In 2016–17, 120 fellowships with full and partial tuition reimbursements (averaging $915 per year), 5 research assistantships with full and partial tuition reimbursements (averaging $2,300 per year), 136 teaching assistantships with full and partial tuition reimbursements (averaging $2,300 per year) were awarded; career-related internships or fieldwork, Federal Work-Study, institutionally sponsored loans, scholarships/grants, tuition waivers (full and partial), and unspecified assistantships also available. Support available to part-time students. Financial award application deadline: 2/15; financial award applicants required to submit FAFSA. *Faculty research:* Nanocrystal polymerization of cellulose using electron microscopy. *Unit head:* Dr. Kevin Lauth, Acting Dean, 718-488-1347, E-mail: kevin.lauth@liu.edu. *Application contact:* Gabrielle Gannon, Director of Graduate Admissions, 718-488-1011, Fax: 718-780-6110, E-mail: bkln-admissions@liu.edu.

**Louisiana State University and Agricultural & Mechanical College,** Graduate School, Manship School of Mass Communication, Baton Rouge, LA 70803. Offers MMC, PhD, JD/MMC. *Accreditation:* ACEJMC.

**Loyola University Maryland,** Graduate Programs, Loyola College of Arts and Sciences, Emerging Media Department, Baltimore, MD 21210-2699. Offers emerging media (MA). *Program availability:* Part-time, online learning. *Faculty:* 65 full-time (40 women), 26 part-time/adjunct (18 women). *Students:* 5 full-time (2 women), 55 part-time (38 women); includes 18 minority (12 Black or African American, non-Hispanic/Latino; 1 Asian, non-Hispanic/Latino; 5 Hispanic/Latino). Average age 30. 18 applicants, 89% accepted, 13 enrolled. In 2016, 4 master's awarded. *Application deadline:* For fall admission, 8/1 for domestic students. Applications are processed on a rolling basis. Application fee: $60. Electronic applications accepted. *Expenses:* Contact institution. *Financial support:* In 2016–17, 8 students received support. Career-related internships or fieldwork, scholarships/grants, and tuition waivers available. Financial award application deadline: 4/15; financial award applicants required to submit FAFSA. *Unit head:* Dr. Elliot King, Chair, 410-617-2819, E-mail: eking@loyola.edu. *Application contact:* Dr. Neil Alperstein, Program Director, 410-617-2548, E-mail: nalperstein@loyola.edu.
Website: http://www.loyola.edu/academic/communication/

**Lynn University,** College of Business and Management, Boca Raton, FL 33431-5598. Offers business administration (MBA), including aviation management, financial valuation and investment management, hospitality management, human resource management, international business management, marketing, media management, sports management. *Program availability:* Part-time, evening/weekend, 100% online, blended/hybrid learning. *Faculty:* 24 full-time (9 women), 24 part-time/adjunct (4 women). *Students:* 265 full-time (125 women), 182 part-time (96 women); includes 100 minority (41 Black or African American, non-Hispanic/Latino; 11 Asian, non-Hispanic/Latino; 42 Hispanic/Latino; 6 Two or more races, non-Hispanic/Latino), 119 international. Average age 28. 280 applicants, 94% accepted, 181 enrolled. In 2016, 219 master's awarded. *Degree requirements:* For master's, strategic management seminar, simulation capstone. *Entrance requirements:* For master's, bachelor's degree from accredited institution, resume, letter of recommendation, official transcripts, essay/personal statement. Additional exam requirements/recommendations for international students: Required—TOEFL (minimum score 550 paper-based; 80 iBT), IELTS (minimum score 6.5). *Application deadline:* For fall admission, 8/18 for domestic students, 8/4 for international students; for spring admission, 12/15 for domestic students, 12/1 for international students; for summer admission, 4/17 for domestic students, 4/3 for international students. Applications are processed on a rolling basis. Application fee: $45. Electronic applications accepted. *Expenses:* $725 per credit. *Financial support:* In 2016–17, 115 students received support. Career-related internships or fieldwork, Federal Work-Study, scholarships/grants, tuition waivers (full and partial), and unspecified assistantships available. Support available to part-time students. Financial award application deadline: 3/1; financial award applicants required to submit FAFSA. *Faculty research:* Market volatility investing, biometric research, sports legal history, organizational leadership, urban economic development and productivity. *Unit head:* Dr. RT Good, Dean of the College of Business and Management, 561-237-7458, E-mail: rgood@lynn.edu. *Application contact:* Steven Pruitt, Director of Graduate and Undergraduate Evening Admission, 561-237-7834, Fax: 561-237-7100, E-mail: spruitt@lynn.edu.
Website: http://www.lynn.edu/academics/colleges/business-and-management

**Lynn University,** Eugene M. and Christine E. Lynn College of International Communication, Boca Raton, FL 33431-5598. Offers communication and media (MS), including digital media, media studies and practice; digital media (Certificate). *Program availability:* Part-time, evening/weekend. *Faculty:* 15 full-time (8 women), 6 part-time/adjunct (3 women). *Students:* 24 full-time (20 women), 15 part-time (14 women); includes 11 minority (7 Black or African American, non-Hispanic/Latino; 2 Asian, non-Hispanic/Latino; 2 Hispanic/Latino), 14 international. Average age 27. 38 applicants, 87% accepted, 17 enrolled. In 2016, 18 master's, 1 other advanced degree awarded. *Degree requirements:* For master's, project or thesis. *Entrance requirements:* For master's, resume, letter of recommendation, official transcripts, bachelor's degree from accredited institution, personal statement. Additional exam requirements/recommendations for international students: Required—TOEFL (minimum score 550 paper-based; 80 iBT), IELTS (minimum score 6.5). *Application deadline:* For fall admission, 8/18 for domestic students, 8/4 for international students; for spring admission, 12/15 for domestic students, 12/1 for international students; for summer admission, 4/17 for domestic students, 4/3 for international students. Applications are processed on a rolling basis. Application fee: $45. Electronic applications accepted. *Expenses:* $725 per credit hour. *Financial support:* In 2016–17, 7 students received support. Career-related internships or fieldwork, Federal Work-Study, institutionally sponsored loans, scholarships/grants, tuition waivers (partial), and unspecified assistantships available. Support available to part-time students. Financial award application deadline: 8/1; financial award applicants required to submit FAFSA. *Unit head:* Dr. David L. Jaffe, Dean, 561-237-7099, Fax: 561-237-7097, E-mail: djaffe@lynn.edu. *Application contact:* Steven Pruitt, Director of Graduate Admission, 561-237-7834, Fax: 561-237-7100, E-mail: admission@lynn.edu.
Website: http://www.lynn.edu/academics/colleges/international-communication

**Massachusetts College of Art and Design,** Graduate Programs, MFA Program, Boston, MA 02115-5882. Offers 2D fine arts (MFA), including painting, printmaking; 3D fine arts (MFA), including ceramics, fibers, glass, jewelry and metalsmithing, sculpture; design (MFA, Postbaccalaureate Certificate), including dynamic media; fine arts (MFA),

*Media Studies*

including interdisciplinary; media arts (MFA, Postbaccalaureate Certificate), including film/video (MFA), photography. *Accreditation:* NASAD. *Faculty:* 40 full-time (19 women), 55 part-time/adjunct (23 women). *Students:* 58 full-time (39 women), 16 part-time (12 women); includes 10 minority (1 Black or African American, non-Hispanic/Latino; 4 Asian, non-Hispanic/Latino; 4 Hispanic/Latino; 1 Native Hawaiian or other Pacific Islander, non-Hispanic/Latino), 28 international. 247 applicants, 52% accepted, 47 enrolled. In 2016, 34 master's, 3 other advanced degrees awarded. *Degree requirements:* For master's, thesis, thesis exhibition (for fine arts programs); thesis project and document (for design/dynamic media program). *Entrance requirements:* For master's, portfolio, college transcripts, resume, statement of purpose, letters of reference, interview, 6 credits of art history taken prior to or during MFA program; for Postbaccalaureate Certificate, portfolio, college transcripts, resume, statement of purpose, letters of reference, interview. Additional exam requirements/recommendations for international students: Required—TOEFL (minimum score 550 paper-based; 85 iBT); Recommended—IELTS (minimum score 6.5). *Application deadline:* For fall admission, 1/4 priority date for domestic and international students; for summer admission, 1/4 priority date for domestic and international students. Application fee: $90. Electronic applications accepted. *Expenses:* $780 per credit tuition. *Financial support:* In 2016–17, 57 students received support, including 33 teaching assistantships (averaging $2,160 per year); fellowships, research assistantships, career-related internships or fieldwork, scholarships/grants, tuition waivers (partial), unspecified assistantships, and 6-8 one-term adjunct co-teaching positions; 27 full-year general assistantships also available. Support available to part-time students. Financial award application deadline: 1/4; financial award applicants required to submit FAFSA. *Faculty research:* Painting and printmaking, sculpture, photography, film and video, dynamic media design. *Unit head:* Paul Paturzo, Dean of Graduate Studies, 617-879-7166, E-mail: pjpaturzo@massart.edu. *Application contact:* Lauren O'Neill, Assistant Director of Graduate Admissions, 617-879-7222, E-mail: gradadmissions@massart.edu. Website: http://www.massart.edu/Admissions/Graduate_Programs.html

**Massachusetts Institute of Technology,** School of Architecture and Planning, Program in Media Arts and Sciences, Cambridge, MA 02139. Offers media arts and sciences (SM, PhD); media technology (SM). *Faculty:* 23 full-time (5 women). *Students:* 173 full-time (62 women), 1 part-time; includes 39 minority (4 Black or African American, non-Hispanic/Latino; 19 Asian, non-Hispanic/Latino; 11 Hispanic/Latino; 5 Two or more races, non-Hispanic/Latino), 77 international. Average age 29. 920 applicants, 8% accepted, 66 enrolled. In 2016, 39 master's, 12 doctorates awarded. Terminal master's awarded for partial completion of doctoral program. *Degree requirements:* For master's, thesis; for doctorate, comprehensive exam, thesis/dissertation. *Entrance requirements:* Additional exam requirements/recommendations for international students: Required—IELTS. *Application deadline:* For fall admission, 12/1 for domestic and international students. Application fee: $75. Electronic applications accepted. *Expenses:* Tuition: Full-time $46,400; part-time $725 per credit. One-time fee: $312 full-time. Full-time tuition and fees vary according to course load and program. *Financial support:* In 2016–17, 163 students received support, including 17 fellowships (averaging $36,200 per year), 153 research assistantships (averaging $37,600 per year); teaching assistantships, Federal Work-Study, institutionally sponsored loans, scholarships/grants, traineeships, health care benefits, unspecified assistantships, and resident tutors also available. Support available to part-time students. Financial award application deadline: 5/1; financial award applicants required to submit FAFSA. *Faculty research:* Human machine interaction; new media technologies; learning and creativity; design and fabrication; biological interfaces. *Total annual research expenditures:* $22.7 million. *Unit head:* Prof. Patricia Maes, Program Head, 617-253-5114, E-mail: mas@media.mit.edu. *Application contact:* 617-253-5114, E-mail: mas@media.mit.edu. Website: http://www.media.mit.edu/admissions/

**Massachusetts Institute of Technology,** School of Humanities, Arts, and Social Sciences, Program in Comparative Media Studies/Writing, Program in Comparative Media Studies, Cambridge, MA 02139. Offers SM. *Faculty:* 8 full-time (2 women). *Students:* 18 full-time (13 women); includes 5 minority (2 Asian, non-Hispanic/Latino; 1 Hispanic/Latino; 2 Two or more races, non-Hispanic/Latino), 7 international. Average age 26. 93 applicants, 12% accepted, 9 enrolled. In 2016, 5 master's awarded. *Degree requirements:* For master's, thesis. *Entrance requirements:* For master's, GRE General Test. Additional exam requirements/recommendations for international students: Required—IELTS. *Application deadline:* For fall admission, 1/1 for domestic and international students. Application fee: $75. Electronic applications accepted. *Expenses:* Tuition: Full-time $46,400; part-time $725 per credit. One-time fee: $312 full-time. Full-time tuition and fees vary according to course load and program. *Financial support:* In 2016–17, 17 students received support, including 18 research assistantships (averaging $34,900 per year); fellowships, teaching assistantships, Federal Work-Study, institutionally sponsored loans, scholarships/grants, traineeships, health care benefits, unspecified assistantships, and resident tutors also available. Support available to part-time students. Financial award application deadline: 5/1; financial award applicants required to submit FAFSA. *Faculty research:* Media history and theory; game design, learning games, and creative computing; civic media; digital humanities; TV/film/Internet studies. *Total annual research expenditures:* $734,000. *Unit head:* Prof. Heather Hendershot, Director, 617-253-3599, Fax: 617-258-5133, E-mail: cmsw@mit.edu. *Application contact:* 617-253-5036, E-mail: cms-admissions@mit.edu. Website: http://cmsw.mit.edu/education/comparative-media-studies/

**Metropolitan College of New York,** Program in Business Administration, New York, NY 10006. Offers financial services (MBA); general management (MBA); health services and risk management (MBA); media management (MBA). *Accreditation:* ACBSP. *Program availability:* Evening/weekend. *Students:* 167 full-time (117 women), 43 part-time (30 women); includes 161 minority (114 Black or African American, non-Hispanic/Latino; 3 American Indian or Alaska Native, non-Hispanic/Latino; 10 Asian, non-Hispanic/Latino; 32 Hispanic/Latino; 2 Two or more races, non-Hispanic/Latino), 26 international. Average age 37. In 2016, 111 master's awarded. *Degree requirements:* For master's, thesis, 10-day study abroad. *Entrance requirements:* For master's, GMAT. Additional exam requirements/recommendations for international students: Required—TOEFL (minimum score 600 paper-based). *Application deadline:* For fall admission, 7/15 priority date for domestic students; for winter admission, 11/15 priority date for domestic students; for spring admission, 3/30 priority date for domestic students. Applications are processed on a rolling basis. Application fee: $45. Electronic applications accepted. *Expenses:* Contact institution. *Financial support:* Scholarships/grants available. Financial award application deadline: 8/15; financial award applicants required to submit FAFSA. *Unit head:* Dr. Tilokie Depoo, Dean and Professor, School for Business, 212-343-1234 Ext. 2204. *Application contact:* Steebo Varghese, Assistant Director of Admissions, 212-343-1234 Ext. 2708, Fax: 212-343-8470.

**Michigan State University,** The Graduate School, College of Communication Arts and Sciences, Department of Telecommunication, Information Studies, and Media, East Lansing, MI 48824. Offers digital media arts and technology (MA); information and telecommunication management (MA); information, policy and society (MA); serious game design (MA). *Entrance requirements:* Additional exam requirements/recommendations for international students: Required—TOEFL. Electronic applications accepted.

**Michigan State University,** The Graduate School, College of Communication Arts and Sciences, Program in Communication Arts and Sciences–Media and Information Studies, East Lansing, MI 48824. Offers PhD. *Entrance requirements:* Additional exam requirements/recommendations for international students: Required—TOEFL. Electronic applications accepted. *Faculty research:* Mass media, comparative media.

**Missouri Western State University,** Program in Digital Media, St. Joseph, MO 64507-2294. Offers MAA. *Program availability:* Part-time. *Students:* 12 full-time (5 women), 5 part-time (1 woman), 9 international. Average age 30. 9 applicants, 56% accepted, 3 enrolled. In 2016, 1 master's awarded. *Entrance requirements:* For master's, minimum GPA of 2.75, curriculum vitae, interview, 3 letters of reference, letter of intent, portfolio. Additional exam requirements/recommendations for international students: Recommended—TOEFL (minimum score 79 iBT), IELTS (minimum score 6). *Application deadline:* For fall admission, 7/15 for domestic and international students; for spring admission, 10/1 for domestic and international students; for summer admission, 3/15 for domestic students. Applications are processed on a rolling basis. Application fee: $50. Electronic applications accepted. *Expenses:* Tuition, state resident: full-time $6548; part-time $327.39 per credit hour. Tuition, nonresident: full-time $11,848; part-time $592.39 per credit hour. *Required fees:* $542; $99 per credit hour. $176 per semester. One-time fee: $50. Tuition and fees vary according to course load and program. *Financial support:* Scholarships/grants and unspecified assistantships available. Support available to part-time students. *Unit head:* Dr. Bob Bergland, Professor, 816-271-4446, E-mail: bergland@missouriwestern.edu. *Application contact:* Dr. Benjamin D. Caldwell, Dean of the Graduate School, 816-271-4394, Fax: 816-271-4525, E-mail: graduate@missouriwestern.edu. Website: http://www.missouriwestern.edu/digitalmedia/

**Monmouth University,** Graduate Studies, Department of Corporate and Public Communication, West Long Branch, NJ 07764-1898. Offers corporate and public communication (MA); human resources management and communication (Certificate); public service communication specialist (Certificate); strategic public relations and new media (Certificate). *Program availability:* Part-time, evening/weekend. *Degree requirements:* For master's, comprehensive exam (for some programs), thesis (for some programs), project. *Entrance requirements:* For master's, GRE, baccalaureate degree with minimum GPA of 3.0 in major, 2.75 overall; two letters of recommendation; personal essay (750 words or less describing preparation for study and personal objectives); digital or hard copy portfolio of select samples of work including a writing sample; resume. Additional exam requirements/recommendations for international students: Required—TOEFL (minimum score 550 paper-based; 79 iBT), IELTS (minimum score 6), Michigan English Language Assessment Battery (minimum score 77). Electronic applications accepted. *Faculty research:* Service-learning, history of television, feminism and the media, executive communication, public relations pedagogy.

**New Mexico Highlands University,** Graduate Studies, College of Arts and Sciences, Department of Computer Sciences, Las Vegas, NM 87701. Offers media arts and computer science (MS), including computer science. *Degree requirements:* For master's, comprehensive exam, thesis. *Entrance requirements:* For master's, minimum undergraduate GPA of 3.0. Additional exam requirements/recommendations for international students: Required—TOEFL (minimum score 540 paper-based). *Faculty research:* Advanced digital compositing, photographic installations and exhibition design, pattern recognition, parallel and distributed computing, computer security education.

**The New School,** Schools of Public Engagement, Program in Media Studies, New York, NY 10003. Offers documentary media studies (Graduate Certificate); media management (MS, Graduate Certificate); media studies (MA). *Program availability:* Part-time, 100% online. *Faculty:* 19 full-time (9 women), 43 part-time/adjunct (13 women). *Students:* 254 full-time (177 women), 142 part-time (94 women); includes 127 minority (58 Black or African American, non-Hispanic/Latino; 2 American Indian or Alaska Native, non-Hispanic/Latino; 13 Asian, non-Hispanic/Latino; 43 Hispanic/Latino; 1 Native Hawaiian or other Pacific Islander, non-Hispanic/Latino; 10 Two or more races, non-Hispanic/Latino), 131 international. Average age 29. 315 applicants, 89% accepted, 125 enrolled. In 2016, 214 master's, 27 other advanced degrees awarded. *Degree requirements:* For master's, thesis, capstone project (for MS); for Graduate Certificate, thesis optional, synthesis paper (for media management). *Entrance requirements:* For master's, two letters of recommendation, statement of purpose, resume, transcripts. Additional exam requirements/recommendations for international students: Required—TOEFL (minimum score 100 iBT), IELTS (minimum score 7), PTE (minimum score 68). *Application deadline:* For fall admission, 2/5 priority date for domestic and international students; for spring admission, 10/15 priority date for domestic and international students. Applications are processed on a rolling basis. Application fee: $50. Electronic applications accepted. *Expenses:* Contact institution. *Financial support:* Research assistantships, teaching assistantships, career-related internships or fieldwork, Federal Work-Study, scholarships/grants, and unspecified assistantships available. Support available to part-time students. Financial award application deadline: 2/1; financial award applicants required to submit FAFSA. *Faculty research:* Media theory and criticism, digital media production, media management, documentary studies and sound studies. *Unit head:* Carol Wilder, Dean, School of Media Studies, 212-229-8903 Ext. 4071, E-mail: wilderc@newschool.edu. *Application contact:* Karl Ramos, Assistant Director of Graduate Admission, 212-229-5630 Ext. 2330, E-mail: ramosk@newschool.edu. Website: http://www.newschool.edu/

**New York University,** Graduate School of Arts and Science, Department of Anthropology, Program in Culture and Media, New York, NY 10012-1019. Offers MA/Advanced Certificate, PhD/Advanced Certificate. *Entrance requirements:* Additional exam requirements/recommendations for international students: Required—TOEFL. *Faculty research:* Critical history of ethnographic film, ethnography of media, indigenous media, politics of reproduction and disability, social movements.

**New York University,** School of Continuing and Professional Studies, Tisch Institute for Sports Management, Media, and Business, New York, NY 10012-1019. Offers global sports media (MS); professional and collegiate sports operations (MS); sports business (Advanced Certificate); sports law (MS); sports marketing and sales (MS). *Program availability:* Part-time, evening/weekend. *Degree requirements:* For master's, thesis. *Entrance requirements:* For master's, GRE or GMAT (only upon request), bachelor's degree, resume with relevant professional work, internship or volunteer experience, two letters of recommendation, statement of purpose. Additional exam requirements/recommendations for international students: Required—TOEFL (minimum score 600 paper-based; 100 iBT), IELTS (minimum score 7). Electronic applications accepted. *Faculty research:* Implications of college football's bowl coalition series from a legal, economic, and academic perspective; social history of sports.

**New York University,** Steinhardt School of Culture, Education, and Human Development, Department of Media, Culture and Communication, New York, NY 10010. Offers media, culture and communication (MA, PhD); MLIS/MA. *Program availability:* Part-time. Terminal master's awarded for partial completion of doctoral program. *Degree requirements:* For master's, thesis (for some programs); for doctorate, thesis/dissertation. *Entrance requirements:* For master's, GRE General Test; for doctorate, GRE General Test, interview. Additional exam requirements/recommendations for international students: Required—TOEFL (minimum score 100 iBT). Electronic applications accepted. *Faculty research:* Digital media and new technologies, media criticism, flow of media and culture transnationally and transculturally.

**Norfolk State University,** School of Graduate Studies, School of Liberal Arts, Department of Media and Communication, Norfolk, VA 23504. Offers MA. *Program availability:* Part-time. *Degree requirements:* For master's, thesis. *Entrance requirements:* For master's, GRE, minimum GPA of 2.5, letters of recommendation. Additional exam requirements/recommendations for international students: Required—TOEFL.

**Northern Kentucky University,** Office of Graduate Programs, College of Informatics, Program in Communication, Highland Heights, KY 41099. Offers communication (MA); communication teaching (Certificate); documentary studies (Certificate); public relations (Certificate); relationships (Certificate). *Program availability:* Part-time, evening/weekend. Terminal master's awarded for partial completion of doctoral program. *Degree requirements:* For master's, comprehensive exams, thesis or applied capstone project. *Entrance requirements:* For master's, GRE, minimum GPA of 3.0, 3 letters of recommendation, letter of intent. Additional exam requirements/recommendations for international students: Required—TOEFL (minimum score 79 iBT); Recommended—IELTS (minimum score 6.5). Electronic applications accepted. *Faculty research:* Mediating effect of health communication, organizational communication, quantitative and qualitative research methods, family and interpersonal communication.

**Northwestern University,** The Graduate School, Kellogg School of Management, Management Programs, Evanston, IL 60208. Offers accounting information and management (MBA, PhD); analytical finance (MBA); business administration (MBA); decision sciences (MBA); entrepreneurship and innovation (MBA); finance (MBA, PhD); health enterprise management (MBA); human resources management (MBA); international business (MBA); management and organizations (MBA, PhD); management and organizations and sociology (PhD); management and strategy (MBA); management studies (MS); managerial analytics (MBA); managerial economics (MBA); managerial economics and strategy (PhD); marketing (MBA, PhD); marketing management (MBA); media management (MBA); operations management (MBA, PhD); real estate (MBA); social enterprise at Kellogg (MBA); JD/MBA. *Program availability:* Part-time, evening/weekend. Terminal master's awarded for partial completion of doctoral program. *Degree requirements:* For doctorate, thesis/dissertation, 2 years of coursework, qualifying (field) exam and candidacy, summer research papers and presentations to faculty, proposal defense, final exam/defense. *Entrance requirements:* For master's, GMAT, GRE, interview, 2 letters of recommendation, college transcripts, resume, essays, Kellogg honor code; for doctorate, GMAT, GRE, statement of purpose, transcripts, 2 letters of recommendation, resume, interview. Additional exam requirements/recommendations for international students: Required—TOEFL, IELTS. Electronic applications accepted. *Expenses:* Contact institution. *Faculty research:* Business cycles and international finance, health policy, networks, non-market strategy, consumer psychology.

**Northwestern University,** The Graduate School, School of Communication, Department of Communication Studies, Evanston, IL 60208. Offers communication studies (PhD), including interaction and social influence, rhetoric and public culture; managerial communication (MSC); media, technology and society (PhD); technology and social behavior (PhD). PhD admissions and degree offered through The Graduate School. Terminal master's awarded for partial completion of doctoral program. *Degree requirements:* For doctorate, thesis/dissertation. *Entrance requirements:* For master's and doctorate, GRE General Test. Additional exam requirements/recommendations for international students: Required—TOEFL. Electronic applications accepted.

**Northwestern University,** The Graduate School, School of Communication, Department of Radio, Television and Film, Evanston, IL 60208. Offers documentary media (MFA); screen cultures (MA, PhD); writing for the screen and stage (MFA). Admissions and degrees offered through The Graduate School. *Program availability:* Part-time. Terminal master's awarded for partial completion of doctoral program. *Degree requirements:* For master's, comprehensive exam or thesis; for doctorate, thesis/dissertation, qualifying exam. *Entrance requirements:* For master's and doctorate, GRE General Test. Additional exam requirements/recommendations for international students: Required—TOEFL. Electronic applications accepted. *Faculty research:* Art and new media, media theory and criticism, gender, media history, documentary.

**Ohio University,** Graduate College, Scripps College of Communication, School of Media Arts and Studies, Athens, OH 45701-2979. Offers mass communication (PhD); media arts and studies (MA). *Degree requirements:* For master's, comprehensive exam (for some programs), thesis or alternative; for doctorate, comprehensive exam, thesis/dissertation. *Entrance requirements:* For master's, GRE General Test or MAT, minimum GPA of 3.0; for doctorate, GRE General Test or MAT. Additional exam requirements/recommendations for international students: Required—TOEFL (minimum score 600 paper-based; 100 iBT) or IELTS (minimum score 7). *Application deadline:* For fall admission, 1/31 priority date for domestic students, 12/31 priority date for international students. Application fee: $50 ($55 for international students). Electronic applications accepted. *Financial support:* Research assistantships with full tuition reimbursements, teaching assistantships with full tuition reimbursements, career-related internships or fieldwork, Federal Work-Study, institutionally sponsored loans, and unspecified assistantships available. Financial award application deadline: 1/31; financial award applicants required to submit FAFSA. *Faculty research:* Media and development communication, new media and society, industry studies. *Unit head:* Dr. Roger Cooper, Director, 740-593-4872, Fax: 740-593-9184, E-mail: cooperr@ohio.edu. *Application contact:* Dr. Gregory Newton, Interim Director for Graduate Studies, 740-593-4870, Fax: 740-593-9184, E-mail: newtong@ohio.edu.
Website: http://www.mediaschool.ohiou.edu

**Ohio University,** Graduate College, Scripps College of Communication, School of Visual Communication, Athens, OH 45701-2979. Offers MA. *Entrance requirements:* For master's, minimum GPA of 2.5, portfolio. Additional exam requirements/recommendations for international students: Required—TOEFL (minimum score 600 paper-based; 100 iBT) or IELTS (minimum score 7). *Application deadline:* For fall admission, 2/1 for domestic students, 12/14 for international students. Application fee: $50 ($55 for international students). Electronic applications accepted. *Financial support:* Federal Work-Study, institutionally sponsored loans, and tuition waivers (partial) available. Financial award applicants required to submit FAFSA. *Faculty research:* Photojournalism (including documentary photography), commercial photography (including illustrative photography), picture editing, informational graphics/publication design, interactive multimedia, visual media management. *Unit head:* Terry Eiler, Director, 740-595-4895, Fax: 740-593-0190, E-mail: eiler@ohio.edu. *Application contact:* Stan Alost, Assistant Director, 740-597-1756, Fax: 740-593-0190, E-mail: alost@ohio.edu.
Website: http://www.viscom.ohiou.edu/

**Pace University,** Dyson College of Arts and Sciences, MA Program in Media and Communication Arts, New York, NY 10038. Offers MA. *Program availability:* Part-time, evening/weekend. *Students:* 13 full-time (11 women), 17 part-time (12 women); includes 12 minority (7 Black or African American, non-Hispanic/Latino; 1 Asian, non-Hispanic/

Latino; 3 Hispanic/Latino; 1 Two or more races, non-Hispanic/Latino), 8 international. Average age 27. In 2016, 18 master's awarded. *Degree requirements:* For master's, comprehensive exam, thesis, internship. *Entrance requirements:* For master's, portfolio containing examples of prior work (press releases, advertisements, presentations, writing samples, etc.) and official transcripts. Additional exam requirements/recommendations for international students: Required—TOEFL (minimum score 100 iBT). *Application deadline:* For fall admission, 8/1 priority date for domestic students, 6/1 for international students; for spring admission, 12/1 priority date for domestic students, 10/1 for international students. Applications are processed on a rolling basis. Application fee: $70. Electronic applications accepted. *Expenses: Tuition:* Part-time $1195 per credit. *Required fees:* $260 per semester. Tuition and fees vary according to degree level, campus/location and program. *Financial support:* Career-related internships or fieldwork, scholarships/grants, and unspecified assistantships available. Financial award application deadline: 2/15; financial award applicants required to submit FAFSA. *Unit head:* Dr. Maria Luskay, Program Director, 914-773-3353, E-mail: mluskay@pace.edu. *Application contact:* Susan Ford-Goldschein, Director of Admissions, 914-422-4283, Fax: 212-346-1585, E-mail: graduateadmission@pace.edu.
Website: http://www.pace.edu/dyson/programs/ma-media-communication-arts-plv

**Paris College of Art,** Graduate Programs, Paris, France. Offers accessories design (MA); fashion design: new materials and technologies (MA); fashion film and photography (MA); interior design (MA); transdisciplinary new media (MA, MFA). *Entrance requirements:* Additional exam requirements/recommendations for international students: Required—TOEFL or IELTS.

**Penn State University Park,** Graduate School, College of Communications, Department of Communications, University Park, PA 16802. Offers mass communications (PhD); media studies (MA). *Unit head:* Dr. Marie C. Hardin, Dean, 814-863-1484, Fax: 814-863-8044. *Application contact:* Lori Hawn, Director, Graduate Student Services, 814-865-1795, Fax: 814-863-4627, E-mail: l-gswww@lists.psu.edu.
Website: http://comm.psu.edu/

**Pepperdine University,** Seaver College, Division of Communication, Malibu, CA 90263. Offers cinematic media production (MFA); strategic communication (MA). *Program availability:* Part-time. *Students:* 7 full-time (3 women), 26 part-time (16 women); includes 11 minority (4 Black or African American, non-Hispanic/Latino; 1 American Indian or Alaska Native, non-Hispanic/Latino; 3 Asian, non-Hispanic/Latino; 2 Hispanic/Latino; 1 Native Hawaiian or other Pacific Islander, non-Hispanic/Latino), 4 international. Average age 27. In 2016, 8 master's awarded. *Entrance requirements:* For master's, GRE General Test, letters of recommendation, writing sample. Additional exam requirements/recommendations for international students: Required—TOEFL. *Application deadline:* For fall admission, 2/1 priority date for domestic students, 2/1 for international students. Applications are processed on a rolling basis. Application fee: $65. Electronic applications accepted. *Financial support:* Research assistantships, teaching assistantships, career-related internships or fieldwork, and scholarships/grants available. Support available to part-time students. Financial award applicants required to submit FAFSA. *Unit head:* Dr. Kenneth E. Waters, Divisional Dean/Professor of Journalism, 310-506-4245, E-mail: ken.waters@pepperdine.edu. *Application contact:* Hayley Wolf, Director of Admission, 310-506-4392,
E-mail: hayley.wolf@pepperdine.edu.

**Pratt Institute,** School of Liberal Arts and Sciences, Program in Media Studies, Brooklyn, NY 11205-3899. Offers MA. *Faculty:* 9 full-time (5 women), 3 part-time/adjunct (1 woman). *Students:* 17 full-time (11 women), 1 part-time (0 women); includes 4 minority (2 Black or African American, non-Hispanic/Latino; 1 Hispanic/Latino; 1 Two or more races, non-Hispanic/Latino), 7 international. Average age 26. 39 applicants, 87% accepted, 8 enrolled. In 2016, 4 master's awarded. *Degree requirements:* For master's, thesis. *Entrance requirements:* For master's, BA, BS, or BFA from accredited institution; statement of purpose; 10-20 pages of relevant writing samples; transcripts of undergraduate coursework; three letters of recommendation. Additional exam requirements/recommendations for international students: Required—TOEFL (minimum score 600 paper-based; 100 iBT). *Application deadline:* For fall admission, 1/5 for domestic and international students; for spring admission, 10/1 for domestic and international students. Application fee: $50 ($90 for international students). Electronic applications accepted. *Expenses:* $29,646 full-time tuition, $1,938 fees. *Financial support:* Career-related internships or fieldwork, Federal Work-Study, institutionally sponsored loans, scholarships/grants, health care benefits, and unspecified assistantships available. Support available to part-time students. Financial award application deadline: 2/1; financial award applicants required to submit FAFSA. *Unit head:* Maria Damon, Chair, 718-636-3790, E-mail: mdamon@pratt.edu. *Application contact:* Natalie Capannelli, Director of Graduate Admissions, 718-636-3551, Fax: 718-399-4242, E-mail: ncapanne@pratt.edu.
Website: https://www.pratt.edu/academics/liberal-arts-and-sciences/graduate-media-studies/

See Display on next page and Close-Up on page 769.

**Queens College of the City University of New York,** Arts and Humanities Division, Department of Media Studies, Queens, NY 11367-1597. Offers MA. *Degree requirements:* For master's, thesis. *Entrance requirements:* For master's, GRE General Test, minimum GPA of 3.0. Additional exam requirements/recommendations for international students: Required—TOEFL. *Expenses:* Tuition, state resident: full-time $5065; part-time $425 per credit. Tuition, nonresident: part-time $780 per credit. *Required fees:* $522; $397 per credit. Part-time tuition and fees vary according to course load and program.

**Rhode Island School of Design,** Graduate Studies, Department of Digital and Media, Providence, RI 02903-2784. Offers MFA. *Faculty:* 4 full-time (2 women), 13 part-time/adjunct (3 women). *Students:* 27 full-time (19 women); includes 6 minority (4 Asian, non-Hispanic/Latino; 1 Hispanic/Latino; 1 Two or more races, non-Hispanic/Latino), 12 international. Average age 28. 140 applicants, 19% accepted, 13 enrolled. In 2016, 14 master's awarded. *Degree requirements:* For master's, thesis, exhibition. *Entrance requirements:* For master's, portfolio, statement of purpose, 3 letters of recommendation. Additional exam requirements/recommendations for international students: Required—TOEFL (minimum score 580 paper-based; 93 iBT). *Application deadline:* For fall admission, 2/1 for domestic and international students. Application fee: $60. Electronic applications accepted. *Expenses: Tuition:* Full-time $46,800. *Required fees:* $310. *Financial support:* Fellowships, research assistantships, teaching assistantships, Federal Work-Study, scholarships/grants, and unspecified assistantships available. Financial award application deadline: 2/15; financial award applicants required to submit FAFSA. *Unit head:* Shona Kitchen, Head, 401-454-6139, Fax: 401-277-4966, E-mail: skitchen@risd.edu. *Application contact:* Molly Pettengil, Assistant Director for Graduate Recruitment, 401-454-6312, Fax: 401-454-6309, E-mail: mpetteng@risd.edu.
Website: http://www.risd.edu/academics/digital-media/

**Robert Morris University Illinois,** Morris Graduate School of Management, Chicago, IL 60605. Offers accounting (MBA); accounting/finance (MBA); business analytics (MIS); design and media (MM); design management (MM); educational technology (MM); health care administration (MM); higher education administration (MM); human resource

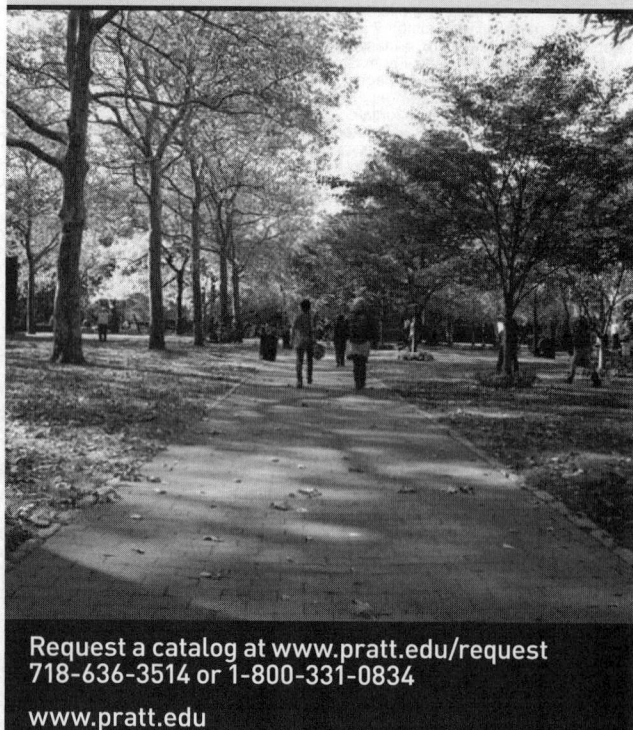
management (MBA); information security (MIS); information systems (MBA, MIS); law enforcement administration (MM); management (MBA); management/finance (MBA); management/human resource management (MBA); mobile computing (MIS); sports administration (MM). *Program availability:* Part-time, evening/weekend. *Faculty:* 4 full-time (1 woman), 25 part-time/adjunct (5 women). *Students:* 196 full-time (98 women), 151 part-time (85 women); includes 200 minority (114 Black or African American, non-Hispanic/Latino; 17 Asian, non-Hispanic/Latino; 67 Hispanic/Latino; 2 Two or more races, non-Hispanic/Latino), 23 international. Average age 33. 174 applicants, 61% accepted, 97 enrolled. In 2016, 190 master's awarded. *Entrance requirements:* For master's, official transcripts and letters of recommendation (for some programs); written personal statement. Additional exam requirements/recommendations for international students: Required—TOEFL (minimum score 550 paper-based). *Application deadline:* Applications are processed on a rolling basis. Application fee: $20 ($100 for international students). Electronic applications accepted. *Expenses: Tuition:* Full-time $16,500; part-time $2750 per course. *Financial support:* In 2016–17, 444 students received support. Federal Work-Study, scholarships/grants, and unspecified assistantships available. Support available to part-time students. Financial award applicants required to submit FAFSA. *Unit head:* Kayed Akkawi, Dean, 312-935-6050, Fax: 312-935-6020, E-mail: kakkawi@robertmorris.edu. *Application contact:* Danielle Naffziger, Vice President of Marketing and Enrollment, 312-935-4812, Fax: 312-935-6020, E-mail: dnaffziger@robertmorris.edu.

**Rochester Institute of Technology,** Graduate Enrollment Services, College of Imaging Arts and Sciences, School of Media Sciences, MS Program in Media Arts and Technology, Rochester, NY 14623-5603. Offers MS. *Program availability:* Part-time, evening/weekend. *Degree requirements:* For master's, capstone project. *Entrance requirements:* For master's, minimum GPA of 3.0 (recommended). Additional exam requirements/recommendations for international students: Required—TOEFL (minimum score 79 iBT), IELTS (minimum score 6.5), PTE (minimum score 58). *Application deadline:* Applications are processed on a rolling basis. Application fee: $60. Electronic applications accepted. *Expenses:* $1,742 per credit hour. *Financial support:* Research assistantships with partial tuition reimbursements, teaching assistantships with partial tuition reimbursements, career-related internships or fieldwork, scholarships/grants, and unspecified assistantships available. Support available to part-time students. Financial award applicants required to submit FAFSA. *Faculty research:* Digital publishing, digital content management, media distribution, consumer preferences, media business transformation. *Unit head:* Christine Heusner, Graduate Program Director, 585-475-4627, E-mail: cxhppr@rit.edu. *Application contact:* Diane Ellison, Associate Vice President, Graduate Enrollment Services, 585-475-2229, Fax: 585-475-7164, E-mail: gradinfo@rit.edu.
Website: http://cias.rit.edu/schools/media-sciences/graduate-media-arts-and-technology

**Rochester Institute of Technology,** Graduate Enrollment Services, College of Liberal Arts, School of Communication, MS Program in Communication and Media Technologies, Rochester, NY 14623. Offers MS. *Program availability:* Part-time. *Students:* 13 full-time (9 women), 9 part-time (5 women); includes 2 minority (1 Black or African American, non-Hispanic/Latino; 1 American Indian or Alaska Native, non-Hispanic/Latino), 10 international. Average age 28. 27 applicants, 48% accepted, 7 enrolled. In 2016, 11 master's awarded. *Degree requirements:* For master's, thesis. *Entrance requirements:* For master's, minimum GPA of 3.0 (recommended), writing sample. Additional exam requirements/recommendations for international students: Required—TOEFL (minimum score 570 paper-based; 88 iBT), IELTS (minimum score 6.5), PTE (minimum score 61). *Application deadline:* For fall admission, 2/15 priority date for domestic and international students; for spring admission, 12/15 priority date for domestic and international students. Applications are processed on a rolling basis. Application fee: $60. Electronic applications accepted. *Expenses:* $1,742 per credit hour. *Financial support:* In 2016–17, 13 students received support. Research assistantships with partial tuition reimbursements available, teaching assistantships with partial tuition reimbursements available, career-related internships or fieldwork, scholarships/grants, and unspecified assistantships available. Support available to part-time students. Financial award applicants required to submit FAFSA. *Faculty research:* Media and culture, visual communication, mass media, technology and media. *Unit head:* Dr. Grant Cos, Graduate Program Director, 585-475-6646, Fax: 585-475-7732, E-mail: communication@rit.edu. *Application contact:* Diane Ellison, Associate Vice President, Graduate Enrollment Services, 585-475-2229, Fax: 585-475-7164, E-mail: gradinfo@rit.edu.
Website: http://www.rit.edu/cla/communication/graduate-programs/ms-communication-media-technologies/overview

**Rowan University,** Graduate School, College of Communication and Creative Arts, Integrated Marketing Communication and New Media Certificate of Graduate Study Program, Glassboro, NJ 08028-1701. Offers CGS. Electronic applications accepted.

**Sacred Heart University,** Graduate Programs, College of Arts and Sciences, School of Communication and Media Arts, Fairfield, CT 06825. Offers corporate communications and public relations (MA Comm); digital multimedia journalism (MA Comm); digital multimedia production (MA Comm); film and television production (MA); media literacy and digital culture (MA), including children, health and media, media and social justice, political action and media production; sports communication and media (MA), including athletic communications and promotions, sports broadcasting. *Program availability:* Part-time, evening/weekend. *Faculty:* 9 full-time (1 woman), 3 part-time/adjunct (2 women). *Students:* 60 full-time (34 women), 44 part-time (23 women); includes 23 minority (14 Black or African American, non-Hispanic/Latino; 7 Hispanic/Latino; 2 Two or more races, non-Hispanic/Latino), 18 international. Average age 26. 135 applicants, 93% accepted, 72 enrolled. In 2016, 69 master's awarded. *Degree requirements:* For master's, thesis or alternative. *Entrance requirements:* For master's, bachelor's degree. Additional exam requirements/recommendations for international students: Required—TOEFL (minimum score 570 paper-based, 80 iBT), TWE, or IELTS (6.5); Recommended—TSE. *Application deadline:* Applications are processed on a rolling basis. Application fee: $75. Electronic applications accepted. *Expenses:* $935 per credit. *Financial support:* Unspecified assistantships available. Financial award applicants required to submit FAFSA. *Unit head:* Dr. Andrew Miller, Chair, 203-396-8087, E-mail: millera@sacredheart.edu. *Application contact:* William Sweeney, Director of Graduate Admissions Operations, 203-365-7619, Fax: 203-365-4732, E-mail: graduatestudies@sacredheart.edu.
Website: http://www.sacredheart.edu/academics/collegeofartsssciences/academicdepartments/communicationmediastudies/

**Saginaw Valley State University,** College of Arts and Behavioral Sciences, Program in Communication and Media Administration, University Center, MI 48710. Offers MA. *Program availability:* Part-time, evening/weekend. *Students:* 27 full-time (15 women), 8 part-time (6 women); includes 2 minority (1 Black or African American, non-Hispanic/Latino; 1 Asian, non-Hispanic/Latino), 24 international. Average age 27. 24 applicants, 46% accepted, 7 enrolled. In 2016, 13 master's awarded. *Degree requirements:* For master's, thesis. *Entrance requirements:* For master's, minimum GPA of 3.0. Additional exam requirements/recommendations for international students: Required—TOEFL (minimum score 540 paper-based; 76 iBT). *Application deadline:* For fall admission, 7/15 for international students; for winter admission, 11/15 for international students; for spring admission, 4/15 for international students. Applications are processed on a rolling basis. Application fee: $30 ($90 for international students). Electronic applications accepted. *Expenses:* Tuition, state resident: full-time $9652; part-time $536 per credit hour. Tuition, nonresident: full-time $12,259; part-time $1022 per credit hour. *Required fees:* $263; $14.60 per credit hour. Tuition and fees vary according to degree level. *Financial support:* Federal Work-Study and scholarships/grants available. Support available to part-time students. Financial award application deadline: 4/1; financial award applicants required to submit FAFSA. *Unit head:* Dr. Robert Drew, Professor of Communication, 989-964-7495, E-mail: rdrew@svsu.edu. *Application contact:* Jenna Briggs, Director, Graduate and International Admissions, 989-964-6096, Fax: 989-964-2788, E-mail: gradadm@svsu.edu.

**San Diego State University,** Graduate and Research Affairs, College of Professional Studies and Fine Arts, School of Communication, San Diego, CA 92182. Offers advertising and public relations (MA); critical-cultural studies (MA); interaction studies (MA); intercultural and international studies (MA); new media studies (MA); news and information studies (MA); telecommunications and media management (MA). *Degree requirements:* For master's, thesis. *Entrance requirements:* For master's, GRE General Test, 3 letters of recommendation. Additional exam requirements/recommendations for international students: Required—TOEFL. Electronic applications accepted.

**San Diego State University,** Graduate and Research Affairs, College of Professional Studies and Fine Arts, School of Theater, Television and Film, Program in Television, Film, and New Media Production, San Diego, CA 92182. Offers MA. *Entrance requirements:* For master's, GRE General Test, 3 letters of recommendation, resume, sample reel, influential book list, influential films list, hobby list. Additional exam requirements/recommendations for international students: Required—TOEFL. Electronic applications accepted. *Faculty research:* Experimental film and television programs, documentary film, television research and production.

**San Francisco State University,** Division of Graduate Studies, College of Liberal and Creative Arts, Department of Broadcast and Electronic Communication Arts, San Francisco, CA 94132-1722. Offers MA. *Expenses:* Tuition, state resident: full-time $6738. Tuition, nonresident: full-time $15,666. *Required fees:* $1012. Tuition and fees vary according to degree level and program. *Unit head:* Dr. Vinay Shrivastava, Chair, 415-338-1787, Fax: 415-338-1168, E-mail: vinay@sfsu.edu. *Application contact:* Dr. Nancy Reist, Graduate Coordinator, 415-338-1787, Fax: 415-338-1168, E-mail: sami@sfsu.edu. Website: http://beca.sfsu.edu/

**San Jose State University,** Graduate Studies and Research, College of Humanities and the Arts, San Jose, CA 95192-0001. Offers art (MA, MFA), including art history and visual culture (MA), digital media art (MFA), photography (MFA), pictorial art (MFA), spatial art (MFA); computational linguistics (Certificate); English (MA, MFA), including creative writing (MA); French (MA); humanities and arts (Certificate); linguistics (MA); music (MA); philosophy (MA); professional and technical communication (Certificate); Spanish (MA); teaching English to speakers of other languages (MA); TESOL (Certificate); theatre arts (MA). Electronic applications accepted.

**Savannah College of Art and Design,** Graduate School, Program in Motion Media Design, Savannah, GA 31402-3146. Offers MA, MFA. *Program availability:* Part-time, 100% online. *Faculty:* 14 full-time (3 women), 7 part-time/adjunct (5 women). *Students:* 56 full-time (35 women), 20 part-time (8 women); includes 12 minority (9 Black or African American, non-Hispanic/Latino; 1 Asian, non-Hispanic/Latino; 2 Hispanic/Latino), 40 international. Average age 30. 51 applicants, 61% accepted, 20 enrolled. In 2016, 22 master's awarded. *Degree requirements:* For master's, final project (for MA); thesis (for MFA). *Entrance requirements:* For master's, GRE (recommended), portfolio (submitted in digital format), audition or writing submission, resume, statement of purpose, two letters of recommendation. Additional exam requirements/recommendations for international students: Required—TOEFL (minimum score 550 paper-based, 85 iBT), IELTS (minimum score 6.5), or ACTFL. *Application deadline:* For fall admission, 4/1 for domestic and international students. Applications are processed on a rolling basis. Application fee: $40. Electronic applications accepted. *Expenses:* Tuition: Full-time $36,045. Tuition and fees vary according to course load. *Financial support:* Career-related internships or fieldwork, Federal Work-Study, and scholarships/grants available. Financial award application deadline: 4/1; financial award applicants required to submit FAFSA. *Unit head:* Kelly Carlton, Chair, Motion Media Design. *Application contact:* Jenny Jaquillard, Executive Director of Admissions, Recruitment and Events, 912-525-5100, Fax: 912-525-5985, E-mail: admission@scad.edu. Website: http://www.scad.edu/academics/programs/motion-media-design

**Savannah College of Art and Design,** Graduate School, Program in Performing Arts, Savannah, GA 31402-3146. Offers MFA. *Faculty:* 13 full-time (5 women), 6 part-time/adjunct (4 women). *Students:* 41 full-time (26 women), 2 part-time (both women); includes 16 minority (13 Black or African American, non-Hispanic/Latino; 1 American Indian or Alaska Native, non-Hispanic/Latino; 2 Hispanic/Latino), 1 international. Average age 26. 92 applicants, 60% accepted, 20 enrolled. In 2016, 28 master's awarded. *Degree requirements:* For master's, thesis. *Entrance requirements:* For master's, GRE (recommended), portfolio (submitted in digital format), audition or writing submission, resume, statement of purpose, two letters of recommendation. Additional exam requirements/recommendations for international students: Required—TOEFL (minimum score 550 paper-based, 85 iBT), IELTS (minimum score 6.5), or ACTFL. *Application deadline:* For fall admission, 4/1 for domestic and international students. Applications are processed on a rolling basis. Application fee: $40. Electronic applications accepted. *Expenses:* Tuition: Full-time $36,045. Tuition and fees vary according to course load. *Financial support:* Career-related internships or fieldwork, Federal Work-Study, and scholarships/grants available. Financial award application deadline: 4/1; financial award applicants required to submit FAFSA. *Unit head:* Mark Tymchyshyn, Chair, Performing Arts. *Application contact:* Jenny Jaquillard, Executive Director of Admissions, Recruitment and Events, 912-525-5100, Fax: 912-525-5985, E-mail: admission@scad.edu. Website: http://www.scad.edu/academics/programs/performing-arts

**Southern Illinois University Carbondale,** Graduate School, College of Mass Communication and Media Arts, Department of Mass Communication and Media Arts, Carbondale, IL 62901-4701. Offers MFA, PhD. *Degree requirements:* For doctorate, thesis/dissertation. *Entrance requirements:* For master's, minimum GPA of 2.7; for doctorate, GRE, minimum GPA of 3.25. Additional exam requirements/recommendations for international students: Required—TOEFL (minimum score 100 iBT).

**Southern Illinois University Carbondale,** Graduate School, College of Mass Communication and Media Arts, Department of Professional Media and Media Management Studies, Carbondale, IL 62901-4701. Offers MS. *Entrance requirements:* Additional exam requirements/recommendations for international students: Required—TOEFL (minimum score 100 iBT).

**Southern Illinois University Carbondale,** Graduate School, College of Mass Communication and Media Arts, Program in Media Theory and Research, Carbondale, IL 62901-4701. Offers MA. *Entrance requirements:* For master's, GRE, minimum GPA of

2.7. Additional exam requirements/recommendations for international students: Required—TOEFL (minimum score 100 iBT).

**Southern Illinois University Edwardsville,** Graduate School, College of Arts and Sciences, Department of Mass Communications, Program in Media Literacy, Edwardsville, IL 62026. Offers Postbaccalaureate Certificate. *Program availability:* Part-time, evening/weekend. *Entrance requirements:* Additional exam requirements/recommendations for international students: Required—TOEFL (minimum score 550 paper-based; 79 iBT), IELTS (minimum score 6.5). Electronic applications accepted.

**Stevens Institute of Technology,** Graduate School, Charles V. Schaefer Jr. School of Engineering and Science, Interdisciplinary Program in Media and Broadcast Engineering, Hoboken, NJ 07030. Offers MS. *Students:* 3 applicants, 33% accepted. *Degree requirements:* For master's, thesis optional, minimum B average in major field and overall. *Entrance requirements:* Additional exam requirements/recommendations for international students: Required—TOEFL (minimum score 74 iBT), IELTS (minimum score 6). *Application deadline:* For fall admission, 6/1 for domestic students, 4/15 for international students; for spring admission, 11/30 for domestic students, 11/1 for international students. *Expenses:* Tuition: Full-time $33,328; part-time $1501 per credit. *Required fees:* $1186; $566 per credit. $283 per semester. *Unit head:* Dr. Keith G. Sheppard, Interim Dean, 201-216-5263. *Application contact:* Graduate Admissions, 888-783-8367, Fax: 888-555-1306, E-mail: graduate@stevens.edu.

**Syracuse University,** S. I. Newhouse School of Public Communications, MA Program in Media Studies, Syracuse, NY 13244. Offers MA. *Students:* Average age 25. *Degree requirements:* For master's, thesis. *Entrance requirements:* For master's, GRE General Test, resume, official transcripts, personal statement, three letters of recommendation. Additional exam requirements/recommendations for international students: Required—TOEFL (minimum score 600 paper-based; 100 iBT). *Application deadline:* For fall admission, 1/15 priority date for domestic and international students. Application fee: $45. Electronic applications accepted. *Expenses:* Tuition: Full-time $25,974; part-time $1443 per credit hour. *Required fees:* $802; $50 per course. Tuition and fees vary according to course load and program. *Financial support:* Fellowships with full tuition reimbursements, research assistantships with partial tuition reimbursements, and teaching assistantships with partial tuition reimbursements available. Financial award application deadline: 1/1. *Faculty research:* Media law, communications theory, global persuasion, mass communications, media and diversity. *Unit head:* Frank Biocca Gorham, Director, 315-443-3372, Fax: 315-443-3946, E-mail: masscomm@syr.edu. *Application contact:* Martha Coria, Graduate Records Office, 315-443-4039, E-mail: pcgrad@syr.edu. Website: http://newhouse.syr.edu/

**Syracuse University,** S. I. Newhouse School of Public Communications, MS Program in New Media Management, Syracuse, NY 13244. Offers MS. *Students:* Average age 24. *Degree requirements:* For master's, thesis optional, capstone course. *Entrance requirements:* For master's, GRE General Test or GMAT, resume, official transcripts, personal statement, three letters of recommendation. Additional exam requirements/recommendations for international students: Required—TOEFL (minimum score 600 paper-based; 100 iBT). *Application deadline:* For summer admission, 1/15 priority date for domestic and international students. Application fee: $45. Electronic applications accepted. *Expenses:* Tuition: Full-time $25,974; part-time $1443 per credit hour. *Required fees:* $802; $50 per course. Tuition and fees vary according to course load and program. *Financial support:* Fellowships with full tuition reimbursements, research assistantships with partial tuition reimbursements, and teaching assistantships with partial tuition reimbursements available. Financial award application deadline: 2/1. *Faculty research:* Emerging enterprise consulting, communications industry frontiers, issues in media management, telecommunications law and policy, media law. *Unit head:* Prof. Stephen Masiclat, Director, 315-443-9243, Fax: 315-443-3946, E-mail: pcgrad@syr.edu. *Application contact:* Martha Coria, Graduate Records Office, 315-443-4039, Fax: 315-334-1834, E-mail: pcgrad@syr.edu. Website: http://newhouse.syr.edu/

**Syracuse University,** S. I. Newhouse School of Public Communications, Program in Television, Radio, and Film, Syracuse, NY 13244. Offers MA. In 2016, 36 master's awarded. *Degree requirements:* For master's, comprehensive exam. *Entrance requirements:* For master's, GRE General Test, resume, official transcripts, personal statement, three letters of recommendation. Additional exam requirements/recommendations for international students: Required—TOEFL (minimum score 600 paper-based; 100 iBT). *Application deadline:* For summer admission, 1/15 priority date for domestic and international students. Application fee: $45. Electronic applications accepted. *Expenses:* Tuition: Full-time $25,974; part-time $1443 per credit hour. *Required fees:* $802; $50 per course. Tuition and fees vary according to course load and program. *Financial support:* Fellowships with full tuition reimbursements, research assistantships with partial tuition reimbursements, and teaching assistantships with partial tuition reimbursements available. Financial award application deadline: 1/15. *Faculty research:* Communications industry frontiers, sound for picture, media studies, television, radio, film. *Unit head:* Michael Schoonmaker, Chair of Television, Radio and Film/Associate Professor, 315-443-9240, E-mail: msschoon@syr.edu. *Application contact:* Martha Coria, Graduate Records Office, 315-443-4039, E-mail: pcgrad@syr.edu. Website: http://newhouse.syr.edu/

**Temple University,** School of Media and Communication, Department of Media Studies and Production, Philadelphia, PA 19122-6096. Offers MA. *Program availability:* Part-time. *Degree requirements:* For master's, thesis optional. *Entrance requirements:* For master's, GRE General Test, minimum GPA of 3.0. Additional exam requirements/recommendations for international students: Required—TOEFL (minimum score 600 paper-based; 100 iBT). Electronic applications accepted. *Expenses:* Contact institution. *Faculty research:* Media institutions, international communications, communication policy, media theory.

**Texas Tech University,** Graduate School, College of Media and Communication, Department of Media and Communication, Lubbock, TX 79409. Offers mass communications (MA, PhD); strategic communication and innovation (MA). *Program availability:* Part-time, evening/weekend, 100% online. *Faculty:* 49 full-time (16 women), 6 part-time/adjunct (3 women). *Students:* 70 full-time (45 women), 100 part-time (72 women); includes 50 minority (11 Black or African American, non-Hispanic/Latino; 2 Asian, non-Hispanic/Latino; 32 Hispanic/Latino; 5 Two or more races, non-Hispanic/Latino), 13 international. Average age 29. 130 applicants, 61% accepted, 65 enrolled. In 2016, 53 master's, 7 doctorates awarded. *Degree requirements:* For master's, thesis optional; for doctorate, comprehensive exam, thesis/dissertation. *Entrance requirements:* For doctorate, GRE. Additional exam requirements/recommendations for international students: Required—TOEFL (minimum score 550 paper-based; 79 iBT), GRE. *Application deadline:* For fall admission, 6/1 priority date for domestic students, 1/15 priority date for international students; for spring admission, 9/1 priority date for domestic students, 6/15 priority date for international students. Applications are processed on a rolling basis. Application fee: $75. Electronic applications accepted. *Expenses:* $315 per credit hour full-time resident tuition; $723 per credit hour full-time non-resident tuition; $50.50 per credit hour fee plus $608 per term fee. *Financial support:* In 2016–17, 82 students received support, including 82 fellowships (averaging

$3,876 per year); research assistantships, teaching assistantships, career-related internships or fieldwork, scholarships/grants, and unspecified assistantships also available. Support available to part-time students. Financial award application deadline: 4/15; financial award applicants required to submit FAFSA. *Faculty research:* Media effects, political communication, health communication, critical/cultural/rhetorical, Hispanic and international communication. *Total annual research expenditures:* $183,606. *Unit head:* Dr. Coy Callison, Graduate Director, 806-834-5344, E-mail: coy.callison@ttu.edu. *Application contact:* Bridget Christopherson, Administrative Assistant, 806-834-1619, E-mail: bridget.christopherson@ttu.edu.

**Trinity College,** Graduate Programs, Program in English, Hartford, CT 06106-3100. Offers literary studies (MA); writing, rhetoric, and media arts (MA). *Program availability:* Part-time, evening/weekend. *Degree requirements:* For master's, thesis (for some programs). *Entrance requirements:* For master's, minimum GPA of 3.0.

**University at Buffalo, the State University of New York,** Graduate School, College of Arts and Sciences, Department of Media Study, Buffalo, NY 14260. Offers film and media study (MAH); media arts production (MFA); media study (PhD); new media design (Certificate); social media (MAH); M Arch/MFA. *Faculty:* 11 full-time (5 women), 3 part-time/adjunct (1 woman). *Students:* 53 full-time (28 women); includes 20 minority (4 Black or African American, non-Hispanic/Latino; 15 Asian, non-Hispanic/Latino; 1 Hispanic/Latino). Average age 26. 82 applicants, 35% accepted, 12 enrolled. In 2016, 14 master's, 1 doctorate, 1 other advanced degree awarded. Terminal master's awarded for partial completion of doctoral program. *Degree requirements:* For master's, thesis, media project; for doctorate, thesis/dissertation, qualifying exam, media project. *Entrance requirements:* For master's, portfolio; for doctorate, GRE, portfolio. Additional exam requirements/recommendations for international students: Required—TOEFL (minimum score 550 paper-based; 79 iBT). *Application deadline:* For fall admission, 1/7 priority date for domestic and international students. Applications are processed on a rolling basis. Application fee: $75. Electronic applications accepted. *Expenses:* $6,673.50 full-time resident tuition and fees, $12,343.50 full-time non-resident tuition and fees. *Financial support:* In 2016–17, 11 students received support, including 11 teaching assistantships with full tuition reimbursements available (averaging $13,733 per year); fellowships, career-related internships or fieldwork, Federal Work-Study, scholarships/grants, health care benefits, and unspecified assistantships also available. Support available to part-time students. Financial award application deadline: 1/7; financial award applicants required to submit FAFSA. *Faculty research:* Digital arts, video, documentary, film, game design, digital poetics, locative media. *Unit head:* Prof. Marc Bohlen, Chair, 716-645-6902, Fax: 716-645-6979, E-mail: mrbohlen@buffalo.edu. *Application contact:* Ann Mangan, Academic Advisor/Graduate Coordinator, 716-645-0945, Fax: 716-645-6979, E-mail: annmanga@buffalo.edu.
Website: http://mediastudy.buffalo.edu/

**University of Bridgeport,** College of Public and International Affairs, Bridgeport, CT 06604. Offers East Asian and Pacific Rim studies (MA); global development and peace (MA); global media and communication studies (MA). *Program availability:* Part-time, evening/weekend. *Degree requirements:* For master's, thesis. *Entrance requirements:* Additional exam requirements/recommendations for international students: Recommended—TOEFL (minimum score 550 paper-based; 80 iBT), IELTS (minimum score 6.5).

**University of California, Los Angeles,** Graduate Division, School of Theater, Film and Television, Department of Film, Television, and Digital Media, Los Angeles, CA 90034. Offers animation (MFA); cinema and media studies (MA, PhD); cinematography (MFA); production (MFA); screenwriting (MFA). *Degree requirements:* For master's, comprehensive exam; for doctorate, one foreign language, thesis/dissertation, oral and written qualifying exams. *Entrance requirements:* For master's, GRE General Test (for MA applicants), bachelor's degree; minimum undergraduate GPA of 3.0 (or its equivalent if letter grade system not used); writing sample (for MA); for doctorate, GRE General Test, master's degree; minimum undergraduate GPA of 3.0 (or its equivalent if letter grade system not used); writing sample. Additional exam requirements/recommendations for international students: Required—TOEFL. Electronic applications accepted. *Expenses:* Contact institution.

**University of California, Santa Barbara,** Graduate Division, College of Letters and Sciences, Division of Humanities and Fine Arts, Department of Film and Media Studies, Santa Barbara, CA 93106-4010. Offers PhD, MA/PhD. Terminal master's awarded for partial completion of doctoral program. *Degree requirements:* For doctorate, one foreign language, comprehensive exam, thesis/dissertation. *Entrance requirements:* For doctorate, GRE, MA in film/media studies or equivalent. Additional exam requirements/recommendations for international students: Required—TOEFL (minimum score 600 paper-based; 100 iBT), IELTS (minimum score 7). Electronic applications accepted. *Faculty research:* Classical film theory, film and television history, historiography, cultural studies, global media, media industries, regulation and policy.

**University of California, Santa Barbara,** Graduate Division, College of Letters and Sciences, Division of Humanities and Fine Arts, Department of Media Arts and Technology, Santa Barbara, CA 93106-6065. Offers MS, PhD. Terminal master's awarded for partial completion of doctoral program. *Degree requirements:* For master's, thesis; for doctorate, comprehensive exam, thesis/dissertation. *Entrance requirements:* For master's and doctorate, GRE. Additional exam requirements/recommendations for international students: Required—TOEFL (minimum score 550 paper-based; 80 iBT), IELTS (minimum score 7). Electronic applications accepted. *Faculty research:* Transarchitectures and world making, virtual and mixed reality, visualization, intelligent space and interactive installation, human-computer interaction.

**University of Chicago,** Division of the Humanities, Department of Cinema and Media Studies, Chicago, IL 60637. Offers PhD. *Students:* 36 full-time (22 women); includes 5 minority (3 Black or African American, non-Hispanic/Latino; 2 Two or more races, non-Hispanic/Latino), 15 international. 99 applicants, 8% accepted, 5 enrolled. In 2016, 4 doctorates awarded. *Degree requirements:* For doctorate, 2 foreign languages, comprehensive exam, thesis/dissertation. *Entrance requirements:* For doctorate, GRE General Test. Additional exam requirements/recommendations for international students: Required—TOEFL (minimum score 104 iBT), IELTS (minimum score 7). *Application deadline:* For fall admission, 12/15 for domestic and international students. Application fee: $90. Electronic applications accepted. *Financial support:* Fellowships with full tuition reimbursements, teaching assistantships with tuition reimbursements, Federal Work-Study, institutionally sponsored loans, scholarships/grants, and health care benefits available. Financial award application deadline: 12/15; financial award applicants required to submit FAFSA. *Unit head:* Daniel Morgan, Chair, 773-702-3317, E-mail: drmorgan@uchicago.edu. *Application contact:* Michael Beetley, Assistant Dean of Students, Admissions and Fellowships, 773-702-1552, Fax: 773-834-9148, E-mail: humanitiesadmissions@uchicago.edu.
Website: http://cms.uchicago.edu/

**University of Chicago,** Division of the Humanities, Master of Arts Program in the Humanities, Chicago, IL 60637. Offers art history (MA); cinema and media studies (MA); classic languages (MA); comparative literature (MA); creative writing (MA); cultural policy studies (MA); digital humanities (MA); East Asian languages and civilizations (MA); English language and literature (MA); gender and sexuality studies (MA);

Germanic studies (MA); linguistics (MA); music (MA); near Eastern languages and civilizations (MA); philosophy (MA); poetics (MA); race, politics and culture (MA); Romance languages and literatures (MA); Slavic languages and literatures (MA); South Asian languages and civilizations (MA); theater and performance studies (MA). *Students:* 80 full-time (43 women), 7 part-time (3 women); includes 20 minority (5 Black or African American, non-Hispanic/Latino; 1 American Indian or Alaska Native, non-Hispanic/Latino; 6 Asian, non-Hispanic/Latino; 5 Hispanic/Latino; 3 Two or more races, non-Hispanic/Latino), 11 international. Average age 26. 706 applicants, 15% accepted, 42 enrolled. In 2016, 92 master's awarded. *Degree requirements:* For master's, thesis. *Entrance requirements:* For master's, GRE General Test. Additional exam requirements/recommendations for international students: Required—TOEFL (minimum score 104 iBT), IELTS (minimum score 7). *Application deadline:* For fall admission, 1/3 for domestic and international students. Application fee: $90. Electronic applications accepted. *Financial support:* In 2016–17, 8 fellowships with partial tuition reimbursements (averaging $12,000 per year) were awarded; Federal Work-Study, institutionally sponsored loans, scholarships/grants, and tuition waivers (partial) also available. Financial award application deadline: 12/15; financial award applicants required to submit FAFSA. *Unit head:* Malynne Sternstein, Co-Director, 773-834-1201, Fax: 773-834-7526. *Application contact:* Program Coordinator, 773-834-1201, Fax: 773-834-7526, E-mail: ma-humanities@uchicago.edu.
Website: http://maph.uchicago.edu/

**University of Colorado Boulder,** Graduate School, College of Engineering and Applied Science, Alliance for Technology, Learning, and Society Program, Boulder, CO 80309. Offers MS, PhD. *Students:* 41 full-time (24 women), 7 part-time (5 women); includes 12 minority (3 Black or African American, non-Hispanic/Latino; 1 American Indian or Alaska Native, non-Hispanic/Latino; 4 Asian, non-Hispanic/Latino; 2 Hispanic/Latino; 2 Two or more races, non-Hispanic/Latino), 4 international. Average age 31. 35 applicants, 57% accepted, 11 enrolled. In 2016, 6 master's, 4 doctorates awarded. *Entrance requirements:* For master's, minimum undergraduate GPA of 3.0. *Application deadline:* For fall admission, 1/9 for domestic students, 12/1 for international students; for spring admission, 11/15 for domestic and international students. Application fee: $60 ($80 for international students). Electronic applications accepted. Application fee is waived when completed online. *Financial support:* In 2016–17, 60 students received support, including 28 fellowships (averaging $8,880 per year), 7 research assistantships with full and partial tuition reimbursements available (averaging $43,213 per year), 1 teaching assistantship with full and partial tuition reimbursement available (averaging $23,713 per year); institutionally sponsored loans, scholarships/grants, health care benefits, and unspecified assistantships also available. Financial award application deadline: 1/15; financial award applicants required to submit FAFSA. *Faculty research:* Evaluation of the Dissector Tool based on the Visible Human Data Project, assessing student outcomes for SENCER (an NSF-sponsored program using civic engagement to increase the interest and learning in undergraduate science at over 300 U.S. universities). *Total annual research expenditures:* $2.9 million. *Application contact:* E-mail: cuatlas@colorado.edu.
Website: http://www.colorado.edu/ATLAS/

**University of Colorado Boulder,** Graduate School, College of Media, Communication and Information, Program in Media Studies, Boulder, CO 80309. Offers PhD. *Faculty:* 7 full-time (2 women). *Students:* 22 full-time (13 women), 1 (woman) part-time; includes 1 minority (Hispanic/Latino), 3 international. Average age 29. 39 applicants, 59% accepted, 10 enrolled. *Entrance requirements:* For doctorate, GRE General Test, minimum undergraduate GPA of 3.25. Additional exam requirements/recommendations for international students: Required—TOEFL. *Application deadline:* For fall admission, 2/15 for domestic and international students; for spring admission, 9/15 for domestic students, 8/15 for international students. Application fee: $60 ($80 for international students). Electronic applications accepted. Application fee is waived when completed online. *Financial support:* In 2016–17, 49 students received support, including 6 fellowships (averaging $1,833 per year), 9 research assistantships with full and partial tuition reimbursements available (averaging $24,570 per year), 15 teaching assistantships with full and partial tuition reimbursements available (averaging $26,084 per year); institutionally sponsored loans, scholarships/grants, health care benefits, and unspecified assistantships also available. Financial award application deadline: 2/1; financial award applicants required to submit FAFSA. *Faculty research:* Mass communication/media, culture, electronic media, cultural/social anthropology, journalism. *Total annual research expenditures:* $11,500. *Application contact:* E-mail: mediastudies@colorado.edu.
Website: http://www.colorado.edu/cmci/academics/media-studies

**University of Denver,** Division of Arts, Humanities and Social Sciences, Department of Media, Film and Journalism Studies, Denver, CO 80208. Offers international and intercultural communication (MA); media and globalization (MA). *Program availability:* Part-time. *Faculty:* 16 full-time (10 women), 5 part-time/adjunct (4 women). *Students:* 8 full-time (7 women), 18 part-time (14 women); includes 8 minority (1 Black or African American, non-Hispanic/Latino; 2 Asian, non-Hispanic/Latino; 5 Hispanic/Latino), 1 international. Average age 27. 54 applicants, 78% accepted, 14 enrolled. In 2016, 21 master's awarded. *Degree requirements:* For master's, thesis (for some programs). *Entrance requirements:* For master's, GRE General Test, bachelor's degree, transcripts, personal statement, three letters of recommendation. Additional exam requirements/recommendations for international students: Required—TOEFL (minimum score 620 paper-based; 105 iBT). *Application deadline:* For fall admission, 2/15 priority date for domestic students, 1/1 priority date for international students. Applications are processed on a rolling basis. Application fee: $65. Electronic applications accepted. *Expenses:* $29,022 per year full-time. *Financial support:* In 2016–17, 16 students received support, including 2 teaching assistantships with tuition reimbursements available (averaging $12,500 per year); career-related internships or fieldwork, Federal Work-Study, institutionally sponsored loans, scholarships/grants, and unspecified assistantships also available. Support available to part-time students. Financial award application deadline: 2/15; financial award applicants required to submit FAFSA. *Faculty research:* Branding; public relations; health communication; social media; international communication. *Unit head:* Dr. Lynn Schofield Clark, Professor and Chair, 303-871-3984, Fax: 303-871-4949, E-mail: lynn.clark@du.edu. *Application contact:* Information Contact, 303-871-2166, E-mail: mfjs@du.edu.
Website: http://www.du.edu/ahss/mfjs

**University of Illinois at Urbana–Champaign,** Graduate College, College of Fine and Applied Arts, School of Art and Design, Program in Design and Media, Champaign, IL 61820. Offers art and design (MFA), including new media; graphic design (MFA); industrial design (MFA). *Accreditation:* NASAD.

**University of Illinois at Urbana–Champaign,** Graduate College, College of Media, Institute of Communications Research, Champaign, IL 61820. Offers communications and media (PhD). *Faculty research:* Feminist cultural studies, media technology, international communications, Latino studies, economics of media.

**The University of Iowa,** Graduate College, College of Liberal Arts and Sciences, Department of Communication Studies, Iowa City, IA 52242-1316. Offers interpersonal communication and relationships (MA, PhD); media studies (MA, PhD); rhetoric and public advocacy (MA, PhD). *Degree requirements:* For master's, thesis optional, exam;

for doctorate, comprehensive exam, thesis/dissertation. *Entrance requirements:* For master's and doctorate, GRE General Test, minimum GPA of 3.0. Additional exam requirements/recommendations for international students: Required—TOEFL (minimum score 550 paper-based; 81 iBT). Electronic applications accepted.

**The University of Iowa,** Graduate College, College of Liberal Arts and Sciences, School of Journalism and Mass Communication, Iowa City, IA 52242-1316. Offers journalism and media communication (MA); mass communication (PhD); strategic communication (MA); JD/MA; JD/PhD. *Degree requirements:* For master's, thesis optional, exam; for doctorate, comprehensive exam, thesis/dissertation. *Entrance requirements:* For master's and doctorate, GRE General Test, minimum GPA of 3.0. Additional exam requirements/recommendations for international students: Required— TOEFL (minimum score 637 paper-based; 110 iBT). Electronic applications accepted. *Faculty research:* Verbal and visual aspects of historical, legal, social, and cross-cultural communication.

**The University of Kansas,** Graduate Studies, College of Liberal Arts and Sciences, Department of Film and Media Studies, Lawrence, KS 66045. Offers MA, PhD. *Students:* 20 full-time (9 women); includes 5 minority (2 Black or African American, non-Hispanic/Latino; 1 American Indian or Alaska Native, non-Hispanic/Latino; 1 Native Hawaiian or other Pacific Islander, non-Hispanic/Latino; 1 Two or more races, non-Hispanic/Latino), 4 international. Average age 32. 16 applicants, 38% accepted, 4 enrolled. In 2016, 2 doctorates awarded. *Entrance requirements:* For master's, GRE General Test, three recent letters of recommendation, current resume, statement of personal goals, writing sample; for doctorate, GRE General Test, MA in film or related field; three recent letters of recommendation; current resume; statement of personal goals; writing sample; minimum GPA of 3.2 undergraduate, 3.5 graduate. Additional exam requirements/recommendations for international students: Required—TOEFL or IELTS. *Application deadline:* For fall admission, 1/1 priority date for domestic and international students. Application fee: $65 ($85 for international students). Electronic applications accepted. *Financial support:* Fellowships, research assistantships, teaching assistantships, scholarships/grants, and unspecified assistantships available. Financial award application deadline: 1/1; financial award applicants required to submit FAFSA. *Faculty research:* Latin American cinema, Japanese and East Asian cinema, new media/cultural geography of media, film history, film theory and visual culture. *Unit head:* Dr. Michael Baskett, Chair, 785-864-1384, E-mail: eiga@ku.edu. *Application contact:* Karla Conrad, Graduate Secretary, 785-864-1340, E-mail: kmconrad@ku.edu. Website: http://film.ku.edu/

**University of Lethbridge,** School of Graduate Studies, Lethbridge, AB T1K 3M4, Canada. Offers addictions counseling (M Sc); agricultural biotechnology (M Sc); agricultural studies (M Sc, MA); anthropology (MA); archaeology (M Sc, MA); art (MA, MFA); biochemistry (M Sc); biological sciences (M Sc); biomolecular science (PhD); biosystems and biodiversity (PhD); Canadian studies (MA); chemistry (M Sc); computer science (M Sc); computer science and geographical information science (M Sc); counseling (MC); counseling psychology (M Ed); dramatic arts (MA); earth, space, and physical science (PhD); economics (MA); education (MA, PhD); educational leadership (M Ed); English (MA); environmental science (M Sc); evolution and behavior (PhD); exercise science (M Sc); French (MA); French/German (MA); French/Spanish (MA); general education (M Ed); geography (M Sc, MA); German (MA); health sciences (M Sc); individualized multidisciplinary (M Sc, MA); kinesiology (M Sc, MA); management (M Sc), including accounting, finance, human resource management and labor relations, information systems, international management, marketing, policy and strategy; mathematics (M Sc); music (M Mus, MA); Native American studies (MA); neuroscience (M Sc, PhD); new media (MA, MFA); nursing (M Sc, MN); philosophy (MA); physics (M Sc); political science (MA); psychology (M Sc, MA); religious studies (MA); sociology (MA); theatre and dramatic arts (MFA); theoretical and computational science (PhD); urban and regional studies (MA); women and gender studies (MA). *Program availability:* Part-time, evening/weekend. *Degree requirements:* For master's, thesis (for some programs); for doctorate, comprehensive exam, thesis/dissertation. *Entrance requirements:* For master's, GMAT (for M Sc in management), bachelor's degree in related field, minimum GPA of 3.0 during previous 20 graded semester courses, 2 years' teaching or related experience (M Ed); for doctorate, master's degree, minimum graduate GPA of 3.5. Additional exam requirements/recommendations for international students: Required—TOEFL (minimum score 580 paper-based; 93 iBT). Electronic applications accepted. *Faculty research:* Movement and brain plasticity, gibberellin physiology, photosynthesis, carbon cycling, molecular properties of main-group ring components.

**University of Maryland, College Park,** Academic Affairs, Phillip Merrill College of Journalism, College Park, MD 20742. Offers broadcast journalism (MA); journalism (MA); journalism and media studies (PhD); online news (MA); public affairs reporting (MA). *Accreditation:* ACEJMC (one or more programs are accredited). *Program availability:* Part-time, evening/weekend. *Degree requirements:* For doctorate, thesis/ dissertation, preliminary written and oral comprehensive exams. *Entrance requirements:* For master's and doctorate, GRE General Test, minimum GPA of 3.0, 3 letters of recommendation. Additional exam requirements/recommendations for international students: Required—TOEFL. Electronic applications accepted. *Faculty research:* Mass communication theory, specialized journalism, new telecommunication technologies, press integration.

**University of Michigan,** Rackham Graduate School, School of Music, Theatre, and Dance, Program in Media Arts, Ann Arbor, MI 48109-2085. Offers MA. *Entrance requirements:* For master's, GRE, portfolio. Additional exam requirements/ recommendations for international students: Required—TOEFL. *Expenses:* Tuition, state resident: full-time $21,466; part-time $1152 per credit hour. Tuition, nonresident: full-time $43,346; part-time $2367 per credit hour. Part-time tuition and fees vary according to course load, degree level and program.

**University of Missouri–St. Louis,** College of Arts and Sciences, Department of Communication and Media, St. Louis, MO 63121. Offers communication (MA). *Program availability:* Part-time, evening/weekend. *Faculty:* 7 full-time (6 women), 1 (woman) part-time/adjunct. *Students:* 4 full-time (all women), 10 part-time (5 women); includes 1 minority (Black or African American, non-Hispanic/Latino), 4 international. Average age 29. 16 applicants, 69% accepted, 6 enrolled. *Degree requirements:* For master's, thesis optional. *Entrance requirements:* For master's, 3 letters of recommendation, minimum GPA of 3.25, BA in communication or related discipline. Additional exam requirements/ recommendations for international students: Required—TOEFL (minimum score 600 paper-based). *Application deadline:* For fall admission, 7/1 for domestic students, 5/1 for international students; for spring admission, 12/1 for domestic students, 10/1 for international students. Application fee: $50 ($40 for international students). Electronic applications accepted. *Financial support:* Teaching assistantships available. Financial award application deadline: 4/1; financial award applicants required to submit FAFSA. *Faculty research:* Theory and methodology: intercultural, interpersonal, and mass organizational. *Unit head:* Dr. Alice Hall, Chair, 314-516-6662, Fax: 314-516-5816, E-mail: halla@umsl.edu. *Application contact:* 314-516-5458, Fax: 314-516-6996, E-mail: gradadm@umsl.edu. Website: http://www.umsl.edu/~comm/

**University of Nevada, Las Vegas,** Graduate College, Greenspun College of Urban Affairs, Hank Greenspun School of Journalism and Media Studies, Las Vegas, NV 89154-5007. Offers MA. *Program availability:* Part-time. *Faculty:* 5 full-time (0 women). *Students:* 6 full-time (5 women), 2 part-time (1 woman); includes 4 minority (2 Black or African American, non-Hispanic/Latino; 1 Hispanic/Latino; 1 Two or more races, non-Hispanic/Latino), 2 international. Average age 28. 10 applicants, 70% accepted, 4 enrolled. In 2016, 6 master's awarded. *Degree requirements:* For master's, comprehensive exam, thesis optional, oral exam. *Entrance requirements:* For master's, GRE General Test, bachelor's degree with minimum GPA 3.0; 3 letters of recommendation; statement of purpose; writing sample. Additional exam requirements/ recommendations for international students: Required—TOEFL (minimum score 550 paper-based; 80 iBT), IELTS (minimum score 7). *Application deadline:* For fall admission, 3/15 for international students. Application fee: $60 ($95 for international students). Electronic applications accepted. *Expenses:* $269.25 per credit, $792 per 3-credit course; $9,634 per year resident; $23,274 per year non-resident; $7,094 fees non-resident (7 credits or more); $1,307 annual health insurance fee. *Financial support:* In 2016–17, 6 teaching assistantships with partial tuition reimbursements (averaging $10,000 per year) were awarded; institutionally sponsored loans, scholarships/grants, health care benefits, and unspecified assistantships also available. Financial award application deadline: 3/15. *Faculty research:* Journalism, mass communication and media history; media law, First Amendment theory, First Amendment law, privacy, obscenity, libel; visual literacy, aesthetics and rhetoric, social psychology of visually-mediated world; global media, audience reception theory and research, video criticism, and advertising; intersection of society and media technologies, emerging technology. *Unit head:* Dr. Joel Lieberman, Interim Director/Professor, 702-895-0249, Fax: 702-895-0252, E-mail: joel.lieberman@unlv.edu. *Application contact:* Dr. Julian Kilker, Graduate Coordinator, 702-895-3729, Fax: 702-895-5189, E-mail: julian.kilker@unlv.edu. Website: http://journalism.unlv.edu/

**The University of North Carolina at Greensboro,** Graduate School, College of Arts and Sciences, Department of Media Studies, Greensboro, NC 27412-5001. Offers film and video production (MFA).

**University of Oregon,** Graduate School, School of Architecture and Allied Arts, Program in Arts and Administration, Eugene, OR 97403. Offers arts management (MA, MS); media management (MA, MS). *Degree requirements:* For master's, summer internship, thesis/project. *Entrance requirements:* For master's, minimum GPA of 3.0; bachelor's degree in history, practice of visual, performing arts or other related degree. Additional exam requirements/recommendations for international students: Required— TOEFL. *Faculty research:* Museum education, arts program evaluation, community arts, information management, arts marketing.

**University of Oregon,** Graduate School, School of Journalism and Communication, Eugene, OR 97403. Offers journalism (MA, MS); media studies (MA, MS, PhD); multimedia journalism (MA, MS); strategic communication (MA, MS). *Accreditation:* ASHA. *Program availability:* Part-time. *Degree requirements:* For master's, thesis or alternative. *Entrance requirements:* For master's, GRE General Test; for doctorate, master's degree. *Faculty research:* Impact of mass communication, media technology, media accountability, craft attitudes, media economics.

**University of South Carolina,** The Graduate School, College of Arts and Sciences, Department of Art, Division of Media Arts, Columbia, SC 29208. Offers MMA. *Degree requirements:* For master's, thesis. *Entrance requirements:* For master's, GRE General Test, interview, portfolio. Additional exam requirements/recommendations for international students: Required—TOEFL. Electronic applications accepted. *Faculty research:* Three dimensional imaging, script writing.

**University of Southern California,** Graduate School, Annenberg School for Communication and Journalism, School of Communication, Program in Communication, Los Angeles, CA 90089. Offers culture and community (PhD); global and transnational communication (PhD); groups, organizations and networks (PhD); health communication and social dynamics (PhD); information, political economy and entertainment (PhD); new media and technology (PhD); rhetoric, politics and public media (PhD). *Students:* 95 full-time (71 women); includes 22 minority (5 Black or African American, non-Hispanic/Latino; 6 Asian, non-Hispanic/Latino; 6 Hispanic/Latino; 5 Two or more races, non-Hispanic/Latino), 36 international. Average age 27. 144 applicants, 15% accepted, 16 enrolled. In 2016, 21 doctorates awarded. *Degree requirements:* For doctorate, thesis/dissertation. *Entrance requirements:* For doctorate, GRE General Test, resume or curriculum vitae, scholarly writing, 3 letters of recommendation, statement of purpose. Additional exam requirements/recommendations for international students: Required—TOEFL (minimum score 114 iBT), IELTS (minimum score 8); Recommended—TWE. *Application deadline:* For fall admission, 12/1 for domestic and international students. Application fee: $90. Electronic applications accepted. *Financial support:* In 2016–17, 16 students received support, including 16 fellowships with full tuition reimbursements available (averaging $5,796 per year); research assistantships, health care benefits, and unspecified assistantships also available. Financial award application deadline: 12/1; financial award applicants required to submit FAFSA. *Faculty research:* Computer-mediated communication, public health campaigns, communication democracy and the public sphere, new communication technologies in organizations, communication and community. *Unit head:* Dr. Peter Monge, Director of the PhD Program, 213-740-0921, E-mail: monge@usc.edu. *Application contact:* Allyson Hill, Associate Dean for Admissions, 213-821-0770, Fax: 213-740-1933, E-mail: ascadm@usc.edu. Website: http://www.annenberg.usc.edu

**University of Southern California,** Graduate School, Annenberg School for Communication and Journalism, School of Communication, Program in Communication Management, Los Angeles, CA 90089. Offers MCM, JD/MCM, MCM/MAJCS. *Program availability:* Part-time, evening/weekend, online learning. *Students:* 153 full-time, 76 part-time; includes 104 minority (31 Black or African American, non-Hispanic/Latino; 29 Asian, non-Hispanic/Latino; 39 Hispanic/Latino; 1 Native Hawaiian or other Pacific Islander, non-Hispanic/Latino; 4 Two or more races, non-Hispanic/Latino), 64 international. Average age 25. 576 applicants, 44% accepted, 161 enrolled. In 2016, 151 master's awarded. *Degree requirements:* For master's, professional project. *Entrance requirements:* For master's, GRE General Test or GMAT, resume, writing samples, recommendation letters, statement of purpose. Additional exam requirements/ recommendations for international students: Required—TOEFL (minimum score 114 iBT), IELTS (minimum score 8). *Application deadline:* For fall admission, 6/5 priority date for domestic students, 1/1 priority date for international students. Applications are processed on a rolling basis. Application fee: $90. Electronic applications accepted. *Financial support:* Career-related internships or fieldwork, Federal Work-Study, and scholarships/grants available. Support available to part-time students. Financial award application deadline: 1/1; financial award applicants required to submit FAFSA. *Faculty research:* Global communication, communication law and policy, entertainment management, marketing communication, strategic and corporate communication management. *Unit head:* Dr. Rebecca Weintraub, Director, 213-821-0764, Fax: 213-740-8036, E-mail: weintrau@usc.edu. *Application contact:* Allyson Hill, Associate Dean for Admissions, 213-821-0770, Fax: 213-740-1933, E-mail: ascadm@usc.edu. Website: http://www.annenberg.usc.edu

*Media Studies*

**University of Southern California**, Graduate School, Annenberg School for Communication and Journalism, School of Communication, Program in Digital Social Media, Los Angeles, CA 90089. Offers MS. *Program availability:* Part-time, evening/weekend. *Students:* 14 full-time (10 women), 1 (woman) part-time; includes 7 minority (2 Asian, non-Hispanic/Latino; 4 Hispanic/Latino; 1 Two or more races, non-Hispanic/Latino), 3 international. Average age 29. 41 applicants, 37% accepted, 13 enrolled. In 2016, 15 master's awarded. *Degree requirements:* For master's, dynamic digital media site or app launch. *Entrance requirements:* For master's, GRE General Test, resume, statement of purpose, writing sample, two letters of recommendation. Additional exam requirements/recommendations for international students: Required—TOEFL (minimum score 114 iBT), IELTS (minimum score 8). *Application deadline:* For fall admission, 1/31 for domestic and international students. Applications are processed on a rolling basis. Application fee: $90. Electronic applications accepted. *Financial support:* Career-related internships or fieldwork and Federal Work-Study available. Financial award application deadline: 11/1; financial award applicants required to submit FAFSA. *Unit head:* Dr. Karen North, Clinical Professor of Communication/Director, Digital Social Media, 310-235-4444, E-mail: knorth@usc.edu. *Application contact:* Allyson Hill, Associate Dean of Admissions, 213-821-0770, E-mail: ascadm@usc.edu.
Website: http://www.annenberg.usc.edu

**University of Southern California**, Graduate School, Dana and David Dornsife College of Letters, Arts and Sciences, Comparative Studies in Literature and Culture Doctoral Program, Los Angeles, CA 90089. Offers comparative literature (PhD); comparative media and culture (PhD); Spanish and Latin American studies (PhD). *Degree requirements:* For doctorate, 2 foreign languages, comprehensive exam, thesis/dissertation. *Entrance requirements:* For doctorate, GRE, competence in language other than English (highly recommended). Additional exam requirements/recommendations for international students: Required—TOEFL. Electronic applications accepted. *Faculty research:* Literary theory, Japanese film and contemporary fiction, Francophone literature and cinema, Latin American and Caribbean literature, Spanish literature and film, nineteenth and twentieth century British and American literature.

**University of Southern California**, Graduate School, School of Cinematic Arts, Interactive Media Division, Los Angeles, CA 90089. Offers interactive media (MFA); media arts and practice (PhD). *Degree requirements:* For master's, thesis, thesis project. *Entrance requirements:* Additional exam requirements/recommendations for international students: Required—TOEFL (minimum score 600 paper-based; 100 iBT). Electronic applications accepted. *Expenses:* Contact institution. *Faculty research:* Immersive media, mobile media, stereoscopic, game design and development, serious games and games for health and learning, experiments in game play.

**University of Southern California**, Graduate School, School of Cinematic Arts, Interdivisional Program in Media Arts and Practice, Los Angeles, CA 90089. Offers PhD. *Degree requirements:* For doctorate, 2 foreign languages, thesis/dissertation. *Entrance requirements:* For doctorate, GRE, portfolio. Additional exam requirements/recommendations for international students: Required—TOEFL. Electronic applications accepted. *Faculty research:* Transmedia, theory and history of emerging technologies; documentary and experimental film and video; interactive media design; telepresence research and mobile media.

**University of South Florida**, College of Arts and Sciences, School of Mass Communications, Tampa, FL 33620-9951. Offers mass communications (MA), including media studies, multimedia journalism, strategic communication management. *Program availability:* Part-time, evening/weekend. *Faculty:* 11 full-time (6 women). *Students:* 27 full-time (23 women), 18 part-time (10 women); includes 5 minority (2 Black or African American, non-Hispanic/Latino; 2 Hispanic/Latino; 1 Native Hawaiian or other Pacific Islander, non-Hispanic/Latino), 25 international. Average age 27. 39 applicants, 82% accepted, 21 enrolled. In 2016, 16 master's awarded. *Degree requirements:* For master's, comprehensive exam, thesis optional. *Entrance requirements:* For master's, GRE General Test, minimum GPA of 3.0 in last 60 hours of course work, three letters of recommendation, letter of intent, resume/curriculum vitae. Additional exam requirements/recommendations for international students: Required—TOEFL (minimum score 550 paper-based; 79 iBT) or IELTS (minimum score 6.5). *Application deadline:* For fall admission, 2/15 for domestic and international students. Application fee: $30. Electronic applications accepted. *Expenses:* Tuition, state resident: full-time $7766; part-time $431.43 per credit hour. Tuition, nonresident: full-time $15,789; part-time $877.17 per credit hour. *Required fees:* $37 per term. *Financial support:* In 2016–17, 5 students received support, including 9 teaching assistantships with tuition reimbursements available (averaging $10,513 per year); unspecified assistantships also available. Financial award application deadline: 2/28. *Faculty research:* First Amendment analysis, civic journalism, public opinion, media ethics, media effects research in sports public relations, public relations management, advertisement, telecommunications. *Total annual research expenditures:* $88,114. *Unit head:* Dr. Jim Andrews, Interim Director/Associate Professor, 813-974-2108, Fax: 813-974-2592, E-mail: jimandrews@usf.edu. *Application contact:* Dr. Michael Mitrook, Assistant Professor, 813-974-8890, Fax: 813-974-2592, E-mail: mmitrook@usf.edu.
Website: http://masscom.usf.edu/grad/

**University of South Florida, St. Petersburg**, College of Arts and Sciences, St. Petersburg, FL 33701. Offers digital journalism and design (MA); environmental science and policy (MA, MS); Florida studies (MLA); journalism and media studies (MA); liberal studies (MLA); psychology (MA). *Program availability:* Part-time, online learning. *Degree requirements:* For master's, comprehensive exam, thesis or project. *Entrance requirements:* For master's, GRE, LSAT, MCAT (varies by program), letter of intent, 3 letters of recommendation, writing samples, bachelor's degree from regionally-accredited institution with minimum GPA of 3.0 overall or in upper two years. Additional exam requirements/recommendations for international students: Required—TOEFL (minimum score 550 paper-based; 79 iBT); Recommended—IELTS. Electronic applications accepted.

**The University of Tennessee**, Graduate School, College of Communication and Information, Knoxville, TN 37996. Offers advertising (MS, PhD); broadcasting (MS, PhD); communications (MS, PhD); information sciences (MS, PhD); journalism (MS, PhD); public relations (MS, PhD); speech communication (MS, PhD). *Program availability:* Part-time, evening/weekend, online learning. *Degree requirements:* For master's, thesis or alternative; for doctorate, thesis/dissertation. *Entrance requirements:* For master's and doctorate, GRE General Test, minimum GPA of 2.7. Additional exam requirements/recommendations for international students: Required—TOEFL. Electronic applications accepted.

**The University of Texas at Austin**, Graduate School, College of Communication, Department of Radio-Television-Film, Austin, TX 78712-1111. Offers film and media production (MFA); media studies (MA, PhD); screenwriting (MFA). *Degree requirements:* For master's, thesis (for some programs); for doctorate, thesis/dissertation. *Entrance requirements:* For master's and doctorate, GRE General Test. Electronic applications accepted. *Faculty research:* International communication, film studies, media and culture, telecommunication and new media, gender and sexuality.

**The University of Western Ontario**, Faculty of Graduate Studies, Faculty of Information and Media Studies, Programs in Media Studies, London, ON N6A 5B8,

Canada. Offers MA, PhD. *Program availability:* Part-time. *Degree requirements:* For master's, thesis; for doctorate, comprehensive exam, thesis/dissertation. *Entrance requirements:* For master's, 2 letters of reference; for doctorate, MA in media studies, communications or related field. Additional exam requirements/recommendations for international students: Required—TOEFL (minimum score 625 paper-based), TWE (minimum score 5). Electronic applications accepted. *Faculty research:* Media cultures, media industries, media technologies.

**University of Wisconsin–Madison**, Graduate School, College of Letters and Science, Department of Communication Arts, Madison, WI 53706-1380. Offers communication science (MA, PhD); film (MA, PhD); media and cultural studies (MA, PhD); rhetoric (MA, PhD). Terminal master's awarded for partial completion of doctoral program. *Degree requirements:* For master's, one foreign language, thesis (for some programs); for doctorate, one foreign language, thesis/dissertation. *Entrance requirements:* For master's and doctorate, GRE General Test, minimum GPA of 3.5. Electronic applications accepted.

**University of Wisconsin–Milwaukee**, Graduate School, College of Letters and Science, Department of English, Milwaukee, WI 53201-0413. Offers English (MA, PhD), including creative writing, literature and cultural theory, media, cinema and digital studies, professional writing, rhetoric and composition. *Students:* 87 full-time (47 women), 50 part-time (27 women); includes 14 minority (4 Asian, non-Hispanic/Latino; 1 Hispanic/Latino; 9 Two or more races, non-Hispanic/Latino), 7 international. Average age 33. 189 applicants, 48% accepted, 31 enrolled. In 2016, 15 master's, 13 doctorates awarded. *Degree requirements:* For master's, thesis or alternative; for doctorate, one foreign language, thesis/dissertation. *Entrance requirements:* For master's, GRE General Test, GRE Subject Test; for doctorate, GRE. Additional exam requirements/recommendations for international students: Required—TOEFL (minimum score 550 paper-based; 79 iBT), IELTS (minimum score 6.5). *Application deadline:* For fall admission, 1/1 priority date for domestic students; for spring admission, 9/1 for domestic students. Applications are processed on a rolling basis. Application fee: $56 ($96 for international students). Electronic applications accepted. *Financial support:* In 2016–17, 4 fellowships, 1 research assistantship, 84 teaching assistantships were awarded; career-related internships or fieldwork, unspecified assistantships, and project assistantships also available. Support available to part-time students. Financial award application deadline: 4/15; financial award applicants required to submit FAFSA. *Unit head:* Mark Netzloff, Department Chair, 414-229-4511, E-mail: netzloff@uwm.edu. *Application contact:* General Information Contact, 414-229-4982, Fax: 414-229-6967, E-mail: gradschool@uwm.edu.
Website: https://uwm.edu/english/

**University of Wisconsin–Milwaukee**, Graduate School, College of Letters and Science, Department of Journalism, Advertising, and Media Studies, Milwaukee, WI 53201-0413. Offers media studies (MA). *Students:* 55 full-time (32 women), 58 part-time (36 women); includes 24 minority (11 Black or African American, non-Hispanic/Latino; 2 Asian, non-Hispanic/Latino; 1 Hispanic/Latino; 10 Two or more races, non-Hispanic/Latino), 13 international. Average age 33. 89 applicants, 61% accepted, 30 enrolled. In 2016, 38 master's awarded. *Degree requirements:* For master's, thesis or alternative. *Entrance requirements:* Additional exam requirements/recommendations for international students: Required—TOEFL (minimum score 550 paper-based; 79 iBT), IELTS (minimum score 6.5). *Application deadline:* For fall admission, 1/1 priority date for domestic students; for spring admission, 9/1 for domestic students. Applications are processed on a rolling basis. Application fee: $56 ($96 for international students). Electronic applications accepted. *Financial support:* In 2016–17, 2 fellowships, 1 research assistantship, 5 teaching assistantships were awarded; career-related internships or fieldwork, unspecified assistantships, and project assistantships also available. Support available to part-time students. Financial award application deadline: 4/15; financial award applicants required to submit FAFSA. *Application contact:* General Information Contact, 414-229-4982, Fax: 414-229-6967, E-mail: gradschool@uwm.edu.

**University of Wisconsin–Stevens Point**, College of Fine Arts and Communication, Division of Communication, Stevens Point, WI 54481-3897. Offers interpersonal communication (MA); media studies (MA); organizational communication (MA); public relations (MA). *Program availability:* Part-time. *Degree requirements:* For master's, thesis or alternative. *Entrance requirements:* For master's, GRE. Additional exam requirements/recommendations for international students: Required—TOEFL (minimum score 575 paper-based). *Faculty research:* Communication theory and research, film history.

**Valparaiso University**, Graduate School and Continuing Education, Program in Media and Communication, Valparaiso, IN 46383. Offers digital media (MS, Certificate); sports media (MS, Certificate). *Program availability:* Part-time, evening/weekend. *Entrance requirements:* For master's, minimum GPA of 3.0, undergraduate minor in communication. Additional exam requirements/recommendations for international students: Required—TOEFL (minimum score 550 paper-based; 80 iBT), IELTS (minimum score 6). Electronic applications accepted. *Expenses:* Tuition: Full-time $11,070; part-time $615 per credit hour. *Required fees:* $116 per semester. Tuition and fees vary according to course load, degree level and program.

**Virginia Commonwealth University**, Graduate School, College of Humanities and Sciences, Department of English, Richmond, VA 23284-9005. Offers creative writing (MFA), including dual genre, fiction, poetry; English (MA), including literature; media, art, and text (PhD). *Program availability:* Part-time. *Degree requirements:* For master's, thesis optional. *Entrance requirements:* For master's, GRE General Test, portfolio (MFA); for doctorate, GRE General Test. Additional exam requirements/recommendations for international students: Required—TOEFL (minimum score 600 paper-based; 100 iBT) or IELTS (minimum score 6.5). *Application deadline:* Applications are processed on a rolling basis. Application fee: $50. Electronic applications accepted. *Financial support:* Fellowships, research assistantships, teaching assistantships, Federal Work-Study, institutionally sponsored loans, and tuition waivers (full and partial) available. Support available to part-time students. Financial award applicants required to submit FAFSA. *Unit head:* Dr. David E. Latane, Chair. *Application contact:* Thom Didato, Director, 804-828-1329, E-mail: tndidato@vcu.edu.
Website: http://www.has.vcu.edu/eng/

**Virginia Commonwealth University**, Graduate School, College of Humanities and Sciences, School of Mass Communications, Program in Media, Art, and Text, Richmond, VA 23284-9005. Offers PhD. *Entrance requirements:* For doctorate, GRE. Additional exam requirements/recommendations for international students: Required—TOEFL (minimum score 600 paper-based; 100 iBT); Recommended—IELTS (minimum score 6.5). *Application deadline:* For fall admission, 1/15 for domestic students. Application fee: $50. Electronic applications accepted. *Unit head:* Dr. Eric G. Garberson, Graduate Program Director, 804-828-7295, E-mail: eggarberson@vcu.edu. *Application contact:* Thom Didato, Graduate Programs Adviser, 804-828-1329, E-mail: tndidato@vcu.edu.

**Virginia State University**, College of Graduate Studies, College of Humanities and Social Sciences, Department of Mass Communications, Petersburg, VA 23806-0001. Offers media management (MA).

**Wayne State University,** College of Fine, Performing and Communication Arts, Department of Communication, Detroit, MI 48202. Offers communication (PhD), including democratic participation and culture, identity and representation, media, society and culture, risk, crisis and conflict, wellness, work life and relationships; communication and new media (Graduate Certificate); communication studies (MA); dispute resolution (MADR, Graduate Certificate); health communication (Graduate Certificate); journalism (MA); media arts (MA); media studies (MA); public relations and organizational communication (MA); JD/MADR. Doctoral program admits for fall only. *Faculty:* 20. *Students:* 59 full-time (32 women), 113 part-time (75 women); includes 69 minority (54 Black or African American, non-Hispanic/Latino; 2 Asian, non-Hispanic/Latino; 7 Hispanic/Latino; 6 Two or more races, non-Hispanic/Latino), 12 international. Average age 34. 154 applicants, 39% accepted, 41 enrolled. In 2016, 31 master's, 10 doctorates, 4 other advanced degrees awarded. *Degree requirements:* For master's, thesis (for some programs), thesis or essay; for doctorate, thesis/dissertation. *Entrance requirements:* For master's, GRE (if undergraduate GPA less than 3.2), personal statement; BA or BS in communication or related field with minimum upper-division GPA of 3.2 and minimum upper-division undergraduate GPA of 3.0, personal statement, and sample of academic writing (for MA); 3 letters of recommendation (for MADR); for doctorate, GRE, MA in communication or related field with minimum GPA of 3.5; three letters of recommendation; personal statement; sample of written scholarship. Additional exam requirements/recommendations for international students: Required—TOEFL (minimum score 600 paper-based; 100 iBT), IELTS, TWE. Application fee: $50. Electronic applications accepted. *Expenses:* $17,240 per year resident tuition and fees, $34,434 per year non-resident tuition and fees. *Financial support:* In 2016–17, 61 students received support, including 4 fellowships with tuition reimbursements available (averaging $16,000 per year), 2 research assistantships with tuition reimbursements available (averaging $19,570 per year), 21 teaching assistantships with tuition reimbursements available (averaging $17,994 per year); scholarships/grants and unspecified assistantships also available. Financial award applicants required to submit FAFSA. *Faculty research:* Rhetorical theory and criticism; mass media theory and research; argumentation; organizational communication; risk and crisis communication; interpersonal, family, and health communication. *Unit head:* Dr. Lillian Black, Professor and Chair, 313-577-2943, E-mail: eh8899@wayne.edu. *Application contact:* E-mail: communication@wayne.edu.
Website: http://comm.wayne.edu/

**Wayne State University,** College of Liberal Arts and Sciences, Department of English, Detroit, MI 48202. Offers English (MA); film and media studies (PhD); literary and cultural studies (PhD); rhetoric and composition studies (PhD). *Faculty:* 30. *Students:* 78 full-time (48 women), 23 part-time (10 women); includes 22 minority (10 Black or African American, non-Hispanic/Latino; 3 Asian, non-Hispanic/Latino; 6 Hispanic/Latino; 3 Two or more races, non-Hispanic/Latino), 7 international. Average age 35. 114 applicants, 33% accepted, 18 enrolled. In 2016, 15 master's, 5 doctorates awarded. Terminal master's awarded for partial completion of doctoral program. *Degree requirements:* For master's, variable foreign language requirement, essay, thesis, or portfolio of work approved by Director of Graduate Studies; for doctorate, one foreign language, comprehensive exam, thesis/dissertation. *Entrance requirements:* For master's, statement of purpose; two academic letters of reference; sample essay from previous English course; for doctorate, GRE General Test, statement of purpose; two academic letters of reference; sample of scholarly or critical writing. Additional exam requirements/recommendations for international students: Required—TOEFL (minimum score 550 paper-based; 79 iBT), TWE (minimum score 5.5), Michigan English Language Assessment Battery (minimum score 85); Recommended—IELTS (minimum score 6.5). *Application deadline:* For fall admission, 1/15 for domestic students. Applications are processed on a rolling basis. Application fee: $50. Electronic applications accepted. *Expenses:* $16,503 per year resident tuition and fees, $33,697 per year non-resident tuition and fees. *Financial support:* In 2016–17, 63 students received support, including 5 fellowships with tuition reimbursements available (averaging $15,800 per year), 30 teaching assistantships with tuition reimbursements available (averaging $17,994 per

year); research assistantships with tuition reimbursements available, scholarships/grants, and unspecified assistantships also available. Financial award applicants required to submit FAFSA. *Faculty research:* Literary and cultural studies, film and new media studies, rhetoric and composition studies, linguistics, and creative writing. *Unit head:* Dr. Kenneth Jackson, Chair and Professor, 313-577-7692, E-mail: ai4054@wayne.edu. *Application contact:* Dr. Carolin Maun, Director of Graduate Studies, 313-577-7694, E-mail: caroline.maun@wayne.edu.
Website: http://clas.wayne.edu/english/

**Webster University,** George Herbert Walker School of Business and Technology, Department of Business, St. Louis, MO 63119-3194. Offers business and organizational security management (MBA); decision support systems (MBA); environmental management (MBA); finance (MBA, MS); forensic accounting (MS); gerontology (MBA); human resources development (MBA); human resources management (MBA); information technology management (MBA); international business (MA, MBA); international relations (MBA); management and leadership (MBA); marketing (MBA); media communications (MBA); procurement and acquisitions management (MBA); Web services (MBA). *Accreditation:* ACBSP. *Program availability:* Part-time, evening/weekend, online learning. *Degree requirements:* For master's, comprehensive exam (for some programs), thesis (for some programs). *Entrance requirements:* Additional exam requirements/recommendations for international students: Required—TOEFL. *Application deadline:* Applications are processed on a rolling basis. Application fee: $35 ($50 for international students). *Expenses: Tuition:* Full-time $21,900; part-time $730 per credit hour. Tuition and fees vary according to campus/location and program. *Financial support:* Federal Work-Study available. Support available to part-time students. Financial award application deadline: 4/1; financial award applicants required to submit FAFSA. *Unit head:* David Porras, Chair, 314-246-8621, E-mail: porrasd@webster.edu. *Application contact:* Sarah Nandor, Director, Graduate and Transfer Admissions, 314-968-7109, E-mail: gadmit@webster.edu.

**Webster University,** School of Communications, Program in Media Communications, St. Louis, MO 63119-3194. Offers MA. *Expenses: Tuition:* Full-time $21,900; part-time $730 per credit hour. Tuition and fees vary according to campus/location and program. *Unit head:* Larry Baden, Program Facilitator, 314-246-7616, E-mail: badenl@webster.edu. *Application contact:* Sarah Nandor, Director, Graduate and Transfer Admissions, 314-968-7109, E-mail: gadmit@webster.edu.

**Webster University,** School of Communications, Program in Media Literacy, St. Louis, MO 63119-3194. Offers MA. *Expenses: Tuition:* Full-time $21,900; part-time $730 per credit hour. Tuition and fees vary according to campus/location and program. *Unit head:* Kit Jenkins, Program Facilitator, 314-246-8638, E-mail: jenkinsk@webster.edu. *Application contact:* Sarah Nandor, Director, Graduate and Transfer Admissions, 314-968-7109, E-mail: gadmit@webster.edu.

**West Virginia State University,** Media Studies Graduate Program, Institute, WV 25112-1000. Offers MA. *Degree requirements:* For master's, thesis, Comprehensive exam may be taken in lieu of a thesis. *Entrance requirements:* For master's, GRE (950), Undergraduate GPA of 3.0, Letters of Recommendation. Additional exam requirements/recommendations for international students: Required—TOEFL (minimum score 550 paper-based). Electronic applications accepted.

**Wilfrid Laurier University,** Faculty of Graduate and Postdoctoral Studies, Faculty of Arts, Department of Communication Studies, Waterloo, ON N2L 3C5, Canada. Offers media, technology and culture (MA); visual communication and culture (MA). *Degree requirements:* For master's, thesis optional. *Entrance requirements:* For master's, honours BA in communication studies or a cognate discipline from an approved university with a minimum B+ overall in last two years of study and in undergraduate major. Additional exam requirements/recommendations for international students: Required—TOEFL (minimum score 89 iBT). Electronic applications accepted. *Faculty research:* Visual communication and culture, media, technology and culture.

# Publishing

**Arizona State University at the Tempe campus,** College of Liberal Arts and Sciences, School of Historical, Philosophical and Religious Studies, Tempe, AZ 85287-4301. Offers European history (MA, PhD); medieval studies (Graduate Certificate); North American history (MA, PhD); philosophy (MA, PhD); public history (MA); religious studies (MA, PhD); Renaissance studies (Graduate Certificate); scholarly publishing (Graduate Certificate). *Program availability:* Part-time. Terminal master's awarded for partial completion of doctoral program. *Degree requirements:* For master's, thesis or alternative, interactive Program of Study (iPOS) submitted before completing 50 percent of required credit hours; for doctorate, variable foreign language requirement, comprehensive exam, thesis/dissertation, interactive Program of Study (iPOS) submitted before completing 50 percent of required credit hours. *Entrance requirements:* For master's and doctorate, GRE, minimum GPA of 3.0 or equivalent in last 2 years of work leading to bachelor's degree. Additional exam requirements/recommendations for international students: Required—TOEFL, IELTS, or PTE. Electronic applications accepted.

**Brown University,** Graduate School, School of Engineering, Providence, RI 02912. Offers biomedical engineering (Sc M, PhD); chemical and biochemical engineering (Sc M, PhD); electrical sciences and computer engineering (Sc M, PhD); fluid and thermal sciences (Sc M, PhD); materials science and engineering (Sc M, PhD); mechanics of solids and structures (Sc M, PhD). *Degree requirements:* For doctorate, thesis/dissertation, preliminary exam.

**Carnegie Mellon University,** Dietrich College of Humanities and Social Sciences, Department of English, Program in Professional Writing, Pittsburgh, PA 15213-3891. Offers editing and publishing (MAPW); policy and non-profit communication (MAPW); public and media relations/corporate communications (MAPW); science or healthcare communication (MAPW); technical writing (MAPW); writing for new media (MAPW); writing for print media (MAPW). *Program availability:* Part-time. *Entrance requirements:* For master's, GRE General Test. Additional exam requirements/recommendations for international students: Required—TOEFL, TWE.

**DePaul University,** College of Liberal Arts and Social Sciences, Chicago, IL 60614. Offers Arabic (MA); Chinese (MA); English (MA); French (MA); German (MA); history (MA); interdisciplinary studies (MA, MS); international public service (MS); international studies (MA); Italian (MA); Japanese (MA); leadership and policy studies (MS); liberal studies (MA); new media studies (MA); nonprofit management (MNM); public administration (MPA); public health (MPH); public service management (MS); social

work (MSW); sociology (MA); Spanish (MA); sustainable urban development (MA); women and gender studies (MA); writing and publishing (MA); writing, rhetoric, and discourse (MA); MA/PhD. *Program availability:* Part-time, evening/weekend, online learning. Terminal master's awarded for partial completion of doctoral program. *Degree requirements:* For master's, variable foreign language requirement, comprehensive exam (for some programs), thesis (for some programs). Electronic applications accepted.

**Emerson College,** Graduate Studies, School of the Arts, Department of Writing, Literature and Publishing, Program in Popular Fiction Writing and Publishing, Boston, MA 02116-4624. Offers MFA. *Program availability:* Online only, 100% online. *Faculty:* 43 full-time (20 women), 6 part-time/adjunct (3 women). *Students:* 11 full-time (7 women), 1 part-time (0 women); includes 6 minority (3 Hispanic/Latino; 3 Two or more races, non-Hispanic/Latino). Average age 27. 31 applicants, 55% accepted, 11 enrolled. *Entrance requirements:* Additional exam requirements/recommendations for international students: Required—TOEFL (minimum score 577 paper-based; 90 iBT), IELTS (minimum score 7). *Application deadline:* Applications are processed on a rolling basis. Application fee: $60 ($75 for international students). Electronic applications accepted. *Financial support:* In 2016–17, 12 students received support. Scholarships/grants available. Financial award applicants required to submit FAFSA. *Application contact:* Leanda Ferland, Office of Graduate Admission, 617-824-8610, Fax: 617-824-8614, E-mail: gradapp@emerson.edu.
Website: http://www.emerson.edu/writing-literature-publishing/mfa-popular-fiction-writing-publishing

**Emerson College,** Graduate Studies, School of the Arts, Department of Writing, Literature and Publishing, Program in Publishing and Writing, Boston, MA 02116-4624. Offers MA. *Program availability:* Part-time, evening/weekend. *Faculty:* 43 full-time (20 women), 6 part-time/adjunct (3 women). *Students:* 84 full-time (77 women), 10 part-time (9 women); includes 18 minority (3 Black or African American, non-Hispanic/Latino; 2 Asian, non-Hispanic/Latino; 12 Hispanic/Latino; 1 Two or more races, non-Hispanic/Latino), 3 international. Average age 25. 100 applicants, 88% accepted, 36 enrolled. In 2016, 45 master's awarded. *Degree requirements:* For master's, thesis or alternative. *Entrance requirements:* For master's, GRE General Test, 15-page writing sample. Additional exam requirements/recommendations for international students: Required—TOEFL (minimum score 550 paper-based; 80 iBT), IELTS (minimum score 6.5). *Application deadline:* For fall admission, 3/1 priority date for domestic and international students. Applications are processed on a rolling basis. Application fee: $60 ($75 for international students). Electronic applications accepted. *Financial support:* In 2016–17, 43 students received support, including 43 fellowships with partial tuition reimbursements available (averaging $5,741 per year); research assistantships with partial tuition reimbursements available, Federal Work-Study, scholarships/grants, and unspecified assistantships also available. Financial award application deadline: 3/1; financial award applicants required to submit FAFSA. *Faculty research:* Publishing. *Application contact:* Leanda Ferland, Director of Graduate Admission, 617-824-8610, Fax: 617-824-8614, E-mail: gradapp@emerson.edu. Website: http://www.emerson.edu/graduate_admission

**The George Washington University,** College of Professional Studies, Program in Publishing, Washington, DC 20052. Offers MPS. Program offered in Alexandria, VA. *Students:* 88 part-time (80 women); includes 17 minority (12 Black or African American, non-Hispanic/Latino; 1 American Indian or Alaska Native, non-Hispanic/Latino; 1 Asian, non-Hispanic/Latino; 3 Hispanic/Latino). Average age 31. 87 applicants, 92% accepted, 45 enrolled. In 2016, 32 master's awarded. *Entrance requirements:* For master's, minimum cumulative GPA of 3.0. *Application deadline:* For fall admission, 4/1 for domestic and international students. Electronic applications accepted. *Unit head:* Dr. Arnold Grossblatt, Director, 202-994-7220, E-mail: arnieg@gwu.edu. *Application contact:* Kristin Williams, Associate Provost, Graduate Enrollment, 202-994-0467, Fax: 202-994-0371, E-mail: ksw@gwu.edu. Website: http://nearyou.gwu.edu/pubs/

**New York University,** School of Continuing and Professional Studies, Center for Publishing, New York, NY 10012-1019. Offers digital and print media (MS). *Program availability:* Part-time, evening/weekend. *Degree requirements:* For master's, thesis. *Entrance requirements:* For master's, GRE or GMAT (only upon request), bachelor's degree, resume with relevant professional work, internship or volunteer experience, two letters of recommendation, statement of purpose. Additional exam requirements/recommendations for international students: Required—TOEFL (minimum score 600 paper-based; 100 iBT), IELTS (minimum score 7). Electronic applications accepted.

**Northwestern University,** Medill School of Journalism, Media, and Integrated Marketing Communications, Evanston, IL 60208. Offers integrated marketing communications (MSIMC), including brand strategy, content marketing, direct and interactive marketing, marketing analytics, strategic communications; interactive publishing (MSJ); magazine writing/editing (MSJ); reporting (MSJ); video/broadcast (MSJ). *Accreditation:* ACEJMC (one or more programs are accredited). *Entrance requirements:* For master's, GRE General Test, GMAT or LSAT (for MSJ). Additional exam requirements/recommendations for international students: Required—TOEFL. Electronic applications accepted. *Expenses:* Contact institution. *Faculty research:* Web business journalism, cultural stereotypes, voter apathy, digital television.

**Pace University,** Dyson College of Arts and Sciences, Program in Publishing, New York, NY 10038. Offers book publishing (Certificate); business side of publishing (Certificate); digital publishing (Certificate); magazine publishing (Certificate); publishing (MS). *Program availability:* Part-time, evening/weekend, 100% online. *Faculty:* 2 full-time (1 woman), 13 part-time/adjunct (7 women). *Students:* 39 full-time (35 women), 30 part-time (26 women); includes 23 minority (8 Black or African American, non-Hispanic/Latino; 3 Asian, non-Hispanic/Latino; 9 Hispanic/Latino; 3 Two or more races, non-Hispanic/Latino), 4 international. Average age 26. In 2016, 36 master's awarded. *Degree requirements:* For master's, internship or thesis. *Entrance requirements:* For master's, GRE General Test, two letters of recommendation, personal statement, resume, all official transcripts. Additional exam requirements/recommendations for international students: Required—TOEFL (minimum score 88 iBT), IELTS (minimum score 7) or PTE (minimum score 60). *Application deadline:* For fall admission, 8/1 priority date for domestic students, 6/1 for international students; for spring admission, 12/1 priority date for domestic students, 10/1 for international students. Applications are processed on a rolling basis. Application fee: $70. Electronic applications accepted. *Expenses: Tuition:* Part-time $1195 per credit. *Required fees:* $260 per semester. Tuition and fees vary according to degree level, campus/location and program. *Financial support:* Research assistantships, career-related internships or fieldwork, scholarships/grants, and unspecified assistantships available. Financial award application deadline: 2/15; financial award applicants required to submit FAFSA. *Unit head:* Prof. Sherman Raskin, MS in Publishing Program Director, 212-346-1431, E-mail: puboffice@pace.edu. *Application contact:* Susan Ford-Goldschein, Director of Graduate Admissions, 212-346-1531, Fax: 212-346-1585, E-mail: graduateadmission@pace.edu. Website: http://www.pace.edu/dyson/academic-departments-and-programs/publishing

**Rosemont College,** Schools of Graduate and Professional Studies, Publishing Program, Rosemont, PA 19010-1699. Offers MA. *Program availability:* Part-time, online learning. *Degree requirements:* For master's, comprehensive exam (for some programs), thesis. *Entrance requirements:* For master's, 3 letters of recommendation. Additional exam requirements/recommendations for international students: Required—TOEFL. Electronic applications accepted. Application fee is waived when completed online.

**Rowan University,** Graduate School, College of Communication and Creative Arts, Program in Editing and Publishing, Glassboro, NJ 08028-1701. Offers CGS. Electronic applications accepted.

**Sam Houston State University,** College of Humanities and Social Sciences, Department of English, Huntsville, TX 77341. Offers creative writing, editing, and publishing (MFA); English (MA). *Program availability:* Part-time. *Degree requirements:* For master's, comprehensive exam, thesis optional. *Entrance requirements:* For master's, GRE General Test, creative writing sample, letters of recommendation. Additional exam requirements/recommendations for international students: Required—TOEFL (minimum score 550 paper-based; 79 iBT), IELTS (minimum score 6.5). Electronic applications accepted.

**Simon Fraser University,** Office of Graduate Studies and Postdoctoral Fellows, Faculty of Communication, Art and Technology, Canadian Institute for Studies in Publishing, Vancouver, BC V6B 5K3, Canada. Offers M Pub. *Faculty:* 4 full-time (2 women). *Students:* 39 full-time (35 women). 49 applicants, 41% accepted, 17 enrolled. In 2016, 18 master's awarded. *Degree requirements:* For master's, internship, internship project report. *Entrance requirements:* For master's, minimum GPA of 3.0 (on scale of 4.33) or 3.33 based on last 60 credits of undergraduate courses. Additional exam requirements/recommendations for international students: Recommended—TOEFL (minimum score 580 paper-based; 93 iBT), IELTS (minimum score 7), TWE (minimum score 5). *Application deadline:* For fall admission, 2/1 for domestic and international students. Application fee: $90 ($125 for international students). Electronic applications accepted. *Expenses:* Contact institution. *Financial support:* In 2016–17, 14 students received support, including 12 fellowships (averaging $4,063 per year); research assistantships, career-related internships or fieldwork, Federal Work-Study, scholarships/grants, and unspecified assistantships also available. *Faculty research:* History of publishing, electronic publishing, editing, multimedia, publication design, communications technology, copyright and intellectual property. *Unit head:* Dr. John Maxwell, Director, Fax: 778-782-5239, E-mail: mpub-grad-chair@sfu.ca. *Application contact:* Jo Anne L. Ray, Program Advisor, 778-782-5242, Fax: 778-782-5239, E-mail: ccsp-info@sfu.ca. Website: http://publishing.sfu.ca/

**University of Baltimore,** Graduate School, Yale Gordon College of Arts and Sciences, Program in Creative Writing and Publishing Arts, Baltimore, MD 21201-5779. Offers MFA. *Program availability:* Part-time, evening/weekend. *Entrance requirements:* Additional exam requirements/recommendations for international students: Required—TOEFL.

**University of Baltimore,** Graduate School, Yale Gordon College of Arts and Sciences, Program in Publications Design, Baltimore, MD 21201-5779. Offers MA. *Program availability:* Part-time, evening/weekend. *Degree requirements:* For master's, seminar project. *Entrance requirements:* For master's, minimum GPA of 3.0, portfolio, interview. Additional exam requirements/recommendations for international students: Required—TOEFL (minimum score 550 paper-based). Electronic applications accepted. *Faculty research:* Communication theory, graphic design, media technology.

**University of Houston–Victoria,** School of Arts and Sciences, Program in Publishing, Victoria, TX 77901-4450. Offers MS. *Entrance requirements:* For master's, GMAT or GRE, 2 letters of recommendation, writing sample. Additional exam requirements/recommendations for international students: Required—TOEFL. Electronic applications accepted.

**Vermont College of Fine Arts,** MFA in Writing and Publishing Program, Montpelier, VT 05602. Offers MFA. *Faculty:* 5 full-time (3 women). *Students:* 18 full-time (13 women); includes 2 minority (1 American Indian or Alaska Native, non-Hispanic/Latino; 1 Two or more races, non-Hispanic/Latino), 1 international. Average age 32. *Degree requirements:* For master's, thesis. *Expenses:* Contact institution. *Financial support:* Fellowships and scholarships/grants available. *Unit head:* Miciah Gault, Director. *Application contact:* David Markow, Director of Enrollment Management, 802-828-8535, E-mail: admissions@vcfa.edu. Website: http://vcfa.edu/writing-publishing

# Rhetoric

**Abilene Christian University,** Graduate Programs, College of Arts and Sciences, Department of English, Abilene, TX 79699. Offers composition/rhetoric (MA); creative writing (MA); literature (MA). *Program availability:* Part-time. *Faculty:* 16 part-time/adjunct (6 women). *Students:* 8 full-time (4 women), 3 part-time (1 woman). 17 applicants, 53% accepted, 4 enrolled. In 2016, 6 master's awarded. *Degree requirements:* For master's, one foreign language, comprehensive exam (for some programs), thesis (for some programs). *Entrance requirements:* For master's, GRE General Test. Additional exam requirements/recommendations for international students: Required—TOEFL (minimum score 80 iBT), IELTS (minimum score 6), PTE. *Application deadline:* For fall admission, 8/11 for domestic students; for spring admission, 11/1 for domestic students. Applications are processed on a rolling basis. Application fee: $50. Electronic applications accepted. *Expenses: Tuition:* Full-time $19,890; part-time $1105 per credit hour. Tuition and fees vary according to course load and program. *Financial support:* In 2016–17, 11 students received support, including 6 teaching assistantships with partial tuition reimbursements available (averaging $5,800 per year); Federal Work-Study and scholarships/grants also available. Support available to part-time students. Financial award application deadline: 4/1; financial award applicants required to submit FAFSA. *Faculty research:* Feminism, Shakespearean dimensions of new literature, poetic consciousness, deconstruction myths. *Unit head:* Dr. William Carroll, Graduate Director, 325-674-2083, Fax: 325-674-2408, E-mail: william.carroll@acu.edu. *Application contact:* Corey Patterson, Director of Graduate Admission and Recruiting, 325-674-6566, Fax: 325-674-6717, E-mail: gradinfo@acu.edu. Website: http://www.acu.edu/graduate/academics/english.html

**Arizona State University at the Tempe campus,** College of Liberal Arts and Sciences, Department of English, Tempe, AZ 85287-0302. Offers applied linguistics (PhD); creative writing (MFA); English (MA, PhD), including comparative literature (MA), linguistics (MA), literature, rhetoric and composition (MA), rhetoric, composition, and linguistics (PhD); film and media studies (MAS), including American media and popular culture; linguistics (Graduate Certificate); teaching English to speakers of other languages (MTESOL); translation studies (Graduate Certificate). Terminal master's awarded for partial completion of doctoral program. *Degree requirements:* For master's, variable foreign language requirement, comprehensive exam (for some programs), thesis (for some programs), interactive Program of Study (iPOS) submitted before completing 50 percent of required credit hours; for doctorate, variable foreign language requirement, comprehensive exam, thesis/dissertation, interactive Program of Study (iPOS) submitted before completing 50 percent of required credit hours. *Entrance requirements:* For master's and doctorate, GRE, minimum GPA of 3.0 or equivalent in last 2 years of work leading to bachelor's degree. Additional exam requirements/recommendations for international students: Required—TOEFL, IELTS, or PTE. Electronic applications accepted.

**Ball State University,** Graduate School, College of Sciences and Humanities, Department of English, Muncie, IN 47306. Offers English (MA, PhD), including composition (MA), creative writing (MA), literature, rhetoric and composition; linguistics (MA), including linguistics, teaching English to speakers of other languages (TESOL) and linguistics. *Program availability:* Part-time. *Degree requirements:* For doctorate, variable foreign language requirement, thesis/dissertation. *Entrance requirements:* For master's, GRE General Test, minimum baccalaureate GPA of 2.75 or 3.0 in latter half of baccalaureate, statement of purpose, writing sample, three letters of recommendation; for doctorate, GRE General Test, GRE Subject Test, minimum graduate GPA of 3.2, statement of purpose, writing sample, three letters of recommendation. Additional exam requirements/recommendations for international students: Required—TOEFL (minimum score 550 paper-based; 79 iBT), IELTS (minimum score 6.5). Electronic applications accepted. *Faculty research:* American literature; literary editing; medieval, Renaissance, and eighteenth-century British literature; rhetoric.

**Bob Jones University,** Graduate Programs, Greenville, SC 29614. Offers accountancy (MS); Bible (MA); Bible translation (MA); Biblical studies (Certificate); broadcast management (MS); business administration (MBA); church history (MA, PhD); church ministries (MA); church music (MM); cinema and video production (MA); counseling (MS); curriculum and instruction (Ed D); divinity (M Div); dramatic production (MA); educational leadership (MS, Ed D, Ed S); elementary education (M Ed, MAT); English (M Ed, MA, MAT); fine arts (MA); graphic design (MA); history (M Ed, MA); illustration (MA); interpretative speech (MA); mathematics (M Ed, MAT); medical missions (Certificate); ministry (MM, D Min); multi-categorical special education (M Ed, MAT); music (M Ed); New Testament interpretation (PhD); Old Testament interpretation (PhD); orchestral instrument performance (MM); organ performance (MM); pastoral studies (MA); personnel services (MS, Ed S); piano pedagogy (MM); piano performance (MM); platform arts (MA); radio and television broadcasting (MS); rhetoric and public address (MA); secondary education (M Ed); studio art (MA); teaching Bible (MA); theology (MA, PhD); voice performance (MM); youth ministries (MA); M Div/MM.

**Boise State University,** College of Arts and Sciences, Department of English, Boise, ID 83725-1525. Offers creative writing (MFA); English (MA); rhetoric and composition (MA); teaching English language (MA); technical communication (MA). *Program availability:* Part-time. *Faculty:* 26. *Students:* 44 full-time (28 women), 38 part-time (29 women); includes 6 minority (2 American Indian or Alaska Native, non-Hispanic/Latino; 2 Asian, non-Hispanic/Latino; 1 Hispanic/Latino; 1 Two or more races, non-Hispanic/Latino), 3 international. Average age 33. 242 applicants, 15% accepted, 28 enrolled. In 2016, 29 master's awarded. *Degree requirements:* For master's, thesis (for some programs). *Entrance requirements:* For master's, GRE General Test, minimum GPA of 3.0. Additional exam requirements/recommendations for international students: Required—TOEFL (minimum score 550 paper-based; 80 iBT), IELTS (minimum score 6). *Application deadline:* For fall admission, 4/15 for domestic and international students; for spring admission, 10/15 for domestic and international students. Application fee: $65 ($95 for international students). Electronic applications accepted. *Expenses:* Tuition, state resident: full-time $6058; part-time $358 per credit hour. Tuition, nonresident: full-time $20,108; part-time $608 per credit hour. *Required fees:* $2108. Tuition and fees vary according to program. *Financial support:* In 2016–17, 10 students received support, including 32 teaching assistantships (averaging $8,109 per year); scholarships/grants and unspecified assistantships also available. Financial award application deadline: 1/15; financial award applicants required to submit FAFSA. *Unit head:* Dr. Michelle Payne, Chair, 208-426-3426, Fax: 208-426-4373, E-mail: mpayne@boisestate.edu. *Application contact:* Dr. Tom Hillard, Director of English, 208-426-2991, E-mail: thomashillard@boisestate.edu.
Website: http://english.boisestate.edu/graduate-programs/

**Bowling Green State University,** Graduate College, College of Arts and Sciences, Department of English, Program in English, Bowling Green, OH 43403. Offers English (MA, PhD); literature (MA); rhetoric and writing (PhD); scientific and technical communication (MA). *Program availability:* Part-time. *Degree requirements:* For master's, thesis or alternative; for doctorate, comprehensive exam, thesis/dissertation, foreign language or proficiency in Old English. *Entrance requirements:* For master's and doctorate, GRE General Test. Additional exam requirements/recommendations for international students: Required—TOEFL. *Application deadline:* For fall admission, 2/15 priority date for domestic students. Applications are processed on a rolling basis. Application fee: $30. Electronic applications accepted. *Financial support:* Fellowships with full tuition reimbursements, research assistantships with full tuition reimbursements, teaching assistantships with full tuition reimbursements, Federal Work-Study, and unspecified assistantships available. Financial award applicants required to submit FAFSA. *Faculty research:* Postmodern literary theory, rhetorical theory, ethnic American literature, literature and culture, composition pedagogy. *Unit head:* Dr. Lawrence Coates, Chair, 419-372-7543, E-mail: coatesl@bgsu.edu. *Application contact:* Dr. Piya Lapinski, Graduate Coordinator, 419-372-6864.

**Brigham Young University,** Graduate Studies, College of Humanities, Department of English, Provo, UT 84602-1001. Offers creative writing (MFA); literature (MA); rhetoric/composition (MA). *Faculty:* 54 full-time (16 women). *Students:* 75 full-time (52 women), 4 part-time (all women); includes 3 minority (1 Asian, non-Hispanic/Latino; 2 Hispanic/Latino). Average age 25. 44 applicants, 64% accepted, 24 enrolled. In 2016, 21 master's awarded. *Degree requirements:* For master's, variable foreign language requirement, comprehensive exam, thesis. *Entrance requirements:* For master's, GRE General Test, creative portfolio (for MFA). *Application deadline:* For fall admission, 1/15 for domestic and international students. Application fee: $50. Electronic applications accepted. *Expenses: Tuition:* Full-time $6680; part-time $393 per credit. Tuition and fees vary according to course load, program and student's religious affiliation. *Financial support:* In 2016–17, 22 students received support, including 10 research assistantships (averaging $4,000 per year), 62 teaching assistantships (averaging $6,000 per year); career-related internships or fieldwork, institutionally sponsored loans, scholarships/grants, and tuition waivers (partial) also available. Support available to part-time students. Financial award application deadline: 3/15. *Faculty research:* English literature, American literature, rhetoric, creative writing. *Unit head:* Prof. Phillip Snyder, Head, 801-422-2487, Fax: 801-422-0221, E-mail: phillip_snyder@byu.edu. *Application contact:* Danielle N. Steed, Graduate Secretary and English Program Manager, 801-422-8673, Fax: 801-422-0221, E-mail: danielle-steed@byu.edu.
Website: http://english.byu.edu/

**California State University, Dominguez Hills,** College of Arts and Humanities, Department of English, Carson, CA 90747-0001. Offers English literature (MA); rhetoric and composition (Certificate); teaching English as a second language (MA, Certificate). *Program availability:* Part-time, evening/weekend. *Degree requirements:* For master's, comprehensive exam (for some programs), thesis or alternative. *Entrance requirements:* For master's, minimum GPA of 3.0 in last 60 units. Additional exam requirements/recommendations for international students: Required—TOEFL (minimum score 550 paper-based). Electronic applications accepted. *Faculty research:* Gender studies, transnationalism, discourse analysis, visual culture, Shakespeare.

**California State University, Fresno,** Division of Research and Graduate Studies, College of Arts and Humanities, Department of English, Fresno, CA 93740-8027. Offers creative writing (MFA); literature (MA); rhetoric and writing studies (MA). *Program availability:* Part-time, evening/weekend. *Degree requirements:* For master's, one foreign language, thesis. *Entrance requirements:* For master's, GRE General Test, minimum GPA of 3.0, writing sample. Additional exam requirements/recommendations for international students: Required—TOEFL. *Application deadline:* For fall admission, 5/1 for domestic and international students; for spring admission, 10/1 for domestic and international students. Applications are processed on a rolling basis. Application fee: $55. Electronic applications accepted. *Financial support:* Teaching assistantships, career-related internships or fieldwork, Federal Work-Study, and scholarships/grants available. Support available to part-time students. Financial award application deadline: 3/1; financial award applicants required to submit FAFSA. *Faculty research:* American literature, Renaissance literature, foreign literature. *Unit head:* Dr. Lisa Weston, Chair, 559-278-2553, Fax: 559-278-7143, E-mail: lisaw@csufresno.edu.
Website: http://www.fresnostate.edu/artshum/english/

**California State University, Northridge,** Graduate Studies, College of Humanities, Department of English, Northridge, CA 91330. Offers creative writing (MA); literature (MA); rhetoric and composition theory (MA). *Program availability:* Part-time, evening/weekend. *Faculty:* 31 full-time (15 women), 104 part-time/adjunct (34 women). *Students:* 34 full-time (18 women), 60 part-time (34 women); includes 35 minority (4 Black or African American, non-Hispanic/Latino; 4 American Indian or Alaska Native, non-Hispanic/Latino; 2 Asian, non-Hispanic/Latino; 21 Hispanic/Latino; 4 Two or more races, non-Hispanic/Latino), 1 international. Average age 33. 49 applicants, 71% accepted, 22 enrolled. *Degree requirements:* For master's, thesis or alternative. *Entrance requirements:* For master's, writing proficiency test, GRE General Test or minimum GPA of 3.0. Additional exam requirements/recommendations for international students: Required—TOEFL. *Application deadline:* For fall admission, 11/30 for domestic students. Application fee: $55. *Expenses:* Tuition, state resident: full-time $4152. *Financial support:* Teaching assistantships available. Financial award application deadline: 3/1. *Faculty research:* Reading improvement, professional writing, Dickens, Shaw, English as a second language. *Unit head:* Kent Baxter, Chair, 818-677-3431.
Website: http://www.csun.edu/english/index.php

**California State University, Stanislaus,** College of Humanities and Social Sciences, Program in English (MA), Turlock, CA 95382. Offers literature (Certificate); rhetoric and teaching writing (MA); teaching English to speakers of other languages (MA). *Program availability:* Part-time. *Degree requirements:* For master's, comprehensive exam, thesis or alternative. *Entrance requirements:* For master's, GRE, minimum GPA of 3.0, 2 letters of reference, personal statement. Additional exam requirements/recommendations for international students: Required—TOEFL (minimum score 575 paper-based), TWE (minimum score 4). Electronic applications accepted. *Faculty research:* Transnational literacies, Renaissance and medieval literature, abolition writings and slave narratives, qualitative writing.

**Carnegie Mellon University,** Dietrich College of Humanities and Social Sciences, Department of English, Pittsburgh, PA 15213-3891. Offers communication planning and design (M Des); literary and cultural studies (MA, PhD); professional writing (MAPW), including editing and publishing, policy and non-profit communication, public and media relations / corporate communications, science or healthcare communication, technical writing, writing for new media, writing for print media; rhetoric (MA, PhD). *Program availability:* Part-time. Terminal master's awarded for partial completion of doctoral program. *Degree requirements:* For doctorate, 2 foreign languages, comprehensive exam, thesis/dissertation. *Entrance requirements:* For master's and doctorate, GRE General Test. Additional exam requirements/recommendations for international students: Required—TOEFL, TWE. *Faculty research:* Cognitive processes in discourse with emphasis on writing, testing, and evaluation.

**The Catholic University of America,** School of Arts and Sciences, Department of English Language and Literature, Washington, DC 20064. Offers English (MA, PhD); rhetoric (Certificate). *Program availability:* Part-time. *Faculty:* 14 full-time (6 women). *Students:* 9 full-time (5 women), 34 part-time (20 women); includes 3 minority (2 Hispanic/Latino; 1 Two or more races, non-Hispanic/Latino), 3 international. Average age 29. 29 applicants, 66% accepted, 8 enrolled. In 2016, 7 master's, 8 doctorates awarded. *Degree requirements:* For master's, one foreign language, comprehensive exam; for doctorate, 2 foreign languages, comprehensive exam, thesis/dissertation. *Entrance requirements:* For master's and doctorate, GRE General Test, statement of purpose, official copies of academic transcripts, three letters of recommendation, writing sample. Additional exam requirements/recommendations for international students: Required—TOEFL (minimum score 550 paper-based; 80 iBT). *Application deadline:* For fall admission, 7/15 priority date for domestic students, 7/1 for international students; for spring admission, 11/15 priority date for domestic students, 11/1 for international students. Applications are processed on a rolling basis. Application fee: $55. Electronic applications accepted. *Expenses:* $42,850 per year; $1,170 per credit; $200 per semester part-time fees. *Financial support:* Fellowships, research assistantships, teaching assistantships, Federal Work-Study, scholarships/grants, tuition waivers (full and partial), and unspecified assistantships available. Financial award application deadline: 2/1; financial award applicants required to submit FAFSA. *Faculty research:* Medieval literature, theory and history of rhetoric, Renaissance literature, religion and literature, English and American drama. *Unit head:* Dr. Glen M. Johnson, Chair, 202-319-5488, Fax: 202-319-4188, E-mail: johnsong@cua.edu. *Application contact:* Director of Graduate Admissions, 202-319-5057, Fax: 202-319-6533, E-mail: cua-admissions@cua.edu.
Website: http://english.cua.edu/

**Clemson University,** Graduate School, College of Architecture, Arts, and Humanities, Program in Rhetorics, Communication, and Information Design, Clemson, SC 29634. Offers PhD. *Faculty:* 6 full-time (3 women). *Students:* 25 full-time (12 women), 9 part-time (7 women); includes 4 minority (2 Black or African American, non-Hispanic/Latino; 2 Hispanic/Latino), 5 international. Average age 34. 25 applicants, 56% accepted, 12 enrolled. In 2016, 5 doctorates awarded. *Degree requirements:* For doctorate, thesis/dissertation. *Entrance requirements:* For doctorate, GRE General Test, unofficial transcripts, letters of recommendation. Additional exam requirements/recommendations for international students: Required—TOEFL (minimum score 80 iBT), IELTS (minimum score 6.5). *Application deadline:* For fall admission, 2/1 priority date for domestic and international students. Applications are processed on a rolling basis. Application fee: $80 ($90 for international students). Electronic applications accepted. *Expenses:* $4,264 per semester full-time resident, $8,485 per semester full-time non-resident, $471 per credit hour part-time resident, $942 per credit hour part-time non-resident. *Financial support:* In 2016–17, 34 students received support, including 1 fellowship with partial tuition reimbursement available (averaging $5,000 per year), 2 research assistantships with partial tuition reimbursements available (averaging $17,500 per year), 38 teaching assistantships with partial tuition reimbursements available (averaging $18,800 per year); career-related internships or fieldwork and unspecified assistantships also available. Financial award application deadline: 2/1. *Faculty research:* Historiography and philology, multimodal writing, health communication, future of the book, readability studies. *Unit head:* Dr. Victor Vitanza, Director, 864-656-6411, E-mail: sophist@clemson.edu.
Website: https://rcid.sites.clemson.edu/

**Colorado State University,** College of Liberal Arts, Department of English, Fort Collins, CO 80523-1773. Offers creative nonfiction (MA); creative writing (MFA); literature (MA); rhetoric and composition (MA); TESL/TEFL (MA). *Program availability:* Part-time. *Faculty:* 31 full-time (21 women), 25 part-time/adjunct (23 women). *Students:* 71 full-time (54 women), 30 part-time (21 women); includes 7 minority (1 Black or African American, non-Hispanic/Latino; 2 Asian, non-Hispanic/Latino; 2 Hispanic/Latino; 2 Two or more races, non-Hispanic/Latino), 13 international. Average age 29. 177 applicants, 42% accepted, 39 enrolled. In 2016, 33 master's awarded. *Degree requirements:* For master's, thesis (for some programs). *Entrance requirements:* For master's, BA/BS or equivalent with minimum cumulative undergraduate GPA of 3.0, transcripts, writing sample, statement of purpose, 3 letters of recommendation. Additional exam requirements/recommendations for international students: Recommended—TOEFL (minimum score 550 paper-based; 80 iBT), IELTS (minimum score 6.5). *Application deadline:* For spring admission, 9/15 for domestic and international students. Application fee: $60 ($70 for international students). Electronic applications accepted. *Expenses:* Tuition, state resident: full-time $9628. Tuition, nonresident: full-time $23,603. *Required fees:* $2253; $528.14 per credit hour. $264.07 per semester. Tuition and fees vary according to course load and program. *Financial support:* In 2016–17, 39 students received support, including 38 teaching assistantships with full and partial tuition reimbursements available (averaging $14,005 per year); scholarships/grants, health care benefits, and unspecified assistantships also available. Financial award application deadline: 1/1. *Faculty research:* Literary texts in historical and cultural contexts; creation and criticism of fiction, poetry, creative nonfiction and hybrid genres; critical literacies, multimodalities, and technologies including pedagogical theory and practice; linguistics, second language acquisition and TEFL/TESOL; rhetoric and social change. *Total annual research expenditures:* $154,039. *Unit head:* Louann Reid, Professor, 970-491-6428, E-mail: louann.reid@colostate.edu. *Application contact:* Marnie Leonard, Administrative Assistant, 970-491-2403, E-mail: marnie.leonard@colostate.edu. Website: http://english.colostate.edu/

**DePaul University,** College of Liberal Arts and Social Sciences, Chicago, IL 60614. Offers Arabic (MA); Chinese (MA); English (MA); French (MA); German (MA); history (MA); interdisciplinary studies (MA, MS); international public service (MS); international studies (MA); Italian (MA); Japanese (MA); leadership and policy studies (MS); liberal studies (MA); new media studies (MA); nonprofit management (MNM); public administration (MPA); public health (MPH); public service management (MS); social work (MSW); sociology (MA); Spanish (MA); sustainable urban development (MA); women and gender studies (MA); writing and publishing (MA); writing, rhetoric, and discourse (MA); MA/PhD. *Program availability:* Part-time, evening/weekend, online learning. Terminal master's awarded for partial completion of doctoral program. *Degree requirements:* For master's, variable foreign language requirement, comprehensive exam (for some programs), thesis (for some programs). Electronic applications accepted.

**Duquesne University,** Graduate School of Liberal Arts, Department of Communication and Rhetorical Studies, Pittsburgh, PA 15282-0001. Offers communication (MA); rhetoric (PhD). *Program availability:* Part-time, evening/weekend, 100% online. *Faculty:* 10 full-time (4 women), 5 part-time/adjunct (3 women). *Students:* 100 full-time (63 women), 7 part-time (all women); includes 9 minority (6 Black or African American, non-Hispanic/Latino; 1 Hispanic/Latino; 2 Two or more races, non-Hispanic/Latino), 22 international. Average age 34. 62 applicants, 90% accepted, 28 enrolled. In 2016, 13 master's, 8 doctorates awarded. Terminal master's awarded for partial completion of doctoral program. *Degree requirements:* For master's, thesis optional, practicum; for doctorate, 2 foreign languages, comprehensive exam, thesis/dissertation. *Entrance requirements:* For master's and doctorate, GRE General Test. Additional exam requirements/recommendations for international students: Required—TOEFL. *Application deadline:* For fall admission, 2/1 priority date for domestic and international students; for spring admission, 11/1 priority date for domestic and international students. Applications are processed on a rolling basis. Application fee: $0. Electronic applications accepted. *Expenses:* Tuition: Full-time $22,212; part-time $1234 per credit. Tuition and fees vary according to program. *Financial support:* In 2016–17, 24 students received support, including 7 research assistantships with full tuition reimbursements available (averaging $8,000 per year), 14 teaching assistantships with full tuition reimbursements available (averaging $17,000 per year); career-related internships or fieldwork, Federal Work-Study, institutionally sponsored loans, scholarships/grants, tuition waivers (full and partial), and unspecified assistantships also available. Financial award application deadline: 5/1. *Unit head:* Dr. Ronald Arnett, Chair, 412-396-5076, E-mail: arnett@duq.edu. *Application contact:* Linda Rendulic, Assistant to the Dean, 412-396-6400, Fax: 412-396-5265, E-mail: rendulic@duq.edu. Website: http://www.duq.edu/academics/schools/liberal-arts/graduate-school/programs/communication-

**East Carolina University,** Graduate School, Thomas Harriot College of Arts and Sciences, Department of English, Greenville, NC 27858-4353. Offers creative writing (MA); English studies (MA); linguistics (MA); literature (MA); multicultural and transnational literatures (MA, Certificate); rhetoric and composition (MA); rhetoric, writing, and professional communication (PhD); teaching English in the two-year college (Certificate); teaching English to speakers of other languages (MA, Certificate); technical and professional communication (MA). *Program availability:* Part-time, evening/weekend. *Students:* 54 full-time (36 women), 95 part-time (77 women); includes 32 minority (19 Black or African American, non-Hispanic/Latino; 3 Asian, non-Hispanic/Latino; 6 Hispanic/Latino; 4 Two or more races, non-Hispanic/Latino), 1 international. Average age 35. 78 applicants, 96% accepted, 50 enrolled. In 2016, 34 master's, 1 doctorate awarded. *Degree requirements:* For master's, one foreign language, comprehensive exam, thesis optional. *Entrance requirements:* For master's, GRE General Test, MAT (for MA Ed). Additional exam requirements/recommendations for international students: Required—TOEFL. *Application deadline:* For fall admission, 6/1 priority date for domestic students; for spring admission, 10/15 for domestic students. Applications are processed on a rolling basis. Application fee: $50. *Financial support:* Research assistantships with partial tuition reimbursements, teaching assistantships with partial tuition reimbursements, and Federal Work-Study available. Support available to part-time students. Financial award application deadline: 6/1. *Unit head:* Dr. Jeffrey Johnson, Chair, 252-328-6041, E-mail: johnsonj@ecu.edu. *Application contact:* Dean of Graduate School, 252-328-6012, Fax: 252-328-6071, E-mail: gradschool@ecu.edu. Website: http://www.ecu.edu/cs-cas/engl/graduate/

**Eastern Washington University,** Graduate Studies, College of Arts, Letters and Education, Department of English, Cheney, WA 99004-2431. Offers literature (MA); rhetoric, composition, and technical communication (MA); teaching English as a second language (MA). *Faculty:* 2 full-time (1 woman), 19 part-time/adjunct (9 women). *Students:* 23 full-time (16 women), 7 part-time (5 women); includes 4 minority (1 Black or African American, non-Hispanic/Latino; 2 Hispanic/Latino; 1 Native Hawaiian or other Pacific Islander, non-Hispanic/Latino), 6 international. Average age 35. 27 applicants, 67% accepted, 13 enrolled. In 2016, 20 master's awarded. *Degree requirements:* For master's, comprehensive exam, thesis or alternative. *Entrance requirements:* For master's, GRE General Test, minimum GPA of 3.0. Additional exam requirements/recommendations for international students: Required—TOEFL (minimum score 580 paper-based; 92 iBT), IELTS (minimum score 7), PTE (minimum score 6). *Application deadline:* For fall admission, 4/1 priority date for domestic students; for spring admission, 1/15 for domestic students. Applications are processed on a rolling basis. Application fee: $50. *Expenses:* Tuition, state resident: full-time $11,000; part-time $5500 per credit. Tuition, nonresident: full-time $24,000; part-time $12,000 per credit. *Required fees:* $1300. One-time fee: $50 full-time. Part-time tuition and fees vary according to course load, campus/location and program. *Financial support:* In 2016–17, 25 teaching assistantships with partial tuition reimbursements (averaging $7,000 per year) were awarded; career-related internships or fieldwork, Federal Work-Study, institutionally sponsored loans, scholarships/grants, health care benefits, tuition waivers (partial), and unspecified assistantships also available. Support available to part-time students. Financial award application deadline: 2/1; financial award applicants required to submit FAFSA. *Unit head:* Dr. Logan Greene, Chair, 509-359-2400, E-mail: lgreene@ewu.edu. *Application contact:* Kathy White, Advisor/Recruiter for Graduate Studies, 509-359-2491, E-mail: gradprograms@ewu.edu. Website: http://www.ewu.edu/CALE/Programs/English.xml

**Florida State University,** The Graduate School, College of Arts and Sciences, Department of English, Tallahassee, FL 32312. Offers creative writing (MFA); English (PhD), including creative writing, literature, rhetoric and composition; literature (MA); rhetoric and composition (MA). *Program availability:* Part-time. *Faculty:* 47 full-time (24 women), 2 part-time/adjunct (1 woman). *Students:* 142 full-time (80 women), 31 part-time (23 women); includes 44 minority (17 Black or African American, non-Hispanic/Latino; 1 American Indian or Alaska Native, non-Hispanic/Latino; 12 Asian, non-Hispanic/Latino; 5 Hispanic/Latino; 9 Two or more races, non-Hispanic/Latino), 9 international. Average age 30. 307 applicants, 20% accepted, 38 enrolled. In 2016, 21 master's, 24 doctorates awarded. *Degree requirements:* For master's, one foreign language, 33 hours of coursework including capstone essay, thesis or portfolio (MA); 45 hours of coursework including 9-12 thesis hours (MFA); for doctorate, one foreign language, comprehensive exam, thesis/dissertation, 27 hours of coursework, 24 hours of dissertation work. *Entrance requirements:* For master's and doctorate, GRE General Test, sample of written work, 3 letters of recommendation, resume. Additional exam requirements/recommendations for international students: Required—TOEFL. *Application deadline:* For fall admission, 1/1 priority date for domestic and international students. Application fee: $30. Electronic applications accepted. *Expenses:* Tuition, state resident: full-time $7263; part-time $403.51 per credit hour. Tuition, nonresident: full-time $18,087; part-time $1004.85 per credit hour. *Required fees:* $1365; $75.81 per credit hour. $20 per semester. Tuition and fees vary according to campus/location. *Financial support:* In 2016–17, 132 students received support, including 5 fellowships with tuition reimbursements available, teaching assistantships with tuition reimbursements available (averaging $13,250 per year); career-related internships or fieldwork, Federal Work-Study, and institutionally sponsored loans also available. Financial award application deadline: 8/1; financial award applicants required to submit FAFSA. *Faculty research:* British and Irish literature, American literature, creative writing, rhetoric and composition, multiethnic transnational literature, history of text technologies. *Unit head:* Dr. Gary Taylor, Chair, 850-644-4230, Fax: 850-644-0811, E-mail: ewalker@fsu.edu. *Application contact:* Ginger Martin, Senior Graduate Academic Coordinator, 850-644-1081, Fax: 850-644-9656, E-mail: vmartin@fsu.edu. Website: http://english.fsu.edu/

**Georgia State University,** College of Arts and Sciences, Department of Communication, Atlanta, GA 30302-3083. Offers film, video, and digital imaging (MA), including critical studies, production, screenwriting; human communication and social influence (MA); mass communication (MA); media and society (PhD); moving image studies (PhD); public communication (PhD); rhetoric and politics (PhD). *Program availability:* Part-time. *Faculty:* 57 full-time (34 women). *Students:* 113 full-time (69 women), 56 part-time (33 women); includes 59 minority (37 Black or African American, non-Hispanic/Latino; 1 American Indian or Alaska Native, non-Hispanic/Latino; 2 Asian, non-Hispanic/Latino; 9 Hispanic/Latino; 10 Two or more races, non-Hispanic/Latino), 18 international. Average age 32. 134 applicants, 58% accepted, 47 enrolled. In 2016, 22 master's, 11 doctorates awarded. *Degree requirements:* For master's, variable foreign language requirement, thesis (for some programs); for doctorate, comprehensive exam, thesis/dissertation. *Entrance requirements:* For master's and doctorate, GRE. Additional exam requirements/recommendations for international students: Required—TOEFL (minimum score 550 paper-based; 80 iBT), IELTS (minimum score 6.5). *Application deadline:* For fall admission, 2/10 for domestic and international students; for spring admission, 10/15 for domestic and international students. Application fee: $50. Electronic applications accepted. *Expenses:* Tuition, state resident: full-time $6876; part-time $382 per credit hour. Tuition, nonresident: full-time $22,374; part-time $1243 per credit hour. *Required fees:* $2128; $1064 per term. Part-time tuition and fees vary according to course load and program. *Financial support:* In 2016–17, fellowships with tuition reimbursements (averaging $15,000 per year), teaching assistantships with tuition reimbursements (averaging $15,000 per year) were awarded; career-related internships or fieldwork and unspecified assistantships also available. Financial award applicants required to submit FAFSA. *Faculty research:* New media, mass media and journalism, rhetoric, film and media studies, film production. *Unit head:* Dr. Greg Lisby, Chair, 404-413-5639, Fax: 404-413-5634, E-mail: glisby@gsu.edu. Website: http://communication.gsu.edu

**Georgia State University,** College of Arts and Sciences, Department of English, Atlanta, GA 30302-3083. Offers creative writing (MA, MFA, PhD), including creative writing (PhD), fiction (MA, MFA), poetry (MA, MFA); English (MA, PhD); literary studies (MA, PhD); rhetoric and composition (MA, PhD). *Program availability:* Part-time. *Faculty:* 47 full-time (24 women). *Students:* 123 full-time (73 women), 73 part-time (52 women); includes 28 minority (17 Black or African American, non-Hispanic/Latino; 5 Asian, non-Hispanic/Latino; 2 Hispanic/Latino; 4 Two or more races, non-Hispanic/Latino), 11 international. Average age 37. 164 applicants, 61% accepted, 38 enrolled. In 2016, 15 master's, 9 doctorates awarded. *Degree requirements:* For master's, one foreign language, thesis, 30 hours of coursework plus 6 hours of thesis credit; for doctorate, one foreign language, comprehensive exam, thesis/dissertation, second exam. *Entrance requirements:* For master's and doctorate, GRE. Additional exam requirements/recommendations for international students: Required—TOEFL (minimum score 550 paper-based; 80 iBT). *Application deadline:* For fall admission, 1/15 for domestic and international students. Application fee: $50. Electronic applications accepted. *Expenses:* Tuition, state resident: full-time $6876; part-time $382 per credit hour. Tuition, nonresident: full-time $22,374; part-time $1243 per credit hour. *Required fees:* $2128; $1064 per term. Part-time tuition and fees vary according to course load and program. *Financial support:* In 2016–17, research assistantships with full tuition reimbursements (averaging $6,000 per year), teaching assistantships with full tuition reimbursements (averaging $15,000 per year) were awarded; career-related internships or fieldwork, traineeships, and health care benefits also available. Financial award application deadline: 2/15. *Faculty research:* British and American literature and transnational literatures in English, literary theory and cultural studies, creative writing (fiction and poetry), rhetoric and composition, new media and digital humanities. *Unit head:* Dr. Lynnee Lewis Gaillet, Chair, 404-413-5842, Fax: 404-413-5830, E-mail: lgaillet@gsu.edu. Website: http://www.english.gsu.edu

**Idaho State University,** Office of Graduate Studies, College of Arts and Letters, Department of Communication and Rhetorical Studies, Pocatello, ID 83209-8115. Offers communication and rhetorical studies (MA). *Program availability:* Part-time. *Degree requirements:* For master's, comprehensive exam, paper or thesis. *Entrance requirements:* For master's, GRE General Test, minimum GPA of 3.0 in all upper-level courses. Additional exam requirements/recommendations for international students: Required—TOEFL (minimum score 550 paper-based; 80 iBT). Electronic applications accepted. *Faculty research:* Metaphor and cognition in organizational groups and teams; rhetorical criticism of contemporary culture, including music, film, television, and advertising; communication pedagogy; the effect of language on organizational identification and commitment; risk communication and crisis communication.

**Indiana University Bloomington,** University Graduate School, College of Arts and Sciences, Department of English, Bloomington, IN 47405. Offers creative writing (MA,

MFA), including fiction (MFA), poetry (MFA); literature (PhD); rhetoric (PhD). *Faculty:* 51 full-time (23 women). *Students:* 132 full-time (87 women), 2 part-time (1 woman); includes 24 minority (4 Black or African American, non-Hispanic/Latino; 11 Asian, non-Hispanic/Latino; 3 Hispanic/Latino; 6 Two or more races, non-Hispanic/Latino), 8 international. Average age 30. 273 applicants, 18% accepted, 21 enrolled. In 2016, 16 master's, 16 doctorates awarded. *Degree requirements:* For master's, 30-36 credit hours plus one language proficiency (for MA); 60 credit hours plus thesis (for MFA); for doctorate, thesis/dissertation, qualifying exam; 90 credit hours; 2nd language proficiency or one language only if acquired at in-depth level. *Entrance requirements:* For master's, GRE General Test, GRE Subject Test (for all but MFA and MA in creative writing), minimum GPA of 3.5; for doctorate, GRE General Test, GRE Subject Test, minimum GPA of 3.7. Additional exam requirements/recommendations for international students: Required—TOEFL (minimum score 550 paper-based; 79 iBT), IELTS (minimum score 6.5). *Application deadline:* For fall admission, 1/2 priority date for domestic students, 12/1 for international students. Application fee: $55 ($65 for international students). Electronic applications accepted. *Financial support:* In 2016–17, 8 students received support, including 8 fellowships with full and partial tuition reimbursements available (averaging $18,000 per year), 98 teaching assistantships with full tuition reimbursements available (averaging $15,750 per year); health care benefits also available. Financial award application deadline: 2/1. *Unit head:* Dr. Patricia Ingham, Chair, 812-855-0521, Fax: 812-855-9535, E-mail: pingham@indiana.edu. *Application contact:* Rae Greiner, Director of Graduate Studies, 812-855-9536, Fax: 812-855-9535, E-mail: drgreine@indiana.edu.
Website: http://www.indiana.edu/~engweb/

**Iowa State University of Science and Technology,** Department of English, Ames, IA 50011. Offers creative writing (MFA); English (MA); rhetoric and professional communication (PhD). *Degree requirements:* For master's, thesis or alternative; for doctorate, thesis/dissertation. *Entrance requirements:* For master's, GRE General Test, sample of written work, resume, portfolio in creative writing; for doctorate, GRE General Test, sample of written work, resume. Additional exam requirements/recommendations for international students: Required—TOEFL (minimum score 600 paper-based; 100 iBT), IELTS (minimum score 7). *Application deadline:* For fall admission, 1/5 priority date for domestic and international students. Application fee: $60 ($90 for international students). Electronic applications accepted. *Faculty research:* Creative writing, literature, rhetoric, composition and professional communication, teaching English as a second language, applied linguistics. *Application contact:* Teresa Smiley, Application Contact, 515-294-2477, Fax: 515-294-6814, E-mail: englgrad@iastate.edu.
Website: http://www.engl.iastate.edu/resources/graduate-studies/

**Iowa State University of Science and Technology,** Program in Rhetoric and Professional Communication, Ames, IA 50011. Offers PhD. *Entrance requirements:* For doctorate, GRE, official academic transcripts, resume, three letters of recommendation, writing sample. Additional exam requirements/recommendations for international students: Required—TOEFL (minimum score 640 paper-based; 111 iBT), IELTS (minimum score 7.5). *Application deadline:* For fall admission, 1/5 for domestic students. Application fee: $60 ($90 for international students). Electronic applications accepted. *Application contact:* Teresa Smiley, Application Contact, 515-294-2477, Fax: 515-294-6814, E-mail: englgrad@iastate.edu.
Website: http://engl.iastate.edu/resources/graduate-studies/

**Iowa State University of Science and Technology,** Program in Rhetoric, Composition, and Professional Communication, Ames, IA 50011. Offers MA. *Entrance requirements:* For master's, GRE, official academic transcripts, resume, three letters of recommendation, writing sample. Additional exam requirements/recommendations for international students: Required—TOEFL (minimum score 600 paper-based; 100 iBT), IELTS (minimum score 7). *Application deadline:* For fall admission, 1/5 for domestic students. Application fee: $60 ($90 for international students). Electronic applications accepted. *Application contact:* Teresa Smiley, Application Contact, 515-294-2477, Fax: 515-294-6814, E-mail: englgrad@iastate.edu.
Website: http://engl.iastate.edu/resources/graduate-studies/

**James Madison University,** The Graduate School, College of Arts and Letters, Program in Writing, Rhetoric, and Technical Communication, Harrisonburg, VA 22802. Offers MA, MS. *Program availability:* Part-time. *Faculty:* 20 full-time (11 women), 1 (woman) part-time/adjunct. *Students:* 10 full-time (9 women), 3 part-time (2 women); includes 3 minority (1 Asian, non-Hispanic/Latino; 1 Hispanic/Latino; 1 Two or more races, non-Hispanic/Latino), 1 international. Average age 30. 12 applicants, 83% accepted, 8 enrolled. In 2016, 6 master's awarded. Application fee: $55. Electronic applications accepted. *Financial support:* In 2016–17, 15 students received support, including 3 teaching assistantships with full tuition reimbursements available (averaging $9,284 per year); fellowships, career-related internships or fieldwork, Federal Work-Study, and 7 assistantships (averaging $7911) also available. Financial award application deadline: 3/1; financial award applicants required to submit FAFSA. *Unit head:* Dr. Traci A. Zimmerman, Director of the School of Writing, Rhetoric and Technical Communication, 540-568-2334, E-mail: zimmerta@jmu.edu. *Application contact:* Lynette D. Michael, Director of Graduate Admissions, 540-568-6131 Ext. 6395, Fax: 540-568-7860, E-mail: michaeld@jmu.edu.
Website: http://www.jmu.edu/wrtc/

**Kent State University,** College of Arts and Sciences, Department of English, Kent, OH 44242-0001. Offers creative writing (MFA); English (MA, PhD); English for teachers (MA); literature and writing (MA); rhetoric and composition (PhD); teaching English as a second language (MA). MFA program offered jointly with Cleveland State University, The University of Akron, and Youngstown State University. *Program availability:* Part-time. *Faculty:* 45 full-time (29 women). *Students:* 111 full-time (75 women), 19 part-time (13 women); includes 8 minority (3 Black or African American, non-Hispanic/Latino; 1 Asian, non-Hispanic/Latino; 2 Hispanic/Latino; 2 Two or more races, non-Hispanic/Latino), 27 international. Average age 30. 98 applicants, 61% accepted, 19 enrolled. In 2016, 30 master's, 8 doctorates awarded. *Degree requirements:* For master's, one foreign language, thesis (for some programs), final portfolio, final exam, or thesis (for MA in teaching English as a second language); for doctorate, one foreign language, comprehensive exam, thesis/dissertation. *Entrance requirements:* For master's and doctorate, GRE General Test, statement of purpose, 3 letters of recommendation, writing sample or undergraduate/graduate paper, transcripts. Additional exam requirements/recommendations for international students: Required—TOEFL (minimum score of 600 paper-based, 100 iBT), IELTS (minimum score of 7.0), Michigan English Language Assessment Battery (minimum score of 85), or PTE (minimum score of 68). *Application deadline:* For fall admission, 1/15 for domestic and international students. Applications are processed on a rolling basis. Application fee: $45 ($70 for international students). Electronic applications accepted. *Expenses:* Tuition, state resident: full-time $10,864; part-time $495 per credit hour. Tuition, nonresident: full-time $18,380; part-time $837 per credit hour. *Financial support:* Fellowships with full tuition reimbursements, teaching assistantships with full tuition reimbursements, and unspecified assistantships available. Financial award application deadline: 1/15. *Unit head:* Dr. Robert Trogdon, Chair, 330-672-2676, E-mail: rtrogdon@kent.edu. *Application contact:* Kevin Floyd, Professor and Graduate Coordinator, 330-672-1708,

E-mail: kfloyd@kent.edu.
Website: http://www.kent.edu/english/

**Michigan State University,** The Graduate School, College of Arts and Letters, Program in Rhetoric and Writing, East Lansing, MI 48824. Offers critical studies in literacy and pedagogy (MA); digital rhetoric and professional writing (MA); rhetoric and writing (PhD). *Entrance requirements:* Additional exam requirements/recommendations for international students: Required—TOEFL. Electronic applications accepted. *Faculty research:* Rhetoric, writing and communication studies; media studies; technical communication, writing for digital environments.

**Michigan Technological University,** Graduate School, College of Sciences and Arts, Department of Humanities, Houghton, MI 49931. Offers rhetoric, theory and culture (MS, PhD). *Program availability:* Part-time. *Faculty:* 35 full-time (22 women), 6 part-time/adjunct (3 women). *Students:* 32 full-time (20 women), 12 part-time (8 women); includes 3 minority (all Two or more races, non-Hispanic/Latino), 14 international. Average age 34. 77 applicants, 31% accepted, 17 enrolled. In 2016, 5 master's, 7 doctorates awarded. Terminal master's awarded for partial completion of doctoral program. *Degree requirements:* For master's, comprehensive exam (for some programs), thesis (for some programs); for doctorate, one foreign language, comprehensive exam, thesis/dissertation. *Entrance requirements:* For master's, GRE, statement of purpose, personal statement, official transcripts, 3 letters of recommendation, resume/curriculum vitae, writing sample (10-15 pages); for doctorate, GRE, statement of purpose, personal statement, official transcripts, 3 letters of recommendation, resume/curriculum vitae, writing sample (10-15 pages), master's degree. Additional exam requirements/recommendations for international students: Required—TOEFL (recommended minimum score 100 iBT) or IELTS. *Application deadline:* For fall admission, 1/15 priority date for domestic and international students. Applications are processed on a rolling basis. Electronic applications accepted. *Expenses:* Tuition, state resident: full-time $16,290; part-time $905 per credit. Tuition, nonresident: full-time $16,290; part-time $905 per credit. Required fees: $248; $124 per term. Tuition and fees vary according to course load and program. *Financial support:* In 2016–17, 33 students received support, including 2 fellowships (averaging $15,242 per year), 27 teaching assistantships with tuition reimbursements available (averaging $15,242 per year); career-related internships or fieldwork, Federal Work-Study, scholarships/grants, health care benefits, unspecified assistantships, and cooperative program also available. Financial award applicants required to submit FAFSA. *Faculty research:* Rhetoric and composition; communication and cultural studies; studies of science, technology, and society; technical communication and digital media. Total annual research expenditures: $6,920. *Unit head:* Dr. Ronald L. Strickland, Chair, 906-487-2376, Fax: 906-487-3559, E-mail: rlstrick@mtu.edu. *Application contact:* Alex Renshaw, Administrative Aide, 906-487-2540, Fax: 906-487-3559, E-mail: ajrensha@mtu.edu.
Website: http://www.mtu.edu/humanities/

**Missouri Western State University,** Program in Assessment, St. Joseph, MO 64507-2294. Offers autism spectrum disorders (MAS, Graduate Certificate); TESOL (MAS, Graduate Certificate); writing (MAS). *Program availability:* Part-time. *Students:* 1 (woman) full-time, 33 part-time (25 women). Average age 37. 9 applicants, 100% accepted, 5 enrolled. In 2016, 6 master's, 1 other advanced degree awarded. *Entrance requirements:* For master's, minimum GPA of 2.75. Additional exam requirements/recommendations for international students: Recommended—TOEFL (minimum score 79 iBT), IELTS (minimum score 6). *Application deadline:* For fall admission, 7/15 for domestic and international students; for spring admission, 10/1 for domestic and international students; for summer admission, 3/15 for domestic students. Applications are processed on a rolling basis. Application fee: $50. Electronic applications accepted. *Expenses:* Tuition, state resident: full-time $6548; part-time $327.39 per credit hour. Tuition, nonresident: full-time $11,848; part-time $592.39 per credit hour. Required fees: $542; $99 per credit hour. One-time fee: $50. Tuition and fees vary according to course load and program. *Financial support:* Scholarships/grants and unspecified assistantships available. Support available to part-time students. *Unit head:* Dr. Susan Bashinski, Director of Graduate Programs in Education, 816-271-5629, E-mail: sbashinski@missouriwestern.edu. *Application contact:* Dr. Benjamin D. Caldwell, Dean of the Graduate School, 816-271-4394, Fax: 816-271-4525, E-mail: graduate@missouriwestern.edu.
Website: https://www.missouriwestern.edu/masa/

**Monmouth University,** Graduate Studies, Department of English, West Long Branch, NJ 07764-1898. Offers creative writing (MA); literature (MA); rhetoric and writing (MA). *Program availability:* Part-time, evening/weekend. *Degree requirements:* For master's, comprehensive exam (for some programs), thesis. *Entrance requirements:* For master's, minimum overall GPA of 2.75, fifteen or more credits in literature or related field, essay of 1000 words describing interest and goals, two letters of recommendation, creative writing sample. Additional exam requirements/recommendations for international students: Required—TOEFL (minimum 550 paper-based, 79 internet-based test), IELTS (minimum score 6), Michigan English Language Assessment Battery (minimum score 77) or CAE (minimum score of B2). Electronic applications accepted. *Faculty research:* Renaissance and medieval literature, nineteenth-century American literature, eighteenth-century British literature and women's studies, Old and Middle English, African diaspora and African post-colonial literature.

**New Mexico Highlands University,** Graduate Studies, College of Arts and Sciences, Department of English, Las Vegas, NM 87701. Offers English (MA), including creative writing, language, rhetoric and composition, literature. *Degree requirements:* For master's, comprehensive exam, thesis. *Entrance requirements:* For master's, minimum undergraduate GPA of 3.0. Additional exam requirements/recommendations for international students: Required—TOEFL (minimum score 540 paper-based). *Faculty research:* Twentieth-century literature, life path writing in homeless shelters, native American philosophy, medieval intellectual and cultural history, creating pedagogical tools for teaching law.

**New Mexico State University,** College of Arts and Sciences, Department of English, Las Cruces, NM 88003. Offers creative writing (MFA); English (MA), including creative writing, English studies for teachers, literature, rhetoric and professional communication; rhetoric and professional communication (PhD). *Program availability:* Part-time. *Faculty:* 19 full-time (9 women), 1 (woman) part-time/adjunct. *Students:* 48 full-time (33 women), 24 part-time (14 women); includes 19 minority (2 Asian, non-Hispanic/Latino; 15 Hispanic/Latino; 2 Two or more races, non-Hispanic/Latino), 6 international. Average age 34. 90 applicants, 32% accepted, 19 enrolled. In 2016, 21 master's, 5 doctorates awarded. *Degree requirements:* For master's, one foreign language, thesis (for some programs); for doctorate, comprehensive exam, thesis/dissertation, internship. *Entrance requirements:* For master's and doctorate, sample of written work. Additional exam requirements/recommendations for international students: Required—TOEFL (minimum score 550 paper-based; 79 iBT), IELTS (minimum score 6.5). *Application deadline:* For fall admission, 2/1 for domestic and international students. Application fee: $40 ($50 for international students). Electronic applications accepted. *Expenses:* Tuition, state resident: full-time $4086. Tuition, nonresident: full-time $14,254. Required fees: $853. Tuition and fees vary according to course load. *Financial support:* In 2016–17, 47 students received support, including 42 teaching assistantships (averaging $17,394 per year); career-related internships or fieldwork, Federal Work-Study, scholarships/grants, traineeships, health care benefits, and unspecified assistantships also available. Support available to part-time students. Financial award application deadline: 3/1. *Faculty research:* Composition research, history and theory of rhetoric, technical/professional communication, creative writing, English and American literature. *Total annual research expenditures:* $10,316. *Unit head:* Dr. Barry L. Thatcher, Department Head, 575-646-3931, Fax: 575-646-7725, E-mail: bathatch@nmsu.edu. *Application contact:* Dr. Tracey Eileen Miller-Tomlinson, Director of Graduate Studies, 575-646-2213, Fax: 575-646-7725, E-mail: tomlin@nmsu.edu. Website: http://english.nmsu.edu

**North Carolina State University,** Graduate School, College of Humanities and Social Sciences, Program in Communication, Rhetoric, and Digital Media, Raleigh, NC 27695. Offers PhD.

★ **North Dakota State University,** College of Graduate and Interdisciplinary Studies, College of Arts, Humanities and Social Sciences, Department of English, Fargo, ND 58102. Offers composition (MA); literature (MA); rhetoric, writing and culture (PhD). *Program availability:* Part-time. *Degree requirements:* For master's, one foreign language, thesis. *Entrance requirements:* Additional exam requirements/recommendations for international students: Required—TOEFL (minimum score 600 paper-based; 100 iBT), IELTS (minimum score 7). Electronic applications accepted. *Faculty research:* American and English literature, women's studies, language attitudes, composition practices, computers and composition.

**See Display below and Close-Up on page 767.**

**Northern Arizona University,** Graduate College, College of Arts and Letters, Department of English, Flagstaff, AZ 86011. Offers applied linguistics (PhD); creative writing (MFA), including creative writing; English (MA), including English education, literature, professional writing, rhetoric, writing, and digital media studies; professional writing (Certificate); teaching English as a second language (MA, Certificate). *Program availability:* Part-time. *Degree requirements:* For master's, comprehensive exam (for some programs), thesis (for some programs), departmental qualifying exam; for doctorate, comprehensive exam, thesis/dissertation, departmental qualifying exam. *Entrance requirements:* For master's, minimum GPA of 3.0 or GRE; for doctorate, GRE General Test. Additional exam requirements/recommendations for international students: Required—TOEFL (minimum score 550 paper-based; 80 iBT), IELTS (minimum score 7), TOEFL (minimum score 600 paper-based; 100 iBT) for PhD; TOEFL (minimum score 570 paper-based; 89 iBT) for MA. Electronic applications accepted. *Expenses:* Tuition, state resident: full-time $8971; part-time $444 per credit hour. Tuition, nonresident: full-time $20,958; part-time $1164 per credit hour. *Required fees:* $1018; $644 per credit hour. Tuition and fees vary according to course load, campus/location and program.

**Northern Kentucky University,** Office of Graduate Programs, College of Arts and Sciences, Program in English, Highland Heights, KY 41099. Offers composition and rhetoric (Certificate); creative writing (Certificate); cultural studies and discourses (Certificate); English (MA); professional writing (Certificate). *Program availability:* Part-time, evening/weekend. *Degree requirements:* For master's, comprehensive exam (for some programs), capstone (thesis, portfolio, project, or exams); 30 hours of credit; for Certificate, 18 hours of credit. *Entrance requirements:* For master's, bachelor's degree in English or related field from regionally-accredited institution with minimum GPA of 3.0 in major or cognate area coursework; official transcripts for all undergraduate and graduate work; two letters of reference; for Certificate, official transcripts for all undergraduate and graduate work; bachelor's degree from regionally-accredited institution; minimum undergraduate GPA of 2.5. Additional exam requirements/recommendations for international students: Required—TOEFL (minimum score 79 iBT); Recommended—IELTS (minimum score 6.5). Electronic applications accepted.

**Northwestern University,** The Graduate School, School of Communication, Department of Communication Studies, Evanston, IL 60208. Offers communication studies (PhD), including interaction and social influence, rhetoric and public culture; managerial communication (MSC); media, technology and society (PhD); technology and social behavior (PhD). PhD admissions and degree offered through The Graduate School. Terminal master's awarded for partial completion of doctoral program. *Degree requirements:* For doctorate, thesis/dissertation. *Entrance requirements:* For master's and doctorate, GRE General Test. Additional exam requirements/recommendations for international students: Required—TOEFL. Electronic applications accepted.

**Ohio University,** Graduate College, Scripps College of Communication, School of Communication Studies, Athens, OH 45701-2979. Offers health communication (PhD); organizational communication (MA); relating and organizing (PhD); rhetoric and public culture (PhD). *Program availability:* Part-time, online learning. Terminal master's awarded for partial completion of doctoral program. *Degree requirements:* For master's, capstone; for doctorate, comprehensive exam, thesis/dissertation. *Entrance requirements:* For master's, GRE; for doctorate, GRE General Test, minimum GPA of 3.0. Additional exam requirements/recommendations for international students: Required—TOEFL (minimum score 550 paper-based; 80 iBT) or IELTS (minimum score 6.5). *Application deadline:* For fall admission, 1/15 priority date for domestic and international students. Application fee: $50 ($55 for international students). Electronic applications accepted. *Financial support:* In 2016–17, 12 students received support. Fellowships with full tuition reimbursements available, research assistantships with full tuition reimbursements available, teaching assistantships with full tuition reimbursements available, career-related internships or fieldwork, Federal Work-Study, and institutionally sponsored loans available. Financial award application deadline: 1/15. *Faculty research:* Rhetoric and public culture, relating and organizing, health communication. *Unit head:* Dr. Claudia Hale, Interim Director, 740-593-4825, E-mail: hale@ohio.edu. *Application contact:* Dr. Benjamin Bates, Associate Director for Graduate Studies, 740-593-9163, Fax: 740-593-4810, E-mail: batesb@ohio.edu. Website: http://www.coms.ohiou.edu/

**Rensselaer Polytechnic Institute,** Graduate School, School of Humanities, Arts, and Social Sciences, Programs in Communication and Rhetoric, Troy, NY 12180-3590. Offers MS, PhD. *Faculty:* 12 full-time (7 women). *Students:* 15 full-time (10 women), 1 part-time (0 women). 19 applicants, 26% accepted, 4 enrolled. In 2016, 1 master's, 2 doctorates awarded. Terminal master's awarded for partial completion of doctoral program. *Degree requirements:* For master's, thesis optional; for doctorate, comprehensive exam, thesis/dissertation. *Entrance requirements:* For master's and doctorate, GRE. Additional exam requirements/recommendations for international students: Required—TOEFL (minimum score 570 paper-based; 88 iBT), IELTS (minimum score 6.5), PTE (minimum score 60). *Application deadline:* For fall admission, 1/1 priority date for domestic and international students; for spring admission, 8/15 priority date for domestic and international students. Applications are processed on a rolling basis. Application fee: $75. Electronic applications accepted. *Expenses: Tuition:* Full-time $49,520; part-time $2060 per credit hour. *Required fees:* $2617. *Financial support:* In 2016–17, research assistantships with full tuition reimbursements (averaging $22,000 per year), teaching assistantships with full tuition reimbursements (averaging $22,000 per year) were awarded; fellowships also available. Financial award application deadline: 1/1. *Faculty research:* Communication, game studies, human computer interaction, literary theory, media studies, rhetoric, visual design, writing studies. *Unit head:* Dr. Audrey Bennett, Graduate Program Director, 518-276-6933, E-mail: bennett@rpi.edu. *Application contact:* Office of Graduate Admissions, 518-276-6216, E-mail: gradadmissions@rpi.edu. Website: http://www.cm.rpi.edu/pl/graduate

**Rowan University,** Graduate School, College of Communication and Creative Arts, Writing, Composition, and Rhetoric Certificate of Graduate Study Program, Glassboro, NJ 08028-1701. Offers CGS.

**Salisbury University,** Department of English, Salisbury, MD 21801-6837. Offers English (MA), including creative writing, film, literature, secondary education, TESOL, writing and rhetoric. *Program availability:* Part-time. *Faculty:* 11 full-time (5 women), 1 (woman) part-time/adjunct. *Students:* 11 full-time (9 women), 24 part-time (19 women); includes 1 minority (Black or African American, non-Hispanic/Latino), 4 international. Average age 33. 18 applicants, 67% accepted, 9 enrolled. In 2016, 17 master's awarded. *Degree requirements:* For master's, comprehensive exam, thesis optional. *Entrance requirements:* Additional exam requirements/recommendations for international students: Required—TOEFL (minimum score 550 paper-based, 79 iBT) or IELTS (6.5). *Application deadline:* For fall admission, 8/1 for domestic and international students; for spring admission, 1/1 for domestic and international students. Application fee: $65. Electronic applications accepted. *Expenses:* $381 per credit hour resident tuition, $670 per credit hour non-resident tuition; $84 per credit hour fees. *Financial support:* In 2016–17, 2 students received support, including 11 teaching assistantships with full tuition reimbursements available (averaging $9,395 per year); career-related internships or fieldwork and scholarships/grants also available. Support available to part-time students. Financial award application deadline: 3/1; financial award applicants required to submit FAFSA. *Faculty research:* Literature; linguistics; film studies; rhetoric and composition; TESOL. *Unit head:* Dr. Christopher Vilmar, Graduate Program Director, English, 410-677-6511, E-mail: csvilmar@salisbury.edu. Website: http://www.salisbury.edu/gsr/gradstudies/ENGpage.html

**San Diego State University,** Graduate and Research Affairs, College of Arts and Letters, Department of Rhetoric and Writing Studies, San Diego, CA 92182. Offers MA. *Program availability:* Part-time. *Degree requirements:* For master's, thesis. *Entrance requirements:* For master's, GRE General Test, writing sample, 3 letters of reference. Additional exam requirements/recommendations for international students: Required—TOEFL. Electronic applications accepted.

**Southern Illinois University Carbondale,** Graduate School, College of Liberal Arts, Department of English, Carbondale, IL 62901-4701. Offers composition (MA, PhD), including composition, literature, rhetoric; creative writing (MFA). *Degree requirements:* For master's, one foreign language, thesis; for doctorate, 2 foreign languages, thesis/dissertation. *Entrance requirements:* For master's, GRE General Test, GRE Subject Test, minimum GPA of 2.7; for doctorate, GRE General Test, GRE Subject Test, minimum GPA of 3.25. Additional exam requirements/recommendations for international students: Required—TOEFL. *Faculty research:* British literature, English literature, modern Continental literature, literary criticism and theory, film studies, Irish studies.

**Syracuse University,** College of Arts and Sciences, PhD Program in Composition and Cultural Rhetoric, Syracuse, NY 13244. Offers PhD. *Degree requirements:* For doctorate, comprehensive exam, thesis/dissertation. *Entrance requirements:* For doctorate, GRE, three letters of recommendation, essay on intellectual history and academic interests, statement about teaching interests and practical experience, resume, transcripts. Additional exam requirements/recommendations for international students: Required—TOEFL (minimum score 100 iBT). *Application deadline:* For fall admission, 1/15 priority date for domestic and international students. Application fee: $75. Electronic applications accepted. *Expenses: Tuition:* Full-time $25,974; part-time $1443 per credit hour. *Required fees:* $802; $50 per course. Tuition and fees vary according to course load and program. *Financial support:* Fellowships with tuition reimbursements, teaching assistantships with tuition reimbursements, and scholarships/grants available. Financial award application deadline: 1/15; financial award applicants required to submit FAFSA. *Faculty research:* American ethnic rhetorics, authorship studies, composition studies and pedagogies, studies of gender and sexuality, transnational rhetorics and globalization. *Unit head:* Prof. Eileen Schell, Associate Professor, Writing and Rhetoric/Director of Graduate Studies, 315-443-1067, E-mail: eeschell@syr.edu. *Application contact:* Kristen Krause, Graduate Program Coordinator, 315-443-5146, E-mail: ccr@syr.edu. Website: http://ccr.syr.edu/

**Syracuse University,** College of Visual and Performing Arts, MA Program in Communication and Rhetorical Studies, Syracuse, NY 13244. Offers MA. *Program availability:* Part-time. *Degree requirements:* For master's, comprehensive exam (for some programs), thesis (for some programs). *Entrance requirements:* For master's, GRE General Test, three letters of recommendation, writing sample, transcripts, personal statement, resume. Additional exam requirements/recommendations for international students: Required—TOEFL (minimum score 100 iBT). *Application deadline:* For fall admission, 2/1 priority date for domestic and international students. Application fee: $75. Electronic applications accepted. *Expenses: Tuition:* Full-time $25,974; part-time $1443 per credit hour. *Required fees:* $802; $50 per course. Tuition and fees vary according to course load and program. *Financial support:* In 2016–17, 9 students received support. Fellowships with full tuition reimbursements available, teaching assistantships with tuition reimbursements available, and tuition waivers available. Financial award application deadline: 1/1; financial award applicants required to submit FAFSA. *Faculty research:* Language and social interaction, communication and critical/cultural studies, rhetorical theory and criticism. *Unit head:* Dr. Dana Cloud, Chair, 315-443-5140, E-mail: dlcloud@syr.edu. *Application contact:* Therese West, Information Contact, 315-443-0137, E-mail: admissg@syr.edu. Website: http://vpa.syr.edu/

**Texas Christian University,** AddRan College of Liberal Arts, Department of English, Fort Worth, TX 76129. Offers English (MA, PhD); rhetoric and composition (PhD). *Faculty:* 16 full-time (11 women), 1 (woman) part-time/adjunct. *Students:* 58 full-time (43 women); includes 12 minority (4 Black or African American, non-Hispanic/Latino; 5 Hispanic/Latino; 3 Two or more races, non-Hispanic/Latino), 2 international. Average age 30. 34 applicants, 41% accepted, 13 enrolled. In 2016, 5 master's, 6 doctorates awarded. *Degree requirements:* For master's, one foreign language, thesis; for doctorate, one foreign language, comprehensive exam, thesis/dissertation. *Entrance requirements:* For master's and doctorate, GRE General Test. Additional exam requirements/recommendations for international students: Required—TOEFL. *Application deadline:* 1/10 for domestic and international students. Application fee: $60. Electronic applications accepted. *Expenses:* Contact institution. *Financial support:* In 2016–17, 55 students received support, including 4 fellowships with full tuition reimbursements available (averaging $21,000 per year), 4 research assistantships with full tuition reimbursements available, 24 teaching assistantships with full tuition reimbursements available (averaging $17,000 per year); Federal Work-Study, tuition waivers (full and partial), and unspecified assistantships also available. Financial award application deadline: 1/10; financial award applicants required to submit FAFSA. *Faculty research:* Literary studies, rhetoric and composition, new media writing, print culture, women and gender studies. *Total annual research expenditures:* $10,000. *Unit head:* Dr. Mona Narain, Director of Graduate Studies, 817-257-7240, Fax: 817-257-6238, E-mail: m.narain@tcu.edu. *Application contact:* Merry Roberts, English Department Office Manager, 817-257-6890, E-mail: m.roberts@tcu.edu. Website: http://www.eng.tcu.edu/

**Texas State University,** The Graduate College, College of Liberal Arts, Program in Rhetoric and Composition, San Marcos, TX 78666. Offers MA. *Program availability:* Part-time. *Faculty:* 4 full-time (2 women). *Students:* 8 full-time (3 women), 7 part-time (5 women); includes 6 minority (1 Black or African American, non-Hispanic/Latino; 1 Asian, non-Hispanic/Latino; 4 Hispanic/Latino). Average age 31. 8 applicants, 75% accepted, 4 enrolled. In 2016, 6 master's awarded. *Degree requirements:* For master's, comprehensive exam, thesis optional. *Entrance requirements:* For master's, baccalaureate degree from regionally-accredited institution with minimum GPA of 2.75 on last 60 undergraduate semester hours, 3.0 in minimum of 12 hours of undergraduate English courses; 3 letters of recommendation; portfolio. Additional exam requirements/recommendations for international students: Required—TOEFL (minimum score 550 paper-based; 78 iBT), IELTS (minimum score 6.5). *Application deadline:* For fall admission, 1/15 priority date for domestic and international students; for spring admission, 11/1 for domestic students, 10/1 for international students; for summer admission, 4/15 for domestic students, 3/15 for international students. Applications are processed on a rolling basis. Application fee: $40 ($90 for international students). Electronic applications accepted. *Expenses:* $4,851 per semester. *Financial support:* In 2016–17, 10 students received support, including 1 research assistantship (averaging $16,755 per year), 5 teaching assistantships (averaging $16,396 per year); Federal Work-Study, institutionally sponsored loans, scholarships/grants, and unspecified assistantships also available. Support available to part-time students. Financial award application deadline: 3/1; financial award applicants required to submit FAFSA. *Unit head:* Dr. Rebecca Jackson, Graduate Advisor, 512-245-8975, E-mail: rj10@txstate.edu. *Application contact:* Dr. Andrea Golato, Dean of Graduate School, 512-245-2581, Fax: 512-245-8365, E-mail: gradcollege@txstate.edu. Website: http://marc.english.txstate.edu/

**Texas Tech University,** Graduate School, College of Arts and Sciences, Department of English, Lubbock, TX 79409-3091. Offers English (MA, PhD); technical communication (MA); technical communication and rhetoric (PhD). *Program availability:* Part-time, 100% online, blended/hybrid learning. *Faculty:* 60 full-time (37 women), 22 part-time/adjunct (11 women). *Students:* 93 full-time (59 women), 86 part-time (58 women); includes 24 minority (8 Black or African American, non-Hispanic/Latino; 1 American Indian or Alaska Native, non-Hispanic/Latino; 3 Asian, non-Hispanic/Latino; 8 Hispanic/Latino; 4 Two or more races, non-Hispanic/Latino), 11 international. Average age 33. 173 applicants, 30% accepted, 36 enrolled. In 2016, 15 master's, 17 doctorates awarded. Terminal master's awarded for partial completion of doctoral program. *Degree requirements:* For master's, variable foreign language requirement, comprehensive exam, thesis optional; for doctorate, variable foreign language requirement, comprehensive exam, thesis/dissertation. *Entrance requirements:* For master's and doctorate, GRE General Test. Additional exam requirements/recommendations for international students: Required—TOEFL (minimum score 550 paper-based; 79 iBT), IELTS (minimum score 6.5). *Application deadline:* For fall admission, 6/1 priority date for domestic students, 1/15 priority date for international students; for spring admission, 9/1 priority date for domestic students, 6/15 priority date for international students. Applications are processed on a rolling basis. Application fee: $75. Electronic applications accepted. *Expenses:* $300 per credit hour full-time resident tuition, $708 per credit hour full-time non-resident tuition; $50.50 per credit hour fee plus $608 per term fee. *Financial support:* In 2016–17, 116 students received support, including 102 fellowships (averaging $3,457 per year), 6 research assistantships (averaging $13,381 per year), 78 teaching assistantships (averaging $15,273 per year); career-related internships or fieldwork, Federal Work-Study, scholarships/grants, and unspecified assistantships also available. Financial award application deadline: 12/15; financial award applicants required to submit FAFSA. *Faculty research:* American, British, and comparative literature; creative writing; linguistics; film; technical communication and rhetoric. *Total annual research expenditures:* $65,992. *Unit head:* Dr. Bruce Clarke, Professor, 806-834-7652, Fax: 806-742-0989, E-mail: bruce.clarke@ttu.edu. *Application contact:* Dr. Kanika Batra, Director of Graduate Studies, 806-834-1246, Fax: 806-742-0989, E-mail: english.gradadvisor@ttu.edu. Website: http://www.english.ttu.edu/

**Texas Woman's University,** Graduate School, College of Arts and Sciences, Department of English, Speech, and Foreign Languages, Denton, TX 76204-5829. Offers English (MA); rhetoric (PhD). *Program availability:* Part-time. *Students:* 10 full-time (8 women), 41 part-time (34 women); includes 14 minority (5 Black or African American, non-Hispanic/Latino; 3 Asian, non-Hispanic/Latino; 3 Hispanic/Latino; 3 Two or more races, non-Hispanic/Latino). Average age 39. In 2016, 6 master's, 2 doctorates awarded. *Degree requirements:* For master's, comprehensive exam, thesis; for doctorate, comprehensive exam, thesis/dissertation. *Entrance requirements:* For master's, GRE General Test (preferred minimum score 153 [500 old version] verbal, 138 [350 old version] quantitative), 3 letters of reference, minimum GPA of 3.0 on previous upper-division and graduate work; for doctorate, GRE General Test (preferred minimum score 153 [500 old version] verbal, 138 [350 old version] quantitative), writing sample, 3 letters of reference, interview (for graduate assistants), minimum GPA of 3.0 on previous upper-division and graduate work. Additional exam requirements/recommendations for international students: Recommended—TOEFL (minimum score 600 paper-based; 100 iBT). *Application deadline:* For fall admission, 2/1 priority date for domestic students, 2/1 for international students; for spring admission, 11/1 priority date for domestic students, 7/1 for international students. Applications are processed on a rolling basis. Application fee: $50 ($75 for international students). Electronic applications accepted. *Expenses:* Tuition, state resident: full-time $9046; part-time $251 per credit hour. Tuition, nonresident: full-time $22,922; part-time $614 per credit hour. *International tuition:* $23,046 full-time. *Required fees:* $2690; $1285 per credit hour. One-time fee: $50. Tuition and fees vary according to course level, course load, program and reciprocity agreements. *Financial support:* Research assistantships, teaching assistantships, career-related internships or fieldwork, Federal Work-Study, institutionally sponsored loans, scholarships/grants, traineeships, health care benefits, and unspecified assistantships available. Support available to part-time students. Financial award application deadline: 3/1; financial award applicants required to submit FAFSA. *Faculty research:* British and American literature, rhetoric: historical and applied, composition studies and technology, literary theory and criticism, women's literature and feminist rhetoric. *Unit head:* Dr. Genevieve West, Chair, 940-898-2324, Fax: 940-898-2297, E-mail: gwest@twu.edu. *Application contact:* Dr. Samuel Wheeler, Assistant Director of Admissions, 940-898-3188, Fax: 940-898-3081, E-mail: wheelersr@twu.edu. Website: http://www.twu.edu/english-speech-foreign-languages/

**The University of Alabama,** Graduate School, College of Arts and Sciences, Department of English, Tuscaloosa, AL 35487. Offers composition and rhetoric (PhD); creative writing (MFA), including fiction, poetry; literature (MA, PhD); rhetoric and composition (MA); teaching English as a second language (MATESOL). *Faculty:* 38 full-time (20 women). *Students:* 129 full-time (69 women), 6 part-time (5 women); includes 23 minority (12 Black or African American, non-Hispanic/Latino; 1 Asian, non-Hispanic/Latino; 7 Hispanic/Latino; 3 Two or more races, non-Hispanic/Latino), 3 international. Average age 29. 406 applicants, 13% accepted, 35 enrolled. In 2016, 31 master's, 4 doctorates awarded. *Degree requirements:* For master's, one foreign language, comprehensive exam, thesis optional; for doctorate, 2 foreign languages, comprehensive exam, thesis/dissertation. *Entrance requirements:* For master's, GRE

## Rhetoric

(minimum score of 300, except for MFA), minimum GPA of 3.0, critical writing sample; for doctorate, GRE (minimum score of 300), minimum GPA of 3.5 on master's or equivalent graduate work, critical writing sample. Additional exam requirements/recommendations for international students: Required—TOEFL (minimum score 550 paper-based; 79 iBT). *Application deadline:* For fall admission, 12/31 priority date for domestic and international students. Application fee: $50 ($60 for international students). Electronic applications accepted. *Expenses:* Tuition, state resident: full-time $10,470. Tuition, nonresident: full-time $26,950. *Financial support:* In 2016–17, 128 students received support, including 11 fellowships with full tuition reimbursements available (averaging $15,000 per year), 13 research assistantships with full tuition reimbursements available (averaging $13,500 per year), 100 teaching assistantships with full tuition reimbursements available (averaging $13,500 per year); career-related internships or fieldwork, scholarships/grants, health care benefits, and unspecified assistantships also available. Financial award application deadline: 12/31. *Faculty research:* American literature, British literature, composition/rhetoric, applied linguistics, creative writing. *Unit head:* Prof. Joel Brouwer, Department Chair, 205-348-5065, Fax: 205-348-1388, E-mail: joel.brouwer@ua.edu. *Application contact:* Jennifer Fuqua, Graduate Coordinator, 205-348-0766, Fax: 205-348-1388, E-mail: jfuqua@ua.edu.

**The University of Alabama at Birmingham,** College of Arts and Sciences, Program in English, Birmingham, AL 35294. Offers creative writing (MA); literature (MA); rhetoric and composition (MA). *Program availability:* Part-time. *Degree requirements:* For master's, one foreign language, comprehensive exam, thesis or alternative. *Entrance requirements:* For master's, GRE General Test or MAT, minimum GPA of 2.75. Electronic applications accepted. Full-time tuition and fees vary according to course load and program.

**The University of Arizona,** College of Humanities, Department of English, Rhetoric, Composition and the Teaching of English Program, Tucson, AZ 85721. Offers MA, PhD. *Accreditation:* NASM. *Degree requirements:* For master's, one foreign language, comprehensive exam; for doctorate, one foreign language, comprehensive exam, thesis/dissertation. *Entrance requirements:* For doctorate, GRE General Test, 3 letters of recommendation, writing sample. Additional exam requirements/recommendations for international students: Required—TOEFL (minimum score 550 paper-based; 79 iBT). Electronic applications accepted.

**University of Arkansas at Little Rock,** Graduate School, College of Social Sciences and Communication, Department of Rhetoric and Writing, Little Rock, AR 72204-1099. Offers professional and technical writing (MA). *Program availability:* Part-time, evening/weekend. *Degree requirements:* For master's, thesis or alternative, oral defense of final project. *Entrance requirements:* For master's, GRE, minimum GPA of 3.0, writing portfolio. *Faculty research:* Writing for industry, science, business, and government; composition and rhetorical theory; writing nonfiction; teaching of writing.

**University of California, Berkeley,** Graduate Division, College of Letters and Science, Department of Rhetoric, Berkeley, CA 94720-1500. Offers PhD. *Students:* 31 full-time (17 women); includes 16 minority (2 Black or African American, non-Hispanic/Latino; 6 Asian, non-Hispanic/Latino; 8 Hispanic/Latino), 3 international. Average age 31. 115 applicants, 3 enrolled. In 2016, 7 doctorates awarded. *Degree requirements:* For doctorate, 2 foreign languages, thesis/dissertation, qualifying exam. *Entrance requirements:* For doctorate, GRE General Test, minimum GPA of 3.0, 3 letters of recommendation. *Application deadline:* For fall admission, 12/5 for domestic students. Application fee: $105 ($125 for international students). Electronic applications accepted. *Financial support:* Fellowships, research assistantships, teaching assistantships, institutionally sponsored loans, health care benefits, and unspecified assistantships available. *Faculty research:* History and theory of rhetoric, public discourse (law, politics, and science), literature and philosophy, film. *Unit head:* Prof. David Bates, Chair, 510-642-1415, E-mail: rfa@berkeley.edu. *Application contact:* Marcus Norman, Student Assistant, 510-642-1416, E-mail: mdn@berkeley.edu.
Website: http://rhetoric.berkeley.edu/

**University of Colorado Denver,** College of Liberal Arts and Sciences, Department of English, Denver, CO 80217. Offers applied linguistics (MA); literature (MA); rhetoric and teaching of writing (MA). *Program availability:* Part-time, evening/weekend. *Faculty:* 22 full-time (13 women). *Students:* 18 full-time (12 women), 13 part-time (10 women); includes 3 minority (1 Black or African American, non-Hispanic/Latino; 2 Hispanic/Latino). Average age 31. 19 applicants, 68% accepted, 6 enrolled. In 2016, 10 master's awarded. *Degree requirements:* For master's, variable foreign language requirement, comprehensive exam (for some programs), thesis (for some programs), minimum of 33 credit hours (for literature program), 30 (for rhetoric and teaching of writing and applied linguistics programs). *Entrance requirements:* For master's, GRE General Test, minimum GPA of 3.0 in undergraduate courses, critical writing sample, letters of recommendation, completion of 24 semester hours in English courses (at least 16 at the upper-division level), statement of purpose. Additional exam requirements/recommendations for international students: Required—TOEFL (minimum score 537 paper-based; 75 iBT); Recommended—IELTS (minimum score 6.5). *Application deadline:* For fall admission, 4/1 for domestic and international students; for spring admission, 10/1 for domestic and international students; for summer admission, 4/1 for domestic and international students. Application fee: $50 ($75 for international students). Electronic applications accepted. *Expenses:* Tuition, state resident: full-time $11,006; part-time $474 per credit. Tuition, nonresident: full-time $28,212; part-time $1264 per credit hour. *Required fees:* $256 per semester. One-time fee: $94.32. Tuition and fees vary according to campus/location and program. *Financial support:* In 2016–17, 9 students received support. Fellowships, research assistantships, teaching assistantships, Federal Work-Study, institutionally sponsored loans, scholarships/grants, traineeships, and unspecified assistantships available. Financial award application deadline: 4/1; financial award applicants required to submit FAFSA. *Faculty research:* Literature, rhetoric, teaching of writing, applied linguistics. *Unit head:* Prof. Nancy Ciccone, Chair, 303-556-8395, E-mail: nancy.ciccone@ucdenver.edu. *Application contact:* Francine Olivas-Zarate, English Department, 303-556-2584, Fax: 303-556-2959.
Website: http://www.ucdenver.edu/academics/colleges/CLAS/Departments/english/Programs/Masters/Pages/Overview.aspx

**University of Dayton,** Department of English, Dayton, OH 45469. Offers literary and cultural studies (MA); teaching English to speakers of other languages (TESOL) (MA); writing and rhetoric (MA). *Program availability:* Part-time. *Faculty:* 22 full-time (11 women). *Students:* 15 full-time (10 women), 2 part-time (1 woman); includes 1 minority (Black or African American, non-Hispanic/Latino), 7 international. Average age 27. 55 applicants, 29% accepted. In 2016, 8 master's awarded. *Degree requirements:* For master's, thesis. *Entrance requirements:* For master's, 24 undergraduate-level semester hours in literature and/or writing; minimum GPA of 3.0; transcripts; personal statement; 8-10 page writing sample; three professional letters of recommendation. Additional exam requirements/recommendations for international students: Required—TOEFL (minimum score 550 paper-based, 80 iBT) or IELTS. *Application deadline:* For fall admission, 6/15 priority date for domestic and international students; for spring admission, 12/15 priority date for domestic and international students. Applications are processed on a rolling basis. Application fee: $0 ($50 for international students). Electronic applications accepted. *Expenses:* $890 per credit hour, $25 registration fee.

*Financial support:* In 2016–17, 9 teaching assistantships with full tuition reimbursements (averaging $11,000 per year) were awarded; institutionally sponsored loans and health care benefits also available. Financial award application deadline: 12/15; financial award applicants required to submit FAFSA. *Faculty research:* Gender and Victorian periodicals; literature and human rights; Paul Lawrence Dunbar; the archetype of the Indian princess; Amish country. *Total annual research expenditures:* $35,000. *Unit head:* Dr. Andrew Slade, Chair, 937-229-3434, Fax: 937-229-3563, E-mail: aslade1@udayton.edu. *Application contact:* Dr. Tereza Szeghi, Director of Graduate Studies, 937-229-3443, E-mail: tszeghi1@udayton.edu.
Website: https://www.udayton.edu/artssciences/academics/english/welcome/index.php

**University of Denver,** Division of Arts, Humanities and Social Sciences, Department of Communication Studies, Denver, CO 80208. Offers culture and communication (MA, PhD); interpersonal and family communication (MA, PhD); rhetoric and communication ethics (MA, PhD). *Program availability:* Part-time. *Faculty:* 11 full-time (7 women), 1 (woman) part-time/adjunct. *Students:* 19 full-time (13 women), 11 part-time (9 women); includes 10 minority (2 Black or African American, non-Hispanic/Latino; 1 Asian, non-Hispanic/Latino; 6 Hispanic/Latino; 1 Two or more races, non-Hispanic/Latino), 4 international. Average age 33. 62 applicants, 37% accepted, 7 enrolled. In 2016, 2 master's, 3 doctorates awarded. *Degree requirements:* For master's, comprehensive exam (for some programs), thesis (for some programs), comprehensive exam or thesis; for doctorate, one foreign language, thesis/dissertation. *Entrance requirements:* For master's, GRE General Test, bachelor's degree in communication or a related field, transcripts, essay, resume or curriculum vitae, three letters of recommendation; for doctorate, GRE General Test, bachelor's or master's degree in communication or related field, transcripts, essay, resume or curriculum vitae, three letters of recommendation. Additional exam requirements/recommendations for international students: Required—TOEFL (minimum score 570 paper-based; 88 iBT). *Application deadline:* For fall admission, 12/15 priority date for domestic and international students; for winter admission, 3/15 priority date for domestic and international students; for spring admission, 6/15 priority date for domestic and international students. Applications are processed on a rolling basis. Application fee: $65. Electronic applications accepted. *Expenses:* $29,022 per year full-time. *Financial support:* In 2016–17, 25 students received support, including 8 teaching assistantships with tuition reimbursements available (averaging $17,500 per year); career-related internships or fieldwork, Federal Work-Study, institutionally sponsored loans, scholarships/grants, and unspecified assistantships also available. Support available to part-time students. Financial award application deadline: 2/15; financial award applicants required to submit FAFSA. *Faculty research:* Successful community collaborative efforts, long-term marriages, cross-ethnic friendships, public dialogue about environmental risk, women's international cooperation. *Unit head:* Dr. Christina R. Foust, Associate Professor and Chair, 303-871-4330, Fax: 303-871-4316, E-mail: cfoust@du.edu. *Application contact:* Dr. Mary Claire Morr Serweicz, Associate Professor and Director of Graduate Studies, 303-871-4332, Fax: 303-871-4316, E-mail: mserewic@du.edu. Website: http://www.du.edu/ahss/comn

**The University of Findlay,** Office of Graduate Admissions, Findlay, OH 45840-3653. Offers applied security and analytics (MSAS); athletic training (MAT); business (MBA), including certified management accountant, certified public accountant, health care management, hospitality management; education (MA Ed, Ed D), including children's literature (MA Ed), curriculum and teaching (MA Ed), education (MA Ed), educational administration (MA Ed), human resource development (MA Ed), reading (MA Ed), science education (MA Ed), superintendent (Ed D), teaching (Ed D), technology (MA Ed); environmental, safety and health management (MSEM); health informatics (MS); occupational therapy (MOT); pharmacy (Pharm D); physical therapy (DPT); physician assistant (MPA); rhetoric and writing (MA); teaching English to speakers of other languages (TESOL) and bilingual education (MA). *Program availability:* Part-time, evening/weekend, 100% online, blended/hybrid learning. *Faculty:* 114 full-time (63 women), 44 part-time/adjunct (18 women). *Students:* 751 full-time (452 women), 573 part-time (323 women); includes 164 minority (82 Black or African American, non-Hispanic/Latino; 1 American Indian or Alaska Native, non-Hispanic/Latino; 27 Asian, non-Hispanic/Latino; 37 Hispanic/Latino; 17 Two or more races, non-Hispanic/Latino), 280 international. Average age 28. 661 applicants, 52% accepted, 288 enrolled. In 2016, 366 master's, 137 doctorates awarded. *Degree requirements:* For master's, comprehensive exam (for some programs), thesis, cumulative project, capstone project; for doctorate, thesis/dissertation. *Entrance requirements:* For master's, GRE (for some programs), bachelor's degree from accredited institution, minimum undergraduate GPA of 3.0 in last 64 hours of course work; for doctorate, MAT, minimum cumulative GPA of 3.0, master's degree. Additional exam requirements/recommendations for international students: Recommended—TOEFL (minimum score 79 iBT), IELTS (minimum score 7). *Application deadline:* For fall admission, 6/15 for international students; for spring admission, 12/1 for international students; for summer admission, 4/1 for international students. Applications are processed on a rolling basis. Electronic applications accepted. *Expenses:* Contact institution. *Financial support:* In 2016–17, 139 students received support, including 15 research assistantships with partial tuition reimbursements available (averaging $7,200 per year), 25 teaching assistantships with partial tuition reimbursements available (averaging $7,200 per year); Federal Work-Study, institutionally sponsored loans, and unspecified assistantships also available. Financial award application deadline: 4/1; financial award applicants required to submit FAFSA. *Unit head:* Christopher M. Harris, Director of Admissions, 419-434-4347, E-mail: harrisc1@findlay.edu. *Application contact:* Madeline Fauser Brennan, Graduate Admissions Counselor, 419-434-4636, Fax: 419-434-4898, E-mail: fauserbrennan@findlay.edu.
Website: http://www.findlay.edu/admissions/graduate/Pages/default.aspx

**University of Houston–Downtown,** College of Humanities and Social Sciences, Department of English, Program in Rhetoric and Composition, Houston, TX 77002. Offers MA. *Program availability:* Part-time, evening/weekend. *Faculty:* 4 full-time (2 women). *Students:* 4 full-time (1 woman), 20 part-time (12 women); includes 13 minority (3 Black or African American, non-Hispanic/Latino; 10 Hispanic/Latino). Average age 38. 15 applicants, 87% accepted, 10 enrolled. In 2016, 2 master's awarded. *Entrance requirements:* For master's, essay, resume, 2 letters of recommendation, transcripts, 10-15 page sample of academic writing. Additional exam requirements/recommendations for international students: Required—TOEFL (minimum score 600 paper-based; 86 iBT). *Application deadline:* For fall admission, 5/15 for domestic and international students; for spring admission, 11/15 for domestic and international students; for summer admission, 4/20 for domestic and international students. Application fee: $35 ($60 for international students). Electronic applications accepted. *Expenses:* $305.50 in-state, per credit; $663.50 out-of-state, per credit. *Financial support:* Federal Work-Study and scholarships/grants available. Financial award application deadline: 4/1; financial award applicants required to submit FAFSA. *Unit head:* Dr. Michelle Moosally, Chair, 713-221-8254, Fax: 713-226-5205, E-mail: moosallym@uhd.edu. *Application contact:* Ceshia Love, Director of Graduate and International Admissions, 713-221-8093, Fax: 713-223-7408, E-mail: gradadmissions@uhd.edu.
Website: https://www.uhd.edu/academics/humanities/graduate-programs/masters-arts-rhetoric-composition/Pages/marc-index.aspx

**The University of Iowa,** Graduate College, College of Liberal Arts and Sciences, Department of Communication Studies, Iowa City, IA 52242-1316. Offers interpersonal communication and relationships (MA, PhD); media studies (MA, PhD); rhetoric and public advocacy (MA, PhD). *Degree requirements:* For master's, thesis optional, exam; for doctorate, comprehensive exam, thesis/dissertation. *Entrance requirements:* For master's and doctorate, GRE General Test, minimum GPA of 3.0. Additional exam requirements/recommendations for international students: Required—TOEFL (minimum score 550 paper-based; 81 iBT). Electronic applications accepted.

**University of Louisiana at Lafayette,** College of Liberal Arts, Department of English, Lafayette, LA 70504. Offers British and American literature (MA), including creative writing, folklore, rhetoric; creative writing (PhD); literature (PhD); rhetoric (PhD). *Program availability:* Part-time. Terminal master's awarded for partial completion of doctoral program. *Degree requirements:* For master's, one foreign language, thesis or alternative; for doctorate, 2 foreign languages, comprehensive exam, thesis/dissertation. *Entrance requirements:* For master's, GRE General Test, minimum GPA of 2.75; for doctorate, GRE General Test, minimum GPA of 3.0. Additional exam requirements/recommendations for international students: Required—TOEFL (minimum score 550 paper-based). Electronic applications accepted. *Faculty research:* Composition theory, Southern literature, medieval literature.

**University of Louisville,** Graduate School, College of Arts and Sciences, Department of English, Louisville, KY 40292. Offers English (MA), including creative writing, literature, rhetoric and composition (MA, PhD); English rhetoric and composition (PhD), including rhetoric and composition (MA, PhD). *Program availability:* Part-time, evening/weekend. *Faculty:* 36 full-time (19 women), 6 part-time/adjunct (3 women). *Students:* 54 full-time (39 women), 17 part-time (12 women); includes 9 minority (3 Black or African American, non-Hispanic/Latino; 1 Asian, non-Hispanic/Latino; 3 Hispanic/Latino; 2 Two or more races, non-Hispanic/Latino), 1 international. Average age 30. 87 applicants, 53% accepted, 20 enrolled. In 2016, 16 master's, 2 doctorates awarded. *Degree requirements:* For master's, one foreign language, thesis optional, culminating project of 25-30 pages; for doctorate, one foreign language, comprehensive exam, thesis/dissertation. *Entrance requirements:* For master's and doctorate, GRE General Test. Additional exam requirements/recommendations for international students: Required—TOEFL (minimum score 600 paper-based) or IELTS (6.5). *Application deadline:* Applications are processed on a rolling basis. Application fee: $60. Electronic applications accepted. *Expenses:* $12,448. *Financial support:* In 2016–17, 3 fellowships with full tuition reimbursements (averaging $20,000 per year), 2 research assistantships (averaging $17,750 per year), 34 teaching assistantships with full tuition reimbursements (averaging $17,750 per year) were awarded; health care benefits and unspecified assistantships also available. Financial award application deadline: 1/5. *Faculty research:* Rhetoric and composition, creative writing, eighteenth- and nineteenth-century British literature, nineteenth-century American literature, critical theory. *Total annual research expenditures:* $124,449. *Unit head:* Dr. Glynis Ridley, Chair, 502-852-6803, E-mail: glynis.ridley@louisville.edu. *Application contact:* Annelise Gray, Senior Program Assistant, 502-852-0505, E-mail: annelise.gray@louisville.edu. Website: http://www.louisville.edu/english/graduate

**University of Massachusetts Amherst,** Graduate School, College of Humanities and Fine Arts, Department of English, Amherst, MA 01003. Offers American studies (PhD); composition and rhetoric (PhD); creative writing (MFA); English and American literature (MA, PhD). *Program availability:* Part-time. Terminal master's awarded for partial completion of doctoral program. *Degree requirements:* For master's, one foreign language, thesis optional; for doctorate, one foreign language, comprehensive exam, thesis/dissertation. *Entrance requirements:* For master's, manuscript; for doctorate, GRE General Test, manuscript. Additional exam requirements/recommendations for international students: Required—TOEFL (minimum score 550 paper-based; 80 iBT), IELTS (minimum score 6.5). Electronic applications accepted.

**University of Michigan–Flint,** College of Arts and Sciences, Program in English Language and Literature, Flint, MI 48502-1950. Offers literature (MA); writing and rhetoric (MA). *Program availability:* Part-time. *Faculty:* 26 full-time (17 women), 1 (woman) part-time/adjunct. *Students:* 2 full-time (1 woman), 17 part-time (14 women); includes 5 minority (1 Black or African American, non-Hispanic/Latino; 2 Hispanic/Latino; 2 Two or more races, non-Hispanic/Latino), 1 international. Average age 34. 12 applicants, 83% accepted, 7 enrolled. In 2016, 14 master's awarded. *Degree requirements:* For master's, thesis optional. *Entrance requirements:* For master's, bachelor's degree with major or significant coursework in English or related fields from regionally-accredited institution; minimum overall undergraduate GPA of 3.0. Additional exam requirements/recommendations for international students: Required—TOEFL (minimum score 84 iBT), IELTS (minimum score 6.5). *Application deadline:* For fall admission, 8/1 for domestic students, 5/1 for international students; for winter admission, 11/15 for domestic students, 9/1 for international students; for spring admission, 3/15 for domestic students, 1/1 for international students; for summer admission, 5/15 for domestic students. Applications are processed on a rolling basis. Application fee: $55. Electronic applications accepted. *Expenses:* Contact institution. *Financial support:* Federal Work-Study, scholarships/grants, and unspecified assistantships available. Support available to part-time students. Financial award application deadline: 3/1; financial award applicants required to submit FAFSA. *Unit head:* Dr. Suzanne Knight, Director, 810-762-0145, E-mail: suknight@umflint.edu. *Application contact:* Bradley T. Maki, Director of Graduate Admissions, 810-762-3171, Fax: 810-766-6789, E-mail: bmaki@umflint.edu.
Website: http://www.umflint.edu/graduateprograms/english-language-and-literature-ma

**University of Nebraska–Lincoln,** Graduate College, College of Arts and Sciences, Department of Communication Studies, Lincoln, NE 68588. Offers instructional communication (MA, PhD); interpersonal communication (MA, PhD); marketing, communication studies, and advertising (MA, PhD); organizational communication (MA, PhD); rhetoric and culture (MA, PhD). *Degree requirements:* For master's, thesis optional; for doctorate, comprehensive exam, thesis/dissertation. *Entrance requirements:* For master's and doctorate, GRE General Test, writing sample. Additional exam requirements/recommendations for international students: Required—TOEFL (minimum score 600 paper-based). Electronic applications accepted. *Faculty research:* Message strategies, gender communication, political communication, organizational communication, instructional communication.

**University of Nebraska–Lincoln,** Graduate College, College of Arts and Sciences, Department of English, Lincoln, NE 68588-0333. Offers composition and rhetoric (MA, PhD); creative writing (MA, PhD); literature studies (MA, PhD). *Degree requirements:* For master's, thesis optional; for doctorate, one foreign language, comprehensive exam, thesis/dissertation. *Entrance requirements:* For master's, writing sample; for doctorate, GRE General Test, writing sample. Additional exam requirements/recommendations for international students: Required—TOEFL (minimum score 600 paper-based). Electronic applications accepted. *Faculty research:* Creative writing, composition and rhetoric, women's studies, North American literature, medieval/Renaissance studies.

**The University of North Carolina at Greensboro,** Graduate School, College of Arts and Sciences, Department of English, Program in English, Greensboro, NC 27412-5001. Offers American literature (PhD); English (M Ed, MA); English literature (PhD); rhetoric and composition (PhD). *Degree requirements:* For master's, comprehensive

exam, thesis or alternative; for doctorate, variable foreign language requirement, thesis/dissertation, preliminary exam. *Entrance requirements:* For master's, GRE General Test, GRE Subject Test, minimum GPA of 3.0; for doctorate, GRE General Test, GRE Subject Test, critical writing sample, minimum GPA of 3.0. Additional exam requirements/recommendations for international students: Required—TOEFL. Electronic applications accepted.

**University of Oklahoma,** College of Arts and Sciences, Department of English, Norman, OK 73019. Offers composition and rhetoric (MA, PhD); literary and cultural studies (MA, PhD). *Program availability:* Part-time. *Faculty:* 31 full-time (15 women). *Students:* 26 full-time (16 women), 18 part-time (9 women); includes 9 minority (2 American Indian or Alaska Native, non-Hispanic/Latino; 2 Asian, non-Hispanic/Latino; 3 Hispanic/Latino; 2 Two or more races, non-Hispanic/Latino), 1 international. Average age 32. 38 applicants, 34% accepted, 3 enrolled. In 2016, 7 master's, 7 doctorates awarded. *Degree requirements:* For master's, one foreign language, comprehensive exam (for some programs), thesis (for some programs), exam or thesis; for doctorate, one foreign language, comprehensive exam, thesis/dissertation. *Entrance requirements:* For master's, BA in English or related field; for doctorate, MA in English or related field. Additional exam requirements/recommendations for international students: Required—TOEFL (minimum score 79 iBT) or IELTS (minimum score 6.5). *Application deadline:* For fall admission, 1/5 priority date for domestic and international students. Application fee: $50 ($100 for international students). Electronic applications accepted. *Expenses:* Tuition, state resident: full-time $4886; part-time $203.60 per credit hour. Tuition, nonresident: full-time $18,989; part-time $791.20 per credit hour. *Required fees:* $3283; $126.25 per credit hour. $126.50 per semester. *Financial support:* In 2016–17, 40 students received support, including 5 research assistantships (averaging $13,011 per year), 32 teaching assistantships (averaging $12,550 per year); fellowships, scholarships/grants, health care benefits, and unspecified assistantships also available. Financial award application deadline: 6/1; financial award applicants required to submit FAFSA. *Faculty research:* American Indian literature and culture; composition and rhetoric; American literature; British literature; postcolonial literature and culture. *Unit head:* Dr. Daniela Garofalo, Professor and Chair, 405-325-4661, Fax: 405-325-0831, E-mail: dg@ou.edu. *Application contact:* Sara Day, Graduate Assistant, 405-325-0489, Fax: 405-325-0831, E-mail: redpanda@ou.edu.
Website: http://cas.ou.edu/english

**University of Southern California,** Graduate School, Annenberg School for Communication and Journalism, School of Communication, Program in Communication, Los Angeles, CA 90089. Offers culture and community (PhD); global and transnational communication (PhD); groups, organizations and networks (PhD); health communication and social dynamics (PhD); information, political economy and entertainment (PhD); new media and technology (PhD); rhetoric, politics and public media (PhD). *Students:* 95 full-time (71 women); includes 22 minority (5 Black or African American, non-Hispanic/Latino; 6 Asian, non-Hispanic/Latino; 6 Hispanic/Latino; 5 Two or more races, non-Hispanic/Latino), 36 international. Average age 27. 144 applicants, 15% accepted, 16 enrolled. In 2016, 21 doctorates awarded. *Degree requirements:* For doctorate, thesis/dissertation. *Entrance requirements:* For doctorate, GRE General Test, resume or curriculum vitae, scholarly writing, 3 letters of recommendation, statement of purpose. Additional exam requirements/recommendations for international students: Required—TOEFL (minimum score 114 iBT), IELTS (minimum score 8); Recommended—TWE. *Application deadline:* For fall admission, 12/1 for domestic and international students. Application fee: $90. Electronic applications accepted. *Financial support:* In 2016–17, 16 students received support, including 16 fellowships with full tuition reimbursements available (averaging $5,796 per year); research assistantships, health care benefits, and unspecified assistantships also available. Financial award application deadline: 12/1; financial award applicants required to submit FAFSA. *Faculty research:* Computer-mediated communication, public health campaigns, communication democracy and the public sphere, new communication technologies in organizations, communication and community. *Unit head:* Dr. Peter Monge, Director of the PhD Program, 213-740-0921, E-mail: monge@usc.edu. *Application contact:* Allyson Hill, Associate Dean for Admissions, 213-821-0770, Fax: 213-740-1933, E-mail: ascadm@usc.edu.
Website: http://www.annenberg.usc.edu

**University of South Florida,** College of Arts and Sciences, Department of English, Tampa, FL 33620-9951. Offers creative writing (MFA), including fiction, poetry; English (MA, PhD), including literature, rhetoric and composition. *Program availability:* Part-time, evening/weekend. *Faculty:* 26 full-time (14 women). *Students:* 73 full-time (50 women), 28 part-time (21 women); includes 17 minority (3 Black or African American, non-Hispanic/Latino; 3 Asian, non-Hispanic/Latino; 9 Hispanic/Latino; 2 Two or more races, non-Hispanic/Latino), 2 international. Average age 33. 114 applicants, 55% accepted, 27 enrolled. In 2016, 12 master's, 10 doctorates awarded. *Degree requirements:* For master's, comprehensive exam, thesis (for MFA); thesis or portfolio (for MA); for doctorate, one foreign language, comprehensive exam, thesis/dissertation. *Entrance requirements:* For master's, GRE General Test, minimum undergraduate GPA of 3.5 (for MA), 3.2 (for MFA); three letters of recommendation; personal statement; writing sample from 10 to 20 pages (depending on genre); for doctorate, GRE General Test, minimum graduate GPA of 3.7; three letters of recommendation; 2-3 page personal statement; 2500-word writing sample from English coursework. Additional exam requirements/recommendations for international students: Required—TOEFL (minimum score 550 paper-based; 79 iBT) or IELTS (minimum score 6.5) for MA and PhD; TOEFL (minimum score 600 paper-based) for MFA. *Application deadline:* For fall admission, 1/1 for domestic and international students. Applications are processed on a rolling basis. Application fee: $30. Electronic applications accepted. *Expenses:* Tuition, state resident: full-time $7766; part-time $431.43 per credit hour. Tuition, nonresident: full-time $15,789; part-time $877.17 per credit hour. *Required fees:* $37 per term. *Financial support:* In 2016–17, 20 students received support, including 2 research assistantships (averaging $17,221 per year), 79 teaching assistantships with tuition reimbursements available (averaging $11,576 per year); unspecified assistantships also available. Financial award application deadline: 6/30; financial award applicants required to submit FAFSA. *Faculty research:* British and American literature, rhetoric and composition, world and comparative literatures, creative writing, gender and sexuality studies, women's literature, film and genre studies, literary theory, popular and visual culture, textual and translation studies. *Total annual research expenditures:* $44,400. *Unit head:* Dr. Hunt Hawkins, Professor and Chairperson, 813-974-9492, Fax: 813-974-2270, E-mail: hhawkins@usf.edu. *Application contact:* Dr. Marty Gould, Associate Professor and Graduate Director, 813-974-9474, Fax: 813-974-2270, E-mail: mgould@usf.edu.
Website: http://english.usf.edu/

**The University of Tennessee at Chattanooga,** Program in English, Chattanooga, TN 37403. Offers creative writing (MA); literary study (MA); rhetoric and writing (MA). *Program availability:* Part-time. *Faculty:* 22 full-time (11 women), 1 (woman) part-time/adjunct. *Students:* 16 full-time (11 women), 21 part-time (16 women); includes 3 minority (1 Asian, non-Hispanic/Latino; 1 Hispanic/Latino; 1 Two or more races, non-Hispanic/Latino). Average age 28. 20 applicants, 100% accepted, 17 enrolled. In 2016, 8 master's awarded. *Degree requirements:* For master's, comprehensive exam, thesis. *Entrance requirements:* For master's, minimum GPA of 3.0 in English, two letters of recommendation. Additional exam requirements/recommendations for international

students: Required—TOEFL (minimum score 550 paper-based; 79 iBT), IELTS (minimum score 6). *Application deadline:* For fall admission, 6/15 priority date for domestic students, 7/1 for international students; for spring admission, 11/1 priority date for domestic students, 11/1 for international students. Applications are processed on a rolling basis. Application fee: $35 ($40 for international students). Electronic applications accepted. *Expenses:* $9,876 full-time in-state; $25,994 full-time out-of-state; $450 per credit part-time in-state; $1,345 per credit part-time out-of-state. *Financial support:* In 2016–17, 4 teaching assistantships were awarded; research assistantships, career-related internships or fieldwork, scholarships/grants, health care benefits, and unspecified assistantships also available. Support available to part-time students. Financial award application deadline: 7/1; financial award applicants required to submit FAFSA. *Faculty research:* Technical writing, African-American literature, Milton, creative writing and poetry, American modernism and gender theory. *Total annual research expenditures:* $6,000. *Unit head:* Dr. Christopher Stuart, Department Head, 423-425-2140, Fax: 423-425-2282, E-mail: chris-stuart@utc.edu. *Application contact:* Dr. Joanne Romagni, Dean of the Graduate School, 423-425-4478, Fax: 423-425-5223, E-mail: joanne-romagni@utc.edu.
Website: http://www.utc.edu/english/

**The University of Texas at El Paso,** Graduate School, College of Liberal Arts, Department of English, El Paso, TX 79968-0001. Offers bilingual professional writing (Certificate); English and American literature (MA); rhetoric and composition (PhD); rhetoric and writing studies (MA); teaching English (MAT). *Program availability:* Part-time, evening/weekend. *Degree requirements:* For master's, thesis optional. *Entrance requirements:* For master's, GRE General Test, minimum GPA of 3.0. Additional exam requirements/recommendations for international students: Required—TOEFL. Electronic applications accepted. *Faculty research:* Literature, creative writing, literary theory.

**The University of Texas Rio Grande Valley,** College of Liberal Arts, Department of Writing and Language Studies, Edinburg, TX 78539. Offers English (MAIS); English as a second language (MA); English: rhetoric, composition and literacy studies (MA). *Program availability:* Part-time. *Degree requirements:* For master's, comprehensive exam, thesis or alternative. *Entrance requirements:* For master's, GRE General Test, minimum GPA of 3.0. Tuition and fees vary according to course load and program. *Faculty research:* Latin American literature, women's literature, Caribbean literature, Latina/o studies, sociolinguistics, applied linguistics, creative writing.

**University of Utah,** Graduate School, College of Humanities, Department of English, Salt Lake City, UT 84112. Offers English (MA, MFA, PhD), including creative writing (MFA, PhD), literature and cultural studies (MA, PhD), rhetoric and composition (MA, PhD). *Faculty:* 28 full-time (11 women), 1 part-time/adjunct (0 women). *Students:* 43 full-time (23 women), 23 part-time (14 women); includes 12 minority (1 Black or African American, non-Hispanic/Latino; 4 Asian, non-Hispanic/Latino; 3 Hispanic/Latino; 4 Two or more races, non-Hispanic/Latino), 3 international. Average age 35. 225 applicants, 17% accepted, 14 enrolled. In 2016, 5 master's, 4 doctorates awarded. Terminal master's awarded for partial completion of doctoral program. *Degree requirements:* For master's, 1 standard-level language; exam (for MA); thesis (for MFA); for doctorate, comprehensive exam, thesis/dissertation, 2 standard-level languages/1 advanced-level language. *Entrance requirements:* For master's and doctorate, GRE General Test, minimum GPA of 3.2. Additional exam requirements/recommendations for international students: Required—TOEFL (minimum score 650 paper-based; 115 iBT); Recommended—IELTS (minimum score 9), TSE. *Application deadline:* For fall admission, 12/15 for domestic and international students. Application fee: $55 ($65 for international students). Electronic applications accepted. *Expenses:* Tuition, state resident: full-time $7011; part-time $3918.24 per credit hour. Tuition, nonresident: full-time $22,154; part-time $11,665.42 per credit hour. *Financial support:* In 2016–17, 39 students received support, including 10 fellowships (averaging $18,000 per year), 29 teaching assistantships with full tuition reimbursements available (averaging $16,500 per year); health care benefits also available. Financial award application deadline: 12/15; financial award applicants required to submit FAFSA. *Faculty research:* Creative writing including poetics and modern poetry, fiction, and experimental forms; nineteenth- and twentieth-century British and American literature; American Studies, the American west, and environmental studies; critical theory and practice; race and gender studies. *Total annual research expenditures:* $126,500. *Unit head:* Prof. Barry L. Weller, Department Chair, 801-581-6168, Fax: 801-585-5167, E-mail: barry.weller@utah.edu. *Application contact:* Prof. Andrew Franta, Director of Graduate Studies, 801-581-7850, Fax: 801-585-5167, E-mail: a.franta@utah.edu.
Website: http://english.utah.edu/

**University of Wisconsin–Madison,** Graduate School, College of Letters and Science, Department of Communication Arts, Madison, WI 53706-1380. Offers communication science (MA, PhD); film (MA, PhD); media and cultural studies (MA, PhD); rhetoric (MA, PhD). Terminal master's awarded for partial completion of doctoral program. *Degree requirements:* For master's, one foreign language, thesis (for some programs); for doctorate, one foreign language, thesis/dissertation. *Entrance requirements:* For master's and doctorate, GRE General Test, minimum GPA of 3.5. Electronic applications accepted.

**University of Wisconsin–Milwaukee,** Graduate School, College of Letters and Science, Department of Communication, Milwaukee, WI 53201-0413. Offers communication (MA, PhD), including interpersonal communication (MA), organizational communication (MA), rhetoric and public communication (MA), rhetorical leadership; rhetorical leadership (Graduate Certificate). *Program availability:* Part-time. *Faculty:* 18 full-time (11 women). *Students:* 24 full-time (14 women), 15 part-time (11 women); includes 5 minority (1 Black or African American, non-Hispanic/Latino; 1 Asian, non-Hispanic/Latino; 1 Hispanic/Latino; 2 Two or more races, non-Hispanic/Latino), 4 international. Average age 34. 44 applicants, 52% accepted, 9 enrolled. In 2016, 2 master's, 8 doctorates awarded. *Degree requirements:* For master's, thesis or alternative; for doctorate, comprehensive exam. *Entrance requirements:* For master's, GRE General Test, minimum GPA of 3.0. Additional exam requirements/recommendations for international students: Required—TOEFL (minimum score 550 paper-based; 79 iBT), IELTS (minimum score 6). *Application deadline:* For fall admission, 1/1 priority date for domestic students; for spring admission, 9/1 for domestic students. Applications are processed on a rolling basis. Application fee: $56. Electronic applications accepted. *Financial support:* In 2016–17, 3 fellowships, 34 teaching assistantships were awarded; research assistantships, career-related internships or fieldwork, unspecified assistantships, and project assistantships also available. Support available to part-time students. Financial award application deadline: 4/15; financial award applicants required to submit FAFSA. *Unit head:* Mike Allen, Department Chair, 414-229-4510, E-mail: mikealle@uwm.edu. *Application contact:* General Information Contact, 414-229-4982, Fax: 414-229-6967, E-mail: gradschool@uwm.edu.
Website: https://uwm.edu/communication/

**University of Wisconsin–Milwaukee,** Graduate School, College of Letters and Science, Department of English, Milwaukee, WI 53201-0413. Offers English (MA, PhD), including creative writing, literature and cultural theory, media, cinema and digital studies, professional writing, rhetoric and composition. *Students:* 87 full-time (47 women), 50 part-time (27 women); includes 14 minority (4 Asian, non-Hispanic/Latino; 1 Hispanic/Latino; 9 Two or more races, non-Hispanic/Latino), 7 international. Average age 33. 189 applicants, 48% accepted, 31 enrolled. In 2016, 15 master's, 13 doctorates awarded. *Degree requirements:* For master's, thesis or alternative; for doctorate, one foreign language, thesis/dissertation. *Entrance requirements:* For master's, GRE General Test, GRE Subject Test; for doctorate, GRE. Additional exam requirements/recommendations for international students: Required—TOEFL (minimum score 550 paper-based; 79 iBT), IELTS (minimum score 6.5). *Application deadline:* For fall admission, 1/1 priority date for domestic students; for spring admission, 9/1 for domestic students. Applications are processed on a rolling basis. Application fee: $56 ($96 for international students). Electronic applications accepted. *Financial support:* In 2016–17, 4 fellowships, 1 research assistantship, 84 teaching assistantships were awarded; career-related internships or fieldwork, unspecified assistantships, and project assistantships also available. Support available to part-time students. Financial award application deadline: 4/15; financial award applicants required to submit FAFSA. *Unit head:* Mark Netzloff, Department Chair, 414-229-4511, E-mail: netzloff@uwm.edu. *Application contact:* General Information Contact, 414-229-4982, Fax: 414-229-6967, E-mail: gradschool@uwm.edu.
Website: https://uwm.edu/english/

**Valdosta State University,** Department of English, Valdosta, GA 31698. Offers literature (MA); rhetoric and composition (MA); studies for language arts teachers (MA). *Program availability:* Part-time, 100% online, blended/hybrid learning. *Degree requirements:* For master's, one foreign language, thesis, comprehensive written and/or oral exams. *Entrance requirements:* For master's, GRE General Test, minimum GPA of 3.0. Additional exam requirements/recommendations for international students: Required—TOEFL (minimum score 523 paper-based); Recommended—IELTS. Electronic applications accepted. *Expenses:* Contact institution. *Faculty research:* American literature, creative writing.

**Virginia Polytechnic Institute and State University,** Graduate School, College of Liberal Arts and Human Sciences, Blacksburg, VA 24061. Offers career and technical education (MS Ed, Ed D, PhD, Ed S); communication (MA); counselor education (MA Ed, Ed D, PhD, Ed S); creative writing (MFA); curriculum and instruction (MA Ed, Ed D, PhD, Ed S); educational leadership and policy studies (MA Ed, Ed D, PhD, Ed S); educational research and evaluation (PhD); English (MA); foreign languages, cultures, and literatures (MA); higher education (PhD); higher education and student affairs (MA Ed); history (MA); human development (MS, PhD); material culture and public humanities (MA); philosophy (MA); political science (MA); rhetoric and writing (PhD); science and technology studies (MS, PhD); social, political, ethical, and cultural thought (PhD); sociology (MS, PhD); theater arts (MFA). *Faculty:* 408 full-time (204 women), 3 part-time/adjunct (2 women). *Students:* 657 full-time (446 women), 457 part-time (292 women); includes 213 minority (114 Black or African American, non-Hispanic/Latino; 3 American Indian or Alaska Native, non-Hispanic/Latino; 29 Asian, non-Hispanic/Latino; 44 Hispanic/Latino; 23 Two or more races, non-Hispanic/Latino), 93 international. Average age 33. 805 applicants, 55% accepted, 328 enrolled. In 2016, 270 master's, 91 doctorates awarded. *Degree requirements:* For master's, comprehensive exam (for some programs), thesis (for some programs); for doctorate, comprehensive exam (for some programs), thesis/dissertation (for some programs). *Entrance requirements:* For master's and doctorate, GRE/GMAT. Additional exam requirements/recommendations for international students: Required—TOEFL (minimum score 80 iBT). *Application deadline:* For fall admission, 8/1 for domestic students, 4/1 for international students; for spring admission, 1/1 for domestic students, 9/1 for international students. Applications are processed on a rolling basis. Application fee: $75. Electronic applications accepted. *Expenses:* Tuition, state resident: full-time $12,467; part-time $692.50 per credit hour. Tuition, nonresident: full-time $25,095; part-time $1394.25 per credit hour. *Required fees:* $2669; $491.50 per semester. Tuition and fees vary according to course load, campus/location and program. *Financial support:* In 2016–17, 23 research assistantships with full tuition reimbursements (averaging $19,817 per year), 237 teaching assistantships with full tuition reimbursements (averaging $15,497 per year) were awarded. Financial award application deadline: 3/1; financial award applicants required to submit FAFSA. *Total annual research expenditures:* $6.6 million. *Unit head:* Rosemary Blieszner, Interim Dean, 540-231-6779, Fax: 540-231-7157, E-mail: liberalartsdean@vt.edu. *Application contact:* Chelsea Blanchet, Executive Assistant, 540-231-6779, Fax: 540-231-7157, E-mail: bchels1@vt.edu.
Website: http://www.liberalarts.vt.edu/

**Wayne State University,** College of Liberal Arts and Sciences, Department of English, Detroit, MI 48202. Offers English (MA); film and media studies (PhD); literary and cultural studies (PhD); rhetoric and composition studies (PhD). *Faculty:* 30. *Students:* 78 full-time (48 women), 23 part-time (10 women); includes 22 minority (10 Black or African American, non-Hispanic/Latino; 3 Asian, non-Hispanic/Latino; 6 Hispanic/Latino; 3 Two or more races, non-Hispanic/Latino), 7 international. Average age 35. 114 applicants, 33% accepted, 18 enrolled. In 2016, 15 master's, 5 doctorates awarded. Terminal master's awarded for partial completion of doctoral program. *Degree requirements:* For master's, variable foreign language requirement, essay, thesis, or portfolio of work approved by Director of Graduate Studies; for doctorate, one foreign language, comprehensive exam, thesis/dissertation. *Entrance requirements:* For master's, statement of purpose; two academic letters of reference; sample essay from previous English course; for doctorate, GRE General Test, statement of purpose; two academic letters of reference; sample of scholarly or critical writing. Additional exam requirements/recommendations for international students: Required—TOEFL (minimum score 550 paper-based; 79 iBT), TWE (minimum score 5.5), Michigan English Language Assessment Battery (minimum score 85); Recommended—IELTS (minimum score 6.5). *Application deadline:* For fall admission, 1/15 for domestic students. Applications are processed on a rolling basis. Application fee: $50. Electronic applications accepted. *Expenses:* $16,503 per year resident tuition and fees, $33,697 per year non-resident tuition and fees. *Financial support:* In 2016–17, 63 students received support, including 5 fellowships with tuition reimbursements available (averaging $15,800 per year), 30 teaching assistantships with tuition reimbursements available (averaging $17,994 per year); research assistantships with tuition reimbursements available, scholarships/grants, and unspecified assistantships also available. Financial award applicants required to submit FAFSA. *Faculty research:* Literary and cultural studies, film and new media studies, rhetoric and composition studies, linguistics, and creative writing. *Unit head:* Dr. Kenneth Jackson, Chair and Professor, 313-577-7692, E-mail: ai4054@wayne.edu. *Application contact:* Dr. Carolin Maun, Director of Graduate Studies, 313-577-7694, E-mail: caroline.maun@wayne.edu.
Website: http://clas.wayne.edu/english/

# Speech and Interpersonal Communication

**Ball State University,** Graduate School, College of Communication, Information, and Media, Department of Communication Studies, Muncie, IN 47306. Offers communication studies (MA), including communication liberal arts and sciences, organization and professional communication development. *Program availability:* Part-time. *Degree requirements:* For master's, comprehensive exam (for some programs), thesis (for some programs). *Entrance requirements:* For master's, GRE General Test, minimum baccalaureate GPA of 2.75 or 3.0 in latter half of baccalauareate, goal statement, writing sample, three letters of reference. Additional exam requirements/recommendations for international students: Required—TOEFL (minimum score 550 paper-based; 79 iBT), IELTS (minimum score 6.5). Electronic applications accepted.

**Bob Jones University,** Graduate Programs, Greenville, SC 29614. Offers accountancy (MS); Bible (MA); Bible translation (MA); Biblical studies (Certificate); broadcast management (MS); business administration (MBA); church history (MA, PhD); church ministries (MA); church music (MM); cinema and video production (MA); counseling (MS); curriculum and instruction (Ed D); divinity (M Div); dramatic production (MA); educational leadership (MS, Ed D, Ed S); elementary education (M Ed, MAT); English (M Ed, MA, MAT); fine arts (MA); graphic design (MA); history (M Ed, MA); illustration (MA); interpretative speech (MA); mathematics (M Ed, MAT); medical missions (Certificate); ministry (MM, D Min); multi-categorical special education (M Ed, MAT); music (M Ed); New Testament interpretation (PhD); Old Testament interpretation (PhD); orchestral instrument performance (MM); organ performance (MM); pastoral studies (MA); personnel services (MS, Ed S); piano pedagogy (MM); piano performance (MM); platform arts (MA); radio and television broadcasting (MS); rhetoric and public address (MA); secondary education (M Ed); studio art (MA); teaching Bible (MA); theology (MA, PhD); voice performance (MM); youth ministries (MA); M Div/MM.

**Brooklyn College of the City University of New York,** School of Humanities and Social Sciences, Department of Speech Communication Arts and Sciences, Brooklyn, NY 11210-2889. Offers audiology (Au D); speech (MA), including public communication; speech-language pathology (MS). Au D offered jointly with Hunter College of the City University of New York. *Accreditation:* ASHA (one or more programs are accredited). *Program availability:* Part-time. Terminal master's awarded for partial completion of doctoral program. *Degree requirements:* For master's, comprehensive exam, NTE. *Entrance requirements:* For master's, GRE, minimum GPA of 3.0, interview, essay. Additional exam requirements/recommendations for international students: Required—TOEFL (minimum score 500 paper-based; 61 iBT). Electronic applications accepted. *Faculty research:* Language and learning disorders, aphasia, auditory disorders, public and business communication, voice and fluency disorders.

**California State University, Fullerton,** Graduate Studies, College of Communications, Department of Human Communication Studies, Fullerton, CA 92834-9480. Offers communication studies (MA); communicative disorders (MA). *Accreditation:* ASHA. *Program availability:* Part-time. *Degree requirements:* For master's, comprehensive exam, thesis or alternative. *Entrance requirements:* For master's, minimum GPA of 3.0 in major. Application fee: $55. *Expenses:* Tuition, state resident: full-time $3369; part-time $1953 per unit. Tuition, nonresident: full-time $3915; part-time $2499 per unit. Tuition and fees vary according to course load, degree level and program. *Financial support:* Teaching assistantships, career-related internships or fieldwork, Federal Work-Study, institutionally sponsored loans, and scholarships/grants available. Support available to part-time students. Financial award application deadline: 3/1; financial award applicants required to submit FAFSA. *Faculty research:* Speech therapy. *Unit head:* Gary Ruud, Chair, 657-278-4198, E-mail: gruud@fullerton.edu. *Application contact:* Admissions/Applications, 657-278-2371.
Website: http://communications.fullerton.edu/hcom/

**California State University, Northridge,** Graduate Studies, College of Arts, Media, and Communication, Department of Communication Studies, Northridge, CA 91330. Offers MA. *Faculty:* 14 full-time (9 women), 55 part-time/adjunct (37 women). *Students:* 26 full-time (17 women), 9 part-time (3 women); includes 15 minority (2 Black or African American, non-Hispanic/Latino; 1 Asian, non-Hispanic/Latino; 8 Hispanic/Latino; 4 Two or more races, non-Hispanic/Latino), 3 international. Average age 27. 51 applicants, 41% accepted, 12 enrolled. *Entrance requirements:* For master's, GRE General Test. Additional exam requirements/recommendations for international students: Required—TOEFL. *Application deadline:* For fall admission, 11/30 for domestic students. Application fee: $55. *Expenses:* Tuition, state resident: full-time $4152. *Financial support:* Teaching assistantships available. Financial award application deadline: 3/1. *Unit head:* Kathryn Sorrells, Chair, 818-677-2853.
Website: http://www.csun.edu/CommunicationStudies/

**Colorado State University,** College of Liberal Arts, Department of Communication Studies, Fort Collins, CO 80523-1783. Offers communication (PhD); communication studies (MA), including deliberative practices. *Faculty:* 12 full-time (5 women). *Students:* 19 full-time (11 women), 9 part-time (8 women); includes 4 minority (1 Black or African American, non-Hispanic/Latino; 3 Hispanic/Latino). Average age 25. 28 applicants, 79% accepted, 11 enrolled. In 2016, 11 master's awarded. *Degree requirements:* For master's, thesis, conference submission, colloquium; for doctorate, comprehensive exam, thesis/dissertation, conference submission, colloquium. *Entrance requirements:* For master's and doctorate, GRE, statement of purpose, writing sample, 3 references, resume/curriculum vitae, transcripts. Additional exam requirements/recommendations for international students: Required—TOEFL (minimum score 550 paper-based; 80 iBT), IELTS. *Application deadline:* For fall admission, 1/5 priority date for domestic and international students. Application fee: $60 ($70 for international students). Electronic applications accepted. *Expenses:* Tuition, state resident: full-time $9628. Tuition, nonresident: full-time $23,603. *Required fees:* $2253; $528.14 per credit hour. $264.07 per semester. Tuition and fees vary according to course load and program. *Financial support:* In 2016–17, 20 students received support, including 21 teaching assistantships with full and partial tuition reimbursements available (averaging $13,932 per year); fellowships with full and partial tuition reimbursements available, scholarships/grants, health care benefits, and travel grants also available. Financial award application deadline: 1/5. *Faculty research:* Rhetoric and civic engagement; media and visual culture; relational and organizational communication. *Total annual research expenditures:* $72,989. *Unit head:* Dr. Greg Dickinson, Department Chair and Professor, 970-491-6140, E-mail: greg.dickinson@colostate.edu. *Application contact:* Carly Hennegan, Graduate Studies Support Coordinator, 970-491-4123, E-mail: carly.hennegan@colostate.edu.
Website: http://communicationstudies.colostate.edu/

**Eastern Illinois University,** Graduate School, College of Arts and Humanities, Department of Communication Studies, Charleston, IL 61920. Offers community college pedagogy (MA). *Program availability:* Part-time, evening/weekend. *Degree requirements:* For master's, comprehensive exam (for some programs), thesis (for some

programs). *Entrance requirements:* For master's, GMAT or GRE. Additional exam requirements/recommendations for international students: Required—TOEFL (minimum score 500 paper-based; 61 iBT), IELTS (minimum score 6). Electronic applications accepted.

**Georgia State University,** College of Arts and Sciences, Department of Communication, Atlanta, GA 30302-3083. Offers film, video, and digital imaging (MA), including critical studies, production, screenwriting; human communication and social influence (MA); mass communication (MA); media and society (PhD); moving image studies (PhD); public communication (PhD); rhetoric and politics (PhD). *Program availability:* Part-time. *Faculty:* 57 full-time (34 women). *Students:* 113 full-time (69 women), 56 part-time (33 women); includes 59 minority (37 Black or African American, non-Hispanic/Latino; 1 American Indian or Alaska Native, non-Hispanic/Latino; 2 Asian, non-Hispanic/Latino; 9 Hispanic/Latino; 10 Two or more races, non-Hispanic/Latino), 18 international. Average age 32. 134 applicants, 58% accepted, 47 enrolled. In 2016, 22 master's, 11 doctorates awarded. *Degree requirements:* For master's, variable foreign language requirement, thesis (for some programs); for doctorate, comprehensive exam, thesis/dissertation. *Entrance requirements:* For master's and doctorate, GRE. Additional exam requirements/recommendations for international students: Required—TOEFL (minimum score 550 paper-based; 80 iBT), IELTS (minimum score 6.5). *Application deadline:* For fall admission, 2/10 for domestic and international students; for spring admission, 10/15 for domestic and international students. Application fee: $50. Electronic applications accepted. *Expenses:* Tuition, state resident: full-time $6876; part-time $382 per credit hour. Tuition, nonresident: full-time $22,374; part-time $1243 per credit hour. *Required fees:* $2128; $1064 per term. Part-time tuition and fees vary according to course load and program. *Financial support:* In 2016–17, fellowships with tuition reimbursements (averaging $15,000 per year), teaching assistantships with tuition reimbursements (averaging $15,000 per year) were awarded; career-related internships or fieldwork and unspecified assistantships also available. Financial award applicants required to submit FAFSA. *Faculty research:* New media, mass media and journalism, rhetoric, film and media studies, film production. *Unit head:* Dr. Greg Lisby, Chair, 404-413-5639, Fax: 404-413-5634, E-mail: glisby@gsu.edu.
Website: http://communication.gsu.edu

**Idaho State University,** Office of Graduate Studies, College of Arts and Letters, Department of Communication and Rhetorical Studies, Pocatello, ID 83209-8115. Offers communication and rhetorical studies (MA). *Program availability:* Part-time. *Degree requirements:* For master's, comprehensive exam, paper or thesis. *Entrance requirements:* For master's, GRE General Test, minimum GPA of 3.0 in all upper-level courses. Additional exam requirements/recommendations for international students: Required—TOEFL (minimum score 550 paper-based; 80 iBT). Electronic applications accepted. *Faculty research:* Metaphor and cognition in organizational groups and teams; rhetorical criticism of contemporary culture, including music, film, television, and advertising; communication pedagogy; the effect of language on organizational identification and commitment; risk communication and crisis communication.

**Marquette University,** Graduate School, College of Communication, Milwaukee, WI 53201-1881. Offers advertising and public relations (MA); communication studies (MA); digital storytelling (Certificate); journalism (MA); mass communication (MA); science, health and environmental communication (MA). *Accreditation:* ACEJMC (one or more programs are accredited). *Program availability:* Part-time, evening/weekend. *Faculty:* 36 full-time (18 women), 45 part-time/adjunct (20 women). *Students:* 25 full-time (22 women), 23 part-time (16 women); includes 9 minority (3 Black or African American, non-Hispanic/Latino; 1 American Indian or Alaska Native, non-Hispanic/Latino; 4 Hispanic/Latino; 1 Two or more races, non-Hispanic/Latino), 4 international. Average age 28. 55 applicants, 62% accepted, 21 enrolled. In 2016, 10 master's, 1 other advanced degree awarded. *Degree requirements:* For master's, comprehensive exam, thesis or alternative. *Entrance requirements:* For master's, GRE, official transcripts from all current and previous colleges/universities except Marquette, three letters of recommendation, statement of academic and professional goals. Additional exam requirements/recommendations for international students: Required—TOEFL (minimum score 530 paper-based). *Application deadline:* Applications are processed on a rolling basis. Electronic applications accepted. *Financial support:* Fellowships, research assistantships, teaching assistantships, career-related internships or fieldwork, scholarships/grants, health care benefits, tuition waivers (full and partial), and unspecified assistantships available. Support available to part-time students. Financial award application deadline: 2/15. *Faculty research:* Urban journalism, gender and communication, intercultural communication, religious communication. *Total annual research expenditures:* $7,941. *Unit head:* Dr. Sarah Feldner, Associate Dean. *Application contact:* Dr. Sarah Bonewits Feldner.
Website: http://diederich.marquette.edu/

**New York University,** Steinhardt School of Culture, Education, and Human Development, Department of Media, Culture and Communication, New York, NY 10010. Offers media, culture and communication (MA, PhD); MLIS/MA. *Program availability:* Part-time. Terminal master's awarded for partial completion of doctoral program. *Degree requirements:* For master's, thesis (for some programs); for doctorate, thesis/dissertation. *Entrance requirements:* For master's, GRE General Test; for doctorate, GRE General Test, interview. Additional exam requirements/recommendations for international students: Required—TOEFL (minimum score 100 iBT). Electronic applications accepted. *Faculty research:* Digital media and new technologies, media criticism, flow of media and culture transnationally and transculturally.

**North Dakota State University,** College of Graduate and Interdisciplinary Studies, College of Arts, Humanities and Social Sciences, Department of Communication, Fargo, ND 58102. Offers communication (PhD); mass communication (MA, MS); speech communication (MA, MS). *Program availability:* Part-time, online learning. Terminal master's awarded for partial completion of doctoral program. *Degree requirements:* For master's, thesis (for some programs); for doctorate, comprehensive exam, thesis/dissertation, 2-3 publications. *Entrance requirements:* For master's, GRE, minimum undergraduate GPA of 3.25; for doctorate, GRE, minimum undergraduate GPA of 3.5. Additional exam requirements/recommendations for international students: Required—TOEFL (minimum score 600 paper-based; 100 iBT), IELTS (minimum score 7). Electronic applications accepted. *Faculty research:* Communication and rhetorical theory, organizational communication, broadcast and print journalism, international communication, public relations and advertising.

**Northeastern Illinois University,** College of Graduate Studies and Research, College of Arts and Sciences, Program in Communication, Media and Theatre, Chicago, IL 60625-4699. Offers MA. *Program availability:* Part-time, evening/weekend. *Degree requirements:* For master's, comprehensive exam, oral exams, thesis or 3 term papers. *Entrance requirements:* For master's, 15 undergraduate hours in speech and performing arts, minimum GPA of 2.75. Additional exam requirements/recommendations for international students: Required—TOEFL (minimum score 550 paper-based; 79 iBT). Electronic applications accepted. *Faculty research:* Creative drama, family communication, fine arts and general education, playwriting techniques, interpersonal communications.

**Northwestern University,** The Graduate School, School of Communication, Department of Performance Studies, Evanston, IL 60208. Offers MA, PhD. Admissions and degrees offered through The Graduate School. *Program availability:* Part-time. Terminal master's awarded for partial completion of doctoral program. *Degree requirements:* For master's, recital; for doctorate, one foreign language, thesis/dissertation, recital. *Entrance requirements:* For master's and doctorate, GRE General Test. Additional exam requirements/recommendations for international students: Required—TOEFL. *Faculty research:* Adaptation/performance of literature, ethnography of performance, critical cultural studies, performance theory, intercultural performance, gender studies.

**Ohio University,** Graduate College, Scripps College of Communication, School of Communication Studies, Athens, OH 45701-2979. Offers health communication (PhD); organizational communication (MA); relating and organizing (PhD); rhetoric and public culture (PhD). *Program availability:* Part-time, online learning. Terminal master's awarded for partial completion of doctoral program. *Degree requirements:* For master's, capstone; for doctorate, comprehensive exam, thesis/dissertation. *Entrance requirements:* For master's, GRE; for doctorate, GRE General Test, minimum GPA of 3.0. Additional exam requirements/recommendations for international students: Required—TOEFL (minimum score 550 paper-based; 80 iBT) or IELTS (minimum score 6.5). *Application deadline:* For fall admission, 1/15 priority date for domestic and international students. Application fee: $50 ($55 for international students). Electronic applications accepted. *Financial support:* In 2016–17, 12 students received support. Fellowships with full tuition reimbursements available, research assistantships with full tuition reimbursements available, teaching assistantships with full tuition reimbursements available, career-related internships or fieldwork, Federal Work-Study, and institutionally sponsored loans available. Financial award application deadline: 1/15. *Faculty research:* Rhetoric and public culture, relating and organizing, health communication. *Unit head:* Dr. Claudia Hale, Interim Director, 740-593-4825, E-mail: hale@ohio.edu. *Application contact:* Dr. Benjamin Bates, Associate Director for Graduate Studies, 740-593-9163, Fax: 740-593-4810, E-mail: batesb@ohio.edu. Website: http://www.coms.ohiou.edu/

**Old Dominion University,** College of Arts and Letters, Program in Lifespan and Digital Communication, Norfolk, VA 23529. Offers MA. *Accreditation:* NASAD. *Program availability:* Part-time, evening/weekend. *Faculty:* 15 full-time (5 women). *Students:* 9 full-time (6 women), 17 part-time (13 women); includes 14 minority (7 Black or African American, non-Hispanic/Latino; 2 Asian, non-Hispanic/Latino; 3 Hispanic/Latino; 2 Two or more races, non-Hispanic/Latino), 1 international. Average age 33. 14 applicants, 86% accepted, 12 enrolled. In 2016, 6 master's awarded. *Degree requirements:* For master's, comprehensive exam or thesis. *Entrance requirements:* For master's, GRE. Additional exam requirements/recommendations for international students: Recommended—TOEFL (minimum score 550 paper-based; 79 iBT). *Application deadline:* For fall admission, 6/15 for domestic students, 4/15 for international students. Applications are processed on a rolling basis. Application fee: $50. Electronic applications accepted. *Expenses:* $8,604 tuition; $346 fees. *Financial support:* In 2016–17, 10 students received support, including 1 research assistantship (averaging $10,000 per year), 7 teaching assistantships (averaging $10,000 per year); 3 assistantships (averaging $5000) also available. Financial award application deadline: 6/15. *Faculty research:* Family communication, digital media studies, lifespan communication, social media, screenwriting. *Unit head:* Dr. Thomas J. Socha, Graduate Program Director, 757-683-3833, E-mail: tsocha@odu.edu. *Application contact:* Dr. David C. Earnest, Associate Dean, 757-683-6077, Fax: 757-683-5746, E-mail: dearnest@odu.edu. Website: http://www.odu.edu/commtheatre/graduate#.VzDZI032bGg

**Portland State University,** Graduate Studies, College of Liberal Arts and Sciences, Department of Communication, Portland, OR 97207-0751. Offers general speech communication (MA, MS, Certificate). *Program availability:* Part-time. *Faculty:* 11 full-time (5 women), 9 part-time/adjunct (2 women). *Students:* 23 full-time (14 women), 5 part-time (4 women); includes 5 minority (1 Black or African American, non-Hispanic/Latino; 1 American Indian or Alaska Native, non-Hispanic/Latino; 1 Hispanic/Latino; 2 Two or more races, non-Hispanic/Latino), 2 international. Average age 30. 31 applicants, 48% accepted, 14 enrolled. In 2016, 9 master's awarded. *Degree requirements:* For master's, variable foreign language requirement, thesis optional. *Entrance requirements:* For master's, GRE (for students who select the thesis option and/or who receive an assistantship), minimum GPA of 3.0 in upper-division course work or 2.75 overall, 3 letters of recommendation, statement of purpose, writing samples. Additional exam requirements/recommendations for international students: Required—TOEFL (minimum score 600 paper-based; 100 iBT). *Application deadline:* For fall admission, 2/1 priority date for domestic and international students. Applications are processed on a rolling basis. Application fee: $65. Electronic applications accepted. *Expenses:* Contact institution. *Financial support:* In 2016–17, 10 teaching assistantships with tuition reimbursements (averaging $6,835 per year) were awarded; research assistantships, career-related internships or fieldwork, Federal Work-Study, scholarships/grants, and unspecified assistantships also available. Support available to part-time students. Financial award application deadline: 3/1; financial award applicants required to submit FAFSA. *Total annual research expenditures:* $64,502. *Unit head:* Dr. Jeffrey Robinson, Chair, 503-725-3599, Fax: 503-725-3599, E-mail: jeffreyr@pdx.edu. *Application contact:* Adriane Bolliger, 503-725-5384, Fax: 503-725-5385, E-mail: adriane@pdx.edu. Website: http://www.pdx.edu/communication/

**Rensselaer Polytechnic Institute,** Graduate School, School of Humanities, Arts, and Social Sciences, Programs in Communication and Rhetoric, Troy, NY 12180-3590. Offers MS, PhD. *Faculty:* 12 full-time (7 women). *Students:* 15 full-time (10 women), 1 part-time (0 women). 19 applicants, 26% accepted, 4 enrolled. In 2016, 1 master's, 2 doctorates awarded. Terminal master's awarded for partial completion of doctoral program. *Degree requirements:* For master's, thesis optional; for doctorate, comprehensive exam, thesis/dissertation. *Entrance requirements:* For master's and doctorate, GRE. Additional exam requirements/recommendations for international students: Required—TOEFL (minimum score 570 paper-based; 88 iBT), IELTS (minimum score 6.5), PTE (minimum score 60). *Application deadline:* For fall admission, 1/1 priority date for domestic and international students; for spring admission, 8/15 priority date for domestic and international students. Applications are processed on a rolling basis. Application fee: $75. Electronic applications accepted. *Expenses:* Tuition: Full-time $49,520; part-time $2060 per credit hour. *Required fees:* $2617. *Financial support:* In 2016–17, research assistantships with full tuition reimbursements (averaging $22,000 per year), teaching assistantships with full tuition reimbursements (averaging $22,000 per year) were awarded; fellowships also available. Financial award application deadline: 1/1. *Faculty research:* Communication, game studies, human computer interaction, literary theory, media studies, rhetoric, visual design, writing studies. *Unit head:* Dr. Audrey Bennett, Graduate Program Director, 518-276-6933,

E-mail: bennett@rpi.edu. *Application contact:* Office of Graduate Admissions, 518-276-6216, E-mail: gradadmissions@rpi.edu. Website: http://www.cm.rpi.edu/pl/graduate

**San Francisco State University,** Division of Graduate Studies, College of Liberal and Creative Arts, Department of Communication Studies, San Francisco, CA 94132-1722. Offers MA. *Program availability:* Part-time. *Application deadline:* Applications are processed on a rolling basis. *Expenses:* Tuition, state resident: full-time $6738. Tuition, nonresident: full-time $15,666. *Required fees:* $1012. Tuition and fees vary according to degree level and program. *Financial support:* Teaching assistantships available. *Unit head:* Dr. Christina Sabee, Chair, 415-338-1597, Fax: 415-338-6159, E-mail: csabee@sfsu.edu. *Application contact:* Prof. Leah Wingard, Graduate Coordinator, 415-338-3171, Fax: 415-338-6159, E-mail: wingard@sfsu.edu. Website: http://communicationstudies.sfsu.edu/

**Seton Hall University,** School of Health and Medical Sciences, Program in Speech-Language Pathology, South Orange, NJ 07079-2697. Offers MS. *Accreditation:* ASHA. *Entrance requirements:* For master's, GRE, bachelor's degree, clinical experience; minimum GPA of 3.0, undergraduate preprofessional coursework in communication sciences and disorders. Additional exam requirements/recommendations for international students: Recommended—TOEFL. Electronic applications accepted. *Faculty research:* Child language disorders, motor speech control, voice disorders, dysphagia, early intervention/teaming.

**Southern Illinois University Carbondale,** Graduate School, College of Liberal Arts, Department of Communication Studies, Carbondale, IL 62901-4701. Offers MA, MS, PhD. *Degree requirements:* For master's, one foreign language, thesis or alternative; for doctorate, one foreign language, thesis/dissertation. *Entrance requirements:* For master's, GRE General Test or MAT, minimum GPA of 2.7; for doctorate, GRE General Test or MAT, minimum GPA of 3.25. Additional exam requirements/recommendations for international students: Required—TOEFL (minimum score 100 iBT).

**Southern Illinois University Edwardsville,** Graduate School, College of Arts and Sciences, Department of Applied Communication Studies, Program in Interpersonal Communication, Edwardsville, IL 62026. Offers MA. *Program availability:* Part-time, evening/weekend. *Degree requirements:* For master's, comprehensive exam (for some programs), thesis (for some programs). *Entrance requirements:* Additional exam requirements/recommendations for international students: Required—TOEFL (minimum score 550 paper-based, 79 iBT), IELTS (minimum score 6.5), Michigan Test of English Language Proficiency or PTE. Electronic applications accepted.

**Texas Christian University,** Bob Schieffer College of Communication, Department of Communication Studies, Fort Worth, TX 76129. Offers MS. *Program availability:* Part-time. *Faculty:* 12 full-time (5 women). *Students:* 11 full-time (10 women); includes 1 minority (Asian, non-Hispanic/Latino). Average age 24. 13 applicants, 62% accepted, 5 enrolled. In 2016, 6 master's awarded. *Degree requirements:* For master's, comprehensive exams or thesis. *Entrance requirements:* For master's, GRE General Test. Additional exam requirements/recommendations for international students: Required—TOEFL (minimum score 550 paper-based; 80 iBT). *Application deadline:* For fall and spring admission, 2/15 for domestic and international students. Application fee: $60. Electronic applications accepted. *Expenses: Tuition:* Full-time $26,640; part-time $1480 per credit hour. *Required fees:* $48. Tuition and fees vary according to program. *Financial support:* In 2016–17, 13 students received support, including 10 teaching assistantships with full tuition reimbursements available (averaging $11,000 per year); tuition waivers (full) also available. Financial award application deadline: 2/15. *Faculty research:* Interpersonal communication, social media, organizational communication, persuasion, instructional communication. *Unit head:* Dr. Melissa Schroeder, Associate Professor/Chair, 817-257-7784, Fax: 817-257-6580, E-mail: m.y.schroeder@tcu.edu. *Application contact:* Dr. Paul Schrodt, Professor and Graduate Director, 817-257-5674, Fax: 817-257-6580, E-mail: p.schrodt@tcu.edu. Website: http://www.commstudies.tcu.edu

**The University of Alabama,** Graduate School, College of Communication and Information Sciences, Department of Communication Studies, Tuscaloosa, AL 35487. Offers MA. *Program availability:* Part-time, 100% online, blended/hybrid learning. *Faculty:* 14 full-time (10 women). *Students:* 19 full-time (12 women), 20 part-time (11 women); includes 11 minority (4 Black or African American, non-Hispanic/Latino; 6 Hispanic/Latino; 1 Two or more races, non-Hispanic/Latino), 3 international. Average age 29. 45 applicants, 56% accepted, 21 enrolled. In 2016, 11 master's awarded. *Degree requirements:* For master's, comprehensive exam (for some programs), thesis (for some programs), colloquium presentation; capstone portfolio (for some programs). *Entrance requirements:* For master's, GRE, MAT, minimum GPA of 3.0. Additional exam requirements/recommendations for international students: Required—TOEFL (minimum score 550 paper-based). *Application deadline:* For fall admission, 5/1 for domestic students, 4/1 for international students; for spring admission, 11/1 for domestic students, 10/1 for international students; for summer admission, 3/1 for domestic and international students. Applications are processed on a rolling basis. Application fee: $50 ($60 for international students). Electronic applications accepted. *Expenses:* Tuition, state resident: full-time $10,470. Tuition, nonresident: full-time $26,950. *Financial support:* In 2016–17, 16 students received support, including 1 fellowship with full tuition reimbursement available, 13 teaching assistantships with full tuition reimbursements available (averaging $12,366 per year); health care benefits, unspecified assistantships, and teaching stipend (one semester $3,000) also available. Financial award application deadline: 3/1. *Faculty research:* Rhetorical studies, organizational communication, interpersonal communication, gender and communication, health communication. *Total annual research expenditures:* $12,229. *Unit head:* Dr. Beth S. Bennett, Department Chair, 205-348-8073, E-mail: bbennett@ua.edu. *Application contact:* Dr. Carol Bishop Mills, Graduate Program Coordinator, 205-348-6165, E-mail: cbmills@ua.edu. Website: http://www.comstudies.ua.edu

**University of Arkansas at Little Rock,** Graduate School, College of Social Sciences and Communication, Department of Speech Communication, Little Rock, AR 72204-1099. Offers applied communication studies (MA). *Program availability:* Part-time, evening/weekend. *Degree requirements:* For master's, comprehensive exam, internship, paper, or thesis. *Entrance requirements:* For master's, GRE General Test, MAT, minimum GPA of 2.7. *Faculty research:* Communication theory and applications, managerial communication, human resource training and development, relational communication.

**University of California, Santa Barbara,** Graduate Division, College of Letters and Sciences, Division of Social Sciences, Department of Sociology, Santa Barbara, CA 93106-9430. Offers interdisciplinary emphasis: Black studies (PhD); interdisciplinary emphasis: environment and society (PhD); interdisciplinary emphasis: feminist studies (PhD); interdisciplinary emphasis: global studies (PhD); interdisciplinary emphasis: language, interaction and social organization (PhD); interdisciplinary emphasis: quantitative methods in the social sciences (PhD); interdisciplinary emphasis: technology and society (PhD); sociology (PhD); MA/PhD. Terminal master's awarded for partial completion of doctoral program. *Degree requirements:* For doctorate, comprehensive exam, thesis/dissertation. *Entrance requirements:* For doctorate, GRE General Test. Additional exam requirements/recommendations for international students: Required—TOEFL (minimum score 550 paper-based; 80 iBT), IELTS (minimum score 7). Electronic applications accepted. *Faculty research:* Gender and sexualities, race/ethnicity, social movements, conversation analysis, global sociology.

**University of Denver,** Division of Arts, Humanities and Social Sciences, Department of Communication Studies, Denver, CO 80208. Offers culture and communication (MA, PhD); interpersonal and family communication (MA, PhD); rhetoric and communication ethics (MA, PhD). *Program availability:* Part-time. *Faculty:* 11 full-time (7 women), 1 (woman) part-time/adjunct. *Students:* 19 full-time (13 women), 11 part-time (9 women); includes 10 minority (2 Black or African American, non-Hispanic/Latino; 1 Asian, non-Hispanic/Latino; 6 Hispanic/Latino; 1 Two or more races, non-Hispanic/Latino), 4 international. Average age 33. 62 applicants, 37% accepted, 7 enrolled. In 2016, 2 master's, 3 doctorates awarded. *Degree requirements:* For master's, comprehensive exam (for some programs), thesis (for some programs), comprehensive exam or thesis; for doctorate, one foreign language, thesis/dissertation. *Entrance requirements:* For master's, GRE General Test, bachelor's degree in communication or a related field, transcripts, essay, resume or curriculum vitae, three letters of recommendation; for doctorate, GRE General Test, bachelor's or master's degree in communication or related field, transcripts, essay, resume or curriculum vitae, three letters of recommendation. Additional exam requirements/recommendations for international students: Required—TOEFL (minimum score 570 paper-based; 88 iBT). *Application deadline:* For fall admission, 12/15 priority date for domestic and international students; for winter admission, 3/15 priority date for domestic and international students; for spring admission, 6/15 priority date for domestic and international students. Applications are processed on a rolling basis. Application fee: $65. Electronic applications accepted. *Expenses:* $29,022 per year full-time. *Financial support:* In 2016–17, 25 students received support, including 8 teaching assistantships with tuition reimbursements available (averaging $17,500 per year); career-related internships or fieldwork, Federal Work-Study, institutionally sponsored loans, scholarships/grants, and unspecified assistantships also available. Support available to part-time students. Financial award application deadline: 2/15; financial award applicants required to submit FAFSA. *Faculty research:* Successful community collaborative efforts, long-term marriages, cross-ethnic friendships, public dialogue about environmental risk, women's international cooperation. *Unit head:* Dr. Christina R. Foust, Associate Professor and Chair, 303-871-4330, Fax: 303-871-4316, E-mail: cfoust@du.edu. *Application contact:* Dr. Mary Claire Morr Serweicz, Associate Professor and Director of Graduate Studies, 303-871-4332, Fax: 303-871-4316, E-mail: mserewic@du.edu.
Website: http://www.du.edu/ahss/comn

**University of Hawaii at Manoa,** Graduate Division, College of Arts and Humanities, Department of Communicology, Honolulu, HI 96822. Offers MA. *Program availability:* Part-time. *Degree requirements:* For master's, thesis optional. *Entrance requirements:* For master's, GRE General Test. Additional exam requirements/recommendations for international students: Required—TOEFL (minimum score 600 paper-based; 100 iBT), IELTS (minimum score 7). *Faculty research:* Social influence, relational management, message processing, intercultural communication.

**University of Houston,** College of Liberal Arts and Social Sciences, Jack J. Valenti School of Communication, Houston, TX 77204. Offers health communication (MA); mass communication studies (MA); public relations studies (MA); speech communication (MA). *Program availability:* Part-time. *Degree requirements:* For master's, comprehensive exam (for some programs), thesis (for some programs), 30-33 hours. *Entrance requirements:* For master's, GRE. Additional exam requirements/recommendations for international students: Required—TOEFL. Electronic applications accepted.

**The University of Iowa,** Graduate College, College of Liberal Arts and Sciences, Department of Communication Studies, Iowa City, IA 52242-1316. Offers interpersonal communication and relationships (MA, PhD); media studies (MA, PhD); rhetoric and public advocacy (MA, PhD). *Degree requirements:* For master's, thesis optional, exam; for doctorate, comprehensive exam, thesis/dissertation. *Entrance requirements:* For master's and doctorate, GRE General Test, minimum GPA of 3.0. Additional exam requirements/recommendations for international students: Required—TOEFL (minimum score 550 paper-based; 81 iBT). Electronic applications accepted.

**University of Louisiana at Monroe,** Graduate School, College of Arts, Education, and Sciences, School of Education, Program in Curriculum and Instruction, Monroe, LA 71209-0001. Offers art education (M Ed); biology education (M Ed); chemistry education (M Ed); curriculum and instruction (Ed D); early childhood education (M Ed); earth science education (M Ed); educational leadership (M Ed); elementary education (1-5) (M Ed); English as a second language (M Ed); English education (M Ed); family and consumer education (M Ed); French education (M Ed); history education (M Ed); math education (M Ed); middle school education (M Ed); music education (M Ed); reading education (K-12) (M Ed); Spanish education (M Ed); special education - academically gifted (M Ed); special education - early intervention (M Ed); special education - educational diagnostician (M Ed); special education - mild/moderate disabilities (M Ed); speech education (M Ed). *Accreditation:* NCATE. *Faculty:* 8 full-time (4 women), 4 part-time/adjunct (3 women). *Students:* 13 full-time (11 women), 80 part-time (65 women); includes 25 minority (19 Black or African American, non-Hispanic/Latino; 1 Asian, non-Hispanic/Latino; 3 Hispanic/Latino; 2 Two or more races, non-Hispanic/Latino). Average age 37. 118 applicants, 30% accepted, 16 enrolled. In 2016, 23 master's, 4 doctorates awarded. *Degree requirements:* For master's, comprehensive exam (for some programs), thesis; for doctorate, thesis/dissertation, internships. *Entrance requirements:* For master's, GRE General Test; for doctorate, GRE General Test; minimum undergraduate GPA of 2.75, graduate 3.25. Additional exam requirements/recommendations for international students: Required—TOEFL (minimum score 500 paper-based; 61 iBT). *Application deadline:* For fall admission, 8/24 priority date for domestic students, 7/1 for international students; for winter admission, 12/14 priority date for domestic students; for spring admission, 1/19 for domestic students, 11/1 for international students. Applications are processed on a rolling basis. Application fee: $20 ($30 for international students). Electronic applications accepted. *Expenses:* Tuition, state resident: full-time $6489. Tuition, nonresident: full-time $18,589. *Required fees:* $8984. Tuition and fees vary according to course level, course load, degree level and program. *Financial support:* Research assistantships, career-related internships or fieldwork, Federal Work-Study, and unspecified assistantships available. Financial award application deadline: 4/1; financial award applicants required to submit FAFSA. *Unit head:* Dr. Dorothy Schween, Director, 318-342-1268, Fax: 318-342-3131, E-mail: schween@ulm.edu.

**University of Maryland, College Park,** Academic Affairs, College of Behavioral and Social Sciences, Department of Hearing and Speech Sciences, College Park, MD 20742. Offers audiology (MA, PhD); hearing and speech sciences (Au D); language pathology (MA, PhD); neuroscience (PhD); speech (MA, PhD). *Accreditation:* ASHA (one or more programs are accredited). *Degree requirements:* For master's, thesis optional; for doctorate, thesis/dissertation, written and oral exams. *Entrance requirements:* For master's, GRE General Test, minimum GPA of 3.5, 3 letters of recommendation; for doctorate, GRE General Test, minimum GPA of 3.5. Additional exam requirements/recommendations for international students: Required—TOEFL.

Electronic applications accepted. *Faculty research:* Speech perception, language acquisition, bilingualism, hearing loss.

**University of Nebraska–Lincoln,** Graduate College, College of Arts and Sciences, Department of Communication Studies, Lincoln, NE 68588. Offers instructional communication (MA, PhD); interpersonal communication (MA, PhD); marketing, communication studies, and advertising (MA, PhD); organizational communication (MA, PhD); rhetoric and culture (MA, PhD). *Degree requirements:* For master's, thesis optional; for doctorate, comprehensive exam, thesis/dissertation. *Entrance requirements:* For master's and doctorate, GRE General Test, writing sample. Additional exam requirements/recommendations for international students: Required—TOEFL (minimum score 600 paper-based). Electronic applications accepted. *Faculty research:* Message strategies, gender communication, political communication, organizational communication, instructional communication.

**University of Nevada, Reno,** Graduate School, College of Liberal Arts, Department of Speech Communications, Reno, NV 89557. Offers MA. *Degree requirements:* For master's, thesis optional. *Entrance requirements:* For master's, GRE General Test, minimum GPA of 2.75. Additional exam requirements/recommendations for international students: Required—TOEFL (minimum score 500 paper-based; 61 iBT), IELTS (minimum score 6). Electronic applications accepted. *Faculty research:* Rhetorical theory and criticism; communications/sex roles; judicial, legal, contextual, and behavioral approaches to communication theory.

**University of South Carolina,** The Graduate School, College of Education, Department of Instruction and Teacher Education, Program in Secondary Education, Columbia, SC 29208. Offers art education (IMA, MAT); business education (IMA, MAT); English (MAT); foreign language (MAT); health education (MAT); mathematics (MAT); science (IMA, MAT); secondary (Ed D); secondary education (MT, PhD); social studies (MAT); theatre and speech (MAT). IMA and MT offered jointly with the subject areas. *Accreditation:* NCATE. *Degree requirements:* For master's, comprehensive exam, thesis (for some programs), foreign language (MA); for doctorate, one foreign language, comprehensive exam, thesis/dissertation. *Entrance requirements:* For master's, GRE General Test or MAT, teaching certificate (IMA, M Ed), interview; for doctorate, GRE General Test or MAT, interview. *Faculty research:* Middle school programs, professional development, school collaboration.

**University of Southern Mississippi,** Graduate School, College of Arts and Letters, Department of Communication Studies, Hattiesburg, MS 39406-5131. Offers MA, PhD. *Program availability:* Part-time. *Degree requirements:* For master's, comprehensive exam, thesis optional; for doctorate, comprehensive exam, thesis/dissertation. *Entrance requirements:* For master's, GRE General Test, minimum GPA of 3.0 in last 60 hours and in major; for doctorate, GRE General Test, minimum GPA of 3.5. Additional exam requirements/recommendations for international students: Required—TOEFL, IELTS. *Application deadline:* For fall admission, 3/1 priority date for domestic students, 3/1 for international students; for spring admission, 1/10 priority date for domestic and international students. Application fee: $60. *Expenses: Tuition, area resident:* Full-time $15,708; part-time $437 per credit hour. *Financial support:* Fellowships with full tuition reimbursements, research assistantships, teaching assistantships with full tuition reimbursements, Federal Work-Study, institutionally sponsored loans, scholarships/grants, health care benefits, and unspecified assistantships available. Financial award application deadline: 3/15; financial award applicants required to submit FAFSA. *Faculty research:* Persuasion and social influence, interpersonal communication, organizational communication, political communication, crisis communication, public advocacy. *Unit head:* Dr. Wendy Atkins-Sayre, Chair, 601-266-4271, Fax: 601-266-4275, E-mail: wendy.atkinssayre@usm.edu. *Application contact:* Dr. John Meyer, Director of Graduate Studies, 601-266-4280, Fax: 601-266-4275, E-mail: john.meyer@usm.edu.
Website: https://www.usm.edu/communication-studies

**The University of Tennessee,** Graduate School, College of Communication and Information, Knoxville, TN 37996. Offers advertising (MS, PhD); broadcasting (MS, PhD); communications (MS, PhD); information sciences (MS, PhD); journalism (MS, PhD); public relations (MS, PhD); speech communication (MS, PhD). *Program availability:* Part-time, evening/weekend, online learning. *Degree requirements:* For master's, thesis or alternative; for doctorate, thesis/dissertation. *Entrance requirements:* For master's and doctorate, GRE General Test, minimum GPA of 2.7. Additional exam requirements/recommendations for international students: Required—TOEFL. Electronic applications accepted.

**University of Wisconsin–Madison,** Graduate School, College of Letters and Science, Department of Communicative Disorders, Madison, WI 53706-1380. Offers normal aspects of speech, language and hearing (MS, PhD); speech-language pathology (MS, PhD); MS/PhD. *Accreditation:* ASHA (one or more programs are accredited). *Degree requirements:* For doctorate, thesis/dissertation. *Entrance requirements:* For master's and doctorate, GRE. Electronic applications accepted. *Faculty research:* Language disorders in children and adults, disorders of speech production, intelligibility, fluency, hearing impairment, deafness.

**University of Wisconsin–Stevens Point,** College of Fine Arts and Communication, Division of Communication, Stevens Point, WI 54481-3897. Offers interpersonal communication (MA); media studies (MA); organizational communication (MA); public relations (MA). *Program availability:* Part-time. *Degree requirements:* For master's, thesis or alternative. *Entrance requirements:* For master's, GRE. Additional exam requirements/recommendations for international students: Required—TOEFL (minimum score 575 paper-based). *Faculty research:* Communication theory and research, film history.

**University of Wisconsin–Superior,** Graduate Division, Department of Communicating Arts, Superior, WI 54880-4500. Offers mass communication (MA); speech communication (MA); theater (MA). *Program availability:* Part-time. *Degree requirements:* For master's, comprehensive exam, thesis or alternative, position paper or project. *Entrance requirements:* For master's, minimum GPA of 2.75. Electronic applications accepted. *Faculty research:* Multimedia technology, ethics in journalism, diversity, electronic portfolio assessment.

**Wake Forest University,** Graduate School of Arts and Sciences, Department of Communication, Winston-Salem, NC 27106. Offers speech communication (MA). *Program availability:* Part-time. *Degree requirements:* For master's, one foreign language, thesis. *Entrance requirements:* For master's, GRE General Test, writing sample. Additional exam requirements/recommendations for international students: Required—TOEFL (minimum score 79 iBT). Electronic applications accepted.

**Washington University in St. Louis,** School of Medicine, Program in Audiology and Communication Sciences, St. Louis, MO 63110. Offers audiology (Au D); deaf education (MS); speech and hearing sciences (PhD). *Accreditation:* ASHA (one or more programs are accredited). *Faculty:* 22 full-time (12 women), 18 part-time/adjunct (12 women). *Students:* 72 full-time (67 women). Average age 24. 101 applicants, 32% accepted, 22 enrolled. In 2016, 8 master's, 14 doctorates awarded. *Degree requirements:* For master's, comprehensive exam, thesis, independent study project, oral exam; for doctorate, comprehensive exam, thesis/dissertation, capstone project. *Entrance requirements:* For master's and doctorate, GRE General Test, minimum B average in previous college/university coursework (recommended). Additional exam requirements/

recommendations for international students: Required—TOEFL (minimum score 100 iBT). *Application deadline:* For fall admission, 2/15 for domestic and international students. Application fee: $60 ($80 for international students). Electronic applications accepted. *Expenses:* Contact institution. *Financial support:* In 2016–17, 72 students received support, including 72 fellowships with full and partial tuition reimbursements available (averaging $16,104 per year), 6 teaching assistantships with partial tuition reimbursements available (averaging $1,000 per year); career-related internships or fieldwork, Federal Work-Study, institutionally sponsored loans, scholarships/grants, traineeships, health care benefits, tuition waivers (partial), and unspecified assistantships also available. Financial award application deadline: 2/15; financial award applicants required to submit FAFSA. *Faculty research:* Audiology, deaf education, speech and hearing sciences, sensory neuroscience. *Unit head:* Dr. William W. Clark, Program Director, 314-747-0104, Fax: 314-747-0105. *Application contact:* Beth Elliott, Director, Finance and Student/Academic Affairs, 314-747-0104, Fax: 314-747-0105, E-mail: elliottb@wustl.edu.
Website: http://pacs.wustl.edu/

**Westfield State University,** College of Graduate and Continuing Education, Department of Education, Westfield, MA 01086. Offers early childhood education (M Ed); elementary education (M Ed); occupational education (M Ed); reading (M Ed), including reading specialist; secondary education (M Ed), including biology teacher education, chemistry teacher education, general science teacher education, history teacher education, mathematics teacher education, physical education teacher education; special education (M Ed). *Accreditation:* NCATE. *Program availability:* Part-time, evening/weekend. *Faculty:* 16 full-time (7 women), 33 part-time/adjunct (24 women). *Students:* 21 full-time (10 women), 168 part-time (126 women); includes 6 minority (2 Black or African American, non-Hispanic/Latino; 2 Hispanic/Latino; 2 Two or more races, non-Hispanic/Latino), 1 international. Average age 32. 47 applicants, 85% accepted, 30 enrolled. In 2016, 51 master's awarded. *Degree requirements:* For master's, comprehensive exam, practicum. *Entrance requirements:* For master's, GRE General Test or MAT, minimum undergraduate GPA of 2.8. Additional exam requirements/recommendations for international students: Recommended—TOEFL (minimum score 550 paper-based; 79 iBT). *Application deadline:* For fall admission, 6/30 for domestic students; for spring admission, 10/31 for domestic students; for summer admission, 3/31 for domestic students. Applications are processed on a rolling basis. Application fee: $50. Electronic applications accepted. *Expenses:* Tuition, state resident: part-time $318 per semester hour. Tuition, nonresident: part-time $318 per semester hour. *Required fees:* $75 per semester. Tuition and fees vary according to course load and program. *Financial support:* Unspecified assistantships and SOS scholarships for education majors only available. Financial award application deadline: 3/1; financial award applicants required to submit FAFSA. *Faculty research:* Collaborative teacher education, developmental early childhood education. *Unit head:* Dr. Sandra Berkowitz, Department Chair, 413-572-5323,
E-mail: sberkowitz@westfield.ma.edu. *Application contact:* Shelly Henrichon, Coordinator of DGCE Admissions, 413-572-8022, Fax: 413-572-5227,
E-mail: mhenrichon@westfield.ma.edu.
Website: http://www.westfield.ma.edu/academics/degrees/education-graduate-programs

# Technical Communication

**Auburn University,** Graduate School, College of Liberal Arts, Department of English, Auburn University, AL 36849. Offers MA, MTPC, PhD, Graduate Certificate. *Program availability:* Part-time. *Faculty:* 61 full-time (31 women), 4 part-time/adjunct (0 women). *Students:* 25 full-time (16 women), 34 part-time (23 women); includes 7 minority (3 Black or African American, non-Hispanic/Latino; 2 Asian, non-Hispanic/Latino; 2 Two or more races, non-Hispanic/Latino), 1 international. Average age 30. 57 applicants, 63% accepted, 19 enrolled. In 2016, 19 master's, 10 doctorates, 2 other advanced degrees awarded. *Degree requirements:* For master's, one foreign language, thesis optional, written exam; for doctorate, 2 foreign languages, thesis/dissertation, oral and written exams. *Entrance requirements:* For master's, GRE General Test, sample of written work; for doctorate, GRE General Test, GRE Subject Test, sample of written work. *Application deadline:* Applications are processed on a rolling basis. Application fee: $50 ($60 for international students). Electronic applications accepted. *Expenses:* Tuition, state resident: full-time $9072; part-time $504 per credit hour. Tuition, nonresident: full-time $27,216; part-time $1512 per credit hour. *Required fees:* $812 per semester. Tuition and fees vary according to degree level and program. *Financial support:* Fellowships, teaching assistantships, and Federal Work-Study available. Support available to part-time students. Financial award application deadline: 3/15; financial award applicants required to submit FAFSA. *Faculty research:* English literature, American literature, linguistics, rhetoric and composition, literary theory. *Unit head:* Dr. Jeremy M. Downes, Chair, 334-844-9079. *Application contact:* Dr. George Flowers, Dean of the Graduate School, 334-844-2125.

**Boise State University,** College of Arts and Sciences, Department of English, Boise, ID 83725-1525. Offers creative writing (MFA); English (MA); rhetoric and composition (MA); teaching English language (MA); technical communication (MA). *Program availability:* Part-time. *Faculty:* 26. *Students:* 44 full-time (28 women), 38 part-time (29 women); includes 6 minority (2 American Indian or Alaska Native, non-Hispanic/Latino; 1 Hispanic/Latino; 1 Two or more races, non-Hispanic/Latino), 3 international. Average age 33. 242 applicants, 15% accepted, 28 enrolled. In 2016, 29 master's awarded. *Degree requirements:* For master's, thesis (for some programs). *Entrance requirements:* For master's, GRE General Test, minimum GPA of 3.0. Additional exam requirements/recommendations for international students: Required—TOEFL (minimum score 550 paper-based; 80 iBT), IELTS (minimum score 6). *Application deadline:* For fall admission, 4/15 for domestic and international students; for spring admission, 10/15 for domestic and international students. Application fee: $65 ($95 for international students). Electronic applications accepted. *Expenses:* Tuition, state resident: full-time $6058; part-time $358 per credit hour. Tuition, nonresident: full-time $20,108; part-time $608 per credit hour. *Required fees:* $2108. Tuition and fees vary according to program. *Financial support:* In 2016–17, 10 students received support, including 32 teaching assistantships (averaging $8,109 per year); scholarships/grants and unspecified assistantships also available. Financial award application deadline: 1/15; financial award applicants required to submit FAFSA. *Unit head:* Dr. Michelle Payne, Chair, 208-426-3426, Fax: 208-426-4373, E-mail: mpayne@boisestate.edu. *Application contact:* Dr. Tom Hillard, Director of English, 208-426-2991, E-mail: thomashillard@boisestate.edu.
Website: http://english.boisestate.edu/graduate-programs/

**Bowling Green State University,** Graduate College, College of Arts and Sciences, Department of English, Program in English, Bowling Green, OH 43403. Offers English (MA, PhD); literature (MA); rhetoric and writing (PhD); scientific and technical communication (MA). *Program availability:* Part-time. *Degree requirements:* For master's, thesis or alternative; for doctorate, comprehensive exam, thesis/dissertation, foreign language or proficiency in Old English. *Entrance requirements:* For master's and doctorate, GRE General Test. Additional exam requirements/recommendations for international students: Required—TOEFL. *Application deadline:* For fall admission, 2/15 priority date for domestic students. Applications are processed on a rolling basis. Application fee: $30. Electronic applications accepted. *Financial support:* Fellowships with full tuition reimbursements, research assistantships with full tuition reimbursements, teaching assistantships with full tuition reimbursements, Federal Work-Study, and unspecified assistantships available. Financial award applicants required to submit FAFSA. *Faculty research:* Postmodern literary theory, rhetorical theory, ethnic American literature, literature and culture, composition pedagogy. *Unit head:* Dr. Lawrence Coates, Chair, 419-372-7543, E-mail: coatesl@bgsu.edu. *Application contact:* Dr. Piya Lapinski, Graduate Coordinator, 419-372-6864.

**Drexel University,** College of Arts and Sciences, Department of Communication, Culture and Media, Program in Communication, Philadelphia, PA 19104-2875. Offers public communication (MS); science communication (MS); technical communication (MS). *Program availability:* Part-time, evening/weekend. *Faculty:* 12 full-time (6 women), 14 part-time/adjunct (8 women). *Students:* 12 full-time (6 women), 27 part-time (21 women); includes 5 minority (2 Black or African American, non-Hispanic/Latino; 1 American Indian or Alaska Native, non-Hispanic/Latino; 1 Asian, non-Hispanic/Latino; 1 Native Hawaiian or other Pacific Islander, non-Hispanic/Latino), 4 international. Average age 30. In 2016, 25 master's awarded. *Degree requirements:* For master's, internship, professional portfolio. *Entrance requirements:* For master's, GRE or minimum GPA of 3.0. Additional exam requirements/recommendations for international students: Required—TOEFL. *Application deadline:* For fall admission, 8/21 for domestic students. Applications are processed on a rolling basis. Application fee: $50. Electronic applications accepted. *Expenses:* Tuition: Full-time $32,184; part-time $1192 per credit hour. *Required fees:* $280. Tuition and fees vary according to campus/location and program. *Financial support:* Research assistantships, teaching assistantships, career-related internships or fieldwork, Federal Work-Study, institutionally sponsored loans, tuition waivers (partial), and unspecified assistantships available. Financial award application deadline: 2/1. *Unit head:* Dr. Douglas Porpora, Head, 215-895-2446, Fax: 215-895-1071. *Application contact:* Director of Graduate Admissions, 215-895-6700, Fax: 215-895-5939, E-mail: enroll@drexel.edu.

**East Carolina University,** Graduate School, Thomas Harriot College of Arts and Sciences, Department of English, Greenville, NC 27858-4353. Offers creative writing (MA); English studies (MA); linguistics (MA); literature (MA); multicultural and transnational literatures (MA, Certificate); rhetoric and composition (MA); rhetoric, writing, and professional communication (PhD); teaching English in the two-year college (Certificate); teaching English to speakers of other languages (MA, Certificate); technical and professional communication (MA). *Program availability:* Part-time, evening/weekend. *Students:* 54 full-time (36 women), 95 part-time (77 women); includes 32 minority (19 Black or African American, non-Hispanic/Latino; 3 Asian, non-Hispanic/Latino; 6 Hispanic/Latino; 4 Two or more races, non-Hispanic/Latino), 1 international. Average age 35. 78 applicants, 96% accepted, 50 enrolled. In 2016, 34 master's, 1 doctorate awarded. *Degree requirements:* For master's, one foreign language, comprehensive exam, thesis optional. *Entrance requirements:* For master's, GRE General Test, MAT (for MA Ed). Additional exam requirements/recommendations for international students: Required—TOEFL. *Application deadline:* For fall admission, 6/1 priority date for domestic students; for spring admission, 10/15 for domestic students. Applications are processed on a rolling basis. Application fee: $50. *Financial support:* Research assistantships with partial tuition reimbursements, teaching assistantships with partial tuition reimbursements, and Federal Work-Study available. Support available to part-time students. Financial award application deadline: 6/1. *Unit head:* Dr. Jeffrey Johnson, Chair, 252-328-6041, E-mail: johnsonj@ecu.edu. *Application contact:* Dean of Graduate School, 252-328-6012, Fax: 252-328-6071, E-mail: gradschool@ecu.edu.
Website: http://www.ecu.edu/cs-cas/engl/graduate/

**Eastern Michigan University,** Graduate School, College of Arts and Sciences, Department of English Language and Literature, Programs in Written Communication, Ypsilanti, MI 48197. Offers technical communication (Graduate Certificate); written communication (MA). *Program availability:* Part-time, evening/weekend, online learning. *Students:* 7 full-time (6 women), 14 part-time (10 women); includes 2 minority (both Black or African American, non-Hispanic/Latino). Average age 31. 13 applicants, 85% accepted, 8 enrolled. In 2016, 5 master's, 2 other advanced degrees awarded. *Entrance requirements:* Additional exam requirements/recommendations for international students: Required—TOEFL. *Application deadline:* Applications are processed on a rolling basis. Application fee: $45. *Financial support:* Fellowships, research assistantships with full tuition reimbursements, teaching assistantships with full tuition reimbursements, career-related internships or fieldwork, Federal Work-Study, institutionally sponsored loans, scholarships/grants, tuition waivers (partial), and unspecified assistantships available. Support available to part-time students. Financial award applicants required to submit FAFSA. *Application contact:* Dr. Steve Benninghoff, Program Coordinator, 734-487-2075, Fax: 734-483-9744, E-mail: steve.benninghoff@emich.edu.

**Eastern Washington University,** Graduate Studies, College of Arts, Letters and Education, Department of English, Cheney, WA 99004-2431. Offers literature (MA); rhetoric, composition, and technical communication (MA); teaching English as a second language (MA). *Faculty:* 2 full-time (1 woman), 19 part-time/adjunct (9 women). *Students:* 23 full-time (16 women), 7 part-time (5 women); includes 4 minority (1 Black or African American, non-Hispanic/Latino; 2 Hispanic/Latino; 1 Native Hawaiian or other Pacific Islander, non-Hispanic/Latino), 6 international. Average age 35. 27 applicants, 67% accepted, 13 enrolled. In 2016, 20 master's awarded. *Degree requirements:* For master's, comprehensive exam, thesis or alternative. *Entrance requirements:* For master's, GRE General Test, minimum GPA of 3.0. Additional exam requirements/recommendations for international students: Required—TOEFL (minimum score 580 paper-based; 92 iBT), IELTS (minimum score 7), PTE (minimum score 6). *Application deadline:* For fall admission, 4/1 priority date for domestic students; for spring admission, 1/15 for domestic students. Applications are processed on a rolling basis.

Application fee: $50. *Expenses:* Tuition, state resident: full-time $11,000; part-time $5500 per credit. Tuition, nonresident: full-time $24,000; part-time $12,000 per credit. *Required fees:* $1300. One-time fee: $50 full-time. Part-time tuition and fees vary according to course load, campus/location and program. *Financial support:* In 2016–17, 25 teaching assistantships with partial tuition reimbursements (averaging $7,000 per year) were awarded; career-related internships or fieldwork, Federal Work-Study, institutionally sponsored loans, scholarships/grants, health care benefits, tuition waivers (partial), and unspecified assistantships also available. Support available to part-time students. Financial award application deadline: 2/1; financial award applicants required to submit FAFSA. *Unit head:* Dr. Logan Greene, Chair, 509-359-2400, E-mail: lgreene@ewu.edu. *Application contact:* Kathy White, Advisor/Recruiter for Graduate Studies, 509-359-2491, E-mail: gradprograms@ewu.edu.
Website: http://www.ewu.edu/CALE/Programs/English.xml

**Harvard University,** Harvard Graduate School of Education, Master's Programs in Education, Cambridge, MA 02138. Offers arts in education (Ed M); education policy and management (Ed M); higher education (Ed M); human development and psychology (Ed M); international education policy (Ed M); language and literacy (Ed M); learning and teaching (Ed M); mind, brain, and education (Ed M); prevention science and practice (Ed M); school leadership (Ed M); special studies (Ed M); teacher education (Ed M); technology, innovation, and education (Ed M). *Program availability:* Part-time. *Entrance requirements:* For master's, GRE General Test, statement of purpose, 3 letters of recommendation, resume, official transcripts. Additional exam requirements/recommendations for international students: Required—TOEFL (minimum score 613 paper-based; 104 iBT), TWE (minimum score 5). Electronic applications accepted. *Faculty research:* Learning and development, educational leadership and organizations, education policy analysis.

**Indiana University–Purdue University Indianapolis,** School of Engineering and Technology, MS in Technology Program, Indianapolis, IN 46202. Offers applied data management and analytics (MS); facilities management (MS); information security and assurance (MS); motorsports (MS); organizational leadership (MS); technical communication (MS). *Program availability:* Online learning.

**Lawrence Technological University,** College of Arts and Sciences, Southfield, MI 48075-1058. Offers bioinformatics (Graduate Certificate); computer science (MS); including data science, big data, and data mining, intelligent systems; instructional design, communication, and presentation (Graduate Certificate); instructional technology (Graduate Certificate); premedical studies (Graduate Certificate); technical and professional communication (MS, Graduate Certificate); writing for the digital age (Graduate Certificate). *Program availability:* Part-time, evening/weekend. *Faculty:* 6 full-time (2 women), 10 part-time/adjunct (5 women). *Students:* 37 part-time (18 women); includes 4 minority (1 Black or African American, non-Hispanic/Latino; 1 Asian, non-Hispanic/Latino; 2 Hispanic/Latino), 8 international. Average age 33. 301 applicants, 23% accepted, 9 enrolled. In 2016, 22 master's, 2 other advanced degrees awarded. *Degree requirements:* For master's, thesis (for some programs). *Entrance requirements:* Additional exam requirements/recommendations for international students: Required—TOEFL (minimum score 550 paper-based; 79 iBT), IELTS (minimum score 6.5). *Application deadline:* For fall admission, 5/22 for international students; for spring admission, 10/11 for international students; for summer admission, 2/16 for international students. Applications are processed on a rolling basis. Application fee: $50. Electronic applications accepted. *Expenses:* Tuition: Full-time $14,868; part-time $1062 per credit. *Required fees:* $75 per semester. Tuition and fees vary according to campus/location. *Financial support:* In 2016–17, 9 students received support. Scholarships/grants and tuition reduction available. Financial award application deadline: 4/1; financial award applicants required to submit FAFSA. *Faculty research:* Computer analysis of visual art, psychology of numbers games, neural basis of moral judgement, synthesis of glycosylated warfarin analogs for potential use as antiviral drugs, observation of chemotaxis behavior in c. elegans. *Total annual research expenditures:* $530,625. *Unit head:* Dr. Hsiao-Ping Moore, Dean, 248-204-3500, Fax: 248-204-3518, E-mail: scidean@itu.edu. *Application contact:* Jane Rohrback, Director of Admissions, 248-204-3160, Fax: 248-204-2228, E-mail: admissions@ltu.edu.

**Minnesota State University Mankato,** College of Graduate Studies and Research, College of Arts and Humanities, Department of English, Mankato, MN 56001. Offers communication and composition (MA); creative writing (MFA); English studies (MA); teaching English as a second language (MA, Certificate); technical communication (MA, Certificate). *Program availability:* Part-time. *Students:* 59 full-time (44 women), 106 part-time (67 women). *Degree requirements:* For master's, one foreign language, comprehensive exam, thesis or alternative. *Entrance requirements:* For master's, minimum GPA of 3.0 during previous 2 years, writing sample (MFA). Additional exam requirements/recommendations for international students: Required—TOEFL (minimum score 500 paper-based; 61 iBT). *Application deadline:* For fall admission, 7/1 for domestic students, 5/1 for international students. Applications are processed on a rolling basis. Application fee: $40. Electronic applications accepted. *Financial support:* Research assistantships with full tuition reimbursements, teaching assistantships with full tuition reimbursements, career-related internships or fieldwork, Federal Work-Study, and unspecified assistantships available. Financial award application deadline: 3/15; financial award applicants required to submit FAFSA. *Unit head:* Matthew Sewell, Chair, 507-389-2117, E-mail: matthew.sewell@mnsu.edu.
Website: http://english.mnsu.edu/

**Missouri Western State University,** Program in Written Communication, St. Joseph, MO 64507-2294. Offers teaching of writing (Graduate Certificate); technical communication (MAA); writing studies (MAA). *Program availability:* Part-time. *Students:* 1 full-time (0 women), 8 part-time (7 women). Average age 33. In 2016, 7 master's, 1 other advanced degree awarded. *Entrance requirements:* For master's, minimum undergraduate GPA of 3.0, portfolio, 3 letters of reference. Additional exam requirements/recommendations for international students: Recommended—TOEFL (minimum score 79 iBT), IELTS (minimum score 6). *Application deadline:* For fall admission, 7/15 for domestic and international students; for spring admission, 10/1 for domestic and international students; for summer admission, 3/15 for domestic students. Applications are processed on a rolling basis. Application fee: $50. Electronic applications accepted. *Expenses:* Tuition, state resident: full-time $6548; part-time $327.39 per credit hour. Tuition, nonresident: full-time $11,848; part-time $592.39 per credit hour. *Required fees:* $542; $99 per credit hour. $176 per semester. One-time fee: $50. Tuition and fees vary according to course load and program. *Financial support:* Scholarships/grants and unspecified assistantships available. Support available to part-time students. *Unit head:* Dr. Cynthia Jeney, Associate Professor/Interim Director of Graduate Studies, 816-271-4447, E-mail: jeney@missouriwestern.edu. *Application contact:* Dr. Benjamin D. Caldwell, Dean of the Graduate School, 816-271-4394, Fax: 816-271-4525, E-mail: graduate@missouriwestern.edu.
Website: https://www.missouriwestern.edu/eml/maawc/

**Montana Tech of The University of Montana,** Department of Technical Communication, Butte, MT 59701-8997. Offers MS. *Program availability:* Part-time. *Faculty:* 8 full-time (4 women), 2 part-time/adjunct (1 woman). *Students:* 2 full-time (1 woman), 6 part-time (3 women); includes 1 minority (Asian, non-Hispanic/Latino). Average age 26. 4 applicants, 100% accepted, 3 enrolled. In 2016, 4 master's awarded.

*Degree requirements:* For master's, project or thesis. *Entrance requirements:* For master's, GRE General Test, minimum GPA of 3.0. Additional exam requirements/recommendations for international students: Required—TOEFL (minimum score 545 paper-based; 78 iBT), IELTS (minimum score 6.5). *Application deadline:* For fall admission, 4/1 priority date for domestic students, 3/1 priority date for international students; for spring admission, 10/1 priority date for domestic students, 6/1 priority date for international students. Applications are processed on a rolling basis. Application fee: $50. Electronic applications accepted. *Expenses:* Tuition, state resident: full-time $2901; part-time $1450.68 per degree program. Tuition, nonresident: full-time $8432; part-time $4215.84 per degree program. *Required fees:* $668; $354 per degree program. Tuition and fees vary according to course load and program. *Financial support:* In 2016–17, 6 students received support, including 5 teaching assistantships with partial tuition reimbursements available (averaging $4,000 per year); research assistantships with partial tuition reimbursements available, career-related internships or fieldwork, tuition waivers (partial), and unspecified assistantships also available. Financial award application deadline: 4/1; financial award applicants required to submit FAFSA. *Faculty research:* Environmental concerns and the Big Hole River, history of Butte mining, African studies, multicultural communications. *Unit head:* Dr. Nicholas Hawthorne, Head, 406-496-4224, Fax: 406-496-4510, E-mail: nhawthorne@mtech.edu. *Application contact:* Daniel Stirling, Administrator, Graduate School, 406-496-4304, Fax: 406-496-4710, E-mail: gradschool@mtech.edu.
Website: http://www.mtech.edu/academics/gradschool/degreeprograms/degrees-technical-communications.htm

**New Jersey Institute of Technology,** College of Science and Liberal Arts, Newark, NJ 07102. Offers applied mathematics (MS); applied physics (M Sc, PhD); applied statistics (MS, Certificate); biology (MS, PhD); biostatistics (MS); chemistry (MS, PhD); computational biology (MS); environmental and sustainability policy (MS); environmental science (MS, PhD); history (MA, MAT); materials science and engineering (MS, PhD); mathematical and computational finance (MS); mathematics science (PhD); pharmaceutical chemistry (MS); practice of technical communications (Certificate); professional and technical communications (MS). *Program availability:* Part-time, evening/weekend. *Faculty:* 166 full-time (39 women), 87 part-time/adjunct (32 women). *Students:* 196 full-time (71 women), 68 part-time (33 women); includes 55 minority (15 Black or African American, non-Hispanic/Latino; 19 Asian, non-Hispanic/Latino; 15 Hispanic/Latino; 6 Two or more races, non-Hispanic/Latino), 140 international. Average age 28. 504 applicants, 64% accepted, 65 enrolled. In 2016, 81 master's, 18 doctorates, 1 other advanced degree awarded. Terminal master's awarded for partial completion of doctoral program. *Degree requirements:* For master's, thesis optional; for doctorate, thesis/dissertation. *Entrance requirements:* For master's, GRE General Test; for doctorate, GRE General Test, minimum graduate GPA of 3.5. Additional exam requirements/recommendations for international students: Required—TOEFL (minimum score 550 paper-based; 79 iBT). *Application deadline:* For fall admission, 6/1 priority date for domestic students, 5/1 priority date for international students; for spring admission, 11/15 priority date for domestic and international students. Applications are processed on a rolling basis. Application fee: $75. Electronic applications accepted. *Expenses:* Contact institution. *Financial support:* In 2016–17, 106 students received support, including 32 research assistantships (averaging $17,108 per year), 74 teaching assistantships (averaging $21,368 per year); fellowships, scholarships/grants, traineeships, and unspecified assistantships also available. Financial award application deadline: 1/15. *Faculty research:* Biophotonics and bioimaging, morphogenetic patterning, embryogenesis, biological fluid dynamics, applied research in the mathematical sciences. *Unit head:* Dr. Kevin Belfield, Dean, 973-596-3676, Fax: 973-565-0586, E-mail: kevin.d.belfield@njit.edu. *Application contact:* Stephen Eck, Director of Admissions, 973-596-3300, Fax: 973-596-3461, E-mail: admissions@njit.edu.
Website: http://csla.njit.edu/

**North Carolina State University,** Graduate School, College of Humanities and Social Sciences, Department of English, Program in Technical Communication, Raleigh, NC 27695. Offers MS. *Degree requirements:* For master's, thesis optional. *Entrance requirements:* For master's, GRE General Test. Electronic applications accepted. *Faculty research:* Workplace writing, organizational socialization and power, integrated and multimedia documentation systems, technical communication management, usability testing theories.

**Northeastern University,** College of Professional Studies, Boston, MA 02115-5096. Offers applied nutrition (MS); college athletics administration (MSL); commerce and economic development (MS); corporate and organizational communication (MS); criminal justice (MS); digital media (MPS); elearning and instructional design (M Ed); elementary education (MAT); geographic information technology (MPS); global studies and international relations (MS); higher education administration (M Ed); homeland security (MA); human services (MS); informatics (MPS); leadership (MS); learning analytics (M Ed); learning and instruction (M Ed); nonprofit management (MS); professional sports administration (MSL); project management (MS); regulatory affairs for drugs, biologics, and medical devices (MS); respiratory care leadership (MS); special education (M Ed); technical communication (MS). *Program availability:* Part-time, evening/weekend, 100% online, blended/hybrid learning. *Faculty:* 82 full-time (51 women), 853 part-time/adjunct (366 women). *Students:* 4,947 part-time (3,076 women). In 2016, 1,456 master's awarded. *Application deadline:* Applications are processed on a rolling basis. Application fee: $0. Electronic applications accepted. *Expenses:* Contact institution. *Financial support:* Applicants required to submit FAFSA. *Unit head:* Dr. Mary Loeffelholz, Interim Dean of the College of Professional Studies.
Website: http://www.cps.neu.edu/

**Texas State University,** The Graduate College, College of Liberal Arts, Program in Technical Communication, San Marcos, TX 78666. Offers MA. *Program availability:* Part-time. *Faculty:* 6 full-time (4 women), 1 part-time/adjunct (0 women). *Students:* 13 full-time (11 women), 17 part-time (9 women); includes 8 minority (2 Black or African American, non-Hispanic/Latino; 6 Hispanic/Latino), 1 international. Average age 31. 14 applicants, 71% accepted, 8 enrolled. In 2016, 14 master's awarded. *Degree requirements:* For master's, comprehensive exam, thesis optional. *Entrance requirements:* For master's, baccalaureate degree from regionally-accredited institution with minimum GPA of 2.75 on last 60 undergraduate semester hours, 3.0 in minimum of 12 hours of undergraduate English courses; portfolio. Additional exam requirements/recommendations for international students: Required—TOEFL (minimum score 550 paper-based; 78 iBT), IELTS (minimum score 6.5). *Application deadline:* For fall admission, 1/15 priority date for domestic and international students; for spring admission, 11/1 for domestic students, 10/1 for international students; for summer admission, 4/15 for domestic students, 3/15 for international students. Applications are processed on a rolling basis. Application fee: $40 ($90 for international students). Electronic applications accepted. *Expenses:* $4,851 per semester. *Financial support:* In 2016–17, 13 students received support, including 2 research assistantships (averaging $14,877 per year), 2 teaching assistantships (averaging $16,213 per year); Federal Work-Study, institutionally sponsored loans, and scholarships/grants also available. Support available to part-time students. Financial award application deadline: 3/1; financial award applicants required to submit FAFSA. *Unit head:* Dr. Miriam Williams, Graduate Advisor, 512-245-3015, Fax: 512-245-8546, E-mail: mw32@txstate.edu. *Application contact:* Dr. Andrea Golato, Dean of Graduate School, 512-245-2581, Fax:

*Technical Communication*

512-245-8365, E-mail: gradcollege@txstate.edu.
Website: http://matc.english.txstate.edu/

**University of Houston–Downtown,** College of Humanities and Social Sciences, Department of English, Program in Technical Communication, Houston, TX 77002. Offers MS. *Program availability:* Part-time, evening/weekend. *Faculty:* 4 full-time (2 women). *Students:* 5 full-time (3 women), 25 part-time (17 women); includes 18 minority (11 Black or African American, non-Hispanic/Latino; 1 American Indian or Alaska Native, non-Hispanic/Latino; 1 Asian, non-Hispanic/Latino; 5 Hispanic/Latino). Average age 36. 16 applicants, 81% accepted, 13 enrolled. In 2016, 6 master's awarded. *Entrance requirements:* For master's, GRE (for students with lower than 3.0 GPA), essay, resume, 2 letters of recommendation, transcripts. Additional exam requirements/recommendations for international students: Required—TOEFL (minimum score 600 paper-based; 86 iBT). *Application deadline:* For fall admission, 7/15 for domestic and international students; for spring admission, 11/15 for domestic and international students. Application fee: $35 ($60 for international students). Electronic applications accepted. *Expenses:* $305.50 in-state, per credit; $663.50 out-of-state, per credit. *Financial support:* Federal Work-Study and scholarships/grants available. Financial award application deadline: 4/1; financial award applicants required to submit FAFSA. *Faculty research:* Environmental rhetoric, instructional design, usability, assessment, presentation slides. *Unit head:* Dr. Michelle Moosally, Chair, 713-221-8254, Fax: 713-226-5205, E-mail: moosallym@uhd.edu. *Application contact:* Ceshia Love, Director of Graduate and International Admissions, 713-221-8093, Fax: 713-223-7408, E-mail: gradadmissions@uhd.edu.
Website: https://www.uhd.edu/academics/humanities/graduate-programs/master-science-technical-communication/Pages/mstc-index.aspx

**University of Nebraska at Omaha,** Graduate Studies, College of Arts and Sciences, Department of English, Omaha, NE 68182. Offers advanced writing (Certificate); English (MA); teaching English to speakers of other languages (Certificate); technical communication (Certificate). *Program availability:* Part-time, evening/weekend. *Faculty:* 10 full-time (6 women). *Students:* 9 full-time (7 women), 43 part-time (24 women); includes 1 minority (Two or more races, non-Hispanic/Latino), 3 international. Average age 32. 39 applicants, 46% accepted, 14 enrolled. In 2016, 21 master's, 12 other advanced degrees awarded. *Degree requirements:* For master's, comprehensive exam, thesis (for some programs). *Entrance requirements:* For master's, GRE or MAT, minimum GPA of 3.0, transcripts, 3 letters of recommendation, statement of purpose, writing sample; for Certificate, minimum GPA of 3.0, transcripts, statement of purpose. Additional exam requirements/recommendations for international students: Required—TOEFL, IELTS, PTE. *Application deadline:* Applications are processed on a rolling basis. Application fee: $45. Electronic applications accepted. *Financial support:* In 2016–17, 15 students received support, including 15 teaching assistantships with tuition reimbursements available; fellowships, research assistantships, Federal Work-Study, institutionally sponsored loans, scholarships/grants, health care benefits, tuition waivers (partial), and unspecified assistantships also available. Support available to part-time students. Financial award application deadline: 3/1; financial award applicants required to submit FAFSA. *Unit head:* Dr. Tracy Bridgeford, Chairperson, 402-554-2341, E-mail: graduate@unomaha.edu. *Application contact:* Dr. Ramon Guerra, Graduate Program Chair, 402-554-2341, E-mail: graduate@unomaha.edu.

**University of Nebraska at Omaha,** Graduate Studies, College of Communication, Fine Arts and Media, School of Communication, Omaha, NE 68182. Offers communication (MA); human resources and training (Certificate); technical communication (Certificate). *Program availability:* Part-time, evening/weekend. *Faculty:* 7 full-time (4 women). *Students:* 6 full-time (4 women), 33 part-time (20 women); includes 9 minority (2 Black or African American, non-Hispanic/Latino; 2 Asian, non-Hispanic/Latino; 2 Hispanic/Latino; 3 Two or more races, non-Hispanic/Latino), 2 international. Average age 31. 14 applicants, 57% accepted, 6 enrolled. In 2016, 11 master's, 5 other advanced degrees awarded. *Degree requirements:* For master's, comprehensive exam, thesis (for some programs). *Entrance requirements:* For master's, minimum GPA of 3.0, 15 undergraduate communication courses, resume, statement of purpose, 3 letters of recommendation. Additional exam requirements/recommendations for international students: Required—TOEFL, IELTS, PTE. *Application deadline:* For fall admission, 3/1 priority date for domestic and international students; for spring admission, 10/1 priority date for domestic and international students. Applications are processed on a rolling basis. Application fee: $45. Electronic applications accepted. *Financial support:* In 2016–17, 13 students received support, including 13 teaching assistantships with tuition reimbursements available; fellowships, research assistantships with tuition reimbursements available, Federal Work-Study, institutionally sponsored loans, scholarships/grants, health care benefits, tuition waivers (partial), and unspecified assistantships also available. Support available to part-time students. Financial award application deadline: 3/1; financial award applicants required to submit FAFSA. *Unit head:* Dr. Hugh Reilly, Director, 402-554-2341, E-mail: graduate@unomaha.edu. *Application contact:* Dr. Adam Tyma, Graduate Program Chair, 402-554-2341, E-mail: graduate@unomaha.edu.

**University of South Florida,** Innovative Education, Tampa, FL 33620-9951. Offers adult, career and higher education (Graduate Certificate), including college teaching, leadership in developing human resources, leadership in higher education; Africana studies (Graduate Certificate), including diasporas and health disparities, genocide and human rights; aging studies (Graduate Certificate), including gerontology; art research (Graduate Certificate), including museum studies; business foundations (Graduate Certificate); chemical and biomedical engineering (Graduate Certificate), including materials science and engineering, water, health and sustainability; child and family studies (Graduate Certificate), including positive behavior support; civil and industrial engineering (Graduate Certificate), including transportation systems analysis; community and family health (Graduate Certificate), including maternal and child health, social marketing and public health, violence and injury: prevention and intervention, women's health; criminology (Graduate Certificate), including criminal justice administration; educational measurement and research (Graduate Certificate), including evaluation; English (Graduate Certificate), including comparative literary studies, creative writing, professional and technical communication; entrepreneurship (Graduate Certificate); environmental health (Graduate Certificate), including safety management; epidemiology and biostatistics (Graduate Certificate), including applied biostatistics, biostatistics, concepts and tools of epidemiology, epidemiology, epidemiology of infectious diseases; geography, environment and planning (Graduate Certificate), including community development, environmental policy and management, geographical information systems; geology (Graduate Certificate), including hydrogeology; global health (Graduate Certificate), including disaster management, global health and Latin American and Caribbean studies, global health practice, humanitarian assistance, infection control; government and international affairs (Graduate Certificate), including Cuban studies, globalization studies; health policy and management (Graduate Certificate), including health management and leadership, public health policy and programs; hearing specialist: early intervention (Graduate Certificate); industrial and management systems engineering (Graduate Certificate), including systems engineering, technology management; information studies (Graduate Certificate), including school library media specialist; information systems/decision sciences (Graduate Certificate), including analytics and business intelligence; instructional technology (Graduate Certificate), including distance education, Florida digital/virtual educator, instructional design, multimedia design, Web design; internal medicine, bioethics and medical humanities (Graduate Certificate), including biomedical ethics; Latin American and Caribbean studies (Graduate Certificate); mass communications (Graduate Certificate), including multimedia journalism; mathematics and statistics (Graduate Certificate), including mathematics; medicine (Graduate Certificate), including aging and neuroscience, bioinformatics, biotechnology, brain fitness and memory management, clinical investigation, health informatics, health sciences, integrative weight management, intellectual property, medicine and gender, metabolic and nutritional medicine, metabolic cardiology, pharmacy sciences; national and competitive intelligence (Graduate Certificate); psychological and social foundations (Graduate Certificate), including career counseling, college teaching, diversity in education, mental health counseling, school counseling; public affairs (Graduate Certificate), including nonprofit management, public management, research administration; public health (Graduate Certificate), including environmental health, health equity, public health generalist, translational research in adolescent behavioral health; public health practices (Graduate Certificate), including planning for healthy communities; rehabilitation and mental health counseling (Graduate Certificate), including integrative mental health care, marriage and family therapy, rehabilitation technology; secondary education (Graduate Certificate), including ESOL, foreign language education: culture and content, foreign language education: professional; social work (Graduate Certificate), including geriatric social work/clinical gerontology; special education (Graduate Certificate), including autism spectrum disorder, disabilities education: severe/profound; world languages (Graduate Certificate), including teaching English as a second language (TESL) or foreign language. *Expenses:* Tuition, state resident: full-time $7766; part-time $431.43 per credit hour. Tuition, nonresident: full-time $15,789; part-time $877.17 per credit hour. *Required fees:* $37 per term. *Unit head:* Kathy Barnes, Interdisciplinary Programs Coordinator, 813-974-8031, Fax: 813-974-7061, E-mail: barnesk@usf.edu. *Application contact:* Karen Tylinski, Metro Initiatives, 813-974-9943, Fax: 813-974-7061, E-mail: ktylinsk@usf.edu.
Website: http://www.usf.edu/innovative-education/

**University of Washington,** Graduate School, College of Engineering, Department of Human Centered Design and Engineering, Seattle, WA 98195-2315. Offers human centered design and engineering (MS, PhD); user centered design (Certificate). *Program availability:* Part-time, evening/weekend. *Faculty:* 9 full-time (3 women). *Students:* 99 full-time (56 women), 118 part-time (68 women); includes 59 minority (7 Black or African American, non-Hispanic/Latino; 35 Asian, non-Hispanic/Latino; 9 Hispanic/Latino; 8 Two or more races, non-Hispanic/Latino), 49 international. 571 applicants, 24% accepted, 94 enrolled. In 2016, 64 master's, 3 doctorates awarded. Terminal master's awarded for partial completion of doctoral program. *Degree requirements:* For master's, thesis or alternative; for doctorate, comprehensive exam, thesis/dissertation, preliminary, general, and final exams. *Entrance requirements:* For master's, minimum GPA of 3.0, transcripts, 3 letters of recommendation, curriculum vitae, personal statement of objectives; for doctorate, GRE General Test, minimum GPA of 3.0, transcripts, 3 letters of recommendation, curriculum vitae, personal statement of objectives. Additional exam requirements/recommendations for international students: Required—TOEFL (minimum score 580 paper-based; 106 iBT), Recommended—IELTS (minimum score 7). *Application deadline:* For fall admission, 1/15 for domestic and international students. Application fee: $85. Electronic applications accepted. *Expenses:* Contact institution. *Financial support:* In 2016–17, 51 students received support, including 2 fellowships with full tuition reimbursements available (averaging $1,512 per year), 30 research assistantships with full tuition reimbursements available (averaging $2,670 per year), 19 teaching assistantships with full tuition reimbursements available (averaging $2,486 per year); career-related internships or fieldwork, institutionally sponsored loans, and tuition waivers (full) also available. Financial award application deadline: 2/28; financial award applicants required to submit FAFSA. *Faculty research:* Usability testing; rhetorical and empirical exploration of basic communication phenomena; computer documentation; technology assessment; educational assessment; Web, multimedia and user interface design. *Total annual research expenditures:* $4.9 million. *Unit head:* Dr. David McDonald, Professor/Chair, 206-685-2945, Fax: 206-543-8858, E-mail: hcdechr@uw.edu. *Application contact:* Pat Reilly, Academic Services Manager, 206-543-1798, Fax: 206-543-8858, E-mail: preilly@uw.edu. Website: http://www.hcde.washington.edu/

**University of Wisconsin–Stout,** Graduate School, College of Arts, Humanities and Social Sciences, Menomonie, WI 54751. Offers design (MFA); technical and professional communication (MS). *Accreditation:* NASAD.

# NORTH DAKOTA STATE UNIVERSITY
## College of Arts, Humanities and Social Sciences

 For more information, visit http://petersons.to/ndstateartshumanities

## Programs of Study

The College of Arts, Humanities and Social Sciences at North Dakota State University equips students with the skills and knowledge to thrive in their professional and personal lives, including the following:

- Ability to think critically
- Ability to effectively communicate in all media
- Understanding the diverse ideas that constitute the intellectual marketplace
- Recognition of the significance of all traditions in creating cultures throughout the world

The college offers several graduate programs through eight of its twelve departments: Architecture and Landscape Architecture; Communication; Criminal Justice and Political Science; Emergency Management; English; History, Philosophy, and Religious Studies; Music; and Sociology and Anthropology.

**Department of Architecture and Landscape Architecture:** The Department of Architecture and Landscape Architecture focuses on the challenges related to designing landscapes and built environments. It offers a nationally accredited Master of Architecture (M.Arch.) program for individuals interested in pursuing advanced careers in the field.

**Department of Communication:** The Department of Communication provides students with the expertise to build rewarding careers in a wide variety of professions. Its graduate programs include the Master of Arts (M.A.) and Master of Science (M.S.) in Mass Communication and in Speech Communication, and the Doctor of Philosophy (Ph.D.) in Communication.

**Department of Criminal Justice and Political Science:** The Department of Criminal Justice and Political Science prepares students for positions that protect and serve people and communities, create and strengthen political and social systems, and enhance quality of life. It offers both M.S. and Ph.D. degrees in Criminal Justice.

**Department of Emergency Management:** The Department of Emergency Management trains students to protect people and communities, and it facilitates research that strengthens theory and practice in the field. It has two graduate programs: the M.S. in Emergency Management and Ph.D. in Emergency Management.

**Department of English:** The Department of English cultivates students' appreciation, knowledge, and understanding of the English language. It offers the following graduate programs: the M.A. in English Composition; M.A. in English Literature; and Ph.D. in English: Rhetoric, Writing, and Culture.

**Department of History, Philosophy, and Religious Studies:** The Department of History, Philosophy, and Religious Studies encourages active learning and provides diverse learning opportunities. It provides the M.A. in History and Ph.D. in History programs.

**Challey School of Music:** The Challey School of Music prepares students for excellence in musical performance and scholarship. It provides a Master of Music program with options in performance, conducting, and music education, as well as a Doctor of Musical Arts program with options in performance and conducting.

**Department of Sociology and Anthropology:** The Department of Sociology and Anthropology provides comprehensive study of human behavior in social settings. It has six graduate programs: the M.A. in Anthropology, M.S. in Anthropology, M.S. in Natural Resources Management (social science option), Ph.D. in Natural Resources Management (social science option), M.S. in Sociology, and an online master's in Community Development.

## Research

Faculty members and students actively engage in research regarding a wide range of subjects. Faculty members are awarded millions of dollars in research grants and contracts annually, and their work is published in more than 100 peer-reviewed publications each year.

Students assist faculty members with their research and conduct individual research that contributes to the body of knowledge in their fields.

## Financial Aid

Graduate students in the College of Arts, Humanities and Social Sciences may receive financial aid from employer tuition reimbursement programs, fellowships, graduate assistantships (teaching or research), loans (through federal programs or private lenders), military and veteran assistance, and scholarships from the university and private funders.

## Cost of Study

The most current information on tuition and fees can be found online at https://www.ndsu.edu/onestop/accounts/tuition/.

## Living and Housing Costs

Information about on-campus housing for graduate students can be found at www.ndsu.edu/reslife/general_apartment_information. While there is no specific residence hall for graduate students, they are able to live in the University apartments. There are also numerous housing options in the Fargo community.

## Faculty

Faculty members, like Stephenson J. Beck, Ph.D., are talented teachers and scholars. Dr. Beck is an associate professor and the director of graduate studies in the Department of Communication. His research focuses on relational communication in groups, communication strategy, and macro-cognition. His goal is to understand how people alter messages to achieve individual and group goals and to examine how this process influences group processes and message perception.

Dr. Beck has authored and co-authored many articles and books about his research. He has also presented his work at several conferences, colloquia, and symposia. In addition, he has served on editorial boards of journals, participated in policy and planning and other committees, and operated a consulting practice.

## Student Life

North Dakota State University provides students with the resources and opportunities to create vibrant and fulfilling college careers. They receive academic, career, support, and wellness services from the Career Center, Graduate Center for Writers, Office of International Student and Study Abroad Services, Office of Multicultural Programs, the Wallman Wellness Center, and others.

Social resources include arts and culture, community outreach, intramural sports, recreational programs, and student organizations.

## North Dakota State University

### Location

North Dakota State University is located on the eastern edge of North Dakota in Fargo, the state's largest community. With its sister city, Moorhead, Minnesota, directly across the Red River, Fargo is one of the largest metropolitan centers between Minneapolis and Seattle and offers a family-friendly environment with excellent schools, safe neighborhoods, and a low crime rate; an active arts and cultural scene, including a symphony, civic opera company, art museums, and community theater; and many places to shop and eat, including numerous restaurants, coffee shops, and a newly refurbished downtown district.

### The University

In 1890, North Dakota State University became North Dakota's first land-grant university. Today, this esteemed research institution offers more than 14,400 students nearly 100 undergraduate majors, 86 master's programs, and 53 doctoral programs.

It is recognized nationally and internationally for providing high quality education, excellent service, and innovative research. In fact, the National Science Foundation determined that several of its programs rank within the top 100.

### Applying

In The North Dakota State University graduate school application procedure places responsibility on the applicant to gather all supporting credentials and verifying that the application file is complete. The deadline for submission is dependent upon the program. If no deadline is listed on the program's bulletin page, all application materials are due at least one month prior the start of the semester.

Prospective students must file their application online. There is a $35 nonrefundable application fee. A statement of purpose—covering reasons for pursing graduate study, special interests within the chosen discipline, and preparation, skills, and experience in the proposed field of study—is required for admission consideration and must be uploaded with the online application. Other requirements include three letters of recommendation; official transcripts from each college or university attended; and official GRE or GMAT scores if required. Some programs may have additional requirements, as stated on the individual program pages.

The online application and additional details regarding the application process are available at https://www.ndsu.edu/gradschool/prospective_students.

### Correspondence and Information

College of Arts, Humanities and Social Sciences
Graduate School
North Dakota State University
Department 2820, P.O. Box 6050
Fargo, North Dakota 58108-6050
Phone: 701-231-7033
      800-608-6378 (toll-free)
E-mail: ndsu.grad.school@ndsu.edu
Website: www.ndsu.edu/gradschool
     facebook.com/ndsugradschool (Facebook)
     @NDSUGradSchool (Twitter)

The College of Arts, Humanities and Social Sciences is at the center of the Liberal and Fine Arts on the campus of NDSU. The departments in this college offer high-quality graduate degree programs in the humanities, social sciences, and the fine arts.

# PRATT INSTITUTE
*School of Liberal Arts*

 For more information, visit http://petersons.to/prattmediastudies

## Programs of Study

Pratt has been educating professionals for productive careers since its founding in 1887. Pratt's School of Liberal Arts offers an outstanding professional art and design education taught by a faculty of working professionals who bring high standards and current practices to the classroom. Faculty members have received more than eighteen Tiffany, Fulbright, and Guggenheim awards as well as other prestigious professional honors.

Pratt offers master's degrees in a variety of programs, including Master of Arts in Media Studies; Master of Fine Arts in Performance and Performance Studies; Master of Fine Arts in Writing, and Master of Art in History of Art and Design. Pratt also offers a dual degree in Art History and Library Science and a dual degree in Art History and Fine Art.

Graduates of Pratt's liberal arts programs have the competitive edge needed to obtain top administrative and creative positions in design studios, businesses, various industries, and arts organizations; Students can choose from a wide array of course offerings, including art and design history, comparative literature, philosophy, foreign languages, and social sciences. The graduate programs require the completion of 30 to 68 credits (75 credits for the M.S./M.F.A. dual-degree program) and last from 1-1/2 to 3 years, depending on the curriculum and the number of prerequisites that have been met at the time of admission. For the granting of degrees, all of the graduate programs require the submission of a thesis or a comparable effort.

Media Studies at Pratt is an intensive 30-credit, three-semester theory and practice M.A., shaped in relation to Pratt's art/design/architecture environment and to the lively social space and theoretical scene of Brooklyn and New York City. Classes in media theory and media practice are small, following seminar and workshop formats, and all are taught by professors on Pratt Institute's Brooklyn campus.

The graduate degree offers students the freedom and flexibility to design their own program of study. The M.A. in Media Studies at Pratt is designed to train students to think and make critically, whether their final destination is a Ph.D. program or a professional career in the arts, media, or communication.

The curriculum emphasizes studies of media in their various forms, including film, video, television, radio, writing, smart phones, and other computerized forms of media convergence. Alongside their theoretical investigations, students are also encouraged to become media makers. Guided by a diverse and exceptional faculty, students study the logics and processes of media, and they explore cultural technologies of expression, representation, and manipulation. Students learn to analyze a variety of media forms (cinema, photography, audio-phonic, and social media), along with the aesthetic, social, economic and political contexts in which these media operate. They also work also work on textual analysis, interpretation, and semiotics and gain expertise in media history and theory.

## Research Facilities

The Pratt Library contains 186,589 bound volumes, serial backfiles, and other material (including government documents); 251,603 audiovisual materials; and 3,996 microforms. The library also subscribes to 925 periodicals.

Pratt maintains numerous studios, shops, and technical facilities for work in all media as well as state-of-the-art computer facilities. Digital arts labs include state-of-the-art Macintosh, PC/NT, and UNIX operating systems as well as digital video and audio systems. Pratt also has extensive gallery space for exhibitions.

## Financial Aid

Financial aid awards are offered through a variety of institutional, state, and federally funded programs. These include Graduate Scholarships awarded by departments to incoming students on the basis of merit, endowed and restricted scholarships for continuing students, and student employment. Assistantships are awarded on a competitive basis to continuing students in all departments. Special alumni-sponsored fellowships are also available.

## Cost of Study

Graduate tuition for 2017–18 is $30,834 per year (full-time, 18 credits, $1,713 per credit) and student fees are $1,974 per year. The cost of books and supplies varies widely, depending on the program in which the student is enrolled.

## Living and Housing Costs

Campus housing continues to be expanded to meet students' needs and is available for single students on a first-come, first-served basis. Housing costs average $18,880 per academic year. Pratt offers limited graduate student housing two blocks away from the campus. There is a plentiful supply of moderately priced rentals in the immediate area and in adjacent neighborhoods for married students seeking housing and for those students choosing to reside off campus.

## Student Group

In educating more than four generations of students to be creative, technically skilled, and adaptable professionals, Pratt has gained an international reputation that attracts about 4,600 undergraduate and graduate students annually from forty-eight states and eighty-one countries.

## Location

Pratt Institute's 25-acre, parklike main campus is situated among the turn-of-the-century mansions, Victorian brownstones, and wide, tree-lined boulevards of Clinton Hill, one of Brooklyn's historic neighborhoods. Midtown Manhattan, the heart of New York City, is only 25 minutes away by subway and offers students a vast array of professional, cultural, and recreational opportunities. Pratt also maintains a satellite facility in Manhattan's Chelsea district. Pratt Manhattan houses the Institute's graduate arts and cultural management, communications/packaging design, design management, facilities management, and library and information science; it also offers Associate of Occupational Studies (A.O.S.) and Associate of Applied Science (A.A.S.) degree programs.

## The Institute

A private, nonsectarian institute of higher education, Pratt Institute was founded by industrialist and philanthropist Charles Pratt. Changing with the needs and requirements of the professional world for which it prepares its graduates, Pratt today educates 3,310 undergraduate and 1,349 graduate students for careers in art and design, architecture, and library and information science.

## Applying

The deadline for applications and all supporting materials, including portfolio, is January 5. Applicants should complete the application process online. Early submission of applications with all necessary credentials is highly desirable. Applications received after these dates are considered if openings exist in a particular program. For applicants who intend to file for financial aid, the FAFSA should be filed by March 1 for fall entrance and by October 1 for spring entrance.

## Correspondence and Information

Graduate Admissions Office
Pratt Institute
200 Willoughby Avenue
Brooklyn, New York 11205
United States
Phone: 718-636-3514
    800-331-0834 (toll-free)
Fax: 718-399-4242
E-mail: admissions@pratt.edu
Websites: www.pratt.edu
    www.pratt.edu/admissions/request-information

## THE FACULTY

**Andrew Barnes, Dean of the School of Liberal Arts and Sciences**
Gloriana Russell, Assistant to the Dean

**HISTORY OF ART AND DESIGN**
**John Decker, Chair; Ph.D., UC Santa Barbara.**
**Evan Neely, Acting Assistant Chair, Adjunct Assistant Professor; Ph.D., Columbia.**
Sonya Abrego, Visiting Assistant Instructor; Ph.D., Bard.
Kira Albinsky, Visiting Instructor; M.A., Rutgers.
Kelly Rae Aldridge, Visiting Instructor; M.A., Stony Brook, SUNY.
Karen Bachmann, Visiting Assistant Professor; M.A., SUNY Purchase.
Lisa Banner, Visiting Associate Professor; Ph.D., NYU.
Agnes Berecz, Visiting Assistant Professor; Ph.D., Universite Paris I.
Sam Bryan, Adjunct Associate Professor; D.A., Carnegie Mellon.
Liam Considine, Visiting Assistant Professor; Ph.D., NYU.
Corey D'Augustine, Visiting Assistant Professor; M.A., NYU.
Edward DeCarbo, Adjunct Associate Professor; Ph.D., Indiana.
Eva Diaz, Associate Professor; Ph.D., Princeton.
Dorothea Dietrich, Professor; Ph.D., Yale.
Mary Douglas Edwards, Adjunct Professor; Ph.D., Columbia.
Charles Eppley, Visiting Instructor; M.A., Stony Brook, SUNY.
Diana Gisolfi, Professor; Ph.D., Chicago.
Dimitri Hazzikostas, Assistant Professor; Ph.D., Columbia.
Frima Fox Hofrichter, Professor; Ph.D., Rutgers.
Heather Horton, Visiting Assistant Professor; Ph.D., NYU.

### Pratt Institute

Susan Karnet, Visiting Instructor; M.F.A., Hunter.
Dara Kiese, Visiting Assistant Professor; Ph.D., CUNY Graduate Center.
Vivien Knussi, Adjunct Instructor; Ph.D., Columbia.
Joseph Reid Kopta, Visiting Instructor; M.S., Pratt.
Gayle Rodda Kurtz, Adjunct Associate Professor; Ph.D., CUNY Graduate Center.
Marilyn Kushner, Visiting Professor; Ph.D., Northwestern.
Thomas La Padula, Adjunct Professor; M.F.A., Syracuse.
Tiffany Lambert, Visiting Instructor.
Anca Lasc, Assistant Professor; Ph.D., USC.
Jacob Lewis, Visiting Instructor; Ph.D., Northwestern.
Rael Lewis, Visiting Assistant Professor; Ph.D., Stanford.
Michele Licalsi, Visiting Assistant Professor; M.A., NYU.
William Lorenzo, Visiting Assistant Professor; B.F.A., CUNY, Brooklyn.
Elizabeth Meggs, Assistant Professor; B.F.A., Virginia Commonwealth.
Juan Monroy, Visiting Assistant Professor; M.A., NYU.
Marsha Morton, Professor; Ph.D., NYU.
Nicholas Parkinson, Visiting Instructor; M.A., Stony Brook, SUNY.
Caterina Pierre, Visiting Associate Professor; Ph.D., The Graduate Center, CUNY.
Joyce Polistena, Adjunct Professor; Ph.D., CUNY Graduate Center, CCE.
Katarina V. Posch, Professor; Ph.D., Tokyo University of Fine Arts and Music.
Elena Rossi-Snook, Visiting Assistant Professor; M.A., University of East Anglia.
Ann Schoenfeld, Adjunct Assistant Professor; Ph.D., CUNY Graduate Center.
Dorothy Shepard, Adjunct Associate Professor; Ph.D., Bryn Mawr.
Elizabeth St. George, Visiting Instructor; M.A., Bard.
Adedoyin Teriba, Visiting Assistant Professor; M.A., Princeton.
Jack Toolin, Visiting Assistant Professor; M.F.A., San Jose State.
Alice Walkiewicz, Visiting Instructor; M.Phil., CUNY Graduate Center.
Bor-Hua Wang, Adjunct Assistant Professor; Ph.D., Columbia.
Sarah Wilkins, Visiting Assistant Professor; Ph.D., Rutgers.
Karyn Zieve, Visiting Assistant Professor; Ph.D., NYU.

### MEDIA STUDIES
**Arlene Keizer, Chair, Ph.D.**
**Kathryn Cullen-DuPont, Assistant Chair, Humanities and Media Studies; M.F.A., Goddard.**
Jonathan Beller, Coordinator of Media Studies program, Professor; Ph.D. Duke.
Allen Feldman, Visiting Professor; Ph.D., New School.
Ira Livingston, Professor; Ph.D., Stanford.
Mendi Obadike, Assistant Professor; Ph.D., Duke.
Minh-Ha Pham, Assistant Professor; Ph.D., Berkeley.
Ethan Spigland, Professor; M.F.A., NYU.
Christopher Vitale, Associate Professor; Ph.D., NYU.

### PERFORMANCE AND PERFORMANCE STUDIES
**Arlene Keizer, Chair, Ph.D.**
Tracie Morris, Coordinator of Performance and Performance Studies program, Professor; Ph.D., NYU.
Donald Andreasen, Adjunct Associate Professor; M.F.A., New School.
Youmna Chlala, Associate Professor; M.F.A., California College of the Arts.
Steven Doloff, Professor; Ph.D., CUNY Graduate Center.
Lisabeth During, Associate Professor; Ph.D., Cambridge (U.K.).
James Hannaham, Associate Professor; M.F.A. Texas at Austin.
Ann Holder, Associate Professor; Ph.D. Boston College.
May Joseph, Professor, Global Studies.
Ira Livingston, Professor; Ph.D., Stanford.
Jennifer Miller, Professor, Founder and Artistic Director of Circus Amok.
Mendi Obadike, Assistant Professor; Ph.D., Duke.
Martha Wilson, Visiting Associate Professor; Artist and Gallery Director.

### WRITING
**Arlene Keizer, Chair, Ph.D.**
Christina Hawkey, Coordinator of Writing program, Professor; M.F.A., Massachusetts Amherst.
Saul Anton, Adjunct Assistant Professor; Ph.D., Princeton.
Emily Beall, Adjunct Assistant Professor with CCE; M.A., Washington (Seattle).
Priscilla Becker, Adjunct Assistant Professor; M.F.A., Columbia.
Jonathan Beller, Professor; Ph.D., Duke.
Caterina Bertolotto, Adjunct Professor; M.A. equivalent. Universita degli Studi di Torino (Turin, Italy).
Christopher Bollen, Visiting Instructor; B.A., Columbia.
Peter Catalanotto, Visiting Associate Professor; B.F.A., Pratt.
Diane Cohen, Visiting Instructor; M.A.. CUNY, Brooklyn.
Gabriel Cohen, Adjunct Assistant Professor; B.A., Wesleyan.
Jon Cotner, Visiting Instructor; M.A., St. John's.
Cameron Crawford, Visiting Assistant Professor; M.F.A., Northwestern.
Kathryn Cullen-DuPont; M.F.A., Goddard.
Maria Damon, Professor; Ph.D., Stanford.
Amanda Davidson, Adjunct Assistant Professor; M.F.A., San Francisco State.
Steven Doloff, Professor; B.A., Stony Brook, SUNY.
Claire Donato, Visiting Assistant Professor; M.F.A., Brown.
Laura Elrick, Associate Professor; M.A., NYU.
Wes Enzinna, Visiting Instructor, M.A. UC Berkeley.
Allen Feldman, Visiting Associate Professor; Ph.D., New School.
John Gendall, Visiting Instructor; M.D.E.S., Harvard.
John Glassie, Visiting Instructor; B.A., Johns Hopkins.
David Gordon, Visiting Instructor; M.F.A., Columbia.
Amy Guggenheim, Adjunct Associate Professor; M.A., NYU, CCE.
Paul Haacke, Visiting Assistant Professor; Ph.D., Berkeley.
James Hannaham, Associate Professor; M.F.A., Texas at Austin.
Christian Hawkey, Professor; M.F.A., University of Massachusetts.
Ryan Fischer-Harbage, Visiting Assistant Professor; M.F.A., Bennington.
Jason Helm, Visiting Assistant Professor; M.F.A., Sarah Lawrence.
Jeffrey Hogrefe, Associate Professor; B.A., Berkeley.

Mary-Beth Hughes, Visiting Assistant Professor; B.A., Marymount Manhattan.
Samantha Hunt, Professor; M.F.A., Warren Wilson.
Lucy Ives, Visiting Assistant Professor; M.F.A., Iowa Writer's Workshop.
Jeff T. Johnson, Visiting Assistant Professor; M.F.A., New School.
Adeena Karasick, Adjunct Associate Professor; Ph.D., Concordia (Montreal).
Caitlin Kelly, Visiting Instructor; B.A., Toronto.
Sean C. Kelly, Visiting Instructor; B.A., Montreal.
Krystal Languell, Adjunct Associate Professor; M.F.A., New Mexico State.
Jennifer W. Leung, Visiting Assistant Professor; M.Arch. I, Princeton.
Ellen Levy, Visiting Associate Professor; Ph.D., Vanderbilt.
Rachel Levitsky, Professor; M.F.A., Naropa.
Ira Livingston, Professor; Ph.D., Stanford.
Robert Lopez, Assistant Adjunct Professor; M.F.A., New School.
Max Ludington, Visiting Instructor; M.F.A., Columbia.
Melissa Milgrom, Visiting Assistant Professor; M.A., Pennsylvania.
Tracie Morris, Professor; Ph.D., NYU.
Anna Moschovakis, Adjunct Associate Professor; M.F.A., Bard.
Cecilia Muhlstein, Adjunct Assistant Professor,Tutor; UCLA.
Bill Obrecht, Adjunct Assistant Professor; B.A., Berklee College of Music.
Shelly Orla, Visiting Professor; M.F.A., Sarah Lawrence.
Matteo Pasquinelli, Visiting Assistant Professor; M.A., Bologna.
Jean-Paul Pecqueur, Adjunct Assistant Professor; M.F.A., Washington (Seattle).
Minh-Ha T. Pham, Assistant Professor; Ph.D., Berkeley.
Evan Rehill, Visiting Assistant Professor; M.F.A., San Francisco State.
Eric Rosenblum, Adjunct Assistant Professor; M.F.A., Syracuse.
Jonathan Santlofer, Visiting Assistant Professor; M.F.A., Pratt.
Eliza Schrader, Visiting Instructor; M.F.A., Columbia.
Adrian Shirk, Visiting Instructor; M.F.A., Wyoming.
Timothy M. Simonds, Visiting Assistant Professor; M.A., Brown.
Ethan Spigland, Professor; M.F.A., NYU.
Justin Taylor, Visiting Assistant Professor; M.F.A., New School.
Holly Tavel, Visiting Instructor; M.F.A., Brown.
Johnny Temple, Visiting Instructor; B.A., Wesleyan.
Barbara Turoff, Adjunct Assistant Professor; Ph.D., NYU.
Suzanne Verderber, Associate Professor; Ph.D., Pennsylvania.
Christopher Vitale, Associate Professor; Ph.D., NYU.
Ellery Washington, Associate Professor; M.A. equivalent, Sorbonne (Paris).
Kyle Waugh, Visiting Instructor; M.A., Kansas.
Marisa Williamson, Visiting Assistant Professor; M.F.A., California Institute of the Arts.
Uljana Wolf, Visting Assistant Professor; M.A., Berlin (Germany).
Thad Ziolkowski, Professor, Coordinator, The Writing Program; Ph.D., Yale.
Gina Zucker, Visiting Assistant Professor; M.F.A., New School.

© 2017 Bob Handelman

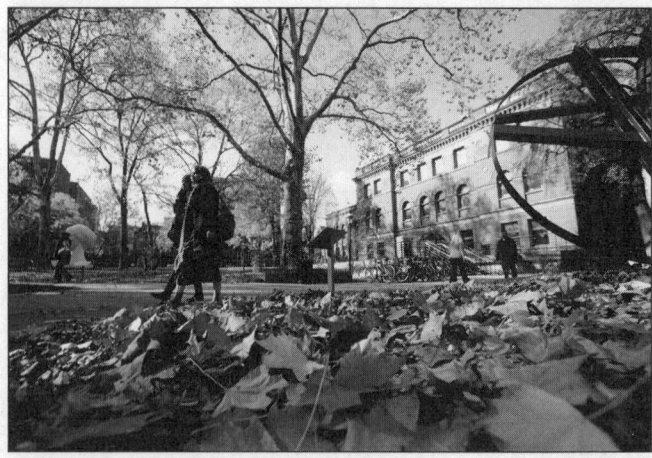

© 2017 Bob Handelman

# Section 17
# Conflict Resolution and Mediation/Peace Studies

This section contains a directory of institutions offering graduate work in conflict resolution and mediation/peace studies, Additional information about programs listed in the directory but not augmented by an in-depth entry may be obtained by writing directly to the dean of a graduate school or chair of a department at the address given in the directory.

For programs offering related work, see also in this book *Political Science and International Affairs* and *Public, Regional, and Industrial Affairs*. In another guide in this series:

**Graduate Programs in Business, Education, Information Studies, Law & Social Work**

See *Business Administration and Management* and *Law*

## CONTENTS

# Conflict Resolution and Mediation/Peace Studies

**Abilene Christian University,** College of Graduate and Professional Studies, Duncum Center for Conflict Resolution, Abilene, TX 79699. Offers conflict resolution (Certificate); conflict resolution and reconciliation (MA). *Program availability:* Part-time, evening/weekend, online learning. *Faculty:* 2 full-time (0 women), 4 part-time/adjunct (3 women). *Students:* 52 full-time (32 women), 12 part-time (7 women); includes 30 minority (20 Black or African American, non-Hispanic/Latino; 1 Asian, non-Hispanic/Latino; 8 Hispanic/Latino; 1 Two or more races, non-Hispanic/Latino), 1 international. 30 applicants, 83% accepted, 16 enrolled. In 2016, 29 master's, 46 other advanced degrees awarded. *Degree requirements:* For master's, practicum. *Entrance requirements:* Additional exam requirements/recommendations for international students: Required—TOEFL (minimum score 80 iBT), IELTS (minimum score 6), PTE. *Application deadline:* For fall admission, 8/11 for domestic students; for winter admission, 10/1 for domestic students; for spring admission, 12/15 for domestic students; for summer admission, 4/15 for domestic students. Applications are processed on a rolling basis. Application fee: $50. Electronic applications accepted. *Expenses:* $831 per credit hour. *Financial support:* In 2016–17, 1 student received support. Available to part-time students. Application deadline: 4/1; applicants required to submit FAFSA. *Unit head:* Dr. Joe Cope, Program Director, 325-674-2015, Fax: 325-674-2427, E-mail: conflictresolution@acu.edu. *Application contact:* Corey Patterson, Director of Graduate Admission and Recruiting, 325-674-6566, Fax: 325-674-6717, E-mail: gradinfo@acu.edu.
Website: http://www.acu.edu/online/academics/conflict-resolution-and-reconciliation.html

**Abilene Christian University,** College of Graduate and Professional Studies, Instructional Leadership Program, Abilene, TX 79699. Offers instructional leadership (M Ed), including conflict resolution, learning with emerging technologies, principalship; learning with emerging technologies (Certificate), including leadership of learning. *Program availability:* Part-time, online learning. *Faculty:* 1 (woman) full-time, 1 part-time/adjunct (0 women). *Students:* 9 full-time (7 women); includes 4 minority (2 Black or African American, non-Hispanic/Latino; 2 Hispanic/Latino). 11 applicants, 100% accepted, 9 enrolled. In 2016, 16 master's awarded. *Degree requirements:* For master's, comprehensive exam, practicum. *Entrance requirements:* Additional exam requirements/recommendations for international students: Required—TOEFL (minimum score 80 iBT), IELTS (minimum score 6), PTE. *Application deadline:* For fall admission, 8/15 priority date for domestic students; for winter admission, 10/1 priority date for domestic students; for spring admission, 12/15 priority date for domestic students; for summer admission, 4/15 for domestic students. Applications are processed on a rolling basis. Application fee: $50. Electronic applications accepted. *Expenses:* $600 per credit hour. *Financial support:* Application deadline: 4/1; applicants required to submit FAFSA. *Unit head:* Dr. Peter Williams, Program Director, 877-698-2793, E-mail: peter.williams@acu.edu. *Application contact:* Graduate Admissions, 855-219-7000, E-mail: gradonline@acu.edu.
Website: http://www.acu.edu/online/academics/master-of-education-in-instructional-leadership.html

**American Public University System,** AMU/APU Graduate Programs, Charles Town, WV 25414. Offers accounting (MBA, MS); applied business analytics (MBA, MS); criminal justice (MA), including business administration, emergency and disaster management, general (MA, MS); educational leadership (M Ed); emergency and disaster management (MA); entrepreneurship (MBA); environmental policy and management (MS), including environmental planning, environmental sustainability, fish and wildlife management, general (MA, MS), global environmental management; finance (MBA); general (MBA); government contracting and acquisition (MBA); health care administration (MBA); health information management (MS); history (MA), including American history, ancient and classical history, European history, global history, public history; homeland security (MA), including business administration, counterterrorism studies, criminal justice, cyber, emergency management and public health, intelligence studies, transportation security; homeland security resource allocation (MBA); humanities (MA); information technology (MS), including digital forensics, enterprise software development, information assurance and security, IT project management; information technology management (MBA); intelligence studies (MA), including criminal intelligence, cyber, general (MA, MS), homeland security, intelligence analysis, intelligence collection, intelligence management, intelligence operations, terrorism studies; international relations and conflict resolution (MA), including comparative and security issues, conflict resolution, international and transnational security issues, peacekeeping; legal studies (MA); management (MA), including strategic consulting; marketing (MBA); military history (MA), including American military history, American Revolution, civil war, war since 1945, World War II; military studies (MA), including joint warfare, strategic leadership; national security studies (MA), including cyber, general (MA, MS), homeland security, regional security studies, security and intelligence analysis, terrorism studies; nonprofit management (MBA); political science (MA), including American politics and government, comparative government and development, general (MA, MS), international relations, public policy; psychology (MA); public administration (MPA), including disaster management, environmental policy, health policy, human resources, national security, organizational management, security management; public health (MPH); reverse logistics management (MA); security management (MA); space studies (MS), including aerospace science, general (MA, MS), planetary science; sports and health sciences (MS); sports management (MBA); teaching (M Ed), including autism spectrum disorder, curriculum and instruction for elementary teachers, elementary reading, English language learners, instructional leadership, online learning, special education, STEAM (STEM plus the arts); transportation and logistics management (MA). *Program availability:* Part-time, evening/weekend, online only, 100% online. *Faculty:* 401 full-time (228 women), 1,678 part-time/adjunct (781 women). *Students:* 378 full-time (184 women), 8,455 part-time (3,484 women); includes 2,972 minority (1,552 Black or African American, non-Hispanic/Latino; 52 American Indian or Alaska Native, non-Hispanic/Latino; 211 Asian, non-Hispanic/Latino; 791 Hispanic/Latino; 70 Native Hawaiian or other Pacific Islander, non-Hispanic/Latino; 296 Two or more races, non-Hispanic/Latino), 109 international. Average age 37. In 2016, 3,185 master's awarded. *Degree requirements:* For master's, comprehensive exam or practicum. *Entrance requirements:* For master's, official transcript showing earned bachelor's degree from institution accredited by recognized accrediting body. Additional exam requirements/recommendations for international students: Required—TOEFL (minimum score 550 paper-based), IELTS (minimum score 6.5). *Application deadline:* Applications are processed on a rolling basis. Application fee: $0. Electronic applications accepted. *Expenses: Tuition:* Part-time $350 per credit hour. *Required fees:* $50 per course. *Financial support:* Scholarships/grants available. Financial award applicants required to submit FAFSA. *Unit head:* Dr. Karan Powell, President, 877-468-6268, Fax: 304-724-3780. *Application contact:* Terry Grant, Vice President of Enrollment Management, 877-468-6268, Fax: 304-724-3780, E-mail: info@apus.edu.
Website: http://www.apus.edu

**American University,** School of International Service, Washington, DC 20016-8071. Offers comparative and regional studies (Certificate); cross-cultural communication (Certificate); development management (MS); ethics, peace, and global affairs (MA); European studies (Certificate); global environmental policy (MA, Certificate); global information technology (Certificate); international affairs (MA), including comparative and international disability policy, comparative and regional studies, international economic relations, international politics, natural resources and sustainable development, U.S. foreign policy; international arts management (Certificate); international communication (MA, Certificate); international development (MA); international economic policy (Certificate); international economic relations (Certificate); international economics (MA); international media (MA); international peace and conflict resolution (MA, Certificate); international politics (Certificate); international relations (MA, PhD); international service (MIS); peacebuilding (Certificate); social enterprise (MA); the Americas (Certificate); United States foreign policy (Certificate); JD/MA. *Program availability:* Part-time, evening/weekend, 100% online. *Faculty:* 116 full-time (53 women), 57 part-time/adjunct (19 women). *Students:* 575 full-time (360 women), 491 part-time (277 women); includes 287 minority (100 Black or African American, non-Hispanic/Latino; 6 American Indian or Alaska Native, non-Hispanic/Latino; 58 Asian, non-Hispanic/Latino; 92 Hispanic/Latino; 1 Native Hawaiian or other Pacific Islander, non-Hispanic/Latino; 30 Two or more races, non-Hispanic/Latino), 151 international. Average age 29. 1,504 applicants, 84% accepted, 403 enrolled. In 2016, 374 master's, 3 doctorates, 1 other advanced degree awarded. Terminal master's awarded for partial completion of doctoral program. *Degree requirements:* For master's, one foreign language, comprehensive exam, thesis or alternative; for doctorate, one foreign language, comprehensive exam, thesis/dissertation. *Entrance requirements:* For master's, GRE, GMAT or GRE (for MA in social enterprise), transcripts, resume, 2 letters of recommendation, statement of purpose; for doctorate, GRE, transcripts, resume, 3 letters of recommendation, statement of purpose. Additional exam requirements/recommendations for international students: Required—TOEFL (minimum score 600 paper-based, 100 iBT), IELTS (minimum score 7 ), or PTE (minimum score of 68). Application fee: $55. Electronic applications accepted. *Expenses:* $1,579 per credit tuition; $1,930 mandatory fees. *Financial support:* Research assistantships, teaching assistantships, institutionally sponsored loans, scholarships/grants, and unspecified assistantships available. Financial award application deadline: 1/15; financial award applicants required to submit FAFSA. *Unit head:* Dr. James Goldgeier, Dean, 202-885-1603, Fax: 202-885-2494, E-mail: goldgeier@american.edu. *Application contact:* Jia Jiang, Associate Director, Graduate Education Enrollment, 202-885-1689, Fax: 202-885-1109, E-mail: jiang@american.edu.
Website: http://www.american.edu/sis/

**The American University of Paris,** Graduate Programs, Paris, France. Offers cross-cultural and sustainable business management (MA); cultural translation (MA); global communications (MA); global communications and civil society (MA); international affairs (MA); international affairs, conflict resolution and civil society development (MA); Middle East and Islamic studies (MA); Middle East and Islamic studies and international affairs (MA); public policy and international affairs (MA); public policy and international law (MA). *Degree requirements:* For master's, thesis (for some programs). *Entrance requirements:* For master's, minimum undergraduate GPA of 3.0. Additional exam requirements/recommendations for international students: Recommended—TOEFL, IELTS. Electronic applications accepted.

**Anabaptist Mennonite Biblical Seminary,** Graduate and Professional Programs, Elkhart, IN 46517-1999. Offers chaplaincy (M Div); Christian faith formation (M Div); Christian formation (MA); Christian spiritual formation (Certificate); divinity (M Div); pastoral ministry (M Div); pastoral theology for financial professionals (Certificate); peace studies (M Div), including environmental sustainability leadership (M Div, MA); theological studies (M Div, Certificate), including peace studies (M Div), theology and ethics (M Div); theology and peace studies (MA), including conflict transformation, environmental sustainability leadership (M Div, MA), international development administration; United Methodist leadership (M Div). Conflict transformation and environmental sustainability leadership concentrations offered in cooperation with Goshen College; international development administration offered in cooperation with Andrews University. *Accreditation:* ACIPE; ATS. *Program availability:* Part-time, 100% online, blended/hybrid learning. *Faculty:* 14 full-time (6 women), 17 part-time/adjunct (8 women). *Students:* 38 full-time (14 women), 60 part-time (33 women); includes 15 minority (4 Black or African American, non-Hispanic/Latino; 5 Asian, non-Hispanic/Latino; 5 Hispanic/Latino; 1 Two or more races, non-Hispanic/Latino), 15 international. Average age 35. 43 applicants, 70% accepted, 29 enrolled. In 2016, 16 master's, 2 other advanced degrees awarded. *Degree requirements:* For master's, variable foreign language requirement, comprehensive exam (for some programs), thesis optional, senior interview. *Entrance requirements:* For master's, undergraduate degree transcripts, 3 letters of reference, essay. Additional exam requirements/recommendations for international students: Required—TOEFL (minimum score 90 iBT); Recommended—IELTS (minimum score 7). *Application deadline:* For fall admission, 6/1 priority date for domestic students, 5/1 priority date for international students. Applications are processed on a rolling basis. Application fee: $25. Electronic applications accepted. *Expenses: Tuition:* Full-time $13,950; part-time $5640 per year. *Required fees:* $900; $300 per unit. $50 per term. *Financial support:* In 2016–17, 40 students received support. Career-related internships or fieldwork, scholarships/grants, unspecified assistantships, and church matching grants available. Support available to part-time students. Financial award application deadline: 4/15; financial award applicants required to submit FAFSA. *Faculty research:* Biblical studies, peace studies, theology, ethics, creation care or environmental ethics, church history, church leadership, mission, ministry, preaching, pastoral leadership, social justice, peacemaking, Jesus Christ, Christianity, Anabaptism, Mennonite, Scripture, Bible, Old Testament, New Testament, spirituality, clinical pastoral education, teaching, faith formation, pastoral care, Koine Greek, Hebrew, Aramaic, Syriac, Ugaritic. *Unit head:* Sara Wenger Shenk, President, 800-964-2627, Fax: 574-295-0092. *Application contact:* Daniel Grimes, Director of Admissions, 574-296-6266, Fax: 574-295-0092, E-mail: admissions@ambs.edu.
Website: http://www.ambs.edu/

**Antioch University Midwest,** Graduate Programs, Individualized Interdisciplinary Studies and Social Sciences Program, Yellow Springs, OH 45387-1609. Offers applied psychology (MA); conflict studies (MA); health and human development (MA); integral studies (MA); peace studies (MA); systems and organizations (MA). *Program availability:* Part-time, evening/weekend, online learning. *Degree requirements:* For master's, thesis or alternative. *Entrance requirements:* For master's, resume, goal

statement, interview. *Application deadline:* For fall admission, 8/1 for domestic students; for winter admission, 12/1 for domestic students; for spring admission, 3/10 for domestic students. Applications are processed on a rolling basis. Application fee: $50. Electronic applications accepted. *Expenses:* $799 per credit hour. *Financial support:* Federal Work-Study available. Financial award applicants required to submit FAFSA. *Application contact:* Deena Kent-Hummel, Director of Admissions, 937-769-1800, Fax: 937-769-1804, E-mail: dkent@antioch.edu.
Website: https://www.antioch.edu/midwest/degrees-programs/business-management-leadership/individualized-master-of-arts-ma/interdisciplinary-studies-and-social-

**Antioch University Midwest,** Graduate Programs, School of Education, Yellow Springs, OH 45387-1609. Offers conflict management (M Ed); dyslexia (M Ed); early childhood education (M Ed); educational leadership (M Ed); intervention specialist, mild to moderate (M Ed); middle childhood education (M Ed); trauma informed education (M Ed). *Accreditation:* NCATE. *Program availability:* Part-time, evening/weekend. *Degree requirements:* For master's, thesis or alternative. *Entrance requirements:* For master's, resume, goal statement, interview. *Application deadline:* For fall admission, 9/7 for domestic students; for winter admission, 12/10 for domestic students; for spring admission, 3/10 for domestic students. Applications are processed on a rolling basis. Application fee: $50. Electronic applications accepted. *Expenses:* $675 per credit hour. *Financial support:* Federal Work-Study available. Financial award applicants required to submit FAFSA. *Unit head:* Dr. Marian Glancy, Director, 937-769-1880, Fax: 937-769-1805, E-mail: mglancy@antioch.edu. *Application contact:* Deena Kent-Hummel, Director of Admissions, 937-769-1823, Fax: 937-769-1804, E-mail: dkent@antioch.edu.
Website: https://www.antioch.edu/midwest/degrees-programs/education-degree/

**Arcadia University,** College of Arts and Sciences, Program in International Peace and Conflict Resolution, Glenside, PA 19038-3295. Offers MA. *Program availability:* Part-time, evening/weekend. *Faculty:* 11 full-time (6 women), 3 part-time/adjunct (0 women). *Students:* 15 full-time (7 women), 7 part-time (4 women); includes 3 minority (2 Black or African American, non-Hispanic/Latino; 1 Two or more races, non-Hispanic/Latino), 3 international. Average age 26. 38 applicants, 66% accepted, 9 enrolled. In 2016, 14 master's awarded. *Degree requirements:* For master's, capstone project. *Entrance requirements:* Additional exam requirements/recommendations for international students: Required—TOEFL or IELTS. *Application deadline:* For fall admission, 4/1 priority date for domestic students. Application fee: $50. *Expenses:* Contact institution. *Unit head:* Amy Cox, Director, 267-620-4752, Fax: 215-572-4049. *Application contact:* 215-572-2910, Fax: 215-572-4049, E-mail: admiss@arcadia.edu.

**Bethany Theological Seminary,** Graduate and Professional Programs, Richmond, IN 47374-4019. Offers biblical studies (MA Th); ministry studies (M Div); peace studies (M Div, MA Th); theological studies (MA Th, CATS); youth ministry (M Div). *Accreditation:* ACIPE; ATS. *Program availability:* Part-time, online learning. *Degree requirements:* For master's, thesis (for some programs). *Entrance requirements:* For master's, letters of reference. Additional exam requirements/recommendations for international students: Required—TOEFL (minimum score 550 paper-based).

**Bethel University,** Graduate Programs, McKenzie, TN 38201. Offers administration and supervision (MA Ed); business administration (MBA); conflict resolution (MA); physician assistant studies (MS). *Program availability:* Part-time, evening/weekend. *Degree requirements:* For master's, thesis (for some programs). *Entrance requirements:* For master's, GRE General Test or MAT, minimum undergraduate GPA of 2.5.

**Brandeis University,** The Heller School for Social Policy and Management, Program in Coexistence and Conflict, Waltham, MA 02454-9110. Offers MA, MA/MA. MA/MA program offered in conjunction with Program in Sustainable International Development. *Degree requirements:* For master's, thesis, internship. *Entrance requirements:* For master's, 3 letters of recommendation, curriculum vitae or resume, 5 years of field experience. Additional exam requirements/recommendations for international students: Required—TOEFL (minimum score 600 paper-based; 100 iBT). Electronic applications accepted. *Faculty research:* Intercommunal conflicts, strategic intervention, conflict resolution, coexistence and conflict, international and inter-governmental organizations.

**California State University, Dominguez Hills,** College of Arts and Humanities, Program in Negotiation, Conflict Resolution and Peacebuilding, Carson, CA 90747-0001. Offers MA. *Program availability:* Part-time, evening/weekend, online learning. *Degree requirements:* For master's, portfolio. *Entrance requirements:* For master's, minimum GPA of 3.0, 3 letters of recommendation. Additional exam requirements/recommendations for international students: Required—TOEFL (minimum score 550 paper-based). Electronic applications accepted. *Faculty research:* Ethnic conflict, mediator ethics, teacher training, global conflict resolution (including role of ombuds), optimal multicultural process.

**Cambridge College,** School of Management, Cambridge, MA 02138-5304. Offers business negotiation and conflict resolution (M Mgt); general business (M Mgt); health care informatics (M Mgt); health care management (M Mgt); leadership in human and organizational dynamics (M Mgt); non-profit and public organization management (M Mgt); small business development (M Mgt); technology management (M Mgt). *Program availability:* Part-time, evening/weekend. *Degree requirements:* For master's, thesis, seminars. *Entrance requirements:* For master's, resume, 2 professional references. Additional exam requirements/recommendations for international students: Required—TOEFL (minimum score 550 paper-based; 79 iBT), Michigan English Language Assessment Battery (minimum score 85); Recommended—IELTS (minimum score 6). Electronic applications accepted. *Expenses:* Contact institution. *Faculty research:* Negotiation, mediation and conflict resolution; leadership; management of diverse organizations; case studies and simulation methodologies for management education, digital as a second language: social networking for digital immigrants, non-profit and public management.

**Carleton University,** Faculty of Graduate Studies, Faculty of Public Affairs and Management, Department of Law, Ottawa, ON K1S 5B6, Canada. Offers conflict resolution (Certificate); legal studies (MA). *Degree requirements:* For master's, thesis. *Entrance requirements:* For master's, honors degree. Additional exam requirements/recommendations for international students: Required—TOEFL. *Faculty research:* Legal and social theory; women, law, and gender relations; law, crime, and social order; political economy of law; international law.

**Champlain College,** Graduate Studies, Burlington, VT 05402-0670. Offers business (MBA); digital forensic science (MS); early childhood education (M Ed); emergent media (MFA, MS); executive leadership (MS); health care administration (MS); information security operations (MS); law (MS); mediation and applied conflict studies (MS). MS in emergent media program held in Shanghai. *Program availability:* Part-time, online learning. *Degree requirements:* For master's, capstone project. *Entrance requirements:* Additional exam requirements/recommendations for international students: Required—TOEFL (minimum score 550 paper-based; 80 iBT). Electronic applications accepted.

**Colgate Rochester Crozer Divinity School,** Graduate and Professional Programs, Rochester, NY 14620-2530. Offers divinity (M Div, MA, Certificate); peace building and interfaith dialogue (D Min); prophetic preaching (D Min); transformative leadership (D Min). *Accreditation:* ACIPE; ATS (one or more programs are accredited). *Program availability:* Part-time, evening/weekend. *Faculty:* 6 full-time (3 women), 8 part-time/adjunct (3 women). *Students:* 85 full-time, 29 part-time; includes 66 minority (56 Black or

African American, non-Hispanic/Latino; 6 Asian, non-Hispanic/Latino; 4 Hispanic/Latino). Average age 43. 33 applicants, 91% accepted, 27 enrolled. In 2016, 12 master's, 3 doctorates awarded. *Degree requirements:* For master's, thesis (for some programs), supervised ministry year (for M Div); for doctorate, thesis/dissertation. *Entrance requirements:* For master's, BA/BS, personal statement, 4 recommendations; for doctorate, M Div, 3 years' professional experience, writing sample, personal statement, curriculum vitae, 4 recommendations. Additional exam requirements/recommendations for international students: Required—TOEFL (minimum score 600 paper-based; 93 iBT). *Application deadline:* For fall admission, 7/1 priority date for domestic students, 3/1 for international students; for spring admission, 12/1 priority date for domestic students, 9/1 for international students. Applications are processed on a rolling basis. Application fee: $35. Electronic applications accepted. *Expenses:* Contact institution. *Financial support:* In 2016–17, 43 students received support. Scholarships/grants available. Financial award application deadline: 9/1; financial award applicants required to submit FAFSA. *Faculty research:* Book of Jeremiah, postcolonial Asian feminist biblical interpretation, Charles Wesley, Christian ethics, black church studies. *Unit head:* Marvin A. McMickle, PhD, President, 585-271-1320 Ext. 680, Fax: 585-271-8013. *Application contact:* Rev. Melissa M. Morral, Vice President for Enrollment Services, 585-340-9633, Fax: 585-340-9644, E-mail: mmorral@crcds.edu.
Website: http://www.crcds.edu

**Colorado Technical University Aurora,** Programs in Business Administration and Management, Aurora, CO 80014. Offers accounting (MBA); business administration (MBA); business administration and management (EMBA); finance (MBA); human resource management (MBA); marketing (MBA); mediation and dispute resolution (MBA); operations management (MBA); project management (MBA); technology management (MBA). *Program availability:* Part-time, evening/weekend. *Degree requirements:* For master's, thesis or alternative. *Entrance requirements:* For master's, minimum undergraduate GPA of 3.0, resume.

**Colorado Technical University Colorado Springs,** Graduate Studies, Program in Management, Colorado Springs, CO 80907. Offers accounting (MBA, MSA); business administration (MBA); finance (MBA); human resources management (MBA); logistics/supply chain management (MBA); management (DM); marketing (MBA); mediation and dispute resolution (MBA); operations management (MBA); project management (MBA); technology management (MBA). *Accreditation:* ACBSP. *Program availability:* Part-time, evening/weekend, online learning. *Degree requirements:* For master's, thesis or alternative; for doctorate, thesis/dissertation. *Entrance requirements:* For doctorate, minimum graduate GPA of 3.0, 5 years of related work experience. *Faculty research:* Sexual harassment, performance evaluation, critical thinking.

**Columbia College,** Graduate Programs, Department of Human Relations, Columbia, SC 29203-5998. Offers organizational change and leadership (MA). *Program availability:* Part-time, evening/weekend, online learning. *Degree requirements:* For master's, thesis, practicum. *Entrance requirements:* For master's, GRE General Test, MAT, 2 letters of recommendation, minimum GPA of 3.2. Additional exam requirements/recommendations for international students: Required—TOEFL. Electronic applications accepted. *Expenses:* Contact institution. *Faculty research:* Envisioning and the resolution of conflict, environmental conflict resolution, crisis negotiation.

**Columbia University,** School of Continuing Education, Program in Negotiation and Conflict Resolution, New York, NY 10027. Offers MS. *Program availability:* Part-time. *Entrance requirements:* For master's, 2 letters of recommendation, professional resume. Electronic applications accepted.

**Cornell University,** Graduate School, Graduate Fields of Architecture, Art and Planning, Field of Regional Science, Ithaca, NY 14853. Offers environmental studies (MA, MS, PhD); international spatial problems (MA, MS, PhD); location theory (MA, MS, PhD); multiregional economic analysis (MA, MS, PhD); peace science (MA, MS, PhD); planning methods (MA, MS, PhD); urban and regional economics (MA, MS, PhD). Terminal master's awarded for partial completion of doctoral program. *Degree requirements:* For master's, thesis; for doctorate, comprehensive exam, thesis/dissertation. *Entrance requirements:* For master's and doctorate, GRE General Test, 2 letters of recommendation. Additional exam requirements/recommendations for international students: Required—TOEFL (minimum score 600 paper-based; 77 iBT). Electronic applications accepted. *Faculty research:* Urban and regional growth, spatial economics, formation of spatial patterns by socioeconomic systems, non-linear dynamics and complex systems, environmental-economic systems.

**Creighton University,** School of Law, Program in Negotiation and Conflict Resolution, Omaha, NE 68178. Offers MS, Certificate. *Program availability:* Part-time, evening/weekend, 100% online, blended/hybrid learning. *Faculty:* 5 full-time (4 women), 10 part-time/adjunct (6 women). *Students:* 32 full-time (19 women), 51 part-time (31 women); includes 9 minority (1 American Indian or Alaska Native, non-Hispanic/Latino; 7 Hispanic/Latino; 1 Two or more races, non-Hispanic/Latino), 2 international. Average age 38. 52 applicants, 87% accepted, 41 enrolled. In 2016, 51 master's, 5 other advanced degrees awarded. *Degree requirements:* For master's, thesis or alternative, practicum. *Entrance requirements:* For master's, baccalaureate degree, two letters of recommendation, statement of purpose (500-750 words), short writing sample, resume, interview with faculty member, transcripts. Additional exam requirements/recommendations for international students: Required—TOEFL (minimum score 90 iBT). *Application deadline:* Applications are processed on a rolling basis. Application fee: $50. Electronic applications accepted. *Expenses:* $828 per credit hour; $1,105 per credit hour (online). *Financial support:* Institutionally sponsored loans available. Financial award applicants required to submit FAFSA. *Faculty research:* Structural violence; online pedagogy; identity conflict; healthcare conflict engagement and inter professional team building; community engagement of difficult conversations. *Unit head:* Dr. Jacqueline Font-Guzman, Director/Professor of Law, 402-280-3883, Fax: 402-280-3756, E-mail: jackiefont@creighton.edu. *Application contact:* Sarah J. Meisinger, Academic Coach, 402-280-3365, Fax: 402-280-3756, E-mail: sarahmeisinger@creighton.edu.
Website: http://law.creighton.edu/werner-institute

**Dallas Baptist University,** College of Business, Business Administration Program, Dallas, TX 75211-9299. Offers accounting (MBA); business communication (MBA); conflict resolution management (MBA); entrepreneurship (MBA); finance (MBA); health care management (MBA); international business (MBA); leading the non-profit organization (MBA); management (MBA); management information systems (MBA); marketing (MBA); project management (MBA); technology and engineering management (MBA). *Accreditation:* ACBSP. *Program availability:* Part-time, evening/weekend, 100% online, blended/hybrid learning. *Application deadline:* Applications are processed on a rolling basis. Application fee: $25. Electronic applications accepted. Application fee is waived when completed online. *Expenses:* Tuition: Full-time $15,408; part-time $856 per credit hour. *Required fees:* $400 per semester. Tuition and fees vary according to course load and degree level. *Unit head:* Dr. Sandra Reid, Chair of Graduate Business Programs, 214-333-5280, E-mail: sandra@dbu.edu. *Application contact:* Bobby Soto, Director of Admissions, 214-333-5242, E-mail: graduate@dbu.edu.
Website: http://www3.dbu.edu/graduate/mba.asp

## Conflict Resolution and Mediation/Peace Studies

**Dallas Baptist University,** College of Business, Management Program, Dallas, TX 75211-9299. Offers conflict resolution management (MA); general management (MA, MS); health care management (MA); human resource management (MA); organizational communication (MA); performance management (MA); professional sales and management optimization (MA). *Program availability:* Part-time, evening/weekend, 100% online, blended/hybrid learning. *Application deadline:* Applications are processed on a rolling basis. Application fee: $25. Electronic applications accepted. Application fee is waived when completed online. *Expenses: Tuition:* Full-time $15,408; part-time $856 per credit hour. *Required fees:* $400 per semester. Tuition and fees vary according to course load and degree level. *Unit head:* Richard Nassar, Director, 214-333-5280, E-mail: richardn@dbu.edu. *Application contact:* Bobby Soto, Director of Admissions, 214-333-5242, E-mail: graduate@dbu.edu.
Website: http://www.dbu.edu/gsb/ma-in-management

**Dominican University,** School of Professional and Continuing Studies, River Forest, IL 60305-1099. Offers conflict resolution (MA). *Program availability:* Part-time, evening/weekend, 100% online, blended/hybrid learning. *Faculty:* 3 part-time/adjunct (2 women). *Students:* 30 full-time (24 women), 15 part-time (11 women); includes 17 minority (11 Black or African American, non-Hispanic/Latino; 5 Hispanic/Latino; 1 Two or more races, non-Hispanic/Latino). Average age 39. 16 applicants, 94% accepted, 15 enrolled. In 2016, 17 master's awarded. *Entrance requirements:* For master's, bachelor's degree in any subject, two letters of recommendation. Additional exam requirements/recommendations for international students: Required—TOEFL (minimum score 550 paper-based; 79 iBT). *Application deadline:* Applications are processed on a rolling basis. Application fee: $25. Electronic applications accepted. *Expenses: Tuition:* Full-time $17,850; part-time $850 per credit hour. *Required fees:* $540; $18 per course. Tuition and fees vary according to course load, degree level and program. *Financial support:* Research assistantships, career-related internships or fieldwork, scholarships/grants, and unspecified assistantships available. Financial award applicants required to submit FAFSA. *Unit head:* Dr. Matthew Hlinak, Assistant Provost for Continuing Studies and Special Initiatives, 708-714-9056, E-mail: mhlinak@dom.edu. *Application contact:* Monica Halloran, Associate Director of Academic Advising, 708-714-9007, Fax: 708-714-9126, E-mail: mhallora@dom.edu.
Website: http://continuingstudies.dom.edu/

**Drew University,** Caspersen School of Graduate Studies, Madison, NJ 07940-1493. Offers conflict resolution and leadership (Certificate), including community leadership, moderation, peace building; history and culture (MA, PhD), including American history, book history, British history, European history, Holocaust and genocide (M Litt, MA, D Litt, PhD), intellectual history, Irish history, print culture, public history; K-12 education (MAT), including art, biology, chemistry, elementary education, English, French, Italian, math, secondary education, special education, teacher of students with disabilities; liberal studies (M Litt, D Litt), including history, Holocaust and genocide (M Litt, MA, D Litt, PhD), Irish/Irish-American studies, literature (M Litt, MMH, D Litt, DMH, CMH), religion, spirituality, teaching in the two-year college, writing; medical humanities (MMH, DMH, CMH), including arts, health, healthcare, literature (M Litt, MMH, D Litt, DMH, CMH), scientific research; poetry (MFA). *Program availability:* Part-time, evening/weekend. *Faculty:* 4 full-time (2 women), 31 part-time/adjunct (16 women). *Students:* 62 full-time (41 women), 199 part-time (130 women); includes 38 minority (17 Black or African American, non-Hispanic/Latino; 3 Asian, non-Hispanic/Latino; 17 Hispanic/Latino; 1 Two or more races, non-Hispanic/Latino), 3 international. Average age 27. 93 applicants, 81% accepted, 46 enrolled. In 2016, 39 master's, 27 doctorates, 26 other advanced degrees awarded. Terminal master's awarded for partial completion of doctoral program. *Degree requirements:* For master's and other advanced degree, thesis (for some programs); for doctorate, one foreign language, comprehensive exam (for some programs), thesis/dissertation. *Entrance requirements:* For master's, PRAXIS Core and Subject Area tests (for MAT), resume, transcripts, writing sample, personal statement, letters of recommendation; for doctorate, GRE (PhD in history and culture), resume, transcripts, writing sample, personal statement, letters of recommendation. Additional exam requirements/recommendations for international students: Required—TOEFL (minimum score 587 paper-based; 94 iBT), IELTS (minimum score 7), TWE (minimum score 4). *Application deadline:* For fall admission, 8/1 for domestic students, 6/1 for international students; for spring admission, 12/1 for domestic students, 10/1 for international students. Applications are processed on a rolling basis. Application fee: $35. Electronic applications accepted. Tuition and fees vary according to program. *Financial support:* Fellowships, research assistantships, teaching assistantships, career-related internships or fieldwork, Federal Work-Study, scholarships/grants, and unspecified assistantships available. Support available to part-time students. Financial award applicants required to submit FAFSA. *Application contact:* Leanne Horinko, Director of Caspersen Admissions, 973-408-3280, E-mail: gradm@drew.edu.
Website: http://www.drew.edu/caspersen

**Eastern Mennonite University,** Program in Conflict Transformation, Harrisonburg, VA 22802-2462. Offers MA, Graduate Certificate. *Program availability:* Part-time. *Degree requirements:* For master's, practicum. *Entrance requirements:* For master's, minimum undergraduate GPA of 2.75. Additional exam requirements/recommendations for international students: Required—TOEFL (minimum score 550 paper-based). Electronic applications accepted. *Expenses:* Contact institution. *Faculty research:* Restorative justice, negotiation, security in an age of terror, trauma recovery, development, peacebuilding.

**Excelsior College,** School of Business and Technology, Albany, NY 12203-5159. Offers business administration (MBA); cybersecurity management (MBA, Graduate Certificate); general business management (MS); health care management (MBA); human performance technology (MBA); human resource management (MS); human resources management (MBA); leadership (MBA, MS); mediation and arbitration (MBA, MS); social media management (MBA); technology management (MBA). *Program availability:* Part-time, evening/weekend, online learning. *Faculty:* 25 part-time/adjunct (9 women). *Students:* 1,801 part-time (487 women); includes 775 minority (424 Black or African American, non-Hispanic/Latino; 5 American Indian or Alaska Native, non-Hispanic/Latino; 58 Asian, non-Hispanic/Latino; 209 Hispanic/Latino; 15 Native Hawaiian or other Pacific Islander, non-Hispanic/Latino; 64 Two or more races, non-Hispanic/Latino), 11 international. Average age 39. In 2016, 288 master's awarded. *Application deadline:* Applications are processed on a rolling basis. Application fee: $50. Electronic applications accepted. *Expenses: Tuition:* Part-time $645 per credit. *Required fees:* $265 per credit. *Financial support:* Scholarships/grants available. *Unit head:* Dr. Lifang Shih, Dean, 888-647-2388. *Application contact:* Admissions, 888-647-2388 Ext. 133, Fax: 518-464-8777, E-mail: admissions@excelsior.edu.

**Excelsior College,** School of Public Service, Albany, NY 12203-5159. Offers criminal justice (MSCI); homeland security and emergency management (MSCJ); justice administration (MSCI); mediation and arbitration (MPA); public administration (MPA). *Program availability:* Part-time, evening/weekend, online learning. *Faculty:* 1 (woman) part-time/adjunct. *Students:* 181 part-time (47 women); includes 78 minority (41 Black or African American, non-Hispanic/Latino; 2 American Indian or Alaska Native, non-Hispanic/Latino; 2 Asian, non-Hispanic/Latino; 25 Hispanic/Latino; 2 Native Hawaiian or other Pacific Islander, non-Hispanic/Latino; 6 Two or more races, non-Hispanic/Latino). Average age 41. In 2016, 30 master's awarded. *Application deadline:* Applications are

processed on a rolling basis. Application fee: $50. Electronic applications accepted. *Expenses: Tuition:* Part-time $645 per credit. *Required fees:* $265 per credit. *Financial support:* Scholarships/grants available. *Unit head:* Dr. Robert Waters, Dean, School of Public Service, 518-464-8500, Fax: 518-464-8777. *Application contact:* Admissions Counselor, 888-647-2388, Fax: 518-464-8777, E-mail: gradadmissions@excelsior.edu.
Website: http://www.excelsior.edu/programs/public-service

**Fresno Pacific University,** Graduate Programs, Program in Peacemaking and Conflict Studies, Fresno, CA 93702-4709. Offers church conflict and peacemaking (Certificate); mediation (Certificate); peacemaking and conflict studies (MA); restorative justice (Certificate). *Program availability:* Part-time, evening/weekend. *Degree requirements:* For master's, thesis. *Entrance requirements:* For master's, GMAT, MAT, GRE, interview, writing sample, three references. Additional exam requirements/recommendations for international students: Required—TOEFL (minimum score 550 paper-based). Electronic applications accepted. *Expenses:* Contact institution.

**George Mason University,** Schar School of Policy and Government, Program in Peace Operations, Arlington, VA 22201. Offers MS. *Faculty:* 7 full-time (3 women), 5 part-time/adjunct (2 women). *Students:* 15 full-time (7 women), 18 part-time (15 women); includes 10 minority (7 Black or African American, non-Hispanic/Latino; 1 Hispanic/Latino; 2 Two or more races, non-Hispanic/Latino), 2 international. Average age 30. 19 applicants, 100% accepted, 11 enrolled. In 2016, 30 master's awarded. *Degree requirements:* For master's, thesis or alternative. *Entrance requirements:* For master's, GRE (for students seeking merit-based scholarships), 750-1000 word goal statement; resume; two copies of official transcript; two letters of recommendation. Additional exam requirements/recommendations for international students: Required—TOEFL (minimum score 575 paper-based; 88 iBT), IELTS (minimum score 6.5), PTE (minimum score 59). *Application deadline:* For fall admission, 2/1 priority date for domestic students. Application fee: $75 ($80 for international students). Electronic applications accepted. *Expenses:* Contact institution. *Financial support:* Career-related internships or fieldwork, Federal Work-Study, and scholarships/grants available. Support available to part-time students. Financial award application deadline: 3/1; financial award applicants required to submit FAFSA. *Unit head:* Enrique Desmond Arias, Director, 703-993-2270, Fax: 703-993-8125, E-mail: earias2@gmu.edu. *Application contact:* Stephanie Ellis, Graduate Admissions Coordinator, 703-993-4478, E-mail: sellis11@gmu.edu.
Website: http://spgia.gmu.edu/programs/graduate-degrees/master-of-science-in-peace-operations/

**George Mason University,** School for Conflict Analysis and Resolution, Arlington, VA 22030. Offers MS, PhD, Certificate. *Program availability:* Part-time, evening/weekend. *Faculty:* 18 full-time (9 women), 21 part-time/adjunct (12 women). *Students:* 116 full-time (63 women), 159 part-time (86 women); includes 92 minority (48 Black or African American, non-Hispanic/Latino; 14 Asian, non-Hispanic/Latino; 23 Hispanic/Latino; 1 Native Hawaiian or other Pacific Islander, non-Hispanic/Latino; 6 Two or more races, non-Hispanic/Latino), 34 international. Average age 35. 224 applicants, 76% accepted, 82 enrolled. In 2016, 75 master's, 8 doctorates, 5 other advanced degrees awarded. *Degree requirements:* For master's, thesis optional; for doctorate, one foreign language, comprehensive exam, thesis/dissertation, oral defense of dissertation. *Entrance requirements:* For master's, 2 official copies of transcripts; 3 letters of recommendation; expanded goals statement; resume; baccalaureate degree from accredited institution with minimum GPA of 3.0; for doctorate, baccalaureate and master's degrees from regionally-accredited institution; minimum GPA of 3.0; 2 official copies of transcripts; expanded goals statement; 3 letters of recommendation; writing sample; resume; for Certificate, baccalaureate degree from accredited institution with minimum GPA of 3.0; 2 official copies of transcripts; letter of intent; 2 letters of recommendation; resume. Additional exam requirements/recommendations for international students: Required—TOEFL (minimum score 575 paper-based; 88 iBT), IELTS (minimum score 6.5), PTE (minimum score 59). Application fee: $75 ($80 for international students). Electronic applications accepted. *Expenses:* Tuition, state resident: full-time $10,628; part-time $443 per credit. Tuition, nonresident: full-time $29,306; part-time $1221 per credit. *Required fees:* $3096; $129 per credit. Tuition and fees vary according to program. *Financial support:* In 2016–17, 38 students received support, including 4 fellowships (averaging $10,814 per year), 24 research assistantships with tuition reimbursements available (averaging $15,919 per year), 11 teaching assistantships with tuition reimbursements available (averaging $10,483 per year); career-related internships or fieldwork, Federal Work-Study, scholarships/grants, unspecified assistantships, and health care benefits (for full-time research or teaching assistantship recipients) also available. Support available to part-time students. Financial award application deadline: 3/1; financial award applicants required to submit FAFSA. *Faculty research:* Preventive diplomacy, conflict/dispute resolution, peace/security, political violence, international terrorism. *Total annual research expenditures:* $1.3 million. *Unit head:* Kevin Avruch, Dean, 703-993-3607, Fax: 703-993-1302, E-mail: kavruch@gmu.edu. *Application contact:* Monique Barner, Assistant Director for Graduate Admissions, 703-993-1300, Fax: 703-993-1302, E-mail: mwilli43@gmu.edu.
Website: http://scar.gmu.edu

**Georgetown University,** Graduate School of Arts and Sciences, Department of Government, Program in Conflict Resolution, Washington, DC 20057. Offers MA.

**Georgetown University,** Graduate School of Arts and Sciences, Walsh School of Foreign Service, Center for Security Studies, Washington, DC 20057. Offers MA, MA/JD, MA/PhD.

**Henley-Putnam University,** Master of Science Program in Strategic Security and Protection Management, San Jose, CA 95131. Offers extremist organizations (MS). *Program availability:* Part-time, online learning. *Degree requirements:* For master's, comprehensive exam, thesis. *Entrance requirements:* For master's, bachelor's degree from institution accredited by an agency recognized by the U.S. Department of Education and/or the Council for Higher Education Accreditation, background check. Additional exam requirements/recommendations for international students: Required—TOEFL (minimum score 650 paper-based; 79 iBT); Recommended—IELTS. *Expenses:* Contact institution.

**Henley-Putnam University,** Master of Science Program in Terrorism and Counterterrorism Studies, San Jose, CA 95131. Offers intelligence operations (MS); protective intelligence (MS). *Program availability:* Part-time, online learning. *Degree requirements:* For master's, thesis. *Entrance requirements:* For master's, bachelor's degree from institution accredited by an agency recognized by the U.S. Department of Education and/or the Council for Higher Education Accreditation, background check. Additional exam requirements/recommendations for international students: Required—TOEFL (minimum score 650 paper-based; 79 iBT); Recommended—IELTS (minimum score 7). *Expenses:* Contact institution.

**Kansas State University,** Graduate School, College of Human Ecology, School of Family Studies and Human Services, Manhattan, KS 66506-1403. Offers applied family sciences (MS); communication sciences and disorders (MS); conflict resolution (Graduate Certificate); couple and family therapy (MS); early childhood education (MS); family and community service (MS); life-span human development (MS); personal financial planning (MS, PhD, Graduate Certificate); youth development (MS, Graduate Certificate). *Accreditation:* AAMFT/COAMFTE; ASHA. *Program availability:* Part-time, online learning. *Faculty:* 43 full-time (30 women), 4 part-time/adjunct (3 women). *Students:* 55 full-time (45 women), 87 part-time (73 women); includes 30 minority (9 Black or African American, non-Hispanic/Latino; 1 American Indian or Alaska Native, non-Hispanic/Latino; 1 Asian, non-Hispanic/Latino; 14 Hispanic/Latino; 1 Native Hawaiian or other Pacific Islander, non-Hispanic/Latino; 4 Two or more races, non-Hispanic/Latino), 6 international. Average age 29. 182 applicants, 29% accepted, 38 enrolled. In 2016, 39 master's, 17 other advanced degrees awarded. *Degree requirements:* For master's, comprehensive exam (for some programs), thesis optional. *Entrance requirements:* For master's, GRE, minimum GPA of 3.0 in last 2 years (60 semester hours) of undergraduate study; for doctorate, GRE. Additional exam requirements/recommendations for international students: Required—TOEFL (minimum score 600 paper-based). *Application deadline:* For fall admission, 2/1 priority date for domestic students, 1/1 priority date for international students; for spring admission, 10/1 priority date for domestic students, 8/1 priority date for international students; for summer admission, 2/1 priority date for domestic students, 12/1 priority date for international students. Applications are processed on a rolling basis. Application fee: $50 ($75 for international students). Electronic applications accepted. *Expenses:* Tuition, state resident: full-time $9670. Tuition, nonresident: full-time $21,828. *Required fees:* $862. *Financial support:* In 2016–17, 35 students received support, including 25 research assistantships (averaging $10,000 per year), 9 teaching assistantships with full tuition reimbursements available (averaging $10,000 per year); unspecified assistantships also available. Financial award application deadline: 3/1. *Faculty research:* Health and security of military families, training in and evaluation of professional human services (marriage and couple therapy, family life education, treatment of speech and swallowing disorders, financial therapy), disorders of communication and swallowing, family and relationship development and health, financial decision-making. *Total annual research expenditures:* $8.4 million. *Unit head:* Dr. Dottie Durband, Director, 785-532-5510, Fax: 785-532-5505, E-mail: dottie@ksu.edu. *Application contact:* Kristi Hageman, Administrative Specialist, 785-532-5510, Fax: 785-532-5505, E-mail: klsmith@ksu.edu. Website: http://www.he.k-state.edu/fshs/

**Kennesaw State University,** College of Humanities and Social Sciences, PhD Program in International Conflict Management, Kennesaw, GA 30144. Offers PhD. *Degree requirements:* For doctorate, one foreign language, thesis/dissertation. *Entrance requirements:* For doctorate, GRE, portfolio of documents, copy of transcripts from all universities previously attended, resume, statement of goals and objectives, academic writing sample, three letters of recommendation. Additional exam requirements/recommendations for international students: Required—TOEFL (minimum score 90 iBT), IELTS (minimum score 7). Electronic applications accepted.

**Kennesaw State University,** College of Humanities and Social Sciences, Program in Conflict Management, Kennesaw, GA 30144. Offers MSCM. *Program availability:* Evening/weekend. *Entrance requirements:* For master's, GMAT, GRE, LSAT. Additional exam requirements/recommendations for international students: Required—TOEFL (minimum score 550 paper-based; 80 iBT), IELTS (minimum score 6.5). Electronic applications accepted.

**Kent State University,** College of Arts and Sciences, Department of Political Science, Kent, OH 44242-0001. Offers political science (MA, PhD), including American politics and policy, conflict analysis and management, transnational and comparative politics and policy; public administration (MPA). *Program availability:* Part-time, online learning. *Faculty:* 18 full-time (5 women). *Students:* 34 full-time (14 women), 62 part-time (31 women); includes 12 minority (5 Black or African American, non-Hispanic/Latino; 1 American Indian or Alaska Native, non-Hispanic/Latino; 2 Asian, non-Hispanic/Latino; 2 Hispanic/Latino; 2 Two or more races, non-Hispanic/Latino), 9 international. Average age 30. 65 applicants, 57% accepted, 21 enrolled. In 2016, 20 master's, 1 doctorate awarded. *Degree requirements:* For master's, thesis (for some programs); for doctorate, comprehensive exam, thesis/dissertation. *Entrance requirements:* For master's and doctorate, GRE, statement of purpose, transcripts, writing sample, 3 letters of recommendation. *Application deadline:* For fall admission, 1/31 for domestic and international students. Applications are processed on a rolling basis. Application fee: $45 ($70 for international students). Electronic applications accepted. *Expenses:* Tuition, state resident: full-time $10,864; part-time $495 per credit hour. Tuition, nonresident: full-time $18,380; part-time $837 per credit hour. *Financial support:* Research assistantships with full tuition reimbursements, teaching assistantships with full tuition reimbursements, health care benefits, and unspecified assistantships available. Financial award application deadline: 1/31. *Unit head:* Dr. Andrew Barnes, Associate Professor and Chair, 330-672-2060, E-mail: abarnes3@kent.edu. *Application contact:* Dr. Ryan L. Claassen, Graduate Coordinator, 330-672-2060, E-mail: rclaasse@kent.edu. Website: http://www.kent.edu/polisci

**Lesley University,** Graduate School of Arts and Social Sciences, Cambridge, MA 02138-2790. Offers clinical mental health counseling (MA), including holistic counseling, school and community counseling, trauma studies; counseling psychology (MA, CAGS), including professional counseling (MA), school counseling (MA); creative writing (MFA); expressive therapies (MA, PhD, CAGS), including art (MA), clinical mental health counseling (MA), dance (MA), expressive therapies (MA), music (MA); independent studies (CAGS); independent study (MA); intercultural relations (MA, CAGS); interdisciplinary studies (MA), including individualized studies, integrative holistic health, mindfulness studies, peace and conflict transformation, trauma sensitive assessment, intervention, and consultation, women's studies; urban environmental leadership (MA). *Program availability:* Part-time, online learning. *Degree requirements:* For master's, internship, practicum, thesis (for expressive therapies); for doctorate, thesis/dissertation, arts apprenticeship, field placement; for CAGS, thesis, internship (for counseling psychology, expressive therapies). *Entrance requirements:* For master's, MAT (counseling psychology), interview, writing samples, art portfolio; for doctorate, GRE or MAT, interview, master's degree; for CAGS, interview, master's degree. Additional exam requirements/recommendations for international students: Required—TOEFL (minimum score 550 paper-based; 80 iBT). Electronic applications accepted. *Faculty research:* Psychotherapy and culture; psychotherapy and psychological trauma; women's issues in art, teaching and psychotherapy; community-based art, psycho-spiritual inquiry.

**Lipscomb University,** College of Business, Nashville, TN 37204-3951. Offers accountancy (M Acc); accounting (MBA); business administration (MM); conflict management (MBA); financial services (MBA); health care informatics (MBA); healthcare management (MBA); information security (MBA); leadership (MBA); nonprofit management (MBA); professional accountancy (Certificate); sports management (MBA); strategic human resources (MBA); sustainability (MBA); MBA/MS; Pharm D/MM. *Accreditation:* ACBSP. *Program availability:* Part-time, evening/weekend. *Faculty:* 22 full-time (4 women), 12 part-time/adjunct (4 women). *Students:* 112 full-time (51 women), 69 part-time (34 women); includes 30 minority (17 Black or African American, non-Hispanic/Latino; 3 Asian, non-Hispanic/Latino; 8 Hispanic/Latino; 2 Two or more races, non-Hispanic/Latino), 5 international. Average age 32. 244 applicants, 55% accepted, 54 enrolled. In 2016, 164 master's awarded. *Entrance requirements:* For master's, GMAT, transcripts, interview, 2 references, resume. Additional exam requirements/recommendations for international students: Required—TOEFL (minimum

score 570 paper-based). *Application deadline:* For fall admission, 6/15 for domestic students, 2/1 for international students; for winter admission, 6/1 for international students; for spring admission, 11/15 for domestic students. Applications are processed on a rolling basis. Application fee: $50 ($75 for international students). Electronic applications accepted. *Expenses:* $1,150-$1,290 per hour, depending on program. *Financial support:* Career-related internships or fieldwork, scholarships/grants, tuition waivers (partial), and unspecified assistantships available. Support available to part-time students. Financial award application deadline: 7/1; financial award applicants required to submit FAFSA. *Faculty research:* Impact of spirituality on organization commitment, women in corporate leadership, psychological empowerment, training. *Unit head:* Allison Duke, Associate Dean of Graduate Business Programs, 615-966-5732, Fax: 615-966-1818, E-mail: allison.duke@lipscomb.edu. *Application contact:* Karen Risley, Manager, Graduate Business Recruiting, 615-966-5145, E-mail: karen.risley@lipscomb.edu. Website: http://www.lipscomb.edu/business/Graduate-Programs

**Lipscomb University,** Institute for Conflict Management, Nashville, TN 37204-3951. Offers MA, Certificate. *Program availability:* Part-time, evening/weekend. *Faculty:* 3 full-time (1 woman), 6 part-time/adjunct (4 women). *Students:* 15 full-time (8 women), 24 part-time (17 women); includes 9 minority (8 Black or African American, non-Hispanic/Latino; 1 Two or more races, non-Hispanic/Latino). Average age 40. In 2016, 13 master's, 9 other advanced degrees awarded. *Degree requirements:* For master's, thesis optional, externship. *Entrance requirements:* For master's, GRE, GMAT, LSAT or equivalent, 3 years of work experience. Additional exam requirements/recommendations for international students: Required—TOEFL (minimum score 570 paper-based; 80 iBT). *Application deadline:* For fall admission, 7/15 for domestic students; for spring admission, 12/15 for domestic students. Applications are processed on a rolling basis. Application fee: $50 ($75 for international students). Electronic applications accepted. *Expenses:* $1,312 per hour. *Financial support:* Tuition waivers (full) available. Financial award applicants required to submit FAFSA. *Faculty research:* Generationally generated conflict, cross-cultural conflict, risk and injury reduction in healthcare, spiritual formation. *Unit head:* Dr. Steve Joiner, Director, 615-966-7141, Fax: 615-966-7143, E-mail: phyllis.hildreth@lipscomb.edu. *Application contact:* Dr. Phyllis Hildreth, Academic Director, 615-966-5695, Fax: 615-966-7143, E-mail: phyllis.hildreth@lipscomb.edu. Website: http://lipscomb.edu/icm

**London Metropolitan University,** Graduate Programs, London, United Kingdom. Offers applied psychology (M Sc); architecture (MA); biomedical science (M Sc); blood science (M Sc); cancer pharmacology (M Sc); computer networking and cyber security (M Sc); computing and information systems (M Sc); conference interpreting (MA); counter-terrorism studies (M Sc); creative, digital and professional writing (MA); crime, violence and prevention (M Sc); criminology (M Sc); curating contemporary art (MA); data analytics (MA); digital media (MA); early childhood studies (MA); education (MA, Ed D); financial services law, regulation and compliance (LL M); food science (M Sc); forensic psychology (M Sc); health and social care management and policy (M Sc); human nutrition (M Sc); human resource management (MA); human rights and international conflict (MA); information technology (M Sc); intelligence and security studies (M Sc); international oil, gas and energy law (LL M); international relations (MA); interpreting (MA); learning and teaching in higher education (MA); legal practice (LL M); media and entertainment law (LL M); organizational and consumer psychology (M Sc); psychological therapy (M Sc); psychology of mental health (M Sc); public health (M Sc); public policy and management (MPA); security studies (M Sc); social work (M Sc); spatial planning and urban design (MA); sports therapy (M Sc); supporting older children and young people with dyslexia (MA); teaching languages (MA), including Arabic, English; translation (MA); woman and child abuse (MA).

**Middlebury Institute of International Studies at Monterey,** Graduate School of International Policy and Management, Program in Nonproliferation and Terrorism Studies, Monterey, CA 93940-2691. Offers MA. *Degree requirements:* For master's, one foreign language. *Entrance requirements:* For master's, minimum GPA of 3.0, proficiency in a foreign language. Additional exam requirements/recommendations for international students: Required—TOEFL (minimum score 550 paper-based; 80 iBT). Application fee is waived when completed online. *Expenses: Tuition:* Full-time $38,250; part-time $1820 per credit. *Required fees:* $78 per semester.

**Montclair State University,** The Graduate School, College of Humanities and Social Sciences, Conflict Management in the Workplace Certificate Program, Montclair, NJ 07043-1624. Offers Certificate. *Expenses:* Tuition, state resident: part-time $553 per credit. Tuition, nonresident: part-time $854 per credit. *Required fees:* $91 per credit. Tuition and fees vary according to program.

**Montclair State University,** The Graduate School, College of Humanities and Social Sciences, MA Program in Law and Governance, Montclair, NJ 07043-1624. Offers conflict management and peace studies (MA); governance, compliance and regulation (MA); intellectual property (MA); law and governance (MA); legal management (MA). *Program availability:* Part-time, evening/weekend. *Degree requirements:* For master's, thesis or comprehensive exam. *Entrance requirements:* For master's, GRE General Test, minimum cumulative GPA of 2.75 for undergraduate work, 2 letters of recommendation, essay. Additional exam requirements/recommendations for international students: Required—TOEFL (minimum score 83 iBT) or IELTS (minimum score 6.5). Electronic applications accepted. *Expenses:* Tuition, state resident: part-time $553 per credit. Tuition, nonresident: part-time $854 per credit. *Required fees:* $91 per credit. Tuition and fees vary according to program.

**Naval Postgraduate School,** Departments and Academic Groups, Department of National Security Affairs, Monterey, CA 93943. Offers national security affairs (MA); security studies (MA), including civil-military relations, combating terrorism: policy and strategy, defense decision-making and planning, Europe and Eurasia, Far East, Southeast Asia, the Pacific, homeland security and defense, Middle East, South Asia, Sub-Saharan Africa, stabilization and reconstruction, western hemisphere. Program only open to commissioned officers of the United States and friendly nations and selected United States federal civilian employees. *Program availability:* Part-time. *Degree requirements:* For master's, thesis (for some programs). *Faculty research:* Privatizing welfare in the Middle East; social construction of Russia's resurgence; institutions, ethnicity and political mobilization in South Africa; Hezbollah; China's strategic interests in Cambodia.

**New York University,** School of Continuing and Professional Studies, Center for Global Affairs, New York, NY 10012-1019. Offers global affairs (MS), including environment/ energy policy, human rights and international law, international development and humanitarian assistance, international relations, peace building, private sector, transnational security; global energy (Advanced Certificate); peacebuilding (Advanced Certificate); transnational security (Advanced Certificate). *Program availability:* Part-time, evening/weekend. *Degree requirements:* For master's, thesis. *Entrance requirements:* For master's, GRE or GMAT (only upon request), bachelor's degree, resume with relevant professional work, internship or volunteer experience, two letters of recommendation, statement of purpose. Additional exam requirements/recommendations for international students: Required—TOEFL (minimum score 600 paper-based; 100 iBT), IELTS (minimum score 7). Electronic applications accepted.

*Conflict Resolution and Mediation/Peace Studies*

**Norwich University,** College of Graduate and Continuing Studies, Master of Arts in Diplomacy Program, Northfield, VT 05663. Offers diplomacy (MA), including cyber diplomacy - policy, cyber diplomacy - technical, international commerce, international conflict management, international terrorism. *Program availability:* Evening/weekend, online only, mostly all online with a week-long residency requirement. *Faculty:* 1 full-time (0 women), 20 part-time/adjunct (3 women). *Students:* 154 full-time (49 women); includes 34 minority (18 Black or African American, non-Hispanic/Latino; 1 Asian, non-Hispanic/Latino; 9 Hispanic/Latino; 6 Two or more races, non-Hispanic/Latino), 1 international. Average age 34. 31 applicants, 100% accepted, 25 enrolled. In 2016, 93 master's awarded. *Degree requirements:* For master's, comprehensive exam, thesis optional. *Entrance requirements:* For master's, minimum undergraduate GPA of 2.75. Additional exam requirements/recommendations for international students: Required—TOEFL (minimum score 550 paper-based; 80 iBT), IELTS (minimum score 6.5). *Application deadline:* For fall admission, 8/14 for domestic and international students; for winter admission, 11/13 for domestic and international students; for spring admission, 2/12 for domestic and international students; for summer admission, 6/5 for domestic and international students. Electronic applications accepted. *Expenses:* Contact institution. *Financial support:* In 2016–17, 75 students received support. Scholarships/grants available. Financial award application deadline: 8/4; financial award applicants required to submit FAFSA. *Unit head:* Dr. Lasha Tchantouridze, Program Director, 802-485-2095, Fax: 802-485-2533, E-mail: ltchanto@norwich.edu. *Application contact:* Admissions Advisor, 800-460-5597 Ext. 3378, Fax: 802-485-2533, E-mail: mdy@online.norwich.edu.
Website: https://online.norwich.edu/degree-programs/masters/master-arts-diplomacy/overview

**Nova Southeastern University,** College of Arts, Humanities, and Social Sciences, Fort Lauderdale, FL 33314-7796. Offers advanced conflict resolution practice (Graduate Certificate); college student affairs (MS); conflict analysis and resolution (MS, PhD); cross-disciplinary studies (MA); family studies (Graduate Certificate); family systems health care (Graduate Certificate); family therapy (MS, PhD); marriage and family therapy (DMFT); peace studies (Graduate Certificate); qualitative research (Graduate Certificate); solution focused coaching (Graduate Certificate). *Accreditation:* AAMFT/COAMFTE (one or more programs are accredited). *Program availability:* Part-time, evening/weekend, 100% online, blended/hybrid learning. *Faculty:* 29 full-time (18 women), 27 part-time/adjunct (21 women). *Students:* 306 full-time (242 women), 889 part-time (683 women); includes 677 minority (403 Black or African American, non-Hispanic/Latino; 2 American Indian or Alaska Native, non-Hispanic/Latino; 20 Asian, non-Hispanic/Latino; 224 Hispanic/Latino; 1 Native Hawaiian or other Pacific Islander, non-Hispanic/Latino; 27 Two or more races, non-Hispanic/Latino), 53 international. Average age 37. 624 applicants, 61% accepted, 285 enrolled. In 2016, 303 master's, 71 doctorates, 34 other advanced degrees awarded. *Degree requirements:* For master's, thesis optional, comprehensive exams, portfolios (for some programs), table-top exams (for some programs); for doctorate, comprehensive exam, thesis/dissertation, qualifying exams, portfolios (for some programs). *Entrance requirements:* For master's, interview, minimum GPA of 3.0, writing sample; for doctorate, interview, minimum GPA of 3.5, master's degree in related field, writing sample; for Graduate Certificate, minimum GPA of 3.0. Additional exam requirements/recommendations for international students: Required—TOEFL. *Application deadline:* For fall admission, 5/17 priority date for domestic and international students; for winter admission, 12/1 priority date for domestic and international students; for spring admission, 4/1 priority date for domestic and international students. Applications are processed on a rolling basis. Application fee: $50. Electronic applications accepted. *Expenses:* $1,005. *Financial support:* In 2016–17, 170 students received support. Career-related internships or fieldwork, Federal Work-Study, scholarships/grants, and unspecified assistantships available. Financial award application deadline: 4/1; financial award applicants required to submit CSS PROFILE. *Faculty research:* Conflict resolution, family therapy, peace research, international conflict, multi-disciplinary studies, college student affairs, national security affairs, health care conflict resolution, family systems health care, advanced family systems, qualitative research, solution-focused coaching. *Unit head:* Dr. Honggang Yang, Dean, 954-262-3016, Fax: 954-262-3968, E-mail: yangh@nova.edu. *Application contact:* Marcia Arango, Student Recruitment Coordinator, 954-262-3006, Fax: 954-262-3968, E-mail: marango@nsu.nova.edu.
Website: http://cahss.nova.edu/

**Old Dominion University,** College of Arts and Letters, Graduate Program in International Studies, Norfolk, VA 23529. Offers conflict and cooperation (MA, PhD); interdependence and transnationalism (MA, PhD); international cultural studies (MA, PhD); international political economy and development (MA, PhD); modeling and simulation (MA, PhD); U.S. foreign policy and international relations (MA, PhD). *Program availability:* Part-time. *Faculty:* 18 full-time (4 women). *Students:* 35 full-time (13 women), 38 part-time (20 women); includes 14 minority (9 Black or African American, non-Hispanic/Latino; 2 Asian, non-Hispanic/Latino; 1 Hispanic/Latino; 2 Two or more races, non-Hispanic/Latino), 19 international. Average age 37. 99 applicants, 54% accepted, 34 enrolled. In 2016, 24 master's, 11 doctorates awarded. Terminal master's awarded for partial completion of doctoral program. *Degree requirements:* For master's, one foreign language, comprehensive exam, thesis optional; for doctorate, one foreign language, comprehensive exam, thesis/dissertation. *Entrance requirements:* For master's, GRE General Test, sample of written work, 2 letters of recommendation; for doctorate, GRE General Test, sample of written work, 3 letters of recommendation. Additional exam requirements/recommendations for international students: Required—TOEFL (minimum score 570 paper-based). *Application deadline:* For fall admission, 1/15 for domestic and international students; for spring admission, 10/15 for domestic and international students. Application fee: $50. Electronic applications accepted. *Expenses:* Contact institution. *Financial support:* In 2016–17, 12 students received support, including 1 fellowship (averaging $15,000 per year), 5 research assistantships with tuition reimbursements available (averaging $15,000 per year), 4 teaching assistantships with tuition reimbursements available (averaging $15,000 per year); career-related internships or fieldwork, institutionally sponsored loans, and unspecified assistantships also available. Financial award application deadline: 1/15; financial award applicants required to submit FAFSA. *Faculty research:* U.S. foreign policy, international security, Transatlantic and Transpacific relations, transnational issues, international political economy and development. *Total annual research expenditures:* $330,391. *Unit head:* Dr. Regina Karp, Graduate Program Director, 757-683-5700, Fax: 757-683-5701, E-mail: rkarp@odu.edu. *Application contact:* Dr. David C. Earnest, Associate Dean, 757-683-6077, Fax: 757-683-5746, E-mail: dearnest@odu.edu.
Website: http://www.odu.edu/gpis

**Pepperdine University,** School of Law, Master of Dispute Resolution Program, Malibu, CA 90263. Offers LL M, MDR, JD/MDR, MDP/MBA, MDR/MPP. *Students:* 41 full-time (25 women), 69 part-time (39 women); includes 24 minority (6 Black or African American, non-Hispanic/Latino; 9 Asian, non-Hispanic/Latino; 7 Hispanic/Latino; 2 Two or more races, non-Hispanic/Latino), 53 international. Average age 35. 120 applicants, 99% accepted, 51 enrolled. In 2016, 30 master's awarded. *Entrance requirements:* For master's, GRE/LSAT, letters of recommendation. *Application deadline:* For fall admission, 2/15 for domestic students; for spring admission, 8/15 for domestic students. Application fee: $60. *Unit head:* Dr. Peter Robinson, Managing Director, Straus Institute

for Dispute Resolution, 310-506-4655, E-mail: peter.robinson@pepperdine.edu. *Application contact:* Seth Hackett, Admissions and Student Services Coordinator, 310-506-4655, E-mail: seth.hackett@pepperdine.edu.
Website: http://law.pepperdine.edu/degrees-programs/master-of-dispute-resolution/

**Portland State University,** Graduate Studies, College of Liberal Arts and Sciences, Program in Conflict Resolution, Portland, OR 97207-0751. Offers MA, MS. *Faculty:* 7 full-time (4 women), 5 part-time/adjunct (2 women). *Students:* 31 full-time (22 women), 22 part-time (14 women); includes 14 minority (4 Black or African American, non-Hispanic/Latino; 2 Asian, non-Hispanic/Latino; 4 Hispanic/Latino; 4 Two or more races, non-Hispanic/Latino), 7 international. Average age 34. 23 applicants, 87% accepted, 12 enrolled. In 2016, 18 master's awarded. *Degree requirements:* For master's, thesis or alternative, practicum. *Entrance requirements:* For master's, 3 letters of recommendation. Additional exam requirements/recommendations for international students: Required—TOEFL (minimum score 550 paper-based; 80 iBT), IELTS (minimum score 6.5). *Application deadline:* For fall admission, 3/30 for domestic students, 3/1 for international students; for winter admission, 9/1 for domestic students, 8/1 for international students; for spring admission, 11/1 for domestic and international students. Application fee: $65. *Expenses:* Contact institution. *Financial support:* In 2016–17, 1 teaching assistantship (averaging $14,250 per year) was awarded; Federal Work-Study also available. *Unit head:* Dr. Harry Anastasiou, Director, 503-725-9711, E-mail: harrya@pdx.edu. *Application contact:* Aislyn Matias, Program Administrator, 503-725-9175, E-mail: aislyn.matias@pdx.edu.
Website: http://www.pdx.edu/conflict-resolution

**Regent University,** Graduate School, School of Law, Virginia Beach, VA 23464-9800. Offers American legal studies (LL M); human rights (LL M); law (MA, JD), including business (MA), criminal justice (MA), general legal studies (MA), human resources management (MA), human rights (MA), mediation (MA), national security (MA), non-profit management (MA), regulatory compliance (MA), wealth management and financial planning (MA); JD/MA; JD/MBA. *Accreditation:* ABA. *Program availability:* Part-time, 100% online, blended/hybrid learning. *Faculty:* 20 full-time (6 women), 67 part-time/adjunct (19 women). *Students:* 364 full-time (219 women), 170 part-time (118 women); includes 213 minority (150 Black or African American, non-Hispanic/Latino; 1 American Indian or Alaska Native, non-Hispanic/Latino; 10 Asian, non-Hispanic/Latino; 34 Hispanic/Latino; 1 Native Hawaiian or other Pacific Islander, non-Hispanic/Latino; 17 Two or more races, non-Hispanic/Latino), 87 international. Average age 34. 834 applicants, 45% accepted, 174 enrolled. In 2016, 48 master's, 85 doctorates awarded. *Entrance requirements:* For master's, college transcripts, resume, personal statement; for doctorate, LSAT, minimum undergraduate GPA of 3.0, official transcripts, 2 letters of recommendation, resume, personal statement. Additional exam requirements/recommendations for international students: Required—TOEFL (minimum score 600 paper-based). *Application deadline:* For fall admission, 3/1 for domestic students. Applications are processed on a rolling basis. Application fee: $50. Electronic applications accepted. *Expenses:* $1,140 per credit (for JD); $650 per credit (for MA); $833 per credit (for LL M); $250 technology fee. *Financial support:* In 2016–17, 319 students received support. Career-related internships or fieldwork, scholarships/grants, and unspecified assistantships available. Support available to part-time students. *Faculty research:* Family law, Constitutional law, law and culture, evidence and practice, intellectual property. *Unit head:* Michael Hernandez, Dean, 757-352-4040, Fax: 757-352-4595, E-mail: michher@regent.edu. *Application contact:* Katie Kerley, Director of Law Admissions, 877-267-5072, Fax: 757-352-4139, E-mail: lawschool@regent.edu.
Website: http://www.regent.edu/law/

**Royal Roads University,** Graduate Studies, Peace and Conflict Studies Program, Victoria, BC V9B 5Y2, Canada. Offers conflict analysis (G Dip); conflict analysis and management (MA); disaster and emergency management (MA); human security and peacebuilding (MA). *Program availability:* Online learning. *Degree requirements:* For master's, thesis. *Entrance requirements:* For master's, 5-7 years of related work experience. Additional exam requirements/recommendations for international students: Required—TOEFL (paper-based 570) or IELTS (7) recommended. Electronic applications accepted. *Faculty research:* Conflict analysis, ethno-political conflict reconciliation, international relations, displaced persons.

**Saint Mary's College of California,** Kalmanovitz School of Education, Leadership Programs, Moraga, CA 94556. Offers coaching and facilitation (MA); organizational leadership and change (MA); peacebuilding and conflict transformation (MA); social justice (MA). *Accreditation:* AACSB. *Program availability:* Part-time, evening/weekend, online learning. *Degree requirements:* For master's, research project. *Entrance requirements:* For master's, letters of recommendation, interview. Electronic applications accepted. *Expenses:* Contact institution. *Faculty research:* Leadership, organizational change, values, adult learning, transformative learning.

**St. Mary's University,** Graduate Studies, Program in International Relations, San Antonio, TX 78228-8507. Offers conflict transformation (Certificate); international conflict resolution (MA); international development (MA); international relations (MA); security policy (MA); JD/MA. *Program availability:* Part-time, evening/weekend, 100% online. *Faculty:* 4 full-time (2 women), 1 part-time/adjunct (0 women). *Students:* 22 full-time (14 women), 59 part-time (18 women); includes 33 minority (5 Black or African American, non-Hispanic/Latino; 2 American Indian or Alaska Native, non-Hispanic/Latino; 6 Asian, non-Hispanic/Latino; 20 Hispanic/Latino), 5 international. Average age 32. 28 applicants, 61% accepted, 6 enrolled. In 2016, 35 master's awarded. *Degree requirements:* For master's, one foreign language, comprehensive exam (for some programs), thesis (for some programs), thesis or comprehensive exam. *Entrance requirements:* For master's, minimum undergraduate cumulative GPA of 3.0. Additional exam requirements/recommendations for international students: Required—TOEFL (minimum score 550 paper-based; 80 iBT), IELTS (minimum score 6). *Application deadline:* For fall admission, 7/1 for domestic students; for spring admission, 11/15 for domestic students; for summer admission, 4/1 for domestic students. Applications are processed on a rolling basis. Application fee: $0. Electronic applications accepted. *Expenses: Tuition:* Full-time $15,600; part-time $865 per credit hour. *Required fees:* $148 per semester. *Financial support:* Research assistantships, Federal Work-Study, tuition waivers (full), unspecified assistantships, and grants for active-duty and retired military, DOD employees, and their spouses available. Financial award application deadline: 3/31; financial award applicants required to submit FAFSA. *Faculty research:* Anthropology and ethics, states in crisis and socioeconomic development, politics and society of south Asia, political psychology, international relations theory. *Unit head:* Dr. Amber Aubone, Graduate International Relations, 210-436-3111, E-mail: aaubone@stmarytx.edu. *Application contact:* Kim Thornton, Director, Graduate and Adult Enrollment Services, 210-436-3101, E-mail: kthornton@stmarytx.edu.

**Saint Paul University,** Faculty of Human Sciences, Program in Conflict Studies, Ottawa, ON K1S 1C4, Canada. Offers MA. *Program availability:* Part-time. *Entrance requirements:* For master's, H=honors BA, B average.

**Salisbury University,** Department of Conflict Analysis and Dispute Resolution, Salisbury, MD 21801-6837. Offers MA. *Program availability:* Part-time. *Faculty:* 6 full-time. *Students:* 38 full-time (26 women), 4 part-time (1 woman); includes 15 minority (10 Black or African American, non-Hispanic/Latino; 1 Asian, non-Hispanic/Latino; 3 Hispanic/Latino; 1 Two or more races, non-Hispanic/Latino), 1 international. Average

age 31. 29 applicants, 72% accepted, 16 enrolled. In 2016, 18 master's awarded. *Degree requirements:* For master's, thesis optional. *Entrance requirements:* Additional exam requirements/recommendations for international students: Required—TOEFL (minimum score 550 paper-based, 79 iBT) or IELTS (6.5). *Application deadline:* For fall admission, 4/14 priority date for domestic and international students. Applications are processed on a rolling basis. Application fee: $65. Electronic applications accepted. *Expenses:* $381 per credit hour resident tuition, $670 per credit hour non-resident tuition; $84 per credit hour fees. *Financial support:* In 2016–17, 8 teaching assistantships with full tuition reimbursements (averaging $8,219 per year) were awarded; career-related internships or fieldwork and scholarships/grants also available. Support available to part-time students. Financial award application deadline: 3/1; financial award applicants required to submit FAFSA. *Faculty research:* Cultural conflict; environmental change and conflicts stemming from ecologic issues and human interactions; international conflict (Africa, South Asia, South America, Middle East); non-violence movement and theories; academic structural issues. *Unit head:* Dr. Vitus Ozoke, Graduate Program Director, Conflict Analysis and Dispute Resolution, 410-677-0276, E-mail: vaozoke@salisbury.edu.
Website: http://www.salisbury.edu/gsr/gradstudies/CADRpage.html

**Salve Regina University,** Program in Humanities, Newport, RI 02840-4192. Offers humanitarian assistance (MA); humanities (PhD); public humanities (MA); religion, peace and justice (MA). *Program availability:* Part-time, evening/weekend, online learning. *Degree requirements:* For master's, thesis optional; for doctorate, one foreign language, comprehensive exam, thesis/dissertation. *Entrance requirements:* For master's, GMAT, GRE General Test, or MAT; for doctorate, GRE General Test. Additional exam requirements/recommendations for international students: Required—TOEFL (minimum score 600 paper-based; 100 iBT) or IELTS. Electronic applications accepted.

**SIT Graduate Institute,** Graduate Programs, Master's Programs in Intercultural Service, Leadership, and Management, Program in Peacebuilding and Conflict Transformation, Brattleboro, VT 05302-0676. Offers MA.

**Southern Methodist University,** Annette Caldwell Simmons School of Education and Human Development, Department of Dispute Resolution and Counseling, Dallas, TX 75275. Offers counseling (MS); dispute resolution (MA). *Program availability:* Part-time. *Degree requirements:* For master's, practica experience, 2 internships (counseling). *Entrance requirements:* For master's, minimum undergraduate GPA of 2.75 (for dispute resolution), 3.0 (for counseling); 3 letters of recommendation. Additional exam requirements/recommendations for international students: Required—TOEFL. Electronic applications accepted.

**Southern New Hampshire University,** School of Business, Manchester, NH 03106-1045. Offers accounting (MBA, MS, Graduate Certificate); accounting finance (MS); accounting/auditing (MS); accounting/forensic accounting (MS); accounting/taxation (MS); athletic administration (MBA, Graduate Certificate); business administration (IMBA, MBA, Certificate, Graduate Certificate), including accounting (Certificate), business administration (MBA), business information systems (Graduate Certificate), human resource management (Certificate); corporate social responsibility (MBA); entrepreneurship (MBA); finance (MBA, MS, Graduate Certificate); finance/corporate finance (MS); finance/investments and securities (MS); forensic accounting (MBA); healthcare informatics (MBA); healthcare management (MBA); human resource management (Graduate Certificate); information technology (MS, Graduate Certificate); information technology management (MBA); international business (Graduate Certificate); international business and information technology (Graduate Certificate); international finance (Graduate Certificate); international sport management (Graduate Certificate); justice studies (MBA); leadership of nonprofit organizations (Graduate Certificate); management (MS); marketing (MBA, MS, Graduate Certificate); operations and project management (MS); operations and supply chain management (MBA, Graduate Certificate); organizational leadership (MS); project management (MBA, Graduate Certificate); Six Sigma (MBA); Six Sigma quality (Graduate Certificate); social media marketing (MBA); sport management (MBA, MS, Graduate Certificate); sustainability and environmental compliance (MBA); workplace conflict management (MBA); MBA/Certificate. *Accreditation:* ACBSP. *Program availability:* Part-time, evening/weekend, online learning. Terminal master's awarded for partial completion of doctoral program. *Degree requirements:* For master's, one foreign language, comprehensive exam (for some programs), thesis or alternative. *Entrance requirements:* For master's, minimum GPA of 2.5. Additional exam requirements/recommendations for international students: Required—TOEFL (minimum score 500 paper-based). Electronic applications accepted.

**Syracuse University,** Maxwell School of Citizenship and Public Affairs, CAS Program in Conflict Resolution, Syracuse, NY 13244. Offers CAS. *Program availability:* Part-time. In 2016, 39 CASs awarded. *Entrance requirements:* For degree, resume, three letters of recommendation, personal statement, official transcripts. Additional exam requirements/recommendations for international students: Required—TOEFL (minimum score 100 iBT). *Application deadline:* For fall admission, 2/1 priority date for domestic and international students; for spring admission, 8/15 priority date for domestic and international students. Applications are processed on a rolling basis. Application fee: $75. Electronic applications accepted. *Expenses: Tuition:* Full-time $25,974; part-time $1443 per credit hour. *Required fees:* $802; $50 per course. Tuition and fees vary according to course load and program. *Financial support:* Application deadline: 2/1. *Faculty research:* Applied dispute resolution and conflict management, advocacy and social movements, collaborative governance, environmental public participation and conflict, transnational conflicts. *Unit head:* Prof. Catherine Gerard, Director, 315-443-2756, E-mail: cgerard@maxwell.syr.edu. *Application contact:* Debbie Toole, 315-443-2367, E-mail: datoole@syr.edu.
Website: https://www.maxwell.syr.edu/exed/certificates/sa-conflict_resolution/overview/

**Trident University International,** College of Business Administration, Program in Business Administration, Cypress, CA 90630. Offers business administration (PhD); conflict and negotiation management (MBA); criminal justice administration (MBA); entrepreneurship (MBA); finance (MBA); general management (MBA); government accounting (MBA); human resource management (MBA); information security and digital assurance management (MBA); information technology management (MBA); international business (MBA); logistics management (MBA); marketing (MBA); project management (MBA); public management (MBA); quality management (MBA); strategic leadership (MBA). *Program availability:* Part-time, evening/weekend, online learning. *Degree requirements:* For doctorate, comprehensive exam, thesis/dissertation, defense of dissertation. *Entrance requirements:* For master's, minimum GPA of 2.5 (students with GPA 3.0 or greater may transfer up to 30% of graduate level credits); for doctorate, minimum GPA of 3.4, curriculum vitae, course work in research methods or statistics. Additional exam requirements/recommendations for international students: Required—TOEFL. Electronic applications accepted.

**Tufts University,** The Fletcher School of Law and Diplomacy, Medford, MA 02155. Offers LL M, MA, MALD, MIB, PhD, DVM/MA, JD/MALD, MALD/MA, MALD/MBA, MALD/MS, MD/MA. *Program availability:* Online learning. *Degree requirements:* For master's, one foreign language, thesis; for doctorate, one foreign language, comprehensive exam, thesis/dissertation, dissertation defense. *Entrance requirements:*

For master's and doctorate, GMAT or GRE General Test. Additional exam requirements/recommendations for international students: Required—TOEFL (minimum score 600 paper-based; 100 iBT), IELTS (minimum score 7). Electronic applications accepted. *Expenses:* Contact institution. *Faculty research:* Negotiation and conflict resolution, international organizations, international business and economic law, security studies, development economics.

**United States International University–Africa,** School of Arts and Sciences, Nairobi, Kenya. Offers counseling psychology (MA), including chemical dependency, health psychology; international relations (MA), including development studies, diplomacy and foreign policy, peace and conflict studies. *Program availability:* Part-time, evening/weekend. *Degree requirements:* For master's, thesis, practicum. *Entrance requirements:* For master's, GRE General Test, 2 letters of recommendation, resume. Additional exam requirements/recommendations for international students: Required—TOEFL. *Faculty research:* Trauma in children, African intellectualism, psychological assessment tools.

**United Theological Seminary of the Twin Cities,** Graduate Programs, New Brighton, MN 55112-2598. Offers advanced theological studies (Diploma); justice and peace studies (M Div, MA); leadership toward racial justice (M Div, MA, Certificate); Methodist studies (M Div, MA, Certificate); ministry (D Min); ministry renewal and professional development (Certificate); pastoral care and counseling (M Div, MA, MARL); religion and theology (MA); theological and religious studies (Certificate); theology and the arts (M Div, MA); urban ministry (M Div, MA, MARL); women's studies: religion, theology and ministry (M Div, MA). *Accreditation:* ACIPE; ATS. *Program availability:* Part-time, evening/weekend. *Degree requirements:* For master's, thesis; for doctorate, comprehensive exam, thesis/dissertation. *Entrance requirements:* For master's, minimum GPA of 2.75; strong analytical, reflective thinking and writing skills; vocational and academic goals compatible with those of Seminary; for doctorate, M Div or equivalent, minimum GPA of 3.0, 3 years experience in professional ministry; for other advanced degree, BA or equivalent life experience; strong analytical, reflective thinking and writing skills (Certificate); proficiency in English language, previous study of theology at a theological school, recommendation of student's denomination (Diploma). Additional exam requirements/recommendations for international students: Required—TOEFL (minimum score 550 paper-based).

**Universidad del Turabo,** Graduate Programs, School of Social Sciences and Humanities, Programs in Public Affairs, Gurabo, PR 00778-3030. Offers arts administration (MPA); conflict and mediation studies (MPA); criminal justice studies (MPA); forensic science (MPA); human services administration (MPA). *Students:* 124 full-time (75 women), 83 part-time (69 women); includes 294 minority (all Hispanic/Latino). Average age 31. 180 applicants, 51% accepted, 74 enrolled. In 2016, 92 master's awarded. *Entrance requirements:* For master's, GRE, EXADEP, interview, essay, official transcript, recommendation letters. *Application deadline:* For fall admission, 8/5 for domestic students. Applications are processed on a rolling basis. Application fee: $25. Electronic applications accepted. *Financial support:* Institutionally sponsored loans available. Financial award applicants required to submit FAFSA. *Unit head:* María del Carmen Santos, Dean, 787-743-7979 Ext. 4232. *Application contact:* Diriee Rodríguez, Admissions Director, 787-743-7979 Ext. 4453, E-mail: admisiones-ut@suagm.edu.
Website: http://ut.suagm.edu/es/sociales

**Université de Sherbrooke,** Faculty of Law, Sherbrooke, QC J1K 2R1, Canada. Offers alternative dispute resolution (LL M, Diploma); business law (Diploma); common law (JD); criminal and penal law (Diploma); health law (LL M, Diploma); international law (LL M); law (LL D); legal management (Diploma); notarial law (Diploma); transnational law (Diploma). *Program availability:* Part-time, evening/weekend. *Degree requirements:* For master's, thesis; for Diploma, one foreign language. *Entrance requirements:* For master's and Diploma, LL B. Electronic applications accepted.

**University of Arkansas at Little Rock,** Graduate School, College of Social Sciences and Communication, Program in Conflict Mediation, Little Rock, AR 72204-1099. Offers Graduate Certificate.

**University of Baltimore,** Graduate School, College of Public Affairs, Program in Negotiations and Conflict Management, Baltimore, MD 21201-5779. Offers MS. *Program availability:* Part-time, evening/weekend. *Degree requirements:* For master's, thesis optional, internship. *Entrance requirements:* For master's, minimum GPA of 3.0. Additional exam requirements/recommendations for international students: Required—TOEFL (minimum score 550 paper-based). Electronic applications accepted. *Faculty research:* Communication and conflict, conflict management systems theory.

**University of Bridgeport,** College of Public and International Affairs, Bridgeport, CT 06604. Offers East Asian and Pacific Rim studies (MA); global development and peace (MA); global media and communication studies (MA). *Program availability:* Part-time, evening/weekend. *Degree requirements:* For master's, thesis. *Entrance requirements:* Additional exam requirements/recommendations for international students: Recommended—TOEFL (minimum score 550 paper-based; 80 iBT), IELTS (minimum score 6.5).

**University of Denver,** Josef Korbel School of International Studies, Program in Conflict Resolution, Denver, CO 80208. Offers MA. *Program availability:* Part-time. *Faculty:* 1 (woman) full-time, 2 part-time/adjunct (1 woman). *Students:* 11 full-time (5 women), 3 part-time (0 women); includes 2 minority (1 Hispanic/Latino; 1 Two or more races, non-Hispanic/Latino). Average age 29. 28 applicants, 86% accepted, 6 enrolled. In 2016, 7 master's awarded. *Degree requirements:* For master's, thesis optional, internship. *Entrance requirements:* For master's, GRE General Test or GMAT, bachelor's degree, transcripts, statement of purpose, writing sample, two letters of recommendation. Additional exam requirements/recommendations for international students: Required—TOEFL (minimum score 587 paper-based; 95 iBT). *Application deadline:* For fall admission, 1/15 priority date for domestic and international students; for winter admission, 11/1 priority date for domestic and international students. Applications are processed on a rolling basis. Application fee: $65. Electronic applications accepted. *Expenses:* $43,458 per year full-time. *Financial support:* In 2016–17, 7 students received support, including 1 research assistantship with tuition reimbursement available (averaging $7,250 per year); career-related internships or fieldwork, Federal Work-Study, scholarships/grants, tuition waivers (partial), and unspecified assistantships also available. Support available to part-time students. Financial award application deadline: 2/15; financial award applicants required to submit FAFSA. *Unit head:* Dr. Karen Feste, Director, 303-871-2418, Fax: 303-871-2456, E-mail: kfeste@du.edu. *Application contact:* Information Contact, 303-871-6477, E-mail: cri@du.edu.
Website: http://www.du.edu/conflictresolution

**University of Hawaii at Manoa,** Graduate Division, College of Social Sciences, Matsunaga Institute for Peace and Conflict Resolution, Honolulu, HI 96822. Offers conflict resolution (Graduate Certificate). *Program availability:* Part-time. *Entrance requirements:* For degree, GRE General Test. Additional exam requirements/recommendations for international students: Required—TOEFL (minimum score 540 paper-based; 76 iBT), IELTS (minimum score 5).

## Conflict Resolution and Mediation/Peace Studies

**University of Idaho,** College of Law, Moscow, ID 83844-2321. Offers business law and entrepreneurship (JD); law (JD); litigation and alternative dispute resolution (JD); Native American law (JD); natural resources and environmental law (JD). *Accreditation:* ABA. *Faculty:* 32 full-time, 11 part-time/adjunct. *Students:* Average age 28. *Entrance requirements:* For doctorate, LSAT, Law School Admission Council Credential Assembly Service (CAS) Report. Additional exam requirements/recommendations for international students: Required—TOEFL. *Application deadline:* For fall admission, 3/15 priority date for domestic students. Applications are processed on a rolling basis. Application fee: $50 ($60 for international students). Electronic applications accepted. *Expenses:* Contact institution. *Financial support:* Career-related internships or fieldwork, Federal Work-Study, and institutionally sponsored loans available. Financial award applicants required to submit FAFSA. *Faculty research:* Transboundary river governance, tribal protection and stewardship, regional water issues, environmental law. *Unit head:* Mark Adams, Dean, 208-885-4977, E-mail: uilaw@uidaho.edu. *Application contact:* Carole Wells, Director of Admissions, 208-885-2300, Fax: 208-885-2252, E-mail: lawadmit@uidaho.edu.
Website: http://www.uidaho.edu/law/

**The University of Manchester,** School of Arts, Histories and Cultures, Manchester, United Kingdom. Offers anthropology, media and performance (PhD); applied theatre professional (PhD); archaeology (PhD); art history and visual studies (PhD); arts management and cultural policy (PhD); classics and ancient history (PhD); composition (PhD); creative writing (PhD); drama (PhD); economic and social history (PhD); electroacoustic composition (PhD); English and American studies (PhD); history (PhD); humanitarianism and conflict response (PhD); museology (PhD); music (PhD); musicology (PhD); religions and theology (PhD).

**University of Massachusetts Amherst,** Graduate School, College of Natural Sciences, Department of Psychological and Brain Sciences, Amherst, MA 01003. Offers clinical psychology (MS, PhD); cognitive psychology (MS, PhD); developmental science (MS, PhD); psychology of peace and violence (MS, PhD); social psychology (MS, PhD). *Accreditation:* APA (one or more programs are accredited). Terminal master's awarded for partial completion of doctoral program. *Degree requirements:* For master's, thesis; for doctorate, comprehensive exam, thesis/dissertation. *Entrance requirements:* For master's and doctorate, GRE General Test, 3 letters of recommendation. Additional exam requirements/recommendations for international students: Required—TOEFL (minimum score 550 paper-based; 80 iBT), IELTS (minimum score 6.5). Electronic applications accepted.

**University of Massachusetts Boston,** John W. McCormack Graduate School of Policy and Global Studies, Program in Conflict Resolution, Boston, MA 02125-3393. Offers MA, Certificate. MA program accepts applications for fall admission only; Certificate program accepts applications for spring admission only. *Faculty:* 8 full-time (4 women), 5 part-time/adjunct (2 women). *Students:* 13 full-time (9 women), 26 part-time (18 women); includes 12 minority (6 Black or African American, non-Hispanic/Latino; 4 Asian, non-Hispanic/Latino; 2 Two or more races, non-Hispanic/Latino), 5 international. Average age 36. 33 applicants, 79% accepted, 17 enrolled. In 2016, 10 master's, 3 other advanced degrees awarded. *Degree requirements:* For master's, practicum, final project. *Entrance requirements:* For master's, MAT or GRE, minimum GPA of 2.75; for Certificate, minimum GPA of 2.75. *Application deadline:* For fall admission, 3/1 for domestic students; for spring admission, 11/1 for domestic students. *Expenses:* Tuition, state resident: full-time $16,863. Tuition, nonresident: full-time $32,913. *Required fees:* $177. *Financial support:* Research assistantships with full tuition reimbursements, teaching assistantships with full tuition reimbursements, career-related internships or fieldwork, Federal Work-Study, and unspecified assistantships available. Support available to part-time students. Financial award application deadline: 3/1. *Faculty research:* Mediation and negotiation, justice and conflict, cross-cultural mediation, environmental fairness, dispute resolution theory and ethics. *Unit head:* Dr. Darren Kew. *Application contact:* Peggy Roldan Patel, Graduate Admissions Coordinator, 617-287-6400, Fax: 617-287-6236, E-mail: bos.gadm@dpc.umassp.edu.

**University of Massachusetts Boston,** John W. McCormack Graduate School of Policy and Global Studies, Program in Global Governance and Human Security, Boston, MA 02125-3393. Offers MA. *Students:* 16 full-time (10 women), 27 part-time (16 women); includes 6 minority (1 Black or African American, non-Hispanic/Latino; 3 Asian, non-Hispanic/Latino; 1 Hispanic/Latino; 1 Two or more races, non-Hispanic/Latino), 20 international. Average age 35. 25 applicants, 48% accepted, 8 enrolled. In 2016, 7 master's awarded. *Expenses:* Tuition, state resident: full-time $16,863. Tuition, nonresident: full-time $32,913. *Required fees:* $177. *Unit head:* Dr. David Cash, Dean. *Application contact:* Peggy Roldan Patel, Graduate Admissions Coordinator, 617-287-6400, Fax: 617-287-6236, E-mail: bos.gadm@dpc.umassp.edu.

**University of Massachusetts Lowell,** College of Fine Arts, Humanities and Social Sciences, Program in Peace and Conflict Studies, Lowell, MA 01854. Offers MA. *Degree requirements:* For master's, practicum, project, or thesis. *Entrance requirements:* For master's, GRE, GMAT, or LSAT, bachelor's degree from accredited college or university, minimum undergraduate GPA of 3.0, 18 credits of peace and conflict studies related coursework, three letters of reference, personal statement, resume or curriculum vitae. Additional exam requirements/recommendations for international students: Required—TOEFL.

**University of Missouri,** Office of Research and Graduate Studies and School of Law, Program in Dispute Resolution, Columbia, MO 65211. Offers LL M, Certificate, Graduate Certificate. *Students:* 7 full-time (5 women); includes 2 minority (both Black or African American, non-Hispanic/Latino), 5 international. Average age 38. *Entrance requirements:* Additional exam requirements/recommendations for international students: Required—TOEFL (minimum score 600 paper-based; 100 iBT). *Application deadline:* For fall admission, 1/1 for domestic students. Applications are processed on a rolling basis. Application fee: $75 ($90 for international students). Electronic applications accepted. *Expenses:* Tuition, state resident: full-time $6347; part-time $352.60 per credit hour. Tuition, nonresident: full-time $17,379; part-time $965.50 per credit hour. *Required fees:* $1035. Tuition and fees vary according to course load, campus/location and program. *Financial support:* Fellowships, research assistantships, teaching assistantships, institutionally sponsored loans, scholarships/grants, health care benefits, and unspecified assistantships available. Support available to part-time students.
Website: http://law.missouri.edu/csdr/llm/

**University of Missouri,** School of Law, Columbia, MO 65211. Offers dispute resolution (LL M); law (JD); JD/MA; JD/MBA; JD/MPA. *Accreditation:* ABA. *Faculty:* 34 full-time (14 women), 5 part-time/adjunct (2 women). *Students:* 304 full-time (123 women), 15 part-time (10 women); includes 54 minority (35 Black or African American, non-Hispanic/Latino; 5 Asian, non-Hispanic/Latino; 5 Hispanic/Latino; 1 Native Hawaiian or other Pacific Islander, non-Hispanic/Latino; 8 Two or more races, non-Hispanic/Latino), 6 international. Average age 26. *Entrance requirements:* For doctorate, LSAT. Additional exam requirements/recommendations for international students: Required—TOEFL (minimum score 600 paper-based; 100 iBT), IELTS (minimum score 7). *Application deadline:* For fall admission, 3/1 priority date for domestic students. Applications are processed on a rolling basis. *Expenses:* Contact institution. *Financial support:* Fellowships, Federal Work-Study, and institutionally sponsored loans available. Financial award application deadline: 3/1; financial award applicants required to submit FAFSA.
Website: http://www.law.missouri.edu/

**University of New Brunswick Fredericton,** School of Graduate Studies, Policy Studies Program, Fredericton, NB E3B 5A3, Canada. Offers citizen engagement/dispute resolution (M Phil); community development (M Phil); international development (M Phil); leadership (M Phil); sustainability/environmental issues (M Phil); worldviews (M Phil). *Program availability:* Part-time. *Degree requirements:* For master's, thesis, report. *Entrance requirements:* For master's, minimum GPA of 3.5. Additional exam requirements/recommendations for international students: Required—TWE (minimum score 5.5), TOEFL (minimum score 600 paper-based; 100 iBT) or IELTS (minimum score 7). Electronic applications accepted. *Faculty research:* International development, worldviews, citizenship/dispute resolution, sustainability/environmental issues, leadership, community development.

**University of New Haven,** Graduate School, College of Arts and Sciences, Program in Industrial and Organizational Psychology, West Haven, CT 06516. Offers conflict management (MA); industrial organizational psychology (MA); industrial-human resources psychology (MA); organizational development and consultation (MA); psychology of conflict management (Graduate Certificate). *Program availability:* Part-time, evening/weekend. *Students:* 72 full-time (49 women), 18 part-time (12 women); includes 20 minority (10 Black or African American, non-Hispanic/Latino; 1 American Indian or Alaska Native, non-Hispanic/Latino; 6 Asian, non-Hispanic/Latino; 2 Hispanic/Latino; 1 Two or more races, non-Hispanic/Latino), 4 international. Average age 26. 117 applicants, 84% accepted, 34 enrolled. In 2016, 59 master's awarded. *Degree requirements:* For master's, thesis or alternative, internship or practicum. *Entrance requirements:* Additional exam requirements/recommendations for international students: Required—TOEFL (minimum score 80 iBT), IELTS, PTE. *Application deadline:* Applications are processed on a rolling basis. Application fee: $50. Electronic applications accepted. Application fee is waived when completed online. *Expenses:* Contact institution. *Financial support:* Research assistantships with partial tuition reimbursements, teaching assistantships with partial tuition reimbursements, career-related internships or fieldwork, Federal Work-Study, scholarships/grants, and unspecified assistantships available. Support available to part-time students. Financial award applicants required to submit FAFSA. *Unit head:* Dr. Eric Marcus, Coordinator, 203-932-1242, E-mail: emarcus@newhaven.edu. *Application contact:* Michelle Mason, Director of Graduate Enrollment, 203-932-7067.
Website: http://www.newhaven.edu/4730/

**The University of North Carolina at Greensboro,** Graduate School, School of Health and Human Sciences, Department of Peace and Conflict Studies, Greensboro, NC 27412-5001. Offers MA, Certificate. Electronic applications accepted.

**The University of North Carolina Wilmington,** College of Arts and Sciences, Department of Public and International Affairs, Wilmington, NC 28403-3297. Offers coastal and ocean policy (MS); conflict management and resolution (MA); public administration (MPA), including coastal management. *Accreditation:* NASPAA. *Program availability:* Part-time. *Faculty:* 17 full-time (8 women). *Students:* 71 full-time (40 women), 63 part-time (38 women); includes 29 minority (16 Black or African American, non-Hispanic/Latino; 1 American Indian or Alaska Native, non-Hispanic/Latino; 2 Asian, non-Hispanic/Latino; 5 Hispanic/Latino; 5 Two or more races, non-Hispanic/Latino), 2 international. Average age 32. 55 applicants, 85% accepted, 32 enrolled. In 2016, 47 master's awarded. *Degree requirements:* For master's, comprehensive exam (for some programs), thesis or alternative, internship, practicum, capstone project. *Entrance requirements:* For master's, GRE, GMAT, 3 letters of recommendation, statement of interest, resume, essay. Additional exam requirements/recommendations for international students: Required—TOEFL (minimum score 79 iBT), IELTS (minimum score 6.5). *Application deadline:* For fall admission, 4/15 for domestic students; for spring admission, 11/15 for domestic students. Applications are processed on a rolling basis. Application fee: $60. Electronic applications accepted. *Expenses:* Contact institution. *Financial support:* Scholarships/grants and unspecified assistantships available. Financial award application deadline: 3/15; financial award applicants required to submit FAFSA. *Unit head:* Dr. Daniel Masters, Chair, 910-962-7583, Fax: 910-962-3286, E-mail: mastersd@uncw.edu. *Application contact:* Dr. Mark Imperial, MPA Program Director, 910-962-7928, Fax: 910-962-3286, E-mail: imperialm@uncw.edu.
Website: http://www.uncw.edu/pia/graduate/index.html

**University of Notre Dame,** Graduate School, College of Arts and Letters, Division of Social Science, Joan B. Kroc Institute for International Peace Studies, Notre Dame, IN 46556. Offers MA, PhD. *Degree requirements:* For master's, one foreign language, comprehensive exam, thesis optional; for doctorate, one foreign language, comprehensive exam, thesis/dissertation. *Entrance requirements:* For master's, GRE General Test. Additional exam requirements/recommendations for international students: Required—TOEFL (minimum score 600 paper-based; 80 iBT). Electronic applications accepted. *Faculty research:* The role of international norms and institutions in peacemaking; the impact of religious, philosophical, and cultural influences on peace; the dynamics of intergroup conflict and conflict transformation; the promotion of social, economic, and environmental justice.

**University of Notre Dame,** Graduate School, Keough School of Global Affairs, Notre Dame, IN 46556. Offers global affairs (MGA); international peace studies (MGA); sustainable development (MGA).

**University of Phoenix–Online Campus,** College of Social Science, Phoenix, AZ 85034-7209. Offers mediation (Certificate); psychology (MS), including behavioral health, industrial-organizational, psychology. *Program availability:* Evening/weekend, online learning. *Entrance requirements:* Additional exam requirements/recommendations for international students: Required—TOEFL, TOEIC (Test of English as an International Communication), Berlitz Online English Proficiency Exam, PTE, or IELTS. Electronic applications accepted. *Expenses:* Contact institution.

**University of San Diego,** Joan B. Kroc School of Peace Studies, San Diego, CA 92110-2492. Offers peace and justice (MA); social innovation (MA). *Faculty:* 5 full-time (2 women), 2 part-time/adjunct (0 women). *Students:* 38 full-time (25 women), 8 part-time (7 women); includes 14 minority (2 Black or African American, non-Hispanic/Latino; 1 Asian, non-Hispanic/Latino; 10 Hispanic/Latino; 1 Two or more races, non-Hispanic/Latino), 8 international. Average age 33. In 2016, 18 master's awarded. *Degree requirements:* For master's, capstone project. *Entrance requirements:* For master's, GRE General Test, minimum GPA of 3.0. Additional exam requirements/recommendations for international students: Required—TOEFL (minimum score 580 paper-based; 83 iBT), TWE. *Application deadline:* For fall admission, 1/15 for domestic and international students. Application fee: $45. Electronic applications accepted. *Financial support:* In 2016–17, 31 students received support. Career-related internships or fieldwork, Federal Work-Study, institutionally sponsored loans, scholarships/grants, and unspecified assistantships available. Support available to part-time students. Financial award application deadline: 4/1; financial award applicants required to submit FAFSA. *Faculty research:* Conflict analysis and resolution, human security and peacebuilding, development and peacebuilding, human rights and transitional justice, religion and peacebuilding. *Unit head:* Dr. Patricia Marquez, Dean, 619-260-7919, E-mail: krocschool@sandiego.edu. *Application contact:* Monica Mahon, Associate

*Conflict Resolution and Mediation/Peace Studies*

Director of Graduate Admissions, 619-260-4524, Fax: 619-260-4158, E-mail: grads@sandiego.edu. Website: http://www.sandiego.edu/peacestudies/

**University of the Sacred Heart,** Graduate Programs, Program in Systems of Justice, San Juan, PR 00914-0383. Offers human rights and anti-discriminatory processes (MASJ); mediation and transformation of conflicts (MASJ).

**University of Victoria,** Faculty of Graduate Studies, Faculty of Human and Social Development, School of Public Administration, Victoria, BC V8W 2Y2, Canada. Offers dispute resolution (MADR); public administration (MPA, PhD); MPA/LL B. *Program availability:* Part-time, evening/weekend, online learning. *Degree requirements:* For master's, thesis (for some programs), report; for doctorate, thesis/dissertation, candidacy exam. *Entrance requirements:* For master's, GMAT or GRE General Test, professional resume; for doctorate, GMAT or GRE General Test. Additional exam requirements/recommendations for international students: Required—TOEFL (minimum score 610 paper-based). Electronic applications accepted. *Faculty research:* Policy analysis, local government, performance management, energy markets, labor markets.

**University of Wisconsin–Milwaukee,** Graduate School, College of Letters and Science, Department of Communication, Milwaukee, WI 53201-0413. Offers communication (MA, PhD), including interpersonal communication (MA), organizational communication (MA), rhetoric and public communication (MA), rhetorical leadership, rhetorical leadership (Graduate Certificate). *Program availability:* Part-time. *Faculty:* 18 full-time (11 women). *Students:* 24 full-time (14 women), 15 part-time (11 women); includes 5 minority (1 Black or African American, non-Hispanic/Latino; 1 Asian, non-Hispanic/Latino; 1 Hispanic/Latino; 2 Two or more races, non-Hispanic/Latino), 4 international. Average age 34. 44 applicants, 52% accepted, 9 enrolled. In 2016, 2 master's, 8 doctorates awarded. *Degree requirements:* For master's, thesis or alternative; for doctorate, comprehensive exam. *Entrance requirements:* For master's, GRE General Test, minimum GPA of 3.0. Additional exam requirements/recommendations for international students: Required—TOEFL (minimum score 550 paper-based; 79 iBT), IELTS (minimum score 6). *Application deadline:* For fall admission, 1/1 priority date for domestic students; for spring admission, 9/1 for domestic students. Applications are processed on a rolling basis. Application fee: $56. Electronic applications accepted. *Financial support:* In 2016–17, 3 fellowships, 34 teaching assistantships were awarded; research assistantships, career-related internships or fieldwork, unspecified assistantships, and project assistantships also available. Support available to part-time students. Financial award application deadline: 4/15; financial award applicants required to submit FAFSA. *Unit head:* Mike Allen, Department Chair, 414-229-4510, E-mail: mikealle@uwm.edu. *Application contact:* General Information Contact, 414-229-4982, Fax: 414-229-6967, E-mail: gradschool@uwm.edu. Website: https://uwm.edu/communication/

**University of Wisconsin–Milwaukee,** Graduate School, College of Letters and Science, Interdepartmental Program in Human Resources and Labor Relations, Milwaukee, WI 53201-0413. Offers human resources and labor relations (MHRLR); international human resources and labor relations (Certificate); mediation and negotiation (Certificate). *Program availability:* Part-time. *Entrance requirements:* For master's, GMAT or GRE General Test. Additional exam requirements/recommendations for international students: Required—TOEFL (minimum score 80 iBT), IELTS (minimum score 6.5). Electronic applications accepted.

**Walden University,** Graduate Programs, School of Public Policy and Administration, Minneapolis, MN 55401. Offers criminal justice (MPA, MPP, MS, Graduate Certificate), including emergency management (MS, PhD), general program (MS), global leadership (MS, PhD), homeland security and policy coordination (MS, PhD), law and public policy (MS, PhD), policy analysis (MS, PhD), public management and leadership (MS, PhD), self-designed (MS), terrorism, mediation, and peace (MS, PhD); criminal justice and executive management (MS), including global leadership (MS, PhD); criminal justice leadership and executive management (MS), including emergency management (MS, PhD), general program, homeland security and policy coordination (MS, PhD), law and public policy (MS, PhD), policy analysis (MS, PhD), public management and leadership (MS, PhD), self-designed, terrorism, mediation, and peace (MS, PhD); emergency management (MPA, MPP, MS), including criminal justice (MS, PhD), general program (MS), homeland security (MS), public management and leadership (MS, PhD), terrorism and emergency management (MS); general program (MPA, MPP); global leadership (MPA, MPP); government management (Graduate Certificate); health policy (MPA, MPP); homeland security (Graduate Certificate); homeland security and policy coordination (MPA, MPP); international nongovernmental organizations (MPA, MPP); law and public policy (MPA, MPP); local government management for sustainable communities (MPA, MPP); nonprofit management (Graduate Certificate); nonprofit management and leadership (MPA, MPP, MS), including global leadership (MS, PhD), international nongovernmental organization (MS), local government for sustainable communities (MS), self designed (MS); online teaching in higher education (Post-Master's Certificate); policy analysis (MPA); public management and leadership (MPA, MPP, Graduate Certificate); public policy (Graduate Certificate); public policy and administration (PhD), including criminal justice (MS, PhD), emergency management (MS, PhD), global leadership (MS, PhD), health policy, homeland security and policy coordination (MS, PhD), international nongovernmental organizations, law and public policy (MS, PhD), local government management for sustainable communities, nonprofit management and leadership, policy analysis (MS, PhD), public management and leadership (MS, PhD), terrorism, mediation, and peace (MS, PhD); strategic planning and public policy (Graduate Certificate); terrorism, mediation, and peace (MPA, MPP). *Program availability:* Part-time, evening/weekend, online only, 100% online. *Degree requirements:* For doctorate, thesis/dissertation, residency. *Entrance requirements:* For master's, bachelor's degree or higher; minimum GPA of 2.5; official transcripts; goal statement (for some programs); access to computer and Internet; for doctorate, master's degree or higher; three years of related professional or academic experience (preferred); minimum GPA of 3.0; goal statement and current resume (for select programs); official transcripts; access to computer and Internet; for other advanced degree, relevant work experience; access to computer and Internet. Additional exam requirements/recommendations for international students: Required—TOEFL (minimum score 550 paper-based, 79 iBT), IELTS (minimum score 6.5), Michigan English Language Assessment Battery (minimum score 82), or PTE (minimum score 53). Electronic applications accepted.

**Walden University,** Graduate Programs, School of Social Work and Human Services, Minneapolis, MN 55401. Offers addictions and social work (DSW); advanced clinical practice (MSW); clinical expertise (DSW); criminal justice (DSW); disaster, crisis, and intervention (DSW); family studies and interventions (DSW); human and social services (PhD), including advanced research, community and social services, community intervention and leadership, conflict management, criminal justice, disaster crisis and intervention, family studies and intervention, gerontology, global social services, higher education, human services and nonprofit administration, mental health facilitation; medical social work (DSW); military social work (MSW); policy practice (DSW); social work (PhD), including addictions and social work, clinical expertise, criminal justice,

disaster, crisis and intervention, family studies and interventions, medical social work, policy practice, social work administration; social work administration (DSW); social work in healthcare (MSW); social work with children and families (MSW). *Accreditation:* CSWE. *Program availability:* Part-time, evening/weekend, online only, 100% online. *Degree requirements:* For master's, residency (for some programs); for doctorate, thesis/dissertation, residency. *Entrance requirements:* For master's, bachelor's degree or higher; minimum GPA of 2.5; official transcripts; goal statement (for some programs); access to computer and Internet; for doctorate, master's degree or higher; three years of related professional or academic experience (preferred); minimum GPA of 3.0; goal statement and current resume (for select programs); official transcripts; access to computer and Internet. Additional exam requirements/recommendations for international students: Required—TOEFL (minimum score 550 paper-based, 79 iBT), IELTS (minimum score 6.5), Michigan English Language Assessment Battery (minimum score 82), or PTE (minimum score 53). Electronic applications accepted.

**Wayne State University,** College of Fine, Performing and Communication Arts, Department of Communication, Detroit, MI 48202. Offers communication (PhD), including democratic participation and culture, identity and representation, media, society and culture, risk, crisis and conflict, wellness, work life and relationships; communication and new media (Graduate Certificate); communication studies (MA); dispute resolution (MADR, Graduate Certificate); health communication (Graduate Certificate); journalism (MA); media arts (MA); media studies (MA); public relations and organizational communication (MA); JD/MADR. Doctoral program admits for fall only. *Faculty:* 20. *Students:* 59 full-time (32 women), 113 part-time (75 women); includes 69 minority (54 Black or African American, non-Hispanic/Latino; 2 Asian, non-Hispanic/Latino; 7 Hispanic/Latino; 6 Two or more races, non-Hispanic/Latino), 12 international. Average age 34. 154 applicants, 39% accepted, 41 enrolled. In 2016, 31 master's, 10 doctorates, 4 other advanced degrees awarded. *Degree requirements:* For master's, thesis (for some programs), thesis or essay; for doctorate, thesis/dissertation. *Entrance requirements:* For master's, GRE (if undergraduate GPA less than 3.2), personal statement; BA or BS in communication or related field with minimum upper-division GPA of 3.2 and minimum upper-division undergraduate GPA of 3.0, personal statement, and sample of academic writing (for MA); 3 letters of recommendation (for MADR); for doctorate, GRE, MA in communication or related field with minimum GPA of 3.5; three letters of recommendation; personal statement; sample of written scholarship. Additional exam requirements/recommendations for international students: Required—TOEFL (minimum score 600 paper-based; 100 iBT), IELTS, TWE. Application fee: $50. Electronic applications accepted. *Expenses:* $17,240 per year resident tuition and fees, $34,434 per year non-resident tuition and fees. *Financial support:* In 2016–17, 61 students received support, including 4 fellowships with tuition reimbursements available (averaging $16,000 per year), 2 research assistantships with tuition reimbursements available (averaging $19,570 per year), 21 teaching assistantships with tuition reimbursements available (averaging $17,994 per year); scholarships/grants and unspecified assistantships also available. Financial award applicants required to submit FAFSA. *Faculty research:* Rhetorical theory and criticism; mass media theory and research; argumentation; organizational communication; risk and crisis communication; interpersonal, family, and health communication. *Unit head:* Dr. Lillian Black, Professor and Chair, 313-577-2943, E-mail: eh8899@wayne.edu. *Application contact:* E-mail: communication@wayne.edu. Website: http://comm.wayne.edu/

**Wayne State University,** College of Liberal Arts and Sciences, Center for Peace and Conflict Studies, Detroit, MI 48202. Offers peace and security studies (Graduate Certificate). *Faculty:* 13. *Degree requirements:* For Graduate Certificate, internship or practicum. *Entrance requirements:* For degree, admission to master's degree program at WSU or University of Windsor, or graduate of master's degree program in approved discipline at an accredited institution. Additional exam requirements/recommendations for international students: Required—TOEFL (minimum score 550 paper-based; 79 iBT), Michigan English Language Assessment Battery (minimum score 85); Recommended—IELTS (minimum score 6.5). *Application deadline:* For fall admission, 6/1 priority date for domestic students, 5/1 priority date for international students; for winter admission, 10/1 priority date for domestic students, 9/1 priority date for international students; for spring admission, 2/1 priority date for domestic students, 1/1 priority date for international students; for summer admission, 2/1 priority date for domestic students, 1/1 priority date for international students. Applications are processed on a rolling basis. Application fee: $50. Electronic applications accepted. *Expenses:* $16,503 per year resident tuition and fees, $33,697 per year non-resident tuition and fees. *Financial support:* Scholarships/grants available. Financial award applicants required to submit FAFSA. *Unit head:* Dr. Fred Pearson, Professor and Program Director, 313-577-3453, E-mail: ab3440@wayne.edu. Website: http://clas.wayne.edu/cpcs/

**Wilfrid Laurier University,** Faculty of Graduate and Postdoctoral Studies, School of International Policy and Governance, Global Governance Program, Waterloo, ON N2L 3C5, Canada. Offers conflict and security (PhD); global environment (PhD); global justice and human rights (PhD); global political economy (PhD); global social governance (PhD); multilateral institutions and diplomacy (PhD). Offered jointly with University of Waterloo. *Degree requirements:* For doctorate, thesis/dissertation. *Entrance requirements:* For doctorate, MA in political science, history, economics, international development studies, international peace studies, globalization studies, environmental studies or related field with minimum A-. Additional exam requirements/recommendations for international students: Required—TOEFL (minimum score 89 iBT). Electronic applications accepted. *Faculty research:* Global political economy, global environment, conflict and security, global justice and human rights, multilateral institutions and diplomacy.

**Willamette University,** College of Law, Salem, OR 97301-3922. Offers dispute resolution (LL M); law (MLS, JD); transnational law (LL M); JD/MBA. *Accreditation:* ABA. *Program availability:* Part-time. *Degree requirements:* For master's, thesis, 25 credit hours (for LL M); 26 credit hours (for MLS); for doctorate, thesis/dissertation, 90 credit hours. *Entrance requirements:* For master's, bachelor's degree (for MLS); domestic or foreign JD (for LL M); for doctorate, LSAT. Additional exam requirements/recommendations for international students: Required—TOEFL (minimum score 480 paper-based; 45 iBT); Recommended—IELTS (minimum score 5). Electronic applications accepted. Application fee is waived when completed online. *Expenses:* Contact institution. *Faculty research:* Dispute resolution, international law, business law, law and government, sustainability.

**Yeshiva University,** Benjamin N. Cardozo School of Law, New York, NY 10003-4301. Offers comparative legal thought (LL M); dispute resolution and advocacy (LL M); general studies (LL M); intellectual property law (LL M); law (JD). *Accreditation:* ABA. *Entrance requirements:* For doctorate, LSAT, 2 letters of recommendation. Electronic applications accepted. *Expenses:* Contact institution. *Faculty research:* Corporate and commercial law, intellectual property law, criminal law and litigation, Constitutional law, legal theory and jurisprudence.

# Section 18
# Criminology and Forensics

This section contains a directory of institutions offering graduate work in criminology and forensics. Additional information about programs listed in the directory but not augmented by an in-depth entry may be obtained by writing directly to the dean of a graduate school or chair of a department at the address given in the directory.

For programs offering related work, see also in this book *Political Science and International Affairs, Psychology and Counseling,* and *Sociology, Anthropology, and Archaeology.* In another guide in this series:

**Graduate Programs in Business, Education, Information Studies, Law & Social Work**

See *Law* and *Social Work*

## CONTENTS

### Program Directories

### Display and Close-Up

### See:

# Criminal Justice and Criminology

**Adler University,** Programs in Psychology, Chicago, IL 60602. Offers advanced Adlerian psychotherapy (Certificate); art therapy (MA); clinical mental health counseling (MA); clinical neuropsychology (Certificate); clinical psychology (Psy D); community psychology (MA); counseling and organizational psychology (MA); counseling psychology (MA); counselor education and supervision (PhD); couple and family therapy (DCFT); criminology (MA); emergency management leadership (MA); forensic psychology (MA); marriage and family counseling (MA); marriage and family therapy (Certificate); military psychology (MA); nonprofit management (MA); organizational psychology (MA); police psychology (MA); public policy and administration (MA); rehabilitation counseling (MA); sport and health psychology (MA); substance abuse counseling (Certificate); Psy D/Certificate; Psy D/MACAT; Psy D/MACP; Psy D/MAMFC; Psy D/MASAC. *Accreditation:* APA. *Program availability:* Part-time, evening/weekend, online learning. Terminal master's awarded for partial completion of doctoral program. *Degree requirements:* For master's, thesis or alternative, oral exam, practicum; for doctorate, thesis/dissertation, clinical exam, internship, oral exam, practicum, written qualifying exam. *Entrance requirements:* For master's, 12 semester hours in psychology, minimum GPA of 3.0; for doctorate, 18 semester hours in psychology, minimum GPA of 3.25; for Certificate, appropriate master's or doctoral degree. Additional exam requirements/recommendations for international students: Required—TOEFL (minimum score 550 paper-based; 79 iBT). Electronic applications accepted.

**See Display on page 982 and Close-Up on page 1225.**

**Adrian College,** Graduate Programs, Adrian, MI 49221-2575. Offers accounting (MS); athletic training (MS); criminal justice (MA). *Degree requirements:* For master's, comprehensive exam (for some programs), thesis (for some programs), thesis, internship or practicum with corresponding in-depth paper and/or presentation. *Entrance requirements:* For master's, appropriate undergraduate degree, minimum cumulative and major GPA of 3.0, personal statement.

**Albany State University,** College of Arts and Humanities, Albany, GA 31705-2717. Offers criminal justice (MS); English education (M Ed); public administration (MPA), including community and economic development, criminal justice administration, health administration and policy, human resources management, public management, public policy, water resources management and policy; social work (MSW). *Program availability:* Part-time. *Degree requirements:* For master's, comprehensive exam, professional portfolio (for MPA), internship, capstone report. *Entrance requirements:* For master's, GRE, MAT, minimum GPA of 3.0, official transcript, pre-medical record/certificate of immunization, letters of reference. *Application deadline:* For fall admission, 6/1 for domestic students, 5/1 for international students; for spring admission, 11/1 for domestic students, 10/1 for international students. Applications are processed on a rolling basis. Application fee: $20. Electronic applications accepted. *Financial support:* Application deadline: 4/15; applicants required to submit FAFSA. *Faculty research:* HIV prevention for minority students. *Unit head:* Dr. Rani George, Dean, 229-430-1877, Fax: 229-430-4296. *Application contact:* Jeffrey Pierce, II, Graduate Admissions Counselor, 229-430-4646, Fax: 229-430-4105, E-mail: jeffrey.pierce@asurams.edu. Website: https://www.asurams.edu/Academics/collegeofarthum/

**Albertus Magnus College,** Master of Science in Criminal Justice Program, New Haven, CT 06511-1189. Offers corrections administration (MS); juvenile justice (MS). *Program availability:* Part-time, evening/weekend, 100% online, blended/hybrid learning. *Students:* 7 full-time (6 women), 7 part-time (5 women); includes 11 minority (8 Black or African American, non-Hispanic/Latino; 1 Hispanic/Latino; 2 Two or more races, non-Hispanic/Latino). Average age 35. *Degree requirements:* For master's, thesis, capstone. *Entrance requirements:* For master's, bachelor's degree from regionally-accredited college or university with minimum GPA of 3.0 in criminal justice, 2.8 overall; undergraduate major in criminal justice or completion of 18 criminal justice credits; interview; two letters of recommendation; one-page personal statement. Additional exam requirements/recommendations for international students: Recommended—TOEFL (minimum score 550 paper-based; 80 iBT). Application fee: $50. *Expenses:* Contact institution. *Financial support:* Federal Work-Study and unspecified assistantships available. Support available to part-time students. Financial award applicants required to submit FAFSA. *Unit head:* John Lawrie, Coordinator, 203-773-6142, E-mail: jnlawrie@albertus.edu. *Application contact:* Dr. Sean O'Connell, Vice President for Academic Affairs, 203-777-8539, Fax: 203-777-3701, E-mail: soconnell@albertus.edu.
Website: http://www.albertus.edu/graduate-degrees/graduate-degree-programs/criminal-justice/

**Alliant International University–San Francisco,** California School of Forensic Studies, Program in Applied Criminology, San Francisco, CA 94133. Offers victimology (MS). *Entrance requirements:* For master's, 3 essays, resume. Additional exam requirements/recommendations for international students: Required—TOEFL (minimum score 550 paper-based; 80 iBT). Electronic applications accepted.

**American Public University System,** AMU/APU Graduate Programs, Charles Town, WV 25414. Offers accounting (MBA, MS); applied business analytics (MBA, MS); criminal justice (MA), including business administration, emergency and disaster management, general (MA, MS); educational leadership (M Ed); emergency and disaster management (MA); entrepreneurship (MBA); environmental policy and management (MS), including environmental planning, environmental sustainability, fish and wildlife management, general (MA, MS); global environmental management; finance (MBA); general (MBA); government contracting and acquisition (MBA); health care administration (MBA); health information management (MS); history (MA), including American history, ancient and classical history, European history, global history, public history; homeland security (MA), including business administration, counterterrorism studies, criminal justice, cyber, emergency management and public health, intelligence studies, transportation security; homeland security resource allocation (MBA); humanities (MA); information technology (MS), including digital forensics, enterprise software development, information assurance and security, IT project management; information technology management (MBA); intelligence studies (MA), including criminal intelligence, cyber, general (MA, MS), homeland security, intelligence analysis, intelligence collection, intelligence management, intelligence operations, terrorism studies; international relations and conflict resolution (MA), including comparative and security issues, conflict resolution, international and transnational security issues, peacekeeping; legal studies (MA); management (MA), including strategic consulting; marketing (MBA); military history (MA), including American military history, American Revolution, civil war, war since 1945, World War II; military studies (MA), including joint warfare, strategic leadership; national security studies (MA), including cyber, general (MA, MS), homeland security, regional security studies, security and intelligence analysis, terrorism studies; nonprofit management (MBA); political science (MA),

including American politics and government, comparative government and development, general (MA, MS), international relations, public policy; psychology (MA); public administration (MPA), including disaster management, environmental policy, health policy, human resources, national security, organizational management, security management; public health (MPH); reverse logistics management (MA); security management (MA); space studies (MS), including aerospace science, general (MA, MS), planetary science; sports and health sciences (MS); sports management (MBA); teaching (M Ed), including autism spectrum disorder, curriculum and instruction for elementary teachers, elementary reading, English language learners, instructional leadership, online learning, special education, STEAM (STEM plus the arts); transportation and logistics management (MA). *Program availability:* Part-time, evening/weekend, online only, 100% online. *Faculty:* 401 full-time (228 women), 1,678 part-time/adjunct (781 women). *Students:* 378 full-time (184 women), 8,455 part-time (3,484 women); includes 2,972 minority (1,552 Black or African American, non-Hispanic/Latino; 52 American Indian or Alaska Native, non-Hispanic/Latino; 211 Asian, non-Hispanic/Latino; 791 Hispanic/Latino; 70 Native Hawaiian or other Pacific Islander, non-Hispanic/Latino; 296 Two or more races, non-Hispanic/Latino), 109 international. Average age 37. In 2016, 3,185 master's awarded. *Degree requirements:* For master's, comprehensive exam or practicum. *Entrance requirements:* For master's, official transcript showing earned bachelor's degree from institution accredited by recognized accrediting body. Additional exam requirements/recommendations for international students: Required—TOEFL (minimum score 550 paper-based), IELTS (minimum score 6.5). *Application deadline:* Applications are processed on a rolling basis. Application fee: $0. Electronic applications accepted. *Expenses:* Tuition: Part-time $350 per credit hour. *Required fees:* $50 per course. *Financial support:* Scholarships/grants available. Financial award applicants required to submit FAFSA. *Unit head:* Dr. Karan Powell, President, 877-468-6268, Fax: 304-724-3780. *Application contact:* Terry Grant, Vice President of Enrollment Management, 877-468-6268, Fax: 304-724-3780, E-mail: info@apus.edu.
Website: http://www.apus.edu

**American University,** School of Public Affairs, Department of Justice, Law and Criminology, Washington, DC 20016-8043. Offers justice, law and criminology (MS, PhD); terrorism, homeland security and policy (MS); JD/MS. *Program availability:* Part-time, evening/weekend. *Faculty:* 20 full-time (10 women), 18 part-time/adjunct (4 women). *Students:* 82 full-time (54 women), 23 part-time (13 women); includes 28 minority (12 Black or African American, non-Hispanic/Latino; 5 Asian, non-Hispanic/Latino; 10 Hispanic/Latino; 1 Two or more races, non-Hispanic/Latino), 6 international. Average age 27. 158 applicants, 75% accepted, 51 enrolled. In 2016, 35 master's, 2 doctorates awarded. *Degree requirements:* For master's, comprehensive exam; for doctorate, comprehensive exam, thesis/dissertation. *Entrance requirements:* For master's, GRE, 2 recommendations, statement of purpose, resume, transcript; for doctorate, GRE, 3 recommendations, statement of purpose, resume, writing sample, transcript. Additional exam requirements/recommendations for international students: Required—TOEFL (minimum score 600 paper-based; 100 iBT), IELTS (minimum score 7), PTE (minimum score 68). *Application deadline:* For fall admission, 2/1 for domestic students, 5/1 for international students; for spring admission, 11/1 for domestic students. Application fee: $55. *Expenses:* $1,579 per credit tuition; $690 mandatory fees. *Financial support:* Research assistantships, teaching assistantships, institutionally sponsored loans, scholarships/grants, and unspecified assistantships available. Financial award application deadline: 2/1; financial award applicants required to submit FAFSA. *Unit head:* Dr. Joseph Young, Department Chair, 202-885-2618, Fax: 202-885-2907, E-mail: jyoung@american.edu. *Application contact:* Rosie Walker, Director, Graduate Enrollment and Recruitment, E-mail: rwalker@american.edu.
Website: http://www.american.edu/spa/jlc/

**American University of Puerto Rico,** Program in Criminal Justice, Bayamon, PR 00960-2037. Offers MA. *Program availability:* Part-time, evening/weekend. *Faculty:* 4 part-time/adjunct (1 woman). *Students:* 1 full-time (0 women), 8 part-time (3 women); all minorities (all Hispanic/Latino). Average age 32. 2 applicants, 100% accepted, 2 enrolled. In 2016, 2 master's awarded. *Degree requirements:* For master's, comprehensive exam. *Entrance requirements:* For master's, interviews; recommendations. *Application deadline:* For fall admission, 8/1 for domestic students; for winter admission, 10/15 for domestic students; for spring admission, 3/22 for domestic students. Applications are processed on a rolling basis. Application fee: $25. *Financial support:* In 2016–17, 8 students received support, including 9 fellowships (averaging $500 per year). Financial award applicants required to submit FAFSA. *Unit head:* Prof. Bolivar Ramirez-Carlo, III, Dean of Faculty, 787-620-2040 Ext. 2011, Fax: 787-785-7377, E-mail: bramirez@aupr.edu. *Application contact:* Keren I. Llanos-Figueroa, Information Contact, 787-620-2040 Ext. 2021, Fax: 787-785-7377, E-mail: kllanos@aupr.edu.

**Anderson University,** Command College of South Carolina, Anderson, SC 29621-4035. Offers criminal justice (MCJ). *Program availability:* Blended/hybrid learning. *Entrance requirements:* For master's, minimum undergraduate GPA of 2.75, 5 years of experience working in criminal justice field, resume. *Expenses:* Contact institution. *Financial support:* Application deadline: 3/1; applicants required to submit FAFSA. *Application contact:* Mallory Knight, Graduate Admission Counselor, 864-231-2182, Fax: 864-231-2115, E-mail: malloryknight@andersonuniversity.edu.
Website: https://www.andersonuniversity.edu/graduate/programs/criminal-justice/command-college

**Angelo State University,** College of Graduate Studies and Research, College of Arts and Humanities, Department of Security Studies and Criminal Justice, San Angelo, TX 76909. Offers criminal justice (MS); homeland security (MS); intelligence, security studies, and analysis (MSS); security studies (MSS). *Program availability:* Part-time, evening/weekend, online learning. *Students:* 75 full-time (31 women), 115 part-time (38 women); includes 65 minority (24 Black or African American, non-Hispanic/Latino; 7 Asian, non-Hispanic/Latino; 31 Hispanic/Latino; 3 Two or more races, non-Hispanic/Latino). Average age 31. *Degree requirements:* For master's, comprehensive exam. *Entrance requirements:* For master's, essay, letters of recommendation. Additional exam requirements/recommendations for international students: Required—TOEFL or IELTS. *Application deadline:* For fall admission, 7/15 priority date for domestic students, 6/10 for international students; for spring admission, 12/1 priority date for domestic students, 11/1 for international students. Applications are processed on a rolling basis. Application fee: $40 ($50 for international students). Electronic applications accepted. *Expenses:* Tuition, state resident: full-time $3726; part-time $2484 per year. Tuition, nonresident: full-time $10,746; part-time $7164 per year. *Required fees:* $2538; $1702 per unit. *Financial support:* Federal Work-Study and scholarships/grants available. Support available to part-time students. Financial award application deadline: 3/1; financial award applicants required to submit FAFSA. *Unit head:* Dr. William A. Taylor, Chair, 325-486-6689, Fax: 325-942-2544, E-mail: william.taylor@angelo.edu.

*Application contact:* Dr. William A. Taylor, Chair, 325-486-6689, Fax: 325-942-2544, E-mail: william.taylor@angelo.edu.
Website: http://www.angelo.edu/dept/security_studies_criminal_justice/

**Anna Maria College,** Graduate Division, Program in Criminal Justice, Paxton, MA 01612. Offers criminal justice (MS). *Program availability:* Part-time, evening/weekend. *Degree requirements:* For master's, capstone project or thesis. *Entrance requirements:* For master's, bachelor's degree in related field, minimum GPA of 2.7. Additional exam requirements/recommendations for international students: Required—TOEFL (minimum score 500 paper-based). Electronic applications accepted.

**Arizona State University at the Tempe campus,** College of Public Programs, School of Criminology and Criminal Justice, Phoenix, AZ 85004. Offers corrections management (Graduate Certificate); criminal justice (MA); criminology and criminal justice (MS, PhD); law enforcement administration (Graduate Certificate). *Program availability:* Part-time, evening/weekend, online learning. Terminal master's awarded for partial completion of doctoral program. *Degree requirements:* For master's, thesis or alternative, policy analysis project, interactive Program of Study (iPOS) submitted before completing 50 percent of required credit hours; for doctorate, comprehensive exam, thesis/dissertation, interactive Program of Study (iPOS) submitted before completing 50 percent of required credit hours. *Entrance requirements:* For master's, GRE (MS), minimum GPA of 3.0 or equivalent in last 2 years of work leading to bachelor's degree; for doctorate, GRE, minimum GPA of 3.0 or equivalent in last 2 years of work leading to bachelor's degree, 2 letters of recommendation, resume, personal statement. Additional exam requirements/recommendations for international students: Required—TOEFL, IELTS, or PTE. Electronic applications accepted.

**Arkansas State University,** Graduate School, College of Humanities and Social Sciences, Department of Criminology, Sociology, and Geography, State University, AR 72467. Offers criminal justice (MA); sociology (MA); sociology education (SCCT). *Program availability:* Part-time. *Degree requirements:* For master's, one foreign language, comprehensive exam, thesis or alternative; for SCCT, comprehensive exam. *Entrance requirements:* For master's, GRE General Test or MAT, appropriate bachelor's degree, letters of recommendation, official transcripts, immunization records; for SCCT, GRE General Test or MAT, interview, master's degree, official transcript, immunization records. Additional exam requirements/recommendations for international students: Required—TOEFL (minimum score 550 paper-based; 79 iBT), IELTS (minimum score 6), PTE (minimum score 56). Electronic applications accepted.

**Armstrong State University,** School of Graduate Studies, Program in Criminal Justice, Savannah, GA 31419-1997. Offers criminal justice (MS); cyber crime (Certificate). *Program availability:* Part-time, online learning. *Faculty:* 6 full-time (4 women), 1 (woman) part-time/adjunct. *Students:* 4 full-time (3 women), 20 part-time (12 women); includes 9 minority (all Black or African American, non-Hispanic/Latino). Average age 29. 42 applicants, 31% accepted, 12 enrolled. In 2016, 5 master's, 11 other advanced degrees awarded. *Degree requirements:* For master's, comprehensive exam, field practicum or thesis. *Entrance requirements:* For master's, GRE General Test (minimum score 150 on verbal, 141 on quantitative, or 4 on analytical section) or MAT, minimum GPA of 2.5, 2 letters of recommendation, letter of intent (500-1000 words). Additional exam requirements/recommendations for international students: Required—TOEFL (minimum score 523 paper-based; 70 iBT). *Application deadline:* For fall admission, 6/1 priority date for domestic students, 5/1 priority date for international students; for spring admission, 11/15 priority date for domestic students, 9/15 priority date for international students; for summer admission, 4/15 priority date for domestic students, 9/15 for international students. Applications are processed on a rolling basis. Application fee: $30. Electronic applications accepted. *Expenses:* Tuition, state resident: full-time $1781; part-time $161.93 per credit hour. Tuition, nonresident: full-time $6482; part-time $589.27 per credit hour. *Required fees:* $1224 per unit. $612 per semester. Tuition and fees vary according to course load, campus/location and program. *Financial support:* In 2016–17, research assistantships with full tuition reimbursements (averaging $5,000 per year) were awarded; career-related internships or fieldwork, Federal Work-Study, scholarships/grants, and unspecified assistantships also available. Support available to part-time students. Financial award application deadline: 3/15; financial award applicants required to submit FAFSA. *Faculty research:* International crime/globalization, cyber-crime, influence of social science research on judicial decision-making. *Unit head:* Dr. Daniel Skidmore-Hess, Department Head, 912-344-2532, Fax: 912-344-3438, E-mail: daniel.skidmore-hess@armstrong.edu. *Application contact:* McKenzie Peterman, Assistant Director of Graduate Admissions, 912-344-2503, Fax: 912-344-3417, E-mail: graduate@armstrong.edu.
Website: https://www.armstrong.edu/academic-departments/cjsps-master-of-science-in-criminal-justice

**Ashworth College,** Graduate Programs, Norcross, GA 30092. Offers business administration (MBA); criminal justice (MS); health care administration (MBA, MS); human resource management (MBA, MS); international business (MBA); management (MS); marketing (MBA, MS).

**Auburn University at Montgomery,** College of Public Policy and Justice, Department of Justice and Public Safety, Montgomery, AL 36124-4023. Offers criminal studies (MSJPS); homeland security (MSJPS); homeland security and emergency management (MS); legal studies (MSJPS); organizational leadership (MSJPS); paralegal (Certificate). *Program availability:* Part-time, evening/weekend. *Degree requirements:* For master's, comprehensive exam, thesis optional. *Entrance requirements:* For master's, GRE General Test or MAT. Electronic applications accepted. *Faculty research:* Law enforcement, corrections, juvenile justice.

**Ball State University,** Graduate School, College of Sciences and Humanities, Department of Political Science, Program in Public Administration, Muncie, IN 47306. Offers public administration (MPA, Certificate), including administrative (MPA), community and economic development (MPA), criminal justice and criminology (MPA), emergency management and homeland security (MPA). *Program availability:* Part-time. *Degree requirements:* For master's, comprehensive exam. *Entrance requirements:* For master's, GRE General Test, minimum baccalaureate GPA of 2.8, two letters of recommendation. Additional exam requirements/recommendations for international students: Required—TOEFL (minimum score 550 paper-based; 79 iBT), IELTS (minimum score 6.5). Electronic applications accepted. *Faculty research:* Employment training programs, personnel and labor relations, planning.

**Bellevue University,** Graduate School, College of Information Technology, Bellevue, NE 68005-3098. Offers computer information systems (MS); cybersecurity (MS); management of information systems (MS); project management (MPM).

**Bellevue University,** Graduate School, College of Professional Studies, Bellevue, NE 68005-3098. Offers instructional design and development (MS); justice administration and criminal management (MS); leadership (MA); organizational performance (MS); public administration (MPA); security management (MS).

**Boise State University,** School of Public Service, Department of Criminal Justice, Boise, ID 83725-1955. Offers MA. *Program availability:* Part-time. *Faculty:* 8. *Students:* 9 full-time (7 women), 12 part-time (6 women); includes 4 minority (1 Asian, non-Hispanic/Latino; 3 Hispanic/Latino). Average age 31. 15 applicants, 53% accepted, 5 enrolled. In 2016, 13 master's awarded. *Degree requirements:* For master's, thesis optional.

*Entrance requirements:* For master's, GRE General Test, minimum GPA of 3.0. Additional exam requirements/recommendations for international students: Required—TOEFL (minimum score 550 paper-based; 80 iBT), IELTS (minimum score 6). *Application deadline:* For fall admission, 4/1 for domestic and international students; for spring admission, 10/1 for domestic and international students. Application fee: $65 ($95 for international students). Electronic applications accepted. *Expenses:* Tuition, state resident: full-time $6058; part-time $358 per credit hour. Tuition, nonresident: full-time $20,108; part-time $608 per credit hour. *Required fees:* $2108. Tuition and fees vary according to program. *Financial support:* In 2016–17, 6 students received support. Scholarships/grants and unspecified assistantships available. Financial award application deadline: 2/15; financial award applicants required to submit FAFSA. *Unit head:* Dr. Lisa Growett Bostaph, Associate Director and Program Coordinator, 208-426-3886, E-mail: lisabostaph@boisestate.edu. *Application contact:* Lisa Growett Bostaph, Program Coordinator, 208-426-3886, E-mail: lisabostaph@boisestate.edu.
Website: http://sps.boisestate.edu/criminaljustice/

**Boston University,** Metropolitan College, Program in Criminal Justice, Boston, MA 02215. Offers MCJ. *Program availability:* Part-time, evening/weekend, online learning. *Faculty:* 5 full-time (2 women), 4 part-time/adjunct (0 women). *Students:* 11 full-time (5 women), 445 part-time (265 women); includes 150 minority (65 Black or African American, non-Hispanic/Latino; 2 American Indian or Alaska Native, non-Hispanic/Latino; 11 Asian, non-Hispanic/Latino; 63 Hispanic/Latino; 1 Native Hawaiian or other Pacific Islander, non-Hispanic/Latino; 8 Two or more races, non-Hispanic/Latino), 24 international. Average age 32. 133 applicants, 83% accepted, 82 enrolled. In 2016, 174 master's awarded. *Degree requirements:* For master's, comprehensive examination (for on-campus program only). *Entrance requirements:* Additional exam requirements/recommendations for international students: Required—TOEFL (minimum score 84 iBT). *Application deadline:* Applications are processed on a rolling basis. Application fee: $85. Electronic applications accepted. *Expenses:* Contact institution. *Financial support:* In 2016–17, 1 student received support, including 8 research assistantships (averaging $4,200 per year); scholarships/grants and unspecified assistantships also available. Support available to part-time students. Financial award applicants required to submit FAFSA. *Faculty research:* Criminal justice administration and planning, criminology, police, corrections, collective violence, juvenile issues, cybersecurity, forensic psychology. *Unit head:* Dr. Daniel P. LeClair, Chair, 617-353-3025, Fax: 617-358-3595, E-mail: dleclair@bu.edu. *Application contact:* Dr. Mary Ellen Mastrorilli, Assistant Professor and Associate Chair, 617-353-3025, E-mail: memastro@bu.edu.
Website: http://www.bu.edu/met/cj/

**Bowling Green State University,** Graduate College, College of Health and Human Services, Program in Criminal Justice, Bowling Green, OH 43403. Offers MSCJ. *Program availability:* Part-time, evening/weekend, online learning. *Degree requirements:* For master's, thesis or alternative. *Entrance requirements:* For master's, GRE General Test. Additional exam requirements/recommendations for international students: Required—TOEFL. *Application deadline:* Applications are processed on a rolling basis. Application fee: $30. Electronic applications accepted. *Financial support:* Research assistantships with full tuition reimbursements, teaching assistantships, and unspecified assistantships available. *Unit head:* Dr. Steven Lab, Head, 419-372-2326. *Application contact:* Dr. William King, Graduate Coordinator, 419-372-2326.

**Bridgewater State University,** College of Graduate Studies, College of Humanities and Social Sciences, Department of Criminal Justice, Bridgewater, MA 02325. Offers MS. *Entrance requirements:* For master's, GRE General Test.

**Buffalo State College, State University of New York,** The Graduate School, Faculty of Applied Science and Education, Department of Criminal Justice, Buffalo, NY 14222-1095. Offers MS. *Program availability:* Part-time, evening/weekend. *Degree requirements:* For master's, comprehensive exam, project. *Entrance requirements:* For master's, minimum GPA of 3.0. Additional exam requirements/recommendations for international students: Required—TOEFL (minimum score 550 paper-based).

**California Coast University,** School of Criminal Justice, Santa Ana, CA 92701. Offers MS.

**California State University, Chico,** Office of Graduate Studies, College of Behavioral and Social Sciences, Political Science and Criminal Justice Department, Chico, CA 95929-0722. Offers political science (MA); public administration (MPA), including health administration, local government management. *Program availability:* Part-time. *Faculty:* 19 full-time (10 women), 24 part-time/adjunct (14 women). *Students:* 32 full-time (18 women), 22 part-time (11 women); includes 19 minority (1 American Indian or Alaska Native, non-Hispanic/Latino; 5 Asian, non-Hispanic/Latino; 10 Hispanic/Latino; 3 Two or more races, non-Hispanic/Latino). 33 applicants, 85% accepted, 18 enrolled. In 2016, 26 master's awarded. *Degree requirements:* For master's, thesis or comprehensive exam. *Entrance requirements:* For master's, two letters of recommendation, statement of purpose. Additional exam requirements/recommendations for international students: Required—TOEFL (minimum score 550 paper-based; 80 iBT), IELTS (minimum score 6.5), PTE. *Application deadline:* For fall admission, 3/1 priority date for domestic students, 3/1 for international students; for spring admission, 9/15 priority date for domestic students, 9/15 for international students. Application fee: $55. Electronic applications accepted. *Financial support:* Fellowships, teaching assistantships, career-related internships or fieldwork, scholarships/grants, traineeships, and unspecified assistantships available. Financial award application deadline: 3/1; financial award applicants required to submit FAFSA. *Unit head:* Mahalley Allen, Chair, 530-898-6506, E-mail: mdallen@csuchico.edu. *Application contact:* Judy L. Morris, Graduate Admissions Coordinator, 530-898-5461, Fax: 530-898-3342, E-mail: jlmorris@csuchico.edu.
Website: http://www.csuchico.edu/pols/

**California State University, Fresno,** Division of Research and Graduate Studies, College of Social Sciences, Department of Criminology, Fresno, CA 93740-8027. Offers MS. *Program availability:* Part-time, evening/weekend. *Degree requirements:* For master's, thesis project or comprehensive examination. *Entrance requirements:* For master's, GRE General Test, minimum GPA of 3.0, personal essay. Additional exam requirements/recommendations for international students: Required—TOEFL. *Application deadline:* For fall admission, 5/1 for domestic and international students; for spring admission, 10/1 for domestic and international students. Applications are processed on a rolling basis. Application fee: $55. Electronic applications accepted. *Financial support:* Career-related internships or fieldwork, Federal Work-Study, scholarships/grants, and unspecified assistantships available. Support available to part-time students. Financial award application deadline: 3/1; financial award applicants required to submit FAFSA. *Faculty research:* Substance abuse, gangs vs. law enforcement, needs of female offenders, battered women, crime victims. *Unit head:* Dr. Emma Hughes, Chair, 559-278-2370, Fax: 559-278-7265, E-mail: emhughes@csufresno.edu. *Application contact:* Dr. Hollianne Marshall, Graduate Coordinator, 559-278-2289, Fax: 559-278-7265, E-mail: holmarshall@csufresno.edu.
Website: http://www.fresnostate.edu/socialsciences/criminology/

**California State University, Long Beach,** Graduate Studies, College of Health and Human Services, Department of Criminal Justice, Long Beach, CA 90840. Offers criminal justice (MS); emergency services administration (MS). *Program availability:*

## Criminal Justice and Criminology

Part-time. *Degree requirements:* For master's, comprehensive course or thesis. *Entrance requirements:* For master's, minimum GPA of 3.0. *Application deadline:* For fall admission, 5/1 for domestic students. Applications are processed on a rolling basis. Application fee: $55. Electronic applications accepted. *Financial support:* Federal Work-Study, institutionally sponsored loans, and scholarships/grants available. Financial award application deadline: 3/2. *Unit head:* Brenda L. Vogel, Director, 562-985-8965.

**California State University, Los Angeles,** Graduate Studies, College of Health and Human Services, Department of Criminal Justice and Criminalistics, Los Angeles, CA 90032-8530. Offers criminal justice (MS); criminalistics (MS). *Program availability:* Part-time, evening/weekend. *Degree requirements:* For master's, thesis. *Entrance requirements:* For master's, minimum GPA of 2.75. Additional exam requirements/recommendations for international students: Required—TOEFL (minimum score 500 paper-based).

**California State University, Sacramento,** Office of Graduate Studies, College of Health and Human Services, Division of Criminal Justice, Sacramento, CA 95819. Offers MS. *Program availability:* Part-time. *Students:* 1 full-time, 29 part-time (21 women); includes 11 minority (3 Black or African American, non-Hispanic/Latino; 2 Asian, non-Hispanic/Latino; 6 Hispanic/Latino). Average age 27. 23 applicants, 65% accepted, 11 enrolled. In 2016, 5 master's awarded. *Degree requirements:* For master's, thesis or project. *Entrance requirements:* For master's, GRE, BA in criminal justice or equivalent; minimum GPA of 3.0 during previous 2 years of course work and in major field. Additional exam requirements/recommendations for international students: Required—TOEFL (minimum score 550 paper-based; 80 iBT). *Application deadline:* For fall admission, 3/1 for domestic and international students; for spring admission, 9/30 for international students. Applications are processed on a rolling basis. Application fee: $55. Electronic applications accepted. *Expenses:* $4,302 full-time tuition and fees per semester, $2,796 part-time. *Financial support:* Career-related internships or fieldwork and Federal Work-Study available. Support available to part-time students. Financial award application deadline: 3/1; financial award applicants required to submit FAFSA. *Unit head:* Dr. Ernest Uwazie, Chair, 916-278-6282, E-mail: uwazieee@csus.edu. *Application contact:* Jose Martinez, Graduate Admissions Supervisor, 916-278-7871, E-mail: martinj@skymail.csus.edu.
Website: http://www.csus.edu/hhs/cj

**California State University, San Bernardino,** Graduate Studies, College of Social and Behavioral Sciences, Program in Criminal Justice, San Bernardino, CA 92407. Offers MA. *Program availability:* Part-time. *Faculty:* 6 full-time (4 women). *Students:* 2 full-time (0 women), 21 part-time (15 women); includes 13 minority (2 Asian, non-Hispanic/Latino; 10 Hispanic/Latino; 1 Two or more races, non-Hispanic/Latino), 2 international. 22 applicants, 68% accepted, 10 enrolled. In 2016, 2 master's awarded. *Entrance requirements:* Additional exam requirements/recommendations for international students: Required—TOEFL. *Application deadline:* For fall admission, 4/1 for domestic students; for winter admission, 9/1 for domestic students; for spring admission, 12/15 for domestic students. Application fee: $55. *Expenses:* Tuition, state resident: full-time $7843; part-time $5011.20 per year. Tuition and fees vary according to course load, degree level, program and reciprocity agreements. *Financial support:* Institutionally sponsored loans available. *Faculty research:* Crime seriousness, fear of crime, victimization, corrections management, crime correlates. *Unit head:* Dr. Larry Gaines, Chair, 909-537-5508, Fax: 909-537-7025, E-mail: lgaines@csusb.edu. *Application contact:* Dr. Francisca Beer, Dean of Graduate Studies, 909-537-5058, E-mail: fbeer@csusb.edu.

**California State University, Stanislaus,** College of Humanities and Social Sciences, Program in Criminal Justice (MA), Turlock, CA 95382. Offers MA. *Program availability:* Part-time. *Degree requirements:* For master's, comprehensive exam, thesis or alternative. *Entrance requirements:* For master's, minimum GPA of 3.0, 3 letters of reference, personal statement. Electronic applications accepted. *Faculty research:* Police gerontology services, hate crimes, juvenile justice, masculinities and modern society, nutrition and criminal behavior.

**California University of Pennsylvania,** School of Graduate Studies and Research, College of Liberal Arts, Department of Criminal Justice, California, PA 15419-1394. Offers applied criminology (MA). *Program availability:* Part-time, evening/weekend. *Degree requirements:* For master's, comprehensive exam, thesis optional. *Entrance requirements:* For master's, MAT, minimum GPA of 3.0. Additional exam requirements/recommendations for international students: Required—TOEFL (minimum score 550 paper-based; 80 iBT). Electronic applications accepted. *Expenses:* Tuition, state resident: full-time $11,592; part-time $483 per credit. Tuition, nonresident: full-time $17,400; part-time $725 per credit. *Required fees:* $3916. Tuition and fees vary according to course load, degree level, campus/location and reciprocity agreements. *Faculty research:* Ethics and law, ethics in police practice, law and morality, police policy, St. Thomas Aquinas and crime.

**California University of Pennsylvania,** School of Graduate Studies and Research, Eberly College of Science and Technology, Department of Professional Studies, California, PA 15419-1394. Offers legal studies (MS), including criminal justice, homeland security, law and public policy. *Program availability:* Part-time, evening/weekend, online learning. *Degree requirements:* For master's, thesis optional. *Entrance requirements:* For master's, interview, minimum GPA of 3.0. Additional exam requirements/recommendations for international students: Required—TOEFL (minimum score 550 paper-based; 80 iBT). Electronic applications accepted. *Expenses:* Tuition, state resident: full-time $11,592; part-time $483 per credit. Tuition, nonresident: full-time $17,400; part-time $725 per credit. *Required fees:* $3916. Tuition and fees vary according to course load, degree level, campus/location and reciprocity agreements. *Faculty research:* Ethics in political practice, ethics and law, law and morality, St. Thomas Aquinas and crime, police policy.

**Calumet College of Saint Joseph,** Program in Public Safety Administration, Whiting, IN 46394-2195. Offers MS.

**Capella University,** School of Public Service Leadership, Doctoral Programs in Healthcare, Minneapolis, MN 55402. Offers criminal justice (PhD); emergency management (PhD); epidemiology (Dr PH); general health administration (DHA); general public administration (DPA); health advocacy and leadership (Dr PH); health care administration (PhD); health care leadership (DHA); health policy advocacy (DHA); multidisciplinary human services (PhD); nonprofit management and leadership (PhD); public safety leadership (PhD); social and community services (PhD).

**Capella University,** School of Public Service Leadership, Master's Programs in Healthcare, Minneapolis, MN 55402. Offers criminal justice (MS); emergency management (MS); general public health (MPH); gerontology (MS); health administration (MHA); health care operations (MHA); health management policy (MPH); health policy (MHA); homeland security (MS); multidisciplinary human services (MS); public administration (MPA); public safety leadership (MS); social and community services (MS); social behavioral sciences (MPH); MS/MPA.

**Caribbean University,** Graduate School, Bayamón, PR 00960-0493. Offers administration and supervision (MA Ed); criminal justice (MA); curriculum and instruction (MA Ed, PhD), including elementary education (MA Ed), English education (MA Ed), history education (MA Ed), mathematics education (MA Ed), primary education (MA Ed),

science education (MA Ed), Spanish education (MA Ed); educational technology in instructional systems (MA Ed); gerontology (MSN); human resources (MBA); museology, archiving and art history (MA Ed); neonatal pediatrics (MSN); physical education (MA Ed); special education (MA Ed). *Entrance requirements:* For master's, interview, minimum GPA of 2.5.

**Carnegie Mellon University,** Heinz College, School of Information Systems and Management, Master of Science in Information Security Policy and Management Program, Pittsburgh, PA 15213-3891. Offers MSISPM. *Entrance requirements:* For master's, GRE or GMAT, college-level course in advanced algebra/pre-calculus; college-level courses in economics and statistics (recommended). Additional exam requirements/recommendations for international students: Required—TOEFL or IELTS.

**The Catholic University of America,** School of Arts and Sciences, Department of Sociology, Washington, DC 20064. Offers crime and justice studies (MA); global and comparative sociology (MA); public policy (MA). *Program availability:* Part-time. *Faculty:* 3 full-time (2 women), 4 part-time/adjunct (0 women). *Students:* 2 full-time (both women), 1 (woman) part-time; includes 2 minority (1 Black or African American, non-Hispanic/Latino; 1 Hispanic/Latino). Average age 22. 7 applicants, 29% accepted, 2 enrolled. In 2016, 2 master's awarded. *Degree requirements:* For master's, comprehensive exam, thesis or alternative, two seminar papers. *Entrance requirements:* For master's, GRE General Test, statement of purpose, official copies of academic transcripts, three letters of recommendation. Additional exam requirements/recommendations for international students: Required—TOEFL (minimum score 550 paper-based; 80 iBT). *Application deadline:* For fall admission, 7/15 priority date for domestic students, 7/1 for international students; for spring admission, 11/15 priority date for domestic students, 11/1 for international students. Applications are processed on a rolling basis. Application fee: $55. Electronic applications accepted. *Expenses:* $42,850 per year; $1,170 per credit; $200 per semester part-time fees. *Financial support:* Fellowships, research assistantships, teaching assistantships, Federal Work-Study, scholarships/grants, tuition waivers (full and partial), and unspecified assistantships available. Financial award application deadline: 2/1; financial award applicants required to submit FAFSA. *Faculty research:* Social movements, gender structure, political sociology, race and ethnic relations, evaluation methodologies. *Total annual research expenditures:* $2,586. *Unit head:* Dr. Enrique S. Pumar, Chair, 202-319-5445, Fax: 202-319-4980, E-mail: pumar@cua.edu. *Application contact:* Director of Graduate Admissions, 202-319-5057, Fax: 202-319-6533, E-mail: cua-admissions@cua.edu.
Website: http://sociology.cua.edu/

**Central Connecticut State University,** School of Graduate Studies, College of Liberal Arts and Social Sciences, Department of Criminology and Criminal Justice, New Britain, CT 06050-4010. Offers criminal justice (MS). *Program availability:* Part-time, evening/weekend. *Faculty:* 9 full-time (4 women). *Students:* 4 full-time (2 women), 35 part-time (22 women); includes 16 minority (6 Black or African American, non-Hispanic/Latino; 5 Asian, non-Hispanic/Latino; 3 Hispanic/Latino; 2 Two or more races, non-Hispanic/Latino). Average age 28. 23 applicants, 78% accepted, 15 enrolled. In 2016, 7 master's awarded. *Degree requirements:* For master's, comprehensive exam, thesis or alternative. *Entrance requirements:* For master's, minimum undergraduate GPA of 3.0, essay, resume. Additional exam requirements/recommendations for international students: Required—TOEFL (minimum score 550 paper-based; 79 iBT). *Application deadline:* For fall admission, 6/1 for domestic students, 5/1 for international students; for spring admission, 11/1 for domestic and international students. Applications are processed on a rolling basis. Application fee: $50. Electronic applications accepted. *Expenses:* Tuition, area resident: Full-time $6497; part-time $606 per credit. Tuition, state resident: full-time $9748; part-time $622 per credit. Tuition, nonresident: full-time $18,102; part-time $622 per credit. *Required fees:* $4459; $246 per credit. *Financial support:* In 2016–17, 3 students received support. Career-related internships or fieldwork, Federal Work-Study, scholarships/grants, and unspecified assistantships available. Support available to part-time students. Financial award application deadline: 3/1; financial award applicants required to submit FAFSA. *Unit head:* Dr. Kathleen Bantley, Chair, 860-832-3005, E-mail: bantleyk@ccsu.edu. *Application contact:* Patricia Gardner, Associate Director of Graduate Studies, 860-832-2350, Fax: 860-832-2362. Website: http://www.ccsu.edu/criminology/index.html

**Chaminade University of Honolulu,** Office of Professional and Continuing Education, Program in Criminal Justice Administration, Honolulu, HI 96816-1578. Offers correctional (MSCJA); criminal justice (MSCJA); law enforcement (MSCJA). *Program availability:* Part-time, evening/weekend, 100% online, blended/hybrid learning. *Faculty:* 3 full-time (1 woman), 3 part-time/adjunct (2 women). *Students:* 46 full-time (21 women), 23 part-time (16 women); includes 52 minority (5 Black or African American, non-Hispanic/Latino; 1 American Indian or Alaska Native, non-Hispanic/Latino; 20 Asian, non-Hispanic/Latino; 4 Hispanic/Latino; 17 Native Hawaiian or other Pacific Islander, non-Hispanic/Latino; 5 Two or more races, non-Hispanic/Latino). Average age 30. 12 applicants, 92% accepted, 11 enrolled. In 2016, 17 master's awarded. *Degree requirements:* For master's, comprehensive exam. *Entrance requirements:* For master's, minimum undergraduate GPA of 3.0, 3 letters of recommendation, interview, resume. Additional exam requirements/recommendations for international students: Required—TOEFL (minimum score 550 paper-based; 79 iBT). *Application deadline:* Applications are processed on a rolling basis. Application fee: $40. Electronic applications accepted. *Expenses:* $775 per credit hour plus $93 fee per online course. *Financial support:* Applicants required to submit FAFSA. *Unit head:* Ronald Becker, Director, 808-735-4703, Fax: 808-739-4614, E-mail: mscja@chaminade.edu. *Application contact:* 808-735-4755, E-mail: gradserv@chaminade.edu.
Website: http://www.chaminade.edu/mscja

**Charleston Southern University,** Department of Criminal Justice, Charleston, SC 29423-8087. Offers MSCJ. *Program availability:* Part-time, evening/weekend. *Degree requirements:* For master's, comprehensive exam, thesis optional. *Entrance requirements:* For master's, GRE or MAT, bachelor's degree in criminal justice. Additional exam requirements/recommendations for international students: Required—TOEFL (minimum score 550 paper-based; 79 iBT).

**Chicago State University,** School of Graduate and Professional Studies, College of Arts and Sciences, Department of Criminal Justice, Philosophy, and Political Science, Chicago, IL 60628. Offers criminal justice (MS). *Program availability:* Part-time, evening/weekend. *Entrance requirements:* For master's, minimum GPA of 2.75. *Faculty research:* Gang crime.

**Clark Atlanta University,** School of Arts and Sciences, Department of Criminal Justice, Atlanta, GA 30314. Offers MA. *Program availability:* Part-time. *Faculty:* 2 full-time (1 woman). *Students:* 9 full-time (7 women), 3 part-time (1 woman); includes 8 minority (all Black or African American, non-Hispanic/Latino), 1 international. Average age 25. 6 applicants, 100% accepted, 6 enrolled. In 2016, 2 master's awarded. *Degree requirements:* For master's, one foreign language, comprehensive exam, thesis. *Entrance requirements:* For master's, GRE General Test, minimum GPA of 2.5. Additional exam requirements/recommendations for international students: Required—TOEFL (minimum score 500 paper-based; 61 iBT). *Application deadline:* For fall admission, 4/1 for domestic and international students; for spring admission, 11/1 for domestic and international students. Applications are processed on a rolling basis.

Application fee: $40 ($55 for international students). *Expenses: Tuition:* Full-time $15,498; part-time $861 per credit hour. *Required fees:* $1326; $1326 per credit hour. Tuition and fees vary according to course load. *Financial support:* Career-related internships or fieldwork, Federal Work-Study, scholarships/grants, and unspecified assistantships available. Support available to part-time students. Financial award application deadline: 4/30; financial award applicants required to submit FAFSA. *Faculty research:* Race and crime, black ex-offenders in the labor market. *Unit head:* Dr. Obie Clayton, Chairperson, 404-880-8681, E-mail: oclayton@cau.edu. *Application contact:* Graduate Program Admissions, 404-880-8483, E-mail: graduateadmissions@cau.edu.

**Clayton State University,** School of Graduate Studies, College of Arts and Sciences, Program in Criminal Justice, Morrow, GA 30260-0285. Offers administration of justice (MS); criminology, law, and society (MS). *Expenses:* Tuition, state resident: full-time $3528; part-time $196 per credit hour. Tuition, nonresident: full-time $13,176; part-time $732 per credit hour. *Required fees:* $1454; $1454 per credit hour. $727 per semester. Tuition and fees vary according to campus/location and program.

**College of Saint Elizabeth,** Program in Justice Administration and Public Service, Morristown, NJ 07960-6989. Offers MA. *Program availability:* Part-time. *Degree requirements:* For master's, thesis or alternative. *Entrance requirements:* For master's, GRE, bachelor's degree from accredited college or university with minimum GPA of 3.0; two letters of recommendation attesting to candidate's ability to perform a high level of academic work as a self-directed learner. Additional exam requirements/recommendations for international students: Required—TOEFL (minimum score 550 paper-based; 79 iBT), IELTS (minimum score 6.5). Electronic applications accepted. Application fee is waived when completed online. *Expenses:* Contact institution.

**Colorado State University–Global Campus,** Graduate Programs, Greenwood Village, CO 80111. Offers criminal justice and law enforcement administration (MS); education leadership (MS); finance (MS); healthcare administration and management (MS); human resource management (MHRM); information technology management (MITM); international management (MS); management (MS); organizational leadership (MS); professional accounting (MPA); project management (MS); teaching and learning (MS). *Accreditation:* ACBSP. *Program availability:* Online learning.

**Colorado Technical University Aurora,** Program in Computer Science, Aurora, CO 80014. Offers computer systems security (MSCS); database systems (MSCS); software engineering (MSCS). *Program availability:* Part-time, evening/weekend. *Degree requirements:* For master's, thesis or alternative. *Entrance requirements:* For master's, minimum undergraduate GPA of 3.0, resume.

**Colorado Technical University Colorado Springs,** Graduate Studies, Program in Criminal Justice, Colorado Springs, CO 80907. Offers MSM. *Program availability:* Online learning.

**Columbia College,** Master of Science in Criminal Justice Program, Columbia, MO 65216-0002. Offers MSCJ. *Program availability:* Part-time, evening/weekend, 100% online, blended/hybrid learning. *Faculty:* 3 full-time (0 women), 14 part-time/adjunct (8 women). *Students:* 7 full-time (3 women), 126 part-time (71 women); includes 43 minority (28 Black or African American, non-Hispanic/Latino; 1 American Indian or Alaska Native, non-Hispanic/Latino; 11 Hispanic/Latino; 1 Native Hawaiian or other Pacific Islander, non-Hispanic/Latino; 2 Two or more races, non-Hispanic/Latino), 1 international. Average age 39. 33 applicants, 97% accepted, 28 enrolled. In 2016, 59 master's awarded. *Degree requirements:* For master's, final exams, culminating experience (intensive writing seminar). *Entrance requirements:* Additional exam requirements/recommendations for international students: Required—TOEFL (minimum score 550 paper-based; 79 iBT). *Application deadline:* For fall admission, 8/9 priority date for domestic and international students; for spring admission, 12/27 priority date for domestic and international students. Applications are processed on a rolling basis. Application fee: $55. Electronic applications accepted. *Expenses:* Contact institution. *Financial support:* Federal Work-Study and scholarships/grants available. Financial award application deadline: 3/1; financial award applicants required to submit FAFSA. *Unit head:* Dr. Mike Lyman, Graduate Program Coordinator, 573-875-7472, E-mail: mlyman@ccis.edu. *Application contact:* Stephanie Johnson, Director of Admissions, 573-875-7352, Fax: 573-875-7506, E-mail: sjohnson@ccis.edu. Website: http://www.ccis.edu/graduate/academics/degrees.asp?MSCJ

**Columbia Southern University,** College of Safety and Emergency Services, Orange Beach, AL 36561. Offers criminal justice administration (MS); emergency services management (MS); occupational safety and health (MS), including environmental management. *Program availability:* Part-time, evening/weekend, online learning. *Entrance requirements:* For master's, bachelor's degree from accredited/approved institution. Additional exam requirements/recommendations for international students: Required—TOEFL. Electronic applications accepted.

**Columbus State University,** Graduate Studies, College of Letters and Sciences, Department of Political Science and Public Administration, Columbus, GA 31907-5645. Offers public administration (MPA), including criminal justice, environmental policy, government administration, health services administration, political campaigning, urban policy. *Program availability:* Part-time, evening/weekend, 100% online, blended/hybrid learning. *Faculty:* 5 full-time (0 women), 5 part-time/adjunct (0 women). *Students:* 38 full-time (22 women), 61 part-time (25 women); includes 52 minority (40 Black or African American, non-Hispanic/Latino; 2 American Indian or Alaska Native, non-Hispanic/Latino; 4 Asian, non-Hispanic/Latino; 4 Hispanic/Latino; 1 Native Hawaiian or other Pacific Islander, non-Hispanic/Latino; 1 Two or more races, non-Hispanic/Latino), 2 international. Average age 32. 69 applicants, 49% accepted, 27 enrolled. In 2016, 55 master's awarded. *Degree requirements:* For master's, comprehensive exam. *Entrance requirements:* For master's, GRE General Test, minimum GPA of 2.75, three letters of recommendation. Additional exam requirements/recommendations for international students: Required—TOEFL (minimum score 550 paper-based; 79 iBT). *Application deadline:* For fall admission, 6/30 for domestic students, 5/1 for international students; for spring admission, 11/1 for domestic and international students; for summer admission, 3/1 for domestic and international students. Applications are processed on a rolling basis. Application fee: $50. Electronic applications accepted. *Expenses:* Tuition, state resident: full-time $4804; part-time $2412 per semester hour. Tuition, nonresident: full-time $19,218; part-time $9612 per semester hour. *Required fees:* $1850; $1850 per semester hour. Tuition and fees vary according to program. *Financial support:* In 2016–17, 5 students received support, including 11 research assistantships with partial tuition reimbursements available (averaging $3,000 per year); career-related internships or fieldwork, Federal Work-Study, institutionally sponsored loans, scholarships/grants, tuition waivers (partial), and unspecified assistantships also available. Support available to part-time students. Financial award application deadline: 5/1; financial award applicants required to submit FAFSA. *Unit head:* Dr. Frederick Gordon, Director, 706-565-7875, E-mail: gordon_frederick@colstate.edu. *Application contact:* Kristin Williams, Director of International and Graduate Recruitment, 706-507-8848, Fax: 706-568-5091, E-mail: williams_kristin@columbusstate.edu. Website: http://politicalscience.columbusstate.edu/

**Concordia University, St. Paul,** College of Health and Science, St. Paul, MN 55104-5494. Offers criminal justice leadership (MA); exercise science (MS); family science (MA); human services (MA); orthotics and prosthetics (MS); physical therapy (DPT);

sports management (MA). *Program availability:* Part-time, evening/weekend, 100% online, blended/hybrid learning. *Faculty:* 7 full-time (2 women), 27 part-time/adjunct (9 women). *Students:* 337 full-time (194 women), 18 part-time (7 women); includes 65 minority (35 Black or African American, non-Hispanic/Latino; 7 Asian, non-Hispanic/Latino; 8 Hispanic/Latino; 4 Native Hawaiian or other Pacific Islander, non-Hispanic/Latino; 11 Two or more races, non-Hispanic/Latino), 3 international. Average age 30. 388 applicants, 40% accepted, 117 enrolled. In 2016, 92 master's awarded. *Degree requirements:* For master's, comprehensive exam (for some programs), thesis (for some programs); for doctorate, at least one 8-12 week clinical rotation outside the St. Paul area. *Entrance requirements:* For master's, official transcripts from regionally-accredited institution stating the conferral of a bachelor's degree with minimum cumulative GPA of 3.0; personal statement; undergraduate degree at accredited college or university in the U.S., English-speaking Canada, the United Kingdom, Ireland, Australia, or New Zealand; for doctorate, undergraduate or graduate degree at accredited college or university in the U.S., English-speaking Canada, the United Kingdom, Ireland, Australia, or New Zealand. Additional exam requirements/recommendations for international students: Recommended—TOEFL (minimum score 547 paper-based; 78 iBT), IELTS (minimum score 6), TSE (minimum score 52). *Application deadline:* For fall admission, 4/1 for domestic students. Applications are processed on a rolling basis. Application fee: $50. Electronic applications accepted. *Expenses:* Contact institution. *Financial support:* In 2016–17, 114 students received support. Scholarships/grants and unspecified assistantships available. Financial award applicants required to submit FAFSA. *Faculty research:* Developmental screening in early childhood, cardiovascular responses to aerobic exercise. *Unit head:* Dr. Katie Fischer, Interim Dean, 651-641-8735, E-mail: fischer@csp.edu. *Application contact:* Kimberly Craig, Associate Vice President, Cohort Enrollment Management, 651-603-6223, Fax: 651-603-6320, E-mail: craig@csp.edu.

**Coppin State University,** Division of Graduate Studies, Division of Arts and Sciences, Department of Criminal Justice and Law Enforcement, Baltimore, MD 21216-3698. Offers criminal justice (MS). *Program availability:* Part-time, evening/weekend. *Degree requirements:* For master's, thesis optional. *Entrance requirements:* For master's, GRE, minimum GPA of 3.0.

**Curry College,** Graduate Studies, Program in Criminal Justice, Milton, MA 02186-9984. Offers MA. *Program availability:* Part-time, evening/weekend. *Degree requirements:* For master's, thesis. *Entrance requirements:* For master's, resume, recommendations, interview. Additional exam requirements/recommendations for international students: Required—TOEFL (minimum score 550 paper-based; 80 iBT). *Expenses:* Contact institution.

**Dallas Baptist University,** Professional Development Program, Dallas, TX 75211-9299. Offers accounting (MA); church leadership (MA); communication (MA); counseling (MA); criminal justice (MA); English as a second language (MA); finance (MA); higher education (MA); leadership studies (MA); management (MA); management information systems (MA); marketing (MA); missions (MA); professional life coaching (MA); training and development (MA). *Program availability:* Part-time, evening/weekend, 100% online, blended/hybrid learning. *Application deadline:* Applications are processed on a rolling basis. Application fee: $25. Electronic applications accepted. Application fee is waived when completed online. *Expenses: Tuition:* Full-time $15,408; part-time $856 per credit hour. *Required fees:* $400 per semester. Tuition and fees vary according to course load and degree level. *Unit head:* Jared Ingram, Director, 214-333-5584, E-mail: jaredi@dbu.edu. *Application contact:* Bobby Soto, Director of Admissions, 214-333-5242, E-mail: graduate@dbu.edu. Website: http://www3.dbu.edu/graduate/mapd.asp

**Delta State University,** Graduate Programs, College of Arts and Sciences, Division of Social Sciences and History, Program in Social Justice and Criminology, Cleveland, MS 38733-0001. Offers MSJC. *Program availability:* Part-time, online learning. *Degree requirements:* For master's, thesis or alternative.

**DeSales University,** Division of Liberal Arts and Social Sciences, Center Valley, PA 18034-9568. Offers criminal justice (MCJ); digital forensics (MCJ, Postbaccalaureate Certificate); education (M Ed), including instructional technology, secondary education, special education, teaching English to speakers of other languages; investigative forensics (MCJ, Postbaccalaureate Certificate). *Program availability:* Part-time, 100% online, blended/hybrid learning. *Faculty:* 5 full-time (3 women), 20 part-time/adjunct (13 women). *Students:* 55 full-time (36 women), 100 part-time (64 women); includes 25 minority (5 Black or African American, non-Hispanic/Latino; 14 Hispanic/Latino; 6 Two or more races, non-Hispanic/Latino). Average age 33. 145 applicants, 80% accepted, 103 enrolled. In 2016, 36 master's awarded. *Entrance requirements:* For master's, bachelor's degree from accredited institution, minimum undergraduate GPA of 3.0, personal statement showing potential of graduate work, three letters of recommendation, professional goal statement. Additional exam requirements/recommendations for international students: Required—TOEFL. *Application deadline:* Applications are processed on a rolling basis. Application fee: $50. Electronic applications accepted. *Expenses: Tuition:* Part-time $815 per credit hour. Tuition and fees vary according to degree level and program. *Financial support:* Applicants required to submit FAFSA. *Unit head:* Dr. Brain Kane, Division Head of Liberal Arts and Social Studies, 610-282-1100 Ext. 1274, E-mail: brian.kane@desales.edu. *Application contact:* Julia Ferraro, Director of Graduate Admissions, 610-282-1100 Ext. 1768, E-mail: gradadmissions@desales.edu.

**East Carolina University,** Graduate School, Thomas Harriot College of Arts and Sciences, Department of Criminal Justice, Greenville, NC 27858-4353. Offers criminal justice (MS); criminal justice education (Certificate); public management and leadership (Certificate); security studies (Certificate). *Program availability:* Part-time, evening/weekend, online learning. *Students:* 24 full-time (12 women), 53 part-time (17 women); includes 27 minority (22 Black or African American, non-Hispanic/Latino; 1 American Indian or Alaska Native, non-Hispanic/Latino; 2 Asian, non-Hispanic/Latino; 2 Hispanic/Latino). Average age 33. 35 applicants, 91% accepted, 24 enrolled. In 2016, 11 master's awarded. *Degree requirements:* For master's, thesis, internship. *Entrance requirements:* For master's, GRE or MAT, bachelor's degree in criminal justice or related field. Additional exam requirements/recommendations for international students: Required—TOEFL. *Application deadline:* For fall admission, 1/15 priority date for domestic students. Application fee: $50. *Financial support:* Research assistantships with tuition reimbursements, career-related internships or fieldwork, Federal Work-Study, institutionally sponsored loans, scholarships/grants, tuition waivers (full), and unspecified assistantships available. Financial award application deadline: 6/1. *Faculty research:* Corrections, policing, international criminal justice, terrorism. *Unit head:* Dr. William P. Bloss, Chair, 252-328-4192, Fax: 252-328-4196, E-mail: blossw@ecu.edu. *Application contact:* Dean of Graduate School, 252-328-6012, Fax: 252-328-6071, E-mail: gradschool@ecu.edu.

**East Carolina University,** Graduate School, Thomas Harriot College of Arts and Sciences, Department of Political Science, Greenville, NC 27858-4353. Offers community health administration (Certificate); public administration (MPA); security studies (Certificate). *Accreditation:* NASPAA. *Program availability:* Part-time, evening/weekend. *Students:* 34 full-time (12 women), 92 part-time (35 women); includes 31 minority (17 Black or African American, non-Hispanic/Latino; 3 Asian, non-Hispanic/Latino; 8 Hispanic/Latino; 3 Two or more races, non-Hispanic/Latino), 2 international.

## Criminal Justice and Criminology

Average age 33. 70 applicants, 91% accepted, 55 enrolled. In 2016, 16 master's awarded. *Degree requirements:* For master's, one foreign language, comprehensive exam. *Entrance requirements:* For master's, GRE General Test. Additional exam requirements/recommendations for international students: Required—TOEFL. *Application deadline:* For fall admission, 6/1 priority date for domestic students; for spring admission, 10/15 for domestic students. Applications are processed on a rolling basis. Application fee: $50. *Financial support:* Research assistantships with partial tuition reimbursements, teaching assistantships with partial tuition reimbursements, and Federal Work-Study available. Support available to part-time students. Financial award application deadline: 6/1. *Unit head:* Dr. Robert Thompson, Interim Chair, 252-328-5686, E-mail: thompsonro@ecu.edu. *Application contact:* Dean of Graduate School, 252-328-6012, Fax: 252-328-6071, E-mail: gradschool@ecu.edu.
Website: http://www.ecu.edu/polsci/mpa/index.html

**East Central University,** School of Graduate Studies, Department of Human Resources, Ada, OK 74820. Offers administration (MSHR); counseling (MSHR); criminal justice (MSHR); human services (MSHR); rehabilitation counseling (MSHR). *Accreditation:* CORE. *Program availability:* Part-time, evening/weekend. *Degree requirements:* For master's, thesis optional. *Entrance requirements:* For master's, GRE General Test, MAT, minimum GPA of 2.5. Electronic applications accepted.

**Eastern Kentucky University,** The Graduate School, College of Justice and Safety, Program in Correctional and Juvenile Justice Studies, Richmond, KY 40475-3102. Offers MS. *Degree requirements:* For master's, comprehensive exam (for some programs), thesis (for some programs). *Entrance requirements:* For master's, GRE.

**Eastern Kentucky University,** The Graduate School, College of Justice and Safety, Program in Criminal Justice and Police Studies, Richmond, KY 40475-3102. Offers criminal justice (MS); criminal justice education (MS); police studies (MS). *Program availability:* Part-time. *Degree requirements:* For master's, thesis optional. *Entrance requirements:* For master's, GRE General Test, minimum GPA of 3.0.

**Eastern Kentucky University,** The Graduate School, College of Justice and Safety, Program in Loss Prevention and Safety, Richmond, KY 40475-3102. Offers MS. *Entrance requirements:* For master's, GRE.

**Eastern Michigan University,** Graduate School, College of Arts and Sciences, Department of Sociology, Anthropology and Criminology, Program in Criminology and Criminal Justice, Ypsilanti, MI 48197. Offers MA. *Students:* 5 full-time (3 women), 13 part-time (10 women); includes 8 minority (5 Black or African American, non-Hispanic/Latino; 1 American Indian or Alaska Native, non-Hispanic/Latino; 2 Hispanic/Latino). Average age 34. 17 applicants, 65% accepted, 6 enrolled. In 2016, 2 master's awarded. Application fee: $45. *Application contact:* Dr. Marilyn Corsianos, Graduate Coordinator, 734-487-0012, Fax: 734-487-9666, E-mail: mcorsiano@emich.edu.

**East Tennessee State University,** School of Graduate Studies, College of Arts and Sciences, Department of Criminal Justice and Criminology, Johnson City, TN 37614. Offers MA, Postbaccalaureate Certificate. *Program availability:* Part-time, evening/weekend. *Degree requirements:* For master's, comprehensive exam, thesis optional; for Postbaccalaureate Certificate, practicum. *Entrance requirements:* For master's, GRE General Test, minimum GPA of 3.0; for Postbaccalaureate Certificate, minimum GPA of 2.5, three letters of recommendation. Additional exam requirements/recommendations for international students: Required—TOEFL (minimum score 550 paper-based; 79 iBT). Electronic applications accepted. *Faculty research:* Adolescent work experience and delinquency, violence against women, prisons and inmates, death penalty, women and crime, juvenile justice and alternative education.

**Excelsior College,** School of Business and Technology, Albany, NY 12203-5159. Offers business administration (MBA); cybersecurity management (MBA, Graduate Certificate); general business management (MS); health care management (MBA); human performance technology (MBA); human resource management (MS); human resources management (MBA); leadership (MBA, MS); mediation and arbitration (MBA, MS); social media management (MBA); technology management (MBA). *Program availability:* Part-time, evening/weekend, online learning. *Faculty:* 25 part-time/adjunct (9 women). *Students:* 1,801 part-time (487 women); includes 775 minority (424 Black or African American, non-Hispanic/Latino; 5 American Indian or Alaska Native, non-Hispanic/Latino; 58 Asian, non-Hispanic/Latino; 209 Hispanic/Latino; 15 Native Hawaiian or other Pacific Islander, non-Hispanic/Latino; 64 Two or more races, non-Hispanic/Latino), 11 international. Average age 39. In 2016, 288 master's awarded. *Application deadline:* Applications are processed on a rolling basis. Application fee: $50. Electronic applications accepted. *Expenses: Tuition:* Part-time $645 per credit. *Required fees:* $265 per credit. *Financial support:* Scholarships/grants available. *Unit head:* Dr. Lifang Shih, Dean, 888-647-2388. *Application contact:* Admissions, 888-647-2388 Ext. 133, Fax: 518-464-8777, E-mail: admissions@excelsior.edu.

**Excelsior College,** School of Public Service, Albany, NY 12203-5159. Offers criminal justice (MSCI); homeland security and emergency management (MSCJ); justice administration (MSCI); mediation and arbitration (MPA); public administration (MPA). *Program availability:* Part-time, evening/weekend, online learning. *Faculty:* 1 (woman) part-time/adjunct. *Students:* 181 part-time (47 women); includes 78 minority (41 Black or African American, non-Hispanic/Latino; 2 American Indian or Alaska Native, non-Hispanic/Latino; 2 Asian, non-Hispanic/Latino; 25 Hispanic/Latino; 2 Native Hawaiian or other Pacific Islander, non-Hispanic/Latino; 6 Two or more races, non-Hispanic/Latino). Average age 41. In 2016, 30 master's awarded. *Application deadline:* Applications are processed on a rolling basis. Application fee: $50. Electronic applications accepted. *Expenses: Tuition:* Part-time $645 per credit. *Required fees:* $265 per credit. *Financial support:* Scholarships/grants available. *Unit head:* Dr. Robert Waters, Dean, School of Public Service, 518-464-8500, Fax: 518-464-8777. *Application contact:* Admissions Counselor, 888-647-2388, Fax: 518-464-8777, E-mail: gradadmissions@excelsior.edu.
Website: http://www.excelsior.edu/programs/public-service

**Fairleigh Dickinson University, Metropolitan Campus,** University College: Arts, Sciences, and Professional Studies, School of Criminal Justice and Legal Studies, Program in Criminal Justice, Teaneck, NJ 07666-1914. Offers MA.

**Fairmont State University,** Program in Criminal Justice, Fairmont, WV 26554. Offers MS. *Program availability:* Part-time, evening/weekend, 100% online. *Faculty:* 5 full-time (2 women). *Students:* 29 full-time (24 women), 13 part-time (6 women); includes 14 minority (7 Black or African American, non-Hispanic/Latino; 1 Asian, non-Hispanic/Latino; 1 Hispanic/Latino; 1 Native Hawaiian or other Pacific Islander, non-Hispanic/Latino; 4 Two or more races, non-Hispanic/Latino). Average age 30. 28 applicants, 61% accepted, 16 enrolled. In 2016, 12 master's awarded. *Degree requirements:* For master's, thesis or comprehensive exam. *Entrance requirements:* For master's, GRE, minimum GPA of 3.0. Additional exam requirements/recommendations for international students: Required—TOEFL (minimum score 80 iBT), IELTS (minimum score 6.5). *Application deadline:* For fall admission, 5/1 for domestic and international students. Applications are processed on a rolling basis. Application fee: $40. Electronic applications accepted. *Expenses: Tuition,* state resident: full-time $7504; part-time $405 per credit hour. Tuition, nonresident: full-time $16,060; part-time $880 per credit hour. Part-time tuition and fees vary according to course load. *Financial support:* In 2016–17, 4 students received support. Research assistantships, teaching assistantships, scholarships/grants, and unspecified assistantships available. Financial award

applicants required to submit FAFSA. *Unit head:* Dr. Jennifer Myers, Director, Graduate Program in Criminal Justice, 304-367-4936, Fax: 304-367-4785, E-mail: jennifer.myers@fairmontstate.edu. *Application contact:* Jack Kirby, Director of Graduate Studies, 304-367-4101, E-mail: jack.kirby@fairmontstate.edu.
Website: http://www.fairmontstate.edu/graduatestudies/CJ_Overview.asp

**Faulkner University,** Alabama Christian College of Arts and Sciences, Department of Criminal Justice, Montgomery, AL 36109-3398. Offers MJA. *Program availability:* Online learning. *Degree requirements:* For master's, research project. *Entrance requirements:* For master's, MAT, GRE or GMAT, minimum overall GPA of 2.5, major 3.0; 3 letters of recommendation; letter of intent; resume.

**Fayetteville State University,** Graduate School, Program in Criminal Justice, Fayetteville, NC 28301-4298. Offers MA. *Program availability:* Part-time. *Faculty:* 14 full-time (8 women). *Students:* 15 full-time (11 women), 35 part-time (25 women); includes 30 minority (27 Black or African American, non-Hispanic/Latino; 3 Hispanic/Latino). Average age 34. 13 applicants, 100% accepted, 13 enrolled. In 2016, 6 master's awarded. *Entrance requirements:* Additional exam requirements/recommendations for international students: Required—TOEFL. *Application deadline:* For fall admission, 4/15 for domestic students; for spring admission, 10/15 for domestic students. Application fee: $40. *Financial support:* Application deadline: 3/1; applicants required to submit FAFSA. *Unit head:* Dr. Joe Brown, Interim Chair, 910-672-1478, Fax: 910-672-1908, E-mail: jbrown25@uncfsu.edu. *Application contact:* Dr. Lori Guevara, Graduate Coordinator, 910-672-2190, Fax: 910-672-1908, E-mail: lguevara@uncfsu.edu.

**Ferris State University,** College of Education and Human Services, School of Criminal Justice, Big Rapids, MI 49307. Offers criminal justice administration (MSCJ). *Program availability:* Part-time, evening/weekend. *Faculty:* 8 full-time (2 women). *Students:* 8 full-time (5 women), 25 part-time (11 women); includes 11 minority (5 Black or African American, non-Hispanic/Latino; 1 American Indian or Alaska Native, non-Hispanic/Latino; 3 Hispanic/Latino; 2 Two or more races, non-Hispanic/Latino). Average age 35. 16 applicants, 88% accepted, 11 enrolled. In 2016, 17 master's awarded. *Degree requirements:* For master's, comprehensive exam or thesis/dissertation. *Entrance requirements:* For master's, bachelor's degree in criminal justice or related field, minimum GPA of 3.0. Additional exam requirements/recommendations for international students: Required—TOEFL (minimum score 500 paper-based; 61 iBT). *Application deadline:* For fall admission, 8/15 for domestic students; for winter admission, 12/15 for domestic students; for spring admission, 3/15 for domestic students. Applications are processed on a rolling basis. Application fee: $0. Electronic applications accepted. Tuition and fees vary according to degree level and program. *Financial support:* In 2016–17, 1 research assistantship (averaging $4,850 per year) was awarded; Federal Work-Study and unspecified assistantships also available. Support available to part-time students. Financial award applicants required to submit FAFSA. *Faculty research:* Policy enactment, health and safety issues, criminological theory, juvenile justice, policy techniques, problem-based learning. *Unit head:* Dr. Nancy L. Hogan, Professor/Graduate Program Coordinator, 231-591-2664, Fax: 231-591-3792, E-mail: hogann@ferris.edu. *Application contact:* Sara P. Rasmussen, Secretary, 231-591-3652, Fax: 231-591-3792, E-mail: sararasmussen@ferris.edu.
Website: http://www.ferris.edu/education/cj/

**Florida Agricultural and Mechanical University,** Division of Graduate Studies, Research, and Continuing Education, College of Social Sciences, Arts and Humanities, Department of History and Political Science, Program in Applied Social Science, Tallahassee, FL 32307-3200. Offers criminal justice (MASS); history (MASS); political science (MASS); public administration (MASS). *Program availability:* Part-time. *Degree requirements:* For master's, thesis optional. *Entrance requirements:* For master's, GRE General Test, minimum GPA of 3.0. *Faculty research:* Southern history, black history, election trends, Presidential history.

**Florida Atlantic University,** College for Design and Social Inquiry, School of Criminology and Criminal Justice, Boca Raton, FL 33431-0991. Offers MS. *Program availability:* Part-time, evening/weekend, online learning. *Faculty:* 9 full-time (2 women). *Students:* 31 full-time (21 women), 38 part-time (26 women); includes 47 minority (27 Black or African American, non-Hispanic/Latino; 3 Asian, non-Hispanic/Latino; 14 Hispanic/Latino; 3 Two or more races, non-Hispanic/Latino). Average age 29. 55 applicants, 55% accepted, 23 enrolled. In 2016, 19 master's awarded. *Degree requirements:* For master's, thesis optional. *Entrance requirements:* For master's, GRE General Test, minimum GPA of 3.0, undergraduate course work in statistics and criminology. Additional exam requirements/recommendations for international students: Required—TOEFL (minimum score 550 paper-based; 61 iBT), IELTS (minimum score 6). *Application deadline:* For fall admission, 5/1 priority date for domestic students, 2/15 for international students; for spring admission, 11/1 priority date for domestic students, 7/15 for international students. Applications are processed on a rolling basis. Application fee: $30. Electronic applications accepted. *Expenses: Tuition,* state resident: full-time $7392; part-time $369.82 per credit hour. Tuition, nonresident: full-time $19,432; part-time $1024.81 per credit hour. *Financial support:* Research assistantships with partial tuition reimbursements, institutionally sponsored loans, scholarships/grants, and unspecified assistantships available. Financial award application deadline: 4/1. *Faculty research:* Restorative, justice corrections, logic modeling, criminal justice management, crime causation. *Unit head:* Sigal Altman, 561-297-4936, E-mail: saltman2013@fau.edu.
Website: http://www.fau.edu/dcj/

**Florida Gulf Coast University,** College of Arts and Sciences, Program in Criminal Justice Studies, Fort Myers, FL 33965-6565. Offers MS. *Faculty:* 238 full-time (97 women), 158 part-time/adjunct (62 women). *Students:* 6 full-time (4 women), 8 part-time (4 women); includes 3 minority (all Black or African American, non-Hispanic/Latino). Average age 26. 10 applicants, 70% accepted, 6 enrolled. In 2016, 3 master's awarded. *Entrance requirements:* For master's, GRE General Test, minimum GPA of 3.0. Additional exam requirements/recommendations for international students: Required—TOEFL (minimum score 550 paper-based). *Application deadline:* For fall admission, 3/1 for domestic students; for spring admission, 11/1 for domestic students. Applications are processed on a rolling basis. Application fee: $30. Electronic applications accepted. *Expenses:* Tuition, state resident: full-time $6721. Tuition, nonresident: full-time $28,170. *Required fees:* $1987. Tuition and fees vary according to course load and degree level. *Financial support:* In 2016–17, 2 students received support. Application deadline: 3/1; applicants required to submit FAFSA. *Unit head:* Shawn Keller, Program Chair, 239-590-4248, E-mail: skeller@fgcu.edu. *Application contact:* Mary Zager, Associate Professor/Chair, Division of Justice Studies, 239-590-7832, Fax: 239-590-7843, E-mail: mzager@fgcu.edu.

**Florida International University,** Steven J. Green School of International and Public Affairs, Department of Criminal Justice, Miami, FL 33199. Offers criminal justice (MS); international crime and justice (PhD). *Program availability:* Part-time, evening/weekend. *Faculty:* 15 full-time (7 women), 28 part-time/adjunct (10 women). *Students:* 46 full-time (31 women), 62 part-time (35 women); includes 83 minority (17 Black or African American, non-Hispanic/Latino; 1 Asian, non-Hispanic/Latino; 64 Hispanic/Latino; 1 Two or more races, non-Hispanic/Latino), 6 international. Average age 28. 133 applicants, 49% accepted, 42 enrolled. In 2016, 28 master's awarded. *Degree requirements:* For master's, thesis optional. *Entrance requirements:* For master's, minimum undergraduate

GPA of 3.0. Additional exam requirements/recommendations for international students: Required—TOEFL (minimum score 550 paper-based; 80 iBT). *Application deadline:* For fall admission, 6/1 for domestic students, 4/1 for international students; for spring admission, 10/1 for domestic students, 9/1 for international students. Applications are processed on a rolling basis. Application fee: $30. Electronic applications accepted. *Expenses:* Tuition, state resident: full-time $8912; part-time $446 per credit hour. Tuition, nonresident: full-time $21,393; part-time $992 per credit hour. *Required fees:* $2185; $195 per semester. Tuition and fees vary according to program. *Financial support:* Institutionally sponsored loans and scholarships/grants available. Financial award application deadline: 3/1; financial award applicants required to submit FAFSA. *Unit head:* Dr. Lisa Stolzenberg, Chair, 305-348-5892, E-mail: stolzenb@fiu.edu. *Application contact:* Nanett Rojas, Manager, Admissions Operations, 305-348-7464, Fax: 305-348-7441, E-mail: gradadm@fiu.edu.
Website: http://cj.fiu.edu/

**Florida State University,** The Graduate School, College of Criminology and Criminal Justice, Tallahassee, FL 32306-1127. Offers criminology and criminal justice (MA, MSC, PhD); MPA/MSC; MS/MSW. *Program availability:* Part-time, 100% online. *Faculty:* 19 full-time (7 women). *Students:* 127 full-time (84 women), 113 part-time (49 women); includes 76 minority (40 Black or African American, non-Hispanic/Latino; 1 American Indian or Alaska Native, non-Hispanic/Latino; 4 Asian, non-Hispanic/Latino; 31 Hispanic/Latino). 151 applicants, 76% accepted, 45 enrolled. In 2016, 56 master's, 7 doctorates awarded. Terminal master's awarded for partial completion of doctoral program. *Degree requirements:* For master's, thesis optional, minimum GPA of 3.0, minimum grade of C in all required courses; for doctorate, comprehensive exam, thesis/dissertation, minimum GPA of 3.0, minimum grade of B in all required courses. *Entrance requirements:* For master's, GRE General Test; for doctorate, GRE General Test, area paper or thesis. Additional exam requirements/recommendations for international students: Required—TOEFL (minimum score 600 paper-based; 100 iBT). *Application deadline:* For fall admission, 7/1 for domestic and international students; for spring admission, 11/1 for domestic and international students. Applications are processed on a rolling basis. Application fee: $30. Electronic applications accepted. *Expenses:* Contact institution. *Financial support:* In 2016–17, 50 students received support, including 3 fellowships with full tuition reimbursements available (averaging $15,000 per year), 23 research assistantships with full tuition reimbursements available (averaging $15,000 per year), 17 teaching assistantships with full tuition reimbursements available (averaging $15,000 per year); career-related internships or fieldwork, institutionally sponsored loans, scholarships/grants, health care benefits, tuition waivers (full), and unspecified assistantships also available. Financial award application deadline: 1/15; financial award applicants required to submit FAFSA. *Faculty research:* Criminological theory, criminal justice administration and planning, criminal justice policy and evaluation, law and social control, biosocial criminology. *Unit head:* Dr. Thomas G. Blomberg, Dean, 850-644-7365, Fax: 850-644-9614. *Application contact:* Margarita Frankeberger, Program Director, 850-644-7373, Fax: 850-644-9614, E-mail: mfrankeberger@fsu.edu.
Website: http://www.criminology.fsu.edu/

**Gannon University,** School of Graduate Studies, College of Humanities, Education, and Social Sciences, School of Humanities, Program in Criminalistics, Erie, PA 16541-0001. Offers MSC. *Program availability:* Online only, 100% online. *Students:* 11 part-time (7 women); includes 2 minority (both Black or African American, non-Hispanic/Latino). Average age 26. 18 applicants, 72% accepted, 11 enrolled. *Entrance requirements:* For master's, bachelor's degree from accredited college or university; transcripts; minimum overall GPA of 2.75, 3.0 in prerequisite courses; resume; three letters of recommendation; background check. Additional exam requirements/recommendations for international students: Required—TOEFL (minimum score 79 iBT). *Application deadline:* Applications are processed on a rolling basis. Application fee: $25. Electronic applications accepted. Application fee is waived when completed online. *Expenses: Tuition:* Full-time $17,370. *Required fees:* $550. Tuition and fees vary according to course load and program. *Financial support:* Application deadline: 7/1; applicants required to submit FAFSA. *Unit head:* Dr. Jerry Clark, Director, 814-871-7121, E-mail: clark120@gannon.edu. *Application contact:* Bridget Philip, Director of Graduate Admissions, 814-871-7412, E-mail: graduate@gannon.edu.

**George Mason University,** College of Humanities and Social Sciences, Department of Criminology, Law and Society, Fairfax, VA 22030. Offers MA, PhD. *Program availability:* Part-time. *Faculty:* 27 full-time (19 women), 44 part-time/adjunct (11 women). *Students:* 32 full-time (23 women), 33 part-time (21 women); includes 14 minority (8 Black or African American, non-Hispanic/Latino; 1 American Indian or Alaska Native, non-Hispanic/Latino; 1 Asian, non-Hispanic/Latino; 4 Hispanic/Latino), 4 international. Average age 31. 68 applicants, 66% accepted, 10 enrolled. In 2016, 6 master's, 5 doctorates awarded. Terminal master's awarded for partial completion of doctoral program. *Degree requirements:* For master's, thesis; for doctorate, thesis/dissertation, two comprehensive exams. *Entrance requirements:* For master's and doctorate, GRE, personal goal statement, transcripts, 3 letters of recommendation, writing sample, resume. Additional exam requirements/recommendations for international students: Required—TOEFL (minimum score 575 paper-based; 88 iBT), IELTS (minimum score 6.5), PTE (minimum score 59). Application fee: $75 ($80 for international students). Electronic applications accepted. *Expenses:* Tuition, state resident: full-time $10,628; part-time $443 per credit. Tuition, nonresident: full-time $29,306; part-time $1221 per credit. *Required fees:* $3096; $129 per credit. Tuition and fees vary according to program. *Financial support:* In 2016–17, 21 students received support, including 16 research assistantships with tuition reimbursements available (averaging $19,722 per year), 5 teaching assistantships with tuition reimbursements available (averaging $17,084 per year); career-related internships or fieldwork, Federal Work-Study, scholarships/grants, unspecified assistantships, and health care benefits (for full-time research or teaching assistantship recipients) also available. Support available to part-time students. Financial award application deadline: 3/1; financial award applicants required to submit FAFSA. *Faculty research:* Health care and justice agencies, public opinion on criminal justice issues and survey methods, police and crime control, police organizations and their reform, crime and place, counterterrorism, social equity and diversity issues, community corrections, prisons and prisoner reentry, evidence-based crime policy, courts and corrections, homeland security, risk and vulnerability assessment, experimental criminology, crime prevention, meta analysis and quantitative research methods. *Total annual research expenditures:* $3.5 million. *Unit head:* David B. Wilson, Chair, 703-993-4701, Fax: 703-993-8316, E-mail: dwilsonb@gmu.edu. *Application contact:* Mary Schifferli, Graduate Coordinator, 703-993-9417, Fax: 703-993-8316, E-mail: mschiffe@gmu.edu.
Website: http://cls.gmu.edu/

**The George Washington University,** Columbian College of Arts and Sciences, Department of Forensic Sciences, Washington, DC 20052. Offers crime scene investigation (MFS); forensic chemistry (MFS); forensic molecular biology (MFS); forensic toxicology (MFS); high-technology crime investigation (MS); security management (MFS). MFS programs in high-technology crime investigation and in security management offered in Arlington, VA. *Program availability:* Part-time, evening/weekend. *Faculty:* 10 full-time (1 woman). *Students:* 72 full-time (51 women), 22 part-time (14 women); includes 37 minority (12 Black or African American, non-Hispanic/Latino; 1 American Indian or Alaska Native, non-Hispanic/Latino; 11 Asian, non-Hispanic/Latino; 11 Hispanic/Latino; 2 Two or more races, non-Hispanic/Latino), 1 international. Average age 27. 162 applicants, 64% accepted, 36 enrolled. In 2016, 36 master's awarded. *Degree requirements:* For master's, comprehensive exam. *Entrance requirements:* For master's, GRE General Test, minimum GPA of 3.0. Additional exam requirements/recommendations for international students: Required—TOEFL (minimum score 550 paper-based; 80 iBT). *Application deadline:* For fall admission, 1/16 priority date for international students; for spring admission, 10/1 priority date for domestic students, 9/1 priority date for international students. Applications are processed on a rolling basis. Application fee: $75. Electronic applications accepted. *Financial support:* In 2016–17, 19 students received support. Fellowships with partial tuition reimbursements available, Federal Work-Study, and tuition waivers available. *Unit head:* Dr. Victor Weedn, Chair, 202-994-6977, E-mail: vweedn@gwu.edu. *Application contact:* 202-994-6210, Fax: 202-994-6213, E-mail: askccas@gwu.edu.
Website: http://forensicsciences.columbian.gwu.edu/

**The George Washington University,** Columbian College of Arts and Sciences, Department of Sociology, Program in Criminology, Washington, DC 20052. Offers MA. *Students:* 10 full-time (all women), 3 part-time (all women); includes 6 minority (4 Black or African American, non-Hispanic/Latino; 1 Hispanic/Latino; 1 Two or more races, non-Hispanic/Latino), 1 international. Average age 25. 18 applicants, 67% accepted, 7 enrolled. In 2016, 4 master's awarded. *Degree requirements:* For master's, comprehensive exam. *Entrance requirements:* For master's, GRE General Test, minimum GPA of 3.0. Additional exam requirements/recommendations for international students: Required—TOEFL (minimum score 550 paper-based). *Application deadline:* For fall admission, 4/1 priority date for domestic and international students; for spring admission, 10/1 priority date for domestic and international students. Applications are processed on a rolling basis. Application fee: $75. Electronic applications accepted. *Financial support:* In 2016–17, fellowships with full tuition reimbursements (averaging $10,000 per year), teaching assistantships (averaging $5,000 per year) were awarded. Financial award application deadline: 2/1. *Unit head:* Ronald Weitzer, Director, 202-994-6895. *Application contact:* Information Contact, 202-994-6345, Fax: 202-994-3239, E-mail: soc@gwu.edu.
Website: http://www.gwu.edu/graduate-programs/criminology

**Georgia College & State University,** Graduate School, College of Arts and Sciences, Department of Government and Sociology, Program in Criminal Justice, Milledgeville, GA 31061. Offers MSCJ. *Program availability:* Part-time, evening/weekend. *Students:* 7 full-time (0 women), 7 part-time (1 woman); includes 7 minority (5 Black or African American, non-Hispanic/Latino; 2 Two or more races, non-Hispanic/Latino). Average age 31. 4 applicants, 100% accepted, 4 enrolled. In 2016, 3 master's awarded. *Degree requirements:* For master's, comprehensive exam, capstone project. *Entrance requirements:* For master's, GRE General Test (minimum score 290), MAT (minimum score 395), or GMAT (minimum score 450) if undergraduate GPA 2.75 - 2.99, minimum GPA of 2.75 in undergraduate work, resume with relevant work experience. *Application deadline:* For fall admission, 7/1 priority date for domestic students, 4/1 priority date for international students; for spring admission, 11/1 priority date for domestic students, 9/1 priority date for international students; for summer admission, 4/1 priority date for domestic students. Applications are processed on a rolling basis. Application fee: $40. Electronic applications accepted. *Expenses:* $288 per credit hour in-state, $1,027 per credit hour out-of-state, $1,990 full-time annual fees. *Financial support:* In 2016–17, 1 student received support. Unspecified assistantships available. Financial award application deadline: 3/1; financial award applicants required to submit FAFSA. *Unit head:* Dr. Sara Doude, Program Coordinator, 478-445-4257, E-mail: sara.doude@gcsu.edu. *Application contact:* Kate Marshall, Graduate Admissions Coordinator, 478-445-1184, Fax: 478-445-1336, E-mail: grad-admit@gcsu.edu.
Website: http://www.gcsu.edu/artsandsciences/gov/criminal-justice-ms

**Georgia State University,** Andrew Young School of Policy Studies, Department of Criminal Justice and Criminology, Atlanta, GA 30302. Offers criminal justice (MS, PhD); public administration (MS). *Program availability:* Part-time. *Faculty:* 14 full-time (5 women). *Students:* 39 full-time (30 women), 5 part-time (all women); includes 21 minority (11 Black or African American, non-Hispanic/Latino; 3 Asian, non-Hispanic/Latino; 4 Hispanic/Latino; 3 Two or more races, non-Hispanic/Latino), 1 international. Average age 29. 56 applicants, 45% accepted, 15 enrolled. In 2016, 8 master's, 2 doctorates awarded. Terminal master's awarded for partial completion of doctoral program. *Degree requirements:* For master's, thesis optional; for doctorate, comprehensive exam, thesis/dissertation. *Entrance requirements:* For master's and doctorate, GRE. Additional exam requirements/recommendations for international students: Required—TOEFL (minimum score 603 paper-based; 100 iBT) or IELTS (minimum score 7). *Application deadline:* For fall admission, 1/15 for domestic and international students. Application fee: $50. Electronic applications accepted. *Expenses:* Tuition, state resident: full-time $6876; part-time $382 per credit hour. Tuition, nonresident: full-time $22,374; part-time $1243 per credit hour. *Required fees:* $2128; $1064 per term. Part-time tuition and fees vary according to course load and program. *Financial support:* In 2016–17, fellowships with full tuition reimbursements (averaging $22,000 per year), research assistantships with full tuition reimbursements (averaging $14,000 per year), teaching assistantships with full tuition reimbursements (averaging $14,000 per year) were awarded; career-related internships or fieldwork, Federal Work-Study, scholarships/grants, traineeships, health care benefits, and unspecified assistantships also available. Financial award application deadline: 2/15. *Faculty research:* Urban violence, drugs, victimization, criminal justice, criminology. *Unit head:* Dr. Richard Wright, Professor of Criminal Justice and Criminology/Department Chair, 404-413-1015, Fax: 404-413-1030, E-mail: rwright28@gsu.edu.
Website: http://aysps.gsu.edu/cj/

**Georgia State University,** Andrew Young School of Policy Studies, Department of Public Management and Policy, Atlanta, GA 30303. Offers criminal justice (MPA); disaster management (Certificate); disaster policy (MPA); environmental policy (PhD); health policy (PhD); management and finance (MPA); nonprofit management (MPA, Certificate); nonprofit policy (MPA); planning and economic development (MPP, Certificate); policy analysis and evaluation (MPA), including planning and economic development; public and nonprofit management (PhD); public finance and budgeting (PhD), including science and technology policy, urban and regional economic development; public finance policy (MPA), including social policy; public health (MPA). *Accreditation:* NASPAA (one or more programs are accredited). *Program availability:* Part-time. *Faculty:* 17 full-time (9 women). *Students:* 123 full-time (77 women), 79 part-time (49 women); includes 84 minority (59 Black or African American, non-Hispanic/Latino; 5 Asian, non-Hispanic/Latino; 14 Hispanic/Latino; 6 Two or more races, non-Hispanic/Latino), 34 international. Average age 30. 237 applicants, 60% accepted, 65 enrolled. In 2016, 59 master's, 4 doctorates, 8 other advanced degrees awarded. Terminal master's awarded for partial completion of doctoral program. *Degree requirements:* For master's, thesis optional; for doctorate, comprehensive exam, thesis/dissertation. *Entrance requirements:* For master's and doctorate, GRE. Additional exam requirements/recommendations for international students: Required—TOEFL (minimum score 603 paper-based; 100 iBT) or IELTS (minimum score 7). *Application deadline:* For fall admission, 1/15 for domestic and international students. Application fee: $50. Electronic applications accepted. *Expenses:* Tuition, state resident: full-time $6876;

## Criminal Justice and Criminology

part-time $382 per credit hour. Tuition, nonresident: full-time $22,374; part-time $1243 per credit hour. *Required fees:* $2128; $1064 per term. Part-time tuition and fees vary according to course load and program. *Financial support:* In 2016–17, fellowships (averaging $8,194 per year), research assistantships (averaging $8,068 per year), teaching assistantships (averaging $3,600 per year) were awarded; institutionally sponsored loans, scholarships/grants, health care benefits, and unspecified assistantships also available. Financial award application deadline: 2/1. *Faculty research:* Public budgeting and finance, public management, nonprofit management, performance measurement and management, urban development. *Unit head:* Dr. Carolyn Bourdeaux, Chair and Professor, 404-413-0013, Fax: 404-413-0104, E-mail: cbourdeaux@gsu.edu.
Website: http://aysps.gsu.edu/pmap/

**Governors State University,** College of Arts and Sciences, Program in Criminal Justice, University Park, IL 60484. Offers MA. *Program availability:* Part-time. *Faculty:* 91 full-time (43 women), 125 part-time/adjunct (64 women). *Students:* 3 full-time (2 women), 30 part-time (12 women); includes 11 minority (10 Black or African American, non-Hispanic/Latino; 1 Hispanic/Latino). Average age 41. 31 applicants, 23% accepted, 5 enrolled. In 2016, 18 master's awarded. *Entrance requirements:* Additional exam requirements/recommendations for international students: Required—TOEFL (minimum score 550 paper-based; 80 iBT), IELTS. *Application deadline:* For fall admission, 4/1 for domestic students. Application fee: $50. Electronic applications accepted. *Expenses:* $307 per credit hour; $38 per term or $76 per credit hour fees. *Financial support:* Application deadline: 5/1; applicants required to submit FAFSA. *Unit head:* Lori Montalbano, Interim Chair, Division of Humanities and Social Science, 708-235-2802, E-mail: lmontalbano@govst.edu. *Application contact:* Yakeea Daniels, Assistant Vice President for Enrollment Services/Director of Admission, 708-534-4510, E-mail: ydaniels@govst.edu.

**The Graduate Center, City University of New York,** Graduate Studies, Program in Criminal Justice, New York, NY 10016-4039. Offers PhD. *Degree requirements:* For doctorate, one foreign language, thesis/dissertation. *Entrance requirements:* For doctorate, GRE General Test, writing sample. Additional exam requirements/recommendations for international students: Required—TOEFL. Electronic applications accepted.

**Grambling State University,** School of Graduate Studies and Research, College of Professional Studies, Department of Criminal Justice, Grambling, LA 71245. Offers MS. *Program availability:* Part-time. *Degree requirements:* For master's, comprehensive exam, thesis optional. *Entrance requirements:* For master's, GRE, minimum GPA of 2.5 on last degree and in four core courses. Additional exam requirements/recommendations for international students: Required—TOEFL (minimum score 500 paper-based; 62 iBT). Electronic applications accepted.

**Grand Valley State University,** College of Community and Public Service, School of Criminal Justice, Allendale, MI 49401-9403. Offers MS. *Program availability:* Part-time, evening/weekend. *Faculty:* 4 full-time (1 woman). *Students:* 6 full-time (4 women), 22 part-time (12 women); includes 9 minority (3 Black or African American, non-Hispanic/Latino; 5 Hispanic/Latino; 1 Two or more races, non-Hispanic/Latino), 1 international. Average age 29. 11 applicants, 100% accepted, 10 enrolled. In 2016, 7 master's awarded. *Degree requirements:* For master's, comprehensive exam or thesis. *Entrance requirements:* For master's, minimum GPA of 3.0, three letters of recommendation, personal statement, essay, oral interview. Additional exam requirements/recommendations for international students: Required—TOEFL. *Application deadline:* For fall admission, 5/1 priority date for domestic students; for winter admission, 11/1 priority date for domestic students; for spring admission, 4/1 priority date for domestic students. Applications are processed on a rolling basis. Application fee: $30. Electronic applications accepted. *Expenses:* $604 per credit hour. *Financial support:* In 2016–17, 10 students received support. Career-related internships or fieldwork, Federal Work-Study, scholarships/grants, and unspecified assistantships available. Financial award application deadline: 5/1. *Faculty research:* Correctional administration, juvenile justice issues/gangs, women's issues, leadership, program/policy evaluation. *Unit head:* Dr. Kathleen Bailey, Director, 616-331-7148, Fax: 616-331-7155, E-mail: baileyk@gvsu.edu. *Application contact:* Christopher Kierkus, Graduate Program Director/Recruiting Contact, 616-331-7132, Fax: 616-331-7155, E-mail: kierkusc@gvsu.edu.
Website: http://www.gvsu.edu/cj/

**Hilbert College,** Program in Criminal Justice Administration, Hamburg, NY 14075-1597. Offers MS. *Program availability:* Evening/weekend, 100% online. *Faculty:* 6 full-time (3 women), 5 part-time/adjunct (2 women). *Students:* 18 full-time (10 women), 3 part-time (2 women); includes 4 minority (2 Black or African American, non-Hispanic/Latino; 2 Two or more races, non-Hispanic/Latino). Average age 28. 7 applicants, 100% accepted, 6 enrolled. In 2016, 11 master's awarded. *Degree requirements:* For master's, final capstone project. *Entrance requirements:* For master's, admissions statement/essay, official transcripts from all prior colleges, two letters of recommendation, current resume, relevant work experience, baccalaureate degree from accredited college or university with minimum cumulative GPA of 3.0, personal interview. Additional exam requirements/recommendations for international students: Recommended—TOEFL. *Application deadline:* Applications are processed on a rolling basis. Application fee: $25. Electronic applications accepted. Application fee is waived when completed online. *Expenses:* Tuition: Full-time $18,600; part-time $775 per credit. *Required fees:* $160; $20 per course. One-time fee: $50. *Financial support:* In 2016–17, 21 students received support. Scholarships/grants and tuition waivers (partial) available. Financial award application deadline: 7/1; financial award applicants required to submit FAFSA. *Unit head:* Kathryn Eskew, Director for Adult and Graduate Studies, 716-649-7900 Ext. 305, Fax: 716-649-0702, E-mail: keskew@hilbert.edu. *Application contact:* Kim Chiarmonte, Director for Adult and Graduate Recruitment, 716-926-8948, Fax: 716-649-0702, E-mail: kchiarmonte@hilbert.edu.
Website: http://www.hilbert.edu/grad/ms-cja

**Holy Family University,** Division of Academic Affairs, Philadelphia, PA 19114. Offers accountancy (MS); business administration (MBA); counseling psychology (MS); criminal justice (MA); education (M Ed); educational leadership (Ed D); nursing (MS). *Accreditation:* ACBSP. *Program availability:* Part-time, evening/weekend. *Faculty:* 28 full-time (19 women), 66 part-time/adjunct (36 women). *Students:* 329 full-time (281 women), 458 part-time (327 women); includes 153 minority (83 Black or African American, non-Hispanic/Latino; 1 American Indian or Alaska Native, non-Hispanic/Latino; 27 Asian, non-Hispanic/Latino; 41 Hispanic/Latino; 1 Native Hawaiian or other Pacific Islander, non-Hispanic/Latino), 4 international. Average age 34. 467 applicants, 69% accepted, 262 enrolled. In 2016, 6 master's, 2 doctorates awarded. *Degree requirements:* For master's, comprehensive exam, thesis or alternative; for doctorate, comprehensive exam, thesis/dissertation. *Entrance requirements:* For master's, minimum GPA of 3.0, interview, essay/professional statement, 2 recommendations, current resume, official transcripts of college or university work. Additional exam requirements/recommendations for international students: Required—TOEFL (minimum score 550 paper-based; 79 iBT), IELTS (minimum score 6). *Application deadline:* For fall admission, 7/1 priority date for domestic and international students; for spring admission, 11/1 priority date for domestic and international students; for summer

admission, 4/1 priority date for domestic and international students. Applications are processed on a rolling basis. Application fee: $25. Electronic applications accepted. *Expenses:* $9,292 per year. *Financial support:* Available to part-time students. Applicants required to submit FAFSA. *Unit head:* Dr. Michael Markowitz, Vice President of Academic Affairs, 267-341-3286, E-mail: mmarkowitz@holyfamily.edu. *Application contact:* Don Reinmold, Director of Graduate Admissions, 267-341-5001 Ext. 3230, Fax: 215-633-0558, E-mail: dreinmold@holyfamily.edu.

**Holy Family University,** Graduate and Professional Programs, School of Arts and Sciences, Program in Criminal Justice, Philadelphia, PA 19114. Offers MA. *Program availability:* Part-time, evening/weekend. *Students:* 8 full-time, 5 part-time. *Degree requirements:* For master's, thesis or alternative. *Entrance requirements:* For master's, 2 letters of recommendation, official transcripts of all college or university work, writing sample. Additional exam requirements/recommendations for international students: Required—TOEFL (minimum score 550 paper-based; 79 iBT), IELTS (minimum score 6), PTE (minimum score 54). *Application deadline:* For fall admission, 7/1 priority date for domestic and international students; for winter admission, 1/1 for domestic students; for spring admission, 11/1 priority date for domestic and international students; for summer admission, 4/1 priority date for domestic and international students. Applications are processed on a rolling basis. Application fee: $25. Electronic applications accepted. *Expenses:* Tuition: Part-time $751 per hour. *Required fees:* $140 per semester. One-time fee: $165 part-time. Part-time tuition and fees vary according to degree level and program. *Financial support:* Available to part-time students. Application deadline: 5/1; applicants required to submit FAFSA. *Unit head:* David Whelan, Associate Professor, 267-341-3416, E-mail: dwhelan@holyfamily.edu. *Application contact:* Gidget Marie Montelibano, Associate Director of Graduate Admissions, 267-341-3558, Fax: 215-637-1478, E-mail: gmontelibano@holyfamily.edu.
Website: http://www.holyfamily.edu/choosing-holy-family-u/academics/schools-of-study/school-of-arts-sciences/graduate-programs/162-criminal-justice

**Howard Payne University,** Program in Criminal Justice, Brownwood, TX 76801-2715. Offers criminal justice (MS), including corrections, law enforcement. *Program availability:* Part-time, evening/weekend, online only, 100% online. *Faculty:* 2 full-time (1 woman). *Entrance requirements:* For master's, baccalaureate degree, minimum cumulative GPA of 3.0, 800–1200 word written essay, official transcripts, three letters of reference. *Application deadline:* Applications are processed on a rolling basis. Electronic applications accepted. *Expenses:* $490 per credit hour plus $50 online fee per course. *Financial support:* Veteran's Administration benefits available. Financial award application deadline: 3/15; financial award applicants required to submit FAFSA. *Unit head:* Lynn Humeniuk, Director, Criminal Justice Program, 325-649-8703, E-mail: lhumeniuk@hputx.edu.
Website: http://www.hputx.edu/academics/schools/school-of-humanities/master-science-criminal-justice/

**Husson University,** Master of Science in Criminal Justice Administration Program, Bangor, ME 04401-2999. Offers MS. *Program availability:* Part-time. *Faculty:* 3 full-time (1 woman), 2 part-time/adjunct (1 woman). *Students:* 11 full-time (1 woman), 6 part-time (0 women); includes 1 minority (Two or more races, non-Hispanic/Latino). Average age 28. 8 applicants, 100% accepted, 5 enrolled. In 2016, 5 master's awarded. *Degree requirements:* For master's, thesis optional. *Entrance requirements:* For master's, letter of recommendation. Additional exam requirements/recommendations for international students: Required—TOEFL (minimum score 550 paper-based; 80 iBT), IELTS (minimum score 6.5). *Application deadline:* For fall admission, 8/1 for domestic students. Applications are processed on a rolling basis. Application fee: $50 ($0 for international students). Electronic applications accepted. *Expenses:* $450 per credit; $450 fees per full-time year. *Financial support:* Career-related internships or fieldwork, scholarships/grants, and unspecified assistantships available. Financial award application deadline: 4/15; financial award applicants required to submit FAFSA. *Faculty research:* Jury's attitudes towards forensic evidence. *Unit head:* John Michaud, Director, School of Legal Studies, 207-941-7037, E-mail: michaudj@husson.edu. *Application contact:* Kristen Card, Director of Graduate Admissions, 207-404-5660, E-mail: cardk@husson.edu.
Website: http://www.husson.edu/college-of-business/school-of-legal-studies/criminal-justice/masterofscienceincriminaljustice

**Illinois State University,** Graduate School, College of Applied Science and Technology, Department of Criminal Justice Sciences, Normal, IL 61790-2200. Offers MA, MS. *Degree requirements:* For master's, thesis or alternative. *Entrance requirements:* For master's, GRE General Test, minimum GPA of 2.6 in last 60 hours of course work. *Faculty research:* Graduate practicum for victim assistance and advocacy, graduate practicum in adult probation cases, graduate practicum in youth intervention program.

**Indiana State University,** College of Graduate and Professional Studies, College of Arts and Sciences, Department of Criminology and Criminal Justice, Terre Haute, IN 47809. Offers MA, MS. *Program availability:* Part-time, online learning. *Degree requirements:* For master's, comprehensive exam, thesis (for some programs). *Entrance requirements:* For master's, minimum GPA of 2.75 in undergraduate work, 3.0 in previous graduate work. Additional exam requirements/recommendations for international students: Required—TOEFL (minimum score 550 paper-based). Electronic applications accepted. *Faculty research:* Violent crime, rape attitudes, classification of offenders, substance abuse, domestic violence.

**Indiana University Bloomington,** University Graduate School, College of Arts and Sciences, Department of Criminal Justice, Bloomington, IN 47405. Offers crime and youth development (MA, PhD); crime, law and psychology (MA, PhD); criminal justice (MA, PhD); criminal justice institutions and practices (MA, PhD); criminology (MA, PhD); developmental criminology (MA, PhD); interdisciplinary studies in crime and punishment (PhD); interdisciplinary studies of crime and punishment (MA); the relationship between crime and gender, race and ethnicity (MA, PhD); theoretical analyses of criminology (MA, PhD). *Program availability:* Part-time. Terminal master's awarded for partial completion of doctoral program. *Degree requirements:* For master's, thesis optional; for doctorate, comprehensive exam, thesis/dissertation, foreign language or research practicum. *Entrance requirements:* For master's and doctorate, GRE General Test. Additional exam requirements/recommendations for international students: Required—TOEFL (minimum score 600 paper-based; 100 iBT); Recommended—TWE. Electronic applications accepted. *Faculty research:* Violence, crime, juveniles, psychology and law, cross-cultural studies.

**Indiana University Northwest,** School of Public and Environmental Affairs, Gary, IN 46408. Offers criminal justice (MPA); environmental affairs (Graduate Certificate); health services (MPA); nonprofit management (Certificate); public management (MPA, Graduate Certificate). *Accreditation:* NASPAA (one or more programs are accredited). *Program availability:* Part-time. *Faculty:* 5 full-time (3 women). *Students:* 10 full-time (8 women), 39 part-time (28 women); includes 25 minority (18 Black or African American, non-Hispanic/Latino; 7 Hispanic/Latino), 1 international. Average age 37. 31 applicants, 97% accepted, 16 enrolled. In 2016, 13 master's, 9 other advanced degrees awarded. *Entrance requirements:* For master's, GRE General Test (minimum combined verbal and quantitative score of 280), GMAT, or LSAT, letters of recommendation. *Application deadline:* For fall admission, 8/15 priority date for domestic students. Applications are processed on a rolling basis. Application fee: $40 ($60 for international students).

Electronic applications accepted. *Financial support:* Career-related internships or fieldwork, Federal Work-Study, and tuition waivers (partial) available. Support available to part-time students. Financial award application deadline: 3/1; financial award applicants required to submit FAFSA. *Faculty research:* Employment in income security policies, evidence in criminal justice, equal employment law, social welfare policy and welfare reform, public finance in developing countries. *Unit head:* Dr. Karl Besel, Assistant Dean and Director, 219-980-6554, Fax: 219-980-6737, E-mail: kbesel@iun.edu.
Website: http://www.iun.edu/spea/index.htm

**Indiana University of Pennsylvania,** School of Graduate Studies and Research, College of Health and Human Services, Department of Criminology, Doctoral Program in Criminology, Indiana, PA 15705. Offers PhD. *Program availability:* Part-time. *Faculty:* 16 full-time (9 women). *Students:* 11 full-time (6 women), 16 part-time (11 women); includes 2 minority (1 Black or African American, non-Hispanic/Latino; 1 Asian, non-Hispanic/Latino), 5 international. Average age 30. 30 applicants, 50% accepted, 5 enrolled. In 2016, 5 doctorates awarded. *Degree requirements:* For doctorate, one foreign language, comprehensive exam, thesis/dissertation. *Entrance requirements:* For doctorate, GRE, 3 letters of recommendation, writing sample. Additional exam requirements/recommendations for international students: Required—TOEFL (minimum score 540 paper-based). *Application deadline:* Applications are processed on a rolling basis. Application fee: $50. Electronic applications accepted. *Expenses:* Contact institution. *Financial support:* In 2016–17, 3 fellowships with full tuition reimbursements (averaging $2,018 per year), 11 research assistantships with tuition reimbursements (averaging $11,909 per year), 4 teaching assistantships with partial tuition reimbursements (averaging $23,305 per year) were awarded; Federal Work-Study, scholarships/grants, and unspecified assistantships also available. Support available to part-time students. Financial award application deadline: 4/15; financial award applicants required to submit FAFSA. *Unit head:* Dr. Erika Frenzel, Graduate Coordinator, 724-357-5976, E-mail: e.frenzel@iup.edu.
Website: http://www.iup.edu/grad/criminologyphd/default.aspx

**Indiana University of Pennsylvania,** School of Graduate Studies and Research, College of Health and Human Services, Department of Criminology, Master's Program in Criminology, Indiana, PA 15705. Offers MA. *Program availability:* Part-time, online learning. *Faculty:* 16 full-time (9 women). *Students:* 42 full-time (22 women), 14 part-time (9 women); includes 11 minority (6 Black or African American, non-Hispanic/Latino; 5 Hispanic/Latino), 2 international. Average age 26. 67 applicants, 70% accepted, 32 enrolled. In 2016, 24 master's awarded. *Degree requirements:* For master's, thesis optional. *Entrance requirements:* For master's, 2 letters of recommendation. Additional exam requirements/recommendations for international students: Required—TOEFL (minimum score 540 paper-based). *Application deadline:* For fall admission, 4/15 priority date for domestic students. Applications are processed on a rolling basis. Application fee: $50. Electronic applications accepted. *Expenses:* Contact institution. *Financial support:* In 2016–17, 17 research assistantships with tuition reimbursements (averaging $2,287 per year) were awarded; fellowships, career-related internships or fieldwork, Federal Work-Study, scholarships/grants, and unspecified assistantships also available. Support available to part-time students. Financial award application deadline: 4/15; financial award applicants required to submit FAFSA. *Unit head:* Dr. Jennifer Gossett, Graduate Coordinator, 724-357-5608, E-mail: jennifer.gossett@iup.edu.
Website: http://www.iup.edu/grad/criminology/default.aspx

**Indiana University–Purdue University Indianapolis,** School of Public and Environmental Affairs, Indianapolis, IN 46202. Offers criminal justice and public safety (MS); homeland security and emergency management (Graduate Certificate); library management (Graduate Certificate); nonprofit management (Graduate Certificate); public affairs (MPA); public management (Graduate Certificate); social entrepreneurship: nonprofit and public benefit organizations (Graduate Certificate); JD/MPA; MLS/NMC; MLS/PMC; MPA/MA. *Accreditation:* CAHME (one or more programs are accredited); NASPAA. *Program availability:* Part-time, evening/weekend, online learning. *Entrance requirements:* For master's, GRE General Test, GMAT or LSAT, minimum GPA of 3.0 (preferred). Additional exam requirements/recommendations for international students: Required—TOEFL (minimum score 93 iBT), IELTS (minimum score 6.5). Electronic applications accepted. *Faculty research:* Nonprofit and public management, public policy, urban policy, sustainability policy, disaster preparedness and recovery, vehicular safety, homicide, offender rehabilitation and re-entry.

**Inter American University of Puerto Rico, Aguadilla Campus,** Graduate School, Aguadilla, PR 00605. Offers accounting (MBA); counseling psychology specializing in family (MS); criminal justice (MA); educative management and leadership (MA); elementary education (M Ed); finance (MBA); human resources (MBA); industrial management (MBA); management information systems (MBA); marketing (MBA). *Program availability:* Part-time, evening/weekend. *Degree requirements:* For master's, comprehensive exam. *Entrance requirements:* For master's, EXADEP, 2 letters of recommendation, minimum GPA of 2.5. Electronic applications accepted.

**Inter American University of Puerto Rico, Metropolitan Campus,** Graduate Programs, Program in Criminal Justice, San Juan, PR 00919-1293. Offers MA. *Program availability:* Part-time, evening/weekend. *Degree requirements:* For master's, comprehensive exam. *Entrance requirements:* For master's, GRE or EXADEP, interview. Electronic applications accepted.

**Inter American University of Puerto Rico, Ponce Campus,** Graduate School, Mercedita, PR 00715-1602. Offers accounting (MBA); biology (M Ed); chemistry (M Ed); criminal justice (MA); elementary education (M Ed); English as a Second Language (M Ed); finance (MBA); history (M Ed); human resources (MBA); marketing (MBA); mathematics (M Ed); Spanish (M Ed). *Entrance requirements:* For master's, minimum GPA of 2.5.

**Iona College,** School of Arts and Science, Department of Criminal Justice, New Rochelle, NY 10801-1890. Offers criminal justice (MS); cybercrime and security (AC); forensic criminology and criminal justice systems (Certificate). *Program availability:* Part-time, evening/weekend. *Faculty:* 2 full-time (0 women), 4 part-time/adjunct (1 woman). *Students:* 8 full-time (6 women), 14 part-time (4 women); includes 9 minority (5 Black or African American, non-Hispanic/Latino; 4 Hispanic/Latino), 1 international. Average age 26. 11 applicants, 100% accepted, 7 enrolled. In 2016, 12 master's, 3 other advanced degrees awarded. *Degree requirements:* For master's, thesis (for some programs), thesis or literature review. *Entrance requirements:* For master's, minimum GPA of 3.0. Additional exam requirements/recommendations for international students: Required—TOEFL (minimum score 500 paper-based; 80 iBT), IELTS (minimum score 6.5). *Application deadline:* For fall admission, 8/1 priority date for domestic students, 5/1 priority date for international students; for spring admission, 1/1 priority date for domestic students, 9/1 priority date for international students. Applications are processed on a rolling basis. Application fee: $50. Electronic applications accepted. *Expenses: Tuition:* Full-time $19,692; part-time $1094 per credit. *Required fees:* $245 per term. Tuition and fees vary according to program. *Financial support:* In 2016–17, 13 students received support. Unspecified assistantships available. Financial award application deadline: 4/15; financial award applicants required to submit FAFSA. *Faculty research:* Juvenile justice, criminology, victimology, policing, social justice, security threat assessment. *Unit head:* Cathryn Lavery, PhD, Chair, 914-633-2597, E-mail: clavery@iona.edu.

*Application contact:* Katelyn Brunck, Assistant Director of Graduate Admissions, 914-633-2451, Fax: 914-633-2277, E-mail: kbrunck@iona.edu.
Website: http://www.iona.edu/Academics/School-of-Arts-Science/Departments/Criminal-Justice/Graduate-Programs.aspx

**Jackson State University,** Graduate School, College of Liberal Arts, Department of Criminal Justice and Sociology, Jackson, MS 39217. Offers criminology and justice services (MA); sociology (MA). *Program availability:* Part-time, evening/weekend. *Degree requirements:* For master's, comprehensive exam, thesis or alternative. *Entrance requirements:* For master's, GRE General Test. Additional exam requirements/recommendations for international students: Required—TOEFL (minimum score 520 paper-based; 67 iBT). *Application deadline:* For fall admission, 3/1 priority date for domestic students, 3/1 for international students; for spring admission, 10/1 for domestic students. Applications are processed on a rolling basis. Application fee: $25. *Expenses:* Tuition, state resident: full-time $7141. Tuition, nonresident: full-time $17,494. *Required fees:* $1080. Tuition and fees vary according to class time, course level, course load, degree level, campus/location, program and student level. *Financial support:* Career-related internships or fieldwork, Federal Work-Study, scholarships/grants, and unspecified assistantships available. Support available to part-time students. Financial award application deadline: 3/1; financial award applicants required to submit FAFSA. *Unit head:* Dr. Etta F. Morgan, Chair, 601-979-2626, E-mail: etta.morgan@jsums.edu. *Application contact:* Fatoumatta Sisay, Manager of Graduate Admissions, 601-979-0342, Fax: 601-979-4325, E-mail: fatoumatta.sisay@jsums.edu.
Website: http://www.jsums.edu/criminaljustice

**Jacksonville State University,** College of Graduate Studies and Continuing Education, College of Arts and Sciences, Department of Criminal Justice, Jacksonville, AL 36265-1602. Offers MS. *Program availability:* Part-time, evening/weekend. *Faculty:* 3 full-time (1 woman), 1 (woman) part-time/adjunct. *Students:* 6 full-time (4 women), 13 part-time (10 women); includes 7 minority (all Black or African American, non-Hispanic/Latino), 1 international. Average age 29. 16 applicants, 69% accepted, 6 enrolled. In 2016, 9 master's awarded. *Degree requirements:* For master's, comprehensive exam, thesis (for some programs). *Entrance requirements:* For master's, GRE General Test or MAT. Additional exam requirements/recommendations for international students: Required—TOEFL (minimum score 500 paper-based; 61 iBT). *Application deadline:* Applications are processed on a rolling basis. Application fee: $35. Electronic applications accepted. *Financial support:* In 2016–17, 3 students received support. Available to part-time students. Application deadline: 4/1; applicants required to submit FAFSA. *Unit head:* Dr. Richard Davis, Head, 256-782-5347, E-mail: rpdavis@jsu.edu. *Application contact:* Dr. Jean Pugliese, Associate Dean, 256-782-5329, Fax: 256-782-5321, E-mail: pugliese@jsu.edu.

**John Jay College of Criminal Justice of the City University of New York,** Graduate Studies, Program in Protection Management, New York, NY 10019. Offers MS. *Program availability:* Part-time, evening/weekend. *Degree requirements:* For master's, thesis or alternative. *Entrance requirements:* For master's, minimum B average. Additional exam requirements/recommendations for international students: Required—TOEFL (minimum score 500 paper-based).

**John Jay College of Criminal Justice of the City University of New York,** Graduate Studies, Programs in Criminal Justice, New York, NY 10019. Offers criminal justice (MA, PhD); criminology and deviance (PhD); forensic psychology (PhD); forensic science (PhD); international crime and justice (MA); law and philosophy (PhD); organizational behavior (PhD); public policy (PhD). *Program availability:* Part-time, evening/weekend. Terminal master's awarded for partial completion of doctoral program. *Degree requirements:* For master's, thesis or alternative; for doctorate, one foreign language, thesis/dissertation. *Entrance requirements:* For master's, GRE General Test, minimum B average; for doctorate, GRE General Test. Additional exam requirements/recommendations for international students: Required—TOEFL (minimum score 500 paper-based).

**Johnson & Wales University,** Graduate Studies, MS Program in Criminal Justice, Providence, RI 02903-3703. Offers MS. *Program availability:* Online learning.

**Kaplan University, Davenport Campus,** School of Criminal Justice, Davenport, IA 52807. Offers corrections (MSCJ); global issues in criminal justice (MSCJ); law (MSCJ); leadership and executive management (MSCJ); policing (MSCJ). *Program availability:* Part-time, evening/weekend, online learning. *Entrance requirements:* Additional exam requirements/recommendations for international students: Required—TOEFL (minimum score 550 paper-based; 80 iBT). Electronic applications accepted.

**Kean University,** College of Business and Public Management, Program in Criminal Justice, Union, NJ 07083. Offers MA. *Program availability:* Part-time. *Faculty:* 14 full-time (4 women). *Students:* 6 full-time (4 women), 6 part-time (3 women); includes 7 minority (4 Black or African American, non-Hispanic/Latino; 1 Asian, non-Hispanic/Latino; 2 Hispanic/Latino). Average age 29. 10 applicants, 40% accepted, 4 enrolled. In 2016, 6 master's awarded. *Degree requirements:* For master's, comprehensive exam, thesis optional. *Entrance requirements:* For master's, GRE (minimum Analytic Writing score of 3.5), 3 reference letters, minimum GPA of 3.0, writing sample, official transcripts from all institutions attended, personal statement, resume, sample of scholarly work from undergraduate studies. Additional exam requirements/recommendations for international students: Required—TOEFL (minimum score 550 paper-based; 79 iBT), IELTS (minimum score 6.5). *Application deadline:* For fall admission, 6/1 for domestic and international students; for spring admission, 12/1 for domestic and international students. Applications are processed on a rolling basis. Application fee: $75. Electronic applications accepted. *Expenses:* Tuition, state resident: full-time $13,156; part-time $640 per credit. Tuition, nonresident: full-time $17,831; part-time $785 per credit. *Required fees:* $3316; $151 per credit. Tuition and fees vary according to course level, course load, degree level and program. *Financial support:* Scholarships/grants and unspecified assistantships available. Financial award applicants required to submit FAFSA. *Unit head:* Dr. Pat McManimon, Program Coordinator, 908-737-4309, E-mail: pmcmanim@kean.edu. *Application contact:* Pedro Lopes, Admissions Counselor, 908-737-7100, E-mail: grad-adm@kean.edu.
Website: http://grad.kean.edu/masters-programs/criminal-justice

**Keiser University,** MA in Criminal Justice-Homeland Security Program, Ft. Lauderdale, FL 33309. Offers MA.

**Keiser University,** MA in Criminal Justice Program, Ft. Lauderdale, FL 33309. Offers MA. *Program availability:* Part-time, online learning.

**Kennesaw State University,** College of Humanities and Social Sciences, Program in Criminal Justice, Kennesaw, GA 30144. Offers MS. *Program availability:* Part-time. *Degree requirements:* For master's, research project or thesis. *Entrance requirements:* For master's, GRE. Additional exam requirements/recommendations for international students: Required—TOEFL (minimum score 550 paper-based; 80 iBT), IELTS (minimum score 6.5). Electronic applications accepted.

**Kent State University,** College of Arts and Sciences, Department of Sociology, Kent, OH 44242-0001. Offers criminology and criminal justice (MA), including corrections, global security, policing, victimology; sociology (MA, PhD). PhD offered jointly with The University of Akron. *Program availability:* Part-time, 100% online. *Faculty:* 31 full-time

(18 women). *Students:* 44 full-time (25 women), 53 part-time (36 women); includes 27 minority (19 Black or African American, non-Hispanic/Latino; 1 Asian, non-Hispanic/Latino; 5 Hispanic/Latino; 2 Two or more races, non-Hispanic/Latino). Average age 30. 71 applicants, 39% accepted, 18 enrolled. In 2016, 4 master's awarded. Terminal master's awarded for partial completion of doctoral program. *Degree requirements:* For master's, capstone project; for doctorate, comprehensive exam, thesis/dissertation. *Entrance requirements:* For master's, minimum GPA of 3.0, transcripts, resume/curriculum vitae, goal statement, 3 letters of recommendation; for doctorate, GRE, minimum GPA of 3.0, transcripts, personal statement, 3 letters of recommendation. Additional exam requirements/recommendations for international students: Required—TOEFL (minimum score of 525 paper-based, 71 iBT), IELTS (minimum score of 6), Michigan English Language Assessment Battery (minimum score of 75), or PTE (minimum score of 48). *Application deadline:* For fall admission, 12/15 for domestic students, 12/1 for international students. Applications are processed on a rolling basis. Application fee: $45 ($70 for international students). Electronic applications accepted. *Expenses:* Tuition, state resident: full-time $10,864; part-time $495 per credit hour. Tuition, nonresident: full-time $18,380; part-time $837 per credit hour. *Financial support:* Research assistantships with full tuition reimbursements, teaching assistantships with full tuition reimbursements, health care benefits, and unspecified assistantships available. Financial award application deadline: 12/15. *Unit head:* Dr. Richard T. Serpe, Professor and Chair, 330-672-2562, E-mail: rserpe@kent.edu. *Application contact:* Dr. William Kalkhoff, Professor and Graduate Coordinator, 330-672-3712, E-mail: wkalkhof@kent.edu.
Website: http://www.kent.edu/sociology/

**Keuka College,** Program in Criminal Justice Administration, Keuka Park, NY 14478. Offers MS. *Program availability:* Part-time, evening/weekend. *Faculty:* 2 full-time, 6 part-time/adjunct (2 women). *Students:* 16 full-time (8 women), 1 (woman) part-time; includes 8 minority (6 Black or African American, non-Hispanic/Latino; 2 Two or more races, non-Hispanic/Latino). Average age 36. 11 applicants, 82% accepted, 6 enrolled. In 2016, 5 master's awarded. *Degree requirements:* For master's, thesis, action research project. *Entrance requirements:* For master's, bachelor's degree from accredited institution, minimum GPA of 3.0, professional experience in field of criminal justice, essay, letter of recommendation. Additional exam requirements/recommendations for international students: Required—TOEFL (minimum score 550 paper-based). *Application deadline:* For fall admission, 8/15 for domestic students; for winter admission, 12/15 for domestic students; for spring admission, 4/15 for domestic students. Applications are processed on a rolling basis. Application fee: $50. Electronic applications accepted. *Expenses:* Contact institution. *Financial support:* Scholarships/grants and tuition waivers (full and partial) available. Financial award applicants required to submit FAFSA. *Faculty research:* Re-entry of mentally ill offenders; mentoring in criminal justice profession; police leadership; police decision making. *Unit head:* Dr. Tom Tremer, Program Director, 315-279-5672, E-mail: ttremer@mail.keuka.edu. *Application contact:* Fred Hoyle, Graduate Admissions, 866-255-3852, Fax: 315-279-5386, E-mail: asapadvisor@keuka.edu.

**Lamar University,** College of Graduate Studies, College of Arts and Sciences, Department of Sociology, Social Work, and Criminal Justice, Beaumont, TX 77710. Offers criminal justice (MS). *Program availability:* Part-time. *Faculty:* 5 full-time (2 women). *Students:* 8 full-time (4 women), 101 part-time (55 women); includes 78 minority (52 Black or African American, non-Hispanic/Latino; 1 Asian, non-Hispanic/Latino; 24 Hispanic/Latino; 1 Two or more races, non-Hispanic/Latino). Average age 36. 93 applicants, 100% accepted, 22 enrolled. In 2016, 70 master's awarded. *Degree requirements:* For master's, thesis or alternative, applied projects. *Entrance requirements:* For master's, GRE General Test. Additional exam requirements/recommendations for international students: Required—TOEFL (minimum score 550 paper-based; 79 iBT), IELTS (minimum score 6.5). *Application deadline:* For fall admission, 8/10 for domestic students, 7/1 for international students; for spring admission, 1/5 for domestic students, 12/1 for international students. Applications are processed on a rolling basis. Application fee: $25 ($50 for international students). Electronic applications accepted. *Expenses:* $8,134 in-state full-time, $5,574 in-state part-time; $15,604 out-of-state full-time, $10,554 out-of-state part-time per year. *Financial support:* Fellowships with partial tuition reimbursements, career-related internships or fieldwork, Federal Work-Study, and scholarships/grants available. Support available to part-time students. Financial award application deadline: 4/1; financial award applicants required to submit FAFSA. *Faculty research:* Corrections, planning and evaluations, juveniles, terrorism, Mexican criminal justice. *Unit head:* Dr. Stuart Wright, Chair, 409-880-8542, Fax: 409-880-2324. *Application contact:* Deidre Mayer, Interim Director, Admissions and Academic Services, 409-880-8888, Fax: 409-880-7419, E-mail: gradmissions@lamar.edu.
Website: http://artssciences.lamar.edu/sociology-social-work-criminal-justice

**Lasell College,** Graduate and Professional Studies in Criminal Justice, Newton, MA 02466. Offers emergency and crisis management (MS, Certificate); homeland security and global justice (MS, Certificate); violence prevention and advocacy (MS, Certificate). *Program availability:* Part-time, evening/weekend, online only, 100% online. *Faculty:* 1 full-time (0 women), 2 part-time/adjunct (both women). *Students:* 5 full-time (2 women), 11 part-time (5 women); includes 2 minority (1 Black or African American, non-Hispanic/Latino; 1 Asian, non-Hispanic/Latino). Average age 30. 23 applicants, 52% accepted, 8 enrolled. *Degree requirements:* For master's, minimum GPA of 3.0; internship or research paper. *Entrance requirements:* For master's, one-page personal statement, 2 letters of recommendation, resume, bachelor's degree transcript; for Certificate, bachelor's transcript, 2 letters of recommendation, 1-page statement, resume. Additional exam requirements/recommendations for international students: Required—TOEFL (minimum score 550 paper-based, 79 iBT) or IELTS (minimum score 6). *Application deadline:* For fall admission, 8/31 priority date for domestic students, 6/30 priority date for international students; for spring admission, 12/31 priority date for domestic students, 10/31 priority date for international students. Applications are processed on a rolling basis. Electronic applications accepted. *Expenses:* $600 per credit. *Financial support:* In 2016–17, 6 students received support. Federal Work-Study, scholarships/grants, and tuition discounts available. Support available to part-time students. Financial award application deadline: 8/31; financial award applicants required to submit FAFSA. *Faculty research:* Children aging out of foster care and the criminal justice system; police departments' attitudes toward the mentally ill and jail diversion programs for those offenders. *Unit head:* Dr. Joan Dolamore, Dean of Graduate and Professional Studies, 617-243-2485, Fax: 617-243-2450, E-mail: gradinfo@lasell.edu. *Application contact:* Adrienne Franciosi, Director of Graduate Enrollment, 617-243-2214, Fax: 617-243-2450, E-mail: gradinfo@lasell.edu.
Website: http://www.lasell.edu/academics/graduate-and-professional-studies/programs-of-study/master-of-science-in-criminal-justice-.html

**Lewis University,** College of Arts and Sciences, Program in Criminal/Social Justice, Romeoville, IL 60446. Offers MS. *Program availability:* Part-time, evening/weekend, 100% online, blended/hybrid learning. *Students:* 7 full-time (6 women), 69 part-time (43 women); includes 26 minority (11 Black or African American, non-Hispanic/Latino; 1 American Indian or Alaska Native, non-Hispanic/Latino; 1 Asian, non-Hispanic/Latino; 10 Hispanic/Latino; 3 Two or more races, non-Hispanic/Latino). Average age 32. *Entrance requirements:* For master's, bachelor's degree or a minimum of 12 related hours in criminal/social justice, 2 letters of recommendation, minimum GPA of 3.0, interview. Additional exam requirements/recommendations for international students: Required—TOEFL (minimum score 550 paper-based; 80 iBT). *Application deadline:* For fall admission, 5/1 priority date for international students; for spring admission, 11/15 priority date for international students. Applications are processed on a rolling basis. Application fee: $40. Electronic applications accepted. *Expenses:* Tuition: Full-time $13,860; part-time $770 per credit hour. *Required fees:* $75 per semester. Tuition and fees vary according to degree level and program. *Financial support:* Federal Work-Study, scholarships/grants, tuition waivers (full and partial), and unspecified assistantships available. Financial award application deadline: 5/1; financial award applicants required to submit FAFSA. *Faculty research:* Community policing, management, terrorism, biological warfare, drugs. *Unit head:* Dr. Calvin Edwards, Chair of Justice, Law and Public Safety Studies, 815-838-0500, Fax: 815-836-5870, E-mail: koloshsa@lewisu.edu. *Application contact:* Michelle Mega, Coordinator, 815-838-0500 Ext. 5342, Fax: 815-836-5342, E-mail: megami@lewisu.edu.
Website: http://www.lewisu.edu/academics/masterscrim/index.htm

**Liberty University,** School of Behavioral Sciences, Lynchburg, VA 24515. Offers clinical mental health counseling (MA); counselor education and supervision (PhD); human services counseling (MA), including addictions and recovery, business, child and family law, Christian ministries, criminal justice, crisis response and trauma, executive leadership, health and wellness, life coaching, marriage and family, military resilience; marriage and family therapy (MA); military resilience (Certificate); professional counseling (MA). *Program availability:* Part-time, online learning. *Students:* 2,041 full-time (1,612 women), 4,970 part-time (3,875 women); includes 1,991 minority (1,678 Black or African American, non-Hispanic/Latino; 33 American Indian or Alaska Native, non-Hispanic/Latino; 48 Asian, non-Hispanic/Latino; 80 Hispanic/Latino; 8 Native Hawaiian or other Pacific Islander, non-Hispanic/Latino; 144 Two or more races, non-Hispanic/Latino), 127 international. Average age 39. 5,496 applicants, 41% accepted, 1257 enrolled. In 2016, 2,813 master's, 11 doctorates, 20 other advanced degrees awarded. *Application deadline:* Applications are processed on a rolling basis. Application fee: $50. Electronic applications accepted. *Financial support:* Applicants required to submit FAFSA. *Unit head:* Dr. Ronald Hawkins, Founding Dean, School of Behavioral Sciences. *Application contact:* Jay Bridge, Director of Admissions, 800-424-9595, Fax: 800-628-7977, E-mail: gradadmissions@liberty.edu.

**Liberty University,** School of Business, Lynchburg, VA 24515. Offers accounting (MBA, MS); business administration (MBA); criminal justice (MBA); cyber security (MS); executive leadership (MA); information systems (MS), including information assurance, technology management; international business (MBA, DBA); leadership (DBA); marketing (MBA, MS, DBA), including digital marketing and advertising (MS), project management (MS), public relations (MS), sports marketing and media (MS); project management (MBA, DBA); public administration (MBA); public relations (MBA). *Program availability:* Part-time, online learning. *Students:* 1,458 full-time (807 women), 4,188 part-time (2,041 women); includes 1,372 minority (1,060 Black or African American, non-Hispanic/Latino; 19 American Indian or Alaska Native, non-Hispanic/Latino; 85 Asian, non-Hispanic/Latino; 75 Hispanic/Latino; 10 Native Hawaiian or other Pacific Islander, non-Hispanic/Latino; 123 Two or more races, non-Hispanic/Latino), 124 international. Average age 35. 5,424 applicants, 45% accepted, 1242 enrolled. In 2016, 1,859 master's, 87 other advanced degrees awarded. *Entrance requirements:* For master's, minimum undergraduate GPA of 3.0, 15 hours of upper-level business courses. Additional exam requirements/recommendations for international students: Required—TOEFL (minimum score 600 paper-based; 100 iBT). *Application deadline:* Applications are processed on a rolling basis. Application fee: $50. Electronic applications accepted. *Expenses:* Contact institution. *Financial support:* Applicants required to submit FAFSA. *Unit head:* Dr. Scott Hicks, Dean, 434-592-4808, Fax: 434-582-2366, E-mail: smhicks@liberty.edu. *Application contact:* Jay Bridge, Director of Graduate Admissions, 800-424-9595, Fax: 800-628-7977, E-mail: gradadmissions@liberty.edu.
Website: http://www.liberty.edu/academics/business/index.cfm?PID-149

**Lincoln University,** Graduate Studies, Jefferson City, MO 65101. Offers business administration (MBA), including accounting, management, management information systems, public administration/policy; elementary teaching (M Ed); environmental science (MS); guidance and counseling (M Ed), including community/agency counseling, elementary school, secondary school; higher education (MA); history (MA); integrated agricultural systems (MS); middle school (M Ed); natural sciences (MS); secondary teaching (M Ed); sociology (MA); sociology/criminal justice (MA). *Program availability:* Part-time, evening/weekend, 100% online, blended/hybrid learning. *Students:* 50 full-time (29 women), 68 part-time (39 women); includes 40 minority (37 Black or African American, non-Hispanic/Latino; 1 Asian, non-Hispanic/Latino; 2 Two or more races, non-Hispanic/Latino), 14 international. Average age 33. 75 applicants, 80% accepted, 34 enrolled. In 2016, 51 master's awarded. *Degree requirements:* For master's, comprehensive exam, thesis optional. *Entrance requirements:* For master's, GRE, MAT or GMAT, minimum GPA of 2.75 overall, 3.0 in courses related to specialization; 3 letters of recommendation; minimum C average in English composition; personal statement of purpose. Additional exam requirements/recommendations for international students: Required—TOEFL (minimum score 500 paper-based; 61 iBT), IELTS (minimum score 5.5), Michigan English Language Assessment Battery (minimum score 80). *Application deadline:* For fall admission, 7/1 priority date for domestic students, 5/1 priority date for international students; for spring admission, 11/1 priority date for domestic students, 10/1 priority date for international students; for summer admission, 6/1 priority date for domestic students. Applications are processed on a rolling basis. Application fee: $30. Electronic applications accepted. *Expenses:* Tuition, state resident: full-time $6840; part-time $5130 per year. Tuition, nonresident: full-time $12,720; part-time $9540 per year. *Required fees:* $852; $811 per unit. Tuition and fees vary according to course load. *Financial support:* In 2016–17, 2 fellowships with tuition reimbursements, 8 research assistantships with tuition reimbursements were awarded; Federal Work-Study, scholarships/grants, and unspecified assistantships also available. Support available to part-time students. Financial award application deadline: 3/1; financial award applicants required to submit FAFSA. *Unit head:* Dr. Rolundus R. Rice, Dean, 573-681-5247, Fax: 573-681-5106, E-mail: gradschool@lincolnu.edu. *Application contact:* Irasema Steck, Administrative Assistant, 573-681-5247, Fax: 573-681-5106, E-mail: gradschool@lincolnu.edu.
Website: http://www.lincolnu.edu/web/graduate-studies/graduate-studies

**Lindenwood University,** Graduate Programs, School of Accelerated Degree Programs, St. Charles, MO 63301-1695. Offers administration (MSA), including management, marketing, project management; business administration (MBA); communications (MA), including digital and multimedia, media management, promotions, training and development; criminal justice and administration (MS); healthcare administration (MS); human resource management (MS); information technology (Certificate); managing information security (MS); managing information technology (MS); managing virtualization and cloud computing (MS); writing (MFA). *Program availability:* Part-time, evening/weekend, 100% online. *Faculty:* 16 full-time (7 women), 75 part-time/adjunct (27 women). *Students:* 609 full-time (386 women), 179 part-time (121 women); includes 257 minority (202 Black or African American, non-Hispanic/Latino; 4 American Indian or Alaska Native, non-Hispanic/Latino; 5 Asian, non-Hispanic/Latino; 28 Hispanic/Latino; 1 Native Hawaiian or other Pacific Islander, non-

Hispanic/Latino; 17 Two or more races, non-Hispanic/Latino), 28 international. Average age 36. 332 applicants, 70% accepted, 205 enrolled. In 2016, 479 master's awarded. *Degree requirements:* For master's, thesis (for some programs), minimum cumulative GPA of 3.0; for Certificate, minimum cumulative GPA of 3.0. *Entrance requirements:* For master's, resume, personal statement, official undergraduate transcript, minimum undergraduate cumulative GPA of 3.0. Additional exam requirements/recommendations for international students: Required—TOEFL (minimum score 550 paper-based; 80 iBT); Recommended—IELTS (minimum score 6.5). *Application deadline:* For fall admission, 9/26 priority date for domestic and international students; for winter admission, 1/3 priority date for domestic and international students; for spring admission, 3/31 priority date for domestic and international students; for summer admission, 7/3 priority date for domestic and international students. Applications are processed on a rolling basis. Application fee: $30 ($100 for international students). Electronic applications accepted. *Expenses: Tuition:* Full-time $15,672; part-time $453 per credit hour. *Required fees:* $205 per semester. Tuition and fees vary according to course level, course load and degree level. *Financial support:* In 2016–17, 467 students received support. Career-related internships or fieldwork, institutionally sponsored loans, scholarships/grants, tuition waivers (partial), and unspecified assistantships available. Financial award application deadline: 6/30; financial award applicants required to submit FAFSA. *Unit head:* Dr. Gina Ganahl, Dean, Accelerated Degree Programs, 636-949-4501, Fax: 636-949-4505, E-mail: gganahl@lindenwood.edu. *Application contact:* Tyler Kostich, Director, Evening and Graduate Admissions, 636-949-4138, Fax: 636-949-4109, E-mail: adultadmissions@lindenwood.edu.
Website: http://www.lindenwood.edu/academics/academic-schools/school-of-accelerated-degree-programs/

**Lindenwood University–Belleville,** Graduate Programs, Belleville, IL 62226. Offers business administration (MBA); communications (MA), including digital and multimedia, media management, promotions, training and development; counseling (MA); criminal justice administration (MS); education (MA); healthcare administration (MS); human resource management (MS); school administration (MA); teaching (MAT).

**Loma Linda University,** School of Behavioral Health, Department of Social Work and Social Ecology, Loma Linda, CA 92350. Offers criminal justice (MS); gerontology (MS); social policy and social research (PhD); social work (MSW). *Accreditation:* CSWE. *Degree requirements:* For master's, comprehensive exam, thesis optional; for doctorate, comprehensive exam, thesis/dissertation. *Entrance requirements:* For master's and doctorate, GRE General Test. Additional exam requirements/recommendations for international students: Required—TOEFL, Michigan English Language Assessment Battery. Electronic applications accepted.

**London Metropolitan University,** Graduate Programs, London, United Kingdom. Offers applied psychology (M Sc); architecture (MA); biomedical science (M Sc); blood science (M Sc); cancer pharmacology (M Sc); computer networking and cyber security (M Sc); computing and information systems (M Sc); conference interpreting (MA); counter-terrorism studies (M Sc); creative, digital and professional writing (MA); crime, violence and prevention (M Sc); criminology (M Sc); curating contemporary art (MA); data analytics (M Sc); digital media (MA); early childhood studies (MA); education (MA, Ed D); financial services law, regulation and compliance (LL M); food science (M Sc); forensic psychology (M Sc); health and social care management and policy (M Sc); human nutrition (M Sc); human resource management (MA); human rights and international conflict (MA); information technology (M Sc); intelligence and security studies (M Sc); international oil, gas and energy law (LL M); international relations (MA); interpreting (MA); learning and teaching in higher education (MA); legal practice (LL M); media and entertainment law (LL M); organizational and consumer psychology (M Sc); psychological therapy (M Sc); psychology of mental health (M Sc); public health (M Sc); public policy and management (MPA); security studies (M Sc); social work (M Sc); spatial planning and urban design (MA); sports therapy (M Sc); supporting older children and young people with dyslexia (MA); teaching languages (MA), including Arabic, English; translation (MA); woman and child abuse (MA).

**Long Island University–LIU Post,** College of Liberal Arts and Sciences, Brookville, NY 11548-1300. Offers applied mathematics (MS); behavior analysis (MA); biology (MS); criminal justice (MS); earth science (MS); English (MA); environmental sustainability (MS); genetic counseling (MS); history (MA); interdisciplinary studies (MA, MS); mathematics for secondary school teachers (MS); mobile GIS application development (Advanced Certificate); political science (MA); psychology (MA). *Program availability:* Part-time, evening/weekend, blended/hybrid learning. *Faculty:* 68 full-time (30 women), 20 part-time/adjunct (13 women). *Students:* 155 full-time (117 women), 125 part-time (82 women); includes 65 minority (17 Black or African American, non-Hispanic/Latino; 14 Asian, non-Hispanic/Latino; 27 Hispanic/Latino; 7 Two or more races, non-Hispanic/Latino), 19 international. 485 applicants, 36% accepted, 77 enrolled. In 2016, 91 master's, 15 other advanced degrees awarded. *Degree requirements:* For master's, comprehensive exam (for some programs), thesis (for some programs). *Entrance requirements:* Additional exam requirements/recommendations for international students: Required—PTE, TOEFL (minimum score 550 paper-based, 75 iBT) or IELTS (6.5). *Application deadline:* Applications are processed on a rolling basis. Application fee: $50. Electronic applications accepted. *Expenses: Tuition:* Full-time $28,272; part-time $1178 per credit. *Required fees:* $451 per term. Tuition and fees vary according to degree level and program. *Financial support:* In 2016–17, 24 teaching assistantships with partial tuition reimbursements (averaging $410 per year) were awarded; fellowships, research assistantships, career-related internships or fieldwork, Federal Work-Study, institutionally sponsored loans, scholarships/grants, tuition waivers (partial), and unspecified assistantships also available. Support available to part-time students. Financial award application deadline: 2/15; financial award applicants required to submit FAFSA. *Faculty research:* Biology, criminal justice, environmental sustainability, mathematics, psychology. *Total annual research expenditures:* $218,000. *Unit head:* Dr. Jeffrey Belnap, Acting Dean, 516-299-2233, Fax: 516-299-4140, E-mail: jeffrey.belnap@liu.edu. *Application contact:* Carol Zerah, Director of Graduate Admissions, 516-299-2900, Fax: 516-299-2137, E-mail: post-enroll@liu.edu.
Website: http://liu.edu/CWPost/Academics/Schools/CLAS

**Loyola University Chicago,** Graduate School, Department of Criminal Justice and Criminology, Chicago, IL 60660. Offers MA. *Program availability:* Part-time, evening/weekend. *Faculty:* 8 full-time (1 woman), 2 part-time/adjunct (1 woman). *Students:* 15 full-time (8 women), 9 part-time (8 women); includes 6 minority (1 Black or African American, non-Hispanic/Latino; 3 Hispanic/Latino; 2 Two or more races, non-Hispanic/Latino). Average age 25. 35 applicants, 57% accepted, 11 enrolled. In 2016, 9 master's awarded. *Degree requirements:* For master's, comprehensive exam or thesis. *Entrance requirements:* For master's, GRE if undergraduate GPA below 3.3, minimum GPA of 3.0. Additional exam requirements/recommendations for international students: Required—TOEFL (minimum score 550 paper-based). *Application deadline:* For fall admission, 2/1 priority date for domestic students. Application fee: $50. Electronic applications accepted. Application fee is waived when completed online. *Expenses:* Contact institution. *Financial support:* In 2016–17, 5 students received support, including 5 research assistantships with partial tuition reimbursements available (averaging $6,000 per year); career-related internships or fieldwork and scholarships/grants also available. Financial award application deadline: 3/1; financial award

applicants required to submit FAFSA. *Faculty research:* Crime and delinquency causation, effectiveness and efficiency of criminal justice system, policy and program evaluation, sentencing, policing, gangs, corrections, ethics. *Total annual research expenditures:* $300,000. *Unit head:* Dr. Donald Stemen, Department Chairperson, 773-508-8505, E-mail: dstemen@luc.edu. *Application contact:* Dr. David Olson, Graduate Program Director, 773-508-8594, E-mail: dolson1@luc.edu.

**Loyola University New Orleans,** College of Arts and Sciences, Program in Criminal Justice, New Orleans, LA 70118-6195. Offers MCJ. *Program availability:* Part-time, evening/weekend. *Faculty:* 5 full-time (2 women), 2 part-time/adjunct (1 woman). *Students:* 10 full-time (8 women), 7 part-time (5 women); includes 4 minority (3 Black or African American, non-Hispanic/Latino; 1 Hispanic/Latino). Average age 32. 36 applicants, 22% accepted, 5 enrolled. In 2016, 33 master's awarded. *Degree requirements:* For master's, comprehensive exam, research and practicum. *Entrance requirements:* For master's, GRE, resume, interview, letters of recommendation, work experience, transcript from accredited university. Additional exam requirements/recommendations for international students: Required—TOEFL (minimum score 550 paper-based). *Application deadline:* For fall admission, 8/15 priority date for domestic and international students; for spring admission, 1/1 priority date for domestic and international students. Applications are processed on a rolling basis. Application fee: $20. Electronic applications accepted. Application fee is waived when completed online. *Expenses:* $818 per credit hour full-time tuition, $883 fees; $409 per credit hour part-time tuition, $527 fees; $275 graduation fee. *Financial support:* In 2016–17, 3 research assistantships (averaging $4,000 per year) were awarded; scholarships/grants and unspecified assistantships also available. Financial award application deadline: 5/1; financial award applicants required to submit FAFSA. *Faculty research:* Physical and social aspects of disasters, reconciling interpretations of gang behaviors and processes with viewpoints of actual gang members, examining the social network dynamics of deviant populations, investigating the future of criminal innovation, navigating racial/ethnic dynamics in criminology, human trafficking, criminology and forensic science. *Unit head:* Dr. Rae Taylor, Chair, 504-865-2041, Fax: 504-865-3883, E-mail: crimjust@loyno.edu. *Application contact:* Clarissa Koederitz, Executive Assistant to the Chair, 504-865-3323, Fax: 504-865-3883, E-mail: crimjust@loyno.edu.
Website: http://cas.loyno.edu/criminologyjustice/master-criminal-justice

**Lynn University,** College of Arts and Sciences, Boca Raton, FL 33431. Offers administration (MS), including criminal justice; applied psychology (MS); mental health counseling (MS). *Program availability:* Part-time, evening/weekend, blended/hybrid learning. *Faculty:* 52 full-time (22 women), 19 part-time/adjunct (11 women). *Students:* 74 full-time (57 women), 39 part-time (28 women); includes 32 minority (20 Black or African American, non-Hispanic/Latino; 2 Asian, non-Hispanic/Latino; 9 Hispanic/Latino; 1 Native Hawaiian or other Pacific Islander, non-Hispanic/Latino), 10 international. Average age 29. 77 applicants, 77% accepted, 39 enrolled. In 2016, 65 master's awarded. *Degree requirements:* For master's, comprehensive exam (for some programs), thesis (for some programs). *Entrance requirements:* For master's, bachelor's degree from accredited institution, resume, letter of recommendation, essay of professional goals, official transcripts. Additional exam requirements/recommendations for international students: Required—TOEFL (minimum score 550 paper-based; 80 iBT), IELTS (minimum score 6.5). *Application deadline:* For fall admission, 8/18 for domestic students, 8/4 for international students; for spring admission, 12/15 for domestic students, 12/1 for international students; for summer admission, 4/17 for domestic students, 4/3 for international students. Applications are processed on a rolling basis. Application fee: $45. Electronic applications accepted. *Expenses:* $725 per credit. *Financial support:* In 2016–17, 25 students received support. Career-related internships or fieldwork, Federal Work-Study, scholarships/grants, tuition waivers (full and partial), and unspecified assistantships available. Support available to part-time students. Financial award application deadline: 3/1; financial award applicants required to submit FAFSA. *Faculty research:* Personality and social media, learning strategies, personal health behaviors and compliance, using drums in substance abuse groups, interpersonal behaviors with individuals with autism, case conceptualization, teaching case conceptualization across the curriculum. *Unit head:* Dr. Katrina Carter-Tellison, Dean, 561-237-7412, E-mail: kcartertellison@lynn.edu. *Application contact:* Steven Pruitt, Director of Graduate Admission, 561-237-7834, Fax: 561-237-7100, E-mail: admissionpm@lynn.edu.
Website: https://www.lynn.edu/academics/colleges-schools/arts-and-sciences

**Madonna University,** School of Business, Livonia, MI 48150-1173. Offers business administration (MBA); international business (MSBA); leadership studies (MSBA); leadership studies in criminal justice (MSBA); quality and operations management (MSBA). *Program availability:* Part-time, evening/weekend, online learning. *Degree requirements:* For master's, thesis (for some programs), foreign language proficiency (international business). *Entrance requirements:* For master's, GMAT, GRE General Test, minimum GPA of 3.0. Electronic applications accepted. *Faculty research:* Management, women in management, future studies.

**Marshall University,** Academic Affairs Division, College of Science, Department of Criminal Justice, Huntington, WV 25755. Offers MS. *Program availability:* Evening/weekend. *Degree requirements:* For master's, thesis optional. *Entrance requirements:* For master's, GRE General Test.

**Marywood University,** Academic Affairs, Munley College of Liberal Arts and Sciences, Department of Social Sciences, Scranton, PA 18509-1598. Offers criminal justice (MS). Electronic applications accepted.

**McNeese State University,** Doré School of Graduate Studies, College of Liberal Arts, Department of Social Sciences, Lake Charles, LA 70609. Offers criminal justice (MS). *Entrance requirements:* For master's, GRE, minimum undergraduate GPA of 3.0, 3 letters of recommendation, autobiography.

**Mercer University,** Graduate Studies, Cecil B. Day Campus, Penfield College, Atlanta, GA 30341. Offers certified rehabilitation counseling (MS); clinical mental health (MS); counselor education and supervision (PhD); criminal justice and public safety leadership (MS); health informatics (MS); human services (MS), including child and adolescent services, gerontology services; organizational leadership (MS); school counseling (MS). *Program availability:* Part-time, evening/weekend, 100% online, blended/hybrid learning. *Faculty:* 15 full-time (8 women), 22 part-time/adjunct (18 women). *Students:* 168 full-time (136 women), 242 part-time (201 women); includes 231 minority (192 Black or African American, non-Hispanic/Latino; 1 American Indian or Alaska Native, non-Hispanic/Latino; 15 Asian, non-Hispanic/Latino; 19 Hispanic/Latino; 1 Native Hawaiian or other Pacific Islander, non-Hispanic/Latino; 3 Two or more races, non-Hispanic/Latino), 2 international. Average age 32. 300 applicants, 45% accepted, 114 enrolled. In 2016, 92 master's, 8 doctorates awarded. *Degree requirements:* For master's, comprehensive exam (for some programs), thesis (for some programs); for doctorate, thesis/dissertation. *Entrance requirements:* For master's, GRE or MAT, Georgia Professional Standards Commission (GPSC) Certification at the SC-5 level; for doctorate, GRE or MAT. Additional exam requirements/recommendations for international students: Recommended—TOEFL (minimum score 550 paper-based; 80 iBT), IELTS (minimum score 6.5). *Application deadline:* For fall admission, 7/1 priority date for domestic and international students; for spring admission, 11/1 priority date for domestic and international students; for summer admission, 4/1 priority date for domestic and

## Criminal Justice and Criminology

international students. Application fee: $35. Electronic applications accepted. Application fee is waived when completed online. *Expenses:* $588 per credit hour. *Financial support:* In 2016–17, 32 students received support. Federal Work-Study, scholarships/grants, and unspecified assistantships available. Financial award applicants required to submit FAFSA. *Faculty research:* Marriage and families issues, leadership and ethics, cyber-bullying, trauma, narrative counseling and theory. *Total annual research expenditures:* $85,000. *Unit head:* Dr. Priscilla R. Danheiser, Dean, 678-547-6028, Fax: 678-547-6008, E-mail: danheiser_p@mercer.edu. Website: http://penfield.mercer.edu/programs/graduate-professional/

**Mercyhurst University,** Graduate Studies, Program in Administration of Justice, Erie, PA 16546. Offers administration of justice (MS). *Program availability:* Part-time, evening/weekend. *Degree requirements:* For master's, thesis optional. *Entrance requirements:* For master's, GRE, resume, essay, three professional references, transcripts. Additional exam requirements/recommendations for international students: Required—TOEFL. Electronic applications accepted. *Faculty research:* Research methods, criminal justice administration, juvenile justice.

**Mercyhurst University,** Graduate Studies, Program in Applied Intelligence, Erie, PA 16546. Offers MS, Certificate. *Program availability:* Online learning. *Degree requirements:* For master's, internship. *Entrance requirements:* For master's, GRE or MAT, resume, essay, three professional references, transcripts. Additional exam requirements/recommendations for international students: Required—TOEFL. Electronic applications accepted.

**Merrimack College,** School of Education and Social Policy, North Andover, MA 01845-5800. Offers community engagement (M Ed), including community organizations, higher education, K-12 education; criminology and criminal justice (MS); curriculum and instruction (M Ed); early childhood education (M Ed); educational leadership (CAGS), including instructional leadership; elementary education (M Ed); English as a second language (PreK-6) (M Ed); high school education (M Ed); higher education (M Ed), including leadership and organizational development, student affairs; middle school education (M Ed); moderate disabilities (PreK-8) (M Ed); school counseling (M Ed). *Program availability:* Part-time, evening/weekend, 100% online courses with immersion events and in-classroom practicum close to home. *Faculty:* 17 full-time, 34 part-time/adjunct. *Students:* 204 full-time (172 women), 83 part-time (67 women); includes 32 minority (4 Black or African American, non-Hispanic/Latino; 2 Asian, non-Hispanic/Latino; 23 Hispanic/Latino; 3 Two or more races, non-Hispanic/Latino), 1 international. Average age 27. 261 applicants, 89% accepted, 200 enrolled. In 2016, 153 master's, 2 other advanced degrees awarded. *Degree requirements:* For master's, practicum, portfolio, and state test (for licensure track); capstone (for higher education, curriculum and instruction, and community engagement tracks). *Entrance requirements:* For master's, Massachusetts Teacher Education Licensure (MTEL), official transcripts from other colleges, resume, personal statement, 2 letters of recommendation. Additional exam requirements/recommendations for international students: Required—TOEFL (minimum score 84 iBT), IELTS (minimum score 6.5), PTE (minimum score 56). *Application deadline:* For fall admission, 8/14 for domestic students, 7/14 for international students; for spring admission, 1/10 for domestic students, 12/10 for international students; for summer admission, 5/10 for domestic students, 4/10 for international students. Applications are processed on a rolling basis. Application fee: $0. Electronic applications accepted. *Expenses:* Contact institution. *Financial support:* Fellowships with full tuition reimbursements, career-related internships or fieldwork, scholarships/grants, and health care benefits available. Support available to part-time students. Financial award application deadline: 5/1; financial award applicants required to submit FAFSA. *Faculty research:* Feminist praxis in higher education, transgender student agency and belonging, campus sexual violence prevention, the scholarship of engagement; community engagement; service learning; diversity education; community-university partnerships, college going behaviors and indicators of success for inner city youth, strategies to increase students pursuit and success in STEM higher education, effective workforce development for displaced or under employed individuals, police reform, e.g. surveillance. *Application contact:* Alyssa Frey, Graduate Admissions Counselor, 978-837-3563, E-mail: freya@merrimack.edu. Website: http://www.merrimack.edu/academics/graduate/education/

**Methodist University,** School of Graduate Studies, Program in Justice Administration, Fayetteville, NC 28311-1498. Offers MJA. *Program availability:* Part-time, evening/weekend. *Entrance requirements:* For master's, bachelor's degree in criminal justice or related discipline with minimum overall GPA of 3.0 from accredited institution. Additional exam requirements/recommendations for international students: Required—TOEFL (minimum score 500 paper-based; 60 iBT).

**Metropolitan State University,** School of Law Enforcement and Criminal Justice, St. Paul, MN 55106-5000. Offers criminal justice (MS). *Program availability:* Part-time, evening/weekend. *Degree requirements:* For master's, thesis. *Entrance requirements:* For master's, resume, letters of reference, minimum GPA of 3.0. Additional exam requirements/recommendations for international students: Required—TOEFL (minimum score 550 paper-based). Electronic applications accepted.

**Michigan State University,** The Graduate School, College of Social Science, School of Criminal Justice, East Lansing, MI 48824. Offers criminal justice (MS, PhD); forensic science (MS); law enforcement intelligence and analysis (MS). *Program availability:* Online learning. *Entrance requirements:* Additional exam requirements/recommendations for international students: Required—TOEFL. Electronic applications accepted.

**Middle Tennessee State University,** College of Graduate Studies, College of Behavioral and Health Sciences, Department of Criminal Justice Administration, Murfreesboro, TN 37132. Offers MCJ. Program offered jointly with Tennessee State University. *Program availability:* Part-time, evening/weekend, online learning. *Degree requirements:* For master's, comprehensive exam, thesis. *Entrance requirements:* For master's, GRE or MAT. Additional exam requirements/recommendations for international students: Required—TOEFL (minimum score 525 paper-based; 71 iBT) or IELTS (minimum score 6). Electronic applications accepted.

**Midwestern State University,** Billie Doris McAda Graduate School, Robert D. and Carol Gunn College of Health Sciences and Human Services, Department of Criminal Justice and Health Services Administration, Wichita Falls, TX 76308. Offers criminal justice (MA); health information management (MHA); health services administration (Graduate Certificate); medical practice management (MHA); public and community sector health care management (MHA); rural and urban hospital management (MHA). *Program availability:* Part-time, evening/weekend. *Degree requirements:* For master's, comprehensive exam, thesis. *Entrance requirements:* For master's, GRE. Additional exam requirements/recommendations for international students: Required—TOEFL (minimum score 550 paper-based). Electronic applications accepted. *Faculty research:* Universal service policy, telehealth, bullying, healthcare financial management, public health ethics.

**Minnesota State University Mankato,** College of Graduate Studies and Research, College of Social and Behavioral Sciences, Department of Sociology and Corrections, Mankato, MN 56001. Offers sociology (MA); sociology: college teaching (MA); sociology: corrections (MS); sociology: human services planning and administration

(MS). *Program availability:* Part-time. *Students:* 9 full-time (5 women), 19 part-time (16 women). *Degree requirements:* For master's, comprehensive exam, thesis or alternative. *Entrance requirements:* For master's, minimum GPA of 3.0 during previous 2 years, 3 letters of reference, resume. Additional exam requirements/recommendations for international students: Required—TOEFL. *Application deadline:* For fall admission, 7/1 priority date for domestic students; for spring admission, 11/1 for domestic students. Applications are processed on a rolling basis. Application fee: $40. Electronic applications accepted. *Financial support:* Research assistantships with full tuition reimbursements, teaching assistantships with full tuition reimbursements, career-related internships or fieldwork, Federal Work-Study, institutionally sponsored loans, and unspecified assistantships available. Support available to part-time students. Financial award application deadline: 3/15; financial award applicants required to submit FAFSA. *Unit head:* Dr. Luis Posas, Chair, 507-389-2257, E-mail: luis.posas@mnsu.edu. *Application contact:* Donald Ebel, Graduate Studies Coordinator, 507-389-5188, Fax: 507-389-5615, E-mail: donald.ebel@mnsu.edu. Website: http://sbs.mnsu.edu/soccorr/

**Mississippi College,** Graduate School, College of Arts and Sciences, School of Humanities and Social Sciences, Department of History, Political Science, Administration of Justice, and Paralegal Studies, Clinton, MS 39058. Offers administration of justice (MSS); history (M Ed, MA, MSS); paralegal studies (Certificate); political science (MSS); social sciences (M Ed, MSS). *Program availability:* Part-time. *Degree requirements:* For master's, one foreign language, comprehensive exam, thesis (for some programs). *Entrance requirements:* For master's, GRE or NTE, minimum GPA of 2.5. Additional exam requirements/recommendations for international students: Recommended—TOEFL, IELTS. Electronic applications accepted.

**Mississippi Valley State University,** Department of Criminal Justice, Itta Bena, MS 38941-1400. Offers MS. *Program availability:* Part-time, evening/weekend. *Faculty:* 5 full-time (2 women), 5 part-time/adjunct (all women). *Students:* 8 full-time (4 women), 46 part-time (27 women); includes 52 minority (all Black or African American, non-Hispanic/Latino). Average age 33. 13 applicants, 100% accepted. In 2016, 26 master's awarded. *Degree requirements:* For master's, 2 foreign languages, thesis optional. *Entrance requirements:* For master's, minimum GPA of 2.5. Additional exam requirements/recommendations for international students: Recommended—TOEFL (minimum score 525 paper-based). *Application deadline:* For fall admission, 4/1 priority date for domestic students; for spring admission, 12/15 priority date for domestic students. Applications are processed on a rolling basis. Application fee: $0. Electronic applications accepted. *Expenses:* Contact institution. *Financial support:* In 2016–17, 12 students received support, including research assistantships with full tuition reimbursements available (averaging $3,640 per year); Federal Work-Study and scholarships/grants also available. Support available to part-time students. Financial award application deadline: 4/15; financial award applicants required to submit FAFSA. *Faculty research:* Police in the criminal justice system, the United States and international terrorism. *Unit head:* Dr. Emmanuel Amadi, Chair, 601-254-3363, Fax: 601-254-3646.

**Missouri Southern State University,** Program in Criminal Justice Administration, Joplin, MO 64801-1595. Offers MS. Program offered jointly with Southeast Missouri State University. *Program availability:* Online learning. *Degree requirements:* For master's, thesis optional. *Entrance requirements:* For master's, minimum undergraduate GPA of 2.5.

**Missouri State University,** Graduate College, College of Humanities and Public Affairs, Department of Criminology and Criminal Justice, Springfield, MO 65897. Offers community corrections (Certificate); criminology and criminal justice (MS); homeland security and defense (Certificate). *Program availability:* Part-time, 100% online, blended/hybrid learning. *Faculty:* 7 full-time (2 women). *Students:* 13 full-time (10 women), 30 part-time (15 women); includes 6 minority (3 Black or African American, non-Hispanic/Latino; 1 Asian, non-Hispanic/Latino; 1 Hispanic/Latino; 1 Two or more races, non-Hispanic/Latino). Average age 31. 38 applicants, 47% accepted, 9 enrolled. In 2016, 12 master's awarded. *Degree requirements:* For master's, comprehensive exam, thesis or alternative. *Entrance requirements:* For master's, bachelor's degree in criminology, criminal justice, or sociology; minimum undergraduate GPA of 3.0. Additional exam requirements/recommendations for international students: Required—TOEFL (minimum score 550 paper-based; 79 iBT), IELTS (minimum score 6). *Application deadline:* For fall admission, 7/20 priority date for domestic students, 5/1 for international students; for spring admission, 12/20 priority date for domestic students, 9/1 for international students; for summer admission, 5/20 priority date for domestic students. Applications are processed on a rolling basis. Application fee: $35 ($50 for international students). Electronic applications accepted. *Expenses:* Tuition, state resident: full-time $5830. Tuition, nonresident: full-time $10,708. *Required fees:* $1130. Tuition and fees vary according to class time, course level, course load and program. *Financial support:* Federal Work-Study, institutionally sponsored loans, and unspecified assistantships available. Financial award application deadline: 3/31; financial award applicants required to submit FAFSA. *Faculty research:* Homeland security initiatives, juvenile policy and programs, law enforcement and drug abuse. *Unit head:* Dr. Brett Garland, Department Head, 417-836-6954, E-mail: brettgarland@missouristate.edu. *Application contact:* Michael Edwards, Coordinator of Graduate Admissions, 417-836-5388, Fax: 417-836-6200, E-mail: michaeledwards@missouristate.edu. Website: http://criminology.missouristate.edu/

**Missouri State University,** Graduate College, Interdisciplinary Program in Professional Studies, Springfield, MO 65897. Offers administrative studies (Certificate); applied communication (MS); criminal justice (MS); environmental management (MS); homeland security (MS); individualized (MS); screenwriting and producing (MS); sports management (MS). *Program availability:* Part-time, evening/weekend, 100% online, blended/hybrid learning. *Students:* 60 full-time (34 women), 66 part-time (29 women); includes 17 minority (7 Black or African American, non-Hispanic/Latino; 1 Asian, non-Hispanic/Latino; 5 Hispanic/Latino; 4 Two or more races, non-Hispanic/Latino), 43 international. Average age 33. 76 applicants, 58% accepted, 38 enrolled. In 2016, 48 master's awarded. *Degree requirements:* For master's, comprehensive exam, thesis or alternative. *Entrance requirements:* For master's, GRE, GMAT (if GPA less than 3.0). Additional exam requirements/recommendations for international students: Required—TOEFL (minimum score 550 paper-based; 79 iBT), IELTS (minimum score 6). *Application deadline:* For fall admission, 7/15 priority date for domestic students; for spring admission, 12/1 priority date for domestic students; for summer admission, 5/1 for domestic students. Applications are processed on a rolling basis. Application fee: $35 ($50 for international students). Electronic applications accepted. *Expenses:* Tuition, state resident: full-time $5830. Tuition, nonresident: full-time $10,708. *Required fees:* $1130. Tuition and fees vary according to class time, course level, course load and program. *Financial support:* Career-related internships or fieldwork, Federal Work-Study, institutionally sponsored loans, scholarships/grants, and unspecified assistantships available. Support available to part-time students. Financial award application deadline: 3/31; financial award applicants required to submit FAFSA. *Unit head:* Dr. Gerald Masterson, Program Director, 417-836-5251, Fax: 417-836-6888, E-mail: mps@missouristate.edu. *Application contact:* Michael Edwards, Coordinator of Graduate Admissions, 417-836-5330, Fax: 417-836-6200, E-mail:

michaeledwards@missouristate.edu.
Website: http://mps.missouristate.edu

**Molloy College,** Criminal Justice Program, Rockville Centre, NY 11571-5002. Offers MS. *Program availability:* Part-time, evening/weekend. *Faculty:* 5 full-time (2 women), 2 part-time/adjunct (0 women). *Students:* 17 full-time (8 women), 18 part-time (8 women); includes 14 minority (7 Black or African American, non-Hispanic/Latino; 2 Asian, non-Hispanic/Latino; 5 Hispanic/Latino). Average age 34. 18 applicants, 78% accepted, 11 enrolled. In 2016, 17 master's awarded. *Entrance requirements:* Additional exam requirements/recommendations for international students: Required—TOEFL (minimum score 550 paper-based; 79 iBT). *Application deadline:* Applications are processed on a rolling basis. Application fee: $60. Electronic applications accepted. *Expenses: Tuition:* Full-time $19,170; part-time $1065 per credit. *Required fees:* $950; $790 per credit. Tuition and fees vary according to course load. *Faculty research:* Performance management; terrorism and global issues; law and policing; understanding crime statistics; juveniles justice. *Unit head:* Dr. John Eterno, Associate Dean/Graduate Program Director, 516-323-3806, E-mail: jeterno@molloy.edu. *Application contact:* Jaclyn Machowicz, Assistant Director for Admissions, 516-323-4010, E-mail: jmachowicz@molloy.edu.

**Monmouth University,** Graduate Studies, Department of Criminal Justice, West Long Branch, NJ 07764-1898. Offers criminal justice (MA), including homeland security; criminal justice administration (Certificate); homeland security (MS, Certificate). *Program availability:* Part-time, evening/weekend, 100% online. *Degree requirements:* For master's, comprehensive exam (for some programs), thesis (for some programs). *Entrance requirements:* For master's and Certificate, baccalaureate degree with minimum GPA of 3.0 in major, 2.5 overall; two letters of recommendation; personal essay. Additional exam requirements/recommendations for international students: Required—TOEFL (minimum score 550 paper-based; 79 iBT), IELTS (minimum score 6), Michigan English Language Assessment Battery (minimum score 77) or Certificate of Advanced English (minimum score B2). Electronic applications accepted. *Faculty research:* Violent crimes, criminal pathology, terrorism, computer crime, comparative criminal justice systems, homeland security.

**Monroe College,** King Graduate School, Bronx, NY 10468. Offers accounting (MS); business administration (MBA), including entrepreneurship, finance, general business administration, healthcare management, human resources, information technology, marketing; computer science (MS); criminal justice (MS); hospitality management (MS); public health (MPH), including biostatistics and epidemiology, community health, health administration and leadership. *Program availability:* Online learning. Application fee: $50.
Website: https://www.monroecollege.edu/Degrees/King-Graduate-School/

**Morehead State University,** Graduate Programs, Caudill College of Arts, Humanities and Social Sciences, Department of Sociology, Social Work and Criminology, Morehead, KY 40351. Offers criminology (MA); general sociology (MA); gerontology (MA); sociology regional analysis (MA); sociology/chemical dependency (MA). *Program availability:* Part-time, evening/weekend. *Degree requirements:* For master's, comprehensive exam, thesis (for some programs). *Entrance requirements:* For master's, GRE General Test, minimum GPA of 3.0 in sociology, 2.75 overall; 18 hours of course work in sociology, writing sample. Additional exam requirements/recommendations for international students: Required—TOEFL (minimum score 500 paper-based). Electronic applications accepted. *Faculty research:* Death and dying; aging, drinking, and drugs; economic development; adult children of alcoholics.

**Mount Mercy University,** Program in Criminal Justice, Cedar Rapids, IA 52402-4797. Offers MA. *Program availability:* Evening/weekend, online learning. *Degree requirements:* For master's, capstone.

**National University,** Academic Affairs, School of Professional Studies, La Jolla, CA 92037-1011. Offers criminal justice (MCJ); digital cinema (MFA); digital journalism (MA); juvenile justice (MS); public administration (MPA), including human resource management. *Program availability:* Part-time, evening/weekend, 100% online, blended/hybrid learning. *Faculty:* 21 full-time (8 women), 35 part-time/adjunct (9 women). *Students:* 280 full-time (155 women), 100 part-time (54 women); includes 226 minority (76 Black or African American, non-Hispanic/Latino; 1 American Indian or Alaska Native, non-Hispanic/Latino; 27 Asian, non-Hispanic/Latino; 102 Hispanic/Latino; 3 Native Hawaiian or other Pacific Islander, non-Hispanic/Latino; 17 Two or more races, non-Hispanic/Latino; 3 international. Average age 37. In 2016, 21 master's awarded. *Degree requirements:* For master's, thesis (for some programs). *Entrance requirements:* For master's, interview, minimum GPA of 2.5. Additional exam requirements/recommendations for international students: Required—TOEFL (minimum score 550 paper-based; 79 iBT), IELTS (minimum score 6). *Application deadline:* Applications are processed on a rolling basis. Application fee: $60 ($65 for international students). Electronic applications accepted. *Financial support:* Career-related internships or fieldwork, institutionally sponsored loans, scholarships/grants, and tuition waivers (partial) available. Support available to part-time students. Financial award application deadline: 6/30; financial award applicants required to submit FAFSA. *Unit head:* School of Professional Studies, 800-628-8648, E-mail: sops@nu.edu. *Application contact:* Brandon Jouganatos, Vice President for Enrollment Services, 800-628-8648, E-mail: advisor@nu.edu.
Website: http://www.nu.edu/OurPrograms/School-of-Professional-Studies.html

**New Charter University,** College of Public Policy and Administration, Program in Criminal Justice, Salt Lake City, UT 84101. Offers MS. *Program availability:* Part-time, evening/weekend, online learning. *Entrance requirements:* For master's, course work in calculus, statistics. Additional exam requirements/recommendations for international students: Required—TOEFL (minimum score 550 paper-based).

**New Jersey City University,** College of Professional Studies, Department of Criminal Justice, Jersey City, NJ 07305-1597. Offers MS. *Program availability:* Part-time, evening/weekend. *Degree requirements:* For master's, thesis or alternative. *Entrance requirements:* Additional exam requirements/recommendations for international students: Required—TOEFL (minimum score 79 iBT).

**New Jersey City University,** College of Professional Studies, Program in National Security Studies, Jersey City, NJ 07305-1597. Offers civil security leadership (D Sc); national security studies (MS, Certificate). *Program availability:* Part-time. *Entrance requirements:* Additional exam requirements/recommendations for international students: Required—TOEFL (minimum score 79 iBT).

**New Mexico State University,** College of Arts and Sciences, Department of Criminal Justice, Las Cruces, NM 88003. Offers MCJ. *Program availability:* Part-time, evening/weekend, 100% online. *Faculty:* 9 full-time (3 women), 1 (woman) part-time/adjunct. *Students:* 22 full-time (11 women), 28 part-time (15 women); includes 40 minority (4 Black or African American, non-Hispanic/Latino; 2 American Indian or Alaska Native, non-Hispanic/Latino; 1 Asian, non-Hispanic/Latino; 33 Hispanic/Latino), 1 international. Average age 31. 28 applicants, 93% accepted, 24 enrolled. In 2016, 14 master's awarded. *Degree requirements:* For master's, comprehensive exam, thesis optional, oral and written exams. *Entrance requirements:* For master's, minimum GPA of 3.0. Additional exam requirements/recommendations for international students: Required—TOEFL (minimum score 550 paper-based; 79 iBT), IELTS (minimum score 6.5).

*Application deadline:* For spring admission, 4/1 priority date for domestic students. Application fee: $40 ($50 for international students). Electronic applications accepted. *Expenses:* Tuition, state resident: full-time $4086. Tuition, nonresident: full-time $14,254. *Required fees:* $853. Tuition and fees vary according to course load. *Financial support:* In 2016–17, 11 students received support, including 9 teaching assistantships (averaging $10,744 per year); career-related internships or fieldwork, Federal Work-Study, scholarships/grants, traineeships, health care benefits, and unspecified assistantships also available. Support available to part-time students. Financial award application deadline: 3/1. *Faculty research:* Juvenile justice, jails and prison administration, courts and legal decision-making, victim studies, policy and evaluation research, narcotics and addiction, research methods, and urban studies, borderland studies, race and identity studies, indigenous jurisprudence, immigration and justice, and diversity in higher education scholarship, statistics, crime theory, race and crime, and street crimes, courts and sentencing, immigration and Latino studies. *Total annual research expenditures:* $4,905. *Unit head:* Dr. Jeffrey Amato, Interim Department Head, 575-646-3316, Fax: 575-646-2827, E-mail: amato@nmsu.edu. *Application contact:* Dr. Francisco Alatorre, Graduate Program Director, 575-646-5159, Fax: 575-646-2827, E-mail: falatorr@nmsu.edu.
Website: http://crimjust.nmsu.edu

**Niagara University,** Graduate Division of Arts and Sciences, Department of Criminal Justice, Niagara University, NY 14109. Offers criminal justice administration (MS). *Program availability:* Part-time. *Students:* 21 full-time (12 women), 14 part-time (3 women); includes 5 minority (4 Black or African American, non-Hispanic/Latino; 1 Hispanic/Latino), 9 international. Average age 31. In 2016, 20 master's awarded. *Entrance requirements:* For master's, GMAT/GRE (minimum score 600). Additional exam requirements/recommendations for international students: Required—TOEFL (minimum score 550 paper-based; 79 iBT), IELTS (minimum score 6). *Application deadline:* For fall admission, 8/1 for domestic students. Applications are processed on a rolling basis. Electronic applications accepted. *Expenses:* $735 per credit hour. *Financial support:* Research assistantships with tuition reimbursements, teaching assistantships with tuition reimbursements, career-related internships or fieldwork, Federal Work-Study, scholarships/grants, and unspecified assistantships available. Support available to part-time students. Financial award application deadline: 4/15; financial award applicants required to submit FAFSA. *Unit head:* Dr. Peter Butera, Interim Dean, 716-286-8061, Fax: 716-286-8061, E-mail: pbutera@niagara.edu. *Application contact:* Ronald Winkley, Director, 716-286-8089, Fax: 716-286-8061, E-mail: rwinkley@niagara.edu.
Website: http://www.niagara.edu/graduate-crj

**Norfolk State University,** School of Graduate Studies, School of Liberal Arts, Department of Sociology, Program in Criminal Justice, Norfolk, VA 23504. Offers MA.

**North Carolina Central University,** College of Behavioral and Social Sciences, Department of Criminal Justice, Durham, NC 27707-3129. Offers MS. *Program availability:* Part-time, evening/weekend. *Degree requirements:* For master's, one foreign language, comprehensive exam, thesis or alternative. *Entrance requirements:* For master's, GRE, minimum GPA of 3.0 in major, 2.5 overall. Additional exam requirements/recommendations for international students: Required—TOEFL.

**North Dakota State University,** College of Graduate and Interdisciplinary Studies, College of Arts, Humanities and Social Sciences, Department of Criminal Justice and Political Science, Fargo, ND 58102. Offers criminal justice (PhD); criminal justice administration (MS). *Program availability:* Part-time. Terminal master's awarded for partial completion of doctoral program. *Degree requirements:* For master's, thesis; for doctorate, comprehensive exam, thesis/dissertation. *Entrance requirements:* For master's, minimum GPA of 3.0 in last 60 credit hours, approved bachelor's degree; course work in research methods and statistics; for doctorate, GRE General Test, minimum GPA of 3.0 over last 60 credit hours, 3 letters of recommendation. Additional exam requirements/recommendations for international students: Required—TOEFL (minimum score 525 paper-based; 71 iBT). *Faculty research:* Corrections, policing, drugs and crime, gender and crime, criminology.

**Northeastern State University,** College of Liberal Arts, Department of Criminal Justice and Legal Studies, Tahlequah, OK 74464-2399. Offers criminal justice (MS). *Program availability:* Part-time, evening/weekend. *Faculty:* 4 full-time (1 woman). *Students:* 18 full-time (14 women), 19 part-time (12 women); includes 18 minority (2 Black or African American, non-Hispanic/Latino; 12 American Indian or Alaska Native, non-Hispanic/Latino; 1 Hispanic/Latino; 3 Two or more races, non-Hispanic/Latino), 1 international. Average age 32. In 2016, 12 master's awarded. *Degree requirements:* For master's, thesis optional, oral exam. *Entrance requirements:* For master's, MAT or GRE, minimum GPA of 2.5. Additional exam requirements/recommendations for international students: Required—TOEFL. *Application deadline:* For fall admission, 6/1 priority date for domestic students. Applications are processed on a rolling basis. Application fee: $25. Electronic applications accepted. *Expenses:* Tuition, state resident: full-time $2816; part-time $216.60 per credit hour. Tuition, nonresident: full-time $6365; part-time $489.60 per credit hour. *Required fees:* $37.40 per credit hour. *Financial support:* Teaching assistantships and Federal Work-Study available. Financial award application deadline: 3/1. *Unit head:* Dr. John Clark, Department Chair, 918-444-3518, E-mail: clarkiii@nsuok.edu. *Application contact:* Josh McCollum, Graduate Coordinator, 918-444-2093, E-mail: mccolluj@nsuok.edu.
Website: http://academics.nsuok.edu/criminaljustice/GraduateStudies.aspx

**Northeastern University,** College of Professional Studies, Boston, MA 02115-5096. Offers applied nutrition (MS); college athletics administration (MSL); commerce and economic development (MS); corporate and organizational communication (MS); criminal justice (MS); digital media (MPS); elearning and instructional design (M Ed); elementary education (MAT); geographic information technology (MPS); global studies and international relations (MS); higher education administration (M Ed); homeland security (MA); human services (MS); informatics (MPS); leadership (MS); learning analytics (M Ed); learning and instruction (M Ed); nonprofit management (MS); professional sports administration (MSL); project management (MS); regulatory affairs for drugs, biologics, and medical devices (MS); respiratory care leadership (MS); special education (M Ed); technical communication (MS). *Program availability:* Part-time, evening/weekend, 100% online, blended/hybrid learning. *Faculty:* 82 full-time (51 women), 853 part-time/adjunct (366 women). *Students:* 4,947 part-time (3,076 women). In 2016, 1,456 master's awarded. *Application deadline:* Applications are processed on a rolling basis. Application fee: $0. Electronic applications accepted. *Expenses:* Contact institution. *Financial support:* Applicants required to submit FAFSA. *Unit head:* Dr. Mary Loeffelholz, Interim Dean of the College of Professional Studies.
Website: http://www.cps.neu.edu/

**Northeastern University,** College of Social Sciences and Humanities, Boston, MA 02115. Offers criminology and criminal justice (MSCJ); criminology and justice policy (PhD); economics (MA, PhD); English (MA, PhD); international affairs (MA); law and public policy (PhD); political science (MA, PhD); public administration (MPA); public history (MA); public policy (MPP); security and resilience studies (MS); sociology (MA, PhD); urban and regional policy (MS); urban informatics (MS); world history (MA, PhD); JD/MS. *Program availability:* Online learning. *Faculty:* 234 full-time (114 women), 55 part-time/adjunct (34 women). *Students:* 427 full-time (239 women), 77 part-time (42

## Criminal Justice and Criminology

women). In 2016, 143 master's, 38 doctorates awarded. *Degree requirements:* For doctorate, variable foreign language requirement, comprehensive exam, thesis/dissertation. *Entrance requirements:* For master's and doctorate, GRE. Additional exam requirements/recommendations for international students: Required—TOEFL, IELTS. Application fee: $75. Electronic applications accepted. *Expenses:* $1,295 per credit. *Financial support:* Teaching assistantships, career-related internships or fieldwork, scholarships/grants, health care benefits, tuition waivers (full and partial), and unspecified assistantships available. Support available to part-time students. Financial award applicants required to submit FAFSA. *Unit head:* Dr. Uta Poiger, Dean, 617-373-5173. *Application contact:* Amber Crowe, Administrative Coordinator, 617-373-5990, Fax: 617-373-7281, E-mail: gradcssh@northeastern.edu.
Website: http://www.northeastern.edu/cssh/graduate

**Northern Arizona University,** Graduate College, College of Social and Behavioral Sciences, Department of Criminology and Criminal Justice, Flagstaff, AZ 86011. Offers applied criminology (MS). *Program availability:* Part-time, online learning. *Degree requirements:* For master's, thesis, internship, comprehensive exam, or practicum. *Entrance requirements:* For master's, minimum GPA of 3.0. Additional exam requirements/recommendations for international students: Required—TOEFL (minimum score 550 paper-based; 80 iBT), IELTS (minimum score 7). Electronic applications accepted. *Expenses:* Tuition, state resident: full-time $8971; part-time $444 per credit hour. Tuition, nonresident: full-time $20,958; part-time $1164 per credit hour. *Required fees:* $1018; $644 per credit hour. Tuition and fees vary according to course load, campus/location and program.

**Northern Michigan University,** Office of Graduate Education and Research, College of Health Sciences and Professional Studies, School of Education, Leadership and Public Service, Marquette, MI 49855-5301. Offers administration and supervision (MAE); elementary education (MAE); higher education in student affairs (MA); instruction (MAE); learning disabilities (MAE); public administration (MPA), including criminal justice administration, human resource administration, public administration, public management, state and local government; reading education (MAE), including reading, reading specialist; science education (MS); secondary education (MAE). *Accreditation:* TEAC. *Program availability:* Part-time, online learning. *Degree requirements:* For master's, thesis (for some programs). *Entrance requirements:* For master's, minimum GPA of 3.0. Additional exam requirements/recommendations for international students: Required—TOEFL (minimum score 550 paper-based; 79 iBT), IELTS (minimum score 6.5). Electronic applications accepted.

**Norwich University,** College of Graduate and Continuing Studies, Master of Public Administration Program, Northfield, VT 05663. Offers criminal justice and public safety (MPA); fiscal management (MPA); international development and influence (MPA); municipal governance (MPA); nonprofit management (MPA); policy analysis and analytics (MPA); public administration leadership and crisis management (MPA); public works and sustainability (MPA). *Program availability:* Evening/weekend, online only, mostly all online with a week-long residency requirement. *Faculty:* 13 part-time/adjunct (5 women). *Students:* 63 full-time (23 women); includes 9 minority (5 Black or African American, non-Hispanic/Latino; 1 Asian, non-Hispanic/Latino; 1 Hispanic/Latino; 2 Two or more races, non-Hispanic/Latino). Average age 38. 23 applicants, 100% accepted, 15 enrolled. In 2016, 38 master's awarded. *Degree requirements:* For master's, capstone. *Entrance requirements:* For master's, minimum undergraduate GPA of 2.75. Additional exam requirements/recommendations for international students: Required—TOEFL (minimum score 550 paper-based; 80 iBT), IELTS (minimum score 6.5). *Application deadline:* For fall admission, 8/14 for domestic and international students; for winter admission, 11/13 for domestic and international students; for spring admission, 2/12 for domestic and international students; for summer admission, 5/15 for domestic and international students. Electronic applications accepted. *Expenses:* Contact institution. *Financial support:* In 2016–17, 21 students received support. Scholarships/grants available. Financial award application deadline: 8/4; financial award applicants required to submit FAFSA. *Unit head:* Dr. Rosemarie Pelletier, Program Director, 802-485-2767, Fax: 802-485-2533, E-mail: rpellet2@norwich.edu. *Application contact:* Admissions Advisor, 800-460-5597 Ext. 3377, Fax: 802-485-2533, E-mail: mpa@online.norwich.edu.
Website: https://online.norwich.edu/degree-programs/masters/master-public-administration/overview

**Norwich University,** College of Graduate and Continuing Studies, Master of Science in Criminal Justice Program, Northfield, VT 05663. Offers MS. *Program availability:* Evening/weekend, online only, mostly all online with a week-long residency requirement. *Entrance requirements:* For master's, minimum GPA of 2.75. Additional exam requirements/recommendations for international students: Required—TOEFL (minimum score 550 paper-based; 80 iBT), IELTS (minimum score 6.5). *Application deadline:* For fall admission, 8/14 for domestic and international students; for winter admission, 11/13 for domestic and international students; for spring admission, 2/12 for domestic and international students; for summer admission, 6/5 for domestic and international students. Electronic applications accepted. *Expenses:* Contact institution. *Financial support:* Scholarships/grants available. Financial award application deadline: 8/4; financial award applicants required to submit FAFSA. *Unit head:* Allison Crowson, Program Manager, 802-485-3304, Fax: 802-485-2533, E-mail: cj@online.norwich.edu. *Application contact:* Admissions Advisor, 866-684-7237, Fax: 802-485-2533, E-mail: cj@online.norwich.edu.
Website: https://online.norwich.edu/degree-programs/masters/master-science-criminal-justice/overview

**Oklahoma City University,** Petree College of Arts and Sciences, Oklahoma City, OK 73106-1402. Offers applied behavioral studies (M Ed); applied sociology: nonprofit leadership (MA); creative writing (MFA); criminology (MS); early childhood education (M Ed); elementary education (M Ed); general studies (MLA); leadership/management (MLA); moving image arts (MFA); professional counseling (M Ed); teaching (MA); teaching English to speakers of other languages (MA). *Program availability:* Part-time, evening/weekend. *Faculty:* 11 full-time (5 women), 15 part-time/adjunct (6 women). *Students:* 77 full-time (55 women), 46 part-time (30 women); includes 32 minority (13 Black or African American, non-Hispanic/Latino; 1 American Indian or Alaska Native, non-Hispanic/Latino; 2 Asian, non-Hispanic/Latino; 12 Hispanic/Latino; 4 Two or more races, non-Hispanic/Latino), 37 international. Average age 34. 92 applicants, 74% accepted, 46 enrolled. In 2016, 72 master's awarded. *Degree requirements:* For master's, capstone/practicum. *Entrance requirements:* For master's, bachelor's degree from accredited institution with minimum GPA of 3.0, essay, recommendation letters. Additional exam requirements/recommendations for international students: Required—TOEFL (minimum score 550 paper-based; 80 iBT). *Application deadline:* Applications are processed on a rolling basis. Application fee: $50. Electronic applications accepted. *Expenses:* Contact institution. *Financial support:* In 2016–17, 16 students received support. Federal Work-Study, institutionally sponsored loans, scholarships/grants, and tuition waivers (full and partial) available. Support available to part-time students. Financial award application deadline: 6/1; financial award applicants required to submit FAFSA. *Unit head:* Dr. Amy Cataldi, Dean, 405-208-5446, Fax: 405-208-5447, E-mail: acataldi@okcu.edu. *Application contact:* Michael Harrington, Director of Graduate

Admissions, 800-633-7242, Fax: 405-208-5356, E-mail: gadmissions@okcu.edu.
Website: http://www.okcu.edu/petree/

**Old Dominion University,** College of Arts and Letters, PhD Program in Criminology and Criminal Justice, Norfolk, VA 23529. Offers criminology and criminal justice (PhD). *Faculty:* 19 full-time (11 women). *Students:* 7 full-time (4 women), 5 part-time (2 women); includes 4 minority (2 Black or African American, non-Hispanic/Latino; 2 Two or more races, non-Hispanic/Latino). Average age 29. 11 applicants, 27% accepted, 2 enrolled. In 2016, 5 doctorates awarded. *Degree requirements:* For doctorate, comprehensive exam, thesis/dissertation. *Entrance requirements:* For doctorate, GRE General Test, MA; minimum graduate GPA of 3.25; theory, methods, and statistics graduate coursework; letters of reference; writing sample. Additional exam requirements/recommendations for international students: Required—TOEFL. *Application deadline:* For fall admission, 1/15 for domestic and international students. Application fee: $50. Electronic applications accepted. *Expenses:* Tuition, state resident: full-time $8604; part-time $478 per credit hour. Tuition, nonresident: full-time $21,510; part-time $1195 per credit hour. *Required fees:* $66 per semester. Tuition and fees vary according to campus/location, program and reciprocity agreements. *Financial support:* In 2016–17, 10 students received support, including 10 teaching assistantships with full tuition reimbursements available (averaging $15,000 per year). Financial award application deadline: 1/15. *Faculty research:* Inequality, crime and justice; domestic violence; community justice; criminological theory; methods; policing; courts and corrections; juvenile justice. *Unit head:* Dr. Scott R. Maggard, Graduate Program Director, 757-683-5528, Fax: 757-683-5634, E-mail: smaggard@odu.edu.
Website: http://al.odu.edu/sociology/phdprogram/index.shtml

**Old Dominion University,** College of Arts and Letters, Program in Applied Sociology, Norfolk, VA 23529. Offers criminal justice (MA); general sociology (MA); women's studies (MA). *Program availability:* Part-time, evening/weekend. *Faculty:* 19 full-time (11 women), 2 part-time (1 woman); includes 6 minority (3 Black or African American, non-Hispanic/Latino; 3 Two or more races, non-Hispanic/Latino). Average age 23. 26 applicants, 65% accepted, 12 enrolled. In 2016, 4 master's awarded. *Degree requirements:* For master's, thesis. *Entrance requirements:* For master's, GRE General Test, minimum GPA of 3.0; 12 credits in criminal justice, sociology, or women's studies. Additional exam requirements/recommendations for international students: Required—TOEFL. *Application deadline:* For fall admission, 3/1 for domestic and international students. Application fee: $50. Electronic applications accepted. *Expenses:* Contact institution. *Financial support:* In 2016–17, 8 students received support, including 2 research assistantships (averaging $10,000 per year), 6 teaching assistantships (averaging $10,000 per year); career-related internships or fieldwork, scholarships/grants, and unspecified assistantships also available. Financial award application deadline: 2/15. *Faculty research:* Quantitative methodology, theory, family, gender/class/race, crime. Total annual research expenditures: $350,000. *Unit head:* Dr. Ingrid Whitaker, Graduate Program Director, 757-683-3811, Fax: 757-683-5634, E-mail: iwhitake@odu.edu. *Application contact:* Dr. David C. Earnest, Associate Dean, 757-683-6077, Fax: 757-683-5746, E-mail: dearnest@odu.edu.
Website: http://al.odu.edu/sociology/gradprogram/graduatehome.shtml

**Penn State Harrisburg,** Graduate School, School of Public Affairs, Middletown, PA 17057. Offers criminal justice (MA); health administration (MHA); health administration: long term care (Certificate); homeland security (Certificate); public administration (MPA, PhD); public administration: non-profit administration (Certificate); public budgeting and financial management (Certificate); public sector human resource management (Certificate). *Accreditation:* NASPAA. *Unit head:* Dr. Mukund S. Kulkarni, Chancellor, 717-948-6105, Fax: 717-948-6452. *Application contact:* Robert W. Coffman, Jr., Director of Enrollment Management, Admissions, 717-948-6250, Fax: 717-948-6325, E-mail: hbgadmit@psu.edu.
Website: https://harrisburg.psu.edu/public-affairs

**Penn State University Park,** Graduate School, College of the Liberal Arts, Department of Sociology and Criminology, University Park, PA 16802. Offers criminology (MA, PhD); sociology (MA, PhD). *Unit head:* Dr. Susan Welch, Dean, 814-865-7691, Fax: 814-863-2085. *Application contact:* Lori Hawn, Director, Graduate Student Services, 814-865-1795, Fax: 814-863-4627, E-mail: l-gswww@lists.psu.edu.
Website: http://sociology.la.psu.edu/

**Point Park University,** School of Arts and Sciences, Department of Criminal Justice and Intelligence Studies, Pittsburgh, PA 15222-1984. Offers criminal justice administration (MS). *Program availability:* Evening/weekend. *Degree requirements:* For master's, comprehensive exam (for some programs), thesis or alternative. *Entrance requirements:* For master's, minimum GPA of 2.75, resume, 2 letters of recommendation. Additional exam requirements/recommendations for international students: Required—TOEFL (minimum score 550 paper-based; 79 iBT). Electronic applications accepted.

**Pontifical Catholic University of Puerto Rico,** College of Graduate Studies in Behavioral Science and Community Affairs, Program in Criminology, Ponce, PR 00717-0777. Offers MA. *Program availability:* Part-time, evening/weekend. *Degree requirements:* For master's, thesis. *Entrance requirements:* For master's, EXADEP, 3 letters of recommendation, interview, minimum GPA of 2.75.

**Pontificia Universidad Catolica Madre y Maestra,** Graduate School, Faculty of Social and Administrative Sciences, Santiago, Dominican Republic. Offers business administration (MBA), including business development, finance, international business, management skills (M Mgmt, MBA), marketing, operations, strategic cost management, strategy, tourist destination planning and management; law (LL M), including civil law, corporate business law, criminal law, international relations, real estate law; management (M Mgmt), including higher financial management, insurance program administration, management skills (M Mgmt, MBA); psychology (MA), including clinical child and adolescent psychology, forensic psychology; strategic human resources (EMBA).

**Portland State University,** Graduate Studies, College of Urban and Public Affairs, Hatfield School of Government, Division of Criminology and Criminal Justice, Portland, OR 97207-0751. Offers MS, PhD. *Program availability:* Part-time. *Faculty:* 13 full-time (6 women), 11 part-time/adjunct (3 women). *Students:* 23 full-time (16 women), 2 part-time (1 woman); includes 7 minority (1 Black or African American, non-Hispanic/Latino; 2 American Indian or Alaska Native, non-Hispanic/Latino; 1 Asian, non-Hispanic/Latino; 2 Hispanic/Latino; 1 Two or more races, non-Hispanic/Latino). Average age 28. 30 applicants, 73% accepted, 17 enrolled. In 2016, 13 master's awarded. *Degree requirements:* For master's, thesis or alternative, comprehensive oral exam; for doctorate, comprehensive exam, thesis/dissertation. *Entrance requirements:* For master's, minimum GPA of 3.2 overall or graduate. Additional exam requirements/recommendations for international students: Required—TOEFL (minimum score 550 paper-based; 80 iBT). *Application deadline:* For fall admission, 2/1 priority date for domestic and international students. Application fee: $65. *Expenses:* Contact institution. *Financial support:* In 2016–17, 16 teaching assistantships with full tuition reimbursements (averaging $6,240 per year) were awarded; research assistantships, career-related internships or fieldwork, Federal Work-Study, scholarships/grants, and unspecified assistantships also available. Support available to part-time students.

Financial award application deadline: 3/1; financial award applicants required to submit FAFSA. *Faculty research:* History of criminal justice, mental health issues, international terrorism, offender assessment, domestic violence. *Total annual research expenditures:* $51,507. *Unit head:* Dr. Kris R. Henning, Chair, 503-725-8520, E-mail: khenning@pdx.edu. *Application contact:* Andrew Nolan, Office Manager, 503-725-9586, E-mail: anolan@pdx.edu.
Website: https://www.pdx.edu/hatfieldschool/criminology-criminal-justice

**Radford University,** College of Graduate Studies and Research, Program in Criminal Justice, Radford, VA 24142. Offers MA, MS, Certificate. *Program availability:* Part-time. *Faculty:* 7 full-time (4 women). *Students:* 17 full-time (13 women), 4 part-time (2 women); includes 4 minority (2 Black or African American, non-Hispanic/Latino; 2 Two or more races, non-Hispanic/Latino), 1 international. Average age 25. 20 applicants, 75% accepted, 14 enrolled. In 2016, 3 master's awarded. *Degree requirements:* For master's, comprehensive exam, thesis optional. *Entrance requirements:* For master's, minimum GPA of 2.9, 2 letters of reference, original writing sample, resume, official transcripts. Additional exam requirements/recommendations for international students: Required—TOEFL (minimum score 550 paper-based; 79 iBT), IELTS (minimum score 6.5). *Application deadline:* For fall admission, 2/15 priority date for domestic students, 12/1 for international students; for spring admission, 7/1 for international students. Applications are processed on a rolling basis. Application fee: $50. Electronic applications accepted. *Expenses:* Tuition, state resident: full-time $7868; part-time $328 per credit hour. Tuition, nonresident: full-time $16,394; part-time $683 per credit hour. *Required fees:* $3090; $130 per credit hour. Tuition and fees vary according to course load and program. *Financial support:* In 2016–17, 13 students received support, including 2 research assistantships (averaging $10,000 per year), 3 teaching assistantships (averaging $10,333 per year); career-related internships or fieldwork, scholarships/grants, and unspecified assistantships also available. Support available to part-time students. Financial award application deadline: 3/1; financial award applicants required to submit FAFSA. *Faculty research:* Spatial issues and crime, gun violence, rural crime, gender and criminal issues, interpersonal violence. *Unit head:* Dr. Nicole Hendrix, Coordinator, 540-831-6148, Fax: 540-831-6075, E-mail: phendrix@radford.edu.
Website: http://www.radford.edu/content/chbs/home/criminal-justice/programs/graduate.html

**Regent University,** Graduate School, School of Law, Virginia Beach, VA 23464-9800. Offers American legal studies (LL M); human rights (LL M); law (MA, JD), including business (MA), criminal justice (MA), general legal studies (MA), human resources management (MA), human rights (MA), mediation (MA), national security (MA), non-profit management (MA), regulatory compliance (MA), wealth management and financial planning (MA); JD/MA; JD/MBA. *Accreditation:* ABA. *Program availability:* Part-time, 100% online, blended/hybrid learning. *Faculty:* 20 full-time (6 women), 67 part-time/adjunct (19 women). *Students:* 364 full-time (219 women), 170 part-time (118 women); includes 213 minority (150 Black or African American, non-Hispanic/Latino; 1 American Indian or Alaska Native, non-Hispanic/Latino; 10 Asian, non-Hispanic/Latino; 34 Hispanic/Latino; 1 Native Hawaiian or other Pacific Islander, non-Hispanic/Latino; 17 Two or more races, non-Hispanic/Latino), 87 international. Average age 34. 834 applicants, 45% accepted, 174 enrolled. In 2016, 48 master's, 85 doctorates awarded. *Entrance requirements:* For master's, college transcripts, resume, personal statement; for doctorate, LSAT, minimum undergraduate GPA of 3.0, official transcripts, 2 letters of recommendation, resume, personal statement. Additional exam requirements/recommendations for international students: Required—TOEFL (minimum score 600 paper-based). *Application deadline:* For fall admission, 3/1 for domestic students. Applications are processed on a rolling basis. Application fee: $50. Electronic applications accepted. *Expenses:* $1,140 per credit (for JD); $650 per credit (for MA); $833 per credit (for LL M); $250 technology fee. *Financial support:* In 2016–17, 319 students received support. Career-related internships or fieldwork, scholarships/grants, and unspecified assistantships available. Support available to part-time students. *Faculty research:* Family law, Constitutional law, law and culture, evidence and practice, intellectual property. *Unit head:* Michael Hernandez, Dean, 757-352-4040, Fax: 757-352-4595, E-mail: michher@regent.edu. *Application contact:* Katie Kerley, Director of Law Admissions, 877-267-5072, Fax: 757-352-4139, E-mail: lawschool@regent.edu.
Website: http://www.regent.edu/law/

**Regis University,** College of Contemporary Liberal Studies, Denver, CO 80221-1099. Offers creative writing (MFA); criminology (M Sc); curriculum, instruction and assessment (M Ed); education - teacher leadership (M Ed); educational leadership (M Ed); elementary education (M Ed); literacy (Certificate); reading (M Ed); secondary education (M Ed); special education (M Ed); teacher academic leadership (Certificate); teacher leadership (MA); teacher/educational leadership (M Ed); teaching the linguistically diverse (M Ed). *Program availability:* Part-time, evening/weekend, 100% online, blended/hybrid learning. *Faculty:* 18 full-time (12 women), 42 part-time/adjunct (26 women). *Students:* 302 full-time (234 women), 270 part-time (218 women); includes 148 minority (33 Black or African American, non-Hispanic/Latino; 3 American Indian or Alaska Native, non-Hispanic/Latino; 13 Asian, non-Hispanic/Latino; 83 Hispanic/Latino; 16 Two or more races, non-Hispanic/Latino), 3 international. Average age 36. 431 applicants, 90% accepted, 110 enrolled. In 2016, 308 master's awarded. *Degree requirements:* For master's, thesis (for some programs). *Entrance requirements:* For master's, official transcript reflecting baccalaureate degree awarded from regionally-accredited college or university, work experience, resume, letters of recommendation. Additional exam requirements/recommendations for international students: Required—TOEFL (minimum score 550 paper-based; 82 iBT). *Application deadline:* For fall admission, 8/15 priority date for domestic students, 7/13 for international students; for winter admission, 10/10 priority date for domestic students, 9/8 for international students; for spring admission, 1/10 priority date for domestic students, 11/17 for international students; for summer admission, 5/1 priority date for domestic students. Applications are processed on a rolling basis. Application fee: $75. Electronic applications accepted. *Expenses:* $485 per credit hour. *Financial support:* Scholarships/grants available. Financial award application deadline: 4/15; financial award applicants required to submit FAFSA. *Unit head:* Dr. Elisa Robyn, Academic Dean. *Application contact:* Cate Clark, Director of Admissions, 303-458-4900, Fax: 303-964-5534, E-mail: ruadmissions@regis.edu.
Website: http://www.regis.edu/CCLS.aspx

**Robert Morris University Illinois,** Morris Graduate School of Management, Chicago, IL 60605. Offers accounting (MBA); accounting/finance (MBA); business analytics (MIS); design and media (MM); design management (MM); educational technology (MM); health care administration (MM); higher education administration (MM); human resource management (MBA); information security (MIS); information systems (MBA, MIS); law enforcement administration (MM); management (MBA); management/finance (MBA); management/human resource management (MBA); mobile computing (MIS); sports administration (MM). *Program availability:* Part-time, evening/weekend. *Faculty:* 4 full-time (1 woman), 25 part-time/adjunct (5 women). *Students:* 196 full-time (98 women), 151 part-time (85 women); includes 200 minority (114 Black or African American, non-Hispanic/Latino; 17 Asian, non-Hispanic/Latino; 67 Hispanic/Latino; 2 Two or more races, non-Hispanic/Latino), 23 international. Average age 33. 174 applicants, 61% accepted, 97 enrolled. In 2016, 190 master's awarded. *Entrance requirements:* For

master's, official transcripts and letters of recommendation (for some programs); written personal statement. Additional exam requirements/recommendations for international students: Required—TOEFL (minimum score 550 paper-based). *Application deadline:* Applications are processed on a rolling basis. Application fee: $20 ($100 for international students). Electronic applications accepted. *Expenses:* Tuition: full-time $16,500; part-time $2750 per course. *Financial support:* In 2016–17, 444 students received support. Federal Work-Study, scholarships/grants, and unspecified assistantships available. Support available to part-time students. Financial award applicants required to submit FAFSA. *Unit head:* Kayed Akkawi, Dean, 312-935-6050, Fax: 312-935-6020, E-mail: kakkawi@robertmorris.edu. *Application contact:* Danielle Naffziger, Vice President of Marketing and Enrollment, 312-935-4812, Fax: 312-935-6020, E-mail: dnaffziger@robertmorris.edu.

**Rochester Institute of Technology,** Graduate Enrollment Services, College of Liberal Arts, Criminal Justice Department, MS Program in Criminal Justice, Rochester, NY 14623. Offers MS. *Program availability:* Part-time. *Students:* 7 full-time (2 women), 4 part-time (3 women); includes 6 minority (4 Black or African American, non-Hispanic/Latino; 2 Asian, non-Hispanic/Latino). Average age 26. 12 applicants, 58% accepted, 5 enrolled. In 2016, 3 master's awarded. *Degree requirements:* For master's, thesis. *Entrance requirements:* For master's, GRE, minimum GPA of 3.0 (recommended). Additional exam requirements/recommendations for international students: Required—TOEFL (minimum score 570 paper-based; 88 iBT), IELTS (minimum score 6.5), PTE (minimum score 58). *Application deadline:* For fall admission, 2/15 priority date for domestic and international students; for spring admission, 12/15 priority date for domestic and international students. Applications are processed on a rolling basis. Application fee: $60. Electronic applications accepted. *Expenses:* $1,742 per credit hour. *Financial support:* In 2016–17, 5 students received support. Research assistantships with partial tuition reimbursements available, teaching assistantships with partial tuition reimbursements available, career-related internships or fieldwork, scholarships/grants, and unspecified assistantships available. Support available to part-time students. Financial award applicants required to submit FAFSA. *Faculty research:* Criminal justice and the deaf and hard of hearing, community-based criminal justice problem-solving, locally relevant action research, strategic partnerships for violence reduction. *Unit head:* Dr. John McCluskey, Graduate Program Director, 585-475-2666, E-mail: jdmgcj@rit.edu. *Application contact:* Diane Ellison, Associate Vice President, Graduate Enrollment Services, 585-475-2229, Fax: 585-475-7164, E-mail: gradinfo@rit.edu.
Website: http://www.rit.edu/cla/criminaljustice/ms/overview

**Roger Williams University,** School of Justice Studies, Bristol, RI 02809. Offers criminal justice (MS); cybersecurity (MS); leadership (MS), including health care administration (MPA, MS); public management (MPA, MS); public administration (MPA), including health care administration (MPA, MS), public management (MPA, MS); MS/JD. *Program availability:* Part-time, evening/weekend, 100% online, blended/hybrid learning. *Faculty:* 10 full-time (5 women), 4 part-time/adjunct (0 women). *Students:* 63 full-time (37 women), 67 part-time (30 women); includes 30 minority (13 Black or African American, non-Hispanic/Latino; 1 American Indian or Alaska Native, non-Hispanic/Latino; 2 Asian, non-Hispanic/Latino; 13 Hispanic/Latino; 1 Native Hawaiian or other Pacific Islander, non-Hispanic/Latino), 3 international. Average age 36. 67 applicants, 96% accepted, 34 enrolled. In 2016, 27 master's awarded. *Degree requirements:* For master's, thesis optional. *Entrance requirements:* For master's, 2 letters of recommendation, college transcript, and resume (for MS in leadership and MPA programs); criminal background check (for MS in cybersecurity). Additional exam requirements/recommendations for international students: Required—TOEFL (minimum score 85 iBT), IELTS (minimum score 6.5). *Application deadline:* For fall admission, 8/1 for domestic students; for spring admission, 1/1 for domestic students. Applications are processed on a rolling basis. Application fee: $50. Electronic applications accepted. Application fee is waived when completed online. *Expenses:* $552 per credit hour tuition (for MS in leadership and MPA); $843 per credit hour tuition (for MS in criminal justice and MS in cybersecurity). *Financial support:* Research assistantships, scholarships/grants, and unspecified assistantships available. Financial award application deadline: 4/1; financial award applicants required to submit FAFSA. *Unit head:* Dr. Stephanie Manzi, Dean, 401-254-3021, Fax: 401-254-3431, E-mail: smanzi@rwu.edu. *Application contact:* Marcus Hanscom, Director of Graduate Admissions, 401-254-6200, Fax: 401-254-3557, E-mail: gradadmit@rwu.edu.
Website: http://www.rwu.edu/academics/departments/criminaljustice.htm#graduate

**Rowan University,** Graduate School, College of Humanities and Social Sciences, Department of Law and Justice Studies, Program in Criminal Justice, Glassboro, NJ 08028-1701. Offers MA. *Program availability:* Part-time, evening/weekend. *Degree requirements:* For master's, thesis. *Entrance requirements:* For master's, GRE General Test. Additional exam requirements/recommendations for international students: Required—TOEFL. Electronic applications accepted.

**Rutgers University–Camden,** Graduate School of Arts and Sciences, Program in Criminal Justice, Camden, NJ 08102. Offers MA, MPA/MA. *Program availability:* Part-time, evening/weekend. *Degree requirements:* For master's, comprehensive exam, thesis optional, 30 credits. *Entrance requirements:* For master's, GRE, 3 letters of recommendation; statement of personal, professional, and academic goals. Additional exam requirements/recommendations for international students: Required—TOEFL, IELTS. Electronic applications accepted. *Faculty research:* Criminal justice policy, public management, children in the criminal justice system, violence, gender and crime.

**Rutgers University–Newark,** Graduate School, School of Criminal Justice, Doctoral Program in Criminal Justice, Newark, NJ 07102. Offers PhD. *Degree requirements:* For doctorate, thesis/dissertation. *Entrance requirements:* Additional exam requirements/recommendations for international students: Required—TOEFL.

**Rutgers University–Newark,** Graduate School, School of Criminal Justice, Master's Program in Criminal Justice, Newark, NJ 07102. Offers MA. *Entrance requirements:* For master's, GRE, minimum undergraduate B average. Additional exam requirements/recommendations for international students: Required—TOEFL.

**Sacred Heart University,** Graduate Programs, College of Arts and Sciences, Department of Criminal Justice, Fairfield, CT 06825. Offers MA. *Program availability:* Part-time, evening/weekend. *Faculty:* 5 full-time (2 women), 2 part-time/adjunct (0 women). *Students:* 14 full-time (6 women), 21 part-time (10 women); includes 15 minority (5 Black or African American, non-Hispanic/Latino; 9 Hispanic/Latino; 1 Two or more races, non-Hispanic/Latino), 1 international. Average age 29. 18 applicants, 94% accepted, 12 enrolled. In 2016, 27 master's awarded. *Degree requirements:* For master's, comprehensive exam, thesis optional. *Entrance requirements:* For master's, BA/BS with minimum GPA of 3.0. Additional exam requirements/recommendations for international students: Required—TOEFL (minimum score 570 paper-based, 80 iBT), TWE, or IELTS (6.5); Recommended—TSE. *Application deadline:* For fall admission, 3/1 for domestic students; for spring admission, 11/1 for domestic students. Applications are processed on a rolling basis. Application fee: $75. Electronic applications accepted. *Expenses:* $790 per credit full-time. *Financial support:* Unspecified assistantships available. Financial award applicants required to submit FAFSA. *Unit head:* Dr. Jim McCabe, Chair, 203-396-8002, E-mail: mccabej@sacredheart.edu. *Application contact:* William Sweeney, Director of Graduate Admissions Operations, 203-365-4827, Fax:

## Criminal Justice and Criminology

203-365-4732, E-mail: gradstudies@sacredheart.edu. Website: http://www.sacredheart.edu/academics/collegeofartssciences/academicdepartments/criminaljustice/masterofartsincriminaljustice/

**St. Ambrose University,** College of Arts and Sciences, Program in Criminal Justice, Davenport, IA 52803-2898. Offers criminal justice (MCJ); juvenile justice education (MCJ). *Program availability:* Part-time, evening/weekend. *Degree requirements:* For master's, thesis (for some programs), practicum or project. *Entrance requirements:* For master's, 2 years of work experience, 2 letters of recommendation, personal interview. Additional exam requirements/recommendations for international students: Required—TOEFL. Electronic applications accepted. *Faculty research:* Community policing.

**St. Cloud State University,** School of Graduate Studies, College of Social Sciences, Department of Criminal Justice, Program in Criminal Justice, St. Cloud, MN 56301-4498. Offers criminal justice administration (MS). *Program availability:* Part-time, evening/weekend, online learning. *Entrance requirements:* For master's, minimum overall GPA in previous undergraduate and graduate records or in last half of undergraduate work. Electronic applications accepted.

**St. John's University,** St. John's College of Liberal Arts and Sciences, Department of Sociology and Anthropology, Queens, NY 11439. Offers criminology and justice (MA); sociology (MA). *Program availability:* Part-time, evening/weekend. *Degree requirements:* For master's, comprehensive exam, thesis optional. *Entrance requirements:* For master's, 18 undergraduate credits in social sciences, minimum GPA of 3.0, bachelor's degree. Additional exam requirements/recommendations for international students: Required—TOEFL (minimum score 600 paper-based; 100 iBT), IELTS (minimum score 7). Electronic applications accepted. *Faculty research:* Community studies and gentrification, global financial crisis, insurance fraud, globalization, immigration and human rights.

**Saint Joseph's University,** College of Arts and Sciences, Department of Criminal Justice, Philadelphia, PA 19131-1395. Offers behavior analysis (MS, Post-Master's Certificate); behavior management (MS); criminal justice (MS); federal law (MS); intelligence and crime (MS). *Program availability:* Part-time, evening/weekend, 100% online, blended/hybrid learning. *Faculty:* 4 full-time (3 women), 43 part-time/adjunct (18 women). *Students:* 23 full-time (13 women), 380 part-time (269 women); includes 116 minority (91 Black or African American, non-Hispanic/Latino; 2 American Indian or Alaska Native, non-Hispanic/Latino; 5 Asian, non-Hispanic/Latino; 16 Hispanic/Latino; 2 Native Hawaiian or other Pacific Islander, non-Hispanic/Latino; 7 international. Average age 31. 214 applicants, 73% accepted, 110 enrolled. In 2016, 141 master's, 34 other advanced degrees awarded. *Degree requirements:* For master's, thesis. *Entrance requirements:* For master's, 2 letters of recommendation, personal statement, resume, official transcripts, minimum GPA of 3.0. Additional exam requirements/recommendations for international students: Required—TOEFL (minimum score 550 paper-based; 80 iBT). *Application deadline:* For fall admission, 7/15 for international students; for spring admission, 11/1 for international students. Applications are processed on a rolling basis. Application fee: $35. Electronic applications accepted. *Expenses:* $853 per credit. *Financial support:* In 2016–17, 5 students received support. Federal Work-Study and unspecified assistantships available. Financial award application deadline: 5/1; financial award applicants required to submit FAFSA. *Faculty research:* Ethics in policing, multiculturalism, behavior analysis. *Total annual research expenditures:* $17,309. *Unit head:* Sylvia DeSantis, Director, 610-660-3131, E-mail: gradcas@sju.edu. *Application contact:* Graduate Admissions, College of Arts and Sciences, 610-660-3131, E-mail: gradcas@sju.edu. Website: http://www.sju.edu/majors-programs/graduate-arts-sciences/masters/criminal-justice-ms

**Saint Leo University,** Graduate Studies in Public Safety Administration, Saint Leo, FL 33574-6665. Offers criminal justice (MS), including corrections, criminal investigation, emergency and disaster management, forensic science, legal studies; emergency and disaster management (MS). *Program availability:* Part-time, evening/weekend, 100% online, blended/hybrid learning. *Faculty:* 7 full-time (2 women), 32 part-time/adjunct (8 women). *Students:* 3 full-time (1 woman), 667 part-time (446 women); includes 355 minority (275 Black or African American, non-Hispanic/Latino; 6 American Indian or Alaska Native, non-Hispanic/Latino; 4 Asian, non-Hispanic/Latino; 56 Hispanic/Latino; 3 Native Hawaiian or other Pacific Islander, non-Hispanic/Latino; 11 Two or more races, non-Hispanic/Latino). Average age 37. 361 applicants, 87% accepted, 177 enrolled. In 2016, 265 master's awarded. *Degree requirements:* For master's, comprehensive project. *Entrance requirements:* For master's, official transcripts, bachelor's degree from regionally-accredited university with minimum GPA of 3.0. Additional exam requirements/recommendations for international students: Required—TOEFL (minimum score 550 paper-based; 80 iBT). *Application deadline:* For fall admission, 7/1 priority date for domestic and international students; for spring admission, 11/1 priority date for domestic and international students. Applications are processed on a rolling basis. Application fee: $80. Electronic applications accepted. *Expenses:* $535 per semester hour (for MS in emergency/disaster management); $555 per semester hour (for MS in criminal justice). *Financial support:* In 2016–17, 14 students received support. Scholarships/grants and health care benefits available. Financial award application deadline: 3/1; financial award applicants required to submit FAFSA. *Unit head:* Dr. Robert Diemer, Director of Graduate Studies in Safety Administration, 352-588-8974, Fax: 352-588-8289, E-mail: graduatepublicsafety@saintleo.edu. *Application contact:* Jennifer Shelley, Senior Associate Director of Graduate Admissions, 800-707-8846, Fax: 352-588-7873, E-mail: grad.admissions@saintleo.edu. Website: http://www.saintleo.edu/academics/graduate

**Saint Mary's University,** Faculty of Arts, Program in Criminology, Halifax, NS B3H 3C3, Canada. Offers MA. *Program availability:* Part-time. *Degree requirements:* For master's, thesis. *Entrance requirements:* For master's, honors degree, official transcripts, sample of academic written work, 2 letters of recommendation. Electronic applications accepted. *Expenses:* Contact institution.

**Saint Peter's University,** Program in Criminal Justice Administration, Jersey City, NJ 07306-5997. Offers federal law enforcement administration (MA); police administration (MA). *Program availability:* Part-time, evening/weekend. *Entrance requirements:* Additional exam requirements/recommendations for international students: Required—TOEFL. Electronic applications accepted.

**St. Thomas University,** School of Business, Department of Management, Miami Gardens, FL 33054-6459. Offers accounting (MBA); general management (MSM, Certificate); health management (MBA, MSM, Certificate); human resource management (MBA, MSM, Certificate); international business (MBA, MIB, MSM, Certificate); justice administration (MSM, Certificate); management accounting (MSM, Certificate); public management (MSM, Certificate); sports administration (MS). *Program availability:* Part-time, evening/weekend. *Degree requirements:* For master's, comprehensive exam. *Entrance requirements:* For master's, interview, minimum GPA of 3.0 or GMAT. Additional exam requirements/recommendations for international students: Required—TOEFL (minimum score 550 paper-based; 79 iBT). Electronic applications accepted.

**Salem State University,** School of Graduate Studies, Program in Criminal Justice, Salem, MA 01970-5353. Offers MS. *Program availability:* Part-time, evening/weekend.

*Entrance requirements:* For master's, GRE or MAT. Additional exam requirements/recommendations for international students: Required—TOEFL (minimum score 550 paper-based; 80 iBT) or IELTS (minimum score 5.5).

**Salve Regina University,** Program in Administration of Justice and Homeland Security, Newport, RI 02840-4192. Offers administration of justice and homeland security (MS); cybersecurity and intelligence (CGS); digital forensics (CGS); leadership in justice (CGS). *Program availability:* Part-time, evening/weekend, online learning. *Entrance requirements:* For master's, GMAT, GRE General Test, or MAT. Additional exam requirements/recommendations for international students: Required—TOEFL (minimum score 600 paper-based; 100 iBT). Electronic applications accepted.

**Sam Houston State University,** College of Criminal Justice, Department of Criminal Justice and Criminology, Huntsville, TX 77341. Offers criminal justice (MS, PhD); criminal justice and criminology (MA); criminal justice leadership and management (MS); victim services management (MS). *Program availability:* Part-time, evening/weekend, online learning. *Degree requirements:* For master's, comprehensive exam (for some programs), thesis (for some programs); for doctorate, comprehensive exam, thesis/dissertation. *Entrance requirements:* For master's, GRE, personal essay, official transcripts, three recommendation letters, resume; for doctorate, GRE, personal essay, official transcripts, three recommendation letters, resume, master's degree. Additional exam requirements/recommendations for international students: Required—TOEFL (minimum score 550 paper-based; 79 iBT), IELTS (minimum score 6.5). Electronic applications accepted.

**San Diego State University,** Graduate and Research Affairs, College of Professional Studies and Fine Arts, School of Public Affairs, Program in Criminal Justice Administration, San Diego, CA 92182. Offers MPA. *Program availability:* Part-time. *Entrance requirements:* For master's, GRE General Test, 2 letters of reference. Additional exam requirements/recommendations for international students: Required—TOEFL. Electronic applications accepted.

**San Diego State University,** Graduate and Research Affairs, College of Professional Studies and Fine Arts, School of Public Affairs, Program in Criminal Justice and Criminology, San Diego, CA 92182. Offers MS. *Entrance requirements:* For master's, GRE General Test, 2 letters of reference. Additional exam requirements/recommendations for international students: Required—TOEFL. Electronic applications accepted.

**San Francisco State University,** Division of Graduate Studies, College of Health and Social Sciences, Public Administration Program, San Francisco, CA 94132-1722. Offers criminal justice administration (MPA); environmental administration and policy (MPA); gerontology (MPA); nonprofit administration (MPA); public management (MPA); public policy (MPA); urban administration (MPA). *Accreditation:* NASPAA. *Expenses:* Tuition, state resident: full-time $6738. Tuition, nonresident: full-time $15,666. *Required fees:* $1012. Tuition and fees vary according to degree level and program. *Unit head:* Dr. Elizabeth Brown, Director of the School of Public Affairs and Civic Engagement, 415-817-4455, Fax: 415-817-4464, E-mail: mpa@sfsu.edu. *Application contact:* Dr. Jennifer Shea, Graduate Coordinator, 415-817-4462, Fax: 415-817-4464, E-mail: jshea@sfsu.edu. Website: http://mpa.sfsu.edu/

**Seattle University,** College of Arts and Sciences, Department of Criminal Justice, Seattle, WA 98122-1090. Offers crime analysis (Certificate); criminal justice (MACJ). *Program availability:* Part-time, evening/weekend. *Faculty:* 8 full-time (2 women), 5 part-time/adjunct (3 women). *Students:* 24 full-time (21 women), 51 part-time (40 women); includes 32 minority (4 Black or African American, non-Hispanic/Latino; 1 American Indian or Alaska Native, non-Hispanic/Latino; 6 Asian, non-Hispanic/Latino; 13 Hispanic/Latino; 1 Native Hawaiian or other Pacific Islander, non-Hispanic/Latino; 7 Two or more races, non-Hispanic/Latino). Average age 28. 71 applicants, 65% accepted, 32 enrolled. In 2016, 22 master's, 2 Certificates awarded. *Degree requirements:* For master's, comprehensive exam or thesis. *Entrance requirements:* For master's, minimum GPA of 3.0; undergraduate degree in criminal justice or related social, behavioral, or physical science, or related coursework and/or volunteer or supervised experience; letters of recommendation; writing sample. Additional exam requirements/recommendations for international students: Required—TOEFL, IELTS. *Application deadline:* For fall admission, 3/15 for domestic and international students. Application fee: $55. Electronic applications accepted. *Financial support:* In 2016–17, 26 students received support. Applicants required to submit FAFSA. *Faculty research:* Criminal justice program evaluation, ex-offender reentry, policing issues, restorative justice, psychopathy. *Unit head:* Dr. Elaine Gunnison, Graduate Program Director, 206-296-2430, E-mail: gunnisone@seattleu.edu. *Application contact:* Janet Shandley, Associate Dean of Graduate Admissions, 206-296-5900, Fax: 206-298-5656, E-mail: grad_admissions@seattleu.edu. Website: https://www.seattleu.edu/artsci/criminal-graduate/

**Shippensburg University of Pennsylvania,** School of Graduate Studies, College of Education and Human Services, Department of Criminal Justice, Shippensburg, PA 17257-2299. Offers administration of justice (MS), including administration of justice, juvenile justice. *Program availability:* Part-time, evening/weekend. *Faculty:* 6 full-time (3 women), 2 part-time/adjunct (1 woman). *Students:* 11 full-time (5 women), 20 part-time (6 women); includes 6 minority (5 Black or African American, non-Hispanic/Latino; 1 Hispanic/Latino). Average age 28. 29 applicants, 76% accepted, 17 enrolled. In 2016, 27 master's awarded. *Degree requirements:* For master's, internship, practicum, or thesis. *Entrance requirements:* For master's, GRE or MAT (if GPA less than 2.75), 500-word statement of interest. Additional exam requirements/recommendations for international students: Required—TOEFL (minimum score 550 paper-based, 68 iBT) or IELTS (minimum score 6). *Application deadline:* For fall admission, 4/30 for international students. Applications are processed on a rolling basis. Application fee: $45. Electronic applications accepted. *Expenses:* Tuition, state resident: part-time $483 per credit. Tuition, nonresident: part-time $725 per credit. *Required fees:* $141 per credit. *Financial support:* In 2016–17, 4 students received support. Career-related internships or fieldwork, scholarships/grants, unspecified assistantships, and resident hall director and student payroll positions available. Support available to part-time students. Financial award application deadline: 3/1; financial award applicants required to submit FAFSA. *Unit head:* Dr. Matthew D. Fetzer, Assistant Professor and Program Coordinator, 717-477-1630, Fax: 717-477-4087, E-mail: mdfetzer@ship.edu. *Application contact:* Megan N. Luft, Assistant Dean of Graduate Admissions, 717-477-1231, Fax: 717-477-4016, E-mail: mnluft@ship.edu. Website: http://www.ship.edu/criminal_justice/

**Simon Fraser University,** Office of Graduate Studies and Postdoctoral Fellows, Faculty of Arts and Social Sciences, School of Criminology, Burnaby, BC V5A 1S6, Canada. Offers applied legal studies (MA); criminology (MA, PhD). *Faculty:* 29 full-time (10 women). *Students:* 154 full-time (97 women), 7 part-time (3 women). 131 applicants, 54% accepted, 56 enrolled. In 2016, 38 master's, 6 doctorates awarded. *Degree requirements:* For master's, thesis or alternative, practicum; for doctorate, thesis/dissertation. *Entrance requirements:* For master's, minimum GPA of 3.0 (on scale of 4.33) or 3.33 based on last 60 credits of undergraduate courses; for doctorate, minimum GPA of 3.5 (on scale of 4.33). Additional exam requirements/recommendations for

international students: Recommended—TOEFL (minimum score 580 paper-based; 93 iBT), IELTS (minimum score 7), TWE (minimum score 5). *Application deadline:* For fall admission, 2/1 for domestic and international students; for spring admission, 2/1 for domestic students. Application fee: $90 ($125 for international students). Electronic applications accepted. *Financial support:* In 2016–17, 51 students received support, including 28 fellowships (averaging $6,500 per year), teaching assistantships (averaging $5,608 per year); research assistantships, career-related internships or fieldwork, Federal Work-Study, and scholarships/grants also available. *Faculty research:* Media and crime, feminist jurisprudence, policy evaluation, forensic entomology, restorative justice. *Unit head:* Dr. Martin Andresen, Associate Director, Graduate Programs, 778-782-7628, Fax: 778-782-4140, E-mail: crim-grad-chair@sfu.ca. *Application contact:* Shaneza Bacchus, Graduate Secretary, 778-782-4762, Fax: 778-782-4140, E-mail: crimgrad@sfu.ca.
Website: http://www.sfu.ca/criminology/

**Simpson College,** Department of Social Sciences, Indianola, IA 50125-1297. Offers criminal justice (MACJ). *Program availability:* Evening/weekend.

**Slippery Rock University of Pennsylvania,** Graduate Studies (Recruitment), College of Liberal Arts, Department of Criminology and Security Studies, Slippery Rock, PA 16057-1383. Offers criminal justice (MA). *Program availability:* Part-time, evening/weekend, online only, 100% online. *Faculty:* 6 full-time (4 women). *Students:* 5 full-time (3 women), 17 part-time (9 women); includes 6 minority (4 Black or African American, non-Hispanic/Latino; 1 Asian, non-Hispanic/Latino; 1 Two or more races, non-Hispanic/Latino). Average age 31. 20 applicants, 60% accepted, 9 enrolled. In 2016, 16 master's awarded. *Degree requirements:* For master's, comprehensive exam (for some programs), thesis (for some programs). *Entrance requirements:* For master's, minimum GPA of 2.75, three letters of recommendation, personal statement. Additional exam requirements/recommendations for international students: Required—TOEFL (minimum score 550 paper-based; 80 iBT). *Application deadline:* For fall admission, 3/1 priority date for domestic students, 5/1 priority date for international students; for spring admission, 10/1 priority date for domestic students, 9/1 priority date for international students. Applications are processed on a rolling basis. Application fee: $25 ($30 for international students). Electronic applications accepted. *Expenses:* $646.50 per credit in-state, $936.80 per credit out-of-state; $581.45 per online credit in-state, $648.65 per online credit out-of-state. *Financial support:* In 2016–17, 3 students received support. Career-related internships or fieldwork, Federal Work-Study, institutionally sponsored loans, scholarships/grants, tuition waivers (partial), and unspecified assistantships available. Support available to part-time students. Financial award application deadline: 5/1; financial award applicants required to submit FAFSA. *Unit head:* Dr. David Champion, Graduate Coordinator, 724-738-4462, Fax: 724-738-4822, E-mail: david.champion@sru.edu. *Application contact:* Brandi Weber-Mortimer, Director of Graduate Admissions, 724-738-2051, Fax: 724-738-2146, E-mail: graduate.admissions@sru.edu.
Website: http://www.sru.edu/academics/graduate-programs/criminal-justice-master-of-arts

**Southeast Missouri State University,** School of Graduate Studies, Department of Criminal Justice and Sociology, Cape Girardeau, MO 63701-4799. Offers criminal justice (MS). *Program availability:* Part-time, online learning. *Faculty:* 6 full-time (3 women), 1 part-time/adjunct (0 women). *Students:* 3 full-time (all women), 41 part-time (21 women); includes 8 minority (6 Black or African American, non-Hispanic/Latino; 2 Hispanic/Latino), 2 international. Average age 33. 23 applicants, 96% accepted, 18 enrolled. In 2016, 10 master's awarded. *Degree requirements:* For master's, thesis, internship, or applied research project. *Entrance requirements:* Additional exam requirements/recommendations for international students: Required—TOEFL (minimum score 550 paper-based; 79 iBT), IELTS (minimum score 6), PTE (minimum score 53). *Application deadline:* For fall admission, 8/1 for domestic students, 6/1 for international students; for spring admission, 11/21 for domestic students, 10/1 for international students; for summer admission, 5/15 for domestic students. Applications are processed on a rolling basis. Application fee: $30 ($40 for international students). Electronic applications accepted. *Expenses:* Tuition, state resident: full-time $3130; part-time $260.80 per credit hour. Tuition, nonresident: full-time $5842; part-time $486.80 per credit hour. Required fees: $33.70 per credit hour. *Financial support:* In 2016–17, 3 students received support. Career-related internships or fieldwork, Federal Work-Study, scholarships/grants, traineeships, tuition waivers (full), and unspecified assistantships available. Financial award application deadline: 6/30; financial award applicants required to submit FAFSA. *Faculty research:* Law enforcement, corrections, courts, marginalized populations, online learning. *Unit head:* Dr. Jeremy Ball, Department Chair, 573-651-2541, Fax: 573-986-6417, E-mail: jball@semo.edu.
Website: http://www.semo.edu/criminaljustice/

**Southern Illinois University Carbondale,** Graduate School, College of Liberal Arts, Department of Criminology and Criminal Justice, Carbondale, IL 62901-4701. Offers MA, PhD. *Degree requirements:* For master's, thesis optional; for doctorate, thesis/dissertation. *Entrance requirements:* For master's, GRE General Test, minimum GPA of 2.7; for doctorate, GRE General Test, minimum GPA of 3.25. Additional exam requirements/recommendations for international students: Required—TOEFL. *Faculty research:* Corrections, criminology, law enforcement, crime prevention, victims of crime.

**Southern University and Agricultural and Mechanical College,** Graduate School, Nelson Mandela School of Public Policy and Urban Affairs, Department of Criminal Justice, Baton Rouge, LA 70813. Offers MS. *Entrance requirements:* Additional exam requirements/recommendations for international students: Required—TOEFL (minimum score 525 paper-based).

**Southern University at New Orleans,** School of Graduate Studies, New Orleans, LA 70126-1009. Offers criminal justice (MA); management information systems (MS); museum studies (MA); social work (MSW). *Accreditation:* CSWE. *Program availability:* Part-time, evening/weekend. *Degree requirements:* For master's, thesis. *Entrance requirements:* For master's, GRE/GMAT. Additional exam requirements/recommendations for international students: Required—TOEFL.

**South University,** Graduate Programs, College of Arts and Sciences, Program in Criminal Justice, Savannah, GA 31406. Offers MS.

**South University,** Graduate Programs, College of Business, Savannah, GA 31406. Offers corrections (MBA); entrepreneurship and small business (MBA); healthcare administration (MBA); hospitality management (MBA); leadership (MS); public administration (MPA); sustainability (MBA).

**South University,** Program in Criminal Justice, Columbia, SC 29203. Offers MS.

**South University,** Program in Criminal Justice, Montgomery, AL 36116-1120. Offers MS.

**South University,** Program in Criminal Justice, Tampa, FL 33614. Offers MS.

**South University,** Program in Criminal Justice, Royal Palm Beach, FL 33411. Offers MS.

**Southwestern College,** Professional Studies Programs, Wichita, KS 67207. Offers business administration (MBA); leadership (MS); management (MS); security administration (MS); specialized ministries (MS). *Program availability:* Part-time,

evening/weekend, online only, 100% online. *Faculty:* 1 full-time (0 women), 12 part-time/adjunct (4 women). *Students:* 81 part-time (26 women); includes 24 minority (10 Black or African American, non-Hispanic/Latino; 4 American Indian or Alaska Native, non-Hispanic/Latino; 1 Asian, non-Hispanic/Latino; 9 Hispanic/Latino). Average age 37. 61 applicants, 75% accepted, 18 enrolled. In 2016, 61 master's awarded. *Degree requirements:* For master's, thesis (for some programs), practicum/capstone project. *Entrance requirements:* For master's, baccalaureate degree; minimum GPA of 3.0. Additional exam requirements/recommendations for international students: Required—TOEFL (minimum score 550 paper-based; 80 iBT). *Application deadline:* Applications are processed on a rolling basis. Application fee: $40. Electronic applications accepted. *Expenses:* Contact institution. *Financial support:* In 2016–17, 9 students received support. Unspecified assistantships and employee tuition benefits available. Financial award applicants required to submit FAFSA. *Unit head:* Dennis Russell, Director of Admissions and Student Services, 888-684-5335 Ext. 3372, Fax: 316-688-5218, E-mail: dennis.russell@sckans.edu.
Website: http://www.southwesterncollege.org

**Southwest University,** Program in Criminal Justice, Kenner, LA 70062. Offers MS.

**Stockton University,** Office of Graduate Studies, Program in Criminal Justice, Galloway, NJ 08205-9441. Offers MA. *Program availability:* Part-time, evening/weekend. *Faculty:* 6 full-time (3 women), 1 part-time/adjunct (0 women). *Students:* 18 full-time (11 women), 9 part-time (8 women); includes 5 minority (2 Black or African American, non-Hispanic/Latino; 3 Hispanic/Latino). Average age 23. 36 applicants, 50% accepted, 13 enrolled. In 2016, 12 master's awarded. *Degree requirements:* For master's, comprehensive exam (for some programs), thesis, student portfolio project. *Entrance requirements:* For master's, GRE General Test, minimum GPA of 3.0. Additional exam requirements/recommendations for international students: Required—TOEFL. *Application deadline:* For fall admission, 7/1 for domestic and international students; for spring admission, 12/1 for domestic students, 11/1 for international students. Applications are processed on a rolling basis. Application fee: $50. Electronic applications accepted. *Expenses:* $772 per credit in-state. *Financial support:* In 2016–17, 9 research assistantships with partial tuition reimbursements were awarded; fellowships, career-related internships or fieldwork, Federal Work-Study, scholarships/grants, and unspecified assistantships also available. Support available to part-time students. Financial award application deadline: 3/1; financial award applicants required to submit FAFSA. *Faculty research:* Homeland security, forensic psychology, corrections, sex crimes, violent crimes. *Unit head:* Dr. Christine Tartaro, 609-626-3640, E-mail: christine.tartaro@stockton.edu. *Application contact:* Tara Williams, Assistant Director of Graduate Enrollment Management, 609-626-3640, Fax: 609-626-6050, E-mail: gradschool@stockton.edu.

**Suffolk University,** College of Arts and Sciences, Department of Sociology, Boston, MA 02108-2770. Offers MSCJS, MSCJS/JD, MSCJS/MPA, MSCJS/MSMHC. *Program availability:* Part-time. *Faculty:* 3 full-time (1 woman), 1 (woman) part-time/adjunct. *Students:* 23 full-time (19 women), 16 part-time (13 women); includes 14 minority (9 Black or African American, non-Hispanic/Latino; 5 Hispanic/Latino), 2 international. Average age 28. 49 applicants, 55% accepted, 17 enrolled. In 2016, 19 master's awarded. *Entrance requirements:* For master's, 2 letters of recommendation, resume. Additional exam requirements/recommendations for international students: Required—TOEFL (minimum score 550 paper-based; 80 iBT). *Application deadline:* For fall admission, 3/15 priority date for domestic students, 3/15 for international students; for spring admission, 10/15 priority date for domestic students, 10/15 for international students. Applications are processed on a rolling basis. Application fee: $50. Electronic applications accepted. *Expenses:* $27,456 per year full-time tuition, $1,144 per credit hour part-time tuition, $52 per year student activity fee. *Financial support:* In 2016–17, 24 students received support, including 25 fellowships (averaging $4,982 per year); career-related internships or fieldwork, Federal Work-Study, institutionally sponsored loans, scholarships/grants, and unspecified assistantships also available. Support available to part-time students. Financial award application deadline: 4/1; financial award applicants required to submit FAFSA. *Faculty research:* Restorative justice, anti-gang initiative, healthcare for female ex-offenders, violence against women, juvenile justice and the courts. *Unit head:* Dr. James Ptacek, Professor/Chair, 617-573-8047, E-mail: jptacek@suffolk.edu. *Application contact:* Mara Marzocchi, Associate Director of Graduate Admissions, 617-573-8302, Fax: 617-305-1733, E-mail: grad.admission@suffolk.edu.
Website: http://www.suffolk.edu/college/graduate/69297.php

**Sul Ross State University,** College of Professional Studies, Department of Criminal Justice, Alpine, TX 79832. Offers criminal justice (MS); homeland security (MS); MS/MA. *Entrance requirements:* For master's, GRE General Test, minimum GPA of 2.5 in last 60 hours of undergraduate work.

**Tarleton State University,** College of Graduate Studies, College of Liberal and Fine Arts, Department of Criminal Justice, Stephenville, TX 76402. Offers criminal justice (MCJ). *Program availability:* Part-time, evening/weekend, 100% online, blended/hybrid learning. *Faculty:* 8 full-time (5 women), 3 part-time/adjunct (0 women). *Students:* 18 full-time (9 women), 132 part-time (62 women); includes 59 minority (25 Black or African American, non-Hispanic/Latino; 3 Asian, non-Hispanic/Latino; 28 Hispanic/Latino; 3 Two or more races, non-Hispanic/Latino), 3 international. 66 applicants, 94% accepted, 49 enrolled. In 2016, 36 master's awarded. *Degree requirements:* For master's, comprehensive exam (for some programs), thesis optional. *Entrance requirements:* For master's, GRE General Test, minimum GPA of 3.0. Additional exam requirements/recommendations for international students: Required—TOEFL (minimum score 550 paper-based; 80 iBT). *Application deadline:* For fall admission, 8/15 priority date for domestic students; for spring admission, 1/7 for domestic students. Applications are processed on a rolling basis. Application fee: $45 ($145 for international students). Electronic applications accepted. *Expenses:* $3,672 tuition; $2,437 fees. *Financial support:* Research assistantships, career-related internships or fieldwork, and Federal Work-Study available. Support available to part-time students. Financial award application deadline: 5/1; financial award applicants required to submit FAFSA. *Unit head:* Dr. Rhonda Dobbs, Department Head, 254-968-9402, E-mail: dobbs@tarleton.edu. *Application contact:* Information Contact, 254-968-9104, Fax: 254-968-9670, E-mail: gradoffice@tarleton.edu.
Website: http://www.tarleton.edu/COLFAWEB/criminaljustice/index.html

**Temple University,** College of Liberal Arts, Department of Criminal Justice, Philadelphia, PA 19122-6096. Offers MA, PhD. *Program availability:* Part-time. Terminal master's awarded for partial completion of doctoral program. *Degree requirements:* For master's, thesis optional; for doctorate, thesis/dissertation, qualifying exams. *Entrance requirements:* For master's, GRE General Test, minimum GPA of 3.0, 3 letters of recommendation; for doctorate, GRE General Test, 3 letters of recommendation. Additional exam requirements/recommendations for international students: Required—TOEFL (minimum score 550 paper-based; 79 iBT). Electronic applications accepted. *Faculty research:* Policy analysis and program evaluation; geography of crime and justice; criminal behavior; rehabilitation and behavioral change; policing, security, and crime prevention; juvenile delinquency and juvenile justice.

**Tennessee State University,** The School of Graduate Studies and Research, College of Liberal Arts, Department of Criminal Justice, Nashville, TN 37209-1561. Offers MCJ.

## Criminal Justice and Criminology

Program offered jointly with Middle Tennessee State University. *Degree requirements:* For master's, thesis. *Entrance requirements:* For master's, GRE General Test or MAT. Electronic applications accepted.

**Texas A&M International University,** Office of Graduate Studies and Research, College of Arts and Sciences, Department of Public Affairs and Social Research, Laredo, TX 78041-1900. Offers criminal justice (MS); history and political thought (MA); political science (MA); public administration (MPA). *Degree requirements:* For master's, comprehensive exam (for some programs), thesis (for some programs). *Entrance requirements:* For master's, GRE General Test. Additional exam requirements/recommendations for international students: Required—TOEFL (minimum score 550 paper-based; 79 iBT).

**Texas A&M University–Central Texas,** Graduate Studies and Research, Killeen, TX 76549. Offers accounting (MS); business administration (MBA); clinical mental health counseling (MS); criminal justice (MCJ); curriculum and instruction (M Ed); educational administration (M Ed); educational psychology - experimental psychology (MS); history (MA); human resource management (MS); information systems (MS); liberal studies (MS); management and leadership (MS); marriage and family therapy (MS); mathematics (MS); political science (MA); school counseling (M Ed); school psychology (Ed S).

**Texas A&M University–Commerce,** College of Humanities, Social Sciences and Arts, Commerce, TX 75429-3011. Offers applied criminology (MS); applied linguistics (MA, MS); art (MA, MFA); Christianity in history (Graduate Certificate); computational linguistics (Graduate Certificate); creative writing (Graduate Certificate); English (MA, MS, PhD); film studies (Graduate Certificate); history (MA, MS); music (MM); political science (MA, MS); public history (Graduate Certificate); sociology (MS); Spanish (MA); studies in children's and adolescent literature and culture (Graduate Certificate); teaching English to speakers of other languages (Graduate Certificate); theater (MA, MS). *Program availability:* Part-time. *Faculty:* 53 full-time (26 women), 7 part-time/adjunct (2 women). *Students:* 87 full-time (55 women), 528 part-time (362 women); includes 198 minority (86 Black or African American, non-Hispanic/Latino; 2 American Indian or Alaska Native, non-Hispanic/Latino; 8 Asian, non-Hispanic/Latino; 84 Hispanic/Latino; 18 Two or more races, non-Hispanic/Latino), 27 international. Average age 37. 333 applicants, 56% accepted, 149 enrolled. In 2016, 66 master's, 8 doctorates awarded. *Degree requirements:* For master's, one foreign language, comprehensive exam, thesis (for some programs); for doctorate, one foreign language, comprehensive exam, thesis/dissertation, departmental qualifying exam. *Entrance requirements:* For master's and doctorate, GRE General Test. Additional exam requirements/recommendations for international students: Required—TOEFL (minimum score 550 paper-based; 79 iBT), IELTS (minimum score 6). *Application deadline:* Applications are processed on a rolling basis. Application fee: $50. Electronic applications accepted. *Expenses:* Contact institution. *Financial support:* In 2016–17, 255 students received support, including 9 research assistantships with partial tuition reimbursements available (averaging $9,000 per year), 68 teaching assistantships with partial tuition reimbursements available (averaging $9,000 per year); Federal Work-Study, institutionally sponsored loans, scholarships/grants, health care benefits, and unspecified assistantships also available. Financial award application deadline: 5/1; financial award applicants required to submit FAFSA. *Unit head:* Dr. Salvatore Attardo, Dean, 903-886-5166, Fax: 903-886-5774, E-mail: salvatore.attardo@tamuc.edu. *Application contact:* Shelby Miller, Graduate Recruiter, 903-468-8123, Fax: 903-886-5774, E-mail: shelby.miller@tamuc.edu.
Website: http://www.tamuc.edu/academics/graduateSchool/programs/humanitiesSocialScienceArts/default.aspx

**Texas A&M University–Kingsville,** College of Graduate Studies, College of Arts and Sciences, Department of Psychology and Sociology, Program in Criminology, Kingsville, TX 78363. Offers MS. *Entrance requirements:* Additional exam requirements/recommendations for international students: Required—TOEFL (minimum score 550 paper-based; 79 iBT); Recommended—IELTS. Electronic applications accepted.

**Texas Christian University,** AddRan College of Liberal Arts, Department of Criminal Justice, Fort Worth, TX 76129. Offers criminal justice and criminology (MS). *Program availability:* Online only, 100% online. *Faculty:* 5 full-time (2 women). *Students:* 29 full-time (17 women); includes 13 minority (3 Black or African American, non-Hispanic/Latino; 9 Hispanic/Latino; 1 Native Hawaiian or other Pacific Islander, non-Hispanic/Latino). Average age 33. 16 applicants, 100% accepted, 15 enrolled. In 2016, 12 master's awarded. *Degree requirements:* For master's, thesis optional. *Entrance requirements:* Additional exam requirements/recommendations for international students: Recommended—TOEFL. *Application deadline:* For fall admission, 4/1 for domestic and international students. Applications are processed on a rolling basis. Application fee: $60. Electronic applications accepted. *Expenses:* $890 per credit hour; $112 fee per online course. *Financial support:* In 2016–17, 9 students received support. Scholarships/grants available. Financial award application deadline: 5/1; financial award applicants required to submit FAFSA. *Faculty research:* Cybercrime, sex offenders, prisoner reentry, criminological theory, policing. *Unit head:* Johnny Nhan, Director/Associate Professor, 626-391-3871, E-mail: j.nhan@tcu.edu. *Application contact:* Pam Carlisle, Administrative Assistant, 817-257-5846, Fax: 817-257-7737, E-mail: p.carlisle@tcu.edu.
Website: http://cj.tcu.edu

**Texas Southern University,** School of Public Affairs, Program in Administration of Justice, Houston, TX 77004-4584. Offers MS, PhD. Electronic applications accepted.

**Texas State University,** The Graduate College, College of Applied Arts, Program in Criminal Justice, San Marcos, TX 78666. Offers MSCJ, PhD. *Program availability:* Part-time, evening/weekend. *Faculty:* 15 full-time (34 women), 35 part-time (15 women); includes 31 minority (7 Black or African American, non-Hispanic/Latino; 1 Asian, non-Hispanic/Latino; 22 Hispanic/Latino; 1 Two or more races, non-Hispanic/Latino), 3 international. Average age 31. 64 applicants, 64% accepted, 21 enrolled. In 2016, 18 master's, 5 doctorates awarded. *Degree requirements:* For master's, comprehensive exam, thesis (for some programs); for doctorate, comprehensive exam, thesis/dissertation. *Entrance requirements:* For master's, GRE, baccalaureate degree in criminal justice or closely-related field from regionally-accredited university with minimum GPA of 3.0 in last 60 hours of course work; for doctorate, GRE (minimum preferred score of 300 with no less than 150 on the verbal section and 150 on the quantitative section), baccalaureate and master's degrees from regionally-accredited university in criminal justice or related field with minimum GPA of 3.5 in graduate courses; 3 letters of recommendation indicating skills and capacity to be successful in a PhD program; statement of personal history and life goals. Additional exam requirements/recommendations for international students: Required—TOEFL (minimum score 550 paper-based; 78 iBT). *Application deadline:* For fall admission, 2/15 priority date for domestic and international students; for spring admission, 8/15 priority date for domestic and international students. Applications are processed on a rolling basis. Application fee: $40 ($90 for international students). Electronic applications accepted. *Expenses:* $9,702 per year. *Financial support:* In 2016–17, 63 students received support, including 5 research assistantships (averaging $25,980 per year), 17 teaching assistantships (averaging $22,900 per year); Federal Work-Study, institutionally sponsored loans, scholarships/grants, and unspecified

assistantships also available. Support available to part-time students. Financial award application deadline: 4/1; financial award applicants required to submit FAFSA. *Faculty research:* Offender decision making, preventing violence against law enforcement, case deconstruction of criminal investigative failures. *Total annual research expenditures:* $1.9 million. *Unit head:* Dr. Mark Stafford, Doctoral Program Director, 512-245-2174, Fax: 512-245-8063, E-mail: ms75@txstate.edu. *Application contact:* Dr. Andrea Golato, Dean of the Graduate College, 512-245-2581, Fax: 512-245-8365, E-mail: gradcollege@txstate.edu.
Website: http://www.cj.txstate.edu/

**Texas State University,** The Graduate College, College of Liberal Arts, Program in Public Administration, San Marcos, TX 78666. Offers international relations (MPA); legal and judicial administration (MPA). *Accreditation:* NASPAA. *Program availability:* Part-time, evening/weekend. *Faculty:* 9 full-time (4 women). *Students:* 36 full-time (14 women), 59 part-time (29 women); includes 53 minority (15 Black or African American, non-Hispanic/Latino; 4 Asian, non-Hispanic/Latino; 32 Hispanic/Latino; 2 Two or more races, non-Hispanic/Latino), 1 international. Average age 31. 41 applicants, 78% accepted, 19 enrolled. In 2016, 22 master's awarded. *Degree requirements:* For master's, comprehensive exam, applied research project. *Entrance requirements:* For master's, baccalaureate degree from regionally-accredited university with minimum GPA of 3.0 on last 60 undergraduate semester hours. Additional exam requirements/recommendations for international students: Required—TOEFL (minimum score 550 paper-based; 78 iBT), IELTS (minimum score 6.5). *Application deadline:* For fall admission, 2/1 priority date for domestic and international students; for spring admission, 10/15 for domestic students, 10/1 for international students; for summer admission, 4/15 for domestic students, 3/15 for international students. Applications are processed on a rolling basis. Application fee: $40 ($90 for international students). Electronic applications accepted. *Expenses:* $4,851 per semester. *Financial support:* In 2016–17, 53 students received support, including 4 research assistantships (averaging $13,336 per year), 10 teaching assistantships (averaging $13,718 per year); career-related internships or fieldwork, Federal Work-Study, institutionally sponsored loans, scholarships/grants, and unspecified assistantships also available. Support available to part-time students. Financial award application deadline: 3/1; financial award applicants required to submit FAFSA. *Unit head:* Dr. Patricia Shields, Graduate Advisor, 512-245-3256, Fax: 512-245-7815, E-mail: ps07@txstate.edu. *Application contact:* Dr. Andrea Golato, Dean of Graduate School, 512-245-2581, Fax: 512-245-8365, E-mail: gradcollege@txstate.edu.
Website: http://www.polisci.txstate.edu/degrees-programs/graduate/MPA.html

**Tiffin University,** Program in Criminal Justice, Tiffin, OH 44883-2161. Offers criminal justice (MS), including crime analysis, criminal behavior, forensic psychology, homeland security administration, justice administration. *Program availability:* Part-time, evening/weekend, 100% online, blended/hybrid learning. *Students:* 83 full-time (61 women), 191 part-time (109 women); includes 85 minority (71 Black or African American, non-Hispanic/Latino; 6 Hispanic/Latino; 1 Native Hawaiian or other Pacific Islander, non-Hispanic/Latino; 7 Two or more races, non-Hispanic/Latino), 6 international. Average age 31. In 2016, 59 master's awarded. *Degree requirements:* For master's, thesis optional. *Entrance requirements:* For master's, minimum undergraduate GPA of 2.5, work experience. Additional exam requirements/recommendations for international students: Required—TOEFL (minimum score 550 paper-based; 79 iBT). *Application deadline:* For fall admission, 9/3 for domestic students, 8/1 for international students; for spring admission, 1/9 priority date for domestic students, 12/1 for international students. Applications are processed on a rolling basis. Application fee: $50. Electronic applications accepted. *Expenses:* Contact institution. *Financial support:* Available to part-time students. Application deadline: 7/31; applicants required to submit FAFSA. *Faculty research:* Terrorism, intelligence, homeland security, guns and crime. *Unit head:* Dr. Kevin Cashen, Dean of Criminal Justice and Security Studies, 419-448-3322, Fax: 419-443-5002, E-mail: cashenk@tiffin.edu. *Application contact:* Nikki Hintze, Director of Graduate and Distance Education Academic Advising, 800-968-6446 Ext. 3596, Fax: 419-443-5002, E-mail: hintzenm@tiffin.edu.
Website: http://www.tiffin.edu

**Trident University International,** College of Business Administration, Program in Business Administration, Cypress, CA 90630. Offers business administration (PhD); conflict and negotiation management (MBA); criminal justice administration (MBA); entrepreneurship (MBA); finance (MBA); general management (MBA); government accounting (MBA); human resource management (MBA); information security and digital assurance management (MBA); information technology management (MBA); international business (MBA); logistics management (MBA); marketing (MBA); project management (MBA); public management (MBA); quality management (MBA); strategic leadership (MBA). *Program availability:* Part-time, evening/weekend, online learning. *Degree requirements:* For doctorate, comprehensive exam, thesis/dissertation, defense of dissertation. *Entrance requirements:* For master's, minimum GPA of 2.5 (students with GPA 3.0 or greater may transfer up to 30% of graduate level credits); for doctorate, minimum GPA of 3.4, curriculum vitae, course work in research methods or statistics. Additional exam requirements/recommendations for international students: Required—TOEFL. Electronic applications accepted.

**Trine University,** Program in Criminal Justice, Angola, IN 46703-1764. Offers emergency management (MS); forensic psychology (MS); law (MS); public administration (MS). *Program availability:* Part-time, evening/weekend. *Entrance requirements:* Additional exam requirements/recommendations for international students: Required—TOEFL. *Expenses: Tuition:* Full-time $13,320. *Required fees:* $460. Tuition and fees vary according to degree level, campus/location, program and student level. *Financial support:* Application deadline: 3/1; applicants required to submit FAFSA. *Unit head:* Craig Laker, Dean, College of Graduate and Professional Studies/Associate Professor, 260-665-4862, E-mail: lakerc@trine.edu.
Website: http://www.trine.edu/academics/majors-and-minors/graduate/criminal-justice/index.aspx

**Troy University,** Graduate School, College of Arts and Sciences, Program in Criminal Justice, Troy, AL 36082. Offers MS. *Program availability:* Part-time, evening/weekend. *Faculty:* 7 full-time (2 women), 9 part-time/adjunct (4 women). *Students:* 32 full-time (18 women), 124 part-time (75 women); includes 73 minority (61 Black or African American, non-Hispanic/Latino; 1 American Indian or Alaska Native, non-Hispanic/Latino; 8 Hispanic/Latino; 3 Two or more races, non-Hispanic/Latino). Average age 35. 104 applicants, 97% accepted, 11 enrolled. In 2016, 136 master's awarded. *Degree requirements:* For master's, comprehensive exam, research course, minimum GPA of 3.0, admission to candidacy. *Entrance requirements:* For master's, GRE (minimum score of 850 on old exam or 290 on new exam), MAT (minimum score of 385) or GMAT (minimum score of 380), bachelor's degree; minimum undergraduate GPA of 2.5 or 3.0 on last 30 semester hours. Additional exam requirements/recommendations for international students: Required—TOEFL (minimum score 523 paper-based; 70 iBT), IELTS (minimum score 6). *Application deadline:* Applications are processed on a rolling basis. Application fee: $50. Electronic applications accepted. *Expenses: Tuition,* state resident: full-time $7146; part-time $397 per credit hour. *Tuition,* nonresident: full-time $14,292; part-time $794 per credit hour. *Required fees:* $802; $50 per semester. Tuition and fees vary according to campus/location and program. *Financial support:*

Fellowships, career-related internships or fieldwork, and scholarships/grants available. Support available to part-time students. Financial award applicants required to submit FAFSA. *Faculty research:* Crime victims, criminal justice personnel issues, disability issues in criminal justice. *Unit head:* Dr. Xiaoli Su, Assistant Chairman, Department of Criminal Justice, 334-808-6571, Fax: 334-808-6487, E-mail: xiaolisiu@troy.edu. *Application contact:* Jessica A. Kimbro, Director of Graduate Admissions, 334-670-3178, E-mail: jacord@troy.edu.

**Troy University,** Graduate School, College of Business, Program in Business Administration, Troy, AL 36082. Offers accounting (EMBA, MBA); criminal justice (EMBA); finance (MBA); general management (EMBA, MBA); healthcare management (EMBA); information systems (EMBA, MBA); international economic development (MBA). *Accreditation:* ACBSP. *Program availability:* Part-time, evening/weekend. *Faculty:* 10 full-time (3 women), 2 part-time/adjunct (0 women). *Students:* 44 full-time (23 women), 131 part-time (69 women); includes 58 minority (38 Black or African American, non-Hispanic/Latino; 13 Asian, non-Hispanic/Latino; 4 Hispanic/Latino; 3 Two or more races, non-Hispanic/Latino). Average age 30. 285 applicants, 91% accepted, 22 enrolled. In 2016, 78 master's awarded. *Degree requirements:* For master's, minimum GPA of 3.0, capstone course, research course. *Entrance requirements:* For master's, GMAT (minimum score 500) or GRE (minimum score 900 on old exam or 294 on new exam), bachelor's degree; minimum undergraduate GPA of 2.5 or 3.0 on last 30 semester hours, letter of recommendation. Additional exam requirements/recommendations for international students: Required—TOEFL (minimum score 523 paper-based; 70 iBT), IELTS (minimum score 6). *Application deadline:* Applications are processed on a rolling basis. Application fee: $50. Electronic applications accepted. *Expenses:* Tuition, state resident: full-time $7146; part-time $397 per credit hour. Tuition, nonresident: full-time $14,292; part-time $794 per credit hour. *Required fees:* $802; $50 per semester. Tuition and fees vary according to campus/location and program. *Financial support:* Fellowships, career-related internships or fieldwork, and scholarships/grants available. Support available to part-time students. Financial award applicants required to submit FAFSA. *Unit head:* Dr. Phillip Mixon, MBA Director, 334-670-3140, Fax: 334-670-3708, E-mail: pamixon@troy.edu. *Application contact:* Jessica A. Kimbro, Director of Graduate Admissions, 334-670-3178, E-mail: jacord@troy.edu.

**Universidad del Este,** Graduate School, Carolina, PR 00984. Offers accounting (MBA); adult education (M Ed); agribusiness (MBA); criminal justice and criminology (MA); curriculum and instruction - early education (M Ed); curriculum and instruction - elementary (M Ed); curriculum and instruction - English (M Ed); curriculum and instruction - Spanish (M Ed); human resources (MBA); information security management (MBA); information technology and Web business development (MBA); management (MBA); public policy (MPA); social work (MA), including clinical social work; special education (M Ed); strategic leadership (MBA).

**Universidad del Turabo,** Graduate Programs, School of Social Sciences and Humanities, Programs in Public Affairs, Program in Criminal Justice Studies, Gurabo, PR 00778-3030. Offers MPA. *Students:* 21 full-time (7 women), 11 part-time (10 women); all minorities (all Hispanic/Latino). Average age 32. 25 applicants, 40% accepted, 9 enrolled. In 2016, 4 master's awarded. *Entrance requirements:* For master's, GRE, EXADEP or GMAT, interview, essay, official transcript, recommendation letters. *Application deadline:* For fall admission, 8/5 for domestic students. Applications are processed on a rolling basis. Application fee: $25. Electronic applications accepted. *Financial support:* Institutionally sponsored loans available. Financial award applicants required to submit FAFSA. *Unit head:* María del Carmen Santos, Dean, 787-743-7979 Ext. 4232. *Application contact:* Diriee Rodríguez, Admissions Director, 787-743-7979 Ext. 4453, E-mail: admisiones-ut@suagm.edu. Website: http://ut.suagm.edu/es/sociales

**Université de Montréal,** Faculty of Arts and Sciences, School of Criminology, Montréal, QC H3C 3J7, Canada. Offers M Sc, PhD. Terminal master's awarded for partial completion of doctoral program. *Degree requirements:* For master's, thesis; for doctorate, thesis/dissertation, general exam. *Entrance requirements:* For master's, B Sc in criminology or the equivalent; for doctorate, M Sc in criminology or equivalent. Electronic applications accepted. *Faculty research:* Criminal behavior, criminality, prison population, victims of crime, female offenders.

**University at Albany, State University of New York,** School of Criminal Justice, Albany, NY 12222-0001. Offers MA, PhD, MSW/MA. *Program availability:* Part-time. *Faculty:* 10 full-time (4 women), 6 part-time/adjunct (5 women). *Students:* 73 full-time (48 women), 37 part-time (22 women); includes 45 minority (19 Black or African American, non-Hispanic/Latino; 1 Asian, non-Hispanic/Latino; 22 Hispanic/Latino; 3 Two or more races, non-Hispanic/Latino), 8 international. 114 applicants, 64% accepted, 25 enrolled. In 2016, 32 master's, 5 doctorates awarded. *Degree requirements:* For doctorate, thesis/dissertation. *Entrance requirements:* For master's and doctorate, GRE General Test. Additional exam requirements/recommendations for international students: Required—TOEFL (minimum score 550 paper-based). *Application deadline:* For fall admission, 7/1 for domestic students, 5/1 for international students. Applications are processed on a rolling basis. Application fee: $75. Electronic applications accepted. *Expenses:* Tuition, state resident: full-time $10,870; part-time $453 per credit hour. Tuition, nonresident: full-time $22,210; part-time $925 per credit hour. *International tuition:* $21,550 full-time. *Required fees:* $1864; $96 per credit hour. *Financial support:* Fellowships, research assistantships, teaching assistantships, career-related internships or fieldwork, Federal Work-Study, and institutionally sponsored loans available. Financial award application deadline: 4/1. *Faculty research:* Causes of delinquency, comparative policing, world crime data, correctional policy, family violence. *Total annual research expenditures:* $916,371. *Unit head:* Alan Lizotte, Dean, 518-442-5214, E-mail: alizotte@albany.edu. *Application contact:* Michael DeRensis, Director, Graduate Admissions, 518-442-3980, Fax: 518-442-3922, E-mail: graduate@albany.edu.

**The University of Alabama,** Graduate School, College of Arts and Sciences, Department of Criminal Justice, Tuscaloosa, AL 35487. Offers MS. *Program availability:* Part-time. *Faculty:* 13 full-time (6 women). *Students:* 20 full-time (13 women), 6 part-time (3 women); includes 7 minority (3 Black or African American, non-Hispanic/Latino; 4 Hispanic/Latino). Average age 26. 25 applicants, 40% accepted, 7 enrolled. In 2016, 7 master's awarded. *Degree requirements:* For master's, comprehensive exam (for some programs), thesis (for some programs), thesis or comprehensive exam. *Entrance requirements:* For master's, GRE. Additional exam requirements/recommendations for international students: Recommended—TOEFL. *Application deadline:* For fall admission, 6/15 for domestic and international students; for winter admission, 11/1 for domestic and international students; for spring admission, 11/15 for domestic and international students. Applications are processed on a rolling basis. Application fee: $50 ($60 for international students). Electronic applications accepted. *Expenses:* Tuition, state resident: full-time $10,470. Tuition, nonresident: full-time $26,950. *Financial support:* In 2016–17, 25 teaching assistantships with partial tuition reimbursements (averaging $6,570 per year) were awarded; fellowships, health care benefits, and unspecified assistantships also available. Financial award application deadline: 6/15. *Faculty research:* Social deviance, sociology of HIV/AIDS, terrorism, cyber crime, juvenile delinquency. *Total annual research expenditures:* $3,049. *Unit head:* Dr. Lesley W. Reid, Department Chair, 205-348-7795, Fax: 205-348-7795, E-mail:

lwreid@ua.edu. *Application contact:* Dr. Adam Lankford, Associate Professor and Director of Graduate Studies, 205-348-9901, Fax: 205-348-9901, E-mail: adam.lankford@ua.edu. Website: http://cj.ua.edu

**The University of Alabama at Birmingham,** College of Arts and Sciences, Program in Criminal Justice, Birmingham, AL 35294. Offers MSCJ. *Program availability:* Part-time, evening/weekend. *Faculty:* 7 full-time (3 women). *Students:* 10 full-time (3 women), 1 part-time (0 women); includes 7 minority (all Black or African American, non-Hispanic/Latino). Average age 30. 8 applicants, 100% accepted, 5 enrolled. In 2016, 3 master's awarded. *Degree requirements:* For master's, thesis or demonstration project that shows proficiency in the subject. *Entrance requirements:* Additional exam requirements/recommendations for international students: Required—TOEFL, TWE. *Application deadline:* For fall admission, 7/1 for domestic and international students; for spring admission, 11/1 for domestic and international students. Application fee: $45 ($60 for international students). Electronic applications accepted. *Expenses:* Contact institution. *Financial support:* In 2016–17, 1 student received support, including 1 research assistantship (averaging $14,280 per year), 1 teaching assistantship (averaging $14,280 per year); career-related internships or fieldwork and scholarships/grants also available. Financial award application deadline: 7/1; financial award applicants required to submit FAFSA. *Faculty research:* Criminology, corrections, police, research methods. *Unit head:* Dr. Heith Copes, Director of Graduate Studies in Criminal Justice, 205-934-2069, Fax: 205-934-2067, E-mail: jhcopes@uab.edu. *Application contact:* Susan Noblitt Banks, Director of Graduate School Operations, 205-934-8227, Fax: 205-934-8413, E-mail: gradschool@uab.edu. Website: http://www.uab.edu/cas/justice-sciences/graduate-programs/master-of-science-in-criminal-justice-mscj

**University of Alaska Fairbanks,** College of Liberal Arts, Department of Justice, Fairbanks, AK 99775-6120. Offers MA. *Program availability:* Part-time, online only, 100% online. *Faculty:* 4 full-time (0 women). *Students:* 15 part-time (9 women); includes 2 minority (1 Black or African American, non-Hispanic/Latino; 1 Hispanic/Latino). Average age 39. 10 applicants, 80% accepted, 8 enrolled. In 2016, 5 master's awarded. *Degree requirements:* For master's, comprehensive exam, oral defense of project or thesis. *Entrance requirements:* For master's, bachelor's degree from accredited institution with minimum cumulative undergraduate and major GPA of 3.0. Additional exam requirements/recommendations for international students: Required—TOEFL (minimum score 550 paper-based; 79 iBT), IELTS (minimum score 6.5). *Application deadline:* For fall admission, 6/1 for domestic students, 3/1 for international students; for spring admission, 10/15 for domestic students, 9/1 for international students. Applications are processed on a rolling basis. Application fee: $60. Electronic applications accepted. *Expenses:* Tuition, state resident: full-time $7992; part-time $444 per credit. Tuition, nonresident: full-time $16,326; part-time $907 per credit. *Required fees:* $39 per credit. $322 per semester. Tuition and fees vary according to course level, course load, campus/location, program and reciprocity agreements. *Financial support:* Federal Work-Study, scholarships/grants, and health care benefits available. Support available to part-time students. Financial award application deadline: 7/1; financial award applicants required to submit FAFSA. *Unit head:* Micheal Daku, Department Chair, 907-474-5500, Fax: 907-474-6510, E-mail: fyjust@uaf.edu. *Application contact:* Mary Kreta, Director of Admissions, 907-474-7500, Fax: 907-474-7097, E-mail: admissions@uaf.edu. Website: http://www.uaf.edu/justice/

**University of Alberta,** Faculty of Graduate Studies and Research, Department of Sociology, Edmonton, AB T6G 2E1, Canada. Offers criminal justice (MA); demography (MA, PhD); sociology (MA, PhD). *Program availability:* Part-time. *Degree requirements:* For master's, thesis (for some programs); for doctorate, thesis/dissertation. *Faculty research:* Criminology, knowledge and culture, methods and theory, population studies, stratification.

**University of Antelope Valley,** Program in Criminal Justice, Lancaster, CA 93534. Offers MS. *Degree requirements:* For master's, capstone project. *Entrance requirements:* For master's, official transcripts documenting earned bachelor's degree from nationally- or regionally-accredited institution with minimum cumulative GPA of 2.0.

**University of Arkansas at Little Rock,** Graduate School, College of Social Sciences and Communication, Department of Criminal Justice, Little Rock, AR 72204-1099. Offers MA, MS, PhD. MS program is offered by distance education. *Program availability:* Part-time, evening/weekend. *Degree requirements:* For master's, thesis defense or written comprehensive exam; for doctorate, thesis/dissertation. *Entrance requirements:* For master's, GRE General Test or MAT, interview, minimum GPA of 2.75. Additional exam requirements/recommendations for international students: Required—TOEFL (minimum score 550 paper-based; 79 iBT). *Faculty research:* Dissemination and analysis of behavioral science knowledge, leadership and managerial skills, philosophy of individual rights and humane treatment.

**University of Baltimore,** Graduate School, College of Public Affairs, Program in Criminal Justice, Baltimore, MD 21201-5779. Offers MS, JD/MS. *Program availability:* Part-time, evening/weekend. *Degree requirements:* For master's, thesis or alternative. *Entrance requirements:* For master's, interview, minimum GPA of 2.8. Additional exam requirements/recommendations for international students: Required—TOEFL (minimum score 550 paper-based). Electronic applications accepted. *Faculty research:* Drugs and violence, police and community policing, women and crime, victimization, correction in community.

**University of California, Irvine,** School of Social Ecology, Department of Criminology, Law and Society, Irvine, CA 92697. Offers MAS, PhD. *Students:* 115 full-time (77 women), 51 part-time (31 women); includes 71 minority (10 Black or African American, non-Hispanic/Latino; 1 American Indian or Alaska Native, non-Hispanic/Latino; 16 Asian, non-Hispanic/Latino; 36 Hispanic/Latino; 8 Two or more races, non-Hispanic/Latino), 25 international. Average age 29. 153 applicants, 68% accepted, 64 enrolled. In 2016, 49 master's, 10 doctorates awarded. *Degree requirements:* For doctorate, thesis/dissertation, research project. *Entrance requirements:* For master's and doctorate, GRE General Test, minimum GPA of 3.0. Additional exam requirements/recommendations for international students: Required—TOEFL (minimum score 550 paper-based). *Application deadline:* For fall admission, 1/15 priority date for domestic and international students. Application fee: $105 ($125 for international students). Electronic applications accepted. *Financial support:* Fellowships, research assistantships with full tuition reimbursements, teaching assistantships, institutionally sponsored loans, traineeships, health care benefits, and unspecified assistantships available. Financial award application deadline: 3/1; financial award applicants required to submit FAFSA. *Faculty research:* White-collar and corporate crime; immigration, the poor, homelessness, and governmental regulation; sentencing, community corrections, and diversion; mathematical and scientific evidence in jury trials; legal and criminological theory development. *Unit head:* Prof. Cheryl Maxon, Department Chair, 949-824-5150, E-mail: cmaxson@uci.edu. *Application contact:* Leslie Noel, Graduate Coordinator, 949-824-1442, Fax: 949-824-3001, E-mail: lknoel@uci.edu. Website: http://cls.soceco.uci.edu/

*Criminal Justice and Criminology*

**University of Central Florida,** College of Health and Public Affairs, Department of Criminal Justice and Legal Studies, Orlando, FL 32816. Offers corrections leadership (Certificate); criminal justice (MS, PhD); juvenile justice leadership (Certificate); police leadership (Certificate). *Program availability:* Part-time, evening/weekend. *Faculty:* 30 full-time (12 women), 13 part-time/adjunct (4 women). *Students:* 88 full-time (57 women), 138 part-time (82 women); includes 95 minority (44 Black or African American, non-Hispanic/Latino; 6 Asian, non-Hispanic/Latino; 40 Hispanic/Latino; 1 Native Hawaiian or other Pacific Islander, non-Hispanic/Latino; 4 Two or more races, non-Hispanic/Latino), 1 international. Average age 31. 184 applicants, 74% accepted, 91 enrolled. In 2016, 69 master's, 25 other advanced degrees awarded. *Degree requirements:* For master's, thesis or alternative. *Entrance requirements:* For master's, minimum GPA of 3.0. Additional exam requirements/recommendations for international students: Required—TOEFL. *Application deadline:* For fall admission, 7/15 for domestic students; for spring admission, 12/1 for domestic students. Application fee: $30. Electronic applications accepted. *Expenses:* Tuition, state resident: part-time $288.16 per credit hour. Tuition, nonresident: part-time $1071.31 per credit hour. *Financial support:* In 2016–17, 17 students received support, including 4 fellowships with partial tuition reimbursements available (averaging $7,250 per year), 11 research assistantships with partial tuition reimbursements available (averaging $11,726 per year), 8 teaching assistantships with partial tuition reimbursements available (averaging $7,441 per year); career-related internships or fieldwork, Federal Work-Study, institutionally sponsored loans, tuition waivers (partial), and unspecified assistantships also available. Financial award application deadline: 3/1; financial award applicants required to submit FAFSA. *Unit head:* Dr. Catherine Kaukinen, Chair, 407-823-2603, E-mail: catherine.kaukinen@ucf.edu. *Application contact:* Assistant Director, Graduate Admissions, 407-823-2766, Fax: 407-823-6442, E-mail: gradadmissions@ucf.edu. Website: https://www2.cohpa.ucf.edu/criminaljustice/

**University of Central Missouri,** The Graduate School, Warrensburg, MO 64093. Offers accountancy (MA); accounting (MBA); applied mathematics (MS); aviation safety (MA); biology (MS); business administration (MBA); career and technical education leadership (MS); college student personnel administration (MS); communication (MA); computer science (MS); counseling (MS); criminal justice (MS); educational leadership (Ed D); educational technology (MS); elementary and early childhood education (MSE); English (MA); environmental studies (MA); finance (MBA); history (MA); human services/educational technology (Ed S); human services/learning resources (Ed S); human services/professional counseling (Ed S); industrial hygiene (MS); industrial management (MS); information systems (MBA); information technology (MS); kinesiology (MS); library science and information services (MS); literacy education (MSE); marketing (MBA); mathematics (MS); music (MA); occupational safety management (MS); psychology (MS); rural family nursing (MS); school administration (MSE); social gerontology (MS); sociology (MA); special education (MSE); speech language pathology (MS); superintendency (Ed S); teaching (MAT); teaching English as a second language (MA); technology (MS); technology management (PhD); theatre (MA). *Program availability:* Part-time, 100% online, blended/hybrid learning. *Degree requirements:* For master's and Ed S, comprehensive exam (for some programs), thesis (for some programs). *Entrance requirements:* Additional exam requirements/recommendations for international students: Required—TOEFL (minimum score 550 paper-based; 79 iBT). Electronic applications accepted.

**University of Central Oklahoma,** The Jackson College of Graduate Studies, College of Liberal Arts, School of Criminal Justice, Edmond, OK 73034-5209. Offers crime and intelligence analysis (MA); criminal justice management and administration (MA). *Program availability:* Part-time. *Entrance requirements:* Additional exam requirements/recommendations for international students: Required—TOEFL (minimum score 550 paper-based; 79 iBT), IELTS (minimum score 6.5). Electronic applications accepted. *Faculty research:* Gender issues, violent offenders.

**University of Cincinnati,** Graduate School, College of Education, Criminal Justice, and Human Services, School of Criminal Justice, Cincinnati, OH 45221. Offers MS, PhD. *Program availability:* Part-time, online learning. *Degree requirements:* For master's, thesis or alternative; for doctorate, thesis/dissertation. *Entrance requirements:* For master's, GRE or MAT, minimum GPA of 3.0; for doctorate, minimum GPA of 3.5. Additional exam requirements/recommendations for international students: Required—TOEFL (minimum score 550 paper-based), OEPT 3. Electronic applications accepted. *Expenses:* Tuition, area resident: Full-time $12,790; part-time $389 per credit hour. Tuition, state resident: full-time $13,290; part-time $419 per credit hour. Tuition, nonresident: full-time $24,532; part-time $976 per credit hour. *International tuition:* $24,832 full-time. *Required fees:* $3958; $140 per credit hour. Tuition and fees vary according to course load, degree level, program and reciprocity agreements.

**University of Colorado Colorado Springs,** School of Public Affairs, Colorado Springs, CO 80918. Offers criminal justice (MCJ); public administration (MPA). *Accreditation:* NASPAA. *Program availability:* Part-time, evening/weekend, 100% online, blended/hybrid learning. *Faculty:* 11 full-time (4 women), 5 part-time/adjunct (3 women). *Students:* 22 full-time (12 women), 142 part-time (79 women); includes 44 minority (6 Black or African American, non-Hispanic/Latino; 1 American Indian or Alaska Native, non-Hispanic/Latino; 4 Asian, non-Hispanic/Latino; 25 Hispanic/Latino; 8 Two or more races, non-Hispanic/Latino). Average age 35. 62 applicants, 94% accepted, 44 enrolled. In 2016, 32 master's awarded. *Degree requirements:* For master's, internship, capstone project, or thesis. *Entrance requirements:* For master's, GRE General Test, GMAT, LSAT, minimum GPA of 3.0. Additional exam requirements/recommendations for international students: Recommended—TOEFL (minimum score 550 paper-based; 80 iBT), IELTS (minimum score 6.5). *Application deadline:* Applications are processed on a rolling basis. Application fee: $60 ($100 for international students). Electronic applications accepted. *Expenses:* Contact institution. *Financial support:* In 2016–17, 36 students received support. Career-related internships or fieldwork, scholarships/grants, and tuition waivers available. Support available to part-time students. Financial award application deadline: 3/1; financial award applicants required to submit FAFSA. *Faculty research:* Antiquated prison environments; public management; intersections of gender, class, race and crime; national security/U.S. foreign policy; leadership, ethics, organizational theory and behavior. *Total annual research expenditures:* $513,691. *Unit head:* Dr. George Reed, Dean, 719-255-4109, E-mail: george.reed@uccs.edu. *Application contact:* Crista Hill, Outreach Student Services Specialist, 719-255-4993, Fax: 719-255-4183, E-mail: chill12@uccs.edu. Website: http://www.uccs.edu/spa/

**University of Colorado Denver,** School of Public Affairs, Program in Criminology and Criminal Justice, Denver, CO 80217. Offers criminal justice (MCJ), including criminal justice, domestic violence, emergency management and homeland security. *Program availability:* Part-time, evening/weekend. *Students:* 23 full-time (15 women), 17 part-time (8 women); includes 5 minority (2 Black or African American, non-Hispanic/Latino; 1 Asian, non-Hispanic/Latino; 1 Hispanic/Latino; 1 Two or more races, non-Hispanic/Latino), 1 international. Average age 30. 13 applicants, 92% accepted, 7 enrolled. In 2016, 26 master's awarded. *Degree requirements:* For master's, thesis or alternative, 36-39 semester credit hours. *Entrance requirements:* For master's, GRE, GMAT, LSAT, recommendations, official transcripts, current resume, essay. Additional exam requirements/recommendations for international students: Required—TOEFL (minimum

score 537 paper-based; 75 iBT); Recommended—IELTS (minimum score 6.5). *Application deadline:* For fall admission, 3/15 priority date for domestic students, 3/1 priority date for international students; for spring admission, 10/15 priority date for domestic students, 10/1 priority date for international students. Application fee: $50 ($75 for international students). Electronic applications accepted. *Expenses:* Contact institution. *Financial support:* In 2016–17, 5 students received support. Fellowships, research assistantships, teaching assistantships, Federal Work-Study, institutionally sponsored loans, scholarships/grants, traineeships, and unspecified assistantships available. Financial award application deadline: 4/1; financial award applicants required to submit FAFSA. *Faculty research:* White collar crime, women and the criminal justice system, applied family violence issues, intimate partner violence and domestic violence interventions, juvenile delinquency. *Unit head:* Dr. Callie Rennison, Program Director, 303-315-2813, Fax: 303-315-2229, E-mail: callie.rennison@ucdenver.edu. *Application contact:* Brendan Hardy, Director of Student Recruitment, 303-315-2227, Fax: 303-315-2229, E-mail: brendan.hardy@ucdenver.edu. Website: http://ucdenver.edu/academics/colleges/SPA/Academics/programs/CriminalJustice/Pages/index.aspx

**University of Colorado Denver,** School of Public Affairs, Program in Public Affairs and Administration, Denver, CO 80127. Offers public administration (MPA), including domestic violence, emergency management and homeland security, environmental policy, management and law, homeland security and defense, local government, nonprofit management, public administration; public affairs (PhD). *Accreditation:* NASPAA. *Program availability:* Part-time, evening/weekend, online learning. *Students:* 241 full-time (146 women), 135 part-time (86 women); includes 61 minority (15 Black or African American, non-Hispanic/Latino; 1 American Indian or Alaska Native, non-Hispanic/Latino; 10 Asian, non-Hispanic/Latino; 26 Hispanic/Latino; 2 Native Hawaiian or other Pacific Islander, non-Hispanic/Latino; 7 Two or more races, non-Hispanic/Latino), 26 international. Average age 36. 240 applicants, 70% accepted, 91 enrolled. In 2016, 158 master's, 8 doctorates awarded. *Degree requirements:* For master's, thesis or alternative, 36-39 credit hours; for doctorate, comprehensive exam, thesis/dissertation, minimum of 66 semester hours, including at least 30 hours of dissertation. *Entrance requirements:* For master's, GRE, GMAT or LSAT, resume, essay, transcripts, recommendations; for doctorate, GRE, resume, essay, transcripts, recommendations. Additional exam requirements/recommendations for international students: Required—TOEFL (minimum score 550 paper-based; 80 iBT); Recommended—IELTS (minimum score 6.5). *Application deadline:* For fall admission, 2/1 priority date for domestic students, 1/15 priority date for international students; for spring admission, 10/15 priority date for domestic students, 10/1 priority date for international students. Application fee: $50 ($75 for international students). Electronic applications accepted. *Expenses:* Contact institution. *Financial support:* In 2016–17, 92 students received support. Fellowships with partial tuition reimbursements available, research assistantships with partial tuition reimbursements available, teaching assistantships with partial tuition reimbursements available, Federal Work-Study, institutionally sponsored loans, scholarships/grants, traineeships, and unspecified assistantships available. Financial award application deadline: 4/1; financial award applicants required to submit FAFSA. *Faculty research:* Housing, education and the social and economic issues of vulnerable populations; nonprofit governance and management; education finance, effectiveness and reform; P-20 education initiatives; municipal government accountability. *Unit head:* Dr. Christine Martell, Director of MPA Program, 303-315-2716, Fax: 303-315-2229, E-mail: christine.martell@ucdenver.edu. *Application contact:* Dawn Savage, Student Services Coordinator, 303-315-2743, Fax: 303-315-2229, E-mail: dawn.savage@ucdenver.edu. Website: http://www.ucdenver.edu/academics/colleges/SPA/Academics/programs/PublicAffairsAdmin/Pages/index.aspx

**University of Delaware,** College of Arts and Sciences, Department of Sociology and Criminal Justice, Newark, DE 19716. Offers criminology (MA, PhD); sociology (MA, PhD). *Degree requirements:* For master's, thesis; for doctorate, comprehensive exam, thesis/dissertation. *Entrance requirements:* For master's and doctorate, GRE, 3 letters of recommendation. Additional exam requirements/recommendations for international students: Required—TOEFL. Electronic applications accepted. *Faculty research:* Sex and gender, criminology/deviance, theory, methods, collective behavior.

**University of Denver,** University College, Denver, CO 80208. Offers arts and culture (MA, Certificate); communication management (MS, Certificate), including translation studies (Certificate); world history and culture (Certificate); environmental policy and management (MS); geographic information systems (MS); global affairs (MA, Certificate), including human capital in organizations (Certificate), philanthropic leadership (Certificate), project management (Certificate), strategic innovation and change (Certificate); healthcare leadership (MS); information communications and technology (MS); leadership and organizations (MS); professional creative writing (MA, Certificate), including emergency planning and response (Certificate), organizational security (Certificate); security management (MS, Certificate); strategic human resources (Certificate). *Program availability:* Part-time, evening/weekend, online learning. *Faculty:* 118 part-time/adjunct (62 women). *Students:* 59 full-time (22 women), 1,285 part-time (750 women); includes 316 minority (111 Black or African American, non-Hispanic/Latino; 8 American Indian or Alaska Native, non-Hispanic/Latino; 39 Asian, non-Hispanic/Latino; 123 Hispanic/Latino; 3 Native Hawaiian or other Pacific Islander, non-Hispanic/Latino; 32 Two or more races, non-Hispanic/Latino), 85 international. Average age 35. 703 applicants, 89% accepted, 390 enrolled. In 2016, 428 master's, 138 other advanced degrees awarded. *Degree requirements:* For master's, capstone project. *Entrance requirements:* For master's, transcripts, two letters of recommendation, personal statement, resume. Additional exam requirements/recommendations for international students: Required—TOEFL (minimum score 550 paper-based; 80 iBT). *Application deadline:* For fall admission, 6/21 priority date for domestic students, 5/1 priority date for international students; for winter admission, 9/14 priority date for domestic students, 9/19 priority date for international students; for spring admission, 1/11 priority date for domestic students, 12/12 priority date for international students; for summer admission, 3/29 priority date for domestic students, 3/6 priority date for international students. Applications are processed on a rolling basis. Application fee: $75. Electronic applications accepted. *Expenses:* $7,236 per year full-time. *Financial support:* In 2016–17, 27 students received support, including 1 teaching assistantship (averaging $1,489 per year). Financial award applicants required to submit FAFSA. *Unit head:* Dr. Michael McGuire, Dean, 303-871-3518, Fax: 303-871-3303, E-mail: mmcguire@du.edu. *Application contact:* Information Contact, 303-871-2291, E-mail: ucoladm@du.edu. Website: http://universitycollege.du.edu/

**University of Detroit Mercy,** College of Liberal Arts and Education, Detroit, MI 48221. Offers addiction counseling (MA); addiction studies (Certificate); clinical mental health counseling (MA); clinical psychology (MA, PhD); computer and information systems (MS); criminal justice (MA); curriculum and instruction (MA); economics (MA); educational administration (MA); financial economics (MA); industrial/organizational psychology (MA); information assurance (MS); intelligence analysis (MA); liberal studies (MALS); religious studies (MA); school counseling (MA, Certificate); school psychology (Spec); security administration (MS); special education: emotionally impaired/behaviorally disordered (MA); special education: learning disabilities (MA). *Program* *availability:* Part-time, evening/weekend. *Degree requirements:* For doctorate, departmental qualifying exam. *Faculty research:* Psychology of aging, history of technology, Renaissance humanism, U.S. and Japanese economic relations.

**University of Florida,** Graduate School, College of Liberal Arts and Sciences, Department of Sociology and Criminology and Law, Gainesville, FL 32611. Offers criminology, law, and society (MA, PhD); sociology (MA, PhD), including sociology, tropical conservation and development, women's and gender studies (PhD); MA/JD. *Program availability:* Part-time. Terminal master's awarded for partial completion of doctoral program. *Degree requirements:* For master's, thesis optional; for doctorate, comprehensive exam, thesis/dissertation. *Entrance requirements:* For master's and doctorate, GRE, minimum GPA of 3.0. Additional exam requirements/recommendations for international students: Required—TOEFL (minimum score 550 paper-based; 80 iBT), IELTS (minimum score 6). Electronic applications accepted. *Faculty research:* Law and society, juvenile justice, criminal investigation procedures, deviance, biosocial criminology, environmental sociology, comparative race and ethnic studies, health and aging, families and gender.

**University of Great Falls,** Graduate Studies, Program in Criminal Justice, Great Falls, MT 59405. Offers MSM. *Program availability:* Part-time, evening/weekend. *Degree requirements:* For master's, thesis optional. *Entrance requirements:* For master's, GRE General Test or MAT, 3 letters of recommendation. Additional exam requirements/recommendations for international students: Required—TOEFL (minimum score 500 paper-based). *Application deadline:* For fall admission, 8/15 priority date for domestic students, 6/15 priority date for international students; for spring admission, 12/15 priority date for domestic students, 10/15 priority date for international students. Applications are processed on a rolling basis. Application fee: $50. Electronic applications accepted. *Expenses: Tuition:* Full-time $14,256; part-time $9504 per semester. *Financial support:* Career-related internships or fieldwork, Federal Work-Study, and institutionally sponsored loans available. Support available to part-time students. Financial award application deadline: 6/1; financial award applicants required to submit FAFSA. *Faculty research:* Delinquency, domestic violence law. *Unit head:* Gail Belfert, Coordinator, 406-791-5338, E-mail: gail.belfert@ugf.edu. *Application contact:* Melanie Houge, Director of Admissions, 406-791-5210, Fax: 406-791-5209, E-mail: melanie.houge@ugf.edu.

**University of Guelph,** Graduate Studies, College of Social and Applied Human Sciences, Department of Criminology and Criminal Justice Policy, Guelph, ON N1G 2W1, Canada. Offers MA. *Degree requirements:* For master's, thesis or major paper. *Entrance requirements:* For master's, minimum B+ average during previous 2 years of coursework. Electronic applications accepted.

**University of Guelph,** Graduate Studies, College of Social and Applied Human Sciences, Department of Sociology and Anthropology, Guelph, ON N1G 2W1, Canada. Offers anthropology (MA); crime and criminal justice policy (MA); sociology (MA, PhD). *Degree requirements:* For master's, thesis or major paper; for doctorate, comprehensive exam, thesis/dissertation. *Entrance requirements:* For master's, minimum B+ average during previous 2 years of course work, honors BA or equivalent; for doctorate, must have an MA in Sociology, must have 80% or higher in graduate level studies. Additional exam requirements/recommendations for international students: Required—TOEFL (minimum score 550 paper-based; 89 iBT) or IELTS (minimum score 6.5). Electronic applications accepted. *Faculty research:* Rural and development sociology; education, employment, and the workplace; race, ethnicity, and native studies; criminology and deviance; social psychology.

**University of Houston–Clear Lake,** School of Human Sciences and Humanities, Programs in Human Sciences, Houston, TX 77058-1002. Offers behavioral sciences (MA), including criminology, cross cultural studies, general psychology, sociology; clinical psychology (MA); criminology (MA); cross cultural studies (MA); family therapy (MA); fitness and human performance (MA); school psychology (MA). *Accreditation:* AAMFT/COAMFTE. *Program availability:* Part-time, evening/weekend, online learning. *Degree requirements:* For master's, thesis or alternative. *Entrance requirements:* For master's, GRE General Test. Additional exam requirements/recommendations for international students: Required—TOEFL (minimum score 550 paper-based). Electronic applications accepted. *Faculty research:* Smoking cessation, adolescent sexuality, white collar crime, serial murder, human factors/human computer interaction.

**University of Houston–Downtown,** College of Public Service, Houston, TX 77002. Offers criminal justice (MS), including criminal justice; urban education (MAT), including curriculum and instruction, elementary and secondary education. *Program availability:* Part-time, evening/weekend, 100% online. *Faculty:* 15 full-time (8 women), 2 part-time/adjunct (1 woman). *Students:* 22 full-time (13 women), 97 part-time (77 women); includes 88 minority (42 Black or African American, non-Hispanic/Latino; 8 Asian, non-Hispanic/Latino; 38 Hispanic/Latino). Average age 34. 67 applicants, 81% accepted, 45 enrolled. In 2016, 37 master's awarded. *Entrance requirements:* Additional exam requirements/recommendations for international students: Required—TOEFL (minimum score 550 paper-based; 80 iBT). Application fee: $35 ($60 for international students). Electronic applications accepted. *Expenses:* $305.50 in-state, per credit; $663.50 out-of-state, per credit. *Financial support:* Federal Work-Study and scholarships/grants available. Financial award application deadline: 4/1; financial award applicants required to submit FAFSA. *Unit head:* Dr. Leigh Van Horn, Interim Dean, 713-221-8991, Fax: 713-226-5274, E-mail: vanhornl@uhd.edu. *Application contact:* Ceshia Love, Director of Graduate and International Admissions, 713-221-8093, Fax: 713-223-7408, E-mail: gradadmissions@uhd.edu.
Website: https://www.uhd.edu/academics/public-service/pages/default.aspx

**University of Houston–Downtown,** Davies College of Business, Master of Security Management Program, Houston, TX 77002. Offers MSM. *Program availability:* Part-time, evening/weekend, online only, 100% online. *Faculty:* 3 full-time (1 woman), 1 part-time/adjunct (0 women). *Students:* 19 part-time (4 women); includes 11 minority (6 Black or African American, non-Hispanic/Latino; 3 Asian, non-Hispanic/Latino; 2 Hispanic/Latino). Average age 43. 3 applicants. In 2016, 12 master's awarded. *Degree requirements:* For master's, capstone project. *Entrance requirements:* For master's, letter of intent, 3 letters of recommendation from supervisors indicating probability of applicant's success in program, proof of three years of paid work experience with supervisory or managerial responsibilities. Additional exam requirements/recommendations for international students: Required—TOEFL (minimum score 550 paper-based; 80 iBT). *Application deadline:* For fall admission, 8/1 for domestic students, 5/1 for international students; for spring admission, 11/15 for domestic students. Application fee: $35 ($60 for international students). Electronic applications accepted. *Expenses:* $305.50 in-state resident per credit; $663.50 non-resident per credit. *Financial support:* Federal Work-Study and scholarships/grants available. Financial award application deadline: 4/1; financial award applicants required to submit FAFSA. *Unit head:* Dr. D. Michael Fields, Dean, Davies College of Business, 713-221-8179, Fax: 713-221-8675, E-mail: fieldsd@uhd.edu. *Application contact:* Ceshia Love, Director of Graduate and International Admissions, 713-221-8093, Fax: 713-223-7408, E-mail: gradadmissions@uhd.edu.
Website: https://www.uhd.edu/academics/business/graduate-programs/Pages/msme-index.aspx

**University of Illinois at Chicago,** College of Liberal Arts and Sciences, Department of Criminology, Law, and Justice, Chicago, IL 60607-7128. Offers MA, PhD. *Program availability:* Evening/weekend. *Degree requirements:* For master's, thesis. *Entrance requirements:* For master's, GRE General Test, minimum GPA of 3.0. Additional exam requirements/recommendations for international students: Required—TOEFL. Electronic applications accepted. *Faculty research:* Sentencing probation, police and court use of scientific evidence, community mediation and conflict resolution.

**University of Louisiana at Monroe,** Graduate School, College of Business and Social Sciences, Department of Criminal Justice, Monroe, LA 71209-0001. Offers MA. *Program availability:* Part-time, evening/weekend. *Faculty:* 2 full-time (1 woman), 1 part-time/adjunct (0 women). *Students:* 15 full-time (10 women), 8 part-time (7 women); includes 16 minority (14 Black or African American, non-Hispanic/Latino; 2 Asian, non-Hispanic/Latino). Average age 28. 56 applicants, 48% accepted, 10 enrolled. In 2016, 7 master's awarded. *Degree requirements:* For master's, thesis optional. *Entrance requirements:* For master's, GRE General Test, minimum GPA of 2.5. Additional exam requirements/recommendations for international students: Required—TOEFL (minimum score 500 paper-based; 61 iBT). *Application deadline:* For fall admission, 8/24 priority date for domestic students, 7/1 for international students; for winter admission, 12/14 priority date for domestic students; for spring admission, 1/19 for domestic students, 11/1 for international students. Applications are processed on a rolling basis. Application fee: $20 ($30 for international students). Electronic applications accepted. *Expenses:* Tuition, state resident: full-time $6489. Tuition, nonresident: full-time $18,589. *Required fees:* $8984. Tuition and fees vary according to course level, course load, degree level and program. *Financial support:* Career-related internships or fieldwork, Federal Work-Study, and unspecified assistantships available. Financial award application deadline: 4/1; financial award applicants required to submit FAFSA. *Unit head:* Dr. Robert D. Hanser, Program Coordinator, 318-342-1443, Fax: 318-342-1458, E-mail: hanser@ulm.edu.
Website: http://www.ulm.edu/criminaljustice

**University of Louisville,** Graduate School, College of Arts and Sciences, Department of Criminal Justice, Louisville, KY 40292. Offers MS, PhD. *Program availability:* Part-time, evening/weekend, 100% online, blended/hybrid learning. *Faculty:* 14 full-time (6 women), 9 part-time/adjunct (1 woman). *Students:* 64 full-time (20 women), 81 part-time (32 women); includes 27 minority (16 Black or African American, non-Hispanic/Latino; 2 Asian, non-Hispanic/Latino; 5 Hispanic/Latino; 4 Two or more races, non-Hispanic/Latino), 2 international. Average age 39. 56 applicants, 63% accepted, 27 enrolled. In 2016, 22 master's, 3 doctorates awarded. *Degree requirements:* For master's, thesis or professional paper; for doctorate, thesis/dissertation, qualifying project. *Entrance requirements:* For master's, GRE General Test, 2 letters of recommendation; personal statement; official transcripts from all colleges attended; for doctorate, GRE General Test, 3 letters of recommendation; personal statement; curriculum vitae or resume; writing sample; official transcripts from all colleges attended. Additional exam requirements/recommendations for international students: Required—TOEFL (minimum score 550 paper-based; 79 iBT), IELTS (minimum score 6.5). *Application deadline:* For fall admission, 7/1 priority date for domestic and international students; for winter admission, 11/1 priority date for domestic students, 11/1 for international students; for spring admission, 11/1 priority date for domestic and international students; for summer admission, 4/1 priority date for domestic and international students. Applications are processed on a rolling basis. Application fee: $60. Electronic applications accepted. *Expenses:* Tuition, state resident: full-time $12,246; part-time $681 per credit hour. Tuition, nonresident: full-time $25,486; part-time $1417 per credit hour. *Required fees:* $196. Tuition and fees vary according to program and reciprocity agreements. *Financial support:* In 2016–17, 2 research assistantships with full tuition reimbursements (averaging $18,000 per year), 8 teaching assistantships with full tuition reimbursements (averaging $18,000 per year) were awarded; health care benefits also available. Financial award application deadline: 2/15; financial award applicants required to submit FAFSA. *Faculty research:* Operations of the elements of the criminal justice system (both theoretical and applied). *Total annual research expenditures:* $152,593. *Unit head:* Dr. Gennaro Vito, Chair, 502-852-6509, Fax: 502-852-0065, E-mail: gfvito01@louisville.edu. *Application contact:* Ginger Brown, Director, Student Services, 502-852-2686, Fax: 502-852-0065, E-mail: vcbrow01@louisville.edu.
Website: https://louisville.edu/justiceadministration/

**University of Management and Technology,** Program in Criminal Justice, Arlington, VA 22209-1609. Offers homeland security (MS). *Program availability:* Part-time, evening/weekend, online learning. *Entrance requirements:* Additional exam requirements/recommendations for international students: Required—TOEFL (minimum score 530 paper-based; 71 iBT).

**University of Management and Technology,** Program in Management, Arlington, VA 22209-1609. Offers acquisition management (MS, AC); criminal justice administration (MS); general management (MS); project management (MS, AC). *Program availability:* Part-time, evening/weekend, online learning. *Entrance requirements:* For master's, 3 recommendations, resume. Additional exam requirements/recommendations for international students: Required—TOEFL (minimum score 530 paper-based; 71 iBT). Electronic applications accepted.

**The University of Manchester,** School of Law, Manchester, United Kingdom. Offers bioethics and medical jurisprudence (PhD); criminology (M Phil, PhD); law (M Phil, PhD).

**University of Maryland, College Park,** Academic Affairs, College of Behavioral and Social Sciences, Department of Criminology and Criminal Justice, College Park, MD 20742. Offers MA, PhD, JD/MA. *Program availability:* Part-time, evening/weekend. Terminal master's awarded for partial completion of doctoral program. *Degree requirements:* For master's, comprehensive exam, thesis optional; for doctorate, comprehensive exam, thesis/dissertation. *Entrance requirements:* For master's, GRE General Test, minimum GPA of 3.0, 3 letters of recommendation; for doctorate, GRE General Test. Additional exam requirements/recommendations for international students: Required—TOEFL. Electronic applications accepted. *Faculty research:* Theory, crime prevention, death penalty, criminal justice technology, policy.

**University of Maryland Eastern Shore,** Graduate Programs, Department of Criminal Justice, Princess Anne, MD 21853-1299. Offers MS. *Program availability:* Part-time, evening/weekend. *Degree requirements:* For master's, comprehensive exam, thesis optional. *Entrance requirements:* For master's, GRE General Test, interview. Additional exam requirements/recommendations for international students: Required—TOEFL (minimum score 80 iBT).

**University of Massachusetts Lowell,** College of Fine Arts, Humanities and Social Sciences, School of Criminology and Justice Studies, Lowell, MA 01854. Offers criminal justice (MA). *Program availability:* Part-time, evening/weekend. *Degree requirements:* For master's, thesis optional. *Entrance requirements:* For master's, GRE General Test or MAT. Electronic applications accepted. *Faculty research:* Family violence, criminal justice management, corrections, policing, delinquency.

**University of Memphis,** Graduate School, College of Arts and Sciences, Department of Criminology and Criminal Justice, Memphis, TN 38103. Offers MA. *Program availability:* Part-time. *Faculty:* 4 full-time (1 woman), 2 part-time/adjunct (1 woman). *Students:* 15

## Criminal Justice and Criminology

full-time (12 women), 11 part-time (4 women); includes 11 minority (10 Black or African American, non-Hispanic/Latino; 1 Hispanic/Latino), 2 international. Average age 32. 21 applicants, 90% accepted, 15 enrolled. In 2016, 8 master's awarded. *Degree requirements:* For master's, comprehensive exam, thesis optional. *Entrance requirements:* For master's, GRE General Test, minimum GPA of 3.0. Additional exam requirements/recommendations for international students: Required—TOEFL (minimum score 550 paper-based; 79 iBT). *Application deadline:* For fall admission, 6/1 for domestic students; for spring admission, 11/1 for domestic students. Application fee: $35 ($60 for international students). Electronic applications accepted. *Expenses:* $5,231.50 per semester full-time in-state, $9,623.50 full-time out-of-state. *Financial support:* In 2016–17, 11 students received support, including 10 research assistantships with full tuition reimbursements available (averaging $13,600 per year); teaching assistantships with full tuition reimbursements available, career-related internships or fieldwork, Federal Work-Study, institutionally sponsored loans, scholarships/grants, tuition waivers (partial), and unspecified assistantships also available. Financial award application deadline: 2/1; financial award applicants required to submit FAFSA. *Faculty research:* Violence, crime prevention, crime analysis, survey research, crisis intervention. *Unit head:* Dr. K. B. Turner, Chair, 901-678-3397, Fax: 901-678-5279, E-mail: kbturner@memphis.edu. *Application contact:* Dr. Bert Burraston, Coordinator of Graduate Studies, 901-678-4767, Fax: 901-678-5279, E-mail: bbrrstom@memphis.edu.
Website: http://www.memphis.edu/cjustice/

**University of Michigan–Dearborn,** College of Arts, Sciences, and Letters, Master of Science in Criminology and Criminal Justice Program, Dearborn, MI 48128. Offers MS. *Program availability:* Part-time, evening/weekend. *Degree requirements:* For master's, thesis optional. *Entrance requirements:* Additional exam requirements/recommendations for international students: Required—TOEFL (minimum score 84 iBT), IELTS (minimum score 6.5). *Application deadline:* For fall admission, 8/1 for domestic students, 5/1 for international students; for winter admission, 12/1 for domestic students, 9/1 for international students; for spring admission, 4/1 for domestic students, 1/1 for international students. Applications are processed on a rolling basis. Application fee: $60. Electronic applications accepted. *Expenses:* Contact institution. *Financial support:* Scholarships/grants available. Financial award application deadline: 3/1; financial award applicants required to submit FAFSA. *Unit head:* Dr. Donald Shelton, JD, Director, 313-593-4681, E-mail: desjd@umich.edu. *Application contact:* Office of Graduate Studies, 313-583-6321, E-mail: umd-graduatestudies@umich.edu.
Website: https://umdearborn.edu/casl/graduate-programs/programs/master-science-criminology-and-criminal-justice

**University of Michigan–Flint,** Graduate Programs, Program in Public Administration, Flint, MI 48502. Offers administration of non-profit agencies (MPA); criminal justice administration (MPA); educational administration (MPA); general public administration (MPA); healthcare administration (MPA). *Program availability:* Part-time. *Faculty:* 1 full-time (0 women), 3 part-time/adjunct (all women). *Students:* 13 full-time (10 women), 97 part-time (59 women); includes 45 minority (35 Black or African American, non-Hispanic/Latino; 1 Asian, non-Hispanic/Latino; 3 Hispanic/Latino; 1 Native Hawaiian or other Pacific Islander, non-Hispanic/Latino; 5 Two or more races, non-Hispanic/Latino), 5 international. Average age 35. 60 applicants, 78% accepted, 38 enrolled. In 2016, 52 master's awarded. *Degree requirements:* For master's, thesis or alternative, internship. *Entrance requirements:* For master's, bachelor's degree from regionally-accredited institution, minimum overall undergraduate GPA of 3.0. Additional exam requirements/recommendations for international students: Required—TOEFL (minimum score 84 iBT), IELTS (minimum score 6.5). *Application deadline:* For fall admission, 8/1 for domestic students, 5/1 for international students; for winter admission, 11/15 for domestic students, 9/1 for international students; for spring admission, 3/15 for domestic students, 1/1 for international students; for summer admission, 5/15 for domestic students. Applications are processed on a rolling basis. Application fee: $55. Electronic applications accepted. *Expenses:* Contact institution. *Financial support:* Career-related internships or fieldwork, Federal Work-Study, and scholarships/grants available. Support available to part-time students. Financial award application deadline: 3/1; financial award applicants required to submit FAFSA. *Unit head:* Dr. Kathryn Schellenberg, Director, 810-762-3340, E-mail: kathsch@umflint.edu. *Application contact:* Bradley T. Maki, Director of Graduate Admissions, 810-762-3171, Fax: 810-766-6789, E-mail: bmaki@umflint.edu.
Website: http://www.umflint.edu/graduateprograms/public-administration-mpa

**University of Minnesota, Duluth,** Graduate School, College of Liberal Arts, Department of Sociology/Anthropology, Program in Criminology, Duluth, MN 55812-2496. Offers MA. *Program availability:* Part-time, evening/weekend. *Degree requirements:* For master's, thesis or alternative. *Entrance requirements:* For master's, minimum GPA of 3.0, letter of recommendation, personal statement. Additional exam requirements/recommendations for international students: Required—TOEFL. *Faculty research:* Restorative justice, juvenile delinquency, social justice, program evaluation.

**University of Missouri–Kansas City,** College of Arts and Sciences, Department of Criminal Justice and Criminology, Kansas City, MO 64110-2499. Offers MS. *Program availability:* Part-time, evening/weekend. *Faculty:* 7 full-time (5 women), 7 part-time/adjunct (3 women). *Students:* 5 full-time (3 women), 22 part-time (15 women); includes 12 minority (6 Black or African American, non-Hispanic/Latino; 3 American Indian or Alaska Native, non-Hispanic/Latino; 1 Asian, non-Hispanic/Latino; 2 Hispanic/Latino). Average age 28. 13 applicants, 69% accepted, 8 enrolled. In 2016, 6 master's awarded. *Degree requirements:* For master's, thesis optional. *Entrance requirements:* For master's, GRE, minimum GPA of 3.0 in major, 2.7 overall. Additional exam requirements/recommendations for international students: Required—TOEFL (minimum score 550 paper-based; 80 iBT). *Application deadline:* For fall admission, 3/1 for domestic and international students; for spring admission, 11/1 for domestic and international students. Applications are processed on a rolling basis. Application fee: $45 ($50 for international students). Electronic applications accepted. *Financial support:* In 2016–17, 1 research assistantship with full tuition reimbursement (averaging $12,000 per year), 4 teaching assistantships with tuition reimbursements (averaging $11,200 per year) were awarded; career-related internships or fieldwork, Federal Work-Study, institutionally sponsored loans, and tuition waivers (partial) also available. Support available to part-time students. Financial award application deadline: 3/1; financial award applicants required to submit FAFSA. *Faculty research:* Death penalty, community corrections, urban community and neighborhoods. *Unit head:* Dr. Kristi Holsinger, Chair, 816-235-1471, Fax: 816-235-5193, E-mail: holsingerk@umkc.edu. *Application contact:* Dr. Lori Sexton, Director, Graduate Program, 816-235-5755, Fax: 816-235-5193, E-mail: sextonl@umkc.edu.
Website: http://cas.umkc.edu/CJC/

**University of Missouri–St. Louis,** College of Arts and Sciences, Department of Criminology and Criminal Justice, St. Louis, MO 63121. Offers MA, PhD. *Faculty:* 16 full-time (6 women), 1 part-time/adjunct (0 women). *Students:* 29 full-time (22 women), 25 part-time (18 women); includes 10 minority (6 Black or African American, non-Hispanic/Latino; 1 Asian, non-Hispanic/Latino; 2 Hispanic/Latino; 1 Two or more races, non-Hispanic/Latino). Average age 29. 90 applicants, 40% accepted, 16 enrolled. *Degree requirements:* For doctorate, thesis/dissertation. *Entrance requirements:* For master's,

essay; 2 letters of recommendation; for doctorate, GRE General Test, writing sample, 3 letters of recommendation. Additional exam requirements/recommendations for international students: Required—TOEFL (minimum score 550 paper-based; 65 iBT), IELTS (minimum score 6.5). *Application deadline:* For fall admission, 2/1 priority date for domestic and international students. Applications are processed on a rolling basis. Application fee: $50 ($40 for international students). Electronic applications accepted. *Financial support:* Fellowships with full tuition reimbursements, research assistantships with tuition reimbursements, teaching assistantships with tuition reimbursements, and career-related internships or fieldwork available. Financial award applicants required to submit FAFSA. *Faculty research:* Crime control, criminological theory, juvenile delinquency, violence, drugs. *Unit head:* Dr. Finn-Aage Esbensen, Chair, 314-516-4619, Fax: 314-516-5048, E-mail: esbensen@umsl.edu. *Application contact:* 314-516-5458, Fax: 314-516-6996, E-mail: gradadm@umsl.edu.
Website: http://www.umsl.edu/ccj/

**University of Montana,** Graduate School, College of Humanities and Sciences, Department of Sociology, Missoula, MT 59812-0002. Offers criminology (MA); inequality and social justice (MA); rural and environmental change (MA); sociology (MA). *Entrance requirements:* For master's, GRE General Test. Additional exam requirements/recommendations for international students: Required—TOEFL. *Faculty research:* Housing, homelessness, hunger, infant mortality, work safety.

**University of Nebraska at Omaha,** Graduate Studies, College of Public Affairs and Community Service, School of Criminology and Criminal Justice, Omaha, NE 68182. Offers criminology and criminal justice (MA, MS, PhD); managing juvenile and adult populations (Certificate). *Program availability:* Part-time, evening/weekend. *Faculty:* 10 full-time (5 women). *Students:* 40 full-time (31 women), 64 part-time (38 women); includes 23 minority (4 Black or African American, non-Hispanic/Latino; 1 American Indian or Alaska Native, non-Hispanic/Latino; 2 Asian, non-Hispanic/Latino; 9 Hispanic/Latino; 7 Two or more races, non-Hispanic/Latino), 8 international. Average age 31. 99 applicants, 52% accepted, 31 enrolled. In 2016, 12 master's, 1 doctorate, 2 other advanced degrees awarded. Terminal master's awarded for partial completion of doctoral program. *Degree requirements:* For master's, comprehensive exam, thesis (for some programs); for doctorate, comprehensive exam, thesis/dissertation. *Entrance requirements:* For master's, GRE General Test, previous course work in criminal justice, statistics, and research methods; minimum GPA of 3.0; official transcripts; statement of purpose; 2 letters of recommendation; for doctorate, GRE General Test, master's degree, minimum undergraduate GPA of 3.0, 3 letters of recommendation, statement of purpose, writing sample, resume. Additional exam requirements/recommendations for international students: Required—TOEFL, IELTS, PTE. *Application deadline:* For fall admission, 1/10 for domestic and international students; for spring admission, 12/1 priority date for domestic and international students; for summer admission, 4/30 for domestic and international students. Applications are processed on a rolling basis. Application fee: $45. Electronic applications accepted. *Financial support:* In 2016–17, 24 students received support, including 17 research assistantships with tuition reimbursements available, 7 teaching assistantships with tuition reimbursements available; career-related internships or fieldwork, Federal Work-Study, institutionally sponsored loans, scholarships/grants, health care benefits, tuition waivers (partial), and unspecified assistantships also available. Support available to part-time students. Financial award application deadline: 3/1; financial award applicants required to submit FAFSA. *Unit head:* Dr. Gaylene Armstrong, Director, 402-554-2341, E-mail: graduate@unomaha.edu. *Application contact:* Lisa Sample, Graduate Program Chair, 402-554-2341, E-mail: graduate@unomaha.edu.

**University of Nevada, Las Vegas,** Graduate College, Greenspun College of Urban Affairs, Department of Criminal Justice, Las Vegas, NV 89154-5009. Offers criminal justice (MA); criminology and criminal justice (PhD). *Program availability:* Part-time. *Faculty:* 8 full-time (5 women). *Students:* 22 full-time (17 women), 9 part-time (7 women); includes 9 minority (1 Black or African American, non-Hispanic/Latino; 4 Hispanic/Latino; 1 Native Hawaiian or other Pacific Islander, non-Hispanic/Latino; 3 Two or more races, non-Hispanic/Latino), 2 international. Average age 28. 34 applicants, 56% accepted, 13 enrolled. In 2016, 8 master's awarded. *Degree requirements:* For master's, comprehensive exam, thesis, oral examination; for doctorate, comprehensive exam, thesis/dissertation. *Entrance requirements:* For master's, GRE General Test, statement of purpose; bachelor's degree; 2 letters of recommendation; for doctorate, GRE General Test (minimum scores: 153 for Quantitative, 155 for Verbal, and 4.5 for Analytical Writing), 3 letters of recommendation; statement of purpose; personal interview. Additional exam requirements/recommendations for international students: Required—TOEFL (minimum score 550 paper-based; 80 iBT), IELTS (minimum score 7). *Application deadline:* For fall admission, 4/15 for domestic students. Application fee: $60 ($95 for international students). Electronic applications accepted. *Expenses:* $269.25 per credit, $792 per 3-credit course; $9,634 per year resident; $23,274 per year non-resident; $7,094 fees non-resident (7 credits or more); $1,307 annual health insurance fee. *Financial support:* In 2016–17, 4 research assistantships with partial tuition reimbursements (averaging $13,688 per year), 14 teaching assistantships with partial tuition reimbursements (averaging $17,875 per year) were awarded; institutionally sponsored loans, scholarships/grants, health care benefits, and unspecified assistantships also available. Financial award application deadline: 3/15. *Faculty research:* Administration of justice, corrections, criminological theory, policing, sociology of law. Total annual research expenditures: $75,716. *Unit head:* Dr. Joel Lieberman, Chair/Associate Professor, 702-895-0249, Fax: 702-895-0252, E-mail: joel.lieberman@unlv.edu. *Application contact:* Dr. Tamara Madensen, Graduate Coordinator, 702-895-5903, Fax: 702-895-0252, E-mail: tamara.madensen@unlv.edu.
Website: http://criminaljustice.unlv.edu/grad/

**University of Nevada, Reno,** Graduate School, College of Liberal Arts, School of Social Research and Justice Studies, Department of Criminal Justice, Reno, NV 89557. Offers MA. *Degree requirements:* For master's, comprehensive exam, thesis optional. *Entrance requirements:* For master's, GRE or LSAT, undergraduate degree in criminal justice with minimum GPA of 3.0. Additional exam requirements/recommendations for international students: Required—TOEFL (minimum score 500 paper-based; 61 iBT), IELTS (minimum score 6). Electronic applications accepted. *Faculty research:* Criminal justice system, social policy interaction.

**University of Nevada, Reno,** Graduate School, College of Liberal Arts, School of Social Research and Justice Studies, Program in Justice Management, Reno, NV 89557. Offers MJM. *Program availability:* Part-time, online learning. *Degree requirements:* For master's, thesis optional. *Entrance requirements:* For master's, minimum GPA of 2.75. Additional exam requirements/recommendations for international students: Required—TOEFL (minimum score 500 paper-based; 61 iBT), IELTS (minimum score 6). Electronic applications accepted. *Faculty research:* Justice administration, adult justice management, juvenile justice management.

**University of New Haven,** Graduate School, Henry C. Lee College of Criminal Justice and Forensic Sciences, Program in Criminal Justice, West Haven, CT 06516. Offers crime analysis (MS); criminal justice (MS, PhD); criminal justice management (MS, Graduate Certificate); forensic computer investigation (MS); forensic psychology (MS); information protection and security (Graduate Certificate); victim advocacy and services management (Graduate Certificate); victimology (MS). *Program availability:* Part-time, evening/weekend, online learning. *Students:* 120 full-time (83 women), 121 part-time (69 women); includes 84 minority (49 Black or African American, non-Hispanic/Latino; 10 Asian, non-Hispanic/Latino; 14 Hispanic/Latino; 1 Native Hawaiian or other Pacific Islander, non-Hispanic/Latino; 10 Two or more races, non-Hispanic/Latino), 10 international. Average age 29. 128 applicants, 90% accepted, 73 enrolled. In 2016, 52 master's, 2 doctorates, 8 other advanced degrees awarded. *Degree requirements:* For master's, thesis or alternative. *Entrance requirements:* Additional exam requirements/recommendations for international students: Required—TOEFL (minimum score 80 iBT), IELTS, PTE (minimum score 53). *Application deadline:* Applications are processed on a rolling basis. Application fee: $50. Electronic applications accepted. Application fee is waived when completed online. *Expenses: Tuition:* Full-time $15,660; part-time $870 per credit hour. *Required fees:* $200; $85 per term. Tuition and fees vary according to program. *Financial support:* Research assistantships with partial tuition reimbursements, teaching assistantships with partial tuition reimbursements, career-related internships or fieldwork, Federal Work-Study, scholarships/grants, and unspecified assistantships available. Support available to part-time students. Financial award applicants required to submit FAFSA. *Application contact:* Michelle Mason, Director of Graduate Enrollment, 203-932-7067, E-mail: mmason@newhaven.edu. Website: http://www.newhaven.edu/5921/

**University of New Haven,** Graduate School, Henry C. Lee College of Criminal Justice and Forensic Sciences, Program in Investigations, West Haven, CT 06516. Offers criminal investigations (MS); financial crimes investigations (MS); forensic computer investigations (MS). *Students:* 29 full-time (16 women), 18 part-time (7 women); includes 16 minority (11 Black or African American, non-Hispanic/Latino; 1 Asian, non-Hispanic/Latino; 2 Hispanic/Latino; 2 Two or more races, non-Hispanic/Latino). Average age 29. 32 applicants, 100% accepted, 27 enrolled. *Application deadline:* Applications are processed on a rolling basis. Application fee: $50. *Expenses: Tuition:* Full-time $15,660; part-time $870 per credit hour. *Required fees:* $200; $85 per term. Tuition and fees vary according to program. *Application contact:* Michelle Mason, Director of Graduate Enrollment, 203-932-7067, E-mail: mmason@newhaven.edu. Website: http://www.newhaven.edu/lee-college/programs/graduate/investigations/

**University of North Alabama,** College of Arts and Sciences, Department of Interdisciplinary and Professional Studies, Florence, AL 35632-0001. Offers professional studies (MPS), including community development, information technology, security and safety leadership. *Program availability:* Part-time. *Faculty:* 1 full-time (0 women), 1 part-time/adjunct (0 women). *Students:* 12 full-time (8 women), 40 part-time (29 women); includes 6 minority (5 Black or African American, non-Hispanic/Latino; 1 Asian, non-Hispanic/Latino), 8 international. Average age 35. 25 applicants, 76% accepted, 15 enrolled. In 2016, 11 master's awarded. *Degree requirements:* For master's, thesis optional. *Entrance requirements:* For master's, ETS PPI, baccalaureate degree from accredited institution; minimum cumulative GPA of 2.75 or 3.0 in last 60 hours of undergraduate study; personal statement. Additional exam requirements/recommendations for international students: Required—TOEFL (minimum score 79 iBT), IELTS (minimum score 6), PTE (minimum score 54). *Application deadline:* Applications are processed on a rolling basis. Application fee: $50 ($100 for international students). Electronic applications accepted. *Expenses: Tuition:* state resident: full-time $2799; part-time $1866 per semester. Tuition, nonresident: full-time $5598; part-time $3732 per semester. *Required fees:* $915; $642 per semester. Tuition and fees vary according to course load. *Financial support:* In 2016–17, 9 students received support. Scholarships/grants and unspecified assistantships available. Financial award application deadline: 12/1; financial award applicants required to submit FAFSA. *Unit head:* Dr. Craig T. Robertson, Director, 256-765-5003, E-mail: ctrobertson@una.edu. *Application contact:* Hillary N. Coats, Graduate Admissions Coordinator, 256-765-4447, E-mail: graduate@una.edu. Website: https://www.una.edu/interdisciplinary-studies/

**University of North Alabama,** College of Arts and Sciences, Department of Politics, Justice, and Law, Florence, AL 35632-0001. Offers criminal justice (MSCJ). *Program availability:* Part-time, 100% online. *Faculty:* 3 full-time (0 women), 2 part-time/adjunct (1 woman). *Students:* 4 full-time (2 women), 21 part-time (9 women); includes 4 minority (3 Black or African American, non-Hispanic/Latino; 1 Hispanic/Latino), 4 international. Average age 30. 13 applicants, 77% accepted, 10 enrolled. In 2016, 3 master's awarded. *Degree requirements:* For master's, comprehensive exam. *Entrance requirements:* For master's, GRE General Test, MAT. Additional exam requirements/recommendations for international students: Required—TOEFL (minimum score 79 iBT), IELTS (minimum score 6), PTE (minimum score 54). *Application deadline:* Applications are processed on a rolling basis. Application fee: $50 ($100 for international students). Electronic applications accepted. *Expenses: Tuition:* state resident: full-time $2799; part-time $1866 per semester. Tuition, nonresident: full-time $5598; part-time $3732 per semester. *Required fees:* $915; $642 per semester. Tuition and fees vary according to course load. *Financial support:* In 2016–17, 2 students received support. Scholarships/grants and unspecified assistantships available. Financial award application deadline: 2/1; financial award applicants required to submit FAFSA. *Unit head:* Dr. Tim Collins, Chair, 256-765-5045, E-mail: jtcollins@una.edu. *Application contact:* Hillary N. Coats, Graduate Admissions Coordinator, 256-765-4447, E-mail: graduate@una.edu. Website: http://www.una.edu/criminaljustice/

**The University of North Carolina at Charlotte,** College of Liberal Arts and Sciences, Department of Criminal Justice and Criminology, Charlotte, NC 28223-0001. Offers MS. *Program availability:* Part-time, evening/weekend. *Faculty:* 15 full-time (8 women). *Students:* 10 full-time (8 women), 8 part-time (7 women); includes 4 minority (2 Black or African American, non-Hispanic/Latino; 1 Hispanic/Latino; 1 Two or more races, non-Hispanic/Latino). Average age 23. 23 applicants, 61% accepted, 9 enrolled. In 2016, 6 master's awarded. *Degree requirements:* For master's, thesis or comprehensive exam. *Entrance requirements:* For master's, GRE, official copies of all undergraduate/graduate transcripts; minimum of three letters of recommendation; personal statement; minimum GPA of 3.0 (preferred). Additional exam requirements/recommendations for international students: Required—TOEFL (minimum score 523 paper-based, 70 iBT) or IELTS (6.5). *Application deadline:* For fall admission, 3/1 priority date for domestic and international students; for spring admission, 10/1 priority date for domestic and international students; for summer admission, 4/1 priority date for domestic and international students. Applications are processed on a rolling basis. Application fee: $75. Electronic applications accepted. *Expenses: Tuition:* state resident: full-time $4252. Tuition, nonresident: full-time $17,423. *Required fees:* $3026. Tuition and fees vary according to course load and program. *Financial support:* In 2016–17, 5 students received support, including 1 research assistantship (averaging $7,500 per year), 4 teaching assistantships (averaging $11,732 per year); career-related internships or fieldwork, Federal Work-Study, institutionally sponsored loans, scholarships/grants, and unspecified assistantships also available. Support available to part-time students. Financial award application deadline: 3/1; financial award applicants required to submit FAFSA. *Total annual research expenditures:* $251,449. *Unit head:* Dr. Michael Turner, Chair, 704-687-0755, E-mail: mgturner@uncc.edu. *Application contact:* Kathy B. Giddings, Director of Graduate Admissions, 704-687-5503, Fax: 704-687-1668, E-mail: gradadm@uncc.edu. Website: http://criminaljustice.uncc.edu/

**The University of North Carolina at Greensboro,** Graduate School, College of Arts and Sciences, Department of Sociology, Greensboro, NC 27412-5001. Offers criminology (MA); sociology (MA). *Program availability:* Part-time. *Degree requirements:* For master's, comprehensive exam, thesis. *Entrance requirements:* For master's, GRE General Test. Additional exam requirements/recommendations for international students: Required—TOEFL. Electronic applications accepted.

**The University of North Carolina Wilmington,** College of Arts and Sciences, Department of Sociology and Criminology, Wilmington, NC 28403-3297. Offers MA. *Program availability:* Part-time. *Faculty:* 15 full-time (9 women). *Students:* 21 full-time (14 women), 6 part-time (5 women); includes 5 minority (1 Black or African American, non-Hispanic/Latino; 2 Hispanic/Latino; 2 Two or more races, non-Hispanic/Latino). Average age 25. 30 applicants, 83% accepted, 16 enrolled. In 2016, 4 master's awarded. *Degree requirements:* For master's, thesis or internship. *Entrance requirements:* For master's, GRE General Test, 3 letters of recommendation, statement of interest, writing sample, minimum GPA of 3.0 in undergraduate work. Additional exam requirements/recommendations for international students: Required—TOEFL (minimum score 79 iBT), IELTS (minimum score 6.5). *Application deadline:* For fall admission, 2/15 for domestic students. Applications are processed on a rolling basis. Application fee: $60. Electronic applications accepted. *Expenses:* Contact institution. *Financial support:* Teaching assistantships, scholarships/grants, and out-of-state tuition award available. Financial award application deadline: 3/15; financial award applicants required to submit FAFSA. *Unit head:* Dr. Mike Maume, Chair, 910-962-7749, Fax: 910-962-7385, E-mail: maume@uncw.edu. *Application contact:* Dr. Daniel Buffington, Graduate Coordinator, 910-962-3434, Fax: 910-962-7385, E-mail: buffingtond@uncw.edu. Website: http://www.uncw.edu/socgrad/index.html

**University of North Dakota,** Graduate School, College of Arts and Sciences, Program in Criminal Justice, Grand Forks, ND 58202. Offers PhD, JD/PhD. *Program availability:* Part-time. *Entrance requirements:* For doctorate, GRE General Test. Additional exam requirements/recommendations for international students: Required—TOEFL (minimum score 550 paper-based; 79 iBT), IELTS (minimum score 6.5). *Application deadline:* For fall admission, 3/31 for domestic and international students; for spring admission, 11/1 for domestic and international students. Application fee: $35. Electronic applications accepted. *Financial support:* Fellowships with partial tuition reimbursements, research assistantships with full and partial tuition reimbursements, teaching assistantships with full and partial tuition reimbursements, Federal Work-Study, scholarships/grants, health care benefits, and unspecified assistantships available. Support available to part-time students. Financial award applicants required to submit FAFSA. *Unit head:* Dr. Michael Meyer, Graduate Director, 701-777-4181, E-mail: michael_meyer2@und.nodak.edu. *Application contact:* Matt Anderson, Admissions Specialist, 701-777-2947, Fax: 701-777-3619, E-mail: matthew.anderson@gradschool.und.edu.

**University of Northern Colorado,** Graduate School, College of Humanities and Social Sciences, Department of Criminology and Criminal Justice, Greeley, CO 80639. Offers criminal justice (MA). *Financial support:* Teaching assistantships available. *Unit head:* Dr. Denise A. Battles, Dean, 970-351-2877, Fax: 970-351-2176. *Application contact:* Linda Sisson, Graduate Student Admission Coordinator, 970-351-1807, Fax: 970-351-2371, E-mail: linda.sisson@unco.edu. Website: http://www.unco.edu/hss/criminology-criminal-justice/

**University of North Florida,** College of Arts and Sciences, Department of Criminology and Criminal Justice, Jacksonville, FL 32224. Offers criminal justice (MS). *Faculty:* 10 full-time (6 women). *Students:* 22 full-time (11 women), 34 part-time (24 women); includes 25 minority (19 Black or African American, non-Hispanic/Latino; 5 Hispanic/Latino; 1 Two or more races, non-Hispanic/Latino). Average age 31. 40 applicants, 55% accepted, 15 enrolled. In 2016, 18 master's awarded. *Degree requirements:* For master's, comprehensive exam, thesis optional. *Entrance requirements:* For master's, GRE General Test, minimum GPA of 3.0 in last 60 hours, letters of recommendation. Additional exam requirements/recommendations for international students: Required—TOEFL (minimum score 500 paper-based; 61 iBT). *Application deadline:* For fall admission, 8/1 priority date for domestic students, 5/1 for international students; for spring admission, 12/1 priority date for domestic students, 10/1 for international students; for summer admission, 4/28 priority date for domestic students, 2/1 for international students. Application fee: $30. Electronic applications accepted. Tuition and fees vary according to course load, campus/location and program. *Financial support:* In 2016–17, 3 students received support, including 5 teaching assistantships (averaging $4,864 per year); research assistantships, Federal Work-Study, scholarships/grants, and unspecified assistantships also available. Financial award application deadline: 4/1; financial award applicants required to submit FAFSA. *Unit head:* Dr. David Forde, Chair, 904-620-2413, E-mail: david.forde@unf.edu. *Application contact:* Dr. Amanda Pascale, Director, The Graduate School, 904-620-1360, Fax: 904-620-1362, E-mail: graduateschool@unf.edu. Website: http://www.unf.edu/coas/ccj/

**University of North Georgia,** Department of Criminal Justice, Dahlonega, GA 30597. Offers MS. *Program availability:* Part-time, evening/weekend, online only, 100% online. *Faculty:* 4 full-time (3 women). *Students:* 5 full-time (all women), 23 part-time (12 women); includes 8 minority (5 Black or African American, non-Hispanic/Latino; 1 Hispanic/Latino; 2 Two or more races, non-Hispanic/Latino). Average age 31. 18 applicants, 67% accepted, 9 enrolled. In 2016, 12 master's awarded. *Degree requirements:* For master's, comprehensive seminar. *Entrance requirements:* For master's, GRE, official transcripts, 3 UNG recommendation forms, letter of intent, professional resume. Additional exam requirements/recommendations for international students: Required—TOEFL (minimum score 550 paper-based; 79 iBT), IELTS (minimum score 6.5). *Application deadline:* For fall admission, 8/10 for domestic students; for spring admission, 12/10 for domestic students; for summer admission, 5/10 for domestic students. Application fee: $40. Electronic applications accepted. *Expenses:* Contact institution. *Financial support:* Fellowships and research assistantships available. Financial award application deadline: 3/17; financial award applicants required to submit FAFSA. *Unit head:* Dr. Brent Paterline, Interim Department Head, 706-864-1914, E-mail: brent.paterline@ung.edu. *Application contact:* Melinda Maxwell, Director of Graduate Admissions, 706-864-1543, E-mail: melinda.maxwell@ung.edu. Website: http://ung.edu/criminal-justice/

**University of North Texas,** Robert B. Toulouse School of Graduate Studies, Denton, TX 76203-5459. Offers accounting (MS); applied anthropology (MA, MS); applied behavior analysis (Certificate); applied geography (MA); applied technology and performance improvement (M Ed, MS); art education (MA); art history (MA); art museum education (Certificate); arts leadership (Certificate); audiology (Au D); behavior analysis (MS); behavioral science (PhD); biochemistry and molecular biology (MS); biology (MA, MS); biomedical engineering (MS); business analysis (MS); chemistry (MS); clinical health psychology (PhD); communication studies (MA, MS); computer engineering (MS); computer science (MS); counseling (M Ed, MS), including clinical mental health counseling (MS), college and university counseling, elementary school counseling, secondary school counseling; creative writing (MA); criminal justice (MS); curriculum and instruction (M Ed); decision sciences (MBA); design (MA, MFA), including fashion design (MFA), innovation studies, interior design (MFA); early childhood studies (MS); economics (MS); educational leadership (M Ed, Ed D); educational psychology (MS,

## Criminal Justice and Criminology

PhD), including family studies (MS), gifted and talented (MS), human development (MS), learning and cognition (MS), research, measurement and evaluation (MS); electrical engineering (MS); emergency management (MPA); engineering technology (MS); English (MA); English as a second language (MA); environmental science (MS); finance (MBA, MS); financial management (MPA); French (MA); health services management (MBA); higher education (M Ed, Ed D); history (MA, MS); hospitality management (MS); human resources management (MPA); information science (MS); information systems (PhD); information technologies (MBA); interdisciplinary studies (MA, MS); international studies (MS); international sustainable tourism (MS); jazz studies (MM); journalism (MA, MJ, Graduate Certificate), including interactive and virtual digital communication (Graduate Certificate), narrative journalism (Graduate Certificate), public relations (Graduate Certificate); kinesiology (MS); linguistics (MA); local government management (MPA); logistics (PhD); logistics and supply chain management (MBA); long-term care, senior housing, and aging services (MA); management (PhD); marketing (MBA); mathematics (MA, MS); mechanical and energy engineering (MS, PhD); music (MA), including ethnomusicology, music theory, musicology, performance; music composition (PhD); music education (MM Ed, PhD); nonprofit management (MPA); operations and supply chain management (MBA); performance (MM, DMA); philosophy (MA); political science (MA); professional and technical communication (MA); radio, television and film (MA, MFA); rehabilitation counseling (Certificate); sociology (MA); Spanish (MA); special education (M Ed); speech-language pathology (MA); strategic management (MBA); studio art (MFA); teaching (M Ed); MBA/MS. *Program availability:* Part-time, evening/weekend, online learning. Terminal master's awarded for partial completion of doctoral program. *Degree requirements:* For master's, variable foreign language requirement, comprehensive exam (for some programs), thesis (for some programs); for doctorate, variable foreign language requirement, comprehensive exam (for some programs), thesis/dissertation; for other advanced degree, variable foreign language requirement, comprehensive exam (for some programs). *Entrance requirements:* For master's and doctorate, GRE, GMAT. Additional exam requirements/recommendations for international students: Required—TOEFL (minimum score 550 paper-based; 79 iBT). Electronic applications accepted.

**University of North Texas at Dallas,** Graduate School, Dallas, TX 75241. Offers accounting (MBA); counseling (M Ed, MS); criminal justice (MS); curriculum and instruction (M Ed); educational administration (M Ed); human resources and organizational behavior (MBA); public leadership (MS); strategic management (MBA).

**University of Oklahoma,** College of Liberal Studies, Norman, OK 73072. Offers administrative leadership (Graduate Certificate); corrections management (Graduate Certificate); criminal justice (MS); government and military leadership (MA); human and health services administration (MA), including human and health services administration, integrated studies; liberal studies (MPS); organizational leadership (MA); restorative justice administration (Graduate Certificate); volunteer and non-profit leadership (MA). *Program availability:* Part-time, online only, 100% online, blended/hybrid learning. *Faculty:* 13 full-time (7 women), 1 part-time/adjunct (0 women). *Students:* 74 full-time (48 women), 598 part-time (289 women); includes 175 minority (45 Black or African American, non-Hispanic/Latino; 39 American Indian or Alaska Native, non-Hispanic/Latino; 8 Asian, non-Hispanic/Latino; 46 Hispanic/Latino; 1 Native Hawaiian or other Pacific Islander, non-Hispanic/Latino; 36 Two or more races, non-Hispanic/Latino), 2 international. Average age 35. 191 applicants, 95% accepted, 120 enrolled. In 2016, 192 master's, 6 other advanced degrees awarded. *Degree requirements:* For master's, comprehensive exam, thesis optional, 33 credit hours; project/internship (for museum studies); for Graduate Certificate, 12 credit hours. *Entrance requirements:* For master's and Graduate Certificate, minimum GPA of 3.0 in last 60 undergraduate hours; statement of goals; resume. Additional exam requirements/recommendations for international students: Required—TOEFL (minimum score 79 iBT) or IELTS (minimum score 6.5). *Application deadline:* For fall admission, 7/1 for domestic and international students; for winter admission, 12/1 for domestic and international students; for spring admission, 5/1 for domestic and international students. Applications are processed on a rolling basis. *Application fee:* $50 ($100 for international students). Electronic applications accepted. *Expenses:* Tuition, state resident: full-time $4886; part-time $203.60 per credit hour. Tuition, nonresident: full-time $18,989; part-time $791.20 per credit hour. *Required fees:* $3283; $126.25 per credit hour. $126.50 per semester. *Financial support:* In 2016–17, 124 students received support. Career-related internships or fieldwork, institutionally sponsored loans, scholarships/grants, health care benefits, and tuition waivers available. Support available to part-time students. Financial award application deadline: 6/1; financial award applicants required to submit FAFSA. *Faculty research:* Management and leadership; policing and corrections management; neuro-psychology of addiction; disproportionate minority contact; ethnic identity and nationalism. *Unit head:* Dr. Martha L. Banz, Associate Provost for Continuing Education/Interim Dean, College of Liberal Studies, 405-325-1061, Fax: 405-325-7132, E-mail: mlbanz@ou.edu. *Application contact:* Michelle Shults, Academic Advisement Services Coordinator, 405-325-2928, Fax: 405-325-7132, E-mail: mshults@ou.edu.
Website: http://www.ou.edu/cls/html

**University of Ottawa,** Faculty of Graduate and Postdoctoral Studies, Faculty of Social Sciences, Department of Criminology, Ottawa, ON K1N 6N5, Canada. Offers MA, MCA, PhD. *Degree requirements:* For master's, thesis or alternative. *Entrance requirements:* For master's, honors bachelor's degree or equivalent, minimum B average. Electronic applications accepted. *Faculty research:* Creation and reform of criminal policies in Canada.

**University of Pennsylvania,** School of Arts and Sciences, Graduate Group in Criminology, Philadelphia, PA 19104. Offers MA, MS, PhD. *Faculty:* 21 full-time (5 women), 1 part-time/adjunct (0 women). *Students:* 23 full-time (17 women), 3 part-time (2 women); includes 5 minority (2 Asian, non-Hispanic/Latino; 2 Hispanic/Latino; 1 Two or more races, non-Hispanic/Latino), 8 international. Average age 26. 179 applicants, 22% accepted, 25 enrolled. In 2016, 14 master's, 3 doctorates awarded. *Expenses: Tuition:* Full-time $31,068; part-time $5762 per course. *Required fees:* $3200; $336 per course. Full-time tuition and fees vary according to degree level, program and student level. Part-time tuition and fees vary according to course load, degree level and program.
Website: http://www.sas.upenn.edu/graduate-division

**University of Phoenix–Augusta Campus,** College of Criminal Justice and Security, Augusta, GA 30909-4583. Offers administration of justice and security (MS).

**University of Phoenix–Bay Area Campus,** College of Criminal Justice and Security, San Jose, CA 95134-1805. Offers administration of justice and security (MS).

**University of Phoenix–Dallas Campus,** College of Criminal Justice and Security, Dallas, TX 75251. Offers administration of justice and security (MS). *Program availability:* Online learning. *Degree requirements:* For master's, thesis (for some programs). *Entrance requirements:* For master's, minimum undergraduate GPA of 2.5, 3 years of work experience. Additional exam requirements/recommendations for international students: Required—TOEFL (minimum score 550 paper-based; 79 iBT). Electronic applications accepted.

**University of Phoenix–Jersey City Campus,** College of Criminal Justice and Security, Jersey City, NJ 07310. Offers administration of justice and security (MS). *Program availability:* Online learning.

**University of Phoenix–Online Campus,** College of Justice and Security, Phoenix, AZ 85034-7209. Offers administration of justice and security (MS), including administration of justice and security, global and homeland security, law enforcement organizations; public administration (MPA). *Program availability:* Evening/weekend, online learning. *Entrance requirements:* Additional exam requirements/recommendations for international students: Required—TOEFL, TOEIC (Test of English as an International Communication), Berlitz Online English Proficiency Exam, PTE, or IELTS. Electronic applications accepted. *Expenses:* Contact institution.

**University of Phoenix–Phoenix Campus,** College of Criminal Justice and Security, Tempe, AZ 85282-2371. Offers administration of justice and security (MS); global and homeland security (MS); law enforcement organizations (MS); public administration (MPA). *Program availability:* Evening/weekend, online learning. *Entrance requirements:* Additional exam requirements/recommendations for international students: Required—TOEFL, TOEIC (Test of English as an International Communication), Berlitz Online English Proficiency Exam, PTE, or IELTS. Electronic applications accepted. *Expenses:* Contact institution.

**University of Phoenix–San Antonio Campus,** College of Criminal Justice and Security, San Antonio, TX 78230. Offers administration of justice and security (MS).

**University of Phoenix–Southern California Campus,** College of Criminal Justice and Security, Costa Mesa, CA 92626. Offers administration of justice and security (MS), including administration of justice and security, global and homeland security, law enforcement organizations; public administration (MPA). *Program availability:* Evening/weekend, online learning. *Entrance requirements:* Additional exam requirements/recommendations for international students: Required—TOEFL, TOEIC (Test of English as an International Communication), Berlitz Online English Proficiency Exam, PTE, or IELTS. Electronic applications accepted. *Expenses:* Contact institution.

**University of Phoenix–Washington D.C. Campus,** College of Criminal Justice and Security, Washington, DC 20001. Offers administration of justice and security (MS).

**University of Phoenix–Western Washington Campus,** College of Criminal Justice and Security, Tukwila, WA 98188. Offers administration of justice and security (MS). *Program availability:* Evening/weekend. *Degree requirements:* For master's, thesis (for some programs). *Entrance requirements:* For master's, minimum undergraduate GPA of 2.5, 3 years of work experience. Additional exam requirements/recommendations for international students: Required—TOEFL (minimum score 550 paper-based; 79 iBT). Electronic applications accepted.

**University of Pittsburgh,** School of Law, Master of Studies in Law Program, Pittsburgh, PA 15260. Offers business law (MSL), including commercial law, corporate law, general business law, international business, tax law; Constitutional law (MSL); criminal law and justice (MSL); disability law (MSL); education law (MSL); elder and estate planning law (MSL); employment and labor law (MSL); energy law (MSL); environmental and real estate law (MSL); family law (MSL); health law (MSL); intellectual property and technology law (MSL); international and human rights law (MSL); jurisprudence (MSL); personal injury and civil litigation (MSL); regulatory law (MSL); self-designed (MSL); sports and entertainment law (MSL). *Program availability:* Part-time. *Faculty:* 48 full-time (21 women), 104 part-time/adjunct (34 women). *Students:* 5 full-time (4 women), 14 part-time (9 women); includes 7 minority (4 Black or African American, non-Hispanic/Latino; 1 Asian, non-Hispanic/Latino; 2 Native Hawaiian or other Pacific Islander, non-Hispanic/Latino). Average age 27. 17 applicants, 53% accepted, 7 enrolled. In 2016, 4 master's awarded. *Entrance requirements:* Additional exam requirements/recommendations for international students: Required—TOEFL (minimum score 600 paper-based; 100 iBT). *Application deadline:* For fall admission, 6/30 for domestic students, 5/1 for international students. Applications are processed on a rolling basis. *Application fee:* $0. Tuition and fees vary according to program. *Faculty research:* Law, health law, business law, contracts, intellectual property, environmental law. *Unit head:* Prof. Alan Meisel, Director, 412-648-1384, Fax: 412-648-2649, E-mail: meisel@pitt.edu. *Application contact:* Beth Ann Pischke, Administrative Coordinator, 412-648-7120, Fax: 412-648-2649, E-mail: pischke@pitt.edu.
Website: http://www.law.pitt.edu/msl

**University of Regina,** Faculty of Graduate Studies and Research, Faculty of Arts, Department of Justice Studies, Regina, SK S4S 0A2, Canada. Offers justice studies (MA); police studies (MA). *Program availability:* Part-time. *Faculty:* 6 full-time (4 women), 9 part-time/adjunct (3 women). *Students:* 2 full-time (1 woman), 2 part-time (both women). 10 applicants, 20% accepted. In 2016, 4 master's awarded. *Degree requirements:* For master's, thesis. *Entrance requirements:* For master's, writing sample. Additional exam requirements/recommendations for international students: Required—TOEFL (minimum score 580 paper-based; 80 iBT), IELTS (minimum score 6.5), PTE (minimum score 59). *Application deadline:* For fall admission, 1/15 for domestic and international students. Application fee: $100. Electronic applications accepted. *Financial support:* In 2016–17, 2 fellowships (averaging $6,000 per year), 1 teaching assistantship (averaging $2,501 per year) were awarded. Financial award application deadline: 6/15. *Faculty research:* Restorative and social justice, policing, public policy, social policy and planning. *Unit head:* Dr. Nick Jones, Department Head, 306-585-4862, Fax: 306-585-4815, E-mail: nick.jones@uregina.ca. *Application contact:* Dr. Michelle Stewart, Graduate Program Coordinator, 306-585-4873, Fax: 306-585-4815, E-mail: michelle.stewart@uregina.ca.
Website: http://www.uregina.ca/arts/justice-studies

**University of St. Thomas,** Graduate Studies, College of Education, Leadership and Counseling, Department of Organization Learning and Development, St. Paul, MN 55105-1096. Offers organization development and change (MA, Ed D); public safety and law enforcement leadership (MA). *Program availability:* Part-time, evening/weekend. *Degree requirements:* For master's, practicum; for doctorate, comprehensive exam, thesis/dissertation. *Entrance requirements:* For master's, minimum GPA of 3.0, 2 letters of reference, personal statement, 2-5 years of organization experience; for doctorate, minimum GPA of 3.5, interview, 5-7 years of organization development or leadership experience. Additional exam requirements/recommendations for international students: Required—TOEFL (minimum score 550 paper-based). *Application deadline:* For fall admission, 7/15 priority date for domestic and international students; for spring admission, 12/9 priority date for domestic and international students; for summer admission, 4/3 priority date for domestic students, 4/3 for international students. Applications are processed on a rolling basis. Electronic applications accepted. *Expenses:* Contact institution. *Financial support:* Fellowships, research assistantships, institutionally sponsored loans, and scholarships/grants available. Support available to part-time students. Financial award application deadline: 8/1; financial award applicants required to submit FAFSA. *Faculty research:* Workplace conflict, physician leaders, virtual teams, technology use in schools/workplace, developing masterful practitioners. *Unit head:* Jean Davidson, Chair, 651-962-4387, Fax: 651-962-4169, E-mail: jmdavidson@stthomas.edu. *Application contact:* Liz G. Knight, Program Manager, 651-962-4459, Fax: 651-962-4169, E-mail: egknight@stthomas.edu.

**University of San Diego,** Division of Professional and Continuing Education, San Diego, CA 92110-2492. Offers cyber security operations and leadership (MS); law enforcement and public safety leadership, (MS). *Program availability:* Part-time-only, evening/weekend, 100% online. *Faculty:* 1 full-time (0 women). *Students:* 200 part-time (44 women); includes 88 minority (10 Black or African American, non-Hispanic/Latino; 22 Asian, non-Hispanic/Latino; 54 Hispanic/Latino; 2 Two or more races, non-Hispanic/Latino). Average age 37. 120 applicants, 88% accepted, 83 enrolled. *Entrance requirements:* For master's, GMAT, GRE, or LSAT if GPA is under 2.75. Additional exam requirements/recommendations for international students: Required—TOEFL (minimum score 90 iBT). *Application deadline:* For fall admission, 8/2 for domestic students; for spring admission, 11/7 for domestic students; for summer admission, 4/11 for domestic students. Applications are processed on a rolling basis. Application fee: $45. Electronic applications accepted. *Financial support:* Application deadline: 4/1; applicants required to submit FAFSA. *Unit head:* Dr. Jason Lemon, Dean, 619-260-4585, E-mail: continuinged@sandiego.edu. *Application contact:* Monica Mahon, Associate Director of Graduate Admissions, 619-260-4524, Fax: 619-260-4158, E-mail: grads@sandiego.edu.
Website: http://pce.sandiego.edu/

**University of South Africa,** College of Law, Pretoria, South Africa. Offers correctional services management (M Tech); criminology (MA, PhD); law (LL M, LL D); penology (MA, PhD); police science (MA, PhD); policing (M Tech); security risk management (M Tech); social science in criminology (MA).

**University of South Carolina,** The Graduate School, College of Arts and Sciences, Department of Criminology and Criminal Justice, Columbia, SC 29208. Offers MA, PhD, JD/MA. *Program availability:* Part-time, evening/weekend. *Degree requirements:* For master's, comprehensive exam, thesis; for doctorate, comprehensive exam, thesis/dissertation. *Entrance requirements:* For master's and doctorate, GRE. Additional exam requirements/recommendations for international students: Required—TOEFL. Electronic applications accepted. *Faculty research:* Juvenile delinquency, substance abuse, policy development, minority issues, law enforcement services.

**The University of South Dakota,** Graduate School, College of Arts and Sciences, Program in Administrative Studies, Vermillion, SD 57069. Offers addiction studies (MSA); criminal justice studies (MSA); health services administration (MSA); human resources (MSA); interdisciplinary studies (MSA); long term care administration (MSA); organizational leadership (MSA). *Program availability:* Part-time, evening/weekend, online learning. *Degree requirements:* For master's, thesis or alternative. *Entrance requirements:* For master's, 3 years of work or experience, minimum GPA of 2.7, resume. Additional exam requirements/recommendations for international students: Required—TOEFL (minimum score 550 paper-based; 79 iBT). Electronic applications accepted.

**University of Southern Mississippi,** Graduate School, College of Science and Technology, School of Criminal Justice, Hattiesburg, MS 39406. Offers criminal justice (MA, MS, PhD); forensic science (MS). *Program availability:* Part-time. *Degree requirements:* For master's, comprehensive exam, thesis; for doctorate, comprehensive exam, thesis/dissertation. *Entrance requirements:* For master's, GRE General Test, minimum GPA of 2.75 in last 60 hours, 3.0 in field of study; for doctorate, GRE General Test, minimum GPA of 3.5. Additional exam requirements/recommendations for international students: Required—TOEFL, IELTS. *Application deadline:* For fall admission, 3/15 priority date for domestic students, 3/15 for international students; for spring admission, 1/10 priority date for domestic and international students. Applications are processed on a rolling basis. Application fee: $60. *Expenses: Tuition, area resident:* Full-time $15,708; part-time $437 per credit hour. *Financial support:* Research assistantships with full tuition reimbursements, teaching assistantships with full tuition reimbursements, career-related internships or fieldwork, Federal Work-Study, institutionally sponsored loans, scholarships/grants, health care benefits, and unspecified assistantships available. Financial award application deadline: 3/15; financial award applicants required to submit FAFSA. *Faculty research:* Crime in the family, police training models, humanities and criminal justice. *Unit head:* Dr. Lisa Nored, Director, 601-266-4509, Fax: 601-266-4391. *Application contact:* Tera Wright, Manager of Graduate Admissions, 601-266-4509, Fax: 601-266-4391.
Website: https://www.usm.edu/criminal-justice

**University of South Florida,** College of Behavioral and Community Sciences, Department of Criminology, Tampa, FL 33620-9951. Offers criminal justice administration (MA); criminology (MA, PhD). *Faculty:* 12 full-time (4 women). *Students:* 35 full-time (23 women), 52 part-time (33 women); includes 27 minority (19 Black or African American, non-Hispanic/Latino; 1 Asian, non-Hispanic/Latino; 6 Hispanic/Latino; 1 Two or more races, non-Hispanic/Latino), 5 international. Average age 30. 111 applicants, 59% accepted, 42 enrolled. In 2016, 25 master's, 7 doctorates awarded. *Degree requirements:* For master's, comprehensive exam, thesis (for some programs); for doctorate, comprehensive exam, thesis/dissertation. *Entrance requirements:* For master's, GRE General Test, statement of purpose; minimum GPA of 3.0 in all upper-division coursework for bachelor's degree, three letters of recommendation, and writing sample (for criminology); minimum undergraduate GPA of 3.0, work experience in the criminal justice field, and two letters of recommendation (for criminal justice administration); for doctorate, GRE General Test, minimum GPA of 3.0 in all upper-division coursework for bachelor's degree or 3.4 in graduate coursework; three letters of recommendation; statement of purpose; sample of academic written work. Additional exam requirements/recommendations for international students: Required—TOEFL (minimum score 550 paper-based; 79 iBT) or IELTS (minimum score 6.5). *Application deadline:* For fall admission, 1/15 for domestic and international students; for spring admission, 9/30 for domestic students, 9/15 for international students. Application fee: $30. Electronic applications accepted. *Expenses: Tuition,* state resident: full-time $7766; part-time $431.43 per credit hour. Tuition, nonresident: full-time $15,789; part-time $877.17 per credit hour. *Required fees:* $37 per term. *Financial support:* In 2016–17, 21 students received support, including 2 research assistantships (averaging $14,172 per year), 15 teaching assistantships with tuition reimbursements available (averaging $11,702 per year). *Faculty research:* Juvenile justice and delinquency, substance use and abuse, macro-level models of criminal behavior, race and social control, violence. *Total annual research expenditures:* $651,010. *Unit head:* Dr. Michael Leiber, Professor and Chair, 813-974-9704, Fax: 813-974-2803, E-mail: mjleiber@usf.edu. *Application contact:* Dr. Ojmarrh Mitchell, Associate Professor and Graduate Director, 813-974-2815, Fax: 813-974-2803, E-mail: omitchell@usf.edu.
Website: http://criminology.cbcs.usf.edu/

**University of South Florida,** Innovative Education, Tampa, FL 33620-9951. Offers adult, career and higher education (Graduate Certificate), including college teaching, leadership in developing human resources, leadership in higher education; Africana studies (Graduate Certificate), including diasporas and health disparities, genocide and human rights; aging studies (Graduate Certificate), including gerontology; art research (Graduate Certificate), including museum studies; business foundations (Graduate Certificate); chemical and biomedical engineering (Graduate Certificate), including materials science and engineering, water, health and sustainability; child and family studies (Graduate Certificate), including positive behavior support; civil and industrial engineering (Graduate Certificate), including transportation systems analysis;

community and family health (Graduate Certificate), including maternal and child health, social marketing and public health, violence and injury: prevention and intervention, women's health; criminology (Graduate Certificate), including criminal justice administration; educational measurement and research (Graduate Certificate), including evaluation; English (Graduate Certificate), including comparative literary studies, creative writing, professional and technical communication; entrepreneurship (Graduate Certificate); environmental health (Graduate Certificate), including safety management; epidemiology and biostatistics (Graduate Certificate), including applied biostatistics, biostatistics, concepts and tools of epidemiology, epidemiology, epidemiology of infectious diseases; geography, environment and planning (Graduate Certificate), including community development, environmental policy and management, geographical information systems; geology (Graduate Certificate), including hydrogeology; global health (Graduate Certificate), including disaster management, global health and Latin American and Caribbean studies, global health practice, humanitarian assistance, infection control; government and international affairs (Graduate Certificate), including Cuban studies, globalization studies; health policy and management (Graduate Certificate), including health management and leadership, public health policy and programs; hearing specialist: early intervention (Graduate Certificate); industrial and management systems engineering (Graduate Certificate), including systems engineering, technology management; information studies (Graduate Certificate), including school library media specialist; information systems/decision sciences (Graduate Certificate), including analytics and business intelligence; instructional technology (Graduate Certificate), including distance education, Florida digital/virtual educator, instructional design, multimedia design, Web design; internal medicine, bioethics and medical humanities (Graduate Certificate), including biomedical ethics; Latin American and Caribbean studies (Graduate Certificate); mass communications (Graduate Certificate), including multimedia journalism; mathematics and statistics (Graduate Certificate), including mathematics; medicine (Graduate Certificate), including aging and neuroscience, bioinformatics, biotechnology, brain fitness and memory management, clinical investigation, health informatics, health sciences, integrative weight management, intellectual property, medicine and gender, metabolic and nutritional medicine, metabolic cardiology, pharmacy sciences; national and competitive intelligence (Graduate Certificate); psychological and social foundations (Graduate Certificate), including career counseling, college teaching, diversity in education, mental health counseling, school counseling; public affairs (Graduate Certificate), including nonprofit management, public management, research administration; public health (Graduate Certificate), including environmental health, health equity, public health generalist, translational research in adolescent behavioral health; public health practices (Graduate Certificate), including planning for healthy communities; rehabilitation and mental health counseling (Graduate Certificate), including integrative mental health care, marriage and family therapy, rehabilitation technology; secondary education (Graduate Certificate), including ESOL, foreign language education: culture and content, foreign language education: professional; social work (Graduate Certificate), including geriatric social work/clinical gerontology; special education (Graduate Certificate), including autism spectrum disorder, disabilities education: severe/profound; world languages (Graduate Certificate), including teaching English as a second language (TESL) or foreign language. *Expenses:* Tuition, state resident: full-time $7766; part-time $431.43 per credit hour. Tuition, nonresident: full-time $15,789; part-time $877.17 per credit hour. *Required fees:* $37 per term. *Unit head:* Kathy Barnes, Interdisciplinary Programs Coordinator, 813-974-8031, Fax: 813-974-7061, E-mail: barnesk@usf.edu. *Application contact:* Karen Tylinski, Metro Initiatives, 813-974-9943, Fax: 813-974-7061, E-mail: ktylinsk@usf.edu.
Website: http://www.usf.edu/innovative-education/

**University of South Florida Sarasota-Manatee,** College of Liberal Arts and Social Sciences, Sarasota, FL 34243. Offers criminal justice (MA); education (MA); educational leadership (M Ed), including curriculum leadership, K-12 public school leadership, non-public/charter school leadership; elementary education (MAT); English education (MA); social work (MSW). *Program availability:* Part-time, 100% online, blended/hybrid learning. *Faculty:* 11 full-time (9 women), 7 part-time/adjunct (5 women). *Students:* 11 full-time (all women), 55 part-time (41 women); includes 18 minority (5 Black or African American, non-Hispanic/Latino; 1 American Indian or Alaska Native, non-Hispanic/Latino; 2 Asian, non-Hispanic/Latino; 10 Hispanic/Latino). Average age 36. 40 applicants, 43% accepted, 17 enrolled. In 2016, 28 master's awarded. *Degree requirements:* For master's, comprehensive exam (for some programs). *Entrance requirements:* Additional exam requirements/recommendations for international students: Required—TOEFL (minimum score 550 paper-based; 79 iBT), IELTS (minimum score 6.5). *Application deadline:* For fall admission, 3/1 priority date for domestic students, 3/1 for international students; for spring admission, 10/1 priority date for domestic students, 10/1 for international students. Applications are processed on a rolling basis. Application fee: $30. Electronic applications accepted. *Expenses:* Contact institution. *Financial support:* In 2016–17, 9 students received support. Career-related internships or fieldwork, institutionally sponsored loans, scholarships/grants, health care benefits, and unspecified assistantships available. Support available to part-time students. Financial award application deadline: 3/1; financial award applicants required to submit FAFSA. *Faculty research:* Educational leadership, secondary education, elementary education, criminal justice, social work. *Unit head:* Dr. Jane Rose, Dean, 941-359-4469, Fax: 941-359-4778, E-mail: jane.rose@sar.usf.edu. *Application contact:* Brandon Avery, Assistant Director, Admissions, 941-359-4331, E-mail: bavery@sar.usf.edu.
Website: http://usfsm.edu/college-of-liberal-arts-sciences/

**The University of Tennessee,** Graduate School, College of Arts and Sciences, Department of Sociology, Knoxville, TN 37996. Offers criminology (MA, PhD); energy, environment, and resource policy (MA, PhD); political economy (MA, PhD). *Program availability:* Part-time. *Degree requirements:* For master's, thesis or alternative; for doctorate, thesis/dissertation. *Entrance requirements:* For master's, GRE General Test, minimum GPA of 3.0; for doctorate, GRE General Test, minimum GPA of 3.5. Additional exam requirements/recommendations for international students: Required—TOEFL. Electronic applications accepted.

**The University of Tennessee at Chattanooga,** Program in Criminal Justice, Chattanooga, TN 37403. Offers MSCJ. *Program availability:* Part-time. *Faculty:* 8 full-time (6 women), 1 part-time/adjunct (0 women). *Students:* 17 full-time (11 women), 18 part-time (9 women); includes 19 minority (13 Black or African American, non-Hispanic/Latino; 3 Hispanic/Latino; 3 Two or more races, non-Hispanic/Latino). Average age 28. 20 applicants, 100% accepted, 13 enrolled. In 2016, 7 master's awarded. *Degree requirements:* For master's, comprehensive exam or thesis. *Entrance requirements:* For master's, GRE General Test or MAT, 2 letters of recommendation. Additional exam requirements/recommendations for international students: Required—TOEFL (minimum score 550 paper-based; 79 iBT), IELTS (minimum score 6). *Application deadline:* For fall admission, 6/15 priority date for domestic students, 7/1 for international students; for spring admission, 11/1 priority date for domestic students, 11/1 for international students. Applications are processed on a rolling basis. Application fee: $35 ($40 for international students). Electronic applications accepted. *Expenses:* $9,876 full-time in-state; $25,994 full-time out-of-state; $450 per credit part-time in-state; $1,345 per credit part-time out-of-state. *Financial support:* In 2016–17, 6 research assistantships were

## Criminal Justice and Criminology

awarded; teaching assistantships, career-related internships or fieldwork, scholarships/grants, and unspecified assistantships also available. Support available to part-time students. Financial award application deadline: 7/1; financial award applicants required to submit FAFSA. *Faculty research:* Violence against women, crime prevention, police accountability, criminal justice privatization, public policy. *Total annual research expenditures:* $77,580. *Unit head:* Dr. Tammy Garland, Graduate Coordinator, 423-425-5245, Fax: 423-425-2228, E-mail: tammy-garland@utc.edu. *Application contact:* Dr. Joanne Romagni, Dean of the Graduate School, 423-425-4478, Fax: 423-425-5223, E-mail: joanne-romagni@utc.edu.
Website: http://www.utc.edu/criminal-justice/criminal-justice-graduate-program/graduate-welcome.php

**The University of Texas at Arlington,** Graduate School, College of Liberal Arts, Department of Criminology and Criminal Justice, Arlington, TX 76019. Offers MA. *Program availability:* Part-time, evening/weekend. *Degree requirements:* For master's, comprehensive exam, thesis or alternative. *Entrance requirements:* For master's, GRE General Test, minimum GPA of 3.0 in last 60 hours of undergraduate course work, 3 letters of recommendation. Additional exam requirements/recommendations for international students: Required—TOEFL (minimum score 550 paper-based). *Application deadline:* For fall admission, 6/15 for domestic students. Applications are processed on a rolling basis. Application fee: $35 ($50 for international students). *Financial support:* Research assistantships and career-related internships or fieldwork available. Financial award application deadline: 6/1; financial award applicants required to submit FAFSA. *Unit head:* Dr. Jaya Davis, Associate Professor and Graduate Programs Director, 817-272-0318, E-mail: jbdavis@uta.edu. *Application contact:* Dr. Rhonda Dobbs, Graduate Advisor, 817-272-3318, E-mail: dobbs@uta.edu.
Website: http://www.uta.edu/criminology

**The University of Texas at Dallas,** School of Economic, Political and Policy Sciences, Program in Criminology, Richardson, TX 75080. Offers criminology (MS, PhD); justice administration and leadership (MS). *Program availability:* Part-time, evening/weekend. *Faculty:* 11 full-time (4 women), 3 part-time/adjunct (1 woman). *Students:* 49 full-time (28 women), 23 part-time (19 women); includes 29 minority (16 Black or African American, non-Hispanic/Latino; 3 Asian, non-Hispanic/Latino; 7 Hispanic/Latino; 3 Two or more races, non-Hispanic/Latino), 3 international. Average age 35. 82 applicants, 38% accepted, 22 enrolled. In 2016, 22 master's, 6 doctorates awarded. *Degree requirements:* For master's, thesis; for doctorate, thesis/dissertation. *Entrance requirements:* For master's, GRE General Test, minimum GPA of 3.0 in upper-level course work in field; for doctorate, GRE (minimum combined verbal and quantitative score of 1200), minimum GPA 3.2 in upper-level course work in field. Additional exam requirements/recommendations for international students: Required—TOEFL (minimum score 550 paper-based). *Application deadline:* For fall admission, 7/15 for domestic students, 5/1 priority date for international students; for spring admission, 11/15 for domestic students, 9/1 priority date for international students. Applications are processed on a rolling basis. Application fee: $50 ($100 for international students). Electronic applications accepted. *Expenses:* Tuition, state resident: full-time $12,418; part-time $690 per semester hour. Tuition, nonresident: full-time $24,150; part-time $1342 per semester hour. Tuition and fees vary according to course load. *Financial support:* In 2016–17, 41 students received support, including 5 research assistantships with partial tuition reimbursements available (averaging $16,800 per year), 8 teaching assistantships with partial tuition reimbursements available (averaging $13,656 per year); career-related internships or fieldwork, Federal Work-Study, institutionally sponsored loans, scholarships/grants, and unspecified assistantships also available. Support available to part-time students. Financial award application deadline: 4/30; financial award applicants required to submit FAFSA. *Faculty research:* Developmental criminology, domestic violence, mental health and violence, the death penalty, corrections. *Unit head:* Dr. Denise Paquette Boots, Program Head, 972-883-6468, Fax: 972-883-2735, E-mail: deniseboots@utdallas.edu. *Application contact:* Rita Medford, Graduate Program Administrator, 972-883-4932, Fax: 972-883-2735, E-mail: rmedford@utdallas.edu.
Website: http://www.utdallas.edu/epps/criminology/

**The University of Texas at San Antonio,** College of Public Policy, Department of Criminal Justice, San Antonio, TX 78207. Offers criminology (MS). *Program availability:* Part-time, evening/weekend. *Faculty:* 5 full-time (2 women). *Students:* 24 full-time (16 women), 24 part-time (13 women); includes 36 minority (2 Black or African American, non-Hispanic/Latino; 1 American Indian or Alaska Native, non-Hispanic/Latino; 1 Asian, non-Hispanic/Latino; 32 Hispanic/Latino). Average age 26. 42 applicants, 60% accepted, 18 enrolled. In 2016, 8 master's awarded. *Degree requirements:* For master's, variable foreign language requirement, minimum of 36 semester credit hours; thesis or written comprehensive exams. *Entrance requirements:* For master's, minimum GPA of 3.0 in last 60 hours of undergraduate course work; 2 letters of recommendation; resume; 18 credit hours in criminal justice, criminology or closely-related discipline. Additional exam requirements/recommendations for international students: Required—TOEFL (minimum score 550 paper-based; 79 iBT), IELTS (minimum score 6.5). *Application deadline:* For fall admission, 7/1 for domestic students, 4/1 for international students; for spring admission, 11/1 for domestic students, 9/1 for international students. Application fee: $45 ($80 for international students). Electronic applications accepted. *Expenses:* Contact institution. *Financial support:* In 2016–17, 7 students received support, including 10 research assistantships (averaging $8,037 per year), 2 teaching assistantships (averaging $8,037 per year). Financial award application deadline: 2/15. *Faculty research:* Criminological theory, crime prevention, administration of justice, correctional interventions, evidence-based practices and program evaluation. *Total annual research expenditures:* $660,434. *Unit head:* Dr. Robert Tillyear, Associate Professor and Chair, 210-458-2679, Fax: 210-458-2680, E-mail: robert.tillyer@utsa.edu. *Application contact:* Dr. Marie Tillyer, Associate Professor/Graduate Advisor of Record, 210-458-2682, Fax: 210-459-2680, E-mail: marie.tillyer@utsa.edu.
Website: http://copp.utsa.edu/department/about-us/

**The University of Texas at Tyler,** College of Arts and Sciences, Department of Social Sciences, Tyler, TX 75799-0001. Offers criminal justice (MS); public administration (MPA); sociology (MS). *Program availability:* Part-time, evening/weekend. *Degree requirements:* For master's, comprehensive exam, thesis optional. *Entrance requirements:* For master's, GRE General Test, minimum GPA of 3.0. Additional exam requirements/recommendations for international students: Required—TOEFL. *Faculty research:* Urban segregation, minority business, violent crime, gender discrimination.

**The University of Texas of the Permian Basin,** Office of Graduate Studies, College of Arts and Sciences, Department of Social Sciences, Program in Criminal Justice Administration, Odessa, TX 79762-0001. Offers MS. *Program availability:* Part-time, evening/weekend. *Degree requirements:* For master's, comprehensive exam (for some programs), thesis (for some programs). *Entrance requirements:* For master's, GRE General Test, 3 letters of recommendation. Additional exam requirements/recommendations for international students: Required—TOEFL (minimum score 550 paper-based).

**The University of Texas Rio Grande Valley,** College of Liberal Arts, Department of Criminal Justice, Edinburg, TX 78539. Offers MS. *Program availability:* Part-time, evening/weekend, online learning. *Degree requirements:* For master's, comprehensive

exam, applied project or thesis. *Entrance requirements:* For master's, minimum undergraduate GPA of 3.0, official transcripts, 250-500 word letter of intent, three letters of recommendation. Additional exam requirements/recommendations for international students: Required—TOEFL (minimum score 550 paper-based; 79 iBT), IELTS (minimum score 6.5). Tuition and fees vary according to course load and program. *Faculty research:* Comparative criminal justice systems, death penalty, community policing, Hispanic women.

**University of the Fraser Valley,** Graduate Studies, Abbotsford, BC V2S 7M8, Canada. Offers criminal justice (MA); social work (MSW). *Program availability:* Evening/weekend. *Faculty:* 23 full-time (13 women). *Students:* 47 full-time (26 women), 2 part-time (1 woman); includes 3 minority (all American Indian or Alaska Native, non-Hispanic/Latino). Average age 37. 79 applicants, 42% accepted, 32 enrolled. In 2016, 19 master's awarded. *Degree requirements:* For master's, thesis optional, major research paper. *Entrance requirements:* For master's, bachelor's degree, work experience in related field. Additional exam requirements/recommendations for international students: Recommended—TOEFL (minimum score 88 iBT), IELTS (minimum score 6.5), TWE. *Application deadline:* For fall admission, 1/31 priority date for domestic students, 4/1 priority date for international students; for winter admission, 9/30 priority date for domestic students, 10/1 priority date for international students; for spring admission, 12/31 priority date for domestic students, 2/1 priority date for international students. Application fee: $45 ($150 for international students). Electronic applications accepted. *Expenses:* Contact institution. *Financial support:* Research assistantships, scholarships/grants, health care benefits, and bursaries available. Financial award application deadline: 5/10. *Faculty research:* Criminal justice, criminology, social work, child welfare. *Unit head:* Dr. Adrienne Chan, Associate Vice President for Research, Engagement and Graduate Studies, 604-504-4074, Fax: 778-880-0356, E-mail: adrienne.chan@ufv.ca. *Application contact:* Educational Advisors, 604-854-4528, Fax: 604-855-7614, E-mail: advising@ufv.ca.
Website: http://www.ufv.ca/Graduate_Studies.htm

**The University of Toledo,** College of Graduate Studies, College of Social Justice and Human Service, Department of Criminal Justice and Social Work, Toledo, OH 43606-3390. Offers child advocacy (Certificate); criminal justice (MA); elder law (Certificate); juvenile justice (Certificate); patient advocacy (Certificate); social work (MSW); JD/MA. *Accreditation:* CSWE. *Program availability:* Part-time. *Degree requirements:* For master's, comprehensive exam, thesis. *Entrance requirements:* For master's and Certificate, minimum cumulative GPA of 2.7 for all previous academic work, letters of recommendation. Additional exam requirements/recommendations for international students: Required—TOEFL (minimum score 550 paper-based; 80 iBT). Electronic applications accepted.

**University of Toronto,** School of Graduate Studies, Faculty of Arts and Science, Centre for Criminology and Sociolegal Studies, Toronto, ON M5S 1A1, Canada. Offers MA, PhD, JD/MA. *Program availability:* Part-time. *Degree requirements:* For doctorate, comprehensive exam, thesis/dissertation. *Entrance requirements:* For master's, 2 letters of reference, bachelor's degree in social science or humanities, minimum B+ average in last 2 years of undergraduate study; for doctorate, 2 letters of reference, MA in criminology or equivalent, minimum A- average. Additional exam requirements/recommendations for international students: Required—TOEFL (minimum score 580 paper-based; 93 iBT), TWE (minimum score 5). Electronic applications accepted.

**University of West Florida,** College of Education and Professional Studies, Department of Criminology and Criminal Justice, Pensacola, FL 32514-5750. Offers criminal justice (MS). *Program availability:* Part-time, evening/weekend. *Faculty:* 2 full-time (0 women). *Students:* 10 full-time (7 women), 22 part-time (9 women); includes 9 minority (4 Black or African American, non-Hispanic/Latino; 1 Asian, non-Hispanic/Latino; 3 Hispanic/Latino; 1 Two or more races, non-Hispanic/Latino), 2 international. Average age 32. 28 applicants, 57% accepted, 12 enrolled. In 2016, 7 master's awarded. *Degree requirements:* For master's, thesis optional. *Entrance requirements:* For master's, GRE or MAT, official transcripts; minimum undergraduate cumulative GPA of 3.0; 3 letters of recommendation; personal statement. Additional exam requirements/recommendations for international students: Required—TOEFL (minimum score 550 paper-based). *Application deadline:* For fall admission, 6/1 for domestic and international students; for spring admission, 10/1 for domestic and international students. Applications are processed on a rolling basis. Electronic applications accepted. *Expenses:* Tuition, state resident: full-time $5316.12. Tuition, nonresident: full-time $11,308. *Required fees:* $583.92. Tuition and fees vary according to course load and program. *Financial support:* In 2016–17, 1 fellowship, 14 research assistantships with partial tuition reimbursements, 2 teaching assistantships with partial tuition reimbursements were awarded; unspecified assistantships also available. *Unit head:* Dr. Diane Scott, Interim Chair, 850-857-6349, E-mail: dscott2@uwf.edu. *Application contact:* Terry McCray, Assistant Director of Graduate Admissions, 850-473-7718, Fax: 850-473-7714, E-mail: gradadmissions@uwf.edu.
Website: http://uwf.edu/ceps/departments/criminology-and-criminal-justice/

**University of West Georgia,** College of Social Sciences, Carrollton, GA 30118. Offers criminology (MA); data analysis and evaluation methods (Postbaccalaureate Certificate); European Union studies (Postbaccalaureate Certificate); integrative health systems (Postbaccalaureate Certificate); nonprofit management and community development (Postbaccalaureate Certificate); psychology (MA, PhD), including consciousness and society (PhD); public administration (MPA); public management (Postbaccalaureate Certificate); sociology (MA). *Program availability:* Part-time, evening/weekend, 100% online, blended/hybrid learning. *Faculty:* 45 full-time (21 women). *Students:* 107 full-time (67 women), 73 part-time (46 women); includes 47 minority (39 Black or African American, non-Hispanic/Latino; 4 Asian, non-Hispanic/Latino; 4 Hispanic/Latino), 10 international. Average age 31. 83 applicants, 88% accepted, 60 enrolled. In 2016, 56 master's, 7 doctorates, 5 other advanced degrees awarded. *Entrance requirements:* Additional exam requirements/recommendations for international students: Required—TOEFL (minimum score 523 paper-based; 69 iBT); Recommended—IELTS (minimum score 6.5). *Application deadline:* For fall admission, 7/15 for domestic students, 6/1 for international students; for spring admission, 11/30 for domestic students, 10/15 for international students; for summer admission, 5/15 for domestic students, 3/30 for international students. Applications are processed on a rolling basis. Application fee: $40. Electronic applications accepted. *Expenses:* Tuition, state resident: full-time $5316; part-time $222 per semester hour. Tuition, nonresident: full-time $20,658; part-time $861 per semester hour. *Required fees:* $1962. Tuition and fees vary according to course load, degree level and program. *Financial support:* Fellowships, research assistantships, teaching assistantships, career-related internships or fieldwork, Federal Work-Study, institutionally sponsored loans, scholarships/grants, and unspecified assistantships available. Support available to part-time students. Financial award application deadline: 4/1; financial award applicants required to submit FAFSA. *Unit head:* Dr. N. Jane McCandless, Dean of Social Sciences, 678-839-5170, Fax: 678-839-5171, E-mail: jmccandl@westga.edu. *Application contact:* Dr. Toby Ziglar, Assistant Dean of the Graduate School, 678-839-1394, Fax: 678-839-1395, E-mail: graduate@westga.edu.
Website: https://www.westga.edu/coss

**University of Windsor,** Faculty of Graduate Studies, Faculty of Arts and Social Sciences, Department of Sociology and Anthropology, Windsor, ON N9B 3P4, Canada. Offers criminology (MA); sociology (MA); sociology-social justice (PhD). *Program availability:* Part-time. *Degree requirements:* For master's, thesis; for doctorate, comprehensive exam, thesis/dissertation. *Entrance requirements:* For master's, minimum B+ average; for doctorate, writing sample, minimum B+ average. Additional exam requirements/recommendations for international students: Required—TOEFL (minimum score 560 paper-based). Electronic applications accepted. *Faculty research:* Power and social change; criminology/deviance; social psychology; comparative development; race and ethnic relations; family, sex, and gender, social justice.

**University of Wisconsin–Milwaukee,** Graduate School, Helen Bader School of Social Welfare, Department of Criminal Justice, Milwaukee, WI 53201-0413. Offers applied data analysis using SAS (Graduate Certificate); crime analytics (MS); criminal justice (MS). *Program availability:* Part-time. *Students:* 20 full-time (11 women), 19 part-time (6 women); includes 12 minority (6 Black or African American, non-Hispanic/Latino; 1 Asian, non-Hispanic/Latino; 5 Two or more races, non-Hispanic/Latino), 1 international. Average age 29. 29 applicants, 76% accepted, 18 enrolled. In 2016, 4 master's, 2 other advanced degrees awarded. *Degree requirements:* For master's, thesis or alternative. *Entrance requirements:* For master's, GRE General Test, MAT. Additional exam requirements/recommendations for international students: Required—TOEFL (minimum score 550 paper-based; 79 iBT), IELTS (minimum score 6.5). *Application deadline:* For fall admission, 1/1 priority date for domestic students; for spring admission, 9/1 for domestic students. Applications are processed on a rolling basis. Application fee: $56 ($96 for international students). Electronic applications accepted. *Financial support:* Fellowships, research assistantships, teaching assistantships with full tuition reimbursements, career-related internships or fieldwork, health care benefits, unspecified assistantships, and project assistantships available. Support available to part-time students. Financial award application deadline: 4/15; financial award applicants required to submit FAFSA. *Application contact:* Mary Russell, Academic Department Specialist, 414-229-2392, E-mail: russelme@uwm.edu.
Website: http://uwm.edu/socialwelfare/academics/criminal-justice-field-placement/

**University of Wisconsin–Platteville,** School of Graduate Studies, Distance Learning Center, Online Master of Science in Criminal Justice Program, Platteville, WI 53818-3099. Offers MS. *Program availability:* Part-time, online learning. *Students:* 2 full-time (both women), 110 part-time (57 women); includes 17 minority (10 Black or African American, non-Hispanic/Latino; 1 Asian, non-Hispanic/Latino; 6 Hispanic/Latino). 68 applicants, 59% accepted, 28 enrolled. In 2016, 20 master's awarded. *Degree requirements:* For master's, thesis or alternative. *Entrance requirements:* Additional exam requirements/recommendations for international students: Required—TOEFL (minimum score 550 paper-based; 79 iBT), IELTS (minimum score 6.5). *Application deadline:* For fall admission, 7/1 priority date for domestic students; for spring admission, 11/1 priority date for domestic students. Applications are processed on a rolling basis. Application fee: $56. Electronic applications accepted. *Expenses:* Contact institution. *Financial support:* Scholarships/grants available. Support available to part-time students. *Unit head:* Cheryl Banachowski-Fuller, Coordinator, 608-342-1652, Fax: 608-342-1986, E-mail: banachoc@uwplatt.edu. *Application contact:* 608-342-1468, Fax: 608-342-1071, E-mail: disted@uwplatt.edu.
Website: http://www.uwplatt.edu/disted/criminal-justice-MS.html

**Urbana University,** College of Social and Behavioral Sciences, Urbana, OH 43078-2091. Offers criminal justice administration (MA). *Entrance requirements:* For master's, 3 letters of recommendation.

**Utica College,** Program in Economic Crime and Fraud Management, Utica, NY 13502-4892. Offers MS. *Program availability:* Part-time, evening/weekend, 100% online. *Faculty:* 7 full-time (0 women). *Students:* 1 full-time (0 women), 96 part-time (53 women); includes 27 minority (19 Black or African American, non-Hispanic/Latino; 1 American Indian or Alaska Native, non-Hispanic/Latino; 2 Asian, non-Hispanic/Latino; 5 Hispanic/Latino). Average age 33. 42 applicants, 93% accepted, 37 enrolled. In 2016, 54 master's awarded. *Entrance requirements:* For master's, BS, minimum GPA of 3.0. Additional exam requirements/recommendations for international students: Required—TOEFL (minimum score 525 paper-based). *Application deadline:* Applications are processed on a rolling basis. Application fee: $50. Electronic applications accepted. *Expenses:* Contact institution. *Financial support:* Career-related internships or fieldwork, scholarships/grants, tuition waivers (partial), and unspecified assistantships available. Support available to part-time students. Financial award application deadline: 3/15; financial award applicants required to submit FAFSA. *Unit head:* Dr. R. Bruce McBride, Director of Economic Crime Graduate Programs, 315-792-3808, E-mail: rmcbride@utica.edu. *Application contact:* John D. Rowe, Director of Graduate Admissions, 315-792-3824, Fax: 315-792-3003, E-mail: jrowe@utica.edu.
Website: http://programs.online.utica.edu/programs/mba-fraud-management.asp

**Utica College,** Program in Economic Crime Management, Utica, NY 13502-4892. Offers MS. *Program availability:* Part-time, evening/weekend, online learning. *Faculty:* 4 full-time (0 women). *Students:* 1 (woman) full-time, 27 part-time (14 women); includes 10 minority (5 Black or African American, non-Hispanic/Latino; 1 Asian, non-Hispanic/Latino; 4 Hispanic/Latino). Average age 39. In 2016, 19 master's awarded. *Degree requirements:* For master's, thesis. *Entrance requirements:* For master's, BS, minimum GPA of 3.0. Additional exam requirements/recommendations for international students: Required—TOEFL (minimum score 525 paper-based). *Application deadline:* Applications are processed on a rolling basis. Application fee: $50. Electronic applications accepted. *Expenses:* Contact institution. *Financial support:* Career-related internships or fieldwork, scholarships/grants, tuition waivers (partial), and unspecified assistantships available. Support available to part-time students. Financial award application deadline: 3/15; financial award applicants required to submit FAFSA. *Unit head:* Dr. R. Bruce McBride, Director of Economic Crime Graduate Programs, 315-792-3808, E-mail: rmcbride@utica.edu. *Application contact:* John D. Rowe, Director of Graduate Admissions, 315-792-3824, Fax: 315-792-3003, E-mail: jrowe@utica.edu.
Website: http://programs.online.utica.edu/programs/masters-financial-crime-compliance-management.asp

**Virginia College in Birmingham,** Virginia College Online, Birmingham, AL 35209. Offers business administration (MBA); criminal justice (MCJ); cybersecurity (MC). *Program availability:* Part-time, evening/weekend, online learning.

**Virginia Commonwealth University,** Graduate School, College of Humanities and Sciences, L. Douglas Wilder School of Government and Public Affairs, Program in Criminal Justice, Richmond, VA 23284-9005. Offers MS, Postbaccalaureate Certificate. *Program availability:* Part-time, evening/weekend. *Degree requirements:* For master's, thesis or comprehensive exam. *Entrance requirements:* For master's, GRE, LSAT or GMAT, minimum cumulative GPA of 3.0. Additional exam requirements/recommendations for international students: Required—TOEFL (minimum score 600 paper-based; 100 iBT); Recommended—IELTS (minimum score 6.5). *Application deadline:* For fall admission, 4/1 for domestic students; for spring admission, 10/1 for domestic students. Applications are processed on a rolling basis. Application fee: $50. Electronic applications accepted. *Financial support:* Federal Work-Study, institutionally sponsored loans, and tuition waivers (full and partial) available. Support available to part-time students. Financial award application deadline: 3/1. *Unit head:* Dr. Jay

Albanese, Chair, 804-827-0844, E-mail: jsalbane@vcu.edu. *Application contact:* Dr. Jill A. Gordon, Associate Dean of Faculty and Academic Affairs, 804-827-0901, Fax: 804-828-1253, E-mail: jagordon@vcu.edu.
Website: http://www.wilder.vcu.edu/programs/criminal-justice/

**Virginia State University,** College of Graduate Studies, College of Humanities and Social Sciences, Department of Sociology and Criminal Justice, Petersburg, VA 23806-0001. Offers criminal justice (MS).

**Walden University,** Graduate Programs, School of Public Policy and Administration, Minneapolis, MN 55401. Offers criminal justice (MPA, MPP, MS, Graduate Certificate), including emergency management (MS, PhD), general program (MS), global leadership (MS, PhD), homeland security and policy coordination (MS, PhD), law and public policy (MS, PhD), policy analysis (MS, PhD), public management and leadership (MS, PhD), self-designed (MS), terrorism, mediation, and peace (MS, PhD); criminal justice and executive management (MS), including global leadership (MS, PhD); criminal justice leadership and executive management (MS), including emergency management (MS, PhD), general program, homeland security and policy coordination (MS, PhD), law and public policy (MS, PhD), policy analysis (MS, PhD), public management and leadership (MS, PhD), self-designed, terrorism, mediation, and peace (MS, PhD); emergency management (MPA, MPP, MS), including criminal justice (MS, PhD), general program (MS), homeland security (MS), public management and leadership (MS, PhD), terrorism and emergency management (MS); general program (MPA, MPP); global leadership (MPA, MPP); government management (Graduate Certificate); health policy (MPA, MPP); homeland security (Graduate Certificate); homeland security and policy coordination (MPA, MPP); international nongovernmental organizations (MPA, MPP); law and public policy (MPA, MPP); local government management for sustainable communities (MPA, MPP); nonprofit management (Graduate Certificate); nonprofit management and leadership (MPA, MPP, MS), including global leadership (MS, PhD), international nongovernmental organization (MS), local government for sustainable communities (MS), self designed (MS); online teaching in higher education (Post-Master's Certificate); policy analysis (MPA); public management and leadership (MPA, MPP, Graduate Certificate); public policy (Graduate Certificate); public policy and administration (PhD), including criminal justice (MS, PhD), emergency management (MS, PhD), global leadership (MS, PhD), health policy, homeland security and policy coordination (MS, PhD), international nongovernmental organizations, law and public policy (MS, PhD), local government management for sustainable communities, nonprofit management and leadership, policy analysis (MS, PhD), public management and leadership (MS, PhD), terrorism, mediation, and peace (MS, PhD); strategic planning and public policy (Graduate Certificate); terrorism, mediation, and peace (MPA, MPP). *Program availability:* Part-time, evening/weekend, online only, 100% online. *Degree requirements:* For doctorate, thesis/dissertation, residency. *Entrance requirements:* For master's, bachelor's degree or higher; minimum GPA of 2.5; official transcripts; goal statement (for some programs); access to computer and Internet; for doctorate, master's degree or higher; three years of related professional or academic experience (preferred); minimum GPA of 3.0; goal statement and current resume (for select programs); official transcripts; access to computer and Internet; for other advanced degree, relevant work experience; access to computer and Internet. Additional exam requirements/recommendations for international students: Required—TOEFL (minimum score 550 paper-based, 79 iBT), IELTS (minimum score 6.5), Michigan English Language Assessment Battery (minimum score 82), or PTE (minimum score 53). Electronic applications accepted.

**Walden University,** Graduate Programs, School of Social Work and Human Services, Minneapolis, MN 55401. Offers addictions and social work (DSW); advanced clinical practice (MSW); clinical expertise (DSW); criminal justice (DSW); disaster, crisis, and intervention (DSW); family studies and interventions (DSW); human and social services (PhD), including advanced research, community and social services, community intervention and leadership, conflict management, criminal justice, disaster crisis and intervention, family studies and intervention, gerontology, global social services, higher education, human services and nonprofit administration, mental health facilitation; medical social work (DSW); military social work (MSW); policy practice (DSW); social work (PhD), including addictions and social work, clinical expertise, criminal justice, disaster, crisis and intervention, family studies and interventions, medical social work, policy practice, social work administration; social work administration (DSW); social work in healthcare (MSW); social work with children and families (MSW). *Accreditation:* CSWE. *Program availability:* Part-time, evening/weekend, online only, 100% online. *Degree requirements:* For master's, residency (for some programs); for doctorate, thesis/dissertation, residency. *Entrance requirements:* For master's, bachelor's degree or higher; minimum GPA of 2.5; official transcripts; goal statement (for some programs); access to computer and Internet; for doctorate, master's degree or higher; three years of related professional or academic experience (preferred); minimum GPA of 3.0; goal statement and current resume (for select programs); official transcripts; access to computer and Internet. Additional exam requirements/recommendations for international students: Required—TOEFL (minimum score 550 paper-based, 79 iBT), IELTS (minimum score 6.5), Michigan English Language Assessment Battery (minimum score 82), or PTE (minimum score 53). Electronic applications accepted.

**Waldorf University,** Program in Organizational Leadership, Forest City, IA 50436. Offers criminal justice leadership (MA); emergency management leadership (MA); fire/rescue executive leadership (MA); human resource development (MA); public administration (MA); sport management (MA); teacher leader (MA).

**Washburn University,** School of Applied Studies, Department of Criminal Justice and Legal Studies, Topeka, KS 66621. Offers MCJ. *Program availability:* Part-time, evening/weekend, online learning. *Degree requirements:* For master's, thesis or alternative, continuous enrollment each fall and spring semester, completion of all program requirements within seven years of entry (MCJ). *Entrance requirements:* For master's, GRE, 3 letters of reference, minimum GPA of 3.0 for undergraduate degree, short biography, official transcripts. Additional exam requirements/recommendations for international students: Required—TOEFL (minimum score 80 iBT). Electronic applications accepted. *Faculty research:* Practitioner behavior, police management and training, field and institutional correction administration, terrorism, police training, sex slaves.

**Washington State University,** College of Arts and Sciences, Department of Criminal Justice and Criminology, Pullman, WA 99164. Offers MA, PhD. MA program also offered at Spokane and Global (online) campuses. *Program availability:* Online learning. *Degree requirements:* For master's, comprehensive exam (for some programs), thesis, oral exam; for doctorate, comprehensive exam, thesis/dissertation, oral or written exam. *Entrance requirements:* For master's, GRE General Test, major in criminal justice, sociology, psychology, liberal arts, or a related field; strong writing and analytical skills; minimum GPA of 3.0; for doctorate, GRE General Test, major in criminal justice, sociology, psychology, liberal arts, or a related field; strong writing and analytical skills. Additional exam requirements/recommendations for international students: Required—TOEFL, IELTS. Electronic applications accepted. *Faculty research:* Community policing, community justice, corrections policy, crime prevention policy, criminal justice management.

## Criminal Justice and Criminology

**Wayland Baptist University,** Graduate Programs, Programs in Behavioral and Social Sciences, Plainview, TX 79072-6998. Offers counseling (MA); criminal justice (MACJ); government administration (MPA); history (MA); homeland security (MPA); humanities (MAH); justice administration (MPA). *Program availability:* Part-time, evening/weekend, online learning. *Degree requirements:* For master's, comprehensive exam. *Entrance requirements:* For master's, GRE, MAT. Additional exam requirements/recommendations for international students: Required—TOEFL (minimum score 500 paper-based; 61 iBT). Electronic applications accepted.

**Waynesburg University,** Graduate and Professional Studies, Canonsburg, PA 15370. Offers business (MBA), including energy management, finance, health systems, human resources, leadership, market development; counseling (MA), including addictions counseling, clinical mental health; counselor education and supervision (PhD); criminal investigation (MA); education (M Ed), including autism, curriculum and instruction, educational leadership, online teaching; nursing (MSN), including administration, education, informatics; nursing practice (DNP); special education (M Ed); technology (M Ed); MSN/MBA. *Accreditation:* AACN. *Program availability:* Part-time, evening/weekend. *Degree requirements:* For doctorate, thesis/dissertation. *Entrance requirements:* Additional exam requirements/recommendations for international students: Required—TOEFL. Electronic applications accepted.

**Wayne State University,** College of Liberal Arts and Sciences, Department of Criminal Justice, Detroit, MI 48202. Offers MS. *Program availability:* 100% online. *Faculty:* 8. *Students:* 3 full-time (1 woman), 42 part-time (30 women); includes 16 minority (12 Black or African American, non-Hispanic/Latino; 3 Hispanic/Latino; 1 Two or more races, non-Hispanic/Latino), 1 international. Average age 29. 68 applicants, 16% accepted, 8 enrolled. In 2016, 13 master's awarded. *Degree requirements:* For master's, comprehensive exam, three-credit essay, thesis, or capstone seminar. *Entrance requirements:* For master's, GRE (for applicants with a GPA of 2.75-2.99), minimum GPA of 3.0 or written statement and writing sample; bachelor's degree from accredited college or university; two letters of recommendation; personal statement. Additional exam requirements/recommendations for international students: Required—TOEFL (minimum score 550 paper-based; 79 iBT), TWE (minimum score 5.5), Michigan English Language Assessment Battery (minimum score 85); Recommended—IELTS (minimum score 6.5). *Application deadline:* For fall admission, 6/1 for domestic students, 5/1 priority date for international students; for winter admission, 10/1 for domestic students, 9/1 priority date for international students. Application fee: $50. Electronic applications accepted. *Expenses:* $16,503 per year resident tuition and fees, $33,697 per year non-resident tuition and fees. *Financial support:* In 2016–17, 15 students received support, including 3 research assistantships with tuition reimbursements available (averaging $16,665 per year), 1 teaching assistantship with tuition reimbursement available (averaging $17,994 per year); fellowships with tuition reimbursements available, scholarships/grants, health care benefits, and unspecified assistantships also available. Financial award applicants required to submit FAFSA. *Faculty research:* Comparative/international criminal justice and criminology, corrections, criminal justice policy, deviant behavior, life-course criminology, juvenile justice, corrections, and delinquency, mental health and crime, policing, positive psychology, suicide, wrongful convictions. *Unit head:* Dr. Shanhe Jiang, Chair, 313-577-2705, E-mail: fx6954@wayne.edu. *Application contact:* Dr. Jennifer Wareham, Associate Professor/Graduate Director, 313-577-3286, Fax: 313-577-9977, E-mail: ay3167@wayne.edu.
Website: http://clas.wayne.edu/CRJ/

**Webber International University,** Graduate School of Business, Babson Park, FL 33827-0096. Offers accounting (MBA); business (MBA); criminal justice management (MBA); international business (MBA); sport business management (MBA). *Program availability:* Part-time, evening/weekend, 100% online. *Faculty:* 11 full-time (3 women), 1 part-time/adjunct (0 women). *Students:* 44 full-time (21 women), 6 part-time (2 women); includes 11 minority (5 Black or African American, non-Hispanic/Latino; 5 Hispanic/Latino; 1 Two or more races, non-Hispanic/Latino), 11 international. Average age 27. 32 applicants, 69% accepted, 18 enrolled. In 2016, 16 master's awarded. *Degree requirements:* For master's, class trip (for international business); practicum (for criminal justice management). *Entrance requirements:* For master's, three recommendation letters, resumé, essay, official transcripts from all colleges and universities attended. Additional exam requirements/recommendations for international students: Recommended—TOEFL (minimum score 500 paper-based; 61 iBT), IELTS (minimum score 6). *Application deadline:* For fall admission, 7/1 for international students. Applications are processed on a rolling basis. Application fee: $50 ($75 for international students). Electronic applications accepted. *Expenses:* $2,013 tuition per course; $207 technology fee per course (for online courses only). *Financial support:* In 2016–17, 11 students received support. Scholarships/grants and unspecified assistantships available. Financial award application deadline: 8/16; financial award applicants required to submit FAFSA. *Unit head:* Dr. Nikos Orphanoudakis, Dean, 863-638-2910, Fax: 863-638-1591, E-mail: orphanoudakisn@webber.edu. *Application contact:* Lacy Edwards, Admissions Counselor and MBA Coordinator, 863-638-2910, Fax: 863-638-1591, E-mail: admissions@webber.edu.

**Webster University,** George Herbert Walker School of Business and Technology, Department of Business, St. Louis, MO 63119-3194. Offers business and organizational security management (MBA); decision support systems (MBA); environmental management (MBA); finance (MBA, MS); forensic accounting (MS); gerontology (MBA); human resources development (MBA); human resources management (MBA); information technology management (MBA); international business (MA, MBA); international relations (MBA); management and leadership (MBA); marketing (MBA); media communications (MBA); procurement and acquisitions management (MBA); Web services (MBA). *Accreditation:* ACBSP. *Program availability:* Part-time, evening/weekend, online learning. *Degree requirements:* For master's, comprehensive exam (for some programs), thesis (for some programs). *Entrance requirements:* Additional exam requirements/recommendations for international students: Required—TOEFL. *Application deadline:* Applications are processed on a rolling basis. Application fee: $35 ($50 for international students). *Expenses: Tuition:* Full-time $21,900; part-time $730 per credit hour. Tuition and fees vary according to campus/location and program. *Financial support:* Federal Work-Study available. Support available to part-time students. Financial award application deadline: 4/1; financial award applicants required to submit FAFSA. *Unit head:* David Porras, Chair, 314-246-8621, E-mail: porrasd@webster.edu. *Application contact:* Sarah Nandor, Director, Graduate and Transfer Admissions, 314-968-7109, E-mail: gadmit@webster.edu.

**Webster University,** George Herbert Walker School of Business and Technology, Department of Management, St. Louis, MO 63119-3194. Offers business and organizational security management (MA); digital marketing management (Graduate Certificate); government contracting (Graduate Certificate); health administration (MHA); health care management (MA); health services management (MA); human resources development (MA); human resources management (MA); information technology management (MA, MS); management (D Mgt); management and leadership (MA); marketing (MA); nonprofit leadership (MA); nonprofit revenue development (Graduate Certificate); organizational development (Graduate Certificate); procurement and acquisitions management (MA); public administration (MPA); space systems operations management (MS). *Program availability:* Part-time, evening/weekend, online learning.

*Degree requirements:* For master's, thesis (for some programs); for doctorate, thesis/dissertation, written exam. *Entrance requirements:* For doctorate, GMAT, 3 years of work experience, MBA. Additional exam requirements/recommendations for international students: Required—TOEFL. *Application deadline:* Applications are processed on a rolling basis. Application fee: $25 ($50 for international students). *Expenses: Tuition:* Full-time $21,900; part-time $730 per credit hour. Tuition and fees vary according to campus/location and program. *Financial support:* Federal Work-Study available. Support available to part-time students. Financial award application deadline: 4/1; financial award applicants required to submit FAFSA. *Unit head:* Barrett Baebler, Chair, 314-246-7940, E-mail: baeblerb@webster.edu. *Application contact:* Sarah Nandor, Director, Graduate and Transfer Admissions, 314-968-7109, E-mail: gadmit@webster.edu.

**West Chester University of Pennsylvania,** College of Business and Public Management, Department of Criminal Justice, West Chester, PA 19383. Offers MS. *Program availability:* Part-time, evening/weekend. *Faculty:* 5 full-time (2 women), 3 part-time/adjunct (all women). *Students:* 8 full-time (4 women), 13 part-time (5 women); includes 2 minority (both Black or African American, non-Hispanic/Latino), 2 international. Average age 32. 48 applicants, 77% accepted, 21 enrolled. In 2016, 18 master's awarded. *Degree requirements:* For master's, 15-credit core (law, research, ethics, theories, and capstone independent research project); 15 additional credits of criminal justice electives. *Entrance requirements:* For master's, minimum GPA of 3.0; two letters of recommendation. Additional exam requirements/recommendations for international students: Required—TOEFL or IELTS. *Application deadline:* For fall admission, 5/15 for international students; for spring admission, 10/15 for international students. Applications are processed on a rolling basis. Application fee: $50. Electronic applications accepted. *Expenses:* Tuition, state resident: full-time $8694; part-time $483 per credit. Tuition, nonresident: full-time $13,050; part-time $725 per credit. *Required fees:* $2399; $119.05 per credit. Tuition and fees vary according to campus/location and program. *Financial support:* Scholarships/grants and unspecified assistantships available. Financial award application deadline: 2/15; financial award applicants required to submit FAFSA. *Faculty research:* Criminal law, criminal procedure, Constitutional interpretation, drug and alcohol prevention, drug courts, mental health courts, legislation related to sex offending, animal cruelty, pharmaceutical battery, terrorism, law enforcement. *Unit head:* Dr. Mary Brewster, Chair, 610-436-2630, Fax: 610-738-0491, E-mail: mbrewster@wcupa.edu. *Application contact:* Dr. Jane Tucker, Graduate Coordinator, 610-436-2648, Fax: 610-738-0491, E-mail: jtucker@wcupa.edu.
Website: http://www.wcupa.edu/business-publicManagement/criminalJustice/

**Western Connecticut State University,** Division of Graduate Studies, Ancell School of Business, Program in Justice Administration, Danbury, CT 06810-6885. Offers MS. *Program availability:* Part-time. *Degree requirements:* For master's, comprehensive exam or research project, completion of program within 6 years. *Entrance requirements:* For master's, GMAT, GRE, LSAT, or MAT. Additional exam requirements/recommendations for international students: Recommended—TOEFL (minimum score 550 paper-based; 79 iBT), IELTS (minimum score 6). *Faculty research:* Examination of prison life as portrayed by the film industry.

**Western Illinois University,** School of Graduate Studies, College of Education and Human Services, School of Law Enforcement and Justice Administration, Macomb, IL 61455-1390. Offers law enforcement and justice administration (MA); police executive administration (Certificate). *Program availability:* Part-time. *Students:* 25 full-time (7 women), 14 part-time (4 women); includes 8 minority (2 Black or African American, non-Hispanic/Latino; 4 Hispanic/Latino; 2 Two or more races, non-Hispanic/Latino). Average age 28. 42 applicants, 93% accepted, 19 enrolled. In 2016, 13 master's, 6 other advanced degrees awarded. *Degree requirements:* For master's, thesis or alternative. *Entrance requirements:* For master's, GRE or MAT, minimum GPA of 3.0. Additional exam requirements/recommendations for international students: Required—TOEFL (minimum score 520 paper-based; 68 iBT). *Application deadline:* Applications are processed on a rolling basis. Application fee: $30. Electronic applications accepted. *Financial support:* In 2016–17, 9 students received support. Unspecified assistantships available. Financial award applicants required to submit FAFSA. *Unit head:* Dr. Jill Myers, Director, 309-298-1038. *Application contact:* Dr. Nancy Parsons, Associate Provost and Director of Graduate Studies, 309-298-1806, Fax: 309-298-2345, E-mail: grad-office@wiu.edu.
Website: http://wiu.edu/leja

**Western Kentucky University,** Graduate Studies, Potter College of Arts and Letters, Department of Sociology, Bowling Green, KY 42101. Offers criminology (MA); sociology (MA). *Program availability:* Online learning. *Degree requirements:* For master's, comprehensive exam, thesis optional, final exam. *Entrance requirements:* For master's, GRE General Test, minimum GPA of 3.0. Additional exam requirements/recommendations for international students: Required—TOEFL (minimum score 555 paper-based; 79 iBT). *Faculty research:* Criminology/delinquency, quantitative and survey research methodology, occupations/professions, sex and gender, demography.

**Western Oregon University,** Graduate Programs, College of Liberal Arts and Sciences, Division of Social Science, Monmouth, OR 97361. Offers criminal justice (MA, MS). *Program availability:* Part-time, evening/weekend. *Degree requirements:* For master's, thesis optional, written exams. *Entrance requirements:* For master's, minimum GPA of 3.0. Additional exam requirements/recommendations for international students: Required—TOEFL (minimum score 550 paper-based; 79 iBT), IELTS (minimum score 6.5). *Faculty research:* Prison to community transition of adult felons, community justice, restorative justice, parole and probation.

**Westfield State University,** College of Graduate and Continuing Education, Department of Criminal Justice, Westfield, MA 01086. Offers MS. *Program availability:* Part-time, evening/weekend. *Faculty:* 5 full-time (0 women). *Students:* 9 full-time (3 women), 22 part-time (9 women); includes 6 minority (1 Black or African American, non-Hispanic/Latino; 3 Hispanic/Latino; 2 Two or more races, non-Hispanic/Latino). Average age 29. 8 applicants, 100% accepted, 5 enrolled. In 2016, 12 master's awarded. *Degree requirements:* For master's, comprehensive exam, thesis (for some programs). *Entrance requirements:* For master's, GRE General Test or MAT, minimum undergraduate GPA of 2.8. Additional exam requirements/recommendations for international students: Recommended—TOEFL (minimum score 550 paper-based; 79 iBT). *Application deadline:* For fall admission, 6/30 for domestic students; for spring admission, 10/31 for domestic students; for summer admission, 3/31 for domestic students. Applications are processed on a rolling basis. Application fee: $50. *Expenses:* Tuition, state resident: part-time $318 per semester hour. Tuition, nonresident: part-time $318 per semester hour. *Required fees:* $75 per semester. Tuition and fees vary according to course load and program. *Financial support:* Unspecified assistantships available. Financial award application deadline: 3/1; financial award applicants required to submit FAFSA. *Unit head:* Dr. Christopher Kudlac, Professor/Graduate Coordinator, 413-572-5728, E-mail: ckudlac@westfield.ma.edu. *Application contact:* Shelly Henrichon, Coordinator of DGCE Admissions, 413-572-8022, Fax: 413-572-5227, E-mail: mhenrichon@westfield.ma.edu.
Website: http://www.westfield.ma.edu/academics/degrees/criminal-justice-graduate-programs

**Westfield State University,** College of Graduate and Continuing Education, Department of Political Science, Westfield, MA 01086. Offers criminal justice administration (MPA); non-profit management (MPA); public management (MPA). *Program availability:* Part-time, evening/weekend. *Faculty:* 2 full-time (1 woman), 4 part-time/adjunct (2 women). *Students:* 13 full-time (6 women), 38 part-time (17 women); includes 11 minority (2 American Indian or Alaska Native, non-Hispanic/Latino; 8 Hispanic/Latino; 1 Two or more races, non-Hispanic/Latino). Average age 29. 16 applicants, 88% accepted, 13 enrolled. In 2016, 17 master's awarded. *Degree requirements:* For master's, comprehensive exam, thesis (for some programs). *Entrance requirements:* For master's, GRE General Test or MAT, minimum undergraduate GPA of 2.8. Additional exam requirements/recommendations for international students: Recommended—TOEFL (minimum score 550 paper-based; 79 iBT). *Application deadline:* For fall admission, 6/30 for domestic students; for spring admission, 10/31 for domestic students; for summer admission, 3/31 for domestic students. Applications are processed on a rolling basis. Application fee: $50. *Expenses:* Tuition, state resident: part-time $318 per semester hour. Tuition, nonresident: part-time $318 per semester hour. *Required fees:* $75 per semester. Tuition and fees vary according to course load and program. *Financial support:* Unspecified assistantships available. Financial award application deadline: 3/1; financial award applicants required to submit FAFSA. *Unit head:* Dr. Hugh Jo, Chair, 413-572-8806, Fax: 413-572-8168, E-mail: hjo@westfield.ma.edu. *Application contact:* Shelly Henrichon, Admissions Coordinator, 413-572-8022, Fax: 413-572-5227, E-mail: mhenrichon@westfield.ma.edu.

**West Liberty University,** School of Professional Studies, West Liberty, WV 26074. Offers justice leadership (MPS); organizational leadership (MPS). *Entrance requirements:* For master's, bachelor's degree from accredited institution, minimum GPA of 2.5. *Application deadline:* Applications are processed on a rolling basis. *Expenses:* Tuition, state resident: full-time $7074; part-time $393 per credit. Tuition, nonresident: full-time $11,124; part-time $618 per credit. *Unit head:* Dr. Thomas Michaud, Dean, 304-217-2800, E-mail: tmichaud@westliberty.edu. Website: http://www.westliberty.edu/highlands/ps/

**West Texas A&M University,** College of Education and Social Sciences, Department of Political Science and Criminal Justice, Canyon, TX 79016-0001. Offers criminal justice (MA). *Program availability:* Part-time, evening/weekend. *Degree requirements:* For master's, comprehensive exam, thesis optional. *Entrance requirements:* For master's, GRE General Test. Additional exam requirements/recommendations for international students: Required—TOEFL. *Application deadline:* For fall admission, 8/1 for domestic students, 6/1 for international students; for spring admission, 12/1 for domestic students, 11/1 for international students; for summer admission, 5/1 for domestic students. Applications are processed on a rolling basis. Application fee: $40 ($75 for international students). Electronic applications accepted. *Financial support:* Application deadline: 2/1; applicants required to submit FAFSA. *Unit head:* Dr. Keith Price, Department Head, 806-651-2418.

**West Virginia State University,** Master of Science Program in Law Enforcement and Administration, Institute, WV 25112-1000. Offers MS. *Degree requirements:* For master's, comprehensive exam, internship, paper. *Entrance requirements:* For master's, GRE (50th Percentile) or MAT (50th Percentile), minimum undergraduate GPA of 2.7, 3 letters of recommendation, completion of course in statistics/research methods, interview. Additional exam requirements/recommendations for international students: Required—TOEFL (minimum score 550 paper-based). Electronic applications accepted.

**Wichita State University,** Graduate School, Fairmount College of Liberal Arts and Sciences, School of Community Affairs, Wichita, KS 67260. Offers criminal justice (MA). *Program availability:* Part-time, 100% online, blended/hybrid learning. *Unit head:* Dr. Michael Birzer, Director, 316-978-7200, Fax: 316-978-3626, E-mail: michael.birzer@wichita.edu. *Application contact:* Jordan Oleson, Admissions Coordinator, 316-978-3095, Fax: 316-978-3253, E-mail: jordan.oleson@wichita.edu. Website: http://www.wichita.edu/cj

**Widener University,** College of Arts and Sciences, Program in Criminal Justice, Chester, PA 19013-5792. Offers MA, Psy D/MA. *Program availability:* Part-time, evening/weekend. *Faculty:* 1 full-time (0 women), 2 part-time/adjunct (0 women). *Students:* 12 part-time (6 women); includes 8 minority (7 Black or African American, non-Hispanic/Latino; 1 Two or more races, non-Hispanic/Latino). Average age 31. 21 applicants, 90% accepted. In 2016, 1 master's awarded. *Degree requirements:* For master's, project. *Entrance requirements:* For master's, interview, minimum undergraduate GPA of 3.0. *Application deadline:* For fall admission, 3/1 priority date for domestic students. Applications are processed on a rolling basis. Application fee: $25

($300 for international students). *Expenses:* Contact institution. *Financial support:* Career-related internships or fieldwork and institutionally sponsored loans available. Support available to part-time students. Financial award application deadline: 5/1. *Faculty research:* Criminal law and procedure, corrections, domestic violence. *Unit head:* Dr. William E. Harver, Director, 610-499-4554, Fax: 510-499-4605, E-mail: william.e.harver@widener.edu.

**Wilfrid Laurier University,** Laurier Brantford, Brantford, ON N3T 2Y3, Canada. Offers criminology (MA), including culture, crime and policy, international crime and justice, media criminology. *Degree requirements:* For master's, thesis. *Entrance requirements:* For master's, honours bachelor's degree with major in criminology or equivalent degree; minimum B+ average in final year and in all criminology courses. Additional exam requirements/recommendations for international students: Required—TOEFL (minimum score 89 iBT). Electronic applications accepted.

**Wilmington University,** College of Social and Behavioral Sciences, New Castle, DE 19720-6491. Offers administration of human services (MS); administration of justice (MS); clinical mental health counseling (MS); homeland security (MS). *Accreditation:* ACA. *Program availability:* Part-time, evening/weekend. *Faculty:* 8 full-time (5 women), 79 part-time/adjunct (35 women). *Students:* 210 full-time (162 women), 444 part-time (325 women); includes 320 minority (285 Black or African American, non-Hispanic/Latino; 12 American Indian or Alaska Native, non-Hispanic/Latino; 9 Asian, non-Hispanic/Latino; 12 Hispanic/Latino; 1 Native Hawaiian or other Pacific Islander, non-Hispanic/Latino; 1 Two or more races, non-Hispanic/Latino), 4 international. Average age 35. 255 applicants, 100% accepted, 255 enrolled. In 2016, 248 master's awarded. *Entrance requirements:* Additional exam requirements/recommendations for international students: Required—TOEFL (minimum score 500 paper-based). *Application deadline:* Applications are processed on a rolling basis. Application fee: $35. Electronic applications accepted. *Expenses:* Tuition: Full-time $8388; part-time $466 per credit. *Required fees:* $25 per semester. Tuition and fees vary according to degree level. *Financial support:* Applicants required to submit FAFSA. *Unit head:* Dr. Edward L. Guthrie, Dean. *Application contact:* Laura Morris, Director of Admissions, 877-967-5464, E-mail: inquire@wilmcoll.edu. Website: http://www.wilmu.edu/behavioralscience/

**Wright State University,** Graduate School, College of Liberal Arts, Program in Applied Behavioral Science, Criminal Justice and Social Problems, Dayton, OH 45435. Offers criminal justice and social problems (MA). *Degree requirements:* For master's, thesis optional. *Entrance requirements:* Additional exam requirements/recommendations for international students: Required—TOEFL. Application fee: $25. *Expenses:* Tuition, state resident: full-time $9952; part-time $622 per credit hour. Tuition, nonresident: full-time $16,960; part-time $1060 per credit hour. *Financial support:* Fellowships, research assistantships, and unspecified assistantships available. Support available to part-time students. Financial award applicants required to submit FAFSA. *Faculty research:* Training and development, criminal justice and social problems, community systems, human factors, industrial/organizational psychology. *Unit head:* Dr. David M. Orenstein, Director, 937-775-2667, Fax: 937-775-4228, E-mail: david.orenstein@wright.edu. *Application contact:* John Kimble, Associate Director of Graduate Admissions and Records, 937-775-2957, Fax: 937-775-2453, E-mail: john.kimble@wright.edu.

**Xavier University,** College of Social Sciences, Health and Education, Department of Criminal Justice, Cincinnati, OH 45207. Offers MS. *Program availability:* Part-time, evening/weekend. *Degree requirements:* For master's, comprehensive exam, thesis. *Entrance requirements:* For master's, MAT, GRE, or LSAT, minimum GPA of 2.7; official transcript; 2 letters of recommendation. Additional exam requirements/recommendations for international students: Required—TOEFL (minimum score 550 paper-based; 79 iBT). Electronic applications accepted. Application fee is waived when completed online. *Expenses:* Contact institution. *Faculty research:* Women and crime, crime policy, policing.

**Youngstown State University,** Graduate School, Bitonte College of Health and Human Services, Department of Criminal Justice, Youngstown, OH 44555-0001. Offers MS. *Program availability:* Part-time, evening/weekend. *Degree requirements:* For master's, thesis optional. *Entrance requirements:* For master's, minimum GPA of 2.7. Additional exam requirements/recommendations for international students: Required—TOEFL. *Faculty research:* Police human resource allocation, police administration, computerized test development, criminal law.

# Forensic Sciences

**Alabama State University,** College of Science, Mathematics and Technology, Department of Physical Sciences, Montgomery, AL 36101-0271. Offers forensic science (MS). *Faculty:* 4 full-time (1 woman). *Students:* 7 full-time (all women), 2 part-time (1 woman); includes 6 minority (all Black or African American, non-Hispanic/Latino), 1 international. Average age 28. 15 applicants, 33% accepted, 2 enrolled. In 2016, 7 master's awarded. *Entrance requirements:* Additional exam requirements/recommendations for international students: Required—TOEFL (minimum score 500 paper-based). *Application deadline:* For fall admission, 4/15 for domestic and international students; for spring admission, 11/15 for domestic and international students; for summer admission, 3/15 for domestic and international students. Application fee: $25. Electronic applications accepted. *Expenses:* Tuition, state resident: full-time $3087; part-time $2744 per credit. Tuition, nonresident: full-time $6174; part-time $5488 per credit. *Required fees:* $2284; $1142 per credit. $571 per semester. Tuition and fees vary according to class time, course level, course load, degree level, program and student level. *Financial support:* Research assistantships and unspecified assistantships available. Financial award application deadline: 6/30; financial award applicants required to submit FAFSA. *Unit head:* Dr. Azriel Gorski, Dean, 334-229-6705, Fax: 334-229-6103, E-mail: agorski@alasu.edu. *Application contact:* Dr. William Person, Dean of Graduate Studies, 334-229-4274, Fax: 334-229-4928, E-mail: wperson@alasu.edu. Website: http://www.alasu.edu/academics/colleges—departments/science-mathematics-technology/physical-sciences/index.aspx

**Alliant International University–Irvine,** California School of Forensic Studies, Irvine, CA 92606. Offers Psy D. *Degree requirements:* For doctorate, comprehensive exam, thesis/dissertation, internship. *Entrance requirements:* For doctorate, minimum GPA of 3.0, recommendations, essay. Additional exam requirements/recommendations for international students: Required—TOEFL (minimum score 80 iBT), TWE (minimum score 5). Electronic applications accepted. *Faculty research:* Detecting deception, psychological safety of undercover police officers, domestic violence, risk assessment, competency evaluations.

**American Public University System,** AMU/APU Graduate Programs, Charles Town, WV 25414. Offers accounting (MBA, MS); applied business analytics (MBA, MS); criminal justice (MA), including business administration, emergency and disaster management, general (MA, MS); educational leadership (M Ed); emergency and disaster management (MA); entrepreneurship (MBA); environmental policy and management (MS), including environmental planning, environmental sustainability, fish and wildlife management, general (MA, MS), global environmental management; finance (MBA); general (MBA); government contracting and acquisition (MBA); health care administration (MBA); health information management (MS); history (MA), including American history, ancient and classical history, European history, global history, public history; homeland security (MA), including business administration, counterterrorism studies, criminal justice, cyber, emergency management and public health, intelligence studies, transportation security; homeland security resource allocation (MBA); humanities (MA); information technology (MS), including digital forensics, enterprise software development, information assurance and security, IT project management; information technology management (MBA); intelligence studies (MA), including criminal intelligence, cyber, general (MA, MS), homeland security, intelligence analysis, intelligence collection, intelligence management, intelligence operations, terrorism studies; international relations and conflict resolution (MA), including comparative and security issues, conflict resolution, international and transnational security issues, peacekeeping; legal studies (MA); management (MA), including strategic consulting; marketing (MBA); military history (MA), including American military history, American Revolution, civil war, war since 1945, World War II; military studies (MA), including joint warfare, strategic leadership; national security studies (MA), including cyber, general (MA, MS), homeland security, regional security studies, security and intelligence analysis, terrorism studies; nonprofit management (MBA); political science (MA), including American politics and government, comparative government and development, general (MA, MS), international relations, public policy; psychology (MA); public administration (MPA), including disaster management, environmental policy, health policy, human resources, national security, organizational management, security

## Forensic Sciences

management; public health (MPH); reverse logistics management (MA); security management (MA); space studies (MS), including aerospace science, general (MA, MS), planetary science; sports and health sciences (MS); sports management (MBA); teaching (M Ed), including autism spectrum disorder, curriculum and instruction for elementary teachers, elementary reading, English language learners, instructional leadership, online learning, special education, STEAM (STEM plus the arts); transportation and logistics management (MA). *Program availability:* Part-time, evening/weekend, online only, 100% online. *Faculty:* 401 full-time (228 women), 1,678 part-time/adjunct (781 women). *Students:* 378 full-time (184 women), 8,455 part-time (3,484 women); includes 2,972 minority (1,552 Black or African American, non-Hispanic/Latino; 52 American Indian or Alaska Native, non-Hispanic/Latino; 211 Asian, non-Hispanic/Latino; 791 Hispanic/Latino; 70 Native Hawaiian or other Pacific Islander, non-Hispanic/Latino; 296 Two or more races, non-Hispanic/Latino), 109 international. Average age 37. In 2016, 3,185 master's awarded. *Degree requirements:* For master's, comprehensive exam or practicum. *Entrance requirements:* For master's, official transcript showing earned bachelor's degree from institution accredited by recognized accrediting body. Additional exam requirements/recommendations for international students: Required—TOEFL (minimum score 550 paper-based), IELTS (minimum score 6.5). *Application deadline:* Applications are processed on a rolling basis. Application fee: $0. Electronic applications accepted. *Expenses: Tuition:* Part-time $350 per credit hour. *Required fees:* $50 per course. *Financial support:* Scholarships/grants available. Financial award applicants required to submit FAFSA. *Unit head:* Dr. Karan Powell, President, 877-468-6268, Fax: 304-724-3780. *Application contact:* Terry Grant, Vice President of Enrollment Management, 877-468-6268, Fax: 304-724-3780, E-mail: info@apus.edu.
Website: http://www.apus.edu

**Arcadia University,** College of Arts and Sciences, Program in Forensic Science, Glenside, PA 19038-3295. Offers MSFS. *Faculty:* 3 full-time (2 women), 13 part-time/adjunct (6 women). *Students:* 26 full-time (19 women), 1 (woman) part-time; includes 1 minority (Asian, non-Hispanic/Latino), 3 international. Average age 24. 45 applicants, 71% accepted, 14 enrolled. In 2016, 14 master's awarded. Application fee: $50. *Expenses:* Contact institution. *Unit head:* Dr. Karen Scott, Program Director, 215-572-2102. *Application contact:* Office of Enrollment Management, 215-572-2910, Fax: 215-572-4049, E-mail: admiss@arcadia.edu.

**Boston University,** School of Medicine, Division of Graduate Medical Sciences, Program in Biomedical Forensic Sciences, Boston, MA 02215. Offers MS. *Program availability:* Part-time, evening/weekend, online learning. *Degree requirements:* For master's, thesis. *Application deadline:* For fall admission, 7/1 for domestic and international students. *Unit head:* Dr. Robin Cotton, Director, 617-638-1950, E-mail: rwcotton@bu.edu. *Application contact:* GMS Admissions Office, 617-638-5255, E-mail: askgms@bu.edu.
Website: http://www.bumc.bu.edu/biomedforensic/

**Boston University,** School of Medicine, Division of Graduate Medical Sciences, Program in Forensic Anthropology, Boston, MA 02215. Offers MS. *Financial support:* Applicants required to submit FAFSA. *Unit head:* Dr. Tara L. Moore, Co-Director, 617-638-4054, Fax: 617-638-4922, E-mail: tlmoore@bu.edu. *Application contact:* GMS Admissions Office, 617-638-5255, E-mail: askgms@bu.edu.
Website: http://www.bumc.bu.edu/gms/forensicanthro-masters-program/

**Carlow University,** College of Leadership and Social Change, MBA Program, Pittsburgh, PA 15213-3165. Offers fraud and forensics (MBA); healthcare management (MBA); human resource management (MBA); leadership and management (MBA); project management (MBA). *Program availability:* Part-time, evening/weekend, 100% online, blended/hybrid learning. *Students:* 87 full-time (65 women), 32 part-time (21 women); includes 31 minority (23 Black or African American, non-Hispanic/Latino; 3 Asian, non-Hispanic/Latino; 2 Hispanic/Latino; 3 Two or more races, non-Hispanic/Latino), 1 international. Average age 33. 54 applicants, 98% accepted, 33 enrolled. In 2016, 29 master's awarded. *Entrance requirements:* For master's, minimum undergraduate GPA of 3.0 (preferred); personal essay; resume; official transcripts; two professional recommendations. Additional exam requirements/recommendations for international students: Required—TOEFL (minimum score 550 paper-based). *Application deadline:* Applications are processed on a rolling basis. Electronic applications accepted. *Expenses: Tuition:* Full-time $11,855; part-time $801 per credit. *Required fees:* $182; $13 per credit. Tuition and fees vary according to course load, degree level and program. *Financial support:* Application deadline: 4/1; applicants required to submit FAFSA. *Unit head:* Dr. Howard Stern, Chair, MBA Program, 412-578-8828, E-mail: hastern@carlow.edu. *Application contact:* 412-578-6059, Fax: 412-578-6321, E-mail: gradstudies@carlow.edu.
Website: http://www.carlow.edu/Business_Administration.aspx

**Cedar Crest College,** Program in Forensic Science, Allentown, PA 18104-6196. Offers MS. *Faculty:* 4 full-time (2 women), 2 part-time/adjunct (1 woman). *Students:* 16 full-time (12 women), 9 part-time (8 women); includes 3 minority (1 Black or African American, non-Hispanic/Latino; 1 American Indian or Alaska Native, non-Hispanic/Latino; 1 Asian, non-Hispanic/Latino). Average age 25. In 2016, 2 master's awarded. *Degree requirements:* For master's, thesis. *Entrance requirements:* For master's, GRE. *Application deadline:* For fall admission, 1/2 priority date for domestic students. Applications are processed on a rolling basis. Electronic applications accepted. *Expenses:* $800 per credit. *Financial support:* In 2016–17, 4 students received support. Unspecified assistantships available. *Faculty research:* Genotyping of low copy number DNA, presumptive and confirmatory testing of gamma hydroxyl butyrate (GHB) and gamma-butyrolactone (GBL). *Unit head:* Dr. Lawrence A. Quarino, Director and Associate Professor, 610-606-4666 Ext. 3507, Fax: 610-740-3787, E-mail: laquarin@cedarcrest.edu. *Application contact:* Mary Ellen Hickes, Director of School of Adult and Graduate Education, 610-606-4666, E-mail: sage@cedarcrest.edu.

**Champlain College,** Graduate Studies, Burlington, VT 05402-0670. Offers business (MBA); digital forensic science (MS); early childhood education (M Ed); emergent media (MFA, MS); executive leadership (MS); health care administration (MS); information security operations (MS); law (MS); mediation and applied conflict studies (MS). MS in emergent media program held in Shanghai. *Program availability:* Part-time, online learning. *Degree requirements:* For master's, capstone project. *Entrance requirements:* Additional exam requirements/recommendations for international students: Required—TOEFL (minimum score 550 paper-based; 80 iBT). Electronic applications accepted.

**The College at Brockport, State University of New York,** School of Business and Management, Brockport, NY 14420-2997. Offers forensic accounting (MS); public administration (MPA, AGC), including arts administration (AGC), nonprofit management (AGC), public administration (MPA). *Program availability:* Part-time. *Faculty:* 5 full-time (1 woman), 1 part-time/adjunct (0 women). *Students:* 13 full-time (5 women), 8 part-time (5 women); includes 4 minority (3 Black or African American, non-Hispanic/Latino; 1 Asian, non-Hispanic/Latino). 29 applicants, 79% accepted, 19 enrolled. In 2016, 17 master's awarded. *Entrance requirements:* For master's, GMAT or GRE General Test. Additional exam requirements/recommendations for international students: Required—TOEFL (minimum score 550 paper-based; 79 iBT), IELTS (minimum score 6.5). *Application deadline:* For fall admission, 7/1 priority date for domestic and international students; for spring admission, 12/1 priority date for domestic and international students. Application fee: $50. Electronic applications accepted. *Expenses:* Contact institution.

*Financial support:* Career-related internships or fieldwork, Federal Work-Study, scholarships/grants, and unspecified assistantships available. Financial award application deadline: 3/15; financial award applicants required to submit FAFSA. *Unit head:* Dr. James Cordeiro, Department Chair, 585-395-5793, Fax: 585-395-2542. *Application contact:* Dr. Donald A. Kent, Graduate Director, 585-395-5521, Fax: 585-395-2515, E-mail: dkent@brockport.edu.
Website: http://www.brockport.edu/academics/school_business_management/

**DeSales University,** Division of Liberal Arts and Social Sciences, Center Valley, PA 18034-9568. Offers criminal justice (MCJ); digital forensics (MCJ, Postbaccalaureate Certificate); education (M Ed), including instructional technology, secondary education, special education, teaching English to speakers of other languages; investigative forensics (MCJ, Postbaccalaureate Certificate). *Program availability:* Part-time, 100% online, blended/hybrid learning. *Faculty:* 5 full-time (3 women), 20 part-time/adjunct (13 women). *Students:* 55 full-time (36 women), 100 part-time (64 women); includes 25 minority (5 Black or African American, non-Hispanic/Latino; 14 Hispanic/Latino; 6 Two or more races, non-Hispanic/Latino). Average age 33. 145 applicants, 80% accepted, 103 enrolled. In 2016, 36 master's awarded. *Entrance requirements:* For master's, bachelor's degree from accredited institution, minimum undergraduate GPA of 3.0, personal statement showing potential of graduate work, three letters of recommendation, professional goal statement. Additional exam requirements/recommendations for international students: Required—TOEFL. *Application deadline:* Applications are processed on a rolling basis. Application fee: $50. Electronic applications accepted. *Expenses: Tuition:* Part-time $815 per credit hour. Tuition and fees vary according to degree level and program. *Financial support:* Applicants required to submit FAFSA. *Unit head:* Dr. Brain Kane, Division Head of Liberal Arts and Social Studies, 610-282-1100 Ext. 1274, E-mail: brian.kane@desales.edu. *Application contact:* Julia Ferraro, Director of Graduate Admissions, 610-282-1100 Ext. 1768, E-mail: gradadmissions@desales.edu.

**DeSales University,** Division of Science and Mathematics, Center Valley, PA 18034-9568. Offers cyber security (Postbaccalaureate Certificate); data analytics (Postbaccalaureate Certificate); information systems (MS), including cyber security, digital forensics, healthcare information management, project management. *Program availability:* Part-time, evening/weekend, 100% online, blended/hybrid learning. *Faculty:* 1 (woman) full-time, 3 part-time/adjunct (0 women). *Students:* 8 full-time (1 woman), 12 part-time (6 women); includes 1 minority (Asian, non-Hispanic/Latino). Average age 34. 20 applicants, 30% accepted, 6 enrolled. In 2016, 7 master's awarded. *Entrance requirements:* For master's, GRE or GMAT, bachelor's degree in computer-related discipline from accredited college or university, minimum undergraduate GPA of 3.0, personal statement, three letters of recommendation. Additional exam requirements/recommendations for international students: Required—TOEFL. *Application deadline:* Applications are processed on a rolling basis. Application fee: $50. Electronic applications accepted. *Expenses:* Contact institution. *Financial support:* Applicants required to submit FAFSA. *Unit head:* Dr. Patricia Riola, MSIS Director/Assistant Professor of Computer Science, 610-282-1100 Ext. 1647, E-mail: patricia.riola@desales.edu. *Application contact:* Julia Ferraro, Director of Graduate Admissions, 610-282-1100 Ext. 1768, E-mail: gradadmissions@desales.edu.
Website: http://www.desales.edu/home/academics/graduate-studies/programs-of-study/msis—master-of-science-in-information-systems

**Duquesne University,** Bayer School of Natural and Environmental Sciences, Program in Forensic Science and Law, Pittsburgh, PA 15282-0001. Offers MS. *Faculty:* 5 full-time (3 women), 15 part-time/adjunct (9 women). *Students:* 21 full-time (18 women); includes 2 minority (1 Hispanic/Latino; 1 Two or more races, non-Hispanic/Latino). Average age 22. In 2016, 10 master's awarded. *Degree requirements:* For master's, comprehensive exam. *Entrance requirements:* For master's, SAT or ACT, recommendation form; minimum total QPA of 3.0, 2.5 in math and science. *Application deadline:* For fall admission, 7/1 for domestic and international students. Applications are processed on a rolling basis. Application fee: $0. Electronic applications accepted. *Expenses:* $1,264 per credit. *Financial support:* In 2016–17, 10 students received support. Career-related internships or fieldwork and scholarships/grants available. Financial award application deadline: 5/1. *Faculty research:* Extraction protocols, mass spectrometry, synthetic fiber analysis, synthetic polymer characterization, trace analysis, amplification of DNA, methods for labeling DNA, construction of a genetic profile, experiential exploration of mitochondrial DNA, the Y-chromosome, amelogenin. *Total annual research expenditures:* $50,419. *Unit head:* Dr. Frederick W. Fochtman, Director, 412-396-6373, E-mail: fochtman@duq.edu. *Application contact:* Valerie L. Lijewski, Assistant Director/Academic Advisor, 412-396-1984, E-mail: lijewski@duq.edu.
Website: http://www.duq.edu/academics/schools/natural-and-environmental-sciences/academic-programs/forensic-science-and-law

**Emporia State University,** Department of Biological Sciences, Emporia, KS 66801-5415. Offers botany (MS); environmental biology (MS); forensic science (MS); general biology (MS); microbial and cellular biology (MS); zoology (MS). *Program availability:* Part-time. *Faculty:* 14 full-time (3 women), 1 part-time/adjunct (0 women). *Students:* 21 full-time (11 women), 16 part-time (8 women); includes 2 minority (1 Hispanic/Latino; 1 Two or more races, non-Hispanic/Latino), 24 international. 33 applicants, 91% accepted, 11 enrolled. In 2016, 9 master's awarded. *Degree requirements:* For master's, comprehensive exam or thesis. *Entrance requirements:* For master's, GRE, appropriate undergraduate degree, interview, letters of reference. Additional exam requirements/recommendations for international students: Required—TOEFL (minimum score 520 paper-based; 68 iBT). *Application deadline:* For fall admission, 8/15 priority date for domestic students. Applications are processed on a rolling basis. Application fee: $30 ($75 for international students). Electronic applications accepted. *Expenses:* Tuition, state resident: full-time $5922; part-time $246.75 per credit hour. Tuition, nonresident: full-time $18,414; part-time $767.25 per credit hour. *Required fees:* $1884; $78.50 per credit hour. *Financial support:* In 2016–17, 5 research assistantships with full tuition reimbursements (averaging $7,344 per year), 10 teaching assistantships with full tuition reimbursements (averaging $7,844 per year) were awarded; career-related internships or fieldwork, Federal Work-Study, institutionally sponsored loans, health care benefits, and unspecified assistantships also available. Financial award application deadline: 3/15; financial award applicants required to submit FAFSA. *Faculty research:* Fisheries, range, and wildlife management; aquatic, plant, grassland, vertebrate, and invertebrate ecology; mammalian and plant systematics, taxonomy, and evolution; immunology, virology, and molecular biology. *Unit head:* Dr. Yixin Eric Yang, Chair, 620-341-5311, Fax: 620-341-5608, E-mail: yyang@emporia.edu.
Website: http://www.emporia.edu/info/degrees-courses/grad/biology

**Emporia State University,** Department of Physical Sciences, Emporia, KS 66801-5415. Offers forensic science (MS); geospatial analysis (Postbaccalaureate Certificate); physical science (MS). *Program availability:* Part-time, online learning. *Faculty:* 15 full-time (5 women), 1 part-time/adjunct (0 women). *Students:* 37 full-time (21 women), 19 part-time (11 women); includes 9 minority (1 Black or African American, non-Hispanic/Latino; 1 Hispanic/Latino; 7 Two or more races, non-Hispanic/Latino), 20 international. 41 applicants, 93% accepted, 17 enrolled. In 2016, 12 master's, 2 other advanced degrees awarded. *Degree requirements:* For master's, comprehensive exam or thesis; qualifying exam. *Entrance requirements:* For master's, appropriate undergraduate

degree. Additional exam requirements/recommendations for international students: Required—TOEFL (minimum score 520 paper-based; 68 iBT). *Application deadline:* For fall admission, 8/15 priority date for domestic students. Applications are processed on a rolling basis. Application fee: $30 ($75 for international students). Electronic applications accepted. *Expenses:* Tuition, state resident: full-time $5922; part-time $246.75 per credit hour. Tuition, nonresident: full-time $18,414; part-time $767.25 per credit hour. *Required fees:* $1884; $78.50 per credit hour. *Financial support:* In 2016–17, 1 research assistantship with full tuition reimbursement (averaging $7,344 per year), 5 teaching assistantships with full tuition reimbursements (averaging $7,844 per year) were awarded; Federal Work-Study, institutionally sponsored loans, health care benefits, and unspecified assistantships also available. Financial award application deadline: 3/15; financial award applicants required to submit FAFSA. *Faculty research:* Bredigite, larnite, and dicalcium silicates from Marble Canyon. *Unit head:* Dr. Kim Simons, Chair, 620-341-5330, Fax: 620-341-6055, E-mail: ksimons@emporia.edu. *Application contact:* Mary Sewell, Admissions Coordinator, 800-950-GRAD, Fax: 620-341-5909, E-mail: msewell@emporia.edu.
Website: http://www.emporia.edu/physci/

**Emporia State University,** Program in Forensic Science, Emporia, KS 66801-5415. Offers MS. *Program availability:* Part-time. *Faculty:* 15 full-time (5 women), 1 part-time/adjunct (0 women). *Students:* 28 full-time (18 women); includes 3 minority (1 Black or African American, non-Hispanic/Latino; 1 Hispanic/Latino; 1 Two or more races, non-Hispanic/Latino), 7 international. 19 applicants, 95% accepted, 9 enrolled. *Entrance requirements:* For master's, bachelor's degree in a natural science or in forensic science (recommended), three letters of reference, official transcripts, minimum undergraduate GPA of 3.0. Additional exam requirements/recommendations for international students: Required—TOEFL. *Application deadline:* For fall admission, 4/15 for domestic students. Applications are processed on a rolling basis. Application fee: $40. Electronic applications accepted. *Expenses:* Tuition, state resident: full-time $5922; part-time $246.75 per credit hour. Tuition, nonresident: full-time $18,414; part-time $767.25 per credit hour. *Required fees:* $1884; $78.50 per credit hour. *Financial support:* In 2016–17, 4 research assistantships (averaging $7,353 per year), 6 teaching assistantships with full tuition reimbursements (averaging $7,335 per year) were awarded; unspecified assistantships also available. Financial award applicants required to submit FAFSA. *Unit head:* Dr. Melissa M. Bailey, Interim Director, 620-341-5619, E-mail: mbailey4@emporia.edu. *Application contact:* April Huddleston, Recruitment and Development Specialist, 800-950-GRAD, Fax: 620-341-5909, E-mail: ahuddles@emporia.edu.
Website: http://www.emporia.edu/physci/forensicscience/

**Florida Gulf Coast University,** College of Arts and Sciences, Program in Criminal Forensic Studies, Fort Myers, FL 33965-6565. Offers MS. *Program availability:* Part-time. *Faculty:* 238 full-time (97 women), 158 part-time/adjunct (62 women). *Students:* 3 part-time (1 woman). Average age 29. In 2016, 2 master's awarded. *Entrance requirements:* For master's, GRE General Test, minimum GPA of 3.0. Additional exam requirements/recommendations for international students: Required—TOEFL (minimum score 550 paper-based). *Application deadline:* For fall admission, 3/1 for domestic students; for spring admission, 11/1 for domestic students. Applications are processed on a rolling basis. Application fee: $30. Electronic applications accepted. *Expenses:* Tuition, state resident: full-time $6721. Tuition, nonresident: full-time $28,170. *Required fees:* $1987. Tuition and fees vary according to course load and degree level. *Financial support:* Application deadline: 3/1; applicants required to submit FAFSA. *Unit head:* Heather Walsh-Haney, Professor, 239-590-7693, Fax: 239-590-7846, E-mail: hwalsh@fgcu.edu. *Application contact:* Debora Haring, Interim Assistant Director, Graduate Studies, 239-590-7908, Fax: 239-590-7843, E-mail: dharing@fgcu.edu.

**Florida International University,** College of Arts, Sciences, and Education, Department of Chemistry and Biochemistry, Miami, FL 33199. Offers chemistry (MS, PhD); forensic science (MS, PSM, PhD). *Program availability:* Part-time, evening/weekend. *Faculty:* 32 full-time (8 women), 6 part-time/adjunct (2 women). *Students:* 133 full-time (71 women), 20 part-time (14 women); includes 55 minority (13 Black or African American, non-Hispanic/Latino; 4 Asian, non-Hispanic/Latino; 37 Hispanic/Latino; 1 Two or more races, non-Hispanic/Latino), 62 international. Average age 28. 223 applicants, 20% accepted, 29 enrolled. In 2016, 14 master's, 16 doctorates awarded. *Degree requirements:* For master's, thesis (for some programs); for doctorate, comprehensive exam, thesis/dissertation. *Entrance requirements:* For master's and doctorate, GRE General Test, minimum GPA of 3.0, 3 letters of recommendation, resume, letter of intent. Additional exam requirements/recommendations for international students: Required—TOEFL (minimum score 550 paper-based; 80 iBT). *Application deadline:* For fall admission, 6/1 for domestic students, 4/1 for international students; for spring admission, 10/1 for domestic students, 9/1 for international students. Applications are processed on a rolling basis. Application fee: $30. Electronic applications accepted. *Expenses:* Tuition, state resident: full-time $8912; part-time $446 per credit hour. Tuition, nonresident: full-time $21,393; part-time $992 per credit hour. *Required fees:* $2185; $195 per semester. Tuition and fees vary according to program. *Financial support:* Institutionally sponsored loans and scholarships/grants available. Financial award application deadline: 3/1; financial award applicants required to submit FAFSA. *Faculty research:* Organic synthesis and reaction catalysis, environmental chemistry, molecular beam studies, organic geochemistry, bioinorganic and organometallic chemistry. *Unit head:* Dr. Yong Cai, Chair, 305-348-6210, Fax: 305-348-3772, E-mail: yong.cai@fiu.edu. *Application contact:* Nanett Rojas, Assistant Director, Graduate Admissions, 305-348-7464, E-mail: gradadm@fiu.edu.

**George Mason University,** College of Science, Program in Forensic Science, Fairfax, VA 22030. Offers MS. *Faculty:* 5 full-time (4 women), 4 part-time/adjunct (2 women). *Students:* 40 full-time (32 women), 42 part-time (31 women); includes 41 minority (13 Black or African American, non-Hispanic/Latino; 7 Asian, non-Hispanic/Latino; 17 Hispanic/Latino; 1 Native Hawaiian or other Pacific Islander, non-Hispanic/Latino; 3 Two or more races, non-Hispanic/Latino), 1 international. Average age 28. 55 applicants, 82% accepted, 26 enrolled. In 2016, 29 master's awarded. *Degree requirements:* For master's, research project or thesis; capstone course. *Entrance requirements:* For master's, BA/BS in related field with minimum GPA of 3.0; 3 letters of recommendation; 2 copies of official transcripts; current resume; expanded goals statement. Additional exam requirements/recommendations for international students: Required—TOEFL (minimum score 575 paper-based; 88 iBT), IELTS (minimum score 6.5), PTE (minimum score 59). *Application deadline:* For fall admission, 2/1 priority date for domestic students. Application fee: $75 ($80 for international students). Electronic applications accepted. *Expenses:* Contact institution. *Financial support:* In 2016–17, 2 students received support, including 1 fellowship (averaging $15,790 per year), 1 teaching assistantship with tuition reimbursement available (averaging $14,500 per year); career-related internships or fieldwork, Federal Work-Study, scholarships/grants, and unspecified assistantships also available. Support available to part-time students. Financial award application deadline: 3/1; financial award applicants required to submit FAFSA. *Faculty research:* Forensic laboratory tests, criminal procedures, forensic chemistry and biology. *Unit head:* Mary E. O'Toole, Director, 703-993-5059, Fax: 703-993-3535, E-mail: motoole2@gmu.edu. *Application contact:* Emily Rancourt, Graduate Program Coordinator, 703-993-5234, Fax: 703-993-1993, E-mail: erancour@gmu.edu.
Website: http://forensicscience.gmu.edu/

**The George Washington University,** Columbian College of Arts and Sciences, Department of Forensic Sciences, Washington, DC 20052. Offers crime scene investigation (MFS); forensic chemistry (MFS); forensic molecular biology (MFS); forensic toxicology (MFS); high-technology crime investigation (MS); security management (MFS). MFS programs in high-technology crime investigation and in security management offered in Arlington, VA. *Program availability:* Part-time, evening/weekend. *Faculty:* 10 full-time (1 woman). *Students:* 72 full-time (51 women), 22 part-time (14 women); includes 37 minority (12 Black or African American, non-Hispanic/Latino; 1 American Indian or Alaska Native, non-Hispanic/Latino; 11 Asian, non-Hispanic/Latino; 11 Hispanic/Latino; 2 Two or more races, non-Hispanic/Latino), 1 international. Average age 27. 162 applicants, 64% accepted, 36 enrolled. In 2016, 36 master's awarded. *Degree requirements:* For master's, comprehensive exam. *Entrance requirements:* For master's, GRE General Test, minimum GPA of 3.0. Additional exam requirements/recommendations for international students: Required—TOEFL (minimum score 550 paper-based; 80 iBT). *Application deadline:* For fall admission, 1/16 priority date for international students; for spring admission, 10/1 priority date for domestic students, 9/1 priority date for international students. Applications are processed on a rolling basis. Application fee: $75. Electronic applications accepted. *Financial support:* In 2016–17, 19 students received support. Fellowships with partial tuition reimbursements available, Federal Work-Study, and tuition waivers available. *Unit head:* Dr. Victor Weedn, Chair, 202-994-6977, E-mail: vweedn@gwu.edu. *Application contact:* 202-994-6210, Fax: 202-994-6213, E-mail: askccas@gwu.edu.
Website: http://forensicsciences.columbian.gwu.edu/

**Georgia State University,** Andrew Young School of Policy Studies, School of Social Work, Atlanta, GA 30294. Offers child welfare leadership (Certificate); community partnerships (MSW); forensic social work (Certificate). *Accreditation:* CSWE. *Program availability:* Part-time. *Faculty:* 17 full-time (12 women). *Students:* 123 full-time (111 women), 4 part-time (2 women); includes 83 minority (65 Black or African American, non-Hispanic/Latino; 12 Hispanic/Latino; 6 Two or more races, non-Hispanic/Latino), 1 international. Average age 30. 123 applicants, 70% accepted, 46 enrolled. In 2016, 49 master's awarded. *Entrance requirements:* For master's and Certificate, GRE. Additional exam requirements/recommendations for international students: Required—TOEFL (minimum score 550 paper-based; 100 iBT) or IELTS (minimum score 7). *Application deadline:* For fall admission, 2/1 priority date for domestic and international students. Application fee: $50. Electronic applications accepted. *Expenses:* Tuition, state resident: full-time $6876; part-time $382 per credit hour. Tuition, nonresident: full-time $22,374; part-time $1243 per credit hour. *Required fees:* $2128; $1064 per term. Part-time tuition and fees vary according to course load and program. *Financial support:* In 2016–17, research assistantships with tuition reimbursements (averaging $4,000 per year), teaching assistantships with tuition reimbursements (averaging $4,000 per year) were awarded; career-related internships or fieldwork, institutionally sponsored loans, scholarships/grants, tuition waivers, and unspecified assistantships also available. Financial award application deadline: 2/1; financial award applicants required to submit FAFSA. *Faculty research:* Community partnership, non-profit organizations, child welfare practice and policy, gerontological practice and policy, restorative justice. *Unit head:* Brian Bride, Director of School of Social Work, 404-413-1052, Fax: 404-413-1075, E-mail: bbride@gsu.edu.
Website: http://aysps.gsu.edu/socialwork

**Golden Gate University,** School of Accounting, San Francisco, CA 94105-2968. Offers accounting (M Ac, MSA, Graduate Certificate); forensic accounting (M Ac, MSA, Graduate Certificate); taxation (M Ac). *Program availability:* Part-time, evening/weekend. *Faculty:* 4 full-time (1 woman), 46 part-time/adjunct (14 women). *Students:* 121 full-time (88 women), 135 part-time (77 women); includes 68 minority (5 Black or African American, non-Hispanic/Latino; 1 American Indian or Alaska Native, non-Hispanic/Latino; 40 Asian, non-Hispanic/Latino; 20 Hispanic/Latino; 1 Native Hawaiian or other Pacific Islander, non-Hispanic/Latino; 1 Two or more races, non-Hispanic/Latino), 107 international. Average age 32. 128 applicants, 71% accepted, 48 enrolled. In 2016, 80 master's awarded. *Entrance requirements:* For master's, minimum GPA of 3.0. Additional exam requirements/recommendations for international students: Required—TOEFL (minimum score 550 paper-based), IELTS (minimum score 6.5). *Application deadline:* For fall admission, 5/15 for international students; for winter admission, 1/15 for international students; for spring admission, 9/15 for international students. Applications are processed on a rolling basis. Application fee: $70 ($100 for international students). Electronic applications accepted. *Expenses:* Contact institution. *Financial support:* In 2016–17, 38 students received support. Career-related internships or fieldwork, Federal Work-Study, institutionally sponsored loans, and scholarships/grants available. Support available to part-time students. Financial award applicants required to submit FAFSA. *Faculty research:* Forensic accounting, audit, tax, CPA exam. *Unit head:* Fred Sroka, Dean, 415-369-5285, Fax: 415-543-2607. *Application contact:* Angela Melero, Enrollment Services, 415-442-7800, Fax: 415-442-7807, E-mail: info@ggu.edu.

**Indiana University–Purdue University Indianapolis,** School of Science, Forensic and Investigative Sciences Program, Indianapolis, IN 46202. Offers MS. *Entrance requirements:* For master's, GRE General Test, bachelor's degree in chemistry, biology, forensic science, pharmacology/toxicology, or related science from accredited institution; minimum GPA of 3.0 for all undergraduate work.

**Iona College,** School of Arts and Science, Department of Criminal Justice, New Rochelle, NY 10801-1890. Offers criminal justice (MS); cybercrime and security (AC); forensic criminology and criminal justice systems (Certificate). *Program availability:* Part-time, evening/weekend. *Faculty:* 2 full-time (0 women), 4 part-time/adjunct (1 woman). *Students:* 8 full-time (6 women), 14 part-time (4 women); includes 9 minority (5 Black or African American, non-Hispanic/Latino; 4 Hispanic/Latino), 1 international. Average age 26. 11 applicants, 100% accepted, 7 enrolled. In 2016, 12 master's, 3 other advanced degrees awarded. *Degree requirements:* For master's, thesis (for some programs), thesis or literature review. *Entrance requirements:* For master's, minimum GPA of 3.0. Additional exam requirements/recommendations for international students: Required—TOEFL (minimum score 550 paper-based; 80 iBT), IELTS (minimum score 6.5). *Application deadline:* For fall admission, 8/1 priority date for domestic students, 5/1 priority date for international students; for spring admission, 1/1 priority date for domestic students, 9/1 priority date for international students. Applications are processed on a rolling basis. Application fee: $50. Electronic applications accepted. *Expenses:* Tuition: Full-time $19,692; part-time $1094 per credit. *Required fees:* $245 per term. Tuition and fees vary according to program. *Financial support:* In 2016–17, 13 students received support. Unspecified assistantships available. Financial award application deadline: 4/15; financial award applicants required to submit FAFSA. *Faculty research:* Juvenile justice, criminology, victimology, policing, social justice, security threat assessment. *Unit head:* Cathryn Lavery, PhD, Chair, 914-633-2597, E-mail: clavery@iona.edu. *Application contact:* Katelyn Brunck, Assistant Director of Graduate Admissions, 914-633-2451, Fax: 914-633-2277, E-mail: kbrunck@iona.edu.
Website: http://www.iona.edu/Academics/School-of-Arts-Science/Departments/Criminal-Justice/Graduate-Programs.aspx

**James Madison University,** The Graduate School, College of Integrated Science and Engineering, Program in Computer Science, Harrisonburg, VA 22802. Offers digital

forensics (MS); information security (MS). *Program availability:* Online learning. *Faculty:* 15 full-time (1 woman), 1 part-time/adjunct (0 women). *Students:* 7 full-time (3 women), 21 part-time (4 women); includes 6 minority (3 Black or African American, non-Hispanic/Latino; 1 Asian, non-Hispanic/Latino; 1 Hispanic/Latino; 1 Two or more races, non-Hispanic/Latino), 3 international. Average age 30. 29 applicants, 97% accepted, 18 enrolled. In 2016, 15 master's awarded. Application fee: $55. Electronic applications accepted. *Financial support:* Fellowships, Federal Work-Study, and 3 assistantships (averaging $7911) available. Financial award application deadline: 3/1; financial award applicants required to submit FAFSA. *Unit head:* Dr. Sharon J. Simmons, Department Head, 540-568-4196, E-mail: simmonsj@jmu.edu. *Application contact:* Lynette D. Michael, Director of Graduate Admissions, 540-568-6131 Ext. 6395, Fax: 540-568-7860, E-mail: michaeld@jmu.edu.
Website: http://www.jmu.edu/cs/

**John Jay College of Criminal Justice of the City University of New York,** Graduate Studies, Program in Forensic Computing, New York, NY 10019. Offers MS. *Program availability:* Part-time, evening/weekend. *Degree requirements:* For master's, thesis or alternative. *Entrance requirements:* For master's, GRE General Test, minimum B average. Additional exam requirements/recommendations for international students: Required—TOEFL (minimum score 500 paper-based).

**John Jay College of Criminal Justice of the City University of New York,** Graduate Studies, Program in Forensic Science, New York, NY 10019. Offers MS. *Program availability:* Part-time, evening/weekend. *Degree requirements:* For master's, thesis. *Entrance requirements:* For master's, GRE, minimum B average. Additional exam requirements/recommendations for international students: Required—TOEFL (minimum score 500 paper-based).

**John Jay College of Criminal Justice of the City University of New York,** Graduate Studies, Programs in Criminal Justice, New York, NY 10019. Offers criminal justice (MA, PhD); criminology and deviance (PhD); forensic psychology (PhD); forensic science (PhD); international crime and justice (MA); law and philosophy (PhD); organizational behavior (PhD); public policy (PhD). *Program availability:* Part-time, evening/weekend. Terminal master's awarded for partial completion of doctoral program. *Degree requirements:* For master's, thesis or alternative; for doctorate, one foreign language, thesis/dissertation. *Entrance requirements:* For master's, GRE General Test, minimum B average; for doctorate, GRE General Test. Additional exam requirements/recommendations for international students: Required—TOEFL (minimum score 500 paper-based).

**La Salle University,** School of Arts and Sciences, Program in Economic Crime Forensics, Philadelphia, PA 19141-1199. Offers corporate fraud (MS); fraud and forensic accounting (Certificate); network security (MS). *Program availability:* Part-time, evening/weekend, online only, 100% online. *Faculty:* 1 (woman) full-time, 5 part-time/adjunct (0 women). *Students:* 3 full-time (1 woman), 65 part-time (39 women); includes 35 minority (25 Black or African American, non-Hispanic/Latino; 1 American Indian or Alaska Native, non-Hispanic/Latino; 5 Asian, non-Hispanic/Latino; 3 Hispanic/Latino; 1 Two or more races, non-Hispanic/Latino), 1 international. Average age 37. 28 applicants, 100% accepted, 18 enrolled. In 2016, 2 master's, 1 other advanced degree awarded. *Entrance requirements:* For master's, minimum GPA of 3.0; professional resume; letters of recommendation; personal interview; for Certificate, professional resume, 200-word essay. Additional exam requirements/recommendations for international students: Required—TOEFL. *Application deadline:* For fall admission, 8/15 priority date for domestic students; for spring admission, 12/15 priority date for domestic students; for summer admission, 4/15 priority date for domestic students. Applications are processed on a rolling basis. Application fee: $35. Electronic applications accepted. Application fee is waived when completed online. *Expenses:* Contact institution. *Financial support:* In 2016–17, 10 students received support. Scholarships/grants available. Support available to part-time students. Financial award application deadline: 8/31; financial award applicants required to submit FAFSA. *Unit head:* Margaret M. McCoey, Director, 215-951-1136, Fax: 215-951-1805, E-mail: mccoey@lasalle.edu. *Application contact:* Elizabeth Heenan, Director, Graduate and Adult Enrollment, 215-951-1100, Fax: 215-951-1462, E-mail: heenan@lasalle.edu.
Website: http://www.lasalle.edu/economic-crime-forensics/

**Long Island University–LIU Brooklyn,** School of Health Professions, Brooklyn, NY 11201-8423. Offers athletic training and sport sciences (MS); community health (MS Ed); exercise science (MS); forensic social work (Advanced Certificate); occupational therapy (MS); physical therapy (DPT); physician assistant (MS); public health (MPH); social work (MSW). *Faculty:* 60 full-time (42 women), 109 part-time/adjunct (62 women). *Students:* 603 full-time (405 women), 69 part-time (52 women); includes 219 minority (117 Black or African American, non-Hispanic/Latino; 1 American Indian or Alaska Native, non-Hispanic/Latino; 38 Asian, non-Hispanic/Latino; 48 Hispanic/Latino; 15 Two or more races, non-Hispanic/Latino), 68 international. 1,127 applicants, 43% accepted, 213 enrolled. In 2016, 192 master's, 42 doctorates awarded. *Degree requirements:* For master's, comprehensive exam (for some programs), thesis (for some programs), research capstone; for doctorate, comprehensive exam, research capstone. *Entrance requirements:* For master's, doctorate, and Advanced Certificate, GRE. Additional exam requirements/recommendations for international students: Required—TOEFL (minimum score 550 paper-based; 79 iBT). *Application deadline:* Applications are processed on a rolling basis. Application fee: $50. Electronic applications accepted. *Expenses: Tuition:* Full-time $28,272; part-time $1178 per credit. *Required fees:* $451 per term. Tuition and fees vary according to degree level, program and student level. *Financial support:* Research assistantships, teaching assistantships, career-related internships or fieldwork, Federal Work-Study, institutionally sponsored loans, scholarships/grants, tuition waivers (partial), and unspecified assistantships available. Support available to part-time students. Financial award application deadline: 2/15; financial award applicants required to submit FAFSA. *Faculty research:* Kinesiology, gender disparities, exercise physiology, gait analysis, social justice. *Unit head:* Dr. Barry S. Eckert, Dean, 718-780-6578, Fax: 718-780-4561, E-mail: barry.eckert@liu.edu. *Application contact:* Dr. Dominick Fortugno, Dean of Admissions, 718-780-6578, Fax: 718-780-4561, E-mail: dominick.fortugno@liu.edu.
Website: http://liu.edu/brooklyn/academics/school-of-health-professions

**Marshall University,** Academic Affairs Division, Forensic Science Center, Huntington, WV 25755. Offers MS, Graduate Certificate. *Degree requirements:* For master's, comprehensive exam, thesis optional. *Entrance requirements:* For master's, GRE General Test, undergraduate degree in a natural science, forensic science, or equivalent course work in a related field; 1 year of undergraduate coursework in general chemistry, organic chemistry, physics and biology, with 1 year of associated laboratory for each course. Additional exam requirements/recommendations for international students: Required—TOEFL. *Expenses:* Contact institution. *Faculty research:* STR analysis of DNA for human identification, forensic analytical chemistry, digital forensics/computer forensics examination, microbial source tracking.

**McGill University,** Faculty of Graduate and Postdoctoral Studies, Faculty of Dentistry, Montréal, QC H3A 2T5, Canada. Offers forensic dentistry (Certificate); oral and maxillofacial surgery (M Sc, PhD).

**Mercyhurst University,** Graduate Studies, Program in Anthropology, Erie, PA 16546. Offers archaeology and geological archaeology (MS); forensic and biological anthropology (MS). *Entrance requirements:* For master's, GRE or MAT, undergraduate degree in related field, interview, resume, essay, three professional references, transcripts. Additional exam requirements/recommendations for international students: Required—TOEFL.

**Michigan State University,** The Graduate School, College of Social Science, School of Criminal Justice, East Lansing, MI 48824. Offers criminal justice (MS, PhD); forensic science (MS); law enforcement intelligence and analysis (MS). *Program availability:* Online learning. *Entrance requirements:* Additional exam requirements/recommendations for international students: Required—TOEFL. Electronic applications accepted.

**Middle Georgia State University,** Office of Graduate Studies, Macon, GA 31206. Offers adult/gerontology acute care nurse practitioner (MSN); information technology (MS), including health informatics, information security and digital forensics, software development. *Entrance requirements:* For master's, GRE. Additional exam requirements/recommendations for international students: Required—TOEFL (minimum score 523 paper-based; 69 iBT). *Expenses:* Contact institution.

**Missouri Western State University,** Program in Forensic Investigations, St. Joseph, MO 64507-2294. Offers MAS, Graduate Certificate. *Program availability:* Part-time. *Students:* 4 full-time (all women), 15 part-time (12 women); includes 5 minority (4 Black or African American, non-Hispanic/Latino; 1 Two or more races, non-Hispanic/Latino), 1 international. Average age 30. 7 applicants, 100% accepted, 6 enrolled. In 2016, 1 master's, 1 other advanced degree awarded. *Entrance requirements:* For master's, minimum GPA of 2.75, personal statement, 2 letters of recommendation. Additional exam requirements/recommendations for international students: Recommended—TOEFL (minimum score 79 iBT), IELTS (minimum score 6). *Application deadline:* For fall admission, 7/15 for domestic and international students; for spring admission, 10/1 for domestic and international students; for summer admission, 3/15 for domestic students. Applications are processed on a rolling basis. Application fee: $50. Electronic applications accepted. *Expenses:* Tuition, state resident: full-time $6548; part-time $327.39 per credit hour. Tuition, nonresident: full-time $11,848; part-time $592.39 per credit hour. *Required fees:* $542; $99 per credit hour. $176 per semester. One-time fee: $50. Tuition and fees vary according to course load and program. *Financial support:* Scholarships/grants and unspecified assistantships available. Support available to part-time students. *Unit head:* Dr. Monty Smith, Forensics Graduate Program Director, 816-271-4434, E-mail: msmith84@missouriwestern.edu. *Application contact:* Dr. Benjamin D. Caldwell, Dean of the Graduate School, 816-271-4394, Fax: 816-271-4525, E-mail: graduate@missouriwestern.edu.
Website: https://www.missouriwestern.edu/cj-ls-swk/forensic-investigation/

**Nebraska Wesleyan University,** University College, Program in Forensic Science, Lincoln, NE 68504-2796. Offers MFS. *Program availability:* Part-time, evening/weekend.

**Oklahoma State University Center for Health Sciences,** Graduate Program in Forensic Sciences, Tulsa, OK 74107-1898. Offers forensic sciences (MS), including arson and explosives investigation, forensic biology/DNA, forensic document examination, forensic pathology/death scene investigations, forensic psychology, forensic science administration, forensic toxicology/trace evidence. *Program availability:* Part-time, evening/weekend, 100% online, blended/hybrid learning. *Degree requirements:* For master's, comprehensive exam, thesis (for some programs), thesis or creative component. *Entrance requirements:* For master's, GRE (for thesis tracks); GRE or MAT (for options in arson and explosives investigation, forensic science administration, and forensic document examination), professional experience (for options in arson and explosives investigation, forensic science administration and forensic document examination). Additional exam requirements/recommendations for international students: Required—TOEFL (minimum score 100 iBT) or IELTS (minimum score 7.0). Electronic applications accepted. *Faculty research:* Studies on the variability in chromosomal DNA; development/enhancement of accessory methods useful for forensic DNA typing; forensic chemistry in the areas of controlled substances, explosives, and technology; research on explosives and IEDs (non-chemistry); therapeutic jurisprudence, issues involving inmates and their families, institutional stress suicide.

**Pace University,** Dyson College of Arts and Sciences, Program in Forensic Science, New York, NY 10038. Offers MS. *Program availability:* Part-time, evening/weekend. *Faculty:* 1 full-time, 5 part-time/adjunct (3 women). *Students:* 16 full-time (11 women), 7 part-time (all women); includes 8 minority (4 Black or African American, non-Hispanic/Latino; 1 Asian, non-Hispanic/Latino; 2 Hispanic/Latino; 1 Two or more races, non-Hispanic/Latino), 2 international. Average age 26. In 2016, 19 master's awarded. *Degree requirements:* For master's, thesis. *Entrance requirements:* For master's, two letters of recommendation, personal statement, resume, official transcripts. Additional exam requirements/recommendations for international students: Required—TOEFL (minimum score 88 iBT). *Application deadline:* For fall admission, 8/1 priority date for domestic students, 6/1 for international students; for spring admission, 12/1 priority date for domestic students, 10/1 for international students. Applications are processed on a rolling basis. Application fee: $70. Electronic applications accepted. *Expenses: Tuition:* Part-time $1195 per credit. *Required fees:* $260 per semester. Tuition and fees vary according to degree level, campus/location and program. *Financial support:* Career-related internships or fieldwork, Federal Work-Study, and scholarships/grants available. Financial award application deadline: 2/15; financial award applicants required to submit FAFSA. *Unit head:* Dr. Demos Athanasopolous, Director, Forensic Science Program, 212-346-1763, E-mail: dathanasopolous@pace.edu. *Application contact:* Susan Ford-Goldschein, Director of Graduate Admissions, 212-346-1531, Fax: 212-346-1585, E-mail: gradnyc@pace.edu.
Website: http://www.pace.edu/dyson/academic-departments-and-programs/forensic-science

**Penn State University Park,** Graduate School, Eberly College of Science, Program in Forensic Science, University Park, PA 16802. Offers MPS.

**Philadelphia College of Osteopathic Medicine,** Graduate and Professional Programs, Programs in Forensic Medicine, Philadelphia, PA 19131-1694. Offers MS. *Program availability:* Evening/weekend. *Faculty:* 2 full-time (0 women), 2 part-time/adjunct (1 woman). *Students:* 79 full-time (61 women); includes 25 minority (9 Black or African American, non-Hispanic/Latino; 16 Two or more races, non-Hispanic/Latino). Average age 28. 44 applicants, 55% accepted, 20 enrolled. In 2016, 37 master's awarded. *Degree requirements:* For master's, capstone project. *Entrance requirements:* For master's, minimum GPA of 3.0; coursework in biology, chemistry, anatomy and physiology or completion of PCOM pathway program. Additional exam requirements/recommendations for international students: Required—TOEFL (minimum score 79 iBT). *Application deadline:* Applications are processed on a rolling basis. Application fee: $75. Electronic applications accepted. *Expenses:* Contact institution. *Financial support:* In 2016–17, 11 students received support. Federal Work-Study, institutionally sponsored loans, and scholarships/grants available. Financial award application deadline: 3/15; financial award applicants required to submit FAFSA. *Unit head:* Dr. Gregory McDonald, Chair, 215-871-6760, Fax: 215-871-6792. *Application contact:* Johnathan Cox,

Associate Director of Admissions, 215-871-6700, Fax: 215-871-6719, E-mail: johnathancox@pcom.edu.
Website: http://www.pcom.edu

**St. Joseph's College, New York,** Program in Forensic Computing, Brooklyn, NY 11205-3688. Offers MS. *Program availability:* Part-time, evening/weekend. *Faculty:* 2 part-time/adjunct (1 woman). *Students:* 3 full-time (all women), 5 part-time (4 women); includes 3 minority (1 Asian, non-Hispanic/Latino; 2 Hispanic/Latino). Average age 27. 9 applicants, 89% accepted, 8 enrolled. *Entrance requirements:* For master's, official transcripts, 2 letters of reference. Additional exam requirements/recommendations for international students: Required—TOEFL (minimum score 80 iBT). *Application deadline:* Applications are processed on a rolling basis. Electronic applications accepted. *Expenses:* Contact institution. *Financial support:* In 2016–17, 2 students received support. *Unit head:* Dr. Joseph Pascarella, Associate Professor, 718-940-5775, E-mail: jpascarella2@sjcny.edu. *Application contact:* Roberto Figueroa, Director, Graduate and Adult Admissions, 718-940-5828, E-mail: rfigueroa@sjcny.edu.
Website: http://www.sjcny.edu

**Saint Leo University,** Graduate Studies in Public Safety Administration, Saint Leo, FL 33574-6665. Offers criminal justice (MS), including corrections, criminal investigation, emergency and disaster management, forensic science, legal studies; emergency and disaster management (MS). *Program availability:* Part-time, evening/weekend, 100% online, blended/hybrid learning. *Faculty:* 7 full-time (2 women), 32 part-time/adjunct (8 women). *Students:* 3 full-time (1 woman), 667 part-time (446 women); includes 355 minority (275 Black or African American, non-Hispanic/Latino; 6 American Indian or Alaska Native, non-Hispanic/Latino; 4 Asian, non-Hispanic/Latino; 56 Hispanic/Latino; 3 Native Hawaiian or other Pacific Islander, non-Hispanic/Latino; 11 Two or more races, non-Hispanic/Latino). Average age 37. 361 applicants, 87% accepted, 177 enrolled. In 2016, 265 master's awarded. *Degree requirements:* For master's, comprehensive project. *Entrance requirements:* For master's, official transcripts, bachelor's degree from regionally-accredited university with minimum GPA of 3.0. Additional exam requirements/recommendations for international students: Required—TOEFL (minimum score 550 paper-based; 80 iBT). *Application deadline:* For fall admission, 7/1 priority date for domestic and international students; for spring admission, 11/1 priority date for domestic and international students. Applications are processed on a rolling basis. Application fee: $80. Electronic applications accepted. *Expenses:* $535 per semester hour (for MS in emergency/disaster management); $555 per semester hour (for MS in criminal justice). *Financial support:* In 2016–17, 14 students received support. Scholarships/grants and health care benefits available. Financial award application deadline: 3/1; financial award applicants required to submit FAFSA. *Unit head:* Dr. Robert Diemer, Director of Graduate Studies in Safety Administration, 352-588-8974, Fax: 352-588-8289, E-mail: graduatepublicsafety@saintleo.edu. *Application contact:* Jennifer Shelley, Senior Associate Director of Graduate Admissions, 800-707-8846, Fax: 352-588-7873, E-mail: grad.admissions@saintleo.edu.
Website: http://www.saintleo.edu/academics/graduate

**Salve Regina University,** Program in Administration of Justice and Homeland Security, Newport, RI 02840-4192. Offers administration of justice and homeland security (MS); cybersecurity and intelligence (CGS); digital forensics (CGS); leadership in justice (CGS). *Program availability:* Part-time, evening/weekend, online learning. *Entrance requirements:* For master's, GMAT, GRE General Test, or MAT. Additional exam requirements/recommendations for international students: Required—TOEFL (minimum score 600 paper-based; 100 iBT). Electronic applications accepted.

**Sam Houston State University,** College of Criminal Justice, Department of Forensic Science, Huntsville, TX 77341. Offers MS. *Program availability:* Part-time. *Degree requirements:* For master's, comprehensive exam. *Entrance requirements:* For master's, GRE, official transcripts, three letters of recommendation, personal essay. Additional exam requirements/recommendations for international students: Required—TOEFL (minimum score 550 paper-based; 79 iBT), IELTS (minimum score 6.5). Electronic applications accepted.

**Sam Houston State University,** College of Sciences, Department of Computer Science, Huntsville, TX 77341. Offers computing and information science (MS); digital forensics (MS); information assurance and security (MS). *Program availability:* Part-time. *Degree requirements:* For master's, comprehensive exam, thesis optional, internship; for doctorate, comprehensive exam, thesis/dissertation. *Entrance requirements:* For master's, GRE General Test, letters of recommendation. Additional exam requirements/recommendations for international students: Required—TOEFL (minimum score 550 paper-based; 79 iBT), IELTS (minimum score 6.5). Electronic applications accepted.

**Seattle University,** College of Arts and Sciences, Department of Criminal Justice, Seattle, WA 98122-1090. Offers crime analysis (Certificate); criminal justice (MACJ). *Program availability:* Part-time, evening/weekend. *Faculty:* 8 full-time (2 women), 5 part-time/adjunct (3 women). *Students:* 24 full-time (21 women), 51 part-time (40 women); includes 32 minority (4 Black or African American, non-Hispanic/Latino; 1 American Indian or Alaska Native, non-Hispanic/Latino; 6 Asian, non-Hispanic/Latino; 13 Hispanic/Latino; 1 Native Hawaiian or other Pacific Islander, non-Hispanic/Latino; 7 Two or more races, non-Hispanic/Latino). Average age 28. 71 applicants, 65% accepted, 32 enrolled. In 2016, 22 master's, 2 Certificates awarded. *Degree requirements:* For master's, comprehensive exam or thesis. *Entrance requirements:* For master's, minimum GPA of 3.0; undergraduate degree in criminal justice or related social, behavioral, or physical science, or related coursework and/or volunteer or supervised experience; letters of recommendation; writing sample. Additional exam requirements/recommendations for international students: Required—TOEFL, IELTS. *Application deadline:* For fall admission, 3/15 for domestic and international students. Application fee: $55. Electronic applications accepted. *Financial support:* In 2016–17, 26 students received support. Applicants required to submit FAFSA. *Faculty research:* Criminal justice program evaluation, ex-offender reentry, policing issues, restorative justice, psychopathy. *Unit head:* Dr. Elaine Gunnison, Graduate Program Director, 206-296-2430, E-mail: gunnisone@seattleu.edu. *Application contact:* Janet Shandley, Associate Dean of Graduate Admissions, 206-296-5900, Fax: 206-298-5656, E-mail: grad_admissions@seattleu.edu.
Website: https://www.seattleu.edu/artsci/criminal-graduate/

**Stevenson University,** Program in Forensic Science, Owings Mills, MD 21117. Offers biology (MS); chemistry (MS); crime scene investigation (MS). Program offered in partnership with Maryland State Police Forensic Sciences Division. *Program availability:* Part-time. *Faculty:* 4 full-time (3 women), 6 part-time/adjunct (3 women). *Students:* 31 full-time (26 women), 20 part-time (16 women); includes 26 minority (20 Black or African American, non-Hispanic/Latino; 1 American Indian or Alaska Native, non-Hispanic/Latino; 1 Asian, non-Hispanic/Latino; 4 Hispanic/Latino). Average age 26. 29 applicants, 90% accepted, 21 enrolled. In 2016, 16 master's awarded. *Degree requirements:* For master's, capstone course. *Entrance requirements:* For master's, bachelor's degree in a natural science from regionally-accredited institution; official college transcripts from all previous academic work; minimum cumulative GPA of 3.0 in past academic work. *Application deadline:* Applications are processed on a rolling basis. Application fee: $0. Electronic applications accepted. *Expenses:* $670 per credit hour. *Financial support:* Unspecified assistantships available. Financial award applicants required to submit

FAFSA. *Unit head:* John Tobin, PhD, Coordinator, 443-352-4142, Fax: 443-394-0538, E-mail: jtobin@stevenson.edu. *Application contact:* William Wellein, Enrollment Counselor, 443-352-5843, Fax: 443-394-0538, E-mail: wwellein@stevenson.edu.
Website: http://www.stevenson.edu

**Stevenson University,** Program in Forensic Studies, Owings Mills, MD 21117. Offers computer forensics (MS); criminalistics (MS); forensic accounting (MS); forensic legal professional (MS); interdisciplinary track (MS); investigations (MS). *Program availability:* Part-time, blended/hybrid learning. *Faculty:* 3 full-time (all women), 12 part-time/adjunct (2 women). *Students:* 21 full-time (17 women), 103 part-time (73 women); includes 59 minority (52 Black or African American, non-Hispanic/Latino; 1 American Indian or Alaska Native, non-Hispanic/Latino; 2 Asian, non-Hispanic/Latino; 4 Hispanic/Latino). Average age 29. 85 applicants, 74% accepted, 43 enrolled. In 2016, 54 master's awarded. *Degree requirements:* For master's, capstone course. *Entrance requirements:* For master's, bachelor's degree from regionally-accredited institution, official college transcripts from all previous academic work, minimum cumulative GPA of 3.0 in past academic work, personal statement (250-350 words). *Application deadline:* Applications are processed on a rolling basis. Application fee: $0. Electronic applications accepted. *Expenses:* $670 per credit hour. *Financial support:* Unspecified assistantships available. Financial award applicants required to submit FAFSA. *Unit head:* Thomas Coogan, JD, Associate Dean, 443-352-4075, Fax: 443-394-0538, E-mail: tcoogan@stevenson.edu. *Application contact:* William Wellein, Enrollment Counselor, 443-352-5843, Fax: 443-394-0538, E-mail: wwellein@stevenson.edu.

**Stratford University,** School of Graduate Studies, Falls Church, VA 22043. Offers accounting (MS); business administration (IMBA, MBA); cyber security (MS); cyber security leadership and policy (MS); digital forensics (MS); enterprise business management (MS); entrepreneurial management (MS); healthcare administration (MS); information systems (MS); international hospitality management (MS); networking and telecommunications (MS); software engineering (MS). *Program availability:* Part-time, evening/weekend, 100% online, blended/hybrid learning. *Students:* 505 full-time (186 women), 172 part-time (88 women); includes 532 minority (165 Black or African American, non-Hispanic/Latino; 18 American Indian or Alaska Native, non-Hispanic/Latino; 324 Asian, non-Hispanic/Latino; 13 Hispanic/Latino; 10 Native Hawaiian or other Pacific Islander, non-Hispanic/Latino; 2 Two or more races, non-Hispanic/Latino). Average age 27. In 2016, 520 master's awarded. *Degree requirements:* For master's, comprehensive exam, capstone project. *Entrance requirements:* For master's, GRE or GMAT, baccalaureate degree. Additional exam requirements/recommendations for international students: Required—TOEFL (minimum score 79 iBT), IELTS (minimum score 6.5), PTE (minimum score 5). *Application deadline:* Applications are processed on a rolling basis. Application fee: $50. Electronic applications accepted. *Expenses: Tuition:* Full-time $4455; part-time $2227.50 per course. One-time fee: $100. *Financial support:* Federal Work-Study and scholarships/grants available. Financial award applicants required to submit FAFSA. *Unit head:* Dr. Richard R. Shurtz, President, 703-539-6890, Fax: 703-539-6960. *Application contact:* Admissions, 800-444-0804, E-mail: fcadmissions@stratford.edu.

**Syracuse University,** College of Arts and Sciences, Programs in Forensic Science, Syracuse, NY 13244. Offers MS, CAS, MS/JD. *Program availability:* Part-time. *Students:* Average age 25. In 2016, 15 master's awarded. *Degree requirements:* For master's, internship. *Entrance requirements:* For master's, GRE General Test, personal statement, three letters of recommendation, transcripts, telephone interview. Additional exam requirements/recommendations for international students: Required—TOEFL (minimum score 100 iBT). *Application deadline:* For fall admission, 2/15 priority date for domestic and international students; for summer admission, 2/15 for domestic students, 2/16 priority date for international students. Applications are processed on a rolling basis. Application fee: $75. Electronic applications accepted. *Expenses: Tuition:* Full-time $25,974; part-time $1443 per credit hour. *Required fees:* $802; $50 per course. Tuition and fees vary according to course load and program. *Financial support:* Fellowships with full tuition reimbursements, research assistantships, teaching assistantships, and scholarships/grants available. Financial award application deadline: 1/1; financial award applicants required to submit FAFSA. *Faculty research:* Chemical analysis, molecular genetics, forensic biochemical analysis, forensic entomology, human osteology. *Unit head:* Dr. Michael M. Sponsler, Director of Curricular Programs for the Forensic and National Security Sciences Institute, 315-443-4347, E-mail: sponsler@syr.edu. *Application contact:* Cassidy Perreault, Administrative Specialist, 315-443-2875, E-mail: forensics@syr.edu.
Website: http://forensics.syr.edu/index.html

**Texas Tech University,** Graduate School, College of Arts and Sciences, Program in Forensic Sciences, Lubbock, TX 79409. Offers MS. *Students:* 13 full-time (8 women), 6 part-time (3 women); includes 6 minority (2 Black or African American, non-Hispanic/Latino; 4 Hispanic/Latino), 2 international. Average age 26. 16 applicants, 38% accepted, 3 enrolled. In 2016, 9 master's awarded. *Degree requirements:* For master's, thesis (for some programs), internship with comprehensive exam. *Entrance requirements:* Additional exam requirements/recommendations for international students: Required—TOEFL (minimum score 550 paper-based; 79 iBT). *Application deadline:* For fall admission, 6/1 priority date for domestic students, 1/15 priority date for international students; for spring admission, 9/1 priority date for domestic students, 6/15 priority date for international students. Applications are processed on a rolling basis. Application fee: $75. Electronic applications accepted. *Expenses:* $300 per credit hour full-time resident tuition, $708 per credit hour full-time non-resident tuition; $50.50 per credit hour fee plus $608 per term fee. *Financial support:* In 2016–17, 8 students received support, including 8 fellowships (averaging $1,964 per year); research assistantships also available. Financial award application deadline: 4/15; financial award applicants required to submit FAFSA. *Faculty research:* Forensic sciences; including toxicology, DNA, chemistry, psychology, and biology. *Unit head:* Dr. Megan A. Thoen, Graduate Program Director, 806-834-1687, Fax: 806-743-7932, E-mail: megan.thoen@ttu.edu.

**Towson University,** Program in Forensic Science, Towson, MD 21252-0001. Offers MS. *Students:* 42 full-time (35 women), 9 part-time (8 women); includes 16 minority (8 Black or African American, non-Hispanic/Latino; 3 Asian, non-Hispanic/Latino; 1 Hispanic/Latino; 4 Two or more races, non-Hispanic/Latino), 3 international. *Entrance requirements:* For master's, minimum GPA of 3.0; bachelor's degree in biological sciences, chemistry, forensic chemistry, or related field. *Application deadline:* Applications are processed on a rolling basis. Application fee: $45. Electronic applications accepted. *Expenses:* Tuition, state resident: full-time $7580; part-time $379 per unit. Tuition, nonresident: full-time $15,700; part-time $785 per unit. *Required fees:* $2480. *Unit head:* Mark Profili, Graduate Program Director, 410-704-2668, E-mail: mprofili@towson.edu. *Application contact:* Coverley Beidleman, Assistant Director of Graduate Admissions, 410-704-2113, Fax: 410-704-3030, E-mail: grads@towson.edu.
Website: http://www.towson.edu/fcsm/departments/chemistry/grad/forensic/

**Universidad del Turabo,** Graduate Programs, School of Social Sciences and Humanities, Programs in Public Affairs, Program in Forensic Science, Gurabo, PR 00778-3030. Offers MPA. *Students:* 71 full-time (44 women), 40 part-time (32 women); all minorities (all Hispanic/Latino). Average age 28. 78 applicants, 67% accepted, 38 enrolled. In 2016, 45 master's awarded. *Entrance requirements:* For master's, GRE,

GMAT or EXADEP, interview, essay, official transcript, recommendation letters. *Application deadline:* Applications are processed on a rolling basis. Application fee: $25. Electronic applications accepted. *Financial support:* Institutionally sponsored loans available. Financial award applicants required to submit FAFSA. *Unit head:* María del Carmen Santos, Dean, 787-743-7979 Ext. 4232. *Application contact:* Diriee Rodríguez, Admissions Director, 787-743-7979 Ext. 4453, E-mail: admisiones-ut@suagm.edu. Website: http://ut.suagm.edu/es/sociales

**University at Albany, State University of New York,** College of Arts and Sciences, Department of Biological Sciences, Albany, NY 12222-0001. Offers forensic biology (MS). *Faculty:* 10 full-time (3 women), 1 part-time/adjunct (0 women). *Students:* 38 full-time (20 women), 26 part-time (16 women); includes 7 minority (1 Black or African American, non-Hispanic/Latino; 4 Asian, non-Hispanic/Latino; 1 Hispanic/Latino; 1 Two or more races, non-Hispanic/Latino), 10 international. 86 applicants, 31% accepted, 17 enrolled. In 2016, 6 master's awarded. *Degree requirements:* For master's, one foreign language. *Entrance requirements:* For master's, GRE General Test. Additional exam requirements/recommendations for international students: Required—TOEFL (minimum score 550 paper-based). *Application deadline:* For fall admission, 2/15 priority date for domestic students, 5/1 for international students; for spring admission, 11/1 for domestic and international students. Applications are processed on a rolling basis. Application fee: $75. Electronic applications accepted. *Expenses:* Tuition, state resident: full-time $10,870; part-time $453 per credit hour. Tuition, nonresident: full-time $22,210; part-time $925 per credit hour. *International tuition:* $21,550 full-time. *Required fees:* $1864; $96 per credit hour. *Financial support:* Fellowships, research assistantships, teaching assistantships, unspecified assistantships, and minority assistantships available. Financial award application deadline: 5/1. *Faculty research:* Interferon, neural development, RNA self-splicing, behavioral ecology, DNA repair enzymes. *Total annual research expenditures:* $2.3 million. *Unit head:* Glyne Griffith, Chair, 518-442-4300, Fax: 518-442-4354, E-mail: ggriffith@albany.edu. *Application contact:* Michael DeRensis, Director, Graduate Admissions, 518-442-3980, Fax: 518-442-3922, E-mail: graduate@albany.edu.
Website: http://www.albany.edu/biology/

**University at Albany, State University of New York,** School of Business, Department of Accounting and Law, Albany, NY 12222-0001. Offers accounting (MS); forensic accounting (MS); professional accounting (MS); tax practice (MS); taxation (MS). *Accreditation:* AACSB. *Faculty:* 9 full-time (2 women), 8 part-time/adjunct (3 women). *Students:* 137 full-time (62 women), 9 part-time (4 women); includes 31 minority (7 Black or African American, non-Hispanic/Latino; 11 Asian, non-Hispanic/Latino; 9 Hispanic/Latino; 4 Two or more races, non-Hispanic/Latino), 22 international. 257 applicants, 67% accepted, 117 enrolled. In 2016, 110 master's awarded. *Degree requirements:* For master's, research project. *Entrance requirements:* For master's, GMAT. Additional exam requirements/recommendations for international students: Required—TOEFL (minimum score 550 paper-based). *Application deadline:* For fall admission, 3/1 priority date for domestic students, 4/1 for international students. Applications are processed on a rolling basis. Application fee: $75. Electronic applications accepted. *Expenses:* Tuition, state resident: full-time $10,870; part-time $453 per credit hour. Tuition, nonresident: full-time $22,210; part-time $925 per credit hour. *International tuition:* $21,550 full-time. *Required fees:* $1864; $96 per credit hour. *Financial support:* Application deadline: 4/1. *Faculty research:* Professional ethics, statistical analysis, cost management systems, accounting theory. *Unit head:* Ingrid Fisher, Chair, 518-956-8365, E-mail: ifisher@albany.edu. *Application contact:* Michael DeRensis, Director, Graduate Admissions, 518-442-3980, Fax: 518-442-3922, E-mail: graduate@albany.edu.
Website: http://www.albany.edu/business/accounting_index.shtml

**The University of Alabama at Birmingham,** College of Arts and Sciences, Program in Computer Forensics and Security Management, Birmingham, AL 35294. Offers MS. Interdisciplinary program offered jointly with College of Arts and Sciences and School of Business. *Degree requirements:* For master's, field practicum (internship). *Entrance requirements:* For master's, GRE General Test (minimum combined score of 320) or GMAT (minimum total score of 550), minimum GPA of 3.0. Electronic applications accepted. Full-time tuition and fees vary according to course load and program.

**The University of Alabama at Birmingham,** College of Arts and Sciences, Program in Forensic Science, Birmingham, AL 35294. Offers MSFS. *Entrance requirements:* For master's, GRE, minimum GPA of 3.0. Additional exam requirements/recommendations for international students: Required—TOEFL, TWE. Electronic applications accepted. Full-time tuition and fees vary according to course load and program.

**University of California, Davis,** Graduate Studies, Graduate Group in Forensic Science, Davis, CA 95616. Offers MS. *Degree requirements:* For master's, thesis. *Entrance requirements:* Additional exam requirements/recommendations for international students: Required—TOEFL (minimum score 550 paper-based), IELTS (minimum score 7). Electronic applications accepted.

**University of Central Florida,** College of Engineering and Computer Science, Department of Electrical Engineering and Computer Science, Program in Computer Science, Orlando, FL 32816. Offers computer science (MS, PhD); digital forensics (MS). *Program availability:* Part-time, evening/weekend. *Students:* 234 full-time (58 women), 126 part-time (24 women); includes 76 minority (15 Black or African American, non-Hispanic/Latino; 13 Asian, non-Hispanic/Latino; 42 Hispanic/Latino; 6 Two or more races, non-Hispanic/Latino), 173 international. Average age 30. 542 applicants, 71% accepted, 141 enrolled. In 2016, 97 master's, 9 doctorates awarded. *Degree requirements:* For master's, thesis or alternative; for doctorate, thesis/dissertation, candidacy exam, departmental qualifying exam. *Entrance requirements:* For master's, GRE General Test, GRE Subject Test, minimum GPA of 3.0 in last 60 hours; for doctorate, GRE Subject Test, minimum GPA of 3.0 in last 60 hours. Additional exam requirements/recommendations for international students: Required—TOEFL. *Application deadline:* For fall admission, 7/15 for domestic students; for spring admission, 12/1 for domestic students. Application fee: $30. Electronic applications accepted. *Expenses:* Tuition, state resident: part-time $288.16 per credit hour. Tuition, nonresident: part-time $1071.31 per credit hour. *Financial support:* In 2016–17, 138 students received support, including 29 fellowships with partial tuition reimbursements available (averaging $10,821 per year), 80 research assistantships with partial tuition reimbursements available (averaging $12,531 per year), 61 teaching assistantships with partial tuition reimbursements available (averaging $11,750 per year); career-related internships or fieldwork, Federal Work-Study, institutionally sponsored loans, tuition waivers (partial), and unspecified assistantships also available. Financial award application deadline: 3/1; financial award applicants required to submit FAFSA. *Faculty research:* Image and video processing, computer vision, AI and machine learning, virtual reality. *Unit head:* Dr. Gary Leavens, Chair, 407-882-0185, E-mail: leavens@ucf.edu. *Application contact:* Assistant Director, Graduate Admissions, 407-823-2766, Fax: 407-823-6442, E-mail: gradadmissions@ucf.edu.
Website: http://web.eecs.ucf.edu/

**University of Central Oklahoma,** The Jackson College of Graduate Studies, College of Liberal Arts, School of Criminal Justice, Edmond, OK 73034-5209. Offers crime and intelligence analysis (MA); criminal justice management and administration (MA). *Program availability:* Part-time. *Entrance requirements:* Additional exam requirements/

recommendations for international students: Required—TOEFL (minimum score 550 paper-based; 79 iBT), IELTS (minimum score 6.5). Electronic applications accepted. *Faculty research:* Gender issues, violent offenders.

**University of Central Oklahoma,** The Jackson College of Graduate Studies, Forensic Science Institute, Edmond, OK 73034-5209. Offers biology/chemistry (MS); forensic science (MS). *Degree requirements:* For master's, thesis. *Entrance requirements:* For master's, GRE, official transcripts. Additional exam requirements/recommendations for international students: Required—TOEFL (minimum score 550 paper-based; 79 iBT), IELTS (minimum score 6.5). Electronic applications accepted.

**University of Charleston,** Master of Forensic Accounting Program, Charleston, WV 25304-1099. Offers EMFA. *Program availability:* Part-time, blended/hybrid learning. *Students:* 23 full-time (16 women); includes 4 minority (2 Black or African American, non-Hispanic/Latino; 1 Hispanic/Latino; 1 Native Hawaiian or other Pacific Islander, non-Hispanic/Latino), 1 international. Average age 36. *Entrance requirements:* Additional exam requirements/recommendations for international students: Required—TOEFL. *Application deadline:* Applications are processed on a rolling basis. Application fee: $50. Electronic applications accepted. *Expenses:* Tuition: Full-time $20,602; part-time $425 per credit. *Required fees:* $200. Tuition and fees vary according to course load, campus/location, program and student level. *Financial support:* Applicants required to submit FAFSA. *Unit head:* Christina Chard, Program Director, 304-352-0033, E-mail: christinachard@ucwv.edu. *Application contact:* Bobby Redd, Admissions Representative, 304-860-5621, E-mail: bobbyredd@ucwv.edu.
Website: http://www.ucwv.edu/Forensic-Accounting/

**University of Colorado Denver,** Business School, Program in Accounting, Denver, CO 80217. Offers accounting and information systems audit control (MS); auditing and forensic accounting (MS); controllership and financial leadership (MS). *Accreditation:* AACSB. *Program availability:* Part-time, evening/weekend. *Students:* 90 full-time (42 women), 54 part-time (32 women); includes 36 minority (1 American Indian or Alaska Native, non-Hispanic/Latino; 21 Asian, non-Hispanic/Latino; 11 Hispanic/Latino; 3 Two or more races, non-Hispanic/Latino), 23 international. Average age 30. 93 applicants, 66% accepted, 38 enrolled. In 2016, 69 master's awarded. *Degree requirements:* For master's, 30 semester hours. *Entrance requirements:* For master's, GMAT (waived for students who already hold a graduate degree, or an undergraduate degree from CU Denver), essay, resume, two letters of recommendation; financial statements (for international students). Additional exam requirements/recommendations for international students: Required—TOEFL (minimum score 537 paper-based; 75 iBT); Recommended—IELTS (minimum score 6.5). *Application deadline:* For fall admission, 4/15 priority date for domestic students, 3/15 priority date for international students; for spring admission, 10/15 priority date for domestic students, 9/15 priority date for international students; for summer admission, 2/15 priority date for domestic students, 1/15 priority date for international students. Applications are processed on a rolling basis. Application fee: $50 ($75 for international students). Electronic applications accepted. *Expenses:* Contact institution. *Financial support:* In 2016–17, 28 students received support. Fellowships, research assistantships, teaching assistantships, Federal Work-Study, institutionally sponsored loans, scholarships/grants, and traineeships available. Financial award application deadline: 4/1; financial award applicants required to submit FAFSA. *Faculty research:* Transportation, energy, communications, healthcare, nano-science and engineering, unmanned aircraft systems, biomedical applications, aerosol mechanics, interface mechanics during rapid evaporation, low SWAP-C inertial navigation systems. *Unit head:* Clifford Young, Associate Dean, 303-315-8000, E-mail: clifford.young@ucdenver.edu. *Application contact:* Admissions Director, Graduate Programs, 303-315-8200, E-mail: bschool.admissions@ucdenver.edu.
Website: http://www.ucdenver.edu/academics/colleges/business/degrees/ms/accounting/Pages/Accounting.aspx

**University of Colorado Denver,** College of Arts and Media, Denver, CO 80217. Offers recording arts (MS), including media forensics, recording arts. *Accreditation:* NASM. *Program availability:* Part-time, evening/weekend. *Faculty:* 34 full-time (12 women), 1 (woman) part-time/adjunct. *Students:* 27 full-time (9 women), 5 part-time (2 women); includes 9 minority (2 Black or African American, non-Hispanic/Latino; 1 Asian, non-Hispanic/Latino; 4 Hispanic/Latino; 2 Two or more races, non-Hispanic/Latino), 2 international. Average age 31. 26 applicants, 92% accepted, 16 enrolled. In 2016, 13 master's awarded. *Degree requirements:* For master's, 34 credits, thesis/portfolio. *Entrance requirements:* For master's, GRE General Test (minimum scores higher than 50th percentile for all sections), minimum undergraduate GPA of 3.0, portfolio, resume, interview, 3 letters of recommendation. Additional exam requirements/recommendations for international students: Required—TOEFL (minimum score 70 iBT). *Application deadline:* For fall admission, 4/1 for domestic students, 3/1 for international students. Application fee: $50 ($75 for international students). Electronic applications accepted. *Expenses:* Contact institution. *Financial support:* In 2016–17, 4 students received support. Federal Work-Study, institutionally sponsored loans, scholarships/grants, traineeships, and unspecified assistantships available. Financial award application deadline: 4/1; financial award applicants required to submit FAFSA. *Faculty research:* Audio forensics, audio pedagogy, concert recordings, digital audio workstations, music law. *Total annual research expenditures:* $10,753. *Unit head:* Laurence D. Kaptain, Dean, College of Arts and Media, 303-556-2279, E-mail: laurence.kaptain@ucdenver.edu. *Application contact:* Lisa Funderburg, Program Assistant, 303-352-3833, E-mail: lisa.funderburg@ucdenver.edu.
Website: http://www.ucdenver.edu/academics/colleges/CAM/programs/meis/masterdegree/Pages/index.aspx

**University of Detroit Mercy,** College of Business Administration, Detroit, MI 48221. Offers business administration (MBA); business fundamentals (Certificate); business turnaround management (Certificate); ethical leadership and change management (Certificate); finance (Certificate); forensic accounting (Certificate); JD/MBA; MBA/MHSA. *Program availability:* Part-time, evening/weekend, 100% online, blended/hybrid learning. *Entrance requirements:* For master's, GMAT, resume, letter of recommendation, transcripts; for Certificate, resume, letter of recommendation, transcripts. Electronic applications accepted. Application fee is waived when completed online. *Expenses:* Contact institution. *Faculty research:* Ethics, international finance, trade policy, leadership, information technology.

**University of Florida,** Graduate School, College of Pharmacy, Programs in Forensic Science, Gainesville, FL 32611. Offers clinical toxicology (Certificate); drug chemistry (Certificate); environmental forensics (Certificate); forensic death investigation (Certificate); forensic DNA and serology (MSP, Certificate); forensic drug chemistry (MSP); forensic science (MSP); forensic toxicology (Certificate). *Program availability:* Part-time, evening/weekend, online learning. *Degree requirements:* For master's, comprehensive exam. *Entrance requirements:* For master's, GRE General Test, minimum GPA of 3.0. Additional exam requirements/recommendations for international students: Required—TOEFL (minimum score 550 paper-based; 80 iBT), IELTS (minimum score 6).

**University of Houston–Victoria,** School of Arts and Sciences, Program in Biomedical Sciences, Victoria, TX 77901-4450. Offers biological sciences (MS); biomedical sciences (MS); forensic science (MS).

**University of Illinois at Chicago,** College of Pharmacy and Graduate College, Graduate Programs in Pharmacy, Program in Forensic Science, Chicago, IL 60607-7128. Offers MS. *Degree requirements:* For master's, thesis. *Entrance requirements:* For master's, GRE General Test. Additional exam requirements/recommendations for international students: Required—TOEFL. *Faculty research:* Interpretation of physical evidence, utilization of physical evidence, analytical toxicology of controlled substances, automated fingerprint systems, dye and ink characterizations.

**University of New Haven,** Graduate School, Henry C. Lee College of Criminal Justice and Forensic Sciences, Program in Criminal Justice, West Haven, CT 06516. Offers crime analysis (MS); criminal justice (MS, PhD); criminal justice management (MS, Graduate Certificate); forensic computer investigation (MS); forensic psychology (MS); information protection and security (Graduate Certificate); victim advocacy and services management (Graduate Certificate); victimology (MS). *Program availability:* Part-time, evening/weekend, online learning. *Students:* 120 full-time (83 women), 121 part-time (69 women); includes 84 minority (49 Black or African American, non-Hispanic/Latino; 10 Asian, non-Hispanic/Latino; 14 Hispanic/Latino; 1 Native Hawaiian or other Pacific Islander, non-Hispanic/Latino; 10 Two or more races, non-Hispanic/Latino), 10 international. Average age 29. 128 applicants, 90% accepted, 73 enrolled. In 2016, 52 master's, 2 doctorates, 8 other advanced degrees awarded. *Degree requirements:* For master's, thesis or alternative. *Entrance requirements:* Additional exam requirements/recommendations for international students: Required—TOEFL (minimum score 80 iBT), IELTS, PTE (minimum score 53). *Application deadline:* Applications are processed on a rolling basis. Application fee: $50. Electronic applications accepted. Application fee is waived when completed online. *Expenses: Tuition:* Full-time $15,660; part-time $870 per credit hour. *Required fees:* $200; $85 per term. Tuition and fees vary according to program. *Financial support:* Research assistantships with partial tuition reimbursements, teaching assistantships with partial tuition reimbursements, career-related internships or fieldwork, Federal Work-Study, scholarships/grants, and unspecified assistantships available. Support available to part-time students. Financial award applicants required to submit FAFSA. *Application contact:* Michelle Mason, Director of Graduate Enrollment, 203-932-7067, E-mail: mmason@newhaven.edu. Website: http://www.newhaven.edu/5921/

**University of New Haven,** Graduate School, Henry C. Lee College of Criminal Justice and Forensic Sciences, Program in Fire Science, West Haven, CT 06516. Offers fire administration (MS); fire science (MS); fire/arson investigation (MS, Graduate Certificate); public safety management (MS, Graduate Certificate). *Program availability:* Part-time, evening/weekend. *Students:* 15 full-time (4 women), 2 part-time (0 women); includes 2 minority (1 Asian, non-Hispanic/Latino; 1 Hispanic/Latino), 10 international. Average age 28. 13 applicants, 100% accepted, 7 enrolled. In 2016, 10 master's, 7 other advanced degrees awarded. *Degree requirements:* For master's, thesis or alternative, research project or internship. *Entrance requirements:* Additional exam requirements/recommendations for international students: Required—TOEFL (minimum score 80 iBT), IELTS, PTE (minimum score 53). *Application deadline:* Applications are processed on a rolling basis. Application fee: $50. Electronic applications accepted. Application fee is waived when completed online. *Expenses: Tuition:* Full-time $15,660; part-time $870 per credit hour. *Required fees:* $200; $85 per term. Tuition and fees vary according to program. *Financial support:* Research assistantships with partial tuition reimbursements, teaching assistantships with partial tuition reimbursements, career-related internships or fieldwork, Federal Work-Study, scholarships/grants, and unspecified assistantships available. Support available to part-time students. Financial award applicants required to submit FAFSA. *Unit head:* Dr. Sorin Iliescu, Director, 203-932-7239, E-mail: silliescu@newhaven.edu. *Application contact:* Michelle Mason, Director of Graduate Enrollment, 203-932-7067, E-mail: mmason@newhaven.edu. Website: http://www.newhaven.edu/5922/

**University of New Haven,** Graduate School, Henry C. Lee College of Criminal Justice and Forensic Sciences, Program in Forensic Science, West Haven, CT 06516. Offers advanced investigation (MS); criminalistics (MS); fire science administration (MS); forensic computer investigation (Graduate Certificate); forensic psychology (Graduate Certificate); forensic science (MS); forensic science/fire science (Graduate Certificate). *Program availability:* Part-time, evening/weekend. *Students:* 68 full-time (52 women), 7 part-time (4 women); includes 16 minority (5 Black or African American, non-Hispanic/Latino; 1 Asian, non-Hispanic/Latino; 9 Hispanic/Latino; 1 Two or more races, non-Hispanic/Latino), 5 international. Average age 25. 101 applicants, 69% accepted, 39 enrolled. In 2016, 31 master's, 3 other advanced degrees awarded. *Degree requirements:* For master's, thesis or alternative, research project or internship. *Entrance requirements:* For master's, GRE. Additional exam requirements/recommendations for international students: Required—TOEFL (minimum score 80 iBT), IELTS, PTE (minimum score 53). *Application deadline:* Applications are processed on a rolling basis. Application fee: $50. Electronic applications accepted. Application fee is waived when completed online. *Expenses: Tuition:* Full-time $15,660; part-time $870 per credit hour. *Required fees:* $200; $85 per term. Tuition and fees vary according to program. *Financial support:* Research assistantships with partial tuition reimbursements, teaching assistantships with partial tuition reimbursements, career-related internships or fieldwork, Federal Work-Study, scholarships/grants, and unspecified assistantships available. Support available to part-time students. Financial award applicants required to submit FAFSA. *Unit head:* Dr. Virginia Maxwell, E-mail: vmaxwell@newhaven.edu. *Application contact:* Michelle Mason, Director of Graduate Enrollment, 203-932-7067, E-mail: mmason@newhaven.edu. Website: http://www.newhaven.edu/5923/

**University of New Haven,** Graduate School, Henry C. Lee College of Criminal Justice and Forensic Sciences, Program in Forensic Technology, West Haven, CT 06516. Offers MS. *Program availability:* Part-time. *Students:* 47 full-time (36 women), 3 part-time (all women); includes 11 minority (3 Black or African American, non-Hispanic/Latino; 7 Hispanic/Latino; 1 Two or more races, non-Hispanic/Latino), 5 international. Average age 25. 48 applicants, 85% accepted, 28 enrolled. *Degree requirements:* For master's, internship or research project. *Application deadline:* Applications are processed on a rolling basis. Application fee: $50. *Expenses: Tuition:* Full-time $15,660; part-time $870 per credit hour. *Required fees:* $200; $85 per term. Tuition and fees vary according to program. *Unit head:* Dr. Lisa Dadio, E-mail: ldadio@newhaven.edu. *Application contact:* Michelle Mason, Director of Graduate Enrollment, 203-932-7067, E-mail: mmason@newhaven.edu. Website: http://www.newhaven.edu/lee-college/programs/graduate/forensic-technology/

**University of North Texas Health Science Center at Fort Worth,** Graduate School of Biomedical Sciences, Fort Worth, TX 76107-2699. Offers anatomy and cell biology (MS, PhD); biochemistry and molecular biology (MS, PhD); biomedical sciences (MS, PhD); biotechnology (MS); forensic genetics (MS); integrative physiology (MS, PhD); medical science (MS); microbiology and immunology (MS, PhD); pharmacology (MS, PhD); science education (MS); DO/MS; DO/PhD. Terminal master's awarded for partial completion of doctoral program. *Degree requirements:* For master's, thesis; for doctorate, thesis/dissertation. *Entrance requirements:* For master's and doctorate, GRE General Test. Additional exam requirements/recommendations for international students: Required—TOEFL. *Expenses:* Contact institution. *Faculty research:* Alzheimer's disease, aging, eye diseases, cancer, cardiovascular disease.

**University of Rhode Island,** Graduate School, College of Arts and Sciences, Department of Computer Science and Statistics, Kingston, RI 02881. Offers computer science (MS, PhD); digital forensics (Graduate Certificate); statistics (MS). *Program availability:* Part-time. *Faculty:* 16 full-time (6 women). *Students:* 32 full-time (13 women), 111 part-time (25 women); includes 26 minority (12 Black or African American, non-Hispanic/Latino; 8 Asian, non-Hispanic/Latino; 5 Hispanic/Latino; 1 Two or more races, non-Hispanic/Latino), 20 international. In 2016, 10 master's, 10 other advanced degrees awarded. *Degree requirements:* For master's, comprehensive exam (for some programs), thesis optional; for doctorate, comprehensive exam, thesis/dissertation. *Entrance requirements:* For master's and doctorate, GRE, 2 letters of recommendation. Additional exam requirements/recommendations for international students: Required—TOEFL. *Application deadline:* For fall admission, 7/15 for domestic students, 2/1 for international students; for spring admission, 11/15 for domestic students, 7/15 for international students; for summer admission, 4/15 for domestic students. Application fee: $65. Electronic applications accepted. *Expenses:* Tuition, state resident: full-time $11,796; part-time $655 per credit. Tuition, nonresident: full-time $24,206; part-time $1345 per credit. *Required fees:* $1546; $44 per credit. One-time fee: $155 full-time; $35 part-time. *Financial support:* In 2016–17, 3 research assistantships with tuition reimbursements (averaging $14,320 per year), 11 teaching assistantships with tuition reimbursements (averaging $17,249 per year) were awarded. Financial award application deadline: 2/1; financial award applicants required to submit FAFSA. *Unit head:* Dr. Joan Peckham, Chair, 401-874-2701, Fax: 401-874-4617, E-mail: joan@cs.uri.edu. *Application contact:* E-mail: grad-inquiries@cs.uri.edu. Website: http://www.cs.uri.edu/

**University of St. Francis,** College of Arts and Sciences, Joliet, IL 60435-6169. Offers forensic social work (Post-Master's Certificate); physician assistant practice (MS); social work (MSW). *Faculty:* 9 full-time (7 women). *Students:* 114 full-time (92 women), 26 part-time (24 women); includes 49 minority (17 Black or African American, non-Hispanic/Latino; 1 American Indian or Alaska Native, non-Hispanic/Latino; 7 Asian, non-Hispanic/Latino; 20 Hispanic/Latino; 1 Native Hawaiian or other Pacific Islander, non-Hispanic/Latino; 3 Two or more races, non-Hispanic/Latino), 1 international. Average age 29. 101 applicants, 38% accepted, 24 enrolled. In 2016, 58 master's awarded. *Entrance requirements:* For master's, GRE (for MS). Additional exam requirements/recommendations for international students: Required—TOEFL (minimum score 550 paper-based; 79 iBT), IELTS (minimum score 6). *Application deadline:* Applications are processed on a rolling basis. Application fee: $30. Electronic applications accepted. Application fee is waived when completed online. *Expenses: Tuition:* Part-time $739 per credit hour. *Required fees:* $125 per semester. Part-time tuition and fees vary according to degree level and program. *Financial support:* In 2016–17, 15 students received support. Career-related internships or fieldwork, scholarships/grants, and unspecified assistantships available. Support available to part-time students. Financial award applicants required to submit FAFSA. *Unit head:* Dr. Robert Kase, Dean, 815-740-3367, Fax: 815-740-6366. *Application contact:* Sandra Sloka, Director of Admissions for Graduate and Degree Completion Programs, 800-735-7500, Fax: 815-740-3431, E-mail: ssloka@stfrancis.edu. Website: http://www.stfrancis.edu/academics/cas

**University of Southern Mississippi,** Graduate School, College of Science and Technology, School of Criminal Justice, Hattiesburg, MS 39406. Offers criminal justice (MA, MS, PhD); forensic science (MS). *Program availability:* Part-time. *Degree requirements:* For master's, comprehensive exam, thesis; for doctorate, comprehensive exam, thesis/dissertation. *Entrance requirements:* For master's, GRE General Test, minimum GPA of 2.75 in last 60 hours, 3.0 in field of study; for doctorate, GRE General Test, minimum GPA of 3.5. Additional exam requirements/recommendations for international students: Required—TOEFL, IELTS. *Application deadline:* For fall admission, 3/15 priority date for domestic students, 3/15 for international students; for spring admission, 1/10 priority date for domestic and international students. Applications are processed on a rolling basis. Application fee: $60. *Expenses: Tuition, area resident:* Full-time $15,708; part-time $437 per credit hour. *Financial support:* Research assistantships with full tuition reimbursements, teaching assistantships with full tuition reimbursements, career-related internships or fieldwork, Federal Work-Study, institutionally sponsored loans, scholarships/grants, health care benefits, and unspecified assistantships available. Financial award application deadline: 3/15; financial award applicants required to submit FAFSA. *Faculty research:* Crime in the family, police training models, humanities and criminal justice. *Unit head:* Dr. Lisa Nored, Director, 601-266-4509, Fax: 601-266-4391. *Application contact:* Tera Wright, Manager of Graduate Admissions, 601-266-4509, Fax: 601-266-4391. Website: https://www.usm.edu/criminal-justice

**University of South Florida,** College of Arts and Sciences, Department of Anthropology, Tampa, FL 33620-9951. Offers applied anthropology (MA, PhD), including archaeological and forensic sciences, biocultural medical anthropology, cultural resource management, heritage studies; medical anthropology (Graduate Certificate). *Program availability:* Part-time. *Faculty:* 23 full-time (14 women). *Students:* 70 full-time (52 women), 41 part-time (28 women); includes 28 minority (6 Black or African American, non-Hispanic/Latino; 2 Asian, non-Hispanic/Latino; 16 Hispanic/Latino; 1 Native Hawaiian or other Pacific Islander, non-Hispanic/Latino; 3 Two or more races, non-Hispanic/Latino), 6 international. Average age 31. 130 applicants, 34% accepted, 18 enrolled. In 2016, 15 master's, 11 doctorates awarded. *Degree requirements:* For master's, one foreign language, comprehensive exam, thesis; for doctorate, one foreign language, comprehensive exam, thesis/dissertation. *Entrance requirements:* For master's and doctorate, GRE, minimum GPA of 3.0, 3 letters of recommendation, statement of purpose, signed research ethics statement, resume or curriculum vitae; for Graduate Certificate, bachelor's degree with minimum GPA of 3.0. Additional exam requirements/recommendations for international students: Required—TOEFL (minimum score 550 paper-based; 79 iBT) or IELTS (minimum score 6.5). *Application deadline:* For fall admission, 12/15 for domestic and international students. Application fee: $30. Electronic applications accepted. *Expenses:* Tuition, state resident: full-time $7766; part-time $431.43 per credit hour. Tuition, nonresident: full-time $15,789; part-time $877.17 per credit hour. *Required fees:* $37 per term. *Financial support:* In 2016–17, 32 students received support, including 14 research assistantships with tuition reimbursements available (averaging $14,475 per year), 52 teaching assistantships with partial tuition reimbursements available (averaging $12,540 per year); scholarships/grants and tuition waivers (partial) also available. Financial award application deadline: 1/15; financial award applicants required to submit FAFSA. *Faculty research:* Biocultural medical anthropology; archaeology and culture resource management in the Americas; community identity and heritage; urban community issues; verbal and nonverbal communications in media and education; global dynamics of sustainable resource management and economic development; social and cultural constructions of race, ethnicity, and gender. *Total annual research expenditures:* $1.1 million. *Unit head:* Dr. David Himmelgreen, Professor/Department Chairperson, 813-974-2138, Fax: 813-974-2668, E-mail: dhimmelg@usf.edu. *Application contact:* Dr. Heide Castaneda, Assistant Professor and Graduate Director, 813-974-2138, Fax: 813-974-2668, E-mail: hcastaneda@usf.edu. Website: http://anthropology.usf.edu/graduate/

*Forensic Sciences*

**University of South Florida,** College of Graduate Studies, Tampa, FL 33620-9951. Offers cybersecurity (MS), including computer security fundamentals, cyber intelligence, digital forensics, information assurance. *Program availability:* Part-time, evening/weekend, online learning. *Faculty:* 1 (woman) full-time. *Students:* 63 full-time (20 women), 199 part-time (55 women); includes 99 minority (33 Black or African American, non-Hispanic/Latino; 1 American Indian or Alaska Native, non-Hispanic/Latino; 9 Asian, non-Hispanic/Latino; 42 Hispanic/Latino; 3 Native Hawaiian or other Pacific Islander, non-Hispanic/Latino; 11 Two or more races, non-Hispanic/Latino), 1 international. Average age 35. 104 applicants, 68% accepted, 49 enrolled. In 2016, 24 master's awarded. Terminal master's awarded for partial completion of doctoral program. *Degree requirements:* For master's, variable foreign language requirement, comprehensive exam, thesis (for some programs), practicum. *Entrance requirements:* For master's, GRE General Test, minimum GPA of 3.0; official transcripts with confirmation that applicant has received bachelor's degree from regionally-accredited university; 250-500 word essay in which student describes academic and professional background, reasons for pursuing degree, and professional goals pertaining to cybersecurity; two letters of recommendation. Additional exam requirements/recommendations for international students: Required—TOEFL (minimum score 550 paper-based; 79 iBT) or IELTS (minimum score 6.5). *Application deadline:* For fall admission, 2/15 for domestic and international students; for spring admission, 10/15 for domestic students, 9/15 for international students; for summer admission, 2/15 for domestic and international students. Application fee: $30. Electronic applications accepted. *Expenses:* Tuition, state resident: full-time $7766; part-time $431.43 per credit hour. Tuition, nonresident: full-time $15,789; part-time $877.17 per credit hour. *Required fees:* $37 per term. *Financial support:* In 2016–17, 5 students received support. Teaching assistantships available. Financial award application deadline: 2/1; financial award applicants required to submit FAFSA. *Faculty research:* Integrated neuroscience, diabetes, sustainability of populations/environment, drug design and delivery, marine science. *Total annual research expenditures:* $625,111. *Unit head:* Dr. Dwayne Smith, Dean, 813-974-7359, Fax: 813-974-5762, E-mail: mdsmith8@usf.edu. *Application contact:* Paul Crawford, Associate Director for Graduate Admissions, 813-974-8800, E-mail: pjcrawford@usf.edu. Website: http://www.grad.usf.edu/

**Utica College,** Program in Cybersecurity, Utica, NY 13502-4892. Offers MS. *Program availability:* Part-time, evening/weekend, 100% online. *Faculty:* 5 full-time (0 women), 8 part-time/adjunct (0 women). *Students:* 3 full-time (2 women), 374 part-time (106 women); includes 108 minority (50 Black or African American, non-Hispanic/Latino; 2 American Indian or Alaska Native, non-Hispanic/Latino; 18 Asian, non-Hispanic/Latino; 28 Hispanic/Latino; 10 Two or more races, non-Hispanic/Latino). Average age 35. 163 applicants, 98% accepted, 155 enrolled. In 2016, 133 master's awarded. *Entrance requirements:* For master's, BS, minimum GPA of 3.0. Additional exam requirements/recommendations for international students: Recommended—TOEFL (minimum score 525 paper-based). *Application deadline:* Applications are processed on a rolling basis. Electronic applications accepted. *Expenses:* Contact institution. *Financial support:* Application deadline: 3/15; applicants required to submit FAFSA. *Faculty research:* Steganography and data hiding, cryptography. *Unit head:* Joseph Giordano, Chair, 315-792-2521. *Application contact:* John D. Rowe, Director of Graduate Admissions, 315-792-3824, Fax: 315-792-3003, E-mail: jrowe@utica.edu. Website: http://programs.online.utica.edu/programs/masters-cybersecurity.asp

**Virginia Commonwealth University,** Graduate School, College of Humanities and Sciences, Department of Forensic Science, Richmond, VA 23284-9005. Offers forensic biology (MS); forensic chemistry/drugs and toxicology (MS); forensic chemistry/trace evidence (MS); forensic physical analysis (MS). *Program availability:* Part-time. *Entrance requirements:* For master's, GRE General Test, bachelor's degree in a natural science discipline, including forensic science, or a degree with equivalent work. Additional exam requirements/recommendations for international students: Required—TOEFL (minimum score 600 paper-based; 100 iBT) or IELTS (minimum score 6.5). *Application deadline:* For fall admission, 3/1 for domestic students. Application fee: $50. Electronic applications accepted. *Financial support:* Federal Work-Study, institutionally sponsored loans, and tuition waivers (full and partial) available. Support available to part-time students. Financial award applicants required to submit FAFSA. *Unit head:* Dr. Tal Simmons, Graduate Program Director, 804-828-3295, E-mail: tlsimmons@vcu.edu. *Application contact:* Dr. Tracey Dawson Cruz, Graduate Director, 804-828-0642, E-mail: tcdawson@vcu.edu. Website: http://forensicscience.vcu.edu/

**Webster University,** George Herbert Walker School of Business and Technology, Department of Business, St. Louis, MO 63119-3194. Offers business and organizational security management (MBA); decision support systems (MBA); environmental management (MBA); finance (MBA, MS); forensic accounting (MS); gerontology (MBA); human resources development (MBA); human resources management (MBA); information technology management (MBA); international business (MA, MBA); international relations (MBA); management and leadership (MBA); marketing (MBA); media communications (MBA); procurement and acquisitions management (MBA); Web services (MBA). *Accreditation:* ACBSP. *Program availability:* Part-time, evening/weekend, online learning. *Degree requirements:* For master's, comprehensive exam (for some programs), thesis (for some programs). *Entrance requirements:* Additional exam requirements/recommendations for international students: Required—TOEFL. *Application deadline:* Applications are processed on a rolling basis. Application fee: $35 ($50 for international students). *Expenses: Tuition:* Full-time $21,900; part-time $730 per credit hour. Tuition and fees vary according to campus/location and program. *Financial support:* Federal Work-Study available. Support available to part-time students. Financial award application deadline: 4/1; financial award applicants required to submit FAFSA. *Unit head:* David Porras, Chair, 314-246-8621, E-mail: porrasd@webster.edu. *Application contact:* Sarah Nandor, Director, Graduate and Transfer Admissions, 314-968-7109, E-mail: gadmit@webster.edu.

**West Virginia University,** Eberly College of Arts and Sciences, Department of Biology, Morgantown, WV 26506. Offers cell and molecular biology (MS, PhD); environmental and evolutionary biology (MS, PhD); forensic biology (MS, PhD); genomic biology (MS, PhD); neurobiology (MS, PhD). Terminal master's awarded for partial completion of doctoral program. *Degree requirements:* For master's, thesis, final exam; for doctorate, thesis/dissertation, preliminary and final exams. *Entrance requirements:* For master's, GRE General Test, GRE Subject Test, minimum GPA of 3.0; for doctorate, GRE General Test, minimum GPA of 3.0. Additional exam requirements/recommendations for international students: Required—TOEFL. *Faculty research:* Environmental biology, genetic engineering, developmental biology, global change, biodiversity.

# Section 19
# Economics

This section contains a directory of institutions offering graduate work in economics. Additional information about programs listed in the directory may be obtained by writing directly to the dean of a graduate school or chair of a department at the address given in the directory.

For programs offering related work, see also in this book *Family and Consumer Sciences, Political Science and International Affairs,* and *Public, Regional, and Industrial Affairs.* In the other guides in this series:

**Graduate Programs in the Physical Sciences, Mathematics, Agricultural Sciences, the Environment & Natural Resources**

See *Agricultural and Food Sciences* and *Mathematical Sciences*

**Graduate Programs in Engineering & Applied Sciences**

See *Computer Science and Information Technology; Geological, Mineral/Mining, and Petroleum Engineering;* and *Industrial Engineering*

**Graduate Programs in Business, Education, Information Studies, Law & Social Work**

See *Business Administration and Management*

## CONTENTS

### Program Directories

### Display and Close-Up

### See:

# Agricultural Economics and Agribusiness

**Alcorn State University,** School of Graduate Studies, School of Agriculture and Applied Science, Lorman, MS 39096-7500. Offers agricultural economics (MS Ag); agronomy (MS Ag); animal science (MS Ag). *Degree requirements:* For master's, thesis optional. *Faculty research:* Aquatic systems, dairy herd improvement, fruit production, alternative farming practices.

**American University of Beirut,** Graduate Programs, Faculty of Agricultural and Food Sciences, Beirut, Lebanon. Offers agricultural economics (MS); animal science (MS); ecosystem management (MSES); food security (MS); food technology (MS); irrigation (MS); nutrition (MS); plant protection (MS); plant science (MS); poultry science (MS); rural community development (MS). *Program availability:* Part-time. *Faculty:* 15 full-time (2 women), 1 part-time/adjunct (0 women). *Students:* 11 full-time (10 women), 63 part-time (46 women); includes 1 minority (Asian, non-Hispanic/Latino). Average age 26. 108 applicants, 76% accepted, 28 enrolled. In 2016, 23 master's awarded. *Degree requirements:* For master's, one foreign language, comprehensive exam, thesis (for some programs). *Entrance requirements:* Additional exam requirements/recommendations for international students: Required—TOEFL (minimum score 600 paper-based; 100 iBT), IELTS (minimum score 7.5). *Application deadline:* For fall admission, 2/10 for domestic and international students; for spring admission, 11/2 for domestic and international students. Application fee: $50. Electronic applications accepted. *Expenses: Tuition:* Full-time $16,740; part-time $930 per credit. *Required fees:* $716. Tuition and fees vary according to course load and program. *Financial support:* In 2016–17, 5 research assistantships with full and partial tuition reimbursements (averaging $1,800 per year), 58 teaching assistantships with full and partial tuition reimbursements (averaging $1,400 per year) were awarded; scholarships/grants, health care benefits, and unspecified assistantships also available. Financial award application deadline: 2/2. *Faculty research:* Noncommunicable disease epidemic; evapotranspiration; rapid poverty assessment; green house biological control strategies; integrated energy planning. *Total annual research expenditures:* $500,000. *Unit head:* Prof. Nahla Chawkat Hwalla, Dean, 961-1350000 Ext. 4400, Fax: 961-1744460, E-mail: nahla@aub.edu.lb. *Application contact:* Dr. Rabih Talhouk, Director, Graduate Council, 961-1350000 Ext. 4386, Fax: 961-1374374, E-mail: graduate.council@aub.edu.lb. Website: http://www.aub.edu.lb/fafs/fafs_home/Pages/index.aspx

**Arizona State University at the Tempe campus,** W. P. Carey School of Business, Morrison School of Agribusiness, Mesa, AZ 85212. Offers PhD. *Program availability:* Part-time, evening/weekend. *Entrance requirements:* Additional exam requirements/recommendations for international students: Required—TOEFL (minimum score 550 paper-based; 80 iBT), IELTS (minimum score 6.5); Recommended—TWE. Electronic applications accepted. *Faculty research:* Consumer behavior and marketing strategies in food markets, supply-chain management, derivatives and risk management, international agricultural trade and policy.

**Auburn University,** Graduate School, College of Agriculture, Department of Agricultural Economics and Rural Sociology, Auburn University, AL 36849. Offers agricultural economics (M Ag). *Program availability:* Part-time. *Faculty:* 14 full-time (5 women). *Students:* 7 full-time (5 women), 2 part-time (1 woman); includes 3 minority (all Black or African American, non-Hispanic/Latino), 5 international. Average age 26. 5 applicants, 60% accepted, 2 enrolled. In 2016, 2 master's awarded. *Degree requirements:* For master's, thesis (for some programs). *Entrance requirements:* For master's, GRE General Test. *Application deadline:* Applications are processed on a rolling basis. Application fee: $50 ($60 for international students). Electronic applications accepted. *Expenses:* Tuition, state resident: full-time $9072; part-time $504 per credit hour. Tuition, nonresident: full-time $27,216; part-time $1512 per credit hour. *Required fees:* $812 per semester. Tuition and fees vary according to degree level and program. *Financial support:* Research assistantships, teaching assistantships, and Federal Work-Study available. Support available to part-time students. Financial award application deadline: 3/15; financial award applicants required to submit FAFSA. *Unit head:* Deacue Fields, Chair, 334-844-4800. *Application contact:* Dr. George Flowers, Dean of the Graduate School, 334-844-2125. Website: http://www.ag.auburn.edu/agec/

**California Polytechnic State University, San Luis Obispo,** College of Agriculture, Food and Environmental Sciences, Department of Agribusiness, San Luis Obispo, CA 93407. Offers MS. *Program availability:* Part-time. In 2016, 2 master's awarded. *Degree requirements:* For master's, comprehensive exam, thesis or alternative. *Entrance requirements:* For master's, GRE. Additional exam requirements/recommendations for international students: Required—TOEFL (minimum score 80 iBT). *Application deadline:* For fall admission, 4/1 for domestic students, 3/1 for international students; for winter admission, 10/1 for domestic students; for spring admission, 1/1 for domestic students. Applications are processed on a rolling basis. Application fee: $55. Electronic applications accepted. *Expenses:* Tuition, state resident: full-time $6738; part-time $3906 per year. Tuition, nonresident: full-time $15,666; part-time $8370 per year. *Required fees:* $3603; $3141 per unit. $1047 per term. *Financial support:* Fellowships, research assistantships, teaching assistantships, career-related internships or fieldwork, institutionally sponsored loans, scholarships/grants, and unspecified assistantships available. Financial award application deadline: 3/2; financial award applicants required to submit FAFSA. Website: http://agb.calpoly.edu/

**Colorado State University,** College of Agricultural Sciences, Department of Agricultural and Resource Economics, Fort Collins, CO 80523-1172. Offers MS, PhD. *Program availability:* Part-time. *Faculty:* 15 full-time (4 women). *Students:* 22 full-time (12 women), 17 part-time (5 women); includes 1 minority (Hispanic/Latino), 12 international. Average age 28. 56 applicants, 73% accepted, 14 enrolled. In 2016, 8 master's, 3 doctorates awarded. Terminal master's awarded for partial completion of doctoral program. *Degree requirements:* For master's, variable foreign language requirement, comprehensive exam (for some programs), thesis optional; for doctorate, variable foreign language requirement, comprehensive exam, thesis/dissertation. *Entrance requirements:* For master's and doctorate, GRE, undergraduate microeconomic theory and econometrics (intermediate). Additional exam requirements/recommendations for international students: Required—TOEFL (minimum score 550 paper-based; 80 iBT). *Application deadline:* For fall admission, 5/1 priority date for domestic students, 5/1 for international students. Applications are processed on a rolling basis. Application fee: $60 ($70 for international students). Electronic applications accepted. *Expenses:* Tuition, state resident: full-time $9628. Tuition, nonresident: full-time $23,603. *Required fees:* $2253; $528.14 per credit hour. $264.07 per semester. Tuition and fees vary according to course load and program. *Financial support:* In 2016–17, 8 students received support, including 2 fellowships with full tuition reimbursements available (averaging $39,039 per year), 14 research assistantships with full tuition reimbursements available (averaging $15,756 per year), 7 teaching assistantships with full tuition reimbursements available (averaging $15,686 per year); scholarships/grants,

health care benefits, tuition waivers (full and partial), and unspecified assistantships also available. Financial award application deadline: 2/15. *Faculty research:* Natural resource and water economics, applied food economics and policy, agribusiness marketing/entrepreneurship. *Total annual research expenditures:* $1.7 million. *Unit head:* Dr. Gregory Perry, Head, 970-491-6955, Fax: 970-491-2067, E-mail: greg.perry@colostate.edu. *Application contact:* Denise Davis, Program Assistant II, 970-491-6955, Fax: 970-491-2067, E-mail: denise.davis@colostate.edu. Website: http://dare.agsci.colostate.edu/

**Cornell University,** Graduate School, Graduate Fields of Agriculture and Life Sciences, Field of Applied Economics and Management, Ithaca, NY 14853. Offers agricultural finance (MS, PhD); applied econometrics and qualitative analysis (MS, PhD); economics of development (MS, PhD); environmental economics (MS, PhD); environmental management (MPS); farm management and production economics (MS, PhD); marketing and food distribution (MS, PhD); public policy analysis (MS, PhD); resource economics (PhD). *Entrance requirements:* For master's and doctorate, GRE. Additional exam requirements/recommendations for international students: Required—TOEFL.

**Cornell University,** Graduate School, Graduate Fields of Agriculture and Life Sciences, Field of Global Development, Ithaca, NY 14853. Offers development policy (MPS); international agriculture and development (MPS); international development (MPS); international nutrition (MPS); international planning (MPS); international population (MPS); science and technology policy (MPS). *Degree requirements:* For master's, project paper. *Entrance requirements:* For master's, GRE General Test (recommended), 2 years of development experience, 2 letters of recommendation. Additional exam requirements/recommendations for international students: Required—TOEFL (minimum score 550 paper-based; 77 iBT). Electronic applications accepted.

**Delaware Valley University,** MBA Program, Doylestown, PA 18901-2697. Offers accounting (MBA); entrepreneurship (MBA); finance (MBA); food and agribusiness (MBA); general business (MBA); global executive leadership (MBA); human resource management (MBA); supply chain management (MBA). *Program availability:* Part-time, evening/weekend, online learning. *Entrance requirements:* For master's, minimum undergraduate GPA of 3.0. Electronic applications accepted. *Expenses:* Contact institution.

**Illinois State University,** Graduate School, College of Applied Science and Technology, Department of Agriculture, Normal, IL 61790-2200. Offers agribusiness (MS). *Degree requirements:* For master's, thesis optional. *Entrance requirements:* For master's, GRE General Test, minimum GPA of 3.0 in last 60 hours. *Faculty research:* Engineering-economic system models for rural ethanol production facilities, development and evaluation of a propane-fueled, production scale, on-site thermal destruction system C-FAR 2007; field scale evaluation and technology transfer of economically, ecologically systems; sound liquid swine manure treatment and application.

**Instituto Centroamericano de Administración de Empresas,** Graduate Programs, La Garita, Costa Rica. Offers agribusiness management (MIAM); business administration (EMBA); finance (MBA); real estate management (MGREM); sustainable development (MBA); technology (MBA). *Degree requirements:* For master's, comprehensive exam, essay. *Entrance requirements:* For master's, GMAT or GRE General Test, fluency in Spanish, interview, letters of recommendation, minimum 1 year of work experience. Additional exam requirements/recommendations for international students: Recommended—TOEFL. Electronic applications accepted. *Faculty research:* Competitiveness, production.

**Iowa State University of Science and Technology,** Department of Economics, Ames, IA 50011. Offers agricultural economics (MS, PhD); economics (MS, PhD); JD/MS; PhD. JD/MS and JD/PhD offered jointly with Drake University and The University of Iowa. *Degree requirements:* For master's, thesis or alternative; for doctorate, thesis/dissertation. *Entrance requirements:* For master's and doctorate, GRE General Test. Additional exam requirements/recommendations for international students: Required—TOEFL (minimum score 570 paper-based; 88 iBT), IELTS (minimum score 6.5). *Application deadline:* For fall admission, 1/31 priority date for domestic and international students. Application fee: $40 ($90 for international students). Electronic applications accepted. *Application contact:* Amy Bainum Emmett, Application Contact, 515-294-2702, E-mail: econgrad@iastate.edu. Website: http://www.econ.iastate.edu/graduate-programs

**Iowa State University of Science and Technology,** Program in Agricultural Economics, Ames, IA 50011. Offers MS, PhD. *Degree requirements:* For master's, thesis or alternative; for doctorate, thesis/dissertation. *Entrance requirements:* For master's and doctorate, GRE General Test. Additional exam requirements/recommendations for international students: Required—TOEFL (minimum score 570 paper-based; 88 iBT), IELTS (minimum score 6.5). *Application deadline:* For fall admission, 1/31 priority date for domestic and international students. Application fee: $60 ($90 for international students). Electronic applications accepted. *Application contact:* Amy Bainum-Emmett, Application Contact, 515-294-2702, E-mail: econgrad@iastate.edu. Website: http://www.econ.iastate.edu/graduate-programs

**Iowa State University of Science and Technology,** Program in Seed Technology and Business, Ames, IA 50011. Offers MS. *Degree requirements:* For master's, thesis or alternative. *Entrance requirements:* For master's, resume, 3 letters of recommendation. Additional exam requirements/recommendations for international students: Required—TOEFL (minimum score 570 paper-based; 85 iBT), IELTS (minimum score 6.5). *Application deadline:* For fall admission, 3/15 priority date for domestic students, 3/15 for international students. Application fee: $60 ($90 for international students). Electronic applications accepted. *Application contact:* Lori Youngberg, Application Contact, 515-294-9137, Fax: 515-294-2014, E-mail: seedgrad@iastate.edu. Website: http://www.seedgrad.iastate.edu/

**Kansas State University,** Graduate School, College of Agriculture, Department of Agricultural Economics, Manhattan, KS 66506. Offers MAB, MS, PhD. *Program availability:* Part-time, online learning. *Faculty:* 39 full-time (7 women), 4 part-time/adjunct (0 women). *Students:* 52 full-time (16 women), 71 part-time (30 women); includes 11 minority (5 Black or African American, non-Hispanic/Latino; 1 Asian, non-Hispanic/Latino; 4 Hispanic/Latino; 1 Two or more races, non-Hispanic/Latino), 40 international. Average age 30. 65 applicants, 46% accepted, 21 enrolled. In 2016, 32 master's, 5 doctorates awarded. Terminal master's awarded for partial completion of doctoral program. *Degree requirements:* For master's, thesis or alternative, oral exam; for doctorate, thesis/dissertation, preliminary exams. *Entrance requirements:* For master's and doctorate, GRE General Test. Additional exam requirements/recommendations for international students: Required—TOEFL (minimum score 550

paper-based; 79 iBT), IELTS (minimum score 6.5). *Application deadline:* For fall admission, 6/1 priority date for domestic students, 1/8 priority date for international students; for spring admission, 10/1 priority date for domestic students, 8/1 priority date for international students. Applications are processed on a rolling basis. Application fee: $50 ($75 for international students). Electronic applications accepted. *Expenses:* Contact institution. *Financial support:* In 2016–17, 45 students received support, including 33 research assistantships with full tuition reimbursements available (averaging $20,738 per year), 10 teaching assistantships with full tuition reimbursements available (averaging $20,738 per year); Federal Work-Study, scholarships/grants, and health care benefits also available. Financial award application deadline: 1/8; financial award applicants required to submit FAFSA. *Faculty research:* Livestock marketing, biofuels research, natural resources, agribusiness industry, international development and trade. *Total annual research expenditures:* $2.9 million. *Unit head:* Dr. Allen Featherstone, Head, 785-532-4441, Fax: 785-532-6925, E-mail: afeather@ksu.edu. *Application contact:* Dr. Jason Bergtold, Director, 785-532-0984, Fax: 785-532-6925, E-mail: bergtold@ksu.edu.
Website: http://www.ageconomics.ksu.edu/

**Louisiana State University and Agricultural & Mechanical College,** Graduate School, College of Agriculture, Department of Agricultural Economics and Agribusiness, Baton Rouge, LA 70803. Offers MS, PhD.

**McGill University,** Faculty of Graduate and Postdoctoral Studies, Faculty of Agricultural and Environmental Sciences, Department of Agricultural Economics, Montréal, QC H3A 2T5, Canada. Offers M Sc.

**Michigan State University,** The Graduate School, College of Agriculture and Natural Resources, Department of Agricultural, Food, and Resource Economics, East Lansing, MI 48824. Offers agricultural economics (MS, PhD); agricultural, food, and resource economics (MS, PhD). *Entrance requirements:* Additional exam requirements/recommendations for international students: Required—TOEFL (minimum score 550 paper-based), Michigan State University ELT ( minimum score 85), Michigan English Language Assessment Battery (minimum score 83). Electronic applications accepted.

**Mississippi State University,** College of Agriculture and Life Sciences, Department of Agricultural Economics, Mississippi State, MS 39762. Offers agricultural economics (MS). MABM offered jointly with College of Business. *Program availability:* Part-time. *Faculty:* 18 full-time (2 women). *Students:* 16 full-time (6 women), 1 part-time (0 women); includes 2 minority (1 Black or African American, non-Hispanic/Latino; 1 Asian, non-Hispanic/Latino), 4 international. Average age 25. 21 applicants, 43% accepted, 4 enrolled. In 2016, 7 master's awarded. *Degree requirements:* For master's, comprehensive exam, thesis (for some programs), thesis defense. *Entrance requirements:* For master's, GRE, minimum GPA of 3.0. Additional exam requirements/recommendations for international students: Required—TOEFL (minimum score 575 paper-based; 84 iBT); Recommended—IELTS (minimum score 7). *Application deadline:* For fall admission, 7/1 for domestic students, 5/1 for international students; for spring admission, 11/1 for domestic students, 9/1 for international students. Applications are processed on a rolling basis. Application fee: $60. Electronic applications accepted. *Expenses:* Tuition, state resident: full-time $7670; part-time $852.50 per credit hour. Tuition, nonresident: full-time $20,790; part-time $2310.50 per credit hour. Part-time tuition and fees vary according to course load. *Financial support:* In 2016–17, 10 research assistantships with full tuition reimbursements (averaging $13,906 per year) were awarded; career-related internships or fieldwork, Federal Work-Study, institutionally sponsored loans, and unspecified assistantships also available. Financial award application deadline: 4/1; financial award applicants required to submit FAFSA. *Faculty research:* Production economics, policy, resource economics, international trade, agribusiness management. *Unit head:* Dr. Keith Coble, Department Head, 662-325-6670, Fax: 662-325-8777, E-mail: coble@aegcon.msstate.edu. *Application contact:* Marina Hunt, Admissions and Enrollment Assistant, 662-325-8188, E-mail: mhunt@grad.msstate.edu.
Website: http://www.agecon.msstate.edu/

**New Mexico State University,** College of Agricultural, Consumer and Environmental Sciences, Department of Agricultural Economics and Agricultural Business, Las Cruces, NM 88003. Offers agribusiness (MBA); economic development (DED); water science management (MS). *Program availability:* Part-time. *Faculty:* 5 full-time (0 women). *Students:* 7 full-time (2 women); includes 3 minority (all Hispanic/Latino), 3 international. Average age 28. 9 applicants, 56% accepted, 2 enrolled. In 2016, 5 master's awarded. *Degree requirements:* For master's, thesis (for some programs); for doctorate, comprehensive exam, thesis/dissertation. *Entrance requirements:* For master's, GRE; GMAT (for MBA), previous course work in intermediate microeconomics, intermediate macroeconomics, college-level calculus, statistics; for doctorate, previous course work in intermediate microeconomics, intermediate macroeconomics, college-level calculus, statistics, related MS or equivalent, minimum GPA of 3.0. Additional exam requirements/recommendations for international students: Required—TOEFL (minimum score 550 paper-based; 79 iBT), IELTS (minimum score 6.5). *Application deadline:* For fall admission, 7/1 priority date for domestic and international students; for spring admission, 11/1 priority date for domestic and international students. Applications are processed on a rolling basis. Application fee: $40 ($50 for international students). Electronic applications accepted. *Expenses:* Tuition, state resident: full-time $4086. Tuition, nonresident: full-time $14,254. *Required fees:* $853. Tuition and fees vary according to course load. *Financial support:* In 2016–17, 5 students received support, including 3 research assistantships (averaging $16,964 per year), 4 teaching assistantships (averaging $14,843 per year); career-related internships or fieldwork, Federal Work-Study, scholarships/grants, traineeships, health care benefits, and unspecified assistantships also available. Support available to part-time students. Financial award application deadline: 3/1. *Faculty research:* Natural resource policy, production economics and farm/ranch management, agribusiness and marketing, international marketing and trade, agricultural risk management. *Total annual research expenditures:* $710,421. *Unit head:* Dr. Jay Lillywhite, Department Head, 575-646-3215, Fax: 575-646-3808, E-mail: lillywhi@nmsu.edu. *Application contact:* Dr. Ram Acharya, Graduate Committee Chair, 575-646-2524, Fax: 575-646-3808, E-mail: acharyar@nmsu.edu.
Website: http://aces.nmsu.edu/academics/aeab/

**New Mexico State University,** College of Business, MBA Program, Las Cruces, NM 88003. Offers agribusiness (MBA); finance (MBA); information systems (MBA). *Accreditation:* AACSB. *Program availability:* Part-time-only, evening/weekend, online with required 2-3 day orientation and 2-3 day concluding session in Las Cruces. *Students:* 55 full-time (23 women), 121 part-time (67 women); includes 97 minority (5 Black or African American, non-Hispanic/Latino; 2 American Indian or Alaska Native, non-Hispanic/Latino; 2 Asian, non-Hispanic/Latino; 85 Hispanic/Latino; 3 Two or more races, non-Hispanic/Latino), 10 international. Average age 32. 139 applicants, 62% accepted, 23 enrolled. In 2016, 46 master's awarded. *Degree requirements:* For master's, comprehensive exam, thesis optional. *Entrance requirements:* For master's, GMAT or GRE (depending upon undergraduate or graduate degree institution and GPA), minimum GPA of 3.5 from AACSB international or ACBSP-accredited institution or graduate degree from regionally-accredited U.S. university (without GMAT or GRE). Additional exam requirements/recommendations for international students: Required—

TOEFL (minimum score 550 paper-based; 79 iBT), IELTS (minimum score 6.5). *Application deadline:* For fall admission, 7/15 priority date for domestic students, 4/15 priority date for international students; for spring admission, 4/15 priority date for domestic students, 9/15 priority date for international students; for summer admission, 4/15 for domestic students, 1/15 for international students. Applications are processed on a rolling basis. Application fee: $40 ($50 for international students). Electronic applications accepted. *Expenses:* Tuition, state resident: full-time $4086. Tuition, nonresident: full-time $14,254. *Required fees:* $853. Tuition and fees vary according to course load. *Financial support:* In 2016–17, 39 students received support, including 1 fellowship (averaging $4,088 per year); Federal Work-Study, institutionally sponsored loans, scholarships/grants, health care benefits, and unspecified assistantships also available. Financial award application deadline: 3/1. *Unit head:* Dr. Kathleen Brook, Associate Dean, 575-646-5431, Fax: 575-646-6155, E-mail: kbrook@nmsu.edu. *Application contact:* John Shonk, MBA Advisor, 575-646-8003, Fax: 575-646-7977, E-mail: mbaprog@nmsu.edu.
Website: http://business.nmsu.edu/mba

**North Carolina Agricultural and Technical State University,** School of Graduate Studies, School of Agriculture and Environmental Sciences, Department of Agribusiness, Applied Economics, and Agriscience Education, Greensboro, NC 27411. Offers agricultural economics (MS); agricultural education (MS). *Accreditation:* NCATE. *Program availability:* Part-time, evening/weekend. *Degree requirements:* For master's, comprehensive exam, thesis or alternative, qualifying exam. *Entrance requirements:* For master's, GRE General Test, minimum GPA of 3.0. *Faculty research:* Aid for small farmers, agricultural technology resources, labor force mobility, agrology.

**North Carolina State University,** Graduate School, College of Agriculture and Life Sciences, Program in Agricultural and Resource Economics, Raleigh, NC 27695. Offers MS. *Program availability:* Part-time. *Degree requirements:* For master's, thesis. *Entrance requirements:* Additional exam requirements/recommendations for international students: Required—TOEFL. Electronic applications accepted. *Faculty research:* Resource economics, international economics, labor economics, econometrics, environmental economics.

**North Dakota State University,** College of Graduate and Interdisciplinary Studies, College of Agriculture, Food Systems, and Natural Resources, Department of Agribusiness and Applied Economics, Fargo, ND 58102. Offers agribusiness and applied economics (MS); international agribusiness (MS). *Program availability:* Part-time. *Degree requirements:* For master's, thesis. *Entrance requirements:* For master's, minimum GPA of 3.0. Additional exam requirements/recommendations for international students: Required—TOEFL (minimum score 525 paper-based; 79 iBT). Electronic applications accepted. *Faculty research:* Agribusiness, transportation, marketing, microeconomics, trade.

**Northwest Missouri State University,** Graduate School, Melvin and Valorie Booth College of Business and Professional Studies, Maryville, MO 64468-6001. Offers agricultural economics (MBA); general management (MBA); human resource management (MBA); marketing (MBA). *Program availability:* Part-time. *Students:* 50 full-time (18 women), 50 part-time (27 women); includes 10 minority (5 Black or African American, non-Hispanic/Latino; 2 Asian, non-Hispanic/Latino; 3 Hispanic/Latino), 16 international. In 2016, 55 master's awarded. *Degree requirements:* For master's, comprehensive exam. *Entrance requirements:* For master's, GMAT, GRE, minimum GPA of 2.5. Additional exam requirements/recommendations for international students: Required—TOEFL (minimum score 550 paper-based). *Application deadline:* For fall admission, 7/1 for domestic and international students; for spring admission, 11/15 for domestic and international students; for summer admission, 4/1 for domestic and international students. Applications are processed on a rolling basis. Application fee: $0 ($50 for international students). Electronic applications accepted. *Expenses:* Tuition, state resident: full-time $3447; part-time $383 per credit hour. Tuition, nonresident: full-time $5724; part-time $636 per credit hour. *Required fees:* $130 per credit hour. *Financial support:* Research assistantships with full tuition reimbursements, teaching assistantships with full tuition reimbursements, career-related internships or fieldwork, and administrative assistantships, tutorial assistantships available. Financial award application deadline: 4/1; financial award applicants required to submit FAFSA. *Unit head:* Dr. Gregory Haddock, Dean of Graduate School, 660-562-1145, Fax: 660-562-1096, E-mail: gradsch@nwmissouri.edu.
Website: http://www.nwmissouri.edu/academics/booth/

**Northwest Missouri State University,** Graduate School, School of Agricultural Sciences, Maryville, MO 64468-6001. Offers agricultural economics (MBA); agricultural education (MS Ed); agriculture (MS); teaching: agriculture (MS Ed). *Program availability:* Part-time. *Students:* 4 full-time (1 woman), 8 part-time (3 women). In 2016, 3 master's awarded. *Degree requirements:* For master's, comprehensive exam, thesis (for some programs). *Entrance requirements:* For master's, GRE General Test, minimum undergraduate GPA of 2.5, writing sample. Additional exam requirements/recommendations for international students: Required—TOEFL (minimum score 550 paper-based). *Application deadline:* For fall admission, 7/1 for domestic and international students; for spring admission, 11/15 for domestic and international students. Applications are processed on a rolling basis. Application fee: $0 ($50 for international students). *Expenses:* Tuition, state resident: full-time $3447; part-time $383 per credit hour. Tuition, nonresident: full-time $5724; part-time $636 per credit hour. *Required fees:* $130 per credit hour. *Financial support:* Research assistantships with full tuition reimbursements, teaching assistantships with full tuition reimbursements, and unspecified assistantships available. Financial award application deadline: 4/1; financial award applicants required to submit FAFSA. *Unit head:* Rodney Barr, Director, 660-562-1620.
Website: http://www.nwmissouri.edu/ag/

**The Ohio State University,** Graduate School, College of Food, Agricultural, and Environmental Sciences, Department of Agricultural, Environmental, and Development Economics, Columbus, OH 43210. Offers MS, PhD. *Faculty:* 22. *Students:* 73 full-time (33 women), 2 part-time (1 woman); includes 5 minority (all Asian, non-Hispanic/Latino), 44 international. Average age 28. In 2016, 25 master's, 14 doctorates awarded. *Degree requirements:* For master's, thesis optional; for doctorate, thesis/dissertation. *Entrance requirements:* For master's, GRE General Test (preferred minimum score: 156 quantitative, 153 verbal), minimum undergraduate GPA of 3.1 (recommended); for doctorate, GRE General Test (minimum score: 163 quantitative, 163 verbal), minimum GPA of 3.3 undergraduate, 3.5 graduate (recommended). Additional exam requirements/recommendations for international students: Required—TOEFL (minimum score 600 paper-based; 100 IBT) for PhD; Recommended—TOEFL (minimum score 550 paper-based; 80 iBT). *Application deadline:* For fall admission, 12/15 priority date for domestic students, 11/30 priority date for international students. Applications are processed on a rolling basis. Application fee: $60 ($70 for international students). Electronic applications accepted. *Financial support:* Fellowships with tuition reimbursements, research assistantships with tuition reimbursements, teaching assistantships with tuition reimbursements, Federal Work-Study, and institutionally sponsored loans available. Support available to part-time students. *Unit head:* Dr. Tim Haab, Chair, 614-292-7911, E-mail: haab.1@osu.edu. *Application contact:* Holly Hall,

### Agricultural Economics and Agribusiness

Graduate Recruitment Coordinator, 614-292-3599, E-mail: aedegradservices@osu.edu. Website: http://aede.osu.edu/

**Oklahoma State University,** College of Agricultural Science and Natural Resources, Department of Agricultural Economics, Stillwater, OK 74078. Offers M Ag, MS, PhD. *Faculty:* 34 full-time (7 women), 1 part-time/adjunct (0 women). *Students:* 29 full-time (11 women), 25 part-time (8 women); includes 3 minority (1 Black or African American, non-Hispanic/Latino; 2 Two or more races, non-Hispanic/Latino), 26 international. Average age 29. 49 applicants, 39% accepted, 11 enrolled. In 2016, 13 master's, 4 doctorates awarded. *Degree requirements:* For master's, thesis or report, oral exam; for doctorate, comprehensive exam, thesis/dissertation. *Entrance requirements:* For master's and doctorate, GRE or GMAT. Additional exam requirements/recommendations for international students: Required—TOEFL (minimum score 550 paper-based; 79 iBT). *Application deadline:* For fall admission, 3/1 priority date for international students; for spring admission, 8/1 priority date for international students. Applications are processed on a rolling basis. Application fee: $40 ($75 for international students). Electronic applications accepted. *Expenses:* Tuition, state resident: full-time $3775; part-time $209.70 per credit hour. Tuition, nonresident: full-time $14,851; part-time $825.05 per credit hour. *Required fees:* $2027; $112.60 per credit hour. Tuition and fees vary according to campus/location. *Financial support:* In 2016–17, 42 research assistantships (averaging $17,637 per year), 4 teaching assistantships (averaging $18,999 per year) were awarded; career-related internships or fieldwork, Federal Work-Study, scholarships/grants, health care benefits, tuition waivers (partial), and unspecified assistantships also available. Support available to part-time students. Financial award application deadline: 3/1; financial award applicants required to submit FAFSA. *Faculty research:* Marketing and agribusiness, production and farm management, policy and natural resources, community and rural development, international trade and development. *Unit head:* Dr. Mike Woods, Department Head, 405-744-6161, Fax: 405-744-8210, E-mail: mike.woods@okstate.edu. Website: http://agecon.okstate.edu

**Penn State University Park,** Graduate School, College of Agricultural Sciences, Department of Agricultural Economics, Sociology, and Education, University Park, PA 16802. Offers agricultural and extension education (M Ed, MS, PhD, Certificate); agricultural, environmental and regional economics (MS, PhD); applied youth, family and community education (M Ed); community and economic development (MPS); rural sociology (MS, PhD). *Unit head:* Dr. Richard T. Roush, Dean, 814-865-2541, Fax: 814-865-3103. *Application contact:* Lori Hawn, Director, Graduate Student Services, 814-865-1795, Fax: 814-863-4627, E-mail: l-gsww@lists.psu.edu. Website: http://aese.psu.edu/

**Presidio Graduate School,** MBA Programs - Seattle, San Francisco, CA 94129. Offers co-operative management (Certificate); food and agriculture systems (Certificate); sustainable business (MBA); sustainable systems (MBA). *Program availability:* Part-time, evening/weekend, blended/hybrid learning. *Students:* Average age 34. *Entrance requirements:* For master's and Certificate, Quantitative Assessment Summary, GRE, or GMAT, resume, two letters of recommendation, essay, transcripts. Additional exam requirements/recommendations for international students: Required—TOEFL (minimum score 90 iBT), IELTS (minimum score 6.5). *Application deadline:* For fall admission, 6/1 priority date for domestic and international students. Applications are processed on a rolling basis. Application fee: $75. Electronic applications accepted. *Financial support:* Scholarships/grants available. Financial award application deadline: 6/15; financial award applicants required to submit FAFSA. *Unit head:* Steven Crane, Provost, 415-651-6555, E-mail: info@presidio.edu. *Application contact:* Kari Dorth, Director of Admissions, 415-655-8912, E-mail: admissions@presidio.edu. Website: https://www.presidio.edu/seattle-mbas-overview/

**Purdue University,** Graduate School, College of Agriculture, Department of Agricultural Economics, West Lafayette, IN 47907. Offers agricultural economics (MS, PhD); food and agricultural business (EMBA). *Program availability:* Part-time. *Faculty:* 47 full-time (6 women), 2 part-time/adjunct (0 women). *Students:* 85 full-time (37 women), 58 part-time (19 women); includes 11 minority (4 Black or African American, non-Hispanic/Latino; 3 Asian, non-Hispanic/Latino; 3 Hispanic/Latino; 1 Two or more races, non-Hispanic/Latino), 57 international. Average age 29. 188 applicants, 47% accepted, 56 enrolled. In 2016, 42 master's, 10 doctorates awarded. Terminal master's awarded for partial completion of doctoral program. *Degree requirements:* For master's, thesis (for some programs); for doctorate, thesis/dissertation. *Entrance requirements:* For master's and doctorate, GRE General Test, minimum undergraduate GPA of 3.0 or equivalent. Additional exam requirements/recommendations for international students: Required— TOEFL (minimum score 550 paper-based; 77 iBT). *Application deadline:* For fall admission, 4/1 priority date for domestic students, 3/1 for international students; for spring admission, 10/1 for domestic students, 8/1 for international students. Applications are processed on a rolling basis. Application fee: $60 ($75 for international students). Electronic applications accepted. *Financial support:* In 2016–17, fellowships with tuition reimbursements (averaging $22,000 per year), research assistantships with tuition reimbursements (averaging $18,000 per year), teaching assistantships with tuition reimbursements (averaging $15,900 per year) were awarded. Financial award application deadline: 3/1; financial award applicants required to submit FAFSA. *Faculty research:* Marketing, international trade, policy and development, production, resources. *Unit head:* Kenneth A. Foster, Interim Head of the Graduate Program, 765-494-1116, E-mail: kfoster@purdue.edu. *Application contact:* Lou Ann Baugh, Graduate Contact, 765-494-4196, E-mail: baughl@purdue.edu. Website: https://ag.purdue.edu/agecon

**Rutgers University–New Brunswick,** Graduate School-New Brunswick, Program in Food and Business Economics, Piscataway, NJ 08854-8097. Offers MS. *Degree requirements:* For master's, comprehensive exam, thesis or alternative. *Entrance requirements:* Additional exam requirements/recommendations for international students: Required—TOEFL. Electronic applications accepted. *Faculty research:* Science policy, land use, nutrition policy, food industry, international development.

**South Carolina State University,** College of Graduate and Professional Studies, School of Business, Orangeburg, SC 29117-0001. Offers agribusiness (MBA); entrepreneurship (MBA); general business administration (MBA); healthcare management (MBA). *Program availability:* Part-time, evening/weekend. *Faculty:* 7 full-time (3 women). *Students:* 19 full-time (11 women), 10 part-time (5 women); includes 27 minority (all Black or African American, non-Hispanic/Latino). Average age 27. 17 applicants, 94% accepted, 15 enrolled. In 2016, 6 master's awarded. *Degree requirements:* For master's, comprehensive exam, business plan. *Entrance requirements:* For master's, GMAT, minimum GPA of 2.8. Additional exam requirements/recommendations for international students: Required—TOEFL. *Application deadline:* For fall admission, 6/15 for domestic and international students; for spring admission, 11/1 for domestic and international students. Application fee: $25. Electronic applications accepted. *Expenses:* Tuition, state resident: full-time $8938; part-time $579 per credit hour. Tuition, nonresident: full-time $19,018; part-time $1139 per credit hour. *Required fees:* $1482; $82 per credit hour. *Financial support:* Fellowships, research assistantships, career-related internships or fieldwork, Federal Work-Study, scholarships/grants, and unspecified assistantships available. Financial award application deadline: 6/1. *Unit head:* Dr. Matthew Guah, Chair, 803-516-4834,

Fax: 803-536-8078, E-mail: mguah@scsu.edu. *Application contact:* Ellen R. Ricoma, MBA Program Director, 803-533-3777, Fax: 803-516-4651, E-mail: ericoma1@scsu.edu.

**Southern Illinois University Carbondale,** Graduate School, College of Agriculture, Department of Agribusiness Economics, Carbondale, IL 62901-4701. Offers MS, MBA/MS. *Program availability:* Part-time. *Degree requirements:* For master's, thesis. *Entrance requirements:* For master's, minimum GPA of 2.7. Additional exam requirements/recommendations for international students: Required—TOEFL (minimum score 550 paper-based; 80 iBT). Electronic applications accepted. *Faculty research:* Agricultural finance and credit, agribusiness management, resource use, rural area economic development, marketing and price analysis.

**Texas A&M University,** College of Agriculture and Life Sciences, Department of Agricultural Economics, College Station, TX 77843. Offers M Agr, MS, PhD. *Program availability:* Part-time. *Students:* 121 full-time (54 women), 16 part-time (9 women); includes 15 minority (2 Asian, non-Hispanic/Latino; 12 Hispanic/Latino; 1 Two or more races, non-Hispanic/Latino), 76 international. Average age 28. 86 applicants, 71% accepted, 27 enrolled. In 2016, 51 master's, 6 doctorates awarded. Terminal master's awarded for partial completion of doctoral program. *Degree requirements:* For master's, comprehensive exam (for some programs); thesis (for some programs); for doctorate, comprehensive exam, thesis/dissertation. *Entrance requirements:* For master's and doctorate, GRE General Test. Additional exam requirements/recommendations for international students: Required—TOEFL (minimum score 550 paper-based; 80 iBT), IELTS (minimum score 6), PTE (minimum score 53). *Application deadline:* For fall admission, 3/1 for domestic students; for spring admission, 8/1 for domestic students. Applications are processed on a rolling basis. Application fee: $50 ($90 for international students). Electronic applications accepted. *Expenses:* Contact institution. *Financial support:* In 2016–17, 111 students received support, including 18 fellowships with tuition reimbursements available (averaging $7,489 per year), 28 research assistantships with tuition reimbursements available (averaging $5,479 per year), 40 teaching assistantships with tuition reimbursements available (averaging $8,049 per year); career-related internships or fieldwork, institutionally sponsored loans, scholarships/grants, traineeships, health care benefits, tuition waivers (full and partial), and unspecified assistantships also available. Support available to part-time students. Financial award application deadline: 3/15; financial award applicants required to submit FAFSA. *Faculty research:* Production economics, agricultural finance, resources, marketing and policy, agribusiness. *Unit head:* Dr. C. Parr Rosson, III, Professor and Head, 979-845-2116, Fax: 979-847-9378, E-mail: prosson@tamu.edu. *Application contact:* Brandi Blankenship, Program Coordinator, 979-845-5222, Fax: 979-862-1563, E-mail: brandi.blankenship@tamu.edu. Website: http://agecon.tamu.edu/

**Texas A&M University–Kingsville,** College of Graduate Studies, Dick and Mary Lewis Kleberg College of Agriculture, Natural Resources and Human Sciences, Department of Agriculture, Agribusiness, and Environmental Sciences, Kingsville, TX 78363. Offers agribusiness (MS); agricultural science (MS); horticulture (PhD); plant and soil science (MS); ranch management (MS). Electronic applications accepted.

**Texas Tech University,** Graduate School, College of Agricultural Sciences and Natural Resources, Department of Agricultural and Applied Economics, Lubbock, TX 79409. Offers agribusiness (MAB); agricultural and applied economics (MS, PhD); JD/MS. *Program availability:* Part-time. *Faculty:* 22 full-time (6 women), 2 part-time/adjunct (0 women). *Students:* 48 full-time (23 women), 11 part-time (6 women); includes 7 minority (6 Hispanic/Latino; 1 Two or more races, non-Hispanic/Latino), 30 international. Average age 30. 50 applicants, 70% accepted, 17 enrolled. In 2016, 18 master's, 6 doctorates awarded. Terminal master's awarded for partial completion of doctoral program. *Degree requirements:* For master's, thesis or alternative; for doctorate, comprehensive exam, thesis/dissertation. *Entrance requirements:* For master's and doctorate, GRE General Test, formal approval from departmental committee. Additional exam requirements/recommendations for international students: Required—TOEFL (minimum score 550 paper-based; 79 iBT). *Application deadline:* For fall admission, 6/1 priority date for domestic students, 1/15 priority date for international students; for spring admission, 9/1 priority date for domestic students, 6/15 priority date for international students. Applications are processed on a rolling basis. Application fee: $75. Electronic applications accepted. *Expenses:* $325 per credit hour full-time resident tuition, $733 per credit hour full-time non-resident tuition; $53.75 per credit hour fee plus $608 per term fee. *Financial support:* In 2016–17, 49 students received support, including 44 fellowships (averaging $2,997 per year), 29 research assistantships (averaging $15,794 per year); teaching assistantships, institutionally sponsored loans, scholarships/grants, health care benefits, and unspecified assistantships also available. Financial award application deadline: 5/1; financial award applicants required to submit FAFSA. *Faculty research:* Economics of the United States cotton and textile industries, natural resource management in semi-arid climates, commodity policy analysis, international trade in agricultural products, agribusiness analysis. *Total annual research expenditures:* $844,410. *Unit head:* Dr. Phillip N. Johnson, Chair, 806-834-0474, Fax: 806-742-1099, E-mail: phil.johnson@ttu.edu. *Application contact:* Dr. Darren Hudson, Graduate Adviser, 806-742-2821, Fax: 806-742-1099, E-mail: darren.hudson@ttu.edu. Website: http://www.aaec.ttu.edu

**Tropical Agriculture Research and Higher Education Center,** Graduate School, Turrialba, Costa Rica. Offers agribusiness management (MS); agroforestry systems (PhD); development practices (MS); ecological agriculture (MS); environmental socioeconomics (MS); forestry in tropical and subtropical zones (PhD); integrated watershed management (MS); international sustainable tourism (MS); management and conservation of tropical rainforests and biodiversity (MS); tropical agriculture (PhD); tropical agroforestry (MS). *Entrance requirements:* For master's, GRE, 2 years of related professional experience, letters of recommendation; for doctorate, GRE, 4 letters of recommendation, letter of support from employing organization, master's degree in agronomy, biological sciences, forestry, natural resources or related field. Additional exam requirements/recommendations for international students: Required—TOEFL (minimum score 550 paper-based). Electronic applications accepted. *Faculty research:* Biodiversity in fragmented landscapes, ecosystem management, integrated pest management, environmental livestock production, biotechnology carbon balances in diverse land uses.

**Tuskegee University,** Graduate Programs, College of Agriculture, Environment and Nutrition Sciences, Department of Agricultural and Environmental Sciences, Program in Agricultural and Resource Economics, Tuskegee, AL 36088. Offers MS. *Degree requirements:* For master's, thesis. *Entrance requirements:* For master's, GRE General Test. Additional exam requirements/recommendations for international students: Required—TOEFL (minimum score 500 paper-based).

**Universidad del Este,** Graduate School, Carolina, PR 00984. Offers accounting (MBA); adult education (M Ed); agribusiness (MBA); criminal justice and criminology (MA); curriculum and instruction - early education (M Ed); curriculum and instruction - elementary (M Ed); curriculum and instruction - English (M Ed); curriculum and instruction - Spanish (M Ed); human resources (MBA); information security management (MBA); information technology and Web business development (MBA); management

(MBA); public policy (MPA); social work (MA), including clinical social work; special education (M Ed); strategic leadership (MBA).

**Université Laval,** Faculty of Agricultural and Food Sciences, Department of Agricultural Economics and Consumer Sciences, Program in Agricultural Economics, Québec, QC G1K 7P4, Canada. Offers M Sc. *Program availability:* Part-time. *Degree requirements:* For master's, thesis (for some programs). *Entrance requirements:* For master's, knowledge of French. Electronic applications accepted.

**University of Alberta,** Faculty of Graduate Studies and Research, Department of Rural Economy, Edmonton, AB T6G 2E1, Canada. Offers agricultural economics (M Ag, M Sc, PhD); forest economics (M Ag, M Sc, PhD); rural sociology (M Ag, M Sc); MBA/M Ag. *Program availability:* Part-time. *Degree requirements:* For doctorate, thesis/dissertation. *Entrance requirements:* Additional exam requirements/recommendations for international students: Required—TOEFL. *Faculty research:* Agroforestry, development, extension education, marketing and trade, natural resources and environment, policy, production economics.

**The University of Arizona,** College of Agriculture and Life Sciences, Department of Agricultural and Resource Economics, Tucson, AZ 85721. Offers MS. *Degree requirements:* For master's, thesis or alternative. *Entrance requirements:* For master's, GRE General Test, 3 letters of recommendation, minimum GPA of 3.0. Additional exam requirements/recommendations for international students: Required—TOEFL (minimum score 550 paper-based; 79 iBT). Electronic applications accepted. *Faculty research:* Natural resources, international development trade, production and marketing, agricultural policy, rural development.

**University of Arkansas,** Graduate School, Dale Bumpers College of Agricultural, Food and Life Sciences, Department of Agricultural Economics, Fayetteville, AR 72701. Offers MS. *Students:* 28 applicants, 100% accepted. In 2016, 26 master's awarded. *Degree requirements:* For master's, thesis optional. *Application deadline:* For fall admission, 4/1 for international students; for spring admission, 10/1 for international students. Applications are processed on a rolling basis. Application fee: $40 ($50 for international students). Electronic applications accepted. *Financial support:* In 2016–17, 8 research assistantships, 1 teaching assistantship were awarded; fellowships with tuition reimbursements, career-related internships or fieldwork, and Federal Work-Study also available. Support available to part-time students. Financial award application deadline: 4/1; financial award applicants required to submit FAFSA. *Unit head:* Dr. Steve A. Halbrook, Chair, 479-575-2281, E-mail: halbrook@uark.edu. *Application contact:* Dr. Daniel Rainey, Graduate Coordinator, 479-575-5584, E-mail: rainey@uark.edu. Website: http://agribus.uark.edu/

**University of California, Berkeley,** Graduate Division, College of Natural Resources, Department of Agricultural and Resource Economics, Berkeley, CA 94720-1500. Offers PhD. *Students:* 70 full-time (28 women); includes 6 minority (1 Black or African American, non-Hispanic/Latino; 3 Asian, non-Hispanic/Latino; 2 Hispanic/Latino), 26 international. Average age 30. 141 applicants, 11 enrolled. In 2016, 14 doctorates awarded. *Degree requirements:* For doctorate, thesis/dissertation, qualifying exam. *Entrance requirements:* For doctorate, GRE General Test, minimum GPA of 3.0, 3 letters of recommendation. *Application deadline:* For fall admission, 12/1 for domestic students. Application fee: $105 ($125 for international students). Electronic applications accepted. *Financial support:* Fellowships, research assistantships, teaching assistantships, institutionally sponsored loans, scholarships/grants, tuition waivers (full and partial), and unspecified assistantships available. Financial award applicants required to submit FAFSA. *Faculty research:* Agricultural economics and policy, environmental and resource economics and policy, international agricultural development and trade. *Unit head:* Prof. David Sunding, Chair, 510-642-3345. *Application contact:* Carmen Karahalios, Student Affairs Officer, 510-642-3347, Fax: 510-643-8911, E-mail: gradadm@are.berkeley.edu. Website: http://are.berkeley.edu/

**University of California, Davis,** Graduate Studies, Program in Agricultural and Resource Economics, Davis, CA 95616. Offers MS, PhD, MBA/MS. Terminal master's awarded for partial completion of doctoral program. *Degree requirements:* For master's, thesis optional; for doctorate, thesis/dissertation. *Entrance requirements:* For master's, GRE General Test, minimum GPA of 3.0; for doctorate, GRE General Test, minimum GPA of 3.3. Additional exam requirements/recommendations for international students: Required—TOEFL (minimum score 550 paper-based). Electronic applications accepted. *Faculty research:* Applied microeconomics, international trade, development, econometrics, environmental economics.

**University of California, Santa Barbara,** Graduate Division, Donald Bren School of Environmental Science and Management, Santa Barbara, CA 93106-5131. Offers economics and environmental science (PhD); environmental science and management (MESM, PhD); technology and society (PhD). *Degree requirements:* For master's, thesis; for doctorate, thesis/dissertation. *Entrance requirements:* For master's and doctorate, GRE. Additional exam requirements/recommendations for international students: Required—TOEFL (minimum score 550 paper-based; 80 iBT), IELTS (minimum score 7). Electronic applications accepted. *Faculty research:* Coastal marine resources management, conservation planning, corporate environmental management, economics and politics of the environment, energy and climate, pollution prevention and remediation, water resources management.

**University of Connecticut,** Graduate School, College of Agriculture, Health and Natural Resources, Department of Agricultural and Resource Economics, Storrs, CT 06269. Offers MS, PhD. Terminal master's awarded for partial completion of doctoral program. *Degree requirements:* For master's, comprehensive exam; for doctorate, thesis/dissertation. *Entrance requirements:* For master's and doctorate, GRE General Test. Additional exam requirements/recommendations for international students: Required—TOEFL (minimum score 550 paper-based). Electronic applications accepted. *Faculty research:* Food marketing, international agricultural development.

**University of Delaware,** College of Agriculture and Natural Resources, Department of Food and Resource Economics, Newark, DE 19716. Offers agricultural and resource economics (MS); agricultural education (MA); operations research (MS); statistics (MS). *Program availability:* Part-time. *Degree requirements:* For master's, thesis. *Entrance requirements:* For master's, GRE General Test, 3 letters of recommendation. Additional exam requirements/recommendations for international students: Required—TOEFL (minimum score 550 paper-based). Electronic applications accepted. *Faculty research:* Experimental economics, environmental and resource economics, land use, law and economics.

**University of Florida,** Graduate School, College of Agricultural and Life Sciences, Department of Food and Resource Economics, Gainesville, FL 32611. Offers agribusiness (MS); food and resource economics (MAB, MS, PhD); hydrologic sciences (MS, PhD); toxicology (MS, PhD); tropical conservation and development (MAB, MS, PhD). *Program availability:* Part-time. *Degree requirements:* For master's, comprehensive exam; for doctorate, comprehensive exam, thesis/dissertation. *Entrance requirements:* For master's, GRE (combined minimum score of 300 overall, 145 on quantitative), minimum GPA of 3.0, minimum B grade in prerequisites; for doctorate, GRE (combined minimum score of 305 overall, 150 on quantitative), minimum GPA of 3.0, minimum B grade in prerequisites. Additional exam requirements/

recommendations for international students: Required—TOEFL (minimum score 550 paper-based; 80 iBT), IELTS (minimum score 6). Electronic applications accepted. *Faculty research:* Economics of agriculture marketing, production, international trade, and policy; environmental and resource economics, development economics.

**University of Georgia,** College of Agricultural and Environmental Sciences, Department of Agricultural and Applied Economics, Athens, GA 30602. Offers agricultural economics (MAE, MS, PhD); environmental economics (MS). *Degree requirements:* For master's, thesis (MS); for doctorate, thesis/dissertation. *Entrance requirements:* For master's and doctorate, GRE General Test. *Application deadline:* For fall admission, 7/1 priority date for domestic students; for spring admission, 11/15 for domestic students. Application fee: $50. Electronic applications accepted. *Financial support:* Fellowships, research assistantships, teaching assistantships, career-related internships or fieldwork, and unspecified assistantships available. *Unit head:* Dr. Octavio A. Ramirez, Interim Head, 706-542-2481, Fax: 706-542-0739, E-mail: oramirez@agecon.uga.edu. *Application contact:* Jeffrey D. Mullen, Graduate Coordinator, 706-543-0767, E-mail: jmullen@uga.edu. Website: http://www.caes.uga.edu/departments/agecon

**University of Guelph,** Graduate Studies, College of Management and Economics, MBA Program, Guelph, ON N1G 2W1, Canada. Offers food and agribusiness management (MBA); hospitality and tourism management (MBA). *Program availability:* Part-time, evening/weekend, online learning. *Entrance requirements:* For master's, minimum B-average, minimum of 3 years of relevant work experience. Additional exam requirements/recommendations for international students: Required—TOEFL (minimum score 550 paper-based). Electronic applications accepted. *Faculty research:* Marketing, operations management, business policy, financial management, organizational behavior.

**University of Guelph,** Graduate Studies, Ontario Agricultural College, Department of Food, Agricultural and Resource Economics, Guelph, ON N1G 2W1, Canada. Offers agricultural economics (M Sc, PhD); MA/M Sc. *Program availability:* Part-time. *Degree requirements:* For master's, thesis; for doctorate, comprehensive exam, thesis/dissertation. *Entrance requirements:* For master's, minimum B- average during previous 2 years of course work; for doctorate, minimum B standing in recognized master's degree. Additional exam requirements/recommendations for international students: Required—TOEFL (minimum score 550 paper-based), IELTS (minimum score 6.5). Electronic applications accepted. *Faculty research:* Agricultural policy, agribusiness, environmental economics, agricultural marketing, production economics.

**University of Idaho,** College of Graduate Studies, College of Agricultural and Life Sciences, Department of Agricultural Economics and Rural Sociology, Moscow, ID 83844. Offers applied economics (MS), including agribusiness, agricultural economics, applied economics. *Faculty:* 5 full-time. *Students:* 7 full-time. Average age 25. In 2016, 7 master's awarded. *Entrance requirements:* For master's, minimum GPA of 3.0. *Application deadline:* For fall admission, 8/1 for domestic students; for spring admission, 12/15 for domestic students. Applications are processed on a rolling basis. Application fee: $60. Electronic applications accepted. *Expenses:* Tuition, state resident: full-time $6460; part-time $414 per credit hour. Tuition, nonresident: full-time $21,268; part-time $1237 per credit hour. *Required fees:* $2070; $60 per credit hour. Full-time tuition and fees vary according to course load and reciprocity agreements. *Financial support:* Research assistantships and teaching assistantships available. Financial award applicants required to submit FAFSA. *Faculty research:* Crops: potatoes, blue grass; livestock: beef, dairy; rural and community development; natural resources and the environment; farm and ranch management. *Unit head:* Dr. Cathy Roheim, Department Head, 208-885-6262, Fax: 208-885-5759, E-mail: cdarby@uidaho.edu. *Application contact:* Sean Scoggin, Graduate Recruitment Coordinator, 208-885-4001, Fax: 208-885-4406, E-mail: graduateadmissions@uidaho.edu. Website: http://www.uidaho.edu/cals/agricultural-economics-and-rural-sociology

**University of Illinois at Urbana–Champaign,** Graduate College, College of Agricultural, Consumer and Environmental Sciences, Department of Agricultural and Consumer Economics, Champaign, IL 61820. Offers agricultural and applied economics (MS, PhD).

**University of Kentucky,** Graduate School, College of Agriculture, Food and Environment, Program in Agricultural Economics, Lexington, KY 40506-0032. Offers MS, PhD. *Degree requirements:* For master's, comprehensive exam, thesis optional; for doctorate, comprehensive exam, thesis/dissertation. *Entrance requirements:* For master's, GRE General Test, minimum undergraduate GPA of 2.75; for doctorate, GRE General Test, minimum graduate GPA of 3.0. Additional exam requirements/recommendations for international students: Required—TOEFL (minimum score 550 paper-based). Electronic applications accepted. *Faculty research:* Food and agricultural marketing, agricultural and food policy, natural resources and environment, rural economic development.

**University of Maine,** Graduate School, College of Natural Sciences, Forestry, and Agriculture, School of Economics, Orono, ME 04469. Offers economics (MA); financial economics (MA); resource economics and policy (MS). *Program availability:* Part-time. *Faculty:* 12 full-time (3 women). *Students:* 21 full-time (6 women), 1 part-time (0 women); includes 1 minority (Two or more races, non-Hispanic/Latino), 8 international. Average age 24. 30 applicants, 90% accepted, 9 enrolled. In 2016, 11 master's awarded. *Degree requirements:* For master's, thesis (for some programs). *Entrance requirements:* For master's, GRE General Test. Additional exam requirements/recommendations for international students: Required—TOEFL (minimum score 580 paper-based; 92 iBT), IELTS (minimum score 8.9). *Application deadline:* For fall admission, 2/15 for domestic students, 2/1 for international students; for spring admission, 9/15 for domestic students, 8/15 for international students. Applications are processed on a rolling basis. Application fee: $65. Electronic applications accepted. *Expenses:* Tuition, state resident: full-time $7524; part-time $2508 per credit. Tuition, nonresident: full-time $24,498; part-time $8166 per credit. *Required fees:* $1148; $571 per credit. *Financial support:* In 2016–17, 21 students received support, including 15 research assistantships (averaging $14,600 per year), 6 teaching assistantships with full tuition reimbursements available (averaging $14,600 per year); career-related internships or fieldwork, Federal Work-Study, institutionally sponsored loans, scholarships/grants, and tuition waivers (full and partial) also available. Support available to part-time students. Financial award application deadline: 3/1. *Faculty research:* Food systems, renewable energy; transportation; water quality; economic development. *Total annual research expenditures:* $881,321. *Unit head:* Dr. Mario Teisl, Director, 207-581-3151, Fax: 207-581-4278. *Application contact:* Scott G. Delcourt, Assistant Vice President for Graduate Studies and Senior Associate Dean, 207-581-3291, Fax: 207-581-3232, E-mail: graduate@maine.edu. Website: http://umaine.edu/soe/

**University of Manitoba,** Faculty of Graduate Studies, Faculty of Agricultural and Food Sciences, Department of Agribusiness and Agricultural Economics, Winnipeg, MB R3T 2N2, Canada. Offers agribusiness (M Sc, PhD). *Degree requirements:* For master's, thesis or alternative; for doctorate, thesis/dissertation.

**University of Maryland, College Park,** Academic Affairs, College of Agriculture and Natural Resources, Department of Agricultural and Resource Economics, College Park,

## Agricultural Economics and Agribusiness

MD 20742. Offers agriculture economics (MS, PhD); resource economics (MS, PhD). *Program availability:* Part-time, evening/weekend. *Degree requirements:* For master's, variable foreign language requirement, thesis optional, oral exam; for doctorate, variable foreign language requirement, oral dissertation defense. *Entrance requirements:* For master's, GRE General Test, minimum GPA of 3.0, course work in microeconomics and calculus, 3 letters of recommendation; for doctorate, GRE General Test. Additional exam requirements/recommendations for international students: Required—TOEFL. Electronic applications accepted. *Faculty research:* Agricultural development, international trade, agricultural marketing, econometrics, farm management and production economics.

**University of Massachusetts Amherst,** Graduate School, College of Social and Behavioral Sciences, Department of Resource Economics, Amherst, MA 01003. Offers MS, PhD. *Program availability:* Part-time. Terminal master's awarded for partial completion of doctoral program. *Degree requirements:* For master's, thesis or alternative; for doctorate, comprehensive exam, thesis/dissertation. *Entrance requirements:* For master's and doctorate, GRE General Test. Additional exam requirements/recommendations for international students: Required—TOEFL (minimum score 550 paper-based; 80 iBT), IELTS (minimum score 6.5). Electronic applications accepted.

**University of Missouri,** Office of Research and Graduate Studies, College of Agriculture, Food and Natural Resources, Department of Agricultural and Applied Economics, Columbia, MO 65211. Offers agricultural economics (MS, PhD); conservation biology (Graduate Certificate). *Faculty:* 21 full-time (5 women). *Students:* 19 full-time (5 women), 14 part-time (6 women); includes 3 minority (1 Black or African American, non-Hispanic/Latino; 1 Asian, non-Hispanic/Latino; 1 Two or more races, non-Hispanic/Latino), 17 international. Average age 33. *Degree requirements:* For doctorate, comprehensive exam, thesis/dissertation. *Entrance requirements:* For master's and doctorate, GRE General Test, minimum GPA of 3.0. Additional exam requirements/recommendations for international students: Required—TOEFL (minimum score 550 paper-based; 80 iBT). *Application deadline:* For fall admission, 2/15 priority date for domestic students, 2/15 for international students; for winter admission, 9/15 for domestic and international students. Applications are processed on a rolling basis. Application fee: $75 ($90 for international students). Electronic applications accepted. *Expenses:* Tuition, state resident: full-time $6347; part-time $352.60 per credit hour. Tuition, nonresident: full-time $17,379; part-time $965.50 per credit hour. *Required fees:* $1035. Tuition and fees vary according to course load, campus/location and program. *Financial support:* Fellowships, research assistantships with tuition reimbursements, teaching assistantships with tuition reimbursements, Federal Work-Study, institutionally sponsored loans, scholarships/grants, health care benefits, and unspecified assistantships available. Financial award application deadline: 3/1; financial award applicants required to submit FAFSA. *Faculty research:* Agribusiness management, contracting and strategy; collective action and cooperative theory; econometrics and price analysis; entrepreneurship; environmental and natural resource economics; food, biofuel and agricultural policy and regulation; international development; regional economics and rural development policy; science policy and innovation; sustainable agriculture and applied ethics.
Website: http://dass.missouri.edu/agecon/grad/

**University of Nebraska–Lincoln,** Graduate College, College of Agricultural Sciences and Natural Resources, Department of Agricultural Economics, Lincoln, NE 68588. Offers agribusiness (MBA); agricultural economics (MS, PhD); community development (M Ag). *Degree requirements:* For master's, thesis optional; for doctorate, comprehensive exam, thesis/dissertation. *Entrance requirements:* For master's and doctorate, GRE General Test. Additional exam requirements/recommendations for international students: Required—TOEFL (minimum score 550 paper-based). Electronic applications accepted. *Faculty research:* Marketing and agribusiness, production economics, resource law, international trade and development, rural policy and revitalization.

**University of Nevada, Reno,** Graduate School, College of Agriculture, Biotechnology and Natural Resources, Department of Resource Economics, Reno, NV 89557. Offers MS, PhD. Terminal master's awarded for partial completion of doctoral program. *Degree requirements:* For master's, thesis optional; for doctorate, thesis/dissertation. *Entrance requirements:* For master's, GRE General Test, minimum GPA of 2.75; for doctorate, GRE General Test, minimum GPA of 3.0. Additional exam requirements/recommendations for international students: Required—TOEFL (minimum score 500 paper-based; 61 iBT), IELTS (minimum score 6). Electronic applications accepted. *Faculty research:* Econometrics, environmental valuation, natural resource and environmental policy analysis, public lands management.

**University of Puerto Rico, Mayagüez Campus,** Graduate Studies, College of Agricultural Sciences, Department of Agricultural Economics and Rural Sociology, Mayagüez, PR 00681-9000. Offers MS. *Program availability:* Part-time. *Faculty:* 15 full-time (7 women). *Students:* 20 full-time (12 women), 2 part-time (0 women); all minorities (all Hispanic/Latino). Average age 25. 8 applicants, 50% accepted, 3 enrolled. In 2016, 1 master's awarded. *Degree requirements:* For master's, comprehensive exam, thesis. *Entrance requirements:* For master's, bachelor's degree in agricultural economics or its equivalent. *Application deadline:* For fall admission, 2/15 for domestic and international students; for spring admission, 9/15 for domestic and international students. Applications are processed on a rolling basis. Application fee: $25. Electronic applications accepted. *Expenses: Tuition, area resident:* Full-time $2466. *International tuition:* $7166 full-time. *Required fees:* $210. One-time fee: $5 full-time. Tuition and fees vary according to course level, campus/location, program and student level. *Financial support:* In 2016–17, 18 students received support, including 15 research assistantships with tuition reimbursements available (averaging $2,477 per year), 10 teaching assistantships with tuition reimbursements available (averaging $2,066 per year); scholarships/grants and unspecified assistantships also available. *Faculty research:* Farm management, agricultural development, agrimarketing, natural resource economics. *Unit head:* Alwin J. Jiménez, PhD, Director, 787-265-3855 Ext. 3860, Fax: 787-265-3860, E-mail: alwin.jimenez@upr.edu. *Application contact:* Margarita Olivencia, Secretary, 787-832-4040 Ext. 2471, Fax: 787-265-3860, E-mail: margarita.olivencia@upr.edu.
Website: http://economia.cca.uprm.edu/

**University of Saskatchewan,** College of Graduate Studies and Research, College of Agriculture, Department of Agricultural Economics, Saskatoon, SK S7N 5A2, Canada. Offers M Ag, M Sc, MA, PhD, PGD. *Degree requirements:* For master's, thesis; for doctorate, comprehensive exam (for some programs), thesis/dissertation. *Entrance requirements:* Additional exam requirements/recommendations for international students: Required—TOEFL (minimum score 80 iBT); Recommended—IELTS (minimum score 6.5).

**University of Saskatchewan,** College of Graduate Studies and Research, Edwards School of Business, Program in Business Administration, Saskatoon, SK S7N 5A2, Canada. Offers agribusiness management (MBA); biotechnology management (MBA); health services management (MBA); indigenous management (MBA); international business management (MBA).

**The University of Tennessee at Martin,** Graduate Programs, College of Business and Global Affairs, Program in Business, Martin, TN 38238. Offers agricultural business (MBA); financial services (MBA); general business (MBA). *Accreditation:* AACSB. *Program availability:* Part-time, online only, 100% online, blended/hybrid learning. *Faculty:* 31. *Students:* 15 full-time (6 women), 79 part-time (28 women); includes 13 minority (6 Black or African American, non-Hispanic/Latino; 2 Asian, non-Hispanic/Latino; 4 Hispanic/Latino; 1 Two or more races, non-Hispanic/Latino). Average age 33. 62 applicants, 40% accepted, 20 enrolled. In 2016, 34 master's awarded. *Degree requirements:* For master's, comprehensive exam. *Entrance requirements:* For master's, GMAT, GRE, minimum GPA of 2.5, resume. Additional exam requirements/recommendations for international students: Required—TOEFL (minimum score 525 paper-based; 71 iBT). *Application deadline:* For fall admission, 7/27 priority date for domestic students, 7/27 for international students; for spring admission, 12/17 priority date for domestic students, 12/17 for international students; for summer admission, 5/10 priority date for domestic and international students. Applications are processed on a rolling basis. Application fee: $30 ($130 for international students). Electronic applications accepted. *Expenses:* Tuition, state resident: full-time $8254; part-time $459 per credit hour. Tuition, nonresident: full-time $22,198; part-time $1234 per credit hour. *Required fees:* $79 per credit hour. Part-time tuition and fees vary according to course load and campus/location. *Financial support:* In 2016–17, 10 students received support, including 5 research assistantships with full tuition reimbursements available (averaging $7,540 per year), 5 teaching assistantships with full tuition reimbursements available (averaging $7,560 per year); career-related internships or fieldwork, scholarships/grants, and unspecified assistantships also available. Support available to part-time students. Financial award application deadline: 2/1; financial award applicants required to submit FAFSA. *Unit head:* Dr. Ashley Kilburn, Coordinator, 731-881-7245, Fax: 731-881-7231, E-mail: mba@utm.edu. *Application contact:* Jolene L. Cunningham, Student Services Specialist, 731-881-7012, Fax: 731-881-7499, E-mail: jcunningham@utm.edu.

**University of Vermont,** Graduate College, College of Agriculture and Life Sciences, Department of Community Development and Applied Economics, Burlington, VT 05405. Offers community development and applied economics (MS); public administration (MPA). *Students:* 16 full-time (10 women); includes 1 minority (Asian, non-Hispanic/Latino). Average age 27. 25 applicants, 84% accepted, 7 enrolled. In 2016, 7 master's awarded. *Degree requirements:* For master's, thesis. *Entrance requirements:* For master's, GRE General Test. Additional exam requirements/recommendations for international students: Required—TOEFL (minimum score 550 paper-based; 80 iBT). *Application deadline:* For fall admission, 4/1 priority date for domestic students, 4/1 for international students; for spring admission, 11/15 for domestic students. Applications are processed on a rolling basis. Application fee: $65. Electronic applications accepted. *Expenses:* Tuition, state resident: full-time $5814. Tuition, nonresident: full-time $14,670. *Financial support:* Fellowships, research assistantships, teaching assistantships, and career-related internships or fieldwork available. Financial award application deadline: 3/1. *Faculty research:* Agricultural production and marketing. *Unit head:* David Conner, 802-656-2001, E-mail: david.conner@uvm.edu.

**University of Wisconsin–Madison,** Graduate School, College of Agricultural and Life Sciences, Department of Agricultural and Applied Economics, Madison, WI 53706. Offers MA, MS, PhD. *Program availability:* Part-time. *Degree requirements:* For doctorate, thesis/dissertation, preliminary exams. *Entrance requirements:* For master's and doctorate, GRE General Test. Additional exam requirements/recommendations for international students: Required—TOEFL (minimum score 580 paper-based; 92 iBT). Electronic applications accepted. *Faculty research:* Environmental and resource economics, international development, community economics, energy economics, agricultural technology, food systems, markets and trade.

**University of Wyoming,** College of Agriculture and Natural Resources, Department of Agricultural and Applied Economics, Laramie, WY 82071. Offers MS. *Program availability:* Part-time. *Degree requirements:* For master's, thesis (for some programs). *Entrance requirements:* For master's, GRE General Test, minimum GPA of 3.0. Additional exam requirements/recommendations for international students: Required—TOEFL. Electronic applications accepted. *Faculty research:* Farm management, agricultural markets, water economics, community development, agricultural business.

**Virginia Polytechnic Institute and State University,** Graduate School, College of Agriculture and Life Sciences, Blacksburg, VA 24061. Offers agricultural and applied economics (MS); agricultural and life sciences (MS); animal and poultry sciences (MS, PhD); crop and soil environmental sciences (MS, PhD); dairy science (MS); entomology (PhD); horticulture (MS, PhD); human nutrition, foods and exercise (MS, PhD); life sciences (MS, PhD); plant pathology, physiology and weed science (PhD). *Faculty:* 235 full-time (69 women). *Students:* 360 full-time (193 women), 150 part-time (89 women); includes 73 minority (30 Black or African American, non-Hispanic/Latino; 15 Asian, non-Hispanic/Latino; 15 Hispanic/Latino; 13 Two or more races, non-Hispanic/Latino), 113 international. Average age 29. 311 applicants, 45% accepted, 106 enrolled. In 2016, 111 master's, 50 doctorates awarded. *Degree requirements:* For master's, comprehensive exam (for some programs), thesis (for some programs); for doctorate, comprehensive exam (for some programs), thesis/dissertation (for some programs). *Entrance requirements:* For master's and doctorate, GRE/GMAT. Additional exam requirements/recommendations for international students: Required—TOEFL (minimum score 80 iBT). *Application deadline:* For fall admission, 8/1 for domestic students, 4/1 for international students; for spring admission, 1/1 for domestic students, 9/1 for international students. Applications are processed on a rolling basis. Application fee: $75. Electronic applications accepted. *Expenses:* Tuition, state resident: full-time $12,467; part-time $692.50 per credit hour. Tuition, nonresident: full-time $25,095; part-time $1394.25 per credit hour. *Required fees:* $2669; $491.50 per semester. Tuition and fees vary according to course load, campus/location and program. *Financial support:* In 2016–17, 258 research assistantships with full tuition reimbursements (averaging $20,636 per year), 107 teaching assistantships with full tuition reimbursements (averaging $20,004 per year) were awarded. Financial award application deadline: 3/1; financial award applicants required to submit FAFSA. *Total annual research expenditures:* $46.9 million. *Unit head:* Dr. Alan L. Grant, Dean, 540-231-4152, Fax: 540-231-4163, E-mail: algrant@vt.edu. *Application contact:* Crystal Tawney, Administrative Assistant, 540-231-4152, Fax: 540-231-4163, E-mail: cdtawney@vt.edu.
Website: http://www.cals.vt.edu/

**Washington State University,** College of Agricultural, Human, and Natural Resource Sciences, School of Economic Sciences, Pullman, WA 99164-6210. Offers agricultural economics (PhD); economics (PhD). Programs offered at the Pullman campus. Terminal master's awarded for partial completion of doctoral program. *Degree requirements:* For master's, comprehensive exam (for some programs), thesis (for some programs), oral exam; for doctorate, comprehensive exam, thesis/dissertation, oral exam, written exam, qualifying exams. *Entrance requirements:* For master's and doctorate, GRE, minimum GPA of 3.0, 3 letters of recommendation. Additional exam requirements/recommendations for international students: Required—TOEFL (minimum score 550 paper-based). Electronic applications accepted. *Faculty research:* Agricultural economics, econometrics, natural resource and environmental economics, industrial organization, health economics.

**West Texas A&M University,** College of Agriculture and Natural Sciences, Department of Agricultural Sciences, Emphasis in Agricultural Business and Economics, Canyon, TX 79016-0001. Offers MS. *Program availability:* Part-time. *Degree requirements:* For master's, comprehensive exam, thesis optional. *Entrance requirements:* For master's, GRE General Test. Additional exam requirements/recommendations for international students: Required—TOEFL (minimum score 550 paper-based). *Application deadline:* For fall admission, 5/1 for international students; for spring admission, 10/30 for international students. Applications are processed on a rolling basis. Application fee: $40 ($75 for international students). Electronic applications accepted. *Financial support:* Research assistantships, teaching assistantships, Federal Work-Study, institutionally sponsored loans, and scholarships/grants available. Support available to part-time students. Financial award applicants required to submit FAFSA. *Faculty research:*

Utilizing expected revenue in selecting optimal marketing alternatives for fixed resource cow/calf operators in the Texas panhandle.
Website: http://www.wtamu.edu/academics/agriculture-graduate-programs-ms.aspx

**West Virginia University,** Davis College of Agriculture, Forestry and Consumer Sciences, Division of Resource Management and Sustainable Development, Program in Agricultural and Resource Economics, Morgantown, WV 26506. Offers MS. *Program availability:* Part-time. *Degree requirements:* For master's, thesis optional. *Entrance requirements:* For master's, GRE General Test, minimum GPA of 2.5, 1 calculus course. Additional exam requirements/recommendations for international students: Required—TOEFL. *Faculty research:* Agricultural production and marketing, rural development, mineral and energy economics, economic development.

# Applied Economics

**Auburn University,** Graduate School, Interdepartmental Programs, Interdepartmental Program in Applied Economics, Auburn University, AL 36849. Offers PhD. *Students:* 20 full-time (10 women), 2 part-time (1 woman), all international. Average age 31. 18 applicants, 22% accepted. In 2016, 6 doctorates awarded. *Expenses:* Tuition, state resident: full-time $9072; part-time $504 per credit hour. Tuition, nonresident: full-time $27,216; part-time $1512 per credit hour. *Required fees:* $812 per semester. Tuition and fees vary according to degree level and program. *Unit head:* Deacue Fields, Chair, 334-844-5614. *Application contact:* Dr. George Flowers, Dean of the Graduate School, 334-844-2125.

**Buffalo State College, State University of New York,** The Graduate School, Faculty of Natural and Social Sciences, Department of Economics and Finance, Buffalo, NY 14222-1095. Offers applied economics (MA). *Degree requirements:* For master's, project. *Entrance requirements:* Additional exam requirements/recommendations for international students: Required—TOEFL (minimum score 550 paper-based).

**Clemson University,** Graduate School, College of Agriculture, Forestry and Life Sciences, Department of Agricultural Sciences, Clemson, SC 29634. Offers agricultural education (M Ag Ed); applied economics (PhD); applied economics and statistics (MS). *Program availability:* Part-time. *Faculty:* 19 full-time (3 women). *Students:* 20 full-time (12 women), 18 part-time (8 women); includes 3 minority (1 Hispanic/Latino; 2 Two or more races, non-Hispanic/Latino), 1 international. Average age 27. 49 applicants, 47% accepted, 14 enrolled. In 2016, 10 master's, 2 doctorates awarded. *Degree requirements:* For master's, thesis optional; for doctorate, comprehensive exam, thesis/dissertation. *Entrance requirements:* For master's and doctorate, GRE General Test, unofficial transcripts, letters of recommendation. Additional exam requirements/recommendations for international students: Required—TOEFL (minimum score 80 iBT), IELTS (minimum score 6.5). *Application deadline:* For fall admission, 6/1 for domestic students, 7/1 for international students; for spring admission, 10/1 for domestic students, 11/1 for international students. Applications are processed on a rolling basis. Application fee: $80 ($90 for international students). Electronic applications accepted. *Expenses:* $4,841 per semester full-time resident, $9,640 per semester full-time non-resident, $612 per credit hour part-time resident, $1,223 per credit hour part-time non-resident. *Financial support:* In 2016–17, 12 students received support, including 2 fellowships with partial tuition reimbursements available (averaging $18,000 per year), 7 research assistantships with partial tuition reimbursements available (averaging $15,071 per year), 5 teaching assistantships with partial tuition reimbursements available (averaging $8,616 per year); career-related internships or fieldwork and unspecified assistantships also available. Financial award application deadline: 6/1. *Unit head:* Dr. George Askew, Dean, 864-656-3013, E-mail: caflsdean-l@clemson.edu. *Application contact:* Dr. Joseph Culin, Associate Dean for Research and Graduate Studies, 864-656-2810, E-mail: jculin@clemson.edu.
Website: http://www.clemson.edu/cafls/departments/agricultural-sciences/index.html

**Cornell University,** Graduate School, Graduate Fields of Agriculture and Life Sciences, Field of Applied Economics and Management, Ithaca, NY 14853. Offers agricultural finance (MS, PhD); applied econometrics and qualitative analysis (MS, PhD); economics of development (MS, PhD); environmental economics (MS, PhD); environmental management (MPS); farm management and production economics (MS, PhD); marketing and food distribution (MS, PhD); public policy analysis (MS, PhD); resource economics (PhD). *Entrance requirements:* For master's and doctorate, GRE. Additional exam requirements/recommendations for international students: Required—TOEFL.

**Cornell University,** Graduate School, Graduate Fields of Arts and Sciences, Field of Economics, Ithaca, NY 14853. Offers applied economics (PhD); basic analytical economics (PhD); econometrics and economic statistics (PhD); economic development and planning (PhD); economic theory (PhD); industrial organization and control (PhD); international economics (PhD); labor economics (PhD); monetary and macro economics (PhD); public finance (PhD). *Degree requirements:* For doctorate, comprehensive exam, thesis/dissertation. *Entrance requirements:* For doctorate, GRE General Test, 3 letters of recommendation. Additional exam requirements/recommendations for international students: Required—TOEFL (minimum score 550 paper-based; 77 iBT). Electronic applications accepted. *Faculty research:* Learning and games, economics of education, political economy, transfer payments, time series and nonparametrics.

**DePaul University,** Kellstadt Graduate School of Business, Chicago, IL 60604. Offers accountancy (M Acc, MS, MSA); applied economics (MBA); banking (MBA); behavioral finance (MBA); brand and product management (MBA); business development (MBA); business information technology (MS); business strategy and decision-making (MBA); computational finance (MS); consumer insights (MBA); corporate finance (MBA); economic policy analysis (MS); entrepreneurship (MBA, MS); finance (MBA, MS); financial analysis (MBA); general business (MBA); health sector management (MBA); hospitality leadership (MBA); hospitality leadership and operational performance (MS); human resource management (MBA); human resources (MS); investment management (MBA); leadership and change management (MBA); management accounting (MBA); marketing (MBA, MS); marketing analysis (MS); marketing strategy and planning (MBA); operations management (MBA); organizational diversity (MBA); real estate (MS); real estate finance and investment (MBA); revenue management (MBA); sports management (MBA); strategic global marketing (MBA); strategy, execution and valuation (MBA); sustainable management (MBA, MS); taxation (MS); wealth management (MS); JD/MBA. *Accreditation:* AACSB. *Program availability:* Part-time, evening/weekend, online learning. *Entrance requirements:* For master's, GMAT, 2 letters of recommendation, resume, essay, official transcripts. Additional exam requirements/recommendations for international students: Required—TOEFL (minimum score 550 paper-based; 80 iBT). Electronic applications accepted. *Expenses:* Contact institution.

**East Carolina University,** Graduate School, Thomas Harriot College of Arts and Sciences, Department of Economics, Greenville, NC 27858-4353. Offers applied and resource economics (MS). *Program availability:* Part-time. *Students:* 10 full-time (1 woman), 1 part-time (0 women), 6 international. Average age 28. 13 applicants, 92% accepted, 9 enrolled. In 2016, 6 master's awarded. *Degree requirements:* For master's, one foreign language, comprehensive exam. *Entrance requirements:* For master's, GRE General Test. Additional exam requirements/recommendations for international students: Required—TOEFL. *Application deadline:* For fall admission, 6/1 priority date for domestic students. Applications are processed on a rolling basis. Application fee: $50. *Financial support:* Research assistantships with partial tuition reimbursements and teaching assistantships with partial tuition reimbursements available. Financial award application deadline: 6/1. *Unit head:* Dr. Richard Ericson, Chair, 252-328-6006, Fax: 252-328-6743, E-mail: ericsonr@ecu.edu. *Application contact:* Dean of Graduate School, 252-328-6012, Fax: 252-328-6071, E-mail: gradschool@ecu.edu.

**Florida State University,** The Graduate School, College of Social Sciences and Public Policy, Department of Economics, Tallahassee, FL 32306-2180. Offers applied economics (MS); economics (PhD); JD/MS. *Program availability:* Part-time. *Faculty:* 32 full-time (4 women), 1 part-time/adjunct (0 women). *Students:* 76 full-time (16 women), 3 part-time (2 women); includes 19 minority (4 Black or African American, non-Hispanic/Latino; 5 Asian, non-Hispanic/Latino; 2 Hispanic/Latino; 8 Two or more races, non-Hispanic/Latino). Average age 26. 155 applicants, 61% accepted, 37 enrolled. In 2016, 23 master's, 5 doctorates awarded. Terminal master's awarded for partial completion of doctoral program. *Degree requirements:* For master's, thesis (for some programs), applied project (for some programs); for doctorate, comprehensive exam, thesis/dissertation, dissertation prospectus, workshops. *Entrance requirements:* For master's, GRE General Test, minimum upper-division undergraduate GPA of 3.0, 3.4 on graduate work; minimum 1 course each in statistics and calculus; principles and sufficient upper-level economics courses; for doctorate, GRE General Test, minimum upper-division undergraduate GPA of 3.0, graduate 3.4; minimum 1 course each in statistics and linear algebra, 2 in calculus. Additional exam requirements/recommendations for international students: Required—TOEFL (minimum score 90 iBT). *Application deadline:* For fall admission, 2/15 priority date for domestic and international students. Applications are processed on a rolling basis. Application fee: $30. Electronic applications accepted. *Expenses:* Tuition, state resident: full-time $7263; part-time $403.51 per credit hour. Tuition, nonresident: full-time $18,087; part-time $1004.85 per credit hour. *Required fees:* $1365; $75.81 per credit hour. $20 per semester. Tuition and fees vary according to campus/location. *Financial support:* In 2016–17, 60 students received support, including 15 fellowships with full tuition reimbursements available (averaging $25,000 per year), 4 research assistantships with full tuition reimbursements available (averaging $19,000 per year), 24 teaching assistantships with full tuition reimbursements available (averaging $19,000 per year); scholarships/grants, tuition waivers (partial), and unspecified assistantships also available. Financial award application deadline: 2/15; financial award applicants required to submit FAFSA. *Faculty research:* Industrial organization, experimental/behavioral, public/urban, law and economics, macroeconomics and financial. *Total annual research expenditures:* $650,000. *Unit head:* Dr. R. Mark Isaac, Chairman, 850-644-5001, Fax: 850-644-4535, E-mail: misaac@fsu.edu. *Application contact:* Dr. Thomas W. Zuehlke, Graduate Director, 850-644-5001, Fax: 850-644-4535, E-mail: tzuehlke@fsu.edu.
Website: http://www.coss.fsu.edu/economics/

**Georgia Southern University,** Jack N. Averitt College of Graduate Studies, College of Business Administration, Program in Applied Economics, Statesboro, GA 30460. Offers applied economics (MS); information systems (Graduate Certificate). *Program availability:* Part-time, evening/weekend, blended/hybrid learning. *Students:* 2 full-time (both women), 21 part-time (6 women); includes 4 minority (2 Black or African American, non-Hispanic/Latino; 1 Asian, non-Hispanic/Latino; 1 Hispanic/Latino), 2 international. Average age 36. 20 applicants, 55% accepted, 9 enrolled. In 2016, 19 master's awarded. *Entrance requirements:* For master's, GRE or GMAT, minimum GPA of 3.0. Additional exam requirements/recommendations for international students: Required—TOEFL (minimum score 550 paper-based; 80 iBT), IELTS (minimum score 6). *Application deadline:* For fall admission, 3/1 for domestic and international students; for spring admission, 10/1 priority date for domestic students, 10/1 for international students. Applications are processed on a rolling basis. Application fee: $50. Electronic applications accepted. *Expenses:* Tuition, state resident: full-time $7236; part-time $277 per semester hour. Tuition, nonresident: full-time $27,118; part-time $1105 per semester hour. *Required fees:* $2092. *Financial support:* Unspecified assistantships available. Financial award application deadline: 4/15; financial award applicants required to submit FAFSA. *Faculty research:* Analytical capabilities in economic development, financial economics, regulatory issues, market analysis, economic development. *Unit head:* Dr. Gordon Smith, Graduate Program Director, 912-478-2357, Fax: 912-478-0710, E-mail: gsmith@georgiasouthern.edu.
Website: http://coba.georgiasouthern.edu/dfe/graduate/master-of-science-in-applied-economics/

**HEC Montreal,** School of Business Administration, Master of Science Programs in Administration, Program in Applied Economics, Montréal, QC H3T 2A7, Canada. Offers M Sc. Most courses are given in French. *Students:* 41 full-time (13 women), 1 (woman) part-time. 28 applicants, 86% accepted, 18 enrolled. In 2016, 9 master's awarded. *Degree requirements:* For master's, one foreign language, thesis. *Entrance requirements:* For master's, Test de francais international (TFI) with minimum score of 850 (for those who have never studied in French), BBA, applied economics degree in another field, degree deemed equivalent by program director and minimum GPA of 3.0 on 4.3 scale. *Application deadline:* For fall admission, 3/15 for domestic and international students; for winter admission, 9/15 for domestic and international

## Applied Economics

students. Application fee: $86 Canadian dollars. Electronic applications accepted. *Expenses: Tuition, area resident:* Part-time $77.80 Canadian dollars per credit. Tuition, state resident: full-time $2797 Canadian dollars; part-time $240.92 Canadian dollars per credit. Tuition, nonresident: full-time $8673 Canadian dollars; part-time $531.43 Canadian dollars per credit. *International tuition:* $19,131 Canadian dollars full-time. *Required fees:* $1699 Canadian dollars; $40.58 Canadian dollars per credit. $67.32 Canadian dollars per term. Tuition and fees vary according to degree level and program. *Financial support:* Research assistantships, teaching assistantships, and scholarships/grants available. Financial award application deadline: 9/2. *Unit head:* Dr. Marie-Helene Jobin, Director, 514-340-6283, E-mail: marie-helene.jobin@hec.ca. *Application contact:* Marianne de Moura, Administrative Director, 514-340-7106, Fax: 514-340-6411, E-mail: marianne.de-moura@hec.ca.
Website: http://www.hec.ca/programmes/maitrises/maitrise-economie-appliquee/index.html

**Johns Hopkins University,** Zanvyl Krieger School of Arts and Sciences, Advanced Academic Programs, Program in Applied Economics, Washington, DC 20036. Offers MA. *Program availability:* Part-time, evening/weekend. *Degree requirements:* For master's, thesis (for some programs). *Entrance requirements:* For master's, minimum GPA of 3.0, coursework in microeconomics and macroeconomics. Additional exam requirements/recommendations for international students: Required—TOEFL (minimum score 100 iBT). Electronic applications accepted.

**Mills College,** Graduate Studies, Lorry I. Lokey Graduate School of Business, Oakland, CA 94613-1000. Offers applied economics (MA); management (MBA). *Program availability:* Part-time. *Faculty:* 3 full-time (all women), 9 part-time/adjunct (5 women). *Students:* 38 full-time (34 women), 20 part-time (16 women); includes 38 minority (15 Black or African American, non-Hispanic/Latino; 3 Asian, non-Hispanic/Latino; 15 Hispanic/Latino; 5 Two or more races, non-Hispanic/Latino), 3 international. Average age 33. 47 applicants, 81% accepted, 22 enrolled. In 2016, 35 master's awarded. *Entrance requirements:* For master's, GRE, SAT, or ACT, 3 letters of recommendation, 2 transcripts. Additional exam requirements/recommendations for international students: Required—TOEFL (minimum score 550 paper-based; 80 iBT) or IELTS (minimum score 6). *Application deadline:* For fall admission, 2/1 priority date for domestic students, 12/15 for international students; for spring admission, 10/1 for domestic students. Applications are processed on a rolling basis. Application fee: $50. *Expenses:* Contact institution. *Financial support:* In 2016–17, 62 students received support, including 62 fellowships with tuition reimbursements available (averaging $8,048 per year); teaching assistantships with tuition reimbursements available, scholarships/grants, and unspecified assistantships also available. Support available to part-time students. Financial award application deadline: 2/1; financial award applicants required to submit FAFSA. *Faculty research:* Diversity and inclusion, applied econometrics, non-profit management, business communication and effective public speaking, social media and Internet marketing. *Unit head:* Dr. Carolyn Sherwood Call, Department Chair, 510-430-3365, Fax: 510-430-2159, E-mail: csherwoodcall@mills.edu. *Application contact:* Robynne Lofton, Director of Admissions, 510-430-3295, Fax: 510-430-2159, E-mail: grad-admission@mills.edu.
Website: http://www.mills.edu/mba

**New York University,** Graduate School of Arts and Science, Department of Economics, New York, NY 10012-1019. Offers applied economic analysis (Advanced Certificate); economics (MA, PhD); JD/MA; MD/PhD. *Program availability:* Part-time, evening/weekend. Terminal master's awarded for partial completion of doctoral program. *Degree requirements:* For master's, thesis; for doctorate, one foreign language, thesis/dissertation, 4 qualifying exams. *Entrance requirements:* For master's and doctorate, GRE General Test. Additional exam requirements/recommendations for international students: Required—TOEFL. *Faculty research:* Economic theory, experimental economics, growth and development, macroeconomics and finance, international trade and international finance.

**North Carolina Agricultural and Technical State University,** School of Graduate Studies, School of Agriculture and Environmental Sciences, Department of Agribusiness, Applied Economics, and Agriscience Education, Greensboro, NC 27411. Offers agricultural economics (MS); agricultural education (MS). *Accreditation:* NCATE. *Program availability:* Part-time, evening/weekend. *Degree requirements:* For master's, comprehensive exam, thesis or alternative, qualifying exam. *Entrance requirements:* For master's, GRE General Test, minimum GPA of 3.0. *Faculty research:* Aid for small farmers, agricultural technology resources, labor force mobility, agrology.

**Ohio University,** Graduate College, College of Arts and Sciences, Department of Economics, Athens, OH 45701-2979. Offers applied economics (MA); financial economics (MFE). *Program availability:* Part-time, evening/weekend. *Degree requirements:* For master's, thesis or alternative. *Entrance requirements:* For master's, GRE or GMAT (recommended), minimum GPA of 3.0. Additional exam requirements/recommendations for international students: Required—TOEFL (minimum score 550 paper-based; 80 iBT) or IELTS (minimum score 6.5). *Application deadline:* For fall admission, 2/15 priority date for domestic and international students; for winter admission, 12/1 for domestic students, 10/1 priority date for international students. Application fee: $50 ($55 for international students). Electronic applications accepted. *Financial support:* Research assistantships with full and partial tuition reimbursements, Federal Work-Study, tuition waivers (partial), and unspecified assistantships available. Financial award application deadline: 2/15. *Faculty research:* Macroeconomics, public finance, international economics and finance, monetary theory, healthcare economics. *Unit head:* Dr. Rosmary Rossiter, Chair, 740-593-2040, E-mail: rossiter@ohio.edu. *Application contact:* Dr. K. Doroodian, Graduate Chair, 740-593-2046, E-mail: doroodia@ohio.edu.
Website: http://www.ohiou.edu/economics/

**Portland State University,** Graduate Studies, College of Urban and Public Affairs, Department of Economics, Portland, OR 97207-0751. Offers applied economics (MA, MS); general economics (MA, MS). *Program availability:* Part-time. *Faculty:* 15 full-time (3 women), 8 part-time/adjunct (4 women). *Students:* 13 full-time (5 women), 4 part-time (1 woman); includes 2 minority (1 Hispanic/Latino; 1 Native Hawaiian or other Pacific Islander, non-Hispanic/Latino), 5 international. Average age 29. 26 applicants, 50% accepted, 11 enrolled. In 2016, 9 master's awarded. *Degree requirements:* For master's, thesis optional; for doctorate, one foreign language, thesis/dissertation. *Entrance requirements:* For master's, minimum GPA of 3.0 in economic course work and overall; course work in calculus. Additional exam requirements/recommendations for international students: Required—TOEFL (minimum score 550 paper-based; 80 iBT). *Application deadline:* For fall admission, 2/1 for domestic and international students; for winter admission, 9/1 for domestic and international students; for spring admission, 12/5 for domestic and international students. Applications are processed on a rolling basis. Application fee: $65. *Expenses:* Contact institution. *Financial support:* In 2016–17, 9 teaching assistantships with full tuition reimbursements (averaging $7,282 per year) were awarded; career-related internships or fieldwork, Federal Work-Study, and unspecified assistantships also available. Support available to part-time students. Financial award application deadline: 3/1; financial award applicants required to submit FAFSA. *Faculty research:* NAFTA, economies of transition, economics of Eastern Europe, artificial intelligence, comparative economic systems. *Total annual research

expenditures:* $181,423. *Unit head:* Dr. Thomas Potiowsky, Chair, 503-725-2288, Fax: 503-725-3945, E-mail: potiowskyt@pdx.edu. *Application contact:* Margie Port, Office Coordinator, 503-725-3974, Fax: 503-725-3974, E-mail: mport@pdx.edu.
Website: https://www.pdx.edu/econ/

**Roosevelt University,** Graduate Division, College of Arts and Sciences, Department of Economics, Chicago, IL 60605. Offers applied economics (MA); economics (MA). *Program availability:* Part-time, evening/weekend. *Degree requirements:* For master's, thesis or alternative. *Entrance requirements:* For master's, minimum GPA of 2.7. *Faculty research:* Labor, gender issues, international trade and development, entrepreneurship, political economy and money.

**St. Cloud State University,** School of Graduate Studies, College of Social Sciences, Department of Economics, Program in Applied Economics, St. Cloud, MN 56301-4498. Offers MS.

**Southern Methodist University,** Dedman College of Humanities and Sciences, Department of Economics, Dallas, TX 75205. Offers applied economics (MA); applied economics and predictive analytics (MS); economics (PhD); law and economics (MA). *Program availability:* Part-time, evening/weekend. Terminal master's awarded for partial completion of doctoral program. *Degree requirements:* For master's, thesis, oral qualifying exam; for doctorate, thesis/dissertation, written exams. *Entrance requirements:* For master's, GRE General Test or GMAT, 12 hours of course work in economics, minimum GPA of 3.0, previous course work in calculus and statistics; for doctorate, GRE General Test, minimum GPA of 3.0; 3 semesters of course work in calculus; 1 semester each of course work in statistics and linear algebra. Additional exam requirements/recommendations for international students: Required—TOEFL (minimum score 550 paper-based). Electronic applications accepted. *Faculty research:* Economic theory, game theory, econometrics, international trade, labor.

**Texas Tech University,** Graduate School, College of Agricultural Sciences and Natural Resources, Department of Agricultural and Applied Economics, Lubbock, TX 79409. Offers agribusiness (MAB); agricultural and applied economics (MS, PhD); JD/MS. *Program availability:* Part-time. *Faculty:* 22 full-time (6 women), 2 part-time/adjunct (0 women). *Students:* 48 full-time (23 women), 11 part-time (6 women); includes 7 minority (6 Hispanic/Latino; 1 Two or more races, non-Hispanic/Latino), 30 international. Average age 30. 50 applicants, 70% accepted, 17 enrolled. In 2016, 18 master's, 6 doctorates awarded. Terminal master's awarded for partial completion of doctoral program. *Degree requirements:* For master's, thesis or alternative; for doctorate, comprehensive exam, thesis/dissertation. *Entrance requirements:* For master's and doctorate, GRE General Test, formal approval from departmental committee. Additional exam requirements/recommendations for international students: Required—TOEFL (minimum score 550 paper-based; 79 iBT). *Application deadline:* For fall admission, 6/1 priority date for domestic students, 1/15 priority date for international students; for spring admission, 9/1 priority date for domestic students, 6/15 priority date for international students. Applications are processed on a rolling basis. Application fee: $75. Electronic applications accepted. *Expenses:* $325 per credit hour full-time resident tuition, $733 per credit hour full-time non-resident tuition; $53.75 per credit hour fee plus $608 per term fee. *Financial support:* In 2016–17, 49 students received support, including 44 fellowships (averaging $2,997 per year), 29 research assistantships (averaging $15,794 per year); teaching assistantships, institutionally sponsored loans, scholarships/grants, health care benefits, and unspecified assistantships also available. Financial award application deadline: 5/1; financial award applicants required to submit FAFSA. *Faculty research:* Economics of the United States cotton and textile industries, natural resource management in semi-arid climates, commodity policy analysis, international trade in agricultural products, agribusiness analysis. *Total annual research expenditures:* $844,410. *Unit head:* Dr. Phillip N. Johnson, Chair, 806-834-0474, Fax: 806-742-1099, E-mail: phil.johnson@ttu.edu. *Application contact:* Dr. Darren Hudson, Graduate Adviser, 806-742-2821, Fax: 806-742-1099, E-mail: darren.hudson@ttu.edu.
Website: http://www.aaec.ttu.edu

**Thomas Jefferson University,** Jefferson School of Population Health, Philadelphia, PA 19107. Offers applied health economics and outcomes research (MS, PhD, Certificate); behavioral health science (PhD); health policy (MS, Certificate); healthcare quality and safety (MS, PhD); population health (Certificate); public health (MPH, Certificate). *Program availability:* Part-time, evening/weekend, online learning. Terminal master's awarded for partial completion of doctoral program. *Degree requirements:* For master's, thesis; for doctorate, comprehensive exam, thesis/dissertation. *Entrance requirements:* For master's, GRE or other graduate entrance exam (MCAT, LSAT, DAT, etc.), two letters of recommendation, curriculum vitae, transcripts from all undergraduate and graduate institutions; for doctorate, GRE (taken within the last 5 years), three letters of recommendation, curriculum vitae, transcripts from all undergraduate and graduate institutions. Additional exam requirements/recommendations for international students: Required—TOEFL. Electronic applications accepted. *Faculty research:* Applied health economics and outcomes research, behavioral and health sciences, chronic disease management, health policy, healthcare quality and patient safety, wellness and prevention.

**University of California, Santa Cruz,** Division of Graduate Studies, Division of Social Sciences, Program in Applied Economics and Finance, Santa Cruz, CA 95064. Offers MS. *Degree requirements:* For master's, thesis or alternative, project. *Entrance requirements:* For master's, GRE General Test, GRE Subject Test. Additional exam requirements/recommendations for international students: Required—TOEFL (minimum score 550 paper-based; 83 iBT); Recommended—IELTS (minimum score 8). Electronic applications accepted. *Faculty research:* Economic decision-making skills for the design and operation of complex institutional systems.

**University of Cincinnati,** Graduate School, Carl H. Lindner College of Business, Program in Applied Economics, Cincinnati, OH 45221. Offers MA. *Program availability:* Part-time, evening/weekend. *Faculty:* 12 full-time (4 women), 2 part-time/adjunct (1 woman). *Students:* 23 full-time (7 women), 14 part-time (7 women); includes 2 minority (1 Black or African American, non-Hispanic/Latino; 1 Two or more races, non-Hispanic/Latino), 19 international. Average age 27. 69 applicants, 45% accepted, 26 enrolled. In 2016, 25 master's awarded. *Degree requirements:* For master's, thesis optional. *Entrance requirements:* For master's, GRE General Test or GMAT, intermediate micro, macro theory, statistics, calculus. Additional exam requirements/recommendations for international students: Required—TOEFL (minimum score 577 paper-based; 90 iBT), IELTS (minimum score 6.5). *Application deadline:* For fall admission, 8/1 priority date for domestic students, 3/15 priority date for international students. Application fee: $65 ($70 for international students). Electronic applications accepted. *Expenses:* Contact institution. *Financial support:* In 2016–17, 23 students received support, including 13 teaching assistantships with full tuition reimbursements available (averaging $4,500 per year); career-related internships or fieldwork, scholarships/grants, tuition waivers (partial), and unspecified assistantships also available. Financial award application deadline: 3/15. *Faculty research:* Econometrics, labor markets, pollution markets, transportation, urban economics. *Unit head:* Dr. David Szymanski, Dean, 513-556-7001, Fax: 513-556-4891, E-mail: david.szymanski@uc.edu. *Application contact:* Dr. Debashis Pal, Academic Director, 513-556-2630, E-mail: debashis.pal@uc.edu.

**University of Georgia,** College of Agricultural and Environmental Sciences, Department of Agricultural and Applied Economics, Athens, GA 30602. Offers agricultural economics (MAE, MS, PhD); environmental economics (MS). *Degree requirements:* For master's, thesis (MS); for doctorate, thesis/dissertation. *Entrance requirements:* For master's and doctorate, GRE General Test. *Application deadline:* For fall admission, 7/1 priority date for domestic students; for spring admission, 11/15 for domestic students. Application fee: $50. Electronic applications accepted. *Financial support:* Fellowships, research assistantships, teaching assistantships, career-related internships or fieldwork, and unspecified assistantships available. *Unit head:* Dr. Octavio A. Ramirez, Interim Head, 706-542-2481, Fax: 706-542-0739, E-mail: oramirez@agecon.uga.edu. *Application contact:* Jeffrey D. Mullen, Graduate Coordinator, 706-543-0767, E-mail: jmullen@uga.edu.
Website: http://www.caes.uga.edu/departments/agecon

**University of Houston,** College of Liberal Arts and Social Sciences, Department of Economics, Houston, TX 77204. Offers applied economics (MA); economics (MA, PhD). Terminal master's awarded for partial completion of doctoral program. *Degree requirements:* For master's, thesis optional; for doctorate, comprehensive exam, thesis/dissertation. *Entrance requirements:* For master's and doctorate, GRE General Test, minimum GPA of 3.0, statement of purpose, three letters of recommendation. Additional exam requirements/recommendations for international students: Required—TOEFL (minimum score 550 paper-based; 79 iBT), IELTS (minimum score 6.5). Electronic applications accepted. *Faculty research:* Econometrics, labor economics, international economics.

**University of Idaho,** College of Graduate Studies, College of Agricultural and Life Sciences, Department of Agricultural Economics and Rural Sociology, Moscow, ID 83844. Offers applied economics (MS), including agribusiness, agricultural economics, applied economics. *Faculty:* 5 full-time. *Students:* 7 full-time. Average age 25. In 2016, 7 master's awarded. *Entrance requirements:* For master's, minimum GPA of 3.0. *Application deadline:* For fall admission, 8/1 for domestic students; for spring admission, 12/15 for domestic students. Applications are processed on a rolling basis. Application fee: $60. Electronic applications accepted. *Expenses:* Tuition, state resident: full-time $6460; part-time $414 per credit hour. Tuition, nonresident: full-time $21,268; part-time $1237 per credit hour. *Required fees:* $2070; $60 per credit hour. Full-time tuition and fees vary according to course load and reciprocity agreements. *Financial support:* Research assistantships and teaching assistantships available. Financial award applicants required to submit FAFSA. *Faculty research:* Crops: potatoes, blue grass; livestock: beef, dairy; rural and community development; natural resources and the environment; farm and ranch management. *Unit head:* Dr. Cathy Roheim, Department Head, 208-885-6262, Fax: 208-885-5759, E-mail: cdarby@uidaho.edu. *Application contact:* Sean Scoggin, Graduate Recruitment Coordinator, 208-885-4001, Fax: 208-885-4406, E-mail: graduateadmissions@uidaho.edu.
Website: http://www.uidaho.edu/cals/agricultural-economics-and-rural-sociology

**University of Illinois at Urbana–Champaign,** Graduate College, College of Agricultural, Consumer and Environmental Sciences, Department of Agricultural and Consumer Economics, Champaign, IL 61820. Offers agricultural and applied economics (MS, PhD).

**University of Massachusetts Boston,** College of Liberal Arts, Program in Applied Economics, Boston, MA 02125-3393. Offers MA. *Faculty:* 22 full-time (9 women), 7 part-time/adjunct (5 women). *Students:* 4 full-time (3 women), 11 part-time (3 women); includes 6 minority (2 Black or African American, non-Hispanic/Latino; 2 Asian, non-Hispanic/Latino; 2 Hispanic/Latino), 2 international. Average age 28. 18 applicants, 56% accepted, 7 enrolled. In 2016, 8 master's awarded. *Expenses:* Tuition, state resident: full-time $16,863. Tuition, nonresident: full-time $32,913. *Required fees:* $177. *Unit head:* Dr. Adugna Lemi, Chair of the Department. *Application contact:* Peggy Roldan Patel, Graduate Admissions Coordinator, 617-287-6400, Fax: 617-287-6236, E-mail: bos.gadm@dpc.umassp.edu.

**University of Michigan,** Rackham Graduate School, College of Literature, Science, and the Arts, Department of Economics, Program in Applied Economics, Ann Arbor, MI 48109. Offers AM. *Program availability:* Part-time. *Entrance requirements:* For master's, GRE General Test. Additional exam requirements/recommendations for international students: Required—TOEFL (minimum score 600 paper-based). *Expenses:* Tuition, state resident: full-time $21,466; part-time $1152 per credit hour. Tuition, nonresident: full-time $43,346; part-time $2367 per credit hour. Part-time tuition and fees vary according to course load, degree level and program. *Faculty research:* Econometric analysis transition, macro.

**University of Minnesota, Twin Cities Campus,** Graduate School, College of Food, Agricultural and Natural Resource Sciences, Applied Economics Graduate Program, Saint Paul, MN 55108. Offers MS, PhD. Terminal master's awarded for partial completion of doctoral program. *Degree requirements:* For master's, comprehensive exam, thesis; for doctorate, comprehensive exam, thesis/dissertation. *Entrance requirements:* For master's and doctorate, GRE, minimum GPA of 3.0 (preferred). Additional exam requirements/recommendations for international students: Required—TOEFL (minimum score 550 paper-based; 79 iBT), IELTS (minimum score 6.5). Electronic applications accepted. *Faculty research:* Consumer behavior, household and labor, policy analysis and health, production and marketing, resource and environmental, trade and development.

**University of Nevada, Las Vegas,** Graduate College, Lee Business School, Department of Management, Entrepreneurship and Technology, Las Vegas, NV 89154-6034. Offers data analytics (Certificate); data analytics and applied economics (MS); management information systems (MS, Certificate); new venture management (Certificate); MS/MS. *Program availability:* Part-time, evening/weekend. *Faculty:* 11 full-time (1 woman). *Students:* 28 full-time (12 women), 45 part-time (19 women); includes 31 minority (6 Black or African American, non-Hispanic/Latino; 9 Asian, non-Hispanic/Latino; 11 Hispanic/Latino; 5 Two or more races, non-Hispanic/Latino), 21 international. Average age 33. 64 applicants, 81% accepted, 30 enrolled. In 2016, 19 master's, 2 other advanced degrees awarded. *Degree requirements:* For master's, thesis optional. *Entrance requirements:* For master's, GMAT or GRE, bachelor's degree with minimum GPA 3.0; 2 letters of recommendation; for Certificate, GMAT or GRE. Additional exam requirements/recommendations for international students: Required—TOEFL (minimum score 550 paper-based; 80 iBT), IELTS (minimum score 7). *Application deadline:* For fall admission, 8/1 for domestic students, 5/1 for international students; for spring admission, 11/15 for domestic students, 10/1 for international students. Application fee: $60 ($95 for international students). Electronic applications accepted. *Expenses:* $269.25 per credit, $792 per 3-credit course; $9,634 per year resident; $23,274 per year non-resident; $7,094 fees non-resident (7 credits or more); $1,307 annual health insurance fee. *Financial support:* In 2016–17, 5 research assistantships with partial tuition reimbursements (averaging $10,000 per year), 5 teaching assistantships with partial tuition reimbursements (averaging $13,000 per year) were awarded; institutionally sponsored loans, scholarships/grants, health care benefits, and unspecified assistantships also available. Financial award application deadline: 3/15. *Faculty research:* Decision-making, publish or perish, ethical issues in information systems, IT-enabled decision making, business ethics. *Unit head:* Dr. Stoney Alder, Chair/Associate Professor, 702-895-2052, Fax: 702-895-4370, E-mail: stoney.alder@unlv.edu. *Application contact:* Dr. Greg Moody, Graduate Coordinator, 702-895-1365, Fax: 702-895-4370, E-mail: gregory.moody@unlv.edu.
Website: https://www.unlv.edu/met

**University of Nevada, Reno,** Graduate School, College of Agriculture, Biotechnology and Natural Resources, Department of Resource Economics, Reno, NV 89557. Offers MS, PhD. Terminal master's awarded for partial completion of doctoral program. *Degree requirements:* For master's, thesis optional; for doctorate, thesis/dissertation. *Entrance requirements:* For master's, GRE General Test, minimum GPA of 2.75; for doctorate, GRE General Test, minimum GPA of 3.0. Additional exam requirements/recommendations for international students: Required—TOEFL (minimum score 500 paper-based; 61 iBT), IELTS (minimum score 6). Electronic applications accepted. *Faculty research:* Econometrics, environmental valuation, natural resource and environmental policy analysis, public lands management.

**University of New Brunswick Fredericton,** School of Graduate Studies, Faculty of Arts, Department of Economics, Fredericton, NB E3B 5A3, Canada. Offers applied economics and finance (M Sc); economics (MA). M Sc offered on Saint John campus. *Entrance requirements:* For master's, minimum GPA of 3.0. Additional exam requirements/recommendations for international students: Required—TWE (minimum score 4), TOEFL (minimum score 580 paper-based) or IELTS (minimum score 7). Electronic applications accepted. *Faculty research:* Epidemiology and population health, micro/macro economics, economics of transportation, regional development, health economics, econometrics.

**The University of North Carolina at Charlotte,** Belk College of Business, Department of Economics, Charlotte, NC 28223-0001. Offers applied econometrics (Graduate Certificate); economics (MS). *Program availability:* Part-time, evening/weekend. *Faculty:* 17 full-time (6 women), 1 part-time/adjunct (0 women). *Students:* 35 full-time (15 women), 30 part-time (3 women); includes 19 minority (8 Black or African American, non-Hispanic/Latino; 3 Asian, non-Hispanic/Latino; 5 Hispanic/Latino; 3 Two or more races, non-Hispanic/Latino), 12 international. Average age 26. 50 applicants, 94% accepted, 24 enrolled. In 2016, 16 master's awarded. *Degree requirements:* For master's, thesis or project. *Entrance requirements:* For master's, GRE General Test, GMAT, undergraduate coursework that includes calculus, econometrics (or equivalent), intermediate macroeconomic theory, intermediate microeconomic theory; for Graduate Certificate, bachelor's degree, or its equivalent, from regionally-accredited college or university; minimum GPA of 2.75 on all previous work completed beyond high school (secondary school); statement of purpose; unofficial transcripts of all college course work. Additional exam requirements/recommendations for international students: Required—TOEFL (minimum score 523 paper-based, 70 iBT) or IELTS (6.5). *Application deadline:* For fall admission, 3/1 priority date for domestic and international students; for spring admission, 10/1 priority date for domestic and international students; for summer admission, 4/1 priority date for domestic and international students. Applications are processed on a rolling basis. Application fee: $75. Electronic applications accepted. *Expenses:* Contact institution. *Financial support:* Career-related internships or fieldwork, institutionally sponsored loans, scholarships/grants, and unspecified assistantships available. Support available to part-time students. Financial award application deadline: 3/1; financial award applicants required to submit FAFSA. *Faculty research:* Health care, taxation, energy, economic growth, monetary policy. *Total annual research expenditures:* $14,012. *Unit head:* Dr. Artie Zillante, Department Chair, 704-687-5375, Fax: 704-687-1384, E-mail: azillant@uncc.edu. *Application contact:* Kathy B. Giddings, Director of Graduate Admissions, 704-687-5503, Fax: 704-687-1668, E-mail: gradadm@uncc.edu.
Website: http://msecon.uncc.edu/

**The University of North Carolina at Greensboro,** Graduate School, Bryan School of Business and Economics, Department of Economics, Program in Applied Economics, Greensboro, NC 27412-5001. Offers MA, MA/PhD. *Degree requirements:* For master's, comprehensive exam, thesis or alternative. *Entrance requirements:* For master's, GRE. Additional exam requirements/recommendations for international students: Required—TOEFL. Electronic applications accepted.

**University of North Dakota,** Graduate School, College of Business and Public Administration, Applied Economics Program, Grand Forks, ND 58202. Offers MSAE. *Program availability:* Part-time, online learning. *Degree requirements:* For master's, comprehensive exam, thesis or alternative. *Entrance requirements:* For master's, GRE General Test. Additional exam requirements/recommendations for international students: Required—TOEFL (minimum score 550 paper-based; 79 iBT), IELTS (minimum score 6.5). *Application deadline:* For fall admission, 8/1 priority date for domestic and international students; for spring admission, 12/1 priority date for domestic and international students. Applications are processed on a rolling basis. Application fee: $35. Electronic applications accepted. *Financial support:* Fellowships with full and partial tuition reimbursements, research assistantships with full and partial tuition reimbursements, teaching assistantships with full and partial tuition reimbursements, Federal Work-Study, scholarships/grants, health care benefits, tuition waivers (full and partial), and unspecified assistantships available. Support available to part-time students. Financial award applicants required to submit FAFSA. *Unit head:* Dr. Cullen Goenner, Graduate Director, 701-777-3353, E-mail: cullen.goenner@mail.business.und.edu. *Application contact:* Matt Anderson, Admissions Specialist, 701-777-2947, Fax: 701-777-3619, E-mail: matthew.anderson@gradschool.und.edu.

**University of Oklahoma,** College of Arts and Sciences, Department of Economics, Norman, OK 73019. Offers applied economics (MA); economics (PhD); managerial economics (MA). *Faculty:* 21 full-time (6 women), 1 part-time/adjunct (0 women). *Students:* 33 full-time (9 women), 38 part-time (8 women); includes 21 minority (7 Black or African American, non-Hispanic/Latino; 1 American Indian or Alaska Native, non-Hispanic/Latino; 5 Asian, non-Hispanic/Latino; 7 Hispanic/Latino; 1 Two or more races, non-Hispanic/Latino), 22 international. Average age 31. 53 applicants, 45% accepted, 20 enrolled. In 2016, 20 master's, 3 doctorates awarded. Terminal master's awarded for partial completion of doctoral program. *Degree requirements:* For master's, comprehensive exam (for some programs); for doctorate, comprehensive exam, thesis/dissertation. *Entrance requirements:* For master's and doctorate, GRE, undergraduate degree in related field. Additional exam requirements/recommendations for international students: Required—TOEFL (minimum score 79 iBT) or IELTS (minimum score 6.5). *Application deadline:* For fall admission, 2/28 priority date for domestic students, 1/30 priority date for international students. Applications are processed on a rolling basis. Application fee: $50 ($100 for international students). Electronic applications accepted. *Expenses:* Tuition, state resident: full-time $4886; part-time $203.60 per credit hour. Tuition, nonresident: full-time $18,989; part-time $791.20 per credit hour. *Required fees:* $3283; $126.25 per credit hour. $126.50 per semester. *Financial support:* In 2016–17, 30 students received support, including 26 teaching assistantships with partial tuition reimbursements available (averaging $14,241 per year); fellowships with partial tuition reimbursements available, research assistantships with partial tuition reimbursements available, scholarships/grants, and health care benefits also available. Financial award application deadline: 6/1; financial award applicants required to submit FAFSA. *Faculty research:* Public economics, development economics, international economics, industrial organization, applied econometrics. *Total annual research expenditures:*

## Applied Economics

$249,871. *Unit head:* Dr. Gary Hoover, Department Chair and Professor of Economics, 405-325-5857, E-mail: ghoover@ou.edu. *Application contact:* Gregory Burge, Director of Graduate Studies/Associate Professor, 405-325-2358, E-mail: gburge@ou.edu. Website: http://cas.ou.edu/economics

**University of Pennsylvania,** Wharton School, Program in Applied Economics, Philadelphia, PA 19104. Offers PhD. *Expenses: Tuition:* Full-time $31,068; part-time $5762 per course. *Required fees:* $3200; $336 per course. Full-time tuition and fees vary according to degree level, program and student level. Part-time tuition and fees vary according to course load, degree level and program.

**University of Regina,** Faculty of Graduate Studies and Research, Faculty of Arts, Department of Economics, Regina, SK S4S 0A2, Canada. Offers applied economics and policy analysis (MA). *Program availability:* Part-time. *Faculty:* 13 full-time (4 women), 6 part-time/adjunct (1 woman). *Students:* 12 full-time (3 women), 5 part-time (1 woman). 49 applicants, 20% accepted. In 2016, 5 master's awarded. *Degree requirements:* For master's, thesis (for some programs), research project. *Entrance requirements:* For master's, writing sample on approved topic. Additional exam requirements/recommendations for international students: Required—TOEFL (minimum score 580 paper-based; 80 iBT), IELTS (minimum score 6.5), PTE (minimum score 59). *Application deadline:* For fall admission, 3/1 for domestic and international students. Application fee: $100. Electronic applications accepted. *Financial support:* In 2016–17, 5 fellowships (averaging $6,400 per year), 11 teaching assistantships (averaging $2,534 per year) were awarded; scholarships/grants also available. *Unit head:* Dr. Monika Cule, Department Head, 306-585-4708, Fax: 306-585-4815, E-mail: monika.cule@uregina.ca. *Application contact:* Dr. Viktoriya Galushko, Graduate Coordinator, 306-585-4191, Fax: 306-585-4815, E-mail: viktoriya.galushko@uregina.ca.
Website: http://www.uregina.ca/arts/economics

**University of Vermont,** Graduate College, College of Agriculture and Life Sciences, Department of Community Development and Applied Economics, Burlington, VT 05405. Offers community development and applied economics (MS); public administration (MPA). *Students:* 16 full-time (10 women); includes 1 minority (Asian, non-Hispanic/Latino). Average age 27. 25 applicants, 84% accepted, 7 enrolled. In 2016, 7 master's awarded. *Degree requirements:* For master's, thesis. *Entrance requirements:* For master's, GRE General Test. Additional exam requirements/recommendations for international students: Required—TOEFL (minimum score 550 paper-based; 80 iBT). *Application deadline:* For fall admission, 4/1 priority date for domestic students, 4/1 for international students; for spring admission, 11/15 for domestic students. Applications are processed on a rolling basis. Application fee: $65. Electronic applications accepted. *Expenses:* Tuition, state resident: full-time $5814. Tuition, nonresident: full-time $14,670. *Financial support:* Fellowships, research assistantships, teaching assistantships, and career-related internships or fieldwork available. Financial award application deadline: 3/1. *Faculty research:* Agricultural production and marketing. *Unit head:* David Conner, 802-656-2001, E-mail: david.conner@uvm.edu.

**University of Wisconsin–Madison,** Graduate School, College of Agricultural and Life Sciences, Department of Agricultural and Applied Economics, Madison, WI 53706. Offers MA, MS, PhD. *Program availability:* Part-time. *Degree requirements:* For doctorate, thesis/dissertation, preliminary exams. *Entrance requirements:* For master's and doctorate, GRE General Test. Additional exam requirements/recommendations for international students: Required—TOEFL (minimum score 580 paper-based; 92 iBT). Electronic applications accepted. *Faculty research:* Environmental and resource economics, international development, community economics, energy economics, agricultural technology, food systems, markets and trade.

**University of Wyoming,** College of Agriculture and Natural Resources, Department of Agricultural and Applied Economics, Laramie, WY 82071. Offers MS. *Program availability:* Part-time. *Degree requirements:* For master's, thesis (for some programs). *Entrance requirements:* For master's, GRE General Test, minimum GPA of 3.0.

Additional exam requirements/recommendations for international students: Required—TOEFL. Electronic applications accepted. *Faculty research:* Farm management, agricultural markets, water economics, community development, agricultural business.

**Utah State University,** School of Graduate Studies, College of Business and College of Agriculture, Department of Economics, Program in Applied Economics, Logan, UT 84322. Offers MS. *Program availability:* Part-time. *Degree requirements:* For master's, thesis optional. *Entrance requirements:* For master's, GRE General Test, minimum GPA of 3.0.

**Virginia Polytechnic Institute and State University,** Graduate School, College of Agriculture and Life Sciences, Blacksburg, VA 24061. Offers agricultural and applied economics (MS); agricultural and life sciences (MS); animal and poultry science (MS, PhD); crop and soil environmental sciences (MS, PhD); dairy science (MS); entomology (PhD); horticulture (MS, PhD); human nutrition, foods and exercise (MS, PhD); life sciences (MS, PhD); plant pathology, physiology and weed science (PhD). *Faculty:* 235 full-time (69 women). *Students:* 360 full-time (193 women), 150 part-time (89 women); includes 73 minority (30 Black or African American, non-Hispanic/Latino; 15 Asian, non-Hispanic/Latino; 15 Hispanic/Latino; 13 Two or more races, non-Hispanic/Latino), 113 international. Average age 29. 311 applicants, 45% accepted, 106 enrolled. In 2016, 111 master's, 50 doctorates awarded. *Degree requirements:* For master's, comprehensive exam (for some programs), thesis (for some programs); for doctorate, comprehensive exam (for some programs), thesis/dissertation (for some programs). *Entrance requirements:* For master's and doctorate, GRE/GMAT. Additional exam requirements/recommendations for international students: Required—TOEFL (minimum score 80 iBT). *Application deadline:* For fall admission, 8/1 for domestic students, 4/1 for international students; for spring admission, 1/1 for domestic students, 9/1 for international students. Applications are processed on a rolling basis. Application fee: $75. Electronic applications accepted. *Expenses:* Tuition, state resident: full-time $12,467; part-time $692.50 per credit hour. Tuition, nonresident: full-time $25,095; part-time $1394.25 per credit hour. *Required fees:* $2669; $491.50 per semester. Tuition and fees vary according to course load, campus/location and program. *Financial support:* In 2016–17, 258 research assistantships with full tuition reimbursements (averaging $20,636 per year), 107 teaching assistantships with full tuition reimbursements (averaging $20,004 per year) were awarded. Financial award application deadline: 3/1; financial award applicants required to submit FAFSA. *Total annual research expenditures:* $46.9 million. *Unit head:* Dr. Alan L. Grant, Dean, 540-231-4152, Fax: 540-231-4163, E-mail: algrant@vt.edu. *Application contact:* Crystal Tawney, Administrative Assistant, 540-231-4152, Fax: 540-231-4163, E-mail: cdtawney@vt.edu. Website: http://www.cals.vt.edu/

**Washington & Jefferson College,** Graduate and Continuing Studies, Washington, PA 15301. Offers applied health care economics and outcomes management (MS); professional accounting (MAC); professional writing (Graduate Certificate); thanatology (Graduate Certificate).

**Western Kentucky University,** Graduate Studies, Gordon Ford College of Business, Program in Applied Economics, Bowling Green, KY 42101. Offers MA.

**Western Michigan University,** Graduate College, College of Arts and Sciences, Department of Economics, Kalamazoo, MI 49008. Offers applied economics (MA, PhD). *Degree requirements:* For master's, thesis; for doctorate, thesis/dissertation.

**Wright State University,** Graduate School, Raj Soin College of Business, Department of Economics, Program in Social and Applied Economics, Dayton, OH 45435. Offers MS. *Expenses:* Tuition, state resident: full-time $9952; part-time $622 per credit hour. Tuition, nonresident: full-time $16,960; part-time $1060 per credit hour. *Unit head:* Dr. Len Kloft, Director, 937-775-2322, Fax: 937-775-2441, E-mail: leonard.kloft@wright.edu. *Application contact:* Dr. Len Kloft, Director, 937-775-2322, Fax: 937-775-2441, E-mail: leonard.kloft@wright.edu.

# Economic Development

**Albany State University,** College of Arts and Humanities, Albany, GA 31705-2717. Offers criminal justice (MS); English education (M Ed); public administration (MPA), including community and economic development, criminal justice administration, health administration and policy, human resources management, public management, public policy, water resources management and policy; social work (MSW). *Program availability:* Part-time. *Degree requirements:* For master's, comprehensive exam, professional portfolio (for MPA), internship, capstone report. *Entrance requirements:* For master's, GRE, MAT, minimum GPA of 3.0, official transcript, pre-medical record/certificate of immunization, letters of reference. *Application deadline:* For fall admission, 6/1 for domestic students, 5/1 for international students; for spring admission, 11/1 for domestic students, 10/1 for international students. Applications are processed on a rolling basis. Application fee: $20. Electronic applications accepted. *Financial support:* Application deadline: 4/15; applicants required to submit FAFSA. *Faculty research:* HIV prevention for minority students. *Unit head:* Dr. Rani George, Dean, 229-430-1877, Fax: 229-430-4296. *Application contact:* Jeffrey Pierce, II, Graduate Admissions Counselor, 229-430-4646, Fax: 229-430-4105, E-mail: jeffrey.pierce@asurams.edu.
Website: https://www.asurams.edu/Academics/collegeofarthum/

**The American University in Cairo,** School of Business, Cairo, Egypt. Offers business administration (MBA); economics (MA); economics in international development (MA, Diploma); finance (MS). *Program availability:* Part-time, evening/weekend. *Faculty:* 24 full-time (4 women), 5 part-time/adjunct (2 women). *Students:* 53 full-time (24 women), 80 part-time (41 women), 1 international. Average age 29. 109 applicants, 45% accepted, 35 enrolled. In 2016, 49 master's awarded. *Degree requirements:* For master's, comprehensive exam (for some programs), thesis (for some programs). *Entrance requirements:* For master's, GMAT, GRE. Additional exam requirements/recommendations for international students: Required—TOEFL (minimum score 450 paper-based; 45 iBT), IELTS (minimum score 5). *Application deadline:* For fall admission, 2/1 priority date for domestic and international students; for spring admission, 10/15 priority date for domestic and international students. Applications are processed on a rolling basis. Application fee: $80. Electronic applications accepted. *Expenses:* Contact institution. *Financial support:* Fellowships with partial tuition reimbursements, scholarships/grants, tuition waivers (partial), and unspecified assistantships available. Financial award application deadline: 3/10. *Faculty research:* Marketing and quality management, banking operations management, economics, finance. *Unit head:* Dr. Nizar Becheikh, Interim Dean, 20-2-2615-2120, E-mail: nbecheikh@aucegypt.edu. *Application contact:* Maha Hegazi, Director of Graduate Admissions, 20-2-2615-1462, E-mail: mahahegazi@aucegypt.edu.
Website: http://www.aucegypt.edu/Business/Pages/default.aspx

**Ball State University,** Graduate School, College of Sciences and Humanities, Department of Political Science, Program in Public Administration, Muncie, IN 47306. Offers public administration (MPA, Certificate), including administrative (MPA), community and economic development (MPA), criminal justice and criminology (MPA), emergency management and homeland security (MPA). *Program availability:* Part-time. *Degree requirements:* For master's, comprehensive exam. *Entrance requirements:* For master's, GRE General Test, minimum bacclaureate GPA of 2.8, two letters of recommendation. Additional exam requirements/recommendations for international students: Required—TOEFL (minimum score 550 paper-based; 79 iBT), IELTS (minimum score 6.5). Electronic applications accepted. *Faculty research:* Employment training programs, personnel and labor relations, planning.

**Ball State University,** Graduate School, Miller College of Business, Interdepartmental Program in Business Administration, Muncie, IN 47306. Offers business administration (MBA); business essentials (Graduate Certificate); community and economic development (Certificate). *Accreditation:* AACSB. *Program availability:* Part-time, 100% online, blended/hybrid learning. *Entrance requirements:* For master's, GMAT or GRE, minimum baccalaureate GPA of 2.75 or 3.0 in latter half of baccalauareate, resume or curriculum vitae, four professional letters of recommendation. Additional exam requirements/recommendations for international students: Required—TOEFL (minimum score 550 paper-based; 79 iBT), IELTS (minimum score 6.5). Electronic applications accepted. *Expenses:* Contact institution.

**Boston University,** Metropolitan College, Department of Administrative Sciences, Boston, MA 02215. Offers applied business analytics (MS); economic development and tourism management (MSAS); enterprise risk management (MS); financial management (MS); global marketing management (MS); innovation and technology (MSAS); insurance management (MSM); project management (MS); supply chain management (MS). *Accreditation:* AACSB. *Program availability:* Part-time, evening/weekend, online learning. *Faculty:* 15 full-time (3 women), 22 part-time/adjunct (3 women). *Students:* 301 full-time (146 women), 934 part-time (501 women); includes 237 minority (81 Black or African American, non-Hispanic/Latino; 5 American Indian or Alaska Native, non-Hispanic/Latino; 60 Asian, non-Hispanic/Latino; 76 Hispanic/Latino; 1 Native Hawaiian or other Pacific Islander, non-Hispanic/Latino; 14 Two or more races, non-Hispanic/Latino), 514 international. Average age 31. 593 applicants, 69% accepted, 260 enrolled. In 2016, 263 master's awarded. *Degree requirements:* For master's, thesis optional. *Entrance requirements:* For master's, 1 year of work experience, minimum GPA of 3.0. Additional exam requirements/recommendations for international students: Required—TOEFL (minimum score 84 iBT). *Application deadline:* Applications are processed on a rolling basis. Application fee: $80. Electronic applications accepted. *Expenses:* Contact institution. *Financial support:* In 2016–17, 15 students received support, including 14 research assistantships (averaging $8,400 per year); career-related internships or fieldwork, Federal Work-Study, and unspecified assistantships also available. *Faculty research:* International business, innovative process. *Unit head:* Dr. John Sullivan, Chair, 617-353-3016, E-mail: adminsc@bu.edu. *Application contact:* Fiona Niven, Administrative Sciences Department, 617-353-3016, E-mail: adminsc@bu.edu. Website: http://www.bu.edu/met/academic-community/departments/administrative-sciences/

**The Catholic University of America,** Busch School of Business and Economics, Washington, DC 20064. Offers accounting (MS); business analysis (MSBA); integral economic development management (MA); integral economic development policy (MA); management (MS), including Federal contract management, human resource management, leadership and management, project management, sales management. *Program availability:* Part-time. *Faculty:* 30 full-time (7 women), 30 part-time/adjunct (5 women). *Students:* 60 full-time (32 women), 26 part-time (14 women); includes 26 minority (11 Black or African American, non-Hispanic/Latino; 8 Asian, non-Hispanic/Latino; 5 Hispanic/Latino; 2 Two or more races, non-Hispanic/Latino), 22 international. Average age 29. 121 applicants, 77% accepted, 64 enrolled. In 2016, 48 master's awarded. *Degree requirements:* For master's, comprehensive exam (for some programs). *Entrance requirements:* For master's, GRE General Test, statement of purpose, official copies of academic transcripts, three letters of recommendation. Additional exam requirements/recommendations for international students: Required—TOEFL (minimum score 550 paper-based; 80 iBT). *Application deadline:* For fall admission, 7/15 priority date for domestic students, 7/1 for international students; for spring admission, 11/15 priority date for domestic students, 11/1 for international students. Applications are processed on a rolling basis. Application fee: $55. Electronic applications accepted. *Expenses:* $42,850 per year; $1,170 per credit; $200 per semester part-time fees. *Financial support:* Fellowships, research assistantships, teaching assistantships, Federal Work-Study, scholarships/grants, tuition waivers (full and partial), and unspecified assistantships available. Financial award application deadline: 2/1; financial award applicants required to submit FAFSA. *Faculty research:* Integrity of the marketing process, economics of energy and the environment, emerging markets, social change, international finance and economic development. *Total annual research expenditures:* $3,698. *Unit head:* Dr. William Bowman, Dean, 202-319-5290, Fax: 202-319-4426, E-mail: otey@cua.edu. *Application contact:* Director of Graduate Admissions, 202-319-5057, Fax: 202-319-6533, E-mail: cua-admissions@cua.edu. Website: http://business.cua.edu/

**Claremont Graduate University,** Graduate Programs, School of Social Science, Policy and Evaluation, Department of Economics, Claremont, CA 91711-6160. Offers behavioral economics and neuroeconomics (PhD); business and financial economics (MA, PhD); economic development (Certificate); international economic and development policy (PhD); international economics policy and development (MA); international money and finance (PhD); political economy and public economics (PhD); political economy and public policy (MA); MBA/PhD. *Program availability:* Part-time. *Faculty:* 5 full-time (1 woman), 2 part-time/adjunct (0 women). *Students:* 92 full-time (31 women), 34 part-time (15 women); includes 14 minority (4 Black or African American, non-Hispanic/Latino; 7 Asian, non-Hispanic/Latino; 2 Hispanic/Latino; 1 Two or more races, non-Hispanic/Latino), 67 international. Average age 33. In 2016, 20 master's, 16 doctorates awarded. *Entrance requirements:* For master's and doctorate, GRE General Test or GMAT. Additional exam requirements/recommendations for international students: Required—TOEFL (minimum score 75 iBT). *Application deadline:* For fall admission, 2/1 priority date for domestic and international students. Applications are processed on a rolling basis. Application fee: $80. Electronic applications accepted. *Expenses:* Tuition: Full-time $44,328; part-time $1847 per unit. *Required fees:* $600; $300 per semester. Tuition and fees vary according to course load and program. *Financial support:* Fellowships, research assistantships, teaching assistantships, Federal Work-Study, institutionally sponsored loans, and scholarships/grants available. Support available to part-time students. Financial award application deadline: 2/15; financial award applicants required to submit FAFSA. *Faculty research:* International and financial economics, law and economics, regulation, public choice economics. *Unit head:* Paul Zak, Chair, 909-621-8788, E-mail: paul.zak@cgu.edu. *Application contact:* Paige Piontkowsky, Senior Assistant Director of Admissions, 909-607-3240, E-mail: paige.piontkowsky@cgu.edu. Website: https://www.cgu.edu/school/ssspe/programs/?areas_of_study=economics

**Cleveland State University,** College of Graduate Studies, Maxine Goodman Levin College of Urban Affairs, Program in Environmental Studies, Cleveland, OH 44115. Offers environmental nonprofit management (MAES); environmental planning (MAES); policy and administration (MAES); sustainable economic development (MAES); urban economic development (Certificate); JD/MAES. *Program availability:* Part-time, evening/weekend. *Faculty:* 16 full-time (8 women), 13 part-time/adjunct (5 women). *Students:* 8 full-time (4 women), 3 part-time (1 woman); includes 2 minority (both Black or African American, non-Hispanic/Latino), 1 international. Average age 28. 10 applicants, 100% accepted, 5 enrolled. In 2016, 1 master's awarded. *Degree requirements:* For master's, thesis or alternative, exit project. *Entrance requirements:* For master's, GRE General Test (minimum score: verbal and quantitative combined 40th percentile, analytical writing 4.0), minimum GPA of 3.0. Additional exam requirements/recommendations for international students: Required—TOEFL (minimum score 550 paper-based; 78 iBT), IELTS (6.0), or International Test of English Proficiency (iTEP). *Application deadline:* For fall admission, 7/1 priority date for domestic students, 5/15 for international students; for spring admission, 11/15 for domestic students, 11/1 for international students; for summer admission, 4/1 for domestic students, 3/15 for international students. Applications are processed on a rolling basis. Application fee: $40. Electronic applications accepted. *Expenses:* Contact institution. *Financial support:* In 2016–17, 4 students received support, including research assistantships with tuition reimbursements available (averaging $7,200 per year), 1 teaching assistantship with partial tuition reimbursement available (averaging $2,400 per year); scholarships/grants, tuition waivers (full and partial), and unspecified assistantships also available. Support available to part-time students. Financial award application deadline: 3/1; financial award applicants required to submit FAFSA. *Faculty research:* Environmental policy and administration, environmental planning, geographic information systems (GIS), urban sustainability planning and management, energy policy, land re-use. *Unit head:* Dr. Sanda Kaufman, Professor/Program Director, 216-687-2367, Fax: 216-687-9239, E-mail: s.kaufman@csuohio.edu. *Application contact:* David Arrighi, Graduate Academic Advisor, 216-523-7522, Fax: 216-687-5398, E-mail: d.arrighi@csuohio.edu. Website: http://urban.csuohio.edu/academics/graduate/maes/

**Cleveland State University,** College of Graduate Studies, Maxine Goodman Levin College of Urban Affairs, Program in Public Administration, Cleveland, OH 44115. Offers economic development (MPA); non-profit management (MPA); public management (MPA); JD/MPA. *Accreditation:* NASPAA. *Program availability:* Part-time, evening/weekend. *Faculty:* 16 full-time (8 women), 13 part-time/adjunct (5 women). *Students:* 19 full-time (12 women), 40 part-time (24 women); includes 18 minority (14 Black or African American, non-Hispanic/Latino; 1 Asian, non-Hispanic/Latino; 1 Hispanic/Latino; 2 Two or more races, non-Hispanic/Latino), 4 international. Average age 31. 79 applicants,

77% accepted, 12 enrolled. In 2016, 29 master's awarded. *Degree requirements:* For master's, thesis or alternative, exit project. *Entrance requirements:* For master's, GRE General Test (minimum scores in 40th percentile verbal and quantitative, 4.0 writing), minimum GPA of 3.0. Additional exam requirements/recommendations for international students: Required—TOEFL (minimum score 550 paper-based; 78 iBT), IELTS (6.0), or International Test of English Proficiency (iTEP). *Application deadline:* For fall admission, 7/1 priority date for domestic students, 5/15 for international students; for spring admission, 11/15 for domestic students, 11/1 for international students; for summer admission, 4/1 for domestic students, 3/15 for international students. Applications are processed on a rolling basis. Application fee: $40. Electronic applications accepted. *Expenses:* Contact institution. *Financial support:* In 2016–17, 16 students received support, including 5 research assistantships with full tuition reimbursements available (averaging $7,200 per year), 1 teaching assistantship with partial tuition reimbursement available (averaging $2,400 per year); scholarships/grants, tuition waivers (full and partial), and unspecified assistantships also available. Support available to part-time students. Financial award application deadline: 3/1; financial award applicants required to submit FAFSA. *Faculty research:* City management, nonprofit management, health care administration, public management, economic development. *Unit head:* Dr. Nicholas Zingale, Director, 216-802-3389, Fax: 216-687-9342, E-mail: n.zingale@csuohio.edu. *Application contact:* David Arrighi, Graduate Academic Advisor, 216-523-7522, Fax: 216-687-5398, E-mail: d.arrighi@csuohio.edu. Website: http://urban.csuohio.edu/academics/graduate/mpa/

**Cleveland State University,** College of Graduate Studies, Maxine Goodman Levin College of Urban Affairs, Program in Urban Planning, Design, and Development, Cleveland, OH 44115. Offers environmental sustainability (MUPDD); housing and neighborhood development (MUPDD); urban economic development (Certificate); JD/MUPDD. *Accreditation:* ACSP. *Program availability:* Part-time, evening/weekend. *Faculty:* 16 full-time (8 women), 13 part-time/adjunct (5 women). *Students:* 8 full-time (3 women), 26 part-time (15 women); includes 4 minority (2 Black or African American, non-Hispanic/Latino; 1 Asian, non-Hispanic/Latino; 1 Two or more races, non-Hispanic/Latino), 2 international. Average age 28. 48 applicants, 56% accepted, 14 enrolled. In 2016, 21 master's awarded. *Degree requirements:* For master's, thesis or alternative, exit project. *Entrance requirements:* For master's, GRE General Test (minimum score: 50th percentile combined verbal and quantitative, 4.0 analytical writing), minimum GPA of 3.0. Additional exam requirements/recommendations for international students: Required—TOEFL (minimum score 550 paper-based; 78 iBT), IELTS (6.0), or International Test of English Proficiency (iTEP). *Application deadline:* For fall admission, 7/1 priority date for domestic students, 5/15 for international students; for spring admission, 11/15 for domestic students, 11/1 for international students; for summer admission, 4/1 for domestic students, 3/15 for international students. Applications are processed on a rolling basis. Application fee: $40. Electronic applications accepted. *Expenses:* Contact institution. *Financial support:* In 2016–17, 10 students received support, including 5 research assistantships with full tuition reimbursements available (averaging $7,200 per year), 3 teaching assistantships with partial tuition reimbursements available (averaging $2,400 per year); scholarships/grants, tuition waivers (full and partial), and unspecified assistantships also available. Support available to part-time students. Financial award application deadline: 3/1; financial award applicants required to submit FAFSA. *Faculty research:* Housing and neighborhood development, urban housing policy, environmental sustainability, economic development, GIS and planning decision support. *Unit head:* Dr. Stephanie Ryberg-Webster, Assistant Professor/Director of MUPD Program, 216-802-3386, Fax: 216-687-2013, E-mail: s.ryberg@csuohio.edu. *Application contact:* David Arrighi, Graduate Academic Advisor, 216-523-7522, Fax: 216-687-5398, E-mail: d.arrighi@csuohio.edu. Website: http://urban.csuohio.edu/academics/graduate/mupdd/

**Concordia University,** School of Graduate Studies, Faculty of Arts and Science, School of Community and Public Affairs, Montréal, QC H3G 1M8, Canada. Offers community economic development (Diploma).

**Cornell University,** Graduate School, Graduate Fields of Agriculture and Life Sciences, Field of Applied Economics and Management, Ithaca, NY 14853. Offers agricultural finance (MS, PhD); applied econometrics and qualitative analysis (MS, PhD); economics of development (MS, PhD); environmental economics (MS, PhD); environmental management (MPS); farm management and production economics (MS, PhD); marketing and food distribution (MS, PhD); public policy analysis (MS, PhD); resource economics (PhD). *Entrance requirements:* For master's and doctorate, GRE. Additional exam requirements/recommendations for international students: Required—TOEFL.

**Cornell University,** Graduate School, Graduate Fields of Architecture, Art and Planning, Field of City and Regional Planning, Ithaca, NY 14853. Offers city and regional planning (MRP, PhD); environmental planning and design (MRP, PhD); historic preservation planning (MA); international development planning (MRP, PhD); planning theory and systems analysis (MRP, PhD); regional economics and development planning (MRP, PhD); regional science (MRP, PhD); social and health systems planning (MRP, PhD); urban and regional theory (MRP, PhD); urban planning history (MRP, PhD). *Accreditation:* ACSP (one or more programs are accredited). *Degree requirements:* For master's, thesis (MA); for doctorate, comprehensive exam, thesis/dissertation. *Entrance requirements:* For master's and doctorate, GRE General Test, 2 letters of recommendation. Additional exam requirements/recommendations for international students: Required—TOEFL (minimum score 600 paper-based; 77 iBT). Electronic applications accepted. *Faculty research:* Land use planning, economic development, international development, historic preservation, community development.

**Cornell University,** Graduate School, Graduate Fields of Arts and Sciences, Field of Economics, Ithaca, NY 14853. Offers applied economics (PhD); basic analytical economics (PhD); econometrics and economic statistics (PhD); economic development and planning (PhD); economic theory (PhD); industrial organization and control (PhD); international economics (PhD); labor economics (PhD); monetary and macro economics (PhD); public finance (PhD). *Degree requirements:* For doctorate, comprehensive exam, thesis/dissertation. *Entrance requirements:* For doctorate, GRE General Test, 3 letters of recommendation. Additional exam requirements/recommendations for international students: Required—TOEFL (minimum score 550 paper-based; 77 iBT). Electronic applications accepted. *Faculty research:* Learning and games, economics of education, political economy, transfer payments, time series and nonparametrics.

**East Carolina University,** Graduate School, Thomas Harriot College of Arts and Sciences, Department of Geography, Planning, and Environment, Greenville, NC 27858-4353. Offers economic development (Certificate); geographic information science and technology (Certificate); geography (MA), including geography, planning, rural development. *Program availability:* Part-time, evening/weekend. *Students:* 15 full-time (8 women), 11 part-time (5 women); includes 6 minority (2 Black or African American, non-Hispanic/Latino; 1 Asian, non-Hispanic/Latino; 3 Hispanic/Latino). Average age 28. 17 applicants, 94% accepted, 9 enrolled. In 2016, 1 master's awarded. *Degree requirements:* For master's, one foreign language, comprehensive exam, thesis optional. *Entrance requirements:* For master's, GRE General Test. Additional exam requirements/recommendations for international students: Required—TOEFL. *Application deadline:* For fall admission, 6/1 priority date for domestic students; for

spring admission, 10/15 for domestic students. Applications are processed on a rolling basis. Application fee: $50. *Financial support:* Research assistantships with partial tuition reimbursements, teaching assistantships with partial tuition reimbursements, and Federal Work-Study available. Support available to part-time students. Financial award application deadline: 6/1. *Unit head:* Dr. Burrell Montz, Chair, 252-328-6086, E-mail: montzb@ecu.edu. *Application contact:* Dean of Graduate School, 252-328-6012, Fax: 252-328-6071, E-mail: gradschool@ecu.edu.
Website: http://www.ecu.edu/geog/

**Eastern University,** School of Leadership and Development, St. Davids, PA 19087-3696. Offers economic development (MBA), including international development, urban development (MA, MBA); international development (MA), including global development, urban development (MA, MBA); nonprofit management (MS); organizational leadership (MA); M Div/MBA. *Program availability:* Part-time, evening/weekend, online learning. *Students:* 59 full-time (32 women), 67 part-time (35 women); includes 40 minority (32 Black or African American, non-Hispanic/Latino; 1 Asian, non-Hispanic/Latino; 5 Hispanic/Latino; 2 Two or more races, non-Hispanic/Latino), 22 international. Average age 33. In 2016, 44 master's awarded. *Entrance requirements:* Additional exam requirements/recommendations for international students: Required—TOEFL (minimum score 550 paper-based; 79 iBT). *Application deadline:* Applications are processed on a rolling basis. Application fee: $35. Electronic applications accepted. Application fee is waived when completed online. *Expenses:* $690 per credit. *Faculty research:* Micro-level economic development, China welfare and economic development, macroethics, micro- and macro-level economic development in transitional economics, organizational effectiveness. *Unit head:* Michael Dziedziak, Executive Director of Enrollment, 800-452-0996, E-mail: gpsadmissions@eastern.edu. Website: http://www.eastern.edu/academics/programs/graduate-programs-leadership-development

**East Tennessee State University,** School of Graduate Studies, College of Arts and Sciences, Department of Political Science, International Affairs and Public Administration, Johnson City, TN 37614. Offers economic development (Postbaccalaureate Certificate); not-for-profit administration (MPA); planning and development (MPA); public financial management (MPA); urban planning (Postbaccalaureate Certificate). *Program availability:* Part-time. *Degree requirements:* For master's, internship. *Entrance requirements:* For master's, GRE General Test, three letters of recommendation; for Postbaccalaureate Certificate, GRE General Test. Additional exam requirements/recommendations for international students: Required—TOEFL (minimum score 550 paper-based; 79 iBT). Electronic applications accepted. *Faculty research:* Labor issues, presidency, public law in American politics, East Asian politics, European politics, Middle Eastern politics, development in comparative politics, international political economy, international relations, world politics in international affairs.

**Fordham University,** Graduate School of Arts and Sciences, Program in International Political Economy and Development, New York, NY 10458. Offers MA, Certificate. *Program availability:* Part-time, evening/weekend. *Students:* 38 full-time (16 women), 13 part-time (10 women); includes 8 minority (1 Black or African American, non-Hispanic/Latino; 4 Asian, non-Hispanic/Latino; 3 Native Hawaiian or other Pacific Islander, non-Hispanic/Latino), 16 international. Average age 27. 207 applicants, 35% accepted, 24 enrolled. In 2016, 24 master's, 1 other advanced degree awarded. *Degree requirements:* For master's, comprehensive exam. *Entrance requirements:* For master's, GRE General Test. Additional exam requirements/recommendations for international students: Required—TOEFL (minimum score 600 paper-based). *Application deadline:* For fall admission, 1/4 priority date for domestic students; for spring admission, 11/1 for domestic students. Application fee: $70. Electronic applications accepted. *Financial support:* In 2016–17, 35 students received support, including 4 fellowships with tuition reimbursements available (averaging $17,014 per year); research assistantships with tuition reimbursements available, career-related internships or fieldwork, institutionally sponsored loans, tuition waivers (full and partial), and unspecified assistantships also available. Financial award application deadline: 1/4; financial award applicants required to submit FAFSA. *Faculty research:* International economics, comparative international politics, international banking and finance, international development, emerging markets and country risk analysis. *Unit head:* Dr. Henry Schwalbenberg, Chair, 718-817-3866, Fax: 718-817-3518. *Application contact:* Bernadette Valentino-Morrison, Director of Graduate Admissions, 718-817-4419, Fax: 718-817-3566, E-mail: valentinomor@fordham.edu.

**Georgetown University,** Graduate School of Arts and Sciences, Department of Economics, Washington, DC 20057. Offers econometrics (PhD); economic development (PhD); economic theory (PhD); industrial organization (PhD); international macro and finance (PhD); international trade (PhD); labor economics (PhD); macroeconomics (PhD); public economics and political economy (PhD); MA/PhD; MS/MA. *Degree requirements:* For doctorate, comprehensive exam, thesis/dissertation. *Entrance requirements:* For doctorate, GRE General Test. Additional exam requirements/recommendations for international students: Required—TOEFL. *Faculty research:* International economics, economic development.

**Georgia Institute of Technology,** Graduate Studies, College of Architecture, School of City and Regional Planning, Atlanta, GA 30332-0001. Offers city and regional planning (PhD); economic development (MCRP); environmental planning and management (MCRP); geographic information systems (MCRP); land and community development (MCRP); land use planning (MCRP); transportation (MCRP); urban design (MCRP); MCP/MSCE. *Accreditation:* ACSP. *Degree requirements:* For master's, thesis, internship. *Entrance requirements:* For master's, GRE General Test, minimum GPA of 2.7. Additional exam requirements/recommendations for international students: Required—TOEFL. Electronic applications accepted.

**Georgia State University,** Andrew Young School of Policy Studies, Department of Public Management and Policy, Atlanta, GA 30303. Offers criminal justice (MPA); disaster management (Certificate); disaster policy (MPA); environmental policy (PhD); health policy (PhD); management and finance (MPA); nonprofit management (MPA, Certificate); nonprofit policy (MPA); planning and economic development (MPP, Certificate); policy analysis and evaluation (MPA), including planning and economic development; public and nonprofit management (PhD); public finance and budgeting (PhD), including science and technology policy, urban and regional economic development; public finance policy (MPA), including social policy; public health (MPA). *Accreditation:* NASPAA (one or more programs are accredited). *Program availability:* Part-time. *Faculty:* 17 full-time (9 women). *Students:* 123 full-time (77 women), 79 part-time (49 women); includes 84 minority (59 Black or African American, non-Hispanic/Latino; 5 Asian, non-Hispanic/Latino; 14 Hispanic/Latino; 6 Two or more races, non-Hispanic/Latino), 34 international. Average age 30. 237 applicants, 60% accepted, 65 enrolled. In 2016, 59 master's, 4 doctorates, 8 other advanced degrees awarded. Terminal master's awarded for partial completion of doctoral program. *Degree requirements:* For master's, thesis optional; for doctorate, comprehensive exam, thesis/dissertation. *Entrance requirements:* For master's and doctorate, GRE. Additional exam requirements/recommendations for international students: Required—TOEFL (minimum score 603 paper-based; 100 iBT) or IELTS (minimum score 7). *Application deadline:* For fall admission, 1/15 for domestic and international students. Application fee: $50.

Electronic applications accepted. *Expenses:* Tuition, state resident: full-time $6876; part-time $382 per credit hour. Tuition, nonresident: full-time $22,374; part-time $1243 per credit hour. *Required fees:* $2128; $1064 per term. Part-time tuition and fees vary according to course load and program. *Financial support:* In 2016–17, fellowships (averaging $8,194 per year), research assistantships (averaging $8,068 per year), teaching assistantships (averaging $3,600 per year) were awarded; institutionally sponsored loans, scholarships/grants, health care benefits, and unspecified assistantships also available. Financial award application deadline: 2/1. *Faculty research:* Public budgeting and finance, public management, nonprofit management, performance measurement and management, urban development. *Unit head:* Dr. Carolyn Bourdeaux, Chair and Professor, 404-413-0013, Fax: 404-413-0104, E-mail: cbourdeaux@gsu.edu.
Website: http://aysps.gsu.edu/pmap/

**Indiana University Bloomington,** School of Public and Environmental Affairs, Public Affairs Programs, Bloomington, IN 47405. Offers economic development (MPA); energy (MPA); environmental policy (PhD); environmental policy and natural resource management (MPA); information systems (MPA); international development (MPA); local government management (MPA); nonprofit management (MPA, Certificate); policy analysis (MPA); public budgeting and financial management (Certificate); public finance (PhD); public financial administration (MPA); public management (MPA, PhD, Certificate); public policy analysis (PhD); social entrepreneurship (Certificate); specialized public affairs (MPA); sustainability and sustainable development (MPA); JD/MPA; MPA/MA; MPA/MIS; MPA/MLS; MSES/MPA. *Accreditation:* NASPAA (one or more programs are accredited). *Program availability:* Part-time. *Degree requirements:* For master's, capstone, internship; for doctorate, comprehensive exam, thesis/dissertation. *Entrance requirements:* For master's, GRE General Test or GMAT, official transcripts, 3 letters of recommendation, resume, personal statement; for doctorate, GRE General Test, official transcripts, 3 letters of recommendation, statement of purpose. Additional exam requirements/recommendations for international students: Required—TOEFL (minimum score 600 paper-based; 96 iBT); Recommended—IELTS (minimum score 7). Electronic applications accepted. *Faculty research:* International development, environmental policy and resource management, policy analysis, public finance, public management, urban management, nonprofit management, energy policy, social policy, public finance.

**New Mexico State University,** College of Business, Department of Economics, Applied Statistics and International Business, Las Cruces, NM 88003. Offers applied statistics (MS); economic development (DED); economics (MA); public utility regulation and economics (Graduate Certificate). *Program availability:* Part-time. *Faculty:* 18 full-time (5 women). *Students:* 41 full-time (14 women), 14 part-time (7 women); includes 15 minority (1 Black or African American, non-Hispanic/Latino; 1 American Indian or Alaska Native, non-Hispanic/Latino; 1 Asian, non-Hispanic/Latino; 10 Hispanic/Latino; 2 Two or more races, non-Hispanic/Latino), 25 international. Average age 35. 73 applicants, 55% accepted, 16 enrolled. In 2016, 19 master's, 5 doctorates, 6 other advanced degrees awarded. Terminal master's awarded for partial completion of doctoral program. *Degree requirements:* For master's, comprehensive exam, thesis or alternative; for doctorate, comprehensive exam, thesis/dissertation, internship. *Entrance requirements:* For master's, minimum GPA of 3.0; for doctorate, appropriate master's degree, minimum GPA of 3.0. Additional exam requirements/recommendations for international students: Required—TOEFL (minimum score 550 paper-based; 79 iBT), IELTS (minimum score 6.5). *Application deadline:* For fall admission, 3/1 priority date for domestic and international students. Applications are processed on a rolling basis. Application fee: $40 ($50 for international students). Electronic applications accepted. *Expenses:* Tuition, state resident: full-time $4086. Tuition, nonresident: full-time $14,254. *Required fees:* $853. Tuition and fees vary according to course load. *Financial support:* In 2016–17, 35 students received support, including 27 teaching assistantships (averaging $13,396 per year); career-related internships or fieldwork, Federal Work-Study, scholarships/grants, traineeships, health care benefits, and unspecified assistantships also available. Support available to part-time students. Financial award application deadline: 3/1. *Faculty research:* Public utilities, environment, linear models, biological sampling, public policy, economic development, energy, regional economics. *Unit head:* Dr. Richard V. Adkisson, 575-646-4988, Fax: 575-646-1915, E-mail: radkisso@nmsu.edu. *Application contact:* 575-646-7211, Fax: 575-646-1915.
Website: http://business.nmsu.edu/departments/economics

**Northeastern University,** College of Professional Studies, Boston, MA 02115-5096. Offers applied nutrition (MS); college athletics administration (MSL); commerce and economic development (MS); corporate and organizational communication (MS); criminal justice (MS); digital media (MPS); elearning and instructional design (M Ed); elementary education (MAT); geographic information technology (MPS); global studies and international relations (MS); higher education administration (M Ed); homeland security (MA); human services (MS); informatics (MPS); leadership (MS); learning analytics (M Ed); learning and instruction (M Ed); nonprofit management (MS); professional sports administration (MSL); project management (MS); regulatory affairs for drugs, biologics, and medical devices (MS); respiratory care leadership (MS); special education (M Ed); technical communication (MS). *Program availability:* Part-time, evening/weekend, 100% online, blended/hybrid learning. *Faculty:* 82 full-time (51 women), 853 part-time/adjunct (366 women). *Students:* 4,947 part-time (3,076 women). In 2016, 1,456 master's awarded. *Application deadline:* Applications are processed on a rolling basis. Application fee: $0. Electronic applications accepted. *Expenses:* Contact institution. *Financial support:* Applicants required to submit FAFSA. *Unit head:* Dr. Mary Loeffelholz, Interim Dean of the College of Professional Studies.
Website: http://www.cps.neu.edu/

**Oregon State University,** College of Agricultural Sciences, Program in Applied Economics, Corvallis, OR 97331. Offers public health economics (MA, MS, PhD); resource and environmental economics (MA); trade and development (MA, MS, PhD); transportation economics (MA, MS). *Program availability:* Part-time. *Faculty:* 14 full-time (3 women), 4 part-time/adjunct (0 women). *Students:* 26 full-time (10 women), 2 part-time (both women); includes 3 minority (1 Asian, non-Hispanic/Latino; 2 Hispanic/Latino), 14 international. Average age 31. 83 applicants, 24% accepted, 5 enrolled. In 2016, 6 master's, 4 doctorates awarded. Terminal master's awarded for partial completion of doctoral program. *Degree requirements:* For master's, thesis (for some programs); for doctorate, thesis/dissertation. *Entrance requirements:* For master's and doctorate, GRE General Test, minimum GPA of 3.0 in last 90 hours. Additional exam requirements/recommendations for international students: Required—TOEFL (minimum score 90 iBT). *Application deadline:* For fall admission, 1/15 for domestic and international students. Application fee: $75 ($85 for international students). *Expenses:* Tuition, state resident: full-time $12,150; part-time $450 per credit. Tuition, nonresident: full-time $21,789; part-time $807 per credit. *Required fees:* $1651; $1507 per credit. One-time fee: $350. Tuition and fees vary according to course load, campus/location and program. *Financial support:* Fellowships, research assistantships, teaching assistantships, career-related internships or fieldwork, Federal Work-Study, and institutionally sponsored loans available. Support available to part-time students. Financial award application deadline: 1/15. *Unit head:* Dr. Larry Lev, Interim Department Head/Professor. *Application contact:* Tjodie Richardson, Applied Economics Advisor,

541-737-1399, E-mail: tjrichardson@oregonstate.edu. Website: http://oregonstate.edu/aecgradprogram/

**Penn State University Park,** Graduate School, College of Agricultural Sciences, Department of Agricultural Economics, Sociology, and Education, University Park, PA 16802. Offers agricultural and extension education (M Ed, MS, PhD, Certificate); agricultural, environmental and regional economics (MS, PhD); applied youth, family and community education (M Ed); community and economic development (MPS); rural sociology (MS, PhD). *Unit head:* Dr. Richard T. Roush, Dean, 814-865-2541, Fax: 814-865-3103. *Application contact:* Lori Hawn, Director, Graduate Student Services, 814-865-1795, Fax: 814-863-4627, E-mail: I-gswww@lists.psu.edu. Website: http://aese.psu.edu/

**State University of New York Empire State College,** School for Graduate Studies, Program in Community and Economic Development, Saratoga Springs, NY 12866-4391. Offers MA. *Program availability:* Part-time, evening/weekend, online learning. *Degree requirements:* For master's, thesis, final project. *Entrance requirements:* For master's, undergraduate-level courses in statistics and macroeconomics, bachelor's degree from regionally-accredited college/university. Additional exam requirements/recommendations for international students: Required—TOEFL (minimum score 600 paper-based). Electronic applications accepted. *Faculty research:* Business history, applied business statistics, labor/management relations, American social problems and business, effect of government economic policies on business.

**Troy University,** Graduate School, College of Business, Program in Business Administration, Troy, AL 36082. Offers accounting (EMBA, MBA); criminal justice (EMBA); finance (MBA); general management (EMBA, MBA); healthcare management (EMBA); information systems (EMBA, MBA); international economic development (MBA). *Accreditation:* ACBSP. *Program availability:* Part-time, evening/weekend. *Faculty:* 10 full-time (3 women), 2 part-time/adjunct (0 women). *Students:* 44 full-time (23 women), 131 part-time (69 women); includes 58 minority (38 Black or African American, non-Hispanic/Latino; 13 Asian, non-Hispanic/Latino; 4 Hispanic/Latino; 3 Two or more races, non-Hispanic/Latino). Average age 30. 285 applicants, 91% accepted, 22 enrolled. In 2016, 78 master's awarded. *Degree requirements:* For master's, minimum GPA of 3.0, capstone course, research course. *Entrance requirements:* For master's, GMAT (minimum score 500) or GRE (minimum score 900 on old exam or 294 on new exam), bachelor's degree; minimum undergraduate GPA of 2.5 or 3.0 on last 30 semester hours, letter of recommendation. Additional exam requirements/recommendations for international students: Required—TOEFL (minimum score 523 paper-based; 70 iBT), IELTS (minimum score 6). *Application deadline:* Applications are processed on a rolling basis. Application fee: $50. Electronic applications accepted. *Expenses:* Tuition, state resident: full-time $7146; part-time $397 per credit hour. Tuition, nonresident: full-time $14,292; part-time $794 per credit hour. *Required fees:* $802; $50 per semester. Tuition and fees vary according to campus/location and program. *Financial support:* Fellowships, career-related internships or fieldwork, and scholarships/grants available. Support available to part-time students. Financial award applicants required to submit FAFSA. *Unit head:* Dr. Phillip Mixon, MBA Director, 334-670-3140, Fax: 334-670-3708, E-mail: pamixon@troy.edu. *Application contact:* Jessica A. Kimbro, Director of Graduate Admissions, 334-670-3178, E-mail: jacord@troy.edu.

**Université de Sherbrooke,** Faculty of Administration, PhD Program in Economic Development, Sherbrooke, QC J1K 2R1, Canada. Offers PhD. *Degree requirements:* For doctorate, one foreign language, comprehensive exam, thesis/dissertation, advanced English as a second language. *Entrance requirements:* For doctorate, letters of recommendation, work experience, formal training. *Faculty research:* Impact analysis of economical policies; productivity, competitivity and international commerce; macroeconometric modelisation; environmental economy.

**University of Central Arkansas,** Graduate School, College of Liberal Arts, Department of Geography, Conway, AR 72035-0001. Offers community and economic development (MS); geographic information systems (MGIS, Certificate). *Program availability:* Part-time, online learning. *Entrance requirements:* Additional exam requirements/recommendations for international students: Required—TOEFL (minimum score 550 paper-based). Electronic applications accepted.

**University of Central Arkansas,** Graduate School, College of Liberal Arts, Program in Community and Economic Development, Conway, AR 72035-0001. Offers community and economic development (MS); geographic and information systems (MGIS, Graduate Certificate). *Program availability:* Part-time, online learning. *Degree requirements:* For master's, comprehensive exam, thesis. *Entrance requirements:* For master's, GRE General Test, minimum GPA of 2.7. Additional exam requirements/recommendations for international students: Required—TOEFL (minimum score 550 paper-based). Electronic applications accepted. *Expenses:* Contact institution.

**University of Colorado Denver,** College of Architecture and Planning, Program in Urban and Regional Planning, Denver, CO 80217. Offers economic and community development planning (MURP); land use and environmental planning (MURP); urban place making (MURP). *Accreditation:* ACSP. *Program availability:* Part-time. *Students:* 93 full-time (62 women), 7 part-time (3 women); includes 27 minority (5 Black or African American, non-Hispanic/Latino; 5 Asian, non-Hispanic/Latino; 14 Hispanic/Latino; 3 Two or more races, non-Hispanic/Latino). Average age 30. 139 applicants, 38% accepted, 34 enrolled. In 2016, 54 master's awarded. *Degree requirements:* For master's, thesis, minimum of 51 semester hours. *Entrance requirements:* For master's, GRE (for students with an undergraduate GPA below 3.0), sample of writing or work project; statement of interest; resume; three letters of recommendation. Additional exam requirements/recommendations for international students: Required—TOEFL (minimum score 75 iBT). *Application deadline:* For fall admission, 2/1 priority date for domestic students, 1/1 priority date for international students; for spring admission, 10/1 for domestic students. Application fee: $50 ($75 for international students). Electronic applications accepted. *Expenses:* Contact institution. *Financial support:* In 2016–17, 37 students received support. Fellowships, research assistantships, teaching assistantships, Federal Work-Study, institutionally sponsored loans, scholarships/grants, and traineeships available. Financial award application deadline: 4/1; financial award applicants required to submit FAFSA. *Faculty research:* Physical planning, environmental planning, economic development planning. *Unit head:* Austin Troy, Professor/Chair, 303-315-1006, E-mail: austin.troy@ucdenver.edu. *Application contact:* Rachael Kuroiwa, Manager of Admissions and Outreach, 303-315-2325, E-mail: rachael.kuroiwa@ucdenver.edu. Website: http://www.ucdenver.edu/academics/colleges/ArchitecturePlanning/Academics/DegreePrograms/MURP/Pages/MURP.aspx

**University of Houston–Victoria,** School of Business Administration, Victoria, TX 77901-4450. Offers accounting (MBA); economic development and entrepreneurship (MS); finance (GMBA, MBA); general business (MBA); international business (MBA); management (GMBA, MBA); marketing (MBA). *Accreditation:* AACSB. *Program availability:* Part-time, evening/weekend, online learning. *Entrance requirements:* For master's, GMAT. Additional exam requirements/recommendations for international students: Required—TOEFL (minimum score 550 paper-based). Electronic applications accepted. *Faculty research:* Economic development, marketing, finance.

**University of Massachusetts Lowell,** College of Fine Arts, Humanities and Social Sciences, Program in Regional Economic and Social Development, Lowell, MA 01854.

Offers MA, Graduate Certificate. *Program availability:* Part-time. *Entrance requirements:* For master's, GRE. Electronic applications accepted.

**University of North Alabama,** College of Arts and Sciences, Department of Interdisciplinary and Professional Studies, Florence, AL 35632-0001. Offers professional studies (MPS), including community development, information technology, security and safety leadership. *Program availability:* Part-time. *Faculty:* 1 full-time (0 women), 1 part-time/adjunct (0 women). *Students:* 12 full-time (8 women), 40 part-time (29 women); includes 6 minority (5 Black or African American, non-Hispanic/Latino; 1 Asian, non-Hispanic/Latino), 8 international. Average age 35. 25 applicants, 76% accepted, 15 enrolled. In 2016, 11 master's awarded. *Degree requirements:* For master's, thesis optional. *Entrance requirements:* For master's, ETS PPI, baccalaureate degree from accredited institution; minimum cumulative GPA of 2.75 or 3.0 in last 60 hours of undergraduate study; personal statement. Additional exam requirements/recommendations for international students: Required—TOEFL (minimum score 79 iBT), IELTS (minimum score 6), PTE (minimum score 54). *Application deadline:* Applications are processed on a rolling basis. Application fee: $50 ($100 for international students). Electronic applications accepted. *Expenses:* Tuition, state resident: full-time $2799; part-time $1866 per semester. Tuition, nonresident: full-time $5598; part-time $3732 per semester. *Required fees:* $915; $642 per semester. Tuition and fees vary according to course load. *Financial support:* In 2016–17, 9 students received support. Scholarships/grants and unspecified assistantships available. Financial award application deadline: 12/1; financial award applicants required to submit FAFSA. *Unit head:* Dr. Craig T. Robertson, Director, 256-765-5003, E-mail: ctrobertson@una.edu. *Application contact:* Hillary N. Coats, Graduate Admissions Coordinator, 256-765-4447, E-mail: graduate@una.edu. Website: https://www.una.edu/interdisciplinary-studies/

**The University of North Carolina at Greensboro,** Graduate School, College of Arts and Sciences, Department of Geography, Greensboro, NC 27412-5001. Offers applied geography (MA); geographic information science (Certificate); geography (PhD); urban and economic development (Certificate). *Degree requirements:* For master's, comprehensive exam, thesis or alternative. *Entrance requirements:* For master's, GRE General Test. Additional exam requirements/recommendations for international students: Required—TOEFL. Electronic applications accepted.

**The University of North Carolina at Greensboro,** Graduate School, College of Arts and Sciences, Department of Political Science, Greensboro, NC 27412-5001. Offers nonprofit management (Certificate); public affairs (MPA); urban and economic development (Certificate). *Accreditation:* NASPAA. *Degree requirements:* For master's, comprehensive exam. *Entrance requirements:* For master's, GRE General Test. Additional exam requirements/recommendations for international students: Required—TOEFL. Electronic applications accepted. *Faculty research:* U.S. Constitution, Canadian parliament, public management, ethical challenge of public service.

**University of Oklahoma,** College of Architecture, Division of Regional and City Planning, Norman, OK 73019. Offers community and economic development (MRCP); physical planning (MRCP); MRCP/MLA. *Accreditation:* ACSP. *Program availability:* Part-time. *Students:* 20 full-time (13 women), 4 part-time (3 women); includes 6 minority (2 Black or African American, non-Hispanic/Latino; 1 American Indian or Alaska Native, non-Hispanic/Latino; 1 Hispanic/Latino; 2 Two or more races, non-Hispanic/Latino), 3 international. Average age 28. 12 applicants, 67% accepted, 5 enrolled. In 2016, 13 master's awarded. Terminal master's awarded for partial completion of doctoral program. *Degree requirements:* For master's, comprehensive exam or thesis. *Entrance requirements:* Additional exam requirements/recommendations for international students: Required—TOEFL (minimum iBT score 79) or IELTS (minimum score 6.5). *Application deadline:* For fall admission, 4/1 priority date for international students. Applications are processed on a rolling basis. Application fee: $50 ($100 for international students). Electronic applications accepted. *Expenses:* Tuition, state resident: full-time $4886; part-time $203.60 per credit hour. Tuition, nonresident: full-time $18,989; part-time $791.20 per credit hour. *Required fees:* $3283; $126.25 per credit hour. $126.50 per semester. *Financial support:* In 2016–17, 26 students received support, including 2 fellowships (averaging $3,750 per year), 3 research assistantships with tuition reimbursements available (averaging $11,915 per year); teaching assistantships, career-related internships or fieldwork, Federal Work-Study, scholarships/grants, health care benefits, tuition waivers, and unspecified assistantships also available. Financial award application deadline: 6/1; financial award applicants required to submit FAFSA. *Faculty research:* Food systems planning, the built environment and public health, community revitalization and minority communities, freight modeling. *Unit head:* Dr. Charles Warnken, Director, 405-325-2444, Fax: 405-325-7558, E-mail: cwarnken@ou.edu. Website: http://rcpl.ou.edu

**University of Oklahoma,** Price College of Business, Program in Business Administration, Norman, OK 73019. Offers accounting (PhD); business administration (MBA, PhD); entrepreneurship and economic development (PhD); finance (PhD); management and international business (PhD); management of information systems (PhD); marketing/supply chain (PhD); JD/MBA; MBA/MS. *Accreditation:* AACSB. *Program availability:* Part-time, evening/weekend. *Students:* 122 full-time (27 women), 146 part-time (30 women); includes 36 minority (5 Black or African American, non-Hispanic/Latino; 6 American Indian or Alaska Native, non-Hispanic/Latino; 8 Asian, non-Hispanic/Latino; 11 Hispanic/Latino; 6 Two or more races, non-Hispanic/Latino), 37 international. Average age 30. 261 applicants, 27% accepted, 59 enrolled. In 2016, 127 master's, 5 doctorates awarded. *Degree requirements:* For doctorate, comprehensive exam, thesis/dissertation. *Entrance requirements:* For master's, GMAT or GRE, resume, statement of goals; for doctorate, GMAT or GRE, resume, statement of goals, 3 letters of recommendation. Additional exam requirements/recommendations for international students: Required—TOEFL (minimum score 100 iBT) or IELTS (minimum score 7). *Application deadline:* For fall admission, 11/15 priority date for domestic and international students; for spring admission, 3/15 priority date for domestic and international students; for summer admission, 5/15 for domestic and international students. Application fee: $50 ($100 for international students). Electronic applications accepted. *Expenses:* Contact institution. *Financial support:* In 2016–17, 107 students received support, including 10 fellowships with partial tuition reimbursements available (averaging $3,295 per year); research assistantships with full and partial tuition reimbursements available, teaching assistantships with full and partial tuition reimbursements available, career-related internships or fieldwork, scholarships/grants, health care benefits, and unspecified assistantships also available. Support available to part-time students. Financial award application deadline: 6/1; financial award applicants required to submit FAFSA. *Faculty research:* Energy finance; international accounting; organizational behavior and entrepreneurship; management information systems; supply chain. *Unit head:* Laku Chidambaram, Associate Dean for Academic Programs and Engagement. *Application contact:* Director of MBA Admissions, 405-325-5623. Website: http://www.ou.edu/content/price/divisions/graduate.html

**University of Pennsylvania,** School of Arts and Sciences, Fels Institute of Government, Philadelphia, PA 19104. Offers economic development and growth (Certificate); government administration (MGA); nonprofit administration (Certificate); organization dynamics (MS); politics (Certificate); public administration (MPA); public

*Economic Development*

finance (Certificate). *Program availability:* Part-time, evening/weekend. *Students:* 49 full-time (29 women), 65 part-time (35 women); includes 28 minority (13 Black or African American, non-Hispanic/Latino; 6 Asian, non-Hispanic/Latino; 6 Hispanic/Latino; 3 Two or more races, non-Hispanic/Latino), 18 international. Average age 30. 371 applicants, 39% accepted, 71 enrolled. In 2016, 52 master's, 17 other advanced degrees awarded. *Expenses: Tuition:* Full-time $31,068; part-time $5762 per course. *Required fees:* $3200; $336 per course. Full-time tuition and fees vary according to degree level, program and student level. Part-time tuition and fees vary according to course load, degree level and program. *Financial support:* Application deadline: 1/1. Website: http://www.fels.upenn.edu/

**University of Puerto Rico, Río Piedras Campus,** Graduate School of Planning, San Juan, PR 00931-3300. Offers economic planning systems (MP); environmental planning (MP); social policy and planning (MP); urban and territorial planning (MP). *Accreditation:* ACSP. *Program availability:* Part-time. *Degree requirements:* For master's, comprehensive exam, thesis, planning project defense. *Entrance requirements:* For master's, PAEG, GRE, minimum GPA of 3.0, 2 letters of recommendation. *Faculty research:* Municipalities, historic Atlas, Puerto Rico, economic future.

**University of Southern California,** Graduate School, Dana and David Dornsife College of Letters, Arts and Sciences, Department of Economics, Los Angeles, CA 90089. Offers economic development programming (MA, PhD); mathematical finance (MS); M PI/MA; MA/JD. Terminal master's awarded for partial completion of doctoral program. *Degree requirements:* For master's, comprehensive exam; for doctorate, comprehensive exam, thesis/dissertation. *Entrance requirements:* For master's and doctorate, GRE. Additional exam requirements/recommendations for international students: Required—TOEFL (minimum score 93 iBT). Electronic applications accepted. *Faculty research:* Macro theory, development economics, econometrics.

**University of Southern Mississippi,** Graduate School, College of Business, Department of Economic Development, Tourism and Sport Management, Hattiesburg, MS 39406. Offers economic development (MS); sport management (MS). *Program availability:* Part-time, evening/weekend. *Degree requirements:* For master's, comprehensive exam, thesis optional, internships. *Entrance requirements:* For master's, GMAT or GRE General Test, minimum GPA of 2.75 in last 60 hours. Additional exam requirements/recommendations for international students: Required—TOEFL, IELTS. *Application deadline:* For fall admission, 8/1 for domestic students, 3/1 for international students; for spring admission, 1/3 for domestic and international students. Applications are processed on a rolling basis. Application fee: $60. Electronic applications accepted. *Expenses: Tuition,* area resident: Full-time $15,708; part-time $437 per credit hour. *Financial support:* Research assistantships with full tuition reimbursements, teaching assistantships with full tuition reimbursements, career-related internships or fieldwork, Federal Work-Study, scholarships/grants, health care benefits, and unspecified assistantships available. Financial award application deadline: 3/1; financial award applicants required to submit FAFSA. *Faculty research:* Economic development, international studies, geography. *Unit head:* Dr. Stacey Hall, Chair, 601-266-6308, Fax: 601-266-6707. *Application contact:* Dr. Chad Miller, Program Coordinator, 601-266-6666, Fax: 601-266-6071. Website: https://www.usm.edu/business/eco-dev-tourism-sport-management

**University of Waterloo,** Graduate Studies, Faculty of Environment, Program in Local Economic Development, Waterloo, ON N2L 3G1, Canada. Offers MAES. *Program availability:* Part-time. *Degree requirements:* For master's, internship, research paper. *Entrance requirements:* Additional exam requirements/recommendations for international students: Required—TOEFL, IELTS, PTE. Electronic applications accepted.

**Vanderbilt University,** Department of Economics, Nashville, TN 37240-1001. Offers economic development (MA); economics (PhD). *Faculty:* 37 full-time (5 women). *Students:* 114 full-time (44 women); includes 11 minority (2 Black or African American, non-Hispanic/Latino; 2 Asian, non-Hispanic/Latino; 2 Hispanic/Latino; 5 Two or more races, non-Hispanic/Latino), 71 international. Average age 26. 621 applicants, 33% accepted, 46 enrolled. In 2016, 39 master's, 7 doctorates awarded. Terminal master's awarded for partial completion of doctoral program. *Degree requirements:* For master's, thesis or alternative; for doctorate, thesis/dissertation, final and qualifying exams. *Entrance requirements:* For master's and doctorate, GRE General Test, GRE Subject Test (recommended). Additional exam requirements/recommendations for international students: Required—TOEFL (minimum score 570 paper-based; 88 iBT). *Application deadline:* For fall admission, 1/15 for domestic and international students; for spring admission, 11/1 for domestic students. Applications are processed on a rolling basis. Electronic applications accepted. *Expenses: Tuition:* Part-time $1854 per credit hour. *Financial support:* Fellowships with tuition reimbursements, teaching assistantships with tuition reimbursements, career-related internships or fieldwork, Federal Work-Study, institutionally sponsored loans, scholarships/grants, and health care benefits available. Financial award application deadline: 1/15; financial award applicants required to submit CSS PROFILE or FAFSA. *Faculty research:* Economic theory, applied fields, developmental economics, environmental economics, health economics and policy. *Unit head:* Dr. Eric Bond, Chair, 615-322-2871, Fax: 615-343-8495, E-mail: k.saggi@vanderbilt.edu. *Application contact:* Jennifer Reinganum, Director of Graduate Studies, 615-322-2871, Fax: 615-343-8495, E-mail: jennifer.f.reinganum@vanderbilt.edu. Website: http://www.vanderbilt.edu/econ/

**Wayne State University,** College of Liberal Arts and Sciences, Department of Political Science, Detroit, MI 48202. Offers political science (MA, PhD); public administration (MPA), including economic development policy and management, health and human services policy and management, human and fiscal resource management, nonprofit policy and management, organizational behavior and management, urban and metropolitan policy and management; JD/MA. *Accreditation:* NASPAA. *Faculty:* 20. *Students:* 64 full-time (20 women), 75 part-time (45 women); includes 48 minority (32 Black or African American, non-Hispanic/Latino; 5 Asian, non-Hispanic/Latino; 4 Hispanic/Latino; 7 Two or more races, non-Hispanic/Latino), 7 international. Average age 33. 105 applicants, 50% accepted, 27 enrolled. In 2016, 25 master's, 5 doctorates

awarded. *Degree requirements:* For master's, comprehensive exam (for some programs), thesis (for some programs); for doctorate, thesis/dissertation. *Entrance requirements:* For master's, GRE General Test, substantial undergraduate preparation in the social sciences, minimum upper-division undergraduate GPA 3.0, two letters of recommendation, personal statement; for doctorate, GRE General Test, 3 letters of recommendation; personal statement; interview. Additional exam requirements/recommendations for international students: Required—TOEFL (minimum score 550 paper-based; 79 iBT), TWE (minimum score 5.5), Michigan English Language Assessment Battery (minimum score 85); Recommended—IELTS (minimum score 6.5). *Application deadline:* For fall admission, 5/15 for domestic students, 5/1 priority date for international students; for winter admission, 10/15 for domestic students, 9/1 priority date for international students. Applications are processed on a rolling basis. Application fee: $50. Electronic applications accepted. *Expenses:* $16,503 per year resident tuition and fees, $33,697 per year non-resident tuition and fees. *Financial support:* In 2016–17, 48 students received support, including 3 fellowships with tuition reimbursements available (averaging $17,333 per year), 13 teaching assistantships with tuition reimbursements available (averaging $18,067 per year); research assistantships with tuition reimbursements available, scholarships/grants, health care benefits, and unspecified assistantships also available. Financial award applicants required to submit FAFSA. *Faculty research:* American government and politics, comparative politics, political methodology, political theory, public administration, public law, public policy, world politics/international relations, formal theory/modeling, gender and politics, international law, peace research, political economy, political psychology, politics of developing countries, race, religion, and ethnicity, urban politics. *Unit head:* Dr. Daniel Geller, Professor and Chair, 313-577-6328, E-mail: dgeller@wayne.edu. *Application contact:* Dr. Sharon Lean, Graduate Director, 313-577-2630, E-mail: gradpolisci@wayne.edu. Website: http://clas.wayne.edu/politicalscience/

**Wayne State University,** College of Liberal Arts and Sciences, Department of Urban Studies and Planning, Detroit, MI 48202. Offers economic development (Graduate Certificate); urban studies and planning (MUP). *Accreditation:* ACSP. *Program availability:* Evening/weekend. *Students:* 17 full-time (7 women), 41 part-time (25 women); includes 23 minority (16 Black or African American, non-Hispanic/Latino; 1 Asian, non-Hispanic/Latino; 3 Hispanic/Latino; 3 Two or more races, non-Hispanic/Latino), 2 international. Average age 29. 67 applicants, 51% accepted, 22 enrolled. In 2016, 15 master's awarded. *Degree requirements:* For master's, thesis or essay. *Entrance requirements:* For degree, graduate degree or actively pursuing a graduate degree at WSU; personal statement of interest. Additional exam requirements/recommendations for international students: Required—TOEFL (minimum score 550 paper-based; 79 iBT), TWE (minimum score 5.5), Michigan English Language Assessment Battery (minimum score 85); Recommended—IELTS (minimum score 6.5). *Application deadline:* For fall admission, 6/1 priority date for domestic students, 5/1 priority date for international students; for winter admission, 10/1 priority date for domestic students, 9/1 priority date for international students; for spring admission, 2/1 priority date for domestic students, 1/1 priority date for international students. Applications are processed on a rolling basis. Application fee: $50. Electronic applications accepted. *Expenses:* $16,503 per year resident tuition and fees, $33,697 per year non-resident tuition and fees. *Financial support:* In 2016–17, 14 students received support, including 2 research assistantships (averaging $14,244 per year); scholarships/grants and unspecified assistantships also available. Financial award applicants required to submit FAFSA. *Faculty research:* Community development, economic development, environmental planning, housing policy, land use planning and policy, local fiscal policy, local planning practices, neighborhood change, sustainable food systems. *Unit head:* Dr. Kami Pothukuchi, Associate Professor and Chair, 313-577-4296, E-mail: k.pothukuchi@wayne.edu. *Application contact:* E-mail: dusp@wayne.edu. Website: http://clas.wayne.edu/dusp/

**Western Illinois University,** School of Graduate Studies, Illinois Institute for Rural Affairs, Macomb, IL 61455-1390. Offers community and economic development (MA). *Students:* 6 full-time (4 women), 1 (woman) part-time; includes 2 minority (1 Hispanic/Latino; 1 Two or more races, non-Hispanic/Latino). Average age 35. 10 applicants, 100% accepted, 7 enrolled. *Application deadline:* Applications are processed on a rolling basis. Application fee: $30. Electronic applications accepted. *Unit head:* Dr. Christopher Merrett, Director, 309-298-2281, E-mail: cd-merrett@wiu.edu. Website: http://www.iira.org

**West Virginia University,** College of Business and Economics, Division of Economics and Finance, Morgantown, WV 26506. Offers business analysis (MA); developmental financial economics (PhD); environmental and resource economics (PhD); international economics (PhD); mathematical economics (MA); monetary economics (PhD); public finance (PhD); public policy (MA); regional and urban economics (PhD); statistics and economics (MA). Terminal master's awarded for partial completion of doctoral program. *Degree requirements:* For master's, thesis optional; for doctorate, comprehensive exam, thesis/dissertation. *Entrance requirements:* For master's and doctorate, GRE General Test, minimum GPA of 3.0; course work in intermediate microeconomics, intermediate macroeconomics, calculus, and statistics. Additional exam requirements/recommendations for international students: Required—TOEFL. Electronic applications accepted. *Faculty research:* Financial economics, regional/urban development, public economics, international trade/international finance/development economics, monetary economics.

**Williams College,** Graduate Program in the History of Art, Williamstown, MA 01267. Offers development economics (MA); history of art (MA). MA in history of art offered jointly with Sterling and Francine Clark Art Institute. *Degree requirements:* For master's, 2 foreign languages, symposium paper and lecture. *Entrance requirements:* For master's, GRE General Test. Additional exam requirements/recommendations for international students: Required—TOEFL. Electronic applications accepted.

**Yale University,** Graduate School of Arts and Sciences, Department of Economics, Program in International and Development Economics, New Haven, CT 06520. Offers MA. *Entrance requirements:* For master's, GRE General Test.

# Economics

**Albany State University,** College of Arts and Humanities, Albany, GA 31705-2717. Offers criminal justice (MS); English education (M Ed); public administration (MPA), including community and economic development, criminal justice administration, health administration and policy, human resources management, public management, public policy, water resources management and policy; social work (MSW). *Program availability:* Part-time. *Degree requirements:* For master's, comprehensive exam,

professional portfolio (for MPA), internship, capstone report. *Entrance requirements:* For master's, GRE, MAT, minimum GPA of 3.0, official transcript, pre-medical record/certificate of immunization, letters of reference. *Application deadline:* For fall admission, 6/1 for domestic students, 5/1 for international students; for spring admission, 11/1 for domestic students, 10/1 for international students. Applications are processed on a rolling basis. Application fee: $20. Electronic applications accepted. *Financial support:*

Application deadline: 4/15; applicants required to submit FAFSA. *Faculty research:* HIV prevention for minority students. *Unit head:* Dr. Rani George, Dean, 229-430-1877, Fax: 229-430-4296. *Application contact:* Jeffrey Pierce, II, Graduate Admissions Counselor, 229-430-4646, Fax: 229-430-4105, E-mail: jeffrey.pierce@asurams.edu.
Website: https://www.asurams.edu/Academics/collegeofarthum/

**American University,** College of Arts and Sciences, Department of Economics, Washington, DC 20016-8029. Offers applied microeconomics (Certificate); economics (MA, PhD); gender analysis in economics (Certificate); international economic relations (Certificate); international economics (MA). *Program availability:* Part-time, evening/weekend, 100% online. *Faculty:* 29 full-time (8 women), 10 part-time/adjunct (3 women). *Students:* 110 full-time (55 women), 71 part-time (32 women); includes 26 minority (9 Black or African American, non-Hispanic/Latino; 6 Asian, non-Hispanic/Latino; 7 Hispanic/Latino; 4 Two or more races, non-Hispanic/Latino), 64 international. Average age 31. 241 applicants, 78% accepted, 48 enrolled. In 2016, 34 master's, 13 doctorates, 5 other advanced degrees awarded. Terminal master's awarded for partial completion of doctoral program. *Degree requirements:* For master's, comprehensive exam, thesis or alternative; for doctorate, comprehensive exam, thesis/dissertation. *Entrance requirements:* For master's and doctorate, GRE, statement of purpose, transcripts, 2 letters of recommendation, resume; for Certificate, bachelor's degree, statement of purpose, transcripts, resume. Additional exam requirements/recommendations for international students: Required—TOEFL (minimum score 100 iBT), IELTS (minimum score 7), PTE (minimum score 68). *Application deadline:* For fall admission, 3/1 for domestic students; for spring admission, 11/1 for domestic students. Applications are processed on a rolling basis. Application fee: $55. Electronic applications accepted. *Expenses:* $1,579 per credit tuition; $690 mandatory fees. *Financial support:* Research assistantships, teaching assistantships, institutionally sponsored loans, and unspecified assistantships available. Financial award application deadline: 2/1; financial award applicants required to submit FAFSA. *Faculty research:* Political economy, development, labor, gender. *Unit head:* Dr. Thomas Husted, Department Chair, 202-885-3773, Fax: 202-885-3790, E-mail: husted@american.edu. *Application contact:* Kathleen Clowery, Associate Director of Graduate Admissions, 202-885-3620, Fax: 202-885-1344, E-mail: clowery@american.edu.
Website: http://www.american.edu/cas/economics/

**American University,** School of International Service, Washington, DC 20016-8071. Offers comparative and regional studies (Certificate); cross-cultural communication (Certificate); development management (MS); ethics, peace, and global affairs (MA); European studies (Certificate); global environmental policy (MA, Certificate); global information technology (Certificate); international affairs (MA), including comparative and international disability policy, comparative and regional studies, international economic relations, international politics, natural resources and sustainable development, U.S. foreign policy; international arts management (Certificate); international communication (MA, Certificate); international development (MA); international economic policy (Certificate); international economic relations (Certificate); international economics (MA); international media (MA); international peace and conflict resolution (MA, Certificate); international politics (Certificate); international relations (MA, PhD); international service (MIS); peacebuilding (Certificate); social enterprise (MA); the Americas (Certificate); United States foreign policy (Certificate); JD/MA. *Program availability:* Part-time, evening/weekend, 100% online. *Faculty:* 116 full-time (53 women), 57 part-time/adjunct (19 women). *Students:* 575 full-time (360 women), 491 part-time (277 women); includes 287 minority (100 Black or African American, non-Hispanic/Latino; 6 American Indian or Alaska Native, non-Hispanic/Latino; 58 Asian, non-Hispanic/Latino; 92 Hispanic/Latino; 1 Native Hawaiian or other Pacific Islander, non-Hispanic/Latino; 30 Two or more races, non-Hispanic/Latino), 151 international. Average age 29. 1,504 applicants, 84% accepted, 403 enrolled. In 2016, 374 master's, 3 doctorates, 1 other advanced degree awarded. Terminal master's awarded for partial completion of doctoral program. *Degree requirements:* For master's, one foreign language, comprehensive exam, thesis or alternative; for doctorate, one foreign language, comprehensive exam, thesis/dissertation. *Entrance requirements:* For master's, GRE, GMAT or GRE (for MA in social enterprise), transcripts, resume, 2 letters of recommendation, statement of purpose; for doctorate, GRE, transcripts, resume, 3 letters of recommendation, statement of purpose. Additional exam requirements/recommendations for international students: Required—TOEFL (minimum score 600 paper-based, 100 iBT), IELTS (minimum score 7 ), or PTE (minimum score of 68). Application fee: $55. Electronic applications accepted. *Expenses:* $1,579 per credit; $1,930 mandatory fees. *Financial support:* Research assistantships, teaching assistantships, institutionally sponsored loans, scholarships/grants, and unspecified assistantships available. Financial award application deadline: 1/15; financial award applicants required to submit FAFSA. *Unit head:* Dr. James Goldgeier, Dean, 202-885-1603, Fax: 202-885-2494, E-mail: goldgeier@american.edu. *Application contact:* Jia Jiang, Associate Director, Graduate Education Enrollment, 202-885-1689, Fax: 202-885-1109, E-mail: jiang@american.edu.
Website: http://www.american.edu/sis/

**The American University in Cairo,** School of Business, Cairo, Egypt. Offers business administration (MBA); economics (MA); economics in international development (MA, Diploma); finance (MS). *Program availability:* Part-time, evening/weekend. *Faculty:* 24 full-time (4 women), 5 part-time/adjunct (2 women). *Students:* 53 full-time (24 women), 80 part-time (41 women), 1 international. Average age 29. 109 applicants, 45% accepted, 35 enrolled. In 2016, 49 master's awarded. *Degree requirements:* For master's, comprehensive exam (for some programs), thesis (for some programs). *Entrance requirements:* For master's, GMAT, GRE. Additional exam requirements/recommendations for international students: Required—TOEFL (minimum score 450 paper-based; 45 iBT), IELTS (minimum score 5). *Application deadline:* For fall admission, 2/1 priority date for domestic and international students; for spring admission, 10/15 priority date for domestic and international students. Applications are processed on a rolling basis. Application fee: $80. Electronic applications accepted. *Expenses:* Contact institution. *Financial support:* Fellowships with partial tuition reimbursements, scholarships/grants, tuition waivers (partial), and unspecified assistantships available. Financial award application deadline: 3/10. *Faculty research:* Marketing and quality management, banking operations management, economics, finance. *Unit head:* Dr. Nizar Becheikh, Interim Dean, 20-2-2615-2120, E-mail: nbecheikh@aucegypt.edu. *Application contact:* Maha Hegazi, Director of Graduate Admissions, 20-2-2615-1462, E-mail: mahahegazi@aucegypt.edu.
Website: http://www.aucegypt.edu/Business/Pages/default.aspx

**American University of Armenia,** Graduate Programs, Yerevan, Armenia. Offers business administration (MBA); computer and information science (MS), including business management, design and manufacturing, energy (ME, MS), industrial engineering and systems management; economics (MS); industrial engineering and systems management (ME), including business, computer aided design/manufacturing, energy (ME, MS), information technology; law (LL M); political science and international affairs (MPSIA); public health (MPH); teaching English as a foreign language (MA). *Program availability:* Part-time, evening/weekend. *Degree requirements:* For master's, thesis (for some programs), capstone/project. *Entrance requirements:* For master's, GRE, GMAT, or LSAT. Additional exam requirements/recommendations for international students: Recommended—TOEFL (minimum score 79 iBT), IELTS (minimum score

6.5). *Faculty research:* Microfinance, finance (rural/development, international, corporate), firm life cycle theory, TESOL, language proficiency testing, public policy, administrative law, economic development, cryptography, artificial intelligence, energy efficiency/renewable energy, computer-aided design/manufacturing, health financing, tuberculosis control, mother/child health, preventive ophthalmology, post-earthquake psychopathological investigations, tobacco control, environmental health risk assessments.

**American University of Beirut,** Graduate Programs, Faculty of Arts and Sciences, Beirut, Lebanon. Offers anthropology (MA); Arab and Middle Eastern history (PhD); Arabic language and literature (MA, PhD); archaeology (MA); art history and curating (MA); biology (MS); cell and molecular biology (PhD); chemistry (MS); clinical psychology (MA); computational sciences (MS); computer science (MS); economics (MA); education (MA); English language (MA); English literature (MA); environmental policy planning (MS); financial economics (MAFE); geology (MS); history (MA); Islamic studies (MA); mathematics (MS); media studies (MA); Middle Eastern studies (MA); physics (MS); political studies (MA); psychology (MA); public administration (MA); public policy and international affairs (MA); sociology (MA); statistics (MA, MS); theoretical physics (PhD); transnational American studies (MA). *Program availability:* Part-time. *Faculty:* 133 full-time (42 women), 6 part-time/adjunct (2 women). *Students:* 240 full-time (172 women), 227 part-time (166 women). Average age 27. 286 applicants, 67% accepted, 108 enrolled. In 2016, 60 master's, 3 doctorates awarded. Terminal master's awarded for partial completion of doctoral program. *Degree requirements:* For master's, one foreign language, comprehensive exam, thesis (for some programs); for doctorate, one foreign language, comprehensive exam, thesis/dissertation. *Entrance requirements:* For master's, GRE (for some MA, MS programs), letters of recommendation; for doctorate, GRE, letters of recommendation. Additional exam requirements/recommendations for international students: Required—TOEFL (minimum score 600 paper-based; 97 iBT), IELTS (minimum score 7). *Application deadline:* For fall admission, 4/3 for domestic students; for winter admission, 11/3 for domestic students. Application fee: $50. Electronic applications accepted. *Expenses:* Contact institution. *Financial support:* In 2016–17, 4 fellowships (averaging $11,200 per year), 18 research assistantships (averaging $5,400 per year) were awarded; teaching assistantships, career-related internships or fieldwork, Federal Work-Study, institutionally sponsored loans, scholarships/grants, traineeships, health care benefits, tuition waivers (full), and unspecified assistantships also available. Support available to part-time students. *Faculty research:* Development economics, spatial econometrics, health economics, labor economics, energy economics, hydrogeology, geophysics, petrophysics, structural geology, mineralogy, petrology, geochemistry, multilingualism, comparative/world literature, translation studies, book histories/ cultures, biocatalysis, molecular recognition, photocatalysis, photophysical and biophysical chemistry, probe chemistry, machine learning, data science. *Unit head:* Dr. Nadia Maria El Cheikh, Dean, Faculty of Arts and Sciences, 961-1374374 Ext. 3800, Fax: 961-1744461, E-mail: nmcheikh@aub.edu.lb. *Application contact:* Dr. Salim Kanaan, Director, Admissions Office, 961-1350000 Ext. 2590, Fax: 961-1750775, E-mail: sk00@aub.edu.lb.
Website: http://www.aub.edu.lb/fas/

**Andrews University,** School of Graduate Studies, School of Business, Graduate Programs in Berrien Springs, MI 49104. Offers MBA, MSA. *Faculty:* 8 full-time (3 women). *Students:* 16 full-time (7 women), 29 part-time (15 women); includes 19 minority (6 Black or African American, non-Hispanic/Latino; 3 Asian, non-Hispanic/Latino; 8 Hispanic/Latino; 2 Two or more races, non-Hispanic/Latino), 12 international. Average age 32. In 2016, 29 master's awarded. *Entrance requirements:* For master's, GMAT. Additional exam requirements/recommendations for international students: Required—TOEFL (minimum score 550 paper-based). Application fee: $40. *Unit head:* Dr. Leonard K. Gashugi, Chair, 769-471-3429, E-mail: gashugi@andrews.edu. *Application contact:* Justina Clayburn, Supervisor of Graduate Admission, 800-253-2874, Fax: 269-471-6321, E-mail: graduate@andrews.edu.

**Arizona State University at the Tempe campus,** W. P. Carey School of Business, Department of Economics, Tempe, AZ 85287-9801. Offers PhD. *Degree requirements:* For doctorate, comprehensive exam, thesis/dissertation, interactive Program of Study (iPOS) submitted before completing 50 percent of required credit hours. *Entrance requirements:* For doctorate, GRE, minimum GPA of 3.0 in last 2 years of work leading to bachelor's degree, 3 letters of recommendation, resume/curriculum vitae, letter of intent, thesis (if applicable), official university transcripts, personal statement. Additional exam requirements/recommendations for international students: Required—TOEFL (minimum score 550 paper-based; 80 iBT), IELTS (minimum score 6.5). Electronic applications accepted. *Faculty research:* Macroeconomics, general equilibrium, business cycles, monetary policy, environmental economics, applied econometrics, economic theory, game theory, procurement and auctions, industrial organization, labor economics, marketing, consumer choice behavior.

**Assumption College,** Business Studies Program, Worcester, MA 01609-1296. Offers accounting (MBA); business studies (CAGS); finance/economics (MBA); human resources (MBA); international business (MBA); management (MBA); marketing (MBA); nonprofit leadership (MBA). *Program availability:* Part-time, evening/weekend. *Faculty:* 4 full-time (1 woman), 19 part-time/adjunct (6 women). *Students:* 44 full-time (16 women), 97 part-time (47 women); includes 20 minority (8 Black or African American, non-Hispanic/Latino; 5 Asian, non-Hispanic/Latino; 6 Hispanic/Latino; 1 Two or more races, non-Hispanic/Latino), 4 international. Average age 29. 34 applicants, 59% accepted, 16 enrolled. In 2016, 97 master's, 1 other advanced degree awarded. *Degree requirements:* For master's, thesis, capstone. *Entrance requirements:* For master's, bachelor's degree, 3 letters of recommendation, official transcripts, personal statement, current resume; for CAGS, MBA or equivalent degree in a closely related field, 3 letters of recommendation, official transcripts, personal statement, current resume. Additional exam requirements/recommendations for international students: Required—TOEFL (minimum score 540 paper-based; 76 iBT), IELTS (minimum score 6). *Application deadline:* For fall admission, 7/1 priority date for domestic and international students; for spring admission, 12/1 priority date for domestic and international students; for summer admission, 4/1 priority date for domestic and international students. Application fee: $30. Electronic applications accepted. *Expenses: Tuition:* Full-time $11,610; part-time $645 per credit. *Required fees:* $70 per term. Tuition and fees vary according to course load and program. *Financial support:* In 2016–17, 19 students received support. Tuition waivers (full and partial), unspecified assistantships, and institutional discounts available. Financial award applicants required to submit FAFSA. *Faculty research:* Workplace diversity, dynamics of team interaction, utilization of leased employees, experiential learning project on due diligence market for prostheses. *Unit head:* Dr. Robin Frkal, Director, 508-767-7622, E-mail: rafrkal@assumption.edu. *Application contact:* Karen Stoyanoff, Director of Recruitment for Graduate Enrollment, 508-767-7442, Fax: 508-799-4412, E-mail: graduate@assumption.edu.
Website: http://graduate.assumption.edu/mba/assumption-mba

**Auburn University,** Graduate School, College of Liberal Arts, Department of Economics, Auburn University, AL 36849. Offers MS. *Program availability:* Part-time. *Faculty:* 15 full-time (5 women), 4 part-time/adjunct (2 women). *Students:* 11 full-time (6 women), 4 part-time (2 women), 11 international. Average age 27. 33 applicants, 33% accepted, 5 enrolled. In 2016, 3 master's awarded. *Degree requirements:* For master's,

## Economics

thesis. *Entrance requirements:* For master's, GMAT, GRE General Test. Additional exam requirements/recommendations for international students: Required—TOEFL. *Application deadline:* Applications are processed on a rolling basis. Application fee: $50 ($60 for international students). Electronic applications accepted. *Expenses:* Tuition, state resident: full-time $9072; part-time $504 per credit hour. Tuition, nonresident: full-time $27,216; part-time $1512 per credit hour. *Required fees:* $812 per semester. Tuition and fees vary according to degree level and program. *Financial support:* Teaching assistantships, career-related internships or fieldwork, and Federal Work-Study available. Support available to part-time students. Financial award application deadline: 3/15; financial award applicants required to submit FAFSA. *Unit head:* Dr. Michael Stern, Interim Chair, 334-844-2982. *Application contact:* Dr. George Flowers, Dean of the Graduate School, 334-844-2125.
Website: http://www.cla.auburn.edu/economics/

**Bard College,** Levy Economics Institute, Annandale-on-Hudson, NY 12504. Offers economic theory and policy (MS).

**Baruch College of the City University of New York,** Zicklin School of Business, Department of Economics and Finance, Program in Economics, New York, NY 10010-5585. Offers MBA. *Program availability:* Part-time, evening/weekend. *Entrance requirements:* For master's, GMAT, 2 letters of recommendation, resume, 2 years of work experience. Additional exam requirements/recommendations for international students: Required—TOEFL (minimum score 590 paper-based), TWE (minimum score 5).

**Baylor University,** Graduate School, Hankamer School of Business, Department of Economics, Waco, TX 76798. Offers MS Eco. *Faculty:* 15 full-time (2 women). *Students:* 14 full-time (6 women), 1 part-time (0 women); includes 2 minority (both Asian, non-Hispanic/Latino), 7 international. In 2016, 5 master's awarded. *Entrance requirements:* For master's, GMAT or GRE General Test. Additional exam requirements/recommendations for international students: Required—TOEFL (minimum score 600 paper-based; 100 iBT), IELTS (minimum score 7). *Application deadline:* For fall admission, 6/15 for domestic and international students. Application fee: $25. Electronic applications accepted. *Expenses: Tuition:* Full-time $28,494; part-time $1583 per credit hour. *Required fees:* $167 per credit hour. Tuition and fees vary according to course load and program. *Financial support:* In 2016–17, 12 students received support. Research assistantships, Federal Work-Study, and institutionally sponsored loans available. Financial award application deadline: 3/1. *Faculty research:* Econometrics, international economics, economic development, comparative economic systems, computational economics, health economics, economics of education, monetary economics, labor economics, experimental economics. *Unit head:* Dr. Van Pham, Graduate Program Director, 254-710-3521, Fax: 254-710-6142, E-mail: van_pham@baylor.edu. *Application contact:* Susan Armstrong, Office Manager, 254-710-6177, Fax: 254-710-6142, E-mail: susan_armstrong@baylor.edu.
Website: http://www.baylor.edu/business/economics/

**Binghamton University, State University of New York,** Graduate School, Harpur College of Arts and Sciences, Department of Economics, Binghamton, NY 13902-6000. Offers MA, PhD. *Program availability:* Part-time. *Faculty:* 25 full-time (7 women), 7 part-time/adjunct (3 women). *Students:* 30 full-time (11 women), 35 part-time (17 women); includes 2 minority (1 Black or African American, non-Hispanic/Latino; 1 Asian, non-Hispanic/Latino), 55 international. Average age 27. 114 applicants, 73% accepted, 19 enrolled. In 2016, 16 master's, 3 doctorates awarded. Terminal master's awarded for partial completion of doctoral program. *Degree requirements:* For doctorate, comprehensive exam, thesis/dissertation. *Entrance requirements:* For master's and doctorate, GRE General Test. Additional exam requirements/recommendations for international students: Required—TOEFL (minimum score 550 paper-based; 80 iBT). *Application deadline:* For fall admission, 2/1 priority date for domestic and international students. Application fee: $75. Electronic applications accepted. *Financial support:* In 2016–17, 32 students received support, including 1 research assistantship with full tuition reimbursement available (averaging $15,000 per year), 29 teaching assistantships with full tuition reimbursements available (averaging $15,000 per year); career-related internships or fieldwork, Federal Work-Study, institutionally sponsored loans, scholarships/grants, health care benefits, tuition waivers (full and partial), and unspecified assistantships also available. Financial award applicants required to submit FAFSA. *Unit head:* Andreas Pape, Director of Graduate Admissions, 607-777-2660, E-mail: apape@binghamton.edu. *Application contact:* Ben Balkaya, Assistant Dean and Director, 607-777-2151, Fax: 607-777-2501, E-mail: balkaya@binghamton.edu.

**Boston College,** Graduate School of Arts and Sciences, Department of Economics, Chestnut Hill, MA 02467-3800. Offers PhD. *Faculty:* 38 full-time. *Students:* 80 full-time (27 women); includes 1 minority (Hispanic/Latino), 63 international. 428 applicants, 6% accepted, 11 enrolled. In 2016, 10 doctorates awarded. *Degree requirements:* For doctorate, comprehensive exam, thesis/dissertation. *Entrance requirements:* For doctorate, GRE General Test, GRE Subject Test. Additional exam requirements/recommendations for international students: Required—TOEFL (minimum score 600 paper-based; 100 iBT), IELTS (minimum score 8). *Application deadline:* For fall admission, 1/2 for domestic and international students. Application fee: $75. Electronic applications accepted. Tuition and fees vary according to program. *Financial support:* In 2016–17, 80 students received support, including fellowships with full tuition reimbursements available (averaging $20,900 per year), research assistantships with full tuition reimbursements available (averaging $21,400 per year), teaching assistantships with full tuition reimbursements available (averaging $21,900 per year); Federal Work-Study, scholarships/grants, health care benefits, and unspecified assistantships also available. Support available to part-time students. Financial award application deadline: 1/2. *Faculty research:* Economic theory, macroeconomics, microeconomics, econometrics, development economics, industrial organization, labor economics, international economics, public sector economics, monetary economics and finance, urban economics. *Unit head:* Dr. Hideo Konishi, Chairperson, 617-552-1209, E-mail: hideo.konishi@bc.edu. *Application contact:* Dr. Dick Tresch, Graduate Program Director, 617-552-3683, E-mail: richard.tresch@bc.edu.
Website: http://www.bc.edu/economics

**Boston University,** Graduate School of Arts and Sciences, Department of Economics, Boston, MA 02215. Offers MA, MAEP, PhD, MBA/MA. *Students:* 342 full-time (150 women), 21 part-time (6 women); includes 14 minority (1 Black or African American, non-Hispanic/Latino; 10 Asian, non-Hispanic/Latino; 2 Hispanic/Latino; 1 Two or more races, non-Hispanic/Latino), 287 international. Average age 25. 1,494 applicants, 41% accepted, 135 enrolled. In 2016, 138 master's, 26 doctorates awarded. Terminal master's awarded for partial completion of doctoral program. *Degree requirements:* For master's, comprehensive exam; for doctorate, comprehensive exam, thesis/dissertation, qualifying exam. *Entrance requirements:* For master's, GRE General Test, 2 letters of recommendation, transcripts, personal statement; for doctorate, GRE General Test, 3 letters of recommendation, transcripts, personal statement. Additional exam requirements/recommendations for international students: Required—TOEFL (minimum score 550 paper-based; 84 iBT). *Application deadline:* For fall admission, 1/5 for domestic and international students; for spring admission, 3/1 for domestic and international students. Application fee: $95. Electronic applications accepted. *Financial support:* In 2016–17, 132 students received support, including 23 fellowships with full tuition reimbursements available (averaging $21,500 per year), 26 research assistantships with full tuition reimbursements available (averaging $21,500 per year), 68 teaching assistantships with full tuition reimbursements available (averaging $21,500 per year); Federal Work-Study, scholarships/grants, and health care benefits also available. Financial award application deadline: 1/5. *Unit head:* Barton Lipman, Chair, 617-353-2995, Fax: 617-353-4449, E-mail: blipman@bu.edu. *Application contact:* Andrew Campolieto, PhD Program Administrator, 617-353-4454, Fax: 617-353-4449, E-mail: acamp@bu.edu.
Website: http://www.bu.edu/econ/

**Brandeis University,** International Business School (IBS), Master of Arts in International Economics and Finance Program, Waltham, MA 02454-9110. Offers business economics (MA). *Faculty:* 29 full-time (10 women), 27 part-time/adjunct (3 women). *Students:* 150 full-time (77 women). Average age 23. 741 applicants, 28% accepted, 68 enrolled. In 2016, 79 master's awarded. *Entrance requirements:* For master's, GMAT or GRE. Additional exam requirements/recommendations for international students: Required—TOEFL (minimum score 600 paper-based; 100 iBT), IELTS (minimum score 7), PTE (minimum score 68). *Application deadline:* For fall admission, 11/1 priority date for domestic and international students; for winter admission, 1/15 priority date for domestic and international students; for spring admission, 3/15 priority date for domestic and international students; for summer admission, 5/15 for domestic and international students. Application fee: $55. Electronic applications accepted. *Expenses:* Contact institution. *Financial support:* In 2016–17, 112 students received support. Institutionally sponsored loans and scholarships/grants available. Financial award application deadline: 3/15; financial award applicants required to submit FAFSA. *Faculty research:* International economic policy analysis, macroeconomics, econometrics, business economics, economic development. *Unit head:* Peter Petri, Dean, 781-736-2256. *Application contact:* Kelly Sugrue, Director of Admissions, 781-736-2252, Fax: 781-736-2263, E-mail: admission@lemberg.brandeis.edu.
Website: http://www.brandeis.edu/global/ma

**Brandeis University,** International Business School (IBS), PhD in International Economics and Finance Program, Waltham, MA 02454-9110. Offers global trade (PhD); macroeconomics (PhD). *Faculty:* 11 full-time (5 women). *Students:* 7 full-time (3 women). Average age 32. 107 applicants, 19% accepted, 7 enrolled. In 2016, 3 doctorates awarded. *Degree requirements:* For doctorate, thesis/dissertation. *Entrance requirements:* Additional exam requirements/recommendations for international students: Required—TOEFL (minimum score 600 paper-based; 100 iBT), IELTS (minimum score 7), PTE (minimum score 68). *Application deadline:* For winter admission, 1/15 priority date for domestic and international students. Application fee: $55. *Expenses:* Contact institution. *Financial support:* In 2016–17, 16 students received support, including 11 fellowships (averaging $9,545 per year), research assistantships (averaging $6,000 per year), teaching assistantships (averaging $6,000 per year); institutionally sponsored loans, scholarships/grants, health care benefits, and tuition waivers (full and partial) also available. Financial award application deadline: 1/15; financial award applicants required to submit FAFSA. *Faculty research:* Global business, global trade, global finance, macroeconomics, development and institutions. *Unit head:* Peter Petri, Interim Dean, 781-736-2256. *Application contact:* Kelly Sugrue, Director of Admissions, 781-736-2252, Fax: 781-736-2263, E-mail: admission@lemberg.brandeis.edu.
Website: https://www.brandeis.edu/global/academics/phd/

**Brock University,** Faculty of Graduate Studies, Faculty of Social Sciences, Program in Business Economics, St. Catharines, ON L2S 3A1, Canada. Offers MBE. *Degree requirements:* For master's, thesis or alternative. *Entrance requirements:* For master's, honours degree. Additional exam requirements/recommendations for international students: Required—TOEFL (minimum score 550 paper-based; 80 iBT), IELTS (minimum score 6.5), TWE (minimum score 4). Electronic applications accepted. *Faculty research:* Microeconomic theory, macroeconomics, econometrics, applied econometrics, economic development.

**Brooklyn College of the City University of New York,** School of Business, Brooklyn, NY 11210-2889. Offers accounting (MS); business administration (MS), including economic analysis, general business, global business and finance. *Program availability:* Part-time, evening/weekend. *Degree requirements:* For master's, comprehensive exam, thesis or alternative. *Entrance requirements:* For master's, GMAT, 2 letters of recommendation. Additional exam requirements/recommendations for international students: Required—TOEFL (minimum score 550 paper-based; 79 iBT). Electronic applications accepted. *Faculty research:* Econometrics, environmental economics, microeconomics, macroeconomics, taxation.

**Brown University,** Graduate School, Department of Economics, Providence, RI 02912. Offers PhD. Terminal master's awarded for partial completion of doctoral program. *Degree requirements:* For doctorate, thesis/dissertation. *Entrance requirements:* For doctorate, GRE General Test.

**Buffalo State College, State University of New York,** The Graduate School, Faculty of Natural and Social Sciences, Department of Economics and Finance, Buffalo, NY 14222-1095. Offers applied economics (MA). *Degree requirements:* For master's, project. *Entrance requirements:* Additional exam requirements/recommendations for international students: Required—TOEFL (minimum score 550 paper-based).

**California Lutheran University,** Graduate Studies, School of Management, Thousand Oaks, CA 91360-2787. Offers business (IMBA); computer science (MS); econometrics (MBA); economics (MS); entrepreneurship (MBA, Certificate); finance (MBA, Certificate); financial planning (MBA, Certificate); information systems and technology (MS); information technology management (MBA, Certificate); international business (MBA, Certificate); management and organization behavior (MBA); management and organizational behavior (Certificate); marketing (MBA, Certificate); microeconomics (MBA); nonprofit and social enterprise (MBA); public policy and administration (MPPA). *Program availability:* Part-time, evening/weekend, 100% online, blended/hybrid learning. *Faculty:* 25 full-time (10 women), 36 part-time/adjunct (12 women). *Students:* 427 full-time (172 women), 189 part-time (87 women); includes 120 minority (14 Black or African American, non-Hispanic/Latino; 2 American Indian or Alaska Native, non-Hispanic/Latino; 19 Asian, non-Hispanic/Latino; 37 Hispanic/Latino; 48 Two or more races, non-Hispanic/Latino), 338 international. Average age 30. 591 applicants, 64% accepted, 131 enrolled. In 2016, 305 master's awarded. *Entrance requirements:* For master's, GMAT, interview, minimum GPA of 3.0. *Application deadline:* Applications are processed on a rolling basis. Application fee: $50. Electronic applications accepted. *Expenses:* Contact institution. *Unit head:* Dr. Gerhard Apfelthaler, Dean, 805-493-3360. *Application contact:* 805-493-3325, Fax: 805-493-3861, E-mail: clugrad@callutheran.edu.
Website: http://www.callutheran.edu/management/

**California Polytechnic State University, San Luis Obispo,** Orfalea College of Business, Program in Economics, San Luis Obispo, CA 93407. Offers MS. *Students:* 13 full-time (3 women), 4 part-time (1 woman); includes 4 minority (2 Asian, non-Hispanic/Latino; 2 Hispanic/Latino), 2 international. Average age 23. In 2016, 10 master's awarded. *Degree requirements:* For master's, comprehensive exam (for some programs), thesis (for some programs). *Entrance requirements:* For master's, GMAT.

Additional exam requirements/recommendations for international students: Required—TOEFL (minimum score 80 iBT). *Application deadline:* For fall admission, 4/1 for domestic students, 3/1 for international students. Applications are processed on a rolling basis. Application fee: $55. Electronic applications accepted. *Expenses:* Tuition, state resident: full-time $6738; part-time $3906 per year. Tuition, nonresident: full-time $15,666; part-time $8370 per year. *Required fees:* $3603; $3141 per unit. $1047 per term. *Financial support:* Fellowships, career-related internships or fieldwork, Federal Work-Study, institutionally sponsored loans, scholarships/grants, and unspecified assistantships available. Support available to part-time students. Financial award application deadline: 3/2; financial award applicants required to submit FAFSA. *Faculty research:* Management of high-tech firms, Pacific Rim, capital market structures, economics of environmental policy, marketing of services. *Unit head:* Dr. Scott Dawson, Dean, 805-756-2705, E-mail: scdawson@calpoly.edu. *Application contact:* Dr. Sanjiv Jaggia, Associate Dean, Graduate Programs, 805-756-7519, E-mail: sjaggia@calpoly.edu.
Website: http://www.cob.calpoly.edu/gradbusiness/degree-programs/ms-economics/

**California State Polytechnic University, Pomona,** Program in Economics, Pomona, CA 91768-2557. Offers MS. *Program availability:* Part-time, evening/weekend. *Students:* 8 full-time (3 women), 32 part-time (15 women); includes 11 minority (1 Black or African American, non-Hispanic/Latino; 1 American Indian or Alaska Native, non-Hispanic/Latino; 3 Asian, non-Hispanic/Latino; 6 Hispanic/Latino), 22 international. Average age 28. 15 applicants, 93% accepted, 11 enrolled. In 2016, 11 master's awarded. *Entrance requirements:* Additional exam requirements/recommendations for international students: Required—TOEFL. *Application deadline:* Applications are processed on a rolling basis. Application fee: $55. Electronic applications accepted. *Expenses:* Contact institution. *Financial support:* Application deadline: 3/2; applicants required to submit FAFSA. *Unit head:* Dr. Gregory Hunter, Graduate Coordinator, 909-869-4888, Fax: 909-869-6987, E-mail: gwhunter@cpp.edu. *Application contact:* Andrew M. Wright, Director of Admissions, 909-869-3130, Fax: 909-869-4529, E-mail: awright@cpp.edu.
Website: http://www.cpp.edu/~class/economics/graduate-students/

**California State University, East Bay,** Office of Graduate Studies, College of Business and Economics, Economics Department, Hayward, CA 94542-3000. Offers MA. *Program availability:* Part-time, evening/weekend. *Students:* 6 full-time (3 women), 25 part-time (9 women); includes 10 minority (2 Black or African American, non-Hispanic/Latino; 4 Asian, non-Hispanic/Latino; 3 Hispanic/Latino; 1 Two or more races, non-Hispanic/Latino), 11 international. Average age 30. 39 applicants, 64% accepted, 9 enrolled. In 2016, 17 master's awarded. *Degree requirements:* For master's, comprehensive exam, project or thesis. *Entrance requirements:* For master's, GMAT, minimum GPA of 2.75 during previous 2 years of course work. Additional exam requirements/recommendations for international students: Required—TOEFL (minimum score 580 paper-based; 92 iBT). *Application deadline:* For fall admission, 6/30 for domestic and international students. Applications are processed on a rolling basis. Application fee: $55. Electronic applications accepted. *Financial support:* Career-related internships or fieldwork, Federal Work-Study, and institutionally sponsored loans available. Support available to part-time students. Financial award application deadline: 3/2; financial award applicants required to submit FAFSA. *Unit head:* Prof. Jed DeVaro, Chair, 510-885-3289, E-mail: jed.devaro@csueastbay.edu. *Application contact:* Christian Roessler, Graduate Program Director, 510-885-2858, E-mail: christian.roessler@csueastbay.edu.
Website: http://www20.csueastbay.edu/cbe/departments/economics/

**California State University, Fullerton,** Graduate Studies, College of Business and Economics, Department of Economics, Fullerton, CA 92834-9480. Offers MA, MBA. *Program availability:* Part-time. *Degree requirements:* For master's, thesis. *Entrance requirements:* For master's, GMAT, GRE General Test. Application fee: $55. *Expenses:* Tuition, state resident: full-time $3369; part-time $1953 per unit. Tuition, nonresident: full-time $3915; part-time $2499 per unit. Tuition and fees vary according to course load, degree level and program. *Financial support:* Career-related internships or fieldwork, Federal Work-Study, institutionally sponsored loans, and scholarships/grants available. Support available to part-time students. Financial award application deadline: 3/1; financial award applicants required to submit FAFSA. *Faculty research:* Environmental and natural resource issues. *Unit head:* Dr. David Wong, Chair, 657-278-3821. *Application contact:* Admissions/Applications, 657-278-2371.

**California State University, Long Beach,** Graduate Studies, College of Liberal Arts, Department of Economics, Long Beach, CA 90840. Offers economics (MA). *Program availability:* Part-time. *Degree requirements:* For master's, comprehensive exam or thesis. *Entrance requirements:* For master's, GRE General Test, GRE Subject Test, minimum GPA of 3.0. *Application deadline:* For fall admission, 4/1 for domestic students. Applications are processed on a rolling basis. Application fee: $55. Electronic applications accepted. *Financial support:* Federal Work-Study, institutionally sponsored loans, and scholarships/grants available. Financial award application deadline: 3/2. *Faculty research:* Trade and development, economic forecasting, resource economics. *Unit head:* Seiji Steimetz, Chair, 562-985-5061, E-mail: econ@csulb.edu.

**California State University, Los Angeles,** Graduate Studies, College of Business and Economics, Department of Economics and Statistics, Los Angeles, CA 90032-8530. Offers financial economics (MA); global economics (MA). *Program availability:* Part-time, evening/weekend. *Degree requirements:* For master's, comprehensive exam or thesis. *Entrance requirements:* For master's, GMAT, minimum GPA of 2.5 during previous 2 years of course work. Additional exam requirements/recommendations for international students: Required—TOEFL (minimum score 550 paper-based). Electronic applications accepted.

**California University of Management and Sciences,** Graduate Programs, Anaheim, CA 92801. Offers business administration (MBA, DBA); computer information systems (MS); economics (MS); international business (MS); sports management (MS).

**Carleton University,** Faculty of Graduate Studies, Faculty of Public Affairs and Management, Department of Economics, Ottawa, ON K1S 5B6, Canada. Offers MA, PhD. PhD program offered jointly with University of Ottawa. *Degree requirements:* For master's, thesis optional; for doctorate, comprehensive exam, thesis/dissertation. *Entrance requirements:* For master's, honors degree; for doctorate, master's degree. Additional exam requirements/recommendations for international students: Required—TOEFL. *Faculty research:* Monetary economics, economic development, public economics, industrial organization, international trade.

**Carleton University,** Faculty of Graduate Studies, Faculty of Public Affairs and Management, Institute of Political Economy, Ottawa, ON K1S 5B6, Canada. Offers MA, PhD. *Degree requirements:* For master's, thesis optional. *Entrance requirements:* For master's, honors degree. Additional exam requirements/recommendations for international students: Required—TOEFL. *Faculty research:* Relationships between economy and politics as they affect the political, social and cultural life of societies; historical processes whereby social change is located in the interaction of the economic, political and cultural, and ideological moments of social life.

**Carnegie Mellon University,** Tepper School of Business, Program in Economics, Pittsburgh, PA 15213-3891. Offers PhD. *Degree requirements:* For doctorate, thesis/

dissertation. *Entrance requirements:* For doctorate, GMAT, GRE General Test. *Faculty research:* Research allocation under asymmetric information, monetary theory, estimation of rational expectations models.

**Central European University,** Department of Economics, Budapest, Hungary. Offers business analytics (M Sc); economic policy in global markets (MA); economics (MA, PhD); global economic relations (MA). *Faculty:* 14 full-time (1 woman), 9 part-time/adjunct (1 woman). *Students:* 122 full-time (44 women). Average age 26. 300 applicants, 24% accepted, 51 enrolled. In 2016, 34 master's, 5 doctorates awarded. *Degree requirements:* For master's, one foreign language, thesis; for doctorate, one foreign language, comprehensive exam, thesis/dissertation. *Entrance requirements:* For master's and doctorate, interview. Additional exam requirements/recommendations for international students: Required—TOEFL (minimum score 570 paper-based); Recommended—IELTS (minimum score 6.5). *Application deadline:* For fall admission, 2/4 for domestic and international students. Application fee: $30. Electronic applications accepted. *Expenses:* Tuition: Full-time 13,500 euros. Tuition and fees vary according to degree level, program and student level. *Financial support:* Fellowships, teaching assistantships, career-related internships or fieldwork, institutionally sponsored loans, scholarships/grants, health care benefits, and tuition waivers (full and partial) available. *Faculty research:* Economic theory (microeconomics and macroeconomics) and econometrics, as well as study of many applied fields, including labor economics, health economics and economics of education, industrial organization, monetary economics, international economics, law and economics, comparative institutional economics, corporate governance, and economics of transition. *Unit head:* Miklos Koren, Head of Department, 36 1 327-3000 Ext. 2212, E-mail: econdept@ceu.edu. *Application contact:* Zsuzsanna Jaszberenyi, Admissions Officer, 361-324-3009, Fax: 367-327-3211, E-mail: admissions@ceu.edu.
Website: http://economics.ceu.edu/

**Central European University,** Department of Legal Studies, Budapest, Hungary. Offers comparative Constitutional law (LL M); human rights (LL M, MA); international business law (LL M); juridical sciences (SJD); law and economics (LL M, MA). *Faculty:* 10 full-time (5 women), 15 part-time/adjunct (3 women). *Students:* 89 full-time (43 women). Average age 27. 420 applicants, 27% accepted, 66 enrolled. In 2016, 52 master's, 4 doctorates awarded. Terminal master's awarded for partial completion of doctoral program. *Degree requirements:* For master's, one foreign language, thesis; for doctorate, one foreign language, comprehensive exam, thesis/dissertation. *Entrance requirements:* For master's and doctorate, LSAT. Additional exam requirements/recommendations for international students: Required—TOEFL (minimum score 570 paper-based); Recommended—IELTS (minimum score 6.5). *Application deadline:* For fall admission, 2/4 for domestic and international students. Application fee: $30. Electronic applications accepted. *Expenses:* Contact institution. *Financial support:* Fellowships, career-related internships or fieldwork, institutionally sponsored loans, scholarships/grants, and tuition waivers (full and partial) available. Financial award application deadline: 2/4. *Faculty research:* Institutional, Constitutional and human rights in European Union law; biomedical law and reproductive rights; data protection law; comparative and international business law and the regulation of business environments;. *Unit head:* Dr. Karoly Bard, Head of Department, 36 1 327-3294, Fax: 361-327-3198, E-mail: legalst@ceu.edu. *Application contact:* Zsuzsanna Jaszberenyi, Department Coordinator, 361-327-3272, Fax: 361-327-3198, E-mail: admissions@ceu.edu.
Website: http://legal.ceu.edu

**Central Michigan University,** College of Graduate Studies, College of Business Administration, Department of Economics, Mount Pleasant, MI 48859. Offers MA. *Program availability:* Part-time. *Degree requirements:* For master's, thesis or alternative. Electronic applications accepted. *Faculty research:* Economic development, industrial organization, international trade, monetary theory, public choice/labor.

**City College of the City University of New York,** Graduate School, Colin Powell School for Civic and Global Leadership, Department of Economics and Business, New York, NY 10031-9198. Offers economics (MA). *Program availability:* Part-time. *Degree requirements:* For master's, comprehensive exam, proficiency in a foreign language or advanced statistics. *Entrance requirements:* Additional exam requirements/recommendations for international students: Required—TOEFL (minimum score 550 paper-based; 79 iBT). Electronic applications accepted. Tuition and fees vary according to course load, degree level and program. *Faculty research:* International economics, health, banking.

**Claremont Graduate University,** Graduate Programs, School of Social Science, Policy and Evaluation, Department of Economics, Claremont, CA 91711-6160. Offers behavioral economics and neuroeconomics (PhD); business and financial economics (MA, PhD); economic development (Certificate); international economic and development policy (PhD); international economics policy and development (MA); international money and finance (PhD); political economy and public economics (PhD); political economy and public policy (MA); MBA/PhD. *Program availability:* Part-time. *Faculty:* 5 full-time (1 woman), 2 part-time/adjunct (0 women). *Students:* 92 full-time (31 women), 34 part-time (15 women); includes 14 minority (4 Black or African American, non-Hispanic/Latino; 7 Asian, non-Hispanic/Latino; 2 Hispanic/Latino; 1 Two or more races, non-Hispanic/Latino), 67 international. Average age 33. In 2016, 20 master's, 16 doctorates awarded. *Entrance requirements:* For master's and doctorate, GRE General Test or GMAT. Additional exam requirements/recommendations for international students: Required—TOEFL (minimum score 75 iBT). *Application deadline:* For fall admission, 2/1 priority date for domestic and international students. Applications are processed on a rolling basis. Application fee: $80. Electronic applications accepted. *Expenses:* Tuition: Full-time $44,328; part-time $1847 per unit. *Required fees:* $600; $300 per semester. Tuition and fees vary according to course load and program. *Financial support:* Fellowships, research assistantships, teaching assistantships, Federal Work-Study, institutionally sponsored loans, and scholarships/grants available. Support available to part-time students. Financial award application deadline: 2/15; financial award applicants required to submit FAFSA. *Faculty research:* International and financial economics, law and economics, regulation, public choice economics. *Unit head:* Paul Zak, Chair, 909-621-8788, E-mail: paul.zak@cgu.edu. *Application contact:* Paige Piontkowsky, Senior Assistant Director of Admissions, 909-607-3240, E-mail: paige.piontkowsky@cgu.edu.
Website: https://www.cgu.edu/school/ssspe/programs/?areas_of_study=economics

**Claremont Graduate University,** Graduate Programs, School of Social Science, Policy and Evaluation, Department of Politics and Policy, Claremont, CA 91711-6160. Offers American politics (MA, PhD); comparative politics (PhD); international political economy (MA); international studies (MA); political philosophy (PhD); political science (PhD); politics, economics and business (MA); public policy (MA, PhD); world politics (PhD); MBA/PhD. *Program availability:* Part-time. *Faculty:* 6 full-time (4 women), 3 part-time/adjunct (0 women). *Students:* 107 full-time (37 women), 32 part-time (10 women); includes 41 minority (6 Black or African American, non-Hispanic/Latino; 10 Asian, non-Hispanic/Latino; 17 Hispanic/Latino; 8 Two or more races, non-Hispanic/Latino), 31 international. Average age 36. In 2016, 21 master's, 14 doctorates awarded. Terminal master's awarded for partial completion of doctoral program. *Entrance requirements:* For master's and doctorate, GRE General Test. Additional exam requirements/recommendations for international students: Required—TOEFL (minimum score 75

## Economics

iBT). *Application deadline:* For fall admission, 2/1 priority date for domestic and international students. Applications are processed on a rolling basis. Application fee: $80. Electronic applications accepted. *Expenses: Tuition:* Full-time $44,328; part-time $1847 per unit. *Required fees:* $600; $300 per semester. Tuition and fees vary according to course load and program. *Financial support:* Fellowships, research assistantships, teaching assistantships, Federal Work-Study, institutionally sponsored loans, and scholarships/grants available. Support available to part-time students. Financial award application deadline: 2/15; financial award applicants required to submit FAFSA. *Faculty research:* Environmental policy, international debt, global democratization, Third World development, public sector discrimination. *Unit head:* Heather Campbell, Chair, 909-621-8689, E-mail: heather.campbell@cgu.edu. *Application contact:* Paige Piontkowsky, Senior Assistant Director of Admissions, 909-607-3240, E-mail: paige.piontkowsky@cgu.edu.
Website: https://www.cgu.edu/school/ssspe/programs/?areas_of_study=politics-and-government

**Claremont Graduate University,** Graduate Programs, School of Social Science, Policy and Evaluation, Program in Politics, Economics, and Business, Claremont, CA 91711-6160. Offers MA. *Program availability:* Part-time. *Students:* 2 full-time (1 woman), 1 part-time (0 women); includes 1 minority (Hispanic/Latino). Average age 31. In 2016, 3 master's awarded. *Entrance requirements:* For master's, GRE General Test. Additional exam requirements/recommendations for international students: Required—TOEFL (minimum score 75 iBT). *Application deadline:* For fall admission, 2/1 priority date for domestic and international students. Applications are processed on a rolling basis. Application fee: $80. Electronic applications accepted. *Expenses: Tuition:* Full-time $44,328; part-time $1847 per unit. *Required fees:* $600; $300 per semester. Tuition and fees vary according to course load and program. *Financial support:* Federal Work-Study, institutionally sponsored loans, and scholarships/grants available. Support available to part-time students. Financial award application deadline: 2/15; financial award applicants required to submit FAFSA. *Unit head:* Stewart Donaldson, Dean, 909-607-8235, E-mail: stewart.donaldson@cgu.edu. *Application contact:* Paige Piontkowsky, Senior Assistant Director of Admissions, 909-607-3240, E-mail: paige.piontkowsky@cgu.edu.
Website: https://www.cgu.edu/academics/program/politics-economics-and-business/

**Clark Atlanta University,** School of Business Administration, Department of Economics, Atlanta, GA 30314. Offers MA. *Program availability:* Part-time. *Faculty:* 2 full-time (0 women). *Students:* 2 full-time (both women), 1 international. Average age 26. 5 applicants. In 2016, 2 master's awarded. *Degree requirements:* For master's, thesis optional. *Entrance requirements:* For master's, GRE General Test, minimum GPA of 2.5. Additional exam requirements/recommendations for international students: Required—TOEFL (minimum score 500 paper-based; 61 iBT). *Application deadline:* For fall admission, 4/1 for domestic and international students; for spring admission, 11/1 for domestic and international students. Applications are processed on a rolling basis. Application fee: $40 ($55 for international students). Electronic applications accepted. *Expenses: Tuition:* Full-time $15,498; part-time $861 per credit hour. *Required fees:* $1326; $1326 per credit hour. Tuition and fees vary according to course load. *Financial support:* Career-related internships or fieldwork, Federal Work-Study, scholarships/grants, and unspecified assistantships available. Support available to part-time students. Financial award application deadline: 4/30; financial award applicants required to submit FAFSA. *Faculty research:* Minority energy demand. *Unit head:* Dr. Young Kim, Chairperson, 404-880-8450, E-mail: ykim@cau.edu. *Application contact:* Graduate Program Admissions, 404-880-8483, E-mail: graduateadmissions@cau.edu.

**Clark University,** Graduate School, Department of Economics, Worcester, MA 01610-1477. Offers PhD. *Faculty:* 9 full-time (3 women), 1 (woman) part-time/adjunct. *Students:* 39 full-time (20 women), 1 (woman) part-time, 31 international. Average age 31. 44 applicants, 61% accepted, 7 enrolled. In 2016, 4 doctorates awarded. *Degree requirements:* For doctorate, thesis/dissertation. *Entrance requirements:* For doctorate, GRE General Test. Additional exam requirements/recommendations for international students: Required—TOEFL. *Application deadline:* For fall admission, 2/1 priority date for domestic students. Applications are processed on a rolling basis. Application fee: $75. Electronic applications accepted. *Expenses: Tuition:* Full-time $44,050. *Required fees:* $80. Tuition and fees vary according to course load and program. *Financial support:* In 2016–17, fellowships with tuition reimbursements (averaging $13,240 per year), 3 research assistantships with tuition reimbursements (averaging $13,240 per year), 12 teaching assistantships with tuition reimbursements (averaging $13,240 per year) were awarded; career-related internships or fieldwork, institutionally sponsored loans, and tuition waivers (full and partial) also available. *Faculty research:* Public finance, economic development, industrial organization, international finance and trade, environmental regulation. *Unit head:* Dr. Jacqueline Geoghegan, Chair, 508-793-7709. *Application contact:* Cindy Rice, Managerial Secretary, 508-793-7226, Fax: 508-793-8849, E-mail: crice@clarku.edu.
Website: http://www.clarku.edu/departments/economics/

**Clemson University,** Graduate School, College of Business, John E. Walker Department of Economics, Clemson, SC 29634. Offers MA, PhD. *Faculty:* 28 full-time (3 women), 4 part-time/adjunct (1 woman). *Students:* 77 full-time (26 women), 4 part-time (2 women); includes 4 minority (1 Black or African American, non-Hispanic/Latino; 1 Hispanic/Latino; 2 Two or more races, non-Hispanic/Latino), 51 international. Average age 28. 139 applicants, 40% accepted, 17 enrolled. In 2016, 19 master's, 18 doctorates awarded. Terminal master's awarded for partial completion of doctoral program. *Degree requirements:* For master's, thesis, 24 course hours, 6 thesis hours; for doctorate, comprehensive exam, thesis/dissertation, 42 course hours, 18 dissertation hours. *Entrance requirements:* For master's and doctorate, GRE General Test or GMAT, unofficial transcripts, letters of recommendation, courses in intermediate microeconomic theory and multivariable calculus. Additional exam requirements/recommendations for international students: Required—TOEFL (minimum score 80 iBT), IELTS (minimum score 6.5). *Application deadline:* For fall admission, 1/15 priority date for domestic and international students. Applications are processed on a rolling basis. Application fee: $80 ($90 for international students). Electronic applications accepted. *Expenses:* $4,264 per semester full-time resident, $8,485 per semester full-time non-resident, $471 per credit hour part-time resident, $942 per credit hour part-time non-resident. *Financial support:* In 2016–17, 72 students received support, including 16 fellowships with partial tuition reimbursements available (averaging $8,926 per year), 19 teaching assistantships with partial tuition reimbursements available (averaging $14,684 per year); unspecified assistantships also available. Financial award application deadline: 1/15. *Faculty research:* Public economics, public choice and political economy; econometrics (focus on data envelope analysis), industrial organization (focus on pricing), labor and development economics, international economics (focus on free trade agreements). *Total annual research expenditures:* $20,956. *Unit head:* Dr. Scott Baier, Interim Department Chair, 864-656-4534, E-mail: sbaier@clemson.edu. *Application contact:* Dr. Curtis Simon, Graduate Program Coordinator, 864-656-3966, E-mail: cjsmn@clemson.edu.
Website: http://economics.clemson.edu/

**Cleveland State University,** College of Graduate Studies, College of Liberal Arts and Social Sciences, Department of Economics, Cleveland, OH 44115. Offers MA. *Program availability:* Part-time, evening/weekend. *Faculty:* 6 full-time (1 woman). *Students:* 8 full-time (2 women), 4 part-time (1 woman); includes 1 minority (Asian, non-Hispanic/Latino), 4 international. Average age 28. 32 applicants, 72% accepted, 7 enrolled. In 2016, 11 master's awarded. *Entrance requirements:* For master's, minimum GPA of 2.75; coursework in micro theory, macro theory, statistics, and calculus. Additional exam requirements/recommendations for international students: Required—TOEFL (minimum score 550 paper-based; 78 iBT), IELTS (minimum score 6). *Application deadline:* For fall admission, 7/1 priority date for domestic students, 5/15 priority date for international students; for spring admission, 11/15 for domestic students, 11/1 for international students; for summer admission, 4/1 for domestic students, 3/15 for international students. Applications are processed on a rolling basis. Application fee: $40. Electronic applications accepted. *Expenses:* Tuition, state resident: full-time $9565. Tuition, nonresident: full-time $17,980. Tuition and fees vary according to program. *Financial support:* In 2016–17, 4 students received support, including 3 teaching assistantships (averaging $30,000 per year). Financial award application deadline: 4/30; financial award applicants required to submit FAFSA. *Faculty research:* Health economics, monetary economics, computational economics, urban economics, financial economics. *Unit head:* Dr. Billy Kosteas, Department Chairperson/Associate Professor, 216-687-4526, Fax: 216-687-9206, E-mail: b.kosteas@csuohio.edu. *Application contact:* Dr. Myong Hun Chang, Professor, 216-687-4523, Fax: 216-687-9206, E-mail: m.chang@csuohio.edu.
Website: http://www.csuohio.edu/class/economics/economics

**Cleveland State University,** College of Graduate Studies, Maxine Goodman Levin College of Urban Affairs, Program in Urban Planning, Design, and Development, Cleveland, OH 44115. Offers environmental sustainability (MUPDD); housing and neighborhood development (MUPDD); urban economic development (Certificate); JD/MUPDD. *Accreditation:* ACSP. *Program availability:* Part-time, evening/weekend. *Faculty:* 16 full-time (8 women), 13 part-time/adjunct (5 women). *Students:* 8 full-time (3 women), 26 part-time (15 women); includes 4 minority (2 Black or African American, non-Hispanic/Latino; 1 Asian, non-Hispanic/Latino; 1 Two or more races, non-Hispanic/Latino), 2 international. Average age 28. 48 applicants, 56% accepted, 14 enrolled. In 2016, 21 master's awarded. *Degree requirements:* For master's, thesis or alternative, exit project. *Entrance requirements:* For master's, GRE General Test (minimum score: 50th percentile combined verbal and quantitative, 4.0 analytical writing), minimum GPA of 3.0. Additional exam requirements/recommendations for international students: Required—TOEFL (minimum score 550 paper-based; 78 iBT), IELTS (6.0), or International Test of English Proficiency (iTEP). *Application deadline:* For fall admission, 7/1 priority date for domestic students, 5/15 for international students; for spring admission, 11/15 for domestic students, 11/1 for international students; for summer admission, 4/1 for domestic students, 3/15 for international students. Applications are processed on a rolling basis. Application fee: $40. Electronic applications accepted. *Expenses:* Contact institution. *Financial support:* In 2016–17, 10 students received support, including 5 research assistantships with full tuition reimbursements available (averaging $7,200 per year), 3 teaching assistantships with partial tuition reimbursements available (averaging $2,400 per year); scholarships/grants, tuition waivers (full and partial), and unspecified assistantships also available. Support available to part-time students. Financial award application deadline: 3/1; financial award applicants required to submit FAFSA. *Faculty research:* Housing and neighborhood development, urban housing policy, environmental sustainability, economic development, GIS and planning decision support. *Unit head:* Dr. Stephanie Ryberg-Webster, Assistant Professor/Director of MUPD Program, 216-802-3386, Fax: 216-687-2013, E-mail: s.ryberg@csuohio.edu. *Application contact:* David Arrighi, Graduate Academic Advisor, 216-523-7522, Fax: 216-687-5398, E-mail: d.arrighi@csuohio.edu.
Website: http://urban.csuohio.edu/academics/graduate/mupdd/

**Colorado State University,** College of Liberal Arts, Department of Economics, Fort Collins, CO 80523-1771. Offers MA, PhD. *Program availability:* Part-time. *Faculty:* 10 full-time (5 women). *Students:* 30 full-time (11 women), 36 part-time (9 women); includes 7 minority (2 Black or African American, non-Hispanic/Latino; 4 Hispanic/Latino; 1 Two or more races, non-Hispanic/Latino), 21 international. Average age 31. 62 applicants, 84% accepted, 12 enrolled. In 2016, 11 master's, 1 doctorate awarded. Terminal master's awarded for partial completion of doctoral program. *Degree requirements:* For master's, thesis; for doctorate, comprehensive exam, thesis/dissertation. *Entrance requirements:* For master's and doctorate, GRE General Test (minimum score of 305 on Verbal plus Quantitative and at least 155 on Quantitative), minimum GPA of 3.0 for last completed degree, evidence of appropriate background course work. Additional exam requirements/recommendations for international students: Required—PTE (minimum score 58), TOEFL (minimum score 550 paper-based, 80 iBT) or IELTS (6.5). *Application deadline:* For fall admission, 5/1 for domestic students, 4/1 priority date for international students. Application fee: $60 ($70 for international students). Electronic applications accepted. *Expenses:* Tuition, state resident: full-time $9628. Tuition, nonresident: full-time $23,603. *Required fees:* $2253; $528.14 per credit hour. $264.07 per semester. Tuition and fees vary according to course load and program. *Financial support:* In 2016–17, 7 students received support, including 2 research assistantships with full tuition reimbursements available (averaging $15,233 per year), 20 teaching assistantships with full tuition reimbursements available (averaging $16,519 per year); health care benefits also available. Financial award application deadline: 2/15. *Faculty research:* Regional economics; political economy; environmental economics; public economics; development and international economics. *Total annual research expenditures:* $187,831. *Unit head:* Dr. Alexandra Bernasek, Professor and Department Chair, 970-491-3321, E-mail: alexandra.bernasek@colostate.edu. *Application contact:* Veronica Nicholson, Program Coordinator, 970-491-6566, E-mail: veronica.nicholson@colostate.edu.
Website: http://economics.colostate.edu/

**Columbia University,** Graduate School of Arts and Sciences, New York, NY 10027. Offers African-American studies (MA); American studies (MA); anthropology (MA, PhD); art history and archaeology (MA, PhD); astronomy (PhD); biological sciences (PhD); biotechnology (MA); chemical physics (PhD); chemistry (PhD); classical studies (MA, PhD); classics (MA, PhD); climate and society (MA); conservation biology (MA); earth and environmental sciences (PhD); East Asia: regional studies (MA); East Asian languages and cultures (MA, PhD); ecology, evolution and environmental biology (MA), including conservation biology; ecology, evolution, and environmental biology (PhD), including ecology and evolutionary biology, evolutionary primatology; economics (MA, PhD); English and comparative literature (MA, PhD); French and Romance philology (MA, PhD); Germanic languages (MA, PhD); global French studies (PhD); global thought (MA); Hispanic cultural studies (MA); history (PhD); history and literature (MA); human rights studies (MA); Islamic studies (MA); Italian (MA, PhD); Japanese pedagogy (MA); Jewish studies (MA); Latin America and the Caribbean: regional studies (MA); Latin American and Iberian cultures (PhD); mathematics (MA, PhD), including finance (MA); medieval and Renaissance studies (MA); Middle Eastern, South Asian, and African studies (MA, PhD); modern art: critical and curatorial studies (MA); modern European studies (MA); museum anthropology (MA); music (DMA, PhD); oral history (MA); philosophical foundations of physics (MA); philosophy (MA, PhD); physics (PhD); political science (MA, PhD); psychology (PhD); quantitative methods in the social sciences (MA); religion (MA, PhD); Russia, Eurasia and East Europe: regional studies (MA); Russian translation (MA); Slavic cultures (MA); Slavic languages (MA, PhD); sociology (MA, PhD); South Asian studies (MA); statistics (MA, PhD); theatre (PhD). Dual-degree programs require admission to both Graduate School of Arts and Sciences and another Columbia school. *Program availability:* Part-time. Terminal master's awarded for partial completion of doctoral program. *Degree requirements:* For master's, variable foreign language requirement, comprehensive exam (for some programs), thesis (for some programs); for doctorate, variable foreign language requirement, comprehensive exam (for some programs), thesis/dissertation. *Entrance requirements:* For master's and doctorate, GRE General Test, GRE Subject Test (for some programs). Additional exam requirements/recommendations for international students: Required—TOEFL, IELTS. Electronic applications accepted.

**Columbia University,** Graduate School of Business, Doctoral Program in Business, New York, NY 10027. Offers business (PhD), including accounting, decision, risk, and operations, finance and economics, management, marketing. *Accreditation:* AACSB. *Degree requirements:* For doctorate, comprehensive exam, thesis/dissertation, major field exam, research paper, thesis proposal. *Entrance requirements:* For doctorate, GMAT or GRE (finance), 2 letters of reference, resume. Additional exam requirements/recommendations for international students: Required—TOEFL. Electronic applications accepted. *Expenses:* Contact institution. *Faculty research:* Human decision making and behavioral research; real estate market and mortgage defaults; financial crisis and corporate governance; international business; security analysis and accounting.

**Columbia University,** Graduate School of Business, MBA Program, New York, NY 10027. Offers accounting (MBA); decision, risk, and operations (MBA); entrepreneurship (MBA); finance and economics (MBA); healthcare and pharmaceutical management (MBA); human resource management (MBA); international business (MBA); leadership and ethics (MBA); management (MBA); marketing (MBA); media (MBA); private equity (MBA); real estate (MBA); social enterprise (MBA); value investing (MBA); DDS/MBA; JD/MBA; MBA/MIA; MBA/MPH; MBA/MS; MD/MBA. *Entrance requirements:* For master's, GMAT, 2 letters of recommendation. Additional exam requirements/recommendations for international students: Required—TOEFL. Electronic applications accepted. *Expenses:* Contact institution. *Faculty research:* Human decision making and behavioral research; real estate market and mortgage defaults; financial crisis and corporate governance; international business; security analysis and accounting.

**Concordia University,** School of Graduate Studies, Faculty of Arts and Science, Department of Economics, Montréal, QC H3G 1M8, Canada. Offers MA, PhD, Diploma. *Degree requirements:* For master's, thesis or alternative, research paper; for doctorate, one foreign language, comprehensive exam, thesis/dissertation, research seminar. *Entrance requirements:* For master's and doctorate, honors degree in economics or equivalent. *Faculty research:* Trade and industrial adjustment, tax policy and reform, environmental policy, economics of migration, economics of telecommunications.

**Copenhagen Business School,** Graduate Programs, Copenhagen, Denmark. Offers business administration (Exec MBA, MBA, PhD); business administration and information systems (M Sc); business, language and culture (M Sc); economics and business administration (M Sc); health management (MHM); international business and politics (M Sc); public administration (MPA); shipping and logistics (Exec MBA); technology, market and organization (MBA).

**Cornell University,** Graduate School, Graduate Fields of Architecture, Art and Planning, Field of Regional Science, Ithaca, NY 14853. Offers environmental studies (MA, MS, PhD); international spatial problems (MA, MS, PhD); location theory (MA, MS, PhD); multiregional economic analysis (MA, MS, PhD); peace science (MA, MS, PhD); planning methods (MA, MS, PhD); urban and regional economics (MA, MS, PhD). Terminal master's awarded for partial completion of doctoral program. *Degree requirements:* For master's, thesis; for doctorate, comprehensive exam, thesis/dissertation. *Entrance requirements:* For master's and doctorate, GRE General Test, 2 letters of recommendation. Additional exam requirements/recommendations for international students: Required—TOEFL (minimum score 600 paper-based; 77 iBT). Electronic applications accepted. *Faculty research:* Urban and regional growth, spatial economics, formation of spatial patterns by socioeconomic systems, non-linear dynamics and complex systems, environmental-economic systems.

**Cornell University,** Graduate School, Graduate Fields of Arts and Sciences, Field of Economics, Ithaca, NY 14853. Offers applied economics (PhD); basic analytical economics (PhD); econometrics and economic statistics (PhD); economic development and planning (PhD); economic theory (PhD); industrial organization and control (PhD); international economics (PhD); labor economics (PhD); monetary and macro economics (PhD); public finance (PhD). *Degree requirements:* For doctorate, comprehensive exam, thesis/dissertation. *Entrance requirements:* For doctorate, GRE General Test, 3 letters of recommendation. Additional exam requirements/recommendations for international students: Required—TOEFL (minimum score 550 paper-based; 77 iBT). Electronic applications accepted. *Faculty research:* Learning and games, economics of education, political economy, transfer payments, time series and nonparametrics.

**Dalhousie University,** Faculty of Science, Department of Economics, Halifax, NS B3H 4R2, Canada. Offers MA, MDE, PhD. *Degree requirements:* For master's, thesis; for doctorate, thesis/dissertation. *Entrance requirements:* For master's and doctorate, GRE (recommended). Additional exam requirements/recommendations for international students: Required—TOEFL, IELTS, CANTEST, CAEL, or Michigan English Language Assessment Battery. Electronic applications accepted. *Faculty research:* Applied econometrics, industrial organization, labor and income distribution, economic theory (micro and macro), resource economics (fishing, forestry).

**DePaul University,** College of Liberal Arts and Social Sciences, Chicago, IL 60614. Offers Arabic (MA); Chinese (MA); English (MA); French (MA); German (MA); history (MA); interdisciplinary studies (MA, MS); international public service (MS); international studies (MA); Italian (MA); Japanese (MA); leadership and policy studies (MS); liberal studies (MA); new media studies (MA); nonprofit management (MNM); public administration (MPA); public health (MPH); public service management (MS); social work (MSW); sociology (MA); Spanish (MA); sustainable urban development (MA); women and gender studies (MA); writing and publishing (MA); writing, rhetoric, and discourse (MA); MA/PhD. *Program availability:* Part-time, evening/weekend, online learning. Terminal master's awarded for partial completion of doctoral program. *Degree requirements:* For master's, variable foreign language requirement, comprehensive exam (for some programs), thesis (for some programs). Electronic applications accepted.

**DePaul University,** Kellstadt Graduate School of Business, Chicago, IL 60604. Offers accountancy (M Acc, MS, MSA); applied economics (MBA); banking (MBA); behavioral finance (MBA); brand and product management (MBA); business development (MBA); business information technology (MS); business strategy and decision-making (MBA); computational finance (MS); consumer insights (MBA); corporate finance (MBA); economic policy analysis (MS); entrepreneurship (MBA); finance (MBA, MS); financial analysis (MBA); general business (MBA); health sector management (MBA); hospitality leadership (MBA); hospitality leadership and operational performance (MS); human resource management (MBA); human resources (MS); investment management (MBA); leadership and change management (MBA); management accounting (MBA);

marketing (MBA, MS); marketing analysis (MS); marketing strategy and planning (MBA); operations management (MBA); organizational diversity (MBA); real estate (MS); real estate finance and investment (MBA); revenue management (MBA); sports management (MBA); strategic global marketing (MBA); strategy, execution and valuation (MBA); sustainable management (MBA, MS); taxation (MS); wealth management (MS); JD/MBA. *Accreditation:* AACSB. *Program availability:* Part-time, evening/weekend, online learning. *Entrance requirements:* For master's, GMAT, 2 letters of recommendation, resume, essay, official transcripts. Additional exam requirements/recommendations for international students: Required—TOEFL (minimum score 550 paper-based; 80 iBT). Electronic applications accepted. *Expenses:* Contact institution.

**Drexel University,** LeBow College of Business, Program in Business Administration, Philadelphia, PA 19104-2875. Offers business administration (MBA, PhD, APC), including accounting (MBA, PhD), decision sciences (PhD), economics (MBA, PhD), finance (MBA, PhD), legal studies (MBA), management (MBA), marketing (MBA, PhD), organizational sciences (PhD), quantitative methods (MBA), strategic management (PhD). *Accreditation:* AACSB. *Program availability:* Part-time, evening/weekend, online learning. *Faculty:* 88 full-time (19 women), 11 part-time/adjunct (2 women). *Students:* 153 full-time (70 women), 388 part-time (168 women); includes 107 minority (31 Black or African American, non-Hispanic/Latino; 1 American Indian or Alaska Native, non-Hispanic/Latino; 48 Asian, non-Hispanic/Latino; 16 Hispanic/Latino; 11 Two or more races, non-Hispanic/Latino), 95 international. Average age 33. In 2016, 174 master's, 8 doctorates, 1 other advanced degree awarded. Terminal master's awarded for partial completion of doctoral program. *Entrance requirements:* For master's, GMAT, minimum GPA of 2.75; for doctorate, GMAT. Additional exam requirements/recommendations for international students: Required—TOEFL. *Application deadline:* For fall admission, 8/21 for domestic students; for spring admission, 3/5 for domestic students. Applications are processed on a rolling basis. Application fee: $50. Electronic applications accepted. *Expenses: Tuition:* Full-time $32,184; part-time $1192 per credit hour. *Required fees:* $280. Tuition and fees vary according to campus/location and program. *Financial support:* Research assistantships, teaching assistantships, career-related internships or fieldwork, and unspecified assistantships available. Financial award application deadline: 2/1. *Faculty research:* Decision support systems, individual and group behavior, operations research, techniques and strategy. *Unit head:* Dr. Thomas Wieckowski, Director of Master's Programs in Business, 215-895-1791, Fax: 215-895-1012. *Application contact:* Director of Graduate Admissions, 215-895-6700, Fax: 215-895-5939, E-mail: enroll@drexel.edu.

**Duke University,** Graduate School, Department of Economics, Durham, NC 27708. Offers AM, PhD, JD/AM. Spring admission applies to AM program only. *Degree requirements:* For doctorate, thesis/dissertation. *Entrance requirements:* For master's and doctorate, GRE General Test. Additional exam requirements/recommendations for international students: Required—TOEFL (minimum score 577 paper-based; 90 iBT) or IELTS (minimum score 7). Electronic applications accepted.

**Duke University,** Graduate School, Program in Economics and Computation, Durham, NC 27708-0097. Offers MS. *Entrance requirements:* For master's, GRE General Test. Additional exam requirements/recommendations for international students: Required—TOEFL (minimum score 577 paper-based; 90 iBT) or IELTS (minimum score 7).

**Duke University,** Graduate School, Program in Statistical and Economic Modeling, Durham, NC 27708. Offers econometrics (MS); financial economics (MS). Program offered jointly by the Departments of Statistical Science and Economics. *Entrance requirements:* For master's, GRE General Test. Additional exam requirements/recommendations for international students: Required—TOEFL (minimum score 577 paper-based; 90 iBT) or IELTS (minimum score 7). Electronic applications accepted.

**Eastern Illinois University,** Graduate School, College of Sciences, Department of Economics, Charleston, IL 61920. Offers MA. *Program availability:* Part-time, evening/weekend. *Degree requirements:* For master's, comprehensive exam (for some programs), thesis (for some programs). *Entrance requirements:* For master's, GMAT or GRE. Additional exam requirements/recommendations for international students: Required—TOEFL (minimum score 500 paper-based; 61 iBT), IELTS (minimum score 6). Electronic applications accepted.

**Eastern Michigan University,** Graduate School, College of Arts and Sciences, Department of Economics, Ypsilanti, MI 48197. Offers MA, Graduate Certificate. *Program availability:* Part-time, evening/weekend, online learning. *Faculty:* 9 full-time (0 women). *Students:* 25 full-time (11 women), 17 part-time (2 women); includes 3 minority (2 Black or African American, non-Hispanic/Latino; 1 Asian, non-Hispanic/Latino), 16 international. Average age 28. 61 applicants, 59% accepted, 13 enrolled. In 2016, 15 master's awarded. *Degree requirements:* For master's, thesis or alternative. *Entrance requirements:* Additional exam requirements/recommendations for international students: Required—TOEFL. *Application deadline:* Applications are processed on a rolling basis. Application fee: $45. *Financial support:* Fellowships, research assistantships with full tuition reimbursements, teaching assistantships with full tuition reimbursements, career-related internships or fieldwork, Federal Work-Study, institutionally sponsored loans, scholarships/grants, tuition waivers (partial), and unspecified assistantships available. Support available to part-time students. Financial award applicants required to submit FAFSA. *Unit head:* Dr. James Saunoris, Interim Department Head, 734-487-3395, Fax: 734-487-9666, E-mail: jsaunori@emich.edu. *Application contact:* Dr. David Crary, Director of Graduate Programs, 734-487-0001, Fax: 734-487-9666, E-mail: dcrary@emich.edu. Website: http://www.emich.edu/economics

**Emory University,** Laney Graduate School, Department of Economics, Atlanta, GA 30322-1100. Offers PhD. *Degree requirements:* For doctorate, comprehensive exam, thesis/dissertation. *Entrance requirements:* For doctorate, GRE General Test. Additional exam requirements/recommendations for international students: Recommended—TOEFL. Electronic applications accepted. *Faculty research:* Applied microeconomics, econometrics, public choice, macroeconomics, law and economics.

**Florida Atlantic University,** College of Business, Department of Economics, Boca Raton, FL 33431-0991. Offers MS. *Program availability:* Part-time, evening/weekend. *Faculty:* 14 full-time (4 women). *Students:* 14 full-time (6 women), 17 part-time (8 women); includes 258 minority (116 Black or African American, non-Hispanic/Latino; 2 Asian, non-Hispanic/Latino; 139 Hispanic/Latino; 1 Two or more races, non-Hispanic/Latino), 53 international. Average age 31. 34 applicants, 62% accepted, 11 enrolled. In 2016, 19 master's awarded. *Degree requirements:* For master's, thesis optional. *Entrance requirements:* For master's, GMAT, GRE General Test, minimum GPA of 3.0. Additional exam requirements/recommendations for international students: Required—TOEFL (minimum score 600 paper-based; 61 iBT), IELTS (minimum score 6). *Application deadline:* For fall admission, 7/1 priority date for domestic students, 2/15 priority date for international students; for spring admission, 4/1 priority date for domestic students, 1/15 priority date for international students. Applications are processed on a rolling basis. Application fee: $30. *Expenses:* Tuition, state resident: full-time $7392; part-time $369.82 per credit hour. Tuition, nonresident: full-time $19,432; part-time $1024.81 per credit hour. *Financial support:* Teaching assistantships with tuition reimbursements, tuition waivers (partial), and unspecified assistantships available.

## Economics

Financial award application deadline: 3/1. *Faculty research:* International trade and finance, decision-making, monetary conditions, economic fluctuations and growth. *Unit head:* Dr. Eric Chiang, Chair, 561-297-3220, E-mail: chiang@fau.edu.
Website: http://business.fau.edu/departments/economics/index.aspx

**Florida International University,** Steven J. Green School of International and Public Affairs, Department of Economics, Miami, FL 33199. Offers MA, PhD. *Program availability:* Part-time, evening/weekend. *Faculty:* 15 full-time (3 women), 8 part-time/adjunct (2 women). *Students:* 33 full-time (10 women), 2 part-time (both women); includes 7 minority (1 Black or African American, non-Hispanic/Latino; 2 Asian, non-Hispanic/Latino; 4 Hispanic/Latino), 26 international. Average age 30. 68 applicants, 35% accepted, 13 enrolled. In 2016, 5 master's, 4 doctorates awarded. *Degree requirements:* For master's, thesis or alternative; for doctorate, comprehensive exam, thesis/dissertation. *Entrance requirements:* For master's, GRE, minimum GPA of 3.0, letters of recommendation; for doctorate, GRE General Test, 3 letters of recommendation, minimum GPA of 3.0. Additional exam requirements/recommendations for international students: Required—TOEFL (minimum score 550 paper-based; 80 iBT). *Application deadline:* For fall admission, 4/1 for domestic and international students. Application fee: $30. Electronic applications accepted. *Expenses:* Tuition, state resident: full-time $8912; part-time $446 per credit hour. Tuition, nonresident: full-time $21,393; part-time $992 per credit hour. *Required fees:* $2185; $195 per semester. Tuition and fees vary according to program. *Financial support:* Federal Work-Study, institutionally sponsored loans, and scholarships/grants available. Financial award application deadline: 3/1; financial award applicants required to submit FAFSA. *Faculty research:* Economic development, international economics, urban/regional economics, Latin American economics. *Unit head:* Dr. Cem Karayalcin, Chair, 305-348-3285, E-mail: ali.karayalcin@fiu.edu. *Application contact:* Nanett Rojas, Manager, Admissions Operations, 305-348-7464, Fax: 305-348-7441, E-mail: gradadm@fiu.edu.
Website: http://economics.fiu.edu/

**Florida State University,** The Graduate School, College of Social Sciences and Public Policy, Department of Economics, Tallahassee, FL 32306-2180. Offers applied economics (MS); economics (PhD); JD/MS. *Program availability:* Part-time. *Faculty:* 32 full-time (4 women), 1 part-time/adjunct (0 women). *Students:* 76 full-time (16 women), 3 part-time (2 women); includes 19 minority (4 Black or African American, non-Hispanic/Latino; 5 Asian, non-Hispanic/Latino; 2 Hispanic/Latino; 8 Two or more races, non-Hispanic/Latino). Average age 26. 155 applicants, 61% accepted, 37 enrolled. In 2016, 23 master's, 5 doctorates awarded. Terminal master's awarded for partial completion of doctoral program. *Degree requirements:* For master's, thesis (for some programs), applied project (for some programs); for doctorate, comprehensive exam, thesis/dissertation, dissertation prospectus, workshops. *Entrance requirements:* For master's, GRE General Test, minimum upper-division undergraduate GPA of 3.0, 3.4 on graduate work; minimum 1 course each in statistics and calculus; principles and sufficient upper-level economics courses; for doctorate, GRE General Test, minimum upper-division undergraduate GPA of 3.0, graduate 3.4; minimum 1 course each in statistics and linear algebra, 2 in calculus. Additional exam requirements/recommendations for international students: Required—TOEFL (minimum score 90 iBT). *Application deadline:* For fall admission, 2/15 priority date for domestic and international students. Applications are processed on a rolling basis. Application fee: $30. Electronic applications accepted. *Expenses:* Tuition, state resident: full-time $7263; part-time $403.51 per credit hour. Tuition, nonresident: full-time $18,087; part-time $1004.85 per credit hour. *Required fees:* $1365; $75.81 per credit hour. $20 per semester. Tuition and fees vary according to campus/location. *Financial support:* In 2016–17, 60 students received support, including 15 fellowships with full tuition reimbursements available (averaging $25,000 per year), 4 research assistantships with full tuition reimbursements available (averaging $19,000 per year), 24 teaching assistantships with full tuition reimbursements available (averaging $19,000 per year); scholarships/grants, tuition waivers (partial), and unspecified assistantships also available. Financial award application deadline: 2/15; financial award applicants required to submit FAFSA. *Faculty research:* Industrial organization, experimental/behavioral, public/urban, law and economics, macroeconomics and financial. *Total annual research expenditures:* $650,000. *Unit head:* Dr. R. Mark Isaac, Chairman, 850-644-5001, Fax: 850-644-4535, E-mail: misaac@fsu.edu. *Application contact:* Dr. Thomas W. Zuehlke, Graduate Director, 850-644-5001, Fax: 850-644-4535, E-mail: tzuehlke@fsu.edu.
Website: http://www.coss.fsu.edu/economics/

**Fordham University,** Graduate School of Arts and Sciences, Department of Economics, New York, NY 10458. Offers MA, PhD. *Program availability:* Part-time, evening/weekend. *Faculty:* 22 full-time (4 women). *Students:* 43 full-time (19 women), 14 part-time (2 women); includes 3 minority (1 American Indian or Alaska Native, non-Hispanic/Latino; 2 Asian, non-Hispanic/Latino), 27 international. Average age 32. 193 applicants, 37% accepted, 15 enrolled. In 2016, 17 master's, 7 doctorates awarded. Terminal master's awarded for partial completion of doctoral program. *Degree requirements:* For master's, comprehensive exam; for doctorate, comprehensive exam, thesis/dissertation. *Entrance requirements:* For master's and doctorate, GRE General Test. Additional exam requirements/recommendations for international students: Required—TOEFL (minimum score 600 paper-based). *Application deadline:* For fall admission, 1/4 priority date for domestic students; for spring admission, 11/1 for domestic students. Application fee: $70. Electronic applications accepted. *Financial support:* In 2016–17, 29 students received support, including 1 fellowship with tuition reimbursement available (averaging $15,000 per year), 16 teaching assistantships with tuition reimbursements available (averaging $24,350 per year); career-related internships or fieldwork, institutionally sponsored loans, tuition waivers (full and partial), and unspecified assistantships also available. Financial award application deadline: 1/4; financial award applicants required to submit FAFSA. *Faculty research:* Developmental economics, econometrics. *Total annual research expenditures:* $129,000. *Unit head:* Dr. Johanna Francis, Associate Chair for Graduate Studies, 718-817-4066, Fax: 718-817-4048, E-mail: ajofrancis@fordham.edu. *Application contact:* Bernadette Valentino-Morrison, Director of Graduate Admissions, 718-817-4419, Fax: 718-817-3566, E-mail: valentinomor@fordham.edu.

**Fordham University,** Graduate School of Arts and Sciences, Program in International Political Economy and Development, New York, NY 10458. Offers MA, Certificate. *Program availability:* Part-time, evening/weekend. *Students:* 38 full-time (16 women), 13 part-time (10 women); includes 8 minority (1 Black or African American, non-Hispanic/Latino; 4 Asian, non-Hispanic/Latino; 3 Native Hawaiian or other Pacific Islander, non-Hispanic/Latino), 16 international. Average age 27. 207 applicants, 35% accepted, 24 enrolled. In 2016, 24 master's, 1 other advanced degree awarded. *Degree requirements:* For master's, comprehensive exam. *Entrance requirements:* For master's, GRE General Test. Additional exam requirements/recommendations for international students: Required—TOEFL (minimum score 600 paper-based). *Application deadline:* For fall admission, 1/4 priority date for domestic students; for spring admission, 11/1 for domestic students. Application fee: $70. Electronic applications accepted. *Financial support:* In 2016–17, 35 students received support, 4 fellowships with tuition reimbursements available (averaging $17,014 per year); research assistantships with tuition reimbursements available, career-related internships or fieldwork, institutionally sponsored loans, tuition waivers (full and partial),

and unspecified assistantships also available. Financial award application deadline: 1/4; financial award applicants required to submit FAFSA. *Faculty research:* International economics, comparative international politics, international banking and finance, international development, emerging markets and country risk analysis. *Unit head:* Dr. Henry Schwalbenberg, Chair, 718-817-3866, Fax: 718-817-3518. *Application contact:* Bernadette Valentino-Morrison, Director of Graduate Admissions, 718-817-4419, Fax: 718-817-3566, E-mail: valentinomor@fordham.edu.

**George Mason University,** Antonin Scalia Law School, Arlington, VA 22201. Offers global antitrust law and economics (LL M); intellectual property (LL M); law (JD); law and economics (LL M); U.S. law (LL M); JD/MA; JD/MPP; JD/PhD. *Accreditation:* ABA. *Program availability:* Part-time, evening/weekend. *Faculty:* 41 full-time (9 women), 84 part-time/adjunct (20 women). *Students:* 382 full-time (172 women), 159 part-time (83 women). 2,587 applicants, 24% accepted, 179 enrolled. *Entrance requirements:* For master's, JD or international equivalent; for doctorate, LSAT, baccalaureate degree or international equivalent. Additional exam requirements/recommendations for international students: Required—TOEFL or IELTS (for LL M applicants only). *Application deadline:* For fall admission, 4/1 for domestic and international students. Applications are processed on a rolling basis. Application fee: $0. Electronic applications accepted. *Expenses:* Contact institution. *Financial support:* Fellowships, research assistantships, career-related internships or fieldwork, scholarships/grants, and tuition waivers (full and partial) available. Support available to part-time students. *Faculty research:* Law and economics; infrastructure protection, including homeland and national security; intellectual property. *Unit head:* Henry N. Butler, Dean, 703-993-8644, Fax: 703-993-8088. *Application contact:* Alison H. Price, Associate Dean for Admissions and Enrollment Management, 703-993-8010, Fax: 703-993-8088, E-mail: lawadmit@gmu.edu.
Website: http://www.law.gmu.edu/

**George Mason University,** College of Humanities and Social Sciences, Department of Economics, Fairfax, VA 22030. Offers MA, PhD. *Faculty:* 29 full-time (1 woman), 15 part-time/adjunct (2 women). *Students:* 140 full-time (38 women), 109 part-time (25 women); includes 35 minority (4 Black or African American, non-Hispanic/Latino; 12 Asian, non-Hispanic/Latino; 15 Hispanic/Latino; 4 Two or more races, non-Hispanic/Latino), 33 international. Average age 30. 191 applicants, 81% accepted, 66 enrolled. In 2016, 45 master's, 14 doctorates awarded. *Degree requirements:* For master's, thesis optional, 2 comprehensive exams; for doctorate, comprehensive exam, thesis/dissertation, 2 preliminary exams, field exams. *Entrance requirements:* For master's, GRE General Test, expanded goals statement; 2 letters of recommendation; undergraduate degree; intermediate microeconomics and macroeconomics; 1 semester of calculus; for doctorate, GRE General Test, 2 letters of recommendation; expanded goals statement; undergraduate degree; intermediate microeconomics and macroeconomics; 1 year of calculus and statistics; 1 semester of matrix algebra and econometrics. Additional exam requirements/recommendations for international students: Required—TOEFL (minimum score 570 paper-based; 80 iBT), IELTS (minimum score 6.5), PTE. *Application deadline:* For fall admission, 3/15 priority date for domestic students. Application fee: $75 ($80 for international students). Electronic applications accepted. *Expenses:* Tuition, state resident: full-time $10,628; part-time $443 per credit. Tuition, nonresident: full-time $29,306; part-time $1221 per credit. *Required fees:* $3096; $129 per credit. Tuition and fees vary according to program. *Financial support:* In 2016–17, 96 students received support, including 35 fellowships (averaging $5,033 per year), 74 research assistantships with tuition reimbursements available (averaging $18,195 per year), 20 teaching assistantships with tuition reimbursements available (averaging $12,711 per year); career-related internships or fieldwork, Federal Work-Study, scholarships/grants, unspecified assistantships, and health care benefits (for full-time research or teaching assistantship recipients) also available. Support available to part-time students. Financial award application deadline: 3/1; financial award applicants required to submit FAFSA. *Faculty research:* Neuroeconomics, experimental economics (computer-based). *Total annual research expenditures:* $2 million. *Unit head:* Daniel Houser, Director/Professor/Chair, 703-993-4856, Fax: 703-993-4851, E-mail: dhouser@gmu.edu. *Application contact:* Mary Jackson, Graduate Coordinator, 703-993-1135, Fax: 703-993-1133, E-mail: mjacksoq@gmu.edu.
Website: http://economics.gmu.edu

**Georgetown University,** Graduate School of Arts and Sciences, Department of Economics, Washington, DC 20057. Offers econometrics (PhD); economic development (PhD); economic theory (PhD); industrial organization (PhD); international macro and finance (PhD); international trade (PhD); labor economics (PhD); macroeconomics (PhD); public economics and political economy (PhD); MA/PhD; MS/MA. *Degree requirements:* For doctorate, comprehensive exam, thesis/dissertation. *Entrance requirements:* For doctorate, GRE General Test. Additional exam requirements/recommendations for international students: Required—TOEFL. *Faculty research:* International economics, economic development.

**The George Washington University,** Columbian College of Arts and Sciences, Department of Economics, Washington, DC 20052. Offers MA, PhD. *Program availability:* Part-time, evening/weekend. *Faculty:* 22 full-time (7 women). *Students:* 85 full-time (40 women), 54 part-time (13 women); includes 13 minority (2 Black or African American, non-Hispanic/Latino; 5 Asian, non-Hispanic/Latino; 4 Hispanic/Latino; 2 Two or more races, non-Hispanic/Latino), 104 international. Average age 28. 538 applicants, 53% accepted, 41 enrolled. In 2016, 23 master's, 12 doctorates awarded. Terminal master's awarded for partial completion of doctoral program. *Degree requirements:* For master's, comprehensive exam, thesis or alternative; for doctorate, thesis/dissertation, general exam. *Entrance requirements:* For master's and doctorate, GRE General Test, minimum GPA of 3.0. Additional exam requirements/recommendations for international students: Required—TOEFL (minimum score 550 paper-based; 80 iBT). *Application deadline:* For fall admission, 1/15 priority date for domestic and international students; for spring admission, 9/1 for international students. Applications are processed on a rolling basis. Application fee: $75. Electronic applications accepted. *Financial support:* In 2016–17, 25 students received support. Fellowships with full tuition reimbursements available, teaching assistantships with tuition reimbursements available, and Federal Work-Study available. Financial award application deadline: 1/15. *Unit head:* Barry R. Chiswick, Chair, 202-994-8680, E-mail: brchis@gwu.edu. *Application contact:* Information Contact, 202-994-6150, Fax: 202-994-6147, E-mail: econgrad@gwu.edu.
Website: http://economics.columbian.gwu.edu/

**Georgia Institute of Technology,** Graduate Studies, Ivan Allen College of Liberal Arts, School of Economics, Atlanta, GA 30332-0001. Offers MS, PhD. *Program availability:* Part-time. Terminal master's awarded for partial completion of doctoral program. *Degree requirements:* For master's, thesis; for doctorate, comprehensive exam, thesis/dissertation, teaching of two undergraduate courses. *Entrance requirements:* For master's and doctorate, GRE. Additional exam requirements/recommendations for international students: Required—TOEFL (minimum score 550 paper-based; 79 iBT). Electronic applications accepted. *Faculty research:* Land use patterns in developing countries, office automation and productivity, dynamic modeling of financial markets.

**Georgia State University,** Andrew Young School of Policy Studies, Department of Economics, Atlanta, GA 30302. Offers economics (MA); environmental economics

(PhD); experimental economics (PhD); labor economics (PhD); policy (MA); public finance (PhD); urban and regional economics (PhD). MA offered through the College of Arts and Sciences. *Program availability:* Part-time. *Faculty:* 26 full-time (4 women). *Students:* 112 full-time (37 women), 10 part-time (3 women); includes 17 minority (8 Black or African American, non-Hispanic/Latino; 3 Asian, non-Hispanic/Latino; 4 Hispanic/Latino; 2 Two or more races, non-Hispanic/Latino), 62 international. Average age 28. 168 applicants, 45% accepted, 31 enrolled. In 2016, 26 master's, 9 doctorates awarded. Terminal master's awarded for partial completion of doctoral program. *Degree requirements:* For master's, thesis optional; for doctorate, comprehensive exam, thesis/dissertation. *Entrance requirements:* For master's and doctorate, GRE. Additional exam requirements/recommendations for international students: Required—TOEFL (minimum score 603 paper-based; 100 iBT) or IELTS (minimum score 7). *Application deadline:* For fall admission, 1/15 for domestic and international students. Application fee: $50. Electronic applications accepted. *Expenses:* Tuition, state resident: full-time $6876; part-time $382 per credit hour. Tuition, nonresident: full-time $22,374; part-time $1243 per credit hour. *Required fees:* $2128; $1064 per term. Part-time tuition and fees vary according to course load and program. *Financial support:* In 2016–17, fellowships with full tuition reimbursements (averaging $11,333 per year), research assistantships with full tuition reimbursements (averaging $9,788 per year), teaching assistantships with full tuition reimbursements (averaging $3,000 per year) were awarded; career-related internships or fieldwork also available. Financial award application deadline: 2/15; financial award applicants required to submit FAFSA. *Faculty research:* Public, experimental, urban/environmental, labor, and health economics. *Unit head:* Dr. Rusty Tchernis, Director of the Doctoral Program, 404-413-0154, Fax: 404-413-0145, E-mail: rtchernis@gsu.edu.
Website: http://economics.gsu.edu/

**Georgia State University,** College of Education and Human Development, Department of Middle and Secondary Education, Atlanta, GA 30302-3083. Offers curriculum and instruction (Ed D); English education (MAT); mathematics education (M Ed, MAT); middle level education (MAT); reading, language and literacy education (M Ed, MAT), including reading instruction (M Ed); science education (M Ed, MAT), including biology (MAT), broad field science (MAT), chemistry (MAT), earth science (MAT), physics (MAT); social studies education (M Ed, MAT), including economics (MAT), geography (MAT), history (MAT), political science (MAT); teaching and learning (PhD), including language and literacy, mathematics education, music education, science education, social studies education, teaching and teacher education. *Accreditation:* NCATE. *Program availability:* Part-time, evening/weekend, online learning. *Faculty:* 24 full-time (18 women). *Students:* 145 full-time (91 women), 151 part-time (102 women); includes 141 minority (104 Black or African American, non-Hispanic/Latino; 1 American Indian or Alaska Native, non-Hispanic/Latino; 16 Asian, non-Hispanic/Latino; 12 Hispanic/Latino; 8 Two or more races, non-Hispanic/Latino), 10 international. Average age 36. 115 applicants, 50% accepted, 41 enrolled. In 2016, 94 master's, 22 doctorates awarded. *Degree requirements:* For master's, comprehensive exam (for some programs), thesis or alternative, exit portfolio; for doctorate, comprehensive exam, thesis/dissertation. *Entrance requirements:* For master's, GRE; GACE I (for initial teacher preparation programs), baccalaureate degree or equivalent, resume, goals statement, two letters of recommendation, minimum undergraduate GPA of 2.5; proof of initial teacher certification in the content area (for M Ed); for doctorate, GRE, resume, goals statement, writing sample, two letters of recommendation, minimum graduate GPA of 3.3, interview. Additional exam requirements/recommendations for international students: Required—TOEFL (minimum score 550 paper-based; 79 iBT) or IELTS (minimum score 6.5). *Application deadline:* For fall admission, 1/15 priority date for domestic and international students; for spring admission, 10/1 for domestic and international students. Application fee: $50. Electronic applications accepted. *Expenses:* Tuition, state resident: full-time $6876; part-time $382 per credit hour. Tuition, nonresident: full-time $22,374; part-time $1243 per credit hour. *Required fees:* $2128; $1064 per term. Part-time tuition and fees vary according to course load and program. *Financial support:* In 2016–17, fellowships with full tuition reimbursements (averaging $19,667 per year), research assistantships with full tuition reimbursements (averaging $5,436 per year), teaching assistantships with full tuition reimbursements (averaging $2,779 per year) were awarded; career-related internships or fieldwork, Federal Work-Study, scholarships/grants, health care benefits, tuition waivers (full and partial), and unspecified assistantships also available. Financial award application deadline: 3/15. *Faculty research:* Teacher education in language and literacy, mathematics, science, and social studies in urban middle and secondary school settings; learning technologies in school, community, and corporate settings; multicultural education and education for social justice; urban education; international education. *Unit head:* Dr. Dana L. Fox, Chair, 404-413-8060, Fax: 404-413-8063, E-mail: dfox@gsu.edu. *Application contact:* Bobbie Turner, Administrative Coordinator I, 404-413-8405, Fax: 404-413-8063, E-mail: bnturner@gsu.edu.
Website: http://mse.education.gsu.edu/

**The Graduate Center, City University of New York,** Graduate Studies, Program in Economics, New York, NY 10016-4039. Offers PhD. *Degree requirements:* For doctorate, thesis/dissertation. *Entrance requirements:* For doctorate, GRE General Test. Additional exam requirements/recommendations for international students: Required—TOEFL. Electronic applications accepted.

**Harvard University,** Graduate School of Arts and Sciences, Committee on Business Economics, Cambridge, MA 02138. Offers PhD. *Degree requirements:* For doctorate, thesis/dissertation. *Entrance requirements:* For doctorate, GMAT or GRE General Test. Additional exam requirements/recommendations for international students: Required—TOEFL.

**Harvard University,** Graduate School of Arts and Sciences, Department of Economics, Cambridge, MA 02138. Offers PhD. *Degree requirements:* For doctorate, thesis/dissertation, oral exam. *Entrance requirements:* For doctorate, GRE General Test, GRE Subject Test. Additional exam requirements/recommendations for international students: Required—TOEFL. *Faculty research:* Industrial organization, macromonetary issues, international economics.

**Hawai`i Pacific University,** College of Business, Program in Business Administration, Honolulu, HI 96813. Offers accounting (MBA); economics (MBA); finance (MBA); hospitality and tourism management (MBA); human resource management (MBA); information systems (MBA); international business (MBA); management (MBA); marketing (MBA); organizational change and development (MBA). *Program availability:* Part-time, evening/weekend, online learning. *Faculty:* 13 full-time (4 women), 1 part-time/adjunct (0 women). *Students:* 106 full-time (47 women), 33 part-time (13 women); includes 66 minority (5 Black or African American, non-Hispanic/Latino; 1 American Indian or Alaska Native, non-Hispanic/Latino; 23 Asian, non-Hispanic/Latino; 11 Hispanic/Latino; 1 Native Hawaiian or other Pacific Islander, non-Hispanic/Latino; 25 Two or more races, non-Hispanic/Latino), 36 international. Average age 33. 77 applicants, 84% accepted, 44 enrolled. In 2016, 78 master's awarded. *Entrance requirements:* For master's, GMAT or GRE. Additional exam requirements/recommendations for international students: Recommended—TOEFL (minimum score 550 paper-based; 80 iBT), IELTS (minimum score 6), TWE (minimum score 5). *Application deadline:* For fall admission, 2/15 priority date for domestic students; for spring admission, 10/15 priority date for domestic students. Applications are processed

on a rolling basis. Application fee: $50. Electronic applications accepted. *Expenses:* Tuition: Full-time $17,190; part-time $955 per credit. *Required fees:* $150; $26 per credit. Tuition and fees vary according to course load and program. *Financial support:* In 2016–17, 27 students received support. Research assistantships, career-related internships or fieldwork, Federal Work-Study, scholarships/grants, tuition waivers, and unspecified assistantships available. Financial award application deadline: 3/1; financial award applicants required to submit FAFSA. *Unit head:* Dr. Warren Wee, Associate Dean/Associate Professor of Accounting, 808-544-9325, E-mail: wwee@hpu.edu. *Application contact:* Danny Lam, Assistant Director of Graduate Admissions, 808-544-1135, E-mail: graduate@hpu.edu.
Website: http://www.hpu.edu/CBA/Graduate/MBA/index.html

**Howard University,** Graduate School, Department of Economics, Washington, DC 20059-0002. Offers MA, PhD. *Program availability:* Part-time. *Degree requirements:* For master's, comprehensive exam, thesis optional; for doctorate, one foreign language, comprehensive exam, thesis/dissertation. *Entrance requirements:* For master's, GRE General Test, minimum GPA of 3.0; for doctorate, GRE General Test, master's degree in economics or related field, minimum GPA of 3.0. Electronic applications accepted. *Faculty research:* Economic development, international trade, urban rentalization.

**Hunter College of the City University of New York,** Graduate School, School of Arts and Sciences, Department of Economics, New York, NY 10065-5085. Offers accounting (MS); economics (MA). *Program availability:* Part-time, evening/weekend. *Students:* 15 full-time (12 women), 41 part-time (17 women); includes 22 minority (7 Black or African American, non-Hispanic/Latino; 11 Asian, non-Hispanic/Latino; 4 Hispanic/Latino), 11 international. Average age 30. 70 applicants, 74% accepted, 28 enrolled. In 2016, 39 master's awarded. *Degree requirements:* For master's, research paper or thesis. *Entrance requirements:* For master's, GMAT or GRE General Test, minimum GPA of 3.0, 18 credits of undergraduate course work in economics (9 in mathematics), 2 letters of recommendation (1 from department member). Additional exam requirements/recommendations for international students: Required—TOEFL. *Application deadline:* For fall admission, 4/1 for domestic students, 2/1 for international students; for spring admission, 11/1 for domestic students, 9/1 for international students. *Financial support:* Fellowships, research assistantships, teaching assistantships, career-related internships or fieldwork, Federal Work-Study, institutionally sponsored loans, and tuition waivers (partial) available. Support available to part-time students. *Faculty research:* Earnings of immigrants and minority groups, taxation and the regional economy. *Unit head:* Dr. Partha Deb, Acting Chairperson, 212-772-5400, E-mail: partha.deb@hunter.cuny.edu.
Website: http://econ.hunter.cuny.edu/

**Illinois State University,** Graduate School, College of Arts and Sciences, Department of Economics, Normal, IL 61790-2200. Offers MA, MS. *Degree requirements:* For master's, thesis or alternative. *Entrance requirements:* For master's, GRE General Test, minimum GPA of 2.6 in last 60 hours of course work. *Faculty research:* Community/economic development; the social, economic and educational correlates of rural school closure; Stevenson Center AmeriCorps project.

**Indiana University Bloomington,** University Graduate School, College of Arts and Sciences, Department of Economics, Bloomington, IN 47405-7104. Offers MS, PhD. *Faculty:* 27 full-time (5 women). *Students:* 72 full-time (24 women), 2 part-time (1 woman); includes 1 minority (Hispanic/Latino), 55 international. Average age 29. 129 applicants, 23% accepted, 14 enrolled. In 2016, 9 master's, 8 doctorates awarded. Terminal master's awarded for partial completion of doctoral program. *Degree requirements:* For doctorate, comprehensive exam, thesis/dissertation, main field exam, two supporting fields, 3rd-year paper, tool skill classes, dissertation proposal presentation, oral defense of dissertation. *Entrance requirements:* For doctorate, GRE General Test, three semesters of calculus, semester of linear algebra, semester of statistics or probability. Additional exam requirements/recommendations for international students: Required—TOEFL (minimum score 600 paper-based; 100 iBT); Recommended—IELTS. *Application deadline:* For fall admission, 1/15 for domestic students, 12/1 for international students. Application fee: $55 ($65 for international students). Electronic applications accepted. *Financial support:* Fellowships with full tuition reimbursements, research assistantships with full tuition reimbursements, teaching assistantships with full tuition reimbursements, institutionally sponsored loans, health care benefits, and unspecified assistantships available. *Faculty research:* Macroeconomics, microeconomic theory, econometrics, experimental economics, economic growth. *Unit head:* Prof. Gerhard Glomm, Chair, 812-855-6160, Fax: 812-855-3736, E-mail: gglomm@indiana.edu. *Application contact:* Brandie Roberts, Graduate Services Assistant, 812-855-8453, Fax: 812-855-3736, E-mail: econgrad@indiana.edu.
Website: https://economics.indiana.edu/

**Indiana University–Purdue University Indianapolis,** School of Liberal Arts, Department of Economics, Indianapolis, IN 46202. Offers MA, MA/MA. *Program availability:* Part-time. *Faculty:* 16 full-time (3 women). *Students:* 25 full-time (12 women), 7 part-time (1 woman); includes 4 minority (1 Black or African American, non-Hispanic/Latino; 2 Asian, non-Hispanic/Latino; 1 Hispanic/Latino), 21 international. Average age 29. 36 applicants, 36% accepted, 11 enrolled. In 2016, 5 master's awarded. *Degree requirements:* For master's, thesis (for some programs). *Entrance requirements:* For master's, GRE, minimum GPA of 3.0; courses in economic theory, statistics, and calculus. Additional exam requirements/recommendations for international students: Required—TOEFL (minimum score 100 iBT), IELTS (minimum score 6.5). Application fee: $60 ($65 for international students). Electronic applications accepted. *Financial support:* In 2016–17, 1 fellowship with partial tuition reimbursement (averaging $22,500 per year) was awarded; research assistantships with partial tuition reimbursements, teaching assistantships with partial tuition reimbursements, career-related internships or fieldwork, health care benefits, tuition waivers, and unspecified assistantships also available. Financial award application deadline: 1/15. *Faculty research:* Charitable giving. *Unit head:* Steve Russell, Chair, 317-278-7214, E-mail: shrusse@iupui.edu. *Application contact:* Terri Crews, Graduate Programs Coordinator, 317-274-8100, E-mail: tcrews@iupui.edu.
Website: http://www.iupui.edu/~econ/

**Instituto Tecnologico de Santo Domingo,** Graduate School, Area of Humanities and Social Sciences, Santo Domingo, Dominican Republic. Offers accounting (Certificate); adult education (Certificate); applied linguistics (MA); economics (MA); education (M Ed); educational psychology (MA, Certificate); gender and development (MA, Certificate); humanistic studies (MA); international marketing management (Certificate); international relations in the Caribbean basin (Certificate); intervention systems in family therapy (MA); linguistic and literary communication (Certificate); pedagogical support (MA); social science education (M Ed); sustainable human development (MA); terminal illness and death psychology (Certificate); youth and adult education (M Ed).

**Instituto Tecnológico y de Estudios Superiores de Monterrey, Campus Ciudad de México,** School of Business Administration, Ciudad de Mexico, Mexico. Offers business administration (EMBA, MBA, PhD); economy (MBA); finance (MBA). EMBA program offered jointly with The University of Texas at Austin. *Program availability:* Part-time, evening/weekend, online learning. *Entrance requirements:* For master's and doctorate, Instituto entrance exam. Additional exam requirements/recommendations for international students: Required—TOEFL.

## SECTION 19: ECONOMICS

*Economics*

**Iowa State University of Science and Technology,** Department of Economics, Ames, IA 50011. Offers agricultural economics (MS, PhD); economics (MS, PhD); JD/MS; JD/PhD. JD/MS and JD/PhD offered jointly with Drake University and The University of Iowa. *Degree requirements:* For master's, thesis or alternative; for doctorate, thesis/dissertation. *Entrance requirements:* For master's and doctorate, GRE General Test. Additional exam requirements/recommendations for international students: Required—TOEFL (minimum score 570 paper-based; 88 iBT), IELTS (minimum score 6.5). *Application deadline:* For fall admission, 1/31 priority date for domestic and international students. Application fee: $40 ($90 for international students). Electronic applications accepted. *Application contact:* Amy Bainum Emmett, Application Contact, 515-294-2702, E-mail: econgrad@iastate.edu.
Website: http://www.econ.iastate.edu/graduate-programs

**Johns Hopkins University,** Zanvyl Krieger School of Arts and Sciences, Department of Economics, Baltimore, MD 21218. Offers PhD. Terminal master's awarded for partial completion of doctoral program. *Degree requirements:* For doctorate, comprehensive exam, thesis/dissertation. *Entrance requirements:* For doctorate, GRE General Test. Additional exam requirements/recommendations for international students: Required—TOEFL (minimum score 600 paper-based), IELTS. Electronic applications accepted. *Faculty research:* General economic theory, econometrics and mathematical economics, trade and development, game theory, urban economics.

**Kansas State University,** Graduate School, College of Arts and Sciences, Department of Economics, Manhattan, KS 66506. Offers MA, PhD. *Faculty:* 14 full-time (4 women), 1 part-time/adjunct (0 women). *Students:* 30 full-time (18 women), 3 part-time (2 women); includes 1 minority (Black or African American, non-Hispanic/Latino), 30 international. Average age 31. 27 applicants, 41% accepted, 4 enrolled. In 2016, 12 master's, 10 doctorates awarded. Terminal master's awarded for partial completion of doctoral program. *Degree requirements:* For master's, comprehensive exam (for some programs), thesis (for some programs), 30 credit hours, including thesis/report or qualifying exams; for doctorate, comprehensive exam, thesis/dissertation, 90 credit hours, including dissertation, qualifying exams, and field exam. *Entrance requirements:* For master's and doctorate, GRE (highly recommended), minimum GPA of 3.0; course work in microeconomics, macroeconomics, calculus and statistics. Additional exam requirements/recommendations for international students: Required—TOEFL (minimum score 550 paper-based; 79 iBT), IELTS (minimum score 6.5), TWE (minimum score 5), PTE (minimum score 58). *Application deadline:* For fall admission, 1/8 priority date for domestic and international students; for spring admission, 8/1 for domestic and international students. Applications are processed on a rolling basis. Application fee: $65 ($75 for international students). Electronic applications accepted. *Expenses:* Tuition, state resident: full-time $9670. Tuition, nonresident: full-time $21,828. *Required fees:* $862. *Financial support:* In 2016–17, 26 students received support, including 26 teaching assistantships with full tuition reimbursements available (averaging $17,000 per year); institutionally sponsored loans, scholarships/grants, and unspecified assistantships also available. Financial award application deadline: 1/8; financial award applicants required to submit FAFSA. *Faculty research:* Macroeconomics, microeconomics and labor economics, development and growth, international economics, industrial organization. *Unit head:* Dr. William Blankenau, Head, 785-532-6340, Fax: 785-532-6919, E-mail: blankenw@ksu.edu. *Application contact:* Crystal Strauss, Administrative Specialist, 785-532-4587, Fax: 785-532-6919, E-mail: strauss@ksu.edu.
Website: http://www.k-state.edu/economics/

**Kent State University,** College of Business Administration, Master of Arts Program in Economics, Kent, OH 44242-0001. Offers MA. *Program availability:* Part-time. *Faculty:* 15 full-time (4 women). *Students:* 24 full-time (11 women), 2 part-time (0 women); includes 1 minority (Black or African American, non-Hispanic/Latino), 18 international. Average age 25. 21 applicants, 95% accepted, 11 enrolled. In 2016, 16 master's awarded. *Entrance requirements:* For master's, GMAT or GRE General Test, minimum GPA of 3.0. Additional exam requirements/recommendations for international students: Required—TOEFL (minimum score 550 paper-based; 80 iBT). *Application deadline:* For fall admission, 2/15 priority date for domestic students, 2/15 for international students; for spring admission, 10/15 for domestic and international students; for summer admission, 5/1 for domestic and international students. Applications are processed on a rolling basis. Application fee: $45 ($70 for international students). Electronic applications accepted. *Expenses:* Tuition, state resident: full-time $10,864; part-time $495 per credit hour. Tuition, nonresident: full-time $18,380; part-time $837 per credit hour. *Financial support:* In 2016–17, 6 students received support, including 6 research assistantships with full tuition reimbursements available (averaging $4,750 per year); fellowships and Federal Work-Study also available. Financial award application deadline: 2/15; financial award applicants required to submit FAFSA. *Faculty research:* Macro and microeconomic theory, labor economics, international economics, quantitative methods. *Unit head:* Dr. Donald R. Williams, Chair and Professor, 330-672-2366, Fax: 330-672-9808, E-mail: dwilliam@kent.edu. *Application contact:* Louise M. Ditchey, Administrative Director, 330-672-2282, Fax: 330-672-7303, E-mail: gradbus@kent.edu.
Website: http://www.kent.edu/business/ma-economics

**Lakehead University,** Graduate Studies, Faculty of Social Sciences and Humanities, Department of Economics, Thunder Bay, ON P7B 5E1, Canada. Offers MA. *Program availability:* Part-time, evening/weekend. *Degree requirements:* For master's, thesis or comprehensive exams, research papers. *Entrance requirements:* For master's, minimum B average. Additional exam requirements/recommendations for international students: Required—TOEFL. *Faculty research:* Public finance, economic history, mathematical economics, quantitative economics.

**Lee University,** Program in Education, Cleveland, TN 37320-3450. Offers art (MAT); curriculum and instruction (M Ed, Ed S); early childhood (MAT); educational leadership (M Ed, Ed S); elementary education (MAT); English and math (MAT); English and science (MAT); English and social studies (MAT); higher education administration (MS); history (MAT); history and economics (MAT); math and science (MAT); math and social studies (MAT); middle grades (MAT); science and social studies (MASW); secondary education (MAT); Spanish (MAT); special education (M Ed, MAT); TESOL (MAT). *Accreditation:* NCATE. *Program availability:* Part-time. *Faculty:* 13 full-time (6 women), 9 part-time/adjunct (4 women). *Students:* 35 full-time (27 women), 50 part-time (32 women); includes 12 minority (5 Black or African American, non-Hispanic/Latino; 5 Hispanic/Latino; 2 Two or more races, non-Hispanic/Latino), 4 international. Average age 30. 43 applicants, 79% accepted, 28 enrolled. In 2016, 42 master's, 6 other advanced degrees awarded. *Degree requirements:* For master's, variable foreign language requirement, thesis optional, internship. *Entrance requirements:* For master's, MAT or GRE General Test, minimum undergraduate GPA of 2.75, 3 letters of recommendation, interview, writing sample, official transcripts, background check; for Ed S, minimum undergraduate and master's GPA of 2.75, official transcripts for undergraduate and master's degrees. Additional exam requirements/recommendations for international students: Required—TOEFL (minimum score 61 iBT). *Application deadline:* For fall admission, 6/1 priority date for domestic and international students; for spring admission, 11/1 priority date for domestic and international students; for summer admission, 4/1 priority date for domestic and international students. Applications are processed on a rolling basis. Application fee: $25. Electronic applications accepted.

*Expenses: Tuition:* Full-time $11,367; part-time $632 per credit hour. *Required fees:* $35 per term. One-time fee: $25. Tuition and fees vary according to program. *Financial support:* In 2016–17, 42 students received support. Career-related internships or fieldwork, Federal Work-Study, institutionally sponsored loans, scholarships/grants, and unspecified assistantships available. Financial award application deadline: 3/1; financial award applicants required to submit FAFSA. *Unit head:* Dr. William Kamm, Director, 423-614-8544, E-mail: wkamm@leeuniversity.edu. *Application contact:* Crystal Keeter, Graduate Education Secretary, 423-614-8544, E-mail: ckeeter@leeuniversity.edu.
Website: http://www.leeuniversity.edu/academics/graduate/education

**Lehigh University,** College of Business and Economics, Department of Economics, Bethlehem, PA 18015. Offers MS, PhD. *Faculty:* 9 full-time (1 woman). *Students:* 34 full-time (15 women), 1 part-time (0 women); includes 1 minority (Asian, non-Hispanic/Latino), 26 international. Average age 25. 91 applicants, 55% accepted, 14 enrolled. In 2016, 14 master's, 5 doctorates awarded. Terminal master's awarded for partial completion of doctoral program. *Degree requirements:* For master's, thesis optional; for doctorate, comprehensive exam, thesis/dissertation, proposal defense. *Entrance requirements:* For master's and doctorate, GMAT or GRE General Test. Additional exam requirements/recommendations for international students: Required—TOEFL (minimum score 600 paper-based; 94 iBT), IELTS (minimum score 7). *Application deadline:* For fall admission, 7/15 for domestic students, 5/1 for international students; for spring admission, 12/1 for domestic students. Application fee: $75. Electronic applications accepted. *Expenses:* Contact institution. *Financial support:* In 2016–17, 18 students received support, including 1 research assistantship with full tuition reimbursement available (averaging $18,900 per year), 13 teaching assistantships with full tuition reimbursements available (averaging $18,000 per year); fellowships and health care benefits also available. Financial award application deadline: 1/15. *Faculty research:* Public finance, investments, applied econometrics, labor economics, health economics. Total annual research expenditures: $23,766. *Unit head:* Dr. James Dearden, Chair, 610-758-5129, Fax: 610-758-4677, E-mail: jad8@lehigh.edu. *Application contact:* Michael Tarantino, Director of Recruitment and Admissions, 610-758-3418, Fax: 610-758-5283, E-mail: mgt215@lehigh.edu.
Website: http://www4.lehigh.edu/business/academics/depts/economics

**Louisiana State University and Agricultural & Mechanical College,** Graduate School, E. J. Ourso College of Business, Department of Economics, Baton Rouge, LA 70803. Offers MS, PhD.

**Louisiana Tech University,** Graduate School, College of Business, Department of Economics and Finance, Ruston, LA 71272. Offers finance (MBA, DBA); finance and economics (DBA). *Program availability:* Part-time. *Degree requirements:* For doctorate, thesis/dissertation. *Entrance requirements:* For master's and doctorate, GMAT. *Application deadline:* For fall admission, 7/29 for domestic students; for spring admission, 2/3 for domestic students. Application fee: $20 ($30 for international students). *Financial support:* Fellowships, research assistantships, and teaching assistantships available. Financial award application deadline: 2/1. *Unit head:* Dr. Otis Gilley, Director, 318-257-4140, Fax: 318-257-4253, E-mail: gilley@latech.edu. *Application contact:* Marilyn J. Robinson, Assistant to the Dean, 318-257-2924, Fax: 318-257-4487.
Website: http://www.business.latech.edu/econ_fin/

**Loyola University Chicago,** Quinlan School of Business, MBA Programs, Chicago, IL 60611. Offers accounting (MBA); business administration (EMBA); business ethics (MBA); economics (MBA); entrepreneurship (MBA); finance (MBA); healthcare management (MBA); human resources management (MBA); international business (MBA); management (MBA); marketing (MBA); operation management (MBA); risk management (MBA); supply chain management (MBA). *Program availability:* Part-time, evening/weekend. *Faculty:* 79 full-time (22 women), 10 part-time/adjunct (6 women). *Students:* 309 full-time (151 women), 65 part-time (31 women); includes 82 minority (25 Black or African American, non-Hispanic/Latino; 27 Asian, non-Hispanic/Latino; 27 Hispanic/Latino; 3 Two or more races, non-Hispanic/Latino), 49 international. Average age 30. 371 applicants, 53% accepted, 114 enrolled. In 2016, 216 master's awarded. *Entrance requirements:* For master's, GMAT or GRE, official transcripts, two letters of recommendation, statement of purpose, resume. Additional exam requirements/recommendations for international students: Required—TOEFL (minimum score 90 iBT) or IELTS (minimum score 6.5). *Application deadline:* For fall admission, 7/15 for domestic and international students; for winter admission, 10/1 for domestic and international students; for spring admission, 1/15 for domestic and international students; for summer admission, 4/1 for domestic and international students. Applications are processed on a rolling basis. Application fee: $50. Electronic applications accepted. Application fee is waived when completed online. *Expenses:* $4,488 per course. *Financial support:* In 2016–17, 83 students received support. Federal Work-Study, scholarships/grants, health care benefits, and unspecified assistantships available. Support available to part-time students. *Faculty research:* Social enterprise and responsibility, emerging markets, supply chain management, risk management. *Unit head:* Katherine Acles, Assistant Dean for Graduate Programs, 312-915-6124, Fax: 312-915-7207, E-mail: kacles@luc.edu. *Application contact:* Lauren Griffin, Enrollment Advisor, Quinlan School of Business Graduate Programs, 312-915-6124, Fax: 312-915-7207, E-mail: lgriffin3@luc.edu.

**Marquette University,** Graduate School of Management, Department of Economics, Milwaukee, WI 53201-1881. Offers business economics (MSAE); financial economics (MSAE); international economics (MSAE); marketing research (MSAE); real estate economics (MSAE). *Program availability:* Part-time, evening/weekend. *Faculty:* 14 full-time (4 women), 2 part-time/adjunct (both women). *Students:* 14 full-time (2 women), 13 part-time (3 women); includes 5 minority (2 Asian, non-Hispanic/Latino; 3 Hispanic/Latino). Average age 26. 27 applicants, 67% accepted, 27 enrolled. In 2016, 17 master's awarded. *Degree requirements:* For master's, comprehensive exam, professional project. *Entrance requirements:* For master's, GMAT or GRE General Test. Additional exam requirements/recommendations for international students: Required—TOEFL, IELTS, PTE. *Application deadline:* For fall admission, 2/15 for domestic and international students. Applications are processed on a rolling basis. Application fee: $50. Electronic applications accepted. *Financial support:* Fellowships, research assistantships, teaching assistantships, Federal Work-Study, institutionally sponsored loans, scholarships/grants, and tuition waivers (full and partial) available. Support available to part-time students. Financial award application deadline: 2/15. *Faculty research:* Monetary and fiscal policy in open economy, housing and regional migration, political economy of taxation and state/local government. *Unit head:* Dr. Brian Till, Dean, 414-288-5724. *Application contact:* Dr. Jeanne Simmons, Associate Dean, 414-288-7145.
Website: http://business.marquette.edu/academics/msae

**Marquette University,** Graduate School of Management, Executive MBA Program, Milwaukee, WI 53201-1881. Offers economics (MBA); finance (MBA); human resources (MBA); international business (MBA); management information systems (MBA); marketing (MBA); operations and supply chain management (MBA); sports business (MBA). *Accreditation:* AACSB. *Students:* 39 full-time (12 women); includes 7 minority (4 Black or African American, non-Hispanic/Latino; 2 Asian, non-Hispanic/Latino; 1 Hispanic/Latino). Average age 38. 25 applicants, 96% accepted, 29 enrolled. In 2016, 14 master's awarded. *Degree requirements:* For master's, international trip. *Entrance*

*requirements:* For master's, GMAT or GRE, two letters of recommendation, official transcripts from current and previous colleges/universities. Additional exam requirements/recommendations for international students: Required—TOEFL (minimum score 550 paper-based; 88 iBT), IELTS (minimum score 6.5), PTE. *Application deadline:* For fall admission, 2/15 for domestic and international students. Application fee: $50. Electronic applications accepted. *Expenses:* Contact institution. *Financial support:* Application deadline: 2/15. *Faculty research:* International trade and finance, customer relationship management, consumer satisfaction, customer service. *Unit head:* Dr. Brian Till, Dean, 414-288-5724. *Application contact:* Dr. Jeanne Simmons, Associate Dean, 414-288-7145.
Website: http://www.busadm.mu.edu/emba/

**Marquette University,** Graduate School of Management, Program in Business Administration, Milwaukee, WI 53201-1881. Offers business administration (MBA); economics (MBA); entrepreneurship (Certificate); finance (MBA); human resources (MBA); international business (MBA); management information systems (MBA); marketing (MBA); operations and supply chain management (MBA); sports business (MBA); JD/MBA; MBA/MA; MBA/MSN. *Accreditation:* AACSB. *Program availability:* Part-time, evening/weekend. *Students:* 25 full-time (12 women), 202 part-time (57 women); includes 17 minority (5 Black or African American, non-Hispanic/Latino; 6 Asian, non-Hispanic/Latino; 2 Hispanic/Latino; 1 Native Hawaiian or other Pacific Islander, non-Hispanic/Latino; 3 Two or more races, non-Hispanic/Latino), 7 international. Average age 31. 107 applicants, 87% accepted, 113 enrolled. In 2016, 107 master's, 5 other advanced degrees awarded. *Degree requirements:* For Certificate, business plan. *Entrance requirements:* For master's, GMAT or GRE, letters of recommendation. Additional exam requirements/recommendations for international students: Required—TOEFL (minimum score 550 paper-based; 88 iBT), IELTS (minimum score 6.5), PTE. *Application deadline:* For fall admission, 2/15 for domestic and international students. Applications are processed on a rolling basis. Application fee: $50. Electronic applications accepted. *Financial support:* Fellowships, research assistantships, teaching assistantships, Federal Work-Study, institutionally sponsored loans, scholarships/grants, and tuition waivers (full and partial) available. Support available to part-time students. Financial award application deadline: 2/15. *Faculty research:* Ethics in the professions, services marketing, technology impact on decision-making, mentoring. *Unit head:* Dr. Brian Till, Dean, 414-288-5724. *Application contact:* Dr. Jeanne Simmons, Associate Dean, 414-288-7145.
Website: http://business.marquette.edu/academics/mba

**Massachusetts Institute of Technology,** School of Humanities, Arts, and Social Sciences, Department of Economics, Cambridge, MA 02139. Offers SM, PhD. *Faculty:* 32 full-time (5 women), 2 part-time/adjunct (0 women). *Students:* 126 full-time (31 women), 2 part-time (0 women); includes 18 minority (11 Asian, non-Hispanic/Latino; 2 Hispanic/Latino; 5 Two or more races, non-Hispanic/Latino), 69 international. Average age 27. 711 applicants, 5% accepted, 24 enrolled. In 2016, 4 master's, 26 doctorates awarded. Terminal master's awarded for partial completion of doctoral program. *Degree requirements:* For master's, thesis; for doctorate, comprehensive exam, thesis/dissertation. *Entrance requirements:* For doctorate, GRE General Test. Additional exam requirements/recommendations for international students: Required—TOEFL, IELTS. *Application deadline:* For fall admission, 12/15 for domestic and international students. Application fee: $75. Electronic applications accepted. *Expenses:* Tuition: Full-time $46,400; part-time $725 per credit. One-time fee: $312 full-time. Full-time tuition and fees vary according to course load and program. *Financial support:* In 2016–17, 106 students received support, including fellowships (averaging $44,100 per year), 13 research assistantships (averaging $41,700 per year), 33 teaching assistantships (averaging $47,800 per year); Federal Work-Study, institutionally sponsored loans, scholarships/grants, traineeships, health care benefits, unspecified assistantships, and resident tutors also available. Support available to part-time students. Financial award application deadline: 5/1; financial award applicants required to submit FAFSA. *Faculty research:* Development economics; econometrics; economic theory; financial economics; industrial organization; health economics; international economics; labor economics; macroeconomics; political economy; public economics/public finance. *Total annual research expenditures:* $12.6 million. *Unit head:* Prof. Glenn Ellison, Department Head, 617-253-3980, Fax: 617-253-1330. *Application contact:* 617-324-5857, E-mail: econ-admit@mit.edu.
Website: http://economics.mit.edu/

**McGill University,** Faculty of Graduate and Postdoctoral Studies, Faculty of Arts, Department of Economics, Montréal, QC H3A 2T5, Canada. Offers economics (MA, PhD); social statistics (MA).

**McMaster University,** School of Graduate Studies, Faculty of Social Sciences, Department of Economics, Hamilton, ON L8S 4M2, Canada. Offers MA, PhD. *Program availability:* Part-time. *Degree requirements:* For doctorate, comprehensive exam, thesis/dissertation. *Entrance requirements:* For master's, GRE (recommended), honors BA in economics; for doctorate, GRE (recommended), B+ average in a master's degree. Additional exam requirements/recommendations for international students: Required—TOEFL (minimum score 580 paper-based). *Faculty research:* Applied microeconomics, econometrics, health economics, labor economics, public finance.

**Memorial University of Newfoundland,** School of Graduate Studies, Department of Economics, St. John's, NL A1C 5S7, Canada. Offers MA. *Degree requirements:* For master's, thesis optional. *Entrance requirements:* For master's, honors degree (minimum 2nd class standing). Electronic applications accepted. *Faculty research:* Public sector economics, natural resource economics.

**Miami University,** Farmer School of Business, Department of Economics, Oxford, OH 45056. Offers MA. *Students:* 14 full-time (3 women), 1 part-time (0 women); includes 2 minority (both Asian, non-Hispanic/Latino), 8 international. Average age 24. In 2016, 19 master's awarded. *Expenses:* Tuition, state resident: full-time $12,890; part-time $564 per credit hour. Tuition, nonresident: full-time $29,604; part-time $1260 per credit hour. *Required fees:* $638. Part-time tuition and fees vary according to course load and program. *Unit head:* George Davis, Chair, 513-529-2836, E-mail: davisgk@miamioh.edu. *Application contact:* Dr. Melissa Thomasson, Director of Graduate Studies, 513-529-2858, E-mail: menketl@miamioh.edu.
Website: http://www.MiamiOH.edu/economics

**Michigan State University,** The Graduate School, College of Social Science, Department of Economics, East Lansing, MI 48824. Offers MA, PhD. *Entrance requirements:* Additional exam requirements/recommendations for international students: Required—TOEFL. Electronic applications accepted.

**Middle Tennessee State University,** College of Graduate Studies, Jennings A. Jones College of Business, Department of Economics and Finance, Murfreesboro, TN 37132. Offers economics (MA, PhD). *Program availability:* Part-time, evening/weekend, online learning. *Degree requirements:* For master's, comprehensive exam, thesis optional; for doctorate, comprehensive exam, thesis/dissertation. *Entrance requirements:* For master's and doctorate, GRE. Additional exam requirements/recommendations for international students: Required—TOEFL (minimum score 525 paper-based; 71 iBT) or IELTS (minimum score 6). Electronic applications accepted.

**Mississippi State University,** College of Business, Department of Finance and Economics, Mississippi State, MS 39762. Offers MA, PhD. PhD in applied economics offered jointly with Department of Agricultural Economics. *Program availability:* Part-time. *Faculty:* 18 full-time (6 women), 1 part-time/adjunct (0 women). *Students:* 6 full-time (3 women), 1 part-time (0 women), 5 international. Average age 29. Terminal master's awarded for partial completion of doctoral program. *Degree requirements:* For master's, comprehensive exam, thesis optional; for doctorate, comprehensive exam, thesis/dissertation, written and oral exams. *Entrance requirements:* For master's, GRE, previously-completed intermediate microeconomics and macroeconomics; for doctorate, GRE, BS with minimum GPA of 3.0 cumulative and over last 60 hours of undergraduate work, 3.25 on all graduate work. Additional exam requirements/recommendations for international students: Required—TOEFL (minimum score 575 paper-based; 84 iBT); Recommended—IELTS (minimum score 6.5). *Application deadline:* For fall admission, 7/1 for domestic students, 5/1 for international students; for spring admission, 11/1 for domestic students, 10/1 for international students. Applications are processed on a rolling basis. Application fee: $60. Electronic applications accepted. *Expenses:* Tuition, state resident: full-time $7670; part-time $852.50 per credit hour. Tuition, nonresident: full-time $20,790; part-time $2310.50 per credit hour. Part-time tuition and fees vary according to course load. *Financial support:* Federal Work-Study, scholarships/grants, health care benefits, and unspecified assistantships available. Financial award application deadline: 4/1; financial award applicants required to submit FAFSA. *Faculty research:* Economics development, mergers, event studies, economic education, bank performance. *Total annual research expenditures:* $979,000. *Unit head:* Dr. Mike Highfield, Department Head, 662-325-3928, Fax: 662-325-1977, E-mail: mhighfield@msstate.edu. *Application contact:* Lakan Drinker, Admissions and Enrollment Assistant, 662-325-8951, E-mail: ldrinker@grad.msstate.edu.
Website: http://www.business.msstate.edu/programs/fe/index.php

**Morgan State University,** School of Graduate Studies, College of Liberal Arts, Department of Economics, Baltimore, MD 21251. Offers MA. *Degree requirements:* For master's, comprehensive exam. *Entrance requirements:* For master's, GRE. Additional exam requirements/recommendations for international students: Required—TOEFL (minimum score 550 paper-based).

**Murray State University,** College of Business and Public Affairs, Program in Economics, Murray, KY 42071. Offers MS. *Program availability:* Part-time. *Entrance requirements:* For master's, GRE General Test or GMAT, economics minor or equivalent, students may be conditionally admitted and fulfill undergraduate requirements. Additional exam requirements/recommendations for international students: Required—TOEFL. *Faculty research:* Economic education, public finance, economic development, banking, telecommunications systems management.

**New Mexico State University,** College of Business, Department of Economics, Applied Statistics and International Business, Las Cruces, NM 88003. Offers applied statistics (MS); economic development (DED); economics (MA); public utility regulation and economics (Graduate Certificate). *Program availability:* Part-time. *Faculty:* 18 full-time (5 women). *Students:* 41 full-time (14 women), 14 part-time (7 women); includes 15 minority (1 Black or African American, non-Hispanic/Latino; 1 American Indian or Alaska Native, non-Hispanic/Latino; 1 Asian, non-Hispanic/Latino; 10 Hispanic/Latino; 2 Two or more races, non-Hispanic/Latino), 25 international. Average age 35. 73 applicants, 55% accepted, 16 enrolled. In 2016, 19 master's, 5 doctorates, 6 other advanced degrees awarded. Terminal master's awarded for partial completion of doctoral program. *Degree requirements:* For master's, comprehensive exam, thesis or alternative; for doctorate, comprehensive exam, thesis/dissertation, internship. *Entrance requirements:* For master's, minimum GPA of 3.0; for doctorate, appropriate master's degree, minimum GPA of 3.0. Additional exam requirements/recommendations for international students: Required—TOEFL (minimum score 550 paper-based; 79 iBT), IELTS (minimum score 6.5). *Application deadline:* For fall admission, 3/1 priority date for domestic and international students. Applications are processed on a rolling basis. Application fee: $40 ($50 for international students). Electronic applications accepted. *Expenses:* Tuition, state resident: full-time $4086. Tuition, nonresident: full-time $14,254. *Required fees:* $853. Tuition and fees vary according to course load. *Financial support:* In 2016–17, 35 students received support, including 27 teaching assistantships (averaging $13,396 per year); career-related internships or fieldwork, Federal Work-Study, scholarships/grants, traineeships, health care benefits, and unspecified assistantships also available. Support available to part-time students. Financial award application deadline: 3/1. *Faculty research:* Public utilities, environment, linear models, biological sampling, public policy, economic development, energy, regional economics. *Unit head:* Dr. Richard V. Adkisson, 575-646-4988, Fax: 575-646-1915, E-mail: radkisso@nmsu.edu. *Application contact:* 575-646-7211, Fax: 575-646-1915.
Website: http://business.nmsu.edu/departments/economics

**The New School,** The New School for Social Research, Department of Economics, New York, NY 10003. Offers economics (M Phil, MA, MS, PhD); global political economy and finance (MA). *Program availability:* Part-time. *Faculty:* 5 full-time (1 woman), 12 part-time/adjunct (4 women). *Students:* 82 full-time (26 women), 21 part-time (6 women); includes 15 minority (5 Black or African American, non-Hispanic/Latino; 4 Asian, non-Hispanic/Latino; 6 Hispanic/Latino), 53 international. Average age 31. 143 applicants, 69% accepted, 18 enrolled. In 2016, 21 master's, 11 doctorates awarded. Terminal master's awarded for partial completion of doctoral program. *Degree requirements:* For master's, mentored research/internship, exam; for doctorate, one foreign language, comprehensive exam, thesis/dissertation. *Entrance requirements:* For master's, GRE, letters of recommendation, writing sample, essays, unofficial transcript; for doctorate, letters of recommendation, writing sample, essays, unofficial transcript. Additional exam requirements/recommendations for international students: Required—TOEFL (minimum score 100 iBT), IELTS (minimum score 7), PTE (minimum score 68). *Application deadline:* For fall admission, 5/5 priority date for domestic and international students; for spring admission, 10/15 priority date for domestic and international students. Applications are processed on a rolling basis. Application fee: $50. Electronic applications accepted. *Expenses:* Contact institution. *Financial support:* Fellowships, research assistantships, teaching assistantships, career-related internships or fieldwork, Federal Work-Study, scholarships/grants, and tuition waivers (full and partial) available. Support available to part-time students. Financial award application deadline: 2/1; financial award applicants required to submit FAFSA. *Faculty research:* Keynesian and post-Keynesian economics; classical political economy of Smith, Ricardo, and Marx; structuralist and institutionalist approaches to economics, and neoclassical economics;. *Unit head:* Dr. William Milberg, Dean, The New School for Social Research, 212-229-5777, E-mail: milbergw@newschool.edu. *Application contact:* Dana Messinger, Director of Graduate Admission, 212-229-5150 Ext. 2300, E-mail: socialresearchadmit@newschool.edu.
Website: http://www.newschool.edu/

**New York University,** Graduate School of Arts and Science, Department of Economics, New York, NY 10012-1019. Offers applied economic analysis (Advanced Certificate); economics (MA, PhD); JD/MA; MD/PhD. *Program availability:* Part-time, evening/weekend. Terminal master's awarded for partial completion of doctoral program. *Degree requirements:* For master's, thesis; for doctorate, one foreign language, thesis/dissertation, 4 qualifying exams. *Entrance requirements:* For master's and doctorate,

## Economics

GRE General Test. Additional exam requirements/recommendations for international students: Required—TOEFL. *Faculty research:* Economic theory, experimental economics, growth and development, macroeconomics and finance, international trade and international finance.

**New York University,** Leonard N. Stern School of Business, Department of Economics, New York, NY 10012-1019. Offers MBA, PhD. *Faculty research:* Applied macroeconomics, macroeconomics and macroeconomic policy, international financial markets, international trade and business, game theory.

**North Carolina State University,** Graduate School, Poole College of Management and College of Agriculture and Life Sciences, Program in Economics, Raleigh, NC 27695. Offers M Econ, MA, PhD. *Program availability:* Part-time. Terminal master's awarded for partial completion of doctoral program. *Degree requirements:* For master's, thesis (for some programs); for doctorate, thesis/dissertation. *Entrance requirements:* For master's and doctorate, GRE General Test. Additional exam requirements/recommendations for international students: Required—TOEFL. Electronic applications accepted. *Faculty research:* Endogenous growth modeling, generalized methods of moments estimation, integration and trade, agricultural policy, path dependence and network externalities.

**Northeastern University,** College of Social Sciences and Humanities, Boston, MA 02115. Offers criminology and criminal justice (MSCJ); criminology and justice policy (PhD); economics (MA, PhD); English (MA, PhD); international affairs (MA); law and public policy (PhD); political science (MA, PhD); public administration (MPA); public history (MA); public policy (MPP); security and resilience studies (MS); sociology (MA, PhD); urban and regional policy (MS); urban informatics (MS); world history (MA, PhD); JD/MS. *Program availability:* Online learning. *Faculty:* 234 full-time (114 women), 55 part-time/adjunct (34 women). *Students:* 427 full-time (239 women), 77 part-time (42 women). In 2016, 143 master's, 38 doctorates awarded. *Degree requirements:* For doctorate, variable foreign language requirement, comprehensive exam, thesis/ dissertation. *Entrance requirements:* For master's and doctorate, GRE. Additional exam requirements/recommendations for international students: Required—TOEFL, IELTS. Application fee: $75. Electronic applications accepted. *Expenses:* $1,295 per credit. *Financial support:* Teaching assistantships, career-related internships or fieldwork, scholarships/grants, health care benefits, tuition waivers (full and partial), and unspecified assistantships available. Support available to part-time students. Financial award applicants required to submit FAFSA. *Unit head:* Dr. Uta Poiger, Dean, 617-373-5173. *Application contact:* Amber Crowe, Administrative Coordinator, 617-373-5990, Fax: 617-373-7281, E-mail: gradcssh@northeastern.edu.
Website: http://www.northeastern.edu/cssh/graduate

**Northern Illinois University,** Graduate School, College of Liberal Arts and Sciences, Department of Economics, De Kalb, IL 60115-2854. Offers MA, PhD. *Program availability:* Part-time. *Faculty:* 15 full-time (3 women). *Students:* 28 full-time (7 women), 5 part-time (2 women); includes 7 minority (1 Black or African American, non-Hispanic/ Latino; 3 Asian, non-Hispanic/Latino; 3 Hispanic/Latino), 21 international. Average age 32. 62 applicants, 50% accepted, 7 enrolled. In 2016, 5 master's, 4 doctorates awarded. Terminal master's awarded for partial completion of doctoral program. *Degree requirements:* For master's, comprehensive exam, thesis or alternative; for doctorate, thesis/dissertation, candidacy exam, dissertation defense, research seminar. *Entrance requirements:* For master's, GRE General Test, minimum GPA of 2.75; for doctorate, GRE General Test, minimum GPA of 2.75 (undergraduate), 3.2 (graduate). Additional exam requirements/recommendations for international students: Required—TOEFL (minimum score 550 paper-based). *Application deadline:* For fall admission, 6/1 for domestic students, 5/1 for international students; for spring admission, 11/1 for domestic students, 10/1 for international students. Applications are processed on a rolling basis. Application fee: $40. Electronic applications accepted. *Financial support:* In 2016–17, 27 teaching assistantships with full tuition reimbursements were awarded; fellowships with full tuition reimbursements, research assistantships with full tuition reimbursements, career-related internships or fieldwork, Federal Work-Study, scholarships/grants, tuition waivers (full), and unspecified assistantships also available. Support available to part-time students. Financial award applicants required to submit FAFSA. *Faculty research:* Unemployment, behavior under uncertainty, effect of debt on compensation and capital utilization, racial inequality of earnings. *Unit head:* Dr. Carl Campbell, Acting Chair, 815-753-6974, Fax: 815-753-1019, E-mail: carlcamp@niu.edu. *Application contact:* Dr. Jeremy Groves, Director, Graduate Studies, 815-753-6957.
Website: http://www.niu.edu/econ/

**Northwestern University,** The Graduate School, Judd A. and Marjorie Weinberg College of Arts and Sciences, Department of Economics, Evanston, IL 60208. Offers PhD, JD/PhD. Admissions and degrees offered through The Graduate School. *Degree requirements:* For doctorate, thesis/dissertation, preliminary written exam. *Entrance requirements:* For doctorate, GRE General Test. Additional exam requirements/ recommendations for international students: Required—TOEFL. *Faculty research:* Organization of industry, behavior of labor markets, effects of monetary policy, theory of markets.

**Northwestern University,** The Graduate School, Kellogg School of Management, Department of Managerial Economics and Decision Sciences, Evanston, IL 60208. Offers PhD. Admissions and degree offered through The Graduate School. *Degree requirements:* For doctorate, comprehensive exam, thesis/dissertation. *Entrance requirements:* For doctorate, GMAT or GRE General Test. Additional exam requirements/recommendations for international students: Required—TOEFL. Electronic applications accepted. *Faculty research:* Competitive strategy and organization, managerial economics, decision sciences, game theory, operations management.

**Oakland University,** Graduate Study and Lifelong Learning, School of Business Administration, Department of Economics, Rochester, MI 48309-4401. Offers economics (MBA, Certificate).

**The Ohio State University,** Graduate School, College of Arts and Sciences, Division of Social and Behavioral Sciences, Department of Economics, Columbus, OH 43210. Offers MA, PhD. *Faculty:* 25. *Students:* 82 full-time (27 women), 63 international. Average age 28. In 2016, 13 master's, 12 doctorates awarded. *Degree requirements:* For doctorate, thesis/dissertation. *Entrance requirements:* For doctorate, GRE. Additional exam requirements/recommendations for international students: Required—TOEFL (minimum score 550 paper-based; 79 iBT), Michigan English Language Assessment Battery (minimum score 82); Recommended—IELTS (minimum score 7). *Application deadline:* For fall admission, 11/30 priority date for domestic and international students. Applications are processed on a rolling basis. Application fee: $60 ($70 for international students). Electronic applications accepted. *Financial support:* Fellowships with tuition reimbursements, research assistantships with tuition reimbursements, teaching assistantships with tuition reimbursements, Federal Work-Study, and institutionally sponsored loans available. Support available to part-time students. *Unit head:* Dr. Trevon Logan, Professor/Chair, 614-292-0762, E-mail: logan.155@osu.edu. *Application contact:* Graduate and Professional Admissions, 614-292-9444, Fax: 614-292-3895, E-mail: gpadmissions@osu.edu.
Website: https://economics.osu.edu/

**Ohio University,** Graduate College, College of Arts and Sciences, Department of Economics, Athens, OH 45701-2979. Offers applied economics (MA); financial economics (MFE). *Program availability:* Part-time, evening/weekend. *Degree requirements:* For master's, thesis or alternative. *Entrance requirements:* For master's, GRE or GMAT (recommended), minimum GPA of 3.0. Additional exam requirements/ recommendations for international students: Required—TOEFL (minimum score 550 paper-based; 80 iBT) or IELTS (minimum score 6.5). *Application deadline:* For fall admission, 2/15 priority date for domestic and international students; for winter admission, 12/1 for domestic students, 10/1 priority date for international students. Application fee: $50 ($55 for international students). Electronic applications accepted. *Financial support:* Research assistantships with full and partial tuition reimbursements, Federal Work-Study, tuition waivers (partial), and unspecified assistantships available. Financial award application deadline: 2/15. *Faculty research:* Macroeconomics, public finance, international economics and finance, monetary theory, healthcare economics. *Unit head:* Dr. Rosmary Rossiter, Chair, 740-593-2040, E-mail: rossiter@ohio.edu. *Application contact:* Dr. K. Doroodian, Graduate Chair, 740-593-2046, E-mail: doroodia@ohio.edu.
Website: http://www.ohiou.edu/economics/

**Oklahoma State University,** Spears School of Business, Department of Economics and Legal Studies in Business, Stillwater, OK 74078. Offers MS, PhD. *Program availability:* Part-time. *Faculty:* 24 full-time (8 women), 2 part-time/adjunct (1 woman). *Students:* 9 full-time (2 women), 8 part-time (2 women); includes 1 minority (Asian, non-Hispanic/Latino), 13 international. Average age 30. 34 applicants, 21% accepted, 5 enrolled. In 2016, 1 master's, 5 doctorates awarded. *Degree requirements:* For master's, thesis or alternative; for doctorate, comprehensive exam, thesis/dissertation. *Entrance requirements:* For master's and doctorate, GRE or GMAT. Additional exam requirements/recommendations for international students: Required—TOEFL (minimum score 550 paper-based; 79 iBT). *Application deadline:* For fall admission, 3/1 priority date for international students; for spring admission, 8/1 priority date for international students. Applications are processed on a rolling basis. Application fee: $40 ($75 for international students). Electronic applications accepted. *Expenses:* Tuition, state resident: full-time $3775; part-time $209.70 per credit hour. Tuition, nonresident: full-time $14,851; part-time $825.05 per credit hour. *Required fees:* $2027; $112.60 per credit hour. Tuition and fees vary according to campus/location. *Financial support:* In 2016–17, 4 research assistantships (averaging $17,217 per year), 18 teaching assistantships (averaging $12,364 per year) were awarded; career-related internships or fieldwork, Federal Work-Study, scholarships/grants, health care benefits, tuition waivers (partial), and unspecified assistantships also available. Support available to part-time students. Financial award application deadline: 3/1; financial award applicants required to submit FAFSA. *Faculty research:* Economics and legal studies in business, regional economic modeling/econometrics, urban/regional economics, monetary economics, international trade/finance/development, environmental economics. *Unit head:* Dr. Lee Adkins, Head, 405-744-5195, Fax: 405-744-5180, E-mail: lee.adkins@okstate.edu. *Application contact:* Dr. Mary Gade, Graduate Coordinator, 405-744-5197, Fax: 405-744-5180, E-mail: mary.gade@okstate.edu.
Website: http://spears.okstate.edu/ecls

**Old Dominion University,** Strome College of Business, Program in Economics, Norfolk, VA 23529. Offers MA. *Program availability:* Part-time, evening/weekend. *Faculty:* 11 full-time (2 women). *Students:* 12 full-time (2 women), 6 part-time (4 women); includes 3 minority (1 Black or African American, non-Hispanic/Latino; 2 Two or more races, non-Hispanic/Latino), 9 international. Average age 28. 50 applicants, 76% accepted, 26 enrolled. In 2016, 14 master's awarded. *Degree requirements:* For master's, comprehensive exam, thesis optional, independent research. *Entrance requirements:* For master's, GMAT or GRE General Test, minimum GPA of 2.5. Additional exam requirements/recommendations for international students: Required—TOEFL (minimum score 520 paper-based; 79 iBT). *Application deadline:* For fall admission, 8/1 priority date for domestic students, 4/15 for international students; for spring admission, 11/1 priority date for domestic students, 10/1 for international students. Applications are processed on a rolling basis. Application fee: $50. Electronic applications accepted. *Expenses:* Contact institution. *Financial support:* In 2016–17, 8 students received support, including 8 research assistantships with partial tuition reimbursements available (averaging $3,200 per year); unspecified assistantships also available. Financial award application deadline: 8/1; financial award applicants required to submit FAFSA. *Faculty research:* International economics, transportation, public economics, macroeconomics, econometrics. *Unit head:* Dr. David Duden Selover, Graduate Program Director, 757-683-3541, Fax: 757-638-5639, E-mail: dselover@odu.edu. *Application contact:* Dr. Ali Ardalan, Associate Dean, 757-683-3520, Fax: 757-683-4076, E-mail: aardalan@odu.edu.
Website: http://www.odu.edu/business/departments/economics

**Oregon State University,** College of Agricultural Sciences, Program in Applied Economics, Corvallis, OR 97331. Offers public health economics (MA, MS, PhD); resource and environmental economics (MA); trade and development (MA, MS, PhD); transportation economics (MA, MS). *Program availability:* Part-time. *Faculty:* 14 full-time (3 women), 4 part-time/adjunct (0 women). *Students:* 26 full-time (10 women), 2 part-time (both women); includes 3 minority (1 Asian, non-Hispanic/Latino; 2 Hispanic/ Latino), 14 international. Average age 31. 83 applicants, 24% accepted, 5 enrolled. In 2016, 6 master's, 4 doctorates awarded. Terminal master's awarded for partial completion of doctoral program. *Degree requirements:* For master's, thesis (for some programs); for doctorate, thesis/dissertation. *Entrance requirements:* For master's and doctorate, GRE General Test, minimum GPA of 3.0 in last 90 hours. Additional exam requirements/recommendations for international students: Required—TOEFL (minimum score 90 iBT). *Application deadline:* For fall admission, 1/15 for domestic and international students. Application fee: $75 ($85 for international students). *Expenses:* Tuition, state resident: full-time $12,150; part-time $450 per credit. Tuition, nonresident: full-time $21,789; part-time $807 per credit. *Required fees:* $1651; $1507 per credit. One-time fee: $350. Tuition and fees vary according to course load, campus/location and program. *Financial support:* Fellowships, research assistantships, teaching assistantships, career-related internships or fieldwork, Federal Work-Study, and institutionally sponsored loans available. Support available to part-time students. Financial award application deadline: 1/15. *Unit head:* Dr. Larry Lev, Interim Department Head/Professor. *Application contact:* Tjodie Richardson, Applied Economics Advisor, 541-737-1399, E-mail: tjrichardson@oregonstate.edu.
Website: http://oregonstate.edu/aecgradprogram/

**Pace University,** Lubin School of Business, Advanced Professional Certificate Program, New York, NY 10038. Offers business economics (APC); e-business (APC); financial management (APC); international business (APC); international economics (APC); investment management (APC); marketing (APC); public accounting (APC). *Program availability:* Evening/weekend. *Students:* 1 applicant, 100% accepted, 1 enrolled. *Entrance requirements:* For degree, MBA or MS in business discipline, relevant professional experience. Additional exam requirements/recommendations for international students: Required—TOEFL (minimum score 90 iBT), IELTS (minimum score 7) or PTE (minimum score 61). *Application deadline:* For fall admission, 8/1 priority date for domestic students, 6/1 for international students; for spring admission, 12/1 for domestic students, 10/1 for international students. Applications are processed

on a rolling basis. Application fee: $70. Electronic applications accepted. *Expenses: Tuition:* Part-time $1195 per credit. *Required fees:* $260 per semester. Tuition and fees vary according to degree level, campus/location and program. *Unit head:* Dr. Jack Yurkiewicz, Director, 212-618-6567, E-mail: jyurkiewicz@pace.edu. *Application contact:* Susan Ford-Goldschein, Director of Graduate Admissions, 212-346-1531, Fax: 212-346-1585, E-mail: graduateadmission@pace.edu.
Website: http://www.pace.edu/lubin/agc

**Penn State University Park,** Graduate School, College of the Liberal Arts, Department of Economics, University Park, PA 16802. Offers MA, PhD. *Unit head:* Dr. Susan Welch, Dean, 814-865-7691, Fax: 814-863-2085. *Application contact:* Lori Hawn, Director, Graduate Student Services, 814-865-1795, Fax: 814-863-4627, E-mail: l-gswww@lists.psu.edu.
Website: http://econ.la.psu.edu/

**Pepperdine University,** School of Public Policy, Malibu, CA 90263. Offers American politics (MPP); economics (MPP); international relations (MPP); state and local policy (MPP); JD/MPP; MBA/MPP; MDR/MPP. *Faculty:* 4 full-time (1 woman), 5 part-time/adjunct (0 women). *Students:* 57 full-time (27 women), 7 part-time (5 women); includes 22 minority (9 Black or African American, non-Hispanic/Latino; 2 American Indian or Alaska Native, non-Hispanic/Latino; 6 Asian, non-Hispanic/Latino; 4 Hispanic/Latino; 1 Two or more races, non-Hispanic/Latino), 10 international. Average age 25. 174 applicants, 55% accepted, 29 enrolled. In 2016, 34 master's awarded. *Entrance requirements:* For master's, GRE or GMAT, 2 letters of recommendation, resume, two essays. Additional exam requirements/recommendations for international students: Required—TOEFL. *Application deadline:* For fall admission, 6/15 for domestic students. Applications are processed on a rolling basis. Application fee: $50. Electronic applications accepted. *Expenses:* $47,710 per academic year; $1,525 per unit (for master's). *Financial support:* Institutionally sponsored loans and scholarships/grants available. Financial award application deadline: 5/1; financial award applicants required to submit FAFSA. *Unit head:* Dr. Pete Peterson, Dean, School of Public Policy, 310-506-7490, Fax: 310-506-7494, E-mail: pete.n.peterson@pepperdine.edu. *Application contact:* Carson Bruno, Assistant Dean for Admission and Program Relations, 310-506-7493, E-mail: carson.bruno@pepperdine.edu.
Website: http://publicpolicy.pepperdine.edu/

**Peru State College,** Graduate Programs, Program in Organizational Management, Peru, NE 68421. Offers MS. Program offered online only. *Program availability:* Part-time, online learning. *Degree requirements:* For master's, thesis (for some programs). *Expenses:* Contact institution. *Faculty research:* Emotional intelligence.

**Portland State University,** Graduate Studies, College of Liberal Arts and Sciences, Systems Science Program, Portland, OR 97207-0751. Offers computational intelligence (Certificate); computer modeling and simulation (Certificate); systems science (MS); systems science/anthropology (PhD); systems science/business administration (PhD); systems science/civil engineering (PhD); systems science/economics (PhD); systems science/engineering management (PhD); systems science/general (PhD); systems science/mathematical sciences (PhD); systems science/mechanical engineering (PhD); systems science/psychology (PhD); systems science/sociology (PhD). *Faculty:* 2 full-time (0 women), 3 part-time/adjunct (1 woman). *Students:* 12 full-time (3 women), 21 part-time (5 women); includes 5 minority (1 Black or African American, non-Hispanic/Latino; 2 Hispanic/Latino; 2 Two or more races, non-Hispanic/Latino). Average age 39. 16 applicants, 69% accepted, 9 enrolled. In 2016, 4 master's, 6 doctorates awarded. *Degree requirements:* For master's, comprehensive exam (for some programs), thesis optional; for doctorate, variable foreign language requirement, comprehensive exam (for some programs), thesis/dissertation. *Entrance requirements:* For master's, GRE/GMAT (recommended), minimum GPA of 3.0 undergraduate or graduate work, 2 letters of recommendation, statement of interest; for doctorate, GMAT, GRE General Test, minimum GPA of 3.0 undergraduate, 3.25 graduate; 2 letters of recommendation; statement of interest. Additional exam requirements/recommendations for international students: Required—TOEFL (minimum score 550 paper-based; 80 iBT). *Application deadline:* For fall admission, 1/15 for domestic and international students; for spring admission, 11/1 for domestic students. Application fee: $65. Electronic applications accepted. *Expenses:* Contact institution. *Financial support:* In 2016–17, 2 research assistantships with tuition reimbursements (averaging $7,830 per year) were awarded; teaching assistantships, career-related internships or fieldwork, Federal Work-Study, scholarships/grants, and unspecified assistantships also available. Support available to part-time students. Financial award application deadline: 3/1; financial award applicants required to submit FAFSA. *Faculty research:* Systems theory and methodology, artificial intelligence neural networks, information theory, nonlinear dynamics/chaos, modeling and simulation. *Unit head:* Dr. Wayne Wakeland, Chair, 503-725-4975, E-mail: wakeland@pdx.edu.
Website: http://www.pdx.edu/sysc/

**Portland State University,** Graduate Studies, College of Urban and Public Affairs, Department of Economics, Portland, OR 97207-0751. Offers applied economics (MA, MS); general economics (MA, MS). *Program availability:* Part-time. *Faculty:* 15 full-time (3 women), 8 part-time/adjunct (4 women). *Students:* 13 full-time (5 women), 4 part-time (1 woman); includes 2 minority (1 Hispanic/Latino; 1 Native Hawaiian or other Pacific Islander, non-Hispanic/Latino), 5 international. Average age 29. 26 applicants, 50% accepted, 11 enrolled. In 2016, 9 master's awarded. *Degree requirements:* For master's, thesis optional; for doctorate, one foreign language, thesis/dissertation. *Entrance requirements:* For master's, minimum GPA of 3.0 in economic course work and overall; course work in calculus. Additional exam requirements/recommendations for international students: Required—TOEFL (minimum score 550 paper-based; 80 iBT). *Application deadline:* For fall admission, 2/1 for domestic and international students; for winter admission, 9/1 for domestic and international students; for spring admission, 12/5 for domestic and international students. Applications are processed on a rolling basis. Application fee: $65. *Expenses:* Contact institution. *Financial support:* In 2016–17, 9 teaching assistantships with full tuition reimbursements (averaging $7,282 per year) were awarded; career-related internships or fieldwork, Federal Work-Study, and unspecified assistantships also available. Support available to part-time students. Financial award application deadline: 3/1; financial award applicants required to submit FAFSA. *Faculty research:* NAFTA, economies of transition, economics of Eastern Europe, artificial intelligence, comparative economic systems. *Total annual research expenditures:* $181,423. *Unit head:* Dr. Thomas Potiowsky, Chair, 503-725-2288, Fax: 503-725-3945, E-mail: potiowskyt@pdx.edu. *Application contact:* Margie Port, Office Coordinator, 503-725-3974, Fax: 503-725-3974, E-mail: mport@pdx.edu.
Website: https://www.pdx.edu/econ/

**Princeton University,** Graduate School, Department of Economics, Princeton, NJ 08544-1019. Offers PhD. *Degree requirements:* For doctorate, thesis/dissertation. *Entrance requirements:* For doctorate, GRE General Test, GRE Subject Test (recommended), working knowledge of multivariate calculus and matrix algebra. Additional exam requirements/recommendations for international students: Required—TOEFL (minimum score 600 paper-based). Electronic applications accepted.

**Princeton University,** Graduate School, Program in Population Studies, Princeton, NJ 08544-1019. Offers demography (PhD, Certificate); economics and demography (PhD); public affairs and demography (PhD); sociology and demography (PhD). *Degree*

*requirements:* For doctorate, thesis/dissertation. *Entrance requirements:* For doctorate, GRE General Test. Additional exam requirements/recommendations for international students: Required—TOEFL (minimum score 600 paper-based). Electronic applications accepted. *Faculty research:* Models, fertility, infant and child mortality, migration.

**Purdue University,** Graduate School, Krannert School of Management, Doctoral Program in Economics, West Lafayette, IN 47907-2056. Offers PhD. *Degree requirements:* For doctorate, comprehensive exam, thesis/dissertation, dissertation proposal in 3rd year of study. *Entrance requirements:* For doctorate, GRE, two semesters of calculus, one semester of linear algebra. Additional exam requirements/recommendations for international students: Required—TOEFL (minimum score 575 paper-based); Recommended—TWE. Electronic applications accepted. *Faculty research:* Econometrics, experimental economics, international economics, macroeconomic theory, industrial organization.

**Queens College of the City University of New York,** Division of Social Sciences, Department of Economics, Queens, NY 11367-1597. Offers risk management-accounting (MS); risk management-dynamic finance analysis (MS); risk management-finance (MS). *Degree requirements:* For master's, thesis. *Entrance requirements:* For master's, minimum GPA of 3.0. Additional exam requirements/recommendations for international students: Required—TOEFL (minimum score 100 iBT), IELTS (minimum score 7). *Expenses:* Tuition, state resident: full-time $5065; part-time $425 per credit. Tuition, nonresident: part-time $780 per credit. *Required fees:* $522; $397 per credit. Part-time tuition and fees vary according to course load and program. *Faculty research:* Business economics, urban economic problems, international economics, economics of nonprofit sector.

**Regis University,** College of Business and Economics, Denver, CO 80221-1099. Offers accounting (MS); executive leadership (Certificate); finance (MS); finance and accounting (MBA); health industry leadership (MBA); human resource management and leadership (MSOL); management (MBA); marketing (MBA); nonprofit leadership (Post-Graduate Certificate); nonprofit management (MNM); nonprofit organizational capacity building (Certificate); operations management (MBA); organizational leadership and management (MSOL); project leadership and management (MS, MSOL); strategic business management (Certificate); strategic human resource integration (Certificate); strategic management (MBA). Programs offered at Colorado Springs Campus, Northwest Denver Campus, Southeast Denver Campus, Fort Collins Campus, Broomfield Campus, Henderson (Nevada) Campus, and Summerlin (Nevada) Campus. *Program availability:* Part-time, evening/weekend, 100% online, blended/hybrid learning. *Faculty:* 15 full-time (5 women), 43 part-time/adjunct (16 women). *Students:* 622 full-time (350 women), 460 part-time (170 women); includes 317 minority (88 Black or African American, non-Hispanic/Latino; 7 American Indian or Alaska Native, non-Hispanic/Latino; 44 Asian, non-Hispanic/Latino; 151 Hispanic/Latino; 1 Native Hawaiian or other Pacific Islander, non-Hispanic/Latino; 26 Two or more races, non-Hispanic/Latino), 44 international. Average age 36. 307 applicants, 73% accepted, 134 enrolled. In 2016, 394 master's awarded. *Degree requirements:* For master's, thesis (for some programs), capstone or final research project. *Entrance requirements:* For master's, official transcript reflecting baccalaureate degree awarded from regionally-accredited college or university, interview, 2 years of full-time related work experience, resume, letters of recommendation. Additional exam requirements/recommendations for international students: Required—TOEFL (minimum score 550 paper-based; 82 iBT). *Application deadline:* For fall admission, 8/15 priority date for domestic students, 8/13 for international students; for winter admission, 10/10 priority date for domestic students, 9/8 for international students; for spring admission, 1/10 priority date for domestic students, 11/17 for international students; for summer admission, 5/1 priority date for domestic students. Applications are processed on a rolling basis. Application fee: $75. Electronic applications accepted. *Expenses:* $780 per credit hour. *Financial support:* Scholarships/grants available. Financial award application deadline: 4/15; financial award applicants required to submit FAFSA. *Faculty research:* Impact of information technology on small business regulation of accounting, international project financing, mineral development, delivery of healthcare to rural indigenous communities. *Unit head:* Dr. Timothy Keane, Academic Dean. *Application contact:* Cate Clark, Director of Admissions, 303-458-4900, Fax: 303-964-5534, E-mail: ruadmissions@regis.edu.
Website: http://www.regis.edu/CBE.aspx

**Rice University,** Graduate Programs, School of Social Sciences, Department of Economics, Houston, TX 77251-1892. Offers economics (PhD); energy economics (MEECON). *Degree requirements:* For doctorate, comprehensive exam, thesis/dissertation. *Entrance requirements:* For doctorate, GRE. Additional exam requirements/recommendations for international students: Required—TOEFL (minimum score 600 paper-based; 90 iBT). Electronic applications accepted.

**Roosevelt University,** Graduate Division, College of Arts and Sciences, Department of Economics, Chicago, IL 60605. Offers applied economics (MA); economics (MA). *Program availability:* Part-time, evening/weekend. *Degree requirements:* For master's, thesis or alternative. *Entrance requirements:* For master's, minimum GPA of 2.7. *Faculty research:* Labor, gender issues, international trade and development, entrepreneurship, political economy and money.

**Rutgers University–Newark,** Graduate School, Program in Economics, Newark, NJ 07102. Offers MA. *Entrance requirements:* For master's, GRE, minimum undergraduate B average.

**Rutgers University–Newark,** Rutgers Business School–Newark and New Brunswick, Doctoral Programs in Management, Newark, NJ 07102. Offers accounting (PhD); accounting information systems (PhD); economics (PhD); finance (PhD); individualized study (PhD); information technology (PhD); international business (PhD); management science (PhD); marketing science (PhD); organizational management (PhD); science, technology and management (PhD); supply chain management (PhD). *Degree requirements:* For doctorate, comprehensive exam, thesis/dissertation. *Entrance requirements:* For doctorate, GRE or GMAT. Additional exam requirements/recommendations for international students: Required—TOEFL (minimum score 550 paper-based; 79 iBT). Electronic applications accepted.

**Rutgers University–New Brunswick,** Graduate School-New Brunswick, Program in Economics, Piscataway, NJ 08854-8097. Offers MA, PhD. Terminal master's awarded for partial completion of doctoral program. *Degree requirements:* For master's, comprehensive exam (for some programs), thesis or alternative; for doctorate, comprehensive exam, thesis/dissertation. *Entrance requirements:* For master's and doctorate, GRE General Test. Additional exam requirements/recommendations for international students: Required—TOEFL. Electronic applications accepted. *Faculty research:* Econometrics, microeconomics, macroeconomics, economichistory.

**St. Cloud State University,** School of Graduate Studies, College of Social Sciences, Department of Economics, St. Cloud, MN 56301-4498. Offers applied economics (MS); public and nonprofit institutions (MS). *Program availability:* Part-time. *Degree requirements:* For master's, thesis or alternative. *Entrance requirements:* For master's, GRE General Test, minimum GPA of 2.75. Additional exam requirements/recommendations for international students: Recommended—TOEFL (minimum score 550 paper-based), IELTS (minimum score 6.5). Electronic applications accepted.

## Economics

**San Diego State University,** Graduate and Research Affairs, College of Arts and Letters, Department of Economics, San Diego, CA 92182. Offers MA. *Entrance requirements:* For master's, GRE General Test, 2 letters of recommendation. Additional exam requirements/recommendations for international students: Required—TOEFL. Electronic applications accepted. *Faculty research:* Financing public education, demand for alternative fuel vehicles, economics of the Gold Rush, interdependence of equity and economic efficiency, economics of welfare.

**San Francisco State University,** Division of Graduate Studies, College of Business, Department of Economics, San Francisco, CA 94132-1722. Offers MA. *Expenses:* Tuition, state resident: full-time $6738. Tuition, nonresident: full-time $15,666. *Required fees:* $1012. Tuition and fees vary according to degree level and program. *Unit head:* Dr. Don Mar, Chair, 415-338-2648, E-mail: dmar@sfsu.edu. *Application contact:* Dr. Lisa Takeyama, Graduate Coordinator, 415-338-2499, E-mail: takeyama@sfsu.edu. Website: http://cob.sfsu.edu/economics

**San Jose State University,** Graduate Studies and Research, College of Social Sciences, San Jose, CA 95192-0001. Offers applications of technology in planning (Certificate); applied anthropology (MA); communication studies (MS); community design and development (Certificate); economics (MA), including applied economics, social sciences; environmental planning (Certificate); geographic information science (Certificate); geography (MA); global citizenship (Certificate); history (MA), including history education, social sciences; Mexican American studies (MA); psychology (MA, MS), including clinical psychology (MS), industrial/organizational psychology (MS); research and experimental psychology (MA); public administration (MA); real estate development (Certificate); social sciences (MPA, MS); sociology (MA); transportation and land use planning (Certificate). *Program availability:* Part-time, evening/weekend. *Entrance requirements:* For master's, minimum GPA of 3.0. Electronic applications accepted.

**Simon Fraser University,** Office of Graduate Studies and Postdoctoral Fellows, Faculty of Arts and Social Sciences, Department of Economics, Burnaby, BC V5A 1S6, Canada. Offers MA, PhD. *Faculty:* 38 full-time (7 women). *Students:* 59 full-time (24 women). 285 applicants, 28% accepted, 21 enrolled. In 2016, 23 master's, 10 doctorates awarded. *Degree requirements:* For master's, thesis (for some programs); for doctorate, comprehensive exam, thesis/dissertation. *Entrance requirements:* For master's, GRE, minimum GPA of 3.0 (on scale of 4.33) or 3.33 based on last 60 credits of undergraduate courses; for doctorate, GRE, minimum GPA of 3.5 (on scale of 4.33). Additional exam requirements/recommendations for international students: Recommended—TOEFL (minimum score 580 paper-based; 93 iBT), IELTS (minimum score 7), TWE (minimum score 5). *Application deadline:* For fall admission, 2/1 priority date for domestic students; for winter admission, 10/1 for domestic students. Application fee: $90 ($125 for international students). *Financial support:* In 2016–17, 28 students received support, including 19 fellowships (averaging $5,303 per year), teaching assistantships (averaging $5,608 per year); research assistantships and scholarships/grants also available. *Faculty research:* Industrial organization, international trade, econometrics, labor, macroeconomics. *Unit head:* Dr. Simon Woodcock, Graduate Chair, 778-782-5813, Fax: 778-782-5944, E-mail: econ-grad-chair@sfu.ca. *Application contact:* Kathleen Vieira-Rebeiro, Graduate Secretary, 778-782-3562, Fax: 778-782-5944, E-mail: econ-grad-sec@sfu.ca.
Website: http://www.sfu.ca/economics/

**South Dakota State University,** Graduate School, College of Agriculture and Biological Sciences, Department of Economics, Brookings, SD 57007. Offers MS. *Degree requirements:* For master's, comprehensive exam, thesis (for some programs), oral exam. *Entrance requirements:* For master's, minimum GPA of 2.75. Additional exam requirements/recommendations for international students: Required—TOEFL (minimum score 550 paper-based; 79 iBT). *Faculty research:* Sustainable agriculture, rural finance, grain and livestock marketing, agricultural policy, applied economics.

**Southern Illinois University Carbondale,** Graduate School, College of Liberal Arts, Department of Economics, Carbondale, IL 62901-4701. Offers MA, MS, PhD. *Degree requirements:* For master's, thesis; for doctorate, thesis/dissertation. *Entrance requirements:* For master's, GRE General Test, minimum GPA of 2.7; for doctorate, GRE General Test, minimum GPA of 3.25. Additional exam requirements/recommendations for international students: Required—TOEFL. *Faculty research:* Advanced economic theory, applied microeconomics, economic development, finance, international economics, monetary theory and policy.

**Southern Illinois University Edwardsville,** Graduate School, School of Business, Department of Economics and Finance, Edwardsville, IL 62026. Offers MA, MS. *Program availability:* Part-time, evening/weekend. *Degree requirements:* For master's, thesis or alternative, final exam, portfolio. *Entrance requirements:* For master's, GMAT or GRE. Additional exam requirements/recommendations for international students: Required—TOEFL (minimum score 550 paper-based; 79 iBT), IELTS (minimum score 6.5). Electronic applications accepted.

**Southern Methodist University,** Dedman College of Humanities and Sciences, Department of Economics, Dallas, TX 75205. Offers applied economics (MA); applied economics and predictive analytics (MS); economics (PhD); law and economics (MA). *Program availability:* Part-time, evening/weekend. Terminal master's awarded for partial completion of doctoral program. *Degree requirements:* For master's, thesis, oral qualifying exam; for doctorate, thesis/dissertation, written exams. *Entrance requirements:* For master's, GRE General Test or GMAT, 12 hours of course work in economics, minimum GPA of 3.0, previous course work in calculus and statistics; for doctorate, GRE General Test, minimum GPA of 3.0; 3 semesters of course work in calculus; 1 semester each of course work in statistics and linear algebra. Additional exam requirements/recommendations for international students: Required—TOEFL (minimum score 550 paper-based). Electronic applications accepted. *Faculty research:* Economic theory, game theory, econometrics, international trade, labor.

**Stanford University,** School of Humanities and Sciences, Department of Economics, Stanford, CA 94305-2004. Offers PhD. *Degree requirements:* For doctorate, comprehensive exam, thesis/dissertation. *Entrance requirements:* For doctorate, GRE General Test. Additional exam requirements/recommendations for international students: Required—TOEFL. Electronic applications accepted. *Expenses:* Tuition: Full-time $47,331. *Required fees:* $609.

**State University of New York College of Environmental Science and Forestry,** Program in Environmental Science, Syracuse, NY 13210-2779. Offers biophysical and ecological economics (MPS); coupled natural and human systems (MPS); ecosystem restoration (MPS); environmental and community land planning (MPS, MS); environmental and natural resources policy (PhD); environmental communication and participatory processes (PhD); environmental monitoring and modeling (MPS); water and wetland resource studies (MPS, MS). *Program availability:* Part-time. *Faculty:* 1 full-time (0 women), 1 (woman) part-time/adjunct. *Students:* 59 full-time (39 women), 16 part-time (10 women); includes 6 minority (1 Black or African American, non-Hispanic/Latino; 1 Asian, non-Hispanic/Latino; 3 Hispanic/Latino; 1 Two or more races, non-Hispanic/Latino), 25 international. Average age 30. 70 applicants, 59% accepted, 20 enrolled. In 2016, 13 master's, 8 doctorates awarded. *Degree requirements:* For master's, thesis (for some programs); for doctorate, comprehensive exam, thesis/

dissertation. *Entrance requirements:* For master's and doctorate, GRE General Test, minimum GPA of 3.0. Additional exam requirements/recommendations for international students: Required—TOEFL (minimum score 550 paper-based; 80 iBT), IELTS (minimum score 6). *Application deadline:* For fall admission, 2/1 priority date for domestic and international students; for spring admission, 11/1 priority date for domestic and international students. Applications are processed on a rolling basis. Application fee: $60. *Expenses:* Tuition, state resident: full-time $10,870; part-time $453 per credit. Tuition, nonresident: full-time $22,210; part-time $925 per credit. *Required fees:* $1075; $89.22 per credit. *Financial support:* In 2016–17, 32 students received support. Application deadline: 6/30; applicants required to submit FAFSA. *Faculty research:* Environmental education/communications, water resources, land resources, waste management. *Unit head:* Dr. Ruth Yanai, Coordinator, 315-470-6955, Fax: 315-470-6700, E-mail: rdyanai@esf.edu. *Application contact:* Scott Shannon, Associate Provost for Instruction/Dean of the Graduate School, 315-470-6599, Fax: 315-470-6978, E-mail: esfgrad@esf.edu.
Website: http://www.esf.edu/environmentalscience/graduate/

**Stony Brook University, State University of New York,** Graduate School, College of Arts and Sciences, Department of Economics, Stony Brook, NY 11794. Offers MA, PhD. *Faculty:* 13 full-time (4 women), 5 part-time/adjunct (1 woman). *Students:* 69 full-time (28 women), 1 part-time (0 women); includes 5 minority (4 Asian, non-Hispanic/Latino; 1 Hispanic/Latino, 60 international. Average age 28. 144 applicants, 57% accepted, 20 enrolled. In 2016, 14 master's, 8 doctorates awarded. *Degree requirements:* For doctorate, comprehensive exam, thesis/dissertation. *Entrance requirements:* For master's and doctorate, GRE General Test. Additional exam requirements/recommendations for international students: Required—TOEFL. *Application deadline:* For fall admission, 1/15 for domestic students; for spring admission, 10/1 for domestic students. Application fee: $100. Electronic applications accepted. *Expenses:* Contact institution. *Financial support:* In 2016–17, 29 teaching assistantships were awarded; fellowships and research assistantships also available. *Faculty research:* Economics, economic theory, macroeconomics, industrial organization, labor economics. *Total annual research expenditures:* $141,794. *Unit head:* Prof. Juan Carlos Conesa, Chair, 631-632-7549, Fax: 631-632-7516, E-mail: juan.conesa@stonybrook.edu. *Application contact:* Maryann Calvacca, Graduate Program Coordinator, 631-632-7537, Fax: 631-632-7516, E-mail: graduate_economics@stonybrook.edu.
Website: http://www.sunysb.edu/economics/

**Syracuse University,** Maxwell School of Citizenship and Public Affairs, Dual MA Program in Economics and International Relations, Syracuse, NY 13244. Offers MA/MA. *Entrance requirements:* Additional exam requirements/recommendations for international students: Required—TOEFL (minimum score 100 iBT). *Application deadline:* For fall admission, 2/1 priority date for domestic and international students. Application fee: $75. Electronic applications accepted. *Expenses: Tuition:* Full-time $25,974; part-time $1443 per credit hour. *Required fees:* $802; $50 per course. Tuition and fees vary according to course load and program. *Financial support:* Fellowships with full tuition reimbursements, research assistantships with tuition reimbursements, and teaching assistantships with tuition reimbursements available. Financial award application deadline: 1/1. *Faculty research:* Economic concepts, urban and regional economics, policy-oriented settings, public and international affairs, comparative foreign policy. *Unit head:* Dr. Robert Bifulco, Associate Dean and Chair, Public Administration and International Affairs, 315-443-3232, E-mail: rbifulco@maxwell.syr.edu. *Application contact:* Christine Omolino, Associate Director, 315-443-4000, Fax: 315-443-3423, E-mail: comolino@syr.edu.
Website: http://www.maxwell.syr.edu/

**Syracuse University,** Maxwell School of Citizenship and Public Affairs, Programs in Economics, Syracuse, NY 13244. Offers MA, PhD. In 2016, 35 master's, 5 doctorates awarded. *Degree requirements:* For doctorate, comprehensive exam, thesis/dissertation. *Entrance requirements:* For master's and doctorate, GRE General Test, personal statement, three letters of recommendation, resume, official transcripts. Additional exam requirements/recommendations for international students: Required—TOEFL (minimum score 100 iBT). *Application deadline:* For fall admission, 1/15 priority date for domestic and international students. Applications are processed on a rolling basis. Application fee: $75. Electronic applications accepted. *Expenses: Tuition:* Full-time $25,974; part-time $1443 per credit hour. *Required fees:* $802; $50 per course. Tuition and fees vary according to course load and program. *Financial support:* Fellowships with full tuition reimbursements, research assistantships with tuition reimbursements, and teaching assistantships with tuition reimbursements available. Financial award application deadline: 1/1. *Faculty research:* International economics, labor economics, public finance, urban economics. *Unit head:* Dr. Stuart Rosenthal, Director of Graduate Studies, 315-443-3809, E-mail: ssrosent@maxwell.syr.edu. *Application contact:* Matthew O'Keefe, Recruiting Contact, 315-443-3843, E-mail: mkokeefe@maxwell.syr.edu.
Website: http://www.maxwell.syr.edu/econ/

**Tarleton State University,** College of Graduate Studies, College of Business Administration, Stephenville, TX 76402. Offers accounting, finance, and economics (M Acc), including accounting; business administration (MBA); management (MS), including human resources management; marketing and computer information systems (MS), including information systems. *Accreditation:* ACBSP. *Program availability:* Part-time, evening/weekend, online learning. *Faculty:* 26 full-time (3 women), 7 part-time/adjunct (2 women). *Students:* 109 full-time (68 women), 350 part-time (204 women); includes 129 minority (39 Black or African American, non-Hispanic/Latino; 1 American Indian or Alaska Native, non-Hispanic/Latino; 10 Asian, non-Hispanic/Latino; 60 Hispanic/Latino; 19 Two or more races, non-Hispanic/Latino), 4 international. Average age 33. 184 applicants, 89% accepted, 126 enrolled. In 2016, 158 master's awarded. *Degree requirements:* For master's, comprehensive exam, thesis optional. *Entrance requirements:* For master's, GMAT or GRE General Test, minimum GPA of 3.0. Additional exam requirements/recommendations for international students: Required—TOEFL (minimum score 550 paper-based; 80 iBT). *Application deadline:* For fall admission, 8/15 priority date for domestic students; for spring admission, 1/7 for domestic students. Applications are processed on a rolling basis. Application fee: $45 ($130 for international students). Electronic applications accepted. *Expenses:* $3,672 tuition; $2,437 fees. *Financial support:* Research assistantships, teaching assistantships, career-related internships or fieldwork, Federal Work-Study, and institutionally sponsored loans available. Support available to part-time students. Financial award application deadline: 5/1; financial award applicants required to submit FAFSA. *Unit head:* Dr. Steve Steed, Dean, 254-968-9645, E-mail: ssteed@tarleton.edu. *Application contact:* Jodie Dearing, Graduate Program Manager, 254-968-9055, E-mail: jdearing@tarleton.edu.
Website: http://www.tarleton.edu/COBAWEB/coba

**Teachers College, Columbia University,** Department of Education Policy and Social Analysis, New York, NY 10027. Offers economics and education (Ed M, MA, PhD); education policy (Ed M, MA, Ed D, PhD); politics and education (Ed M, MA, Ed D, PhD); sociology and education (Ed M, MA, Ed D, PhD). *Students:* 148 full-time (110 women), 107 part-time (85 women); includes 95 minority (40 Black or African American, non-Hispanic/Latino; 23 Asian, non-Hispanic/Latino; 26 Hispanic/Latino; 6 Two or more

races, non-Hispanic/Latino), 74 international. 516 applicants, 54% accepted, 98 enrolled. *Expenses: Tuition:* Full-time $36,288; part-time $1512 per credit. *Required fees:* $438 per semester. One-time fee: $510 full-time. Full-time tuition and fees vary according to course load. *Unit head:* Dr. Jeffrey Henig, Chair, 212-678-8313, Fax: 212-678-3589, E-mail: henig@tc.columbia.edu. *Application contact:* David Estrella, Director of Admissions, 212-678-3305, E-mail: estrella@tc.columbia.edu.
Website: http://www.tc.columbia.edu/education-policy-and-social-analysis/

**Temple University,** College of Liberal Arts, Department of Economics, Philadelphia, PA 19122-6096. Offers MA, PhD. *Program availability:* Part-time, evening/weekend. *Entrance requirements:* For master's and doctorate, GRE, minimum GPA of 3.0, 3 letters of recommendation. Additional exam requirements/recommendations for international students: Required—TOEFL (minimum score 550 paper-based; 79 iBT). Electronic applications accepted. *Faculty research:* Applied econometrics, health economics, labor economics, macroeconomic theory, microeconomic theory.

**Texas A&M University,** College of Liberal Arts, Department of Economics, College Station, TX 77843. Offers MS, PhD. *Program availability:* Part-time. *Faculty:* 28. *Students:* 232 full-time (103 women), 13 part-time (6 women); includes 13 minority (3 Black or African American, non-Hispanic/Latino; 6 Asian, non-Hispanic/Latino; 3 Hispanic/Latino; 1 Two or more races, non-Hispanic/Latino), 203 international. Average age 26. 397 applicants, 47% accepted, 91 enrolled. In 2016, 85 master's, 12 doctorates awarded. Terminal master's awarded for partial completion of doctoral program. *Degree requirements:* For master's, comprehensive exam, thesis optional; for doctorate, comprehensive exam, thesis/dissertation. *Entrance requirements:* For master's and doctorate, GRE General Test. Additional exam requirements/recommendations for international students: Required—TOEFL (minimum score 550 paper-based; 80 iBT), IELTS (minimum score 6), PTE (minimum score 53). *Application deadline:* For fall admission, 3/1 for domestic students. Applications are processed on a rolling basis. Application fee: $50 ($90 for international students). Electronic applications accepted. *Expenses:* Contact institution. *Financial support:* In 2016–17, 139 students received support, including 12 fellowships with tuition reimbursements available (averaging $1,129 per year), 22 research assistantships with tuition reimbursements available (averaging $4,827 per year), 53 teaching assistantships with tuition reimbursements available (averaging $10,558 per year); career-related internships or fieldwork, institutionally sponsored loans, scholarships/grants, traineeships, health care benefits, tuition waivers (full and partial), and unspecified assistantships also available. Support available to part-time students. Financial award application deadline: 3/15; financial award applicants required to submit FAFSA. *Faculty research:* Tax policy, state tax, labor, international economics, macroeconomics. *Unit head:* Dr. Timothy Gronberg, Head, 979-845-7351, E-mail: tjg@econmail.tamu.edu. *Application contact:* Dr. Dennis W. Jansen, Director of Doctoral Program, 979-845-7351, Fax: 979-847-8557, E-mail: d-jansen@tamu.edu.
Website: http://econ.tamu.edu/

**Texas Tech University,** Graduate School, College of Arts and Sciences, Department of Economics, Lubbock, TX 79409. Offers MA, PhD. *Faculty:* 13 full-time (1 woman). *Students:* 47 full-time (19 women), 6 part-time (1 woman); includes 2 minority (both Hispanic/Latino), 48 international. Average age 31. 50 applicants, 42% accepted, 11 enrolled. In 2016, 4 master's, 1 doctorate awarded. Terminal master's awarded for partial completion of doctoral program. *Degree requirements:* For master's, variable foreign language requirement, comprehensive exam (for some programs), thesis (for some programs); for doctorate, variable foreign language requirement, comprehensive exam, thesis/dissertation. *Entrance requirements:* Additional exam requirements/recommendations for international students: Required—TOEFL (minimum score 550 paper-based; 79 iBT). *Application deadline:* For fall admission, 6/1 priority date for domestic students, 1/15 priority date for international students; for spring admission, 9/1 priority date for domestic students, 6/15 priority date for international students. Applications are processed on a rolling basis. Application fee: $75. Electronic applications accepted. *Expenses:* $300 per credit hour full-time resident tuition, $708 per credit hour full-time non-resident tuition; $50.50 per credit hour fee plus $608 per term fee. *Financial support:* In 2016–17, 40 students received support, including 37 fellowships (averaging $1,838 per year), 40 teaching assistantships (averaging $14,150 per year); research assistantships, scholarships/grants, unspecified assistantships, and partial tuition and fee waivers also available. Financial award application deadline: 3/1; financial award applicants required to submit FAFSA. *Faculty research:* Industrial organization, labor economics, public finance, monetary economics, international economics. *Total annual research expenditures:* $1,411. *Unit head:* Dr. Klaus G. Becker, Associate Professor/Chair, 806-834-7275, Fax: 806-742-1137, E-mail: klaus.becker@ttu.edu. *Application contact:* Rosie Carrillo, Business Manager, 806-742-2201, Fax: 806-742-1137, E-mail: rosie.carrillo@ttu.edu.
Website: http://www.depts.ttu.edu/economics/

**Troy University,** Graduate School, College of Business, Program in Economics, Troy, AL 36082. Offers MA. *Program availability:* Part-time, evening/weekend. *Faculty:* 6 full-time (1 woman). *Students:* 6 full-time (0 women), 2 part-time (1 woman). 10 applicants, 70% accepted. *Degree requirements:* For master's, thesis or alternative, minimum GPA of 3.0, capstone course, research course, admission to candidacy. *Entrance requirements:* For master's, GRE (minimum score of 850 on old exam or 290 on new exam), GMAT (minimum score of 380) or MAT (minimum score of 385), official transcripts; bachelor's degree; minimum GPA of 2.5 in all undergraduate work or 3.0 for last 30 semester hours; letter of recommendation. Additional exam requirements/recommendations for international students: Required—TOEFL (minimum score 523 paper-based; 70 iBT), IELTS (minimum score 6). *Application deadline:* Applications are processed on a rolling basis. Application fee: $50. Electronic applications accepted. *Expenses:* Tuition, state resident: full-time $7146; part-time $397 per credit hour. Tuition, nonresident: full-time $14,292; part-time $794 per credit hour. *Required fees:* $802; $50 per semester. Tuition and fees vary according to campus/location and program. *Financial support:* Fellowships, career-related internships or fieldwork, and scholarships/grants available. Support available to part-time students. Financial award applicants required to submit FAFSA. *Unit head:* Dr. Stephen Miller, Chairman, Economics, 334-670-3525, Fax: 334-670-3708, E-mail: scmiller@troy.edu. *Application contact:* Jessica A. Kimbro, Director of Graduate Admissions, 334-670-3178, Fax: 334-670-3733, E-mail: bcamp@troy.edu.

**Tufts University,** Graduate School of Arts and Sciences, Department of Economics, Medford, MA 02155. Offers MS. *Program availability:* Part-time. *Students:* 33 full-time (17 women); includes 5 minority (1 Black or African American, non-Hispanic/Latino; 2 Asian, non-Hispanic/Latino; 2 Hispanic/Latino), 25 international. Average age 24. 217 applicants, 49% accepted, 28 enrolled. In 2016, 23 master's awarded. *Degree requirements:* For master's, thesis optional. *Entrance requirements:* For master's, GRE General Test. Additional exam requirements/recommendations for international students: Required—TOEFL (minimum score 550 paper-based; 80 iBT), IELTS (minimum score 6.5). *Application deadline:* For fall admission, 2/15 for domestic and international students. Applications are processed on a rolling basis. Application fee: $85. Electronic applications accepted. *Expenses:* $49,982 full-time tuition (for MS). *Financial support:* In 2016–17, 31 students received support. Teaching assistantships, Federal Work-Study, scholarships/grants, tuition waivers (full and partial), and

unspecified assistantships available. Financial award application deadline: 1/15. *Unit head:* Dr. Jeffrey Zabel, Graduate Program Director. *Application contact:* Office of Graduate Admissions, 617-627-3395, E-mail: gradadmissions@tufts.edu.
Website: http://ase.tufts.edu/econ

**Tulane University,** School of Liberal Arts, Department of Economics, New Orleans, LA 70118-5669. Offers MA, PhD. *Degree requirements:* For master's, thesis or alternative; for doctorate, one foreign language, thesis/dissertation. *Entrance requirements:* For master's, GRE General Test, minimum B average in undergraduate course work; for doctorate, GRE General Test. Additional exam requirements/recommendations for international students: Required—TOEFL. Electronic applications accepted. *Expenses: Tuition:* Full-time $50,920; part-time $2829 per credit hour. *Required fees:* $2040; $44.50 per credit hour. $580 per term. Tuition and fees vary according to course load, degree level and program. *Faculty research:* Economic development, public finance, labor economics, international and regional economics, industrial organization.

**Universidad de las Américas Puebla,** Division of Graduate Studies, School of Social Sciences, Program in Economics, Puebla, Mexico. Offers economics (MA); finance (M Adm). *Program availability:* Part-time, evening/weekend. *Degree requirements:* For master's, one foreign language, thesis. *Faculty research:* Economic models (mathematics), industrial organization, assets and values market.

**Université de Moncton,** Faculty of Arts and Social Sciences, Department of Economics, Moncton, NB E1A 3E9, Canada. Offers MA. *Degree requirements:* For master's, one foreign language, thesis. *Entrance requirements:* For master's, minimum GPA of 3.0. *Faculty research:* Free trade, public finance, small and medium size businesses, regional development, demography and development.

**Université de Montréal,** Faculty of Arts and Sciences, Department of Economic Sciences, Montréal, QC H3C 3J7, Canada. Offers economics (M Sc, PhD); mathematical and computational finance (M Sc). *Degree requirements:* For master's, one foreign language, thesis; for doctorate, one foreign language, thesis/dissertation, general exam. Electronic applications accepted. *Faculty research:* Applied and economic theory, public choice, international trade, labor economics, industrial organization.

**Université de Sherbrooke,** Faculty of Administration, Program in Economics, Sherbrooke, QC J1K 2R1, Canada. Offers M Sc. Terminal master's awarded for partial completion of doctoral program. *Degree requirements:* For master's, one foreign language, thesis. *Entrance requirements:* For master's, minimum GPA of 3.0 (on 4.3 scale). Electronic applications accepted. *Faculty research:* Poverty and inequality analysis, wellbeing analysis, international trade, econometrics.

**Université de Sherbrooke,** Faculty of Letters and Human Sciences, Department of Economics, Sherbrooke, QC J1K 2R1, Canada. Offers MA. *Degree requirements:* For master's, thesis. *Faculty research:* Economic development, public finance, macroeconomics.

**Université du Québec à Montréal,** Graduate Programs, Program in Economics, Montréal, QC H3C 3P8, Canada. Offers M Sc, PhD. *Program availability:* Part-time. *Degree requirements:* For master's, thesis; for doctorate, thesis/dissertation. *Entrance requirements:* For master's, appropriate bachelor's degree or equivalent, proficiency in French; for doctorate, appropriate master's degree or equivalent, proficiency in French.

**Université Laval,** Faculty of Social Sciences, Department of Economics, Programs in Economics, Québec, QC G1K 7P4, Canada. Offers MA, PhD. Terminal master's awarded for partial completion of doctoral program. *Degree requirements:* For master's, thesis (for some programs); for doctorate, comprehensive exam, thesis/dissertation. *Entrance requirements:* For master's and doctorate, knowledge of French. Electronic applications accepted.

**University at Albany, State University of New York,** College of Arts and Sciences, Department of Economics, Albany, NY 12222-0001. Offers economic forecasting (MA); economics (MA, PhD). *Program availability:* Part-time. *Faculty:* 11 full-time (1 woman), 1 part-time/adjunct (0 women). *Students:* 49 full-time (19 women), 42 part-time (22 women); includes 10 minority (1 Black or African American, non-Hispanic/Latino; 5 Asian, non-Hispanic/Latino; 3 Hispanic/Latino; 1 Two or more races, non-Hispanic/Latino), 66 international. 157 applicants, 46% accepted, 30 enrolled. In 2016, 17 master's, 5 doctorates awarded. Terminal master's awarded for partial completion of doctoral program. *Degree requirements:* For doctorate, one foreign language, thesis/dissertation. *Entrance requirements:* For doctorate, GRE General Test, GRE Subject Test. Additional exam requirements/recommendations for international students: Required—TOEFL (minimum score 550 paper-based). *Application deadline:* For fall admission, 2/15 for domestic students, 5/1 for international students. Applications are processed on a rolling basis. Application fee: $75. Electronic applications accepted. *Expenses:* Tuition, state resident: full-time $10,870; part-time $453 per credit hour. Tuition, nonresident: full-time $22,210; part-time $925 per credit hour. International tuition: $21,550 full-time. *Required fees:* $1864; $96 per credit hour. *Financial support:* Fellowships, research assistantships, teaching assistantships, career-related internships or fieldwork, institutionally sponsored loans, and lectureships available. Financial award application deadline: 2/15. *Faculty research:* Expectations of inflation and interest rates, diffusion of new technology, labor markets in developing countries, government deficits and international exchange markets. *Total annual research expenditures:* $40,525. *Unit head:* Betty Daniel, Chair, 518-442-4735, Fax: 518-442-4736, E-mail: bdaniel@albany.edu. *Application contact:* Michael DeRensis, Director, Graduate Admissions, 518-442-3980, Fax: 518-442-3922, E-mail: graduate@albany.edu.
Website: http://www.albany.edu/econ/

**University at Albany, State University of New York,** Nelson A. Rockefeller College of Public Affairs and Policy, Department of Public Administration and Policy, Albany, NY 12222-0001. Offers financial management and public economics (MPA); financial market regulation (MPA); health policy (MPA); healthcare management (MPA); homeland security (MPA); human resources management (MPA); information strategy and management (MPA); local government management (MPA); nonprofit management (MPA); nonprofit management and leadership (Certificate); organizational behavior and theory (MPA, PhD); planning and policy analysis (CAS); policy analysis (MPA); politics and administration (PhD); public finance (PhD); public management (PhD); public policy (PhD); public sector management (Certificate); women and public policy (Certificate); JD/MPA. JD/MPA offered jointly with Albany Law School. *Accreditation:* NASPAA (one or more programs are accredited). *Faculty:* 23 full-time (8 women), 14 part-time/adjunct (7 women). *Students:* 117 full-time (65 women), 95 part-time (46 women); includes 41 minority (12 Black or African American, non-Hispanic/Latino; 8 Asian, non-Hispanic/Latino; 19 Hispanic/Latino; 2 Two or more races, non-Hispanic/Latino), 38 international. 223 applicants, 70% accepted, 81 enrolled. In 2016, 52 master's, 10 doctorates, 16 other advanced degrees awarded. *Degree requirements:* For doctorate, one foreign language, thesis/dissertation. *Entrance requirements:* For doctorate, GRE General Test. Additional exam requirements/recommendations for international students: Required—TOEFL (minimum score 550 paper-based). *Application deadline:* For fall admission, 2/1 priority date for domestic students, 5/1 for international students; for spring admission, 12/1 for domestic students. Applications are processed on a rolling basis. Application fee: $75. Electronic applications accepted. *Expenses:* Tuition, state resident: full-time

## Economics

$10,870; part-time $453 per credit hour. Tuition, nonresident: full-time $22,210; part-time $925 per credit hour. *International tuition:* $21,550 full-time. *Required fees:* $1864; $96 per credit hour. *Financial support:* Application deadline: 2/1. *Total annual research expenditures:* $847,949. *Unit head:* Victor Asal, Chair, 518-591-8729, E-mail: vasal@albany.edu.
Website: http://www.albany.edu/rockefeller/pad.shtml

**University at Buffalo, the State University of New York,** Graduate School, College of Arts and Sciences, Department of Economics, Buffalo, NY 14260. Offers economics (MA, MS, PhD); financial economics (Certificate); health services (Certificate); information and Internet economics (Certificate); international economics (Certificate); law and regulation (Certificate); urban and regional economics (Certificate). *Program availability:* Part-time. Terminal master's awarded for partial completion of doctoral program. *Degree requirements:* For master's, comprehensive exam; for doctorate, comprehensive exam, thesis/dissertation, field and theory exams. *Entrance requirements:* For master's, GRE General Test or GMAT; for doctorate, GRE General Test. Additional exam requirements/recommendations for international students: Required—TOEFL (minimum score 550 paper-based; 79 iBT), TWE. Electronic applications accepted. *Faculty research:* Human capital, international economics, econometrics, applied economics, urban economics, economic growth and development.

**University at Buffalo, the State University of New York,** Graduate School, Graduate School of Education, Department of Educational Leadership and Policy, Buffalo, NY 14260. Offers economics and education policy analysis (MA); education studies (Ed M); educational administration (Ed M, Ed D, PhD); educational culture, policy and society (PhD); higher education administration (Ed M, PhD); school building leadership (Certificate); school business and human resource administration (Certificate); school district business leadership (Certificate); school district leadership (Certificate). *Program availability:* Part-time, evening/weekend. *Faculty:* 15 full-time (9 women), 8 part-time/adjunct (6 women). *Students:* 77 full-time (51 women), 122 part-time (76 women); includes 30 minority (23 Black or African American, non-Hispanic/Latino; 4 Asian, non-Hispanic/Latino; 3 Hispanic/Latino), 22 international. Average age 34. 144 applicants, 75% accepted, 63 enrolled. In 2016, 59 master's, 11 doctorates, 29 other advanced degrees awarded. *Degree requirements:* For master's, comprehensive exam (for some programs), thesis optional; for doctorate, comprehensive exam, thesis/dissertation. *Entrance requirements:* For master's, interview, letters of reference; for doctorate, GRE General Test or MAT, writing sample, letters of reference. Additional exam requirements/recommendations for international students: Required—TOEFL (minimum score 550 paper-based; 79 iBT). *Application deadline:* For fall admission, 2/1 priority date for domestic students, 2/1 for international students; for spring admission, 11/15 priority date for domestic students, 10/1 for international students. Applications are processed on a rolling basis. Application fee: $50. Electronic applications accepted. *Financial support:* In 2016–17, 13 fellowships (averaging $6,862 per year), 32 research assistantships with tuition reimbursements (averaging $10,496 per year) were awarded; career-related internships or fieldwork, Federal Work-Study, institutionally sponsored loans, scholarships/grants, health care benefits, tuition waivers (full and partial), and unspecified assistantships also available. Financial award application deadline: 3/15; financial award applicants required to submit FAFSA. *Faculty research:* College access and choice, school leadership preparation and practice, public policy, curriculum and pedagogy, comparative and international education. *Total annual research expenditures:* $435,404. *Unit head:* Dr. Janina C. Brutt-Griffler, Chair, 716-645-2471, Fax: 716-645-2481, E-mail: bruttg@buffalo.edu. *Application contact:* Veronica Kase, Admission Assistant, 716-645-2110, Fax: 716-645-7937, E-mail: vakase@buffalo.edu.
Website: http://gse.buffalo.edu/elp

**The University of Akron,** Graduate School, College of Business Administration, Department of Economics, Akron, OH 44325. Offers MA. *Program availability:* Part-time. *Faculty:* 5 full-time (2 women), 3 part-time/adjunct (0 women). *Students:* 12 full-time (1 woman); includes 1 minority (Hispanic/Latino), 8 international. Average age 26. 16 applicants, 63% accepted, 6 enrolled. In 2016, 5 master's awarded. *Degree requirements:* For master's, thesis optional. *Entrance requirements:* For master's, three letters of recommendation (preferably from academics), statement of purpose, resume. Additional exam requirements/recommendations for international students: Required—TOEFL (minimum score 550 paper-based; 79 iBT), IELTS (minimum score 6.5), GRE. *Application deadline:* For fall admission, 2/15 priority date for domestic and international students; for spring admission, 10/15 priority date for domestic and international students. Application fee: $45 ($70 for international students). Electronic applications accepted. *Expenses:* Tuition, state resident: full-time $8618; part-time $359 per credit hour. Tuition, nonresident: full-time $17,149; part-time $715 per credit hour. *Required fees:* $1652. *Financial support:* In 2016–17, 11 teaching assistantships with full and partial tuition reimbursements were awarded; instructional support assistantships also available. Financial award application deadline: 2/15. *Faculty research:* Regional economic performance, effects of addiction on labor market outcomes, programmatic assessment, regional trading arrangements, agriculture production in early twentieth-century South. *Total annual research expenditures:* $3,323. *Unit head:* Dr. Michael Nelson, Chair, 330-972-7939, E-mail: nelson2@uakron.edu. *Application contact:* Dr. Sucharita Ghosh, Director of Graduate Studies, 330-972-7549, E-mail: sghosh@uakron.edu.
Website: http://www.uakron.edu/economics/

**The University of Alabama,** Graduate School, Manderson Graduate School of Business, Economics, Finance and Legal Studies Department, Tuscaloosa, AL 35487. Offers economics (MA, PhD); finance (MS, PhD). *Faculty:* 25 full-time (3 women). *Students:* 47 full-time (15 women), 7 part-time (1 woman); includes 2 minority (1 Asian, non-Hispanic/Latino; 1 Two or more races, non-Hispanic/Latino), 32 international. Average age 28. 178 applicants, 29% accepted, 13 enrolled. In 2016, 36 master's, 6 doctorates awarded. Terminal master's awarded for partial completion of doctoral program. *Degree requirements:* For master's, comprehensive exam (MA), thesis (MS); for doctorate, comprehensive exam, thesis/dissertation. *Entrance requirements:* For master's, GMAT, GRE; for doctorate, GRE or GMAT. Additional exam requirements/recommendations for international students: Required—TOEFL (minimum score 550 paper-based; 79 iBT). *Application deadline:* For fall admission, 7/1 priority date for domestic students, 1/15 for international students; for spring admission, 11/1 priority date for domestic students, 6/1 for international students. Applications are processed on a rolling basis. Application fee: $50 ($60 for international students). Electronic applications accepted. *Expenses:* Tuition, state resident: full-time $10,470. Tuition, nonresident: full-time $26,950. *Financial support:* In 2016–17, 43 students received support, including 24 research assistantships with tuition reimbursements available (averaging $15,000 per year), 19 teaching assistantships with tuition reimbursements available (averaging $15,000 per year); fellowships, Federal Work-Study, institutionally sponsored loans, and unspecified assistantships also available. Financial award application deadline: 1/15. *Faculty research:* Taxation, futures market, monetary theory and policy, income distribution. *Unit head:* Dr. Laura Razzolini, Department Head, 205-348-6683, E-mail: kcwise@cba.ua.edu. *Application contact:* Debra F. Wheatley, Graduate Programs Secretary, 205-348-6683, Fax: 205-348-0590, E-mail: dwheatle@cba.ua.edu.
Website: http://www.cba.ua.edu/

**University of Alaska Fairbanks,** School of Management, Department of Economics, Fairbanks, AK 99775-6080. Offers resource and applied economics (MS). *Program availability:* Part-time. *Faculty:* 6 full-time (1 woman). *Students:* 9 full-time (1 woman), 4 part-time (2 women); includes 2 minority (1 Asian, non-Hispanic/Latino; 1 Hispanic/Latino). Average age 28. 12 applicants, 50% accepted, 4 enrolled. In 2016, 5 master's awarded. *Degree requirements:* For master's, comprehensive exam, oral defense of project or thesis. *Entrance requirements:* For master's, bachelor's degree from accredited institution with minimum cumulative undergraduate and major GPA of 3.0, intermediate microeconomics, intermediate macroeconomics, basic statistics, calculus. Additional exam requirements/recommendations for international students: Required—TOEFL (minimum score 550 paper-based; 79 iBT), IELTS (minimum score 6.5). *Application deadline:* For fall admission, 3/1 priority date for domestic students, 3/1 for international students; for spring admission, 9/1 priority date for domestic students, 9/1 for international students. Applications are processed on a rolling basis. Application fee: $60. Electronic applications accepted. *Expenses:* $533 per credit resident tuition, $673 per semester resident fees; $1,088 per credit non-resident tuition, $835 per semester non-resident fees. *Financial support:* In 2016–17, 9 teaching assistantships with full tuition reimbursements (averaging $14,820 per year) were awarded; fellowships with full tuition reimbursements, research assistantships with full tuition reimbursements, career-related internships or fieldwork, Federal Work-Study, scholarships/grants, health care benefits, and unspecified assistantships also available. Support available to part-time students. Financial award application deadline: 2/15; financial award applicants required to submit FAFSA. *Faculty research:* Statistics; resource and agriculture economics; oil, gas, and energy; sustainability; public land management. *Total annual research expenditures:* $191,000. *Unit head:* Dr. Joe Little, Program Director, 907-474-2711, Fax: 907-474-5219, E-mail: jmlittle2@alaska.edu. *Application contact:* Mary Kreta, Director of Admissions, 907-474-7500, Fax: 907-474-7097, E-mail: admissions@uaf.edu.
Website: http://www.uaf.edu/som/degrees/graduate/msecon/

**University of Alberta,** Faculty of Graduate Studies and Research, Department of Economics, Edmonton, AB T6G 2E1, Canada. Offers economics (MA, PhD); economics and finance (MA); environmental and natural resource economics (PhD). *Program availability:* Part-time. *Degree requirements:* For doctorate, thesis/dissertation. *Entrance requirements:* For master's and doctorate, GRE. Additional exam requirements/recommendations for international students: Required—TOEFL. *Faculty research:* Public finance, international trade, industrial organization, Pacific Rim economics, monetary economics.

**The University of Arizona,** Eller College of Management, Department of Economics, Tucson, AZ 85721. Offers MA, PhD. Terminal master's awarded for partial completion of doctoral program. *Degree requirements:* For master's, comprehensive exam; for doctorate, thesis/dissertation. *Entrance requirements:* For doctorate, GRE General Test, 3 letters of recommendation. Additional exam requirements/recommendations for international students: Required—TOEFL (minimum score 550 paper-based; 79 iBT). Electronic applications accepted. *Faculty research:* Applied microeconomics, experimental economics, economic history, microeconomic theory, property rights, industrial organization.

**University of Arkansas,** Graduate School, Sam M. Walton College of Business Administration, Department of Economics, Fayetteville, AR 72701. Offers MA, PhD. In 2016, 4 master's, 1 doctorate awarded. *Degree requirements:* For doctorate, variable foreign language requirement, thesis/dissertation. *Entrance requirements:* For master's and doctorate, GRE General Test. Application fee: $40 ($50 for international students). *Financial support:* In 2016–17, 5 research assistantships, 8 teaching assistantships were awarded; fellowships with tuition reimbursements, career-related internships or fieldwork, and Federal Work-Study also available. Support available to part-time students. Financial award application deadline: 4/1; financial award applicants required to submit FAFSA. *Unit head:* Dr. Bill Curington, Chair, 479-575-3266, E-mail: bcecon@uark.edu. *Application contact:* 479-575-2851, E-mail: gsb@walton.uark.edu.
Website: http://gsb.uark.edu/

**The University of British Columbia,** Faculty of Arts, Vancouver School of Economics, Vancouver, BC V6T 1Z1, Canada. Offers MA, PhD. *Degree requirements:* For master's, thesis (for some programs); for doctorate, comprehensive exam, thesis/dissertation. *Entrance requirements:* For master's and doctorate, GRE General Test. Additional exam requirements/recommendations for international students: Required—TOEFL. Application fee: $100 Canadian dollars ($162 Canadian dollars for international students). Electronic applications accepted. *Expenses:* $4,802 per year tuition and fees, $8,436 per year international. *Financial support:* Fellowships, research assistantships, teaching assistantships, and tuition waivers (partial) available. *Faculty research:* Economic theory, international economics, labor economics, public finance, economic development. *Application contact:* Maureen Chin, Graduate Admissions, 604-822-4616, Fax: 604-822-5915, E-mail: econ.grad@ubc.ca.
Website: http://www.econ.ubc.ca/

**University of Calgary,** Faculty of Graduate Studies, Faculty of Arts, Department of Economics, Calgary, AB T2N 1N4, Canada. Offers MA, PhD. *Program availability:* Part-time, evening/weekend. *Degree requirements:* For master's, thesis (for some programs); for doctorate, thesis/dissertation, candidacy exam. *Entrance requirements:* Additional exam requirements/recommendations for international students: Required—TOEFL. *Faculty research:* Energy economics, public finance/public choice, resource economics, international trade, monetary economics.

**University of California, Berkeley,** Graduate Division, College of Letters and Science, Department of Economics, Berkeley, CA 94720-1500. Offers PhD, JD/MA. *Students:* 124 full-time (36 women); includes 20 minority (4 Black or African American, non-Hispanic/Latino; 10 Asian, non-Hispanic/Latino; 6 Hispanic/Latino), 68 international. Average age 29. 763 applicants, 19 enrolled. In 2016, 17 doctorates awarded. *Degree requirements:* For doctorate, thesis/dissertation, final exams, oral qualifying exam. *Entrance requirements:* For doctorate, GRE General Test, minimum GPA of 3.0, 3 letters of recommendation. Additional exam requirements/recommendations for international students: Required—TOEFL (minimum score 570 paper-based; 90 iBT). *Application deadline:* For fall admission, 12/1 for domestic students. Application fee: $105 ($125 for international students). Electronic applications accepted. *Financial support:* Fellowships, research assistantships, teaching assistantships, institutionally sponsored loans, health care benefits, and unspecified assistantships available. *Unit head:* Prof. Shachar Kariv, Chair, 510-642-3581, E-mail: econchair@berkeley.edu. *Application contact:* Patrick G. Allen, Graduate Advisor, 510-642-0824, Fax: 510-642-6615, E-mail: gradofc@econ.berkeley.edu. Website: https://www.econ.berkeley.edu

**University of California, Davis,** Graduate Studies, Program in Economics, Davis, CA 95616. Offers MA, PhD. Terminal master's awarded for partial completion of doctoral program. *Degree requirements:* For master's, comprehensive exam (for some programs), thesis (for some programs); for doctorate, thesis/dissertation. *Entrance requirements:* For master's, GRE General Test, minimum GPA of 3.0; for doctorate, GRE General Test, minimum GPA of 3.25. Additional exam requirements/recommendations for international students: Required—TOEFL (minimum score 550 paper-based). Electronic applications accepted. *Faculty research:* Applied microeconomics, macroeconomics, international studies, economic theory, economic history.

**University of California, Irvine,** School of Social Sciences, Department of Economics, Irvine, CA 92697. Offers economics (MA, PhD); public choice (MA, PhD); transportation economics (MA, PhD). *Students:* 89 full-time (25 women); includes 23 minority (1 Black or African American, non-Hispanic/Latino; 9 Asian, non-Hispanic/Latino; 9 Hispanic/Latino; 4 Two or more races, non-Hispanic/Latino), 27 international. Average age 28. 224 applicants, 26% accepted, 25 enrolled. In 2016, 17 master's, 16 doctorates awarded. *Degree requirements:* For doctorate, thesis/dissertation. *Entrance requirements:* For master's and doctorate, GRE General Test, minimum GPA of 3.0. Additional exam requirements/recommendations for international students: Required—TOEFL (minimum score 550 paper-based). *Application deadline:* For fall admission, 1/15 priority date for domestic and international students. Applications are processed on a rolling basis. Application fee: $105 ($125 for international students). Electronic applications accepted. *Financial support:* Fellowships, research assistantships with full tuition reimbursements, teaching assistantships, institutionally sponsored loans, traineeships, health care benefits, and unspecified assistantships available. Financial award application deadline: 3/1; financial award applicants required to submit FAFSA. *Faculty research:* Econometrics, urban economics, applied microeconomics. *Unit head:* Prof. Jan Brueckner, Chair, 949-824-0083, E-mail: jkbrueck@uci.edu. *Application contact:* Prof. John Duffy, Graduate Program Director, 949-824-8341, E-mail: duffy@uci.edu.
Website: http://www.economics.uci.edu/

**University of California, Los Angeles,** Graduate Division, College of Letters and Science, Department of Economics, Los Angeles, CA 90095. Offers MA, PhD. Terminal master's awarded for partial completion of doctoral program. *Degree requirements:* For master's, comprehensive exam; for doctorate, thesis/dissertation, oral and written qualifying exams. *Entrance requirements:* For doctorate, GRE General Test, bachelor's degree; minimum undergraduate GPA of 3.0 (or its equivalent if letter grade system not used). Additional exam requirements/recommendations for international students: Required—TOEFL. Electronic applications accepted.

**University of California, Riverside,** Graduate Division, Department of Economics, Riverside, CA 92521-0102. Offers MA, PhD. Terminal master's awarded for partial completion of doctoral program. *Degree requirements:* For master's, comprehensive exam; for doctorate, thesis/dissertation, qualifying exams. *Entrance requirements:* For master's and doctorate, GRE General Test, minimum GPA of 3.2. Additional exam requirements/recommendations for international students: Required—TOEFL (minimum score 550 paper-based; 80 iBT). Electronic applications accepted. *Expenses:* Tuition, state resident: full-time $16,666. Tuition, nonresident: full-time $31,768. *Required fees:* $11,055.54 per quarter. $3685.18 per quarter. Tuition and fees vary according to campus/location and program. *Faculty research:* Advanced political economy; resource and environmental economics; advanced econometrics; labor economics; advanced microeconomics theory; advanced macroeconomics theory; development economics; economic history; international trade theory; money, credit and business cycles; public economics.

**University of California, San Diego,** Graduate Division, Department of Economics, La Jolla, CA 92093. Offers PhD. *Students:* 122 full-time (43 women), 4 part-time (1 woman). 761 applicants, 11% accepted, 21 enrolled. In 2016, 14 doctorates awarded. *Degree requirements:* For doctorate, comprehensive exam, thesis/dissertation. *Entrance requirements:* For doctorate, GRE General Test, minimum GPA of 3.5, letters of recommendation. Additional exam requirements/recommendations for international students: Required—TOEFL (minimum score 550 paper-based; 80 iBT), IELTS (minimum score 7), PTE. *Application deadline:* For fall admission, 12/14 for domestic students. Application fee: $105 ($125 for international students). Electronic applications accepted. *Expenses:* Tuition, state resident: full-time $11,220. Tuition, nonresident: full-time $26,322. *Required fees:* $1864. *Financial support:* Fellowships, research assistantships, teaching assistantships, and scholarships/grants available. Financial award applicants required to submit FAFSA. *Faculty research:* Behavioral/experimental economics, development economics, econometrics, environment and resource economics, finance, health economics, industrial organization, international, labor, macroeconomics, microeconomic theory, public economics. *Unit head:* Eli Berman, Chair, 858-534-2858, E-mail: econchair@ucsd.edu. *Application contact:* Cathy Pugh, Graduate Coordinator, 858-534-1864, E-mail: econ-phdadmissions@ucsd.edu.
Website: http://economics.ucsd.edu

**University of California, Santa Barbara,** Graduate Division, College of Letters and Sciences, Division of Social Sciences, Department of Economics, Santa Barbara, CA 93106-9210. Offers economics (MA); mathematical economics (PhD); public finance (PhD); MA/PhD. Terminal master's awarded for partial completion of doctoral program. *Degree requirements:* For master's, comprehensive exam; for doctorate, comprehensive exam, thesis/dissertation. *Entrance requirements:* For master's and doctorate, GRE General Test, 3 letters of recommendation, statement of purpose, personal achievements/contributions statement, resume/curriculum vitae, transcripts for post-secondary institutions attended. Additional exam requirements/recommendations for international students: Required—TOEFL (minimum score 550 paper-based; 80 iBT), IELTS (minimum score 7), TOEFL (minimum score 600 paper-based or 100 iBT) for PhD. Electronic applications accepted. *Faculty research:* Labor economics, econometrics, macroeconomic theory and policy, environmental and natural resources economics, experimental and behavioral economics.

**University of California, Santa Barbara,** Graduate Division, College of Letters and Sciences, Division of Social Sciences, Department of Global Studies, Santa Barbara, CA 93106-7065. Offers global culture, ideology, and religion (MA, PhD); global government, human rights, and civil society (MA, PhD); political economy, sustainable development, and the environment (MA, PhD). *Degree requirements:* For master's, one foreign language, thesis, 2 years of a second language; for doctorate, one foreign language, thesis/dissertation, reading proficiency in at least one language other than English. *Entrance requirements:* For master's, GRE, 2 years of a second language with minimum B grade in the final term, statement of purpose, resume or curriculum vitae, 3 letters of recommendation, transcripts (from all post-secondary institutions attended), writing sample (15-20 pages); for doctorate, GRE, statement of purpose, personal achievements/contributions statement, resume or curriculum vitae, 3 letters of recommendation, transcripts from all post-secondary institutions attended, writing sample (15-20 pages). Additional exam requirements/recommendations for international students: Required—TOEFL (minimum score 600 paper-based; 94 iBT), IELTS (minimum score 7). Electronic applications accepted.

**University of California, Santa Barbara,** Graduate Division, Donald Bren School of Environmental Science and Management, Santa Barbara, CA 93106-5131. Offers economics and environmental science (PhD); environmental science and management (MESM, PhD); technology and society (PhD). *Degree requirements:* For master's, thesis; for doctorate, thesis/dissertation. *Entrance requirements:* For master's and doctorate, GRE. Additional exam requirements/recommendations for international students: Required—TOEFL (minimum score 550 paper-based; 80 iBT), IELTS (minimum score 7). Electronic applications accepted. *Faculty research:* Coastal marine resources management, conservation planning, corporate environmental management, economics and politics of the environment, energy and climate, pollution prevention and remediation, water resources management.

**University of California, Santa Cruz,** Division of Graduate Studies, Division of Social Sciences, Program in International Economics, Santa Cruz, CA 95064. Offers PhD. *Degree requirements:* For doctorate, thesis/dissertation, 4 field exams, field papers, econometrics project, qualifying exams. *Entrance requirements:* For doctorate, GRE General Test. Additional exam requirements/recommendations for international students: Required—TOEFL (minimum score 550 paper-based; 83 iBT); Recommended—IELTS (minimum score 8). Electronic applications accepted. *Faculty research:* Current and emerging issues in taxation, industrial policy, environmental regulation, market structure, labor economics focus on behavior and adjustment in an interdependent world economy.

**University of Central Arkansas,** Graduate School, College of Liberal Arts, Program in Community and Economic Development, Conway, AR 72035-0001. Offers community and economic development (MS); geographic and information systems (MGIS, Graduate Certificate). *Program availability:* Part-time, online learning. *Degree requirements:* For master's, comprehensive exam, thesis. *Entrance requirements:* For master's, GRE General Test, minimum GPA of 2.7. Additional exam requirements/recommendations for international students: Required—TOEFL (minimum score 550 paper-based). Electronic applications accepted. *Expenses:* Contact institution.

**University of Chicago,** Booth School of Business, Full-Time MBA Program, Chicago, IL 60637. Offers accounting (MBA); analytic finance (MBA); analytic management (MBA); econometrics and statistics (MBA); economics (MBA); entrepreneurship (MBA); finance (MBA); general management (MBA); health administration and policy (Certificate); international business (MBA); managerial and organizational behavior (MBA); marketing analytics (MBA); marketing management (MBA); operations management (MBA); strategic management (MBA); MBA/AM; MBA/JD; MBA/MA; MBA/MD; MBA/MPP. *Accreditation:* AACSB. *Students:* 1,151 full-time (443 women), 17 part-time (9 women). Terminal master's awarded for partial completion of doctoral program. *Entrance requirements:* For master's, GMAT or GRE, transcripts, resume, 2 letters of recommendation, essay, interview. Additional exam requirements/recommendations for international students: Required—TOEFL (minimum score 600 paper-based; 104 iBT), IELTS (minimum score 7), PTE (minimum score 70). *Application deadline:* For spring admission, 4/1 for domestic and international students. Electronic applications accepted. *Expenses:* Contact institution. *Unit head:* Stacey Kole, Deputy Dean, 773-702-7121. *Application contact:* Full-time MBA Program Admissions, 773-702-7369, Fax: 773-702-9085, E-mail: admissions@chicagobooth.edu.
Website: https://www.chicagobooth.edu/programs/full-time

**University of Chicago,** Division of the Social Sciences, Department of Economics, Chicago, IL 60637. Offers PhD. *Students:* 189 full-time (39 women); includes 14 minority (7 Asian, non-Hispanic/Latino; 3 Hispanic/Latino; 4 Two or more races, non-Hispanic/Latino), 135 international. 612 applicants, 15% accepted, 35 enrolled. In 2016, 17 doctorates awarded. *Degree requirements:* For doctorate, one foreign language, thesis/dissertation, written exams in 2 fields. *Entrance requirements:* For doctorate, GRE General Test. Additional exam requirements/recommendations for international students: Required—TOEFL (minimum score 104 iBT), IELTS (minimum score 7). *Application deadline:* For fall admission, 12/15 for domestic and international students. Application fee: $135. Electronic applications accepted. *Financial support:* In 2016–17, 30 students received support, including 19 fellowships with full tuition reimbursements available (averaging $24,000 per year); Federal Work-Study, institutionally sponsored loans, scholarships/grants, health care benefits, and tuition waivers (full) also available. Financial award application deadline: 12/15. *Unit head:* Prof. John List, Chair, 773-702-8176. *Application contact:* Office of the Dean of Students, 773-702-8415, E-mail: admissions@ssd.uchicago.edu.
Website: http://economics.uchicago.edu

**University of Cincinnati,** Graduate School, Carl H. Lindner College of Business, PhD Programs, Cincinnati, OH 45211. Offers accounting (PhD); economics (PhD); finance (PhD); information systems (PhD); management (PhD); marketing (PhD); operations and business analytics (PhD). *Faculty:* 72 full-time (18 women). *Students:* 37 full-time (19 women); includes 4 minority (1 Black or African American, non-Hispanic/Latino; 3 Asian, non-Hispanic/Latino), 19 international. Average age 30. 92 applicants, 16% accepted, 7 enrolled. In 2016, 4 doctorates awarded. *Degree requirements:* For doctorate, comprehensive exam, thesis/dissertation. *Entrance requirements:* For doctorate, GMAT, GRE, transcripts, essays, resume, letters of recommendation. Additional exam requirements/recommendations for international students: Required—TOEFL (minimum score 600 paper-based; 100 iBT), IELTS (minimum score 7). *Application deadline:* For fall admission, 1/15 for domestic and international students. Application fee: $65 ($70 for international students). Electronic applications accepted. *Expenses:* Contact institution. *Financial support:* In 2016–17, 38 students received support, including 25 research assistantships with tuition reimbursements available (averaging $23,250 per year); scholarships/grants, tuition waivers (full and partial), and unspecified assistantships also available. Financial award application deadline: 1/15; financial award applicants required to submit FAFSA. *Faculty research:* Bayesian Prediction Theory, organizational fairness, consumer insight and market research, EGARCH idiosyncratic volatility and expected stock returns, consumer insight and market research, density estimation from correlated data. *Unit head:* Dr. Suzanne Masterson, Director, 513-556-7125, Fax: 513-556-5499, E-mail: suzanne.masterson@uc.edu. *Application contact:* Angel Elvin, Assistant Director, 513-556-7190, Fax: 513-558-7006, E-mail: angel.elvin@uc.edu.
Website: http://www.business.uc.edu/phd

**University of Colorado Boulder,** Graduate School, College of Arts and Sciences, Department of Economics, Boulder, CO 80309. Offers MA, PhD. *Faculty:* 34 full-time (7 women). *Students:* 60 full-time (19 women), 3 part-time (1 woman); includes 9 minority (6 Asian, non-Hispanic/Latino; 2 Hispanic/Latino; 1 Two or more races, non-Hispanic/Latino), 14 international. Average age 29. 127 applicants, 8% accepted, 10 enrolled. In 2016, 11 master's, 6 doctorates awarded. Terminal master's awarded for partial completion of doctoral program. *Degree requirements:* For master's, comprehensive exam, thesis or alternative; for doctorate, comprehensive exam, thesis/dissertation, preliminary exam. *Entrance requirements:* For master's, GRE General Test, minimum undergraduate GPA of 2.75; for doctorate, GRE General Test. Additional exam requirements/recommendations for international students: Required—TOEFL. *Application deadline:* For fall admission, 1/15 for domestic students, 12/1 for international students. Applications are processed on a rolling basis. Application fee: $60 ($80 for international students). Electronic applications accepted. Application fee is waived when completed online. *Financial support:* In 2016–17, 175 students received support, including 29 fellowships (averaging $4,919 per year), 2 research assistantships with full and partial tuition reimbursements available (averaging $35,749 per year), 56 teaching assistantships with full and partial tuition reimbursements available (averaging $39,827 per year); institutionally sponsored loans, scholarships/grants, health care benefits, and unspecified assistantships also available. Financial award application deadline: 2/1; financial award applicants required to submit FAFSA. *Faculty research:* Economics, microeconomics, labor economics, international economics, economics of the environment. *Total annual research expenditures:* $151,297. *Application contact:* E-mail: econ@colorado.edu.
Website: http://www.colorado.edu/Economics/graduate/index.html

## Economics

**University of Colorado Denver,** Business School, Program in Finance, Denver, CO 80217. Offers economics (MS); finance (MS); financial analysis and management (MS); financial and commodities risk management (MS); risk management and insurance (MS); MS/MA; MS/MBA. *Program availability:* Part-time, evening/weekend. *Students:* 59 full-time (19 women), 25 part-time (4 women); includes 11 minority (1 Black or African American, non-Hispanic/Latino; 4 Asian, non-Hispanic/Latino; 5 Hispanic/Latino; 1 Two or more races, non-Hispanic/Latino), 12 international. Average age 31. 85 applicants, 35% accepted, 12 enrolled. In 2016, 45 master's awarded. *Degree requirements:* For master's, 30 semester hours (18 of required core courses, 9 of finance electives, and 3 of free elective). *Entrance requirements:* For master's, GMAT, essay, resume, and letters of recommendation; financial statements (for international students). Additional exam requirements/recommendations for international students: Required—TOEFL (minimum score 537 paper-based; 75 iBT); Recommended—IELTS (minimum score 6.5). *Application deadline:* For fall admission, 4/15 priority date for domestic students, 3/15 priority date for international students; for spring admission, 10/15 priority date for domestic students, 9/15 priority date for international students; for summer admission, 2/15 priority date for domestic students, 1/15 priority date for international students. Applications are processed on a rolling basis. Application fee: $50 ($75 for international students). Electronic applications accepted. *Expenses:* Contact institution. *Financial support:* In 2016–17, 27 students received support. Teaching assistantships, Federal Work-Study, institutionally sponsored loans, scholarships/grants, and traineeships available. Financial award application deadline: 4/1; financial award applicants required to submit FAFSA. *Faculty research:* Corporate governance, debt maturity policies, regulation and financial markets, option management strategies. *Unit head:* Jian Yang, Director of the Finance Program, 303-315-8423, E-mail: jian.yang@ucdenver.edu. *Application contact:* 303-315-8200, E-mail: bschool.admissions@ucdenver.edu. Website: http://www.ucdenver.edu/academics/colleges/business/degrees/ms/finance/Pages/Finance.aspx

**University of Colorado Denver,** College of Liberal Arts and Sciences, Department of Economics, Denver, CO 80217. Offers MA. *Program availability:* Part-time, evening/weekend. *Faculty:* 13 full-time (3 women), 2 part-time/adjunct (1 woman). *Students:* 29 full-time (9 women), 12 part-time (4 women); includes 8 minority (2 Black or African American, non-Hispanic/Latino; 2 Asian, non-Hispanic/Latino; 2 Hispanic/Latino; 2 Two or more races, non-Hispanic/Latino), 8 international. Average age 29. 59 applicants, 54% accepted, 10 enrolled. In 2016, 13 master's awarded. *Degree requirements:* For master's, thesis or alternative, 30 credit hours, including 21 of core courses and 9 of electives. *Entrance requirements:* For master's, GRE General Test, 15 hours of course work in economics, minimum GPA of 2.5, three letters of recommendation, calculus and statistics course. Additional exam requirements/recommendations for international students: Required—TOEFL (minimum score 537 paper-based; 75 iBT); Recommended—IELTS (minimum score 6.5). *Application deadline:* For fall admission, 6/1 priority date for domestic and international students; for spring admission, 11/1 priority date for domestic and international students. Applications are processed on a rolling basis. Application fee: $50 ($75 for international students). Electronic applications accepted. *Expenses:* Tuition, state resident: full-time $11,006; part-time $474 per credit. Tuition, nonresident: full-time $28,212; part-time $1264 per credit hour. *Required fees:* $256 per semester. One-time fee: $94.32. Tuition and fees vary according to campus/location and program. *Financial support:* In 2016–17, 3 students received support. Fellowships, research assistantships, teaching assistantships, Federal Work-Study, institutionally sponsored loans, scholarships/grants, traineeships, and unspecified assistantships available. Financial award application deadline: 4/1; financial award applicants required to submit FAFSA. *Faculty research:* Economic/income inequality, poverty and mobility measurement; international finance and monetary policy; economics of philanthropy; history of economic thought; health and labor economics. *Unit head:* Dr. Buhong Zheng, Department Chair, 303-315-2034, Fax: 303-315-2048, E-mail: buhong.zheng@ucdenver.edu. *Application contact:* Brian Duncan, Graduate Admissions Advisor, 303-315-2041, E-mail: brian.duncan@ucdenver.edu. Website: http://www.ucdenver.edu/academics/colleges/CLAS/Departments/economics/Programs/MasterofArts/Pages/Overview.aspx

**University of Connecticut,** Graduate School, College of Liberal Arts and Sciences, Department of Economics, Storrs, CT 06269-1063. Offers MA, PhD. Terminal master's awarded for partial completion of doctoral program. *Degree requirements:* For master's, comprehensive exam; for doctorate, thesis/dissertation. *Entrance requirements:* For master's and doctorate, GRE General Test, GRE Subject Test. Additional exam requirements/recommendations for international students: Required—TOEFL (minimum score 550 paper-based). Electronic applications accepted.

**University of Delaware,** Alfred Lerner College of Business and Economics, Department of Economics, Newark, DE 19716. Offers economic education (PhD); economics (MA, MS, PhD); economics for entrepreneurship and educators (MA); MA/MBA. *Program availability:* Part-time. *Degree requirements:* For master's, comprehensive exam, thesis (for some programs), mathematics review exam, research project; for doctorate, comprehensive exam, thesis/dissertation, field exam. *Entrance requirements:* For master's, GMAT or GRE General Test, minimum GPA of 2.5; for doctorate, GRE General Test, minimum GPA of 3.5 in graduate economics course work. Additional exam requirements/recommendations for international students: Required—TOEFL (minimum score 550 paper-based). Electronic applications accepted. *Faculty research:* Applied quantitative economics, industrial organization, resource economics, monetary economics, labor economics.

**University of Denver,** Division of Arts, Humanities and Social Sciences, Department of Economics, Denver, CO 80208. Offers MA. *Program availability:* Part-time. *Faculty:* 10 full-time (3 women), 1 part-time/adjunct (0 women). *Students:* 4 full-time (2 women), 5 part-time (3 women); includes 3 minority (2 Black or African American, non-Hispanic/Latino; 1 Hispanic/Latino), 9 international. Average age 26. 23 applicants, 91% accepted, 7 enrolled. In 2016, 4 master's awarded. *Degree requirements:* For master's, thesis. *Entrance requirements:* For master's, GRE General Test, bachelor's degree with major or minor in economics, 20 quarter hours of economics coursework, or departmental waiver; transcripts; personal statement; three letters of recommendation. Additional exam requirements/recommendations for international students: Required—TOEFL (minimum score 550 paper-based; 80 iBT). *Application deadline:* For fall admission, 2/15 priority date for domestic and international students. Applications are processed on a rolling basis. Application fee: $65. Electronic applications accepted. *Expenses:* $29,022 per year full-time. *Financial support:* In 2016–17, 7 students received support, including 2 teaching assistantships with tuition reimbursements available (averaging $7,500 per year); career-related internships or fieldwork, Federal Work-Study, scholarships/grants, and unspecified assistantships also available. Support available to part-time students. Financial award application deadline: 2/15; financial award applicants required to submit FAFSA. *Faculty research:* Trade and policy effects on economic development; income distribution, inequality, and the macroeconomy; history of economic thought; the Chinese economy; problems of neo-liberalism. *Unit head:* Dr. Peter Sai-Wing Ho, Associate Professor and Chair, 303-871-2259, Fax: 303-871-2605, E-mail: peter.ho@du.edu. *Application contact:* Marisela Calderon, Assistant to the Chair, 303-871-2685, Fax: 303-871-2605, E-mail: econ04@denver.du.edu. Website: http://www.du.edu/ahss/economics

**University of Detroit Mercy,** College of Liberal Arts and Education, Detroit, MI 48221. Offers addiction counseling (MA); addiction studies (Certificate); clinical mental health counseling (MA); clinical psychology (MA, PhD); computer and information systems (MS); criminal justice (MA); curriculum and instruction (MA); economics (MA); educational administration (MA); financial economics (MA); industrial/organizational psychology (MA); information assurance (MS); intelligence analysis (MA); liberal studies (MALS); religious studies (MA); school counseling (MA, Certificate); school psychology (Spec); security administration (MS); special education: emotionally impaired/behaviorally disordered (MA); special education: learning disabilities (MA). *Program availability:* Part-time, evening/weekend. *Degree requirements:* For doctorate, departmental qualifying exam. *Faculty research:* Psychology of aging, history of technology, Renaissance humanism, U.S. and Japanese economic relations.

**University of Florida,** Graduate School, Warrington College of Business Administration, Hough Graduate School of Business, Department of Economics, Gainesville, FL 32611. Offers MA, PhD. Terminal master's awarded for partial completion of doctoral program. *Degree requirements:* For master's, thesis optional; for doctorate, comprehensive exam, thesis/dissertation. *Entrance requirements:* For master's and doctorate, GMAT (minimum score of 465) or GRE General Test, minimum GPA of 3.0. Additional exam requirements/recommendations for international students: Required—TOEFL (minimum score 550 paper-based; 80 iBT), IELTS (minimum score 6). Electronic applications accepted. *Faculty research:* Econometrics, international economics, industrial organization, public finance, economic theory.

**University of Georgia,** Terry College of Business, Department of Economics, Athens, GA 30602. Offers MA, PhD. *Degree requirements:* For master's, thesis; for doctorate, thesis/dissertation. *Entrance requirements:* For master's and doctorate, GRE General Test. *Application deadline:* For fall admission, 7/1 priority date for domestic students; for spring admission, 11/15 for domestic students. Application fee: $50. Electronic applications accepted. *Financial support:* Fellowships, research assistantships, and teaching assistantships available. *Unit head:* Dr. Christopher M. Cornwell, Head, 706-542-3670, Fax: 706-542-3376, E-mail: cornwl@terry.uga.edu. *Application contact:* Josh Kinsler, Graduate Coordinator, 706-542-3696, Fax: 706-542-3376, E-mail: econgc@uga.edu. Website: http://www.terry.uga.edu/economics/

**University of Guelph,** Graduate Studies, College of Management and Economics, Department of Economics, Guelph, ON N1G 2W1, Canada. Offers MA, PhD. *Program availability:* Part-time. *Degree requirements:* For master's, thesis or alternative; for doctorate, comprehensive exam, thesis/dissertation. *Entrance requirements:* For master's, minimum B+ average during previous 2 years of course work; for doctorate, minimum A- average, MA in economics. Additional exam requirements/recommendations for international students: Required—TOEFL (minimum score 550 paper-based; 89 iBT), IELTS (minimum score 6.5). Electronic applications accepted. *Faculty research:* Resource and environmental economics, econometrics, labor economics, micro and macro economics.

**University of Hawaii at Manoa,** Graduate Division, College of Social Sciences, Department of Economics, Honolulu, HI 96822. Offers MA, PhD. *Program availability:* Part-time. Terminal master's awarded for partial completion of doctoral program. *Degree requirements:* For master's, thesis optional; for doctorate, comprehensive exam, thesis/dissertation. *Entrance requirements:* For master's and doctorate, GRE General Test. Additional exam requirements/recommendations for international students: Required—TOEFL (minimum score 500 paper-based; 61 iBT), IELTS (minimum score 5). *Faculty research:* Trade, development, demography, labor, resource economics.

**University of Houston,** College of Liberal Arts and Social Sciences, Department of Economics, Houston, TX 77204. Offers applied economics (MA); economics (MA, PhD). Terminal master's awarded for partial completion of doctoral program. *Degree requirements:* For master's, thesis optional; for doctorate, comprehensive exam, thesis/dissertation. *Entrance requirements:* For master's and doctorate, GRE General Test, minimum GPA of 3.0, statement of purpose, three letters of recommendation. Additional exam requirements/recommendations for international students: Required—TOEFL (minimum score 550 paper-based; 79 iBT), IELTS (minimum score 6.5). Electronic applications accepted. *Faculty research:* Econometrics, labor economics, international economics.

**University of Illinois at Chicago,** College of Liberal Arts and Sciences, Department of Economics, Chicago, IL 60607-7128. Offers MA, PhD, MBA/MA. Terminal master's awarded for partial completion of doctoral program. *Degree requirements:* For master's, comprehensive exam; for doctorate, thesis/dissertation. *Entrance requirements:* For master's and doctorate, GRE General Test, minimum GPA of 2.75. Additional exam requirements/recommendations for international students: Required—TOEFL. Electronic applications accepted. *Faculty research:* International, labor, and urban economics.

**University of Illinois at Urbana–Champaign,** Graduate College, College of Liberal Arts and Sciences, Department of Economics, Champaign, IL 61820. Offers economics (MS, PhD); policy economics (MS). Terminal master's awarded for partial completion of doctoral program.

**The University of Iowa,** Henry B. Tippie College of Business, Department of Economics, Iowa City, IA 52242-1316. Offers PhD. *Faculty:* 20 full-time (5 women), 9 part-time/adjunct (3 women). *Students:* 31 full-time (16 women); includes 1 minority (Asian, non-Hispanic/Latino), 19 international. Average age 27. 148 applicants, 14% accepted, 5 enrolled. In 2016, 3 doctorates awarded. *Degree requirements:* For doctorate, comprehensive exam, thesis/dissertation. *Entrance requirements:* For doctorate, GRE General Test. Additional exam requirements/recommendations for international students: Required—TOEFL (minimum score 100 iBT). *Application deadline:* For fall admission, 1/15 priority date for domestic and international students. Application fee: $60 ($100 for international students). Electronic applications accepted. *Financial support:* In 2016–17, 31 students received support, including 3 fellowships (averaging $1,000 per year), 2 research assistantships with full tuition reimbursements available (averaging $18,809 per year), 29 teaching assistantships with full tuition reimbursements available (averaging $18,809 per year); health care benefits and unspecified assistantships also available. Financial award application deadline: 1/15. *Faculty research:* Political economy, macroeconomics, econometrics, game theory, economic development. *Unit head:* Prof. Jarjisu Sa-Aadu, Interim Department Executive Officer, 319-335-0829, Fax: 319-335-1956, E-mail: jsa-aadu@uiowa.edu. *Application contact:* Renea L. Jay, Associate Director, Non-MBA Graduate Programs, 319-335-0830, Fax: 319-335-1956, E-mail: renea-jay@uiowa.edu. Website: https://tippie.uiowa.edu/economics

**The University of Kansas,** Graduate Studies, College of Liberal Arts and Sciences, Department of Economics, Lawrence, KS 66045. Offers MA, PhD, JD/MA. *Program availability:* Part-time. *Students:* 57 full-time (24 women), 2 part-time (1 woman); includes 2 minority (1 Asian, non-Hispanic/Latino; 1 Two or more races, non-Hispanic/Latino), 47 international. Average age 28. 112 applicants, 38% accepted, 12 enrolled. In 2016, 18 master's, 8 doctorates awarded. Terminal master's awarded for partial completion of doctoral program. *Degree requirements:* For doctorate, thesis/dissertation or alternative. *Entrance requirements:* For master's and doctorate, statement of

personal goals, resume or curriculum vitae, official transcripts, three letters of recommendation. Additional exam requirements/recommendations for international students: Required—TOEFL, IELTS. *Application deadline:* For fall admission, 2/1 priority date for domestic and international students; for spring admission, 11/1 priority date for domestic and international students. Application fee: $65 ($85 for international students). Electronic applications accepted. *Financial support:* Fellowships, research assistantships, teaching assistantships, institutionally sponsored loans, scholarships/grants, health care benefits, and unspecified assistantships available. Financial award application deadline: 2/1. *Faculty research:* Macroeconomics, econometrics, industrial organization, microeconomics, economic development, international economics, financial economics. *Unit head:* Ted Juhl, Chair, 785-864-2849, E-mail: juhl@ku.edu. *Application contact:* Michelle Huslig-Lowrance, Graduate Secretary, 785-864-2841, E-mail: econgrad@ku.edu.
Website: http://www.economics.ku.edu/

**University of Kentucky,** Graduate School, Gatton College of Business and Economics, Program in Economics, Lexington, KY 40506-0032. Offers MS, PhD. *Degree requirements:* For master's, comprehensive exam; for doctorate, comprehensive exam, thesis/dissertation. *Entrance requirements:* For master's, GMAT, minimum undergraduate GPA of 2.75; for doctorate, GMAT, minimum undergraduate GPA of 3.0. Additional exam requirements/recommendations for international students: Required—TOEFL (minimum score 550 paper-based). Electronic applications accepted. *Faculty research:* Public economics, international economics and economic development, labor economics, environmental economics, industrial economics.

**University of Lethbridge,** School of Graduate Studies, Lethbridge, AB T1K 3M4, Canada. Offers addictions counseling (M Sc); agricultural biotechnology (M Sc); agricultural studies (M Sc, MA); anthropology (MA); archaeology (M Sc, MA); art (MA, MFA); biochemistry (M Sc); biological sciences (M Sc); biomolecular science (PhD); biosystems and biodiversity (PhD); Canadian studies (MA); chemistry (M Sc); computer science (M Sc); computer science and geographical information science (M Sc); counseling (MC); counseling psychology (M Ed); dramatic arts (MA); earth, space, and physical science (PhD); economics (MA); education (MA, PhD); educational leadership (M Ed); English (MA); environmental science (M Sc); evolution and behavior (PhD); exercise science (M Sc); French (MA); French/German (MA); French/Spanish (MA); general education (M Ed); geography (M Sc, MA); German (MA); health sciences (M Sc); individualized multidisciplinary (M Sc, MA); kinesiology (M Sc, MA); management (M Sc), including accounting, finance, human resource management and labor relations, information systems, international management, marketing, policy and strategy; mathematics (M Sc); music (M Mus, MA); Native American studies (MA); neuroscience (M Sc, PhD); new media (MA, MFA); nursing (M Sc, MN); philosophy (MA); physics (M Sc); political science (MA); psychology (M Sc, MA); religious studies (MA); sociology (MA); theatre and dramatic arts (MFA); theoretical and computational science (PhD); urban and regional studies (MA); women and gender studies (MA). *Program availability:* Part-time, evening/weekend. *Degree requirements:* For master's, thesis (for some programs); for doctorate, comprehensive exam, thesis/dissertation. *Entrance requirements:* For master's, GMAT (for M Sc in management), bachelor's degree in related field, minimum GPA of 3.0 during previous 20 graded semester courses, 2 years' teaching or related experience (M Ed); for doctorate, master's degree, minimum graduate GPA of 3.5. Additional exam requirements/recommendations for international students: Required—TOEFL (minimum score 580 paper-based; 93 iBT). Electronic applications accepted. *Faculty research:* Movement and brain plasticity, gibberellin physiology, photosynthesis, carbon cycling, molecular properties of main-group ring components.

**University of Maine,** Graduate School, College of Natural Sciences, Forestry, and Agriculture, School of Economics, Orono, ME 04469. Offers economics (MA); financial economics (MA); resource economics and policy (MS). *Program availability:* Part-time. *Faculty:* 12 full-time (3 women). *Students:* 21 full-time (6 women), 1 part-time (0 women); includes 1 minority (Two or more races, non-Hispanic/Latino), 8 international. Average age 24. 30 applicants, 90% accepted, 9 enrolled. In 2016, 11 master's awarded. *Degree requirements:* For master's, thesis (for some programs). *Entrance requirements:* For master's, GRE General Test. Additional exam requirements/recommendations for international students: Required—TOEFL (minimum score 580 paper-based; 92 iBT), IELTS (minimum score 8.9). *Application deadline:* For fall admission, 2/15 for domestic and 2/1 for international students; for spring admission, 9/15 for domestic and 8/15 for international students. Applications are processed on a rolling basis. Application fee: $65. Electronic applications accepted. *Expenses:* Tuition, state resident: full-time $7524; part-time $2508 per credit. Tuition, nonresident: full-time $24,498; part-time $8166 per credit. *Required fees:* $1148; $571 per credit. *Financial support:* In 2016–17, 21 students received support, including 15 research assistantships (averaging $14,600 per year), 6 teaching assistantships with full tuition reimbursements available (averaging $14,600 per year); career-related internships or fieldwork, Federal Work-Study, institutionally sponsored loans, scholarships/grants, and tuition waivers (full and partial) also available. Support available to part-time students. Financial award application deadline: 3/1. *Faculty research:* Food systems, renewable energy; transportation; water quality; economic development. *Total annual research expenditures:* $881,321. *Unit head:* Dr. Mario Teisl, Director, 207-581-3151, Fax: 207-581-4278. *Application contact:* Scott G. Delcourt, Assistant Vice President for Graduate Studies and Senior Associate Dean, 207-581-3291, Fax: 207-581-3232, E-mail: graduate@maine.edu.
Website: http://umaine.edu/soe/

**The University of Manchester,** School of Arts, Histories and Cultures, Manchester, United Kingdom. Offers anthropology, media and performance (PhD); applied theatre professional (PhD); archaeology (PhD); art history and visual studies (PhD); arts management and cultural policy (PhD); classics and ancient history (PhD); composition (PhD); creative writing (PhD); drama (PhD); economic and social history (PhD); electroacoustic composition (PhD); English and American studies (PhD); history (PhD); humanitarianism and conflict response (PhD); museology (PhD); music (PhD); musicology (PhD); religions and theology (PhD).

**University of Manitoba,** Faculty of Graduate Studies, Faculty of Arts, Department of Economics, Winnipeg, MB R3T 2N2, Canada. Offers MA, PhD. *Degree requirements:* For master's, thesis or alternative; for doctorate, one foreign language, thesis/dissertation.

**University of Maryland, Baltimore County,** The Graduate School, College of Arts, Humanities and Social Sciences, Department of Economics, Program in Economic Policy Analysis, Baltimore, MD 21250. Offers MA. *Program availability:* Part-time. *Faculty:* 17 full-time (6 women), 4 part-time/adjunct (2 women). *Students:* 5 full-time (2 women), 6 part-time (3 women); includes 2 minority (1 Black or African American, non-Hispanic/Latino; 1 Asian, non-Hispanic/Latino), 4 international. Average age 29. 16 applicants, 63% accepted, 5 enrolled. In 2016, 6 master's awarded. *Degree requirements:* For master's, comprehensive exam, capstone research project. *Entrance requirements:* For master's, GRE General Test, undergraduate coursework in economic theory, econometrics, and calculus; letters of reference; statement of purpose; transcripts. Additional exam requirements/recommendations for international students: Required—TOEFL. *Application deadline:* For fall admission, 7/1 priority date for domestic students, 3/1 priority date for international students; for spring admission, 1/1 priority date for domestic students, 9/15 priority date for international students. Applications are processed on a rolling basis. Application fee: $45. Electronic applications accepted. *Expenses:* Tuition, state resident: full-time $13,294. Tuition, nonresident: full-time $20,286. *Financial support:* In 2016–17, 6 students received support, including 5 research assistantships with tuition reimbursements available (averaging $12,560 per year), 1 teaching assistantship with partial tuition reimbursement available (averaging $6,500 per year); Federal Work-Study, health care benefits, tuition waivers (full and partial), and unspecified assistantships also available. Support available to part-time students. Financial award application deadline: 4/15; financial award applicants required to submit FAFSA. *Faculty research:* Health and hospital policy evaluation, environmental policy analysis, economics of education, economic growth and development, cost-benefit and risk analysis. *Total annual research expenditures:* $28,539. *Unit head:* Dr. David F. Mitch, Chair, 410-455-2157, Fax: 410-455-1054, E-mail: mitch@umbc.edu. *Application contact:* Dr. Tim H. Gindling, Graduate Program Director, 410-455-3629, Fax: 410-455-1054, E-mail: econ-masters@umbc.edu.
Website: http://www.umbc.edu/economics/grad_intro.html

**University of Maryland, Baltimore County,** The Graduate School, College of Arts, Humanities and Social Sciences, School of Public Policy, Baltimore, MD 21250. Offers public policy (MPP, PhD), including economics (PhD), educational policy, emergency services (PhD), environmental policy, evaluation and analytical methods, health policy, policy history (PhD), public management, urban policy. *Program availability:* Part-time, evening/weekend. *Faculty:* 10 full-time (4 women), 1 part-time/adjunct (0 women). *Students:* 48 full-time (23 women), 66 part-time (36 women); includes 23 minority (14 Black or African American, non-Hispanic/Latino; 4 Asian, non-Hispanic/Latino; 3 Hispanic/Latino; 1 Native Hawaiian or other Pacific Islander, non-Hispanic/Latino; 1 Two or more races, non-Hispanic/Latino), 6 international. Average age 37. 49 applicants, 65% accepted, 16 enrolled. In 2016, 15 master's, 6 doctorates awarded. Terminal master's awarded for partial completion of doctoral program. *Degree requirements:* For master's, thesis, policy analysis paper, internship for pre-service; for doctorate, thesis/dissertation, comprehensive and field qualifying exams. *Entrance requirements:* For master's and doctorate, GRE General Test, 3 academic letters of reference, resume, research paper, official transcripts. Additional exam requirements/recommendations for international students: Required—TOEFL (minimum score 550 paper-based; 80 iBT). *Application deadline:* For fall admission, 1/15 priority date for domestic students, 1/1 priority date for international students; for spring admission, 11/1 priority date for domestic students, 5/1 priority date for international students. Applications are processed on a rolling basis. Application fee: $50. Electronic applications accepted. *Expenses:* $733 per credit hour in-state tuition and fees, $1,127 per credit hour out-of-state; $27,321 tuition and fees in-state, $41,899 out-of-state (for MPP); $38,316 tuition and fees in-state, $58,804 out-of-state (PhD). *Financial support:* In 2016–17, 25 students received support, including 2 fellowships with full tuition reimbursements available (averaging $14,000 per year), 23 research assistantships with full tuition reimbursements available (averaging $20,000 per year); career-related internships or fieldwork, Federal Work-Study, scholarships/grants, health care benefits, and unspecified assistantships also available. Financial award application deadline: 1/15; financial award applicants required to submit FAFSA. *Faculty research:* Education policy, health policy, urban policy, public management, evaluation and analytical method. *Unit head:* Dr. Donald F. Norris, Director, 410-455-3201, Fax: 410-455-1172, E-mail: norris@umbc.edu. *Application contact:* Sally F. Helms, Administrator of Academic Affairs, 410-455-3202, Fax: 410-455-1172, E-mail: gradpubpol@umbc.edu.
Website: http://publicpolicy.umbc.edu/

**University of Maryland, College Park,** Academic Affairs, College of Behavioral and Social Sciences, Department of Economics, College Park, MD 20742. Offers MA, PhD. *Program availability:* Part-time, evening/weekend. Terminal master's awarded for partial completion of doctoral program. *Degree requirements:* For master's, comprehensive exam, thesis optional; for doctorate, comprehensive exam, thesis/dissertation, exams. *Entrance requirements:* For master's, GRE General Test, minimum GPA of 3.0, course work in calculus and mathematics, 3 letters of recommendation; for doctorate, GRE General Test, calculus background. Additional exam requirements/recommendations for international students: Required—TOEFL. Electronic applications accepted. *Faculty research:* International economics, natural resource and environmental economics, forecasting and policy analysis, economic growth, demography of inequality.

**University of Maryland, College Park,** Academic Affairs, College of Behavioral and Social Sciences, Department of Government and Politics, College Park, MD 20742. Offers American politics (PhD); comparative politics (PhD); international relations (PhD); political economy (PhD); political theory (PhD). *Program availability:* Part-time, evening/weekend. *Degree requirements:* For doctorate, comprehensive exam, thesis/dissertation, written exams in 2 fields. *Entrance requirements:* For doctorate, GRE General Test, minimum GPA of 3.5, writing sample. Additional exam requirements/recommendations for international students: Required—TOEFL. Electronic applications accepted. *Faculty research:* International development/conflict, international security, post-communist society, public service, dynamics of conflict and conflict resolution.

**University of Massachusetts Amherst,** Graduate School, College of Social and Behavioral Sciences, Department of Economics, Amherst, MA 01003. Offers MA, PhD. *Program availability:* Part-time. Terminal master's awarded for partial completion of doctoral program. *Degree requirements:* For master's, thesis or alternative; for doctorate, comprehensive exam, thesis/dissertation. *Entrance requirements:* For master's and doctorate, GRE General Test. Additional exam requirements/recommendations for international students: Required—TOEFL (minimum score 550 paper-based; 80 iBT), IELTS (minimum score 6.5). Electronic applications accepted.

**University of Massachusetts Lowell,** College of Fine Arts, Humanities and Social Sciences, Program in Regional Economic and Social Development, Lowell, MA 01854. Offers MA, Graduate Certificate. *Program availability:* Part-time. *Entrance requirements:* For master's, GRE. Electronic applications accepted.

**University of Memphis,** Graduate School, Fogelman College of Business and Economics, Department of Economics, Memphis, TN 38103. Offers MA, PhD. *Program availability:* Part-time. *Faculty:* 8 full-time (1 woman). *Students:* 6 full-time (1 woman), 6 part-time (1 woman); includes 2 minority (1 Asian, non-Hispanic/Latino; 1 Two or more races, non-Hispanic/Latino), 1 international. Average age 31. 14 applicants, 71% accepted, 7 enrolled. In 2016, 7 master's awarded. Terminal master's awarded for partial completion of doctoral program. *Degree requirements:* For master's, comprehensive exam, thesis or alternative; for doctorate, comprehensive exam, thesis/dissertation, paper presentation. *Entrance requirements:* For master's, GMAT or GRE General Test, previous course work in statistics, intermediate micro and macro theory; one semester of calculus and statistics and matrix or linear algebra; for doctorate, GMAT or GRE, two letters of reference, personal statement, curriculum vitae, interview, minimum GPA of 3.4. Additional exam requirements/recommendations for international students: Required—TOEFL (minimum score 550 paper-based; 79 iBT). *Application deadline:* For fall admission, 8/1 for domestic students; for spring admission, 12/1 for domestic students. Application fee: $35 ($60 for international students). Electronic applications accepted. *Expenses:* $5,231.50 per semester full-time in-state, $9,623.50

## Economics

full-time out-of-state. *Financial support:* In 2016–17, 3 students received support, including 11 research assistantships with full tuition reimbursements available (averaging $16,546 per year), 2 teaching assistantships with full tuition reimbursements available (averaging $6,500 per year); Federal Work-Study, scholarships/grants, and unspecified assistantships also available. Financial award application deadline: 2/1; financial award applicants required to submit FAFSA. *Faculty research:* Tax research, medical economics, law and economics, labor economics, U.S. and Japanese economic relations. *Unit head:* Dr. William Smith, Chair, 901-678-2785, E-mail: wtsmith@memphis.edu. *Application contact:* Dr. Albert Okunade, PhD Program Coordinator, 901-678-2672, Fax: 901-678-4705, E-mail: aokunade@memphis.edu. Website: http://economics.memphis.edu/

**University of Memphis,** Graduate School, Fogelman College of Business and Economics, Program in Business Administration, Memphis, TN 38152. Offers accounting (MBA, PhD); business administration (IMBA); economics (PhD); executive business administration (MBA); finance (PhD); management (PhD); marketing (MS); marketing and supply chain management (PhD); real estate development (MS); JD/MBA. *Accreditation:* AACSB. *Faculty:* 44 full-time (9 women), 5 part-time/adjunct (0 women). *Students:* 167 full-time (64 women), 341 part-time (119 women); includes 154 minority (80 Black or African American, non-Hispanic/Latino; 1 American Indian or Alaska Native, non-Hispanic/Latino; 43 Asian, non-Hispanic/Latino; 12 Hispanic/Latino; 1 Native Hawaiian or other Pacific Islander, non-Hispanic/Latino; 17 Two or more races, non-Hispanic/Latino), 96 international. Average age 33. 306 applicants, 64% accepted, 154 enrolled. In 2016, 273 master's, 7 doctorates awarded. *Degree requirements:* For master's, comprehensive exam; for doctorate, comprehensive exam, thesis/dissertation. *Entrance requirements:* For master's, GMAT, resume; for doctorate, GMAT, interview, minimum GPA of 3.4, resume, letter of recommendation. Additional exam requirements/recommendations for international students: Required—TOEFL (minimum score 550 paper-based). *Application deadline:* For fall admission, 8/1 for domestic students; for spring admission, 12/1 for domestic students. Application fee: $35 ($60 for international students). *Expenses:* Tuition, state resident: full-time $10,463; part-time $9483 per year. Tuition, nonresident: full-time $19,247; part-time $17,291 per year. *Required fees:* $821.50 per semester. Tuition and fees vary according to course load and program. *Financial support:* In 2016–17, 164 students received support. Research assistantships with full tuition reimbursements available, teaching assistantships with full tuition reimbursements available, career-related internships or fieldwork, Federal Work-Study, scholarships/grants, and unspecified assistantships available. Financial award application deadline: 2/15; financial award applicants required to submit FAFSA. *Faculty research:* Competitive business strategy, finance microstructures, supply chain management innovations, health care economics, litigation risks and corporate audits. *Unit head:* Dr. Rajiv Grover, Dean, 901-678-3759, E-mail: rgrover@memphis.edu. *Application contact:* Dr. Carol V. Danehower, Associate Dean, 901-678-5402, Fax: 901-678-3579, E-mail: fcbegp@memphis.edu. Website: https://web0.memphis.edu/gradcatalog/degreeprog/fcbe/fcbe.php

**University of Michigan,** Rackham Graduate School, College of Literature, Science, and the Arts, Department of Economics, Ann Arbor, MI 48109. Offers applied economics (AM, PhD); economics (AM, PhD); public policy and economics (PhD); social work and economics (PhD); JD/PhD; MPP/AM. Terminal master's awarded for partial completion of doctoral program. *Degree requirements:* For doctorate, comprehensive exam, thesis/dissertation, oral defense of dissertation; preliminary exams in microeconomics, macroeconomics, and 2 fields. *Entrance requirements:* For master's and doctorate, GRE General Test. Additional exam requirements/recommendations for international students: Required—TOEFL (minimum score 600 paper-based; 100 iBT). Electronic applications accepted. *Expenses:* Tuition, state resident: full-time $21,466; part-time $1152 per credit hour. Tuition, nonresident: full-time $43,346; part-time $2367 per credit hour. Part-time tuition and fees vary according to course load, degree level and program. *Faculty research:* Econometric analysis, finance, industrial organization, international trade, public finance, economic development, economic history, health, labor, natural resources, population studies, macro theory, micro theory.

**University of Michigan,** School of Social Work, Interdisciplinary PhD Program in Social Work and Social Science, Ann Arbor, MI 48109-1106. Offers social work and anthropology (PhD); social work and economics (PhD); social work and political science (PhD); social work and psychology (PhD); social work and sociology (PhD). Programs offered through the Rackham Graduate School. *Faculty:* 50 full-time (29 women), 62 part-time/adjunct (48 women). *Students:* 59 full-time (42 women); includes 30 minority (14 Black or African American, non-Hispanic/Latino; 9 Asian, non-Hispanic/Latino; 7 Hispanic/Latino). Average age 32. 114 applicants, 7% accepted, 8 enrolled. In 2016, 8 doctorates awarded. *Degree requirements:* For doctorate, thesis/dissertation, oral defense of dissertation, preliminary exam. *Entrance requirements:* For doctorate, GRE General Test. Additional exam requirements/recommendations for international students: Required—TOEFL (minimum score 620 paper-based, 88 iBT) or IELTS. *Application deadline:* For fall admission, 12/1 for domestic and international students. Application fee: $75 ($90 for international students). Electronic applications accepted. *Expenses:* $42,016 fall/winter tuition. *Financial support:* In 2016–17, 59 students received support, including 20 fellowships with full tuition reimbursements available (averaging $15,200 per year), 8 research assistantships with full tuition reimbursements available (averaging $19,737 per year), 17 teaching assistantships with full tuition reimbursements available (averaging $19,737 per year); career-related internships or fieldwork, scholarships/grants, traineeships, health care benefits, tuition waivers (full and partial), and unspecified assistantships also available. Financial award application deadline: 12/1; financial award applicants required to submit FAFSA. *Faculty research:* Children and family, aging, community organization, health and mental health, police and evaluation. *Total annual research expenditures:* $3.8 million. *Unit head:* Dr. Daphne C. Watkins, Director, 734-763-5768, E-mail: daphnew@umich.edu. *Application contact:* Todd Huynh, Graduate Coordinator, 734-647-2554, Fax: 734-615-3192, E-mail: ssw.phd.info@umich.edu. Website: https://ssw.umich.edu/offices/phd

**University of Minnesota, Twin Cities Campus,** Graduate School, College of Liberal Arts, Department of Economics, Minneapolis, MN 55455. Offers MA, PhD. *Faculty:* 19 full-time (3 women), 6 part-time/adjunct (3 women). *Students:* 116 full-time (25 women), 3 part-time (1 woman); includes 9 minority (5 Asian, non-Hispanic/Latino; 3 Hispanic/Latino; 1 Two or more races, non-Hispanic/Latino), 84 international. Average age 27. 358 applicants, 21% accepted, 22 enrolled. In 2016, 18 doctorates awarded. Terminal master's awarded for partial completion of doctoral program. *Degree requirements:* For master's, comprehensive exam; for doctorate, comprehensive exam, thesis/dissertation, preliminary exams. *Entrance requirements:* For doctorate, GRE General Test. Additional exam requirements/recommendations for international students: Required—TOEFL (minimum score 100 iBT), IELTS (minimum score 7). *Application deadline:* For fall admission, 12/12 priority date for domestic and international students. Application fee: $75 ($95 for international students). Electronic applications accepted. *Expenses:* Contact institution. *Financial support:* In 2016–17, 90 students received support, including 16 fellowships with full tuition reimbursements available (averaging $23,000 per year), 4 research assistantships with full tuition reimbursements available (averaging $17,500 per year), 71 teaching assistantships with full tuition reimbursements available (averaging $17,500 per year); scholarships/grants and unspecified assistantships also

available. Financial award application deadline: 12/12. *Faculty research:* Macroeconomics, monetary economics, econometrics, mathematical economics, industrial organization, applied microeconomic theory. *Unit head:* Prof. Christopher Phelan, Chair, 612-625-6353, Fax: 612-624-0209. *Application contact:* Prof. Amil Petrin, Director of Graduate Studies, 612-625-6833, Fax: 612-624-0209, E-mail: econdgs@umn.edu. Website: https://cla.umn.edu/economics

**University of Mississippi,** Graduate School, College of Liberal Arts, University, MS 38677. Offers anthropology (MA); biology (MS, PhD); chemistry (MS, PhD); economics (MA, PhD); English (MA, PhD); experimental psychology (PhD); history (MA, PhD); mathematics (MS, PhD); modern languages (MA); music (MM); philosophy (MA); physics (MA, MS, PhD); political science (MA, PhD); studio art (MFA). *Program availability:* Part-time. *Faculty:* 472 full-time (263 women), 75 part-time/adjunct (35 women). *Students:* 415 full-time (210 women), 57 part-time (20 women); includes 70 minority (35 Black or African American, non-Hispanic/Latino; 13 Asian, non-Hispanic/Latino; 14 Hispanic/Latino; 8 Two or more races, non-Hispanic/Latino), 102 international. Average age 27. *Degree requirements:* For doctorate, thesis/dissertation. *Entrance requirements:* For master's, GRE General Test, minimum GPA of 3.0; for doctorate, GRE General Test. Additional exam requirements/recommendations for international students: Required—TOEFL. *Application deadline:* For fall admission, 4/1 for domestic students; for spring admission, 10/1 for domestic students. Applications are processed on a rolling basis. Application fee: $40. Electronic applications accepted. *Financial support:* Fellowships, research assistantships, teaching assistantships, career-related internships or fieldwork, Federal Work-Study, institutionally sponsored loans, scholarships/grants, and unspecified assistantships available. Financial award application deadline: 3/1; financial award applicants required to submit FAFSA. *Unit head:* Dr. Lee Michael Cohen, Dean, 662-915-7177, Fax: 662-915-5792, E-mail: libarts@olemiss.edu. *Application contact:* Dr. Christy M. Wyandt, Associate Dean of Graduate School, 662-915-7474, Fax: 662-915-7577, E-mail: cwyandt@olemiss.edu. Website: https://www.olemiss.edu

**University of Missouri,** Office of Research and Graduate Studies, College of Arts and Science, Department of Economics, Columbia, MO 65211. Offers MA, PhD. *Faculty:* 23 full-time (3 women), 2 part-time/adjunct (0 women). *Students:* 40 full-time (16 women), 25 part-time (6 women). Terminal master's awarded for partial completion of doctoral program. *Degree requirements:* For doctorate, comprehensive exam, thesis/dissertation. *Entrance requirements:* For master's, GRE General Test (minimum score 700 quantitative, 400 verbal), minimum GPA of 3.0; bachelor's degree in any field; for doctorate, GRE General Test (minimum score 700 quantitative, 400 verbal), minimum GPA of 3.0. Additional exam requirements/recommendations for international students: Required—TOEFL (minimum score 550 paper-based; 80 iBT), IELTS (minimum score 6.5). *Application deadline:* For fall admission, 1/1 priority date for domestic and international students; for winter admission, 10/1 priority date for domestic and international students; for spring admission, 3/1 for domestic students. Application fee: $75 ($90 for international students). Electronic applications accepted. *Expenses:* Tuition, state resident: full-time $6347; part-time $352.60 per credit hour. Tuition, nonresident: full-time $17,379; part-time $965.50 per credit hour. *Required fees:* $1035. Tuition and fees vary according to course load, campus/location and program. *Financial support:* Fellowships with tuition reimbursements, research assistantships with full tuition reimbursements, teaching assistantships with full tuition reimbursements, institutionally sponsored loans, health care benefits, and unspecified assistantships available. *Faculty research:* Monetary economics, econometrics, macroeconomics, public economics, industrial organization, game theory, labor economics, microeconomic theory, teacher labor markets, international trade. Website: http://economics.missouri.edu/graduate/index.shtml

**University of Missouri–Kansas City,** College of Arts and Sciences, Department of Economics, Kansas City, MO 64110-2499. Offers MA, PhD. PhD (interdisciplinary) offered through the School of Graduate Studies. *Program availability:* Part-time, evening/weekend. *Faculty:* 10 full-time (2 women), 2 part-time/adjunct (0 women). *Students:* 16 full-time (5 women), 21 part-time (5 women); includes 6 minority (4 Black or African American, non-Hispanic/Latino; 2 Hispanic/Latino), 8 international. Average age 30. 61 applicants, 34% accepted, 13 enrolled. In 2016, 32 master's awarded. *Degree requirements:* For doctorate, comprehensive exam, thesis/dissertation. *Entrance requirements:* For master's, GRE or minimum undergraduate GPA of 2.5; for doctorate, GRE, master's degree in economics or equivalent. Additional exam requirements/recommendations for international students: Required—TOEFL (minimum score 550 paper-based; 80 iBT). *Application deadline:* For fall admission, 2/1 priority date for domestic and international students; for spring admission, 9/1 priority date for domestic and international students. Applications are processed on a rolling basis. Application fee: $45 ($50 for international students). Electronic applications accepted. *Financial support:* In 2016–17, 18 teaching assistantships with partial tuition reimbursements (averaging $12,833 per year) were awarded; research assistantships with partial tuition reimbursements, career-related internships or fieldwork, Federal Work-Study, institutionally sponsored loans, and tuition waivers (full and partial) also available. Support available to part-time students. Financial award application deadline: 3/1; financial award applicants required to submit FAFSA. *Faculty research:* International trade, general theory, institutions/utilities, forensic economics, human resources. *Unit head:* Karen Vorst, Chair, 816-235-2838, Fax: 816-238-2836, E-mail: vorstk@umkc.edu. *Application contact:* Erik Olsen, Graduate Advisor, 816-235-5715, E-mail: olsenek@umkc.edu. Website: http://cas.umkc.edu/econ/

**University of Missouri–St. Louis,** College of Arts and Sciences, Department of Economics, St. Louis, MO 63121. Offers MA. *Program availability:* Part-time, evening/weekend. *Faculty:* 12 full-time (3 women), 2 part-time/adjunct (1 woman). *Students:* 10 full-time (2 women), 10 part-time (2 women); includes 3 minority (1 Black or African American, non-Hispanic/Latino; 2 Asian, non-Hispanic/Latino), 2 international. Average age 28. 9 applicants, 67% accepted, 3 enrolled. *Entrance requirements:* For master's, GRE General Test, 2 letters of recommendation. Additional exam requirements/recommendations for international students: Required—TOEFL (minimum score 550 paper-based; 79 iBT), IELTS (minimum score 6.5). *Application deadline:* For fall admission, 7/1 priority date for domestic and international students; for spring admission, 12/1 priority date for domestic and international students. Applications are processed on a rolling basis. Application fee: $50 ($40 for international students). Electronic applications accepted. *Financial support:* Research assistantships and teaching assistantships with tuition reimbursements available. Financial award applicants required to submit FAFSA. *Faculty research:* Health economics, public policy analysis, econometrics, public choice, telecommunications and forensic economics. *Unit head:* Anne Winkler, Chair, 314-516-5553, Fax: 314-516-5562, E-mail: awinkler@umsl.edu. *Application contact:* 314-516-5458, Fax: 314-516-6996, E-mail: gradadm@umsl.edu. Website: http://www.umsl.edu/~econ/

**University of Montana,** Graduate School, College of Humanities and Sciences, Department of Economics, Missoula, MT 59812-0002. Offers MA. *Degree requirements:* For master's, thesis. *Entrance requirements:* For master's, GRE General Test.

Additional exam requirements/recommendations for international students: Required—TOEFL (minimum score 525 paper-based). *Faculty research:* Resource economics, public policy, environmental economics, economic development, regional economics.

**University of Nebraska at Omaha,** Graduate Studies, College of Business Administration, Department of Economics, Omaha, NE 68182. Offers MA, MS. *Program availability:* Part-time, evening/weekend. *Faculty:* 6 full-time (2 women). *Students:* 24 full-time (4 women), 14 part-time (5 women); includes 9 minority (4 Black or African American, non-Hispanic/Latino; 2 Asian, non-Hispanic/Latino; 1 Hispanic/Latino; 2 Two or more races, non-Hispanic/Latino), 17 international. Average age 30. 34 applicants, 56% accepted, 12 enrolled. In 2016, 27 master's awarded. *Degree requirements:* For master's, comprehensive exam, thesis (for some programs). *Entrance requirements:* For master's, minimum GPA of 2.7, official transcripts. Additional exam requirements/recommendations for international students: Required—TOEFL, IELTS, PTE. *Application deadline:* For fall admission, 7/15 priority date for domestic students, 6/1 priority date for international students; for spring admission, 12/1 priority date for domestic students, 11/1 priority date for international students; for summer admission, 4/15 for domestic students, 3/1 for international students. Applications are processed on a rolling basis. Application fee: $45. Electronic applications accepted. *Financial support:* In 2016–17, 6 students received support, including 5 research assistantships with tuition reimbursements available, 1 teaching assistantship with tuition reimbursement available; Federal Work-Study, scholarships/grants, health care benefits, and unspecified assistantships also available. Support available to part-time students. Financial award application deadline: 3/1; financial award applicants required to submit FAFSA. *Unit head:* Dr. Christopher Decker, Chairperson, 402-554-2341, E-mail: graduate@unomaha.edu. *Application contact:* Dr. Catherine Co, Graduate Program Chair, 402-554-2341, E-mail: graduate@unomaha.edu.

**University of Nebraska–Lincoln,** Graduate College, College of Business Administration, Department of Economics, Lincoln, NE 68588. Offers MA, PhD, JD/MA. *Degree requirements:* For master's, thesis optional; for doctorate, comprehensive exam, thesis/dissertation. *Entrance requirements:* For master's and doctorate, GRE General Test. Additional exam requirements/recommendations for international students: Required—TOEFL (minimum score 550 paper-based). Electronic applications accepted. *Faculty research:* Applied microeconomics, economic education, international trade and finance, public finance, regional and institutional economics.

**University of Nevada, Las Vegas,** Graduate College, Lee Business School, Department of Economics, Las Vegas, NV 89154-6005. Offers MA, MA/MS. *Program availability:* Part-time. *Faculty:* 7 full-time (1 woman), 1 part-time/adjunct (0 women). *Students:* 10 full-time (0 women), 15 part-time (3 women); includes 7 minority (2 Black or African American, non-Hispanic/Latino; 3 Asian, non-Hispanic/Latino; 1 Hispanic/Latino; 1 Two or more races, non-Hispanic/Latino), 3 international. Average age 31. 17 applicants, 88% accepted, 7 enrolled. In 2016, 7 master's awarded. *Degree requirements:* For master's, thesis optional, oral defense of thesis; internship. *Entrance requirements:* For master's, GRE General Test or GMAT, bachelor's degree with minimum GPA 3.0. Additional exam requirements/recommendations for international students: Required—TOEFL (minimum score 550 paper-based; 80 iBT), IELTS (minimum score 7). *Application deadline:* For fall admission, 6/15 for domestic students, 5/1 for international students; for spring admission, 11/15 for domestic students, 10/1 for international students. Application fee: $60 ($95 for international students). Electronic applications accepted. *Expenses:* $269.25 per credit, $792 per 3-credit course; $9,634 per year resident; $23,274 per year non-resident; $7,094 fees non-resident (7 credits or more); $1,307 annual health insurance fee. *Financial support:* In 2016–17, 4 research assistantships with partial tuition reimbursements (averaging $10,000 per year), 6 teaching assistantships with partial tuition reimbursements (averaging $10,000 per year) were awarded; institutionally sponsored loans, scholarships/grants, health care benefits, and unspecified assistantships also available. Financial award application deadline: 3/15. *Faculty research:* Labor economics/industrial organization; real estate economics; macroeconomics and credit markets; urban, regional and environmental economics; public finance/public policy. *Total annual research expenditures:* $55,474. *Unit head:* Dr. Jeff Waddoups, Chair/Professor, 702-895-3497, Fax: 702-895-1354, E-mail: jeffrey.waddoups@unlv.edu. *Application contact:* Dr. Mary Riddel, Graduate Coordinator, 702-895-2792, Fax: 702-895-1354, E-mail: mary.riddel@unlv.edu. Website: http://business.unlv.edu/economics/

**University of Nevada, Reno,** Graduate School, College of Business Administration, Department of Economics, Reno, NV 89557. Offers MA, MS. *Degree requirements:* For master's, thesis. *Entrance requirements:* For master's, GMAT or GRE, minimum GPA of 2.75. Additional exam requirements/recommendations for international students: Required—TOEFL (minimum score 500 paper-based; 61 iBT), IELTS (minimum score 6). Electronic applications accepted. *Faculty research:* Applied microeconomics, public finance, development, labor.

**University of New Brunswick Fredericton,** School of Graduate Studies, Faculty of Arts, Department of Economics, Fredericton, NB E3B 5A3, Canada. Offers applied economics and finance (M Sc); economics (MA). M Sc offered on Saint John campus. *Entrance requirements:* For master's, minimum GPA of 3.0. Additional exam requirements/recommendations for international students: Required—TWE (minimum score 4), TOEFL (minimum score 580 paper-based) or IELTS (minimum score 7). Electronic applications accepted. *Faculty research:* Epidemiology and population health, micro/macro economics, economics of transportation, regional development, health economics, econometrics.

**University of New Hampshire,** Graduate School, Peter T. Paul College of Business and Economics, Department of Economics, Durham, NH 03824. Offers MA, PhD. *Program availability:* Part-time. Terminal master's awarded for partial completion of doctoral program. *Degree requirements:* For master's, thesis or alternative; for doctorate, one foreign language, thesis/dissertation. *Entrance requirements:* For master's and doctorate, GRE General Test. Additional exam requirements/recommendations for international students: Required—TOEFL (minimum score 550 paper-based; 80 iBT). Electronic applications accepted. *Faculty research:* Labor economics, international development, econometrics, finance, political economy.

**University of New Mexico,** Graduate Studies, College of Arts and Sciences, Program in Economics, Albuquerque, NM 87131-2039. Offers econometrics (MA); economic theory (MA); environmental/natural resource economics (MA, PhD); international/development and sustainability economics (MA, PhD); public economics (MA, PhD). *Program availability:* Part-time. *Faculty:* 11 full-time (5 women). *Students:* 34 full-time (11 women), 19 part-time (7 women); includes 9 minority (1 Black or African American, non-Hispanic/Latino; 1 Asian, non-Hispanic/Latino; 6 Hispanic/Latino; 1 Two or more races, non-Hispanic/Latino), 29 international. Average age 32. 58 applicants, 24% accepted, 11 enrolled. In 2016, 7 master's, 4 doctorates awarded. Terminal master's awarded for partial completion of doctoral program. *Degree requirements:* For master's, comprehensive exam, thesis (for some programs); for doctorate, comprehensive exam, thesis/dissertation. *Entrance requirements:* For master's and doctorate, GRE General Test, 3 letters of recommendation, letter of intent, curriculum vitae. Additional exam requirements/recommendations for international students: Required—TOEFL (minimum score 520 paper-based; 68 iBT). *Application deadline:* For fall admission, 3/1 priority date for domestic students, 3/1 for international students. Applications are processed on a rolling basis. Application fee: $50. Electronic applications accepted. *Financial support:* Fellowships with tuition reimbursements, research assistantships with tuition reimbursements, teaching assistantships with tuition reimbursements, career-related internships or fieldwork, Federal Work-Study, scholarships/grants, health care benefits, and unspecified assistantships available. Support available to part-time students. Financial award application deadline: 3/1; financial award applicants required to submit FAFSA. *Faculty research:* Core theory, econometrics, public finance, international/development economics, labor/human resource economics, environmental/natural resource economics. *Total annual research expenditures:* $167,690. *Unit head:* Dr. Janie Chermak, Chair, 505-277-2037, Fax: 505-277-9445, E-mail: jchermak@unm.edu. *Application contact:* Jeff Newcomer Miller, Academic Advisor, 505-277-3056, Fax: 505-277-9445, E-mail: econgrad@unm.edu. Website: http://econ.unm.edu

**University of New Orleans,** Graduate School, College of Business Administration, Department of Economics and Finance, Program in Financial Economics, New Orleans, LA 70148. Offers PhD. Terminal master's awarded for partial completion of doctoral program. *Degree requirements:* For doctorate, one foreign language, comprehensive exam, thesis/dissertation, general exams. *Entrance requirements:* For doctorate, GRE General Test, minimum GPA of 3.0. Additional exam requirements/recommendations for international students: Required—TOEFL (minimum score 550 paper-based; 79 iBT). Electronic applications accepted. *Faculty research:* Urban and regional economics, economic development, monetary theory and policy, international finance.

**The University of North Carolina at Chapel Hill,** Graduate School, College of Arts and Sciences, Department of Economics, Chapel Hill, NC 27599. Offers MS, PhD. Terminal master's awarded for partial completion of doctoral program. *Degree requirements:* For master's, comprehensive exam, thesis or alternative; for doctorate, comprehensive exam, thesis/dissertation. *Entrance requirements:* For master's, GRE General Test, minimum GPA of 3.0; for doctorate, GRE General Test, minimum GPA of 3.5. Additional exam requirements/recommendations for international students: Required—TOEFL (minimum score 550 paper-based). Electronic applications accepted. *Faculty research:* Health economics, micro theory/IO, labor economics, economic history, financial econometrics.

**The University of North Carolina at Charlotte,** Belk College of Business, Department of Economics, Charlotte, NC 28223-0001. Offers applied econometrics (Graduate Certificate); economics (MS). *Program availability:* Part-time, evening/weekend. *Faculty:* 17 full-time (6 women), 1 part-time/adjunct (0 women). *Students:* 35 full-time (15 women), 30 part-time (3 women); includes 19 minority (8 Black or African American, non-Hispanic/Latino; 3 Asian, non-Hispanic/Latino; 5 Hispanic/Latino; 3 Two or more races, non-Hispanic/Latino), 12 international. Average age 26. 50 applicants, 94% accepted, 24 enrolled. In 2016, 16 master's awarded. *Degree requirements:* For master's, thesis or project. *Entrance requirements:* For master's, GRE General Test, GMAT, undergraduate coursework that includes calculus, econometrics (or equivalent), intermediate macroeconomic theory, intermediate microeconomic theory; for Graduate Certificate, bachelor's degree, or its equivalent, from regionally-accredited college or university; minimum GPA of 2.75 on all previous work completed beyond high school (secondary school); statement of purpose; unofficial transcripts of all college course work. Additional exam requirements/recommendations for international students: Required—TOEFL (minimum score 523 paper-based, 70 iBT) or IELTS (6.5). *Application deadline:* For fall admission, 3/1 priority date for domestic and international students; for spring admission, 10/1 priority date for domestic and international students; for summer admission, 4/1 priority date for domestic and international students. Applications are processed on a rolling basis. Application fee: $75. Electronic applications accepted. *Expenses:* Contact institution. *Financial support:* Career-related internships or fieldwork, institutionally sponsored loans, scholarships/grants, and unspecified assistantships available. Support available to part-time students. Financial award application deadline: 3/1; financial award applicants required to submit FAFSA. *Faculty research:* Health care, taxation, energy, economic growth, monetary policy. *Total annual research expenditures:* $14,012. *Unit head:* Dr. Artie Zillante, Department Chair, 704-687-5375, Fax: 704-687-1384, E-mail: azillant@uncc.edu. *Application contact:* Kathy B. Giddings, Director of Graduate Admissions, 704-687-5503, Fax: 704-687-1668, E-mail: gradadm@uncc.edu. Website: http://msecon.uncc.edu/

**The University of North Carolina at Greensboro,** Graduate School, Bryan School of Business and Economics, Department of Economics, Program in Economics, Greensboro, NC 27412-5001. Offers PhD. *Degree requirements:* For doctorate, comprehensive exam, thesis/dissertation. *Entrance requirements:* Additional exam requirements/recommendations for international students: Required—TOEFL. Electronic applications accepted.

**University of North Florida,** Coggin College of Business, MBA Program, Jacksonville, FL 32224. Offers accounting (MBA); construction management (MBA); e-commerce (MBA); economics (MBA); finance (MBA); human resource management (MBA); international business (MBA); logistics (MBA); management applications (MBA). *Accreditation:* AACSB. *Program availability:* Part-time, evening/weekend. *Faculty:* 16 full-time (4 women), 1 (woman) part-time/adjunct. *Students:* 105 full-time (50 women), 162 part-time (68 women); includes 57 minority (14 Black or African American, non-Hispanic/Latino; 1 American Indian or Alaska Native, non-Hispanic/Latino; 17 Asian, non-Hispanic/Latino; 18 Hispanic/Latino; 7 Two or more races, non-Hispanic/Latino), 41 international. Average age 28. 231 applicants, 46% accepted, 84 enrolled. In 2016, 114 master's awarded. *Entrance requirements:* For master's, GMAT or GRE, U.S. bachelor's degree from regionally-accredited university or equivalent foreign degree. Additional exam requirements/recommendations for international students: Required—TOEFL (minimum score 550 paper-based; 79 iBT). *Application deadline:* For fall admission, 8/1 priority date for domestic students, 5/1 for international students; for spring admission, 12/1 priority date for domestic students, 10/1 for international students; for summer admission, 4/29 priority date for domestic students, 2/1 for international students. Application fee: $30. Tuition and fees vary according to course load, campus/location and program. *Financial support:* In 2016–17, 22 students received support, including 1 research assistantship (averaging $2,501 per year); teaching assistantships, Federal Work-Study, and tuition waivers (partial) also available. Support available to part-time students. Financial award application deadline: 4/1; financial award applicants required to submit FAFSA. *Faculty research:* Performance measures, costing, and inventory issues in logistics and supply chain management; inter-organizational systems; international management and marketing practices; e-commerce; organizational learning and socialization processes. *Total annual research expenditures:* $17,654. *Unit head:* Dr. Parvez Ahmed, Graduate Program Director, 904-620-1678, E-mail: pahmed@unf.edu. *Application contact:* Amy Bishop, MSM Advisor, 904-620-2575, Fax: 904-620-2832, E-mail: coggin.students@unf.edu. Website: http://www.unf.edu/graduateschool/academics/programs/MBA.aspx

**University of North Texas,** Robert B. Toulouse School of Graduate Studies, Denton, TX 76203-5459. Offers accounting (MS); applied anthropology (MA, MS); applied behavior analysis (Certificate); applied geography (MA); applied technology and performance improvement (M Ed, MS); art education (MA); art history (MA); art museum education (Certificate); arts leadership (Certificate); audiology (Au D); behavior analysis

*Economics*

(MS); behavioral science (PhD); biochemistry and molecular biology (MS); biology (MA, MS); biomedical engineering (MS); business analysis (MS); chemistry (MS); clinical health psychology (PhD); communication studies (MA, MS); computer engineering (MS); computer science (MS); counseling (M Ed, MS), including clinical mental health counseling (MS), college and university counseling, elementary school counseling, secondary school counseling; creative writing (MA); criminal justice (MS); curriculum and instruction (M Ed); decision sciences (MBA); design (MA, MFA), including fashion design (MFA), innovation studies, interior design (MFA); early childhood studies (MS); economics (MA); educational leadership (M Ed, Ed D); educational psychology (MS, PhD), including family studies (MS), gifted and talented (MS), human development (MS), learning and cognition (MS), research, measurement and evaluation (MS); electrical engineering (MS); emergency management (MPA); engineering technology (MS); English (MA); English as a second language (MA); environmental science (MS); finance (MBA, MS); financial management (MPA); French (MA); health services management (MBA); higher education (M Ed, Ed D); history (MA, MS); hospitality management (MS); human resources management (MPA); information science (MS); information systems (PhD); information technologies (MBA); interdisciplinary studies (MA, MS); international studies (MA); international sustainable tourism (MS); jazz studies (MM); journalism (MA, MJ, Graduate Certificate), including interactive and virtual digital communication (Graduate Certificate), narrative journalism (Graduate Certificate), public relations (Graduate Certificate); kinesiology (MS); linguistics (MA); local government management (MPA); logistics (PhD); logistics and supply chain management (MBA); long-term care, senior housing, and aging services (MA); management (PhD); marketing (MBA); mathematics (MA, MS); mechanical and energy engineering (MS, PhD); music (MA), including ethnomusicology, music theory, musicology, performance; music composition (PhD); music education (MM Ed, PhD); nonprofit management (MPA); operations and supply chain management (MBA); performance (MM, DMA); philosophy (MA); political science (MA); professional and technical communication (MA); radio, television and film (MA, MFA); rehabilitation counseling (Certificate); sociology (MA); Spanish (MA); special education (M Ed); speech-language pathology (MS); strategic management (MBA); studio art (MFA); teaching (M Ed); MBA/MS. *Program availability:* Part-time, evening/weekend, online learning. Terminal master's awarded for partial completion of doctoral program. *Degree requirements:* For master's, variable foreign language requirement, comprehensive exam (for some programs), thesis (for some programs); for doctorate, variable foreign language requirement, comprehensive exam (for some programs), thesis/dissertation; for other advanced degree, variable foreign language requirement, comprehensive exam (for some programs). *Entrance requirements:* For master's and doctorate, GRE, GMAT. Additional exam requirements/recommendations for international students: Required—TOEFL (minimum score 550 paper-based; 79 iBT). Electronic applications accepted.

**University of Notre Dame,** Graduate School, College of Arts and Letters, Division of Social Science, Department of Economics and Econometrics, Notre Dame, IN 46556. Offers MA, PhD. Terminal master's awarded for partial completion of doctoral program. *Degree requirements:* For master's, comprehensive exam (for some programs), thesis optional; for doctorate, thesis/dissertation, candidacy exam. *Entrance requirements:* For doctorate, GRE General Test. Additional exam requirements/recommendations for international students: Required—TOEFL (minimum score 600 paper-based; 80 iBT). Electronic applications accepted.

**University of Oklahoma,** College of Arts and Sciences, Department of Economics, Norman, OK 73019. Offers applied economics (MA); economics (PhD); managerial economics (MA). *Faculty:* 21 full-time (6 women), 1 part-time/adjunct (0 women). *Students:* 33 full-time (9 women), 38 part-time (8 women); includes 21 minority (7 Black or African American, non-Hispanic/Latino; 1 American Indian or Alaska Native, non-Hispanic/Latino; 5 Asian, non-Hispanic/Latino; 7 Hispanic/Latino; 1 Two or more races, non-Hispanic/Latino), 22 international. Average age 31. 53 applicants, 45% accepted, 20 enrolled. In 2016, 20 master's, 3 doctorates awarded. Terminal master's awarded for partial completion of doctoral program. *Degree requirements:* For master's, comprehensive exam (for some programs); for doctorate, comprehensive exam, thesis/dissertation. *Entrance requirements:* For master's and doctorate, GRE, undergraduate degree in related field. Additional exam requirements/recommendations for international students: Required—TOEFL (minimum score 79 iBT) or IELTS (minimum score 6.5). *Application deadline:* For fall admission, 2/28 priority date for domestic students, 1/30 priority date for international students. Applications are processed on a rolling basis. Application fee: $50 ($100 for international students). Electronic applications accepted. *Expenses:* Tuition, state resident: full-time $4886; part-time $203.60 per credit hour. Tuition, nonresident: full-time $18,989; part-time $791.20 per credit hour. *Required fees:* $3283; $126.25 per credit hour. $126.50 per semester. *Financial support:* In 2016–17, 30 students received support, including 26 teaching assistantships with partial tuition reimbursements available (averaging $14,241 per year); fellowships with partial tuition reimbursements available, research assistantships with partial tuition reimbursements available, scholarships/grants, and health care benefits also available. Financial award application deadline: 6/1; financial award applicants required to submit FAFSA. *Faculty research:* Public economics, development economics, international economics, industrial organization, applied econometrics. *Total annual research expenditures:* $249,871. *Unit head:* Dr. Gary Hoover, Department Chair and Professor of Economics, 405-325-5857, E-mail: ghoover@ou.edu. *Application contact:* Gregory Burge, Director of Graduate Studies/Associate Professor, 405-325-2358, E-mail: gburge@ou.edu. Website: http://cas.ou.edu/economics

**University of Oklahoma,** College of International Studies, Norman, OK 73019. Offers economics and development (MAIS), including global economics and development, global security studies (MA, MAIS); global affairs (MA), including economics and development, global security studies (MA, MAIS); JD/MAIS; MAIS/MSW. *Program availability:* Part-time, online courses with an 8-10 day study abroad. *Faculty:* 18 full-time (6 women), 1 part-time/adjunct (0 women). *Students:* 48 full-time (21 women), 231 part-time (53 women); includes 85 minority (21 Black or African American, non-Hispanic/Latino; 2 American Indian or Alaska Native, non-Hispanic/Latino; 13 Asian, non-Hispanic/Latino; 33 Hispanic/Latino; 3 Native Hawaiian or other Pacific Islander, non-Hispanic/Latino; 13 Two or more races, non-Hispanic/Latino), 4 international. Average age 32. 60 applicants, 88% accepted, 36 enrolled. In 2016, 68 master's awarded. Terminal master's awarded for partial completion of doctoral program. *Degree requirements:* For master's, variable foreign language requirement, 36 credit hours (33 online); thesis, policy paper or internship project; faculty-led overseas travel program of 8-10 days that will vary in location (online). *Entrance requirements:* For master's, GRE. Additional exam requirements/recommendations for international students: Required—TOEFL (minimum score 79 iBT) or IELTS (minimum score 6.5). *Application deadline:* For fall admission, 2/15 for domestic and international students. Application fee: $50 ($100 for international students). Electronic applications accepted. *Expenses:* Tuition, state resident: full-time $4886; part-time $203.60 per credit hour. Tuition, nonresident: full-time $18,989; part-time $791.20 per credit hour. *Required fees:* $3283; $126.25 per credit hour. $126.50 per semester. *Financial support:* In 2016–17, 27 students received support, including 7 research assistantships with full tuition reimbursements available (averaging $13,500 per year), 3 teaching assistantships with full tuition reimbursements available (averaging $13,500 per year); fellowships with full tuition reimbursements available, career-related internships or fieldwork, scholarships/grants, health care

benefits, and unspecified assistantships also available. Financial award application deadline: 6/1; financial award applicants required to submit FAFSA. *Faculty research:* Area studies, including the Middle East, China, East and South Asia, Latin America, and Europe; political economy and development; international security; identity and nationalism; global history and culture. *Unit head:* Dr. Mitchell Smith, Professor/Associate Dean for Academic Affairs, 405-325-1584, Fax: 405-325-7738, E-mail: mps@ou.edu. *Application contact:* Katie Watkins, Academic Advisor, 405-325-2337, Fax: 405-325-7738, E-mail: kwatkins@ou.edu.
Website: http://www.ou.edu/dais

**University of Oregon,** Graduate School, College of Arts and Sciences, Department of Economics, Eugene, OR 97403. Offers MA, MS, PhD. Terminal master's awarded for partial completion of doctoral program. *Degree requirements:* For master's, thesis or alternative; for doctorate, thesis/dissertation, qualifying exam. *Entrance requirements:* For master's and doctorate, GRE General Test, minimum GPA of 3.0. Additional exam requirements/recommendations for international students: Required—TOEFL. *Faculty research:* Labor economics, macroeconomics, international economics, industrial organization, public finance.

**University of Ottawa,** Faculty of Graduate and Postdoctoral Studies, Faculty of Social Sciences, Department of Economics, Ottawa, ON K1N 6N5, Canada. Offers MA, PhD. PhD offered jointly with Carleton University. *Program availability:* Part-time. *Degree requirements:* For master's, thesis or alternative; for doctorate, comprehensive exam, thesis/dissertation. *Entrance requirements:* For master's, honors bachelor's degree or equivalent, minimum B average; for doctorate, master's degree, minimum B+ average. Electronic applications accepted. *Faculty research:* Public economics, industrial organizations, monetary economics, international economics, economic development.

**University of Pennsylvania,** School of Arts and Sciences, Graduate Group in Economics, Philadelphia, PA 19104. Offers AM, PhD, JD/AM, JD/PhD. *Faculty:* 40 full-time (5 women), 5 part-time/adjunct (0 women). *Students:* 108 full-time (25 women); includes 5 minority (1 Black or African American, non-Hispanic/Latino; 2 Asian, non-Hispanic/Latino; 1 Hispanic/Latino; 1 Two or more races, non-Hispanic/Latino), 86 international. Average age 28. 707 applicants, 16% accepted, 24 enrolled. In 2016, 11 master's, 13 doctorates awarded. *Degree requirements:* For doctorate, thesis/dissertation. *Entrance requirements:* For doctorate, GRE General Test. *Expenses:* Tuition: Full-time $31,068; part-time $5762 per course. *Required fees:* $3200; $336 per course. Full-time tuition and fees vary according to degree level, program and student level. Part-time tuition and fees vary according to course load, degree level and program. Website: http://economics.sas.upenn.edu/graduate-program

**University of Pittsburgh,** Dietrich School of Arts and Sciences, Department of Economics, Pittsburgh, PA 15260. Offers MA, PhD. *Faculty:* 24 full-time (8 women). *Students:* 50 full-time (20 women); includes 29 minority (27 Asian, non-Hispanic/Latino; 2 Hispanic/Latino). Average age 27. 303 applicants, 8% accepted, 14 enrolled. *Degree requirements:* For doctorate, comprehensive exam, thesis/dissertation, comprehensive research paper. *Entrance requirements:* For doctorate, GRE, 3 letters of recommendation. Additional exam requirements/recommendations for international students: Required—TOEFL (minimum score 90 iBT). *Application deadline:* For fall admission, 1/15 for domestic and international students. Application fee: $50. Electronic applications accepted. Tuition and fees vary according to program. *Financial support:* In 2016–17, 8 fellowships with full tuition reimbursements (averaging $21,692 per year), 4 research assistantships with full tuition reimbursements (averaging $17,910 per year), 24 teaching assistantships with full tuition reimbursements (averaging $17,910 per year) were awarded; tuition waivers (full) also available. Financial award application deadline: 1/15. *Faculty research:* Game theory, experimental economics, econometrics, labor, international trade. *Total annual research expenditures:* $101,679. *Unit head:* Dr. Lise Vesterlund, Chair, 412-648-1732, Fax: 412-648-7038, E-mail: vester@pitt.edu. *Application contact:* Dr. Werner Troesken, Director of Graduate Studies, 412-648-2823, E-mail: troesken@pitt.edu.
Website: http://www.econ.pitt.edu/

**University of Pittsburgh,** Dietrich School of Arts and Sciences, Program in Computational Modeling and Simulation, Pittsburgh, PA 15260. Offers biological science (PhD); chemistry (PhD); computer science (PhD); economics (PhD); geology and environmental sciences (PhD); mathematics (PhD); physics and astronomy (PhD); psychology (PhD); statistics (PhD). *Program availability:* Part-time. *Faculty:* 4 full-time (1 woman). *Students:* 3 full-time (1 woman), 1 part-time (0 women); includes 1 minority (Asian, non-Hispanic/Latino). Average age 23. 7 applicants, 43% accepted, 2 enrolled. *Degree requirements:* For doctorate, comprehensive exam, thesis/dissertation, preliminary exam. *Entrance requirements:* For doctorate, GRE, statement of purpose, transcripts for all college-level institutions attended, three letters of reference. Additional exam requirements/recommendations for international students: Required—TOEFL (minimum score 90 iBT), IELTS (minimum score 7). *Application deadline:* For fall admission, 1/15 for domestic and international students. Applications are processed on a rolling basis. Application fee: $0 ($50 for international students). Electronic applications accepted. *Expenses:* Contact institution. *Financial support:* In 2016–17, 3 students received support, including 2 fellowships with full tuition reimbursements available (averaging $28,500 per year), 2 research assistantships with full tuition reimbursements available (averaging $23,000 per year); tuition waivers (full) also available. Financial award application deadline: 4/15. *Faculty research:* Econometric modeling, developing reduced-scaling first principles approaches for expedited predictions of molecular and materials properties, developing computational models to quantitatively describe origins of reactivity and selectivity in organ catalytic reactions, image retrieval, human-machine communication. *Unit head:* Dr. Holger Hoock, Associate Dean, 412-624-3939, Fax: 412-624-6855. *Application contact:* Wendy G. Janocha, Graduate Administrator, 412-648-7251, E-mail: wgj1@pitt.edu.
Website: http://cmsp.pitt.edu/

**University of Pittsburgh,** Graduate School of Public and International Affairs, Master of Public and International Affairs Program, Pittsburgh, PA 15260. Offers human security (MPIA); international political economy (MPIA); security and intelligence studies (MPIA); JD/MPIA; MBA/MPIA; MPH/MPIA; MPIA/MSW; MSIS/MPIA. *Program availability:* Part-time, evening/weekend. *Faculty:* 34 full-time (12 women), 18 part-time/adjunct (5 women). *Students:* 98 full-time (42 women), 17 part-time (8 women); includes 17 minority (8 Black or African American, non-Hispanic/Latino; 2 Asian, non-Hispanic/Latino; 6 Hispanic/Latino; 1 Two or more races, non-Hispanic/Latino), 20 international. Average age 26. 181 applicants, 91% accepted, 48 enrolled. In 2016, 70 master's awarded. *Degree requirements:* For master's, thesis optional, capstone seminar. *Entrance requirements:* For master's, GRE General Test or GMAT, 2 letters of recommendation, resume, undergraduate transcripts, personal statement. Additional exam requirements/recommendations for international students: Required—TOEFL (minimum score 80 iBT); Recommended—IELTS (minimum score 7). *Application deadline:* For fall admission, 2/1 for domestic students, 1/15 for international students; for spring admission, 11/1 for domestic students, 8/1 for international students. Application fee: $50. Electronic applications accepted. *Expenses:* $22,578 per year in-state; $36,734 per year out-of-state. *Financial support:* In 2016–17, 47 students received support, including 2 fellowships with full tuition reimbursements available (averaging $18,000 per year), 3 research assistantships with full tuition reimbursements available (averaging $14,620 per year); career-related internships or fieldwork and scholarships/grants also available. Financial award application deadline: 2/1; financial award applicants required to submit FAFSA. *Faculty research:* International political economy, human security, security and intelligence. *Total annual research expenditures:* $1.3 million. *Unit head:* Dr. John T.S. Keeler, Dean, 412-648-7605, E-mail: keeler@pitt.edu. *Application contact:* Dr. Michael T. Rizzi, Director of Student Services, 412-648-7640, Fax: 412-648-7641, E-mail: rizzim@pitt.edu. Website: http://www.gspia.pitt.edu/

**University of Puerto Rico, Río Piedras Campus,** College of Social Sciences, Department of Economics, San Juan, PR 00931-3300. Offers MA. *Program availability:* Part-time. *Degree requirements:* For master's, comprehensive exam, thesis. *Entrance requirements:* For master's, GRE, PAEG, interview, minimum GPA of 3.0, letter of recommendation.

**University of Regina,** Faculty of Graduate Studies and Research, Johnson-Shoyama Graduate School of Public Policy, Regina, SK S4S 0A2, Canada. Offers economic analysis for public policy (Master's Certificate); health administration (MHA); health systems management (Master's Certificate); public management (MPA, Master's Certificate); public policy (MPA, MPP, PhD); public policy analysis (Master's Certificate). *Program availability:* Part-time. *Faculty:* 9 full-time (4 women), 15 part-time/adjunct (4 women). *Students:* 88 full-time (56 women), 159 part-time (103 women). 202 applicants, 43% accepted. In 2016, 43 master's, 20 other advanced degrees awarded. *Degree requirements:* For master's, thesis (for some programs); for doctorate, thesis/dissertation. *Entrance requirements:* For doctorate, master's degree, intended research program in an area of public policy. Additional exam requirements/recommendations for international students: Required—TOEFL (minimum score 580 paper-based; 80 iBT), IELTS (minimum score 6.5), PTE (minimum score 59). *Application deadline:* For fall admission, 2/1 for domestic and international students. Application fee: $100. Electronic applications accepted. *Expenses:* Contact institution. *Financial support:* In 2016–17, 17 fellowships (averaging $6,059 per year), 19 teaching assistantships (averaging $2,507 per year) were awarded; career-related internships or fieldwork and scholarships/grants also available. Financial award application deadline: 6/15. *Faculty research:* Governance and administration, public finance, public policy analysis, non-governmental organizations and alternative service delivery, micro-economics for policy analysis. *Unit head:* Dr. Kathleen McNutt, Executive Director, Main Campus, 306-585-4759, Fax: 306-585-5461, E-mail: kathy.mcnutt@uregina.ca. *Application contact:* Constance Heshka-Argue, Manager, Main Campus, 306-585-5462, Fax: 306-585-5461, E-mail: connie.heska-argue@uregina.ca. Website: http://www.schoolofpublicpolicy.sk.ca/

**University of Rhode Island,** Graduate School, College of the Environment and Life Sciences, Department of Environmental and Natural Resource Economics, Kingston, RI 02881. Offers MESM, MS, PhD. *Program availability:* Part-time. *Faculty:* 7 full-time (2 women). *Students:* 22 full-time (8 women), 5 part-time (1 woman), 11 international. In 2016, 8 master's, 3 doctorates awarded. *Degree requirements:* For master's, comprehensive exam (for some programs), thesis optional; for doctorate, comprehensive exam, thesis/dissertation. *Entrance requirements:* For master's and doctorate, GRE, 3 letters of recommendation. Additional exam requirements/recommendations for international students: Required—TOEFL. *Application deadline:* For fall admission, 7/15 for domestic students, 2/1 for international students; for spring admission, 11/15 for domestic students, 7/15 for international students; for summer admission, 4/15 for domestic students. Application fee: $65. Electronic applications accepted. *Expenses:* Tuition, state resident: full-time $11,796; part-time $655 per credit. Tuition, nonresident: full-time $24,206; part-time $1345 per credit. *Required fees:* $1546; $44 per credit. One-time fee: $155 full-time; $35 part-time. *Financial support:* In 2016–17, 18 research assistantships (averaging $14,124 per year), 1 teaching assistantship (averaging $18,296 per year) were awarded. Financial award application deadline: 7/15; financial award applicants required to submit FAFSA. *Unit head:* Dr. James Opaluch, Chair, 401-874-4590, Fax: 401-874-4766, E-mail: jimo@uri.edu. *Application contact:* Graduate Admission, 401-874-2872, E-mail: gradadm@etal.uri.edu. Website: http://web.uri.edu/enre/

**University of Rochester,** School of Arts and Sciences, Department of Economics, Rochester, NY 14627. Offers PhD. *Faculty:* 17 full-time (6 women). *Students:* 51 full-time (14 women), 1 part-time (0 women), 42 international. Average age 27. 347 applicants, 22% accepted, 17 enrolled. In 2016, 13 doctorates awarded. *Degree requirements:* For doctorate, thesis/dissertation, qualifying exam. *Entrance requirements:* For doctorate, GRE General Test, transcripts, three letters of recommendation. Additional exam requirements/recommendations for international students: Required—TOEFL (minimum score 600 paper-based; 100 iBT). *Application deadline:* For fall admission, 1/3 for domestic and international students. Application fee: $60. Electronic applications accepted. *Expenses:* $1,538 per credit. *Financial support:* In 2016–17, 35 students received support, including 35 teaching assistantships with full tuition reimbursements available (averaging $20,000 per year); scholarships/grants also available. Financial award application deadline: 1/3. *Unit head:* Srihari Govindan, Chair, 585-275-7241, E-mail: s.govindan@rochester.edu. *Application contact:* Kerri Hoppe, Administrative Assistant, 585-275-8625, E-mail: khoppe@rochester.edu. Website: http://www.econ.rochester.edu/

**University of San Francisco,** College of Arts and Sciences, Economics Program, San Francisco, CA 94117-1080. Offers MA, MS, MSB/MBA. *Program availability:* Part-time, evening/weekend. *Faculty:* 8 full-time (2 women), 1 part-time/adjunct (0 women). *Students:* 39 full-time (22 women), 1 part-time (0 women); includes 5 minority (4 Asian, non-Hispanic/Latino; 1 Two or more races, non-Hispanic/Latino), 30 international. Average age 26. 91 applicants, 76% accepted, 19 enrolled. In 2016, 16 master's awarded. *Degree requirements:* For master's, comprehensive exam, thesis or alternative. *Entrance requirements:* For master's, GRE General Test (recommended), BA in economics (preferred). Additional exam requirements/recommendations for international students: Required—TOEFL, IELTS, PTE. *Application deadline:* For fall admission, 3/1 for domestic and international students. Applications are processed on a rolling basis. Application fee: $55 ($65 for international students). *Expenses: Tuition:* Full-time $23,310; part-time $1295 per credit. Tuition and fees vary according to course load, degree level, campus/location and program. *Financial support:* In 2016–17, 14 students received support. Fellowships, teaching assistantships, and career-related internships or fieldwork available. Financial award application deadline: 3/2; financial award applicants required to submit FAFSA. *Faculty research:* Economic development, forecasting and planning, labor markets, Pacific Rim, financial markets. *Unit head:* Courtney Arguello, Program Manager, 415-422-2711, Fax: 415-422-5784. *Application contact:* Mark Landerghini, Information Contact, 415-422-5101, Fax: 415-422-2217, E-mail: asgraduate@usfca.edu. Website: https://www.usfca.edu/arts-sciences/graduate-programs/economics

**University of Saskatchewan,** College of Graduate Studies and Research, College of Arts and Science, Department of Economics, Saskatoon, SK S7N 5A2, Canada. Offers MA, Diploma. *Degree requirements:* For master's, thesis (for some programs). *Entrance requirements:* Additional exam requirements/recommendations for international students: Required—TOEFL (minimum score 80 iBT); Recommended—IELTS (minimum score 6.5). Electronic applications accepted.

**University of South Africa,** College of Economic and Management Sciences, Pretoria, South Africa. Offers accounting (D Admin, D Com); accounting science (DA); auditing (D Admin, D Com); business administration (M Tech); business economics (D Admin); business leadership (DBL); business management (D Admin, D Com); economic management analysis (M Tech); economics (D Admin, D Com, PhD); human resource development (M Tech); industrial psychology (D Admin, D Com, PhD); logistics (D Com); marketing (M Tech); public administration (D Admin, D Com, DPA, PhD); public management (M Tech); quantitative management (D Admin, D Com); real estate (M Tech); statistics (D Admin, PhD); tourism management (D Admin, D Com); transport economics (D Admin, D Com).

**University of South Carolina,** The Graduate School, Darla Moore School of Business, Doctoral Program in Business Administration, Columbia, SC 29208. Offers business administration (PhD); economics (PhD). *Degree requirements:* For doctorate, thesis/dissertation, qualifying and comprehensive exams. *Entrance requirements:* For doctorate, GRE or GMAT. Additional exam requirements/recommendations for international students: Required—TOEFL (minimum score 600 paper-based; 100 iBT), IELTS (minimum score 7). Electronic applications accepted. *Expenses:* Contact institution. *Faculty research:* International competitiveness of U.S. textiles, international compensation, exchange rates, international finance.

**University of South Carolina,** The Graduate School, Darla Moore School of Business, Master of Arts in Economics Program, Columbia, SC 29208. Offers MA, JD/MA. *Degree requirements:* For master's, thesis optional. *Entrance requirements:* For master's, GMAT or GRE General Test. Additional exam requirements/recommendations for international students: Required—TOEFL (minimum score 100 iBT); Recommended—IELTS. Electronic applications accepted. *Faculty research:* Monetary theory, labor economics, international economics, industrial organization.

**University of Southern California,** Graduate School, Dana and David Dornsife College of Letters, Arts and Sciences, Department of Economics, Los Angeles, CA 90089. Offers economic development programming (MA, PhD); mathematical finance (MS); M PI/MA; MA/JD. Terminal master's awarded for partial completion of doctoral program. *Degree requirements:* For master's, comprehensive exam; for doctorate, comprehensive exam, thesis/dissertation. *Entrance requirements:* For master's and doctorate, GRE. Additional exam requirements/recommendations for international students: Required—TOEFL (minimum score 93 iBT). Electronic applications accepted. *Faculty research:* Macro theory, development economics, econometrics.

**University of Southern Mississippi,** Graduate School, College of Business, Department of Economic Development, Tourism and Sport Management, Hattiesburg, MS 39406. Offers economic development (MS); sport management (MS). *Program availability:* Part-time, evening/weekend. *Degree requirements:* For master's, comprehensive exam, thesis optional, internships. *Entrance requirements:* For master's, GMAT or GRE General Test, minimum GPA of 2.75 in last 60 hours. Additional exam requirements/recommendations for international students: Required—TOEFL, IELTS. *Application deadline:* For fall admission, 8/1 for domestic students, 3/1 for international students; for spring admission, 1/3 for domestic and international students. Applications are processed on a rolling basis. Application fee: $60. Electronic applications accepted. *Expenses: Tuition, area resident:* Full-time $15,708; part-time $437 per credit hour. *Financial support:* Research assistantships with full tuition reimbursements, teaching assistantships with full tuition reimbursements, career-related internships or fieldwork, Federal Work-Study, scholarships/grants, health care benefits, and unspecified assistantships available. Financial award application deadline: 3/1; financial award applicants required to submit FAFSA. *Faculty research:* Economic development, international studies, geography. *Unit head:* Dr. Stacey Hall, Chair, 601-266-6308, Fax: 601-266-6707. *Application contact:* Dr. Chad Miller, Program Coordinator, 601-266-6666, Fax: 601-266-6071. Website: https://www.usm.edu/business/eco-dev-tourism-sport-management

**University of South Florida,** College of Arts and Sciences, Department of Economics, Tampa, FL 33620-9951. Offers MA, PhD. *Program availability:* Part-time, evening/weekend. *Faculty:* 12 full-time (3 women). *Students:* 32 full-time (9 women), 14 part-time (4 women); includes 7 minority (2 Black or African American, non-Hispanic/Latino; 2 Asian, non-Hispanic/Latino; 3 Hispanic/Latino), 17 international. Average age 28. 67 applicants, 57% accepted, 13 enrolled. In 2016, 10 master's, 2 doctorates awarded. *Degree requirements:* For master's, comprehensive exam, oral exam; for doctorate, comprehensive exam, thesis/dissertation. *Entrance requirements:* For master's, GRE General Test, minimum GPA of 3.0 in last 60 hours of course work; minimum B grade in calculus, statistics, undergraduate-level intermediate microeconomics, and undergraduate-level intermediate macroeconomics; for doctorate, GRE General Test, minimum GPA of 3.0 in last 60 hours of undergraduate and graduate coursework; minimum B grade in calculus (two courses), probability and statistics, undergraduate intermediate-level microeconomics and undergraduate intermediate-level macroeconomics. Additional exam requirements/recommendations for international students: Required—TOEFL (minimum score 550 paper-based; 79 iBT) or IELTS (minimum score 6.5). *Application deadline:* For fall admission, 1/31 for domestic and international students; for spring admission, 10/15 for domestic students, 9/15 for international students. Applications are processed on a rolling basis. Application fee: $30. Electronic applications accepted. *Expenses:* Tuition, state resident: full-time $7766; part-time $431.43 per credit hour. Tuition, nonresident: full-time $15,789; part-time $877.17 per credit hour. *Required fees:* $37 per term. *Financial support:* In 2016–17, 14 students received support, including 1 research assistantship (averaging $13,082 per year), 15 teaching assistantships with tuition reimbursements available (averaging $11,393 per year); unspecified assistantships also available. Financial award application deadline: 2/1; financial award applicants required to submit FAFSA. *Faculty research:* Applied microeconomics, health economics, industrial organization, development economics, public economics. *Unit head:* Dr. Bradley Kamp, Associate Professor and Chairperson, 813-974-6549, Fax: 813-974-6510, E-mail: bkamp@usf.edu. *Application contact:* Dr. Michael Loewy, Associate Professor and Graduate Director, 813-974-6532, Fax: 813-974-6510, E-mail: mloewy@usf.edu. Website: http://www.economics.usf.edu

**The University of Tennessee,** Graduate School, College of Arts and Sciences, Department of Sociology, Knoxville, TN 37996. Offers criminology (MA, PhD); energy, environment, and resource policy (MA, PhD); political economy (MA, PhD). *Program availability:* Part-time. *Degree requirements:* For master's, thesis or alternative; for doctorate, thesis/dissertation. *Entrance requirements:* For master's, GRE General Test, minimum GPA of 3.0; for doctorate, GRE General Test, minimum GPA of 3.5. Additional exam requirements/recommendations for international students: Required—TOEFL. Electronic applications accepted.

**The University of Tennessee,** Graduate School, College of Business Administration, Department of Economics, Knoxville, TN 37996. Offers MA, PhD. *Degree requirements:* For master's, thesis or alternative; for doctorate, thesis/dissertation. *Entrance requirements:* For master's and doctorate, GRE General Test or GMAT, minimum GPA of 2.7. Additional exam requirements/recommendations for international students: Required—TOEFL. Electronic applications accepted.

## Economics

**The University of Texas at Arlington,** Graduate School, College of Business, Economics Department, Arlington, TX 76019. Offers MA. *Program availability:* Part-time, evening/weekend. *Degree requirements:* For master's, thesis optional. *Entrance requirements:* For master's, GMAT or GRE. Additional exam requirements/recommendations for international students: Required—TOEFL (minimum score 550 paper-based; 79 iBT). *Application deadline:* For fall admission, 6/1 for domestic students, 4/1 for international students; for spring admission, 10/15 for domestic students, 9/15 for international students. Applications are processed on a rolling basis. Application fee: $40 ($70 for international students). *Financial support:* Teaching assistantships, career-related internships or fieldwork, scholarships/grants, and unspecified assistantships available. Support available to part-time students. Financial award application deadline: 6/1; financial award applicants required to submit FAFSA. *Unit head:* Dr. Roger Meiners, Chair, 817-272-3061, Fax: 817-272-2073, E-mail: meiners@uta.edu. *Application contact:* Dr. Tim Wunder, Graduate Advisor, 817-272-3253, Fax: 817-272-3145, E-mail: tim.wunder@uta.edu.
Website: http://wweb.uta.edu/economics/

**The University of Texas at Austin,** Graduate School, College of Liberal Arts, Department of Economics, Austin, TX 78712-1111. Offers MA, MS Econ, PhD. *Program availability:* Part-time. *Degree requirements:* For master's, thesis; for doctorate, comprehensive exam, thesis/dissertation. *Entrance requirements:* For master's and doctorate, GRE General Test, minimum GPA of 3.5 (based on upper-division undergraduate and graduate course work). Additional exam requirements/recommendations for international students: Required—TOEFL. Electronic applications accepted. *Faculty research:* Industrial organization, game theory, monetary economics, labor economics, public economics.

**The University of Texas at Dallas,** School of Economic, Political and Policy Sciences, Program in Economics, Richardson, TX 75080. Offers MS, PhD. *Program availability:* Part-time, evening/weekend. *Faculty:* 13 full-time (4 women), 1 part-time/adjunct (0 women). *Students:* 49 full-time (13 women), 9 part-time (3 women); includes 16 minority (6 Black or African American, non-Hispanic/Latino; 4 Asian, non-Hispanic/Latino; 3 Hispanic/Latino; 3 Two or more races, non-Hispanic/Latino), 33 international. Average age 30. 86 applicants, 49% accepted, 17 enrolled. In 2016, 15 master's, 3 doctorates awarded. *Degree requirements:* For master's, internship; for doctorate, thesis/dissertation. *Entrance requirements:* For master's, GRE (minimum combined verbal and quantitative score of 1200), minimum GPA of 3.0 in upper-level course work in field; for doctorate, GRE (minimum combined verbal and quantitative score of 1200, writing 4.5), minimum GPA of 3.25 in upper-level and graduate course work in field. Additional exam requirements/recommendations for international students: Required—TOEFL (minimum score 550 paper-based). *Application deadline:* For fall admission, 7/15 for domestic students, 5/1 priority date for international students; for spring admission, 11/15 for domestic students, 9/1 priority date for international students. Applications are processed on a rolling basis. Application fee: $50 ($100 for international students). Electronic applications accepted. *Expenses:* Tuition, state resident: full-time $12,418; part-time $690 per semester hour. Tuition, nonresident: full-time $24,150; part-time $1342 per semester hour. Tuition and fees vary according to course load. *Financial support:* In 2016–17, 34 students received support, including 3 research assistantships with partial tuition reimbursements available (averaging $19,158 per year), 16 teaching assistantships with partial tuition reimbursements available (averaging $13,100 per year); career-related internships or fieldwork, Federal Work-Study, institutionally sponsored loans, scholarships/grants, and unspecified assistantships also available. Support available to part-time students. Financial award application deadline: 4/30; financial award applicants required to submit FAFSA. *Faculty research:* Bargaining and negotiation, experimental economics, judgment and decision-making, game theory, terrorism. *Unit head:* Dr. Daniel G. Arce, Program Head, 972-883-6857, Fax: 972-883-2735, E-mail: darce@utdallas.edu. *Application contact:* Judy Du, Graduate Program Administrator, 972-883-4964, Fax: 972-883-2735, E-mail: judy.du@utdallas.edu.
Website: http://www.utdallas.edu/epps/economics/

**The University of Texas at Dallas,** School of Economic, Political and Policy Sciences, Program in Public Policy and Political Economy, Richardson, TX 75080. Offers international political economy (MS); public policy (MPP); public policy and political economy (PhD); social data analytics and research (MS). *Program availability:* Part-time, evening/weekend. *Faculty:* 24 full-time (2 women), 2 part-time/adjunct (1 woman). *Students:* 47 full-time (24 women), 30 part-time (14 women); includes 20 minority (4 Black or African American, non-Hispanic/Latino; 1 American Indian or Alaska Native, non-Hispanic/Latino; 3 Asian, non-Hispanic/Latino; 11 Hispanic/Latino; 1 Two or more races, non-Hispanic/Latino), 25 international. Average age 35. 55 applicants, 55% accepted, 12 enrolled. In 2016, 13 master's, 9 doctorates awarded. *Degree requirements:* For doctorate, thesis/dissertation. *Entrance requirements:* For master's and doctorate, GRE General Test, minimum GPA of 3.0 in upper-level course work in field. Additional exam requirements/recommendations for international students: Required—TOEFL (minimum score 550 paper-based). *Application deadline:* For fall admission, 7/15 for domestic students, 5/1 priority date for international students; for spring admission, 11/15 for domestic students, 9/1 priority date for international students. Applications are processed on a rolling basis. Application fee: $50 ($100 for international students). Electronic applications accepted. *Expenses:* Tuition, state resident: full-time $12,418; part-time $690 per semester hour. Tuition, nonresident: full-time $24,150; part-time $1342 per semester hour. Tuition and fees vary according to course load. *Financial support:* In 2016–17, 45 students received support, including 13 research assistantships with partial tuition reimbursements available (averaging $18,538 per year), 14 teaching assistantships with partial tuition reimbursements available (averaging $13,100 per year); career-related internships or fieldwork, Federal Work-Study, institutionally sponsored loans, scholarships/grants, and unspecified assistantships also available. Support available to part-time students. Financial award application deadline: 4/30; financial award applicants required to submit FAFSA. *Faculty research:* Ethnicity, community and local public good provision; community mental health policy; Texas Schools Project; biological and chemical arms control; cross-disciplinary applications of quantitative methodology. *Unit head:* Dr. Jennifer Holmes, Program Head, 972-883-6843, Fax: 972-883-6297, E-mail: jholmes@utdallas.edu. *Application contact:* Betsy Albritton, Graduate Program Administrator, 972-883-6406, Fax: 972-883-6297, E-mail: betsy.albritton@utdallas.edu.
Website: http://www.utdallas.edu/epps/public-policy-and-political-economy/

**The University of Texas at El Paso,** Graduate School, College of Business Administration, Department of Economics and Finance, El Paso, TX 79968-0001. Offers economics (MS). *Program availability:* Part-time, evening/weekend. *Degree requirements:* For master's, thesis optional, at least 24 credit hours with minimum cumulative GPA of 3.0. *Entrance requirements:* For master's, GRE, undergraduate degree from accredited college or university. Additional exam requirements/recommendations for international students: Required—TOEFL. Electronic applications accepted. *Faculty research:* Border economics, public utility economics, urban economics, international economics, applied econometrics.

**The University of Texas at San Antonio,** College of Business, Department of Economics, San Antonio, TX 78249-0617. Offers business economics (MBA); economics (MA). *Program availability:* Part-time, evening/weekend. *Faculty:* 9 full-time

(3 women), 1 part-time/adjunct (0 women). *Students:* 23 full-time (2 women), 15 part-time (5 women); includes 15 minority (1 Black or African American, non-Hispanic/Latino; 1 Asian, non-Hispanic/Latino; 11 Hispanic/Latino; 2 Two or more races, non-Hispanic/Latino), 3 international. Average age 29. 32 applicants, 78% accepted, 18 enrolled. In 2016, 6 master's awarded. *Degree requirements:* For master's, comprehensive exam, thesis optional. *Entrance requirements:* For master's, GMAT or GRE, transcripts, statement of purpose. Additional exam requirements/recommendations for international students: Required—TOEFL (minimum score 550 paper-based; 79 iBT), IELTS (minimum score 6.5). *Application deadline:* For fall admission, 7/1 for domestic students, 4/1 for international students; for spring admission, 11/1 for domestic students, 9/1 for international students. Applications are processed on a rolling basis. Application fee: $45 ($80 for international students). Electronic applications accepted. *Faculty research:* Game theory, international trade, monetary policy, panel data, exchange and interest rates. *Total annual research expenditures:* $223,875. *Unit head:* Dr. Melody Lo, Department Chair, 210-458-4315, Fax: 210-458-5837, E-mail: melody.lo@utsa.edu. *Application contact:* Katherine Pope, Economics Graduate Advisor of Record, 210-458-7316, Fax: 210-458-4398, E-mail: katherine.pope@utsa.edu.
Website: http://business.utsa.edu/economics/

**The University of Toledo,** College of Graduate Studies, College of Languages, Literature and Social Sciences, Department of Economics, Toledo, OH 43606-3390. Offers applied econometric specialization (MA); economics (MA). *Program availability:* Part-time. *Degree requirements:* For master's, comprehensive exam, paper or thesis. *Entrance requirements:* For master's, GRE General Test, minimum cumulative GPA of 2.7 on all previous academic work, three letters of recommendation, statement of purpose, transcripts from all prior institutions attended. Additional exam requirements/recommendations for international students: Required—TOEFL (minimum score 550 paper-based; 80 iBT). Electronic applications accepted. *Faculty research:* Economic development.

**The University of Toledo,** College of Graduate Studies, Judith Herb College of Education, Department of Curriculum and Instruction, Toledo, OH 43606-3390. Offers art education (ME); career and technical education (ME, Ed S); curriculum and instruction (ME, PhD, Ed S); early childhood education (Ed S); education and anthropology (MAE); education and biology (MES); education and chemistry (MES); education and classics (MAE); education and economics (MAE); education and English (MAE); education and French (MAE); education and geology (MES); education and German (MAE); education and history (MAE); education and mathematics (MAE, MES); education and physics (MES); education and political science (MAE); education and sociology (MAE); education and Spanish (MAE); educational media (PhD); educational technology (ME); educational technology: virtual educator (Certificate); elementary education (PhD); English as a second language (MAE); gifted and talented education (PhD); middle childhood education (ME); secondary education (ME, PhD); special education (PhD). *Accreditation:* NCATE. *Program availability:* Part-time, evening/weekend. *Degree requirements:* For master's, comprehensive exam, thesis or alternative; for doctorate, comprehensive exam, thesis/dissertation; for other advanced degree, thesis optional. *Entrance requirements:* For master's, doctorate, and other advanced degree, minimum cumulative GPA of 2.7 for all previous academic work, letters of recommendation. Additional exam requirements/recommendations for international students: Required—TOEFL (minimum score 550 paper-based; 80 iBT). Electronic applications accepted.

**University of Toronto,** School of Graduate Studies, Faculty of Arts and Science, Department of Economics, Toronto, ON M5S 1A1, Canada. Offers economics (MA, PhD); financial economics (MFE); JD/MA; JD/PhD. *Program availability:* Part-time. *Degree requirements:* For doctorate, comprehensive exam, thesis/dissertation. *Entrance requirements:* For master's, GRE (for applicants without a degree from a Canadian university), minimum B average in final year, 2 letters of reference; for doctorate, GRE (for applicants without a degree from a Canadian university), master's degree in economics, minimum B+ average, 3 letters of reference. Additional exam requirements/recommendations for international students: Required—TOEFL (minimum 580 paper-based; 93 iBT), IELTS (minimum score 7), TWE (minimum score 5), or Michigan English Language Assessment Battery (minimum score 85). Electronic applications accepted.

**University of Utah,** Graduate School, College of Social and Behavioral Science, Department of Economics, Salt Lake City, UT 84112. Offers econometrics (M Stat); economics (M Phil, MA, MS, PhD). *Faculty:* 16 full-time (4 women), 7 part-time/adjunct (1 woman). *Students:* 19 full-time (5 women), 3 part-time (1 woman); includes 15 minority (2 Black or African American, non-Hispanic/Latino; 5 Asian, non-Hispanic/Latino; 7 Hispanic/Latino; 1 Two or more races, non-Hispanic/Latino), 36 international. Average age 33. 106 applicants, 28% accepted, 12 enrolled. In 2016, 17 master's, 7 doctorates awarded. Terminal master's awarded for partial completion of doctoral program. *Degree requirements:* For master's, thesis or alternative, exam, oral presentation, research project; for doctorate, comprehensive exam, thesis/dissertation, qualifying exams. *Entrance requirements:* For master's, GRE General Test; GRE Subject Test (for M Stat), undergraduate course work in economics, minimum GPA of 3.0; for doctorate, GRE General Test, minimum GPA of 3.0, course work in calculus and statistics. Additional exam requirements/recommendations for international students: Required—TOEFL (minimum score 500 paper-based; 61 iBT) or IELTS (minimum score 6). *Application deadline:* For fall admission, 2/1 priority date for domestic and international students. Application fee: $55 ($65 for international students). Electronic applications accepted. *Expenses:* Tuition, state resident: full-time $7011; part-time $3918.24 per credit hour. Tuition, nonresident: full-time $22,154; part-time $11,665.42 per credit hour. *Financial support:* In 2016–17, 27 students received support, including 4 fellowships with full tuition reimbursements available (averaging $14,500 per year), 5 research assistantships (averaging $2,000 per year), 32 teaching assistantships with full tuition reimbursements available (averaging $14,500 per year); scholarships/grants, traineeships, health care benefits, tuition waivers, and unspecified assistantships also available. Financial award application deadline: 2/1. *Faculty research:* Globalization, inequality, sustainability, development, history. *Total annual research expenditures:* $162,736. *Unit head:* Dr. Thomas Maloney, Chair, 801-581-7481, E-mail: maloney@economics.utah.edu. *Application contact:* Nicole O'Shea, Academic Advisor, 801-581-7481, E-mail: grad-advising@economics.utah.edu.
Website: http://www.economics.utah.edu

**University of Utah,** Graduate School, Interdepartmental Program in Statistics, Salt Lake City, UT 84112-1107. Offers biostatistics (M Stat); econometrics (M Stat); educational psychology (M Stat); mathematics (M Stat); sociology (M Stat). *Program availability:* Part-time. *Students:* 30 full-time (9 women), 29 part-time (8 women); includes 10 minority (7 Asian, non-Hispanic/Latino; 3 Hispanic/Latino), 12 international. Average age 31. 50 applicants, 70% accepted, 27 enrolled. In 2016, 20 master's awarded. *Degree requirements:* For master's, comprehensive exam (for some programs), projects. *Entrance requirements:* For master's, GRE General Test (for all but biostatistics); GRE Subject Test (for mathematics), minimum GPA of 3.0; course work in calculus, matrix theory, statistics. Additional exam requirements/recommendations for international students: Required—TOEFL (minimum score 500 paper-based; 61 iBT). *Application deadline:* For fall admission, 7/1 for domestic students, 4/1 for international

students. Applications are processed on a rolling basis. Application fee: $55 ($65 for international students). Electronic applications accepted. *Expenses:* Tuition, state resident: full-time $7011; part-time $3918.24 per credit hour. Tuition, nonresident: full-time $22,154; part-time $11,665.42 per credit hour. *Financial support:* In 2016–17, 10 students received support, including 10 research assistantships with tuition reimbursements available (averaging $1,000 per year); career-related internships or fieldwork, scholarships/grants, and unspecified assistantships also available. *Faculty research:* Biostatistics, sociology, economics, educational psychology, mathematics. *Unit head:* Xiaoming Sheng, Chair, University Statistics Committee, 801-213-3729, E-mail: xiaoming.sheng@utah.edu. *Application contact:* Laura Egbert, Coordinator, 801-585-6853, E-mail: laura.egbert@utah.edu.
Website: http://www.mstat.utah.edu

**University of Victoria,** Faculty of Graduate Studies, Faculty of Social Sciences, Department of Economics, Victoria, BC V8W 2Y2, Canada. Offers MA, PhD. *Program availability:* Part-time. *Degree requirements:* For master's, comprehensive exam (for some programs), thesis optional; for doctorate, comprehensive exam, thesis/dissertation, candidacy exam. *Entrance requirements:* For master's and doctorate, GRE. Additional exam requirements/recommendations for international students: Required—TOEFL (minimum score 575 paper-based), IELTS (minimum score 7). Electronic applications accepted. *Faculty research:* Industrial organization, cost/benefit, applied economics, econometrics, airline economics, health economics.

**University of Virginia,** College and Graduate School of Arts and Sciences, Department of Economics, Charlottesville, VA 22903. Offers MA, PhD. *Faculty:* 31 full-time (4 women), 3 part-time/adjunct (1 woman). *Students:* 88 full-time (37 women); includes 4 minority (2 Asian, non-Hispanic/Latino; 2 Two or more races, non-Hispanic/Latino), 58 international. Average age 27. 482 applicants, 10% accepted, 20 enrolled. In 2016, 20 master's, 8 doctorates awarded. *Degree requirements:* For master's, comprehensive exam (for some programs), thesis (for some programs), thesis or comprehensive exam; for doctorate, comprehensive exam, thesis/dissertation. *Entrance requirements:* For master's and doctorate, GRE General Test. Additional exam requirements/recommendations for international students: Required—TOEFL (minimum score 600 paper-based; 90 iBT), IELTS (minimum score 7). *Application deadline:* For fall admission, 4/1 for domestic and international students. Applications are processed on a rolling basis. Application fee: $60. Electronic applications accepted. *Expenses:* Tuition, state resident: full-time $15,026; part-time $834 per credit hour. Tuition, nonresident: full-time $25,168; part-time $1378 per credit hour. *Required fees:* $2654. *Financial support:* Fellowships, research assistantships, teaching assistantships, and tuition waivers (full and partial) available. Financial award application deadline: 2/1; financial award applicants required to submit FAFSA. *Faculty research:* Macroeconomics, public economics, labor, industrial organization, economic history. *Unit head:* John Pepper, Chair, 434-924-3177, Fax: 434-982-2904, E-mail: econ@virginia.edu. *Application contact:* Sheetal Sekhri, Graduate Director, 434-924-3177, Fax: 434-982-2904, E-mail: ss5mj@virginia.edu.
Website: http://economics.virginia.edu/

**University of Washington,** Graduate School, College of Arts and Sciences, Department of Economics, Seattle, WA 98195. Offers PhD. Terminal master's awarded for partial completion of doctoral program. *Degree requirements:* For doctorate, comprehensive exam, thesis/dissertation. *Entrance requirements:* For doctorate, GRE General Test, minimum GPA of 3.0. Additional exam requirements/recommendations for international students: Required—TOEFL. Electronic applications accepted. *Faculty research:* Microeconomic theory; macroeconomic theory; econometrics; natural resource economics; international, development, and industrial organization.

**University of Washington,** Graduate School, School of Public Health, Department of Health Services, Seattle, WA 98195. Offers clinical research (MS); community-oriented public health practice (MPH); evaluative sciences and statistics (PhD); health behavior and social determinants of health (PhD); health economics (PhD); health informatics and health information management (MHIHIM); health services (MS, PhD); health services administration (EMHA, MHA); health systems and policy (MPH); health systems research (PhD); maternal and child health (MPH); social and behavioral sciences (MPH); JD/MHA; MHA/MBA; MHA/MD; MHA/MPA; MPH/JD; MPH/MD; MPH/MN; MPH/MPA; MPH/MS; MPH/MSD; MPH/MSW; MPH/PhD. *Program availability:* Online learning. Terminal master's awarded for partial completion of doctoral program. *Degree requirements:* For master's, thesis (for some programs), practicum (MPH); for doctorate, comprehensive exam, thesis/dissertation. *Entrance requirements:* For master's and doctorate, GRE General Test, minimum GPA of 3.0. Additional exam requirements/recommendations for international students: Required—TOEFL (minimum score 580 paper-based; 92 iBT), IELTS (minimum score 7). Electronic applications accepted. *Expenses:* Contact institution. *Faculty research:* Public health practice, health promotion and disease prevention, maternal and child health, organizational behavior and culture, health policy.

**University of Waterloo,** Graduate Studies, Faculty of Arts, Department of Economics, Waterloo, ON N2L 3G1, Canada. Offers MA, PhD. *Program availability:* Part-time. *Entrance requirements:* For master's, honors degree, minimum B average. Additional exam requirements/recommendations for international students: Required—TOEFL, IELTS, PTE. Electronic applications accepted. *Faculty research:* Applied microeconomics, applied macroeconomics, public finance, international trade and finance, wage inflation and consumer problems.

**The University of Western Ontario,** Faculty of Graduate Studies, Social Sciences Division, Department of Economics, London, ON N6A 5B8, Canada. Offers MA, PhD. *Degree requirements:* For doctorate, thesis/dissertation. *Entrance requirements:* For master's, GRE, honours BA with B+ average. Additional exam requirements/recommendations for international students: Required—TOEFL.

**University of Windsor,** Faculty of Graduate Studies, Faculty of Science, Department of Economics, Windsor, ON N9B 3P4, Canada. Offers MA. *Program availability:* Part-time. *Degree requirements:* For master's, thesis or alternative. *Entrance requirements:* For master's, minimum B average. Additional exam requirements/recommendations for international students: Required—TOEFL (minimum score 560 paper-based). Electronic applications accepted. *Faculty research:* International trade, economic growth, microeconomic theory.

**University of Wisconsin–Madison,** Graduate School, College of Letters and Science, Department of Economics, Madison, WI 53706-1380. Offers PhD. *Degree requirements:* For doctorate, thesis/dissertation. *Entrance requirements:* For doctorate, GRE General Test, 3 semesters of course work in calculus, 1 semester of course work in algebra and mathematics/statistics. Electronic applications accepted.

**University of Wisconsin–Milwaukee,** Graduate School, College of Letters and Science, Department of Economics, Milwaukee, WI 53201-0413. Offers economics (MA, PhD), including advanced econometrics, development econometrics, industrial economics, international economics, labor economics, monetary theory and policy. *Students:* 40 full-time (10 women), 10 part-time (2 women); includes 4 minority (1 Black or African American, non-Hispanic/Latino; 3 Asian, non-Hispanic/Latino), 29 international. Average age 31. 77 applicants, 53% accepted, 16 enrolled. In 2016, 13 master's, 6 doctorates awarded. *Degree requirements:* For master's, comprehensive

exam; for doctorate, comprehensive exam, thesis/dissertation. *Entrance requirements:* For master's, GRE General Test; for doctorate, GRE General Test, GRE Subject Test, minimum GPA 3.0. Additional exam requirements/recommendations for international students: Required—TOEFL (minimum score 550 paper-based; 79 iBT), IELTS (minimum score 6.5). *Application deadline:* For fall admission, 1/1 priority date for domestic students; for spring admission, 9/1 for domestic students. Applications are processed on a rolling basis. Application fee: $56 ($96 for international students). *Financial support:* In 2016–17, 28 teaching assistantships were awarded; career-related internships or fieldwork and unspecified assistantships also available. Support available to part-time students. Financial award application deadline: 4/15; financial award applicants required to submit FAFSA. *Unit head:* Scott J. Adams, Department Chair, 414-229-4811, E-mail: sjadams@uwm.edu. *Application contact:* General Information Contact, 414-229-4982, Fax: 414-229-6967, E-mail: gradschool@uwm.edu.
Website: https://www.uwm.edu/economics/

**University of Wyoming,** College of Business, Department of Economics and Finance, Program in Economics, Laramie, WY 82071. Offers MS, PhD. *Program availability:* Part-time. *Degree requirements:* For master's, thesis; for doctorate, comprehensive exam, thesis/dissertation. *Entrance requirements:* For master's, GRE General Test or GMAT, minimum GPA of 3.0; for doctorate, GRE General Test, minimum GPA of 3.0. Additional exam requirements/recommendations for international students: Required—TOEFL (minimum score 525 paper-based). *Faculty research:* Resource and environmental economics, industrial organization, regulation.

**University of Wyoming,** College of Business, Department of Economics and Finance, Program in Economics and Finance, Laramie, WY 82071. Offers MS. *Degree requirements:* For master's, thesis. *Entrance requirements:* For master's, GRE, minimum GPA of 3.0. Additional exam requirements/recommendations for international students: Required—TOEFL (minimum score 540 paper-based; 76 iBT). *Faculty research:* Financial economics.

**Utah State University,** School of Graduate Studies, College of Business and College of Agriculture, Department of Economics, Logan, UT 84322. Offers applied economics (MS); economics (MA, MS, PhD). Terminal master's awarded for partial completion of doctoral program. *Degree requirements:* For master's, thesis (for some programs); for doctorate, comprehensive exam, thesis/dissertation. *Entrance requirements:* For master's, GRE General Test, GMAT, minimum GPA of 3.0, TOEFL for international; for doctorate, GRE General Test, minimum GPA of 3.0, TOEFL. Additional exam requirements/recommendations for international students: Required—TOEFL. Electronic applications accepted. *Faculty research:* Resource economics, economic theory, international trade, industrial organization, development.

**Vanderbilt University,** Department of Economics, Nashville, TN 37240-1001. Offers economic development (MA); economics (PhD). *Faculty:* 37 full-time (5 women). *Students:* 114 full-time (44 women); includes 11 minority (2 Black or African American, non-Hispanic/Latino; 2 Asian, non-Hispanic/Latino; 2 Hispanic/Latino; 5 Two or more races, non-Hispanic/Latino), 71 international. Average age 26. 621 applicants, 33% accepted, 46 enrolled. In 2016, 39 master's, 7 doctorates awarded. Terminal master's awarded for partial completion of doctoral program. *Degree requirements:* For master's, thesis or alternative; for doctorate, thesis/dissertation, final and qualifying exams. *Entrance requirements:* For master's and doctorate, GRE General Test, GRE Subject Test (recommended). Additional exam requirements/recommendations for international students: Required—TOEFL (minimum score 570 paper-based; 88 iBT). *Application deadline:* For fall admission, 1/15 for domestic and international students; for spring admission, 11/1 for domestic students. Applications are processed on a rolling basis. Electronic applications accepted. *Expenses:* Tuition: Part-time $1854 per credit hour. *Financial support:* Fellowships with tuition reimbursements, teaching assistantships with tuition reimbursements, career-related internships or fieldwork, Federal Work-Study, institutionally sponsored loans, scholarships/grants, and health care benefits available. Financial award application deadline: 1/15; financial award applicants required to submit CSS PROFILE or FAFSA. *Faculty research:* Economic theory, applied fields, developmental economics, environmental economics, health economics and policy. *Unit head:* Dr. Eric Bond, Chair, 615-322-2871, Fax: 615-343-8495, E-mail: k.saggi@vanderbilt.edu. *Application contact:* Jennifer Reinganum, Director of Graduate Studies, 615-322-2871, Fax: 615-343-8495, E-mail: jennifer.f.reinganum@vanderbilt.edu.
Website: http://www.vanderbilt.edu/econ/

**Vanderbilt University,** Vanderbilt Law School, Nashville, TN 37203. Offers law (LL M, JD); law and economics (PhD); JD/M Div; JD/MA; JD/MBA; JD/MD; JD/MPP; JD/MTS; JD/PhD; LL M/MA. *Accreditation:* ABA. *Faculty:* 37 full-time (14 women), 51 part-time/adjunct (21 women). *Students:* 572 full-time (292 women); includes 128 minority (60 Black or African American, non-Hispanic/Latino; 3 American Indian or Alaska Native, non-Hispanic/Latino; 25 Asian, non-Hispanic/Latino; 34 Hispanic/Latino; 6 Two or more races, non-Hispanic/Latino), 17 international. Average age 23. 4,380 applicants, 32% accepted, 204 enrolled. In 2016, 35 master's, 195 doctorates awarded. *Degree requirements:* For doctorate, comprehensive exam (for some programs), thesis/dissertation (for some programs), 72 hours of coursework and research (for PhD). *Entrance requirements:* For master's, foreign law degree; for doctorate, GRE (for PhD), LSAT, advanced undergraduate economics (for PhD). Additional exam requirements/recommendations for international students: Required—TOEFL. *Application deadline:* For fall admission, 4/1 for domestic and international students. Applications are processed on a rolling basis. Application fee: $50. Electronic applications accepted. *Expenses:* Contact institution. *Financial support:* In 2016–17, 486 students received support. Career-related internships or fieldwork, Federal Work-Study, institutionally sponsored loans, scholarships/grants, and health care benefits available. Financial award application deadline: 2/15; financial award applicants required to submit FAFSA. *Unit head:* G. Todd Morton, Assistant Dean of Admissions, 615-322-6452, Fax: 615-322-1531, E-mail: admissions@law.vanderbilt.edu. *Application contact:* Admissions Office, 615-322-6452, Fax: 615-322-1531, E-mail: admissions@law.vanderbilt.edu.
Website: http://law.vanderbilt.edu/

**Virginia Commonwealth University,** Graduate School, School of Business, Program in Economics, Richmond, VA 23284-9005. Offers MA. *Degree requirements:* For master's, thesis optional. *Entrance requirements:* For master's, GRE General Test (preferred) or GMAT. Additional exam requirements/recommendations for international students: Required—TOEFL (minimum score 600 paper-based; 100 iBT). *Application deadline:* For fall admission, 7/1 for domestic students; for spring admission, 11/1 for domestic students. Applications are processed on a rolling basis. Application fee: $50. Electronic applications accepted. *Financial support:* Fellowships, research assistantships, teaching assistantships, Federal Work-Study, institutionally sponsored loans, and tuition waivers (full and partial) available. Financial award application deadline: 3/15; financial award applicants required to submit FAFSA. *Unit head:* Dr. Edward L. Millner, Chair, 804-828-1717, Fax: 804-828-1719, E-mail: elmillne@vcu.edu. *Application contact:* Colleen A. Davis, Graduate Program Director, 804-828-4622, E-mail: androvichcm@vcu.edu.
Website: http://www.business.vcu.edu/graduate.html

**Virginia Polytechnic Institute and State University,** Graduate School, College of Science, Blacksburg, VA 24061. Offers biological sciences (MS, PhD); biomedical

## Economics

technology development and management (MS); chemistry (MS, PhD); data analysis and applied statistics (MA); economics (MA, PhD); geosciences (MS, PhD); mathematics (MS, PhD); physics (MS, PhD); psychology (MS, PhD); statistics (MS, PhD). *Faculty:* 299 full-time (92 women), 1 part-time/adjunct (0 women). *Students:* 567 full-time (222 women), 47 part-time (19 women); includes 66 minority (14 Black or African American, non-Hispanic/Latino; 12 Asian, non-Hispanic/Latino; 29 Hispanic/Latino; 11 Two or more races, non-Hispanic/Latino), 247 international. Average age 27. 956 applicants, 17% accepted, 118 enrolled. In 2016, 75 master's, 71 doctorates awarded. *Degree requirements:* For master's, comprehensive exam (for some programs), thesis (for some programs); for doctorate, comprehensive exam (for some programs), thesis/dissertation (for some programs). *Entrance requirements:* For master's and doctorate, GRE/GMAT. Additional exam requirements/recommendations for international students: Required—TOEFL (minimum score 80 iBT). *Application deadline:* For fall admission, 8/1 for domestic students, 4/1 for international students; for spring admission, 1/1 for domestic students, 9/1 for international students. Applications are processed on a rolling basis. Application fee: $75. Electronic applications accepted. *Expenses:* Tuition, state resident: full-time $12,467; part-time $692.50 per credit hour. Tuition, nonresident: full-time $25,095; part-time $1394.25 per credit hour. *Required fees:* $2669; $491.50 per semester. Tuition and fees vary according to course load, campus/location and program. *Financial support:* In 2016–17, 156 research assistantships with full tuition reimbursements (averaging $21,863 per year), 379 teaching assistantships with full tuition reimbursements (averaging $18,980 per year) were awarded. Financial award application deadline: 3/1; financial award applicants required to submit FAFSA. *Total annual research expenditures:* $22.3 million. *Unit head:* Dr. Sally C. Morton, Dean, 540-231-5422, Fax: 540-231-3380, E-mail: scmorton@vt.edu. *Application contact:* Teresa Price, Executive Assistant to the Dean and Grants Specialist, 540-231-6394, Fax: 540-231-3380, E-mail: tfprice@vt.edu. Website: http://www.science.vt.edu/

**Virginia State University,** College of Graduate Studies, College of Humanities and Social Sciences, Department of Political Science, Public Administration and Economics, Petersburg, VA 23806-0001. Offers economics (MA). *Degree requirements:* For master's, thesis optional. *Entrance requirements:* For master's, GRE General Test.

**Washington State University,** College of Agricultural, Human, and Natural Resource Sciences, School of Economic Sciences, Pullman, WA 99164-6210. Offers agricultural economics (PhD); economics (PhD). Programs offered at the Pullman campus. Terminal master's awarded for partial completion of doctoral program. *Degree requirements:* For master's, comprehensive exam (for some programs), thesis (for some programs), oral exam; for doctorate, comprehensive exam, thesis/dissertation, oral exam, written exam, qualifying exams. *Entrance requirements:* For master's and doctorate, GRE, minimum GPA of 3.0, 3 letters of recommendation. Additional exam requirements/recommendations for international students: Required—TOEFL (minimum score 550 paper-based). Electronic applications accepted. *Faculty research:* Agricultural economics, econometrics, natural resource and environmental economics, industrial organization, health economics.

**Washington University in St. Louis,** The Graduate School, Department of Economics, St. Louis, MO 63130-4899. Offers PhD. Terminal master's awarded for partial completion of doctoral program. *Degree requirements:* For doctorate, one foreign language, thesis/dissertation. *Entrance requirements:* For doctorate, GRE General Test. Additional exam requirements/recommendations for international students: Required—TOEFL. Electronic applications accepted. *Faculty research:* Economic theory; industrial organization; political economy; public economics; macroeconomics; public finance, development economics.

**Wayne State University,** College of Liberal Arts and Sciences, Department of Economics, Detroit, MI 48202. Offers advanced macroeconomics (PhD); econometrics (MA); health economics (MA, PhD); industrial organization (MA, PhD); international economics (MA, PhD); labor and human resources (MA); labor economics (PhD); macroeconomics (MA); microeconomics (MA); JD/MA. *Faculty:* 13. *Students:* 38 full-time (11 women), 7 part-time (3 women); includes 8 minority (5 Black or African American, non-Hispanic/Latino; 1 Asian, non-Hispanic/Latino; 1 Hispanic/Latino; 1 Two or more races, non-Hispanic/Latino), 22 international. Average age 33. 97 applicants, 36% accepted, 8 enrolled. In 2016, 10 master's, 7 doctorates awarded. *Degree requirements:* For master's, comprehensive exam; for doctorate, comprehensive exam, thesis/dissertation, oral examination on research, completion of course work in quantitative methods, final lecture. *Entrance requirements:* For master's, minimum upper-division GPA of 3.0; prior coursework in intermediate microeconomic and macroeconomic theory, statistics, and elementary calculus; for doctorate, GRE, minimum upper-division GPA of 3.0, prior coursework in intermediate microeconomic and macroeconomic theory, statistics, two courses in calculus, three letters of recommendation from officials or teaching staff at institution(s) most recently attended, statement of purpose. Additional exam requirements/recommendations for international students: Required—TOEFL (minimum score 550 paper-based; 79 iBT), TWE (minimum score 5.5), Michigan English Language Assessment Battery (minimum score 85); Recommended—IELTS (minimum score 6.5). *Application deadline:* For fall admission, 5/1 for domestic and international students; for winter admission, 10/1 priority date for domestic students, 9/1 priority date for international students; for spring admission, 1/1 priority date for domestic and international students. Applications are processed on a rolling basis. Application fee: $50. Electronic applications accepted. *Expenses:* $16,503 per year resident tuition and fees, $33,697 per year non-resident tuition and fees. *Financial support:* In 2016–17, 26 students received support, including 2 fellowships with tuition reimbursements available (averaging $16,000 per year), 17 teaching assistantships with tuition reimbursements available (averaging $17,994 per year); research assistantships with tuition reimbursements available, scholarships/grants, health care benefits, and unspecified assistantships also available. Support available to part-time students. Financial award applicants required to submit FAFSA. *Faculty research:* Health economics, international economics, macro economics, urban and labor economics, econometrics. *Unit head:* Dr. Stephen J. Spurr, Professor and Chair, 313-577-3232, Fax: 313-577-9564, E-mail: sspurr@wayne.edu. *Application contact:* Dr. Allen Charles Goodman, Graduate Director, 313-577-3235, Fax: 313-577-9564, E-mail: allen.goodman@wayne.edu.
Website: http://clas.wayne.edu/economics/

**Western Illinois University,** School of Graduate Studies, College of Business and Technology, Department of Economics and Decision Sciences, Program in Economics, Macomb, IL 61455-1390. Offers MA. *Students:* 23 full-time (8 women), 2 part-time (1 woman); includes 9 minority (4 Black or African American, non-Hispanic/Latino; 3 Asian, non-Hispanic/Latino; 1 Hispanic/Latino; 1 Two or more races, non-Hispanic/Latino), 11 international. Average age 31. 33 applicants, 58% accepted, 11 enrolled. In 2016, 12 master's awarded. *Application deadline:* Applications are processed on a rolling basis. Application fee: $30. Electronic applications accepted. *Financial support:* In 2016–17, 20 students received support. Unspecified assistantships available. *Unit head:* Dr. Tej Kaul, Chairperson, 309-298-1153. *Application contact:* Dr. Nancy Parsons, Assistant Director of Graduate Studies, 309-298-1806, Fax: 309-298-2345, E-mail: grad-office@wiu.edu.
Website: http://www.wiu.edu/cbt/eds/graduate-economics.php

**Western Michigan University,** Graduate College, College of Arts and Sciences, Department of Economics, Kalamazoo, MI 49008. Offers applied economics (MA, PhD). *Degree requirements:* For master's, thesis; for doctorate, thesis/dissertation.

**West Texas A&M University,** College of Business, Department of Accounting, Economics and Finance, Program in Finance and Economics, Canyon, TX 79016-0001. Offers MS. *Program availability:* Part-time, evening/weekend, 100% online, blended/hybrid learning. *Degree requirements:* For master's, comprehensive exam, thesis optional. *Entrance requirements:* For master's, GMAT. Additional exam requirements/recommendations for international students: Required—TOEFL (minimum score 550 paper-based). *Application deadline:* For fall admission, 8/1 for domestic students, 5/1 for international students; for spring admission, 12/1 for domestic students, 10/30 for international students; for summer admission, 5/1 for domestic students. Applications are processed on a rolling basis. Application fee: $40 ($75 for international students). Electronic applications accepted. *Financial support:* Research assistantships, teaching assistantships with partial tuition reimbursements, Federal Work-Study, institutionally sponsored loans, and tuition waivers (partial) available. Support available to part-time students. Financial award applicants required to submit CSS PROFILE or FAFSA. *Faculty research:* International trade composition, cycle of poverty, trade effects in Asian countries, structural problems in Japanese economy, reform and the U.S. sugar program-Nebraska. *Unit head:* Dr. LaVelle Mills, Associate Dean, 806-651-3866, E-mail: lmills@wtamu.edu. *Application contact:* Dr. Jonathan Shaffer, Associate Professor, 806-651-2489, E-mail: jshaffer@wtamu.edu.
Website: http://www.wtamu.edu/academics/finance-economics-graduate-program.aspx

**West Virginia University,** College of Business and Economics, Division of Economics and Finance, Morgantown, WV 26506. Offers business analysis (MA); developmental financial economics (PhD); environmental and resource economics (PhD); international economics (PhD); mathematical economics (MA); monetary economics (PhD); public finance (PhD); public policy (MA); regional and urban economics (PhD); statistics and economics (MA). Terminal master's awarded for partial completion of doctoral program. *Degree requirements:* For master's, thesis optional; for doctorate, comprehensive exam, thesis/dissertation. *Entrance requirements:* For master's and doctorate, GRE General Test, minimum GPA of 3.0; course work in intermediate microeconomics, intermediate macroeconomics, calculus, and statistics. Additional exam requirements/recommendations for international students: Required—TOEFL. Electronic applications accepted. *Faculty research:* Financial economics, regional/urban development, public economics, international trade/international finance/development economics, monetary economics.

**Wichita State University,** Graduate School, W. Frank Barton School of Business, Department of Economics, Wichita, KS 67260. Offers economic analysis (MA); financial economics (MA); international economics (MA). *Program availability:* Part-time, evening/weekend. *Unit head:* Dr. Jen-Chi Cheng, Chair, 316-978-3220, Fax: 316-978-3845, E-mail: jenchi.cheng@wichita.edu. *Application contact:* Jordan Oleson, Admissions Coordinator, 316-978-3095, Fax: 316-978-3253, E-mail: jordan.oleson@wichita.edu.
Website: http://www.wichita.edu/econ

**Wilfrid Laurier University,** Faculty of Graduate and Postdoctoral Studies, School of Business and Economics, Department of Business, Waterloo, ON N2L 3C5, Canada. Offers accounting (PhD); finance (M Fin); financial economics (PhD); marketing (PhD); operations and supply chain management (PhD); organizational behavior and human resource management (M Sc); organizational behaviour and human resource management (PhD); supply chain management (M Sc); technology management (EMTM). *Accreditation:* AACSB. *Program availability:* Part-time, evening/weekend. *Degree requirements:* For master's, thesis optional; for doctorate, comprehensive exam, thesis/dissertation. *Entrance requirements:* For master's, GMAT, 4-year honors degree with minimum B+ average; for doctorate, GMAT, master's degree, minimum B+ average. Additional exam requirements/recommendations for international students: Required—TOEFL (minimum score 89 iBT). Electronic applications accepted. *Faculty research:* Financial economics, management and organizational behavior, operations and supply chain management.

**Wilfrid Laurier University,** Faculty of Graduate and Postdoctoral Studies, School of Business and Economics, Department of Economics, Waterloo, ON N2L 3C5, Canada. Offers MA. *Entrance requirements:* For master's, honors BA or the equivalent in economics, minimum B average in undergraduate course work. Additional exam requirements/recommendations for international students: Required—TOEFL (minimum score 89 iBT). Electronic applications accepted. *Faculty research:* Economic forecasting, economic policy analysis, industry and market studies, financial economics, strategic planning, public policy and business.

**Wilfrid Laurier University,** Faculty of Graduate and Postdoctoral Studies, School of International Policy and Governance, Global Governance Program, Waterloo, ON N2L 3C5, Canada. Offers conflict and security (PhD); global environment (PhD); global justice and human rights (PhD); global political economy (PhD); global social governance (PhD); multilateral institutions and diplomacy (PhD). Offered jointly with University of Waterloo. *Degree requirements:* For doctorate, thesis/dissertation. *Entrance requirements:* For doctorate, MA in political science, history, economics, international development studies, international peace studies, globalization studies, environmental studies or related field with minimum A-. Additional exam requirements/recommendations for international students: Required—TOEFL (minimum score 89 iBT). Electronic applications accepted. *Faculty research:* Global political economy, global environment, conflict and security, global justice and human rights, multilateral institutions and diplomacy.

**Wright State University,** Graduate School, Raj Soin College of Business, Department of Economics, Dayton, OH 45435. Offers social and applied economics (MS). *Entrance requirements:* For master's, GRE General Test. Additional exam requirements/recommendations for international students: Required—TOEFL. Application fee: $25. *Expenses:* Tuition, state resident: full-time $9952; part-time $622 per credit hour. Tuition, nonresident: full-time $16,960; part-time $1060 per credit hour. *Financial support:* Fellowships, research assistantships, teaching assistantships, career-related internships or fieldwork, and unspecified assistantships available. Support available to part-time students. Financial award applicants required to submit FAFSA. *Unit head:* Dr. Joseph Eisenhauer, Chair, 937-775-3070, Fax: 937-775-2441, E-mail: joseph.eisenhauer@wright.edu. *Application contact:* Dr. Len Kloft, Director, 937-775-2322, Fax: 937-775-2441, E-mail: leonard.kloft@wright.edu.

**Yale University,** Graduate School of Arts and Sciences, Department of Economics, New Haven, CT 06520. Offers economics (PhD); international and development economics (MA). *Degree requirements:* For doctorate, thesis/dissertation. *Entrance requirements:* For master's, GRE General Test; for doctorate, GRE General Test, GRE Subject Test. *Faculty research:* Economic history of Western Europe, environmental economics, economic growth and development.

**Yeshiva University,** Graduate Programs in Arts and Sciences, New York, NY 10033-3201. Offers mathematical sciences (PhD); mathematics (MA); quantitative economics (MS); speech-language pathology (MS).

**York University,** Faculty of Graduate Studies, Faculty of Liberal Arts and Professional Studies, Program in Economics, Toronto, ON M3J 1P3, Canada. Offers MA, PhD.

*Program availability:* Part-time. *Degree requirements:* For doctorate, comprehensive exam, thesis/dissertation. Electronic applications accepted.

**Youngstown State University,** Graduate School, College of Liberal Arts and Social Sciences, Department of Economics, Youngstown, OH 44555-0001. Offers economics (MA); financial economics (MA). *Program availability:* Part-time. *Degree requirements:*

For master's, comprehensive exam, thesis optional. *Entrance requirements:* For master's, minimum GPA of 2.7, 21 hours in economics. Additional exam requirements/recommendations for international students: Required—TOEFL. *Faculty research:* Forecasting, applied econometrics, labor economics, applied macroeconomics, industrial organization.

# International Economics

**American University,** College of Arts and Sciences, Department of Economics, Washington, DC 20016-8029. Offers applied microeconomics (Certificate); economics (MA, PhD); gender analysis in economics (Certificate); international economic relations (Certificate); international economics (MA). *Program availability:* Part-time, evening/weekend, 100% online. *Faculty:* 29 full-time (8 women), 10 part-time/adjunct (3 women). *Students:* 110 full-time (55 women), 71 part-time (32 women); includes 26 minority (9 Black or African American, non-Hispanic/Latino; 6 Asian, non-Hispanic/Latino; 7 Hispanic/Latino; 4 Two or more races, non-Hispanic/Latino), 64 international. Average age 31. 241 applicants, 78% accepted, 48 enrolled. In 2016, 34 master's, 13 doctorates, 5 other advanced degrees awarded. Terminal master's awarded for partial completion of doctoral program. *Degree requirements:* For master's, comprehensive exam, thesis or alternative; for doctorate, comprehensive exam, thesis/dissertation. *Entrance requirements:* For master's and doctorate, GRE, statement of purpose, transcripts, 2 letters of recommendation, resume; for Certificate, bachelor's degree, statement of purpose, transcripts, resume. Additional exam requirements/recommendations for international students: Required—TOEFL (minimum score 100 iBT), IELTS (minimum score 7), PTE (minimum score 68). *Application deadline:* For fall admission, 3/1 for domestic students; for spring admission, 11/1 for domestic students. Applications are processed on a rolling basis. Application fee: $55. Electronic applications accepted. *Expenses:* $1,579 per credit tuition; $690 mandatory fees. *Financial support:* Research assistantships, teaching assistantships, institutionally sponsored loans, and unspecified assistantships available. Financial award application deadline: 2/1; financial award applicants required to submit FAFSA. *Faculty research:* Political economy, development, labor, gender. *Unit head:* Dr. Thomas Husted, Department Chair, 202-885-3773, Fax: 202-885-3790, E-mail: husted@american.edu. *Application contact:* Kathleen Clowery, Associate Director of Graduate Admissions, 202-885-3620, Fax: 202-885-1344, E-mail: clowery@american.edu.
Website: http://www.american.edu/cas/economics/

**American University,** School of International Service, Washington, DC 20016-8071. Offers comparative and regional studies (Certificate); cross-cultural communication (Certificate); development management (MS); ethics, peace, and global affairs (MA); European studies (Certificate); global environmental policy (MA, Certificate); global information technology (Certificate); international affairs (MA), including comparative and international disability policy, comparative and regional studies, international economic relations, international politics, natural resources and sustainable development, U.S. foreign policy; international arts management (Certificate); international communication (MA, Certificate); international development (MA); international economic policy (Certificate); international economic relations (Certificate); international economics (MA); international media (MA); international peace and conflict resolution (MA, Certificate); international politics (Certificate); international relations (MA, PhD); international service (MIS); peacebuilding (Certificate); social enterprise (MA); the Americas (Certificate); United States foreign policy (Certificate); JD/MA. *Program availability:* Part-time, evening/weekend, 100% online. *Faculty:* 116 full-time (53 women), 57 part-time/adjunct (19 women). *Students:* 575 full-time (360 women), 491 part-time (277 women); includes 287 minority (100 Black or African American, non-Hispanic/Latino; 6 American Indian or Alaska Native, non-Hispanic/Latino; 58 Asian, non-Hispanic/Latino; 92 Hispanic/Latino; 1 Native Hawaiian or other Pacific Islander, non-Hispanic/Latino; 30 Two or more races, non-Hispanic/Latino), 151 international. Average age 29. 1,504 applicants, 84% accepted, 403 enrolled. In 2016, 374 master's, 3 doctorates, 1 other advanced degree awarded. Terminal master's awarded for partial completion of doctoral program. *Degree requirements:* For master's, one foreign language, comprehensive exam, thesis or alternative; for doctorate, one foreign language, comprehensive exam, thesis/dissertation. *Entrance requirements:* For master's, GRE, GMAT or GRE (for MA in social enterprise), transcripts, resume, 2 letters of recommendation, statement of purpose; for doctorate, GRE, transcripts, resume, 3 letters of recommendation, statement of purpose. Additional exam requirements/recommendations for international students: Required—TOEFL (minimum score 600 paper-based, 100 iBT), IELTS (minimum score 7), or PTE (minimum score of 68). Application fee: $55. Electronic applications accepted. *Expenses:* $1,579 per credit tuition; $1,930 mandatory fees. *Financial support:* Research assistantships, teaching assistantships, institutionally sponsored loans, scholarships/grants, and unspecified assistantships available. Financial award application deadline: 1/15; financial award applicants required to submit FAFSA. *Unit head:* Dr. James Goldgeier, Dean, 202-885-1603, Fax: 202-885-2494, E-mail: goldgeier@american.edu. *Application contact:* Jia Jiang, Associate Director, Graduate Education Enrollment, 202-885-1689, Fax: 202-885-1109, E-mail: jiang@american.edu.
Website: http://www.american.edu/sis/

**Baruch College of the City University of New York,** Austin W. Marxe School of Public and International Affairs, Program in International Affairs, New York, NY 10010-5585. Offers international nongovernmental organizations (MIA); trade policy and global economic governance (MIA); Western Hemisphere affairs (MIA). *Program availability:* Part-time.

See Display on page 931 and Close-Up on page 977.

**Bryant University,** Graduate School of Business, Smithfield, RI 02917. Offers accounting (MPAC); business administration (MBA), including general management, global finance, global supply chain management, international business; business analytics (Graduate Certificate); taxation (MST). *Program availability:* Part-time, evening/weekend. *Faculty:* 16 full-time (3 women), 2 part-time/adjunct (0 women). *Students:* 71 full-time (23 women), 83 part-time (32 women); includes 17 minority (5 Black or African American, non-Hispanic/Latino; 4 Asian, non-Hispanic/Latino; 5 Hispanic/Latino; 3 Two or more races, non-Hispanic/Latino), 17 international. Average age 27. 165 applicants, 57% accepted, 66 enrolled. In 2016, 106 master's, 12 other advanced degrees awarded. *Degree requirements:* For master's, comprehensive exam (for some programs). *Entrance requirements:* For master's, GMAT, resume, recommendation, college transcripts. Additional exam requirements/recommendations for international students: Required—TOEFL (minimum score 580 paper-based; 95 iBT). *Application deadline:* For fall admission, 7/15 for domestic and international students; for spring admission, 11/15 for domestic and international students; for summer admission,

4/15 for domestic and international students. Applications are processed on a rolling basis. Application fee: $80. Electronic applications accepted. *Expenses:* Contact institution. *Financial support:* Research assistantships, scholarships/grants, and unspecified assistantships available. Support available to part-time students. Financial award application deadline: 2/15; financial award applicants required to submit FAFSA. *Faculty research:* International business, public sector auditing, taxation of partnerships, information systems security, financial markets microstructure. *Unit head:* Bjorn Carlsson, Graduate Program Director, 401-232-6707, E-mail: bcarlsson@bryant.edu. *Application contact:* Terri Rogers, Admissions Assistant, 401-232-6230, Fax: 401-232-6494, E-mail: graduateprograms@bryant.edu.
Website: http://gradschool.bryant.edu/business/

**Claremont Graduate University,** Graduate Programs, School of Social Science, Policy and Evaluation, Department of Economics, Claremont, CA 91711-6160. Offers behavioral economics and neuroeconomics (PhD); business and financial economics (MA, PhD); economic development (Certificate); international economic and development policy (PhD); international economics policy and development (MA); international money and finance (PhD); political economy and public economics (PhD); political economy and public policy (MA); MBA/PhD. *Program availability:* Part-time. *Faculty:* 5 full-time (1 woman), 2 part-time/adjunct (0 women). *Students:* 92 full-time (31 women), 34 part-time (15 women); includes 14 minority (4 Black or African American, non-Hispanic/Latino; 7 Asian, non-Hispanic/Latino; 2 Hispanic/Latino; 1 Two or more races, non-Hispanic/Latino), 67 international. Average age 33. In 2016, 20 master's, 16 doctorates awarded. *Entrance requirements:* For master's and doctorate, GRE General Test or GMAT. Additional exam requirements/recommendations for international students: Required—TOEFL (minimum score 75 iBT). *Application deadline:* For fall admission, 2/1 priority date for domestic and international students. Applications are processed on a rolling basis. Application fee: $80. Electronic applications accepted. *Expenses:* Tuition: Full-time $44,328; part-time $1847 per unit. *Required fees:* $600; $300 per semester. Tuition and fees vary according to course load and program. *Financial support:* Fellowships, research assistantships, teaching assistantships, Federal Work-Study, institutionally sponsored loans, and scholarships/grants available. Support available to part-time students. Financial award application deadline: 2/15; financial award applicants required to submit FAFSA. *Faculty research:* International and financial economics, law and economics, regulation, public choice economics. *Unit head:* Paul Zak, Chair, 909-621-8788, E-mail: paul.zak@cgu.edu. *Application contact:* Paige Piontkowsky, Senior Assistant Director of Admissions, 909-607-3240, E-mail: paige.piontkowsky@cgu.edu.
Website: https://www.cgu.edu/school/ssspe/programs/?areas_of_study=economics

**Cleveland State University,** College of Graduate Studies, College of Liberal Arts and Social Sciences, Department of Political Science, Cleveland, OH 44115. Offers global interactions (MA), including global business interactions, global political interactions. *Faculty:* 3 full-time (1 woman). *Students:* 12 full-time (3 women), 10 part-time (1 woman); includes 9 minority (3 Black or African American, non-Hispanic/Latino; 3 Hispanic/Latino; 3 Two or more races, non-Hispanic/Latino), 3 international. Average age 27. 33 applicants, 100% accepted, 5 enrolled. In 2016, 6 master's awarded. *Degree requirements:* For master's, exit project. *Entrance requirements:* For master's, minimum undergraduate GPA of 3.0 or GRE (50th percentile or above); two letters of recommendation; undergraduate degree in economics, political science, international relations, or a related discipline; completion of undergraduate macro and micro economics course. Additional exam requirements/recommendations for international students: Required—TOEFL (minimum score 550 paper-based; 78 iBT). *Application deadline:* For fall admission, 7/1 for domestic students, 5/15 for international students; for spring admission, 11/15 for domestic students, 11/1 for international students; for summer admission, 4/1 for domestic students, 3/15 for international students. Applications are processed on a rolling basis. Application fee: $40. Electronic applications accepted. *Expenses:* Contact institution. *Financial support:* In 2016–17, 3 research assistantships with full tuition reimbursements (averaging $13,214 per year) were awarded; tuition waivers (full) and unspecified assistantships also available. Financial award applicants required to submit FAFSA. *Faculty research:* International political economy, globalization, new regionalism, European integration, adaptation to climate change. *Unit head:* Dr. Rodger M. Govea, Associate Professor/Chairperson, 216-687-4554, E-mail: r.govea@csuohio.edu. *Application contact:* Janice McCowan, Public Inquiries Assistant, 216-523-7473, Fax: 216-687-9210, E-mail: j.c.mccowan@csuohio.edu.
Website: http://www.csuohio.edu/class/politicalscience/

**Fordham University,** Gabelli School of Business, New York, NY 10023. Offers accounting (MBA, MS); applied statistics and decision-making (MS); business administration (EMBA); business analytics (MS); communications and media management (MBA); electronic business (MBA); entrepreneurship (MBA); finance (MBA); global finance (MS); global sustainability (MBA); healthcare management (MBA); information systems (MBA, MS); investor relations (MS); management (MBA, MS); marketing (MBA); marketing intelligence (MS); media management (MS); nonprofit leadership (MS); quantitative finance (MS); taxation (MS); JD/MBA; MS/MBA. *Accreditation:* AACSB. *Program availability:* Part-time, evening/weekend. *Faculty:* 132 full-time (44 women), 51 part-time/adjunct (7 women). *Students:* 1,117 full-time (668 women), 553 part-time (282 women); includes 207 minority (44 Black or African American, non-Hispanic/Latino; 92 Asian, non-Hispanic/Latino; 69 Hispanic/Latino; 2 Native Hawaiian or other Pacific Islander, non-Hispanic/Latino), 1,088 international. Average age 27. 4,745 applicants, 46% accepted, 752 enrolled. In 2016, 996 master's awarded. Terminal master's awarded for partial completion of doctoral program. *Degree requirements:* For master's, internships (required for MS in quantitative finance, recommended for MBA). *Entrance requirements:* For master's, GMAT/GRE, 2 letters of recommendation, resume, 2 essays, transcripts. Additional exam requirements/recommendations for international students: Required—TOEFL (minimum score 100 iBT), IELTS (minimum score 7). *Application deadline:* For fall admission, 11/15 priority date for domestic and international students; for winter admission, 1/15 priority date for domestic students, 1/1 priority date for international students; for spring admission, 3/1 for domestic and international students; for summer admission, 6/1 for domestic

## International Economics

students. Application fee: $130. Electronic applications accepted. *Expenses:* $1,397 per credit. *Financial support:* In 2016–17, 78 students received support. Career-related internships or fieldwork, institutionally sponsored loans, scholarships/grants, and unspecified assistantships available. Support available to part-time students. Financial award application deadline: 6/30; financial award applicants required to submit FAFSA. *Unit head:* Dr. Donna Rapaccioli, Dean, 212-636-6165, Fax: 212-307-1779, E-mail: rapaccioli@fordham.edu. *Application contact:* Lawrence Murray, Senior Assistant Dean of Graduate Admissions and Advising, 212-636-6200, Fax: 212-636-7076, E-mail: admissionsgb@fordham.edu.
Website: http://www.fordham.edu/gabelli

**Fordham University,** Graduate School of Arts and Sciences, Program in International Political Economy and Development, New York, NY 10458. Offers MA, Certificate. *Program availability:* Part-time, evening/weekend. *Students:* 38 full-time (16 women), 13 part-time (10 women); includes 8 minority (1 Black or African American, non-Hispanic/Latino; 4 Asian, non-Hispanic/Latino; 3 Native Hawaiian or other Pacific Islander, non-Hispanic/Latino), 16 international. Average age 27. 207 applicants, 35% accepted, 24 enrolled. In 2016, 24 master's, 1 other advanced degree awarded. *Degree requirements:* For master's, comprehensive exam. *Entrance requirements:* For master's, GRE General Test. Additional exam requirements/recommendations for international students: Required—TOEFL (minimum score 600 paper-based). *Application deadline:* For fall admission, 1/4 priority date for domestic students; for spring admission, 11/1 for domestic students. Application fee: $70. Electronic applications accepted. *Financial support:* In 2016–17, 35 students received support, including 4 fellowships with tuition reimbursements available (averaging $17,014 per year); research assistantships with tuition reimbursements available, career-related internships or fieldwork, institutionally sponsored loans, tuition waivers (full and partial), and unspecified assistantships also available. Financial award application deadline: 1/4; financial award applicants required to submit FAFSA. *Faculty research:* International economics, comparative international politics, international banking and finance, international development, emerging markets and country risk analysis. *Unit head:* Dr. Henry Schwalbenberg, Chair, 718-817-3866, Fax: 718-817-3518. *Application contact:* Bernadette Valentino-Morrison, Director of Graduate Admissions, 718-817-4419, Fax: 718-817-3566, E-mail: valentinomor@fordham.edu.

**Johns Hopkins University,** School of Advanced International Studies, Washington, DC 20036. Offers global risk (MA); international development (MA, Certificate), including international economics (MA); international economics and finance (MA); international public policy (MIPP); international relations (PhD); international studies (Certificate); Japan studies (MA), including international economics; Korea studies (MA), including international economics; South Asia studies (MA), including international economics; Southeast Asia studies (MA), including international economics; JD/MA; MBA/MA; MHS/MA. Terminal master's awarded for partial completion of doctoral program. *Degree requirements:* For master's, 4-6 international economics courses, 5-6 functional or regional concentration courses, 2 core examinations, proficiency in language other than native language, capstone project; for doctorate, 2 foreign languages, thesis/dissertation, 3 comprehensive exams, economics, quantitative and qualitative course, dissertation prospectus and defense. *Entrance requirements:* For master's, GMAT or GRE General Test, previous course work in economics, foreign language, undergraduate degree; for doctorate, GRE General Test, master's degree. Additional exam requirements/recommendations for international students: Required—TOEFL (minimum score 600 paper-based; 100 iBT) or IELTS (minimum score 7). Electronic applications accepted. *Expenses:* Contact institution. *Faculty research:* Regional studies, international relations, international economics, energy and environment, international development.

**The New School,** The New School for Social Research, Department of Economics, New York, NY 10003. Offers economics (M Phil, MA, MS, PhD); global political economy and finance (MA). *Program availability:* Part-time. *Faculty:* 5 full-time (1 woman), 12 part-time/adjunct (4 women). *Students:* 82 full-time (26 women), 21 part-time (6 women); includes 15 minority (5 Black or African American, non-Hispanic/Latino; 4 Asian, non-Hispanic/Latino; 6 Hispanic/Latino), 53 international. Average age 31. 143 applicants, 69% accepted, 18 enrolled. In 2016, 21 master's, 11 doctorates awarded. Terminal master's awarded for partial completion of doctoral program. *Degree requirements:* For master's, mentored research/internship, exam; for doctorate, one foreign language, comprehensive exam, thesis/dissertation. *Entrance requirements:* For master's, GRE, letters of recommendation, writing sample, essays, unofficial transcript; for doctorate, letters of recommendation, writing sample, essays, unofficial transcript. Additional exam requirements/recommendations for international students: Required—TOEFL (minimum score 100 iBT), IELTS (minimum score 7), PTE (minimum score 68). *Application deadline:* For fall admission, 5/5 priority date for domestic and international students; for spring admission, 10/15 priority date for domestic and international students. Applications are processed on a rolling basis. Application fee: $50. Electronic applications accepted. *Expenses:* Contact institution. *Financial support:* Fellowships, research assistantships, teaching assistantships, career-related internships or fieldwork, Federal Work-Study, scholarships/grants, and tuition waivers (full and partial) available. Support available to part-time students. Financial award application deadline: 2/1; financial award applicants required to submit FAFSA. *Faculty research:* Keynesian and post-Keynesian economics; classical political economy of Smith, Ricardo, and Marx; structuralist and institutionalist approaches to economics, and neoclassical economics;. *Unit head:* Dr. William Milberg, Dean, The New School for Social Research, 212-229-5777, E-mail: milbergw@newschool.edu. *Application contact:* Dana Messinger, Director of Graduate Admission, 212-229-5150 Ext. 2300, E-mail: socialresearchadmit@newschool.edu.
Website: http://www.newschool.edu/

**Pace University,** Lubin School of Business, Advanced Professional Certificate Program, New York, NY 10038. Offers business economics (APC); e-business (APC); financial management (APC); international business (APC); international economics (APC); investment management (APC); marketing (APC); public accounting (APC). *Program availability:* Evening/weekend. *Students:* 1 applicant, 100% accepted, 1 enrolled. *Entrance requirements:* For degree, MBA or MS in business discipline, relevant professional experience. Additional exam requirements/recommendations for international students: Required—TOEFL (minimum score 90 iBT), IELTS (minimum score 7) or PTE (minimum score 61). *Application deadline:* For fall admission, 8/1 priority date for domestic students, 6/1 for international students; for spring admission, 12/1 for domestic students, 10/1 for international students. Applications are processed on a rolling basis. Application fee: $70. Electronic applications accepted. *Expenses: Tuition:* Part-time $1195 per credit. *Required fees:* $260 per semester. Tuition and fees vary according to degree level, campus/location and program. *Unit head:* Dr. Jack Yurkiewicz, Director, 212-618-6567, E-mail: jyurkiewicz@pace.edu. *Application contact:* Susan Ford-Goldschein, Director of Graduate Admissions, 212-346-1531, Fax: 212-346-1585, E-mail: graduateadmission@pace.edu.
Website: http://www.pace.edu/lubin/agc

**University of California, San Diego,** Graduate Division, School of Global Policy and Strategy, Master of International Affairs Program, La Jolla, CA 92093. Offers international development and nonprofit management (MIA); international economics

(MIA); international environmental policy (MIA); international management (MIA); international politics (MIA). Students will choose one of the following country/regional specializations: China, Japan, Korea, Latin America, or Southeast Asia. *Faculty:* 33 full-time (9 women), 20 part-time/adjunct (4 women). *Students:* 300 full-time (150 women). Average age 24. 460 applicants, 120 enrolled. In 2016, 120 master's awarded. *Degree requirements:* For master's, one foreign language. *Entrance requirements:* For master's, GMAT or GRE General Test. Additional exam requirements/recommendations for international students: Required—TOEFL (minimum score 90 iBT), IELTS (minimum score 7). *Application deadline:* For fall admission, 1/15 for domestic and international students. Applications are processed on a rolling basis. Application fee: $90 ($110 for international students). Electronic applications accepted. *Expenses:* Tuition, state resident: full-time $11,220. Tuition, nonresident: full-time $26,322. *Required fees:* $1864. *Financial support:* In 2016–17, 140 students received support, including 60 fellowships with full and partial tuition reimbursements available (averaging $50,000 per year), 15 research assistantships with full tuition reimbursements available (averaging $20,000 per year), 20 teaching assistantships with full tuition reimbursements available (averaging $20,000 per year); career-related internships or fieldwork, scholarships/grants, and unspecified assistantships also available. Financial award application deadline: 1/15. *Unit head:* Sonja Steinbrech, Director of Enrollment, 858-534-7162, E-mail: ssteinbrech@ucsd.edu. *Application contact:* Admissions Representative, 858-534-5914, E-mail: gps-apply@uscd.edu.
Website: http://gps.ucsd.edu/academics/mia.html

**University of New Mexico,** Graduate Studies, College of Arts and Sciences, Program in Economics, Albuquerque, NM 87131-2039. Offers econometrics (MA); economic theory (MA); environmental/natural resource economics (MA, PhD); international/development and sustainability economics (MA, PhD); public economics (MA, PhD). *Program availability:* Part-time. *Faculty:* 11 full-time (5 women). *Students:* 34 full-time (11 women), 19 part-time (7 women); includes 9 minority (1 Black or African American, non-Hispanic/Latino; 1 Asian, non-Hispanic/Latino; 6 Hispanic/Latino; 1 Two or more races, non-Hispanic/Latino), 29 international. Average age 32. 58 applicants, 24% accepted, 11 enrolled. In 2016, 7 master's, 4 doctorates awarded. Terminal master's awarded for partial completion of doctoral program. *Degree requirements:* For master's, comprehensive exam, thesis (for some programs); for doctorate, comprehensive exam, thesis/dissertation. *Entrance requirements:* For master's and doctorate, GRE General Test, 3 letters of recommendation, letter of intent, curriculum vitae. Additional exam requirements/recommendations for international students: Required—TOEFL (minimum score 520 paper-based; 68 iBT). *Application deadline:* For fall admission, 3/1 priority date for domestic students, 3/1 for international students. Applications are processed on a rolling basis. Application fee: $50. Electronic applications accepted. *Financial support:* Fellowships with tuition reimbursements, research assistantships with tuition reimbursements, teaching assistantships with tuition reimbursements, career-related internships or fieldwork, Federal Work-Study, scholarships/grants, health care benefits, and unspecified assistantships available. Support available to part-time students. Financial award application deadline: 3/1; financial award applicants required to submit FAFSA. *Faculty research:* Core theory, econometrics, public finance, international/development economics, labor/human resource economics, environmental/natural resource economics. *Total annual research expenditures:* $167,690. *Unit head:* Dr. Janie Chermak, Chair, 505-277-2037, Fax: 505-277-9445, E-mail: jchermak@unm.edu. *Application contact:* Jeff Newcomer Miller, Academic Advisor, 505-277-3056, Fax: 505-277-9445, E-mail: econgrad@unm.edu.
Website: http://econ.unm.edu

**University of Wisconsin–Milwaukee,** Graduate School, College of Letters and Science, Department of Economics, Milwaukee, WI 53201-0413. Offers economics (MA, PhD), including advanced econometrics, development econometrics, industrial economics, international economics, labor economics, monetary theory and policy. *Students:* 40 full-time (10 women), 10 part-time (2 women); includes 4 minority (1 Black or African American, non-Hispanic/Latino; 3 Asian, non-Hispanic/Latino), 29 international. Average age 31. 77 applicants, 53% accepted, 16 enrolled. In 2016, 13 master's, 6 doctorates awarded. *Degree requirements:* For master's, comprehensive exam; for doctorate, comprehensive exam, thesis/dissertation. *Entrance requirements:* For master's, GRE General Test; for doctorate, GRE General Test, GRE Subject Test, minimum GPA of 3.0. Additional exam requirements/recommendations for international students: Required—TOEFL (minimum score 550 paper-based; 79 iBT), IELTS (minimum score 6.5). *Application deadline:* For fall admission, 1/1 priority date for domestic students; for spring admission, 9/1 for domestic students. Applications are processed on a rolling basis. Application fee: $56 ($96 for international students). *Financial support:* In 2016–17, 28 teaching assistantships were awarded; career-related internships or fieldwork and unspecified assistantships also available. Support available to part-time students. Financial award application deadline: 4/15; financial award applicants required to submit FAFSA. *Unit head:* Scott J. Adams, Department Chair, 414-229-4811, E-mail: sjadams@uwm.edu. *Application contact:* General Information Contact, 414-229-4982, Fax: 414-229-6967, E-mail: gradschool@uwm.edu.
Website: https://uwm.edu/economics/

**Valparaiso University,** Graduate School and Continuing Education, Program in International Economics and Finance, Valparaiso, IN 46383. Offers MS. *Program availability:* Part-time, evening/weekend. *Entrance requirements:* For master's, 1 semester of college-level calculus; 1 statistics or quantitative methods class; 2 semesters of introductory economics (course content in introductory economics must include both introductory microeconomics and macroeconomics); 1 introductory accounting course; minimum undergraduate GPA of 3.0; 2 letters of recommendation. Additional exam requirements/recommendations for international students: Required—TOEFL (minimum score 550 paper-based; 80 iBT), IELTS (minimum score 6). *Expenses: Tuition:* Full-time $11,070; part-time $615 per credit hour. *Required fees:* $116 per semester. Tuition and fees vary according to course load, degree level and program.

**Wayne State University,** College of Liberal Arts and Sciences, Department of Economics, Detroit, MI 48202. Offers advanced macroeconomics (PhD); econometrics (MA); health economics (MA, PhD); industrial organization (MA, PhD); international economics (MA, PhD); labor and human resources (MA); labor economics (PhD); macroeconomics (MA); microeconomics (MA); JD/MA. *Faculty:* 13. *Students:* 38 full-time (11 women), 7 part-time (3 women); includes 8 minority (5 Black or African American, non-Hispanic/Latino; 1 Asian, non-Hispanic/Latino; 1 Hispanic/Latino; 1 Two or more races, non-Hispanic/Latino), 22 international. Average age 33. 97 applicants, 36% accepted, 8 enrolled. In 2016, 10 master's, 7 doctorates awarded. *Degree requirements:* For master's, comprehensive exam; for doctorate, comprehensive exam, thesis/dissertation, oral examination on research, completion of course work in quantitative methods, final lecture. *Entrance requirements:* For master's, minimum upper-division GPA of 3.0; prior coursework in intermediate microeconomic and macroeconomic theory, statistics, and elementary calculus; for doctorate, GRE, minimum upper-division GPA of 3.0, prior coursework in intermediate microeconomic and macroeconomic theory, statistics, two courses in calculus, three letters of recommendation from officials or teaching staff at institution(s) most recently attended, statement of purpose. Additional exam requirements/recommendations for international students: Required—TOEFL (minimum score 550 paper-based; 79 iBT), TWE (minimum

score 5.5), Michigan English Language Assessment Battery (minimum score 85); Recommended—IELTS (minimum score 6.5). *Application deadline:* For fall admission, 5/1 for domestic and international students; for winter admission, 10/1 priority date for domestic students, 9/1 priority date for international students; for spring admission, 1/1 priority date for domestic and international students. Applications are processed on a rolling basis. Application fee: $50. Electronic applications accepted. *Expenses:* $16,503 per year resident tuition and fees, $33,697 per year non-resident tuition and fees. *Financial support:* In 2016–17, 26 students received support, including 2 fellowships with tuition reimbursements available (averaging $16,000 per year), 17 teaching assistantships with tuition reimbursements available (averaging $17,994 per year); research assistantships with tuition reimbursements available, scholarships/grants, health care benefits, and unspecified assistantships also available. Support available to part-time students. Financial award applicants required to submit FAFSA. *Faculty research:* Health economics, international economics, macro economics, urban and labor economics, econometrics. *Unit head:* Dr. Stephen J. Spurr, Professor and Chair, 313-577-3232, Fax: 313-577-9564, E-mail: sspurr@wayne.edu. *Application contact:* Dr. Allen Charles Goodman, Graduate Director, 313-577-3235, Fax: 313-577-9564, E-mail: allen.goodman@wayne.edu.
Website: http://clas.wayne.edu/economics/

**West Virginia University,** College of Business and Economics, Division of Economics and Finance, Morgantown, WV 26506. Offers business analysis (MA); developmental financial economics (PhD); environmental and resource economics (PhD); international economics (PhD); mathematical economics (MA); monetary economics (PhD); public finance (PhD); public policy (MA); regional and urban economics (PhD); statistics and economics (MA). Terminal master's awarded for partial completion of doctoral program. *Degree requirements:* For master's, thesis optional; for doctorate, comprehensive exam, thesis/dissertation. *Entrance requirements:* For master's and doctorate, GRE General

Test, minimum GPA of 3.0; course work in intermediate microeconomics, intermediate macroeconomics, calculus, and statistics. Additional exam requirements/recommendations for international students: Required—TOEFL. Electronic applications accepted. *Faculty research:* Financial economics, regional/urban development, public economics, international trade/international finance/development economics, monetary economics.

**Wichita State University,** Graduate School, W. Frank Barton School of Business, Department of Economics, Wichita, KS 67260. Offers economic analysis (MA); financial economics (MA); international economics (MA). *Program availability:* Part-time, evening/weekend. *Unit head:* Dr. Jen-Chi Cheng, Chair, 316-978-3220, Fax: 316-978-3845, E-mail: jenchi.cheng@wichita.edu. *Application contact:* Jordan Oleson, Admissions Coordinator, 316-978-3095, Fax: 316-978-3253, E-mail: jordan.oleson@wichita.edu. Website: http://www.wichita.edu/econ

**Wilfrid Laurier University,** Faculty of Graduate and Postdoctoral Studies, School of International Policy and Governance, International Public Policy Program, Waterloo, ON N2L 3C5, Canada. Offers global governance (MIPP); human security (MIPP); international economic relations (MIPP); international environmental policy (MIPP). Offered jointly with University of Waterloo. *Entrance requirements:* For master's, honours BA with minimum B average. Additional exam requirements/recommendations for international students: Required—TOEFL (minimum score 89 iBT). Electronic applications accepted. *Faculty research:* International environmental policy, international economic relations, human security, global governance.

**Yale University,** Graduate School of Arts and Sciences, Department of Economics, Program in International and Development Economics, New Haven, CT 06520. Offers MA. *Entrance requirements:* For master's, GRE General Test.

# Mineral Economics

**Colorado School of Mines,** Office of Graduate Studies, Department of Economics and Business, Golden, CO 80401. Offers engineering and technology management (MS); mineral economics (PhD); operations research and engineering (PhD). *Program availability:* Part-time. *Degree requirements:* For master's, thesis (for some programs); for doctorate, comprehensive exam, thesis/dissertation. *Entrance requirements:* For master's and doctorate, GRE General Test. Additional exam requirements/recommendations for international students: Required—TOEFL (minimum score 550 paper-based; 80 iBT). Electronic applications accepted. *Expenses:* Tuition, state resident: full-time $15,690. Tuition, nonresident: full-time $34,020. *Required fees:* $2152. Tuition and fees vary according to course load. *Faculty research:* International trade, resource and environmental economics, energy economics, operations research.

**Michigan Technological University,** Graduate School, School of Business and Economics, Houghton, MI 49931. Offers accounting (MS); applied natural resource economics (MS); business administration (MBA). *Accreditation:* AACSB. *Program availability:* Part-time, evening/weekend. *Faculty:* 23 full-time (7 women), 1 part-time/adjunct. *Students:* 18 full-time (8 women), 23 part-time (12 women); includes 3 minority (1 Black or African American, non-Hispanic/Latino; 1 Asian, non-Hispanic/Latino; 1 Hispanic/Latino), 10 international. Average age 29. 122 applicants, 30% accepted, 16 enrolled. In 2016, 27 master's awarded. *Degree requirements:* For master's, thesis (for some programs). *Entrance requirements:* For master's, GMAT/GRE (recommended minimum score in the 50th percentile), statement of purpose, personal statement, official transcripts, 2 letters of recommendation, resume/curriculum vitae. Additional exam

requirements/recommendations for international students: Required—TOEFL (recommended minimum score 95 iBT) or IELTS (minimum score 7). *Application deadline:* For fall admission, 7/1 for domestic and international students; for spring admission, 12/1 for domestic and international students. Applications are processed on a rolling basis. Electronic applications accepted. *Expenses:* Tuition, state resident: full-time $16,290; part-time $905 per credit. Tuition, nonresident: full-time $16,290; part-time $905 per credit. *Required fees:* $248; $124 per term. Tuition and fees vary according to course load and program. *Financial support:* In 2016–17, 13 students received support. Health care benefits and unspecified assistantships available. Financial award application deadline: 2/1; financial award applicants required to submit FAFSA. *Faculty research:* Natural resource and mineral economics, entrepreneurship, management of technology and innovation, engineering management, management information systems. *Unit head:* Dr. Dean Johnson, Dean, 906-487-2668, Fax: 906-487-1863, E-mail: dean@mtu.edu. *Application contact:* Carol T. Wingerson, Administrative Aide, 906-487-2328, Fax: 906-487-2284, E-mail: gradadms@mtu.edu.
Website: http://www.mtu.edu/business/

**The University of Texas at Austin,** Graduate School, Cockrell School of Engineering, Department of Petroleum and Geosystems Engineering, Program in Energy and Earth Resources, Austin, TX 78712-1111. Offers MA. *Degree requirements:* For master's, thesis, seminar. *Entrance requirements:* For master's, GRE General Test. Additional exam requirements/recommendations for international students: Required—TOEFL. Electronic applications accepted.

# Section 20
# Family and Consumer Sciences

This section contains a directory of institutions offering graduate work in family and consumer sciences, followed by an in-depth entry submitted by an institution that chose to prepare a detailed program description. Additional information about programs listed in the directory but not augmented by an in-depth entry may be obtained by writing directly to the dean of a graduate school or chair of a department at the address given in the directory.

For programs offering related work, see also in this book *Economics, Psychology and Counseling,* and *Sociology, Anthropology, and Archaeology.* In another guide in this series:

**Graduate Programs in Business, Education, Health, Information Studies, Law & Social Work**
See *Social Work*

## CONTENTS

# Family and Consumer Sciences-General

**Alabama Agricultural and Mechanical University,** School of Graduate Studies, College of Agricultural, Life and Natural Sciences, Department of Family and Consumer Sciences, Huntsville, AL 35811. Offers apparel, merchandising and design (MS); family and consumer sciences (MS); human development and family studies (MS); nutrition and hospitality management (MS). *Program availability:* Part-time, evening/weekend. *Degree requirements:* For master's, comprehensive exam, thesis optional. *Entrance requirements:* For master's, GRE General Test. Additional exam requirements/recommendations for international students: Required—TOEFL (minimum score 500 paper-based; 61 iBT). *Application deadline:* For fall admission, 5/1 for domestic students. Applications are processed on a rolling basis. Application fee: $25. Electronic applications accepted. *Expenses:* Tuition, nonresident: part-time $826 per credit hour. Full-time tuition and fees vary according to course load and program. *Financial support:* Research assistantships with tuition reimbursements, teaching assistantships with tuition reimbursements, career-related internships or fieldwork, Federal Work-Study, and traineeships available. Financial award application deadline: 4/1. *Faculty research:* Food biotechnology, nutrition, food microbiology, food engineering, food chemistry. *Unit head:* Dr. Cynthia Smith, Chair, 256-372-4172, Fax: 256-372-5433, E-mail: cynthia.smith@aamu.edu.
Website: http://www.aamu.edu/academics/alns/consumersciences/

**Ball State University,** Graduate School, College of Applied Sciences and Technology, Department of Family and Consumer Sciences, Muncie, IN 47306. Offers family and consumer science (MS), including apparel design (MA, MS), fashion merchandising (MA, MS), interior design (MA, MS), residential property management (MA, MS); family and consumer sciences (MA), including apparel design (MA, MS), fashion merchandising (MA, MS), interior design (MA, MS), residential property management (MA, MS); nutrition and dietetics (MA, MS). *Program availability:* Part-time, evening/weekend, 100% online. *Degree requirements:* For master's, thesis or alternative. *Entrance requirements:* For master's, letter of intent, resume, two letters of recommendation, portfolio (for interior design option). Additional exam requirements/recommendations for international students: Required—TOEFL (minimum score 550 paper-based; 79 iBT), IELTS (minimum score 6.5). Electronic applications accepted. *Faculty research:* Maternal and infant nutrition, nutrition education.

**California State University, Northridge,** Graduate Studies, College of Health and Human Development, Department of Family and Consumer Sciences, Northridge, CA 91330. Offers MS. *Program availability:* Part-time, evening/weekend. *Faculty:* 15 full-time (1 woman), 31 part-time/adjunct (3 women). *Students:* 36 full-time (30 women), 34 part-time (all women); includes 33 minority (6 Black or African American, non-Hispanic/Latino; 8 Asian, non-Hispanic/Latino; 17 Hispanic/Latino; 2 Two or more races, non-Hispanic/Latino), 12 international. Average age 32. 21 applicants, 86% accepted, 10 enrolled. *Degree requirements:* For master's, thesis, project, or comprehensive exam. *Entrance requirements:* For master's, GRE General Test or minimum GPA of 3.0. Additional exam requirements/recommendations for international students: Required—TOEFL. *Application deadline:* For fall admission, 11/30 for domestic students. Application fee: $55. *Expenses:* Tuition, state resident: full-time $4152. *Financial support:* Teaching assistantships, career-related internships or fieldwork, Federal Work-Study, and institutionally sponsored loans available. Financial award application deadline: 3/1. *Unit head:* Dr. Yi Cai, Chair, 818-677-3051, E-mail: yi.cai@csun.edu.
Website: http://www.csun.edu/hhd/fcs/

**Central Michigan University,** College of Graduate Studies, College of Education and Human Services, Department of Human Environmental Studies, Mount Pleasant, MI 48859. Offers apparel product development and merchandising technology (MS); gerontology (Graduate Certificate); human development and family studies (MA); nutrition and dietetics (MS). *Program availability:* Part-time, evening/weekend. *Degree requirements:* For master's, thesis or alternative. Electronic applications accepted. *Faculty research:* Human growth and development, family studies and human sexuality, human nutrition and dietetics, apparel and textile retailing, computer-aided design for apparel.

**Central Washington University,** Graduate Studies and Research, College of Education and Professional Studies, Department of Family and Consumer Sciences, Ellensburg, WA 98926. Offers career and technical education (MS); family and consumer sciences education (MS); family studies (MS). *Program availability:* Part-time. *Degree requirements:* For master's, thesis or alternative. *Entrance requirements:* For master's, minimum GPA of 3.0. Additional exam requirements/recommendations for international students: Required—TOEFL (minimum score 550 paper-based; 79 iBT). Electronic applications accepted.

**Clemson University,** Graduate School, College of Behavioral, Social and Health Sciences, Department of Youth, Family and Community Studies, Clemson, SC 29634. Offers PhD, Certificate. *Program availability:* Part-time-only, online only, blended/hybrid learning. *Faculty:* 7 full-time (4 women), 4 part-time/adjunct (3 women). *Students:* 14 full-time (12 women), 19 part-time (17 women); includes 2 minority (1 Asian, non-Hispanic/Latino; 1 Hispanic/Latino), 14 international. Average age 38. 37 applicants, 27% accepted, 9 enrolled. In 2016, 5 doctorates, 2 other advanced degrees awarded. *Degree requirements:* For doctorate, comprehensive exam, thesis/dissertation. *Entrance requirements:* For doctorate, GRE General Test, unofficial transcripts, personal statement, writing sample, letters of recommendation. Additional exam requirements/recommendations for international students: Required—TOEFL (minimum score 80 iBT), IELTS (minimum score 6.5). *Application deadline:* For fall admission, 2/1 priority date for domestic and international students. Application fee: $80 ($90 for international students). Electronic applications accepted. *Expenses:* $3,431 per semester full-time resident, $6,875 per semester full-time non-resident, $387 per credit hour part-time resident, $770 per credit hour part-time non-resident, $3,428 per credit hour (for online courses). *Financial support:* In 2016–17, 15 students received support, including 1 fellowship with partial tuition reimbursement available (averaging $5,000 per year), 12 research assistantships with partial tuition reimbursements available (averaging $20,917 per year), 1 teaching assistantship with partial tuition reimbursement available (averaging $20,000 per year); career-related internships or fieldwork and unspecified assistantships also available. Financial award application deadline: 2/1. *Faculty research:* Community development and engagement, health and human rights, bullying prevention, suicidal behavior, dating violence. *Total annual research expenditures:* $1 million. *Unit head:* Dr. Mark Small, Department Chair, 864-656-6286, E-mail: msmall@clemson.edu. *Application contact:* Shelli Charles, Graduate Student Administrative Coordinator, 864-656-3410, E-mail: shellic@clemson.edu.
Website: http://www.clemson.edu/cbshs/departments/family-community-studies/index.html

**East Carolina University,** Graduate School, College of Education, Department of Elementary and Middle Grades Education, Greenville, NC 27858-4353. Offers elementary education (MA Ed, MAT); English education (MAT); family and consumer science (MAT); health education (MAT); Hispanic studies (MAT); history education (MAT); middle grades education (MA Ed, MAT); music education (MAT); science education (MAT); special education (MAT), including general curriculum; vocational education (MAT). *Accreditation:* NCATE. *Program availability:* Part-time, evening/weekend, online learning. *Students:* 5 full-time (4 women), 18 part-time (16 women); includes 4 minority (3 Black or African American, non-Hispanic/Latino; 1 Hispanic/Latino). Average age 31. 19 applicants, 95% accepted, 13 enrolled. In 2016, 8 master's awarded. *Degree requirements:* For master's, comprehensive exam, thesis optional. *Entrance requirements:* For master's, GRE or MAT, minimum GPA of 2.5, bachelor's degree in related field, teaching license (MA Ed). Additional exam requirements/recommendations for international students: Required—TOEFL. *Application deadline:* For fall admission, 6/1 priority date for domestic students. Applications are processed on a rolling basis. Application fee: $70. *Financial support:* Federal Work-Study available. Support available to part-time students. Financial award application deadline: 6/1. *Unit head:* Dr. Ann Bullock, Chair, 252-328-1126, E-mail: bullockv@ecu.edu. *Application contact:* Dean of Graduate School, 252-328-6012, Fax: 252-328-6071, E-mail: gradschool@ecu.edu.
Website: http://www.ecu.edu/cs-educ/elmid/index.cfm

**Eastern Illinois University,** Graduate School, Lumpkin College of Business and Applied Sciences, School of Family and Consumer Sciences, Program in Family and Consumer Sciences, Charleston, IL 61920. Offers MS. *Program availability:* Part-time, evening/weekend, online learning. *Degree requirements:* For master's, comprehensive exam (for some programs), thesis (for some programs). *Entrance requirements:* For master's, GMAT or GRE. Additional exam requirements/recommendations for international students: Required—TOEFL (minimum score 500 paper-based; 61 iBT), IELTS (minimum score 6). Electronic applications accepted.

**Florida State University,** The Graduate School, College of Human Sciences, Tallahassee, FL 32306-1490. Offers MS, PhD. *Accreditation:* AAMFT/COAMFTE. *Program availability:* Part-time. *Faculty:* 40 full-time (22 women). *Students:* 119 full-time (74 women), 16 part-time (12 women); includes 34 minority (12 Black or African American, non-Hispanic/Latino; 2 Asian, non-Hispanic/Latino; 10 Hispanic/Latino; 1 Native Hawaiian or other Pacific Islander, non-Hispanic/Latino; 9 Two or more races, non-Hispanic/Latino), 17 international. 171 applicants, 47% accepted, 50 enrolled. In 2016, 38 master's, 6 doctorates awarded. *Degree requirements:* For master's, comprehensive exam (for some programs), thesis optional; for doctorate, thesis/dissertation. *Entrance requirements:* For master's, GRE General Test, minimum upper-division GPA of 3.0; for doctorate, GRE General Test, minimum upper-division GPA of 3.0, master's degree. Additional exam requirements/recommendations for international students: Required—TOEFL (minimum score 550 paper-based; 80 iBT). *Application deadline:* For fall admission, 4/1 for domestic and international students; for spring admission, 10/1 for domestic and international students. Applications are processed on a rolling basis. Application fee: $30. Electronic applications accepted. *Expenses:* Tuition, state resident: full-time $7263; part-time $403.51 per credit hour. Tuition, nonresident: full-time $18,087; part-time $1004.85 per credit hour. *Required fees:* $1365; $75.81 per credit hour. $20 per semester. Tuition and fees vary according to campus/location. *Financial support:* In 2016–17, 88 students received support, including 34 research assistantships with full tuition reimbursements available (averaging $7,796 per year), 78 teaching assistantships with full tuition reimbursements available (averaging $8,976 per year); career-related internships or fieldwork, Federal Work-Study, scholarships/grants, and unspecified assistantships also available. Financial award application deadline: 1/15; financial award applicants required to submit FAFSA. *Faculty research:* Body composition, functional food, chronic disease and aging response; food safety, food allergy, and safety/quality detection methods; sports nutrition, energy balance and human performance; cardiovascular function, families at risk, relational interventions, parenting, martial process and family therapy; merchandising and product development. *Total annual research expenditures:* $1.8 million. *Unit head:* Dr. Michael D. Delp, Dean, 850-644-1281, Fax: 850-644-0700, E-mail: mdelp@fsu.edu. *Application contact:* Tara L. Hartman, Academic Program Specialist, 850-644-7221, Fax: 850-644-0700, E-mail: thartman@fsu.edu.
Website: http://humansciences.fsu.edu

**Fontbonne University,** Graduate Programs, St. Louis, MO 63105-3098. Offers accounting (MBA, MS); art (MA); art (K-12) (MAT); business (MBA); computer science (MS); deaf education (MA); early intervention in deaf education (MA); education (MA), including autism spectrum disorders, curriculum and instruction, diverse learners, early childhood education, reading, special education; elementary education (MAT); family and consumer sciences (MA), including multidisciplinary health communication studies; fine arts (MFA); instructional design and technology (MS); management and leadership (MM); middle school education (MAT); secondary education (MAT); special education (MAT); speech-language pathology (MS); supply chain management (MS); theatre (MA). *Program availability:* Part-time, evening/weekend, online learning. *Faculty:* 32 full-time (24 women), 43 part-time/adjunct (26 women). *Students:* 456 full-time (313 women), 102 part-time (77 women); includes 138 minority (118 Black or African American, non-Hispanic/Latino; 1 American Indian or Alaska Native, non-Hispanic/Latino; 7 Asian, non-Hispanic/Latino; 9 Hispanic/Latino; 3 Two or more races, non-Hispanic/Latino), 37 international. *Degree requirements:* For master's, comprehensive exam (for some programs), thesis (for some programs). *Entrance requirements:* Additional exam requirements/recommendations for international students: Required—TOEFL (minimum score 500 paper-based; 65 iBT). *Application deadline:* For fall admission, 8/1 for international students; for spring admission, 12/1 for international students. Applications are processed on a rolling basis. Application fee: $25 ($30 for international students). Electronic applications accepted. *Expenses:* Full-time $8436; part-time $703 per credit hour. *Required fees:* $18 per credit hour. Tuition and fees vary according to course load. *Financial support:* Teaching assistantships with partial tuition reimbursements and scholarships/grants available. Support available to part-time students. Financial award application deadline: 4/1; financial award applicants required to submit FAFSA. *Unit head:* Dr. Carey Adams, Vice President for Academic Affairs, 314-719-3609, E-mail: cadams@fontbonne.edu. *Application contact:* Lauryn Filip, Coordinator, Graduate Admission and Professional Studies, 314-889-4650, E-mail: admissions@fontbonne.edu.
Website: https://www.fontbonne.edu/academics/graduate-programs/

**Hofstra University,** School of Education, Programs in Teacher Education, Hempstead, NY 11549. Offers bilingual education (MA, Advanced Certificate); bilingual extension (Advanced Certificate), including education/speech language pathology; business education (MS Ed); early childhood and childhood education (MS Ed); early childhood education (MA, MS Ed); education technology (Advanced Certificate); elementary education (MA, MS Ed), including science, technology, engineering, and mathematics

(STEM) (MA); English education (MS Ed); family and consumer science (MS Ed); fine arts and music education (Advanced Certificate); fine arts education (MS Ed); foreign language and TESOL (MS Ed); foreign language education (MS Ed), including French, German, Russian, Spanish; learning and teaching (Ed D), including applied linguistics, art education, arts and humanities, early childhood education, English education, human development, math education, math, science, and technology, multicultural education, physical education, science education, social studies education, special education; mathematics education (MA, MS Ed); middle school extension (Advanced Certificate), including grades 5-6, grades 7-9; music education (MA, MS Ed); science education (MA, MS Ed), including biology, chemistry, earth science, geology, physics; secondary education (Advanced Certificate); social studies education (MA, MS Ed); teaching languages other than English and TESOL (MS Ed); TESOL (MS Ed, Advanced Certificate). *Program availability:* Part-time, evening/weekend, blended/hybrid learning. *Students:* 139 full-time (97 women), 145 part-time (106 women); includes 60 minority (15 Black or African American, non-Hispanic/Latino; 1 American Indian or Alaska Native, non-Hispanic/Latino; 12 Asian, non-Hispanic/Latino; 31 Hispanic/Latino; 1 Two or more races, non-Hispanic/Latino), 21 international. Average age 29. 255 applicants, 86% accepted, 122 enrolled. In 2016, 101 master's, 4 doctorates, 43 other advanced degrees awarded. *Degree requirements:* For master's, comprehensive exam, thesis (for some programs), exit project, student teaching, fieldwork, electronic portfolio, curriculum project, minimum GPA of 3.0; for doctorate, thesis/dissertation; for Advanced Certificate, 3 foreign languages, comprehensive exam (for some programs), thesis project. *Entrance requirements:* For master's, GRE, MAT, 2 letters of recommendation, portfolio, teacher certification (MA), interview, essay; for doctorate, GMAT, GRE, LSAT, or MAT; for Advanced Certificate, 2 letters of recommendation, essay, interview and/or portfolio, teaching certificate. Additional exam requirements/recommendations for international students: Required—TOEFL (minimum score 550 paper-based; 80 iBT). *Application deadline:* Applications are processed on a rolling basis. Application fee: $75. Electronic applications accepted. *Expenses: Tuition:* Full-time $1240. *Required fees:* $970. Tuition and fees vary according to program. *Financial support:* In 2016–17, 149 students received support, including 58 fellowships with full and partial tuition reimbursements available (averaging $5,309 per year), 5 research assistantships with full and partial tuition reimbursements available (averaging $7,073 per year); career-related internships or fieldwork, Federal Work-Study, institutionally sponsored loans, scholarships/grants, traineeships, tuition waivers (full and partial), and unspecified assistantships also available. Support available to part-time students. Financial award applicants required to submit FAFSA. *Faculty research:* Educational interventions that foster critical-thinking skills; teachers' attitudes about professional development; threats to teacher quality. *Unit head:* Dr. Eustace Thompson, Chairperson, 516-463-5749, Fax: 516-463-6275, E-mail: eustace.g.thompson@hofstra.edu. *Application contact:* Sunil Samuel, Assistant Vice President of Admissions, 516-463-4723, Fax: 516-463-4664, E-mail: graduateadmission@hofstra.edu.
Website: http://www.hofstra.edu/education/

**Illinois State University,** Graduate School, College of Applied Science and Technology, Department of Family and Consumer Sciences, Normal, IL 61790-2200. Offers MA, MS. *Degree requirements:* For master's, thesis or alternative. *Entrance requirements:* For master's, GRE General Test, minimum GPA of 2.8 in last 60 hours of course work. *Faculty research:* Graduate practicum assistantships, startup for Jump Start of McLean County grant, providing low-income preschool children with early literacy experiences, generations of Hope-ICI replication.

**Iowa State University of Science and Technology,** Program in Family and Consumer Sciences, Ames, IA 50011. Offers MFCS. *Degree requirements:* For master's, thesis or alternative. *Entrance requirements:* For master's, GRE General Test. Additional exam requirements/recommendations for international students: Required—TOEFL (minimum score 550 paper-based; 79 iBT), IELTS (minimum score 6.5). *Application deadline:* For fall admission, 4/15 priority date for domestic and international students; for spring admission, 10/15 priority date for domestic and international students. Application fee: $60 ($90 for international students). Electronic applications accepted. *Application contact:* Karen Smidt, Application Contact, 515-294-5397, E-mail: mfcsinfo@iastate.edu.
Website: http://www.hs.iastate.edu/odeet/students/programs/comprehensive.php

**Kansas State University,** Graduate School, College of Human Ecology, Manhattan, KS 66506. Offers MS, PhD, Graduate Certificate. *Program availability:* Part-time, online learning. *Faculty:* 64 full-time (41 women), 10 part-time/adjunct (7 women). *Students:* 147 full-time (104 women), 167 part-time (131 women); includes 53 minority (17 Black or African American, non-Hispanic/Latino; 1 American Indian or Alaska Native, non-Hispanic/Latino; 5 Asian, non-Hispanic/Latino; 23 Hispanic/Latino; 1 Native Hawaiian or other Pacific Islander, non-Hispanic/Latino; 6 Two or more races, non-Hispanic/Latino), 45 international. Average age 33. 285 applicants, 35% accepted, 63 enrolled. In 2016, 82 master's, 18 doctorates, 20 other advanced degrees awarded. *Degree requirements:* For master's, residency; for doctorate, thesis/dissertation, residency. *Application deadline:* For fall admission, 2/1 priority date for domestic and international students; for spring admission, 8/1 priority date for domestic and international students. Applications are processed on a rolling basis. Application fee: $50 ($75 for international students). Electronic applications accepted. *Expenses:* Tuition, state resident: full-time $9670. Tuition, nonresident: full-time $21,828. *Required fees:* $862. *Financial support:* In 2016–17, 71 research assistantships (averaging $13,454 per year), 50 teaching assistantships with full and partial tuition reimbursements (averaging $13,202 per year) were awarded; career-related internships or fieldwork, Federal Work-Study, institutionally sponsored loans, scholarships/grants, and tuition waivers (full) also available. Support available to part-time students. Financial award application deadline: 3/1; financial award applicants required to submit FAFSA. *Faculty research:* Apparel and textiles, food service and hospitality management, life span human development, family life education and consultation, marriage and family therapy. *Total annual research expenditures:* $12.4 million. *Unit head:* Dr. John Buckwalter, Dean, 785-532-5500, Fax: 785-532-5504, E-mail: jbb3@ksu.edu. *Application contact:* Mary Anne Andrews, Director, Academic and Student Services, 785-532-5500, Fax: 785-532-5504, E-mail: mandrews@ksu.edu.
Website: http://www.he.k-state.edu/

**Lamar University,** College of Graduate Studies, College of Education and Human Development, Department of Family and Consumer Sciences, Beaumont, TX 77710. Offers MS. *Program availability:* Part-time, evening/weekend. *Faculty:* 6 full-time (all women). *Students:* 22 full-time (19 women), 6 part-time (5 women); includes 9 minority (4 Black or African American, non-Hispanic/Latino; 2 Asian, non-Hispanic/Latino; 2 Hispanic/Latino; 1 Two or more races, non-Hispanic/Latino), 6 international. Average age 29. 17 applicants, 100% accepted, 16 enrolled. In 2016, 10 master's awarded. *Degree requirements:* For master's, thesis optional. *Entrance requirements:* For master's, GRE General Test. Additional exam requirements/recommendations for international students: Required—TOEFL (minimum score 550 paper-based; 79 iBT), IELTS (minimum score 6.5). *Application deadline:* For fall admission, 8/10 for domestic students, 7/1 for international students; for spring admission, 1/5 for domestic students, 12/1 for international students. Applications are processed on a rolling basis. Application fee: $25 ($50 for international students). Electronic applications accepted. *Expenses:* $8,134 in-state full-time, $5,574 in-state part-time; $15,604 out-of-state full-time,

$10,554 out-of-state part-time per year. *Financial support:* Fellowships, research assistantships, teaching assistantships, career-related internships or fieldwork, Federal Work-Study, and institutionally sponsored loans available. Support available to part-time students. Financial award application deadline: 4/1; financial award applicants required to submit FAFSA. *Faculty research:* Maternal and infant nutrition, eating disorders, sports nutrition, human sexuality, family violence. *Unit head:* Dr. Tammy Henderson, Chair, 409-880-8668, Fax: 409-880-8666. *Application contact:* Deidre Mayer, Interim Director, Admissions and Academic Services, 409-880-8888, Fax: 409-880-7419, E-mail: gradmissions@lamar.edu.
Website: http://education.lamar.edu/family-and-consumer-sciences

**Louisiana State University and Agricultural & Mechanical College,** Graduate School, College of Agriculture, School of Human Ecology, Baton Rouge, LA 70803. Offers MS, PhD.

**Louisiana Tech University,** Graduate School, College of Applied and Natural Sciences, School of Human Ecology, Ruston, LA 71272. Offers nutrition and dietetics (MS). *Program availability:* Part-time. *Degree requirements:* For master's, comprehensive exam, thesis or alternative, Registered Dietician Exam eligibility. *Entrance requirements:* For master's, GRE General Test, minimum overall GPA of 2.75. *Application deadline:* For fall admission, 7/29 priority date for domestic students; for spring admission, 2/3 for domestic students. Applications are processed on a rolling basis. Application fee: $20 ($30 for international students). *Financial support:* Fellowships, research assistantships, career-related internships or fieldwork, and Federal Work-Study available. Financial award application deadline: 2/1. *Unit head:* Dr. Ethel G. Jones, Director, 318-257-3727, Fax: 318-257-4014.
Website: http://ans.latech.edu/human-ecology.html

**New Mexico State University,** College of Agricultural, Consumer and Environmental Sciences, Department of Family and Consumer Sciences, Las Cruces, NM 88003. Offers clothing, textiles, and merchandising (MS); family and child science (MS); family and consumer science education (MS); family and consumer sciences (MS); food science and technology (MS); hotel, restaurant, and tourism management (MS); human nutrition and dietetic sciences (MS). *Program availability:* Part-time. *Faculty:* 9 full-time (6 women), 1 (woman) part-time/adjunct. *Students:* 32 full-time (28 women), 6 part-time (5 women); includes 17 minority (2 Black or African American, non-Hispanic/Latino; 1 American Indian or Alaska Native, non-Hispanic/Latino; 14 Hispanic/Latino), 1 international. Average age 27. 23 applicants, 91% accepted, 15 enrolled. In 2016, 16 master's awarded. *Degree requirements:* For master's, comprehensive exam (for some programs), thesis (for some programs), oral exam. *Entrance requirements:* For master's, GRE, 3 letters of reference from faculty members or employers, resume, letter of interest. Additional exam requirements/recommendations for international students: Required—TOEFL (minimum score 550 paper-based; 79 iBT), IELTS (minimum score 6.5). *Application deadline:* For fall admission, 2/1 priority date for domestic and international students; for spring admission, 10/1 for domestic and international students. Applications are processed on a rolling basis. Application fee: $40 ($50 for international students). Electronic applications accepted. *Expenses:* Tuition, state resident: full-time $4086. Tuition, nonresident: full-time $14,254. *Required fees:* $853. Tuition and fees vary according to course load. *Financial support:* In 2016–17, 27 students received support, including 4 research assistantships (averaging $14,844 per year), 10 teaching assistantships (averaging $10,707 per year); career-related internships or fieldwork, Federal Work-Study, scholarships/grants, traineeships, health care benefits, and unspecified assistantships also available. Support available to part-time students. Financial award application deadline: 3/1. *Faculty research:* Food product analysis, childhood obesity, dietary decision-making, military families, equine assisted psychotherapy. *Total annual research expenditures:* $401,869. *Unit head:* Dr. Esther L. Devall, Department Head, 575-646-1161, Fax: 575-646-1889, E-mail: edevall@nmsu.edu. *Application contact:* Dr. Kourtney Vaillancourt, Graduate Program Contact, 575-646-3383, Fax: 575-646-1889, E-mail: kvaillan@nmsu.edu.
Website: http://aces.nmsu.edu/academics/fcs

**North Dakota State University,** College of Graduate and Interdisciplinary Studies, College of Human Development and Education, School of Education, Program in Family and Consumer Sciences Education, Fargo, ND 58102. Offers M Ed, MS. *Accreditation:* NCATE. *Program availability:* Part-time. *Degree requirements:* For master's, comprehensive exam, thesis or alternative. *Entrance requirements:* For master's, MAT. Additional exam requirements/recommendations for international students: Required—TOEFL. *Faculty research:* Needs of beginning teachers, learning styles and achievement, school-level variables and curriculum change.

**The Ohio State University,** Graduate School, College of Education and Human Ecology, Department of Human Sciences, Columbus, OH 43210. Offers consumer sciences (MS, PhD); human development and family science (PhD); human nutrition (MS, PhD); kinesiology (MA, PhD). *Program availability:* Part-time. *Faculty:* 54. *Students:* 128 full-time (77 women), 8 part-time (6 women); includes 21 minority (7 Black or African American, non-Hispanic/Latino; 8 Hispanic/Latino; 6 Two or more races, non-Hispanic/Latino), 30 international. Average age 27. In 2016, 27 master's, 17 doctorates awarded. *Degree requirements:* For master's, thesis optional; for doctorate, thesis/dissertation. *Entrance requirements:* For master's and doctorate, GRE. Additional exam requirements/recommendations for international students: Required—TOEFL (minimum score 550 paper-based; 79 iBT), Michigan English Language Assessment Battery (minimum score 82); Recommended—IELTS (minimum score 7). *Application deadline:* For fall admission, 12/1 priority date for domestic and international students. Applications are processed on a rolling basis. Application fee: $60 ($70 for international students). Electronic applications accepted. *Financial support:* Fellowships with tuition reimbursements, research assistantships with tuition reimbursements, teaching assistantships with tuition reimbursements, Federal Work-Study, and institutionally sponsored loans available. Support available to part-time students. *Unit head:* Dr. Joe Wheaton, Interim Chair, E-mail: wheaton.3@osu.edu. *Application contact:* Graduate and Professional Admissions, 614-292-9444, Fax: 614-292-3895, E-mail: gpadmissions@osu.edu.
Website: http://ehe.osu.edu/human-sciences/

**Oklahoma State University,** College of Human Sciences, Department of Human Development and Family Science, Stillwater, OK 74078. Offers human development and family science (MS, PhD), including family financial planning (MS), human environmental sciences; marriage and family therapy (MS). *Accreditation:* AAMFT/COAMFTE (one or more programs are accredited). *Program availability:* Online learning. *Faculty:* 31 full-time (22 women), 11 part-time/adjunct (9 women). *Students:* 26 full-time (23 women), 35 part-time (30 women); includes 16 minority (7 Black or African American, non-Hispanic/Latino; 1 American Indian or Alaska Native, non-Hispanic/Latino; 5 Hispanic/Latino; 3 Two or more races, non-Hispanic/Latino), 1 international. Average age 30. 47 applicants, 55% accepted, 22 enrolled. In 2016, 27 master's, 2 doctorates awarded. *Degree requirements:* For master's, thesis (for some programs); for doctorate, comprehensive exam, thesis/dissertation. *Entrance requirements:* For master's and doctorate, GRE or GMAT. Additional exam requirements/recommendations for international students: Required—TOEFL (minimum score 550 paper-based; 79 iBT). *Application deadline:* For fall admission, 3/1 priority date for international students; for spring admission, 8/1 priority date for international students.

## Family and Consumer Sciences-General

Applications are processed on a rolling basis. Application fee: $40 ($75 for international students). Electronic applications accepted. *Expenses:* Tuition, state resident: full-time $3775; part-time $209.70 per credit hour. Tuition, nonresident: full-time $14,851; part-time $825.05 per credit hour. *Required fees:* $2027; $112.60 per credit hour. Tuition and fees vary according to campus/location. *Financial support:* In 2016–17, 37 research assistantships (averaging $4,670 per year), 31 teaching assistantships (averaging $4,921 per year) were awarded; career-related internships or fieldwork, Federal Work-Study, scholarships/grants, health care benefits, tuition waivers (partial), and unspecified assistantships also available. Support available to part-time students. Financial award application deadline: 3/1; financial award applicants required to submit FAFSA. *Faculty research:* Family relations and child development, consequences of adolescent parenting, family stress and coping, impacts of sexual abuse on families, children's social cognition and self-competence, gerontology and health care. *Unit head:* Dr. Sissy Osteen, Department Head, 405-744-4741, Fax: 405-744-6344, E-mail: sissy.osteen@okstate.edu. *Application contact:* Dr. Michael Criss, Graduate Coordinator, 405-744-5057, Fax: 405-744-6344, E-mail: michael.criss@okstate.edu. Website: http://humansciences.okstate.edu/hdfs/

**Purdue University,** Graduate School, College of Health and Human Sciences, West Lafayette, IN 47907. Offers MS, Au D, PhD. *Program availability:* Part-time. *Faculty:* 212 full-time (119 women), 16 part-time/adjunct (11 women). *Students:* 417 full-time (312 women), 97 part-time (71 women); includes 64 minority (16 Black or African American, non-Hispanic/Latino; 1 American Indian or Alaska Native, non-Hispanic/Latino; 17 Asian, non-Hispanic/Latino; 17 Hispanic/Latino; 13 Two or more races, non-Hispanic/Latino; 121 international. Average age 28. 1,035 applicants, 34% accepted, 168 enrolled. In 2016, 53 master's, 118 doctorates awarded. *Degree requirements:* For doctorate, thesis/dissertation. *Entrance requirements:* Additional exam requirements/recommendations for international students: Required—TOEFL. *Application deadline:* Applications are processed on a rolling basis. Application fee: $60 ($75 for international students). Electronic applications accepted. *Financial support:* Fellowships, research assistantships, teaching assistantships, and career-related internships or fieldwork available. Support available to part-time students. Financial award applicants required to submit FAFSA. *Unit head:* Dr. Christine M. Ladisch, Inaugural Dean, 765-494-8210. *Application contact:* Graduate School Admissions, 765-494-2600, Fax: 765-494-0136, E-mail: gradinfo@purdue.edu. Website: http://www.purdue.edu/hhs/

**Queens College of the City University of New York,** Mathematics and Natural Sciences Division, Department of Family, Nutrition and Exercise Sciences, Queens, NY 11367-1597. Offers exercise science specialist (MS); family and consumer science (K-12) (AC); family and consumer science/teaching curriculum (K-12) (MS Ed); nutrition and exercise science (MS); nutrition specialist (MS); physical education (K-12) (AC); physical education/teaching curriculum (pre K-12) (MS Ed). *Program availability:* Part-time, evening/weekend. *Faculty:* 16 full-time (14 women), 46 part-time/adjunct (32 women). *Students:* 16 full-time (6 women), 157 part-time (86 women); includes 67 minority (19 Black or African American, non-Hispanic/Latino; 1 American Indian or Alaska Native, non-Hispanic/Latino; 18 Asian, non-Hispanic/Latino; 27 Hispanic/Latino; 2 Two or more races, non-Hispanic/Latino), 9 international. Average age 30. 95 applicants, 76% accepted, 45 enrolled. In 2016, 34 master's, 14 other advanced degrees awarded. *Degree requirements:* For master's, research project. *Entrance requirements:* For master's, minimum GPA of 3.0. Additional exam requirements/recommendations for international students: Required—TOEFL, IELTS. *Application deadline:* For fall admission, 4/1 for domestic students; for spring admission, 11/1 for domestic students. Applications are processed on a rolling basis. Application fee: $125. Electronic applications accepted. *Expenses:* Tuition, state resident: full-time $5065; part-time $425 per credit. Tuition, nonresident: part-time $780 per credit. *Required fees:* $522; $397 per credit. Part-time tuition and fees vary according to course load and program. *Financial support:* Career-related internships or fieldwork and unspecified assistantships available. Financial award application deadline: 4/1; financial award applicants required to submit FAFSA. *Unit head:* Dr. Michael Toner, Chairperson, 718-997-4168, E-mail: michael.toner@qc.cuny.edu.

**Sam Houston State University,** College of Health Sciences, Department of Family and Consumer Sciences, Huntsville, TX 77341. Offers dietetics (MS); family and consumer sciences (MS). *Program availability:* Part-time, evening/weekend. *Degree requirements:* For master's, comprehensive exam, thesis optional, internship. *Entrance requirements:* For master's, GRE General Test, letters of recommendation, personal statement, writing sample. Additional exam requirements/recommendations for international students: Required—TOEFL (minimum score 550 paper-based; 79 iBT), IELTS (minimum score 6.5). Electronic applications accepted.

**San Francisco State University,** Division of Graduate Studies, College of Health and Social Sciences, Department of Consumer and Family Studies/Dietetics, San Francisco, CA 94132-1722. Offers MA. *Program availability:* Part-time. *Application deadline:* Applications are processed on a rolling basis. *Expenses:* Tuition, state resident: full-time $6738. Tuition, nonresident: full-time $15,666. *Required fees:* $1012. Tuition and fees vary according to degree level and program. *Unit head:* Dr. Connie Ulasewicz, Chair, 415-338-2060, Fax: 415-338-0947, E-mail: cbu@sfsu.edu. *Application contact:* Kelly Vuong, Academic Office Coordinator, 415-338-1219, Fax: 415-338-0947, E-mail: kvuong@sfsu.edu. Website: http://cfsd.sfsu.edu/

**South Carolina State University,** College of Graduate and Professional Studies, Department of Family and Consumer Sciences, Orangeburg, SC 29117-0001. Offers individual and family development (MS); nutritional sciences (MS). *Program availability:* Part-time, evening/weekend. *Faculty:* 3 full-time (all women), 1 (woman) part-time/adjunct. *Students:* 7 full-time (5 women), 6 part-time (all women); all minorities (all Black or African American, non-Hispanic/Latino). Average age 33. 10 applicants, 90% accepted, 9 enrolled. In 2016, 5 master's awarded. *Degree requirements:* For master's, comprehensive exam, thesis optional, departmental qualifying exam. *Entrance requirements:* For master's, GRE, MAT, or NTE, minimum GPA of 2.7. *Application deadline:* For fall admission, 6/15 priority date for domestic students, 6/15 for international students; for spring admission, 11/1 for domestic and international students. Application fee: $25. Electronic applications accepted. *Expenses:* Tuition, state resident: full-time $8938; part-time $579 per credit hour. Tuition, nonresident: full-time $19,018; part-time $1139 per credit hour. *Required fees:* $1482; $82 per credit hour. *Financial support:* Fellowships, Federal Work-Study, and scholarships/grants available. Financial award application deadline: 6/1. *Unit head:* Dr. William H. Whitaker, Chair, Department of Family and Consumer Sciences, 803-536-8958, Fax: 803-533-3268, E-mail: wwhitak3@scsu.edu. *Application contact:* Curtis Foskey, Coordinator of Graduate Admission, 803-536-8419, Fax: 803-536-8812, E-mail: cfoskey@scsu.edu.

**South Dakota State University,** Graduate School, College of Education and Human Sciences, Department of Consumer Sciences, Brookings, SD 57007. Offers family financial planning (MS); merchandising (MS). *Entrance requirements:* For master's, resume. Additional exam requirements/recommendations for international students: Required—TOEFL (minimum score 525 paper-based).

**Stephen F. Austin State University,** Graduate School, College of Education, Department of Human Sciences, Nacogdoches, TX 75962. Offers MS. *Degree*

*requirements:* For master's, comprehensive exam, thesis or alternative. *Entrance requirements:* For master's, GRE General Test. Additional exam requirements/recommendations for international students: Required—TOEFL. *Faculty research:* Consumer economics, nutrition education, clothing and textiles, family, interior design.

**Tennessee State University,** The School of Graduate Studies and Research, College of Agriculture, Human and Natural Sciences, Nashville, TN 37209-1561. Offers agricultural sciences (MS), including agribusiness, agricultural and extension education, animal science, plant and soil science; biological sciences (MS, PhD); biotechnology (PhD); chemistry (MS). *Program availability:* Part-time, evening/weekend. *Degree requirements:* For master's, thesis. *Entrance requirements:* For master's, GRE General Test, GRE Subject Test, MAT. *Faculty research:* Small farm economics, ornamental horticulture, beef cattle production, rural elderly.

**Texas A&M University–Kingsville,** College of Graduate Studies, Dick and Mary Lewis Kleberg College of Agriculture, Natural Resources and Human Sciences, Department of Human Sciences, Kingsville, TX 78363. Offers MS. *Degree requirements:* For master's, variable foreign language requirement, comprehensive exam, thesis (for some programs). *Entrance requirements:* For master's, GRE, MAT, GMAT. Additional exam requirements/recommendations for international students: Required—TOEFL (minimum score 550 paper-based; 79 iBT). Electronic applications accepted. *Faculty research:* Mexican-American families, abuse in families, nontraditional students.

**Texas Southern University,** College of Liberal Arts and Behavioral Sciences, Department of Human Services and Consumer Sciences, Houston, TX 77004-4584. Offers MS. *Program availability:* Part-time, evening/weekend. *Degree requirements:* For master's, comprehensive exam, thesis (for some programs). *Entrance requirements:* For master's, GRE General Test, minimum GPA of 2.5. Additional exam requirements/recommendations for international students: Required—TOEFL. Electronic applications accepted. *Faculty research:* Food radiation/food for space travel, adolescent parenting, gerontology/grandparenting.

**Texas State University,** The Graduate College, College of Applied Arts, Program in Merchandising and Consumer Studies, San Marcos, TX 78666. Offers MS. *Program availability:* Part-time. *Faculty:* 4 full-time (all women). *Students:* 7 full-time (all women), 2 part-time (both women); includes 5 minority (1 Black or African American, non-Hispanic/Latino; 3 Hispanic/Latino; 1 Two or more races, non-Hispanic/Latino), 1 international. Average age 27. 7 applicants, 86% accepted, 1 enrolled. In 2016, 9 master's awarded. *Degree requirements:* For master's, thesis optional. *Entrance requirements:* For master's, GRE (minimum preferred score of 300 verbal plus quantitative), baccalaureate degree from regionally-accredited institution with minimum GPA of 3.0 on last 60 hours of undergraduate coursework; two letters of recommendation; statement of purpose describing professional goals and rationale for pursuing graduate study; resume. Additional exam requirements/recommendations for international students: Required—TOEFL (minimum score 550 paper-based; 78 iBT), IELTS (minimum score 6.5). *Application deadline:* For fall admission, 6/15 priority date for domestic students, 6/1 priority date for international students; for spring admission, 10/15 priority date for domestic students, 10/1 priority date for international students; for summer admission, 4/15 priority date for domestic students, 3/15 priority date for international students. Applications are processed on a rolling basis. Application fee: $40 ($90 for international students). Electronic applications accepted. *Expenses:* $4,851 per semester. *Financial support:* In 2016–17, 6 students received support, including 4 research assistantships (averaging $9,963 per year), 2 teaching assistantships (averaging $13,502 per year); scholarships/grants also available. Financial award application deadline: 3/1; financial award applicants required to submit FAFSA. *Faculty research:* Developing sustainability curriculum. *Total annual research expenditures:* $26,761. *Unit head:* Dr. Jiyun Kang, Graduate Advisor, 512-245-2534, E-mail: jk53@txstate.edu. *Application contact:* Dr. Andrea Golato, Dean of the Graduate College, 512-245-2581, Fax: 512-245-8365, E-mail: gradcollege@txstate.edu. Website: http://www.fcs.txstate.edu/degrees-programs/fm/fm_grad.html

**Texas Tech University,** Graduate School, College of Human Sciences, Lubbock, TX 79409-1162. Offers MS, PhD, JD/MS. *Program availability:* Part-time, 100% online, blended/hybrid learning. *Faculty:* 109 full-time (71 women), 23 part-time/adjunct (19 women). *Students:* 294 full-time (173 women), 118 part-time (82 women); includes 86 minority (14 Black or African American, non-Hispanic/Latino; 1 American Indian or Alaska Native, non-Hispanic/Latino; 3 Asian, non-Hispanic/Latino; 55 Hispanic/Latino; 13 Two or more races, non-Hispanic/Latino), 108 international. Average age 30. 364 applicants, 53% accepted, 122 enrolled. In 2016, 96 master's, 37 doctorates awarded. *Degree requirements:* For master's, comprehensive exam, thesis (for some programs); for doctorate, comprehensive exam, thesis/dissertation. *Entrance requirements:* Additional exam requirements/recommendations for international students: Required—TOEFL (minimum score 550 paper-based; 79 iBT). *Application deadline:* For fall admission, 6/1 priority date for domestic students, 1/15 priority date for international students; for spring admission, 9/1 priority date for domestic students, 6/15 priority date for international students. Applications are processed on a rolling basis. Application fee: $75. Electronic applications accepted. *Expenses:* $315 per credit hour full-time resident tuition, $723 per credit hour full-time non-resident tuition; $50.50 per credit hour fee plus $608 per term fee. *Financial support:* In 2016–17, 342 students received support, including 323 fellowships (averaging $4,316 per year), 90 research assistantships (averaging $9,852 per year), 128 teaching assistantships (averaging $11,940 per year); institutionally sponsored loans, scholarships/grants, and unspecified assistantships also available. Financial award application deadline: 2/1; financial award applicants required to submit FAFSA. *Faculty research:* Adult and childhood obesity; addiction and recovery sciences; rural health and wellbeing-both community and clinical perspectives; retirement planning, disability and the living environment; and developmental problems for children and families. *Total annual research expenditures:* $2.3 million. *Unit head:* Dr. Linda C. Hoover, Dean, 806-742-3031, Fax: 806-742-1849, E-mail: linda.hoover@ttu.edu. *Application contact:* Prof. Mitzi Lauderdale, Associate Dean for Students, 806-834-0529, Fax: 806-742-1849, E-mail: mitzi.lauderdale@ttu.edu. Website: http://www.hs.ttu.edu

**Tufts University,** Graduate School of Arts and Sciences, Eliot-Pearson Department of Child Study and Human Development, Medford, MA 02155. Offers child study and human development (MA, PhD); early childhood education (MAT). *Program availability:* Part-time. *Faculty:* 21 full-time (16 women), 15 part-time/adjunct (13 women). *Students:* 81 full-time (70 women), 6 part-time (5 women); includes 19 minority (6 Black or African American, non-Hispanic/Latino; 7 Asian, non-Hispanic/Latino; 3 Hispanic/Latino; 3 Two or more races, non-Hispanic/Latino), 16 international. Average age 27. 129 applicants, 59% accepted, 37 enrolled. In 2016, 19 master's, 5 doctorates awarded. *Degree requirements:* For master's, thesis (for some programs); for doctorate, comprehensive exam, thesis/dissertation. *Entrance requirements:* For master's and doctorate, GRE General Test. Additional exam requirements/recommendations for international students: Required—TOEFL (minimum score 550 paper-based; 80 iBT), IELTS (minimum score 6.5). *Application deadline:* For fall admission, 12/1 priority date for domestic and international students. Applications are processed on a rolling basis. Application fee: $85. Electronic applications accepted. *Expenses:* $49,982 full-time tuition (for MA); $29,936 full-time tuition (for PhD). *Financial support:* In 2016–17, 78 students received support. Fellowships, research assistantships, teaching assistantships, Federal Work-Study, scholarships/grants, tuition waivers (full and partial), and unspecified assistantships available. Support available to part-time students. Financial award application deadline: 1/15. *Faculty research:* Reading and language, developmental technologies, cognitive and social development, policy and program evaluation. *Unit head:* Dr. David Henry Feldman, Graduate Program Director. *Application contact:* Office of Graduate Admissions, 617-627-3395, E-mail: gradadmissions@tufts.edu. Website: http://ase.tufts.edu/epcd

**The University of Alabama,** Graduate School, College of Human Environmental Sciences, Tuscaloosa, AL 35487. Offers MA, MS, MSHES, PhD. *Program availability:* Part-time, evening/weekend, online learning. *Faculty:* 52 full-time (38 women), 3 part-time/adjunct (2 women). *Students:* 213 full-time (138 women), 392 part-time (278 women); includes 142 minority (105 Black or African American, non-Hispanic/Latino; 3 American Indian or Alaska Native, non-Hispanic/Latino; 4 Asian, non-Hispanic/Latino; 17 Hispanic/Latino; 2 Native Hawaiian or other Pacific Islander, non-Hispanic/Latino; 11 Two or more races, non-Hispanic/Latino), 5 international. Average age 33. 147 applicants, 82% accepted, 112 enrolled. In 2016, 90 master's awarded. *Degree requirements:* For doctorate, thesis/dissertation. *Entrance requirements:* For master's, GRE General Test or MAT (minimum score: 50th percentile), minimum GPA of 3.0; for doctorate, GRE General Test or MAT, minimum GPA of 3.0. *Application deadline:* For fall admission, 7/6 for domestic students. Applications are processed on a rolling basis. Application fee: $50 ($60 for international students). Electronic applications accepted. *Expenses:* Tuition, state resident: full-time $10,470. Tuition, nonresident: full-time $26,950. *Financial support:* In 2016–17, 2 research assistantships with full tuition reimbursements (averaging $9,000 per year) were awarded; fellowships with tuition reimbursements, teaching assistantships with full tuition reimbursements, career-related internships or fieldwork, Federal Work-Study, institutionally sponsored loans, and scholarships/grants also available. *Faculty research:* Students' use of credit, determinants of income differential: comparing Asians with blacks and whites, expenditure patterns of Chinese, racial and ethnic differences in the likelihood of charitable contributions, health insurance coverage and precautionary behavior savings. *Total annual research expenditures:* $122,639. *Unit head:* Dr. Milla D. Boschung, Dean, 205-348-6250, Fax: 205-348-1786, E-mail: mboschun@ches.ua.edu. *Application contact:* Patrick D. Fuller, Admissions Officer, 205-348-5923, Fax: 205-348-0400, E-mail: patrick.d.fuller@ua.edu. Website: http://www.ches.ua.edu/

**University of Alberta,** Faculty of Graduate Studies and Research, Department of Human Ecology, Edmonton, AB T6G 2E1, Canada. Offers family ecology and practice (M Sc, PhD); textiles and clothing (M Sc, MA, PhD). *Program availability:* Online learning. *Degree requirements:* For master's, thesis (for some programs); for doctorate, comprehensive exam, thesis/dissertation. *Entrance requirements:* For master's and doctorate, minimum GPA of 7.0 on a 9.0 scale. Additional exam requirements/recommendations for international students: Required—TOEFL (minimum score 580 paper-based). *Faculty research:* Families and aging, family and child poverty, paid and unpaid work of families, textiles and clothing, parent-child relationships.

**The University of Arizona,** College of Agriculture and Life Sciences, School of Family and Consumer Sciences, Tucson, AZ 85721. Offers PhD. *Program availability:* Part-time. *Entrance requirements:* For doctorate, GRE General Test, minimum GPA of 3.0. Additional exam requirements/recommendations for international students: Required—TOEFL (minimum score 550 paper-based; 79 iBT). Electronic applications accepted. *Faculty research:* Interpersonal relationships, human development, retailing management, consumer behaviors.

**University of Arkansas,** Graduate School, Dale Bumpers College of Agricultural, Food and Life Sciences, School of Human Environmental Sciences, Fayetteville, AR 72701. Offers MS. *Program availability:* Part-time, online learning. In 2016, 8 master's awarded. *Degree requirements:* For master's, comprehensive exam, thesis (for some programs). *Application deadline:* For fall admission, 4/1 for international students; for spring admission, 10/1 for international students. Applications are processed on a rolling basis. Application fee: $40 ($50 for international students). Electronic applications accepted. *Financial support:* In 2016–17, 14 research assistantships were awarded; fellowships, teaching assistantships, and Federal Work-Study also available. Support available to part-time students. Financial award application deadline: 4/1; financial award applicants required to submit FAFSA. *Unit head:* Dr. Betsy Garrison, Department Head, 479-575-4305, E-mail: megarris@uark.edu. *Application contact:* Graduate Admissions, 479-575-6246, Fax: 479-575-5908, E-mail: gradinfo@uark.edu. Website: http://hesc.uark.edu/

**University of Central Arkansas,** Graduate School, College of Health and Behavioral Sciences, Department of Family and Consumer Sciences, Conway, AR 72035-0001. Offers MS. *Program availability:* Part-time, evening/weekend, online learning. *Degree requirements:* For master's, comprehensive exam, thesis optional. *Entrance requirements:* For master's, GRE General Test, minimum GPA of 2.7. Additional exam requirements/recommendations for international students: Required—TOEFL (minimum score 550 paper-based). Electronic applications accepted. *Expenses:* Contact institution. *Faculty research:* Neurology, developmental disabilities, diet consequences.

**University of Central Oklahoma,** The Jackson College of Graduate Studies, College of Education and Professional Studies, Department of Human Environmental Sciences, Edmond, OK 73034-5209. Offers family and child studies (MS), including family life education, infant/child specialist, marriage and family therapy; nutrition-food management (MS). *Program availability:* Part-time. *Degree requirements:* For master's, comprehensive exam (for some programs), thesis (for some programs). *Entrance requirements:* For master's, GRE, essay, physical, CPR and First Aid training. Additional exam requirements/recommendations for international students: Required—TOEFL (minimum score 550 paper-based; 79 iBT), IELTS (minimum score 6.5). Electronic applications accepted.

**University of Florida,** Graduate School, College of Agricultural and Life Sciences, Department of Family, Youth, and Community Sciences, Gainesville, FL 32611. Offers community studies (MS); family and youth development (MS); family, youth and community sciences (MS); nonprofit organization development (MS). *Program availability:* Part-time, online learning. *Degree requirements:* For master's, comprehensive exam (for some programs), thesis (for some programs). *Entrance requirements:* For master's, GRE General Test, minimum GPA of 3.0. Additional exam requirements/recommendations for international students: Required—TOEFL (minimum score 550 paper-based; 80 iBT), IELTS (minimum score 6). Electronic applications accepted. *Faculty research:* Adolescent risk behaviors, family risk and resilience, family financial management, community-based organizations/interventions, nutrition and wellness.

**University of Georgia,** College of Family and Consumer Sciences, Athens, GA 30602. Offers MS. *Degree requirements:* For doctorate, thesis/dissertation. *Entrance requirements:* For master's and doctorate, GRE General Test. *Application deadline:* For fall admission, 7/1 priority date for domestic students; for spring admission, 11/15 for domestic students. Application fee: $50. Electronic applications accepted. *Financial support:* Fellowships, research assistantships, teaching assistantships, and unspecified assistantships available. Website: http://www.fcs.uga.edu/

**University of Houston,** College of Technology, Department of Human Development and Consumer Science, Houston, TX 77204. Offers future studies in commerce (MS); human resources development (MS). *Program availability:* Part-time. *Degree requirements:* For master's, project or thesis. *Entrance requirements:* For master's, GMAT, MAT. Additional exam requirements/recommendations for international students: Required—TOEFL (minimum score 550 paper-based; 79 iBT). Electronic applications accepted.

**University of Louisiana at Monroe,** Graduate School, College of Arts, Education, and Sciences, School of Education, Program in Curriculum and Instruction, Monroe, LA 71209-0001. Offers art education (M Ed); biology education (M Ed); chemistry education (M Ed); curriculum and instruction (Ed D); early childhood education (M Ed); earth science education (M Ed); educational leadership (M Ed); elementary education (1-5) (M Ed); English as a second language (M Ed); English education (M Ed); family and consumer education (M Ed); French education (M Ed); history education (M Ed); math education (M Ed); middle school education (M Ed); music education (M Ed); reading education (K-12) (M Ed); Spanish education (M Ed); special education - academically gifted (M Ed); special education - early intervention (M Ed); special education - educational diagnostician (M Ed); special education - mild/moderate disabilities (M Ed); speech education (M Ed). *Accreditation:* NCATE. *Faculty:* 8 full-time (4 women), 4 part-time/adjunct (3 women). *Students:* 13 full-time (11 women), 80 part-time (65 women); includes 25 minority (19 Black or African American, non-Hispanic/Latino; 1 Asian, non-Hispanic/Latino; 3 Hispanic/Latino; 2 Two or more races, non-Hispanic/Latino). Average age 37. 118 applicants, 30% accepted, 16 enrolled. In 2016, 23 master's, 4 doctorates awarded. *Degree requirements:* For master's, comprehensive exam (for some programs), thesis; for doctorate, thesis/dissertation, internships. *Entrance requirements:* For master's, GRE General Test; for doctorate, GRE General Test, minimum undergraduate GPA of 2.75, graduate 3.25. Additional exam requirements/recommendations for international students: Required—TOEFL (minimum score 500 paper-based; 61 iBT). *Application deadline:* For fall admission, 8/24 priority date for domestic students, 7/1 for international students; for winter admission, 12/14 priority date for domestic students; for spring admission, 1/19 for domestic students, 11/1 for international students. Applications are processed on a rolling basis. Application fee: $20 ($30 for international students). Electronic applications accepted. *Expenses:* Tuition, state resident: full-time $6489. Tuition, nonresident: full-time $18,589. *Required fees:* $8984. Tuition and fees vary according to course level, course load, degree level and program. *Financial support:* Research assistantships, career-related internships or fieldwork, Federal Work-Study, and unspecified assistantships available. Financial award application deadline: 4/1; financial award applicants required to submit FAFSA. *Unit head:* Dr. Dorothy Schween, Director, 318-342-1268, Fax: 318-342-3131, E-mail: schween@ulm.edu.

**University of Manitoba,** Faculty of Graduate Studies, Faculty of Human Ecology, Winnipeg, MB R3T 2N2, Canada. Offers M Sc. *Degree requirements:* For master's, thesis.

**University of Maryland, College Park,** Academic Affairs, School of Public Health, Department of Family Science, College Park, MD 20742. Offers family studies (PhD); marriage and family therapy (MS); maternal and child health (PhD). *Accreditation:* AAMFT/COAMFTE. *Program availability:* Part-time, evening/weekend. *Degree requirements:* For master's, thesis or alternative; for doctorate, comprehensive exam, thesis/dissertation, oral defense. *Entrance requirements:* For master's, GRE General Test, minimum GPA of 3.0, 3 letters of recommendation; for doctorate, GRE General Test, minimum GPA of 3.0, 3 letters of recommendation, research sample. Electronic applications accepted. *Faculty research:* Family life quality, interracial couples, child support, homeless families, family and child well-being.

**University of Missouri,** Office of Research and Graduate Studies, College of Human Environmental Sciences, Columbia, MO 65211. Offers MA, MS, PhD, Certificate, Graduate Certificate. *Accreditation:* AND. *Program availability:* Part-time. *Faculty:* 63 full-time (41 women). *Students:* 83 full-time (57 women), 87 part-time (64 women); includes 22 minority (8 Black or African American, non-Hispanic/Latino; 4 Asian, non-Hispanic/Latino; 7 Hispanic/Latino; 3 Two or more races, non-Hispanic/Latino), 33 international. Average age 33. *Degree requirements:* For doctorate, thesis/dissertation. *Entrance requirements:* For master's and doctorate, GRE General Test, minimum GPA of 3.0. Additional exam requirements/recommendations for international students: Required—TOEFL (minimum score 550 paper-based; 80 iBT), IELTS (minimum score 6.5). *Application deadline:* Applications are processed on a rolling basis. Application fee: $75 ($90 for international students). *Expenses:* Tuition, state resident: full-time $6347; part-time $352.60 per credit hour. Tuition, nonresident: full-time $17,379; part-time $965.50 per credit hour. *Required fees:* $1035. Tuition and fees vary according to course load, campus/location and program. *Financial support:* Fellowships with tuition reimbursements, research assistantships with tuition reimbursements, teaching assistantships with tuition reimbursements, institutionally sponsored loans, scholarships/grants, traineeships, health care benefits, and unspecified assistantships available. Support available to part-time students. Website: http://hes.missouri.edu/

**University of Nebraska–Lincoln,** Graduate College, College of Education and Human Sciences, Department of Child, Youth and Family Studies, Lincoln, NE 68588. Offers child development/early childhood education (MS, PhD); child, youth and family studies (MS); family and consumer sciences education (MS, PhD); family financial planning (MS); family science (MS, PhD); gerontology (PhD); human sciences (PhD), including child, youth and family studies, gerontology, medical family therapy; marriage and family therapy (MS); medical family therapy (PhD); youth development (MS). *Accreditation:* AAMFT/COAMFTE (one or more programs are accredited). *Program availability:* Online learning. *Degree requirements:* For master's, thesis optional. *Entrance requirements:* For master's, GRE. Additional exam requirements/recommendations for international students: Required—TOEFL (minimum score 550 paper-based). Electronic applications accepted. *Faculty research:* Marriage and family therapy, child development/early childhood education, family financial management.

**University of Puerto Rico, Río Piedras Campus,** College of Education, Program in Family Ecology and Nutrition, San Juan, PR 00931-3300. Offers M Ed. *Program availability:* Part-time. *Degree requirements:* For master's, thesis. *Entrance requirements:* For master's, PAEG or GRE, minimum GPA of 3.0, letter of recommendation.

**University of South Africa,** College of Agriculture and Environmental Sciences, Pretoria, South Africa. Offers agriculture (MS); consumer science (MCS); environmental management (MA, MS, PhD); environmental science (MA, MS, PhD); geography (MA, MS, PhD); horticulture (M Tech); human ecology (MHE); life sciences (MS); nature conservation (M Tech).

**The University of Tennessee,** Graduate School, College of Education, Health and Human Sciences, Program in Human Ecology, Knoxville, TN 37996. Offers child and family studies (PhD); community health (PhD); nutrition science (PhD); retailing and consumer sciences (PhD); textile science (PhD). *Degree requirements:* For doctorate, thesis/dissertation. *Entrance requirements:* For doctorate, GRE General Test, minimum

GPA of 2.7. Additional exam requirements/recommendations for international students: Required—TOEFL. Electronic applications accepted.

**The University of Tennessee at Martin,** Graduate Programs, College of Agriculture and Applied Sciences, Department of Family and Consumer Sciences, Martin, TN 38238. Offers dietetics (MSFCS); general family and consumer sciences (MSFCS). *Program availability:* Part-time, 100% online. *Faculty:* 10. *Students:* 5 full-time (all women), 34 part-time (32 women); includes 9 minority (8 Black or African American, non-Hispanic/Latino; 1 Two or more races, non-Hispanic/Latino). Average age 28. 58 applicants, 71% accepted, 15 enrolled. In 2016, 11 master's awarded. *Degree requirements:* For master's, comprehensive exam, thesis optional. *Entrance requirements:* For master's, GRE General Test, minimum GPA of 2.5. Additional exam requirements/recommendations for international students: Required—TOEFL (minimum score 525 paper-based; 71 iBT). *Application deadline:* For fall admission, 7/27 priority date for domestic and international students; for spring admission, 12/17 priority date for domestic and international students; for summer admission, 5/10 priority date for domestic and international students. Applications are processed on a rolling basis. Application fee: $30 ($130 for international students). Electronic applications accepted. *Expenses:* Tuition, state resident: full-time $8254; part-time $459 per credit hour. Tuition, nonresident: full-time $22,198; part-time $1234 per credit hour. *Required fees:* $79 per credit hour. Part-time tuition and fees vary according to course load and campus/location. *Financial support:* In 2016–17, 4 students received support, including 1 research assistantship (averaging $6,283 per year), 3 teaching assistantships with full tuition reimbursements available (averaging $8,001 per year); scholarships/grants and unspecified assistantships also available. Financial award application deadline: 2/1; financial award applicants required to submit FAFSA. *Faculty research:* Children with developmental disabilities, regional food product development and marketing, parent education. *Unit head:* Dr. Lisa LeBleu, Coordinator, 731-881-7116, Fax: 731-881-7106, E-mail: llebleu@utm.edu. *Application contact:* Jolene L. Cunningham, Student Services Specialist, 731-881-7012, Fax: 731-881-7499, E-mail: jcunningham@utm.edu. Website: http://www.utm.edu/departments/caas/fcs/index.php

**The University of Texas at Austin,** Graduate School, College of Natural Sciences, School of Human Ecology, Austin, TX 78712-1111. Offers human development and family sciences (MA, PhD); nutritional sciences (MA, PhD), including nutrition (MA); nutritional sciences (PhD); textile and apparel technology (MS). *Degree requirements:*

For master's, thesis; for doctorate, thesis/dissertation. *Entrance requirements:* For master's and doctorate, GRE General Test. Electronic applications accepted.

**University of Wisconsin–Madison,** Graduate School, School of Human Ecology, Madison, WI 53706. Offers consumer behavior and family economics (MS, PhD); design studies (MFA, MS, PhD); human development and family studies (MS, PhD). Terminal master's awarded for partial completion of doctoral program. *Degree requirements:* For master's, thesis (for some programs); for doctorate, comprehensive exam, thesis/dissertation. *Entrance requirements:* For master's, GRE General Test, portfolio (design studies), 3 letters of recommendation; for doctorate, GRE General Test. Additional exam requirements/recommendations for international students: Required—TOEFL (minimum score 580 paper-based; 92 iBT). Electronic applications accepted.

**University of Wisconsin–Stevens Point,** College of Professional Studies, School of Health Promotion and Human Development, Program in Human and Community Resources, Stevens Point, WI 54481-3897. Offers MS. *Program availability:* Part-time. *Degree requirements:* For master's, thesis or alternative. *Entrance requirements:* For master's, minimum GPA of 2.75.

**Utah State University,** School of Graduate Studies, Emma Eccles Jones College of Education and Human Services, Department of Family, Consumer, and Human Development, Logan, UT 84322. Offers family and human development (MFHD); family, consumer, and human development (MS, PhD), including adolescence/youth (MS), adult development/aging (MS), consumer science (MS), infancy/childhood (MS), marriage and family relations (MS), marriage and family therapy (MS). *Accreditation:* AAMFT/COAMFTE (one or more programs are accredited). *Program availability:* Part-time, evening/weekend, online learning. *Degree requirements:* For master's, thesis; for doctorate, comprehensive exam, thesis/dissertation, competencies. *Entrance requirements:* For master's, GRE General Test or MAT, minimum GPA of 3.0, 3 letters of recommendation; for doctorate, GRE, minimum GPA of 3.0, 3 letters of recommendation. Additional exam requirements/recommendations for international students: Required—TOEFL. Electronic applications accepted. *Faculty research:* Marriage and family relations, adolescent problem behavior, family financial management, early literacy, mental health in the elderly, parent child attachment.

**Western Michigan University,** Graduate College, College of Education and Human Development, Department of Family and Consumer Sciences, Kalamazoo, MI 49008. Offers career and technical education (MA); family and consumer sciences (MA).

# Child and Family Studies

**Alabama Agricultural and Mechanical University,** School of Graduate Studies, College of Agricultural, Life and Natural Sciences, Department of Family and Consumer Sciences, Huntsville, AL 35811. Offers apparel, merchandising and design (MS); family and consumer sciences (MS); human development and family studies (MS); nutrition and hospitality management (MS). *Program availability:* Part-time, evening/weekend. *Degree requirements:* For master's, comprehensive exam, thesis optional. *Entrance requirements:* For master's, GRE General Test. Additional exam requirements/recommendations for international students: Required—TOEFL (minimum score 500 paper-based; 61 iBT). *Application deadline:* For fall admission, 5/1 for domestic students. Applications are processed on a rolling basis. Application fee: $25. Electronic applications accepted. *Expenses:* Tuition, nonresident: part-time $826 per credit hour. Full-time tuition and fees vary according to course load and program. *Financial support:* Research assistantships with tuition reimbursements, teaching assistantships with tuition reimbursements, career-related internships or fieldwork, Federal Work-Study, and traineeships available. Financial award application deadline: 4/1. *Faculty research:* Food biotechnology, nutrition, food microbiology, food engineering, food chemistry. *Unit head:* Dr. Cynthia Smith, Chair, 256-372-4172, Fax: 256-372-5433, E-mail: cynthia.smith@aamu.edu. Website: http://www.aamu.edu/academics/alns/consumersciences/

**Amberton University,** Graduate School, Program in Family Studies, Garland, TX 75041-5595. Offers MS.

**Arizona State University at the Tempe campus,** College of Liberal Arts and Sciences, School of Social and Family Dynamics, Tempe, AZ 85287-3701. Offers family and human development (MS, PhD); infant-family practice (MAS); marriage and family therapy (MAS); sociology (MA, PhD). Terminal master's awarded for partial completion of doctoral program. *Degree requirements:* For master's, thesis or alternative, interactive Program of Study (iPOS) submitted before completing 50 percent of required credit hours; for doctorate, thesis/dissertation, interactive Program of Study (iPOS) submitted before completing 50 percent of required credit hours. *Entrance requirements:* For master's and doctorate, GRE, minimum GPA of 3.0 or equivalent in last 2 years of work leading to bachelor's degree. Additional exam requirements/recommendations for international students: Required—TOEFL, IELTS, or PTE. Electronic applications accepted. *Expenses:* Contact institution.

**Asbury University,** School of Graduate and Professional Studies, Master of Social Work Program, Wilmore, KY 40390-1198. Offers child and family services (MSW). *Accreditation:* CSWE. *Degree requirements:* For master's, comprehensive exam, 954 praticum hours completed in agency. *Entrance requirements:* For master's, prerequisite courses in psychology, sociology, and statistics. Additional exam requirements/recommendations for international students: Required—TOEFL. Electronic applications accepted. *Expenses:* Contact institution. *Faculty research:* Integration of faith and practice, survivors of family violence, program evaluation, cross-cultural counseling.

**Assumption College,** Clinical Counseling Psychology Program, Worcester, MA 01609-1296. Offers child and family interventions (MA); clinical counseling (CAGS); cognitive-behavioral therapies (MA). *Program availability:* Part-time, evening/weekend. *Faculty:* 4 full-time (2 women), 7 part-time/adjunct (2 women). *Students:* 40 full-time (31 women), 29 part-time (26 women); includes 11 minority (1 Black or African American, non-Hispanic/Latino; 1 American Indian or Alaska Native, non-Hispanic/Latino; 4 Asian, non-Hispanic/Latino; 5 Hispanic/Latino). Average age 27. 63 applicants, 51% accepted, 20 enrolled. In 2016, 25 master's awarded. *Degree requirements:* For master's, comprehensive exam, internship, practicum; for CAGS, comprehensive exam. *Entrance requirements:* For master's, bachelor's degree and at least 6 psychology courses completed with minimum GPA of 3.0 both overall and in the psychology courses; 3 letters of recommendation; official transcripts; personal statement; current resume; for CAGS, master's degree in clinical counseling psychology or mental health counseling, or baccalaureate degree and at least 6 psychology courses with minimum GPA of 3.0 overall and in psychology courses; 3 letters of recommendation; official transcripts; personal statement; current resume; interview. Additional exam requirements/recommendations for international students: Required—TOEFL (minimum score 540

paper-based; 76 iBT), IELTS (minimum score 6). *Application deadline:* For fall admission, 3/7 priority date for domestic and international students; for spring admission, 10/5 for domestic and international students; for summer admission, 2/8 for domestic and international students. Application fee: $30. Electronic applications accepted. *Expenses: Tuition:* Full-time $11,610; part-time $645 per credit. *Required fees:* $70 per term. Tuition and fees vary according to course load and program. *Financial support:* In 2016–17, 17 students received support, including 12 fellowships with full tuition reimbursements available; tuition waivers (full and partial), unspecified assistantships, and institutional discounts also available. Financial award application deadline: 3/7; financial award applicants required to submit FAFSA. *Faculty research:* Mood disorders, adjustment to life-threatening illness, perception of movement, socioemotional development of young children, discovery versus disclosure. *Unit head:* Dr. Leonard A. Doerfler, Director, 508-767-7549, Fax: 508-767-7263, E-mail: doerfler@assumption.edu. *Application contact:* Karen Stoyanoff, Director of Recruitment for Graduate Enrollment, 508-767-7442, Fax: 508-799-4412, E-mail: graduate@assumption.edu. Website: http://graduate.assumption.edu/counseling-psychology/ma-clinical-counseling-psychology-overview

**Auburn University,** Graduate School, College of Human Sciences, Department of Human Development and Family Studies, Auburn University, AL 36849. Offers MS, PhD. *Accreditation:* AAMFT/COAMFTE (one or more programs are accredited). *Program availability:* Part-time. *Faculty:* 24 full-time (15 women). *Students:* 22 full-time (18 women), 11 part-time (9 women); includes 9 minority (6 Black or African American, non-Hispanic/Latino; 1 Asian, non-Hispanic/Latino; 2 Hispanic/Latino). Average age 26. 52 applicants, 27% accepted, 11 enrolled. In 2016, 8 master's, 6 doctorates awarded. *Degree requirements:* For master's, thesis, oral exam; for doctorate, thesis/dissertation. *Entrance requirements:* For master's, GRE General Test; for doctorate, GRE General Test, master's degree. *Application deadline:* Applications are processed on a rolling basis. Application fee: $50 ($60 for international students). *Expenses:* Tuition, state resident: full-time $9072; part-time $504 per credit hour. Tuition, nonresident: full-time $27,216; part-time $1512 per credit hour. *Required fees:* $812 per semester. Tuition and fees vary according to degree level and program. *Financial support:* Research assistantships, teaching assistantships, and Federal Work-Study available. Support available to part-time students. Financial award application deadline: 3/15; financial award applicants required to submit FAFSA. *Faculty research:* Family influences on personality and social development, parent-child relations, infancy, day care, parent education. *Unit head:* Dr. Joe F. Pittman, Jr., Head, 334-844-3242, E-mail: mbradbar@humsci.auburn.edu. *Application contact:* Dr. George Flowers, Dean of the Graduate School, 334-844-2125. Website: http://www.humsci.auburn.edu/hdfs/

**Bank Street College of Education,** Graduate School, Program in Child Life, New York, NY 10025. Offers MS. *Degree requirements:* For master's, thesis. *Entrance requirements:* For master's, interview, essays, 100 hours of volunteer experience in a child life setting. Additional exam requirements/recommendations for international students: Required—TOEFL (minimum score 600 paper-based; 100 iBT), IELTS (minimum score 7). *Faculty research:* Therapeutic play in child life setting, child advocacy, psychosocial and educational intervention with care of sick children.

**Bank Street College of Education,** Graduate School, Program in Infant and Family Development and Early Intervention, New York, NY 10025. Offers infant and family development (MS Ed); infant and family early childhood special and general education (MS Ed); infant and family/early childhood special education (Ed M). *Degree requirements:* For master's, thesis. *Entrance requirements:* For master's, interview, essays. Additional exam requirements/recommendations for international students: Required—TOEFL (minimum score 600 paper-based; 100 iBT), IELTS (minimum score 7). Electronic applications accepted. *Faculty research:* Early intervention, early attachment practice in infant and toddler childcare, parenting skills in adolescents.

**Brandeis University,** The Heller School for Social Policy and Management, Program in Public Policy, Waltham, MA 02454-9110. Offers aging (MPP); behavioral health (MPP);

children, youth and families (MPP); general social policy (MPP); health (MPP); poverty alleviation and development (MPP); MPP/MA. *Degree requirements:* For master's, thesis. *Entrance requirements:* For master's, GRE, 3 letters of recommendation, statement of purpose, 3 to 5 years of professional experience. Additional exam requirements/recommendations for international students: Required—TOEFL (minimum score 600 paper-based; 100 iBT). Electronic applications accepted. *Faculty research:* Health and behavioral health, children and families, disabilities, aging policy, substance abuse, work, inequality and social change, women/gender, poverty alleviation.

**Brandeis University,** The Heller School for Social Policy and Management, Program in Social Policy, Waltham, MA 02454-9110. Offers assets and inequalities (PhD); children, youth and families (PhD); global health and development (PhD); health and behavioral health (PhD). *Degree requirements:* For doctorate, comprehensive exam, thesis/ dissertation, qualifying paper, 2-year residency. *Entrance requirements:* For doctorate, GRE General Test, 3 letters of recommendation, statement of purpose, writing sample, at least 3-5 years of professional experience. Additional exam requirements/ recommendations for international students: Required—TOEFL (minimum score 600 paper-based; 100 iBT). Electronic applications accepted. *Faculty research:* Health; mental health; substance abuse; children, youth, and families; aging; international and community development; disabilities; work and inequality; hunger and poverty.

**Brigham Young University,** Graduate Studies, College of Family, Home, and Social Sciences, Program in Marriage, Family and Human Development, Provo, UT 84602. Offers MS, PhD. *Accreditation:* AAMFT/COAMFTE. *Faculty:* 24 full-time (5 women). *Students:* 27 full-time (15 women); includes 4 minority (1 American Indian or Alaska Native, non-Hispanic/Latino; 2 Asian, non-Hispanic/Latino; 1 Native Hawaiian or other Pacific Islander, non-Hispanic/Latino), 3 international. Average age 27. 24 applicants, 54% accepted, 11 enrolled. In 2016, 5 master's, 4 doctorates awarded. *Degree requirements:* For master's, thesis; for doctorate, comprehensive exam, thesis/ dissertation. *Entrance requirements:* For master's and doctorate, GRE General Test, minimum GPA of 3.0 in last 60 semester hours, letters of recommendation. Additional exam requirements/recommendations for international students: Required—TOEFL (minimum score 580 paper-based; 85 iBT), IELTS (minimum score 7). *Application deadline:* For fall admission, 1/10 for domestic and international students. Application fee: $50. Electronic applications accepted. *Expenses: Tuition:* Full-time $6680; part-time $393 per credit. Tuition and fees vary according to course load, program and student's religious affiliation. *Financial support:* In 2016–17, 23 students received support, including 23 research assistantships with full and partial tuition reimbursements available (averaging $8,560 per year), 1 teaching assistantship with tuition reimbursement available (averaging $2,800 per year); scholarships/grants and unspecified assistantships also available. Financial award application deadline: 3/25. *Faculty research:* Family studies and family process, marriage, adolescence and emerging adulthood, adult development and aging, child development. *Unit head:* Dr. Dean M. Busby, Director, School of Life, 801-422-2069, Fax: 801-422-0230, E-mail: dean_busby@byu.edu. *Application contact:* Graduate Secretary, 801-422-2060, E-mail: mfhdgrad@byu.edu.
Website: http://mfhd.byu.edu

**Brock University,** Faculty of Graduate Studies, Faculty of Social Sciences, Program in Child and Youth Studies, St. Catharines, ON L2S 3A1, Canada. Offers MA. *Program availability:* Part-time. *Degree requirements:* For master's, thesis. *Entrance requirements:* For master's, honors BA. Additional exam requirements/ recommendations for international students: Required—TOEFL (minimum score 550 paper-based; 80 iBT), IELTS (minimum score 6.5), TWE (minimum score 4). Electronic applications accepted. *Faculty research:* Cognitive mechanisms, youth resilience, developmental disabilities, parent-child interactions and communication.

**California State University, East Bay,** Office of Graduate Studies, College of Letters, Arts, and Social Sciences, Department of Social Work, Hayward, CA 94542-3000. Offers children, youth, and family services (MSW); community mental health services (MSW). *Accreditation:* CSWE. *Students:* 129 full-time (106 women), 2 part-time (both women); includes 102 minority (33 Black or African American, non-Hispanic/Latino; 1 American Indian or Alaska Native, non-Hispanic/Latino; 20 Asian, non-Hispanic/Latino; 43 Hispanic/Latino; 5 Two or more races, non-Hispanic/Latino), 1 international. Average age 31. 394 applicants, 21% accepted, 68 enrolled. In 2016, 125 master's awarded. *Degree requirements:* For master's, comprehensive exam. *Entrance requirements:* For master's, minimum GPA of 2.8; courses in statistics and either human biology, physiology, or anatomy; liberal arts or social science baccalaureate degree; 3 letters of recommendation; personal statement; criminal background check; student professional liability insurance. Additional exam requirements/recommendations for international students: Required—TOEFL (minimum score 550 paper-based). *Application deadline:* For fall admission, 3/15 for domestic and international students. Applications are processed on a rolling basis. Application fee: $55. Electronic applications accepted. *Financial support:* Fellowships, career-related internships or fieldwork, Federal Work-Study, institutionally sponsored loans, and scholarships/grants available. Support available to part-time students. Financial award application deadline: 3/2; financial award applicants required to submit FAFSA. *Unit head:* Dr. Holly Vugia, Interim Chair, 510-885-2121, E-mail: holly.vugia@csueastbay.edu. *Application contact:* Dr. Donna Wiley, Interim Associate Vice President for Academic Programs and Graduate Studies, 510-885-3716, Fax: 510-885-4777, E-mail: donna.wiley@csueastbay.edu.
Website: http://www20.csueastbay.edu/class/departments/socialwork/

**California State University, Los Angeles,** Graduate Studies, College of Health and Human Services, Department of Child and Family Studies, Los Angeles, CA 90032-8530. Offers child development (MA). *Program availability:* Part-time, evening/weekend. *Degree requirements:* For master's, comprehensive exam, project or thesis. *Entrance requirements:* Additional exam requirements/recommendations for international students: Required—TOEFL (minimum score 500 paper-based). *Faculty research:* Nutrition education, laundry product and fabric durability, computer usage in public school home economics.

**California State University, San Marcos,** College of Education, Health and Human Services, Department of Social Work, San Marcos, CA 92096-0001. Offers behavioral health (MSW); children, youth and families (MSW). *Accreditation:* CSWE. *Degree requirements:* For master's, thesis, capstone project. *Expenses:* Contact institution.

**Capella University,** Harold Abel School of Social and Behavioral Science, Master's Programs in Counseling, Minneapolis, MN 55402. Offers child and adolescent development (MS); general addiction counseling (MS); general marriage and family counseling/therapy (MS); general mental health counseling (MS); general school counseling (MS).

**Central Michigan University,** College of Graduate Studies, College of Education and Human Services, Department of Human Environmental Studies, Mount Pleasant, MI 48859. Offers apparel product development and merchandising technology (MS); gerontology (Graduate Certificate); human development and family studies (MA); nutrition and dietetics (MS). *Program availability:* Part-time, evening/weekend. *Degree requirements:* For master's, thesis or alternative. Electronic applications accepted. *Faculty research:* Human growth and development, family studies and human sexuality,

human nutrition and dietetics, apparel and textile retailing, computer-aided design for apparel.

**Central Washington University,** Graduate Studies and Research, College of Education and Professional Studies, Department of Family and Consumer Sciences, Ellensburg, WA 98926. Offers career and technical education (MS); family and consumer sciences education (MS); family studies (MS). *Program availability:* Part-time. *Degree requirements:* For master's, thesis or alternative. *Entrance requirements:* For master's, minimum GPA of 3.0. Additional exam requirements/recommendations for international students: Required—TOEFL (minimum score 550 paper-based; 79 iBT). Electronic applications accepted.

**Colorado State University,** College of Health and Human Sciences, Department of Human Development and Family Studies, Fort Collins, CO 80523-1570. Offers applied developmental science (PhD); family and developmental studies (MS); marriage and family therapy (MS). *Accreditation:* AAMFT/COAMFTE. *Faculty:* 18 full-time (15 women), 3 part-time/adjunct (0 women). *Students:* 34 full-time (30 women), 4 part-time (3 women); includes 6 minority (2 Asian, non-Hispanic/Latino; 4 Hispanic/Latino), 1 international. Average age 27. 64 applicants, 38% accepted, 14 enrolled. In 2016, 6 master's, 3 doctorates awarded. Terminal master's awarded for partial completion of doctoral program. *Degree requirements:* For master's, thesis; for doctorate, comprehensive exam, thesis/dissertation. *Entrance requirements:* For master's and doctorate, GRE General Test, 3 letters of recommendation; minimum GPA of 3.0. Additional exam requirements/recommendations for international students: Required—TOEFL (minimum score 550 paper-based; 80 iBT), IELTS (minimum score 6.5), PTE (minimum score 58). *Application deadline:* For fall admission, 1/2 priority date for domestic and international students. Application fee: $60 ($70 for international students). Electronic applications accepted. *Expenses: Tuition,* state resident: full-time $9628. Tuition, nonresident: full-time $23,603. *Required fees:* $2253; $528.14 per credit hour. $264.07 per semester. Tuition and fees vary according to course load and program. *Financial support:* In 2016–17, 35 students received support, including 14 research assistantships with full and partial tuition reimbursements available (averaging $10,449 per year), 13 teaching assistantships with full and partial tuition reimbursements available (averaging $8,038 per year); fellowships with full and partial tuition reimbursements available, Federal Work-Study, scholarships/grants, health care benefits, and unspecified assistantships also available. Financial award application deadline: 1/2; financial award applicants required to submit FAFSA. *Faculty research:* Risk, resilience, and developmental psychopathology; treatment, intervention, and prevention science; emotion, regulation, and relational processes; adult development and aging; cultural context and diversity. *Total annual research expenditures:* $1.2 million. *Unit head:* Dr. Lise Youngblade, Department Head, 970-491-3581, Fax: 970-491-7975, E-mail: lise.youngblade@colostate.edu. *Application contact:* Mary Daughtrey, Administrative Assistant III, 970-491-2872, Fax: 970-491-7975, E-mail: mary.daughtrey@colostate.edu.
Website: http://www.hdfs.chhs.colostate.edu/

**Concordia University,** School of Graduate Studies, Faculty of Arts and Science, Department of Education, Program in Child Studies, Montréal, QC H3G 1M8, Canada. Offers MA. *Degree requirements:* For master's, one foreign language, thesis optional. *Entrance requirements:* For master's, minimum B average in undergraduate course work. *Faculty research:* Development and family relations, children and technology, cooperative learning strategies, exceptional children, second language acquisition.

**Concordia University, St. Paul,** College of Health and Science, St. Paul, MN 55104-5494. Offers criminal justice leadership (MA); exercise science (MS); family science (MA); human services (MA); orthotics and prosthetics (MS); physical therapy (DPT); sports management (MA). *Program availability:* Part-time, evening/weekend, 100% online, blended/hybrid learning. *Faculty:* 7 full-time (2 women), 27 part-time/adjunct (9 women). *Students:* 337 full-time (194 women), 18 part-time (7 women); includes 65 minority (35 Black or African American, non-Hispanic/Latino; 7 Asian, non-Hispanic/Latino; 8 Hispanic/Latino; 4 Native Hawaiian or other Pacific Islander, non-Hispanic/Latino; 11 Two or more races, non-Hispanic/Latino), 3 international. Average age 30. 388 applicants, 40% accepted, 117 enrolled. In 2016, 92 master's awarded. *Degree requirements:* For master's, comprehensive exam (for some programs), thesis (for some programs); for doctorate, at least one 8-12 week clinical rotation outside the St. Paul area. *Entrance requirements:* For master's, official transcripts from regionally-accredited institution stating the conferral of a bachelor's degree with minimum cumulative GPA of 3.0; personal statement; undergraduate degree at accredited college or university in the U.S., English-speaking Canada, the United Kingdom, Ireland, Australia, or New Zealand; for doctorate, undergraduate or graduate degree at accredited college or university in the U.S., English-speaking Canada, the United Kingdom, Ireland, Australia, or New Zealand. Additional exam requirements/recommendations for international students: Recommended—TOEFL (minimum score 547 paper-based; 78 iBT), IELTS (minimum score 6), TSE (minimum score 52). *Application deadline:* For fall admission, 4/1 for domestic students. Applications are processed on a rolling basis. Application fee: $50. Electronic applications accepted. *Expenses:* Contact institution. *Financial support:* In 2016–17, 114 students received support. Scholarships/grants and unspecified assistantships available. Financial award applicants required to submit FAFSA. *Faculty research:* Developmental screening in early childhood, cardiovascular responses to aerobic exercise. *Unit head:* Dr. Katie Fischer, Interim Dean, 651-641-8735, E-mail: fischer@csp.edu. *Application contact:* Kimberly Craig, Associate Vice President, Cohort Enrollment Management, 651-603-6223, Fax: 651-603-6320, E-mail: craig@csp.edu.

**Concordia University Wisconsin,** Graduate Programs, Department of Education, Program in Family Studies, Mequon, WI 53097-2402. Offers MS Ed. *Degree requirements:* For master's, comprehensive exam, thesis or alternative. *Entrance requirements:* For master's, minimum GPA of 3.0. Additional exam requirements/ recommendations for international students: Required—TOEFL. Application fee: $35. *Financial support:* Application deadline: 8/1. *Unit head:* Dr. Val Keiper, Head, 262-243-4266, E-mail: val.keiper@cuw.edu. *Application contact:* Graduate Admissions, 262-243-4248, Fax: 262-243-4428, E-mail: val.keiper@cuw.edu.

**Cornell University,** Graduate School, Graduate Fields of Human Ecology, Field of Human Development, Ithaca, NY 14853. Offers developmental psychology (MA, PhD), including cognitive development, developmental psychopathology, ecology of human development, social and personality development; human development and family studies (MA, PhD), including ecology of human development, family studies and the life course. *Degree requirements:* For doctorate, comprehensive exam, thesis/dissertation, pre-doctoral research project, teaching experience. *Entrance requirements:* For doctorate, GRE General Test, 2 letters of recommendation. Additional exam requirements/recommendations for international students: Required—TOEFL (minimum score 550 paper-based; 77 iBT). Electronic applications accepted. *Faculty research:* Cognitive development, developmental psychopathology, ecology of human development, family studies and the life course, social and personality development.

**Dallas Theological Seminary,** Graduate Programs, Dallas, TX 75204-6499. Offers adult education (Th M); apologetics (Th M); Bible backgrounds (Th M); Bible translation (Th M); Biblical and theological studies (Certificate); biblical counseling (MA); biblical exegesis and linguistics (MA); biblical exposition (PhD); biblical studies (MA); Biblical theology (Th M); children's education (Th M); Christian education (MA, D Min); Christian

## Child and Family Studies

leadership (MA); cross-cultural ministries (MA); educational administration (Th M); educational leadership (Th M); evangelism and discipleship (Th M); exposition of Biblical books (Th M); family life education (Th M); general studies (Th M); Hebrew and cognate studies (Th M); hermeneutics (Th M); historical theology (Th M); homiletics (Th M); intercultural ministries (Th M); Jesus studies (Th M); leadership studies (Th M); media and communication (MA); media arts (Th M); ministry (D Min); ministry with women (Th M); New Testament studies (Th M, PhD); Old Testament studies (Th M, PhD); parachurch ministries (Th M); pastoral care and counseling (Th M); pastoral theology and practice (Th M); philosophy (Th M); sacred theology (STM); spiritual formation (Th M); systematic theology (Th M); teaching in Christian institutions (Th M); theological studies (PhD); urban ministries (Th M); worship studies (Th M); youth education (Th M). *Program availability:* Part-time, online learning. *Degree requirements:* For master's, variable foreign language requirement, thesis (for some programs); for doctorate, 2 foreign languages, thesis/dissertation. *Entrance requirements:* For master's, GRE or MAT (if minimum undergraduate cumulative GPA is below 2.5 or undergraduate degree is unaccredited). Additional exam requirements/recommendations for international students: Required—TOEFL (minimum score 575 paper-based; 85 iBT), TWE. Electronic applications accepted.

**East Carolina University,** Graduate School, College of Health and Human Performance, Department of Human Development and Family Science, Greenville, NC 27858-4353. Offers birth through kindergarten education (MA Ed); child development and family relations (MS); marriage and family therapy (MS); medical family therapy (PhD). *Accreditation:* AAMFT/COAMFTE. *Program availability:* Part-time. *Students:* 67 full-time (62 women), 25 part-time (23 women); includes 22 minority (13 Black or African American, non-Hispanic/Latino; 2 American Indian or Alaska Native, non-Hispanic/Latino; 1 Asian, non-Hispanic/Latino; 3 Hispanic/Latino; 1 Native Hawaiian or other Pacific Islander, non-Hispanic/Latino; 2 Two or more races, non-Hispanic/Latino), 1 international. Average age 29. 126 applicants, 49% accepted, 43 enrolled. In 2016, 24 master's, 4 doctorates awarded. *Degree requirements:* For master's, comprehensive exam, thesis optional. *Application deadline:* For fall admission, 1/15 for domestic students; for spring admission, 10/15 for domestic students. Applications are processed on a rolling basis. Application fee: $50. *Financial support:* Research assistantships, teaching assistantships, career-related internships or fieldwork, Federal Work-Study, institutionally sponsored loans, and scholarships/grants available. Support available to part-time students. Financial award application deadline: 6/1. *Faculty research:* Child care quality, mental health delivery systems for children, family violence. *Unit head:* Dr. Sharon Ballard, Interim Chair, 252-328-1356, E-mail: ballards@ecu.edu. *Application contact:* Dean of Graduate School, 252-328-6012, Fax: 252-328-6071, E-mail: gradschool@ecu.edu.
Website: http://www.ecu.edu/cs-hhp/hdfs/

**Eastern University,** Program in Marriage and Family Therapy Studies, St. Davids, PA 19087-3696. Offers marriage and family studies (DA); marriage and family therapy (PhD). *Program availability:* Evening/weekend, online learning. *Students:* 60 full-time (43 women); includes 41 minority (37 Black or African American, non-Hispanic/Latino; 1 Asian, non-Hispanic/Latino; 2 Hispanic/Latino; 1 Two or more races, non-Hispanic/Latino), 1 international. Average age 43. In 2016, 8 doctorates awarded. *Degree requirements:* For doctorate, thesis/dissertation. *Entrance requirements:* Additional exam requirements/recommendations for international students: Required—TOEFL (minimum score 550 paper-based; 79 iBT). *Application deadline:* Applications are processed on a rolling basis. Application fee: $75. Electronic applications accepted. Application fee is waived when completed online. *Expenses:* $785 per credit. *Unit head:* Michael Dziedziak, Executive Director of Enrollment, 800-452-0996, E-mail: gpsadmissions@eastern.edu.
Website: http://www.eastern.edu/academics/programs/da-marriage-and-family/da-marriage-and-family

**Fairfield University,** Graduate School of Education and Allied Professions, Fairfield, CT 06824. Offers applied behavior analysis (ATC); applied psychology (MA); clinical mental health counseling (MA, CAS); educational technology (MA); elementary education (MA, CAS); family studies (MA); integration of spirituality and religion in counseling (ATC); marriage and family therapy (MA); reading and language development (Sixth Year Certificate); school counseling (MA, CAS); school psychology (MA, CAS); school-based marriage and family therapy (ATC); secondary education (MA); special education (MA, CAS); substance abuse counseling (ATC); teaching (Certificate); teaching and foundations (MA, CAS); TESOL, world languages, and bilingual education (MA, CAS). *Accreditation:* NCATE. *Program availability:* Part-time, evening/weekend. *Faculty:* 19 full-time (15 women), 38 part-time/adjunct (26 women). *Students:* 153 full-time (132 women), 302 part-time (252 women); includes 97 minority (24 Black or African American, non-Hispanic/Latino; 12 Asian, non-Hispanic/Latino; 55 Hispanic/Latino; 6 Two or more races, non-Hispanic/Latino), 6 international. Average age 32. 283 applicants, 61% accepted, 97 enrolled. In 2016, 130 master's awarded. *Degree requirements:* For master's, comprehensive exam. *Entrance requirements:* For master's, minimum GPA of 3.0, 2 recommendations, resume. Additional exam requirements/recommendations for international students: Required—TOEFL (minimum score 550 paper-based; 84 iBT) or IELTS (minimum score 7.5). *Application deadline:* For fall admission, 2/15 for international students; for spring admission, 10/1 for international students. Application fee: $60. Electronic applications accepted. *Expenses:* $725 per credit hour. *Financial support:* In 2016–17, 42 students received support. Career-related internships or fieldwork and unspecified assistantships available. Support available to part-time students. Financial award applicants required to submit FAFSA. *Faculty research:* Reading and literacy, writing, social justice and inequality in education, addictions and mental health issues, therapeutic relationships and clinical supervision. *Unit head:* Dr. Robert D. Hannafin, Dean, 203-254-4250, Fax: 203-254-4241, E-mail: rhannafin@fairfield.edu. *Application contact:* Marianne Gumpper, Director of Graduate Admission, 203-254-4184, Fax: 203-254-4073, E-mail: gradadmis@fairfield.edu.
Website: http://www.fairfield.edu/gseap

**Florida State University,** The Graduate School, College of Human Sciences, Department of Family and Child Sciences, Tallahassee, FL 32306. Offers family and child sciences (MS); family relations (PhD); marriage and family therapy (PhD). *Accreditation:* AAMFT/COAMFTE. *Program availability:* Part-time. *Faculty:* 14 full-time (9 women). *Students:* 30 full-time (20 women), 3 part-time (all women); includes 13 minority (7 Black or African American, non-Hispanic/Latino; 1 Asian, non-Hispanic/Latino; 2 Hispanic/Latino; 1 Native Hawaiian or other Pacific Islander, non-Hispanic/Latino; 2 Two or more races, non-Hispanic/Latino), 1 international. 38 applicants, 37% accepted, 10 enrolled. In 2016, 6 master's, 4 doctorates awarded. Terminal master's awarded for partial completion of doctoral program. *Degree requirements:* For master's, thesis optional; for doctorate, thesis/dissertation, preliminary examination; clinical examination (for marriage and family therapy). *Entrance requirements:* For master's and doctorate, GRE General Test, writing assessment, minimum GPA of 3.0. Additional exam requirements/recommendations for international students: Required—TOEFL (minimum score 550 paper-based; 80 iBT). *Application deadline:* For fall admission, 12/1 for domestic and international students. Applications are processed on a rolling basis. Application fee: $30. Electronic applications accepted. *Expenses:* Tuition, state resident: full-time $7263; part-time $403.51 per credit hour. Tuition, nonresident: full-

time $18,087; part-time $1004.85 per credit hour. *Required fees:* $1365; $75.81 per credit hour. $20 per semester. Tuition and fees vary according to campus/location. *Financial support:* In 2016–17, 31 students received support, including 8 research assistantships with full tuition reimbursements available (averaging $11,647 per year), 23 teaching assistantships with full tuition reimbursements available (averaging $10,594 per year); fellowships with partial tuition reimbursements available, career-related internships or fieldwork, Federal Work-Study, institutionally sponsored loans, scholarships/grants, health care benefits, and unspecified assistantships also available. Financial award application deadline: 1/5; financial award applicants required to submit FAFSA. *Faculty research:* Family therapy, parent-child relations, distressed families and foster care, marital processes, relational interventions, family structural complexity. *Total annual research expenditures:* $889,003. *Unit head:* Dr. Joseph Grzywacz, Department Chair, 850-644-3217, Fax: 850-644-3439, E-mail: jgrzywacz@fsu.edu. *Application contact:* Donna Romano, Office Administrator, 850-644-3217, Fax: 850-644-3439, E-mail: dromano@fsu.edu.
Website: http://www.chs.fsu.edu/Departments/Family-Child-Sciences

**Indiana University–Purdue University Indianapolis,** School of Liberal Arts, Department of Sociology, Indianapolis, IN 46202. Offers family/gender studies (MA); medical sociology (MA); work/occupations (MA).

**Iowa State University of Science and Technology,** Department of Human Development and Family Studies, Ames, IA 50011. Offers human development and family studies (MFCS, MS, PhD). *Degree requirements:* For master's, thesis; for doctorate, thesis/dissertation. *Entrance requirements:* For master's and doctorate, GRE General Test. Additional exam requirements/recommendations for international students: Required—TOEFL (minimum score 550 paper-based; 79 iBT), IELTS (minimum score 6.5). *Application deadline:* For fall admission, 1/15 priority date for domestic and international students. Application fee: $60 ($90 for international students). Electronic applications accepted. *Faculty research:* Child development, early childhood education, family resource management and housing, life span studies. *Application contact:* Brenda Nelson, Application Contact, 515-294-6321, Fax: 515-294-2502, E-mail: hdfs-grad-adm@iastate.edu.
Website: http://www.hdfs.hs.iastate.edu/graduate/

**Kansas State University,** Graduate School, College of Human Ecology, Doctorate in Human Ecology Program, Manhattan, KS 66506-1407. Offers apparel and textiles (PhD); applied family sciences (PhD); couple and family therapy (PhD); hospitality administration (PhD); kinesiology (PhD); life-span human development (PhD). *Program availability:* Part-time. *Faculty:* 36 full-time (23 women). *Students:* 44 full-time (26 women), 16 part-time (10 women); includes 9 minority (3 Black or African American, non-Hispanic/Latino; 2 Asian, non-Hispanic/Latino; 2 Hispanic/Latino; 2 Two or more races, non-Hispanic/Latino), 18 international. Average age 30. 43 applicants, 35% accepted, 8 enrolled. In 2016, 13 doctorates awarded. *Degree requirements:* For doctorate, thesis/dissertation. *Entrance requirements:* Additional exam requirements/recommendations for international students: Required—TOEFL. *Application deadline:* For fall admission, 2/1 priority date for domestic and international students; for spring admission, 8/1 priority date for domestic and international students. Applications are processed on a rolling basis. Application fee: $50 ($75 for international students). Electronic applications accepted. *Expenses:* Tuition, state resident: full-time $9670. Tuition, nonresident: full-time $21,828. *Required fees:* $862. *Financial support:* In 2016–17, research assistantships with partial tuition reimbursements (averaging $12,000 per year), teaching assistantships with partial tuition reimbursements (averaging $12,000 per year) were awarded. Financial award application deadline: 3/1. *Total annual research expenditures:* $1.8 million. *Unit head:* Dr. John Buckwalter, Dean, 785-532-5500, Fax: 785-532-5504, E-mail: jbb3@ksu.edu. *Application contact:* Dr. Bronwyn Fees, Associate Dean for Academic Affairs, 785-532-5500, Fax: 785-532-5504, E-mail: fees@ksu.edu.

**Kansas State University,** Graduate School, College of Human Ecology, School of Family Studies and Human Services, Manhattan, KS 66506-1403. Offers applied family sciences (MS); communication sciences and disorders (MS); conflict resolution (Graduate Certificate); couple and family therapy (MS); early childhood education (MS); family and community service (MS); life-span human development (MS); personal financial planning (MS, PhD, Graduate Certificate); youth development (MS, Graduate Certificate). *Accreditation:* AAMFT/COAMFTE; ASHA. *Program availability:* Part-time, online learning. *Faculty:* 43 full-time (30 women), 4 part-time/adjunct (3 women). *Students:* 55 full-time (45 women), 87 part-time (73 women); includes 30 minority (9 Black or African American, non-Hispanic/Latino; 1 American Indian or Alaska Native, non-Hispanic/Latino; 1 Asian, non-Hispanic/Latino; 14 Hispanic/Latino; 1 Native Hawaiian or other Pacific Islander, non-Hispanic/Latino; 4 Two or more races, non-Hispanic/Latino), 6 international. Average age 29. 182 applicants, 29% accepted, 38 enrolled. In 2016, 39 master's, 17 other advanced degrees awarded. *Degree requirements:* For master's, comprehensive exam (for some programs), thesis optional. *Entrance requirements:* For master's, GRE, minimum GPA of 3.0 in last 2 years (60 semester hours) of undergraduate study; for doctorate, GRE. Additional exam requirements/recommendations for international students: Required—TOEFL (minimum score 600 paper-based). *Application deadline:* For fall admission, 2/1 priority date for domestic students, 1/1 priority date for international students; for spring admission, 10/1 priority date for domestic students, 8/1 priority date for international students; for summer admission, 2/1 priority date for domestic students, 12/1 priority date for international students. Applications are processed on a rolling basis. Application fee: $50 ($75 for international students). Electronic applications accepted. *Expenses:* Tuition, state resident: full-time $9670. Tuition, nonresident: full-time $21,828. *Required fees:* $862. *Financial support:* In 2016–17, 35 students received support, including 25 research assistantships (averaging $10,000 per year), 9 teaching assistantships with full tuition reimbursements available (averaging $10,000 per year); unspecified assistantships also available. Financial award application deadline: 3/1. *Faculty research:* Health and security of military families, training in and evaluation of professional human services (marriage and couple therapy, family life education, treatment of speech and swallowing disorders, financial therapy), disorders of communication and swallowing, family and relationship development and health, financial decision-making. *Total annual research expenditures:* $8.4 million. *Unit head:* Dr. Dottie Durband, Director, 785-532-5510, Fax: 785-532-5505, E-mail: dottie@ksu.edu. *Application contact:* Kristi Hageman, Administrative Specialist, 785-532-5510, Fax: 785-532-5505, E-mail: klsmith@ksu.edu.
Website: http://www.he.k-state.edu/fshs/

**Kean University,** College of Education, Program in Early Childhood Education, Union, NJ 07083. Offers administration in early childhood and family studies (MA); advanced curriculum and teaching (MA); classroom instruction - P-3 certification (MA). *Accreditation:* NCATE. *Program availability:* Part-time. *Faculty:* 15 full-time (9 women). *Students:* 1 full-time (0 women), 13 part-time (12 women); includes 7 minority (3 Black or African American, non-Hispanic/Latino; 3 Asian, non-Hispanic/Latino; 1 Hispanic/Latino). Average age 37. 42 applicants, 71% accepted, 30 enrolled. In 2016, 3 master's awarded. *Entrance requirements:* For master's, GRE General Test, PRAXIS Early Childhood Content Knowledge (for some programs), minimum GPA of 3.0, 2 letters of recommendation, teacher certification (for some programs), personal statement, official

transcripts, resume. Additional exam requirements/recommendations for international students: Required—TOEFL (minimum score 550 paper-based; 79 iBT), IELTS (minimum score 6.5). *Application deadline:* For fall admission, 6/1 for domestic and international students; for spring admission, 12/1 for domestic and international students. Applications are processed on a rolling basis. Application fee: $75. Electronic applications accepted. *Expenses:* Tuition, state resident: full-time $13,156; part-time $640 per credit. Tuition, nonresident: full-time $17,831; part-time $785 per credit. *Required fees:* $3316; $151 per credit. Tuition and fees vary according to course level, course load, degree level and program. *Financial support:* Scholarships/grants and unspecified assistantships available. Financial award applicants required to submit FAFSA. *Unit head:* Dr. Polly Ashelman, Program Coordinator, 908-737-3785, E-mail: pashelma@kean.edu. *Application contact:* Brittany Gerstenhaber, Admissions Counselor, 908-737-7100, E-mail: grad-adm@kean.edu.
Website: http://grad.kean.edu/masters-programs/administration-early-childhood-family-studies

**Kent State University,** College of Education, Health and Human Services, School of Lifespan Development and Educational Sciences, Program in Human Development and Family Studies, Kent, OH 44242-0001. Offers MA. *Degree requirements:* For master's, thesis optional. *Entrance requirements:* For master's, minimum undergraduate GPA of 3.0, 3 letters of reference, goals statement. Additional exam requirements/recommendations for international students: Required—TOEFL (minimum score 550 paper-based; 80 iBT). *Expenses:* Tuition, state resident: full-time $10,864; part-time $495 per credit hour. Tuition, nonresident: full-time $18,380; part-time $837 per credit hour.

**Liberty University,** School of Behavioral Sciences, Lynchburg, VA 24515. Offers clinical mental health counseling (MA); counselor education and supervision (PhD); human services counseling (MA), including addictions and recovery, business, child and family law, Christian ministries, crisis response and trauma, executive leadership, health and wellness, life coaching, marriage and family, military resilience; marriage and family therapy (MA); military resilience (Certificate); professional counseling (MA). *Program availability:* Part-time, online learning. *Students:* 2,041 full-time (1,612 women), 4,970 part-time (3,875 women); includes 1,991 minority (1,678 Black or African American, non-Hispanic/Latino; 33 American Indian or Alaska Native, non-Hispanic/Latino; 48 Asian, non-Hispanic/Latino; 80 Hispanic/Latino; 8 Native Hawaiian or other Pacific Islander, non-Hispanic/Latino; 144 Two or more races, non-Hispanic/Latino), 127 international. Average age 39. 5,496 applicants, 41% accepted, 1257 enrolled. In 2016, 2,813 master's, 11 doctorates, 20 other advanced degrees awarded. *Application deadline:* Applications are processed on a rolling basis. Application fee: $50. Electronic applications accepted. *Financial support:* Applicants required to submit FAFSA. *Unit head:* Dr. Ronald Hawkins, Founding Dean, School of Behavioral Sciences. *Application contact:* Jay Bridge, Director of Admissions, 800-424-9595, Fax: 800-628-7977, E-mail: gradadmissions@liberty.edu.

**Loma Linda University,** School of Behavioral Health, Department of Counseling and Family Sciences, Loma Linda, CA 92350. Offers child life specialist (MS); clinical mediation (Certificate); counseling (MS); drug and alcohol counseling (Certificate); family life education (Certificate); marital and family therapy (DMFT); school counseling (Certificate). *Degree requirements:* For master's, comprehensive exam, thesis optional; for doctorate, comprehensive exam, thesis/dissertation (for some programs). *Entrance requirements:* For master's, minimum GPA of 3.0; for doctorate, GRE. Additional exam requirements/recommendations for international students: Required—TOEFL (minimum score 550 paper-based). Electronic applications accepted.

**London Metropolitan University,** Graduate Programs, London, United Kingdom. Offers applied psychology (M Sc); architecture (MA); biomedical science (M Sc); blood science (M Sc); cancer pharmacology (M Sc); computer networking and cyber security (M Sc); computing and information systems (M Sc); conference interpreting (MA); counter-terrorism studies (M Sc); creative, digital and professional writing (MA); crime, violence and prevention (M Sc); criminology (M Sc); curating contemporary art (MA); data analytics (M Sc); digital media (MA); early childhood studies (MA); education (MA, Ed D); financial services law, regulation and compliance (LL M); food science (M Sc); forensic psychology (M Sc); health and social care management and policy (M Sc); human nutrition (M Sc); human resource management (MA); human rights and international conflict (MA); information technology (M Sc); intelligence and security studies (M Sc); international oil, gas and energy law (LL M); international relations (MA); interpreting (MA); learning and teaching in higher education (MA); legal practice (LL M); media and entertainment law (LL M); organizational and consumer psychology (M Sc); psychological therapy (M Sc); psychology of mental health (M Sc); public health (M Sc); public policy and management (MPA); security studies (M Sc); social work (M Sc); spatial planning and urban design (MA); sports therapy (M Sc); supporting older children and young people with dyslexia (MA); teaching languages (MA), including Arabic, English; translation (MA); woman and child abuse (MA).

**Miami University,** College of Education, Health and Society, Department of Family Studies and Social Work, Oxford, OH 45056. Offers MA. *Students:* 28 full-time (26 women), 4 part-time (3 women); includes 8 minority (7 Black or African American, non-Hispanic/Latino; 1 Two or more races, non-Hispanic/Latino), 1 international. Average age 28. In 2016, 16 master's awarded. *Expenses:* Tuition, state resident: full-time $12,890; part-time $564 per credit hour. Tuition, nonresident: full-time $29,604; part-time $1260 per credit hour. *Required fees:* $638. Part-time tuition and fees vary according to course load and program. *Unit head:* Dr. Elise Radina, Professor and Chair, 513-529-3314, E-mail: kargerhj@miamioh.edu. *Application contact:* Kellie Bottoms, Graduate Secretary, 513-529-2323, E-mail: penninka@miamioh.edu.
Website: http://www.MiamiOH.edu/fsw

**Michigan State University,** The Graduate School, College of Social Science, Department of Family and Child Ecology, East Lansing, MI 48824. Offers child development (MA); community services (MS); family and child ecology (PhD); family studies (MA); marriage and family therapy (MA); youth development (MA). *Accreditation:* AAMFT/COAMFTE (one or more programs are accredited). *Entrance requirements:* For master's, GRE General Test, minimum GPA of 3.0 in last 2 years of undergraduate course work, 3 letters of recommendation; for doctorate, GRE General Test, minimum GPA of 3.0, 3 letters of recommendation, background in behavioral sciences. Additional exam requirements/recommendations for international students: Required—TOEFL. Electronic applications accepted.

**Mississippi State University,** College of Agriculture and Life Sciences, School of Human Sciences, Mississippi State, MS 39762. Offers agriculture and extension education (MS, PhD), including agriculture and extension education (PhD), leadership (MS), teaching (MS); human development and family studies (MS, PhD). *Accreditation:* NCATE (one or more programs are accredited). *Program availability:* Part-time. *Faculty:* 23 full-time (13 women), 1 part-time/adjunct (0 women). *Students:* 35 full-time (25 women), 61 part-time (45 women); includes 19 minority (15 Black or African American, non-Hispanic/Latino; 2 Hispanic/Latino; 2 Two or more races, non-Hispanic/Latino), 5 international. Average age 35. 22 applicants, 73% accepted, 12 enrolled. In 2016, 8 master's, 4 doctorates awarded. *Degree requirements:* For master's, thesis optional, comprehensive oral or written exam. *Entrance requirements:* For master's, GRE, minimum GPA of 2.75 in last 4 semesters of course work; for doctorate, minimum GPA

of 3.0 on prior graduate work. Additional exam requirements/recommendations for international students: Required—TOEFL (minimum score 477 paper-based; 53 iBT); Recommended—IELTS (minimum score 4.5). *Application deadline:* For fall admission, 7/1 for domestic students, 5/1 for international students; for spring admission, 11/1 for domestic students, 9/1 for international students. Applications are processed on a rolling basis. Application fee: $60. Electronic applications accepted. *Expenses:* Tuition, state resident: full-time $7670; part-time $852.50 per credit hour. Tuition, nonresident: full-time $20,790; part-time $2310.50 per credit hour. Part-time tuition and fees vary according to course load. *Financial support:* Federal Work-Study, institutionally sponsored loans, and unspecified assistantships available. Financial award application deadline: 4/1; financial award applicants required to submit FAFSA. *Faculty research:* Animal welfare, agro science, information technology, learning styles, problem solving. *Unit head:* Dr. Michael Newman, Director and Professor, 662-325-2950, E-mail: mnewman@humansci.msstate.edu. *Application contact:* Marina Hunt, Admissions and Enrollment Assistant, 662-325-5188, E-mail: mhunt@grad.msstate.edu.
Website: http://www.humansci.msstate.edu

**Missouri State University,** Graduate College, College of Education, Department of Childhood Education and Family Studies, Program in Early Childhood and Family Development, Springfield, MO 65897. Offers MS. *Program availability:* Part-time, 100% online, blended/hybrid learning. *Faculty:* 69 full-time. *Students:* 9 full-time (8 women), 37 part-time (all women); includes 6 minority (3 Black or African American, non-Hispanic/Latino; 1 Asian, non-Hispanic/Latino; 1 Hispanic/Latino; 1 Two or more races, non-Hispanic/Latino), 2 international. Average age 31. 28 applicants, 79% accepted, 16 enrolled. In 2016, 18 master's awarded. *Entrance requirements:* For master's, GRE, minimum GPA of 3.0. Additional exam requirements/recommendations for international students: Required—TOEFL (minimum score 550 paper-based; 79 iBT), IELTS (minimum score 6). *Application deadline:* For fall admission, 7/20 priority date for domestic students, 5/1 for international students; for spring admission, 12/20 priority date for domestic students, 9/1 for international students; for summer admission, 5/20 priority date for domestic students. Applications are processed on a rolling basis. Application fee: $35 ($50 for international students). Electronic applications accepted. *Expenses:* Tuition, state resident: full-time $5830. Tuition, nonresident: full-time $10,708. *Required fees:* $1130. Tuition and fees vary according to class time, course level, course load and program. *Financial support:* Federal Work-Study, institutionally sponsored loans, scholarships/grants, and unspecified assistantships available. Financial award application deadline: 3/31; financial award applicants required to submit FAFSA. *Unit head:* Dr. Denise Cunningham, Department Head, 417-836-8915, Fax: 417-836-8900, E-mail: cefs@missouristate.edu. *Application contact:* Michael Edwards, Coordinator of Graduate Admissions, 417-836-5300, Fax: 417-836-6200, E-mail: michaeledwards@missouristate.edu.
Website: http://education.missouristate.edu/ecfd/

**Montclair State University,** The Graduate School, College of Education and Human Services, Doctoral Program in Family Studies, Montclair, NJ 07043-1624. Offers PhD. *Program availability:* Part-time, evening/weekend. *Degree requirements:* For doctorate, comprehensive exam, thesis/dissertation. *Entrance requirements:* For doctorate, GRE General Test, interview, 3 letters of recommendation, essay. Additional exam requirements/recommendations for international students: Required—TOEFL (minimum score 83 iBT), IELTS (minimum score 6.5). Electronic applications accepted. *Expenses:* Tuition, state resident: part-time $553 per credit. Tuition, nonresident: part-time $854 per credit. *Required fees:* $91 per credit. Tuition and fees vary according to program.

**Montclair State University,** The Graduate School, College of Education and Human Services, Program in Family and Child Studies, Montclair, NJ 07043-1624. Offers MA. *Program availability:* Part-time, evening/weekend. *Degree requirements:* For master's, comprehensive exam, thesis or alternative. *Entrance requirements:* For master's, GRE General Test, essay, 2 letters of recommendation. Additional exam requirements/recommendations for international students: Required—TOEFL (minimum score 83 iBT), IELTS (minimum score 6.5). Electronic applications accepted. *Expenses:* Tuition, state resident: part-time $553 per credit. Tuition, nonresident: part-time $854 per credit. *Required fees:* $91 per credit. Tuition and fees vary according to program.

**Montclair State University,** The Graduate School, College of Humanities and Social Sciences, Adolescent Advocacy Certificate Program, Montclair, NJ 07043-1624. Offers Certificate. *Expenses:* Tuition, state resident: part-time $553 per credit. Tuition, nonresident: part-time $854 per credit. *Required fees:* $91 per credit. Tuition and fees vary according to program.

**Montclair State University,** The Graduate School, College of Humanities and Social Sciences, Child Advocacy and Policy Certificate Program, Montclair, NJ 07043-1624. Offers Certificate. *Expenses:* Tuition, state resident: part-time $553 per credit. Tuition, nonresident: part-time $854 per credit. *Required fees:* $91 per credit. Tuition and fees vary according to program.

**Mount Saint Vincent University,** Graduate Programs, Department of Child and Youth Study, Halifax, NS B3M 2J6, Canada. Offers MA. *Program availability:* Part-time, evening/weekend. *Degree requirements:* For master's, thesis. *Entrance requirements:* For master's, bachelor's degree in related field, minimum B+ average, professional experience. Electronic applications accepted.

**Mount Saint Vincent University,** Graduate Programs, Department of Family Studies and Gerontology, Halifax, NS B3M 2J6, Canada. Offers MA. *Program availability:* Part-time, online learning. *Degree requirements:* For master's, thesis. *Entrance requirements:* For master's, minimum GPA of 3.0; course work in statistics, research methods, family and social theories.

**North Carolina Agricultural and Technical State University,** School of Graduate Studies, School of Agriculture and Environmental Sciences, Department of Family and Consumer Sciences, Greensboro, NC 27411. Offers child development early education and family studies (MAT); family and consumer sciences (MAT); food and nutrition (MS). *Program availability:* Part-time, evening/weekend. *Degree requirements:* For master's, comprehensive exam, thesis or alternative, qualifying exam. *Entrance requirements:* For master's, GRE General Test, minimum GPA of 2.6.

★ **North Dakota State University,** College of Graduate and Interdisciplinary Studies, College of Human Development and Education, Department of Human Development and Family Science, Fargo, ND 58102. Offers couple and family therapy (PhD); developmental science (PhD); family financial planning (MS, Certificate); gerontology (MS, Certificate); youth development (MS). *Accreditation:* AAMFT/COAMFTE. *Program availability:* Part-time, evening/weekend, online learning. *Degree requirements:* For master's, thesis or alternative; for doctorate, thesis/dissertation. *Entrance requirements:* Additional exam requirements/recommendations for international students: Required—TOEFL (minimum score 525 paper-based; 71 iBT). *Faculty research:* Family therapy, resilience, parenting, adolescent development, mental health.
**See Display on next page and Close-Up on page 895.**

**Northern Illinois University,** Graduate School, College of Health and Human Sciences, School of Family, Consumer and Nutrition Sciences, De Kalb, IL 60115-2854. Offers applied family and child studies (MS); nutrition and dietetics (MS). *Accreditation:*

## Child and Family Studies

AAMFT/COAMFTE. *Program availability:* Part-time. *Faculty:* 16 full-time (14 women), 2 part-time/adjunct (1 woman). *Students:* 53 full-time (50 women), 17 part-time (16 women); includes 11 minority (8 Hispanic/Latino; 3 Two or more races, non-Hispanic/Latino), 1 international. Average age 26. 79 applicants, 53% accepted, 21 enrolled. In 2016, 28 master's awarded. *Degree requirements:* For master's, comprehensive exam, internship, thesis (for nutrition and dietetics). *Entrance requirements:* For master's, GRE General Test, minimum GPA of 2.75. Additional exam requirements/recommendations for international students: Required—TOEFL (minimum score 550 paper-based). *Application deadline:* For fall admission, 6/1 for domestic students, 5/1 for international students; for spring admission, 11/1 for domestic students, 10/1 for international students. Applications are processed on a rolling basis. Application fee: $40. Electronic applications accepted. *Financial support:* In 2016–17, 8 research assistantships with full tuition reimbursements, 33 teaching assistantships with full tuition reimbursements were awarded; fellowships with full tuition reimbursements, career-related internships or fieldwork, Federal Work-Study, scholarships/grants, tuition waivers (full), and staff assistantships also available. Support available to part-time students. Financial award applicants required to submit FAFSA. *Faculty research:* Preliminary child development, hospitality administration in Asia, sports nutrition, eating disorders. *Unit head:* Dr. Thomas Pavkov, Chair, 815-753-6342, Fax: 815-753-1321, E-mail: tpavkov@niu.edu. *Application contact:* Graduate School Office, 815-753-0395, E-mail: gradsch@niu.edu. Website: http://www.fcns.niu.edu/

**The Ohio State University,** Graduate School, College of Education and Human Ecology, Department of Human Sciences, Columbus, OH 43210. Offers consumer sciences (MS, PhD); human development and family science (PhD); human nutrition (MS, PhD); kinesiology (MA, PhD). *Program availability:* Part-time. *Faculty:* 54. *Students:* 128 full-time (77 women), 8 part-time (6 women); includes 21 minority (7 Black or African American, non-Hispanic/Latino; 8 Hispanic/Latino; 6 Two or more races, non-Hispanic/Latino), 30 international. Average age 27. In 2016, 27 master's, 17 doctorates awarded. *Degree requirements:* For master's, thesis optional; for doctorate, thesis/dissertation. *Entrance requirements:* For master's and doctorate, GRE. Additional exam requirements/recommendations for international students: Required—TOEFL (minimum score 550 paper-based; 79 iBT), Michigan English Language Assessment Battery (minimum score 82); Recommended—IELTS (minimum score 7). *Application deadline:* For fall admission, 12/1 priority date for domestic and international students. Applications are processed on a rolling basis. Application fee: $60 ($70 for international students). Electronic applications accepted. *Financial support:* Fellowships with tuition reimbursements, research assistantships with tuition reimbursements, teaching assistantships with tuition reimbursements, Federal Work-Study, and institutionally sponsored loans available. Support available to part-time students. *Unit head:* Dr. Joe Wheaton, Interim Chair, E-mail: wheaton.3@osu.edu. *Application contact:* Graduate and Professional Admissions, 614-292-9444, Fax: 614-292-3895, E-mail: gpadmissions@osu.edu. Website: http://ehe.osu.edu/human-sciences/

**Ohio University,** Graduate College, College of Health Sciences and Professions, Department of Social and Public Health, Athens, OH 45701-2979. Offers early child development and family life (MS); family studies (MS); health administration (MHA); public health (MPH); social work (MSW). *Accreditation:* CEPH. *Program availability:* Part-time, evening/weekend, online learning. *Degree requirements:* For master's, capstone (MPH). *Entrance requirements:* For master's, GMAT, GRE General Test, previous course work in accounting, management, and statistics, previous public health background (MHA, MPH). Additional exam requirements/recommendations for international students: Required—TOEFL (minimum score 550 paper-based; 80 iBT) or IELTS (minimum score 6.5). *Application deadline:* Applications are processed on a rolling basis. Application fee: $50 ($55 for international students). Electronic applications

accepted. *Expenses:* Contact institution. *Financial support:* Research assistantships with full tuition reimbursements, career-related internships or fieldwork, Federal Work-Study, institutionally sponsored loans, and unspecified assistantships available. Financial award applicants required to submit FAFSA. *Faculty research:* Health care management, health policy, managed care, health behavior, disease prevention. *Unit head:* Dr. Matthew Adeyanju, School Director, 740-593-1849, Fax: 740-593-0555, E-mail: adeyanju@ohio.edu. *Application contact:* Dr. Ruth Ann Althaus, Graduate Coordinator, Master of Health Administration Program, 740-597-2981, E-mail: althaus@ohio.edu. Website: http://www.ohio.edu/chsp/sph/

**Oklahoma State University,** College of Human Sciences, Department of Human Development and Family Science, Stillwater, OK 74078. Offers human development and family science (MS, PhD), including family financial planning (MS), human environmental sciences; marriage and family therapy (MS). *Accreditation:* AAMFT/COAMFTE (one or more programs are accredited). *Program availability:* Online learning. *Faculty:* 31 full-time (22 women), 11 part-time/adjunct (9 women). *Students:* 26 full-time (23 women), 35 part-time (30 women); includes 16 minority (7 Black or African American, non-Hispanic/Latino; 1 American Indian or Alaska Native, non-Hispanic/Latino; 5 Hispanic/Latino; 3 Two or more races, non-Hispanic/Latino), 1 international. Average age 30. 47 applicants, 55% accepted, 22 enrolled. In 2016, 27 master's, 2 doctorates awarded. *Degree requirements:* For master's, thesis (for some programs); for doctorate, comprehensive exam, thesis/dissertation. *Entrance requirements:* For master's and doctorate, GRE or GMAT. Additional exam requirements/recommendations for international students: Required—TOEFL (minimum score 550 paper-based; 79 iBT). *Application deadline:* For fall admission, 3/1 priority date for international students; for spring admission, 8/1 priority date for international students. Applications are processed on a rolling basis. Application fee: $40 ($75 for international students). Electronic applications accepted. *Expenses:* Tuition, state resident: full-time $3775; part-time $209.70 per credit hour. Tuition, nonresident: full-time $14,851; part-time $825.05 per credit hour. *Required fees:* $2027; $112.60 per credit hour. Tuition and fees vary according to campus/location. *Financial support:* In 2016–17, 37 research assistantships (averaging $4,670 per year), 31 teaching assistantships (averaging $4,921 per year) were awarded; career-related internships or fieldwork, Federal Work-Study, scholarships/grants, health care benefits, tuition waivers (partial), and unspecified assistantships also available. Support available to part-time students. Financial award application deadline: 3/1; financial award applicants required to submit FAFSA. *Faculty research:* Family relations and child development, consequences of adolescent parenting, family stress and coping, impacts of sexual abuse on families, children's social cognition and self-competence, gerontology and health care. *Unit head:* Dr. Sissy Osteen, Department Head, 405-744-4741, Fax: 405-744-6344, E-mail: sissy.osteen@okstate.edu. *Application contact:* Dr. Michael Criss, Graduate Coordinator, 405-744-5057, Fax: 405-744-6344, E-mail: michael.criss@okstate.edu. Website: http://humansciences.okstate.edu/hdfs/

**Oregon State University,** College of Public Health and Human Sciences, Program in Human Development and Family Studies, Corvallis, OR 97331. Offers MS, PhD. *Faculty:* 15 full-time (13 women), 2 part-time/adjunct (both women). *Students:* 29 full-time (24 women), 4 part-time (3 women); includes 8 minority (1 Black or African American, non-Hispanic/Latino; 2 American Indian or Alaska Native, non-Hispanic/Latino; 2 Asian, non-Hispanic/Latino; 2 Hispanic/Latino; 1 Two or more races, non-Hispanic/Latino), 2 international. Average age 32. 20 applicants, 40% accepted, 6 enrolled. In 2016, 2 master's, 7 doctorates awarded. *Entrance requirements:* For master's, GRE; for doctorate, GRE, master's degree (including thesis). Additional exam requirements/recommendations for international students: Required—TOEFL (minimum score 80 iBT), IELTS (minimum score 6.5). *Application deadline:* For fall admission, 4/15

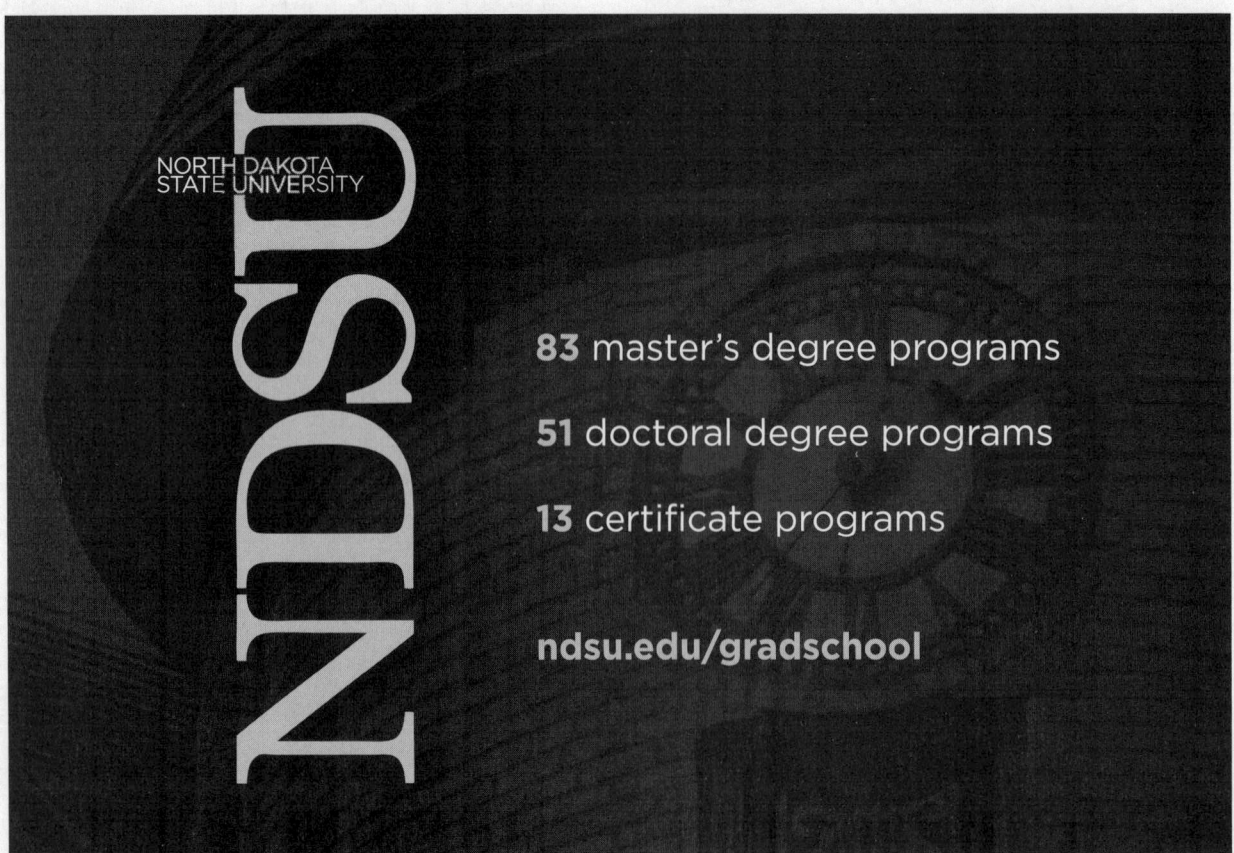

NORTH DAKOTA STATE UNIVERSITY

**83** master's degree programs

**51** doctoral degree programs

**13** certificate programs

ndsu.edu/gradschool

for domestic and international students. *Expenses:* Tuition, state resident: full-time $12,150; part-time $450 per credit. Tuition, nonresident: full-time $21,789; part-time $807 per credit. *Required fees:* $1651; $1507 per credit. One-time fee: $350. Tuition and fees vary according to course load, campus/location and program. *Financial support:* Fellowships, research assistantships, and teaching assistantships available. Financial award application deadline: 1/2. *Unit head:* Dr. Robert Stawski, Associate Professor. *Application contact:* Megan Ferris, Doctoral Programs Manager, E-mail: megan.ferris@oregonstate.edu.
Website: http://health.oregonstate.edu/degrees/graduate/hdfs

**Oxford Graduate School,** Graduate Programs, Dayton, TN 37321-6736. Offers family life education (M Litt); integration of religion and society (D Phil); organizational leadership (M Litt). *Faculty:* 10 full-time (2 women), 22 part-time/adjunct (7 women). *Students:* 105 full-time (40 women). *Entrance requirements:* For master's, official transcripts, three letters of recommendation, bachelor's degree or its equivalent, minimum undergraduate GPA of 3.0, minimum of 3 years of professional experience; for doctorate, official transcripts, three letters of recommendation, master's degree with minimum GPA of 3.0, minimum of 5 years of professional experience. *Expenses:* $7,875 per year (for D Phil); $6,000 per year (for M Litt). *Application contact:* Gwen Ballant, Director of Admissions, 423-775-6596, Fax: 423-775-6599, E-mail: oxfordgraduateschool@ogs.edu.

**Penn State University Park,** Graduate School, College of Health and Human Development, Department of Human Development and Family Studies, University Park, PA 16802. Offers MS, PhD. *Unit head:* Dr. Ann C. Crouter, Dean, 814-865-1420, Fax: 814-865-3282. *Application contact:* Lori Hawn, Director, Graduate Student Services, 814-865-1795, Fax: 814-863-4627, E-mail: l-gswww@lists.psu.edu.
Website: http://hhd.psu.edu/hdfs/

**Purdue University,** Graduate School, College of Health and Human Sciences, Department of Child Development and Family Studies, West Lafayette, IN 47907. Offers developmental studies (MS, PhD); family studies (MS, PhD); marriage and family therapy (MS, PhD). *Accreditation:* AAMFT/COAMFTE (one or more programs are accredited). *Program availability:* Part-time. *Faculty:* 19 full-time (11 women), 1 (woman) part-time/adjunct. *Students:* 22 full-time (21 women), 1 (woman) part-time; includes 3 minority (1 Black or African American, non-Hispanic/Latino; 1 Hispanic/Latino; 1 Two or more races, non-Hispanic/Latino), 5 international. Average age 26. 41 applicants, 29% accepted, 8 enrolled. In 2016, 4 master's, 3 doctorates awarded. Terminal master's awarded for partial completion of doctoral program. *Degree requirements:* For master's, thesis; for doctorate, thesis/dissertation. *Entrance requirements:* For master's and doctorate, GRE General Test (minimum score 1000 combined verbal and quantitative), minimum undergraduate GPA of 3.0 or equivalent. Additional exam requirements/recommendations for international students: Required—TOEFL (minimum score 600 paper-based; 90 iBT), TWE (minimum score 4). *Application deadline:* For fall admission, 1/4 for domestic and international students. Applications are processed on a rolling basis. Application fee: $60 ($75 for international students). Electronic applications accepted. *Financial support:* Fellowships with full tuition reimbursements, research assistantships with full tuition reimbursements, teaching assistantships with full tuition reimbursements, and career-related internships or fieldwork available. Support available to part-time students. Financial award application deadline: 1/15; financial award applicants required to submit FAFSA. *Faculty research:* Inclusion of children with special needs, families as learning environments, relationships in child care, work-family relations, AIDS prevention. *Unit head:* Dr. Doran C. French, Head, 765-494-9511, E-mail: dcfrench@purdue.edu. *Application contact:* Tina Putz, Graduate Contact, 765-496-3816, E-mail: tputz@purdue.edu.
Website: http://www.purdue.edu/hhs/hdfs/

**Purdue University Northwest,** Graduate Studies Office, School of Liberal Arts and Social Sciences, Department of Behavioral Sciences, Hammond, IN 46323-2094. Offers child development and family studies (MS); marriage and family therapy (MS). *Accreditation:* AAMFT/COAMFTE. *Program availability:* Part-time. *Degree requirements:* For master's, thesis. *Entrance requirements:* For master's, GRE, interview. Additional exam requirements/recommendations for international students: Required—TOEFL. *Faculty research:* Substance abuse, sexual abuse, couple therapy, professional issues, adolescent therapy.

**Queens College of the City University of New York,** Mathematics and Natural Sciences Division, Department of Family, Nutrition and Exercise Sciences, Queens, NY 11367-1597. Offers exercise science specialist (MS); family and consumer science (K-12) (AC); family and consumer science/teaching curriculum (K-12) (MS Ed); nutrition and exercise science (MS); nutrition specialist (MS); physical education (K-12) (AC); physical education/teaching curriculum (pre K-12) (MS Ed). *Program availability:* Part-time, evening/weekend. *Faculty:* 16 full-time (14 women), 46 part-time/adjunct (32 women). *Students:* 16 full-time (6 women), 157 part-time (86 women); includes 67 minority (19 Black or African American, non-Hispanic/Latino; 1 American Indian or Alaska Native, non-Hispanic/Latino; 18 Asian, non-Hispanic/Latino; 27 Hispanic/Latino; 2 Two or more races, non-Hispanic/Latino), 9 international. Average age 30. 95 applicants, 76% accepted, 45 enrolled. In 2016, 34 master's, 14 other advanced degrees awarded. *Degree requirements:* For master's, research project. *Entrance requirements:* For master's, minimum GPA of 3.0. Additional exam requirements/recommendations for international students: Required—TOEFL, IELTS. *Application deadline:* For fall admission, 4/1 for domestic students; for spring admission, 11/1 for domestic students. Applications are processed on a rolling basis. Application fee: $125. Electronic applications accepted. *Expenses:* Tuition, state resident: full-time $5065; part-time $425 per credit. Tuition, nonresident: part-time $780 per credit. *Required fees:* $522; $397 per credit. Part-time tuition and fees vary according to course load and program. *Financial support:* Career-related internships or fieldwork and unspecified assistantships available. Financial award application deadline: 4/1; financial award applicants required to submit FAFSA. *Unit head:* Dr. Michael Toner, Chairperson, 718-997-4168, E-mail: michael.toner@qc.cuny.edu.

**Roberts Wesleyan College,** Department of Social Work, Rochester, NY 14624-1997. Offers child and family practice (MSW); mental health practice (MSW). *Accreditation:* CSWE. *Entrance requirements:* For master's, minimum GPA of 2.75. *Faculty research:* Religion and social work, family studies, values and ethics.

**St. Cloud State University,** School of Graduate Studies, School of Education, Department of Child and Family Studies, St. Cloud, MN 56301-4498. Offers MS. *Degree requirements:* For master's, thesis or alternative. *Entrance requirements:* For master's, GRE General Test, minimum GPA of 2.75. Additional exam requirements/recommendations for international students: Required—Michigan English Language Assessment Battery; Recommended—TOEFL (minimum score 550 paper-based), IELTS (minimum score 6.5). Electronic applications accepted.

**San Diego State University,** Graduate and Research Affairs, College of Education, Department of Child and Family Development, San Diego, CA 92182. Offers child development (MS). *Program availability:* Part-time. *Degree requirements:* For master's, thesis. *Entrance requirements:* For master's, GRE General Test, 3 letters of recommendation, interview. Additional exam requirements/recommendations for international students: Required—TOEFL. Electronic applications accepted.

**South Carolina State University,** College of Graduate and Professional Studies, Department of Family and Consumer Sciences, Orangeburg, SC 29117-0001. Offers individual and family development (MS); nutritional sciences (MS). *Program availability:* Part-time, evening/weekend. *Faculty:* 3 full-time (all women), 1 (woman) part-time/adjunct. *Students:* 7 full-time (5 women), 6 part-time (all women); all minorities (all Black or African American, non-Hispanic/Latino). Average age 33. 10 applicants, 90% accepted, 9 enrolled. In 2016, 5 master's awarded. *Degree requirements:* For master's, comprehensive exam, thesis optional, departmental qualifying exam. *Entrance requirements:* For master's, GRE, MAT, or NTE, minimum GPA of 2.7. *Application deadline:* For fall admission, 6/15 priority date for domestic students, 6/15 for international students; for spring admission, 11/1 for domestic and international students. Application fee: $25. Electronic applications accepted. *Expenses:* Tuition, state resident: full-time $8938; part-time $579 per credit hour. Tuition, nonresident: full-time $19,018; part-time $1139 per credit hour. *Required fees:* $1482; $82 per credit hour. *Financial support:* Fellowships, Federal Work-Study, and scholarships/grants available. Financial award application deadline: 6/1. *Unit head:* Dr. William H. Whitaker, Chair, Department of Family and Consumer Sciences, 803-536-8958, Fax: 803-533-3268, E-mail: wwhitak3@scsu.edu. *Application contact:* Curtis Foskey, Coordinator of Graduate Admission, 803-536-8419, Fax: 803-536-8812, E-mail: cfoskey@scsu.edu.

**Spring Arbor University,** School of Human Services, Spring Arbor, MI 49283-9799. Offers counseling (MAC); family studies (MAFS); nursing (MSN). *Program availability:* Part-time, evening/weekend, online learning. *Entrance requirements:* For master's, bachelor's degree from regionally-accredited college or university, minimum GPA of 3.0 for at least the last two years of the bachelor's degree, at least two recommendations from professional/academic individuals. Additional exam requirements/recommendations for international students: Required—TOEFL (minimum score 600 paper-based). Electronic applications accepted.

**State University of New York at Oswego,** Graduate Studies, School of Education, Department of Vocational Teacher Preparation, Oswego, NY 13126. Offers agriculture (MS Ed); business and marketing (MS Ed); family and consumer sciences (MS Ed); health careers (MS Ed); technical education (MS Ed); trade education (MS Ed). *Accreditation:* NCATE. *Program availability:* Part-time, evening/weekend. *Degree requirements:* For master's, comprehensive exam, thesis or alternative. *Entrance requirements:* Additional exam requirements/recommendations for international students: Required—TOEFL (minimum score 560 paper-based).

**Syracuse University,** David B. Falk College of Sport and Human Dynamics, Programs in Child and Family Studies, Syracuse, NY 13244. Offers MA, MS, PhD. *Accreditation:* AAMFT/COAMFTE (one or more programs are accredited). *Program availability:* Part-time. *Degree requirements:* For master's, comprehensive exam (for some programs), thesis; for doctorate, comprehensive exam, thesis/dissertation. *Entrance requirements:* For master's and doctorate, GRE General Test, personal statement, official transcripts, three letters of recommendation, resume. Additional exam requirements/recommendations for international students: Required—TOEFL (minimum score 100 iBT). *Application deadline:* For fall admission, 2/15 priority date for domestic and international students; for spring admission, 11/15 priority date for domestic and international students. Application fee: $75. Electronic applications accepted. *Expenses:* Tuition: Full-time $25,974; part-time $1443 per credit hour. *Required fees:* $802; $50 per course. Tuition and fees vary according to course load and program. *Financial support:* Fellowships with full tuition reimbursements, research assistantships with tuition reimbursements, teaching assistantships with tuition reimbursements, career-related internships or fieldwork, and tuition waivers available. Financial award application deadline: 1/1. *Faculty research:* Family and child theories, research methods, family dynamics, child development. *Unit head:* Dr. Rachel R. Razza, Associate Professor/Graduate Program Director, 315-443-7377, Fax: 315-443-9402, E-mail: rrazza@syr.edu. *Application contact:* Felicia Otero, Director of Admissions, 315-443-5555, E-mail: falk@syr.edu.
Website: http://falk.syr.edu/ChildFamilyStudies/Default.aspx

**Texas State University,** The Graduate College, College of Applied Arts, Program in Family and Child Studies, San Marcos, TX 78666. Offers MS. *Program availability:* Part-time. *Faculty:* 6 full-time (5 women), 3 part-time/adjunct (all women). *Students:* 21 full-time (all women), 21 part-time (all women); includes 11 minority (2 Asian, non-Hispanic/Latino; 7 Hispanic/Latino; 2 Two or more races, non-Hispanic/Latino). Average age 26. 75 applicants, 39% accepted, 13 enrolled. In 2016, 20 master's awarded. *Degree requirements:* For master's, comprehensive exam, thesis (for some programs), competitive child life internship (for some programs). *Entrance requirements:* For master's, GRE (minimum preferred combined score of 285 on the verbal/quantitative sections with no less than 145 on the verbal and 140 on the quantitative), baccalaureate degree from regionally-accredited institution with minimum GPA of 3.0 on last 60 undergraduate hours, three letters of recommendation, 500-word statement of purpose, resume. Additional exam requirements/recommendations for international students: Required—TOEFL (minimum score 550 paper-based; 78 iBT). *Application deadline:* For fall admission, 2/15 for domestic and international students. Applications are processed on a rolling basis. Application fee: $40 ($90 for international students). Electronic applications accepted. *Expenses:* $4,851 per semester. *Financial support:* In 2016–17, 17 students received support, including 9 research assistantships (averaging $13,591 per year), 4 teaching assistantships (averaging $13,675 per year); scholarships/grants and unspecified assistantships also available. Financial award application deadline: 4/1; financial award applicants required to submit FAFSA. *Faculty research:* Mexican-origin student success, academic identity and its role in predicting post-secondary achievement, strengthening relationships/strengthening families. *Total annual research expenditures:* $863,318. *Unit head:* Dr. Melissa Delgado, Graduate Advisor, 512-245-2904, Fax: 512-245-3829, E-mail: msfamilyandchild@txstate.edu. *Application contact:* Dr. Andrea Golato, Dean of the Graduate College, 512-245-2581, Fax: 512-245-8365, E-mail: er15@txstate.edu.
Website: http://www.fcs.txstate.edu/degrees-programs/fcd/fcdgrad.html

**Texas Tech University,** Graduate School, College of Human Sciences, Department of Human Development and Family Studies, Lubbock, TX 79409-1230. Offers human development and family studies (MS, PhD), including gerontology (MS). *Accreditation:* AAMFT/COAMFTE (one or more programs are accredited). *Faculty:* 24 full-time (21 women), 7 part-time/adjunct (all women). *Students:* 28 full-time (23 women), 20 part-time (14 women); includes 12 minority (3 Black or African American, non-Hispanic/Latino; 1 American Indian or Alaska Native, non-Hispanic/Latino; 7 Hispanic/Latino; 1 Two or more races, non-Hispanic/Latino), 12 international. Average age 33. 34 applicants, 44% accepted, 4 enrolled. In 2016, 5 master's, 4 doctorates awarded. *Degree requirements:* For master's, thesis; for doctorate, comprehensive exam, thesis/dissertation. *Entrance requirements:* For master's and doctorate, GRE General Test. Additional exam requirements/recommendations for international students: Required—TOEFL (minimum score 550 paper-based; 79 iBT). *Application deadline:* For fall admission, 6/1 priority date for domestic students, 1/15 priority date for international students; for spring admission, 9/1 priority date for domestic students, 6/15 priority date for international students. Applications are processed on a rolling basis. Application fee: $75. Electronic applications accepted. *Expenses:* $315 per credit hour full-time resident tuition, $723 per credit hour full-time non-resident tuition; $50.50 per credit hour fee plus

## Child and Family Studies

$608 per term fee. *Financial support:* In 2016–17, 38 students received support, including 35 fellowships (averaging $4,579 per year), 24 research assistantships (averaging $8,526 per year), 23 teaching assistantships (averaging $9,522 per year); scholarships/grants and unspecified assistantships also available. Financial award application deadline: 4/15; financial award applicants required to submit FAFSA. *Faculty research:* 34226. *Total annual research expenditures:* $64,339. *Unit head:* Dr. Ann M. Mastergeorge, Chairperson, 806-834-7162, Fax: 806-742-3042, E-mail: ann.mastergeorge@ttu.edu. *Application contact:* Dr. Malinda Colwell, Graduate Program Director, 806-742-3000 Ext. 250, Fax: 806-742-0285, E-mail: malinda.colwell@ttu.edu.
Website: http://www.depts.ttu.edu/hdfs

**Texas Woman's University,** Graduate School, College of Professional Education, Department of Family Sciences, Denton, TX 76204-5769. Offers child development (MS); counseling and development (MS); early childhood development and education (PhD); early childhood education (M Ed); family studies (MS, PhD); family therapy (MS, PhD). *Accreditation:* ACA (one or more programs are accredited). *Program availability:* Part-time, evening/weekend. *Students:* Average age 34. In 2016, 99 master's, 9 doctorates awarded. Terminal master's awarded for partial completion of doctoral program. *Degree requirements:* For master's, comprehensive exam (for some programs), thesis (for some programs); for doctorate, comprehensive exam, thesis/ dissertation. *Entrance requirements:* Additional exam requirements/recommendations for international students: Required—TOEFL (minimum score 550 paper-based; 79 iBT). *Application deadline:* For fall admission, 7/1 priority date for domestic students, 2/15 for international students; for spring admission, 9/15 priority date for domestic students, 7/1 for international students. Applications are processed on a rolling basis. Application fee: $50 ($75 for international students). Electronic applications accepted. *Expenses:* Tuition, state resident: full-time $9046; part-time $251 per credit hour. Tuition, nonresident: full-time $22,922; part-time $614 per credit hour. *International tuition:* $23,046 full-time. *Required fees:* $2690; $1285 per credit hour. One-time fee: $50. Tuition and fees vary according to course level, course load, program and reciprocity agreements. *Financial support:* Research assistantships, teaching assistantships, career-related internships or fieldwork, Federal Work-Study, institutionally sponsored loans, scholarships/grants, traineeships, health care benefits, and unspecified assistantships available. Support available to part-time students. Financial award application deadline: 3/1; financial award applicants required to submit FAFSA. *Faculty research:* Parenting/parent education, military families, play therapy, family sexuality, diversity, healthy relationships/healthy marriages, childhood obesity, male communication. *Unit head:* Dr. Karen Petty, Chair, 940-898-2685, Fax: 940-898-2676, E-mail: famsci@twu.edu. *Application contact:* Dr. Samuel Wheeler, Assistant Director of Admissions, 940-898-3188, Fax: 940-898-3081, E-mail: wheelersr@twu.edu.
Website: http://www.twu.edu/family-sciences/

**Towson University,** Program in Child Life, Administration and Family Collaboration, Towson, MD 21252-0001. Offers MS. *Students:* 13 full-time (12 women), 11 part-time (all women); includes 4 minority (1 Black or African American, non-Hispanic/Latino; 2 Asian, non-Hispanic/Latino; 1 Hispanic/Latino). *Entrance requirements:* For master's, bachelor's degree; minimum GPA of 3.0; minimum of 40 hours of volunteer or paid work experience with children with special health care needs in a child life department under the direct supervision of a Certified Child Life Specialist; essay; volunteer/work experience verification form. Application fee: $45. Electronic applications accepted. *Expenses:* Tuition, state resident: full-time $7580; part-time $379 per unit. Tuition, nonresident: full-time $15,700; part-time $785 per unit. *Required fees:* $2480. *Unit head:* Prof. Lisa Martinelli Beasley, Graduate Program Director, 410-704-3766, E-mail: lmartinelli@towson.edu. *Application contact:* Coverley Beidleman, Assistant Director of Graduate Admissions, 410-704-2113, Fax: 410-704-3030, E-mail: grads@towson.edu.
Website: http://www.towson.edu/cla/departments/familystudies/grad/childlife/

**Towson University,** Program in Family-Professional Collaboration, Towson, MD 21252-0001. Offers Postbaccalaureate Certificate. *Students:* 15 full-time (14 women), 13 part-time (all women); includes 6 minority (3 Black or African American, non-Hispanic/Latino; 2 Asian, non-Hispanic/Latino; 1 Hispanic/Latino). *Entrance requirements:* For degree, minimum GPA of 3.0; bachelor's degree; resume; interview with program director. *Application deadline:* Applications are processed on a rolling basis. Application fee: $45. Electronic applications accepted. *Expenses:* Tuition, state resident: full-time $7580; part-time $379 per unit. Tuition, nonresident: full-time $15,700; part-time $785 per unit. *Required fees:* $2480. *Unit head:* Dr. Catherine Breneman, Graduate Program Director, 410-704-4871, E-mail: cbreneman@towson.edu. *Application contact:* Coverley Beidleman, Assistant Director of Graduate Admissions, 410-704-2113, Fax: 410-704-3030, E-mail: grads@towson.edu.
Website: http://www.towson.edu/cla/departments/familystudies/grad/famprofessionalpbc/index.html

**Tufts University,** Graduate School of Arts and Sciences, Eliot-Pearson Department of Child Study and Human Development, Medford, MA 02155. Offers child study and human development (MA, PhD); early childhood education (MAT). *Program availability:* Part-time. *Faculty:* 21 full-time (16 women), 15 part-time/adjunct (13 women). *Students:* 81 full-time (70 women), 6 part-time (5 women); includes 19 minority (6 Black or African American, non-Hispanic/Latino; 7 Asian, non-Hispanic/Latino; 3 Hispanic/Latino; 3 Two or more races, non-Hispanic/Latino), 16 international. Average age 27. 129 applicants, 59% accepted, 37 enrolled. In 2016, 19 master's, 5 doctorates awarded. *Degree requirements:* For master's, thesis (for some programs); for doctorate, comprehensive exam, thesis/dissertation. *Entrance requirements:* For master's and doctorate, GRE General Test. Additional exam requirements/recommendations for international students: Required—TOEFL (minimum score 550 paper-based; 80 iBT), IELTS (minimum score 6.5). *Application deadline:* For fall admission, 12/1 priority date for domestic and international students. Applications are processed on a rolling basis. Application fee: $85. Electronic applications accepted. *Expenses:* $49,982 full-time tuition (for MA); $29,936 full-time tuition (for PhD). *Financial support:* In 2016–17, 78 students received support. Fellowships, research assistantships, teaching assistantships, Federal Work-Study, scholarships/grants, tuition waivers (full and partial), and unspecified assistantships available. Support available to part-time students. Financial award application deadline: 1/15. *Faculty research:* Reading and language, developmental technologies, cognitive and social development, policy and program evaluation. *Unit head:* Dr. David Henry Feldman, Graduate Program Director. *Application contact:* Office of Graduate Admissions, 617-627-3395, E-mail: gradadmissions@tufts.edu.
Website: http://ase.tufts.edu/epcd

**The University of Akron,** Graduate School, Buchtel College of Arts and Sciences, School of Family and Consumer Sciences, Akron, OH 44325. Offers child and family development (MA), including child development, family development; clothing, textiles and interiors (MA). *Program availability:* Part-time, evening/weekend. *Faculty:* 4 full-time (all women), 16 part-time/adjunct (10 women). *Degree requirements:* For master's, comprehensive exam, thesis optional. *Entrance requirements:* For master's, GRE, minimum GPA of 2.75, three letters of recommendation, statement of purpose. Additional exam requirements/recommendations for international students: Required— TOEFL (minimum score 550 paper-based; 79 iBT), IELTS (minimum score 6.5).

*Application deadline:* For fall admission, 3/1 priority date for domestic and international students; for spring admission, 10/1 priority date for domestic and international students. Application fee: $45 ($70 for international students). Electronic applications accepted. *Expenses:* Tuition, state resident: full-time $8618; part-time $359 per credit hour. Tuition, nonresident: full-time $17,149; part-time $715 per credit hour. *Required fees:* $1652. *Financial support:* In 2016–17, 1 teaching assistantship with full tuition reimbursement was awarded. *Faculty research:* Nutritional health wellness/sports nutrition; historical/cultural aspects of clothing, textiles, interiors; family and consumer sciences (FCS) curriculum development; life span gender roles; families in international and historical perspectives. *Unit head:* Dr. Virginia Gunn, Interim Director, 330-972-7729, E-mail: vgunn@uakron.edu. *Application contact:* Dr. Shannon Zentall, Graduate Director, 330-972-6049, E-mail: szentall@uakron.edu.
Website: http://www.uakron.edu/fcs/

**The University of Alabama,** Graduate School, College of Human Environmental Sciences, Department of Human Development and Family Studies, Tuscaloosa, AL 35487. Offers human development and family studies (MSHES); marriage and family therapy (MSHES); parent and family life education (MSHES). *Faculty:* 10 full-time (8 women). *Students:* 23 full-time (22 women), 6 part-time (all women); includes 6 minority (5 Black or African American, non-Hispanic/Latino; 1 Two or more races, non-Hispanic/ Latino). Average age 25. 25 applicants, 72% accepted, 10 enrolled. In 2016, 10 master's awarded. Terminal master's awarded for partial completion of doctoral program. *Degree requirements:* For master's, comprehensive exam (for some programs), thesis (for some programs). *Entrance requirements:* For master's, GRE General Test or MAT, minimum GPA of 3.0. Additional exam requirements/recommendations for international students: Required—TOEFL (minimum score 79 iBT), IELTS (minimum score 6.5). *Application deadline:* For fall admission, 12/15 priority date for domestic and international students. Applications are processed on a rolling basis. Application fee: $50 ($60 for international students). Electronic applications accepted. *Expenses:* Tuition, state resident: full-time $10,470. Tuition, nonresident: full-time $26,950. *Financial support:* In 2016–17, 8 students received support, including 3 research assistantships with full tuition reimbursements available (averaging $13,140 per year), 5 teaching assistantships (averaging $13,140 per year); fellowships, career-related internships or fieldwork, Federal Work-Study, scholarships/grants, health care benefits, and unspecified assistantships also available. Financial award application deadline: 3/15. *Faculty research:* Parent/child relationships, preschool curricula and quality measures for child care programs, family strengths and adolescent behaviors, depression in mothers and infants, word association and word learning in young children, bullying behaviors in children, attachment parenting, medical play therapy, socialization of young children, impact of daily experiences on relationship quality, re-entry of service members into civilian roles. *Total annual research expenditures:* $1,650. *Unit head:* Dr. Carroll M. Tingle, Chair, 205-348-6158, Fax: 205-348-8153, E-mail: ctingle@ches.ua.edu. *Application contact:* Dr. Maria Hernandez-Reif, Professor, 205-348-5894, Fax: 205-348-8153, E-mail: mhernandez-reif@ches.ua.edu.
Website: http://www.hdfs.ches.ua.edu/

**The University of Arizona,** College of Education, Department of Disability and Psychoeducational Studies, Tucson, AZ 85721. Offers counseling and mental health (MA), including rehabilitation counseling, school counseling; family studies and human development (M Ed); rehabilitation counseling (PhD); school counseling (MA); school psychology (PhD, Ed S); special education (MA, PhD), including cross-categorical special education (MA), deaf and hard of hearing (MA), learning disabilities (MA), severe and multiple disabilities (MA), special education (PhD), visual impairment (MA). *Accreditation:* CORE. *Program availability:* Part-time. Terminal master's awarded for partial completion of doctoral program. *Degree requirements:* For master's, comprehensive exam, thesis optional; for doctorate, comprehensive exam, thesis/ dissertation. *Entrance requirements:* For master's, statement of purpose; for doctorate, GRE General Test (minimum score 1100) or MAT, 3 letters of recommendation. Additional exam requirements/recommendations for international students: Required— TOEFL (minimum score 550 paper-based; 79 iBT).

**University of Central Oklahoma,** The Jackson College of Graduate Studies, College of Education and Professional Studies, Department of Human Environmental Sciences, Edmond, OK 73034-5209. Offers family and child studies (MS), including family life education, infant/child specialist, marriage and family therapy; nutrition-food management (MS). *Program availability:* Part-time. *Degree requirements:* For master's, comprehensive exam (for some programs), thesis (for some programs). *Entrance requirements:* For master's, GRE, essay, physical, CPR and First Aid training. Additional exam requirements/recommendations for international students: Required—TOEFL (minimum score 550 paper-based; 79 iBT), IELTS (minimum score 6.5). Electronic applications accepted.

**University of Connecticut,** Graduate School, College of Liberal Arts and Sciences, Department of Human Development and Family Studies, Storrs, CT 06269. Offers MA, PhD. *Accreditation:* AAMFT/COAMFTE (one or more programs are accredited). Terminal master's awarded for partial completion of doctoral program. *Degree requirements:* For master's, comprehensive exam; for doctorate, thesis/dissertation. *Entrance requirements:* For doctorate, GRE General Test. Additional exam requirements/recommendations for international students: Required—TOEFL (minimum score 550 paper-based). Electronic applications accepted.

**University of Delaware,** College of Education and Human Development, Department of Human Development and Family Studies, Newark, DE 19716. Offers MS, PhD. *Program availability:* Part-time. Terminal master's awarded for partial completion of doctoral program. *Degree requirements:* For master's, thesis or alternative; for doctorate, comprehensive exam, thesis/dissertation. *Entrance requirements:* For master's and doctorate, GRE General Test, 3 letters of recommendation. Additional exam requirements/recommendations for international students: Required—TOEFL. Electronic applications accepted. *Faculty research:* Early childhood inclusive education, relationships, family risk and resilience, disability issues, program development and evaluation.

**University of Denver,** Morgridge College of Education, Denver, CO 80208. Offers child, family and school psychology (MA, PhD, Ed S); counseling psychology (MA, PhD); curriculum and instruction (MA, Ed D, PhD); curriculum instruction and teaching (Certificate); early childhood special education (MA, Certificate); educational leadership and policy studies (MA, Ed D, PhD, Certificate); higher education (Ed D, PhD); library and information science (MLIS); research methods and statistics (MA, PhD). *Accreditation:* ALA; APA (one or more programs are accredited). *Program availability:* Part-time, evening/weekend, online learning. *Faculty:* 39 full-time (29 women), 60 part-time/adjunct (42 women). *Students:* 498 full-time (392 women), 362 part-time (282 women); includes 223 minority (63 Black or African American, non-Hispanic/Latino; 6 American Indian or Alaska Native, non-Hispanic/Latino; 20 Asian, non-Hispanic/Latino; 102 Hispanic/Latino; 1 Native Hawaiian or other Pacific Islander, non-Hispanic/Latino; 31 Two or more races, non-Hispanic/Latino), 40 international. Average age 32. 1,027 applicants, 69% accepted, 386 enrolled. In 2016, 252 master's, 36 doctorates, 141 other advanced degrees awarded. Terminal master's awarded for partial completion of doctoral program. *Degree requirements:* For master's, comprehensive exam; for doctorate, 2 foreign languages, comprehensive exam, thesis/dissertation. *Entrance*

*requirements:* For master's and doctorate, GRE General Test or GMAT. Additional exam requirements/recommendations for international students: Required—TOEFL (minimum score 550 paper-based; 80 iBT). *Application deadline:* Applications are processed on a rolling basis. Application fee: $65. Electronic applications accepted. *Expenses:* $29,022 per year full-time. *Financial support:* In 2016–17, 697 students received support, including 37 research assistantships with tuition reimbursements available (averaging $11,209 per year), 66 teaching assistantships with tuition reimbursements available (averaging $3,742 per year); career-related internships or fieldwork, Federal Work-Study, institutionally sponsored loans, scholarships/grants, and unspecified assistantships also available. Support available to part-time students. Financial award application deadline: 2/15; financial award applicants required to submit FAFSA. *Faculty research:* Early childhood education, access and equity, educational leadership, family and school partnerships, neurodevelopmental disorders. *Total annual research expenditures:* $3.3 million. *Unit head:* Dr. Karen Riley, Dean, 303-871-3665, Fax: 303-871-4456, E-mail: karen.riley@du.edu. *Application contact:* Jodi Dye, Director of Admissions, 303-871-2510, Fax: 303-871-4456, E-mail: jodi.dye@du.edu.
Website: http://morgridge.du.edu

**University of Georgia,** College of Family and Consumer Sciences, Department of Human Development and Family Science, Athens, GA 30602. Offers child and family development (MS). *Accreditation:* AAMFT/COAMFTE. *Degree requirements:* For master's, thesis (MS). *Entrance requirements:* For master's, GRE General Test. *Application deadline:* For fall admission, 7/1 priority date for domestic students; for spring admission, 11/15 for domestic students. Application fee: $50. Electronic applications accepted. *Financial support:* Fellowships, research assistantships, teaching assistantships, and unspecified assistantships available. *Unit head:* Dr. Jay Mancini, Head, 706-542-4844, Fax: 706-542-4389, E-mail: mancini@fcs.uga.edu. *Application contact:* Emilie Smith, Graduate Coordinator, 706-542-4844, E-mail: emilie.smith@uga.edu.
Website: http://www.fcs.uga.edu/hdfs/

**University of Guelph,** Graduate Studies, College of Social and Applied Human Sciences, Department of Family Relations and Applied Nutrition, Guelph, ON N1G 2W1, Canada. Offers applied nutrition (MAN); family relations and human development (M Sc, PhD), including applied human nutrition, couple and family therapy (M Sc), family relations and human development. *Accreditation:* AAMFT/COAMFTE (one or more programs are accredited). *Program availability:* Part-time. *Degree requirements:* For master's, thesis (for some programs); for doctorate, comprehensive exam, thesis/dissertation. *Entrance requirements:* For master's, minimum B+ average; for doctorate, master's degree in family relations and human development or related field with a minimum B+ average or master's degree in applied human nutrition. Additional exam requirements/recommendations for international students: Required—TOEFL (minimum score 600 paper-based). Electronic applications accepted. *Faculty research:* Child and adolescent development, social gerontology, family roles and relations, couple and family therapy, applied human nutrition.

**University of Illinois at Springfield,** Graduate Programs, College of Education and Human Services, Program in Human Services, Springfield, IL 62703-5407. Offers alcohol and substance abuse (Graduate Certificate); alcoholism and substance abuse (MA); child and family services (MA); gerontology (MA); social services administration (MA). *Program availability:* Part-time, evening/weekend, 100% online, blended/hybrid learning. *Faculty:* 4 full-time (all women), 2 part-time/adjunct (1 woman). *Students:* 10 full-time (8 women), 62 part-time (53 women); includes 28 minority (23 Black or African American, non-Hispanic/Latino; 3 Hispanic/Latino; 2 Two or more races, non-Hispanic/Latino). Average age 34. 37 applicants, 46% accepted, 16 enrolled. In 2016, 32 master's, 3 other advanced degrees awarded. *Degree requirements:* For master's, internship; capstone project or thesis. *Entrance requirements:* For master's, minimum undergraduate GPA of 3.0, 2 letters of recommendation from professional or academic sources, statement of intent, interview. Additional exam requirements/recommendations for international students: Required—TOEFL (minimum score 500 paper-based; 61 iBT). *Application deadline:* Applications are processed on a rolling basis. Application fee: $60 ($75 for international students). Electronic applications accepted. *Expenses:* Tuition, state resident: part-time $329 per credit hour. Tuition, nonresident: part-time $675 per credit hour. *Financial support:* In 2016–17, fellowships with full tuition reimbursements (averaging $9,900 per year), research assistantships with full tuition reimbursements (averaging $9,991 per year), teaching assistantships with full tuition reimbursements (averaging $10,059 per year) were awarded; career-related internships or fieldwork, Federal Work-Study, scholarships/grants, health care benefits, and unspecified assistantships also available. Support available to part-time students. Financial award application deadline: 11/15; financial award applicants required to submit FAFSA. *Unit head:* Dr. Carolyn Peck, Program Administrator, 217-206-7577, Fax: 217-206-6775, E-mail: peck.carolyn@uis.edu. *Application contact:* Dr. Cecelia Cornell, Associate Vice Chancellor for Graduate Education, 217-206-7230, E-mail: ccorn1@uis.edu.
Website: http://www.uis.edu/humanservices

**University of Kentucky,** Graduate School, College of Agriculture, Food and Environment, Program in Family Studies, Human Development, and Resource Management, Lexington, KY 40506-0032. Offers MS, PhD. *Accreditation:* AAMFT/COAMFTE. *Degree requirements:* For master's, comprehensive exam, thesis optional. *Entrance requirements:* For master's, GRE General Test, minimum undergraduate GPA of 2.75; for doctorate, GRE General Test, minimum undergraduate GPA of 3.0. Additional exam requirements/recommendations for international students: Required—TOEFL (minimum score 550 paper-based). Electronic applications accepted. *Faculty research:* Early childhood education, family therapy, family resource management and consumer studies, human development.

**University of La Verne,** LaFetra College of Education, Programs in Child Development/Child Life, La Verne, CA 91750-4443. Offers child development (MS); child life (MS). *Program availability:* Part-time. *Students:* 36 full-time (all women), 68 part-time (67 women); includes 53 minority (6 Black or African American, non-Hispanic/Latino; 1 Asian, non-Hispanic/Latino; 47 Hispanic/Latino), 5 international. Average age 31. *Entrance requirements:* For master's, minimum GPA of 3.0, 3 letters of reference, writing sample. Additional exam requirements/recommendations for international students: Required—TOEFL (minimum score 550 paper-based). *Application deadline:* Applications are processed on a rolling basis. Application fee: $50. *Expenses:* Contact institution. *Financial support:* Scholarships/grants and traineeships available. Financial award application deadline: 3/2; financial award applicants required to submit FAFSA. *Unit head:* Laurie Schroeder, Chairperson, 909-448-4653, E-mail: lschroeder3@laverne.edu. *Application contact:* Christy Ranells, Program and Admission Specialist, 909-448-4644, Fax: 909-971-2295, E-mail: cranells@laverne.edu.
Website: http://www.laverne.edu/education/

**University of Manitoba,** Faculty of Graduate Studies, Faculty of Human Ecology, Department of Family Social Sciences, Winnipeg, MB R3T 2N2, Canada. Offers M Sc. *Degree requirements:* For master's, thesis.

**University of Maryland, College Park,** Academic Affairs, School of Public Health, Department of Family Science, College Park, MD 20742. Offers family studies (PhD); marriage and family therapy (MS); maternal and child health (PhD). *Accreditation:* AAMFT/COAMFTE. *Program availability:* Part-time, evening/weekend. *Degree*

*requirements:* For master's, thesis or alternative; for doctorate, comprehensive exam, thesis/dissertation, oral defense. *Entrance requirements:* For master's, GRE General Test, minimum GPA of 3.0, 3 letters of recommendation; for doctorate, GRE General Test, minimum GPA of 3.0, 3 letters of recommendation, research sample. Electronic applications accepted. *Faculty research:* Family life quality, interracial couples, child support, homeless families, family and child well-being.

**University of Massachusetts Amherst,** Graduate School, College of Education, Program in Education, Amherst, MA 01003. Offers bilingual, English as a second language, and multicultural education (M Ed, Ed S); child study and early education (M Ed); children, families and schools (Ed D, Ed S); early childhood and elementary teacher education (M Ed); educational leadership (M Ed); educational policy and leadership (Ed D); higher education (M Ed); international education (M Ed); language, literacy and culture (Ed D); learning, media and technology (M Ed, Ed S); mathematics, science, and learning technologies (Ed D); reading and writing (M Ed); research, educational measurement and psychometrics (Ed D); school counselor education (M Ed, Ed S); school psychology (Ed S); science education (Ed S); secondary teacher education (M Ed); social justice education (M Ed, Ed D, Ed S); special education (M Ed, Ed D, Ed S); teacher education and school improvement (Ed D, Ed S). *Accreditation:* NCATE. *Program availability:* Part-time, online learning. Terminal master's awarded for partial completion of doctoral program. *Degree requirements:* For doctorate, comprehensive exam, thesis/dissertation. *Entrance requirements:* Additional exam requirements/recommendations for international students: Required—TOEFL (minimum score 550 paper-based; 80 iBT), IELTS (minimum score 6.5). Electronic applications accepted.

**University of Minnesota, Twin Cities Campus,** Graduate School, College of Education and Human Development, Department of Family Social Science, Minneapolis, MN 55455-0213. Offers family education (M Ed); marriage and family therapy (MA, PhD); prevention science (MA). *Accreditation:* AAMFT/COAMFTE (one or more programs are accredited). *Faculty:* 19 full-time (13 women). *Students:* 54 full-time (44 women), 34 part-time (32 women); includes 19 minority (4 Black or African American, non-Hispanic/Latino; 8 Asian, non-Hispanic/Latino; 5 Hispanic/Latino; 2 Two or more races, non-Hispanic/Latino), 8 international. Average age 34. 31 applicants, 42% accepted, 13 enrolled. In 2016, 46 master's, 12 doctorates awarded. *Degree requirements:* For master's, thesis; for doctorate, thesis/dissertation. *Entrance requirements:* For master's and doctorate, GRE General Test, minimum undergraduate GPA of 3.0 (preferred). Additional exam requirements/recommendations for international students: Required—TOEFL. *Application deadline:* For fall admission, 12/15 for domestic students. Application fee: $75 ($95 for international students). *Financial support:* In 2016–17, 5 fellowships, 27 research assistantships (averaging $10,744 per year), 16 teaching assistantships (averaging $8,454 per year) were awarded; career-related internships or fieldwork, Federal Work-Study, institutionally sponsored loans, and tuition waivers (partial) also available. Financial award application deadline: 6/30; financial award applicants required to submit FAFSA. *Faculty research:* Ethnicity, culture and diverse families in social context; family stress, loss, and trauma; family finances; parenting; family transitions, and child adjustment in a family context. *Total annual research expenditures:* $2.2 million. *Unit head:* Dr. Lynne Borden, Head, 612-625-1900, Fax: 612-625-4227, E-mail: lmborden@umn.edu. *Application contact:* Dr. Jodi Dworkin, Director of Graduate Studies, 612-624-3732, Fax: 612-625-4227, E-mail: jdworkin@umn.edu.
Website: http://www.cehd.umn.edu/fsos/

**University of Missouri,** Office of Research and Graduate Studies, College of Human Environmental Sciences, Department of Human Development and Family Studies, Columbia, MO 65211. Offers MA, MS, PhD. *Entrance requirements:* For master's, GRE General Test, minimum GPA of 3.0. Additional exam requirements/recommendations for international students: Required—TOEFL (minimum score 550 paper-based; 80 iBT). Electronic applications accepted. *Expenses:* Tuition, state resident: full-time $6347; part-time $352.60 per credit hour. Tuition, nonresident: full-time $17,379; part-time $965.50 per credit hour. *Required fees:* $1035. Tuition and fees vary according to course load, campus/location and program.

**University of Montana,** Graduate School, Phyllis J. Washington College of Education and Human Sciences, Department of Counselor Education, Missoula, MT 59812-0002. Offers clinical mental health counseling (MA); counseling and supervision (Ed D); counselor education (Ed S); intercultural youth and family development (MA); school counseling (MA). *Accreditation:* ACA. *Degree requirements:* For doctorate, thesis/dissertation. *Entrance requirements:* For master's, doctorate, and Ed S, GRE General Test. Additional exam requirements/recommendations for international students: Required—TOEFL.

**University of Nebraska–Lincoln,** Graduate College, College of Education and Human Sciences, Department of Child, Youth and Family Studies, Lincoln, NE 68588. Offers child development/early childhood education (MS, PhD); child, youth and family studies (MS); family and consumer sciences education (MS, PhD); family financial planning (MS); family science (MS, PhD); gerontology (PhD); human sciences (PhD), including child, youth and family studies, gerontology, medical family therapy; marriage and family therapy (MS); medical family therapy (PhD); youth development (MS). *Accreditation:* AAMFT/COAMFTE (one or more programs are accredited). *Program availability:* Online learning. *Degree requirements:* For master's, thesis optional. *Entrance requirements:* For master's, GRE. Additional exam requirements/recommendations for international students: Required—TOEFL (minimum score 550 paper-based). Electronic applications accepted. *Faculty research:* Marriage and family therapy, child development/early childhood education, family financial management.

**University of Nevada, Reno,** Graduate School, College of Education, Department of Human Development and Family Studies, Reno, NV 89557. Offers MS. *Degree requirements:* For master's, thesis optional. *Entrance requirements:* For master's, GRE General Test, minimum GPA of 2.75. Additional exam requirements/recommendations for international students: Required—TOEFL (minimum score 500 paper-based; 61 iBT), IELTS (minimum score 6). Electronic applications accepted. *Faculty research:* Early childhood/adolescent development, family studies.

**University of New Hampshire,** Graduate School, College of Health and Human Services, Department of Human Development and Family Studies, Durham, NH 03824. Offers adolescent development (Postbaccalaureate Certificate); human development and family studies (MS); marriage and family therapy (MS). Program offered in fall only. *Accreditation:* AAMFT/COAMFTE. *Program availability:* Part-time. *Degree requirements:* For master's, thesis or alternative. *Entrance requirements:* For master's, GRE General Test. Additional exam requirements/recommendations for international students: Required—TOEFL (minimum score 550 paper-based; 80 iBT). Electronic applications accepted.

**University of New Mexico,** Graduate Studies, College of Education, Program in Family Studies, Albuquerque, NM 87131-2039. Offers family life education (MA); family relations (MA); family studies (PhD); human development in families (MA). *Program availability:* Part-time, evening/weekend. *Faculty:* 4 full-time (1 woman). *Students:* 18 full-time (15 women), 14 part-time (12 women); includes 19 minority (2 Black or African American, non-Hispanic/Latino; 1 American Indian or Alaska Native, non-Hispanic/

## Child and Family Studies

Latino; 16 Hispanic/Latino), 4 international. Average age 38. 11 applicants, 91% accepted, 10 enrolled. In 2016, 2 master's, 1 doctorate awarded. *Degree requirements:* For master's, comprehensive exam, thesis (for some programs); for doctorate, comprehensive exam, thesis/dissertation. *Entrance requirements:* For master's, written paper, 3 letters of recommendation, personal statement; for doctorate, GRE General Test, written paper, 3 letters of recommendation, personal statement, interview. Additional exam requirements/recommendations for international students: Required—TOEFL (minimum score 550 paper-based). *Application deadline:* For fall admission, 3/15 priority date for domestic and international students; for spring admission, 10/15 priority date for domestic and international students. Applications are processed on a rolling basis. Application fee: $50. Electronic applications accepted. *Financial support:* Fellowships, teaching assistantships with tuition reimbursements, and unspecified assistantships available. Financial award application deadline: 3/1; financial award applicants required to submit FAFSA. *Faculty research:* Home, community and school relations; multicultural issues; parent-child interactions; grandparents as primary caretakers for grandchildren; fathering; early childhood evaluation; early childhood development; globalization and indigenous cultures. *Unit head:* Dr. Ziarat Hossain, Program Coordinator, 505-277-4162, Fax: 505-277-8361, E-mail: zhossain@unm.edu. *Application contact:* Cynthia Salas, Department Administrator, 505-277-4535, Fax: 505-277-8361, E-mail: divbse@unm.edu.
Website: https://coe.unm.edu/departments-programs/ifce/family-studies/

**University of North Alabama,** College of Arts and Sciences, Department of Sociology and Family Studies, Florence, AL 35632-0001. Offers family studies (MS). *Program availability:* Part-time, 100% online. *Faculty:* 3 full-time (all women). *Students:* 1 (woman) full-time, 9 part-time (all women); includes 4 minority (all Black or African American, non-Hispanic/Latino). Average age 34. 6 applicants, 83% accepted, 4 enrolled. In 2016, 3 master's awarded. *Degree requirements:* For master's, project or thesis. *Entrance requirements:* For master's, GRE or MAT, three professional references, writing sample. Additional exam requirements/recommendations for international students: Required—TOEFL (minimum score 79 iBT), IELTS (minimum score 6), PTE (minimum score 54). *Application deadline:* For fall admission, 7/1 for domestic and international students; for spring admission, 11/1 for domestic and international students; for summer admission, 4/1 for domestic and international students. Applications are processed on a rolling basis. Application fee: $50 ($100 for international students). Electronic applications accepted. *Expenses:* Tuition, state resident: full-time $2799; part-time $1866 per semester. Tuition, nonresident: full-time $5598; part-time $3732 per semester. *Required fees:* $915; $642 per semester. Tuition and fees vary according to course load. *Financial support:* In 2016–17, 1 student received support. Scholarships/grants and unspecified assistantships available. Financial award application deadline: 2/1. *Unit head:* Dr. Yaschica Williams, Chair, 256-765-4200, E-mail: ywilliams@una.edu. *Application contact:* Hillary N. Coats, Graduate Admissions Coordinator, 256-765-4447, E-mail: graduate@una.edu.
Website: https://www.una.edu/sociology/

**The University of North Carolina at Charlotte,** Cato College of Education, Department of Special Education and Child Development, Charlotte, NC 28223-0001. Offers academically or intellectually gifted (Graduate Certificate); autism spectrum disorders (Graduate Certificate); child and family development: birth through kindergarten (Graduate Certificate); child and family studies: early education (M Ed); special education (M Ed, PhD, Graduate Certificate), including academically or intellectually gifted (M Ed). *Program availability:* Part-time, 100% online, blended/hybrid learning. *Faculty:* 25 full-time (18 women), 8 part-time/adjunct (6 women). *Students:* 21 full-time (17 women), 106 part-time (101 women); includes 11 minority (8 Black or African American, non-Hispanic/Latino; 1 Hispanic/Latino; 2 Two or more races, non-Hispanic/Latino), 4 international. Average age 34. 83 applicants, 95% accepted, 66 enrolled. In 2016, 6 master's, 7 doctorates, 42 other advanced degrees awarded. *Degree requirements:* For master's, thesis or alternative, research project; for doctorate, thesis/dissertation, portfolio; for Graduate Certificate, internship. *Entrance requirements:* For master's, GRE or MAT, personal statement, letters of recommendation; for doctorate, GRE or MAT, 2 official transcripts of all academic work attempted since high school indicating minimum GPA of 3.5 in graduate degree program; at least 3 references of someone who knows applicant's current work and/or academic achievements in previous degree work; two-page essay; current resume or curriculum vitae; writing sample; documentation of teaching; for Graduate Certificate, undergraduate degree from regionally-accredited four-year institution; minimum cumulative undergraduate GPA of 3.0; three recommendations from persons knowledgeable of applicant's interaction with children and families; statement of purpose; clear criminal background check. Additional exam requirements/recommendations for international students: Required—TOEFL (minimum score 523 paper-based, 70 iBT) or IELTS (6.5). *Application deadline:* For fall admission, 12/1 for domestic and international students; for spring admission, 10/1 priority date for domestic and international students; for summer admission, 4/1 priority date for domestic and international students. Applications are processed on a rolling basis. Application fee: $75. Electronic applications accepted. *Expenses:* Tuition, state resident: full-time $4252. Tuition, nonresident: full-time $17,423. *Required fees:* $3026. Tuition and fees vary according to course load and program. *Financial support:* In 2016–17, 11 students received support, including 10 research assistantships (averaging $9,195 per year), 1 teaching assistantship (averaging $16,848 per year); career-related internships or fieldwork, institutionally sponsored loans, scholarships/grants, and unspecified assistantships also available. Support available to part-time students. Financial award application deadline: 3/1; financial award applicants required to submit FAFSA. *Total annual research expenditures:* $4 million. *Unit head:* Dr. Belva Collins, Chair, 704-687-8828, E-mail: belva.collins@uncc.edu. *Application contact:* Kathy B. Giddings, Director of Graduate Admissions, 704-687-5503, Fax: 704-687-1668, E-mail: gradadm@uncc.edu.
Website: http://spcd.uncc.edu/

**The University of North Carolina at Charlotte,** Cato College of Education, Interdisciplinary Education Programs, Charlotte, NC 28223-0001. Offers art education (Graduate Certificate); child and family development: early childhood education (MAT); curriculum and instruction (PhD); elementary education (MAT); foreign language education (MAT); middle grades education (MAT); secondary education (MAT); special education (MAT); teaching (Graduate Certificate); teaching English as a second language (MAT); theatre education (Graduate Certificate). *Program availability:* Part-time, 100% online, blended/hybrid learning. *Students:* 78 full-time (59 women), 619 part-time (484 women); includes 255 minority (186 Black or African American, non-Hispanic/Latino; 1 American Indian or Alaska Native, non-Hispanic/Latino; 16 Asian, non-Hispanic/Latino; 37 Hispanic/Latino; 15 Two or more races, non-Hispanic/Latino), 10 international. Average age 33. 380 applicants, 92% accepted, 264 enrolled. In 2016, 93 master's, 8 doctorates, 176 other advanced degrees awarded. *Degree requirements:* For master's, thesis or alternative, research project/exam. *Entrance requirements:* For master's, GRE or MAT, bachelor's degree, or its U.S. equivalent, from regionally-accredited college or university; minimum overall GPA of 3.0 on all previous work beyond high school; statement of purpose (essay); at least three recommendation forms; for doctorate, GRE or MAT, bachelor's degree (or its U.S. equivalent) from regionally-accredited college or university; minimum overall GPA of 3.5 in master's degree program; for Graduate Certificate, bachelor's degree from regionally-accredited

university; minimum GPA of 2.75 on all post-secondary work attempted; transcripts; personal statement outlining why the applicant seeks admission to the program. Additional exam requirements/recommendations for international students: Required—TOEFL (minimum score 523 paper-based) or IELTS (6.5). *Application deadline:* For fall admission, 3/1 priority date for domestic and international students; for spring admission, 10/1 priority date for domestic and international students; for summer admission, 4/1 priority date for domestic and international students. Applications are processed on a rolling basis. Application fee: $75. Electronic applications accepted. *Expenses:* Tuition, state resident: full-time $4252. Tuition, nonresident: full-time $17,423. *Required fees:* $3026. Tuition and fees vary according to course load and program. *Financial support:* Career-related internships or fieldwork, institutionally sponsored loans, scholarships/grants, and unspecified assistantships available. Support available to part-time students. Financial award application deadline: 3/1; financial award applicants required to submit FAFSA. *Unit head:* Dr. Ellen McIntyre, Dean, 704-687-8722, E-mail: ellen.mcintyre@uncc.edu. *Application contact:* Kathy B. Giddings, Director of Graduate Admissions, 704-687-5503, Fax: 704-687-1668, E-mail: gradadm@uncc.edu.
Website: http://education.uncc.edu/academic-programs

**The University of North Carolina at Greensboro,** Graduate School, School of Health and Human Sciences, Department of Human Development and Family Studies, Greensboro, NC 27412-5001. Offers M Ed, MS, PhD. *Degree requirements:* For master's, one foreign language; for doctorate, one foreign language, thesis/dissertation. *Entrance requirements:* For master's and doctorate, GRE General Test. Additional exam requirements/recommendations for international students: Required—TOEFL. Electronic applications accepted. *Expenses:* Contact institution. *Faculty research:* Adolescent mothers, multi-handicapped, older adults.

**University of North Texas,** Robert B. Toulouse School of Graduate Studies, Denton, TX 76203-5459. Offers accounting (MS); applied anthropology (MA, MS); applied behavior analysis (Certificate); applied geography (MA); applied technology and performance improvement (M Ed, MS); art education (MA); art history (MA); art museum education (Certificate); arts leadership (Certificate); audiology (Au D); behavior analysis (MS); behavioral science (PhD); biochemistry and molecular biology (MS); biology (MA, MS); biomedical engineering (MS); business analysis (MS); chemistry (MS); clinical health psychology (PhD); communication studies (MA, MS); computer engineering (MS); computer science (MS); counseling (M Ed, MS), including clinical mental health counseling (MS), college and university counseling, elementary school counseling, secondary school counseling; creative writing (MA); criminal justice (MS); curriculum and instruction (M Ed); decision sciences (MBA); design (MA, MFA), including fashion design (MFA), innovation studies, interior design (MFA); early childhood studies (MS); economics (MS); educational leadership (M Ed, Ed D); educational psychology (MS, PhD), including family studies (MS), gifted and talented (MS), human development (MS), learning and cognition (MS), research, measurement and evaluation (MS); electrical engineering (MS); emergency management (MPA); engineering technology (MS); English (MA); English as a second language (MA); environmental science (MS); finance (MBA, MS); financial management (MPA); French (MA); health services management (MBA); higher education (M Ed, Ed D); history (MA, MS); hospitality management (MS); human resources management (MPA); information science (MS); information systems (PhD); information technologies (MBA); interdisciplinary studies (MA, MS); international studies (MA); international sustainable tourism (MS); jazz studies (MM); journalism (MA, MJ, Graduate Certificate), including interactive and virtual digital communication (Graduate Certificate), narrative journalism (Graduate Certificate), public relations (Graduate Certificate); kinesiology (MS); linguistics (MA); local government management (MPA); logistics (PhD); logistics and supply chain management (MBA); long-term care, senior housing, and aging services (MA); management (PhD); marketing (MBA); mathematics (MA, MS); mechanical and energy engineering (MS, PhD); music (MA), including ethnomusicology, music theory, musicology, performance; music composition (PhD); music education (MM Ed, PhD); nonprofit management (MPA); operations and supply chain management (MBA); performance (MM, DMA); philosophy (MA); political science (MA); professional and technical communication (MA); radio, television and film (MA, MFA); rehabilitation counseling (Certificate); sociology (MA); Spanish (MA); special education (M Ed); speech-language pathology (MA); strategic management (MBA); studio art (MFA); teaching (M Ed); MBA/MS. *Program availability:* Part-time, evening/weekend, online learning. Terminal master's awarded for partial completion of doctoral program. *Degree requirements:* For master's, variable foreign language requirement, comprehensive exam (for some programs), thesis (for some programs); for doctorate, variable foreign language requirement, comprehensive exam (for some programs), thesis/dissertation; for other advanced degree, variable foreign language requirement, comprehensive exam (for some programs). *Entrance requirements:* For master's and doctorate, GRE, GMAT. Additional exam requirements/recommendations for international students: Required—TOEFL (minimum score 550 paper-based; 79 iBT). Electronic applications accepted.

**University of Rhode Island,** Graduate School, College of Health Sciences, Department of Human Development and Family Studies, Kingston, RI 02881. Offers college student personnel (MS); human development and family studies (MS); marriage and family therapy (MS). *Accreditation:* AAMFT/COAMFTE. *Program availability:* Part-time. *Faculty:* 15 full-time (10 women). *Students:* 43 full-time (28 women), 14 part-time (10 women); includes 11 minority (7 Black or African American, non-Hispanic/Latino; 1 Asian, non-Hispanic/Latino; 1 Hispanic/Latino; 2 Two or more races, non-Hispanic/Latino). In 2016, 26 master's awarded. *Degree requirements:* For master's, comprehensive exam (for some programs), thesis optional. *Entrance requirements:* For master's, GRE or MAT, 2 letters of recommendation; resume (for college student personnel specialization). Additional exam requirements/recommendations for international students: Required—TOEFL. *Application deadline:* For fall admission, 1/15 for domestic and international students. Application fee: $65. Electronic applications accepted. *Expenses:* Tuition, state resident: full-time $11,796; part-time $655 per credit. Tuition, nonresident: full-time $24,206; part-time $1345 per credit. *Required fees:* $1546; $44 per credit. One-time fee: $155 full-time; $35 part-time. *Financial support:* In 2016–17, 2 research assistantships (averaging $8,592 per year), 4 teaching assistantships (averaging $11,456 per year) were awarded. Financial award application deadline: 1/15; financial award applicants required to submit FAFSA. *Unit head:* Dr. Karen McCurdy, Chair, 401-874-5960, Fax: 401-874-4020, E-mail: kmccurdy@uri.edu. *Application contact:* Graduate Admissions, 401-874-2872, E-mail: gradadm@etal.uri.edu.
Website: http://www.uri.edu/hss/hdf/

**University of Southern California,** Graduate School, School of Social Work, Los Angeles, CA 90089. Offers community organization, planning and administration (MSW); families and children (MSW); health (MSW); mental health (MSW); military social work and veterans services (MSW); older adults (MSW); public child welfare (MSW); school settings (MSW); social work (MSW, PhD); systems of mental illness recovery (MSW); work and life (MSW); JD/MSW; M PI/MSW; MPA/MSW; MSW/MBA; MSW/MJCS; MSW/MS. *Accreditation:* CSWE (one or more programs are accredited). *Degree requirements:* For doctorate, comprehensive exam, thesis/dissertation, qualifying exam/publishable paper. *Entrance requirements:* For doctorate, GRE General Test. Additional exam requirements/recommendations for international students:

Required—TOEFL (minimum score 600 paper-based; 100 iBT), ESL exam. Electronic applications accepted. *Faculty research:* Department of Defense Educational Activity, detection/treatment of depression among older adults, health/aging, psychosocial adaptation to extreme environments/man made disasters; mental health needs of older adults.

**University of Southern Mississippi,** Graduate School, College of Education and Psychology, Department of Child and Family Studies, Hattiesburg, MS 39406. Offers child and family studies (MS); marriage and family therapy (MS); school counseling (M Ed). *Accreditation:* AAMFT/COAMFTE (one or more programs are accredited). *Program availability:* Part-time, online learning. *Degree requirements:* For master's, comprehensive exam, thesis optional. *Entrance requirements:* For master's, GRE General Test, minimum GPA of 2.75 on last 60 hours. Additional exam requirements/recommendations for international students: Required—TOEFL. *Application deadline:* For fall admission, 3/1 priority date for domestic students, 3/1 for international students; for spring admission, 1/1 priority date for domestic and international students. Applications are processed on a rolling basis. Application fee: $60. Electronic applications accepted. *Expenses: Tuition, area resident:* Full-time $15,708; part-time $437 per credit hour. *Financial support:* Fellowships, research assistantships with full tuition reimbursements, career-related internships or fieldwork, Federal Work-Study, institutionally sponsored loans, scholarships/grants, health care benefits, and unspecified assistantships available. Financial award application deadline: 3/15; financial award applicants required to submit FAFSA. *Faculty research:* School food service, teen pregnancy, diet and cholesterol metabolism. *Unit head:* Pat Sims, Chair, 601-266-6990, Fax: 601-266-4680. *Application contact:* Shonna Breland, Manager of Graduate Admissions, 601-266-6563, Fax: 601-266-5138.
Website: https://www.usm.edu/family-studies-child-development

**University of South Florida,** College of Behavioral and Community Sciences, Department of Child and Family Studies, Tampa, FL 33620-9951. Offers applied behavior analysis (MA, MS, PhD); behavioral and community sciences (PhD); child and adolescent behavioral health (MS), including developmental disabilities, leadership in child and adolescent health, translational research and evaluation, youth and behavioral health; rehabilitation and mental health counseling (MA), including addictions and substance abuse counseling, marriage and family therapy. *Accreditation:* ACA. *Faculty:* 15 full-time (10 women), 1 (woman) part-time/adjunct. *Students:* 146 full-time (127 women), 90 part-time (74 women); includes 92 minority (22 Black or African American, non-Hispanic/Latino; 12 Asian, non-Hispanic/Latino; 49 Hispanic/Latino; 9 Two or more races, non-Hispanic/Latino), 3 international. Average age 28. 267 applicants, 51% accepted, 93 enrolled. In 2016, 63 master's awarded. *Degree requirements:* For master's, comprehensive exam, thesis (for some programs); for doctorate, comprehensive exam, thesis/dissertation, Behavior Analyst Board Certification Exam. *Entrance requirements:* For master's, GRE General Test, minimum GPA of 3.0 in last 60 hours of coursework; letters of recommendation; one-page narrative describing experience, interest, and career goals in applied behavior analysis; resume or curriculum vitae (varies by program); for doctorate, GRE General Test, master's degree in behavioral analysis or closely-related field; minimum GPA of 3.5 in graduate course work; three letters of recommendation; campus visit with faculty interview; personal statement; curriculum vitae; evidence of research experiences and expertise. Additional exam requirements/recommendations for international students: Required—TOEFL (minimum score 550 paper-based; 79 iBT) or IELTS (minimum score 6.5). *Application deadline:* For fall admission, 12/5 for domestic and international students. Application fee: $30. *Expenses:* Tuition, state resident: full-time $7766; part-time $431.43 per credit hour. Tuition, nonresident: full-time $15,789; part-time $877.17 per credit hour. *Required fees:* $37 per term. *Financial support:* In 2016–17, 50 students received support. Unspecified assistantships available. *Faculty research:* Applied behavior analysis, autism, behavior management, behavioral intervention, children, developmental disabilities, experimental analysis of behavior, functional assessment, positive behavior support. *Total annual research expenditures:* $16.4 million. *Application contact:* Dr. Raymond G. Miltenberger, Professor/Director of Master's Program, 813-974-5079, Fax: 813-974-6115, E-mail: miltenbe@usf.edu.
Website: http://cfs.cbcs.usf.edu/

**University of South Florida,** Innovative Education, Tampa, FL 33620-9951. Offers adult, career and higher education (Graduate Certificate), including college teaching, leadership in developing human resources, leadership in higher education; Africana studies (Graduate Certificate), including diasporas and health disparities, genocide and human rights; aging studies (Graduate Certificate), including gerontology; art research (Graduate Certificate), including museum studies; business foundations (Graduate Certificate); chemical and biomedical engineering (Graduate Certificate), including materials science and engineering, water, health and sustainability; child and family studies (Graduate Certificate), including positive behavior support; civil and industrial engineering (Graduate Certificate), including transportation systems analysis; community and family health (Graduate Certificate), including maternal and child health, social marketing and public health, violence and injury: prevention and intervention, women's health; criminology (Graduate Certificate), including criminal justice administration; educational measurement and research (Graduate Certificate), including evaluation; English (Graduate Certificate), including comparative literary studies, creative writing, professional and technical communication; entrepreneurship (Graduate Certificate); environmental health (Graduate Certificate), including safety management; epidemiology and biostatistics (Graduate Certificate), including applied biostatistics, biostatistics, concepts and tools of epidemiology, epidemiology, epidemiology of infectious diseases; geography, environment and planning (Graduate Certificate), including community development, environmental policy and management, geographical information systems; geology (Graduate Certificate), including hydrogeology; global health (Graduate Certificate), including disaster management, global health and Latin American and Caribbean studies, global health practice, humanitarian assistance, infection control; government and international affairs (Graduate Certificate), including Cuban studies, globalization studies; health policy and management (Graduate Certificate), including health management and leadership, public health policy and programs; hearing specialist: early intervention (Graduate Certificate); industrial and management systems engineering (Graduate Certificate), including systems engineering, technology management; information studies (Graduate Certificate), including school library media specialist; information systems/decision sciences (Graduate Certificate), including analytics and business intelligence; instructional technology (Graduate Certificate), including distance education, Florida digital/virtual educator, instructional design, multimedia design, Web design; internal medicine, bioethics and medical humanities (Graduate Certificate), including biomedical ethics; Latin American and Caribbean studies (Graduate Certificate), including mass communications (Graduate Certificate), including multimedia journalism; mathematics and statistics (Graduate Certificate), including mathematics; medicine (Graduate Certificate), including aging and neuroscience, bioinformatics, biotechnology, brain fitness and memory management, clinical investigation, health informatics, health sciences, integrative weight management, intellectual property, medicine and gender, metabolic and nutritional medicine, metabolic cardiology, pharmacy sciences; national and competitive intelligence (Graduate Certificate); psychological and social foundations (Graduate Certificate), including career counseling, college teaching, diversity in

education, mental health counseling, school counseling; public affairs (Graduate Certificate), including nonprofit management, public management, research administration; public health (Graduate Certificate), including environmental health, health equity, public health generalist, translational research in adolescent behavioral health; public health practices (Graduate Certificate), including planning for healthy communities; rehabilitation and mental health counseling (Graduate Certificate), including integrative mental health care, marriage and family therapy, rehabilitation technology; secondary education (Graduate Certificate), including ESOL, foreign language education: culture and content, foreign language education: professional; social work (Graduate Certificate), including geriatric social work/clinical gerontology; special education (Graduate Certificate), including autism spectrum disorder, disabilities education: severe/profound; world languages (Graduate Certificate), including teaching English as a second language (TESL) or foreign language. *Expenses:* Tuition, state resident: full-time $7766; part-time $431.43 per credit hour. Tuition, nonresident: full-time $15,789; part-time $877.17 per credit hour. *Required fees:* $37 per term. *Unit head:* Kathy Barnes, Interdisciplinary Programs Coordinator, 813-974-8031, Fax: 813-974-7061, E-mail: barnesk@usf.edu. *Application contact:* Karen Tylinski, Metro Initiatives, 813-974-9943, Fax: 813-974-7061, E-mail: ktylinsk@usf.edu.
Website: http://www.usf.edu/innovative-education/

**The University of Tennessee,** Graduate School, College of Education, Health and Human Sciences, Department of Child and Family Studies, Knoxville, TN 37996. Offers child and family studies (MS); early childhood education (MS). *Program availability:* Part-time. *Degree requirements:* For master's, thesis or alternative. *Entrance requirements:* For master's, GRE General Test, minimum GPA of 2.7. Additional exam requirements/recommendations for international students: Required—TOEFL. Electronic applications accepted.

**The University of Tennessee,** Graduate School, College of Education, Health and Human Sciences, Program in Human Ecology, Knoxville, TN 37996. Offers child and family studies (PhD); community health (PhD); nutrition science (PhD); retailing and consumer sciences (PhD); textile science (PhD). *Degree requirements:* For doctorate, thesis/dissertation. *Entrance requirements:* For doctorate, GRE General Test, minimum GPA of 2.7. Additional exam requirements/recommendations for international students: Required—TOEFL. Electronic applications accepted.

**The University of Tennessee at Martin,** Graduate Programs, College of Agriculture and Applied Sciences, Department of Family and Consumer Sciences, Martin, TN 38238. Offers dietetics (MSFCS); general family and consumer sciences (MSFCS). *Program availability:* Part-time, 100% online. *Faculty:* 10. *Students:* 5 full-time (all women), 34 part-time (32 women); includes 9 minority (8 Black or African American, non-Hispanic/Latino; 1 Two or more races, non-Hispanic/Latino). Average age 28. 58 applicants, 71% accepted, 15 enrolled. In 2016, 11 master's awarded. *Degree requirements:* For master's, comprehensive exam, thesis optional. *Entrance requirements:* For master's, GRE General Test, minimum GPA of 2.5. Additional exam requirements/recommendations for international students: Required—TOEFL (minimum score 525 paper-based; 71 iBT). *Application deadline:* For fall admission, 7/27 priority date for domestic and international students; for spring admission, 12/17 priority date for domestic and international students; for summer admission, 5/10 priority date for domestic and international students. Applications are processed on a rolling basis. Application fee: $30 ($130 for international students). Electronic applications accepted. *Expenses:* Tuition, state resident: full-time $8254; part-time $459 per credit hour. Tuition, nonresident: full-time $22,198; part-time $1234 per credit hour. *Required fees:* $79 per credit hour. Part-time tuition and fees vary according to course load and campus/location. *Financial support:* In 2016–17, 4 students received support, including 1 research assistantship (averaging $6,283 per year), 3 teaching assistantships with full tuition reimbursements available (averaging $8,001 per year); scholarships/grants and unspecified assistantships also available. Financial award application deadline: 2/1; financial award applicants required to submit FAFSA. *Faculty research:* Children with developmental disabilities, regional food product development and marketing, parent education. *Unit head:* Dr. Lisa LeBleu, Coordinator, 731-881-7116, Fax: 731-881-7106, E-mail: llebleu@utm.edu. *Application contact:* Jolene L. Cunningham, Student Services Specialist, 731-881-7012, Fax: 731-881-7499, E-mail: jcunningham@utm.edu.
Website: http://www.utm.edu/departments/caas/fcs/index.php

**The University of Texas at Austin,** Graduate School, College of Natural Sciences, School of Human Ecology, Program in Human Development and Family Sciences, Austin, TX 78712-1111. Offers MA, PhD. *Degree requirements:* For master's, thesis; for doctorate, thesis/dissertation. *Entrance requirements:* For master's and doctorate, GRE General Test. Additional exam requirements/recommendations for international students: Required—TOEFL. Electronic applications accepted. *Faculty research:* Marriage and family relationships, parenting, impact of television on children, courtship, family policy.

**The University of Texas at Dallas,** School of Behavioral and Brain Sciences, Program in Psychological Sciences, Richardson, TX 75080. Offers early childhood disorders (MS); psychological sciences (MS, PhD). *Program availability:* Part-time, evening/weekend. *Faculty:* 16 full-time (11 women), 4 part-time/adjunct (all women). *Students:* 66 full-time (54 women), 14 part-time (10 women); includes 32 minority (6 Black or African American, non-Hispanic/Latino; 8 Asian, non-Hispanic/Latino; 16 Hispanic/Latino; 2 Two or more races, non-Hispanic/Latino), 4 international. Average age 27. 148 applicants, 36% accepted, 36 enrolled. In 2016, 23 master's, 2 doctorates awarded. *Degree requirements:* For master's, directed project or internship; for doctorate, thesis/dissertation. *Entrance requirements:* For master's and doctorate, GRE General Test, minimum GPA of 3.0 in upper-level course work. Additional exam requirements/recommendations for international students: Required—TOEFL (minimum score 550 paper-based). *Application deadline:* For fall admission, 7/15 for domestic students, 5/1 priority date for international students; for spring admission, 11/15 for domestic students, 9/1 priority date for international students. Applications are processed on a rolling basis. Application fee: $50 ($100 for international students). Electronic applications accepted. *Expenses:* Tuition, state resident: full-time $12,418; part-time $690 per semester hour. Tuition, nonresident: full-time $24,150; part-time $1342 per semester hour. Tuition and fees vary according to course load. *Financial support:* In 2016–17, 64 students received support, including 6 research assistantships with partial tuition reimbursements available (averaging $25,546 per year), 21 teaching assistantships with partial tuition reimbursements available (averaging $17,091 per year); fellowships, career-related internships or fieldwork, Federal Work-Study, scholarships/grants, and unspecified assistantships also available. Support available to part-time students. Financial award application deadline: 4/30; financial award applicants required to submit FAFSA. *Faculty research:* Neurocognitive development in young adulthood, infant learning, infant and toddler eye tracking, social aggression. *Unit head:* Dr. Shayla Holub, Program Head, Psychological Sciences, 972-883-4475, Fax: 972-883-2491, E-mail: sholub@utdallas.edu. *Application contact:* Jasmin Stubblefield, Program Coordinator, 972-883-2697, Fax: 972-883-2491, E-mail: psysciencesphd@utdallas.edu.
Website: http://www.utdallas.edu/bbs/degrees/psy-degrees/

**University of Utah,** Graduate School, College of Social and Behavioral Science, Department of Family and Consumer Studies, Salt Lake City, UT 84112-0080. Offers human development and social policy (MS). *Program availability:* Part-time. *Faculty:* 15

## Child and Family Studies

full-time (7 women), 5 part-time/adjunct (all women). *Students:* 8 full-time (all women), 2 part-time (both women). Average age 25. 12 applicants, 67% accepted, 7 enrolled. In 2016, 7 master's awarded. *Degree requirements:* For master's, comprehensive exam (for some programs), thesis (for some programs), thesis or project. *Entrance requirements:* For master's, GRE General Test, minimum undergraduate GPA of 3.0, courses in research methods and statistics. Additional exam requirements/recommendations for international students: Required—TOEFL (minimum score 550 paper-based). *Application deadline:* For fall admission, 2/1 priority date for domestic and international students. Applications are processed on a rolling basis. Application fee: $55 ($65 for international students). Electronic applications accepted. *Expenses:* Contact institution. *Financial support:* In 2016–17, 6 students received support, including 1 research assistantship with full tuition reimbursement available (averaging $14,000 per year), 4 teaching assistantships with full tuition reimbursements available (averaging $14,000 per year). Financial award application deadline: 5/1. *Faculty research:* Social, physical, educational and economic contexts of individuals, families and communities. *Unit head:* Prof. Lori Kowaleski-Jones, PhD, Chair, 801-585-0074, Fax: 801-581-5156, E-mail: lk2700@fcs.utah.edu. *Application contact:* Prof. Sonia Salari, PhD, Graduate Director, 801-581-5725, E-mail: sonia.salari@fcs.utah.edu. Website: http://fcs.utah.edu/

**University of Victoria,** Faculty of Graduate Studies, Faculty of Human and Social Development, School of Child and Youth Care, Victoria, BC V8W 2Y2, Canada. Offers MA, PhD. *Program availability:* Part-time. *Degree requirements:* For master's, thesis. *Entrance requirements:* For master's, resume, professional references, sample of academic writing. Additional exam requirements/recommendations for international students: Required—TOEFL (minimum score 575 paper-based), IELTS (minimum score 7). Electronic applications accepted.

**University of Wisconsin–Madison,** Graduate School, School of Human Ecology, Program in Human Development and Family Studies, Madison, WI 53706-1380. Offers MS, PhD. *Program availability:* Part-time. Terminal master's awarded for partial completion of doctoral program. *Degree requirements:* For master's, thesis; for doctorate, comprehensive exam, thesis/dissertation. *Entrance requirements:* For master's, GRE General Test, 3 letters of recommendation; for doctorate, GRE General Test, MS or MA, 3 letters of recommendation. Additional exam requirements/recommendations for international students: Required—TOEFL (minimum score 580 paper-based; 92 iBT). Electronic applications accepted. *Faculty research:* Human development, adolescence, adulthood, prevention, intervention.

**Utah State University,** School of Graduate Studies, Emma Eccles Jones College of Education and Human Services, Department of Family, Consumer, and Human Development, Logan, UT 84322. Offers family and human development (MFHD); family, consumer, and human development (MS, PhD), including adolescence/youth (MS), adult development/aging (MS), consumer science (MS), infancy/childhood (MS), marriage and family relations (MS), marriage and family therapy (MS). *Accreditation:* AAMFT/COAMFTE (one or more programs are accredited). *Program availability:* Part-time, evening/weekend, online learning. *Degree requirements:* For master's, thesis; for doctorate, comprehensive exam, thesis/dissertation, competencies. *Entrance requirements:* For master's, GRE General Test or MAT, minimum GPA of 3.0, 3 letters of recommendation; for doctorate, GRE, minimum GPA of 3.0, 3 letters of recommendation. Additional exam requirements/recommendations for international students: Required—TOEFL. Electronic applications accepted. *Faculty research:* Marriage and family relations, adolescent problem behavior, family financial management, early literacy, mental health in the elderly, parent child attachment.

**Vanderbilt University,** Peabody College, Department of Psychology and Human Development, Nashville, TN 37240-1001. Offers child studies (M Ed); clinical psychological assessment (M Ed); quantitative methods (M Ed). *Accreditation:* APA. *Program availability:* Part-time. *Faculty:* 36 full-time (23 women), 11 part-time/adjunct (8 women). *Students:* 51 full-time (46 women), 6 part-time (4 women); includes 11 minority (4 Black or African American, non-Hispanic/Latino; 1 Asian, non-Hispanic/Latino; 5 Hispanic/Latino; 1 Two or more races, non-Hispanic/Latino), 10 international. Average age 25. 195 applicants, 34% accepted, 33 enrolled. In 2016, 21 master's awarded. *Degree requirements:* For master's, comprehensive exam, thesis optional. *Entrance requirements:* For master's, GRE General Test. Additional exam requirements/recommendations for international students: Required—TOEFL (minimum score 550 paper-based; 80 iBT). *Application deadline:* For fall admission, 12/31 for domestic and international students; for spring admission, 11/1 for domestic and international students. Applications are processed on a rolling basis. Application fee: $0. Electronic applications accepted. *Expenses:* Tuition: Part-time $1854 per credit hour. *Financial support:* Fellowships with partial tuition reimbursements, research assistantships with partial tuition reimbursements, teaching assistantships with partial tuition reimbursements, Federal Work-Study, institutionally sponsored loans, scholarships/grants, tuition waivers (partial), and unspecified assistantships available. Financial award application deadline: 1/15; financial award applicants required to submit FAFSA. *Faculty research:* Child clinical psychology and developmental psychopathology; cognitive psychology, language and social development; educational and developmental neuroscience; quantitative methods and evaluation. *Unit head:* Dr. Amy Needham, Chair, 615-322-8141, Fax: 615-343-9494, E-mail: amy.needham@vanderbilt.edu. *Application contact:* Ally Armstead, Educational Coordinator, 615-343-4963, Fax: 615-343-9494, E-mail: ally.armstead@vanderbilt.edu. Website: http://peabody.vanderbilt.edu/departments/psych/index.php

**Walden University,** Graduate Programs, School of Counseling, Minneapolis, MN 55401. Offers addiction counseling (MS), including addictions and public health, child and adolescent counseling, family studies and interventions, forensic counseling, general program, military families and culture, trauma and crisis counseling; clinical mental health counseling (MS), including addiction counseling, forensic counseling, military families and culture, trauma and crisis counseling; counselor education and supervision (PhD), including consultation, counseling and social change, forensic mental health counseling, leadership and program evaluation, trauma and crisis; marriage,

couple, and family counseling (MS), including addiction counseling, career counseling, forensic counseling, military families and culture, trauma and crisis counseling; school counseling (MS), including addiction counseling, career counseling, crisis and trauma, military families and culture. *Accreditation:* ACA. *Program availability:* Part-time, evening/weekend, online only, 100% online. *Degree requirements:* For master's, residency, field experience, professional development plan, licensure plan; for doctorate, thesis/dissertation, residency, practicum, internship. *Entrance requirements:* For master's, bachelor's degree or higher; minimum GPA of 2.5; official transcripts; goal statement (for some programs); access to computer and Internet; for doctorate, master's degree or higher; three years of related professional or academic experience (preferred); minimum GPA of 3.0; goal statement and current resume (for select programs); official transcripts; access to computer and Internet. Additional exam requirements/recommendations for international students: Required—TOEFL (minimum score 550 paper-based, 79 iBT), IELTS (minimum score 6.5), Michigan English Language Assessment Battery (minimum score 82), or PTE (minimum score 53). Electronic applications accepted.

**Walden University,** Graduate Programs, School of Social Work and Human Services, Minneapolis, MN 55401. Offers addictions and social work (DSW); advanced clinical practice (MSW); clinical expertise (DSW); criminal justice (DSW); disaster, crisis, and intervention (DSW); family studies and interventions (DSW); human and social services (PhD), including advanced research, community and social services, community intervention and leadership, conflict management, criminal justice, disaster crisis and intervention, family studies and intervention, gerontology, global social services, higher education, human services and nonprofit administration, mental health facilitation; medical social work (DSW); military social work (MSW); policy practice (DSW); social work (PhD), including addictions and social work, clinical expertise, criminal justice, disaster, crisis and intervention, family studies and interventions, medical social work, policy practice, social work administration; social work administration (DSW); social work in healthcare (MSW); social work with children and families (MSW). *Accreditation:* CSWE. *Program availability:* Part-time, evening/weekend, online only, 100% online. *Degree requirements:* For master's, residency (for some programs); for doctorate, thesis/dissertation, residency. *Entrance requirements:* For master's, bachelor's degree or higher; minimum GPA of 2.5; official transcripts; goal statement (for some programs); access to computer and Internet; for doctorate, master's degree or higher; three years of related professional or academic experience (preferred); minimum GPA of 3.0; goal statement and current resume (for select programs); official transcripts; access to computer and Internet. Additional exam requirements/recommendations for international students: Required—TOEFL (minimum score 550 paper-based, 79 iBT), IELTS (minimum score 6.5), Michigan English Language Assessment Battery (minimum score 82), or PTE (minimum score 53). Electronic applications accepted.

**Washington University in St. Louis,** Brown School, St. Louis, MO 63110. Offers American Indian/Alaska native (MSW); children, youth and families (MSW); epidemiology/biostatistics (MPH); health (MSW); health policy analysis (MPH); individualized (MSW), including health; mental health (MSW); older adults and aging societies (MSW); public health sciences (PhD); social and economic development (MSW); social work (PhD); violence and injury prevention (MSW); JD/MSW; M Arch/MSW; MPH/MBA; MSW/M Div; MSW/M Ed; MSW/MAPS; MSW/MBA; MSW/MPH; MUD/MSW. MSW/M Div and MSW/MAPS offered in partnership with Eden Theological Seminary. *Accreditation:* CSWE (one or more programs are accredited). *Faculty:* 54 full-time (31 women), 87 part-time/adjunct (61 women). *Students:* 281 full-time (235 women); includes 105 minority (37 Black or African American, non-Hispanic/Latino; 14 American Indian or Alaska Native, non-Hispanic/Latino; 20 Asian, non-Hispanic/Latino; 15 Hispanic/Latino; 1 Native Hawaiian or other Pacific Islander, non-Hispanic/Latino; 18 Two or more races, non-Hispanic/Latino), 47 international. Average age 25. 1,003 applicants, 281 enrolled. In 2016, 239 master's, 5 doctorates awarded. *Degree requirements:* For master's, 60 credit hours (for MSW); 52 credit hours (for MPH); practicum; for doctorate, comprehensive exam, thesis/dissertation. *Entrance requirements:* For master's, GRE (preferred), GMAT, LSAT, MCAT, PCAT, or United States Medical Licensing Exam (for MPH); for doctorate, GRE. Additional exam requirements/recommendations for international students: Required—TOEFL (minimum score 100 iBT) or IELTS. *Application deadline:* For fall admission, 12/15 priority date for domestic and international students; for winter admission, 3/1 priority date for domestic and international students. Applications are processed on a rolling basis. Electronic applications accepted. *Expenses:* Contact institution. *Financial support:* In 2016–17, 267 students received support, including 35 fellowships, 48 research assistantships; Federal Work-Study, scholarships/grants, and unspecified assistantships also available. Support available to part-time students. Financial award applicants required to submit FAFSA. *Faculty research:* Mental health, social policy, health policy, epidemiology, social and economic development. *Unit head:* Jamie L. Adkisson, Director of Admissions and Recruitment, 314-935-3524, Fax: 314-935-4859, E-mail: jadkisson@wustl.edu. *Application contact:* Office of Admissions and Recruitment, 314-935-6676, Fax: 314-935-4859, E-mail: brownadmissions@wustl.edu. Website: http://brownschool.wustl.edu

**West Virginia University,** College of Education and Human Services, Department of Technology, Learning and Culture, Program in Child Development and Family Studies, Morgantown, WV 26506. Offers MA. *Program availability:* Part-time. *Degree requirements:* For master's, thesis. *Entrance requirements:* For master's, GRE General Test, minimum GPA of 3.0, interview. Additional exam requirements/recommendations for international students: Required—TOEFL. Electronic applications accepted.

**Wheelock College,** Graduate Programs, Division of Child and Family Studies, Boston, MA 02215. Offers family studies (MS); family support and parent education (MS); family, culture, and society (MS). *Program availability:* Part-time, online learning. *Degree requirements:* For master's, comprehensive exam. Electronic applications accepted. *Faculty research:* Cross-cultural studies of parenting, effects of chronic illness on families, parenting education.

# Child Development

**California State University, Los Angeles,** Graduate Studies, College of Health and Human Services, Department of Child and Family Studies, Los Angeles, CA 90032-8530. Offers child development (MA). *Program availability:* Part-time, evening/weekend. *Degree requirements:* For master's, comprehensive exam, project or thesis. *Entrance requirements:* Additional exam requirements/recommendations for international students: Required—TOEFL (minimum score 500 paper-based). *Faculty research:*

Nutrition education, laundry product and fabric durability, computer usage in public school home economics.

**California State University, Sacramento,** Office of Graduate Studies, College of Education, Department of Graduate and Professional Studies in Education, Sacramento, CA 95819. Offers child development (MA); counseling (MS); curriculum and instruction (MA); education (Ed D); education leadership and policy studies (MA), including higher education, PreK-12; educational technology (MA); gender equity (MA);

language and literacy (MA); multicultural education (MA); school psychology (MA); special education (MA); workforce development advocacy (MA). *Program availability:* Part-time. *Students:* 446 full-time (335 women), 125 part-time (97 women); includes 298 minority (39 Black or African American, non-Hispanic/Latino; 3 American Indian or Alaska Native, non-Hispanic/Latino; 97 Asian, non-Hispanic/Latino; 153 Hispanic/Latino; 6 Native Hawaiian or other Pacific Islander, non-Hispanic/Latino). Average age 32. 540 applicants, 76% accepted, 250 enrolled. In 2016, 107 master's, 7 doctorates awarded. *Degree requirements:* For master's, thesis or project; writing proficiency exam. *Entrance requirements:* For master's, minimum GPA of 2.5, 3.0 in last 60 units. Additional exam requirements/recommendations for international students: Required—TOEFL (minimum score 550 paper-based; 80 iBT). *Application deadline:* For fall admission, 2/15 for domestic students, 1/15 for international students. Applications are processed on a rolling basis. Application fee: $55. Electronic applications accepted. *Expenses:* $4,302 full-time tuition and fees per semester, $2,796 part-time. *Financial support:* Career-related internships or fieldwork and Federal Work-Study available. Support available to part-time students. Financial award application deadline: 3/1; financial award applicants required to submit FAFSA. *Unit head:* Dr. Susan Heredia, Chair, 916-278-5942, E-mail: coe@csus.edu. *Application contact:* Jose Martinez, Graduate Admissions Supervisor, 916-278-7871, E-mail: martinj@skymail.csus.edu.
Website: http://www.csus.edu/coe/academics/graduate/index.html

**California State University, San Bernardino,** Graduate Studies, College of Social and Behavioral Sciences, Department of Psychology, San Bernardino, CA 92407. Offers child development (MA); clinical/counseling psychology (MS); general/experimental psychology (MA); industrial/organizational psychology (MS). *Faculty:* 21 full-time (11 women). *Students:* 59 full-time (43 women), 15 part-time (9 women); includes 47 minority (2 Black or African American, non-Hispanic/Latino; 3 Asian, non-Hispanic/Latino; 33 Hispanic/Latino; 9 Two or more races, non-Hispanic/Latino; 3 international. 217 applicants, 18% accepted, 32 enrolled. In 2016, 38 master's awarded. *Degree requirements:* For master's, comprehensive exam, thesis (for some programs). *Entrance requirements:* Additional exam requirements/recommendations for international students: Required—TOEFL. Application fee: $55. *Expenses:* Tuition, state resident: full-time $7843; part-time $5011.20 per year. Tuition and fees vary according to course load, degree level, program and reciprocity agreements. *Financial support:* Fellowships, research assistantships, and teaching assistantships available. *Faculty research:* Perceptual development, human memory, psychopharmacology, psychology of women, language acquisition. *Unit head:* Dr. Robert Ricco, Chair, 909-537-5485, Fax: 909-537-7003, E-mail: rricco@csusb.edu. *Application contact:* Dr. Francisca Beer, Dean of Graduate Studies, 909-537-5058, E-mail: fbeer@csusb.edu.
Website: http://psychology.csusb.edu/

**California State University, San Bernardino,** Graduate Studies, College of Social and Behavioral Sciences, Program in Child Development, San Bernardino, CA 92407. Offers psychology-life span (MA). *Faculty:* 1 full-time (0 women). *Students:* 3 full-time (all women), 21 part-time (18 women); includes 12 minority (10 Hispanic/Latino; 2 Two or more races, non-Hispanic/Latino; 1 international. 21 applicants, 67% accepted, 11 enrolled. In 2016, 8 master's awarded. *Degree requirements:* For master's, comprehensive exam. *Entrance requirements:* Additional exam requirements/recommendations for international students: Required—TOEFL. *Application deadline:* For fall admission, 5/1 for domestic students. Application fee: $55. *Expenses:* Tuition, state resident: full-time $7843; part-time $5011.20 per year. Tuition and fees vary according to course load, degree level, program and reciprocity agreements. *Unit head:* Dr. Sharon Ward, Director, 909-537-7304, E-mail: sward@csusb.edu. *Application contact:* Dr. Francisca Beer, Dean of Graduate Studies, 909-537-5058, E-mail: fbeer@csusb.edu.

**Chaminade University of Honolulu,** Office of Professional and Continuing Education, Program in Education, Honolulu, HI 96816-1578. Offers child development (M Ed); early childhood education (MAT); educational leadership (M Ed); elementary education (MAT); instructional leadership (M Ed); Montessori (M Ed); secondary education (MAT); special education (MAT). *Program availability:* Part-time, evening/weekend, 100% online, blended/hybrid learning. *Faculty:* 7 full-time (4 women), 8 part-time/adjunct (6 women). *Students:* 98 full-time (80 women), 82 part-time (62 women); includes 110 minority (6 Black or African American, non-Hispanic/Latino; 2 American Indian or Alaska Native, non-Hispanic/Latino; 51 Asian, non-Hispanic/Latino; 9 Hispanic/Latino; 41 Native Hawaiian or other Pacific Islander, non-Hispanic/Latino; 1 Two or more races, non-Hispanic/Latino), 1 international. Average age 35. 38 applicants, 100% accepted, 29 enrolled. In 2016, 79 master's awarded. *Degree requirements:* For master's, thesis or alternative. *Entrance requirements:* For master's, PRAXIS (for MAT), minimum GPA of 2.75 (for M Ed), 3.0 (for MAT); 2 letters of recommendation, resume, writing sample (for MAT). Additional exam requirements/recommendations for international students: Required—TOEFL (minimum score 550 paper-based; 79 iBT). *Application deadline:* Applications are processed on a rolling basis. Application fee: $40. Electronic applications accepted. *Expenses:* $740 per credit hour plus $93 fee per online course. *Financial support:* Applicants required to submit FAFSA. *Unit head:* Dr. Dale Fryxell, Interim Dean, 808-739-4684, Fax: 808-739-4607, E-mail: edu-advising@chaminade.edu. *Application contact:* 808-735-4755, E-mail: gradserv@chaminade.edu.
Website: http://www.chaminade.edu/education

**East Carolina University,** Graduate School, College of Health and Human Performance, Department of Human Development and Family Science, Greenville, NC 27858-4353. Offers birth through kindergarten education (MA Ed); child development and family relations (MS); marriage and family therapy (MS); medical family therapy (PhD). *Accreditation:* AAMFT/COAMFTE. *Program availability:* Part-time. *Students:* 67 full-time (62 women), 25 part-time (23 women); includes 22 minority (13 Black or African American, non-Hispanic/Latino; 2 American Indian or Alaska Native, non-Hispanic/Latino; 1 Asian, non-Hispanic/Latino; 3 Hispanic/Latino; 1 Native Hawaiian or other Pacific Islander, non-Hispanic/Latino; 2 Two or more races, non-Hispanic/Latino), 1 international. Average age 29. 126 applicants, 49% accepted, 43 enrolled. In 2016, 24 master's, 4 doctorates awarded. *Degree requirements:* For master's, comprehensive exam, thesis optional. *Application deadline:* For fall admission, 1/15 for domestic students; for spring admission, 10/15 for domestic students. Applications are processed on a rolling basis. Application fee: $50. *Financial support:* Research assistantships, teaching assistantships, career-related internships or fieldwork, Federal Work-Study, institutionally sponsored loans, and scholarships/grants available. Support available to part-time students. Financial award application deadline: 6/1. *Faculty research:* Child care quality, mental health delivery systems for children, family violence. *Unit head:* Dr. Sharon Ballard, Interim Chair, 252-328-1356, E-mail: ballards@ecu.edu. *Application contact:* Dean of Graduate School, 252-328-6012, Fax: 252-328-6071, E-mail: gradschool@ecu.edu.
Website: http://www.ecu.edu/cs-hhp/hdfs/

**Erikson Institute,** Academic Programs, Program in Child Development, Chicago, IL 60654. Offers MS. *Degree requirements:* For master's, comprehensive exam, internship. *Entrance requirements:* For master's, 3 letters of recommendation, minimum GPA of 2.75. Additional exam requirements/recommendations for international students: Required—TOEFL.

**Fielding Graduate University,** Graduate Programs, School of Leadership Studies, Programs in Infant and Early Childhood Development, Santa Barbara, CA 93105-3814. Offers infant and early childhood development (PhD); reflective practice/supervision (Certificate). *Faculty:* 1 (woman) full-time, 27 part-time/adjunct (21 women). *Students:* 71 full-time (65 women); includes 26 minority (8 Black or African American, non-Hispanic/Latino; 2 American Indian or Alaska Native, non-Hispanic/Latino; 5 Asian, non-Hispanic/Latino; 7 Hispanic/Latino; 4 Two or more races, non-Hispanic/Latino), 1 international. Average age 45. 18 applicants, 100% accepted, 10 enrolled. *Degree requirements:* For doctorate, thesis/dissertation. *Entrance requirements:* For doctorate, bachelor's or master's degree from regionally-accredited U.S. institution or equivalent, curriculum vitae, statement of purpose, critical thinking writing sample, 2 letters of recommendation, official transcript. *Application deadline:* For fall admission, 7/16 for domestic and international students; for spring admission, 11/1 for domestic and international students; for summer admission, 3/1 for domestic and international students. Application fee: $75. Electronic applications accepted. *Expenses:* $8,275 per term (for PhD); $570 per credit (for Graduate Certificate). *Financial support:* In 2016–17, 1 student received support. Scholarships/grants available. Financial award applicants required to submit FAFSA. *Unit head:* Dr. Barbara Mink, Program Director, E-mail: bmink@fielding.edu. *Application contact:* Enrollment Coordinator, 800-340-1099 Ext. 4098, Fax: 805-687-9793, E-mail: hodadmission@fielding.edu.
Website: http://www.fielding.edu/our-programs/school-of-leadership-studies/phd-infant-early-childhood-development/

**Kansas State University,** Graduate School, College of Human Ecology, School of Family Studies and Human Services, Manhattan, KS 66506-1403. Offers applied family sciences (MS); communication sciences and disorders (MS); conflict resolution (Graduate Certificate); couple and family therapy (MS); early childhood education (MS); family and community service (MS); life-span human development (MS); personal financial planning (MS, PhD, Graduate Certificate); youth development (MS, Graduate Certificate). *Accreditation:* AAMFT/COAMFTE; ASHA. *Program availability:* Part-time, online learning. *Faculty:* 43 full-time (30 women), 4 part-time/adjunct (3 women). *Students:* 55 full-time (45 women), 87 part-time (73 women); includes 30 minority (9 Black or African American, non-Hispanic/Latino; 1 American Indian or Alaska Native, non-Hispanic/Latino; 1 Asian, non-Hispanic/Latino; 14 Hispanic/Latino; 1 Native Hawaiian or other Pacific Islander, non-Hispanic/Latino; 4 Two or more races, non-Hispanic/Latino), 6 international. Average age 29. 182 applicants, 29% accepted, 38 enrolled. In 2016, 39 master's, 17 other advanced degrees awarded. *Degree requirements:* For master's, comprehensive exam (for some programs), thesis optional. *Entrance requirements:* For master's, GRE, minimum GPA of 3.0 in last 2 years (60 semester hours) of undergraduate study; for doctorate, GRE. Additional exam requirements/recommendations for international students: Required—TOEFL (minimum score 600 paper-based). *Application deadline:* For fall admission, 2/1 priority date for domestic students, 1/1 priority date for international students; for spring admission, 10/1 priority date for domestic students, 8/1 priority date for international students; for summer admission, 2/1 priority date for domestic students, 12/1 priority date for international students. Applications are processed on a rolling basis. Application fee: $50 ($75 for international students). Electronic applications accepted. *Expenses:* Tuition, state resident: full-time $9670. Tuition, nonresident: full-time $21,828. *Required fees:* $862. *Financial support:* In 2016–17, 35 students received support, including 25 research assistantships (averaging $10,000 per year), 9 teaching assistantships with full tuition reimbursements available (averaging $10,000 per year); unspecified assistantships also available. Financial award application deadline: 3/1. *Faculty research:* Health and security of military families, training in and evaluation of professional human services (marriage and couple therapy, family life education, treatment of speech and swallowing disorders, financial therapy), disorders of communication and swallowing, family and relationship development and health, financial decision-making. *Total annual research expenditures:* $8.4 million. *Unit head:* Dr. Dottie Durband, Director, 785-532-5510, Fax: 785-532-5505, E-mail: dottie@ksu.edu. *Application contact:* Kristi Hageman, Administrative Specialist, 785-532-5510, Fax: 785-532-5505, E-mail: klsmith@ksu.edu.
Website: http://www.he.k-state.edu/fshs/

**Lee University,** Graduate Studies in Counseling, Cleveland, TN 37320-3450. Offers holistic child development (MS); marriage and family studies (MS); marriage and family therapy (MS); school counseling (MS). *Program availability:* Part-time, 100% online. *Faculty:* 8 full-time (3 women), 3 part-time/adjunct (0 women). *Students:* 86 full-time (65 women), 27 part-time (18 women); includes 46 minority (9 Black or African American, non-Hispanic/Latino; 1 American Indian or Alaska Native, non-Hispanic/Latino; 1 Asian, non-Hispanic/Latino; 33 Hispanic/Latino; 2 Two or more races, non-Hispanic/Latino), 8 international. Average age 31. 34 applicants, 65% accepted, 18 enrolled. In 2016, 31 master's awarded. *Degree requirements:* For master's, variable foreign language requirement, comprehensive exam (for some programs), thesis (for some programs), internship. *Entrance requirements:* For master's, GRE General Test or MAT (waived if undergraduate GPA is greater than 3.0 or if applicant already has a graduate degree), minimum undergraduate GPA of 3.0, 3 letters of recommendation, interview, official transcripts, essay. Additional exam requirements/recommendations for international students: Required—TOEFL (minimum score 61 iBT). *Application deadline:* For fall admission, 4/1 priority date for domestic and international students; for spring admission, 11/1 priority date for domestic and international students. Applications are processed on a rolling basis. Application fee: $25. Electronic applications accepted. *Expenses:* Tuition: Full-time $11,367; part-time $632 per credit hour. *Required fees:* $35 per term. One-time fee: $25. Tuition and fees vary according to program. *Financial support:* In 2016–17, 25 students received support. Career-related internships or fieldwork, Federal Work-Study, institutionally sponsored loans, scholarships/grants, and unspecified assistantships available. Financial award application deadline: 3/1; financial award applicants required to submit FAFSA. *Unit head:* Dr. Trevor Milliron, Director, 423-614-8126, Fax: 423-614-8124, E-mail: tmilliron@leeuniversity.edu. *Application contact:* 
Website: http://www.leeuniversity.edu/academics/graduate/counseling/

**Michigan State University,** The Graduate School, College of Social Science, Department of Family and Child Ecology, East Lansing, MI 48824. Offers child development (MA); community services (MS); family and child ecology (PhD); family studies (MA); marriage and family therapy (MA); youth development (MA). *Accreditation:* AAMFT/COAMFTE (one or more programs are accredited). *Entrance requirements:* For master's, GRE General Test, minimum GPA of 3.0 in last 2 years of undergraduate course work, 3 letters of recommendation; for doctorate, GRE General Test, minimum GPA of 3.0, 3 letters of recommendation, background in behavioral sciences. Additional exam requirements/recommendations for international students: Required—TOEFL. Electronic applications accepted.

**Montclair State University,** The Graduate School, College of Education and Human Services, Infant and Early Childhood Mental Health Certificate Program, Montclair, NJ 07043-1624. Offers Certificate. *Expenses:* Tuition, state resident: part-time $553 per credit. Tuition, nonresident: part-time $854 per credit. *Required fees:* $91 per credit. Tuition and fees vary according to program.

**Montclair State University,** The Graduate School, College of Humanities and Social Sciences, MA Program in Child Advocacy and Policy, Montclair, NJ 07043-1624. Offers

*Child Development*

MA. *Program availability:* Online learning. *Degree requirements:* For master's, seminar. *Entrance requirements:* For master's, minimum GPA of 3.0 in undergraduate major, interview, writing sample. *Expenses:* Tuition, state resident: part-time $553 per credit. Tuition, nonresident: part-time $854 per credit. *Required fees:* $91 per credit. Tuition and fees vary according to program.

**Mount Saint Mary College,** Division of Education, Newburgh, NY 12550-3494. Offers adolescence and special education (MS Ed); childhood education (MS Ed); literacy education (MS Ed); middle school (7-9) (MS Ed). *Accreditation:* NCATE. *Program availability:* Part-time, evening/weekend. *Faculty:* 12 full-time (10 women), 3 part-time/adjunct (all women). *Students:* 27 full-time (19 women), 78 part-time (59 women); includes 12 minority (1 Black or African American, non-Hispanic/Latino; 1 Asian, non-Hispanic/Latino; 7 Hispanic/Latino; 3 Two or more races, non-Hispanic/Latino). Average age 28. 30 applicants, 100% accepted, 16 enrolled. In 2016, 62 master's awarded. *Entrance requirements:* Additional exam requirements/recommendations for international students: Required—TOEFL (minimum score 80 iBT). *Application deadline:* Applications are processed on a rolling basis. Application fee: $45. Electronic applications accepted. Application fee is waived when completed online. *Expenses:* Tuition: Full-time $13,914; part-time $773 per credit. *Required fees:* $82 per semester. *Financial support:* In 2016–17, 18 students received support. Unspecified assistantships available. Financial award application deadline: 4/15; financial award applicants required to submit FAFSA. *Faculty research:* Learning and teaching styles, computers in special education, language development. *Unit head:* Dr. Monica Merritt, Graduate Coordinator, 845-569-3430, Fax: 845-569-3535, E-mail: monica.merritt@msmc.edu. *Application contact:* Lisa Gallina, Director of Admissions for Graduate Programs and Adult Degree Completion, 845-569-3166, Fax: 845-569-3450, E-mail: lisa.gallina@msmc.edu.
Website: http://www.msmc.edu/Academics/Graduate_Programs/Master_of_Science_in_Education

**North Carolina Agricultural and Technical State University,** School of Graduate Studies, School of Agriculture and Environmental Sciences, Department of Family and Consumer Sciences, Greensboro, NC 27411. Offers child development early education and family studies (MAT); family and consumer sciences (MAT); food and nutrition (MS). *Program availability:* Part-time, evening/weekend. *Degree requirements:* For master's, comprehensive exam, thesis or alternative, qualifying exam. *Entrance requirements:* For master's, GRE General Test, minimum GPA of 2.6.

**North Dakota State University,** College of Graduate and Interdisciplinary Studies, College of Human Development and Education, Department of Human Development and Family Science, Program in Youth Development, Fargo, ND 58102. Offers MS. *Degree requirements:* For master's, comprehensive exam, thesis. *Entrance requirements:* Additional exam requirements/recommendations for international students: Required—TOEFL (minimum score 525 paper-based; 71 iBT). *Faculty research:* Gerontology, wellness, counselor education.

**Ohio University,** Graduate College, College of Health Sciences and Professions, Department of Social and Public Health, Athens, OH 45701-2979. Offers early child development and family life (MS); family studies (MS); health administration (MHA); public health (MPH); social work (MSW). *Accreditation:* CEPH. *Program availability:* Part-time, evening/weekend, online learning. *Degree requirements:* For master's, capstone (MPH). *Entrance requirements:* For master's, GMAT, GRE General Test, previous course work in accounting, management, and statistics, previous public health background (MHA, MPH). Additional exam requirements/recommendations for international students: Required—TOEFL (minimum score 550 paper-based; 80 iBT) or IELTS (minimum score 6.5). *Application deadline:* Applications are processed on a rolling basis. Application fee: $50 ($55 for international students). Electronic applications accepted. *Expenses:* Contact institution. *Financial support:* Research assistantships with full tuition reimbursements, career-related internships or fieldwork, Federal Work-Study, institutionally sponsored loans, and unspecified assistantships available. Financial award applicants required to submit FAFSA. *Faculty research:* Health care management, health policy, managed care, health behavior, disease prevention. *Unit head:* Dr. Matthew Adeyanju, School Director, 740-593-1849, Fax: 740-593-0555, E-mail: adeyanju@ohio.edu. *Application contact:* Dr. Ruth Ann Althaus, Graduate Coordinator, Master of Health Administration Program, 740-597-2981, E-mail: althaus@ohio.edu.
Website: http://www.ohio.edu/chsp/sph/

**Purdue University,** Graduate School, College of Health and Human Sciences, Department of Child Development and Family Studies, West Lafayette, IN 47907. Offers developmental studies (MS, PhD); family studies (MS, PhD); marriage and family therapy (MS, PhD). *Accreditation:* AAMFT/COAMFTE (one or more programs are accredited). *Program availability:* Part-time. *Faculty:* 19 full-time (11 women), 1 (woman) part-time/adjunct. *Students:* 22 full-time (21 women), 1 (woman) part-time; includes 3 minority (1 Black or African American, non-Hispanic/Latino; 1 Hispanic/Latino; 1 Two or more races, non-Hispanic/Latino), 5 international. Average age 26. 41 applicants, 29% accepted, 8 enrolled. In 2016, 4 master's, 3 doctorates awarded. Terminal master's awarded for partial completion of doctoral program. *Degree requirements:* For master's, thesis; for doctorate, thesis/dissertation. *Entrance requirements:* For master's and doctorate, GRE General Test (minimum score 1000 combined verbal and quantitative), minimum undergraduate GPA of 3.0 or equivalent. Additional exam requirements/recommendations for international students: Required—TOEFL (minimum score 600 paper-based; 90 iBT), TWE (minimum score 4). *Application deadline:* For fall admission, 1/4 for domestic and international students. Applications are processed on a rolling basis. Application fee: $60 ($75 for international students). Electronic applications accepted. *Financial support:* Fellowships with full tuition reimbursements, research assistantships with full tuition reimbursements, teaching assistantships with full tuition reimbursements, and career-related internships or fieldwork available. Support available to part-time students. Financial award application deadline: 1/15; financial award applicants required to submit FAFSA. *Faculty research:* Inclusion of children with special needs, families as learning environments, relationships in child care, work-family relations, AIDS prevention. *Unit head:* Dr. Doran C. French, Head, 765-494-9511, E-mail: dcfrench@purdue.edu. *Application contact:* Tina Putz, Graduate Contact, 765-496-3816, E-mail: tputz@purdue.edu.
Website: http://www.purdue.edu/hhs/hdfs/

**Purdue University Northwest,** Graduate Studies Office, School of Liberal Arts and Social Sciences, Department of Behavioral Sciences, Hammond, IN 46323-2094. Offers child development and family studies (MS); marriage and family therapy (MS). *Accreditation:* AAMFT/COAMFTE. *Program availability:* Part-time. *Degree requirements:* For master's, thesis. *Entrance requirements:* For master's, GRE, interview. Additional exam requirements/recommendations for international students: Required—TOEFL. *Faculty research:* Substance abuse, sexual abuse, couple therapy, professional issues, adolescent therapy.

**Rutgers University–Camden,** Graduate School of Arts and Sciences, Program in Childhood Studies, Camden, NJ 08102. Offers MA, PhD. *Program availability:* Part-time, evening/weekend. *Degree requirements:* For master's, comprehensive exam, thesis (for some programs), 30 credits; for doctorate, comprehensive exam, thesis/dissertation, 60 credits. *Entrance requirements:* For master's and doctorate, GRE, 3 letters of recommendation; statement of personal, professional and academic goals. Additional exam requirements/recommendations for international students: Required—TOEFL, IELTS. Electronic applications accepted. *Faculty research:* Children's consumer culture, moral development, development of personality and social relations, children's literature, commodification of childhood.

**San Diego State University,** Graduate and Research Affairs, College of Education, Department of Child and Family Development, San Diego, CA 92182. Offers child development (MS). *Program availability:* Part-time. *Degree requirements:* For master's, thesis. *Entrance requirements:* For master's, GRE General Test, 3 letters of recommendation, interview. Additional exam requirements/recommendations for international students: Required—TOEFL. Electronic applications accepted.

**San Jose State University,** Graduate Studies and Research, Connie L. Lurie College of Education, San Jose, CA 95192-0001. Offers child and adolescent development (MA); common core mathematics (K-8) (Certificate, Credential); education (MA, Credential), including counseling and student personnel (MA); speech pathology (MA); educational leadership (MA, Ed D, Credential), including administration and supervision (MA), higher education (MA), preliminary administrative services (Credential); professional administrative services (Credential); elementary education (MA), including curriculum and instruction; K-12 school counseling (Credential); K-12 school counseling internship (Credential); school child welfare attendance (Credential); single subject (Credential). *Accreditation:* NCATE. *Program availability:* Evening/weekend. Electronic applications accepted.

**Sarah Lawrence College,** Graduate Studies, Program in Child Development, Bronxville, NY 10708-5999. Offers MA. *Program availability:* Part-time. *Degree requirements:* For master's, thesis, fieldwork. *Entrance requirements:* For master's, minimum B average in undergraduate coursework. Additional exam requirements/recommendations for international students: Required—TOEFL. Electronic applications accepted.

**Southern New Hampshire University,** School of Education, Manchester, NH 03106-1045. Offers business education (M Ed); child development (M Ed); curriculum and instruction (M Ed), including education leadership, reading, special education, technology integration; education (M Ed); educational leadership (M Ed, Ed D); educational studies (M Ed); elementary education (M Ed); English (MAT); English for speakers of other languages (M Ed); reading and writing specialist (M Ed); school business administration (Certificate); secondary education (M Ed); special education (M Ed); technology integration specialist (M Ed). *Program availability:* Part-time, evening/weekend, online learning. *Degree requirements:* For master's, comprehensive exam (for some programs), thesis or alternative. *Entrance requirements:* For master's, PRAXIS I, minimum GPA of 2.75. Additional exam requirements/recommendations for international students: Required—TOEFL (minimum score 550 paper-based). Electronic applications accepted. *Expenses:* Contact institution.

**Texas Woman's University,** Graduate School, College of Professional Education, Department of Family Sciences, Denton, TX 76204-5769. Offers child development (MS); counseling and development (MS); early childhood development and education (PhD); early childhood education (M Ed); family studies (MS, PhD); family therapy (MS, PhD). *Accreditation:* ACA (one or more programs are accredited). *Program availability:* Part-time, evening/weekend. *Students:* Average age 34. In 2016, 99 master's, 9 doctorates awarded. Terminal master's awarded for partial completion of doctoral program. *Degree requirements:* For master's, comprehensive exam (for some programs), thesis (for some programs); for doctorate, comprehensive exam, thesis/dissertation. *Entrance requirements:* Additional exam requirements/recommendations for international students: Required—TOEFL (minimum score 550 paper-based; 79 iBT). *Application deadline:* For fall admission, 7/1 priority date for domestic students, 2/15 for international students; for spring admission, 9/15 priority date for domestic students, 7/1 for international students. Applications are processed on a rolling basis. Application fee: $50 ($75 for international students). Electronic applications accepted. *Expenses:* Tuition, state resident: full-time $9046; part-time $251 per credit hour. Tuition, nonresident: full-time $22,922; part-time $614 per credit hour. International student: $23,046 full-time. *Required fees:* $2690; $1285 per credit hour. One-time fee: $50. Tuition and fees vary according to course level, course load, program and reciprocity agreements. *Financial support:* Research assistantships, teaching assistantships, career-related internships or fieldwork, Federal Work-Study, institutionally sponsored loans, scholarships/grants, traineeships, health care benefits, and unspecified assistantships available. Support available to part-time students. Financial award application deadline: 3/1; financial award applicants required to submit FAFSA. *Faculty research:* Parenting/parent education, military families, play therapy, family sexuality, diversity, healthy relationships/healthy marriages, childhood obesity, male communication. *Unit head:* Dr. Karen Petty, Chair, 940-898-2685, Fax: 940-898-2676, E-mail: famsci@twu.edu. *Application contact:* Dr. Samuel Wheeler, Assistant Director of Admissions, 940-898-3188, Fax: 940-898-3081, E-mail: wheelersr@twu.edu.
Website: http://www.twu.edu/family-sciences/

**Tufts University,** Graduate School of Arts and Sciences, Eliot-Pearson Department of Child Study and Human Development, Medford, MA 02155. Offers child study and human development (MA, PhD); early childhood education (MAT). *Program availability:* Part-time. *Faculty:* 21 full-time (16 women), 15 part-time/adjunct (13 women). *Students:* 81 full-time (70 women), 6 part-time (5 women); includes 19 minority (6 Black or African American, non-Hispanic/Latino; 7 Asian, non-Hispanic/Latino; 3 Hispanic/Latino; 3 Two or more races, non-Hispanic/Latino), 16 international. Average age 27. 129 applicants, 59% accepted, 37 enrolled. In 2016, 19 master's, 5 doctorates awarded. *Degree requirements:* For master's, thesis (for some programs); for doctorate, comprehensive exam, thesis/dissertation. *Entrance requirements:* For master's and doctorate, GRE General Test. Additional exam requirements/recommendations for international students: Required—TOEFL (minimum score 550 paper-based; 80 iBT), IELTS (minimum score 6.5). *Application deadline:* For fall admission, 12/1 priority date for domestic and international students. Applications are processed on a rolling basis. Application fee: $85. Electronic applications accepted. *Expenses:* $49,982 full-time tuition (for MA); $29,936 full-time tuition (for PhD). *Financial support:* In 2016–17, 78 students received support. Fellowships, research assistantships, teaching assistantships, Federal Work-Study, scholarships/grants, tuition waivers (full and partial), and unspecified assistantships available. Support available to part-time students. Financial award application deadline: 1/15. *Faculty research:* Reading and language, developmental technologies, cognitive and social development, policy and program evaluation. *Unit head:* Dr. David Henry Feldman, Graduate Program Director. *Application contact:* Office of Graduate Admissions, 617-627-3395, E-mail: gradadmissions@tufts.edu.
Website: http://ase.tufts.edu/epcd

**The University of Akron,** Graduate School, Buchtel College of Arts and Sciences, School of Family and Consumer Sciences, Akron, OH 44325. Offers child and family development (MA), including child development, family development; clothing, textiles and interiors (MA). *Program availability:* Part-time, evening/weekend. *Faculty:* 4 full-time (all women), 16 part-time/adjunct (10 women). *Degree requirements:* For master's, comprehensive exam, thesis optional. *Entrance requirements:* For master's, GRE, minimum GPA of 2.75, three letters of recommendation, statement of purpose.

Additional exam requirements/recommendations for international students: Required—TOEFL (minimum score 550 paper-based; 79 iBT), IELTS (minimum score 6.5). *Application deadline:* For fall admission, 3/1 priority date for domestic and international students; for spring admission, 10/1 priority date for domestic and international students. Application fee: $45 ($70 for international students). Electronic applications accepted. *Expenses:* Tuition, state resident: full-time $8618; part-time $359 per credit hour. Tuition, nonresident: full-time $17,149; part-time $715 per credit hour. *Required fees:* $1652. *Financial support:* In 2016–17, 1 teaching assistantship with full tuition reimbursement was awarded. *Faculty research:* Nutritional health wellness/sports nutrition; historical/cultural aspects of clothing, textiles, interiors; family and consumer sciences (FCS) curriculum development; life span gender roles; families in international and historical perspectives. *Unit head:* Dr. Virginia Gunn, Interim Director, 330-972-7729, E-mail: vgunn@uakron.edu. *Application contact:* Dr. Shannon Zentall, Graduate Director, 330-972-6049, E-mail: szentall@uakron.edu. Website: http://www.uakron.edu/fcs/

**University of California, Davis,** Graduate Studies, Graduate Group in Child Development, Davis, CA 95616. Offers MS. *Degree requirements:* For master's, comprehensive exam (for some programs), thesis (for some programs). *Entrance requirements:* For master's, GRE General Test, minimum GPA of 3.0. Additional exam requirements/recommendations for international students: Required—TOEFL (minimum score 550 paper-based). Electronic applications accepted. *Faculty research:* Cognitive development, socio-emotional development, early childhood.

**University of Central Florida,** College of Education and Human Performance, Department of Child, Family and Community Sciences, Orlando, FL 32816. Offers early childhood development and education (MS); exceptional student education (M Ed, MA, Certificate), including autism spectrum disorders (Certificate), exceptional student education (M Ed), exceptional student education K-12 (MA), intervention specialist (Certificate), pre-kindergarten disabilities (Certificate), severe or profound disabilities (Certificate), special education (Certificate). *Program availability:* Part-time, evening/weekend. *Faculty:* 34 full-time (22 women), 40 part-time/adjunct (31 women). *Students:* 75 full-time (47 women), 187 part-time (153 women); includes 89 minority (26 Black or African American, non-Hispanic/Latino; 1 American Indian or Alaska Native, non-Hispanic/Latino; 6 Asian, non-Hispanic/Latino; 55 Hispanic/Latino; 1 Two or more races, non-Hispanic/Latino), 3 international. Average age 32. 205 applicants, 67% accepted, 86 enrolled. In 2016, 87 master's, 64 other advanced degrees awarded. *Degree requirements:* For master's, thesis or alternative, research project; for Certificate, thesis or alternative. *Entrance requirements:* For master's, GRE General Test; for Certificate, GRE General Test, minimum GPA of 3.0. Additional exam requirements/recommendations for international students: Required—TOEFL. *Application deadline:* For fall admission, 7/15 for domestic students; for spring admission, 11/15 for domestic students. Application fee: $30. Electronic applications accepted. *Expenses:* Tuition, state resident: part-time $288.16 per credit hour. Tuition, nonresident: part-time $1071.31 per credit hour. *Financial support:* In 2016–17, 5 students received support, including 6 research assistantships with partial tuition reimbursements available (averaging $5,881 per year), 2 teaching assistantships with partial tuition reimbursements available (averaging $9,252 per year); fellowships, career-related internships or fieldwork, Federal Work-Study, institutionally sponsored loans, and unspecified assistantships also available. Financial award application deadline: 3/1; financial award applicants required to submit FAFSA. *Unit head:* Dr. Glenn Lambie, Chair, 407-823-6106, E-mail: glenn.lambie@ucf.edu. *Application contact:* Assistant Director, Graduate Admissions, 407-823-2766, Fax: 407-823-6442, E-mail: gradadmissions@ucf.edu. Website: http://education.ucf.edu/cfcs/

**University of Florida,** Graduate School, College of Agricultural and Life Sciences, Department of Family, Youth, and Community Sciences, Gainesville, FL 32611. Offers community studies (MS); family and youth development (MS); family, youth and community sciences (MS); nonprofit organization development (MS). *Program availability:* Part-time, online learning. *Degree requirements:* For master's, comprehensive exam (for some programs), thesis (for some programs). *Entrance requirements:* For master's, GRE General Test, minimum GPA of 3.0. Additional exam requirements/recommendations for international students: Required—TOEFL (minimum score 550 paper-based; 80 iBT), IELTS (minimum score 6). Electronic applications accepted. *Faculty research:* Adolescent risk behaviors, family risk and resilience, family financial management, community-based organizations/interventions, nutrition and wellness.

**University of La Verne,** LaFetra College of Education, Programs in Child Development/Child Life, La Verne, CA 91750-4443. Offers child development (MS); child life (MS). *Program availability:* Part-time. *Students:* 36 full-time (all women), 68 part-time (67 women); includes 53 minority (5 Black or African American, non-Hispanic/Latino; 1 Asian, non-Hispanic/Latino; 47 Hispanic/Latino), 5 international. Average age 31. *Entrance requirements:* For master's, minimum GPA of 3.0, 3 letters of reference, writing sample. Additional exam requirements/recommendations for international students: Required—TOEFL (minimum score 550 paper-based). *Application deadline:* Applications are processed on a rolling basis. Application fee: $50. *Expenses:* Contact institution. *Financial support:* Scholarships/grants and traineeships available. Financial award application deadline: 3/2; financial award applicants required to submit FAFSA. *Unit head:* Laurie Schroeder, Chairperson, 909-448-4653, E-mail: lschroeder3@laverne.edu. *Application contact:* Christy Ranells, Program and Admission Specialist, 909-448-4644, Fax: 909-971-2295, E-mail: cranells@laverne.edu. Website: http://www.laverne.edu/education/

**University of Minnesota, Twin Cities Campus,** Graduate School, College of Education and Human Development, Institute of Child Development, Minneapolis, MN 55455-0213. Offers applied child and adolescent development (MA); child psychology (PhD); early childhood education (M Ed). *Faculty:* 17 full-time (8 women). *Students:* 65 full-time (59 women), 16 part-time (15 women); includes 19 minority (5 Black or African American, non-Hispanic/Latino; 4 Asian, non-Hispanic/Latino; 7 Hispanic/Latino; 3 Two or more races, non-Hispanic/Latino), 2 international. Average age 28. 132 applicants, 23% accepted, 30 enrolled. In 2016, 26 master's, 9 doctorates awarded. Application fee: $75 ($95 for international students). *Financial support:* In 2016–17, 26 fellowships, 21 research assistantships with full tuition reimbursements (averaging $13,750 per year), 20 teaching assistantships with full tuition reimbursements (averaging $10,832 per year) were awarded. *Faculty research:* Developmental affective and cognitive neuroscience; developmental psychopathology; intervention and prevention science; social and emotional development; cognitive, language, and perceptual development. *Total annual research expenditures:* $7.2 million. *Unit head:* Dr. Megan Gunnar, Director, 612-624-2713, E-mail: gunnar@umn.edu. *Application contact:* Dr. Kathleen Thomas, Director of Graduate Studies, 612-625-3389, E-mail: thoma114@umn.edu. Website: http://www.cehd.umn.edu/ICD

**University of Nebraska–Lincoln,** Graduate College, College of Education and Human Sciences, Department of Child, Youth and Family Studies, Lincoln, NE 68588. Offers child development/early childhood education (MS, PhD); child, youth and family studies (MS); family and consumer sciences education (MS, PhD); family financial planning (MS); family science (MS, PhD); gerontology (PhD); human sciences (PhD), including child, youth and family studies, gerontology, medical family therapy; marriage and family therapy (MS); medical family therapy (PhD); youth development (MS). *Accreditation:* AAMFT/COAMFTE (one or more programs are accredited). *Program availability:* Online learning. *Degree requirements:* For master's, thesis optional. *Entrance requirements:* For master's, GRE. Additional exam requirements/recommendations for international students: Required—TOEFL (minimum score 550 paper-based). Electronic applications accepted. *Faculty research:* Marriage and family therapy, child development/early childhood education, family financial management.

**The University of North Carolina at Charlotte,** Cato College of Education, Department of Special Education and Child Development, Charlotte, NC 28223-0001. Offers academically or intellectually gifted (Graduate Certificate); autism spectrum disorders (Graduate Certificate); child and family development: birth through kindergarten (Graduate Certificate); child and family studies: early education (M Ed); special education (M Ed, PhD, Graduate Certificate), including academically or intellectually gifted (M Ed). *Program availability:* Part-time, 100% online, blended/hybrid learning. *Faculty:* 25 full-time (18 women), 8 part-time/adjunct (6 women). *Students:* 21 full-time (17 women), 106 part-time (101 women); includes 11 minority (8 Black or African American, non-Hispanic/Latino; 1 Hispanic/Latino; 2 Two or more races, non-Hispanic/Latino), 4 international. Average age 34. 83 applicants, 95% accepted, 66 enrolled. In 2016, 6 master's, 7 doctorates, 42 other advanced degrees awarded. *Degree requirements:* For master's, thesis or alternative, research project; for doctorate, thesis/dissertation, portfolio; for Graduate Certificate, internship. *Entrance requirements:* For master's, GRE or MAT, personal statement, letters of recommendation; for doctorate, GRE or MAT, 2 official transcripts of all academic work attempted since high school indicating minimum GPA of 3.5 in graduate degree program; at least 3 references of someone who knows applicant's current work and/or academic achievements in previous degree work; two-page essay; current resume or curriculum vitae; writing sample; documentation of teaching; for Graduate Certificate, undergraduate degree from regionally-accredited four-year institution; minimum cumulative undergraduate GPA of 3.0; three recommendations from persons knowledgeable of applicant's interaction with children and families; statement of purpose; clear criminal background check. Additional exam requirements/recommendations for international students: Required—TOEFL (minimum score 523 paper-based, 70 iBT) or IELTS (6.5). *Application deadline:* For fall admission, 12/1 for domestic and international students; for spring admission, 10/1 priority date for domestic and international students; for summer admission, 4/1 priority date for domestic and international students. Applications are processed on a rolling basis. Application fee: $75. Electronic applications accepted. *Expenses:* Tuition, state resident: full-time $4252. Tuition, nonresident: full-time $17,423. *Required fees:* $3026. Tuition and fees vary according to course load and program. *Financial support:* In 2016–17, 11 students received support, including 10 research assistantships (averaging $9,195 per year), 1 teaching assistantship (averaging $16,848 per year); career-related internships or fieldwork, institutionally sponsored loans, scholarships/grants, and unspecified assistantships also available. Support available to part-time students. Financial award application deadline: 3/1; financial award applicants required to submit FAFSA. *Total annual research expenditures:* $4 million. *Unit head:* Dr. Belva Collins, Chair, 704-687-8828, E-mail: belva.collins@uncc.edu. *Application contact:* Kathy B. Giddings, Director of Graduate Admissions, 704-687-5503, Fax: 704-687-1668, E-mail: gradadm@uncc.edu. Website: http://spcd.uncc.edu/

**The University of Tennessee at Martin,** Graduate Programs, College of Agriculture and Applied Sciences, Department of Family and Consumer Sciences, Martin, TN 38238. Offers dietetics (MSFCS); general family and consumer sciences (MSFCS). *Program availability:* Part-time, 100% online. *Faculty:* 10. *Students:* 5 full-time (all women), 34 part-time (32 women); includes 9 minority (8 Black or African American, non-Hispanic/Latino; 1 Two or more races, non-Hispanic/Latino). Average age 28. 58 applicants, 71% accepted, 15 enrolled. In 2016, 11 master's awarded. *Degree requirements:* For master's, comprehensive exam, thesis optional. *Entrance requirements:* For master's, GRE General Test, minimum GPA of 2.5. Additional exam requirements/recommendations for international students: Required—TOEFL (minimum score 525 paper-based; 71 iBT). *Application deadline:* For fall admission, 7/27 priority date for domestic and international students; for spring admission, 12/17 priority date for domestic and international students; for summer admission, 5/10 priority date for domestic and international students. Applications are processed on a rolling basis. Application fee: $30 ($130 for international students). Electronic applications accepted. *Expenses:* Tuition, state resident: full-time $8254; part-time $459 per credit hour. Tuition, nonresident: full-time $22,198; part-time $1234 per credit hour. *Required fees:* $79 per credit hour. Part-time tuition and fees vary according to course load and campus/location. *Financial support:* In 2016–17, 4 students received support, including 1 research assistantship (averaging $6,283 per year), 3 teaching assistantships with full tuition reimbursements available (averaging $8,001 per year); scholarships/grants and unspecified assistantships also available. Financial award application deadline: 2/1; financial award applicants required to submit FAFSA. *Faculty research:* Children with developmental disabilities, regional food product development and marketing, parent education. *Unit head:* Dr. Lisa LeBleu, Coordinator, 731-881-7116, Fax: 731-881-7106, E-mail: llebleu@utm.edu. *Application contact:* Jolene L. Cunningham, Student Services Specialist, 731-881-7012, Fax: 731-881-7499, E-mail: jcunningham@utm.edu. Website: http://www.utm.edu/departments/caas/fcs/index.php

**The University of Texas at Austin,** Graduate School, College of Natural Sciences, School of Human Ecology, Austin, TX 78712-1111. Offers human development and family sciences (MA, PhD); nutritional sciences (MA, PhD), including nutrition (MA); nutritional sciences (PhD); textile and apparel technology (MS). *Degree requirements:* For master's, thesis; for doctorate, thesis/dissertation. *Entrance requirements:* For master's and doctorate, GRE General Test. Electronic applications accepted.

**The University of West Alabama,** School of Graduate Studies, College of Education, Departments of Instructional Leadership and Support/Curriculum and Instruction, Program in Early Childhood Education, Livingston, AL 35470. Offers early childhood development (M Ed); early childhood education (Ed S); early childhood education P-3 (M Ed). *Accreditation:* NCATE. *Program availability:* Part-time, evening/weekend, 100% online. *Faculty:* 5 full-time (all women), 22 part-time/adjunct (16 women). *Students:* 72 (70 women); includes 23 minority (all Black or African American, non-Hispanic/Latino). Average age 34. 27 applicants, 85% accepted, 18 enrolled. In 2016, 7 master's, 4 Ed Ss awarded. *Degree requirements:* For master's, comprehensive exam, thesis optional; for Ed S, comprehensive exam. *Entrance requirements:* For master's, GRE General Test, MAT, minimum GPA of 2.75. Additional exam requirements/recommendations for international students: Required—TOEFL (minimum score 500 paper-based; 61 iBT). *Application deadline:* Applications are processed on a rolling basis. Application fee: $40. Electronic applications accepted. *Expenses:* Tuition, state resident: part-time $355 per credit hour. Tuition, nonresident: part-time $710 per credit hour. *Required fees:* $130 per semester. *Financial support:* Teaching assistantships, Federal Work-Study, scholarships/grants, and unspecified assistantships available. Support available to part-time students. Financial award applicants required to submit FAFSA. *Unit head:* Dr. Jodie Winship, Chair of Curriculum and Instruction, 205-652-5415, Fax: 205-652-3706, E-mail: jwinship@uwa.edu. *Application contact:* Dr. B. J. Kimbrough, Dean of Graduate Studies, 205-652-3647, Fax: 205-652-3706, E-mail: bkimbrough@uwa.edu. Website: http://www.uwa.edu/earlychildhoodeducationp3.aspx

*Child Development*

**University of Wyoming,** College of Agriculture and Natural Resources, Department of Family and Consumer Sciences, Laramie, WY 82071. Offers early childhood development (MS); family and consumer sciences (MS); food science and human nutrition (MS). *Program availability:* Part-time. *Degree requirements:* For master's, thesis, project. *Entrance requirements:* For master's, GRE General Test or MCAT, minimum GPA of 3.0. Additional exam requirements/recommendations for international students: Required—TOEFL (minimum score 540 paper-based; 76 iBT). Electronic applications accepted. *Faculty research:* Asthma, obesity and healthy weights, nutrition concerns of children with special health care needs, food product development, food safety, postpartum health, exercise nutrition.

**Whittier College,** Graduate Programs, Department of Education and Child Development, Whittier, CA 90608-0634. Offers educational administration (MA Ed); elementary education (MA Ed); secondary education (MA Ed). *Program availability:* Part-time, evening/weekend. *Degree requirements:* For master's, thesis. *Entrance requirements:* For master's, GRE General Test, MAT, minimum GPA of 3.5, academic writing sample.

# Clothing and Textiles

**Alabama Agricultural and Mechanical University,** School of Graduate Studies, College of Agricultural, Life and Natural Sciences, Department of Family and Consumer Sciences, Huntsville, AL 35811. Offers apparel, merchandising and design (MS); family and consumer sciences (MS); human development and family studies (MS); nutrition and hospitality management (MS). *Program availability:* Part-time, evening/weekend. *Degree requirements:* For master's, comprehensive exam, thesis optional. *Entrance requirements:* For master's, GRE General Test. Additional exam requirements/recommendations for international students: Required—TOEFL (minimum score 500 paper-based; 61 iBT). *Application deadline:* For fall admission, 5/1 for domestic students. Applications are processed on a rolling basis. Application fee: $25. Electronic applications accepted. *Expenses:* Tuition, nonresident: part-time $826 per credit hour. Full-time tuition and fees vary according to course load and program. *Financial support:* Research assistantships with tuition reimbursements, teaching assistantships with tuition reimbursements, career-related internships or fieldwork, Federal Work-Study, and traineeships available. Financial award application deadline: 4/1. *Faculty research:* Food biotechnology, nutrition, food microbiology, food engineering, food chemistry. *Unit head:* Dr. Cynthia Smith, Chair, 256-372-4172, Fax: 256-372-5433, E-mail: cynthia.smith@aamu.edu. Website: http://www.aamu.edu/academics/alns/consumersciences/

**Auburn University,** Graduate School, College of Human Sciences, Department of Consumer Affairs, Auburn University, AL 36849. Offers MS, PhD. *Program availability:* Part-time. *Faculty:* 16 full-time (15 women). *Students:* 17 full-time (12 women), 11 part-time (all women); includes 4 minority (2 Black or African American, non-Hispanic/Latino; 1 Asian, non-Hispanic/Latino; 1 Two or more races, non-Hispanic/Latino), 14 international. Average age 30. 19 applicants, 68% accepted, 6 enrolled. In 2016, 4 master's awarded. *Degree requirements:* For master's, thesis (for some programs). *Entrance requirements:* For master's, GRE General Test. *Application deadline:* Applications are processed on a rolling basis. Application fee: $50 ($60 for international students). Electronic applications accepted. *Expenses:* Tuition, state resident: full-time $9072; part-time $504 per credit hour. Tuition, nonresident: full-time $27,216; part-time $1512 per credit hour. *Required fees:* $812 per semester. Tuition and fees vary according to degree level and program. *Financial support:* Fellowships, research assistantships, teaching assistantships, career-related internships or fieldwork, and Federal Work-Study available. Support available to part-time students. Financial award application deadline: 3/15; financial award applicants required to submit FAFSA. *Faculty research:* Merchandising, consumer behavior, international marketing of textiles and apparel, apparel product development. *Unit head:* Dr. Carol Warfield, Head, 334-844-1329, E-mail: cwarfiel@humsci.auburn.edu. *Application contact:* Dr. George Flowers, Dean of the Graduate School, 334-844-2125.

**Central Michigan University,** College of Graduate Studies, College of Education and Human Services, Department of Human Environmental Studies, Mount Pleasant, MI 48859. Offers apparel product development and merchandising technology (MS); gerontology (Graduate Certificate); human development and family studies (MA); nutrition and dietetics (MS). *Program availability:* Part-time, evening/weekend. *Degree requirements:* For master's, thesis or alternative. Electronic applications accepted. *Faculty research:* Human growth and development, family studies and human sexuality, human nutrition and dietetics, apparel and textile retailing, computer-aided design for apparel.

**Cornell University,** Graduate School, Graduate Fields of Human Ecology, Field of Fiber Science and Apparel Design, Ithaca, NY 14853. Offers apparel design (MA, MPS); fiber science (MS, PhD); polymer science (MS, PhD); textile science (MS, PhD). *Degree requirements:* For master's, thesis (MA, MS), project paper (MPS); for doctorate, comprehensive exam, thesis/dissertation. *Entrance requirements:* For master's, GRE General Test, 2 letters of recommendation, portfolio (for functional apparel design); for doctorate, GRE General Test, 2 letters of recommendation. Additional exam requirements/recommendations for international students: Required—TOEFL (minimum score 600 paper-based; 77 iBT). Electronic applications accepted. *Faculty research:* Apparel design, consumption, mass customization, 3-D body scanning.

**Eastern Michigan University,** Graduate School, College of Technology, School of Visual and Built Environments, Program in Apparel Textiles and Merchandising, Ypsilanti, MI 48197. Offers MS. *Program availability:* Part-time, evening/weekend, online learning. *Students:* 2 full-time (both women), 14 part-time (11 women); includes 4 minority (2 Black or African American, non-Hispanic/Latino; 1 Hispanic/Latino; 1 Two or more races, non-Hispanic/Latino), 6 international. Average age 30. 15 applicants, 67% accepted, 7 enrolled. In 2016, 4 master's awarded. *Entrance requirements:* Additional exam requirements/recommendations for international students: Required—TOEFL. *Application deadline:* Applications are processed on a rolling basis. Application fee: $45. *Financial support:* Fellowships, research assistantships with full tuition reimbursements, teaching assistantships with full tuition reimbursements, career-related internships or fieldwork, Federal Work-Study, institutionally sponsored loans, scholarships/grants, tuition waivers (partial), and unspecified assistantships available. Support available to part-time students. Financial award applicants required to submit FAFSA. *Application contact:* Dr. Subhas Ghosh, Program Coordinator, 734-487-2476, Fax: 734-487-7690, E-mail: sghosh@emich.edu.

**Fashion Institute of Technology,** School of Graduate Studies, Program in Fashion and Textile Studies: History, Theory, Museum Practice, New York, NY 10001-5992. Offers MA. *Accreditation:* NASAD. *Students:* 36. 49 applicants, 31% accepted, 14 enrolled. *Degree requirements:* For master's, one foreign language, thesis, internship. *Entrance requirements:* For master's, GRE General Test or GRE Subject Test, previous course work in art history and chemistry, 4 semesters of a foreign language. Additional exam requirements/recommendations for international students: Required—TOEFL (minimum score 550 paper-based). *Application deadline:* For fall admission, 2/15 priority date for domestic and international students. Applications are processed on a rolling basis. Application fee: $50. Electronic applications accepted. *Expenses:* Tuition, state resident: full-time $10,870; part-time $453 per credit. Tuition, nonresident: full-time $22,210; part-time $925 per credit. *Required fees:* $745. *Financial support:* Federal Work-Study and scholarships/grants available. Financial award applicants required to submit FAFSA. *Unit head:* Denyse Montegut, Associate Chair, 212-217-4308. *Application contact:* Administrative Coordinator, 212-217-4300, E-mail: gradinfo@fitnyc.edu. Website: http://www.fitnyc.edu/fashion-textile-history/
**See Display on page 184 and Close-Up on page 205.**

**Fashion Institute of Technology,** School of Graduate Studies, Program in Fashion Design, New York, NY 10001-5992. Offers MFA. *Entrance requirements:* For master's, portfolio. *Expenses:* Tuition, state resident: full-time $10,870; part-time $453 per credit. Tuition, nonresident: full-time $22,210; part-time $925 per credit. *Required fees:* $745.
**See Display on next page and Close-Up on page 893.**

**Georgia State University,** College of Arts and Sciences, Ernest G. Welch School of Art and Design, Program in Studio Art, Atlanta, GA 30302-3083. Offers ceramics (MFA); drawing and painting (MFA); graphic design (MFA); interior design (MFA); photography (MFA); printmaking (MFA); sculpture (MFA); textiles (MFA). *Accreditation:* NASAD. *Degree requirements:* For master's, thesis. *Application deadline:* For fall admission, 1/6 for domestic and international students; for spring admission, 1/15 priority date for domestic and international students. Application fee: $50. Electronic applications accepted. *Expenses:* Tuition, state resident: full-time $6876; part-time $382 per credit hour. Tuition, nonresident: full-time $22,374; part-time $1243 per credit hour. *Required fees:* $2128; $1064 per term. Part-time tuition and fees vary according to course load and program. *Financial support:* In 2016–17, fellowships with full tuition reimbursements (averaging $11,000 per year), teaching assistantships with full tuition reimbursements (averaging $7,000 per year) were awarded; research assistantships, scholarships/grants, and unspecified assistantships also available. Financial award application deadline: 4/15; financial award applicants required to submit FAFSA. *Faculty research:* Advertising and typography, new media, traditional media, three-dimensional art, architectural and environmental design. *Unit head:* Michael White, Director, Welch School of Art and Design, 404-413-5221, Fax: 404-413-5261, E-mail: mwhite@gsu.edu. *Application contact:* Hubert Stanley Anderson, Director of Graduate Studies, 404-413-5229, Fax: 404-413-5261, E-mail: artgrad@gsu.edu. Website: http://artdesign.gsu.edu/graduate/admissions/masters-of-fine-arts-in-studio/

**Iowa State University of Science and Technology,** Department of Apparel, Events, and Hospitality Management, Ames, IA 50011-1078. Offers apparel, merchandising, and design (MS, PhD); hospitality management (MS, PhD). *Program availability:* Online learning. *Degree requirements:* For doctorate, thesis/dissertation. *Entrance requirements:* For master's and doctorate, GRE General Test. Additional exam requirements/recommendations for international students: Required—TOEFL (minimum score 550 paper-based; 79 iBT), IELTS (minimum score 6.5). *Application deadline:* For fall admission, 2/1 priority date for domestic and international students. Application fee: $40 ($90 for international students). Electronic applications accepted. *Application contact:* Ann Marie Fiore, Director of Graduate Education, 515-294-9303, E-mail: amfiore@iastate.edu. Website: http://www.aeshm.hs.iastate.edu/graduate-programs/amd/

**Iowa State University of Science and Technology,** Program in Apparel, Merchandising, and Design, Ames, IA 50011. Offers MS, PhD. *Degree requirements:* For master's, thesis; for doctorate, thesis/dissertation. *Entrance requirements:* Additional exam requirements/recommendations for international students: Required—TOEFL (minimum score 550 paper-based; 79 iBT), IELTS (minimum score 6.5). *Application deadline:* For fall admission, 2/1 priority date for domestic and international students. Application fee: $60 ($90 for international students). Electronic applications accepted. *Application contact:* Ann Marie Fiore, Application Contact, 515-294-9303, E-mail: amfiore@iastate.edu. Website: http://www.aeshm.hs.iastate.edu/graduate-programs/amd/

**Kansas State University,** Graduate School, College of Human Ecology, Department of Apparel, Textiles, and Interior Design, Manhattan, KS 66506. Offers apparel and textiles (MS), including general apparel and textiles, merchandising. Merchandising option offered online through the Great Plains Interactive Distance Education Alliance, including Oklahoma State University, North Dakota State University, and South Dakota State University. *Program availability:* Online learning. *Faculty:* 12 full-time (9 women). *Students:* 3 full-time (2 women), 8 part-time (all women); includes 4 minority (2 Black or African American, non-Hispanic/Latino; 1 Asian, non-Hispanic/Latino; 1 Hispanic/Latino), 2 international. Average age 31. 9 applicants, 22% accepted, 2 enrolled. In 2016, 5 master's awarded. *Degree requirements:* For master's, comprehensive exam (for some programs), thesis (for some programs). *Entrance requirements:* For master's, GRE General Test (except for merchandising applicants), minimum undergraduate GPA of 3.0. Additional exam requirements/recommendations for international students: Required—TOEFL (minimum score 550 paper-based; 79 iBT), IELTS (minimum score 6.1). *Application deadline:* For fall admission, 1/1 priority date for domestic and international students; for spring admission, 8/1 priority date for domestic and international students; for summer admission, 12/1 priority date for domestic and international students. Applications are processed on a rolling basis. Application fee: $50 ($75 for international students). Electronic applications accepted. *Expenses:* Contact institution. *Financial support:* In 2016–17, 5 students received support, including 2 research assistantships (averaging $21,000 per year), 3 teaching assistantships with full tuition reimbursements available (averaging $17,616 per year); institutionally sponsored loans, scholarships/grants, and unspecified assistantships also available. Financial award application deadline: 2/1; financial award applicants required to submit FAFSA. *Faculty research:* Apparel marketing and consumer behavior, social and environmental responsibility, apparel design, new product development. *Total annual research expenditures:* $222,454. *Unit head:* Prof. Barbara G. Anderson, Head, 785-532-6993, Fax: 785-532-3796, E-mail: barbara@ksu.edu. *Application contact:* Gina Jackson, Application Contact, 785-532-6993, Fax: 785-532-3796, E-mail: gjackson@ksu.edu. Website: http://www.he.k-state.edu/atid/

**Kansas State University,** Graduate School, College of Human Ecology, Doctorate in Human Ecology Program, Manhattan, KS 66506-1407. Offers apparel and textiles (PhD); applied family sciences (PhD); couple and family therapy (PhD); hospitality administration (PhD); kinesiology (PhD); life-span human development (PhD). *Program availability:* Part-time. *Faculty:* 36 full-time (23 women). *Students:* 44 full-time (26 women), 16 part-time (10 women); includes 9 minority (3 Black or African American, non-Hispanic/Latino; 2 Asian, non-Hispanic/Latino; 2 Hispanic/Latino; 2 Two or more races, non-Hispanic/Latino), 18 international. Average age 30. 43 applicants, 35% accepted, 8 enrolled. In 2016, 13 doctorates awarded. *Degree requirements:* For doctorate, thesis/dissertation. *Entrance requirements:* Additional exam requirements/recommendations for international students: Required—TOEFL. *Application deadline:* For fall admission, 2/1 priority date for domestic and international students; for spring admission, 8/1 priority date for domestic and international students. Applications are processed on a rolling basis. Application fee: $50 ($75 for international students). Electronic applications accepted. *Expenses:* Tuition, state resident: full-time $9670. Tuition, nonresident: full-time $21,828. *Required fees:* $862. *Financial support:* In 2016–17, research assistantships with partial tuition reimbursements (averaging $12,000 per year), teaching assistantships with partial tuition reimbursements (averaging $12,000 per year) were awarded. Financial award application deadline: 3/1. *Total annual research expenditures:* $1.8 million. *Unit head:* Dr. John Buckwalter, Dean, 785-532-5500, Fax: 785-532-5504, E-mail: jbb3@ksu.edu. *Application contact:* Dr. Bronwyn Fees, Associate Dean for Academic Affairs, 785-532-5500, Fax: 785-532-5504, E-mail: fees@ksu.edu.

**LIM College,** MPS Program, New York, NY 10022-5268. Offers fashion marketing (MPS); fashion merchandising and retail management (MPS); visual merchandising (MPS). *Accreditation:* ACBSP.

**New Mexico State University,** College of Agricultural, Consumer and Environmental Sciences, Department of Family and Consumer Sciences, Las Cruces, NM 88003. Offers clothing, textiles, and merchandising (MS); family and child science (MS); family and consumer science education (MS); family and consumer sciences (MS); food science and technology (MS); hotel, restaurant, and tourism management (MS); human nutrition and dietetic sciences (MS). *Program availability:* Part-time. *Faculty:* 9 full-time (6 women), 1 (woman) part-time/adjunct. *Students:* 32 full-time (28 women), 6 part-time (5 women); includes 17 minority (2 Black or African American, non-Hispanic/Latino; 1 American Indian or Alaska Native, non-Hispanic/Latino; 14 Hispanic/Latino), 1 international. Average age 27. 23 applicants, 91% accepted, 15 enrolled. In 2016, 16 master's awarded. *Degree requirements:* For master's, comprehensive exam (for some programs), thesis (for some programs), oral exam. *Entrance requirements:* For master's, GRE, 3 letters of reference from faculty members or employers, resume, letter of interest. Additional exam requirements/recommendations for international students: Required—TOEFL (minimum score 550 paper-based; 79 iBT), IELTS (minimum score 6.5). *Application deadline:* For fall admission, 2/1 priority date for domestic and international students; for spring admission, 10/1 for domestic and international students. Applications are processed on a rolling basis. Application fee: $40 ($50 for international students). Electronic applications accepted. *Expenses:* Tuition, state resident: full-time $4086. Tuition, nonresident: full-time $14,254. *Required fees:* $853. Tuition and fees vary according to course load. *Financial support:* In 2016–17, 27 students received support, including 4 research assistantships (averaging $14,844 per year), 10 teaching assistantships (averaging $10,707 per year); career-related internships or fieldwork, Federal Work-Study, scholarships/grants, traineeships, health care benefits, and unspecified assistantships also available. Support available to part-time students. Financial award application deadline: 3/1. *Faculty research:* Food product analysis, childhood obesity, dietary decision-making, military families, equine assisted psychotherapy. *Total annual research expenditures:* $401,869. *Unit head:* Dr. Esther L.

Devall, Department Head, 575-646-1161, Fax: 575-646-1889, E-mail: edevall@nmsu.edu. *Application contact:* Dr. Kourtney Vaillancourt, Graduate Program Contact, 575-646-3383, Fax: 575-646-1889, E-mail: kvaillan@nmsu.edu. Website: http://aces.nmsu.edu/academics/fcs

**The New School,** Parsons Paris, Program in Fashion Studies, New York, NY 10011. Offers MA. *Program availability:* Part-time. *Faculty:* 5 full-time (2 women). *Students:* 8 full-time (7 women); includes 2 minority (1 Black or African American, non-Hispanic/Latino; 1 Two or more races, non-Hispanic/Latino), 5 international. Average age 27. 19 applicants, 100% accepted, 8 enrolled. *Degree requirements:* For master's, one foreign language, thesis optional. *Entrance requirements:* For master's, transcripts, resume, statement of purpose, recommendation letters, interview. Additional exam requirements/recommendations for international students: Required—TOEFL (minimum score 92 iBT), IELTS (minimum score 7), PTE (minimum score 63). *Application deadline:* Applications are processed on a rolling basis. Application fee: $50. Electronic applications accepted. *Expenses:* Contact institution. *Financial support:* Research assistantships, teaching assistantships, and career-related internships or fieldwork available. *Faculty research:* Fashion history, communication. *Unit head:* Marco Pecorari, Coordinator, 33-176217661, E-mail: pecorarm@newschool.edu. *Application contact:* Mike Fakih, Director of Admissions, Parsons Paris, 33 176 21 76 67, E-mail: thinkparsonsparis@newschool.edu.

**North Carolina State University,** Graduate School, College of Textiles, Program in Textile Technology Management, Raleigh, NC 27695. Offers PhD. *Degree requirements:* For doctorate, one foreign language, thesis/dissertation, cumulative exams. *Entrance requirements:* For doctorate, GRE or GMAT. Electronic applications accepted. *Faculty research:* Niche markets, supply chain, globalization, logistics.

**North Dakota State University,** College of Graduate and Interdisciplinary Studies, College of Human Development and Education, Department of Apparel, Design, and Hospitality Management, Fargo, ND 58102. Offers merchandising (MS, Certificate). *Program availability:* Online learning. *Degree requirements:* For master's, practicum and/or thesis. Electronic applications accepted.

**Oklahoma State University,** College of Human Sciences, Department of Design, Housing and Merchandising, Stillwater, OK 74078. Offers MS, PhD. *Faculty:* 16 full-time (12 women). *Students:* 5 full-time (3 women), 7 part-time (all women); includes 1 minority (Black or African American, non-Hispanic/Latino), 6 international. Average age 27. 18 applicants, 39% accepted, 7 enrolled. In 2016, 1 master's awarded. *Degree requirements:* For master's, thesis (for some programs); for doctorate, comprehensive exam, thesis/dissertation. *Entrance requirements:* For master's and doctorate, GRE or GMAT. Additional exam requirements/recommendations for international students: Required—TOEFL (minimum score 550 paper-based; 79 iBT). *Application deadline:* For fall admission, 3/1 priority date for international students; for spring admission, 8/1 priority date for international students. Applications are processed on a rolling basis. Application fee: $40 ($75 for international students). Electronic applications accepted. *Expenses:* Tuition, state resident: full-time $3775; part-time $209.70 per credit hour. Tuition, nonresident: full-time $14,851; part-time $825.05 per credit hour. *Required fees:* $2027; $112.60 per credit hour. Tuition and fees vary according to campus/location. *Financial support:* In 2016–17, 6 research assistantships (averaging $5,203 per year), 6 teaching assistantships (averaging $9,894 per year) were awarded; career-related internships or fieldwork, Federal Work-Study, scholarships/grants, health care benefits, tuition waivers (partial), and unspecified assistantships also available. Support available to part-time students. Financial award application deadline: 3/1; financial award applicants required to submit FAFSA. *Faculty research:* Environmental sciences design, housing and merchandising; creativity and physical environment; product development, production and evaluation; experimental learning and critical thinking; technology

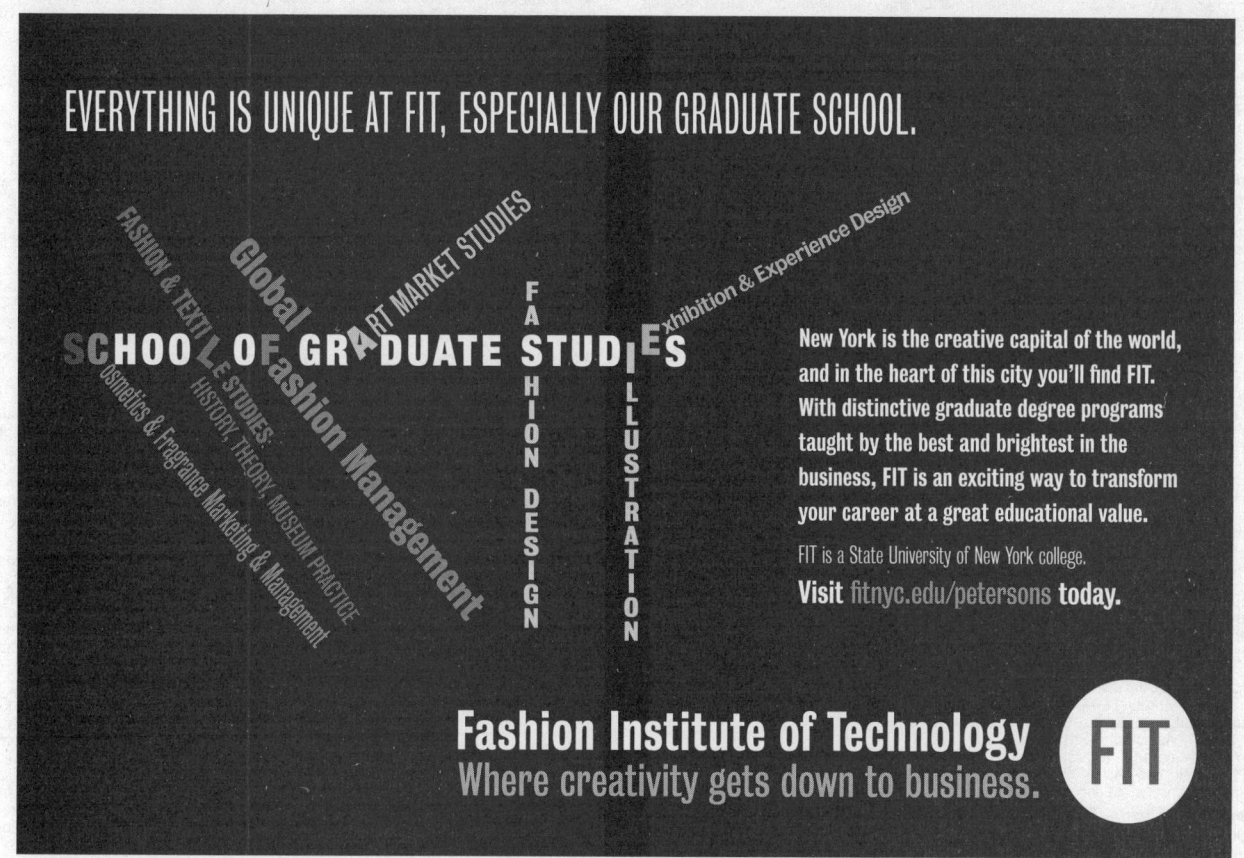

## Clothing and Textiles

strategies and assessment; customer expectation and satisfaction. *Unit head:* Dr. Jane Swinney, Interim Department Head, 405-744-6552, Fax: 405-744-6910, E-mail: jane.swinney@okstate.edu. *Application contact:* Dr. Christine Johnson, Associate Dean for Research and Graduate Studies, 405-744-1744, E-mail: christine.johnson@okstate.edu.
Website: http://humansciences.okstate.edu/dhm/

**Oregon State University,** College of Business, Program in Design and Human Environment, Corvallis, OR 97331. Offers MA, MS, PhD. *Program availability:* Part-time. *Faculty:* 6 full-time (all women). *Students:* 4 full-time (2 women), 4 part-time (all women); includes 3 minority (1 Asian, non-Hispanic/Latino; 1 Hispanic/Latino; 1 Two or more races, non-Hispanic/Latino), 3 international. Average age 43. In 2016, 2 master's, 1 doctorate awarded. Terminal master's awarded for partial completion of doctoral program. *Entrance requirements:* For master's and doctorate, GRE General Test, minimum GPA of 3.0 in last 90 hours. Additional exam requirements/recommendations for international students: Required—TOEFL (minimum score 80 iBT), IELTS (minimum score 6.5). Application fee: $75 ($85 for international students). *Expenses:* Tuition, state resident: full-time $12,150; part-time $450 per credit. Tuition, nonresident: full-time $21,789; part-time $807 per credit. *Required fees:* $1651; $1507 per credit. One-time fee: $350. Tuition and fees vary according to course load, campus/location and program. *Financial support:* Research assistantships, teaching assistantships, career-related internships or fieldwork, Federal Work-Study, and institutionally sponsored loans available. Support available to part-time students. Financial award application deadline: 1/15.
Website: http://business.oregonstate.edu/graduate-programs

**Philadelphia University,** School of Business Administration, Program in Global Fashion Enterprise, Philadelphia, PA 19144. Offers MS. *Program availability:* Part-time. *Entrance requirements:* For master's, GRE or GMAT, minimum GPA of 2.8, official transcripts, two letters of recommendation, essay. Additional exam requirements/recommendations for international students: Required—TOEFL (minimum score 550 paper-based; 79 iBT). Electronic applications accepted.

**Rutgers University–Newark,** Rutgers Business School–Newark and New Brunswick, Program in Business of Fashion, Newark, NJ 07102. Offers MBA.

**Savannah College of Art and Design,** Graduate School, Program in Accessory Design, Savannah, GA 31402-3146. Offers MA, MFA. *Program availability:* Part-time. *Faculty:* 5 full-time (3 women). *Students:* 14 full-time (12 women), 2 part-time (both women); includes 4 minority (1 Asian, non-Hispanic/Latino; 3 Hispanic/Latino), 7 international. Average age 27. 15 applicants, 40% accepted, 4 enrolled. In 2016, 4 master's awarded. *Degree requirements:* For master's, final project (for MA); thesis (for MFA). *Entrance requirements:* For master's, GRE (recommended), portfolio (submitted in digital format), audition or writing submission, resume, statement of purpose, two letters of recommendation. Additional exam requirements/recommendations for international students: Required—TOEFL (minimum score 550 paper-based, 85 iBT), IELTS (minimum score 6.5), or ACTFL. *Application deadline:* For fall admission, 4/1 for domestic and international students. Applications are processed on a rolling basis. Application fee: $40. Electronic applications accepted. *Expenses: Tuition:* Full-time $36,045. Tuition and fees vary according to course load. *Financial support:* Career-related internships or fieldwork and Federal Work-Study available. Financial award application deadline: 4/1; financial award applicants required to submit FAFSA. *Unit head:* Michael Fink, Dean, School of Fashion. *Application contact:* Jenny Jaquillard, Executive Director of Admissions, Recruitment and Events, 912-525-5100, Fax: 912-525-5985, E-mail: admission@scad.edu.
Website: http://www.scad.edu/academics/programs/accessory-design

**The University of Akron,** Graduate School, Buchtel College of Arts and Sciences, School of Family and Consumer Sciences, Akron, OH 44325. Offers child and family development (MA), including child development, family development; clothing, textiles and interiors (MA). *Program availability:* Part-time, evening/weekend. *Faculty:* 4 full-time (all women), 16 part-time/adjunct (10 women). *Degree requirements:* For master's, comprehensive exam, thesis optional. *Entrance requirements:* For master's, GRE, minimum GPA of 2.75, three letters of recommendation, statement of purpose. Additional exam requirements/recommendations for international students: Required—TOEFL (minimum score 550 paper-based), IELTS (minimum score 6.5). *Application deadline:* For fall admission, 3/1 priority date for domestic and international students; for spring admission, 10/1 priority date for domestic and international students. Application fee: $45 ($70 for international students). Electronic applications accepted. *Expenses:* Tuition, state resident: full-time $8618; part-time $359 per credit hour. Tuition, nonresident: full-time $17,149; part-time $715 per credit hour. *Required fees:* $1652. *Financial support:* In 2016–17, 1 teaching assistantship with full tuition reimbursement was awarded. *Faculty research:* Nutritional health wellness/sports nutrition; historical/cultural aspects of clothing, textiles, interiors; family and consumer sciences (FCS) curriculum development; life span gender roles; families in international and historical perspectives. *Unit head:* Dr. Virginia Gunn, Interim Director, 330-972-7729, E-mail: vgunn@uakron.edu. *Application contact:* Dr. Shannon Zentall, Graduate Director, 330-972-6049, E-mail: szentall@uakron.edu.
Website: http://www.uakron.edu/fcs/

**The University of Alabama,** Graduate School, College of Human Environmental Sciences, Department of Clothing, Textiles, and Interior Design, Tuscaloosa, AL 35487. Offers apparel and textiles (MSHES). *Faculty:* 6 full-time (all women). *Students:* 3 full-time (2 women), 1 (woman) part-time; includes 1 minority (Black or African American, non-Hispanic/Latino), 1 international. Average age 28. 3 applicants. *Degree requirements:* For master's, comprehensive exam (for some programs), thesis optional. *Entrance requirements:* For master's, GRE General Test or MAT, minimum GPA of 3.0. Additional exam requirements/recommendations for international students: Required—TOEFL. *Application deadline:* For fall admission, 7/1 for domestic students; for spring admission, 10/30 for domestic students; for summer admission, 4/30 for domestic students. Applications are processed on a rolling basis. Application fee: $50 ($60 for international students). Electronic applications accepted. *Expenses:* Tuition, state resident: full-time $10,470. Tuition, nonresident: full-time $26,950. *Financial support:* In 2016–17, 3 students received support, including 1 research assistantship with full tuition reimbursement available (averaging $12,000 per year), 2 teaching assistantships with partial tuition reimbursements available (averaging $6,000 per year); fellowships, career-related internships or fieldwork, Federal Work-Study, scholarships/grants, and health care benefits also available. Financial award application deadline: 4/15. *Faculty research:* Archeological and historic textiles with material culture analysis, textile science sustainability issues and fibers, scholarship of engagement in higher education, international marketing and trade with soft goods branding management, apparel design with sustainability and zero-waste pattern development. *Unit head:* Dr. Shirley Foster, Chair and Assistant Professor, 205-348-6176, Fax: 205-348-0022, E-mail: sfoster@ches.ua.edu. *Application contact:* Patrick D. Fuller, Admissions Officer, 205-348-5923, Fax: 205-348-0400, E-mail: patrick.d.fuller@ua.edu.
Website: http://www.ctd.ches.ua.edu/

**University of Alberta,** Faculty of Graduate Studies and Research, Department of Human Ecology, Edmonton, AB T6G 2E1, Canada. Offers family ecology and practice (M Sc, PhD); textiles and clothing (M Sc, MA, PhD). *Program availability:* Online

learning. *Degree requirements:* For master's, thesis (for some programs); for doctorate, comprehensive exam, thesis/dissertation. *Entrance requirements:* For master's and doctorate, minimum GPA of 7.0 on a 9.0 scale. Additional exam requirements/recommendations for international students: Required—TOEFL (minimum score 580 paper-based). *Faculty research:* Families and aging, family and child poverty, paid and unpaid work of families, textiles and clothing, parent-child relationships.

**University of California, Davis,** Graduate Studies, Graduate Group in Textiles, Davis, CA 95616. Offers MS. *Degree requirements:* For master's, comprehensive exam (for some programs), thesis (for some programs). *Entrance requirements:* For master's, GRE General Test, minimum GPA of 3.0. Additional exam requirements/recommendations for international students: Required—TOEFL (minimum score 550 paper-based). Electronic applications accepted. *Faculty research:* Fiber science, social psychology, consumer psychology, chemical and physical properties of fibrous and polymeric materials.

**University of Delaware,** College of Arts and Sciences, Department of Fashion and Apparel Studies, Newark, DE 19716. Offers MS.

**University of Georgia,** College of Family and Consumer Sciences, Department of Textiles, Merchandising, and Interiors, Athens, GA 30602. Offers historical and cultural aspects of dress and textiles (MS); interior environments (MS); international merchandising (PhD); merchandising and international trade (MS); polymer, fiber and textile science (MS); polymer, fiber, and textile sciences (PhD). *Degree requirements:* For master's, thesis; for doctorate, thesis/dissertation. *Entrance requirements:* For master's and doctorate, GRE General Test. *Application deadline:* For fall admission, 7/1 priority date for domestic students; for spring admission, 11/15 for domestic students. Application fee: $50. Electronic applications accepted. *Financial support:* Fellowships, research assistantships, teaching assistantships, and unspecified assistantships available. *Unit head:* Dr. Patricia K. Hunt-Hurst, Department Head, 706-542-4891, Fax: 706-542-4862, E-mail: phunt@fcs.uga.edu. *Application contact:* Suraj Sharma, Graduate Coordinator, 706-542-7353, E-mail: ssharma@uga.edu.
Website: http://www.fcs.uga.edu/tmi/

**The University of Manchester,** School of Materials, Manchester, United Kingdom. Offers advanced aerospace materials engineering (M Sc); advanced metallic systems (PhD); biomedical materials (M Phil, M Sc, PhD); ceramics and glass (M Phil, M Sc, PhD); composite materials (M Sc, PhD); corrosion and protection (M Phil, M Sc, PhD); materials (M Phil, PhD); metallic materials (M Phil, M Sc, PhD); nanostructural materials (M Phil, M Sc, PhD); paper science (M Phil, M Sc, PhD); polymer science and engineering (M Phil, M Sc, PhD); technical textiles (M Sc); textile design, fashion and management (M Phil, M Sc, PhD); textile science and technology (M Phil, M Sc, PhD); textiles (M Phil, PhD); textiles and fashion (M Ent).

**University of Manitoba,** Faculty of Graduate Studies, Faculty of Human Ecology, Department of Textile Sciences, Winnipeg, MB R3T 2N2, Canada. Offers M Sc. *Degree requirements:* For master's, thesis.

**University of Minnesota, Twin Cities Campus,** Graduate School, College of Design, Department of Design, Housing, and Apparel, Minneapolis, MN 55455-0213. Offers apparel (MA, MS, PhD); design communication (MA, MS, PhD); housing studies (MA, MS, PhD, Postbaccalaureate Certificate); interactive design (MFA); interior design (MA, MS, PhD). *Program availability:* Part-time. *Degree requirements:* For master's and Postbaccalaureate Certificate, comprehensive exam, thesis (for some programs); for doctorate, comprehensive exam, thesis/dissertation. *Entrance requirements:* For master's, GRE General Test, minimum GPA of 3.0 (preferred), portfolio, 3 letters of recommendation; for doctorate, GRE General Test, minimum GPA of 3.0 (preferred), portfolio, 3 letters of recommendation, writing sample; for Postbaccalaureate Certificate, GRE General Test, minimum GPA of 3.0 (preferred). Additional exam requirements/recommendations for international students: Required—TOEFL (minimum score 550 paper-based; 79 iBT). Electronic applications accepted. *Faculty research:* Housing policy and community development; consumer behavior; interactive design; design history; social, cultural, and behavioral issues related to designed environments.

**University of Missouri,** Office of Research and Graduate Studies, College of Human Environmental Sciences, Department of Textile and Apparel Management, Columbia, MO 65211. Offers MS, PhD. *Entrance requirements:* For master's, GRE General Test, minimum GPA of 3.0. Additional exam requirements/recommendations for international students: Required—TOEFL (minimum score 550 paper-based; 80 iBT). Electronic applications accepted. *Expenses:* Tuition, state resident: full-time $6347; part-time $352.60 per credit hour. Tuition, nonresident: full-time $17,379; part-time $965.50 per credit hour. *Required fees:* $1035. Tuition and fees vary according to course load, campus/location and program.

**University of Nebraska–Lincoln,** Graduate College, College of Education and Human Sciences, Department of Textiles, Clothing and Design, Lincoln, NE 68588. Offers human sciences (PhD), including textiles, clothing and design (MS, PhD); merchandising (MS); textile history/quilt studies (MA); textile science (MS); textile-apparel (MA); textiles, clothing and design (MA, MS), including textiles, clothing and design (MS, PhD). *Program availability:* Part-time, online learning. *Degree requirements:* For master's, thesis optional. *Entrance requirements:* For master's, GRE General Test. Additional exam requirements/recommendations for international students: Required—TOEFL (minimum score 550 paper-based). Electronic applications accepted. *Faculty research:* Merchandising, textile science, fiber arts, textile history, quilt studies.

**The University of Tennessee,** Graduate School, College of Education, Health and Human Sciences, Department of Consumer and Industry Services Management, Program in Consumer Services Management, Knoxville, TN 37996. Offers retail and consumer sciences (MS); textile science (MS). *Program availability:* Part-time. *Degree requirements:* For master's, thesis or alternative. *Entrance requirements:* For master's, GRE General Test, minimum GPA of 2.7. Additional exam requirements/recommendations for international students: Required—TOEFL. Electronic applications accepted.

**The University of Tennessee,** Graduate School, College of Education, Health and Human Sciences, Program in Human Ecology, Knoxville, TN 37996. Offers child and family studies (PhD); community health (PhD); nutrition science (PhD); retailing and consumer sciences (PhD); textile science (PhD). *Degree requirements:* For doctorate, thesis/dissertation. *Entrance requirements:* For doctorate, GRE General Test, minimum GPA of 2.7. Additional exam requirements/recommendations for international students: Required—TOEFL. Electronic applications accepted.

**University of the Incarnate Word,** School of Graduate Studies and Research, School of Media and Design, San Antonio, TX 78209-6397. Offers communication arts (MA); fashion design (MA). *Program availability:* Part-time, evening/weekend. *Faculty:* 8 full-time (4 women), 7 part-time/adjunct (4 women). *Students:* 27 full-time (20 women), 6 part-time (5 women); includes 17 minority (1 Black or African American, non-Hispanic/Latino; 16 Hispanic/Latino), 5 international. In 2016, 14 master's awarded. *Degree requirements:* For master's, thesis or alternative, capstone. *Entrance requirements:* For master's, GRE, interview, writing sample. Additional exam requirements/recommendations for international students: Required—TOEFL (minimum score 560 paper-based; 83 iBT). *Application deadline:* Applications are processed on a rolling

basis. Application fee: $20. Electronic applications accepted. *Expenses: Tuition:* Full-time $7965; part-time $885 per credit hour. *Required fees:* $40 per credit hour. Tuition and fees vary according to course load, degree level, campus/location, program and student level. *Financial support:* Federal Work-Study, scholarships/grants, tuition waivers (partial), and unspecified assistantships available. Financial award applicants required to submit FAFSA. *Unit head:* Dr. Sharon Welkey, Dean, 210-829-6091, Fax: 210-829-3196, E-mail: welkey@uiwtx.edu. *Application contact:* Johnny Garcia, Graduate Admissions Counselor, 210-805-3554, Fax: 210-829-3921, E-mail: admis@uiwtx.edu.
Website: http://www.uiw.edu/simd/index.htm

**Washington State University,** College of Agricultural, Human, and Natural Resource Sciences, Department of Apparel, Merchandising, Design, and Textiles, Pullman, WA 99164-2020. Offers MA. Programs offered at the Pullman campus. *Program availability:* Part-time. *Degree requirements:* For master's, comprehensive exam (for some programs), thesis, oral exam. *Entrance requirements:* For master's, minimum GPA of 3.0, 2 writing samples, 2 letters of recommendation. Additional exam requirements/recommendations for international students: Required—TOEFL, IELTS. Electronic applications accepted. *Faculty research:* Product development, supply chain management, cultural diversity, consumer behavior, functional design.

# Consumer Economics

**Colorado State University,** College of Health and Human Sciences, Department of Design and Merchandising, Fort Collins, CO 80523-1574. Offers apparel and merchandising (MS); interior design (MS). *Program availability:* Part-time. *Faculty:* 7 full-time (all women). *Students:* 10 full-time (7 women), 9 part-time (all women), 4 international. Average age 31. 12 applicants, 100% accepted, 5 enrolled. In 2016, 11 master's awarded. *Degree requirements:* For master's, thesis or alternative. *Entrance requirements:* For master's, minimum cumulative undergraduate GPA of 3.0; bachelor's degree from four-year, accredited institution. Additional exam requirements/recommendations for international students: Required—TOEFL (minimum score 550 paper-based; 80 iBT). *Application deadline:* For fall admission, 3/1 priority date for domestic and international students; for spring admission, 10/15 priority date for domestic and international students. Applications are processed on a rolling basis. Application fee: $60 ($70 for international students). Electronic applications accepted. *Expenses:* Tuition, state resident: full-time $9628. Tuition, nonresident: full-time $23,603. *Required fees:* $2253; $528.14 per credit hour. $264.07 per semester. Tuition and fees vary according to course load and program. *Financial support:* In 2016–17, 9 students received support, including 5 research assistantships with full and partial tuition reimbursements available (averaging $6,966 per year), 2 teaching assistantships with full and partial tuition reimbursements available (averaging $8,708 per year); fellowships with full and partial tuition reimbursements available, Federal Work-Study, scholarships/grants, health care benefits, and unspecified assistantships also available. Financial award application deadline: 3/1. *Faculty research:* Consumer behavior, creativity and innovation, design/product development, social responsibility, social/cultural/historical aspects of the near environment. *Total annual research expenditures:* $41,861. *Unit head:* Dr. Nancy Miller, Professor and Department Head, 970-491-5811, Fax: 970-491-4855, E-mail: nancy.miller@colostate.edu. *Application contact:* Dr. Jennifer Ogle, Professor and Graduate Coordinator, 970-491-3794, Fax: 970-491-4855, E-mail: jennifer.ogle@colostate.edu.
Website: http://www.dm.chhs.colostate.edu/

**Cornell University,** Graduate School, Graduate Fields of Human Ecology, Field of Policy Analysis and Management, Ithaca, NY 14853. Offers consumer policy (PhD); family and social welfare policy (PhD); health administration (MHA); health management and policy (PhD); public policy (PhD). *Degree requirements:* For master's, thesis; for doctorate, thesis/dissertation. *Entrance requirements:* For master's, GRE General Test or GMAT, 2 letters of recommendation; for doctorate, GRE General Test, 2 letters of recommendation. Additional exam requirements/recommendations for international students: Required—TOEFL (minimum score 550 paper-based; 77 iBT). Electronic applications accepted. *Faculty research:* Health policy, family policy, social welfare policy, program evaluation, consumer policy.

**Kansas State University,** Graduate School, College of Human Ecology, Department of Food, Nutrition, Dietetics and Health, Manhattan, KS 66506. Offers dietetics (MS); human nutrition (PhD); nutrition, dietetics and sensory sciences (MS); nutritional sciences (PhD); public health nutrition (PhD); public health physical activity (PhD); sensory analysis and consumer behavior (PhD). *Program availability:* Part-time. *Faculty:* 17 full-time (11 women), 11 part-time/adjunct (3 women). *Students:* 27 full-time (20 women), 32 part-time (26 women); includes 5 minority (2 Black or African American, non-Hispanic/Latino; 1 Asian, non-Hispanic/Latino; 2 Hispanic/Latino), 17 international. Average age 31. 18 applicants, 50% accepted, 5 enrolled. In 2016, 15 master's, 5 doctorates awarded. *Degree requirements:* For master's, thesis or alternative, residency; for doctorate, thesis/dissertation, residency. *Entrance requirements:* For master's, GRE General Test, minimum undergraduate GPA of 3.0; for doctorate, GRE General Test, minimum graduate GPA of 3.0. Additional exam requirements/recommendations for international students: Required—TOEFL (minimum score 550 paper-based; 79 iBT), IELTS (minimum score 6.5). *Application deadline:* For fall admission, 2/1 priority date for domestic and international students; for spring admission, 8/1 priority date for domestic and international students. Applications are processed on a rolling basis. Application fee: $50 ($75 for international students). Electronic applications accepted. *Expenses:* Tuition, state resident: full-time $9670. Tuition, nonresident: full-time $21,828. *Required fees:* $862. *Financial support:* In 2016–17, 29 students received support, including 16 research assistantships with full and partial tuition reimbursements available (averaging $15,711 per year), 6 teaching assistantships with full and partial tuition reimbursements available (averaging $10,167 per year); career-related internships or fieldwork, Federal Work-Study, institutionally sponsored loans, scholarships/grants, health care benefits, and tuition waivers (full and partial) also available. Support available to part-time students. Financial award application deadline: 3/1; financial award applicants required to submit FAFSA. *Faculty research:* Cancer and immunology, obesity, sensory analysis and consumer behavior, nutrient metabolism, clinical and community interventions. *Total annual research expenditures:* $1.1 million. *Unit head:* Dr. Mark Haub, Head, 785-532-5508, Fax: 785-532-3132, E-mail: haub@ksu.edu. *Application contact:* Karen Rogers, Administrative Assistant, 785-532-0124, E-mail: karen39@k-state.edu.
Website: http://www.he.k-state.edu/fndh/

**Kansas State University,** Graduate School, College of Human Ecology, School of Family Studies and Human Services, Manhattan, KS 66506-1403. Offers applied family sciences (MS); communication sciences and disorders (MS); conflict resolution (Graduate Certificate); couple and family therapy (MS); early childhood education (MS); family and community service (MS); life-span human development (MS); personal financial planning (MS, PhD, Graduate Certificate); youth development (MS, Graduate Certificate). *Accreditation:* AAMFT/COAMFTE; ASHA. *Program availability:* Part-time, online learning. *Faculty:* 43 full-time (30 women), 4 part-time/adjunct (3 women). *Students:* 55 full-time (45 women), 87 part-time (73 women); includes 30 minority (9 Black or African American, non-Hispanic/Latino; 1 American Indian or Alaska Native, non-Hispanic/Latino; 1 Asian, non-Hispanic/Latino; 14 Hispanic/Latino; 1 Native Hawaiian or other Pacific Islander, non-Hispanic/Latino; 4 Two or more races, non-

Hispanic/Latino), 6 international. Average age 29. 182 applicants, 29% accepted, 38 enrolled. In 2016, 39 master's, 17 other advanced degrees awarded. *Degree requirements:* For master's, comprehensive exam (for some programs), thesis optional. *Entrance requirements:* For master's, GRE, minimum GPA of 3.0 in last 2 years (60 semester hours) of undergraduate study; for doctorate, GRE. Additional exam requirements/recommendations for international students: Required—TOEFL (minimum score 600 paper-based). *Application deadline:* For fall admission, 2/1 priority date for domestic students, 1/1 priority date for international students; for spring admission, 10/1 priority date for domestic students, 8/1 priority date for international students; for summer admission, 2/1 priority date for domestic students, 12/1 priority date for international students. Applications are processed on a rolling basis. Application fee: $50 ($75 for international students). Electronic applications accepted. *Expenses:* Tuition, state resident: full-time $9670. Tuition, nonresident: full-time $21,828. *Required fees:* $862. *Financial support:* In 2016–17, 35 students received support, including 25 research assistantships (averaging $10,000 per year), 9 teaching assistantships with full tuition reimbursements available (averaging $10,000 per year); unspecified assistantships also available. Financial award application deadline: 3/1. *Faculty research:* Health and security of military families, training in and evaluation of professional human services (marriage and couple therapy, family life education, treatment of speech and swallowing disorders, financial therapy), disorders of communication and swallowing, family and relationship development and health, financial decision-making. *Total annual research expenditures:* $8.4 million. *Unit head:* Dr. Dottie Durband, Director, 785-532-5510, Fax: 785-532-5505, E-mail: dottie@ksu.edu. *Application contact:* Kristi Hageman, Administrative Specialist, 785-532-5510, Fax: 785-532-5505, E-mail: klsmith@ksu.edu.
Website: http://www.he.k-state.edu/fshs/

**North Carolina Agricultural and Technical State University,** School of Graduate Studies, School of Agriculture and Environmental Sciences, Department of Family and Consumer Sciences, Greensboro, NC 27411. Offers child development early education and family studies (MAT); family and consumer sciences (MAT); food and nutrition (MS). *Program availability:* Part-time, evening/weekend. *Degree requirements:* For master's, comprehensive exam, thesis or alternative, qualifying exam. *Entrance requirements:* For master's, GRE General Test, minimum GPA of 2.6.

**North Dakota State University,** College of Graduate and Interdisciplinary Studies, College of Human Development and Education, Department of Human Development and Family Science, Program in Family Financial Planning, Fargo, ND 58102. Offers MS, Certificate. Electronic applications accepted.

**Ohio University,** Graduate College, College of Health Sciences and Professions, School of Applied Health Sciences and Wellness, Program in Food and Nutrition, Athens, OH 45701-2979. Offers human and consumer sciences (MS). *Unit head:* Dhiraj G. Vattem, Director and Professor, E-mail: vattem@ohio.edu. *Application contact:* Marnie Miller, Student Services Coordinator, 740-593-2800, Fax: 740-593-4625, E-mail: graduate@ohio.edu.
Website: http://www.ouchsp.org/foods-and-nutrition

**Oklahoma State University,** College of Human Sciences, Department of Human Development and Family Science, Stillwater, OK 74078. Offers human development and family science (MS, PhD), including family financial planning (MS), human environmental sciences; marriage and family therapy (MS). *Accreditation:* AAMFT/COAMFTE (one or more programs are accredited). *Program availability:* Online learning. *Faculty:* 31 full-time (22 women), 11 part-time/adjunct (9 women). *Students:* 26 full-time (23 women), 35 part-time (30 women); includes 16 minority (7 Black or African American, non-Hispanic/Latino; 1 American Indian or Alaska Native, non-Hispanic/Latino; 5 Hispanic/Latino; 3 Two or more races, non-Hispanic/Latino), 1 international. Average age 30. 47 applicants, 55% accepted, 22 enrolled. In 2016, 27 master's, 2 doctorates awarded. *Degree requirements:* For master's, thesis (for some programs); for doctorate, comprehensive exam, thesis/dissertation. *Entrance requirements:* For master's and doctorate, GRE or GMAT. Additional exam requirements/recommendations for international students: Required—TOEFL (minimum score 550 paper-based; 79 iBT). *Application deadline:* For fall admission, 3/1 priority date for international students; for spring admission, 8/1 priority date for international students. Applications are processed on a rolling basis. Application fee: $40 ($75 for international students). Electronic applications accepted. *Expenses:* Tuition, state resident: full-time $3775; part-time $209.70 per credit hour. Tuition, nonresident: full-time $14,851; part-time $825.05 per credit hour. *Required fees:* $2027; $112.60 per credit hour. Tuition and fees vary according to campus/location. *Financial support:* In 2016–17, 37 research assistantships (averaging $4,670 per year), 31 teaching assistantships (averaging $4,921 per year) were awarded; career-related internships or fieldwork, Federal Work-Study, scholarships/grants, health care benefits, tuition waivers (partial), and unspecified assistantships also available. Support available to part-time students. Financial award application deadline: 3/1; financial award applicants required to submit FAFSA. *Faculty research:* Family relations and child development, consequences of adolescent parenting, family stress and coping, impacts of sexual abuse on families, children's social cognition and self-competence, gerontology and health care. *Unit head:* Dr. Sissy Osteen, Department Head, 405-744-4741, Fax: 405-744-6344, E-mail: sissy.osteen@okstate.edu. *Application contact:* Dr. Michael Criss, Graduate Coordinator, 405-744-5057, Fax: 405-744-6344, E-mail: michael.criss@okstate.edu.
Website: http://humansciences.okstate.edu/hdfs/

**Purdue University,** Graduate School, College of Health and Human Sciences, Department of Consumer Sciences and Retailing, West Lafayette, IN 47907. Offers consumer behavior (MS, PhD); family and consumer economics (MS, PhD). *Program availability:* Part-time. *Faculty:* 13 full-time (6 women). *Students:* 15 full-time (8 women), 6 part-time (2 women); includes 5 minority (1 Black or African American, non-Hispanic/Latino; 2 Asian, non-Hispanic/Latino; 2 Hispanic/Latino), 11 international. Average age

29. 28 applicants, 50% accepted, 7 enrolled. In 2016, 5 master's, 4 doctorates awarded. *Degree requirements:* For master's, thesis, oral presentation, final examination; for doctorate, comprehensive exam, thesis/dissertation, oral presentation, final examination. *Entrance requirements:* For master's, GMAT or GRE General Test (minimum 50th percentile), minimum undergraduate GPA of 3.0 or equivalent; for doctorate, GMAT or GRE General Test (minimum 50th percentile), minimum undergraduate GPA of 3.0 or equivalent; master's degree with minimum GPA of 3.25 or equivalent. Additional exam requirements/recommendations for international students: Required—TOEFL (minimum score 550 paper-based; 77 iBT). *Application deadline:* For fall admission, 2/15 priority date for domestic students, 2/15 for international students. Applications are processed on a rolling basis. Application fee: $60 ($75 for international students). Electronic applications accepted. *Financial support:* Fellowships, research assistantships with tuition reimbursements, teaching assistantships with tuition reimbursements, and career-related internships or fieldwork available. Support available to part-time students. Financial award applicants required to submit FAFSA. *Faculty research:* Family financial resources, retail management and patronage, chemical analysis of textile dyes and finishes. *Unit head:* Richard A. Feinberg, Head of the Graduate Program, 765-494-8301, E-mail: xdjl@purdue.edu. *Application contact:* Kaitee Hardesty, Graduate Coordinator, 765-494-2600, Fax: 765-494-8317, E-mail: hardestk@purdue.edu.
Website: http://www.purdue.edu/hhs/csr/

**South Dakota State University,** Graduate School, College of Education and Human Sciences, Department of Consumer Sciences, Brookings, SD 57007. Offers family financial planning (MS); merchandising (MS). *Entrance requirements:* For master's, resume. Additional exam requirements/recommendations for international students: Required—TOEFL (minimum score 525 paper-based).

**State University of New York at Oswego,** Graduate Studies, School of Education, Department of Vocational Teacher Preparation, Oswego, NY 13126. Offers agriculture (MS Ed); business and marketing (MS Ed); family and consumer sciences (MS Ed); health careers (MS Ed); technical education (MS Ed); trade education (MS Ed). *Accreditation:* NCATE. *Program availability:* Part-time, evening/weekend. *Degree requirements:* For master's, comprehensive exam, thesis or alternative. *Entrance requirements:* Additional exam requirements/recommendations for international students: Required—TOEFL (minimum score 560 paper-based).

**Texas Tech University,** Graduate School, College of Human Sciences, Department of Personal Financial Planning, Lubbock, TX 79409-1210. Offers MS, PhD, JD/MS. *Program availability:* Part-time, online learning. *Faculty:* 11 full-time (6 women), 5 part-time/adjunct (2 women). *Students:* 96 full-time (35 women), 28 part-time (15 women); includes 35 minority (5 Black or African American, non-Hispanic/Latino; 1 Asian, non-Hispanic/Latino; 23 Hispanic/Latino; 6 Two or more races, non-Hispanic/Latino), 31 international. Average age 31. 120 applicants, 67% accepted, 44 enrolled. In 2016, 30 master's, 5 doctorates awarded. Terminal master's awarded for partial completion of doctoral program. *Degree requirements:* For master's, thesis or alternative; for doctorate, comprehensive exam, thesis/dissertation. *Entrance requirements:* For doctorate, GRE, GMAT, or LSAT. Additional exam requirements/recommendations for international students: Required—TOEFL (minimum score 550 paper-based; 79 iBT). *Application deadline:* For fall admission, 6/1 priority date for domestic students, 1/15 priority date for international students; for spring admission, 9/1 priority date for domestic students, 6/15 priority date for international students. Applications are processed on a rolling basis. Application fee: $75. Electronic applications accepted. *Expenses:* $315 per credit hour full-time resident tuition, $723 per credit hour full-time non-resident tuition; $50.50 per credit hour fee plus $608 per term fee. *Financial support:* In 2016–17, 106 students received support, including 101 fellowships (averaging $3,582 per year), 5 research assistantships (averaging $9,615 per year), 31 teaching assistantships (averaging $14,229 per year); Federal Work-Study, scholarships/grants, health care benefits, and unspecified assistantships also available. Financial award application deadline: 1/15; financial award applicants required to submit FAFSA. *Faculty research:* Financial literacy, retirement planning and living, financial risk tolerance, charitable financial planning, reverse mortgages. *Total annual research expenditures:* $88,900. *Unit head:* Dr. Vickie Hampton, Department Chair, 806-834-1824, Fax: 806-742-5033, E-mail: vickie.hampton@ttu.edu. *Application contact:* Dr. John Gilliam, MS Program Director, 806-834-8864, Fax: 806-742-5033, E-mail: john.gilliam@ttu.edu.
Website: http://www.pfp.ttu.edu

**Université Laval,** Faculty of Agricultural and Food Sciences, Department of Agricultural Economics and Consumer Sciences, Program in Consumer Sciences, Québec, QC G1K 7P4, Canada. Offers Diploma. *Program availability:* Part-time. *Entrance requirements:* For degree, knowledge of French and English. Electronic applications accepted.

**The University of Alabama,** Graduate School, College of Human Environmental Sciences, Department of Consumer Sciences, Tuscaloosa, AL 35487-0158. Offers MS. *Program availability:* Part-time, evening/weekend, online learning. *Faculty:* 11 full-time (6 women), 2 part-time/adjunct (1 woman). *Students:* 14 full-time (8 women), 46 part-time (19 women); includes 15 minority (10 Black or African American, non-Hispanic/Latino; 3 Hispanic/Latino; 2 Two or more races, non-Hispanic/Latino). Average age 36. 40 applicants, 70% accepted, 27 enrolled. In 2016, 16 master's awarded. *Degree requirements:* For master's, capstone. *Entrance requirements:* For master's, GRE or GMAT (50th percentile or higher), minimum GPA of 3.0. Additional exam requirements/recommendations for international students: Required—TOEFL. *Application deadline:* For fall admission, 7/1 priority date for domestic and international students; for winter admission, 1/1 priority date for domestic and international students. Applications are processed on a rolling basis. Application fee: $50 ($60 for international students). Electronic applications accepted. *Expenses:* Tuition, state resident: full-time $10,470. Tuition, nonresident: full-time $26,950. *Financial support:* In 2016–17, 1 research assistantship with full tuition reimbursement (averaging $13,000 per year), 1 teaching assistantship with full tuition reimbursement (averaging $13,000 per year) were awarded. Financial award application deadline: 3/15. *Faculty research:* Consumer economics, financial planning, policy evaluation, retirement preparedness, financial wellness. *Unit head:* Dr. Milla D. Boschung, Chair, 205-348-6250, Fax: 205-348-3789, E-mail: mboschun@ches.ua.edu. *Application contact:* Lauren Creel, Departmental Assistant, 205-348-6178, Fax: 205-348-3789, E-mail: lcreel@ches.ua.edu.
Website: http://www.csm.ches.ua.edu/

**University of Guelph,** Graduate Studies, College of Management and Economics, Department of Marketing and Consumer Studies, Guelph, ON N1G 2W1, Canada. Offers M Sc. *Degree requirements:* For master's, thesis. *Entrance requirements:* For master's, GMAT or GRE General Test, minimum B average during previous 2 years of course work. Additional exam requirements/recommendations for international students: Required—TOEFL (minimum score 575 paper-based). Electronic applications accepted. *Faculty research:* Marketing, quality management, consumer economics, housing and real estate management, problem gambling.

**University of Idaho,** College of Graduate Studies, College of Agricultural and Life Sciences, Margaret Ritchie School of Family and Consumer Sciences, Moscow, ID 83844-3183. Offers MS. *Faculty:* 9 full-time, 1 part-time/adjunct. *Students:* 14 full-time, 1 part-time. Average age 28. In 2016, 3 master's awarded. *Entrance requirements:* For

master's, minimum GPA of 3.0. Additional exam requirements/recommendations for international students: Required—TOEFL. *Application deadline:* For fall admission, 8/1 for domestic students; for spring admission, 12/15 for domestic students. Application fee: $60. *Expenses:* Tuition, state resident: full-time $6460; part-time $414 per credit hour. Tuition, nonresident: full-time $21,268; part-time $1237 per credit hour. *Required fees:* $2070; $60 per credit hour. Full-time tuition and fees vary according to course load and reciprocity agreements. *Financial support:* Research assistantships and teaching assistantships available. *Faculty research:* Food and nutrition; clothing, textiles and design; child, family and consumer studies; early childhood development. *Unit head:* Dr. Sonya Sue Meyer, Interim Chair, 208-885-6546, E-mail: famcon@uidaho.edu. *Application contact:* Sean Scoggin, Graduate Recruitment Coordinator, 208-885-4001, Fax: 208-885-4406, E-mail: graduateadmissions@uidaho.edu.
Website: http://www.uidaho.edu/cals/family-and-consumer-sciences

**University of Illinois at Urbana–Champaign,** Graduate College, College of Agricultural, Consumer and Environmental Sciences, Department of Agricultural and Consumer Economics, Champaign, IL 61820. Offers agricultural and applied economics (MS, PhD).

**University of Missouri,** Office of Research and Graduate Studies, College of Human Environmental Sciences, Department of Personal Financial Planning, Columbia, MO 65211. Offers MS, PhD, Certificate, Graduate Certificate. *Entrance requirements:* For master's, GRE General Test, minimum GPA of 3.0. Additional exam requirements/recommendations for international students: Required—TOEFL (minimum score 550 paper-based; 80 iBT). Electronic applications accepted. *Expenses:* Tuition, state resident: full-time $6347; part-time $352.60 per credit hour. Tuition, nonresident: full-time $17,379; part-time $965.50 per credit hour. *Required fees:* $1035. Tuition and fees vary according to course load, campus/location and program.

**University of Nebraska–Lincoln,** Graduate College, College of Education and Human Sciences, Department of Child, Youth and Family Studies, Lincoln, NE 68588. Offers child development/early childhood education (MS, PhD); child, youth and family studies (MS); family and consumer sciences education (MS, PhD); family financial planning (MS); family science (MS, PhD); gerontology (PhD); human sciences (PhD), including child, youth and family studies, gerontology, medical family therapy; marriage and family therapy (MS); medical family therapy (PhD); youth development (MS). *Accreditation:* AAMFT/COAMFTE (one or more programs are accredited). *Program availability:* Online learning. *Degree requirements:* For master's, thesis optional. *Entrance requirements:* For master's, GRE. Additional exam requirements/recommendations for international students: Required—TOEFL (minimum score 550 paper-based). Electronic applications accepted. *Faculty research:* Marriage and family therapy, child development/early childhood education, family financial management.

**University of South Carolina,** The Graduate School, College of Hospitality, Retail, and Sport Management, Department of Retailing, Columbia, SC 29208. Offers MR. *Program availability:* Part-time. *Degree requirements:* For master's, comprehensive exam, internship or thesis. *Entrance requirements:* For master's, GMAT or GRE General Test, minimum GPA of 3.0. Additional exam requirements/recommendations for international students: Required—TOEFL (minimum score 80 iBT). Electronic applications accepted. *Faculty research:* Retail technology, retail strategy, international retailing.

**The University of Tennessee,** Graduate School, College of Education, Health and Human Sciences, Department of Consumer and Industry Services Management, Program in Consumer Services Management, Knoxville, TN 37996. Offers retail and consumer sciences (MS); textile science (MS). *Program availability:* Part-time. *Degree requirements:* For master's, thesis or alternative. *Entrance requirements:* For master's, GRE General Test, minimum GPA of 2.7. Additional exam requirements/recommendations for international students: Required—TOEFL. Electronic applications accepted.

**The University of Tennessee,** Graduate School, College of Education, Health and Human Sciences, Program in Human Ecology, Knoxville, TN 37996. Offers child and family studies (PhD); community health (PhD); nutrition science (PhD); retailing and consumer sciences (PhD); textile science (PhD). *Degree requirements:* For doctorate, thesis/dissertation. *Entrance requirements:* For doctorate, GRE General Test, minimum GPA of 2.7. Additional exam requirements/recommendations for international students: Required—TOEFL. Electronic applications accepted.

**University of Utah,** Graduate School, College of Social and Behavioral Science, Department of Family and Consumer Studies, Salt Lake City, UT 84112-0080. Offers human development and social policy (MS). *Program availability:* Part-time. *Faculty:* 15 full-time (7 women), 5 part-time/adjunct (all women). *Students:* 8 full-time (all women), 2 part-time (both women). Average age 25. 12 applicants, 67% accepted, 7 enrolled. In 2016, 7 master's awarded. *Degree requirements:* For master's, comprehensive exam (for some programs), thesis (for some programs), thesis or project. *Entrance requirements:* For master's, GRE General Test, minimum undergraduate GPA of 3.0, courses in research methods and statistics. Additional exam requirements/recommendations for international students: Required—TOEFL (minimum score 550 paper-based). *Application deadline:* For fall admission, 2/1 priority date for domestic and international students. Applications are processed on a rolling basis. Application fee: $55 ($65 for international students). Electronic applications accepted. *Expenses:* Contact institution. *Financial support:* In 2016–17, 6 students received support, including 1 research assistantship with full tuition reimbursement available (averaging $14,000 per year), 4 teaching assistantships with full tuition reimbursements available (averaging $14,000 per year). Financial award application deadline: 5/1. *Faculty research:* Social, physical, educational and economic contexts of individuals, families and communities. *Unit head:* Prof. Lori Kowaleski-Jones, PhD, Chair, 801-585-0074, Fax: 801-581-5156, E-mail: lk2700@fcs.utah.edu. *Application contact:* Prof. Sonia Salari, PhD, Graduate Director, 801-581-5725, E-mail: sonia.salari@fcs.utah.edu.
Website: http://fcs.utah.edu/

**University of Wisconsin–Madison,** Graduate School, School of Human Ecology, Program in Consumer Behavior and Family Economics, Madison, WI 53706-1380. Offers MS, PhD. Terminal master's awarded for partial completion of doctoral program. *Degree requirements:* For master's, thesis optional; for doctorate, comprehensive exam, thesis/dissertation. *Entrance requirements:* For master's and doctorate, GRE General Test, 3 letters of recommendation. Additional exam requirements/recommendations for international students: Required—TOEFL (minimum score 580 paper-based; 92 iBT). Electronic applications accepted. *Faculty research:* Economic well-being of elderly, finance, financial planning, health care policy, consumer behavior.

**University of Wyoming,** College of Agriculture and Natural Resources, Department of Family and Consumer Sciences, Laramie, WY 82071. Offers early childhood development (MS); family and consumer sciences (MS); food science and human nutrition (MS). *Program availability:* Part-time. *Degree requirements:* For master's, thesis, project. *Entrance requirements:* For master's, GRE General Test or MCAT, minimum GPA of 3.0. Additional exam requirements/recommendations for international students: Required—TOEFL (minimum score 540 paper-based; 76 iBT). Electronic applications accepted. *Faculty research:* Asthma, obesity and healthy weights, nutrition concerns of children with special health care needs, food product development, food safety, postpartum health, exercise nutrition.

**Utah State University,** School of Graduate Studies, College of Agriculture, Department of Agricultural Systems Technology and Education, Logan, UT 84322. Offers agricultural systems technology (MS), including agricultural extension education, agricultural mechanization, international agricultural extension, secondary and postsecondary agricultural education; family and consumer sciences education (MS). *Program availability:* Part-time, online learning. *Degree requirements:* For master's, comprehensive exam (for some programs), thesis (for some programs). *Entrance requirements:* For master's, GRE General Test, MAT, BS in agricultural education, agricultural extension, or related agricultural or science discipline; minimum GPA of 3.0. Additional exam requirements/recommendations for international students: Required—TOEFL. *Faculty research:* Extension and adult education; structures and environment; low-input agriculture; farm safety, systems, and mechanizations.

# Gerontology

**Adelphi University,** Ruth S. Ammon School of Education, Program in Physical Education and Human Performance Science, Garden City, NY 11530-0701. Offers aging (Certificate); physical/educational human performance science (MA). *Program availability:* Part-time, evening/weekend. *Students:* 67 full-time (31 women), 95 part-time (33 women); includes 56 minority (22 Black or African American, non-Hispanic/Latino; 2 Asian, non-Hispanic/Latino; 29 Hispanic/Latino; 3 Two or more races, non-Hispanic/Latino), 3 international. Average age 27. 140 applicants, 84% accepted, 69 enrolled. In 2016, 40 master's awarded. *Degree requirements:* For master's, internship. *Entrance requirements:* For master's, 3 letters of recommendation, resume. Additional exam requirements/recommendations for international students: Required—TOEFL (minimum score 550 paper-based; 80 iBT), IELTS (minimum score 6.5). *Application deadline:* For fall admission, 4/1 for international students; for spring admission, 11/1 for international students. Applications are processed on a rolling basis. Application fee: $50. Electronic applications accepted. *Expenses:* Contact institution. *Financial support:* Research assistantships, teaching assistantships, career-related internships or fieldwork, institutionally sponsored loans, scholarships/grants, traineeships, and unspecified assistantships available. Support available to part-time students. Financial award application deadline: 2/15; financial award applicants required to submit FAFSA. *Faculty research:* Physical education for the handicapped, sport sociology, sport pedagogy. *Unit head:* Dr. Ronald Feingold, Chair, 516-877-4764, E-mail: feingold@adelphi.edu. *Application contact:* Christine Murphy, Director of Admissions, 516-877-3050, Fax: 516-877-3039, E-mail: graduateadmissions@adelphi.edu.

**Alliant International University–Los Angeles,** California School of Professional Psychology, Program in Couple and Family Therapy, Alhambra, CA 91803. Offers chemical dependency (MA); gerontology (MA); Latin American family therapy (MA). *Accreditation:* AAMFT/COAMFTE. *Program availability:* Part-time, evening/weekend. Terminal master's awarded for partial completion of doctoral program. *Degree requirements:* For master's, comprehensive exam, 50 hours of professional development activities. *Entrance requirements:* Additional exam requirements/recommendations for international students: Required—TOEFL (minimum score 550 paper-based). Electronic applications accepted. *Faculty research:* Foster care, therapy with minority couples, parenting, marriage, trauma.

**Arizona State University at the Tempe campus,** College of Public Programs, School of Social Work, Phoenix, AZ 85004-0689. Offers advanced direct practice (MSW); assessment of integrative health modalities (Graduate Certificate); gerontology (Graduate Certificate); Latino cultural competency (Graduate Certificate); planning, administration and community practice (MSW); social work (PhD); trauma and bereavement (Graduate Certificate); MPA/MSW. *Accreditation:* CSWE (one or more programs are accredited). *Program availability:* Part-time. Terminal master's awarded for partial completion of doctoral program. *Degree requirements:* For master's, thesis or alternative, capstone project, interactive Program of Study (iPOS) submitted before completing 50 percent of required credit hours; for doctorate, comprehensive exam, thesis/dissertation, interactive Program of Study (iPOS) submitted before completing 50 percent of required credit hours. *Entrance requirements:* For master's, GRE or MAT, minimum GPA of 3.2 or equivalent in last 2 years of work leading to bachelor's degree; for doctorate, GRE, minimum GPA of 3.0 or equivalent in last 2 years of work leading to bachelor's degree, 3 letters of recommendation, resume, samples of professional writing, personal statement. Additional exam requirements/recommendations for international students: Required—TOEFL, IELTS, or PTE. Electronic applications accepted. *Expenses:* Contact institution.

**Arkansas State University,** Graduate School, College of Nursing and Health Professions, School of Nursing, State University, AR 72467. Offers aging studies (Graduate Certificate); health care management (Graduate Certificate); health sciences (MS); health sciences education (Graduate Certificate); nurse anesthesia (MSN); nursing (MSN); nursing practice (DNP). *Accreditation:* AANA/CANAEP (one or more programs are accredited); ACEN. *Program availability:* Part-time. *Degree requirements:* For master's and Graduate Certificate, comprehensive exam, thesis or alternative; for doctorate, comprehensive exam, thesis/dissertation. *Entrance requirements:* For master's, GRE General Test or MAT, appropriate bachelor's degree, current Arkansas nursing license, CPR certification, physical examination, professional liability insurance, critical care experience, ACLS Certification, PALS Certification, interview, immunization records, personal goal statement, health assessment; for doctorate, GRE or MAT, NCLEX-RN Exam, appropriate master's degree, current Arkansas nursing license, CPR certification, physical examination, professional liability insurance, critical care experience, ACLS Certification, PALS Certification, interview, immunization records, personal goal statement, health assessment, TB skin test, background check; for Graduate Certificate, GRE or MAT, appropriate bachelor's degree, official transcripts, immunization records, proof of employment in healthcare, TB Skin Test, TB Mask Fit Test, CPR Certification. Additional exam requirements/recommendations for international students: Required—TOEFL (minimum score 550 paper-based; 79 iBT), IELTS (minimum score 6), PTE (minimum score 56). Electronic applications accepted. *Expenses:* Contact institution.

**California State University, Fullerton,** Graduate Studies, College of Humanities and Social Sciences, Program in Gerontology, Fullerton, CA 92834-9480. Offers MS. *Program availability:* Part-time. *Expenses:* Tuition, state resident: full-time $3369; part-time $1953 per unit. Tuition, nonresident: full-time $3915; part-time $2499 per unit. Tuition and fees vary according to course load, degree level and program. *Financial support:* Career-related internships or fieldwork, Federal Work-Study, institutionally sponsored loans, and scholarships/grants available. Financial award application deadline: 3/1; financial award applicants required to submit FAFSA. *Unit head:* Dr. Barbara Cherry, Coordinator, 657-278-3035. *Application contact:* Admissions/Applications, 657-278-2371.

**California State University, Long Beach,** Graduate Studies, College of Health and Human Services, Program in Gerontology, Long Beach, CA 90840. Offers MS. *Program availability:* Part-time. *Degree requirements:* For master's, thesis optional. *Application deadline:* For fall admission, 7/1 for domestic students. Applications are processed on a rolling basis. Application fee: $55. Electronic applications accepted. *Financial support:* Federal Work-Study, institutionally sponsored loans, and scholarships/grants available. Financial award application deadline: 3/2. *Unit head:* Maria Claver, Director, 562-985-4495, Fax: 562-985-4414, E-mail: maria.claver@csulb.edu.

**Capella University,** School of Public Service Leadership, Master's Programs in Healthcare, Minneapolis, MN 55402. Offers criminal justice (MS); emergency management (MS); general public health (MPH); gerontology (MS); health administration (MHA); health care operations (MHA); health management policy (MPH); health policy (MHA); homeland security (MS); multidisciplinary human services (MS); public administration (MPA); public safety leadership (MS); social and community services (MS); social behavioral sciences (MPH); MS/MPA.

**Central Michigan University,** College of Graduate Studies, College of Education and Human Services, Department of Human Environmental Studies, Mount Pleasant, MI 48859. Offers apparel product development and merchandising technology (MS); gerontology (Graduate Certificate); human development and family studies (MA); nutrition and dietetics (MS). *Program availability:* Part-time, evening/weekend. *Degree requirements:* For master's, thesis or alternative. Electronic applications accepted. *Faculty research:* Human growth and development, family studies and human sexuality, human nutrition and dietetics, apparel and textile retailing, computer-aided design for apparel.

**The College at Brockport, State University of New York,** School of Education, Health, and Human Services, Greater Rochester Collaborative Master of Social Work Program, Brockport, NY 14420-2997. Offers family and community practice (MSW); gerontology (AGC); interdisciplinary health practice (MSW). Program offered jointly with Nazareth College of Rochester. *Accreditation:* CSWE. *Program availability:* Part-time. *Faculty:* 6 full-time (4 women), 6 part-time/adjunct (4 women). *Students:* 46 full-time (41 women), 142 part-time (121 women); includes 39 minority (20 Black or African American, non-Hispanic/Latino; 2 American Indian or Alaska Native, non-Hispanic/Latino; 3 Asian, non-Hispanic/Latino; 6 Hispanic/Latino; 1 Native Hawaiian or other Pacific Islander, non-Hispanic/Latino; 7 Two or more races, non-Hispanic/Latino), 1 international. 158 applicants, 79% accepted, 81 enrolled. In 2016, 90 master's, 10 other advanced degrees awarded. *Degree requirements:* For master's, thesis or alternative. *Entrance requirements:* For master's, minimum GPA of 3.0, letters of recommendation, statement of objectives. Additional exam requirements/recommendations for international students: Required—TOEFL (minimum score 550 paper-based; 79 iBT), IELTS (minimum score 6.5). *Application deadline:* For fall admission, 1/15 priority date for domestic and international students; for summer admission, 1/15 priority date for domestic and international students. Application fee: $50. Electronic applications accepted. *Expenses:* Contact institution. *Financial support:* Federal Work-Study, scholarships/grants, and unspecified assistantships available. Support available to part-time students. Financial award application deadline: 3/15; financial award applicants required to submit FAFSA. *Faculty research:* Care giving, child welfare, gerontological social work, home-school-community partnerships, domestic violence. *Unit head:* Debra Fromm Faria, Co-Director, 585-395-8455, Fax: 585-395-8603, E-mail: grcmsw@brockport.edu. *Application contact:* Brad Snyder, Coordinator of Admissions, 585-395-3845, Fax: 585-395-8603, E-mail: bsynder@brockport.edu. Website: http://www.brockport.edu/grcmsw

**Concordia University Chicago,** College of Graduate and Innovative Programs, Program in Gerontology, River Forest, IL 60305-1499. Offers MA. *Program availability:* Part-time, evening/weekend. *Degree requirements:* For master's, comprehensive exam, thesis. *Entrance requirements:* For master's, minimum GPA of 2.9. Additional exam requirements/recommendations for international students: Required—TOEFL (minimum score 550 paper-based). Electronic applications accepted.

**DeSales University,** Division of Healthcare, Center Valley, PA 18034-9568. Offers adult-gerontology acute care (Post Master's Certificate); adult-gerontology acute care nurse practitioner (MSN); adult-gerontology acute certified nurse practitioner (Post Master's Certificate); adult-gerontology clinical nurse specialist (MSN, Post Master's Certificate); clinical leadership (DNP); family nurse practitioner (MSN, Post Master's Certificate); general nursing practice (DNP); nurse anesthetist (MSN); nurse educator (Post Master's Certificate, Postbaccalaureate Certificate); nurse midwife (MSN); nurse practitioner (MSN); psychiatric-mental health nurse practitioner (MSN, Post Master's Certificate); DNP/MBA. *Accreditation:* ACEN. *Program availability:* Part-time. *Faculty:* 22 full-time (14 women), 37 part-time/adjunct (29 women). *Students:* 274 full-time (206 women), 78 part-time (68 women); includes 40 minority (9 Black or African American, non-Hispanic/Latino; 14 Asian, non-Hispanic/Latino; 11 Hispanic/Latino; 6 Two or more races, non-Hispanic/Latino). Average age 34. 2,430 applicants, 6% accepted, 129 enrolled. In 2016, 76 master's, 6 doctorates awarded. *Degree requirements:* For master's, minimum GPA of 3.0, portfolio; for doctorate, minimum GPA of 3.0, scholarly capstone project. *Entrance requirements:* For master's, GRE or MAT (waived if applicant has an undergraduate GPA of 3.0 or higher), BSN from ACEN- or CCNE-accredited program, minimum undergraduate GPA of 3.0, active RN license or eligibility, two letters of recommendation, essay, health care experience, personal interview; for doctorate, BSN or MSN from ACEN- or CCNE-accredited institution, minimum GPA of 3.3 in graduate program, current licensure as an RN. Additional exam requirements/recommendations for international students: Required—TOEFL (minimum score 104 iBT). *Application deadline:* Applications are processed on a rolling basis. Application fee: $50. Electronic applications accepted. *Expenses:* Contact institution. *Financial support:* Applicants required to submit FAFSA. *Unit head:* Fr. Dr. Peter Leonard, OSFS, Dean of Graduate Education, 610-282-1100 Ext. 1289, E-mail: peter.leonard@desales.edu. *Application contact:* Julia Ferraro, Director of Graduate Admissions, 610-282-1100 Ext. 1768, E-mail: gradadmissions@desales.edu.

**Duke University,** School of Nursing, Durham, NC 27708-0586. Offers acute care pediatric nurse practitioner (MSN, Post-Graduate Certificate); adult-gerontology nurse practitioner (MSN, Post-Graduate Certificate), including acute care, primary care; family nurse practitioner (MSN, Post-Graduate Certificate); neonatal nurse practitioner (MSN); nurse anesthesia (DNP); nurse practitioner (DNP); nursing (PhD); nursing and health care leadership (MSN); nursing education (MSN); nursing informatics (MSN); pediatric nurse practitioner (MSN), including primary care (MSN, Post-Graduate Certificate);

## *Gerontology*

women's health nurse practitioner (MSN). *Accreditation:* AACN; AANA/CANAEP. *Program availability:* Part-time, evening/weekend, online learning. *Faculty:* 73 full-time (62 women). *Students:* 161 full-time (138 women), 598 part-time (532 women); includes 161 minority (58 Black or African American, non-Hispanic/Latino; 4 American Indian or Alaska Native, non-Hispanic/Latino; 43 Asian, non-Hispanic/Latino; 30 Hispanic/Latino; 26 Two or more races, non-Hispanic/Latino), 9 international. Average age 34. 648 applicants, 48% accepted, 231 enrolled. In 2016, 216 master's, 56 doctorates, 19 other advanced degrees awarded. Terminal master's awarded for partial completion of doctoral program. *Degree requirements:* For master's, thesis optional; for doctorate, capstone project. *Entrance requirements:* For master's, GRE General Test (waived if undergraduate GPA of 3.4 or higher), 1 year of nursing experience (recommended), BSN, minimum GPA of 3.0, previous course work in statistics; for doctorate, GRE General Test (waived if undergraduate GPA of 3.4 or higher), BSN or MSN, minimum GPA of 3.0, resume, personal statement, undergraduate statistics course, current licensure as a registered nurse, transcripts from all post-secondary institutions; for Post-Graduate Certificate, MSN, licensure or eligibility as a professional nurse, transcripts from all post-secondary institutions, previous course work in statistics. Additional exam requirements/recommendations for international students: Required—TOEFL (minimum score 100 iBT), IELTS (minimum score 7). *Application deadline:* For fall admission, 12/1 for domestic and international students; for spring admission, 5/1 for domestic and international students. Application fee: $50. Electronic applications accepted. *Expenses:* Contact institution. *Financial support:* Institutionally sponsored loans, scholarships/grants, and traineeships available. Support available to part-time students. Financial award applicants required to submit FAFSA. *Faculty research:* Cardiovascular disease, caregiver skill training, data mining, prostate cancer, neonatal immune system. *Unit head:* Dr. Marion E. Broome, Dean/Vice Chancellor for Nursing Affairs/Associate Vice President for Academic Affairs for Nursing, 919-684-9446, Fax: 919-684-9414, E-mail: marion.broome@duke.edu. *Application contact:* Dr. Ernie Rushing, Director of Admissions and Recruitment, 919-668-6274, Fax: 919-668-4693, E-mail: ernie.rushing@dm.duke.edu.
Website: http://www.nursing.duke.edu/

**East Carolina University,** Graduate School, College of Health and Human Performance, School of Social Work, Greenville, NC 27858-4353. Offers gerontology (Certificate); social work (MSW); substance abuse (Certificate). *Accreditation:* CSWE. *Program availability:* Online learning. *Students:* 99 full-time (90 women), 38 part-time (32 women); includes 63 minority (51 Black or African American, non-Hispanic/Latino; 3 Asian, non-Hispanic/Latino; 7 Hispanic/Latino; 2 Two or more races, non-Hispanic/Latino). Average age 31. 129 applicants, 77% accepted, 66 enrolled. In 2016, 82 master's awarded. *Degree requirements:* For master's, comprehensive exam. *Entrance requirements:* For master's, GRE or MAT. Additional exam requirements/recommendations for international students: Required—TOEFL. *Application deadline:* For fall admission, 2/1 priority date for domestic and international students. Application fee: $50. *Financial support:* Fellowships and research assistantships available. Financial award application deadline: 6/1. *Faculty research:* Social research, gerontology, women's issues, social services in schools, human behavior. *Unit head:* Dr. Shelia Bunch, Director, 252-328-4202, E-mail: bunchs@ecu.edu. *Application contact:* Dean of Graduate School, 252-328-6012, Fax: 252-328-6071, E-mail: gradschool@ecu.edu.
Website: http://www.ecu.edu/cs-hhp/socw/

**Eastern Illinois University,** Graduate School, Lumpkin College of Business and Applied Sciences, School of Family and Consumer Sciences, Program in Aging Studies, Charleston, IL 61920. Offers MA. *Program availability:* Part-time, evening/weekend. *Degree requirements:* For master's, comprehensive exam (for some programs), thesis (for some programs). *Entrance requirements:* For master's, GMAT or GRE. Additional exam requirements/recommendations for international students: Required—TOEFL (minimum score 500 paper-based; 61 iBT), IELTS (minimum score 6). Electronic applications accepted.

**Eastern Michigan University,** Graduate School, College of Health and Human Services, School of Health Sciences, Programs in Gerontology and Dementia, Ypsilanti, MI 48197. Offers dementia (Graduate Certificate); gerontology (Graduate Certificate). *Students:* 1 (woman) full-time, 4 part-time (3 women), 1 international. Average age 44. 7 applicants, 57% accepted, 1 enrolled. In 2016, 3 Graduate Certificates awarded. Application fee: $45. *Application contact:* Dr. Andrea Gossett Zakrajsek, Director, Aging Studies Program, 734-487-3220, Fax: 734-487-4095, E-mail: azakrajs@emich.edu.

**Georgia State University,** College of Arts and Sciences, Gerontology Institute, Atlanta, GA 30302-3083. Offers MA, Certificate. *Program availability:* Part-time. *Faculty:* 4 full-time (all women). *Students:* 18 full-time (15 women), 17 part-time (14 women); includes 21 minority (15 Black or African American, non-Hispanic/Latino; 3 Asian, non-Hispanic/Latino; 2 Hispanic/Latino; 1 Two or more races, non-Hispanic/Latino), 1 international. Average age 45. 22 applicants, 100% accepted, 15 enrolled. In 2016, 10 master's, 3 other advanced degrees awarded. *Degree requirements:* For master's, thesis (for some programs), internship/capstone project; for Certificate, thesis, internship. *Entrance requirements:* For master's, GRE. Additional exam requirements/recommendations for international students: Required—TOEFL. *Application deadline:* For fall admission, 4/15 for domestic and international students; for spring admission, 10/15 for domestic and international students. Applications are processed on a rolling basis. Application fee: $50. Electronic applications accepted. *Expenses:* Tuition, state resident: full-time $6876; part-time $382 per credit hour. Tuition, nonresident: full-time $22,374; part-time $1243 per credit hour. *Required fees:* $2128; $1064 per term. Part-time tuition and fees vary according to course load and program. *Financial support:* In 2016–17, research assistantships with full tuition reimbursements (averaging $6,000 per year) were awarded; career-related internships or fieldwork, scholarships/grants, and unspecified assistantships also available. Financial award application deadline: 4/15; financial award applicants required to submit FAFSA. *Faculty research:* Long term care and assisted living, aging workforce, health disparities and aging, sexuality and relationships over the life course, caregiving and social relationships with age. *Unit head:* Dr. Elizabeth O. Burgess, Director, 404-413-5210, Fax: 404-413-5219, E-mail: eburgess@gsu.edu. *Application contact:* Dr. Candace L. Kemp, Director of Graduate Studies, 404-413-5210, Fax: 404-413-5219, E-mail: ckemp@gsu.edu.
Website: http://gerontology.gsu.edu/students/graduate/

**Kansas State University,** Graduate School, College of Human Ecology, Center on Aging, Manhattan, KS 66506. Offers gerontology (MS, Graduate Certificate). *Program availability:* Part-time, online learning. *Faculty:* 2 full-time (both women), 2 part-time/adjunct (both women). *Students:* 3 full-time (2 women), 26 part-time (22 women). Average age 45. 9 applicants, 78% accepted, 5 enrolled. In 2016, 8 master's, 2 other advanced degrees awarded. *Degree requirements:* For master's, comprehensive exam. *Entrance requirements:* For master's, bachelor's degree with minimum GPA of 3.0 from college or university accredited by the cognizant regional accrediting agency. *Application deadline:* For fall admission, 2/1 priority date for domestic students, 1/1 for international students; for spring admission, 9/1 priority date for domestic students, 8/1 for international students; for summer admission, 2/1 priority date for domestic students, 12/1 for international students. Applications are processed on a rolling basis. Application fee: $50 ($75 for international students). Electronic applications accepted. *Expenses:*

Contact institution. *Financial support:* Teaching assistantships available. *Faculty research:* Long-term care, environments and aging, sexuality and aging, aging in rural America. *Unit head:* Dr. Gayle Marie Doll, Director, 785-532-5945, Fax: 785-532-5504, E-mail: gdoll@ksu.edu. *Application contact:* Pamela Kay Evans, Administrative Officer, 785-532-5945, Fax: 785-532-5504, E-mail: gerontology@k-state.edu.
Website: http://www.he.k-state.edu/aging/

**Kent State University,** College of Arts and Sciences, Department of Psychological Sciences, Kent, OH 44242-0001. Offers clinical psychology (MA, PhD), including gerontology (MA), psychological sciences (MA); experimental psychology (MA, PhD), including gerontology (MA), psychological sciences (MA). *Accreditation:* APA (one or more programs are accredited). *Program availability:* Part-time. *Faculty:* 29 full-time (15 women). *Students:* 29 full-time (24 women); includes 9 minority (4 Black or African American, non-Hispanic/Latino; 2 Asian, non-Hispanic/Latino; 2 Hispanic/Latino; 1 Two or more races, non-Hispanic/Latino), 1 international. Average age 31. 323 applicants, 5% accepted, 17 enrolled. Terminal master's awarded for partial completion of doctoral program. *Degree requirements:* For master's, thesis; for doctorate, thesis/dissertation. *Entrance requirements:* For master's and doctorate, GRE General Test, personal statement, transcripts, 3 letters of recommendation. Additional exam requirements/recommendations for international students: Required—TOEFL (minimum score of 525 paper-based, 71 iBT), IELTS (minimum score of 6), Michigan English Language Assessment Battery (minimum score of 75), or PTE (minimum score of 48). *Application deadline:* For fall admission, 12/1 for domestic and international students. Applications are processed on a rolling basis. Application fee: $45 ($70 for international students). Electronic applications accepted. *Expenses:* Tuition, state resident: full-time $10,864; part-time $495 per credit hour. Tuition, nonresident: full-time $18,380; part-time $837 per credit hour. *Financial support:* Unspecified assistantships available. Financial award application deadline: 12/1. *Unit head:* Dr. Maria S. Zaragoza, Professor and Chair, 330-672-2166, E-mail: mzaragoz@kent.edu. *Application contact:* Dr. John A. Updegraff, Professor and Graduate Coordinator, 330-672-2166, E-mail: jupdegr1@kent.edu.
Website: http://www.kent.edu/psychology/graduate-programs

**Lakehead University,** Graduate Studies, Department of History, Thunder Bay, ON P7B 5E1, Canada. Offers gerontology (MA); history (MA); women's studies (MA). *Program availability:* Part-time. *Degree requirements:* For master's, one foreign language, thesis. *Entrance requirements:* For master's, minimum B average. Additional exam requirements/recommendations for international students: Required—TOEFL. *Faculty research:* Canadian history, British history, Russian/German history, women's studies.

**Lakehead University,** Graduate Studies, Faculty of Education, Thunder Bay, ON P7B 5E1, Canada. Offers educational studies (PhD); gerontology (M Ed); women's studies (M Ed). *Program availability:* Part-time, evening/weekend. *Degree requirements:* For master's, project or thesis. *Entrance requirements:* For master's, minimum B average. Additional exam requirements/recommendations for international students: Required—TOEFL. *Faculty research:* Art education, AIDS education, language arts education, gerontology, women's studies.

**Lakehead University,** Graduate Studies, Faculty of Social Sciences and Humanities, Department of Sociology, Thunder Bay, ON P7B 5E1, Canada. Offers gerontology (MA); health services and policy research (MA); sociology (MA); women's studies (MA). *Program availability:* Part-time, evening/weekend. *Degree requirements:* For master's, research project or thesis. *Entrance requirements:* For master's, minimum B average. Additional exam requirements/recommendations for international students: Required—TOEFL. *Faculty research:* Sociology of medicine, cultural and social change, health human resources, gerontology, women's studies.

**Lakehead University,** Graduate Studies, Gerontology Collaborative Program-Northern Educational Center for Aging and Health, Thunder Bay, ON P7B 5E1, Canada. Offers gerontology (M Ed, M Sc, MA, MSW). *Program availability:* Part-time. *Degree requirements:* For master's, thesis (for some programs). *Entrance requirements:* Additional exam requirements/recommendations for international students: Required—TOEFL. *Faculty research:* Integrated health information systems.

**Lakehead University,** Graduate Studies, School of Kinesiology, Thunder Bay, ON P7B 5E1, Canada. Offers kinesiology (M Sc); kinesiology and gerontology (M Sc). *Program availability:* Part-time. *Degree requirements:* For master's, thesis. *Entrance requirements:* For master's, minimum B average. Additional exam requirements/recommendations for international students: Required—TOEFL. *Faculty research:* Social psychology and physical education, sport history, sports medicine, exercise physiology, gerontology.

**Lakehead University,** Graduate Studies, School of Social Work, Thunder Bay, ON P7B 5E1, Canada. Offers gerontology (MSW); social work (MSW); women's studies (MSW). *Program availability:* Part-time. *Degree requirements:* For master's, thesis or project. *Entrance requirements:* For master's, minimum B average. Additional exam requirements/recommendations for international students: Required—TOEFL. *Faculty research:* Clinical psychology, social work and practice theory, long-term care, health care for frail elderly, women's studies.

**La Salle University,** School of Nursing and Health Sciences, Program in Nursing, Philadelphia, PA 19141-1199. Offers adult gerontology primary care nurse practitioner (MSN, Certificate); adult health and illness clinical nurse specialist (MSN); adult-gerontology clinical nurse specialist (MSN, Certificate); clinical nurse leader (MSN); family primary care nurse practitioner (MSN, Certificate); gerontology (Certificate); nurse anesthetist (MSN, Certificate); nursing (MSN, Certificate); nursing administration (MSN, Certificate); nursing education (Certificate); nursing practice (DNP); nursing service administration (MSN); public health nursing (MSN, Certificate); school nursing (Certificate); MSN/MBA; MSN/MPH. *Accreditation:* AACN; AANA/CANAEP. *Program availability:* Part-time, evening/weekend, 100% online. *Faculty:* 13 full-time (12 women), 18 part-time/adjunct (15 women). *Students:* 2 full-time (1 woman), 361 part-time (296 women); includes 102 minority (54 Black or African American, non-Hispanic/Latino; 1 American Indian or Alaska Native, non-Hispanic/Latino; 25 Asian, non-Hispanic/Latino; 13 Hispanic/Latino; 1 Native Hawaiian or other Pacific Islander, non-Hispanic/Latino; 8 Two or more races, non-Hispanic/Latino), 4 international. Average age 37. 87 applicants, 67% accepted, 44 enrolled. In 2016, 86 master's, 2 doctorates, 9 other advanced degrees awarded. *Degree requirements:* For doctorate, minimum of 1,000 hours of post baccalaureate clinical practice supervised by preceptors. *Entrance requirements:* For master's, GRE, MAT, or GMAT (for students with BSN GPA of less than 3.2), baccalaureate degree in nursing from an NLNAC- or CCNE-accredited program or an MSN Bridge program; Pennsylvania RN license; 2 letters of reference; resume; statement of philosophy articulating professional values and future educational goal; 1 year of work experience as a registered nurse; for doctorate, GRE (waived for applicants with MSN cumulative GPA of 3.7 or above), MSN from nationally-accredited program or master's degree, MBA or MHA from nationally-accredited program; resume or curriculum vitae; 2 letters of reference; interview; for Certificate, GRE, MAT, or GMAT (for students with BSN GPA of less than 3.2, baccalaureate degree in nursing from an NLNAC- or CCNE-accredited program or an MSN Bridge program; Pennsylvania RN license; 2 letters of reference; resume; statement of philosophy articulating professional values and future educational goal; 1 year of work experience as a registered nurse. Additional exam requirements/recommendations for international students: Required—

TOEFL. *Application deadline:* For fall admission, 8/15 priority date for domestic students, 7/15 for international students; for spring admission, 12/15 priority date for domestic students, 11/15 for international students; for summer admission, 4/15 priority date for domestic students, 3/15 for international students. Applications are processed on a rolling basis. Application fee: $35. Electronic applications accepted. Application fee is waived when completed online. *Expenses:* Contact institution. *Financial support:* In 2016–17, 8 students received support. Scholarships/grants and traineeships available. Support available to part-time students. Financial award application deadline: 8/31; financial award applicants required to submit FAFSA. *Unit head:* Dr. Patricia M. Dillon, Director, 215-951-1322, Fax: 215-951-1896, E-mail: msnapn@lasalle.edu. *Application contact:* Elizabeth Heenan, Director, Graduate and Adult Enrollment, 215-951-1100, Fax: 215-951-1462, E-mail: heenan@lasalle.edu.
Website: http://www.lasalle.edu/nursing/program-options/

**Loma Linda University,** School of Behavioral Health, Department of Social Work and Social Ecology, Loma Linda, CA 92350. Offers criminal justice (MS); gerontology (MS); social policy and social research (PhD); social work (MSW). *Accreditation:* CSWE. *Degree requirements:* For master's, comprehensive exam, thesis optional; for doctorate, comprehensive exam, thesis/dissertation. *Entrance requirements:* For master's and doctorate, GRE General Test. Additional exam requirements/recommendations for international students: Required—TOEFL, Michigan English Language Assessment Battery. Electronic applications accepted.

**Long Island University–LIU Brooklyn,** School of Business, Public Administration and Information Sciences, Brooklyn, NY 11201-8423. Offers accounting (MBA); accounting (MS); business administration (MBA); computer science (MS); gerontology (Advanced Certificate); health administration (MPA); human resources management (MS); not-for-profit management (Advanced Certificate); public administration (MPA); taxation (MS). *Program availability:* Part-time, evening/weekend, blended/hybrid learning. *Faculty:* 18 full-time (9 women), 32 part-time/adjunct (10 women). *Students:* 275 full-time (150 women), 238 part-time (161 women); includes 281 minority (200 Black or African American, non-Hispanic/Latino; 2 American Indian or Alaska Native, non-Hispanic/Latino; 38 Asian, non-Hispanic/Latino; 36 Hispanic/Latino; 1 Native Hawaiian or other Pacific Islander, non-Hispanic/Latino; 4 Two or more races, non-Hispanic/Latino), 140 international. 796 applicants, 66% accepted, 143 enrolled. In 2016, 185 master's, 17 other advanced degrees awarded. *Entrance requirements:* Additional exam requirements/recommendations for international students: Required—TOEFL (minimum score 527 paper-based; 75 iBT). *Application deadline:* Applications are processed on a rolling basis. Application fee: $50. Electronic applications accepted. *Expenses: Tuition:* Full-time $28,272; part-time $1178 per credit. *Required fees:* $451 per term. Tuition and fees vary according to degree level, program and student level. *Financial support:* In 2016–17, 94 students received support. Career-related internships or fieldwork, Federal Work-Study, institutionally sponsored loans, scholarships/grants, and unspecified assistantships available. Support available to part-time students. Financial award application deadline: 2/15; financial award applicants required to submit FAFSA. *Faculty research:* Corporate social responsibility; executive compensation and corporate governance; combinatorics; secure mobile coding; social equity and justice, particularly among the Latino population; public and healthcare finance. *Unit head:* Dr. Edward Rogoff, Dean, 718-488-1159, E-mail: edward.rogoff@liu.edu. *Application contact:* Gabrielle Gannon, Director of Graduate Admissions, 718-488-1011, Fax: 718-780-6110, E-mail: bkln-admissions@liu.edu.
Website: http://liu.edu/Brooklyn/Academics/School-of-Business-Public-Administration-and-Information-Sciences

**Long Island University–LIU Post,** School of Health Professions and Nursing, Brookville, NY 11548-1300. Offers cardiovascular perfusion (MS); clinical lab sciences (MS); clinical laboratory management (MS); dietetic internship (Advanced Certificate); family nurse practitioner (MS, Advanced Certificate); forensic social work (Advanced Certificate); gerontology (Advanced Certificate); health administration (MPA); medical biology (MS); non-profit management (Advanced Certificate); nursing education (MS); nutrition (MS); public administration (MPA); social work (MSW). *Program availability:* Part-time, evening/weekend, blended/hybrid learning. *Faculty:* 27 full-time (20 women), 43 part-time/adjunct (32 women). *Students:* 251 full-time (184 women), 243 part-time (197 women); includes 179 minority (76 Black or African American, non-Hispanic/Latino; 55 Asian, non-Hispanic/Latino; 42 Hispanic/Latino; 1 Native Hawaiian or other Pacific Islander, non-Hispanic/Latino; 5 Two or more races, non-Hispanic/Latino), 79 international. 581 applicants, 67% accepted, 168 enrolled. In 2016, 185 master's, 29 other advanced degrees awarded. *Degree requirements:* For master's, comprehensive exam (for some programs), thesis (for some programs); for Advanced Certificate, comprehensive exam (for some programs). *Entrance requirements:* Additional exam requirements/recommendations for international students: Required—TOEFL (minimum score 550 paper-based, 75 iBT) or IELTS. *Application deadline:* Applications are processed on a rolling basis. Application fee: $50. Electronic applications accepted. *Expenses: Tuition:* Full-time $28,272; part-time $1178 per credit. *Required fees:* $451 per term. Tuition and fees vary according to degree level and program. *Financial support:* In 2016–17, 5 research assistantships with partial tuition reimbursements (averaging $725 per year), 3 teaching assistantships with partial tuition reimbursements (averaging $800 per year) were awarded; career-related internships or fieldwork, Federal Work-Study, institutionally sponsored loans, scholarships/grants, and unspecified assistantships also available. Support available to part-time students. Financial award application deadline: 2/15; financial award applicants required to submit FAFSA. *Faculty research:* Cancer gene regulation, childhood obesity, host-pathogen interaction, interprofessional simulation, interstitial cystitis. *Total annual research expenditures:* $35,000. *Unit head:* Dr. Stacy Gropack, Dean, 516-299-2485, Fax: 516-299-2527, E-mail: post-shpn@liu.edu. *Application contact:* Carol Zerah, Director of Graduate Admissions, 516-299-2900, Fax: 516-299-2137, E-mail: post-enroll@liu.edu.
Website: http://liu.edu/post/health

**Marywood University,** Academic Affairs, College of Health and Human Services, School of Social Work, Program in Gerontology, Scranton, PA 18509-1598. Offers MS. *Program availability:* Part-time. Electronic applications accepted.

**McDaniel College,** Graduate and Professional Studies, Program in Gerontology, Westminster, MD 21157-4390. Offers MS, Postbaccalaureate Certificate. *Program availability:* Part-time, evening/weekend, online only, 100% online. *Faculty:* 1 (woman) full-time, 3 part-time/adjunct (2 women). *Students:* 7 full-time (5 women), 11 part-time (10 women); includes 3 minority (2 Black or African American, non-Hispanic/Latino; 1 Hispanic/Latino). Average age 32. 6 applicants, 100% accepted. In 2016, 3 master's, 1 other advanced degree awarded. *Degree requirements:* For master's, portfolio. *Entrance requirements:* For master's, 3 recommendations. Additional exam requirements/recommendations for international students: Required—TOEFL (minimum score 79 iBT), IELTS (minimum score 6). *Application deadline:* For fall admission, 6/1 priority date for domestic students; for spring admission, 11/1 priority date for domestic students; for summer admission, 3/1 priority date for domestic students. Applications are processed on a rolling basis. Application fee: $75. Electronic applications accepted. *Expenses: Tuition:* Full-time $8370; part-time $465 per credit. *Required fees:* $75 per semester. Tuition and fees vary according to course load, program and reciprocity agreements. *Financial support:* Application deadline: 3/1; applicants required to submit

FAFSA. *Unit head:* Fax: 410-857-2515, E-mail: gradadms@mcdaniel.edu. *Application contact:* Penny Pfeiffer, Senior Graduate Enrollment Management Specialist, 410-857-2513, Fax: 410-857-2515, E-mail: ppfeiffer@mcdaniel.edu.

**Mercer University,** Graduate Studies, Cecil B. Day Campus, Penfield College, Atlanta, GA 30341. Offers certified rehabilitation counseling (MS); clinical mental health (MS); counselor education and supervision (PhD); criminal justice and public safety leadership (MS); health informatics (MS); human services (MS), including child and adolescent services, gerontology services; organizational leadership (MS); school counseling (MS). *Program availability:* Part-time, evening/weekend, 100% online, blended/hybrid learning. *Faculty:* 15 full-time (8 women), 22 part-time/adjunct (18 women). *Students:* 168 full-time (136 women), 242 part-time (201 women); includes 231 minority (192 Black or African American, non-Hispanic/Latino; 1 American Indian or Alaska Native, non-Hispanic/Latino; 15 Asian, non-Hispanic/Latino; 19 Hispanic/Latino; 1 Native Hawaiian or other Pacific Islander, non-Hispanic/Latino; 3 Two or more races, non-Hispanic/Latino), 2 international. Average age 32. 300 applicants, 45% accepted, 114 enrolled. In 2016, 92 master's, 8 doctorates awarded. *Degree requirements:* For master's, comprehensive exam (for some programs), thesis (for some programs); for doctorate, thesis/dissertation. *Entrance requirements:* For master's, GRE or MAT, Georgia Professional Standards Commission (GPSC) Certification at the SC-5 level; for doctorate, GRE or MAT. Additional exam requirements/recommendations for international students: Recommended—TOEFL (minimum score 550 paper-based; 80 iBT), IELTS (minimum score 6.5). *Application deadline:* For fall admission, 7/1 priority date for domestic and international students; for spring admission, 11/1 priority date for domestic and international students; for summer admission, 4/1 priority date for domestic and international students. Application fee: $35. Electronic applications accepted. Application fee is waived when completed online. *Expenses:* $588 per credit hour. *Financial support:* In 2016–17, 32 students received support. Federal Work-Study, scholarships/grants, and unspecified assistantships available. Financial award applicants required to submit FAFSA. *Faculty research:* Marriage and families issues, leadership and ethics, cyber-bullying, trauma, narrative counseling and theory. *Total annual research expenditures:* $85,000. *Unit head:* Dr. Priscilla R. Danheiser, Dean, 678-547-6028, Fax: 678-547-6008, E-mail: danheiser_p@mercer.edu.
Website: http://penfield.mercer.edu/programs/graduate-professional/

**Miami University,** College of Arts and Science, Department of Sociology and Gerontology, Oxford, OH 45056. Offers gerontology (MGS); population and social gerontology (MPSG); social gerontology (PhD). *Students:* 29 full-time (25 women), 11 part-time (8 women); includes 3 minority (1 Black or African American, non-Hispanic/Latino; 1 Asian, non-Hispanic/Latino; 1 Hispanic/Latino), 12 international. Average age 33. In 2016, 14 master's, 3 doctorates awarded. *Expenses:* Tuition, state resident: full-time $12,890; part-time $564 per credit hour. Tuition, nonresident: full-time $29,604; part-time $1260 per credit hour. *Required fees:* $638. Part-time tuition and fees vary according to course load and program. *Unit head:* Dr. Stephen Lippman, Chair and Associate Professor, 513-529-8515, E-mail: lippmas@miamioh.edu. *Application contact:* Dr. Jennifer Kinney, Director of Graduate Studies, 513-529-2915, E-mail: kinneyjm@miamioh.edu.
Website: http://www.MiamiOH.edu/sociology/

**Middle Tennessee State University,** College of Graduate Studies, College of Liberal Arts, Program in Gerontology, Murfreesboro, TN 37132. Offers Graduate Certificate. *Program availability:* Part-time, evening/weekend, online learning. *Entrance requirements:* Additional exam requirements/recommendations for international students: Required—TOEFL (minimum score 525 paper-based; 71 iBT) or IELTS (minimum score 6). Electronic applications accepted.

**Minnesota State University Mankato,** College of Graduate Studies and Research, College of Social and Behavioral Sciences, Program in Aging Studies, Mankato, MN 56001. Offers MS. *Students:* 4 full-time (all women), 6 part-time (4 women). *Degree requirements:* For master's, comprehensive exam, thesis optional. *Entrance requirements:* For master's, GRE, minimum GPA of 3.0 during previous 2 years, letters of recommendation. Additional exam requirements/recommendations for international students: Required—TOEFL. *Application deadline:* For fall admission, 7/1 priority date for domestic students; for spring admission, 11/1 for domestic students. Applications are processed on a rolling basis. Application fee: $40. Electronic applications accepted. *Financial support:* Federal Work-Study, scholarships/grants, and unspecified assistantships available. Support available to part-time students. Financial award application deadline: 3/15; financial award applicants required to submit FAFSA.
Website: http://sbs.mnsu.edu/agingstudies/graduate.html

**Morehead State University,** Graduate Programs, Caudill College of Arts, Humanities and Social Sciences, Department of Sociology, Social Work and Criminology, Morehead, KY 40351. Offers criminology (MA); general sociology (MA); gerontology (MA); sociology regional analysis (MA); sociology/chemical dependency (MA). *Program availability:* Part-time, evening/weekend. *Degree requirements:* For master's, comprehensive exam, thesis (for some programs). *Entrance requirements:* For master's, GRE General Test, minimum GPA of 3.0 in sociology, 2.75 overall; 18 hours of course work in sociology, writing sample. Additional exam requirements/recommendations for international students: Required—TOEFL (minimum score 500 paper-based). Electronic applications accepted. *Faculty research:* Death and dying; aging, drinking, and drugs; economic development; adult children of alcoholics.

**Mount Saint Vincent University,** Graduate Programs, Department of Family Studies and Gerontology, Halifax, NS B3M 2J6, Canada. Offers MA. *Program availability:* Part-time, online learning. *Degree requirements:* For master's, thesis. *Entrance requirements:* For master's, minimum GPA of 3.0; course work in statistics, research methods, family and social theories.

**North Dakota State University,** College of Graduate and Interdisciplinary Studies, College of Human Development and Education, Department of Human Development and Family Science, Program in Gerontology, Fargo, ND 58102. Offers MS, Certificate. Electronic applications accepted.

**Northeastern Illinois University,** College of Graduate Studies and Research, College of Arts and Sciences, Program in Gerontology, Chicago, IL 60625-4699. Offers MA. *Program availability:* Part-time, evening/weekend. *Degree requirements:* For master's, comprehensive exam, paper and project or thesis, practicum. *Entrance requirements:* For master's, 15 hours in social sciences (3 hours in gerontology), 1 course in research methods or statistics, minimum GPA of 2.75. Additional exam requirements/recommendations for international students: Required—TOEFL (minimum score 550 paper-based; 79 iBT). Electronic applications accepted. *Faculty research:* Later life development, cultural diversity, humanities and aging, elder abuse, AIDS and aging, computer training.

**Oregon Health & Science University,** School of Nursing, Program in Nursing Education, Portland, OR 97239-3098. Offers MN, Post Master's Certificate. *Program availability:* Part-time, online only, 100% online. *Faculty:* 2 full-time (both women), 1 (woman) part-time/adjunct. *Students:* 13 full-time (12 women); includes 1 minority (Asian, non-Hispanic/Latino). Average age 38. 14 applicants, 93% accepted, 10 enrolled. In 2016, 14 master's awarded. *Entrance requirements:* For master's, minimum cumulative GPA of 3.0, 3 letters of recommendation, essay, RN license or eligibility, BS

## Gerontology

with major in nursing or BSN, statistics taken in last 5 years with minimum B- grade; for Post Master's Certificate, minimum cumulative GPA of 3.0, 3 letters of recommendation, essay, RN license or eligibility, master's degree in nursing, statistics taken in last 5 years with minimum B- grade. Additional exam requirements/recommendations for international students: Required—TOEFL (minimum score 83 iBT). *Application deadline:* For fall admission, 5/31 for domestic and international students. Applications are processed on a rolling basis. Application fee: $65. Electronic applications accepted. *Expenses:* $583 per credit in-state tuition, $755 out-of-state. *Financial support:* In 2016–17, 2 students received support. Federal Work-Study, institutionally sponsored loans, and scholarships/grants available. Financial award application deadline: 3/1; financial award applicants required to submit FAFSA. *Faculty research:* Quality of end-of-life care in long-term settings, ethical issues in studying dying people and their families, strategies for improving clinical judgement. *Application contact:* Office of Recruitment, 503-494-7725, Fax: 503-494-4350, E-mail: proginfo@ohsu.edu.

**Portland State University,** Graduate Studies, OHSU-PSU School of Public Health, Health Promotion Program, Portland, OR 97207-0751. Offers aging (Certificate); community health (PhD); health education (MA, MS); health promotion (MPH); health studies (MPA, MPH), including health administration. MPH offered jointly with Oregon Health & Science University. *Program availability:* Part-time. *Faculty:* 25 full-time (19 women), 4 part-time/adjunct (2 women). *Students:* 22 full-time (19 women), 27 part-time (23 women); includes 14 minority (2 American Indian or Alaska Native, non-Hispanic/Latino; 2 Asian, non-Hispanic/Latino; 4 Hispanic/Latino; 1 Native Hawaiian or other Pacific Islander, non-Hispanic/Latino; 5 Two or more races, non-Hispanic/Latino), 1 international. Average age 32. 35 applicants, 20% accepted, 5 enrolled. In 2016, 19 master's, 1 doctorate awarded. *Degree requirements:* For master's, comprehensive exam (for some programs), thesis (for some programs), internship/praticum, oral and written exams (depending on program; for doctorate, comprehensive exam, thesis/dissertation. *Entrance requirements:* For master's, GRE (for MPH program), 3 letters of recommendation, minimum GPA of 3.0, resume; for doctorate, GRE, transcripts, personal statement, resume, writing sample, 3 letters of recommendation. Additional exam requirements/recommendations for international students: Required—TOEFL (minimum score 550 paper-based; 80 iBT). *Application deadline:* For fall admission, 2/1 for domestic and international students. Applications are processed on a rolling basis. Application fee: $65. *Expenses:* Contact institution. *Financial support:* In 2016–17, 9 research assistantships with tuition reimbursements (averaging $7,556 per year) were awarded; teaching assistantships, career-related internships or fieldwork, Federal Work-Study, scholarships/grants, and unspecified assistantships also available. Support available to part-time students. Financial award application deadline: 3/1; financial award applicants required to submit FAFSA. *Unit head:* Dr. David Bangsberg, Founding Dean, 503-282-7537. *Application contact:* Dr. Jill Rissi, Dean for Academic Affairs, E-mail: jrissi@pdx.edu.
Website: http://www.healthed.pdx.edu/

**Sage Graduate School,** School of Management, Program in Health Services Administration, Troy, NY 12180-4115. Offers gerontology (MS). *Program availability:* Part-time, evening/weekend. *Faculty:* 3 full-time (2 women), 13 part-time/adjunct (4 women). *Students:* 9 full-time (7 women), 32 part-time (23 women); includes 3 minority (1 Black or African American, non-Hispanic/Latino; 1 Asian, non-Hispanic/Latino; 1 Hispanic/Latino). Average age 32. 49 applicants, 41% accepted, 14 enrolled. In 2016, 16 master's awarded. *Entrance requirements:* For master's, minimum GPA of 2.75, resume, 2 letters of recommendation. Additional exam requirements/recommendations for international students: Required—TOEFL (minimum score 550 paper-based). *Application deadline:* Applications are processed on a rolling basis. Application fee: $40. Electronic applications accepted. *Expenses: Tuition:* Full-time $12,240; part-time $680 per credit hour. Tuition and fees vary according to degree level and program. *Financial support:* Fellowships, research assistantships, Federal Work-Study, scholarships/grants, and unspecified assistantships available. Support available to part-time students. Financial award application deadline: 3/1; financial award applicants required to submit FAFSA. *Unit head:* Dr. Kimberly Fredericks, Dean, School of Management, 518-292-1782, Fax: 518-292-1964, E-mail: fredek1@sage.edu. *Application contact:* Wendy D. Diefendorf, Director of Graduate and Adult Admission, 518-244-2443, Fax: 518-244-6880, E-mail: diefew@sage.edu.

**St. Cloud State University,** School of Graduate Studies, School of Health and Human Services, Program in Gerontology, St. Cloud, MN 56301-4498. Offers MS. *Program availability:* Part-time. *Degree requirements:* For master's, thesis or alternative. *Entrance requirements:* For master's, GRE General Test, minimum GPA of 2.75. Additional exam requirements/recommendations for international students: Required—Michigan English Language Assessment Battery; Recommended—TOEFL (minimum score 550 paper-based), IELTS (minimum score 6.5). Electronic applications accepted.

**San Diego State University,** Graduate and Research Affairs, College of Health and Human Services, Department of Gerontology, San Diego, CA 92182. Offers MS. *Program availability:* Part-time, evening/weekend. *Degree requirements:* For master's, thesis. *Entrance requirements:* For master's, GRE General Test. Additional exam requirements/recommendations for international students: Required—TOEFL. Electronic applications accepted.

**San Francisco State University,** Division of Graduate Studies, College of Health and Social Sciences, Gerontology Program, San Francisco, CA 94132-1722. Offers MA. *Program availability:* Part-time. *Application deadline:* Applications are processed on a rolling basis. *Expenses:* Tuition, state resident: full-time $6738. Tuition, nonresident: full-time $15,666. *Required fees:* $1012. Tuition and fees vary according to degree level and program. *Financial support:* Career-related internships or fieldwork and unspecified assistantships available. *Unit head:* Dr. Darlene Yee-Melichar, Program Coordinator, 415-338-1684, Fax: 415-338-3556, E-mail: dyee@sfsu.edu.
Website: http://gerontology.sfsu.edu/

**San Francisco State University,** Division of Graduate Studies, College of Health and Social Sciences, Public Administration Program, San Francisco, CA 94132-1722. Offers criminal justice administration (MPA); environmental administration and policy (MPA); gerontology (MPA); nonprofit administration (MPA); public management (MPA); public policy (MPA); urban administration (MPA). *Accreditation:* NASPAA. *Expenses:* Tuition, state resident: full-time $6738. Tuition, nonresident: full-time $15,666. *Required fees:* $1012. Tuition and fees vary according to degree level and program. *Unit head:* Dr. Elizabeth Brown, Director of the School of Public Affairs and Civic Engagement, 415-817-4455, Fax: 415-817-4464, E-mail: mpa@sfsu.edu. *Application contact:* Dr. Jennifer Shea, Graduate Coordinator, 415-817-4462, Fax: 415-817-4464, E-mail: jshea@sfsu.edu.
Website: http://mpa.sfsu.edu/

**Simon Fraser University,** Office of Graduate Studies and Postdoctoral Fellows, Faculty of Arts and Social Sciences, Department of Gerontology, Vancouver, BC V6B 5K3, Canada. Offers MA, PhD. *Program availability:* Part-time. *Faculty:* 5 full-time (1 woman). *Students:* 23 full-time (19 women). 11 applicants, 64% accepted, 6 enrolled. In 2016, 5 master's awarded. *Degree requirements:* For master's, thesis or alternative, internship; for doctorate, comprehensive exam, thesis/dissertation. *Entrance requirements:* For master's, minimum GPA of 3.0 (on scale of 4.33) or 3.33 based on last 60 credits of undergraduate courses; for doctorate, minimum GPA of 3.5 (on scale of 4.33).

Additional exam requirements/recommendations for international students: Recommended—TOEFL (minimum score 580 paper-based; 93 iBT), IELTS (minimum score 7), TWE (minimum score 5). *Application deadline:* For fall admission, 1/30 for domestic and international students; for winter admission, 8/30 for domestic and international students. Application fee: $90 ($125 for international students). Electronic applications accepted. *Financial support:* In 2016–17, 15 students received support, including 8 fellowships (averaging $6,500 per year), teaching assistantships (averaging $5,608 per year); research assistantships, career-related internships or fieldwork, Federal Work-Study, scholarships/grants, and unspecified assistantships also available. Support available to part-time students. *Faculty research:* Aging and the built environment, changing demography and lifestyles, health promotion/population health and aging, prevention of victimization and exploitation of older persons, technology and aging. *Unit head:* Dr. Sean Markey, Graduate Chair, 778-782-7635, Fax: 778-782-5066, E-mail: gero-grad-chair@sfu.ca. *Application contact:* Roslyn McKoen, Graduate Secretary, 778-782-5065, Fax: 778-782-5066, E-mail: gero@sfu.ca.
Website: http://www.sfu.ca/gerontology/

**Temple University,** College of Public Health, Department of Nursing, Philadelphia, PA 19122. Offers adult-gerontology primary care (DNP); family-individual across the lifespan (DNP); nursing (DNP). *Accreditation:* AACN. *Program availability:* Part-time. *Degree requirements:* For doctorate, evidence-based practice project. *Entrance requirements:* For doctorate, GRE General Test or MAT, 2 letters of reference, RN license, interview, statement of purpose, resume. Additional exam requirements/recommendations for international students: Required—TOEFL (minimum score 600 paper-based; 100 iBT). Electronic applications accepted. *Expenses:* Contact institution. *Faculty research:* Health promotion, chronic illness, family support systems, primary care, health policy, community health services, evidence-based practice.

**Texas Christian University,** Harris College of Nursing and Health Sciences, Doctor of Nursing Practice Program, Fort Worth, TX 76109. Offers advanced practice registered nurse (DNP); clinical nurse specialist - adult/gerontology nursing (DNP); clinical nurse specialist - pediatrics (DNP); family nurse practitioner (DNP); nursing administration (DNP). *Accreditation:* AACN. *Program availability:* Part-time. *Faculty:* 23 full-time (20 women), 2 part-time/adjunct (both women). *Students:* 45 full-time (40 women), 13 part-time (11 women); includes 13 minority (6 Black or African American, non-Hispanic/Latino; 2 Asian, non-Hispanic/Latino; 5 Hispanic/Latino). Average age 43. 33 applicants, 79% accepted, 24 enrolled. In 2016, 18 doctorates awarded. *Degree requirements:* For doctorate, thesis/dissertation or alternative, practicum. *Entrance requirements:* For doctorate, three reference letters, essay, resume, two official transcripts from each institution attended, APRN recognition or MSN with experience in nursing administration. *Application deadline:* For summer admission, 11/15 for domestic and international students. Application fee: $60. Electronic applications accepted. *Expenses:* $1,480 per credit hour tuition plus $112 per course fee. *Financial support:* Teaching assistantships and scholarships/grants available. Financial award application deadline: 2/15; financial award applicants required to submit FAFSA. *Faculty research:* Geriatrics, cancer survivorship, health literacy, endothelial cells, clinical simulation outcomes. *Unit head:* Dr. Kenneth Lowrance, Director, 817-257-6729, Fax: 817-257-8383, E-mail: k.w.lowrance@tcu.edu. *Application contact:* Mary Jane Allred, Administrative Program Specialist, 817-257-6726, Fax: 817-257-8383, E-mail: m.allred@tcu.edu.
Website: http://dnp.tcu.edu/

**Texas State University,** The Graduate College, College of Liberal Arts, Program in Dementia and Aging Studies, San Marcos, TX 78666. Offers MS. *Program availability:* Part-time, evening/weekend. *Faculty:* 20 full-time (10 women). *Students:* 17 full-time (13 women), 20 part-time (16 women); includes 12 minority (2 Black or African American, non-Hispanic/Latino; 2 Asian, non-Hispanic/Latino; 8 Hispanic/Latino). Average age 35. 16 applicants, 75% accepted, 7 enrolled. In 2016, 2 master's awarded. *Degree requirements:* For master's, comprehensive exam, thesis (for some programs). *Entrance requirements:* For master's, baccalaureate degree from regionally-accredited university with minimum GPA of 3.0 on last 60 undergraduate semester hours. Additional exam requirements/recommendations for international students: Required—TOEFL (minimum score 550 paper-based; 78 iBT), IELTS (minimum score 6.5). *Application deadline:* For fall admission, 3/1 priority date for domestic and international students; for spring admission, 10/15 for domestic students, 10/1 for international students; for summer admission, 4/15 for domestic students, 3/15 for international students. Applications are processed on a rolling basis. Application fee: $40 ($90 for international students). Electronic applications accepted. *Expenses:* $4,851 per semester. *Financial support:* In 2016–17, 15 students received support. Research assistantships, teaching assistantships, career-related internships or fieldwork, Federal Work-Study, institutionally sponsored loans, scholarships/grants, and unspecified assistantships available. Support available to part-time students. Financial award application deadline: 3/1; financial award applicants required to submit FAFSA. *Unit head:* Dr. Patti Giuffre, Graduate Advisor, 512-245-8983, Fax: 512-245-8362, E-mail: pg07@txstate.edu. *Application contact:* Dr. Andrea Golato, Dean of Graduate School, 512-245-2581, Fax: 512-245-8365, E-mail: gradcollege@txstate.edu.
Website: http://www.soci.txstate.edu/

**Texas Tech University,** Graduate School, College of Human Sciences, Department of Human Development and Family Studies, Lubbock, TX 79409-1230. Offers human development and family studies (MS, PhD), including gerontology (MS). *Accreditation:* AAMFT/COAMFTE (one or more programs are accredited). *Faculty:* 24 full-time (21 women), 7 part-time/adjunct (all women). *Students:* 28 full-time (23 women), 20 part-time (14 women); includes 12 minority (3 Black or African American, non-Hispanic/Latino; 1 American Indian or Alaska Native, non-Hispanic/Latino; 7 Hispanic/Latino; 1 Two or more races, non-Hispanic/Latino), 12 international. Average age 33. 34 applicants, 44% accepted, 4 enrolled. In 2016, 5 master's, 4 doctorates awarded. *Degree requirements:* For master's, thesis; for doctorate, comprehensive exam, thesis/dissertation. *Entrance requirements:* For master's and doctorate, GRE General Test. Additional exam requirements/recommendations for international students: Required—TOEFL (minimum score 550 paper-based; 79 iBT). *Application deadline:* For fall admission, 6/1 priority date for domestic students, 1/15 priority date for international students; for spring admission, 9/1 priority date for domestic students, 6/15 priority date for international students. Applications are processed on a rolling basis. Application fee: $75. Electronic applications accepted. *Expenses:* $315 per credit hour full-time resident tuition, $723 per credit hour full-time non-resident tuition; $50.50 per credit hour fee plus $608 per term fee. *Financial support:* In 2016–17, 38 students received support, including 35 fellowships (averaging $4,579 per year), 24 research assistantships (averaging $8,526 per year), 23 teaching assistantships (averaging $9,522 per year); scholarships/grants and unspecified assistantships also available. Financial award application deadline: 4/15; financial award applicants required to submit FAFSA. *Faculty research:* 34226. *Total annual research expenditures:* $64,339. *Unit head:* Dr. Ann M. Mastergeorge, Chairperson, 806-834-7162, Fax: 806-742-3042, E-mail: ann.mastergeorge@ttu.edu. *Application contact:* Dr. Malinda Colwell, Graduate Program Director, 806-742-3000 Ext. 250, Fax: 806-742-0285, E-mail: malinda.colwell@ttu.edu.
Website: http://www.depts.ttu.edu/hdfs

**Université de Sherbrooke,** Faculty of Letters and Human Sciences, Department of Psychology, Sherbrooke, QC J1K 2R1, Canada. Offers gerontology (MA). *Degree requirements:* For master's, thesis. *Faculty research:* Human relations.

**Université Laval,** Faculty of Medicine, Post-Professional Programs in Medical Studies, Québec, QC G1K 7P4, Canada. Offers anatomy–pathology (DESS); anesthesiology (DESS); cardiology (DESS); care of older people (Diploma); clinical research (DESS); community health (DESS); dermatology (DESS); diagnostic radiology (DESS); emergency medicine (Diploma); family medicine (DESS); general surgery (DESS); geriatrics (DESS); hematology (DESS); internal medicine (DESS); maternal and fetal medicine (Diploma); medical biochemistry (DESS); medical microbiology and infectious diseases (DESS); medical oncology (DESS); nephrology (DESS); neurology (DESS); neurosurgery (DESS); obstetrics and gynecology (DESS); ophthalmology (DESS); orthopedic surgery (DESS); oto-rhino-laryngology (DESS); palliative medicine (Diploma); pediatrics (DESS); plastic surgery (DESS); psychiatry (DESS); pulmonary medicine (DESS); radiology–oncology (DESS); thoracic surgery (DESS); urology (DESS). *Degree requirements:* For other advanced degree, comprehensive exam. *Entrance requirements:* For degree, knowledge of French. Electronic applications accepted.

**The University of Akron,** Graduate School, Buchtel College of Arts and Sciences, Department of Psychology, Program in Adult Development and Aging, Akron, OH 44325. Offers PhD. *Students:* 10 full-time (8 women), 1 part-time (0 women); includes 1 minority (Two or more races, non-Hispanic/Latino), 1 international. Average age 27. 17 applicants, 24% accepted, 4 enrolled. *Degree requirements:* For doctorate, one foreign language, comprehensive exam, thesis/dissertation. *Entrance requirements:* For doctorate, GRE, minimum graduate GPA of 3.25, three letters of recommendation, personal statement, resume. Additional exam requirements/recommendations for international students: Required—TOEFL (minimum score 550 paper-based; 79 iBT), IELTS (minimum score 6.5). *Application deadline:* For fall admission, 1/15 for domestic and international students. Application fee: $45 ($70 for international students). Electronic applications accepted. *Expenses:* Tuition, state resident: full-time $8618; part-time $359 per credit hour. Tuition, nonresident: full-time $17,149; part-time $715 per credit hour. *Required fees:* $1652. *Financial support:* Fellowships with full tuition reimbursements, research assistantships with full tuition reimbursements, and teaching assistantships with full tuition reimbursements available. *Faculty research:* Changes in memory and cognition with age, automaticity and effects of training, models of visual word recognition, experimental neuropsychology. *Unit head:* Dr. Paul Levy, Department Chair, 330-972-8369, E-mail: plevy@uakron.edu.
Website: http://www.uakron.edu/psychology/academics/adult-development-and-aging/index.dot

**University of Arkansas at Little Rock,** Graduate School, College of Education and Health Professions, School of Social Work, Program in Gerontology, Little Rock, AR 72204-1099. Offers Graduate Certificate.

**University of Central Missouri,** The Graduate School, Warrensburg, MO 64093. Offers accountancy (MA); accounting (MBA); applied mathematics (MS); aviation safety (MA); biology (MS); business administration (MBA); career and technical education leadership (MS); college student personnel administration (MS); communication (MA); computer science (MS); counseling (MS); criminal justice (MS); educational leadership (Ed D); educational technology (MS); elementary and early childhood education (MSE); English (MA); environmental studies (MA); finance (MBA); history (MA); human services/educational technology (Ed S); human services/learning resources (Ed S); human services/professional counseling (Ed S); industrial hygiene (MS); industrial management (MS); information systems (MBA); information technology (MS); kinesiology (MS); library science and information services (MS); literacy education (MSE); marketing (MBA); mathematics (MS); music (MA); occupational safety management (MS); psychology (MS); rural family nursing (MS); school administration (MSE); social gerontology (MS); sociology (MA); special education (MSE); speech language pathology (MS); superintendency (Ed S); teaching (MAT); teaching English as a second language (MA); technology (MS); technology management (PhD); theatre (MA). *Program availability:* Part-time, 100% online, blended/hybrid learning. *Degree requirements:* For master's and Ed S, comprehensive exam (for some programs), thesis (for some programs). *Entrance requirements:* Additional exam requirements/recommendations for international students: Required—TOEFL (minimum score 550 paper-based; 79 iBT). Electronic applications accepted.

**University of Central Oklahoma,** The Jackson College of Graduate Studies, College of Liberal Arts, Department of Sociology, Gerontology, and Substance Abuse Studies, Edmond, OK 73034-5209. Offers gerontology (MA); sociology (MA), including substance abuse studies. *Program availability:* Part-time. *Degree requirements:* For master's, variable foreign language requirement, comprehensive exam (for some programs), thesis (for some programs). *Entrance requirements:* For master's, GRE. Additional exam requirements/recommendations for international students: Required—TOEFL (minimum score 550 paper-based; 79 iBT), IELTS (minimum score 6.5). Electronic applications accepted.

**University of Georgia,** College of Public Health, Institute of Gerontology, Athens, GA 30602. Offers Certificate. *Application contact:* Mary Ann Johnson, Graduate Coordinator, 706-542-4286, E-mail: noahnet@geron.uga.edu.

**University of Illinois at Springfield,** Graduate Programs, College of Education and Human Services, Program in Human Services, Springfield, IL 62703-5407. Offers alcohol and substance abuse (Graduate Certificate); alcoholism and substance abuse (MA); child and family services (MA); gerontology (MA); social services administration (MA). *Program availability:* Part-time, evening/weekend, 100% online, blended/hybrid learning. *Faculty:* 4 full-time (all women), 2 part-time/adjunct (1 woman). *Students:* 10 full-time (8 women), 62 part-time (53 women); includes 28 minority (23 Black or African American, non-Hispanic/Latino; 3 Hispanic/Latino; 2 Two or more races, non-Hispanic/Latino). Average age 34. 37 applicants, 46% accepted, 16 enrolled. In 2016, 32 master's, 3 other advanced degrees awarded. *Degree requirements:* For master's, internship; capstone project or thesis. *Entrance requirements:* For master's, minimum undergraduate GPA of 3.0, 2 letters of recommendation from professional or academic sources, statement of intent, interview. Additional exam requirements/recommendations for international students: Required—TOEFL (minimum score 500 paper-based; 61 iBT). *Application deadline:* Applications are processed on a rolling basis. Application fee: $60 ($75 for international students). Electronic applications accepted. *Expenses:* Tuition, state resident: part-time $329 per credit hour. Tuition, nonresident: part-time $675 per credit hour. *Financial support:* In 2016–17, fellowships with full tuition reimbursements (averaging $9,900 per year), research assistantships with full tuition reimbursements (averaging $9,991 per year), teaching assistantships with full tuition reimbursements (averaging $10,059 per year) were awarded; career-related internships or fieldwork, Federal Work-Study, scholarships/grants, health care benefits, and unspecified assistantships also available. Support available to part-time students. Financial award application deadline: 11/15; financial award applicants required to submit FAFSA. *Unit head:* Dr. Carolyn Peck, Program Administrator, 217-206-7577, Fax: 217-206-6775, E-mail: peck.carolyn@uis.edu. *Application contact:* Dr. Cecelia Cornell, Associate Vice Chancellor for Graduate Education, 217-206-7230, E-mail: ccorn1@uis.edu.
Website: http://www.uis.edu/humanservices

**University of Indianapolis,** Graduate Programs, Center for Aging and Community, Indianapolis, IN 46227-3697. Offers gerontology (MS, Certificate). *Program availability:* Part-time, evening/weekend, online learning. *Degree requirements:* For master's, capstone course. *Entrance requirements:* For master's, 3 letters of recommendation. Additional exam requirements/recommendations for international students: Required—TOEFL (minimum score 550 paper-based).

**University of Indianapolis,** Graduate Programs, School of Nursing, Indianapolis, IN 46227-3697. Offers advanced practice nursing (DNP); family nurse practitioner (MSN); gerontological nurse practitioner (MSN); neonatal nurse practitioner (MSN); nurse-midwifery (MSN); nursing (MSN); nursing and health systems leadership (MSN); nursing education (MSN); women's health nurse practitioner (MSN); MBA/MSN. *Accreditation:* AACN. *Entrance requirements:* For master's, minimum GPA of 3.0, interview, letters of recommendation, resume, IN nursing license, 1 year of professional practice; for doctorate, graduate of NLNAC- or CCNE-accredited nursing program; MSN or MA with nursing major and minimum cumulative GPA of 3.25; unencumbered RN license with eligibility for licensure in Indiana; completion of graduate-level statistics course within last 5 years with minimum grade of B; resume; essay; official transcripts from all academic institutions. Additional exam requirements/recommendations for international students: Required—TOEFL (minimum score 550 paper-based). Electronic applications accepted.

**The University of Kansas,** Graduate Studies, College of Liberal Arts and Sciences, Program in Gerontology, Lawrence, KS 66045. Offers PhD. *Students:* 2 full-time (both women), 1 international. Average age 37. 33 applicants, 36% accepted, 8 enrolled. *Entrance requirements:* For doctorate, GRE, 3 letters of recommendation, resume, personal statement, transcripts, list of all courses taken in relevant areas such as sociology, psychology, human development, social welfare, biology, and health services. Additional exam requirements/recommendations for international students: Required—TOEFL. *Application deadline:* For fall admission, 1/15 priority date for domestic and international students. Application fee: $65 ($85 for international students). Electronic applications accepted. *Financial support:* Fellowships, research assistantships, career-related internships or fieldwork, traineeships, and unspecified assistantships available. Financial award application deadline: 1/15. *Faculty research:* Communication and aging, work and retirement, cognitive aging, dementia, environmental gerontology. *Unit head:* Tamara Baker, Interim Director, 785-864-2633, E-mail: tbakerthomas@ku.edu. *Application contact:* Graduate Admissions Contact, 785-864-4130, Fax: 785-864-2666, E-mail: gerontology@ku.edu.
Website: http://www.gerontology.ku.edu/

**University of Kentucky,** Graduate School, College of Public Health, Program in Gerontology, Lexington, KY 40506-0032. Offers PhD, Graduate Certificate. *Degree requirements:* For doctorate, comprehensive exam, thesis/dissertation. *Entrance requirements:* For doctorate, GRE General Test, minimum undergraduate GPA of 2.75, graduate 3.0. Additional exam requirements/recommendations for international students: Required—TOEFL (minimum score 550 paper-based). Electronic applications accepted.

**University of La Verne,** College of Business and Public Management, Program in Gerontology, La Verne, CA 91750-4443. Offers geriatric care management (MS); gerontology (Certificate); gerontology administration (MS); health services management (MS). *Program availability:* Part-time. *Students:* 6 full-time (all women), 11 part-time (9 women); includes 11 minority (2 Black or African American, non-Hispanic/Latino; 9 Hispanic/Latino), 4 international. Average age 34. *Entrance requirements:* For master's, bachelor's degree, minimum preferred GPA of 2.75, 2 recommendations, personal statement. Additional exam requirements/recommendations for international students: Required—TOEFL (minimum score 550 paper-based). *Application deadline:* Applications are processed on a rolling basis. Application fee: $50. *Expenses:* Contact institution. *Financial support:* Federal Work-Study, institutionally sponsored loans, and scholarships/grants available. Financial award application deadline: 3/2; financial award applicants required to submit FAFSA. *Unit head:* Kelly Niles-Yokum, Program Director, 909-448-1584, E-mail: kniles-yokum@laverne.edu. *Application contact:* Barbara Cox, Program and Admissions Specialist, 909-448-4004, Fax: 909-971-2295, E-mail: bcox@laverne.edu.
Website: http://laverne.edu/business-and-public-administration/m-s-in-gerontology/

**University of Louisiana at Monroe,** Graduate School, College of Health and Pharmaceutical Sciences, Department of Gerontology, Monroe, LA 71209-0001. Offers aging studies (MA); gerontology (CGS); program administration (MA). *Program availability:* Part-time. *Faculty:* 3 part-time/adjunct (1 woman). *Students:* 2 full-time (both women), 4 part-time (3 women); includes 3 minority (all Black or African American, non-Hispanic/Latino). Average age 34. 7 applicants, 43% accepted, 3 enrolled. In 2016, 5 master's awarded. *Degree requirements:* For master's, thesis (for some programs), internship. *Entrance requirements:* For master's and CGS, GRE General Test, minimum cumulative undergraduate GPA of 2.75. Additional exam requirements/recommendations for international students: Required—TOEFL (minimum score 500 paper-based; 61 iBT). *Application deadline:* For fall admission, 8/24 priority date for domestic students, 7/1 for international students; for winter admission, 12/14 priority date for domestic students; for spring admission, 1/19 for domestic students, 11/1 for international students. Applications are processed on a rolling basis. Application fee: $20 ($30 for international students). Electronic applications accepted. *Expenses:* Tuition, state resident: full-time $6489. Tuition, nonresident: full-time $18,589. *Required fees:* $8984. Tuition and fees vary according to course level, course load, degree level and program. *Financial support:* Career-related internships or fieldwork, Federal Work-Study, and unspecified assistantships available. Financial award application deadline: 4/1; financial award applicants required to submit FAFSA. *Unit head:* Dr. Karen Kopera-Frye, Head, 318-342-1467, E-mail: frye@ulm.edu.
Website: http://www.ulm.edu/gerontology/

**University of Louisville,** Graduate School, Raymond A. Kent School of Social Work, Louisville, KY 40292-0001. Offers marriage and family therapy (PMC), including mental health; social work (MSSW, PhD), including alcohol and drug counseling (MSSW), gerontology (MSSW), marriage and family (PhD), school social work (MSSW). *Accreditation:* AAMFT/COAMFTE; CSWE (one or more programs are accredited). *Program availability:* Part-time, evening/weekend, 100% online, blended/hybrid learning. *Faculty:* 29 full-time (19 women), 51 part-time/adjunct (42 women). *Students:* 384 full-time (324 women), 81 part-time (65 women); includes 116 minority (65 Black or African American, non-Hispanic/Latino; 7 Asian, non-Hispanic/Latino; 18 Hispanic/Latino; 1 Native Hawaiian or other Pacific Islander, non-Hispanic/Latino; 25 Two or more races, non-Hispanic/Latino), 7 international. Average age 31. 419 applicants, 63% accepted, 184 enrolled. In 2016, 191 master's, 2 doctorates awarded. *Degree requirements:* For doctorate, comprehensive exam, thesis/dissertation. *Entrance requirements:* For master's, GRE or minimum GPA of 2.75; for doctorate, GRE General Test, interview, writing sample. Additional exam requirements/recommendations for international students: Required—TOEFL (minimum score 550 paper-based; 79 iBT), IELTS (minimum score 6.5). *Application deadline:* For fall admission, 5/30 for domestic and international students; for spring admission, 9/30 for domestic and international students; for summer admission, 2/28 for domestic and international students. Applications are processed on a rolling basis. Application fee: $60. Electronic

*Gerontology*

applications accepted. *Expenses:* Contact institution. *Financial support:* In 2016–17, 12 research assistantships with full tuition reimbursements (averaging $21,500 per year) were awarded; health care benefits and unspecified assistantships also available. Financial award application deadline: 5/15; financial award applicants required to submit FAFSA. *Faculty research:* Equipping young children with skills, assisting abused or neglected children, helping juveniles with sexual behavioral problems, illuminating the contributions that men and women make to their families, managing chronic conditions, enhance trauma-informed services, address social and health issues of older adults, palliative and end-of-life care. *Total annual research expenditures:* $4.8 million. *Unit head:* Dr. David Jenkins, Dean, 502-852-3944, E-mail: dajenk03@exchange.louisville.edu. *Application contact:* Misty Kupka, Program Manager for Admissions and Recruitment, 502-852-0414, Fax: 502-852-0422, E-mail: misty.kupka@louisville.edu.
Website: http://www.louisville.edu/kent

**University of Maryland, Baltimore,** Graduate School, Graduate Program in Life Sciences, Program in Gerontology, Baltimore, MD 21201. Offers PhD. *Students:* 8 full-time (7 women), 4 part-time (all women); includes 4 minority (1 Black or African American, non-Hispanic/Latino; 2 Hispanic/Latino; 1 Two or more races, non-Hispanic/Latino), 2 international. Average age 30. 7 applicants, 57% accepted, 3 enrolled. In 2016, 2 doctorates awarded. *Degree requirements:* For doctorate, comprehensive exam, thesis/dissertation. *Entrance requirements:* For doctorate, GRE General Test. Additional exam requirements/recommendations for international students: Required—TOEFL (minimum score 550 paper-based; 80 iBT); Recommended—IELTS (minimum score 7). *Application deadline:* For fall admission, 1/15 for domestic and international students. Application fee: $75. Electronic applications accepted. Tuition and fees vary according to program. *Financial support:* Fellowships, research assistantships, and health care benefits available. Financial award application deadline: 3/1; financial award applicants required to submit FAFSA. *Faculty research:* Aging policy issues; epidemiology of aging; social, cultural, behavioral sciences. *Unit head:* Dr. Denise Orwig, Professor and Program Director, 410-706-4926, E-mail: dorwig@epi.umaryland.edu. *Application contact:* Justine Golden, Coordinator, 410-706-1733, E-mail: jgolden@epi.umaryland.edu.
Website: http://www.gerontologyphd.umaryland.edu/

**University of Maryland, Baltimore,** School of Medicine, Department of Epidemiology and Public Health, Baltimore, MD 21201. Offers biostatistics (MS); clinical research (MS); epidemiology and preventive medicine (MPH, MS, PhD); gerontology (PhD); human genetics and genomic medicine (MS, PhD); molecular epidemiology (MS, PhD); toxicology (MS, PhD); JD/MS; MD/PhD; MS/PhD. *Accreditation:* CEPH. *Program availability:* Part-time. *Students:* 86 full-time (64 women), 43 part-time (25 women); includes 47 minority (20 Black or African American, non-Hispanic/Latino; 14 Asian, non-Hispanic/Latino; 7 Hispanic/Latino; 6 Two or more races, non-Hispanic/Latino), 19 international. Average age 31. In 2016, 64 master's, 44 doctorates awarded. *Degree requirements:* For doctorate, comprehensive exam, thesis/dissertation. *Entrance requirements:* For master's and doctorate, GRE General Test. Additional exam requirements/recommendations for international students: Required—TOEFL (minimum score 550 paper-based; 80 iBT); Recommended—IELTS (minimum score 7). *Application deadline:* For fall admission, 1/15 for domestic and international students. Application fee: $75. Electronic applications accepted. *Expenses:* Contact institution. *Financial support:* In 2016–17, research assistantships with partial tuition reimbursements (averaging $26,000 per year) were awarded; fellowships, Federal Work-Study, scholarships/grants, and unspecified assistantships also available. Financial award application deadline: 3/1; financial award applicants required to submit FAFSA. *Unit head:* Dr. Laura Hungerford, Program Director, 410-706-8492, Fax: 410-706-4225. *Application contact:* Jessica Kelley, Program Coordinator, 410-706-8492, Fax: 410-706-4225, E-mail: jkelley@som.umaryland.edu.
Website: http://lifesciences.umaryland.edu/epidemiology/

**University of Maryland, Baltimore County,** The Graduate School, College of Arts, Humanities and Social Sciences, Doctoral Program in Gerontology at UMB/UMBC, Baltimore, MD 21201. Offers aging policy issues (PhD); epidemiology of aging (PhD); social, cultural, and behavioral sciences (PhD); MA/PhD; MS/PhD. Program offered with University of Maryland, Baltimore. *Program availability:* Part-time. *Faculty:* 17 part-time/adjunct (13 women). *Students:* 9 full-time (8 women), 12 part-time (10 women); includes 7 minority (3 Black or African American, non-Hispanic/Latino; 2 Asian, non-Hispanic/Latino; 2 Hispanic/Latino), 3 international. Average age 35. 13 applicants, 31% accepted, 3 enrolled. In 2016, 4 doctorates awarded. *Degree requirements:* For doctorate, comprehensive exam, thesis/dissertation. *Entrance requirements:* For doctorate, GRE General Test. Additional exam requirements/recommendations for international students: Required—TOEFL, TWE. *Application deadline:* For spring admission, 1/15 for domestic and international students. Application fee: $45. Electronic applications accepted. *Expenses:* Tuition, state resident: full-time $13,294. Tuition, nonresident: full-time $20,286. *Financial support:* Dissertation awards available. Financial award application deadline: 2/1; financial award applicants required to submit FAFSA. *Faculty research:* Aging and health policy, behavioral aspects of aging, epidemiology of aging. *Total annual research expenditures:* $13.5 million. *Unit head:* Dr. John Schumacher, Co-Director, UMBC Campus, 410-455-2074, Fax: 410-455-3184, E-mail: jschuma@umbc.edu. *Application contact:* Justine Golden, Academic Coordinator, 410-706-4926, Fax: 410-706-4433, E-mail: jgold002@umaryland.edu.
Website: http://lifesciences.umaryland.edu/gerontologyphd/

**University of Maryland, Baltimore County,** The Graduate School, Erickson School of Aging Studies, Baltimore, MD 21228. Offers management of aging services (MA). *Program availability:* Part-time. *Faculty:* 4 full-time (1 woman), 7 part-time/adjunct (1 woman). *Students:* 18 full-time (11 women); includes 9 minority (8 Black or African American, non-Hispanic/Latino; 1 Hispanic/Latino). Average age 30. 23 applicants, 91% accepted, 18 enrolled. In 2016, 13 master's awarded. *Entrance requirements:* For master's, essays. *Application deadline:* Applications are processed on a rolling basis. Application fee: $50. Electronic applications accepted. *Expenses:* $790 per credit hour. *Financial support:* In 2016–17, 15 students received support, including 1 teaching assistantship with full tuition reimbursement available (averaging $21,600 per year). Financial award applicants required to submit FAFSA. *Faculty research:* Policy implications of entitlement programs, demographic impact of aging population, person-centered care for dementia, changing culture in long-term care. *Unit head:* Bill Holman, Graduate Program Director, 443-543-5603, E-mail: holman1@umbc.edu. *Application contact:* Michelle Howell, Administrative Assistant, 443-543-5607, E-mail: mhowell@umbc.edu.
Website: http://www.umbc.edu/erickson/

**University of Massachusetts Boston,** John W. McCormack Graduate School of Policy and Global Studies, Program in Gerontology, Boston, MA 02125-3393. Offers gerontology (PhD). *Program availability:* Part-time. *Faculty:* 10 full-time (7 women), 1 (woman) part-time/adjunct. *Students:* 29 full-time (23 women), 100 part-time (85 women); includes 23 minority (11 Black or African American, non-Hispanic/Latino; 9 Asian, non-Hispanic/Latino; 1 Hispanic/Latino; 2 Two or more races, non-Hispanic/Latino), 15 international. Average age 38. 49 applicants, 73% accepted, 23 enrolled. In 2016, 40 master's, 7 doctorates, 5 other advanced degrees awarded. *Degree requirements:* For doctorate, comprehensive exam, thesis/dissertation. *Entrance requirements:* For doctorate, GRE General Test, minimum GPA of 3.0. *Application deadline:* For fall admission, 2/1 for domestic students. *Expenses:* Tuition, state resident: full-time $16,863. Tuition, nonresident: full-time $32,913. *Required fees:* $177. *Financial support:* Research assistantships with full tuition reimbursements, teaching assistantships with full tuition reimbursements, career-related internships or fieldwork, Federal Work-Study, and unspecified assistantships available. Support available to part-time students. Financial award application deadline: 3/1; financial award applicants required to submit FAFSA. *Faculty research:* Aging with a chronic disability, pension policy and social security system, elderly minorities, health services research, living arrangements. *Unit head:* Dr. Jeffrey Burr, Chair of the Department. *Application contact:* Peggy Roldan Patel, Graduate Admissions Coordinator, 617-287-6400, Fax: 617-287-6236, E-mail: bos.gadm@dpc.umassp.edu.

**University of Michigan–Flint,** School of Nursing, Flint, MI 48502. Offers adult-gerontology acute care (DNP); adult-gerontology primary care (DNP); family nurse practitioner (DNP); nursing (MSN); psychiatric mental health (DNP); psychiatric mental health nurse practitioner (Certificate). *Accreditation:* AACN. *Program availability:* Part-time, evening/weekend, 100% online. *Faculty:* 31 full-time (29 women), 82 part-time/adjunct (75 women). *Students:* 166 full-time (148 women), 106 part-time (89 women); includes 68 minority (33 Black or African American, non-Hispanic/Latino; 2 American Indian or Alaska Native, non-Hispanic/Latino; 14 Asian, non-Hispanic/Latino; 8 Hispanic/Latino; 11 Two or more races, non-Hispanic/Latino), 2 international. Average age 37. 106 applicants, 84% accepted, 62 enrolled. In 2016, 34 doctorates, 5 other advanced degrees awarded. *Entrance requirements:* For master's, BSN from regionally-accredited college; minimum GPA of 3.2; current unencumbered RN license in the United States; three or more credits in college-level chemistry or statistics with minimum C grade; for doctorate, BSN or MSN (with APRN certification) from regionally-accredited college or university with minimum overall undergraduate GPA of 3.2; college-level statistics with minimum C grade; for Certificate, completion of nurse practitioner program with MS from regionally-accredited college or university with minimum overall GPA of 3.2; current unencumbered RN license in the United States; current unencumbered license as nurse practitioner; current certification as nurse practitioner in specialty other than discipline of study. Additional exam requirements/recommendations for international students: Required—TOEFL (minimum score 84 iBT), IELTS (minimum score 6.5). *Application deadline:* For fall admission, 7/1 for domestic students, 4/1 for international students; for winter admission, 11/1 for domestic students, 9/1 for international students; for spring admission, 3/15 for domestic students, 1/1 for international students. Applications are processed on a rolling basis. Application fee: $55. Electronic applications accepted. *Expenses:* Contact institution. *Financial support:* Federal Work-Study, scholarships/grants, and unspecified assistantships available. Support available to part-time students. Financial award application deadline: 3/1; financial award applicants required to submit FAFSA. *Faculty research:* Family system stress, self breast exam, family roads evaluation, causal model testing for psycho social development, basic needs, nurse preparation training. *Unit head:* Dr. Constance J. Creech, Director, 810-762-3420, Fax: 810-766-6851, E-mail: ccreech@umflint.edu. *Application contact:* Bradley T. Maki, Director of Graduate Admissions, 810-762-3171, Fax: 810-766-6789, E-mail: bmaki@umflint.edu.
Website: https://www.umflint.edu/nursing

**University of Missouri,** Office of Research and Graduate Studies, School of Social Work, Columbia, MO 65211. Offers gerontological social work (Certificate); military social work (Certificate); social work (MSW, PhD). *Accreditation:* CSWE. *Program availability:* Part-time. *Faculty:* 15 full-time (10 women). *Students:* 84 full-time (77 women), 138 part-time (127 women); includes 21 minority (11 Black or African American, non-Hispanic/Latino; 6 Hispanic/Latino; 4 Two or more races, non-Hispanic/Latino), 2 international. Average age 29. *Entrance requirements:* For master's, GRE General Test, minimum GPA of 3.0. Additional exam requirements/recommendations for international students: Required—TOEFL (minimum score 90 iBT), IELTS (minimum score 7). *Application deadline:* For fall admission, 1/15 priority date for domestic and international students. Applications are processed on a rolling basis. Application fee: $75 ($90 for international students). Electronic applications accepted. *Expenses:* Tuition, state resident: full-time $6347; part-time $352.60 per credit hour. Tuition, nonresident: full-time $17,379; part-time $965.50 per credit hour. *Required fees:* $1035. Tuition and fees vary according to course load, campus/location and program. *Financial support:* Fellowships with tuition reimbursements, research assistantships with tuition reimbursements, teaching assistantships with tuition reimbursements, institutionally sponsored loans, scholarships/grants, health care benefits, and unspecified assistantships available. Support available to part-time students.
Website: http://ssw.missouri.edu/

**University of Missouri–St. Louis,** College of Arts and Sciences, Program in Gerontology, St. Louis, MO 63121. Offers MS, Certificate. *Program availability:* Part-time, evening/weekend. *Faculty:* 2 full-time (both women), 2 part-time/adjunct (1 woman). *Entrance requirements:* For master's, 3 letters of recommendation, personal statement. Additional exam requirements/recommendations for international students: Required—TOEFL (minimum score 550 paper-based; 79 iBT), IELTS (minimum score 6.5). *Application deadline:* For fall admission, 7/1 priority date for domestic and international students; for spring admission, 12/1 priority date for domestic and international students. Applications are processed on a rolling basis. Application fee: $50 ($40 for international students). Electronic applications accepted. *Financial support:* Research assistantships with tuition reimbursements, teaching assistantships, career-related internships or fieldwork, and Federal Work-Study available. Financial award applicants required to submit FAFSA. *Faculty research:* Health care policy, social support and stress, retirement policy health behavior, ethnic differences in aging. *Unit head:* Thomas Meuser, Director, 314-516-5421, Fax: 314-516-5210, E-mail: meusert@umsl.edu. *Application contact:* Fax: 314-516-6996, E-mail: gradadm@umsl.edu.
Website: http://www.umsl.edu/gerontology/

**University of Nebraska at Omaha,** Graduate Studies, College of Public Affairs and Community Service, Department of Gerontology, Omaha, NE 68182. Offers gerontology (PhD, Certificate); social gerontology (MA). *Program availability:* Part-time, evening/weekend. *Faculty:* 6 full-time (4 women). *Students:* 3 full-time (all women), 39 part-time (36 women); includes 4 minority (2 Black or African American, non-Hispanic/Latino; 2 Hispanic/Latino). Average age 36. 17 applicants, 65% accepted, 9 enrolled. In 2016, 11 master's, 4 other advanced degrees awarded. *Degree requirements:* For master's, comprehensive exam, thesis. *Entrance requirements:* For master's, minimum GPA of 3.0, official transcripts, 2 letters of recommendation; for Certificate, minimum GPA of 3.0, official transcripts, 3 letters of recommendation. Additional exam requirements/recommendations for international students: Required—TOEFL (minimum score 550 paper-based), IELTS (minimum score 5.5), PTE (minimum score 44). *Application deadline:* For fall admission, 7/1 for domestic students; for spring admission, 12/1 for domestic students. Applications are processed on a rolling basis. Application fee: $45. Electronic applications accepted. *Financial support:* In 2016–17, 2 students received support, including 1 research assistantship, 1 teaching assistantship; fellowships, career-related internships or fieldwork, Federal Work-Study, institutionally sponsored loans, scholarships/grants, health care benefits, and tuition waivers (partial) also

available. Support available to part-time students. Financial award application deadline: 3/1; financial award applicants required to submit FAFSA. *Unit head:* Dr. Julie Masters, Chairperson, 402-554-2341, E-mail: graduate@unomaha.edu. *Application contact:* Dr. Chris Kelly, Graduate Program Chair, 402-554-2341, E-mail: graduate@unomaha.edu.

**University of Nebraska–Lincoln,** Graduate College, College of Education and Human Sciences, Department of Child, Youth and Family Studies, Lincoln, NE 68588. Offers child development/early childhood education (MS, PhD); child, youth and family studies (MS); family and consumer sciences education (MS, PhD); family financial planning (MS); family science (MS, PhD); gerontology (PhD); human sciences (PhD), including child, youth and family studies, gerontology, medical family therapy; marriage and family therapy (MS); medical family therapy (PhD); youth development (MS). *Accreditation:* AAMFT/COAMFTE (one or more programs are accredited). *Program availability:* Online learning. *Degree requirements:* For master's, thesis optional. *Entrance requirements:* For master's, GRE. Additional exam requirements/recommendations for international students: Required—TOEFL (minimum score 550 paper-based). Electronic applications accepted. *Faculty research:* Marriage and family therapy, child development/early childhood education, family financial management.

**The University of North Carolina at Charlotte,** College of Liberal Arts and Sciences, Interdisciplinary Liberal Arts and Sciences Programs, Charlotte, NC 28223-0001. Offers gender, sexuality, and women's studies (Graduate Certificate); gerontology (MA, Graduate Certificate); Latin American studies (MA); liberal studies (MA); organizational science (PhD); public policy (PhD). *Program availability:* Part-time, evening/weekend. *Faculty:* 1 (woman) part-time/adjunct. *Students:* 65 full-time (49 women), 61 part-time (50 women); includes 31 minority (11 Black or African American, non-Hispanic/Latino; 1 American Indian or Alaska Native, non-Hispanic/Latino; 2 Asian, non-Hispanic/Latino; 16 Hispanic/Latino; 1 Two or more races, non-Hispanic/Latino), 15 international. Average age 32. 128 applicants, 41% accepted, 40 enrolled. In 2016, 15 master's, 12 doctorates, 7 other advanced degrees awarded. *Degree requirements:* For master's, comprehensive exam (for some programs), thesis (for some programs), practicum, project; for doctorate, comprehensive exam, thesis/dissertation; for Graduate Certificate, practicum (for gerontology). *Entrance requirements:* For master's, GRE General Test or MAT, bachelor's degree from accredited college or university; official transcripts of all previous academic work attempted beyond high school; minimum overall GPA of 3.0 on applicant's previous work beyond high school; statement of purpose; recommendation letters; for doctorate, GRE or GMAT, statement of purpose discussing interest in program and objectives for pursuing degree, current resume or curriculum vitae, unofficial transcripts; for Graduate Certificate, bachelor's degree from accredited university and either be enrolled in and in good standing in a graduate degree program at UNC Charlotte or have a minimum undergraduate GPA of 3.0. Additional exam requirements/recommendations for international students: Required—TOEFL (minimum score 523 paper-based, 70 iBT) or IELTS (6.5). *Application deadline:* For fall admission, 2/15 for domestic and international students; for spring admission, 10/1 for domestic and international students; for summer admission, 4/1 for domestic and international students. Applications are processed on a rolling basis. Application fee: $75. Electronic applications accepted. *Expenses:* Tuition, state resident: full-time $4252. Tuition, nonresident: full-time $17,423. *Required fees:* $3026. Tuition and fees vary according to course load and program. *Financial support:* In 2016–17, 26 students received support, including 17 research assistantships (averaging $12,840 per year), 7 teaching assistantships (averaging $14,442 per year); career-related internships or fieldwork, institutionally sponsored loans, scholarships/grants, unspecified assistantships, and administrative assistantships also available. Support available to part-time students. Financial award application deadline: 3/1; financial award applicants required to submit FAFSA. *Unit head:* Dr. Nancy A. Gutierrez, Dean, 704-687-0081, E-mail: ngutierr@uncc.edu. *Application contact:* Kathy B. Giddings, Director of Graduate Admissions, 704-687-5503, Fax: 704-687-3279, E-mail: gradadm@uncc.edu. Website: http://clas.uncc.edu/academics

**The University of North Carolina at Greensboro,** Graduate School, School of Health and Human Sciences, Program in Gerontology, Greensboro, NC 27412-5001. Offers MS, Certificate, MS/MBA. Electronic applications accepted.

**The University of North Carolina Wilmington,** School of Health and Applied Human Sciences, Wilmington, NC 28403-3297. Offers applied gerontology (MS); gerontology (Postbaccalaureate Certificate). *Program availability:* Part-time, online learning. *Faculty:* 13 full-time (7 women), 2 part-time (both women); includes 1 minority (Black or African American, non-Hispanic/Latino). Average age 33. 6 applicants, 100% accepted, 6 enrolled. In 2016, 1 master's awarded. *Degree requirements:* For master's, thesis or alternative, practicum, final project. *Entrance requirements:* For master's, GRE, minimum undergraduate B average, 3 recommendations. Additional exam requirements/recommendations for international students: Required—TOEFL (minimum score 79 iBT), IELTS (minimum score 6.5). *Application deadline:* For fall admission, 6/15 for domestic students; for spring admission, 11/15 for domestic students; for summer admission, 3/15 for domestic students. Applications are processed on a rolling basis. Application fee: $60. Electronic applications accepted. *Expenses:* Contact institution. *Financial support:* Scholarships/grants and unspecified assistantships available. Financial award application deadline: 3/15; financial award applicants required to submit FAFSA. *Unit head:* Dr. Chris Lantz, Director, 910-962-2364, Fax: 910-962-7073, E-mail: lantzc@uncw.edu. *Application contact:* Dr. Anne Glass, Program Coordinator, 910-962-7816, E-mail: glassa@uncw.edu. Website: http://www.uncw.edu/shahs

**University of Northern Colorado,** Graduate School, College of Natural and Health Sciences, School of Human Sciences, Program in Gerontology, Greeley, CO 80639. Offers MA. *Program availability:* Part-time. *Degree requirements:* For master's, comprehensive exam. *Entrance requirements:* For master's, GRE General Test or MAT, 2 letters of recommendation. *Application deadline:* Applications are processed on a rolling basis. Application fee: $50 ($60 for international students). Electronic applications accepted. *Financial support:* Fellowships, research assistantships, teaching assistantships, and unspecified assistantships available. Financial award application deadline: 3/1; financial award applicants required to submit FAFSA. *Unit head:* Dr. Susan Collins, Program Coordinator, 970-351-2403. *Application contact:* Linda Sisson, Graduate Student Admission Coordinator, 970-351-1807, Fax: 970-351-2371, E-mail: linda.sisson@unco.edu. Website: http://www.unco.edu/nhs/gerontology/

**University of Northern Colorado,** Graduate School, College of Natural and Health Sciences, School of Nursing, Greeley, CO 80639. Offers adult gerontology acute care nurse practitioner (MS, DNP); family nurse practitioner (DNP); nursing practice (DNP). *Accreditation:* AACN. *Program availability:* Online learning. *Degree requirements:* For master's, comprehensive exam, thesis or alternative; for doctorate, comprehensive exam, thesis/dissertation. *Entrance requirements:* For master's and doctorate, GRE General Test, minimum GPA of 3.0 in last 60 hours, BS in nursing, 2 letters of recommendation. *Application deadline:* Applications are processed on a rolling basis. Application fee: $50 ($60 for international students). Electronic applications accepted. *Financial support:* Fellowships, research assistantships, teaching assistantships, and unspecified assistantships available. Financial award application deadline: 3/1; financial

award applicants required to submit FAFSA. *Unit head:* Dr. Kathleen Bradshaw LaSala, Director, 970-351-2293, Fax: 970-351-1707. *Application contact:* Linda Sisson, Graduate Student Admission Coordinator, 970-351-1807, Fax: 970-351-2371, E-mail: linda.sisson@unco.edu. Website: http://www.unco.edu/nhs/nursing/

**University of North Texas,** Robert B. Toulouse School of Graduate Studies, Denton, TX 76203-5459. Offers accounting (MS); applied anthropology (MA, MS); applied behavior analysis (Certificate); applied geography (MA); applied technology and performance improvement (M Ed, MS); art education (MA); art history (MA); art museum education (Certificate); arts leadership (Certificate); audiology (Au D); behavior analysis (MS); behavioral science (PhD); biochemistry and molecular biology (MS); biology (MA, MS); biomedical engineering (MS); business analysis (MS); chemistry (MS); clinical health psychology (PhD); communication studies (MA, MS); computer engineering (MS); computer science (MS); counseling (M Ed, MS), including clinical mental health counseling (MS), college and university counseling, elementary school counseling, secondary school counseling; creative writing (MA); criminal justice (MS); curriculum and instruction (M Ed); decision sciences (MBA); design (MA, MFA), including fashion design (MFA), innovation studies, interior design (MFA); early childhood studies (MS); economics (MS); educational leadership (M Ed, Ed D); educational psychology (MS, PhD), including family studies (MS), gifted and talented (MS), human development (MS), learning and cognition (MS), research, measurement and evaluation (MS); electrical engineering (MS); emergency management (MPA); engineering technology (MS); English (MA); English as a second language (MA); environmental science (MS); finance (MBA, MS); financial management (MPA); French (MA); health services management (MBA); higher education (M Ed, Ed D); history (MA, MS); hospitality management (MS); human resources management (MPA); information science (MS); information systems (PhD); information technologies (MBA); interdisciplinary studies (MA, MS); international studies (MA); international sustainable tourism (MS); jazz studies (MM); journalism (MA, MJ, Graduate Certificate), including interactive and virtual digital communication (Graduate Certificate), narrative journalism (Graduate Certificate), public relations (Graduate Certificate); kinesiology (MS); linguistics (MA); local government management (MPA); logistics (PhD); logistics and supply chain management (MBA); long-term care, senior housing, and aging services (MA); management (PhD); marketing (MBA); mathematics (MA, MS); mechanical and energy engineering (MS, PhD); music (MA), including ethnomusicology, music theory, musicology, performance; music composition (PhD); music education (MM Ed, PhD); nonprofit management (MPA); operations and supply chain management (MBA); performance (MM, DMA); philosophy (MA); political science (MA); professional and technical communication (MA); radio, television and film (MA, MFA); rehabilitation counseling (Certificate); sociology (MA); Spanish (MA); special education (M Ed); speech-language pathology (MA); strategic management (MBA); studio art (MFA); teaching (M Ed); MBA/MS. *Program availability:* Part-time, evening/weekend, online learning. Terminal master's awarded for partial completion of doctoral program. *Degree requirements:* For master's, variable foreign language requirement, comprehensive exam (for some programs), thesis (for some programs); for doctorate, variable foreign language requirement, comprehensive exam (for some programs), thesis/dissertation; for other advanced degree, variable foreign language requirement, comprehensive exam (for some programs). *Entrance requirements:* For master's and doctorate, GRE, GMAT. Additional exam requirements/recommendations for international students: Required—TOEFL (minimum score 550 paper-based; 79 iBT). Electronic applications accepted.

**University of Phoenix–Central Valley Campus,** College of Nursing, Fresno, CA 93720-1552. Offers education (MHA); gerontology (MHA); health administration (MHA); nursing (MSN); MSN/MBA.

**University of Phoenix–Charlotte Campus,** College of Nursing, Charlotte, NC 28273-3409. Offers education (MHA); gerontology (MHA); health administration (MHA); informatics (MHA, MSN); nursing (MSN); nursing/health care education (MSN). *Program availability:* Evening/weekend. *Degree requirements:* For master's, thesis (for some programs). *Entrance requirements:* For master's, minimum undergraduate GPA of 2.5, 3 years work experience. Additional exam requirements/recommendations for international students: Required—TOEFL (minimum score 550 paper-based; 79 iBT). Electronic applications accepted.

**University of Phoenix–Colorado Springs Downtown Campus,** College of Nursing, Colorado Springs, CO 80903. Offers education (MHA); gerontology (MHA); health administration (MHA); nursing (MSN); MSN/MBA. *Program availability:* Evening/weekend. *Degree requirements:* For master's, thesis (for some programs). *Entrance requirements:* For master's, minimum undergraduate GPA of 2.5, 3 years of work experience, RN license. Additional exam requirements/recommendations for international students: Required—TOEFL (minimum score 550 paper-based; 79 iBT). Electronic applications accepted.

**University of Phoenix–Hawaii Campus,** College of Nursing, Honolulu, HI 96813-3800. Offers education (MHA); family nurse practitioner (MSN); gerontology (MHA); health administration (MHA); nursing (MSN); nursing/health care education (MSN); MSN/MBA. *Program availability:* Evening/weekend. *Degree requirements:* For master's, thesis (for some programs). *Entrance requirements:* For master's, minimum undergraduate GPA of 2.5, 3 years of work experience, RN license. Additional exam requirements/recommendations for international students: Required—TOEFL (minimum score 550 paper-based; 79 iBT). Electronic applications accepted.

**University of Phoenix–Washington D.C. Campus,** College of Nursing, Washington, DC 20001. Offers education (MHA); gerontology (MHA); health administration (MHA, DHA); informatics (MHA, MSN); nursing (MSN, PhD); nursing/health care education (MSN); MSN/MBA; MSN/MHA.

**University of Puerto Rico, Medical Sciences Campus,** Graduate School of Public Health, Department of Human Development, Program in Gerontology, San Juan, PR 00936-5067. Offers MPH, Certificate. *Program availability:* Part-time, evening/weekend. *Entrance requirements:* For master's, GRE, previous course work in social sciences, biology, psychology, and algebra.

**University of Regina,** Faculty of Graduate Studies and Research, Faculty of Arts, Program in Gerontology, Regina, SK S4S 0A2, Canada. Offers M Sc, MA. *Program availability:* Part-time. *Students:* 1 (woman) full-time, 1 (woman) part-time. 3 applicants, 33% accepted. In 2016, 1 master's awarded. *Degree requirements:* For master's, thesis. *Entrance requirements:* Additional exam requirements/recommendations for international students: Required—TOEFL (minimum score 580 paper-based; 80 iBT), IELTS (minimum score 6.5), PTE (minimum score 59). *Application deadline:* For fall admission, 3/31 for domestic and international students. Application fee: $100. Electronic applications accepted. *Financial support:* In 2016–17, 3 teaching assistantships (averaging $2,501 per year) were awarded; fellowships and scholarships/grants also available. Financial award application deadline: 6/15. *Faculty research:* Health economics and policy; aging, society, and human service work; end-of-life issues for human service workers; physiology of aging; ethical decision-making in kinesiology and health care administration. *Unit head:* Abigail Wickson-Griffiths, Program Coordinator, 306-337-2132, E-mail: abigail.wickson-griffiths@uregina.ca.

## Gerontology

**University of Saint Joseph,** Program in Gerontology, West Hartford, CT 06117-2700. Offers Certificate. *Program availability:* Part-time, evening/weekend. *Entrance requirements:* For degree, 2 letters of recommendation, letter of intent. Electronic applications accepted. Application fee is waived when completed online. *Expenses:* Tuition: Full-time $14,580; part-time $729 per credit hour. *Required fees:* $920; $46 per credit hour. Tuition and fees vary according to course load, degree level and program.

**University of South Carolina,** The Graduate School, Program in Gerontology, Columbia, SC 29208. Offers Certificate. *Program availability:* Part-time. *Degree requirements:* For Certificate, practicum. Electronic applications accepted.

**University of Southern California,** Graduate School, Davis School of Gerontology, Los Angeles, CA 90089. Offers aging services management (MASM); biology of aging (PhD); gerontology (MA, MS, PhD, Graduate Certificate); long term care administration (MLTCA); DDS/MS; JD/MS; M PI/MS; MBA/MS; MHA/MS; MPA/MS; MS/MA; MS/MSW; Pharm D/MS. PhD in biology of aging offered jointly with Buck Institute for Research on Aging. *Program availability:* Part-time, online learning. Terminal master's awarded for partial completion of doctoral program. *Degree requirements:* For master's, thesis or alternative; for doctorate, comprehensive exam, thesis/dissertation. *Entrance requirements:* For master's, GRE (recommended); for doctorate, GRE. Additional exam requirements/recommendations for international students: Recommended—TOEFL. Electronic applications accepted. *Faculty research:* Sex steroids and Alzheimer's disease, memory, cognition and brain plasticity, environment and injury prevention, antioxidants, stress and aging, inflammation and aging, euthanasia, caloric restriction and chemotherapy, biodemographic of aging, health outcomes research, families and intergenerational relatives, care-giving of elderly, biology, psychology, sociology, policy.

**University of Southern California,** Graduate School, School of Social Work, Los Angeles, CA 90089. Offers community organization, planning and administration (MSW); families and children (MSW); health (MSW); mental health (MSW); military social work and veterans services (MSW); older adults (MSW); public child welfare (MSW); school settings (MSW); social work (MSW, PhD); systems of mental illness recovery (MSW); work and life (MSW); JD/MSW; M PI/MSW; MPA/MSW; MSW/MBA; MSW/MJCS; MSW/MS. *Accreditation:* CSWE (one or more programs are accredited). *Degree requirements:* For doctorate, comprehensive exam, thesis/dissertation, qualifying exam/publishable paper. *Entrance requirements:* For doctorate, GRE General Test. Additional exam requirements/recommendations for international students: Required—TOEFL (minimum score 600 paper-based; 100 iBT), ESL exam. Electronic applications accepted. *Faculty research:* Department of Defense Educational Activity, detection/treatment of depression among older adults, health/aging, psychosocial adaptation to extreme environments/man made disasters; mental health needs of older adults.

**University of Southern Indiana,** Graduate Studies, College of Nursing and Health Professions, Program in Nursing, Evansville, IN 47712-3590. Offers adult-gerontology acute care nurse practitioner (MSN, PMC); adult-gerontology clinical nurse specialist (MSN, PMC); adult-gerontology primary care nurse practitioner (MSN, PMC); advanced nursing practice (DNP); family nurse practitioner (MSN, PMC); nursing education (MSN, PMC); nursing management and leadership (MSN, PMC); organizational and systems leadership (DNP); psychiatric mental health nurse practitioner (MSN, PMC). *Accreditation:* AACN. *Program availability:* Part-time, online learning. *Faculty:* 11 full-time (10 women), 3 part-time/adjunct (all women). *Students:* 70 full-time (63 women), 368 part-time (328 women); includes 45 minority (24 Black or African American, non-Hispanic/Latino; 1 American Indian or Alaska Native, non-Hispanic/Latino; 5 Asian, non-Hispanic/Latino; 12 Hispanic/Latino; 3 Two or more races, non-Hispanic/Latino). Average age 36. In 2016, 107 master's, 20 doctorates, 8 other advanced degrees awarded. *Entrance requirements:* For master's, BSN from nationally-accredited school; minimum cumulative GPA of 3.0; satisfactory completion of a course in undergraduate statistics (minimum grade C); one year of full-time experience or 2,000 hours of clinical practice as an RN (recommended); unencumbered U.S. RN license; for doctorate, minimum GPA of 3.0, completion of graduate research course with minimum B grade, unencumbered RN license, resume/curriculum vitae, three professional references, 1-2 page narrative of practice experience and professional goals, Capstone Project Information form. Additional exam requirements/recommendations for international students: Required—TOEFL (minimum score 550 paper-based; 79 iBT), IELTS (minimum score 6). *Application deadline:* For fall admission, 2/1 for domestic students, 1/1 priority date for international students. Applications are processed on a rolling basis. Application fee: $40. Electronic applications accepted. *Expenses:* Contact institution. *Financial support:* Federal Work-Study, scholarships/grants, tuition waivers (full and partial), and unspecified assistantships available. Financial award application deadline: 3/1; financial award applicants required to submit FAFSA. *Unit head:* Dr. Mellisa A. Hall, Chair of the Master of Science in Nursing Program, 812-465-1168, E-mail: mrowser@usi.edu. *Application contact:* Dr. Mayola Rowser, Director, Graduate Studies, 812-465-7015, Fax: 812-464-1956, E-mail: mrowser@usi.edu.
Website: https://www.usi.edu/health/nursing

**University of South Florida,** College of Behavioral and Community Sciences, School of Aging Studies, Tampa, FL 33620-9951. Offers aging studies (PhD); gerontology (MA). *Program availability:* Part-time, evening/weekend. *Faculty:* 9 full-time (4 women). *Students:* 27 full-time (21 women), 5 part-time (all women); includes 13 minority (4 Black or African American, non-Hispanic/Latino; 1 Asian, non-Hispanic/Latino; 6 Hispanic/Latino; 2 Two or more races, non-Hispanic/Latino), 1 international. Average age 29. 35 applicants, 31% accepted, 7 enrolled. In 2016, 5 master's, 4 doctorates awarded. *Degree requirements:* For master's, comprehensive exam, thesis optional; for doctorate, comprehensive exam, thesis/dissertation. *Entrance requirements:* For master's, GRE General Test, minimum GPA of 3.0; for doctorate, GRE General Test, minimum GPA of 3.25, three letters of recommendation, summary of career goals, single-authored writing sample. Additional exam requirements/recommendations for international students: Required—TOEFL (minimum score 79 iBT). *Application deadline:* For fall admission, 12/11 priority date for domestic and international students; for spring admission, 10/15 for domestic students, 9/15 for international students; for summer admission, 2/15 for domestic students, 1/15 for international students. Application fee: $30. Electronic applications accepted. *Expenses:* Tuition, state resident: full-time $7766; part-time $431.43 per credit hour. Tuition, nonresident: full-time $15,789; part-time $877.17 per credit hour. *Required fees:* $37 per term. *Financial support:* In 2016–17, 9 students received support, including 2 research assistantships with tuition reimbursements available (averaging $15,690 per year), 13 teaching assistantships with tuition reimbursements available (averaging $13,503 per year). Financial award application deadline: 2/3. *Faculty research:* Aging and mental health, public policy and long-term care, minority aging, care-giving, guardianship, cognitive aging, Alzheimer's disease. *Total annual research expenditures:* $520,684. *Unit head:* Dr. Cathy L. McEvoy, Director and Professor, 813-974-1940, Fax: 813-974-9754, E-mail: cmcevoy@usf.edu. *Application contact:* Brent Small, Professor, 813-974-9746, Fax: 813-974-9754, E-mail: bsmall@usf.edu.
Website: http://agingstudies.cbcs.usf.edu/aprog/

**University of South Florida,** Innovative Education, Tampa, FL 33620-9951. Offers adult, career and higher education (Graduate Certificate), including college teaching, leadership in developing human resources, leadership in higher education; Africana studies (Graduate Certificate), including diasporas and health disparities, genocide and human rights; aging studies (Graduate Certificate), including gerontology; art research (Graduate Certificate), including museum studies; business foundations (Graduate Certificate); chemical and biomedical engineering (Graduate Certificate), including materials science and engineering, water, health and sustainability; child and family studies (Graduate Certificate), including positive behavior support; civil and industrial engineering (Graduate Certificate), including transportation systems analysis; community and family health (Graduate Certificate), including maternal and child health, social marketing and public health, violence and injury: prevention and intervention, women's health; criminology (Graduate Certificate), including criminal justice administration; educational measurement and research (Graduate Certificate), including evaluation; English (Graduate Certificate), including comparative literary studies, creative writing, professional and technical communication; entrepreneurship (Graduate Certificate); environmental health (Graduate Certificate), including safety management; epidemiology and biostatistics (Graduate Certificate), including applied biostatistics, biostatistics, concepts and tools of epidemiology, epidemiology, epidemiology of infectious diseases; geography, environment and planning (Graduate Certificate), including community development, environmental policy and management, geographical information systems; geology (Graduate Certificate), including hydrogeology; global health (Graduate Certificate), including disaster management, global health and Latin American and Caribbean studies, global health practice, humanitarian assistance, infection control; government and international affairs (Graduate Certificate), including Cuban studies, globalization studies; health policy and management (Graduate Certificate), including health management and leadership, public health policy and programs; hearing specialist: early intervention (Graduate Certificate); industrial and management systems engineering (Graduate Certificate), including systems engineering, technology management; information studies (Graduate Certificate), including school library media specialist; information systems/decision sciences (Graduate Certificate), including analytics and business intelligence; instructional technology (Graduate Certificate), including distance education, Florida digital/virtual educator, instructional design, multimedia design, Web design; internal medicine, bioethics and medical humanities (Graduate Certificate), including biomedical ethics; Latin American and Caribbean studies (Graduate Certificate); mass communications (Graduate Certificate), including multimedia journalism; mathematics and statistics (Graduate Certificate), including mathematics; medicine (Graduate Certificate), including aging and neuroscience, bioinformatics, biotechnology, brain fitness and memory management, clinical investigation, health informatics, health sciences, integrative weight management, intellectual property, medicine and gender, metabolic and nutritional medicine, metabolic cardiology, pharmacy sciences; national and competitive intelligence (Graduate Certificate); psychological and social foundations (Graduate Certificate), including career counseling, college teaching, diversity in education, mental health counseling, school counseling; public affairs (Graduate Certificate), including nonprofit management, public management, research administration; public health (Graduate Certificate), including environmental health, health equity, public health generalist, translational research in adolescent behavioral health; public health practices (Graduate Certificate), including planning for healthy communities; rehabilitation and mental health counseling (Graduate Certificate), including integrative mental health care, marriage and family therapy, rehabilitation technology; secondary education (Graduate Certificate), including ESOL, foreign language education: culture and content, foreign language education: professional; social work (Graduate Certificate), including geriatric social work/clinical gerontology; special education (Graduate Certificate), including autism spectrum disorder, disabilities education: severe/profound; world languages (Graduate Certificate), including teaching English as a second language (TESL) or foreign language. *Expenses:* Tuition, state resident: full-time $7766; part-time $431.43 per credit hour. Tuition, nonresident: full-time $15,789; part-time $877.17 per credit hour. *Required fees:* $37 per term. *Unit head:* Kathy Barnes, Interdisciplinary Programs Coordinator, 813-974-8031, Fax: 813-974-7061, E-mail: barnesk@usf.edu. *Application contact:* Karen Tylinski, Metro Initiatives, 813-974-9943, Fax: 813-974-7061, E-mail: ktylinsk@usf.edu.
Website: http://www.usf.edu/innovative-education/

**University of South Florida,** Morsani College of Medicine and College of Graduate Studies, Graduate Programs in Medical Sciences, Tampa, FL 33620-9951. Offers advanced athletic training (MS); athletic training (MS); bioinformatics and computational biology (MSBCB); biotechnology (MSB); health informatics (MSHI); medical sciences (MSMS, PhD), including aging and neuroscience (MSMS), allergy, immunology and infectious disease (PhD), anatomy, biochemistry and molecular biology, clinical and translational research, health science (MSMS), interdisciplinary medical sciences (MSMS), medical microbiology and immunology (MSMS), metabolic and nutritional medicine (MSMS), microbiology and immunology (PhD), molecular medicine, molecular pharmacology and physiology (PhD), neuroscience (PhD), pathology and cell biology (PhD), women's health (MSMS). *Students:* 454 full-time (239 women), 273 part-time (173 women); includes 347 minority (110 Black or African American, non-Hispanic/Latino; 1 American Indian or Alaska Native, non-Hispanic/Latino; 99 Asian, non-Hispanic/Latino; 113 Hispanic/Latino; 1 Native Hawaiian or other Pacific Islander, non-Hispanic/Latino; 23 Two or more races, non-Hispanic/Latino), 61 international. Average age 27. 7,242 applicants, 8% accepted, 395 enrolled. In 2016, 374 master's, 13 doctorates awarded. Terminal master's awarded for partial completion of doctoral program. *Degree requirements:* For master's, comprehensive exam, thesis; for doctorate, comprehensive exam, thesis/dissertation. *Entrance requirements:* For master's, GRE General Test or GMAT, bachelor's degree or equivalent from regionally-accredited university with minimum GPA of 3.0 in upper-division sciences coursework; prerequisites in general biology, general chemistry, general physics, organic chemistry, quantitative analysis, and integral and differential calculus; for doctorate, GRE General Test, bachelor's degree from regionally-accredited university with minimum GPA of 3.0 in upper-division sciences coursework; 3 letters of recommendation; personal interview; 1-2 page personal statement; prerequisites in biology, chemistry, physics, organic chemistry, quantitative analysis, and integral/differential calculus. Additional exam requirements/recommendations for international students: Required—TOEFL (minimum score 550 paper-based; 79 iBT) or IELTS (minimum score 6.5). *Application deadline:* For fall admission, 2/1 for domestic and international students. Application fee: $30. Electronic applications accepted. *Expenses:* Contact institution. *Financial support:* In 2016–17, 116 students received support. *Faculty research:* Anatomy, biochemistry, cancer biology, cardiovascular disease, cell biology, immunology, microbiology, molecular biology, neuroscience, pharmacology, physiology. *Total annual research expenditures:* $42.3 million. *Unit head:* Dr. Michael Barber, Professor/Associate Dean for Graduate and Postdoctoral Affairs, 813-974-9908, Fax: 813-974-4317, E-mail: mbarber@health.usf.edu. *Application contact:* Dr. Eric Bennett, Graduate Director, PhD Program in Medical Sciences, 813-974-1545, Fax: 813-974-4317, E-mail: esbennet@health.usf.edu.
Website: http://health.usf.edu/nocms/medicine/graduatestudies/

**The University of Tennessee,** Graduate School, College of Education, Health and Human Sciences, Program in Public Health, Knoxville, TN 37996. Offers community health education (MPH); gerontology (MPH); health planning/administration (MPH); MS/MPH. *Accreditation:* CEPH. *Degree requirements:* For master's, thesis optional.

*Entrance requirements:* For master's, minimum GPA of 2.7. Additional exam requirements/recommendations for international students: Required—TOEFL. Electronic applications accepted.

**The University of Toledo,** College of Graduate Studies, College of Medicine and Life Sciences, Department of Public Health and Preventative Medicine, Toledo, OH 43606-3390. Offers biostatistics and epidemiology (Certificate); contemporary gerontological practice (Certificate); environmental and occupational health and safety (MPH); epidemiology (Certificate); global public health (Certificate); health promotion and education (MPH); industrial hygiene (MSOH); medical and health science teaching and learning (Certificate); occupational health (Certificate); public health administration (MPH); public health and emergency response (Certificate); public health epidemiology (MPH); public health nutrition (MPH); MD/MPH. *Program availability:* Part-time, evening/weekend. *Degree requirements:* For master's, thesis or alternative. *Entrance requirements:* For master's, GRE, minimum undergraduate GPA of 3.0, three letters of recommendation, statement of purpose, transcripts from all prior institutions attended, resume; for Certificate, minimum undergraduate GPA of 3.0, three letters of recommendation, statement of purpose, transcripts from all prior institutions attended, resume. Additional exam requirements/recommendations for international students: Required—TOEFL (minimum score 550 paper-based; 80 iBT), IELTS (minimum score 6.5). Electronic applications accepted.

**University of Utah,** Graduate School, College of Nursing, Gerontology Interdisciplinary Program, Salt Lake City, UT 84112. Offers MS, Certificate. *Program availability:* Part-time, evening/weekend, online only. *Faculty:* 10 full-time (9 women). *Students:* 6 full-time (all women), 2 part-time (1 woman). Average age 39. 11 applicants, 91% accepted, 7 enrolled. In 2016, 6 master's awarded. *Degree requirements:* For master's, thesis or project. *Entrance requirements:* For master's, GRE General Test (if cumulative GPA is less than 3.2), minimum undergraduate GPA of 3.0. Additional exam requirements/recommendations for international students: Required—TOEFL (minimum score 500 paper-based; 85 iBT). *Application deadline:* For fall admission, 1/15 for domestic and international students. Application fee: $55 ($65 for international students). Electronic applications accepted. *Expenses:* $7,635 resident tuition and fees; $18,904 non-resident tuition and fees. *Financial support:* In 2016–17, 8 students received support, including 5 fellowships with partial tuition reimbursements available (averaging $6,339 per year), 2 teaching assistantships with partial tuition reimbursements available (averaging $10,308 per year); scholarships/grants and health care benefits also available. Support available to part-time students. Financial award application deadline: 1/15; financial award applicants required to submit FAFSA. *Faculty research:* Spousal bereavement, family caregiving, health promotion and self-care, geriatric care management, technology and aging. *Unit head:* Kara Dassel, Director, 801-585-7438, Fax: 801-587-7697, E-mail: kara.dassel@nurs.utah.edu. *Application contact:* Arminka Zeljkovic, Program Manager, 801-581-8198, Fax: 801-585-9705, E-mail: arminka.zeljkovic@nurs.utah.edu. Website: http://www.nursing.utah.edu/gerontology/

**University of Wisconsin–Milwaukee,** Graduate School, Helen Bader School of Social Welfare, Department of Social Work, Milwaukee, WI 53201-0413. Offers applied gerontology (Certificate); marriage and family therapy (Certificate); non-profit management (Certificate); social welfare (PhD); social work (MSW, PhD). *Accreditation:* CSWE. *Program availability:* Part-time. *Students:* 232 full-time (194 women), 84 part-time (69 women); includes 79 minority (43 Black or African American, non-Hispanic/Latino; 1 American Indian or Alaska Native, non-Hispanic/Latino; 6 Asian, non-Hispanic/Latino; 2 Hispanic/Latino; 27 Two or more races, non-Hispanic/Latino), 2 international. Average age 30. 383 applicants, 57% accepted, 129 enrolled. In 2016, 126 master's, 2 doctorates, 6 other advanced degrees awarded. *Degree requirements:* For master's, thesis or alternative. *Entrance requirements:* For doctorate, GRE, bachelor's degree. Additional exam requirements/recommendations for international students: Required—TOEFL (minimum score 550 paper-based; 79 iBT), IELTS (minimum score 6.5). *Application deadline:* For fall admission, 1/1 priority date for domestic students; for spring admission, 9/1 for domestic students. Applications are processed on a rolling basis. Application fee: $56 ($96 for international students). Electronic applications accepted. *Financial support:* Fellowships, research assistantships, teaching assistantships, career-related internships or fieldwork, health care benefits, unspecified assistantships, and project assistantships available. Support available to part-time students. Financial award application deadline: 4/15; financial award applicants required to submit FAFSA. *Application contact:* Deb Padgett, Associate Professor, Social Work, 414-229-6452, E-mail: dpadgett@uwm.edu. Website: http://uwm.edu/socialwelfare/academics/

**Virginia Commonwealth University,** Graduate School, School of Allied Health Professions, Department of Gerontology, Richmond, VA 23284-9005. Offers gerontology (MS). *Program availability:* Part-time. *Entrance requirements:* For master's, GRE General Test or MAT. Additional exam requirements/recommendations for international students: Required—TOEFL (minimum score 600 paper-based; 100 iBT); Recommended—IELTS (minimum score 6.5). Application fee: $50. Electronic applications accepted. *Financial support:* Career-related internships or fieldwork available. Financial award applicants required to submit FAFSA. *Faculty research:* Alzheimer's disease, age-related alcoholism and suicide, pain perception, curriculum development and evaluation in gerontology/geriatrics. *Unit head:* Dr. E. Ayn Welleford, Chair, 804-828-1565, E-mail: ewellefo@vcu.edu. *Application contact:* Monica L. White, Director of Student Services, 804-828-3273, Fax: 804-828-8656, E-mail: mlwhite1@vcu.edu.
Website: http://www.sahp.vcu.edu/gerontology/

**Virginia Commonwealth University,** Graduate School, School of Allied Health Professions, Doctoral Program in Health Related Sciences, Richmond, VA 23284-9005. Offers clinical laboratory sciences (PhD); gerontology (PhD); health administration (PhD); nurse anesthesia (PhD); occupational therapy (PhD); physical therapy (PhD); radiation sciences (PhD); rehabilitation leadership (PhD). *Entrance requirements:* For doctorate, GRE General Test or MAT, minimum GPA of 3.3 in master's degree. Additional exam requirements/recommendations for international students: Required—TOEFL (minimum score 600 paper-based; 100 iBT); Recommended—IELTS (minimum score 6.5). *Application deadline:* For fall admission, 3/15 for domestic students. Application fee: $50. Electronic applications accepted. *Unit head:* Dr. Paula K. Kupstas, Director, Health Related Sciences Program, 804-828-1914, E-mail: pkupstas@vcu.edu. *Application contact:* Monica L. White, Director of Student Services, 804-828-3273, Fax: 804-828-8656, E-mail: mlwhite1@vcu.edu.
Website: http://www.pubapps.vcu.edu/BULLETINS/prog_search/?did-20005

**Walden University,** Graduate Programs, School of Social Work and Human Services, Minneapolis, MN 55401. Offers addictions and social work (DSW); advanced clinical practice (MSW); clinical expertise (DSW); criminal justice (DSW); disaster, crisis, and intervention (DSW); family studies and interventions (DSW); human and social services (PhD), including advanced research, community and social services, community intervention and leadership, conflict management, criminal justice, disaster crisis and intervention, family studies and intervention, gerontology, global social services, higher education, human services and nonprofit administration, mental health facilitation; medical social work (DSW); military social work (MSW); policy practice (DSW); social work (PhD), including addictions and social work, clinical expertise, criminal justice,

disaster, crisis and intervention, family studies and interventions, medical social work, policy practice, social work administration; social work administration (DSW); social work in healthcare (MSW); social work with children and families (MSW). *Accreditation:* CSWE. *Program availability:* Part-time, evening/weekend, online only, 100% online. *Degree requirements:* For master's, residency (for some programs); for doctorate, thesis/dissertation, residency. *Entrance requirements:* For master's, bachelor's degree or higher; minimum GPA of 2.5; official transcripts; goal statement (for some programs); access to computer and Internet; for doctorate, master's degree or higher; three years of related professional or academic experience (preferred); minimum GPA of 3.0; goal statement and current resume (for select programs); official transcripts; access to computer and Internet. Additional exam requirements/recommendations for international students: Required—TOEFL (minimum score 550 paper-based, 79 iBT), IELTS (minimum score 6.5), Michigan English Language Assessment Battery (minimum score 82), or PTE (minimum score 53). Electronic applications accepted.

**Washington University in St. Louis,** Brown School, St. Louis, MO 63110. Offers American Indian/Alaska native (MSW); children, youth and families (MSW); epidemiology/biostatistics (MPH); health (MSW); health policy analysis (MPH); individualized (MSW), including health; mental health (MSW); older adults and aging societies (MSW); public health sciences (PhD); social and economic development (MSW); social work (PhD); violence and injury prevention (MSW); JD/MSW; M Arch/MSW; MPH/MBA; MSW/M Div; MSW/M Ed; MSW/MAPS; MSW/MBA; MSW/MPH; MUD/MSW. MSW/M Div and MSW/MAPS offered in partnership with Eden Theological Seminary. *Accreditation:* CSWE (one or more programs are accredited). *Faculty:* 54 full-time (31 women), 87 part-time/adjunct (61 women). *Students:* 281 full-time (235 women); includes 105 minority (37 Black or African American, non-Hispanic/Latino; 14 American Indian or Alaska Native, non-Hispanic/Latino; 20 Asian, non-Hispanic/Latino; 15 Hispanic/Latino; 1 Native Hawaiian or other Pacific Islander, non-Hispanic/Latino; 18 Two or more races, non-Hispanic/Latino), 47 international. Average age 25. 1,003 applicants, 281 enrolled. In 2016, 239 master's, 5 doctorates awarded. *Degree requirements:* For master's, 60 credit hours (for MSW); 52 credit hours (for MPH); practicum; for doctorate, comprehensive exam, thesis/dissertation. *Entrance requirements:* For master's, GRE (preferred), GMAT, LSAT, MCAT, PCAT, or United States Medical Licensing Exam (for MPH); for doctorate, GRE. Additional exam requirements/recommendations for international students: Required—TOEFL (minimum score 100 iBT) or IELTS. *Application deadline:* For fall admission, 12/15 priority date for domestic and international students; for winter admission, 3/1 priority date for domestic and international students. Applications are processed on a rolling basis. Electronic applications accepted. *Expenses:* Contact institution. *Financial support:* In 2016–17, 267 students received support, including 35 fellowships, 48 research assistantships; Federal Work-Study, scholarships/grants, and unspecified assistantships also available. Support available to part-time students. Financial award applicants required to submit FAFSA. *Faculty research:* Mental health, social policy, health policy, epidemiology, social and economic development. *Unit head:* Jamie L. Adkisson, Director of Admissions and Recruitment, 314-935-3524, Fax: 314-935-4859, E-mail: jadkisson@wustl.edu. *Application contact:* Office of Admissions and Recruitment, 314-935-6676, Fax: 314-935-4859, E-mail: brownadmissions@wustl.edu.
Website: http://brownschool.wustl.edu

**Washington University in St. Louis,** The Graduate School, Department of Psychological and Brain Sciences, St. Louis, MO 63130-4899. Offers aging and development (PhD). Terminal master's awarded for partial completion of doctoral program. *Degree requirements:* For doctorate, thesis/dissertation. *Entrance requirements:* For doctorate, GRE General Test. Additional exam requirements/recommendations for international students: Required—TOEFL. Electronic applications accepted. *Faculty research:* Behavior/brain/cognition; clinical; aging/development; social/personality.

**Wayne State University,** School of Social Work, Detroit, MI 48202. Offers alcohol and drug abuse studies (Certificate); clinical social work theory and practice (Certificate); disabilities (Certificate); gerontology (Certificate); social welfare research and evaluation (Certificate); social work (MSW, PhD); social work and anthropology (PhD); social work and gerontology (PhD); social work and infant mental health (MSW, PhD); social work practice with families and couples (Certificate). Application deadlines: April 1 for MSW, December 19 for PhD. *Accreditation:* CSWE (one or more programs are accredited). *Program availability:* Part-time, evening/weekend. *Faculty:* 24. *Students:* 515 full-time (442 women), 150 part-time (128 women); includes 251 minority (179 Black or African American, non-Hispanic/Latino; 4 American Indian or Alaska Native, non-Hispanic/Latino; 11 Asian, non-Hispanic/Latino; 29 Hispanic/Latino; 1 Native Hawaiian or other Pacific Islander, non-Hispanic/Latino; 27 Two or more races, non-Hispanic/Latino), 17 international. Average age 31. 809 applicants, 36% accepted, 200 enrolled. In 2016, 356 master's, 2 doctorates, 20 other advanced degrees awarded. *Degree requirements:* For master's, filed work; for doctorate, variable foreign language requirement, comprehensive exam, thesis/dissertation. *Entrance requirements:* For master's, personal interest statement, resume, 3 references; for doctorate, GRE (minimum combined score of 1000 on Verbal and Quantitative components), minimum undergraduate GPA of 3.5, MSW from CSWE-accredited institution (or working towards one), resume, three letters of reference, personal statement, summary of relevant research and professional experience, writing sample, interview; for Certificate, MSW or actively enrolled in advanced portion of MSW program. Additional exam requirements/recommendations for international students: Required—TOEFL (minimum score 550 paper-based; 79 iBT), TWE (minimum score 5.5), Michigan English Language Assessment Battery (minimum score 85); Recommended—IELTS (minimum score 6.5). *Application deadline:* Applications are processed on a rolling basis. Application fee: $50. Electronic applications accepted. *Expenses:* $16,503 per year resident tuition and fees, $33,697 per year non-resident tuition and fees. *Financial support:* In 2016–17, 119 students received support, including 5 fellowships with tuition reimbursements available (averaging $18,800 per year), 2 research assistantships with tuition reimbursements available (averaging $21,593 per year), 2 teaching assistantships with tuition reimbursements available (averaging $17,994 per year); scholarships/grants and unspecified assistantships also available. Financial award applicants required to submit FAFSA. *Faculty research:* Aging, child welfare, health and behavioral health, interpersonal violence, community development, policy and program development. *Unit head:* Dr. Jerrold Brandell, Interim Dean, 313-577-4409, E-mail: aa4537@wayne.edu. *Application contact:* Shantalea Johns, Interim Director of Admissions, 313-577-4409, E-mail: shantalea@wayne.edu.
Website: http://socialwork.wayne.edu/

**Webster University,** College of Arts and Sciences, Department of Psychology, St. Louis, MO 63119-3194. Offers counseling psychology (MS); gerontology (MS). *Program availability:* Part-time. *Entrance requirements:* Additional exam requirements/recommendations for international students: Required—TOEFL. *Application deadline:* Applications are processed on a rolling basis. Application fee: $35 ($50 for international students). *Expenses:* Tuition: Full-time $21,900; part-time $730 per credit hour. Tuition and fees vary according to campus/location and program. *Financial support:* Federal Work-Study available. Support available to part-time students. Financial award application deadline: 4/1; financial award applicants required to submit FAFSA.

## Gerontology

*Application contact:* Debi Aholt, Department Manager, 314-246-6970, Fax: 314-246-6094, E-mail: aholtda@webster.edu.

**Webster University,** George Herbert Walker School of Business and Technology, Department of Business, St. Louis, MO 63119-3194. Offers business and organizational security management (MBA); decision support systems (MBA); environmental management (MBA); finance (MBA, MS); forensic accounting (MS); gerontology (MBA); human resources development (MBA); human resources management (MBA); information technology management (MBA); international business (MA, MBA); international relations (MBA); management and leadership (MBA); marketing (MBA); media communications (MBA); procurement and acquisitions management (MBA); Web services (MBA). *Accreditation:* ACBSP. *Program availability:* Part-time, evening/weekend, online learning. *Degree requirements:* For master's, comprehensive exam (for some programs), thesis (for some programs). *Entrance requirements:* Additional exam requirements/recommendations for international students: Required—TOEFL. *Application deadline:* Applications are processed on a rolling basis. Application fee: $35 ($50 for international students). *Expenses: Tuition:* Full-time $21,900; part-time $730 per credit hour. Tuition and fees vary according to campus/location and program. *Financial support:* Federal Work-Study available. Support available to part-time students. Financial award application deadline: 4/1; financial award applicants required to submit FAFSA. *Unit head:* David Porras, Chair, 314-246-8621, E-mail: porrasd@webster.edu. *Application contact:* Sarah Nandor, Director, Graduate and Transfer Admissions, 314-968-7109, E-mail: gadmit@webster.edu.

**West Chester University of Pennsylvania,** College of Health Sciences, Department of Health, West Chester, PA 19383. Offers emergency preparedness (Certificate); gerontology (Certificate); health care management (Certificate); integrative health (Certificate); public health (MPH); school health (M Ed). *Accreditation:* CEPH. *Program availability:* Part-time, evening/weekend. *Faculty:* 13 full-time (8 women), 5 part-time/adjunct (3 women). *Students:* 89 full-time (70 women), 94 part-time (62 women); includes 76 minority (65 Black or African American, non-Hispanic/Latino; 6 Asian, non-Hispanic/Latino; 5 Hispanic/Latino), 17 international. Average age 30. 119 applicants, 89% accepted, 63 enrolled. In 2016, 64 master's, 2 other advanced degrees awarded. *Degree requirements:* For master's, research report (for M Ed); major project and practicum (for MPH); for Certificate, 18 credits (for gerontology). *Entrance requirements:* For master's, undergraduate introduction to statistics course; for Certificate, goal statement, two letters of recommendation, resume, and official transcripts from all previously completed coursework (for gerontology). Additional exam requirements/recommendations for international students: Required—TOEFL or IELTS. *Application deadline:* For fall admission, 5/15 for international students; for spring admission, 10/15 for international students. Applications are processed on a rolling basis. Application fee: $50. Electronic applications accepted. *Expenses:* Tuition, state resident: full-time $8694; part-time $483 per credit. Tuition, nonresident: full-time $13,050; part-time $725 per credit. *Required fees:* $2399; $119.05 per credit. Tuition and fees vary according to campus/location and program. *Financial support:* Scholarships/grants and unspecified assistantships available. Financial award application deadline: 2/15; financial award applicants required to submit FAFSA. *Faculty research:* Healthy school communities, community health issues and evidence-based programs, environment and health, nutrition and health, integrative health. *Unit head:* Dr. Bethann Cinelli, Chair, 610-436-2267, E-mail: bcinelli@wcupa.edu. *Application contact:* Dr. Lynn Carson, Graduate Coordinator, 610-436-2138, E-mail: lcarson@wcupa.edu.
Website: http://www.wcupa.edu/HealthSciences/health/

**Wichita State University,** Graduate School, College of Health Professions, Department of Public Health Sciences, Wichita, KS 67260. Offers aging studies (MA). *Program availability:* Part-time, 100% online, blended/hybrid learning. *Unit head:* Dr. Nicole Rogers, Chairperson, 316-978-3060, Fax: 316-978-3072, E-mail: nicole.rogers@wichita.edu. *Application contact:* Jordan Oleson, Admissions Coordinator, 316-978-3095, Fax: 316-978-3253, E-mail: jordan.oleson@wichita.edu.
Website: http://www.wichita.edu/phs

**Youngstown State University,** Graduate School, College of Liberal Arts and Social Sciences, Program in Gerontology, Youngstown, OH 44555-0001. Offers MA. *Program availability:* Part-time, evening/weekend, online learning. *Degree requirements:* For master's, thesis optional. *Entrance requirements:* For master's, GRE, minimum GPA of 3.0, three letters of recommendation, letter of intent, resume or curriculum vitae, social statistics course at undergraduate or graduate level, minimum of 9 credit hours of aging-related coursework at undergraduate or graduate level.

# FASHION INSTITUTE OF TECHNOLOGY
## College of Art and Design

## Programs of Study

The Fashion Institute of Technology (FIT), a State University of New York (SUNY) college of art and design, business, and technology, is home to a mix of innovative achievers, creative thinkers, and industry pioneers. FIT fosters interdisciplinary initiatives, advances research, and provides access to an international network of professionals. With a reputation for excellence, FIT offers its diverse student body access to world-class faculty, dynamic and relevant curricula, and a superior education at an affordable cost. It offers seven programs of graduate study. The programs in Art Market Studies; Exhibition and Experience Design; and Fashion and Textile Studies: History, Theory, Museum Practice lead to the Master of Arts (M.A.) degree. The Illustration and Fashion Design programs lead to the Master of Fine Arts (M.F.A.) degree. The Master of Professional Studies (M.P.S.) degree programs are Cosmetics and Fragrance Marketing and Management and Global Fashion Management.

Fashion Design is a two-year, full-time, 60-credit M.F.A. program that invites students to embark on a highly mentored personal journey into their own ideas and philosophies around fashion and design. They are encouraged and supported to innovate in design, fit, cut, construction, silhouette, and materiality, all with intention and meaning. Students are required to reflect with critical distance on their own work as well as contribute as an active participant in the critique space in a collaborative studio environment to gain new perspectives on their own ideas, concepts, philosophies, and ideologies, and to give feedback and insight to others on theirs.

## Research Facilities

The School of Graduate Studies is primarily located in the campus's Shirley Goodman Resource Center, which also houses the Gladys Marcus Library and The Museum at FIT. School of Graduate Studies facilities include conference rooms; a fully equipped conservation laboratory; a multipurpose laboratory for conservation projects and the dressing of mannequins; storage facilities for costume and textile materials; a graduate student lounge with computer and printer access; a graduate student library reading room with computers, reference materials, and copies of past classes' qualifying and thesis papers; specialized wireless classrooms; traditional and digital illustration studios; and classrooms equipped with model stands, easels, and drafting tables.

The Gladys Marcus Library houses more than 300,000 volumes of print, nonprint, and digital resources. Specialized holdings include industry reference materials, manufacturers' catalogs, original fashion sketches and scrapbooks, photographs, portfolios of plates, and sample books. The FIT Digital Library provides access to over 90 searchable online databases.

The Museum at FIT houses one of the world's most important collections of clothing and textiles and is the only museum in New York City dedicated to the art of fashion. The permanent collection encompasses more than 50,000 garments and accessories dating from the eighteenth century to the present, with particular strength in twentieth-century fashion, as well as 30,000 textiles and 100,000 textile swatches. Each year, nearly 100,000 visitors are drawn to the museum's award-winning exhibitions and public programs.

## Financial Aid

FIT directly administers its institutional grants, scholarships, and loans. Federal funding administered by the college may include Federal Perkins Loans, federally subsidized and unsubsidized Direct Loans for students, Grad PLUS loans, and the Federal Work-Study Program. Priority for institutionally administered funds is given to students enrolled and designated as full-time.

## Cost of Study

Tuition for New York State residents is $5,603 per semester, or $467 per credit. Out-of-state residents' tuition is $11,449 per semester, or $954 per credit. Tuition and fees are subject to change at the discretion of FIT's Board of Trustees. Additional expenses—for class materials, textbooks, and travel—may apply and vary per program.

## Living and Housing Costs

On-campus housing is available to graduate students. Traditional residence hall accommodations (including meal plan) cost from $5,887 to $7,074 per semester. Apartment-style housing options (not including meal plan) cost from $6,299 to $10,495 per semester.

*Fashion Institute of Technology*

## Student Group

Enrollment in the School of Graduate Studies is approximately 200 students per academic year, allowing considerable individual advisement. Students come to FIT from throughout the country and around the world.

## Student Outcomes

Fashion Design graduates will have gained a new level of design fluency and creative confidence, a mastery of their own specialized craft:OLOGY, and an understanding of their place as a maker and influencer in fashion history/ futures. They enter personally defined industries as articulate, vocal, and formidable design specialists, not design generalists, and are expected to populate a mix of large-scale, high-end design houses, smaller ateliers, entrepreneurial ventures, experimental think tanks, and consultancies, or to engage in continued study at the M.Phil. or Ph.D. level.

## Location

FIT is located in Manhattan's Chelsea neighborhood, at the heart of the advertising, visual arts, marketing, fashion, business, design, and communications industries. Students are connected to New York City and gain unparalleled exposure to their field through guest lectures, field trips, internships, and sponsored competitions. The location provides access to major museums, galleries, and auction houses as well as dining, entertainment, and shopping options. The campus is near subway, bus, and commuter rail lines.

## Applying

Applicants to all School of Graduate Studies programs must hold a baccalaureate degree in an appropriate major from a college or university, with a cumulative GPA of 3.0 or higher. International students from non-English-speaking countries are required to submit minimum TOEFL scores of 550 on the written test, 213 on the computer test, or 80 on the Internet test. Each major has additional, specialized prerequisites for admission; for detailed information, students should visit the School of Graduate Studies on FIT's website.

Domestic and international students use the same application when seeking admission. The deadline for completed applications with transcripts and supplemental materials is March 15 for the Fashion Design program. After the deadline date, applicants are considered on a rolling admissions basis. Candidates may apply online at fitnyc.edu/gradstudies.

## Correspondence and Information

School of Graduate Studies
Shirley Goodman Resource Center, Room E315
Fashion Institute of Technology
227 West 27 Street
New York, New York 10001-5992
Phone: 212-217-4300
Fax: 212-217-4301
E-mail: gradinfo@fitnyc.edu
Websites: fitnyc.edu/gradstudies
fitnyc.edu/fashion-design-mfa

## THE FACULTY

A partial list of faculty members is below. Guest lecturers are not included.

Jonathan Kyle Farmer, Chair, M.A., Royal College of Art (London).
Ammar Belal, B.A., Clark.
Sarah C. Byrd, M.A., Fashion Institute of Technology.
Kira Craft, M.A., Parsons.
Ariele Elia, M.A., Fashion Institute of Technology.
Julian Guthrie, M.F.A., Parsons.
James Mendolia, Master in International Business Innovation (I.M.B.I), Universidad de Murcia
Aura Taylor, M.F.A., Academy of Art University.
Vasilija Zivanic, M.F.A., Boston University.

# NORTH DAKOTA STATE UNIVERSITY
## College of Human Development and Education

**NDSU** GRADUATE SCHOOL

 For more information, visit http://petersons.to/ndstatehumandevelopmenteducation

## Programs of Study

The College of Human Development and Education at North Dakota State University educates and trains students who want to make a difference in others' lives. Its rigorous programs and innovative research focus on people and how they interact in educational, living, and work environments.

The college's fifteen master's degree programs and seven doctoral degree programs are provided through four departments:

- Apparel, Design, and Hospitality Management
- School of Education
- Health, Nutrition, and Exercise Sciences
- Human Development and Family Science

The college provides a student-focused, friendly community where students are actively involved in the learning process. As a result, they acquire the knowledge and skills to improve the lives of individuals within communities, families, and the workplace.

**Online Master of Science (M.S.) program in Human Development and Family Science:** The M.S. in Human Development and Family Science is a 36-credit, online program with three options: youth development, gerontology, and family financial planning.

**The y**outh development option trains individuals to develop and implement programs and services that promote the positive development of adolescents. The gerontology option provides in-depth knowledge of the social, physical, and mental changes associated with aging. The family financial planning option provides extensive knowledge of family and personal financial management and eligibility to take the CFP® Certification Examination.

**Doctor of Philosophy (Ph.D.) programs in Human Development and Family Science:** The College of Human Development and Education also offers Ph.D. programs in developmental science and in couple and family therapy.

The 60-credit Ph.D. in Developmental Science program focuses on human development across the lifespan. It integrates the biological, cognitive, and socio-emotional aspects of development and incorporates the cultural, familial, institutional, and social contexts in which development occurs.

The 81-credit Ph.D. in Couple and Family Therapy program focuses on feminist and social justice principles. This foundation prepares students for clinical, research, and supervisory work with diverse and marginalized populations and communities.

**Graduate programs in Health, Nutrition, and Exercise Sciences:** The Department of Health, Nutrition, and Exercise Sciences offers six graduate programs, including the M.S. in Health, Nutrition, and Exercise Sciences and the Ph.D. in Exercise Science and Nutrition.

M.S. programs in Health, Nutrition, and Exercise Sciences prepare students for advanced positions in exercise science, health promotion, nutrition/dietetics, physical activity, and physical education teaching and coaching. There are three options: the 31-credit exercise and nutrition option; the 30-credit, online leadership in physical education and sport option; and the 36-credit, online dietetics option.

The 60-credit Ph.D. program in Exercise Science and Nutrition prepares students for leadership positions in community settings, government agencies, professional agencies and organizations, and universities.

## Research

The College of Human Development and Education provides many resources and opportunities for students to engage in cutting-edge research, including state-of-the-art equipment, modern labs, and dedicated teachers.

Graduate students work closely with faculty members to investigate issues relevant to their field, develop academic and grant-writing skills, and publish articles in periodicals. They coauthored more than twenty refereed journal articles and gave numerous presentations at professional conferences during the 2015–16 academic year.

Faculty members are dedicated to conducting research that improves people's lives and strengthens communities. Their accomplishments during the 2015–16 academic year include the following:

- Thirty-one faculty members (52 percent) received external research funding.
- Thirty-five tenured/tenure-track faculty members (58 percent) published refereed journal articles.
- Faculty members published 68 refereed journal articles in 2015–16 for a total of 212 for a three-year period.
- Forty faculty members (73 percent) made presentations at international conferences in countries such as the Czech Republic, Lithuania, Australia, France, Japan, Spain, and other locations.

## Financial Aid

Graduate students in the College of Human Development and Education may qualify for the following financial assistance programs: graduate assistantships (teaching or research), scholarships (from the University and private funders), grants, fellowships, loans (through federal programs or private lenders), military and veteran assistance, and employer tuition reimbursement programs.

Applicants should consult with their academic departments and the Office of Financial Aid and Scholarships to learn about their financial aid options.

## Cost of Study

The most current information on tuition and fees can be found online at https://www.ndsu.edu/onestop/accounts/tuition/.

## Living and Housing Costs

Information about on-campus housing for graduate students can be found at www.ndsu.edu/reslife/general_apartment_information. While there is no specific residence hall for graduate students, they are able to live in the University apartments. There are also numerous housing options in the Fargo community.

*North Dakota State University*

### The Faculty

Faculty members like James Deal, Ph.D. are accomplished teachers, scholars, and leaders. They bring cutting-edge research to their classrooms, serve on editorial boards of scholarly journals, and serve as officers of professional organizations, among other endeavors.

Professor Deal joined the Department of Human Development and Family Science in 1993. He has received several grants and published numerous articles in his areas of interest: whole family function, quantitative research methods, and personality development in children.

### Student Life

Graduate students at North Dakota State University join a warm and opportunity-rich community where they can achieve their educational, personal, research, and social goals. Academic, wellness, and support resources include the Counseling Center, Graduate Center for Writers, Office of International Students and Study Abroad Services, Office of Multicultural Programs, Wallman Wellness Center, and more.

Additional amenities include banking services, childcare, on-campus housing, graphic services, and meeting rooms. Social resources include affinity groups, recreational programs, arts and culture, and student organizations.

### Location

North Dakota State University is located on the eastern edge of North Dakota in Fargo, the state's largest community. With its sister city, Moorhead, Minnesota, directly across the Red River, Fargo is one of the largest metropolitan centers between Minneapolis and Seattle and offers a family-friendly environment with excellent schools, safe neighborhoods, and a low crime rate; an active arts and cultural scene, including a symphony, civic opera company, art museums, and community theater; and many places to shop and eat, including numerous restaurants, coffee shops, and a newly refurbished downtown district.

### The University

Established in 1890, North Dakota State University is a student-focused, land-grant, research institution known nationally and internationally for excellence in education and research. Its vibrant campus community includes more than 14,400 students (approximately 2,100 of whom are graduate students), more than 1,000 faculty members and educators, and approximately 4,000 staff members. It offers students nearly 100 undergraduate majors, 86 master's programs, and 53 doctoral programs.

The National Science Foundation ranks a number of North Dakota State University's programs among the top 100 in the country.

### Applying

The North Dakota State University graduate school application procedure places responsibility on the applicant to gather all supporting credentials and verifying that the application file is complete. The deadline for submission is dependent upon the program. If no deadline is listed on the program's bulletin page, all application materials are due at least one month prior the start of the semester.

Prospective students must file their application online. There is a $35 nonrefundable application fee. A statement of purpose—covering reasons for pursing graduate study, special interests within the chosen discipline, and preparation, skills, and experience in the proposed field of study—is required for admission consideration and must be uploaded with the online application. Other requirements include three letters of recommendation; official transcripts from each college or university attended; and official GRE or GMAT scores if required. Some programs may have additional requirements, as stated on the individual program pages.

The online application and additional details regarding the application process are available at https://www.ndsu.edu/gradschool/prospective_students.

### Correspondence and Information

College of Human Development and Education
Graduate School
North Dakota State University
Dept. 2820, P.O. Box 6050
Fargo, North Dakota 58108-6050
Phone: 701-231-7033
     800-608-6378 (toll-free)
E-mail: ndsu.grad.school@ndsu.edu
Website: www.ndsu.edu/gradschool
     facebook.com/ndsugradschool (Facebook)
     @NDSUGradSchool (Twitter)

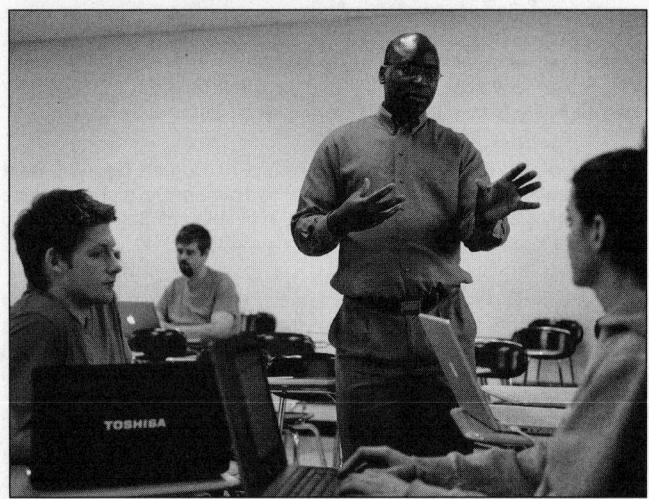

The College of Human Development and Education offers graduate programs that focus on people. These nationally recognized programs conduct research and other scholarly activities that focus on individuals as they interact at work and in educational and living environments.

# Section 21
# Geography

This section contains a directory of institutions offering graduate work in geography. Additional information about programs listed in the directory may be obtained by writing directly to the dean of a graduate school or chair of a department at the address given in the directory.

For programs offering related work, see also in this book *Area and Cultural Studies* and *Humanities*. In another guide in this series:

**Graduate Programs in the Physical Sciences, Mathematics, Agricultural Sciences, the Environment & Natural Resources**
See *Geosciences*

## CONTENTS

### Program Directories

# Geographic Information Systems

**Acadia University,** Faculty of Pure and Applied Science, Program in Applied Geomatics, Wolfville, NS B4P 2R6, Canada. Offers M Sc. Program offered jointly with Nova Scotia Community College. *Degree requirements:* For master's, thesis optional. *Entrance requirements:* Additional exam requirements/recommendations for international students: Required—TOEFL (minimum score 580 paper-based; 93 iBT), IELTS (minimum score 6.5).

**Appalachian State University,** Cratis D. Williams Graduate School, Department of Geography and Planning, Boone, NC 28608. Offers geography (MA), including geographic information science. *Program availability:* Part-time, online learning. *Degree requirements:* For master's, comprehensive exam, thesis or alternative. *Entrance requirements:* For master's, GRE General Test, 3 letters of recommendation. Additional exam requirements/recommendations for international students: Required—TOEFL (minimum score 570 paper-based; 79 iBT), IELTS (minimum score 6.5). *Application deadline:* For fall admission, 3/15 priority date for domestic students, 2/1 for international students; for spring admission, 11/1 for domestic students, 7/1 for international students. Applications are processed on a rolling basis. Application fee: $55. Electronic applications accepted. *Expenses:* Tuition, state resident: full-time $4744. Tuition, nonresident: full-time $17,913. Full-time tuition and fees vary according to program. *Financial support:* Fellowships, research assistantships, teaching assistantships, career-related internships or fieldwork, Federal Work-Study, scholarships/grants, and unspecified assistantships available. Financial award application deadline: 4/1; financial award applicants required to submit FAFSA. *Faculty research:* Global change, climatology, production cartography, geographic information systems, North Carolina geography, Latin America. *Unit head:* Dr. Kathleen Schroeder, Chairperson, 828-262-3000, Fax: 828-262-3067, E-mail: schroederk@appstate.edu. *Application contact:* Dr. Baker Perry, Graduate Program Director, E-mail: perrylb@appstate.edu. Website: http://www.geo.appstate.edu

**Arizona State University at the Tempe campus,** College of Liberal Arts and Sciences, School of Geographical Sciences and Urban Planning, Tempe, AZ 85287-5302. Offers geographic information systems (MAS); geographical information science (Graduate Certificate); geography (MA, PhD); transportation systems (Graduate Certificate); urban and environmental planning (MUEP); urban planning (PhD). *Accreditation:* ACSP. Terminal master's awarded for partial completion of doctoral program. *Degree requirements:* For master's, thesis, interactive Program of Study (iPOS) submitted before completing 50 percent of required credit hours; for doctorate, comprehensive exam, thesis/dissertation, interactive Program of Study (iPOS) submitted before completing 50 percent of required credit hours. *Entrance requirements:* For master's and doctorate, GRE, minimum GPA of 3.0 or equivalent in last 2 years of work leading to bachelor's degree. Additional exam requirements/recommendations for international students: Required—TOEFL, IELTS, or PTE. Electronic applications accepted. *Expenses:* Contact institution.

**Auburn University at Montgomery,** College of Public Policy and Justice, Department of Sociology, Anthropology and Geography, Montgomery, AL 36124-4023. Offers geographic information systems (MS).

**Ball State University,** Graduate School, College of Sciences and Humanities, Department of Geography, Muncie, IN 47306. Offers geographic information systems (Certificate); geography (MS); professional meteorology and climatology (Certificate). *Program availability:* Part-time. *Degree requirements:* For master's, thesis. *Entrance requirements:* For master's, minimum baccalaureate GPA of 2.75 or 3.0 in latter half of baccalaureate, letter of interest, three letters of recommendation, resume or curriculum vitae, official transcripts. Additional exam requirements/recommendations for international students: Required—TOEFL (minimum score 550 paper-based; 79 iBT), IELTS (minimum score 6.5). Electronic applications accepted. *Faculty research:* Remote sensing, tourism and recreation, Latin American urbanization.

**Boston University,** Graduate School of Arts and Sciences, Department of Earth and Environment, Boston, MA 02215. Offers earth and environment (PhD); earth sciences (MA, PhD); energy and environment (MA); geography (MA, PhD); global development policy (MA); international relations and environmental policy (MA); remote sensing and geospatial sciences (MA). *Students:* 66 full-time (30 women), 3 part-time (1 woman); includes 4 minority (1 Asian, non-Hispanic/Latino; 3 Hispanic/Latino), 31 international. Average age 27. 163 applicants, 35% accepted, 18 enrolled. In 2016, 11 master's, 13 doctorates awarded. Terminal master's awarded for partial completion of doctoral program. *Degree requirements:* For master's, comprehensive exam (for some programs), thesis (for some programs); for doctorate, comprehensive exam, thesis/dissertation. *Entrance requirements:* For master's and doctorate, GRE General Test, 3 letters of recommendation, official transcripts, personal statement, writing sample (for geography). Additional exam requirements/recommendations for international students: Required—TOEFL (minimum score 550 paper-based; 84 iBT). *Application deadline:* For fall admission, 1/31 for domestic and international students; for winter admission, 10/15 for domestic and international students. Application fee: $95. Electronic applications accepted. *Financial support:* In 2016–17, 39 students received support, including 4 fellowships with full tuition reimbursements available (averaging $21,500 per year), 14 research assistantships with full tuition reimbursements available (averaging $21,500 per year), 15 teaching assistantships with full tuition reimbursements available (averaging $21,500 per year); Federal Work-Study, scholarships/grants, traineeships, and health care benefits also available. Financial award application deadline: 1/31. *Faculty research:* Biogeosciences, climate and surface processes; energy, environment and society; geographical sciences; geology, geochemistry and geophysics. *Unit head:* David Marchant, Chair, 617-353-3236, E-mail: marchant@bu.edu. *Application contact:* Alissa Beideck, Graduate Program Coordinator, 617-353-2529, Fax: 617-353-8399, E-mail: abeideck@bu.edu. Website: http://www.bu.edu/earth/

**Central Michigan University,** College of Graduate Studies, College of Science and Technology, Department of Geography, Mount Pleasant, MI 48859. Offers geographic information sciences (MS). *Degree requirements:* For master's, thesis optional. *Entrance requirements:* For master's, GRE.

**Chicago State University,** School of Graduate and Professional Studies, College of Arts and Sciences, Department of Geography, Sociology, History, African-American Studies and Anthropology, Chicago, IL 60628. Offers geographic information systems (MA); geography (MA); history (MA). *Entrance requirements:* For master's, minimum GPA of 3.0.

**Claremont Graduate University,** Graduate Programs, Center for Information Systems and Technology, Claremont, CA 91711-6160. Offers cybersecurity and networking (MS); data science and analytics (MS); electronic commerce (PhD); geographic information systems (MS); health informatics (MS); information systems (Certificate); IT strategy and innovation (MS); knowledge management (PhD); systems development (PhD);

telecommunications and networking (PhD); MBA/MS. *Program availability:* Part-time. *Faculty:* 8 full-time (1 woman), 1 part-time/adjunct (0 women). *Students:* 60 full-time (18 women), 81 part-time (27 women); includes 34 minority (7 Black or African American, non-Hispanic/Latino; 18 Asian, non-Hispanic/Latino; 7 Hispanic/Latino; 1 Native Hawaiian or other Pacific Islander, non-Hispanic/Latino; 1 Two or more races, non-Hispanic/Latino), 80 international. Average age 35. In 2016, 21 master's, 10 doctorates awarded. *Degree requirements:* For doctorate, comprehensive exam, thesis/dissertation, portfolio. *Entrance requirements:* For master's and doctorate, GMAT, GRE General Test. Additional exam requirements/recommendations for international students: Required—TOEFL (minimum score 75 iBT). *Application deadline:* For fall admission, 2/1 priority date for domestic and international students. Applications are processed on a rolling basis. Application fee: $80. Electronic applications accepted. *Expenses: Tuition:* Full-time $44,328; part-time $1847 per unit. *Required fees:* $600; $300 per semester. Tuition and fees vary according to course load and program. *Financial support:* Fellowships, research assistantships, teaching assistantships, Federal Work-Study, institutionally sponsored loans, and scholarships/grants available. Support available to part-time students. Financial award application deadline: 2/15; financial award applicants required to submit FAFSA. *Faculty research:* Man-machine interaction, organizational aspects of computing, implementation of information systems, information systems practice. *Unit head:* Lorne Olfman, Acting Director, 909-607-3035, E-mail: lorne.olfman@cgu.edu. *Application contact:* Jake Campbell, Senior Assistant Director of Admissions, 909-607-3024, E-mail: jake.campbell@cgu.edu. Website: https://www.cgu.edu/school/center-for-information-systems-and-technology/

**Clark University,** Graduate School, Department of International Development, Community, and Environment, Program in Geographic Information Science for Development and Environment, Worcester, MA 01610-1477. Offers MS. *Students:* 50 full-time (24 women), 2 part-time (1 woman); includes 5 minority (1 Black or African American, non-Hispanic/Latino; 2 Asian, non-Hispanic/Latino; 2 Two or more races, non-Hispanic/Latino), 28 international. Average age 26. 96 applicants, 69% accepted, 22 enrolled. In 2016, 17 master's awarded. *Degree requirements:* For master's, thesis. *Entrance requirements:* For master's, 3 references, resume or curriculum vitae. Additional exam requirements/recommendations for international students: Required—TOEFL (minimum score 575 paper-based; 90 iBT) or IELTS (minimum score 6.5). *Application deadline:* For fall admission, 1/15 for domestic students. Application fee: $75. *Expenses: Tuition:* Full-time $44,050. *Required fees:* $80. Tuition and fees vary according to course load and program. *Financial support:* Fellowships with partial tuition reimbursements, research assistantships with partial tuition reimbursements, teaching assistantships with partial tuition reimbursements, institutionally sponsored loans, and scholarships/grants available. *Faculty research:* Land-use change, the effects of environmental influences on child health and development, quantitative methods, watershed management, brownfields redevelopment, human/environment interactions, biodiversity conservation, climate change. *Unit head:* Dr. Jie Tian, Coordinator, 508-793-7527, Fax: 508-793-8820. *Application contact:* Sawsan Berjawi, Manager of Academic and Student Affairs, 508-421-3846, Fax: 508-793-8820, E-mail: sberjawi@clarku.edu. Website: http://www.clarku.edu/programs/masters-geographic-information-science-development-and-environment

**The College of William and Mary,** Faculty of Arts and Sciences, Department of Applied Science, Williamsburg, VA 23185. Offers accelerator science (PhD); applied mathematics (PhD); applied mechanics (PhD); applied robotics (PhD); applied science (MS); atmospheric and environmental science (PhD); computational neuroscience (PhD); interface, thin film and surface science (PhD); lasers and optics (PhD); magnetic resonance (PhD); materials science and engineering (PhD); mathematical and computational biology (PhD); medical imaging (PhD); nanotechnology (PhD); neuroscience (PhD); non-destructive evaluation (PhD); polymer chemistry (PhD); remote sensing (PhD). *Program availability:* Part-time. *Faculty:* 8 full-time (2 women), 2 part-time/adjunct (0 women). *Students:* 30 full-time (11 women), 4 part-time (0 women); includes 16 minority (2 Black or African American, non-Hispanic/Latino; 12 Asian, non-Hispanic/Latino; 2 Hispanic/Latino), 12 international. Average age 28. 37 applicants, 27% accepted, 7 enrolled. In 2016, 6 doctorates awarded. Terminal master's awarded for partial completion of doctoral program. *Degree requirements:* For master's, comprehensive exam, thesis; for doctorate, comprehensive exam, thesis/dissertation, 4 core courses. *Entrance requirements:* For master's and doctorate, GRE General Test, GRE Subject Test. Additional exam requirements/recommendations for international students: Required—TOEFL, IELTS. *Application deadline:* For fall admission, 2/3 priority date for domestic students, 2/3 for international students; for spring admission, 10/15 priority date for domestic students, 10/14 for international students. Applications are processed on a rolling basis. Application fee: $45. Electronic applications accepted. *Expenses:* Contact institution. *Financial support:* In 2016–17, 7 students received support, including 27 research assistantships (averaging $25,000 per year), 1 teaching assistantship (averaging $9,500 per year); fellowships, scholarships/grants, health care benefits, tuition waivers (full), and unspecified assistantships also available. Financial award application deadline: 4/15; financial award applicants required to submit FAFSA. *Faculty research:* Computational biology, non-destructive evaluation, neurophysiology, laser spectroscopy, nanotechnology. *Total annual research expenditures:* $536,220. *Unit head:* Dr. Christopher Del Negro, Chair, 757-221-7808, Fax: 757-221-2050, E-mail: cadeln@wm.edu. *Application contact:* Lianne Rios Ashburne, Graduate Program Coordinator, 757-221-2563, Fax: 757-221-2050, E-mail: lrashburne@wm.edu. Website: http://www.wm.edu/as/appliedscience

**East Carolina University,** Graduate School, Thomas Harriot College of Arts and Sciences, Department of Geography, Planning, and Environment, Greenville, NC 27858-4353. Offers economic development (Certificate); geographic information science and technology (Certificate); geography (MA), including geography, planning, rural development. *Program availability:* Part-time, evening/weekend. *Students:* 15 full-time (8 women), 11 part-time (5 women); includes 6 minority (2 Black or African American, non-Hispanic/Latino; 1 Asian, non-Hispanic/Latino; 3 Hispanic/Latino). Average age 28. 17 applicants, 94% accepted, 9 enrolled. In 2016, 1 master's awarded. *Degree requirements:* For master's, one foreign language, comprehensive exam, thesis optional. *Entrance requirements:* For master's, GRE General Test. Additional exam requirements/recommendations for international students: Required—TOEFL. *Application deadline:* For fall admission, 6/1 priority date for domestic students; for spring admission, 10/15 for domestic students. Applications are processed on a rolling basis. Application fee: $50. *Financial support:* Research assistantships with partial tuition reimbursements, teaching assistantships with partial tuition reimbursements, and Federal Work-Study available. Support available to part-time students. Financial award application deadline: 6/1. *Unit head:* Dr. Burrell Montz, Chair, 252-328-6086, E-mail: montzb@ecu.edu. *Application contact:* Dean of Graduate School, 252-328-6012, Fax:

252-328-6071, E-mail: gradschool@ecu.edu.
Website: http://www.ecu.edu/geog/

**Eastern Illinois University,** Graduate School, College of Sciences, Department of Geology/Geography, Charleston, IL 61920. Offers MS. *Program availability:* Part-time, evening/weekend. *Entrance requirements:* For master's, GMAT or GRE. Additional exam requirements/recommendations for international students: Required—TOEFL (minimum score 500 paper-based; 61 iBT), IELTS (minimum score 6). Electronic applications accepted.

**Eastern Michigan University,** Graduate School, College of Arts and Sciences, Department of Geography and Geology, Programs in Geographic Information Systems, Ypsilanti, MI 48197. Offers geographic information systems (MS); geographic information systems for educators (Graduate Certificate); geographic information systems for professionals (Graduate Certificate). *Students:* 9 full-time (2 women), 19 part-time (3 women), 16 international. Average age 28. 24 applicants, 83% accepted, 9 enrolled. In 2016, 6 master's, 2 other advanced degrees awarded. Application fee: $45. *Application contact:* Dr. Hugh Semple, Program Advisor, 734-487-8169, Fax: 734-487-6979, E-mail: hsemple@emich.edu.

**Elizabeth City State University,** School of Mathematics, Science and Technology, Master of Science in Mathematics Program, Elizabeth City, NC 27909-7806. Offers applied mathematics (MS); community college teaching (MS); mathematics education (MS); remote sensing (MS). *Program availability:* Part-time, evening/weekend. *Degree requirements:* For master's, thesis. *Entrance requirements:* For master's, MAT and/or GRE, minimum GPA of 3.0, 3 letters of recommendation, two official transcripts from all undergraduate/graduate schools attended, typewritten one-page request for entry into program that includes description of student's educational preparation. Additional exam requirements/recommendations for international students: Required—TOEFL (minimum score 550 paper-based, 80 iBT) or IELTS (minimum score 6.5). Electronic applications accepted. *Faculty research:* Oceanic temperature effects, mathematics strategies in elementary schools, multimedia, Antarctic temperature mapping, computer networks, water quality, remote sensing, polar ice, satellite imagery.

**Elmhurst College,** Graduate Programs, Program in Geographic Information Systems, Elmhurst, IL 60126-3296. Offers MS. *Program availability:* Part-time, evening/weekend, 100% online. *Faculty:* 3 part-time/adjunct (1 woman). *Students:* 19 part-time (10 women); includes 2 minority (1 American Indian or Alaska Native, non-Hispanic/Latino; 1 Hispanic/Latino). Average age 32. 26 applicants, 54% accepted, 11 enrolled. *Entrance requirements:* For master's, 3 recommendations, resume, statement of purpose. Additional exam requirements/recommendations for international students: Required—TOEFL (minimum score 550 paper-based; 79 iBT). *Application deadline:* Applications are processed on a rolling basis. Application fee: $0. Electronic applications accepted. *Expenses:* $725 per semester hour. *Financial support:* In 2016–17, 7 students received support. Scholarships/grants available. Support available to part-time students. Financial award application deadline: 3/1; financial award applicants required to submit FAFSA. *Unit head:* Judy Bock. *Application contact:* Timothy J. Panfil, Director of Enrollment Management, School for Professional Studies, 630-617-3300 Ext. 3256, Fax: 630-617-6471, E-mail: panfilt@elmhurst.edu.
Website: http://www.elmhurst.edu/applied_geospatial_sciences

**Florida State University,** The Graduate School, College of Social Sciences and Public Policy, Department of Geography, Tallahassee, FL 32306. Offers geographic information science (MS); geography (MA, MS, PhD). *Program availability:* Part-time. *Faculty:* 11 full-time (4 women), 4 part-time/adjunct (2 women). *Students:* 64 full-time (31 women), 6 part-time (3 women); includes 21 minority (4 Black or African American, non-Hispanic/Latino; 10 Asian, non-Hispanic/Latino; 7 Two or more races, non-Hispanic/Latino). Average age 30. 70 applicants, 73% accepted, 30 enrolled. In 2016, 15 master's, 6 doctorates awarded. Terminal master's awarded for partial completion of doctoral program. *Degree requirements:* For master's, thesis (for some programs); for doctorate, comprehensive exam, thesis/dissertation. *Entrance requirements:* For master's and doctorate, GRE General Test, minimum GPA of 3.0. Additional exam requirements/recommendations for international students: Required—TOEFL (minimum score 80 iBT). *Application deadline:* For fall admission, 3/1 priority date for domestic and international students; for spring admission, 10/1 priority date for domestic and international students. Applications are processed on a rolling basis. Application fee: $30. Electronic applications accepted. *Expenses:* Contact institution. *Financial support:* In 2016–17, 50 students received support, including 7 research assistantships with full tuition reimbursements available (averaging $17,000 per year), 43 teaching assistantships with full tuition reimbursements available (averaging $17,000 per year); career-related internships or fieldwork, Federal Work-Study, institutionally sponsored loans, scholarships/grants, health care benefits, tuition waivers (full and partial), and unspecified assistantships also available. Financial award application deadline: 3/1; financial award applicants required to submit FAFSA. *Faculty research:* Society-nature interactions, geographic information science, environmental studies, hurricanes, remote sensing, urban, transportation. *Total annual research expenditures:* $159,022. *Unit head:* Prof. James Elsner, Chair, 850-644-1706, Fax: 850-644-5913, E-mail: jelsner@fsu.edu. *Application contact:* Prof. Victor Mesev, Graduate Director, 850-645-2498, Fax: 850-644-5193, E-mail: vmesev@fsu.edu.
Website: http://geography.fsu.edu/

**George Mason University,** College of Science, Department of Geography and Geoinformation Science, Fairfax, VA 22030. Offers earth system science (MS); earth systems and geoinformation sciences (PhD); geography and geoinformation science (Certificate). *Faculty:* 18 full-time (2 women), 6 part-time/adjunct (0 women). *Students:* 75 full-time (22 women), 106 part-time (23 women); includes 26 minority (6 Black or African American, non-Hispanic/Latino; 9 Asian, non-Hispanic/Latino; 7 Hispanic/Latino; 4 Two or more races, non-Hispanic/Latino), 34 international. Average age 35. 87 applicants, 93% accepted, 42 enrolled. In 2016, 31 master's, 8 doctorates, 18 other advanced degrees awarded. *Degree requirements:* For master's, thesis optional. *Entrance requirements:* For master's, GRE (waived for those who have earned a master's degree from U.S. institution), bachelor's degree with minimum GPA of 3.0; 2 copies of official transcripts; current resume; expanded goals statement; 3 letters of recommendation; for doctorate, GRE (waived for those who have earned a master's degree from U.S. institution), bachelor's degree with minimum GPA of 3.0; 2 copies of official transcripts; 3 letters of recommendation; resume; expanded goals statement; for Certificate, GRE (waived for those who have earned a master's degree from U.S. institution), baccalaureate degree with minimum GPA of 3.0; 2 official copies of transcripts; expanded goals statement; 3 letters of recommendation; resume. Additional exam requirements/recommendations for international students: Required—TOEFL (minimum score 575 paper-based; 88 iBT), IELTS (minimum score 6.5), PTE (minimum score 59). *Application deadline:* For fall admission, 2/1 priority date for domestic students. Application fee: $75 ($80 for international students). Electronic applications accepted. *Expenses:* Tuition, state resident: full-time $10,628; part-time $443 per credit. Tuition, nonresident: full-time $29,306; part-time $1221 per credit. *Required fees:* $3096; $129 per credit. Tuition and fees vary according to program. *Financial support:* In 2016–17, 34 students received support, including 24 research assistantships with tuition reimbursements available (averaging $18,740 per year), 10 teaching assistantships with tuition reimbursements available (averaging $12,089 per year);

career-related internships or fieldwork, Federal Work-Study, scholarships/grants, unspecified assistantships, and health care benefits (for full-time research or teaching assistantship recipients) also available. Support available to part-time students. Financial award application deadline: 3/1; financial award applicants required to submit FAFSA. *Faculty research:* Global environment climate monitoring, gender and earth science, earth science education, remote sensing, planetary geology, hydrology, theoretical issues of geographic information data acquisition and processing. *Total annual research expenditures:* $1.7 million. *Unit head:* Anthony Stefanidis, Acting Chair, 703-993-9237, Fax: 703-993-9230, E-mail: astefani@gmu.edu. *Application contact:* Samantha Cooke, Department Manager, 703-993-1212, E-mail: scooke4@gmu.edu.
Website: http://ggs.gmu.edu/

**Georgia Institute of Technology,** Graduate Studies, College of Architecture, School of City and Regional Planning, Atlanta, GA 30332-0001. Offers city and regional planning (PhD); economic development (MCRP); environmental planning and management (MCRP); geographic information systems (MCRP); land and community development (MCRP); land use planning (MCRP); transportation (MCRP); urban design (MCRP); MCP/MSCE. *Accreditation:* ACSP. *Degree requirements:* For master's, thesis, internship. *Entrance requirements:* For master's, GRE General Test, minimum GPA of 2.7. Additional exam requirements/recommendations for international students: Required—TOEFL. Electronic applications accepted.

**Georgia State University,** College of Arts and Sciences, Department of Geosciences, Program in Geographic Information Systems, Atlanta, GA 30302-3083. Offers Certificate. *Program availability:* Part-time. *Entrance requirements:* For degree, GRE. Additional exam requirements/recommendations for international students: Required—TOEFL (minimum score 550 paper-based; 80 iBT). *Application deadline:* For fall admission, 4/15 for domestic and international students; for spring admission, 11/15 for domestic and international students. Electronic applications accepted. *Expenses:* Tuition, state resident: full-time $6876; part-time $382 per credit hour. Tuition, nonresident: full-time $22,374; part-time $1243 per credit hour. *Required fees:* $2128; $1064 per term. Part-time tuition and fees vary according to course load and program. *Financial support:* Career-related internships or fieldwork available. *Faculty research:* Geographic information science. *Unit head:* Dr. W. Crawford Elliott, Chair, 404-413-5756, E-mail: wcelliott@gsu.edu.
Website: http://geosciences.gsu.edu/grad-programs/

**Hunter College of the City University of New York,** Graduate School, School of Arts and Sciences, Department of Geography, New York, NY 10065-5085. Offers geographic information science (Certificate); geography (MA); geoinformatics (MS). *Program availability:* Part-time, evening/weekend. *Students:* 2 full-time (1 woman), 43 part-time (10 women); includes 14 minority (5 Black or African American, non-Hispanic/Latino; 5 Asian, non-Hispanic/Latino; 4 Hispanic/Latino), 4 international. Average age 30. 26 applicants, 81% accepted, 20 enrolled. In 2016, 11 master's, 12 other advanced degrees awarded. *Degree requirements:* For master's, comprehensive exam or thesis. *Entrance requirements:* For master's, GRE General Test, minimum B average in major, B- overall; 18 credits of course work in geography; 2 letters of recommendation; for Certificate, minimum B average in major, B- overall. Additional exam requirements/recommendations for international students: Required—TOEFL. *Application deadline:* For fall admission, 4/1 for domestic students; for spring admission, 11/1 for domestic students. Applications are processed on a rolling basis. *Financial support:* Fellowships, research assistantships, teaching assistantships, career-related internships or fieldwork, Federal Work-Study, institutionally sponsored loans, and unspecified assistantships available. Financial award application deadline: 3/1. *Faculty research:* Urban geography, economic geography, geographic information science, demographic methods, climate change. *Unit head:* Prof. Allan Frei, Chair, 212-772-5322, Fax: 212-772-5322, E-mail: afrei@hunter.cuny.edu. *Application contact:* Hongmian Gong, Graduate Advisor, 212-772-4658, Fax: 212-772-5268, E-mail: gong@hunter.cuny.edu.
Website: http://www.geo.hunter.cuny.edu/

**Idaho State University,** Office of Graduate Studies, College of Science and Engineering, Department of Geosciences, Pocatello, ID 83209-8072. Offers geographic information science (MS); geology (MNS, MS); geology with emphasis in environmental geoscience (MS); geophysics/hydrology/geology (MS); geotechnology (Postbaccalaureate Certificate). *Program availability:* Part-time. *Degree requirements:* For master's, comprehensive exam, thesis, oral colloquium; for Postbaccalaureate Certificate, thesis optional, minimum 19 credits. *Entrance requirements:* For master's, GRE General Test (minimum 50th percentile in 2 sections), 3 letters of recommendation; for Postbaccalaureate Certificate, GRE General Test, 3 letters of recommendation, bachelor's degree, statement of goals. Additional exam requirements/recommendations for international students: Required—TOEFL (minimum score 550 paper-based; 80 iBT). Electronic applications accepted. *Faculty research:* Quantitative field mapping and sampling: microscopic, geochemical, and isotopic analysis of rocks, minerals and water; remote sensing, geographic information systems, and global positioning systems: environmental and watershed management; surficial and fluvial processes: landscape change; regional tectonics, structural geology; planetary geology.

**Indiana University of Pennsylvania,** School of Graduate Studies and Research, College of Humanities and Social Sciences, Department of Geography and Regional Planning, Geographic Information Science/Cartography Track, Indiana, PA 15705. Offers MS. *Program availability:* Part-time. *Faculty:* 9 full-time (2 women). *Students:* 5 full-time (1 woman); includes 1 minority (Asian, non-Hispanic/Latino). Average age 29. 4 applicants, 100% accepted, 2 enrolled. In 2016, 3 master's awarded. *Degree requirements:* For master's, thesis optional. *Entrance requirements:* Additional exam requirements/recommendations for international students: Required—TOEFL (minimum score 550 paper-based). *Application deadline:* Applications are processed on a rolling basis. Application fee: $50. Electronic applications accepted. *Expenses:* Tuition, state resident: full-time $8694; part-time $483 per credit. Tuition, nonresident: full-time $13,050; part-time $725 per credit. *Required fees:* $157 per credit. $50 per term. Tuition and fees vary according to course load and program. *Financial support:* In 2016–17, 4 research assistantships with tuition reimbursements (averaging $5,198 per year) were awarded; career-related internships or fieldwork, Federal Work-Study, scholarships/grants, and unspecified assistantships also available. Financial award application deadline: 4/15; financial award applicants required to submit FAFSA. *Unit head:* Dr. Richard Hoch, Graduate Coordinator, 724-357-5990, E-mail: richard.hoch@iup.edu.
Website: http://www.iup.edu/georegionalplan/grad/default.aspx

**Indiana University of Pennsylvania,** School of Graduate Studies and Research, College of Humanities and Social Sciences, Department of Geography and Regional Planning, Program in Geographic Information Science and Geospatial Techniques, Indiana, PA 15705. Offers Certificate. *Faculty:* 10 full-time (1 woman), 1 (woman) part-time/adjunct. In 2016, 5 Certificates awarded. *Entrance requirements:* Additional exam requirements/recommendations for international students: Required—TOEFL (minimum score 550 paper-based). *Application deadline:* Applications are processed on a rolling basis. Application fee: $50. Electronic applications accepted. *Expenses:* Tuition, state resident: full-time $8694; part-time $483 per credit. Tuition, nonresident: full-time $13,050; part-time $725 per credit. *Required fees:* $157 per credit. $50 per term. Tuition and fees vary according to course load and program. *Financial support:* Application deadline: 4/15; applicants required to submit FAFSA. *Unit head:* Dr. Richard Hoch,

## Geographic Information Systems

Graduate Coordinator, 724-357-5990, E-mail: richard.hoch@iup.edu. Website: http://www.iup.edu/georegionalplan/grad/default.aspx

**Indiana University–Purdue University Indianapolis,** School of Liberal Arts, Department of Geography, Indianapolis, IN 46202. Offers geographic information systems (MS, Certificate). *Program availability:* Part-time. *Faculty:* 5 full-time (1 woman). *Students:* 6 full-time (4 women), 12 part-time (3 women); includes 5 minority (2 Black or African American, non-Hispanic/Latino; 1 American Indian or Alaska Native, non-Hispanic/Latino; 1 Asian, non-Hispanic/Latino; 1 Hispanic/Latino). Average age 34. 9 applicants, 100% accepted, 5 enrolled. In 2016, 3 master's, 6 other advanced degrees awarded. *Degree requirements:* For master's, variable foreign language requirement, thesis; for Certificate, variable foreign language requirement. *Entrance requirements:* For master's, GRE (minimum verbal or quantitative score of 600, with the other score above 500), minimum GPA of 3.0; for Certificate, minimum GPA of 3.0. Additional exam requirements/recommendations for international students: Required—TOEFL (minimum score 550 paper-based), IELTS. Application fee: $60 ($65 for international students). Electronic applications accepted. *Expenses:* $12,104 resident tuition and fees, $29,546 non-resident. *Financial support:* In 2016–17, 2 students received support. Institutionally sponsored loans, scholarships/grants, health care benefits, tuition waivers (full and partial), and unspecified assistantships available. Financial award applicants required to submit CSS PROFILE or FAFSA. *Faculty research:* Remote sensing, geographic information systems, epidemiology, public health, weather and climate, soils. *Unit head:* Dr. Daniel P. Johnson, Chair, 317-278-5536, Fax: 317-278-5220, E-mail: dpjohnso@iupui.edu. *Application contact:* Dr. Owen Dwyer III, Graduate Advisor, 317-274-8808, E-mail: odwyer@iupui.edu.
Website: http://liberalarts.iupui.edu/geography/

**Johns Hopkins University,** Zanvyl Krieger School of Arts and Sciences, Advanced Academic Programs, Program in Environmental Sciences and Policy, Washington, DC 20036. Offers energy policy and climate (MS); environmental sciences (MS); geographic information systems (MS, Certificate). *Program availability:* Part-time, evening/weekend, online learning. *Degree requirements:* For master's, thesis (for some programs). *Entrance requirements:* For master's, minimum GPA of 3.0, coursework in chemistry and calculus. Additional exam requirements/recommendations for international students: Required—TOEFL (minimum score 100 iBT). Electronic applications accepted.

**Kansas State University,** Graduate School, College of Arts and Sciences, Department of Geography, Manhattan, KS 66506. Offers geographic information science (Graduate Certificate); geography (MA, PhD). *Faculty:* 12 full-time (3 women), 1 part-time/adjunct (0 women). *Students:* 32 full-time (15 women), 13 part-time (5 women); includes 7 minority (3 Asian, non-Hispanic/Latino; 2 Hispanic/Latino; 2 Two or more races, non-Hispanic/Latino), 16 international. Average age 30. 18 applicants, 56% accepted, 7 enrolled. In 2016, 3 master's, 2 doctorates, 2 other advanced degrees awarded. *Degree requirements:* For master's, thesis optional, oral exam; for doctorate, one foreign language, thesis/dissertation. *Entrance requirements:* For master's and doctorate, GRE General Test, minimum GPA of 3.0. *Application deadline:* For fall admission, 2/1 priority date for domestic and international students; for spring admission, 8/1 priority date for domestic and international students. Applications are processed on a rolling basis. Application fee: $50 ($75 for international students). Electronic applications accepted. *Expenses:* Tuition, state resident: full-time $9670. Tuition, nonresident: full-time $21,828. *Required fees:* $862. *Financial support:* In 2016–17, 2 research assistantships (averaging $18,770 per year), 18 teaching assistantships with full tuition reimbursements (averaging $13,158 per year) were awarded; Federal Work-Study, institutionally sponsored loans, and scholarships/grants also available. Support available to part-time students. Financial award application deadline: 3/1; financial award applicants required to submit FAFSA. *Faculty research:* Human environment interaction, health and population, culture and landscape, physical geography, geospatial analysis and applications. *Total annual research expenditures:* $294,540. *Unit head:* Charles Martin, Head, 785-532-0136, Fax: 785-532-7310, E-mail: cwmgeog@ksu.edu. *Application contact:* Douglas Goodin, Director, 785-532-3411, Fax: 785-532-7310, E-mail: dgoodin@ksu.edu.
Website: http://www.k-state.edu/geography/

**Kent State University,** College of Arts and Sciences, Department of Geography, Kent, OH 44242-0001. Offers geographic information science (MGIS), including cyber geographic information science, environmental geographic information science, geographic information science and health; geography (MA, PhD). *Program availability:* Part-time. *Faculty:* 12 full-time (5 women). *Students:* 41 full-time (13 women), 7 part-time (2 women); includes 3 minority (1 Black or African American, non-Hispanic/Latino; 1 Hispanic/Latino; 1 Two or more races, non-Hispanic/Latino), 14 international. Average age 31. 49 applicants, 59% accepted, 21 enrolled. In 2016, 3 master's, 4 doctorates awarded. *Degree requirements:* For master's, thesis; for doctorate, comprehensive exam, thesis/dissertation. *Entrance requirements:* For master's and doctorate, GRE (minimum score of 300 verbal and quantitative on new scale), minimum GPA of 3.0, minor in geography, transcripts, letters of recommendation. Additional exam requirements/recommendations for international students: Required—TOEFL (minimum score of 525 paper-based, 71 iBT), IELTS (minimum score of 6), Michigan English Language Assessment Battery (minimum score of 75), or PTE (minimum score of 48). *Application deadline:* For fall admission, 2/1 for domestic and international students; for spring admission, 11/1 for domestic and international students; for summer admission, 4/1 for domestic and international students. Applications are processed on a rolling basis. Application fee: $45 ($70 for international students). Electronic applications accepted. *Expenses:* Tuition, state resident: full-time $10,864; part-time $495 per credit hour. Tuition, nonresident: full-time $18,380; part-time $837 per credit hour. *Financial support:* Fellowships with full tuition reimbursements, research assistantships with full tuition reimbursements, teaching assistantships with full tuition reimbursements, Federal Work-Study, scholarships/grants, and unspecified assistantships available. Financial award application deadline: 2/1. *Unit head:* Dr. Scott Sheridan, Professor/Acting Chair, 330-672-3224, Fax: 330-672-4304, E-mail: ssherid1@kent.edu. *Application contact:* Dr. David H. Kaplan, Professor and Graduate Coordinator, 330-672-3221, E-mail: dkaplan@kent.edu.
Website: https://www.kent.edu/geography

**Long Island University–LIU Post,** College of Liberal Arts and Sciences, Brookville, NY 11548-1300. Offers applied mathematics (MS); behavior analysis (MA); biology (MS); criminal justice (MS); earth science (MS); English (MA); environmental sustainability (MS); genetic counseling (MS); history (MA); interdisciplinary studies (MA, MS); mathematics for secondary school teachers (MS); mobile GIS application development (Advanced Certificate); political science (MA); psychology (MA). *Program availability:* Part-time, evening/weekend, blended/hybrid learning. *Faculty:* 68 full-time (30 women), 20 part-time/adjunct (13 women). *Students:* 155 full-time (117 women), 125 part-time (82 women); includes 65 minority (17 Black or African American, non-Hispanic/Latino; 14 Asian, non-Hispanic/Latino; 27 Hispanic/Latino; 7 Two or more races, non-Hispanic/Latino), 19 international. 485 applicants, 36% accepted, 77 enrolled. In 2016, 91 master's, 15 other advanced degrees awarded. *Degree requirements:* For master's, comprehensive exam (for some programs), thesis (for some programs). *Entrance requirements:* Additional exam requirements/recommendations for international

students: Required—PTE, TOEFL (minimum score 550 paper-based, 75 iBT) or IELTS (6.5). *Application deadline:* Applications are processed on a rolling basis. Application fee: $50. Electronic applications accepted. *Expenses: Tuition:* Full-time $28,272; part-time $1178 per credit. *Required fees:* $451 per term. Tuition and fees vary according to degree level and program. *Financial support:* In 2016–17, 24 teaching assistantships with partial tuition reimbursements (averaging $410 per year) were awarded; fellowships, research assistantships, career-related internships or fieldwork, Federal Work-Study, institutionally sponsored loans, scholarships/grants, tuition waivers (partial), and unspecified assistantships also available. Support available to part-time students. Financial award application deadline: 2/15; financial award applicants required to submit FAFSA. *Faculty research:* Biology, criminal justice, environmental sustainability, mathematics, psychology. *Total annual research expenditures:* $218,000. *Unit head:* Dr. Jeffrey Belnap, Acting Dean, 516-299-2233, Fax: 516-299-4140, E-mail: jeffrey.belnap@liu.edu. *Application contact:* Carol Zerah, Director of Graduate Admissions, 516-299-2900, Fax: 516-299-2137, E-mail: post-enroll@liu.edu.
Website: http://liu.edu/CWPost/Academics/Schools/CLAS

**Michigan Technological University,** Graduate School, School of Technology, Houghton, MI 49931. Offers integrated geospatial technology (MS); medical informatics (MS). *Program availability:* Part-time, 100% online, blended/hybrid learning. *Faculty:* 26 full-time, 4 part-time/adjunct. *Students:* 11 full-time (6 women), 9 part-time (4 women); includes 2 minority (1 Black or African American, non-Hispanic/Latino; 1 American Indian or Alaska Native, non-Hispanic/Latino), 8 international. Average age 36. 53 applicants, 43% accepted, 7 enrolled. In 2016, 6 master's awarded. *Degree requirements:* For master's, comprehensive exam (for some programs), thesis (for some programs), thesis or comprehensive exam. *Entrance requirements:* For master's, GRE (for some programs), statement of purpose, personal statement, official transcripts, 2-3 letters of recommendation, resume/curriculum vitae. Additional exam requirements/recommendations for international students: Required—TOEFL (recommended minimum score 79 iBT) or IELTS. *Application deadline:* Applications are processed on a rolling basis. Electronic applications accepted. *Expenses:* Tuition, state resident: full-time $16,290; part-time $905 per credit. Tuition, nonresident: full-time $16,290; part-time $905 per credit. *Required fees:* $248; $124 per term. Tuition and fees vary according to course load and program. *Financial support:* In 2016–17, 6 students received support, including 1 research assistantship (averaging $15,242 per year); career-related internships or fieldwork, Federal Work-Study, scholarships/grants, and health care benefits also available. Financial award applicants required to submit FAFSA. *Faculty research:* Cybersecurity, medical image processing, sensory data fusion, architectural and archaeological laser scanning, high resolution remote sensing. *Total annual research expenditures:* $437,518. *Unit head:* Dr. James O. Frendewey, Dean, 906-487-2260, Fax: 906-487-2583, E-mail: jimf@mtu.edu. *Application contact:* Peggy A. Gorton, Executive Assistant, 906-487-2260, Fax: 906-487-2583, E-mail: pagorton@mtu.edu.
Website: http://www.mtu.edu/technology/

**Millersville University of Pennsylvania,** College of Graduate Studies and Adult Learning, College of Science and Technology, Department of Earth Sciences, Program in Integrated Scientific Applications: GeoInformatics Option, Millersville, PA 17551-0302. Offers MS. *Program availability:* Part-time, evening/weekend. *Faculty:* 4 full-time (2 women), 1 part-time/adjunct (0 women). *Students:* 2 full-time (1 woman), 2 part-time (0 women); includes 1 minority (Hispanic/Latino). Average age 28. 3 applicants, 67% accepted, 2 enrolled. *Degree requirements:* For master's, thesis optional, internship, applied research. *Entrance requirements:* For master's, GRE, MAT or GMAT (if cumulative GPA is lower than 3.0), official transcript, three professional letters of recommendation, academic and professional goals statement, current resume, interview with program coordinator. Additional exam requirements/recommendations for international students: Required—TOEFL (minimum score 600 paper-based), IELTS (minimum score 6). *Application deadline:* Applications are processed on a rolling basis. Application fee: $40. Electronic applications accepted. *Expenses:* $483 per credit resident tuition; $725 per credit non-resident tuition. *Financial support:* In 2016–17, 2 students received support. Unspecified assistantships available. Financial award application deadline: 3/15; financial award applicants required to submit FAFSA. *Faculty research:* Climatology and meteorology, remote sensing, geoinformatics, environmental economics and policy, business management, business operations analysis, finance and accounting, statistical applications, satellite data analytics. *Unit head:* Dr. Richard D. Clark, Coordinator, 717-871-7434, Fax: 717-871-7918, E-mail: richard.clark@millersville.edu. *Application contact:* Dr. Victor S. DeSantis, Dean of College of Graduate Studies and Adult Learning/Associate Provost for Civic and Community Engagement, 717-871-7619, Fax: 717-871-7954, E-mail: victor.desantis@millersville.edu.
Website: http://www.millersville.edu/esci/msisa/geoinformatics.php

**Montclair State University,** The Graduate School, College of Science and Mathematics, Geographic Information Science Certificate Program, Montclair, NJ 07043-1624. Offers Certificate. *Expenses:* Tuition, state resident: part-time $553 per credit. Tuition, nonresident: part-time $854 per credit. *Required fees:* $91 per credit. Tuition and fees vary according to program.

**Naval Postgraduate School,** Departments and Academic Groups, Department of Information Sciences, Monterey, CA 93943. Offers electronic warfare systems engineering (MS); information sciences (PhD); information systems and operations (MS); information technology management (MS); information warfare systems engineering (MS); knowledge superiority (Certificate); remote sensing intelligence (MS); system technology (command, control and communications) (MS). Program open only to commissioned officers of the United States and friendly nations and selected United States federal civilian employees. *Program availability:* Part-time. *Degree requirements:* For master's, thesis (for some programs); for doctorate, thesis/dissertation. *Faculty research:* Designing inter-organisational collectivities for dynamic fit: stability, manoeuvrability and application in disaster relief endeavours; system self-awareness and related methods for Improving the use and understanding of data within DoD; evaluating a macrocognition model of team collaboration using real-world data from the Haiti relief effort; cyber distortion in command and control; performance and QoS in service-based systems.

**North Carolina State University,** Graduate School, College of Natural Resources, Department of Parks, Recreation and Tourism Management, Raleigh, NC 27695. Offers natural resource management (MPRTM, MS); park and recreation management (MPRTM, MS); parks, recreation and tourism management (PhD); recreational sport management (MPRTM, MS); spatial information science (MPRTM, MS); tourism policy and development (MPRTM, MS). *Degree requirements:* For master's, thesis (for some programs); for doctorate, thesis/dissertation. *Entrance requirements:* For master's and doctorate, GRE General Test. Additional exam requirements/recommendations for international students: Required—TOEFL. Electronic applications accepted. *Faculty research:* Tourism policy and development, spatial information systems, natural resource management, recreational sports management, park and recreation management.

**Northeastern University,** College of Professional Studies, Boston, MA 02115-5096. Offers applied nutrition (MS); college athletics administration (MSL); commerce and economic development (MS); corporate and organizational communication (MS); criminal justice (MS); digital media (MPS); elearning and instructional design (M Ed); elementary education (MAT); geographic information technology (MPS); global studies and international relations (MS); higher education administration (M Ed); homeland security (MA); human services (MS); informatics (MPS); leadership (MS); learning analytics (M Ed); learning and instruction (M Ed); nonprofit management (MS); professional sports administration (MSL); project management (MS); regulatory affairs for drugs, biologics, and medical devices (MS); respiratory care leadership (MS); special education (M Ed); technical communication (MS). *Program availability:* Part-time, evening/weekend, 100% online, blended/hybrid learning. *Faculty:* 82 full-time (51 women), 853 part-time/adjunct (366 women). *Students:* 4,947 part-time (3,076 women). In 2016, 1,456 master's awarded. *Application deadline:* Applications are processed on a rolling basis. Application fee: $0. Electronic applications accepted. *Expenses:* Contact institution. *Financial support:* Applicants required to submit FAFSA. *Unit head:* Dr. Mary Loeffelholz, Interim Dean of the College of Professional Studies. Website: http://www.cps.neu.edu/

**Northern Arizona University,** Graduate College, College of Social and Behavioral Sciences, Department of Geography, Planning, and Recreation, Flagstaff, AZ 86011. Offers applied geospatial sciences (MS); community planning (Certificate); geographic information systems (Certificate). *Program availability:* Online learning. *Degree requirements:* For master's, thesis optional. *Entrance requirements:* For master's, GRE General Test. Additional exam requirements/recommendations for international students: Required—TOEFL (minimum score 550 paper-based; 80 iBT), IELTS (minimum score 7). Electronic applications accepted. *Expenses:* Tuition, state resident: full-time $8971; part-time $444 per credit hour. Tuition, nonresident: full-time $20,958; part-time $1164 per credit hour. *Required fees:* $1018; $644 per credit hour. Tuition and fees vary according to course load, campus/location and program.

**Northern Kentucky University,** Office of Graduate Programs, College of Informatics, Department of Computer Science, Highland Heights, KY 41099. Offers computer science (MSCS); geographic information systems (Certificate); secure software engineering (Certificate). *Program availability:* Part-time, evening/weekend. *Degree requirements:* For master's, thesis optional. *Entrance requirements:* For master's, GRE, minimum GPA of 3.0, at least 4 semesters of undergraduate study in computer science including intermediate computer programming and data structures, one year of calculus, one course in discrete mathematics. Additional exam requirements/recommendations for international students: Required—TOEFL (minimum score 550 paper-based; 79 iBT). Recommended—IELTS (minimum score 6.5). Electronic applications accepted. *Faculty research:* Data privacy, data mining, wireless security, secure software engineering, secure networking.

**Northwest Missouri State University,** Graduate School, College of Arts and Sciences, Maryville, MO 64468-6001. Offers biology (MS); elementary mathematics specialist (MS Ed); English (MA); English education (MS Ed); English pedagogy (MA); geographic information science (MS, Certificate); history (MS Ed); mathematics (MS); mathematics education (MS Ed); teaching: science (MS Ed). *Program availability:* Part-time. *Students:* 12 full-time (8 women), 69 part-time (31 women). *Degree requirements:* For master's, comprehensive exam. *Entrance requirements:* For master's, GRE General Test, writing sample. Additional exam requirements/recommendations for international students: Required—TOEFL (minimum score 550 paper-based). *Application deadline:* For fall admission, 7/1 for domestic and international students; for spring admission, 11/15 for domestic and international students. Applications are processed on a rolling basis. Application fee: $0 ($50 for international students). Electronic applications accepted. *Expenses:* Tuition, state resident: full-time $3447; part-time $383 per credit hour. Tuition, nonresident: full-time $5724; part-time $636 per credit hour. *Required fees:* $130 per credit hour. *Financial support:* Research assistantships with full tuition reimbursements, teaching assistantships with full tuition reimbursements, and administrative assistantships, tutorial assistantships available. Financial award application deadline: 4/1; financial award applicants required to submit FAFSA. *Unit head:* Dr. Michael Steiner, Dean, 660-562-1197. Website: http://www.nwmissouri.edu/academics/arts/

**Oregon State University,** College of Forestry, Program in Natural Resources, Corvallis, OR 97331. Offers fisheries management (MNR); forests and climate change (MNR); geographic information science (MNR); sustainable natural resources (MNR); urban forestry (MNR); water conflict management and transformation (MNR); wildlife management (MNR). *Program availability:* Part-time, online only, 100% online. *Students:* 7 full-time (5 women), 43 part-time (23 women); includes 8 minority (2 American Indian or Alaska Native, non-Hispanic/Latino; 2 Asian, non-Hispanic/Latino; 4 Hispanic/Latino). Average age 36. 18 applicants, 22% accepted, 3 enrolled. In 2016, 15 master's awarded. *Entrance requirements:* For master's, GRE. Additional exam requirements/recommendations for international students: Required—TOEFL (minimum score 80 iBT), IELTS (minimum score 6.5). Application fee: $75 ($85 for international students). *Expenses:* $521 per credit. *Unit head:* Dr. Badege Bishaw, Director, Master of Natural Resources and Sustainable Natural Resource Program, 541-737-9495, E-mail: badege.bishaw@oregonstate.edu. Website: http://ecampus.oregonstate.edu/online-degrees/graduate/natural-resources/

**Penn State University Park,** Graduate School, College of Earth and Mineral Sciences, Department of Geography, University Park, PA 16802. Offers geographic information systems (MGIS); geography (MS, PhD). *Unit head:* Dr. William E. Easterling, III, Dean, 814-865-7482, Fax: 814-863-7708. *Application contact:* Lori Hawn, Director, Graduate Student Services, 814-865-1795, Fax: 814-863-4627, E-mail: l-gswww@lists.psu.edu. Website: http://geog.psu.edu/

**Saint Louis University,** Graduate Education, College of Education and Public Service, Department of Public Policy Studies, St. Louis, MO 63103. Offers geographic information systems (Certificate); organizational development (Certificate); public administration (MAPA); public policy analysis (PhD); urban affairs (MAUA); urban planning and real estate development (MUPRED). *Program availability:* Part-time. *Degree requirements:* For master's, comprehensive exam (for some programs), thesis (for some programs); for doctorate, comprehensive exam, thesis/dissertation, preliminary exams. *Entrance requirements:* For master's, GMAT, GRE General Test, or LSAT, letters of recommendation, resume; for doctorate, GMAT, GRE General Test, or LSAT, letters of recommendation, resumé, interview, transcripts, goal statement. Additional exam requirements/recommendations for international students: Required—TOEFL (minimum score 525 paper-based). Electronic applications accepted. *Faculty research:* Urban politics, brown fields, e-government, and administration, evaluation research, community development, electronic government and governance.

**Saint Mary's University of Minnesota,** Schools of Graduate and Professional Programs, Graduate School of Business and Technology, Geographic Information Science Program, Winona, MN 55987-1399. Offers MS, Certificate. Tuition and fees vary according to degree level and program. *Unit head:* John Ebert, Director, 507-457-6961, E-mail: jebert@smumn.edu. *Application contact:* Jami Spitzer, Information Contact, 507-457-7500, E-mail: jspitzer@smumn.edu. Website: http://www.smumn.edu/graduate-home/areas-of-study/graduate-school-of-business-technology/ms-in-geographic-information-science

**Salisbury University,** Program in Geographic Information Systems Management, Salisbury, MD 21801-6837. Offers MS. *Program availability:* Part-time, evening/weekend, online only, 100% online. *Faculty:* 2 full-time (2 women). *Students:* 4 full-time (2 women), 14 part-time (4 women); includes 1 minority (Black or African American, non-Hispanic/Latino), 2 international. Average age 34. 2 applicants, 50% accepted, 1 enrolled. In 2016, 3 master's awarded. *Entrance requirements:* Additional exam requirements/recommendations for international students: Required—TOEFL (minimum score 550 paper-based, 79 iBT) or IELTS (6.5). *Application deadline:* For fall admission, 7/1 priority date for domestic and international students; for spring admission, 10/1 priority date for domestic and international students; for summer admission, 3/1 priority date for domestic and international students. Applications are processed on a rolling basis. Application fee: $65. Electronic applications accepted. *Expenses:* $750 per credit hour (online). *Financial support:* In 2016–17, 2 teaching assistantships with full tuition reimbursements (averaging $9,000 per year) were awarded; career-related internships or fieldwork and scholarships/grants also available. Support available to part-time students. Financial award application deadline: 3/1; financial award applicants required to submit FAFSA. *Faculty research:* GIS management; parallel processing; LIDAR; environmental modeling; GIS. *Unit head:* Dr. Stuart Hamilton, Graduate Program Director, Geographic Information Systems Management, 410-543-6456, E-mail: sehamilton@salisbury.edu. *Application contact:* Jennifer Gordy, Program Management Specialist, 410-543-6460, E-mail: jlgordy@salisbury.edu. Website: http://www.salisbury.edu/gsr/gradstudies/GISpage.html

**Sam Houston State University,** College of Sciences, Department of Geography and Geology, Huntsville, TX 77341. Offers applied geographic information science (MS); geographic information science (Certificate). *Program availability:* Part-time. *Degree requirements:* For master's, comprehensive exam, thesis (for some programs). *Entrance requirements:* For master's, GRE General Test, letters of recommendation. Additional exam requirements/recommendations for international students: Required—TOEFL (minimum score 550 paper-based; 79 iBT), IELTS (minimum score 6.5). Electronic applications accepted.

**San Francisco State University,** Division of Graduate Studies, College of Science and Engineering, Department of Geography and Environment, San Francisco, CA 94132-1722. Offers geographic information science (MS); geography (MA); resource management and environmental planning (MA). *Expenses:* Tuition, state resident: full-time $6738. Tuition, nonresident: full-time $15,666. *Required fees:* $1012. Tuition and fees vary according to degree level and program. *Unit head:* Dr. Jerry Davis, Chair, 415-338-2983, Fax: 415-338-6243, E-mail: jerry@sfsu.edu. *Application contact:* Dr. Nancy Wilkinson, Graduate Coordinator, 415-338-1439, Fax: 415-338-6243, E-mail: nancyw@sfsu.edu. Website: http://geog.sfsu.edu/

**State University of New York College of Environmental Science and Forestry,** Department of Environmental Resources Engineering, Syracuse, NY 13210-2779. Offers ecological engineering (MPS, MS, PhD); environmental management (MPS); environmental resources engineering (MPS, MS, PhD); geospatial information science and engineering (MPS, MS, PhD); water resources engineering (MPS, MS, PhD). *Program availability:* Part-time. *Faculty:* 8 full-time (1 woman), 9 part-time/adjunct (3 women). *Students:* 34 full-time (13 women), 13 part-time (2 women); includes 3 minority (1 Black or African American, non-Hispanic/Latino; 1 Asian, non-Hispanic/Latino; 1 Hispanic/Latino), 21 international. Average age 28. 44 applicants, 48% accepted, 10 enrolled. In 2016, 8 master's, 1 doctorate awarded. *Degree requirements:* For master's, thesis (for some programs); for doctorate, comprehensive exam, thesis/dissertation. *Entrance requirements:* For master's and doctorate, GRE General Test, minimum GPA of 3.0. Additional exam requirements/recommendations for international students: Required—TOEFL (minimum score 550 paper-based; 80 iBT), IELTS (minimum score 6). *Application deadline:* For fall admission, 1/15 priority date for domestic and international students; for spring admission, 11/1 priority date for domestic and international students. Applications are processed on a rolling basis. Application fee: $60. *Expenses:* Tuition, state resident: full-time $10,870; part-time $453 per credit. Tuition, nonresident: full-time $22,210; part-time $925 per credit. *Required fees:* $1075; $89.22 per credit. *Financial support:* In 2016–17, 7 students received support. Application deadline: 6/30; applicants required to submit FAFSA. *Faculty research:* Ecological engineering, environmental resources engineering, geospatial information science and engineering, water resources engineering, environmental science. *Unit head:* Dr. Theodore Endreny, Chair, 315-470-6565, Fax: 315-470-6958, E-mail: te@esf.edu. *Application contact:* Scott Shannon, Associate Provost for Instruction/Dean of the Graduate School, 315-470-6599, Fax: 315-470-6978, E-mail: esfgrad@esf.edu. Website: http://www.esf.edu/ere

**Stony Brook University, State University of New York,** Graduate School, School of Marine and Atmospheric Sciences, Sustainability Studies Program, Stony Brook, NY 11794-3352. Offers geospatial sciences (Graduate Certificate). *Faculty:* 7 full-time (4 women), 4 part-time/adjunct (1 woman). *Students:* 1 full-time (0 women), 6 part-time (1 woman); includes 1 minority (Two or more races, non-Hispanic/Latino). Average age 29. 4 applicants, 100% accepted, 4 enrolled. In 2016, 9 Graduate Certificates awarded. *Entrance requirements:* For degree, personal statement, letters of recommendation, official transcripts. Additional exam requirements/recommendations for international students: Required—TOEFL. *Application deadline:* For fall admission, 1/15 for domestic students. Application fee: $100. *Expenses:* Contact institution. *Financial support:* Teaching assistantships available. *Unit head:* Dr. Heidi Hutner, Director, 631-632-5360, E-mail: heidi.hutner@stonybrook.edu. *Application contact:* Kim Knoll, Staff Assistant, 631-632-8656, Fax: 631-632-5375, E-mail: kim.knoll@stonybrook.edu. Website: http://www.stonybrook.edu/commcms/sustainability/

**Temple University,** College of Liberal Arts, Department of Geography and Urban Studies, Philadelphia, PA 19122-6096. Offers geographic information systems (PSM, Graduate Certificate); geography and urban studies (MA, PhD). *Degree requirements:* For master's, comprehensive exam, thesis or alternative. *Entrance requirements:* For master's, GRE General Test, minimum GPA of 3.0, 3 letters of recommendation; for doctorate, GRE, minimum GPA of 3.0, 3 letters of recommendation. Additional exam requirements/recommendations for international students: Required—TOEFL (minimum score 575 paper-based; 88 iBT). Electronic applications accepted. *Faculty research:* Social justice, sustainability, globalization, geographic methods, urban processes.

**Texas State University,** The Graduate College, College of Liberal Arts, Doctoral Program in Geographic Information Science, San Marcos, TX 78666. Offers PhD. *Program availability:* Part-time, evening/weekend. *Faculty:* 25 full-time (9 women). *Students:* 10 full-time (6 women), 9 part-time (4 women); includes 3 minority (2 Asian, non-Hispanic/Latino; 1 Hispanic/Latino), 11 international. Average age 34. 21 applicants, 71% accepted, 9 enrolled. In 2016, 2 doctorates awarded. *Degree requirements:* For doctorate, comprehensive exam, thesis/dissertation. *Entrance requirements:* For doctorate, GRE (minimum preferred score of 303 verbal and quantitative), master's degree in geography or related field from regionally-accredited institution with minimum GPA of 3.5 on all graduate coursework, 3 letters of recommendation, statement of purpose, curriculum vitae. Additional exam requirements/recommendations for international students: Required—TOEFL (minimum score 550 paper-based; 78 iBT), IELTS (minimum score 6.5). *Application deadline:* For fall

## Geographic Information Systems

admission, 1/15 priority date for domestic and international students. Applications are processed on a rolling basis. Application fee: $40 ($90 for international students). Electronic applications accepted. *Expenses:* $4,851 per semester. *Financial support:* In 2016–17, 27 students received support, including 10 teaching assistantships (averaging $30,380 per year); research assistantships, career-related internships or fieldwork, Federal Work-Study, institutionally sponsored loans, and scholarships/grants also available. Support available to part-time students. Financial award application deadline: 3/1; financial award applicants required to submit FAFSA. *Faculty research:* Earth science and remote sensing; image science and analysis. *Total annual research expenditures:* $238,516. *Unit head:* Dr. Yongmei Lu, PhD Program Director, 512-245-1337, Fax: 512-245-8353, E-mail: yl10@txstate.edu. *Application contact:* Dr. Andrea Golato, Dean of Graduate School, 512-245-2581, Fax: 512-245-8365, E-mail: gradcollege@txstate.edu.
Website: http://www.geo.txstate.edu/

**Université du Québec à Montréal,** Graduate Programs, Program in Geographical Information Systems, Montréal, QC H3C 3P8, Canada. Offers Diploma. *Program availability:* Part-time. *Entrance requirements:* For degree, appropriate bachelor's degree or equivalent, proficiency in French.

**Université Laval,** Faculty of Administrative Sciences, Programs in Business Administration, Québec, QC G1K 7P4, Canada. Offers accounting (MBA); agri-food management (MBA); electronic business (MBA, Diploma); factory management and logistics (MBA); finance (MBA); firm management (MBA); geomatic management (MBA); information technology management (MBA); international management (MBA); management (MBA); management accounting (MBA, Diploma); marketing (MBA); modeling and organizational decision (MBA); occupational health and safety management (MBA); pharmacy management (MBA); social and environmental responsibility (MBA); technological entrepreneurship (Diploma). *Accreditation:* AACSB. *Program availability:* Part-time, evening/weekend, online learning. *Entrance requirements:* For master's and Diploma, knowledge of French and English. Electronic applications accepted.

**University at Albany, State University of New York,** College of Arts and Sciences, Department of Geography and Planning, Albany, NY 12222-0001. Offers geographic information science (Certificate); geography (MA); regional planning (MRP); urban policy (Certificate). *Program availability:* Part-time. *Faculty:* 8 full-time (2 women), 6 part-time/adjunct (3 women). *Students:* 40 full-time (13 women), 20 part-time (8 women); includes 9 minority (5 Black or African American, non-Hispanic/Latino; 2 Asian, non-Hispanic/Latino; 1 Hispanic/Latino; 1 Two or more races, non-Hispanic/Latino), 10 international. 48 applicants, 85% accepted, 18 enrolled. In 2016, 34 master's, 10 other advanced degrees awarded. *Entrance requirements:* Additional exam requirements/recommendations for international students: Required—TOEFL (minimum score 550 paper-based). *Application deadline:* For fall admission, 3/1 for domestic students, 5/1 for international students; for spring admission, 11/1 for international students. Applications are processed on a rolling basis. Application fee: $75. Electronic applications accepted. *Expenses:* Tuition, state resident: full-time $10,870; part-time $453 per credit hour. Tuition, nonresident: full-time $22,210; part-time $925 per credit hour. *International tuition:* $21,550 full-time. *Required fees:* $1864; $96 per credit hour. *Financial support:* Fellowships, teaching assistantships, career-related internships or fieldwork, Federal Work-Study, and institutionally sponsored loans available. Financial award application deadline: 3/1. *Faculty research:* Urban geography, social/cultural geography, urban planning, remote sensing, spatial analysis/geographic information systems. *Total annual research expenditures:* $1.1 million. *Unit head:* Catherine Lawson, Chair, 518-442-4636, Fax: 518-442-4742, E-mail: lawsonc@albany.edu. *Application contact:* Michael DeRensis, Director, Graduate Admissions, 518-442-3980, Fax: 518-442-3922, E-mail: graduate@albany.edu.
Website: http://www.albany.edu/gp/

**University at Buffalo, the State University of New York,** Graduate School, College of Arts and Sciences, Department of Geography, Buffalo, NY 14214. Offers earth systems science (MA, MS); economic geography and business geographics (MS); environmental modeling and analysis (MA); geographic information science (MA, MS); geography (MA, PhD); health geography (MS); international trade (MA); urban and regional analysis (MA). *Program availability:* Part-time. *Faculty:* 18 full-time (8 women), 1 part-time/adjunct (0 women). *Students:* 45 full-time (29 women), 51 part-time (15 women); includes 64 minority (1 Black or African American, non-Hispanic/Latino; 61 Asian, non-Hispanic/Latino; 2 Hispanic/Latino), 41 international. Average age 28. 167 applicants, 34% accepted, 28 enrolled. In 2016, 23 master's, 7 doctorates awarded. Terminal master's awarded for partial completion of doctoral program. *Degree requirements:* For master's, thesis (for some programs), project or portfolio; for doctorate, thesis/dissertation. *Entrance requirements:* For master's, GRE General Test, minimum GPA of 2.9; for doctorate, GRE General Test, minimum GPA of 3.0. Additional exam requirements/recommendations for international students: Required—TOEFL (minimum score 550 paper-based; 79 iBT). *Application deadline:* For fall admission, 5/1 priority date for domestic students, 3/10 priority date for international students; for spring admission, 11/1 priority date for domestic students, 9/1 priority date for international students. Applications are processed on a rolling basis. Application fee: $75. Electronic applications accepted. *Expenses:* Contact institution. *Financial support:* In 2016–17, 15 students received support, including 7 fellowships with full tuition reimbursements available (averaging $3,070 per year), 7 research assistantships with full tuition reimbursements available (averaging $14,000 per year), 15 teaching assistantships with full tuition reimbursements available (averaging $14,080 per year); career-related internships or fieldwork, Federal Work-Study, institutionally sponsored loans, traineeships, health care benefits, and unspecified assistantships also available. Financial award application deadline: 1/10. *Faculty research:* International business and world trade, geographic information systems and cartography, transportation, urban and regional analysis, physical and environmental geography. *Total annual research expenditures:* $2.6 million. *Unit head:* Dr. Sean Bennett, Chairman, 716-645-0490, Fax: 716-645-2329, E-mail: seanb@buffalo.edu. *Application contact:* Wendy Zitzka, Graduate Secretary, 716-645-0471, Fax: 716-645-2329, E-mail: wzitzka@buffalo.edu.
Website: http://www.geog.buffalo.edu/

**The University of Alabama,** Graduate School, College of Arts and Sciences, Department of Geography, Tuscaloosa, AL 35487. Offers earth system science (MS, PhD); environment and natural resources (MS, PhD); environment and society (MS, PhD); geographic information science (MS, PhD). *Program availability:* Part-time. *Faculty:* 14 full-time (2 women). *Students:* 26 full-time (11 women), 5 part-time (1 woman); includes 1 minority (Hispanic/Latino), 8 international. Average age 26. 46 applicants, 35% accepted, 11 enrolled. In 2016, 10 master's awarded. *Degree requirements:* For master's, comprehensive exam, thesis; for doctorate, comprehensive exam, thesis/dissertation. *Entrance requirements:* For master's, GRE, minimum GPA of 3.0. Additional exam requirements/recommendations for international students: Required—TOEFL (minimum score 550 paper-based; 79 iBT). *Application deadline:* For fall admission, 2/15 priority date for domestic and international students; for spring admission, 10/1 priority date for domestic and international students. Applications are processed on a rolling basis. Application fee: $50 ($60 for international students). Electronic applications accepted. *Expenses:* Tuition, state resident: full-time $10,470.

Tuition, nonresident: full-time $26,950. *Financial support:* In 2016–17, 20 students received support, including fellowships with full tuition reimbursements available (averaging $15,000 per year), 4 research assistantships with full tuition reimbursements available (averaging $14,013 per year), 18 teaching assistantships with full tuition reimbursements available (averaging $14,013 per year); career-related internships or fieldwork, health care benefits, and unspecified assistantships also available. Financial award application deadline: 2/15. *Faculty research:* Earth system science; geographic information science; environment and natural resources; environment and society. *Total annual research expenditures:* $347,176. *Unit head:* Dr. Douglas Sherman, Chair, 205-348-5047, Fax: 205-348-2278, E-mail: douglas.j.sherman@ua.edu. *Application contact:* Dr. Justin Hart, Associate Professor, 205-348-5047, Fax: 205-348-2278, E-mail: hart013@ua.edu.
Website: http://geography.ua.edu

**University of Alaska Fairbanks,** College of Natural Sciences and Mathematics, Department of Geosciences, Fairbanks, AK 99775-5780. Offers geophysics (MS), including remote sensing geophysics, snow, ice, and permafrost geophysics, solid-earth geophysics. *Program availability:* Part-time. *Faculty:* 12 full-time (3 women), 1 part-time/adjunct (0 women). *Students:* 50 full-time (25 women), 26 part-time (10 women); includes 3 minority (1 Asian, non-Hispanic/Latino; 1 Hispanic/Latino; 1 Two or more races, non-Hispanic/Latino), 16 international. Average age 30. 75 applicants, 16% accepted, 12 enrolled. In 2016, 8 master's awarded. *Degree requirements:* For master's, comprehensive exam, thesis, oral defense of thesis. *Entrance requirements:* For master's, GRE General Test, bachelor's degree in geology, geophysics, or an appropriate physical science or engineering with minimum cumulative undergraduate and major GPA of 3.0. Additional exam requirements/recommendations for international students: Required—TOEFL (minimum score 550 paper-based; 79 iBT), IELTS (minimum score 6.5). *Application deadline:* For fall admission, 6/1 for domestic students, 3/1 for international students; for spring admission, 10/15 for domestic students, 9/1 for international students. Applications are processed on a rolling basis. Application fee: $60. Electronic applications accepted. *Expenses:* Tuition, state resident: full-time $7992; part-time $444 per credit. Tuition, nonresident: full-time $16,326; part-time $907 per credit. *Required fees:* $39 per credit. $322 per semester. Tuition and fees vary according to course level, course load, campus/location, program and reciprocity agreements. *Financial support:* In 2016–17, 30 research assistantships with full tuition reimbursements (averaging $16,975 per year), 15 teaching assistantships with full tuition reimbursements (averaging $11,787 per year) were awarded; fellowships with full tuition reimbursements, Federal Work-Study, scholarships/grants, health care benefits, and unspecified assistantships also available. Support available to part-time students. Financial award application deadline: 2/15; financial award applicants required to submit FAFSA. *Faculty research:* Glacial surging, volcanology, geochronology, impact cratering, permafrost geophysics. *Unit head:* Dr. Paul McCarthy, Department Chair, 907-474-7565, Fax: 907-474-5163, E-mail: geology@uaf.edu. *Application contact:* Mary Kreta, Director of Admissions, 907-474-7500, Fax: 907-474-7097, E-mail: admissions@uaf.edu.
Website: http://www.uaf.edu/geology/

**The University of Arizona,** College of Social and Behavioral Sciences, School of Geography and Development, Tucson, AZ 85721. Offers geographic information systems technology (MA); geography (PhD). *Program availability:* Part-time. Terminal master's awarded for partial completion of doctoral program. *Degree requirements:* For master's, thesis or additional course work; for doctorate, variable foreign language requirement, thesis/dissertation. *Entrance requirements:* For master's, GRE General Test, 2 letters of recommendation; for doctorate, GRE General Test, statement of purpose, 2 letters of recommendation, master's degree. Additional exam requirements/recommendations for international students: Required—TOEFL (minimum score 550 paper-based; 79 iBT). Electronic applications accepted. *Faculty research:* Population, Latin America, Anglo-America, the former Soviet Union, the Middle East.

**University of Central Arkansas,** Graduate School, College of Liberal Arts, Department of Geography, Conway, AR 72035-0001. Offers community and economic development (MS); geographic information systems (MGIS, Certificate). *Program availability:* Part-time, online learning. *Entrance requirements:* Additional exam requirements/recommendations for international students: Required—TOEFL (minimum score 550 paper-based). Electronic applications accepted.

**University of Central Arkansas,** Graduate School, College of Liberal Arts, Program in Community and Economic Development, Conway, AR 72035-0001. Offers community and economic development (MS); geographic and information systems (MGIS, Graduate Certificate). *Program availability:* Part-time, online learning. *Degree requirements:* For master's, comprehensive exam, thesis. *Entrance requirements:* For master's, GRE General Test, minimum GPA of 2.7. Additional exam requirements/recommendations for international students: Required—TOEFL (minimum score 550 paper-based). Electronic applications accepted. *Expenses:* Contact institution.

**University of Central Florida,** College of Graduate Studies, Program in Interdisciplinary Studies, Orlando, FL 32816. Offers geographic information systems (Certificate); interdisciplinary studies (MA, MS). *Students:* 7 full-time (4 women), 25 part-time (17 women); includes 9 minority (3 Black or African American, non-Hispanic/Latino; 1 Asian, non-Hispanic/Latino; 4 Hispanic/Latino; 1 Two or more races, non-Hispanic/Latino). Average age 32. 38 applicants, 82% accepted, 27 enrolled. In 2016, 7 master's awarded. *Degree requirements:* For master's, thesis or alternative. *Entrance requirements:* For master's, GRE General Test, minimum GPA of 3.0 in last 60 hours. Additional exam requirements/recommendations for international students: Required—TOEFL. *Application deadline:* For fall admission, 7/15 for domestic students; for spring admission, 12/1 for domestic students. Application fee: $30. Electronic applications accepted. *Expenses:* Tuition, state resident: part-time $288.16 per credit hour. Tuition, nonresident: part-time $1071.31 per credit hour. *Financial support:* Teaching assistantships available. Financial award application deadline: 3/1; financial award applicants required to submit FAFSA. *Unit head:* Dr. John Weishampel, Associate Dean, 407-823-6634, E-mail: john.weishampel@ucf.edu. *Application contact:* Assistant Director, Graduate Admissions, 407-823-2766, Fax: 407-823-6442, E-mail: gradadmissions@ucf.edu.
Website: https://www.graduate.ucf.edu/IDS/

**University of Colorado Denver,** Business School, Program in Information Systems, Denver, CO 80217. Offers accounting and information systems audit and control (MS); business intelligence systems (MS); digital health entrepreneurship (MS); enterprise risk management (MS); enterprise technology management (MS); geographic information systems (MS); health information technology (MS); technology innovation and entrepreneurship (MS); Web and mobile computing (MS). *Program availability:* Part-time, evening/weekend, online learning. *Students:* 110 full-time (44 women), 33 part-time (11 women); includes 19 minority (1 Black or African American, non-Hispanic/Latino; 8 Asian, non-Hispanic/Latino; 6 Hispanic/Latino; 4 Two or more races, non-Hispanic/Latino), 79 international. Average age 29. 140 applicants, 71% accepted, 38 enrolled. In 2016, 50 master's awarded. *Degree requirements:* For master's, 30 credit hours. *Entrance requirements:* For master's, GMAT, resume, essay, two letters of recommendation, financial statements (for international applicants). Additional exam requirements/recommendations for international students: Required—TOEFL (minimum

score 525 paper-based; 71 iBT); Recommended—IELTS (minimum score 6.5). *Application deadline:* For fall admission, 4/15 priority date for domestic students, 3/15 priority date for international students; for spring admission, 10/15 priority date for domestic students, 9/15 priority date for international students; for summer admission, 2/15 priority date for domestic students, 1/15 priority date for international students. Applications are processed on a rolling basis. Application fee: $50 ($75 for international students). Electronic applications accepted. *Expenses:* Contact institution. *Financial support:* In 2016–17, 24 students received support. Fellowships, research assistantships, teaching assistantships, Federal Work-Study, institutionally sponsored loans, scholarships/grants, and traineeships available. Financial award application deadline: 4/1; financial award applicants required to submit FAFSA. *Faculty research:* Human-computer interaction, expert systems, database management, electronic commerce, object-oriented software development. *Unit head:* Dr. Jahangir Karimi, Director of Information Systems Programs, 303-315-8430, E-mail: jahangir.karimi@ucdenver.edu. *Application contact:* 303-315-8200, E-mail: bschool.admissions@ucdenver.edu.
Website: http://www.ucdenver.edu/academics/colleges/business/degrees/ms/IS/Pages/Information-Systems.aspx

**University of Colorado Denver,** College of Engineering and Applied Science, Department of Civil Engineering, Denver, CO 80217. Offers civil engineering (EASPh D); civil engineering systems (PhD); environmental and sustainability engineering (MS, PhD); geographic information systems (MS); geotechnical engineering (MS, PhD); hydrology and hydraulics (MS, PhD); structural engineering (MS, PhD); transportation engineering (MS, PhD). *Program availability:* Part-time, evening/weekend. *Faculty:* 15 full-time (3 women), 9 part-time/adjunct (0 women). *Students:* 50 full-time (15 women), 33 part-time (7 women); includes 10 minority (1 Black or African American, non-Hispanic/Latino; 2 Asian, non-Hispanic/Latino; 6 Hispanic/Latino; 1 Two or more races, non-Hispanic/Latino), 31 international. Average age 30. 105 applicants, 51% accepted, 14 enrolled. In 2016, 29 master's, 2 doctorates awarded. *Degree requirements:* For master's, comprehensive exam, 30 credit hours, project or thesis; for doctorate, comprehensive exam, thesis/dissertation, 60 credit hours (30 of which are dissertation research). *Entrance requirements:* For master's, GRE, statement of purpose, transcripts, three references; for doctorate, GRE, statement of purpose, transcripts, references, letter of support from faculty stating willingness to serve as dissertation advisor and outlining plan for financial support. Additional exam requirements/recommendations for international students: Required—TOEFL (minimum score 537 paper-based; 75 iBT); Recommended—IELTS (minimum score 6.5). *Application deadline:* For fall admission, 5/1 for domestic students, 4/1 for international students; for spring admission, 10/1 for domestic students, 9/1 for international students; for summer admission, 2/15 for domestic students, 1/15 for international students. Application fee: $50 ($75 for international students). Electronic applications accepted. *Expenses:* Contact institution. *Financial support:* In 2016–17, 62 students received support. Fellowships, research assistantships, teaching assistantships, career-related internships or fieldwork, Federal Work-Study, institutionally sponsored loans, scholarships/grants, traineeships, and unspecified assistantships available. Financial award application deadline: 4/1; financial award applicants required to submit FAFSA. *Faculty research:* Earthquake source physics, environmental biotechnology, hydrologic and hydraulic engineering, sustainability assessments, transportation energy use and greenhouse gas emissions. *Unit head:* Dr. Kevin Rens, Chair, 303-556-8017, E-mail: kevin.rens@ucdenver.edu. *Application contact:* Roxanne Pizano, Program Coordinator, 303-556-6274, E-mail: roxanne.pizano@ucdenver.edu.
Website: http://www.ucdenver.edu/academics/colleges/Engineering/Programs/Civil-Engineering/Pages/CivilEngineering.aspx

**University of Colorado Denver,** College of Engineering and Applied Science, Master of Engineering Program, Denver, CO 80217-3364. Offers civil engineering (M Eng), including civil engineering, geographic information systems, transportation systems; electrical engineering (M Eng); mechanical engineering (M Eng). *Program availability:* Part-time. *Students:* 35 full-time (9 women), 23 part-time (7 women); includes 5 minority (1 American Indian or Alaska Native, non-Hispanic/Latino; 2 Hispanic/Latino; 2 Two or more races, non-Hispanic/Latino), 11 international. Average age 31. 75 applicants, 63% accepted, 13 enrolled. In 2016, 17 master's awarded. *Degree requirements:* For master's, comprehensive exam, 27 credit hours of course work, 3 credit hours of report or thesis work. *Entrance requirements:* For master's, GRE (for those with GPA below 2.75), transcripts, references, statement of purpose. Additional exam requirements/recommendations for international students: Required—TOEFL (minimum score 537 paper-based; 75 iBT); Recommended—IELTS (minimum score 6.5). *Application deadline:* For fall admission, 4/1 for domestic students, 3/1 for international students; for spring admission, 10/1 for domestic students, 9/15 for international students. Applications are processed on a rolling basis. Application fee: $50 ($75 for international students). Electronic applications accepted. *Expenses:* Contact institution. *Financial support:* In 2016–17, 120 students received support. Fellowships, research assistantships, teaching assistantships, Federal Work-Study, institutionally sponsored loans, scholarships/grants, traineeships, and unspecified assistantships available. Financial award application deadline: 4/1; financial award applicants required to submit FAFSA. *Faculty research:* Civil, electrical and mechanical engineering. *Application contact:* Graduate School Admissions, 303-315-2179, E-mail: ceasgaapplications@ucdenver.edu.
Website: http://www.ucdenver.edu/academics/colleges/Engineering/admissions/Masters/Pages/MastersAdmissions.aspx

**University of Colorado Denver,** College of Liberal Arts and Sciences, Department of Geography and Environmental Sciences, Denver, CO 80217. Offers environmental sciences (MS), including air quality, ecosystems, environmental health, environmental science education, geospatial analysis, urban agriculture, water quality. *Program availability:* Part-time, evening/weekend. *Faculty:* 13 full-time (4 women), 5 part-time/adjunct (2 women). *Students:* 47 full-time (24 women), 6 part-time (2 women); includes 10 minority (1 Black or African American, non-Hispanic/Latino; 2 Asian, non-Hispanic/Latino; 5 Hispanic/Latino; 2 Two or more races, non-Hispanic/Latino), 1 international. Average age 30. 57 applicants, 72% accepted, 18 enrolled. In 2016, 23 master's awarded. *Degree requirements:* For master's, thesis or alternative, 30 credits including 21 of core requirements and 9 of environmental science electives. *Entrance requirements:* For master's, GRE General Test, BA in one of the natural/physical sciences or engineering (or equivalent background); prerequisite coursework in calculus and physics (one semester each); general chemistry with lab and general biology with lab (two semesters each); three letters of recommendation. Additional exam requirements/recommendations for international students: Required—TOEFL (minimum score 537 paper-based; 75 iBT); Recommended—IELTS (minimum score 6.5). *Application deadline:* For fall admission, 1/20 for domestic and international students; for spring admission, 10/1 for domestic and international students. Application fee: $50 ($75 for international students). Electronic applications accepted. *Expenses:* Tuition, state resident: full-time $11,006; part-time $474 per credit. Tuition, nonresident: full-time $28,212; part-time $1264 per credit hour. *Required fees:* $256 per semester. One-time fee: $94.32. Tuition and fees vary according to campus/location and program. *Financial support:* In 2016–17, 6 students received support. Fellowships, research assistantships, teaching assistantships, Federal Work-Study, institutionally sponsored loans,

scholarships/grants, and traineeships available. Financial award application deadline: 4/1; financial award applicants required to submit FAFSA. *Faculty research:* Air quality, environmental health, ecosystems, hazardous waste, water quality, geospatial analysis and environmental science education. *Unit head:* Anne Chinn, Director of MS in Environmental Sciences Program, 303-556-3958, E-mail: ges@ucdenver.edu. *Application contact:* Sue Eddleman, Program Assistant, 303-352-3698, E-mail: sue.eddleman@ucdenver.edu.
Website: http://www.ucdenver.edu/academics/colleges/CLAS/Departments/ges/Programs/MasterofScience/Pages/MasterofScience.aspx

**University of Denver,** University College, Denver, CO 80208. Offers arts and culture (MA, Certificate); communication management (MS, Certificate), including translation studies (Certificate), world history and culture (Certificate); environmental policy and management (MS); geographic information systems (MS); global affairs (MA, Certificate), including human capital in organizations (Certificate), philanthropic leadership (Certificate), project management (Certificate), strategic innovation and change (Certificate); healthcare leadership (MS); information communications and technology (MS); leadership and organizations (MS); professional creative writing (MA, Certificate), including emergency planning and response (Certificate), organizational security (Certificate); security management (MS, Certificate); strategic human resources (Certificate). *Program availability:* Part-time, evening/weekend, online learning. *Faculty:* 118 part-time/adjunct (62 women). *Students:* 59 full-time (22 women), 1,285 part-time (750 women); includes 316 minority (111 Black or African American, non-Hispanic/Latino; 8 American Indian or Alaska Native, non-Hispanic/Latino; 39 Asian, non-Hispanic/Latino; 123 Hispanic/Latino; 3 Native Hawaiian or other Pacific Islander, non-Hispanic/Latino; 32 Two or more races, non-Hispanic/Latino), 85 international. Average age 35. 703 applicants, 89% accepted, 390 enrolled. In 2016, 428 master's, 138 other advanced degrees awarded. *Degree requirements:* For master's, capstone project. *Entrance requirements:* For master's, transcripts, two letters of recommendation, personal statement, resume. Additional exam requirements/recommendations for international students: Required—TOEFL (minimum score 550 paper-based; 80 iBT). *Application deadline:* For fall admission, 6/21 priority date for domestic students, 5/1 priority date for international students; for winter admission, 9/14 priority date for domestic students, 9/19 priority date for international students; for spring admission, 1/11 priority date for domestic students, 12/12 priority date for international students; for summer admission, 3/29 priority date for domestic students, 3/6 priority date for international students. Applications are processed on a rolling basis. Application fee: $75. Electronic applications accepted. *Expenses:* $7,236 per year full-time. *Financial support:* In 2016–17, 27 students received support, including 1 teaching assistantship (averaging $1,489 per year). Financial award applicants required to submit FAFSA. *Unit head:* Dr. Michael McGuire, Dean, 303-871-3518, Fax: 303-871-3303, E-mail: mmcguire@du.edu. *Application contact:* Information Contact, 303-871-2291, E-mail: ucoladm@du.edu.
Website: http://universitycollege.du.edu/

**University of Florida,** Graduate School, College of Liberal Arts and Sciences, Department of Geography, Gainesville, FL 32611. Offers applications of geographic technologies (MA, MS); geographic information systems (MA, MS, PhD); geography (MA, MS, PhD); hydrologic sciences (MS, PhD); tropical conservation and development (MA, MS, PhD); wetland sciences (MA, MS, PhD). *Degree requirements:* For master's, thesis; for doctorate, comprehensive exam, thesis/dissertation. *Entrance requirements:* For master's and doctorate, GRE General Test, minimum GPA of 3.0. Additional exam requirements/recommendations for international students: Required—TOEFL (minimum score 550 paper-based; 80 iBT), IELTS (minimum score 6). Electronic applications accepted. *Faculty research:* Economic development, physical geography, hydrology, climatology, tropical agriculture.

**The University of Iowa,** Graduate College, Program in Informatics, Iowa City, IA 52242-1316. Offers bioinformatics (MS, PhD); bioinformatics and computational biology (Certificate); geoinformatics (MS, PhD, Certificate); health informatics (MS, PhD, Certificate); information science (MS, PhD, Certificate). *Degree requirements:* For master's, thesis optional; for doctorate, comprehensive exam, thesis/dissertation. *Entrance requirements:* For master's and doctorate, GRE General Test, minimum GPA of 3.0. Additional exam requirements/recommendations for international students: Required—TOEFL (minimum score 550 paper-based; 81 iBT). Electronic applications accepted.

**The University of Kansas,** Graduate Studies, College of Liberal Arts and Sciences, Department of Geography, Lawrence, KS 66045-7613. Offers atmospheric science (MS); geographic information science (Graduate Certificate); geography (MA, PhD); MUP/MA. *Program availability:* Part-time. *Students:* 48 full-time (19 women), 18 part-time (7 women); includes 9 minority (7 American Indian or Alaska Native, non-Hispanic/Latino; 1 Asian, non-Hispanic/Latino; 1 Hispanic/Latino), 7 international. Average age 33. 55 applicants, 33% accepted, 9 enrolled. In 2016, 15 master's, 6 doctorates awarded. *Entrance requirements:* For master's and doctorate, GRE General Test, 3 letters of reference, transcripts, statement of interests, resume. Additional exam requirements/recommendations for international students: Required—TOEFL. *Application deadline:* For fall admission, 1/15 priority date for domestic and international students; for spring admission, 11/1 for domestic and international students; for summer admission, 4/1 for domestic and international students. Application fee: $65 ($85 for international students). Electronic applications accepted. *Financial support:* Fellowships, research assistantships, teaching assistantships, and unspecified assistantships available. Financial award application deadline: 1/15. *Faculty research:* Physical geography, human/cultural/regional geography, geographic information science, atmospheric science. *Unit head:* Nathaniel Brunsell, Chair, 785-864-2021, E-mail: brunsell@ku.edu. *Application contact:* Beverly Koerner, Graduate Admission Contact, 785-864-7706, E-mail: koerner@ku.edu.
Website: http://www.geog.ku.edu/

**University of Lethbridge,** School of Graduate Studies, Lethbridge, AB T1K 3M4, Canada. Offers addictions counseling (M Sc); agricultural biotechnology (M Sc); agricultural studies (M Sc, MA); anthropology (MA); archaeology (M Sc, MA); art (MA, MFA); biochemistry (M Sc); biological sciences (M Sc); biomolecular science (PhD); biosystems and biodiversity (PhD); Canadian studies (MA); chemistry (M Sc); computer science (M Sc); computer science and geographical information science (M Sc); counseling (MC); counseling psychology (M Ed); dramatic arts (MA); earth, space, and physical science (PhD); economics (MA); education (MA, PhD); educational leadership (M Ed); English (MA); environmental science (M Sc); evolution and behavior (PhD); exercise science (M Sc); French (MA); French/German (MA); French/Spanish (MA); general education (M Ed); geography (M Sc, MA); German (MA); health sciences (M Sc); individualized multidisciplinary (M Sc, MA); kinesiology (M Sc, MA); management (M Sc), including accounting, finance, human resource management and labor relations, information systems, international management, marketing, policy and strategy; mathematics (M Sc); music (M Mus, MA); Native American studies (MA); neuroscience (M Sc, PhD); new media (MA, MFA); nursing (M Sc, MN); philosophy (MA); physics (M Sc); political science (MA); psychology (M Sc, MA); religious studies (MA); sociology (MA); theatre and dramatic arts (MFA); theoretical and computational science (PhD); urban and regional studies (MA); women and gender studies (MA).

## Geographic Information Systems

*Program availability:* Part-time, evening/weekend. *Degree requirements:* For master's, thesis (for some programs); for doctorate, comprehensive exam, thesis/dissertation. *Entrance requirements:* For master's, GMAT (for M Sc in management), bachelor's degree in related field, minimum GPA of 3.0 during previous 20 graded semester courses, 2 years' teaching or related experience (M Ed); for doctorate, master's degree, minimum graduate GPA of 3.5. Additional exam requirements/recommendations for international students: Required—TOEFL (minimum score 580 paper-based; 93 iBT). Electronic applications accepted. *Faculty research:* Movement and brain plasticity, gibberellin physiology, photosynthesis, carbon cycling, molecular properties of main-group ring components.

**University of Maryland, Baltimore County,** The Graduate School, College of Arts, Humanities and Social Sciences, Department of Geography and Environmental Systems, Program in Geographic Information Systems, Rockville, MD 20850. Offers MPS, Certificate. *Program availability:* Part-time, evening/weekend. *Faculty:* 13 part-time/adjunct (3 women). *Students:* 8 full-time (2 women), 21 part-time (6 women); includes 9 minority (4 Black or African American, non-Hispanic/Latino; 2 Asian, non-Hispanic/Latino; 2 Hispanic/Latino; 1 Two or more races, non-Hispanic/Latino), 8 international. Average age 33. 17 applicants, 71% accepted, 6 enrolled. In 2016, 14 master's, 8 Certificates awarded. *Entrance requirements:* Additional exam requirements/recommendations for international students: Required—TOEFL (minimum score 80 iBT), IELTS (minimum score 6.5). *Application deadline:* For fall admission, 8/1 for domestic students, 6/1 for international students; for spring admission, 12/1 for domestic students, 11/1 for international students. Applications are processed on a rolling basis. Application fee: $50. Electronic applications accepted. *Expenses:* Contact institution. *Faculty research:* Enterprise GIS. *Unit head:* Dr. Erwin Villiger, Program Director, 301-738-6087, E-mail: villiger@umbc.edu. *Application contact:* Rickeysha Jones, Program Coordinator, 301-738-6285, E-mail: rcjones@umbc.edu. Website: http://www.umbc.edu/gis

**University of Memphis,** Graduate School, College of Arts and Sciences, Department of Earth Sciences, Memphis, TN 38152. Offers earth sciences (MA, MS, PhD), including archaeology (MS), geography (MS), geology (MS), geophysics (MS), interdisciplinary studies (MS); geographic information systems (Graduate Certificate), including geographic information systems, GIS educator, GIS planning, GIS professional. *Program availability:* Part-time, evening/weekend. *Faculty:* 17 full-time (3 women), 5 part-time/adjunct (0 women). *Students:* 37 full-time (10 women), 25 part-time (6 women); includes 3 minority (2 Black or African American, non-Hispanic/Latino; 1 Two or more races, non-Hispanic/Latino), 22 international. Average age 33. 30 applicants, 60% accepted, 12 enrolled. In 2016, 21 master's, 5 doctorates, 6 other advanced degrees awarded. Terminal master's awarded for partial completion of doctoral program. *Degree requirements:* For master's, comprehensive exam, thesis, seminar presentation; for doctorate, comprehensive exam, thesis/dissertation, qualifying exam, submission of two manuscripts for publication in peer-reviewed journal or books. *Entrance requirements:* For master's, GRE General Test, 3 letters of recommendation, statement of research interests; for doctorate, GRE General Test, 2 letters of recommendation, resume, personal statement. Additional exam requirements/recommendations for international students: Required—TOEFL (minimum score 550 paper-based; 79 iBT). *Application deadline:* For fall admission, 1/15 for domestic students; for spring admission, 11/1 for domestic students. Applications are processed on a rolling basis. Application fee: $35 ($60 for international students). Electronic applications accepted. *Expenses:* $5,231.50 per semester full-time in-state, $9,623.50 full-time out-of-state. *Financial support:* In 2016–17, 18 students received support, including 4 research assistantships with full tuition reimbursements available (averaging $13,960 per year), 11 teaching assistantships with full tuition reimbursements available (averaging $18,864 per year); fellowships with full tuition reimbursements available, Federal Work-Study, scholarships/grants, and unspecified assistantships also available. Financial award application deadline: 2/1; financial award applicants required to submit FAFSA. *Faculty research:* Hazards, active tectonics, geophysics, hydrology and water resources, spatial analysis. *Unit head:* Dr. Daniel Larsen, Chair, 901-678-4538, Fax: 901-678-2178, E-mail: dlarsen@memphis.edu. *Application contact:* Dr. Randel T. Cox, Graduate Coordinator, 901-678-4361, Fax: 901-678-2178, E-mail: randycox@memphis.edu. Website: http://www.memphis.edu/earthsciences

**University of Minnesota, Twin Cities Campus,** Graduate School, College of Food, Agricultural and Natural Resource Sciences, Program in Natural Resources Science and Management, St. Paul, MN 55108. Offers assessment, monitoring, and geospatial analysis (MS, PhD); economics, policy, management, and society (MS, PhD); forest hydrology and watershed management (MS, PhD); forest products (MS, PhD); forests: biology, ecology, conservation, and management (MS, PhD); natural resources science and management (MS, PhD); paper science and engineering (MS, PhD); recreation resources, tourism, and environmental education (MS, PhD); wildlife ecology and management (MS, PhD). *Program availability:* Part-time. *Faculty:* 71 full-time (28 women), 52 part-time/adjunct (7 women). *Students:* 79 full-time (46 women), 27 part-time (14 women); includes 11 minority (2 Black or African American, non-Hispanic/Latino; 3 American Indian or Alaska Native, non-Hispanic/Latino; 3 Asian, non-Hispanic/Latino; 3 Hispanic/Latino), 9 international. Average age 31. 63 applicants, 57% accepted, 26 enrolled. In 2016, 19 master's, 3 doctorates awarded. Terminal master's awarded for partial completion of doctoral program. *Degree requirements:* For master's, comprehensive exam, thesis (for some programs); for doctorate, comprehensive exam, thesis/dissertation. *Entrance requirements:* For master's and doctorate, GRE General Test. Additional exam requirements/recommendations for international students: Required—TOEFL (minimum score 550 paper-based; 79 iBT), IELTS (minimum score 6.5). *Application deadline:* For fall admission, 12/16 priority date for domestic and international students; for spring admission, 10/15 for domestic and international students. Applications are processed on a rolling basis. Application fee: $75 ($95 for international students). Electronic applications accepted. *Financial support:* In 2016–17, 5 students received support, including fellowships with full tuition reimbursements available (averaging $40,000 per year), research assistantships with full tuition reimbursements available (averaging $40,000 per year), teaching assistantships with full tuition reimbursements available (averaging $40,000 per year); scholarships/grants, health care benefits, and unspecified assistantships also available. *Faculty research:* Forest hydrology, biology, ecology, conservation, and management; recreation resources and environmental education; wildlife ecology; economics, policy, and society; geographic information systems (GIS); forest products and paper science. *Unit head:* Dr. Mae Davenport, Interim Director of Graduate Studies, 612-624-2721, E-mail: mdaven@umn.edu. *Application contact:* Toni Abts, Graduate Program Coordinator, 612-624-7683, Fax: 612-625-5212, E-mail: twheeler@umn.edu. Website: http://www.nrsm.umn.edu

**University of Minnesota, Twin Cities Campus,** Graduate School, College of Liberal Arts, Program in Geographic Information Science, Minneapolis, MN 55455-0213. Offers MGIS. *Program availability:* Part-time. *Degree requirements:* For master's, comprehensive exam, capstone project. *Entrance requirements:* For master's, minimum GPA of 3.0; course work in college-level math, statistics, and computer programming. Additional exam requirements/recommendations for international students: Required—TOEFL (minimum score 600 paper-based; 100 iBT). *Expenses:* Contact institution.

*Faculty research:* Geographic information science and society, spatial analysis and modeling, spatial databases, remote sensing, geovisualization.

**University of Missouri,** Office of Research and Graduate Studies, College of Agriculture, Food and Natural Resources, School of Natural Resources, Columbia, MO 65211. Offers agroforestry (MS, Certificate); conservation biology (Certificate); fisheries and wildlife sciences (MS, PhD); forestry (MS, PhD); geographical information science (Certificate); human dimensions of natural resources (MS, PhD); parks, recreation and tourism (MS); society and ecosystems (Certificate); soil, environmental and atmospheric sciences (MS, PhD); water resources (MS, PhD). *Program availability:* Part-time. *Faculty:* 34 full-time (7 women). *Students:* 55 full-time (19 women), 75 part-time (32 women); includes 8 minority (2 Black or African American, non-Hispanic/Latino; 3 Hispanic/Latino; 3 Two or more races, non-Hispanic/Latino), 26 international. Average age 30. *Degree requirements:* For doctorate, thesis/dissertation. *Entrance requirements:* For master's and doctorate, GRE General Test (minimum score 1200 Verbal and Quantitative), minimum GPA of 3.2. Additional exam requirements/recommendations for international students: Required—TOEFL (minimum score 550 paper-based; 80 iBT), IELTS (minimum score 6.5). *Application deadline:* For fall admission, 5/15 for domestic and international students; for spring admission, 10/15 for domestic and international students; for summer admission, 3/15 for domestic and international students. Applications are processed on a rolling basis. Application fee: $75 ($90 for international students). Electronic applications accepted. *Expenses:* Tuition, state resident: full-time $6347; part-time $352.60 per credit hour. Tuition, nonresident: full-time $17,379; part-time $965.50 per credit hour. *Required fees:* $1035. Tuition and fees vary according to course load, campus/location and program. *Financial support:* Fellowships with tuition reimbursements, research assistantships with tuition reimbursements, teaching assistantships with tuition reimbursements, institutionally sponsored loans, scholarships/grants, health care benefits, and unspecified assistantships available. Support available to part-time students. Website: http://www.snr.missouri.edu/

**University of Missouri,** Office of Research and Graduate Studies, College of Arts and Science, Department of Geography, Columbia, MO 65211. Offers geographic information science (Graduate Certificate); geography (MA). *Faculty:* 9 full-time (0 women). *Students:* 10 full-time (5 women), 1 part-time (0 women). *Degree requirements:* For master's, thesis or alternative. *Entrance requirements:* For master's, GRE General Test (minimum score 1000 verbal and quantitative), minimum GPA of 3.0. Additional exam requirements/recommendations for international students: Required—TOEFL (minimum score 500 paper-based; 61 iBT). *Application deadline:* For fall admission, 1/15 priority date for domestic and international students; for winter admission, 10/1 for domestic students; for spring admission, 4/1 for domestic students. Applications are processed on a rolling basis. Application fee: $75 ($90 for international students). Electronic applications accepted. *Expenses:* Tuition, state resident: full-time $6347; part-time $352.60 per credit hour. Tuition, nonresident: full-time $17,379; part-time $965.50 per credit hour. *Required fees:* $1035. Tuition and fees vary according to course load, campus/location and program. *Financial support:* Fellowships with full tuition reimbursements, research assistantships with full tuition reimbursements, teaching assistantships with full tuition reimbursements, institutionally sponsored loans, health care benefits, and unspecified assistantships available. *Faculty research:* Human geography, nature/society relationships, the physical environment, application of geographic information sciences. Website: http://www.geog.missouri.edu/?q-grad/graduate-program

**University of Nebraska at Omaha,** Graduate Studies, College of Arts and Sciences, Department of Geography and Geology, Omaha, NE 68182. Offers geographic information science (Certificate); geography (MA). *Program availability:* Part-time. *Faculty:* 5 full-time (2 women). *Students:* 11 full-time (2 women), 14 part-time (6 women); includes 3 minority (2 Hispanic/Latino; 1 Two or more races, non-Hispanic/Latino), 2 international. Average age 32. 16 applicants, 69% accepted, 9 enrolled. In 2016, 9 master's, 3 other advanced degrees awarded. *Degree requirements:* For master's, comprehensive exam, thesis (for some programs). *Entrance requirements:* For master's, GRE, minimum GPA of 3.0, 15 undergraduate geography hours, transcripts, resume, statement of purpose, 2 letters of recommendation; for Certificate, minimum GPA of 3.0, transcripts, resume, statement of purpose, 2 letters of recommendation. Additional exam requirements/recommendations for international students: Required—TOEFL, IELTS, PTE. *Application deadline:* For fall admission, 7/1 priority date for domestic and international students; for spring admission, 12/1 priority date for domestic and international students; for summer admission, 5/1 for domestic and international students. Applications are processed on a rolling basis. Application fee: $45. Electronic applications accepted. *Financial support:* In 2016–17, 10 students received support, including 1 research assistantship with tuition reimbursement available, 9 teaching assistantships with tuition reimbursements available; fellowships, Federal Work-Study, institutionally sponsored loans, scholarships/grants, health care benefits, tuition waivers (partial), and unspecified assistantships also available. Support available to part-time students. Financial award application deadline: 3/1; financial award applicants required to submit FAFSA. *Unit head:* Dr. Rex Cammack, Chairperson, 402-554-2341, E-mail: graduate@unomaha.edu. *Application contact:* Dr. Christina Dando, Graduate Program Chair, 402-554-2341, E-mail: graduate@unomaha.edu.

**University of New Hampshire,** Graduate School, Interdisciplinary Programs, Program in Geospatial Science, Durham, NH 03824. Offers Postbaccalaureate Certificate. *Entrance requirements:* For degree, official transcripts, 2 letters of recommendation, personal statement/essay. Additional exam requirements/recommendations for international students: Required—TOEFL (minimum score 550 paper-based; 80 iBT). Electronic applications accepted.

**University of New Haven,** Graduate School, College of Arts and Sciences, Program in Environmental Science, West Haven, CT 06516. Offers environmental ecology (MS); environmental education (MS); environmental geoscience (MS); environmental health and management (MS); environmental science (MS); geographical information systems (MS, Graduate Certificate). *Program availability:* Part-time, evening/weekend. *Students:* 25 full-time (16 women), 10 part-time (5 women); includes 4 minority (1 Black or African American, non-Hispanic/Latino; 1 Asian, non-Hispanic/Latino; 1 Hispanic/Latino; 1 Two or more races, non-Hispanic/Latino), 8 international. Average age 26. 36 applicants, 83% accepted, 15 enrolled. In 2016, 13 master's awarded. *Degree requirements:* For master's, thesis optional, research project. *Entrance requirements:* Additional exam requirements/recommendations for international students: Required—TOEFL (minimum score 80 iBT), IELTS, PTE. *Application deadline:* Applications are processed on a rolling basis. Application fee: $50. Electronic applications accepted. Application fee is waived when completed online. *Expenses: Tuition:* Full-time $15,660; part-time $870 per credit hour. *Required fees:* $200; $85 per term. Tuition and fees vary according to program. *Financial support:* Research assistantships with partial tuition reimbursements, teaching assistantships with partial tuition reimbursements, career-related internships or fieldwork, Federal Work-Study, scholarships/grants, and unspecified assistantships available. Support available to part-time students. Financial award applicants required to submit FAFSA. *Unit head:* Dr. Roman Zajac, Coordinator, 203-932-7114, E-mail: rzajac@newhaven.edu. *Application contact:* Michelle Mason, Director of Graduate

Enrollment, 203-932-7067, E-mail: mmason@newhaven.edu.
Website: http://www.newhaven.edu/4728/

**University of North Alabama,** College of Arts and Sciences, Department of Geography, Florence, AL 35632-0001. Offers geospatial science (MS). *Program availability:* Part-time, 100% online. *Faculty:* 7 full-time (2 women). *Students:* 7 full-time (1 woman), 7 part-time (1 woman); includes 1 minority (Asian, non-Hispanic/Latino), 2 international. Average age 29. 5 applicants, 100% accepted, 4 enrolled. In 2016, 3 master's awarded. *Degree requirements:* For master's, comprehensive exam (for some programs), thesis optional. *Entrance requirements:* For master's, GRE, 3 letters of recommendation, personal statement, letter of intent. Additional exam requirements/recommendations for international students: Required—TOEFL (minimum score 79 iBT), IELTS (minimum score 6), PTE (minimum score 54). *Application deadline:* Applications are processed on a rolling basis. Application fee: $50 ($100 for international students). Electronic applications accepted. *Expenses:* Tuition, state resident: full-time $2799; part-time $1866 per semester. Tuition, nonresident: full-time $5598; part-time $3732 per semester. *Required fees:* $915; $642 per semester. Tuition and fees vary according to course load. *Financial support:* In 2016–17, 8 students received support. Scholarships/grants and unspecified assistantships available. Financial award application deadline: 2/1; financial award applicants required to submit FAFSA. *Unit head:* Dr. Francis T. Koti, Chair, 256-765-4219, E-mail: ftkoti@una.edu. *Application contact:* Hillary N. Coats, Graduate Admissions Coordinator, 256-765-4447, E-mail: graduate@una.edu.
Website: http://www.una.edu/geography/

**The University of North Carolina at Charlotte,** College of Liberal Arts and Sciences, Department of Geography and Earth Sciences, Charlotte, NC 28223-0001. Offers earth sciences (MS); geography (MA), including community planning, geographic information science and technologies, location analysis, transportation studies, urban-regional analysis; geography and urban regional analysis (PhD). *Program availability:* Part-time, evening/weekend. *Faculty:* 30 full-time (12 women), 1 part-time/adjunct (0 women). *Students:* 55 full-time (25 women), 29 part-time (15 women); includes 14 minority (4 Black or African American, non-Hispanic/Latino; 3 Asian, non-Hispanic/Latino; 3 Hispanic/Latino; 4 Two or more races, non-Hispanic/Latino), 18 international. Average age 29. 78 applicants, 72% accepted, 25 enrolled. In 2016, 18 master's, 4 doctorates awarded. Terminal master's awarded for partial completion of doctoral program. *Degree requirements:* For master's, comprehensive exam, thesis or alternative, project; for doctorate, thesis/dissertation. *Entrance requirements:* For master's, GRE General Test or MAT, minimum GPA of 2.75, 3.0 for junior and senior years, transcripts, letters of recommendation, and personal essays (for MS); minimum overall GPA of 3.1 or for the last 2 years, 3.2 in major, three letters of reference, and personal essay (for MA); for doctorate, GRE, MA or MS in geography or a field related to the primary emphases of the program; minimum master's-level GPA of 3.5; GIS proficiency. Additional exam requirements/recommendations for international students: Required—TOEFL (minimum score 523 paper-based, 70 iBT) or IELTS (6.5). *Application deadline:* For fall admission, 2/1 for domestic and international students; for spring admission, 9/30 for domestic and international students. Applications are processed on a rolling basis. Application fee: $75. Electronic applications accepted. *Expenses:* Tuition, state resident: full-time $4252. Tuition, nonresident: full-time $17,423. *Required fees:* $3026. Tuition and fees vary according to course load and program. *Financial support:* In 2016–17, 49 students received support, including 1 fellowship (averaging $35,000 per year), 8 research assistantships (averaging $7,500 per year), 40 teaching assistantships (averaging $9,277 per year); career-related internships or fieldwork, institutionally sponsored loans, scholarships/grants, and unspecified assistantships also available. Support available to part-time students. Financial award application deadline: 3/1; financial award applicants required to submit FAFSA. *Total annual research expenditures:* $401,921. *Unit head:* Dr. Craig Allan, Chair, 704-687-5999, E-mail: ges@uncc.edu. *Application contact:* Kathy B. Giddings, Director of Graduate Admissions, 704-687-5503, Fax: 704-687-1668, E-mail: gradadm@uncc.edu.
Website: https://geoearth.uncc.edu/

**The University of North Carolina at Greensboro,** Graduate School, College of Arts and Sciences, Department of Geography, Greensboro, NC 27412-5001. Offers applied geography (MA); geographic information science (Certificate); geography (PhD); urban and economic development (Certificate). *Degree requirements:* For master's, comprehensive exam, thesis or alternative. *Entrance requirements:* For master's, GRE General Test. Additional exam requirements/recommendations for international students: Required—TOEFL. Electronic applications accepted.

**University of North Dakota,** Graduate School, College of Arts and Sciences, Department of Geography and Geographic Information Science, Grand Forks, ND 58202. Offers MA, MS. *Program availability:* Part-time. *Degree requirements:* For master's, comprehensive exam, thesis or alternative. *Entrance requirements:* For master's, minimum GPA of 3.0. Additional exam requirements/recommendations for international students: Required—TOEFL (minimum score 550 paper-based; 79 iBT), IELTS (minimum score 6.5). *Application deadline:* For fall admission, 8/1 priority date for domestic students, 5/1 priority date for international students; for spring admission, 12/1 priority date for domestic students, 9/1 priority date for international students. Applications are processed on a rolling basis. Application fee: $35. Electronic applications accepted. *Financial support:* Fellowships with full and partial tuition reimbursements, research assistantships with full and partial tuition reimbursements, teaching assistantships with full and partial tuition reimbursements, Federal Work-Study, institutionally sponsored loans, scholarships/grants, health care benefits, tuition waivers (full and partial), and unspecified assistantships available. Support available to part-time students. Financial award application deadline: 3/15; financial award applicants required to submit FAFSA. *Faculty research:* Regional and urban development, environmental geography, geographic education, geographic techniques. *Unit head:* Dr. Douglas Munski, Graduate Director, 701-777-6195, Fax: 701-777-6195, E-mail: douglas_munski@und.nodak.edu. *Application contact:* Matt Anderson, Admissions Specialist, 701-777-2947, Fax: 701-777-3619, E-mail: matthew.anderson@gradschool.und.edu.
Website: http://www.und.edu/dept/geog/grad.html

**University of Pennsylvania,** School of Design, Department of City and Regional Planning, Philadelphia, PA 19104. Offers city and regional planning (PhD); city planning (MCP); GIS and spatial analysis (Certificate); land preservation (Certificate); urban design (Certificate); urban redevelopment (Certificate); urban spatial analytics (MUSA). *Accreditation:* ACSP (one or more programs are accredited). *Program availability:* Part-time. *Faculty:* 13 full-time (5 women), 4 part-time/adjunct (0 women). *Students:* 136 full-time (77 women), 15 part-time (11 women); includes 22 minority (5 Black or African American, non-Hispanic/Latino; 8 Asian, non-Hispanic/Latino; 6 Hispanic/Latino; 1 Native Hawaiian or other Pacific Islander, non-Hispanic/Latino; 2 Two or more races, non-Hispanic/Latino), 56 international. Average age 27. 419 applicants, 58% accepted, 90 enrolled. In 2016, 76 master's, 8 doctorates awarded. *Degree requirements:* For doctorate, thesis/dissertation. *Entrance requirements:* Additional exam requirements/recommendations for international students: Required—TOEFL (minimum score 100 iBT); Recommended—IELTS (minimum score 7), TSE (minimum score 68). *Application deadline:* For spring admission, 1/12 for domestic students. Application fee: $80.

Electronic applications accepted. *Expenses: Tuition:* Full-time $31,068; part-time $5762 per course. *Required fees:* $3200; $336 per course. Full-time tuition and fees vary according to degree level, program and student level. Part-time tuition and fees vary according to course load, degree level and program. *Financial support:* In 2016–17, 39 teaching assistantships (averaging $2,000 per year) were awarded; fellowships, research assistantships, and Federal Work-Study also available. Financial award application deadline: 2/15; financial award applicants required to submit FAFSA. *Faculty research:* Transportation planning, community and economic development, public private development, land use and environmental planning, urban design. *Unit head:* Dr. John Landis, Department Chair, 215-746-2340, E-mail: jlan@design.upenn.edu. *Application contact:* Roslynne Carter, Administrative Assistant, 215-898-8330, Fax: 215-898-5730, E-mail: admissions@design.upenn.edu.
Website: https://www.design.upenn.edu/city-regional-planning

**University of Pittsburgh,** Dietrich School of Arts and Sciences, Department of Geology and Environmental Science, Pittsburgh, PA 15260. Offers geographical information systems and remote sensing (Pro-MS); geology and environmental science (MS, PhD). *Program availability:* Part-time. *Faculty:* 12 full-time (3 women). *Students:* 34 full-time (20 women), 2 part-time (both women); includes 5 minority (1 Black or African American, non-Hispanic/Latino; 4 Asian, non-Hispanic/Latino), 3 international. Average age 30. 72 applicants, 64% accepted, 29 enrolled. In 2016, 5 master's, 3 doctorates awarded. *Degree requirements:* For master's, thesis; for doctorate, comprehensive exam, thesis/dissertation, public presentation. *Entrance requirements:* For master's and doctorate, GRE. Additional exam requirements/recommendations for international students: Required—TOEFL (minimum score 100 iBT); Recommended—IELTS (minimum score 7). *Application deadline:* For fall admission, 1/15 for domestic and international students. Application fee: $50. Electronic applications accepted. *Expenses:* $36,734 tuition and fees. *Financial support:* In 2016–17, 27 students received support, including 4 fellowships (averaging $23,191 per year), 31 research assistantships with full tuition reimbursements available (averaging $7,006 per year), 20 teaching assistantships with full tuition reimbursements available (averaging $8,815 per year); scholarships/grants, health care benefits, and unspecified assistantships also available. Financial award application deadline: 1/15. *Faculty research:* Volcanology; sedimentary geochemistry; hydrology; geophysics; geomorphology; remote sensing. *Total annual research expenditures:* $1.3 million. *Unit head:* Cindy Niznik, Administrative Officer, 412-624-9070, E-mail: niznik@pitt.edu. *Application contact:* Annemarie Vranesevic, Academic Coordinator, 412-624-8779, E-mail: gpsgrad@pitt.edu.
Website: http://geology.pitt.edu/

**University of Redlands,** College of Arts and Sciences, Program in Geographic Information Systems, Redlands, CA 92373-0999. Offers MS. *Entrance requirements:* For master's, 2 years of professional experience using GIS or 2 university-level GIS courses plus internship, minimum undergraduate GPA of 3.0, 2 letters of recommendation. Additional exam requirements/recommendations for international students: Required—TOEFL (minimum score 550 paper-based); Recommended—IELTS (minimum score 5.5). Electronic applications accepted. *Expenses:* Contact institution.

**University of Southern California,** Graduate School, Dana and David Dornsife College of Letters, Arts and Sciences, Spatial Sciences Institute, Los Angeles, CA 90089. Offers geographic information science and technology (MS, Graduate Certificate). *Program availability:* Part-time, evening/weekend, online learning. Terminal master's awarded for partial completion of doctoral program. *Degree requirements:* For master's, thesis. *Entrance requirements:* For master's, GRE. Additional exam requirements/recommendations for international students: Required—TOEFL. Electronic applications accepted. *Faculty research:* Geocoding, geocomputation, GIS, environmental exposure estimation, spatial data accuracy and uncertainty.

**University of South Florida,** College of Arts and Sciences, School of Geosciences, Tampa, FL 33620-9951. Offers environmental science and policy (MS); geography (MA), including environmental geography, geographic information science and spatial analysis, human geography; geography and environmental science and policy (PhD); geology (MS, PhD); urban and regional planning (MURP). *Program availability:* Part-time, evening/weekend. *Faculty:* 31 full-time (6 women). *Students:* 88 full-time (42 women), 44 part-time (17 women); includes 16 minority (7 Black or African American, non-Hispanic/Latino; 5 Asian, non-Hispanic/Latino; 3 Hispanic/Latino; 1 Two or more races, non-Hispanic/Latino), 34 international. Average age 32. 133 applicants, 51% accepted, 34 enrolled. In 2016, 28 master's, 7 doctorates awarded. *Degree requirements:* For master's, comprehensive exam, thesis (for some programs); for doctorate, comprehensive exam, thesis/dissertation. *Entrance requirements:* For master's, GRE General Test, minimum GPA of 3.0 for last 60 credits of undergraduate degree, letter of intent, letters of recommendation; for doctorate, GRE General Test, minimum GPA of 3.0 (for geology), 3.2 (for environmental science and policy and geography); letter of intent; letters of recommendation. Additional exam requirements/recommendations for international students: Required—TOEFL (minimum score 550 paper-based; 79 iBT) or IELTS (minimum score 6.5) for MA and MURP; TOEFL (minimum score 600 paper-based) for MS and PhD. *Application deadline:* For fall admission, 2/15 for domestic and international students; for spring admission, 10/15 for domestic students, 9/15 for international students. Application fee: $30. Electronic applications accepted. *Expenses:* Tuition, state resident: full-time $7766; part-time $431.43 per credit hour. Tuition, nonresident: full-time $15,789; part-time $877.17 per credit hour. *Required fees:* $37 per term. *Financial support:* In 2016–17, 47 students received support, including 3 research assistantships (averaging $12,345 per year), 25 teaching assistantships with tuition reimbursements available (averaging $12,807 per year); unspecified assistantships also available. Financial award application deadline: 3/1. *Faculty research:* Geography: human geography, environmental geography, geographic information science and spatial analysis, urban geography, social theory; environmental science, policy, and planning: water resources, wildlife ecology, Karst and wetland environments, natural hazards, soil contamination, meteorology and climatology, environmental sustainability and policy, urban and regional planning. *Total annual research expenditures:* $3.3 million. *Unit head:* Dr. Jayajit Chakraborty, Professor and Chair, Geography Division, 813-974-8188, Fax: 813-974-5911, E-mail: jchakrab@usf.edu. *Application contact:* Dr. Jennifer Collins, Associate Professor and Graduate Program Coordinator, 813-974-4242, Fax: 813-974-5911, E-mail: collinsjm@usf.edu.
Website: http://hennarot.forest.usf.edu/main/depts/geosci

**University of South Florida,** Innovative Education, Tampa, FL 33620-9951. Offers adult, career and higher education (Graduate Certificate), including college teaching, leadership in developing human resources, leadership in higher education; Africana studies (Graduate Certificate), including diasporas and health disparities, genocide and human rights; aging studies (Graduate Certificate), including gerontology; art research (Graduate Certificate), including museum studies; business foundations (Graduate Certificate); chemical and biomedical engineering (Graduate Certificate), including materials science and engineering, water, health and sustainability; child and family studies (Graduate Certificate), including positive behavior support; civil and industrial engineering (Graduate Certificate), including transportation systems analysis; community and family health (Graduate Certificate), including maternal and child health,

## Geographic Information Systems

social marketing and public health, violence and injury: prevention and intervention, women's health; criminology (Graduate Certificate), including criminal justice administration; educational measurement and research (Graduate Certificate), including evaluation; English (Graduate Certificate), including comparative literary studies, creative writing, professional and technical communication; entrepreneurship (Graduate Certificate); environmental health (Graduate Certificate), including safety management; epidemiology and biostatistics (Graduate Certificate), including applied biostatistics, biostatistics, concepts and tools of epidemiology, epidemiology, epidemiology of infectious diseases; geography, environment and planning (Graduate Certificate), including community development, environmental policy and management, geographical information systems; geology (Graduate Certificate), including hydrogeology; global health (Graduate Certificate), including disaster management, global health and Latin American and Caribbean studies, global health practice, humanitarian assistance, infection control; government and international affairs (Graduate Certificate), including Cuban studies, globalization studies; health policy and management (Graduate Certificate), including health management and leadership, public health policy and programs; hearing specialist: early intervention (Graduate Certificate); industrial and management systems engineering (Graduate Certificate), including systems engineering, technology management; information studies (Graduate Certificate), including school library media specialist; information systems/decision sciences (Graduate Certificate), including analytics and business intelligence; instructional technology (Graduate Certificate), including distance education, Florida digital/virtual educator, instructional design, multimedia design, Web design; internal medicine, bioethics and medical humanities (Graduate Certificate), including biomedical ethics; Latin American and Caribbean studies (Graduate Certificate); mass communications (Graduate Certificate), including multimedia journalism; mathematics and statistics (Graduate Certificate), including mathematics; medicine (Graduate Certificate), including aging and neuroscience, bioinformatics, biotechnology, brain fitness and memory management, clinical investigation, health informatics, health sciences, integrative weight management, intellectual property, medicine and gender, metabolic and nutritional medicine, metabolic cardiology, pharmacy sciences; national and competitive intelligence (Graduate Certificate), including career counseling, college teaching, diversity in education, mental health counseling, school counseling; public affairs (Graduate Certificate), including nonprofit management, public management, research administration; public health (Graduate Certificate), including environmental health, health equity, public health generalist, translational research in adolescent behavioral health; public health practices (Graduate Certificate), including planning for healthy communities; rehabilitation and mental health counseling (Graduate Certificate), including integrative mental health care, marriage and family therapy, rehabilitation technology; secondary education (Graduate Certificate), including ESOL, foreign language education: culture and content, foreign language education: professional; social work (Graduate Certificate), including geriatric social work/clinical gerontology; special education (Graduate Certificate), including autism spectrum disorder, disabilities education: severe/profound; world languages (Graduate Certificate), including teaching English as a second language (TESL) or foreign language. *Expenses:* Tuition, state resident: full-time $7766; part-time $431.43 per credit hour. Tuition, nonresident: full-time $15,789; part-time $877.17 per credit hour. *Required fees:* $37 per term. *Unit head:* Kathy Barnes, Interdisciplinary Programs Coordinator, 813-974-8031, Fax: 813-974-7061, E-mail: barnesk@usf.edu. *Application contact:* Karen Tylinski, Metro Initiatives, 813-974-9943, Fax: 813-974-7061, E-mail: ktylinsk@usf.edu.
Website: http://www.usf.edu/innovative-education/

**The University of Texas at Dallas,** School of Economic, Political and Policy Sciences, Program in Geospatial Information Sciences, Richardson, TX 75080. Offers MS, PhD. *Program availability:* Part-time, evening/weekend. *Faculty:* 9 full-time (1 woman). *Students:* 61 full-time (22 women), 34 part-time (15 women); includes 14 minority (3 Black or African American, non-Hispanic/Latino; 4 Asian, non-Hispanic/Latino; 5 Hispanic/Latino; 2 Two or more races, non-Hispanic/Latino), 45 international. Average age 31. 102 applicants, 72% accepted, 45 enrolled. In 2016, 12 master's, 1 doctorate awarded. *Degree requirements:* For master's, thesis (for some programs), project or thesis; internship; for doctorate, comprehensive exam, thesis/dissertation. *Entrance requirements:* For master's and doctorate, GRE General Test, minimum GPA of 3.0 in upper-level coursework in field. Additional exam requirements/recommendations for international students: Required—TOEFL (minimum score 550 paper-based). *Application deadline:* For fall admission, 7/15 for domestic students, 5/1 priority date for international students; for spring admission, 11/15 for domestic students, 9/1 priority date for international students. Applications are processed on a rolling basis. Application fee: $50 ($100 for international students). Electronic applications accepted. *Expenses:* Tuition, state resident: full-time $12,418; part-time $690 per semester hour. Tuition, nonresident: full-time $24,150; part-time $1342 per semester hour. Tuition and fees vary according to course load. *Financial support:* In 2016–17, 27 students received support, including 5 fellowships (averaging $2,500 per year), 4 research assistantships with partial tuition reimbursements available (averaging $19,075 per year), 9 teaching assistantships with partial tuition reimbursements available (averaging $13,100 per year); career-related internships or fieldwork, Federal Work-Study, institutionally sponsored loans, scholarships/grants, and unspecified assistantships also available. Support available to part-time students. Financial award application deadline: 4/30; financial award applicants required to submit FAFSA. *Faculty research:* Urban and regional development, artificial intelligence techniques for geospatial investigation, improvement of current spatial analysis and modeling techniques, demographic studies. *Unit head:* Dr. Fang Qiu, Program Head, 972-883-4134, Fax: 972-883-2735, E-mail: ffqiu@utdallas.edu. *Application contact:* Katie Doctor, Graduate Program Administrator, 972-883-4936, Fax: 972-883-6297, E-mail: kdoctor@utdallas.edu.
Website: http://www.utdallas.edu/epps/geospatial-science/

**The University of Toledo,** College of Graduate Studies, College of Languages, Literature and Social Sciences, Department of Geography and Planning, Toledo, OH 43606-3390. Offers geographic information science and applied geographics (Certificate); geography and planning (MA); spatially-integrated social science (PhD). *Program availability:* Part-time. *Degree requirements:* For master's, comprehensive exam, thesis; for doctorate, thesis/dissertation. *Entrance requirements:* For master's and doctorate, GRE General Test, minimum cumulative point-hour ratio of 2.7 for all previous academic work, three letters of recommendation; for Certificate, minimum cumulative point-hour ratio of 2.7 for all previous academic work, three letters of recommendation. Additional exam requirements/recommendations for international students: Required—TOEFL (minimum score 550 paper-based; 80 iBT). Electronic applications accepted.

**University of Utah,** Graduate School, College of Social and Behavioral Science, Department of Geography, Salt Lake City, UT 84112-9155. Offers geographic information science (MS); geography (MS, PhD). *Program availability:* Part-time. *Faculty:* 13 full-time (4 women), 21 part-time/adjunct (8 women). *Students:* 39 full-time (22 women), 16 part-time (3 women); includes 7 minority (1 Black or African American, non-Hispanic/Latino; 1 Asian, non-Hispanic/Latino; 4 Hispanic/Latino; 1 Two or more races, non-Hispanic/Latino), 5 international. Average age 30. 62 applicants, 63% accepted, 10 enrolled. In 2016, 10 master's, 1 doctorate awarded. *Degree requirements:*

For master's, thesis (for some programs), 6 research hours (for MS in geography); skills portfolio (for MS in geographic information science); for doctorate, comprehensive exam, thesis/dissertation, 14 research hours, 2 consecutive full-time semesters. *Entrance requirements:* For master's, GRE General Test (except for MS in geographic information science), minimum undergraduate GPA of 3.0; for doctorate, GRE General Test, minimum undergraduate GPA of 3.0. Additional exam requirements/recommendations for international students: Required—TOEFL (minimum score 550 paper-based; 80 iBT), IELTS (minimum score 6.5). *Application deadline:* For fall admission, 1/10 priority date for domestic and international students; for spring admission, 10/1 for domestic and international students. Application fee: $55 ($65 for international students). Electronic applications accepted. *Expenses:* $3,763.51 per semester resident tuition (10 credit hours for 4 semesters); $11,951.20 per semester non-resident tuition (10 credit hours for 4 semesters); $25-$120 lab fees (for some courses). *Financial support:* In 2016–17, 36 students received support, including 2 fellowships with full tuition reimbursements available (averaging $17,500 per year), 12 research assistantships with full tuition reimbursements available (averaging $17,423 per year), 11 teaching assistantships with full tuition reimbursements available (averaging $15,727 per year); career-related internships or fieldwork, scholarships/grants, health care benefits, and unspecified assistantships also available. Financial award application deadline: 1/10. *Faculty research:* Urban-economic geography, earth system science, geographic information science and remote sensing, paleo environmental studies, hazards. *Total annual research expenditures:* $1.2 million. *Unit head:* Dr. Andrea R. Brunelle, Chair, 801-581-8218, Fax: 801-581-8219, E-mail: andrea.brunelle@geog.utah.edu. *Application contact:* Dr. Philip E. Dennison, Director of Graduate Studies, 801-581-8218, Fax: 801-581-8219, E-mail: dennison@geog.utah.edu.
Website: http://www.geog.utah.edu

**University of West Georgia,** College of Science and Mathematics, Carrollton, GA 30118. Offers biology (MS); computer science (MS); geographic information systems (Postbaccalaureate Certificate); mathematics (MS). *Program availability:* Part-time, evening/weekend, 100% online, blended/hybrid learning. *Faculty:* 49 full-time (17 women). *Students:* 15 full-time (7 women), 61 part-time (26 women); includes 19 minority (14 Black or African American, non-Hispanic/Latino; 1 American Indian or Alaska Native, non-Hispanic/Latino; 3 Asian, non-Hispanic/Latino; 1 Two or more races, non-Hispanic/Latino), 6 international. Average age 33. 64 applicants, 86% accepted, 43 enrolled. In 2016, 21 master's, 4 other advanced degrees awarded. *Entrance requirements:* Additional exam requirements/recommendations for international students: Required—TOEFL (minimum score 523 paper-based; 69 iBT); Recommended—IELTS (minimum score 6.5). *Application deadline:* For fall admission, 6/1 for domestic and international students; for spring admission, 11/15 for domestic students, 10/15 for international students; for summer admission, 4/1 for domestic students, 3/30 for international students. Applications are processed on a rolling basis. Application fee: $40. Electronic applications accepted. *Expenses:* Tuition, state resident: full-time $5316; part-time $222 per semester hour. Tuition, nonresident: full-time $20,658; part-time $861 per semester hour. *Required fees:* $1962. Tuition and fees vary according to course load, degree level and program. *Financial support:* Fellowships, research assistantships, teaching assistantships, career-related internships or fieldwork, Federal Work-Study, institutionally sponsored loans, scholarships/grants, and unspecified assistantships available. Support available to part-time students. Financial award application deadline: 4/1; financial award applicants required to submit FAFSA. *Unit head:* Dr. Lok C. Lew Yan Voon, Dean of Science and Mathematics, 678-839-5190, Fax: 678-839-5191, E-mail: lokl@westga.edu. *Application contact:* Dr. Toby Ziglar, Assistant Dean of the Graduate School, 678-839-1394, Fax: 678-839-1395, E-mail: graduate@westga.edu.
Website: http://www.westga.edu/cosm

**University of Wisconsin–Madison,** Graduate School, College of Letters and Science, Department of Geography, Madison, WI 53706-1380. Offers cartography and geographic information systems (MS); geographic information systems (Certificate); geography (MS, PhD). *Program availability:* Part-time. *Degree requirements:* For master's, thesis; for doctorate, thesis/dissertation; for Certificate, internship. *Entrance requirements:* For master's and doctorate, GRE General Test, minimum GPA of 3.25. Electronic applications accepted. *Faculty research:* Physical geography, urban/historical geography, people-environment, history of cartography, GIS.

**University of Wisconsin–Milwaukee,** Graduate School, School of Architecture and Urban Planning, Department of Architecture, Milwaukee, WI 53201-0413. Offers architecture (M Arch, MS Arch, PhD); geographic information systems (Graduate Certificate). *Students:* 114 full-time (51 women), 15 part-time (4 women); includes 18 minority (3 Black or African American, non-Hispanic/Latino; 1 American Indian or Alaska Native, non-Hispanic/Latino; 6 Asian, non-Hispanic/Latino; 2 Hispanic/Latino; 6 Two or more races, non-Hispanic/Latino), 21 international. Average age 30. 131 applicants, 59% accepted, 42 enrolled. In 2016, 65 master's, 1 doctorate, 11 other advanced degrees awarded. *Degree requirements:* For master's, comprehensive exam, thesis; for doctorate, comprehensive exam, thesis/dissertation. *Entrance requirements:* For master's, GRE General Test, portfolio. Additional exam requirements/recommendations for international students: Required—TOEFL (minimum score 600 paper-based; 100 iBT), IELTS (minimum score 7). *Application deadline:* For fall admission, 1/1 priority date for domestic students; for spring admission, 9/1 for domestic students. Applications are processed on a rolling basis. Application fee: $56 ($96 for international students). Electronic applications accepted. *Financial support:* In 2016–17, 3 fellowships, 20 teaching assistantships were awarded; career-related internships or fieldwork, health care benefits, unspecified assistantships, and project assistantships also available. Support available to part-time students. Financial award application deadline: 4/15; financial award applicants required to submit FAFSA. *Unit head:* Robert Greenstreet, Dean. *Application contact:* Student Advising Office, 414-229-4015, E-mail: sarup-grad@uwm.edu.
Website: https://uwm.edu/sarup/architecture/

**Virginia Commonwealth University,** Graduate School, College of Humanities and Sciences, L. Douglas Wilder School of Government and Public Affairs, Department of Urban Studies and Planning, Program in Geographic Information Systems, Richmond, VA 23284-9005. Offers Certificate. *Entrance requirements:* Additional exam requirements/recommendations for international students: Required—TOEFL (minimum score 600 paper-based; 100 iBT); Recommended—IELTS (minimum score 6.5). *Application deadline:* Applications are processed on a rolling basis. Application fee: $50. Electronic applications accepted. *Unit head:* Dr. Meghan Z. Gough, Graduate Program Director, 804-827-0869, E-mail: mzgough@vcu.edu. *Application contact:* Dr. Richard R. Huff, Director of Graduate Advising, 804-827-1430, E-mail: rrhuff@vcu.edu.
Website: http://www.wilder.vcu.edu/academic/certificate/index.html

**Virginia Polytechnic Institute and State University,** Graduate School, College of Natural Resources and Environment, Blacksburg, VA 24061. Offers fisheries and wildlife (MS, PhD); forestry and forest products (MF, MS, PhD); geography (MS); geospatial and environmental analysis (MNR); natural resources (MNR). *Faculty:* 74 full-time (17 women). *Students:* 174 full-time (85 women), 67 part-time (37 women); includes 22 minority (4 Black or African American, non-Hispanic/Latino; 4 Asian, non-Hispanic/

Latino; 12 Hispanic/Latino; 2 Two or more races, non-Hispanic/Latino), 36 international. Average age 31. 103 applicants, 61% accepted, 57 enrolled. In 2016, 102 master's, 20 doctorates awarded. *Degree requirements:* For master's, comprehensive exam (for some programs), thesis (for some programs); for doctorate, comprehensive exam (for some programs), thesis/dissertation (for some programs). *Entrance requirements:* For master's and doctorate, GRE/GMAT. Additional exam requirements/recommendations for international students: Required—TOEFL (minimum score 80 iBT). *Application deadline:* For fall admission, 8/1 for domestic students, 4/1 for international students; for spring admission, 1/1 for domestic students, 9/1 for international students. Applications are processed on a rolling basis. Application fee: $75. Electronic applications accepted. *Expenses:* Tuition, state resident: full-time $12,467; part-time $692.50 per credit hour. Tuition, nonresident: full-time $25,095; part-time $1394.25 per credit hour. *Required fees:* $2669; $491.50 per semester. Tuition and fees vary according to course load, campus/location and program. *Financial support:* In 2016–17, 1 fellowship (averaging $24,256 per year), 23 research assistantships with full tuition reimbursements (averaging $26,209 per year), 26 teaching assistantships with full tuition reimbursements (averaging $22,466 per year) were awarded. Financial award application deadline: 3/1; financial award applicants required to submit FAFSA. *Total annual research expenditures:* $15.8 million. *Unit head:* Dr. Paul M. Winistorfer, Dean, 540-231-5481, Fax: 540-231-7664, E-mail: pstorfer@vt.edu. *Application contact:* Arlice Banks, Executive Assistant, 540-231-7051, Fax: 540-231-7664, E-mail: arbanks@vt.edu.
Website: http://cnre.vt.edu/

**West Chester University of Pennsylvania,** College of Business and Public Management, Department of Geography and Planning, West Chester, PA 19383. Offers geographic information systems (Certificate); geography (MS); geography and planning (MURP); urban and regional planning (MPA, Certificate). *Program availability:* Part-time, evening/weekend. *Faculty:* 5 full-time (2 women). *Students:* 8 full-time (4 women), 13 part-time (5 women); includes 2 minority (both Black or African American, non-Hispanic/Latino), 2 international. Average age 32. 14 applicants, 100% accepted, 8 enrolled. In 2016, 8 master's, 1 other advanced degree awarded. *Degree requirements:* For master's, thesis optional, 48 credits: 27 credits required, 21 credits electives (for MURP); 33 credits or 11 courses (for MS); for Certificate, 12 credits or 4 courses (for geographic information systems); 18 credits or 6 courses (for urban and regional planning). *Entrance requirements:* For master's and Certificate, minimum GPA of 2.8, resume, two letters of recommendation. Additional exam requirements/recommendations for international students: Required—TOEFL or IELTS. *Application deadline:* For fall admission, 5/15 for international students; for spring admission, 10/15 for international students. Applications are processed on a rolling basis. Application fee: $50. Electronic applications accepted. *Expenses:* Tuition, state resident: full-time $8694; part-time $483 per credit. Tuition, nonresident: full-time $13,050; part-time $725 per credit. *Required fees:* $2399; $119.05 per credit. Tuition and fees vary according to campus/location and program. *Financial support:* Scholarships/grants and unspecified assistantships available. Financial award application deadline: 2/15; financial award applicants required to submit FAFSA. *Faculty research:* Sustainability and environmental conservation, land use/suburban planning, geographic information systems, transportation planning, housing, economic development. *Unit head:* Dr. Dottie Ives Dewey, Chair/Graduate Coordinator for GIS Certificate Program, 610-436-2746, Fax: 610-436-2889, E-mail: divesdewey@wcupa.edu. *Application contact:* Dr. Matin Katirai, Graduate Coordinator, 610-436-2392, Fax: 610-436-2889, E-mail: mkatirai@wcupa.edu.
Website: http://www.wcupa.edu/business-publicManagement/geographyPlanning/

**Western Illinois University,** School of Graduate Studies, College of Arts and Sciences, Department of Biological Sciences, Macomb, IL 61455-1390. Offers biology (MS); environmental GIS (Certificate); zoo and aquarium studies (Certificate). *Program availability:* Part-time. *Students:* 52 full-time (29 women), 27 part-time (22 women); includes 5 minority (1 Black or African American, non-Hispanic/Latino; 2 Hispanic/Latino; 2 Two or more races, non-Hispanic/Latino), 32 international. Average age 28. 39 applicants, 77% accepted, 10 enrolled. In 2016, 29 master's, 10 other advanced degrees awarded. *Degree requirements:* For master's, thesis or alternative. *Entrance requirements:* Additional exam requirements/recommendations for international students: Required—TOEFL (minimum score 550 paper-based; 80 iBT);

Recommended—IELTS. *Application deadline:* Applications are processed on a rolling basis. Application fee: $30. Electronic applications accepted. *Financial support:* In 2016–17, 13 research assistantships with full tuition reimbursements (averaging $7,544 per year), 19 teaching assistantships with full tuition reimbursements (averaging $8,688 per year) were awarded; unspecified assistantships also available. Financial award applicants required to submit FAFSA. *Unit head:* Dr. Richard Musser, Chairperson, 309-298-1546. *Application contact:* Dr. Nancy Parsons, Associate Provost and Director of Graduate Studies, 309-298-1806, Fax: 309-298-2345, E-mail: grad-office@wiu.edu.
Website: http://www.wiu.edu/biology

**Western Illinois University,** School of Graduate Studies, College of Arts and Sciences, Department of Geography, Macomb, IL 61455-1390. Offers community development and planning (Certificate); geography (MA); GIS analysis: GIS applications (Certificate). *Program availability:* Part-time. *Students:* 7 full-time (2 women), 5 part-time (2 women); includes 3 minority (2 Black or African American, non-Hispanic/Latino; 1 Asian, non-Hispanic/Latino), 1 international. Average age 30. 10 applicants, 80% accepted, 4 enrolled. In 2016, 9 master's, 3 other advanced degrees awarded. *Degree requirements:* For master's, thesis or alternative. *Entrance requirements:* Additional exam requirements/recommendations for international students: Required—TOEFL (minimum score 550 paper-based; 80 iBT). *Application deadline:* Applications are processed on a rolling basis. Application fee: $30. Electronic applications accepted. *Financial support:* In 2016–17, 6 students received support, including research assistantships with full tuition reimbursements available (averaging $7,544 per year); unspecified assistantships also available. Financial award applicants required to submit FAFSA. *Unit head:* Dr. Sam Thompson, Chairperson, 309-298-1648. *Application contact:* Dr. Nancy Parsons, Associate Provost and Director of Graduate School, 309-298-1806, Fax: 309-298-2345, E-mail: grad-office@wiu.edu.
Website: http://www.wiu.edu/cas/geography/

**Western Michigan University,** Graduate College, College of Arts and Sciences, Department of Geography, Kalamazoo, MI 49008. Offers geographic information science (Graduate Certificate); geography (MA). *Degree requirements:* For master's, thesis.

**West Virginia University,** Eberly College of Arts and Sciences, Department of Geology and Geography, Program in Geography, Morgantown, WV 26506. Offers energy and environmental resources (MA); geographic information systems (PhD); geography-regional development (PhD); GIS/cartographic analysis (MA); regional development (MA). *Program availability:* Part-time. *Degree requirements:* For master's, thesis, oral and written exams; for doctorate, comprehensive exam, thesis/dissertation, oral and written exams. *Entrance requirements:* For master's and doctorate, GRE General Test, minimum GPA of 3.0. Additional exam requirements/recommendations for international students: Required—TOEFL. Electronic applications accepted. *Faculty research:* Space, place and development, geographic information science, environmental geography.

**Wilmington University,** College of Technology, New Castle, DE 19720-6491. Offers geographic information systems (MS); information assurance (MS); information systems technologies (MS); Internet/Web design (MS); management and management information systems (MS). *Program availability:* Part-time, evening/weekend. *Faculty:* 5 full-time (1 woman), 114 part-time/adjunct (31 women). *Students:* 1,316 full-time (321 women), 263 part-time (79 women); includes 71 minority (53 Black or African American, non-Hispanic/Latino; 5 American Indian or Alaska Native, non-Hispanic/Latino; 8 Asian, non-Hispanic/Latino; 4 Hispanic/Latino; 1 Two or more races, non-Hispanic/Latino), 1,437 international. Average age 26. 856 applicants, 100% accepted, 332 enrolled. In 2016, 756 master's awarded. *Entrance requirements:* Additional exam requirements/recommendations for international students: Required—TOEFL (minimum score 500 paper-based). *Application deadline:* Applications are processed on a rolling basis. Application fee: $35. Electronic applications accepted. *Expenses:* Tuition: Full-time $8388; part-time $466 per credit. *Required fees:* $25 per semester. Tuition and fees vary according to degree level. *Unit head:* Dr. Mary Ann K. Westerfield, Dean. *Application contact:* Laura Morris, Director of Admissions, 877-967-5464, E-mail: infocenter@wilmu.edu.
Website: http://www.wilmu.edu/technology/

# Geography

**Appalachian State University,** Cratis D. Williams Graduate School, Department of Geography and Planning, Boone, NC 28608. Offers geography (MA), including geographic information science. *Program availability:* Part-time, online learning. *Degree requirements:* For master's, comprehensive exam, thesis or alternative. *Entrance requirements:* For master's, GRE General Test, 3 letters of recommendation. Additional exam requirements/recommendations for international students: Required—TOEFL (minimum score 570 paper-based; 79 iBT), IELTS (minimum score 6.5). *Application deadline:* For fall admission, 3/15 priority date for domestic students, 2/1 for international students; for spring admission, 11/1 for domestic students, 7/1 for international students. Applications are processed on a rolling basis. Application fee: $55. Electronic applications accepted. *Expenses:* Tuition, state resident: full-time $4744. Tuition, nonresident: full-time $17,913. Full-time tuition and fees vary according to program. *Financial support:* Fellowships, research assistantships, teaching assistantships, career-related internships or fieldwork, Federal Work-Study, scholarships/grants, and unspecified assistantships available. Financial award application deadline: 4/1; financial award applicants required to submit FAFSA. *Faculty research:* Global change, climatology, production cartography, geographic information systems, North Carolina geography, Latin America. *Unit head:* Dr. Kathleen Schroeder, Chairperson, 828-262-3000, Fax: 828-262-3067, E-mail: schroederk@appstate.edu. *Application contact:* Dr. Baker Perry, Graduate Program Director, E-mail: perrylb@appstate.edu.
Website: http://www.geo.appstate.edu

**Arizona State University at the Tempe campus,** College of Liberal Arts and Sciences, School of Geographical Sciences and Urban Planning, Tempe, AZ 85287-5302. Offers geographic information systems (MAS); geographic information science (Graduate Certificate); geography (MA, PhD); transportation systems (Graduate Certificate); urban and environmental planning (MUEP); urban planning (PhD). *Accreditation:* ACSP. Terminal master's awarded for partial completion of doctoral program. *Degree requirements:* For master's, thesis, interactive Program of Study (iPOS) submitted before completing 50 percent of required credit hours; for doctorate, comprehensive exam, thesis/dissertation, interactive Program of Study (iPOS) submitted before completing 50 percent of required credit hours. *Entrance requirements:* For master's and doctorate, GRE, minimum GPA of 3.0 or equivalent in last 2 years of work leading to bachelor's degree. Additional exam requirements/recommendations for international

students: Required—TOEFL, IELTS, or PTE. Electronic applications accepted. *Expenses:* Contact institution.

**Auburn University,** Graduate School, College of Sciences and Mathematics, Department of Geology and Geography, Auburn University, AL 36849. Offers MS. *Program availability:* Part-time. *Faculty:* 18 full-time (5 women), 1 part-time/adjunct (0 women). *Students:* 23 full-time (8 women), 11 part-time (4 women); includes 4 minority (3 Hispanic/Latino; 1 Two or more races, non-Hispanic/Latino), 10 international. Average age 25. 45 applicants, 38% accepted, 12 enrolled. In 2016, 11 master's awarded. *Degree requirements:* For master's, computer language or geographic information systems, field camp. *Entrance requirements:* For master's, GRE General Test. *Application deadline:* Applications are processed on a rolling basis. Application fee: $50 ($60 for international students). Electronic applications accepted. *Expenses:* Tuition, state resident: full-time $9072; part-time $504 per credit hour. Tuition, nonresident: full-time $27,216; part-time $1512 per credit hour. *Required fees:* $812 per semester. Tuition and fees vary according to degree level and program. *Financial support:* Research assistantships, teaching assistantships, and Federal Work-Study available. Support available to part-time students. Financial award application deadline: 3/15; financial award applicants required to submit FAFSA. *Faculty research:* Empirical magma dynamics and melt migration, ore mineralogy, role of terrestrial plant biomass in deposition, metamorphic petrology and isotope geochemistry, reef development, crinoid topology. *Unit head:* Dr. Mark Steltenpohl, Chair, 334-844-4893. *Application contact:* Dr. George Flowers, Dean of the Graduate School, 334-844-2125.

**Ball State University,** Graduate School, College of Sciences and Humanities, Department of Geography, Muncie, IN 47306. Offers geographic information systems (Certificate); geography (MS); professional meteorology and climatology (Certificate). *Program availability:* Part-time. *Degree requirements:* For master's, thesis. *Entrance requirements:* For master's, minimum baccalaureate GPA of 2.75 or 3.0 in latter half of baccalaureate, letter of interest, three letters of recommendation, resume or curriculum vitae, official transcripts. Additional exam requirements/recommendations for international students: Required—TOEFL (minimum score 550 paper-based; 79 iBT), IELTS (minimum score 6.5). Electronic applications accepted. *Faculty research:* Remote sensing, tourism and recreation, Latin American urbanization.

# Geography

**Binghamton University, State University of New York,** Graduate School, Harpur College of Arts and Sciences, Department of Geography, Binghamton, NY 13902-6000. Offers MA. *Program availability:* Part-time. *Faculty:* 11 full-time (4 women), 6 part-time/adjunct (4 women). *Students:* 26 full-time (10 women), 7 part-time (3 women); includes 9 minority (2 Black or African American, non-Hispanic/Latino; 1 Asian, non-Hispanic/Latino; 4 Hispanic/Latino; 2 Two or more races, non-Hispanic/Latino), 15 international. Average age 25. 33 applicants, 97% accepted, 12 enrolled. In 2016, 9 master's awarded. *Degree requirements:* For master's, one foreign language, thesis (for some programs). *Entrance requirements:* For master's, GRE General Test. Additional exam requirements/recommendations for international students: Required—TOEFL (minimum score 550 paper-based; 80 iBT). *Application deadline:* For fall admission, 5/15 priority date for domestic and international students; for spring admission, 1/15 priority date for domestic and international students. Application fee: $75. Electronic applications accepted. *Financial support:* In 2016–17, 19 students received support, including 8 teaching assistantships with full tuition reimbursements available (averaging $15,000 per year); career-related internships or fieldwork, Federal Work-Study, institutionally sponsored loans, scholarships/grants, health care benefits, tuition waivers (full and partial), and unspecified assistantships also available. Financial award application deadline: 1/15; financial award applicants required to submit FAFSA. *Unit head:* John Frazier, Director of Graduate Studies, 607-777-6179, E-mail: frazier@binghamton.edu. *Application contact:* Ben Balkaya, Assistant Dean and Director, 607-777-2151, Fax: 607-777-2501, E-mail: balkaya@binghamton.edu.

**Boston University,** Graduate School of Arts and Sciences, Department of Earth and Environment, Boston, MA 02215. Offers earth and environment (PhD); earth sciences (MA, PhD); energy and environment (MA); geography (MA, PhD); global development policy (MA); international relations and environmental policy (MA); remote sensing and geospatial sciences (MA). *Students:* 66 full-time (30 women), 3 part-time (1 woman); includes 4 minority (1 Asian, non-Hispanic/Latino; 3 Hispanic/Latino), 31 international. Average age 27. 163 applicants, 35% accepted, 18 enrolled. In 2016, 11 master's, 13 doctorates awarded. Terminal master's awarded for partial completion of doctoral program. *Degree requirements:* For master's, comprehensive exam (for some programs), thesis (for some programs); for doctorate, comprehensive exam, thesis/dissertation. *Entrance requirements:* For master's and doctorate, GRE General Test, 3 letters of recommendation, official transcripts, personal statement, writing sample (for geography). Additional exam requirements/recommendations for international students: Required—TOEFL (minimum score 550 paper-based; 84 iBT). *Application deadline:* For fall admission, 1/31 for domestic and international students; for winter admission, 10/15 for domestic and international students. Application fee: $95. Electronic applications accepted. *Financial support:* In 2016–17, 39 students received support, including 4 fellowships with full tuition reimbursements available (averaging $21,500 per year), 14 research assistantships with full tuition reimbursements available (averaging $21,500 per year), 15 teaching assistantships with full tuition reimbursements available (averaging $21,500 per year); Federal Work-Study, scholarships/grants, traineeships, and health care benefits also available. Financial award application deadline: 1/31. *Faculty research:* Biogeosciences, climate and surface processes; energy, environment and society; geographical sciences; geology, geochemistry and geophysics. *Unit head:* David Marchant, Chair, 617-353-3236, E-mail: marchant@bu.edu. *Application contact:* Alissa Beideck, Graduate Program Coordinator, 617-353-2529, Fax: 617-353-8399, E-mail: abeideck@bu.edu.
Website: http://www.bu.edu/earth/

**Brock University,** Faculty of Graduate Studies, Faculty of Social Sciences, Program in Geography, St. Catharines, ON L2S 3A1, Canada. Offers MA. *Program availability:* Part-time. *Degree requirements:* For master's, thesis optional. *Entrance requirements:* For master's, honors degree. Additional exam requirements/recommendations for international students: Required—TOEFL (minimum score 550 paper-based; 80 iBT), IELTS (minimum score 6.5), TWE (minimum score 4).

**California State University, East Bay,** Office of Graduate Studies, College of Letters, Arts, and Social Sciences, Department of Anthropology, Geography and Environmental Studies, Hayward, CA 94542-3000. Offers anthropology (MA); geography (MA). *Program availability:* Part-time. *Students:* 1 (woman) full-time, 7 part-time (all women); includes 3 minority (all Hispanic/Latino). Average age 38. In 2016, 5 master's awarded. *Degree requirements:* For master's, variable foreign language requirement, project or thesis. *Entrance requirements:* For master's, minimum GPA of 3.0 in field. Additional exam requirements/recommendations for international students: Required—TOEFL (minimum score 550 paper-based). *Application deadline:* For fall admission, 6/30 for domestic and international students. Applications are processed on a rolling basis. Application fee: $55. Electronic applications accepted. *Financial support:* Fellowships, teaching assistantships, career-related internships or fieldwork, Federal Work-Study, institutionally sponsored loans, and scholarships/grants available. Support available to part-time students. Financial award application deadline: 3/2; financial award applicants required to submit FAFSA. *Faculty research:* Sustainability, water resources, geographic information systems (GIS), mapping. *Unit head:* Dr. David Larson, Chair, 510-885-3192, E-mail: david.larson@csueastbay.edu. *Application contact:* Prof. David Woo, Graduate Advisor for Geography, 510-885-3160, Fax: 510-885-2353, E-mail: david.woo@csueastbay.edu.
Website: http://www20.csueastbay.edu/class/departments/ages/index.html

**California State University, Fullerton,** Graduate Studies, College of Humanities and Social Sciences, Department of Geography, Fullerton, CA 92834-9480. Offers MA. *Program availability:* Part-time. *Degree requirements:* For master's, comprehensive exam or thesis. *Entrance requirements:* For master's, minimum GPA of 3.0, 18 undergraduate credits in field. Application fee: $55. *Expenses:* Tuition, state resident: full-time $3369; part-time $1953 per unit. Tuition, nonresident: full-time $3915; part-time $2499 per unit. Tuition and fees vary according to course load, degree level and program. *Financial support:* Career-related internships or fieldwork, Federal Work-Study, institutionally sponsored loans, and scholarships/grants available. Support available to part-time students. Financial award application deadline: 3/1; financial award applicants required to submit FAFSA. *Faculty research:* Human geography, physical geography. *Unit head:* Mark Drayse, Chair, 657-278-7593, E-mail: mdrayse@fullerton.edu. *Application contact:* Admissions/Applications, 657-278-2371.

**California State University, Long Beach,** Graduate Studies, College of Liberal Arts, Department of Geography, Long Beach, CA 90840. Offers MA, MS. *Program availability:* Part-time. *Degree requirements:* For master's, thesis. *Application deadline:* For fall admission, 4/15 for domestic students; for spring admission, 10/15 for domestic students. Applications are processed on a rolling basis. Application fee: $55. Electronic applications accepted. *Financial support:* Career-related internships or fieldwork, Federal Work-Study, institutionally sponsored loans, and scholarships/grants available. Financial award application deadline: 3/2. *Faculty research:* Demography, geographic information systems, world landforms and societies. *Unit head:* Paul Laris, 562-985-4977, Fax: 562-985-8432, E-mail: vdelcasi@csulb.edu. *Application contact:* Dr. Christine Rodrigue, Graduate Advisor, 562-985-2358, Fax: 562-985-8993, E-mail: rodrigue@csulb.edu.

**California State University, Los Angeles,** Graduate Studies, College of Natural and Social Sciences, Department of Geography and Urban Analysis, Los Angeles, CA 90032-8530. Offers geography (MA). *Program availability:* Part-time, evening/weekend. *Degree requirements:* For master's, one foreign language, comprehensive exam or thesis. *Entrance requirements:* Additional exam requirements/recommendations for international students: Required—TOEFL (minimum score 500 paper-based). Electronic applications accepted. *Faculty research:* Technique focus-air photography, cartography, location analysis.

**California State University, Northridge,** Graduate Studies, College of Social and Behavioral Sciences, Department of Geography, Northridge, CA 91330. Offers MA. *Program availability:* Part-time. *Faculty:* 13 full-time (8 women), 14 part-time/adjunct (5 women). *Students:* 9 full-time (3 women), 19 part-time (9 women); includes 12 minority (2 Black or African American, non-Hispanic/Latino; 5 Asian, non-Hispanic/Latino; 5 Hispanic/Latino). Average age 32. 25 applicants, 64% accepted, 9 enrolled. *Degree requirements:* For master's, one foreign language, thesis. *Entrance requirements:* For master's, GRE General Test or minimum GPA of 3.0. Additional exam requirements/recommendations for international students: Required—TOEFL. *Application deadline:* For fall admission, 11/30 for domestic students. Application fee: $55. *Expenses:* Tuition, state resident: full-time $4152. *Financial support:* Teaching assistantships available. Financial award application deadline: 3/1. *Unit head:* Edward Jackiewicz, Chair, 818-677-3532.
Website: http://www.csun.edu/csbs/departments/geography/index.html

**Carleton University,** Faculty of Graduate Studies, Faculty of Arts and Social Sciences, Department of Geography and Environmental Studies, Ottawa, ON K1S 5B6, Canada. Offers geography (M Sc, MA, PhD). *Degree requirements:* For master's, thesis, seminar; for doctorate, one foreign language, thesis/dissertation, 2 comprehensive exams. *Entrance requirements:* For master's, honors degree; for doctorate, master's degree in geography. Additional exam requirements/recommendations for international students: Required—TOEFL. *Faculty research:* Human dimensions of global environmental change, winter environments, population studies, historical geography, globalization.

**Central Connecticut State University,** School of Graduate Studies, College of Liberal Arts and Social Sciences, Department of Geography, New Britain, CT 06050-4010. Offers MS. *Program availability:* Part-time, evening/weekend. *Faculty:* 5 full-time (1 woman). *Students:* 8 full-time (5 women), 18 part-time (8 women); includes 3 minority (1 Black or African American, non-Hispanic/Latino; 1 Hispanic/Latino; 1 Two or more races, non-Hispanic/Latino). Average age 32. 12 applicants, 92% accepted, 8 enrolled. In 2016, 3 master's awarded. *Degree requirements:* For master's, comprehensive exam, thesis or alternative, special project. *Entrance requirements:* For master's, minimum undergraduate GPA of 3.0, essay. Additional exam requirements/recommendations for international students: Required—TOEFL (minimum score 550 paper-based; 79 iBT). *Application deadline:* For fall admission, 6/1 for domestic students, 5/1 for international students; for spring admission, 11/1 for domestic and international students. Applications are processed on a rolling basis. Application fee: $50. Electronic applications accepted. *Expenses: Tuition, area resident:* Full-time $6497; part-time $606 per credit. Tuition, state resident: full-time $9748; part-time $622 per credit. Tuition, nonresident: full-time $18,102; part-time $622 per credit. *Required fees:* $4459; $246 per credit. *Financial support:* In 2016–17, 3 students received support. Career-related internships or fieldwork, Federal Work-Study, scholarships/grants, and unspecified assistantships available. Support available to part-time students. Financial award application deadline: 3/1; financial award applicants required to submit FAFSA. *Faculty research:* Regional planning, environmental protection, tourism, computer mapping and geographic information systems. *Unit head:* Dr. Richard Benfield, Chair, 860-832-2785, E-mail: benfieldr@ccsu.edu. *Application contact:* Patricia Gardner, Associate Director of Graduate Studies, 860-832-2350, Fax: 860-832-2362.
Website: http://www.ccsu.edu/geography/index.html

**Chicago State University,** School of Graduate and Professional Studies, College of Arts and Sciences, Department of Geography, Sociology, History, African-American Studies and Anthropology, Chicago, IL 60628. Offers geographic information systems (MA); geography (MA); history (MA). *Entrance requirements:* For master's, minimum GPA of 3.0.

**Clark University,** Graduate School, School of Geography, Worcester, MA 01610-1477. Offers geography (PhD). *Faculty:* 17 full-time (6 women). *Students:* 56 full-time (27 women), 1 (woman) part-time; includes 7 minority (2 Black or African American, non-Hispanic/Latino; 2 Asian, non-Hispanic/Latino; 3 Hispanic/Latino), 23 international. Average age 31. 103 applicants, 28% accepted, 20 enrolled. In 2016, 7 doctorates awarded. *Degree requirements:* For doctorate, thesis/dissertation. *Entrance requirements:* For doctorate, GRE General Test. Additional exam requirements/recommendations for international students: Required—TOEFL. *Application deadline:* For fall admission, 12/31 priority date for domestic and international students. Applications are processed on a rolling basis. Application fee: $75. *Expenses: Tuition:* Full-time $44,050. *Required fees:* $80. Tuition and fees vary according to course load and program. *Financial support:* In 2016–17, 3 fellowships with full tuition reimbursements (averaging $17,325 per year), 12 research assistantships with full tuition reimbursements (averaging $17,325 per year), 16 teaching assistantships with full tuition reimbursements (averaging $17,325 per year) were awarded; career-related internships or fieldwork and tuition waivers (full) also available. *Faculty research:* Global environmental change, geographic information systems, natural and technological hazards, water resources, urbanization. *Total annual research expenditures:* $749,059. *Unit head:* Dr. Anthony Bebbington, Director, 508-793-7370. *Application contact:* Brenda Nikas-Hayes, Admission Coordinator, 508-793-7336, Fax: 508-793-8881, E-mail: geography@clarku.edu.
Website: http://www.clarku.edu/departments/geography/

**Concordia University,** School of Graduate Studies, Faculty of Arts and Science, Department of Geography, Planning and Environment, Montréal, QC H3G 1M8, Canada. Offers environmental assessment (M Env, Diploma); geography, urban and environmental studies (M Sc, PhD).

**Concordia University,** School of Graduate Studies, Faculty of Arts and Science, Department of Political Science, Montréal, QC H3G 1M8, Canada. Offers political science (PhD); public policy and public administration (MA), including geography. *Degree requirements:* For master's, one foreign language, comprehensive exam, thesis optional, internship. *Entrance requirements:* For master's, honors degree or equivalent. Additional exam requirements/recommendations for international students: Required—TOEFL. *Faculty research:* International public policy and administration, Quebec public administration, public policy and social/political theory, geography and public policy, public administration and decision making.

**East Carolina University,** Graduate School, Thomas Harriot College of Arts and Sciences, Department of Geography, Planning, and Environment, Greenville, NC 27858-4353. Offers economic development (Certificate); geographic information science and technology (Certificate); geography (MA), including geography, planning, rural development. *Program availability:* Part-time, evening/weekend. *Students:* 15 full-time (8 women), 11 part-time (5 women); includes 6 minority (2 Black or African American, non-Hispanic/Latino; 1 Asian, non-Hispanic/Latino; 3 Hispanic/Latino). Average age 28. 17 applicants, 94% accepted, 9 enrolled. In 2016, 1 master's awarded. *Degree*

*requirements:* For master's, one foreign language, comprehensive exam, thesis optional. *Entrance requirements:* For master's, GRE General Test. Additional exam requirements/recommendations for international students: Required—TOEFL. *Application deadline:* For fall admission, 6/1 priority date for domestic students; for spring admission, 10/15 for domestic students. Applications are processed on a rolling basis. Application fee: $50. *Financial support:* Research assistantships with partial tuition reimbursements, teaching assistantships with partial tuition reimbursements, and Federal Work-Study. Support available to part-time students. Financial award application deadline: 6/1. *Unit head:* Dr. Burrell Montz, Chair, 252-328-6086, E-mail: montzb@ecu.edu. *Application contact:* Dean of Graduate School, 252-328-6012, Fax: 252-328-6071, E-mail: gradschool@ecu.edu.
Website: http://www.ecu.edu/geog/

**East Stroudsburg University of Pennsylvania,** Graduate and Extended Studies, College of Arts and Sciences, Department of History and Geography, East Stroudsburg, PA 18301-2999. Offers M Ed, MA, MS. *Program availability:* Part-time, evening/weekend. *Students:* 13 full-time (2 women), 10 part-time (1 woman), 8 international. *Degree requirements:* For master's, comprehensive exam, thesis, thesis defense. *Entrance requirements:* For master's, Commonwealth of Pennsylvania Department of Education certification requirements (M Ed). Additional exam requirements/recommendations for international students: Recommended—TOEFL (minimum score 560 paper-based; 83 iBT), IELTS. *Application deadline:* For fall admission, 7/31 priority date for domestic students, 6/30 priority date for international students; for spring admission, 11/30 for domestic students, 10/31 for international students. Applications are processed on a rolling basis. Application fee: $50. Electronic applications accepted. *Expenses:* Tuition, state resident: full-time $8694; part-time $5796 per year. Tuition, nonresident: full-time $13,050; part-time $8700 per year. *Required fees:* $2550; $1690 per unit. $845 per semester. Tuition and fees vary according to course load, campus/location and program. *Financial support:* Research assistantships with tuition reimbursements, Federal Work-Study, and unspecified assistantships available. Support available to part-time students. Financial award application deadline: 3/1; financial award applicants required to submit FAFSA. *Unit head:* Martin Wilson, Graduate Coordinator, 570-422-3536, Fax: 570-422-3937, E-mail: mwilson@esu.edu. *Application contact:* Kevin Quintero, Associate Director, Graduate and Extended Studies, 570-422-3890, Fax: 570-422-2711, E-mail: kquintero@esu.edu.

**Florida State University,** The Graduate School, College of Social Sciences and Public Policy, Department of Geography, Tallahassee, FL 32306. Offers geographic information science (MS); geography (MA, MS, PhD). *Program availability:* Part-time. *Faculty:* 11 full-time (4 women), 4 part-time/adjunct (2 women). *Students:* 64 full-time (31 women), 6 part-time (3 women); includes 21 minority (4 Black or African American, non-Hispanic/Latino; 10 Asian, non-Hispanic/Latino; 7 Two or more races, non-Hispanic/Latino). Average age 30. 70 applicants, 73% accepted, 30 enrolled. In 2016, 15 master's, 6 doctorates awarded. Terminal master's awarded for partial completion of doctoral program. *Degree requirements:* For master's, thesis (for some programs); for doctorate, comprehensive exam, thesis/dissertation. *Entrance requirements:* For master's and doctorate, GRE General Test, minimum GPA of 3.0. Additional exam requirements/recommendations for international students: Required—TOEFL (minimum score 80 iBT). *Application deadline:* For fall admission, 3/1 priority date for domestic and international students; for spring admission, 10/1 priority date for domestic and international students. Applications are processed on a rolling basis. Application fee: $30. Electronic applications accepted. *Expenses:* Contact institution. *Financial support:* In 2016–17, 50 students received support, including 7 research assistantships with full tuition reimbursements available (averaging $17,000 per year), 43 teaching assistantships with full tuition reimbursements available (averaging $17,000 per year); career-related internships or fieldwork, Federal Work-Study, institutionally sponsored loans, scholarships/grants, health care benefits, tuition waivers (full and partial), and unspecified assistantships also available. Financial award application deadline: 3/1; financial award applicants required to submit FAFSA. *Faculty research:* Society-nature interactions, geographic information science, environmental studies, hurricanes, remote sensing, urban, transportation. *Total annual research expenditures:* $159,022. *Unit head:* Prof. James Elsner, Chair, 850-644-1706, Fax: 850-644-5913, E-mail: jelsner@fsu.edu. *Application contact:* Prof. Victor Mesev, Graduate Director, 850-645-2498, Fax: 850-644-5193, E-mail: vmesev@fsu.edu.
Website: http://geography.fsu.edu/

**Fort Hays State University,** Graduate School, College of Science, Technology and Mathematics, Department of Geosciences, Program in Geosciences, Hays, KS 67601-4099. Offers geography (MS); geology (MS). *Degree requirements:* For master's, comprehensive exam, thesis. *Entrance requirements:* For master's, GRE General Test. Additional exam requirements/recommendations for international students: Required—TOEFL (minimum score 550 paper-based). Electronic applications accepted. *Faculty research:* Cretaceous and late Cenozoic stratigraphy, sedimentation, paleontology.

**George Mason University,** College of Science, Department of Geography and Geoinformation Science, Fairfax, VA 22030. Offers earth system science (MS); earth systems and geoinformation sciences (PhD); geography and geoinformation science (Certificate). *Faculty:* 18 full-time (2 women), 6 part-time/adjunct (0 women). *Students:* 75 full-time (22 women), 106 part-time (23 women); includes 26 minority (6 Black or African American, non-Hispanic/Latino; 9 Asian, non-Hispanic/Latino; 7 Hispanic/Latino; 4 Two or more races, non-Hispanic/Latino), 34 international. Average age 35. 87 applicants, 93% accepted, 42 enrolled. In 2016, 31 master's, 8 doctorates, 18 other advanced degrees awarded. *Degree requirements:* For master's, thesis optional. *Entrance requirements:* For master's, GRE (waived for those who have earned a master's degree from U.S. institution), bachelor's degree with minimum GPA of 3.0; 2 copies of official transcripts; current resume; expanded goals statement; 3 letters of recommendation; for doctorate, GRE (waived for those who have earned a master's degree from U.S. institution), bachelor's degree with minimum GPA of 3.0; 2 copies of official transcripts; 3 letters of recommendation; resume; expanded goals statement; for Certificate, GRE (waived for those who have earned a master's degree from U.S. institution), baccalaureate degree with minimum GPA of 3.0; 2 official copies of transcripts; expanded goals statement; 3 letters of recommendation; resume. Additional exam requirements/recommendations for international students: Required—TOEFL (minimum score 575 paper-based; 88 iBT), IELTS (minimum score 6.5), PTE (minimum score 59). *Application deadline:* For fall admission, 2/1 priority date for domestic students. Application fee: $75 ($80 for international students). Electronic applications accepted. *Expenses:* Tuition, state resident: full-time $10,628; part-time $443 per credit. Tuition, nonresident: full-time $29,306; part-time $1221 per credit. *Required fees:* $3096; $129 per credit. Tuition and fees vary according to program. *Financial support:* In 2016–17, 34 students received support, including 24 research assistantships with tuition reimbursements available (averaging $18,740 per year), 10 teaching assistantships with tuition reimbursements available (averaging $12,089 per year); career-related internships or fieldwork, Federal Work-Study, scholarships/grants, unspecified assistantships, and health care benefits for full-time research or teaching assistantship recipients) also available. Support available to part-time students. Financial award application deadline: 3/1; financial award applicants required to submit FAFSA. *Faculty research:* Global environment climate monitoring, gender and earth science, earth science education, remote sensing, planetary geology, hydrology,

theoretical issues of geographic information data acquisition and processing. *Total annual research expenditures:* $1.7 million. *Unit head:* Anthony Stefanidis, Acting Chair, 703-993-9237, Fax: 703-993-9230, E-mail: astefani@gmu.edu. *Application contact:* Samantha Cooke, Department Manager, 703-993-1212, E-mail: scooke4@gmu.edu.
Website: http://ggs.gmu.edu/

**The George Washington University,** Columbian College of Arts and Sciences, Department of Geography, Washington, DC 20052. Offers MA, Graduate Certificate. *Faculty:* 11 full-time (5 women). *Students:* 19 full-time (9 women), 18 part-time (9 women); includes 8 minority (3 Black or African American, non-Hispanic/Latino; 3 Asian, non-Hispanic/Latino; 1 Hispanic/Latino; 1 Two or more races, non-Hispanic/Latino), 1 international. Average age 26. 62 applicants, 79% accepted, 17 enrolled. In 2016, 12 master's, 21 other advanced degrees awarded. *Degree requirements:* For master's, comprehensive exam, thesis or alternative. *Entrance requirements:* For master's, GRE General Test, BA in geography or related field, minimum GPA of 3.0. Additional exam requirements/recommendations for international students: Required—TOEFL (minimum score 550 paper-based; 80 iBT). *Application deadline:* For fall admission, 4/1 priority date for domestic students, 1/15 priority date for international students; for spring admission, 10/1 priority date for domestic students, 9/1 priority date for international students. Applications are processed on a rolling basis. Application fee: $75. Electronic applications accepted. *Financial support:* In 2016–17, 10 students received support. Fellowships with tuition reimbursements available, teaching assistantships with tuition reimbursements available, Federal Work-Study, institutionally sponsored loans, and tuition waivers available. Financial award application deadline: 1/15. *Unit head:* Dr. Marie Price, Chair, 202-994-6187. *Application contact:* Information Contact, 202-994-6185, Fax: 202-994-2484.
Website: http://geography.columbian.gwu.edu/

**Georgia State University,** College of Arts and Sciences, Department of Geosciences, Program in Geography, Atlanta, GA 30302-3083. Offers MS. *Program availability:* Part-time. *Degree requirements:* For master's, one foreign language, thesis or alternative, written and oral exams. *Entrance requirements:* For master's, GRE General Test. Additional exam requirements/recommendations for international students: Required—TOEFL. *Application deadline:* For fall admission, 4/15 for domestic and international students; for spring admission, 10/15 for domestic and international students. Applications are processed on a rolling basis. Application fee: $50. Electronic applications accepted. *Expenses:* Tuition, state resident: full-time $6876; part-time $382 per credit hour. Tuition, nonresident: full-time $22,374; part-time $1243 per credit hour. *Required fees:* $2128; $1064 per term. Part-time tuition and fees vary according to course load and program. *Financial support:* Research assistantships with full tuition reimbursements and teaching assistantships with full tuition reimbursements available. *Faculty research:* Urban economics, biogeography, cartography, geographic information science. *Unit head:* Dr. W. Crawford Elliott, Chair, 404-413-5756, E-mail: wcelliott@gsu.edu.
Website: http://geosciences.gsu.edu/grad-programs/

**Georgia State University,** College of Education and Human Development, Department of Middle and Secondary Education, Atlanta, GA 30302-3083. Offers curriculum and instruction (Ed D); English education (MAT); mathematics education (M Ed, MAT); middle level education (MAT); reading, language and literacy education (M Ed, MAT), including reading instruction (M Ed); science education (M Ed, MAT), including biology (MAT), broad field science (MAT), chemistry (MAT), earth science (MAT), physics (MAT); social studies education (M Ed, MAT), including economics (MAT), geography (MAT), history (MAT), political science (MAT); teaching and learning (PhD), including language and literacy, mathematics education, music education, science education, social studies education, teaching and teacher education. *Accreditation:* NCATE. *Program availability:* Part-time, evening/weekend, online learning. *Faculty:* 24 full-time (18 women). *Students:* 145 full-time (91 women), 151 part-time (102 women); includes 141 minority (104 Black or African American, non-Hispanic/Latino; 1 American Indian or Alaska Native, non-Hispanic/Latino; 16 Asian, non-Hispanic/Latino; 12 Hispanic/Latino; 8 Two or more races, non-Hispanic/Latino), 10 international. Average age 36. 115 applicants, 50% accepted, 41 enrolled. In 2016, 94 master's, 22 doctorates awarded. *Degree requirements:* For master's, comprehensive exam (for some programs), thesis or alternative, exit portfolio; for doctorate, comprehensive exam, thesis/dissertation. *Entrance requirements:* For master's, GRE; GACE I (for initial teacher preparation programs), baccalaureate degree or equivalent, resume, goals statement, two letters of recommendation, minimum undergraduate GPA of 2.5; proof of initial teacher certification in the content area (for M Ed); for doctorate, GRE, resume, goals statement, writing sample, two letters of recommendation, minimum graduate GPA of 3.3, interview. Additional exam requirements/recommendations for international students: Required—TOEFL (minimum score 550 paper-based; 79 iBT) or IELTS (minimum score 6.5). *Application deadline:* For fall admission, 1/15 priority date for domestic and international students; for spring admission, 10/1 for domestic and international students. Application fee: $50. Electronic applications accepted. *Expenses:* Tuition, state resident: full-time $6876; part-time $382 per credit hour. Tuition, nonresident: full-time $22,374; part-time $1243 per credit hour. *Required fees:* $2128; $1064 per term. Part-time tuition and fees vary according to course load and program. *Financial support:* In 2016–17, fellowships with full tuition reimbursements (averaging $19,667 per year), research assistantships with full tuition reimbursements (averaging $5,436 per year), teaching assistantships with full tuition reimbursements (averaging $2,779 per year) were awarded; career-related internships or fieldwork, Federal Work-Study, scholarships/grants, health care benefits, tuition waivers (full and partial), and unspecified assistantships also available. Financial award application deadline: 3/15. *Faculty research:* Teacher education in language and literacy, mathematics, science, and social studies in urban middle and secondary school settings; learning technologies in school, community, and corporate settings; multicultural education and education for social justice; urban education; international education. *Unit head:* Dr. Dana L. Fox, Chair, 404-413-8060, Fax: 404-413-8063, E-mail: dfox@gsu.edu. *Application contact:* Bobbie Turner, Administrative Coordinator I, 404-413-8405, Fax: 404-413-8063, E-mail: bnturner@gsu.edu.
Website: http://mse.education.gsu.edu/

**Hunter College of the City University of New York,** Graduate School, School of Arts and Sciences, Department of Geography, New York, NY 10065-5085. Offers geographic information science (Certificate); geography (MA); geoinformatics (MS). *Program availability:* Part-time, evening/weekend. *Students:* 2 full-time (1 woman), 43 part-time (10 women); includes 14 minority (5 Black or African American, non-Hispanic/Latino; 5 Asian, non-Hispanic/Latino; 4 Hispanic/Latino), 4 international. Average age 30. 26 applicants, 81% accepted, 20 enrolled. In 2016, 11 master's, 12 other advanced degrees awarded. *Degree requirements:* For master's, comprehensive exam or thesis. *Entrance requirements:* For master's, GRE General Test, minimum B average in major, B- overall; 18 credits of course work in geography; 2 letters of recommendation; for Certificate, minimum B average in major, B- overall. Additional exam requirements/recommendations for international students: Required—TOEFL. *Application deadline:* For fall admission, 4/1 for domestic students; for spring admission, 11/1 for domestic students. Applications are processed on a rolling basis. *Financial support:* Fellowships, research assistantships, teaching assistantships, career-related internships or fieldwork, Federal Work-Study, institutionally sponsored loans, and unspecified assistantships available. Financial award application deadline: 3/1. *Faculty research:* Urban geography,

## Geography

economic geography, geographic information science, demographic methods, climate change. *Unit head:* Prof. Allan Frei, Chair, 212-772-5322, Fax: 212-772-5322, E-mail: afrei@hunter.cuny.edu. *Application contact:* Hongmian Gong, Graduate Advisor, 212-772-4658, Fax: 212-772-5268, E-mail: gong@hunter.cuny.edu.
Website: http://www.geo.hunter.cuny.edu/

**Indiana University Bloomington,** University Graduate School, College of Arts and Sciences, Department of Geography, Bloomington, IN 47405. Offers PhD. *Faculty:* 11 full-time (2 women), 14 part-time/adjunct (3 women). *Students:* 20 full-time (7 women), 4 part-time (3 women); includes 4 minority (1 Black or African American, non-Hispanic/Latino; 2 Asian, non-Hispanic/Latino; 1 Hispanic/Latino), 4 international. Average age 30. 29 applicants, 55% accepted, 6 enrolled. In 2016, 4 doctorates awarded. *Degree requirements:* For doctorate, comprehensive exam, thesis/dissertation. *Entrance requirements:* For doctorate, GRE General Test, minimum GPA of 3.0. Additional exam requirements/recommendations for international students: Required—TOEFL (minimum score 620 paper-based; 105 iBT), IELTS (minimum score 7). *Application deadline:* For fall admission, 1/15 priority date for domestic students, 12/1 priority date for international students; for spring admission, 11/15 priority date for domestic students, 11/1 priority date for international students. Application fee: $55 ($65 for international students). Electronic applications accepted. *Financial support:* In 2016–17, 3 fellowships with full and partial tuition reimbursements (averaging $19,333 per year), 2 research assistantships with full tuition reimbursements (averaging $16,039 per year), 15 teaching assistantships with full tuition reimbursements (averaging $15,750 per year) were awarded; health care benefits also available. Financial award application deadline: 12/15; financial award applicants required to submit FAFSA. *Faculty research:* Statistical climatology, dendrochronology, land-change science, cultural and political ecology, cultural geography, economic geography, geographic information science, spatial data analysis and modeling. *Unit head:* Dr. Daniel Knudsen, Chair and Professor, 812-855-6303, Fax: 812-855-1661, E-mail: knudsen@indiana.edu. *Application contact:* Susan White, Graduate Secretary, 812-855-6303, Fax: 812-855-1661, E-mail: suswhite@indiana.edu.
Website: http://www.iub.edu/~geog/

**Indiana University of Pennsylvania,** School of Graduate Studies and Research, College of Humanities and Social Sciences, Department of Geography and Regional Planning, MA Program in Geography, Indiana, PA 15705. Offers MA. *Program availability:* Part-time. *Faculty:* 9 full-time (2 women). *Degree requirements:* For master's, thesis optional. *Entrance requirements:* For master's, GRE, 2 letters of recommendation. Additional exam requirements/recommendations for international students: Required—TOEFL (minimum score 540 paper-based). *Application deadline:* Applications are processed on a rolling basis. Application fee: $50. Electronic applications accepted. *Expenses:* Tuition, state resident: full-time $8694; part-time $483 per credit. Tuition, nonresident: full-time $13,050; part-time $725 per credit. *Required fees:* $157 per credit. $50 per term. Tuition and fees vary according to course load and program. *Financial support:* Federal Work-Study, scholarships/grants, and unspecified assistantships available. Support available to part-time students. Financial award application deadline: 4/15; financial award applicants required to submit FAFSA. *Unit head:* Dr. Richard Hoch, Graduate Coordinator, 724-357-5990, E-mail: richard.hoch@iup.edu.
Website: http://www.iup.edu/georegionalplan/grad/default.aspx

**Kansas State University,** Graduate School, College of Arts and Sciences, Department of Geography, Manhattan, KS 66506. Offers geographic information science (Graduate Certificate); geography (MA, PhD). *Faculty:* 12 full-time (3 women), 1 part-time/adjunct (0 women). *Students:* 32 full-time (15 women), 13 part-time (5 women); includes 7 minority (3 Asian, non-Hispanic/Latino; 2 Hispanic/Latino; 2 Two or more races, non-Hispanic/Latino), 16 international. Average age 30. 18 applicants, 56% accepted, 7 enrolled. In 2016, 3 master's, 2 doctorates, 2 other advanced degrees awarded. *Degree requirements:* For master's, thesis optional, oral exam; for doctorate, one foreign language, thesis/dissertation. *Entrance requirements:* For master's and doctorate, GRE General Test, minimum GPA of 3.0. *Application deadline:* For fall admission, 2/1 priority date for domestic and international students; for spring admission, 8/1 priority date for domestic and international students. Applications are processed on a rolling basis. Application fee: $50 ($75 for international students). Electronic applications accepted. *Expenses:* Tuition, state resident: full-time $9670. Tuition, nonresident: full-time $21,828. *Required fees:* $862. *Financial support:* In 2016–17, 2 research assistantships (averaging $18,770 per year), 18 teaching assistantships with full tuition reimbursements (averaging $13,158 per year) were awarded; Federal Work-Study, institutionally sponsored loans, and scholarships/grants also available. Support available to part-time students. Financial award application deadline: 3/1; financial award applicants required to submit FAFSA. *Faculty research:* Human environment interaction, health and population, culture and landscape, physical geography, geospatial analysis and applications. *Total annual research expenditures:* $294,540. *Unit head:* Charles Martin, Head, 785-532-0136, Fax: 785-532-7310, E-mail: cwmgeog@ksu.edu. *Application contact:* Douglas Goodin, Director, 785-532-3411, Fax: 785-532-7310, E-mail: dgoodin@ksu.edu.
Website: http://www.k-state.edu/geography/

**Kent State University,** College of Arts and Sciences, Department of Geography, Kent, OH 44242-0001. Offers geographic information science (MGIS), including cyber geographic information science, environmental geographic information science, geographic information science and health; geography (MA, PhD). *Program availability:* Part-time. *Faculty:* 12 full-time (5 women). *Students:* 41 full-time (13 women), 7 part-time (2 women); includes 3 minority (1 Black or African American, non-Hispanic/Latino; 1 Hispanic/Latino; 1 Two or more races, non-Hispanic/Latino), 14 international. Average age 31. 49 applicants, 59% accepted, 21 enrolled. In 2016, 3 master's, 4 doctorates awarded. *Degree requirements:* For master's, thesis; for doctorate, comprehensive exam, thesis/dissertation. *Entrance requirements:* For master's and doctorate, GRE (minimum score of 300 verbal and quantitative on new scale), minimum GPA of 3.0, minor in geography, transcripts, letters of recommendation. Additional exam requirements/recommendations for international students: Required—TOEFL (minimum score of 525 paper-based, 71 iBT), IELTS (minimum score of 6), Michigan English Language Assessment Battery (minimum score of 75), or PTE (minimum score of 48). *Application deadline:* For fall admission, 2/1 for domestic and international students; for spring admission, 11/1 for domestic and international students; for summer admission, 4/1 for domestic and international students. Applications are processed on a rolling basis. Application fee: $45 ($70 for international students). Electronic applications accepted. *Expenses:* Tuition, state resident: full-time $10,864; part-time $495 per credit hour. Tuition, nonresident: full-time $18,380; part-time $837 per credit hour. *Financial support:* Fellowships with full tuition reimbursements, research assistantships with full tuition reimbursements, teaching assistantships with full tuition reimbursements, Federal Work-Study, scholarships/grants, and unspecified assistantships available. Financial award application deadline: 2/1. *Unit head:* Dr. Scott Sheridan, Professor/Acting Chair, 330-672-3224, Fax: 330-672-4304, E-mail: ssherid1@kent.edu. *Application contact:* Dr. David H. Kaplan, Professor and Graduate Coordinator, 330-672-3221, E-mail: dkaplan@kent.edu.
Website: https://www.kent.edu/geography

**Louisiana State University and Agricultural & Mechanical College,** Graduate School, College of Humanities and Social Sciences, Department of Geography and Anthropology, Baton Rouge, LA 70803. Offers geography (MA, MS); geography and anthropology (PhD).

**Marshall University,** Academic Affairs Division, College of Liberal Arts, Department of Geography, Huntington, WV 25755. Offers MA, MS, Certificate. *Entrance requirements:* For master's, thesis optional. *Entrance requirements:* For master's, GRE General Test (for MS).

**McGill University,** Faculty of Graduate and Postdoctoral Studies, Faculty of Science, Department of Geography, Montréal, QC H3A 2T5, Canada. Offers geography (M Sc, MA, PhD); neo-tropical environment (MA, PhD); social statistics (MA).

**McMaster University,** School of Graduate Studies, Faculty of Science, School of Geography and Earth Sciences, Hamilton, ON L8S 4M2, Canada. Offers geochemistry (PhD); geology (M Sc, PhD); human geography (MA, PhD); physical geography (M Sc, PhD). *Program availability:* Part-time. Terminal master's awarded for partial completion of doctoral program. *Degree requirements:* For master's, thesis; for doctorate, comprehensive exam, thesis/dissertation. *Entrance requirements:* For master's, minimum B+ average. Additional exam requirements/recommendations for international students: Required—TOEFL (minimum score 550 paper-based).

**Memorial University of Newfoundland,** School of Graduate Studies, Department of Geography, St. John's, NL A1C 5S7, Canada. Offers M Sc, MA, PhD. *Program availability:* Part-time. *Degree requirements:* For master's, thesis; for doctorate, comprehensive exam, thesis/dissertation, seminar, oral defense of thesis. *Entrance requirements:* For master's, 2nd class degree; for doctorate, master's degree. Electronic applications accepted. *Faculty research:* Cultural/historical geography, physical geography, economic geography, cartography, geographical information systems.

**Miami University,** College of Arts and Science, Department of Geography, Oxford, OH 45056. Offers MA. *Students:* 10 full-time (4 women), 1 (woman) part-time; includes 1 minority (Two or more races, non-Hispanic/Latino), 3 international. Average age 30. In 2016, 4 master's awarded. *Expenses:* Tuition, state resident: full-time $12,890; part-time $564 per credit hour. Tuition, nonresident: full-time $29,604; part-time $1260 per credit hour. *Required fees:* $638. Part-time tuition and fees vary according to course load and program. *Unit head:* Dr. Bruce D'Arcus, Department Chair/Associate Professor of Geography, 513-529-1521, E-mail: darcusb@miamioh.edu. *Application contact:* Department of Geography, 513-529-5010, E-mail: geography@miamioh.edu.
Website: http://www.MiamiOH.edu/geography/

**Michigan State University,** The Graduate School, College of Social Science, Department of Geography, East Lansing, MI 48824. Offers geographic information science (MS); geography (MS, PhD). *Degree requirements:* For master's, comprehensive exam, thesis (for some programs), presentation of poster/paper or oral defense of thesis; for doctorate, comprehensive exam, thesis/dissertation, presentation of poster/paper, presentation and defense of dissertation proposal, oral exam in defense of dissertation. *Entrance requirements:* Additional exam requirements/recommendations for international students: Required—TOEFL (minimum score 600 paper-based). Electronic applications accepted.

**Minnesota State University Mankato,** College of Graduate Studies and Research, College of Social and Behavioral Sciences, Department of Geography, Mankato, MN 56001. Offers MS. *Program availability:* Part-time. *Students:* 7 full-time (4 women), 21 part-time (3 women). *Degree requirements:* For master's, one foreign language, comprehensive exam, thesis optional. *Entrance requirements:* For master's, minimum GPA of 3.0. *Application deadline:* For fall admission, 3/1 priority date for domestic students. Applications are processed on a rolling basis. Application fee: $40. Electronic applications accepted. *Financial support:* Research assistantships, teaching assistantships with full tuition reimbursements, career-related internships or fieldwork, Federal Work-Study, institutionally sponsored loans, and unspecified assistantships available. Support available to part-time students. Financial award application deadline: 3/15; financial award applicants required to submit FAFSA. *Unit head:* Dr. Woo Jang, Graduate Coordinator, 507-389-1466, E-mail: woo-suk.jang@mnsu.edu.
Website: http://sbs.mnsu.edu/geography/

**Mississippi State University,** College of Arts and Sciences, Department of Geosciences, Mississippi State, MS 39762. Offers applied meteorology (MS); broadcast meteorology (MS); earth and atmospheric science (PhD); environmental geosciences (MS); geography (MS); geology (MS); geospatial sciences (MS); professional meteorology (MS); teachers in geosciences (MS). *Program availability:* Blended/hybrid learning. *Faculty:* 21 full-time (5 women), 1 part-time/adjunct (0 women). *Students:* 61 full-time (22 women), 162 part-time (73 women); includes 29 minority (5 Black or African American, non-Hispanic/Latino; 1 American Indian or Alaska Native, non-Hispanic/Latino; 2 Asian, non-Hispanic/Latino; 16 Hispanic/Latino; 1 Native Hawaiian or other Pacific Islander, non-Hispanic/Latino; 4 Two or more races, non-Hispanic/Latino), 12 international. Average age 33. 138 applicants, 72% accepted, 77 enrolled. In 2016, 69 master's, 3 doctorates awarded. *Degree requirements:* For master's, thesis (for some programs), comprehensive oral or written exam; for doctorate, thesis/dissertation, comprehensive oral or written exam. *Entrance requirements:* For master's, GRE (for on-campus applicants), minimum undergraduate GPA of 2.75; for doctorate, thesis-based MS with background in one department emphasis area. Additional exam requirements/recommendations for international students: Required—TOEFL (minimum score 477 paper-based; 53 iBT); Recommended—IELTS (minimum score 4.5). *Application deadline:* For fall admission, 7/1 for domestic students, 5/1 for international students; for spring admission, 11/1 for domestic students, 9/1 for international students. Applications are processed on a rolling basis. Application fee: $60. Electronic applications accepted. *Expenses:* Tuition, state resident: full-time $7670; part-time $852.50 per credit hour. Tuition, nonresident: full-time $20,790; part-time $2310.50 per credit hour. Part-time tuition and fees vary according to course load. *Financial support:* In 2016–17, 3 research assistantships with full tuition reimbursements (averaging $14,000 per year), 31 teaching assistantships with full tuition reimbursements (averaging $14,516 per year) were awarded; Federal Work-Study, institutionally sponsored loans, scholarships/grants, tuition waivers (partial), and unspecified assistantships also available. Financial award application deadline: 4/1; financial award applicants required to submit FAFSA. *Faculty research:* Climatology, hydrogeology, sedimentology, meteorology. *Total annual research expenditures:* $2.4 million. *Unit head:* Dr. William Cooke, Department Head, 662-325-1393, Fax: 662-325-9423, E-mail: whc5@geosci.msstate.edu. *Application contact:* Nathan Drake, Admissions and Enrollment Assistant, 662-325-3804, E-mail: ndrake@grad.msstate.edu.
Website: http://www.geosciences.msstate.edu

**Missouri State University,** Graduate College, College of Natural and Applied Sciences, Department of Geography, Geology, and Planning, Springfield, MO 65897. Offers natural and applied science (MNAS), including geography, geology and planning; secondary education (MS Ed), including earth science, physical geography. *Program availability:* Part-time, evening/weekend. *Faculty:* 18 full-time (4 women), 1 part-time/adjunct (0 women). *Students:* 18 full-time (6 women), 13 part-time (9 women); includes 2 minority (both Hispanic/Latino), 4 international. Average age 30. 36 applicants, 67% accepted, 19 enrolled. In 2016, 5 master's awarded. *Degree requirements:* For master's,

comprehensive exam, thesis (for some programs). *Entrance requirements:* For master's, GRE General Test (MS, MNAS), minimum undergraduate GPA of 3.0 (MS, MNAS), 9-12 teacher certification (MS Ed). Additional exam requirements/recommendations for international students: Required—TOEFL (minimum score 550 paper-based; 79 iBT), IELTS (minimum score 6). *Application deadline:* For fall admission, 7/20 priority date for domestic students, 5/1 for international students; for spring admission, 12/20 priority date for domestic students, 9/1 for international students. Applications are processed on a rolling basis. Application fee: $35 ($50 for international students). Electronic applications accepted. *Expenses:* Tuition, state resident: full-time $5830. Tuition, nonresident: full-time $10,708. *Required fees:* $1130. Tuition and fees vary according to class time, course level, course load and program. *Financial support:* In 2016–17, 3 research assistantships with full tuition reimbursements (averaging $11,574 per year), 15 teaching assistantships with full tuition reimbursements (averaging $9,365 per year) were awarded; career-related internships or fieldwork, Federal Work-Study, institutionally sponsored loans, scholarships/grants, and unspecified assistantships also available. Financial award application deadline: 3/31; financial award applicants required to submit FAFSA. *Faculty research:* Stratigraphy and ancient meteorite impacts, environmental geochemistry of karst, hyperspectral image processing, water quality, small town planning. *Unit head:* Dr. Toby Dogwiler, Department Head, 417-836-5800, Fax: 417-836-6934, E-mail: tobydogwiler@missouristate.edu. *Application contact:* Michael Edwards, Coordinator of Graduate Admissions, 417-836-5330, Fax: 417-836-6200, E-mail: michaeledwards@missouristate.edu.
Website: http://geosciences.missouristate.edu/

**New Mexico State University,** College of Arts and Sciences, Department of Geography, Las Cruces, NM 88003. Offers applied geography (MAG). *Program availability:* Part-time. *Faculty:* 6 full-time (2 women). *Students:* 13 full-time (7 women), 16 part-time (6 women); includes 10 minority (all Hispanic/Latino). Average age 35. 8 applicants, 50% accepted, 3 enrolled. In 2016, 5 master's awarded. *Degree requirements:* For master's, comprehensive exam, thesis or residency paper. *Entrance requirements:* For master's, bachelor's degree in geography or related field. Additional exam requirements/recommendations for international students: Required—TOEFL (minimum score 550 paper-based; 79 iBT), IELTS (minimum score 6.5). *Application deadline:* For spring admission, 2/1 for domestic students, 2/1 for international students. Applications are processed on a rolling basis. Application fee: $40 ($50 for international students). Electronic applications accepted. *Expenses:* Tuition, state resident: full-time $4086. Tuition, nonresident: full-time $14,254. *Required fees:* $853. Tuition and fees vary according to course load. *Financial support:* In 2016–17, 9 students received support, including 4 fellowships (averaging $4,088 per year), 6 teaching assistantships (averaging $16,997 per year); career-related internships or fieldwork, Federal Work-Study, scholarships/grants, traineeships, health care benefits, and unspecified assistantships also available. Support available to part-time students. Financial award application deadline: 3/1. *Faculty research:* Landscape ecology, land use, geomorphology, Latin America and the U.S.-Mexico border, geographic information systems, geographic education, biogeography, water resources research. *Total annual research expenditures:* $56,609. *Unit head:* Dr. Carol Campbell, Department Head, 575-646-3509, Fax: 575-646-7430, E-mail: geobird@nmsu.edu. *Application contact:* Dr. Daniel P. Dugas, Graduate Advisor, 575-646-1045, Fax: 575-646-7430, E-mail: ddugas@nmsu.edu.
Website: http://geography.nmsu.edu

**Northeastern Illinois University,** College of Graduate Studies and Research, College of Arts and Sciences, Program in Geography and Environmental Studies, Chicago, IL 60625-4699. Offers MA. *Program availability:* Part-time, evening/weekend. *Degree requirements:* For master's, comprehensive exam, thesis optional. *Entrance requirements:* For master's, undergraduate minor in geography or environmental studies, minimum GPA of 2.75. Additional exam requirements/recommendations for international students: Required—TOEFL (minimum score 550 paper-based; 79 iBT). Electronic applications accepted. *Faculty research:* Segregation and urbanization of minority groups in the Chicago area, scale dependence and parameterization in nonpoint source pollution modeling, ecological land classification and mapping, ecosystem restoration, soil-vegetation relationships.

**Northern Arizona University,** Graduate College, College of Social and Behavioral Sciences, Department of Geography, Planning, and Recreation, Flagstaff, AZ 86011. Offers applied geospatial sciences (MS); community planning (Certificate); geographic information systems (Certificate). *Program availability:* Online learning. *Degree requirements:* For master's, thesis optional. *Entrance requirements:* For master's, GRE General Test. Additional exam requirements/recommendations for international students: Required—TOEFL (minimum score 550 paper-based; 80 iBT), IELTS (minimum score 7). Electronic applications accepted. *Expenses:* Tuition, state resident: full-time $8971; part-time $444 per credit hour. Tuition, nonresident: full-time $20,958; part-time $1164 per credit hour. *Required fees:* $1018; $644 per credit hour. Tuition and fees vary according to course load, campus/location and program.

**Northern Illinois University,** Graduate School, College of Liberal Arts and Sciences, Department of Geography, De Kalb, IL 60115-2854. Offers MS, PhD. *Program availability:* Part-time. *Faculty:* 8 full-time (2 women). *Students:* 13 full-time (4 women), 10 part-time (4 women); includes 3 minority (1 Asian, non-Hispanic/Latino; 1 Hispanic/Latino; 1 Two or more races, non-Hispanic/Latino), 2 international. Average age 31. 21 applicants, 67% accepted, 3 enrolled. In 2016, 8 master's awarded. *Degree requirements:* For master's, comprehensive exam, thesis optional, research seminar. *Entrance requirements:* For master's, GRE General Test, minimum GPA of 2.75; for doctorate, master's degree. Additional exam requirements/recommendations for international students: Required—TOEFL (minimum score 550 paper-based). *Application deadline:* For fall admission, 2/1 priority date for domestic students, 5/1 for international students; for spring admission, 10/1 priority date for domestic students, 10/1 for international students. Applications are processed on a rolling basis. Application fee: $40. Electronic applications accepted. *Financial support:* In 2016–17, 1 research assistantship with full tuition reimbursement, 15 teaching assistantships with full tuition reimbursements were awarded; fellowships with full tuition reimbursements, career-related internships or fieldwork, Federal Work-Study, scholarships/grants, tuition waivers (full), and unspecified assistantships also available. Support available to part-time students. Financial award applicants required to submit FAFSA. *Faculty research:* Synoptic meteorology, human impacts on soil properties, plant-soil relationships, hydrological cycle, climate variability. *Unit head:* Dr. David Changnon, Chair, 815-753-6826, Fax: 815-753-6872, E-mail: dchangnon@niu.edu. *Application contact:* Dr. Michael Konen, Coordinator of Graduate Studies, 815-753-0631, E-mail: mkonen@niu.edu.
Website: http://globe.geog.niu.edu/

**The Ohio State University,** Graduate School, College of Arts and Sciences, Division of Social and Behavioral Sciences, Department of Geography, Columbus, OH 43210. Offers atmospheric sciences (MS, PhD); geography (MA, PhD). *Faculty:* 22. *Students:* 36 full-time (17 women), 2 part-time (1 woman), 19 international. Average age 27. In 2016, 9 master's, 6 doctorates awarded. *Degree requirements:* For doctorate, variable foreign language requirement, thesis/dissertation. *Entrance requirements:* For master's and doctorate, GRE. Additional exam requirements/recommendations for international students: Required—Michigan English Language Assessment Battery (minimum score 86); Recommended—TOEFL (minimum score 600 paper-based; 100 iBT), IELTS (minimum score 8). *Application deadline:* For fall admission, 12/13 priority date for domestic students, 11/30 priority date for international students. Applications are processed on a rolling basis. Application fee: $60 ($70 for international students). Electronic applications accepted. *Financial support:* Fellowships with tuition reimbursements, research assistantships with tuition reimbursements, teaching assistantships with tuition reimbursements, Federal Work-Study, and institutionally sponsored loans available. Support available to part-time students. *Unit head:* Dr. Morton O'Kelly, Professor and Chair, 614-292-8744, E-mail: okelly.1@osu.edu. *Application contact:* Graduate and Professional Admissions, 614-292-9444, Fax: 614-292-3895, E-mail: gpadmissions@osu.edu.
Website: http://www.geography.osu.edu/

**Ohio University,** Graduate College, College of Arts and Sciences, Department of Geography, Athens, OH 45701-2979. Offers MA, MS. *Program availability:* Part-time. *Degree requirements:* For master's, thesis or alternative. *Entrance requirements:* For master's, GRE General Test, minimum GPA of 3.0. Additional exam requirements/recommendations for international students: Required—TOEFL (minimum score 600 paper-based; 100 iBT) or IELTS (minimum score 8). *Application deadline:* For fall admission, 2/15 priority date for domestic and international students. Application fee: $50 ($55 for international students). Electronic applications accepted. *Financial support:* Research assistantships with full tuition reimbursements, teaching assistantships with full tuition reimbursements, Federal Work-Study, institutionally sponsored loans, tuition waivers (partial), and unspecified assistantships available. Financial award application deadline: 2/15. *Faculty research:* Environmental geography, cartography and geographic information systems, cultural ecology, area studies, historical geography. *Unit head:* Dr. James Dyer, Graduate Chair, 740-593-1142, E-mail: dyer@ohio.edu. *Application contact:* Dr. Dorothy Sack, Graduate Chair, 740-593-1149, E-mail: sack@ohio.edu.
Website: http://www.ohio.edu/geography/

**Oklahoma State University,** College of Arts and Sciences, Department of Geography, Stillwater, OK 74078. Offers MS, PhD. *Faculty:* 17 full-time (7 women), 2 part-time/adjunct (0 women). *Students:* 11 full-time (5 women), 19 part-time (9 women), 8 international. Average age 31. 13 applicants, 38% accepted, 5 enrolled. In 2016, 7 master's, 2 doctorates awarded. *Degree requirements:* For master's, thesis or alternative; for doctorate, comprehensive exam, thesis/dissertation. *Entrance requirements:* For master's and doctorate, GRE. Additional exam requirements/recommendations for international students: Required—TOEFL (minimum score 550 paper-based; 79 iBT). *Application deadline:* For fall admission, 3/1 priority date for international students; for spring admission, 8/1 priority date for international students. Applications are processed on a rolling basis. Application fee: $40 ($75 for international students). Electronic applications accepted. *Expenses:* Tuition, state resident: full-time $3775; part-time $209.70 per credit hour. Tuition, nonresident: full-time $14,851; part-time $825.05 per credit hour. *Required fees:* $2027; $112.60 per credit hour. Tuition and fees vary according to campus/location. *Financial support:* In 2016–17, 12 research assistantships (averaging $13,580 per year), 15 teaching assistantships (averaging $17,879 per year) were awarded; career-related internships or fieldwork, Federal Work-Study, scholarships/grants, health care benefits, tuition waivers (partial), and unspecified assistantships also available. Support available to part-time students. Financial award application deadline: 3/1; financial award applicants required to submit FAFSA. *Faculty research:* Cultural ecology, resource management, historical/cultural geography, central Asia, geographic information systems. *Unit head:* Dr. Dale Lightfoot, Department Head, 405-744-6250, Fax: 405-744-5620, E-mail: d.lightfoot@okstate.edu.
Website: http://geog.okstate.edu

**Oregon State University,** College of Earth, Ocean, and Atmospheric Sciences, Program in Geography, Corvallis, OR 97331. Offers geographic information science (MA, MS, PhD); physical geography (MA, MS, PhD); resource geography (MA, MS, PhD). *Faculty:* 6 full-time (3 women), 1 (woman) part-time/adjunct. *Students:* 20 full-time (10 women), 2 part-time (1 woman); includes 1 minority (Hispanic/Latino), 2 international. Average age 31. 73 applicants, 18% accepted, 8 enrolled. In 2016, 5 master's, 5 doctorates awarded. Terminal master's awarded for partial completion of doctoral program. *Entrance requirements:* For master's and doctorate, GRE, minimum GPA of 3.0 in last 90 hours. Additional exam requirements/recommendations for international students: Required—TOEFL (minimum score 80 iBT), IELTS (minimum score 6.5). *Application deadline:* For fall admission, 1/5 for domestic students. Application fee: $75 ($85 for international students). *Expenses:* Tuition, state resident: full-time $12,150; part-time $450 per credit. Tuition, nonresident: full-time $21,789; part-time $807 per credit. *Required fees:* $1651; $1507 per credit. One-time fee: $350. Tuition and fees vary according to course load, campus/location and program. *Financial support:* Fellowships, research assistantships, teaching assistantships, Federal Work-Study, and institutionally sponsored loans available. Support available to part-time students. Financial award application deadline: 1/5. *Faculty research:* Resources, physical geography, cartography, remote sensing. *Unit head:* Dr. Julia Jones, Professor. *Application contact:* Lori Hartline, Geography Advisor, 541-737-5188, E-mail: hartline@coas.oregonstate.edu.
Website: http://ceoas.oregonstate.edu/academics/geography/

**Penn State University Park,** Graduate School, College of Earth and Mineral Sciences, Department of Geography, University Park, PA 16802. Offers geographic information systems (MGIS); geography (MS, PhD). *Unit head:* Dr. William E. Easterling, III, Dean, 814-865-7482, Fax: 814-863-7708. *Application contact:* Lori Hawn, Director, Graduate Student Services, 814-865-1795, Fax: 814-863-4627, E-mail: l-gswww@lists.psu.edu.
Website: http://geog.psu.edu/

**Philadelphia University,** College of Architecture and the Built Environment, Program in Geodesign, Philadelphia, PA 19144. Offers MS. *Program availability:* Part-time.

**Portland State University,** Graduate Studies, College of Liberal Arts and Sciences, Department of Geography, Portland, OR 97207-0751. Offers MA, MAT, MS, MST, PhD. *Program availability:* Part-time. *Faculty:* 10 full-time (3 women), 8 part-time/adjunct (1 woman). *Students:* 22 full-time (9 women), 27 part-time (11 women); includes 9 minority (2 Asian, non-Hispanic/Latino; 4 Hispanic/Latino; 3 Two or more races, non-Hispanic/Latino), 1 international. Average age 31. 55 applicants, 47% accepted, 22 enrolled. In 2016, 6 master's awarded. *Degree requirements:* For master's, thesis (for some programs). *Entrance requirements:* For master's, GRE General Test (minimum score of 297), geography degree with minimum GPA of 3.0 overall, 3 letters of recommendation. Additional exam requirements/recommendations for international students: Required—TOEFL (minimum score 550 paper-based; 80 iBT), IELTS (minimum score 6.5), PTE (minimum score 60). *Application deadline:* For fall admission, 1/15 priority date for domestic and international students. Applications are processed on a rolling basis. Application fee: $65. *Expenses:* Contact institution. *Financial support:* In 2016–17, 4 research assistantships with tuition reimbursements (averaging $13,985 per year), 10 teaching assistantships with tuition reimbursements (averaging $9,732 per year) were awarded; career-related internships or fieldwork, Federal Work-Study, scholarships/grants, and unspecified assistantships also available. Support available to part-time students. Financial award application deadline: 3/1; financial award applicants required to submit FAFSA. *Faculty research:* Geographic information systems, natural lands,

## Geography

Latin American subsistence farming, climatic change, urban perspectives. *Total annual research expenditures:* $205,101. *Unit head:* Dr. Heejun Chang, Chair, 503-725-3162, Fax: 503-725-3162, E-mail: changh@pdx.edu. *Application contact:* Dr. Barbara Brower, Graduate Committee Chair, 503-725-8044, Fax: 503-725-3166, E-mail: browerb@pdx.edu.
Website: http://www.pdx.edu/geography/

**Queen's University at Kingston,** School of Graduate Studies, Faculty of Arts and Sciences, Department of Geography, Kingston, ON K7L 3N6, Canada. Offers M Sc, MA, PhD. *Degree requirements:* For master's, thesis; for doctorate, comprehensive exam, thesis/dissertation. *Entrance requirements:* Additional exam requirements/ recommendations for international students: Required—TOEFL. *Faculty research:* Urban and economic geography, historical-cultural geography, earth system science.

**Rutgers University–New Brunswick,** Graduate School-New Brunswick, Program in Geography, Piscataway, NJ 08854-8097. Offers MA, MS, PhD. Terminal master's awarded for partial completion of doctoral program. *Degree requirements:* For master's, thesis or alternative; for doctorate, comprehensive exam, thesis/dissertation. *Entrance requirements:* For master's and doctorate, GRE General Test. Additional exam requirements/recommendations for international students: Required—TOEFL. *Faculty research:* Urban social theory, climate, political biology, hazards, economic development.

**St. Cloud State University,** School of Graduate Studies, College of Social Sciences, Department of Geography and Planning, St. Cloud, MN 56301-4498. Offers MS. *Degree requirements:* For master's, comprehensive exam (for some programs), thesis or alternative. *Entrance requirements:* For master's, GRE General Test, minimum GPA of 2.75. Additional exam requirements/recommendations for international students: Required—Michigan English Language Assessment Battery; Recommended—TOEFL (minimum score 550 paper-based), IELTS (minimum score 6.5). Electronic applications accepted.

**Salem State University,** School of Graduate Studies, Program in Geo-Information Science, Salem, MA 01970-5353. Offers MS. *Program availability:* Part-time, evening/ weekend. *Degree requirements:* For master's, thesis optional. *Entrance requirements:* For master's, GRE or MAT. Additional exam requirements/recommendations for international students: Required—TOEFL (minimum score 550 paper-based; 80 iBT) or IELTS (minimum score 5.5).

**San Diego State University,** Graduate and Research Affairs, College of Arts and Letters, Department of Geography, San Diego, CA 92182. Offers MA, PhD. PhD offered jointly with University of California, Santa Barbara. *Degree requirements:* For master's, thesis; for doctorate, thesis/dissertation. *Entrance requirements:* For master's, GRE General Test, bachelor's degree in related field, 3 letters of recommendation. Additional exam requirements/recommendations for international students: Required—TOEFL. Electronic applications accepted. *Faculty research:* Physical geography, human geography, biogeography, environmental resources, geographic analysis.

**San Francisco State University,** Division of Graduate Studies, College of Science and Engineering, Department of Geography and Environment, San Francisco, CA 94132-1722. Offers geographic information science (MS); geography (MA); resource management and environmental planning (MA). *Expenses:* Tuition, state resident: full-time $6738. Tuition, nonresident: full-time $15,666. *Required fees:* $1012. Tuition and fees vary according to degree level and program. *Unit head:* Dr. Jerry Davis, Chair, 415-338-2983, Fax: 415-338-6243, E-mail: jerry@sfsu.edu. *Application contact:* Dr. Nancy Wilkinson, Graduate Coordinator, 415-338-1439, Fax: 415-338-6243, E-mail: nancyw@sfsu.edu.
Website: http://geog.sfsu.edu/

**San Jose State University,** Graduate Studies and Research, College of Social Sciences, San Jose, CA 95192-0001. Offers applications of technology in planning (Certificate); applied anthropology (MA); communication studies (MS); community design and development (Certificate); economics (MA), including applied economics, social sciences; environmental planning (Certificate); geographic information science (Certificate); geography (MA); global citizenship (Certificate); history (MA), including history education, social sciences; Mexican American studies (MA); psychology (MA, MS), including clinical psychology (MS), industrial/organizational psychology (MS); research and experimental psychology (MA); public administration (MA); real estate development (Certificate); social sciences (MPA, MS); sociology (MA); transportation and land use planning (Certificate). *Program availability:* Part-time, evening/weekend. *Entrance requirements:* For master's, minimum GPA of 3.0. Electronic applications accepted.

**Shippensburg University of Pennsylvania,** School of Graduate Studies, College of Education and Human Services, Department of Teacher Education, Shippensburg, PA 17257-2299. Offers curriculum and instruction (M Ed), including biology, early childhood education, elementary and middle level education, elementary education, geography/ earth science, history, mathematics, middle school education, modern languages; literacy studies (Certificate); online instruction, learning, and technology (Certificate); reading (M Ed); teaching English as a second language (Certificate). *Accreditation:* NCATE. *Program availability:* Part-time, evening/weekend, 100% online, blended/hybrid learning. *Faculty:* 14 full-time (9 women), 5 part-time/adjunct (all women). *Students:* 11 full-time (10 women), 88 part-time (81 women); includes 8 minority (3 Black or African American, non-Hispanic/Latino; 2 Asian, non-Hispanic/Latino; 3 Hispanic/Latino), 4 international. Average age 32. 57 applicants, 60% accepted, 28 enrolled. In 2016, 18 master's awarded. *Degree requirements:* For master's, comprehensive exam (for some programs), thesis optional, practicum or internship; capstone seminar (for some programs). *Entrance requirements:* For master's, MAT or GRE (if GPA less than 2.75), interview, 3 letters of reference, questionnaire of teaching background and future goals, resume. Additional exam requirements/recommendations for international students: Required—TOEFL (minimum score 550 paper-based, 68 iBT) or IELTS (minimum score 6). *Application deadline:* For fall admission, 4/1 priority date for domestic students, 4/30 for international students; for spring admission, 9/1 priority date for domestic students, 9/ 30 for international students; for summer admission, 2/1 priority date for domestic students. Applications are processed on a rolling basis. Application fee: $45. Electronic applications accepted. *Expenses:* Tuition, state resident: part-time $483 per credit. Tuition, nonresident: part-time $725 per credit. *Required fees:* $141 per credit. *Financial support:* In 2016–17, 3 students received support. Career-related internships or fieldwork, scholarships/grants, unspecified assistantships, and resident hall director and student payroll positions available. Support available to part-time students. Financial award application deadline: 3/1; financial award applicants required to submit FAFSA. *Unit head:* Dr. Christine A. Royce, Chairperson, 717-477-1688, Fax: 717-477-4046, E-mail: caroyc@ship.edu. *Application contact:* Megan N. Luft, Assistant Dean of Graduate Admissions, 717-477-1231, Fax: 717-477-4016, E-mail: mnluft@ship.edu.
Website: http://www.ship.edu/teacher/

**Simon Fraser University,** Office of Graduate Studies and Postdoctoral Fellows, Faculty of Environment, Department of Geography, Burnaby, BC V5A 1S6, Canada. Offers M Sc, MA, PhD. *Faculty:* 20 full-time (7 women). *Students:* 51 full-time (20 women). 35 applicants, 43% accepted, 9 enrolled. In 2016, 7 master's, 5 doctorates awarded. *Degree requirements:* For master's, one foreign language, thesis; for doctorate, one

foreign language, comprehensive exam, thesis/dissertation. *Entrance requirements:* For master's, minimum GPA of 3.0 (on scale of 4.33) or 3.33 based on last 60 credits of undergraduate courses; for doctorate, minimum GPA of 3.5 (on scale of 4.33). Additional exam requirements/recommendations for international students: Recommended—TOEFL (minimum score 580 paper-based; 93 iBT), IELTS (minimum score 7), TWE (minimum score 5). *Application deadline:* For fall admission, 1/22 for domestic and international students; for winter admission, 9/15 for domestic and international students. Application fee: $90 ($125 for international students). Electronic applications accepted. *Financial support:* In 2016–17, 31 students received support, including 17 fellowships (averaging $6,500 per year), teaching assistantships (averaging $5,608 per year); research assistantships and scholarships/grants also available. *Faculty research:* Theoretical and systematic aspects of geography, ginseng research, geographic information sciences, tourism and community planning, geomorphology. *Unit head:* Dr. Nadine Schuurman, Graduate Chair, 778-782-3320, E-mail: geog-grad-chair@sfu.ca. *Application contact:* Odessa Cadieux-Rey, Graduate Secretary, 778-782-3322, E-mail: geog-grad-sec@sfu.ca.
Website: http://www.sfu.ca/geography/

**South Dakota State University,** Graduate School, College of Arts and Science, Department of Geography, Brookings, SD 57007. Offers MS. *Program availability:* Part-time. *Degree requirements:* For master's, thesis, oral exam. *Entrance requirements:* Additional exam requirements/recommendations for international students: Required— TOEFL (minimum score 525 paper-based; 71 iBT). *Faculty research:* Contemporary agriculture and rural land use, geography of Indian casino gambling, geography of illegal drug trade, geography of crop circles.

**Southern Illinois University Carbondale,** Graduate School, College of Liberal Arts, Department of Geography, Carbondale, IL 62901-4701. Offers MS, PhD. *Degree requirements:* For master's, thesis; for doctorate, thesis/dissertation. *Entrance requirements:* For master's, GRE (recommended), minimum GPA of 2.7; for doctorate, minimum GPA of 3.25. Additional exam requirements/recommendations for international students: Required—TOEFL. *Faculty research:* Natural resources management emphasizing water resources and environmental quality of air, water, and land systems.

**Southern Illinois University Edwardsville,** Graduate School, College of Arts and Sciences, Department of Geography, Edwardsville, IL 62026. Offers MS. *Program availability:* Part-time, evening/weekend. *Degree requirements:* For master's, thesis optional, final exam. *Entrance requirements:* For master's, GRE (for applicants with a GPA less than 2.8). Additional exam requirements/recommendations for international students: Required—TOEFL (minimum score 550 paper-based; 79 iBT), IELTS (minimum score 6.5). Electronic applications accepted.

**Syracuse University,** Maxwell School of Citizenship and Public Affairs, Programs in Geography, Syracuse, NY 13244. Offers MA, PhD. *Program availability:* Part-time, evening/weekend. *Degree requirements:* For master's, thesis or alternative; for doctorate, comprehensive exam, thesis/dissertation. *Entrance requirements:* For master's and doctorate, GRE General Test, personal statement, three letters of recommendation, official transcripts, resume. Additional exam requirements/ recommendations for international students: Required—TOEFL (minimum score 100 iBT). *Application deadline:* For fall admission, 1/5 priority date for domestic and international students. Application fee: $75. Electronic applications accepted. *Expenses: Tuition:* Full-time $25,974; part-time $1443 per credit hour. *Required fees:* $802; $50 per course. Tuition and fees vary according to course load and program. *Financial support:* Fellowships with full tuition reimbursements, research assistantships with tuition reimbursements, and teaching assistantships with tuition reimbursements available. Financial award application deadline: 1/1. *Faculty research:* Biogeography, geomorphology, human impacts on vegetation and land forms, geographic information systems, remote sensing. *Unit head:* Dr. Tom Perreault, Director of Graduate Studies, 315-443-9467, E-mail: taperrea@maxwell.syr.edu.
Website: http://www.maxwell.syr.edu/geo/

**Temple University,** College of Liberal Arts, Department of Geography and Urban Studies, Philadelphia, PA 19122-6096. Offers geographic information systems (PSM, Graduate Certificate); geography and urban studies (MA, PhD). *Degree requirements:* For master's, comprehensive exam, thesis or alternative. *Entrance requirements:* For master's, GRE General Test, minimum GPA of 3.0, 3 letters of recommendation; for doctorate, GRE, minimum GPA of 3.0, 3 letters of recommendation. Additional exam requirements/recommendations for international students: Required—TOEFL (minimum score 575 paper-based; 88 iBT). Electronic applications accepted. *Faculty research:* Social justice, sustainability, globalization, geographic methods, urban processes.

**Texas A&M University,** College of Geosciences, Department of Geography, College Station, TX 77843. Offers MS, PhD. *Program availability:* Part-time. *Faculty:* 18. *Students:* 73 full-time (34 women), 19 part-time (11 women); includes 12 minority (2 Black or African American, non-Hispanic/Latino; 3 Asian, non-Hispanic/Latino; 7 Hispanic/Latino), 28 international. Average age 28. 111 applicants, 42% accepted, 26 enrolled. In 2016, 7 master's, 6 doctorates awarded. *Degree requirements:* For master's, thesis optional; for doctorate, thesis/dissertation. *Entrance requirements:* For master's and doctorate, GRE General Test. Additional exam requirements/recommendations for international students: Required—TOEFL (minimum score 550 paper-based; 80 iBT), IELTS (minimum score 6), PTE (minimum score 53). *Application deadline:* For fall admission, 1/1 priority date for domestic students. Applications are processed on a rolling basis. Application fee: $50 ($90 for international students). Electronic applications accepted. *Expenses:* Contact institution. *Financial support:* In 2016–17, 77 students received support, including 25 fellowships with tuition reimbursements available (averaging $4,909 per year), 27 research assistantships with tuition reimbursements available (averaging $6,003 per year), 27 teaching assistantships with tuition reimbursements available (averaging $9,679 per year); career-related internships or fieldwork, institutionally sponsored loans, scholarships/grants, traineeships, health care benefits, tuition waivers (full and partial), and unspecified assistantships also available. Support available to part-time students. Financial award application deadline: 3/15; financial award applicants required to submit FAFSA. *Faculty research:* Geomorphology, historical geography, urban-economic geography, geographic education and technology, human-environment interaction. *Unit head:* Dr. David M. Cairns, Department Head, 979-845-2783, E-mail: cairns@tamu.edu. *Application contact:* Dr. Steven M. Quiring, Associate Professor and Director of Graduate Programs, 979-458-1712, Fax: 979-862-4487, E-mail: squiring@tamu.edu.
Website: http://geography.tamu.edu

**Texas State University,** The Graduate College, College of Liberal Arts, Doctoral Program in Geographic Education, San Marcos, TX 78666. Offers PhD. *Program availability:* Part-time, evening/weekend. *Faculty:* 25 full-time (9 women). *Students:* 4 full-time (2 women), 1 (woman) part-time; includes 1 minority (Hispanic/Latino), 2 international. Average age 33. 4 applicants, 50% accepted, 2 enrolled. In 2016, 2 doctorates awarded. *Degree requirements:* For doctorate, comprehensive exam, thesis/ dissertation. *Entrance requirements:* For doctorate, GRE General Test (minimum preferred score of 303 verbal and quantitative), master's degree in geography or related field with minimum GPA of 3.5 on all graduate coursework, 3 letters of recommendation, statement of purpose, curriculum vitae. Additional exam requirements/recommendations for international students: Required—TOEFL (minimum score 550 paper-based; 78 iBT),

IELTS (minimum score 6.5). *Application deadline:* For fall admission, 1/1 priority date for domestic students, 1/15 priority date for international students. Applications are processed on a rolling basis. Application fee: $40 ($90 for international students). Electronic applications accepted. *Expenses:* $4,851 per semester. *Financial support:* In 2016–17, 4 students received support, including 1 research assistantship (averaging $30,648 per year), 3 teaching assistantships (averaging $29,764 per year); career-related internships or fieldwork, Federal Work-Study, and institutionally sponsored loans also available. Support available to part-time students. Financial award application deadline: 3/1; financial award applicants required to submit FAFSA. *Faculty research:* Exploring Texas with digital data maps; image science analysis; remote sensing of urban growth; qualification of alligator gar recruitment dynamics. *Total annual research expenditures:* $238,516. *Unit head:* Dr. Yongmei Lu, PhD Program Director, 512-245-1337, Fax: 512-245-8353, E-mail: yl10@txstate.edu. *Application contact:* Dr. Andrea Golato, Dean of Graduate School, 512-245-2581, Fax: 512-245-8365, E-mail: gradcollege@txstate.edu.
Website: http://www.geo.txstate.edu/

**Texas State University,** The Graduate College, College of Liberal Arts, Doctoral Program in Geography, San Marcos, TX 78666. Offers PhD. *Program availability:* Part-time. *Faculty:* 25 full-time (9 women). *Students:* 16 full-time (6 women), 5 part-time (3 women); includes 3 minority (all Hispanic/Latino), 6 international. Average age 35. 53 applicants, 77% accepted, 10 enrolled. *Degree requirements:* For doctorate, comprehensive exam, thesis/dissertation. *Entrance requirements:* For doctorate, GRE (minimum preferred score of 303 verbal and quantitative), master's degree in geography or related field from regionally-accredited institution with minimum GPA of 3.5 in completed graduate course work, 3 letters of recommendation, statement of purpose, curriculum vitae. Additional exam requirements/recommendations for international students: Required—TOEFL (minimum score 550 paper-based; 78 iBT), IELTS (minimum score 6.5). *Application deadline:* For fall admission, 1/15 priority date for domestic and international students. Applications are processed on a rolling basis. Application fee: $40 ($90 for international students). Electronic applications accepted. *Expenses:* $4,851. *Financial support:* In 2016–17, 7 students received support, including 2 research assistantships (averaging $34,444 per year), 14 teaching assistantships (averaging $29,639 per year); career-related internships or fieldwork, Federal Work-Study, and institutionally sponsored loans also available. Support available to part-time students. Financial award application deadline: 3/1; financial award applicants required to submit FAFSA. *Faculty research:* Image analysis; earth science remote imaging. *Total annual research expenditures:* $238,516. *Unit head:* Dr. Yongmei Lu, PhD Program Director, 512-245-1337, Fax: 512-245-8353, E-mail: yl10@txstate.edu. *Application contact:* Dr. Andrea Golato, Dean of Graduate School, 512-245-2581, Fax: 512-245-8365, E-mail: gradcollege@txstate.edu.
Website: http://www.geo.txstate.edu/

**Texas State University,** The Graduate College, College of Liberal Arts, Master's Program in Geography, San Marcos, TX 78666. Offers MAG, MS. *Program availability:* Evening/weekend. *Faculty:* 29 full-time (10 women), 3 part-time/adjunct (1 woman). *Students:* 45 full-time (21 women), 18 part-time (8 women); includes 16 minority (2 Black or African American, non-Hispanic/Latino; 2 Asian, non-Hispanic/Latino; 11 Hispanic/Latino; 1 Two or more races, non-Hispanic/Latino), 6 international. Average age 29. 84 applicants, 77% accepted, 28 enrolled. In 2016, 23 master's awarded. *Degree requirements:* For master's, comprehensive exam, thesis (for some programs). *Entrance requirements:* For master's, GRE General Test (minimum preferred score of 300 verbal and quantitative), baccalaureate degree from regionally-accredited institution with minimum GPA of 3.2 in last 60 hours of course work (for MAG), 3.4 (for MS); 2 letters of recommendation; statement of purpose; current resume. Additional exam requirements/recommendations for international students: Required—TOEFL (minimum score 550 paper-based; 78 iBT), IELTS (minimum score 6.5). *Application deadline:* For fall admission, 2/1 priority date for domestic and international students; for spring admission, 10/15 priority date for domestic students, 10/1 for international students. Applications are processed on a rolling basis. Application fee: $40 ($90 for international students). Electronic applications accepted. *Expenses:* $4,851 per semester. *Financial support:* In 2016–17, 41 students received support, including 6 research assistantships (averaging $14,212 per year), 13 teaching assistantships (averaging $14,720 per year); career-related internships or fieldwork, Federal Work-Study, institutionally sponsored loans, and scholarships/grants also available. Support available to part-time students. Financial award application deadline: 3/1; financial award applicants required to submit FAFSA. *Faculty research:* Air pollution exposure health effects indicators; mining data to ID risk factors; building capacity for learning progressions research in geography; land management impacts on water quality in New Zealand; cross-scale interactions among climate, land use and river water quality; geospatial resources, materials and tools for STEM teacher preparation; exploring Texas with digital story maps. *Total annual research expenditures:* $238,516. *Unit head:* Dr. Yongmei Lu, Graduate Adviser, 512-245-1337, Fax: 512-245-8353, E-mail: yl10@txstate.edu. *Application contact:* Dr. Andrea Golato, Dean of Graduate School, 512-245-2581, Fax: 512-245-8365, E-mail: gradcollege@txstate.edu.
Website: http://www.geo.txstate.edu/

**Texas Tech University,** Graduate School, College of Arts and Sciences, Department of Geosciences, Lubbock, TX 79409-1053. Offers atmospheric science (MS); geography (MS); geosciences (MS, PhD). *Program availability:* Part-time. *Faculty:* 32 full-time (4 women), 4 part-time/adjunct (1 woman). *Students:* 77 full-time (28 women), 13 part-time (6 women); includes 15 minority (1 Black or African American, non-Hispanic/Latino; 1 Asian, non-Hispanic/Latino; 10 Hispanic/Latino; 3 Two or more races, non-Hispanic/Latino), 22 international. Average age 27. 155 applicants, 16% accepted, 21 enrolled. In 2016, 21 master's, 4 doctorates awarded. *Degree requirements:* For master's, thesis; for doctorate, comprehensive exam, thesis/dissertation. *Entrance requirements:* For master's and doctorate, GRE General Test. Additional exam requirements/recommendations for international students: Required—TOEFL (minimum score 550 paper-based; 79 iBT). *Application deadline:* For fall admission, 6/1 priority date for domestic students, 1/15 priority date for international students; for spring admission, 9/1 priority date for domestic students, 6/15 priority date for international students. Applications are processed on a rolling basis. Application fee: $75. Electronic applications accepted. *Expenses:* $300 per credit hour full-time resident tuition, $708 per credit hour full-time non-resident tuition; $50.50 per credit hour fee plus $608 per term fee. *Financial support:* In 2016–17, 82 students received support, including 60 fellowships (averaging $3,017 per year), 35 research assistantships (averaging $14,365 per year), 59 teaching assistantships (averaging $12,766 per year); Federal Work-Study, scholarships/grants, health care benefits, tuition waivers (partial), and unspecified assistantships also available. Financial award application deadline: 2/15; financial award applicants required to submit FAFSA. *Faculty research:* Geology, geophysics, geochemistry, geospatial technology, atmospheric sciences. *Total annual research expenditures:* $6.7 million. *Unit head:* Dr. Jeffrey A. Lee, Chairman, 806-834-8228, Fax: 806-742-0100, E-mail: jeff.lee@ttu.edu. *Application contact:* Dr. Callum Hetherington, Associate Professor, 806-834-3110, Fax: 806-724-0100, E-mail: callum.hetherington@ttu.edu.
Website: http://www.geosciences.ttu.edu

**Towson University,** Program in Geography and Environmental Planning, Towson, MD 21252-0001. Offers MA. *Program availability:* Part-time, evening/weekend. *Students:* 7 full-time (2 women), 12 part-time (4 women); includes 3 minority (2 Black or African American, non-Hispanic/Latino; 1 Two or more races, non-Hispanic/Latino), 1 international. *Degree requirements:* For master's, thesis optional. *Entrance requirements:* For master's, bachelor's degree with minimum of 9 credits of course work in geography, minimum GPA of 3.0 overall and in all geography courses, 2 letters of recommendation, essay. *Application deadline:* Applications are processed on a rolling basis. Application fee: $45. Electronic applications accepted. *Expenses:* Tuition, state resident: full-time $7580; part-time $379 per unit. Tuition, nonresident: full-time $15,700; part-time $785 per unit. *Required fees:* $2480. *Financial support:* Application deadline: 4/1. *Unit head:* Dr. Charles Schmitz, Graduate Program Director, 410-704-2966, E-mail: cschmitz@towson.edu. *Application contact:* Coverley Beidleman, Assistant Director of Graduate Admissions, 410-704-2113, Fax: 410-704-3030, E-mail: grads@towson.edu. Website: http://www.towson.edu/cla/departments/geography/gradgeography/

**Trent University,** Graduate Studies, Program in Applications of Modeling in the Natural and Social Sciences, Peterborough, ON K9J 7B8, Canada. Offers applications of modeling in the natural and social sciences (MA); biology (M Sc, PhD); chemistry (M Sc); computer studies (M Sc); geography (M Sc, PhD); physics (M Sc). *Program availability:* Part-time. *Degree requirements:* For master's, thesis. *Entrance requirements:* For master's, honours degree. *Faculty research:* Computation of heat transfer, atmospheric physics, statistical mechanics, stress and coping, evolutionary ecology.

**Trent University,** Graduate Studies, Program in Environmental and Life Sciences and Program in Applications of Modeling in the Natural and Social Sciences, Department of Geography, Peterborough, ON K9J 7B8, Canada. Offers M Sc, PhD. *Program availability:* Part-time. *Degree requirements:* For master's, thesis; for doctorate, thesis/dissertation. *Entrance requirements:* For master's, honors degree; for doctorate, master's degree. *Faculty research:* Hydrometeorology, snow and ice, urban hydrology, fluvial geomorphology.

**Université de Montréal,** Faculty of Arts and Sciences, Department of Geography, Montréal, QC H3C 3J7, Canada. Offers environment and durable development (DESS); geography (M Sc, PhD, DESS). *Degree requirements:* For master's, 2 foreign languages, thesis (for some programs); for doctorate, 3 foreign languages, thesis/dissertation, general exam. *Entrance requirements:* For master's, bachelor's degree in related field; for doctorate, MA in geography or related field. Electronic applications accepted. *Faculty research:* Cartography, palynology, geomorphology, economic geography, regional and urban development.

**Université de Sherbrooke,** Faculty of Letters and Human Sciences, Department of Geography and Remote Sensing, Sherbrooke, QC J1K 2R1, Canada. Offers M Sc, PhD. *Degree requirements:* For master's, one foreign language, thesis; for doctorate, thesis/dissertation. *Faculty research:* Cartography.

**Université du Québec à Montréal,** Graduate Programs, Program in Geography, Montréal, QC H3C 3P8, Canada. Offers M Sc. *Program availability:* Part-time. *Degree requirements:* For master's, thesis optional. *Entrance requirements:* For master's, appropriate bachelor's degree or equivalent and proficiency in French.

**Université Laval,** Faculty of Forestry, Geography and Geomatics, Department of Geography, Program in Geographical Sciences, Québec, QC G1K 7P4, Canada. Offers M Sc Geogr, PhD. Terminal master's awarded for partial completion of doctoral program. *Degree requirements:* For master's, thesis; for doctorate, comprehensive exam, thesis/dissertation. *Entrance requirements:* For master's, knowledge of French; for doctorate, knowledge of French, knowledge of a second language. Electronic applications accepted.

**University at Albany, State University of New York,** College of Arts and Sciences, Department of Geography and Planning, Program in Geography, Albany, NY 12222-0001. Offers MA. *Degree requirements:* For master's, thesis or alternative. *Entrance requirements:* Additional exam requirements/recommendations for international students: Required—TOEFL (minimum score 550 paper-based). *Application deadline:* For fall admission, 3/1 for domestic students, 5/1 for international students; for spring admission, 11/1 for international students. Applications are processed on a rolling basis. Application fee: $75. Electronic applications accepted. *Expenses:* Tuition, state resident: full-time $10,870; part-time $453 per credit hour. Tuition, nonresident: full-time $22,210; part-time $925 per credit hour. International tuition: $21,550 full-time. *Required fees:* $1864; $96 per credit hour. *Financial support:* Fellowships, teaching assistantships, Federal Work-Study, and institutionally sponsored loans available. Financial award application deadline: 6/1. *Faculty research:* Remote sensing, cultural/social geography, urban geography. *Unit head:* Andrei Lapenas, Director, 518-442-4191, E-mail: andreil@albany.edu. *Application contact:* Michael DeRensis, Director, Graduate Admissions, 518-442-3980, Fax: 518-442-3922, E-mail: graduate@albany.edu.
Website: http://www.albany.edu/gp/masters_geography_and_planning.php

**University at Buffalo, the State University of New York,** Graduate School, College of Arts and Sciences, Department of Geography, Buffalo, NY 14214. Offers earth systems science (MA, MS); economic geography and business geographics (MS); environmental modeling and analysis (MA); geographic information science (MA, MS); geography (MA, PhD); health geography (MS); international trade (MA); urban and regional analysis (MA). *Program availability:* Part-time. *Faculty:* 18 full-time (8 women), 1 part-time/adjunct (0 women). *Students:* 45 full-time (29 women), 51 part-time (15 women); includes 64 minority (1 Black or African American, non-Hispanic/Latino; 61 Asian, non-Hispanic/Latino; 2 Hispanic/Latino), 41 international. Average age 28. 167 applicants, 34% accepted, 28 enrolled. In 2016, 23 master's, 7 doctorates awarded. Terminal master's awarded for partial completion of doctoral program. *Degree requirements:* For master's, thesis (for some programs), project or portfolio; for doctorate, thesis/dissertation. *Entrance requirements:* For master's, GRE General Test, minimum GPA of 2.9; for doctorate, GRE General Test, minimum GPA of 3.0. Additional exam requirements/recommendations for international students: Required—TOEFL (minimum score 550 paper-based; 79 iBT). *Application deadline:* For fall admission, 5/1 priority date for domestic students, 3/10 priority date for international students; for spring admission, 11/1 priority date for domestic students, 9/1 priority date for international students. Applications are processed on a rolling basis. Application fee: $75. Electronic applications accepted. *Expenses:* Contact institution. *Financial support:* In 2016–17, 15 students received support, including 7 fellowships with full tuition reimbursements available (averaging $3,070 per year), 7 research assistantships with full tuition reimbursements available (averaging $14,000 per year), 15 teaching assistantships with full tuition reimbursements available (averaging $14,080 per year); career-related internships or fieldwork, Federal Work-Study, institutionally sponsored loans, traineeships, health care benefits, and unspecified assistantships also available. Financial award application deadline: 1/10. *Faculty research:* International business and world trade, geographic information systems and cartography, transportation, urban and regional analysis, physical and environmental geography. *Total annual research expenditures:* $2.6 million. *Unit head:* Dr. Sean Bennett, Chairman, 716-645-0490, Fax: 716-645-2329, E-mail: seanb@buffalo.edu. *Application contact:* Wendy Zitzka,

# Geography

Graduate Secretary, 716-645-0471, Fax: 716-645-2329, E-mail: wzitzka@buffalo.edu. Website: http://www.geog.buffalo.edu/

**The University of Alabama,** Graduate School, College of Arts and Sciences, Department of Geography, Tuscaloosa, AL 35487. Offers earth system science (MS, PhD); environment and natural resources (MS, PhD); environment and society (MS, PhD); geographic information science (MS, PhD). *Program availability:* Part-time. *Faculty:* 14 full-time (2 women). *Students:* 26 full-time (11 women), 5 part-time (1 woman); includes 1 minority (Hispanic/Latino), 8 international. Average age 26. 46 applicants, 35% accepted, 11 enrolled. In 2016, 10 master's awarded. *Degree requirements:* For master's, comprehensive exam, thesis; for doctorate, comprehensive exam, thesis/dissertation. *Entrance requirements:* For master's, GRE, minimum GPA of 3.0. Additional exam requirements/recommendations for international students: Required—TOEFL (minimum score 550 paper-based; 79 iBT). *Application deadline:* For fall admission, 2/15 priority date for domestic and international students; for spring admission, 10/1 priority date for domestic and international students. Applications are processed on a rolling basis. Application fee: $50 ($60 for international students). Electronic applications accepted. *Expenses:* Tuition, state resident: full-time $10,470. Tuition, nonresident: full-time $26,950. *Financial support:* In 2016–17, 20 students received support, including fellowships with full tuition reimbursements available (averaging $15,000 per year), 4 research assistantships with full tuition reimbursements available (averaging $14,013 per year), 18 teaching assistantships with full tuition reimbursements available (averaging $14,013 per year); career-related internships or fieldwork, health care benefits, and unspecified assistantships also available. Financial award application deadline: 2/15. *Faculty research:* Earth system science; geographic information science; environment and natural resources; environment and society. *Total annual research expenditures:* $347,176. *Unit head:* Dr. Douglas Sherman, Chair, 205-348-5047, Fax: 205-348-2278, E-mail: douglas.j.sherman@ua.edu. *Application contact:* Dr. Justin Hart, Associate Professor, 205-348-5047, Fax: 205-348-2278, E-mail: hart013@ua.edu.
Website: http://geography.ua.edu

**The University of Arizona,** College of Social and Behavioral Sciences, School of Geography and Development, Tucson, AZ 85721. Offers geographic information systems technology (MA); geography (PhD). *Program availability:* Part-time. Terminal master's awarded for partial completion of doctoral program. *Degree requirements:* For master's, thesis or additional course work; for doctorate, variable foreign language requirement, thesis/dissertation. *Entrance requirements:* For master's, GRE General Test, 2 letters of recommendation; for doctorate, GRE General Test, statement of purpose, 2 letters of recommendation, master's degree. Additional exam requirements/recommendations for international students: Required—TOEFL (minimum score 550 paper-based; 79 iBT). Electronic applications accepted. *Faculty research:* Population, Latin America, Anglo-America, the former Soviet Union, the Middle East.

**University of Arkansas,** Graduate School, J. William Fulbright College of Arts and Sciences, Department of Geosciences, Program in Geography, Fayetteville, AR 72701. Offers MA. *Program availability:* Part-time. In 2016, 6 master's awarded. *Degree requirements:* For master's, thesis. *Application deadline:* For fall admission, 4/1 for international students; for spring admission, 10/1 for international students. Applications are processed on a rolling basis. Application fee: $40 ($50 for international students). Electronic applications accepted. *Financial support:* In 2016–17, 7 research assistantships, 5 teaching assistantships were awarded; fellowships, career-related internships or fieldwork, and Federal Work-Study also available. Support available to part-time students. Financial award application deadline: 4/1; financial award applicants required to submit FAFSA. *Unit head:* Dr. Chris Liner, Chair, 479-575-3355, Fax: 479-575-3469, E-mail: liner@uark.edu. *Application contact:* Dr. Fiona Davidson, Graduate Coordinator, 479-575-3879, E-mail: fdavidso@uark.edu.
Website: http://geosciences.uark.edu/

**The University of British Columbia,** Faculty of Arts and Faculty of Graduate Studies, Department of Geography, Vancouver, BC V6T 1Z2, Canada. Offers M Sc, MA, PhD. *Program availability:* Part-time. Terminal master's awarded for partial completion of doctoral program. *Degree requirements:* For master's, thesis; for doctorate, comprehensive exam, thesis/dissertation. *Entrance requirements:* For master's and doctorate, minimum B average, 2nd class honors, upper division (class II, division I). Additional exam requirements/recommendations for international students: Required—TOEFL. *Application deadline:* Applications are processed on a rolling basis. Application fee: $100 Canadian dollars ($162 Canadian dollars for international students). Electronic applications accepted. *Expenses:* $4,802 per year tuition and fees, $8,436 per year international. *Financial support:* Fellowships, research assistantships, teaching assistantships, and career-related internships or fieldwork available. Financial award application deadline: 2/1. *Faculty research:* Earth system science, environmental geography, historical geography, social geography, urban geography. *Application contact:* Danny Wong, Graduate Program Staff, 604-822-2663, Fax: 604-822-6150, E-mail: graduate.program@geog.ubc.ca.
Website: http://www.geog.ubc.ca/

**University of Calgary,** Faculty of Graduate Studies, Faculty of Arts, Department of Geography, Calgary, AB T2N 1N4, Canada. Offers M Sc, MA, MGIS, PhD. *Program availability:* Part-time. *Degree requirements:* For master's, departmental conference; for doctorate, thesis/dissertation, candidacy exam, departmental conference. *Entrance requirements:* For master's, minimum undergraduate GPA of 3.0 during last 2 years; for doctorate, minimum GPA of 3.0 during previous 2 years, master's degree. Additional exam requirements/recommendations for international students: Required—TOEFL (minimum score 550 paper-based). Electronic applications accepted. *Faculty research:* Geographic information systems, remote sensing, geomorphology, earth system processes, urban and required environmental health research.

**University of California, Berkeley,** Graduate Division, College of Letters and Science, Department of Geography, Berkeley, CA 94720-1500. Offers PhD. *Students:* 44 full-time (25 women); includes 13 minority (4 Black or African American, non-Hispanic/Latino; 1 American Indian or Alaska Native, non-Hispanic/Latino; 4 Asian, non-Hispanic/Latino; 4 Hispanic/Latino), 6 international. Average age 32. 80 applicants, 8 enrolled. In 2016, 7 doctorates awarded. *Degree requirements:* For doctorate, thesis/dissertation, qualifying exam. *Entrance requirements:* For doctorate, GRE General Test, minimum GPA of 3.0, 3 letters of recommendation. Additional exam requirements/recommendations for international students: Required—TOEFL (minimum score 570 paper-based; 90 iBT). *Application deadline:* For fall admission, 12/1 for domestic students. Application fee: $105 ($125 for international students). Electronic applications accepted. *Financial support:* Fellowships, research assistantships, teaching assistantships, institutionally sponsored loans, health care benefits, and unspecified assistantships available. *Unit head:* Prof. Nathan Sayre, Chair, 510-642-3903, Fax: 510-642-3370. *Application contact:* Marjorie Ensor, Graduate Assistant for Admission, 510-642-3904, Fax: 510-642-3370, E-mail: ensor@berkeley.edu.
Website: http://geography.berkeley.edu

**University of California, Davis,** Graduate Studies, Graduate Group in Geography, Davis, CA 95616. Offers MA, PhD. Terminal master's awarded for partial completion of doctoral program. *Degree requirements:* For master's, comprehensive exam (for some programs), thesis (for some programs); for doctorate, thesis/dissertation. *Entrance*

*requirements:* For master's, GRE General Test, minimum GPA of 3.0; for doctorate, GRE General Test, master's degree, minimum GPA of 3.0. Additional exam requirements/recommendations for international students: Required—TOEFL (minimum score 550 paper-based). Electronic applications accepted. *Faculty research:* Cultural agrosystems, mountain society habitat and South Asia.

**University of California, Los Angeles,** Graduate Division, College of Letters and Science, Department of Geography, Los Angeles, CA 90095. Offers MA, PhD. Terminal master's awarded for partial completion of doctoral program. *Degree requirements:* For master's, thesis; for doctorate, thesis/dissertation, oral and written qualifying exams. *Entrance requirements:* For doctorate, GRE General Test, bachelor's degree; minimum undergraduate GPA of 3.3, 3.5 in graduate work (or its equivalent if letter grade system not used); writing sample. Additional exam requirements/recommendations for international students: Required—TOEFL. Electronic applications accepted.

**University of California, Santa Barbara,** Graduate Division, College of Letters and Sciences, Division of Mathematics, Life, and Physical Sciences, Department of Geography, Santa Barbara, CA 93106-4060. Offers cognitive science (PhD); geography (MA, PhD); global studies (PhD); quantitative methods in the social sciences (PhD); technology and society (PhD); transportation (PhD); MA/PhD. Terminal master's awarded for partial completion of doctoral program. *Degree requirements:* For master's, comprehensive exam (for some programs), thesis or alternative; for doctorate, comprehensive exam, thesis/dissertation, 1 quarter of teaching assistantship. *Entrance requirements:* For master's and doctorate, GRE (minimum combined verbal and quantitative scores above 1100 in old scoring system or 301 in new scoring system). Additional exam requirements/recommendations for international students: Required—TOEFL (minimum score 550 paper-based; 80 iBT), IELTS (minimum score 7). Electronic applications accepted. *Faculty research:* Earth system science; human environment relations; modeling, measurement, and computation.

**University of Central Arkansas,** Graduate School, College of Liberal Arts, Department of Geography, Conway, AR 72035-0001. Offers community and economic development (MS); geographic information systems (MGIS, Certificate). *Program availability:* Part-time, online learning. *Entrance requirements:* Additional exam requirements/recommendations for international students: Required—TOEFL (minimum score 550 paper-based). Electronic applications accepted.

**University of Cincinnati,** Graduate School, McMicken College of Arts and Sciences, Department of Geography, Cincinnati, OH 45221. Offers MA, PhD. Terminal master's awarded for partial completion of doctoral program. *Degree requirements:* For master's, thesis optional; for doctorate, one foreign language, comprehensive exam, thesis/dissertation. *Entrance requirements:* For master's and doctorate, GRE General Test. Additional exam requirements/recommendations for international students: Required—TOEFL. Electronic applications accepted. *Expenses: Tuition, area resident:* Full-time $12,790; part-time $389 per credit hour. Tuition, state resident: full-time $13,290; part-time $419 per credit hour. Tuition, nonresident: full-time $24,532; part-time $976 per credit hour. *International tuition:* $24,832 full-time. *Required fees:* $3958; $140 per credit hour. Tuition and fees vary according to course load, degree level, program and reciprocity agreements. *Faculty research:* Urban-economics, GIS, physical-environmental.

**University of Colorado Boulder,** Graduate School, College of Arts and Sciences, Department of Geography, Boulder, CO 80309. Offers MA, PhD. *Faculty:* 24 full-time (8 women). *Students:* 77 full-time (35 women), 4 part-time (all women); includes 5 minority (2 Hispanic/Latino; 3 Two or more races, non-Hispanic/Latino), 13 international. Average age 32. 117 applicants, 23% accepted, 14 enrolled. In 2016, 4 master's, 8 doctorates awarded. Terminal master's awarded for partial completion of doctoral program. *Degree requirements:* For master's, thesis; for doctorate, one foreign language, comprehensive exam, thesis/dissertation. *Entrance requirements:* For master's, GRE General Test, minimum undergraduate GPA of 3.0; for doctorate, GRE General Test. *Application deadline:* For fall admission, 12/1 for domestic and international students. Application fee: $60 ($80 for international students). Electronic applications accepted. Application fee is waived when completed online. *Financial support:* In 2016–17, 164 students received support, including 18 fellowships (averaging $15,236 per year), 20 research assistantships with full and partial tuition reimbursements available (averaging $37,537 per year), 39 teaching assistantships with full and partial tuition reimbursements available (averaging $39,149 per year); institutionally sponsored loans, scholarships/grants, health care benefits, and unspecified assistantships also available. Financial award application deadline: 1/15; financial award applicants required to submit FAFSA. *Faculty research:* Hydrology, physical geography, political geography, earth sciences, cultural geography. *Total annual research expenditures:* $47.4 million. *Application contact:* E-mail: geoggrad@colorado.edu.
Website: http://geography.colorado.edu

**University of Colorado Colorado Springs,** College of Letters, Arts and Sciences, Department of Geography and Environmental Studies, Colorado Springs, CO 80918. Offers MA. *Program availability:* Part-time. *Faculty:* 8 full-time (3 women), 1 (woman) part-time/adjunct. *Students:* 2 full-time (1 woman), 12 part-time (8 women); includes 5 minority (1 Asian, non-Hispanic/Latino; 4 Hispanic/Latino). Average age 32. 9 applicants, 89% accepted, 3 enrolled. In 2016, 6 master's awarded. *Degree requirements:* For master's, comprehensive exam (for some programs), thesis (for some programs). *Entrance requirements:* For master's, GRE (recommended minimum combined score for the verbal and quantitative tests of 1000), minimum undergraduate GPA of 3.0, statement of intent (essay). Additional exam requirements/recommendations for international students: Recommended—TOEFL (minimum score 550 paper-based; 80 iBT), IELTS (minimum score 6.5). *Application deadline:* For fall admission, 2/1 priority date for domestic and international students. Applications are processed on a rolling basis. Application fee: $60 ($100 for international students). *Expenses:* Tuition, state resident: full-time $9983. Tuition, nonresident: full-time $20,153. Tuition and fees vary according to course load, degree level, program and reciprocity agreements. *Financial support:* In 2016–17, 9 students received support. Federal Work-Study, scholarships/grants, health care benefits, and unspecified assistantships available. Support available to part-time students. Financial award application deadline: 3/1; financial award applicants required to submit FAFSA. *Faculty research:* Socio-ecological implications of conservation strategies, cultural geography, militarized spaces, geovisualization, geographic information systems, hydrology, biogeography, human-environment interactions, geomorphology, population. *Total annual research expenditures:* $124,548. *Unit head:* Dr. Kelli Klebe, Dean of the Graduate School, 719-255-3779, Fax: 719-255-3045, E-mail: kklebe@uccs.edu. *Application contact:* David Havlick, Associate Professor, 719-255-4906, E-mail: dhavlick@uccs.edu.
Website: http://www.uccs.edu/geography/

**University of Connecticut,** Graduate School, College of Liberal Arts and Sciences, Department of Geography, Storrs, CT 06269. Offers MA, PhD. *Degree requirements:* For master's, comprehensive exam; for doctorate, thesis/dissertation. *Entrance requirements:* For master's and doctorate, GRE General Test. Additional exam requirements/recommendations for international students: Required—TOEFL (minimum score 550 paper-based). Electronic applications accepted.

**University of Delaware,** College of Earth, Ocean, and Environment, Department of Geography, Newark, DE 19716. Offers MA, MS, PhD. *Degree requirements:* For master's, thesis; for doctorate, thesis/dissertation. *Entrance requirements:* For master's and doctorate, GRE General Test. Additional exam requirements/recommendations for international students: Required—TOEFL. Electronic applications accepted. *Faculty research:* Permafrost, glaciers, climatology, physical geography, human geography.

**University of Florida,** Graduate School, College of Liberal Arts and Sciences, Department of Geography, Gainesville, FL 32611. Offers applications of geographic technologies (MA, MS); geographic information systems (MA, MS, PhD); geography (MA, MS, PhD); hydrologic sciences (MS, PhD); tropical conservation and development (MA, MS, PhD); wetland sciences (MA, MS, PhD). *Degree requirements:* For master's, thesis; for doctorate, comprehensive exam, thesis/dissertation. *Entrance requirements:* For master's and doctorate, GRE General Test, minimum GPA of 3.0. Additional exam requirements/recommendations for international students: Required—TOEFL (minimum score 550 paper-based; 80 iBT), IELTS (minimum score 6). Electronic applications accepted. *Faculty research:* Economic development, physical geography, hydrology, climatology, tropical agriculture.

**University of Georgia,** Franklin College of Arts and Sciences, Department of Geography, Athens, GA 30602. Offers MA, MS, PhD. *Degree requirements:* For master's, one foreign language, thesis; for doctorate, one foreign language, thesis/dissertation. *Entrance requirements:* For master's and doctorate, GRE General Test. *Application deadline:* For fall admission, 7/1 priority date for domestic students; for spring admission, 11/15 for domestic students. Application fee: $50. Electronic applications accepted. *Financial support:* Fellowships, research assistantships, teaching assistantships, and unspecified assistantships available. *Unit head:* Dr. Thomas Mote, Head, 706-542-2856, Fax: 706-542-2388, E-mail: tmote@uga.edu. *Application contact:* Xiaobai Yao, Graduate Coordinator, 706-543-0326, E-mail: xyao@uga.edu.
Website: http://www.ggy.uga.edu/

**University of Guelph,** Graduate Studies, College of Social and Applied Human Sciences, Department of Geography, Guelph, ON N1G 2W1, Canada. Offers M Sc, MA, PhD. *Program availability:* Part-time. *Degree requirements:* For master's, thesis (for some programs); for doctorate, comprehensive exam, thesis/dissertation. *Entrance requirements:* For master's, minimum B average during previous 2 years of course work; for doctorate, minimum A- average. Additional exam requirements/recommendations for international students: Required—TOEFL (minimum score 550 paper-based). Electronic applications accepted. *Faculty research:* Rural resource evaluation, environmental analysis, biophysical process, rural settlement and land use, resource assessment.

**University of Hawaii at Manoa,** Graduate Division, College of Social Sciences, Department of Geography, Honolulu, HI 96822. Offers geography (MA, PhD); ocean policy (Graduate Certificate). *Program availability:* Part-time. *Degree requirements:* For master's, one foreign language, comprehensive exam, thesis; for doctorate, one foreign language, comprehensive exam, thesis/dissertation. *Entrance requirements:* For master's, GRE General Test; for doctorate, GRE General Test, sample of written work. Additional exam requirements/recommendations for international students: Required—TOEFL (minimum score 500 paper-based; 61 iBT), IELTS (minimum score 5). *Faculty research:* Physical geography, human geography, methodology.

**University of Idaho,** College of Graduate Studies, College of Science, Department of Geography, Moscow, ID 83844. Offers MS, PhD. *Faculty:* 7 full-time. *Students:* 13 full-time, 2 part-time. Average age 33. In 2016, 8 master's, 1 doctorate awarded. *Degree requirements:* For doctorate, thesis/dissertation. *Entrance requirements:* For master's and doctorate, minimum GPA of 3.0. Additional exam requirements/recommendations for international students: Required—TOEFL. *Application deadline:* For fall admission, 8/1 for domestic students; for spring admission, 12/15 for domestic students. Applications are processed on a rolling basis. Application fee: $60. Electronic applications accepted. *Expenses:* Tuition, state resident: full-time $6460; part-time $414 per credit hour. Tuition, nonresident: full-time $21,268; part-time $1237 per credit hour. *Required fees:* $2070; $60 per credit hour. Full-time tuition and fees vary according to course load and reciprocity agreements. *Financial support:* Research assistantships and teaching assistantships available. Financial award applicants required to submit FAFSA. *Faculty research:* Land cover land use changes, rural development, geographic trade models, climate change and effects on ecosystems, migration and regional development. *Unit head:* Dr. Leslie Baker, Chair, 208-885-6216, E-mail: geography@uidaho.edu. *Application contact:* Sean Scoggin, Graduate Recruitment Coordinator, 208-885-4723, Fax: 208-885-4406, E-mail: graduateadmissions@uidaho.edu.
Website: https://www.uidaho.edu/sci/geography

**University of Illinois at Chicago,** College of Liberal Arts and Sciences, Department of Anthropology, Program in Environmental and Urban Geography, Chicago, IL 60607-7128. Offers MA. *Program availability:* Part-time. *Degree requirements:* For master's, thesis. *Entrance requirements:* For master's, GRE General Test, minimum GPA of 2.75. Additional exam requirements/recommendations for international students: Required—TOEFL. Electronic applications accepted.

**University of Illinois at Urbana–Champaign,** Graduate College, College of Liberal Arts and Sciences, School of Earth, Society and Environment, Department of Geography and Geographic Information Science, Champaign, IL 61820. Offers MA, MS, PhD.

**The University of Iowa,** Graduate College, College of Liberal Arts and Sciences, Department of Geographical and Sustainability Sciences, Iowa City, IA 52242-1316. Offers MA, PhD, Certificate. *Degree requirements:* For master's, thesis optional, exam; for doctorate, comprehensive exam, thesis/dissertation. *Entrance requirements:* For master's and doctorate, GRE General Test, minimum GPA of 3.0. Additional exam requirements/recommendations for international students: Required—TOEFL (minimum score 550 paper-based; 81 iBT). Electronic applications accepted.

**The University of Kansas,** Graduate Studies, College of Liberal Arts and Sciences, Department of Geography, Lawrence, KS 66045-7613. Offers atmospheric science (MS); geographic information science (Graduate Certificate); geography (MA, PhD); MUP/MA. *Program availability:* Part-time. *Students:* 48 full-time (19 women), 18 part-time (7 women); includes 9 minority (7 American Indian or Alaska Native, non-Hispanic/Latino; 1 Asian, non-Hispanic/Latino; 1 Hispanic/Latino), 7 international. Average age 33. 55 applicants, 33% accepted, 9 enrolled. In 2016, 15 master's, 6 doctorates awarded. *Entrance requirements:* For master's and doctorate, GRE General Test, 3 letters of reference, transcripts, statement of interests, resume. Additional exam requirements/recommendations for international students: Required—TOEFL. *Application deadline:* For fall admission, 1/15 priority date for domestic and international students; for spring admission, 11/1 for domestic and international students; for summer admission, 4/1 for domestic and international students. Application fee: $65 ($85 for international students). Electronic applications accepted. *Financial support:* Fellowships, research assistantships, teaching assistantships, and unspecified assistantships available. Financial award application deadline: 1/15. *Faculty research:* Physical geography, human/cultural/regional geography, geographic information science, atmospheric science. *Unit head:* Nathaniel Brunsell, Chair, 785-864-2021, E-mail: brunsell@ku.edu. *Application contact:* Beverly Koerner, Graduate Admission

Contact, 785-864-7706, E-mail: koerner@ku.edu.
Website: http://www.geog.ku.edu/

**University of Kentucky,** Graduate School, College of Arts and Sciences, Program in Geography, Lexington, KY 40506-0032. Offers MA, PhD. *Degree requirements:* For master's, comprehensive exam, thesis optional; for doctorate, one foreign language, comprehensive exam, thesis/dissertation. *Entrance requirements:* For master's, GRE General Test, minimum undergraduate GPA of 2.75; for doctorate, GRE General Test, minimum graduate GPA of 3.0. Additional exam requirements/recommendations for international students: Required—TOEFL (minimum score 550 paper-based). Electronic applications accepted. *Faculty research:* Cultural, industrial, medical, political, social, population, and transportation geography; geographic analysis; Third World (especially Southeast Asia theory); Eastern Europe.

**University of Lethbridge,** School of Graduate Studies, Lethbridge, AB T1K 3M4, Canada. Offers addictions counseling (M Sc); agricultural biotechnology (M Sc); agricultural studies (M Sc, MA); anthropology (MA); archaeology (M Sc, MA); art (MA, MFA); biochemistry (M Sc); biological sciences (M Sc); biomolecular science (PhD); biosystems and biodiversity (PhD); Canadian studies (MA); chemistry (M Sc); computer science (M Sc); computer science and geographical information science (M Sc); counseling (MC); counseling psychology (M Ed); dramatic arts (MA); earth, space, and physical science (PhD); economics (MA); education (MA, PhD); educational leadership (M Ed); English (MA); environmental science (M Sc); evolution and behavior (PhD); exercise science (M Sc); French (MA); French/German (MA); French/Spanish (MA); general education (M Ed); geography (M Sc, MA); German (MA); health sciences (M Sc); individualized multidisciplinary (M Sc, MA); kinesiology (M Sc, MA); management (M Sc), including accounting, finance, human resource management and labor relations, information systems, international management, marketing, policy and strategy; mathematics (M Sc); music (M Mus, MA); Native American studies (MA); neuroscience (M Sc, PhD); new media (MA, MFA); nursing (M Sc, MN); philosophy (MA); physics (M Sc); political science (MA); psychology (M Sc, MA); religious studies (MA); sociology (MA); theatre and dramatic arts (MFA); theoretical and computational science (PhD); urban and regional studies (MA); women and gender studies (MA). *Program availability:* Part-time, evening/weekend. *Degree requirements:* For master's, thesis (for some programs); for doctorate, comprehensive exam, thesis/dissertation. *Entrance requirements:* For master's, GMAT (for M Sc in management), bachelor's degree in related field, minimum GPA of 3.0 during previous 20 graded semester courses, 2 years' teaching or related experience (M Ed); for doctorate, master's degree, minimum graduate GPA of 3.5. Additional exam requirements/recommendations for international students: Required—TOEFL (minimum score 580 paper-based; 93 iBT). Electronic applications accepted. *Faculty research:* Movement and brain plasticity, gibberellin physiology, photosynthesis, carbon cycling, molecular properties of main-group ring components.

**University of Louisville,** Graduate School, College of Arts and Sciences, Department of Geography and Geosciences, Louisville, KY 40292-0001. Offers applied geography (MS). *Program availability:* Part-time. *Faculty:* 12 full-time (4 women). *Students:* 6 full-time (1 woman), 8 part-time (0 women). Average age 29. 5 applicants, 80% accepted, 4 enrolled. In 2016, 6 master's awarded. *Degree requirements:* For master's, thesis. *Entrance requirements:* For master's, GRE (minimum combined score of 1000), BA/BS with minimum cumulative GPA of 3.0. Additional exam requirements/recommendations for international students: Required—TOEFL (minimum score 550 paper-based; 79 iBT). *Application deadline:* For fall admission, 11/1 for domestic students, 5/1 priority date for international students; for spring admission, 4/1 for domestic students, 11/1 priority date for international students; for summer admission, 4/1 priority date for international students. Applications are processed on a rolling basis. Application fee: $60. Electronic applications accepted. *Expenses:* Tuition, state resident: full-time $12,246; part-time $681 per credit hour. Tuition, nonresident: full-time $25,486; part-time $1417 per credit hour. *Required fees:* $196. Tuition and fees vary according to program and reciprocity agreements. *Financial support:* Scholarships/grants available. Financial award application deadline: 4/1. *Faculty research:* Climatology and global climate change, physical geography, human geography, medical and population geography, geographic information systems, remote sensing and spatial statistics. *Total annual research expenditures:* $71,096. *Unit head:* Dr. David A. Howarth, Professor and Chair of Geography and Geosciences, 502-852-2693. *Application contact:* Dr. Carol L. Hanchette, Director, Graduate Admissions, 502-852-2699, Fax: 502-852-4560, E-mail: carol.hanchette@louisville.edu.
Website: http://louisville.edu/geography/

**The University of Manchester,** School of Environment and Development, Manchester, United Kingdom. Offers architecture (M Phil, PhD); development policy and management (M Phil, PhD); human geography (M Phil, PhD); physical geography (M Phil, PhD); planning and landscape (M Phil, PhD).

**The University of Manchester,** School of Nursing, Midwifery and Social Work, Manchester, United Kingdom. Offers nursing (M Phil, PhD); social work (M Phil, PhD).

**University of Manitoba,** Faculty of Graduate Studies, Clayton H. Riddell Faculty of Environment, Earth, and Resources, Department of Environment and Geography, Winnipeg, MB R3T 2N2, Canada. Offers environment (M Env); environment and geography (M Sc); geography (MA, PhD). *Degree requirements:* For master's, thesis; for doctorate, one foreign language, thesis/dissertation.

**University of Maryland, Baltimore County,** The Graduate School, College of Arts, Humanities and Social Sciences, Department of Geography and Environmental Systems, Program in Geography and Environmental Systems, Baltimore, MD 21250. Offers MS, PhD. *Program availability:* Part-time. *Faculty:* 14 full-time (5 women), 11 part-time/adjunct (2 women). *Students:* 12 full-time (8 women), 4 part-time (0 women); includes 3 minority (2 Asian, non-Hispanic/Latino; 1 Hispanic/Latino), 1 international. Average age 30. 25 applicants, 44% accepted, 6 enrolled. In 2016, 4 master's, 1 doctorate awarded. Terminal master's awarded for partial completion of doctoral program. *Degree requirements:* For master's, thesis optional, annual faculty evaluation, research paper; for doctorate, comprehensive exam, thesis/dissertation, annual faculty evaluation, qualifying exams, proposal and dissertation defense. *Entrance requirements:* For master's and doctorate, GRE, minimum GPA of 3.0 overall, 3.3 in major. Additional exam requirements/recommendations for international students: Required—TOEFL (minimum score 550 paper-based; 80 iBT); Recommended—IELTS. *Application deadline:* For fall admission, 2/1 for domestic students, 1/1 for international students. Application fee: $50. Electronic applications accepted. *Expenses:* $13,194 per year resident. *Financial support:* In 2016–17, 16 students received support, including 5 research assistantships with full tuition reimbursements available (averaging $19,700 per year), 11 teaching assistantships with full tuition reimbursements available (averaging $19,700 per year); fellowships, scholarships/grants, traineeships, health care benefits, and unspecified assistantships also available. Financial award application deadline: 2/1. *Faculty research:* Watershed processes; political ecology; land change and land use; conservation and development; urbanization; economic geography; climate and weather systems; ecology and biogeography; landscape ecology; urban sustainability; environmental health; environmental policy; geographic information science and remote sensing. *Unit head:* Dr. David Lansing, Graduate Program Director, 410-455-2971, E-mail: dlansing@umbc.edu. *Application contact:* Kathryn Nee,

*Geography*

Coordinator of Domestic Admissions, 410-455-2944, E-mail: nee@umbc.edu. Website: http://ges.umbc.edu/graduate/

**University of Maryland, College Park,** Academic Affairs, College of Behavioral and Social Sciences, Department of Geography, College Park, MD 20742. Offers MA, PhD, MA/MLS. *Program availability:* Part-time, evening/weekend. Terminal master's awarded for partial completion of doctoral program. *Degree requirements:* For master's, thesis, oral exam; for doctorate, comprehensive exam, thesis/dissertation. *Entrance requirements:* For master's, GRE General Test, minimum GPA of 3.0, 3 letters of recommendation; for doctorate, GRE General Test. Additional exam requirements/recommendations for international students: Required—TOEFL, TWE. Electronic applications accepted. *Faculty research:* Cartography and automated mapping, environmental systems analysis, metropolitan analysis and planning, historical and human geography, coastal geomorphology.

**University of Massachusetts Amherst,** Graduate School, College of Natural Sciences, Department of Geosciences, Program in Geography, Amherst, MA 01003. Offers MS. *Program availability:* Part-time. *Degree requirements:* For master's, thesis or alternative. *Entrance requirements:* For master's, GRE General Test. Additional exam requirements/ recommendations for international students: Required—TOEFL (minimum score 550 paper-based; 80 iBT), IELTS (minimum score 6.5). Electronic applications accepted.

**University of Memphis,** Graduate School, College of Arts and Sciences, Department of Earth Sciences, Memphis, TN 38152. Offers earth sciences (MA, MS, PhD), including archaeology (MS), geography (MS), geology (MS), geophysics (MS), interdisciplinary studies (MS); geographic information systems (Graduate Certificate), including geographic information systems, GIS educator, GIS planning, GIS professional. *Program availability:* Part-time, evening/weekend. *Faculty:* 17 full-time (3 women), 5 part-time/adjunct (0 women). *Students:* 37 full-time (10 women), 25 part-time (6 women); includes 3 minority (2 Black or African American, non-Hispanic/Latino; 1 Two or more races, non-Hispanic/Latino), 22 international. Average age 33. 30 applicants, 60% accepted, 12 enrolled. In 2016, 21 master's, 5 doctorates, 6 other advanced degrees awarded. Terminal master's awarded for partial completion of doctoral program. *Degree requirements:* For master's, comprehensive exam, thesis, seminar presentation; for doctorate, comprehensive exam, thesis/dissertation, qualifying exam, submission of two manuscripts for publication in peer-reviewed journal or books. *Entrance requirements:* For master's, GRE General Test, 3 letters of recommendation, statement of research interests; for doctorate, GRE General Test, 2 letters of recommendation, resume, personal statement. Additional exam requirements/recommendations for international students: Required—TOEFL (minimum score 550 paper-based; 79 iBT). *Application deadline:* For fall admission, 1/15 for domestic students; for spring admission, 11/1 for domestic students. Applications are processed on a rolling basis. Application fee: $35 ($60 for international students). Electronic applications accepted. *Expenses:* $5,231.50 per semester full-time in-state, $9,623.50 full-time out-of-state. *Financial support:* In 2016–17, 18 students received support, including 4 research assistantships with full tuition reimbursements available (averaging $13,960 per year), 11 teaching assistantships with full tuition reimbursements available (averaging $18,864 per year); fellowships with full tuition reimbursements available, Federal Work-Study, scholarships/grants, and unspecified assistantships also available. Financial award application deadline: 2/1; financial award applicants required to submit FAFSA. *Faculty research:* Hazards, active tectonics, geophysics, hydrology and water resources, spatial analysis. *Unit head:* Dr. Daniel Larsen, Chair, 901-678-4538, Fax: 901-678-2178, E-mail: dlarsen@memphis.edu. *Application contact:* Dr. Randel T. Cox, Graduate Coordinator, 901-678-4361, Fax: 901-678-2178, E-mail: randycox@memphis.edu. Website: http://www.memphis.edu/earthsciences/

**University of Miami,** Graduate School, College of Arts and Sciences, Department of Geography and Regional Studies, Coral Gables, FL 33124. Offers geography (MA). *Program availability:* Part-time. *Degree requirements:* For master's, thesis. *Entrance requirements:* For master's, GRE, 3 letters of recommendation, official transcripts. Additional exam requirements/recommendations for international students: Required—TOEFL. Electronic applications accepted. *Faculty research:* Urbanization, globalization, environmental change.

**University of Minnesota, Twin Cities Campus,** Graduate School, College of Liberal Arts, Department of Geography, Environment and Society, Minneapolis, MN 55455. Offers MA, PhD. *Faculty:* 19 full-time (4 women), 8 part-time/adjunct (3 women). *Students:* 51 full-time (26 women); includes 8 minority (2 Black or African American, non-Hispanic/Latino; 4 Asian, non-Hispanic/Latino; 1 Hispanic/Latino; 1 Two or more races, non-Hispanic/Latino), 10 international. 64 applicants, 28% accepted, 9 enrolled. In 2016, 2 master's awarded. Terminal master's awarded for partial completion of doctoral program. *Degree requirements:* For master's, comprehensive exam, thesis or 3 papers; for doctorate, comprehensive exam, thesis/dissertation. *Entrance requirements:* For master's and doctorate, GRE General Test, minimum GPA of 3.5. Additional exam requirements/recommendations for international students: Required—TOEFL (minimum score 600 paper-based; 100 iBT), IELTS (minimum score 7), Michigan English Language Assessment Battery (minimum score 84). *Application deadline:* For fall admission, 12/15 for domestic and international students. Application fee: $75 ($95 for international students). Electronic applications accepted. *Financial support:* In 2016–17, 37 students received support, including 7 fellowships with full tuition reimbursements available (averaging $22,500 per year), 3 research assistantships with full tuition reimbursements available (averaging $16,000 per year), 21 teaching assistantships with full tuition reimbursements available (averaging $16,000 per year); career-related internships or fieldwork, scholarships/grants, traineeships, health care benefits, tuition waivers (full), and unspecified assistantships also available. Financial award application deadline: 12/15. *Faculty research:* Geovisualization; geographic information systems; spatial analysis and modeling; spatial databases; remote sensing; biogeography; international labor migrations; political globalization and uneven development; governance, citizenship and justice; environmental change; culture, place and flow; nature and society; health geography; dendrochronology. *Total annual research expenditures:* $597,826. *Unit head:* Abdi I. Samatar, Chair, 612-625-6080, Fax: 612-624-1044, E-mail: samat001@umn.edu. *Application contact:* Sara C. Braun, Graduate Program Coordinator, 612-625-6080, Fax: 612-624-1044, E-mail: geog-dgs@umn.edu. Website: http://www.geog.umn.edu/

**University of Missouri,** Office of Research and Graduate Studies, College of Arts and Science, Department of Geography, Columbia, MO 65211. Offers geographic information science (Graduate Certificate); geography (MA). *Faculty:* 9 full-time (0 women). *Students:* 10 full-time (5 women), 1 part-time (0 women). *Entrance requirements:* For master's, thesis or alternative. *Entrance requirements:* For master's, GRE General Test (minimum score 1000 verbal and quantitative), minimum GPA of 3.0. Additional exam requirements/recommendations for international students: Required—TOEFL (minimum score 500 paper-based; 61 iBT). *Application deadline:* For fall admission, 1/15 priority date for domestic and international students; for winter admission, 10/1 for domestic students; for spring admission, 4/1 for domestic students. Applications are processed on a rolling basis. Application fee: $75 ($90 for international students). Electronic applications accepted. *Expenses:* Tuition, state resident: full-time $6347; part-time $352.60 per credit hour. Tuition, nonresident: full-time $17,379; part-time $965.50 per credit hour. *Required fees:* $1035. Tuition and fees vary according to

course load, campus/location and program. *Financial support:* Fellowships with full tuition reimbursements, research assistantships with full tuition reimbursements, teaching assistantships with full tuition reimbursements, institutionally sponsored loans, health care benefits, and unspecified assistantships available. *Faculty research:* Human geography, nature/society relationships, the physical environment, application of geographic information sciences. Website: http://www.geog.missouri.edu/?q-grad/graduate-program

**University of Montana,** Graduate School, College of Humanities and Sciences, Department of Geography, Missoula, MT 59812-0002. Offers community and environmental planning (MA); geography (MA, MS). *Entrance requirements:* For master's, GRE General Test. Additional exam requirements/recommendations for international students: Required—TOEFL.

**University of Nebraska at Omaha,** Graduate Studies, College of Arts and Sciences, Department of Geography and Geology, Omaha, NE 68182. Offers geographic information science (Certificate); geography (MA). *Program availability:* Part-time. *Faculty:* 5 full-time (2 women). *Students:* 11 full-time (2 women), 14 part-time (6 women); includes 3 minority (2 Hispanic/Latino; 1 Two or more races, non-Hispanic/Latino), 2 international. Average age 32. 16 applicants, 69% accepted, 9 enrolled. In 2016, 9 master's, 3 other advanced degrees awarded. *Degree requirements:* For master's, comprehensive exam, thesis (for some programs). *Entrance requirements:* For master's, GRE, minimum GPA of 3.0, 15 undergraduate geography hours, transcripts, resume, statement of purpose, 2 letters of recommendation; for Certificate, minimum GPA of 3.0, transcripts, resume, statement of purpose, 2 letters of recommendation. Additional exam requirements/recommendations for international students: Required—TOEFL, IELTS, PTE. *Application deadline:* For fall admission, 7/1 priority date for domestic and international students; for spring admission, 12/1 priority date for domestic and international students; for summer admission, 5/1 for domestic and international students. Applications are processed on a rolling basis. Application fee: $45. Electronic applications accepted. *Financial support:* In 2016–17, 10 students received support, including 1 research assistantship with tuition reimbursement available, 9 teaching assistantships with tuition reimbursements available; fellowships, Federal Work-Study, institutionally sponsored loans, scholarships/grants, health care benefits, tuition waivers (partial), and unspecified assistantships also available. Support available to part-time students. Financial award application deadline: 3/1; financial award applicants required to submit FAFSA. *Unit head:* Dr. Rex Cammack, Chairperson, 402-554-2341, E-mail: graduate@unomaha.edu. *Application contact:* Dr. Christina Dando, Graduate Program Chair, 402-554-2341, E-mail: graduate@unomaha.edu.

**University of Nebraska–Lincoln,** Graduate College, College of Arts and Sciences, Department of Anthropology and Geography, Program in Geography, Lincoln, NE 68588. Offers MA, PhD. *Degree requirements:* For master's, thesis optional; for doctorate, comprehensive exam, thesis/dissertation. *Entrance requirements:* For master's and doctorate, GRE General Test. Additional exam requirements/recommendations for international students: Required—TOEFL (minimum score 550 paper-based). Electronic applications accepted. *Faculty research:* Climatology, historical-cultural geography, geographic information systems/cartography/remote sensing, human geography, Great Plains studies.

**University of Nevada, Reno,** Graduate School, College of Science, Mackay School of Earth Sciences and Engineering, Department of Geography, Program in Geography, Reno, NV 89557. Offers MS, PhD. Terminal master's awarded for partial completion of doctoral program. *Degree requirements:* For master's, comprehensive exam, thesis; for doctorate, comprehensive exam, thesis/dissertation. *Entrance requirements:* For master's and doctorate, GRE General Test, minimum GPA of 2.75. Additional exam requirements/recommendations for international students: Required—TOEFL (minimum score 500 paper-based; 61 iBT), IELTS (minimum score 6). Electronic applications accepted. *Faculty research:* Natural resources, education, climatology, biogeography, ethnic/cultural geography.

**University of New Mexico,** Graduate Studies, College of Arts and Sciences, Program in Geography and Environmental Studies, Albuquerque, NM 87131-2039. Offers MS. *Program availability:* Part-time. *Faculty:* 9 full-time (3 women). *Students:* 9 full-time (7 women), 11 part-time (3 women); includes 3 minority (1 American Indian or Alaska Native, non-Hispanic/Latino; 2 Hispanic/Latino). Average age 30. 13 applicants, 62% accepted, 6 enrolled. In 2016, 6 master's awarded. *Degree requirements:* For master's, comprehensive exam (for some programs), thesis (for some programs). *Entrance requirements:* For master's, GRE. Additional exam requirements/recommendations for international students: Required—TOEFL. *Application deadline:* For fall admission, 2/1 priority date for domestic students, 1/1 priority date for international students; for spring admission, 11/15 for domestic and international students. Application fee: $50. Electronic applications accepted. *Financial support:* Research assistantships with full tuition reimbursements, teaching assistantships with full tuition reimbursements, health care benefits, and tuition waivers (full and partial) available. Financial award applicants required to submit FAFSA. *Faculty research:* Geographic information science, environmental management. *Unit head:* Dr. Scott M. Freundschuh, Chair, 505-277-0058, Fax: 505-277-3614, E-mail: sfreunds@unm.edu. *Application contact:* Dr. K. Maria D. Lane, Director of Graduate Studies, 505-277-4075, Fax: 505-277-3614, E-mail: mdlane@unm.edu. Website: http://geography.unm.edu

**University of New Orleans,** Graduate School, College of Liberal Arts, Department of Geography, New Orleans, LA 70148. Offers MA. *Entrance requirements:* For master's, GRE General Test. Additional exam requirements/recommendations for international students: Required—TOEFL (minimum score 550 paper-based; 79 iBT). Electronic applications accepted.

**The University of North Carolina at Chapel Hill,** Graduate School, College of Arts and Sciences, Department of Geography, Chapel Hill, NC 27599. Offers MA, PhD. *Degree requirements:* For master's, one foreign language, comprehensive exam, thesis; for doctorate, 2 foreign languages, comprehensive exam, thesis/dissertation. *Entrance requirements:* For master's and doctorate, GRE General Test, minimum GPA of 3.0. *Faculty research:* Geographic information systems, climatology, hydrology, population research, Latino immigration.

**The University of North Carolina at Charlotte,** College of Liberal Arts and Sciences, Department of Geography and Earth Sciences, Charlotte, NC 28223-0001. Offers earth sciences (MS); geography (MA), including community planning, geographic information science and technologies, location analysis, transportation studies, urban-regional analysis; geography and urban regional analysis (PhD). *Program availability:* Part-time, evening/weekend. *Faculty:* 30 full-time (12 women), 1 part-time/adjunct (0 women). *Students:* 55 full-time (25 women), 29 part-time (15 women); includes 14 minority (4 Black or African American, non-Hispanic/Latino; 3 Asian, non-Hispanic/Latino; 3 Hispanic/Latino; 4 Two or more races, non-Hispanic/Latino), 18 international. Average age 29. 78 applicants, 72% accepted, 25 enrolled. In 2016, 18 master's, 4 doctorates awarded. Terminal master's awarded for partial completion of doctoral program. *Degree requirements:* For master's, comprehensive exam, thesis or alternative, project; for doctorate, thesis/dissertation. *Entrance requirements:* For master's, GRE General Test or MAT, minimum GPA of 2.75, 3.0 for junior and senior years, transcripts, letters of recommendation, and personal essays (for MS); minimum overall GPA of 3.1 or for the last 2 years, 3.2 in major, three letters of reference, and personal essay (for MA); for doctorate, GRE, MA or MS in geography or a field related to the primary emphases of the program; minimum master's-level GPA of 3.5; GIS proficiency. Additional exam requirements/recommendations for international students: Required—TOEFL (minimum score 523 paper-based, 70 iBT) or IELTS (6.5). *Application deadline:* For fall admission, 2/1 for domestic and international students; for spring admission, 9/30 for domestic and international students. Applications are processed on a rolling basis. Application fee: $75. Electronic applications accepted. *Expenses:* Tuition, state resident: full-time $4252. Tuition, nonresident: full-time $17,423. *Required fees:* $3026. Tuition and fees vary according to course load and program. *Financial support:* In 2016–17, 49 students received support, including 1 fellowship (averaging $35,000 per year), 8 research assistantships (averaging $7,500 per year), 40 teaching assistantships (averaging $9,277 per year); career-related internships or fieldwork, institutionally sponsored loans, scholarships/grants, and unspecified assistantships also available. Support available to part-time students. Financial award application deadline: 3/1; financial award applicants required to submit FAFSA. *Total annual research expenditures:* $401,921. *Unit head:* Dr. Craig Allan, Chair, 704-687-5999, E-mail: ges@uncc.edu. *Application contact:* Kathy B. Giddings, Director of Graduate Admissions, 704-687-5503, Fax: 704-687-1668, E-mail: gradadm@uncc.edu. Website: https://geoearth.uncc.edu/

**The University of North Carolina at Greensboro,** Graduate School, College of Arts and Sciences, Department of Geography, Greensboro, NC 27412-5001. Offers applied geography (MA); geographic information science (Certificate); geography (PhD); urban and economic development (Certificate). *Degree requirements:* For master's, comprehensive exam, thesis or alternative. *Entrance requirements:* For master's, GRE General Test. Additional exam requirements/recommendations for international students: Required—TOEFL. Electronic applications accepted.

**University of North Dakota,** Graduate School, College of Arts and Sciences, Department of Geography and Geographic Information Science, Grand Forks, ND 58202. Offers MA, MS. *Program availability:* Part-time. *Degree requirements:* For master's, comprehensive exam, thesis or alternative. *Entrance requirements:* For master's, minimum GPA of 3.0. Additional exam requirements/recommendations for international students: Required—TOEFL (minimum score 550 paper-based; 79 iBT), IELTS (minimum score 6.5). *Application deadline:* For fall admission, 8/1 priority date for domestic students, 5/1 priority date for international students; for spring admission, 12/1 priority date for domestic students, 9/1 priority date for international students. Applications are processed on a rolling basis. Application fee: $35. Electronic applications accepted. *Financial support:* Fellowships with full and partial tuition reimbursements, research assistantships with full and partial tuition reimbursements, teaching assistantships with full and partial tuition reimbursements, Federal Work-Study, institutionally sponsored loans, scholarships/grants, health care benefits, tuition waivers (full and partial), and unspecified assistantships available. Support available to part-time students. Financial award application deadline: 3/15; financial award applicants required to submit FAFSA. *Faculty research:* Regional and urban development, environmental geography, geographic education, geographic techniques. *Unit head:* Dr. Douglas Munski, Graduate Director, 701-777-6195, Fax: 701-777-6195, E-mail: douglas_munski@und.nodak.edu. *Application contact:* Matt Anderson, Admissions Specialist, 701-777-2947, Fax: 701-777-3619, E-mail: matthew.anderson@gradschool.und.edu. Website: http://www.und.edu/dept/geog/grad.html

**University of Northern Iowa,** Graduate College, College of Social and Behavioral Sciences, Department of Geography, Cedar Falls, IA 50614. Offers MA. *Program availability:* Part-time. *Degree requirements:* For master's, thesis or alternative. *Entrance requirements:* For master's, minimum GPA of 3.0; 2 letters of recommendation; brief statement about professional interests and career objectives. Additional exam requirements/recommendations for international students: Required—TOEFL (minimum score 500 paper-based; 61 iBT). Electronic applications accepted.

**University of North Texas,** Robert B. Toulouse School of Graduate Studies, Denton, TX 76203-5459. Offers accounting (MS); applied anthropology (MA, MS); applied behavior analysis (Certificate); applied geography (MA); applied technology and performance improvement (M Ed, MS); art education (MA); art history (MA); art museum education (Certificate); arts leadership (Certificate); audiology (Au D); behavior analysis (MS); behavioral science (PhD); biochemistry and molecular biology (MS); biology (MA, MS); biomedical engineering (MS); business analysis (MS); chemistry (MS); clinical health psychology (PhD); communication studies (MA, MS); computer engineering (MS); computer science (MS); counseling (M Ed, MS), including clinical mental health counseling (MS), college and university counseling, elementary school counseling, secondary school counseling; creative writing (MA); criminal justice (MS); curriculum and instruction (M Ed); decision sciences (MBA); design (MA, MFA), including fashion design (MFA), innovation studies, interior design (MFA); early childhood studies (MS); economics (MS); educational leadership (M Ed, Ed D); educational psychology (MS, PhD), including family studies (MS), gifted and talented (MS), human development (MS), learning and cognition (MS), research, measurement and evaluation (MS); electrical engineering (MS); emergency management (MPA); engineering technology (MS); English (MA); English as a second language (MA); environmental science (MS); finance (MBA, MS); financial management (MPA); French (MA); health services management (MBA); higher education (M Ed, Ed D); history (MA, MS); hospitality management (MS); human resources management (MPA); information science (MS); information systems (PhD); information technologies (MBA); interdisciplinary studies (MA, MS); international studies (MA); international sustainable tourism (MS); jazz studies (MM); journalism (MA, MJ, Graduate Certificate), including interactive and virtual digital communication (Graduate Certificate), narrative journalism (Graduate Certificate), public relations (Graduate Certificate); kinesiology (MS); linguistics (MA); local government management (MPA); logistics (PhD); logistics and supply chain management (MBA); long-term care, senior housing, and aging services (MA); management (PhD); marketing (MBA); mathematics (MA, MS); mechanical and energy engineering (MS, PhD); music (MA), including ethnomusicology, music theory, musicology, performance; music composition (PhD); music education (MM Ed, PhD); nonprofit management (MPA); operations and supply chain management (MBA); performance (MM, DMA); philosophy (MA); political science (MA); professional and technical communication (MA); radio, television and film (MA, MFA); rehabilitation counseling (Certificate); sociology (MA); Spanish (MA); special education (M Ed); speech-language pathology (MA); strategic management (MBA); studio art (MFA); teaching (M Ed); MBA/MS. *Program availability:* Part-time, evening/weekend, online learning. Terminal master's awarded for partial completion of doctoral program. *Degree requirements:* For master's, variable foreign language requirement, comprehensive exam (for some programs), thesis (for some programs); for doctorate, variable foreign language requirement, comprehensive exam (for some programs), thesis/dissertation; for other advanced degree, variable foreign language requirement, comprehensive exam (for some programs). *Entrance requirements:* For master's and doctorate, GRE, GMAT. Additional exam requirements/recommendations for international students: Required—TOEFL (minimum score 550 paper-based; 79 iBT). Electronic applications accepted.

**University of Oklahoma,** College of Atmospheric and Geographic Sciences, Department of Geography and Environmental Sustainability, Norman, OK 73019. Offers environmental sustainability (MS); geography (MA, MS, PhD), including geospatial technologies (MS), physical geography (MS). *Program availability:* Part-time. *Faculty:* 23 full-time (7 women). *Students:* 22 full-time (18 women), 10 part-time (3 women); includes 4 minority (1 American Indian or Alaska Native, non-Hispanic/Latino; 2 Hispanic/Latino; 1 Two or more races, non-Hispanic/Latino), 4 international. Average age 29. 16 applicants, 31% accepted, 4 enrolled. In 2016, 7 master's, 3 doctorates awarded. *Degree requirements:* For master's, comprehensive exam (for some programs), thesis (for some programs); for doctorate, comprehensive exam (for some programs), thesis/dissertation (for some programs). *Entrance requirements:* For master's and doctorate, GRE, personal statement, transcripts, two letters of recommendation, writing sample. Additional exam requirements/recommendations for international students: Required—TOEFL (minimum score 79 iBT) or IELTS (minimum score 6.5). *Application deadline:* For fall admission, 1/15 for domestic and international students; for spring admission, 9/1 for domestic students, 11/1 for international students. Application fee: $50 ($100 for international students). Electronic applications accepted. *Expenses:* Tuition, state resident: full-time $4886; part-time $203.60 per credit hour. Tuition, nonresident: full-time $18,989; part-time $791.20 per credit hour. *Required fees:* $3283; $126.25 per credit hour. $126.50 per semester. *Financial support:* In 2016–17, 36 students received support, including 2 fellowships with full tuition reimbursements available (averaging $3,500 per year), 8 research assistantships with full tuition reimbursements available (averaging $14,928 per year), 11 teaching assistantships with full tuition reimbursements available (averaging $13,952 per year); Federal Work-Study, scholarships/grants, and unspecified assistantships also available. Financial award application deadline: 6/1; financial award applicants required to submit FAFSA. *Faculty research:* Land cover land use change; economic geography; landscape ecology; environmental economics; renewable energy. *Total annual research expenditures:* $1.2 million. *Unit head:* Dr. Kristen de Beurs, Associate Professor and Chair, 405-325-5325, E-mail: kdebeurs@ou.edu. *Application contact:* Travis Gliedt, Graduate Liaison, 405-325-5325, E-mail: tgliedt@ou.edu. Website: http://geography.ou.edu

**University of Oregon,** Graduate School, College of Arts and Sciences, Department of Geography, Eugene, OR 97403. Offers MA, MS, PhD. *Degree requirements:* For master's, one foreign language, thesis; for doctorate, one foreign language, thesis/dissertation. *Entrance requirements:* For master's and doctorate, GRE General Test, minimum GPA of 3.0. Additional exam requirements/recommendations for international students: Required—TOEFL. *Faculty research:* Place-name research, past climates, quaternary environments, plant diffusions, population redistributions.

**University of Ottawa,** Faculty of Graduate and Postdoctoral Studies, Faculty of Arts, Department of Geography, Ottawa, ON K1N 6N5, Canada. Offers M Geog, M Sc, MA, PhD. *Degree requirements:* For master's, one foreign language, thesis; for doctorate, one foreign language, comprehensive exam, thesis/dissertation. *Entrance requirements:* For master's, honors degree or equivalent, minimum B average; for doctorate, master's degree, minimum B+ average. Electronic applications accepted. *Faculty research:* The physical geography of cold environment; space, place and society, environmental change.

**University of Prince Edward Island,** Faculty of Arts, Charlottetown, PE C1A 4P3, Canada. Offers island studies (MA). *Program availability:* Part-time. *Degree requirements:* For master's, thesis. *Entrance requirements:* Additional exam requirements/recommendations for international students: Required—TOEFL (minimum score 550 paper-based; 80 iBT), Canadian Academic English Language Assessment, Michigan English Language Assessment Battery, Canadian Test of English for Scholars and Trainees. *Faculty research:* International island studies.

**University of Regina,** Faculty of Graduate Studies and Research, Faculty of Arts, Department of Geography, Regina, SK S4S 0A2, Canada. Offers M Sc, MA, PhD. Offered as a special case program. *Program availability:* Part-time. *Faculty:* 9 full-time (4 women), 4 part-time/adjunct (1 woman). *Students:* 4 full-time (2 women). 1 applicant. In 2016, 8 master's, 4 doctorates awarded. *Degree requirements:* For master's, thesis; for doctorate, thesis/dissertation. *Entrance requirements:* Additional exam requirements/recommendations for international students: Required—TOEFL (minimum score 580 paper-based; 80 iBT), IELTS (minimum score 6.5), PTE (minimum score 59). *Application deadline:* For fall admission, 3/1 for domestic and international students; for winter admission, 10/1 for domestic and international students. Applications are processed on a rolling basis. Application fee: $100. Electronic applications accepted. *Financial support:* In 2016–17, 1 fellowship (averaging $7,000 per year), 1 teaching assistantship (averaging $2,623 per year) were awarded; scholarships/grants also available. Financial award application deadline: 6/15. *Faculty research:* Cultural, historical, economic, rural, urban, population, and prairie geography; thematic and atlas cartography; climatology and meteorology; geomorphology; biogeography. *Unit head:* Dr. Kyle Hodder, Department Head, 306-585-5127, Fax: 306-585-4815, E-mail: kyle.hodder@uregina.ca. Website: http://www.uregina.ca/arts/geography

**University of Saskatchewan,** College of Graduate Studies and Research, College of Arts and Science, Department of Geography, Saskatoon, SK S7N 5A2, Canada. Offers M Sc, MA, PhD. *Degree requirements:* For master's, thesis; for doctorate, comprehensive exam (for some programs), thesis/dissertation. *Entrance requirements:* Additional exam requirements/recommendations for international students: Required—TOEFL (minimum score 80 iBT); Recommended—IELTS (minimum score 6.5). Electronic applications accepted.

**University of South Africa,** College of Agriculture and Environmental Sciences, Pretoria, South Africa. Offers agriculture (MS); consumer science (MCS); environmental management (MA, MS, PhD); environmental science (MA, MS, PhD); geography (MA, MS, PhD); horticulture (M Tech); human ecology (MHE); life sciences (MS); nature conservation (M Tech).

**University of South Carolina,** The Graduate School, College of Arts and Sciences, Department of Geography, Columbia, SC 29208. Offers geography (MA, MS, PhD); geography education (IMA). IMA and MAT offered in cooperation with the College of Education. *Program availability:* Part-time. *Degree requirements:* For master's, comprehensive exam, thesis (for some programs); for doctorate, comprehensive exam, thesis/dissertation. *Entrance requirements:* For master's, GRE General Test; for doctorate, GRE General Test, master's degree. Electronic applications accepted. *Faculty research:* Geographic information processing; economic, cultural, physical, and environmental geography.

**University of Southern California,** Graduate School, Dana and David Dornsife College of Letters, Arts and Sciences, Spatial Sciences Institute, Los Angeles, CA 90089. Offers geographic information science and technology (MS, Graduate Certificate). *Program availability:* Part-time, evening/weekend, online learning. Terminal master's awarded for partial completion of doctoral program. *Degree requirements:* For master's, thesis. *Entrance requirements:* For master's, GRE. Additional exam requirements/recommendations for international students: Required—TOEFL. Electronic applications accepted. *Faculty research:* Geocoding, geocomputation, GIS, environmental exposure estimation, spatial data accuracy and uncertainty.

## Geography

**University of Southern Mississippi,** Graduate School, College of Science and Technology, Department of Geography and Geology, Hattiesburg, MS 39406. Offers geography (MS, PhD); geology (MS); professional geology (MS). *Program availability:* Part-time. *Degree requirements:* For master's, comprehensive exam, thesis (for some programs), internships; for doctorate, comprehensive exam, thesis/dissertation. *Entrance requirements:* For master's, GMAT, GRE General Test, minimum GPA of 3.0 for last 60 hours; for doctorate, GRE, minimum GPA of 3.5. Additional exam requirements/recommendations for international students: Required—TOEFL, IELTS. *Application deadline:* For fall admission, 3/15 for domestic and international students; for spring admission, 1/3 for domestic students. Applications are processed on a rolling basis. Application fee: $60. Electronic applications accepted. *Expenses: Tuition, area resident:* Full-time $15,708; part-time $437 per credit hour. *Financial support:* Fellowships with full tuition reimbursements, research assistantships with tuition reimbursements, teaching assistantships with full tuition reimbursements, career-related internships or fieldwork, Federal Work-Study, scholarships/grants, health care benefits, and unspecified assistantships available. Financial award application deadline: 3/15; financial award applicants required to submit FAFSA. *Faculty research:* City and regional planning, geographic techniques, physical geography, human geography. *Unit head:* Dr. David Cochran, Chair, 601-266-4728, Fax: 601-266-6219. *Application contact:* Shonna Breland, Manager of Graduate School Admissions, 601-266-6567, Fax: 601-266-5138.
Website: https://www.usm.edu/geography-geology

**University of South Florida,** Innovative Education, Tampa, FL 33620-9951. Offers adult, career and higher education (Graduate Certificate), including college teaching, leadership in developing human resources, leadership in higher education; Africana studies (Graduate Certificate), including diasporas and health disparities, genocide and human rights; aging studies (Graduate Certificate), including gerontology; art research (Graduate Certificate), including museum studies; business foundations (Graduate Certificate); chemical and biomedical engineering (Graduate Certificate), including materials science and engineering, water, health and sustainability; child and family studies (Graduate Certificate), including positive behavior support; civil and industrial engineering (Graduate Certificate), including transportation systems analysis; community and family health (Graduate Certificate), including maternal and child health, social marketing and public health, violence and injury: prevention and intervention, women's health; criminology (Graduate Certificate), including criminal justice administration; educational measurement and research (Graduate Certificate), including evaluation; English (Graduate Certificate), including comparative literary studies, creative writing, professional and technical communication; entrepreneurship (Graduate Certificate); environmental health (Graduate Certificate), including safety management; epidemiology and biostatistics (Graduate Certificate), including applied biostatistics, biostatistics, concepts and tools of epidemiology, epidemiology, epidemiology of infectious diseases; geography, environment and planning (Graduate Certificate), including community development, environmental policy and management, geographical information systems; geology (Graduate Certificate), including hydrogeology; global health (Graduate Certificate), including disaster management, global health and Latin American and Caribbean studies, global health practice, humanitarian assistance, infection control; government and international affairs (Graduate Certificate), including Cuban studies, globalization studies; health policy and management (Graduate Certificate), including health management and leadership, public health policy and programs; hearing specialist: early intervention (Graduate Certificate); industrial and management systems engineering (Graduate Certificate), including systems engineering, technology management; information studies (Graduate Certificate), including school library media specialist; information systems/decision sciences (Graduate Certificate), including analytics and business intelligence; instructional technology (Graduate Certificate), including distance education, Florida digital/virtual educator, instructional design, multimedia design, Web design; internal medicine, bioethics and medical humanities (Graduate Certificate), including biomedical ethics; Latin American and Caribbean studies (Graduate Certificate); mass communications (Graduate Certificate), including multimedia journalism; mathematics and statistics (Graduate Certificate), including mathematics; medicine (Graduate Certificate), including aging and neuroscience, bioinformatics, biotechnology, brain fitness and memory management, clinical investigation, health informatics, health sciences, integrative weight management, intellectual property, medicine and gender, metabolic and nutritional medicine, metabolic cardiology, pharmacy sciences; national and competitive intelligence (Graduate Certificate); psychological and social foundations (Graduate Certificate), including career counseling, college teaching, diversity in education, mental health counseling, school counseling; public affairs (Graduate Certificate), including nonprofit management, public management, research administration; public health (Graduate Certificate), including environmental health, health equity, public health generalist, translational research in adolescent behavioral health; public health practices (Graduate Certificate), including planning for healthy communities; rehabilitation and mental health counseling (Graduate Certificate), including integrative mental health care, marriage and family therapy, rehabilitation technology; secondary education (Graduate Certificate), including ESOL, foreign language education: culture and content, foreign language education: professional; social work (Graduate Certificate), including geriatric social work/clinical gerontology; special education (Graduate Certificate), including autism spectrum disorder, disabilities education: severe/profound; world languages (Graduate Certificate), including teaching English as a second language (TESL) or foreign language. *Expenses:* Tuition, state resident: full-time $7766; part-time $431.43 per credit hour. Tuition, nonresident: full-time $15,789; part-time $877.17 per credit hour. *Required fees:* $37 per term. *Unit head:* Kathy Barnes, Interdisciplinary Programs Coordinator, 813-974-8031, Fax: 813-974-7061, E-mail: barnesk@usf.edu. *Application contact:* Karen Tylinski, Metro Initiatives, 813-974-9943, Fax: 813-974-7061, E-mail: ktylinsk@usf.edu.
Website: http://www.usf.edu/innovative-education/

**The University of Tennessee,** Graduate School, College of Arts and Sciences, Department of Geography, Knoxville, TN 37996. Offers MS, PhD. *Degree requirements:* For master's, thesis or alternative; for doctorate, thesis/dissertation. *Entrance requirements:* For master's and doctorate, GRE General Test, minimum GPA of 2.7. Additional exam requirements/recommendations for international students: Required—TOEFL. Electronic applications accepted.

**The University of Texas at Austin,** Graduate School, College of Liberal Arts, Department of Geography and the Environment, Austin, TX 78712-1111. Offers MA, PhD. *Degree requirements:* For master's, thesis or alternative; for doctorate, thesis/dissertation. *Entrance requirements:* For master's and doctorate, GRE General Test. Additional exam requirements/recommendations for international students: Required—TOEFL. Electronic applications accepted. *Faculty research:* Cultural and historical geography, environmental and physical geography, human-environment interactions, electronic technology and hypermedia, international area studies.

**The University of Texas at Dallas,** School of Economic, Political and Policy Sciences, Program in Geospatial Information Sciences, Richardson, TX 75080. Offers MS, PhD. *Program availability:* Part-time, evening/weekend. *Faculty:* 9 full-time (1 woman). *Students:* 61 full-time (22 women), 34 part-time (15 women); includes 14 minority (3 Black or African American, non-Hispanic/Latino; 4 Asian, non-Hispanic/Latino; 5

Hispanic/Latino; 2 Two or more races, non-Hispanic/Latino), 45 international. Average age 31. 102 applicants, 72% accepted, 45 enrolled. In 2016, 12 master's, 1 doctorate awarded. *Degree requirements:* For master's, thesis (for some programs), project or thesis; internship; for doctorate, comprehensive exam, thesis/dissertation. *Entrance requirements:* For master's and doctorate, GRE General Test, minimum GPA of 3.0 in upper-level coursework in field. Additional exam requirements/recommendations for international students: Required—TOEFL (minimum score 550 paper-based). *Application deadline:* For fall admission, 7/15 for domestic students, 5/1 priority date for international students; for spring admission, 11/15 for domestic students, 9/1 priority date for international students. Applications are processed on a rolling basis. Application fee: $50 ($100 for international students). Electronic applications accepted. *Expenses:* Tuition, state resident: full-time $12,418; part-time $690 per semester hour. Tuition, nonresident: full-time $24,150; part-time $1342 per semester hour. Tuition and fees vary according to course load. *Financial support:* In 2016-17, 27 students received support, including 5 fellowships (averaging $2,500 per year), 4 research assistantships with partial tuition reimbursements available (averaging $19,075 per year), 9 teaching assistantships with partial tuition reimbursements available (averaging $13,100 per year); career-related internships or fieldwork, Federal Work-Study, institutionally sponsored loans, scholarships/grants, and unspecified assistantships also available. Support available to part-time students. Financial award application deadline: 4/30; financial award applicants required to submit FAFSA. *Faculty research:* Urban and regional development, artificial intelligence techniques for geospatial investigation, improvement of current spatial analysis and modeling techniques, demographic studies. *Unit head:* Dr. Fang Qiu, Program Head, 972-883-4134, Fax: 972-883-2735, E-mail: ffqiu@utdallas.edu. *Application contact:* Katie Doctor, Graduate Program Administrator, 972-883-4936, Fax: 972-883-6297, E-mail: kdoctor@utdallas.edu.
Website: http://www.utdallas.edu/epps/geospatial-science/

**The University of Toledo,** College of Graduate Studies, College of Languages, Literature and Social Sciences, Department of Geography and Planning, Toledo, OH 43606-3390. Offers geographic information science and applied geographics (Certificate); geography and planning (MA); spatially-integrated social science (PhD). *Program availability:* Part-time. *Degree requirements:* For master's, comprehensive exam, thesis; for doctorate, thesis/dissertation. *Entrance requirements:* For master's and doctorate, GRE General Test, minimum cumulative point-hour ratio of 2.7 for all previous academic work, three letters of recommendation; for Certificate, minimum cumulative point-hour ratio of 2.7 for all previous academic work, three letters of recommendation. Additional exam requirements/recommendations for international students: Required—TOEFL (minimum score 550 paper-based; 80 iBT). Electronic applications accepted.

**University of Toronto,** School of Graduate Studies, Faculty of Arts and Science, Department of Geography, Toronto, ON M5S 1A1, Canada. Offers geography (M Sc, MA, PhD); planning (M Sc Pl, MUDS, PhD); urban design (MUD). *Program availability:* Part-time. *Degree requirements:* For master's, thesis optional; for doctorate, thesis/dissertation. *Entrance requirements:* For master's, bachelor's degree or equivalent in geography or a closely related field, minimum B+ average in each of 2 final years of degree, 3 letters of reference; for doctorate, master of geography degree, minimum A-average. Additional exam requirements/recommendations for international students: Required—TOEFL (minimum score 580 paper-based; 93 iBT), TWE (minimum score 5). Electronic applications accepted. *Faculty research:* Spatial statistics, computer cartography, climatology, hydrology, biogeography.

**University of Utah,** Graduate School, College of Social and Behavioral Science, Department of Geography, Salt Lake City, UT 84112-9155. Offers geographic information science (MS); geography (MS, PhD). *Program availability:* Part-time. *Faculty:* 13 full-time (4 women), 21 part-time/adjunct (8 women). *Students:* 39 full-time (22 women), 16 part-time (3 women); includes 7 minority (1 Black or African American, non-Hispanic/Latino; 1 Asian, non-Hispanic/Latino; 4 Hispanic/Latino; 1 Two or more races, non-Hispanic/Latino), 5 international. Average age 30. 62 applicants, 63% accepted, 10 enrolled. In 2016, 10 master's, 1 doctorate awarded. *Degree requirements:* For master's, thesis (for some programs), 6 research hours (for MS in geography); skills portfolio (for MS in geographic information science); for doctorate, comprehensive exam, thesis/dissertation, 14 research hours, 2 consecutive full-time semesters. *Entrance requirements:* For master's, GRE General Test (except for MS in geographic information science), minimum undergraduate GPA of 3.0; for doctorate, GRE General Test, minimum undergraduate GPA of 3.0. Additional exam requirements/recommendations for international students: Required—TOEFL (minimum score 550 paper-based; 80 iBT), IELTS (minimum score 6.5). *Application deadline:* For fall admission, 1/10 priority date for domestic and international students; for spring admission, 10/1 for domestic and international students. Application fee: $55 ($65 for international students). Electronic applications accepted. *Expenses:* $3,763.51 per semester resident tuition (10 credit hours for 4 semesters); $11,951.20 per semester non-resident tuition (10 credit hours for 4 semesters); $25-$120 lab fees (for some courses). *Financial support:* In 2016-17, 36 students received support, including 2 fellowships with full tuition reimbursements available (averaging $17,500 per year), 12 research assistantships with full tuition reimbursements available (averaging $17,423 per year), 11 teaching assistantships with full tuition reimbursements available (averaging $15,727 per year); career-related internships or fieldwork, scholarships/grants, health care benefits, and unspecified assistantships also available. Financial award application deadline: 1/10. *Faculty research:* Urban-economic geography, earth system science, geographic information science and remote sensing, paleo environmental studies, hazards. *Total annual research expenditures:* $1.2 million. *Unit head:* Dr. Andrea R. Brunelle, Chair, 801-581-8218, Fax: 801-581-8219, E-mail: andrea.brunelle@geog.utah.edu. *Application contact:* Dr. Philip E. Dennison, Director of Graduate Studies, 801-581-8218, Fax: 801-581-8219, E-mail: dennison@geog.utah.edu.
Website: http://www.geog.utah.edu

**University of Victoria,** Faculty of Graduate Studies, Faculty of Social Sciences, Department of Geography, Victoria, BC V8W 2Y2, Canada. Offers M Sc, MA, PhD. *Program availability:* Part-time. *Degree requirements:* For master's, thesis; for doctorate, comprehensive exam, thesis/dissertation, candidacy exam. *Entrance requirements:* For master's, minimum B+ average in undergraduate course work; for doctorate, master's degree. Additional exam requirements/recommendations for international students: Required—TOEFL (minimum score 575 paper-based), IELTS (minimum score 7). Electronic applications accepted. *Faculty research:* Resources and protected areas, remote sensing and forestry, geographic information systems and cartography, urban regional planning, physical climatology.

**University of Washington,** Graduate School, College of Arts and Sciences, Department of Geography, Seattle, WA 98195. Offers MA, PhD. *Degree requirements:* For master's, thesis; for doctorate, thesis/dissertation. *Entrance requirements:* For master's and doctorate, GRE General Test. Additional exam requirements/recommendations for international students: Required—TOEFL. Electronic applications accepted. *Faculty research:* Globalization and social theory, nature and society, regional economic development, urban patterns and processes, geographic information systems.

**University of Waterloo,** Graduate Studies, Faculty of Environment, Department of Geography and Environmental Management, Waterloo, ON N2L 3G1, Canada. Offers MA, PhD. MA, PhD offered jointly with Wilfrid Laurier University. *Degree requirements:* For master's, thesis optional; for doctorate, one foreign language, comprehensive exam, thesis/dissertation. *Entrance requirements:* For master's, honors degree, minimum B average; for doctorate, master's degree, minimum A- average. Additional exam requirements/recommendations for international students: Required—TOEFL, IELTS, PTE. Electronic applications accepted. *Faculty research:* Urban economic geography; physical geography; resource management; cultural, regional, historical geography; spatial data.

**The University of Western Ontario,** Faculty of Graduate Studies, Social Sciences Division, Department of Geography, London, ON N6A 5B8, Canada. Offers M Sc, MA, PhD. *Degree requirements:* For master's, thesis; for doctorate, thesis/dissertation. *Entrance requirements:* For master's, GRE, honors degree, minimum B average; for doctorate, honors degree, minimum B average. Additional exam requirements/ recommendations for international students: Required—TOEFL.

**University of Wisconsin–Madison,** Graduate School, College of Letters and Science, Department of Geography, Madison, WI 53706-1380. Offers cartography and geographic information systems (MS); geographic information systems (Certificate); geography (MS, PhD). *Program availability:* Part-time. *Degree requirements:* For master's, thesis; for doctorate, thesis/dissertation; for Certificate, internship. *Entrance requirements:* For master's and doctorate, GRE General Test, minimum GPA of 3.25. Electronic applications accepted. *Faculty research:* Physical geography, urban/historical geography, people-environment, history of cartography, GIS.

**University of Wisconsin–Milwaukee,** Graduate School, College of Letters and Science, Department of Geography, Milwaukee, WI 53201-0413. Offers international interests (MA, MS, PhD); physical geography and environmental studies (MA, MS, PhD); urban development (MA, MS, PhD). *Students:* 14 full-time (6 women), 7 part-time (6 women); includes 4 minority (1 Black or African American, non-Hispanic/Latino; 2 Asian, non-Hispanic/Latino; 1 Two or more races, non-Hispanic/Latino), 7 international. Average age 34. 25 applicants, 56% accepted, 5 enrolled. In 2016, 5 master's, 3 doctorates awarded. *Degree requirements:* For master's, comprehensive exam, thesis; for doctorate, thesis/dissertation. *Entrance requirements:* For master's and doctorate, GRE. Additional exam requirements/recommendations for international students: Required—TOEFL (minimum score 550 paper-based; 79 iBT), IELTS (minimum score 6.5). *Application deadline:* For fall admission, 1/1 priority date for domestic students; for spring admission, 9/1 for domestic students. Applications are processed on a rolling basis. Application fee: $56 ($96 for international students). Electronic applications accepted. *Financial support:* Fellowships, research assistantships, teaching assistantships, career-related internships or fieldwork, unspecified assistantships, and project assistantships available. Support available to part-time students. Financial award application deadline: 4/15; financial award applicants required to submit FAFSA. *Unit head:* Mark Schwartz, Department Chair, 414-229-3740, E-mail: mds@uwm.edu. *Application contact:* General Information Contact, 414-229-4982, Fax: 414-229-6967, E-mail: gradschool@uwm.edu.
Website: http://www4.uwm.edu/letsci/geography/

**University of Wyoming,** College of Arts and Sciences, Department of Geography, Laramie, WY 82071. Offers geography (MA, MP, MST); geography/water resources (MA); rural planning and natural resources (MP), including community and regional planning and natural resources. *Program availability:* Online learning. *Degree requirements:* For master's, thesis optional. *Entrance requirements:* For master's, GRE General Test, minimum GPA of 3.0. Additional exam requirements/recommendations for international students: Required—TOEFL. Electronic applications accepted. *Faculty research:* Landscape ecology, landscape change, public land management, rural and small town planning, GIS.

**Utah State University,** School of Graduate Studies, College of Natural Resources, Department of Environment and Society, Logan, UT 84322. Offers bioregional planning (MS); geography (MA, MS); human dimensions of ecosystem science and management (MS, PhD); recreation resource management (MS, PhD). *Degree requirements:* For master's, comprehensive exam, thesis (for some programs). *Entrance requirements:* For master's and doctorate, GRE General Test, minimum GPA of 3.0. Additional exam requirements/recommendations for international students: Required—TOEFL. Electronic applications accepted. *Faculty research:* Geographic information systems/ geographic and environmental education, bioregional planning, natural resource and environmental policy, outdoor recreation and tourism, natural resource and environmental management.

**Virginia Polytechnic Institute and State University,** Graduate School, College of Natural Resources and Environment, Blacksburg, VA 24061. Offers fisheries and wildlife (MS, PhD); forestry and forest products (MF, MS, PhD); geography (MS); geospatial and environmental analysis (PhD); natural resources (MNR). *Faculty:* 74 full-time (17 women). *Students:* 174 full-time (85 women), 67 part-time (37 women); includes 22 minority (4 Black or African American, non-Hispanic/Latino; 4 Asian, non-Hispanic/ Latino; 12 Hispanic/Latino; 2 Two or more races, non-Hispanic/Latino), 36 international. Average age 31. 103 applicants, 61% accepted, 57 enrolled. In 2016, 102 master's, 20 doctorates awarded. *Degree requirements:* For master's, comprehensive exam (for some programs), thesis (for some programs); for doctorate, comprehensive exam (for some programs), thesis/dissertation (for some programs). *Entrance requirements:* For master's and doctorate, GRE/GMAT. Additional exam requirements/recommendations for international students: Required—TOEFL (minimum score 80 iBT). *Application deadline:* For fall admission, 8/1 for domestic students, 4/1 for international students; for spring admission, 1/1 for domestic students, 9/1 for international students. Applications are processed on a rolling basis. Application fee: $75. Electronic applications accepted. *Expenses:* Tuition, state resident: full-time $12,467; part-time $692.50 per credit hour. Tuition, nonresident: full-time $25,095; part-time $1394.25 per credit hour. *Required fees:* $2669; $491.50 per semester. Tuition and fees vary according to course load, campus/location and program. *Financial support:* In 2016–17, 1 fellowship (averaging $24,256 per year), 23 research assistantships with full tuition reimbursements (averaging $26,209 per year), 26 teaching assistantships with full tuition reimbursements (averaging $22,466 per year) were awarded. Financial award application deadline: 3/1; financial award applicants required to submit FAFSA. *Total annual research expenditures:* $15.8 million. *Unit head:* Dr. Paul M. Winistorfer, Dean, 540-231-5481, Fax: 540-231-7664, E-mail: pstorfer@vt.edu. *Application contact:* Arlice Banks, Executive Assistant, 540-231-7051, Fax: 540-231-7664,

E-mail: arbanks@vt.edu.
Website: http://cnre.vt.edu/

**West Chester University of Pennsylvania,** College of Business and Public Management, Department of Geography and Planning, West Chester, PA 19383. Offers geographic information systems (Certificate); geography (MS); geography and planning (MURP); urban and regional planning (MPA, Certificate). *Program availability:* Part-time, evening/weekend. *Faculty:* 5 full-time (2 women). *Students:* 8 full-time (4 women), 13 part-time (5 women); includes 2 minority (both Black or African American, non-Hispanic/ Latino), 2 international. Average age 32. 14 applicants, 100% accepted, 8 enrolled. In 2016, 8 master's, 1 other advanced degree awarded. *Degree requirements:* For master's, thesis optional, 48 credits: 27 credits required, 21 credits electives (for MURP); 33 credits or 11 courses (for MS); for Certificate, 12 credits or 4 courses (for geographic information systems); 18 credits or 6 courses (for urban and regional planning). *Entrance requirements:* For master's and Certificate, minimum GPA of 2.8, resume, two letters of recommendation. Additional exam requirements/recommendations for international students: Required—TOEFL or IELTS. *Application deadline:* For fall admission, 5/15 for international students; for spring admission, 10/15 for international students. Applications are processed on a rolling basis. Application fee: $50. Electronic applications accepted. *Expenses:* Tuition, state resident: full-time $8694; part-time $483 per credit. Tuition, nonresident: full-time $13,050; part-time $725 per credit. *Required fees:* $2399; $119.05 per credit. Tuition and fees vary according to campus/location and program. *Financial support:* Scholarships/grants and unspecified assistantships available. Financial award application deadline: 2/15; financial award applicants required to submit FAFSA. *Faculty research:* Sustainability and environmental conservation, land use/suburban planning, geographic information systems, transportation planning, housing, economic development. *Unit head:* Dr. Dottie Ives Dewey, Chair/Graduate Coordinator for GIS Certificate Program, 610-436-2746, Fax: 610-436-2889, E-mail: divesdewey@wcupa.edu. *Application contact:* Dr. Matin Katirai, Graduate Coordinator, 610-436-2392, Fax: 610-436-2889, E-mail: mkatirai@wcupa.edu.
Website: http://www.wcupa.edu/business-publicManagement/geographyPlanning/

**Western Illinois University,** School of Graduate Studies, College of Arts and Sciences, Department of Geography, Macomb, IL 61455-1390. Offers community development and planning (Certificate); geography (MA); GIS analysis: GIS applications (Certificate). *Program availability:* Part-time. *Students:* 7 full-time (2 women), 5 part-time (2 women); includes 3 minority (2 Black or African American, non-Hispanic/Latino; 1 Asian, non-Hispanic/Latino), 1 international. Average age 30. 10 applicants, 80% accepted, 4 enrolled. In 2016, 9 master's, 3 other advanced degrees awarded. *Degree requirements:* For master's, thesis or alternative. *Entrance requirements:* Additional exam requirements/recommendations for international students: Required—TOEFL (minimum score 550 paper-based; 80 iBT). *Application deadline:* Applications are processed on a rolling basis. Application fee: $30. Electronic applications accepted. *Financial support:* In 2016–17, 6 students received support, including research assistantships with full tuition reimbursements available (averaging $7,544 per year); unspecified assistantships also available. Financial award applicants required to submit FAFSA. *Unit head:* Dr. Sam Thompson, Chairperson, 309-298-1648. *Application contact:* Dr. Nancy Parsons, Associate Provost and Director of Graduate School, 309-298-1806, Fax: 309-298-2345, E-mail: grad-office@wiu.edu.
Website: http://www.wiu.edu/cas/geography/

**Western Michigan University,** Graduate College, College of Arts and Sciences, Department of Geography, Kalamazoo, MI 49008. Offers geographic information science (Graduate Certificate); geography (MA). *Degree requirements:* For master's, thesis.

**Western Michigan University,** Graduate College, College of Arts and Sciences, Department of Interdisciplinary Arts and Sciences, Kalamazoo, MI 49008. Offers science education (MA, PhD), including biological sciences (PhD), chemistry (PhD), geosciences (PhD), physical geography (PhD), physics (PhD), science education (PhD). *Degree requirements:* For doctorate, thesis/dissertation.

**Western Washington University,** Graduate School, Huxley College of the Environment, Department of Environmental Studies, Program in Geography, Bellingham, WA 98225-5996. Offers MS. *Entrance requirements:* Additional exam requirements/recommendations for international students: Required—TOEFL (minimum score 567 paper-based). Electronic applications accepted.

**West Virginia University,** Eberly College of Arts and Sciences, Department of Geology and Geography, Program in Geography, Morgantown, WV 26506. Offers energy and environmental resources (MA); geographic information systems (PhD); geography-regional development (PhD); GIS/cartographic analysis (MA); regional development (MA). *Program availability:* Part-time. *Degree requirements:* For master's, thesis, oral and written exams; for doctorate, comprehensive exam, thesis/dissertation, oral and written exams. *Entrance requirements:* For master's and doctorate, GRE General Test, minimum GPA of 3.0. Additional exam requirements/recommendations for international students: Required—TOEFL. Electronic applications accepted. *Faculty research:* Space, place and development, geographic information science, environmental geography.

**Wilfrid Laurier University,** Faculty of Graduate and Postdoctoral Studies, Faculty of Arts, Department of Geography and Environmental Studies, Waterloo, ON N2L 3C5, Canada. Offers environmental and resource management (MA, MES, PhD); environmental science (M Sc, MES, PhD); geomatics (M Sc, MES, PhD); human geography (MES, PhD). *Program availability:* Part-time. *Degree requirements:* For master's, thesis optional; for doctorate, thesis/dissertation. *Entrance requirements:* For master's, honors BA in geography, minimum B average in undergraduate course work; honors BSc with minimum B+ or honors BES or BA in physical geography, environmental or earth sciences or the equivalent; for doctorate, MA in geography, minimum A- average. Additional exam requirements/recommendations for international students: Required—TOEFL (minimum score 89 iBT). Electronic applications accepted. *Faculty research:* Resources management, urban, economic, physical, cultural, earth surfaces, geomatics, historical, regional, spatial data handling.

**York University,** Faculty of Graduate Studies, Faculty of Liberal Arts and Professional Studies, Program in Geography, Toronto, ON M3J 1P3, Canada. Offers M Sc, MA, PhD. *Program availability:* Part-time. *Degree requirements:* For master's, thesis or alternative; for doctorate, comprehensive exam, thesis/dissertation. Electronic applications accepted.

# Section 22
# Military and Defense Studies

This section contains a directory of institutions offering graduate work in military and defense studies. Additional information about programs listed in the directory may be obtained by writing directly to the dean of a graduate school or chair of a department at the address given in the directory.

For programs offering related work, see also in this book *History* and *Political Science and International Affairs.*

## CONTENTS

### Program Directories

# Military and Defense Studies

**American Public University System,** AMU/APU Graduate Programs, Charles Town, WV 25414. Offers accounting (MBA, MS); applied business analytics (MBA, MS); criminal justice (MA), including business administration, emergency and disaster management, general (MA, MS); educational leadership (M Ed); emergency and disaster management (MA); entrepreneurship (MBA); environmental policy and management (MS), including environmental planning, environmental sustainability, fish and wildlife management, general (MA, MS), global environmental management; finance (MBA); general (MBA); government contracting and acquisition (MBA); health care administration (MBA); health information management (MS); history (MA), including American history, ancient and classical history, European history, global history, public history; homeland security (MA), including business administration, counterterrorism studies, criminal justice, cyber, emergency management and public health, intelligence studies, transportation security; homeland security resource allocation (MBA); humanities (MA); information technology (MS), including digital forensics, enterprise software development, information assurance and security, IT project management; information technology management (MBA); intelligence studies (MA), including criminal intelligence, cyber, general (MA, MS), homeland security, intelligence analysis, intelligence collection, intelligence management, intelligence operations, terrorism studies; international relations and conflict resolution (MA), including comparative and security issues, conflict resolution, international and transnational security issues, peacekeeping; legal studies (MA); management (MA), including strategic consulting; marketing (MBA); military history (MA), including American military history, American Revolution, civil war, war since 1945, World War II; military studies (MA), including joint warfare, strategic leadership; national security studies (MA), including cyber, general (MA, MS), homeland security, regional security studies, security and intelligence analysis, terrorism studies; nonprofit management (MBA); political science (MA), including American politics and government, comparative government and development, general (MA, MS), international relations, public policy; psychology (MA); public administration (MPA), including disaster management, environmental policy, health policy, human resources, national security, organizational management, security management; public health (MPH); reverse logistics management (MA); security management (MA); space studies (MS), including aerospace science, general (MA, MS), planetary science; sports and health sciences (MS); sports management (MBA); teaching (M Ed), including autism spectrum disorder, curriculum and instruction for elementary teachers, elementary reading, English language learners, instructional leadership, online learning, special education, STEAM (STEM plus the arts); transportation and logistics management (MA). *Program availability:* Part-time, evening/weekend, online only, 100% online. *Faculty:* 401 full-time (228 women), 1,678 part-time/adjunct (781 women). *Students:* 378 full-time (184 women), 8,455 part-time (3,484 women); includes 2,972 minority (1,552 Black or African American, non-Hispanic/Latino; 52 American Indian or Alaska Native, non-Hispanic/Latino; 211 Asian, non-Hispanic/Latino; 791 Hispanic/Latino; 70 Native Hawaiian or other Pacific Islander, non-Hispanic/Latino; 296 Two or more races, non-Hispanic/Latino), 109 international. Average age 37. In 2016, 3,185 master's awarded. *Degree requirements:* For master's, comprehensive exam or practicum. *Entrance requirements:* For master's, official transcript showing earned bachelor's degree from institution accredited by recognized accrediting body. Additional exam requirements/recommendations for international students: Required—TOEFL (minimum score 550 paper-based), IELTS (minimum score 6.5). *Application deadline:* Applications are processed on a rolling basis. Application fee: $0. Electronic applications accepted. *Expenses: Tuition:* Part-time $350 per credit hour. *Required fees:* $50 per course. *Financial support:* Scholarships/grants available. Financial award applicants required to submit FAFSA. *Unit head:* Dr. Karan Powell, President, 877-468-6268, Fax: 304-724-3780. *Application contact:* Terry Grant, Vice President of Enrollment Management, 877-468-6268, Fax: 304-724-3780, E-mail: info@apus.edu. Website: http://www.apus.edu

**Austin Peay State University,** College of Graduate Studies, College of Arts and Letters, Department of History and Philosophy, Clarksville, TN 37044. Offers military history (MA). *Program availability:* Part-time, online learning. *Faculty:* 9 full-time (1 woman), 1 part-time/adjunct (0 women). *Students:* 10 full-time (5 women), 15 part-time (2 women). Average age 39. 12 applicants, 83% accepted, 7 enrolled. In 2016, 11 master's awarded. *Degree requirements:* For master's, comprehensive exam, thesis optional. *Entrance requirements:* For master's, GRE General Test, minimum undergraduate GPA of 2.75, 3 letters of recommendation. Additional exam requirements/recommendations for international students: Required—TOEFL (minimum score 500 paper-based). *Application deadline:* For fall admission, 8/9 priority date for domestic students. Applications are processed on a rolling basis. Application fee: $45 ($50 for international students). Electronic applications accepted. *Expenses: Tuition,* state resident: full-time $8300; part-time $415 per credit hour. Tuition, nonresident: full-time $22,280; part-time $1114 per credit hour. *Required fees:* $1473; $73.65 per credit hour. *Financial support:* Research assistantships with full tuition reimbursements, career-related internships or fieldwork, Federal Work-Study, institutionally sponsored loans, scholarships/grants, and unspecified assistantships available. Support available to part-time students. Financial award application deadline: 4/1; financial award applicants required to submit FAFSA. *Faculty research:* Russia, eastern Europe, diplomatic military history, gilded age, foreign relations. *Unit head:* Dr. Cameron Sutt, Chair, 931-221-7919, Fax: 931-221-7917, E-mail: suttc@apsu.edu. *Application contact:* Brad Averitt, Coordinator of Graduate Admissions, 800-859-4723, Fax: 931-221-7662, E-mail: gradadmissions@apsu.edu. Website: http://www.apsu.edu/history/

**Bellevue University,** Graduate School, College of Arts and Sciences, Bellevue, NE 68005-3098. Offers clinical counseling (MS); healthcare administration (MHA); human services (MA); international security and intelligence studies (MS); managerial communication (MA). *Program availability:* Online learning.

**The Citadel, The Military College of South Carolina,** Citadel Graduate College, Department of Leadership Studies, Charleston, SC 29409. Offers MS, Graduate Certificate. *Program availability:* Part-time, evening/weekend, 100% online, blended/hybrid learning. *Faculty:* 1 full-time (0 women), 2 part-time/adjunct (0 women). *Students:* 7 full-time (3 women), 40 part-time (16 women); includes 9 minority (4 Black or African American, non-Hispanic/Latino; 2 Asian, non-Hispanic/Latino; 3 Hispanic/Latino), 1 international. In 2016, 7 master's, 9 other advanced degrees awarded. *Entrance requirements:* For master's, GRE (minimum verbal and quantitative combination of 290) or MAT (minimum of 396), official transcript reflecting highest degree earned from regionally-accredited college or university; for Graduate Certificate, official transcript for baccalaureate degree from regionally-accredited college or university. Additional exam requirements/recommendations for international students: Required—TOEFL (minimum score 550 paper-based; 79 iBT). *Application deadline:* Applications are processed on a rolling basis. Application fee: $40. Electronic applications accepted. *Expenses: Tuition,* state resident: full-time $5121; part-time $569 per credit hour. Tuition, nonresident: full-time $8613; part-time $957 per credit hour. *Required fees:* $90 per term. *Financial support:* Fellowships and unspecified assistantships available. Support available to part-time students. Financial award application deadline: 7/1; financial award applicants required to submit FAFSA. *Unit head:* Dr. Benjamin P. Dean, Department Head, 843-953-9679, E-mail: bdean@citadel.edu. *Application contact:* Dr. Jaye Goosby Smith, Program Director, 843-953-5165, E-mail: jsmith53@citadel.edu. Website: http://www.citadel.edu/root/leadershipstudies

**The Citadel, The Military College of South Carolina,** Citadel Graduate College, School of Humanities and Social Sciences, Department of Criminal Justice, Charleston, SC 29409. Offers homeland security (Graduate Certificate); intelligence analysis (Graduate Certificate); intelligence and security studies (MA). *Program availability:* Part-time, evening/weekend, 100% online, blended/hybrid learning. *Faculty:* 1 (woman) full-time. *Students:* 5 full-time (1 woman), 8 part-time (27 women); includes 1 minority (Two or more races, non-Hispanic/Latino). In 2016, 2 master's, 11 other advanced degrees awarded. *Entrance requirements:* For master's, GRE or MAT, writing sample that demonstrates strong critical thinking and communication skills. Additional exam requirements/recommendations for international students: Required—TOEFL (minimum score 550 paper-based; 79 iBT). *Application deadline:* Applications are processed on a rolling basis. Application fee: $40. Electronic applications accepted. *Expenses:* Tuition, state resident: full-time $5121; part-time $569 per credit hour. Tuition, nonresident: full-time $8613; part-time $957 per credit hour. *Required fees:* $90 per term. *Financial support:* Fellowships and unspecified assistantships available. Support available to part-time students. Financial award application deadline: 7/1; financial award applicants required to submit FAFSA. *Unit head:* Dr. Sean P. Griffin, Department Head, 843-953-0319, E-mail: sean.griffin@citadel.edu. *Application contact:* Dr. Carl Jensen, Director of Intelligence and Security Studies Program, 843-953-9680, E-mail: cjensen1@citadel.edu. Website: http://www.citadel.edu/root/criminaljustice

**East Carolina University,** Graduate School, Thomas Harriot College of Arts and Sciences, Department of History, Greenville, NC 27858-4353. Offers American history (MA); Atlantic world (MA); European history (MA); history education (MA Ed); maritime studies (MA); military history (MA); public history (MA). *Program availability:* Part-time, evening/weekend. *Students:* 44 full-time (21 women), 48 part-time (27 women); includes 8 minority (1 Black or African American, non-Hispanic/Latino; 5 Hispanic/Latino; 2 Two or more races, non-Hispanic/Latino), 2 international. Average age 29. 46 applicants, 80% accepted, 23 enrolled. In 2016, 24 master's awarded. *Degree requirements:* For master's, one foreign language, comprehensive exam, thesis. *Entrance requirements:* For master's, GRE General Test, GRE Subject Test. Additional exam requirements/recommendations for international students: Required—TOEFL. *Application deadline:* For fall admission, 6/1 priority date for domestic students; for spring admission, 10/15 for domestic students. Applications are processed on a rolling basis. Application fee: $50. *Financial support:* Fellowships, research assistantships with partial tuition reimbursements, teaching assistantships with partial tuition reimbursements, and Federal Work-Study available. Support available to part-time students. Financial award application deadline: 6/1. *Unit head:* Dr. Gerry Prokopowicz, Chair, 252-328-6587, E-mail: prokopowiczg@ecu.edu. Website: http://www.ecu.edu/cs-cas/history/graduatedegrees.cfm

**Embry-Riddle Aeronautical University–Prescott,** Security and Intelligence Studies Program, Prescott, AZ 86301-3720. Offers security and intelligence studies (MSSIS). *Program availability:* Part-time. *Faculty:* 7 full-time (0 women), 1 part-time/adjunct (0 women). *Students:* 30 full-time (7 women), 5 part-time (2 women); includes 8 minority (2 Black or African American, non-Hispanic/Latino; 2 Asian, non-Hispanic/Latino; 3 Hispanic/Latino; 1 Two or more races, non-Hispanic/Latino), 3 international. Average age 27. 50 applicants, 70% accepted, 14 enrolled. In 2016, 3 master's awarded. *Degree requirements:* For master's, experimental research project, thesis, or comprehensive examination. *Entrance requirements:* For master's, GRE (taken within the last 5 years). Additional exam requirements/recommendations for international students: Required—TOEFL (minimum score 550 paper-based, 79 iBT) or IELTS (6). *Application deadline:* For fall admission, 1/15 priority date for domestic students; for spring admission, 11/1 priority date for domestic students; for summer admission, 4/1 priority date for domestic students. Applications are processed on a rolling basis. Application fee: $50. Electronic applications accepted. *Expenses: Tuition:* Full-time $16,296; part-time $1358 per credit hour. *Required fees:* $1234; $617 per semester. One-time fee: $100 full-time. Tuition and fees vary according to course load. *Financial support:* Research assistantships, career-related internships or fieldwork, scholarships/grants, and unspecified assistantships available. Financial award application deadline: 3/15; financial award applicants required to submit FAFSA. *Faculty research:* New applications and storage methods that will prevent the leakage of sensitive information in the commercial world as well as in government. *Unit head:* Philip Jones, PhD, Dean and Professor, College of Security and Intelligence, 928-777-6992, E-mail: philip.e.jones@erau.edu. *Application contact:* Graduate Admissions, 928-777-6600, E-mail: prescott@erau.edu. Website: http://prescott.erau.edu/degrees/master/security-intelligence/

**The George Washington University,** Elliott School of International Affairs, Program in Security Policy Studies, Washington, DC 20052. Offers MA. *Program availability:* Part-time. *Students:* 99 full-time (44 women), 60 part-time (23 women); includes 50 minority (8 Black or African American, non-Hispanic/Latino; 14 Asian, non-Hispanic/Latino; 16 Hispanic/Latino; 12 Two or more races, non-Hispanic/Latino), 7 international. Average age 27. 293 applicants, 76% accepted, 74 enrolled. In 2016, 43 master's awarded. *Degree requirements:* For master's, one foreign language, capstone project. *Entrance requirements:* For master's, GRE General Test, 2 semesters of introductory economics, 2 years of a modern foreign language or 1 semester of statistics. Additional exam requirements/recommendations for international students: Required—TOEFL (minimum score 100 iBT), IELTS (minimum score 7). *Application deadline:* For fall admission, 1/15 priority date for domestic and international students; for spring admission, 10/1 for domestic and international students. Application fee: $75. Electronic applications accepted. *Financial support:* In 2016–17, 22 students received support. Fellowships with partial tuition reimbursements available, Federal Work-Study, and scholarships/grants available. Financial award application deadline: 1/15; financial award applicants required to submit FAFSA. *Faculty research:* U.S. arms transfer policies, military balance in the Third World, U.S. foreign policy, technology and security policy. *Unit head:* Joanna Spear, Director, 202-994-7003, E-mail: security@gwu.edu. *Application contact:* Nicole A. Campbell, Director of Graduate Admissions, 202-994-7050, Fax: 202-994-9537, E-mail: esiagrad@gwu.edu. Website: http://elliott.gwu.edu/academics/graduate/sps

**Hawai'i Pacific University,** College of Liberal Arts, Program in Diplomacy and Military Studies, Honolulu, HI 96813. Offers MA. *Program availability:* Part-time, evening/weekend. *Faculty:* 4 full-time (0 women). *Students:* 27 full-time (6 women), 38 part-time

(12 women); includes 25 minority (3 Black or African American, non-Hispanic/Latino; 13 Asian, non-Hispanic/Latino; 3 Hispanic/Latino; 2 Native Hawaiian or other Pacific Islander, non-Hispanic/Latino; 4 Two or more races, non-Hispanic/Latino), 5 international. Average age 35. 37 applicants, 89% accepted, 20 enrolled. In 2016, 27 master's awarded. *Entrance requirements:* Additional exam requirements/recommendations for international students: Recommended—TOEFL (minimum score 550 paper-based; 80 iBT), IELTS (minimum score 6), TWE (minimum score 5). *Application deadline:* For fall admission, 2/15 priority date for domestic students; for spring admission, 10/15 priority date for domestic students. Applications are processed on a rolling basis. Application fee: $50. Electronic applications accepted. *Expenses: Tuition:* Full-time $17,190; part-time $955 per credit. *Required fees:* $150; $26 per credit. Tuition and fees vary according to course load and program. *Financial support:* In 2016–17, 4 students received support. Career-related internships or fieldwork, Federal Work-Study, scholarships/grants, tuition waivers, and unspecified assistantships available. Financial award application deadline: 3/1; financial award applicants required to submit FAFSA. *Unit head:* Dr. Russell Hart, Director, 808-544-8043, E-mail: rhart@hpu.edu. *Application contact:* Danny Lam, Assistant Director of Graduate Admissions, 808-544-1135, E-mail: graduate@hpu.edu. Website: http://www.hpu.edu/CHSS/History/GraduateDegree/MADMS/MADMSmain.html

**Henley-Putnam University,** Master of Science Program in Intelligence Management, San Jose, CA 95131. Offers MS. *Program availability:* Part-time, online learning. *Degree requirements:* For master's, thesis. *Entrance requirements:* For master's, bachelor's degree from an institution accredited by an agency recognized by the U.S. Department of Education and/or the Council for Higher Education Accreditation; background check. Additional exam requirements/recommendations for international students: Required—TOEFL (minimum score 650 paper-based; 79 iBT); Recommended—IELTS (minimum score 7). *Expenses:* Contact institution.

**Henley-Putnam University,** Master of Science Program in Strategic Security and Protection Management, San Jose, CA 95131. Offers extremist organizations (MS). *Program availability:* Part-time, online learning. *Degree requirements:* For master's, comprehensive exam, thesis. *Entrance requirements:* For master's, bachelor's degree from institution accredited by an agency recognized by the U.S. Department of Education and/or the Council for Higher Education Accreditation, background check. Additional exam requirements/recommendations for international students: Required—TOEFL (minimum score 650 paper-based; 79 iBT); Recommended—IELTS. *Expenses:* Contact institution.

**Henley-Putnam University,** Master of Science Program in Terrorism and Counterterrorism Studies, San Jose, CA 95131. Offers intelligence operations (MS); protective intelligence (MS). *Program availability:* Part-time, online learning. *Degree requirements:* For master's, thesis. *Entrance requirements:* For master's, bachelor's degree from institution accredited by an agency recognized by the U.S. Department of Education and/or the Council for Higher Education Accreditation; background check. Additional exam requirements/recommendations for international students: Required—TOEFL (minimum score 650 paper-based; 79 iBT); Recommended—IELTS (minimum score 7). *Expenses:* Contact institution.

**The Institute of World Politics,** Graduate Programs in National Security, Intelligence, and International Affairs, Washington, DC 20036. Offers American foreign policy (Certificate); comparative political culture (Certificate); counterintelligence (Certificate); democracy building (Certificate); intelligence (Certificate); international politics (Certificate); national security affairs (Certificate); public diplomacy and political warfare (Certificate); statecraft and national security affairs (MA); statecraft and world politics (MA); strategic intelligence studies (MA). *Program availability:* Part-time, evening/weekend. *Degree requirements:* For master's, comprehensive exam, thesis optional. *Entrance requirements:* For master's, GRE General Test. Additional exam requirements/recommendations for international students: Required—TOEFL. Electronic applications accepted. *Faculty research:* Intelligence, national security, statecraft.

**Johns Hopkins University,** School of Education, Master's Programs in Education, Baltimore, MD 21218. Offers counseling (MS), including clinical mental health counseling, school counseling; education (MS), including educational studies, gifted education, reading, school administration and supervision, technology for educators; elementary education (MAT); health professions (M Ed); intelligence analysis (MS); organizational leadership (MS); secondary education (MAT), including biology, chemistry, earth/space science, English, physics, social studies; special education (MS), including early childhood special education, general special education studies, mild to moderate disabilities, severe disabilities. *Program availability:* Part-time, evening/weekend, 100% online, blended/hybrid learning. *Students:* 345 full-time (265 women), 1,601 part-time (1,245 women); includes 837 minority (392 Black or African American, non-Hispanic/Latino; 7 American Indian or Alaska Native, non-Hispanic/Latino; 14 Asian, non-Hispanic/Latino; 207 Hispanic/Latino; 7 Native Hawaiian or other Pacific Islander, non-Hispanic/Latino; 83 Two or more races, non-Hispanic/Latino), 55 international. Average age 27. 1,352 applicants, 76% accepted, 819 enrolled. In 2016, 642 master's awarded. *Degree requirements:* For master's, comprehensive exam (for some programs), portfolio, capstone project and/or internship; PRAXIS II (subject area assessments) for initial teacher preparation programs that lead to licensure. *Entrance requirements:* For master's, GRE (for full-time programs only); PRAXIS I/core or state-approved alternative (for initial teacher preparation programs that lead to licensure), minimum of bachelor's degree from regionally- or nationally-accredited institution; minimum GPA of 3.0 in all previous programs of study; official transcripts from all post-secondary institutions attended; essay; curriculum vitae/resume; letters of recommendation (3 for full-time programs, 2 for part-time programs); dispositions survey. Additional exam requirements/recommendations for international students: Required—TOEFL (minimum score 600 paper-based; 100 iBT), IELTS (minimum score 7). *Application deadline:* For fall admission, 4/1 priority date for domestic students, 4/1 for international students; for spring admission, 10/1 priority date for domestic students, 10/1 for international students; for summer admission, 2/1 priority date for domestic students, 2/1 for international students. Applications are processed on a rolling basis. Application fee: $80. Electronic applications accepted. *Expenses:* Contact institution. *Financial support:* Application deadline: 4/1; applicants required to submit FAFSA. *Unit head:* Dr. Christopher C. Morphew, Dean. *Application contact:* Elisabeth Woodward, Director of Admissions, 410-516-9796, Fax: 410-516-9817, E-mail: soe.info@jhu.edu. Website: http://education.jhu.edu

**The Judge Advocate General's School, U.S. Army,** Graduate Programs, Charlottesville, VA 22903-1781. Offers LL M. Program available only to active duty military lawyers. *Accreditation:* ABA. *Degree requirements:* For master's, thesis optional. *Entrance requirements:* For master's, active duty military lawyer, international military officer, or DOD civilian attorney; JD or LL B. *Faculty research:* Criminal law, administrative and civil law, contract law, international law, legal research and writing.

**Liberty University,** School of Divinity, Lynchburg, VA 24515. Offers Biblical studies (M Div); church history (MAR, Th M); discipleship and church ministry (M Div, MAR, MCM); evangelism and church planting (M Div, MAR, MCM); global studies (M Div, MCM, MGS); homiletics (M Div, MAR, Th M, D Min); leadership (M Div, D Min); marketplace chaplaincy (M Div, MCM); ministry (D Min); pastoral counseling (M Div,

MA, MAR, D Min), including addictions and recovery (MA), crisis response and trauma (MA), discipleship and church ministries (MA), leadership (MA), life coaching (MA), marketplace chaplaincy (MA), marriage and family (MA), military resilience (MA), pastoral counseling (MA); pastoral ministries (M Div, MCM); religious education (MRE); theology (M Div, MAR, MTS); theology and apologetics (PhD); worship (M Div, MAR, MCM, D Min). *Program availability:* Part-time, online learning. *Students:* 2,140 full-time (615 women), 3,020 part-time (906 women); includes 1,312 minority (1,016 Black or African American, non-Hispanic/Latino; 9 American Indian or Alaska Native, non-Hispanic/Latino; 100 Asian, non-Hispanic/Latino; 90 Hispanic/Latino; 7 Native Hawaiian or other Pacific Islander, non-Hispanic/Latino; 90 Two or more races, non-Hispanic/Latino), 158 international. Average age 42. 3,651 applicants, 37% accepted, 909 enrolled. In 2016, 1,551 master's, 39 doctorates, 168 other advanced degrees awarded. *Degree requirements:* For master's, 2 foreign languages, thesis (for some programs); for doctorate, 2 foreign languages, thesis/dissertation. *Entrance requirements:* For master's, minimum undergraduate GPA of 2.0; for doctorate, GRE General Test or MAT, minimum graduate GPA of 3.0. Additional exam requirements/recommendations for international students: Required—TOEFL (minimum score 600 paper-based; 100 iBT). *Application deadline:* For fall admission, 6/1 for domestic students; for spring admission, 11/1 for domestic students. Applications are processed on a rolling basis. Application fee: $50. Electronic applications accepted. *Expenses:* Contact institution. *Financial support:* Teaching assistantships with tuition reimbursements, career-related internships or fieldwork, and Federal Work-Study available. Financial award applicants required to submit FAFSA. *Unit head:* Dr. Ed Hindson, Dean, 434-592-4140, Fax: 434-522-0415, E-mail: ehindson@liberty.edu. *Application contact:* Jay Bridge, Director of Graduate Admissions, 800-424-9595, Fax: 800-628-7977, E-mail: gradadmissions@liberty.edu. Website: https://www.liberty.edu/divinity/

**London Metropolitan University,** Graduate Programs, London, United Kingdom. Offers applied psychology (M Sc); architecture (MA); biomedical science (M Sc); blood science (M Sc); cancer pharmacology (M Sc); computer networking and cyber security (M Sc); computing and information systems (M Sc); conference interpreting (MA); counter-terrorism studies (M Sc); creative, digital and professional writing (MA); crime, violence and prevention (M Sc); criminology (M Sc); curating contemporary art (MA); data analytics (M Sc); digital media (MA); early childhood studies (MA); education (MA, Ed D); financial services law, regulation and compliance (LL M); food science (M Sc); forensic psychology (M Sc); health and social care management and policy (M Sc); human nutrition (M Sc); human resource management (MA); human rights and international conflict (MA); information technology (M Sc); intelligence and security studies (M Sc); international oil, gas and energy law (LL M); international relations (MA); interpreting (MA); learning and teaching in higher education (MA); legal practice (LL M); media and entertainment law (LL M); organizational and consumer psychology (M Sc); psychological therapy (MA); psychology of mental health (M Sc); public health (MA); public policy and management (MPA); security studies (M Sc); social work (M Sc); spatial planning and urban design (MA); sports therapy (M Sc); supporting older children and young people with dyslexia (MA); teaching languages (MA), including Arabic, English; translation (MA); woman and child abuse (MA).

**Missouri State University,** Graduate College, College of Humanities and Public Affairs, Department of Defense and Strategic Studies, Fairfax, VA 22031. Offers defense and strategic studies (Certificate); general weapons of mass destruction (MS). *Program availability:* Part-time. *Faculty:* 2 full-time (0 women), 19 part-time/adjunct (5 women). *Students:* 25 full-time (9 women), 59 part-time (16 women); includes 20 minority (6 Black or African American, non-Hispanic/Latino; 1 American Indian or Alaska Native, non-Hispanic/Latino; 2 Asian, non-Hispanic/Latino; 5 Hispanic/Latino; 6 Two or more races, non-Hispanic/Latino), 1 international. Average age 26. 50 applicants, 80% accepted, 37 enrolled. In 2016, 35 master's awarded. *Degree requirements:* For master's, comprehensive exam, thesis or alternative. *Entrance requirements:* For master's, GRE, minimum GPA of 2.75, 3 letters of recommendation. Additional exam requirements/recommendations for international students: Required—TOEFL (minimum score 550 paper-based; 79 iBT), IELTS (minimum score 6). *Application deadline:* For fall admission, 4/15 priority date for domestic students, 4/15 for international students. Applications are processed on a rolling basis. Application fee: $35 ($50 for international students). Electronic applications accepted. *Expenses:* Tuition, state resident: full-time $5830. Tuition, nonresident: full-time $10,708. *Required fees:* $1130. Tuition and fees vary according to class time, course level, course load and program. *Financial support:* Career-related internships or fieldwork, Federal Work-Study, institutionally sponsored loans, scholarships/grants, and unspecified assistantships available. Financial award application deadline: 3/31; financial award applicants required to submit FAFSA. *Faculty research:* Middle East, terrorism, arms control, U.S.-Soviet military balance, strategic defense initiative. *Unit head:* Dr. Keith Payne, Head, 703-218-3565, Fax: 703-218-3568, E-mail: kbpayne@missouristate.edu. *Application contact:* Michael Edwards, Coordinator of Graduate Admissions, 417-836-5330, Fax: 417-836-6200, E-mail: michaeledwards@missouristate.edu. Website: http://dss.missouristate.edu

**National Defense University,** The Dwight D. Eisenhower School for National Security and Resource Strategy, Washington, DC 20319-5066. Offers national resource strategy (MS). Open only to Department of Defense employees and specific federal agencies. *Degree requirements:* For master's, comprehensive exam. *Entrance requirements:* Additional exam requirements/recommendations for international students: Required—TOEFL. *Faculty research:* Industrial base and relation to national security, acquisition and relation to national security, resourcing the national security strategy.

**National Defense University,** Joint Advanced Warfighting School, Norfolk, VA 23511. Offers joint campaign planning and strategy (MS). Open only to Department of Defense employees and specific federal agencies. *Degree requirements:* For master's, thesis. *Faculty research:* Irregular warfare, national policy and strategy, international organizations and policies, modern military history and applications of lessons learned, historical military leadership relating to present-day environments.

**National Defense University,** National War College, Washington, DC 20319-5066. Offers national security strategy (MS). Open only to Department of Defense employees and specific federal agencies. *Degree requirements:* For master's, comprehensive exam. *Entrance requirements:* Additional exam requirements/recommendations for international students: Required—TOEFL. *Faculty research:* National security policy, regional security, U.S. national security strategy, U.S. military, strategy.

**National Intelligence University,** Graduate Program, Washington, DC 20340-5100. Offers MSSI. Open only to federal government employees. *Program availability:* Part-time, evening/weekend. *Degree requirements:* For master's, thesis. *Entrance requirements:* For master's, MAT, authorized nomination. *Faculty research:* Law and intelligence, intelligence and higher education, low-intensity conflict, intelligence information systems.

**Naval Postgraduate School,** Departments and Academic Groups, Department of Computer Science, Monterey, CA 93943. Offers computer science (MS, PhD); identity management and cyber security (MA); modeling of virtual environments and simulations (MS, PhD); software engineering (MS, PhD). Program only open to commissioned officers of the United States and friendly nations and selected United States federal civilian employees. *Program availability:* Part-time, online learning. *Degree requirements:* For master's, thesis; for doctorate, thesis/dissertation.

## Military and Defense Studies

**Naval Postgraduate School,** Departments and Academic Groups, Department of Defense Analysis, Monterey, CA 93943. Offers command and control (MS); communications (MS); defense analysis (MS), including astronautics; financial management (MS); information operations (MS); irregular warfare (MS); national security affairs (MS); operations analysis (MS); special operations (MA, MS), including command and control (MS), communications (MS), financial management (MS), information operations (MS), irregular warfare (MS), national security affairs, operations analysis (MS), tactile missiles (MS), terrorist operations and financing (MS); tactile missiles (MS); terrorist operations and financing (MS). Program only open to commissioned officers of the United States and friendly nations and selected United States federal civilian employees. *Program availability:* Part-time. *Degree requirements:* For master's, thesis. *Faculty research:* CTF Global Ecco Project, Afghanistan endgames, core lab Philippines project, Defense Manpower Data Center (DMDC) data vulnerability.

**Naval Postgraduate School,** Departments and Academic Groups, Department of National Security Affairs, Monterey, CA 93943. Offers national security affairs (MA); security studies (MA), including civil-military relations, combating terrorism: policy and strategy, defense decision-making and planning, Europe and Eurasia, Far East, Southeast Asia, the Pacific, homeland security and defense, Middle East, South Asia, Sub-Saharan Africa, stabilization and reconstruction, western hemisphere. Program only open to commissioned officers of the United States and friendly nations and selected United States federal civilian employees. *Program availability:* Part-time. *Degree requirements:* For master's, thesis (for some programs). *Faculty research:* Privatizing welfare in the Middle East; social construction of Russia's resurgence; institutions, ethnicity and political mobilization in South Africa; Hezbollah; China's strategic interests in Cambodia.

**Naval Postgraduate School,** Departments and Academic Groups, Graduate School of Business and Public Policy, Monterey, CA 93943. Offers acquisition and contract management (MBA); business administration (EMBA, MBA); contract management (MS); defense business management (MBA); defense systems analysis (MS), including management; defense systems management (international) (MBA); financial management (MBA); information management (MBA); manpower systems analysis (MS); material logistics support management (MBA); program management (MS); resource planning and management for international defense (MBA); supply chain management (MBA); systems acquisition management (MBA); transportation management (MBA). Program only open to commissioned officers of the United States and friendly nations and selected United States federal civilian employees. *Accreditation:* AACSB; NASPAA. *Program availability:* Part-time, online learning. *Degree requirements:* For master's, thesis (for some programs), terminal project/capstone (for some programs). *Faculty research:* U.S. and European public procurement policies for small and medium-sized enterprises, examining external validity criticisms in the choice of students as subjects in accounting experiment studies, assurance of learning in contract management education, contracting for cloud computing: opportunities and risks, NPS, Apple App Store as a business model supporting U. S. Navy requirements.

**Naval Postgraduate School,** Departments and Academic Groups, Undersea Warfare Academic Group, Monterey, CA 93943. Offers applied mathematics (MS); applied physics (MS); applied science (MS), including acoustics, operations research, physical oceanography, signal processing; electrical engineering (MS); engineering acoustics (MS, PhD); engineering science (MS), including electrical engineering, mechanical engineering; mechanical engineer (ME); mechanical engineering (MS, MSME); meteorology (MS); operations research (MS); physical oceanography (MS). Program only open to commissioned officers of the United States and friendly nations and selected United States federal civilian employees. *Program availability:* Part-time. *Degree requirements:* For master's, thesis. *Faculty research:* Unmanned/autonomous vehicles, sea mines and countermeasures, submarine warfare in the twentieth and twenty-first centuries.

**Norwich University,** College of Graduate and Continuing Studies, Master of Arts in Military History Program, Northfield, VT 05663. Offers MA. *Program availability:* Evening/weekend, online only, mostly all online with a week-long residency requirement. *Faculty:* 23 part-time/adjunct (3 women). *Students:* 110 full-time (12 women); includes 6 minority (1 Black or African American, non-Hispanic/Latino; 1 Asian, non-Hispanic/Latino; 1 Hispanic/Latino; 3 Two or more races, non-Hispanic/Latino). Average age 38. 34 applicants, 97% accepted, 25 enrolled. In 2016, 52 master's awarded. *Degree requirements:* For master's, thesis optional, capstone. *Entrance requirements:* For master's, minimum undergraduate GPA of 2.75. Additional exam requirements/recommendations for international students: Required—TOEFL (minimum score 550 paper-based; 80 iBT), IELTS (minimum score 6.5). *Application deadline:* For fall admission, 8/14 for domestic and international students; for winter admission, 11/13 for domestic and international students; for spring admission, 2/12 for domestic and international students; for summer admission, 6/5 for domestic and international students. Electronic applications accepted. *Expenses:* Contact institution. *Financial support:* In 2016–17, 39 students received support. Scholarships/grants available. Financial award application deadline: 8/4; financial award applicants required to submit FAFSA. *Unit head:* Dr. James Ehrman, Program Director, 802-485-2567, Fax: 802-485-2533, E-mail: jehrman@norwich.edu. *Application contact:* Admissions Advisor, 800-460-5597 Ext. 3372, Fax: 802-485-2533, E-mail: mmh@online.norwich.edu.
Website: https://online.norwich.edu/degree-programs/masters/master-arts-military-history/overview

**Royal Military College of Canada,** Division of Graduate Studies and Research, Continuing Studies, Department of History, Kingston, ON K7K 7B4, Canada. Offers defense management and policy (MA); history (PhD); war studies (MA). *Degree requirements:* For master's, thesis. *Entrance requirements:* For master's, honours degree with second-class standing; for doctorate, master's degree. Electronic applications accepted.

**School of Advanced Air and Space Studies,** Program in Airpower Art and Science, Maxwell AFB, AL 36112-6424. Offers MA. Available to active duty military officers only. *Degree requirements:* For master's, comprehensive exam, thesis. *Entrance requirements:* For master's, less than 16 years total of active commissioned service; master's degree or undergraduate degree with a minimum GPA of 2.75. Additional exam requirements/recommendations for international students: Required—TOEFL. *Faculty research:* Military history, political science, international relations, social history, technology.

**United States Army Command and General Staff College,** Graduate Program, Fort Leavenworth, KS 66027-2301. Offers military art and science (MMAS). Only career military officers are selected to attend United States Army Command and General Staff College; Graduate Program is voluntary for first-year students, but mandatory for second-year students.

**University of Calgary,** Faculty of Graduate Studies, Centre for Military and Strategic Studies, Calgary, AB T2N 1N4, Canada. Offers MSS, PhD. PhD offered in special cases only. *Program availability:* Part-time. *Degree requirements:* For master's, thesis; for doctorate, comprehensive exam, thesis/dissertation. *Entrance requirements:* For master's, minimum GPA of 3.4. Additional exam requirements/recommendations for international students: Recommended—TOEFL (minimum score 550 paper-based). *Faculty research:* Military history, Israeli studies, strategic studies, int'l relations, Arctic security.

**University of Colorado Denver,** School of Public Affairs, Program in Public Affairs and Administration, Denver, CO 80127. Offers public administration (MPA), including domestic violence, emergency management and homeland security, environmental policy, management and law, homeland security and defense, local government, nonprofit management, public administration; public affairs (PhD). *Accreditation:* NASPAA. *Program availability:* Part-time, evening/weekend, online learning. *Students:* 241 full-time (146 women), 135 part-time (86 women); includes 61 minority (15 Black or African American, non-Hispanic/Latino; 1 American Indian or Alaska Native, non-Hispanic/Latino; 10 Asian, non-Hispanic/Latino; 26 Hispanic/Latino; 2 Native Hawaiian or other Pacific Islander, non-Hispanic/Latino; 7 Two or more races, non-Hispanic/Latino), 26 international. Average age 36. 240 applicants, 70% accepted, 91 enrolled. In 2016, 158 master's, 8 doctorates awarded. *Degree requirements:* For master's, thesis or alternative, 36-39 credit hours; for doctorate, comprehensive exam, thesis/dissertation, minimum of 66 semester hours, including at least 30 hours of dissertation. *Entrance requirements:* For master's, GRE, GMAT or LSAT, resume, essay, transcripts, recommendations; for doctorate, GRE, resume, essay, transcripts, recommendations. Additional exam requirements/recommendations for international students: Required—TOEFL (minimum score 550 paper-based; 80 iBT); Recommended—IELTS (minimum score 6.5). *Application deadline:* For fall admission, 2/1 priority date for domestic students, 1/15 priority date for international students; for spring admission, 10/15 priority date for domestic students, 10/1 priority date for international students. Application fee: $50 ($75 for international students). Electronic applications accepted. *Expenses:* Contact institution. *Financial support:* In 2016–17, 92 students received support. Fellowships with partial tuition reimbursements available, research assistantships with partial tuition reimbursements available, teaching assistantships with partial tuition reimbursements available, Federal Work-Study, institutionally sponsored loans, scholarships/grants, traineeships, and unspecified assistantships available. Financial award application deadline: 4/1; financial award applicants required to submit FAFSA. *Faculty research:* Housing, education and the social and economic issues of vulnerable populations; nonprofit governance and management; education finance, effectiveness and reform; P-20 education initiatives; municipal government accountability. *Unit head:* Dr. Christine Martell, Director of MPA Program, 303-315-2716, Fax: 303-315-2229, E-mail: christine.martell@ucdenver.edu. *Application contact:* Dawn Savage, Student Services Coordinator, 303-315-2743, Fax: 303-315-2229, E-mail: dawn.savage@ucdenver.edu.
Website: http://www.ucdenver.edu/academics/colleges/SPA/Academics/programs/PublicAffairsAdmin/Pages/index.aspx

**University of Pittsburgh,** Graduate School of Public and International Affairs, Master of Public and International Affairs Program, Pittsburgh, PA 15260. Offers human security (MPIA); international political economy (MPIA); security and intelligence studies (MPIA); JD/MPIA; MBA/MPIA; MPH/MPIA; MPIA/MSW; MSIS/MPIA. *Program availability:* Part-time, evening/weekend. *Faculty:* 34 full-time (12 women), 17 part-time/adjunct (5 women). *Students:* 98 full-time (42 women), 17 part-time (8 women); includes 17 minority (8 Black or African American, non-Hispanic/Latino; 2 Asian, non-Hispanic/Latino; 6 Hispanic/Latino; 1 Two or more races, non-Hispanic/Latino), 20 international. Average age 26. 181 applicants, 91% accepted, 48 enrolled. In 2016, 70 master's awarded. *Degree requirements:* For master's, thesis optional, capstone seminar. *Entrance requirements:* For master's, GRE General Test or GMAT, 2 letters of recommendation, resume, undergraduate transcripts, personal statement. Additional exam requirements/recommendations for international students: Required—TOEFL (minimum score 80 iBT); Recommended—IELTS (minimum score 7). *Application deadline:* For fall admission, 2/1 for domestic students, 1/15 for international students; for spring admission, 11/1 for domestic students, 8/1 for international students. Application fee: $50. Electronic applications accepted. *Expenses:* $22,578 per year in-state; $36,734 per year out-of-state. *Financial support:* In 2016–17, 47 students received support, including 2 fellowships with full tuition reimbursements available (averaging $18,000 per year), 3 research assistantships with full tuition reimbursements available (averaging $14,620 per year); career-related internships or fieldwork and scholarships/grants also available. Financial award application deadline: 2/1; financial award applicants required to submit FAFSA. *Faculty research:* International political economy, human security, security and intelligence. *Total annual research expenditures:* $1.3 million. *Unit head:* Dr. John T.S. Keeler, Dean, 412-648-7605, E-mail: keeler@pitt.edu. *Application contact:* Dr. Michael T. Rizzi, Director of Student Services, 412-648-7640, Fax: 412-648-7641, E-mail: rizzim@pitt.edu.
Website: http://www.gspia.pitt.edu/

# National Security

**American Public University System,** AMU/APU Graduate Programs, Charles Town, WV 25414. Offers accounting (MBA, MS); applied business analytics (MBA, MS); criminal justice (MA), including business administration, emergency and disaster management, general (MA, MS); educational leadership (M Ed); emergency and disaster management (MA); entrepreneurship (MBA); environmental policy and management (MS), including environmental planning, environmental sustainability, fish and wildlife management, general (MA, MS), global environmental management; finance (MBA); general (MBA); government contracting and acquisition (MBA); health care administration (MBA); health information management (MS); history (MA), including American history, ancient and classical history, European history, global history, public history; homeland security (MA), including business administration, counterterrorism studies, criminal justice, cyber, emergency management and public health, intelligence studies, transportation security; homeland security resource allocation (MBA); humanities (MA); information technology (MS), including digital forensics, enterprise

software development, information assurance and security, IT project management; information technology management (MBA); intelligence studies (MA), including criminal intelligence, cyber, general (MA, MS), homeland security, intelligence analysis, intelligence collection, intelligence management, intelligence operations, terrorism studies; international relations and conflict resolution (MA), including comparative and security issues, conflict resolution, international and transnational security issues, peacekeeping; legal studies (MA); management (MA), including strategic consulting; marketing (MBA); military history (MA), including American military history, American Revolution, civil war, war since 1945, World War II; military studies (MA), including joint warfare, strategic leadership; national security studies (MA), including cyber, general (MA, MS), homeland security, regional security studies, security and intelligence analysis, terrorism studies; nonprofit management (MBA); political science (MA), including American politics and government, comparative government and development, general (MA, MS), international relations, public policy; psychology (MA); public administration (MPA), including disaster management, environmental policy, health policy, human resources, national security, organizational management, security management; public health (MPH); reverse logistics management (MA); security management (MA); space studies (MS), including aerospace science, general (MA, MS), planetary science; sports and health sciences (MS); sports management (MBA); teaching (M Ed), including autism spectrum disorder, curriculum and instruction for elementary teachers, elementary reading, English language learners, instructional leadership, online learning, special education, STEAM (STEM plus the arts); transportation and logistics management (MA). *Program availability:* Part-time, evening/weekend, online only, 100% online. *Faculty:* 401 full-time (228 women), 1,678 part-time/adjunct (781 women). *Students:* 378 full-time (184 women), 8,455 part-time (3,484 women); includes 2,972 minority (1,552 Black or African American, non-Hispanic/Latino; 52 American Indian or Alaska Native, non-Hispanic/Latino; 211 Asian, non-Hispanic/Latino; 791 Hispanic/Latino; 70 Native Hawaiian or other Pacific Islander, non-Hispanic/Latino; 296 Two or more races, non-Hispanic/Latino), 109 international. Average age 37. In 2016, 3,185 master's awarded. *Degree requirements:* For master's, comprehensive exam or practicum. *Entrance requirements:* For master's, official transcript showing earned bachelor's degree from institution accredited by recognized accrediting body. Additional exam requirements/recommendations for international students: Required—TOEFL (minimum score 550 paper-based), IELTS (minimum score 6.5). *Application deadline:* Applications are processed on a rolling basis. Application fee: $0. Electronic applications accepted. *Expenses: Tuition:* Part-time $350 per credit hour. *Required fees:* $50 per course. *Financial support:* Scholarships/grants available. Financial award applicants required to submit FAFSA. *Unit head:* Dr. Karan Powell, President, 877-468-6268, Fax: 304-724-3780. *Application contact:* Terry Grant, Vice President of Enrollment Management, 877-468-6268, Fax: 304-724-3780, E-mail: info@apus.edu.
Website: http://www.apus.edu

**Angelo State University,** College of Graduate Studies and Research, College of Arts and Humanities, Department of Security Studies and Criminal Justice, San Angelo, TX 76909. Offers criminal justice (MS); homeland security (MS); intelligence, security studies, and analysis (MSS); security studies (MSS). *Program availability:* Part-time, evening/weekend, online learning. *Students:* 75 full-time (31 women), 115 part-time (38 women); includes 65 minority (24 Black or African American, non-Hispanic/Latino; 7 Asian, non-Hispanic/Latino; 31 Hispanic/Latino; 3 Two or more races, non-Hispanic/Latino). Average age 31. *Degree requirements:* For master's, comprehensive exam. *Entrance requirements:* For master's, essay, letters of recommendation. Additional exam requirements/recommendations for international students: Required—TOEFL or IELTS. *Application deadline:* For fall admission, 7/15 priority date for domestic students, 6/10 for international students; for spring admission, 12/1 priority date for domestic students, 11/1 for international students. Applications are processed on a rolling basis. Application fee: $40 ($50 for international students). Electronic applications accepted. *Expenses:* Tuition, state resident: full-time $3726; part-time $2484 per year. Tuition, nonresident: full-time $10,746; part-time $7164 per year. *Required fees:* $2538; $1702 per unit. *Financial support:* Federal Work-Study and scholarships/grants available. Support available to part-time students. Financial award application deadline: 3/1; financial award applicants required to submit FAFSA. *Unit head:* Dr. William A. Taylor, Chair, 325-486-6689, Fax: 325-942-2544, E-mail: william.taylor@angelo.edu. *Application contact:* Dr. William A. Taylor, Chair, 325-486-6689, Fax: 325-942-2544, E-mail: william.taylor@angelo.edu.
Website: http://www.angelo.edu/dept/security_studies_criminal_justice/

**Bellevue University,** Graduate School, College of Arts and Sciences, Bellevue, NE 68005-3098. Offers clinical counseling (MS); healthcare administration (MHA); human services (MA); international security and intelligence studies (MS); managerial communication (MA). *Program availability:* Online learning.

**California State University, San Bernardino,** Graduate Studies, College of Social and Behavioral Sciences, Program in National Security Studies, San Bernardino, CA 92407. Offers MA. *Program availability:* Part-time, evening/weekend. *Students:* 9 full-time (4 women), 24 part-time (9 women); includes 14 minority (1 Black or African American, non-Hispanic/Latino; 1 Asian, non-Hispanic/Latino; 11 Hispanic/Latino; 1 Two or more races, non-Hispanic/Latino), 2 international. 18 applicants, 89% accepted, 12 enrolled. In 2016, 16 master's awarded. *Degree requirements:* For master's, comprehensive exam. *Entrance requirements:* Additional exam requirements/recommendations for international students: Required—TOEFL. *Application deadline:* For fall admission, 4/15 for domestic students; for winter admission, 10/16 for domestic students; for spring admission, 1/22 for domestic students. Application fee: $55. *Expenses:* Tuition, state resident: full-time $7843; part-time $5011.20 per year. Tuition and fees vary according to course load, degree level, program and reciprocity agreements. *Unit head:* Dr. Mark Clark, Director, 909-537-5491, Fax: 909-537-7018, E-mail: mtclark@csusb.edu. *Application contact:* Dr. Francisca Beer, Dean of Graduate Studies, 909-537-5058, E-mail: fbeer@csusb.edu.

**The Citadel, The Military College of South Carolina,** Citadel Graduate College, School of Humanities and Social Sciences, Department of Criminal Justice, Charleston, SC 29409. Offers homeland security (Graduate Certificate); intelligence analysis (Graduate Certificate); intelligence and security studies (MA). *Program availability:* Part-time, evening/weekend, 100% online, blended/hybrid learning. *Faculty:* 1 (woman) full-time. *Students:* 5 full-time (1 woman), 8 part-time (5 women); includes 1 minority (Two or more races, non-Hispanic/Latino). In 2016, 2 master's, 11 other advanced degrees awarded. *Entrance requirements:* For master's, GRE or MAT, writing sample that demonstrates strong critical thinking and communication skills. Additional exam requirements/recommendations for international students: Required—TOEFL (minimum score 550 paper-based; 79 iBT). *Application deadline:* Applications are processed on a rolling basis. Application fee: $40. Electronic applications accepted. *Expenses:* Tuition, state resident: full-time $5121; part-time $569 per credit hour. Tuition, nonresident: full-time $8613; part-time $957 per credit hour. *Required fees:* $90 per term. *Financial support:* Fellowships and unspecified assistantships available. Support available to part-time students. Financial award application deadline: 7/1; financial award applicants required to submit FAFSA. *Unit head:* Dr. Sean P. Griffin, Department Head, 843-953-0319, E-mail: sean.griffin@citadel.edu. *Application contact:* Dr. Carl Jensen, Director of Intelligence and Security Studies Program, 843-953-9680, E-mail:

cjensen1@citadel.edu.
Website: http://www.citadel.edu/root/criminaljustice

**George Mason University,** Schar School of Policy and Government, Program in Biodefense, Arlington, VA 22201. Offers MS, PhD, Certificate. *Faculty:* 3 full-time (1 woman), 10 part-time/adjunct (4 women). *Students:* 13 full-time (9 women), 42 part-time (24 women); includes 8 minority (3 Asian, non-Hispanic/Latino; 2 Hispanic/Latino; 3 Two or more races, non-Hispanic/Latino), 2 international. Average age 31. 36 applicants, 69% accepted, 16 enrolled. In 2016, 13 master's, 5 doctorates, 1 other advanced degree awarded. *Entrance requirements:* For master's, GRE (taken in the past five years), transcripts from all previous institutions attended in the U.S.; goals statement; two letters of recommendation; current resume; writing sample; for doctorate, GRE (taken in the past five years), official transcript from all colleges and universities attended; current resume; two letters of recommendation; statement of goals (not to exceed 500 words); writing sample (approximately 10-25 pages in length). Additional exam requirements/ recommendations for international students: Required—TOEFL (minimum score 575 paper-based; 88 iBT), IELTS (minimum score 6.5), PTE (minimum score 59). *Application deadline:* For fall admission, 2/1 priority date for domestic students. Application fee: $75 ($80 for international students). Electronic applications accepted. *Expenses:* Tuition, state resident: full-time $10,628; part-time $443 per credit. Tuition, nonresident: full-time $29,306; part-time $1221 per credit. *Required fees:* $3096; $129 per credit. Tuition and fees vary according to program. *Financial support:* In 2016–17, 3 students received support, including 3 research assistantships with tuition reimbursements available (averaging $16,752 per year); career-related internships or fieldwork, Federal Work-Study, scholarships/grants, unspecified assistantships, and health care benefits (for full-time research or teaching assistantship recipients) also available. Support available to part-time students. *Unit head:* Gregory Koblentz, 703-993-1266, Fax: 703-993-1399, E-mail: gkoblent@gmu.edu. *Application contact:* Stephanie Ellis, Graduate Admissions Coordinator, 703-993-4478, E-mail: sellis11@gmu.edu.
Website: http://spgia.gmu.edu/programs/graduate-degrees/ms-in-biodefense/

**The George Washington University,** Law School, Washington, DC 20052. Offers law (SJD); national security and U.S. foreign relations (LL M). *Accreditation:* ABA. *Program availability:* Part-time, evening/weekend. *Faculty:* 84 full-time (33 women). *Students:* 1,622 full-time (867 women), 315 part-time (150 women); includes 482 minority (164 Black or African American, non-Hispanic/Latino; 15 American Indian or Alaska Native, non-Hispanic/Latino; 234 Asian, non-Hispanic/Latino; 55 Hispanic/Latino; 4 Native Hawaiian or other Pacific Islander, non-Hispanic/Latino; 10 Two or more races, non-Hispanic/Latino), 222 international. Average age 27. 223 applicants, 100% accepted, 133 enrolled. In 2016, 166 master's, 1 doctorate awarded. *Degree requirements:* For doctorate, thesis/dissertation (for some programs). *Entrance requirements:* For master's, JD or equivalent; for doctorate, LSAT (for JD), LL M or equivalent (for SJD). *Application deadline:* For fall admission, 3/1 for domestic students. Applications are processed on a rolling basis. Application fee: $75. *Expenses:* Contact institution. *Financial support:* Research assistantships, career-related internships or fieldwork, Federal Work-Study, institutionally sponsored loans, scholarships/grants, and tuition waivers (full and partial) available. Support available to part-time students. Financial award application deadline: 3/1; financial award applicants required to submit CSS PROFILE or FAFSA. *Unit head:* Blake D. Morant, Dean, E-mail: bmorant@law.gwu.edu. *Application contact:* Sophia Sim, Assistant Dean of Admissions and Financial Aid, 202-994-7235, Fax: 202-739-0624, E-mail: ssim@law.gwu.edu.
Website: http://www.law.gwu.edu/

**Henley-Putnam University,** Doctorate Program in Strategic Security, San Jose, CA 95131. Offers DSS. *Program availability:* Part-time, online learning. *Degree requirements:* For doctorate, thesis/dissertation. *Entrance requirements:* For doctorate, 5 years of strategic security experience; background check; interview with dean; copy of master's thesis; master's or bachelor's degree with equivalent of 30 graduate-level semester hours in strategic security or related field from accredited institution. Additional exam requirements/recommendations for international students: Required—TOEFL (minimum score 650 paper-based; 79 iBT); Recommended—IELTS (minimum score 7). *Expenses:* Contact institution.

**The Institute of World Politics,** Graduate Programs in National Security, Intelligence, and International Affairs, Washington, DC 20036. Offers American foreign policy (Certificate); comparative political culture (Certificate); counterintelligence (Certificate); democracy building (Certificate); intelligence (Certificate); international politics (Certificate); national security affairs (Certificate); public diplomacy and political warfare (Certificate); statecraft and national security affairs (MA); statecraft and world politics (MA); strategic intelligence studies (MA). *Program availability:* Part-time, evening/ weekend. *Degree requirements:* For master's, comprehensive exam, thesis optional. *Entrance requirements:* For master's, GRE General Test. Additional exam requirements/ recommendations for international students: Required—TOEFL. Electronic applications accepted. *Faculty research:* Intelligence, national security, statecraft.

**Kansas State University,** Graduate School, College of Arts and Sciences, Security Studies Program, Manhattan, KS 66506. Offers MA, PhD. *Program availability:* Part-time. *Faculty:* 18 full-time (3 women), 38 part-time (6 women); includes 7 minority (4 Black or African American, non-Hispanic/Latino; 2 Asian, non-Hispanic/Latino; 1 Two or more races, non-Hispanic/Latino), 4 international. Average age 38. 45 applicants, 38% accepted, 13 enrolled. In 2016, 11 master's, 1 doctorate awarded. Terminal master's awarded for partial completion of doctoral program. *Degree requirements:* For doctorate, comprehensive exam, thesis/ dissertation. *Entrance requirements:* For doctorate, GRE. Additional exam requirements/recommendations for international students: Required—TOEFL (minimum score 550 paper-based; 79 iBT), IELTS (minimum score 6.5), PTE (minimum score 58). *Application deadline:* For fall admission, 2/1 for domestic students, 1/1 for international students; for spring admission, 10/15 for domestic students, 8/1 for international students; for summer admission, 2/1 for domestic students. Application fee: $50 ($75 for international students). Electronic applications accepted. *Expenses:* Tuition, state resident: full-time $9670. Tuition, nonresident: full-time $21,828. *Required fees:* $862. *Financial support:* Teaching assistantships with full tuition reimbursements available. Financial award application deadline: 4/1. *Faculty research:* International conflict and security, military history. *Unit head:* Dr. Andrew Long, Director, 785-532-3786, E-mail: aglong@ksu.edu. *Application contact:* Bri Beck, Administrative Assistant, 785-532-3786, E-mail: securstu@ksu.edu.
Website: http://www.k-state.edu/securitystudies/

**National Defense University,** College of International Security Affairs, Washington, DC 20319-5066. Offers strategic security studies (MA), including counterterrorism, homeland defense, international security studies. *Program availability:* Part-time, evening/weekend. *Degree requirements:* For master's, thesis. *Entrance requirements:* Additional exam requirements/recommendations for international students: Required—TOEFL.

**National Defense University,** National War College, Washington, DC 20319-5066. Offers national security strategy (MS). Open only to Department of Defense employees and specific federal agencies. *Degree requirements:* For master's, comprehensive exam. *Entrance requirements:* Additional exam requirements/recommendations for

## National Security

international students: Required—TOEFL. *Faculty research:* National security policy, regional security, U.S. national security strategy, U.S. military, strategy.

**Naval Postgraduate School,** Departments and Academic Groups, Department of Defense Analysis, Monterey, CA 93943. Offers command and control (MS); communications (MS); defense analysis (MS), including astronautics; financial management (MS); information operations (MS); irregular warfare (MS); national security affairs (MS); operations analysis (MS); special operations (MA, MS), including command and control (MS), communications (MS), financial management (MS), information operations (MS), irregular warfare (MS), national security affairs, operations analysis (MS), tactile missiles (MS); terrorist operations and financing (MS); tactile missiles (MS); terrorist operations and financing (MS). Program only open to commissioned officers of the United States and friendly nations and selected United States federal civilian employees. *Program availability:* Part-time. *Degree requirements:* For master's, thesis. *Faculty research:* CTF Global Ecco Project, Afghanistan endgames, core lab Philippines project, Defense Manpower Data Center (DMDC) data vulnerability.

**Naval Postgraduate School,** Departments and Academic Groups, Department of National Security Affairs, Monterey, CA 93943. Offers national security affairs (MA); security studies (MA), including civil-military relations, combating terrorism: policy and strategy, defense decision-making and planning, Europe and Eurasia, Far East, Southeast Asia, the Pacific, homeland security and defense, Middle East, South Asia, Sub-Saharan Africa, stabilization and reconstruction, western hemisphere. Program only open to commissioned officers of the United States and friendly nations and selected United States federal civilian employees. *Program availability:* Part-time. *Degree requirements:* For master's, thesis (for some programs). *Faculty research:* Privatizing welfare in the Middle East; social construction of Russia's resurgence; institutions, ethnicity and political mobilization in South Africa; Hezbollah; China's strategic interests in Cambodia.

**Naval Postgraduate School,** Departments and Academic Groups, Global Public Policy Academic Group, Monterey, CA 93943. Offers stability, security, and development in complex operations (Certificate). *Degree requirements:* For Certificate, certificate hybrid course (requiring short biographical essay and short introductory session with instructor during the distributed learning component). *Faculty research:* Implementing program budgeting in the Serbian Ministry of Defense, recognizing patterns of anomie that set the conditions for insurgency.

**Naval War College,** Program in National Security and Strategic Studies, Newport, RI 02841-1207. Offers MA. Program open only to full-time military personnel.

**New Jersey City University,** College of Professional Studies, Program in National Security Studies, Jersey City, NJ 07305-1597. Offers civil security leadership (D Sc); national security studies (MS, Certificate). *Program availability:* Part-time. *Entrance requirements:* Additional exam requirements/recommendations for international students: Required—TOEFL (minimum score 79 iBT).

**New York University,** School of Continuing and Professional Studies, Center for Global Affairs, New York, NY 10012-1019. Offers global affairs (MS), including environment/ energy policy, human rights and international law, international development and humanitarian assistance, international relations, peace building, private sector, transnational security; global energy (Advanced Certificate); peacebuilding (Advanced Certificate); transnational security (Advanced Certificate). *Program availability:* Part-time, evening/weekend. *Degree requirements:* For master's, thesis. *Entrance requirements:* For master's, GRE or GMAT (only upon request), bachelor's degree, resume with relevant professional work, internship or volunteer experience, two letters of recommendation, statement of purpose. Additional exam requirements/ recommendations for international students: Required—TOEFL (minimum score 600 paper-based; 100 iBT), IELTS (minimum score 7). Electronic applications accepted.

**Regent University,** Graduate School, Robertson School of Government, Virginia Beach, VA 23464-9800. Offers government (MA), including American government, healthcare policy and ethics (MA, MPA), international relations, law and public policy, national security studies, political communication, political theory, religion and politics; public administration (MPA), including emergency management and homeland security, federal government, general public administration, healthcare policy and ethics (MA, MPA), law, nonprofit administration and faith-based organizations, public leadership and management, servant leadership. *Program availability:* Part-time, evening/weekend, 100% online, blended/hybrid learning. *Faculty:* 8 full-time (1 woman), 19 part-time/ adjunct (3 women). *Students:* 40 full-time (27 women), 119 part-time (69 women); includes 73 minority (47 Black or African American, non-Hispanic/Latino; 3 Asian, non-Hispanic/Latino; 15 Hispanic/Latino; 8 Two or more races, non-Hispanic/Latino), 6 international. Average age 35. 253 applicants, 41% accepted, 70 enrolled. In 2016, 34 master's awarded. *Degree requirements:* For master's, thesis optional, internship. *Entrance requirements:* For master's, GRE General Test or LSAT, personal essay, writing sample, resume, college transcripts. Additional exam requirements/ recommendations for international students: Required—TOEFL (minimum score 577 paper-based). *Application deadline:* For fall admission, 5/1 priority date for domestic students; for spring admission, 11/1 priority date for domestic students. Applications are processed on a rolling basis. Application fee: $50. Electronic applications accepted. *Expenses:* $650 per credit (MA/MPA); $250 per semester technology fee. *Financial support:* In 2016–17, 78 students received support. Career-related internships or fieldwork, scholarships/grants, and unspecified assistantships available. Support available to part-time students. *Faculty research:* International relations and politics, public administration, leadership and ethics, Biblical law, Constitutional law and Supreme Court. *Unit head:* Dr. Eric Patterson, Dean, 757-352-4616, Fax: 757-352-4735, E-mail: epatterson@regent.edu. *Application contact:* Heidi Cece, Assistant Vice President of Enrollment Management, 800-373-5504, Fax: 757-352-4381, E-mail: admissions@regent.edu.
Website: http://www.regent.edu/rsg/

**Regent University,** Graduate School, School of Law, Virginia Beach, VA 23464-9800. Offers American legal studies (LL M); human rights (LL M); law (MA, JD), including business (MA), criminal justice (MA), general legal studies (MA), human resources management (MA), human rights (MA), mediation (MA), national security (MA), non-profit management (MA), regulatory compliance (MA), wealth management and financial planning (MA); JD/MA; JD/MBA. *Accreditation:* ABA. *Program availability:* Part-time, 100% online, blended/hybrid learning. *Faculty:* 20 full-time (6 women), 67 part-time/ adjunct (19 women). *Students:* 364 full-time (219 women), 170 part-time (118 women); includes 213 minority (150 Black or African American, non-Hispanic/Latino; 1 American Indian or Alaska Native, non-Hispanic/Latino; 10 Asian, non-Hispanic/Latino; 34 Hispanic/Latino; 1 Native Hawaiian or other Pacific Islander, non-Hispanic/Latino; 17 Two or more races, non-Hispanic/Latino), 87 international. Average age 34. 834 applicants, 45% accepted, 174 enrolled. In 2016, 48 master's, 85 doctorates awarded. *Entrance requirements:* For master's, college transcripts, resume, personal statement; for doctorate, LSAT, minimum undergraduate GPA of 3.0, official transcripts, 2 letters of recommendation, resume, personal statement. Additional exam requirements/ recommendations for international students: Required—TOEFL (minimum score 600 paper-based). *Application deadline:* For fall admission, 3/1 for domestic students.

Applications are processed on a rolling basis. Application fee: $50. Electronic applications accepted. *Expenses:* $1,140 per credit (for JD); $650 per credit (for MA); $833 per credit (for LL M); $250 technology fee. *Financial support:* In 2016–17, 319 students received support. Career-related internships or fieldwork, scholarships/grants, and unspecified assistantships available. Support available to part-time students. *Faculty research:* Family law, Constitutional law, law and culture, evidence and practice, intellectual property. *Unit head:* Michael Hernandez, Dean, 757-352-4040, Fax: 757-352-4595, E-mail: michher@regent.edu. *Application contact:* Katie Kerley, Director of Law Admissions, 877-267-5072, Fax: 757-352-4139, E-mail: lawschool@regent.edu.
Website: http://www.regent.edu/law/

**Texas A&M University,** Bush School of Government and Public Service, College Station, TX 77840. Offers homeland security (Certificate); international affairs (MIA, Certificate); national security affairs (Certificate); non-profit management (Certificate); public service and administration (MPSA). *Accreditation:* NASPAA. *Faculty:* 68. *Students:* 324 full-time (165 women), 26 part-time (10 women); includes 89 minority (19 Black or African American, non-Hispanic/Latino; 4 Asian, non-Hispanic/Latino; 58 Hispanic/Latino; 1 Native Hawaiian or other Pacific Islander, non-Hispanic/Latino; 7 Two or more races, non-Hispanic/Latino), 44 international. Average age 27. 261 applicants, 96% accepted, 165 enrolled. In 2016, 164 master's awarded. *Degree requirements:* For master's, summer internship. *Entrance requirements:* For master's, GRE (preferred) or GMAT. Additional exam requirements/recommendations for international students: Required—TOEFL (minimum score 550 paper-based; 80 iBT), IELTS (minimum score 6), PTE (minimum score 53). *Application deadline:* For fall admission, 1/15 for domestic and international students. Application fee: $50 ($90 for international students). Electronic applications accepted. *Expenses:* Contact institution. *Financial support:* In 2016–17, 413 students received support, including 16 fellowships with tuition reimbursements available (averaging $18,236 per year), 61 research assistantships with tuition reimbursements available (averaging $5,904 per year), 1 teaching assistantship (averaging $4,025 per year); career-related internships or fieldwork, institutionally sponsored loans, scholarships/grants, traineeships, health care benefits, tuition waivers (full and partial), and unspecified assistantships also available. Support available to part-time students. Financial award application deadline: 3/15; financial award applicants required to submit FAFSA. *Faculty research:* Public policy, Presidential studies, public leadership, economic policy, social policy. *Unit head:* Dr. Mark Welsh, Dean, 979-862-8007, E-mail: mwelsh@tamu.edu. *Application contact:* Kathryn Meyer, Director of Recruitment and Admissions, 979-458-4767, Fax: 979-845-4155, E-mail: bushschooladmissions@tamu.edu.
Website: http://bush.tamu.edu/

**Trinity Washington University,** School of Business and Graduate Studies, Washington, DC 20017-1094. Offers business administration (MBA); communication (MA); international security studies (MA); organizational management (MSA), including federal program management, human resource management, nonprofit management, organizational development, public and community health. *Program availability:* Part-time, evening/weekend. *Degree requirements:* For master's, thesis (for some programs), capstone project (MSA). *Entrance requirements:* For master's, minimum GPA of 2.5. Additional exam requirements/recommendations for international students: Required— TOEFL (minimum score 550 paper-based).

**University of Central Florida,** College of Sciences, Department of Political Science, Orlando, FL 32816. Offers intelligence and national security (Certificate); political science (MA); security studies (PhD). *Program availability:* Part-time, evening/weekend. *Faculty:* 39 full-time (12 women), 11 part-time/adjunct (2 women). *Students:* 38 full-time (11 women), 19 part-time (9 women); includes 16 minority (4 Black or African American, non-Hispanic/Latino; 2 Asian, non-Hispanic/Latino; 8 Hispanic/Latino; 2 Two or more races, non-Hispanic/Latino), 11 international. Average age 31. 44 applicants, 68% accepted, 18 enrolled. In 2016, 14 master's, 1 other advanced degree awarded. *Degree requirements:* For master's, comprehensive exam, thesis; for doctorate, one foreign language, thesis/dissertation, oral qualifying examination, written candidacy exam. *Entrance requirements:* For master's, GRE General Test, minimum GPA of 3.0 in last 60 hours; for doctorate, GRE General Test, master's degree or its equivalent in political science, international politics, international relations, or related discipline. Additional exam requirements/recommendations for international students: Required—TOEFL. *Application deadline:* For fall admission, 7/15 for domestic students; for spring admission, 12/1 for domestic students. Application fee: $30. Electronic applications accepted. *Expenses:* Tuition, state resident: part-time $288.16 per credit hour. Tuition, nonresident: part-time $1071.31 per credit hour. *Financial support:* In 2016–17, 21 students received support, including 6 fellowships with partial tuition reimbursements available (averaging $5,667 per year), 3 research assistantships with partial tuition reimbursements available (averaging $18,661 per year), 16 teaching assistantships with partial tuition reimbursements available (averaging $11,617 per year); career-related internships or fieldwork, Federal Work-Study, institutionally sponsored loans, tuition waivers (partial), and unspecified assistantships also available. Financial award application deadline: 3/1; financial award applicants required to submit FAFSA. *Faculty research:* Environment, international relations, security studies, comparative politics. *Unit head:* Dr. Kerstin Hamann, Chair, 407-823-2085, Fax: 407-823-0051, E-mail: kerstin.hamann@ucf.edu. *Application contact:* Assistant Director, Graduate Admissions, 407-823-2766, Fax: 407-823-6442, E-mail: gradadmissions@ucf.edu.
Website: http://politicalscience.cos.ucf.edu/

**University of Nebraska at Omaha,** Graduate Studies, College of Arts and Sciences, Department of Political Science, Omaha, NE 68182. Offers American government (Certificate); global information operations (Certificate); intelligence and national security (Certificate); political science (MS). *Program availability:* Part-time, evening/weekend, online learning. *Faculty:* 7 full-time (3 women). *Students:* 8 full-time (4 women), 58 part-time (19 women); includes 9 minority (4 Black or African American, non-Hispanic/Latino; 1 Asian, non-Hispanic/Latino; 2 Hispanic/Latino; 2 Two or more races, non-Hispanic/ Latino), 1 international. Average age 34. 53 applicants, 74% accepted, 25 enrolled. In 2016, 30 master's awarded. *Degree requirements:* For master's, comprehensive exam, thesis (for some programs). *Entrance requirements:* For master's, 15 undergraduate political science hours, minimum undergraduate GPA of 3.0, 2 letters of recommendation, official transcripts. Additional exam requirements/recommendations for international students: Required—TOEFL, IELTS, PTE. *Application deadline:* For fall admission, 7/15 priority date for domestic and international students; for spring admission, 11/15 priority date for domestic and international students; for summer admission, 4/15 for domestic and international students. Applications are processed on a rolling basis. Application fee: $45. Electronic applications accepted. *Financial support:* In 2016–17, 5 students received support, including 2 research assistantships with tuition reimbursements available, 3 teaching assistantships with tuition reimbursements available; fellowships, Federal Work-Study, scholarships/grants, health care benefits, tuition waivers (partial), and unspecified assistantships also available. Financial award application deadline: 3/1; financial award applicants required to submit FAFSA. *Unit head:* Dr. Jody Neathery-Castro, Chairperson, 402-554-2341, E-mail: graduate@unomaha.edu. *Application contact:* Dr. Gregory Petrow, Graduate Program Chair, 402-554-2341, E-mail: graduate@unomaha.edu.

**University of New Haven,** Graduate School, Henry C. Lee College of Criminal Justice and Forensic Sciences, Program in National Security, West Haven, CT 06516. Offers information protection and security (MS); national security (MS, Graduate Certificate); national security administration (Graduate Certificate). *Program availability:* Part-time, evening/weekend. *Students:* 43 full-time (20 women), 34 part-time (13 women); includes 19 minority (6 Black or African American, non-Hispanic/Latino; 1 Asian, non-Hispanic/Latino; 9 Hispanic/Latino; 3 Two or more races, non-Hispanic/Latino), 6 international. Average age 31. 41 applicants, 98% accepted, 27 enrolled. In 2016, 27 master's, 2 other advanced degrees awarded. *Degree requirements:* For master's, thesis or alternative, research project or internship. *Entrance requirements:* Additional exam requirements/recommendations for international students: Required—TOEFL (minimum score 70 iBT), IELTS, or PTE (minimum score of 53). *Application deadline:* Applications are processed on a rolling basis. Application fee: $50. Electronic applications accepted. Application fee is waived when completed online. *Expenses: Tuition:* Full-time $15,660; part-time $870 per credit hour. *Required fees:* $200; $85 per term. Tuition and fees vary according to program. *Financial support:* Research assistantships with partial tuition reimbursements, teaching assistantships with partial tuition reimbursements, career-related internships or fieldwork, Federal Work-Study, scholarships/grants, and unspecified assistantships available. Support available to part-time students. Financial award applicants required to submit FAFSA. *Unit head:* Dr. Jibey Asthappan, Director, 203-479-4147, E-mail: jasthappan@newhaven.edu. *Application contact:* Michelle Mason, Director of Graduate Enrollment, 203-932-7067, E-mail: mmason@newhaven.edu.
Website: http://www.newhaven.edu/5924/

**Virginia Polytechnic Institute and State University,** VT Online, Blacksburg, VA 24061. Offers advanced transportation systems (Certificate); aerospace engineering (MS); agricultural and life sciences (MSLFS); business information systems (Graduate Certificate); career and technical education (MS); civil engineering (MS); computer engineering (M Eng, MS); decision support systems (Graduate Certificate); eLearning leadership (MA); electrical engineering (M Eng, MS); engineering administration (MEA); environmental engineering (Certificate); environmental politics and policy (Graduate Certificate); environmental sciences and engineering (MS); foundations of political analysis (Graduate Certificate); health product risk management (Graduate Certificate); industrial and systems engineering (MS); information policy and society (Graduate Certificate); information security (Graduate Certificate); information technology (MIT); instructional technology (MA); integrative STEM education (MA Ed); liberal arts (Graduate Certificate); life sciences: health product risk management (MS); natural resources (MNR, Graduate Certificate); networking (Graduate Certificate); nonprofit and nongovernmental organization management (Graduate Certificate); ocean engineering (MS); political science (MA); security studies (Graduate Certificate); software development (Graduate Certificate). *Expenses:* Tuition, state resident: full-time $12,467; part-time $692.50 per credit hour. Tuition, nonresident: full-time $25,095; part-time $1394.25 per credit hour. *Required fees:* $2669; $491.50 per semester. Tuition and fees vary according to course load, campus/location and program.

**Western Michigan University Thomas M. Cooley Law School,** Graduate Programs, Lansing, MI 48901-3038. Offers administrative law (public law) (JD); business transactions (JD); Canadian law practice (JD); constitutional law/civil rights (public law) (JD); corporate law and finance (LL M); environmental law (public law) (JD); general practice (JD), including solo and small firm; homeland and national security law (LL M); insurance law (LL M); intellectual property (JD); intellectual property law (LL M); international law (JD); litigation (JD); self-directed (LL M, JD); tax law (LL M); taxation (JD); U.S. legal studies for foreign attorneys (LL M); JD/LL M; JD/MBA; JD/MPA; JD/MSW. *Program availability:* Part-time, evening/weekend, 100% online, blended/hybrid learning. *Degree requirements:* For master's, thesis optional; for doctorate, minimum of 3 credits of clinical experience. *Entrance requirements:* For master's, JD or LL B; for doctorate, LSAT. Additional exam requirements/recommendations for international students: Required—TOEFL (for U.S. legal studies for foreign attorneys LL M program); Recommended—TOEFL. Electronic applications accepted. *Faculty research:* Wrongful convictions, civil rights, environmental law, litigation techniques, data mining, intellectual property, practical and skills-based legal education.

# Section 23
# Political Science and International Affairs

This section contains a directory of institutions offering graduate work in political science and international affairs. Additional information about programs listed in the directory but not augmented by an in-depth entry may be obtained by writing directly to the dean of a graduate school or chair of a department at the address given in the directory.

For programs offering related work, see also in this book *Area and Cultural Studies, History, Language and Literature,* and *Public, Regional, and Industrial Affairs.* In another guide in this series:
**Graduate Programs in Business, Education, Information Studies, Law & Social Work**
See *International Business*

## CONTENTS

### Program Directories

### Displays and Close-Ups

# International Affairs

**American Graduate School in Paris,** Program in International Relations and Diplomacy, Paris, France. Offers MA, PhD.

**American Public University System,** AMU/APU Graduate Programs, Charles Town, WV 25414. Offers accounting (MBA, MS); applied business analytics (MBA, MS); criminal justice (MA), including business administration, emergency and disaster management, general (MA, MS); educational leadership (M Ed); emergency and disaster management (MA); entrepreneurship (MBA); environmental policy and management (MS), including environmental planning, environmental sustainability, fish and wildlife management, general (MA, MS), global environmental management; finance (MBA); general (MBA); government contracting and acquisition (MBA); health care administration (MBA); health information management (MS); history (MA), including American history, ancient and classical history, European history, global history, public history; homeland security (MA), including business administration, counterterrorism studies, criminal justice, cyber, emergency management and public health, intelligence studies, transportation security; homeland security resource allocation (MBA); humanities (MA); information technology (MS), including digital forensics, enterprise software development, information assurance and security, IT project management; information technology management (MBA); intelligence studies (MA), including criminal intelligence, cyber, general (MA, MS), homeland security, intelligence analysis, intelligence collection, intelligence management, intelligence operations, terrorism studies; international relations and conflict resolution (MA), including comparative and security issues, conflict resolution, international and transnational security issues, peacekeeping; legal studies (MA); management (MA), including strategic consulting; marketing (MBA); military history (MA), including American military history, American Revolution, civil war, war since 1945, World War II; military studies (MA), including joint warfare, strategic leadership; national security studies (MA), including cyber, general (MA, MS), homeland security, regional security studies, security and intelligence analysis, terrorism studies; nonprofit management (MBA); political science (MA), including American politics and government, comparative government and development, general (MA, MS), international relations, public policy; psychology (MA); public administration (MPA), including disaster management, environmental policy, health policy, human resources, national security, organizational management, security management; public health (MPH); reverse logistics management (MA); security management (MA); space studies (MS), including aerospace science, general (MA, MS), planetary science; sports and health sciences (MS); sports management (MBA); teaching (M Ed), including autism spectrum disorder, curriculum and instruction for elementary teachers, elementary reading, English language learners, instructional leadership, online learning, special education, STEAM (STEM plus the arts); transportation and logistics management (MA). *Program availability:* Part-time, evening/weekend, online only, 100% online. *Faculty:* 401 full-time (228 women), 1,678 part-time/adjunct (781 women). *Students:* 378 full-time (184 women), 8,455 part-time (3,484 women); includes 2,972 minority (1,552 Black or African American, non-Hispanic/Latino; 52 American Indian or Alaska Native, non-Hispanic/Latino; 211 Asian, non-Hispanic/Latino; 791 Hispanic/Latino; 70 Native Hawaiian or other Pacific Islander, non-Hispanic/Latino; 296 Two or more races, non-Hispanic/Latino), 109 international. Average age 37. In 2016, 3,185 master's awarded. *Degree requirements:* For master's, comprehensive exam or practicum. *Entrance requirements:* For master's, official transcript showing earned bachelor's degree from institution accredited by recognized accrediting body. Additional exam requirements/recommendations for international students: Required—TOEFL (minimum score 550 paper-based), IELTS (minimum score 6.5). *Application deadline:* Applications are processed on a rolling basis. Application fee: $0. Electronic applications accepted. *Expenses: Tuition:* Part-time $350 per credit hour. *Required fees:* $50 per course. *Financial support:* Scholarships/grants available. Financial award applicants required to submit FAFSA. *Unit head:* Dr. Karan Powell, President, 877-468-6268, Fax: 304-724-3780. *Application contact:* Terry Grant, Vice President of Enrollment Management, 877-468-6268, Fax: 304-724-3780, E-mail: info@apus.edu. Website: http://www.apus.edu

**American University,** School of International Service, Washington, DC 20016-8071. Offers comparative and regional studies (Certificate); cross-cultural communication (Certificate); development management (MS); ethics, peace, and global affairs (MA); European studies (Certificate); global environmental policy (MA, Certificate); global information technology (Certificate); international affairs (MA), including comparative and international disability policy, comparative and regional studies, international economic relations, international politics, natural resources and sustainable development, U.S. foreign policy; international arts management (Certificate); international communication (MA, Certificate); international development (MA); international economic policy (Certificate); international economic relations (Certificate); international economics (MA); international media (MA); international peace and conflict resolution (MA, Certificate); international politics (Certificate); international relations (MA, PhD); international service (MIS); peacebuilding (Certificate); social enterprise (MA); the Americas (Certificate); United States foreign policy (Certificate); JD/MA. *Program availability:* Part-time, evening/weekend, 100% online. *Faculty:* 116 full-time (53 women), 57 part-time/adjunct (19 women). *Students:* 575 full-time (360 women), 491 part-time (277 women); includes 287 minority (100 Black or African American, non-Hispanic/Latino; 6 American Indian or Alaska Native, non-Hispanic/Latino; 58 Asian, non-Hispanic/Latino; 92 Hispanic/Latino; 1 Native Hawaiian or other Pacific Islander, non-Hispanic/Latino; 30 Two or more races, non-Hispanic/Latino), 151 international. Average age 29. 1,504 applicants, 84% accepted, 403 enrolled. In 2016, 374 master's, 3 doctorates, 1 other advanced degree awarded. Terminal master's awarded for partial completion of doctoral program. *Degree requirements:* For master's, one foreign language, comprehensive exam, thesis or alternative; for doctorate, one foreign language, comprehensive exam, thesis/dissertation. *Entrance requirements:* For master's, GRE, GMAT or GRE (for MA in social enterprise), transcripts, resume, 2 letters of recommendation, statement of purpose; for doctorate, GRE, transcripts, resume, 3 letters of recommendation, statement of purpose. Additional exam requirements/recommendations for international students: Required—TOEFL (minimum score 600 paper-based, 100 iBT), IELTS (minimum score 7 ), or PTE (minimum score of 68). Application fee: $55. Electronic applications accepted. *Expenses:* $1,579 per credit tuition; $1,930 mandatory fees. *Financial support:* Research assistantships, teaching assistantships, institutionally sponsored loans, scholarships/grants, and unspecified assistantships available. Financial award application deadline: 1/15; financial award applicants required to submit FAFSA. *Unit head:* Dr. James Goldgeier, Dean, 202-885-1603, Fax: 202-885-2494, E-mail: goldgeier@american.edu. *Application contact:* Jia Jiang, Associate Director, Graduate Education Enrollment, 202-885-1689, Fax: 202-885-1109, E-mail: jiang@american.edu. Website: http://www.american.edu/sis/

**American University of Armenia,** Graduate Programs, Yerevan, Armenia. Offers business administration (MBA); computer and information science (MS), including business management, design and manufacturing, energy (ME, MS), industrial engineering and systems management; economics (MS); industrial engineering and systems management (ME), including business, computer aided design/manufacturing, energy (ME, MS), information technology; law (LL M); political science and international affairs (MPSIA); public health (MPH); teaching English as a foreign language (MA). *Program availability:* Part-time, evening/weekend. *Degree requirements:* For master's, thesis (for some programs), capstone/project. *Entrance requirements:* For master's, GRE, GMAT, or LSAT. Additional exam requirements/recommendations for international students: Recommended—TOEFL (minimum score 79 iBT), IELTS (minimum score 6.5). *Faculty research:* Microfinance, finance (rural/development, international, corporate), firm life cycle theory, TESOL, language proficiency testing, public policy, administrative law, economic development, cryptography, artificial intelligence, energy efficiency/renewable energy, computer-aided design/manufacturing, health financing, tuberculosis control, mother/child health, preventive ophthalmology, post-earthquake psychopathological investigations, tobacco control, environmental health risk assessments.

**American University of Beirut,** Graduate Programs, Faculty of Arts and Sciences, Beirut, Lebanon. Offers anthropology (MA); Arab and Middle Eastern history (PhD); Arabic language and literature (MA, PhD); archaeology (MA); art history and curating (MA); biology (MS); cell and molecular biology (PhD); chemistry (MS); clinical psychology (MA); computational sciences (MS); computer science (MS); economics (MA); education (MA); English language (MA); English literature (MA); environmental policy planning (MS); financial economics (MAFE); geology (MS); history (MA); Islamic studies (MA); mathematics (MA); media studies (MA); Middle Eastern studies (MA); physics (MS); political studies (MA); psychology (MA); public administration (MA); public policy and international affairs (MA); sociology (MA); statistics (MA, MS); theoretical physics (PhD); transnational American studies (MA). *Program availability:* Part-time. *Faculty:* 133 full-time (42 women), 6 part-time/adjunct (2 women). *Students:* 240 full-time (172 women), 227 part-time (166 women). Average age 27. 286 applicants, 67% accepted, 108 enrolled. In 2016, 60 master's, 3 doctorates awarded. Terminal master's awarded for partial completion of doctoral program. *Degree requirements:* For master's, one foreign language, comprehensive exam, thesis (for some programs); for doctorate, one foreign language, comprehensive exam, thesis/dissertation. *Entrance requirements:* For master's, GRE (for some MA, MS programs), letters of recommendation; for doctorate, GRE, letters of recommendation. Additional exam requirements/recommendations for international students: Required—TOEFL (minimum score 600 paper-based; 97 iBT), IELTS (minimum score 7). *Application deadline:* For fall admission, 4/3 for domestic students; for winter admission, 11/3 for domestic students. Application fee: $50. Electronic applications accepted. *Expenses:* Contact institution. *Financial support:* In 2016–17, 4 fellowships (averaging $11,200 per year), 18 research assistantships (averaging $5,400 per year) were awarded; teaching assistantships, career-related internships or fieldwork, Federal Work-Study, institutionally sponsored loans, scholarships/grants, traineeships, health care benefits, tuition waivers (full), and unspecified assistantships also available. Support available to part-time students. *Faculty research:* Development economics, spatial econometrics, health economics, labor economics, energy economics, hydrogeology, geophysics, petrophysics, structural geology, mineralogy, petrology, geochemistry, multilingualism, comparative/world literature, translation studies, book histories/ cultures, biocatalysis, molecular recognition, photocatalysis, photophysical and biophysical chemistry, probe chemistry, machine learning, data science. *Unit head:* Dr. Nadia Maria El Cheikh, Dean, Faculty of Arts and Sciences, 961-1374374 Ext. 3800, Fax: 961-1744461, E-mail: nmcheikh@aub.edu.lb. *Application contact:* Dr. Salim Kanaan, Director, Admissions Office, 961-1350000 Ext. 2590, Fax: 961-1750775, E-mail: sk00@aub.edu.lb. Website: http://www.aub.edu.lb/fas/

**The American University of Paris,** Graduate Programs, Paris, France. Offers cross-cultural and sustainable business management (MA); cultural translation (MA); global communications (MA); global communications and civil society (MA); international affairs (MA); international affairs, conflict resolution and civil society development (MA); Middle East and Islamic studies (MA); Middle East and Islamic studies and international affairs (MA); public policy and international affairs (MA); public policy and international law (MA). *Degree requirements:* For master's, thesis (for some programs). *Entrance requirements:* For master's, minimum undergraduate GPA of 3.0. Additional exam requirements/recommendations for international students: Recommended—TOEFL, IELTS. Electronic applications accepted.

**Anabaptist Mennonite Biblical Seminary,** Graduate and Professional Programs, Elkhart, IN 46517-1999. Offers chaplaincy (M Div); Christian faith formation (M Div); Christian formation (MA); Christian spiritual formation (Certificate); divinity (M Div); pastoral ministry (M Div); pastoral theology for financial professionals (Certificate); peace studies (M Div), including environmental sustainability leadership (M Div, MA); theological studies (M Div, Certificate), including peace studies (M Div), theology and ethics (M Div); theology and peace studies (MA), including conflict transformation, environmental sustainability leadership (M Div, MA), international development administration; United Methodist leadership (M Div). Conflict transformation and environmental sustainability leadership concentrations offered in cooperation with Goshen College; international development administration offered in cooperation with Andrews University. *Accreditation:* ACIPE; ATS. *Program availability:* Part-time, 100% online, blended/hybrid learning. *Faculty:* 14 full-time (6 women), 17 part-time/adjunct (8 women). *Students:* 38 full-time (14 women), 60 part-time (33 women); includes 15 minority (4 Black or African American, non-Hispanic/Latino; 5 Asian, non-Hispanic/Latino; 5 Hispanic/Latino; 1 Two or more races, non-Hispanic/Latino), 15 international. Average age 35. 43 applicants, 70% accepted, 29 enrolled. In 2016, 16 master's, 2 other advanced degrees awarded. *Degree requirements:* For master's, variable foreign language requirement, comprehensive exam (for some programs), thesis optional, senior interview. *Entrance requirements:* For master's, undergraduate degree transcripts, 3 letters of reference, essay. Additional exam requirements/recommendations for international students: Required—TOEFL (minimum score 90 iBT); Recommended—IELTS (minimum score 7). *Application deadline:* For fall admission, 6/1 priority date for domestic students, 5/1 priority date for international students. Applications are processed on a rolling basis. Application fee: $25. Electronic applications accepted. *Expenses: Tuition:* Full-time $13,950; part-time $5640 per year. *Required fees:* $900; $300 per unit. $50 per term. *Financial support:* In 2016–17, 40 students received support. Career-related internships or fieldwork, scholarships/grants, unspecified assistantships, and church matching grants available. Support available to part-time students. Financial award application deadline: 4/15; financial award applicants required to submit FAFSA. *Faculty research:* Biblical studies, peace studies,

theology, ethics, creation care or environmental ethics, church history, church leadership, mission, ministry, preaching, pastoral leadership, social justice, peacemaking, Jesus Christ, Christianity, Anabaptism, Mennonite, Scripture, Bible, Old Testament, New Testament, spirituality, clinical pastoral education, teaching, faith formation, pastoral care, Koine Greek, Hebrew, Aramaic, Syriac, Ugaritic. *Unit head:* Sara Wenger Shenk, President, 800-964-2627, Fax: 574-295-0092. *Application contact:* Daniel Grimes, Director of Admissions, 574-296-6266, Fax: 574-295-0092, E-mail: admissions@ambs.edu.
Website: http://www.ambs.edu/

**Arcadia University,** College of Arts and Sciences, Program in International Public Relations, Glenside, PA 19038-3295. Offers MA. *Students:* 4 full-time (2 women), 5 part-time (3 women); includes 2 minority (1 Black or African American, non-Hispanic/Latino; 1 Asian, non-Hispanic/Latino), 5 international. Average age 29. In 2016, 5 master's awarded. *Degree requirements:* For master's, thesis, internship. *Expenses:* Contact institution. *Application contact:* Office of Enrollment Management, 215-572-2910, Fax: 215-572-4049, E-mail: admiss@arcadia.edu.

**Auburn University at Montgomery,** College of Public Policy and Justice, Department of Political Science and Public Administration, Montgomery, AL 36124-4023. Offers international relations (MIR); nonprofit management and leadership (Certificate); political science (MPS); public administration (MPA); public administration and public policy (PhD); public health care administration and policy (Certificate). PhD offered jointly with Auburn University. *Accreditation:* NASPAA (one or more programs are accredited). *Program availability:* Part-time, evening/weekend. *Degree requirements:* For master's, comprehensive exam; for doctorate, thesis/dissertation. *Entrance requirements:* For master's, GRE General Test or MAT; for doctorate, GRE General Test. Electronic applications accepted.

**Azusa Pacific University,** School of Behavioral and Applied Sciences, Department of Leadership and Organizational Psychology, Azusa, CA 91702-7000. Offers college student affairs (M Ed); global leadership (MA); organizational leadership (MA).

⭐ **Baruch College of the City University of New York,** Austin W. Marxe School of Public and International Affairs, Program in International Affairs, New York, NY 10010-5585. Offers international nongovernmental organizations (MIA); trade policy and global economic governance (MIA); Western Hemisphere affairs (MIA). *Program availability:* Part-time.
**See Display on this page and Close-Up on page 977.**

**Baylor University,** Graduate School, College of Arts and Sciences, Department of Political Science, Waco, TX 76798. Offers international studies (MA); political science (MA, PhD); public policy and administration (MPPA); JD/MPPA. *Faculty:* 18 full-time (3 women), 1 part-time/adjunct (0 women). *Students:* 29 full-time (11 women), 2 part-time (both women); includes 3 minority (all Hispanic/Latino), 2 international. Average age 26. 27 applicants, 22% accepted, 4 enrolled. In 2016, 6 master's, 2 doctorates awarded. Terminal master's awarded for partial completion of doctoral program. *Degree requirements:* For master's, variable foreign language requirement, comprehensive exam (for some programs), thesis (for some programs); for doctorate, variable foreign language requirement, comprehensive exam, thesis/dissertation. *Entrance requirements:* For master's and doctorate, GRE General Test. Additional exam requirements/recommendations for international students: Required—TOEFL. *Application deadline:* For fall admission, 12/20 for domestic and international students. Application fee: $25. Electronic applications accepted. *Expenses: Tuition:* Full-time $28,494; part-time $1583 per credit hour. *Required fees:* $167 per credit hour. Tuition and fees vary according to course load and program. *Financial support:* In 2016–17, 17 students received support, including 17 research assistantships with full tuition reimbursements available (averaging $16,000 per year); career-related internships or fieldwork, Federal Work-Study, and institutionally sponsored loans also available. Financial award application deadline: 12/20; financial award applicants required to submit FAFSA. *Unit head:* Dr. Timothy Burns, Graduate Program Director, 254-710-6237, Fax: 254-710-3122, E-mail: timothy_burns@baylor.edu. *Application contact:* Jenice Langston, Office Manager, 254-710-3161, Fax: 254-710-3122, E-mail: jenice_langston@baylor.edu.
Website: http://www.baylor.edu/political_science/

**Baylor University,** Graduate School, Hankamer School of Business, Department of Economics, Waco, TX 76798. Offers MS Eco. *Faculty:* 15 full-time (2 women). *Students:* 14 full-time (6 women), 1 part-time (0 women); includes 2 minority (both Asian, non-Hispanic/Latino), 7 international. In 2016, 5 master's awarded. *Entrance requirements:* For master's, GMAT or GRE General Test. Additional exam requirements/recommendations for international students: Required—TOEFL (minimum score 600 paper-based; 100 iBT), IELTS (minimum score 7). *Application deadline:* For fall admission, 6/15 for domestic and international students. Application fee: $25. Electronic applications accepted. *Expenses: Tuition:* Full-time $28,494; part-time $1583 per credit hour. *Required fees:* $167 per credit hour. Tuition and fees vary according to course load and program. *Financial support:* In 2016–17, 12 students received support. Research assistantships, Federal Work-Study, and institutionally sponsored loans available. Financial award application deadline: 3/1. *Faculty research:* Econometrics, international economics, economic development, comparative economic systems, computational economics, health economics, economics of education, monetary economics, labor economics, experimental economics. *Unit head:* Dr. Van Pham, Graduate Program Director, 254-710-3521, Fax: 254-710-6142, E-mail: van_pham@baylor.edu. *Application contact:* Susan Armstrong, Office Manager, 254-710-6177, Fax: 254-710-6142, E-mail: susan_armstrong@baylor.edu.
Website: http://www.baylor.edu/business/economics/

⭐ **Boston University,** Graduate School of Arts and Sciences, Frederick S. Pardee School of Global Studies, Boston, MA 02215. Offers MA, MA/JD, MBA/MA. *Faculty:* 33 full-time (8 women), 10 part-time/adjunct (4 women). *Students:* 83 full-time (46 women), 18 part-time (11 women); includes 15 minority (5 Black or African American, non-Hispanic/Latino; 4 Asian, non-Hispanic/Latino; 5 Hispanic/Latino; 1 Two or more races, non-Hispanic/Latino), 37 international. Average age 26. 360 applicants, 73% accepted, 35 enrolled. In 2016, 35 master's awarded. *Degree requirements:* For master's, one foreign language, thesis (for some programs), capstone. *Entrance requirements:* For master's, GRE General Test, 3 letters of recommendation, transcript of all prior college coursework, personal statement, resume or curriculum vitae (recommended). Additional exam requirements/recommendations for international students: Required—TOEFL (minimum score 550 paper-based; 84 iBT). *Application deadline:* For fall admission, 4/15 for domestic and international students; for spring admission, 10/15 for domestic and international students. Applications are processed on a rolling basis. Application fee: $95. Electronic applications accepted. *Financial support:* In 2016–17, 30 students received support. Federal Work-Study, scholarships/grants, and unspecified assistantships available. Financial award application deadline: 1/15. *Faculty research:* International relations, area studies, political economy, global development policy, global climate. *Unit head:* Adil Najam, Dean, 617-358-0988, Fax: 617-353-9290, E-mail: anajam@bu.edu. *Application contact:* Michael Williams, Graduate Program Administrator, 617-353-9349,

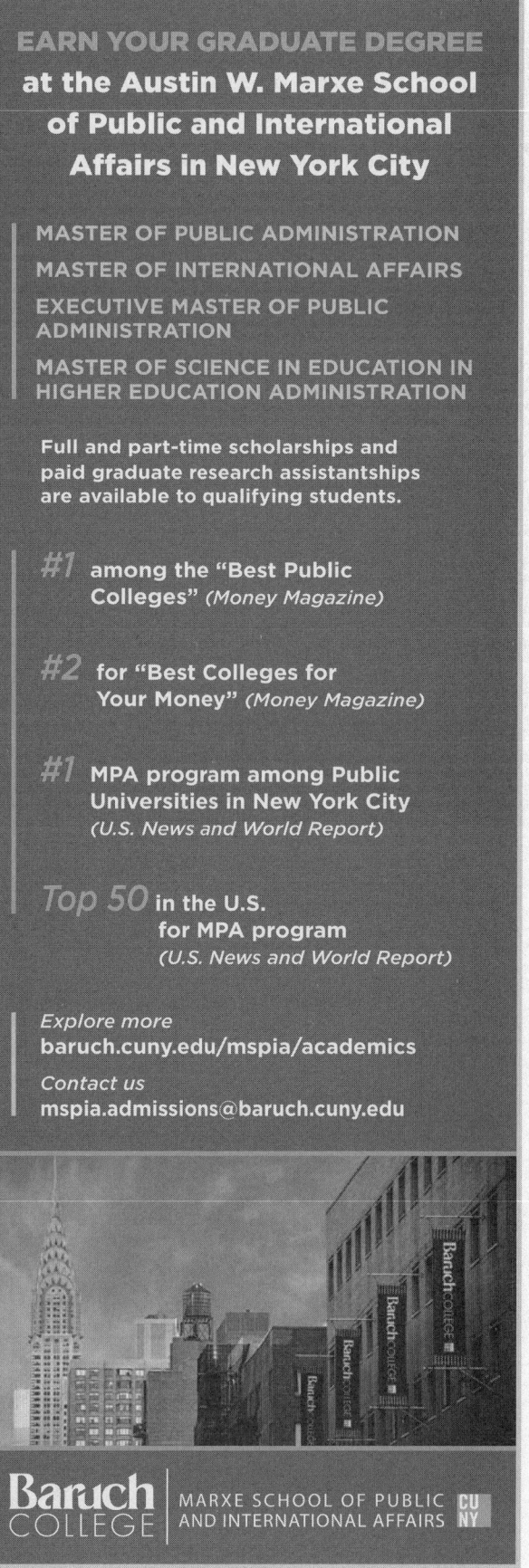

## International Affairs

Fax: 617-353-9290, E-mail: psgsgrad@bu.edu.
Website: http://www.bu.edu/PardeeSchool

**See Display below and Close-Up on page 979.**

**Brandeis University,** Graduate School of Arts and Sciences, Graduate Program in Global Studies, Waltham, MA 02454-9110. Offers MA. *Program availability:* Part-time. *Faculty:* 12 full-time (4 women), 2 part-time/adjunct (both women). *Students:* 12 full-time (8 women), 2 part-time (both women); includes 1 minority (Two or more races, non-Hispanic/Latino), 6 international. 29 applicants, 86% accepted, 12 enrolled. In 2016, 5 master's awarded. *Degree requirements:* For master's, one foreign language, thesis. *Entrance requirements:* For master's, GRE, official transcript(s), 2 recommendation letters, curriculum vitae or resume, statement of purpose, writing sample. Additional exam requirements/recommendations for international students: Required—TOEFL (minimum score 600 paper-based; 100 iBT); Recommended—IELTS (minimum score 7), TSE (minimum score 68). *Application deadline:* For fall admission, 5/1 for domestic students. Application fee: $75. Electronic applications accepted. *Financial support:* In 2016–17, 12 students received support, including 6 teaching assistantships with partial tuition reimbursements available (averaging $3,200 per year); Federal Work-Study, scholarships/grants, and tuition waivers (partial) also available. Support available to part-time students. Financial award application deadline: 4/15; financial award applicants required to submit FAFSA. *Faculty research:* Globalization; global service: preparing for work with non-profits; emerging powers; transnational security and migration. *Unit head:* Prof. Kristen Lucken, Director of Graduate Studies, 781-736-2234, Fax: 781-736-2232, E-mail: klucken@brandeis.edu. *Application contact:* Mangok Bol, Department Administrator, 781-736-2234, Fax: 781-736-2232, E-mail: mbol@brandeis.edu.
Website: http://www.brandeis.edu/gsas

**Brigham Young University,** Graduate Studies, Marriott School of Management, Master of Business Administration Program, Provo, UT 84602. Offers entrepreneurship (MBA); finance (MBA); global supply chain management (MBA); marketing (MBA); strategic human resources (MBA); JD/MBA; MBA/MS. *Accreditation:* AACSB. *Students:* 321 full-time (63 women); includes 16 minority (1 Black or African American, non-Hispanic/Latino; 9 Asian, non-Hispanic/Latino; 6 Hispanic/Latino), 69 international. Average age 31. 397 applicants, 49% accepted, 154 enrolled. In 2016, 146 master's awarded. *Entrance requirements:* For master's, GMAT or GRE, minimum GPA of 3.0 in last 60 hours. Additional exam requirements/recommendations for international students: Required—TOEFL (minimum score 590 paper-based; 94 iBT), IELTS (minimum score 7). *Application deadline:* For fall admission, 5/1 for domestic students, 1/15 for international students. Applications are processed on a rolling basis. Application fee: $50. Electronic applications accepted. *Expenses:* Contact institution. *Financial support:* In 2016–17, 247 students received support. Research assistantships, teaching assistantships, career-related internships or fieldwork, institutionally sponsored loans, and scholarships/grants available. Financial award application deadline: 3/1; financial award applicants required to submit FAFSA. *Faculty research:* Finance, marketing, supply chain management, entrepreneurship, strategic human resources. *Unit head:* Dr. Grant McQueen, Director, 801-422-3500, Fax: 801-422-0513, E-mail: mba@byu.edu. *Application contact:* Yvette Anderson, MBA Program Admissions Director, 801-422-3500, Fax: 801-422-0513, E-mail: mba@byu.edu.
Website: http://mba.byu.edu

**Brock University,** Faculty of Graduate Studies, Faculty of Social Sciences, Program in Political Science, St. Catharines, ON L2S 3A1, Canada. Offers Canadian politics (MA); comparative politics (MA); international relations (MA); political theory or philosophy (MA); public policy (MA). *Program availability:* Part-time. *Degree requirements:* For master's, thesis optional. *Entrance requirements:* For master's, honors degree.

Additional exam requirements/recommendations for international students: Required—TOEFL (minimum score 550 paper-based; 80 iBT), IELTS (minimum score 6.5), TWE (minimum score 4). Electronic applications accepted. *Faculty research:* Public administration reform, economic and social justice, politics of societies, Canadian politics, international relations.

**Brooklyn College of the City University of New York,** School of Humanities and Social Sciences, Department of Political Science, Brooklyn, NY 11210-2889. Offers international affairs (MA); political science (MA); urban policy and administration (MA). *Program availability:* Part-time, evening/weekend. *Degree requirements:* For master's, comprehensive exam (for some programs), thesis or alternative, foreign language exam (for international affairs program). *Entrance requirements:* For master's, 2 letters of recommendation, personal statement. Additional exam requirements/recommendations for international students: Required—TOEFL (minimum score 500 paper-based; 61 iBT). *Faculty research:* Ethics and politics, politics of criminal justice, Western Europe, international law and politics, labor politics.

**California State University, Stanislaus,** College of Humanities and Social Sciences, Program in History (MA), Turlock, CA 95382. Offers history (MA); international relations (MA); secondary school teachers (MA). *Program availability:* Part-time. *Degree requirements:* For master's, comprehensive exam, thesis or alternative. *Entrance requirements:* For master's, GRE, minimum GPA of 3.0, personal statement. Additional exam requirements/recommendations for international students: Required—TOEFL (minimum score 575 paper-based). Electronic applications accepted. *Faculty research:* History of Ancient Greece, history and ecology of the Central Valley, acculturation and gender.

**Carleton University,** Faculty of Graduate Studies, Faculty of Public Affairs and Management, Norman Paterson School of International Affairs, Ottawa, ON K1S 5B6, Canada. Offers MA. *Program availability:* Part-time. *Degree requirements:* For master's, one foreign language, comprehensive exam, thesis optional. *Entrance requirements:* For master's, honors degree. Additional exam requirements/recommendations for international students: Required—TOEFL. *Faculty research:* International conflict, development, political economy, conflict analysis.

**The Catholic University of America,** School of Arts and Sciences, Department of Politics, Washington, DC 20064. Offers American government (MA, PhD); Congressional and Presidential studies (MA); international affairs (MA); international political economics (MA); political theory (MA, PhD); world politics (MA, PhD); MA/JD. MA/JD offered jointly with Law School. *Program availability:* Part-time. *Faculty:* 14 full-time (2 women), 1 (woman) part-time/adjunct. *Students:* 24 full-time (7 women), 44 part-time (11 women); includes 10 minority (3 Black or African American, non-Hispanic/Latino; 2 Asian, non-Hispanic/Latino; 3 Hispanic/Latino; 2 Two or more races, non-Hispanic/Latino), 11 international. Average age 32. 40 applicants, 78% accepted, 13 enrolled. In 2016, 16 master's, 6 doctorates awarded. *Degree requirements:* For master's, one foreign language, comprehensive exam, thesis or alternative; for doctorate, variable foreign language requirement, comprehensive exam, thesis/dissertation. *Entrance requirements:* For master's, GRE General Test, statement of purpose, official copies of academic transcripts, three letters of recommendation, minimum GPA of 3.0; for doctorate, GRE General Test, statement of purpose, official copies of academic transcripts, three letters of recommendation. Additional exam requirements/recommendations for international students: Required—TOEFL (minimum score 550 paper-based; 80 iBT). *Application deadline:* For fall admission, 7/15 priority date for domestic students, 7/1 for international students; for spring admission, 11/15 priority date for domestic students, 11/1 for international students. Applications are processed on a rolling basis. Application fee: $55. Electronic applications accepted. *Expenses:* $42,850 per year; $1,170 per credit; $200 per semester part-time fees.

*Financial support:* Fellowships, research assistantships, teaching assistantships, Federal Work-Study, scholarships/grants, tuition waivers (full and partial), and unspecified assistantships available. Financial award application deadline: 2/1; financial award applicants required to submit FAFSA. *Faculty research:* Political philosophy, American political institutions and processes, political economy, international relations, U.S. political leadership since 1789. *Unit head:* Dr. Dennis Coyle, Chair, 202-319-5813, Fax: 202-319-6289, E-mail: coyle@cua.edu. *Application contact:* Director of Graduate Admissions, 202-319-5057, Fax: 202-319-6533, E-mail: cua-admissions@cua.edu. Website: http://politics.cua.edu/

**Central Connecticut State University,** School of Graduate Studies, College of Liberal Arts and Social Sciences, Program in International Studies, New Britain, CT 06050-4010. Offers MS. *Program availability:* Part-time, evening/weekend. *Faculty:* 3 full-time (0 women). *Students:* 13 full-time (8 women), 13 part-time (6 women); includes 6 minority (4 Black or African American, non-Hispanic/Latino; 2 Hispanic/Latino), 2 international. Average age 33. 17 applicants, 71% accepted, 10 enrolled. In 2016, 3 master's awarded. *Degree requirements:* For master's, thesis or alternative, special project. *Entrance requirements:* For master's, minimum undergraduate GPA of 3.0, essay, resume. Additional exam requirements/recommendations for international students: Required—TOEFL (minimum score 550 paper-based; 79 iBT). *Application deadline:* For fall admission, 5/1 for domestic and international students; for spring admission, 11/1 for domestic and international students. Applications are processed on a rolling basis. Application fee: $50. Electronic applications accepted. *Expenses: Tuition, area resident:* Full-time $6497; part-time $606 per credit. Tuition, state resident: full-time $9748; part-time $622 per credit. Tuition, nonresident: full-time $18,102; part-time $622 per credit. *Required fees:* $4459; $246 per credit. *Financial support:* In 2016–17, 4 students received support. Career-related internships or fieldwork, Federal Work-Study, scholarships/grants, and unspecified assistantships available. Support available to part-time students. Financial award application deadline: 3/1; financial award applicants required to submit FAFSA. *Unit head:* Dr. Paul Petterson, Program Director, 860-832-2969, E-mail: pettersonp@ccsu.edu. *Application contact:* Patricia Gardner, Associate Director of Graduate Studies, 860-832-2350, Fax: 860-832-2362. Website: http://www.ccsu.edu/internationalstudies/

**Central European University,** Department of International Relations, Budapest, Hungary. Offers global economic relations (MA); international relations (MA, PhD). *Faculty:* 11 full-time (3 women), 4 part-time/adjunct (1 woman). *Students:* 76 full-time (40 women), 2 part-time (1 woman). Average age 28. 650 applicants, 15% accepted, 60 enrolled. In 2016, 40 master's, 4 doctorates awarded. *Degree requirements:* For master's, one foreign language, thesis; for doctorate, one foreign language, comprehensive exam, thesis/dissertation. *Entrance requirements:* For master's, 500-word essay, statement of purpose; for doctorate, interview. Additional exam requirements/recommendations for international students: Required—TOEFL (minimum score 570 paper-based); Recommended—IELTS (minimum score 6.5). *Application deadline:* For fall admission, 2/4 for domestic and international students. Application fee: $30. Electronic applications accepted. *Expenses: Tuition:* Full-time 13,500 euros. Tuition and fees vary according to degree level, program and student level. *Financial support:* In 2016–17, 71 students received support. Fellowships, career-related internships or fieldwork, scholarships/grants, health care benefits, and tuition waivers (full and partial) available. *Faculty research:* International relations theory, in both its traditional and critical forms, and to the two major sub-disciplines of security studies and international political economy, forms the foundation of the program, complemented by a multidisciplinary approach to the study of the EU and its role as a global actor. *Unit head:* Matteo Fumagalli, Head of Department, 36 1 327-3243 Ext. 2219, E-mail: fumagallim@ceu.edu. *Application contact:* Zsuzsanna Jaszberenyi, Admissions Officer, 361-324-3009, Fax: 367-327-3211, E-mail: admissions@ceu.edu. Website: http://ir.ceu.edu/

**Central Michigan University,** Central Michigan University Global Campus, Program in Administration, Mount Pleasant, MI 48859. Offers acquisitions administration (MSA, Certificate); engineering management administration (MSA, Certificate); general administration (MSA, Certificate); health services administration (MSA, Certificate); human resources administration (MSA, Certificate); information resource management (MSA); information resource management administration (Certificate); international administration (MSA, Certificate); leadership (MSA, Certificate); philanthropy and fundraising administration (MSA, Certificate); public administration (MSA, Certificate); recreation and park administration (MSA); research administration (MSA, Certificate). *Program availability:* Part-time, evening/weekend, online learning. *Faculty:* 21 full-time (5 women), 168 part-time/adjunct (43 women). *Students:* 3,059 (1,741 women); includes 1,392 minority (1,003 Black or African American, non-Hispanic/Latino; 27 American Indian or Alaska Native, non-Hispanic/Latino; 93 Asian, non-Hispanic/Latino; 49 Hispanic/Latino; 10 Native Hawaiian or other Pacific Islander, non-Hispanic/Latino; 210 Two or more races, non-Hispanic/Latino). Average age 38. In 2016, 289 master's awarded. *Entrance requirements:* For master's, minimum GPA of 2.7 in major. *Application deadline:* Applications are processed on a rolling basis. Application fee: $50. Electronic applications accepted. *Financial support:* Scholarships/grants available. Support available to part-time students. Financial award applicants required to submit FAFSA. *Unit head:* Dr. Patricia Chase, Director, 989-774-6525, E-mail: chase1pb@cmich.edu. *Application contact:* 877-268-4636, E-mail: cmuglobal@cmich.edu.

**Chapman University,** Wilkinson College of Arts, Humanities, and Social Sciences, International Studies Program, Orange, CA 92866. Offers MA. *Program availability:* Part-time, evening/weekend. *Faculty:* 8 full-time (6 women), 1 part-time/adjunct (0 women). *Students:* 5 full-time (4 women), 4 part-time (2 women); includes 4 minority (1 Black or African American, non-Hispanic/Latino; 1 Asian, non-Hispanic/Latino; 2 Hispanic/Latino). Average age 26. 14 applicants, 71% accepted, 4 enrolled. In 2016, 7 master's awarded. *Degree requirements:* For master's, thesis. *Entrance requirements:* For master's, GRE (if undergraduate GPA less than 3.0), minimum undergraduate GPA of 2.5. Additional exam requirements/recommendations for international students: Required—TOEFL (minimum score 550 paper-based, 80 iBT), IELTS (6.5), PTE Academic (53), or CAE. *Application deadline:* For fall admission, 2/1 priority date for domestic students. Applications are processed on a rolling basis. Application fee: $60. Electronic applications accepted. *Expenses:* Contact institution. *Financial support:* Fellowships, Federal Work-Study, scholarships/grants, and unspecified assistantships available. Financial award applicants required to submit FAFSA. *Unit head:* Dr. Lynn Horton, Director, 714-997-6976, E-mail: horton@chapman.edu. *Application contact:* Jon Hernandez, Graduate Admission Counselor, 714-997-6770, E-mail: jonherna@chapman.edu. Website: http://www.chapman.edu/wilkinson/graduate-studies/ma-international-studies/index.aspx

**City College of the City University of New York,** Graduate School, Colin Powell School for Civic and Global Leadership, Program in International Relations, New York, NY 10031-9198. Offers MA. *Program availability:* Part-time. *Degree requirements:* For master's, one foreign language, thesis. *Entrance requirements:* For master's, GRE, 3 letters of recommendation. Additional exam requirements/recommendations for international students: Required—TOEFL (minimum score 600 paper-based; 100 iBT).

Electronic applications accepted. Tuition and fees vary according to course load, degree level and program. *Faculty research:* International finance, international economics, European diplomatic history, area studies, international politics and diplomacy.

**Claremont Graduate University,** Graduate Programs, School of Social Science, Policy and Evaluation, Department of Politics and Policy, Claremont, CA 91711-6160. Offers American politics (MA, PhD); comparative politics (PhD); international political economy (MA); international studies (MA); political philosophy (PhD); political science (PhD); politics, economics and business (MA); public policy (MA, PhD); world politics (PhD); MBA/PhD. *Program availability:* Part-time. *Faculty:* 6 full-time (4 women), 3 part-time/adjunct (0 women). *Students:* 107 full-time (37 women), 32 part-time (10 women); includes 41 minority (6 Black or African American, non-Hispanic/Latino; 10 Asian, non-Hispanic/Latino; 17 Hispanic/Latino; 8 Two or more races, non-Hispanic/Latino), 31 international. Average age 36. In 2016, 21 master's, 14 doctorates awarded. Terminal master's awarded for partial completion of doctoral program. *Entrance requirements:* For master's and doctorate, GRE General Test. Additional exam requirements/recommendations for international students: Required—TOEFL (minimum score 75 iBT). *Application deadline:* For fall admission, 2/1 priority date for domestic and international students. Applications are processed on a rolling basis. Application fee: $80. Electronic applications accepted. *Expenses: Tuition:* Full-time $44,328; part-time $1847 per unit. *Required fees:* $600; $300 per semester. Tuition and fees vary according to course load and program. *Financial support:* Fellowships, research assistantships, teaching assistantships, Federal Work-Study, institutionally sponsored loans, and scholarships/grants available. Support available to part-time students. Financial award application deadline: 2/15; financial award applicants required to submit FAFSA. *Faculty research:* Environmental policy, international debt, global democratization, Third World development, public sector discrimination. *Unit head:* Heather Campbell, Chair, 909-621-8689, E-mail: heather.campbell@cgu.edu. *Application contact:* Paige Piontkowsky, Senior Assistant Director of Admissions, 909-607-3240, E-mail: paige.piontkowsky@cgu.edu. Website: https://www.cgu.edu/school/ssspe/programs/?areas_of_study=politics-and-government

**Cleveland State University,** College of Graduate Studies, College of Liberal Arts and Social Sciences, Department of Political Science, Cleveland, OH 44115. Offers global interactions (MA), including global business interactions, global political interactions. *Faculty:* 3 full-time (1 woman). *Students:* 12 full-time (3 women), 10 part-time (1 woman); includes 9 minority (3 Black or African American, non-Hispanic/Latino; 3 Hispanic/Latino; 3 Two or more races, non-Hispanic/Latino), 3 international. Average age 27. 33 applicants, 100% accepted, 5 enrolled. In 2016, 6 master's awarded. *Degree requirements:* For master's, exit project. *Entrance requirements:* For master's, minimum undergraduate GPA of 3.0 or GRE (50th percentile or above); two letters of recommendation; undergraduate degree in economics, political science, international relations, or a related discipline; completion of undergraduate macro and micro economics course. Additional exam requirements/recommendations for international students: Required—TOEFL (minimum score 550 paper-based; 78 iBT). *Application deadline:* For fall admission, 7/1 for domestic students, 5/15 for international students; for spring admission, 11/15 for domestic students, 11/1 for international students; for summer admission, 4/1 for domestic students, 3/15 for international students. Applications are processed on a rolling basis. Application fee: $40. Electronic applications accepted. *Expenses:* Contact institution. *Financial support:* In 2016–17, 3 research assistantships with full tuition reimbursements (averaging $13,214 per year) were awarded; tuition waivers (full) and unspecified assistantships also available. Financial award applicants required to submit FAFSA. *Faculty research:* International political economy, globalization, new regionalism, European integration, adaptation to climate change. *Unit head:* Dr. Rodger M. Govea, Associate Professor/Chairperson, 216-687-4554, E-mail: r.govea@csuohio.edu. *Application contact:* Janice McCowan, Public Inquiries Assistant, 216-523-7473, Fax: 216-687-9210, E-mail: j.c.mccowan@csuohio.edu. Website: http://www.csuohio.edu/class/politicalscience/

**Colorado School of Mines,** Office of Graduate Studies, Department of Liberal Arts and International Studies, Golden, CO 80401. Offers international political economy (Graduate Certificate); science and technology policy (Graduate Certificate). *Program availability:* Part-time. *Entrance requirements:* Additional exam requirements/recommendations for international students: Required—TOEFL (minimum score 550 paper-based; 80 iBT). Electronic applications accepted. *Expenses:* Tuition, state resident: full-time $15,690. Tuition, nonresident: full-time $34,020. *Required fees:* $2152. Tuition and fees vary according to course load.

**Columbia University,** Graduate School of Arts and Sciences, New York, NY 10027. Offers African-American studies (MA); American studies (MA); anthropology (MA, PhD); art history and archaeology (MA, PhD); astronomy (PhD); biological sciences (PhD); biotechnology (MA); chemical physics (PhD); chemistry (PhD); classical studies (MA, PhD); classics (MA, PhD); climate and society (MA); conservation biology (MA); earth and environmental sciences (PhD); East Asia: regional studies (MA); East Asian languages and cultures (MA, PhD); ecology, evolution and environmental biology (MA), including conservation biology; ecology, evolution, and environmental biology (PhD), including ecology and evolutionary biology, evolutionary primatology; economics (MA, PhD); English and comparative literature (MA, PhD); French and Romance philology (MA, PhD); Germanic languages (MA, PhD); global French studies (MA); global thought (MA); Hispanic cultural studies (MA); history (PhD); history and literature (MA); human rights studies (MA); Islamic studies (MA); Italian (MA, PhD); Japanese pedagogy (MA); Jewish studies (MA); Latin America and the Caribbean: regional studies (MA); Latin American and Iberian cultures (PhD); mathematics (MA, PhD), including finance (MA); medieval and Renaissance studies (MA); Middle Eastern, South Asian, and African studies (MA, PhD); modern art: critical and curatorial studies (MA); modern European studies (MA); museum anthropology (MA); music (DMA, PhD); oral history (MA); philosophical foundations of physics (MA); philosophy (MA, PhD); physics (PhD); political science (MA, PhD); psychology (PhD); quantitative methods in the social sciences (MA); religion (MA, PhD); Russia, Eurasia and East Europe: regional studies (MA); Russian translation (MA); Slavic cultures (MA); Slavic languages (MA, PhD); sociology (MA, PhD); South Asian studies (MA); statistics (MA, PhD); theatre (PhD). Dual-degree programs require admission to both Graduate School of Arts and Sciences and another Columbia school. *Program availability:* Part-time. Terminal master's awarded for partial completion of doctoral program. *Degree requirements:* For master's, variable foreign language requirement, comprehensive exam (for some programs), thesis (for some programs); for doctorate, variable foreign language requirement, comprehensive exam (for some programs), thesis/dissertation. *Entrance requirements:* For master's and doctorate, GRE General Test, GRE Subject Test (for some programs). Additional exam requirements/recommendations for international students: Required—TOEFL, IELTS. Electronic applications accepted.

**Columbia University,** School of International and Public Affairs, Program in International Affairs, New York, NY 10027. Offers MIA, JD/MIA, MBA/MIA, MIA/MS, MPH/MIA, MSJ/MIA. *Faculty:* 70 full-time (18 women), 203 part-time/adjunct (80 women). *Students:* Average age 27. *Degree requirements:* For master's, one foreign language, comprehensive exam. *Entrance requirements:* For master's, GRE General

*International Affairs*

Test. Additional exam requirements/recommendations for international students: Required—TOEFL (minimum score 600 paper-based; 100 iBT), IELTS (minimum score 7), PTE (minimum score 68). *Application deadline:* For fall admission, 1/5 for domestic and international students; for spring admission, 10/15 for domestic and international students. Application fee: $95. Electronic applications accepted. *Financial support:* Fellowships, research assistantships, teaching assistantships, career-related internships or fieldwork, Federal Work-Study, and institutionally sponsored loans available. Financial award application deadline: 1/5; financial award applicants required to submit FAFSA. *Application contact:* Grace Han, Executive Director of Admissions and Financial Aid, 212-854-6216, Fax: 212-854-3010,
E-mail: sipa_admission@columbia.edu.
Website: www.sipa.columbia.edu

**Concordia University Irvine,** School of Professional Studies, Irvine, CA 92612-3299. Offers healthcare administration (MHA); international studies (MAIS), including Africa, China; nursing (MSN).
**See Display below.**

**Cornell University,** Graduate School, Graduate Fields of Arts and Sciences, Field of Government, Ithaca, NY 14853. Offers American politics (PhD); comparative politics (PhD); international relations (PhD); political methodology (PhD); political thought (PhD); public policy (PhD). *Degree requirements:* For doctorate, comprehensive exam, thesis/dissertation. *Entrance requirements:* For doctorate, GRE General Test, sample of written work, 3 letters of recommendation. Additional exam requirements/recommendations for international students: Required—TOEFL (minimum score 550 paper-based; 77 iBT). Electronic applications accepted. *Faculty research:* Political theory, American politics, comparative politics, international relations, methodology.

**Creighton University,** Graduate School, College of Arts and Sciences, Program in International Relations, Omaha, NE 68178-0001. Offers MA. *Program availability:* Part-time, evening/weekend. *Faculty:* 9 full-time (2 women). *Students:* 2 full-time (1 woman), 2 part-time (both women), 1 international. Average age 24. 1 applicant, 100% accepted. In 2016, 10 master's awarded. *Degree requirements:* For master's, comprehensive exam, thesis optional. *Entrance requirements:* For master's, GRE General Test, 3 letters of recommendation. Additional exam requirements/recommendations for international students: Required—TOEFL (minimum score 90 iBT). *Application deadline:* For fall admission, 3/1 priority date for domestic and international students; for winter admission, 12/1 priority date for domestic students, 7/1 priority date for international students; for spring admission, 4/1 priority date for domestic students, 9/1 priority date for international students; for summer admission, 3/1 for domestic and international students. Applications are processed on a rolling basis. Application fee: $50. Electronic applications accepted. *Expenses: Tuition:* Full-time $14,400; part-time $800 per credit hour. *Required fees:* $158 per semester. Tuition and fees vary according to course load, campus/location, program, reciprocity agreements and student's religious affiliation. *Financial support:* In 2016–17, 4 fellowships with full tuition reimbursements (averaging $11,465 per year) were awarded; scholarships/grants and health care benefits also available. Support available to part-time students. Financial award application deadline: 5/1; financial award applicants required to submit FAFSA. *Unit head:* Dr. Erika Moreno, Chair, 402-280-2368, E-mail: erikamoreno@creighton.edu. *Application contact:* Lindsay Johnson, Director of Graduate and Adult Recruitment, 402-280-2703, Fax: 402-280-2423, E-mail: gradschool@creighton.edu.

**Dallas Baptist University,** Gary Cook School of Leadership, Program in International Studies, Dallas, TX 75211-9299. Offers East Asian studies (MA); European studies (MA); general international studies (MA); global business (MA); international immersion (MA); international ministry (MA); international relations (MA). *Program availability:* Part-time, evening/weekend. *Application deadline:* Applications are processed on a rolling

basis. Application fee: $25. Electronic applications accepted. Application fee is waived when completed online. *Expenses: Tuition:* Full-time $15,408; part-time $856 per credit hour. *Required fees:* $400 per semester. Tuition and fees vary according to course load and degree level. *Unit head:* Dr. Brent A. Thomason, Director, 214-333-5236, E-mail: brentt@dbu.edu. *Application contact:* Bobby Soto, Director of Admissions, 214-333-5242, E-mail: graduate@dbu.edu.
Website: http://www4.dbu.edu/leadership/mainternational

**DePaul University,** College of Liberal Arts and Social Sciences, Chicago, IL 60614. Offers Arabic (MA); Chinese (MA); English (MA); French (MA); German (MA); history (MA); interdisciplinary studies (MA, MS); international public service (MS); international studies (MA); Italian (MA); Japanese (MA); leadership and policy studies (MS); liberal studies (MA); new media studies (MA); nonprofit management (MNM); public administration (MPA); public health (MPH); public service management (MS); social work (MSW); sociology (MA); Spanish (MA); sustainable urban development (MA); women and gender studies (MA); writing and publishing (MA); writing, rhetoric, and discourse (MA); MA/PhD. *Program availability:* Part-time, evening/weekend, online learning. Terminal master's awarded for partial completion of doctoral program. *Degree requirements:* For master's, variable foreign language requirement, comprehensive exam (for some programs), thesis (for some programs). Electronic applications accepted.

**East Carolina University,** Graduate School, Thomas Harriot College of Arts and Sciences, Program in International Studies, Greenville, NC 27858-4353. Offers MA. *Program availability:* Part-time. *Degree requirements:* For master's, one foreign language, comprehensive exam, thesis optional, international field experience. *Entrance requirements:* For master's, GRE General Test. Additional exam requirements/recommendations for international students: Required—TOEFL. *Application deadline:* Applications are processed on a rolling basis. Application fee: $50. *Financial support:* Research assistantships with partial tuition reimbursements available. Financial award application deadline: 6/1. *Unit head:* Dr. David L. Smith, Director, 252-328-5524, E-mail: smithdav@ecu.edu. *Application contact:* Dean of Graduate School, 252-328-6012, Fax: 252-328-6071, E-mail: gradschool@ecu.edu.
Website: http://www.ecu.edu/cs-cas/international/maisindex.cfm

**Embry-Riddle Aeronautical University–Worldwide,** Department of Security and Emergency Services, Daytona Beach, FL 32114-3900. Offers cybersecurity management and policy (MSCMP); human security and resilience (MSHSR). *Program availability:* Part-time, evening/weekend, 100% online, blended/hybrid learning, EagleVision Classroom (between classrooms), EagleVision Home (faculty and students at home), and a blend of Classroom or Home. *Faculty:* 4 full-time (3 women), 5 part-time/adjunct (1 woman). *Students:* 2 full-time (both women), 5 part-time (2 women); includes 27 minority (10 Black or African American, non-Hispanic/Latino; 3 Asian, non-Hispanic/Latino; 2 Hispanic/Latino; 12 Two or more races, non-Hispanic/Latino), 1 international. Average age 37. *Degree requirements:* For master's, capstone project. *Entrance requirements:* Additional exam requirements/recommendations for international students: Required—TOEFL (minimum score 550 paper-based, 79 iBT) or IELTS (6). *Application deadline:* Applications are processed on a rolling basis. Application fee: $50. Electronic applications accepted. *Expenses:* $620 per credit (for civilians), $530 per credit (for military). *Financial support:* Career-related internships or fieldwork and scholarships/grants available. Financial award applicants required to submit FAFSA. *Unit head:* Ronald Wakeham, Department Chair, E-mail: ronald.wakeham@erau.edu. *Application contact:* Worldwide Campus, 800-522-6787, E-mail: worldwide@erau.edu.
Website: http://worldwide.erau.edu/colleges/arts-sciences/department-emergency-services

**Fairleigh Dickinson University, Metropolitan Campus,** University College: Arts, Sciences, and Professional Studies, School of History, Political and International Studies, Program in International Studies, Teaneck, NJ 07666-1914. Offers MA.

**Florida International University,** Steven J. Green School of International and Public Affairs, Department of Politics and International Relations, Miami, FL 33199. Offers international relations (MA, PhD), including international relations (PhD), international studies (MA); political science (MA, PhD). Ph D program has fall admissions only. *Program availability:* Part-time, evening/weekend. *Faculty:* 30 full-time (12 women), 24 part-time/adjunct (5 women). *Students:* 158 full-time (85 women), 40 part-time (10 women); includes 100 minority (13 Black or African American, non-Hispanic/Latino; 5 Asian, non-Hispanic/Latino; 78 Hispanic/Latino; 4 Two or more races, non-Hispanic/Latino), 47 international. Average age 29. 187 applicants, 57% accepted, 73 enrolled. In 2016, 47 master's, 5 doctorates awarded. *Degree requirements:* For master's, one foreign language, thesis optional; for doctorate, one foreign language, comprehensive exam, thesis/dissertation. *Entrance requirements:* For master's and doctorate, GRE General Test, minimum GPA of 3.0, letters of recommendation. Additional exam requirements/recommendations for international students: Required—TOEFL (minimum score 550 paper-based; 80 iBT). *Application deadline:* For fall admission, 3/15 for domestic and international students; for spring admission, 8/15 for domestic and international students. Application fee: $30. Electronic applications accepted. *Expenses:* Tuition, state resident: full-time $8912; part-time $446 per credit hour. Tuition, nonresident: full-time $21,393; part-time $992 per credit hour. *Required fees:* $2185; $195 per semester. Tuition and fees vary according to program. *Financial support:* Institutionally sponsored loans, scholarships/grants, and unspecified assistantships available. Financial award application deadline: 3/1; financial award applicants required to submit FAFSA. *Unit head:* Dr. John Clark, Chair, 305-348-2227, Fax: 305-348-3765, E-mail: john.clark@fiu.edu. *Application contact:* Nanett Rojas, Manager, Admissions Operations, 305-348-7464, E-mail: nanett.rojas@fiu.edu.
Website: http://pir.fiu.edu

**Florida State University,** The Graduate School, College of Social Sciences and Public Policy, Program in International Affairs, Tallahassee, FL 32306. Offers MA, MS, JD/MA, JD/MS. *Program availability:* Part-time. *Faculty:* 4 full-time (all women), 4 part-time/adjunct. *Students:* 38 full-time (16 women), 19 part-time (11 women); includes 21 minority (4 Black or African American, non-Hispanic/Latino; 3 Asian, non-Hispanic/Latino; 3 Hispanic/Latino; 11 Two or more races, non-Hispanic/Latino). Average age 25. 55 applicants, 87% accepted, 23 enrolled. In 2016, 27 master's awarded. *Degree requirements:* For master's, one foreign language, comprehensive exam, thesis optional. *Entrance requirements:* For master's, GRE General Test, minimum GPA of 3.0. Additional exam requirements/recommendations for international students: Required—TOEFL (minimum score 550 paper-based, 80 iBT) or IELTS (6.5). *Application deadline:* For fall admission, 7/1 for domestic and international students; for spring admission, 11/1 for domestic and international students; for summer admission, 3/1 for domestic and international students. Applications are processed on a rolling basis. Application fee: $30. Electronic applications accepted. *Expenses:* Contact institution. *Financial support:* In 2016–17, 7 students received support, including 5 research assistantships with full tuition reimbursements available (averaging $5,000 per year), 2 teaching assistantships with full tuition reimbursements available (averaging $5,000 per year); career-related internships or fieldwork, Federal Work-Study, institutionally sponsored loans, scholarships/grants, and unspecified assistantships also available. Financial award application deadline: 2/1; financial award applicants required to submit FAFSA. *Faculty research:* Deception in World War II. *Unit head:* Dr. Lee K. Metcalf, Director, 850-644-4418, Fax: 850-645-4981, E-mail: lmetcalf@fsu.edu. *Application contact:* Sam Bandak, Academic Program Specialist, 850-644-4418, Fax: 850-645-4981, E-mail: sbandak@fsu.edu.
Website: http://coss.fsu.edu/inaprog/programs/graduate/g-IA

**Fordham University,** Graduate School of Arts and Sciences, Program in International Political Economy and Development, New York, NY 10458. Offers MA, Certificate. *Program availability:* Part-time, evening/weekend. *Students:* 38 full-time (16 women), 13 part-time (10 women); includes 8 minority (1 Black or African American, non-Hispanic/Latino; 4 Asian, non-Hispanic/Latino; 3 Native Hawaiian or other Pacific Islander, non-Hispanic/Latino), 16 international. Average age 27. 207 applicants, 35% accepted, 24 enrolled. In 2016, 24 master's, 1 other advanced degree awarded. *Degree requirements:* For master's, comprehensive exam. *Entrance requirements:* For master's, GRE General Test. Additional exam requirements/recommendations for international students: Required—TOEFL (minimum score 600 paper-based). *Application deadline:* For fall admission, 1/4 priority date for domestic students; for spring admission, 11/1 for domestic students. Application fee: $70. Electronic applications accepted. *Financial support:* In 2016–17, 35 students received support, including 4 fellowships with tuition reimbursements available (averaging $17,014 per year); research assistantships with tuition reimbursements available, career-related internships or fieldwork, institutionally sponsored loans, tuition waivers (full and partial), and unspecified assistantships also available. Financial award application deadline: 1/4; financial award applicants required to submit FAFSA. *Faculty research:* International economics, comparative international politics, international banking and finance, international development, emerging markets and country risk analysis. *Unit head:* Dr. Henry Schwalbenberg, Chair, 718-817-3866, Fax: 718-817-3518. *Application contact:* Bernadette Valentino-Morrison, Director of Graduate Admissions, 718-817-4419, Fax: 718-817-3566, E-mail: valentinomor@fordham.edu.

**George Mason University,** Schar School of Policy and Government, Program in International Commerce and Policy, Arlington, VA 22201. Offers MA. *Faculty:* 12 full-time (3 women), 7 part-time/adjunct (2 women). *Students:* 27 full-time (13 women), 61 part-time (31 women); includes 34 minority (11 Black or African American, non-Hispanic/Latino; 12 Asian, non-Hispanic/Latino; 10 Hispanic/Latino; 1 Two or more races, non-Hispanic/Latino), 9 international. Average age 29. 52 applicants, 85% accepted, 25 enrolled. In 2016, 64 master's awarded. *Degree requirements:* For master's, thesis or alternative. *Entrance requirements:* For master's, GRE/GMAT (for students seeking merit-based scholarships), bachelor's degree with minimum of GPA of 3.0; expanded goals statement; current resume; 2 official copies of transcripts; 2 letters of recommendation. Additional exam requirements/recommendations for international students: Required—TOEFL (minimum score 575 paper-based; 88 iBT), IELTS (minimum score 6.5), PTE (minimum score 59). *Application deadline:* For fall admission, 2/1 priority date for domestic students. Application fee: $75 ($80 for international students). Electronic applications accepted. *Expenses:* Contact institution. *Financial support:* Career-related internships or fieldwork, Federal Work-Study, and scholarships/grants available. Financial award application deadline: 3/1; financial award applicants required to submit FAFSA. *Unit head:* Kenneth Reinert, Director, 703-993-8212, Fax: 703-993-8215, E-mail: kreinert@gmu.edu. *Application contact:* Stephanie Ellis, Graduate Admissions Coordinator, 703-993-4478, E-mail: sellis11@gmu.edu.
Website: http://spgia.gmu.edu/programs/graduate-degrees/international-commerce-and-policy-icp/

**Georgetown University,** Graduate School of Arts and Sciences, School of Continuing Studies, Washington, DC 20057. Offers American studies (MALS); Catholic studies (MALS); classical civilizations (MALS); emergency and disaster management (MPS); ethics and the professions (MALS); global strategic communications (MPS); hospitality management (MPS); human resources management (MPS); humanities (MALS); individualized study (MALS); integrated marketing communications (MPS); international affairs (MALS); Islam and Muslim-Christian relations (MALS); journalism (MPS); liberal studies (DLS); literature and society (MALS); medieval and early modern European studies (MALS); public relations and corporate communications (MPS); real estate (MPS); religious studies (MALS); social and public policy (MALS); sports industry management (MPS); systems engineering management (MPS); technology management (MPS); the theory and practice of American democracy (MALS); urban and regional planning (MPS); visual culture (MALS). MPS in systems engineering management offered jointly with Stevens Institute of Technology. *Entrance requirements:* Additional exam requirements/recommendations for international students: Required—TOEFL.

**Georgetown University,** Graduate School of Arts and Sciences, Walsh School of Foreign Service, BMW Center for German and European Studies, Washington, DC 20057. Offers MA, MA/JD, MA/PhD. *Degree requirements:* For master's, 2 foreign languages, comprehensive exam. *Entrance requirements:* For master's, GRE General Test. Additional exam requirements/recommendations for international students: Required—TOEFL. Electronic applications accepted. *Faculty research:* Transatlantic relations, European Union, German and European Studies.

**Georgetown University,** Graduate School of Arts and Sciences, Walsh School of Foreign Service, Master of Science in Foreign Service Program, Washington, DC 20057. Offers global business and finance (MS); global politics and security (MS); international development (MS); self design (MS); JD/MS; MA/MS; MBA/MS; MPP/MS. *Faculty:* 28 full-time (7 women), 41 part-time/adjunct (6 women). *Students:* 203 full-time (105 women); includes 42 minority (9 Black or African American, non-Hispanic/Latino; 1 American Indian or Alaska Native, non-Hispanic/Latino; 14 Asian, non-Hispanic/Latino; 11 Hispanic/Latino; 7 Two or more races, non-Hispanic/Latino), 53 international. Average age 27. 729 applicants. In 2016, 105 master's awarded. *Degree requirements:* For master's, one foreign language, comprehensive exam, internship. *Entrance requirements:* For master's, GRE General Test or GMAT (for students with undergraduate degree from English-speaking institution), one semester each of micro and macroeconomics with minimum B- grade; two to three years of experience with a second language besides native tongue. Additional exam requirements/recommendations for international students: Required—TOEFL (minimum score 100 iBT) or IELTS (minimum score 7). *Application deadline:* For fall admission, 1/15 for domestic and international students. Application fee: $90. Electronic applications accepted. *Expenses:* Contact institution. *Financial support:* In 2016–17, 87 students received support, including 4 research assistantships (averaging $5,000 per year), 4 teaching assistantships (averaging $5,000 per year); career-related internships or fieldwork, scholarships/grants, tuition waivers (partial), and unspecified assistantships also available. Financial award application deadline: 1/15. *Faculty research:* International business diplomacy, political risk analysis, science and technology, intercultural perspectives on contemporary issues. *Unit head:* Dr. Anthony Arend, Director, 202-687-5763. *Application contact:* MSFS Admissions, 202-687-5763, E-mail: msfsinfo@georgetown.edu.
Website: http://msfs.georgetown.edu/

**Georgetown University,** Law Center, Washington, DC 20001. Offers environmental law (LL M); global health law (LL M); global health law and international institutions (LL M); individualized study (LL M); international business and economic law (LL M); law (JD, SJD); national security law (LL M); securities and financial regulation (LL M); taxation (LL M); JD/LL M; JD/MA; JD/MBA; JD/MPH; JD/PhD. *Accreditation:* ABA. *Program availability:* Part-time, evening/weekend. *Degree requirements:* For master's, thesis; for doctorate, thesis/dissertation (for some programs). *Entrance requirements:* For master's, JD, LL B, or first law degree earned in country of origin; for doctorate, LSAT (for JD). Additional exam requirements/recommendations for international students: Required—TOEFL. *Expenses:* Contact institution. *Faculty research:* Constitutional law, legal history, jurisprudence.

**The George Washington University,** Elliott School of International Affairs, Program in International Affairs, Washington, DC 20052. Offers MA. *Program availability:* Part-time. *Faculty:* 72 full-time (23 women). *Students:* 514 full-time (300 women), 252 part-time (150 women); includes 237 minority (59 Black or African American, non-Hispanic/Latino; 67 Asian, non-Hispanic/Latino; 81 Hispanic/Latino; 30 Two or more races, non-Hispanic/Latino), 109 international. Average age 27. 1,417 applicants, 81% accepted, 325 enrolled. In 2016, 305 master's awarded. *Degree requirements:* For master's, one foreign language, capstone project. *Entrance requirements:* For master's, GRE General Test, 2 years of a modern foreign language, 2 semesters of introductory economics. Additional exam requirements/recommendations for international students: Required—TOEFL (minimum score 100 iBT), IELTS (minimum score 7). *Application deadline:* For fall admission, 1/15 priority date for domestic and international students; for spring admission, 10/1 for domestic students. Application fee: $75. Electronic applications accepted. *Financial support:* In 2016–17, 61 students received support. Fellowships with partial tuition reimbursements available and Federal Work-Study available. Financial award application deadline: 1/15; financial award applicants required to submit FAFSA. *Faculty research:* Area studies, international economics, national security policy studies, international economic development, Sino-Soviet studies. *Unit head:* Dr. Marcus King, Director, 202-994-7137, E-mail: maia@gwu.edu. *Application contact:* Nicole A. Campbell, Director of Graduate Admissions, 202-994-7050, Fax: 202-994-9537, E-mail: esiagrad@gwu.edu.
Website: http://elliott.gwu.edu/international-affairs-masters

**The George Washington University,** Elliott School of International Affairs, Program in International Policy and Practice, Washington, DC 20052. Offers MIPP. *Program availability:* Part-time. *Students:* 19 full-time (8 women), 23 part-time (12 women); includes 12 minority (8 Black or African American, non-Hispanic/Latino; 1 Asian, non-Hispanic/Latino; 3 Hispanic/Latino), 7 international. Average age 35. 51 applicants, 86% accepted, 17 enrolled. In 2016, 26 master's awarded. *Degree requirements:* For master's, one foreign language. *Entrance requirements:* For master's, GRE (recommended), advanced degree or 8 years of experience plus BA, introductory microeconomics and macroeconomics. Additional exam requirements/recommendations for international students: Required—TOEFL (minimum score 100 iBT), IELTS (minimum score 7). *Application deadline:* For fall admission, 1/15 priority date for domestic and international students; for spring admission, 10/1 for domestic and international students. Application fee: $75. Electronic applications accepted. *Financial support:* In 2016–17, 13 students received support. Fellowships with partial tuition reimbursements available, Federal Work-Study, and scholarships/grants available. Financial award application deadline: 1/15; financial award applicants required to submit FAFSA. *Unit head:* Prof. Matthew Levinger, Director, 202-994-9946, E-mail: mippgw@gwu.edu. *Application contact:* Nicole A. Campbell, Director of Graduate Admissions, 202-994-7050, Fax: 202-994-9537, E-mail: esiagrad@gwu.edu.
Website: http://elliott.gwu.edu/international-policy-and-practice

**The George Washington University,** Elliott School of International Affairs, Program in International Studies, Washington, DC 20052. Offers MIS. *Program availability:* Part-time. *Degree requirements:* For master's, one foreign language. *Entrance requirements:*

## International Affairs

For master's, 2 years (or equivalent) of a modern, spoken foreign language; introductory microeconomics/macroeconomics coursework. Additional exam requirements/recommendations for international students: Required—TOEFL (minimum score 600 paper-based; 100 iBT), IELTS (minimum score 7). *Application deadline:* For fall admission, 1/15 priority date for domestic and international students; for spring admission, 10/1 for domestic students. Application fee: $75. Electronic applications accepted. *Financial support:* Fellowships with partial tuition reimbursements, Federal Work-Study, and scholarships/grants available. Financial award application deadline: 1/15; financial award applicants required to submit FAFSA. *Unit head:* Lisa Stephenson, Associate Dean for Academic Programs, 202-994-6034, E-mail: lstephen@gwu.edu. *Application contact:* Nicole A. Campbell, Director of Graduate Admissions, 202-994-7050, Fax: 202-994-9537, E-mail: esiagrad@gwu.edu.
Website: http://elliott.gwu.edu/international-studies-masters

**The George Washington University,** Law School, Washington, DC 20052. Offers law (SJD); national security and U.S. foreign relations (LL M). *Accreditation:* ABA. *Program availability:* Part-time, evening/weekend. *Faculty:* 84 full-time (33 women). *Students:* 1,622 full-time (867 women), 315 part-time (150 women); includes 482 minority (164 Black or African American, non-Hispanic/Latino; 15 American Indian or Alaska Native, non-Hispanic/Latino; 234 Asian, non-Hispanic/Latino; 55 Hispanic/Latino; 4 Native Hawaiian or other Pacific Islander, non-Hispanic/Latino; 10 Two or more races, non-Hispanic/Latino), 222 international. Average age 27. 223 applicants, 100% accepted, 133 enrolled. In 2016, 166 master's, 1 doctorate awarded. *Degree requirements:* For doctorate, thesis/dissertation (for some programs). *Entrance requirements:* For master's, JD or equivalent; for doctorate, LSAT (for JD), LL M or equivalent (for SJD). *Application deadline:* For fall admission, 3/1 for domestic students. Applications are processed on a rolling basis. Application fee: $75. *Expenses:* Contact institution. *Financial support:* Research assistantships, career-related internships or fieldwork, Federal Work-Study, institutionally sponsored loans, scholarships/grants, and tuition waivers (full and partial) available. Support available to part-time students. Financial award application deadline: 3/1; financial award applicants required to submit CSS PROFILE or FAFSA. *Unit head:* Blake D. Morant, Dean, E-mail: bmorant@law.gwu.edu. *Application contact:* Sophia Sim, Assistant Dean of Admissions and Financial Aid, 202-994-7235, Fax: 202-739-0624, E-mail: ssim@law.gwu.edu.
Website: http://www.law.gwu.edu/

**Georgia Institute of Technology,** Graduate Studies, Ivan Allen College of Liberal Arts, Sam Nunn School of International Affairs, Atlanta, GA 30332-0001. Offers MS. *Program availability:* Part-time. Terminal master's awarded for partial completion of doctoral program. *Degree requirements:* For master's, one foreign language, thesis optional, minimum GPA of 3.0, literacy in economics and technology. *Entrance requirements:* For master's, GRE. Additional exam requirements/recommendations for international students: Required—TOEFL (minimum score 600 paper-based; 100 iBT). Electronic applications accepted. *Faculty research:* International political economy, international security, Asian and European studies.

**Harvard University,** Graduate School of Arts and Sciences, Department of Government, Cambridge, MA 02138. Offers political science (PhD), including American politics, comparative politics, international relations, political thought, quantitative methods. *Degree requirements:* For doctorate, one foreign language, thesis/dissertation, general exams. *Entrance requirements:* For doctorate, GRE General Test. Additional exam requirements/recommendations for international students: Required—TOEFL.

**Harvard University,** Law School, Professional Programs in Law, Cambridge, MA 02138. Offers international and comparative law (JD); law and business (JD); law and government (JD); law and social change (JD); law, science and technology (JD); JD/MALD; JD/MBA; JD/MPH; JD/MPP; JD/PhD. *Accreditation:* ABA. *Degree requirements:* For doctorate, 3rd-year paper. *Entrance requirements:* For doctorate, LSAT. *Faculty research:* Constitutional law, voting rights law, cyber law.

**Indiana University South Bend,** College of Liberal Arts and Sciences, South Bend, IN 46634-7111. Offers advanced computer programming (Graduate Certificate); applied informatics (Graduate Certificate); applied mathematics and computer science (MS); behavior modification (Graduate Certificate); computer applications (Graduate Certificate); computer programming (Graduate Certificate); correctional management and supervision (Graduate Certificate); English (MA); health systems management (Graduate Certificate); international studies (Graduate Certificate); liberal studies (MLS); nonprofit management (Graduate Certificate); paralegal studies (Graduate Certificate); professional writing (Graduate Certificate); public affairs (MPA); public management (Graduate Certificate); social and cultural diversity (Graduate Certificate); strategic sustainability leadership (Graduate Certificate); technology for administration (Graduate Certificate). *Program availability:* Part-time, evening/weekend. *Faculty:* 79 full-time (33 women). *Students:* 31 full-time (11 women), 92 part-time (53 women); includes 28 minority (9 Black or African American, non-Hispanic/Latino; 8 Asian, non-Hispanic/Latino; 5 Hispanic/Latino; 6 Two or more races, non-Hispanic/Latino), 19 international. Average age 38. 51 applicants, 84% accepted, 31 enrolled. In 2016, 30 master's, 6 other advanced degrees awarded. *Degree requirements:* For master's, variable foreign language requirement, thesis (for some programs). *Entrance requirements:* For master's, minimum GPA of 3.0. Additional exam requirements/recommendations for international students: Required—TOEFL (minimum score 550 paper-based; 80 iBT). *Application deadline:* For fall admission, 7/31 priority date for domestic students, 7/1 priority date for international students; for spring admission, 3/31 priority date for domestic students, 11/1 priority date for international students. Applications are processed on a rolling basis. Application fee: $40 ($60 for international students). *Expenses:* $276.98 per credit hour in-state; $652.54 per credit hour out-of-state. *Financial support:* In 2016–17, 5 teaching assistantships were awarded; Federal Work-Study also available. Support available to part-time students. Financial award application deadline: 3/10. *Faculty research:* Artificial intelligence, bioinformatics, English language and literature, creative writing, computer networks. *Total annual research expenditures:* $127,000. *Unit head:* Dr. Elizabeth E. Dunn, Dean, 574-520-4290, E-mail: elizdunn@iusb.edu. *Application contact:* Admissions Counselor, 574-520-4839, Fax: 574-520-4834, E-mail: graduate@iusb.edu.
Website: https://www.iusb.edu/clas/

**Instituto Tecnologico de Santo Domingo,** Graduate School, Area of Humanities and Social Sciences, Santo Domingo, Dominican Republic. Offers accounting (Certificate); adult education (Certificate); applied linguistics (MA); economics (MA); education (M Ed); educational psychology (MA, Certificate); gender and development (MA, Certificate); humanistic studies (MA); international marketing management (Certificate); international relations in the Caribbean basin (Certificate); intervention systems in family therapy (MA); linguistic and literary communication (Certificate); pedagogical support (MA); social science education (M Ed); sustainable human development (MA); terminal illness and death psychology (Certificate); youth and adult education (M Ed).

**Instituto Tecnológico y de Estudios Superiores de Monterrey, Campus Ciudad Obregón,** Program in International Relations, Ciudad Obregón, Mexico. Offers MIR.

**International University in Geneva,** Leadership Programs, Geneva, Switzerland. Offers international relations and diplomacy (MIRD); media and communication (MA);

public administration (DPA). *Degree requirements:* For master's, comprehensive exam. *Entrance requirements:* Additional exam requirements/recommendations for international students: Required—TOEFL. Electronic applications accepted.

**Johns Hopkins University,** School of Advanced International Studies, Washington, DC 20036. Offers global risk (MA); international development (MA, Certificate), including international economics and finance (MA); international economics and finance (MA); international public policy (MIPP); international relations (PhD); international studies (Certificate); Japan studies (MA), including international economics; Korea studies (MA), including international economics; South Asia studies (MA), including international economics; Southeast Asia studies (MA), including international economics; JD/MA; MBA/MA; MHS/MA. Terminal master's awarded for partial completion of doctoral program. *Degree requirements:* For master's, 4-6 international economics courses, 5-6 functional or regional concentration courses, 2 core examinations, proficiency in language other than native language, capstone project; for doctorate, 2 foreign languages, thesis/dissertation, 3 comprehensive exams, economics, quantitative and qualitative course, dissertation prospectus and defense. *Entrance requirements:* For master's, GMAT or GRE General Test, previous course work in economics, foreign language, undergraduate degree; for doctorate, GRE General Test, master's degree. Additional exam requirements/recommendations for international students: Required—TOEFL (minimum score 600 paper-based; 100 iBT) or IELTS (minimum score 7). Electronic applications accepted. *Expenses:* Contact institution. *Faculty research:* Regional studies, international relations, international economics, energy and environment, international development.

**Kennesaw State University,** College of Humanities and Social Sciences, Program in International Policy Management, Kennesaw, GA 30144. Offers MS. *Program availability:* Online learning. *Degree requirements:* For master's, practicum or thesis. *Entrance requirements:* For master's, GRE, resume, letters of recommendation, writing sample. Additional exam requirements/recommendations for international students: Required—TOEFL (minimum score 550 paper-based; 80 iBT), IELTS (minimum score 6.5). Electronic applications accepted.

**Lebanese American University,** School of Arts and Sciences, Beirut, Lebanon. Offers computer science (MS); international affairs (MA).

**Lesley University,** Graduate School of Arts and Social Sciences, Cambridge, MA 02138-2790. Offers clinical mental health counseling (MA), including holistic counseling, school and community counseling, trauma studies; counseling psychology (MA, CAGS); creative writing (MFA); expressive therapies (MA, PhD, CAGS), including art (MA), clinical mental health counseling (MA), dance (MA), expressive therapies (MA), music (MA); independent studies (CAGS); independent study (MA); intercultural relations (MA, CAGS); interdisciplinary studies (MA), including individualized studies, integrative holistic health, mindfulness studies, peace and conflict transformation, trauma sensitive assessment, intervention, and consultation, women's studies; urban environmental leadership (MA). *Program availability:* Part-time, online learning. *Degree requirements:* For master's, internship, practicum, thesis (for expressive therapies); for doctorate, thesis/dissertation, arts apprenticeship, field placement; for CAGS, thesis, internship (for counseling psychology, expressive therapies). *Entrance requirements:* For master's, MAT (counseling psychology), interview, writing samples, art portfolio; for doctorate, GRE or MAT, interview, master's degree; for CAGS, interview, master's degree. Additional exam requirements/recommendations for international students: Required—TOEFL (minimum score 550 paper-based; 80 iBT). Electronic applications accepted. *Faculty research:* Psychotherapy and culture; psychotherapy and psychological trauma; women's issues in art, teaching and psychotherapy; community-based art, psycho-spiritual inquiry.

**Liberty University,** School of Divinity, Lynchburg, VA 24515. Offers Biblical studies (M Div); church history (MAR, Th M); discipleship and church ministry (M Div, MAR, MCM); evangelism and church planting (M Div, MAR, MCM); global studies (M Div, MCM, MGS); homiletics (M Div, MAR, Th M, D Min); leadership (M Div, D Min); marketplace chaplaincy (M Div, MCM); ministry (D Min); pastoral counseling (M Div, MA, MAR, D Min), including addictions and recovery (MA), crisis response and trauma (MA), discipleship and church ministries (MA), leadership (MA), life coaching (MA), marketplace chaplaincy (MA), marriage and family (MA), military resilience (MA), pastoral counseling (MA); pastoral ministries (M Div, MCM); religious education (MRE); theology (M Div, MAR, MTS); theology and apologetics (PhD); worship (M Div, MAR, MCM, D Min). *Program availability:* Part-time, online learning. *Students:* 2,140 full-time (615 women), 3,020 part-time (906 women); includes 1,312 minority (1,016 Black or African American, non-Hispanic/Latino; 9 American Indian or Alaska Native, non-Hispanic/Latino; 100 Asian, non-Hispanic/Latino; 90 Hispanic/Latino; 7 Native Hawaiian or other Pacific Islander, non-Hispanic/Latino; 90 Two or more races, non-Hispanic/Latino), 158 international. Average age 42. 3,651 applicants, 37% accepted, 909 enrolled. In 2016, 1,551 master's, 39 doctorates, 168 other advanced degrees awarded. *Degree requirements:* For master's, 2 foreign languages, thesis (for some programs); for doctorate, 2 foreign languages, thesis/dissertation. *Entrance requirements:* For master's, minimum undergraduate GPA of 2.0; for doctorate, GRE General Test or MAT, minimum graduate GPA of 3.0. Additional exam requirements/recommendations for international students: Required—TOEFL (minimum score 600 paper-based; 100 iBT). *Application deadline:* For fall admission, 6/1 for domestic students; for spring admission, 11/1 for domestic students. Applications are processed on a rolling basis. Application fee: $50. Electronic applications accepted. *Expenses:* Contact institution. *Financial support:* Teaching assistantships with tuition reimbursements, career-related internships or fieldwork, and Federal Work-Study available. Financial award applicants required to submit FAFSA. *Unit head:* Dr. Ed Hindson, Dean, 434-592-4140, Fax: 434-522-0415, E-mail: ehindson@liberty.edu. *Application contact:* Jay Bridge, Director of Graduate Admissions, 800-424-9595, Fax: 800-628-7977, E-mail: gradadmissions@liberty.edu.
Website: https://www.liberty.edu/divinity/

**London Metropolitan University,** Graduate Programs, London, United Kingdom. Offers applied psychology (M Sc); architecture (MA); biomedical science (M Sc); blood science (M Sc); cancer pharmacology (M Sc); computer networking and cyber security (M Sc); computing and information systems (M Sc); conference interpreting (MA); counter-terrorism studies (M Sc); creative, digital and professional writing (MA); crime, violence and prevention (M Sc); criminology (M Sc); curating contemporary art (MA); data analytics (M Sc); digital media (MA); early childhood studies (MA, Ed D); financial services law, regulation and compliance (LL M); food science (M Sc); forensic psychology (M Sc); health and social care management and policy (M Sc); human nutrition (M Sc); human resource management (MA); human rights and international conflict (MA); information technology (M Sc); intelligence and security studies (M Sc); international oil, gas and energy law (LL M); international relations (MA); interpreting (MA); learning and teaching in higher education (MA); legal practice (LL M); media and entertainment law (LL M); organizational and consumer psychology (M Sc); psychological therapy (M Sc); psychology of mental health (M Sc); public health (M Sc); public policy and management (MPA); security studies (M Sc); social work (M Sc); spatial planning and urban design (MA); sports therapy (M Sc); supporting older children and young people with dyslexia (MA); teaching languages (MA), including Arabic, English; translation (MA); woman and child abuse (MA).

**Marquette University,** Graduate School, College of Arts and Sciences, Department of History, Milwaukee, WI 53201-1881. Offers European history (MA, PhD); global studies (MA); United States history (MA, PhD). *Program availability:* Part-time. *Faculty:* 22 full-time (7 women), 2 part-time/adjunct (0 women). *Students:* 29 full-time (10 women), 8 part-time (3 women); includes 2 minority (1 Hispanic/Latino; 1 Two or more races, non-Hispanic/Latino), 2 international. Average age 32. 26 applicants, 85% accepted, 13 enrolled. In 2016, 10 master's, 2 doctorates awarded. *Degree requirements:* For master's, comprehensive exam, essay, 2 classes of research seminars (6 hours); for doctorate, one foreign language, comprehensive exam, thesis/dissertation, 2 research seminars, dissertation seminar. *Entrance requirements:* For master's, GRE General Test, official transcripts from all current and previous colleges/universities except Marquette, one-page statement of purpose, three letters of recommendation from former teachers; for doctorate, GRE General Test, official transcripts from all current and previous colleges/universities except Marquette, one-page statement of purpose, three letters of recommendation from former teachers, writing sample. Additional exam requirements/recommendations for international students: Required—TOEFL. *Application deadline:* For fall admission, 12/31 for domestic and international students. Application fee: $50. Electronic applications accepted. *Financial support:* Fellowships with partial tuition reimbursements, research assistantships with full tuition reimbursements, teaching assistantships with full tuition reimbursements, scholarships/grants, health care benefits, tuition waivers (full and partial), and unspecified assistantships available. Support available to part-time students. Financial award application deadline: 2/15. *Faculty research:* Children's history, Soviet and post-Soviet history, modern Ireland and Britain, Japan and martial arts, American Catholicism. *Unit head:* Dr. James Marten, Chair, 414-288-7901, Fax: 414-288-1578. *Application contact:* Dr. Angela Sorby.
Website: http://www.marquette.edu/history/grad.shtml

**Marquette University,** Graduate School, College of Arts and Sciences, Department of Political Science, Milwaukee, WI 53201-1881. Offers international affairs (MA); political science (MA); public service (MA); JD/MA; MA/MBA. *Program availability:* Part-time. *Faculty:* 17 full-time (7 women), 6 part-time/adjunct (2 women). *Students:* 22 full-time (11 women), 5 part-time (3 women); includes 4 minority (3 Hispanic/Latino; 1 Two or more races, non-Hispanic/Latino). Average age 26. 32 applicants, 78% accepted, 27 enrolled. In 2016, 16 master's awarded. *Degree requirements:* For master's, comprehensive exam, thesis optional. *Entrance requirements:* For master's, GRE General Test, official transcripts from all current and previous colleges/universities except Marquette, three letters of recommendation, statement of purpose. Additional exam requirements/recommendations for international students: Required—TOEFL (minimum score 530 paper-based). *Application deadline:* For fall admission, 2/15 for domestic and international students. Application fee: $50. Electronic applications accepted. *Financial support:* Fellowships with partial tuition reimbursements, research assistantships with full tuition reimbursements, scholarships/grants, health care benefits, tuition waivers (full and partial), and unspecified assistantships available. Support available to part-time students. Financial award application deadline: 2/15. *Faculty research:* Public opinion and electoral behavior, public policy analysis, Congress and the Presidency, judicial behavior, political system transitions. *Total annual research expenditures:* $617. *Unit head:* Dr. Lowell Barrington, Chair, 414-288-5234. *Application contact:* Dr. Julia Azari.
Website: http://www.marquette.edu/polisci/grad.shtml

**McMaster University,** School of Graduate Studies, Faculty of Humanities and Faculty of Social Sciences, Institute on Globalization and the Human Condition, Hamilton, ON L8S 4M2, Canada. Offers globalization studies (MA).

**McMaster University,** School of Graduate Studies, Faculty of Social Sciences, Department of Political Science, Hamilton, ON L8S 4M2, Canada. Offers international relations (PhD); political science (MA); public and the global economy (MA); public policy (PhD); public policy and administration (MA). MA program in public policy and administration offered jointly with University of Guelph. *Program availability:* Part-time. *Degree requirements:* For master's, thesis or alternative. *Entrance requirements:* For master's, minimum B+ average. Additional exam requirements/recommendations for international students: Required—TOEFL (minimum score 580 paper-based). *Faculty research:* Organizational theory, internationalization of public policy, water resource policies, political interest intermediation, comparative politics.

**Middlebury Institute of International Studies at Monterey,** Graduate School of International Policy and Management, Program in International Policy and Development, Monterey, CA 93940-2691. Offers MA. *Degree requirements:* For master's, one foreign language. *Entrance requirements:* For master's, minimum GPA of 3.0, proficiency in a foreign language. Additional exam requirements/recommendations for international students: Required—TOEFL (minimum score 550 paper-based; 80 iBT). Electronic applications accepted. *Expenses: Tuition:* Full-time $38,250; part-time $1820 per credit. *Required fees:* $78 per semester.

**Middle Tennessee State University,** College of Graduate Studies, College of Liberal Arts, Department of Political Science, Murfreesboro, TN 37132. Offers international affairs (MA). *Program availability:* Part-time, evening/weekend, online learning. *Entrance requirements:* Additional exam requirements/recommendations for international students: Required—TOEFL (minimum score 525 paper-based; 71 iBT) or IELTS (minimum score 6). Electronic applications accepted.

**Missouri State University,** Graduate College, College of Humanities and Public Affairs, Department of Political Science, Program in Global Studies, Springfield, MO 65897. Offers MGS. *Program availability:* Part-time. *Students:* 13 full-time (5 women), 5 part-time (2 women); includes 1 minority (Two or more races, non-Hispanic/Latino), 6 international. Average age 25. 13 applicants, 38% accepted, 2 enrolled. In 2016, 6 master's awarded. *Degree requirements:* For master's, 2 foreign languages, comprehensive exam, thesis or alternative. *Entrance requirements:* For master's, GRE, minimum GPA of 3.0. Additional exam requirements/recommendations for international students: Required—TOEFL (minimum score 550 paper-based; 79 iBT), IELTS (minimum score 6). *Application deadline:* For fall admission, 7/20 priority date for domestic students, 5/1 for international students; for spring admission, 12/20 priority date for domestic students, 9/1 for international students; for summer admission, 5/20 priority date for domestic students. Applications are processed on a rolling basis. Application fee: $35 ($50 for international students). Electronic applications accepted. *Expenses:* Tuition, state resident: full-time $5830. Tuition, nonresident: full-time $10,708. *Required fees:* $1130. Tuition and fees vary according to class time, course level, course load and program. *Financial support:* Federal Work-Study, institutionally sponsored loans, scholarships/grants, and unspecified assistantships available. Support available to part-time students. Financial award application deadline: 3/31; financial award applicants required to submit FAFSA. *Faculty research:* U.S.-China policy, Eastern European politics, South American political reform, landmine use policy. *Unit head:* Dr. George Connor, Department Head, 417-836-5630, Fax: 417-836-6655, E-mail: georgeconnor@missouristate.edu. *Application contact:* Michael Edwards, Coordinator of Graduate Admissions, 417-836-5330, Fax: 417-836-6200, E-mail: michaeledwards@missouristate.edu.
Website: http://polsci.missouristate.edu/mgs/

**Morgan State University,** School of Graduate Studies, College of Liberal Arts, Department of World Languages and International Studies, Baltimore, MD 21251. Offers international studies (MA). *Program availability:* Part-time, evening/weekend. *Degree requirements:* For master's, one foreign language, comprehensive exam, thesis. *Entrance requirements:* For master's, GRE. Additional exam requirements/recommendations for international students: Required—TOEFL (minimum score 550 paper-based).

**New England College,** Program in Management, Henniker, NH 03242-3293. Offers accounting (MSA); healthcare administration (MS); international relations (MA); marketing management (MS); nonprofit leadership (MS); project management (MS); strategic leadership (MS). *Program availability:* Part-time, evening/weekend. *Degree requirements:* For master's, independent research project. Electronic applications accepted.

**The New School,** Schools of Public Engagement, Program in International Affairs, New York, NY 10011. Offers MA, MS. *Program availability:* Part-time. *Faculty:* 34 full-time (16 women), 14 part-time/adjunct (3 women). *Students:* 152 full-time (103 women), 51 part-time (35 women); includes 81 minority (28 Black or African American, non-Hispanic/Latino; 1 American Indian or Alaska Native, non-Hispanic/Latino; 14 Asian, non-Hispanic/Latino; 30 Hispanic/Latino; 8 Two or more races, non-Hispanic/Latino), 55 international. Average age 28. 222 applicants, 91% accepted, 59 enrolled. In 2016, 117 master's awarded. *Degree requirements:* For master's, thesis or alternative. *Entrance requirements:* For master's, academic writing sample, two letters of recommendation, statement of purpose, resume, transcripts. Additional exam requirements/recommendations for international students: Required—TOEFL (minimum score 100 iBT), IELTS (minimum score 7), PTE (minimum score 68). *Application deadline:* For fall admission, 1/15 priority date for domestic and international students; for spring admission, 10/15 priority date for domestic and international students. Applications are processed on a rolling basis. Application fee: $50. Electronic applications accepted. *Expenses:* Contact institution. *Financial support:* Research assistantships, career-related internships or fieldwork, Federal Work-Study, scholarships/grants, and unspecified assistantships available. Support available to part-time students. Financial award application deadline: 2/1; financial award applicants required to submit FAFSA. *Faculty research:* Cities and social justice, conflict and security development, governance and rights, media and culture. *Unit head:* Stephen Collier, Chair, 212-229-5400 Ext. 2432, E-mail: colliers@newschool.edu. *Application contact:* Sharon Greenidge, Assistant Director of Admission, 212-229-5400 Ext. 1103, E-mail: greenids@newschool.edu.
Website: http://www.newschool.edu/

**New York University,** Graduate School of Arts and Science, Department of Politics, New York, NY 10012-1019. Offers political campaign management (MA); politics (MA, PhD); JD/MA; MBA/MA. *Program availability:* Part-time. Terminal master's awarded for partial completion of doctoral program. *Degree requirements:* For master's, one foreign language, thesis or alternative; for doctorate, 2 foreign languages, comprehensive exam, thesis/dissertation. *Entrance requirements:* For master's and doctorate, GRE General Test. Additional exam requirements/recommendations for international students: Required—TOEFL. *Faculty research:* Comparative politics, democratic theory and practice, rational choice, political economy, international relations.

**New York University,** School of Continuing and Professional Studies, Center for Global Affairs, New York, NY 10012-1019. Offers global affairs (MS), including environment/energy policy, human rights and international law, international development and humanitarian assistance, international relations, peace building, private sector, transnational security; global energy (Advanced Certificate); peacebuilding (Advanced Certificate); transnational security (Advanced Certificate). *Program availability:* Part-time, evening/weekend. *Degree requirements:* For master's, thesis. *Entrance requirements:* For master's, GRE or GMAT (only upon request), bachelor's degree, resume with relevant professional work, internship or volunteer experience, two letters of recommendation, statement of purpose. Additional exam requirements/recommendations for international students: Required—TOEFL (minimum score 600 paper-based; 100 iBT), IELTS (minimum score 7). Electronic applications accepted.

**North Carolina State University,** Graduate School, College of Humanities and Social Sciences, School of Public and International Affairs, Program in International Studies, Raleigh, NC 27695. Offers MIS. *Degree requirements:* For master's, thesis optional. *Entrance requirements:* For master's, GRE General Test, minimum GPA of 3.0 during previous 2 years. Electronic applications accepted. *Faculty research:* Global environmental policy and climate change, drug policy and the Caribbean, U.S. national security politics, local responses to globalization, the political economy of the European Union.

**Northeastern University,** College of Professional Studies, Boston, MA 02115-5096. Offers applied nutrition (MS); college athletics administration (MSL); commerce and economic development (MS); corporate and organizational communication (MS); criminal justice (MS); digital media (MPS); elearning and instructional design (M Ed); elementary education (MAT); geographic information technology (MPS); global studies and international relations (MS); higher education administration (M Ed); homeland security (MA); human services (MS); informatics (MPS); leadership (MS); learning analytics (M Ed); learning and instruction (M Ed); nonprofit management (MS); professional sports administration (MSL); project management (MS); regulatory affairs for drugs, biologics, and medical devices (MS); respiratory care leadership (MS); special education (M Ed); technical communication (MS). *Program availability:* Part-time, evening/weekend, 100% online, blended/hybrid learning. *Faculty:* 82 full-time (51 women), 853 part-time/adjunct (366 women). *Students:* 4,947 part-time (3,076 women). In 2016, 1,456 master's awarded. *Application deadline:* Applications are processed on a rolling basis. Application fee: $0. Electronic applications accepted. *Expenses:* Contact institution. *Financial support:* Applicants required to submit FAFSA. *Unit head:* Dr. Mary Loeffelholz, Interim Dean of the College of Professional Studies.
Website: http://www.cps.neu.edu/

**Northeastern University,** College of Social Sciences and Humanities, Boston, MA 02115. Offers criminology and criminal justice (MSCJ); criminology and justice policy (PhD); economics (MA, PhD); English (MA, PhD); international affairs (MA); law and public policy (PhD); political science (MA, PhD); public administration (MPA); public history (MA); public policy (MPP); security and resilience studies (MS); sociology (MA, PhD); urban and regional policy (MS); urban informatics (MS); world history (MA, PhD); JD/MS. *Program availability:* Online learning. *Faculty:* 234 full-time (114 women), 55 part-time/adjunct (34 women). *Students:* 427 full-time (239 women), 77 part-time (42 women). In 2016, 143 master's, 38 doctorates awarded. *Degree requirements:* For doctorate, variable foreign language requirement, comprehensive exam, thesis/dissertation. *Entrance requirements:* For master's and doctorate, GRE. Additional exam requirements/recommendations for international students: Required—TOEFL, IELTS. Application fee: $75. Electronic applications accepted. *Expenses:* $1,295 per credit. *Financial support:* Teaching assistantships, career-related internships or fieldwork, scholarships/grants, health care benefits, tuition waivers (full and partial), and unspecified assistantships available. Support available to part-time students. Financial award applicants required to submit FAFSA. *Unit head:* Dr. Uta Poiger, Dean, 617-373-5173. *Application contact:* Amber Crowe, Administrative Coordinator, 617-373-5990,

## International Affairs

Fax: 617-373-7281, E-mail: gradcssh@northeastern.edu.
Website: http://www.northeastern.edu/cssh/graduate

**Northwestern University,** The Graduate School, Center for International and Comparative Studies, Evanston, IL 60208. Offers Certificate.

**Northwestern University,** Pritzker School of Law, Chicago, IL 60611-3069. Offers international human rights (LL M); law (JD); law and business (LL M); science law (MSL); tax (LL M in Tax); JD/LL M; JD/MBA; JD/PhD; LL M/Certificate. Executive LL M programs offered in Madrid (Spain), Seoul (South Korea), and Tel Aviv (Israel). *Accreditation:* ABA. *Entrance requirements:* For master's, law degree or equivalent, letter of recommendation, resume; for doctorate, LSAT, 1 letter of recommendation, resume. Additional exam requirements/recommendations for international students: Required—TOEFL. Electronic applications accepted. *Expenses:* Contact institution. *Faculty research:* Constitutional law, corporate law, international law, law and social policy, ethical studies.

**Norwich University,** College of Graduate and Continuing Studies, Master of Arts in Diplomacy Program, Northfield, VT 05663. Offers diplomacy (MA), including cyber diplomacy - policy, cyber diplomacy - technical, international commerce, international conflict management, international terrorism. *Program availability:* Evening/weekend, online only, mostly all online with a week-long residency requirement. *Faculty:* 1 full-time (0 women), 20 part-time/adjunct (3 women). *Students:* 154 full-time (49 women); includes 34 minority (18 Black or African American, non-Hispanic/Latino; 1 Asian, non-Hispanic/Latino; 9 Hispanic/Latino; 6 Two or more races, non-Hispanic/Latino), 1 international. Average age 34. 31 applicants, 100% accepted, 25 enrolled. In 2016, 93 master's awarded. *Degree requirements:* For master's, comprehensive exam, thesis optional. *Entrance requirements:* For master's, minimum undergraduate GPA of 2.75. Additional exam requirements/recommendations for international students: Required—TOEFL (minimum score 550 paper-based; 80 iBT), IELTS (minimum score 6.5). *Application deadline:* For fall admission, 8/14 for domestic and international students; for winter admission, 11/13 for domestic and international students; for spring admission, 2/12 for domestic and international students; for summer admission, 6/5 for domestic and international students. Electronic applications accepted. *Expenses:* Contact institution. *Financial support:* In 2016–17, 75 students received support. Scholarships/grants available. Financial award application deadline: 8/4; financial award applicants required to submit FAFSA. *Unit head:* Dr. Lasha Tchantouridze, Program Director, 802-485-2095, Fax: 802-485-2533, E-mail: ltchanto@norwich.edu. *Application contact:* Admissions Advisor, 800-460-5597 Ext. 3378, Fax: 802-485-2533, E-mail: mdy@online.norwich.edu.
Website: https://online.norwich.edu/degree-programs/masters/master-arts-diplomacy/overview

**Norwich University,** College of Graduate and Continuing Studies, Master of Arts in International Relations Program, Northfield, VT 05663. Offers international relations (MA), including cyber diplomacy-policy, cyber diplomacy-technical, international development, international security, national security, regions of the world. *Program availability:* Evening/weekend, online only, mostly all online with a week-long residency requirement. *Faculty:* 9 part-time/adjunct (3 women). *Students:* 51 full-time (18 women); includes 11 minority (8 Black or African American, non-Hispanic/Latino; 2 Asian, non-Hispanic/Latino; 1 Two or more races, non-Hispanic/Latino). Average age 34. 33 applicants, 100% accepted, 22 enrolled. *Degree requirements:* For master's, research paper. *Entrance requirements:* For master's, minimum undergraduate GPA of 2.75. Additional exam requirements/recommendations for international students: Required—TOEFL (minimum score 550 paper-based; 80 iBT), IELTS (minimum score 6.5). *Application deadline:* For fall admission, 8/14 for domestic and international students; for winter admission, 11/13 for domestic and international students; for spring admission, 2/12 for domestic and international students; for summer admission, 6/5 for domestic and international students. Electronic applications accepted. *Expenses:* Contact institution. *Financial support:* In 2016–17, 24 students received support. Scholarships/grants available. Financial award application deadline: 8/4; financial award applicants required to submit FAFSA. *Unit head:* Dr. Lasha Tchantouridze, Director, 802-485-2095, Fax: 802-485-2533, E-mail: ltchanto@norwich.edu. *Application contact:* Admissions Office, 800-460-5597 Ext. 3392, E-mail: mair@online.norwich.edu.
Website: https://online.norwich.edu/degree-programs/masters/master-arts-international-relations/overview

**Ohio University,** Graduate College, Center for International Studies, Program in Communications and Development Studies, Athens, OH 45701-2979. Offers MA. *Program availability:* Part-time. *Degree requirements:* For master's, one foreign language, thesis optional, internship. *Entrance requirements:* For master's, minimum GPA of 3.0. Additional exam requirements/recommendations for international students: Required—TOEFL (minimum score 550 paper-based; 80 iBT), IELTS (minimum score 6.5). *Application deadline:* For fall admission, 1/1 for domestic and international students. Application fee: $50 ($55 for international students). Electronic applications accepted. *Financial support:* Research assistantships with full tuition reimbursements, Federal Work-Study, institutionally sponsored loans, and tuition waivers (partial) available. Financial award application deadline: 1/1. *Faculty research:* National development processes, public relations and participatory research, audio and video production, health communication, urban development. *Unit head:* Dr. Lawrence Wood, Director, 740-593-1833, E-mail: woodl@ohio.edu. *Application contact:* Patti Malloy, Administrative Assistant, 740-593-1836, Fax: 740-593-1837, E-mail: malloyp@ohio.edu.
Website: http://www.ohio.edu/commdev/

**Oklahoma State University,** Graduate College, Stillwater, OK 74078. Offers aerospace security (Graduate Certificate); bioenergy and sustainable technology (Graduate Certificate); business data mining (Graduate Certificate); business sustainability (Graduate Certificate); environmental science (MS); international studies (MS); non-profit management (Graduate Certificate); teaching English to speakers of other languages (Graduate Certificate); telecommunications management (MS). Programs are interdisciplinary. *Students:* 50 full-time (28 women), 109 part-time (63 women); includes 23 minority (4 Black or African American, non-Hispanic/Latino; 5 American Indian or Alaska Native, non-Hispanic/Latino; 4 Asian, non-Hispanic/Latino; 4 Hispanic/Latino; 6 Two or more races, non-Hispanic/Latino), 58 international. Average age 29. 363 applicants, 81% accepted, 71 enrolled. In 2016, 56 master's, 9 doctorates awarded. *Degree requirements:* For master's, thesis (for some programs); for doctorate, comprehensive exam, thesis/dissertation. *Entrance requirements:* For master's and doctorate, GRE or GMAT. Additional exam requirements/recommendations for international students: Required—TOEFL (minimum score 550 paper-based; 79 iBT). *Application deadline:* For fall admission, 3/1 priority date for domestic and international students; for spring admission, 8/1 priority date for domestic and international students. Applications are processed on a rolling basis. Application fee: $40 ($75 for international students). Electronic applications accepted. *Expenses:* Tuition, state resident: full-time $3775; part-time $209.70 per credit hour. Tuition, nonresident: full-time $14,851; part-time $825.05 per credit hour. *Required fees:* $2027; $112.60 per credit hour. Tuition and fees vary according to campus/location. *Financial support:* Research assistantships, career-related internships or fieldwork, Federal Work-Study, scholarships/grants, health care benefits, tuition waivers (partial), and unspecified assistantships available. Support available to part-time students. Financial award application deadline: 3/1; financial

award applicants required to submit FAFSA. *Unit head:* Dr. Sheryl Tucker, Dean, 405-744-6368, Fax: 405-744-0355, E-mail: gradi@okstate.edu. *Application contact:* Dr. Susan Mathew, Assistant Director of Graduate Admissions, 405-744-6368, Fax: 405-744-0355, E-mail: gradi@okstate.edu.
Website: http://gradcollege.okstate.edu/

**Old Dominion University,** College of Arts and Letters, Graduate Program in International Studies, Norfolk, VA 23529. Offers conflict and cooperation (MA, PhD); interdependence and transnationalism (MA, PhD); international cultural studies (MA, PhD); international political economy and development (MA, PhD); modeling and simulation (MA, PhD); U.S. foreign policy and international relations (MA, PhD). *Program availability:* Part-time. *Faculty:* 18 full-time (4 women). *Students:* 35 full-time (13 women), 38 part-time (20 women); includes 14 minority (9 Black or African American, non-Hispanic/Latino; 2 Asian, non-Hispanic/Latino; 1 Hispanic/Latino; 2 Two or more races, non-Hispanic/Latino), 19 international. Average age 37. 99 applicants, 54% accepted, 34 enrolled. In 2016, 24 master's, 11 doctorates awarded. Terminal master's awarded for partial completion of doctoral program. *Degree requirements:* For master's, one foreign language, comprehensive exam, thesis optional; for doctorate, one foreign language, comprehensive exam, thesis/dissertation. *Entrance requirements:* For master's, GRE General Test, sample of written work, 2 letters of recommendation; for doctorate, GRE General Test, sample of written work, 3 letters of recommendation. Additional exam requirements/recommendations for international students: Required—TOEFL (minimum score 570 paper-based). *Application deadline:* For fall admission, 1/15 for domestic and international students; for spring admission, 10/15 for domestic and international students. Application fee: $50. Electronic applications accepted. *Expenses:* Contact institution. *Financial support:* In 2016–17, 12 students received support, including 1 fellowship (averaging $15,000 per year), 5 research assistantships with tuition reimbursements available (averaging $15,000 per year), 4 teaching assistantships with tuition reimbursements available (averaging $15,000 per year); career-related internships or fieldwork, institutionally sponsored loans, and unspecified assistantships also available. Financial award application deadline: 1/15; financial award applicants required to submit FAFSA. *Faculty research:* U.S. foreign policy, international security, Transatlantic and Transpacific relations, transnational issues, international political economy and development. *Total annual research expenditures:* $330,391. *Unit head:* Dr. Regina Karp, Graduate Program Director, 757-683-5700, Fax: 757-683-5701, E-mail: rkarp@odu.edu. *Application contact:* Dr. David C. Earnest, Associate Dean, 757-683-6077, Fax: 757-683-5746, E-mail: dearnest@odu.edu.
Website: http://www.odu.edu/gpis

**Penn State University Park,** Graduate School, School of International Affairs, University Park, PA 16802. Offers MIA. *Students:* 83 full-time (47 women), 4 part-time (3 women). Average age 25. 166 applicants, 82% accepted, 49 enrolled. In 2016, 40 master's awarded. *Entrance requirements:* Additional exam requirements/recommendations for international students: Required—TOEFL (minimum score 550 paper-based; 80 iBT), IELTS. *Application deadline:* Applications are processed on a rolling basis. Application fee: $65. Electronic applications accepted. *Financial support:* Fellowships, research assistantships, teaching assistantships, career-related internships or fieldwork, Federal Work-Study, scholarships/grants, traineeships, health care benefits, and unspecified assistantships available. Support available to part-time students. Financial award application deadline: 3/1; financial award applicants required to submit FAFSA. *Unit head:* Hari M. Osofsky, Dean, 814-863-1521, Fax: 814-863-7274. *Application contact:* Lori Hawn, Director, Graduate Student Services, 814-865-1795, Fax: 814-863-4627, E-mail: l-gswww@lists.psu.edu.
Website: http://sia.psu.edu/

**Pepperdine University,** Graduate School of Education and Psychology, Division of Education, Los Angeles, CA 90045. Offers administration and preliminary administrative services (MS); education (MA); educational leadership, administration, and policy (Ed D); global leadership and change (PhD); learning technologies (MA, Ed D); organizational leadership (Ed D); social entrepreneurship and change (MA); teaching (MA); teaching: TESOL (MA). *Program availability:* Part-time, evening/weekend, online learning. *Students:* 262 full-time (169 women), 385 part-time (264 women); includes 286 minority (123 Black or African American, non-Hispanic/Latino; 4 American Indian or Alaska Native, non-Hispanic/Latino; 59 Asian, non-Hispanic/Latino; 77 Hispanic/Latino; 6 Native Hawaiian or other Pacific Islander, non-Hispanic/Latino; 17 Two or more races, non-Hispanic/Latino), 46 international. Average age 38. 372 applicants, 95% accepted, 200 enrolled. In 2016, 142 master's, 66 doctorates awarded. *Degree requirements:* For doctorate, thesis/dissertation. *Entrance requirements:* For master's, GRE General Test; for doctorate, GRE General Test, MAT. Additional exam requirements/recommendations for international students: Required—TOEFL. *Application deadline:* Applications are processed on a rolling basis. Application fee: $55. *Expenses:* $1,165 per unit (for master's); $1,460 per unit (for doctorate). *Financial support:* Research assistantships, teaching assistantships, career-related internships or fieldwork, institutionally sponsored loans, and scholarships/grants available. Support available to part-time students. Financial award application deadline: 7/1; financial award applicants required to submit FAFSA. *Unit head:* Dr. Martine Jago, Associate Dean, Education Division, 310-568-2828, E-mail: martine.jago@pepperdine.edu. *Application contact:* Chris Costa, Director of Enrollment, 310-568-2850, E-mail: chris.costa@pepperdine.edu.
Website: http://gsep.pepperdine.edu/masters-education/

**Pepperdine University,** School of Public Policy, Malibu, CA 90263. Offers American politics (MPP); economics (MPP); international relations (MPP); state and local policy (MPP); JD/MPP; MBA/MPP; MDR/MPP. *Faculty:* 4 full-time (1 woman), 5 part-time/adjunct (0 women). *Students:* 57 full-time (27 women), 7 part-time (5 women); includes 22 minority (9 Black or African American, non-Hispanic/Latino; 2 American Indian or Alaska Native, non-Hispanic/Latino; 6 Asian, non-Hispanic/Latino; 4 Hispanic/Latino; 1 Two or more races, non-Hispanic/Latino), 10 international. Average age 25. 174 applicants, 55% accepted, 29 enrolled. In 2016, 34 master's awarded. *Entrance requirements:* For master's, GRE or GMAT, 2 letters of recommendation, resume, two essays. Additional exam requirements/recommendations for international students: Required—TOEFL. *Application deadline:* For fall admission, 6/15 for domestic students. Applications are processed on a rolling basis. Application fee: $50. Electronic applications accepted. *Expenses:* $47,710 per academic year; $1,525 per unit (for master's). *Financial support:* Institutionally sponsored loans and scholarships/grants available. Financial award application deadline: 5/1; financial award applicants required to submit FAFSA. *Unit head:* Dr. Pete Peterson, Dean, School of Public Policy, 310-506-7490, Fax: 310-506-7494, E-mail: pete.n.peterson@pepperdine.edu. *Application contact:* Carson Bruno, Assistant Dean for Admission and Program Relations, 310-506-7493, E-mail: carson.bruno@pepperdine.edu.
Website: http://publicpolicy.pepperdine.edu/

**Pontificia Universidad Catolica Madre y Maestra,** Graduate School, Faculty of Social and Administrative Sciences, Santiago, Dominican Republic. Offers business administration (MBA), including business development, finance, international business, management skills (M Mgmt, MBA), marketing, operations, strategic cost management, strategy, tourist destination planning and management; law (LL M), including civil law, corporate business law, criminal law, international relations, real estate law;

management (M Mgmt), including higher financial management, insurance program administration, management skills (M Mgmt, MBA); psychology (MA), including clinical child and adolescent psychology, forensic psychology; strategic human resources (EMBA).

**Princeton University,** Graduate School, Woodrow Wilson School of Public and International Affairs, Princeton, NJ 08544-1019. Offers public affairs (MPA, PhD); public policy (MPP); JD/MPA. JD/MPA offered jointly with Columbia University, New York University, Stanford University. Terminal master's awarded for partial completion of doctoral program. *Degree requirements:* For master's, internship; for doctorate, one foreign language, thesis/dissertation. *Entrance requirements:* For master's, GRE General Test, original policy memo; for doctorate, GRE General Test. Additional exam requirements/recommendations for international students: Required—TOEFL (minimum score 600 paper-based). Electronic applications accepted.

**Queen's University at Kingston,** School of Graduate Studies, Faculty of Arts and Sciences, Department of Political Studies, Kingston, ON K7L 3N6, Canada. Offers Canadian politics (PhD); comparative politics (PhD); gender and politics (PhD); international relations (PhD); political theory (PhD). *Degree requirements:* For master's, thesis or alternative; for doctorate, one foreign language, thesis/dissertation, qualifying exams. *Entrance requirements:* Additional exam requirements/recommendations for international students: Required—TOEFL (minimum score 600 paper-based). *Faculty research:* Canadian politics, comparative politics, political thought, international politics, women and politics.

**Regent's University London,** Webster Graduate School, London, United Kingdom. Offers business (MBA); finance (MS); human resources (MA); information technology management (MA); international business (MA); international non-governmental organizations (MA); international relations (MA); management and leadership (MA); marketing (MA). *Program availability:* Part-time.

**Regent University,** Graduate School, Robertson School of Government, Virginia Beach, VA 23464-9800. Offers government (MA), including American government, healthcare policy and ethics (MA, MPA), international relations, law and public policy, national security studies, political communication, political theory, religion and politics; public administration (MPA), including emergency management and homeland security, federal government, general public administration, healthcare policy and ethics (MA, MPA), law, nonprofit administration and faith-based organizations, public leadership and management, servant leadership. *Program availability:* Part-time, evening/weekend, 100% online, blended/hybrid learning. *Faculty:* 8 full-time (1 woman), 19 part-time/adjunct (3 women). *Students:* 40 full-time (27 women), 119 part-time (69 women); includes 73 minority (47 Black or African American, non-Hispanic/Latino; 3 Asian, non-Hispanic/Latino; 15 Hispanic/Latino; 8 Two or more races, non-Hispanic/Latino), 6 international. Average age 35. 253 applicants, 41% accepted, 70 enrolled. In 2016, 34 master's awarded. *Degree requirements:* For master's, thesis optional, internship. *Entrance requirements:* For master's, GRE General Test or LSAT, personal essay, writing sample, resume, college transcripts. Additional exam requirements/recommendations for international students: Required—TOEFL (minimum score 577 paper-based). *Application deadline:* For fall admission, 5/1 priority date for domestic students; for spring admission, 11/1 priority date for domestic students. Applications are processed on a rolling basis. Application fee: $50. Electronic applications accepted. *Expenses:* $650 per credit (MA/MPA); $250 per semester technology fee. *Financial support:* In 2016–17, 78 students received support. Career-related internships or fieldwork, scholarships/grants, and unspecified assistantships available. Support available to part-time students. *Faculty research:* International relations and politics, public administration, leadership and ethics, Biblical law, Constitutional law and Supreme Court. *Unit head:* Dr. Eric Patterson, Dean, 757-352-4616, Fax: 757-352-4735, E-mail: epatterson@regent.edu. *Application contact:* Heidi Cece, Assistant Vice President of Enrollment Management, 800-373-5504, Fax: 757-352-4381, E-mail: admissions@regent.edu.
Website: http://www.regent.edu/rsg/

**Richmond, The American International University in London,** MA in International Relations Program, Richmond, United Kingdom. Offers MA. *Program availability:* Part-time. *Entrance requirements:* Additional exam requirements/recommendations for international students: Required—TOEFL, IELTS. Electronic applications accepted.

**Rutgers University–Camden,** Graduate School of Arts and Sciences, Department of Public Policy and Administration, Camden, NJ 08102. Offers education policy and leadership (MPA); international public service and development (MPA); public management (MPA); JD/MPA; MPA/MA. *Accreditation:* NASPAA. *Program availability:* Part-time, evening/weekend. *Degree requirements:* For master's, directed study, research workshop, 42 credits. *Entrance requirements:* For master's, GRE General Test, GMAT or LSAT, 3 letters of recommendation; resume. Additional exam requirements/recommendations for international students: Required—TOEFL (minimum score 550 paper-based), IELTS. Electronic applications accepted. *Faculty research:* Nonprofit management, county and municipal administration, health and human services, government communication, administrative law, educational finance.

**Rutgers University–Newark,** Graduate School, Division of Global Affairs, Newark, NJ 07102. Offers MS, PhD. *Program availability:* Part-time, evening/weekend. *Degree requirements:* For master's, one foreign language, thesis optional. *Entrance requirements:* For master's and doctorate, GRE General Test, minimum B average. Electronic applications accepted. *Faculty research:* International organizations, diplomacy, world history, international political economy, global environment.

**Rutgers University–Newark,** Graduate School, Program in Political Science, Newark, NJ 07102. Offers American political system (MA); international relations (MA); JD/MA. *Program availability:* Part-time, evening/weekend. *Degree requirements:* For master's, comprehensive exam, thesis optional. *Entrance requirements:* For master's, GRE, minimum undergraduate B average. Electronic applications accepted. *Faculty research:* Policymaking and policy evaluation in the United States; government and politics in Europe, Middle East, Asia, Africa, and Latin America.

**Rutgers University–New Brunswick,** Graduate School-New Brunswick, Department of Political Science, Piscataway, NJ 08854-8097. Offers American politics (PhD); comparative politics (PhD); international relations (PhD); political theory (PhD); public law (PhD); United Nations and global policy studies (MA); women and politics (PhD). *Degree requirements:* For doctorate, one foreign language, comprehensive exam, thesis/dissertation. *Entrance requirements:* For master's, bachelor's degree from accredited U.S. college or university or a comparable institution in another country; for doctorate, GRE General Test. Additional exam requirements/recommendations for international students: Required—TOEFL.

**Rutgers University–New Brunswick,** Graduate School-New Brunswick, Program in Global and Comparative History, New Brunswick, NJ 08901. Offers MA. *Entrance requirements:* For master's, GRE, minimum GPA of 3.0, official transcripts, two letters of recommendation, 1-2 page personal statement, 10-15 page writing sample. Electronic applications accepted.

**St. John's University,** College of Professional Studies, Department of Mass Communications, Queens, NY 11439. Offers international communications (MS).

*Program availability:* Part-time, evening/weekend. *Degree requirements:* For master's, one foreign language, thesis optional. *Entrance requirements:* For master's, GRE, official transcript showing conferral of bachelor's degree, 2 letters of recommendation, proficiency in a foreign language, minimum GPA of 3.0. Additional exam requirements/recommendations for international students: Required—TOEFL (minimum score 600 paper-based; 100 iBT), IELTS (minimum score 7). Electronic applications accepted.

**St. John's University,** St. John's College of Liberal Arts and Sciences, Department of Government and Politics, Queens, NY 11439. Offers government and politics (MA, Adv C), including government and politics (MA), international law and diplomacy (Adv C); public administration (Adv C); international law and diplomacy (Adv C); JD/MA; MA/MS. *Program availability:* Part-time, evening/weekend. *Degree requirements:* For master's, comprehensive exam, thesis optional. *Entrance requirements:* For master's, minimum GPA of 3.0, 18 undergraduate credits in government and politics. Additional exam requirements/recommendations for international students: Required—TOEFL (minimum score 600 paper-based; 100 iBT), IELTS (minimum score 7). Electronic applications accepted. *Faculty research:* Presidential leadership, morality and politics, U.S. foreign policy, U.S. national security policy, New York state and local government and politics, state building and social policy, public opinion, campaigns and elections, education politics, North African politics, energy and European Union politics.

**St. Mary's University,** Graduate Studies, Program in International Relations, San Antonio, TX 78228-8507. Offers conflict transformation (Certificate); international conflict resolution (MA); international development (MA); international relations (MA); security policy (MA). *Program availability:* Part-time, evening/weekend, 100% online. *Faculty:* 4 full-time (2 women), 1 part-time/adjunct (0 women). *Students:* 22 full-time (14 women), 59 part-time (18 women); includes 33 minority (5 Black or African American, non-Hispanic/Latino; 2 American Indian or Alaska Native, non-Hispanic/Latino; 6 Asian, non-Hispanic/Latino; 20 Hispanic/Latino), 5 international. Average age 32. 28 applicants, 61% accepted, 6 enrolled. In 2016, 35 master's awarded. *Degree requirements:* For master's, one foreign language, comprehensive exam (for some programs), thesis (for some programs), thesis or comprehensive exam. *Entrance requirements:* For master's, minimum undergraduate cumulative GPA of 3.0. Additional exam requirements/recommendations for international students: Required—TOEFL (minimum score 550 paper-based; 80 iBT), IELTS (minimum score 6). *Application deadline:* For fall admission, 7/1 for domestic students; for spring admission, 11/15 for domestic students; for summer admission, 4/1 for domestic students. Applications are processed on a rolling basis. Application fee: $0. Electronic applications accepted. *Expenses: Tuition:* Full-time $15,600; part-time $865 per credit hour. *Required fees:* $148 per semester. *Financial support:* Research assistantships, Federal Work-Study, tuition waivers (full), unspecified assistantships, and grants for active-duty and retired military, DOD employees, and their spouses available. Financial award application deadline: 3/31; financial award applicants required to submit FAFSA. *Faculty research:* Anthropology and ethics, states in crisis and socioeconomic development, politics and society of south Asia, political psychology, international relations theory. *Unit head:* Dr. Amber Aubone, Graduate International Relations, 210-436-3111, E-mail: aaubone@stmarytx.edu. *Application contact:* Kim Thornton, Director, Graduate and Adult Enrollment Services, 210-436-3101, E-mail: kthornton@stmarytx.edu.

**Salve Regina University,** Program in International Relations, Newport, RI 02840-4192. Offers MA, Certificate. *Program availability:* Part-time, evening/weekend, online learning. *Entrance requirements:* For master's, GMAT, GRE General Test, MAT or LSAT. Additional exam requirements/recommendations for international students: Required—TOEFL (minimum score 600 paper-based; 100 iBT) or IELTS. Electronic applications accepted.

**San Francisco State University,** Division of Graduate Studies, College of Liberal and Creative Arts, Department of International Relations, San Francisco, CA 94132-1722. Offers MA. *Expenses:* Tuition, state resident: full-time $6738. Tuition, nonresident: full-time $15,666. *Required fees:* $1012. Tuition and fees vary according to degree level and program. *Unit head:* Dr. Mahmood Monshipouri, Chair, 415-338-2239, Fax: 415-338-6159, E-mail: mmonship@sfsu.edu. *Application contact:* Dr. Burcu Akan Ellis, Graduate Coordinator, 415-405-2694, Fax: 415-338-6159, E-mail: bellis@sfsu.edu.
Website: http://internationalrelations.sfsu.edu/

**Schiller International University,** Program in International Relations and Diplomacy, Paris, France. Offers MA. *Program availability:* Part-time, evening/weekend. *Degree requirements:* For master's, one foreign language, final comprehensive exam or thesis. *Entrance requirements:* For master's, undergraduate mathematics (strongly advised). Additional exam requirements/recommendations for international students: Required—TOEFL (minimum score 550 paper-based).

**Seton Hall University,** School of Diplomacy and International Relations, South Orange, NJ 07079-2697. Offers diplomacy and international relations (MA); global health management (Graduate Certificate); post-conflict state reconstruction and sustainability (Graduate Certificate); United Nations studies (Graduate Certificate); JD/MA; MA/MA; MBA/MA; MPA/MA. *Program availability:* Part-time, evening/weekend, 100% online, blended/hybrid learning. *Degree requirements:* For master's, thesis (for some programs), 45 credits; for Graduate Certificate, 15 credits. *Entrance requirements:* For master's, GRE, GMAT, or LSAT. Additional exam requirements/recommendations for international students: Required—TOEFL. Electronic applications accepted. *Expenses:* Contact institution. *Faculty research:* International economics and development, global health, United Nations, conflict negotiation, foreign policy analysis, international security, energy politics, Eastern and Central Europe, Latin America, Africa, peacemaking, genocide prevention, international organizations, international political economy, U.S.-China relations, democratization, international law, research methods.

**Simon Fraser University,** Office of Graduate Studies and Postdoctoral Fellows, Faculty of Arts and Social Sciences, School for International Studies, Burnaby, BC V5A 1S6, Canada. Offers MA. *Faculty:* 11 full-time (3 women). *Students:* 18 full-time (13 women). 46 applicants, 28% accepted, 7 enrolled. In 2016, 10 master's awarded. *Entrance requirements:* Additional exam requirements/recommendations for international students: Required—TOEFL (minimum score 580 paper-based; 93 iBT), IELTS (minimum score 7), TWE (minimum score 5). *Application deadline:* For spring admission, 1/3 for domestic and international students. Application fee: $90 ($125 for international students). Electronic applications accepted. *Financial support:* In 2016–17, 9 students received support, including 11 fellowships (averaging $6,500 per year), 8 teaching assistantships (averaging $6,000 per year). *Faculty research:* Peace and security, international development, human rights and international law, governance and civil society. *Unit head:* Gerardo Otero, Associate Professor, 778-782-8837, E-mail: mais-grad-chair@sfu.ca. *Application contact:* Joel Blok, Graduate Secretary, 778-782-7148, E-mail: intst@sfu.ca.
Website: http://www.sfu.ca/internationalstudies.html

**SIT Graduate Institute,** Graduate Programs, Master's Programs in Intercultural Service, Leadership, and Management, Brattleboro, VT 05302-0676. Offers intercultural service, leadership, and management (self-designed) (MA); international education (MA); peacebuilding and conflict transformation (MA); sustainable development (MA). *Program availability:* Online learning. *Degree requirements:* For master's, one foreign language, thesis. *Entrance requirements:* For master's, 3 letters of reference. Additional

## International Affairs

exam requirements/recommendations for international students: Required—TOEFL, IELTS. *Faculty research:* Intercultural communication, conflict resolution, international education, world issues, international affairs.

**Syracuse University,** Maxwell School of Citizenship and Public Affairs, Dual MA Program in Economics and International Relations, Syracuse, NY 13244. Offers MA/MA. *Entrance requirements:* Additional exam requirements/recommendations for international students: Required—TOEFL (minimum score 100 iBT). *Application deadline:* For fall admission, 2/1 priority date for domestic and international students. Application fee: $75. Electronic applications accepted. *Expenses: Tuition:* Full-time $25,974; part-time $1443 per credit hour. *Required fees:* $802; $50 per course. Tuition and fees vary according to course load and program. *Financial support:* Fellowships with full tuition reimbursements, research assistantships with tuition reimbursements, and teaching assistantships with tuition reimbursements available. Financial award application deadline: 1/1. *Faculty research:* Economic concepts, urban and regional economics, policy-oriented settings, public and international affairs, comparative foreign policy. *Unit head:* Dr. Robert Bifulco, Associate Dean and Chair, Public Administration and International Affairs, 315-443-3232, E-mail: rbifulco@maxwell.syr.edu. *Application contact:* Christine Omolino, Associate Director, 315-443-4000, Fax: 315-443-3423, E-mail: comolino@syr.edu.
Website: http://www.maxwell.syr.edu/

**Syracuse University,** Maxwell School of Citizenship and Public Affairs, Dual MPA/IR Program in Public Administration and International Relations, Syracuse, NY 13244. Offers MPA/MA. *Students:* Average age 27. *Entrance requirements:* Additional exam requirements/recommendations for international students: Required—TOEFL (minimum score 100 iBT). *Application deadline:* For fall admission, 2/1 priority date for domestic and international students. Application fee: $75. Electronic applications accepted. *Expenses: Tuition:* Full-time $25,974; part-time $1443 per credit hour. *Required fees:* $802; $50 per course. Tuition and fees vary according to course load and program. *Financial support:* Fellowships with full tuition reimbursements, research assistantships with tuition reimbursements, and teaching assistantships with tuition reimbursements available. Financial award application deadline: 1/1; financial award applicants required to submit FAFSA. *Faculty research:* Economics for public decisions, comparative foreign policy, international and development administration, public and nonprofit management, quantitative analysis. *Unit head:* Dr. Robert Bifulco, Associate Dean and Chair, Department of Public Administration and International Affairs, 315-443-3232, E-mail: rbifulco@maxwell.syr.edu. *Application contact:* Christine Omolino, 315-443-4000, E-mail: comolino@syr.edu.
Website: http://www.maxwell.syr.edu/

**Syracuse University,** Maxwell School of Citizenship and Public Affairs, EMIR Program of International Relations, Syracuse, NY 13244. Offers EMIR. *Program availability:* Part-time. *Entrance requirements:* For master's, resume, personal statement, official transcripts, three letters of recommendation, proof of competence in a second language. Additional exam requirements/recommendations for international students: Required—TOEFL (minimum score 100 iBT). *Application deadline:* For fall admission, 2/1 priority date for domestic and international students; for spring admission, 8/1 priority date for domestic and international students. Applications are processed on a rolling basis. Application fee: $75. Electronic applications accepted. *Expenses: Tuition:* Full-time $25,974; part-time $1443 per credit hour. *Required fees:* $802; $50 per course. Tuition and fees vary according to course load and program. *Financial support:* Application deadline: 2/1. *Unit head:* Steven Lux, Director of Executive Education, 315-443-3759, E-mail: sjlux@maxwell.syr.edu. *Application contact:* Margaret Lane, Assistant Director, 315-443-8708, E-mail: melane02@maxwell.syr.edu.
Website: http://www.maxwell.syr.edu/exed/degree_programs/emir/overview/

**Syracuse University,** Maxwell School of Citizenship and Public Affairs, MA/MS Program in Public Diplomacy, Syracuse, NY 13244. Offers MS/MA. *Students:* Average age 26. *Entrance requirements:* Additional exam requirements/recommendations for international students: Required—TOEFL (minimum score 100 iBT). *Application deadline:* For fall admission, 2/1 for domestic students, 2/1 priority date for international students. Application fee: $75. Electronic applications accepted. *Expenses: Tuition:* Full-time $25,974; part-time $1443 per credit hour. *Required fees:* $802; $50 per course. Tuition and fees vary according to course load and program. *Financial support:* Fellowships with full tuition reimbursements, research assistantships, and teaching assistantships available. Financial award application deadline: 1/1. *Faculty research:* Public diplomacy and communications, economic dimensions of global power, comparative foreign policy, development and sustainability, culture in world affairs. *Unit head:* Dr. Robert Bifulco, Associate Dean and Chair, Public Administration and International Affairs, 315-443-3232, E-mail: rbifulco@maxwell.syr.edu. *Application contact:* Martha Coria, Program Contact, 315-443-5749, Fax: 315-443-1834, E-mail: pcgrad@syr.edu.
Website: http://www.maxwell.syr.edu/

**Syracuse University,** Maxwell School of Citizenship and Public Affairs, MA Program in International Relations, Syracuse, NY 13244. Offers MA. *Program availability:* Part-time, evening/weekend. *Degree requirements:* For master's, thesis or alternative. *Entrance requirements:* For master's, GRE General Test, resume, personal statement, three letters of recommendation, official transcripts. Additional exam requirements/recommendations for international students: Required—TOEFL (minimum score 100 iBT). *Application deadline:* For fall admission, 2/1 priority date for domestic and international students. Application fee: $75. Electronic applications accepted. *Expenses: Tuition:* Full-time $25,974; part-time $1443 per credit hour. *Required fees:* $802; $50 per course. Tuition and fees vary according to course load and program. *Financial support:* Fellowships with full tuition reimbursements, research assistantships with tuition reimbursements, and teaching assistantships with tuition reimbursements available. Financial award application deadline: 1/1. *Faculty research:* International actors and issues, challenges of international management and leadership, comparative foreign policy, economic dimensions of global power, development and sustainability. *Unit head:* Dr. Robert Bifulco, Associate Dean and Chair, Public Administration and International Affairs, 315-443-3232, E-mail: rbifulco@maxwell.syr.edu. *Application contact:* Christine Omolino, 315-443-4000, E-mail: comolino@syr.edu.
Website: http://www.maxwell.syr.edu/IR/

**Teachers College, Columbia University,** Department of Arts and Humanities, New York, NY 10027. Offers applied linguistics (MA, Ed D); art and art education (Ed M, MA, Ed D, Ed DCT); arts administration (MA); bilingual and bicultural education (MA); global competence (Certificate); history and education (Ed D, PhD); music and music education (Ed DCT); philosophy and education (MA, Ed D, PhD); social studies education (Ed M, PhD); teaching English to speakers of other languages (Ed M); teaching of English and English education (Ed M, MA, Ed D, PhD), including English education (Ed M, Ed D, PhD), teaching of English (MA); teaching of social studies (MA); TESOL (MA, Ed D). *Program availability:* Part-time, evening/weekend. *Students:* 429 full-time (329 women), 467 part-time (332 women); includes 268 minority (62 Black or African American, non-Hispanic/Latino; 1 American Indian or Alaska Native, non-Hispanic/Latino; 108 Asian, non-Hispanic/Latino; 76 Hispanic/Latino; 21 Two or more races, non-Hispanic/Latino), 212 international. 1,068 applicants, 53% accepted, 272 enrolled. Terminal master's awarded for partial completion of doctoral program.

*Expenses: Tuition:* Full-time $36,288; part-time $1512 per credit. *Required fees:* $438 per semester. One-time fee: $510 full-time. Full-time tuition and fees vary according to course load. *Financial support:* Fellowships, research assistantships, teaching assistantships, career-related internships or fieldwork, Federal Work-Study, institutionally sponsored loans, tuition waivers (full and partial), and unspecified assistantships available. Support available to part-time students. *Unit head:* Prof. William Gaudelli, Department Chair, 212-678-3150, E-mail: wg74@columbia.edu. *Application contact:* David Estrella, Director of Admissions, 212-678-3305, Fax: 212-678-4171, E-mail: estrella@tc.columbia.edu.
Website: http://www.tc.edu/a%26h/

**Texas A&M University,** Bush School of Government and Public Service, College Station, TX 77840. Offers homeland security (Certificate); international affairs (MIA, Certificate); national security affairs (Certificate); non-profit management (Certificate); public service and administration (MPSA). *Accreditation:* NASPAA. *Faculty:* 68. *Students:* 324 full-time (165 women), 26 part-time (10 women); includes 89 minority (19 Black or African American, non-Hispanic/Latino; 4 Asian, non-Hispanic/Latino; 58 Hispanic/Latino; 1 Native Hawaiian or other Pacific Islander, non-Hispanic/Latino; 7 Two or more races, non-Hispanic/Latino), 44 international. Average age 27. 261 applicants, 96% accepted, 165 enrolled. In 2016, 164 master's awarded. *Degree requirements:* For master's, summer internship. *Entrance requirements:* For master's, GRE (preferred) or GMAT. Additional exam requirements/recommendations for international students: Required—TOEFL (minimum score 550 paper-based; 80 iBT), IELTS (minimum score 6), PTE (minimum score 53). *Application deadline:* For fall admission, 1/15 for domestic and international students. Application fee: $50 ($90 for international students). Electronic applications accepted. *Expenses:* Contact institution. *Financial support:* In 2016–17, 413 students received support, including 16 fellowships with tuition reimbursements available (averaging $18,236 per year), 61 research assistantships with tuition reimbursements available (averaging $5,904 per year), 1 teaching assistantship (averaging $4,025 per year); career-related internships or fieldwork, institutionally sponsored loans, scholarships/grants, traineeships, health care benefits, tuition waivers (full and partial), and unspecified assistantships also available. Support available to part-time students. Financial award application deadline: 3/15; financial award applicants required to submit FAFSA. *Faculty research:* Public policy, Presidential studies, public leadership, economic policy, social policy. *Unit head:* Dr. Mark Welsh, Dean, 979-862-8007, E-mail: mwelsh@tamu.edu. *Application contact:* Kathryn Meyer, Director of Recruitment and Admissions, 979-458-4767, Fax: 979-845-4155, E-mail: bushschooladmissions@tamu.edu.
Website: http://bush.tamu.edu/

**Texas State University,** The Graduate College, College of Liberal Arts, Program in International Studies, San Marcos, TX 78666. Offers MA. *Program availability:* Part-time. *Faculty:* 12 full-time (4 women). *Students:* 14 full-time (5 women), 8 part-time (5 women); includes 8 minority (2 Black or African American, non-Hispanic/Latino; 4 Hispanic/Latino; 2 Two or more races, non-Hispanic/Latino), 3 international. Average age 28. 32 applicants, 69% accepted, 10 enrolled. In 2016, 18 master's awarded. *Degree requirements:* For master's, comprehensive exam, thesis (for some programs). *Entrance requirements:* For master's, minimum GPA of 3.0 in last 60 hours leading to bachelor's degree. Additional exam requirements/recommendations for international students: Required—TOEFL (minimum score 550 paper-based; 78 iBT), IELTS (minimum score 6.5). *Application deadline:* For fall admission, 2/15 priority date for domestic students, 2/15 for international students; for spring admission, 10/15 for domestic students, 10/1 for international students; for summer admission, 4/15 for domestic students, 3/15 for international students. Applications are processed on a rolling basis. Application fee: $40 ($90 for international students). *Expenses:* $4,851 per semester. *Financial support:* In 2016–17, 15 students received support, including 3 teaching assistantships (averaging $13,637 per year); research assistantships, Federal Work-Study, institutionally sponsored loans, scholarships/grants, health care benefits, and unspecified assistantships also available. Support available to part-time students. Financial award application deadline: 3/1; financial award applicants required to submit FAFSA. *Unit head:* Dr. Dennis Dunn, Graduate Advisor, 512-245-2107, E-mail: dd05@txstate.edu. *Application contact:* Dr. Andrea Golato, Dean of Graduate School, 512-245-2581, Fax: 512-245-8365, E-mail: gradcollege@txstate.edu.
Website: http://www.txstate.edu/internationalstudies

**Texas State University,** The Graduate College, College of Liberal Arts, Program in Public Administration, San Marcos, TX 78666. Offers international relations (MPA); legal and judicial administration (MPA). *Accreditation:* NASPAA. *Program availability:* Part-time, evening/weekend. *Faculty:* 9 full-time (4 women). *Students:* 36 full-time (14 women), 59 part-time (29 women); includes 53 minority (15 Black or African American, non-Hispanic/Latino; 4 Asian, non-Hispanic/Latino; 32 Hispanic/Latino; 2 Two or more races, non-Hispanic/Latino), 1 international. Average age 31. 41 applicants, 78% accepted, 19 enrolled. In 2016, 22 master's awarded. *Degree requirements:* For master's, comprehensive exam, applied research project. *Entrance requirements:* For master's, baccalaureate degree from regionally-accredited university with minimum GPA of 3.0 on last 60 undergraduate semester hours. Additional exam requirements/recommendations for international students: Required—TOEFL (minimum score 550 paper-based; 78 iBT), IELTS (minimum score 6.5). *Application deadline:* For fall admission, 2/1 priority date for domestic and international students; for spring admission, 10/15 for domestic students, 10/1 for international students; for summer admission, 4/15 for domestic students, 3/15 for international students. Applications are processed on a rolling basis. Application fee: $40 ($90 for international students). Electronic applications accepted. *Expenses:* $4,851 per semester. *Financial support:* In 2016–17, 53 students received support, including 4 research assistantships (averaging $13,336 per year), 10 teaching assistantships (averaging $13,718 per year); career-related internships or fieldwork, Federal Work-Study, institutionally sponsored loans, scholarships/grants, and unspecified assistantships also available. Support available to part-time students. Financial award application deadline: 3/1; financial award applicants required to submit FAFSA. *Unit head:* Dr. Patricia Shields, Graduate Advisor, 512-245-3256, Fax: 512-245-7815, E-mail: ps07@txstate.edu. *Application contact:* Dr. Andrea Golato, Dean of Graduate School, 512-245-2581, Fax: 512-245-8365, E-mail: gradcollege@txstate.edu.
Website: http://www.polisci.txstate.edu/degrees-programs/graduate/MPA.html

**Troy University,** Graduate School, College of Arts and Sciences, Program in International Relations, Troy, AL 36082. Offers MS. *Program availability:* Part-time, evening/weekend, 100% online, blended/hybrid learning. *Faculty:* 13 full-time (1 woman), 9 part-time/adjunct (0 women). *Students:* 52 full-time (20 women), 229 part-time (61 women); includes 47 minority (18 Black or African American, non-Hispanic/Latino; 3 American Indian or Alaska Native, non-Hispanic/Latino; 4 Asian, non-Hispanic/Latino; 10 Hispanic/Latino; 6 Native Hawaiian or other Pacific Islander, non-Hispanic/Latino; 6 Two or more races, non-Hispanic/Latino). Average age 30. 189 applicants, 93% accepted, 12 enrolled. In 2016, 87 master's awarded. *Degree requirements:* For master's, comprehensive exam (for some programs), thesis (for some programs), comprehensive exam or thesis, minimum GPA of 3.0, admission to candidacy, minimum B grade on research. *Entrance requirements:* For master's, GRE (minimum score of 920 on old exam or 294 on new exam), MAT (minimum score of 396) or GMAT (minimum score of 490), bachelor's degree; minimum undergraduate GPA of 2.5 or 3.0 on last 30 semester hours. Additional exam requirements/recommendations for international students: Required—TOEFL (minimum score 523 paper-based; 70 iBT), IELTS (minimum score 6). *Application deadline:* Applications are processed on a rolling basis. Application fee: $50. Electronic applications accepted. *Expenses:* Tuition, state resident: full-time $7146; part-time $397 per credit hour. Tuition, nonresident: full-time $14,292; part-time $794 per credit hour. *Required fees:* $802; $50 per semester. Tuition and fees vary according to campus/location and program. *Financial support:* Fellowships, career-related internships or fieldwork, and scholarships/grants available. Support available to part-time students. Financial award applicants required to submit FAFSA. *Faculty research:* Elections, religion and world politics, terrorism. *Unit head:* Dr. M. Slobodchikoff, Director, International Relations, 334-670-3420, Fax: 334-670-5647, E-mail: mslobodchikoff@troy.edu. *Application contact:* Jessica A. Kimbro, Director of Graduate Admissions, 334-670-3178, Fax: 334-670-3733, E-mail: jacord@troy.edu.

**Tufts University,** The Fletcher School of Law and Diplomacy, Medford, MA 02155. Offers LL M, MA, MALD, MIB, PhD, DVM/MA, JD/MALD, MALD/MA, MALD/MBA, MALD/MS, MD/MA. *Program availability:* Online learning. *Degree requirements:* For master's, one foreign language, thesis; for doctorate, one foreign language, comprehensive exam, thesis/dissertation, dissertation defense. *Entrance requirements:* For master's and doctorate, GMAT or GRE General Test. Additional exam requirements/recommendations for international students: Required—TOEFL (minimum score 600 paper-based; 100 iBT), IELTS (minimum score 7). Electronic applications accepted. *Expenses:* Contact institution. *Faculty research:* Negotiation and conflict resolution, international organizations, international business and economic law, security studies, development economics.

**Tufts University,** Graduate School of Arts and Sciences, Department of History, Medford, MA 02155. Offers history (MA, PhD), including global history (PhD); history and museum studies (MA). *Students:* 23 full-time (16 women); includes 4 minority (1 Black or African American, non-Hispanic/Latino; 2 Asian, non-Hispanic/Latino; 1 Two or more races, non-Hispanic/Latino), 5 international. Average age 26. 57 applicants, 42% accepted, 7 enrolled. In 2016, 4 master's awarded. Terminal master's awarded for partial completion of doctoral program. *Degree requirements:* For master's, one foreign language, thesis optional; for doctorate, 2 foreign languages, comprehensive exam, thesis/dissertation. *Entrance requirements:* For master's and doctorate, GRE General Test, writing sample. Additional exam requirements/recommendations for international students: Required—TOEFL (minimum score 550 paper-based; 80 iBT), IELTS (minimum score 6.5). *Application deadline:* For fall admission, 1/15 for domestic and international students. Applications are processed on a rolling basis. Application fee: $85. Electronic applications accepted. *Expenses:* $49,982 full-time tuition (for MA); $29,936 full-time tuition (for PhD). *Financial support:* In 2016–17, 20 students received support. Teaching assistantships, Federal Work-Study, scholarships/grants, tuition waivers (full and partial), and unspecified assistantships available. Financial award application deadline: 1/15. *Unit head:* Dr. Steven Marrone, Graduate Program Director. *Application contact:* Office of Graduate Admissions, 617-627-3395, E-mail: gradadmissions@tufts.edu.
Website: http://www.ase.tufts.edu/history/

**United States International University–Africa,** School of Arts and Sciences, Nairobi, Kenya. Offers counseling psychology (MA), including chemical dependency, health psychology; international relations (MA), including development studies, diplomacy and foreign policy, peace and conflict studies. *Program availability:* Part-time, evening/weekend. *Degree requirements:* For master's, thesis, practicum. *Entrance requirements:* For master's, GRE General Test, 2 letters of recommendation, resume. Additional exam requirements/recommendations for international students: Required—TOEFL. *Faculty research:* Trauma in children, African intellectualism, psychological assessment tools.

**Universidad de las Americas, A.C.,** Program in International Organizations and Institutions, Mexico City, Mexico. Offers MA.

**Universidad Nacional Pedro Henriquez Urena,** Graduate School, Santo Domingo, Dominican Republic. Offers agricultural diversity (MS), including horticultural/fruit production, tropical animal production; conservation of monuments and cultural assets (M Arch); ecology and environment (MS); environmental engineering (MEE); international relations (MA); natural resource management (MS); political science (MA); project optimization (MPM); project feasibility (MPM); project management (MPM); sanitation engineering (ME); science for teachers (MS); tropical Caribbean architecture (M Arch).

**Université de Montréal,** Faculty of Arts and Sciences, Programs in International Studies, Montréal, QC H3C 3J7, Canada. Offers M Sc, DESS.

**Université Laval,** Québec Institute for Advanced International Studies, Program in International Relations, Québec, QC G1K 7P4, Canada. Offers MA, PhD. *Degree requirements:* For master's, thesis (for some programs). *Entrance requirements:* For master's, English exam, French exam. Electronic applications accepted.

**University of Bridgeport,** College of Public and International Affairs, Bridgeport, CT 06604. Offers East Asian and Pacific Rim studies (MA); global development and peace (MA); global media and communication studies (MA). *Program availability:* Part-time, evening/weekend. *Degree requirements:* For master's, thesis. *Entrance requirements:* Additional exam requirements/recommendations for international students: Recommended—TOEFL (minimum score 550 paper-based; 80 iBT), IELTS (minimum score 6.5).

**The University of British Columbia,** Institute of Asian Research, Vancouver, BC V6T 1Z2, Canada. Offers Asia Pacific policy studies (MAAPPS); public policy and global affairs (MPPGA). *Degree requirements:* For master's, thesis optional. *Entrance requirements:* Additional exam requirements/recommendations for international students: Required—TOEFL. Application fee: $100 ($162 for international students). Electronic applications accepted. *Expenses:* $26,842 per year tuition and fees, $42,648 per year international. *Financial support:* Fellowships with tuition reimbursements, research assistantships, career-related internships or fieldwork, institutionally sponsored loans, scholarships/grants, and tuition waivers (partial) available. *Faculty research:* Social cohesion, globalization, social safety nets, policy research, research and development alliances, knowledge-based workshops on Asia-Pacific studies. *Application contact:* Kerry Ross, Graduate Program Staff, 604-822-4571, E-mail: mppga.program@ubc.ca.
Website: http://iar.ubc.ca/

**University of California, Berkeley,** Graduate Division, Program in Global Studies, Berkeley, CA 94720-1500. Offers MA. *Students:* 2 full-time (both women). *Application deadline:* For fall admission, 1/31 for domestic students. Application fee: $105 ($125 for international students). Electronic applications accepted. *Financial support:* Fellowships, research assistantships, teaching assistantships, institutionally sponsored loans, health care benefits, and unspecified assistantships available. *Unit head:* Prof. Maximilian Aufhammer, Chair, 510-642-4466.
Website: http://globalstudies.berkeley.edu

**University of California, San Diego,** Graduate Division, Department of Political Science, La Jolla, CA 92093. Offers political science (PhD); political science and

international affairs (PhD). *Students:* 68 full-time (22 women). 365 applicants, 10% accepted, 7 enrolled. In 2016, 17 doctorates awarded. *Degree requirements:* For doctorate, comprehensive exam, thesis/dissertation. *Entrance requirements:* For doctorate, GRE General Test, letters of recommendation. Additional exam requirements/recommendations for international students: Required—TOEFL (minimum score 600 paper-based; 100 iBT), IELTS. *Application deadline:* For fall admission, 12/13 for domestic students. Application fee: $105 ($125 for international students). Electronic applications accepted. *Expenses:* Tuition, state resident: full-time $11,220. Tuition, nonresident: full-time $26,322. *Required fees:* $1864. *Financial support:* Fellowships, research assistantships, teaching assistantships, and scholarships/grants available. Financial award applicants required to submit FAFSA. *Faculty research:* American politics, comparative politics, international relations, methodology, political theory. *Unit head:* Thad Kousser, Chair, 858-534-3239, E-mail: tkousser@ucsd.edu. *Application contact:* Aubrey Rudd, Graduate Coordinator, 858-534-2705, E-mail: psgradadmissions@ucsd.edu.
Website: http://polisci.ucsd.edu/

**University of California, San Diego,** Graduate Division, School of Global Policy and Strategy, Master of International Affairs Program, La Jolla, CA 92093. Offers international development and nonprofit management (MIA); international economics (MIA); international environmental policy (MIA); international management (MIA); international politics (MIA). Students will choose one of the following country/regional specializations: China, Japan, Korea, Latin America, or Southeast Asia. *Faculty:* 33 full-time (9 women), 20 part-time/adjunct (4 women). *Students:* 300 full-time (150 women). Average age 24. 460 applicants, 120 enrolled. In 2016, 120 master's awarded. *Degree requirements:* For master's, one foreign language. *Entrance requirements:* For master's, GMAT or GRE General Test. Additional exam requirements/recommendations for international students: Required—TOEFL (minimum score 90 iBT), IELTS (minimum score 7). *Application deadline:* For fall admission, 1/15 for domestic and international students. Applications are processed on a rolling basis. Application fee: $90 ($110 for international students). Electronic applications accepted. *Expenses:* Tuition, state resident: full-time $11,220. Tuition, nonresident: full-time $26,322. *Required fees:* $1864. *Financial support:* In 2016–17, 140 students received support, including 60 fellowships with full and partial tuition reimbursements available (averaging $50,000 per year), 15 research assistantships with full tuition reimbursements available (averaging $20,000 per year), 20 teaching assistantships with full tuition reimbursements available (averaging $20,000 per year); career-related internships or fieldwork, scholarships/grants, and unspecified assistantships also available. Financial award application deadline: 1/15. *Unit head:* Sonja Steinbrech, Director of Enrollment, 858-534-7162, E-mail: ssteinbrech@ucsd.edu. *Application contact:* Admissions Representative, 858-534-5914, E-mail: gps-apply@uscd.edu.
Website: http://gps.ucsd.edu/academics/mia.html

**University of California, Santa Barbara,** Graduate Division, College of Letters and Sciences, Division of Humanities and Fine Arts, Department of English, Santa Barbara, CA 93106-3170. Offers English (PhD), including environment and society, European medieval studies, feminist studies, global studies, technology and society, translation studies, writing studies; MA/PhD. Terminal master's awarded for partial completion of doctoral program. *Degree requirements:* For doctorate, one foreign language, comprehensive exam, thesis/dissertation. *Entrance requirements:* For doctorate, GRE General Test, GRE Subject Test (English literature). Additional exam requirements/recommendations for international students: Required—TOEFL (minimum score 550 paper-based; 80 iBT), IELTS (minimum score 7). Electronic applications accepted. *Faculty research:* Medieval, Romantic and Victorian studies; gender studies and feminist theory; literature and the mind; American literature; literature and new media/information culture.

**University of California, Santa Barbara,** Graduate Division, College of Letters and Sciences, Division of Humanities and Fine Arts, Department of History, Santa Barbara, CA 93106-9410. Offers European medieval studies (PhD); global studies (PhD); public historical studies (PhD); technology and society (PhD); women's studies (PhD); MA/PhD. *Degree requirements:* For doctorate, variable foreign language requirement, comprehensive exam, thesis/dissertation. *Entrance requirements:* For doctorate, GRE. Additional exam requirements/recommendations for international students: Required—TOEFL (minimum score 550 paper-based; 80 iBT), IELTS (minimum score 7). Electronic applications accepted. *Faculty research:* Europe, United States, Latin America, Africa, Middle East, East Asia.

**University of California, Santa Barbara,** Graduate Division, College of Letters and Sciences, Division of Humanities and Fine Arts, Department of Religious Studies, Santa Barbara, CA 93106-3130. Offers ancient Mediterranean studies (PhD); cognitive science (PhD); European medieval studies (PhD); feminist studies (PhD); global studies (PhD); religious studies (MA, PhD); translation studies (PhD); MA/PhD. Terminal master's awarded for partial completion of doctoral program. *Degree requirements:* For master's, one foreign language, comprehensive exam (for some programs), thesis (for some programs); for doctorate, 2 foreign languages, thesis/dissertation, methodology. *Entrance requirements:* For master's and doctorate, GRE General Test. Additional exam requirements/recommendations for international students: Required—TOEFL (minimum score 550 paper-based; 80 iBT), IELTS (minimum score 7). Electronic applications accepted. *Faculty research:* Area studies; religious traditions; theory and method in the study of religion; religion, culture, and politics; spirituality and religious experience.

**University of California, Santa Barbara,** Graduate Division, College of Letters and Sciences, Division of Humanities and Fine Arts, Program in Comparative Literature, Santa Barbara, CA 93106-4130. Offers comparative literature (PhD); East Asian literatures (PhD); feminist studies (PhD); French (PhD); global studies (PhD); translation studies (PhD); MA/PhD. *Degree requirements:* For doctorate, 2 foreign languages, comprehensive exam, thesis/dissertation. *Entrance requirements:* For doctorate, GRE. Additional exam requirements/recommendations for international students: Required—TOEFL (minimum score 550 paper-based; 80 iBT), IELTS (minimum score 7). Electronic applications accepted. *Faculty research:* Comparative literary studies in global context, critical theory, translation studies, media technological studies, trauma studies.

**University of California, Santa Barbara,** Graduate Division, College of Letters and Sciences, Division of Mathematics, Life, and Physical Sciences, Department of Geography, Santa Barbara, CA 93106-4060. Offers cognitive science (PhD); geography (MA, PhD); global studies (PhD); quantitative methods in the social sciences (PhD); technology and society (PhD); transportation (PhD); MA/PhD. Terminal master's awarded for partial completion of doctoral program. *Degree requirements:* For master's, comprehensive exam (for some programs), thesis or alternative; for doctorate, comprehensive exam, thesis/dissertation, 1 quarter of teaching assistantship. *Entrance requirements:* For master's and doctorate, GRE (minimum combined verbal and quantitative scores above 1100 in old scoring system or 301 in new scoring system). Additional exam requirements/recommendations for international students: Required—TOEFL (minimum score 550 paper-based; 80 iBT), IELTS (minimum score 7). Electronic applications accepted. *Faculty research:* Earth system science; human environment relations; modeling, measurement, and computation.

**University of California, Santa Barbara,** Graduate Division, College of Letters and Sciences, Division of Social Sciences, Department of Global Studies, Santa Barbara,

## International Affairs

CA 93106-7065. Offers global culture, ideology, and religion (MA, PhD); global government, human rights, and civil society (MA, PhD); political economy, sustainable development, and the environment (MA, PhD). *Degree requirements:* For master's, one foreign language, thesis, 2 years of a second language; for doctorate, one foreign language, thesis/dissertation, reading proficiency in at least one language other than English. *Entrance requirements:* For master's, GRE, 2 years of a second language with minimum B grade in the final term, statement of purpose, resume or curriculum vitae, 3 letters of recommendation, transcripts (from all post-secondary institutions attended), writing sample (15-20 pages); for doctorate, GRE, statement of purpose, personal achievements/contributions statement, resume or curriculum vitae, 3 letters of recommendation, transcripts from all post-secondary institutions attended, writing sample (15-20 pages). Additional exam requirements/recommendations for international students: Required—TOEFL (minimum score 600 paper-based; 94 iBT), IELTS (minimum score 7). Electronic applications accepted.

**University of California, Santa Barbara,** Graduate Division, College of Letters and Sciences, Division of Social Sciences, Department of Sociology, Santa Barbara, CA 93106-9430. Offers interdisciplinary emphasis: Black studies (PhD); interdisciplinary emphasis: environment and society (PhD); interdisciplinary emphasis: feminist studies (PhD); interdisciplinary emphasis: global studies (PhD); interdisciplinary emphasis: language, interaction and social organization (PhD); interdisciplinary emphasis: quantitative methods in the social sciences (PhD); interdisciplinary emphasis: technology and society (PhD); sociology (PhD); MA/PhD. Terminal master's awarded for partial completion of doctoral program. *Degree requirements:* For doctorate, comprehensive exam, thesis/dissertation. *Entrance requirements:* For doctorate, GRE General Test. Additional exam requirements/recommendations for international students: Required—TOEFL (minimum score 550 paper-based; 80 iBT), IELTS (minimum score 7). Electronic applications accepted. *Faculty research:* Gender and sexualities, race/ethnicity, social movements, conversation analysis, global sociology.

**University of California, Santa Cruz,** Division of Graduate Studies, Division of Social Sciences, Program in International Economics, Santa Cruz, CA 95064. Offers PhD. *Degree requirements:* For doctorate, thesis/dissertation, 4 field exams, field papers, econometrics project, qualifying exams. *Entrance requirements:* For doctorate, GRE General Test. Additional exam requirements/recommendations for international students: Required—TOEFL (minimum score 550 paper-based; 83 iBT); Recommended—IELTS (minimum score 8). Electronic applications accepted. *Faculty research:* Current and emerging issues in taxation, industrial policy, environmental regulation, market structure, labor economics focus on behavior and adjustment in an interdependent world economy.

**University of Central Oklahoma,** The Jackson College of Graduate Studies, College of Liberal Arts, Department of Political Science, Edmond, OK 73034-5209. Offers international affairs (MA); political science (MA); public administration (MPA). *Program availability:* Part-time. *Degree requirements:* For master's, comprehensive exam (for some programs), thesis (for some programs). *Entrance requirements:* For master's, GRE, 18 undergraduate hours in political science. Additional exam requirements/recommendations for international students: Required—TOEFL (minimum score 550 paper-based; 79 iBT), IELTS (minimum score 6.5). Electronic applications accepted.

**University of Chicago,** Division of the Social Sciences, Committee on International Relations, Chicago, IL 60637. Offers MA. *Students:* 51 full-time (21 women); includes 11 minority (2 Black or African American, non-Hispanic/Latino; 4 Asian, non-Hispanic/Latino; 5 Hispanic/Latino), 10 international. Average age 24. 185 applicants, 58% accepted, 34 enrolled. In 2016, 49 master's awarded. *Degree requirements:* For master's, thesis. *Entrance requirements:* For master's, GRE General Test. Additional exam requirements/recommendations for international students: Required—TOEFL (minimum score 104 iBT), IELTS (minimum score 7). *Application deadline:* For fall admission, 1/5 for domestic and international students. Application fee: $90. Electronic applications accepted. *Financial support:* In 2016–17, 42 students received support. Federal Work-Study, institutionally sponsored loans, and scholarships/grants available. Financial award application deadline: 1/5. *Unit head:* Prof. Mark Bradley, Chair, 773-702-3558. *Application contact:* Office of the Dean of Students, 773-702-8415, E-mail: admissions@ssd.uchicago.edu.
Website: http://cir.uchicago.edu

**University of Colorado Denver,** College of Liberal Arts and Sciences, Program in Humanities, Denver, CO 80217. Offers community health science (MSS); humanities (MH); international studies (MSS); philosophy and theory (MH); social justice (MSS); society and the environment (MSS); visual studies (MH); women's and gender studies (MSS). *Program availability:* Part-time, evening/weekend. *Faculty:* 3 full-time (1 woman). *Students:* 12 full-time (6 women), 15 part-time (7 women); includes 6 minority (1 American Indian or Alaska Native, non-Hispanic/Latino; 3 Hispanic/Latino; 2 Two or more races, non-Hispanic/Latino). Average age 41. 4 applicants, 100% accepted, 4 enrolled. In 2016, 5 master's awarded. *Degree requirements:* For master's, 36 credit hours, project or thesis. *Entrance requirements:* For master's, writing sample, statement of purpose/letter of intent, three letters of recommendation. Additional exam requirements/recommendations for international students: Required—TOEFL (minimum score 537 paper-based; 75 iBT); Recommended—IELTS (minimum score 6.5). *Application deadline:* For fall admission, 5/15 for domestic students, 5/15 priority date for international students; for spring admission, 10/15 for domestic students, 10/15 priority date for international students; for summer admission, 3/15 for domestic and international students. Application fee: $50 ($75 for international students). Electronic applications accepted. *Expenses:* Tuition, state resident: full-time $11,006; part-time $474 per credit. Tuition, nonresident: full-time $28,212; part-time $1264 per credit hour. *Required fees:* $256 per semester. One-time fee: $94.32. Tuition and fees vary according to campus/location and program. *Financial support:* In 2016–17, 2 students received support. Fellowships, research assistantships, teaching assistantships, Federal Work-Study, institutionally sponsored loans, scholarships/grants, and traineeships available. Financial award application deadline: 4/1; financial award applicants required to submit FAFSA. *Faculty research:* Women and gender in the classical Mediterranean, communication theory and democracy, relationship between psychology and philosophy. *Unit head:* Margaret Woodhull, Director of Humanities, 303-315-3568, E-mail: margaret.woodhull@ucdenver.edu. *Application contact:* Angela Beale, Program Assistant, 303-315-3565, E-mail: mastershs@ucdenver.edu.
Website: http://www.ucdenver.edu/academics/colleges/CLAS/Programs/HumanitiesSocialSciences/Programs/Pages/MasterofHumanities.aspx

**University of Connecticut,** Graduate School, College of Liberal Arts and Sciences, Field of International Studies, Program in International Studies, Storrs, CT 06269. Offers European studies (MA); Italian history and culture (MA); Latino and Latin American studies (MA). *Degree requirements:* For master's, comprehensive exam. *Entrance requirements:* For master's, GRE General Test. Additional exam requirements/recommendations for international students: Required—TOEFL (minimum score 550 paper-based). Electronic applications accepted.

**University of Delaware,** College of Arts and Sciences, Department of Political Science and International Relations, Newark, DE 19716. Offers MA, PhD. Terminal master's awarded for partial completion of doctoral program. *Degree requirements:* For master's, research paper; for doctorate, one foreign language, comprehensive exam, thesis/

dissertation. *Entrance requirements:* For master's and doctorate, GRE General Test, minimum GPA of 3.2 in major, 3.0 overall. Additional exam requirements/recommendations for international students: Required—TOEFL (minimum score 600 paper-based). Electronic applications accepted. *Faculty research:* Social constructivism, international migration, international security, democratization, human rights.

**University of Denver,** Division of Arts, Humanities and Social Sciences, Department of Media, Film and Journalism Studies, Denver, CO 80208. Offers international and intercultural communication (MA); media and globalization (MA). *Program availability:* Part-time. *Faculty:* 16 full-time (10 women), 5 part-time/adjunct (4 women). *Students:* 8 full-time (7 women), 18 part-time (14 women); includes 8 minority (1 Black or African American, non-Hispanic/Latino; 2 Asian, non-Hispanic/Latino; 5 Hispanic/Latino), 1 international. Average age 27. 54 applicants, 78% accepted, 14 enrolled. In 2016, 21 master's awarded. *Degree requirements:* For master's, thesis (for some programs). *Entrance requirements:* For master's, GRE General Test, bachelor's degree, transcripts, personal statement, three letters of recommendation. Additional exam requirements/recommendations for international students: Required—TOEFL (minimum score 620 paper-based; 105 iBT). *Application deadline:* For fall admission, 2/15 priority date for domestic students, 1/1 priority date for international students. Applications are processed on a rolling basis. Application fee: $65. Electronic applications accepted. *Expenses:* $29,022 per year full-time. *Financial support:* In 2016–17, 16 students received support, including 2 teaching assistantships with tuition reimbursements available (averaging $12,500 per year); career-related internships or fieldwork, Federal Work-Study, institutionally sponsored loans, scholarships/grants, and unspecified assistantships also available. Support available to part-time students. Financial award application deadline: 2/15; financial award applicants required to submit FAFSA. *Faculty research:* Branding; public relations; health communication; social media; international communication. *Unit head:* Dr. Lynn Schofield Clark, Professor and Chair, 303-871-3984, Fax: 303-871-4949, E-mail: lynn.clark@du.edu. *Application contact:* Information Contact, 303-871-2166, E-mail: mfjs@du.edu.
Website: http://www.du.edu/ahss/mfjs

**University of Denver,** Josef Korbel School of International Studies, Denver, CO 80208. Offers conflict resolution (MA); global business and corporate social responsibility (Certificate); global finance, trade and economic integration (MA); global health affairs (Certificate); homeland security (Certificate); humanitarian assistance (Certificate); international administration (MA); international development (MA); international human rights (MA); international security (MA); international studies (MA, PhD); public policy studies (MPP); religion and international affairs (Certificate). *Program availability:* Part-time. *Faculty:* 46 full-time (16 women), 28 part-time/adjunct (8 women). *Students:* 368 full-time (204 women), 26 part-time (10 women); includes 82 minority (15 Black or African American, non-Hispanic/Latino; 2 American Indian or Alaska Native, non-Hispanic/Latino; 11 Asian, non-Hispanic/Latino; 43 Hispanic/Latino; 11 Two or more races, non-Hispanic/Latino), 38 international. Average age 27. 764 applicants, 82% accepted, 138 enrolled. In 2016, 197 master's, 10 doctorates, 28 other advanced degrees awarded. *Degree requirements:* For master's, one foreign language, thesis (for some programs); for doctorate, one foreign language, comprehensive exam, thesis/dissertation, two extended research papers. *Entrance requirements:* For master's, GRE General Test, bachelor's degree, transcripts, two letters of recommendation, statement of purpose, resume or curriculum vitae; for doctorate, GRE General Test, master's degree, transcripts, three letters of recommendation, statement of purpose, resume or curriculum vitae, writing sample; for Certificate, bachelor's degree, transcripts, two letters of recommendation, statement of purpose, resume or curriculum vitae. Additional exam requirements/recommendations for international students: Required—TOEFL (minimum score 587 paper-based; 95 iBT). *Application deadline:* For fall admission, 1/15 priority date for domestic and international students; for winter admission, 11/1 for domestic and international students. Applications are processed on a rolling basis. Application fee: $65. Electronic applications accepted. *Expenses:* $43,458 per year full-time. *Financial support:* In 2016–17, 244 students received support, including 1 research assistantship with tuition reimbursement available (averaging $7,250 per year), 5 teaching assistantships with tuition reimbursements available (averaging $2,842 per year); career-related internships or fieldwork, Federal Work-Study, institutionally sponsored loans, scholarships/grants, and unspecified assistantships also available. Support available to part-time students. Financial award application deadline: 2/15; financial award applicants required to submit FAFSA. *Faculty research:* Human rights and international security, international politics and economics, economic-social and political development, international technology analysis and management. *Unit head:* Dr. Christopher R. Hill, Dean, 303-871-2359, Fax: 303-871-2456, E-mail: christopher.r.hill@du.edu. *Application contact:* Admissions Contact, E-mail: korbeladm@du.edu.
Website: http://www.du.edu/korbel

**University of Denver,** University College, Denver, CO 80208. Offers arts and culture (MA, Certificate); communication management (MS, Certificate), including translation studies (Certificate), world history and culture (Certificate); environmental policy and management (MS); geographic information systems (MS); global affairs (MA, Certificate), including human capital in organizations (Certificate), philanthropic leadership (Certificate), project management (Certificate), strategic innovation and change (Certificate); healthcare leadership (MS); information communications and technology (MS); leadership and organizations (MA, Certificate), including emergency planning and response (Certificate), organizational security (Certificate); security management (MS, Certificate); strategic human resources (Certificate). *Program availability:* Part-time, evening/weekend, online learning. *Faculty:* 118 part-time/adjunct (62 women). *Students:* 59 full-time (22 women), 1,285 part-time (750 women); includes 316 minority (111 Black or African American, non-Hispanic/Latino; 8 American Indian or Alaska Native, non-Hispanic/Latino; 39 Asian, non-Hispanic/Latino; 123 Hispanic/Latino; 3 Native Hawaiian or other Pacific Islander, non-Hispanic/Latino; 32 Two or more races, non-Hispanic/Latino), 85 international. Average age 35. 703 applicants, 89% accepted, 390 enrolled. In 2016, 428 master's, 138 other advanced degrees awarded. *Degree requirements:* For master's, capstone project. *Entrance requirements:* For master's, transcripts, two letters of recommendation, personal statement, resume. Additional exam requirements/recommendations for international students: Required—TOEFL (minimum score 550 paper-based; 80 iBT). *Application deadline:* For fall admission, 6/21 priority date for domestic students, 5/1 priority date for international students; for winter admission, 9/14 priority date for domestic students, 9/19 priority date for international students; for spring admission, 1/11 priority date for domestic students, 12/12 priority date for international students; for summer admission, 3/29 priority date for domestic students, 3/6 priority date for international students. Applications are processed on a rolling basis. Application fee: $75. Electronic applications accepted. *Expenses:* $7,236 per year full-time. *Financial support:* In 2016–17, 27 students received support, including 1 teaching assistantship (averaging $1,489 per year). Financial award applicants required to submit FAFSA. *Unit head:* Dr. Michael McGuire, Dean, 303-871-3518, Fax: 303-871-3303, E-mail: mmcguire@du.edu. *Application contact:* Information Contact, 303-871-2291, E-mail: ucoladm@du.edu.
Website: http://universitycollege.du.edu/

**University of Florida,** Graduate School, College of Liberal Arts and Sciences, Department of Political Science, Program in International Relations, Gainesville, FL 32611. Offers MA, MAT. *Degree requirements:* For master's, comprehensive exam (for some programs), thesis optional. *Entrance requirements:* For master's, GRE General Test, minimum GPA of 3.0. Additional exam requirements/recommendations for international students: Required—TOEFL (minimum score 550 paper-based; 80 iBT), IELTS (minimum score 6). Electronic applications accepted. *Faculty research:* International relations theory, international political economy, feminist international relations, international security, international organization.

**University of Georgia,** School of Public and International Affairs, Department of International Affairs, Athens, GA 30602. Offers MA, MIP, PhD. *Unit head:* Dr. Markus Crepaz, Head, 706-542-6705, E-mail: mcrepaz@uga.edu. *Application contact:* Amanda Murdie, Graduate Coordinator, 706-425-9659, E-mail: murdie@uga.edu. Website: http://intl.uga.edu/

**University of Georgia,** School of Public and International Affairs, Program in Political Science/International Affairs, Athens, GA 30602. Offers MA, PhD. *Degree requirements:* For master's, one foreign language, thesis; for doctorate, one foreign language, thesis/dissertation. *Entrance requirements:* For master's and doctorate, GRE General Test. *Application deadline:* For fall admission, 7/1 priority date for domestic students; for spring admission, 11/15 for domestic students. Application fee: $50. Electronic applications accepted. *Financial support:* Fellowships, research assistantships, teaching assistantships, and unspecified assistantships available. *Unit head:* Dr. John A. Maltese, Head, 706-542-4147, E-mail: jmaltese@uga.edu. *Application contact:* Michael Lynch, Graduate Coordinator, 706-543-4421, E-mail: mlynch@uga.edu. Website: http://www.uga.edu/pol-sci/

**University of Hawaii at Manoa,** Graduate Division, International Cultural Studies Graduate Certificate Program, Honolulu, HI 96822. Offers Graduate Certificate. *Program availability:* Part-time. *Entrance requirements:* For degree, GRE General Test. Additional exam requirements/recommendations for international students: Required—TOEFL (minimum score 540 paper-based; 76 iBT), IELTS (minimum score 5).

**University of Indianapolis,** Graduate Programs, College of Arts and Sciences, Department of History and Political Science, Indianapolis, IN 46227-3697. Offers history (MA); international relations (MA). *Program availability:* Part-time, evening/weekend. *Degree requirements:* For master's, thesis optional. *Entrance requirements:* For master's, GRE Subject Test, minimum GPA of 3.0, 3 letters of recommendation. Additional exam requirements/recommendations for international students: Required—TOEFL (minimum score 550 paper-based). Electronic applications accepted.

**The University of Kansas,** Graduate Studies, College of Liberal Arts and Sciences, Center for Global and International Studies, Lawrence, KS 66045. Offers MA. *Program availability:* Part-time, evening/weekend. *Students:* 31 full-time (8 women), 11 part-time (3 women); includes 8 minority (1 Black or African American, non-Hispanic/Latino; 1 American Indian or Alaska Native, non-Hispanic/Latino; 3 Asian, non-Hispanic/Latino; 1 Hispanic/Latino; 2 Two or more races, non-Hispanic/Latino), 2 international. Average age 34. 30 applicants, 93% accepted, 24 enrolled. In 2016, 28 master's awarded. *Entrance requirements:* For master's, GRE, minimum GPA of 3.0, 2 letters of reference, curriculum vitae, reflective essay, 300-500 word statement of interest describing relevant aspects of background and addressing how program will help meet academic and professional goals. Additional exam requirements/recommendations for international students: Required—TOEFL (minimum score 80 iBT). *Application deadline:* For fall admission, 4/1 priority date for domestic and international students; for spring admission, 10/1 priority date for domestic and international students. Application fee: $65 ($85 for international students). Electronic applications accepted. *Financial support:* Research assistantships, teaching assistantships, scholarships/grants, health care benefits, and unspecified assistantships available. Support available to part-time students. *Faculty research:* Globalization, environmental sociology, economic development, comparative government, international relations. *Unit head:* Shannon O'Lear, Director, 785-864-2041, E-mail: olear@ku.edu. *Application contact:* Alyssa McDonald, Graduate Admissions Contact, 785-864-9814, E-mail: mcdonalda@ku.edu. Website: http://global.ku.edu/

**University of Kentucky,** Graduate School, Patterson School of Diplomacy and International Commerce, Lexington, KY 40506-0027. Offers MA. *Degree requirements:* For master's, one foreign language, comprehensive exam, statistics. *Entrance requirements:* For master's, GRE General Test, minimum undergraduate GPA of 3.0. Additional exam requirements/recommendations for international students: Required—TOEFL (minimum score 550 paper-based; 79 iBT). Electronic applications accepted. *Faculty research:* International relations, foreign and defense policy, cross-cultural negotiation, international science and technology, diplomacy, international economics and development, geopolitical modeling.

**University of Maine,** Graduate School, College of Liberal Arts and Sciences, School of Policy and International Affairs, Orono, ME 04469. Offers global policy (MA). *Faculty:* 4 full-time (1 woman), 6 part-time/adjunct (0 women). *Students:* 30 full-time (13 women), 2 part-time (1 woman); includes 3 minority (1 Black or African American, non-Hispanic/Latino; 1 Hispanic/Latino; 1 Two or more races, non-Hispanic/Latino), 8 international. Average age 27. 34 applicants, 91% accepted, 13 enrolled. In 2016, 7 master's awarded. *Entrance requirements:* For master's, GRE. Additional exam requirements/recommendations for international students: Required—TOEFL (minimum score 80 iBT), IELTS (minimum score 6.5). *Application deadline:* Applications are processed on a rolling basis. Application fee: $65. Electronic applications accepted. *Expenses:* Tuition, state resident: full-time $7524; part-time $2508 per credit. Tuition, nonresident: full-time $24,498; part-time $8166 per credit. *Required fees:* $1148; $571 per credit. *Financial support:* In 2016–17, 10 students received support, including 3 fellowships (averaging $19,600 per year), 1 teaching assistantship (averaging $14,600 per year); career-related internships or fieldwork, Federal Work-Study, scholarships/grants, and unspecified assistantships also available. Financial award application deadline: 3/1. *Faculty research:* International political economy; international environmental policy; dynamics of political conflict; international development; foreign direct investment. *Unit head:* Capt. James Settele, Director, 207-581-3153, E-mail: james.settele@umit.maine.edu. *Application contact:* Scott G. Delcourt, Assistant Vice President for Graduate Studies and Senior Associate Dean, 207-581-3291, Fax: 207-581-3232, E-mail: graduate@maine.edu. Website: http://spia.umaine.edu/

**The University of Manchester,** School of Arts, Histories and Cultures, Manchester, United Kingdom. Offers anthropology, media and performance (PhD); applied theatre professional (PhD); archaeology (PhD); art history and visual studies (PhD); arts management and cultural policy (PhD); classics and ancient history (PhD); composition (PhD); creative writing (PhD); drama (PhD); economic and social history (PhD); electroacoustic composition (PhD); English and American studies (PhD); history (PhD); humanitarianism and conflict response (PhD); museology (PhD); music (PhD); musicology (PhD); religions and theology (PhD).

**University of Massachusetts Boston,** John W. McCormack Graduate School of Policy and Global Studies, Program in Global Governance and Human Security, Boston, MA 02125-3393. Offers MA. *Students:* 16 full-time (10 women), 27 part-time (16 women); includes 6 minority (1 Black or African American, non-Hispanic/Latino; 3 Asian, non-Hispanic/Latino; 1 Hispanic/Latino; 1 Two or more races, non-Hispanic/Latino), 20 international. Average age 35. 25 applicants, 48% accepted, 8 enrolled. In 2016, 7 master's awarded. *Expenses:* Tuition, state resident: full-time $16,863. Tuition, nonresident: full-time $32,913. *Required fees:* $177. *Unit head:* Dr. David Cash, Dean. *Application contact:* Peggy Roldan Patel, Graduate Admissions Coordinator, 617-287-6400, Fax: 617-287-6236, E-mail: bos.gadm@dpc.umassp.edu.

**University of Miami,** Graduate School, College of Arts and Sciences, Department of International Studies, Coral Gables, FL 33124. Offers MA, PhD. *Degree requirements:* For master's, one foreign language, comprehensive exam; for doctorate, one foreign language, comprehensive exam, thesis/dissertation. *Entrance requirements:* For master's, GRE General Test, minimum GPA of 3.0; for doctorate, GRE General Test. Additional exam requirements/recommendations for international students: Required—TOEFL. Electronic applications accepted. *Faculty research:* Latin American studies, international economics, international security and conflict, comparative development, international health policy.

**University of Miami,** Graduate School, Program in International Administration, Coral Gables, FL 33124. Offers MAIA. *Program availability:* Part-time, evening/weekend. *Degree requirements:* For master's, practicum. *Entrance requirements:* For master's, GRE General Test. Additional exam requirements/recommendations for international students: Required—TOEFL (minimum score 550 paper-based), IELTS (minimum score 6.5). Electronic applications accepted.

**University of Michigan–Flint,** College of Arts and Sciences, Program in Social Sciences, Flint, MI 48502-1950. Offers gender studies (MA); global studies (MA); U.S. history and politics (MA). *Program availability:* Part-time. *Faculty:* 9 full-time (1 woman), 1 (woman) part-time/adjunct. *Students:* 4 full-time (1 woman), 21 part-time (14 women); includes 12 minority (9 Black or African American, non-Hispanic/Latino; 2 Hispanic/Latino; 1 Two or more races, non-Hispanic/Latino). Average age 39. 17 applicants, 82% accepted, 7 enrolled. In 2016, 7 master's awarded. *Entrance requirements:* For master's, bachelor's degree from regionally-accredited institution, minimum overall undergraduate GPA of 3.0. Additional exam requirements/recommendations for international students: Required—TOEFL (minimum score 84 iBT), IELTS (minimum score 6.5). *Application deadline:* For fall admission, 8/1 for domestic students, 5/1 for international students; for winter admission, 11/15 for domestic students, 9/1 for international students; for spring admission, 3/15 for domestic students, 1/1 for international students; for summer admission, 5/15 for domestic students. Applications are processed on a rolling basis. Application fee: $55. Electronic applications accepted. *Financial support:* Federal Work-Study, scholarships/grants, and unspecified assistantships available. Support available to part-time students. Financial award application deadline: 3/1; financial award applicants required to submit FAFSA. *Unit head:* Dr. Adam Lutzker, Director, 810-762-3470, Fax: 810-762-3281, E-mail: alutzker@umflint.edu. *Application contact:* Bradley T. Maki, Director of Graduate Admissions, 810-762-3171, Fax: 810-766-6789, E-mail: bmaki@umflint.edu. Website: http://www.umflint.edu/graduateprograms/social-sciences-ma

**University of Northern British Columbia,** Office of Graduate Studies, Prince George, BC V2N 4Z9, Canada. Offers business administration (Diploma); community health science (M Sc); disability management (MA); education (M Ed); first nations studies (MA); gender studies (MA); history (MA); interdisciplinary studies (MA); international studies (MA); mathematical, computer and physical sciences (M Sc); natural resources and environmental studies (M Sc, MA, MNRES, PhD); political science (MA); psychology (M Sc, PhD); social work (MSW). *Program availability:* Part-time, evening/weekend, online learning. *Degree requirements:* For master's, thesis; for doctorate, thesis/dissertation. *Entrance requirements:* For master's, GRE, minimum B average in undergraduate course work; for doctorate, candidacy exam, minimum A average in graduate course work.

**University of North Georgia,** Program in International Affairs, Dahlonega, GA 30597. Offers MAIA. *Program availability:* Part-time, evening/weekend, 100% online. *Faculty:* 9 full-time (1 woman). *Students:* 8 full-time (7 women), 31 part-time (13 women); includes 8 minority (6 Black or African American, non-Hispanic/Latino; 1 Asian, non-Hispanic/Latino; 1 Two or more races, non-Hispanic/Latino). Average age 32. 29 applicants, 76% accepted, 11 enrolled. In 2016, 11 master's awarded. *Degree requirements:* For master's, thesis optional. *Entrance requirements:* For master's, GRE or GMAT, minimum undergraduate GPA of 2.5, 3 letters of recommendation. Additional exam requirements/recommendations for international students: Required—TOEFL (minimum score 550 paper-based; 79 iBT), IELTS (minimum score 6.5). *Application deadline:* For fall admission, 8/1 priority date for domestic students; for spring admission, 12/1 priority date for domestic students; for summer admission, 5/1 priority date for domestic students. Applications are processed on a rolling basis. Application fee: $40. Electronic applications accepted. *Expenses:* Contact institution. *Financial support:* Career-related internships or fieldwork, scholarships/grants, and unspecified assistantships available. Financial award application deadline: 3/17; financial award applicants required to submit CSS PROFILE or FAFSA. *Unit head:* Dr. Cristian Harris, Department Head, 706-867-3251, E-mail: cristian.harris@ung.edu. *Application contact:* Melinda Maxwell, Director of Graduate Admissions, 706-864-1543, E-mail: melinda.maxwell@ung.edu. Website: http://ung.edu/political-science-international-affairs/

**University of North Texas,** Robert B. Toulouse School of Graduate Studies, Denton, TX 76203-5459. Offers accounting (MS); applied anthropology (MA, MS); applied behavior analysis (Certificate); applied geography (MA); applied technology and performance improvement (M Ed, MS); art education (MA); art history (MA); art museum education (Certificate); arts leadership (Certificate); audiology (Au D); behavior analysis (MS); behavioral science (PhD); biochemistry and molecular biology (MS); biology (MA, MS); biomedical engineering (MS); business analysis (MS); chemistry (MS); clinical health psychology (PhD); communication studies (MA, MS); computer engineering (MS); computer science (MS); counseling (M Ed, MS), including clinical mental health counseling (MS), college and university counseling, elementary school counseling, secondary school counseling; creative writing (MA); criminal justice (MS); curriculum and instruction (M Ed); decision sciences (MBA); design (MA, MFA), including fashion design (MFA), innovation studies, interior design (MFA); early childhood studies (MS); economics (MS); educational leadership (M Ed, Ed D); educational psychology (MS, PhD), including family studies (MS), gifted and talented (MS), human development (MS), learning and cognition (MS), research, measurement and evaluation (MS); electrical engineering (MS); emergency management (MPA); engineering technology (MS); English (MA); English as a second language (MA); environmental science (MS); finance (MBA, MS); financial management (MPA); French (MA); health services management (MBA); higher education (M Ed, Ed D); history (MA, MS); hospitality management (MS); human resources management (MPA); information science (MS); information systems (PhD); information technologies (MBA); interdisciplinary studies (MA, MS); international studies (MA); international sustainable tourism (MS); jazz studies (MM); journalism (MA, MJ, Graduate Certificate), including interactive and virtual digital communication (Graduate Certificate), narrative journalism (Graduate Certificate), public relations (Graduate Certificate); kinesiology (MS); linguistics (MA); local government management (MPA); logistics (PhD); logistics and supply chain management (MBA); long-term care, senior housing, and aging services (MA); management (PhD); marketing

*International Affairs*

(MBA); mathematics (MA, MS); mechanical and energy engineering (MS, PhD); music (MA), including ethnomusicology, music theory, musicology, performance; music composition (PhD); music education (MM Ed, PhD); nonprofit management (MPA); operations and supply chain management (MBA); performance (MM, DMA); philosophy (MA); political science (MA); professional and technical communication (MA); radio, television and film (MA, MFA); rehabilitation counseling (Certificate); sociology (MA); Spanish (MA); special education (M Ed); speech-language pathology (MA); strategic management (MBA); studio art (MFA); teaching (M Ed); MBA/MS. *Program availability:* Part-time, evening/weekend, online learning. Terminal master's awarded for partial completion of doctoral program. *Degree requirements:* For master's, variable foreign language requirement, comprehensive exam (for some programs), thesis (for some programs); for doctorate, variable foreign language requirement, comprehensive exam (for some programs), thesis/dissertation; for other advanced degree, variable foreign language requirement, comprehensive exam (for some programs). *Entrance requirements:* For master's and doctorate, GRE, GMAT. Additional exam requirements/recommendations for international students: Required—TOEFL (minimum score 550 paper-based; 79 iBT). Electronic applications accepted.

**University of Notre Dame,** Graduate School, Keough School of Global Affairs, Notre Dame, IN 46556. Offers global affairs (MGA); international peace studies (MGA); sustainable development (MGA).

**University of Oklahoma,** College of International Studies, Norman, OK 73019. Offers economics and development (MAIS), including global economics and development, global security studies (MA, MAIS); global affairs (MA), including economics and development, global security studies (MA, MAIS); JD/MAIS; MAIS/MSW. *Program availability:* Part-time, online courses with an 8-10 day study abroad. *Faculty:* 18 full-time (6 women), 1 part-time/adjunct (0 women). *Students:* 48 full-time (21 women), 231 part-time (53 women); includes 85 minority (21 Black or African American, non-Hispanic/Latino; 2 American Indian or Alaska Native, non-Hispanic/Latino; 13 Asian, non-Hispanic/Latino; 33 Hispanic/Latino; 3 Native Hawaiian or other Pacific Islander, non-Hispanic/Latino; 13 Two or more races, non-Hispanic/Latino), 4 international. Average age 32. 60 applicants, 88% accepted, 36 enrolled. In 2016, 68 master's awarded. Terminal master's awarded for partial completion of doctoral program. *Degree requirements:* For master's, variable foreign language requirement, 36 credit hours (33 online); thesis, policy paper or internship project; faculty-led overseas travel program of 8-10 days that will vary in location (online). *Entrance requirements:* For master's, GRE. Additional exam requirements/recommendations for international students: Required—TOEFL (minimum score 79 iBT) or IELTS (minimum score 6.5). *Application deadline:* For fall admission, 2/15 for domestic and international students. Application fee: $50 ($100 for international students). Electronic applications accepted. *Expenses:* Tuition, state resident: full-time $4886; part-time $203.60 per credit hour. Tuition, nonresident: full-time $18,989; part-time $791.20 per credit hour. *Required fees:* $3283; $126.25 per credit hour. $126.50 per semester. *Financial support:* In 2016–17, 27 students received support, including 7 research assistantships with full tuition reimbursements available (averaging $13,500 per year), 3 teaching assistantships with full tuition reimbursements available (averaging $13,500 per year); fellowships with full tuition reimbursements available, career-related internships or fieldwork, scholarships/grants, health care benefits, and unspecified assistantships also available. Financial award application deadline: 6/1; financial award applicants required to submit FAFSA. *Faculty research:* Area studies, including the Middle East, China, East and South Asia, Latin America, and Europe; political economy and development; international security; identity and nationalism; global history and culture. *Unit head:* Dr. Mitchell Smith, Professor/Associate Dean for Academic Affairs, 405-325-1584, Fax: 405-325-7738, E-mail: mps@ou.edu. *Application contact:* Katie Watkins, Academic Advisor, 405-325-2337, Fax: 405-325-7738, E-mail: kwatkins@ou.edu.
Website: http://www.ou.edu/dais

**University of Oregon,** Graduate School, College of Arts and Sciences, Program in International Studies, Eugene, OR 97403. Offers MA. *Program availability:* Part-time. *Degree requirements:* For master's, one foreign language, thesis, internship. *Entrance requirements:* For master's, minimum GPA of 3.0. Additional exam requirements/recommendations for international students: Required—TOEFL. *Faculty research:* International development studies; environmental studies; cross-cultural communications; planning, public policy, and management; several world regions.

**University of Pennsylvania,** School of Arts and Sciences, Graduate Group in International Studies, Philadelphia, PA 19104. Offers AM. *Faculty:* 7 full-time (1 woman), 5 part-time/adjunct (1 woman). *Students:* 11 full-time (6 women); includes 3 minority (2 Asian, non-Hispanic/Latino; 1 Hispanic/Latino), 4 international. Average age 32. In 2016, 74 master's awarded. Application fee: $70. *Expenses:* Tuition: Full-time $31,068; part-time $5762 per course. *Required fees:* $3200; $336 per course. Full-time tuition and fees vary according to degree level, program and student level. Part-time tuition and fees vary according to course load, degree level and program.
Website: http://www.sas.upenn.edu/graduate-division

**University of Pittsburgh,** Graduate School of Public and International Affairs, Doctoral Program in Public and International Affairs, Pittsburgh, PA 15260. Offers international affairs (PhD); international development (PhD); public administration (PhD); public policy (PhD). *Program availability:* Part-time, evening/weekend. *Faculty:* 34 full-time (12 women), 17 part-time/adjunct (5 women). *Students:* 29 full-time (12 women), 1 part-time (0 women); includes 4 minority (2 Asian, non-Hispanic/Latino; 2 Hispanic/Latino), 5 international. Average age 37. 60 applicants, 18% accepted, 5 enrolled. In 2016, 3 doctorates awarded. *Degree requirements:* For doctorate, comprehensive exam, thesis/dissertation, mid-term evaluation, preliminary exam, annual review. *Entrance requirements:* For doctorate, GRE or GMAT, 2 letters of recommendation, resume, undergraduate transcripts, personal statement, writing sample. Additional exam requirements/recommendations for international students: Required—TOEFL (minimum score 80 iBT); Recommended—IELTS (minimum score 7). *Application deadline:* For fall admission, 1/15 for domestic and international students. Application fee: $50. Electronic applications accepted. *Expenses:* $22,578 per year in-state; $36,734 per year out-of-state. *Financial support:* In 2016–17, 16 students received support, including 16 research assistantships with partial tuition reimbursements available (averaging $14,620 per year); fellowships also available. Financial award application deadline: 1/15; financial award applicants required to submit FAFSA. *Faculty research:* International development, international security and intelligence, human rights, urban affairs and planning, energy and environmental policy, nonprofit management, public management. *Total annual research expenditures:* $1.3 million. *Unit head:* Dr. John T.S. Keeler, Dean, 412-648-7605, Fax: 412-648-2605, E-mail: keeler@pitt.edu. *Application contact:* Dr. Michael T. Rizzi, Director of Student Services, 412-648-7640, Fax: 412-648-7641, E-mail: rizzim@pitt.edu.
Website: http://www.gspia.pitt.edu/

**University of Pittsburgh,** Graduate School of Public and International Affairs, Master of Public Administration Program, Pittsburgh, PA 15260. Offers energy and environment (MPA); governance and international public management (MPA); policy research and analysis (MPA); public and nonprofit management (MPA); urban affairs and planning (MPA); JD/MPA; MPH/MPA; MSIS/MPA; MSW/MPA. *Accreditation:* NASPAA. *Program availability:* Part-time, evening/weekend. *Faculty:* 34 full-time (12 women), 17 part-time/

adjunct (5 women). *Students:* 93 full-time (66 women), 21 part-time (16 women); includes 8 minority (4 Black or African American, non-Hispanic/Latino; 1 Asian, non-Hispanic/Latino; 3 Hispanic/Latino), 61 international. Average age 26. 200 applicants, 81% accepted, 49 enrolled. In 2016, 62 master's awarded. *Degree requirements:* For master's, thesis optional, capstone seminar. *Entrance requirements:* For master's, GRE General Test or GMAT, 2 letters of recommendation, resume, undergraduate transcripts, personal statement. Additional exam requirements/recommendations for international students: Required—TOEFL (minimum score 80 iBT); Recommended—IELTS (minimum score 7). *Application deadline:* For fall admission, 2/1 priority date for domestic students, 1/15 for international students; for spring admission, 11/1 for domestic students, 8/1 for international students. Application fee: $50. Electronic applications accepted. *Expenses:* $22,578 per year in-state; $36,734 per year out-of-state. *Financial support:* In 2016–17, 10 students received support, including 2 research assistantships with full tuition reimbursements available (averaging $14,620 per year); fellowships with full tuition reimbursements available, career-related internships or fieldwork, scholarships/grants, health care benefits, and unspecified assistantships also available. Financial award application deadline: 2/1; financial award applicants required to submit FAFSA. *Faculty research:* Urban affairs and planning, governance and international public management, nonprofit management, policy research and analysis, energy and environmental policy. *Total annual research expenditures:* $1.3 million. *Unit head:* Dr. John T.S. Keeler, Dean, 412-648-7605, Fax: 412-648-2605, E-mail: keeler@pitt.edu. *Application contact:* Dr. Michael T. Rizzi, Director of Student Services, 412-648-7640, Fax: 412-648-7641, E-mail: rizzim@pitt.edu.
Website: http://www.gspia.pitt.edu/

**University of Pittsburgh,** Graduate School of Public and International Affairs, Master of Public and International Affairs Program, Pittsburgh, PA 15260. Offers human security (MPIA); international political economy (MPIA); security and intelligence studies (MPIA); JD/MPIA; MBA/MPIA; MPH/MPIA; MPIA/MSW; MSIS/MPIA. *Program availability:* Part-time, evening/weekend. *Faculty:* 34 full-time (12 women), 17 part-time/adjunct (5 women). *Students:* 98 full-time (42 women), 17 part-time (8 women); includes 17 minority (8 Black or African American, non-Hispanic/Latino; 2 Asian, non-Hispanic/Latino; 6 Hispanic/Latino; 1 Two or more races, non-Hispanic/Latino), 20 international. Average age 26. 181 applicants, 91% accepted, 48 enrolled. In 2016, 70 master's awarded. *Degree requirements:* For master's, thesis optional, capstone seminar. *Entrance requirements:* For master's, GRE General Test or GMAT, 2 letters of recommendation, resume, undergraduate transcripts, personal statement. Additional exam requirements/recommendations for international students: Required—TOEFL (minimum score 80 iBT); Recommended—IELTS (minimum score 7). *Application deadline:* For fall admission, 2/1 for domestic students, 1/15 for international students; for spring admission, 11/1 for domestic students, 8/1 for international students. Application fee: $50. Electronic applications accepted. *Expenses:* $22,578 per year in-state; $36,734 per year out-of-state. *Financial support:* In 2016–17, 47 students received support, including 2 fellowships with full tuition reimbursements available (averaging $18,000 per year), 3 research assistantships with full tuition reimbursements available (averaging $14,620 per year); career-related internships or fieldwork and scholarships/grants also available. Financial award application deadline: 2/1; financial award applicants required to submit FAFSA. *Faculty research:* International political economy, human security, security and intelligence. *Total annual research expenditures:* $1.3 million. *Unit head:* Dr. John T.S. Keeler, Dean, 412-648-7605, E-mail: keeler@pitt.edu. *Application contact:* Dr. Michael T. Rizzi, Director of Student Services, 412-648-7640, Fax: 412-648-7641, E-mail: rizzim@pitt.edu.
Website: http://www.gspia.pitt.edu/

**University of Pittsburgh,** Katz Graduate School of Business, MBA/Master of Public and International Affairs Dual-Degree Program, Pittsburgh, PA 15260. Offers MBA/MPIA. *Accreditation:* AACSB. *Program availability:* Part-time, evening/weekend. *Faculty:* 88 full-time (27 women), 42 part-time/adjunct (15 women). *Students:* 3 applicants, 33% accepted. *Entrance requirements:* Additional exam requirements/recommendations for international students: Required—TOEFL (minimum score 100 iBT) or IELTS (minimum score 7.0). *Application deadline:* For fall admission, 4/1 priority date for domestic students, 2/1 priority date for international students. Application fee: $50. Electronic applications accepted. Tuition and fees vary according to program. *Financial support:* Scholarships/grants available. Financial award application deadline: 6/1; financial award applicants required to submit FAFSA. *Faculty research:* Accounting systems/financial reporting, corporate finance, shopper marketing/consumer behavior, management information systems, organizational behavior and entrepreneurship. *Total annual research expenditures:* $493,036. *Unit head:* Dr. Arjang A. Assad, Dean, 412-648-1556, Fax: 412-648-1552, E-mail: aassad@katz.pitt.edu. *Application contact:* Thomas Keller, Director of MBA Admissions, 412-648-1700, Fax: 412-648-1659, E-mail: mba@katz.pitt.edu.
Website: http://www.business.pitt.edu/katz/mba/academics/programs/mba-mpia.php

**University of Pittsburgh,** University Center for International Studies, Pittsburgh, PA 15260. Offers African studies (Certificate); Asian studies (Certificate); European Union studies (Certificate); global studies (Certificate); Latin American studies (Certificate); Russian and East European studies (Certificate); West European studies (Certificate). *Program availability:* Part-time, evening/weekend, online learning. *Students:* 175 full-time (105 women), 14 part-time (10 women); includes 78 minority (5 Black or African American, non-Hispanic/Latino; 30 Asian, non-Hispanic/Latino; 42 Hispanic/Latino; 1 Two or more races, non-Hispanic/Latino). Average age 29. *Degree requirements:* For Certificate, one foreign language, comprehensive exam (for some programs), thesis (for some programs). *Entrance requirements:* Additional exam requirements/recommendations for international students: Required—TOEFL. *Expenses:* Contact institution. *Financial support:* In 2016–17, 22 fellowships with full tuition reimbursements (averaging $17,878 per year) were awarded; scholarships/grants, traineeships, health care benefits, tuition waivers, and unspecified assistantships also available. *Unit head:* Dr. Ariel Armony, Director, 412-648-7374, Fax: 412-624-4672, E-mail: armony@pitt.edu.
Website: http://www.ucis.pitt.edu

**University of Rhode Island,** Graduate School, College of Arts and Sciences, Department of Political Science, Kingston, RI 02881. Offers political science (MA), including American politics, comparative government, international relations, public policy; public policy and administration (MPA). *Program availability:* Part-time. *Faculty:* 12 full-time (5 women). *Students:* 20 full-time (9 women), 37 part-time (20 women); includes 11 minority (4 Black or African American, non-Hispanic/Latino; 2 American Indian or Alaska Native, non-Hispanic/Latino; 1 Asian, non-Hispanic/Latino; 3 Hispanic/Latino; 1 Two or more races, non-Hispanic/Latino), 1 international. In 2016, 15 master's awarded. *Degree requirements:* For master's, comprehensive exam (for some programs), thesis optional. *Entrance requirements:* For master's, GRE, GMAT, or MAT if undergraduate GPA below 3.0, 2 letters of recommendation. Additional exam requirements/recommendations for international students: Required—TOEFL. *Application deadline:* For fall admission, 2/1 for international students; for spring admission, 7/15 for international students. Application fee: $65. Electronic applications accepted. *Expenses:* Tuition, state resident: full-time $11,796; part-time $655 per credit. Tuition, nonresident: full-time $24,206; part-time $1345 per credit. *Required fees:* $1546; $44 per credit. One-time fee: $155 full-time; $35 part-time. *Financial support:* In 2016–17, 6 teaching assistantships with tuition reimbursements (averaging $15,753 per

year) were awarded; research assistantships also available. Financial award application deadline: 7/15; financial award applicants required to submit FAFSA. *Unit head:* Dr. Brian Krueger, Department Chair, 401-874-4058, Fax: 401-874-4072, E-mail: bkrueger@uri.edu. *Application contact:* Dr. Marc Hutchison, Director/Associate Professor, 401-874-4054, Fax: 401-874-4072, E-mail: mlhutch@uri.edu.
Website: http://www.uri.edu/artsci/psc/

**University of Rochester,** School of Arts and Sciences, Department of History, Rochester, NY 14627. Offers American history (MA, PhD); European history (MA, PhD); global history (MA, PhD). *Faculty:* 19 full-time (4 women). *Students:* 28 full-time (12 women); includes 2 minority (1 Asian, non-Hispanic/Latino; 1 Two or more races, non-Hispanic/Latino), 2 international. Average age 31. 32 applicants, 28% accepted, 5 enrolled. In 2016, 5 master's, 4 doctorates awarded. Terminal master's awarded for partial completion of doctoral program. *Degree requirements:* For master's, one foreign language, thesis or alternative; for doctorate, 2 foreign languages, thesis/dissertation, comprehensive oral exam, qualifying exam. *Entrance requirements:* For master's and doctorate, GRE General Test, sample of written work. Additional exam requirements/recommendations for international students: Required—TOEFL. *Application deadline:* For fall admission, 1/15 for domestic and international students. Application fee: $60. Electronic applications accepted. *Expenses:* $1,538 per credit. *Financial support:* In 2016–17, 24 students received support, including 7 fellowships (averaging $20,000 per year); tuition waivers (full and partial) also available. Financial award application deadline: 1/15. *Unit head:* Matthew Lenoe, Chair, 585-275-9355, E-mail: matthew.lenoe@rochester.edu. *Application contact:* Alissa Clark, Secretary, 585-275-2053.
Website: http://www.rochester.edu/College/HIS/

**University of San Diego,** College of Arts and Sciences, Master of Arts Program in International Relations, San Diego, CA 92110-2492. Offers MA, JD/MA. *Program availability:* Part-time, evening/weekend. *Faculty:* 5 full-time (2 women). *Students:* 10 full-time (4 women), 17 part-time (10 women); includes 8 minority (1 Asian, non-Hispanic/Latino; 7 Hispanic/Latino), 4 international. Average age 32. 43 applicants, 58% accepted, 10 enrolled. In 2016, 15 master's awarded. *Degree requirements:* For master's, comprehensive exam. *Entrance requirements:* For master's, GRE General Test (minimum scores: 153 verbal/147 quantitative/4.5 analytical writing), minimum GPA of 3.2; 24 units in political science, history and/or economics. Additional exam requirements/recommendations for international students: Required—TOEFL (minimum score 580 paper-based; 83 iBT), TWE. *Application deadline:* For fall admission, 3/1 priority date for domestic and international students; for spring admission, 10/1 priority date for domestic and international students. Applications are processed on a rolling basis. Application fee: $45. Electronic applications accepted. *Financial support:* In 2016–17, 27 students received support. Institutionally sponsored loans and unspecified assistantships available. Support available to part-time students. Financial award application deadline: 4/1; financial award applicants required to submit FAFSA. *Faculty research:* Comparative politics, international relations, international security, foreign policy, and international development. *Unit head:* Dr. Randy Willoughby, Graduate Program Director, 619-260-4014, Fax: 619-260-6840, E-mail: mair@sandiego.edu. *Application contact:* Monica Mahon, Associate Director of Graduate Admissions, 619-260-4524, Fax: 619-260-4158, E-mail: grads@sandiego.edu.
Website: http://www.sandiego.edu/cas/mair/

**University of San Francisco,** College of Arts and Sciences, International Studies Program, San Francisco, CA 94117-1080. Offers MA. *Program availability:* Part-time. *Faculty:* 6 full-time (3 women), 1 part-time/adjunct (0 women). *Students:* 36 full-time (30 women), 31 part-time (17 women); includes 29 minority (5 Black or African American, non-Hispanic/Latino; 9 Asian, non-Hispanic/Latino; 10 Hispanic/Latino; 5 Two or more races, non-Hispanic/Latino), 20 international. Average age 26. 143 applicants, 92% accepted, 36 enrolled. In 2016, 49 master's awarded. *Entrance requirements:* Additional exam requirements/recommendations for international students: Required—TOEFL, IELTS, PTE. *Application deadline:* For fall admission, 2/1 for domestic and international students. Electronic applications accepted. *Expenses: Tuition:* Full-time $23,310; part-time $1295 per credit. Tuition and fees vary according to course load, degree level, campus/location and program. *Financial support:* In 2016–17, 26 students received support. Tuition waivers available. Financial award applicants required to submit FAFSA. *Unit head:* Christie Meno, Administrative Director, 415-422-5122. *Application contact:* Mark Landerghini, Information Contact, 415-422-5101, Fax: 415-422-2217, E-mail: asgraduate@usfca.edu.
Website: https://www.usfca.edu/arts-sciences/graduate-programs/international-studies

**University of San Francisco,** College of Arts and Sciences, Program in Migration Studies, San Francisco, CA 94117-1080. Offers MMS. *Faculty:* 3 full-time (2 women). *Students:* 11 full-time (10 women); includes 6 minority (all Hispanic/Latino). Average age 25. 37 applicants, 95% accepted, 11 enrolled. *Entrance requirements:* For master's, statement of purpose. Additional exam requirements/recommendations for international students: Required—TOEFL, IELTS, PTE. *Application deadline:* For fall admission, 2/1 priority date for domestic students, 2/1 for international students. Applications are processed on a rolling basis. Electronic applications accepted. *Expenses: Tuition:* Full-time $23,310; part-time $1295 per credit. Tuition and fees vary according to course load, degree level, campus/location and program. *Financial support:* In 2016–17, 10 students received support. Applicants required to submit FAFSA. *Unit head:* Dr. Lois Lorenzen, Faculty Director, 415-422-5543, E-mail: migrationstudies@usfca.edu. *Application contact:* Mark Landerghini, Information Contact, 415-422-5101, Fax: 415-422-2217, E-mail: asgraduate@usfca.edu.
Website: https://www.usfca.edu/arts-sciences/graduate-programs/migration-studies

**University of South Carolina,** The Graduate School, College of Arts and Sciences, Department of Political Science, Program in International Studies, Columbia, SC 29208. Offers MA, PhD. *Program availability:* Part-time. Terminal master's awarded for partial completion of doctoral program. *Degree requirements:* For master's, one foreign language, thesis or alternative; for doctorate, one foreign language, comprehensive exam, thesis/dissertation. *Entrance requirements:* For master's, GRE General Test, minimum GPA of 3.3; for doctorate, GRE General Test, minimum GPA of 3.5. Additional exam requirements/recommendations for international students: Required—TOEFL. Electronic applications accepted. *Faculty research:* International relations, international organization, foreign policy, comparative politics.

**University of Southern California,** Graduate School, Annenberg School for Communication and Journalism, School of Communication, Program in Public Diplomacy, Los Angeles, CA 90089. Offers MPD. *Program availability:* Part-time. *Students:* 33 full-time (22 women), 4 part-time; includes 9 minority (1 Black or African American, non-Hispanic/Latino; 2 Asian, non-Hispanic/Latino; 5 Hispanic/Latino; 1 Two or more races, non-Hispanic/Latino), 8 international. Average age 26. 45 applicants, 60% accepted, 19 enrolled. In 2016, 23 master's awarded. *Degree requirements:* For master's, thesis. *Entrance requirements:* For master's, GRE, resume, writing samples, statement of purpose, recommendation letters. Additional exam requirements/recommendations for international students: Required—TOEFL (minimum score 114 iBT), IELTS (minimum score 8). *Application deadline:* For fall admission, 1/15 priority date for domestic and international students. Application fee: $90. Electronic applications accepted. *Financial support:* In 2016–17, 6 fellowships (averaging $15,000

per year) were awarded; career-related internships or fieldwork, Federal Work-Study, and scholarships/grants also available. Support available to part-time students. Financial award application deadline: 1/15; financial award applicants required to submit FAFSA. *Unit head:* Dr. Nicholas Cull, Director, 213-821-4080, E-mail: cull@usc.edu. *Application contact:* Allyson Hill, Associate Dean for Admissions, 213-821-0770, Fax: 213-740-1933, E-mail: ascadm@usc.edu.
Website: http://www.annenberg.usc.edu

**University of Southern California,** Graduate School, Dana and David Dornsife College of Letters, Arts and Sciences, Political Science and International Relations PhD Program, Los Angeles, CA 90089. Offers PhD. *Degree requirements:* For doctorate, variable foreign language requirement, comprehensive exam, thesis/dissertation. *Entrance requirements:* For doctorate, GRE (minimum score 1000). Additional exam requirements/recommendations for international students: Required—TOEFL (minimum score 600 paper-based; 100 iBT). Electronic applications accepted. *Faculty research:* American politics, foreign policy analysis, international political economy, race/ethics politics, security studies.

**University of Southern California,** Graduate School, School of Policy, Planning, and Development, Master of International Public Policy and Management Program, Los Angeles, CA 90089. Offers MPPM. *Program availability:* Part-time. *Entrance requirements:* Additional exam requirements/recommendations for international students: Required—TOEFL (minimum score 71 iBT). Electronic applications accepted. *Expenses:* Contact institution. *Faculty research:* International development, economic development, social policy problems, issues of developing countries, international and comparative.

**University of South Florida,** College of Arts and Sciences, Department of Government and International Affairs, Tampa, FL 33620-9951. Offers government (PhD); Latin American, Caribbean and Latino studies (MA); political science (MA), including comparative government and politics; public administration (MPA). *Program availability:* Part-time, evening/weekend. *Faculty:* 15 full-time (3 women). *Students:* 47 full-time (26 women), 40 part-time (22 women); includes 15 minority (6 Black or African American, non-Hispanic/Latino; 1 Asian, non-Hispanic/Latino; 7 Hispanic/Latino; 1 Two or more races, non-Hispanic/Latino), 15 international. Average age 32. 59 applicants, 58% accepted, 21 enrolled. In 2016, 30 master's, 3 doctorates awarded. *Degree requirements:* For master's, comprehensive exam, thesis; for doctorate, comprehensive exam, thesis/dissertation. *Entrance requirements:* For master's, GRE General Test, minimum GPA of 3.0 in upper-division undergraduate course work; letters of recommendation (2 for MPA, 3 for MS); 500-word personal statement and undergraduate background in political science or related fields (for MS); one-page career statement (for MPA); for doctorate, GRE General Test, 500-word personal statement, three letters of recommendation, transcripts of MA/BA coursework, writing sample. Additional exam requirements/recommendations for international students: Required—TOEFL (minimum score 550 paper-based; 79 iBT) or IELTS (minimum score 6.5). *Application deadline:* For fall admission, 1/5 for domestic and international students; for spring admission, 10/15 for domestic students, 9/15 for international students. Applications are processed on a rolling basis. Application fee: $30. Electronic applications accepted. *Expenses:* Tuition, state resident: full-time $7766; part-time $431.43 per credit hour. Tuition, nonresident: full-time $15,789; part-time $877.17 per credit hour. *Required fees:* $37 per term. *Financial support:* In 2016–17, 1 student received support, including 18 teaching assistantships with tuition reimbursements available (averaging $12,390 per year); unspecified assistantships also available. Financial award application deadline: 4/1. *Faculty research:* Citizenship and identity, social movements, global governance, American politics, public policy. *Total annual research expenditures:* $222,648. *Unit head:* Dr. Steven Tauber, Associate Professor/Interim Chair, 813-974-2278, Fax: 813-974-0832, E-mail: stauber@usf.edu. *Application contact:* Dr. Bernd Reiter, Associate Professor and Director of Graduate Studies, 813-974-3583, Fax: 813-974-0832, E-mail: breiter@usf.edu.
Website: http://gia.usf.edu/

**University of South Florida,** Innovative Education, Tampa, FL 33620-9951. Offers adult, career and higher education (Graduate Certificate), including college teaching, leadership in developing human resources, leadership in higher education; Africana studies (Graduate Certificate), including diasporas and health disparities, genocide and human rights; aging studies (Graduate Certificate), including gerontology; art research (Graduate Certificate), including museum studies; business foundations (Graduate Certificate); chemical and biomedical engineering (Graduate Certificate), including materials science and engineering, water, health and sustainability; child and family studies (Graduate Certificate), including positive behavior support; civil and industrial engineering (Graduate Certificate), including transportation systems analysis; community and family health (Graduate Certificate), including maternal and child health, social marketing and public health, violence and injury: prevention and intervention, women's health; criminology (Graduate Certificate), including criminal justice administration; educational measurement and research (Graduate Certificate), including evaluation; English (Graduate Certificate), including comparative literary studies, creative writing, professional and technical communication; entrepreneurship (Graduate Certificate); environmental health (Graduate Certificate), including safety management; epidemiology and biostatistics (Graduate Certificate), including applied biostatistics, biostatistics, concepts and tools of epidemiology, epidemiology, epidemiology of infectious diseases; geography, environment and planning (Graduate Certificate), including community development, environmental policy and management, geographical information systems; geology (Graduate Certificate), including hydrogeology; global health (Graduate Certificate), including disaster management, global health and Latin American and Caribbean studies, global health practice, humanitarian assistance, infection control; government and international affairs (Graduate Certificate), including Cuban studies, globalization studies; health policy and management (Graduate Certificate), including health management and leadership, public health policy and programs; hearing specialist: early intervention (Graduate Certificate); industrial and management systems engineering (Graduate Certificate), including systems engineering, technology management; information studies (Graduate Certificate), including school library media specialist; information systems/decision sciences (Graduate Certificate), including analytics and business intelligence; instructional technology (Graduate Certificate), including distance education, Florida digital/virtual educator, instructional design, multimedia design, Web design; internal medicine, bioethics and medical humanities (Graduate Certificate), including biomedical ethics; Latin American and Caribbean studies (Graduate Certificate); mass communications (Graduate Certificate), including multimedia journalism; mathematics and statistics (Graduate Certificate), including mathematics; medicine (Graduate Certificate), including aging and neuroscience, bioinformatics, biotechnology, brain fitness and memory management, clinical investigation, health informatics, health sciences, integrative weight management, intellectual property, medicine and gender, metabolic and nutritional medicine, metabolic cardiology, pharmacy sciences; national and competitive intelligence (Graduate Certificate); psychological and social foundations (Graduate Certificate), including career counseling, college teaching, diversity in education, mental health counseling, school counseling; public affairs (Graduate Certificate), including nonprofit management, public management, research administration; public health (Graduate Certificate), including environmental health,

## International Affairs

health equity, public health generalist, translational research in adolescent behavioral health; public health practices (Graduate Certificate), including planning for healthy communities; rehabilitation and mental health counseling (Graduate Certificate), including integrative mental health care, marriage and family therapy, rehabilitation technology; secondary education (Graduate Certificate), including ESOL, foreign language education: culture and content, foreign language education: professional; social work (Graduate Certificate), including geriatric social work/clinical gerontology; special education (Graduate Certificate), including autism spectrum disorder, disabilities education: severe/profound; world languages (Graduate Certificate), including teaching English as a second language (TESL) or foreign language. *Expenses:* Tuition, state resident: full-time $7766; part-time $431.43 per credit hour. Tuition, nonresident: full-time $15,789; part-time $877.17 per credit hour. *Required fees:* $37 per term. *Unit head:* Kathy Barnes, Interdisciplinary Programs Coordinator, 813-974-8031, Fax: 813-974-7061, E-mail: barnesk@usf.edu. *Application contact:* Karen Tylinski, Metro Initiatives, 813-974-9943, Fax: 813-974-7061, E-mail: ktylinsk@usf.edu.
Website: http://www.usf.edu/innovative-education/

**University of the Pacific,** McGeorge School of Law, Sacramento, CA 95817. Offers advocacy (JD); international water resources law (JSD); public policy and law (LL M); JD/MBA; JD/MPPA. *Accreditation:* ABA. *Program availability:* Part-time, evening weekend. *Faculty:* 38 full-time (17 women), 40 part-time/adjunct (11 women). *Students:* 365 full-time (195 women), 188 part-time (105 women); includes 187 minority (24 Black or African American, non-Hispanic/Latino; 3 American Indian or Alaska Native, non-Hispanic/Latino; 43 Asian, non-Hispanic/Latino; 114 Hispanic/Latino; 1 Native Hawaiian or other Pacific Islander, non-Hispanic/Latino; 2 Two or more races, non-Hispanic/Latino), 1 international. Average age 28. In 2016, 4 master's, 158 doctorates awarded. *Degree requirements:* For master's, thesis (for some programs); for doctorate, thesis/dissertation (for some programs). *Entrance requirements:* For master's, JD; for doctorate, LSAT (for JD), LL M (for JSD). Additional exam requirements/recommendations for international students: Required—TOEFL (minimum score 600 paper-based; 100 iBT). *Application deadline:* For fall admission, 3/15 priority date for domestic students. Applications are processed on a rolling basis. Application fee: $50. Electronic applications accepted. *Expenses:* Contact institution. *Financial support:* Fellowships, research assistantships, teaching assistantships, career-related internships or fieldwork, Federal Work-Study, institutionally sponsored loans, and scholarships/grants available. Support available to part-time students. Financial award applicants required to submit FAFSA. *Faculty research:* International legal studies, public policy and law, advocacy, intellectual property law, taxation, criminal law. *Unit head:* Francis Jay Mootz, III, Dean, 916-739-7151, E-mail: jmootz@pacific.edu. *Application contact:* 916-739-7105, Fax: 916-739-7301, E-mail: mcgeorge@pacific.edu. Website: http://www.mcgeorge.edu/

**University of Toronto,** School of Graduate Studies, Munk School of Global Affairs, Toronto, ON M5S 1A1, Canada. Offers European, Russian and Eurasian studies (MA); global affairs (MGA); JD/MA. *Entrance requirements:* For master's, GRE General Test, GMAT, or LSAT, Honours (4-year) BA or equivalent, minimum cumulative and final year GPA of 3.5. Additional exam requirements/recommendations for international students: Required—TOEFL (minimum score 100 iBT), TWE (minimum score 5). Electronic applications accepted.

**University of Utah,** Graduate School, College of Social and Behavioral Science, Department of Political Science, Program in Political Science, Salt Lake City, UT 84112. Offers American politics (MA, MS, PhD); comparative politics (MA, MS, PhD); international relations (MA, MS, PhD); political theory (MA, MS, PhD); public administration (MA, MS, PhD). *Faculty:* 31 full-time (8 women), 10 part-time/adjunct (3 women). *Students:* 45 full-time (16 women), 19 part-time (9 women); includes 6 minority (2 Asian, non-Hispanic/Latino; 2 Hispanic/Latino; 2 Two or more races, non-Hispanic/Latino), 4 international. Average age 35. 37 applicants, 49% accepted, 7 enrolled. In 2016, 2 master's, 4 doctorates awarded. Terminal master's awarded for partial completion of doctoral program. *Degree requirements:* For master's, variable foreign language requirement, thesis or research paper; for doctorate, comprehensive exam, thesis/dissertation. *Entrance requirements:* For master's and doctorate, GRE General Test, minimum GPA of 3.2. Additional exam requirements/recommendations for international students: Required—TOEFL (minimum score 580 paper-based; 61 iBT), IELTS (minimum score 6). *Application deadline:* For fall admission, 1/15 priority date for domestic and international students. Application fee: $55 ($65 for international students). Electronic applications accepted. *Expenses:* Contact institution. *Financial support:* In 2016–17, 10 students received support, including 5 fellowships with full tuition reimbursements available (averaging $15,250 per year), 13 teaching assistantships with full tuition reimbursements available (averaging $15,000 per year); career-related internships or fieldwork, scholarships/grants, health care benefits, and unspecified assistantships also available. Financial award application deadline: 1/15; financial award applicants required to submit FAFSA. *Faculty research:* International politics, comparative politics, political theory, American politics, public administration. *Total annual research expenditures:* $15,000. *Unit head:* Mark Button, Chair, 801-585-7987, Fax: 801-585-6492, E-mail: mark.button@poli-sci.utah.edu. *Application contact:* Sandy Hiskey, Graduate Academic Advisor, 801-581-8608, Fax: 801-585-6492, E-mail: sandy.hiskey@utah.edu.
Website: http://www.poli-sci.utah.edu/

**University of Utah,** Graduate School, College of Social and Behavioral Science, Master of Science in International Affairs and Global Enterprise Program, Salt Lake City, UT 84112. Offers MS. *Program availability:* Part-time. *Students:* 17 full-time (8 women), 10 part-time (6 women); includes 7 minority (1 Black or African American, non-Hispanic/Latino; 4 Hispanic/Latino; 2 Two or more races, non-Hispanic/Latino), 1 international. Average age 28. 29 applicants, 76% accepted, 18 enrolled. In 2016, 9 master's awarded. *Degree requirements:* For master's, one foreign language, comprehensive exam (for some programs), thesis or alternative, major research paper. *Entrance requirements:* For master's, GMAT, LSAT, or GRE, undergraduate coursework in statistics, microeconomics theory and macroeconomics theory. Additional exam requirements/recommendations for international students: Required—TOEFL (minimum score 600 paper-based; 100 iBT). *Application deadline:* For fall admission, 3/1 for domestic and international students; for spring admission, 9/1 for domestic and international students; for summer admission, 1/15 for domestic and international students. Application fee: $55 ($65 for international students). Electronic applications accepted. *Expenses:* Contact institution. *Financial support:* In 2016–17, 5 students received support, including 4 fellowships with partial tuition reimbursements available (averaging $2,000 per year); unspecified assistantships also available. Financial award application deadline: 2/15. *Unit head:* Dr. Stephen Reynolds, Director, 801-581-8620, Fax: 801-585-5081, E-mail: stephen.reynolds@csbs.utah.edu. *Application contact:* Elizabeth Henke, Program Manager, 801-585-7722, Fax: 801-587-7861, E-mail: elizabeth.henke@cppa.utah.edu.
Website: http://www.miage.utah.edu

**University of Virginia,** College and Graduate School of Arts and Sciences, Department of Politics, Program in Foreign Affairs, Charlottesville, VA 22903. Offers MA, PhD; JD/MA, MBA/MA. *Students:* 30 full-time (13 women); includes 4 minority (1 Black or African American, non-Hispanic/Latino; 1 Asian, non-Hispanic/Latino; 1 Hispanic/Latino; 1 Two

or more races, non-Hispanic/Latino), 10 international. Average age 30. 107 applicants, 18% accepted, 7 enrolled. In 2016, 3 master's, 3 doctorates awarded. *Degree requirements:* For master's, one foreign language, 2 research/statistics courses or thesis; for doctorate, variable foreign language requirement, thesis/dissertation, 2 research/statistics courses. *Entrance requirements:* For master's and doctorate, GRE General Test, long writing sample; 2 letters of recommendation. Additional exam requirements/recommendations for international students: Required—TOEFL (minimum score 600 paper-based; 90 iBT), IELTS (minimum score 7). *Application deadline:* For fall admission, 12/4 for domestic and international students. Applications are processed on a rolling basis. Application fee: $60. Electronic applications accepted. *Expenses:* Tuition, state resident: full-time $15,026; part-time $834 per credit hour. Tuition, nonresident: full-time $25,168; part-time $1378 per credit hour. *Required fees:* $2654. *Financial support:* Fellowships and teaching assistantships available. Financial award application deadline: 12/4; financial award applicants required to submit FAFSA. *Unit head:* David Leblang, Chair, 434-924-3192, Fax: 434-924-3359, E-mail: dal7w@virginia.edu. *Application contact:* Jeffery A. Jenkins, Director of Graduate Studies, 434-924-3192, Fax: 434-924-3359, E-mail: jaj7d@virginia.edu.
Website: http://politics.virginia.edu/

**University of Washington,** Graduate School, College of Arts and Sciences, Henry M. Jackson School of International Studies, International Studies PhD Program, Seattle, WA 98195. Offers PhD. *Degree requirements:* For doctorate, variable foreign language requirement, comprehensive exam, thesis/dissertation, research tutorial with capstone presentation; dissertation prospectus defense; final examination. *Entrance requirements:* For doctorate, GRE General Test, master's degree. Additional exam requirements/recommendations for international students: Required—TOEFL (minimum score 500 paper-based; 92 iBT), IELTS (minimum score 7).

**University of Waterloo,** Graduate Studies, Faculty of Arts, Department of Political Science, Waterloo, ON N2L 3G1, Canada. Offers global governance (MA, PhD). *Program availability:* Part-time. *Degree requirements:* For master's, thesis (for some programs), research paper. *Entrance requirements:* For master's, honors degree, minimum B average, writing sample. Additional exam requirements/recommendations for international students: Required—TOEFL, IELTS, PTE. Electronic applications accepted. *Faculty research:* Conflict and conflict resolution, political economy, contemporary political theory, Canadian state and society.

**University of Waterloo,** Graduate Studies, Faculty of Arts, Global Governance Program, Waterloo, ON N2L 3G1, Canada. Offers MA, PhD. *Entrance requirements:* For doctorate, MA. Additional exam requirements/recommendations for international students: Required—TOEFL, IELTS, PTE. Electronic applications accepted. *Faculty research:* Global political economy, global environment, peace and security, global justice and human rights, multilateral institutions and diplomacy.

**University of Wyoming,** College of Arts and Sciences, Program in International Studies, Laramie, WY 82071. Offers international peace corps (MA); international studies (MA). *Program availability:* Part-time. *Degree requirements:* For master's, one foreign language, thesis. *Entrance requirements:* For master's, GRE General Test, minimum GPA of 3.0. Additional exam requirements/recommendations for international students: Required—TOEFL (minimum score 525 paper-based). Electronic applications accepted. *Faculty research:* International political economy, comparative social institutions, foreign policy, economic development.

**Virginia International University,** School of Public and International Affairs, Fairfax, VA 22030. Offers international relations (MS); public administration (MPA).

**Virginia Polytechnic Institute and State University,** Graduate School, College of Architecture and Urban Studies, Blacksburg, VA 24061. Offers architecture (MS Arch); architecture and design research (PhD); building/construction science and management (MS); creative technologies (MFA); environmental design and planning (PhD); landscape architecture (MLA); planning, governance, and globalization (PhD); public administration (MPA); public administration/public affairs (PhD, Certificate); public and international affairs (MPIA); urban and regional planning (MURP). *Accreditation:* ASLA (one or more programs are accredited). *Faculty:* 136 full-time (53 women). *Students:* 371 full-time (185 women), 210 part-time (104 women); includes 118 minority (49 Black or African American, non-Hispanic/Latino; 1 American Indian or Alaska Native, non-Hispanic/Latino; 30 Asian, non-Hispanic/Latino; 32 Hispanic/Latino; 6 Two or more races, non-Hispanic/Latino), 137 international. Average age 31. 566 applicants, 55% accepted, 160 enrolled. In 2016, 137 master's, 24 doctorates awarded. *Degree requirements:* For master's, comprehensive exam (for some programs), thesis (for some programs); for doctorate, comprehensive exam (for some programs), thesis/dissertation (for some programs). *Entrance requirements:* For master's and doctorate, GRE/GMAT. Additional exam requirements/recommendations for international students: Required—TOEFL (minimum score 80 iBT). *Application deadline:* For fall admission, 8/1 for domestic students, 4/1 for international students; for spring admission, 1/1 for domestic students, 9/1 for international students. Applications are processed on a rolling basis. Application fee: $75. Electronic applications accepted. *Expenses:* Tuition, state resident: full-time $12,467; part-time $692.50 per credit hour. Tuition, nonresident: full-time $25,095; part-time $1394.25 per credit hour. *Required fees:* $2669; $491.50 per semester. Tuition and fees vary according to course load, campus/location and program. *Financial support:* In 2016–17, 11 research assistantships with full tuition reimbursements (averaging $19,474 per year), 45 teaching assistantships with full tuition reimbursements (averaging $16,014 per year) were awarded. Financial award application deadline: 3/1; financial award applicants required to submit FAFSA. *Total annual research expenditures:* $3.6 million. *Unit head:* Dr. A. J. Davis, Dean, 540-231-6416, Fax: 540-231-6332, E-mail: davisa@vt.edu. *Application contact:* Christine Mattsson-Coon, Executive Assistant, 540-231-6416, Fax: 540-231-6332, E-mail: cmattsso@vt.edu.
Website: http://www.caus.vt.edu/

**Walden University,** Graduate Programs, School of Public Policy and Administration, Minneapolis, MN 55401. Offers criminal justice (MPA, MPP, MS, Graduate Certificate), including emergency management (MS, PhD), general program (MS), global leadership (MS, PhD), homeland security and policy coordination (MS, PhD), law and public policy (MS, PhD), policy analysis (MS, PhD), public management and leadership (MS, PhD), self-designed (MS), terrorism, mediation, and peace (MS, PhD); criminal justice and executive management (MS), including global leadership (MS, PhD); criminal justice leadership and executive management (MS), including emergency management (MS, PhD), general program, homeland security and policy coordination (MS, PhD), law and public policy (MS, PhD), policy analysis (MS, PhD), public management and leadership (MS, PhD), self-designed, terrorism, mediation, and peace (MS, PhD); emergency management (MPA, MPP, MS), including criminal justice (MS, PhD), general program (MS), homeland security (MS), general program (MPA, MPP), global leadership (MPA, MPP); government management (Graduate Certificate); health policy (MPA, MPP); homeland security (MPA, MPP); homeland security and policy coordination (MPA, MPP); international nongovernmental organizations (MPA, MPP); law and public policy (MPA, MPP); local government management for sustainable communities (MPA, MPP); nonprofit management (Graduate Certificate); nonprofit management and leadership (MPA, MPP, MS), including global leadership (MS, PhD), international nongovernmental organization (MS), local government for sustainable communities (MS), self designed (MS); online teaching in higher education (Post-Master's Certificate); policy analysis (MPA); public management and leadership (MPA, MPP, Graduate Certificate); public policy (Graduate Certificate); public policy and administration (PhD), including criminal justice (MS, PhD), emergency management (MS, PhD), global leadership (MS, PhD), health policy, homeland security and policy coordination (MS, PhD), international nongovernmental organizations, law and public policy (MS, PhD), local government management for sustainable communities, nonprofit management and leadership, policy analysis (MS, PhD), public management and leadership (MS, PhD), terrorism, mediation, and peace (MS, PhD); strategic planning and public policy (Graduate Certificate); terrorism, mediation, and peace (MPA, MPP). *Program availability:* Part-time, evening/weekend, online only, 100% online. *Degree requirements:* For doctorate, thesis/dissertation, residency. *Entrance requirements:* For master's, bachelor's degree or higher; minimum GPA of 2.5; official transcripts; goal statement (for some programs); access to computer and Internet; for doctorate, master's degree or higher; three years of related professional or academic experience (preferred); minimum GPA of 3.0; goal statement and current resume (for select programs); official transcripts; access to computer and Internet; for other advanced degree, relevant work experience; access to computer and Internet. Additional exam requirements/recommendations for international students: Required—TOEFL (minimum score 550 paper-based, 79 iBT), IELTS (minimum score 6.5), Michigan English Language Assessment Battery (minimum score 82), or PTE (minimum score 53). Electronic applications accepted.

**Webster University,** College of Arts and Sciences, Department of History, Politics and International Relations, St. Louis, MO 63119-3194. Offers international nongovernmental organizations (MA), including global international relations, international relations; international relations (GM Acc). *Program availability:* Part-time, evening/weekend, online learning. *Degree requirements:* For master's, thesis optional. *Entrance requirements:* Additional exam requirements/recommendations for international students: Required—TOEFL. *Application deadline:* Applications are processed on a rolling basis. Application fee: $25 ($50 for international students). *Expenses: Tuition:* Full-time $21,900; part-time $730 per credit hour. Tuition and fees vary according to campus/location and program. *Financial support:* Career-related internships or fieldwork and Federal Work-Study available. Support available to part-time students. Financial award application deadline: 4/1; financial award applicants required to submit FAFSA. *Faculty research:* International law, political economy, international organizations, Latin American law, public policy and human rights. *Unit head:* Daniel C. Hellinger, Chair, 314-968-7064, Fax: 314-968-7403, E-mail: hellindc@webster.edu.

**Webster University,** College of Arts and Sciences, Institute for Human Rights and Humanitarian Studies, St. Louis, MO 63119-3194. Offers international human rights (MA). *Expenses: Tuition:* Full-time $21,900; part-time $730 per credit hour. Tuition and fees vary according to campus/location and program. *Unit head:* Dr. David Carl Wilson, Dean, 314-968-7160, Fax: 314-963-6043, E-mail: wilson@webster.edu. *Application contact:* Sarah Nandor, Director, Graduate and Transfer Admissions, 314-968-7109, E-mail: gadmit@webster.edu.

**Webster University,** George Herbert Walker School of Business and Technology, Department of Business, St. Louis, MO 63119-3194. Offers business and organizational security management (MBA); decision support systems (MBA); environmental management (MBA); finance (MBA, MS); forensic accounting (MS); gerontology (MBA); human resources development (MBA); human resources management (MBA); information technology management (MBA); international business (MA, MBA); international relations (MBA); management and leadership (MBA); marketing (MBA); media communications (MBA); procurement and acquisitions management (MBA); Web services (MBA). *Accreditation:* ACBSP. *Program availability:* Part-time, evening/weekend, online learning. *Degree requirements:* For master's, comprehensive exam (for some programs), thesis (for some programs). *Entrance requirements:* Additional exam requirements/recommendations for international students: Required—TOEFL. *Application deadline:* Applications are processed on a rolling basis. Application fee: $35 ($50 for international students). *Expenses: Tuition:* Full-time $21,900; part-time $730 per credit hour. Tuition and fees vary according to campus/location and program. *Financial support:* Federal Work-Study available. Support available to part-time students. Financial award application deadline: 4/1; financial award applicants required to submit FAFSA. *Unit head:* David Porras, Chair, 314-246-8621, E-mail: porrasd@webster.edu. *Application contact:* Sarah Nandor, Director, Graduate and Transfer Admissions, 314-968-7109, E-mail: gadmit@webster.edu.

**Western Michigan University,** Graduate College, College of Arts and Sciences, Department of Political Science, Kalamazoo, MI 49008. Offers international development administration (MIDA), including Peace Corps; political science (MA, PhD). *Degree requirements:* For master's, thesis optional; for doctorate, thesis/dissertation.

**West Virginia University,** Eberly College of Arts and Sciences, Department of Political Science, Morgantown, WV 26506. Offers American public policy and politics (MA); international and comparative public policy and politics (MA); political science (PhD); public policy analysis (PhD). Terminal master's awarded for partial completion of doctoral program. *Degree requirements:* For master's, thesis optional; for doctorate, comprehensive exam, thesis/dissertation. *Entrance requirements:* For master's, GRE General Test, minimum GPA of 2.75; for doctorate, GRE General Test, minimum GPA of 3.0. Additional exam requirements/recommendations for international students: Required—TOEFL. *Faculty research:* Public policy, research methods, foreign policy analysis, judicial politics, environmental and energy policy.

**Wilfrid Laurier University,** Faculty of Graduate and Postdoctoral Studies, Faculty of Arts, Department of Political Science, Waterloo, ON N2L 3C5, Canada. Offers Canadian political studies (MA); comparative politics/international relations (MA). *Program availability:* Part-time. *Degree requirements:* For master's, thesis optional. *Entrance requirements:* For master's, honors bachelor's degree or the equivalent in political science, minimum B average in undergraduate course work. Additional exam requirements/recommendations for international students: Required—TOEFL (minimum score 89 iBT). Electronic applications accepted. *Faculty research:* Political behavior/political psychology, Canadian political studies, comparative, politics/relations, public opinion and electoral studies, international.

**Wilfrid Laurier University,** Faculty of Graduate and Postdoctoral Studies, School of International Policy and Governance, Global Governance Program, Waterloo, ON N2L 3C5, Canada. Offers conflict and security (PhD); global environment (PhD); global justice and human rights (PhD); global political economy (PhD); global social governance (PhD); multilateral institutions and diplomacy (PhD). Offered jointly with University of Waterloo. *Degree requirements:* For doctorate, thesis/dissertation. *Entrance requirements:* For doctorate, MA in political science, history, economics, international development studies, international peace studies, globalization studies, environmental studies or related field with minimum A-. Additional exam requirements/recommendations for international students: Required—TOEFL (minimum score 89 iBT). Electronic applications accepted. *Faculty research:* Global political economy, global environment, conflict and security, global justice and human rights, multilateral institutions and diplomacy.

**Wilfrid Laurier University,** Faculty of Graduate and Postdoctoral Studies, School of International Policy and Governance, International Public Policy Program, Waterloo, ON N2L 3C5, Canada. Offers global governance (MIPP); human security (MIPP); international economic relations (MIPP); international environmental policy (MIPP). Offered jointly with University of Waterloo. *Entrance requirements:* For master's, honours BA with minimum B average. Additional exam requirements/recommendations for international students: Required—TOEFL (minimum score 89 iBT). Electronic applications accepted. *Faculty research:* International environmental policy, international economic relations, human security, global governance.

**Wilfrid Laurier University,** Laurier Brantford, Brantford, ON N3T 2Y3, Canada. Offers criminology (MA), including culture, crime and policy, international crime and justice, media criminology. *Degree requirements:* For master's, thesis. *Entrance requirements:* For master's, honours bachelor's degree with major in criminology or equivalent degree; minimum B+ average in final year and in all criminology courses. Additional exam requirements/recommendations for international students: Required—TOEFL (minimum score 89 iBT). Electronic applications accepted.

**Yale University,** Graduate School of Arts and Sciences, Department of Economics, Program in International and Development Economics, New Haven, CT 06520. Offers MA. *Entrance requirements:* For master's, GRE General Test.

**Yale University,** Graduate School of Arts and Sciences, Graduate Program in Global Affairs, New Haven, CT 06520-8359. Offers MA, JD/MA, MBA/MA, MEM/MA, MF/MA, MFS/MA, MPH/MA. *Faculty:* 241. *Students:* 61 full-time (29 women); includes 9 minority (1 Black or African American, non-Hispanic/Latino; 2 Asian, non-Hispanic/Latino; 3 Hispanic/Latino; 3 Two or more races, non-Hispanic/Latino), 25 international. Average age 28. 377 applicants, 12% accepted, 29 enrolled. In 2016, 33 master's awarded. *Degree requirements:* For master's, one foreign language, summer internship or project. *Entrance requirements:* For master's, GRE General Test, professional experience and introductory coursework in microeconomics and macroeconomics (strongly preferred). Additional exam requirements/recommendations for international students: Required—TOEFL (minimum score 102 iBT) or IELTS (minimum score 7.5). *Application deadline:* For fall admission, 1/2 for domestic and international students. Application fee: $105. Electronic applications accepted. *Expenses:* Contact institution. *Financial support:* In 2016–17, 49 students received support, including 23 fellowships with full and partial tuition reimbursements available (averaging $18,091 per year), 37 teaching assistantships (averaging $6,595 per year); research assistantships, career-related internships or fieldwork, institutionally sponsored loans, scholarships/grants, tuition waivers (full and partial), unspecified assistantships, and competitive summer fellowships for unpaid internships and projects also available. Financial award application deadline: 1/2. *Faculty research:* International security studies, global health, international economic development, political economy, policy. *Unit head:* James Levinsohn, Director, Jackson Institute for Global Affairs, 203-432-6253, Fax: 203-432-9886, E-mail: jackson.institute@yale.edu. *Application contact:* Cristin Siebert, Director of Student Affairs and Admissions, Jackson Institute for Global Affairs, 203-432-5954, Fax: 203-432-9886, E-mail: cristin.siebert@yale.edu.
Website: http://jackson.yale.edu/ma-degree

**York University,** Faculty of Graduate Studies, Glendon Campus, Program in Public and International Affairs, Toronto, ON M3J 1P3, Canada. Offers MA.

# International Development

**American University,** School of International Service, Washington, DC 20016-8071. Offers comparative and regional studies (Certificate); cross-cultural communication (Certificate); development management (MS); ethics, peace, and global affairs (MA); European studies (Certificate); global environmental policy (MA, Certificate); global information technology (Certificate); international affairs (MA), including comparative and international disability policy, comparative and regional studies, international economic relations, international politics, natural resources and sustainable development, U.S. foreign policy; international arts management (Certificate); international communication (MA, Certificate); international development (MA); international economic policy (Certificate); international economic relations (Certificate); international economics (MA); international media (MA); international peace and conflict resolution (MA, Certificate); international politics (Certificate); international relations (MA, PhD); international service (MIS); peacebuilding (Certificate); social enterprise (MA); the Americas (Certificate); United States foreign policy (Certificate); JD/MA. *Program availability:* Part-time, evening/weekend, 100% online. *Faculty:* 116 full-time (53 women), 57 part-time/adjunct (19 women). *Students:* 575 full-time (360 women), 491 part-time (277 women); includes 287 minority (100 Black or African American, non-Hispanic/Latino; 6 American Indian or Alaska Native, non-Hispanic/Latino; 58 Asian, non-Hispanic/Latino; 92 Hispanic/Latino; 1 Native Hawaiian or other Pacific Islander, non-Hispanic/Latino; 30 Two or more races, non-Hispanic/Latino), 151 international. Average age 29. 1,504 applicants, 84% accepted, 403 enrolled. In 2016, 374 master's, 3 doctorates, 1 other advanced degree awarded. Terminal master's awarded for partial completion of doctoral program. *Degree requirements:* For master's, one foreign language, comprehensive exam, thesis or alternative; for doctorate, one foreign language, comprehensive exam, thesis/dissertation. *Entrance requirements:* For master's, GRE; GMAT or GRE (for MA in social enterprise), transcripts, resume, 2 letters of recommendation, statement of purpose; for doctorate, GRE, transcripts, resume, 3 letters of recommendation, statement of purpose. Additional exam requirements/recommendations for international students: Required—TOEFL (minimum score 600 paper-based, 100 iBT), IELTS (minimum score 7 ), or PTE (minimum score of 68). Application fee: $55. Electronic applications accepted. *Expenses:* $1,579 per credit tuition; $1,930 mandatory fees. *Financial support:* Research assistantships, teaching assistantships, institutionally sponsored loans, scholarships/grants, and unspecified assistantships available. Financial award application deadline: 1/15; financial award

## International Development

applicants required to submit FAFSA. *Unit head:* Dr. James Goldgeier, Dean, 202-885-1603, Fax: 202-885-2494, E-mail: goldgeier@american.edu. *Application contact:* Jia Jiang, Associate Director, Graduate Education Enrollment, 202-885-1689, Fax: 202-885-1109, E-mail: jjiang@american.edu.
Website: http://www.american.edu/sis/

**Andrews University,** School of Graduate Studies, College of Arts and Sciences, Department of Behavioral Science, Program in International Development, Berrien Springs, MI 49104. Offers community and international development (MSCID). *Program availability:* Online learning. *Faculty:* 10 full-time (2 women), 1 part-time/adjunct (0 women). *Students:* 15 full-time (13 women), 6 part-time (3 women); includes 9 minority (4 Black or African American, non-Hispanic/Latino; 2 Asian, non-Hispanic/Latino; 3 Hispanic/Latino), 8 international. Average age 32. In 2016, 12 master's awarded. *Entrance requirements:* For master's, GRE General Test. Additional exam requirements/recommendations for international students: Required—TOEFL (minimum score 550 paper-based). Application fee: $40. *Unit head:* Dr. Duane C. McBride, Director, 269-471-3152. *Application contact:* Justina Clayburn, Supervisor of Graduate Admission, 800-253-2874, Fax: 269-471-6321, E-mail: graduate@andrews.edu.
Website: http://www.andrews.edu/grad/programs/community-and-international-development-off-campus.html

**Athabasca University,** Centre for Interdisciplinary Studies, Athabasca, AB T9S 3A3, Canada. Offers adult education (MA); community studies (MA); cultural studies (MA); educational studies (MA); global change (MA); heritage resource management (Postbaccalaureate Certificate); legislative drafting (Postbaccalaureate Certificate); work, organization, and leadership (MA). *Program availability:* Part-time, evening/weekend, online learning. *Degree requirements:* For master's, project. *Entrance requirements:* Additional exam requirements/recommendations for international students: Required—TOEFL (minimum score 560 paper-based). Electronic applications accepted. *Faculty research:* Women's history, literature and culture studies, sustainable development, labor and education.

**Clark University,** Graduate School, Department of International Development, Community, and Environment, Program in International Development and Social Change, Worcester, MA 01610-1477. Offers MA. *Students:* 45 full-time (32 women), 10 part-time (6 women); includes 12 minority (6 Black or African American, non-Hispanic/Latino; 3 Asian, non-Hispanic/Latino; 3 Two or more races, non-Hispanic/Latino), 11 international. Average age 28. 116 applicants, 83% accepted, 27 enrolled. In 2016, 22 master's awarded. *Degree requirements:* For master's, thesis. *Entrance requirements:* For master's, 3 references, resume or curriculum vitae. Additional exam requirements/recommendations for international students: Required—TOEFL (minimum score 575 paper-based; 90 iBT) or IELTS (minimum score 6.5). *Application deadline:* For fall admission, 1/15 for domestic students. Application fee: $75. *Expenses: Tuition:* Full-time $44,050. *Required fees:* $80. Tuition and fees vary according to course load and program. *Financial support:* Fellowships with partial tuition reimbursements, research assistantships with partial tuition reimbursements, teaching assistantships with partial tuition reimbursements, institutionally sponsored loans, and scholarships/grants available. *Faculty research:* Community action research, gender analysis, land-use planning, geographic information systems, HIV and AIDS, global health and social justice, environmental health, climate change and sustainability. *Unit head:* Dr. David Bell, Coordinator, 508-793-7568, Fax: 508-793-8820. *Application contact:* Sawsan Berjawi, Manager of Academic and Student Affairs, 508-421-3846, E-mail: sberjawi@clarku.edu.
Website: http://www.clarku.edu/programs/masters-international-development-and-social-change

**Colorado State University,** College of Liberal Arts, Department of Anthropology, Fort Collins, CO 80523-1787. Offers anthropology of health and well-being (MA); humans and the environment (MA); international development (MA); professional methods and techniques (MA). *Program availability:* Part-time. *Faculty:* 9 full-time (3 women), 1 (woman) part-time/adjunct. *Students:* 25 full-time (15 women), 21 part-time (14 women); includes 3 minority (1 Asian, non-Hispanic/Latino; 2 Hispanic/Latino), 6 international. Average age 29. 50 applicants, 54% accepted, 17 enrolled. In 2016, 10 master's awarded. *Degree requirements:* For master's, thesis (for some programs), professional portfolio. *Entrance requirements:* For master's, GRE General Test, minimum GPA of 3.0, BA/BS, transcripts, statement of purpose, writing sample, 3 letters of recommendation. Additional exam requirements/recommendations for international students: Required—TOEFL (minimum score 550 paper-based; 80 iBT). *Application deadline:* For fall admission, 2/1 for domestic and international students. Application fee: $60 ($70 for international students). Electronic applications accepted. *Expenses:* Tuition, state resident: full-time $9628. Tuition, nonresident: full-time $23,603. *Required fees:* $2253; $528.14 per credit hour. $264.07 per semester. Tuition and fees vary according to course load and program. *Financial support:* In 2016–17, 15 students received support, including 14 teaching assistantships with full and partial tuition reimbursements available (averaging $13,932 per year); scholarships/grants and unspecified assistantships also available. Financial award application deadline: 3/1; financial award applicants required to submit FAFSA. *Faculty research:* Archaeology, cultural anthropology, biological anthropology, geography. *Total annual research expenditures:* $329,999. *Unit head:* Dr. Michelle M. Glantz, Professor and Chair, 970-491-4635, Fax: 970-491-7597, E-mail: mica.glantz@colostate.edu. *Application contact:* Dr. Mary Van Buren, Graduate Program Coordinator, 970-491-3781, Fax: 970-491-7597, E-mail: mary.vanburen@colostate.edu.
Website: http://anthropology.colostate.edu/

**Dalhousie University,** Faculty of Arts and Social Science, Department of International Development Studies, Halifax, NS B3H 4R2, Canada. Offers MA. *Entrance requirements:* Additional exam requirements/recommendations for international students: Required—TOEFL, IELTS, CANTEST, CAEL, or Michigan English Language Assessment Battery. Electronic applications accepted.

**Duke University,** Sanford School of Public Policy, Master of International Development Policy Program, Durham, NC 27708-0237. Offers MIDP. *Faculty:* 12 full-time (5 women), 9 part-time/adjunct (2 women). *Students:* 76 full-time (27 women); includes 5 minority (1 Black or African American, non-Hispanic/Latino; 1 American Indian or Alaska Native, non-Hispanic/Latino; 2 Hispanic/Latino; 1 Native Hawaiian or other Pacific Islander, non-Hispanic/Latino), 70 international. Average age 33. 156 applicants, 39 enrolled. In 2016, 60 master's awarded. *Degree requirements:* For master's, thesis, internship, project. *Entrance requirements:* For master's, minimum five years of professional experience in a development-related field. Additional exam requirements/recommendations for international students: Required—TOEFL (minimum score 577 paper-based; 90 iBT), IELTS (minimum score 7), PTE (minimum score 64). *Application deadline:* For fall admission, 1/5 priority date for domestic and international students. Applications are processed on a rolling basis. Application fee: $80. Electronic applications accepted. *Expenses:* $37,574 estimated tuition $10,805 estimated remaining fees. *Financial support:* In 2016–17, 60 students received support, including teaching assistantships (averaging $4,000 per year); fellowships, research assistantships, career-related internships or fieldwork, scholarships/grants, tuition waivers (partial), and unspecified assistantships also available. Financial award application deadline: 1/5; financial award applicants required to submit FAFSA. *Faculty research:* Economic development, social

policy and development, peace and conflict resolution, public finance, international taxation. *Unit head:* Dr. Corinne Krupp, Director of Graduate Studies, 919-613-9221, Fax: 919-684-2861, E-mail: midpinfo@duke.edu. *Application contact:* Cheryl Bailey, Assistant Director, Admissions, 919-613-9281, Fax: 919-684-2861, E-mail: midinfo@duke.edu.
Website: http://dcid.sanford.duke.edu/academics/midp

**Eastern University,** School of Leadership and Development, St. Davids, PA 19087-3696. Offers economic development (MBA), including international development, urban development (MA, MBA); international development (MA), including global development, urban development (MA, MBA); nonprofit management (MS); organizational leadership (MA); M Div/MBA. *Program availability:* Part-time, evening/weekend, online learning. *Students:* 59 full-time (32 women), 67 part-time (35 women); includes 40 minority (32 Black or African American, non-Hispanic/Latino; 1 Asian, non-Hispanic/Latino; 5 Hispanic/Latino; 2 Two or more races, non-Hispanic/Latino), 22 international. Average age 33. In 2016, 44 master's awarded. *Entrance requirements:* Additional exam requirements/recommendations for international students: Required—TOEFL (minimum score 550 paper-based; 79 iBT). *Application deadline:* Applications are processed on a rolling basis. Application fee: $35. Electronic applications accepted. Application fee is waived when completed online. *Expenses:* $690 per credit. *Faculty research:* Micro-level economic development, China welfare and economic development, macroethics, micro- and macro-level economic development in transitional economics, organizational effectiveness. *Unit head:* Michael Dziedziak, Executive Director of Enrollment, 800-452-0996, E-mail: gpsadmissions@eastern.edu.
Website: http://www.eastern.edu/academics/programs/graduate-programs-leadership-development

**Fordham University,** Graduate School of Arts and Sciences, Program in International Political Economy and Development, New York, NY 10458. Offers MA, Certificate. *Program availability:* Part-time, evening/weekend. *Students:* 38 full-time (16 women), 13 part-time (10 women); includes 8 minority (1 Black or African American, non-Hispanic/Latino; 4 Asian, non-Hispanic/Latino; 3 Native Hawaiian or other Pacific Islander, non-Hispanic/Latino), 16 international. Average age 27. 207 applicants, 35% accepted, 24 enrolled. In 2016, 24 master's, 1 other advanced degree awarded. *Degree requirements:* For master's, comprehensive exam. *Entrance requirements:* For master's, GRE General Test. Additional exam requirements/recommendations for international students: Required—TOEFL (minimum score 600 paper-based). *Application deadline:* For fall admission, 1/4 priority date for domestic students; for spring admission, 11/1 for domestic students. Application fee: $70. Electronic applications accepted. *Financial support:* In 2016–17, 35 students received support, including 4 fellowships with tuition reimbursements available (averaging $17,014 per year); research assistantships with tuition reimbursements available, career-related internships or fieldwork, institutionally sponsored loans, tuition waivers (full and partial), and unspecified assistantships also available. Financial award application deadline: 1/4; financial award applicants required to submit FAFSA. *Faculty research:* International economics, comparative international politics, international banking and finance, international development, emerging markets and country risk analysis. *Unit head:* Dr. Henry Schwalbenberg, Chair, 718-817-3866, Fax: 718-817-3518. *Application contact:* Bernadette Valentino-Morrison, Director of Graduate Admissions, 718-817-4419, Fax: 718-817-3566, E-mail: valentinomor@fordham.edu.

**Georgetown University,** Graduate School of Arts and Sciences, McCourt School of Public Policy, Washington, DC 20057. Offers data science for public policy (MDSPP); international development policy (MIDP); policy leadership (EMPL); policy management (MPM); public policy (MPP); MBA/MPP; MPP/JD; MPA/MA; MPP/MSFS; MPP/PhD. *Entrance requirements:* For master's, GRE General Test, minimum B average. Additional exam requirements/recommendations for international students: Required—TOEFL. *Faculty research:* Social policy, government, private sector.

**The George Washington University,** Columbian College of Arts and Sciences, Department of Anthropology, Washington, DC 20052. Offers anthropology (MA, PhD); international development (MA); medical anthropology (MA); museum training (MA). *Program availability:* Part-time, evening/weekend. *Faculty:* 15 full-time (6 women). *Students:* 27 full-time (20 women), 11 part-time (8 women); includes 12 minority (1 Black or African American, non-Hispanic/Latino; 2 Asian, non-Hispanic/Latino; 5 Hispanic/Latino; 4 Two or more races, non-Hispanic/Latino), 6 international. Average age 28. 86 applicants, 33% accepted, 9 enrolled. In 2016, 10 master's awarded. *Degree requirements:* For master's, one foreign language, comprehensive exam, thesis or alternative. *Entrance requirements:* For master's, GRE General Test, minimum GPA of 3.0. Additional exam requirements/recommendations for international students: Required—TOEFL (minimum score 550 paper-based; 80 iBT). *Application deadline:* For fall admission, 1/15 priority date for international students; for spring admission, 9/15 priority date for domestic students, 9/1 priority date for international students. Applications are processed on a rolling basis. Application fee: $75. Electronic applications accepted. *Financial support:* In 2016–17, 8 students received support. Fellowships, teaching assistantships, career-related internships or fieldwork, and Federal Work-Study available. Financial award application deadline: 1/15. *Unit head:* Richard Grinker, Chair, 202-994-6984, E-mail: rgrink@email.gwu.edu. *Application contact:* Information Contact, 202-994-6075, E-mail: anth@gwu.edu.
Website: http://anthropology.columbian.gwu.edu/

**The George Washington University,** Elliott School of International Affairs, Program in International Development Studies, Washington, DC 20052. Offers MA. *Program availability:* Part-time. *Students:* 63 full-time (53 women), 32 part-time (29 women); includes 34 minority (10 Black or African American, non-Hispanic/Latino; 15 Asian, non-Hispanic/Latino; 6 Hispanic/Latino; 3 Two or more races, non-Hispanic/Latino), 15 international. Average age 27. 209 applicants, 86% accepted, 32 enrolled. In 2016, 46 master's awarded. *Degree requirements:* For master's, one foreign language, capstone project. *Entrance requirements:* For master's, GRE General Test, 2 years (or the equivalent) of a modern foreign language, introductory courses in microeconomics and macroeconomics. Additional exam requirements/recommendations for international students: Required—TOEFL (minimum score 100 iBT), IELTS (minimum score 7). *Application deadline:* For fall admission, 1/15 priority date for domestic and international students; for spring admission, 10/1 for domestic students. Application fee: $75. Electronic applications accepted. *Financial support:* In 2016–17, 27 students received support. Fellowships with partial tuition reimbursements available, Federal Work-Study, and scholarships/grants available. Financial award application deadline: 1/15; financial award applicants required to submit FAFSA. *Faculty research:* Development, anthropology, health and development, political science, education. *Unit head:* Prof. Sean Roberts, Director, 202-994-5767, E-mail: ids@gwu.edu. *Application contact:* Nicole A. Campbell, Director of Graduate Admissions, 202-994-7050, Fax: 202-994-9537, E-mail: esiagrad@gwu.edu.
Website: http://elliott.gwu.edu/international-development-studies

**Harvard University,** John F. Kennedy School of Government, Master in Public Administration in International Development Program, Cambridge, MA 02138. Offers MPAID. *Students:* 131 full-time (55 women); includes 9 minority (1 Black or African American, non-Hispanic/Latino; 4 Asian, non-Hispanic/Latino; 3 Hispanic/Latino; 1 Two or more races, non-Hispanic/Latino), 100 international. Average age 29. 241 applicants,

36% accepted, 67 enrolled. In 2016, 64 master's awarded. *Entrance requirements:* For master's, one course each in microeconomics and macroeconomics; two college-level calculus courses (one must contain multivariable calculus); bachelor's degree; 2-3 years of professional experience in development (strongly encouraged). Additional exam requirements/recommendations for international students: Required—TOEFL (minimum score 600 paper-based; 100 iBT). *Application deadline:* For fall admission, 12/1 for domestic students. Application fee: $100. Electronic applications accepted. *Financial support:* In 2016–17, 87 fellowships (averaging $42,906 per year) were awarded; research assistantships, teaching assistantships, career-related internships or fieldwork, Federal Work-Study, institutionally sponsored loans, scholarships/grants, health care benefits, and unspecified assistantships also available. Financial award application deadline: 2/24; financial award applicants required to submit CSS PROFILE or FAFSA. *Unit head:* Carol Finney, Director, 617-495-7799, E-mail: carol_finney@harvard.edu. *Application contact:* 617-495-2133, E-mail: mpaid_program@hks.harvard.edu. Website: http://www.hks.harvard.edu/degrees/masters/mpa-id

**Hope International University,** School of Graduate and Professional Studies, Program in Business Administration, Fullerton, CA 92831-3138. Offers general management (MBA, MSM); international development (MBA, MSM); marketing management (MBA, MSM); non-profit management (MBA, MSM). *Program availability:* Part-time, online learning. *Degree requirements:* For master's, comprehensive exam (for some programs), thesis (for some programs), project. *Entrance requirements:* For master's, minimum GPA of 3.0; 2 references. Additional exam requirements/recommendations for international students: Required—TOEFL (minimum score 550 paper-based; 86 iBT); Recommended—IELTS (minimum score 6.5). Electronic applications accepted. *Expenses:* Contact institution.

**Indiana University Bloomington,** School of Public and Environmental Affairs, Public Affairs Programs, Bloomington, IN 47405. Offers economic development (MPA); energy (MPA); environmental policy (PhD); environmental policy and natural resource management (MPA); information systems (MPA); international development (MPA); local government management (MPA); nonprofit management (MPA, Certificate); policy analysis (MPA); public budgeting and financial management (Certificate); public finance (PhD); public financial administration (MPA); public management (MPA, PhD, Certificate); public policy analysis (PhD); social entrepreneurship (Certificate); specialized public affairs (MPA); sustainability and sustainable development (MPA); JD/MPA; MPA/MA; MPA/MIS; MPA/MLS; MSES/MPA. *Accreditation:* NASPAA (one or more programs are accredited). *Program availability:* Part-time. *Degree requirements:* For master's, capstone, internship; for doctorate, comprehensive exam, thesis/dissertation. *Entrance requirements:* For master's, GRE General Test or GMAT, official transcripts, 3 letters of recommendation, resume, personal statement; for doctorate, GRE General Test, official transcripts, 3 letters of recommendation, statement of purpose. Additional exam requirements/recommendations for international students: Required—TOEFL (minimum score 600 paper-based; 96 iBT); Recommended—IELTS (minimum score 7). Electronic applications accepted. *Faculty research:* International development, environmental policy and resource management, policy analysis, public finance, public management, urban management, nonprofit management, energy policy, social policy, public finance.

**Johns Hopkins University,** School of Advanced International Studies, Washington, DC 20036. Offers global risk (MA); international development (MA, Certificate), including international economics (MA); international economics and finance (MA); international public policy (MIPP); international relations (PhD); international studies (Certificate); Japan studies (MA), including international economics; Korea studies (MA), including international economics; South Asia studies (MA), including international economics; Southeast Asia studies (MA), including international economics; JD/MA; MBA/MA; MHS/MA. Terminal master's awarded for partial completion of doctoral program. *Degree requirements:* For master's, 4-6 international economics courses, 5-6 functional or regional concentration courses, 2 core examinations, proficiency in language other than native language, capstone project; for doctorate, 2 foreign languages, thesis/dissertation, 3 comprehensive exams, economics, quantitative and qualitative course, dissertation prospectus and defense. *Entrance requirements:* For master's, GMAT or GRE General Test, previous course work in economics, foreign language, undergraduate degree; for doctorate, GRE General Test, master's degree. Additional exam requirements/recommendations for international students: Required—TOEFL (minimum score 600 paper-based; 100 iBT) or IELTS (minimum score 7). Electronic applications accepted. *Expenses:* Contact institution. *Faculty research:* Regional studies, international relations, international economics, energy and environment, international development.

**Lehigh University,** College of Education, Program in Comparative and International Education, Bethlehem, PA 18015. Offers comparative and international education (MA, PhD); globalization and educational change (M Ed); international development in education (Certificate). *Program availability:* Part-time, blended/hybrid learning. *Faculty:* 4 full-time (2 women), 1 part-time/adjunct (0 women). *Students:* 25 full-time (20 women), 29 part-time (24 women); includes 4 minority (1 Black or African American, non-Hispanic/Latino; 1 Asian, non-Hispanic/Latino; 2 Hispanic/Latino), 13 international. Average age 34. 77 applicants, 66% accepted, 10 enrolled. In 2016, 14 master's awarded. *Degree requirements:* For master's, thesis (MA); for doctorate, comprehensive exam, thesis/dissertation. *Entrance requirements:* For master's, 2 letters of recommendation, transcripts, essays, resume; for doctorate, GRE, transcripts, 2 letters of recommendation, essay, curriculum vitae, 2 writing samples. Additional exam requirements/recommendations for international students: Required—TOEFL (minimum score 93 iBT). *Application deadline:* For fall and spring admission, 2/1 for domestic and international students. Application fee: $65. Electronic applications accepted. *Expenses:* $565 per credit. *Financial support:* In 2016–17, 1 research assistantship with full tuition reimbursement was awarded; fellowships, scholarships/grants, health care benefits, tuition waivers, and unspecified assistantships also available. Financial award application deadline: 1/31; financial award applicants required to submit FAFSA. *Faculty research:* Comparative education, rural education, gender equity in education, educational borrowing, comparing education systems, education policy and globalization, family-school relationships, China, international testing, social inequities, European Education Policy and school-work transition. *Total annual research expenditures:* $24,949. *Unit head:* Dr. Arpana Inman, Program Director/Professor, 610-758-4443, Fax: 610-758-6223, E-mail: agi2@lehigh.edu. *Application contact:* Sharon Y. Warden, Coordinator, 610-758-3256, Fax: 610-758-6223, E-mail: sy00@lehigh.edu. Website: http://ed.lehigh.edu

**Marymount California University,** Program in Leadership and Global Development, Rancho Palos Verdes, CA 90275-6299. Offers MS.

**McGill University,** Faculty of Graduate and Postdoctoral Studies, Desautels Faculty of Management, Montréal, QC H3A 2T5, Canada. Offers administration (PhD); entrepreneurial studies (MBA); finance (MBA); general management (Post Master's Certificate); information systems (MBA); international business (MBA); international practicing management (MM); management (MBA); management for development (MBA); manufacturing management (MMM); marketing (MBA); operations management (MBA); public accountancy (Diploma); strategic management (MBA); MBA/LL B; MD/

MBA. MMM offered jointly with Faculty of Engineering; PhD with Concordia University, HEC Montreal, Université de Montréal, Université du Québec à Montréal.

**Middlebury Institute of International Studies at Monterey,** Graduate School of International Policy and Management, Program in International Policy and Development, Monterey, CA 93940-2691. Offers MA. *Degree requirements:* For master's, one foreign language. *Entrance requirements:* For master's, minimum GPA of 3.0, proficiency in a foreign language. Additional exam requirements/recommendations for international students: Required—TOEFL (minimum score 550 paper-based; 80 iBT). Electronic applications accepted. *Expenses: Tuition:* Full-time $38,250; part-time $1820 per credit. *Required fees:* $78 per semester.

**New York University,** School of Continuing and Professional Studies, Center for Global Affairs, New York, NY 10012-1019. Offers global affairs (MS), including environment/energy policy, human rights and international law, international development and humanitarian assistance, international relations, peace building, private sector, transnational security; global energy (Advanced Certificate); peacebuilding (Advanced Certificate); transnational security (Advanced Certificate). *Program availability:* Part-time, evening/weekend. *Degree requirements:* For master's, thesis. *Entrance requirements:* For master's, GRE or GMAT (only upon request), bachelor's degree, resume with relevant professional work, internship or volunteer experience, two letters of recommendation, statement of purpose. Additional exam requirements/recommendations for international students: Required—TOEFL (minimum score 600 paper-based; 100 iBT), IELTS (minimum score 7). Electronic applications accepted.

**Norwich University,** College of Graduate and Continuing Studies, Master of Arts in International Relations Program, Northfield, VT 05663. Offers international relations (MA), including cyber diplomacy-policy, cyber diplomacy-technical, international development, international security, national security, regions of the world. *Program availability:* Evening/weekend, online only, mostly all online with a week-long residency requirement. *Faculty:* 9 part-time/adjunct (3 women). *Students:* 51 full-time (18 women); includes 11 minority (8 Black or African American, non-Hispanic/Latino; 2 Asian, non-Hispanic/Latino; 1 Two or more races, non-Hispanic/Latino). Average age 34. 33 applicants, 100% accepted, 22 enrolled. *Degree requirements:* For master's, research paper. *Entrance requirements:* For master's, minimum undergraduate GPA of 2.75. Additional exam requirements/recommendations for international students: Required—TOEFL (minimum score 550 paper-based; 80 iBT), IELTS (minimum score 6.5). *Application deadline:* For fall admission, 8/14 for domestic and international students; for winter admission, 11/13 for domestic and international students; for spring admission, 2/12 for domestic and international students; for summer admission, 6/5 for domestic and international students. Electronic applications accepted. *Expenses:* Contact institution. *Financial support:* In 2016–17, 24 students received support. Scholarships/grants available. Financial award application deadline: 8/4; financial award applicants required to submit FAFSA. *Unit head:* Dr. Lasha Tchantouridze, Director, 802-485-2095, Fax: 802-485-2533, E-mail: ltchanto@norwich.edu. *Application contact:* Admissions Office, 800-460-5597 Ext. 3392, E-mail: mair@online.norwich.edu. Website: https://online.norwich.edu/degree-programs/masters/master-arts-international-relations/overview

**Norwich University,** College of Graduate and Continuing Studies, Master of Public Administration Program, Northfield, VT 05663. Offers criminal justice and public safety (MPA); fiscal management (MPA); international development and influence (MPA); municipal governance (MPA); nonprofit management (MPA); policy analysis and analytics (MPA); public administration leadership and crisis management (MPA); public works and sustainability (MPA). *Program availability:* Evening/weekend, online only, mostly all online with a week-long residency requirement. *Faculty:* 13 part-time/adjunct (5 women). *Students:* 63 full-time (23 women); includes 9 minority (5 Black or African American, non-Hispanic/Latino; 1 Asian, non-Hispanic/Latino; 1 Hispanic/Latino; 2 Two or more races, non-Hispanic/Latino). Average age 38. 23 applicants, 100% accepted, 15 enrolled. In 2016, 38 master's awarded. *Degree requirements:* For master's, capstone. *Entrance requirements:* For master's, minimum undergraduate GPA of 2.75. Additional exam requirements/recommendations for international students: Required—TOEFL (minimum score 550 paper-based; 80 iBT), IELTS (minimum score 6.5). *Application deadline:* For fall admission, 8/14 for domestic and international students; for winter admission, 11/13 for domestic and international students; for spring admission, 2/12 for domestic and international students; for summer admission, 5/15 for domestic and international students. Electronic applications accepted. *Expenses:* Contact institution. *Financial support:* In 2016–17, 21 students received support. Scholarships/grants available. Financial award application deadline: 8/4; financial award applicants required to submit FAFSA. *Unit head:* Dr. Rosemarie Pelletier, Program Director, 802-485-2767, Fax: 802-485-2533, E-mail: rpellet2@norwich.edu. *Application contact:* Admissions Advisor, 800-460-5597 Ext. 3377, Fax: 802-485-2533, E-mail: mpa@online.norwich.edu. Website: https://online.norwich.edu/degree-programs/masters/master-public-administration/overview

**Ohio University,** Graduate College, Center for International Studies, Program in International Development Studies, Athens, OH 45701-2979. Offers MA. *Program availability:* Part-time. *Degree requirements:* For master's, one foreign language, thesis optional. *Entrance requirements:* For master's, minimum GPA of 3.0. Additional exam requirements/recommendations for international students: Required—TOEFL (minimum score 550 paper-based; 80 iBT), IELTS (minimum score 6.5). *Application deadline:* For fall admission, 1/1 for domestic and international students. Application fee: $50 ($55 for international students). Electronic applications accepted. *Financial support:* Research assistantships with full tuition reimbursements, career-related internships or fieldwork, Federal Work-Study, institutionally sponsored loans, tuition waivers (partial), and unspecified assistantships available. Financial award application deadline: 1/1. *Faculty research:* Problems and issues in social, economic, political, health and environmental development. *Unit head:* Brandon Kendhammer, Director, 740-593-1841, Fax: 740-593-1837, E-mail: kendhamm@ohio.edu. *Application contact:* Patti Malloy, Administrative Assistant, 740-593-1836, Fax: 740-593-1837, E-mail: malloyp@ohio.edu. Website: http://www.ohio.edu/developmentstudies/

**Old Dominion University,** College of Arts and Letters, Graduate Program in International Studies, Norfolk, VA 23529. Offers conflict and cooperation (MA, PhD); interdependence and transnationalism (MA, PhD); international cultural studies (MA, PhD); international political economy and development (MA, PhD); modeling and simulation (MA, PhD); U.S. foreign policy and international relations (MA, PhD). *Program availability:* Part-time. *Faculty:* 18 full-time (4 women). *Students:* 35 full-time (13 women), 38 part-time (20 women); includes 14 minority (9 Black or African American, non-Hispanic/Latino; 2 Asian, non-Hispanic/Latino; 1 Hispanic/Latino; 2 Two or more races, non-Hispanic/Latino), 19 international. Average age 37. 99 applicants, 54% accepted, 34 enrolled. In 2016, 24 master's, 11 doctorates awarded. Terminal master's awarded for partial completion of doctoral program. *Degree requirements:* For master's, one foreign language, comprehensive exam, thesis optional; for doctorate, one foreign language, comprehensive exam, thesis/dissertation. *Entrance requirements:* For master's, GRE General Test, sample of written work, 2 letters of recommendation; for doctorate, GRE General Test, sample of written work, 3 letters of recommendation. Additional exam requirements/recommendations for international students: Required—

*International Development*

TOEFL (minimum score 570 paper-based). *Application deadline:* For fall admission, 1/15 for domestic and international students; for spring admission, 10/15 for domestic and international students. Application fee: $50. Electronic applications accepted. *Expenses:* Contact institution. *Financial support:* In 2016–17, 12 students received support, including 1 fellowship (averaging $15,000 per year), 5 research assistantships with tuition reimbursements available (averaging $15,000 per year), 4 teaching assistantships with tuition reimbursements available (averaging $15,000 per year); career-related internships or fieldwork, institutionally sponsored loans, and unspecified assistantships also available. Financial award application deadline: 1/15; financial award applicants required to submit FAFSA. *Faculty research:* U.S. foreign policy, international security, Transatlantic and Transpacific relations, transnational issues, international political economy and development. *Total annual research expenditures:* $330,391. *Unit head:* Dr. Regina Karp, Graduate Program Director, 757-683-5700, Fax: 757-683-5701, E-mail: rkarp@odu.edu. *Application contact:* Dr. David C. Earnest, Associate Dean, 757-683-6077, Fax: 757-683-5746, E-mail: dearnest@odu.edu. Website: http://www.odu.edu/gpis

**Rutgers University–Camden,** Graduate School of Arts and Sciences, Department of Public Policy and Administration, Camden, NJ 08102. Offers education policy and leadership (MPA); international public service and development (MPA); public management (MPA); JD/MPA; MPA/MA. *Accreditation:* NASPAA. *Program availability:* Part-time, evening/weekend. *Degree requirements:* For master's, directed study, research workshop, 42 credits. *Entrance requirements:* For master's, GRE General Test, GMAT or LSAT, 3 letters of recommendation; resume. Additional exam requirements/recommendations for international students: Required—TOEFL (minimum score 550 paper-based), IELTS. Electronic applications accepted. *Faculty research:* Nonprofit management, county and municipal administration, health and human services, government communication, administrative law, educational finance.

**Saint Mary's University,** Faculty of Arts, International Development Studies Program, Halifax, NS B3H 3C3, Canada. Offers MA, Graduate Diploma. *Program availability:* Part-time. *Degree requirements:* For master's, thesis. *Entrance requirements:* For master's, honors degree. *Faculty research:* Dynamics of global development, gender and development, policy analysis, models and strategies for development, Latin American and Caribbean development.

**St. Mary's University,** Graduate Studies, Program in International Relations, San Antonio, TX 78228-8507. Offers conflict transformation (Certificate); international conflict resolution (MA); international development (MA); international relations (MA); security policy (MA); JD/MA. *Program availability:* Part-time, evening/weekend, 100% online. *Faculty:* 4 full-time (2 women), 1 part-time/adjunct (0 women). *Students:* 22 full-time (14 women), 59 part-time (18 women); includes 33 minority (5 Black or African American, non-Hispanic/Latino; 2 American Indian or Alaska Native, non-Hispanic/Latino; 6 Asian, non-Hispanic/Latino; 20 Hispanic/Latino), 5 international. Average age 32. 28 applicants, 61% accepted, 6 enrolled. In 2016, 35 master's awarded. *Degree requirements:* For master's, one foreign language, comprehensive exam (for some programs), thesis (for some programs), thesis or comprehensive exam. *Entrance requirements:* For master's, minimum undergraduate cumulative GPA of 3.0. Additional exam requirements/recommendations for international students: Required—TOEFL (minimum score 550 paper-based; 80 iBT), IELTS (minimum score 6). *Application deadline:* For fall admission, 7/1 for domestic students; for spring admission, 11/15 for domestic students; for summer admission, 4/1 for domestic students. Applications are processed on a rolling basis. Application fee: $0. Electronic applications accepted. *Expenses: Tuition:* Full-time $15,600; part-time $865 per credit hour. *Required fees:* $148 per semester. *Financial support:* Research assistantships, Federal Work-Study, tuition waivers (full), unspecified assistantships, and grants for active-duty and retired military, DOD employees, and their spouses available. Financial award application deadline: 3/31; financial award applicants required to submit FAFSA. *Faculty research:* Anthropology and ethics, states in crisis and socioeconomic development, politics and society of south Asia, political psychology, international relations theory. *Unit head:* Dr. Amber Aubone, Graduate International Relations, 210-436-3111, E-mail: aaubone@stmarytx.edu. *Application contact:* Kim Thornton, Director, Graduate and Adult Enrollment Services, 210-436-3101, E-mail: kthornton@stmarytx.edu.

**Saint Mary's University of Minnesota,** Schools of Graduate and Professional Programs, Graduate School of Business and Technology, International Development Program, Winona, MN 55987-1399. Offers MA. *Program availability:* Online learning. Tuition and fees vary according to degree level and program. *Unit head:* Matt Bluem, Director, 612-238-4535, E-mail: mbluem@smumn.edu. *Application contact:* James Callinan, Director of Admissions for Graduate and Professional Programs, 612-728-5185, Fax: 612-728-5121, E-mail: jcallina@smumn.edu. Website: http://onlineprograms.smumn.edu/maid/master-of-arts-in-international-development

**Tufts University,** The Fletcher School of Law and Diplomacy, Medford, MA 02155. Offers LL M, MA, MALD, MIB, PhD, DVM/MA, JD/MALD, MALD/MA, MALD/MBA, MALD/MS, MD/MA. *Program availability:* Online learning. *Degree requirements:* For master's, one foreign language, thesis; for doctorate, one foreign language, comprehensive exam, thesis/dissertation, dissertation defense. *Entrance requirements:* For master's and doctorate, GMAT or GRE General Test. Additional exam requirements/recommendations for international students: Required—TOEFL (minimum score 600 paper-based; 100 iBT), IELTS (minimum score 7). Electronic applications accepted. *Expenses:* Contact institution. *Faculty research:* Negotiation and conflict resolution, international organizations, international business and economic law, security studies, development economics.

**Tufts University,** Graduate School of Arts and Sciences, Department of Urban and Environmental Policy and Planning, Medford, MA 02155. Offers community development (MA); environmental policy (MA); health and human welfare (MA); housing policy (MA); international environment/development policy (MA); public policy (MPP); MA/JD; MA/MBA; MA/MPH; MA/MS; MALD/MA. MALD/MA offered in connection with The Fletcher School of Law and Diplomacy; MA/MPH with School of Medicine; MA/MS with School of Nutrition Science and Policy or School of Engineering; MA/MBA with Boston College, Carroll School of Management; MA/JD with Boston College Law School. *Accreditation:* ACSP (one or more programs are accredited). *Program availability:* Part-time. *Students:* 94 full-time (73 women), 18 part-time (14 women); includes 29 minority (11 Black or African American, non-Hispanic/Latino; 9 Asian, non-Hispanic/Latino; 6 Hispanic/Latino; 3 Two or more races, non-Hispanic/Latino), 18 international. Average age 30. 153 applicants, 78% accepted, 51 enrolled. In 2016, 20 master's awarded. *Degree requirements:* For master's, thesis or alternative, internship. *Entrance requirements:* For master's, GRE General Test. Additional exam requirements/recommendations for international students: Required—TOEFL (minimum score 550 paper-based; 80 iBT), IELTS (minimum score 6.5). *Application deadline:* For fall admission, 1/15 for domestic and international students. Applications are processed on a rolling basis. Application fee: $85. Electronic applications accepted. *Expenses:* $49,982 full-time tuition (for MPP); $34,932 full-time tuition (for MA). *Financial support:* Fellowships, research assistantships, teaching assistantships, career-related internships or fieldwork, Federal Work-Study, scholarships/grants, tuition waivers (full and partial), and unspecified assistantships available. Support available to part-time

students. Financial award application deadline: 1/15. *Unit head:* Dr. Mary Davis, Graduate Program Director. *Application contact:* Office of Graduate Admissions, 617-627-3395, E-mail: gradadmissions@tufts.edu. Website: http://ase.tufts.edu/uep/

**Tulane University,** School of Law, The Payson Center for International Development, New Orleans, LA 70118. Offers international development (MS, PhD); law and development (LL M); JD/MS. *Program availability:* Part-time. Terminal master's awarded for partial completion of doctoral program. *Degree requirements:* For master's, comprehensive exam (for some programs), thesis optional; for doctorate, comprehensive exam, thesis/dissertation. *Entrance requirements:* For master's, GRE General Test, minimum 3.0 GPA in undergraduate course work; for doctorate, GRE. Additional exam requirements/recommendations for international students: Required—TOEFL (minimum score 600 paper-based; 90 iBT). Electronic applications accepted. *Expenses:* Contact institution. *Faculty research:* Poverty and inequality, sustainability, health and human development, GIS for development, monitoring and evaluation.

**University of California, San Diego,** Graduate Division, School of Global Policy and Strategy, Master of International Affairs Program, La Jolla, CA 92093. Offers international development and nonprofit management (MIA); international economics (MIA); international environmental policy (MIA); international management (MIA); international politics (MIA). Students will choose one of the following country/regional specializations: China, Japan, Korea, Latin America, or Southeast Asia. *Faculty:* 33 full-time (9 women), 20 part-time/adjunct (4 women). *Students:* 300 full-time (150 women). Average age 24. 460 applicants, 120 enrolled. In 2016, 120 master's awarded. *Degree requirements:* For master's, one foreign language. *Entrance requirements:* For master's, GMAT or GRE General Test. Additional exam requirements/recommendations for international students: Required—TOEFL (minimum score 90 iBT), IELTS (minimum score 7). *Application deadline:* For fall admission, 1/15 for domestic and international students. Applications are processed on a rolling basis. Application fee: $90 ($110 for international students). Electronic applications accepted. *Expenses:* Tuition, state resident: full-time $11,220. Tuition, nonresident: full-time $26,322. *Required fees:* $1864. *Financial support:* In 2016–17, 140 students received support, including 60 fellowships with full and partial tuition reimbursements available (averaging $50,000 per year), 15 research assistantships with full tuition reimbursements available (averaging $20,000 per year), 20 teaching assistantships with full tuition reimbursements available (averaging $20,000 per year); career-related internships or fieldwork, scholarships/grants, and unspecified assistantships also available. Financial award application deadline: 1/15. *Unit head:* Sonja Steinbrech, Director of Enrollment, 858-534-7162, E-mail: ssteinbrech@ucsd.edu. *Application contact:* Admissions Representative, 858-534-5914, E-mail: gps-apply@uscd.edu. Website: http://gps.ucsd.edu/academics/mia.html

**University of Denver,** Josef Korbel School of International Studies, Denver, CO 80208. Offers conflict resolution (MA); global business and corporate social responsibility (Certificate); global finance, trade and economic integration (MA); global health affairs (Certificate); homeland security (Certificate); humanitarian assistance (Certificate); international administration (MA); international development (MA); international human rights (MA); international security (MA); international studies (MA, PhD); public policy studies (MPP); religion and international affairs (Certificate). *Program availability:* Part-time. *Faculty:* 46 full-time (16 women), 28 part-time/adjunct (8 women). *Students:* 368 full-time (204 women), 26 part-time (10 women); includes 82 minority (15 Black or African American, non-Hispanic/Latino; 2 American Indian or Alaska Native, non-Hispanic/Latino; 11 Asian, non-Hispanic/Latino; 43 Hispanic/Latino; 11 Two or more races, non-Hispanic/Latino), 38 international. Average age 27. 764 applicants, 82% accepted, 138 enrolled. In 2016, 197 master's, 10 doctorates, 28 other advanced degrees awarded. *Degree requirements:* For master's, one foreign language, thesis (for some programs); for doctorate, one foreign language, comprehensive exam, thesis/dissertation, two extended research papers. *Entrance requirements:* For master's, GRE General Test, bachelor's degree, transcripts, two letters of recommendation, statement of purpose, resume or curriculum vitae; for doctorate, GRE General Test, master's degree, transcripts, three letters of recommendation, statement of purpose, resume or curriculum vitae, writing sample; for Certificate, bachelor's degree, transcripts, two letters of recommendation, statement of purpose, resume or curriculum vitae. Additional exam requirements/recommendations for international students: Required—TOEFL (minimum score 587 paper-based; 95 iBT). *Application deadline:* For fall admission, 1/15 priority date for domestic and international students; for winter admission, 11/1 for domestic and international students. Applications are processed on a rolling basis. Application fee: $65. Electronic applications accepted. *Expenses:* $43,458 per year full-time. *Financial support:* In 2016–17, 244 students received support, including 1 research assistantship with tuition reimbursement available (averaging $7,250 per year), 5 teaching assistantships with tuition reimbursements available (averaging $2,842 per year); career-related internships or fieldwork, Federal Work-Study, institutionally sponsored loans, scholarships/grants, and unspecified assistantships also available. Support available to part-time students. Financial award application deadline: 2/15; financial award applicants required to submit FAFSA. *Faculty research:* Human rights and international security, international politics and economics, economic-social and political development, international technology analysis and management. *Unit head:* Dr. Christopher R. Hill, Dean, 303-871-2359, Fax: 303-871-2456, E-mail: christopher.r.hill@du.edu. *Application contact:* Admissions Contact, E-mail: korbeladm@du.edu. Website: http://www.du.edu/korbel

**University of Florida,** Graduate School, College of Liberal Arts and Sciences, Department of Political Science, Gainesville, FL 32611. Offers educational policy (PhD); international development policy and administration (MA, Certificate); international relations (MA, MAT); political campaigning (MA, Certificate); political science (MA, PhD); public affairs (MA, Certificate); tropical conservation and development (MA, PhD); JD/MA. Terminal master's awarded for partial completion of doctoral program. *Degree requirements:* For master's, variable foreign language requirement, comprehensive exam (for some programs), thesis or alternative, internship (for some programs); for doctorate, variable foreign language requirement, comprehensive exam, thesis/dissertation. *Entrance requirements:* For master's and doctorate, GRE General Test (minimum score: 308 combined verbal/quantitative), minimum GPA of 3.5. Additional exam requirements/recommendations for international students: Required—TOEFL (minimum score 550 paper-based; 80 iBT), IELTS (minimum score 6). Electronic applications accepted. *Faculty research:* American electoral politics and political institutions, comparative democratization and development, theories of international relation, and political theory.

**University of Guelph,** Graduate Studies, Collaborative International Development Studies, Guelph, ON N1G 2W1, Canada. Offers M Eng, M Sc, MA, MBA, PhD. *Program availability:* Part-time. *Degree requirements:* For master's, thesis (for some programs), seminar; for doctorate, comprehensive exam (for some programs), thesis/dissertation. *Entrance requirements:* For master's, honour's degree with courses in economics, social science, and empirical methods. *Faculty research:* Transformation of developing societies, regional differences, national and international processes of development, long-term change.

**University of Hawaii at Manoa,** Graduate Division, College of Social Sciences, Department of Urban and Regional Planning, Honolulu, HI 96822. Offers community planning (MURP); disaster management and humanitarian assistance (Graduate Certificate); environmental planning and sustainability (MURP); international development planning (MURP); land use, transportation and infrastructure planning (MURP); planning studies (Graduate Certificate); urban and regional planning (PhD, Graduate Certificate). *Accreditation:* ACSP. *Program availability:* Part-time. *Entrance requirements:* For master's, GRE General Test, minimum GPA of 3.0; for doctorate, GRE General Test. Additional exam requirements/recommendations for international students: Required—TOEFL (minimum score 500 paper-based; 61 iBT), IELTS (minimum score 5).

**The University of Manchester,** School of Environment and Development, Manchester, United Kingdom. Offers architecture (M Phil, PhD); development policy and management (M Phil, PhD); human geography (M Phil, PhD); physical geography (M Phil, PhD); planning and landscape (M Phil, PhD).

**University of Massachusetts Boston,** Graduate School of Global Inclusion and Social Development, Program in Global Inclusion and Social Development, Boston, MA 02125-3393. Offers MA, PhD. *Students:* 28 full-time (24 women), 18 part-time (15 women); includes 10 minority (5 Black or African American, non-Hispanic/Latino; 2 Hispanic/Latino; 1 Native Hawaiian or other Pacific Islander, non-Hispanic/Latino; 2 Two or more races, non-Hispanic/Latino), 9 international. Average age 37. 46 applicants, 50% accepted, 11 enrolled. *Expenses:* Tuition, state resident: full-time $16,863. Tuition, nonresident: full-time $32,913. *Required fees:* $177. *Unit head:* Dr. Kristy Alster, Associate Provost, 617-287-5700, Fax: 617-287-5699, E-mail: kristine.alster@umb.edu. *Application contact:* Peggy Roldan Patel, Graduate Admissions Coordinator, 617-287-6400, Fax: 617-287-6236, E-mail: bos.gadm@dpc.umassp.edu.

**University of Minnesota, Twin Cities Campus,** Graduate School, Hubert H. Humphrey School of Public Affairs, Master of Development Practice Program, Minneapolis, MN 55455. Offers MDP. Program offered jointly with Interdisciplinary Center for the Study of Global Change. *Degree requirements:* For master's, thesis or alternative, international field experience. *Entrance requirements:* For master's, GRE. Additional exam requirements/recommendations for international students: Required—TOEFL (minimum score 600 paper-based; 100 iBT), IELTS (minimum score 7). Electronic applications accepted. *Expenses:* Contact institution. *Faculty research:* Policy analysis and management, health and education, natural sciences, social sciences, interdisciplinary research methods.

**University of New Brunswick Fredericton,** School of Graduate Studies, Policy Studies Program, Fredericton, NB E3B 5A3, Canada. Offers citizen engagement/dispute resolution (M Phil); community development (M Phil); international development (M Phil); leadership (M Phil); sustainability/environmental issues (M Phil); worldviews (M Phil). *Program availability:* Part-time. *Degree requirements:* For master's, thesis, report. *Entrance requirements:* For master's, minimum GPA of 3.5. Additional exam requirements/recommendations for international students: Required—TWE (minimum score 5.5), TOEFL (minimum score 600 paper-based; 100 iBT) or IELTS (minimum score 7). Electronic applications accepted. *Faculty research:* International development, worldviews, citizenship/dispute resolution, sustainability/environmental issues, leadership, community development.

**University of New Mexico,** Graduate Studies, College of Arts and Sciences, Program in Economics, Albuquerque, NM 87131-2039. Offers econometrics (MA); economic theory (MA); environmental/natural resource economics (MA, PhD); international/development and sustainability economics (MA, PhD); public economics (MA, PhD). *Program availability:* Part-time. *Faculty:* 11 full-time (5 women). *Students:* 34 full-time (11 women), 19 part-time (7 women); includes 9 minority (1 Black or African American, non-Hispanic/Latino; 1 Asian, non-Hispanic/Latino; 6 Hispanic/Latino; 1 Two or more races, non-Hispanic/Latino), 29 international. Average age 32. 58 applicants, 24% accepted, 11 enrolled. In 2016, 7 master's, 4 doctorates awarded. Terminal master's awarded for partial completion of doctoral program. *Degree requirements:* For master's, comprehensive exam, thesis (for some programs); for doctorate, comprehensive exam, thesis/dissertation. *Entrance requirements:* For master's and doctorate, GRE General Test, 3 letters of recommendation, letter of intent, curriculum vitae. Additional exam requirements/recommendations for international students: Required—TOEFL (minimum score 520 paper-based; 68 iBT). *Application deadline:* For fall admission, 3/1 priority date for domestic students, 3/1 for international students. Applications are processed on a rolling basis. Application fee: $50. Electronic applications accepted. *Financial support:* Fellowships with tuition reimbursements, research assistantships with tuition reimbursements, teaching assistantships with tuition reimbursements, career-related internships or fieldwork, Federal Work-Study, scholarships/grants, health care benefits, and unspecified assistantships available. Support available to part-time students. Financial award application deadline: 3/1; financial award applicants required to submit FAFSA. *Faculty research:* Core theory, econometrics, public finance, international/development economics, labor/human resource economics, environmental/natural resource economics. *Total annual research expenditures:* $167,690. *Unit head:* Dr. Janie Chermak, Chair, 505-277-2037, Fax: 505-277-9445, E-mail: jchermak@unm.edu. *Application contact:* Jeff Newcomer Miller, Academic Advisor, 505-277-3056, Fax: 505-277-9445, E-mail: econgrad@unm.edu.
Website: http://econ.unm.edu

**University of Ottawa,** Faculty of Graduate and Postdoctoral Studies, Program in Globalization and International Development, Ottawa, ON K1N 6N5, Canada. Offers MA. *Degree requirements:* For master's, thesis or alternative. *Entrance requirements:* For master's, honours bachelor's degree or equivalent, minimum B average.

**University of Pittsburgh,** Graduate School of Public and International Affairs, Doctoral Program in Public and International Affairs, Pittsburgh, PA 15260. Offers international affairs (PhD); international development (PhD); public administration (PhD); public policy (PhD). *Program availability:* Part-time, evening/weekend. *Faculty:* 34 full-time (12 women), 17 part-time/adjunct (5 women). *Students:* 29 full-time (12 women), 1 part-time (0 women); includes 4 minority (2 Asian, non-Hispanic/Latino; 2 Hispanic/Latino), 14 international. Average age 37. 60 applicants, 18% accepted, 5 enrolled. In 2016, 3 doctorates awarded. *Degree requirements:* For doctorate, comprehensive exam, thesis/dissertation, mid-term evaluation, preliminary exam, annual review. *Entrance requirements:* For doctorate, GRE or GMAT, 2 letters of recommendation, resume, undergraduate transcripts, personal statement, writing sample. Additional exam requirements/recommendations for international students: Required—TOEFL (minimum score 80 iBT); Recommended—IELTS (minimum score 7). *Application deadline:* For fall admission, 1/15 for domestic and international students. Application fee: $50. Electronic applications accepted. *Expenses:* $22,578 per year in-state; $36,734 per year out-of-state. *Financial support:* In 2016–17, 16 students received support, including 16 research assistantships with partial tuition reimbursements available (averaging $14,620 per year); fellowships also available. Financial award application deadline: 1/15; financial award applicants required to submit FAFSA. *Faculty research:* International development, international security and intelligence, human rights, urban affairs and planning, energy and environmental policy, nonprofit management, public management. *Total annual research expenditures:* $1.3 million. *Unit head:* Dr. John T.S. Keeler, Dean, 412-648-7605, Fax: 412-648-2605, E-mail: keeler@pitt.edu. *Application contact:* Dr.

Michael T. Rizzi, Director of Student Services, 412-648-7640, Fax: 412-648-7641, E-mail: rizzim@pitt.edu.
Website: http://www.gspia.pitt.edu/

**University of Pittsburgh,** Graduate School of Public and International Affairs, Master of International Development Program, Pittsburgh, PA 15260. Offers energy and environment (MID); governance and international public management (MID); human security (MID); nongovernmental organizations and civil society (MID); urban affairs and planning (MID); MID/JD; MID/MBA; MID/MPH; MID/MSIS; MID/MSW. *Program availability:* Part-time, evening/weekend. *Faculty:* 34 full-time (12 women), 17 part-time/adjunct (5 women). *Students:* 47 full-time (32 women), 10 part-time (8 women); includes 13 minority (7 Black or African American, non-Hispanic/Latino; 3 Asian, non-Hispanic/Latino; 2 Hispanic/Latino; 1 Two or more races, non-Hispanic/Latino), 12 international. Average age 28. 107 applicants, 87% accepted, 29 enrolled. In 2016, 29 master's awarded. *Degree requirements:* For master's, thesis optional, capstone seminar. *Entrance requirements:* For master's, GRE General Test or GMAT, 2 letters of recommendation; undergraduate transcripts; resume; personal statement. Additional exam requirements/recommendations for international students: Required—TOEFL (minimum score 80 iBT); Recommended—IELTS (minimum score 7). *Application deadline:* For fall admission, 2/1 priority date for domestic students, 1/15 for international students; for spring admission, 11/1 priority date for domestic students, 8/1 for international students. Application fee: $50. Electronic applications accepted. *Expenses:* $22,578 per year in-state; $36,734 per year out-of-state. *Financial support:* In 2016–17, 28 students received support, including 4 fellowships with full tuition reimbursements available (averaging $18,000 per year), 4 research assistantships with full tuition reimbursements available (averaging $14,620 per year); career-related internships or fieldwork, scholarships/grants, health care benefits, and unspecified assistantships also available. Financial award application deadline: 2/1; financial award applicants required to submit FAFSA. *Faculty research:* Nongovernmental organizations, energy and environmental policy, human security, urban affairs and planning, governance and international management. *Total annual research expenditures:* $1.3 million. *Unit head:* Dr. John T.S. Keeler, Dean, 412-648-7605, Fax: 412-648-2605, E-mail: keeler@pitt.edu. *Application contact:* Dr. Michael T. Rizzi, Director of Student Services, 412-648-7640, Fax: 412-648-7641, E-mail: rizzim@pitt.edu.
Website: http://www.gspia.pitt.edu/

**University of Pittsburgh,** Katz Graduate School of Business, MBA/Master of International Development Joint Degree Program, Pittsburgh, PA 15260. Offers MID/MBA. *Accreditation:* AACSB. *Program availability:* Part-time, evening/weekend. *Faculty:* 88 full-time (27 women), 42 part-time/adjunct (9 women). *Students:* 1 (woman) full-time. Average age 26. 6 applicants, 33% accepted, 1 enrolled. *Entrance requirements:* Additional exam requirements/recommendations for international students: Required—TOEFL (minimum score 100 iBT) or IELTS (minimum score 7.0). *Application deadline:* For fall admission, 4/1 priority date for domestic students, 2/1 priority date for international students. Application fee: $50. Electronic applications accepted. Tuition and fees vary according to program. *Financial support:* Scholarships/grants available. Financial award application deadline: 6/1; financial award applicants required to submit FAFSA. *Faculty research:* Accounting systems/financial reporting, corporate finance, shopper marketing/consumer behavior, management information systems, organizational behavior and entrepreneurship. *Total annual research expenditures:* $493,036. *Unit head:* Dr. Arjang A. Assad, Dean, 412-648-1556, Fax: 412-648-1552, E-mail: aassad@katz.pitt.edu. *Application contact:* Thomas Keller, Director of MBA Admissions, 412-648-1700, Fax: 412-648-1659, E-mail: mba@katz.pitt.edu.
Website: http://www.business.pitt.edu/katz/mba/academics/programs/mba-mid.php

**University of San Francisco,** College of Arts and Sciences, International and Development Economics Program, San Francisco, CA 94117-1080. Offers MA. *Faculty:* 8 full-time (2 women), 2 part-time/adjunct (1 woman). *Students:* 43 full-time (19 women), 1 part-time (0 women); includes 7 minority (4 Black or African American, non-Hispanic/Latino; 2 Asian, non-Hispanic/Latino; 1 Two or more races, non-Hispanic/Latino), 24 international. Average age 27. 79 applicants, 91% accepted, 21 enrolled. In 2016, 14 master's awarded. *Application deadline:* For fall admission, 3/1 for domestic students. *Expenses:* Tuition: Full-time $23,310; part-time $1295 per credit. Tuition and fees vary according to course load, degree level, campus/location and program. *Financial support:* In 2016–17, 19 students received support. *Unit head:* Courtney Arguello, Program Manager, 415-422-2711, Fax: 415-422-6983. *Application contact:* Mark Landerghini, Information Contact, 415-422-5101, Fax: 415-422-6983, E-mail: asgraduate@usfca.edu.
Website: https://www.usfca.edu/arts-sciences/graduate-programs/international-development-economics

**University of Southern Mississippi,** Graduate School, College of Arts and Letters, Department of Political Science, International Development and International Affairs, Hattiesburg, MS 39406. Offers international development (PhD); political science (MA). *Program availability:* Part-time, evening/weekend, online learning. *Degree requirements:* For master's, comprehensive exam, thesis (for some programs); for doctorate, comprehensive exam, thesis/dissertation. *Entrance requirements:* For master's, GRE General Test, minimum GPA of 2.75 in last 2 years, 3.0 in field of study; for doctorate, GRE General Test, minimum GPA of 3.5. Additional exam requirements/recommendations for international students: Required—TOEFL, IELTS. *Application deadline:* For fall admission, 3/1 priority date for domestic students, 3/1 for international students. Applications are processed on a rolling basis. Application fee: $60. *Expenses:* Tuition, area resident: Full-time $15,708; part-time $437 per credit hour. *Financial support:* Research assistantships with full and partial tuition reimbursements, teaching assistantships with full tuition reimbursements, career-related internships or fieldwork, Federal Work-Study, scholarships/grants, health care benefits, and unspecified assistantships available. Financial award application deadline: 3/15; financial award applicants required to submit FAFSA. *Faculty research:* American politics, international politics, political theory, comparative politics, public law. *Unit head:* Edward Sayre, Chair, 601-266-4310. *Application contact:* Marek Steedman, Director, Graduate Studies, 601-266-4317, Fax: 601-266-4172.
Website: https://www.usm.edu/political-science-international-development-affairs

**Walden University,** Graduate Programs, School of Public Policy and Administration, Minneapolis, MN 55401. Offers criminal justice (MPA, MPP, MS, Graduate Certificate), including emergency management (MS, PhD), general program (MS), global leadership (MS, PhD), homeland security and policy coordination (MS, PhD), law and public policy (MS, PhD), policy analysis (MS, PhD), public management and leadership (MS, PhD), self-designed (MS), terrorism, mediation, and peace (MS, PhD); criminal justice and executive management (MS), including global leadership (MS, PhD); criminal justice leadership and executive management (MS), including emergency management (MS, PhD), general program, homeland security and policy coordination (MS, PhD), law and public policy (MS, PhD), policy analysis (MS, PhD), public management and leadership (MS, PhD), self-designed, terrorism, mediation, and peace (MS, PhD); emergency management (MPA, MPP, MS), including criminal justice (MS, PhD), general program (MS), homeland security (MS), public management and leadership (MS, PhD), terrorism and emergency management (MS); general program (MPA, MPP); global leadership (MPA, MPP); government management (Graduate Certificate); health policy (MPA,

MPP); homeland security (Graduate Certificate); homeland security and policy coordination (MPA, MPP); international nongovernmental organizations (MPA, MPP); law and public policy (MPA, MPP); local government management for sustainable communities (MPA, MPP); nonprofit management (Graduate Certificate); nonprofit management and leadership (MPA, MPP, MS), including global leadership (MS, PhD), international nongovernmental organization (MS), local government for sustainable communities (MS), self designed (MS); online teaching in higher education (Post-Master's Certificate); policy analysis (MPA); public management and leadership (MPA, MPP, Graduate Certificate); public policy (Graduate Certificate); public policy and administration (PhD), including criminal justice (MS, PhD), emergency management (MS, PhD), global leadership (MS, PhD), health policy, homeland security and policy coordination (MS, PhD), international nongovernmental organizations, law and public policy (MS, PhD), local government management for sustainable communities, nonprofit management and leadership, policy analysis (MS, PhD), public management and

leadership (MS, PhD), terrorism, mediation, and peace (MS, PhD); strategic planning and public policy (Graduate Certificate); terrorism, mediation, and peace (MPA, MPP). *Program availability:* Part-time, evening/weekend, online only, 100% online. *Degree requirements:* For doctorate, thesis/dissertation, residency. *Entrance requirements:* For master's, bachelor's degree or higher; minimum GPA of 2.5; official transcripts; goal statement (for some programs); access to computer and Internet; for doctorate, master's degree or higher; three years of related professional or academic experience (preferred); minimum GPA of 3.0; goal statement and current resume (for select programs); official transcripts; access to computer and Internet; for other advanced degree, relevant work experience; access to computer and Internet. Additional exam requirements/recommendations for international students: Required—TOEFL (minimum score 550 paper-based, 79 iBT), IELTS (minimum score 6.5), Michigan English Language Assessment Battery (minimum score 82), or PTE (minimum score 53). Electronic applications accepted.

# International Trade Policy

**Baruch College of the City University of New York,** Austin W. Marxe School of Public and International Affairs, Program in International Affairs, New York, NY 10010-5585. Offers international nongovernmental organizations (MIA); trade policy and global economic governance (MIA); Western Hemisphere affairs (MIA). *Program availability:* Part-time.
**See Display on page 931 and Close-Up on page 977.**

**The George Washington University,** Elliott School of International Affairs, Program in International Trade and Investment Policy, Washington, DC 20052. Offers MA. *Program availability:* Part-time. *Students:* 30 full-time (12 women), 12 part-time (7 women); includes 15 minority (4 Black or African American, non-Hispanic/Latino; 3 Asian, non-Hispanic/Latino; 7 Hispanic/Latino; 1 Two or more races, non-Hispanic/Latino), 15 international. Average age 28. 61 applicants, 87% accepted. In 2016, 19 master's awarded. *Degree requirements:* For master's, one foreign language, capstone project. *Entrance requirements:* For master's, GRE General Test, 2 years of a modern foreign language, 2 semesters of introductory economics. Additional exam requirements/recommendations for international students: Required—TOEFL (minimum score 100 iBT), IELTS (minimum score 7). *Application deadline:* For fall admission, 1/15 priority date for domestic and international students; for spring admission, 10/1 for domestic students. Application fee: $75. Electronic applications accepted. *Financial support:* In 2016–17, 11 students received support. Fellowships with partial tuition reimbursements available, Federal Work-Study, and scholarships/grants available.

Financial award application deadline: 1/15. *Unit head:* Prof. Michael Moore, Director, 202-994-5230, E-mail: itip@gwu.edu. *Application contact:* Nicole A. Campbell, Director of Graduate Admissions, 202-994-7050, Fax: 202-994-9537, E-mail: esiagrad@gwu.edu.
Website: http://elliott.gwu.edu/international-trade-investment-policy

**Middlebury Institute of International Studies at Monterey,** Graduate School of International Policy and Management, Program in International Trade and Economic Diplomacy, Monterey, CA 93940-2691. Offers MA. *Entrance requirements:* For master's, statement of purpose, resume or curriculum vitae, undergraduate transcripts, 2 letters of recommendation, interview. Additional exam requirements/recommendations for international students: Required—TOEFL or IELTS. *Expenses: Tuition:* Full-time $38,250; part-time $1820 per credit. *Required fees:* $78 per semester.

**Valparaiso University,** Graduate School and Continuing Education, Program in International Commerce and Policy, Valparaiso, IN 46383. Offers MS, JD/MS. *Program availability:* Part-time, evening/weekend. *Entrance requirements:* For master's, minimum GPA of 3.0. Additional exam requirements/recommendations for international students: Required—TOEFL (minimum score 550 paper-based; 80 iBT), IELTS (minimum score 6). Electronic applications accepted. *Expenses: Tuition:* Full-time $11,070; part-time $615 per credit hour. *Required fees:* $116 per semester. Tuition and fees vary according to course load, degree level and program.

# Political Science

**Acadia University,** Faculty of Arts, Department of Political Science, Wolfville, NS B4P 2R6, Canada. Offers MA. *Degree requirements:* For master's, thesis. *Entrance requirements:* For master's, honors degree or equivalent. Additional exam requirements/recommendations for international students: Required—TOEFL (minimum score 580 paper-based; 93 iBT), IELTS (minimum score 6.5). *Faculty research:* Atlantic Canada, international relations and organization, human rights, Canadian politics, political thought, technology.

**American Public University System,** AMU/APU Graduate Programs, Charles Town, WV 25414. Offers accounting (MBA, MS); applied business analytics (MBA, MS); criminal justice (MA), including business administration, emergency and disaster management, general (MA, MS); educational leadership (M Ed); emergency and disaster management (MA); entrepreneurship (MBA); environmental policy and management (MS), including environmental planning, environmental sustainability, fish and wildlife management, general (MA, MS), global environmental management; finance (MBA); general (MBA); government contracting and acquisition (MBA); health care administration (MBA); health information management (MS); history (MA), including American history, ancient and classical history, European history, global history, public history; homeland security (MA), including business administration, counterterrorism studies, criminal justice, cyber, emergency management and public health, intelligence studies, transportation security; homeland security resource allocation (MBA); humanities (MA); information technology (MS), including digital forensics, enterprise software development, information assurance and security, IT project management; information technology management (MBA); intelligence studies (MA), including criminal intelligence, cyber, general (MA, MS), homeland security, intelligence analysis, intelligence collection, intelligence management, intelligence operations, terrorism studies; international relations and conflict resolution (MA), including comparative and security issues, conflict resolution, international and transnational security issues, peacekeeping; legal studies (MA); management (MA), including strategic consulting; marketing (MBA); military history (MA), including American military history, American Revolution, civil war, war since 1945, World War II; military studies (MA), including joint warfare, strategic leadership; national security studies (MA), including cyber, general (MA, MS), homeland security, regional security studies, security and intelligence analysis, terrorism studies; nonprofit management (MBA); political science (MA), including American politics and government, comparative government and development, general (MA, MS), international relations, public policy; psychology (MA); public administration (MPA), including disaster management, environmental policy, health policy, human resources, national security, organizational management, security management; public health (MPH); reverse logistics management (MA); security management (MA); space studies (MS), including aerospace science, general (MA, MS), planetary science; sports and health sciences (MS); sports management (MBA); teaching (M Ed), including autism spectrum disorder, curriculum and instruction for elementary teachers, elementary reading, English language learners, instructional leadership, online learning, special education, STEAM (STEM plus the arts); transportation and logistics management (MA). *Program availability:* Part-time, evening/weekend, online only, 100% online. *Faculty:* 401 full-time (228 women), 1,678 part-time/adjunct (781 women). *Students:* 378 full-time (184 women), 8,455 part-time (3,484 women); includes 2,972 minority (1,552 Black or African American, non-Hispanic/Latino; 52 American Indian or Alaska Native, non-Hispanic/Latino; 211 Asian, non-Hispanic/

Latino; 791 Hispanic/Latino; 70 Native Hawaiian or other Pacific Islander, non-Hispanic/Latino; 296 Two or more races, non-Hispanic/Latino), 109 international. Average age 37. In 2016, 3,185 master's awarded. *Degree requirements:* For master's, comprehensive exam or practicum. *Entrance requirements:* For master's, official transcript showing earned bachelor's degree from institution accredited by recognized accrediting body. Additional exam requirements/recommendations for international students: Required—TOEFL (minimum score 550 paper-based), IELTS (minimum score 6.5). *Application deadline:* Applications are processed on a rolling basis. Application fee: $0. Electronic applications accepted. *Expenses: Tuition:* Part-time $350 per credit hour. *Required fees:* $50 per course. *Financial support:* Scholarships/grants available. Financial award applicants required to submit FAFSA. *Unit head:* Dr. Karan Powell, President, 877-468-6268, Fax: 304-724-3780. *Application contact:* Terry Grant, Vice President of Enrollment Management, 877-468-6268, Fax: 304-724-3780, E-mail: info@apus.edu.
Website: http://www.apus.edu

**American University,** School of Communication, Program in Political Communication, Washington, DC 20016-8001. Offers MA. *Program availability:* Part-time. *Students:* 24 full-time (14 women), 7 part-time (5 women); includes 8 minority (3 Black or African American, non-Hispanic/Latino; 5 Hispanic/Latino), 2 international. 36 applicants, 92% accepted, 15 enrolled. In 2016, 11 master's awarded. *Degree requirements:* For master's, comprehensive exam, thesis or alternative. *Entrance requirements:* For master's, GRE General Test. Additional exam requirements/recommendations for international students: Required—TOEFL (minimum score 600 paper-based; 100 iBT), IELTS (minimum score 7). *Application deadline:* For fall admission, 2/1 priority date for domestic and international students; for spring admission, 11/1 for domestic and international students. Applications are processed on a rolling basis. Application fee: $55. Electronic applications accepted. *Expenses: Tuition:* Full-time $28,422; part-time $1579 per credit hour. *Required fees:* $690; $200 per term. Tuition and fees vary according to course load, degree level and program. *Financial support:* In 2016–17, 3 research assistantships with full tuition reimbursements (averaging $15,000 per year) were awarded; career-related internships or fieldwork, Federal Work-Study, institutionally sponsored loans, scholarships/grants, tuition waivers (partial), and unspecified assistantships also available. Financial award application deadline: 2/1; financial award applicants required to submit FAFSA. *Faculty research:* Polling and public opinion, political polling, advocacy communication, entertainment and politics, communication research and management, political communication theory, campaign ethics. *Unit head:* Prof. Molly O'Rourke, Executive in Residence, 202-885-2968, Fax: 202-885-2019, E-mail: morourke@american.edu. *Application contact:* Christine Rials, Assistant Director for Graduate Admissions, 202-885-2040, Fax: 202-885-2019, E-mail: crials@american.edu.
Website: http://www.american.edu/soc/communication/degrees/MA-POLC-SOC.cfm

**American University,** School of International Service, Washington, DC 20016-8071. Offers comparative and regional studies (Certificate); cross-cultural communication (Certificate); development management (MS); ethics, peace, and global affairs (MA); European studies (Certificate); global environmental policy (MA, Certificate); global information technology (Certificate); international affairs (MA), including comparative and international disability policy, comparative and regional studies, international economic relations, international politics, natural resources and sustainable development, U.S. foreign policy; international arts management (Certificate);

international communication (MA, Certificate); international development (MA); international economic policy (Certificate); international economic relations (Certificate); international economics (MA); international media (MA); international peace and conflict resolution (MA, Certificate); international politics (Certificate); international relations (MA, PhD); international service (MIS); peacebuilding (Certificate); social enterprise (MA); the Americas (Certificate); United States foreign policy (Certificate); JD/MA. *Program availability:* Part-time, evening/weekend, 100% online. *Faculty:* 116 full-time (53 women), 57 part-time/adjunct (19 women). *Students:* 575 full-time (360 women), 491 part-time (277 women); includes 287 minority (100 Black or African American, non-Hispanic/Latino; 6 American Indian or Alaska Native, non-Hispanic/Latino; 58 Asian, non-Hispanic/Latino; 1 Native Hawaiian or other Pacific Islander, non-Hispanic/Latino; 30 Two or more races, non-Hispanic/Latino), 151 international. Average age 29. 1,504 applicants, 84% accepted, 403 enrolled. In 2016, 374 master's, 3 doctorates, 1 other advanced degree awarded. Terminal master's awarded for partial completion of doctoral program. *Degree requirements:* For master's, one foreign language, comprehensive exam, thesis or alternative; for doctorate, one foreign language, comprehensive exam, thesis/dissertation. *Entrance requirements:* For master's, GRE; GMAT or GRE (for MA in social enterprise), transcripts, resume, 2 letters of recommendation, statement of purpose; for doctorate, GRE, transcripts, resume, 3 letters of recommendation, statement of purpose. Additional exam requirements/recommendations for international students: Required—TOEFL (minimum score 600 paper-based, 100 iBT), IELTS (minimum score 7), or PTE (minimum score of 68). Application fee: $55. Electronic applications accepted. *Expenses:* $1,579 per credit tuition; $1,930 mandatory fees. *Financial support:* Research assistantships, teaching assistantships, institutionally sponsored loans, scholarships/grants, and unspecified assistantships available. Financial award application deadline: 1/15; financial award applicants required to submit FAFSA. *Unit head:* Dr. James Goldgeier, Dean, 202-885-1603, Fax: 202-885-2494, E-mail: goldgeier@american.edu. *Application contact:* Jia Jiang, Associate Director, Graduate Education Enrollment, 202-885-1689, Fax: 202-885-1109, E-mail: jiang@american.edu.
Website: http://www.american.edu/sis/

**American University,** School of Public Affairs, Department of Government, Washington, DC 20016-8130. Offers political communication (MA); political science (MA, PhD), including American politics (MA), applied politics (MA); women, policy and political leadership (Certificate). *Program availability:* Part-time, evening/weekend. *Faculty:* 31 full-time (13 women), 24 part-time/adjunct (7 women). *Students:* 44 full-time (27 women), 10 part-time (2 women); includes 16 minority (5 Black or African American, non-Hispanic/Latino; 5 Asian, non-Hispanic/Latino; 6 Hispanic/Latino), 7 international. Average age 28. 107 applicants, 52% accepted, 19 enrolled. In 2016, 24 master's, 3 doctorates, 1 other advanced degree awarded. Terminal master's awarded for partial completion of doctoral program. *Expenses:* $1,579 per credit tuition; $690 mandatory fees. *Financial support:* Research assistantships, teaching assistantships, and institutionally sponsored loans available. Financial award application deadline: 2/1; financial award applicants required to submit FAFSA. *Unit head:* Thomas Merrill, Chair, Government, 202-885-6246, Fax: 202-885-2967, E-mail: merrill@american.edu. *Application contact:* Rosie Walker, Director, Graduate Enrollment and Recruitment, E-mail: rwalker@american.edu.
Website: http://www.american.edu/spa/gov/

**American University of Armenia,** Graduate Programs, Yerevan, Armenia. Offers business administration (MBA); computer and information science (MS), including business management, design and manufacturing, energy (ME, MS), industrial engineering and systems management; economics (MS); industrial engineering and systems management (ME), including business, computer aided design/manufacturing, energy (ME, MS), information technology; law (LL M); political science and international affairs (MPSIA); public health (MPH); teaching English as a foreign language (MA). *Program availability:* Part-time, evening/weekend. *Degree requirements:* For master's, thesis (for some programs), capstone/project. *Entrance requirements:* For master's, GRE, GMAT, or LSAT. Additional exam requirements/recommendations for international students: Recommended—TOEFL (minimum score 79 iBT), IELTS (minimum score 6.5). *Faculty research:* Microfinance, finance (rural/development, international, corporate), firm life cycle theory, TESOL, language proficiency testing, public policy, administrative law, economic development, cryptography, artificial intelligence, energy efficiency/renewable energy, computer-aided design/manufacturing, health financing, tuberculosis control, mother/child health, preventive ophthalmology, post-earthquake psychopathological investigations, tobacco control, environmental health risk assessments.

**American University of Beirut,** Graduate Programs, Faculty of Arts and Sciences, Beirut, Lebanon. Offers anthropology (MA); Arab and Middle Eastern history (PhD); Arabic language and literature (MA, PhD); archaeology (MA); art history and curating (MA); biology (MS); cell and molecular biology (PhD); chemistry (MS); clinical psychology (MA); computational sciences (MS); computer science (MS); economics (MA); education (MA); English language (MA); English literature (MA); environmental policy planning (MS); financial economics (MAFE); geology (MS); history (MA); Islamic studies (MA); mathematics (MS); media studies (MA); Middle Eastern studies (MA); physics (MS); political studies (MA); psychology (MA); public administration (MA); public policy and international affairs (MA); sociology (MA); statistics (MA, MS); theoretical physics (PhD); transnational American studies (MA). *Program availability:* Part-time. *Faculty:* 133 full-time (42 women), 6 part-time/adjunct (2 women). *Students:* 240 full-time (172 women), 227 part-time (166 women). Average age 27. 286 applicants, 67% accepted, 108 enrolled. In 2016, 60 master's, 3 doctorates awarded. Terminal master's awarded for partial completion of doctoral program. *Degree requirements:* For master's, one foreign language, comprehensive exam, thesis (for some programs); for doctorate, one foreign language, comprehensive exam, thesis/dissertation. *Entrance requirements:* For master's, GRE (for some MA, MS programs), letters of recommendation; for doctorate, GRE, letters of recommendation. Additional exam requirements/recommendations for international students: Required—TOEFL (minimum score 600 paper-based; 97 iBT), IELTS (minimum score 7). *Application deadline:* For fall admission, 4/3 for domestic students; for winter admission, 11/3 for domestic students. Application fee: $50. Electronic applications accepted. *Expenses:* Contact institution. *Financial support:* In 2016–17, 4 fellowships (averaging $11,200 per year), 18 research assistantships (averaging $5,400 per year) were awarded; teaching assistantships, career-related internships or fieldwork, Federal Work-Study, institutionally sponsored loans, scholarships/grants, traineeships, health care benefits, tuition waivers (full), and unspecified assistantships also available. Support available to part-time students. *Faculty research:* Development economics, spatial econometrics, health economics, labor economics, energy economics, hydrogeology, geophysics, petrophysics, structural geology, mineralogy, petrology, geochemistry, multilingualism, comparative/world literature, translation studies, book histories/ cultures, biocatalysis, molecular recognition, photocatalysis, photophysical and biophysical chemistry, probe chemistry, machine learning, data science. *Unit head:* Dr. Nadia Maria El Cheikh, Dean, Faculty of Arts and Sciences, 961-1374374 Ext. 3800, Fax: 961-1744461, E-mail: nmcheikh@aub.edu.lb. *Application contact:* Dr. Salim Kanaan, Director, Admissions Office, 961-1350000 Ext. 2590, Fax: 961-1750775, E-mail: sk00@aub.edu.lb.
Website: http://www.aub.edu.lb/fas/

**Appalachian State University,** Cratis D. Williams Graduate School, Department of Government and Justice Studies, Boone, NC 28608. Offers political science (MA), including American government; public administration (MPA), including public management. *Program availability:* Part-time, online learning. *Degree requirements:* For master's, variable foreign language requirement, comprehensive exam, thesis optional. *Entrance requirements:* For master's, GRE General Test, 3 letters of recommendation. Additional exam requirements/recommendations for international students: Required—TOEFL (minimum score 570 paper-based; 79 iBT), IELTS (minimum score 6.5). *Application deadline:* For fall admission, 3/15 priority date for domestic students, 2/1 for international students; for spring admission, 11/1 for domestic students, 7/1 for international students. Applications are processed on a rolling basis. Application fee: $55. Electronic applications accepted. *Expenses:* Tuition, state resident: full-time $4744. Tuition, nonresident: full-time $17,913. Full-time tuition and fees vary according to program. *Financial support:* Fellowships, research assistantships, teaching assistantships, career-related internships or fieldwork, Federal Work-Study, scholarships/grants, and unspecified assistantships available. Financial award application deadline: 4/1; financial award applicants required to submit FAFSA. *Faculty research:* Campaign finance, emerging democracies, bureaucratic politics, judicial behavior, administration of justice. *Unit head:* Dr. Brian Ellison, Chairperson, 828-262-3085, E-mail: ellisonba@appstate.edu. *Application contact:* Dr. Brad Bradbury, Program Director, 828-262-7913, E-mail: bradburymd@appstate.edu.
Website: http://www.pscj.appstate.edu

**Arizona State University at the Tempe campus,** College of Liberal Arts and Sciences, School of Politics and Global Studies, Tempe, AZ 85287-3902. Offers political science (MA, PhD). *Program availability:* Part-time. Terminal master's awarded for partial completion of doctoral program. *Degree requirements:* For master's, thesis or alternative, interactive Program of Study (iPOS) submitted before completing 50 percent of required credit hours; for doctorate, comprehensive exam, thesis/dissertation, interactive Program of Study (iPOS) submitted before completing 50 percent of required credit hours. *Entrance requirements:* For master's and doctorate, GRE, minimum GPA of 3.0 or equivalent in last 2 years of work leading to bachelor's degree. Additional exam requirements/recommendations for international students: Required—TOEFL, IELTS, or PTE. Electronic applications accepted.

**Arkansas State University,** Graduate School, College of Humanities and Social Sciences, Department of Political Science, State University, AR 72467. Offers political science (MA); political science education (SCCT); public administration (MPA). *Accreditation:* NASPAA (one or more programs are accredited). *Program availability:* Part-time. *Degree requirements:* For master's, comprehensive exam, thesis or alternative; for SCCT, comprehensive exam. *Entrance requirements:* For master's, GRE General Test or MAT, GMAT, appropriate bachelor's degree, letters of recommendation, official transcripts, immunization records, statement of purpose; for SCCT, GRE General Test or MAT, GMAT, interview, master's degree, official transcript, letters of recommendation, immunization records. Additional exam requirements/recommendations for international students: Required—TOEFL (minimum score 550 paper-based; 79 iBT), IELTS (minimum score 6), PTE (minimum score 56). Electronic applications accepted.

**Ashland University,** College of Arts and Sciences, Program in American History and Government, Ashland, OH 44805-3702. Offers MAHG. *Program availability:* Part-time. *Degree requirements:* For master's, capstone project or thesis. *Entrance requirements:* For master's, minimum undergraduate GPA of 2.75, 3.0 graduate. *Application deadline:* Applications are processed on a rolling basis. Application fee: $30. Electronic applications accepted. *Expenses:* Contact institution. *Financial support:* Fellowships and research assistantships available. Financial award application deadline: 4/1. *Faculty research:* American founding, United States Civil War, Progressive Era. *Unit head:* Dr. Peter W. Schramm, Chair, 419-289-5411, Fax: 419-289-5425, E-mail: pschramm@ashland.edu. *Application contact:* Christian A. Pascarella, Director, 419-289-5411, Fax 419-289-5425, E-mail: cpascare@ashland.edu.
Website: http://mahg.ashland.edu

**Auburn University,** Graduate School, College of Liberal Arts, Department of Political Science, Auburn University, AL 36849. Offers public administration (MPA, PhD, Graduate Certificate); MPA/MCP. *Program availability:* Part-time. *Faculty:* 27 full-time (14 women), 4 part-time/adjunct (2 women). *Students:* 54 full-time (33 women), 40 part-time (22 women); includes 22 minority (18 Black or African American, non-Hispanic/Latino; 2 American Indian or Alaska Native, non-Hispanic/Latino; 1 Asian, non-Hispanic/Latino; 1 Hispanic/Latino), 18 international. Average age 34. 64 applicants, 53% accepted, 22 enrolled. In 2016, 13 master's, 7 doctorates awarded. *Degree requirements:* For doctorate, thesis/dissertation. *Entrance requirements:* For master's, GRE General Test, minimum GPA of 3.0 in political science, 2.5 overall; for doctorate, GRE General Test. *Application deadline:* Applications are processed on a rolling basis. Application fee: $50 ($60 for international students). Electronic applications accepted. *Expenses:* Tuition, state resident: full-time $9072; part-time $504 per credit hour. Tuition, nonresident: full-time $27,216; part-time $1512 per credit hour. *Required fees:* $812 per semester. Tuition and fees vary according to degree level and program. *Financial support:* Fellowships, research assistantships, teaching assistantships, career-related internships or fieldwork, and Federal Work-Study available. Support available to part-time students. Financial award application deadline: 3/15; financial award applicants required to submit FAFSA. *Faculty research:* Policy evaluation, political economy, privatization, participation, election administration. *Unit head:* Cynthia Bowling, Chair, 334-844-5370. *Application contact:* Dr. George Flowers, Dean of the Graduate School, 334-844-2125.
Website: http://cla.auburn.edu/polisci/

**Auburn University at Montgomery,** College of Public Policy and Justice, Department of Political Science and Public Administration, Montgomery, AL 36124-4023. Offers international relations (MIR); nonprofit management and leadership (Certificate); political science (MPS); public administration (MPA); public administration and public policy (PhD); public health care administration and policy (Certificate). PhD offered jointly with Auburn University. *Accreditation:* NASPAA (one or more programs are accredited). *Program availability:* Part-time, evening/weekend. *Degree requirements:* For master's, comprehensive exam; for doctorate, thesis/dissertation. *Entrance requirements:* For master's, GRE General Test or MAT; for doctorate, GRE General Test. Electronic applications accepted.

**Ball State University,** Graduate School, College of Sciences and Humanities, Department of Political Science, Program in Political Science, Muncie, IN 47306. Offers MA. *Program availability:* Part-time. *Degree requirements:* For master's, comprehensive exam. *Entrance requirements:* For master's, GRE General Test, minimum baccalaureate GPA of 2.8. Additional exam requirements/recommendations for international students: Required—TOEFL (minimum score 550 paper-based; 79 iBT), IELTS (minimum score 6.5). Electronic applications accepted. *Faculty research:* Survey research, public policy.

**Baylor University,** Graduate School, College of Arts and Sciences, Department of Political Science, Waco, TX 76798. Offers international studies (MA); political science (MA, PhD); public policy and administration (MPPA); JD/MPPA. *Faculty:* 18 full-time (3 women), 1 part-time/adjunct (0 women). *Students:* 29 full-time (11 women), 2 part-time

## Political Science

(both women); includes 3 minority (all Hispanic/Latino), 2 international. Average age 26. 27 applicants, 22% accepted, 4 enrolled. In 2016, 6 master's, 2 doctorates awarded. Terminal master's awarded for partial completion of doctoral program. *Degree requirements:* For master's, variable foreign language requirement, comprehensive exam (for some programs), thesis (for some programs); for doctorate, variable foreign language requirement, comprehensive exam, thesis/dissertation. *Entrance requirements:* For master's and doctorate, GRE General Test. Additional exam requirements/recommendations for international students: Required—TOEFL. *Application deadline:* For fall admission, 12/20 for domestic and international students. Application fee: $25. Electronic applications accepted. *Expenses: Tuition:* Full-time $28,494; part-time $1583 per credit hour. *Required fees:* $167 per credit hour. Tuition and fees vary according to course load and program. *Financial support:* In 2016–17, 17 students received support, including 17 research assistantships with full tuition reimbursements available (averaging $16,000 per year); career-related internships or fieldwork, Federal Work-Study, and institutionally sponsored loans also available. Financial award application deadline: 12/20; financial award applicants required to submit FAFSA. *Unit head:* Dr. Timothy Burns, Graduate Program Director, 254-710-6237, Fax: 254-710-3122, E-mail: timothy_burns@baylor.edu. *Application contact:* Jenice Langston, Office Manager, 254-710-3161, Fax: 254-710-3122, E-mail: jenice_langston@baylor.edu.
Website: http://www.baylor.edu/political_science/

**Binghamton University, State University of New York,** Graduate School, Harpur College of Arts and Sciences, Department of Political Science, Binghamton, NY 13902-6000. Offers MA, PhD. *Program availability:* Part-time. *Faculty:* 19 full-time (6 women), 3 part-time/adjunct (2 women). *Students:* 18 full-time (9 women), 20 part-time (9 women); includes 5 minority (1 Black or African American, non-Hispanic/Latino; 1 American Indian or Alaska Native, non-Hispanic/Latino; 3 Hispanic/Latino), 15 international. Average age 31. 46 applicants, 52% accepted, 7 enrolled. In 2016, 8 master's, 6 doctorates awarded. Terminal master's awarded for partial completion of doctoral program. *Degree requirements:* For master's, comprehensive exam (for some programs), thesis (for some programs); for doctorate, variable foreign language requirement, comprehensive exam, thesis/dissertation. *Entrance requirements:* For master's and doctorate, GRE General Test. Additional exam requirements/recommendations for international students: Required—TOEFL (minimum score 550 paper-based; 80 iBT). *Application deadline:* For fall admission, 1/15 priority date for domestic and international students. Application fee: $75. Electronic applications accepted. *Financial support:* In 2016–17, 26 students received support, including 4 research assistantships with full tuition reimbursements available (averaging $15,000 per year), 19 teaching assistantships with full tuition reimbursements available (averaging $15,000 per year); career-related internships or fieldwork, Federal Work-Study, institutionally sponsored loans, scholarships/grants, health care benefits, tuition waivers (full and partial), and unspecified assistantships also available. Financial award applicants required to submit FAFSA. *Unit head:* Dr. David H. Clark, Chairperson, 607-777-2675, E-mail: dclark@binghamton.edu. *Application contact:* Ben Balkaya, Assistant Dean and Director, 607-777-2151, Fax: 607-777-2501, E-mail: balkaya@binghamton.edu.

**Boise State University,** School of Public Service, Department of Political Science, Boise, ID 83725-1935. Offers MA. *Program availability:* Part-time. *Faculty:* 4. *Students:* 11 full-time (4 women), 4 part-time (1 woman); includes 2 minority (1 Hispanic/Latino; 1 Native Hawaiian or other Pacific Islander, non-Hispanic/Latino), 1 international. Average age 37. 18 applicants, 67% accepted, 10 enrolled. *Degree requirements:* For master's, comprehensive exam, thesis (for some programs), thesis or professional project. *Entrance requirements:* For master's, GRE General Test. Additional exam requirements/recommendations for international students: Required—TOEFL (minimum score 550 paper-based; 80 iBT), IELTS (minimum score 6). *Application deadline:* For fall admission, 5/1 for domestic and international students. Application fee: $65 ($94 for international students). Electronic applications accepted. *Expenses: Tuition,* state resident: full-time $6058; part-time $358 per credit hour. Tuition, nonresident: full-time $20,108; part-time $608 per credit hour. *Required fees:* $2108. Tuition and fees vary according to program. *Financial support:* In 2016–17, 4 students received support, including 2 research assistantships (averaging $4,083 per year); scholarships/grants and unspecified assistantships also available. Financial award application deadline: 2/15; financial award applicants required to submit FAFSA. *Unit head:* Dr. Brian Wampler, Chair, 208-426-2650, E-mail: bwampler@boisestate.edu. *Application contact:* Dr. Michael Allen, Graduate Program Coordinator, 208-426-2518, E-mail: michaelaallen@boisestate.edu.
Website: https://sps.boisestate.edu/politicalscience/

**Boston College,** Graduate School of Arts and Sciences, Department of Political Science, Chestnut Hill, MA 02467-3800. Offers MA, PhD. *Faculty:* 26 full-time. *Students:* 44 full-time (14 women); includes 1 minority (Two or more races, non-Hispanic/Latino), 10 international. 130 applicants, 45% accepted, 13 enrolled. In 2016, 15 master's, 4 doctorates awarded. Terminal master's awarded for partial completion of doctoral program. *Degree requirements:* For master's, thesis or alternative; for doctorate, one foreign language, thesis/dissertation. *Entrance requirements:* For master's and doctorate, GRE General Test. Additional exam requirements/recommendations for international students: Required—TOEFL (minimum score 600 paper-based; 100 iBT), IELTS (minimum score 8). *Application deadline:* For fall admission, 1/2 for domestic and international students. Application fee: $75. Electronic applications accepted. Tuition and fees vary according to program. *Financial support:* In 2016–17, 30 students received support, including fellowships with full tuition reimbursements available (averaging $21,400 per year), research assistantships with full tuition reimbursements available (averaging $21,400 per year), teaching assistantships with full tuition reimbursements available (averaging $21,400 per year); Federal Work-Study, scholarships/grants, health care benefits, tuition waivers (full and partial), and unspecified assistantships also available. Support available to part-time students. Financial award application deadline: 3/1; financial award applicants required to submit FAFSA. *Faculty research:* Political theory, American politics, international politics, comparative politics. *Unit head:* Dr. Susan Shell, Chairperson, 617-552-4161, E-mail: susan.shell@bc.edu. *Application contact:* Dr. Nasser Behnegar, Graduate Program Director, 617-552-1897, E-mail: nasser.behnegar@bc.edu.
Website: http://www.bc.edu/polisci

**Boston University,** Graduate School of Arts and Sciences, Department of Political Science, Boston, MA 02215. Offers PhD. *Students:* 46 full-time (21 women), 5 part-time (3 women); includes 6 minority (3 Asian, non-Hispanic/Latino; 2 Hispanic/Latino; 1 Two or more races, non-Hispanic/Latino), 24 international. Average age 32. 88 applicants, 16% accepted, 4 enrolled. In 2016, 7 doctorates awarded. Terminal master's awarded for partial completion of doctoral program. *Degree requirements:* For doctorate, comprehensive exam, thesis/dissertation. *Entrance requirements:* For doctorate, GRE General Test, 3 letters of recommendation, transcripts, personal statement, curriculum vitae. Additional exam requirements/recommendations for international students: Required—TOEFL (minimum score 600 paper-based; 100 iBT). *Application deadline:* For fall admission, 12/1 for domestic and international students. Application fee: $95. Electronic applications accepted. *Financial support:* In 2016–17, 41 students received support, including 5 fellowships with full tuition reimbursements available (averaging

$21,500 per year), 1 research assistantship with full tuition reimbursement available (averaging $21,500 per year), 17 teaching assistantships with full tuition reimbursements available (averaging $21,500 per year); career-related internships or fieldwork, Federal Work-Study, scholarships/grants, and health care benefits also available. Support available to part-time students. Financial award application deadline: 12/1. *Unit head:* David Mayers, Chair, 617-353-2540, Fax: 617-353-5508, E-mail: dmayers@bu.edu. *Application contact:* Cady Steinberg, Graduate Program Coordinator, 617-353-2540, Fax: 617-353-5508, E-mail: pograd@bu.edu.
Website: http://www.bu.edu/polisci

**Brandeis University,** Graduate School of Arts and Sciences, Department of Politics, Waltham, MA 02454-9110. Offers MA, PhD. *Faculty:* 13 full-time (3 women), 2 part-time/adjunct (1 woman). *Students:* 15 full-time (7 women); includes 1 minority (Hispanic/Latino), 4 international. 82 applicants, 15% accepted, 7 enrolled. In 2016, 3 master's, 3 doctorates awarded. Terminal master's awarded for partial completion of doctoral program. *Degree requirements:* For master's, thesis or alternative, proseminar; for doctorate, one foreign language, comprehensive exam, thesis/dissertation, proseminar; teaching requirement; research tools requirement; qualifying exams. *Entrance requirements:* For master's and doctorate, GRE General Test, sample of written work, resume, 3 letters of recommendation, statement of purpose, transcript(s). Additional exam requirements/recommendations for international students: Required—TOEFL (minimum score 600 paper-based; 100 iBT); Recommended—IELTS (minimum score 7), TSE (minimum score 68). *Application deadline:* For fall admission, 1/15 priority date for domestic and international students. Application fee: $75. Electronic applications accepted. *Financial support:* In 2016–17, 11 students received support, including 10 fellowships with full tuition reimbursements available (averaging $24,000 per year), 3 teaching assistantships with partial tuition reimbursements available (averaging $1,600 per year); Federal Work-Study, scholarships/grants, health care benefits, and tuition waivers (full and partial) also available. Financial award application deadline: 4/15; financial award applicants required to submit FAFSA. *Faculty research:* American political development and contemporary politics, international law and foreign policy, political theory, comparative politics, European politics. *Unit head:* Dr. Kerry Chase, Director of Graduate Studies, 781-736-2725, Fax: 781-736-2777, E-mail: chase@brandeis.edu. *Application contact:* Rosanne Colocouris, Department Administrator, 781-736-2755, Fax: 781-736-2777, E-mail: colocour@brandeis.edu.
Website: http://www.brandeis.edu/gsas

**Brigham Young University,** Graduate Studies, Marriott School of Management, Master of Public Administration Program, Provo, UT 84602. Offers federal government (MPA); health care (MPA); local government management (MPA); nonprofit management (MPA); JD/MPA. *Accreditation:* NASPAA. *Students:* 98 full-time (54 women); includes 16 minority (2 Black or African American, non-Hispanic/Latino; 2 Asian, non-Hispanic/Latino; 10 Hispanic/Latino; 2 Native Hawaiian or other Pacific Islander, non-Hispanic/Latino), 20 international. Average age 29. 77 applicants, 81% accepted, 49 enrolled. In 2016, 42 master's awarded. *Entrance requirements:* For master's, GMAT or GRE, minimum GPA of 3.0, MPA Excel prep course. Additional exam requirements/recommendations for international students: Required—TOEFL (minimum score 580 paper-based; 85 iBT). *Application deadline:* For fall admission, 1/15 for domestic and international students. Application fee: $50. Electronic applications accepted. *Expenses:* Contact institution. *Financial support:* In 2016–17, 99 students received support. Research assistantships, teaching assistantships, career-related internships or fieldwork, institutionally sponsored loans, and scholarships/grants available. Financial award application deadline: 4/15; financial award applicants required to submit FAFSA. *Faculty research:* Taxes, budgeting, nonprofit, ethics, decision modeling, work balance, organizational behavior. *Unit head:* Dr. Jeffery Thompson, Director, 801-422-4221, Fax: 801-422-0311, E-mail: mpa@byu.edu. *Application contact:* Catherine Cooper, Associate Director, 801-422-4221, Fax: 801-422-0311, E-mail: mpa@byu.edu.
Website: http://mpa.byu.edu

**Brock University,** Faculty of Graduate Studies, Faculty of Social Sciences, Program in Political Science, St. Catharines, ON L2S 3A1, Canada. Offers Canadian politics (MA); comparative politics (MA); international relations (MA); political theory or philosophy (MA); public policy (MA). *Program availability:* Part-time. *Degree requirements:* For master's, thesis optional. *Entrance requirements:* For master's, honors degree. Additional exam requirements/recommendations for international students: Required—TOEFL (minimum score 550 paper-based; 80 iBT), IELTS (minimum score 6.5), TWE (minimum score 4). Electronic applications accepted. *Faculty research:* Public administration reform, economic and social justice, politics of societies, Canadian politics, international relations.

**Brooklyn College of the City University of New York,** School of Humanities and Social Sciences, Department of Political Science, Brooklyn, NY 11210-2889. Offers international affairs (MA); political science (MA); urban policy and administration (MA). *Program availability:* Part-time, evening/weekend. *Degree requirements:* For master's, comprehensive exam (for some programs), thesis or alternative, foreign language exam (for international affairs program). *Entrance requirements:* For master's, 2 letters of recommendation, personal statement. Additional exam requirements/recommendations for international students: Required—TOEFL (minimum score 500 paper-based; 61 iBT). *Faculty research:* Ethics and politics, politics of criminal justice, Western Europe, international law and politics, labor politics.

**Brown University,** Graduate School, Department of Political Science, Providence, RI 02912. Offers PhD. *Degree requirements:* For doctorate, thesis/dissertation. *Entrance requirements:* For doctorate, GRE General Test.

**California Polytechnic State University, San Luis Obispo,** College of Liberal Arts, Department of Political Science, San Luis Obispo, CA 93407. Offers MPP. *Program availability:* Part-time. *Faculty:* 4 full-time (3 women). *Students:* 2 full-time (0 women), 14 part-time (9 women); includes 5 minority (3 Hispanic/Latino; 2 Two or more races, non-Hispanic/Latino). Average age 31. 27 applicants, 74% accepted, 9 enrolled. In 2016, 9 master's awarded. *Degree requirements:* For master's, comprehensive exam. *Entrance requirements:* For master's, GRE. Additional exam requirements/recommendations for international students: Required—TOEFL (minimum score 80 iBT). *Application deadline:* For fall admission, 4/1 for domestic students, 3/1 for international students. Application fee: $55. *Expenses:* Tuition, state resident: full-time $6738; part-time $3906 per year. Tuition, nonresident: full-time $15,666; part-time $8370 per year. *Required fees:* $3603; $3141 per unit. $1047 per term. *Financial support:* Fellowships, research assistantships, career-related internships or fieldwork, Federal Work-Study, and scholarships/grants available. Support available to part-time students. Financial award application deadline: 3/2; financial award applicants required to submit FAFSA. *Faculty research:* Public policy analysis, public finance, policy internship. *Unit head:* Dr. Michael Latner, Graduate Coordinator, 805-756-6402, E-mail: mlatner@calpoly.edu.
Website: http://mpp.calpoly.edu/

**California State University, Chico,** Office of Graduate Studies, College of Behavioral and Social Sciences, Political Science and Criminal Justice Department, Program in Political Science, Chico, CA 95929-0722. Offers MA. *Program availability:* Part-time. *Students:* 8 full-time (3 women), 10 part-time (4 women); includes 5 minority (all Hispanic/Latino). 15 applicants, 100% accepted, 9 enrolled. *Degree requirements:* For master's, thesis or comprehensive examination. *Entrance requirements:* For master's, 2

letters of recommendation, statement of purpose. Additional exam requirements/recommendations for international students: Required—TOEFL (minimum score 550 paper-based; 80 iBT), IELTS (minimum score 6.5), PTE (minimum score 59). *Application deadline:* For fall admission, 3/1 priority date for domestic students, 3/1 for international students; for spring admission, 9/15 priority date for domestic students, 9/15 for international students. Application fee: $55. Electronic applications accepted. *Financial support:* Career-related internships or fieldwork available. Financial award application deadline: 3/1; financial award applicants required to submit FAFSA. *Unit head:* Mahalley Allen, Chair, 530-898-6506, Fax: 530-898-6910, E-mail: mdallen@csuchico.edu. *Application contact:* Judy L. Rice, School of Graduate, International, and Interdisciplinary Studies, 530-898-5416, Fax: 530-898-3342, E-mail: jlrice@csuchico.edu.
Website: http://catalog.csuchico.edu/viewer/11/POLS/POLSNONEMA.html

**California State University, Fullerton,** Graduate Studies, College of Humanities and Social Sciences, Division of Politics, Administration, and Justice, Fullerton, CA 92834-9480. Offers political science (MA); public administration (MPA). *Accreditation:* NASPAA (one or more programs are accredited). *Program availability:* Part-time. *Degree requirements:* For master's, comprehensive exam, project or thesis. *Entrance requirements:* For master's, minimum GPA of 2.5 in last 60 units of course work, 12 units of course work in social sciences. Application fee: $55. *Expenses:* Tuition, state resident: full-time $3369; part-time $1953 per unit. Tuition, nonresident: full-time $3915; part-time $2499 per unit. Tuition and fees vary according to course load, degree level and program. *Financial support:* Career-related internships or fieldwork, Federal Work-Study, institutionally sponsored loans, and scholarships/grants available. Support available to part-time students. Financial award application deadline: 3/1; financial award applicants required to submit FAFSA. *Faculty research:* Emergency management plans. *Unit head:* Dr. Stephen Stambough, Chair, 657-278-2933. *Application contact:* Admissions/Applications, 657-278-2371.

**California State University, Long Beach,** Graduate Studies, College of Liberal Arts, Department of Political Science, Long Beach, CA 90840. Offers MA. *Program availability:* Part-time. *Degree requirements:* For master's, one foreign language, comprehensive exam or thesis. *Entrance requirements:* For master's, GRE General Test, minimum GPA of 3.0 in field. *Application deadline:* For fall admission, 4/1 for domestic students. Applications are processed on a rolling basis. Application fee: $55. Electronic applications accepted. *Financial support:* In 2016–17, 6 students received support. Teaching assistantships, Federal Work-Study, institutionally sponsored loans, and scholarships/grants available. Financial award application deadline: 3/2. *Faculty research:* Social welfare policy, international political economy, Marxism, voting behavior. *Unit head:* Dr. Teresa Wright, Chair, 562-985-4704, Fax: 562-985-4979, E-mail: twright@csulb.edu. *Application contact:* Dr. Liesl Haas, Graduate Advisor, 562-985-5860, Fax: 562-985-4979, E-mail: lhaas@csulb.edu.

**California State University, Los Angeles,** Graduate Studies, College of Natural and Social Sciences, Department of Political Science, Los Angeles, CA 90032-8530. Offers political science (MA); public administration (MS). *Program availability:* Part-time, evening/weekend. *Degree requirements:* For master's, comprehensive exam or thesis. *Entrance requirements:* Additional exam requirements/recommendations for international students: Required—TOEFL (minimum score 500 paper-based). Electronic applications accepted. *Faculty research:* Government; public policy and law; international, political, and economic relations; comparative politics.

**California State University, Northridge,** Graduate Studies, College of Social and Behavioral Sciences, Department of Political Science, Northridge, CA 91330. Offers MA. *Faculty:* 14 full-time (8 women), 9 part-time/adjunct (7 women). *Students:* 9 full-time (6 women), 8 part-time (5 women); includes 9 minority (2 Asian, non-Hispanic/Latino; 6 Hispanic/Latino; 1 Two or more races, non-Hispanic/Latino), 3 international. Average age 33. 491 applicants, 71% accepted, 2 enrolled. *Degree requirements:* For master's, comprehensive exam. *Entrance requirements:* For master's, GRE (if cumulative undergraduate GPA less than 3.0), 2 letters of recommendation. Additional exam requirements/recommendations for international students: Required—TOEFL. *Application deadline:* For fall admission, 11/30 for domestic students. Application fee: $55. *Expenses:* Tuition, state resident: full-time $4152. *Financial support:* Application deadline: 3/1. *Unit head:* Dr. Lawrence Becker, Chair, 818-677-3488.
Website: http://www.csun.edu/csbs/departments/political_science/index.html

**California State University, Sacramento,** Office of Graduate Studies, College of Social Sciences and Interdisciplinary Studies, Department of Government, Sacramento, CA 95819. Offers MA. *Program availability:* Part-time. *Students:* 4 full-time (2 women), 22 part-time (9 women); includes 10 minority (4 Black or African American, non-Hispanic/Latino; 1 Asian, non-Hispanic/Latino; 5 Hispanic/Latino). Average age 28. 14 applicants, 93% accepted, 10 enrolled. In 2016, 6 master's awarded. *Degree requirements:* For master's, thesis, project or comprehensive exam; writing proficiency exam. *Entrance requirements:* For master's, GRE, minimum GPA of 3.0 during previous 2 years. Additional exam requirements/recommendations for international students: Required—TOEFL (minimum score 550 paper-based; 80 iBT). *Application deadline:* For fall admission, 3/1 for domestic and international students; for spring admission, 9/30 for international students. Applications are processed on a rolling basis. Application fee: $55. Electronic applications accepted. *Expenses:* $4,302 full-time tuition and fees per semester, $2,796 part-time. *Financial support:* Career-related internships or fieldwork and Federal Work-Study available. Support available to part-time students. Financial award application deadline: 3/1; financial award applicants required to submit FAFSA. *Unit head:* Dr. Jim Cox, Professor and Graduate Coordinator, 916-278-6378, E-mail: jhcox@csus.edu. *Application contact:* Jose Martinez, Graduate Admissions Supervisor, 916-278-7871, E-mail: martinj@skymail.csus.edu.
Website: http://www.csus.edu/govt

**Carleton University,** Faculty of Graduate Studies, Faculty of Public Affairs and Management, Department of Political Science, Ottawa, ON K1S 5B6, Canada. Offers MA, PhD. *Degree requirements:* For master's, one foreign language, comprehensive exam, thesis optional; for doctorate, one foreign language, comprehensive exam, thesis/dissertation. *Entrance requirements:* For master's, honors degree in political science, minimum B average; for doctorate, master's degree in political science. Additional exam requirements/recommendations for international students: Required—TOEFL. *Faculty research:* Canadian politics, comparative politics, international relations, public administration and policy analysis, political theory.

**Carleton University,** Faculty of Graduate Studies, Faculty of Public Affairs and Management, Institute of Political Economy, Ottawa, ON K1S 5B6, Canada. Offers MA, PhD. *Degree requirements:* For master's, thesis optional. *Entrance requirements:* For master's, honors degree. Additional exam requirements/recommendations for international students: Required—TOEFL. *Faculty research:* Relationships between economy and politics as they affect the political, social and cultural life of societies; historical processes whereby social change is located in the interaction of the economic, political and cultural, and ideological moments of social life.

**Case Western Reserve University,** School of Graduate Studies, Department of Political Science, Cleveland, OH 44106. Offers MA, PhD. *Faculty:* 8 full-time (4 women), 5 part-time/adjunct (0 women). *Students:* 1 full-time (0 women). Average age 30. 8

applicants, 50% accepted, 1 enrolled. Terminal master's awarded for partial completion of doctoral program. *Degree requirements:* For master's, comprehensive exam (for some programs), thesis (for some programs); for doctorate, thesis/dissertation. *Entrance requirements:* For master's and doctorate, GRE General Test, undergraduate degree in political science, three letters of recommendation, statement of objectives. Additional exam requirements/recommendations for international students: Required—TOEFL (minimum score 577 paper-based; 90 iBT); Recommended—IELTS (minimum score 7). *Application deadline:* For fall admission, 5/1 priority date for domestic students; for spring admission, 11/1 for domestic students. Applications are processed on a rolling basis. Application fee: $50. Electronic applications accepted. *Expenses: Tuition:* Full-time $42,576; part-time $1774 per credit hour. *Required fees:* $34. Tuition and fees vary according to course load and program. *Financial support:* Federal Work-Study and institutionally sponsored loans available. Financial award application deadline: 2/15; financial award applicants required to submit CSS PROFILE or FAFSA. *Faculty research:* American political institutions, elections and political parties both in the United States and abroad; legislative politics; international relations with an emphasis on international political economy; the development and decline of nation-states; the politics of gender; public policy and public organizations; research methods; comparative politics with regional concentrations including Western Europe, Africa, Central Asia and the Middle East. *Unit head:* Karen Beckwith, Professor and Chair, Department of Political Science, 216-368-4129, Fax: 216-368-4681, E-mail: karen.beckwith@case.edu. *Application contact:* Jessica Jurcak, Department Assistant, 216-368-2424, Fax: 216-368-4681, E-mail: jessica.jurcak@case.edu.
Website: http://politicalscience.case.edu/

**The Catholic University of America,** School of Arts and Sciences, Department of Politics, Washington, DC 20064. Offers American government (MA, PhD); Congressional and Presidential studies (MA); international affairs (MA); international political economics (MA); political theory (MA, PhD); world politics (MA, PhD); MA/JD. MA/JD offered jointly with Law School. *Program availability:* Part-time. *Faculty:* 14 full-time (2 women), 1 (woman) part-time/adjunct. *Students:* 24 full-time (7 women), 44 part-time (11 women); includes 10 minority (3 Black or African American, non-Hispanic/Latino; 2 Asian, non-Hispanic/Latino; 3 Hispanic/Latino; 2 Two or more races, non-Hispanic/Latino), 11 international. Average age 32. 40 applicants, 78% accepted, 13 enrolled. In 2016, 16 master's, 6 doctorates awarded. *Degree requirements:* For master's, one foreign language, comprehensive exam, thesis or alternative; for doctorate, variable foreign language requirement, comprehensive exam, thesis/dissertation. *Entrance requirements:* For master's, GRE General Test, statement of purpose, official copies of academic transcripts, three letters of recommendation, minimum GPA of 3.0; for doctorate, GRE General Test, statement of purpose, official copies of academic transcripts, three letters of recommendation. Additional exam requirements/recommendations for international students: Required—TOEFL (minimum score 550 paper-based; 80 iBT). *Application deadline:* For fall admission, 7/15 priority date for domestic students, 7/1 for international students; for spring admission, 11/1 priority date for domestic students, 11/1 for international students. Applications are processed on a rolling basis. Application fee: $55. Electronic applications accepted. *Expenses:* $42,850 per year; $1,170 per credit; $200 per semester part-time fees. *Financial support:* Fellowships, research assistantships, teaching assistantships, Federal Work-Study, scholarships/grants, tuition waivers (full and partial), and unspecified assistantships available. Financial award application deadline: 2/1; financial award applicants required to submit FAFSA. *Faculty research:* Political philosophy, American political institutions and processes, political economy, international relations, U.S. political leadership since 1789. *Unit head:* Dr. Dennis Coyle, Chair, 202-319-5813, Fax: 202-319-6289, E-mail: coyle@cua.edu. *Application contact:* Director of Graduate Admissions, 202-319-5057, Fax: 202-319-6533, E-mail: cua-admissions@cua.edu.
Website: http://politics.cua.edu/

**Central European University,** Department of Political Science, Budapest, Hungary. Offers MA, PhD. *Faculty:* 16 full-time (5 women), 6 part-time/adjunct (2 women). *Students:* 108 full-time (42 women). Average age 27. 340 applicants, 26% accepted, 54 enrolled. In 2016, 47 master's, 10 doctorates awarded. *Degree requirements:* For master's, one foreign language, thesis; for doctorate, one foreign language, comprehensive exam, thesis/dissertation. *Entrance requirements:* For master's and doctorate, interview. Additional exam requirements/recommendations for international students: Required—TOEFL (minimum score 570 paper-based); Recommended—IELTS (minimum score 6.5). *Application deadline:* For fall admission, 2/4 for domestic and international students. Application fee: $30. Electronic applications accepted. *Expenses: Tuition:* Full-time 13,500 euros. Tuition and fees vary according to degree level, program and student level. *Financial support:* Fellowships, teaching assistantships, career-related internships or fieldwork, scholarships/grants, health care benefits, and tuition waivers (full and partial) available. *Faculty research:* Comparative and international political economy, public policy analysis, public understanding of genetics, legislation on abortion and euthanasia, democratization and elite change, rational choice theory, experimental economics (behavioral game theory), Cold War history, gender and politics. *Unit head:* Dr. Carsten Q. Schneider, Head of Department, 36 1 235-6164, E-mail: polsci@ceu.edu. *Application contact:* Zsuzsanna Jaszberenyi, Admissions Officer, 361-324-3009, Fax: 367-327-3211, E-mail: admissions@ceu.edu.
Website: http://politicalscience.ceu.edu

**Central European University,** Nationalism Studies Program, Budapest, Hungary. Offers MA. *Faculty:* 5 full-time (1 woman), 5 part-time/adjunct (3 women). *Students:* 32 full-time (22 women). Average age 26. 116 applicants, 28% accepted, 24 enrolled. In 2016, 22 master's awarded. *Degree requirements:* For master's, one foreign language, thesis. *Entrance requirements:* For master's, interview. Additional exam requirements/recommendations for international students: Required—TOEFL (minimum score 570 paper-based); Recommended—IELTS (minimum score 6.5). *Application deadline:* For fall admission, 2/4 for domestic and international students. Application fee: $30. Electronic applications accepted. *Expenses: Tuition:* Full-time 13,500 euros. Tuition and fees vary according to degree level, program and student level. *Financial support:* In 2016–17, 32 students received support. Fellowships, scholarships/grants, health care benefits, and tuition waivers (full and partial) available. *Faculty research:* Issues of territory, power, and identity; comparative welfare state studies; social history of social policy in Central and Eastern Europe; gender and ethnic aspects of old and new poverty; ethnic minorities, Jewish studies. *Unit head:* Dr. Michael Laurence Miller, Program Director, 36 1 327-3081, E-mail: nationalism@ceu.edu. *Application contact:* Zsuzsanna Jaszberenyi, Admissions Officer, 361-324-3009, Fax: 367-327-3211, E-mail: admissions@ceu.edu.
Website: http://nationalism.ceu.edu

**Central Michigan University,** Central Michigan University Global Campus, Program in Public Administration, Mount Pleasant, MI 48859. Offers general public administration (MPA); public management (MPA); state and local government (MPA). *Accreditation:* NASPAA. *Program availability:* Part-time, evening/weekend. *Faculty:* 4 full-time (1 woman), 5 part-time/adjunct (1 woman). *Students:* 50 (31 women); includes 30 minority (22 Black or African American, non-Hispanic/Latino; 4 American Indian or Alaska Native, non-Hispanic/Latino; 1 Asian, non-Hispanic/Latino; 3 Two or more races, non-Hispanic/Latino). Average age 39. In 2016, 7 master's awarded. *Entrance requirements:* For master's, minimum GPA of 2.8. Additional exam requirements/recommendations for

*Political Science*

international students: Required—TOEFL. Electronic applications accepted. *Financial support:* Scholarships/grants available. Support available to part-time students. *Unit head:* Dr. Lawrence Sych, Program Director, 989-774-3316, E-mail: sych1l@cmich.edu. *Application contact:* 877-268-4636, E-mail: cmuglobal@cmich.edu.

**Central Michigan University,** College of Graduate Studies, College of Humanities and Social and Behavioral Sciences, Department of Political Science, Program in Political Science, Mount Pleasant, MI 48859. Offers American politics (MA), including American politics, comparative/international politics. *Program availability:* Part-time. *Degree requirements:* For master's, thesis or alternative. Electronic applications accepted.

**Central Michigan University,** College of Graduate Studies, College of Humanities and Social and Behavioral Sciences, Department of Political Science, Program in Public Administration, Mount Pleasant, MI 48859. Offers professional development in public administration (Graduate Certificate); public administration (MPA); public management (MPA); state and local government (MPA). *Program availability:* Part-time. *Degree requirements:* For master's, thesis or alternative. Electronic applications accepted.

**The Citadel, The Military College of South Carolina,** Citadel Graduate College, School of Humanities and Social Sciences, Department of Political Science, Charleston, SC 29409. Offers international politics and military affairs (MA); social science (MA). *Program availability:* Part-time, evening/weekend, 100% online, blended/hybrid learning. *Faculty:* 5 full-time (1 woman). *Students:* 19 full-time (7 women), 22 part-time (14 women); includes 11 minority (9 Black or African American, non-Hispanic/Latino; 1 Hispanic/Latino; 1 Two or more races, non-Hispanic/Latino). 24 applicants, 79% accepted, 9 enrolled. In 2016, 6 master's awarded. *Entrance requirements:* For master's, GRE (minimum combined score of 290 verbal and quantitative), MAT (minimum raw score of 396), written statement of purpose setting forth intentions, goals, and preparation for graduate study; at least 2 academic letters of recommendation addressing ability to undertake coursework at graduate level. Additional exam requirements/recommendations for international students: Required—TOEFL (minimum score 550 paper-based; 79 iBT). *Application deadline:* Applications are processed on a rolling basis. Application fee: $40. Electronic applications accepted. *Expenses:* Tuition, state resident: full-time $5121; part-time $569 per credit hour. Tuition, nonresident: full-time $8613; part-time $957 per credit hour. *Required fees:* $90 per term. *Financial support:* Fellowships and unspecified assistantships available. Support available to part-time students. Financial award application deadline: 7/1; financial award applicants required to submit FAFSA. *Unit head:* Dr. DuBose Kapeluck, Department Head, 843-953-2037, E-mail: dubose.kapeluck@citadel.edu. *Application contact:* Dr. Terry Mays, Associate Professor, 843-953-5069, E-mail: terry.mays@citadel.edu.
Website: http://www.citadel.edu/root/politicalscience

**Claremont Graduate University,** Graduate Programs, School of Social Science, Policy and Evaluation, Department of Politics and Policy, Claremont, CA 91711-6160. Offers American politics (MA, PhD); comparative politics (PhD); international political economy (MA); international studies (MA); political philosophy (PhD); political science (PhD); politics, economics and business (MA); public policy (MA, PhD); world politics (PhD); MBA/PhD. *Program availability:* Part-time. *Faculty:* 6 full-time (4 women), 3 part-time/adjunct (0 women). *Students:* 107 full-time (37 women), 32 part-time (10 women); includes 41 minority (6 Black or African American, non-Hispanic/Latino; 10 Asian, non-Hispanic/Latino; 17 Hispanic/Latino; 8 Two or more races, non-Hispanic/Latino), 31 international. Average age 36. In 2016, 21 master's, 14 doctorates awarded. Terminal master's awarded for partial completion of doctoral program. *Entrance requirements:* For master's and doctorate, GRE General Test. Additional exam requirements/recommendations for international students: Required—TOEFL (minimum score 75 iBT). *Application deadline:* For fall admission, 2/1 priority date for domestic and international students. Applications are processed on a rolling basis. Application fee: $80. Electronic applications accepted. *Expenses:* Tuition: Full-time $44,328; part-time $1847 per unit. *Required fees:* $600; $300 per semester. Tuition and fees vary according to course load and program. *Financial support:* Fellowships, research assistantships, teaching assistantships, Federal Work-Study, institutionally sponsored loans, and scholarships/grants available. Support available to part-time students. Financial award application deadline: 2/15; financial award applicants required to submit FAFSA. *Faculty research:* Environmental policy, international debt, global democratization, Third World development, public sector discrimination. *Unit head:* Heather Campbell, Chair, 909-621-8689, E-mail: heather.campbell@cgu.edu. *Application contact:* Paige Piontkowsky, Senior Assistant Director of Admissions, 909-607-3240, E-mail: paige.piontkowsky@cgu.edu.
Website: https://www.cgu.edu/school/ssspe/programs/?areas_of_study=politics-and-government

**Claremont Graduate University,** Graduate Programs, School of Social Science, Policy and Evaluation, Program in Politics, Economics, and Business, Claremont, CA 91711-6160. Offers MA. *Program availability:* Part-time. *Students:* 2 full-time (1 woman), 1 part-time (0 women); includes 1 minority (Hispanic/Latino). Average age 31. In 2016, 3 master's awarded. *Entrance requirements:* For master's, GRE General Test. Additional exam requirements/recommendations for international students: Required—TOEFL (minimum score 75 iBT). *Application deadline:* For fall admission, 2/1 priority date for domestic and international students. Applications are processed on a rolling basis. Application fee: $80. Electronic applications accepted. *Expenses:* Tuition: Full-time $44,328; part-time $1847 per unit. *Required fees:* $600; $300 per semester. Tuition and fees vary according to course load and program. *Financial support:* Federal Work-Study, institutionally sponsored loans, and scholarships/grants available. Support available to part-time students. Financial award application deadline: 2/15; financial award applicants required to submit FAFSA. *Unit head:* Stewart Donaldson, Dean, 909-607-8235, E-mail: stewart.donaldson@cgu.edu. *Application contact:* Paige Piontkowsky, Senior Assistant Director of Admissions, 909-607-3240, E-mail: paige.piontkowsky@cgu.edu.
Website: https://www.cgu.edu/academics/program/politics-economics-and-business/

**Clark Atlanta University,** School of Arts and Sciences, Department of Political Science, Atlanta, GA 30314. Offers MA, PhD. *Program availability:* Part-time. *Faculty:* 5 full-time (1 woman), 2 part-time/adjunct (0 women). *Students:* 7 full-time (4 women), 28 part-time (17 women); includes 31 minority (all Black or African American, non-Hispanic/Latino). Average age 39. 8 applicants, 100% accepted, 6 enrolled. In 2016, 1 master's, 1 doctorate awarded. Terminal master's awarded for partial completion of doctoral program. *Degree requirements:* For master's, one foreign language, comprehensive exam, thesis; for doctorate, 2 foreign languages, comprehensive exam, thesis/dissertation. *Entrance requirements:* For master's, GRE General Test, minimum GPA of 2.5; for doctorate, GRE General Test, minimum graduate GPA of 3.0. Additional exam requirements/recommendations for international students: Required—TOEFL (minimum score 500 paper-based; 61 iBT). *Application deadline:* For fall admission, 4/1 for domestic and international students; for spring admission, 11/1 for domestic and international students. Applications are processed on a rolling basis. Application fee: $40 ($55 for international students). *Expenses:* Tuition: Full-time $15,498; part-time $861 per credit hour. *Required fees:* $1326; $1326 per credit hour. Tuition and fees vary according to course load. *Financial support:* Fellowships, scholarships/grants, and unspecified assistantships available. Financial award application deadline: 4/30; financial award applicants required to submit FAFSA. *Faculty research:* Public policy

and education, rural politics, women and state economic programs, reconstruction after war in Africa, environmental policies. *Unit head:* Dr. Henry Elonge, Chairperson, 404-880-6653, Fax: 404-880-8717, E-mail: helonge@cau.edu. *Application contact:* Graduate Program Admissions, 404-880-8483, E-mail: graduateadmissions@cau.edu.

**Clemson University,** Graduate School, College of Behavioral, Social and Health Sciences, Program in Public Administration, Clemson, SC 29634. Offers public administration (MPA, Certificate), including emergency management (MPA), homeland defense and security (MPA), local government (MPA), non-profit management (MPA), sustainable development (MPA). *Program availability:* Part-time, evening/weekend, online only, 100% online. *Faculty:* 4 full-time (2 women), 11 part-time/adjunct (5 women). *Students:* 8 full-time (5 women), 54 part-time (30 women); includes 16 minority (13 Black or African American, non-Hispanic/Latino; 2 Hispanic/Latino; 1 Two or more races, non-Hispanic/Latino). Average age 36. 25 applicants, 80% accepted, 18 enrolled. In 2016, 18 master's awarded. *Degree requirements:* For master's, comprehensive exam, thesis or alternative. *Entrance requirements:* For master's, GRE General Test, two letters of recommendation, unofficial transcripts, personal statement of purpose, documentation and explanation of related professional experience, resume. Additional exam requirements/recommendations for international students: Required—TOEFL (minimum score 80 iBT), IELTS (minimum score 6.5). *Application deadline:* For fall admission, 4/1 for domestic students, 3/1 for international students; for spring admission, 11/1 for domestic students, 10/1 for international students. Applications are processed on a rolling basis. Application fee: $80 ($90 for international students). Electronic applications accepted. *Expenses:* $4,264 per semester full-time resident, $8,485 per semester full-time non-resident, $695 per credit hour. *Faculty research:* Economic development, community vitality, entrepreneurship, broadband infrastructure, public health innovations and communities. *Total annual research expenditures:* $11,485. *Unit head:* Dr. Lori Dickes, Program Coordinator, 864-656-7831, E-mail: lorid@clemson.edu.
Website: https://www.clemson.edu/cbshs/departments/mpa/

**Colorado State University,** College of Liberal Arts, Department of Political Science, Fort Collins, CO 80523-1782. Offers environmental politics and policy (PhD); political science (MA). *Program availability:* Part-time. *Faculty:* 11 full-time (4 women). *Students:* 21 full-time (14 women), 13 part-time (8 women); includes 3 minority (2 Asian, non-Hispanic/Latino; 1 Hispanic/Latino), 1 international. Average age 29. 23 applicants, 52% accepted, 7 enrolled. In 2016, 7 master's awarded. Terminal master's awarded for partial completion of doctoral program. *Degree requirements:* For master's, variable foreign language requirement, comprehensive exam (for some programs), thesis or alternative; for doctorate, variable foreign language requirement, comprehensive exam, thesis/dissertation. *Entrance requirements:* For master's, GRE or LSAT, minimum GPA of 3.0; for doctorate, GRE General Test, minimum GPA of 3.5, master's or law degree. Additional exam requirements/recommendations for international students: Required—TOEFL (minimum score 600 paper-based), IELTS, TWE, PTE. *Application deadline:* For fall admission, 2/15 priority date for domestic and international students; for spring admission, 10/15 priority date for domestic students, 8/1 priority date for international students. Applications are processed on a rolling basis. Application fee: $60 ($70 for international students). Electronic applications accepted. *Expenses:* Tuition, state resident: full-time $9628. Tuition, nonresident: full-time $23,603. *Required fees:* $2253; $528.14 per credit hour. $264.07 per semester. Tuition and fees vary according to course load and program. *Financial support:* In 2016–17, 26 students received support, including 24 teaching assistantships with full tuition reimbursements available (averaging $16,294 per year). Financial award application deadline: 2/15. *Faculty research:* Environmental politics and policy, government and governance, state and local government, social justice and equity. *Total annual research expenditures:* $4,707. *Unit head:* Dr. Michele Betsill, Professor and Chair, 970-491-5157, E-mail: m.betsill@colostate.edu. *Application contact:* April Lindgren, Program Assistant, 970-491-5157, E-mail: april.lindgren@colostate.edu.
Website: http://polisci.colostate.edu/

**Columbia University,** Graduate School of Arts and Sciences, New York, NY 10027. Offers African-American studies (MA); American studies (MA); anthropology (MA, PhD); art history and archaeology (MA, PhD); astronomy (PhD); biological sciences (PhD); biotechnology (MA); chemical physics (PhD); chemistry (PhD); classical studies (MA, PhD); classics (MA, PhD); climate and society (MA); conservation biology (MA); earth and environmental sciences (PhD); East Asia: regional studies (MA); East Asian languages and cultures (MA, PhD); ecology, evolution and environmental biology (MA), including conservation biology; ecology, evolution, and environmental biology (PhD), including ecology and evolutionary biology, evolutionary primatology; economics (MA, PhD); English and comparative literature (MA, PhD); French and Romance philology (MA, PhD); Germanic languages (MA, PhD); global French studies (MA); global thought (MA); Hispanic cultural studies (MA); history (PhD); history and literature (MA); human rights studies (MA); Islamic studies (MA); Italian (MA, PhD); Japanese pedagogy (MA); Jewish studies (MA); Latin America and the Caribbean: regional studies (MA); Latin American and Iberian cultures (PhD); mathematics (MA, PhD), including finance (MA); medieval and Renaissance studies (MA); Middle Eastern, South Asian, and African studies (MA, PhD); modern art: critical and curatorial studies (MA); modern European studies (MA); museum anthropology (MA); music (DMA, PhD); oral history (MA); philosophical foundations of physics (MA); philosophy (MA, PhD); physics (PhD); political science (MA, PhD); psychology (PhD); quantitative methods in the social sciences (MA); religion (MA, PhD); Russia, Eurasia and East Europe: regional studies (MA); Russian translation (MA); Slavic cultures (MA); Slavic languages (MA, PhD); sociology (MA, PhD); South Asian studies (MA); statistics (MA, PhD); theatre (PhD). Dual-degree programs require admission to both Graduate School of Arts and Sciences and another Columbia school. *Program availability:* Part-time. Terminal master's awarded for partial completion of doctoral program. *Degree requirements:* For master's, variable foreign language requirement, comprehensive exam (for some programs), thesis (for some programs); for doctorate, variable foreign language requirement, comprehensive exam (for some programs), thesis/dissertation. *Entrance requirements:* For master's and doctorate, GRE General Test, GRE Subject Test (for some programs). Additional exam requirements/recommendations for international students: Required—TOEFL, IELTS. Electronic applications accepted.

**Columbus State University,** Graduate Studies, College of Letters and Sciences, Department of Political Science and Public Administration, Columbus, GA 31907-5645. Offers public administration (MPA), including criminal justice, environmental policy, government administration, health services administration, political campaigning, urban policy. *Program availability:* Part-time, evening/weekend, 100% online, blended/hybrid learning. *Faculty:* 5 full-time (0 women), 5 part-time/adjunct (0 women). *Students:* 38 full-time (22 women), 61 part-time (25 women); includes 52 minority (40 Black or African American, non-Hispanic/Latino; 2 American Indian or Alaska Native, non-Hispanic/Latino; 4 Asian, non-Hispanic/Latino; 4 Hispanic/Latino; 1 Native Hawaiian or other Pacific Islander, non-Hispanic/Latino; 1 Two or more races, non-Hispanic/Latino), 2 international. Average age 32. 69 applicants, 49% accepted, 27 enrolled. In 2016, 55 master's awarded. *Degree requirements:* For master's, comprehensive exam. *Entrance requirements:* For master's, GRE General Test, minimum GPA of 2.75, three letters of recommendation. Additional exam requirements/recommendations for international students: Required—TOEFL (minimum score 550 paper-based; 79 iBT). *Application*

*deadline:* For fall admission, 6/30 for domestic students, 5/1 for international students; for spring admission, 11/1 for domestic and international students; for summer admission, 3/1 for domestic and international students. Applications are processed on a rolling basis. Application fee: $50. Electronic applications accepted. *Expenses:* Tuition, state resident: full-time $4804; part-time $2412 per semester hour. Tuition, nonresident: full-time $19,218; part-time $9612 per semester hour. *Required fees:* $1850; $1850 per semester hour. Tuition and fees vary according to program. *Financial support:* In 2016–17, 5 students received support, including 11 research assistantships with partial tuition reimbursements available (averaging $3,000 per year); career-related internships or fieldwork, Federal Work-Study, institutionally sponsored loans, scholarships/grants, tuition waivers (partial), and unspecified assistantships also available. Support available to part-time students. Financial award application deadline: 5/1; financial award applicants required to submit FAFSA. *Unit head:* Dr. Frederick Gordon, Director, 706-565-7875, E-mail: gordon_frederick@colstate.edu. *Application contact:* Kristin Williams, Director of International and Graduate Recruitment, 706-507-8848, Fax: 706-568-5091, E-mail: williams_kristin@columbusstate.edu.
Website: http://politicalscience.columbusstate.edu/

**Concordia University,** School of Graduate Studies, Faculty of Arts and Science, Department of Political Science, Montréal, QC H3G 1M8, Canada. Offers political science (PhD); public policy and public administration (MA), including geography. *Degree requirements:* For master's, one foreign language, comprehensive exam, thesis optional, internship. *Entrance requirements:* For master's, honors degree or equivalent. Additional exam requirements/recommendations for international students: Required—TOEFL. *Faculty research:* International public policy and administration, Quebec public administration, public policy and social/political theory, geography and public policy, public administration and decision making.

**Converse College,** School of Education and Graduate Studies, Program in Liberal Arts, Spartanburg, SC 29302. Offers English (MLA); history (MLA); political science (MLA). *Degree requirements:* For master's, capstone paper. *Entrance requirements:* For master's, minimum GPA of 3.0, 2 recommendations. *Application deadline:* For fall admission, 5/1 priority date for domestic students; for spring admission, 1/30 for domestic students. Application fee: $40. *Expenses: Tuition:* Full-time $3600; part-time $400 per credit hour. *Required fees:* $70 per term. *Unit head:* Dr. Kathy Good, Dean of the School of Education and Graduate Studies, 864-596-9082, E-mail: kathy.good@converse.edu. *Application contact:* Dr. Thomas McDaniel, Director of Master of Liberal Arts Program, 864-596-9015, E-mail: tom.mcdaniel@converse.edu.

**Cornell University,** Graduate School, Graduate Fields of Arts and Sciences, Field of Government, Ithaca, NY 14853. Offers American politics (PhD); comparative politics (PhD); international relations (PhD); political methodology (PhD); political thought (PhD); public policy (PhD). *Degree requirements:* For doctorate, comprehensive exam, thesis/dissertation. *Entrance requirements:* For doctorate, GRE General Test, sample of written work, 3 letters of recommendation. Additional exam requirements/recommendations for international students: Required—TOEFL (minimum score 550 paper-based; 77 iBT). Electronic applications accepted. *Faculty research:* Political theory, American politics, comparative politics, international relations, methodology.

**Dalhousie University,** Faculty of Arts and Social Science, Department of Political Science, Halifax, NS B3H 4R2, Canada. Offers MA, PhD. *Entrance requirements:* Additional exam requirements/recommendations for international students: Required—TOEFL, IELTS, CANTEST, CAEL, or Michigan English Language Assessment Battery. Electronic applications accepted. *Faculty research:* Canadian political behavior and institutions, international politics, foreign policy, African politics, liberalism and modern political theory.

**Dominican University of California,** School of Arts, Humanities and Social Sciences, Humanities Program, San Rafael, CA 94901-2298. Offers applied music (MA); art history (MA); creative writing (MA); gender studies (MA); history (MA); literature (MA); philosophy (MA); political theory (MA); religion (MA). *Program availability:* Part-time. *Degree requirements:* For master's, thesis or alternative. *Entrance requirements:* For master's, minimum GPA of 3.0, interview. Additional exam requirements/recommendations for international students: Required—TOEFL (minimum score 550 paper-based; 80 iBT), IELTS (minimum score 6.5). Electronic applications accepted. Application fee is waived when completed online. *Expenses:* Contact institution.

**Duke University,** Graduate School, Department of Political Science, Durham, NC 27708. Offers AM, PhD, JD/AM. Terminal master's awarded for partial completion of doctoral program. *Degree requirements:* For doctorate, 2 foreign languages, thesis/dissertation. *Entrance requirements:* For master's and doctorate, GRE General Test. Additional exam requirements/recommendations for international students: Required—TOEFL (minimum score 577 paper-based; 90 iBT) or IELTS (minimum score 7). Electronic applications accepted.

**East Carolina University,** Graduate School, Thomas Harriot College of Arts and Sciences, Department of Political Science, Greenville, NC 27858-4353. Offers community health administration (Certificate); public administration (MPA); security studies (Certificate). *Accreditation:* NASPAA. *Program availability:* Part-time, evening/weekend. *Students:* 34 full-time (12 women), 92 part-time (35 women); includes 31 minority (17 Black or African American, non-Hispanic/Latino; 3 Asian, non-Hispanic/Latino; 8 Hispanic/Latino; 3 Two or more races, non-Hispanic/Latino), 2 international. Average age 33. 70 applicants, 91% accepted, 55 enrolled. In 2016, 16 master's awarded. *Degree requirements:* For master's, one foreign language, comprehensive exam. *Entrance requirements:* For master's, GRE General Test. Additional exam requirements/recommendations for international students: Required—TOEFL. *Application deadline:* For fall admission, 6/1 priority date for domestic students; for spring admission, 10/15 for domestic students. Applications are processed on a rolling basis. Application fee: $50. *Financial support:* Research assistantships with partial tuition reimbursements, teaching assistantships with partial tuition reimbursements, and Federal Work-Study available. Support available to part-time students. Financial award application deadline: 6/1. *Unit head:* Dr. Robert Thompson, Interim Chair, 252-328-5686, E-mail: thompsonro@ecu.edu. *Application contact:* Dean of Graduate School, 252-328-6012, Fax: 252-328-6071, E-mail: gradschool@ecu.edu.
Website: http://www.ecu.edu/polsci/mpa/index.html

**Eastern Illinois University,** Graduate School, College of Sciences, Department of Political Science, Charleston, IL 61920. Offers MA. *Program availability:* Part-time, evening/weekend. *Degree requirements:* For master's, comprehensive exam (for some programs), thesis (for some programs). *Entrance requirements:* For master's, GMAT or GRE. Additional exam requirements/recommendations for international students: Required—TOEFL (minimum score 500 paper-based; 61 iBT), IELTS (minimum score 6). Electronic applications accepted.

**Eastern Kentucky University,** The Graduate School, College of Arts and Sciences, Department of Government, Program in Political Science, Richmond, KY 40475-3102. Offers MA. *Entrance requirements:* For master's, GRE General Test, minimum GPA of 2.5.

**East Stroudsburg University of Pennsylvania,** Graduate and Extended Studies, College of Arts and Sciences, Department of Political Science and Economics, East Stroudsburg, PA 18301-2999. Offers management and leadership in public administration (MS); political science (MA). *Program availability:* Part-time, evening/weekend. *Students:* 15 full-time (6 women), 8 part-time (1 woman); includes 4 minority (3 Black or African American, non-Hispanic/Latino; 1 Hispanic/Latino), 3 international. *Degree requirements:* For master's, variable foreign language requirement, comprehensive exam, thesis or alternative. *Entrance requirements:* Additional exam requirements/recommendations for international students: Required—TOEFL (minimum score 560 paper-based; 83 iBT) or IELTS. *Application deadline:* For fall admission, 7/31 priority date for domestic students, 6/30 priority date for international students; for spring admission, 11/30 for domestic students, 10/31 for international students. Applications are processed on a rolling basis. Application fee: $50. Electronic applications accepted. *Expenses:* Tuition, state resident: full-time $8694; part-time $5796 per year. Tuition, nonresident: full-time $13,050; part-time $8700 per year. *Required fees:* $2550; $1690 per unit. $845 per semester. Tuition and fees vary according to course load, campus/location and program. *Financial support:* Research assistantships with tuition reimbursements, Federal Work-Study, and unspecified assistantships available. Support available to part-time students. Financial award application deadline: 3/1; financial award applicants required to submit FAFSA. *Unit head:* Samuel Quainoo, Chair, 570-422-3275, Fax: 570-422-3506. *Application contact:* Kevin Quintero, Associate Director, Graduate and Extended Studies, 570-422-3890, Fax: 570-422-2711, E-mail: kquintero@esu.edu.
Website: http://www.esu.edu/academics/departments/polisci-econ/index.cfm

**East Tennessee State University,** School of Graduate Studies, College of Arts and Sciences, Department of Political Science, International Affairs and Public Administration, Johnson City, TN 37614. Offers economic development (Postbaccalaureate Certificate); not-for-profit administration (MPA); planning and development (MPA); public financial management (MPA); urban planning (Postbaccalaureate Certificate). *Program availability:* Part-time. *Degree requirements:* For master's, internship. *Entrance requirements:* For master's, GRE General Test, three letters of recommendation; for Postbaccalaureate Certificate, GRE General Test. Additional exam requirements/recommendations for international students: Required—TOEFL (minimum score 550 paper-based; 79 iBT). Electronic applications accepted. *Faculty research:* Labor issues, presidency, public law in American politics, East Asian politics, European politics, Middle Eastern politics, development in comparative politics, international political economy, international relations, world politics in international affairs.

**Edinboro University of Pennsylvania,** Department of History, Politics, Languages and Cultures, Edinboro, PA 16444. Offers social sciences (MA), including anthropology, history. *Program availability:* Part-time, evening/weekend. *Degree requirements:* For master's, thesis or alternative, competency exam. *Entrance requirements:* For master's, GRE or MAT, minimum QPA of 2.5. Electronic applications accepted.

**Emory University,** Laney Graduate School, Department of Political Science, Atlanta, GA 30322-1100. Offers PhD. *Degree requirements:* For doctorate, comprehensive exam, thesis/dissertation. *Entrance requirements:* For doctorate, GRE General Test, minimum GPA of 3.0. Additional exam requirements/recommendations for international students: Required—TOEFL. Electronic applications accepted. *Faculty research:* Post-Soviet politics, comparative politics, international politics, judicial politics and methodology, American national political institutions.

**Fairleigh Dickinson University, Metropolitan Campus,** University College: Arts, Sciences, and Professional Studies, School of History, Political and International Studies, Program in Political Science, Teaneck, NJ 07666-1914. Offers MA.

**Florida Agricultural and Mechanical University,** Division of Graduate Studies, Research, and Continuing Education, College of Social Sciences, Arts and Humanities, Department of History and Political Science, Program in Applied Social Science, Tallahassee, FL 32307-3200. Offers criminal justice (MASS); history (MASS); political science (MASS); public administration (MASS). *Program availability:* Part-time. *Degree requirements:* For master's, thesis optional. *Entrance requirements:* For master's, GRE General Test, minimum GPA of 3.0. *Faculty research:* Southern history, black history, election trends, Presidential history.

**Florida Atlantic University,** Dorothy F. Schmidt College of Arts and Letters, Department of Political Science, Boca Raton, FL 33431-0991. Offers MA. *Program availability:* Part-time. *Faculty:* 15 full-time (3 women). *Students:* 14 full-time (6 women), 11 part-time (2 women); includes 10 minority (2 Black or African American, non-Hispanic/Latino; 1 Asian, non-Hispanic/Latino; 7 Hispanic/Latino). Average age 30. 28 applicants, 64% accepted, 13 enrolled. In 2016, 11 master's awarded. *Degree requirements:* For master's, one foreign language, thesis or alternative. *Entrance requirements:* For master's, GRE General Test, minimum GPA of 3.0 during last 60 hours of course work. Additional exam requirements/recommendations for international students: Required—TOEFL (minimum score 500 paper-based; 61 iBT), IELTS (minimum score 6). *Application deadline:* For fall admission, 7/1 for domestic students, 2/15 for international students; for spring admission, 11/1 for domestic students, 7/15 for international students. Applications are processed on a rolling basis. Application fee: $30. Electronic applications accepted. *Expenses:* Tuition, state resident: full-time $7392; part-time $369.82 per credit hour. Tuition, nonresident: full-time $19,432; part-time $1024.81 per credit hour. *Financial support:* Research assistantships, teaching assistantships with partial tuition reimbursements, career-related internships or fieldwork, Federal Work-Study, and institutionally sponsored loans available. Support available to part-time students. Financial award application deadline: 4/16. *Faculty research:* Public policy, comparative policy affecting women, Congress, international system, urban policy. *Unit head:* Dr. Kevin K. Wagner, 561-297-3218, E-mail: kwagne15@fau.edu.
Website: http://www.fau.edu/politicalscience/

**Florida International University,** Steven J. Green School of International and Public Affairs, Department of Politics and International Relations, Miami, FL 33199. Offers international relations (MA, PhD), including international relations (PhD), international studies (MA); political science (MA, PhD). Ph D program has fall admissions only. *Program availability:* Part-time, evening/weekend. *Faculty:* 30 full-time (12 women), 24 part-time/adjunct (5 women). *Students:* 158 full-time (85 women), 40 part-time (10 women); includes 100 minority (13 Black or African American, non-Hispanic/Latino; 5 Asian, non-Hispanic/Latino; 78 Hispanic/Latino; 4 Two or more races, non-Hispanic/Latino), 47 international. Average age 29. 187 applicants, 57% accepted, 73 enrolled. In 2016, 47 master's, 5 doctorates awarded. *Degree requirements:* For master's, one foreign language, thesis optional; for doctorate, one foreign language, comprehensive exam, thesis/dissertation. *Entrance requirements:* For master's and doctorate, GRE General Test, minimum GPA of 3.0, letters of recommendation. Additional exam requirements/recommendations for international students: Required—TOEFL (minimum score 550 paper-based; 80 iBT). *Application deadline:* For fall admission, 3/15 for domestic and international students; for spring admission, 8/15 for domestic and international students. Application fee: $30. Electronic applications accepted. *Expenses:* Tuition, state resident: full-time $8912; part-time $446 per credit hour. Tuition, nonresident: full-time $21,393; part-time $992 per credit hour. *Required fees:* $2185; $195 per semester. Tuition and fees vary according to program. *Financial support:* Institutionally sponsored loans, scholarships/grants, and unspecified assistantships available. Financial award application deadline: 3/1; financial award applicants required

to submit FAFSA. *Unit head:* Dr. John Clark, Chair, 305-348-2227, Fax: 305-348-3765, E-mail: john.clark@fiu.edu. *Application contact:* Nanett Rojas, Manager, Admissions Operations, 305-348-7464, E-mail: nanett.rojas@fiu.edu.
Website: http://pir.fiu.edu

**Florida State University,** The Graduate School, College of Social Sciences and Public Policy, Department of Political Science, Tallahassee, FL 32306-2230. Offers applied American politics and policy (MA, MS); political science (PhD). *Program availability:* Part-time. *Faculty:* 22 full-time (5 women), 1 part-time/adjunct (0 women). *Students:* 58 full-time (26 women), 26 part-time (11 women); includes 20 minority (4 Black or African American, non-Hispanic/Latino; 2 Asian, non-Hispanic/Latino; 4 Hispanic/Latino; 10 Two or more races, non-Hispanic/Latino). Average age 25. 77 applicants, 58% accepted, 29 enrolled. In 2016, 24 master's, 5 doctorates awarded. Terminal master's awarded for partial completion of doctoral program. *Degree requirements:* For master's, thesis optional; for doctorate, comprehensive exam, thesis/dissertation. *Entrance requirements:* For master's, GRE General Test, minimum undergraduate GPA of 3.0; for doctorate, GRE General Test, minimum graduate GPA of 3.5, undergraduate 3.0. Additional exam requirements/recommendations for international students: Required—TOEFL (minimum score 600 paper-based; 100 iBT). *Application deadline:* For fall admission, 1/15 priority date for domestic and international students. Applications are processed on a rolling basis. Application fee: $30. Electronic applications accepted. *Expenses:* Tuition, state resident: full-time $7263; part-time $403.51 per credit hour. Tuition, nonresident: full-time $18,087; part-time $1004.85 per credit hour. *Required fees:* $1365; $75.81 per credit hour. $20 per semester. Tuition and fees vary according to campus/location. *Financial support:* In 2016–17, 38 students received support, including 2 fellowships with full tuition reimbursements available (averaging $20,000 per year), 32 research assistantships with full tuition reimbursements available (averaging $17,000 per year), 4 teaching assistantships with full tuition reimbursements available (averaging $17,000 per year), Federal Work-Study, institutionally sponsored loans, scholarships/grants, and unspecified assistantships also available. Financial award application deadline: 1/15; financial award applicants required to submit FAFSA. *Faculty research:* American government, international relations, comparative government, public policy. *Total annual research expenditures:* $130,000. *Unit head:* Dr. Mark Souva, Director of Graduate Studies, 850-644-7315, Fax: 850-644-1367, E-mail: msouva@fsu.edu. *Application contact:* Jeremiah J. Fisher, Academic Coordinator, 850-644-7305, Fax: 850-644-1367, E-mail: jeremiah.fisher@fsu.edu.
Website: http://coss.fsu.edu/polisci/

**Fordham University,** Graduate School of Arts and Sciences, Program in Elections and Campaign Management, New York, NY 10458. Offers MA. *Students:* 5 full-time (3 women), 7 part-time (2 women); includes 1 minority (Black or African American, non-Hispanic/Latino), 3 international. Average age 29. 37 applicants, 49% accepted, 7 enrolled. In 2016, 13 master's awarded. Application fee: $70. *Unit head:* Dr. Costas Panagopoulos, Director, 718-817-3967, E-mail: campaigns@fordham.edu. *Application contact:* Bernadette Valentino-Morrison, Director of Graduate Admissions, 718-817-4419, Fax: 718-817-3566, E-mail: valentinomor@fordham.edu.
Website: http://www.fordham.edu/academics/programs_at_fordham_/elections__campaign_/

**George Mason University,** Schar School of Policy and Government, Program in Political Science, Arlington, VA 22201. Offers MA, PhD. *Faculty:* 20 full-time (6 women), 5 part-time/adjunct (1 woman). *Students:* 32 full-time (15 women), 36 part-time (15 women); includes 13 minority (4 Black or African American, non-Hispanic/Latino; 1 Asian, non-Hispanic/Latino; 6 Hispanic/Latino; 2 Two or more races, non-Hispanic/Latino), 6 international. Average age 32. 74 applicants, 46% accepted, 13 enrolled. In 2016, 21 master's, 5 doctorates awarded. *Entrance requirements:* For master's, GRE (taken in the past five years), transcripts from all previous institutions attended in the U.S.; goals statement; two letters of recommendation; current resume; writing sample; for doctorate, GRE (taken in the past five years), official transcript from all colleges and universities attended; current resume; three letters of recommendation; statement of professional goals; writing sample (approximately 10-25 pages in length). Additional exam requirements/recommendations for international students: Required—TOEFL (minimum score 575 paper-based; 88 iBT), IELTS (minimum score 6.5), PTE (minimum score 59). Application fee: $75 ($80 for international students). Electronic applications accepted. *Expenses:* Tuition, state resident: full-time $10,628; part-time $443 per credit. Tuition, nonresident: full-time $29,306; part-time $1221 per credit. *Required fees:* $3096; $129 per credit. Tuition and fees vary according to program. *Financial support:* In 2016–17, 18 students received support, including 3 fellowships (averaging $7,636 per year), 3 research assistantships with tuition reimbursements available (averaging $21,000 per year), 14 teaching assistantships with tuition reimbursements available (averaging $16,446 per year); career-related internships or fieldwork, Federal Work-Study, scholarships/grants, unspecified assistantships, and health care benefits (for full-time research or teaching assistantship recipients) also available. Support available to part-time students. Financial award applicants required to submit FAFSA. *Unit head:* Ming Wan, Director, 703-993-2955, Fax: 703-993-1399, E-mail: mwan@gmu.edu. *Application contact:* Stephanie Ellis, Graduate Admissions Coordinator, 703-993-4478, E-mail: sellis11@gmu.edu.
Website: http://spgia.gmu.edu/programs/graduate-degrees/ma-in-political-science/

**Georgetown University,** Graduate School of Arts and Sciences, Department of Government, Program in Democracy and Governance, Washington, DC 20057. Offers MA.

**Georgetown University,** Graduate School of Arts and Sciences, School of Continuing Studies, Washington, DC 20057. Offers American studies (MALS); Catholic studies (MALS); classical civilizations (MALS); emergency and disaster management (MPS); ethics and the professions (MALS); global strategic communications (MPS); hospitality management (MPS); human resources management (MPS); humanities (MALS); individualized study (MALS); integrated marketing communications (MPS); international affairs (MALS); Islam and Muslim-Christian relations (MALS); journalism (MPS); liberal studies (DLS); literature and society (MALS); medieval and early modern European studies (MALS); public relations and corporate communications (MPS); real estate (MPS); religious studies (MALS); social and public policy (MALS); sports industry management (MPS); systems engineering management (MPS); technology management (MPS); the theory and practice of American democracy (MALS); urban and regional planning (MPS); visual culture (MALS). MPS in systems engineering management offered jointly with Stevens Institute of Technology. *Entrance requirements:* Additional exam requirements/recommendations for international students: Required—TOEFL.

**The George Washington University,** College of Professional Studies, Graduate School of Political Management, Program in Legislative Affairs, Washington, DC 20052. Offers MPS. *Program availability:* Part-time, evening/weekend. *Students:* 32 full-time (8 women), 39 part-time (17 women); includes 14 minority (6 Black or African American, non-Hispanic/Latino; 1 Asian, non-Hispanic/Latino; 6 Hispanic/Latino; 1 Native Hawaiian or other Pacific Islander, non-Hispanic/Latino), 3 international. Average age 31. 51 applicants, 98% accepted, 39 enrolled. In 2016, 60 master's awarded. *Degree requirements:* For master's, comprehensive exam. *Entrance requirements:* For master's, GRE General Test, minimum GPA of 3.0. Additional exam requirements/

recommendations for international students: Required—TOEFL (minimum score 550 paper-based). *Application deadline:* For fall admission, 4/1 priority date for domestic and international students; for spring admission, 10/1 priority date for domestic and international students. Applications are processed on a rolling basis. Application fee: $75. Electronic applications accepted. *Financial support:* Application deadline: 2/1. *Unit head:* Dr. Steven E. Billet, Director, 202-994-6000, E-mail: sbillet@gwu.edu. *Application contact:* Information Contact, 202-994-6000, Fax: 202-994-6006, E-mail: gspmmail@gwu.edu.
Website: http://www.gwu.edu/~gspm/academics/mala.shtml

**The George Washington University,** Columbian College of Arts and Sciences, Department of Political Science, Washington, DC 20052. Offers legal institutions and theory (MA); political science (MA). *Program availability:* Part-time, evening/weekend. *Faculty:* 29 full-time (9 women). *Students:* 34 full-time (10 women), 50 part-time (22 women); includes 13 minority (2 Black or African American, non-Hispanic/Latino; 5 Asian, non-Hispanic/Latino; 5 Hispanic/Latino; 1 Two or more races, non-Hispanic/Latino), 19 international. Average age 31. 317 applicants, 15% accepted, 13 enrolled. In 2016, 12 master's, 12 doctorates awarded. Terminal master's awarded for partial completion of doctoral program. *Degree requirements:* For master's, one foreign language, comprehensive exam, thesis or alternative; for doctorate, 2 foreign languages, thesis/dissertation, general exam. *Entrance requirements:* For master's and doctorate, GRE General Test, minimum GPA of 3.0. Additional exam requirements/recommendations for international students: Required—TOEFL (minimum score 550 paper-based; 80 iBT). *Application deadline:* For fall admission, 1/15 priority date for domestic students; for spring admission, 10/1 priority date for domestic students. Applications are processed on a rolling basis. Application fee: $75. Electronic applications accepted. *Financial support:* In 2016–17, 43 students received support. Fellowships with tuition reimbursements available, teaching assistantships with tuition reimbursements available, Federal Work-Study, and tuition waivers available. *Unit head:* Christopher J. Deering, Chair, 202-994-6564, E-mail: rocket@gwu.edu. *Application contact:* 202-994-6210, Fax: 202-994-6213, E-mail: askccas@gwu.edu.
Website: http://politicalscience.columbian.gwu.edu/

**The George Washington University,** Elliott School of International Affairs, Program in Security Policy Studies, Washington, DC 20052. Offers MA. *Program availability:* Part-time. *Students:* 99 full-time (44 women), 60 part-time (23 women); includes 50 minority (8 Black or African American, non-Hispanic/Latino; 14 Asian, non-Hispanic/Latino; 16 Hispanic/Latino; 12 Two or more races, non-Hispanic/Latino), 7 international. Average age 27. 293 applicants, 76% accepted, 74 enrolled. In 2016, 43 master's awarded. *Degree requirements:* For master's, one foreign language, capstone project. *Entrance requirements:* For master's, GRE General Test, 2 semesters of introductory economics, 2 years of a modern foreign language or 1 semester of statistics. Additional exam requirements/recommendations for international students: Required—TOEFL (minimum score 100 iBT), IELTS (minimum score 7). *Application deadline:* For fall admission, 1/15 priority date for domestic and international students; for spring admission, 10/1 priority date for domestic and international students. Application fee: $75. Electronic applications accepted. *Financial support:* In 2016–17, 22 students received support. Fellowships with partial tuition reimbursements available, Federal Work-Study, and scholarships/grants available. Financial award application deadline: 1/15; financial award applicants required to submit FAFSA. *Faculty research:* U.S. arms transfer policies, military balance in the Third World, U.S. foreign policy, technology and security policy. *Unit head:* Joanna Spear, Director, 202-994-7003, E-mail: security@gwu.edu. *Application contact:* Nicole A. Campbell, Director of Graduate Admissions, 202-994-7050, Fax: 202-994-9537, E-mail: esiagrad@gwu.edu.
Website: http://elliott.gwu.edu/academics/graduate/sps

**Georgia State University,** College of Arts and Sciences, Department of Communication, Atlanta, GA 30302-3083. Offers film, video, and digital imaging (MA), including critical studies, production, screenwriting; human communication and social influence (MA); mass communication (MA); media and society (PhD); moving image studies (PhD); public communication (PhD); rhetoric and politics (PhD). *Program availability:* Part-time. *Faculty:* 57 full-time (34 women). *Students:* 113 full-time (69 women), 56 part-time (33 women); includes 59 minority (37 Black or African American, non-Hispanic/Latino; 1 American Indian or Alaska Native, non-Hispanic/Latino; 2 Asian, non-Hispanic/Latino; 9 Hispanic/Latino; 10 Two or more races, non-Hispanic/Latino), 18 international. Average age 32. 134 applicants, 58% accepted, 47 enrolled. In 2016, 22 master's, 11 doctorates awarded. *Degree requirements:* For master's, variable foreign language requirement, thesis (for some programs); for doctorate, comprehensive exam, thesis/dissertation. *Entrance requirements:* For master's and doctorate, GRE. Additional exam requirements/recommendations for international students: Required—TOEFL (minimum score 550 paper-based; 80 iBT), IELTS (minimum score 6.5). *Application deadline:* For fall admission, 2/10 for domestic and international students; for spring admission, 10/15 for domestic and international students. Application fee: $50. Electronic applications accepted. *Expenses:* Tuition, state resident: full-time $6876; part-time $382 per credit hour. Tuition, nonresident: full-time $22,374; part-time $1243 per credit hour. *Required fees:* $2128; $1064 per term. Part-time tuition and fees vary according to course load and program. *Financial support:* In 2016–17, fellowships with tuition reimbursements (averaging $15,000 per year), teaching assistantships with tuition reimbursements (averaging $15,000 per year) were awarded; career-related internships or fieldwork and unspecified assistantships also available. Financial award applicants required to submit FAFSA. *Faculty research:* New media, mass media and journalism, rhetoric, film and media studies, film production. *Unit head:* Dr. Greg Lisby, Chair, 404-413-5639, Fax: 404-413-5634, E-mail: glisby@gsu.edu.
Website: http://communication.gsu.edu

**Georgia State University,** College of Arts and Sciences, Department of Political Science, Atlanta, GA 30302-3083. Offers MA, PhD. *Program availability:* Part-time, evening/weekend. *Faculty:* 26 full-time (8 women). *Students:* 65 full-time (32 women), 14 part-time (6 women); includes 18 minority (11 Black or African American, non-Hispanic/Latino; 3 Asian, non-Hispanic/Latino; 3 Hispanic/Latino; 1 Two or more races, non-Hispanic/Latino), 20 international. Average age 32. 68 applicants, 82% accepted, 31 enrolled. In 2016, 21 master's, 3 doctorates awarded. Terminal master's awarded for partial completion of doctoral program. *Degree requirements:* For master's, thesis (for some programs); for doctorate, one foreign language, comprehensive exam, thesis/dissertation. *Entrance requirements:* For master's and doctorate, GRE. Additional exam requirements/recommendations for international students: Required—TOEFL (minimum score 550 paper-based; 80 iBT) or IELTS (minimum score 6.5). *Application deadline:* For fall admission, 2/1 priority date for domestic and international students; for spring admission, 10/15 for domestic and international students. Applications are processed on a rolling basis. Application fee: $50. Electronic applications accepted. *Expenses:* Tuition, state resident: full-time $6876; part-time $382 per credit hour. Tuition, nonresident: full-time $22,374; part-time $1243 per credit hour. *Required fees:* $2128; $1064 per term. Part-time tuition and fees vary according to course load and program. *Financial support:* In 2016–17, fellowships with full tuition reimbursements (averaging $19,000 per year), research assistantships with full tuition reimbursements (averaging $14,000 per year), teaching assistantships with full tuition reimbursements (averaging $4,000 per year) were awarded; career-related internships or fieldwork and health care benefits also available. Financial award application deadline: 2/1; financial award applicants required to submit FAFSA. *Faculty research:* Political behavior and attitudes, judicial politics and policymaking, comparative democratization, international governance, national and international political institutions and structures. *Unit head:* Dr. Carrie Manning, Chair, 404-413-6162, Fax: 404-413-6156, E-mail: cmanning2@gsu.edu. *Application contact:* Dr. Amy Steigerwalt, Director of Graduate Studies, 404-413-6162, Fax: 404-413-6156, E-mail: asteigerwalt@gsu.edu. Website: http://politicalscience.gsu.edu/home/graduate/degree-requirements/

**Georgia State University,** College of Education and Human Development, Department of Middle and Secondary Education, Atlanta, GA 30302-3083. Offers curriculum and instruction (Ed D); English education (MAT); mathematics education (M Ed, MAT); middle level education (MAT); reading, language and literacy education (M Ed, MAT), including reading instruction (M Ed); science education (M Ed, MAT), including biology (MAT), broad field science (MAT), chemistry (MAT), earth science (MAT), physics (MAT); social studies education (M Ed, MAT), including economics (MAT), geography (MAT), history (MAT), political science (MAT); teaching and learning (PhD), including language and literacy, mathematics education, music education, science education, social studies education, teaching and teacher education. *Accreditation:* NCATE. *Program availability:* Part-time, evening/weekend, online learning. *Faculty:* 24 full-time (18 women). *Students:* 145 full-time (91 women), 151 part-time (102 women); includes 141 minority (104 Black or African American, non-Hispanic/Latino; 1 American Indian or Alaska Native, non-Hispanic/Latino; 16 Asian, non-Hispanic/Latino; 12 Hispanic/Latino; 8 Two or more races, non-Hispanic/Latino), 10 international. Average age 36. 115 applicants, 50% accepted, 41 enrolled. In 2016, 94 master's, 22 doctorates awarded. *Degree requirements:* For master's, comprehensive exam (for some programs), thesis or alternative, exit portfolio; for doctorate, comprehensive exam, thesis/dissertation. *Entrance requirements:* For master's, GRE; GACE I (for initial teacher preparation programs), baccalaureate degree or equivalent, resume, goals statement, two letters of recommendation, minimum undergraduate GPA of 2.5; proof of initial teacher certification in the content area (for M Ed); for doctorate, GRE, resume, goals statement, writing sample, two letters of recommendation, minimum graduate GPA of 3.3, interview. Additional exam requirements/recommendations for international students: Required—TOEFL (minimum score 550 paper-based; 79 iBT) or IELTS (minimum score 6.5). *Application deadline:* For fall admission, 1/15 priority date for domestic and international students; for spring admission, 10/1 for domestic and international students. Application fee: $50. Electronic applications accepted. *Expenses:* Tuition, state resident: full-time $6876; part-time $382 per credit hour. Tuition, nonresident: full-time $22,374; part-time $1243 per credit hour. *Required fees:* $2128; $1064 per term. Part-time tuition and fees vary according to course load and program. *Financial support:* In 2016–17, fellowships with full tuition reimbursements (averaging $19,667 per year), research assistantships with full tuition reimbursements (averaging $5,436 per year), teaching assistantships with full tuition reimbursements (averaging $2,779 per year) were awarded; career-related internships or fieldwork, Federal Work-Study, scholarships/grants, health care benefits, tuition waivers (full and partial), and unspecified assistantships also available. Financial award application deadline: 3/15. *Faculty research:* Teacher education in language and literacy, mathematics, science, and social studies in urban middle and secondary school settings; learning technologies in school, community, and corporate settings; multicultural education and education for social justice; urban education; international education. *Unit head:* Dr. Dana L. Fox, Chair, 404-413-8060, Fax: 404-413-8063, E-mail: dfox@gsu.edu. *Application contact:* Bobbie Turner, Administrative Coordinator I, 404-413-8405, Fax: 404-413-8063, E-mail: bnturner@gsu.edu. Website: http://mse.education.gsu.edu/

**Governors State University,** College of Arts and Sciences, Program in Political and Justice Studies, University Park, IL 60484. Offers MA. *Program availability:* Part-time. *Faculty:* 91 full-time (43 women), 125 part-time/adjunct (64 women). *Students:* 6 full-time (4 women), 21 part-time (11 women); includes 16 minority (all Black or African American, non-Hispanic/Latino), 1 international. Average age 37. 29 applicants, 66% accepted, 16 enrolled. In 2016, 13 master's awarded. *Entrance requirements:* Additional exam requirements/recommendations for international students: Required—TOEFL (minimum score 550 paper-based; 80 iBT), IELTS. *Application deadline:* For fall admission, 4/1 for domestic students. Application fee: $50. Electronic applications accepted. *Expenses:* $307 per credit hour; $38 per term or $76 per credit hour fees. *Financial support:* Application deadline: 5/1; applicants required to submit FAFSA. *Unit head:* Lori Montalbano, Chair, Division of Humanities and Social Science, 708-235-2802, E-mail: lmontalbano@govst.edu. *Application contact:* Yakeea Daniels, Assistant Vice President for Enrollment Services/Director of Admission, 708-534-4510, E-mail: ydaniels@govst.edu.

**The Graduate Center, City University of New York,** Graduate Studies, Program in Political Science, New York, NY 10016-4039. Offers MA, PhD. Terminal master's awarded for partial completion of doctoral program. *Degree requirements:* For master's, one foreign language, thesis; for doctorate, one foreign language, thesis/dissertation. *Entrance requirements:* For master's and doctorate, GRE General Test. Additional exam requirements/recommendations for international students: Required—TOEFL. Electronic applications accepted.

**Grambling State University,** School of Graduate Studies and Research, College of Arts and Sciences, Department of Political Science and Public Administration, Grambling, LA 71270. Offers health services administration (MPA); human resource management (MPA); public management (MPA); state and local government (MPA). *Accreditation:* NASPAA. *Program availability:* Part-time. *Degree requirements:* For master's, comprehensive exam (for some programs), thesis optional. *Entrance requirements:* For master's, GRE, minimum GPA of 2.75 on last degree. Additional exam requirements/recommendations for international students: Required—TOEFL (minimum score 500 paper-based; 62 iBT). Electronic applications accepted.

**Harvard University,** Graduate School of Arts and Sciences, Committee on Political Economy and Government, Cambridge, MA 02138. Offers PhD. *Entrance requirements:* For doctorate, GRE General Test or GMAT. Additional exam requirements/recommendations for international students: Required—TOEFL.

**Harvard University,** Graduate School of Arts and Sciences, Department of Government, Cambridge, MA 02138. Offers political science (PhD), including American politics, comparative politics, international relations, political thought, quantitative methods. *Degree requirements:* For doctorate, one foreign language, thesis/dissertation, general exams. *Entrance requirements:* For doctorate, GRE General Test. Additional exam requirements/recommendations for international students: Required—TOEFL.

**Harvard University,** John F. Kennedy School of Government, Cambridge, MA 02138. Offers MPA, MPAID, MPP, PhD, JD/MPP, MBA/MPP, MD/MPP. *Students:* 927 full-time (512 women), 6 part-time (2 women); includes 159 minority (34 Black or African American, non-Hispanic/Latino; 1 American Indian or Alaska Native, non-Hispanic/Latino; 69 Asian, non-Hispanic/Latino; 37 Hispanic/Latino; 1 Native Hawaiian or other Pacific Islander, non-Hispanic/Latino; 17 Two or more races, non-Hispanic/Latino), 430 international. Average age 31. 2,722 applicants, 33% accepted, 628 enrolled. In 2016, 540 master's awarded. *Degree requirements:* For master's, thesis/dissertation. *Entrance requirements:* For master's, GMAT or GRE General Test; for doctorate, GRE General Test. Additional exam requirements/recommendations for international

students: Required—TOEFL (minimum score 600 paper-based; 100 iBT), TWE. *Application deadline:* For fall admission, 12/1 for domestic students. Application fee: $100. Electronic applications accepted. *Financial support:* Fellowships, research assistantships, teaching assistantships, career-related internships or fieldwork, Federal Work-Study, institutionally sponsored loans, scholarships/grants, and unspecified assistantships available. Support available to part-time students. Financial award application deadline: 2/24; financial award applicants required to submit CSS PROFILE or FAFSA. *Unit head:* Douglas W. Elmendorf, Dean, 617-495-1122. *Application contact:* 617-495-1155, Fax: 617-496-1165, E-mail: hks_admissions@harvard.edu. Website: http://www.hks.harvard.edu/

**Hillsdale College,** Van Andel Graduate School of Statesmanship, Hillsdale, MI 49242. Offers politics (MA, PhD). *Entrance requirements:* For master's and doctorate, GRE. Additional exam requirements/recommendations for international students: Required—TOEFL. *Application deadline:* For fall admission, 12/15 priority date for domestic and international students; for spring admission, 10/15 priority date for domestic and international students. Electronic applications accepted. *Expenses: Tuition:* Full-time $23,420; part-time $1280 per credit hour. *Unit head:* Dr. Ronald J. Pestritto, Dean, 517-607-2483, E-mail: gradschool@hillsdale.edu. Website: http://gradschool.hillsdale.edu

**Howard University,** Graduate School, Department of Political Science, Program in Political Science, Washington, DC 20059-0002. Offers MA, PhD. *Degree requirements:* For master's, comprehensive exam. *Entrance requirements:* For master's, GRE General Test, minimum GPA of 3.0; for doctorate, GRE General Test, minimum GPA of 2.8.

**Idaho State University,** Office of Graduate Studies, College of Arts and Letters, Department of Political Science, Pocatello, ID 83209-8073. Offers political science (MA, DA); public administration (MPA). *Program availability:* Part-time. *Degree requirements:* For master's, comprehensive exam, thesis optional; for doctorate, comprehensive exam, thesis/dissertation, teaching internship. *Entrance requirements:* For master's, GRE General Test, minimum GPA of 3.0 in last 2 years of undergraduate study, 3 letters of recommendation; for doctorate, GRE General Test, major field of American politics, minimum GPA of 3.0 in last 2 years of undergraduate study, 3 letters of recommendation. Additional exam requirements/recommendations for international students: Required—TOEFL (minimum score 550 paper-based; 80 iBT). Electronic applications accepted. *Faculty research:* International affairs, environmental policy, decision making, Constitution, executive/legislative relations.

**Illinois State University,** Graduate School, College of Arts and Sciences, Department of Politics and Government, Normal, IL 61790-2200. Offers MA, MS. *Degree requirements:* For master's, thesis or alternative. *Entrance requirements:* For master's, GRE General Test, minimum GPA of 3.0 in last 60 hours of course work, 15 hours of course work in political science. *Faculty research:* Political tolerance in a democracy under external threats: a survey of public opinion.

**Indiana University Bloomington,** University Graduate School, College of Arts and Sciences, Department of Political Science, Bloomington, IN 47405-7000. Offers MA, PhD. Terminal master's awarded for partial completion of doctoral program. *Degree requirements:* For master's, thesis, 30 credit hours; for doctorate, comprehensive exam, thesis/dissertation. *Entrance requirements:* For master's, GRE, personal statement, transcripts, 3 letters of recommendation; for doctorate, GRE, sample of written work, 3 letters of recommendation, personal statement. Additional exam requirements/recommendations for international students: Required—TOEFL (minimum score 640 paper-based; 112 iBT). Electronic applications accepted. *Faculty research:* American politics, international relations, public policy, political theory, comparative politics, theory and methodology.

**Indiana University–Purdue University Indianapolis,** School of Liberal Arts, Department of Political Science, Indianapolis, IN 46202. Offers MA, Certificate.

**Institute for Christian Studies,** Graduate Programs, Toronto, ON M5T 1R4, Canada. Offers education (M Phil F, PhD); history of philosophy (M Phil F, PhD); philosophical aesthetics (M Phil F, PhD); philosophy of religion (M Phil F, PhD); political theory (M Phil F, PhD); systematic philosophy (M Phil F, PhD); theology (M Phil F, PhD); worldview studies (MWS). *Program availability:* Part-time, online learning. *Degree requirements:* For master's, one foreign language, thesis; for doctorate, 2 foreign languages, thesis/dissertation. *Entrance requirements:* For master's and doctorate, philosophy background. Additional exam requirements/recommendations for international students: Required—TOEFL (minimum score 600 paper-based). *Faculty research:* Human rights, anthropology of self, medieval discourse, gender and body, post-modern thought; biblical hermeneutics, creational aesthetics, ecumenism, epistemology, political theory and public policy, relational psychotherapy.

**The Institute of World Politics,** Graduate Programs in National Security, Intelligence, and International Affairs, Washington, DC 20036. Offers American foreign policy (Certificate); comparative political culture (Certificate); counterintelligence (Certificate); democracy building (Certificate); intelligence (Certificate); international politics (Certificate); national security affairs (Certificate); public diplomacy and political warfare (Certificate); statecraft and national security affairs (MA); statecraft and world politics (MA); strategic intelligence studies (MA). *Program availability:* Part-time, evening/weekend. *Degree requirements:* For master's, comprehensive exam, thesis optional. *Entrance requirements:* For master's, GRE General Test. Additional exam requirements/recommendations for international students: Required—TOEFL. Electronic applications accepted. *Faculty research:* Intelligence, national security, statecraft.

**Iowa State University of Science and Technology,** Department of Political Science, Ames, IA 50011. Offers political science (MA); public administration (MPA); JD/MA. JD/MA offered jointly with Drake University. *Degree requirements:* For master's, thesis (for some programs). *Entrance requirements:* For master's, GRE General Test, GMAT or LSAT. Additional exam requirements/recommendations for international students: Required—TOEFL (minimum score 570 paper-based; 80 iBT), IELTS (minimum score 6.5). *Application deadline:* For fall admission, 1/1 priority date for domestic and international students; for spring admission, 10/1 for domestic and international students. Application fee: $60 ($90 for international students). Electronic applications accepted. *Application contact:* Alex Tuckness, Application Contact, 515-294-8910, Fax: 515-294-1003, E-mail: tuckness@iastate.edu. Website: http://www.pols.iastate.edu

**Jackson State University,** Graduate School, College of Liberal Arts, Department of Political Science, Jackson, MS 39217. Offers MA. *Program availability:* Part-time, evening/weekend. *Degree requirements:* For master's, comprehensive exam, thesis or alternative. *Entrance requirements:* For master's, GRE General Test. Additional exam requirements/recommendations for international students: Required—TOEFL (minimum score 520 paper-based; 67 iBT). *Application deadline:* For fall admission, 3/1 priority date for domestic students, 3/1 for international students; for spring admission, 10/1 for domestic and international students. Applications are processed on a rolling basis. Application fee: $25. *Expenses:* Tuition, state resident: full-time $7141. Tuition, nonresident: full-time $17,494. *Required fees:* $1080. Tuition and fees vary according to class time, course level, course load, degree level, campus/location, program and student level. *Financial support:* Career-related internships or fieldwork, Federal Work-Study, scholarships/grants, and unspecified assistantships available. Support available

## Political Science

to part-time students. Financial award application deadline: 3/1; financial award applicants required to submit FAFSA. *Unit head:* Dr. Rickey Hill, Chair, 601-979-2822, Fax: 601-979-2904, E-mail: rickey.hill@jsums.edu. *Application contact:* Fatoumatta Sisay, Manager of Graduate Admissions, 601-979-0342, Fax: 601-979-4325, E-mail: fatoumatta.sisay@jsums.edu. Website: http://www.jsums.edu/polisci/

**Jacksonville State University,** College of Graduate Studies and Continuing Education, College of Arts and Sciences, Department of Political Science, Jacksonville, AL 36265-1602. Offers MPA. *Program availability:* Part-time, evening/weekend. *Faculty:* 7 full-time (1 woman). *Students:* 18 full-time (8 women), 45 part-time (27 women); includes 11 minority (all Black or African American, non-Hispanic/Latino), 5 international. Average age 31. 44 applicants, 59% accepted, 22 enrolled. In 2016, 13 master's awarded. *Degree requirements:* For master's, comprehensive exam, thesis (for some programs). *Entrance requirements:* For master's, GRE General Test or MAT. Additional exam requirements/recommendations for international students: Required—TOEFL (minimum score 61 iBT). *Application deadline:* Applications are processed on a rolling basis. Application fee: $35. Electronic applications accepted. *Financial support:* In 2016–17, 19 students received support. Available to part-time students. Application deadline: 4/1; applicants required to submit FAFSA. *Unit head:* Dr. Paul Hathaway, Head, 256-782-5652, E-mail: phathaway@jsu.edu. *Application contact:* Dr. Jean Pugliese, Associate Dean, 256-782-8278, Fax: 256-782-5321, E-mail: pugliese@jsu.edu.

**James Madison University,** The Graduate School, College of Arts and Letters, Program in Political Science, Harrisonburg, VA 22807. Offers political science (MA), including European Union policy studies. *Students:* 10 full-time (8 women); includes 4 minority (1 Black or African American, non-Hispanic/Latino; 1 Asian, non-Hispanic/Latino; 2 Hispanic/Latino). Average age 30. 19 applicants, 100% accepted, 12 enrolled. In 2016, 14 master's awarded. Application fee: $55. Electronic applications accepted. *Financial support:* Application deadline: 3/1; applicants required to submit FAFSA. *Unit head:* Dr. Charles Blake, Academic Unit Head, 540-568-6344, Fax: 540-568-8021, E-mail: blakech@jmu.edu. *Application contact:* Lynette D. Michael, Director of Graduate Admissions, 540-568-6131 Ext. 6395, Fax: 540-568-7860, E-mail: michaeld@jmu.edu. Website: http://www.jmu.edu/eeurounionpolicy.shtml

**Johns Hopkins University,** Zanvyl Krieger School of Arts and Sciences, Advanced Academic Programs, Program in Government, Washington, DC 20036. Offers global security studies (MA); government (MA); national securities study (Certificate); nonprofit management (Certificate); public management (MA); research administration (MS); MA/MBA. *Program availability:* Part-time, evening/weekend, online learning. *Degree requirements:* For master's, thesis. *Entrance requirements:* For master's, minimum GPA of 3.0. Additional exam requirements/recommendations for international students: Required—TOEFL (minimum score 100 iBT). Electronic applications accepted.

**Johns Hopkins University,** Zanvyl Krieger School of Arts and Sciences, Department of Political Science, Baltimore, MD 21218. Offers MA, PhD. *Degree requirements:* For doctorate, one foreign language, comprehensive exam, thesis/dissertation. *Entrance requirements:* For doctorate, GRE General Test. Additional exam requirements/recommendations for international students: Required—TOEFL (minimum score 600 paper-based; 100 iBT), IELTS. Electronic applications accepted. *Faculty research:* American politics, comparative politics, international relations, political theory, urban politics.

**Kansas State University,** Graduate School, College of Arts and Sciences, Department of Political Science, Manhattan, KS 66506. Offers political science (MA), including political science; public administration (MPA). *Program availability:* Part-time. *Faculty:* 18 full-time (5 women). *Students:* 6 full-time (2 women), 4 part-time (1 woman); includes 1 minority (Black or African American, non-Hispanic/Latino), 1 international. Average age 35. 6 applicants, 67% accepted, 2 enrolled. In 2016, 1 master's awarded. *Degree requirements:* For master's, comprehensive exam, thesis or alternative. *Entrance requirements:* For master's, GRE (recommended), minimum GPA of 3.0. Additional exam requirements/recommendations for international students: Required—TOEFL (minimum score 550 paper-based; 79 iBT); Recommended—IELTS (minimum score 6.5), TSE (minimum score 58). *Application deadline:* For fall admission, 2/1 priority date for domestic and international students; for spring admission, 8/1 priority date for domestic and international students. Applications are processed on a rolling basis. Application fee: $50 ($75 for international students). Electronic applications accepted. *Expenses:* Tuition, state resident: full-time $9670. Tuition, nonresident: full-time $21,828. *Required fees:* $862. *Financial support:* In 2016–17, 14 students received support, including 9 teaching assistantships with tuition reimbursements available (averaging $14,000 per year); fellowships, research assistantships, career-related internships or fieldwork, Federal Work-Study, institutionally sponsored loans, and scholarships/grants also available. Support available to part-time students. Financial award application deadline: 3/1; financial award applicants required to submit FAFSA. *Faculty research:* Armed conflict, civil military relations, comparative public administration and policy, electoral competition, legislative studies. *Unit head:* Dr. Jeff Pickering, Head, 785-532-0454, Fax: 785-532-2339, E-mail: jjp@ksu.edu. *Application contact:* Dr. James Franke, Director, 785-532-0451, Fax: 785-532-2339, E-mail: jfranke@ksu.edu. Website: http://www.k-state.edu/polsci/

**Kaplan University, Davenport Campus,** School of Legal Studies, Davenport, IA 52807. Offers health care delivery (MS); pathway to paralegal (Postbaccalaureate Certificate); state and local government (MS). *Program availability:* Part-time, evening/weekend, online learning. *Entrance requirements:* Additional exam requirements/recommendations for international students: Required—TOEFL (minimum score 550 paper-based; 80 iBT).

**Kent State University,** College of Arts and Sciences, Department of Political Science, Kent, OH 44242-0001. Offers political science (MA, PhD), including American politics and policy, conflict analysis and management, transnational and comparative politics and policy; public administration (MPA). *Program availability:* Part-time, online learning. *Faculty:* 18 full-time (5 women). *Students:* 34 full-time (14 women), 62 part-time (31 women); includes 12 minority (5 Black or African American, non-Hispanic/Latino; 1 American Indian or Alaska Native, non-Hispanic/Latino; 2 Asian, non-Hispanic/Latino; 2 Hispanic/Latino; 2 Two or more races, non-Hispanic/Latino), 9 international. Average age 30. 65 applicants, 57% accepted, 21 enrolled. In 2016, 20 master's, 1 doctorate awarded. *Degree requirements:* For master's, thesis (for some programs); for doctorate, comprehensive exam, thesis/dissertation. *Entrance requirements:* For master's and doctorate, GRE, statement of purpose, transcripts, writing sample, 3 letters of recommendation. *Application deadline:* For fall admission, 1/31 for domestic and international students. Applications are processed on a rolling basis. Application fee: $45 ($70 for international students). Electronic applications accepted. *Expenses:* Tuition, state resident: full-time $10,864; part-time $495 per credit hour. Tuition, nonresident: full-time $18,380; part-time $837 per credit hour. *Financial support:* Research assistantships with full tuition reimbursements, teaching assistantships with full tuition reimbursements, health care benefits, and unspecified assistantships available. Financial award application deadline: 1/31. *Unit head:* Dr. Andrew Barnes, Associate Professor and Chair, 330-672-2060, E-mail: abarnes3@kent.edu. *Application contact:* Dr. Ryan L. Claassen, Graduate Coordinator, 330-672-2060, E-mail: rclaasse@kent.edu. Website: http://www.kent.edu/polisci

**Lamar University,** College of Graduate Studies, College of Arts and Sciences, Department of Political Science, Beaumont, TX 77710. Offers public administration (MPA). *Program availability:* Part-time. *Faculty:* 3 full-time (2 women). *Students:* 5 full-time (1 woman), 9 part-time (4 women); includes 9 minority (8 Black or African American, non-Hispanic/Latino; 1 Hispanic/Latino), 3 international. Average age 31. 8 applicants, 100% accepted, 5 enrolled. In 2016, 5 master's awarded. *Entrance requirements:* For master's, GRE General Test. Additional exam requirements/recommendations for international students: Required—TOEFL (minimum score 550 paper-based; 79 iBT), IELTS (minimum score 6.5). *Application deadline:* For fall admission, 8/10 for domestic students, 7/1 for international students; for spring admission, 1/5 for domestic students, 12/1 for international students. Applications are processed on a rolling basis. Application fee: $25 ($50 for international students). Electronic applications accepted. *Expenses:* $8,134 in-state full-time, $5,574 in-state part-time; $15,604 out-of-state full-time, $10,554 out-of-state part-time per year. *Financial support:* Fellowships, research assistantships, teaching assistantships, career-related internships or fieldwork, Federal Work-Study, and institutionally sponsored loans available. Financial award application deadline: 4/1; financial award applicants required to submit FAFSA. *Faculty research:* Political activities of administrators, administrative response to Hurricane Rita, budgeting, environmental politics, urban planning. *Unit head:* Dr. Terri Davis, Chair, 409-880-8285, Fax: 409-880-8710. *Application contact:* Deidre Mayer, Interim Director, Admissions and Academic Services, 409-880-8888, Fax: 409-880-7419, E-mail: gradmissions@lamar.edu. Website: http://artssciences.lamar.edu/political-science

**Lehigh University,** College of Arts and Sciences, Department of Political Science, Bethlehem, PA 18015. Offers politics and policy (MA), including political theory. *Program availability:* Part-time. *Faculty:* 14 full-time (7 women). *Students:* 9 full-time (6 women), 1 (woman) part-time; includes 4 minority (1 Black or African American, non-Hispanic/Latino; 2 Asian, non-Hispanic/Latino; 1 Hispanic/Latino), 3 international. Average age 26. 14 applicants, 79% accepted, 5 enrolled. In 2016, 11 master's awarded. *Degree requirements:* For master's, thesis optional, extended paper. *Entrance requirements:* Additional exam requirements/recommendations for international students: Required—TOEFL. *Application deadline:* For fall admission, 6/1 for domestic and international students. Application fee: $75. Electronic applications accepted. *Expenses:* $1,420 per credit. *Financial support:* In 2016–17, 6 students received support, including 2 teaching assistantships with full tuition reimbursements available; career-related internships or fieldwork and tuition waivers (partial) also available. Financial award application deadline: 3/15. *Faculty research:* American politics and institutions, comparative politics, public policy, political theory. *Unit head:* Dr. Saladin Ambar, Chairman, 610-758-3338, Fax: 610-758-3348, E-mail: sma409@lehigh.edu. *Application contact:* Dr. Janet Laible, Director, Graduate Studies, 610-758-5879, Fax: 610-758-3348, E-mail: jml6@lehigh.edu. Website: http://polisci.cas2.lehigh.edu/

**Long Island University–LIU Brooklyn,** Richard L. Conolly College of Liberal Arts and Sciences, Brooklyn, NY 11201-8423. Offers biology (MS); chemistry (MS); clinical psychology (PhD); communication sciences and disorders (MS); creative writing (MFA); English (MA); media arts (MA, MFA); political science (MA); psychology (MA); social science (MS); sociology (MA); speech-language pathology (MS); United Nations (Advanced Certificate); urban studies (MA); writing and production for television (MFA). *Program availability:* Part-time, evening/weekend. *Faculty:* 90 full-time (35 women), 125 part-time/adjunct (67 women). *Students:* 355 full-time (276 women), 220 part-time (161 women); includes 245 minority (119 Black or African American, non-Hispanic/Latino; 32 Asian, non-Hispanic/Latino; 80 Hispanic/Latino; 1 Native Hawaiian or other Pacific Islander, non-Hispanic/Latino; 13 Two or more races, non-Hispanic/Latino), 85 international. 792 applicants, 41% accepted, 141 enrolled. In 2016, 154 master's, 18 doctorates, 4 other advanced degrees awarded. *Degree requirements:* For master's, comprehensive exam (for some programs), thesis (for some programs); for doctorate, comprehensive exam (for some programs), thesis/dissertation (for some programs). *Entrance requirements:* For master's and doctorate, GRE. Additional exam requirements/recommendations for international students: Recommended—TOEFL (minimum score 550 paper-based; 79 iBT). *Application deadline:* Applications are processed on a rolling basis. Application fee: $50. Electronic applications accepted. *Expenses: Tuition:* Full-time $28,272; part-time $1178 per credit. *Required fees:* $451 per term. Tuition and fees vary according to degree level, program and student level. *Financial support:* In 2016–17, 120 fellowships with full and partial tuition reimbursements (averaging $915 per year), 5 research assistantships with full and partial tuition reimbursements (averaging $2,300 per year), 136 teaching assistantships with full and partial tuition reimbursements (averaging $2,300 per year) were awarded; career-related internships or fieldwork, Federal Work-Study, institutionally sponsored loans, scholarships/grants, tuition waivers (full and partial), and unspecified assistantships also available. Support available to part-time students. Financial award application deadline: 2/15; financial award applicants required to submit FAFSA. *Faculty research:* Nanocrystal polymerization of cellulose using electron microscopy. *Unit head:* Dr. Kevin Lauth, Acting Dean, 718-488-1347, E-mail: kevin.lauth@liu.edu. *Application contact:* Gabrielle Gannon, Director of Graduate Admissions, 718-488-1011, Fax: 718-780-6110, E-mail: bkln-admissions@liu.edu.

**Long Island University–LIU Post,** College of Liberal Arts and Sciences, Brookville, NY 11548-1300. Offers applied mathematics (MS); behavior analysis (MA); biology (MS); criminal justice (MS); earth science (MS); English (MA); environmental sustainability (MS); genetic counseling (MS); history (MA); interdisciplinary studies (MA, MS); mathematics for secondary school teachers (MS); mobile GIS application development (Advanced Certificate); political science (MA); psychology (MA). *Program availability:* Part-time, evening/weekend, blended/hybrid learning. *Faculty:* 68 full-time (30 women), 20 part-time/adjunct (13 women). *Students:* 155 full-time (117 women), 125 part-time (82 women); includes 65 minority (17 Black or African American, non-Hispanic/Latino; 14 Asian, non-Hispanic/Latino; 27 Hispanic/Latino; 7 Two or more races, non-Hispanic/Latino), 19 international. 485 applicants, 36% accepted, 77 enrolled. In 2016, 91 master's, 15 other advanced degrees awarded. *Degree requirements:* For master's, comprehensive exam (for some programs), thesis (for some programs). *Entrance requirements:* Additional exam requirements/recommendations for international students: Required—PTE, TOEFL (minimum score 550 paper-based, 75 iBT) or IELTS (6.5). *Application deadline:* Applications are processed on a rolling basis. Application fee: $50. Electronic applications accepted. *Expenses: Tuition:* Full-time $28,272; part-time $1178 per credit. *Required fees:* $451 per term. Tuition and fees vary according to degree level and program. *Financial support:* In 2016–17, 24 teaching assistantships with partial tuition reimbursements (averaging $410 per year) were awarded; fellowships, research assistantships, career-related internships or fieldwork, Federal Work-Study, institutionally sponsored loans, scholarships/grants, tuition waivers (partial), and unspecified assistantships also available. Support available to part-time students. Financial award application deadline: 2/15; financial award applicants required to submit FAFSA. *Faculty research:* Biology, criminal justice, environmental sustainability, mathematics, psychology. *Total annual research expenditures:* $218,000. *Unit head:* Dr. Jeffrey Belnap, Acting Dean, 516-299-2233, Fax: 516-299-4140, E-mail: jeffrey.belnap@liu.edu. *Application contact:* Carol Zerah, Director of Graduate

Admissions, 516-299-2900, Fax: 516-299-2137, E-mail: post-enroll@liu.edu. Website: http://liu.edu/CWPost/Academics/Schools/CLAS

**Louisiana State University and Agricultural & Mechanical College,** Graduate School, College of Humanities and Social Sciences, Department of Political Science, Baton Rouge, LA 70803. Offers MA, PhD.

**Loyola University Chicago,** Graduate School, Department of Political Science, Chicago, IL 60611. Offers MA, PhD. *Program availability:* Part-time, evening/weekend. *Faculty:* 19 full-time (5 women). *Students:* 21 full-time (10 women), 3 part-time (1 woman); includes 1 minority (Black or African American, non-Hispanic/Latino), 6 international. Average age 30. 40 applicants, 43% accepted, 6 enrolled. In 2016, 6 master's, 2 doctorates awarded. Terminal master's awarded for partial completion of doctoral program. *Degree requirements:* For master's, comprehensive exam, thesis or alternative; for doctorate, comprehensive exam, thesis/dissertation. *Entrance requirements:* For master's and doctorate, GRE General Test. Additional exam requirements/recommendations for international students: Required—TOEFL (minimum score 550 paper-based; 79 iBT). *Application deadline:* For fall admission, 6/1 for domestic and international students; for spring admission, 10/1 for domestic and international students. Applications are processed on a rolling basis. Application fee: $0. Electronic applications accepted. *Expenses:* Tuition: Full-time $18,594. *Required fees:* $848. Part-time tuition and fees vary according to course load, degree level and program. *Financial support:* In 2016–17, 9 students received support, including 9 fellowships with full tuition reimbursements available (averaging $18,000 per year), 9 research assistantships with full tuition reimbursements available (averaging $18,000 per year); Federal Work-Study, institutionally sponsored loans, scholarships/grants, tuition waivers (full and partial), and unspecified assistantships also available. Financial award application deadline: 2/15. *Faculty research:* American elections, parties and political institutions; comparative politics; foreign policy analysis; international relations theory; modern and contemporary political thought. *Unit head:* Prof. Peter Sanchez, Graduate Program Director, 773-508-8658, Fax: 773-508-3131, E-mail: psanche@luc.edu. *Application contact:* Ron Martin, Assistant Director of Enrollment Management, 312-915-8950, Fax: 312-915-8905, E-mail: gradapp@luc.edu. Website: http://www.luc.edu/politicalscience/

**Marquette University,** Graduate School, College of Arts and Sciences, Department of Political Science, Milwaukee, WI 53201-1881. Offers international affairs (MA); political science (MA); public service (MA); JD/MA; MA/MBA. *Program availability:* Part-time. *Faculty:* 17 full-time (7 women), 6 part-time/adjunct (2 women). *Students:* 22 full-time (11 women), 5 part-time (3 women); includes 4 minority (3 Hispanic/Latino; 1 Two or more races, non-Hispanic/Latino). Average age 26. 32 applicants, 78% accepted, 27 enrolled. In 2016, 16 master's awarded. *Degree requirements:* For master's, comprehensive exam, thesis optional. *Entrance requirements:* For master's, GRE General Test, official transcripts from all current and previous colleges/universities except Marquette, three letters of recommendation, statement of purpose. Additional exam requirements/recommendations for international students: Required—TOEFL (minimum score 530 paper-based). *Application deadline:* For fall admission, 2/15 for domestic and international students. Application fee: $50. Electronic applications accepted. *Financial support:* Fellowships with partial tuition reimbursements, research assistantships with full tuition reimbursements, scholarships/grants, health care benefits, tuition waivers (full and partial), and unspecified assistantships available. Support available to part-time students. Financial award application deadline: 2/15. *Faculty research:* Public opinion and electoral behavior, public policy analysis, Congress and the Presidency, judicial behavior, political system transitions. *Total annual research expenditures:* $617. *Unit head:* Dr. Lowell Barrington, Chair, 414-288-5234. *Application contact:* Dr. Julia Azari. Website: http://www.marquette.edu/polisci/grad.shtml

**Marshall University,** Academic Affairs Division, College of Liberal Arts, Department of Political Science, Huntington, WV 25755. Offers MA, MPA. *Degree requirements:* For master's, thesis optional. *Entrance requirements:* For master's, GRE General Test.

**Massachusetts Institute of Technology,** School of Humanities, Arts, and Social Sciences, Department of Political Science, Cambridge, MA 02139. Offers SM, PhD. *Faculty:* 28 full-time (8 women), 1 (woman) part-time/adjunct. *Students:* 64 full-time (28 women); includes 6 minority (2 Asian, non-Hispanic/Latino; 1 Hispanic/Latino; 3 Two or more races, non-Hispanic/Latino), 29 international. Average age 29. 412 applicants, 7% accepted, 9 enrolled. In 2016, 3 master's, 5 doctorates awarded. Terminal master's awarded for partial completion of doctoral program. *Degree requirements:* For master's, thesis, minimum GPA of 3.5 in all subjects; for doctorate, one foreign language, comprehensive exam, thesis/dissertation. *Entrance requirements:* For master's and doctorate, GRE General Test. Additional exam requirements/recommendations for international students: Required—TOEFL, IELTS. *Application deadline:* For fall admission, 12/15 for domestic and international students. Application fee: $75. Electronic applications accepted. *Expenses:* Tuition: Full-time $46,400; part-time $725 per credit. One-time fee: $312 full-time. Full-time tuition and fees vary according to course load and program. *Financial support:* In 2016–17, 61 students received support, including 20 fellowships (averaging $38,600 per year), 25 research assistantships (averaging $39,600 per year), 11 teaching assistantships (averaging $40,300 per year); Federal Work-Study, institutionally sponsored loans, scholarships/grants, traineeships, health care benefits, unspecified assistantships, and resident tutors also available. Support available to part-time students. Financial award application deadline: 5/1; financial award applicants required to submit FAFSA. *Faculty research:* International relations, security studies, American politics, comparative politics, political economy, models and methods. *Total annual research expenditures:* $1.9 million. *Unit head:* Prof. Andrea Campbell, Department Head, 617-253-5262, Fax: 617-258-6164, E-mail: politicalscience@mit.edu. *Application contact:* 617-253-8336, E-mail: twarog@mit.edu. Website: http://web.mit.edu/polisci/

**McGill University,** Faculty of Graduate and Postdoctoral Studies, Faculty of Arts, Department of Political Science, Montréal, QC H3A 2T5, Canada. Offers MA, PhD.

**McMaster University,** School of Graduate Studies, Faculty of Social Sciences, Department of Political Science, Hamilton, ON L8S 4M2, Canada. Offers international relations (PhD); political science (MA); public and the global economy (MA); public policy (PhD); public policy and administration (MA). MA program in public policy and administration offered jointly with University of Guelph. *Program availability:* Part-time. *Degree requirements:* For master's, thesis or alternative. *Entrance requirements:* For master's, minimum B+ average. Additional exam requirements/recommendations for international students: Required—TOEFL (minimum score 580 paper-based). *Faculty research:* Organizational theory, internationalization of public policy, water resource policies, political interest intermediation, comparative politics.

**Memorial University of Newfoundland,** School of Graduate Studies, Department of Political Science, St. John's, NL A1C 5S7, Canada. Offers MA. *Program availability:* Part-time, evening/weekend. *Degree requirements:* For master's, thesis optional. *Entrance requirements:* For master's, minimum 2nd class bachelor's degree. Electronic applications accepted. *Faculty research:* Comparative politics, Canadian government and politics, Newfoundland politics, and the politics of multi-level systems.

**Miami University,** College of Arts and Science, Department of Political Science, Oxford, OH 45056. Offers MA. *Students:* 10 full-time (6 women); includes 1 minority (Black or African American, non-Hispanic/Latino), 2 international. Average age 27. In 2016, 5 master's awarded. *Expenses:* Tuition, state resident: full-time $12,890; part-time $564 per credit hour. Tuition, nonresident: full-time $29,604; part-time $1260 per credit hour. *Required fees:* $638. Part-time tuition and fees vary according to course load and program. *Unit head:* Dr. Patrick Haney, Interim Chair, 513-529-4321, E-mail: haneypk@miamioh.edu. *Application contact:* Dr. Brian Dannoff, Associate Professor and Graduate Studies Director, 513-529-0160, E-mail: danoffbf@miamioh.edu. Website: http://miamioh.edu/cas/academics/departments/political-science/academics/graduate-studies/

**Michigan State University,** The Graduate School, College of Social Science, Department of Political Science, East Lansing, MI 48824. Offers political science (MA, PhD); public policy (MPP). *Degree requirements:* For master's, practicum; for doctorate, comprehensive exam, presentation of dissertation. *Entrance requirements:* Additional exam requirements/recommendations for international students: Required—TOEFL. Electronic applications accepted.

**Middle Tennessee State University,** College of Graduate Studies, College of Liberal Arts, Department of Political Science, Murfreesboro, TN 37132. Offers international affairs (MA). *Program availability:* Part-time, evening/weekend, online learning. *Entrance requirements:* Additional exam requirements/recommendations for international students: Required—TOEFL (minimum score 525 paper-based; 71 iBT) or IELTS (minimum score 6). Electronic applications accepted.

**Midwestern State University,** Billie Doris McAda Graduate School, Prothro-Yeager College of Humanities and Social Sciences, Department of Political Science, Wichita Falls, TX 76308. Offers MA. *Degree requirements:* For master's, one foreign language, comprehensive exam, thesis optional. *Entrance requirements:* For master's, GRE General Test/GMAT/MAT, bachelor's degree from regionally-accredited institution, minimum GPA of 3.0 on last 60 hours of undergraduate work. Additional exam requirements/recommendations for international students: Required—TOEFL (minimum score 550 paper-based). Electronic applications accepted. *Faculty research:* American politics, political behavior, political research methods, conflict processes, Latin American politics.

**Mississippi College,** Graduate School, College of Arts and Sciences, School of Humanities and Social Sciences, Department of History, Political Science, Administration of Justice, and Paralegal Studies, Clinton, MS 39058. Offers administration of justice (MSS); history (M Ed, MA, MSS); paralegal studies (Certificate); political science (MSS); social sciences (M Ed, MSS). *Program availability:* Part-time. *Degree requirements:* For master's, one foreign language, comprehensive exam, thesis (for some programs). *Entrance requirements:* For master's, GRE or NTE, minimum GPA of 2.5. Additional exam requirements/recommendations for international students: Recommended—TOEFL, IELTS. Electronic applications accepted.

**Mississippi State University,** College of Arts and Sciences, Department of Political Science and Public Administration, Mississippi State, MS 39762. Offers political science (MA); public policy and administration (MPPA, PhD). *Accreditation:* NASPAA (one or more programs are accredited). *Program availability:* Evening/weekend, blended/hybrid learning. *Faculty:* 14 full-time (4 women), 1 part-time/adjunct (0 women). *Students:* 34 full-time (18 women), 35 part-time (18 women); includes 26 minority (22 Black or African American, non-Hispanic/Latino; 1 American Indian or Alaska Native, non-Hispanic/Latino; 3 Hispanic/Latino), 4 international. Average age 31. 33 applicants, 61% accepted, 18 enrolled. In 2016, 22 master's, 7 doctorates awarded. *Degree requirements:* For master's, thesis, optional, comprehensive oral or written exam; for doctorate, thesis/dissertation, comprehensive oral and written exam. *Entrance requirements:* For master's, GRE, minimum GPA of 3.0 on the last two years of undergraduate courses or graduate work; for doctorate, GRE General Test, minimum graduate GPA of 3.35. Additional exam requirements/recommendations for international students: Required—TOEFL (minimum score 600 paper-based; 100 iBT); Recommended—IELTS (minimum score 7.5). *Application deadline:* For fall admission, 8/1 priority date for domestic students, 5/1 for international students; for spring admission, 12/1 priority date for domestic students, 9/1 for international students. Applications are processed on a rolling basis. Application fee: $60. Electronic applications accepted. *Expenses:* Tuition, state resident: full-time $7670; part-time $852.50 per credit hour. Tuition, nonresident: full-time $20,790; part-time $2310.50 per credit hour. Part-time tuition and fees vary according to course load. *Financial support:* In 2016–17, 6 research assistantships with full tuition reimbursements (averaging $9,085 per year), 2 teaching assistantships with full tuition reimbursements (averaging $8,920 per year) were awarded; Federal Work-Study, institutionally sponsored loans, scholarships/grants, and unspecified assistantships also available. Financial award application deadline: 4/1; financial award applicants required to submit FAFSA. *Faculty research:* American politics, international relations, state and local government, comparative government, public administration. *Total annual research expenditures:* $977,000. *Unit head:* Dr. P. Edward French, Interim Department Head, 662-325-2711, Fax: 662-325-2716, E-mail: efrench@pspa.msstate.edu. *Application contact:* Nathan Drake, Admissions and Enrollment Assistant, 662-325-3804, E-mail: ndrake@grad.msstate.edu. Website: http://www.pspa.msstate.edu/

**Missouri State University,** Graduate College, College of Humanities and Public Affairs, Department of Political Science, Springfield, MO 65897. Offers global studies (MGS); public administration (MPA); public management (Certificate). *Program availability:* Part-time. *Faculty:* 14 full-time (2 women). *Students:* 24 full-time (9 women), 13 part-time (7 women); includes 1 minority (Two or more races, non-Hispanic/Latino), 10 international. Average age 28. 29 applicants, 59% accepted, 9 enrolled. In 2016, 16 master's awarded. *Degree requirements:* For master's, variable foreign language requirement, comprehensive exam, thesis or alternative. *Entrance requirements:* For master's, GRE, minimum GPA of 3.0. Additional exam requirements/recommendations for international students: Required—TOEFL (minimum score 550 paper-based; 79 iBT), IELTS (minimum score 6). *Application deadline:* For fall admission, 7/20 priority date for domestic students, 5/1 for international students; for spring admission, 12/20 priority date for domestic students, 9/1 for international students. Applications are processed on a rolling basis. Application fee: $35 ($50 for international students). Electronic applications accepted. *Expenses:* Tuition, state resident: full-time $5830. Tuition, nonresident: full-time $10,708. *Required fees:* $1130. Tuition and fees vary according to class time, course level, course load and program. *Financial support:* Career-related internships or fieldwork, Federal Work-Study, scholarships/grants, and unspecified assistantships available. Support available to part-time students. Financial award application deadline: 3/31; financial award applicants required to submit FAFSA. *Faculty research:* Public procurement; Missouri politics; international relations of East Asia, law of church and state. *Unit head:* Dr. George Connor, Department Head, 417-836-5630, Fax: 417-836-6655, E-mail: georgeconnor@missouristate.edu. *Application contact:* Michael Edwards, Coordinator of Graduate Admissions, 417-836-5330, Fax: 417-836-6200, E-mail: michaeledwards@missouristate.edu. Website: http://polsci.missouristate.edu

*Political Science*

**Montclair State University,** The Graduate School, College of Humanities and Social Sciences, MA Program in Law and Governance, Montclair, NJ 07043-1624. Offers conflict management and peace studies (MA); governance, compliance and regulation (MA); intellectual property (MA); law and governance (MA); legal management (MA). *Program availability:* Part-time, evening/weekend. *Degree requirements:* For master's, thesis or comprehensive exam. *Entrance requirements:* For master's, GRE General Test, minimum cumulative GPA of 2.75 for undergraduate work, 2 letters of recommendation, essay. Additional exam requirements/recommendations for international students: Required—TOEFL (minimum score 83 iBT) or IELTS (minimum score 6.5). Electronic applications accepted. *Expenses:* Tuition, state resident: part-time $553 per credit. Tuition, nonresident: part-time $854 per credit. *Required fees:* $91 per credit. Tuition and fees vary according to program.

**New Mexico Highlands University,** Graduate Studies, College of Arts and Sciences, Department of History, Political Science, and Languages and Culture, Las Vegas, NM 87701. Offers public affairs (MA), including historical and cross-cultural perspectives, history/political science, political and governmental processes. *Degree requirements:* For master's, comprehensive exam, thesis or alternative. *Entrance requirements:* Additional exam requirements/recommendations for international students: Required—TOEFL (minimum score 540 paper-based).

**New Mexico State University,** College of Arts and Sciences, Department of Government, Las Cruces, NM 88003. Offers government (MA); public administration (MPA). *Accreditation:* NASPAA (one or more programs are accredited). *Program availability:* Part-time. *Faculty:* 8 full-time (4 women), 1 (woman) part-time/adjunct. *Students:* 22 full-time (9 women), 13 part-time (7 women); includes 22 minority (3 Black or African American, non-Hispanic/Latino; 18 Hispanic/Latino; 1 Two or more races, non-Hispanic/Latino), 1 international. Average age 31. 17 applicants, 65% accepted, 7 enrolled. In 2016, 14 master's awarded. *Degree requirements:* For master's, comprehensive exam (for some programs), thesis optional. *Entrance requirements:* For master's, GRE (if GPA less than 3.0), writing sample, 3 letters of recommendation, resume. Additional exam requirements/recommendations for international students: Required—TOEFL (minimum score 550 paper-based; 79 iBT), IELTS (minimum score 6.5). *Application deadline:* For fall admission, 10/1 for domestic and international students; for spring admission, 3/1 for domestic and international students; for summer admission, 3/1 for domestic and international students. Application fee: $40 ($50 for international students). Electronic applications accepted. *Expenses:* Tuition, state resident: full-time $4086. Tuition, nonresident: full-time $14,254. *Required fees:* $853. Tuition and fees vary according to course load. *Financial support:* In 2016–17, 15 students received support, including 10 teaching assistantships (averaging $12,723 per year); career-related internships or fieldwork, Federal Work-Study, scholarships/grants, health care benefits, and unspecified assistantships also available. Support available to part-time students. Financial award application deadline: 3/1. *Faculty research:* U.S.-Mexico border studies, public administration and policy, international relations, Latin America, American politics and theory. *Total annual research expenditures:* $6,605. *Unit head:* Dr. Neil Harvey, Department Head, 575-646-4935, Fax: 575-646-2052, E-mail: nharvey@nmsu.edu. *Application contact:* Dr. Neil Harvey, Director, Master of Arts in Government Program, 575-646-4935, Fax: 575-646-2052, E-mail: nharvey@nmsu.edu. Website: http://deptofgov.nmsu.edu

**The New School,** The New School for Social Research, Department of Political Science, New York, NY 10003. Offers politics (M Phil, MA, PhD). *Program availability:* Part-time, evening/weekend. *Faculty:* 5 full-time (2 women), 12 part-time/adjunct (4 women). *Students:* 97 full-time (47 women), 9 part-time (1 woman); includes 12 minority (1 Black or African American, non-Hispanic/Latino; 1 Asian, non-Hispanic/Latino; 7 Hispanic/Latino; 3 Two or more races, non-Hispanic/Latino), 45 international. Average age 33. 118 applicants, 68% accepted, 15 enrolled. In 2016, 29 master's, 2 doctorates awarded. Terminal master's awarded for partial completion of doctoral program. *Degree requirements:* For master's, thesis or alternative, paper; for doctorate, variable foreign language requirement, comprehensive exam, thesis/dissertation. *Entrance requirements:* For master's, GRE, letters of recommendation, writing sample, essays, unofficial transcripts; for doctorate, letters of recommendation, writing sample, essays, unofficial transcripts. Additional exam requirements/recommendations for international students: Required—TOEFL (minimum score 100 iBT), IELTS (minimum score 7), PTE (minimum score 68). *Application deadline:* For fall admission, 8/1 priority date for domestic and international students; for spring admission, 10/15 priority date for domestic and international students. Applications are processed on a rolling basis. Application fee: $50. Electronic applications accepted. *Expenses:* Contact institution. *Financial support:* Fellowships, research assistantships, teaching assistantships, Federal Work-Study, scholarships/grants, and tuition waivers (full and partial) available. Support available to part-time students. Financial award application deadline: 2/1; financial award applicants required to submit FAFSA. *Faculty research:* Democracies in theory and practice; political thought and its history; international politics; politics in economic and social context; political development in historical perspective; institutions, policy, and governance. *Unit head:* Dr. William Milberg, Dean, The New School for Social Research, 212-229-5777, E-mail: milbergw@newschool.edu. *Application contact:* Dana Messinger, Director of Graduate Admission, 212-229-5150 Ext. 2300, E-mail: socialresearchadmit@newschool.edu.
Website: http://www.newschool.edu/nssr/politics/

**New York University,** Graduate School of Arts and Science, Department of Politics, New York, NY 10012-1019. Offers political campaign management (MA); politics (MA, PhD); JD/MA; MBA/MA. *Program availability:* Part-time. Terminal master's awarded for partial completion of doctoral program. *Degree requirements:* For master's, one foreign language, thesis or alternative; for doctorate, 2 foreign languages, comprehensive exam, thesis/dissertation. *Entrance requirements:* For master's and doctorate, GRE General Test. Additional exam requirements/recommendations for international students: Required—TOEFL. *Faculty research:* Comparative politics, democratic theory and practice, rational choice, political economy, international relations.

**Northeastern Illinois University,** College of Graduate Studies and Research, College of Arts and Sciences, Program in Political Science, Chicago, IL 60625-4699. Offers MA. *Program availability:* Part-time, evening/weekend. *Degree requirements:* For master's, comprehensive exam, thesis optional. *Entrance requirements:* For master's, minimum GPA of 2.75. Additional exam requirements/recommendations for international students: Required—TOEFL (minimum score 550 paper-based; 79 iBT). Electronic applications accepted. *Faculty research:* Chinese politics, Latin American democratization, Jewish feminism, administration and delegation.

**Northeastern University,** College of Social Sciences and Humanities, Boston, MA 02115. Offers criminology and criminal justice (MSCJ); criminology and justice policy (PhD); economics (MA, PhD); English (MA, PhD); international affairs (MA); law and public policy (PhD); political science (MA, PhD); public administration (MPA); public history (MA); public policy (MPP); security and resilience studies (MS); sociology (MA, PhD); urban and regional planning (MS); urban informatics (MS); world history (MA, PhD); JD/MS. *Program availability:* Online learning. *Faculty:* 234 full-time (114 women), 55 part-time/adjunct (34 women). *Students:* 427 full-time (239 women), 77 part-time (42 women). In 2016, 143 master's, 38 doctorates awarded. *Degree requirements:* For doctorate, variable foreign language requirement, comprehensive exam, thesis/ dissertation. *Entrance requirements:* For master's and doctorate, GRE. Additional exam requirements/recommendations for international students: Required—TOEFL, IELTS. Application fee: $75. Electronic applications accepted. *Expenses:* $1,295 per credit. *Financial support:* Teaching assistantships, career-related internships or fieldwork, scholarships/grants, health care benefits, tuition waivers (full and partial), and unspecified assistantships available. Support available to part-time students. Financial award applicants required to submit FAFSA. *Unit head:* Dr. Uta Poiger, Dean, 617-373-5173. *Application contact:* Amber Crowe, Administrative Coordinator, 617-373-5990, Fax: 617-373-7281, E-mail: gradcssh@northeastern.edu.
Website: http://www.northeastern.edu/cssh/graduate

**Northern Arizona University,** Graduate College, College of Social and Behavioral Sciences, Department of Politics and International Affairs, Flagstaff, AZ 86011. Offers political science (MA, PhD); public administration (MPA); public management (Certificate). *Program availability:* Part-time. *Degree requirements:* For master's, comprehensive exam (for some programs), thesis optional; for doctorate, one foreign language, comprehensive exam, thesis/dissertation. *Entrance requirements:* For master's, GRE (minimum 70th percentile ranking in each testing area preferred); for doctorate, GRE (minimum score in 70th percentile in each testing area preferred). Additional exam requirements/recommendations for international students: Required—TOEFL (minimum score 550 paper-based; 80 iBT), IELTS (minimum score 7). Electronic applications accepted. *Expenses:* Tuition, state resident: full-time $8971; part-time $444 per credit hour. Tuition, nonresident: full-time $20,958; part-time $1164 per credit hour. *Required fees:* $1018; $644 per credit hour. Tuition and fees vary according to course load, campus/location and program.

**Northern Illinois University,** Graduate School, College of Liberal Arts and Sciences, Department of Political Science, De Kalb, IL 60115-2854. Offers MA, PhD. *Program availability:* Part-time, evening/weekend. *Faculty:* 24 full-time (5 women), 8 part-time/ adjunct (2 women). *Students:* 78 full-time (27 women), 55 part-time (21 women); includes 27 minority (7 Black or African American, non-Hispanic/Latino; 3 Asian, non-Hispanic/Latino; 14 Hispanic/Latino; 3 Two or more races, non-Hispanic/Latino), 19 international. Average age 32. 42 applicants, 48% accepted, 6 enrolled. In 2016, 34 master's, 6 doctorates awarded. Terminal master's awarded for partial completion of doctoral program. *Degree requirements:* For master's, comprehensive exam, thesis optional; for doctorate, variable foreign language requirement, thesis/dissertation, candidacy exam, dissertation defense. *Entrance requirements:* For master's, GRE General Test, minimum GPA of 2.75, 9 hours of course work in political science; for doctorate, GRE General Test, minimum GPA of 2.75 (undergraduate), 3.2 (graduate); undergraduate major in related field. Additional exam requirements/recommendations for international students: Required—TOEFL (minimum score 550 paper-based). *Application deadline:* For fall admission, 3/1 priority date for domestic students, 5/1 for international students; for spring admission, 11/1 for domestic students, 10/1 for international students. Applications are processed on a rolling basis. Application fee: $40. Electronic applications accepted. *Financial support:* In 2016–17, 20 teaching assistantships with full tuition reimbursements were awarded; fellowships with full tuition reimbursements, research assistantships with full tuition reimbursements, career-related internships or fieldwork, Federal Work-Study, scholarships/grants, tuition waivers (full), and unspecified assistantships also available. Support available to part-time students. Financial award applicants required to submit FAFSA. *Faculty research:* Terrorism and dynamics of trade, U.S. foreign policy, political economy of development, biopolitical theory, women and politics. *Unit head:* Dr. Scott Schraufnagel, Chair, 815-753-7046, Fax: 815-753-6302, E-mail: sschrauf@niu.edu. *Application contact:* Dr. Scot Schraufnagel, Director, Graduate Studies, 815-753-7054, E-mail: sschrauf@niu.edu. Website: http://polisci.niu.edu/

**Northwestern University,** The Graduate School, Judd A. and Marjorie Weinberg College of Arts and Sciences, Department of Political Science, Evanston, IL 60208. Offers PhD, JD/PhD. Admissions and degrees offered through The Graduate School. Terminal master's awarded for partial completion of doctoral program. *Degree requirements:* For doctorate, thesis/dissertation, qualifying exams. *Entrance requirements:* For doctorate, GRE General Test, sample of written work. Additional exam requirements/recommendations for international students: Required—TOEFL. *Faculty research:* Formal theory/formal political economy, political economy of development/state-business relations, labor market institutions and welfare policy, public opinion and political behavior, feminist political theory.

**The Ohio State University,** Graduate School, College of Arts and Sciences, Division of Social and Behavioral Sciences, Department of Political Science, Columbus, OH 43210. Offers PhD. *Faculty:* 32. *Students:* 77 full-time (23 women), 4 part-time (2 women), 18 international. Average age 28. In 2016, 7 doctorates awarded. Terminal master's awarded for partial completion of doctoral program. *Degree requirements:* For doctorate, thesis/dissertation. *Entrance requirements:* For doctorate, GRE General Test. Additional exam requirements/recommendations for international students: Recommended—TOEFL (minimum score 600 paper-based; 100 iBT), IELTS (minimum score 8). *Application deadline:* For fall admission, 12/15 priority date for domestic students, 11/30 priority date for international students. Applications are processed on a rolling basis. Application fee: $60 ($70 for international students). Electronic applications accepted. *Financial support:* Fellowships with tuition reimbursements, research assistantships with tuition reimbursements, teaching assistantships with tuition reimbursements, Federal Work-Study, and institutionally sponsored loans available. Support available to part-time students. *Faculty research:* American, comparative, and international politics; political theory. *Unit head:* Dr. Richard Hermann, Chair, 614-292-2880, Fax: 614-292-1146, E-mail: hermann.1@osu.edu. *Application contact:* Graduate and Professional Admissions, 614-292-9444, Fax: 614-292-3895, E-mail: gpadmissions@osu.edu. Website: http://polisci.osu.edu/

**Ohio University,** Graduate College, College of Arts and Sciences, Department of Political Science, Athens, OH 45701-2979. Offers MA. *Program availability:* Part-time, evening/weekend. *Degree requirements:* For master's, comprehensive exam, thesis or alternative. *Entrance requirements:* For master's, GRE General Test, minimum GPA of 3.0. Additional exam requirements/recommendations for international students: Required—TOEFL (minimum score 550 paper-based; 80 iBT) or IELTS (minimum score 6.5). *Application deadline:* For fall admission, 2/15 priority date for domestic and international students. Applications are processed on a rolling basis. Application fee: $50 ($55 for international students). Electronic applications accepted. *Financial support:* Research assistantships with full tuition reimbursements, teaching assistantships with full tuition reimbursements, career-related internships or fieldwork, Federal Work-Study, institutionally sponsored loans, and tuition waivers (partial) available. Financial award application deadline: 2/15. *Faculty research:* International relations, Latin American politics, public policy, economic development, political theory. *Unit head:* Dr. Judith Grant, Chair, 740-593-4369, Fax: 740-593-0394, E-mail: grantj1@ohio.edu. *Application contact:* Dr. Sarah Poggione, Graduate Chair, 740-597-1348, Fax: 740-593-0394, E-mail: poggione@ohio.edu.
Website: http://www.ohiou.edu/pols/

**Oklahoma State University,** College of Arts and Sciences, Department of Political Science, Stillwater, OK 74078. Offers fire and emergency management administration (MS, PhD); political science (MA). *Faculty:* 23 full-time (9 women), 3 part-time/adjunct (1

woman). *Students:* 24 full-time (2 women), 46 part-time (12 women); includes 10 minority (1 Black or African American, non-Hispanic/Latino; 1 Asian, non-Hispanic/Latino; 8 Hispanic/Latino), 11 international. Average age 36. 46 applicants, 65% accepted, 20 enrolled. In 2016, 17 master's, 3 doctorates awarded. *Degree requirements:* For master's, comprehensive exam, thesis or creative component; for doctorate, comprehensive exam, thesis/dissertation. *Entrance requirements:* For master's and doctorate, GRE. Additional exam requirements/recommendations for international students: Required—TOEFL (minimum score 550 paper-based; 79 iBT). *Application deadline:* For fall admission, 3/1 priority date for international students; for spring admission, 8/1 priority date for international students. Applications are processed on a rolling basis. Application fee: $40 ($75 for international students). Electronic applications accepted. *Expenses:* Tuition, state resident: full-time $3775; part-time $209.70 per credit hour. Tuition, nonresident: full-time $14,851; part-time $825.05 per credit hour. *Required fees:* $2027; $112.60 per credit hour. Tuition and fees vary according to campus/location. *Financial support:* In 2016–17, 7 teaching assistantships (averaging $14,035 per year) were awarded; research assistantships, career-related internships or fieldwork, Federal Work-Study, scholarships/grants, health care benefits, tuition waivers (partial), and unspecified assistantships also available. Support available to part-time students. Financial award application deadline: 3/1; financial award applicants required to submit FAFSA. *Faculty research:* Fire and emergency management, environmental dispute resolution, voting and elections, women and politics, urban politics. *Unit head:* Dr. Jeanette Mendez, Department Head, 405-744-5607, E-mail: jeanette.mendez@okstate.edu.
Website: http://polsci.okstate.edu

**Penn State University Park,** Graduate School, College of the Liberal Arts, Department of Political Science, University Park, PA 16802. Offers MA, PhD. *Unit head:* Dr. Susan Welch, Dean, 814-865-7691, Fax: 814-863-2085. *Application contact:* Lori Hawn, Director, Graduate Student Services, 814-865-1795, Fax: 814-863-4627, E-mail: l-gswww@lists.psu.edu.
Website: http://polsci.la.psu.edu/

**Pepperdine University,** School of Public Policy, Malibu, CA 90263. Offers American politics (MPP); economics (MPP); international relations (MPP); state and local policy (MPP); JD/MPP; MBA/MPP; MDR/MPP. *Faculty:* 4 full-time (1 woman), 5 part-time/adjunct (0 women). *Students:* 57 full-time (27 women), 7 part-time (5 women); includes 22 minority (9 Black or African American, non-Hispanic/Latino; 2 American Indian or Alaska Native, non-Hispanic/Latino; 6 Asian, non-Hispanic/Latino; 4 Hispanic/Latino; 1 Two or more races, non-Hispanic/Latino), 10 international. Average age 25. 174 applicants, 55% accepted, 29 enrolled. In 2016, 34 master's awarded. *Entrance requirements:* For master's, GRE or GMAT, 2 letters of recommendation, resume, two essays. Additional exam requirements/recommendations for international students: Required—TOEFL. *Application deadline:* For fall admission, 6/15 for domestic students. Applications are processed on a rolling basis. Application fee: $50. Electronic applications accepted. *Expenses:* $47,710 per academic year; $1,525 per unit (for master's). *Financial support:* Institutionally sponsored loans and scholarships/grants available. Financial award application deadline: 5/1; financial award applicants required to submit FAFSA. *Unit head:* Dr. Pete Peterson, Dean, School of Public Policy, 310-506-7490, Fax: 310-506-7494, E-mail: pete.n.peterson@pepperdine.edu. *Application contact:* Carson Bruno, Assistant Dean for Admission and Program Relations, 310-506-7493, E-mail: carson.bruno@pepperdine.edu.
Website: http://publicpolicy.pepperdine.edu/

**Portland State University,** Graduate Studies, College of Urban and Public Affairs, Hatfield School of Government, Division of Political Science, Portland, OR 97207-0751. Offers MA, MAT, MS, MST, PhD. *Program availability:* Part-time. *Faculty:* 12 full-time (4 women), 9 part-time/adjunct (2 women). *Students:* 8 full-time (4 women), 7 part-time (2 women); includes 3 minority (1 Hispanic/Latino; 2 Two or more races, non-Hispanic/Latino), 1 international. Average age 36. 9 applicants, 67% accepted, 4 enrolled. In 2016, 4 master's awarded. *Degree requirements:* For master's, one foreign language, comprehensive exam, thesis; for doctorate, comprehensive exam, thesis/dissertation. *Entrance requirements:* For master's, GRE General Test or MAT, minimum GPA of 3.1, 2 letters of recommendation. Additional exam requirements/recommendations for international students: Required—TOEFL (minimum score 550 paper-based; 90 iBT). *Application deadline:* For fall admission, 4/1 priority date for domestic students, 3/1 priority date for international students; for spring admission, 11/1 for domestic and international students. Application fee: $65. *Expenses:* Contact institution. *Financial support:* In 2016–17, 8 research assistantships with tuition reimbursements (averaging $3,572 per year), 3 teaching assistantships with tuition reimbursements (averaging $7,314 per year) were awarded; career-related internships or fieldwork, Federal Work-Study, and unspecified assistantships also available. Support available to part-time students. Financial award application deadline: 3/1; financial award applicants required to submit FAFSA. *Faculty research:* Congress, presidency, political reform, international environment, hate speech. *Total annual research expenditures:* $326. *Unit head:* Christopher Shortell, Chair, 503-725-5139, Fax: 503-725-8444, E-mail: shortell@pdx.edu.
Website: https://www.pdx.edu/hatfieldschool/political-science

**Princeton University,** Graduate School, Department of Politics, Princeton, NJ 08544-1019. Offers political philosophy (PhD); politics (PhD). *Degree requirements:* For doctorate, comprehensive exam, thesis/dissertation, teaching experience. *Entrance requirements:* For doctorate, GRE General Test, sample of written work, letters of recommendation. Additional exam requirements/recommendations for international students: Required—TOEFL (minimum score 600 paper-based). Electronic applications accepted. *Faculty research:* American politics, comparative politics, formal and quantitative methods, international relations, public law, political theory.

**Purdue University,** Graduate School, College of Liberal Arts, Department of Political Science, West Lafayette, IN 47907. Offers MA, PhD. *Program availability:* Part-time, evening/weekend. *Faculty:* 21 full-time (9 women), 1 part-time/adjunct (0 women). *Students:* 32 full-time (12 women), 16 part-time (7 women); includes 4 minority (2 Black or African American, non-Hispanic/Latino; 2 Hispanic/Latino), 14 international. Average age 31. 19 applicants, 63% accepted, 9 enrolled. In 2016, 5 master's, 2 doctorates awarded. Terminal master's awarded for partial completion of doctoral program. *Degree requirements:* For master's, comprehensive exam; for doctorate, comprehensive exam, thesis/dissertation. *Entrance requirements:* For master's and doctorate, GRE General Test (minimum score of 160 verbal, 600 on old scoring), minimum undergraduate GPA of 3.0. Additional exam requirements/recommendations for international students: Required—TOEFL (minimum score 600 paper-based; 90 iBT). *Application deadline:* For fall admission, 12/15 priority date for domestic and international students; for spring admission, 10/15 for domestic and international students. Applications are processed on a rolling basis. Application fee: $60 ($75 for international students). Electronic applications accepted. *Financial support:* Fellowships, research assistantships, teaching assistantships, and career-related internships or fieldwork available. Support available to part-time students. Financial award application deadline: 2/1; financial award applicants required to submit FAFSA. *Faculty research:* International relations, political behavior and institutions, comparative politics, political theory, public policy. *Unit head:* Rosalee A. Clawson, Head of the Graduate Program, 765-494-4162, E-mail: clawsonr@purdue.edu. *Application contact:* Annie Wheeldon, Graduate Contact, 765-494-4163, E-mail: polgradcoordinator@purdue.edu.
Website: http://www.polsci.purdue.edu/

**Queen's University at Kingston,** School of Graduate Studies, Faculty of Arts and Sciences, Department of Political Studies, Kingston, ON K7L 3N6, Canada. Offers Canadian politics (PhD); comparative politics (PhD); gender and politics (PhD); international relations (PhD); political theory (PhD). *Degree requirements:* For master's, thesis or alternative; for doctorate, one foreign language, thesis/dissertation, qualifying exams. *Entrance requirements:* Additional exam requirements/recommendations for international students: Required—TOEFL (minimum score 600 paper-based). *Faculty research:* Canadian politics, comparative politics, political thought, international politics, women and politics.

**Regent University,** Graduate School, Robertson School of Government, Virginia Beach, VA 23464-9800. Offers government (MA), including American government, healthcare policy and ethics (MA, MPA), international relations, law and public policy, national security studies, political communication, political theory, religion and politics; public administration (MPA), including emergency management and homeland security, federal government, general public administration, healthcare policy and ethics (MA, MPA), law, nonprofit administration and faith-based organizations, public leadership and management, servant leadership. *Program availability:* Part-time, evening/weekend, 100% online, blended/hybrid learning. *Faculty:* 8 full-time (1 woman), 19 part-time/adjunct (3 women). *Students:* 40 full-time (27 women), 119 part-time (69 women); includes 73 minority (47 Black or African American, non-Hispanic/Latino; 3 Asian, non-Hispanic/Latino; 15 Hispanic/Latino; 8 Two or more races, non-Hispanic/Latino), 6 international. Average age 35. 253 applicants, 41% accepted, 70 enrolled. In 2016, 34 master's awarded. *Degree requirements:* For master's, thesis optional, internship. *Entrance requirements:* For master's, GRE General Test or LSAT, personal essay, writing sample, resume, college transcripts. Additional exam requirements/recommendations for international students: Required—TOEFL (minimum score 577 paper-based). *Application deadline:* For fall admission, 5/1 priority date for domestic students; for spring admission, 11/1 priority date for domestic students. Applications are processed on a rolling basis. Application fee: $50. Electronic applications accepted. *Expenses:* $650 per credit (MA/MPA); $250 per semester technology fee. *Financial support:* In 2016–17, 78 students received support. Career-related internships or fieldwork, scholarships/grants, and unspecified assistantships available. Support available to part-time students. *Faculty research:* International relations and politics, public administration, leadership and ethics, Biblical law, Constitutional law and Supreme Court. *Unit head:* Dr. Eric Patterson, Dean, 757-352-4616, Fax: 757-352-4735, E-mail: epatterson@regent.edu. *Application contact:* Heidi Cece, Assistant Vice President of Enrollment Management, 800-373-5504, Fax: 757-352-4381, E-mail: admissions@regent.edu.
Website: http://www.regent.edu/rsg/

**Rice University,** Graduate Programs, School of Social Sciences, Department of Political Science, Houston, TX 77251-1892. Offers PhD. Terminal master's awarded for partial completion of doctoral program. *Degree requirements:* For doctorate, comprehensive exam, thesis/dissertation, 42 hours of coursework. *Entrance requirements:* For doctorate, GRE General Test. Additional exam requirements/recommendations for international students: Required—TOEFL (minimum score 600 paper-based; 90 iBT). Electronic applications accepted. *Faculty research:* Comparative government in Western Europe and the former Soviet Union, international relations, Congress and public policy in American government, minority politics.

**Roosevelt University,** Graduate Division, College of Arts and Sciences, Department of Political Science and Public Administration, Program in Political Science, Chicago, IL 60605. Offers MA. *Program availability:* Part-time, evening/weekend. *Degree requirements:* For master's, thesis or alternative. *Entrance requirements:* For master's, minimum GPA of 2.7. *Faculty research:* Metropolitan social movements, American politics, comparative politics, political theory.

**Rutgers University–Newark,** Graduate School, Program in Political Science, Newark, NJ 07102. Offers American political system (MA); international relations (MA); JD/MA. *Program availability:* Part-time, evening/weekend. *Degree requirements:* For master's, comprehensive exam, thesis optional. *Entrance requirements:* For master's, GRE, minimum undergraduate B average. Electronic applications accepted. *Faculty research:* Policymaking and policy evaluation in the United States; government and politics in Europe, Middle East, Asia, Africa, and Latin America.

**Rutgers University–New Brunswick,** Graduate School-New Brunswick, Department of Political Science, Piscataway, NJ 08854-8097. Offers American politics (PhD); comparative politics (PhD); international relations (PhD); political theory (PhD); public law (PhD); United Nations and global policy studies (MA); women and politics (PhD). *Degree requirements:* For doctorate, one foreign language, comprehensive exam, thesis/dissertation. *Entrance requirements:* For master's, bachelor's degree from accredited U.S. college or university or a comparable institution in another country; for doctorate, GRE General Test. Additional exam requirements/recommendations for international students: Required—TOEFL.

**St. John's University,** St. John's College of Liberal Arts and Sciences, Department of Government and Politics and Division of Library and Information Science, Program in Government and Library and Information Science, Queens, NY 11439. Offers MA/MS. *Program availability:* Part-time, evening/weekend. *Entrance requirements:* Additional exam requirements/recommendations for international students: Required—TOEFL (minimum score 600 paper-based; 100 iBT), IELTS (minimum score 7). Electronic applications accepted.

**St. John's University,** St. John's College of Liberal Arts and Sciences, Department of Government and Politics, Program in Government and Politics, Queens, NY 11439. Offers government and politics (MA); public administration (Adv C); JD/MA. *Program availability:* Part-time, evening/weekend. *Degree requirements:* For master's, comprehensive exam, thesis optional. *Entrance requirements:* For master's, minimum GPA of 3.0, 18 credits at undergraduate level in government and politics. Additional exam requirements/recommendations for international students: Required—TOEFL (minimum score 600 paper-based; 100 iBT), IELTS (minimum score 7). Electronic applications accepted.

**Saint Louis University,** Graduate Education, College of Arts and Sciences and Graduate Education, Department of Political Science, St. Louis, MO 63103. Offers MA. *Program availability:* Part-time. *Entrance requirements:* For master's, GRE or LSAT, letters of recommendation, resume, writing sample. Additional exam requirements/recommendations for international students: Required—TOEFL (minimum score 525 paper-based). Electronic applications accepted. *Faculty research:* Part of Asia, Africa, Latin America, and Russia; international political economy; diplomacy and international organization; theories of democracy and justice; American political institutions.

**Sam Houston State University,** College of Humanities and Social Sciences, Department of Political Science, Huntsville, TX 77341. Offers political science (MA); public administration (MPA). *Program availability:* Part-time, online learning. *Degree requirements:* For master's, comprehensive exam, thesis optional, internship. *Entrance requirements:* For master's, GRE General Test, GMAT, writing sample of scholarly work, letters of recommendation, statement of purpose, resume. Additional exam requirements/recommendations for international students: Required—TOEFL (minimum score 550 paper-based; 79 iBT), IELTS (minimum score 6.5). Electronic applications accepted.

**San Diego State University,** Graduate and Research Affairs, College of Arts and Letters, Department of Political Science, San Diego, CA 92182. Offers MA. *Program availability:* Part-time. *Degree requirements:* For master's, thesis. *Entrance requirements:* For master's, GRE General Test, minimum GPA of 3.0, 2 letters of reference. Additional exam requirements/recommendations for international students: Required—TOEFL. Electronic applications accepted.

**San Francisco State University,** Division of Graduate Studies, College of Liberal and Creative Arts, Department of Political Science, San Francisco, CA 94132-1722. Offers MA. *Expenses:* Tuition, state resident: full-time $6738. Tuition, nonresident: full-time $15,666. *Required fees:* $1012. Tuition and fees vary according to degree level and program. *Financial support:* Research assistantships and teaching assistantships available. *Unit head:* Dr. James Martel, Interim Chair, 415-405-2162, Fax: 415-338-2391, E-mail: jmartel@sfsu.edu. *Application contact:* Prof. Katherine Gordy, Graduate Coordinator, 415-338-7528, Fax: 415-338-2391, E-mail: kgordy@sfsu.edu. Website: http://politicalscience.sfsu.edu/

**Simon Fraser University,** Office of Graduate Studies and Postdoctoral Fellows, Faculty of Arts and Social Sciences, Department of Political Science, Burnaby, BC V5A 1S6, Canada. Offers MA, PhD. *Faculty:* 17 full-time (3 women). *Students:* 34 full-time (15 women). 68 applicants, 38% accepted, 13 enrolled. In 2016, 10 master's, 2 doctorates awarded. *Degree requirements:* For master's, thesis or alternative, field exams; for doctorate, one foreign language, comprehensive exam, thesis/dissertation. *Entrance requirements:* For master's, minimum GPA of 3.0 (on scale of 4.33) or 3.33 based on last 60 credits of undergraduate courses; for doctorate, minimum GPA of 3.5 (on scale of 4.33). Additional exam requirements/recommendations for international students: Recommended—TOEFL (minimum score 580 paper-based; 93 iBT), IELTS (minimum score 7), TWE (minimum score 5). *Application deadline:* For fall admission, 1/15 for domestic and international students. Application fee: $90 ($125 for international students). Electronic applications accepted. *Financial support:* In 2016–17, 12 students received support, including 11 fellowships (averaging $5,909 per year), teaching assistantships (averaging $5,608 per year); research assistantships and scholarships/grants also available. *Faculty research:* Political theory and methodology, Canadian politics, comparative politics, international relations, urban politics, public policy, and public administration. *Unit head:* Dr. Genevieve Johnson, Graduate Chair, 778-782-3145, Fax: 778-782-4786, E-mail: pol-gradchair@sfu.ca. *Application contact:* Katherine Ensslen, Graduate Secretary, 778-782-5487, Fax: 778-782-4786, E-mail: polgrad@sfu.ca. Website: http://www.sfu.ca/politics/

**Sonoma State University,** School of Social Sciences, Department of Political Science, Rohnert Park, CA 94928. Offers administration of nonprofit agencies (Certificate); public administration (MPA). *Program availability:* Part-time, evening/weekend. *Degree requirements:* For master's, thesis or alternative. *Entrance requirements:* For master's, GRE General Test, minimum GPA of 3.0. Additional exam requirements/recommendations for international students: Required—TOEFL (minimum score 500 paper-based). *Application deadline:* For fall admission, 11/30 for domestic students; for spring admission, 8/31 for domestic students. Application fee: $55. *Expenses:* Tuition, state resident: full-time $6738; part-time $3906 per unit. *Required fees:* $1916; $1916 per year. Tuition and fees vary according to course load, degree level and program. *Financial support:* Research assistantships, teaching assistantships, career-related internships or fieldwork, and Federal Work-Study available. Support available to part-time students. Financial award application deadline: 3/2; financial award applicants required to submit FAFSA. *Unit head:* Catherine Nelson, Chair, 707-664-2179, E-mail: catherine.nelson@sonoma.edu. *Application contact:* Diane Brown, Graduate Program Coordinator, 707-664-2875, Fax: 707-664-3920, E-mail: diane.brown@sonoma.edu. Website: http://www.sonoma.edu/polisci/

**Southern Connecticut State University,** School of Graduate Studies, School of Arts and Sciences, Department of Political Science, New Haven, CT 06515-1355. Offers MS. *Program availability:* Part-time, evening/weekend. *Faculty:* 3 full-time (1 woman). *Students:* 8 full-time (1 woman), 9 part-time (6 women); includes 6 minority (5 Black or African American, non-Hispanic/Latino; 1 Hispanic/Latino), 1 international. Average age 38. 9 applicants, 33% accepted, 3 enrolled. In 2016, 4 master's awarded. *Degree requirements:* For master's, thesis or alternative. *Entrance requirements:* For master's, interview. *Application deadline:* For fall admission, 7/15 priority date for domestic students. Applications are processed on a rolling basis. Application fee: $50. Electronic applications accepted. *Expenses:* Tuition, state resident: full-time $6497; part-time $519 per credit hour. Tuition, nonresident: full-time $18,102; part-time $535 per credit hour. *Required fees:* $4722; $55 per semester. Tuition and fees vary according to program. *Financial support:* Career-related internships or fieldwork, scholarships/grants, and unspecified assistantships available. Financial award application deadline: 4/15; financial award applicants required to submit FAFSA. *Unit head:* Dr. Kevin Buterbaugh, Chairperson, 203-392-5662, Fax: 203-392-5670, E-mail: buterbaughk1@southernct.edu. *Application contact:* Lisa Galvin, Director of Graduate Admissions, 203-392-5240, Fax: 203-392-5235, E-mail: galvinl1@southernct.edu.

**Southern Illinois University Carbondale,** Graduate School, College of Liberal Arts, Department of Political Science, Program in Political Science, Carbondale, IL 62901-4701. Offers MA, PhD, JD/PhD. *Program availability:* Part-time. *Degree requirements:* For doctorate, thesis/dissertation. *Entrance requirements:* For master's, GRE General Test, minimum GPA of 2.7; for doctorate, GRE General Test, minimum GPA of 3.5. Additional exam requirements/recommendations for international students: Required—TOEFL. *Faculty research:* Public law, international relations, comparative government, American government.

**Southern University and Agricultural and Mechanical College,** Graduate School, Nelson Mandela School of Public Policy and Urban Affairs, Department of Political Science and Geography, Baton Rouge, LA 70813. Offers social sciences (MA). *Degree requirements:* For master's, thesis. *Entrance requirements:* For master's, GMAT or GRE General Test, minimum GPA of 3.0. Additional exam requirements/recommendations for international students: Required—TOEFL. *Faculty research:* Redistricting, comparative studies, environmental politics, political geography, mayoral elections.

**Stanford University,** School of Humanities and Sciences, Department of Political Science, Stanford, CA 94305-2004. Offers MA, PhD. Terminal master's awarded for partial completion of doctoral program. *Degree requirements:* For doctorate, one foreign language, thesis/dissertation, oral exam. *Entrance requirements:* For master's and doctorate, GRE General Test. Additional exam requirements/recommendations for international students: Required—TOEFL. Electronic applications accepted. *Expenses:* Tuition: Full-time $47,331. *Required fees:* $609.

**Stony Brook University, State University of New York,** Graduate School, College of Arts and Sciences, Department of Political Science, Stony Brook, NY 11794. Offers political science (MA, PhD); public policy (MAPP); public policy and urban development (MA). *Program availability:* Evening/weekend. *Faculty:* 19 full-time (5 women), 8 part-

time/adjunct (2 women). *Students:* 55 full-time (24 women), 17 part-time (4 women); includes 11 minority (4 Black or African American, non-Hispanic/Latino; 4 Asian, non-Hispanic/Latino; 3 Hispanic/Latino), 19 international. Average age 27. 111 applicants, 60% accepted, 37 enrolled. In 2016, 34 master's, 8 doctorates awarded. *Degree requirements:* For doctorate, thesis/dissertation. *Entrance requirements:* For master's and doctorate, GRE General Test. Additional exam requirements/recommendations for international students: Required—TOEFL (minimum score 90 iBT). *Application deadline:* For fall admission, 1/15 for domestic students; for spring admission, 10/1 for domestic students. Application fee: $100. Electronic applications accepted. *Expenses:* Contact institution. *Financial support:* In 2016–17, 13 teaching assistantships were awarded; fellowships and research assistantships also available. *Faculty research:* Public opinion, political methodology, political science, political parties, political behavior. *Total annual research expenditures:* $110,424. *Unit head:* Dr. Jeffrey Segal, Chair, 631-632-7662, Fax: 631-632-4116, E-mail: jeffrey.segal@stonybrook.edu. *Application contact:* Carri Ann Horner, Coordinator, 631-632-7667, Fax: 631-632-4116, E-mail: carri.horner@stonybrook.edu. Website: http://www.sunysb.edu/polsci/

**Suffolk University,** College of Arts and Sciences, Department of Government, Boston, MA 02108-2770. Offers international relations (MSPS); political science (MSPS); professional politics (MSPS, CAGS); MPA/MSPS. *Program availability:* Part-time, evening/weekend. *Faculty:* 5 full-time (2 women), 2 part-time/adjunct (0 women). *Students:* 14 full-time (8 women), 11 part-time (5 women); includes 10 minority (5 Black or African American, non-Hispanic/Latino; 5 Hispanic/Latino), 5 international. Average age 27. 39 applicants, 77% accepted, 17 enrolled. In 2016, 3 master's awarded. *Degree requirements:* For master's, thesis optional. *Entrance requirements:* For master's, GRE General Test or MAT, 2 letters of recommendation, resume. Additional exam requirements/recommendations for international students: Required—TOEFL (minimum score 550 paper-based; 80 iBT). *Application deadline:* For fall admission, 3/15 priority date for domestic and international students; for spring admission, 10/15 priority date for domestic and international students. Applications are processed on a rolling basis. Application fee: $50. Electronic applications accepted. *Expenses:* $28,368 per year full-time tuition, $1,182 per credit hour part-time tuition, $52 per year student activity fee. *Financial support:* In 2016–17, 19 students received support, including 19 fellowships (averaging $5,453 per year); career-related internships or fieldwork, Federal Work-Study, and institutionally sponsored loans also available. Support available to part-time students. Financial award application deadline: 4/1; financial award applicants required to submit FAFSA. *Faculty research:* Political marketing, social movements and political parties, election administration, urban resilience, the regulatory state. *Unit head:* Rachel Cobb, Department Chair, 617-305-6380, E-mail: rcobb@suffolk.edu. *Application contact:* Mara Marzocchi, Associate Director of Graduate Admissions, 617-573-8302, Fax: 617-305-1733, E-mail: grad.admission@suffolk.edu. Website: http://www.cas.suffolk.edu/government

**Suffolk University,** Sawyer Business School, Department of Public Administration, Boston, MA 02108-2770. Offers community health (MPA); information systems, performance management, and big data analytics (MPA); nonprofit management (MPA); state and local government (MPA); JD/MPA; MPA/MS; MPA/MSCJ; MPA/MSMHC; MPA/MSPS. *Accreditation:* NASPAA (one or more programs are accredited). *Program availability:* Part-time, evening/weekend. *Faculty:* 4 full-time (1 woman), 2 part-time/adjunct (both women). *Students:* 26 full-time (13 women), 96 part-time (58 women); includes 42 minority (18 Black or African American, non-Hispanic/Latino; 5 Asian, non-Hispanic/Latino; 18 Hispanic/Latino; 1 Two or more races, non-Hispanic/Latino), 4 international. Average age 34. 133 applicants, 85% accepted, 53 enrolled. In 2016, 47 degrees awarded. *Entrance requirements:* Additional exam requirements/recommendations for international students: Required—TOEFL (minimum score 550 paper-based; 80 iBT). *Application deadline:* For fall admission, 3/15 priority date for domestic and international students; for spring admission, 10/15 priority date for domestic and international students. Applications are processed on a rolling basis. Application fee: $50. Electronic applications accepted. *Expenses:* Tuition: Full-time $41,490; part-time $1383 per credit hour. *Required fees:* $52; $52 per credit hour. Part-time tuition and fees vary according to course load and program. *Financial support:* In 2016–17, 82 students received support, including 78 fellowships (averaging $6,546 per year); career-related internships or fieldwork, Federal Work-Study, institutionally sponsored loans, and scholarships/grants also available. Support available to part-time students. Financial award application deadline: 4/1; financial award applicants required to submit FAFSA. *Faculty research:* Local government, health care, federal policy, mental health, HIV/AIDS. *Unit head:* Brenda Bond, Director/Department Chair, 617-305-1768, E-mail: bbond@suffolk.edu. *Application contact:* Mara Marzocchi, Associate Director of Graduate Admissions, 617-573-8302, Fax: 617-305-1733, E-mail: grad.admission@suffolk.edu. Website: http://www.suffolk.edu/mpa

**Sul Ross State University,** College of Arts and Sciences, Department of Behavioral and Social Sciences, Program in Political Science, Alpine, TX 79832. Offers MA. *Program availability:* Part-time, evening/weekend. *Degree requirements:* For master's, thesis optional. *Entrance requirements:* For master's, GRE General Test, minimum undergraduate GPA of 2.5 in last 60 hours. *Faculty research:* Local government, state government, borderland studies, British studies.

**Syracuse University,** Maxwell School of Citizenship and Public Affairs, Programs in Political Science, Syracuse, NY 13244. Offers MA, PhD, JD/MA, JD/PhD, MAIR/PhD. *Students:* Average age 31. *Degree requirements:* For doctorate, comprehensive exam, thesis/dissertation. *Entrance requirements:* For master's and doctorate, GRE General Test, three letters of recommendation, personal statement, official transcripts, resume. Additional exam requirements/recommendations for international students: Required—TOEFL (minimum score 100 iBT). *Application deadline:* For fall admission, 1/15 priority date for domestic and international students. Application fee: $75. Electronic applications accepted. *Expenses:* Tuition: Full-time $25,974; part-time $1443 per credit hour. *Required fees:* $802; $50 per course. Tuition and fees vary according to course load and program. *Financial support:* Fellowships with full tuition reimbursements, research assistantships with tuition reimbursements, and teaching assistantships with tuition reimbursements available. Financial award application deadline: 1/1. *Faculty research:* Comparative politics, political theory and methods, international relations, public administration and policy. *Unit head:* Dr. Seth Jolly, Director of Graduate Studies in Political Science, 315-443-2113, E-mail: skjolly@maxwell.syr.edu. *Application contact:* Candy Brooks, Recruiting Contact, 315-443-2238, E-mail: cbrooks01@syr.edu. Website: http://www.maxwell.syr.edu/psc/

**Syracuse University,** School of Information Studies, CAS Program in E-Government Management and Leadership, Syracuse, NY 13244. Offers CAS. *Program availability:* Part-time. *Entrance requirements:* For degree, resume, personal statement, official transcripts, three letters of recommendation. Additional exam requirements/recommendations for international students: Required—TOEFL (minimum score 100 iBT). *Application deadline:* For fall admission, 2/1 priority date for domestic students; for spring admission, 8/15 priority date for domestic and international students. Applications are processed on a rolling basis. Application fee: $75. Electronic applications accepted. *Expenses:* Tuition: Full-time $25,974; part-time $1443 per credit hour. *Required fees:*

$802; $50 per course. Tuition and fees vary according to course load and program. *Faculty research:* Information strategy and management in the public sector, enterprise technologies, policy analysis, networked governance. *Unit head:* Carsten Østerlund, Program Director, E-mail: costerlu@syr.edu. *Application contact:* Margaret Lane, Assistant Director, Executive Education, 315-443-8708, E-mail: melane02@maxwell.syr.edu.
Website: https://ischool.syr.edu/academics/graduate/cas/cas-e-government-management-and-leadership/

**Tarleton State University,** College of Graduate Studies, College of Liberal and Fine Arts, Department of Social Sciences, Stephenville, TX 76402. Offers history (MA). *Program availability:* Part-time, evening/weekend. *Faculty:* 5 full-time (1 woman). *Students:* 9 part-time (7 women); includes 2 minority (both Hispanic/Latino). 6 applicants, 100% accepted, 3 enrolled. In 2016, 2 master's awarded. *Degree requirements:* For master's, variable foreign language requirement, comprehensive exam, thesis optional. *Entrance requirements:* For master's, GRE General Test, minimum GPA of 3.0. Additional exam requirements/recommendations for international students: Required—TOEFL (minimum score 550 paper-based; 80 iBT). *Application deadline:* For fall admission, 8/15 priority date for domestic students; for spring admission, 1/7 for domestic students. Applications are processed on a rolling basis. Application fee: $45 ($145 for international students). Electronic applications accepted. *Expenses:* $3,672 tuition; $2,437 fees. *Financial support:* Research assistantships, teaching assistantships, career-related internships or fieldwork, and Federal Work-Study available. Support available to part-time students. Financial award application deadline: 5/1; financial award applicants required to submit FAFSA. *Unit head:* Dr. Eric Morrow, Department Head, 254-968-9626, E-mail: morrow@tarleton.edu. *Application contact:* Information Contact, 254-968-9104, Fax: 254-968-9670, E-mail: gradoffice@tarleton.edu.

**Teachers College, Columbia University,** Department of Education Policy and Social Analysis, New York, NY 10027. Offers economics and education (Ed M, MA, PhD); education policy (Ed M, MA, Ed D, PhD); politics and education (Ed M, MA, Ed D, PhD); sociology and education (Ed M, MA, Ed D, PhD). *Students:* 148 full-time (110 women), 107 part-time (85 women); includes 95 minority (40 Black or African American, non-Hispanic/Latino; 23 Asian, non-Hispanic/Latino; 26 Hispanic/Latino; 6 Two or more races, non-Hispanic/Latino), 74 international. 516 applicants, 54% accepted, 98 enrolled. *Expenses: Tuition:* Full-time $36,288; part-time $1512 per credit. *Required fees:* $438 per semester. One-time fee: $510 full-time. Full-time tuition and fees vary according to course load. *Unit head:* Dr. Jeffrey Henig, Chair, 212-678-8313, Fax: 212-678-3589, E-mail: henig@tc.columbia.edu. *Application contact:* David Estrella, Director of Admissions, 212-678-3305, E-mail: estrella@tc.columbia.edu.
Website: http://www.tc.columbia.edu/education-policy-and-social-analysis/

**Temple University,** College of Liberal Arts, Department of Political Science, Philadelphia, PA 19122-6096. Offers MA, PhD. *Program availability:* Part-time. Terminal master's awarded for partial completion of doctoral program. *Degree requirements:* For master's, comprehensive exam; for doctorate, thesis/dissertation, preliminary and oral exams. *Entrance requirements:* For master's and doctorate, GRE General Test, minimum GPA of 3.0, 3 letters of recommendation. Additional exam requirements/recommendations for international students: Required—TOEFL (minimum score 600 paper-based; 100 iBT). Electronic applications accepted. *Faculty research:* American politics, international relations, comparative politics, political theory, public policy.

**Texas A&M International University,** Office of Graduate Studies and Research, College of Arts and Sciences, Department of Humanities, Laredo, TX 78041-1900. Offers English (MA); Hispanic studies (PhD); history and political thought (MA); language, literature and translation (MA). *Degree requirements:* For master's, comprehensive exam (for some programs), thesis (for some programs). *Entrance requirements:* For master's, GRE General Test. Additional exam requirements/recommendations for international students: Required—TOEFL (minimum score 550 paper-based; 79 iBT).

**Texas A&M International University,** Office of Graduate Studies and Research, College of Arts and Sciences, Department of Public Affairs and Social Research, Laredo, TX 78041-1900. Offers criminal justice (MS); history and political thought (MA); political science (MA); public administration (MPA). *Degree requirements:* For master's, comprehensive exam (for some programs), thesis (for some programs). *Entrance requirements:* For master's, GRE General Test. Additional exam requirements/recommendations for international students: Required—TOEFL (minimum score 550 paper-based; 79 iBT).

**Texas A&M University,** College of Liberal Arts, Department of Political Science, College Station, TX 77843. Offers MA, PhD. *Faculty:* 33. *Students:* 48 full-time (20 women), 2 part-time (both women); includes 9 minority (2 Black or African American, non-Hispanic/Latino; 6 Hispanic/Latino; 1 Two or more races, non-Hispanic/Latino), 16 international. Average age 28. 61 applicants, 25% accepted, 15 enrolled. In 2016, 3 master's, 7 doctorates awarded. *Degree requirements:* For doctorate, comprehensive exam, thesis/dissertation. *Entrance requirements:* For doctorate, GRE General Test, minimum GPA of 3.4. Additional exam requirements/recommendations for international students: Required—TOEFL (minimum score 550 paper-based; 80 iBT), IELTS (minimum score 6), PTE (minimum score 53). *Application deadline:* For fall admission, 12/22 for domestic and international students. Application fee: $50 ($90 for international students). Electronic applications accepted. *Expenses:* Contact institution. *Financial support:* In 2016–17, 48 students received support, including 4 fellowships with tuition reimbursements available (averaging $22,146 per year), 38 research assistantships with tuition reimbursements available (averaging $5,374 per year), 17 teaching assistantships with tuition reimbursements available (averaging $9,689 per year); career-related internships or fieldwork, institutionally sponsored loans, scholarships/grants, traineeships, health care benefits, tuition waivers (full and partial), unspecified assistantships, and assistant lecturer positions also available. Support available to part-time students. Financial award application deadline: 3/15; financial award applicants required to submit FAFSA. *Faculty research:* American politics, international relations, comparative politics, political theory, public policy. *Unit head:* Dr. William Clark, Department Head, 979-845-2827, E-mail: wrclark@tamu.edu. *Application contact:* Dr. Alex C. Pacek, Director of Graduate Studies, 979-845-3229, Fax: 979-847-8924, E-mail: a-pacek@tamu.edu.
Website: http://pols.tamu.edu/

**Texas A&M University–Central Texas,** Graduate Studies and Research, Killeen, TX 76549. Offers accounting (MS); business administration (MBA); clinical mental health counseling (MS); criminal justice (MCJ); curriculum and instruction (M Ed); educational administration (M Ed); educational psychology - experimental psychology (MS); history (MA); human resource management (MS); information systems (MS); liberal studies (MS); management and leadership (MS); marriage and family therapy (MS); mathematics (MS); political science (MA); school counseling (M Ed); school psychology (Ed S).

**Texas A&M University–Commerce,** College of Humanities, Social Sciences and Arts, Commerce, TX 75429-3011. Offers applied criminology (MS); applied linguistics (MA, MS); art (MA, MFA); Christianity in history (Graduate Certificate); computational linguistics (Graduate Certificate); creative writing (Graduate Certificate); English (MA, MS, PhD); film studies (Graduate Certificate); history (MA, MS); music (MM); political science (MA, MS); public history (Graduate Certificate); sociology (MS); Spanish (MA); studies in children's and adolescent literature and culture (Graduate Certificate); teaching English to speakers of other languages (Graduate Certificate); theater (MA, MS). *Program availability:* Part-time. *Students:* 87 full-time (55 women), 528 part-time (362 women); includes 198 minority (86 Black or African American, non-Hispanic/Latino; 2 American Indian or Alaska Native, non-Hispanic/Latino; 8 Asian, non-Hispanic/Latino; 84 Hispanic/Latino; 18 Two or more races, non-Hispanic/Latino), 27 international. Average age 37. 333 applicants, 56% accepted, 149 enrolled. In 2016, 66 master's, 8 doctorates awarded. *Degree requirements:* For master's, one foreign language, comprehensive exam, thesis (for some programs); for doctorate, one foreign language, comprehensive exam, thesis/dissertation, departmental qualifying exam. *Entrance requirements:* For master's and doctorate, GRE General Test. Additional exam requirements/recommendations for international students: Required—TOEFL (minimum score 550 paper-based; 79 iBT), IELTS (minimum score 6). *Application deadline:* Applications are processed on a rolling basis. Application fee: $50. Electronic applications accepted. *Expenses:* Contact institution. *Financial support:* In 2016–17, 255 students received support, including 9 research assistantships with partial tuition reimbursements available (averaging $9,000 per year), 68 teaching assistantships with partial tuition reimbursements available (averaging $9,000 per year); Federal Work-Study, institutionally sponsored loans, scholarships/grants, health care benefits, and unspecified assistantships also available. Financial award application deadline: 5/1; financial award applicants required to submit FAFSA. *Unit head:* Dr. Salvatore Attardo, Dean, 903-886-5166, Fax: 903-886-5774, E-mail: salvatore.attardo@tamuc.edu. *Application contact:* Shelby Miller, Graduate Recruiter, 903-468-8123, Fax: 903-886-5774, E-mail: shelby.miller@tamuc.edu.
Website: http://www.tamuc.edu/academics/graduateSchool/programs/humanitiesSocialScienceArts/default.aspx

**Texas State University,** The Graduate College, College of Liberal Arts, Program in Political Science, San Marcos, TX 78666. Offers MA. *Program availability:* Part-time, evening/weekend. *Faculty:* 13 full-time (2 women). *Students:* 18 full-time (12 women), 13 part-time (3 women); includes 13 minority (2 Black or African American, non-Hispanic/Latino; 9 Hispanic/Latino; 2 Two or more races, non-Hispanic/Latino), 1 international. Average age 32. 24 applicants, 75% accepted, 11 enrolled. In 2016, 13 master's awarded. *Degree requirements:* For master's, comprehensive exam, thesis optional. *Entrance requirements:* For master's, baccalaureate degree in political science from regionally-accredited university; minimum GPA of 3.0 on last 60 undergraduate semester hours of letter-grade work earned at a four-year college or university before receipt of the bachelor's (plus any previously completed graduate work). Additional exam requirements/recommendations for international students: Required—TOEFL (minimum score 550 paper-based; 78 iBT), IELTS (minimum score 6.5). *Application deadline:* For fall admission, 2/15 priority date for domestic and international students; for spring admission, 10/15 for domestic students, 10/1 for international students; for summer admission, 4/15 for domestic students, 3/15 for international students. Applications are processed on a rolling basis. Application fee: $40 ($90 for international students). Electronic applications accepted. *Expenses:* $4,851 per semester. *Financial support:* In 2016–17, 17 students received support, including 6 teaching assistantships (averaging $13,878 per year); research assistantships, career-related internships or fieldwork, Federal Work-Study, institutionally sponsored loans, scholarships/grants, and unspecified assistantships also available. Support available to part-time students. Financial award application deadline: 3/1; financial award applicants required to submit FAFSA. *Unit head:* Dr. Cecilia Castillio, Graduate Adviser, 512-245-2143, Fax: 512-345-7815, E-mail: cr09@txstate.edu. *Application contact:* Dr. Andrea Golato, Dean of Graduate School, 512-245-2581, Fax: 512-245-8365, E-mail: gradcollege@txstate.edu.
Website: http://www.polisci.txstate.edu/degrees-programs/graduate.html

**Texas Tech University,** Graduate School, College of Arts and Sciences, Department of Political Science, Lubbock, TX 79409-1015. Offers political science (MA, PhD); public administration (MPA); JD/MPA. *Accreditation:* NASPAA (one or more programs are accredited). *Program availability:* Online learning. *Faculty:* 32 full-time (7 women). *Students:* 53 full-time (21 women), 25 part-time (11 women); includes 13 minority (3 Black or African American, non-Hispanic/Latino; 1 Asian, non-Hispanic/Latino; 8 Hispanic/Latino; 1 Two or more races, non-Hispanic/Latino), 20 international. Average age 31. 66 applicants, 61% accepted, 27 enrolled. In 2016, 17 master's, 5 doctorates awarded. *Degree requirements:* For master's, thesis or alternative; for doctorate, thesis/dissertation. *Entrance requirements:* For master's and doctorate, GRE General Test, 3 letters of reference. Additional exam requirements/recommendations for international students: Required—TOEFL (minimum score 550 paper-based; 79 iBT). *Application deadline:* For fall admission, 6/1 priority date for domestic students, 1/15 priority date for international students; for spring admission, 9/1 priority date for domestic students, 6/15 priority date for international students. Applications are processed on a rolling basis. Application fee: $75. Electronic applications accepted. *Expenses:* $300 per credit hour full-time resident tuition, $708 per credit hour full-time non-resident tuition; $50.50 per credit hour fee plus $608 per term fee. *Financial support:* In 2016–17, 60 students received support, including 46 fellowships (averaging $2,133 per year), 4 research assistantships (averaging $8,661 per year), 51 teaching assistantships (averaging $11,454 per year); tuition waivers and grader positions also available. Financial award application deadline: 4/15; financial award applicants required to submit FAFSA. *Faculty research:* State politics, American institutions and behavior, Asian politics, international and comparative political relations and economics, public administration and organizations. *Total annual research expenditures:* $177,690. *Unit head:* Dr. Dennis Patterson, Chair, 806-742-3121, Fax: 806-742-0850, E-mail: dennis.patterson@ttu.edu. *Application contact:* Dr. David Lektzian, Associate Chair, 806-742-3121, Fax: 806-742-0850, E-mail: david.lektzian@ttu.edu.
Website: http://www.depts.ttu.edu/politicalscience

**Texas Woman's University,** Graduate School, College of Arts and Sciences, Department of History and Government, Denton, TX 76201. Offers government (MA); history (MA). *Program availability:* Part-time, evening/weekend. *Students:* 4 full-time (1 woman), 23 part-time (21 women); includes 8 minority (2 Black or African American, non-Hispanic/Latino; 1 Asian, non-Hispanic/Latino; 4 Hispanic/Latino; 1 Two or more races, non-Hispanic/Latino), 2 international. Average age 35. In 2016, 7 master's awarded. *Degree requirements:* For master's, comprehensive exam, thesis. *Entrance requirements:* For master's, minimum GPA of 3.25, written statement of purpose, 2 letters of reference. Additional exam requirements/recommendations for international students: Required—TOEFL (minimum score 550 paper-based; 79 iBT). *Application deadline:* For fall admission, 7/1 priority date for domestic students, 3/1 for international students; for spring admission, 12/1 priority date for domestic students, 7/1 for international students. Applications are processed on a rolling basis. Application fee: $50 ($75 for international students). Electronic applications accepted. *Expenses:* Tuition, state resident: full-time $9046; part-time $251 per credit hour. Tuition, nonresident: full-time $22,922; part-time $614 per credit hour. *International tuition:* $23,046 full-time. *Required fees:* $2690; $1285 per credit hour. One-time fee: $50. Tuition and fees vary according to course level, course load, program and reciprocity

agreements. *Financial support:* Research assistantships, teaching assistantships, career-related internships or fieldwork, Federal Work-Study, institutionally sponsored loans, scholarships/grants, traineeships, health care benefits, and unspecified assistantships available. Support available to part-time students. Financial award application deadline: 3/1; financial award applicants required to submit FAFSA. *Faculty research:* U.S. history, politics, and law; global history, politics, and law; Latin American and Caribbean history; legal studies; women in history, politics, and law. *Unit head:* Dr. Jonathan Olsen, Chair, 940-898-2156, Fax: 940-898-2130, E-mail: jolsen1@twu.edu. *Application contact:* Dr. Samuel Wheeler, Assistant Director of Admissions, 940-898-3188, Fax: 940-898-3081, E-mail: wheelersr@twu.edu.
Website: http://www.twu.edu/history-government/

**Tulane University,** School of Liberal Arts, Department of Political Science, New Orleans, LA 70118-5669. Offers PhD. *Degree requirements:* For doctorate, 2 foreign languages, thesis/dissertation. *Entrance requirements:* For doctorate, GRE General Test. Additional exam requirements/recommendations for international students: Required—TOEFL. Electronic applications accepted. *Expenses: Tuition:* Full-time $50,920; part-time $2829 per credit hour. *Required fees:* $2040; $44.50 per credit hour. $580 per term. Tuition and fees vary according to course load, degree level and program.

**Universidad Nacional Pedro Henriquez Urena,** Graduate School, Santo Domingo, Dominican Republic. Offers agricultural diversity (MS), including horticultural/fruit production, tropical animal production; conservation of monuments and cultural assets (M Arch); ecology and environment (MS); environmental engineering (MEE); international relations (MA); natural resource management (MS); political science (MA); project optimization (MPM); project feasibility (MPM); project management (MPM); sanitation engineering (ME); science for teachers (MS); tropical Caribbean architecture (M Arch).

**Université de Montréal,** Faculty of Arts and Sciences, Department of Political Science, Montréal, QC H3C 3J7, Canada. Offers M Sc, PhD. *Degree requirements:* For master's, thesis; for doctorate, thesis/dissertation, general exam. *Entrance requirements:* For master's, minimum GPA of 2.8; for doctorate, master's degree, minimum GPA of 3.0. Electronic applications accepted.

**Université du Québec à Montréal,** Graduate Programs, Program in Political Science, Montréal, QC H3C 3P8, Canada. Offers MA, PhD. *Program availability:* Part-time. *Degree requirements:* For master's, thesis; for doctorate, thesis/dissertation. *Entrance requirements:* For master's, appropriate bachelor's degree or equivalent, proficiency in French; for doctorate, appropriate master's degree or equivalent, proficiency in French.

**Université Laval,** Faculty of Social Sciences, Department of Political Science, Program in Policy Analysis, Québec, QC G1K 7P4, Canada. Offers MA. *Degree requirements:* For master's, thesis (for some programs). *Entrance requirements:* For master's, knowledge of French, comprehension of written English. Electronic applications accepted.

**Université Laval,** Faculty of Social Sciences, Department of Political Science, Programs in Political Science, Québec, QC G1K 7P4, Canada. Offers MA, PhD. Terminal master's awarded for partial completion of doctoral program. *Degree requirements:* For master's, thesis (for some programs); for doctorate, comprehensive exam, thesis/dissertation. *Entrance requirements:* For master's, knowledge of French; for doctorate, knowledge of French, comprehension of written English. Electronic applications accepted.

**University at Albany, State University of New York,** Nelson A. Rockefeller College of Public Affairs and Policy, Department of Political Science, Albany, NY 12222-0001. Offers MA, PhD. *Faculty:* 22 full-time (8 women), 7 part-time/adjunct (2 women). *Students:* 16 full-time (8 women), 24 part-time (10 women); includes 3 minority (1 Asian, non-Hispanic/Latino; 1 Hispanic/Latino; 1 Two or more races, non-Hispanic/Latino), 9 international. Average age 34. 37 applicants, 59% accepted, 7 enrolled. In 2016, 4 master's, 5 doctorates awarded. *Degree requirements:* For doctorate, one foreign language, thesis/dissertation. *Entrance requirements:* For doctorate, GRE General Test. Additional exam requirements/recommendations for international students: Required—TOEFL (minimum score 550 paper-based). *Application deadline:* For fall admission, 2/1 priority date for domestic students, 5/1 for international students; for spring admission, 11/1 for international students. Applications are processed on a rolling basis. Application fee: $75. Electronic applications accepted. *Expenses:* Tuition, state resident: full-time $10,870; part-time $453 per credit hour. Tuition, nonresident: full-time $22,210; part-time $925 per credit hour. *International tuition:* $21,550 full-time. *Required fees:* $1864; $96 per credit hour. *Financial support:* Fellowships available. Financial award application deadline: 2/1. *Total annual research expenditures:* $938,742. *Unit head:* Julie Novkov, Chair, 518-442-5256, E-mail: jnovkov@albany.edu.
Website: http://www.albany.edu/rockefeller/pos/index.htm

**University at Buffalo, the State University of New York,** Graduate School, College of Arts and Sciences, Department of Political Science, Buffalo, NY 14214. Offers MA, PhD. *Faculty:* 14 full-time (4 women), 2 part-time/adjunct (0 women). *Students:* 20 full-time (8 women), 9 part-time (5 women); includes 3 minority (all Black or African American, non-Hispanic/Latino), 1 international. Average age 28. 26 applicants, 88% accepted, 4 enrolled. In 2016, 11 master's, 4 doctorates awarded. Terminal master's awarded for partial completion of doctoral program. *Degree requirements:* For master's, comprehensive exam, thesis or alternative, paper, project, portfolio; for doctorate, comprehensive exam, thesis/dissertation. *Entrance requirements:* For master's, GRE General Test, minimum GPA of 3.0; for doctorate, GRE General Test, minimum GPA of 3.3. Additional exam requirements/recommendations for international students: Required—TOEFL (minimum score 550 paper-based; 79 iBT), IELTS (minimum score 6.5), PTE (minimum score 55). *Application deadline:* For fall admission, 8/1 priority date for domestic students, 3/1 for international students; for spring admission, 11/1 priority date for domestic students, 10/1 for international students. Applications are processed on a rolling basis. Application fee: $75. Electronic applications accepted. *Financial support:* In 2016–17, 12 students received support, including 2 fellowships with full tuition reimbursements available (averaging $6,000 per year), 12 teaching assistantships with full tuition reimbursements available (averaging $13,500 per year); research assistantships, career-related internships or fieldwork, Federal Work-Study, health care benefits, tuition waivers (full), and unspecified assistantships also available. Financial award application deadline: 1/1; financial award applicants required to submit FAFSA. *Faculty research:* American politics, public law, comparative politics, international politics. *Unit head:* Dr. Harvey Palmer, Chairman, 716-645-8449, Fax: 716-645-2166, E-mail: hpalmer@buffalo.edu. *Application contact:* Mary E. O'Brien, Graduate Coordinator, 716-645-3441, Fax: 716-645-2166, E-mail: meobrien@buffalo.edu.
Website: http://www.polsci.buffalo.edu/graduate/

**The University of Akron,** Graduate School, Buchtel College of Arts and Sciences, Department of Political Science, Akron, OH 44325. Offers MA, MAP, JD/MAP. *Program availability:* Part-time. *Faculty:* 10 full-time (1 woman), 11 part-time/adjunct (3 women). *Students:* 20 full-time (7 women), 7 part-time (3 women); includes 3 minority (2 Black or African American, non-Hispanic/Latino; 1 Two or more races, non-Hispanic/Latino), 4 international. Average age 28. 20 applicants, 90% accepted, 9 enrolled. In 2016, 13 master's awarded. *Degree requirements:* For master's, comprehensive exam, essay,

seminars (political science), portfolio (applied politics). *Entrance requirements:* For master's, minimum GPA of 3.0, three letters of recommendation (two of which must be from faculty members), statement of purpose. Additional exam requirements/recommendations for international students: Required—TOEFL (minimum score 550 paper-based; 79 iBT), IELTS (minimum score 6.5). *Application deadline:* For fall admission, 4/1 for domestic and international students; for spring admission, 12/1 for domestic and international students. Applications are processed on a rolling basis. Application fee: $45 ($70 for international students). Electronic applications accepted. *Expenses:* Tuition, state resident: full-time $8618; part-time $359 per credit hour. Tuition, nonresident: full-time $17,149; part-time $715 per credit hour. *Required fees:* $1652. *Financial support:* In 2016–17, 16 teaching assistantships with partial tuition reimbursements were awarded. *Faculty research:* Public opinion and public policy, international/comparative politics, the politics of criminal justice, conflict management. *Total annual research expenditures:* $139,335. *Unit head:* Dr. Nancy Marion, Interim Chair, 330-972-5551, E-mail: nmarion@uakron.edu. *Application contact:* Dr. Stephen Brooks, Graduate Director, 330-972-7944.
Website: http://www.uakron.edu/polisci/

**The University of Alabama,** Graduate School, College of Arts and Sciences, Department of Political Science, Tuscaloosa, AL 35487. Offers political science (MA, PhD); public administration (MPA). *Program availability:* Part-time. *Faculty:* 16 full-time (4 women). *Students:* 48 full-time (16 women), 17 part-time (3 women); includes 12 minority (9 Black or African American, non-Hispanic/Latino; 1 American Indian or Alaska Native, non-Hispanic/Latino; 1 Asian, non-Hispanic/Latino; 1 Two or more races, non-Hispanic/Latino), 6 international. Average age 30. 44 applicants, 70% accepted, 16 enrolled. In 2016, 16 master's, 6 doctorates awarded. Terminal master's awarded for partial completion of doctoral program. *Degree requirements:* For master's, comprehensive exam, thesis optional; for doctorate, comprehensive exam, thesis/dissertation. *Entrance requirements:* For master's and doctorate, GRE, minimum undergraduate GPA of 3.0. Additional exam requirements/recommendations for international students: Required—TOEFL. *Application deadline:* For fall admission, 6/30 for domestic and international students; for spring admission, 10/15 for domestic and international students. Applications are processed on a rolling basis. Application fee: $50 ($60 for international students). Electronic applications accepted. *Expenses:* Tuition, state resident: full-time $10,470. Tuition, nonresident: full-time $26,950. *Financial support:* In 2016–17, 15 students received support, including 3 fellowships with full tuition reimbursements available (averaging $15,000 per year), teaching assistantships with full tuition reimbursements available (averaging $12,500 per year); career-related internships or fieldwork and Federal Work-Study also available. Financial award application deadline: 2/15. *Faculty research:* American politics, comparative politics, international relations, public policy and administration, political theory. *Total annual research expenditures:* $5,000. *Unit head:* Dr. Joseph Smith, Chair and Professor, 205-348-5981, E-mail: josmith@bama.ua.edu. *Application contact:* Dr. Douglas Gibler, Graduate Advisor, 205-348-5528, Fax: 205-348-5298, E-mail: dmgibler@bama.ua.edu.
Website: http://www.as.ua.edu/psc/

**University of Alberta,** Faculty of Graduate Studies and Research, Department of Political Science, Edmonton, AB T6G 2E1, Canada. Offers MA, PhD. *Program availability:* Part-time. *Degree requirements:* For master's, thesis (for some programs); for doctorate, one foreign language, thesis/dissertation. *Entrance requirements:* Additional exam requirements/recommendations for international students: Required—TOEFL. *Faculty research:* Canadian politics, international relations, globalization, classical and contemporary political theory, gender and politics.

**The University of Arizona,** College of Social and Behavioral Sciences, Department of Political Science, Tucson, AZ 85721. Offers MA, PhD. Terminal master's awarded for partial completion of doctoral program. *Degree requirements:* For master's, thesis or alternative; for doctorate, variable foreign language requirement, comprehensive exam, thesis/dissertation. *Entrance requirements:* For master's, GRE General Test, minimum GPA of 3.2, 3 letters of recommendation, writing sample; for doctorate, GRE General Test, minimum GPA of 3.2, 3 letters of recommendation, statement of purpose, writing sample. Additional exam requirements/recommendations for international students: Required—TOEFL (minimum score 550 paper-based; 79 iBT). Electronic applications accepted. *Faculty research:* Voting behavior, political participation, Soviet domestic and Sino-Soviet relations, presidential leadership and congressional behavior.

**University of Arkansas,** Graduate School, J. William Fulbright College of Arts and Sciences, Department of Political Science, Program in Political Science, Fayetteville, AR 72701. Offers MA. In 2016, 9 master's awarded. *Degree requirements:* For master's, thesis or alternative. *Entrance requirements:* For master's, GRE General Test. *Application deadline:* For fall admission, 4/1 for international students; for spring admission, 10/1 for international students. Applications are processed on a rolling basis. Application fee: $40 ($50 for international students). Electronic applications accepted. *Financial support:* In 2016–17, 1 research assistantship, 6 teaching assistantships were awarded; fellowships, career-related internships or fieldwork, and Federal Work-Study also available. Support available to part-time students. Financial award application deadline: 4/1; financial award applicants required to submit FAFSA. *Unit head:* Dr. John Gaber, 479-575-3356, E-mail: jgaber@uark.edu. *Application contact:* Dr. Pearl Dowe, Graduate Coordinator, 479-575-6434, E-mail: pkford@uark.edu.
Website: http://plsc.uark.edu/

**The University of British Columbia,** Faculty of Arts, Department of Political Science, Vancouver, BC V6T 1Z1, Canada. Offers MA, PhD. *Program availability:* Part-time. *Degree requirements:* For master's, thesis; for doctorate, comprehensive exam, thesis/dissertation. *Entrance requirements:* For master's, BA in political science; for doctorate, GRE, BA and MA in political science. Additional exam requirements/recommendations for international students: Required—TOEFL, TWE. Application fee: $100 Canadian dollars ($162 Canadian dollars for international students). Electronic applications accepted. *Expenses:* $4,802 per year tuition and fees, $8,436 per year international. *Financial support:* Fellowships, research assistantships, teaching assistantships, scholarships/grants, and unspecified assistantships available. Financial award application deadline: 10/1. *Faculty research:* Canadian politics, international relations, political theory, comparative politics, public policy. *Unit head:* Barbara Arneil, Head, 604-822-9551, E-mail: arneil@mail.ubc.ca. *Application contact:* Josephine Calazan, Graduate Program Assistant, 604-822-2717, Fax: 604-822-5540, E-mail: poli.grad@ubc.ca.
Website: http://politics.ubc.ca/

**University of Calgary,** Faculty of Graduate Studies, Faculty of Arts, Department of Political Science, Calgary, AB T2N 1N4, Canada. Offers MA, PhD. *Degree requirements:* For master's, thesis; for doctorate, one foreign language, comprehensive exam, thesis/dissertation, prospectus, oral and written candidacy exams. *Entrance requirements:* For master's, minimum GPA of 3.4; for doctorate, minimum GPA of 3.7. Additional exam requirements/recommendations for international students: Required—TOEFL (minimum score 620 paper-based). Electronic applications accepted. *Faculty research:* Canadian politics, international relations, comparative politics, theory, public policy.

**University of California, Berkeley,** Graduate Division, College of Letters and Science, Charles and Louise Travers Department of Political Science, Berkeley, CA 94720-1500. Offers PhD. *Faculty:* 44 full-time, 1 part-time/adjunct. *Students:* 93 full-time (37 women); includes 15 minority (3 Black or African American, non-Hispanic/Latino; 10 Asian, non-Hispanic/Latino; 2 Hispanic/Latino), 14 international. Average age 31. 465 applicants, 13 enrolled. In 2016, 21 doctorates awarded. *Degree requirements:* For doctorate, thesis/dissertation, oral qualifying exams. *Entrance requirements:* For doctorate, GRE General Test, minimum GPA of 3.0, 3 letters of recommendation. Additional exam requirements/recommendations for international students: Required—TOEFL (minimum score 570 paper-based; 90 iBT). *Application deadline:* For fall admission, 12/1 for domestic students. Application fee: $105 ($125 for international students). Electronic applications accepted. *Financial support:* Fellowships, research assistantships, teaching assistantships, health care benefits, and unspecified assistantships available. Financial award applicants required to submit FAFSA. *Unit head:* Prof. Eric Schickler, Chair, 510-643-4408, E-mail: ch_politicalscience@ls.berkeley.edu. *Application contact:* 510-643-4408, E-mail: pscadmit@berkeley.edu. Website: http://www.polisci.berkeley.edu/

**University of California, Davis,** Graduate Studies, Program in Political Science, Davis, CA 95616. Offers MA, PhD. Terminal master's awarded for partial completion of doctoral program. *Degree requirements:* For master's, thesis; for doctorate, thesis/dissertation. *Entrance requirements:* For master's and doctorate, GRE General Test, minimum GPA of 3.0, writing sample. Additional exam requirements/recommendations for international students: Required—TOEFL (minimum score 550 paper-based). Electronic applications accepted. *Faculty research:* American government and politics, political theory, comparative politics, international relations, public law.

**University of California, Irvine,** School of Social Sciences, Department of Political Science, Irvine, CA 92697. Offers political psychology (PhD); political sciences (PhD); public choice (PhD). *Students:* 53 full-time (22 women), 4 part-time (all women); includes 15 minority (9 Asian, non-Hispanic/Latino; 5 Hispanic/Latino; 1 Two or more races, non-Hispanic/Latino), 6 international. Average age 31. 113 applicants, 29% accepted, 14 enrolled. In 2016, 11 doctorates awarded. *Degree requirements:* For doctorate, thesis/dissertation. *Entrance requirements:* For doctorate, GRE General Test, minimum GPA of 3.0. Additional exam requirements/recommendations for international students: Required—TOEFL (minimum score 550 paper-based). *Application deadline:* For fall admission, 1/15 priority date for domestic students, 1/15 for international students. Applications are processed on a rolling basis. Application fee: $105 ($125 for international students). Electronic applications accepted. *Financial support:* Fellowships, research assistantships with full tuition reimbursements, teaching assistantships, institutionally sponsored loans, traineeships, health care benefits, and unspecified assistantships available. Financial award application deadline: 3/1; financial award applicants required to submit FAFSA. *Faculty research:* Political behavior, political economy, international relations. *Unit head:* Jeffrey Kopstein, Chair, 949-824-4012, E-mail: kopstein@uci.edu. *Application contact:* Robert Uriu, Graduate Program Director, 949-824-1868, E-mail: rmuriu@uci.edu. Website: http://www.polisci.uci.edu/

**University of California, Los Angeles,** Graduate Division, College of Letters and Science, Department of Political Science, Los Angeles, CA 90095. Offers MA, PhD. Terminal master's awarded for partial completion of doctoral program. *Degree requirements:* For master's, comprehensive exam; for doctorate, one foreign language, thesis/dissertation, oral and written qualifying exams. *Entrance requirements:* For doctorate, GRE General Test, bachelor's degree; minimum undergraduate GPA of 3.0 (or its equivalent if letter grade system not used); writing sample. Additional exam requirements/recommendations for international students: Required—TOEFL. Electronic applications accepted.

**University of California, Riverside,** Graduate Division, Department of Political Science, Riverside, CA 92521-0102. Offers MA, PhD. *Program availability:* Part-time. Terminal master's awarded for partial completion of doctoral program. *Degree requirements:* For master's, comprehensive exams or thesis; for doctorate, thesis/dissertation, qualifying exams. *Entrance requirements:* For master's and doctorate, GRE General Test, minimum GPA of 3.2. Additional exam requirements/recommendations for international students: Required—TOEFL (minimum score 550 paper-based; 80 iBT). Electronic applications accepted. *Expenses:* Tuition, state resident: full-time $16,666. Tuition, nonresident: full-time $31,768. *Required fees:* $11,055.54 per quarter. $3685.18 per quarter. Tuition and fees vary according to campus/location and program. *Faculty research:* American politics, mass political behavior, comparative politics, international relations, political theory.

**University of California, San Diego,** Graduate Division, Department of Political Science, La Jolla, CA 92093. Offers political science (PhD); political science and international affairs (PhD). *Students:* 68 full-time (22 women). 365 applicants, 10% accepted, 7 enrolled. In 2016, 17 doctorates awarded. *Degree requirements:* For doctorate, comprehensive exam, thesis/dissertation. *Entrance requirements:* For doctorate, GRE General Test, letters of recommendation. Additional exam requirements/recommendations for international students: Required—TOEFL (minimum score 600 paper-based; 100 iBT), IELTS. *Application deadline:* For fall admission, 12/13 for domestic students. Application fee: $105 ($125 for international students). Electronic applications accepted. *Expenses:* Tuition, state resident: full-time $11,220. Tuition, nonresident: full-time $26,322. *Required fees:* $1864. *Financial support:* Fellowships, research assistantships, teaching assistantships, and scholarships/grants available. Financial award applicants required to submit FAFSA. *Faculty research:* American politics, comparative politics, international relations, methodology, political theory. *Unit head:* Thad Kousser, Chair, 858-534-3239, E-mail: tkousser@ucsd.edu. *Application contact:* Aubrey Rudd, Graduate Coordinator, 858-534-2705, E-mail: psgradadmissions@ucsd.edu. Website: http://polisci.ucsd.edu/

**University of California, San Diego,** Graduate Division, School of Global Policy and Strategy, La Jolla, CA 92093. Offers Chinese economic and political affairs (MCEPA), including Chinese economy, Chinese environment, Chinese foreign relations and security, Chinese politics and public policy; international affairs (MAS, MIA), including international development and nonprofit management (MIA), international economics (MIA), international environmental policy (MIA), international management (MIA), international politics (MIA); political science and international affairs (PhD); public policy (MPP), including American policy in global context, business, government and regulation, energy and environmental policy, health policy, program design and evaluation, security policy. *Program availability:* Part-time. *Faculty:* 33 full-time (9 women), 20 part-time/adjunct (4 women). *Students:* 390 full-time, 6 part-time. Average age 26. 590 applicants, 165 enrolled. In 2016, 160 master's, 3 doctorates awarded. *Degree requirements:* For master's, language capstone (for MIA and MCEPA); for doctorate, thesis/dissertation. *Entrance requirements:* For master's, GMAT or GRE General Test; for doctorate, GRE General Test. Additional exam requirements/recommendations for international students: Required—TOEFL (minimum score 90 iBT), IELTS (minimum score 7). *Application deadline:* For fall admission, 1/15 for domestic and international students. Applications are processed on a rolling basis. Application fee: $102 ($125 for international students). Electronic applications accepted.

*Expenses:* Contact institution. *Financial support:* In 2016–17, 140 students received support, including 60 fellowships with full and partial tuition reimbursements available (averaging $50,000 per year), 15 research assistantships with full tuition reimbursements available (averaging $20,000 per year), 20 teaching assistantships with full tuition reimbursements available (averaging $20,000 per year); career-related internships or fieldwork, scholarships/grants, and unspecified assistantships also available. Financial award application deadline: 1/15. *Faculty research:* Public policy; international management, finance and trade; international development; international politics in Latin America, China, Korea, Japan, and Southeast Asia; international environmental policy. *Unit head:* Sonja Steinbrech, Director of Enrollment, 858-534-7162, E-mail: ssteinbrech@ucsd.edu. *Application contact:* Admissions Representative, 858-534-5914, Fax: 858-534-5914, E-mail: gps-apply@uscd.edu. Website: http://gps.ucsd.edu

**University of California, Santa Barbara,** Graduate Division, College of Letters and Sciences, Division of Social Sciences, Department of Global Studies, Santa Barbara, CA 93106-7065. Offers global culture, ideology, and religion (MA, PhD); global government, human rights, and civil society (MA, PhD); political economy, sustainable development, and the environment (MA, PhD). *Degree requirements:* For master's, one foreign language, thesis, 2 years of a second language; for doctorate, one foreign language, thesis/dissertation, reading proficiency in at least one language other than English. *Entrance requirements:* For master's, GRE, 2 years of a second language with minimum B grade in the final term, statement of purpose, resume or curriculum vitae, 3 letters of recommendation, transcripts (from all post-secondary institutions attended), writing sample (15-20 pages); for doctorate, GRE, statement of purpose, personal achievements/contributions statement, resume or curriculum vitae, 3 letters of recommendation, transcripts from all post-secondary institutions attended, writing sample (15-20 pages). Additional exam requirements/recommendations for international students: Required—TOEFL (minimum score 600 paper-based; 94 iBT), IELTS (minimum score 7). Electronic applications accepted.

**University of California, Santa Barbara,** Graduate Division, College of Letters and Sciences, Division of Social Sciences, Department of Political Science, Santa Barbara, CA 93106-9420. Offers PhD, MA/PhD. Terminal master's awarded for partial completion of doctoral program. *Degree requirements:* For doctorate, one foreign language, thesis/dissertation, 2 comprehensive exams or 1 exam and field paper. *Entrance requirements:* For doctorate, GRE General Test. Additional exam requirements/recommendations for international students: Required—TOEFL (minimum score 600 paper-based; 100 iBT), IELTS. Electronic applications accepted. *Faculty research:* American politics, comparative politics, international relations, political theory.

**University of California, Santa Cruz,** Division of Graduate Studies, Division of Social Sciences, Politics Department, Santa Cruz, CA 95064. Offers PhD. *Degree requirements:* For doctorate, qualifying exam. *Entrance requirements:* For doctorate, GRE. Additional exam requirements/recommendations for international students: Required—TOEFL (minimum score 550 paper-based; 83 iBT); Recommended—IELTS (minimum score 8). Electronic applications accepted. *Faculty research:* Political and social thought, political institutions, political economy, political and social forces.

**University of Central Florida,** College of Sciences, Department of Political Science, Orlando, FL 32816. Offers intelligence and national security (Certificate); political science (MA); security studies (PhD). *Program availability:* Part-time, evening/weekend. *Faculty:* 39 full-time (12 women), 11 part-time/adjunct (2 women). *Students:* 38 full-time (11 women), 19 part-time (9 women); includes 16 minority (4 Black or African American, non-Hispanic/Latino; 2 Asian, non-Hispanic/Latino; 8 Hispanic/Latino; 2 Two or more races, non-Hispanic/Latino), 11 international. Average age 31. 44 applicants, 68% accepted, 18 enrolled. In 2016, 14 master's, 1 other advanced degree awarded. *Degree requirements:* For master's, comprehensive exam, thesis; for doctorate, one foreign language, thesis/dissertation, oral qualifying examination, written candidacy exam. *Entrance requirements:* For master's, GRE General Test, minimum GPA of 3.0 in last 60 hours; for doctorate, GRE General Test, master's degree or its equivalent in political science, international politics, international relations, or related discipline. Additional exam requirements/recommendations for international students: Required—TOEFL. *Application deadline:* For fall admission, 7/15 for domestic students; for spring admission, 12/1 for domestic students. Application fee: $30. Electronic applications accepted. *Expenses:* Tuition, state resident: part-time $288.16 per credit hour. Tuition, nonresident: part-time $1071.31 per credit hour. *Financial support:* In 2016–17, 21 students received support, including 6 fellowships with partial tuition reimbursements available (averaging $5,667 per year), 3 research assistantships with partial tuition reimbursements available (averaging $18,661 per year), 16 teaching assistantships with partial tuition reimbursements available (averaging $11,617 per year); career-related internships or fieldwork, Federal Work-Study, institutionally sponsored loans, tuition waivers (partial), and unspecified assistantships also available. Financial award application deadline: 3/1; financial award applicants required to submit FAFSA. *Faculty research:* Environment, international relations, security studies, comparative politics. *Unit head:* Dr. Kerstin Hamann, Chair, 407-823-2085, Fax: 407-823-0051, E-mail: kerstin.hamann@ucf.edu. *Application contact:* Assistant Director, Graduate Admissions, 407-823-2766, Fax: 407-823-6442, E-mail: gradadmissions@ucf.edu. Website: http://politicalscience.cos.ucf.edu/

**University of Central Oklahoma,** The Jackson College of Graduate Studies, College of Liberal Arts, Department of Political Science, Edmond, OK 73034-5209. Offers international affairs (MA); political science (MA); public administration (MPA). *Program availability:* Part-time. *Degree requirements:* For master's, comprehensive exam (for some programs), thesis (for some programs). *Entrance requirements:* For master's, GRE, 18 undergraduate hours in political science. Additional exam requirements/recommendations for international students: Required—TOEFL (minimum score 550 paper-based; 79 iBT), IELTS (minimum score 6.5). Electronic applications accepted.

**University of Chicago,** Division of the Social Sciences, Department of Political Science, Chicago, IL 60637. Offers PhD. *Students:* 123 full-time (52 women); includes 42 minority (19 Black or African American, non-Hispanic/Latino; 1 American Indian or Alaska Native, non-Hispanic/Latino; 6 Asian, non-Hispanic/Latino; 10 Hispanic/Latino; 6 Two or more races, non-Hispanic/Latino), 32 international. 456 applicants, 8% accepted, 14 enrolled. In 2016, 16 doctorates awarded. *Degree requirements:* For doctorate, one foreign language, thesis/dissertation, exam, qualifying paper. *Entrance requirements:* For doctorate, GRE General Test. Additional exam requirements/recommendations for international students: Required—TOEFL (minimum score 104 iBT), IELTS (minimum score 7). *Application deadline:* For fall admission, 12/15 for domestic and international students. Application fee: $90. Electronic applications accepted. *Financial support:* In 2016–17, 14 students received support, including 14 fellowships with full tuition reimbursements available (averaging $23,000 per year); career-related internships or fieldwork, Federal Work-Study, institutionally sponsored loans, scholarships/grants, and health care benefits also available. Financial award application deadline: 12/15. *Faculty research:* Political philosophy, international political economy, strategic studies, public policy and race relations, comparative politics (China, Middle East, Soviet Union, Africa, India, Japan). *Unit head:* John Mark Hansen, Interim Chair, 773-702-5476, E-mail: jhansen@uchicago.edu. *Application contact:* Office of the Dean of Students, 773-702-

## Political Science

8415, E-mail: admissions@ssd.uchicago.edu.
Website: http://political-science.uchicago.edu

**University of Cincinnati,** Graduate School, McMicken College of Arts and Sciences, Department of Political Science, Cincinnati, OH 45221. Offers MA, PhD. Terminal master's awarded for partial completion of doctoral program. *Degree requirements:* For master's, thesis (for some programs); for doctorate, thesis/dissertation. *Entrance requirements:* For master's and doctorate, GRE General Test, GRE Subject Test. Additional exam requirements/recommendations for international students: Required—TOEFL. Electronic applications accepted. *Expenses: Tuition, area resident:* Full-time $12,790; part-time $389 per credit hour. Tuition, state resident: full-time $13,290; part-time $419 per credit hour. Tuition, nonresident: full-time $24,532; part-time $976 per credit hour. *International tuition:* $24,832 full-time. *Required fees:* $140 per credit hour. Tuition and fees vary according to course load, degree level, program and reciprocity agreements. *Faculty research:* International security, methodology, American politics, comparative politics.

**University of Colorado Boulder,** Graduate School, College of Arts and Sciences, Department of Political Science, Boulder, CO 80309. Offers MA, PhD. *Faculty:* 26 full-time (8 women). *Students:* 49 full-time (23 women); includes 5 minority (1 Asian, non-Hispanic/Latino; 3 Hispanic/Latino; 1 Two or more races, non-Hispanic/Latino), 6 international. Average age 30. 106 applicants, 31% accepted, 9 enrolled. In 2016, 10 master's, 7 doctorates awarded. Terminal master's awarded for partial completion of doctoral program. *Degree requirements:* For master's, comprehensive exam, thesis; for doctorate, one foreign language, thesis/dissertation. *Entrance requirements:* For master's, GRE General Test, minimum undergraduate GPA of 3.0; for doctorate, GRE General Test, minimum GPA of 3.5 (undergraduate), 3.0 (graduate). *Application deadline:* For fall admission, 12/15 for domestic and international students. Application fee: $60 ($80 for international students). Electronic applications accepted. Application fee is waived when completed online. *Financial support:* In 2016–17, 134 students received support, including 26 fellowships (averaging $2,041 per year), 3 research assistantships with full and partial tuition reimbursements available (averaging $27,548 per year), 45 teaching assistantships with full and partial tuition reimbursements available (averaging $40,725 per year); institutionally sponsored loans, scholarships/grants, health care benefits, and unspecified assistantships also available. Financial award application deadline: 12/31; financial award applicants required to submit FAFSA. *Faculty research:* Political science, democracy, comparative government, political economics/economy, international relations/diplomacy. *Total annual research expenditures:* $471,434. *Application contact:* E-mail: pscigrad@colorado.edu. Website: http://polsci.colorado.edu/

**University of Colorado Denver,** College of Liberal Arts and Sciences, Department of Political Science, Denver, CO 80217. Offers MA. *Program availability:* Part-time, evening/weekend. *Faculty:* 12 full-time (4 women), 2 part-time/adjunct (0 women). *Students:* 31 full-time (13 women), 31 part-time (12 women); includes 18 minority (6 Black or African American, non-Hispanic/Latino; 3 American Indian or Alaska Native, non-Hispanic/Latino; 1 Asian, non-Hispanic/Latino; 8 Hispanic/Latino), 3 international. Average age 33. 17 applicants, 71% accepted, 7 enrolled. In 2016, 26 master's awarded. *Degree requirements:* For master's, project or thesis, minimum of 30 credit hours. *Entrance requirements:* For master's, 18 hours of course work in political science; minimum GPA of 3.0 (3.2 preferred); statement of purpose; academic writing sample. Additional exam requirements/recommendations for international students: Required—TOEFL (minimum score 537 paper-based; 75 iBT); Recommended—IELTS (minimum score 6.5). *Application deadline:* For fall admission, 3/1 for domestic students, 3/1 priority date for international students; for spring admission, 10/1 for domestic students, 10/1 priority date for international students. Application fee: $50 ($75 for international students). Electronic applications accepted. *Expenses:* Tuition, state resident: full-time $11,006; part-time $474 per credit. Tuition, nonresident: full-time $28,212; part-time $1264 per credit hour. *Required fees:* $256 per semester. One-time fee: $94.32. Tuition and fees vary according to campus/location and program. *Financial support:* In 2016–17, 2 students received support. Fellowships, research assistantships, teaching assistantships, Federal Work-Study, institutionally sponsored loans, scholarships/grants, and traineeships available. Financial award application deadline: 4/1; financial award applicants required to submit FAFSA. *Faculty research:* Indigenous peoples in the international legal and political arena; political developments in Europe and the former Soviet Union; early Chinese industrialization, modern Chinese political and economic development, and human rights; Congressional oversight and Congressional-executive relations. *Unit head:* Dr. Anthony Robinson, Chair, 303-556-2746, E-mail: tony.robinson@ucdenver.edu. *Application contact:* Political Science Department, 303-556-3556.
Website: http://www.ucdenver.edu/academics/colleges/CLAS/Departments/PoliticalScience/Programs/Masters/Pages/MasterofArts.aspx

**University of Colorado Denver,** School of Public Affairs, Program in Public Affairs and Administration, Denver, CO 80127. Offers public administration (MPA), including domestic violence, emergency management and homeland security, environmental policy, management and law, homeland security and defense, local government, nonprofit management, public administration; public affairs (PhD). *Accreditation:* NASPAA. *Program availability:* Part-time, evening/weekend, online learning. *Students:* 241 full-time (146 women), 135 part-time (86 women); includes 61 minority (15 Black or African American, non-Hispanic/Latino; 1 American Indian or Alaska Native, non-Hispanic/Latino; 10 Asian, non-Hispanic/Latino; 26 Hispanic/Latino; 2 Native Hawaiian or other Pacific Islander, non-Hispanic/Latino; 7 Two or more races, non-Hispanic/Latino), 26 international. Average age 36. 240 applicants, 70% accepted, 91 enrolled. In 2016, 158 master's, 8 doctorates awarded. *Degree requirements:* For master's, thesis or alternative, 36-39 credit hours; for doctorate, comprehensive exam, thesis/dissertation, minimum of 66 semester hours, including at least 30 hours of dissertation. *Entrance requirements:* For master's, GRE, GMAT or LSAT, resume, essay, transcripts, recommendations; for doctorate, GRE, resume, essay, transcripts, recommendations. Additional exam requirements/recommendations for international students: Required—TOEFL (minimum score 550 paper-based; 80 iBT); Recommended—IELTS (minimum score 6.5). *Application deadline:* For fall admission, 2/1 priority date for domestic students, 1/15 priority date for international students; for spring admission, 10/15 priority date for domestic students, 10/1 priority date for international students. Application fee: $50 ($75 for international students). Electronic applications accepted. *Expenses:* Contact institution. *Financial support:* In 2016–17, 92 students received support. Fellowships with partial tuition reimbursements available, research assistantships with partial tuition reimbursements available, teaching assistantships with partial tuition reimbursements available, Federal Work-Study, institutionally sponsored loans, scholarships/grants, traineeships, and unspecified assistantships available. Financial award application deadline: 4/1; financial award applicants required to submit FAFSA. *Faculty research:* Housing, education and the social and economic issues of vulnerable populations; nonprofit governance and management; education finance, effectiveness and reform; P-20 education initiatives; municipal government accountability. *Unit head:* Dr. Christine Martell, Director of MPA Program, 303-315-2716, Fax: 303-315-2229, E-mail: christine.martell@ucdenver.edu. *Application contact:* Dawn Savage, Student Services Coordinator, 303-315-2743, Fax: 303-315-2229, E-mail: dawn.savage@ucdenver.edu.

Website: http://www.ucdenver.edu/academics/colleges/SPA/Academics/programs/PublicAffairsAdmin/Pages/index.aspx

**University of Connecticut,** Graduate School, College of Liberal Arts and Sciences, Department of Political Science, Storrs, CT 06269. Offers MA, PhD. Terminal master's awarded for partial completion of doctoral program. *Degree requirements:* For master's, comprehensive exam; for doctorate, 2 foreign languages, thesis/dissertation. *Entrance requirements:* For master's and doctorate, GRE General Test. Additional exam requirements/recommendations for international students: Required—TOEFL (minimum score 550 paper-based). Electronic applications accepted.

**University of Dallas,** Braniff Graduate School of Liberal Arts, Institute of Philosophic Studies, Doctoral Program in Politics, Irving, TX 75062-4736. Offers PhD. *Degree requirements:* For doctorate, 2 foreign languages, comprehensive exam, thesis/dissertation. *Entrance requirements:* For doctorate, GRE General Test. Additional exam requirements/recommendations for international students: Required—TOEFL. *Faculty research:* Classical, medieval, and modern political philosophy; American political thought and institutions; politics and literature.

**University of Dallas,** Braniff Graduate School of Liberal Arts, Master's Program in Politics, Irving, TX 75062-4736. Offers M Pol, MA. *Program availability:* Part-time. *Degree requirements:* For master's, one foreign language, comprehensive exam, thesis. *Entrance requirements:* For master's, GRE General Test. Additional exam requirements/recommendations for international students: Required—TOEFL. *Faculty research:* Classical, medieval, and modern political philosophy; American political thought and institutions; politics and literature.

**University of Delaware,** College of Arts and Sciences, Department of Political Science and International Relations, Newark, DE 19716. Offers MA, PhD. Terminal master's awarded for partial completion of doctoral program. *Degree requirements:* For master's, research paper; for doctorate, one foreign language, comprehensive exam, thesis/dissertation. *Entrance requirements:* For master's and doctorate, GRE General Test, minimum GPA of 3.2 in major, 3.0 overall. Additional exam requirements/recommendations for international students: Required—TOEFL (minimum score 600 paper-based). Electronic applications accepted. *Faculty research:* Social constructivism. international migration, international security, democratization, human rights.

**University of Florida,** Graduate School, College of Liberal Arts and Sciences, Department of Political Science, Gainesville, FL 32611. Offers educational policy (PhD); international development policy and administration (MA, Certificate); international relations (MA, MAT); political campaigning (MA, Certificate); political science (MA, PhD); public affairs (MA, Certificate); tropical conservation and development (MA, PhD); JD/MA. Terminal master's awarded for partial completion of doctoral program. *Degree requirements:* For master's, variable foreign language requirement, comprehensive exam (for some programs), thesis or alternative, internship (for some programs); for doctorate, variable foreign language requirement, comprehensive exam, thesis/dissertation. *Entrance requirements:* For master's and doctorate, GRE General Test (minimum score: 308 combined verbal/quantitative), minimum GPA of 3.5. Additional exam requirements/recommendations for international students: Required—TOEFL (minimum score 550 paper-based; 80 iBT), IELTS (minimum score 6). Electronic applications accepted. *Faculty research:* American electoral politics and political institutions, comparative democratization and development, theories of international relation, and political theory.

**University of Georgia,** School of Public and International Affairs, Program in Political Science/International Affairs, Athens, GA 30602. Offers MA, PhD. *Degree requirements:* For master's, one foreign language, thesis; for doctorate, one foreign language, thesis/dissertation. *Entrance requirements:* For master's and doctorate, GRE General Test. *Application deadline:* For fall admission, 7/1 priority date for domestic students; for spring admission, 11/15 for domestic students. Application fee: $50. Electronic applications accepted. *Financial support:* Fellowships, research assistantships, teaching assistantships, and unspecified assistantships available. *Unit head:* Dr. John A. Maltese, Head, 706-542-4147, E-mail: jmaltese@uga.edu. *Application contact:* Michael Lynch, Graduate Coordinator, 706-543-4421, E-mail: mlynch@uga.edu.
Website: http://www.uga.edu/pol-sci/

**University of Guelph,** Graduate Studies, College of Social and Applied Human Sciences, Department of Political Science, Guelph, ON N1G 2W1, Canada. Offers comparative politics (MA); international development (MA); political science (MA); public policy and public administration (MA); the Americas (Canada emphasis) (MA). MA in public policy and public administration offered in collaboration with Department of Political Science of McMaster University. *Degree requirements:* For master's, thesis or paper. *Entrance requirements:* For master's, minimum B average during previous 2 years of course work, 4 year Honours Degree in Political Science. Additional exam requirements/recommendations for international students: Required—TOEFL. Electronic applications accepted. *Faculty research:* Political ethics, constitutional power.

**University of Hawaii at Manoa,** Graduate Division, College of Social Sciences, Department of Political Science, Honolulu, HI 96822. Offers MA, PhD. *Program availability:* Part-time. Terminal master's awarded for partial completion of doctoral program. *Degree requirements:* For master's, thesis optional; for doctorate, comprehensive exam, thesis/dissertation. *Entrance requirements:* Additional exam requirements/recommendations for international students: Required—TOEFL (minimum score 540 paper-based; 76 iBT), IELTS (minimum score 5). *Faculty research:* Asia/Pacific, political economy, human rights, futures, postmodernism.

**University of Houston,** College of Liberal Arts and Social Sciences, Department of Political Science, Houston, TX 77204. Offers political science (MA, PhD); public administration (MA). *Program availability:* Part-time. Terminal master's awarded for partial completion of doctoral program. *Degree requirements:* For master's, thesis optional; for doctorate, thesis/dissertation. *Entrance requirements:* For master's and doctorate, GRE. Additional exam requirements/recommendations for international students: Required—TOEFL (minimum score 550 paper-based; 79 iBT). *Faculty research:* American politics, political theory, judicial process, public policy, comparative politics.

**University of Idaho,** College of Graduate Studies, College of Letters, Arts and Social Sciences, Department of Politics and Philosophy, Moscow, ID 83844. Offers political science (MA, PhD); public administration (MPA). *Faculty:* 9 full-time. *Students:* 8 full-time, 12 part-time. Average age 35. In 2016, 7 master's awarded. *Entrance requirements:* For master's, minimum GPA of 3.0. Additional exam requirements/recommendations for international students: Required—TOEFL. *Expenses:* Tuition, state resident: full-time $6460; part-time $414 per credit hour. Tuition, nonresident: full-time $21,268; part-time $1237 per credit hour. *Required fees:* $2070; $60 per credit hour. Full-time tuition and fees vary according to course load and reciprocity agreements. *Unit head:* Dr. Brian Ellison, Chair, 208-885-6328, E-mail: politicsphilosophy@uidaho.edu. *Application contact:* Sean Scoggin, Graduate Recruitment Coordinator, 208-885-4723, E-mail: graduateadmissions@uidaho.edu. Website: https://www.uidaho.edu/class/politics-and-philosophy

**University of Illinois at Chicago,** College of Liberal Arts and Sciences, Department of Political Science, Chicago, IL 60607-7128. Offers MA, PhD. *Program availability:* Part-time. Terminal master's awarded for partial completion of doctoral program. *Degree requirements:* For master's, thesis or comprehensive exam. *Entrance requirements:* For master's, GRE General Test, minimum GPA of 3.0. Additional exam requirements/recommendations for international students: Required—TOEFL. Electronic applications accepted. *Faculty research:* Policy analysis/national urban politics and policy, electoral behavior.

**University of Illinois at Springfield,** Graduate Programs, College of Public Affairs and Administration, Department of Political Science, Springfield, IL 62703-5407. Offers MA. *Program availability:* Part-time, evening/weekend, 100% online, blended/hybrid learning. *Faculty:* 5 full-time (2 women), 2 part-time/adjunct (1 woman). *Students:* 10 full-time (3 women), 52 part-time (17 women); includes 10 minority (7 Black or African American, non-Hispanic/Latino; 1 Asian, non-Hispanic/Latino; 2 Hispanic/Latino). Average age 33. 54 applicants, 63% accepted, 20 enrolled. In 2016, 12 master's awarded. *Degree requirements:* For master's, comprehensive exam, participant/observer case study, or thesis. *Entrance requirements:* For master's, minimum undergraduate GPA of 3.0. Additional exam requirements/recommendations for international students: Required—TOEFL (minimum score 500 paper-based; 61 iBT). *Application deadline:* Applications are processed on a rolling basis. Application fee: $60 ($75 for international students). Electronic applications accepted. *Expenses:* Tuition, state resident: part-time $329 per credit hour. Tuition, nonresident: part-time $675 per credit hour. *Financial support:* In 2016–17, fellowships with full tuition reimbursements (averaging $9,900 per year), research assistantships with full tuition reimbursements (averaging $9,991 per year), teaching assistantships with full tuition reimbursements (averaging $10,059 per year) were awarded; career-related internships or fieldwork, Federal Work-Study, scholarships/grants, health care benefits, and unspecified assistantships also available. Support available to part-time students. Financial award application deadline: 11/15; financial award applicants required to submit FAFSA. *Unit head:* Dr. Richard Gilman-Opalsky, Program Administrator, 217-206-8328, E-mail: rgilm3@uis.edu. *Application contact:* Dr. Cecelia Cornell, Associate Vice Chancellor for Graduate Education, 217-206-7230, E-mail: ccorn1@uis.edu.
Website: http://www.uis.edu/politicalstudies/

**University of Illinois at Urbana–Champaign,** Graduate College, College of Liberal Arts and Sciences, Department of Political Science, Champaign, IL 61820. Offers MA, PhD, PhD/JD.

**The University of Iowa,** Graduate College, College of Liberal Arts and Sciences, Department of Political Science, Iowa City, IA 52242-1316. Offers PhD. *Degree requirements:* For doctorate, comprehensive exam, thesis/dissertation. *Entrance requirements:* For doctorate, GRE General Test, minimum GPA of 3.0. Additional exam requirements/recommendations for international students: Required—TOEFL (minimum score 600 paper-based; 100 iBT). Electronic applications accepted.

**The University of Kansas,** Graduate Studies, College of Liberal Arts and Sciences, Department of Political Science, Lawrence, KS 66045. Offers MA, PhD, DMA/PhD. *Program availability:* Part-time. *Students:* 34 full-time (13 women), 7 part-time (3 women); includes 5 minority (2 Black or African American, non-Hispanic/Latino; 1 American Indian or Alaska Native, non-Hispanic/Latino; 1 Hispanic/Latino; 1 Two or more races, non-Hispanic/Latino), 8 international. Average age 32. 44 applicants, 70% accepted, 12 enrolled. In 2016, 7 master's, 4 doctorates awarded. Terminal master's awarded for partial completion of doctoral program. *Entrance requirements:* For master's, GRE General Test, 3 letters of recommendation, curriculum vitae, transcripts, personal statement; for doctorate, GRE General Test, 3 letters of recommendation, transcripts, personal statement, curriculum vitae. Additional exam requirements/recommendations for international students: Required—TOEFL. *Application deadline:* For fall admission, 4/15 for domestic and international students. Application fee: $65 ($85 for international students). Electronic applications accepted. *Financial support:* Fellowships, research assistantships, teaching assistantships, scholarships/grants, health care benefits, and unspecified assistantships available. Financial award application deadline: 1/7. *Faculty research:* Latino politics, gender politics, Middle East and North African politics, American politics/voting behavior, environmental policy. *Unit head:* Don Haider-Markel, Chair, 785-864-9034, E-mail: dhmarkel@ku.edu. *Application contact:* Graduate Coordinator, 785-864-3523, E-mail: gradpols@ku.edu.
Website: https://kups.ku.edu/

**University of Kentucky,** Graduate School, College of Arts and Sciences, Program in Political Science, Lexington, KY 40506-0032. Offers MA, PhD. *Degree requirements:* For master's, comprehensive exam, thesis optional; for doctorate, comprehensive exam, thesis/dissertation. *Entrance requirements:* For master's, GRE General Test, minimum undergraduate GPA of 2.75; for doctorate, GRE General Test, minimum graduate GPA of 3.0. Additional exam requirements/recommendations for international students: Required—TOEFL (minimum score 550 paper-based). Electronic applications accepted. *Faculty research:* International political economy, critical policy studies, regional conflict and integration, race and American politics, media studies.

**University of Lethbridge,** School of Graduate Studies, Lethbridge, AB T1K 3M4, Canada. Offers addictions counseling (M Sc); agricultural biotechnology (M Sc); agricultural studies (M Sc, MA); anthropology (MA); archaeology (M Sc, MA); art (MA, MFA); biochemistry (M Sc); biological sciences (M Sc); biomolecular science (PhD); biosystems and biodiversity (PhD); Canadian studies (MA); chemistry (M Sc); computer science (M Sc); computer science and geographical information science (M Sc); counseling (MC); counseling psychology (M Ed); dramatic arts (MA); earth, space, and physical science (PhD); economics (MA); education (MA, PhD); educational leadership (M Ed); English (MA); environmental science (M Sc); evolution and behavior (PhD); exercise science (M Sc); French (MA); French/German (MA); French/Spanish (MA); general education (M Ed); geography (M Sc, MA); German (MA); health sciences (M Sc); individualized multidisciplinary (M Sc, MA); kinesiology (M Sc, MA); management (M Sc), including accounting, finance, human resource management and labor relations, information systems, international management, marketing, policy and strategy; mathematics (M Sc); music (M Mus, MA); Native American studies (MA); neuroscience (M Sc, PhD); new media (MA, MFA); nursing (M Sc, MN); philosophy (MA); physics (M Sc); political science (MA); psychology (M Sc, MA); religious studies (MA); sociology (MA); theatre and dramatic arts (MFA); theoretical and computational science (PhD); urban and regional studies (MA); women and gender studies (MA). *Program availability:* Part-time, evening/weekend. *Degree requirements:* For master's, thesis (for some programs); for doctorate, comprehensive exam, thesis/dissertation. *Entrance requirements:* For master's, GMAT (for M Sc in management), bachelor's degree in related field, minimum GPA of 3.0 during previous 20 graded semester courses, 2 years' teaching or related experience (M Ed); for doctorate, master's degree, minimum graduate GPA of 3.5. Additional exam requirements/recommendations for international students: Required—TOEFL (minimum score 580 paper-based; 93 iBT). Electronic applications accepted. *Faculty research:* Movement and brain plasticity, gibberellin physiology, photosynthesis, carbon cycling, molecular properties of main-group ring components.

**University of Louisville,** Graduate School, College of Arts and Sciences, Department of Political Science, Louisville, KY 40292-0001. Offers digital politics (MA); political science (MA). *Program availability:* Part-time, evening/weekend. *Faculty:* 20 full-time (8 women), 7 part-time/adjunct (2 women). *Students:* 7 full-time (2 women), 4 part-time (1 woman); includes 3 minority (2 Black or African American, non-Hispanic/Latino; 1 Asian, non-Hispanic/Latino), 3 international. Average age 30. 10 applicants, 80% accepted, 3 enrolled. In 2016, 6 master's awarded. *Degree requirements:* For master's, thesis optional. *Entrance requirements:* For master's, GRE (minimum scores: 153 verbal, 144 quantitative, 4.0 analytic writing), minimum overall undergraduate GPA of 3.0 or 3.2 in final two years of undergraduate study. Additional exam requirements/recommendations for international students: Required—TOEFL (minimum score 550 paper-based; 79 iBT), IELTS (minimum score 6.5). *Application deadline:* For fall admission, 7/15 for domestic and international students; for spring admission, 11/15 for domestic and international students. Applications are processed on a rolling basis. Application fee: $65. Electronic applications accepted. Application fee is waived when completed online. *Expenses:* Tuition, state resident: full-time $12,246; part-time $681 per credit hour. Tuition, nonresident: full-time $25,486; part-time $1417 per credit hour. *Required fees:* $196. Tuition and fees vary according to program and reciprocity agreements. *Financial support:* In 2016–17, 2 teaching assistantships with full tuition reimbursements (averaging $12,000 per year) were awarded; health care benefits and unspecified assistantships also available. Financial award application deadline: 4/1. *Faculty research:* American politics, public policy, international relations, comparative politics, internet and politics. *Total annual research expenditures:* $397,905. *Unit head:* Dr. Rodger A. Payne, Chair, 502-852-3316, E-mail: r.payne@louisvile.edu. *Application contact:* Betty Younis, Graduate Program Assistant, 502-852-1009, Fax: 502-852-7923, E-mail: betty.younis@louisvile.edu.
Website: http://louisville.edu/politicalscience

**The University of Manchester,** School of Social Sciences, Manchester, United Kingdom. Offers ethnographic documentary (M Phil); interdisciplinary study of culture (PhD); philosophy (PhD); politics (PhD); social anthropology (PhD); social anthropology with visual media (PhD); social change (PhD); social statistics (PhD); sociology (PhD); visual anthropology (M Phil).

**University of Manitoba,** Faculty of Graduate Studies, Faculty of Arts, Department of Political Studies, Winnipeg, MB R3T 2N2, Canada. Offers political studies (MA); public administration (MPA). *Degree requirements:* For master's, one foreign language, thesis or alternative.

**University of Maryland, College Park,** Academic Affairs, College of Behavioral and Social Sciences, Department of Government and Politics, College Park, MD 20742. Offers American politics (PhD); comparative politics (PhD); international relations (PhD); political economy (PhD); political theory (PhD). *Program availability:* Part-time, evening/weekend. *Degree requirements:* For doctorate, comprehensive exam, thesis/dissertation, written exams in 2 fields. *Entrance requirements:* For doctorate, GRE General Test, minimum GPA of 3.5, writing sample. Additional exam requirements/recommendations for international students: Required—TOEFL. Electronic applications accepted. *Faculty research:* International development/conflict, international security, post-communist society, public service, dynamics of conflict and conflict resolution.

**University of Massachusetts Amherst,** Graduate School, College of Social and Behavioral Sciences, Department of Political Science, Amherst, MA 01003. Offers MA, PhD. *Program availability:* Part-time. Terminal master's awarded for partial completion of doctoral program. *Degree requirements:* For master's, one foreign language, thesis or alternative; for doctorate, one foreign language, comprehensive exam, thesis/dissertation. *Entrance requirements:* For master's and doctorate, GRE General Test, writing sample, 3 letters of recommendation. Additional exam requirements/recommendations for international students: Required—TOEFL (minimum score 550 paper-based; 80 iBT), IELTS (minimum score 6.5). Electronic applications accepted.

**University of Memphis,** Graduate School, College of Arts and Sciences, Department of Political Science, Memphis, TN 38152. Offers MA. *Faculty:* 4 full-time (1 woman). *Students:* 9 full-time (4 women), 2 part-time (1 woman); includes 2 minority (both Black or African American, non-Hispanic/Latino). Average age 26. 4 applicants, 100% accepted, 2 enrolled. In 2016, 13 master's awarded. *Degree requirements:* For master's, comprehensive exam (for some programs), thesis or alternative, internship. *Entrance requirements:* For master's, GRE General Test or LSAT, minimum GPA of 3.0, letters of recommendation, statement of career goals and interests. *Application deadline:* For fall admission, 8/1 for domestic students; for spring admission, 12/1 for domestic students. Applications are processed on a rolling basis. Application fee: $35 ($60 for international students). Electronic applications accepted. *Expenses:* $5,231.50 per semester full-time in-state, $9,623.50 full-time out-of-state. *Financial support:* In 2016–17, 10 students received support, including 8 research assistantships with full tuition reimbursements available (averaging $17,000 per year); Federal Work-Study, scholarships/grants, and unspecified assistantships also available. Financial award application deadline: 2/1; financial award applicants required to submit FAFSA. *Faculty research:* Political philosophy, comparative judicial studies, conflict studies, legislative studies, foreign policy. *Unit head:* Dr. Matthias Kaelberer, Chair, 901-678-2395, Fax: 901-678-2983, E-mail: mkaelbrr@memphis.edu. *Application contact:* Dr. Nicole Detraz, Graduate Studies Coordinator, 901-678-2395, Fax: 901-678-2983, E-mail: ndetraz@memphis.edu.
Website: http://www.memphis.edu/polisci/

**University of Miami,** Graduate School, College of Arts and Sciences, Department of Political Science, Coral Gables, FL 33124. Offers MPA, MPA/JD, MPA/MPH. *Program availability:* Part-time, evening/weekend. *Degree requirements:* For master's, thesis optional. *Entrance requirements:* For master's, GRE General Test. Additional exam requirements/recommendations for international students: Required—TOEFL (minimum score 550 paper-based; 80 iBT). Electronic applications accepted. *Faculty research:* Financial management, non-profit management, human resource management, public service ethics, information technology management.

**University of Michigan,** Rackham Graduate School, College of Literature, Science, and the Arts, Department of Political Science, Ann Arbor, MI 48109. Offers political science (PhD); political science and public policy (PhD); social work and political science (PhD). *Faculty:* 48 full-time (17 women), 6 part-time/adjunct (4 women). *Students:* 104 full-time (42 women); includes 17 minority (5 Black or African American, non-Hispanic/Latino; 4 Asian, non-Hispanic/Latino; 6 Hispanic/Latino; 2 Two or more races, non-Hispanic/Latino), 29 international. Average age 29. 397 applicants, 12% accepted, 17 enrolled. In 2016, 27 doctorates awarded. Terminal master's awarded for partial completion of doctoral program. *Degree requirements:* For doctorate, comprehensive exam, thesis/dissertation, oral defense of dissertation, preliminary exams. *Entrance requirements:* For doctorate, GRE General Test. Additional exam requirements/recommendations for international students: Required—TOEFL. *Application deadline:* For fall admission, 12/15 for domestic and international students. Application fee: $75 ($90 for international students). Electronic applications accepted. *Expenses:* Tuition, state resident: full-time $21,466; part-time $1152 per credit hour. Tuition, nonresident: full-time $43,346; part-time $2367 per credit hour. Part-time tuition and fees vary according to course load, degree level and program. *Financial support:* In 2016–17, 100 students received support, including 17 fellowships with full tuition reimbursements available (averaging $19,737 per year), 12 research assistantships with full tuition reimbursements available (averaging $19,737 per year), 35 teaching assistantships with full tuition reimbursements available (averaging $19,737 per year); health care benefits, tuition waivers (full), and unspecified assistantships also available. Financial award

## Political Science

application deadline: 12/15. *Faculty research:* Political theory; American politics; world politics; comparative politics; research methods; law, courts, and politics. *Unit head:* Nancy Burns, Chair, 734-764-6313, Fax: 734-764-3522. *Application contact:* Nicole Rutherford, Academic Program Manager, 734-764-6313, Fax: 734-764-3522, E-mail: psgradinfo@umich.edu. Website: http://www.lsa.umich.edu/polisci

**University of Michigan,** School of Social Work, Interdisciplinary PhD Program in Social Work and Social Science, Ann Arbor, MI 48109-1106. Offers social work and anthropology (PhD); social work and economics (PhD); social work and political science (PhD); social work and psychology (PhD); social work and sociology (PhD). Programs offered through the Rackham Graduate School. *Faculty:* 50 full-time (29 women), 62 part-time/adjunct (48 women). *Students:* 59 full-time (42 women); includes 30 minority (14 Black or African American, non-Hispanic/Latino; 9 Asian, non-Hispanic/Latino; 7 Hispanic/Latino). Average age 32. 114 applicants, 7% accepted, 8 enrolled. In 2016, 8 doctorates awarded. *Degree requirements:* For doctorate, thesis/dissertation, oral defense of dissertation, preliminary exam. *Entrance requirements:* For doctorate, GRE General Test. Additional exam requirements/recommendations for international students: Required—TOEFL (minimum score 620 paper-based; 88 iBT) or IELTS. *Application deadline:* For fall admission, 12/1 for domestic and international students. Application fee: $75 ($90 for international students). Electronic applications accepted. *Expenses:* $42,016 fall/winter tuition. *Financial support:* In 2016–17, 59 students received support, including 20 fellowships with full tuition reimbursements available (averaging $15,200 per year), 8 research assistantships with full tuition reimbursements available (averaging $19,737 per year), 17 teaching assistantships with full tuition reimbursements available (averaging $19,737 per year); career-related internships or fieldwork, scholarships/grants, traineeships, health care benefits, tuition waivers (full and partial), and unspecified assistantships also available. Financial award application deadline: 12/1; financial award applicants required to submit FAFSA. *Faculty research:* Children and family, aging, community organization, health and mental health, police and evaluation. *Total annual research expenditures:* $3.8 million. *Unit head:* Dr. Daphne C. Watkins, Director, 734-763-5768, E-mail: daphnew@umich.edu. *Application contact:* Todd Huynh, Graduate Coordinator, 734-647-2554, Fax: 734-615-3192, E-mail: ssw.phd.info@umich.edu. Website: https://ssw.umich.edu/offices/phd

**University of Michigan–Flint,** College of Arts and Sciences, Program in Social Sciences, Flint, MI 48502-1950. Offers gender studies (MA); global studies (MA); U.S. history and politics (MA). *Program availability:* Part-time. *Faculty:* 9 full-time (1 woman), 1 (woman) part-time/adjunct. *Students:* 4 full-time (1 woman), 21 part-time (14 women); includes 12 minority (9 Black or African American, non-Hispanic/Latino; 2 Hispanic/Latino; 1 Two or more races, non-Hispanic/Latino). Average age 39. 17 applicants, 82% accepted, 7 enrolled. In 2016, 7 master's awarded. *Entrance requirements:* For master's, bachelor's degree from regionally-accredited institution, minimum overall undergraduate GPA of 3.0. Additional exam requirements/recommendations for international students: Required—TOEFL (minimum score 84 iBT), IELTS (minimum score 6.5). *Application deadline:* For fall admission, 8/1 for domestic students, 5/1 for international students; for winter admission, 11/15 for domestic students, 9/1 for international students; for spring admission, 3/15 for domestic students, 1/1 for international students; for summer admission, 5/15 for domestic students. Applications are processed on a rolling basis. Application fee: $55. Electronic applications accepted. *Financial support:* Federal Work-Study, scholarships/grants, and unspecified assistantships available. Support available to part-time students. Financial award application deadline: 3/1; financial award applicants required to submit FAFSA. *Unit head:* Dr. Adam Lutzker, Director, 810-762-3470, Fax: 810-762-3281, E-mail: alutzker@umflint.edu. *Application contact:* Bradley T. Maki, Director of Graduate Admissions, 810-762-3171, Fax: 810-766-6789, E-mail: bmaki@umflint.edu. Website: http://www.umflint.edu/graduateprograms/social-sciences-ma

**University of Minnesota, Twin Cities Campus,** Graduate School, College of Liberal Arts, Department of Political Science, Minneapolis, MN 55455. Offers PhD. *Degree requirements:* For doctorate, thesis/dissertation, 1 foreign language or statistics. *Entrance requirements:* For doctorate, GRE. Additional exam requirements/recommendations for international students: Required—TOEFL; Recommended—IELTS. Electronic applications accepted. *Faculty research:* American politics, comparative politics, international relations, political theory, research methodology.

**University of Mississippi,** Graduate School, College of Liberal Arts, University, MS 38677. Offers anthropology (MA); biology (MS, PhD); chemistry (MS, PhD); economics (MA, PhD); English (MA, PhD); experimental psychology (PhD); history (MA, PhD); mathematics (MS, PhD); modern languages (MA); music (MM); philosophy (MA); physics (MA, MS, PhD); political science (MA, PhD); studio art (MFA). *Program availability:* Part-time. *Faculty:* 472 full-time (263 women), 75 part-time/adjunct (35 women). *Students:* 415 full-time (210 women), 57 part-time (20 women); includes 70 minority (35 Black or African American, non-Hispanic/Latino; 13 Asian, non-Hispanic/Latino; 14 Hispanic/Latino; 8 Two or more races, non-Hispanic/Latino), 102 international. Average age 27. *Degree requirements:* For doctorate, thesis/dissertation. *Entrance requirements:* For master's, GRE General Test, minimum GPA of 3.0; for doctorate, GRE General Test. Additional exam requirements/recommendations for international students: Required—TOEFL. *Application deadline:* For fall admission, 4/1 for domestic students; for spring admission, 10/1 for domestic students. Applications are processed on a rolling basis. Application fee: $40. Electronic applications accepted. *Financial support:* Fellowships, research assistantships, teaching assistantships, career-related internships or fieldwork, Federal Work-Study, institutionally sponsored loans, scholarships/grants, and unspecified assistantships available. Financial award application deadline: 3/1; financial award applicants required to submit FAFSA. *Unit head:* Dr. Lee Michael Cohen, Dean, 662-915-7177, Fax: 662-915-5792, E-mail: libarts@olemiss.edu. *Application contact:* Dr. Christy M. Wyandt, Associate Dean of Graduate School, 662-915-7474, Fax: 662-915-7577, E-mail: cwyandt@olemiss.edu. Website: https://www.olemiss.edu

**University of Missouri,** Office of Research and Graduate Studies, College of Arts and Science, Department of Political Science, Columbia, MO 65211. Offers MA, PhD. *Faculty:* 16 full-time (2 women). *Students:* 45 full-time (18 women), 1 (woman) part-time. Terminal master's awarded for partial completion of doctoral program. *Degree requirements:* For doctorate, one foreign language, comprehensive exam, thesis/dissertation. *Entrance requirements:* For master's, GRE General Test (minimum combined score 1000 Verbal and Quantitative), minimum GPA of 3.0 in last 60 hours and in political science courses; at least 12 hours of upper-level course work in political science; for doctorate, GRE General Test (minimum combined score 1200 Verbal and Quantitative), minimum GPA of 3.0 in last 60 hours and in political science courses; at least 12 hours of upper-level course work in political science. Additional exam requirements/recommendations for international students: Required—TOEFL (minimum score 570 paper-based; 88 iBT). *Application deadline:* For fall admission, 2/1 priority date for domestic and international students; for winter admission, 10/1 for domestic and international students. Applications are processed on a rolling basis. Application fee: $75 ($90 for international students). Electronic applications accepted. *Expenses:* Tuition, state resident: full-time $6347; part-time $352.60 per credit hour. Tuition, nonresident: full-time $17,379; part-time $965.50 per credit hour. *Required fees:* $1035. Tuition and fees vary according to course load, campus/location and program. *Financial*

support: Fellowships with tuition reimbursements, research assistantships with tuition reimbursements, teaching assistantships with full tuition reimbursements, institutionally sponsored loans, health care benefits, and unspecified assistantships available. *Faculty research:* American politics, comparative politics, international relations, public policy and administration. Website: http://politicalscience.missouri.edu/grad/index.shtml

**University of Missouri–Kansas City,** College of Arts and Sciences, Department of Political Science, Kansas City, MO 64110-2499. Offers MA, PhD (interdisciplinary) offered through the School of Graduate Studies. *Program availability:* Part-time, evening/weekend. *Faculty:* 7 full-time (4 women), 3 part-time/adjunct (0 women). *Students:* 3 full-time (1 woman). Average age 32. 10 applicants, 30% accepted, 2 enrolled. Terminal master's awarded for partial completion of doctoral program. *Degree requirements:* For master's, thesis optional. *Entrance requirements:* For master's, GRE, minimum GPA of 3.0, course work in political science, 2 letters of recommendation. Additional exam requirements/recommendations for international students: Required—TOEFL (minimum score 550 paper-based; 80 iBT). *Application deadline:* For fall admission, 4/1 priority date for domestic and international students; for spring admission, 11/1 priority date for domestic and international students. Applications are processed on a rolling basis. Application fee: $45 ($50 for international students). Electronic applications accepted. *Financial support:* In 2016–17, 2 teaching assistantships (averaging $6,300 per year) were awarded; career-related internships or fieldwork and institutionally sponsored loans also available. Financial award application deadline: 3/1; financial award applicants required to submit FAFSA. *Faculty research:* Sex and gender, Chinese politics, voting behavior, politics of Presidency and social security, public law. *Unit head:* Dr. Elizabeth Vonnahme, Chair, 816-235-5844, Fax: 816-235-5594, E-mail: vonnehmeb@umkc.edu. *Application contact:* Tamara Byland, Director of Admissions, 816-235-1111, Fax: 816-235-5544, E-mail: admit@umkc.edu. Website: http://cas.umkc.edu/polisci/

**University of Missouri–St. Louis,** College of Arts and Sciences, Department of Political Science, St. Louis, MO 63121. Offers American politics (MA); comparative politics (MA); international politics (MA); political process and behavior (MA); political science (PhD); public administration and public policy (MA); urban and regional politics (MA). *Program availability:* Part-time, evening/weekend. *Faculty:* 17 full-time (5 women), 8 part-time/adjunct (4 women). *Students:* 28 full-time (8 women), 30 part-time (12 women); includes 8 minority (7 Black or African American, non-Hispanic/Latino; 1 Two or more races, non-Hispanic/Latino), 5 international. 17 applicants, 82% accepted, 9 enrolled. Terminal master's awarded for partial completion of doctoral program. *Degree requirements:* For master's, thesis optional; for doctorate, thesis/dissertation. *Entrance requirements:* For master's, GRE General Test, 2 letters of recommendation, statement of purpose; for doctorate, GRE General Test, 3 letters of recommendation, statement of purpose. Additional exam requirements/recommendations for international students: Required—TOEFL (minimum score 550 paper-based; 79 iBT), IELTS (minimum score 6.5). *Application deadline:* For fall admission, 2/15 priority date for domestic and international students; for winter admission, 10/15 for domestic and international students; for spring admission, 10/15 priority date for domestic and international students. Applications are processed on a rolling basis. Application fee: $50 ($40 for international students). Electronic applications accepted. *Financial support:* Fellowships, research assistantships with tuition reimbursements, teaching assistantships with tuition reimbursements, and career-related internships or fieldwork available. Support available to part-time students. Financial award application deadline: 3/15; financial award applicants required to submit FAFSA. *Faculty research:* Public policy, urban politics and administration, American government. *Unit head:* Dave Robertson, Chair, 314-516-5521, Fax: 314-516-7236. *Application contact:* 314-516-5458, Fax: 314-516-6996, E-mail: gradadm@umsl.edu. Website: http://www.umsl.edu/~polisci/

**University of Montana,** Graduate School, College of Humanities and Sciences, Department of Political Science, Program in Political Science, Missoula, MT 59812-0002. Offers MA. *Degree requirements:* For master's, thesis. *Entrance requirements:* For master's, GRE General Test.

**University of Nebraska at Omaha,** Graduate Studies, College of Arts and Sciences, Department of Political Science, Omaha, NE 68182. Offers American government (Certificate); global information operations (Certificate); intelligence and national security (Certificate); political science (MS). *Program availability:* Part-time, evening/weekend, online learning. *Faculty:* 7 full-time (3 women). *Students:* 8 full-time (4 women), 58 part-time (19 women); includes 9 minority (4 Black or African American, non-Hispanic/Latino; 1 Asian, non-Hispanic/Latino; 2 Hispanic/Latino; 2 Two or more races, non-Hispanic/Latino), 1 international. Average age 34. 53 applicants, 74% accepted, 25 enrolled. In 2016, 30 master's awarded. *Degree requirements:* For master's, comprehensive exam, thesis (for some programs). *Entrance requirements:* For master's, 15 undergraduate political science hours, minimum undergraduate GPA of 3.0, 2 letters of recommendation, official transcripts. Additional exam requirements/recommendations for international students: Required—TOEFL, IELTS, PTE. *Application deadline:* For fall admission, 7/15 priority date for domestic and international students; for spring admission, 11/15 priority date for domestic and international students; for summer admission, 4/15 for domestic and international students. Applications are processed on a rolling basis. Application fee: $45. Electronic applications accepted. *Financial support:* In 2016–17, 5 students received support, including 2 research assistantships with tuition reimbursements available, 3 teaching assistantships with tuition reimbursements available; fellowships, Federal Work-Study, scholarships/grants, health care benefits, tuition waivers (partial), and unspecified assistantships also available. Financial award application deadline: 3/1; financial award applicants required to submit FAFSA. *Unit head:* Dr. Jody Neathery-Castro, Chairperson, 402-554-2341, E-mail: graduate@unomaha.edu. *Application contact:* Dr. Gregory Petrow, Graduate Program Chair, 402-554-2341, E-mail: graduate@unomaha.edu.

**University of Nebraska–Lincoln,** Graduate College, College of Arts and Sciences, Department of Political Science, Lincoln, NE 68588. Offers political science (MA, PhD); public policy analysis (Graduate Certificate). *Degree requirements:* For master's, thesis optional; for doctorate, variable foreign language requirement, comprehensive exam, thesis/dissertation. *Entrance requirements:* For master's and doctorate, GRE General Test, writing sample. Additional exam requirements/recommendations for international students: Required—TOEFL (minimum score 600 paper-based). Electronic applications accepted. *Faculty research:* Public policy; comparative politics; international relations; political theory, behavior, and methodology; American politics.

**University of Nevada, Las Vegas,** Graduate College, College of Liberal Arts, Department of Political Science, Las Vegas, NV 89154-5029. Offers MA, PhD. *Program availability:* Part-time. *Faculty:* 11 full-time (3 women). *Students:* 18 full-time (7 women), 18 part-time (2 women); includes 10 minority (3 Black or African American, non-Hispanic/Latino; 1 Asian, non-Hispanic/Latino; 4 Hispanic/Latino; 2 Two or more races, non-Hispanic/Latino), 1 international. Average age 34. 17 applicants, 71% accepted, 8 enrolled. In 2016, 1 master's, 1 doctorate awarded. *Degree requirements:* For master's, thesis, professional paper; for doctorate, one foreign language, comprehensive exam, thesis/dissertation, oral examination. *Entrance requirements:* For master's, GRE General Test, 2 letters of recommendation; personal statement; bachelor's degree; minimum GPA of 3.0; for doctorate, GRE General Test, minimum GPA of 3.3 in BA, 3.5 in MA; 12 credits of course work; 3 letters of recommendations; personal statement;

writing sample. Additional exam requirements/recommendations for international students: Required—TOEFL (minimum score 550 paper-based; 80 iBT), IELTS (minimum score 7). *Application deadline:* For fall admission, 2/1 for domestic students. Application fee: $60 ($95 for international students). Electronic applications accepted. *Expenses:* $269.25 per credit, $792 per 3-credit course; $9,634 per year resident; $23,274 per year non-resident; $7,094 fees non-resident (7 credits or more); $1,307 annual health insurance fee. *Financial support:* In 2016–17, 5 research assistantships with partial tuition reimbursements (averaging $14,850 per year), 10 teaching assistantships with partial tuition reimbursements (averaging $15,707 per year) were awarded; institutionally sponsored loans, scholarships/grants, health care benefits, and unspecified assistantships also available. Financial award application deadline: 3/15. *Faculty research:* International political economy and security, religion and politics, democratization, demographic change and its consequences, international security and political violence, ancient political philosophy, political behavior, political institutions. *Total annual research expenditures:* $86,830. *Unit head:* Dr. John P. Tuman, Chair and Professor, 702-895-5258, Fax: 702-895-1065, E-mail: john.tuman@unlv.edu. *Application contact:* Dr. David Damore, Graduate Coordinator, 702-895-3217, Fax: 702-895-1065, E-mail: david.damore@unlv.edu.
Website: http://liberalarts.unlv.edu/Political_Science/

**University of Nevada, Reno,** Graduate School, College of Liberal Arts, Department of Political Science, Program in Political Science, Reno, NV 89557. Offers MA, PhD. Terminal master's awarded for partial completion of doctoral program. *Degree requirements:* For master's, comprehensive exam, oral exam/thesis or professional paper; for doctorate, thesis/dissertation, 2 field exams, oral exam. *Entrance requirements:* For master's, GRE General Test, GMAT, LSAT, minimum GPA of 2.75; for doctorate, GRE General Test, GMAT, LSAT, minimum GPA of 3.0. Additional exam requirements/recommendations for international students: Required—TOEFL (minimum score 500 paper-based; 61 iBT), IELTS (minimum score 6). Electronic applications accepted. *Faculty research:* Analysis of political processes, institutions, and policies.

**University of New Brunswick Fredericton,** School of Graduate Studies, Faculty of Arts, Department of Political Science, Fredericton, NB E3B 5A3, Canada. Offers MA. *Program availability:* Part-time. *Degree requirements:* For master's, thesis (for some programs). *Entrance requirements:* For master's, minimum cumulative GPA of 3.3; 4-year bachelor's degree, or equivalent, in political science. Additional exam requirements/recommendations for international students: Required—TOEFL. Electronic applications accepted. *Faculty research:* Political theory, public policy, gender and politics, global political economy and Canadian politics.

**University of New Hampshire,** Graduate School, College of Liberal Arts, Department of Political Science, Program in Political Science, Durham, NH 03824. Offers political science (MA); sustainability politics and policy (Postbaccalaureate Certificate). *Program availability:* Part-time. *Degree requirements:* For master's, thesis. *Entrance requirements:* For master's, GRE General Test. Additional exam requirements/recommendations for international students: Required—TOEFL (minimum score 550 paper-based; 80 iBT). Electronic applications accepted.

**University of New Mexico,** Graduate Studies, College of Arts and Sciences, Program in Political Science, Albuquerque, NM 87131-2039. Offers MA, PhD. *Program availability:* Part-time. *Faculty:* 9 full-time (6 women). *Students:* 19 full-time (8 women), 12 part-time (4 women); includes 10 minority (1 Black or African American, non-Hispanic/Latino; 7 Hispanic/Latino; 2 Two or more races, non-Hispanic/Latino), 7 international. Average age 31. 33 applicants, 48% accepted, 8 enrolled. In 2016, 7 master's, 2 doctorates awarded. Terminal master's awarded for partial completion of doctoral program. *Degree requirements:* For master's, comprehensive exam, thesis optional; for doctorate, comprehensive exam, thesis/dissertation, field research paper, minimum cumulative GPA of 3.5. *Entrance requirements:* For master's and doctorate, GRE General Test, 3 letters of recommendation, writing sample, letter of intent. Additional exam requirements/recommendations for international students: Required—TOEFL. *Application deadline:* For fall admission, 1/15 priority date for domestic and international students. Application fee: $50. Electronic applications accepted. *Financial support:* Fellowships with full tuition reimbursements, research assistantships with full tuition reimbursements, teaching assistantships with full tuition reimbursements, scholarships/grants, health care benefits, and unspecified assistantships available. Financial award application deadline: 1/15; financial award applicants required to submit FAFSA. *Faculty research:* Latin American politics, American politics, comparative politics, public policy, international relations, methodology. *Unit head:* Dr. William Stanley, Chair, 505-277-5104, Fax: 505-277-2821, E-mail: wstanley@unm.edu. *Application contact:* Shoshana Handel, Graduate Program Assistant, 505-277-5104, Fax: 505-277-2821, E-mail: shandel@unm.edu.
Website: http://polisci.unm.edu/index.html

**University of New Orleans,** Graduate School, College of Liberal Arts, Department of Political Science, New Orleans, LA 70148. Offers political science (MA, PhD); public administration (MPA). *Program availability:* Evening/weekend. *Degree requirements:* For master's, one foreign language, thesis or alternative; for doctorate, one foreign language, thesis/dissertation. *Entrance requirements:* For master's, GRE General Test; for doctorate, GRE General Test, GRE Subject Test. Additional exam requirements/recommendations for international students: Required—TOEFL (minimum score 550 paper-based; 79 iBT), IELTS (minimum score 6.5). Electronic applications accepted. *Faculty research:* Judicial politics, public policy, voting rights, Southern politics, presidential-congressional relations.

**University of North Alabama,** College of Arts and Sciences, Department of Politics, Justice, and Law, Florence, AL 35632-0001. Offers criminal justice (MSCJ). *Program availability:* Part-time, 100% online. *Faculty:* 3 full-time (0 women), 2 part-time/adjunct (1 woman). *Students:* 4 full-time (2 women), 21 part-time (9 women); includes 4 minority (3 Black or African American, non-Hispanic/Latino; 1 Hispanic/Latino), 4 international. Average age 30. 13 applicants, 77% accepted, 10 enrolled. In 2016, 3 master's awarded. *Degree requirements:* For master's, comprehensive exam. *Entrance requirements:* For master's, GRE General Test, MAT. Additional exam requirements/recommendations for international students: Required—TOEFL (minimum score 79 iBT), IELTS (minimum score 6), PTE (minimum score 54). *Application deadline:* Applications are processed on a rolling basis. Application fee: $50 ($100 for international students). Electronic applications accepted. *Expenses:* Tuition, state resident: full-time $2799; part-time $1866 per semester. Tuition, nonresident: full-time $5598; part-time $3732 per semester. *Required fees:* $915; $642 per semester. Tuition and fees vary according to course load. *Financial support:* In 2016–17, 2 students received support. Scholarships/grants and unspecified assistantships available. Financial award application deadline: 2/1; financial award applicants required to submit FAFSA. *Unit head:* Dr. Tim Collins, Chair, 256-765-5045, E-mail: jtcollins@una.edu. *Application contact:* Hillary N. Coats, Graduate Admissions Coordinator, 256-765-4447, E-mail: graduate@una.edu. Website: http://www.una.edu/criminaljustice/

**The University of North Carolina at Chapel Hill,** Graduate School, College of Arts and Sciences, Department of Political Science, Chapel Hill, NC 27599. Offers Latin American studies (Certificate); political science (MA, PhD); trans-Atlantic studies (MA). *Degree requirements:* For master's, comprehensive exam; for doctorate, one foreign language, comprehensive exam, thesis/dissertation. *Entrance requirements:* For master's and doctorate, GRE General Test, minimum GPA of 3.0 recommended. Electronic applications accepted.

**The University of North Carolina at Greensboro,** Graduate School, College of Arts and Sciences, Department of Political Science, Greensboro, NC 27412-5001. Offers nonprofit management (Certificate); public affairs (MPA); urban and economic development (Certificate). *Accreditation:* NASPAA. *Degree requirements:* For master's, comprehensive exam. *Entrance requirements:* For master's, GRE General Test. Additional exam requirements/recommendations for international students: Required—TOEFL. Electronic applications accepted. *Faculty research:* U.S. Constitution, Canadian parliament, public management, ethical challenge of public service.

**University of Northern British Columbia,** Office of Graduate Studies, Prince George, BC V2N 4Z9, Canada. Offers business administration (Diploma); community health science (M Sc); disability management (MA); education (M Ed); first nations studies (MA); gender studies (MA); history (MA); interdisciplinary studies (MA); international studies (MA); mathematical, computer and physical sciences (M Sc); natural resources and environmental studies (M Sc, MA, MNRES, PhD); political science (MA); psychology (M Sc, PhD); social work (MSW). *Program availability:* Part-time, evening/weekend, online learning. *Degree requirements:* For master's, thesis; for doctorate, thesis/dissertation. *Entrance requirements:* For master's, GRE, minimum B average in undergraduate course work; for doctorate, candidacy exam, minimum A average in graduate course work.

**University of North Texas,** Robert B. Toulouse School of Graduate Studies, Denton, TX 76203-5459. Offers accounting (MS); applied anthropology (MA, MS); applied behavior analysis (Certificate); applied geography (MS); applied technology and performance improvement (M Ed, MS); art education (MA); art history; art museum education (Certificate); arts leadership (Certificate); audiology (Au D); behavior analysis (MS); behavioral science (PhD); biochemistry and molecular biology (MS); biology (MA, MS); biomedical engineering (MS); business analysis (MS); chemistry (MS); clinical health psychology (PhD); communication studies (MA, MS); computer engineering (MS); computer science (MS); counseling (M Ed, MS), including clinical mental health counseling (MS), college and university counseling, elementary school counseling, secondary school counseling; creative writing (MA); criminal justice (MS); curriculum and instruction (M Ed); decision sciences (MBA); design (MA, MFA), including fashion design (MFA), innovation studies, interior design (MFA); early childhood studies (MS); economics (MS); educational leadership (M Ed, Ed D); educational psychology (MS, PhD), including family studies (MS), gifted and talented (MS), human development (MS), learning and cognition (MS), research, measurement and evaluation (MS); electrical engineering (MS); emergency management (MPA); engineering technology (MS); English (MA); English as a second language (MA); environmental science (MS); finance (MBA, MS); financial management (MPA); French (MA); health services management (MBA); higher education (M Ed, Ed D); history (MA, MS); hospitality management (MS); human resources management (MPA); information science (MS); information systems (PhD); information technologies (MBA); interdisciplinary studies (MA, MS); international studies (MA); international sustainable tourism (MS); jazz studies (MM); journalism (MA, MJ, Graduate Certificate), including interactive and virtual digital communication (Graduate Certificate), narrative journalism (Graduate Certificate), public relations (Graduate Certificate); kinesiology (MS); linguistics (MA); local government management (MPA); logistics (PhD); logistics and supply chain management (MBA); long-term care, senior housing, and aging services (MA); management (PhD); marketing (MBA); mathematics (MA, MS); mechanical and energy engineering (MS, PhD); music (MA), including ethnomusicology, music theory, musicology, performance; music composition (PhD); music education (MM Ed, PhD); nonprofit management (MPA); operations and supply chain management (MBA); performance (MM, DMA); philosophy (MA); political science (MA); professional and technical communication (MA); radio, television and film (MA, MFA); rehabilitation counseling (Certificate); sociology (MA); Spanish (MA); special education (M Ed); speech-language pathology (MA); strategic management (MBA); studio art (MFA); teaching (M Ed); MBA/MS. *Program availability:* Part-time, evening/weekend, online learning. Terminal master's awarded for partial completion of doctoral program. *Degree requirements:* For master's, variable foreign language requirement, comprehensive exam (for some programs), thesis (for some programs); for doctorate, variable foreign language requirement, comprehensive exam (for some programs), thesis/dissertation; for other advanced degree, variable foreign language requirement, comprehensive exam (for some programs). *Entrance requirements:* For master's and doctorate, GRE, GMAT. Additional exam requirements/recommendations for international students: Required—TOEFL (minimum score 550 paper-based; 79 iBT). Electronic applications accepted.

**University of Notre Dame,** Graduate School, College of Arts and Letters, Division of Social Science, Department of Political Science, Notre Dame, IN 46556. Offers PhD. *Degree requirements:* For doctorate, one foreign language, comprehensive exam, thesis/dissertation, candidacy exam. *Entrance requirements:* For doctorate, GRE General Test. Additional exam requirements/recommendations for international students: Required—TOEFL (minimum score 600 paper-based; 80 iBT). Electronic applications accepted. *Faculty research:* American government, comparative politics, international relations, political theory.

**University of Oklahoma,** College of Arts and Sciences, Department of Political Science, Program in Political Science, Norman, OK 73019. Offers MA, PhD. *Students:* 26 full-time (6 women), 18 part-time (8 women); includes 3 minority (1 Black or African American, non-Hispanic/Latino; 2 Hispanic/Latino), 9 international. Average age 32. 18 applicants, 56% accepted, 5 enrolled. In 2016, 3 master's, 1 doctorate awarded. Terminal master's awarded for partial completion of doctoral program. *Degree requirements:* For master's, comprehensive exam, thesis optional, 36 hours; for doctorate, comprehensive exam, thesis/dissertation, 90 hours. *Entrance requirements:* For master's and doctorate, GRE, statement of purpose, writing sample, three letters of recommendation. Additional exam requirements/recommendations for international students: Required—TOEFL (minimum score 100 iBT) or IELTS (minimum score 7). *Application deadline:* For fall admission, 2/1 priority date for domestic and international students. Application fee: $50 ($100 for international students). Electronic applications accepted. *Expenses:* Tuition, state resident: full-time $4886; part-time $203.60 per credit hour. Tuition, nonresident: full-time $18,989; part-time $791.20 per credit hour. *Required fees:* $3283; $126.25 per credit hour. $126.50 per semester. *Financial support:* In 2016–17, 32 students received support. Research assistantships with full tuition reimbursements available, teaching assistantships with full tuition reimbursements available, scholarships/grants, health care benefits, unspecified assistantships, and travel and conference attendance funding available. Financial award application deadline: 6/1; financial award applicants required to submit FAFSA. *Faculty research:* American and comparative politics, public administration and policy, international relations, political theory and research methods. *Unit head:* Prof. Keith Gaddie, Chair, 405-325-2061, Fax: 405-325-0718, E-mail: pscgradprog@ou.edu. *Application contact:* Jeff Alexander, Graduate Programs Coordinator, 405-325-1845, Fax: 405-325-0718, E-mail: pscgradprog@ou.edu.
Website: http://psc.ou.edu/graduate-programs

**University of Oregon,** Graduate School, College of Arts and Sciences, Department of Political Science, Eugene, OR 97403. Offers MA, MS, PhD. Terminal master's awarded for partial completion of doctoral program. *Degree requirements:* For master's, thesis or alternative; for doctorate, thesis/dissertation. *Entrance requirements:* For master's and doctorate, GRE General Test, minimum GPA of 3.0. Additional exam requirements/recommendations for international students: Required—TOEFL. *Faculty research:* Public policy, public choice, comparative politics, political economy, international relations.

**University of Ottawa,** Faculty of Graduate and Postdoctoral Studies, Faculty of Social Sciences, Department of Political Studies, Ottawa, ON K1N 6N5, Canada. Offers MA, PhD. *Degree requirements:* For master's, thesis or alternative, fluency in English and French; for doctorate, comprehensive exam, thesis/dissertation. *Entrance requirements:* For master's, honors bachelor's degree or equivalent, minimum B average; for doctorate, master's degree, minimum B+ average. Electronic applications accepted. *Faculty research:* Political thought and analysis of ideologies, Canadian and Québécois policies, international and comparative policies.

**University of Pennsylvania,** School of Arts and Sciences, Fels Institute of Government, Philadelphia, PA 19104. Offers economic development and growth (Certificate); government administration (MGA); nonprofit administration (Certificate); organization dynamics (MS); politics (Certificate); public administration (MPA); public finance (Certificate). *Program availability:* Part-time, evening/weekend. *Students:* 49 full-time (29 women), 65 part-time (35 women); includes 28 minority (13 Black or African American, non-Hispanic/Latino; 6 Asian, non-Hispanic/Latino; 6 Hispanic/Latino; 3 Two or more races, non-Hispanic/Latino), 18 international. Average age 30. 371 applicants, 39% accepted, 71 enrolled. In 2016, 52 master's, 17 other advanced degrees awarded. *Expenses: Tuition:* Full-time $31,068; part-time $5762 per course. *Required fees:* $3200; $336 per course. Full-time tuition and fees vary according to degree level, program and student level. Part-time tuition and fees vary according to course load, degree level and program. *Financial support:* Application deadline: 1/1. Website: http://www.fels.upenn.edu/

**University of Pennsylvania,** School of Arts and Sciences, Graduate Group in Political Science, Philadelphia, PA 19104. Offers AM, PhD, MGA/AM. *Faculty:* 31 full-time (10 women), 2 part-time/adjunct (1 woman). *Students:* 67 full-time (28 women), 2 part-time (1 woman); includes 11 minority (2 Black or African American, non-Hispanic/Latino; 2 Asian, non-Hispanic/Latino; 3 Hispanic/Latino; 4 Two or more races, non-Hispanic/Latino), 16 international. Average age 29. 276 applicants, 11% accepted, 13 enrolled. In 2016, 10 master's, 11 doctorates awarded. Terminal master's awarded for partial completion of doctoral program. *Expenses: Tuition:* Full-time $31,068; part-time $5762 per course. *Required fees:* $3200; $336 per course. Full-time tuition and fees vary according to degree level, program and student level. Part-time tuition and fees vary according to course load, degree level and program. *Financial support:* Teaching assistantships available. Website: http://www.sas.upenn.edu/polisci/content/graduate-program

**University of Pittsburgh,** Dietrich School of Arts and Sciences, Department of Political Science, Pittsburgh, PA 15260. Offers MA, PhD. *Faculty:* 21 full-time (7 women). *Students:* 57 full-time (20 women); includes 21 minority (12 Asian, non-Hispanic/Latino; 9 Hispanic/Latino). Average age 30. 91 applicants, 31% accepted, 12 enrolled. In 2016, 8 master's, 3 doctorates awarded. Terminal master's awarded for partial completion of doctoral program. *Degree requirements:* For master's and doctorate, comprehensive exam. *Entrance requirements:* For doctorate, GRE General Test, minimum QPA of 3.0. Additional exam requirements/recommendations for international students: Required—TOEFL (minimum score 90 iBT). *Application deadline:* For fall admission, 1/8 for domestic and international students. Applications are processed on a rolling basis. Application fee: $50. Electronic applications accepted. Tuition and fees vary according to program. *Financial support:* In 2016–17, 17 fellowships with full tuition reimbursements (averaging $21,692 per year), 11 research assistantships with full tuition reimbursements (averaging $17,910 per year), 10 teaching assistantships with full tuition reimbursements (averaging $17,910 per year) were awarded; tuition waivers (partial) also available. Financial award application deadline: 1/8. *Total annual research expenditures:* $253,422. *Unit head:* Dr. Steven Finkel, Chair, 412-648-7290, E-mail: finkel@pitt.edu. *Application contact:* Dr. Daniela Donno, Director of Graduate Students, 412-648-7275, E-mail: donno@pitt.edu. Website: http://www.polisci.pitt.edu/

**University of Pittsburgh,** Graduate School of Public and International Affairs, Master of Public and International Affairs Program, Pittsburgh, PA 15260. Offers human security (MPIA); international political economy (MPIA); security and intelligence studies (MPIA); JD/MPIA; MBA/MPIA; MPH/MPIA; MPIA/MSW; MSIS/MPIA. *Program availability:* Part-time, evening/weekend. *Faculty:* 34 full-time (12 women), 17 part-time/adjunct (5 women). *Students:* 98 full-time (42 women), 17 part-time (8 women); includes 17 minority (8 Black or African American, non-Hispanic/Latino; 2 Asian, non-Hispanic/Latino; 6 Hispanic/Latino; 1 Two or more races, non-Hispanic/Latino), 20 international. Average age 26. 181 applicants, 91% accepted, 48 enrolled. In 2016, 70 master's awarded. *Degree requirements:* For master's, thesis optional, capstone seminar. *Entrance requirements:* For master's, GRE General Test or GMAT, 2 letters of recommendation, resume, undergraduate transcripts, personal statement. Additional exam requirements/recommendations for international students: Required—TOEFL (minimum score 80 iBT); Recommended—IELTS (minimum score 7). *Application deadline:* For fall admission, 2/1 for domestic students, 1/15 for international students; for spring admission, 11/1 for domestic students, 8/1 for international students. Application fee: $50. Electronic applications accepted. *Expenses:* $22,578 per year in-state; $36,734 per year out-of-state. *Financial support:* In 2016–17, 47 students received support, including 2 fellowships with full tuition reimbursements available (averaging $18,000 per year), 3 research assistantships with full tuition reimbursements available (averaging $14,620 per year); career-related internships or fieldwork and scholarships/grants also available. Financial award application deadline: 2/1; financial award applicants required to submit FAFSA. *Faculty research:* International political economy, human security, security and intelligence. *Total annual research expenditures:* $1.3 million. *Unit head:* Dr. John T.S. Keeler, Dean, 412-648-7605, E-mail: keeler@pitt.edu. *Application contact:* Dr. Michael T. Rizzi, Director of Student Services, 412-648-7640, Fax: 412-648-7641, E-mail: rizzim@pitt.edu. Website: http://www.gspia.pitt.edu/

**University of Regina,** Faculty of Graduate Studies and Research, Faculty of Arts, Program in Social and Political Thought, Regina, SK S4S 0A2, Canada. Offers MA. *Program availability:* Part-time. *Faculty:* 11 full-time (4 women). *Students:* 6 full-time (2 women), 6 part-time (2 women). 12 applicants, 33% accepted. *Degree requirements:* For master's, thesis. *Entrance requirements:* Additional exam requirements/recommendations for international students: Required—TOEFL (minimum score 580 paper-based; 80 iBT), IELTS (minimum score 6.5), PTE (minimum score 59). *Application deadline:* For fall admission, 3/30 for domestic and international students. Application fee: $100. Electronic applications accepted. *Financial support:* In 2016–17, 2 fellowships (averaging $6,000 per year), 2 teaching assistantships (averaging $2,501 per year) were awarded; scholarships/grants also available. Financial award application deadline: 6/15. *Faculty research:* Liberalism and freedom, neo-conservatism, Aristotle's ethics, Kant's ethical theory and political philosophy, Hegel's philosophy of right. *Unit head:* Dr. Lee Ward, Graduate Coordinator, 306-359-1259, E-mail:

lee.ward@uregina.ca. *Application contact:* Doreen Thompson, Administrative Assistant, 306-585-4332, E-mail: doreen.thompson@uregina.ca.

**University of Rhode Island,** Graduate School, College of Arts and Sciences, Department of Political Science, Kingston, RI 02881. Offers political science (MA), including American politics, comparative government, international relations, public policy; public policy and administration (MPA). *Program availability:* Part-time. *Faculty:* 12 full-time (5 women). *Students:* 20 full-time (9 women), 37 part-time (20 women); includes 11 minority (4 Black or African American, non-Hispanic/Latino; 2 American Indian or Alaska Native, non-Hispanic/Latino; 1 Asian, non-Hispanic/Latino; 3 Hispanic/Latino; 1 Two or more races, non-Hispanic/Latino), 1 international. In 2016, 15 master's awarded. *Degree requirements:* For master's, comprehensive exam (for some programs), thesis optional. *Entrance requirements:* For master's, GRE, GMAT, or MAT if undergraduate GPA below 3.0, 2 letters of recommendation. Additional exam requirements/recommendations for international students: Required—TOEFL. *Application deadline:* For fall admission, 2/1 for international students; for spring admission, 7/15 for international students. Application fee: $65. Electronic applications accepted. *Expenses:* Tuition, state resident: full-time $11,796; part-time $655 per credit. Tuition, nonresident: full-time $24,206; part-time $1345 per credit. *Required fees:* $1546; $44 per credit. One-time fee: $155 full-time; $35 part-time. *Financial support:* In 2016–17, 6 teaching assistantships with tuition reimbursements (averaging $15,753 per year) were awarded; research assistantships also available. Financial award application deadline: 7/15; financial award applicants required to submit FAFSA. *Unit head:* Dr. Brian Krueger, Department Chair, 401-874-4058, Fax: 401-874-4072, E-mail: bkrueger@uri.edu. *Application contact:* Dr. Marc Hutchison, Director/Associate Professor, 401-874-4058, Fax: 401-874-4072, E-mail: mlhutch@uri.edu. Website: http://www.uri.edu/artsci/psc/

**University of Rochester,** School of Arts and Sciences, Department of Political Science, Rochester, NY 14627. Offers PhD. *Faculty:* 20 full-time (4 women). *Students:* 45 full-time (17 women); includes 5 minority (1 Asian, non-Hispanic/Latino; 3 Hispanic/Latino; 1 Two or more races, non-Hispanic/Latino), 24 international. Average age 28. 102 applicants, 21% accepted, 7 enrolled. In 2016, 3 doctorates awarded. *Degree requirements:* For doctorate, thesis/dissertation, qualifying exam. *Entrance requirements:* For doctorate, GRE General Test, writing sample. Additional exam requirements/recommendations for international students: Required—TOEFL (minimum score 600 paper-based; 100 iBT). *Application deadline:* For fall admission, 1/8 for domestic and international students. Application fee: $60. Electronic applications accepted. *Expenses:* $1,538 per credit. *Financial support:* In 2016–17, 35 students received support. Research assistantships, teaching assistantships, scholarships/grants, health care benefits, and tuition waivers (full and partial) available. Support available to part-time students. Financial award application deadline: 4/15. *Unit head:* Gretchen Helmke, Chair, 585-275-5236. *Application contact:* AnneMarie Tyll, Department Secretary, 585-275-8745, E-mail: atyll@ur.rochester.edu. Website: http://www.sas.rochester.edu/psc/

**University of Saskatchewan,** College of Graduate Studies and Research, College of Arts and Science, Department of Political Studies, Saskatoon, SK S7N 5A2, Canada. Offers MA. *Degree requirements:* For master's, thesis. *Entrance requirements:* Additional exam requirements/recommendations for international students: Required—TOEFL (minimum score 80 iBT); Recommended—IELTS (minimum score 6.5). Electronic applications accepted.

**University of South Africa,** College of Human Sciences, Pretoria, South Africa. Offers adult education (M Ed); African languages (MA, PhD); African politics (MA, PhD); Afrikaans (MA, PhD); ancient history (MA, PhD); ancient Near Eastern studies (MA, PhD); anthropology (MA, PhD); applied linguistics (MA); Arabic (MA, PhD); archaeology (MA); art history (MA); Biblical archaeology (MA); Biblical studies (M Th, D Th, PhD); Christian spirituality (M Th, D Th); church history (M Th, D Th); classical studies (MA, PhD); clinical psychology (MA); communication (MA, PhD); comparative education (M Ed, Ed D); consulting psychology (D Admin, D Com, PhD); curriculum studies (M Ed, Ed D); development studies (M Admin, MA, D Admin, PhD); didactics (M Ed, Ed D); education (M Tech); education management (M Ed, Ed D); educational psychology (M Ed); English (MA); environmental education (M Ed); French (MA, PhD); German (MA, PhD); Greek (MA); guidance and counseling (M Ed); health studies (MA, PhD), including health sciences education (MA), health services management (MA), medical and surgical nursing science (critical care general) (MA), midwifery and neonatal nursing science (MA), trauma and emergency care (MA); history (MA, PhD); history of education (Ed D); inclusive education (M Ed, Ed D); information and communications technology policy and regulation (MA); information science (MA, MIS, PhD); international politics (MA, PhD); Islamic studies (MA, PhD); Italian (MA, PhD); Judaica (MA, PhD); linguistics (MA, PhD); mathematical education (M Ed); mathematics education (MA); missiology (M Th, D Th); modern Hebrew (MA, PhD); musicology (MA, MMus, D Mus, PhD); natural science education (M Ed); New Testament (M Th, D Th); Old Testament (D Th); pastoral therapy (M Th, D Th); philosophy (MA); philosophy of education (M Ed, Ed D); politics (MA, PhD); Portuguese (MA, PhD); practical theology (M Th, D Th); psychology (MA, MS, PhD); psychology of education (M Ed, Ed D); public health (MA); religious studies (MA, D Th, PhD); Romance languages (MA); Russian (MA, PhD); Semitic languages (MA, PhD); social behavior studies in HIV/AIDS (MA); social science (mental health) (MA); social science in development studies (MA); social science in psychology (MA); social science in social work (MA); social science in sociology (MA); social work (MSW, DSW, PhD); socio-education (M Ed, Ed D); sociolinguistics (MA); sociology (MA, PhD); Spanish (MA, PhD); systematic theology (M Th, D Th); TESOL (teaching English to speakers of other languages) (MA); theological ethics (M Th, D Th); theory of literature (MA, PhD); urban ministries (D Th); urban ministry (M Th).

**University of South Carolina,** The Graduate School, College of Arts and Sciences, Department of Political Science, Program in Political Science, Columbia, SC 29208. Offers MA, PhD. *Program availability:* Part-time. Terminal master's awarded for partial completion of doctoral program. *Degree requirements:* For master's, one foreign language, thesis; for doctorate, one foreign language, comprehensive exam, thesis/dissertation. *Entrance requirements:* For master's and doctorate, GRE General Test, minimum GPA of 3.5. Additional exam requirements/recommendations for international students: Required—TOEFL. Electronic applications accepted. *Faculty research:* American government and politics, comparative politics, political theory, international politics, public administration and policy.

**The University of South Dakota,** Graduate School, College of Arts and Sciences, Department of Political Science, Vermillion, SD 57069. Offers American political institutions (PhD); American politics and public policy (MA); political science (EMPA, MA); public administration (MPA, PhD); public policy (PhD); JD/MA. *Accreditation:* NASPAA (one or more programs are accredited). *Program availability:* Part-time, online learning. *Degree requirements:* For master's, comprehensive exam, thesis (for some programs). *Entrance requirements:* For master's, GRE or LSAT (for MPA), GRE General Test (for MA), minimum GPA of 3.0. Additional exam requirements/recommendations for international students: Required—TOEFL (minimum score 550 paper-based; 79 iBT). Electronic applications accepted.

**University of Southern California,** Graduate School, Annenberg School for Communication and Journalism, School of Communication, Program in Public

Diplomacy, Los Angeles, CA 90089. Offers MPD. *Program availability:* Part-time. *Students:* 33 full-time (22 women), 4 part-time; includes 9 minority (1 Black or African American, non-Hispanic/Latino; 2 Asian, non-Hispanic/Latino; 5 Hispanic/Latino; 1 Two or more races, non-Hispanic/Latino), 8 international. Average age 26. 45 applicants, 60% accepted, 19 enrolled. In 2016, 23 master's awarded. *Degree requirements:* For master's, thesis. *Entrance requirements:* For master's, GRE, resume, writing samples, statement of purpose, recommendation letters. Additional exam requirements/recommendations for international students: Required—TOEFL (minimum score 114 iBT), IELTS (minimum score 8). *Application deadline:* For fall admission, 1/15 priority date for domestic and international students. Application fee: $90. Electronic applications accepted. *Financial support:* In 2016–17, 6 fellowships (averaging $15,000 per year) were awarded; career-related internships or fieldwork, Federal Work-Study, and scholarships/grants also available. Support available to part-time students. Financial award application deadline: 1/15; financial award applicants required to submit FAFSA. *Unit head:* Dr. Nicholas Cull, Director, 213-821-4080, E-mail: cull@usc.edu. *Application contact:* Allyson Hill, Associate Dean for Admissions, 213-821-0770, Fax: 213-740-1933, E-mail: ascadm@usc.edu.
Website: http://www.annenberg.usc.edu

**University of Southern California,** Graduate School, Dana and David Dornsife College of Letters, Arts and Sciences, Political Science and International Relations PhD Program, Los Angeles, CA 90089. Offers PhD. *Degree requirements:* For doctorate, variable foreign language requirement, comprehensive exam, thesis/dissertation. *Entrance requirements:* For doctorate, GRE (minimum score 1000). Additional exam requirements/recommendations for international students: Required—TOEFL (minimum score 600 paper-based; 100 iBT). Electronic applications accepted. *Faculty research:* American politics, foreign policy analysis, international political economy, race/ethics politics, security studies.

**University of Southern Mississippi,** Graduate School, College of Arts and Letters, Department of Political Science, International Development and International Affairs, Hattiesburg, MS 39406. Offers international development (PhD); political science (MA). *Program availability:* Part-time, evening/weekend, online learning. *Degree requirements:* For master's, comprehensive exam, thesis (for some programs); for doctorate, comprehensive exam, thesis/dissertation. *Entrance requirements:* For master's, GRE General Test, minimum GPA of 2.75 in last 2 years, 3.0 in field of study; for doctorate, GRE General Test, minimum GPA of 3.5. Additional exam requirements/recommendations for international students: Required—TOEFL, IELTS. *Application deadline:* For fall admission, 3/1 priority date for domestic students, 3/1 for international students. Applications are processed on a rolling basis. Application fee: $60. *Expenses: Tuition, area resident:* Full-time $15,708; part-time $437 per credit hour. *Financial support:* Research assistantships with full and partial tuition reimbursements, teaching assistantships with full tuition reimbursements, career-related internships or fieldwork, Federal Work-Study, scholarships/grants, health care benefits, and unspecified assistantships available. Financial award application deadline: 3/15; financial award applicants required to submit FAFSA. *Faculty research:* American politics, international politics, political theory, comparative politics, public law. *Unit head:* Edward Sayre, Chair, 601-266-4310. *Application contact:* Marek Steedman, Director, Graduate Studies, 601-266-4317, Fax: 601-266-4172.
Website: https://www.usm.edu/political-science-international-development-affairs

**University of South Florida,** College of Arts and Sciences, Department of Government and International Affairs, Tampa, FL 33620-9951. Offers government (PhD); Latin American, Caribbean and Latino studies (MA); political science (MA), including comparative government and politics; public administration (MPA). *Program availability:* Part-time, evening/weekend. *Faculty:* 15 full-time (3 women). *Students:* 47 full-time (26 women), 40 part-time (22 women); includes 15 minority (6 Black or African American, non-Hispanic/Latino; 1 Asian, non-Hispanic/Latino; 7 Hispanic/Latino; 1 Two or more races, non-Hispanic/Latino), 15 international. Average age 32. 59 applicants, 58% accepted, 21 enrolled. In 2016, 30 master's, 3 doctorates awarded. *Degree requirements:* For master's, comprehensive exam, thesis; for doctorate, comprehensive exam, thesis/dissertation. *Entrance requirements:* For master's, GRE General Test, minimum GPA of 3.0 in upper-division undergraduate course work; letters of recommendation (2 for MPA, 3 for MS); 500-word personal statement and undergraduate background in political science or related fields (for MS); one-page career statement (for MPA); for doctorate, GRE General Test, 500-word personal statement, three letters of recommendation, transcripts of MA/BA coursework, writing sample. Additional exam requirements/recommendations for international students: Required—TOEFL (minimum score 550 paper-based; 79 iBT) or IELTS (minimum score 6.5). *Application deadline:* For fall admission, 1/5 for domestic and international students; for spring admission, 10/15 for domestic students, 9/15 for international students. Applications are processed on a rolling basis. Application fee: $30. Electronic applications accepted. *Expenses:* Tuition, state resident: full-time $7766; part-time $431.43 per credit hour. Tuition, nonresident: full-time $15,789; part-time $877.17 per credit hour. *Required fees:* $37 per term. *Financial support:* In 2016–17, 1 student received support, including 18 teaching assistantships with tuition reimbursements available (averaging $12,390 per year); unspecified assistantships also available. Financial award application deadline: 4/1. *Faculty research:* Citizenship and identity, social movements, global governance, American politics, public policy. *Total annual research expenditures:* $222,648. *Unit head:* Dr. Steven Tauber, Associate Professor/Interim Chair, 813-974-2278, Fax: 813-974-0832, E-mail: stauber@usf.edu. *Application contact:* Dr. Bernd Reiter, Associate Professor and Director of Graduate Studies, 813-974-3583, Fax: 813-974-0832, E-mail: breiter@usf.edu.
Website: http://gia.usf.edu/

**University of South Florida,** Innovative Education, Tampa, FL 33620-9951. Offers adult, career and higher education (Graduate Certificate), including college teaching, leadership in developing human resources, leadership in higher education; Africana studies (Graduate Certificate), including diasporas and health disparities, genocide and human rights; aging studies (Graduate Certificate), including gerontology; art research (Graduate Certificate), including museum studies; business foundations (Graduate Certificate); chemical and biomedical engineering (Graduate Certificate), including materials science and engineering, water, health and sustainability; child and family studies (Graduate Certificate), including positive behavior support; civil and industrial engineering (Graduate Certificate), including transportation systems analysis; community and family health (Graduate Certificate), including maternal and child health, social marketing and public health, violence and injury: prevention and intervention, women's health; criminology (Graduate Certificate), including criminal justice administration; educational measurement and research (Graduate Certificate), including evaluation; English (Graduate Certificate), including comparative literary studies, creative writing, professional and technical communication; entrepreneurship (Graduate Certificate); environmental health (Graduate Certificate), including safety management; epidemiology and biostatistics (Graduate Certificate), including applied biostatistics, biostatistics, concepts and tools of epidemiology, epidemiology, epidemiology of infectious diseases; geography, environment and planning (Graduate Certificate), including community development, environmental policy and management, geographical information systems; geology (Graduate Certificate), including hydrogeology; global health (Graduate Certificate), including disaster management,

global health and Latin American and Caribbean studies, global health practice, humanitarian assistance, infection control; government and international affairs (Graduate Certificate), including Cuban studies, globalization studies; health policy and management (Graduate Certificate), including health management and leadership, public health policy and programs; hearing specialist: early intervention (Graduate Certificate); industrial and management systems engineering (Graduate Certificate), including systems engineering, technology management; information studies (Graduate Certificate), including school library media specialist; information systems/decision sciences (Graduate Certificate), including analytics and business intelligence; instructional technology (Graduate Certificate), including distance education, Florida digital/virtual educator, instructional design, multimedia design, Web design; internal medicine, bioethics and medical humanities (Graduate Certificate), including biomedical ethics; Latin American and Caribbean studies (Graduate Certificate); mass communications (Graduate Certificate), including multimedia journalism; mathematics and statistics (Graduate Certificate), including mathematics; medicine (Graduate Certificate), including aging and neuroscience, bioinformatics, biotechnology, brain fitness and memory management, clinical investigation, health informatics, health sciences, integrative weight management, intellectual property, medicine and gender, metabolic and nutritional medicine, metabolic cardiology, pharmacy sciences; national and competitive intelligence (Graduate Certificate); psychological and social foundations (Graduate Certificate), including career counseling, college teaching, diversity in education, mental health counseling, school counseling; public affairs (Graduate Certificate), including nonprofit management, public management, research administration; public health (Graduate Certificate), including environmental health, health equity, public health generalist, translational research in adolescent behavioral health; public health practices (Graduate Certificate), including planning for healthy communities; rehabilitation and mental health counseling (Graduate Certificate), including integrative mental health care, marriage and family therapy, rehabilitation technology; secondary education (Graduate Certificate), including ESOL, foreign language education: culture and content, foreign language education: professional; social work (Graduate Certificate), including geriatric social work/clinical gerontology; special education (Graduate Certificate), including autism spectrum disorder, disabilities education: severe/profound; world languages (Graduate Certificate), including teaching English as a second language (TESL) or foreign language. *Expenses:* Tuition, state resident: full-time $7766; part-time $431.43 per credit hour. Tuition, nonresident: full-time $15,789; part-time $877.17 per credit hour. *Required fees:* $37 per term. *Unit head:* Kathy Barnes, Interdisciplinary Programs Coordinator, 813-974-8031, Fax: 813-974-7061, E-mail: barnesk@usf.edu. *Application contact:* Karen Tylinski, Metro Initiatives, 813-974-9943, Fax: 813-974-7061, E-mail: ktylinsk@usf.edu.
Website: http://www.usf.edu/innovative-education/

**The University of Tennessee,** Graduate School, College of Arts and Sciences, Department of Political Science, Program in Political Science, Knoxville, TN 37996. Offers MA, PhD. *Program availability:* Part-time. *Degree requirements:* For master's, thesis or alternative; for doctorate, one foreign language, thesis/dissertation. *Entrance requirements:* For master's and doctorate, GRE General Test, minimum GPA of 2.7. Additional exam requirements/recommendations for international students: Required—TOEFL. Electronic applications accepted.

**The University of Tennessee,** Graduate School, College of Arts and Sciences, Department of Sociology, Knoxville, TN 37996. Offers criminology (MA, PhD); energy, environment, and resource policy (MA, PhD); political economy (MA, PhD). *Program availability:* Part-time. *Degree requirements:* For master's, thesis or alternative; for doctorate, thesis/dissertation. *Entrance requirements:* For master's, GRE General Test, minimum GPA of 3.0; for doctorate, GRE General Test, minimum GPA of 3.5. Additional exam requirements/recommendations for international students: Required—TOEFL. Electronic applications accepted.

**The University of Tennessee at Chattanooga,** Department of Political Science and Public Service, Chattanooga, TN 37403. Offers local government management (MPA); non profit management (MPA); public administration (MPA); public administration and non-profit management (Postbaccalaureate Certificate). *Program availability:* Part-time, evening/weekend. *Faculty:* 5 full-time (2 women). *Students:* 8 full-time (2 women), 14 part-time (11 women); includes 6 minority (4 Black or African American, non-Hispanic/Latino; 1 Asian, non-Hispanic/Latino; 1 Two or more races, non-Hispanic/Latino). Average age 31. 14 applicants, 86% accepted, 7 enrolled. In 2016, 11 master's awarded. *Degree requirements:* For master's, comprehensive exam, thesis or alternative, internship. *Entrance requirements:* For master's, GRE General Test. Additional exam requirements/recommendations for international students: Required—TOEFL (minimum score 550 paper-based; 79 iBT), IELTS (minimum score 6). *Application deadline:* For fall admission, 6/15 priority date for domestic students, 7/1 for international students; for spring admission, 11/1 priority date for domestic students, 11/1 for international students. Applications are processed on a rolling basis. Application fee: $35 ($40 for international students). Electronic applications accepted. *Expenses:* $9,876 full-time in-state; $25,994 full-time out-of-state; $450 per credit part-time in-state; $1,345 per credit part-time out-of-state. *Financial support:* In 2016–17, 2 research assistantships were awarded; career-related internships or fieldwork, scholarships/grants, and unspecified assistantships also available. Support available to part-time students. Financial award application deadline: 7/1; financial award applicants required to submit FAFSA. *Faculty research:* Organizational cultures and renewal, management theory, public policy, policy analysis, nonprofit organization. *Total annual research expenditures:* $1,700. *Unit head:* Dr. Michelle D. Deardorf, Department Head, 423-425-4231, Fax: 423-425-2373, E-mail: michelle-deardorff@utc.edu. *Application contact:* Dr. Joanne Romagni, Dean of the Graduate School, 423-425-4478, Fax: 423-425-5223, E-mail: joanne-romagni@utc.edu.
Website: http://www.utc.edu/political-science-public-service/

**The University of Texas at Arlington,** Graduate School, College of Liberal Arts, Department of Political Science, Arlington, TX 76019. Offers MA. *Program availability:* Part-time, evening/weekend. *Degree requirements:* For master's, comprehensive exam, thesis optional. *Entrance requirements:* For master's, GRE, minimum GPA of 3.0 in last 60 hours of course work. Additional exam requirements/recommendations for international students: Required—TOEFL (minimum score 550 paper-based). *Application deadline:* For fall admission, 6/15 for domestic students. Applications are processed on a rolling basis. Application fee: $35 ($50 for international students). Electronic applications accepted. *Financial support:* Fellowships with full tuition reimbursements, teaching assistantships, career-related internships or fieldwork, institutionally sponsored loans, and scholarships/grants available. Support available to part-time students. Financial award application deadline: 6/1; financial award applicants required to submit FAFSA. *Unit head:* Dr. Rebecca Deen, Chair, 817-272-2991, Fax: 817-272-2525, E-mail: deen@uta.edu. *Application contact:* Dr. Brent Boyea, Graduate Advisor, 817-272-2991, E-mail: boyea@uta.edu.
Website: http://www.uta.edu/pols/

**The University of Texas at Austin,** Graduate School, College of Liberal Arts, Department of Government, Austin, TX 78712-1111. Offers MA, PhD, PhD/JD. *Degree requirements:* For master's, thesis; for doctorate, comprehensive exam, thesis/

## Political Science

dissertation. *Entrance requirements:* For master's and doctorate, GRE General Test. Electronic applications accepted.

**The University of Texas at Dallas,** School of Economic, Political and Policy Sciences, Program in Political Science, Richardson, TX 75080. Offers Constitutional law (MA); legislative studies (MA); political science (MA, PhD). *Program availability:* Part-time, evening/weekend. *Faculty:* 12 full-time (2 women). *Students:* 27 full-time (7 women), 15 part-time (10 women); includes 11 minority (7 Black or African American, non-Hispanic/Latino; 1 Asian, non-Hispanic/Latino; 3 Hispanic/Latino), 9 international. Average age 35. 27 applicants, 59% accepted, 11 enrolled. In 2016, 9 master's, 4 doctorates awarded. Terminal master's awarded for partial completion of doctoral program. *Degree requirements:* For master's, thesis optional, independent study; for doctorate, thesis/dissertation, practicum research. *Entrance requirements:* For master's, GRE (minimum combined verbal and quantitative score of 1100, minimum undergraduate GPA of 3.0; for doctorate, GRE (minimum combined verbal and quantitative score of 1200, writing 4.5), minimum undergraduate GPA of 3.2. Additional exam requirements/recommendations for international students: Required—TOEFL (minimum score 550 paper-based). *Application deadline:* For fall admission, 7/15 for domestic students, 5/1 priority date for international students; for spring admission, 11/15 for domestic students, 9/1 priority date for international students. Applications are processed on a rolling basis. Application fee: $50 ($100 for international students). Electronic applications accepted. *Expenses:* Tuition, state resident: full-time $12,418; part-time $690 per semester hour. Tuition, nonresident: full-time $24,150; part-time $1342 per semester hour. Tuition and fees vary according to course load. *Financial support:* In 2016–17, 25 students received support, including 1 research assistantship with partial tuition reimbursement available (averaging $20,000 per year), 16 teaching assistantships with partial tuition reimbursements available (averaging $13,100 per year); career-related internships or fieldwork, Federal Work-Study, institutionally sponsored loans, and scholarships/grants also available. Support available to part-time students. Financial award application deadline: 4/30; financial award applicants required to submit FAFSA. *Faculty research:* Terrorism and democratic stability, redistricting and representation, trust and social exchange, how economic ideas impact political thought and public policy. *Unit head:* Dr. Jennifer Holmes, Program Head, 972-883-6843, Fax: 972-883-2735, E-mail: jholmes@utdallas.edu. *Application contact:* Cheryl Berry, Graduate Program Administrator, 972-883-2932, Fax: 972-883-2735, E-mail: politicalscience@utdallas.edu. Website: http://www.utdallas.edu/epps/political-science/

**The University of Texas at Dallas,** School of Economic, Political and Policy Sciences, Program in Public Policy and Political Economy, Richardson, TX 75080. Offers international political economy (MS); public policy (MPP); public policy and political economy (PhD); social data analytics and research (MS). *Program availability:* Part-time, evening/weekend. *Faculty:* 24 full-time (2 women), 2 part-time/adjunct (1 woman). *Students:* 47 full-time (24 women), 30 part-time (14 women); includes 20 minority (4 Black or African American, non-Hispanic/Latino; 1 American Indian or Alaska Native, non-Hispanic/Latino; 3 Asian, non-Hispanic/Latino; 11 Hispanic/Latino; 1 Two or more races, non-Hispanic/Latino), 25 international. Average age 35. 55 applicants, 55% accepted, 12 enrolled. In 2016, 13 master's, 9 doctorates awarded. *Degree requirements:* For doctorate, thesis/dissertation. *Entrance requirements:* For master's and doctorate, GRE General Test, minimum GPA of 3.0 in upper-level course work in field. Additional exam requirements/recommendations for international students: Required—TOEFL (minimum score 550 paper-based). *Application deadline:* For fall admission, 7/15 for domestic students, 5/1 priority date for international students; for spring admission, 11/15 for domestic students, 9/1 priority date for international students. Applications are processed on a rolling basis. Application fee: $50 ($100 for international students). Electronic applications accepted. *Expenses:* Tuition, state resident: full-time $12,418; part-time $690 per semester hour. Tuition, nonresident: full-time $24,150; part-time $1342 per semester hour. Tuition and fees vary according to course load. *Financial support:* In 2016–17, 45 students received support, including 13 research assistantships with partial tuition reimbursements available (averaging $18,538 per year), 14 teaching assistantships with partial tuition reimbursements available (averaging $13,100 per year); career-related internships or fieldwork, Federal Work-Study, institutionally sponsored loans, scholarships/grants, and unspecified assistantships also available. Support available to part-time students. Financial award application deadline: 4/30; financial award applicants required to submit FAFSA. *Faculty research:* Ethnicity, community and local public good provision; community mental health policy; Texas Schools Project; biological and chemical arms control; cross-disciplinary applications of quantitative methodology. *Unit head:* Dr. Jennifer Holmes, Program Head, 972-883-6843, Fax: 972-883-6297, E-mail: jholmes@utdallas.edu. *Application contact:* Betsy Albritton, Graduate Program Administrator, 972-883-6406, Fax: 972-883-6297, E-mail: betsy.albritton@utdallas.edu. Website: http://www.utdallas.edu/epps/public-policy-and-political-economy/

**The University of Texas at El Paso,** Graduate School, College of Liberal Arts, Department of Political Science, El Paso, TX 79968-0001. Offers MA. *Program availability:* Part-time, evening/weekend. *Degree requirements:* For master's, thesis optional. *Entrance requirements:* For master's, GRE, letters of recommendation, personal statement, transcripts. Additional exam requirements/recommendations for international students: Required—TOEFL; Recommended—IELTS. Electronic applications accepted. *Faculty research:* Democracy and democratization, political institutions, regional integration, international security, presidential and legislative politics.

**The University of Texas at San Antonio,** College of Liberal and Fine Arts, Department of Political Science and Geography, San Antonio, TX 78249-0617. Offers political science (MA). *Program availability:* Part-time, evening/weekend. *Faculty:* 13 full-time (3 women). *Students:* 11 full-time (7 women), 16 part-time (6 women); includes 11 minority (1 Asian, non-Hispanic/Latino; 9 Hispanic/Latino; 1 Two or more races, non-Hispanic/Latino), 1 international. Average age 30. 13 applicants, 92% accepted, 6 enrolled. In 2016, 3 master's awarded. *Degree requirements:* For master's, comprehensive exam (for some programs), thesis optional. *Entrance requirements:* For master's, GRE General Test or LSAT, 18 semester credit hours in upper-division undergraduate or graduate-level courses in political science or directly-related fields in the social or behavioral sciences; 3 letters of recommendation; statement of purpose. Additional exam requirements/recommendations for international students: Required—TOEFL (minimum score 550 paper-based; 79 iBT), IELTS (minimum score 6.5). *Application deadline:* For fall admission, 7/1 for domestic students, 4/1 for international students; for spring admission, 11/1 for domestic students, 9/1 for international students. Application fee: $45 ($80 for international students). *Financial support:* Applicants required to submit FAFSA. *Faculty research:* Minority representation and legislation, comparative welfare policy, strategic conflict in India and Pakistan, homeland security, global governance, American political behavior. *Total annual research expenditures:* $1,968. *Unit head:* Dr. Daniel Engster, Chair, 210-458-5645, E-mail: daniel.engster@utsa.edu. *Application contact:* Dr. James Calder, Graduate Advisor of Record, 210-458-7671, Fax: 210-458-7671, E-mail: james.calder@utsa.edu. Website: http://colfa.utsa.edu/Polisci/

**The University of Texas at Tyler,** College of Arts and Sciences, Department of Political Science, Tyler, TX 75799-0001. Offers MA. *Program availability:* Part-time, evening/weekend. *Degree requirements:* For master's, comprehensive exam, thesis optional.

*Entrance requirements:* Additional exam requirements/recommendations for international students: Required—TOEFL. *Faculty research:* American politics, comparative politics, international relations, political theory and philosophy.

**The University of Texas of the Permian Basin,** Office of Graduate Studies, College of Arts and Sciences, Department of Social Sciences, Odessa, TX 79762-0001. Offers criminal justice administration (MS); political science (MPA). *Program availability:* Part-time, evening/weekend. *Degree requirements:* For master's, comprehensive exam (for some programs), thesis (for some programs). *Entrance requirements:* For master's, GRE General Test. Additional exam requirements/recommendations for international students: Required—TOEFL (minimum score 550 paper-based).

**The University of Toledo,** College of Graduate Studies, College of Languages, Literature and Social Sciences, Department of Political Science and Public Administration, Toledo, OH 43606-3390. Offers health care policy and administration (Certificate); management of non-profit organizations (Certificate); municipal administration (Certificate); political science (MA); public administration (MPA); JD/MPA. *Accreditation:* NASPAA. *Program availability:* Part-time. *Degree requirements:* For master's, comprehensive exam (for some programs), thesis. *Entrance requirements:* For master's, GRE General Test, minimum cumulative point-hour ratio of 2.7 (3.0 for MPA) for all previous academic work, three letters of recommendation, statement of purpose, transcripts from all prior institutions attended; for Certificate, minimum cumulative point-hour ratio of 2.7 for all previous academic work, three letters of recommendation, statement of purpose, transcripts from all prior institutions attended. Additional exam requirements/recommendations for international students: Required—TOEFL (minimum score 550 paper-based; 80 iBT). Electronic applications accepted. *Faculty research:* Economic development, health care, Third World, criminal justice, Eastern Europe.

**University of Toronto,** School of Graduate Studies, Faculty of Arts and Science, Department of Political Science, Toronto, ON M5S 1A1, Canada. Offers MA, PhD, JD/MA, JD/PhD. *Program availability:* Part-time. *Degree requirements:* For master's, thesis optional; for doctorate, one foreign language, thesis/dissertation, reading competency in a language other than English. *Entrance requirements:* For master's, 3 letters of recommendation, writing sample, statement of scholarly intent, minimum cumulative GPA of B+ in a four-year bachelor's program including B+ average over five to eight suitably-distributed full-year political science courses; for doctorate, 4 letters of recommendation, writing sample, minimum A- in most recent political science (or equivalent) degree. Additional exam requirements/recommendations for international students: Required—TOEFL (minimum score 580 paper-based; 93 iBT), TWE (minimum score 5). Electronic applications accepted.

**University of Utah,** Graduate School, College of Humanities, Program in Middle East Studies, Salt Lake City, UT 84112. Offers Arabic (MA, PhD); Hebrew (MA); history (MA, PhD); Persian (MA, PhD); political science (MA, PhD). *Students:* 3 part-time (2 women); includes 1 minority (Asian, non-Hispanic/Latino), 1 international. In 2016, 2 master's awarded. Terminal master's awarded for partial completion of doctoral program. *Degree requirements:* For master's, 2 foreign languages, comprehensive exam, thesis optional; for doctorate, 3 foreign languages, comprehensive exam, thesis/dissertation. *Entrance requirements:* For master's, GRE General Test, minimum GPA of 3.2; for doctorate, GRE General Test, MA in Middle East studies or equivalent, minimum GPA of 3.2. Additional exam requirements/recommendations for international students: Required—TOEFL (minimum score 580 paper-based; 92 iBT); Recommended—IELTS (minimum score 7). *Application deadline:* For fall admission, 1/15 priority date for domestic and international students. Application fee: $55 ($65 for international students). Electronic applications accepted. *Expenses:* Tuition, state resident: full-time $7011; part-time $3918.24 per credit hour. Tuition, nonresident: full-time $22,154; part-time $11,665.42 per credit hour. *Financial support:* In 2016–17, 5 students received support, including 2 teaching assistantships with full tuition reimbursements available (averaging $13,500 per year); fellowships and unspecified assistantships also available. Financial award application deadline: 1/15. *Faculty research:* Islamic studies; Middle Eastern history; political science; Judaic studies; anthropology; Arabic, Persian, Hebrew, and Turkish language and literature. *Unit head:* Johanna Watzinger-Tharp, Director, 801-581-7148, Fax: 801-581-6105, E-mail: j.tharp@utah.edu. *Application contact:* Kellie Hubbard, Academic Advisor, 801-581-5362, Fax: 801-581-6105, E-mail: kellie.hubbard@utah.edu. Website: http://www.mec.utah.edu

**University of Utah,** Graduate School, College of Social and Behavioral Science, Department of Political Science, Program in Political Science, Salt Lake City, UT 84112. Offers American politics (MA, MS, PhD); comparative politics (MA, MS, PhD); international relations (MA, MS, PhD); political theory (MA, MS, PhD); public administration (MA, MS, PhD). *Faculty:* 31 full-time (8 women), 10 part-time/adjunct (3 women). *Students:* 45 full-time (16 women), 19 part-time (9 women); includes 6 minority (2 Asian, non-Hispanic/Latino; 2 Hispanic/Latino; 2 Two or more races, non-Hispanic/Latino), 4 international. Average age 35. 37 applicants, 49% accepted, 7 enrolled. In 2016, 2 master's, 4 doctorates awarded. Terminal master's awarded for partial completion of doctoral program. *Degree requirements:* For master's, variable foreign language requirement, thesis or research paper; for doctorate, comprehensive exam, thesis/dissertation. *Entrance requirements:* For master's and doctorate, GRE General Test, minimum GPA of 3.2. Additional exam requirements/recommendations for international students: Required—TOEFL (minimum score 580 paper-based; 61 iBT), IELTS (minimum score 6). *Application deadline:* For fall admission, 1/15 priority date for domestic and international students. Application fee: $55 ($65 for international students). Electronic applications accepted. *Expenses:* Contact institution. *Financial support:* In 2016–17, 10 students received support, including 5 fellowships with full tuition reimbursements available (averaging $15,250 per year), 13 teaching assistantships with full tuition reimbursements available (averaging $15,000 per year); career-related internships or fieldwork, scholarships/grants, health care benefits, and unspecified assistantships also available. Financial award application deadline: 1/15; financial award applicants required to submit FAFSA. *Faculty research:* International politics, comparative politics, political theory, American politics, public administration. *Total annual research expenditures:* $15,000. *Unit head:* Mark Button, Chair, 801-585-7987, Fax: 801-585-6492, E-mail: mark.button@poli-sci.utah.edu. *Application contact:* Sandy Hiskey, Graduate Academic Advisor, 801-581-8608, Fax: 801-585-6492, E-mail: sandy.hiskey@utah.edu. Website: http://www.poli-sci.utah.edu/

**University of Victoria,** Faculty of Graduate Studies, Faculty of Social Sciences, Department of Political Science, Victoria, BC V8W 2Y2, Canada. Offers MA, PhD. *Program availability:* Part-time. *Degree requirements:* For master's, thesis; for doctorate, thesis/dissertation, candidacy exam. *Entrance requirements:* For master's, minimum B+ average in last 2 years of undergraduate course work. Additional exam requirements/recommendations for international students: Required—TOEFL (minimum score 600 paper-based). Electronic applications accepted. *Faculty research:* Political theory, political parties, international political economy, comparative public policy, British Columbian politics.

**University of Virginia,** College and Graduate School of Arts and Sciences, Department of Politics, Program in Government, Charlottesville, VA 22903. Offers MA, PhD, JD/MA, MBA/MA. *Students:* 24 full-time (6 women); includes 2 minority (1 Asian, non-Hispanic/

Latino; 1 Two or more races, non-Hispanic/Latino), 3 international. Average age 28. 63 applicants, 24% accepted, 4 enrolled. In 2016, 2 master's, 6 doctorates awarded. *Degree requirements:* For master's, 2 research/statistics courses or thesis; for doctorate, variable foreign language requirement, thesis/dissertation, 2 research/statistics courses. *Entrance requirements:* For master's and doctorate, GRE General Test, long writing sample; 2 letters of recommendation. Additional exam requirements/recommendations for international students: Required—TOEFL (minimum score 600 paper-based; 90 iBT), IELTS (minimum score 7). *Application deadline:* For fall admission, 12/4 for domestic and international students. Applications are processed on a rolling basis. Application fee: $60. Electronic applications accepted. *Expenses:* Tuition, state resident: full-time $15,026; part-time $834 per credit hour. Tuition, nonresident: full-time $25,168; part-time $1378 per credit hour. *Required fees:* $2654. *Financial support:* Fellowships and teaching assistantships available. Financial award application deadline: 12/4; financial award applicants required to submit FAFSA. *Unit head:* David Leblang, Chair, 434-924-3192, Fax: 434-924-3159, E-mail: dal7w@virginia.edu. *Application contact:* Jeffery A. Jenkins, Director of Graduate Studies, 434-924-3192, Fax: 434-924-3159, E-mail: jaj7d@virginia.edu. Website: http://politics.virginia.edu/

**University of Washington,** Graduate School, College of Arts and Sciences, Department of Political Science, Seattle, WA 98195. Offers MA, PhD. *Degree requirements:* For doctorate, thesis/dissertation. *Entrance requirements:* For master's and doctorate, GRE General Test, minimum GPA of 3.0. Additional exam requirements/recommendations for international students: Required—TOEFL. Electronic applications accepted. *Faculty research:* American politics, comparative politics, international relations, political theory, political economy.

**University of Waterloo,** Graduate Studies, Faculty of Arts, Department of Political Science, Waterloo, ON N2L 3G1, Canada. Offers global governance (MA, PhD). *Program availability:* Part-time. *Degree requirements:* For master's, thesis (for some programs), research paper. *Entrance requirements:* For master's, honors degree, minimum B average, writing sample. Additional exam requirements/recommendations for international students: Required—TOEFL, IELTS, PTE. Electronic applications accepted. *Faculty research:* Conflict and conflict resolution, political economy, contemporary political theory, Canadian state and society.

**University of Waterloo,** Graduate Studies, Faculty of Arts, Global Governance Program, Waterloo, ON N2L 3G1, Canada. Offers MA, PhD. *Entrance requirements:* For doctorate, MA. Additional exam requirements/recommendations for international students: Required—TOEFL, IELTS, PTE. Electronic applications accepted. *Faculty research:* Global political economy, global environment, peace and security, global justice and human rights, multilateral institutions and diplomacy.

**The University of Western Ontario,** Faculty of Graduate Studies, Social Sciences Division, Department of Political Science, London, ON N6A 5B8, Canada. Offers MA, MPA, PhD. *Program availability:* Part-time. *Degree requirements:* For master's, thesis; for doctorate, comprehensive exam, thesis/dissertation. *Entrance requirements:* For master's, minimum B average, honors BA in political science or equivalent, sample of written work; for doctorate, MA in political science or equivalent. *Faculty research:* Political theory, Canadian politics, local government, comparative politics, international relations.

**University of West Florida,** College of Arts, Social Sciences, and Humanities, Department of Government, Pensacola, FL 32514-5750. Offers political science (MA), including political science, security and diplomacy. *Program availability:* Part-time, evening/weekend. *Faculty:* 5 full-time (2 women), 1 part-time/adjunct (0 women). *Students:* 9 full-time (5 women), 9 part-time (6 women). Average age 28. 24 applicants, 75% accepted, 9 enrolled. In 2016, 3 master's awarded. *Degree requirements:* For master's, thesis or alternative. *Entrance requirements:* For master's, GRE, official transcripts; minimum GPA of 3.0; 500-word writing sample in form of letter of intent; resume. Additional exam requirements/recommendations for international students: Required—TOEFL (minimum score 550 paper-based). *Application deadline:* For fall admission, 6/1 for domestic and international students; for spring admission, 10/1 for domestic and international students. Applications are processed on a rolling basis. Application fee: $30. *Expenses:* Tuition, state resident: full-time $5316.12. Tuition, nonresident: full-time $11,308. *Required fees:* $583.92. Tuition and fees vary according to course load and program. *Financial support:* In 2016–17, 6 fellowships with partial tuition reimbursements (averaging $175 per year), 5 research assistantships with partial tuition reimbursements (averaging $3,280 per year), 1 teaching assistantship with partial tuition reimbursement (averaging $5,000 per year) were awarded; unspecified assistantships also available. Financial award application deadline: 4/15; financial award applicants required to submit FAFSA. *Faculty research:* Political campaigns, elections, law enforcement, growth management. *Unit head:* Michelle Hale Williams, Chair, 850-474-2347, E-mail: govt@uwf.edu. *Application contact:* Terry McCray, Assistant Director of Graduate Admissions, 850-473-7718, Fax: 850-473-7714, E-mail: gradadmissions@uwf.edu. Website: http://uwf.edu/cassh/departments/government/

**University of Windsor,** Faculty of Graduate Studies, Faculty of Arts and Social Sciences, Department of Political Science, Windsor, ON N9B 3P4, Canada. Offers MA. *Program availability:* Part-time. *Entrance requirements:* For master's, minimum B+ average. Additional exam requirements/recommendations for international students: Required—TOEFL (minimum score 600 paper-based). Electronic applications accepted. *Faculty research:* Canadian politics and government, local government, comparative political Canadian public administration, public policy.

**University of Wisconsin–Madison,** Graduate School, College of Letters and Science, Department of Political Science, Madison, WI 53706-1380. Offers PhD. *Degree requirements:* For doctorate, thesis/dissertation. *Entrance requirements:* For doctorate, GRE General Test. Electronic applications accepted. *Faculty research:* Comparative politics, American politics, international relations, political theory, political methodology.

**University of Wisconsin–Milwaukee,** Graduate School, College of Letters and Science, Department of Political Science, Milwaukee, WI 53201-0413. Offers MA, PhD. *Students:* 16 full-time (8 women), 1 (woman) part-time, 6 international. Average age 31. 30 applicants, 60% accepted, 6 enrolled. In 2016, 4 master's, 2 doctorates awarded. *Degree requirements:* For master's, thesis or alternative; for doctorate, one foreign language, thesis/dissertation. *Entrance requirements:* For master's and doctorate, GRE General Test, minimum GPA of 3.0. Additional exam requirements/recommendations for international students: Required—TOEFL (minimum score 550 paper-based; 79 iBT), IELTS (minimum score 6.5). *Application deadline:* For fall admission, 1/1 priority date for domestic students; for spring admission, 9/1 for domestic students. Applications are processed on a rolling basis. Application fee: $56 ($96 for international students). Electronic applications accepted. *Financial support:* In 2016–17, 1 fellowship, 2 research assistantships, 21 teaching assistantships were awarded; career-related internships or fieldwork, unspecified assistantships, and project assistantships also available. Support available to part-time students. Financial award application deadline: 4/15; financial award applicants required to submit FAFSA. *Unit head:* Thomas Holbrook, Department Chair, 414-229-4221, E-mail: holbroot@uwm.edu. *Application contact:* General Information Contact, 414-229-4982, Fax: 414-229-6967, E-mail: gradschool@uwm.edu. Website: http://www.uwm.edu/dept/polsci/

**University of Wyoming,** College of Arts and Sciences, Department of Political Science, Program in Political Science, Laramie, WY 82071. Offers MA. *Program availability:* Part-time. *Degree requirements:* For master's, thesis or alternative. *Entrance requirements:* For master's, GRE General Test, bachelor's degree in political science, minimum GPA of 3.0. Additional exam requirements/recommendations for international students: Required—TOEFL (minimum score 525 paper-based). Electronic applications accepted. *Faculty research:* American government, public law, judicial politics, political theory, international relations.

**Utah State University,** School of Graduate Studies, College of Humanities, Arts and Social Sciences, Department of Political Science, Logan, UT 84322. Offers MA, MS. *Program availability:* Part-time. *Degree requirements:* For master's, one foreign language, thesis. *Entrance requirements:* For master's, GRE General Test, minimum GPA of 3.0. Additional exam requirements/recommendations for international students: Required—TOEFL. *Faculty research:* Political parties; social choice; international political economics; foreign policy; politics, markets, and public policy.

**Vanderbilt University,** Department of Political Science, Nashville, TN 37240-1001. Offers MA, MAT, PhD. *Faculty:* 26 full-time (11 women). *Students:* 32 full-time (12 women), 2 part-time (both women); includes 4 minority (1 Black or African American, non-Hispanic/Latino; 1 Asian, non-Hispanic/Latino; 1 Hispanic/Latino; 1 Two or more races, non-Hispanic/Latino), 10 international. Average age 28. 170 applicants, 13% accepted, 7 enrolled. In 2016, 6 master's, 6 doctorates awarded. Terminal master's awarded for partial completion of doctoral program. *Degree requirements:* For master's, thesis; for doctorate, thesis/dissertation, final and qualifying exams. *Entrance requirements:* For master's and doctorate, GRE General Test, writing sample. Additional exam requirements/recommendations for international students: Required—TOEFL (minimum score 570 paper-based; 88 iBT). *Application deadline:* For fall admission, 1/15 for domestic and international students. Electronic applications accepted. *Expenses:* Tuition: Part-time $1854 per credit hour. *Financial support:* Fellowships with full tuition reimbursements, research assistantships with full tuition reimbursements, teaching assistantships with full tuition reimbursements, Federal Work-Study, institutionally sponsored loans, scholarships/grants, and health care benefits available. Financial award application deadline: 1/15; financial award applicants required to submit CSS PROFILE or FAFSA. *Faculty research:* American politics, comparative politics, international politics, political theory, political culture and life. *Unit head:* Dr. David Lewis, Chair, 615-322-6222, Fax: 615-343-6003, E-mail: david.lewis@vanderbilt.edu. *Application contact:* Jon Hiskey, Director of Graduate Studies, 615-322-6222, Fax: 615-343-6003, E-mail: j.hiskey@vanderbilt.edu. Website: http://www.vanderbilt.edu/political-science/

**Villanova University,** Graduate School of Liberal Arts and Sciences, Department of Political Science, Villanova, PA 19085-1699. Offers MA. *Program availability:* Part-time, evening/weekend, online learning. *Faculty:* 6. *Students:* 23 full-time (7 women), 6 part-time (3 women); includes 3 minority (2 Black or African American, non-Hispanic/Latino; 1 Hispanic/Latino), 6 international. Average age 28. 15 applicants, 80% accepted, 11 enrolled. In 2016, 10 master's awarded. *Degree requirements:* For master's, comprehensive exam (for some programs). *Entrance requirements:* For master's, GRE, minimum GPA of 3.0. Additional exam requirements/recommendations for international students: Required—TOEFL. *Application deadline:* For fall admission, 5/1 priority date for international students; for spring admission, 10/15 for international students. Applications are processed on a rolling basis. Application fee: $50. Electronic applications accepted. *Financial support:* Research assistantships, scholarships/grants, and unspecified assistantships available. Financial award applicants required to submit FAFSA. *Unit head:* Dr. Markus Kreuzer, Director, 610-519-4710. Website: http://www.psc.villanova.edu/gradwww.htm

**Virginia Commonwealth University,** Graduate School, College of Humanities and Sciences, L. Douglas Wilder School of Government and Public Affairs, Richmond, VA 23284-9005. Offers MA, MPA, MS, MURP, PhD, Certificate, Graduate Certificate, Postbaccalaureate Certificate. *Unit head:* Dr. Niraj Verma, Director, L. Douglas Wilder School of Government and Public Affairs, 804-828-2292. *Application contact:* Dr. Sarah J. Brubaker, Associate Director, 804-827-2400, E-mail: sbrubaker@vcu.edu. Website: http://www.wilder.vcu.edu/

**Virginia Polytechnic Institute and State University,** Graduate School, College of Liberal Arts and Human Sciences, Blacksburg, VA 24061. Offers career and technical education (MS Ed, Ed D, PhD, Ed S); communication (MA); counselor education (MA Ed, Ed D, PhD, Ed S); creative writing (MFA); curriculum and instruction (MA Ed, Ed D, PhD, Ed S); educational leadership and policy studies (MA Ed, Ed D, PhD, Ed S); educational research and evaluation (PhD); English (MA); foreign languages, cultures, and literatures (MA); higher education (PhD); higher education and student affairs (MA Ed); history (MA); human development (MS, PhD); material culture and public humanities (MA); philosophy (MA); political science (MA); rhetoric and writing (PhD); science and technology studies (MS, PhD); social, political, ethical, and cultural thought (PhD); sociology (MS, PhD); theater arts (MFA). *Faculty:* 408 full-time (204 women), 3 part-time/adjunct (2 women). *Students:* 657 full-time (446 women), 457 part-time (292 women); includes 213 minority (114 Black or African American, non-Hispanic/Latino; 3 American Indian or Alaska Native, non-Hispanic/Latino; 29 Asian, non-Hispanic/Latino; 44 Hispanic/Latino; 23 Two or more races, non-Hispanic/Latino), 93 international. Average age 33. 805 applicants, 55% accepted, 328 enrolled. In 2016, 270 master's, 91 doctorates awarded. *Degree requirements:* For master's, comprehensive exam (for some programs), thesis (for some programs); for doctorate, comprehensive exam (for some programs), thesis/dissertation (for some programs). *Entrance requirements:* For master's and doctorate, GRE/GMAT. Additional exam requirements/recommendations for international students: Required—TOEFL (minimum score 80 iBT). *Application deadline:* For fall admission, 8/1 for domestic students, 4/1 for international students; for spring admission, 1/1 for domestic students, 9/1 for international students. Applications are processed on a rolling basis. Application fee: $75. Electronic applications accepted. *Expenses:* Tuition, state resident: full-time $12,467; part-time $692.50 per credit hour. Tuition, nonresident: full-time $25,095; part-time $1394.25 per credit hour. *Required fees:* $2669; $491.50 per semester. Tuition and fees vary according to course load, campus/location and program. *Financial support:* In 2016–17, 23 research assistantships with full tuition reimbursements (averaging $19,817 per year), 237 teaching assistantships with full tuition reimbursements (averaging $15,497 per year) were awarded. Financial award application deadline: 3/1; financial award applicants required to submit FAFSA. *Total annual research expenditures:* $6.6 million. *Unit head:* Rosemary Blieszner, Interim Dean, 540-231-6779, Fax: 540-231-7157, E-mail: liberalartsdean@vt.edu. *Application contact:* Chelsea Blanchet, Executive Assistant, 540-231-6779, Fax: 540-231-7157, E-mail: bchels1@vt.edu. Website: http://www.liberalarts.vt.edu/

**Virginia Polytechnic Institute and State University,** VT Online, Blacksburg, VA 24061. Offers advanced transportation systems (Certificate); aerospace engineering (MS); agricultural and life sciences (MSLFS); business information systems (Graduate Certificate); career and technical education (MS); civil engineering (MS); computer engineering (M Eng, MS); decision support systems (Graduate Certificate); eLearning leadership (MA); electrical engineering (M Eng, MS); engineering administration (MEA); environmental engineering (Certificate); environmental politics and policy (Graduate

### Political Science

Certificate); environmental sciences and engineering (MS); foundations of political analysis (Graduate Certificate); health product risk management (Graduate Certificate); industrial and systems engineering (MS); information policy and society (Graduate Certificate); information security (Graduate Certificate); information technology (MIT); instructional technology (MA); integrative STEM education (MA Ed); liberal arts (Graduate Certificate); life sciences: health product risk management (MS); natural resources (MNR, Graduate Certificate); networking (Graduate Certificate); nonprofit and nongovernmental organization management (Graduate Certificate); ocean engineering (MS); political science (MA); security studies (Graduate Certificate); software development (Graduate Certificate). *Expenses:* Tuition, state resident: full-time $12,467; part-time $692.50 per credit hour. Tuition, nonresident: full-time $25,095; part-time $1394.25 per credit hour. *Required fees:* $2669; $491.50 per semester. Tuition and fees vary according to course load, campus/location and program.

**Walden University,** Graduate Programs, School of Public Policy and Administration, Minneapolis, MN 55401. Offers criminal justice (MPA, MPP, MS, Graduate Certificate), including emergency management (MS, PhD), general program (MS), global leadership (MS, PhD), homeland security and policy coordination (MS, PhD), law and public policy (MS, PhD), policy analysis (MS, PhD), public management and leadership (MS, PhD), self-designed (MS), terrorism, mediation, and peace (MS, PhD); criminal justice and executive management (MS), including global leadership (MS, PhD); criminal justice leadership and executive management (MS), including emergency management (MS, PhD), general program, homeland security and policy coordination (MS, PhD), law and public policy (MS, PhD), policy analysis (MS, PhD), public management and leadership (MS, PhD), self-designed, terrorism, mediation, and peace (MS, PhD); emergency management (MPA, MPP, MS), including criminal justice (MS, PhD); general program (MS), homeland security (MS); public management and leadership (MS, PhD), terrorism and emergency management (MS); general program (MPA, MPP); global leadership (MPA, MPP); government management (Graduate Certificate); health policy (MPA, MPP); homeland security (Graduate Certificate); homeland security and policy coordination (MPA, MPP); international nongovernmental organizations (MPA, MPP); law and public policy (MPA, MPP); local government management for sustainable communities (MPA, MPP); nonprofit management (Graduate Certificate); nonprofit management and leadership (MPA, MPP, MS), including global leadership (MS, PhD); international nongovernmental organization (MS); local government for sustainable communities (MS); self designed (MS); online teaching in higher education (Post-Master's Certificate); policy analysis (MPA); public management and leadership (MPA, MPP, Graduate Certificate); public policy (Graduate Certificate); public policy and administration (PhD), including criminal justice (MS, PhD); emergency management (MS, PhD), global leadership (MS, PhD), health policy, homeland security and policy coordination (MS, PhD), international nongovernmental organizations, law and public policy (MS, PhD), local government management for sustainable communities, nonprofit management and leadership, policy analysis (MS, PhD), public management and leadership (MS, PhD), terrorism, mediation, and peace (MS, PhD); strategic planning and public policy (Graduate Certificate); terrorism, mediation, and peace (MPA, MPP). *Program availability:* Part-time, evening/weekend, online only, 100% online. *Degree requirements:* For doctorate, thesis/dissertation, residency. *Entrance requirements:* For master's, bachelor's degree or higher; minimum GPA of 2.5; official transcripts; goal statement (for some programs); access to computer and Internet; for doctorate, master's degree or higher; three years of related professional or academic experience (preferred); minimum GPA of 3.0; goal statement and current resume (for select programs); official transcripts; access to computer and Internet; for other advanced degree, relevant work experience; access to computer and Internet. Additional exam requirements/recommendations for international students: Required—TOEFL (minimum score 550 paper-based, 79 iBT), IELTS (minimum score 6.5), Michigan English Language Assessment Battery (minimum score 82), or PTE (minimum score 53). Electronic applications accepted.

**Washington State University,** College of Arts and Sciences, School of Politics, Philosophy and Public Affairs, Pullman, WA 99164-4880. Offers bioethics (Graduate Certificate); political science (MA, PhD); public affairs (MPA). MPA, MA, and PhD programs also offered at the Vancouver campus; Graduate Certificate offered through Global (online) campus. *Accreditation:* NASPAA. *Program availability:* Online learning. Terminal master's awarded for partial completion of doctoral program. *Degree requirements:* For master's, comprehensive exam (for some programs), thesis, oral exam; for doctorate, comprehensive exam, thesis/dissertation, oral exam, written exam. *Entrance requirements:* For master's, GRE General Test, minimum GPA of 3.0; for doctorate, GRE General Test, minimum GPA of 3.5. Additional exam requirements/recommendations for international students: Required—TOEFL. Electronic applications accepted. *Faculty research:* Political psychology and image theory, grass roots environmental policy, federal juvenile policy.

**Washington University in St. Louis,** The Graduate School, Department of Political Science, St. Louis, MO 63130-4899. Offers PhD. *Degree requirements:* For doctorate, thesis/dissertation. *Entrance requirements:* For doctorate, GRE General Test. Additional exam requirements/recommendations for international students: Required—TOEFL. Electronic applications accepted. *Faculty research:* American politics (including law and courts); comparative politics; formal theory; international politics; normative theory; political methodology.

**Wayne State University,** College of Liberal Arts and Sciences, Department of Political Science, Detroit, MI 48202. Offers political science (MA, PhD); public administration (MPA), including economic development policy and management, health and human services policy and management, human and fiscal resource management, nonprofit policy and management, organizational behavior and management, urban and metropolitan policy and management; JD/MA. *Accreditation:* NASPAA. *Faculty:* 20. *Students:* 64 full-time (20 women), 75 part-time (45 women); includes 48 minority (32 Black or African American, non-Hispanic/Latino; 5 Asian, non-Hispanic/Latino; 4 Hispanic/Latino; 7 Two or more races, non-Hispanic/Latino), 7 international. Average age 33. 105 applicants, 50% accepted, 27 enrolled. In 2016, 25 master's, 5 doctorates awarded. *Degree requirements:* For master's, comprehensive exam (for some programs), thesis (for some programs); for doctorate, thesis/dissertation. *Entrance requirements:* For master's, GRE General Test, substantial undergraduate preparation in the social sciences, minimum upper-division undergraduate GPA of 3.0, two letters of recommendation, personal statement; for doctorate, GRE General Test, 3 letters of recommendation; personal statement; interview. Additional exam requirements/recommendations for international students: Required—TOEFL (minimum score 550 paper-based; 79 iBT), TWE (minimum score 5.5), Michigan English Language Assessment Battery (minimum score 85); Recommended—IELTS (minimum score 6.5). *Application deadline:* For fall admission, 5/15 for domestic students, 5/1 priority date for international students; for winter admission, 10/15 for domestic students, 9/1 priority date for international students. Applications are processed on a rolling basis. Application fee: $50. Electronic applications accepted. *Expenses:* $16,503 per year resident tuition and fees, $33,697 per year non-resident tuition and fees. *Financial support:* In 2016–17, 48 students received support, including 3 fellowships with tuition reimbursements available (averaging $17,333 per year), 13 teaching assistantships with tuition reimbursements available (averaging $18,067 per year); research assistantships with tuition reimbursements available, scholarships/grants, health care benefits, and unspecified assistantships also available. Financial award applicants required to submit FAFSA. *Faculty research:* American government and politics, comparative politics, political methodology, political theory, public administration, public law, public policy, world politics/international relations, formal theory/modeling, gender and politics, international law, peace research, political economy, political psychology, politics of developing countries, race, religion, and ethnicity, urban politics. *Unit head:* Dr. Daniel Geller, Professor and Chair, 313-577-6328, E-mail: dgeller@wayne.edu. *Application contact:* Dr. Sharon Lean, Graduate Director, 313-577-2630, E-mail: gradpolisci@wayne.edu. Website: http://clas.wayne.edu/politicalscience/

**Western Illinois University,** School of Graduate Studies, College of Arts and Sciences, Department of Political Science, Macomb, IL 61455-1390. Offers MA. *Program availability:* Part-time. *Students:* 12 full-time (5 women), 8 part-time (2 women); includes 8 minority (5 Black or African American, non-Hispanic/Latino; 1 Asian, non-Hispanic/Latino; 2 Hispanic/Latino), 5 international. Average age 29. 15 applicants, 87% accepted, 7 enrolled. In 2016, 16 master's awarded. *Degree requirements:* For master's, comprehensive exam, thesis or alternative. *Entrance requirements:* Additional exam requirements/recommendations for international students: Required—TOEFL (minimum score 550 paper-based; 80 iBT). *Application deadline:* Applications are processed on a rolling basis. Application fee: $30. Electronic applications accepted. *Financial support:* In 2016–17, 12 students received support. Unspecified assistantships available. Financial award applicants required to submit FAFSA. *Unit head:* Dr. Keith Boeckelman, Chairperson, 309-298-1055. *Application contact:* Dr. Nancy Parsons, Associate Provost and Director of Graduate Studies, 309-298-1806, Fax: 309-298-2345, E-mail: grad-office@wiu.edu. Website: http://www.wiu.edu/cas/Political_Science/

**Western Kentucky University,** Graduate Studies, Potter College of Arts and Letters, Department of Political Science, Bowling Green, KY 42101. Offers MPA. *Accreditation:* NASPAA. *Program availability:* Part-time, evening/weekend. *Degree requirements:* For master's, comprehensive exam, final exam. *Entrance requirements:* For master's, GRE General Test, minimum GPA of 2.75. Additional exam requirements/recommendations for international students: Required—TOEFL (minimum score 555 paper-based; 79 iBT). *Faculty research:* Role of non-profits, comparative policy analysis, social welfare policy, rural administration, ethics and bureaucracy.

**Western Michigan University,** Graduate College, College of Arts and Sciences, Department of Political Science, Kalamazoo, MI 49008. Offers international development administration (MIDA), including Peace Corps; political science (MA, PhD). *Degree requirements:* For master's, thesis optional; for doctorate, thesis/dissertation.

**Western Washington University,** Graduate School, College of Humanities and Social Sciences, Department of Political Science, Bellingham, WA 98225-5996. Offers MA. *Program availability:* Part-time. *Degree requirements:* For master's, comprehensive exam, thesis (for some programs). *Entrance requirements:* For master's, GRE General Test, minimum GPA of 3.0 in last 60 semester hours or last 90 quarter hours. Additional exam requirements/recommendations for international students: Required—TOEFL (minimum score 567 paper-based). Electronic applications accepted. *Faculty research:* Elections, environment, identity, international relations.

**West Virginia University,** Eberly College of Arts and Sciences, Department of Political Science, Morgantown, WV 26506. Offers American public policy and politics (MA); international and comparative public policy and politics (MA); political science (PhD); public policy analysis (PhD). Terminal master's awarded for partial completion of doctoral program. *Degree requirements:* For master's, thesis optional; for doctorate, comprehensive exam, thesis/dissertation. *Entrance requirements:* For master's, GRE General Test, minimum GPA of 2.75; for doctorate, GRE General Test, minimum GPA of 3.0. Additional exam requirements/recommendations for international students: Required—TOEFL. *Faculty research:* Public policy, research methods, foreign policy analysis, judicial politics, environmental and energy policy.

**Wilfrid Laurier University,** Faculty of Graduate and Postdoctoral Studies, Faculty of Arts, Department of Political Science, Waterloo, ON N2L 3C5, Canada. Offers Canadian political studies (MA); comparative politics/international relations (MA). *Program availability:* Part-time. *Degree requirements:* For master's, thesis optional. *Entrance requirements:* For master's, honors bachelor's degree or the equivalent in political science, minimum B average in undergraduate course work. Additional exam requirements/recommendations for international students: Required—TOEFL (minimum score 89 iBT). Electronic applications accepted. *Faculty research:* Political behavior/political psychology, Canadian political studies, comparative, politics/relations, public opinion and electoral studies, international.

**Wilfrid Laurier University,** Faculty of Graduate and Postdoctoral Studies, School of International Policy and Governance, Global Governance Program, Waterloo, ON N2L 3C5, Canada. Offers conflict and security (PhD); global environment (PhD); global justice and human rights (PhD); global political economy (PhD); global social governance (PhD); multilateral institutions and diplomacy (PhD). Offered jointly with University of Waterloo. *Degree requirements:* For doctorate, thesis/dissertation. *Entrance requirements:* For doctorate, MA in political science, history, economics, international development studies, international peace studies, globalization studies, environmental studies or related field with minimum A-. Additional exam requirements/recommendations for international students: Required—TOEFL (minimum score 89 iBT). Electronic applications accepted. *Faculty research:* Global political economy, global environment, conflict and security, global justice and human rights, multilateral institutions and diplomacy.

**Wilfrid Laurier University,** Faculty of Graduate and Postdoctoral Studies, School of International Policy and Governance, International Public Policy Program, Waterloo, ON N2L 3C5, Canada. Offers global governance (MIPP); human security (MIPP); international economic relations (MIPP); international environmental policy (MIPP). Offered jointly with University of Waterloo. *Entrance requirements:* For master's, honours BA with minimum B average. Additional exam requirements/recommendations for international students: Required—TOEFL (minimum score 89 iBT). Electronic applications accepted. *Faculty research:* International environmental policy, international economic relations, human security, global governance.

**Yale University,** Graduate School of Arts and Sciences, Department of Political Science, New Haven, CT 06520. Offers PhD. *Degree requirements:* For doctorate, one foreign language, thesis/dissertation. *Entrance requirements:* For doctorate, GRE General Test. *Faculty research:* U.N. and international security.

**York University,** Faculty of Graduate Studies, Faculty of Liberal Arts and Professional Studies, Program in Political Science, Toronto, ON M3J 1P3, Canada. Offers MA, PhD. *Program availability:* Part-time. *Degree requirements:* For master's, thesis or alternative; for doctorate, one foreign language, comprehensive exam, thesis/dissertation. Electronic applications accepted.

**York University,** Faculty of Graduate Studies, Program in Social and Political Thought, Toronto, ON M3J 1P3, Canada. Offers MA, PhD. *Program availability:* Part-time. *Degree requirements:* For master's, one foreign language, thesis or alternative, oral exams; for doctorate, one foreign language, comprehensive exam, thesis/dissertation. Electronic applications accepted.

# AUSTIN W. MARXE SCHOOL OF PUBLIC AND INTERNATIONAL AFFAIRS AT BARUCH COLLEGE

*School of International Affairs*

 For more information, visit http://petersons.to/baruchaustinwmarxe

## Programs of Study

Austin W. Marxe School of Public and International Affairs at Baruch College provides "education that makes a difference." It's the only public graduate school in New York City dedicated to public affairs. It provides a variety of programs including undergraduate and graduate programs in public policy and administration, master's programs in higher education administration and educational leadership, and certificate programs in several areas.

It draws from the largest public affairs faculty in the country. Faculty members include award-winning scholars and former New York City commissioners as well as a member of the National Academy of Public Administration and a presidential professor.

The school takes an interdisciplinary approach to professional development, research, and teaching and develops new programs to provide the most relevant education and training. In addition, it provides a forum to discuss public policy and maintains research centers to conduct innovative studies concerning matters of the public interest.

**Master of Public Administration (M.P.A.):** The M.P.A. program at Austin W. Marxe School of Public and International Affairs is one of the top programs in country. Its curriculum, which can be completed on a full-time or part-time basis, has a minimum of 42 credits for students with administrative experience. Students without this experience complete an additional three-credit internship. Specializations are offered in five areas: health care policy, nonprofit administration, policy analysis and evaluation, public management, and urban development and sustainability.

The M.P.A. has two nontraditional delivery models: Executive M.P.A. and National Urban Fellows M.P.A. The 42-credit Executive M.P.A. was created for mid-career professionals who want to develop analytical and leadership skills. The 33-credit National Urban Fellows M.P.A. is offered in collaboration with National Urban Fellows, Inc. It enables people from underrepresented communities to earn M.P.A. degrees through a combination of full-time study and internships.

**Master of International Affairs (M.I.A.):** The two-year Master of International Affairs program provides multidisciplinary analysis and understanding of global policy and governance in the international setting. Its curriculum has 42 credits of core and concentration courses. Concentrations include international nongovernmental organizations, western hemisphere affairs, trade policy and global economic governance, and special concentration.
Students also receive advanced training in key techniques of policy analysis, budgeting, assessment of political culture, global communication strategies, regionally specific issues, and comparative methods. The program offers opportunities for study in a variety of substantial social and public policy areas (e.g., welfare and social security, international development, housing, migration, health), across a range of national, regional (Latin America, Asia, Africa, and the European Union), and global settings. While our concentration in Western Hemisphere Affairs will focus on that region, the M.I.A. program is committed to analyzing problems in a global context. The School has relationships with educational institutions in Europe, Latin America, and Asia and students will have the opportunity to do internships or study abroad.

**Master of Science in Higher Education Administration:** This M.S.Ed. program was created for higher education professionals. It offers two programs: generalist and institutional research and assessment specialization.

The 36-credit generalist program provides skills and knowledge in higher education management with a focus on student services. It has 21 credits of core courses including a capstone course and 15 credits of electives. Students without administrative experience must also complete a three-credit internship.

The institutional research and assessment specialization also has 36 credits (27 credits of core and 9 credits of elective courses). It builds upon capstone and core courses in the generalist program. Its curriculum includes research and analysis requirements and electives in budgeting, institutional research, and program evaluation.

## Research Opportunities

The Austin W. Marxe School of Public and International Affairs supports public policy through civic engagement and applied research. Its innovative policy and research programs promote public affairs education and social advocacy. It has seven centers:

- Baruch College Survey Research
- Center for Educational Leadership
- Center on Equality Pluralism and Policy
- Center for Nonprofit Strategy and Management
- CUNY Institute for Demographic Research
- International Comparative Policy Analysis Forum
- New York Federal Statistical Research Data Center

These centers provide in-depth knowledge about a wide array of policy topics as well as hands-on experience that can be applied to career pursuits and research projects.

## Financial Aid

Baruch College offers graduate students who reside in New York State competitive tuition rates in comparison to many other universities and colleges in the New York City metropolitan area. Financial aid in the forms of federal loans, graduate research assistantships, and scholarships helps students fund their education. There are competitive fellowship and scholarship packages available to qualified incoming and continuing students. Some of the fellowship opportunities provide full tuition coverage.

## Cost of Study

For the 2017–18 academic year, tuition for the M.P.A. and M.I.A. programs, $6,005 per semester for New York State residents and $950 per credit for out-of-state residents and international students. Tuition for the M.S.Ed. program is $5,225 per semester for New York State residents and $805 per credit for out-of-state residents and international students. Fees for all programs total $680 per semester.

## Student Group

In fall 2016, there were 815 graduate students enrolled in programs through the Marxe School of Public and International Affairs. Of that group, 550 were enrolled in the M.P.A. program, 115 in the M.S.Ed. program. The student body in the School is 36 percent male and 64 percent female. There are more than 8,000 alumni of the School.

*Austin W. Marxe School of Public and International Affairs at Baruch College*

## Location

Baruch College is located in New York City, New York in the northeastern region of the United States. Its vibrant campus provides many academic and social resources, including easy access to Midtown; Wall Street; and the international headquarters of major companies, cultural institutions, and nonprofit organizations. This gives student numerous career, internship, and networking opportunities. Students also have access to New York City's diverse array of cultural, dining, entertainment, and outdoor recreational options.

## The College

A member of the City University of New York, Baruch College was founded in 1847 as the Free Academy. It was the first free public college in the country. Today, it continues the tradition of providing academic excellence and opportunity for students in New York City, the metropolitan region, and the world.

The college educates one of the most diverse student bodies in the United States. It has over 18,000 students who speak more than 130 languages and trace their roots to 170-plus countries. It offers 29 undergraduate majors, 56 undergraduate minors, 53 graduate programs, and two doctoral programs. U.S. News & World Report, Forbes, and the Princeton Review rank Baruch College among the nation's top colleges.

## Faculty

The faculty of the Marxe School of Public and International Affairs is among the largest and most globally diverse in the country. Accomplished and widely recognized in their fields, each member brings a wealth of experience in advising or leading cabinet-level agencies, political leaders, and major health, nonprofit, or government organizations around the world. Their goal is to help students grow both personally and professionally while addressing today's most pressing public policy challenges and providing guidance on course work, development opportunities, and careers.

Faculty members bring expertise and scholarship in numerous areas to the classroom. For example, Professor Cristina Balboa examines comparative policy, international relations, and organization theory to explain the relationship between organizations' internal characteristics and external accountability, effectiveness, and legitimacy. She's also an administrator for the Global Issues/Transnational Actors interest group, which is part of the Association for Research on Nonprofit Organizations and Voluntary Action. A complete staff listing is available online at http://www.baruch.cuny.edu/mspia/faculty-and-staff/index.html.

## Applying

Graduate program sin the Austin W. Marxe School of Public and International Affairs attract students from all over the world, representing a wide range of backgrounds, cultures, and professions. They come to engage, interact, and be part of theSchool's interdisciplinary approach to learning and professional development.

Students interested in the M.P.A., Executive MPA, M.I.A., or M.S.Ed. program should apply online at https://app.applyyourself.com/AYApplicantLogin/fl_ApplicantConnectLogin.asp?id=baruch-spa.

## Correspondence and Information

The Austin W. Marxe School of Public and International Affairs
Young Hah, Director of Graduate Admissions and Enrollment Services
Baruch College, CUNY
One Bernard Baruch Way, Box D-0901
New York, New York 10010-5585
Phone: 646-660-6750
E-mail: mspia.admissions@baruch.cuny.edu
Website: http://www.baruch.cuny.edu/mspia

Baruch College Newman Library'

Neighborhood around Baruch College'

# BOSTON UNIVERSITY
## The Frederick S. Pardee School of Global Studies

 For more information, visit http://petersons.to/bostonu_globalstudies

**Boston University** Frederick S. Pardee School of Global Studies

## Programs of Study

The Frederick S. Pardee School of Global Studies at Boston University (www.bu.edu/pardeeschool) is dedicated to advancing human progress. Through rigorous and creative undergraduate, graduate, and professional education; path-breaking research; and active engagement in innovative initiatives, students apply their education and knowledge to make a real-world difference in the critical challenges humanity faces.

The School has one of the largest programs in international relations in the United States, as well as one of the largest graduate programs within the College of Arts and Sciences at Boston University (BU). It offers more courses on intelligence than any other civilian school in the nation. Other strengths include security, development, environment, religion, regional studies, and cross-cultural studies. Additional information can be found online at www.bu.edu/pardeeschool/academics/undergraduate/international-relations.

Each program is designed to educate and train students for a variety of international relations careers, including positions related to diplomacy, sustainable development, foreign policy analysis, intelligence, international communication, environmental policy, and the corporate sector.

**Master of Arts Programs:** The Pardee School offers six Master of Arts (M.A.) programs with eight functional specializations, two dual-degree programs, one regional degree, and two graduate certificates (www.bu.edu/pardeeschool/academics/graduate).

In addition to the flagship two-year M.A. in International Affairs program, the Pardee School offers degrees in Global Policy (MGP), Latin American Studies (LAS M.A.), and a rigorous five-year B.A. in International Relations/M.A. in International Affairs program. An accelerated one-year International Relations program is available for both civilian professionals and military officers looking to advance their international affairs careers. Dual degrees are offered in International Relations and Master of Business Administration (IR/M.B.A. Dual Degree) and International Relations and Juris Doctor (IR/J.D. Dual Degree). Students can also choose to complete a graduate certificate in African Studies or Asian Studies in conjunction with their degree.

These programs provide students with dynamic opportunities to learn about global issues through course work not only in the Pardee School but also in related departments at BU, enabling students to tailor their program to fit their individual career goals and interests. By providing a wide-ranging and comprehensive set of analytical tools, the School's multidisciplinary approach gives students the skills they need to analyze diverse real-world situations.

**Off-Campus Programs:** The Pardee School offers a range of high-quality study-abroad options that provide M.A. students opportunities to study and intern in some of the most interesting and important places on the planet. All programs are conducted in English. Unless otherwise noted, programs are open to all Pardee students, including Geneva: Global Governance, Economic Development, and Human Rights; Brussels: The EU in the 21st Century; Geneva and London: International Conflict Resolution; London: Mass Communication; London: Journalism; Kenya: Field Practicum in Public Health and Environment; and Washington, D.C.: Journalism. More information is available at www.bu.edu/pardeeschool/academics/graduate ma-study-abroad-programs.

## Related Programs and Centers

The Pardee School complements and enhances the BU educational experience by sponsoring a range of conferences and seminars, bringing dynamic, prominent guest speakers to the school. Regional and Thematic Studies Centers within the Pardee School include the African Studies Center, the Center for the Study of Asia, the Center for the Study of Europe, the Institute for the Study of Muslim Societies and Civilizations, the Latin American Studies Program, the Middle East and North Africa Studies Program, and the Institute on Culture, Religion, & World Affairs. For more information, visit www.bu.edu/pardeeschool/research/centers-programs. BU's various schools and departments offer numerous opportunities to attend sponsored talks and participate in research related to a variety of international affairs issues.

## Financial Aid

Boston University provides $26.2 million in financial aid annually through its comprehensive financial aid services. Students have access to a number of graduate scholarships, fellowships, and assistantships, including the Martin Luther King Jr. Fellowship for students committed to community involvement and social justice, the Whitney M. Young Jr. Fellowship for students studying race relations and urban problems, and graduate research assistantships. Over 50 percent of the 2016 incoming class was offered scholarship aid. Federal Work-Study and other funds are also available. Further details are available at schoohttp://www.bu.edu/cas/prospective-students/graduate-admissions/graduate-financial-aid.

## Cost of Study

Most students attend full-time (16–18 credits per term) while completing course work, and pay full-time tuition accordingly. It is also possible to take course work on a part-time basis, in which case students pay by the class. Some students require an extra term after finishing their course work to write the capstone M.A. Paper, during which time they pay a modest continuing student fee, equivalent to the cost of a 2-credit class.

The most up-to-date information on tuition and fees can be found online at http://www.bu.edu/cas/prospective-students/graduate-admissions/graduate-financial-aid.

### Living and Housing Opportunities

The Boston University Real Estate office rents apartments owned by Boston University to full-time Boston University graduate students, current faculty, and staff only. Apartments are not be rented to undergraduate students or those not affiliated with Boston University. Graduate students often choose BU on-campus apartments because of the wide selection of options in price, size, and location and convenience to campus and area amenities.

### The University and The School

With a foundation dating back to 1839, Boston University remains one of the most dynamic universities in the world. Nearly one in seven students is classified as an international student, with students hailing from more than 139 nations. Boston University has satellite campuses and exchange programs in more than 30 cities on six continents.

The combination of cutting-edge research and instruction in global studies with the deep resources of BU is what gives Pardee School students their advantage in the workforce and on the world stage. From the class of 2014, 87 percent of graduates are working full time in government offices, NGOs, and the private sector.

### Experienced, Dedicated Faculty

The Pardee School offers a world-class array of faculty members with backgrounds in diplomacy, intelligence, academia, the military, and more. Moreover, the Pardee School prides itself on being a teaching school, with students rating the accessibility and engagement of their professors at the highest levels.

Faculty members of BU have been recipients of a wide range of awards and honors, including the Nobel Prize, Presidential Citizens Medal, Pulitzer Prize, and Guggenheim Fellowships, as well as recognition from the American Academy of Arts and Sciences, American Academy of Arts and Letters, and National Academy of Sciences.

More information about the faculty is available on the School's website at http://www.bu.edu/pardeeschool/academics/faculty.

### Applying

Applicants to the Pardee School M.A. programs apply through the Graduate School of Arts & Sciences. The application is online and all materials must be submitted electronically; no application materials should be sent directly to the Pardee School. Applicants interested in the IR/J.D. or IR/M.B.A. programs need to apply twice,

both to the Pardee School and partner school. For applications to the partner schools, applicants must follow all policies, procedures, and deadlines of those schools.

Applications should include the Application Form, transcripts of all prior university studies, three letters of recommendation, official GRE general scores, a personal statement, a resume or CV (recommended, not required), and official TOEFL Scores (for most international students).

Application deadlines are April 15 for fall enrollment and October 15 for spring enrollment. The application system opens to accept new applications on September 1. Priority deadline for aid consideration is January 15.

### Correspondence and Information
Graduate Office
Boston University
154 Bay State Road
Boston, Massachusetts 02215
United States
Phone: 617-353-9349
E-mail: psgsgrad@bu.edu
Website: bu.edu/pardeeschool

# Section 24
# Psychology and Counseling

This section contains a directory of institutions offering graduate work in psychology and counseling, followed by in-depth entries submitted by institutions that chose to prepare detailed program descriptions. Additional information about programs listed in the directory but not augmented by an in-depth entry may be obtained by writing directly to the dean of a graduate school or chair of a department at the address given in the directory.

For programs offering related work, see also in this book *Criminology and Forensics, Family and Consumer Sciences,* and *Sociology, Anthropology, and Archaeology.* In the other guides in this series:
**Graduate Programs in the Biological/Biomedical Sciences & Health-Related Medical Professions**
See *Biological and Biomedical Sciences; Genetics, Developmental Biology, and Reproductive Biology; Neuroscience and Neurobiology; Nursing (Psychiatric Nursing); Pharmacy and Pharmaceutical Sciences; Pharmacology and Toxicology;* and *Public Health*
**Graduate Programs in Business, Education, Information Studies, Law & Social Work**
See *Education* and *Social Work*

## CONTENTS

### Program Directories

### Displays and Close-Ups

# Psychology—General

**Abilene Christian University,** Graduate Programs, College of Arts and Sciences, Department of Psychology, Program in Psychology, Abilene, TX 79699. Offers MS. *Students:* 8 full-time (5 women); includes 1 minority (Hispanic/Latino). 8 applicants, 50% accepted, 3 enrolled. In 2016, 2 master's awarded. *Degree requirements:* For master's, comprehensive exam, thesis. *Entrance requirements:* Additional exam requirements/ recommendations for international students: Required—TOEFL (minimum score 80 iBT), IELTS (minimum score 6), PTE. *Application deadline:* For fall admission, 3/30 priority date for domestic students; for spring admission, 11/1 for domestic students. Applications are processed on a rolling basis. Application fee: $50. Electronic applications accepted. *Expenses: Tuition:* Full-time $19,890; part-time $1105 per credit hour. Tuition and fees vary according to course load and program. *Financial support:* In 2016–17, 4 students received support. Federal Work-Study and scholarships/grants available. Support available to part-time students. Financial award application deadline: 4/1; financial award applicants required to submit FAFSA. *Unit head:* Dr. Cherisse Flangan, Graduate Director, 325-674-4826, Fax: 325-674-6968, E-mail: cherisse.flanagan@acu.edu. *Application contact:* Corey Patterson, Director of Graduate Admission and Recruiting, 325-674-6566, Fax: 325-674-6717, E-mail: gradinfo@acu.edu.
Website: http://www.acu.edu/graduate/academics/psychology.html

**Acadia University,** Faculty of Pure and Applied Science, Department of Psychology, Wolfville, NS B4P 2R6, Canada. Offers clinical psychology (M Sc). *Degree requirements:* For master's, thesis. *Entrance requirements:* For master's, GRE General Test, GRE Subject Test, honors degree or equivalent. Additional exam requirements/ recommendations for international students: Required—TOEFL (minimum score 580 paper-based; 93 iBT), IELTS (minimum score 6.5). *Faculty research:* Social psychology, job stress, psychotherapy, cognition perception, development.

**Adelphi University,** Gordon F. Derner School of Psychology, Program in General Psychology, Garden City, NY 11530-0701. Offers MA. *Students:* 50 full-time (42 women), 16 part-time (13 women); includes 40 minority (18 Black or African American, non-Hispanic/Latino; 5 Asian, non-Hispanic/Latino; 15 Hispanic/Latino; 2 Two or more races, non-Hispanic/Latino), 12 international. Average age 27. 107 applicants, 79% accepted, 36 enrolled. In 2016, 58 master's awarded. *Degree requirements:* For master's, comprehensive exam. *Entrance requirements:* For master's, 2 letters of recommendation; minimum GPA of 3.0; course work in psychology including developmental psychology, psychopathology, and research design or experimental psychology; personal essay; transcripts from all previously-attended schools. Additional exam requirements/recommendations for international students: Required—TOEFL (minimum score 550 paper-based; 80 iBT). *Application deadline:* For fall admission, 5/1 priority date for international students; for spring admission, 11/1 priority date for international students. Applications are processed on a rolling basis. Application fee: $50. Electronic applications accepted. *Expenses:* Contact institution. *Financial support:* Research assistantships with full and partial tuition reimbursements, teaching assistantships, career-related internships or fieldwork, institutionally sponsored loans, scholarships/grants, traineeships, and unspecified assistantships available. Support available to part-time students. Financial award application deadline: 2/15; financial award applicants required to submit FAFSA. *Unit head:* Dr. Errol Rodriguez, Assistant Dean, 516-237-8572, E-mail: erodriguez@adelphi.edu. *Application contact:* Christine Murphy, Director of Admissions, 516-877-3050, Fax: 516-877-3039, E-mail: graduateadmissions@adelphi.edu.
Website: http://derner.adelphi.edu/psychology/graduate/ma-general-psychology/

**Adler University,** Programs in Psychology, Chicago, IL 60602. Offers advanced Adlerian psychotherapy (Certificate); art therapy (MA); clinical mental health counseling (MA); clinical neuropsychology (Certificate); clinical psychology (Psy D); community psychology (MA); counseling and organizational psychology (MA); counseling psychology (MA); counselor education and supervision (PhD); couple and family therapy (DCFT); criminology (MA); emergency management leadership (MA); forensic psychology (MA); marriage and family counseling (MA); marriage and family therapy (Certificate); military psychology (MA); nonprofit management (MA); organizational psychology (MA); police psychology (MA); public policy and administration (MA); rehabilitation counseling (MA); sport and health psychology (MA); substance abuse counseling (Certificate); Psy D/Certificate; Psy D/MACAT; Psy D/MACP; Psy D/MAMFC; Psy D/MASAC. *Accreditation:* APA. *Program availability:* Part-time, evening/weekend, online learning. Terminal master's awarded for partial completion of doctoral program. *Degree requirements:* For master's, thesis or alternative, oral exam, practicum; for doctorate, thesis/dissertation, clinical exam, internship, oral exam, practicum, written qualifying exam. *Entrance requirements:* For master's, 12 semester hours in psychology, minimum GPA of 3.0; for doctorate, 18 semester hours in psychology, minimum GPA of 3.25; for Certificate, appropriate master's or doctoral degree. Additional exam requirements/recommendations for international students: Required—TOEFL (minimum score 550 paper-based; 79 iBT). Electronic applications accepted.

**See Display below and Close-Up on page 1225.**

**Alabama Agricultural and Mechanical University,** School of Graduate Studies, College of Education, Humanities, and Behavioral Sciences, Department of Social Work, Psychology and Counseling, Huntsville, AL 35811. Offers psychology and counseling (MS, Ed S), including clinical psychology (MS), counseling psychology (MS), guidance and counseling, rehabilitation counseling (MS), school counseling (MS), school psychology (MS), school psychometry (MS); social work (MSW). *Accreditation:* CORE; NCATE. *Program availability:* Part-time, evening/weekend. *Degree requirements:* For master's, comprehensive exam. *Entrance requirements:* For master's, GRE General Test. Additional exam requirements/recommendations for international students: Required—TOEFL (minimum score 500 paper-based; 61 iBT). *Application deadline:* For fall admission, 5/1 for domestic students. Application fee: $15 ($20 for international students). *Expenses:* Tuition, nonresident: part-time $826 per credit hour. Full-time tuition and fees vary according to course load and program. *Financial support:* Career-related internships or fieldwork available. Support available to part-time students. Financial award application deadline: 4/1. *Faculty research:* Increasing numbers of minorities in special education and speech-language pathology. *Unit head:* Dr. Shirley King, Chair, 256-372-5520, Fax: 256-372-5526.

**Alliant International University–Fresno,** California School of Professional Psychology, Fresno, CA 93727. Offers MA, PhD, Psy D, MA/PhD, Psy D/MA. *Accreditation:* APA. *Degree requirements:* For doctorate, comprehensive exam, thesis/dissertation. *Entrance requirements:* For doctorate, minimum GPA of 3.0, letters of recommendation, essay, interview. Additional exam requirements/recommendations for international

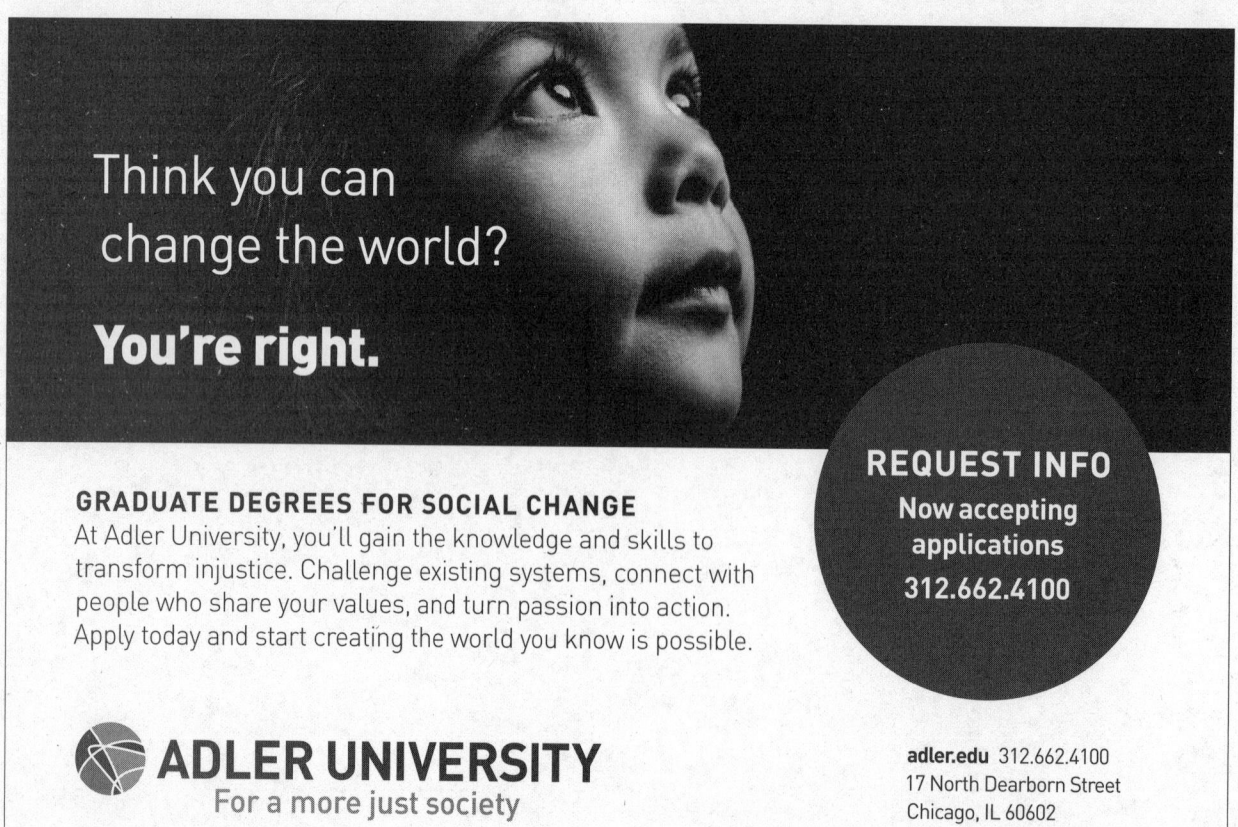

students: Required—TOEFL (minimum score 550 paper-based), TWE (minimum score 5). Electronic applications accepted. *Faculty research:* Parent-child relationships, LGBT families, social justice, women's health, neurocognitive functioning.

**Alliant International University–Los Angeles,** California School of Professional Psychology, Alhambra, CA 91803. Offers MA, PhD, Psy D. *Accreditation:* APA. *Degree requirements:* For doctorate, comprehensive exam, thesis/dissertation. *Entrance requirements:* For doctorate, interview, minimum GPA of 3.0 in psychology and overall, letters of recommendation. Additional exam requirements/recommendations for international students: Required—TOEFL (minimum score 600 paper-based), TWE (minimum score 5). Electronic applications accepted. *Faculty research:* Family therapy, multi-cultural psychology, post-traumatic stress, assessment, community mental health.

**Alliant International University–Sacramento,** California School of Professional Psychology, Sacramento, CA 95833. Offers MA, Psy D. *Program availability:* Part-time. *Degree requirements:* For doctorate, comprehensive exam, thesis/dissertation. *Entrance requirements:* For master's and doctorate, minimum GPA of 3.0, recommendations, essay. Additional exam requirements/recommendations for international students: Required—TOEFL (minimum score 600 paper-based), TWE (minimum score 5). Electronic applications accepted. *Faculty research:* International research testing a model of health behavior change for the developing world, immigration stress, addiction, issues facing LGBTQI community life.

**Alliant International University–San Diego,** California School of Professional Psychology, San Diego, CA 92131. Offers MA, MS, PhD, Psy D. *Accreditation:* APA. *Program availability:* Part-time. Terminal master's awarded for partial completion of doctoral program. *Degree requirements:* For master's, practicum; for doctorate, comprehensive exam, thesis/dissertation, internship or practicum. *Entrance requirements:* For master's and doctorate, minimum GPA of 3.0, essay, letters of recommendation, interview. Additional exam requirements/recommendations for international students: Required—TOEFL (minimum score 550 paper-based; 80 iBT), TWE (minimum score 5). *Faculty research:* Couples therapy, depression, multicultural and international issues, evidence-based practice, neuropsychology of autism, ADHD.

**Alliant International University–San Francisco,** California School of Professional Psychology, San Francisco, CA 94133. Offers MA, Post-Doctoral MS, PhD, Psy D, Certificate. *Accreditation:* APA (one or more programs are accredited). *Degree requirements:* For doctorate, comprehensive exam, thesis/dissertation, internship. *Entrance requirements:* For master's and doctorate, minimum GPA of 3.0, recommendations, essay, interview. Additional exam requirements/recommendations for international students: Required—TOEFL (minimum score 550 paper-based; 80 iBT), TWE (minimum score 5). Electronic applications accepted. *Faculty research:* Multicultural issues, lesbian/gay/bisexual/transgender issues, health psychology, family systems, substance abuse.

**American International College,** School of Business, Arts and Sciences, Springfield, MA 01109-3189. Offers accounting and taxation (MS); business administration (MBA); clinical psychology (MA); educational psychology (Ed D); forensic psychology (MS); general psychology (MA, CAGS); management (CAGS); resort and casino management (MBA, CAGS). *Program availability:* Part-time, evening/weekend. *Degree requirements:* For master's, comprehensive exam (for some programs), thesis (for some programs), practicum; for doctorate, comprehensive exam (for some programs), thesis/dissertation; for CAGS, comprehensive exam (for some programs), thesis (for some programs). *Entrance requirements:* For master's, BS or BA; for doctorate, interview. Additional exam requirements/recommendations for international students: Required—TOEFL (minimum score 550 paper-based; 80 iBT). *Expenses: Tuition:* Full-time $7902; part-time $750 per semester hour. *Required fees:* $60; $60 per semester hour. $30 per semester. One-time fee: $100. Tuition and fees vary according to course load, degree level, campus/location and program.

**American Public University System,** AMU/APU Graduate Programs, Charles Town, WV 25414. Offers accounting (MBA, MS); applied business analytics (MBA, MS); criminal justice (MA), including business administration, emergency and disaster management, general (MA, MS); educational leadership (M Ed); emergency and disaster management (MA); entrepreneurship (MBA); environmental policy and management (MS), including environmental planning, environmental sustainability, fish and wildlife management, general (MA, MS), global environmental management; finance (MBA); general (MBA); government contracting and acquisition (MBA); health care administration (MBA); health information management (MS); history (MA), including American history, ancient and classical history, European history, global history, public history; homeland security (MA), including business administration, counterterrorism studies, criminal justice, cyber, emergency management and public health, intelligence studies, transportation security; homeland security resource allocation (MBA); humanities (MA); information technology (MS), including digital forensics, enterprise software development, information assurance and security, IT project management; information technology management (MBA); intelligence studies (MA), including criminal intelligence, cyber, general (MA, MS), homeland security, intelligence analysis, intelligence collection, intelligence management, intelligence operations, terrorism studies; international relations and conflict resolution (MA), including comparative and security issues, conflict resolution, international and transnational security issues, peacekeeping; legal studies (MA); management (MA), including strategic consulting; marketing (MBA); military history (MA), including American military history, American Revolution, civil war, war since 1945, World War II; military studies (MA), including joint warfare, strategic leadership; national security studies (MA), including cyber, general (MA, MS), homeland security, regional security studies, security and intelligence analysis, terrorism studies; nonprofit management (MBA); political science (MA), including American politics and government, comparative government and development, general (MA, MS), international relations, public policy; psychology (MA); public administration (MPA), including disaster management, environmental policy, health policy, human resources, national security, organizational management, security management; public health (MPH); reverse logistics management (MA); security management (MA); space studies (MS), including aerospace science, general (MA, MS), planetary science; sports and health sciences (MS); sports management (MBA); teaching (M Ed), including autism spectrum disorder, curriculum and instruction for elementary teachers, elementary reading, English language learners, instructional leadership, online learning, special education, STEAM (STEM plus the arts); transportation and logistics management (MA). *Program availability:* Part-time, evening/weekend, online only, 100% online. *Faculty:* 401 full-time (228 women), 1,678 part-time/adjunct (781 women). *Students:* 378 full-time (184 women), 8,455 part-time (3,484 women); includes 2,972 minority (1,552 Black or African American, non-Hispanic/Latino; 52 American Indian or Alaska Native, non-Hispanic/Latino; 211 Asian, non-Hispanic/Latino; 791 Hispanic/Latino; 70 Native Hawaiian or other Pacific Islander, non-Hispanic/Latino; 296 Two or more races, non-Hispanic/Latino), 109 international. Average age 37. In 2016, 3,185 master's awarded. *Degree requirements:* For master's, comprehensive exam or practicum. *Entrance requirements:* For master's, official transcript showing earned bachelor's degree from institution accredited by recognized accrediting body. Additional exam requirements/recommendations for international students: Required—TOEFL (minimum score 550 paper-based), IELTS (minimum score 6.5). *Application deadline:* Applications are processed on a rolling basis. Application fee: $0. Electronic

applications accepted. *Expenses: Tuition:* Part-time $350 per credit hour. *Required fees:* $50 per course. *Financial support:* Scholarships/grants available. Financial award applicants required to submit FAFSA. *Unit head:* Dr. Karan Powell, President, 877-468-6268, Fax: 304-724-3780. *Application contact:* Terry Grant, Vice President of Enrollment Management, 877-468-6268, Fax: 304-724-3780, E-mail: info@apus.edu. Website: http://www.apus.edu

**American University,** College of Arts and Sciences, Department of Psychology, Washington, DC 22016-8062. Offers addiction and addictive behavior (Certificate); behavior, cognition, and neuroscience (PhD); clinical psychology (PhD); psychobiology of healing (Certificate); psychology (MA). *Accreditation:* APA. *Program availability:* Part-time. *Faculty:* 22 full-time (9 women), 11 part-time/adjunct (3 women). *Students:* 86 full-time (72 women), 12 part-time (9 women); includes 15 minority (5 Black or African American, non-Hispanic/Latino; 4 Asian, non-Hispanic/Latino; 4 Hispanic/Latino; 2 Two or more races, non-Hispanic/Latino), 6 international. Average age 28. 479 applicants, 12% accepted, 34 enrolled. In 2016, 27 master's, 13 doctorates awarded. *Degree requirements:* For master's, comprehensive exam, thesis or alternative; for doctorate, comprehensive exam, thesis/dissertation. *Entrance requirements:* For master's, GRE General Test, GRE Subject Test, statement of purpose, transcripts, 2 letters of recommendation; for doctorate, GRE General Test, GRE Subject Test, 3 letters of recommendation, statement of purpose, transcripts, resume. Additional exam requirements/recommendations for international students: Required—TOEFL (minimum score 100 iBT), IELTS (minimum score 7), PTE (minimum score 68). Application fee: $55. *Expenses:* $1,579 per credit tuition; $690 mandatory fees. *Financial support:* Research assistantships, teaching assistantships, institutionally sponsored loans, scholarships/grants, and unspecified assistantships available. Financial award application deadline: 2/1; financial award applicants required to submit FAFSA. *Unit head:* Dr. David Haaga, Department Chair, 202-885-1718, Fax: 202-885-1023, E-mail: ahrens@american.edu. *Application contact:* Kathleen Clowery, Associate Director, Graduate Admission, 202-885-3620, Fax: 202-885-1344, E-mail: clowery@american.edu. Website: http://www.american.edu/CAS/Psychology/

**The American University in Cairo,** School of Humanities and Social Sciences, Cairo, Egypt. Offers Arab and Islamic civilizations (Graduate Diploma); Arabic studies (MA); comparative literary studies (Graduate Diploma); Egyptology and Coptology (MA); English and comparative literature (MA); humanities and social sciences (Graduate Diploma); philosophy (MA); psychology (MA); sociology and anthropology (MA); teaching Arabic as a foreign language (MA); teaching English to speakers of other languages (MA). *Program availability:* Part-time, evening/weekend. *Faculty:* 51 full-time (29 women), 4 part-time/adjunct (2 women). *Students:* 65 full-time (47 women), 179 part-time (138 women), 32 international. Average age 30. 221 applicants, 45% accepted, 54 enrolled. In 2016, 95 master's awarded. *Degree requirements:* For master's, comprehensive exam (for some programs), thesis (for some programs). *Entrance requirements:* Additional exam requirements/recommendations for international students: Required—TOEFL (minimum score 450 paper-based; 45 iBT), IELTS (minimum score 5). *Application deadline:* For fall admission, 2/1 priority date for domestic and international students; for spring admission, 10/15 priority date for domestic and international students. Applications are processed on a rolling basis. Application fee: $80. Electronic applications accepted. *Expenses:* Contact institution. *Financial support:* Fellowships with partial tuition reimbursements, scholarships/grants, tuition waivers (partial), and unspecified assistantships available. Financial award application deadline: 3/10. *Faculty research:* English literature, political science, psychology, sociology, anthropology and Egyptology, teaching English for non-speakers, teaching Arabic as a foreign language, philosophy, Arabic studies. *Unit head:* Dr. Nathaniel Bowditch, Dean, 20-2-2615-1788, E-mail: nbowditch@aucegypt.edu. *Application contact:* Maha Hegazi, Director for Graduate Admissions, 20-2-2615-1462, E-mail: mahahegazi@aucegypt.edu. Website: http://www.aucegypt.edu/huss/Pages/default.aspx

**American University of Beirut,** Graduate Programs, Faculty of Arts and Sciences, Beirut, Lebanon. Offers anthropology (MA); Arab and Middle Eastern history (PhD); Arabic language and literature (MA, PhD); archaeology (MA); art history and curating (MA); biology (MS); cell and molecular biology (PhD); chemistry (MS); clinical psychology (MA); computational sciences (MS); computer science (MS); economics (MA); education (MA); English language (MA); English literature (MA); environmental policy planning (MS); financial economics (MAFE); geology (MS); history (MA); Islamic studies (MA); mathematics (MS); media studies (MA); Middle Eastern studies (MA); physics (MS); political studies (MA); psychology (MA); public administration (MA); public policy and international affairs (MA); sociology (MA); statistics (MA, MS); theoretical physics (PhD); transnational American studies (MA). *Program availability:* Part-time. *Faculty:* 133 full-time (42 women), 6 part-time/adjunct (2 women). *Students:* 240 full-time (172 women), 227 part-time (166 women). Average age 27. 286 applicants, 67% accepted, 108 enrolled. In 2016, 60 master's, 3 doctorates awarded. Terminal master's awarded for partial completion of doctoral program. *Degree requirements:* For master's, one foreign language, comprehensive exam, thesis (for some programs); for doctorate, one foreign language, comprehensive exam, thesis/dissertation. *Entrance requirements:* For master's, GRE (for some MA, MS programs), letters of recommendation; for doctorate, GRE, letters of recommendation. Additional exam requirements/recommendations for international students: Required—TOEFL (minimum score 600 paper-based; 97 iBT), IELTS (minimum score 7). *Application deadline:* For fall admission, 4/3 for domestic students; for winter admission, 11/3 for domestic students. Application fee: $50. Electronic applications accepted. *Expenses:* Contact institution. *Financial support:* In 2016–17, 4 fellowships (averaging $11,200 per year), 18 research assistantships (averaging $5,400 per year) were awarded; teaching assistantships, career-related internships or fieldwork, Federal Work-Study, institutionally sponsored loans, scholarships/grants, traineeships, health care benefits, tuition waivers (full), and unspecified assistantships also available. Support available to part-time students. *Faculty research:* Development economics, spatial econometrics, health economics, labor economics, energy economics, hydrogeology, geophysics, petrophysics, structural geology, mineralogy, petrology, geochemistry, multilingualism, comparative/world literature, translation studies, book histories/ cultures, biocatalysis, molecular recognition, photocatalysis, photophysical and biophysical chemistry, probe chemistry, machine learning, data science. *Unit head:* Dr. Nadia Maria El Cheikh, Dean, Faculty of Arts and Sciences, 961-1374374 Ext. 3800, Fax: 961-1744461, E-mail: nmcheikh@aub.edu.lb. *Application contact:* Dr. Salim Kanaan, Director, Admissions Office, 961-1350000 Ext. 2590, Fax: 961-1750775, E-mail: sk00@aub.edu.lb. Website: http://www.aub.edu.lb/fas/

**Andrews University,** School of Graduate Studies, School of Education, Department of Graduate Psychology and Counseling, Berrien Springs, MI 49104. Offers community counseling (MA), including clinical mental health counseling, community counseling; counseling psychology (PhD); educational and developmental psychology (MA, Ed D, PhD), including educational and developmental psychology (MA), educational psychology (Ed D, PhD); school counseling (MA); school psychology (Ed S); special education (MS). *Accreditation:* ACA (one or more programs are accredited). *Program availability:* Part-time. *Faculty:* 12 full-time (5 women), 4 part-time/adjunct (2 women). *Students:* 67 full-time (49 women), 15 part-time (12 women); includes 27 minority (19

## Psychology—General

Black or African American, non-Hispanic/Latino; 7 Hispanic/Latino; 1 Two or more races, non-Hispanic/Latino), 17 international. Average age 35. In 2016, 26 master's, 3 doctorates, 2 other advanced degrees awarded. Terminal master's awarded for partial completion of doctoral program. *Degree requirements:* For master's, thesis optional; for doctorate, thesis/dissertation. *Entrance requirements:* For master's, GRE Subject Test, minimum GPA of 2.6; for doctorate, GRE General Test, MA, minimum GPA of 3.5, sample of research. Additional exam requirements/recommendations for international students: Required—TOEFL (minimum score 550 paper-based). *Application deadline:* Applications are processed on a rolling basis. Application fee: $40. *Faculty research:* Testing methods, temperament, African-American studies, counseling process, multicultural issues. *Unit head:* Dr. Rudi Bailey, Chair, 269-471-3473. *Application contact:* Justina Clayburn, Supervisor of Graduate Admission, 800-253-2874, Fax: 269-471-6321, E-mail: graduate@andrews.edu.
Website: https://www.andrews.edu/sed/gpc/

**Angelo State University,** College of Graduate Studies and Research, Archer College of Health and Human Services, Department of Psychology, Sociology and Social Work, San Angelo, TX 76909. Offers applied psychology (MS); counseling psychology (MS); industrial-organizational psychology (MS). *Program availability:* Part-time, evening/weekend. *Students:* 73 full-time (53 women), 33 part-time (22 women); includes 36 minority (5 Black or African American, non-Hispanic/Latino; 31 Hispanic/Latino), 5 international. Average age 32. *Degree requirements:* For master's, comprehensive exam, thesis optional. *Entrance requirements:* For master's, GRE General Test (for industrial and organizational psychology only), essay, letters of recommendation (for industrial and organizational psychology only). Additional exam requirements/recommendations for international students: Required—TOEFL or IELTS. *Application deadline:* For fall admission, 7/15 priority date for domestic students, 6/10 for international students; for spring admission, 12/1 priority date for domestic students, 11/1 for international students. Applications are processed on a rolling basis. Application fee: $40 ($50 for international students). Electronic applications accepted. *Expenses:* Tuition, state resident: full-time $3726; part-time $2484 per year. Tuition, nonresident: full-time $10,746; part-time $7164 per year. *Required fees:* $2538; $1702 per unit. *Financial support:* Teaching assistantships, career-related internships or fieldwork, Federal Work-Study, scholarships/grants, and unspecified assistantships available. Support available to part-time students. Financial award application deadline: 3/1; financial award applicants required to submit FAFSA. *Unit head:* Dr. James N. Forbes, Chair, 325-486-6120, Fax: 325-942-2290, E-mail: james.forbes@angelo.edu. *Application contact:* Dr. James N. Forbes, Chair, 325-486-6120, Fax: 325-942-2290, E-mail: james.forbes@angelo.edu.
Website: http://www.angelo.edu/dept/psychology_sociology/

**Antioch University Los Angeles,** Graduate Programs, Program in Psychology, Culver City, CA 90230. Offers clinical psychology (MA); psychology (MA). *Program availability:* Part-time. *Degree requirements:* For master's, thesis (for some programs), internship. *Entrance requirements:* For master's, interview. Additional exam requirements/recommendations for international students: Required—TOEFL. *Faculty research:* Creativity and humor, ethnic humor, adult development, Jungian theory, psychoanalytic theory.

**Antioch University Seattle,** Graduate Programs, Program in Psychology, Seattle, WA 98121-1814. Offers counseling (MA); psychology (MA, Psy D). *Program availability:* Part-time, evening/weekend. *Degree requirements:* For master's, internship; for doctorate, thesis/dissertation. Electronic applications accepted. *Faculty research:* Trauma and post-traumatic stress disorders, workplace harassment and violence, multicultural issues and diversity.

**Appalachian State University,** Cratis D. Williams Graduate School, Department of Psychology, Boone, NC 28608. Offers clinical health psychology (MA). *Program availability:* Part-time. *Degree requirements:* For master's, comprehensive exam, thesis optional, exit exam. *Entrance requirements:* For master's, GRE General Test, 3 letters of recommendation. Additional exam requirements/recommendations for international students: Required—TOEFL (minimum score 550 paper-based; 79 iBT) or IELTS (minimum score 6.5). *Application deadline:* For fall admission, 2/15 for domestic students, 2/1 for international students. Applications are processed on a rolling basis. Application fee: $55. Electronic applications accepted. *Expenses:* Tuition, state resident: full-time $4744. Tuition, nonresident: full-time $17,913. Full-time tuition and fees vary according to program. *Financial support:* Fellowships, research assistantships, teaching assistantships, career-related internships or fieldwork, Federal Work-Study, scholarships/grants, and unspecified assistantships available. Financial award application deadline: 4/1; financial award applicants required to submit FAFSA. *Faculty research:* Eating disorders, school-based consultations, organizational behavior management, brain mechanisms of sound localization, parenting styles. *Unit head:* Dr. James Denniston, Chair, 828-262-2272, Fax: 828-262-2272, E-mail: dennistonjc@appstate.edu. *Application contact:* Dr. Twila Wingrove, Program Director, 828-262-2272 Ext. 440, E-mail: wingroveta@appstate.edu.
Website: http://www.psych.appstate.edu/

**Arcadia University,** College of Arts and Sciences, Department of Psychology, Glenside, PA 19038-3295. Offers applied behavior analysis (MA); autism (MAC); child/family therapy (MAC); community public health (MAC); counseling/international peace and conflict resolution dual degree (MAC); mental health counseling (MAC); trauma (MAC). *Program availability:* Part-time. *Faculty:* 14 full-time (9 women), 10 part-time/adjunct (9 women). *Students:* 33 full-time (27 women), 39 part-time (30 women); includes 22 minority (13 Black or African American, non-Hispanic/Latino; 2 Asian, non-Hispanic/Latino; 1 Hispanic/Latino; 6 Two or more races, non-Hispanic/Latino), 1 international. Average age 30. 61 applicants, 64% accepted, 24 enrolled. In 2016, 41 master's awarded. *Degree requirements:* For master's, practicum. *Entrance requirements:* For master's, GRE General Test or MAT. *Application deadline:* For fall admission, 1/15 for domestic students; for spring admission, 9/15 for domestic students. Applications are processed on a rolling basis. Application fee: $50. *Expenses:* Contact institution. *Financial support:* Research assistantships, career-related internships or fieldwork, and unspecified assistantships available. Support available to part-time students. Financial award application deadline: 8/15. *Unit head:* Dr. Steven Robbins, Chair, 215-572-2987. *Application contact:* 215-572-2925, Fax: 215-572-2126, E-mail: grad@arcadia.edu.

**Arcadia University,** School of Education, Glenside, PA 19038-3295. Offers art education (M Ed); computer education (CAS); curriculum (CAS); curriculum studies (M Ed); early childhood education (M Ed), including individualized, master teacher, research in child development; educational leadership (M Ed, Ed D, CAS); elementary education (M Ed); English education (MA Ed); environmental education (MA Ed); instructional technology (M Ed); language arts (M Ed); library science (M Ed); mathematics education (M Ed, MA Ed); music education (MA Ed); psychology (MA Ed); reading (M Ed, CAS); science education (M Ed, CAS); secondary education (M Ed, CAS); special education (M Ed, Ed D, CAS); theater arts (MA Ed); written communication (MA Ed). *Accreditation:* NASAD. *Program availability:* Part-time, evening/weekend, online learning. *Faculty:* 19 full-time (13 women), 3 part-time/adjunct (all women). *Students:* 22 full-time (16 women), 356 part-time (284 women); includes 84 minority (55 Black or African American, non-Hispanic/Latino; 2 American Indian or

Alaska Native, non-Hispanic/Latino; 13 Asian, non-Hispanic/Latino; 11 Hispanic/Latino; 3 Two or more races, non-Hispanic/Latino), 4 international. Average age 34. 145 applicants, 73% accepted, 80 enrolled. In 2016, 95 master's, 11 doctorates awarded. *Application deadline:* Applications are processed on a rolling basis. Application fee: $50. Electronic applications accepted. *Expenses:* Contact institution. *Financial support:* Career-related internships or fieldwork, tuition waivers (partial), and unspecified assistantships available. *Unit head:* John T Groves, Interim Dean of the School of Education, 215-572-2940. *Application contact:* 215-572-2925, Fax: 215-572-2126, E-mail: grad@arcadia.edu.

**Argosy University, Atlanta,** Georgia School of Professional Psychology, Atlanta, GA 30328. Offers clinical psychology (MA, Psy D, Postdoctoral Respecialization Certificate), including child and family psychology (Psy D), general adult clinical (Psy D), health psychology (Psy D), neuropsychology/geropsychology (Psy D); community counseling (MA), including marriage and family therapy; counselor education and supervision (Ed D); forensic psychology (MA); industrial organizational psychology (MA); marriage and family therapy (Certificate); sport-exercise psychology (MA). *Accreditation:* APA.

**Argosy University, Chicago,** Illinois School of Professional Psychology, Chicago, IL 60601. Offers clinical psychology (MA, Psy D), including child and adolescent psychology (Psy D), client-centered and experiential psychotherapies (Psy D), diversity and multicultural psychology (Psy D), family psychology (Psy D), forensic psychology (Psy D), health psychology (Psy D), neuropsychology (Psy D), organizational consulting (Psy D), psychoanalytic psychology (Psy D), psychology and spirituality (Psy D); community counseling (MA); counseling psychology (Ed D), including counselor education and supervision; counselor education and supervision (Ed D); industrial organizational psychology (MA). *Accreditation:* APA (one or more programs are accredited). *Program availability:* Online learning.

**Argosy University, Dallas,** College of Psychology and Behavioral Sciences, Farmers Branch, TX 75244. Offers MA, Ed D, Psy D.

**Argosy University, Denver,** College of Psychology and Behavioral Sciences, Denver, CO 80231. Offers clinical mental health counseling (MA); clinical psychology (MA, Psy D); counseling psychology (Ed D); counselor education and supervision (Ed D); forensic psychology (MA); industrial organizational psychology (MA); marriage and family therapy (MA, DMFT).

**Argosy University, Hawai`i,** Hawai'i School of Professional Psychology, Honolulu, HI 96813. Offers MA, MS, Ed D, Psy D, Certificate, Postdoctoral Respecialization Certificate. *Accreditation:* APA.

**Argosy University, Inland Empire,** College of Psychology and Behavioral Sciences, Ontario, CA 91761. Offers clinical psychology/marriage and family therapy (MA); counseling psychology (Ed D); counseling psychology/marriage and family therapy (MA); forensic psychology (MA); industrial organizational psychology (MA); sport-exercise psychology (MA).

**Argosy University, Los Angeles,** College of Psychology and Behavioral Sciences, Santa Monica, CA 90045. Offers clinical psychology/marriage and family therapy (MA); counseling psychology (Ed D); counseling psychology/marriage and family therapy (MA); forensic psychology (MA).

**Argosy University, Nashville,** College of Psychology and Behavioral Sciences, Nashville, TN 37214. Offers counselor education and supervision (Ed D); mental health counseling (MA).

**Argosy University, Northern Virginia,** American School of Professional Psychology, Arlington, VA 22209. Offers clinical psychology (MA, Psy D), including child and family psychology (Psy D), diversity and multicultural psychology (Psy D), forensic psychology (Psy D), health and neuropsychology (Psy D); community counseling (MA); counseling psychology (Ed D), including counselor education and supervision; counselor education and supervision (Ed D); forensic psychology (MA).

**Argosy University, Orange County,** American School of Professional Psychology, Orange, CA 92868. Offers MA, Ed D, Psy D. *Accreditation:* APA. *Program availability:* Part-time, evening/weekend. *Degree requirements:* For master's, comprehensive exam; for doctorate, comprehensive exam, thesis/dissertation. *Entrance requirements:* For master's and doctorate, 3 letters of recommendation, interview, resume. Additional exam requirements/recommendations for international students: Required—TOEFL. Electronic applications accepted. *Faculty research:* The psychological aspects of infertility medicine, depression, psychoanalytic therapy, experiential approaches to teaching.

**Argosy University, Phoenix,** Arizona School of Professional Psychology, Phoenix, AZ 85021. Offers MA, Psy D.

**Argosy University, Salt Lake City,** College of Psychology and Behavioral Sciences, Draper, UT 84020. Offers counseling psychology (Ed D); counselor education and supervision (Ed D); forensic psychology (MA); marriage and family therapy (MA, DMFT); mental health counseling (MA).

**Argosy University, San Diego,** College of Psychology and Behavioral Sciences, San Diego, CA 92108. Offers clinical psychology/marriage and family therapy (MA); counseling psychology (Ed D); counseling psychology/marriage and family therapy (MA); forensic psychology (MA).

**Argosy University, San Francisco Bay Area,** American School of Professional Psychology, Alameda, CA 94501. Offers clinical psychology (MA, Psy D); counseling psychology (MA, Ed D); forensic psychology (MA); sport-exercise psychology (MA). *Accreditation:* APA (one or more programs are accredited).

**Argosy University, Sarasota,** College of Psychology and Behavioral Sciences, Sarasota, FL 34235. Offers community counseling (MA); counseling psychology (Ed D); counselor education and supervision (Ed D); forensic psychology (MA); marriage and family therapy (MA); mental health counseling (MA); pastoral community counseling (Ed D).

**Argosy University, Schaumburg,** College of Behavioral Sciences, Schaumburg, IL 60173-5403. Offers clinical mental health counseling (MA); forensic psychology (MA, Post-Graduate Certificate); industrial organizational psychology (MA); sport-exercise psychology (MA). *Accreditation:* ACA; APA.

**Argosy University, Seattle,** College of Psychology and Behavioral Sciences, Seattle, WA 98121. Offers MA, Ed D, Psy D, Postdoctoral Respecialization Certificate.

**Argosy University, Tampa,** Florida School of Professional Psychology, Tampa, FL 33607. Offers clinical psychology (MA, Psy D), including clinical psychology; counselor education and supervision (Ed D); industrial organizational psychology (MA); marriage and family therapy (MA); mental health counseling (MA).

**Argosy University, Twin Cities,** Minnesota School of Professional Psychology, Eagan, MN 55121. Offers clinical psychology (MA, Psy D), including child and family psychology (Psy D), forensic psychology (Psy D), health and neuropsychology (Psy D), trauma (Psy D); forensic counseling (Post-Graduate Certificate); forensic psychology (MA); industrial organizational psychology (MA); marriage and family therapy (MA, DMFT), including forensic counseling (MA). *Accreditation:* AAMFT; AAMFT/COAMFTE; APA.

**Arizona State University at the Tempe campus,** College of Liberal Arts and Sciences, Department of Psychology, Tempe, AZ 85287-1104. Offers applied behavior analysis (MS); behavioral neuroscience (PhD); clinical psychology (PhD); cognitive science (PhD); developmental psychology (PhD); quantitative psychology (PhD); social psychology (PhD). *Accreditation:* APA. *Degree requirements:* For doctorate, comprehensive exam, thesis/dissertation, interactive Program of Study (iPOS) submitted before completing 50 percent of required credit hours. *Entrance requirements:* For doctorate, GRE General Test, GRE Subject Test, minimum GPA of 3.0 or equivalent in last 2 years of work leading to bachelor's degree. Additional exam requirements/recommendations for international students: Required—TOEFL, IELTS, or PTE. Electronic applications accepted.

**Arizona State University at the Tempe campus,** New College of Interdisciplinary Arts and Sciences, Program in Psychology, Phoenix, AZ 85069-7100. Offers MS. *Program availability:* Part-time, evening/weekend. *Degree requirements:* For master's, thesis or applied project, interactive Program of Study (iPOS) submitted before completing 50 percent of required credit hours. *Entrance requirements:* For master's, GRE, bachelor's degree in psychology or related field; minimum cumulative GPA of 3.0; successful completion of undergraduate statistics and research methods courses; three letters of recommendation from faculty; personal statement of research interests and goals. Additional exam requirements/recommendations for international students: Required—TOEFL, IELTS, or PTE. Electronic applications accepted. *Faculty research:* Emotion; stress; social identity, intergroup relations and prejudice; psychology and the legal system; discursive psychology; cognitive neuroscience, bilingualism and cognition; social psychology and bullying; health related decision-making; psychophysiology; attention, eye-tracking and natural behavior.

**Arkansas Tech University,** College of Arts and Humanities, Russellville, AR 72801. Offers applied sociology (MS); English (M Ed, MA); history (MA); liberal arts (MLA); multi-media journalism (MA); psychology (MS); teaching English as a second language (MA). *Program availability:* Part-time. *Students:* 56 full-time (42 women), 121 part-time (85 women); includes 23 minority (7 Black or African American, non-Hispanic/Latino; 1 Asian, non-Hispanic/Latino; 11 Hispanic/Latino; 4 Two or more races, non-Hispanic/Latino), 34 international. Average age 32. In 2016, 90 master's awarded. *Degree requirements:* For master's, comprehensive exam (for some programs), thesis (for some programs), project. *Entrance requirements:* For master's, GRE General Test or GMAT. Additional exam requirements/recommendations for international students: Required—TOEFL (minimum score 550 paper-based; 79 iBT), IELTS (minimum score 6). *Application deadline:* For fall admission, 3/1 priority date for domestic students, 5/1 priority date for international students; for spring admission, 10/1 priority date for domestic and international students. Applications are processed on a rolling basis. Application fee: $25 ($75 for international students). Electronic applications accepted. *Expenses:* Tuition, state resident: full-time $4932; part-time $274 per credit hour. Tuition, nonresident: full-time $9864; part-time $548 per credit hour. *Required fees:* $513 per semester. Tuition and fees vary according to course load. *Financial support:* In 2016–17, research assistantships with full tuition reimbursements (averaging $4,800 per year), teaching assistantships with full tuition reimbursements (averaging $4,800 per year) were awarded; career-related internships or fieldwork, Federal Work-Study, scholarships/grants, health care benefits, and unspecified assistantships also available. Support available to part-time students. Financial award application deadline: 4/15; financial award applicants required to submit FAFSA. *Unit head:* Dr. Jeffrey Woods, Dean, 479-968-0274, Fax: 479-964-0812, E-mail: jwoods@atu.edu. *Application contact:* Dr. Mary B. Gunter, Dean of Graduate College, 479-968-0398, Fax: 479-964-0542, E-mail: gradcollege@atu.edu.
Website: http://www.atu.edu/humanities/

**Auburn University,** Graduate School, College of Liberal Arts, Department of Psychology, Auburn University, AL 36849. Offers MS, PhD. *Accreditation:* APA (one or more programs are accredited). *Program availability:* Part-time. *Faculty:* 25 full-time (9 women), 1 (woman) part-time/adjunct. *Students:* 46 full-time (33 women), 29 part-time (19 women); includes 9 minority (1 Black or African American, non-Hispanic/Latino; 2 Asian, non-Hispanic/Latino; 4 Hispanic/Latino; 2 Two or more races, non-Hispanic/Latino), 4 international. Average age 27. 367 applicants, 5% accepted, 19 enrolled. In 2016, 26 master's, 18 doctorates awarded. *Degree requirements:* For doctorate, thesis/dissertation. *Entrance requirements:* For master's, GRE General Test, GRE Subject Test, minimum GPA of 3.25 in psychology, 3.0 overall; for doctorate, GRE General Test, GRE Subject Test. *Application deadline:* Applications are processed on a rolling basis. Application fee: $50 ($60 for international students). Electronic applications accepted. *Expenses:* Tuition, state resident: full-time $9072; part-time $504 per credit hour. Tuition, nonresident: full-time $27,216; part-time $1512 per credit hour. *Required fees:* $812 per semester. Tuition and fees vary according to degree level and program. *Financial support:* Research assistantships, teaching assistantships, and Federal Work-Study available. Support available to part-time students. Financial award application deadline: 3/15; financial award applicants required to submit FAFSA. *Faculty research:* Clinical psychology, learning, industrial psychology, organizational psychology. *Unit head:* Dr. Peter Chen, Head, 334-844-4412. *Application contact:* Dr. George Flowers, Dean of the Graduate School, 334-844-2125.

**Auburn University at Montgomery,** College of Arts and Sciences, Department of Psychology, Montgomery, AL 36124-4023. Offers clinical psychology (MS). *Program availability:* Part-time, evening/weekend. *Degree requirements:* For master's, comprehensive exam, thesis optional. *Entrance requirements:* For master's, GRE General Test or MAT. Electronic applications accepted. *Faculty research:* Community service, diagnosis, behavior modification.

**Augusta University,** The Graduate School, College of Science and Mathematics, Department of Psychological Sciences, Augusta, GA 30912. Offers MS. *Program availability:* Part-time. *Degree requirements:* For master's, thesis optional, written/oral exam. *Entrance requirements:* For master's, GRE General Test, minimum GPA of 3.0, bachelor's degree in psychology or equivalent course work, three letters of recommendation. Additional exam requirements/recommendations for international students: Required—TOEFL. Electronic applications accepted. *Faculty research:* Developmental, cognitive, gender and aging issues, consumer behavior, conditioned taste aversions, circadian rhythms, use of slang and offensive language.

**Austin Peay State University,** College of Graduate Studies, College of Behavioral and Health Sciences, Department of Psychology, Clarksville, TN 37044. Offers industrial-organizational psychology (MS); mental health counseling (MS), including clinical mental health, school counseling; school counseling (MS). *Program availability:* Part-time, online learning. *Faculty:* 9 full-time (6 women), 2 part-time/adjunct (1 woman). *Students:* 49 full-time (41 women), 18 part-time (12 women); includes 17 minority (13 Black or African American, non-Hispanic/Latino; 2 Hispanic/Latino; 2 Two or more races, non-Hispanic/Latino), 1 international. Average age 30. 59 applicants, 59% accepted, 21 enrolled. In 2016, 25 master's awarded. *Degree requirements:* For master's, comprehensive exam, thesis (for some programs). *Entrance requirements:* For master's, GRE General Test, minimum undergraduate GPA of 2.5, 3 letters of recommendation, bachelor's degree. Additional exam requirements/recommendations for international students: Required—TOEFL (minimum score 500 paper-based). *Application deadline:* For fall admission, 8/9 priority date for domestic students. Applications are processed on

a rolling basis. Application fee: $45 ($50 for international students). Electronic applications accepted. *Expenses:* Tuition, state resident: full-time $8300; part-time $415 per credit hour. Tuition, nonresident: full-time $22,280; part-time $1114 per credit hour. *Required fees:* $1473; $73.65 per credit hour. *Financial support:* Research assistantships with full tuition reimbursements, career-related internships or fieldwork, Federal Work-Study, institutionally sponsored loans, scholarships/grants, and unspecified assistantships available. Support available to part-time students. Financial award application deadline: 4/1; financial award applicants required to submit FAFSA. *Unit head:* Dr. Nicole Knickmeyer, Chair, 931-221-7232, Fax: 931-221-6267, E-mail: knickmeyer@apsu.edu. *Application contact:* Brad Averitt, Coordinator of Graduate Admissions, 800-859-4723, Fax: 931-221-7641, E-mail: gradadmissions@apsu.edu.
Website: http://www.apsu.edu/psychology

**Avila University,** Department of Psychology, Kansas City, MO 64145-1698. Offers counseling psychology (MS); psychology (MS). *Program availability:* Part-time. *Faculty:* 7 full-time (6 women), 10 part-time/adjunct (4 women). *Students:* 92 full-time (78 women), 22 part-time (20 women); includes 39 minority (25 Black or African American, non-Hispanic/Latino; 1 American Indian or Alaska Native, non-Hispanic/Latino; 3 Asian, non-Hispanic/Latino; 8 Hispanic/Latino; 2 Two or more races, non-Hispanic/Latino), 1 international. Average age 34. 93 applicants, 43% accepted, 30 enrolled. In 2016, 48 master's awarded. *Degree requirements:* For master's, thesis optional, capstone project. *Entrance requirements:* For master's, bachelor's degree, minimum GPA of 3.0 in all previous undergraduate and graduate coursework, 2 letters of recommendation, letter of intent, resume. Additional exam requirements/recommendations for international students: Required—TOEFL (minimum score 80 iBT). *Application deadline:* Applications are processed on a rolling basis. Application fee: $0. Electronic applications accepted. *Expenses:* $583 per credit hour. *Financial support:* In 2016–17, 15 students received support, including 5 research assistantships with partial tuition reimbursements available; career-related internships or fieldwork, scholarships/grants, and unspecified assistantships also available. Support available to part-time students. Financial award applicants required to submit FAFSA. *Faculty research:* Emotional regulation, embodied cognition, trauma and restorative justice, psychophysiology of public speaking anxiety. *Unit head:* Aaron R. Coffey, Director of Graduate Psychology Enrollment Management, 816-501-0419, Fax: 816-501-2455, E-mail: aaron.coffey@avila.edu. *Application contact:* Tamika Doolin, Graduate Admissions Advisor, 816-501-3661, Fax: 816-501-2455, E-mail: gradpsych@avila.edu.
Website: https://www.avila.edu/psychology/

**Azusa Pacific University,** School of Behavioral and Applied Sciences, Department of Graduate Psychology, Azusa, CA 91702-7000. Offers clinical psychology (MA, Psy D), including family therapy (MA). *Accreditation:* APA (one or more programs are accredited). *Program availability:* Part-time, evening/weekend. *Degree requirements:* For master's, comprehensive exam, 250 hours of clinical experience, individual and group therapy. *Entrance requirements:* For master's, interview, minimum GPA of 3.0, Minnesota Multiphasic Personality Inventory. Additional exam requirements/recommendations for international students: Required—TOEFL (minimum score 600 paper-based).

**Azusa Pacific University,** School of Behavioral and Applied Sciences, Department of Psychology, Azusa, CA 91702-7000. Offers MS.

**Ball State University,** Graduate School, College of Sciences and Humanities, Department of Psychological Science, Muncie, IN 47306. Offers clinical psychology (MA); cognitive and social processes (MA). *Program availability:* Part-time. *Entrance requirements:* For master's, GRE General Test, minimum baccalaureate GPA of 2.75 or 3.0 in latter half of baccalaureate, goals statements, curriculum vitae, letters of recommendation. Additional exam requirements/recommendations for international students: Required—TOEFL (minimum score 550 paper-based; 79 iBT), IELTS (minimum score 6.5). Electronic applications accepted.

**Barry University,** College of Arts and Sciences, Department of Psychology, Miami Shores, FL 33161-6695. Offers clinical psychology (MS); school psychology (MS, SSP). *Program availability:* Part-time, evening/weekend. *Degree requirements:* For master's, thesis, practicum. *Entrance requirements:* For master's, GRE General Test, minimum GPA of 3.0, course work in psychology. Electronic applications accepted. *Faculty research:* Closed head injury, memory and aging, infant/mother interaction, evolutionary aspects of behavior, gender roles.

**Baylor University,** Graduate School, College of Arts and Sciences, Department of Psychology and Neuroscience, Program in Psychology, Waco, TX 76798. Offers MA, PhD. *Faculty:* 16 full-time (4 women). *Students:* 23 full-time (16 women); includes 7 minority (1 Asian, non-Hispanic/Latino; 3 Hispanic/Latino; 3 Two or more races, non-Hispanic/Latino), 1 international. Average age 25. 60 applicants, 8% accepted, 5 enrolled. In 2016, 1 master's, 4 doctorates awarded. Terminal master's awarded for partial completion of doctoral program. *Degree requirements:* For master's, thesis; for doctorate, comprehensive exam, thesis/dissertation. *Entrance requirements:* For master's and doctorate, GRE General Test. Additional exam requirements/recommendations for international students: Required—TOEFL. *Application deadline:* For fall admission, 1/15 for domestic and international students. Application fee: $50. Electronic applications accepted. *Expenses:* Tuition: Full-time $28,494; part-time $1583 per credit hour. *Required fees:* $167 per credit hour. Tuition and fees vary according to course load and program. *Financial support:* In 2016–17, 20 students received support, including 4 research assistantships with full tuition reimbursements available (averaging $21,000 per year), 16 teaching assistantships with full tuition reimbursements available (averaging $21,000 per year); health care benefits also available. *Faculty research:* Animal learning/behavior, psychopharmacology, memory and cognition, health psychology, psychology of religion. *Unit head:* Dr. Jim H. Patton, Graduate Program Director, 254-710-2237, Fax: 254-710-3033, E-mail: jim_patton@baylor.edu. *Application contact:* Laura Sumrall, Graduate Studies Coordinator, 254-710-2961, Fax: 254-710-3033, E-mail: laura_sumrall@baylor.edu.
Website: http://www.baylor.edu/psychologyneuroscience/

**Binghamton University, State University of New York,** Graduate School, Harpur College of Arts and Sciences, Department of Psychology, Binghamton, NY 13902-6000. Offers behavioral neuroscience (PhD); clinical psychology (PhD); cognitive and behavioral science (PhD). *Accreditation:* APA. *Program availability:* Part-time. *Faculty:* 34 full-time (17 women), 9 part-time/adjunct (5 women). *Students:* 42 full-time (23 women), 45 part-time (30 women); includes 16 minority (3 Black or African American, non-Hispanic/Latino; 7 Asian, non-Hispanic/Latino; 4 Hispanic/Latino; 2 Two or more races, non-Hispanic/Latino), 2 international. Average age 28. 197 applicants, 15% accepted, 16 enrolled. In 2016, 10 doctorates awarded. Terminal master's awarded for partial completion of doctoral program. *Degree requirements:* For doctorate, comprehensive exam (for some programs), thesis/dissertation. *Entrance requirements:* For doctorate, GRE General Test. Additional exam requirements/recommendations for international students: Required—TOEFL (minimum score 550 paper-based; 80 iBT). Application fee: $75. Electronic applications accepted. *Financial support:* In 2016–17, 67 students received support, including 15 research assistantships with full tuition reimbursements available (averaging $17,500 per year), 40 teaching assistantships with full tuition reimbursements available (averaging $17,500 per year); career-related internships or fieldwork, Federal Work-Study, institutionally sponsored loans,

## Psychology—General

scholarships/grants, health care benefits, tuition waivers (full and partial), and unspecified assistantships also available. Financial award applicants required to submit FAFSA. *Unit head:* Dr. Matthew D. Johnson, Chair, 607-777-2370, E-mail: mjohnson@binghamton.edu. *Application contact:* Ben Balkaya, Assistant Dean and Director, 607-777-2151, Fax: 607-777-2501, E-mail: balkaya@binghamton.edu.

**Biola University,** Rosemead School of Psychology, La Mirada, CA 90639-0001. Offers clinical psychology (PhD, Psy D). *Accreditation:* APA. *Degree requirements:* For doctorate, comprehensive exam, thesis/dissertation. *Entrance requirements:* For doctorate, GRE General Test, interview, 30 undergraduate semester hours of credits in psychology, minimum GPA of 3.0. Additional exam requirements/recommendations for international students: Required—TOEFL (minimum score 600 paper-based; 100 iBT). Electronic applications accepted. *Expenses:* Contact institution. *Faculty research:* Integration of psychology and theology, psychology of child/adolescent, psychology of marriage, psychology of gender, psychology of trauma, psychology of forensics, multi-cultural studies and mental health.

**Boston College,** Graduate School of Arts and Sciences, Department of Psychology, Chestnut Hill, MA 02467-3800. Offers PhD. *Faculty:* 21 full-time. *Students:* 21 full-time (17 women); includes 3 minority (1 Asian, non-Hispanic/Latino; 1 Hispanic/Latino; 1 Two or more races, non-Hispanic/Latino), 5 international. 287 applicants, 3% accepted, 6 enrolled. In 2016, 3 doctorates awarded. *Degree requirements:* For doctorate, thesis/dissertation, fieldwork. *Entrance requirements:* For doctorate, GRE General Test, GRE Subject Test. Additional exam requirements/recommendations for international students: Required—TOEFL (minimum score 600 paper-based; 100 iBT), IELTS (minimum score 8). *Application deadline:* For fall admission, 12/15 for domestic and international students. Application fee: $75. Electronic applications accepted. Tuition and fees vary according to program. *Financial support:* In 2016–17, 21 students received support, including fellowships with full tuition reimbursements available (averaging $23,200 per year), research assistantships with full tuition reimbursements available (averaging $23,200 per year), teaching assistantships with full tuition reimbursements available (averaging $23,200 per year); career-related internships or fieldwork, health care benefits, and unspecified assistantships also available. Support available to part-time students. Financial award application deadline: 3/1; financial award applicants required to submit FAFSA. *Faculty research:* Behavioral neuroscience, cognitive neuroscience, developmental psychology, quantitative psychology and social psychology. *Unit head:* Dr. Ellen Winner, Chairperson, 617-552-4100, E-mail: winner@bc.edu. *Application contact:* Dr. Scott Slotnick, Graduate Program Director, 617-552-4100, E-mail: slotnics@bc.edu.
Website: http://www.bc.edu/psychology

**Boston Graduate School of Psychoanalysis,** BGSP-New Jersey, Brookline, MA 02446-4602. Offers psychoanalysis (MA); psychoanalytic counseling (MA). Programs offered in conjunction with Academic of Clinical and Applied Psychoanalysis in Livingston, NJ.

**Boston Graduate School of Psychoanalysis,** New York Graduate School of Psychoanalysis, New York, NY 10011. Offers MA. *Program availability:* Part-time. *Degree requirements:* For master's, thesis. *Entrance requirements:* For master's, interview, BA, writing sample, letters of recommendation. Additional exam requirements/recommendations for international students: Required—TOEFL.

**Boston University,** Graduate School of Arts and Sciences, Department of Psychological and Brain Sciences, Boston, MA 02215. Offers MA, PhD. *Accreditation:* APA (one or more programs are accredited). *Students:* 101 full-time (78 women), 6 part-time (3 women); includes 27 minority (4 Black or African American, non-Hispanic/Latino; 9 Asian, non-Hispanic/Latino; 11 Hispanic/Latino; 3 Two or more races, non-Hispanic/Latino), 13 international. Average age 27. 964 applicants, 13% accepted, 40 enrolled. In 2016, 33 master's, 10 doctorates awarded. Terminal master's awarded for partial completion of doctoral program. *Degree requirements:* For master's, thesis or alternative, research apprenticeship; for doctorate, comprehensive exam, thesis/dissertation. *Entrance requirements:* For master's and doctorate, GRE General Test, GRE Subject Test (recommended), three letters of recommendation, transcripts, personal statement, curriculum vitae. Additional exam requirements/recommendations for international students: Required—TOEFL (minimum score 550 paper-based; 84 iBT). *Application deadline:* For fall admission, 12/1 for domestic and international students. Application fee: $95. Electronic applications accepted. *Financial support:* In 2016–17, 66 students received support, including 2 fellowships with full tuition reimbursements available (averaging $21,500 per year), 27 research assistantships with full tuition reimbursements available (averaging $21,500 per year), 27 teaching assistantships with full tuition reimbursements available (averaging $21,500 per year); career-related internships or fieldwork, Federal Work-Study, scholarships/grants, traineeships, and health care benefits also available. Financial award application deadline: 12/1; financial award applicants required to submit FAFSA. *Unit head:* David Somers, Chairman, 617-358-1372, Fax: 617-353-6933, E-mail: somers@bu.edu. *Application contact:* Martin Gastmann, Assistant Director of Admissions and Financial Aid, 617-353-2696, Fax: 617-358-5492, E-mail: grs@bu.edu.
Website: http://www.bu.edu/psych/

**Boston University,** School of Medicine, Division of Graduate Medical Sciences, Program in Mental Health Counseling and Behavioral Medicine, Boston, MA 02215. Offers MA. *Faculty research:* HIV/AIDS, trauma, behavioral medicine (obesity, breast cancer), neurosciences, autism, serious mental illness, sports psychology. *Unit head:* Dr. Stephen Brady, Director, 617-414-2320, Fax: 617-414-2323, E-mail: sbrady@bu.edu. *Application contact:* GMS Admissions Office, 617-638-5255, E-mail: askgms@bu.edu.
Website: http://www.bumc.bu.edu/mhbm/

**Bowling Green State University,** Graduate College, College of Arts and Sciences, Department of Psychology, Bowling Green, OH 43403. Offers clinical psychology (MA, PhD); developmental psychology (MA, PhD); experimental psychology (MA, PhD); industrial/organizational psychology (MA, PhD); quantitative psychology (MA, PhD). *Accreditation:* APA (one or more programs are accredited). *Degree requirements:* For doctorate, thesis/dissertation. *Entrance requirements:* For doctorate, GRE General Test, GRE Subject Test. Additional exam requirements/recommendations for international students: Required—TOEFL. *Application deadline:* For fall admission, 1/1 for domestic students. Application fee: $30. Electronic applications accepted. *Financial support:* Fellowships with full tuition reimbursements, research assistantships with full tuition reimbursements, teaching assistantships with full tuition reimbursements, career-related internships or fieldwork, Federal Work-Study, institutionally sponsored loans, tuition waivers (full), and unspecified assistantships available. Financial award applicants required to submit FAFSA. *Faculty research:* Personnel psychology, developmental-mathematical models, behavioral medication, brain process, child/adolescent social cognition. *Unit head:* Dr. Mike Zickar, Chair, 419-372-2301, E-mail: mzickar@bgsu.edu. *Application contact:* Dr. Terry L. Lawrence, Assistant Dean for Graduate Admissions and Studies, 419-372-7713, Fax: 419-372-8569, E-mail: tlawren@bgnet.bgsu.edu.

**Brandeis University,** Graduate School of Arts and Sciences, Department of Psychology, Waltham, MA 02454-9110. Offers brain, body and behavior (PhD); cognitive neuroscience (PhD); general psychology (MA); social/developmental

psychology (PhD). *Program availability:* Part-time. *Faculty:* 14 full-time (7 women), 4 part-time/adjunct (3 women). *Students:* 40 full-time (27 women), 1 (woman) part-time; includes 5 minority (1 Black or African American, non-Hispanic/Latino; 2 Asian, non-Hispanic/Latino; 2 Hispanic/Latino), 9 international. 148 applicants, 23% accepted, 15 enrolled. In 2016, 8 master's, 3 doctorates awarded. Terminal master's awarded for partial completion of doctoral program. *Degree requirements:* For master's, thesis or alternative; for doctorate, thesis/dissertation, research reports. *Entrance requirements:* For master's and doctorate, GRE General Test; GRE Subject Test (recommended), 3 letters of recommendation, statement of purpose, transcript(s), resume. Additional exam requirements/recommendations for international students: Required—TOEFL (minimum score 600 paper-based; 100 iBT); Recommended—IELTS (minimum score 7), TSE (minimum score 68). *Application deadline:* For fall admission, 1/15 priority date for domestic and international students. Application fee: $75. Electronic applications accepted. *Financial support:* In 2016–17, 22 students received support, including 22 fellowships with full tuition reimbursements available (averaging $24,000 per year), 34 teaching assistantships with partial tuition reimbursements available (averaging $3,200 per year); Federal Work-Study, scholarships/grants, health care benefits, and tuition waivers (full and partial) also available. Support available to part-time students. Financial award application deadline: 4/15; financial award applicants required to submit FAFSA. *Faculty research:* Brain, body, and behavior across the lifespan; face perception and nonverbal communication; learning and memory; motor control and spatial orientation; neurophysiology of learning and decision making; personality and cognition in adulthood and old age; social, cultural and affective neuroscience; social relations and health physiology; speech comprehension and memory; taste physiology and psychophysics; visual perception. *Unit head:* Prof. Paul DiZio, Department Chair, 781-736-3300, Fax: 781-736-3291, E-mail: dizio@brandeis.edu. *Application contact:* Phil Gnatowski, Department Administrator, 781-736-3302, Fax: 781-736-3291, E-mail: gnat@brandeis.edu.
Website: http://www.brandeis.edu/departments/psych/

**Brandman University,** School of Arts and Sciences, Irvine, CA 92618. Offers psychology (MA), including counseling, marriage and family therapy, professional clinical counseling. *Expenses: Tuition:* Full-time $14,880; part-time $620 per credit hour. Tuition and fees vary according to degree level and program. *Unit head:* Dr. Jeremy Korr, Dean, 949-341-9831.
Website: https://www.brandman.edu/arts-sciences

**Brenau University,** Sydney O. Smith Graduate School, College of Health Sciences, Gainesville, GA 30501. Offers family nurse practitioner (MSN); nurse educator (MSN); nursing management (MSN); occupational therapy (MS); psychology (MS). *Accreditation:* AOTA. *Program availability:* Part-time, evening/weekend. *Degree requirements:* For master's, comprehensive exam (for some programs), thesis (for some programs), clinical practicum hours. *Entrance requirements:* For master's, GRE General Test or MAT (for some programs), interview, writing sample, references (for some programs). Additional exam requirements/recommendations for international students: Required—TOEFL (minimum score 500 paper-based; 61 iBT); Recommended—IELTS (minimum score 5). Electronic applications accepted. *Expenses:* Contact institution.

**Bridgewater State University,** College of Graduate Studies, College of Humanities and Social Sciences, Department of Psychology, Bridgewater, MA 02325. Offers MA. *Program availability:* Part-time, evening/weekend. *Entrance requirements:* For master's, GRE General Test.

**Brigham Young University,** Graduate Studies, College of Family, Home, and Social Sciences, Department of Psychology, Provo, UT 84602. Offers applied social psychology (PhD); clinical psychology (PhD); cognitive and behavioral neuroscience (PhD); developmental psychology (PhD). *Accreditation:* APA. *Faculty:* 29 full-time (7 women), 8 part-time/adjunct (2 women). *Students:* 59 full-time (34 women); includes 9 minority (2 Black or African American, non-Hispanic/Latino; 4 Asian, non-Hispanic/Latino; 2 Hispanic/Latino; 1 Native Hawaiian or other Pacific Islander, non-Hispanic/Latino). Average age 29. 49 applicants, 33% accepted, 11 enrolled. In 2016, 12 doctorates awarded. *Degree requirements:* For doctorate, comprehensive exam (for some programs), thesis/dissertation, publishable paper. *Entrance requirements:* For doctorate, GRE General Test, minimum GPA of 3.0. Additional exam requirements/recommendations for international students: Required—TOEFL (minimum score 580 paper-based; 85 iBT). *Application deadline:* For fall admission, 12/1 for domestic and international students. Application fee: $50. Electronic applications accepted. *Expenses:* Contact institution. *Financial support:* In 2016–17, 41 students received support, including 32 research assistantships with partial tuition reimbursements available (averaging $12,000 per year), 5 teaching assistantships with partial tuition reimbursements available (averaging $12,000 per year); career-related internships or fieldwork, scholarships/grants, tuition waivers (partial), and unspecified assistantships also available. Financial award application deadline: 5/31. *Faculty research:* Psychotherapy process, Alzheimer's disease/dementia, psychology and law, health, psychology, developmental. *Total annual research expenditures:* $73,281. *Unit head:* Dr. Dawson Hedges, Chair, 801-422-6357, Fax: 801-422-0602, E-mail: dawson_hedges@byu.edu. *Application contact:* Leesa D. Scott, Coordinator of Student Programs, 801-422-4560, Fax: 801-422-0602, E-mail: leesa_scott@byu.edu.
Website: http://psychology.byu.edu/

**Brock University,** Faculty of Graduate Studies, Faculty of Social Sciences, Program in Psychology, St. Catharines, ON L2S 3A1, Canada. Offers behavioral neuroscience (MA, PhD); life span development (MA, PhD); social personality (MA, PhD). *Program availability:* Part-time. *Degree requirements:* For master's, thesis; for doctorate, thesis/dissertation. *Entrance requirements:* For master's, GRE, honors degree; for doctorate, GRE, master's degree. Additional exam requirements/recommendations for international students: Required—TOEFL (minimum score 550 paper-based; 80 iBT), IELTS (minimum score 6.5), TWE (minimum score 4). Electronic applications accepted. *Faculty research:* Social personality, behavioral neuroscience, life-span development.

**Brooklyn College of the City University of New York,** School of Natural and Behavioral Sciences, Department of Psychology, Brooklyn, NY 11210-2889. Offers experimental psychology (MA); industrial and organizational psychology (MA), including human relations, organizational behavior; mental health counseling (MA); psychology (PhD). *Program availability:* Part-time. *Degree requirements:* For master's, comprehensive exam, thesis (for some programs). *Entrance requirements:* For master's, minimum GPA of 3.0, 2 letters of recommendation, essay; for doctorate, GRE. Additional exam requirements/recommendations for international students: Required—TOEFL (minimum score 520 paper-based; 69 iBT). Electronic applications accepted.

**Brown University,** Graduate School, Department of Cognitive, Linguistic and Psychological Sciences, Providence, RI 02912. Offers cognitive science (Sc M, PhD); linguistics (AM, PhD); psychology (PhD). *Degree requirements:* For master's, one foreign language, thesis or alternative; for doctorate, 2 foreign languages, thesis/dissertation.

**Bucknell University,** Graduate Studies, College of Arts and Sciences, Department of Psychology, Lewisburg, PA 17837. Offers MS. *Degree requirements:* For master's, thesis. *Entrance requirements:* For master's, GRE General Test, GRE Subject Test, minimum GPA of 3.0. Additional exam requirements/recommendations for international

students: Required—TOEFL (minimum score 600 paper-based). *Application deadline:* For fall admission, 2/1 priority date for domestic students, 1/1 priority date for international students. Application fee: $25. *Expenses: Tuition, area resident:* Part-time $5475 per course. *Financial support:* Research assistantships and unspecified assistantships available. Financial award application deadline: 2/1. *Unit head:* Dr. Bill Flack, Chair, 570-577-1200. *Application contact:* Gretchen H. Fegley, Coordinator, 570-577-3655, Fax: 570-577-3760, E-mail: gfegley@bucknell.edu.
Website: http://www.bucknell.edu/Psychology

**California Coast University,** School of Behavioral Science, Santa Ana, CA 92701. Offers psychology (MS). *Program availability:* Online learning.

**California Institute of Integral Studies,** School of Consciousness and Transformation, San Francisco, CA 94103. Offers anthropology and social change (MA, PhD); Asian philosophies and cultures (MA); creative inquiry/interdisciplinary arts (MFA); East-West psychology (MA, PhD); integral and transpersonal psychology (PhD); philosophy and religion (PhD), including ecology, spirituality, and religion, philosophy, cosmology, and consciousness, women's spirituality; theater and performance making (MFA); transformative leadership (MA); transformative studies (PhD); women, gender, spirituality and social justice (MA); writing and consciousness (MFA). *Program availability:* Part-time, evening/weekend, 100% online, blended/hybrid learning. *Students:* 390 full-time (256 women), 121 part-time (84 women); includes 135 minority (39 Black or African American, non-Hispanic/Latino; 2 American Indian or Alaska Native, non-Hispanic/Latino; 22 Asian, non-Hispanic/Latino; 40 Hispanic/Latino; 2 Native Hawaiian or other Pacific Islander, non-Hispanic/Latino; 30 Two or more races, non-Hispanic/Latino), 51 international. Average age 38. 195 applicants, 92% accepted, 124 enrolled. In 2016, 35 master's, 41 doctorates awarded. Terminal master's awarded for partial completion of doctoral program. *Degree requirements:* For master's, thesis optional; for doctorate, comprehensive exam, thesis/dissertation, 1 foreign language (for Asian philosophies and cultures). *Entrance requirements:* For master's, minimum GPA of 3.0, letters of recommendation, writing sample; for doctorate, master's degree, minimum GPA of 3.0, letters of recommendation, writing sample. Additional exam requirements/recommendations for international students: Required—TOEFL. *Application deadline:* For fall admission, 2/1 priority date for domestic and international students; for spring admission, 10/15 priority date for domestic and international students. Applications are processed on a rolling basis. Application fee: $65. Electronic applications accepted. *Expenses: Tuition:* Full-time $19,728; part-time $1098 per semester hour. *Required fees:* $320; $320 per semester hour. *Financial support:* Research assistantships, teaching assistantships, career-related internships or fieldwork, Federal Work-Study, and scholarships/grants available. Support available to part-time students. Financial award application deadline: 4/15; financial award applicants required to submit FAFSA. *Faculty research:* Ecology and sustainability, philosophy and religion, East-West psychology, integrative health, social and cultural anthropology, transformative leadership. *Application contact:* Ellen Durst, Director of Admissions, 415-575-6100, Fax: 415-575-1268, E-mail: admissions@ciis.edu.
Website: http://www.ciis.edu/

**California Institute of Integral Studies,** School of Professional Psychology and Health, San Francisco, CA 94103. Offers clinical psychology (Psy D); community mental health (MA); drama therapy (MA); expressive arts therapy (MA); human sexuality (PhD); integral counseling psychology (MA); integrative health studies (MA); psychological studies (MA); somatic psychology (MA). *Program availability:* Part-time, evening/weekend, 100% online, blended/hybrid learning. *Students:* 526 full-time (408 women), 113 part-time (96 women); includes 173 minority (34 Black or African American, non-Hispanic/Latino; 5 American Indian or Alaska Native, non-Hispanic/Latino; 31 Asian, non-Hispanic/Latino; 58 Hispanic/Latino; 1 Native Hawaiian or other Pacific Islander, non-Hispanic/Latino; 44 Two or more races, non-Hispanic/Latino), 52 international. Average age 38. 319 applicants, 85% accepted, 164 enrolled. In 2016, 157 master's, 21 doctorates awarded. *Degree requirements:* For doctorate, comprehensive exam, thesis/dissertation. *Entrance requirements:* For master's, minimum GPA of 3.0, letters of recommendation, writing sample; for doctorate, GRE, MA in psychology or social work with appropriate practical experience for advanced standing, or BA with a minimum GPA of 3.1; letters of recommendation; writing sample. Additional exam requirements/recommendations for international students: Required—TOEFL. *Application deadline:* For fall admission, 2/1 priority date for domestic and international students; for spring admission, 10/15 priority date for domestic and international students. Applications are processed on a rolling basis. Application fee: $65. Electronic applications accepted. *Expenses: Tuition:* Full-time $19,728; part-time $1098 per semester hour. *Required fees:* $320; $320 per semester hour. *Financial support:* Research assistantships with tuition reimbursements, teaching assistantships with tuition reimbursements, career-related internships or fieldwork, Federal Work-Study, and scholarships/grants available. Support available to part-time students. Financial award application deadline: 4/15; financial award applicants required to submit FAFSA. *Faculty research:* Transpersonal psychology, somatic psychology, expressive arts therapy, drama therapy, community mental health, ecopsychology, integrative health, human sexuality. *Application contact:* Ellen Durst, Director of Admissions, 415-575-6100, Fax: 415-575-1268, E-mail: admissions@ciis.edu.

**California Lutheran University,** Graduate Studies, Department of Psychology, Thousand Oaks, CA 91360-2787. Offers clinical psychology (MS, Psy D); marital and family therapy (MS). *Accreditation:* APA. *Program availability:* Part-time. *Faculty:* 11 full-time (6 women), 15 part-time/adjunct (13 women). *Students:* 133 full-time (109 women), 37 part-time (32 women); includes 63 minority (2 Black or African American, non-Hispanic/Latino; 2 American Indian or Alaska Native, non-Hispanic/Latino; 4 Asian, non-Hispanic/Latino; 30 Hispanic/Latino; 25 Two or more races, non-Hispanic/Latino), 9 international. Average age 30. 234 applicants, 50% accepted, 73 enrolled. In 2016, 60 master's, 7 doctorates awarded. *Degree requirements:* For master's, thesis or comprehensive exams; for doctorate, thesis/dissertation, internship. *Entrance requirements:* For master's, GRE General Test, interview, minimum GPA of 3.0; for doctorate, GRE General Test. *Application deadline:* For fall admission, 12/1 priority date for domestic and international students. Applications are processed on a rolling basis. Application fee: $50. Electronic applications accepted. *Unit head:* Dr. Richard Holigrock, Dean, 805-493-3723. *Application contact:* 805-493-3325, Fax: 805-493-3861, E-mail: clugrad@callutheran.edu.

**California Polytechnic State University, San Luis Obispo,** College of Liberal Arts, Department of Psychology and Child Development, San Luis Obispo, CA 93407. Offers psychology (MS). *Program availability:* Part-time. *Faculty:* 5 full-time (2 women), 1 (woman) part-time/adjunct. *Students:* 29 full-time (25 women), 4 part-time (3 women); includes 7 minority (1 Asian, non-Hispanic/Latino; 5 Hispanic/Latino; 1 Two or more races, non-Hispanic/Latino). Average age 26. 51 applicants, 53% accepted, 14 enrolled. In 2016, 19 master's awarded. *Degree requirements:* For master's, comprehensive exam (for some programs), thesis (for some programs). *Entrance requirements:* For master's, GRE. Additional exam requirements/recommendations for international students: Required—TOEFL (minimum score 80 iBT). *Application deadline:* For fall admission, 1/1 for domestic and international students. Application fee: $55. Electronic applications accepted. *Expenses: Tuition, state resident:* full-time $6738; part-time $3906 per year. Tuition, nonresident: full-time $15,666; part-time $8370 per year.

*Required fees:* $3603; $3141 per unit. $1047 per term. *Financial support:* Fellowships, research assistantships, career-related internships or fieldwork, Federal Work-Study, and institutionally sponsored loans available. Support available to part-time students. Financial award application deadline: 3/2; financial award applicants required to submit FAFSA. *Faculty research:* Eating disorders, mood disorders, neuropsychology, forensic psychology, group therapy. *Unit head:* Dr. Lisa Sweatt, Graduate Coordinator, 805-756-6123, E-mail: lsweatt@calpoly.edu.
Website: http://psycd.calpoly.edu/graduate/?pid-3

**California State Polytechnic University, Pomona,** Program in Psychology, Pomona, CA 91768-2557. Offers MS. *Program availability:* Part-time, evening/weekend. *Students:* 31 full-time (26 women); includes 23 minority (1 Black or African American, non-Hispanic/Latino; 4 Asian, non-Hispanic/Latino; 16 Hispanic/Latino; 2 Two or more races, non-Hispanic/Latino), 1 international. Average age 24. 16 applicants, 100% accepted, 16 enrolled. In 2016, 15 master's awarded. *Entrance requirements:* Additional exam requirements/recommendations for international students: Required—TOEFL. *Application deadline:* Applications are processed on a rolling basis. Application fee: $55. Electronic applications accepted. *Expenses:* Contact institution. *Financial support:* Application deadline: 3/2; applicants required to submit FAFSA. *Unit head:* Dr. Jeffery Mio, Director of Graduate Studies, 909-869-3899, Fax: 909-869-4930, E-mail: jsmio@cpp.edu. *Application contact:* Andrew M. Wright, Director of Admissions, 909-869-3130, Fax: 909-869-4529, E-mail: awright@cpp.edu.
Website: http://www.cpp.edu/~class/psychology-sociology/psychology/masters-program.shtml

**California State University, Chico,** Office of Graduate Studies, College of Behavioral and Social Sciences, Department of Psychology, Program in Psychological Science, Chico, CA 95929-0722. Offers MA. *Students:* 7 full-time (5 women), 9 part-time (6 women); includes 6 minority (1 Black or African American, non-Hispanic/Latino; 2 Asian, non-Hispanic/Latino; 2 Hispanic/Latino; 1 Two or more races, non-Hispanic/Latino). 17 applicants, 47% accepted, 5 enrolled. *Degree requirements:* For master's, thesis. *Entrance requirements:* For master's, GRE General Test or MAT, 3 letters of recommendation, statement of purpose. Additional exam requirements/recommendations for international students: Required—TOEFL (minimum score 550 paper-based; 80 iBT), IELTS (minimum score 6.5), PTE (minimum score 59). *Application deadline:* For fall admission, 3/1 for domestic and international students. Application fee: $55. Electronic applications accepted. *Financial support:* Research assistantships available. Financial award application deadline: 3/1; financial award applicants required to submit FAFSA. *Unit head:* Dr. Brian Oppy, Chair, 530-898-4609, Fax: 530-898-4740, E-mail: psy@csuchico.edu. *Application contact:* Judy L. Morris, Graduate Admissions Coordinator, 530-898-5416, Fax: 530-898-3342, E-mail: jlmorris@csuchico.edu.
Website: http://www.csuchico.edu/psy/graduate/psyScience.shtml

**California State University, Dominguez Hills,** College of Natural and Behavioral Sciences, Department of Psychology, Carson, CA 90747-0001. Offers clinical psychology (MA); health psychology (MA). *Program availability:* Part-time, evening/weekend. Terminal master's awarded for partial completion of doctoral program. *Degree requirements:* For master's, comprehensive exam, thesis optional. *Entrance requirements:* For master's, GRE General Test or MAT, interview, minimum GPA of 3.0, prerequisite psychology courses. Additional exam requirements/recommendations for international students: Required—TOEFL (minimum score 550 paper-based). Electronic applications accepted. *Faculty research:* Culture and health, neuropsychology and HIV, psychohistory of the Holocaust, community and adolescents, malingering.

**California State University, Fresno,** Division of Research and Graduate Studies, College of Science and Mathematics, Department of Psychology, Fresno, CA 93740-8027. Offers applied behavior analysis (MA); general/experimental psychology (MA); school psychology (Ed S). *Degree requirements:* For master's, thesis. *Entrance requirements:* For master's, GRE General Test, GRE Subject Test, minimum GPA of 3.0. Additional exam requirements/recommendations for international students: Required—TOEFL. *Application deadline:* For fall admission, 5/1 for domestic and international students; for spring admission, 10/1 for domestic and international students. Applications are processed on a rolling basis. Application fee: $55. Electronic applications accepted. *Financial support:* Teaching assistantships, career-related internships or fieldwork, Federal Work-Study, scholarships/grants, and unspecified assistantships available. Support available to part-time students. Financial award application deadline: 3/1; financial award applicants required to submit FAFSA. *Faculty research:* Oncology prediction, parenting stress, wellness, aging and memory, retrieval inhibition, anger, minority mental health. *Unit head:* Dr. Constance Jones, Chair, 559-278-2691, Fax: 559-278-7910, E-mail: conniej@csufresno.edu. *Application contact:* Dr. Marilyn Wilson, Ed S Program Coordinator, 559-278-5129, Fax: 559-278-7910, E-mail: marilynw@csufresno.edu.
Website: http://www.fresnostate.edu/csm/psych/

**California State University, Fresno,** Division of Research and Graduate Studies, Kremen School of Education and Human Development, Department of Counselor Education and Rehabilitation, Program in Clinical Rehabilitation and Mental Health Counseling, Fresno, CA 93740-8027. Offers MS. *Accreditation:* CORE. *Program availability:* Part-time, evening/weekend. *Degree requirements:* For master's, internship; project, thesis, or comprehensive exam. *Entrance requirements:* For master's, GRE General Test, MAT, minimum GPA of 3.0, official transcripts. Additional exam requirements/recommendations for international students: Required—TOEFL. *Application deadline:* For fall admission, 5/1 for domestic and international students; for spring admission, 10/1 for domestic and international students. Applications are processed on a rolling basis. Application fee: $55. Electronic applications accepted. *Financial support:* Career-related internships or fieldwork, Federal Work-Study, scholarships/grants, and research awards available. Support available to part-time students. Financial award application deadline: 3/1; financial award applicants required to submit FAFSA. *Faculty research:* Aging, career development, job retention, rehabilitation administration. *Unit head:* Dr. Steve Koobatian, Coordinator, 559-278-0316, Fax: 559-278-0045, E-mail: skoobatian@csufresno.edu.
Website: http://www.fresnostate.edu/kremen/graduate-counseling/ms-rehab-coun.html

**California State University, Fullerton,** Graduate Studies, College of Humanities and Social Sciences, Department of Psychology, Fullerton, CA 92834-9480. Offers clinical psychology (MS); psychology (MA). *Program availability:* Part-time. *Degree requirements:* For master's, thesis. *Entrance requirements:* For master's, GRE General Test, GRE Subject Test, undergraduate major in psychology or related field. Application fee: $55. *Expenses:* Tuition, state resident: full-time $3369; part-time $1953 per unit. Tuition, nonresident: full-time $3915; part-time $2499 per unit. Tuition and fees vary according to course load, degree level and program. *Financial support:* Career-related internships or fieldwork, Federal Work-Study, institutionally sponsored loans, and scholarships/grants available. Support available to part-time students. Financial award application deadline: 3/1; financial award applicants required to submit FAFSA. *Unit head:* Eriko Self, Chair, 657-278-3514, Fax: 657-278-7134. *Application contact:* Admissions/Applications, 657-278-2371.

**California State University, Long Beach,** Graduate Studies, College of Liberal Arts, Department of Psychology, Long Beach, CA 90840. Offers human factors (MS);

industrial/organizational psychology (MS); psychology (MA). *Program availability:* Part-time, evening/weekend. *Degree requirements:* For master's, comprehensive exam, thesis. *Entrance requirements:* For master's, GRE General Test, GRE Subject Test. *Application deadline:* For fall admission, 3/1 for domestic students. Applications are processed on a rolling basis. Application fee: $55. Electronic applications accepted. *Financial support:* Federal Work-Study, institutionally sponsored loans, and scholarships/grants available. Financial award application deadline: 3/2. *Faculty research:* Physiological psychology, social and personality psychology, community-clinical psychology, industrial-organizational psychology, developmental psychology. *Unit head:* David J. Whitney, Chair, 562-985-5001, Fax: 562-985-8004. *Application contact:* Dr. Mark Wiley, Associate Dean, 562-985-5381, Fax: 562-985-2463, E-mail: mwiley@csulb.edu.

**California State University, Los Angeles,** Graduate Studies, College of Natural and Social Sciences, Department of Psychology, Los Angeles, CA 90032-8530. Offers MA, MS. *Program availability:* Part-time, evening/weekend. *Degree requirements:* For master's, comprehensive exam or thesis. *Entrance requirements:* Additional exam requirements/recommendations for international students: Required—TOEFL (minimum score 500 paper-based). Electronic applications accepted. *Faculty research:* Binaural resolution of the size of an acoustic array, response and generalization of matching to sample in children.

**California State University, Northridge,** Graduate Studies, College of Social and Behavioral Sciences, Department of Psychology, Northridge, CA 91330. Offers clinical psychology (MA); general experimental psychology (MA). *Faculty:* 27 full-time (9 women), 32 part-time/adjunct (13 women). *Students:* 52 full-time (37 women), 6 part-time (4 women); includes 33 minority (2 Black or African American, non-Hispanic/Latino; 6 Asian, non-Hispanic/Latino; 24 Hispanic/Latino; 1 Two or more races, non-Hispanic/Latino), 2 international. Average age 25. 275 applicants, 23% accepted, 27 enrolled. *Degree requirements:* For master's, thesis. *Entrance requirements:* For master's, GRE General Test, GRE Subject Test, minimum GPA of 3.0, letters of recommendation. Additional exam requirements/recommendations for international students: Required—TOEFL. *Application deadline:* For fall admission, 11/30 for domestic students. Application fee: $55. *Expenses:* Tuition, state resident: full-time $4152. *Financial support:* Application deadline: 3/1. *Unit head:* Jill Razani, Chair, 818-677-3506. Website: http://www.csun.edu/csbs/departments/psychology/index.html

**California State University, Sacramento,** Office of Graduate Studies, College of Social Sciences and Interdisciplinary Studies, Department of Psychology, Sacramento, CA 95819. Offers applied behavior analysis (MA); counseling psychology (MA); industrial/organizational psychology (MA). *Program availability:* Part-time. *Students:* 13 full-time (9 women), 11 part-time (9 women); includes 6 minority (3 Asian, non-Hispanic/Latino; 3 Hispanic/Latino). Average age 27. 74 applicants, 16% accepted, 11 enrolled. In 2016, 7 master's awarded. *Degree requirements:* For master's, thesis, writing proficiency exam. *Entrance requirements:* For master's, GRE, minimum GPA of 3.0 during previous 2 years. Additional exam requirements/recommendations for international students: Required—TOEFL (minimum score 550 paper-based; 80 iBT). *Application deadline:* For fall admission, 3/1 for domestic and international students; for spring admission, 9/30 for international students. Applications are processed on a rolling basis. Application fee: $55. Electronic applications accepted. *Expenses:* $4,302 full-time tuition and fees per semester, $2,796 part-time. *Financial support:* Career-related internships or fieldwork and Federal Work-Study available. Support available to part-time students. Financial award application deadline: 2/1; financial award applicants required to submit FAFSA. *Unit head:* Dr. Rebecca Cameron, Interim Department Chair, 916-278-6254, E-mail: cameron@csus.edu. *Application contact:* Jose Martinez, Graduate Admissions Supervisor, 916-278-7871, E-mail: martinj@skymail.csus.edu. Website: http://www.csus.edu/psyc

**California State University, San Bernardino,** Graduate Studies, College of Social and Behavioral Sciences, Department of Psychology, San Bernardino, CA 92407. Offers child development (MA); clinical/counseling psychology (MS); general/experimental psychology (MA); industrial/organizational psychology (MS). *Faculty:* 21 full-time (11 women). *Students:* 59 full-time (43 women), 15 part-time (9 women); includes 47 minority (2 Black or African American, non-Hispanic/Latino; 3 Asian, non-Hispanic/Latino; 33 Hispanic/Latino; 9 Two or more races, non-Hispanic/Latino), 3 international. 217 applicants, 18% accepted, 32 enrolled. In 2016, 38 master's awarded. *Degree requirements:* For master's, comprehensive exam, thesis (for some programs). *Entrance requirements:* Additional exam requirements/recommendations for international students: Required—TOEFL. Application fee: $55. *Expenses:* Tuition, state resident: full-time $7843; part-time $5011.20 per year. Tuition and fees vary according to course load, degree level, program and reciprocity agreements. *Financial support:* Fellowships, research assistantships, and teaching assistantships available. *Faculty research:* Perceptual development, human memory, psychopharmacology, psychology of women, language acquisition. *Unit head:* Dr. Robert Ricco, Chair, 909-537-5485, Fax: 909-537-7003, E-mail: rricco@csusb.edu. *Application contact:* Dr. Francisca Beer, Dean of Graduate Studies, 909-537-5058, E-mail: fbeer@csusb.edu. Website: http://psychology.csusb.edu

**California State University, San Marcos,** College of Humanities, Arts, Behavioral and Social Sciences, Program in Psychology, San Marcos, CA 92096-0001. Offers MA. *Degree requirements:* For master's, thesis. *Entrance requirements:* For master's, GRE General Test, GRE Subject Test in psychology (recommended), 3 letters of recommendation. Additional exam requirements/recommendations for international students: Required—TOEFL (minimum score 550 paper-based). Electronic applications accepted. *Expenses:* Tuition, state resident: full-time $6738. Tuition, nonresident: full-time $13,434. *Required fees:* $1906. Tuition and fees vary according to campus/location and program. *Faculty research:* Psychopharmacology, recovery from major surgery, computer literacy in children, neuropsychology of hemispheric differences, conservation psychology.

**California State University, Stanislaus,** College of Human and Health Sciences, Program in Psychology (MA/MS), Turlock, CA 95382. Offers behavior analysis (MS); counseling psychology (MS); psychology (MA). *Program availability:* Part-time. *Degree requirements:* For master's, thesis. *Entrance requirements:* For master's, GRE, minimum GPA of 3.0, 3 letters of reference, 16 psychology prerequisites, personal statement. Additional exam requirements/recommendations for international students: Required—TOEFL (minimum score 550 paper-based). Electronic applications accepted. *Faculty research:* Hedonic tone judgment, syntax and autism, early literacy assessment and native and non-native languages.

**Cambridge College,** School of Psychology and Counseling, Cambridge, MA 02138-5304. Offers addiction counseling (M Ed); alcohol and drug counseling (Certificate); counseling psychology (M Ed, CAGS); counseling psychology: forensic counseling (M Ed); marriage and family therapy (M Ed); mental health and addiction counseling (M Ed); mental health counseling (M Ed); mental health counseling for school guidance counselors (Post Master's Certificate); psychological studies (M Ed); school adjustment and mental health counseling (M Ed); school adjustment, mental health and addiction counseling (M Ed); school guidance counselor (M Ed); trauma studies (Certificate). *Program availability:* Part-time, evening/weekend. *Degree requirements:* For master's and other advanced degree, thesis, practicum/internship. *Entrance requirements:* For master's, resume, 2 professional references; for other advanced degree, official transcripts, documents for transfer credit evaluation, resume, written personal statement/essay, 2 professional references, health insurance, immunizations form. Additional exam requirements/recommendations for international students: Required—TOEFL (minimum score 550 paper-based; 79 iBT), Michigan English Language Assessment Battery (minimum score 85); Recommended—IELTS (minimum score 6). Electronic applications accepted. *Expenses:* Contact institution. *Faculty research:* Trauma, drug and alcohol counseling, cross-cultural issues, school counseling, trauma in schools.

**Cameron University,** Office of Graduate Studies, Program in Behavioral Sciences, Lawton, OK 73505-6377. Offers MS. *Program availability:* Part-time, evening/weekend. *Degree requirements:* For master's, comprehensive exam, thesis optional. *Entrance requirements:* Additional exam requirements/recommendations for international students: Required—TOEFL (minimum score 550 paper-based). Electronic applications accepted. *Faculty research:* Student burnout, attention deficit hyperactivity disorder, group decision making, counseling outcomes, smoking cessation.

**Capella University,** Harold Abel School of Social and Behavioral Science, Doctoral Programs in Psychology, Minneapolis, MN 55402. Offers addiction psychology (PhD); clinical psychology (Psy D); educational psychology (PhD); general advanced studies in human behavior (PhD); general psychology (PhD); industrial/organizational psychology (PhD); school psychology (Psy D).

**Capella University,** Harold Abel School of Social and Behavioral Science, Master's Programs in Psychology, Minneapolis, MN 55402. Offers applied behavior analysis (MS); clinical psychology (MS); counseling psychology (MS); educational psychology (MS); evaluation, research, and measurement (MS); general advanced studies in human behavior (MS); general psychology (MS); industrial/organizational psychology (MS); leadership coaching psychology (MS); school psychology (MS); sport psychology (MS).

**Cardinal Stritch University,** College of Arts and Sciences, Department of Psychology, Milwaukee, WI 53217-3985. Offers clinical psychology (MA). *Program availability:* Part-time, evening/weekend. *Faculty:* 5. *Students:* 11 full-time (8 women), 17 part-time (12 women); includes 6 minority (2 Black or African American, non-Hispanic/Latino; 3 Hispanic/Latino; 1 Two or more races, non-Hispanic/Latino), 5 international. Average age 27. 54 applicants, 87% accepted, 11 enrolled. In 2016, 25 master's awarded. *Degree requirements:* For master's, thesis, portfolio, clinical practicum. *Entrance requirements:* For master's, interview, minimum GPA of 3.0, 3 letters of recommendation. Additional exam requirements/recommendations for international students: Required—TOEFL (minimum score 79 iBT), IELTS (minimum score 6.5). *Application deadline:* For fall admission, 7/15 priority date for domestic students; for spring admission, 12/15 priority date for domestic students. Applications are processed on a rolling basis. Electronic applications accepted. *Expenses: Tuition:* Full-time $11,890; part-time $765 per credit hour. Tuition and fees vary according to class time, course load, degree level, program and student's religious affiliation. *Financial support:* Research assistantships with partial tuition reimbursements, career-related internships or fieldwork, Federal Work-Study, and scholarships/grants available. Financial award applicants required to submit FAFSA. *Unit head:* Dr. Trevor Hyde, Chair, 414-410-4489, E-mail: tfhyde@stritch.edu. *Application contact:* Graduate Admissions, 800-347-8822 Ext. 4042, E-mail: admissions@stritch.edu.

**Carleton University,** Faculty of Graduate Studies, Faculty of Arts and Social Sciences, Department of Psychology, Ottawa, ON K1S 5B6, Canada. Offers neuroscience (M Sc); psychology (MA, PhD). *Program availability:* Part-time. *Degree requirements:* For master's, thesis; for doctorate, comprehensive exam, thesis/dissertation. *Entrance requirements:* For master's, honors degree; for doctorate, GRE, master's degree. Additional exam requirements/recommendations for international students: Required—TOEFL. *Faculty research:* Behavioral neuroscience, social and personality psychology, cognitive/perception, developmental psychology, computer user research and evaluation, forensic psychology, health psychology.

**Carlos Albizu University,** Graduate Programs, San Juan, PR 00901. Offers clinical psychology (MS, PhD, Psy D); general psychology (PhD); industrial/organizational psychology (MS, PhD); speech and language pathology (MS). *Accreditation:* APA (one or more programs are accredited). *Program availability:* Part-time, evening/weekend. Terminal master's awarded for partial completion of doctoral program. *Degree requirements:* For master's, one foreign language, comprehensive exam, thesis; for doctorate, one foreign language, comprehensive exam, thesis/dissertation, written qualifying exams. *Entrance requirements:* For master's, GRE General Test or EXADEP, interview; minimum GPA of 2.8 (industrial/organizational psychology); for doctorate, GRE General Test or EXADEP, interview; minimum GPA of 3.0 (PhD in industrial/organizational psychology and clinical psychology), 3.25 (Psy D). *Faculty research:* Psychotherapeutic techniques for Hispanics, psychology of the aged, school dropouts, stress, violence.

**Carlos Albizu University, Miami Campus,** Graduate Programs, Miami, FL 33172-2209. Offers clinical psychology (PhD, Psy D); entrepreneurship (MBA); exceptional student education (MS); human services (PhD); industrial/organizational psychology (MS); marriage and family therapy (MS); mental health counseling (MS); nonprofit management (MBA); organizational management (MBA); psychology (MS); school counseling (MS); speech and language pathology (MS); teaching English for speakers of other languages (MS). *Accreditation:* APA. *Program availability:* Part-time, evening/weekend, 100% online. *Faculty:* 28 full-time (22 women), 31 part-time/adjunct (19 women). *Students:* 475 full-time (396 women), 191 part-time (161 women); includes 560 minority (56 Black or African American, non-Hispanic/Latino; 1 American Indian or Alaska Native, non-Hispanic/Latino; 4 Asian, non-Hispanic/Latino; 494 Hispanic/Latino; 5 Two or more races, non-Hispanic/Latino), 15 international. Average age 34. 335 applicants, 46% accepted, 122 enrolled. In 2016, 143 master's, 48 doctorates awarded. Terminal master's awarded for partial completion of doctoral program. *Degree requirements:* For master's, comprehensive exam, integrative project (for MBA); research project (for exceptional student education, teaching English as a second language); for doctorate, comprehensive exam, thesis/dissertation, internship, project. *Entrance requirements:* For master's, 3 letters of recommendation, interview, minimum GPA of 3.0, resume, statement of purpose, official transcripts; for doctorate, 3 letters of recommendation, minimum GPA of 3.0, resume, interview, statement of purpose, official transcripts. Additional exam requirements/recommendations for international students: Required—Michigan Test of English Language Proficiency. *Application deadline:* For fall admission, 4/1 priority date for domestic students, 5/1 priority date for international students; for spring admission, 11/1 priority date for domestic students, 9/1 priority date for international students. Applications are processed on a rolling basis. Application fee: $50. Electronic applications accepted. *Expenses:* Contact institution. *Financial support:* In 2016–17, 131 students received support. Federal Work-Study, scholarships/grants, unspecified assistantships, and tuition discounts available. Financial award application deadline: 6/1; financial award applicants required to submit FAFSA. *Faculty research:* Psychotherapy, forensic psychology, neuropsychology, marketing strategy, entrepreneurship, special education, speech-language pathology. *Unit head:* Dr. Etiony Aldarondo, Provost, 305-593-1223 Ext. 3138, Fax: 305-592-7930, E-mail: ealdarondo@albizu.edu. *Application contact:* Sonia Feliciano, Institutional Director of

Student Recruitment, 305-593-1223 Ext. 3108, Fax: 305-477-8983, E-mail: sfeliciano@albizu.edu.

**Carnegie Mellon University,** Dietrich College of Humanities and Social Sciences, Department of Psychology, Pittsburgh, PA 15213-3891. Offers cognitive neuroscience (PhD); cognitive psychology (PhD); developmental psychology (PhD); social/personality/health psychology (PhD). *Degree requirements:* For doctorate, comprehensive exam, thesis/dissertation. *Entrance requirements:* For doctorate, GRE General Test. Additional exam requirements/recommendations for international students: Required—TOEFL. *Faculty research:* Artificial intelligence, stress and the immune system, children's learning strategies, neural basis of cognition.

**Case Western Reserve University,** School of Graduate Studies, Psychological Sciences Department, Cleveland, OH 44106. Offers clinical psychology (PhD); communication sciences (MA, PhD), including speech-language pathology; experimental psychology (PhD). *Accreditation:* APA (one or more programs are accredited). *Program availability:* Part-time. *Faculty:* 18 full-time (13 women), 6 part-time/adjunct (4 women). *Students:* 54 full-time (43 women), 1 (woman) part-time; includes 8 minority (3 Black or African American, non-Hispanic/Latino; 1 Asian, non-Hispanic/Latino; 3 Hispanic/Latino; 1 Two or more races, non-Hispanic/Latino). Average age 27. 340 applicants, 5% accepted, 16 enrolled. In 2016, 14 master's, 4 doctorates awarded. Terminal master's awarded for partial completion of doctoral program. *Degree requirements:* For master's, comprehensive exam, thesis optional; for doctorate, thesis/dissertation, internship. *Entrance requirements:* For doctorate, GRE General Test, GRE Subject Test, personal statement; curriculum vitae. Additional exam requirements/recommendations for international students: Required—TOEFL (minimum score 577 paper-based; 90 iBT); Recommended—IELTS (minimum score 7). *Application deadline:* For fall admission, 12/1 priority date for domestic students. Application fee: $50. Electronic applications accepted. *Expenses: Tuition:* Full-time $42,576; part-time $1774 per credit hour. *Required fees:* $34. Tuition and fees vary according to course load and program. *Financial support:* Fellowships, research assistantships, teaching assistantships, and tuition waivers (full and partial) available. Financial award application deadline: 12/1. *Faculty research:* Adolescent suicide, cognitive processing, repressive responses, visual perception, impact of HIV infection, neuropsychology; traumatic brain injury, phonological disorders, child language disorders, communication problems in the aged and Alzheimer's patients, cleft palate, voice disorders. *Unit head:* Dr. Lee Thompson, Professor and Chair, Department of Psychological Sciences, 216-368-6477, Fax: 216-368-4891, E-mail: cwrupsych@gmail.com. *Application contact:* Dr. Norah Feeny, Director of Clinical Training, 216-368-2695, Fax: 216-368-4891, E-mail: cwrupsych@gmail.com.
Website: http://psychsciences.case.edu/

**Castleton University,** Division of Graduate Studies, Department of Psychology, Castleton, VT 05735. Offers forensic psychology (MA). *Degree requirements:* For master's, thesis. *Entrance requirements:* For master's, GRE General Test, minimum undergraduate GPA of 3.5, previous course work in research methodology and statistics. Additional exam requirements/recommendations for international students: Required—TOEFL. *Faculty research:* Psychology and law, juvenile delinquency, criminal psychology, correctional psychology, police psychology.

**The Catholic University of America,** School of Arts and Sciences, Department of Psychology, Washington, DC 20064. Offers applied experimental psychology (PhD); clinical psychology (PhD); general psychology (MA); human development psychology (PhD); human factors (MA); MA/JD. MA/JD offered jointly with Columbus School of Law. *Accreditation:* APA (one or more programs are accredited). *Program availability:* Part-time. *Faculty:* 11 full-time (6 women), 5 part-time/adjunct (2 women). *Students:* 40 full-time (26 women), 36 part-time (29 women); includes 19 minority (3 Black or African American, non-Hispanic/Latino; 5 Asian, non-Hispanic/Latino; 4 Hispanic/Latino; 7 Two or more races, non-Hispanic/Latino), 8 international. Average age 28. 230 applicants, 27% accepted, 23 enrolled. In 2016, 15 master's, 6 doctorates awarded. *Degree requirements:* For master's, comprehensive exam, thesis (for some programs); for doctorate, comprehensive exam, thesis/dissertation. *Entrance requirements:* For master's, GRE General Test, statement of purpose, official copies of academic transcripts, three letters of recommendation; for doctorate, GRE General Test, GRE Subject Test, statement of purpose, official copies of academic transcripts, three letters of recommendation. Additional exam requirements/recommendations for international students: Required—TOEFL (minimum score 550 paper-based; 80 iBT). *Application deadline:* For fall admission, 7/15 priority date for domestic students, 7/1 for international students; for spring admission, 11/15 priority date for domestic students, 11/1 for international students. Applications are processed on a rolling basis. Application fee: $55. Electronic applications accepted. *Expenses:* $42,850 per year; $1,170 per credit; $200 per semester part-time fees. *Financial support:* Fellowships, research assistantships, teaching assistantships, Federal Work-Study, scholarships/grants, tuition waivers (full and partial), and unspecified assistantships available. Financial award application deadline: 2/1; financial award applicants required to submit FAFSA. *Faculty research:* Clinical psychology, applied cognitive science, psychopathology, cognitive neuroscience, psychotherapy. *Total annual research expenditures:* $936,581. *Unit head:* Dr. Marc M. Sebrechts, Chair, 202-319-5750, Fax: 202-319-6263, E-mail: sebrechts@cua.edu. *Application contact:* Director of Graduate Admissions, 202-319-5057, Fax: 202-319-6533, E-mail: cua-admissions@cua.edu.
Website: http://psychology.cua.edu/

**Central Connecticut State University,** School of Graduate Studies, College of Liberal Arts and Social Sciences, Department of Psychological Science, New Britain, CT 06050-4010. Offers MA. *Program availability:* Part-time, evening/weekend. *Faculty:* 12 full-time (8 women). *Students:* 20 full-time (14 women), 11 part-time (9 women); includes 9 minority (3 Black or African American, non-Hispanic/Latino; 2 Asian, non-Hispanic/Latino; 3 Hispanic/Latino; 1 Two or more races, non-Hispanic/Latino). Average age 26. 41 applicants, 51% accepted, 13 enrolled. In 2016, 12 master's awarded. *Degree requirements:* For master's, thesis or alternative. *Entrance requirements:* For master's, minimum undergraduate GPA of 2.7, letters of recommendation, personal statement. Additional exam requirements/recommendations for international students: Required—TOEFL (minimum score 550 paper-based; 79 iBT). *Application deadline:* For fall admission, 4/1 for domestic and international students; for spring admission, 11/1 for domestic and international students. Applications are processed on a rolling basis. Application fee: $50. Electronic applications accepted. *Expenses: Tuition, area resident:* Full-time $6497; part-time $606 per credit. Tuition, state resident: full-time $9748; part-time $622 per credit. Tuition, nonresident: full-time $18,102; part-time $622 per credit. *Required fees:* $4459; $246 per credit. *Financial support:* In 2016–17, 3 students received support. Career-related internships or fieldwork, Federal Work-Study, scholarships/grants, and unspecified assistantships available. Support available to part-time students. Financial award application deadline: 3/1; financial award applicants required to submit FAFSA. *Faculty research:* Clinical psychology, general psychology, child development, cognitive development, drugs/behavior. *Unit head:* Dr. Carolyn Fallahi, Chair, 860-832-3100, E-mail: fallahic@ccsu.edu. *Application contact:* Patricia Gardner, Associate Director of Graduate Studies, 860-832-2350, Fax: 860-832-2362.
Website: http://www.ccsu.edu/psychology/index.html

**Central Michigan University,** College of Graduate Studies, College of Humanities and Social and Behavioral Sciences, Department of Psychology, Mount Pleasant, MI 48859. Offers clinical psychology (PhD); experimental psychology (MS, PhD), including applied experimental psychology (PhD), experimental psychology (MS); industrial and organizational psychology (MA, PhD), including industrial and organizational psychology, occupational health psychology (PhD); neuroscience (MS, PhD); school psychology (PhD, S Psy S), including psychological services (S Psy S), school psychology (PhD). *Accreditation:* APA (one or more programs are accredited). Terminal master's awarded for partial completion of doctoral program. *Degree requirements:* For master's, thesis or alternative; for doctorate, thesis/dissertation; for S Psy S, thesis. *Entrance requirements:* For doctorate, GRE. Electronic applications accepted. *Faculty research:* Experimental psychology, clinical psychology, industrial/organizational psychology, school psychology, neuroscience.

**Central Washington University,** Graduate Studies and Research, College of the Sciences, Department of Psychology, Ellensburg, WA 98926. Offers experimental psychology (MS); mental health counseling (MS); school counseling (M Ed); school psychology (M Ed). *Program availability:* Evening/weekend. *Degree requirements:* For master's, thesis. *Entrance requirements:* For master's, GRE General Test, minimum GPA of 3.0. Additional exam requirements/recommendations for international students: Required—TOEFL (minimum score 550 paper-based; 79 iBT). Electronic applications accepted.

**Chestnut Hill College,** School of Graduate Studies, Division of Psychology, Philadelphia, PA 19118-2693. Offers clinical and counseling psychology (MS, CAS), including clinical and counseling psychology; clinical psychology (Psy D), including clinical psychology. *Program availability:* Part-time, evening/weekend. *Degree requirements:* For master's, thesis optional, practica; for doctorate, comprehensive exam, thesis/dissertation, internship, practica, clinical competency exam. *Entrance requirements:* For master's, GRE General Test, writing sample, letters of recommendation; for doctorate, GRE General Test, master's degree in counseling/clinical psychology or closely-related field, official transcripts, letters of recommendation, statement of professional goals, writing sample; for CAS, GRE General Test, official transcripts, letters of recommendation, statement of professional goals, writing sample. Additional exam requirements/recommendations for international students: Required—TOEFL (minimum score 500 paper-based), IELTS (minimum score 6.0), or TWE (minimum score 22). *Expenses:* Contact institution. *Faculty research:* Lifespan development, trauma and sexual abuse, cultural diversity, family psychology and family therapy, psychodynamic therapy.

**The Chicago School of Professional Psychology,** Program in Business Psychology, Chicago, IL 60610. Offers business psychology (PhD); industrial and organizational business psychology (Psy D); industrial and organizational psychology (MA); organizational leadership (MA, PhD). *Degree requirements:* For doctorate, thesis/dissertation optional. *Entrance requirements:* For doctorate, GRE. Additional exam requirements/recommendations for international students: Required—TOEFL.

**The Chicago School of Professional Psychology at Irvine,** Program in Psychology, Irvine, CA 92612. Offers generalist (Psy D); psychodynamic psychotherapy (Psy D).

**The Chicago School of Professional Psychology: Online,** Program in International Psychology, Chicago, IL 60654. Offers PhD.

**The Chicago School of Professional Psychology: Online,** Program in Psychology, Chicago, IL 60654. Offers child and adolescent psychology (MA); generalist (MA); gerontology (MA); international psychology (MA); organizational leadership (MA); sport and exercise psychology (MA).

**The Citadel, The Military College of South Carolina,** Citadel Graduate College, School of Humanities and Social Sciences, Department of Psychology, Charleston, SC 29409. Offers psychology (MA), including clinical counseling; school psychology (Ed S). *Program availability:* Part-time, evening/weekend. *Faculty:* 4 full-time (1 woman), 4 part-time/adjunct (3 women). *Students:* 50 full-time (41 women), 50 part-time (45 women); includes 14 minority (6 Black or African American, non-Hispanic/Latino; 5 Hispanic/Latino; 1 Native Hawaiian or other Pacific Islander, non-Hispanic/Latino; 2 Two or more races, non-Hispanic/Latino). In 2016, 20 master's, 9 other advanced degrees awarded. *Degree requirements:* For master's, comprehensive exam, practicum; internship (written and oral presentation of a case study as part of internship); for Ed S, comprehensive exam, thesis (for some programs), practicum, internship. *Entrance requirements:* For master's, GRE (minimum combined score of 297, 150 on verbal reasoning and 141 on quantitative reasoning) or MAT (minimum score of 410), minimum undergraduate GPA of 3.0; 12 credit hours in psychology or minimum score on GRE Subject Test in psychology of 600; 2 letters of recommendation; for Ed S, GRE (minimum combined score of 297, 150 on verbal reasoning and 147 on quantitative reasoning) or MAT (minimum score of 410), minimum undergraduate or graduate GPA of 3.0; 2 letters of recommendation. Additional exam requirements/recommendations for international students: Required—TOEFL (minimum score 550 paper-based; 79 iBT). *Application deadline:* Applications are processed on a rolling basis. Application fee: $40. Electronic applications accepted. *Expenses:* Tuition, state resident: full-time $5121; part-time $569 per credit hour. Tuition, nonresident: full-time $8613; part-time $957 per credit hour. *Required fees:* $90 per term. *Financial support:* Fellowships and unspecified assistantships available. Support available to part-time students. Financial award application deadline: 7/1; financial award applicants required to submit FAFSA. *Unit head:* Dr. Steve A. Nida, Department Head, 843-953-5320, E-mail: steve.nida@citadel.edu. *Application contact:* Dr. Genelle K. Sawyer, Director of the MA in Clinical Counseling Program, 843-953-5427, E-mail: genelle.sawyer@citadel.edu.
Website: http://www.citadel.edu/root/psychology-graduateprograms

**City College of the City University of New York,** Graduate School, Colin Powell School for Civic and Global Leadership, Department of Psychology, New York, NY 10031-9198. Offers clinical psychology (PhD); general psychology (MA); mental health counseling (MA). PhD program offered jointly with Graduate School and University Center of the City University of New York. *Accreditation:* APA (one or more programs are accredited). *Program availability:* Part-time. *Degree requirements:* For master's, one foreign language, comprehensive exam, thesis. *Entrance requirements:* For master's, GRE. Additional exam requirements/recommendations for international students: Required—TOEFL (minimum score 550 paper-based; 79 iBT). Electronic applications accepted. Tuition and fees vary according to course load, degree level and program. *Faculty research:* Social/personality psychology, physiological psychology, cognition and development.

**Claremont Graduate University,** Graduate Programs, School of Social Science, Policy and Evaluation, Department of Psychology, Claremont, CA 91711-6160. Offers advanced study in evaluation (Certificate); cognitive psychology (MA, PhD); developmental psychology (MA, PhD); evaluation and applied research methods (MA, PhD); health behavior research and evaluation (MA, PhD); human resource development and evaluation (MA); industrial/organizational psychology (MA, PhD); organizational behavior (MA, PhD); organizational psychology (MA, PhD); social psychology (MA, PhD); MBA/PhD. *Program availability:* Part-time. *Faculty:* 19 full-time (9 women), 1 part-time/adjunct (0 women). *Students:* 244 full-time (160 women), 66 part-time (38 women); includes 93 minority (15 Black or African American, non-Hispanic/

*Psychology—General*

Latino; 2 American Indian or Alaska Native, non-Hispanic/Latino; 29 Asian, non-Hispanic/Latino; 31 Hispanic/Latino; 2 Native Hawaiian or other Pacific Islander, non-Hispanic/Latino; 14 Two or more races, non-Hispanic/Latino; 41 international. Average age 30. In 2016, 61 master's, 23 doctorates, 5 other advanced degrees awarded. Terminal master's awarded for partial completion of doctoral program. *Entrance requirements:* For master's and doctorate, GRE General Test. Additional exam requirements/recommendations for international students: Required—TOEFL (minimum score 75 iBT). *Application deadline:* For fall admission, 1/15 priority date for domestic and international students. Applications are processed on a rolling basis. Application fee: $80. Electronic applications accepted. *Expenses: Tuition:* Full-time $44,328; part-time $1847 per unit. *Required fees:* $600; $300 per semester. Tuition and fees vary according to course load and program. *Financial support:* Fellowships, research assistantships, teaching assistantships, Federal Work-Study, institutionally sponsored loans, scholarships/grants, and tuition waivers (full and partial) available. Support available to part-time students. Financial award application deadline: 2/15; financial award applicants required to submit FAFSA. *Faculty research:* Social intervention, diversity in organizations, eyewitness memory, aging and cognition, drug policy. *Unit head:* William Crano, Chair, 909-607-3311, E-mail: william.crano@cgu.edu. *Application contact:* Paige Piontkowsky, Senior Assistant Director of Admissions, 909-607-3240, E-mail: paige.piontkowsky@cgu.edu.
Website: https://www.cgu.edu/school/sssspe/programs/?areas_of_study=psychology

**Clayton State University,** School of Graduate Studies, College of Arts and Sciences, Program in Psychology, Morrow, GA 30260-0285. Offers applied developmental psychology (MS); clinical/counseling psychology (MS). *Entrance requirements:* For master's, GRE, 2 official transcripts; 3 letters of recommendation; statement of purpose; on-campus interview; background check. Additional exam requirements/recommendations for international students: Required—TOEFL (minimum score 550 paper-based). Electronic applications accepted. *Expenses:* Tuition, state resident: full-time $3528; part-time $196 per credit hour. Tuition, nonresident: full-time $13,176; part-time $732 per credit hour. *Required fees:* $1454; $1454 per credit hour. $727 per semester. Tuition and fees vary according to campus/location and program.

**Clemson University,** Graduate School, College of Behavioral, Social and Health Sciences, Department of Psychology, Program in Human Factors Psychology, Clemson, SC 29634. Offers PhD. *Faculty:* 29 full-time (11 women), 1 (woman) part-time/adjunct. *Students:* 17 full-time (7 women); includes 1 minority (Two or more races, non-Hispanic/Latino). Average age 27. 31 applicants, 10% accepted, 3 enrolled. In 2016, 1 doctorate awarded. *Degree requirements:* For doctorate, comprehensive exam, thesis/dissertation. *Entrance requirements:* For doctorate, GRE General Test, unofficial transcripts, letters of recommendation, statement of intent. Additional exam requirements/recommendations for international students: Required—TOEFL (minimum score 80 iBT), IELTS (minimum score 6.5). *Application deadline:* For fall admission, 1/15 priority date for domestic and international students. Application fee: $80 ($90 for international students). Electronic applications accepted. *Expenses:* $5,617 per semester full-time resident, $11,194 per semester full-time non-resident, $697 per credit hour part-time resident, $1,392 per credit hour part-time non-resident. *Financial support:* In 2016–17, 14 students received support, including 1 fellowship with partial tuition reimbursement available (averaging $5,000 per year), 2 research assistantships with partial tuition reimbursements available (averaging $17,768 per year), 15 teaching assistantships with partial tuition reimbursements available (averaging $13,733 per year); career-related internships or fieldwork also available. Financial award application deadline: 1/15. *Faculty research:* Transportation safety, human factors in health care, human-computer interaction, ergonomics, vision and visual performance. *Unit head:* Dr. Patrick Raymark, Chair, 864-656-4715, Fax: 864-656-0358, E-mail: praymar@clemson.edu. *Application contact:* Dr. Robert Sinclair, Graduate Program Coordinator, 864-656-3931, E-mail: rsincla@clemson.edu.
Website: http://www.clemson.edu/cbshs/departments/psychology/graduate/hfphd.html

**Cleveland State University,** College of Graduate Studies, College of Sciences and Health Professions, Department of Psychology, Cleveland, OH 44115. Offers MA, PhD, Psy S. *Accreditation:* APA. *Faculty:* 9 full-time (3 women), 14 part-time/adjunct (5 women). *Students:* 64 full-time (46 women), 30 part-time (24 women); includes 18 minority (14 Black or African American, non-Hispanic/Latino; 4 Hispanic/Latino), 3 international. Average age 27. 167 applicants, 44% accepted, 36 enrolled. In 2016, 44 master's, 2 doctorates, 6 other advanced degrees awarded. Terminal master's awarded for partial completion of doctoral program. *Degree requirements:* For master's, comprehensive exam (for some programs), thesis (for some programs); for doctorate, comprehensive exam, thesis/dissertation; for Psy S, internship. *Entrance requirements:* For master's and doctorate, GRE General Test. Additional exam requirements/recommendations for international students: Required—TOEFL (minimum score 550 paper-based; 78 iBT). *Application deadline:* For fall admission, 2/1 priority date for domestic and international students. Application fee: $40. Electronic applications accepted. *Expenses:* Tuition, state resident: full-time $9565. Tuition, nonresident: full-time $17,980. Tuition and fees vary according to program. *Financial support:* In 2016–17, 40 students received support, including 4 research assistantships with full tuition reimbursements available (averaging $15,500 per year), 4 teaching assistantships with full tuition reimbursements available (averaging $15,500 per year); career-related internships or fieldwork, Federal Work-Study, scholarships/grants, tuition waivers (partial), and unspecified assistantships also available. Financial award application deadline: 3/1; financial award applicants required to submit FAFSA. *Faculty research:* Cognition and language, neuropsychological functioning and assessment, academic and behavioral interventions for schoolchildren, dementia care giving, emotional regulation. *Total annual research expenditures:* $68,057. *Unit head:* Dr. Kathleen M. McNamara, Chairperson, 216-687-2545, Fax: 216-687-9294, E-mail: k.mcnamara@csuohio.edu. *Application contact:* Barbara E. Durfey, Administrative Secretary, 216-687-2544, Fax: 216-687-9294, E-mail: b.durfey@csuohio.edu.
Website: http://www.csuohio.edu/sciences/dept/psychology/

**The College at Brockport, State University of New York,** School of Arts and Sciences, Department of Psychology, Brockport, NY 14420-2997. Offers MA. *Program availability:* Part-time. *Faculty:* 10 full-time (7 women), 1 (woman) part-time/adjunct. *Students:* 11 full-time (8 women), 4 part-time (2 women); includes 2 minority (both Two or more races, non-Hispanic/Latino). 27 applicants, 30% accepted, 7 enrolled. In 2016, 8 master's awarded. *Degree requirements:* For master's, thesis optional. *Entrance requirements:* For master's, GRE General Test, letters of recommendation, interview, minimum GPA of 3.0. Additional exam requirements/recommendations for international students: Required—TOEFL (minimum score 550 paper-based; 79 iBT), IELTS (minimum score 6.5). *Application deadline:* For fall admission, 4/1 priority date for domestic and international students. Application fee: $50. Electronic applications accepted. *Expenses:* Contact institution. *Financial support:* In 2016–17, 3 teaching assistantships with full tuition reimbursements (averaging $6,000 per year) were awarded; Federal Work-Study, scholarships/grants, and unspecified assistantships also available. Support available to part-time students. Financial award application deadline: 3/15; financial award applicants required to submit FAFSA. *Faculty research:* Positive psychology, decision-making and applied behavior analysis, family processes and close relationships, cognition and neuropsychology, social/personality and industrial/organizational psychology. *Unit head:* Dr. Sara Margolin, 585-395-2908, Fax: 585-395-

2116, E-mail: smargoli@brockport.edu. *Application contact:* Danielle A. Welch, Graduate Counselor, 585-295-5430, Fax: 585-395-2115, E-mail: dwelch@brockport.edu.
Website: http://www.brockport.edu/math/grad/

**College of Saint Elizabeth,** Department of Psychology, Morristown, NJ 07960-6989. Offers counseling psychology (MA); forensic psychology (MA); mental health counseling (Certificate); psychology (Psy D); student affairs in higher education (Certificate). *Program availability:* Part-time. *Degree requirements:* For master's, thesis or alternative. *Entrance requirements:* For master's, minimum GPA of 3.0, BA in psychology (preferred), 12 credits of course work in psychology; for doctorate, GRE, 3 letters of recommendation from professionals who can comment on the applicant's qualifications for doctoral study; master's degree in counseling psychology, forensic psychology and counseling, or its equivalent. Additional exam requirements/recommendations for international students: Required—TOEFL (minimum score 550 paper-based; 79 iBT), IELTS (minimum score 6.5). Electronic applications accepted. *Expenses:* Contact institution.

**College of St. Joseph,** Graduate Programs, Division of Psychology and Human Services, Rutland, VT 05701-3899. Offers alcohol and substance abuse counseling (MS); clinical mental health counseling (MS); clinical psychology (MS); community counseling (MS); school guidance counseling (MS). *Program availability:* Part-time, evening/weekend. *Degree requirements:* For master's, comprehensive exam, thesis optional. *Entrance requirements:* For master's, official college transcripts; 2 letters of reference. Additional exam requirements/recommendations for international students: Required—TOEFL (minimum score 550 paper-based). *Application deadline:* Applications are processed on a rolling basis. Application fee: $35. Electronic applications accepted. *Expenses: Tuition, area resident:* Full-time $13,800; part-time $560 per credit. *Required fees:* $75 per semester. Full-time tuition and fees vary according to course load. *Financial support:* Teaching assistantships with tuition reimbursements, career-related internships or fieldwork, Federal Work-Study, and unspecified assistantships available. Support available to part-time students. Financial award application deadline: 3/1. *Unit head:* Dr. Craig Knapp, Chair, 802-773-5900 Ext. 3219, Fax: 802-776-5258, E-mail: cknapp@csj.edu. *Application contact:* Alan Young, Dean of Admissions, 802-773-5900 Ext. 3227, Fax: 802-776-5310, E-mail: alanyoung@csj.edu.

**The College of William and Mary,** Faculty of Arts and Sciences, Department of Psychological Sciences, Williamsburg, VA 23187-8795. Offers MS. *Faculty:* 24 full-time (11 women), 5 part-time/adjunct (2 women). *Students:* 17 full-time (10 women); includes 1 minority (Asian, non-Hispanic/Latino), 3 international. Average age 26. 107 applicants, 7% accepted, 7 enrolled. In 2016, 7 master's awarded. *Degree requirements:* For master's, thesis. *Entrance requirements:* For master's, GRE, course in statistics and research methods. Additional exam requirements/recommendations for international students: Required—TOEFL, IELTS. *Application deadline:* For fall admission, 2/1 for domestic and international students. Application fee: $45. Electronic applications accepted. *Expenses:* Contact institution. *Financial support:* In 2016–17, 17 students received support, including 1 research assistantship with full tuition reimbursement available (averaging $13,500 per year), 16 teaching assistantships with full tuition reimbursements available (averaging $13,500 per year). *Faculty research:* Personality, developmental, clinical and neuroscience, social psychology. *Total annual research expenditures:* $249,023. *Unit head:* Dr. Josh Burk, Chair, 757-221-3870, E-mail: jabur2@wm.edu. *Application contact:* Lynnette Bolden, Administrator of Graduate Student Services, 757-221-3870, Fax: 757-221-3896, E-mail: lbbolden@wm.edu.
Website: http://www.wm.edu/as/psychology

**Colorado State University,** College of Natural Sciences, Department of Psychology, Fort Collins, CO 80523-1876. Offers psychology (PhD). *Accreditation:* APA. *Program availability:* Online only, 100% online. *Faculty:* 31 full-time (19 women), 2 part-time/adjunct (1 woman). *Students:* 51 full-time (36 women), 81 part-time (47 women); includes 25 minority (2 Black or African American, non-Hispanic/Latino; 1 American Indian or Alaska Native, non-Hispanic/Latino; 3 Asian, non-Hispanic/Latino; 14 Hispanic/Latino; 5 Two or more races, non-Hispanic/Latino), 2 international. Average age 29. 31 applicants, 97% accepted, 28 enrolled. In 2016, 24 master's, 16 doctorates awarded. *Degree requirements:* For master's, comprehensive exam, thesis; for doctorate, comprehensive exam, thesis/dissertation. *Entrance requirements:* For master's, GRE General Test, GRE Subject Test (for some programs; minimum scores within 50th percentile), minimum GPA of 3.2, 3 letters of recommendation, resume/curriculum vitae; for doctorate, GRE General Test; GRE Subject Test (for some programs, minimum scores within 50th percentile), minimum GPA of 3.6, 3 letters of recommendation, resume/curriculum vitae, transcripts. Additional exam requirements/recommendations for international students: Required—TOEFL (minimum score 550 paper-based; 80 iBT); Recommended—IELTS (minimum score 6.5), TSE (minimum score 58). *Application deadline:* For fall admission, 12/1 for domestic and international students. Application fee: $60 ($70 for international students). Electronic applications accepted. *Expenses:* $659-$713 per credit hour (for online programs). *Financial support:* In 2016–17, 75 students received support, including 3 research assistantships with full tuition reimbursements available (averaging $11,554 per year), 52 teaching assistantships with full tuition reimbursements available (averaging $13,420 per year); fellowships with full tuition reimbursements available, scholarships/grants, and traineeships also available. Financial award application deadline: 12/1; financial award applicants required to submit FAFSA. *Faculty research:* Occupational health psychology; developmental disabilities; memory and aging; understanding well-being and meaning of life; embodied perception and cognition. *Total annual research expenditures:* $2.8 million. *Unit head:* Dr. Don Rojas, Department Chair, E-mail: don.rojas@colostate.edu. *Application contact:* Linda Thornton, Administrative Assistant II, 970-491-5212, E-mail: linda.thornton@colostate.edu.
Website: http://www.colostate.edu/Depts/Psychology/

**Columbia University,** Graduate School of Arts and Sciences, New York, NY 10027. Offers African-American studies (MA); American studies (MA); anthropology (MA, PhD); art history and archaeology (MA, PhD); astronomy (PhD); biological sciences (PhD); biotechnology (MA); chemical physics (PhD); chemistry (PhD); classical studies (MA, PhD); classics (MA); climate and society (MA); conservation biology (MA); earth and environmental sciences (PhD); East Asia: regional studies (MA); East Asian languages and cultures (MA, PhD); ecology, evolution and environmental biology (MA), including conservation biology; ecology, evolution, and environmental biology (PhD), including ecology and evolutionary biology, evolutionary primatology; economics (MA, PhD); English and comparative literature (MA, PhD); French and Romance philology (MA, PhD); Germanic languages (MA, PhD); global French studies (MA); global thought (MA); Hispanic cultural studies (MA); history (PhD); history and literature (MA); human rights studies (MA); Islamic studies (MA); Italian (MA, PhD); Japanese pedagogy (MA); Jewish studies (MA); Latin America and the Caribbean: regional studies (MA); Latin American and Iberian cultures (PhD); mathematics (MA, PhD), including finance (MA); medieval and Renaissance studies (MA); Middle Eastern, South Asian, and African studies (MA, PhD); modern art: critical and curatorial studies (MA); modern European studies (MA); museum anthropology (MA); music (DMA, PhD); oral history (MA); philosophical foundations of physics (MA); philosophy (MA, PhD); physics (PhD);

political science (MA, PhD); psychology (PhD); quantitative methods in the social sciences (MA); religion (MA, PhD); Russia, Eurasia and East Europe: regional studies (MA); Russian translation (MA); Slavic cultures (MA); Slavic languages (MA, PhD); sociology (MA, PhD); South Asian studies (MA); statistics (MA, PhD); theatre (PhD). Dual-degree programs require admission to both Graduate School of Arts and Sciences and another Columbia school. *Program availability:* Part-time. Terminal master's awarded for partial completion of doctoral program. *Degree requirements:* For master's, variable foreign language requirement, comprehensive exam (for some programs), thesis (for some programs); for doctorate, variable foreign language requirement, comprehensive exam (for some programs), thesis/dissertation. *Entrance requirements:* For master's and doctorate, GRE General Test, GRE Subject Test (for some programs). Additional exam requirements/recommendations for international students: Required—TOEFL, IELTS. Electronic applications accepted.

**Concordia University,** School of Graduate Studies, Faculty of Arts and Science, Department of Psychology, MA Program in Psychology, Montréal, QC H3G 1M8, Canada. Offers MA. *Degree requirements:* For master's, comprehensive exam, thesis. *Entrance requirements:* For master's, GRE General Test, GRE Subject Test, honors degree in psychology or equivalent. *Faculty research:* Appetitive motivation and drug dependence, human information processing, psychology of physical activity.

**Concordia University Chicago,** College of Graduate and Innovative Programs, Program in Psychology, River Forest, IL 60305-1499. Offers MA. *Program availability:* Part-time, evening/weekend. *Degree requirements:* For master's, comprehensive exam, thesis optional. *Entrance requirements:* For master's, minimum GPA of 2.9. Additional exam requirements/recommendations for international students: Required—TOEFL (minimum score 550 paper-based). Electronic applications accepted. *Faculty research:* Lutheran high school counseling research.

**Cornell University,** Graduate School, Graduate Fields of Arts and Sciences, Field of Psychology, Ithaca, NY 14853. Offers biopsychology (PhD); human experimental psychology (PhD); personality and social psychology (PhD). *Degree requirements:* For doctorate, comprehensive exam, thesis/dissertation, 2 semesters of teaching experience. *Entrance requirements:* For doctorate, GRE General Test, 3 letters of recommendation. Additional exam requirements/recommendations for international students: Required—TOEFL (minimum score 550 paper-based; 77 iBT). Electronic applications accepted. *Faculty research:* Sensory and perceptual systems, social cognition, cognitive development, quantitative and computational modeling, behavioral neuroscience.

**Dalhousie University,** Faculty of Science, Department of Psychology, Halifax, NS B3H 4R2, Canada. Offers clinical psychology (PhD); psychology (M Sc, PhD); psychology/neuroscience (M Sc, PhD). *Degree requirements:* For master's, thesis; for doctorate, thesis/dissertation. *Entrance requirements:* For doctorate, GRE General Test. Additional exam requirements/recommendations for international students: Required—TOEFL, IELTS, CANTEST, CAEL, or Michigan English Language Assessment Battery. Electronic applications accepted. *Faculty research:* Physiological psychology, psychology of learning, learning and behavior, forensic clinical health psychology, development perception and cognition.

**Dartmouth College,** School of Graduate and Advanced Studies, Department of Psychological and Brain Sciences, Hanover, NH 03755. Offers cognitive neuroscience (PhD); psychology (PhD). *Faculty:* 24 full-time (5 women), 5 part-time/adjunct (3 women). *Students:* 43 full-time (22 women); includes 5 minority (1 American Indian or Alaska Native, non-Hispanic/Latino; 1 Asian, non-Hispanic/Latino; 3 Hispanic/Latino), 5 international. Average age 27. 92 applicants, 15% accepted, 10 enrolled. In 2016, 5 doctorates awarded. *Degree requirements:* For doctorate, thesis/dissertation. *Entrance requirements:* For doctorate, GRE General Test, GRE Subject Test. Additional exam requirements/recommendations for international students: Required—TOEFL. *Application deadline:* For fall admission, 11/30 for domestic students. Application fee: $50. Electronic applications accepted. *Faculty research:* Behavioral neuroscience, cognitive neuroscience, cognitive science, social/personality psychology. *Unit head:* Dr. David Bucci, Chair, 603-646-3439. *Application contact:* Julia Abraham, Department Administrator, 603-646-2744, E-mail: julia.s.abraham@dartmouth.edu. Website: http://www.dartmouth.edu/~psych/graduate/

**DePaul University,** College of Science and Health, Chicago, IL 60614. Offers applied mathematics (MS); applied statistics (MS); biological sciences (MA, MS); chemistry (MS); mathematics education (MA); mathematics for teaching (MS); nursing (MS); nursing practice (DNP); physics (MS); psychology (MS); pure mathematics (MS); science education (MS); MA/PhD. *Accreditation:* AACN. Electronic applications accepted.

**Drexel University,** College of Arts and Sciences, Department of Psychology, Philadelphia, PA 19104-2875. Offers clinical psychology (PhD), including clinical psychology, forensic psychology, health psychology, neuropsychology; psychology (MS); JD/PhD. *Accreditation:* APA (one or more programs are accredited). *Faculty:* 27 full-time (17 women), 8 part-time/adjunct (7 women). *Students:* 83 full-time (70 women), 8 part-time (5 women); includes 16 minority (4 Black or African American, non-Hispanic/Latino; 5 Asian, non-Hispanic/Latino; 3 Hispanic/Latino; 4 Two or more races, non-Hispanic/Latino), 4 international. Average age 27. In 2016, 21 master's, 10 doctorates awarded. *Degree requirements:* For doctorate, thesis/dissertation, internship. *Entrance requirements:* For doctorate, GRE General Test. Additional exam requirements/recommendations for international students: Required—TOEFL. *Application deadline:* For fall admission, 2/1 for domestic students. Applications are processed on a rolling basis. Application fee: $50. Electronic applications accepted. *Expenses:* Contact institution. *Financial support:* Research assistantships, teaching assistantships, career-related internships or fieldwork, Federal Work-Study, institutionally sponsored loans, tuition waivers (full and partial), unspecified assistantships, and practicum positions available. Financial award application deadline: 2/1. *Faculty research:* Neurosciences, rehabilitation psychology, cognitive science, neurological assessment. *Total annual research expenditures:* $3.9 million. *Unit head:* Dr. Kirk Heilbrun, Head, 215-895-2402, Fax: 215-895-1333. *Application contact:* Director of Graduate Admissions, 215-895-6700, Fax: 215-895-5939, E-mail: enroll@drexel.edu.

**Duke University,** Graduate School, Department of Psychology and Neuroscience, Durham, NC 27708. Offers biological psychology (PhD); clinical psychology (PhD); cognitive psychology (PhD); developmental psychology (PhD); experimental psychology (PhD); health psychology (PhD); human social development (PhD); JD/MA. *Accreditation:* APA (one or more programs are accredited). *Degree requirements:* For doctorate, thesis/dissertation. *Entrance requirements:* For doctorate, GRE General Test. Additional exam requirements/recommendations for international students: Required—TOEFL (minimum score 577 paper-based; 90 iBT) or IELTS (minimum score 7). Electronic applications accepted.

**Duquesne University,** Graduate School of Liberal Arts, Department of Psychology, Pittsburgh, PA 15282-0001. Offers clinical psychology (PhD). *Accreditation:* APA. *Faculty:* 13 full-time (7 women). *Students:* 45 full-time (29 women); includes 7 minority (2 Black or African American, non-Hispanic/Latino; 1 Asian, non-Hispanic/Latino; 4 Hispanic/Latino), 6 international. Average age 31. 94 applicants, 7% accepted, 7 enrolled. In 2016, 5 doctorates awarded. *Degree requirements:* For doctorate,

comprehensive exam, thesis/dissertation. *Entrance requirements:* For doctorate, GRE General Test, MA in psychology. Additional exam requirements/recommendations for international students: Required—TOEFL. *Application deadline:* For fall admission, 12/15 for domestic and international students. Application fee: $0. Electronic applications accepted. *Expenses: Tuition:* Full-time $22,212; part-time $1234 per credit. Tuition and fees vary according to program. *Financial support:* In 2016–17, 38 students received support, including 28 teaching assistantships with full tuition reimbursements available (averaging $17,000 per year); career-related internships or fieldwork, scholarships/grants, tuition waivers (partial), and unspecified assistantships also available. Financial award application deadline: 5/1. *Faculty research:* Emotion, language motivation, imagination, development. *Unit head:* Dr. Leswin Laubscher, Chair, 412-396-1843, E-mail: laubscherl@duq.edu. *Application contact:* Linda Rendulic, Assistant to the Dean, 412-396-6400, Fax: 412-396-5265, E-mail: rendulic@duq.edu. Website: http://www.duq.edu/academics/schools/liberal-arts/graduate-school/programs/clinical-psychology

**East Central University,** School of Graduate Studies, Department of Psychology, Ada, OK 74820. Offers MSPS. *Program availability:* Part-time, evening/weekend. *Entrance requirements:* For master's, GRE General Test, MAT. Electronic applications accepted.

**Eastern Illinois University,** Graduate School, College of Sciences, Department of Psychology, Charleston, IL 61920. Offers clinical psychology (MA); school psychology (SSP). *Program availability:* Part-time, evening/weekend. *Degree requirements:* For master's, comprehensive exam, thesis; for SSP, thesis. *Entrance requirements:* For master's and SSP, GMAT or GRE. Additional exam requirements/recommendations for international students: Required—TOEFL (minimum score 500 paper-based; 61 iBT), IELTS (minimum score 6). Electronic applications accepted.

**Eastern Kentucky University,** The Graduate School, College of Arts and Sciences, Department of Psychology, Richmond, KY 40475-3102. Offers clinical psychology (MS); industrial/organizational psychology (MS); school psychology (Psy S). *Program availability:* Part-time. *Entrance requirements:* For master's and Psy S, GRE General Test, minimum GPA of 2.5. *Faculty research:* Autism, social psychology, parenting, assessment of depression/anxiety, reading.

**Eastern Michigan University,** Graduate School, College of Arts and Sciences, Department of Psychology, Ypsilanti, MI 48197. Offers clinical behavioral psychology (MS); clinical psychology (MS); general clinical psychology (PhD); general experimental psychology (MS). *Accreditation:* APA. *Faculty:* 25 full-time (15 women). *Students:* 39 full-time (34 women), 49 part-time (38 women); includes 20 minority (3 Black or African American, non-Hispanic/Latino; 1 American Indian or Alaska Native, non-Hispanic/Latino; 5 Asian, non-Hispanic/Latino; 5 Hispanic/Latino; 6 Two or more races, non-Hispanic/Latino), 1 international. Average age 27. 273 applicants, 14% accepted, 31 enrolled. In 2016, 29 master's, 10 doctorates awarded. *Degree requirements:* For master's, 600-hour practicum; for doctorate, 1500-hour practicum; 2000-hour internship. *Entrance requirements:* For master's and doctorate, GRE. *Application deadline:* For fall admission, 2/15 for domestic students. Application fee: $45. *Financial support:* Fellowships available. *Unit head:* Dr. Carol Freedman-Doan, Department Head, 734-487-1155, Fax: 734-487-6553, E-mail: cfreedman@emich.edu.

**Eastern Washington University,** Graduate Studies, College of Social Sciences, Department of Psychology, Cheney, WA 99004-2431. Offers clinical psychology (MS); experimental psychology (MS); mental health counseling (MS), including applied psychology, mental health counseling; school counseling (MS), including applied psychology, school counseling; school psychology (Ed S). *Faculty:* 10 full-time (2 women), 3 part-time/adjunct (0 women). *Students:* 22 full-time (16 women), 2 part-time (1 woman); includes 7 minority (3 Asian, non-Hispanic/Latino; 4 Hispanic/Latino), 2 international. Average age 29. 66 applicants, 18% accepted, 12 enrolled. In 2016, 9 master's awarded. *Degree requirements:* For master's, comprehensive exam, thesis or alternative. *Entrance requirements:* For master's, GRE General Test, minimum GPA of 3.0. Additional exam requirements/recommendations for international students: Required—TOEFL (minimum score 580 paper-based; 92 iBT), IELTS (minimum score 7), PTE (minimum score 63). *Application deadline:* For fall admission, 3/1 for domestic students. Applications are processed on a rolling basis. Application fee: $75. Electronic applications accepted. *Expenses:* Tuition, state resident: full-time $11,000; part-time $5500 per credit. Tuition, nonresident: full-time $24,000; part-time $12,000 per credit. *Required fees:* $1300. One-time fee: $50 full-time. Part-time tuition and fees vary according to course load, campus/location and program. *Financial support:* In 2016–17, 6 teaching assistantships with partial tuition reimbursements (averaging $10,000 per year) were awarded; career-related internships or fieldwork, Federal Work-Study, institutionally sponsored loans, scholarships/grants, health care benefits, tuition waivers (partial), and unspecified assistantships also available. Support available to part-time students. Financial award application deadline: 2/1; financial award applicants required to submit FAFSA. *Unit head:* Dr. Nick Jackson, Chair, 509-359-4302, E-mail: njackson@ewu.edu. *Application contact:* Kathy White, Advisor/Recruiter for Graduate Studies, 509-359-6297, Fax: 509-359-6044, E-mail: gradprograms@ewu.edu.

**East Tennessee State University,** School of Graduate Studies, College of Arts and Sciences, Department of Psychology, Johnson City, TN 37614. Offers PhD. *Accreditation:* APA. Terminal master's awarded for partial completion of doctoral program. *Degree requirements:* For doctorate, thesis/dissertation, externship. *Entrance requirements:* For doctorate, GRE General Test, minimum GPA of 3.0, three letters of recommendation, interview. Additional exam requirements/recommendations for international students: Required—TOEFL (minimum score 550 paper-based; 79 iBT). Electronic applications accepted. *Faculty research:* Women's issues, prenatal stress, childhood obesity, suicide prevention, behavioral pediatrics, self-control, substance dependence, violence.

**Emory University,** Laney Graduate School, Department of Psychology, Atlanta, GA 30322-1100. Offers clinical psychology (PhD); cognition and development (PhD); neuroscience and animal behavior (PhD). *Accreditation:* APA. *Degree requirements:* For doctorate, comprehensive exam, thesis/dissertation. *Entrance requirements:* For doctorate, GRE General Test, minimum GPA of 3.25. Additional exam requirements/recommendations for international students: Required—TOEFL. Electronic applications accepted. *Faculty research:* Neuroscience and animal behavior; adult and child psychopathology, cognition development assessment.

**Emporia State University,** Program in Psychology, Emporia, KS 66801-5415. Offers general psychology (MS); industrial/organizational psychology (MS). *Program availability:* Part-time. *Faculty:* 8 full-time (4 women). *Students:* 10 full-time (7 women), 9 part-time (6 women); includes 2 minority (both Black or African American, non-Hispanic/Latino), 2 international. 16 applicants, 94% accepted, 4 enrolled. In 2016, 8 master's awarded. *Degree requirements:* For master's, comprehensive exam or thesis, internship. *Entrance requirements:* For master's, GRE General Test or MAT, essay exam, appropriate bachelor's degree, letters of recommendation. Additional exam requirements/recommendations for international students: Required—TOEFL (minimum score 520 paper-based; 68 iBT). *Application deadline:* For fall admission, 6/1 priority date for domestic students; for spring admission, 10/1 for domestic students. Applications are processed on a rolling basis. Application fee: $30 ($75 for international students). Electronic applications accepted. *Expenses:* Tuition, state resident: full-time

## Psychology—General

$5922; part-time $246.75 per credit hour. Tuition, nonresident: full-time $18,414; part-time $767.25 per credit hour. *Required fees:* $1884; $78.50 per credit hour. *Financial support:* In 2016–17, 8 research assistantships with full tuition reimbursements (averaging $7,353 per year), 4 teaching assistantships with full tuition reimbursements (averaging $7,344 per year) were awarded; career-related internships or fieldwork, Federal Work-Study, institutionally sponsored loans, health care benefits, and unspecified assistantships also available. Financial award application deadline: 3/15; financial award applicants required to submit FAFSA. *Faculty research:* Driving under the influence (DUI) personality, lifestyles and imposter phenomenon. *Unit head:* Dr. Jim Persinger, Chair, 620-341-5317, E-mail: jpersing@emporia.edu. *Application contact:* Mary Sewell, Admissions Coordinator, 800-950-GRAD, Fax: 620-341-5909, E-mail: msewell@emporia.edu.

**Evangel University,** Department of Behavioral Sciences, Springfield, MO 65802. Offers clinical mental health counseling (MS). *Program availability:* Part-time. *Faculty:* 6 full-time (5 women), 5 part-time/adjunct (all women). *Students:* 35 full-time (26 women), 10 part-time (7 women); includes 5 minority (2 Black or African American, non-Hispanic/Latino; 2 Hispanic/Latino; 1 Two or more races, non-Hispanic/Latino). Average age 33. 27 applicants, 85% accepted, 20 enrolled. In 2016, 34 master's awarded. *Degree requirements:* For master's, comprehensive exam, thesis optional. *Entrance requirements:* For master's, GRE General Test, minimum undergraduate GPA of 3.0. Additional exam requirements/recommendations for international students: Required—TOEFL (minimum score 550 paper-based). *Application deadline:* For fall admission, 7/15 priority date for domestic students, 8/1 for international students; for spring admission, 11/15 priority date for domestic students, 12/1 for international students. Applications are processed on a rolling basis. Application fee: $25. Electronic applications accepted. Application fee is waived when completed online. *Expenses: Tuition:* Part-time $400 per credit hour. *Required fees:* $148 per trimester. One-time fee: $25. Tuition and fees vary according to course load, degree level and program. *Financial support:* In 2016–17, 6 students received support. Unspecified assistantships available. Financial award application deadline: 4/1; financial award applicants required to submit FAFSA. *Unit head:* Christine Arnzen, Program Coordinator, 417-865-2815 Ext. 8618, E-mail: arnzenc@evangel.edu. *Application contact:* Matt Petry, Admissions Representative, Graduate Studies, 417-865-2815 Ext. 7416, Fax: 417-575-5484, E-mail: benitezk@evangel.edu.
Website: https://www.evangel.edu/departments/behavioral-social-sciences/about-the-department/

**Fairleigh Dickinson University, College at Florham,** Maxwell Becton College of Arts and Sciences, Department of Psychology, Madison, NJ 07940-1099. Offers clinical mental health counseling (MA); counseling (MA); industrial/organizational psychology (MA); organizational behavior (MA, Certificate), including organizational behavior (MA), organizational leadership (Certificate); MA/MBA.

**Fairleigh Dickinson University, Metropolitan Campus,** University College: Arts, Sciences, and Professional Studies, School of Psychology, Teaneck, NJ 07666-1914. Offers clinical psychology (MA, PhD); clinical psychopharmacology (MA); forensic psychology (MA); general-theoretical psychology (MA, Certificate); school psychology (MA, Psy D). *Accreditation:* APA (one or more programs are accredited).

**Fayetteville State University,** Graduate School, Program in Psychology, Fayetteville, NC 28301-4298. Offers MA. *Program availability:* Part-time, evening/weekend. *Faculty:* 13 full-time (6 women). *Students:* 23 full-time (19 women), 3 part-time (1 woman); includes 11 minority (8 Black or African American, non-Hispanic/Latino; 2 Asian, non-Hispanic/Latino; 1 Hispanic/Latino). Average age 32. 11 applicants, 100% accepted, 11 enrolled. In 2016, 6 master's awarded. *Degree requirements:* For master's, comprehensive exam, internship. *Entrance requirements:* For master's, GRE. Additional exam requirements/recommendations for international students: Required—TOEFL. *Application deadline:* For fall admission, 4/15 for domestic students. Applications are processed on a rolling basis. Application fee: $40. Electronic applications accepted. *Financial support:* Application deadline: 3/1; applicants required to submit FAFSA. *Faculty research:* Psychopathology and psychotherapy, psychological assessment, psychological disorders and behaviors, cognitive, psychophysiology, social epidemiology. *Unit head:* Dr. Timothy O. Moore, Interim Chair, 910-672-1413, Fax: 910-672-1043, E-mail: tmoore40@uncfsu.edu. *Application contact:* Dr. David Wallace, Graduate Coordinator for Experimental Track, 910-672-1419, Fax: 910-672-1043, E-mail: dwallace@uncfsu.edu.

**Fielding Graduate University,** Graduate Programs, School of Psychology, Santa Barbara, CA 93105-3814. Offers clinical psychology (PhD, Post-Doctoral Certificate, Postbaccalaureate Certificate), including clinical psychology (Postbaccalaureate Certificate), forensic psychology (PhD), health psychology (PhD), neuropsychology (PhD), parent-infant mental health (PhD), respecialization in clinical psychology (Post-Doctoral Certificate), violence prevention and control (PhD); media psychology (MA, PhD, Certificate); neuropsychology (Post-Doctoral Certificate). *Accreditation:* APA. *Program availability:* Part-time, 100% online, blended/hybrid learning. *Faculty:* 32 full-time (22 women), 44 part-time/adjunct (21 women). *Students:* 485 full-time (372 women), 82 part-time (59 women); includes 202 minority (87 Black or African American, non-Hispanic/Latino; 2 American Indian or Alaska Native, non-Hispanic/Latino; 19 Asian, non-Hispanic/Latino; 68 Hispanic/Latino; 26 Two or more races, non-Hispanic/Latino), 5 international. Average age 41. 320 applicants, 49% accepted, 106 enrolled. In 2016, 9 master's, 46 doctorates, 68 other advanced degrees awarded. Terminal master's awarded for partial completion of doctoral program. *Degree requirements:* For master's, thesis or alternative, capstone project; for doctorate, comprehensive exam, thesis/dissertation. *Entrance requirements:* For master's, BA from regionally-accredited institution or equivalent, minimum GPA of 2.5; for doctorate, BA or MA from regionally-accredited institution or equivalent, writing sample, minimum GPA of 3.0. *Application deadline:* For fall admission, 1/24 for domestic and international students; for spring admission, 11/1 for domestic and international students; for summer admission, 3/1 for domestic and international students. Application fee: $75. Electronic applications accepted. *Expenses: Tuition:* Full-time $27,180; part-time $720 per credit. Tuition and fees vary according to course load, degree level and program. *Financial support:* In 2016–17, 32 students received support, including 2 research assistantships (averaging $884 per year), 18 teaching assistantships (averaging $1,889 per year); scholarships/grants and health care benefits also available. Support available to part-time students. Financial award applicants required to submit FAFSA. *Unit head:* Dr. Gerald Porter, Provost and Senior Vice President, 805-898-2940, E-mail: gporter@fielding.edu. *Application contact:* Enrollment Coordinator, 800-340-1099 Ext. 4098, Fax: 805-687-9793, E-mail: psyadmission@fielding.edu.
Website: http://www.fielding.edu/our-programs/school-of-psychology/

**Fisk University,** Division of Graduate Studies, Department of Psychology, Nashville, TN 37208-3051. Offers clinical psychology (MA); psychology (MA). *Degree requirements:* For master's, thesis. *Entrance requirements:* For master's, GRE General Test, GRE Subject Test, minimum GPA of 3.0. Electronic applications accepted. *Faculty research:* Ethnic and gender identity, development, female adolescent development, juvenile delinquency prevention.

**Fitchburg State University,** Division of Graduate and Continuing Education, Program in Interdisciplinary Studies, Fitchburg, MA 01420-2697. Offers applied communications

(CAGS); counseling/psychology (CAGS); individualized track (CAGS); reading specialist (CAGS). *Program availability:* Part-time, evening/weekend. *Entrance requirements:* Additional exam requirements/recommendations for international students: Required—TOEFL (minimum score 550 paper-based; 79 iBT). Electronic applications accepted. *Expenses:* Tuition, state resident: full-time $2871; part-time $1914 per year. Tuition, nonresident: full-time $2871; part-time $1914 per year. *Required fees:* $3828. Tuition and fees vary according to program.

**Florida Agricultural and Mechanical University,** Division of Graduate Studies, Research, and Continuing Education, College of Social Sciences, Arts and Humanities, Department of Psychology, Tallahassee, FL 32307-3200. Offers community psychology (MS). *Degree requirements:* For master's, thesis. *Entrance requirements:* For master's, GRE General Test, minimum GPA of 3.0. Additional exam requirements/recommendations for international students: Required—TOEFL.

**Florida Atlantic University,** Charles E. Schmidt College of Science, Department of Psychology, Boca Raton, FL 33431-0991. Offers MA. *Faculty:* 20 full-time (6 women). *Students:* 43 full-time (18 women), 19 part-time (11 women); includes 21 minority (2 Black or African American, non-Hispanic/Latino; 3 Asian, non-Hispanic/Latino; 16 Hispanic/Latino), 5 international. Average age 28. 76 applicants, 30% accepted, 23 enrolled. In 2016, 8 master's awarded. Terminal master's awarded for partial completion of doctoral program. *Degree requirements:* For master's, one foreign language, thesis or alternative. *Entrance requirements:* For master's, GRE General Test, minimum GPA of 3.0 during previous 2 years. Additional exam requirements/recommendations for international students: Required—TOEFL (minimum score 500 paper-based; 61 iBT), IELTS (minimum score 6). *Application deadline:* For fall admission, 5/1 for domestic students, 5/15 for international students. Application fee: $30. Electronic applications accepted. *Expenses:* Tuition, state resident: full-time $7392; part-time $369.82 per credit hour. Tuition, nonresident: full-time $19,432; part-time $1024.81 per credit hour. *Financial support:* Research assistantships with partial tuition reimbursements, teaching assistantships with partial tuition reimbursements, Federal Work-Study, institutionally sponsored loans, scholarships/grants, and unspecified assistantships available. Financial award application deadline: 3/1; financial award applicants required to submit FAFSA. *Faculty research:* Cognition, psychobiology, developmental psychology, social psychology, neuroscience.
Website: http://psy.fau.edu/

**Florida Institute of Technology,** College of Psychology and Liberal Arts, Melbourne, FL 32901-6975. Offers MA, MS, PhD, Psy D. *Program availability:* Part-time, evening/weekend, 100% online. *Faculty:* 34 full-time (17 women), 9 part-time/adjunct (4 women). *Students:* 350 full-time (278 women), 35 part-time (29 women); includes 91 minority (14 Black or African American, non-Hispanic/Latino; 1 American Indian or Alaska Native, non-Hispanic/Latino; 15 Asian, non-Hispanic/Latino; 44 Hispanic/Latino; 17 Two or more races, non-Hispanic/Latino), 30 international. Average age 29. 735 applicants, 36% accepted, 138 enrolled. In 2016, 144 master's, 28 doctorates awarded. Terminal master's awarded for partial completion of doctoral program. *Degree requirements:* For master's, comprehensive exam (for some programs), thesis or final exam; for doctorate, comprehensive exam, thesis/dissertation optional, internship. *Entrance requirements:* For master's, GRE General Test, minimum GPA of 3.0, 2 letters of recommendation, resume, statement of objectives; for doctorate, GRE General Test, GRE Subject Test, 3 letters of recommendation, minimum GPA of 3.2, resume, statement of objectives. Additional exam requirements/recommendations for international students: Required—TOEFL (minimum score 550 paper-based; 79 iBT). *Application deadline:* For fall admission, 4/1 for international students; for spring admission, 9/30 for international students. Applications are processed on a rolling basis. Electronic applications accepted. *Expenses: Tuition:* Full-time $22,338; part-time $1241 per credit hour. *Required fees:* $250. Tuition and fees vary according to degree level, campus/location and program. *Financial support:* In 2016–17, 68 research assistantships with partial tuition reimbursements, 31 teaching assistantships with partial tuition reimbursements (averaging $8,002 per year) were awarded; fellowships, career-related internships or fieldwork, institutionally sponsored loans, tuition waivers (partial), unspecified assistantships, and tuition remissions also available. Support available to part-time students. Financial award application deadline: 3/1; financial award applicants required to submit FAFSA. *Unit head:* Dr. Mary Beth Kenkel, Dean, 321-674-8142, Fax: 321-674-7105, E-mail: mkenkel@fit.edu. *Application contact:* Cheryl A. Brown, Associate Director of Graduate Admissions, 321-674-7581, Fax: 321-723-9468, E-mail: cbrown@fit.edu.
Website: http://cpla.fit.edu

**Florida International University,** College of Arts, Sciences, and Education, Department of Psychology, Miami, FL 33199. Offers behavioral analysis (MS); clinical science (PhD); cognitive neuroscience (PhD); counseling psychology (MS); developmental science (MS, PhD); legal psychology (MS, PhD); organizational psychology (MS, PhD). Program has fall admissions only. *Accreditation:* APA. *Program availability:* Part-time, evening/weekend. *Faculty:* 44 full-time (27 women), 41 part-time/adjunct (30 women). *Students:* 150 full-time (115 women), 17 part-time (10 women); includes 89 minority (8 Black or African American, non-Hispanic/Latino; 5 Asian, non-Hispanic/Latino; 75 Hispanic/Latino; 1 Two or more races, non-Hispanic/Latino), 10 international. Average age 27. 287 applicants, 24% accepted, 57 enrolled. In 2016, 35 master's, 11 doctorates awarded. Terminal master's awarded for partial completion of doctoral program. *Degree requirements:* For master's, thesis; for doctorate, comprehensive exam, thesis/dissertation. *Entrance requirements:* For master's, GRE General Test, minimum GPA of 3.0, resume, 3 letters of recommendation; for doctorate, GRE General Test, 3 letters of recommendation, resume, letter of intent, two writing samples, minimum GPA of 3.0. Additional exam requirements/recommendations for international students: Required—TOEFL (minimum score 550 paper-based; 80 iBT). *Application deadline:* For fall admission, 12/15 for domestic and international students. Application fee: $30. Electronic applications accepted. *Expenses:* Tuition, state resident: full-time $8912; part-time $446 per credit hour. Tuition, nonresident: full-time $21,393; part-time $992 per credit hour. *Required fees:* $2185; $195 per semester. Tuition and fees vary according to program. *Financial support:* Institutionally sponsored loans and scholarships/grants available. Financial award application deadline: 3/1. *Faculty research:* Legal psychology, organizational and industrial psychology, child behavior psychology. *Unit head:* Dr. William Pelham, Chair, 305-348-3002, Fax: 305-348-3646, E-mail: wpelham@fiu.edu. *Application contact:* Nanett Rojas, Assistant Director, Graduate Admissions, 305-348-7464, Fax: 305-348-7441, E-mail: gradadm@fiu.edu.

**Florida State University,** The Graduate School, College of Arts and Sciences, Department of Psychology, Tallahassee, FL 32306-4301. Offers applied behavior analysis (MS); clinical psychology (PhD); cognitive psychology (PhD); developmental psychology (PhD); neuroscience (MS, PhD), including neuroscience (PhD); psychobiology (MS); social psychology (PhD). *Accreditation:* APA (one or more programs are accredited). *Faculty:* 45 full-time (20 women). *Students:* 154 full-time (115 women), 10 part-time (5 women); includes 32 minority (4 Black or African American, non-Hispanic/Latino; 4 Asian, non-Hispanic/Latino; 17 Hispanic/Latino; 7 Two or more races, non-Hispanic/Latino), 3 international. Average age 28. 512 applicants, 13% accepted, 44 enrolled. In 2016, 35 master's, 21 doctorates awarded. Terminal master's awarded for partial completion of doctoral program. *Degree requirements:* For master's, comprehensive exam (for some programs), thesis (for some programs); for doctorate, comprehensive exam, thesis/dissertation. *Entrance requirements:* For master's, GRE General Test, minimum GPA of 3.0; for doctorate, GRE General Test. Additional exam requirements/recommendations for international students: Required—TOEFL (minimum score 80 iBT). Application fee: $30. Electronic applications accepted. *Expenses:* Tuition, state resident: full-time $7263; part-time $403.51 per credit hour. Tuition, nonresident: full-time $18,087; part-time $1004.85 per credit hour. *Required fees:* $1365; $75.81 per credit hour. $20 per semester. Tuition and fees vary according to campus/location. *Financial support:* In 2016–17, 150 students received support, including 15 fellowships with full tuition reimbursements available (averaging $22,815 per year), 41 research assistantships with full tuition reimbursements available (averaging $23,815 per year), 94 teaching assistantships with full tuition reimbursements available (averaging $18,315 per year); career-related internships or fieldwork and health care benefits also available. Financial award applicants required to submit FAFSA. *Total annual research expenditures:* $13.1 million. *Unit head:* Dr. Jeanette Taylor, Chairman, 850-644-2040, Fax: 850-644-7739, E-mail: taylor@psy.fsu.edu. *Application contact:* Lynda L. Gibson, Graduate Program Associate, 850-644-2499, Fax: 850-644-7739, E-mail: grad-info@psy.fsu.edu. Website: http://www.psy.fsu.edu/

**Fordham University,** Graduate School of Arts and Sciences, Department of Psychology, New York, NY 10458. Offers applied developmental psychology (PhD); applied psychological methods (MS); clinical psychology (PhD); psychometrics (PhD). *Faculty:* 25 full-time (8 women), 3 part-time/adjunct (2 women). *Students:* 94 full-time (70 women), 21 part-time (14 women); includes 23 minority (9 Black or African American, non-Hispanic/Latino; 1 American Indian or Alaska Native, non-Hispanic/Latino; 13 Asian, non-Hispanic/Latino), 15 international. Average age 31. 981 applicants, 6% accepted, 24 enrolled. In 2016, 15 master's, 15 doctorates awarded. Terminal master's awarded for partial completion of doctoral program. *Degree requirements:* For master's, comprehensive exam; for doctorate, comprehensive exam, thesis/dissertation. *Entrance requirements:* For doctorate, GRE General Test, GRE Subject Test. Additional exam requirements/recommendations for international students: Required—TOEFL (minimum score 600 paper-based). *Application deadline:* For fall admission, 12/14 for domestic students. Application fee: $70. Electronic applications accepted. *Financial support:* In 2016–17, 73 students received support, including 16 fellowships with tuition reimbursements available (averaging $24,561 per year), 12 research assistantships with tuition reimbursements available (averaging $15,170 per year), 11 teaching assistantships with tuition reimbursements available (averaging $12,286 per year); career-related internships or fieldwork, institutionally sponsored loans, tuition waivers (full and partial), and unspecified assistantships also available. Financial award application deadline: 12/14; financial award applicants required to submit FAFSA. *Total annual research expenditures:* $2.8 million. *Unit head:* Dr. Barry Rosenfeld, Chair, 718-817-3794, Fax: 718-817-3699, E-mail: rosenfeld@fordham.edu. *Application contact:* Bernadette Valentino-Morrison, Director of Graduate Admissions, 718-817-4419, Fax: 718-817-3566, E-mail: valentinomor@fordham.edu.

**Fort Hays State University,** Graduate School, College of Arts and Sciences, Department of Psychology, Hays, KS 67601-4099. Offers psychology (MS); school psychology (Ed S). *Degree requirements:* For master's and Ed S, comprehensive exam, thesis. *Entrance requirements:* For master's, GRE General Test. Additional exam requirements/recommendations for international students: Required—TOEFL (minimum score 550 paper-based). Electronic applications accepted. *Faculty research:* Memory, learning, motivation, clinical and experimental psychology, history and systems of psychological stressors in rural environments.

**Framingham State University,** Continuing Education, Program in Counseling Psychology, Framingham, MA 01701-9101. Offers MA. *Program availability:* Part-time, evening/weekend.

**Francis Marion University,** Graduate Programs, Department of Psychology, Florence, SC 29502-0547. Offers applied psychology (MS), including clinical/counseling psychology, school psychology; school psychology (SSP). *Program availability:* Part-time, evening/weekend. *Degree requirements:* For master's, internship. *Entrance requirements:* For master's, GRE General Test, official transcripts, two letters of recommendation. Additional exam requirements/recommendations for international students: Required—TOEFL (minimum score 550 paper-based; 79 iBT). *Expenses:* Tuition, state resident: full-time $10,100; part-time $505 per credit hour. Tuition, nonresident: full-time $20,196; part-time $1009.80 per credit hour. *Required fees:* $14.80 per credit hour. $73 per semester. Tuition and fees vary according to course load and program. *Faculty research:* Parenting and family relationships, child development, applied behavioral analysis, post-traumatic stress disorder, clinical psychology in adults.

**Frostburg State University,** Graduate School, College of Liberal Arts and Sciences, Department of Psychology, Frostburg, MD 21532-1099. Offers counseling psychology (MS). *Program availability:* Part-time, evening/weekend. *Degree requirements:* For master's, internship. *Entrance requirements:* For master's, GRE General Test or MAT, interview, minimum GPA of 3.0, resume. Additional exam requirements/recommendations for international students: Required—TOEFL. Electronic applications accepted.

**Gardner-Webb University,** Graduate School, School of Psychology, Boiling Springs, NC 28017. Offers mental health counseling (MA); school counseling (MA). *Program availability:* Part-time, evening/weekend. *Faculty:* 5 full-time (4 women), 4 part-time/adjunct (2 women). *Students:* 11 full-time (all women), 60 part-time (57 women); includes 16 minority (13 Black or African American, non-Hispanic/Latino; 3 Hispanic/Latino). Average age 29. 116 applicants, 31% accepted, 36 enrolled. In 2016, 401 master's awarded. *Degree requirements:* For master's, comprehensive exam. *Entrance requirements:* For master's, GRE General Test, MAT, minimum GPA of 2.7. *Application deadline:* For fall admission, 7/1 priority date for domestic students. Applications are processed on a rolling basis. Electronic applications accepted. *Expenses:* Contact institution. *Financial support:* Unspecified assistantships available. *Unit head:* Dr. David Carscaddon, Chair, 704-406-4437, Fax: 704-406-4329, E-mail: dcarscaddon@gardner-webb.edu. *Application contact:* Office of Graduate Admissions, 877-498-4723, Fax: 704-406-3895, E-mail: gradinfo@gardner-webb.edu.

**Geneva College,** Master of Arts in Counseling Program, Beaver Falls, PA 15010-3599. Offers clinical mental health counseling (MA); marriage and family counseling (MA); school counseling (MA). *Accreditation:* ACA. *Program availability:* Part-time, evening/weekend. *Faculty:* 6 full-time (3 women), 3 part-time/adjunct (2 women). *Students:* 35 full-time (28 women), 32 part-time (23 women); includes 11 minority (9 Black or African American, non-Hispanic/Latino; 2 Hispanic/Latino). Average age 34. 42 applicants, 71% accepted, 21 enrolled. In 2016, 24 master's awarded. *Degree requirements:* For master's, comprehensive exam, 50-60 credits (depending on program), practicum, internship. *Entrance requirements:* For master's, minimum GPA of 3.0 (preferred), 3 letters of recommendation, essay on career goals, resume of educational and professional experiences. Additional exam requirements/recommendations for international students: Required—TOEFL. *Application deadline:* For fall admission, 9/1 for domestic students; for spring admission, 1/10 for domestic students. Applications are processed on a rolling basis. Electronic applications accepted. *Expenses:* $670 per credit. *Financial support:* In 2016–17, 3 students received support. Research assistantships, teaching assistantships, career-related internships or fieldwork, and unspecified assistantships available. Financial award application deadline: 8/1; financial award applicants required to submit FAFSA. *Faculty research:* Blended family counseling; premarital and newlywed couples; religion in clinical supervision; conceptual mapping in research, supervision, and clinical work. *Unit head:* Dr. Shannan Shiderly, Program Director, 724-847-6649, Fax: 724-847-6101, E-mail: slshider@geneva.edu. *Application contact:* Marina Frazier, Graduate Program Manager, 724-847-6697, E-mail: counseling@geneva.edu.
Website: http://www.geneva.edu/page/grad_counseling

**George Mason University,** College of Humanities and Social Sciences, Department of Psychology, Fairfax, VA 22030. Offers applied developmental psychology (Certificate); cognitive and behavioral neuroscience (MA); industrial/organizational psychology (PhD). *Accreditation:* APA. *Faculty:* 42 full-time (20 women), 13 part-time/adjunct (11 women). *Students:* 160 full-time (105 women), 57 part-time (30 women); includes 36 minority (9 Black or African American, non-Hispanic/Latino; 8 Asian, non-Hispanic/Latino; 12 Hispanic/Latino; 1 Native Hawaiian or other Pacific Islander, non-Hispanic/Latino; 6 Two or more races, non-Hispanic/Latino), 14 international. Average age 26. 742 applicants, 15% accepted, 57 enrolled. In 2016, 59 master's, 21 doctorates, 7 other advanced degrees awarded. *Degree requirements:* For master's, comprehensive exam, thesis (for biopsychology); for doctorate, comprehensive exam, thesis/dissertation, 2nd-year project. *Entrance requirements:* For master's, GRE, 2 official transcripts; goals statement; 15 undergraduate credits in concentration for which the applicant is applying; for doctorate, GRE, 3 letters of recommendation; resume; goals statement; minimum GPA of 3.0 overall for last 60 undergraduate credits, 3.25 in psychology courses; 15 undergraduate credits in concentration for which the applicant is applying; 2 official transcripts; for Certificate, GRE, 2 official transcripts; expanded goals statement; 3 letters of recommendation. Additional exam requirements/recommendations for international students: Required—TOEFL (minimum score 575 paper-based; 88 iBT), IELTS (minimum score 6.5), PTE (minimum score 59). Application fee: $75 ($80 for international students). Electronic applications accepted. *Expenses:* Tuition, state resident: full-time $10,628; part-time $443 per credit. Tuition, nonresident: full-time $29,306; part-time $1221 per credit. *Required fees:* $3096; $129 per credit. Tuition and fees vary according to program. *Financial support:* In 2016–17, 116 students received support, including 7 fellowships (averaging $11,348 per year), 42 research assistantships with tuition reimbursements available (averaging $14,292 per year), 88 teaching assistantships with tuition reimbursements available (averaging $13,815 per year); career-related internships or fieldwork, Federal Work-Study, scholarships/grants, tuition waivers (partial), unspecified assistantships, and health care benefits (for full-time research or teaching assistantship recipients) also available. Support available to part-time students. Financial award application deadline: 3/1; financial award applicants required to submit FAFSA. *Faculty research:* Applied developmental psychology, biopsychology, clinical psychology, human factors/applied cognition psychology, industrial/organizational psychology, school psychology. *Total annual research expenditures:* $5.6 million. *Unit head:* Reeshad Dalal, Department Chair, 703-993-9487, Fax: 703-993-1359, E-mail: rdalal@gmu.edu. *Application contact:* Michael Hock, Graduate Program Coordinator, 703-993-1548, Fax: 703-993-1359, E-mail: mhock2@gmu.edu.
Website: http://psychology.gmu.edu

**Georgetown University,** Graduate School of Arts and Sciences, Department of Psychology, Washington, DC 20057. Offers PhD, JD/MPP. *Degree requirements:* For doctorate, thesis/dissertation. *Entrance requirements:* For doctorate, GRE General Test, GRE Subject Test. Additional exam requirements/recommendations for international students: Required—TOEFL.

**The George Washington University,** Columbian College of Arts and Sciences, Department of Psychology, Washington, DC 20052. Offers applied social psychology (PhD); clinical psychology (PhD); cognitive neuroscience (PhD). *Accreditation:* APA. *Program availability:* Part-time, evening/weekend. *Faculty:* 25 full-time (14 women). *Students:* 39 full-time (28 women), 30 part-time (21 women); includes 21 minority (9 Black or African American, non-Hispanic/Latino; 4 Asian, non-Hispanic/Latino; 6 Hispanic/Latino; 2 Two or more races, non-Hispanic/Latino), 7 international. Average age 28. 442 applicants, 5% accepted, 12 enrolled. In 2016, 12 doctorates awarded. *Degree requirements:* For doctorate, thesis/dissertation or alternative, general exam. *Entrance requirements:* For doctorate, GRE General Test, minimum GPA of 3.0. Additional exam requirements/recommendations for international students: Required—TOEFL (minimum score 550 paper-based; 80 iBT). *Application deadline:* For fall admission, 1/15 for domestic and international students. Application fee: $75. *Financial support:* In 2016–17, 62 students received support. Fellowships with tuition reimbursements available, teaching assistantships with tuition reimbursements available, career-related internships or fieldwork, Federal Work-Study, and tuition waivers available. *Unit head:* Dr. Paul Poppen, Chair, 202-994-6324, E-mail: pjp@gwu.edu. *Application contact:* Information Contact, 202-994-6320, Fax: 202-994-1602, E-mail: psydept@gwu.edu.
Website: http://psychology.columbian.gwu.edu/

**The George Washington University,** Columbian College of Arts and Sciences, Program in Professional Psychology, Washington, DC 20052. Offers MA, Psy D, Graduate Certificate. *Accreditation:* APA. *Faculty:* 10 full-time (3 women). *Students:* 141 full-time (118 women), 100 part-time (71 women); includes 58 minority (17 Black or African American, non-Hispanic/Latino; 7 Asian, non-Hispanic/Latino; 28 Hispanic/Latino; 6 Two or more races, non-Hispanic/Latino), 16 international. Average age 28. 325 applicants, 46% accepted, 85 enrolled. In 2016, 82 master's, 25 doctorates, 11 other advanced degrees awarded. *Entrance requirements:* For doctorate, GRE General Test, interview, minimum GPA of 3.0. Additional exam requirements/recommendations for international students: Required—TOEFL (minimum score 550 paper-based; 80 iBT). *Application deadline:* For fall admission, 12/1 priority date for domestic students. Applications are processed on a rolling basis. Application fee: $75. Electronic applications accepted. *Financial support:* Fellowships with partial tuition reimbursements available. *Unit head:* Dr. Loring Ingraham, Director, 202-496-4712, Fax: 202-496-6263, E-mail: ingraham@gwu.edu. *Application contact:* 202-496-6210, Fax: 202-994-6213, E-mail: askccas@gwu.edu.
Website: http://psyd.columbian.gwu.edu/

**Georgia Institute of Technology,** Graduate Studies, College of Sciences, School of Psychology, Atlanta, GA 30332-0001. Offers MS, PhD. *Program availability:* Part-time. Terminal master's awarded for partial completion of doctoral program. *Degree requirements:* For master's, thesis; for doctorate, thesis/dissertation. *Entrance requirements:* For master's and doctorate, GRE General Test, GRE Subject Test. Additional exam requirements/recommendations for international students: Required—TOEFL (minimum score 550 paper-based; 79 iBT). Electronic applications accepted. *Faculty research:* Experimental, industrial-organizational, and engineering psychology; cognitive aging and processes; leadership; human factors.

**Georgia Southern University,** Jack N. Averitt College of Graduate Studies, College of Liberal Arts and Social Sciences, Program in Psychology, Statesboro, GA 30460. Offers clinical psychology (Psy D); psychology (MS). *Students:* 53 full-time (35 women), 15

*Psychology—General*

part-time (10 women); includes 14 minority (3 Black or African American, non-Hispanic/Latino; 3 Asian, non-Hispanic/Latino; 5 Hispanic/Latino; 3 Two or more races, non-Hispanic/Latino), 1 international. Average age 27. 118 applicants, 27% accepted, 18 enrolled. In 2016, 11 master's, 3 doctorates awarded. Terminal master's awarded for partial completion of doctoral program. *Degree requirements:* For master's, comprehensive exam, thesis (for some programs), terminal exam; for doctorate, comprehensive exam, thesis/dissertation, clinical qualifying exam, practicum, internship. *Entrance requirements:* For master's, GRE General Test, minimum GPA of 3.0, introductory courses in psychology and statistics, letters of recommendation; for doctorate, GRE General Test; GRE Subject Test (if no undergraduate degree in psychology), minimum undergraduate GPA of 3.25; 3 letters of reference; statement of purpose. Additional exam requirements/recommendations for international students: Required—TOEFL (minimum score 550 paper-based; 80 iBT), IELTS (minimum score 6). *Application deadline:* For fall admission, 1/15 priority date for domestic students, 1/15 for international students. Application fee: $50. Electronic applications accepted. *Expenses:* Tuition, state resident: full-time $7236; part-time $277 per semester hour. Tuition, nonresident: full-time $27,118; part-time $1105 per semester hour. *Required fees:* $2092. *Financial support:* In 2016–17, 39 students received support, including 4 fellowships with full tuition reimbursements available (averaging $7,750 per year), 6 research assistantships with full tuition reimbursements available (averaging $7,750 per year), 17 teaching assistantships with full tuition reimbursements available (averaging $7,750 per year); career-related internships or fieldwork, Federal Work-Study, scholarships/grants, tuition waivers (full), and unspecified assistantships also available. Support available to part-time students. Financial award application deadline: 4/15; financial award applicants required to submit FAFSA. *Faculty research:* Clinical psychology, cognitive psychology, social psychology, developmental psychology, teaching and psychology, social judgment and behavior, psychology of religion. *Unit head:* Dr. Michael Nielsen, Graduate Director, 912-478-5539, Fax: 912-478-0751, E-mail: mnielsen@georgiasouthern.edu. Website: http://class.georgiasouthern.edu/psychology/

**Georgia State University,** College of Arts and Sciences, Department of Psychology, Atlanta, GA 30302-3083. Offers clinical (PhD); cognitive sciences (PhD); community (PhD); developmental (PhD); neuropsychology and behavioral neuroscience (PhD). *Accreditation:* APA. *Faculty:* 40 full-time (80 women), 2 part-time (both women); includes 25 minority (8 Black or African American, non-Hispanic/Latino; 9 Asian, non-Hispanic/Latino; 3 Hispanic/Latino; 5 Two or more races, non-Hispanic/Latino), 7 international. Average age 28. 517 applicants, 6% accepted, 17 enrolled. In 2016, 19 doctorates awarded. *Degree requirements:* For doctorate, comprehensive exam, thesis/dissertation, residency year (for clinical only). *Entrance requirements:* For doctorate, GRE. Additional exam requirements/recommendations for international students: Required—TOEFL (minimum score 550 paper-based; 80 iBT). *Application deadline:* For fall admission, 12/1 for domestic and international students. Application fee: $50. Electronic applications accepted. *Expenses:* Tuition, state resident: full-time $6876; part-time $382 per credit hour. Tuition, nonresident: full-time $22,374; part-time $1243 per credit hour. *Required fees:* $2128; $1064 per term. Part-time tuition and fees vary according to course load and program. *Financial support:* In 2016–17, fellowships with full tuition reimbursements (averaging $19,282 per year), research assistantships with full tuition reimbursements (averaging $5,173 per year), teaching assistantships with full tuition reimbursements (averaging $6,389 per year) were awarded; scholarships/grants, traineeships, health care benefits, and unspecified assistantships also available. Financial award applicants required to submit FAFSA. *Faculty research:* Clinical psychology, developmental psychology, community psychology, neuropsychology and behavioral neuroscience, cognitive sciences. *Unit head:* Dr. Lisa Armistead, Chair, 404-413-6205, Fax: 404-413-6207, E-mail: lparmistead@gsu.edu. *Application contact:* Dr. Lindsey Cohen, Director of Graduate Studies, 404-413-6263, Fax: 404-413-6207, E-mail: llcohen@gsu.edu.

**Goddard College,** Graduate Division, Master of Arts in Psychology Program, Plainfield, VT 05667-9432. Offers expressive arts therapy (MA); psychology (MA); sexual orientation (MA). *Program availability:* Part-time, online learning. *Degree requirements:* For master's, thesis or alternative, clinical internship. *Entrance requirements:* For master's, eight specific undergraduate prerequisite courses taken within previous five years (or preparatory semester at Goddard), statement of purpose, 3 letters of recommendation, interview. Electronic applications accepted.

**Golden Gate University,** Ageno School of Business, San Francisco, CA 94105-2968. Offers accounting (MBA); business administration (EMBA, MBA, PMBA, DBA); business analytics (MS); finance (MBA, MS, Certificate); financial planning (MS, Certificate); healthcare information systems (Certificate); human resource management (MBA, MS); human resources management (Certificate); information systems (MS); information technology (MBA); information technology management (Certificate); integrated marketing and communications (MS, Certificate); international business (MBA); management (MBA); marketing (MBA, MS, Certificate); operations supply chain management (Certificate); psychology (MA, Certificate); public administration (EMPA); public relations (MS, Certificate); technical market analysis (Certificate); JD/MBA. *Program availability:* Part-time, evening/weekend. *Faculty:* 18 full-time (3 women), 117 part-time/adjunct (44 women). *Students:* 458 full-time (254 women), 664 part-time (331 women); includes 346 minority (75 Black or African American, non-Hispanic/Latino; 2 American Indian or Alaska Native, non-Hispanic/Latino; 132 Asian, non-Hispanic/Latino; 105 Hispanic/Latino; 9 Native Hawaiian or other Pacific Islander, non-Hispanic/Latino; 23 Two or more races, non-Hispanic/Latino), 354 international. Average age 34. 905 applicants, 83% accepted, 165 enrolled. In 2016, 350 master's, 2 doctorates awarded. *Degree requirements:* For doctorate, thesis/dissertation, qualifying examination. *Entrance requirements:* For master's, GMAT (for MBA), minimum GPA of 2.5 (MS). Additional exam requirements/recommendations for international students: Required—TOEFL (minimum score 550 paper-based; 79 iBT). *Application deadline:* For fall admission, 5/15 for domestic and international students; for winter admission, 1/15 for domestic and international students; for spring admission, 9/15 for domestic and international students. Applications are processed on a rolling basis. Application fee: $70 ($110 for international students). Electronic applications accepted. *Expenses:* Contact institution. *Financial support:* In 2016–17, 372 students received support. Career-related internships or fieldwork, Federal Work-Study, institutionally sponsored loans, and scholarships/grants available. Support available to part-time students. Financial award applicants required to submit FAFSA. *Unit head:* Dr. Gordon Swartz, Dean, 415-442-7027, Fax: 415-442-6579, E-mail: gswartz@ggu.edu. *Application contact:* Angela Melero, Enrollment Services, 415-442-7800, Fax: 415-442-7807, E-mail: info@ggu.edu. Website: http://www.ggu.edu/programs/business-and-management

**Governors State University,** College of Education, Program in Psychology, University Park, IL 60484. Offers MA. *Program availability:* Part-time. *Faculty:* 47 full-time (31 women), 49 part-time/adjunct (39 women). *Students:* 22 full-time (21 women), 50 part-time (43 women); includes 30 minority (20 Black or African American, non-Hispanic/Latino; 7 Hispanic/Latino; 3 Two or more races, non-Hispanic/Latino), 3 international. Average age 34. 65 applicants, 40% accepted, 26 enrolled. In 2016, 15 master's awarded. *Entrance requirements:* Additional exam requirements/recommendations for international students: Required—TOEFL (minimum score 550 paper-based; 80 iBT).

IELTS. *Application deadline:* For fall admission, 4/1 for domestic students. Application fee: $50. Electronic applications accepted. *Expenses:* $307 per credit hour; $38 per term or $76 per credit hour fees; $367 per credit hour tuition (for school psychology doctoral). *Financial support:* Application deadline: 5/1; applicants required to submit FAFSA. *Unit head:* Shannon Dermer, Chair, Division of Psychology and Counseling, 708-534-3142, E-mail: sdermer@govst.edu. *Application contact:* Yakeea Daniels, Assistant Vice President for Enrollment Services/Director of Admission, 708-534-4510, E-mail: ydaniels@govst.edu.

**The Graduate Center, City University of New York,** Graduate Studies, Program in Psychology, New York, NY 10016-4039. Offers basic applied neurocognition (PhD); biopsychology (PhD); clinical psychology (PhD); developmental psychology (PhD); environmental psychology (PhD); experimental psychology (PhD); industrial psychology (PhD); learning processes (PhD); neuropsychology (PhD); psychology (PhD); social personality (PhD). *Degree requirements:* For doctorate, one foreign language, thesis/dissertation. *Entrance requirements:* For doctorate, GRE General Test. Additional exam requirements/recommendations for international students: Required—TOEFL. Electronic applications accepted.

**Grand Canyon University,** College of Doctoral Studies, Phoenix, AZ 85017-1097. Offers data analytics (DBA); general psychology (PhD), including cognition and instruction, industrial and organizational psychology, integrating technology, learning, and psychology, performance psychology; management (DBA); marketing (DBA); organizational leadership (Ed D), including behavioral health, Christian ministry, health care administration, organizational development. *Degree requirements:* For doctorate, comprehensive exam, thesis/dissertation. *Entrance requirements:* For doctorate, minimum GPA of 3.4 on earned advanced degree from regionally-accredited institution; transcripts; goals statement. Application fee: $0. *Unit head:* Michael Berger, Dean, 602-639-7255. *Application contact:* Michael Berger, Dean, 602-639-7255. Website: https://www.gcu.edu/college-of-doctoral-studies.php

**Hardin-Simmons University,** Graduate School, Cynthia Ann Parker College of Liberal Arts, Department of Psychology, Abilene, TX 79698-0001. Offers clinical counseling and marriage and family therapy (MA). *Program availability:* Part-time. *Faculty:* 6 full-time (3 women). *Students:* 14 full-time (all women), 2 part-time (both women); includes 5 minority (all Hispanic/Latino). Average age 29. In 2016, 13 master's awarded. *Degree requirements:* For master's, comprehensive exam, clinical experience, project. *Entrance requirements:* For master's, 21 semester hours of course work in psychology (18 in upper-division classes); minimum undergraduate GPA of 3.0 in major, 2.7 overall; writing sample; letters of recommendation. Additional exam requirements/recommendations for international students: Required—TOEFL (minimum score 550 paper-based; 75 iBT). *Application deadline:* For fall admission, 8/15 priority date for domestic students, 4/1 for international students; for spring admission, 1/5 priority date for domestic students, 9/1 for international students. Applications are processed on a rolling basis. Application fee: $50. Electronic applications accepted. *Expenses:* Tuition: Full-time $12,510; part-time $695 per credit hour. *Required fees:* $325; $110 per semester. *Financial support:* In 2016–17, 14 students received support, including 8 fellowships (averaging $1,750 per year); career-related internships or fieldwork and scholarships/grants also available. Support available to part-time students. Financial award application deadline: 6/30; financial award applicants required to submit FAFSA. *Faculty research:* Spirituality in marriage, intimacy and sexuality in marriage, sex education in the church, role of faith in marital satisfaction, family stress management. *Unit head:* Dr. Lori Copeland, Department Head, 325-670-1295, Fax: 325-670-1458, E-mail: lcope@hsutx.edu. *Application contact:* Dr. Nancy Kucinski, Dean of Graduate Studies, 325-670-1298, Fax: 325-670-1564, E-mail: gradoff@hsutx.edu. Website: http://www.hsutx.edu/academics/cap/psychology/

**Harvard University,** Graduate School of Arts and Sciences, Department of Psychology, Cambridge, MA 02138. Offers psychology (PhD), including behavior and decision analysis, cognition, developmental psychology, experimental psychology, personality, psychobiology, psychopathology; social psychology (PhD). *Accreditation:* APA. *Degree requirements:* For doctorate, thesis/dissertation, general exams. *Entrance requirements:* For doctorate, GRE General Test. Additional exam requirements/recommendations for international students: Required—TOEFL.

**Hofstra University,** College of Liberal Arts and Sciences, Programs in Psychology, Hempstead, NY 11549. Offers applied organizational psychology (PhD); clinical psychology (PhD); industrial/organizational psychology (MA); school-community psychology (Psy D). *Accreditation:* APA. *Program availability:* Part-time, evening/weekend. *Students:* 195 full-time (130 women), 32 part-time (18 women); includes 43 minority (9 Black or African American, non-Hispanic/Latino; 2 American Indian or Alaska Native, non-Hispanic/Latino; 8 Asian, non-Hispanic/Latino; 21 Hispanic/Latino; 2 Native Hawaiian or other Pacific Islander, non-Hispanic/Latino; 1 Two or more races, non-Hispanic/Latino), 21 international. Average age 27. 299 applicants, 40% accepted, 54 enrolled. In 2016, 51 master's, 36 doctorates awarded. *Degree requirements:* For master's, comprehensive exam, thesis optional, internship, minimum GPA of 3.0; for doctorate, comprehensive exam, thesis/dissertation, 1st year qualifying examination, 2nd year research project, successful practicum/externship placements, written presentation and successful oral defense of dissertation, completion of full-time internship. *Entrance requirements:* For master's, GRE General Test, minimum GPA of 3.0, essay, interview; for doctorate, GRE General Test, GRE Subject Test (psychology), 3 letters of recommendation, interview, essay, curriculum vitae. Additional exam requirements/recommendations for international students: Required—TOEFL (minimum score 550 paper-based; 80 iBT). *Application deadline:* For fall admission, 12/31 for domestic and international students. Application fee: $75. Electronic applications accepted. *Expenses: Tuition:* Full-time $1240. *Required fees:* $970. Tuition and fees vary according to program. *Financial support:* In 2016–17, 119 students received support, including 112 fellowships with full and partial tuition reimbursements available (averaging $8,418 per year), 4 research assistantships with full and partial tuition reimbursements available (averaging $5,940 per year); career-related internships or fieldwork, Federal Work-Study, institutionally sponsored loans, scholarships/grants, traineeships, tuition waivers (full and partial), and unspecified assistantships also available. Support available to part-time students. Financial award applicants required to submit FAFSA. *Faculty research:* PTSD, secondary trauma, childhood adjustment problems, the impact of exercise on emotional states treatment of anxiety disorders and depression, cognitive appraisal and emotion, evolutionary psychology - implications for clinical psychology (evolutionary psychopathology, theory of human nature), treatment of phobic and post-traumatic stress disorders with exposure therapies, self-help and motivational interviewing. *Unit head:* Dr. Craig Johnson, Chairperson, 516-463-5636, E-mail: craig.a.johnson@hofstra.edu. *Application contact:* Sunil Samuel, Assistant Vice President of Admissions, 516-463-4723, Fax: 516-463-4664, E-mail: graduateadmission@hofstra.edu. Website: http://www.hofstra.edu/hclas

**Hood College,** Graduate School, Programs in Human Sciences, Frederick, MD 21701-8575. Offers human sciences (MA), including psychology. *Program availability:* Part-time, evening/weekend. *Faculty:* 5 full-time, 3 part-time/adjunct. *Students:* 11 full-time (8 women), 25 part-time (18 women); includes 6 minority (3 Black or African American, non-Hispanic/Latino; 1 Asian, non-Hispanic/Latino; 2 Two or more races, non-Hispanic/

Latino), 1 international. Average age 38. 20 applicants, 95% accepted, 16 enrolled. In 2016, 29 master's awarded. *Degree requirements:* For master's, comprehensive exam, thesis optional, capstone/research project. *Entrance requirements:* For master's, minimum GPA of 2.75, essay. Additional exam requirements/recommendations for international students: Required—TOEFL (minimum score 575 paper-based; 89 iBT), IELTS (minimum score 6.5). *Application deadline:* For fall admission, 8/15 priority date for domestic students, 8/5 for international students; for spring admission, 12/1 priority date for domestic students, 12/1 for international students; for summer admission, 5/1 priority date for domestic students, 4/15 for international students. Applications are processed on a rolling basis. Application fee: $35. Electronic applications accepted. *Expenses:* $450 per credit hour; $105 comprehensive fee per semester. *Financial support:* Research assistantships with full tuition reimbursements, tuition waivers (partial), and unspecified assistantships available. Financial award applicants required to submit FAFSA. *Faculty research:* Mind-body medicine and multicultural healing, the New Orleans jazz funeral, death practices in African-American culture, bereavement theories and gender differences, Piaget's theory of cognitive development as a formal mathematical model. *Unit head:* April Boulton, Interim Dean of the Graduate School, 301-696-3600, E-mail: gofurther@hood.edu. *Application contact:* Jan Marcus, Assistant Director of Graduate Admissions, 301-696-3600, E-mail: gofurther@hood.ed.
Website: http://www.hood.edu/graduate

**Houston Baptist University,** College of Education and Behavioral Sciences, Program in Psychology, Houston, TX 77074-3298. Offers school psychology (MAP). *Program availability:* Part-time, evening/weekend. *Students:* 42 full-time (38 women), 61 part-time (53 women); includes 67 minority (38 Black or African American, non-Hispanic/Latino; 8 Asian, non-Hispanic/Latino; 20 Hispanic/Latino; 1 Two or more races, non-Hispanic/Latino), 3 international. Average age 30. 162 applicants, 33% accepted, 26 enrolled. In 2016, 27 master's awarded. *Degree requirements:* For master's, comprehensive exam, thesis. *Entrance requirements:* For master's, GRE (waived with a cumulative GPA of 3.0 or higher), minimum GPA of 2.5, two recommendations, resume, bachelor's degree conferred transcript. Additional exam requirements/recommendations for international students: Required—TOEFL (minimum score 80 iBT), IELTS (minimum score 6.5). *Application deadline:* For fall admission, 8/1 for domestic students, 6/1 for international students; for spring admission, 1/1 for domestic students, 11/1 for international students; for summer admission, 5/1 for domestic students, 3/1 for international students. Applications are processed on a rolling basis. Application fee: $0 ($100 for international students). Electronic applications accepted. Application fee is waived when completed online. *Expenses:* $1,650 per 3-hour course; $1,275 annual general fee; $1,060 annual technology fee. *Financial support:* In 2016–17, 2 students received support. Federal Work-Study and scholarships/grants available. Support available to part-time students. Financial award application deadline: 4/1; financial award applicants required to submit FAFSA. *Faculty research:* Drug and alcohol abuse in relation to delinquency, mental health and school factors, chronic stress, coping strategies. *Unit head:* Dr. Renata Nero, Chair, 281-649-3171, Fax: 281-649-3361, E-mail: rnero@hbu.edu. *Application contact:* Victoria Humphreys, Administrative Assistant to the Dean, 281-649-3131, E-mail: vhumphreys@hbu.edu.
Website: http://www.hbu.edu/MAP

**Howard University,** Graduate School, Department of Psychology, Washington, DC 20059-0002. Offers clinical psychology (PhD); developmental psychology (PhD); experimental psychology (PhD); neuropsychology (PhD); personality psychology (PhD); psychology (MS); social psychology (PhD). *Accreditation:* APA (one or more programs are accredited). *Program availability:* Part-time. *Degree requirements:* For master's, thesis; for doctorate, comprehensive exam, thesis/dissertation, qualifying exam. *Entrance requirements:* For master's, GRE General Test, minimum GPA of 2.5, bachelor's degree in psychology or related field; for doctorate, GRE General Test, minimum GPA of 3.0. *Faculty research:* Personality and psychophysiology, educational and social development of African-American children, child and adult psychopathology.

**Humboldt State University,** Academic Programs, College of Professional Studies, Department of Psychology, Arcata, CA 95521-8299. Offers psychology (MA), including biological psychology, counseling, developmental psychopathology, school psychology, social and environmental psychology. *Degree requirements:* For master's, thesis. *Entrance requirements:* For master's, appropriate bachelor's degree, minimum GPA of 2.5. Additional exam requirements/recommendations for international students: Required—TOEFL (minimum score 500 paper-based). *Expenses:* Tuition, state resident: full-time $6738; part-time $1953 per semester. Tuition, nonresident: full-time $13,434; part-time $3813 per semester. *Required fees:* $1738; $653 per semester. Tuition and fees vary according to program. *Faculty research:* School psychology, counseling, eating disorders, mood induction, depression.

**Hunter College of the City University of New York,** Graduate School, School of Arts and Sciences, Department of Psychology, New York, NY 10065-5085. Offers animal behavior and conservation (MA, Certificate); general psychology (MA). *Program availability:* Part-time, evening/weekend. *Students:* 6 full-time (5 women), 79 part-time (59 women); includes 17 minority (5 Black or African American, non-Hispanic/Latino; 5 Asian, non-Hispanic/Latino; 7 Hispanic/Latino), 5 international. Average age 29. 145 applicants, 42% accepted, 38 enrolled. In 2016, 27 master's, 11 other advanced degrees awarded. *Degree requirements:* For master's, comprehensive exam, thesis. *Entrance requirements:* For master's, GRE General Test, minimum 12 credits of course work in psychology, including statistics and experimental psychology; 2 letters of recommendation. Additional exam requirements/recommendations for international students: Required—TOEFL. *Application deadline:* For fall admission, 4/1 for domestic students, 2/1 for international students; for spring admission, 11/1 for domestic students, 9/1 for international students. Applications are processed on a rolling basis. *Financial support:* Federal Work-Study, scholarships/grants, and tuition waivers (partial) available. Support available to part-time students. *Faculty research:* Personality, cognitive and linguistic development, hormonal and neural control of behavior, gender and culture, social cognition of health and attitudes. *Unit head:* Christopher B. Braun, Chair, 212-772-5554, Fax: 212-772-5620, E-mail: psychadv@hunter.cuny.edu. *Application contact:* Milena Solo, Graduate Admissions Director, 212-772-4288, Fax: 212-650-3336, E-mail: milena.solo@hunter.cuny.edu.
Website: http://www.hunter.cuny.edu/psychology/

**Idaho State University,** Office of Graduate Studies, College of Arts and Letters, Department of Psychology, Pocatello, ID 83209-8112. Offers clinical psychology (PhD); experimental psychology (PhD). *Accreditation:* APA. *Program availability:* Part-time. *Degree requirements:* For doctorate, comprehensive exam, thesis/dissertation, 1 year full-time clinical internship. *Entrance requirements:* For doctorate, GRE General Test, GRE Subject Test, MS in psychology, recommendation from Clinical Admissions Committee. Additional exam requirements/recommendations for international students: Required—TOEFL (minimum score 550 paper-based; 80 iBT). Electronic applications accepted. *Faculty research:* Substance abuse, sexual decision making, trauma, behavioral pharmacology, developmental psychopathology, working memory and strategies, goal setting, person perception, developmental psychobiology, parent-child interactions.

**Illinois Institute of Technology,** Graduate College, Lewis College of Human Sciences, Department of Psychology, Chicago, IL 60616. Offers clinical psychology (PhD);

industrial and organizational psychology (PhD); personnel and human resource development (MS); rehabilitation and mental health counseling (MS); rehabilitation counseling education (PhD). *Accreditation:* APA (one or more programs are accredited); CORE. *Program availability:* Part-time, evening/weekend. Terminal master's awarded for partial completion of doctoral program. *Degree requirements:* For master's, thesis (for some programs); for doctorate, comprehensive exam, thesis/dissertation, minimum of 107 credit hours, 1-year full-time internship. *Entrance requirements:* For master's, GRE General Test (minimum score 298 Quantitative and Verbal, 3.0 Analytical Writing), minimum GPA of 3.0; 3 letters of recommendation; bachelor's degree from accredited institution (for personnel and human resource development); for doctorate, GRE General Test (minimum score 298 Quantitative and Verbal, 3.0 Analytical Writing), bachelor's or master's degree from accredited institution, recommendations. Additional exam requirements/recommendations for international students: Required—TOEFL (minimum score 550 paper-based; 80 iBT). Electronic applications accepted. *Faculty research:* Clinical psychology, rehabilitation and mental health counseling, industrial organizational psychology.

**Illinois State University,** Graduate School, College of Arts and Sciences, Department of Psychology, Normal, IL 61790-2200. Offers psychology (MA, MS), including clinical-counseling psychology, cognitive and behavioral sciences, developmental psychology, industrial/organizational-social psychology; school psychology (PhD, SSP). *Accreditation:* APA. *Degree requirements:* For master's, thesis or alternative; for doctorate, variable foreign language requirement, thesis/dissertation, 2 terms of residency, internship, practicum. *Entrance requirements:* For master's, GRE General Test, GRE Subject Test, minimum GPA of 3.0 in last 60 hours of course work; for doctorate, GRE General Test. *Faculty research:* Comprehensive evaluation system for the central region professional development grant, Illinois school psychology internship consortium, for children's sake.

**Immaculata University,** College of Graduate Studies, Department of Psychology, Immaculata, PA 19345. Offers clinical mental health counseling (MA); clinical psychology (Psy D); forensic psychology (Graduate Certificate); integrative psychotherapy (Graduate Certificate); neuropsychology (Graduate Certificate); psychodynamic psychotherapy (Graduate Certificate); psychological testing (Graduate Certificate); school counseling (MA, Graduate Certificate); school psychology (MA). *Accreditation:* APA. *Program availability:* Part-time, evening/weekend. Terminal master's awarded for partial completion of doctoral program. *Degree requirements:* For master's, comprehensive exam, thesis optional; for doctorate, comprehensive exam, thesis/dissertation. *Entrance requirements:* For master's, GRE General Test or MAT, minimum GPA of 3.0; for doctorate, GRE General Test or MAT, minimum GPA of 3.5. Additional exam requirements/recommendations for international students: Required—TOEFL, IELTS. Electronic applications accepted. *Faculty research:* Supervision ethics, psychology of teaching, gender.

**Indiana State University,** College of Graduate and Professional Studies, College of Arts and Sciences, Department of Psychology, Terre Haute, IN 47809. Offers clinical psychology (Psy D); general psychology (MA, MS). *Accreditation:* APA (one or more programs are accredited). Terminal master's awarded for partial completion of doctoral program. *Degree requirements:* For master's, thesis (for some programs); for doctorate, comprehensive exam, thesis/dissertation, internship, professional research project. *Entrance requirements:* For master's, GRE General Test, 12 semester hours of course work in psychology, minimum GPA of 2.75; for doctorate, GRE General Test, minimum GPA of 3.0. Additional exam requirements/recommendations for international students: Required—TOEFL (minimum score 550 paper-based). Electronic applications accepted.

**Indiana Tech,** Program in Psychology, Fort Wayne, IN 46803-1297. Offers MS.

**Indiana University Bloomington,** University Graduate School, College of Arts and Sciences, Department of Psychological and Brain Sciences, Bloomington, IN 47405. Offers clinical science (PhD); cognitive neuroscience (PhD); cognitive psychology (PhD); developmental psychology (PhD); methods of behavior (PhD); molecular systems neuroscience (PhD); social psychology (PhD). *Accreditation:* APA. *Degree requirements:* For doctorate, comprehensive exam, 90 credit hours, 2 advanced statistics/methods courses, 2 written research projects, the teaching of psychology course, teaching 1 semester of undergraduate methods course, qualifying examination, minor or a second major, first-year research seminar course, dissertation defense, written dissertation. *Entrance requirements:* For doctorate, GRE. Additional exam requirements/recommendations for international students: Required—TOEFL (minimum score 550 paper-based; 79 iBT). Electronic applications accepted. *Faculty research:* Clinical science, cognitive neuroscience, cognitive psychology, developmental psychology, mechanisms of behavior, molecular and systems neuroscience, social psychology.

**Indiana University of Pennsylvania,** School of Graduate Studies and Research, College of Natural Sciences and Mathematics, Department of Psychology, Indiana, PA 15705. Offers clinical psychology (Psy D); psychology (MA). *Accreditation:* APA (one or more programs are accredited). *Program availability:* Part-time. *Faculty:* 13 full-time (7 women). *Students:* 43 full-time (29 women), 22 part-time (15 women); includes 9 minority (3 Asian, non-Hispanic/Latino; 5 Hispanic/Latino; 1 Two or more races, non-Hispanic/Latino), 2 international. Average age 26. 227 applicants, 13% accepted, 15 enrolled. In 2016, 10 master's, 10 doctorates awarded. Terminal master's awarded for partial completion of doctoral program. *Degree requirements:* For doctorate, comprehensive exam, thesis/dissertation, internship, practicum. *Entrance requirements:* For doctorate, GRE General Test, minimum GPA of 3.0, interview, 3 letters of recommendation. Additional exam requirements/recommendations for international students: Required—TOEFL (minimum score 540 paper-based). *Application deadline:* Applications are processed on a rolling basis. Application fee: $50. Electronic applications accepted. *Expenses:* Tuition, state resident: full-time $8694; part-time $483 per credit. Tuition, nonresident: full-time $13,050; part-time $725 per credit. *Required fees:* $157 per credit. $50 per term. Tuition and fees vary according to course load and program. *Financial support:* In 2016–17, 13 fellowships with full tuition reimbursements (averaging $522 per year), 45 research assistantships with tuition reimbursements (averaging $2,625 per year), 2 teaching assistantships with partial tuition reimbursements (averaging $23,305 per year) were awarded; career-related internships or fieldwork, Federal Work-Study, scholarships/grants, and unspecified assistantships also available. Support available to part-time students. Financial award application deadline: 4/15; financial award applicants required to submit FAFSA. *Unit head:* Dr. Raymond Pavloski, Chairperson, 724-357-2426, E-mail: pavloski@iup.edu. *Application contact:* Dr. David LaPorte, Graduate Coordinator, 724-357-2426, E-mail: laporte@iup.edu.
Website: http://www.iup.edu/psychology

**Indiana University–Purdue University Indianapolis,** School of Science, Department of Psychology, Indianapolis, IN 46202-3275. Offers clinical psychology (MS); industrial/organizational psychology (MS); psychobiology of addictions (MS). *Accreditation:* APA (one or more programs are accredited). Terminal master's awarded for partial completion of doctoral program. *Degree requirements:* For master's, thesis; for doctorate, thesis/dissertation. *Entrance requirements:* For master's, GRE General Test, minimum undergraduate GPA of 3.0; for doctorate, GRE General Test, GRE Subject Test (clinical psychology), minimum undergraduate GPA of 3.2. Additional exam

## Psychology—General

requirements/recommendations for international students: Required—TOEFL (minimum score 567 paper-based; 86 iBT), IELTS (minimum score 6.5). Electronic applications accepted. *Faculty research:* Severe mental illness, health psychology, neurological research, alcoholism and psychopathology, functional activities within organizations.

**Inter American University of Puerto Rico, Metropolitan Campus,** Graduate Programs, Program in Psychology, San Juan, PR 00919-1293. Offers counseling psychology (MA, PhD); industrial/organizational psychology (MA, PhD); labor relations (MA); school psychology (MA, PhD). *Degree requirements:* For master's, comprehensive exam. *Entrance requirements:* For master's, GRE or EXADEP, interview. Electronic applications accepted.

**Inter American University of Puerto Rico, San Germán Campus,** Graduate Studies Center, Program in Psychology, San Germán, PR 00683-5008. Offers counseling psychology (MA, PhD); school psychology (MA, PhD). *Program availability:* Part-time, evening/weekend. *Degree requirements:* For master's, comprehensive exam, thesis; for doctorate, comprehensive exam, thesis/dissertation. *Entrance requirements:* For master's, GRE General Test or EXADEP, minimum GPA of 3.0; for doctorate, GRE, EXADEP or MAT, minimum GPA of 3.0.

**Iona College,** School of Arts and Science, Department of Psychology, New Rochelle, NY 10801-1890. Offers general-experimental psychology (MA); human resources (Certificate); industrial-organizational psychology (MA); mental health counseling (MA); organizational behavior (Certificate); psychology (MA); school psychology (MA). *Program availability:* Part-time. *Faculty:* 9 full-time (5 women), 6 part-time/adjunct (5 women). *Students:* 61 full-time (42 women), 32 part-time (23 women); includes 40 minority (8 Black or African American, non-Hispanic/Latino; 3 Asian, non-Hispanic/Latino; 28 Hispanic/Latino; 1 Two or more races, non-Hispanic/Latino), 2 international. Average age 25. 91 applicants, 80% accepted, 37 enrolled. In 2016, 18 master's awarded. *Degree requirements:* For master's, thesis (for some programs), literature review (for some programs). *Entrance requirements:* For master's, BA in psychology including 3 credits each in psychology statistics and experimental research methods, or 9 credits in psychology including 3 credits in psychology statistics, 3 credits in psychology research methods and 3 credits of upper-level coursework. Additional exam requirements/recommendations for international students: Required—TOEFL (minimum score 550 paper-based), IELTS (minimum score 6.5). *Application deadline:* For fall admission, 8/15 for domestic students, 5/1 for international students; for spring admission, 1/15 for domestic students, 9/1 for international students. Applications are processed on a rolling basis. Application fee: $50. Electronic applications accepted. *Expenses: Tuition:* Full-time $19,692; part-time $1094 per credit. *Required fees:* $245 per term. Tuition and fees vary according to program. *Financial support:* In 2016–17, 49 students received support. Research assistantships with partial tuition reimbursements available, tuition waivers (partial), and unspecified assistantships available. Support available to part-time students. Financial award application deadline: 4/15; financial award applicants required to submit FAFSA. *Faculty research:* Non-suicidal self-injury, trauma response, performance appraisal and evaluation, diversity infusion, assessment and treatment of sexual offenders. *Unit head:* Patricia Oswald, PhD, Chair, 914-633-2374, E-mail: poswald@iona.edu. *Application contact:* Katelyn Brunck, Assistant Director, Graduate Admissions, 914-633-2451, Fax: 914-633-2277, E-mail: kbrunck@iona.edu.
Website: http://www.iona.edu/Academics/School-of-Arts-Science/Departments/Psychology/Graduate-Programs.aspx

**Iowa State University of Science and Technology,** Department of Psychology, Ames, IA 50011. Offers cognitive psychology (PhD); counseling psychology (PhD); psychology (MS, PhD); social psychology (PhD). *Accreditation:* APA (one or more programs are accredited). *Entrance requirements:* For doctorate, GRE General Test, GRE Subject Test (psychology), 3 letters of recommendation. Additional exam requirements/recommendations for international students: Required—TOEFL (minimum score 560 paper-based; 79 iBT), IELTS (minimum score 6.5). *Application deadline:* For fall admission, 1/2 priority date for domestic and international students. Application fee: $60 ($90 for international students). Electronic applications accepted. *Faculty research:* Counseling psychology, cognitive psychology, social psychology, health psychology, psychology and public policy. *Application contact:* Sarah Kallsen, Application Contact, 515-294-1742, Fax: 515-294-6424, E-mail: psychadm@iastate.edu.
Website: http://www.psychology.iastate.edu/

**Jackson State University,** Graduate School, College of Liberal Arts, Department of Psychology, Jackson, MS 39217. Offers clinical psychology (PhD). *Accreditation:* APA. *Degree requirements:* For doctorate, comprehensive exam, thesis/dissertation. *Entrance requirements:* For doctorate, MAT, GRE. Additional exam requirements/recommendations for international students: Required—TOEFL (minimum score 520 paper-based; 67 iBT). *Application deadline:* For fall admission, 1/15 for domestic and international students. Application fee: $25. *Expenses:* Tuition, state resident: full-time $7141. Tuition, nonresident: full-time $17,494. *Required fees:* $1080. Tuition and fees vary according to class time, course level, course load, degree level, campus/location, program and student level. *Financial support:* Fellowships, research assistantships, teaching assistantships, career-related internships or fieldwork, Federal Work-Study, scholarships/grants, tuition waivers (full), and unspecified assistantships available. Support available to part-time students. Financial award application deadline: 3/1; financial award applicants required to submit FAFSA. *Unit head:* Dr. Pamela G. Banks, Chair, 601-979-3378, Fax: 601-979-3947, E-mail: pbanks@jsums.edu. *Application contact:* Fatoumatta Sisay, Manager of Graduate Admissions, 601-979-0342, Fax: 601-977-4325, E-mail: fatoumatta.sisay@jsums.edu.
Website: http://www.jsums.edu/psychology/

**Jacksonville State University,** College of Graduate Studies and Continuing Education, College of Arts and Sciences, Department of Psychology, Jacksonville, AL 36265-1602. Offers MS. *Program availability:* Part-time, evening/weekend. *Faculty:* 5 full-time (4 women). *Students:* 12 full-time (11 women), 3 part-time (2 women). Average age 27. 24 applicants, 33% accepted, 6 enrolled. In 2016, 7 master's awarded. *Degree requirements:* For master's, comprehensive exam, thesis (for some programs). *Entrance requirements:* For master's, GRE General Test or MAT. Additional exam requirements/recommendations for international students: Required—TOEFL (minimum score 500 paper-based; 61 iBT). *Application deadline:* Applications are processed on a rolling basis. Application fee: $35. Electronic applications accepted. *Financial support:* In 2016–17, 9 students received support. Available to part-time students. Application deadline: 4/1; applicants required to submit FAFSA. *Unit head:* Dr. Paige McKerchar, Interim Department Head, 256-782-5808, E-mail: pmckerchar@jsu.edu. *Application contact:* Dr. Jean Pugliese, Associate Dean, 256-782-8278, Fax: 256-782-5321, E-mail: pugliese@jsu.edu.

**James Madison University,** The Graduate School, College of Health and Behavioral Sciences, Program in Psychological Sciences, Harrisonburg, VA 22807. Offers applied research (MA); behavior analysis (MA); experimental psychology (MA); quantitative psychology (MA). *Program availability:* Part-time, evening/weekend. *Students:* 21 full-time (10 women), 3 part-time (2 women); includes 3 minority (1 American Indian or Alaska Native, non-Hispanic/Latino; 1 Native Hawaiian or other Pacific Islander, non-Hispanic/Latino; 1 Two or more races, non-Hispanic/Latino). Average age 30. 58 applicants, 31% accepted, 14 enrolled. In 2016, 14 master's awarded. Application fee:

$55. Electronic applications accepted. *Financial support:* In 2016–17, 2 teaching assistantships with full tuition reimbursements (averaging $9,284 per year) were awarded; career-related internships or fieldwork, Federal Work-Study, and 19 assistantships (averaging $7911) also available. Financial award application deadline: 3/1; financial award applicants required to submit FAFSA. *Unit head:* Dr. Jeff S. Dyche, Graduate Program Director, 540-568-4965, E-mail: dychejs@jmu.edu. *Application contact:* Lynette D. Michael, Director of Graduate Admissions, 540-568-6131 Ext. 6395, Fax: 540-568-7860, E-mail: michaeld@jmu.edu.
Website: http://www.psyc.jmu.edu/psycsciences/

**John F. Kennedy University,** Graduate School of Holistic Studies, Department of Integral Studies, Program in Integral Psychology, Pleasant Hill, CA 94523-4817. Offers dream studies (Certificate); integral psychology (MA); life coaching (Certificate). *Program availability:* Part-time, evening/weekend.

**John F. Kennedy University,** Graduate School of Professional Psychology, Pleasant Hill, CA 94523-4817. Offers MA, Psy D, Certificate. *Accreditation:* APA. *Program availability:* Part-time, evening/weekend. *Degree requirements:* For master's, thesis or alternative. *Entrance requirements:* For master's, interview. Additional exam requirements/recommendations for international students: Required—TOEFL.

**Johns Hopkins University,** Zanvyl Krieger School of Arts and Sciences, Department of Psychological and Brain Sciences, Baltimore, MD 21218. Offers PhD. *Degree requirements:* For doctorate, thesis/dissertation, research project, teaching experience. *Entrance requirements:* For doctorate, GRE General Test. Additional exam requirements/recommendations for international students: Required—TOEFL (minimum score 600 paper-based; 100 iBT), IELTS (minimum score 7). Electronic applications accepted. *Faculty research:* Biopsychology, cognitive psychology, cognitive neuroscience, developmental psychology, neurobiology.

**Kansas State University,** Graduate School, College of Arts and Sciences, Department of Psychological Sciences, Manhattan, KS 66506. Offers MS, PhD. *Program availability:* Part-time. *Faculty:* 15 full-time (5 women), 3 part-time/adjunct (0 women). *Students:* 31 full-time (15 women), 49 part-time (34 women); includes 14 minority (2 Black or African American, non-Hispanic/Latino; 1 American Indian or Alaska Native, non-Hispanic/Latino; 3 Asian, non-Hispanic/Latino; 4 Hispanic/Latino; 4 Two or more races, non-Hispanic/Latino), 2 international. Average age 31. 108 applicants, 24% accepted, 19 enrolled. In 2016, 20 master's, 8 doctorates awarded. *Degree requirements:* For master's, thesis or alternative; for doctorate, thesis/dissertation, preliminary exam. *Entrance requirements:* For master's, GRE General Test, minimum undergraduate GPA of 3.0; for doctorate, GRE General Test, minimum GPA of 3.0. Additional exam requirements/recommendations for international students: Required—TOEFL (minimum score 600 paper-based). *Application deadline:* For fall admission, 1/15 priority date for domestic and international students; for spring admission, 8/1 for domestic and international students. Applications are processed on a rolling basis. Application fee: $50 ($75 for international students). Electronic applications accepted. *Expenses:* Tuition, state resident: full-time $9670. Tuition, nonresident: full-time $21,828. *Required fees:* $862. *Financial support:* In 2016–17, 33 students received support, including 1 fellowship with full tuition reimbursement available (averaging $34,000 per year), 11 research assistantships (averaging $18,000 per year), 21 teaching assistantships with full tuition reimbursements available (averaging $15,315 per year); career-related internships or fieldwork, institutionally sponsored loans, and scholarships/grants also available. Support available to part-time students. Financial award application deadline: 3/1; financial award applicants required to submit FAFSA. *Faculty research:* Personal and occupational health, neurological bases of drug use and abuse, measurement and reduction of prejudice, judgment and decision-making, visual perception. *Total annual research expenditures:* $556,470. *Unit head:* Prof. Michael Young, Head, 785-532-0602, Fax: 785-532-5401, E-mail: michaelyoung@ksu.edu. *Application contact:* Prof. Gary L. Brase, Director, 785-532-0609, Fax: 785-532-5401, E-mail: gbrase@ksu.edu.
Website: http://www.k-state.edu/psych

**Kean University,** College of Liberal Arts, Program in Psychology, Union, NJ 07083. Offers forensic psychology (MA); human behavior and organizational psychology (MA); psychological services (MA). *Program availability:* Part-time. *Faculty:* 18 full-time (14 women). *Students:* 45 full-time (35 women), 39 part-time (25 women); includes 48 minority (21 Black or African American, non-Hispanic/Latino; 8 Asian, non-Hispanic/Latino; 16 Hispanic/Latino; 1 Native Hawaiian or other Pacific Islander, non-Hispanic/Latino; 2 Two or more races, non-Hispanic/Latino), 2 international. Average age 27. 54 applicants, 91% accepted, 44 enrolled. In 2016, 25 master's awarded. *Degree requirements:* For master's, comprehensive exam, research component, two semesters of advanced seminar. *Entrance requirements:* For master's, GRE General Test, minimum GPA of 3.0; official transcripts from all institutions attended; two letters of recommendation; professional resume/curriculum vitae; 12 credits in behavioral sciences on the undergraduate level. Additional exam requirements/recommendations for international students: Required—TOEFL (minimum score 550 paper-based; 79 iBT), IELTS (minimum score 6.5). *Application deadline:* For fall admission, 6/1 for domestic and international students; for spring admission, 12/1 for domestic and international students. Applications are processed on a rolling basis. Application fee: $75. Electronic applications accepted. *Expenses:* Tuition, state resident: full-time $13,156; part-time $640 per credit. Tuition, nonresident: full-time $17,831; part-time $785 per credit. *Required fees:* $3316; $151 per credit. Tuition and fees vary according to course level, course load, degree level and program. *Financial support:* Scholarships/grants and unspecified assistantships available. Financial award applicants required to submit FAFSA. *Unit head:* Dr. Muriel Singer, Program Coordinator, 908-737-5886, E-mail: msinger@kean.edu. *Application contact:* Amy Clark, Program Assistant, 908-737-7100, E-mail: grad-adm@kean.edu.
Website: http://grad.kean.edu/masters-programs/psychological-services

**Keiser University,** MS in Psychology Program, Ft. Lauderdale, FL 33309. Offers MS.

**Keiser University,** PhD in Psychology Program, Ft. Lauderdale, FL 33309. Offers PhD.

**Kent State University,** College of Arts and Sciences, Department of Psychological Sciences, Kent, OH 44242-0001. Offers clinical psychology (MA, PhD), including gerontology (MA), psychological sciences (MA); experimental psychology (MA, PhD), including gerontology (MA), psychological sciences (MA). *Accreditation:* APA (one or more programs are accredited). *Program availability:* Part-time. *Faculty:* 29 full-time (15 women). *Students:* 29 full-time (24 women); includes 9 minority (4 Black or African American, non-Hispanic/Latino; 2 Asian, non-Hispanic/Latino; 2 Hispanic/Latino; 1 Two or more races, non-Hispanic/Latino), 1 international. Average age 31. 323 applicants, 5% accepted, 17 enrolled. Terminal master's awarded for partial completion of doctoral program. *Degree requirements:* For master's, thesis; for doctorate, thesis/dissertation. *Entrance requirements:* For master's and doctorate, GRE General Test, personal statement, transcripts, 3 letters of recommendation. Additional exam requirements/recommendations for international students: Required—TOEFL (minimum score of 525 paper-based, 71 iBT), IELTS (minimum score of 6), Michigan English Language Assessment Battery (minimum score of 75), or PTE (minimum score of 48). *Application deadline:* For fall admission, 12/1 for domestic and international students. Applications are processed on a rolling basis. Application fee: $45 ($70 for international students). Electronic applications accepted. *Expenses:* Tuition, state resident: full-time $10,864;

part-time $495 per credit hour. Tuition, nonresident: full-time $18,380; part-time $837 per credit hour. *Financial support:* Unspecified assistantships available. Financial award application deadline: 12/1. *Unit head:* Dr. Maria S. Zaragoza, Professor and Chair, 330-672-2166, E-mail: mzaragoz@kent.edu. *Application contact:* Dr. John A. Updegraff, Professor and Graduate Coordinator, 330-672-2166, E-mail: jupdegr1@kent.edu. Website: http://www.kent.edu/psychology/graduate-programs

**Kent State University,** College of Public Health, Kent, OH 44242-0001. Offers public health (MPH, PhD), including biostatistics (MPH), environmental health sciences (MPH), epidemiology, health policy and management, prevention science (PhD), social and behavioral sciences (MPH). *Accreditation:* CEPH. *Program availability:* Part-time, online learning. *Faculty:* 28 full-time (16 women). *Students:* 131 full-time (104 women), 133 part-time (102 women); includes 56 minority (36 Black or African American, non-Hispanic/Latino; 1 American Indian or Alaska Native, non-Hispanic/Latino; 5 Asian, non-Hispanic/Latino; 8 Hispanic/Latino; 6 Two or more races, non-Hispanic/Latino), 35 international. Average age 33. 216 applicants, 59% accepted, 80 enrolled. In 2016, 55 master's, 1 doctorate awarded. *Degree requirements:* For master's, comprehensive exam, 300 hours' placement at public health agency, final portfolio and presentation; for doctorate, comprehensive exam, thesis/dissertation. *Entrance requirements:* For master's, GRE, minimum GPA of 3.0, transcripts, goal statement, 3 letters of recommendation; for doctorate, GRE, minimum GPA of 3.0, personal statement, resume, interview, 3 letters of recommendation. *Application deadline:* For fall admission, 6/15 for domestic and international students; for spring admission, 10/15 for domestic and international students; for summer admission, 3/15 for domestic and international students. Applications are processed on a rolling basis. Application fee: $45 ($70 for international students). Electronic applications accepted. *Expenses:* Tuition, state resident: full-time $10,864; part-time $495 per credit hour. Tuition, nonresident: full-time $18,380; part-time $837 per credit hour. *Financial support:* Unspecified assistantships available. *Unit head:* Dr. Sonia Alemagno, Dean and Professor of Health Policy and Management, 330-672-6500, E-mail: salemagn@kent.edu. *Application contact:* Dr. Mark A. James, Professor/Chair/Graduate Advisor, 330-672-6506, E-mail: mjames22@kent.edu.
Website: http://www.kent.edu/publichealth/

**Kentucky State University,** College of Arts and Sciences, Frankfort, KY 40601. Offers interdisciplinary behavioral sciences (MA). *Program availability:* Part-time, evening/weekend, blended/hybrid learning. *Faculty:* 3 full-time (2 women). *Students:* 2 full-time (1 woman), 4 part-time (all women); includes 5 minority (all Black or African American, non-Hispanic/Latino). Average age 29. 5 applicants, 40% accepted, 2 enrolled. In 2016, 2 master's awarded. *Degree requirements:* For master's, comprehensive exam, thesis optional. *Entrance requirements:* For master's, GRE, statement of educational goals and career objectives, essay, resume, 3 letters of reference. Additional exam requirements/recommendations for international students: Required—TOEFL (minimum score 500 paper-based; 61 iBT). *Application deadline:* For fall admission, 7/1 for domestic students, 4/1 for international students; for spring admission, 11/15 for domestic students, 8/15 for international students; for summer admission, 5/1 for domestic students, 2/1 for international students. Applications are processed on a rolling basis. Application fee: $30 ($100 for international students). Electronic applications accepted. *Expenses:* Tuition, state resident: full-time $7524; part-time $418 per credit hour. Tuition, nonresident: full-time $11,322; part-time $629 per credit hour. Tuition and fees vary according to course load. *Financial support:* In 2016–17, 5 students received support. Research assistantships, scholarships/grants, tuition waivers (partial), and unspecified assistantships available. Financial award application deadline: 4/15; financial award applicants required to submit FAFSA. *Faculty research:* Validity and reliability of forensic science; cognitive human factors in forensic science; judicial decision-making; education, training, and certification of forensic science practitioners; sex and race effects on offender sentence; job satisfaction; policing; victimology; perceptions versus realities; cultural capital; educational deficits; community-based participatory research; American race relations; race and fear; social media and political awareness. *Total annual research expenditures:* $134,183. *Unit head:* Dr. Tierra Freeman, Chair of Behavioral and Social Sciences, 502-597-5932, E-mail: tierra.freeman@kysu.edu. *Application contact:* Dr. James Obielodan, Director of Graduate Studies, 502-597-4723, E-mail: james.obielodan@kysu.edu.

**Lakehead University,** Graduate Studies, Department of Psychology, Thunder Bay, ON P7B 5E1, Canada. Offers clinical psychology (PhD); experimental psychology (MA). *Program availability:* Part-time, evening/weekend. *Degree requirements:* For master's, thesis optional; for doctorate, thesis/dissertation, 2 comprehensive exams, internship. *Entrance requirements:* For master's, GRE, honors degree in psychology, advanced course work in statistics, minimum B average; for doctorate, GRE, minimum B average. Additional exam requirements/recommendations for international students: Required—TOEFL. *Faculty research:* Chaos theory, health psychology, counseling psychology, gerontology, women's studies.

**Lamar University,** College of Graduate Studies, College of Arts and Sciences, Department of Psychology, Beaumont, TX 77710. Offers clinical psychology (MS); industrial/organizational psychology (MS). *Program availability:* Part-time. *Faculty:* 6 full-time (4 women). *Students:* 8 full-time (6 women), 8 part-time (6 women); includes 5 minority (1 Black or African American, non-Hispanic/Latino; 3 Hispanic/Latino; 1 Two or more races, non-Hispanic/Latino), 1 international. Average age 28. 15 applicants, 100% accepted, 3 enrolled. In 2016, 6 master's awarded. *Degree requirements:* For master's, thesis, practicum. *Entrance requirements:* For master's, GRE General Test, minimum GPA of 2.75 in last 60 hours of undergraduate course work. Additional exam requirements/recommendations for international students: Required—TOEFL (minimum score 550 paper-based; 79 iBT), IELTS (minimum score 6.5). *Application deadline:* For fall admission, 8/10 for domestic students, 7/1 for international students; for spring admission, 1/5 for domestic students, 12/1 for international students. Application fee: $25 ($50 for international students). *Expenses:* $8,134 in-state full-time, $5,574 in-state part-time; $15,604 out-of-state full-time, $10,554 out-of-state part-time per year. *Financial support:* In 2016–17, 12 students received support. Fellowships, research assistantships, teaching assistantships, career-related internships or fieldwork, Federal Work-Study, scholarships/grants, and tuition waivers (partial) available. Support available to part-time students. Financial award application deadline: 4/1. *Faculty research:* Group think, health psychology, school psychology, behavioral neuroscience. *Unit head:* Dr. Edythe E. Kirk, Chair, 409-880-8285, Fax: 409-880-1710. *Application contact:* Deidre Mayer, Interim Director, Admissions and Academic Services, 409-880-8888, Fax: 409-880-7419, E-mail: gradmission@lamar.edu.
Website: http://artssciences.lamar.edu/psychology

**La Salle University,** School of Arts and Sciences, Program in Clinical Psychology, Philadelphia, PA 19141-1199. Offers child clinical psychology (Psy D); clinical health psychology (Psy D); clinical psychology (MA); general practice psychology (Psy D). *Accreditation:* AAMFT/COAMFTE. *Program availability:* Part-time, evening/weekend. *Faculty:* 9 full-time (7 women), 6 part-time/adjunct (3 women). *Students:* 77 full-time (62 women), 37 part-time (28 women); includes 15 minority (2 Black or African American, non-Hispanic/Latino; 6 Asian, non-Hispanic/Latino; 4 Hispanic/Latino; 3 Two or more races, non-Hispanic/Latino), 4 international. Average age 27. 301 applicants, 22% accepted, 17 enrolled. In 2016, 20 master's, 17 doctorates awarded. Terminal master's awarded for partial completion of doctoral program. *Degree requirements:* For doctorate, comprehensive exam, thesis/dissertation. *Entrance requirements:* For doctorate, GRE (minimum scores of 148 on both the Verbal Reasoning and Quantitative Reasoning sections strongly recommended); GRE Subject Test in psychology (for those entering with bachelor's degree), baccalaureate degree from accredited institution with major in psychology or related discipline; minimum undergraduate GPA of 3.0, 3.2 graduate; three letters of recommendation; statement of interest and intent; curriculum vitae or resume; personal interview. Additional exam requirements/recommendations for international students: Required—TOEFL. *Application deadline:* For fall admission, 1/15 for domestic students, 1/1 for international students. Application fee: $35. Electronic applications accepted. Application fee is waived when completed online. *Expenses:* Contact institution. *Financial support:* In 2016–17, 26 students received support. Scholarships/grants and unspecified assistantships available. Financial award application deadline: 8/31; financial award applicants required to submit FAFSA. *Unit head:* Dr. Randy Fingerhut, Director, 215-951-1284, Fax: 215-951-5140, E-mail: psyd@lasalle.edu. *Application contact:* Elizabeth Heenan, Director, Graduate and Adult Enrollment, 215-951-1100, Fax: 215-951-1462, E-mail: heenan@lasalle.edu.
Website: http://www.lasalle.edu/doctor-of-psychology/

**Laurentian University,** School of Graduate Studies and Research, Programme in Psychology, Sudbury, ON P3E 2C6, Canada. Offers applied psychology (MA); experimental psychology (MA).

**Lehigh University,** College of Arts and Sciences, Department of Psychology, Bethlehem, PA 18015. Offers MS, PhD. *Faculty:* 13 full-time (8 women). *Students:* 16 full-time (11 women); includes 3 minority (2 Black or African American, non-Hispanic/Latino; 1 Asian, non-Hispanic/Latino), 5 international. Average age 27. 67 applicants, 13% accepted, 3 enrolled. In 2016, 1 master's, 3 doctorates awarded. Terminal master's awarded for partial completion of doctoral program. *Degree requirements:* For master's, thesis; for doctorate, comprehensive exam, thesis/dissertation. *Entrance requirements:* For master's and doctorate, GRE General Test. Additional exam requirements/recommendations for international students: Required—TOEFL. *Application deadline:* For fall admission, 1/1 for domestic and international students. Application fee: $75. Electronic applications accepted. *Expenses:* $1,420 per credit. *Financial support:* In 2016–17, 14 students received support, including 2 research assistantships with full tuition reimbursements available (averaging $20,000 per year), 12 teaching assistantships with full tuition reimbursements available (averaging $20,000 per year); fellowships also available. Financial award application deadline: 1/1. *Faculty research:* Cognition, memory, language, and their development; prosocial cognition, emotion, and action; conflict and cooperation between and within groups; self-control of cognition and emotion; optimizing developmental and relational outcomes. *Total annual research expenditures:* $360,280. *Unit head:* Dr. Gordon Moskowitz, Chairperson, 610-758-3624, Fax: 610-758-6277, E-mail: gbm4@lehigh.edu. *Application contact:* Dr. Almut Hupbach, Program Director, 610-758-6762, Fax: 610-758-6277, E-mail: alh309@lehigh.edu.
Website: http://psychology.cas2.lehigh.edu/

**Lesley University,** Graduate School of Arts and Social Sciences, Cambridge, MA 02138-2790. Offers clinical mental health counseling (MA), including holistic counseling, school and community counseling, trauma studies; counseling psychology (MA, CAGS), including professional counseling (MA), school counseling (MA); creative writing (MFA); expressive therapies (MA, PhD, CAGS), including art (MA), clinical mental health counseling (MA), dance (MA), expressive therapies (MA), music (MA); independent studies (CAGS); independent study (MA); intercultural relations (MA, CAGS); interdisciplinary studies (MA), including individualized studies, integrative holistic health, mindfulness studies, peace and conflict transformation, trauma sensitive assessment, intervention, and consultation, women's studies; urban environmental leadership (MA). *Program availability:* Part-time, online learning. *Degree requirements:* For master's, internship, practicum, thesis (for expressive therapies); for doctorate, thesis/dissertation, arts apprenticeship, field placement; for CAGS, thesis, internship (for counseling psychology, expressive therapies). *Entrance requirements:* For master's, MAT (counseling psychology), interview, writing samples, art portfolio; for doctorate, GRE or MAT, interview, master's degree; for CAGS, interview, master's degree. Additional exam requirements/recommendations for international students: Required—TOEFL (minimum score 550 paper-based; 80 iBT). Electronic applications accepted. *Faculty research:* Psychotherapy and culture; psychotherapy and psychological trauma; women's issues in art, teaching and psychotherapy; community-based art, psycho-spiritual inquiry.

**LeTourneau University,** Graduate Programs, Longview, TX 75607-7001. Offers business (MBA); counseling (MA), including licensed professional counselor, marriage and family therapy, school counseling; curriculum and instruction (M Ed); educational administration (M Ed); engineering (ME, MS); engineering management (MEM); health care administration (MS); marriage and family therapy (MA); psychology (MA); strategic leadership (MSL); teacher leadership (M Ed); teaching and learning (M Ed). *Program availability:* Part-time, 100% online, blended/hybrid learning. *Faculty:* 24 full-time (7 women), 40 part-time/adjunct (15 women). *Students:* 82 full-time (48 women), 428 part-time (331 women); includes 234 minority (138 Black or African American, non-Hispanic/Latino; 5 American Indian or Alaska Native, non-Hispanic/Latino; 5 Asian, non-Hispanic/Latino; 50 Hispanic/Latino; 36 Two or more races, non-Hispanic/Latino), 15 international. Average age 37. 257 applicants, 60% accepted, 141 enrolled. In 2016, 136 master's awarded. *Degree requirements:* For master's, thesis (for some programs). *Entrance requirements:* Additional exam requirements/recommendations for international students: Required—TOEFL. *Application deadline:* For fall admission, 8/22 for domestic students, 8/29 for international students; for winter admission, 10/10 for domestic students; for spring admission, 1/2 for domestic students, 1/10 for international students; for summer admission, 5/1 for domestic and international students. Applications are processed on a rolling basis. Electronic applications accepted. *Expenses:* $10,890–$18,450 tuition per year (depending on program). *Financial support:* Research assistantships, institutionally sponsored loans, and unspecified assistantships available. Financial award applicants required to submit FAFSA. *Application contact:* Chris Fontaine, Assistant Vice President for Enrollment Services and Global Admissions, 903-233-4312, E-mail: chrisfontaine@letu.edu.
Website: http://www.letu.edu

**Lipscomb University,** Department of Graduate Psychology and Counseling, Nashville, TN 37204-3951. Offers clinical mental health counseling (MS); counseling psychology (Certificate); marriage and family therapy (MMFT); psychology (MS). *Program availability:* Part-time, evening/weekend. *Faculty:* 13 full-time (5 women), 10 part-time/adjunct (6 women). *Students:* 120 full-time (92 women), 30 part-time (27 women); includes 38 minority (22 Black or African American, non-Hispanic/Latino; 1 American Indian or Alaska Native, non-Hispanic/Latino; 1 Asian, non-Hispanic/Latino; 11 Hispanic/Latino; 3 Two or more races, non-Hispanic/Latino), 2 international. Average age 28. In 2016, 44 master's, 1 other advanced degree awarded. *Degree requirements:* For master's, thesis (for some programs), practicum, internship, capstone. *Entrance requirements:* For master's, GRE, resume, 3 reference letters, transcripts, goals statement. Additional exam requirements/recommendations for international students: Required—TOEFL (minimum score 570 paper-based; 80 iBT). *Application deadline:* For fall admission, 7/1 for domestic students; for spring admission, 11/1 for domestic students. Applications are processed on a rolling basis. Application fee: $50 ($75 for

## *Psychology—General*

international students). Electronic applications accepted. *Expenses:* $898 per hour. *Financial support:* Scholarships/grants and unspecified assistantships available. Financial award applicants required to submit FAFSA. *Faculty research:* Cognitive psychology, neuroscience, health psychology, grief issues. *Unit head:* Dr. Shanna Ray, Director/Professor of Psychology, 615-966-5833, E-mail: shanna.ray@lipscomb.edu. *Application contact:* Kathi Johnson, Recruiting and Marketing Coordinator, 615-966-5237, E-mail: kathi.johnson@lipscomb.edu.
Website: http://www.lipscomb.edu/psychology/graduate-programs

**Loma Linda University,** School of Behavioral Health, Department of Psychology, Loma Linda, CA 92350. Offers clinical psychology (PhD, Psy D). *Accreditation:* APA. *Degree requirements:* For doctorate, comprehensive exam, thesis/dissertation. *Entrance requirements:* For doctorate, GRE General Test, three letters of recommendation. Additional exam requirements/recommendations for international students: Required—TOEFL (minimum score 550 paper-based; 80 iBT). Electronic applications accepted.

**Long Island University–LIU Brooklyn,** Richard L. Conolly College of Liberal Arts and Sciences, Brooklyn, NY 11201-8423. Offers biology (MS); chemistry (MS); clinical psychology (PhD); communication sciences and disorders (MS); creative writing (MFA); English (MA); media arts (MA, MFA); political science (MA); psychology (MA); social science (MS); sociology (MA); speech-language pathology (MS); United Nations (Advanced Certificate); urban studies (MA); writing and production for television (MFA). *Program availability:* Part-time, evening/weekend. *Faculty:* 90 full-time (35 women), 125 part-time/adjunct (67 women). *Students:* 355 full-time (276 women), 220 part-time (161 women); includes 245 minority (119 Black or African American, non-Hispanic/Latino; 32 Asian, non-Hispanic/Latino; 80 Hispanic/Latino; 1 Native Hawaiian or other Pacific Islander, non-Hispanic/Latino; 13 Two or more races, non-Hispanic/Latino), 85 international. 792 applicants, 41% accepted, 141 enrolled. In 2016, 154 master's, 18 doctorates, 4 other advanced degrees awarded. *Degree requirements:* For master's, comprehensive exam (for some programs), thesis (for some programs); for doctorate, comprehensive exam (for some programs), thesis/dissertation (for some programs). *Entrance requirements:* For master's and doctorate, GRE. Additional exam requirements/recommendations for international students: Recommended—TOEFL (minimum score 550 paper-based; 79 iBT). *Application deadline:* Applications are processed on a rolling basis. Application fee: $50. Electronic applications accepted. *Expenses: Tuition:* Full-time $28,272; part-time $1178 per credit. *Required fees:* $451 per term. Tuition and fees vary according to degree level, program and student level. *Financial support:* In 2016–17, 120 fellowships with full and partial tuition reimbursements (averaging $915 per year), 5 research assistantships with full and partial tuition reimbursements (averaging $2,300 per year), 136 teaching assistantships with full and partial tuition reimbursements (averaging $2,300 per year) were awarded; career-related internships or fieldwork, Federal Work-Study, institutionally sponsored loans, scholarships/grants, tuition waivers (full and partial), and unspecified assistantships also available. Support available to part-time students. Financial award application deadline: 2/15; financial award applicants required to submit FAFSA. *Faculty research:* Nanocrystal polymerization of cellulose using electron microscopy. *Unit head:* Dr. Kevin Lauth, Acting Dean, 718-488-1347, E-mail: kevin.lauth@liu.edu. *Application contact:* Gabrielle Gannon, Director of Graduate Admissions, 718-488-1011, Fax: 718-780-6110, E-mail: bkln-admissions@liu.edu.

**Long Island University–LIU Post,** College of Liberal Arts and Sciences, Brookville, NY 11548-1300. Offers applied mathematics (MS); behavior analysis (MA); biology (MS); criminal justice (MS); earth science (MS); English (MA); environmental sustainability (MS); genetic counseling (MS); history (MA); interdisciplinary studies (MA, MS); mathematics for secondary school teachers (MS); mobile GIS application development (Advanced Certificate); political science (MA); psychology (MA). *Program availability:* Part-time, evening/weekend, blended/hybrid learning. *Faculty:* 68 full-time (30 women), 20 part-time/adjunct (13 women). *Students:* 155 full-time (117 women), 125 part-time (82 women); includes 65 minority (17 Black or African American, non-Hispanic/Latino; 14 Asian, non-Hispanic/Latino; 27 Hispanic/Latino; 7 Two or more races, non-Hispanic/Latino), 19 international. 485 applicants, 36% accepted, 77 enrolled. In 2016, 91 master's, 15 other advanced degrees awarded. *Degree requirements:* For master's, comprehensive exam (for some programs), thesis (for some programs). *Entrance requirements:* Additional exam requirements/recommendations for international students: Required—PTE, TOEFL (minimum score 550 paper-based, 75 iBT) or IELTS (6.5). *Application deadline:* Applications are processed on a rolling basis. Application fee: $50. Electronic applications accepted. *Expenses: Tuition:* Full-time $28,272; part-time $1178 per credit. *Required fees:* $451 per term. Tuition and fees vary according to degree level and program. *Financial support:* In 2016–17, 24 teaching assistantships with partial tuition reimbursements (averaging $410 per year) were awarded; fellowships, research assistantships, career-related internships or fieldwork, Federal Work-Study, institutionally sponsored loans, scholarships/grants, tuition waivers (partial), and unspecified assistantships also available. Support available to part-time students. Financial award application deadline: 2/15; financial award applicants required to submit FAFSA. *Faculty research:* Biology, criminal justice, environmental sustainability, mathematics, psychology. *Total annual research expenditures:* $218,000. *Unit head:* Dr. Jeffrey Belnap, Acting Dean, 516-299-2233, Fax: 516-299-4140, E-mail: jeffrey.belnap@liu.edu. *Application contact:* Carol Zerah, Director of Graduate Admissions, 516-299-2900, Fax: 516-299-2137, E-mail: post-enroll@liu.edu.
Website: http://liu.edu/CWPost/Academics/Schools/CLAS

**Louisiana State University and Agricultural & Mechanical College,** Graduate School, College of Humanities and Social Sciences, Department of Psychology, Baton Rouge, LA 70803. Offers biological psychology (MA, PhD); clinical psychology (MA, PhD); cognitive psychology (MA, PhD); developmental psychology (MA, PhD); school psychology (MA, PhD). *Accreditation:* APA (one or more programs are accredited).

**Louisiana Tech University,** Graduate School, College of Education, Department of Psychology and Behavioral Sciences, Ruston, LA 71272. Offers counseling and guidance (MA); counseling psychology (PhD); industrial and organizational psychology (MA, PhD). *Accreditation:* APA (one or more programs are accredited). *Program availability:* Part-time. *Degree requirements:* For master's, thesis or alternative; for doctorate, thesis/dissertation. *Entrance requirements:* For master's and doctorate, GRE General Test. *Application deadline:* For fall admission, 7/29 for domestic students; for spring admission, 2/3 for domestic students. Application fee: $20 ($30 for international students). *Financial support:* Fellowships, research assistantships, teaching assistantships, and career-related internships or fieldwork available. Financial award application deadline: 2/1. *Unit head:* Dr. Donna Thomas, Chair, 318-257-5066, Fax: 318-257-2379, E-mail: dthomas@latech.edu. *Application contact:* Dr. Cathy Stockton, Associate Dean of Graduate Studies, 318-257-3229, Fax: 318-257-2379, E-mail: cstock@latech.edu.
Website: http://education.latech.edu/departments/psychology/

**Loyola University Chicago,** Graduate School, Programs in Non-Clinical Psychology, Chicago, IL 60660. Offers developmental psychology (PhD). *Faculty:* 7 full-time (2 women), 1 (woman) part-time/adjunct. *Students:* 40 full-time (31 women), 5 part-time (all women); includes 14 minority (6 Black or African American, non-Hispanic/Latino; 4 Hispanic/Latino; 4 Two or more races, non-Hispanic/Latino), 2 international. Average age 29. 92 applicants, 17% accepted, 14 enrolled. In 2016, 9 master's, 9 doctorates awarded. Terminal master's awarded for partial completion of doctoral program. *Degree requirements:* For master's, thesis; for doctorate, comprehensive exam, thesis/dissertation, internship. *Entrance requirements:* For master's and doctorate, GRE General Test, sample of written work. Additional exam requirements/recommendations for international students: Required—TOEFL. *Application deadline:* For fall admission, 1/15 for domestic and international students. Application fee: $50. Electronic applications accepted. Application fee is waived when completed online. *Expenses: Tuition:* Full-time $18,594. *Required fees:* $848. Part-time tuition and fees vary according to course load, degree level and program. *Financial support:* In 2016–17, 1 fellowship with tuition reimbursement (averaging $16,000 per year), 5 research assistantships with tuition reimbursements (averaging $16,000 per year), 1 teaching assistantship with tuition reimbursement (averaging $16,000 per year) were awarded; career-related internships or fieldwork, Federal Work-Study, and scholarships/grants also available. Financial award application deadline: 12/15; financial award applicants required to submit FAFSA. *Faculty research:* Program evaluation, attitudes and prejudice, psychological well-being, self esteem and relationships, groups and organizations. *Total annual research expenditures:* $150,000. *Unit head:* Dr. Christine Li-Grine, Graduate Department Head, 773-508-8225, Fax: 773-508-8713, E-mail: cligrining@luc.edu. *Application contact:* Ron Martin, Assistant Director of Enrollment Management, 312-915-8950, Fax: 312-915-8905, E-mail: gradapp@luc.edu.

**Loyola University Maryland,** Graduate Programs, Loyola College of Arts and Sciences, Department of Psychology, Baltimore, MD 21210-2699. Offers clinical psychology (MS, Psy D, CAS); counseling psychology (MS, CAS). *Accreditation:* APA. *Program availability:* Part-time, evening/weekend. *Faculty:* 65 full-time (40 women), 26 part-time/adjunct (18 women). *Students:* 188 full-time (155 women), 54 part-time (40 women); includes 67 minority (22 Black or African American, non-Hispanic/Latino; 1 American Indian or Alaska Native, non-Hispanic/Latino; 13 Asian, non-Hispanic/Latino; 22 Hispanic/Latino; 9 Two or more races, non-Hispanic/Latino), 9 international. Average age 26. 630 applicants, 36% accepted, 93 enrolled. In 2016, 36 master's, 12 doctorates awarded. *Degree requirements:* For doctorate, thesis/dissertation. *Entrance requirements:* For master's, GRE, essay, 3 letters of recommendation, transcript. Additional exam requirements/recommendations for international students: Required—TOEFL (minimum score 550 paper-based), IELTS (minimum score 7). *Application deadline:* For fall admission, 12/1 for domestic students, 3/1 for international students. Application fee: $60. Electronic applications accepted. *Expenses:* Contact institution. *Financial support:* In 2016–17, 11 students received support. Scholarships/grants and unspecified assistantships available. Financial award application deadline: 4/15; financial award applicants required to submit FAFSA. *Unit head:* Traci Martino, 410-617-2175, E-mail: ayu@loyola.edu.

**Madonna University,** Department of Psychology, Livonia, MI 48150-1173. Offers clinical psychology (MSCP). *Program availability:* Part-time, evening/weekend. *Degree requirements:* For master's, thesis or alternative. *Entrance requirements:* Additional exam requirements/recommendations for international students: Required—TOEFL. Electronic applications accepted.

**Mansfield University of Pennsylvania,** Graduate Studies, Program in Organizational Leadership, Mansfield, PA 16933. Offers MA. *Program availability:* Online learning.

**Marietta College,** Program in Psychology, Marietta, OH 45750-4000. Offers MAP. *Program availability:* Part-time. *Faculty:* 5 part-time/adjunct (2 women). *Students:* 10 full-time (6 women), 1 (woman) part-time; includes 1 minority (Black or African American, non-Hispanic/Latino), 1 international. Average age 24. 12 applicants, 83% accepted, 7 enrolled. In 2016, 1 master's awarded. *Degree requirements:* For master's, thesis. *Entrance requirements:* For master's, GRE, transcripts, essay, two letters of recommendation. *Application deadline:* Applications are processed on a rolling basis. Application fee: $25. *Expenses:* $775 per credit hour. *Financial support:* Unspecified assistantships available. *Unit head:* Dr. Chris Klein, Director, 740-376-4795, E-mail: clk002@marietta.edu.

**Marist College,** Graduate Programs, School of Social and Behavioral Sciences, Poughkeepsie, NY 12601-1387. Offers education (M Ed, MA); mental health counseling (MA); school psychology (MA, Adv C). *Program availability:* Part-time, evening/weekend. *Degree requirements:* For master's, thesis optional. *Entrance requirements:* For master's, GRE General Test, letters of recommendation, minimum undergraduate GPA of 3.0, interview. Additional exam requirements/recommendations for international students: Required—TOEFL (minimum score 550 paper-based; 80 iBT); Recommended—IELTS (minimum score 6.5). Electronic applications accepted. *Faculty research:* AIDS prevention, educational intervention, humanistic counseling research, aging and development, neuroimaging.

**Marquette University,** Graduate School, College of Arts and Sciences, Department of Psychology, Milwaukee, WI 53201-1881. Offers PhD. *Accreditation:* APA. *Faculty:* 17 full-time (7 women), 1 part-time/adjunct (0 women). *Students:* 35 full-time (29 women); includes 8 minority (6 Hispanic/Latino; 2 Two or more races, non-Hispanic/Latino), 1 international. Average age 26. 178 applicants, 8% accepted, 5 enrolled. In 2016, 8 doctorates awarded. Terminal master's awarded for partial completion of doctoral program. *Degree requirements:* For doctorate, thesis/dissertation, internship, qualifying exam. *Entrance requirements:* For doctorate, GRE General Test, sample of scholarly writing, official transcripts from all current and previous colleges/universities except Marquette, personal statement, three letters of reference. Additional exam requirements/recommendations for international students: Required—TOEFL (minimum score 530 paper-based). *Application deadline:* For fall admission, 12/1 for domestic and international students. Application fee: $50. Electronic applications accepted. *Financial support:* Fellowships, research assistantships, scholarships/grants, health care benefits, tuition waivers (full and partial), and unspecified assistantships available. Support available to part-time students. Financial award application deadline: 2/15. *Faculty research:* Mental imagery, moral development, organizational behavior, depression, psychotherapy outcomes. *Total annual research expenditures:* $354,067. *Unit head:* Dr. John Grych, Chair, 414-288-7460. *Application contact:* Dr. Alyson Gerdes.
Website: http://www.marquette.edu/psyc/graduate.shtml

**Marshall University,** Academic Affairs Division, College of Liberal Arts, Department of Psychology, Huntington, WV 25755. Offers clinical psychology (Certificate); psychology (MA, Psy D). *Accreditation:* APA. *Degree requirements:* For master's, thesis optional. *Entrance requirements:* For master's, GRE General Test or MAT.

**Martin University,** Division of Psychology, Indianapolis, IN 46218-3867. Offers community psychology (MS). *Program availability:* Part-time, evening/weekend. *Degree requirements:* For master's, thesis. *Entrance requirements:* For master's, GRE General Test, GRE Subject Test.

**Marywood University,** Academic Affairs, Reap College of Education and Human Development, Department of Psychology and Counseling, Program in Psychology, Scranton, PA 18509-1598. Offers clinical services (MA); general theoretical psychology (MA). *Program availability:* Part-time. Electronic applications accepted.

**McGill University,** Faculty of Graduate and Postdoctoral Studies, Faculty of Medicine, Department of Psychiatry, Montréal, QC H3A 2T5, Canada. Offers M Sc.

**McGill University,** Faculty of Graduate and Postdoctoral Studies, Faculty of Science, Department of Psychology, Montréal, QC H3A 2T5, Canada. Offers clinical psychology (PhD); experimental psychology (M Sc, MA, PhD).

**McMaster University,** School of Graduate Studies, Faculty of Science, Department of Psychology, Hamilton, ON L8S 4M2, Canada. Offers M Sc, PhD. *Degree requirements:* For doctorate, comprehensive exam, thesis/dissertation. *Entrance requirements:* For doctorate, GRE General Test, honors degree, minimum B+ average. Additional exam requirements/recommendations for international students: Required—TOEFL (minimum score 550 paper-based).

**McNeese State University,** Doré School of Graduate Studies, Burton College of Education, Department of Psychology, Lake Charles, LA 70609. Offers addiction treatment (MA); applied behavior analysis (MA); counseling psychology (MA); general/experimental psychology (MA). *Program availability:* Evening/weekend. *Entrance requirements:* For master's, GRE.

**Medaille College,** Programs in Psychology, Buffalo, NY 14214-2695. Offers clinical psychology (Psy D); marriage and family therapy (MA); mental health counseling (MA); psychology (MA). *Accreditation:* ACA. *Program availability:* Part-time, evening/weekend. *Degree requirements:* For master's, comprehensive exam (for some programs), thesis (for some programs). *Entrance requirements:* For master's, GRE General Test (psychology), minimum GPA of 2.75 (psychology). Additional exam requirements/recommendations for international students: Required—TOEFL (minimum score 550 paper-based). Electronic applications accepted. *Faculty research:* Schizophrenia, Parkinson's Disease, eyewitness testimony, methodology.

**Memorial University of Newfoundland,** School of Graduate Studies, Department of Psychology, St. John's, NL A1C 5S7, Canada. Offers applied psychological sciences (MAPS); clinical psychology (Psy D); experimental psychology (M Sc, PhD). *Program availability:* Part-time. *Degree requirements:* For master's, workterms (MASP), thesis (M Sc); for doctorate, comprehensive exam, thesis/dissertation, oral thesis defense. *Entrance requirements:* For master's, GRE, honors bachelor's degree of high second class standing or equivalent; for doctorate, GRE, master's or honors degree. Electronic applications accepted. *Faculty research:* Behavioral neuroscience, cognition, theory and research on abnormal behavior.

**Mercy College,** School of Social and Behavioral Sciences, Program in Psychology, Dobbs Ferry, NY 10522-1189. Offers MS. *Program availability:* Part-time, evening/weekend, 100% online, blended/hybrid learning. *Students:* 29 full-time (23 women), 26 part-time (19 women); includes 39 minority (15 Black or African American, non-Hispanic/Latino; 7 Asian, non-Hispanic/Latino; 16 Hispanic/Latino; 1 Native Hawaiian or other Pacific Islander, non-Hispanic/Latino; 1 international. Average age 34. 49 applicants, 39% accepted, 14 enrolled. In 2016, 16 master's awarded. *Degree requirements:* For master's, thesis (for some programs), written comprehensive exam or 6-credit thesis. *Entrance requirements:* For master's, essay, interview, resume, letter of recommendation, undergraduate transcript with minimum GPA of 3.0. Additional exam requirements/recommendations for international students: Required—TOEFL (minimum score 600 paper-based; 100 iBT), IELTS (minimum score 8). *Application deadline:* For fall admission, 8/1 for international students. Applications are processed on a rolling basis. Application fee: $40. Electronic applications accepted. *Expenses:* Tuition: Full-time $15,156; part-time $842 per credit hour. *Required fees:* $620; $155 per term. Tuition and fees vary according to course load and program. *Financial support:* Career-related internships or fieldwork, Federal Work-Study, scholarships/grants, and unspecified assistantships available. Support available to part-time students. Financial award applicants required to submit FAFSA. *Unit head:* Dr. Karol Dean, Dean, School of Social and Behavioral Sciences, 914-674-7517, E-mail: kdean@mercy.edu. *Application contact:* Allison Gurdineer, Senior Director of Admissions, 877-637-2946, Fax: 914-674-7382, E-mail: admissions@mercy.edu.
Website: https://www.mercy.edu/degrees-programs/ms-psychology

**Metropolitan State University,** College of Health, Community and Professional Studies, St. Paul, MN 55106-5000. Offers advanced dental therapy (MS); leadership and management (MSN); nurse educator (MSN); nursing (DNP); psychology (MA). *Accreditation:* AACN. *Program availability:* Part-time. *Degree requirements:* For master's, thesis or alternative; for doctorate, thesis/dissertation or alternative. *Entrance requirements:* For master's, GRE General Test, minimum GPA of 3.0, RN license, BS/BA; for doctorate, minimum GPA of 3.0; RN license, MSN. Additional exam requirements/recommendations for international students: Required—TOEFL (minimum score 550 paper-based). *Faculty research:* Women's health, gerontology.

**Miami University,** College of Arts and Science, Department of Psychology, Oxford, OH 45056. Offers MA, PhD. *Accreditation:* APA (one or more programs are accredited). *Students:* 68 full-time (48 women); includes 14 minority (2 Black or African American, non-Hispanic/Latino; 4 Asian, non-Hispanic/Latino; 7 Hispanic/Latino; 1 Two or more races, non-Hispanic/Latino), 5 international. Average age 27. In 2016, 7 master's, 9 doctorates awarded. *Expenses:* Tuition, state resident: full-time $12,890; part-time $564 per credit hour. Tuition, nonresident: full-time $29,604; part-time $1260 per credit hour. *Required fees:* $638. Part-time tuition and fees vary according to course load and program. *Unit head:* Dr. Cecilia Shore, Professor and Interim Chair, 513-529-4929, E-mail: shorec@miamioh.edu. *Application contact:* 513-529-2400, E-mail: psychology@miamioh.edu.
Website: http://www.MiamiOH.edu/psychology/

**Michigan School of Professional Psychology,** MA and Psy D Programs in Clinical Psychology, Farmington Hills, MI 48334. Offers MA, Psy D. *Accreditation:* APA. *Program availability:* Part-time. *Faculty:* 8 full-time (4 women), 13 part-time/adjunct (11 women). *Students:* 84 full-time (66 women), 56 part-time (46 women); includes 42 minority (29 Black or African American, non-Hispanic/Latino; 2 Asian, non-Hispanic/Latino; 5 Hispanic/Latino; 6 Two or more races, non-Hispanic/Latino), 1 international. Average age 34. 155 applicants, 54% accepted, 61 enrolled. In 2016, 42 master's, 17 doctorates awarded. *Degree requirements:* For master's, practicum; for doctorate, comprehensive exam, thesis/dissertation, internship, practicum. *Entrance requirements:* For master's, undergraduate degree from accredited institution with minimum GPA of 2.5; major in psychology, social work, or counseling; for doctorate, GRE General Test, undergraduate degree from accredited institution with minimum GPA of 2.5; graduate degree in psychology, social work, or counseling from accredited institution with minimum GPA of 3.25; graduate-level practicum. Additional exam requirements/recommendations for international students: Required—TOEFL (minimum score 550 paper-based; 79 iBT). *Application deadline:* For fall admission, 8/15 for domestic students; for winter admission, 12/1 for domestic students; for spring admission, 4/3 for domestic students. Applications are processed on a rolling basis. Application fee: $75. Electronic applications accepted. *Expenses:* Contact institution. *Financial support:* In 2016–17, 6 students received support, including 1 research assistantship, 5 teaching assistantships (averaging $14,436 per year); institutionally sponsored loans, scholarships/grants, and unspecified assistantships also available. Financial award application deadline: 8/30; financial award applicants required to submit FAFSA. *Faculty research:* Health psychology, trauma. *Unit head:* Dr. Frances Brown, Program Director, 248-476-1122, Fax: 248-476-1125. *Application contact:* Carrie Hauser, Coordinator of Admissions and Student Engagement, 248-476-1122 Ext. 117, Fax: 248-476-1125,

E-mail: chauser@mispp.edu.
Website: http://www.mispp.edu

**Michigan State University,** The Graduate School, College of Social Science, Department of Psychology, East Lansing, MI 48824. Offers MA, PhD. *Accreditation:* APA (one or more programs are accredited). *Entrance requirements:* Additional exam requirements/recommendations for international students: Required—TOEFL (minimum score 550 paper-based), Michigan State University ELT ( minimum score 85), Michigan English Language Assessment Battery (minimum score 83). Electronic applications accepted.

**Middle Tennessee State University,** College of Graduate Studies, College of Behavioral and Health Sciences, Department of Psychology, Murfreesboro, TN 37132. Offers clinical psychology (MA); experimental psychology (MA); industrial/organizational psychology (MA); psychology (MA, Ed S); quantitative psychology (MA); school psychology (MA). *Program availability:* Part-time, evening/weekend, online learning. *Degree requirements:* For master's, comprehensive exam, thesis. *Entrance requirements:* For master's, GRE. Additional exam requirements/recommendations for international students: Required—TOEFL (minimum score 525 paper-based; 71 iBT) or IELTS (minimum score 6). Electronic applications accepted. *Faculty research:* Health psychology, industrial/organizational psychology, experimental psychology.

**Millersville University of Pennsylvania,** College of Graduate Studies and Adult Learning, College of Education and Human Services, Department of Psychology, Millersville, PA 17551-0302. Offers clinical psychology (MS); school counseling (M Ed); school psychology (MS). *Program availability:* Part-time, evening/weekend. *Faculty:* 19 full-time (13 women). *Students:* 54 full-time (45 women), 57 part-time (52 women); includes 15 minority (4 Black or African American, non-Hispanic/Latino; 1 American Indian or Alaska Native, non-Hispanic/Latino; 1 Asian, non-Hispanic/Latino; 7 Hispanic/Latino; 2 Two or more races, non-Hispanic/Latino), 1 international. Average age 27. 78 applicants, 78% accepted, 36 enrolled. In 2016, 33 master's awarded. *Degree requirements:* For master's, comprehensive exam (for some programs), thesis optional, internship, practicum, portfolio. *Entrance requirements:* For master's, GRE or MAT (if cumulative GPA is lower than 3.0), at least 1 academic reference; interview. Additional exam requirements/recommendations for international students: Required—TOEFL (minimum score 600 paper-based), IELTS (minimum score 6). Application fee: $40. Electronic applications accepted. *Expenses:* $483 per credit resident tuition; $725 per credit non-resident tuition. *Financial support:* In 2016–17, 37 students received support. Unspecified assistantships available. Financial award application deadline: 3/15; financial award applicants required to submit FAFSA. *Faculty research:* Correlates of creativity, mindfulness training with special needs children, preference assessments with young children, memory and aging, contingency management and behavioral economics, implicit stereotypes. *Unit head:* Dr. Frederick S. Foster-Clark, Chair, 717-871-7265, Fax: 717-871-7946, E-mail: frederick.foster-clark@millersville.edu. *Application contact:* Dr. Victor S. DeSantis, Dean of College of Graduate Studies and Adult Learning/Associate Provost for Civic and Community Engagement, 717-871-7619, Fax: 717-871-7954, E-mail: victor.desantis@millersville.edu.
Website: http://www.millersville.edu/psychology

**Minnesota State University Mankato,** College of Graduate Studies and Research, College of Social and Behavioral Sciences, Department of Psychology, Mankato, MN 56001. Offers clinical psychology (MA); industrial/organizational psychology (MA); school psychology (Psy D). *Program availability:* Part-time. *Students:* 51 full-time (34 women), 12 part-time (11 women). *Degree requirements:* For master's, one foreign language, comprehensive exam, thesis (for some programs). *Entrance requirements:* For master's, GRE General Test, GRE Subject Test (clinical psychology), minimum GPA of 3.0 during previous 2 years, 3 letters of reference. Additional exam requirements/recommendations for international students: Required—TOEFL. *Application deadline:* For fall admission, 1/1 priority date for domestic students. Applications are processed on a rolling basis. Application fee: $40. Electronic applications accepted. *Financial support:* Research assistantships, teaching assistantships with full tuition reimbursements, career-related internships or fieldwork, Federal Work-Study, institutionally sponsored loans, and unspecified assistantships available. Support available to part-time students. Financial award application deadline: 3/15; financial award applicants required to submit FAFSA.
Website: http://sbs.mnsu.edu/psych/

**Mississippi State University,** College of Arts and Sciences, Department of Psychology, Mississippi State, MS 39762. Offers applied cognitive science (PhD); clinical psychology (PhD), including clinical psychology; psychology (MS). *Accreditation:* APA. *Faculty:* 21 full-time (9 women), 2 part-time/adjunct (1 woman). *Students:* 33 full-time (21 women), 6 part-time (5 women); includes 6 minority (3 Black or African American, non-Hispanic/Latino; 2 Asian, non-Hispanic/Latino; 1 Two or more races, non-Hispanic/Latino), 2 international. Average age 27. 53 applicants, 23% accepted, 8 enrolled. In 2016, 1 master's, 3 doctorates awarded. Terminal master's awarded for partial completion of doctoral program. *Degree requirements:* For master's, comprehensive exam, thesis; for doctorate, thesis/dissertation, qualifying exam, comprehensive written and oral exam. *Entrance requirements:* For master's, GRE General Test, minimum GPA of 2.75 on last two years of undergraduate courses; for doctorate, GRE General Test, proficiency in at least 1 computer language, minimum GPA of 3.0. Additional exam requirements/recommendations for international students: Required—TOEFL (minimum score 477 paper-based; 53 iBT); Recommended—IELTS (minimum score 4.5). *Application deadline:* For fall admission, 1/15 priority date for domestic students, 5/1 for international students; for spring admission, 11/1 priority date for domestic students, 9/1 for international students. Applications are processed on a rolling basis. Application fee: $60. Electronic applications accepted. *Expenses:* Tuition, state resident: full-time $7670; part-time $852.50 per credit hour. Tuition, nonresident: full-time $20,790; part-time $2310.50 per credit hour. Part-time tuition and fees vary according to course load. *Financial support:* In 2016–17, 5 research assistantships with full tuition reimbursements (averaging $13,441 per year), 21 teaching assistantships with full tuition reimbursements (averaging $10,291 per year) were awarded; career-related internships or fieldwork, Federal Work-Study, institutionally sponsored loans, scholarships/grants, and unspecified assistantships also available. Financial award application deadline: 4/1; financial award applicants required to submit FAFSA. *Faculty research:* Personality type, alcoholism, blindness and low vision, mental retardation, language comprehension. *Total annual research expenditures:* $1.7 million. *Unit head:* Dr. Mitchell E. Berman, Department Head, 662-325-3202, Fax: 662-325-7212, E-mail: mberman@psychology.msstate.edu. *Application contact:* Lakan Drinker, Admissions and Enrollment Assistant, 662-325-8951, E-mail: ldrinker@grad.msstate.edu.
Website: http://www.psychology.msstate.edu

**Missouri State University,** Graduate College, College of Health and Human Services, Department of Psychology, Springfield, MO 65897. Offers applied behavior analysis (MS); clinical psychology (MS); experimental psychology (MS); forensic child psychology (Certificate); industrial/organizational psychology (MS). *Faculty:* 25 full-time (11 women), 4 part-time/adjunct (0 women). *Students:* 65 full-time (49 women), 7 part-time (5 women); includes 12 minority (1 Black or African American, non-Hispanic/Latino; 3 American Indian or Alaska Native, non-Hispanic/Latino; 3 Asian, non-Hispanic/Latino; 2 Hispanic/Latino; 3 Two or more races, non-Hispanic/Latino), 6 international. Average

age 25. 159 applicants, 25% accepted, 31 enrolled. In 2016, 22 master's awarded. *Degree requirements:* For master's, comprehensive exam, thesis. *Entrance requirements:* For master's, GRE General Test, GRE Subject Test, minimum GPA of 3.25 in major, 3.0 overall; 20 hours of course work in psychology. Additional exam requirements/recommendations for international students: Required—TOEFL (minimum score 550 paper-based; 79 iBT), IELTS (minimum score 6). *Application deadline:* For fall admission, 2/15 priority date for domestic and international students. Application fee: $35 ($50 for international students). Electronic applications accepted. *Expenses:* Tuition, state resident: full-time $5830. Tuition, nonresident: full-time $10,708. *Required fees:* $1130. Tuition and fees vary according to class time, course level, course load and program. *Financial support:* In 2016–17, 9 research assistantships with full tuition reimbursements (averaging $8,772 per year), 8 teaching assistantships with full tuition reimbursements (averaging $8,772 per year) were awarded; career-related internships or fieldwork, Federal Work-Study, institutionally sponsored loans, scholarships/grants, and unspecified assistantships also available. Financial award application deadline: 3/31; financial award applicants required to submit FAFSA. *Faculty research:* Work-family conflict, child forensic psychology, sports psychology, body image assessment, visual learning. *Unit head:* Dr. Paul Deal, Department Head, 417-836-5797, Fax: 417-836-8330, E-mail: psychology@missouristate.edu. *Application contact:* Michael Edwards, Coordinator of Graduate Admissions, 417-836-5330, Fax: 417-836-6200, E-mail: michaeledwards@missouristate.edu.
Website: http://psychology.missouristate.edu/

**Monmouth University,** Graduate Studies, Department of Psychological Counseling, West Long Branch, NJ 07764-1898. Offers professional counseling (MS, PMC); psychological counseling (MA), including addiction studies, psychological counseling. *Accreditation:* ACA. *Program availability:* Part-time, evening/weekend. *Degree requirements:* For master's, comprehensive exam (for some programs), thesis optional, fieldwork. *Entrance requirements:* For master's, GRE, minimum GPA of 3.0 overall, 12 credits in psychology or closely-related field, two Monmouth University psychological counseling recommendation forms, narrative essay; for PMC, degree or current enrollment in CACREP-accredited master's program in counseling with minimum cumulative GPA of 3.0. Additional exam requirements/recommendations for international students: Required—TOEFL (minimum score 550 paper-based; 79 iBT), IELTS (minimum score 5), Michigan English Language Assessment Battery (minimum score 77) or Certificate of Advanced English (minimum score B2). Electronic applications accepted. *Faculty research:* Violent crime, single parenting, the African-American male, counseling older women, successful behavior for under-achieving youth.

**Montana State University,** The Graduate School, College of Letters and Science, Department of Psychology, Bozeman, MT 59717. Offers MS. *Program availability:* Part-time. *Degree requirements:* For master's, comprehensive exam, thesis (for some programs). *Entrance requirements:* For master's, GRE General Test. Additional exam requirements/recommendations for international students: Required—TOEFL (minimum score 550 paper-based). Electronic applications accepted. *Faculty research:* Psychological study of social cognitive, neuro and eating behaviors.

**Montana State University Billings,** College of Arts and Sciences, Department of Psychology, Billings, MT 59101. Offers MS. *Program availability:* Part-time. *Faculty:* 4 full-time. *Students:* 21. *Degree requirements:* For master's, thesis optional. *Entrance requirements:* For master's, GRE General Test, 3 letters of recommendation, resume. Additional exam requirements/recommendations for international students: Required—TOEFL (minimum score 79 iBT), IELTS (minimum score 6.5). *Application deadline:* For fall admission, 3/15 for domestic students, 7/15 for international students; for spring admission, 12/1 for international students. Applications are processed on a rolling basis. Application fee: $40. Electronic applications accepted. *Expenses:* Tuition, state resident: full-time $5265; part-time $3436 per year. Tuition, nonresident: full-time $14,030; part-time $9280 per year. International tuition: $19,295 full-time. Tuition and fees vary according to degree level, campus/location and program. *Financial support:* Research assistantships with partial tuition reimbursements, teaching assistantships with partial tuition reimbursements, career-related internships or fieldwork, Federal Work-Study, institutionally sponsored loans, scholarships/grants, tuition waivers (partial), and unspecified assistantships available. Support available to part-time students. Financial award application deadline: 5/1; financial award applicants required to submit FAFSA. *Unit head:* Dr. Mike Havens, Chair, 406-657-2248, E-mail: mhavens@msubillings.edu. *Application contact:* David M. Sullivan, Graduate Studies Counselor, 406-657-2053, Fax: 406-657-2299, E-mail: dsullivan@msubillings.edu.

**Montclair State University,** The Graduate School, College of Humanities and Social Sciences, Program in Psychology, Montclair, NJ 07043-1624. Offers MA. *Program availability:* Part-time, evening/weekend. *Degree requirements:* For master's, thesis. *Entrance requirements:* For master's, GRE General Test, 2 letters of recommendation, essay. Additional exam requirements/recommendations for international students: Required—TOEFL (minimum score 83 iBT), IELTS (minimum score 6.5). Electronic applications accepted. *Expenses:* Tuition, state resident: part-time $553 per credit. Tuition, nonresident: part-time $854 per credit. *Required fees:* $91 per credit. Tuition and fees vary according to program. *Faculty research:* Information processing, cerebral lateralization, hedonics.

**Morehead State University,** Graduate Programs, College of Science and Technology, Department of Psychology, Morehead, KY 40351. Offers clinical/counseling psychology (MS); general/experimental psychology (MS). *Program availability:* Part-time, evening/weekend. *Degree requirements:* For master's, comprehensive exam, thesis optional. *Entrance requirements:* For master's, GRE General Test, 18 undergraduate hours in psychology, minimum GPA of 3.0, 3 letters of recommendation. Additional exam requirements/recommendations for international students: Required—TOEFL (minimum score 500 paper-based). Electronic applications accepted. *Faculty research:* Mood induction effects, serotonin receptor activity, stress, perceptual processes.

**Morgan State University,** School of Graduate Studies, College of Liberal Arts, Department of Psychology, Baltimore, MD 21251. Offers psychometrics (MS, PhD). *Entrance requirements:* For master's and doctorate, GRE.

**Mount Aloysius College,** Program in Psychology, Cresson, PA 16630-1999. Offers MS. *Program availability:* Part-time, evening/weekend. *Entrance requirements:* For master's, GRE General Test. Additional exam requirements/recommendations for international students: Required—IELTS (minimum score 6.5); Recommended—TOEFL. *Application deadline:* Applications are processed on a rolling basis. Application fee: $30. Electronic applications accepted. Application fee is waived when completed online. *Expenses: Tuition:* Full-time $6750; part-time $750 per credit. *Required fees:* $285 per semester. *Financial support:* Unspecified assistantships available. *Application contact:* Matthew P. Bodenschatz, Director of Graduate and Continuing Education Admissions, 814-886-6556, Fax: 814-886-6441, E-mail: mbodenschatz@mtaloy.edu.

**Murray State University,** College of Humanities and Fine Arts, Program in Psychology, Murray, KY 42071. Offers clinical psychology (MA, MS); psychology (MA, MS). *Program availability:* Part-time. *Degree requirements:* For master's, one foreign language, comprehensive exam (for some programs), thesis. *Entrance requirements:* For master's,

GRE General Test. Additional exam requirements/recommendations for international students: Required—TOEFL.

**National Louis University,** College of Arts and Sciences, Chicago, IL 60603. Offers adult education (Ed D); counseling and human services (MS); language and academic development (M Ed, Certificate); psychology (MA, PhD, Certificate); public policy (MA); written communication (MS, Certificate). *Program availability:* Part-time, evening/weekend, online learning. *Degree requirements:* For master's and Certificate, comprehensive exam (for some programs), thesis (for some programs); for doctorate, thesis/dissertation. *Entrance requirements:* For master's, MAT or GRE, 3 professional or academic references, interview, minimum GPA of 3.0; for doctorate, GRE General Test, MAT, or Watson-Glaser Critical Thinking Appraisal, three professional or academic references, statement of academic and professional goals, 3 years of experience in field, interview, master's degree, resume, writing sample; for Certificate, GRE, MAT, or Watson-Glaser Critical Thinking Appraisal, three professional or academic references, statement of academic and professional goals, interview, minimum GPA of 3.0. Additional exam requirements/recommendations for international students: Required—Department of Language Studies Assessment or TOEFL (minimum score 550 paper-based; 79 iBT). Electronic applications accepted.

**New Mexico Highlands University,** Graduate Studies, College of Arts and Sciences, Department of Social and Behavioral Sciences, Las Vegas, NM 87701. Offers psychology (MS), including clinical psychology/counseling, general psychology; public affairs (MA), including applied sociology; Southwest studies (MA), including anthropology. *Program availability:* Part-time. *Degree requirements:* For master's, comprehensive exam, thesis or alternative. *Entrance requirements:* For master's, minimum undergraduate GPA of 3.0. Additional exam requirements/recommendations for international students: Required—TOEFL (minimum score 540 paper-based). *Faculty research:* Southwest Native American resettlement development, community-level interventions, neurochemistry of personality, comparative criminal justice, social theory and activism.

**New Mexico State University,** College of Arts and Sciences, Department of Psychology, Las Cruces, NM 88003. Offers engineering psychology (PhD); psychology (MA). *Program availability:* Part-time. *Faculty:* 12 full-time (4 women). *Students:* 29 full-time (14 women), 5 part-time (2 women); includes 9 minority (2 Asian, non-Hispanic/Latino; 5 Hispanic/Latino; 2 Two or more races, non-Hispanic/Latino), 3 international. Average age 30. 36 applicants, 17% accepted, 4 enrolled. In 2016, 4 master's, 1 doctorate awarded. *Degree requirements:* For master's, thesis; for doctorate, comprehensive exam, thesis/dissertation, work-related experience (teaching or internship). *Entrance requirements:* For master's, GRE General Test, letters of recommendation, curriculum vitae, personal statement; for doctorate, GRE General Test, letters of recommendation, master's thesis, curriculum vitae, personal statement. Additional exam requirements/recommendations for international students: Required—TOEFL (minimum score 550 paper-based; 79 iBT), IELTS (minimum score 6.5). *Application deadline:* For fall admission, 2/1 priority date for domestic students, 2/1 for international students. Applications are processed on a rolling basis. Application fee: $40 ($50 for international students). Electronic applications accepted. *Expenses:* Tuition, state resident: full-time $4086. Tuition, nonresident: full-time $14,254. *Required fees:* $853. Tuition and fees vary according to course load. *Financial support:* In 2016–17, 30 students received support, including 4 fellowships (averaging $4,088 per year), 2 research assistantships (averaging $12,723 per year), 18 teaching assistantships (averaging $14,251 per year); career-related internships or fieldwork, Federal Work-Study, scholarships/grants, traineeships, health care benefits, and unspecified assistantships also available. Support available to part-time students. Financial award application deadline: 3/1. *Faculty research:* Engineering, cognitive, and social psychology; human/computer interaction; cognitive science. *Total annual research expenditures:* $137,762. *Unit head:* Dr. Dominic A. Simon, Department Head, 575-646-2502, Fax: 575-646-6212, E-mail: domsimon@nmsu.edu. *Application contact:* Dr. Laura J. Madson, Chair of Graduate Committee, 575-646-6207, Fax: 575-646-6212, E-mail: lmadson@nmsu.edu.
Website: http://psych.nmsu.edu

**The New School,** The New School for Social Research, Department of Psychology, New York, NY 10003. Offers clinical psychology (PhD); cognitive, social, and developmental psychology (PhD); psychology (MA). *Accreditation:* APA (one or more programs are accredited). *Program availability:* Part-time. *Faculty:* 16 full-time (6 women), 12 part-time/adjunct (4 women). *Students:* 115 full-time (85 women), 99 part-time (77 women); includes 36 minority (9 Black or African American, non-Hispanic/Latino; 1 American Indian or Alaska Native, non-Hispanic/Latino; 11 Asian, non-Hispanic/Latino; 12 Hispanic/Latino; 3 Two or more races, non-Hispanic/Latino), 32 international. Average age 29. 247 applicants, 84% accepted, 60 enrolled. In 2016, 57 master's, 19 doctorates awarded. Terminal master's awarded for partial completion of doctoral program. *Degree requirements:* For master's, comprehensive exam, thesis (for some programs); for doctorate, comprehensive exam, thesis/dissertation. *Entrance requirements:* For master's, GRE, letters of recommendation, writing sample, essays, unofficial transcripts; for doctorate, letters of recommendation, writing sample, essays, unofficial transcripts. Additional exam requirements/recommendations for international students: Required—TOEFL (minimum score 100 iBT), IELTS (minimum score 7), PTE (minimum score 68). *Application deadline:* For fall admission, 8/1 priority date for domestic and international students; for spring admission, 10/15 priority date for domestic and international students. Applications are processed on a rolling basis. Application fee: $50. Electronic applications accepted. *Expenses:* Contact institution. *Financial support:* Fellowships, research assistantships, teaching assistantships, career-related internships or fieldwork, Federal Work-Study, scholarships/grants, and tuition waivers (full and partial) available. Support available to part-time students. Financial award application deadline: 2/1; financial award applicants required to submit FAFSA. *Faculty research:* Cognitive, social, and developmental psychology; clinical psychology; mental health and substance abuse counseling. *Unit head:* Dr. William Milberg, Dean, The New School for Social Research, 212-229-5777, E-mail: milbergw@newschool.edu. *Application contact:* Dana Messinger, Director of Graduate Admission, 212-229-5150 Ext. 2300, E-mail: socialresearchadmit@newschool.edu.

**New York Medical College,** School of Health Sciences and Practice, Valhalla, NY 10595. Offers behavioral sciences and health promotion (MPH); biostatistics (MS); children with special health care (Graduate Certificate); emergency preparedness (Graduate Certificate); environmental health science (MPH); epidemiology (MPH, MS); global health (Graduate Certificate); health education (Graduate Certificate); health policy and management (MPH, Dr PH); industrial hygiene (Graduate Certificate); pediatric dysphagia (Post-Graduate Certificate); physical therapy (DPT); public health (Graduate Certificate); speech-language pathology (MS). *Accreditation:* CEPH. *Program availability:* Part-time, evening/weekend, 100% online, blended/hybrid learning. *Faculty:* 42 full-time (31 women), 236 part-time/adjunct (138 women). *Students:* 235 full-time (165 women), 252 part-time (185 women); includes 188 minority (83 Black or African American, non-Hispanic/Latino; 1 American Indian or Alaska Native, non-Hispanic/Latino; 62 Asian, non-Hispanic/Latino; 36 Hispanic/Latino; 6 Two or more races, non-Hispanic/Latino), 26 international. Average age 27. In 2016, 110 master's, 37 doctorates awarded. *Degree requirements:* For master's, comprehensive exam (for some

programs), thesis (for some programs); for doctorate, thesis/dissertation. *Expenses:* $1,070 per credit tuition, $105 fees. *Unit head:* Ben Watson, PhD, Vice Dean, 914-594-4531, E-mail: ben_watson@nymc.edu. *Application contact:* Veronica Jarek-Prinz, Associate Dean for Admissions and Enrollment Management, 914-594-3941, E-mail: veronica_jarekprinz@nymc.edu.
Website: http://www.nymc.edu/school-of-health-sciences-and-practice-shsp/

**New York University,** Graduate School of Arts and Science, Department of Psychology, New York, NY 10012-1019. Offers cognition and perception (PhD); community psychology (PhD); general psychology (MA); industrial/organizational psychology (MA); psychotherapy and psychoanalysis (Advanced Certificate); social/personality psychology (PhD). *Program availability:* Part-time. Terminal master's awarded for partial completion of doctoral program. *Degree requirements:* For master's, comprehensive exam, thesis or alternative; for doctorate, thesis/dissertation. *Entrance requirements:* For master's and doctorate, GRE General Test. Additional exam requirements/recommendations for international students: Required—TOEFL. *Faculty research:* Vision, memory, social cognition, social and cognitive development, relationships.

**New York University,** Steinhardt School of Culture, Education, and Human Development, Department of Applied Psychology, Programs in Educational and Developmental Psychology, New York, NY 10003. Offers developmental psychology (PhD); human development and social intervention (MA); psychology and social intervention (PhD). *Accreditation:* APA (one or more programs are accredited). *Program availability:* Part-time. *Degree requirements:* For master's, thesis (for some programs); for doctorate, thesis/dissertation. *Entrance requirements:* For doctorate, GRE General Test, interview. Additional exam requirements/recommendations for international students: Required—TOEFL. Electronic applications accepted. *Faculty research:* Schools and communities, self-regulation and academic achievement, intervention and social change, trauma and resilience, cognition.

**Norfolk State University,** School of Graduate Studies, School of Liberal Arts, Department of Psychology, Norfolk, VA 23504. Offers community/clinical psychology (MA); psychology (Psy D). Psy D offered through the Virginia Consortium for Professional Psychology. *Program availability:* Part-time. *Degree requirements:* For master's, comprehensive exam, thesis or alternative; for doctorate, comprehensive exam, thesis/dissertation. *Entrance requirements:* For master's, minimum GPA of 2.7.

**North Carolina Central University,** College of Behavioral and Social Sciences, Department of Psychology, Durham, NC 27707-3129. Offers MA. *Program availability:* Part-time, evening/weekend. *Degree requirements:* For master's, one foreign language, comprehensive exam, thesis. *Entrance requirements:* For master's, GRE, minimum GPA of 3.0 in major, 2.5 overall. Additional exam requirements/recommendations for international students: Required—TOEFL.

**North Carolina State University,** Graduate School, College of Humanities and Social Sciences, Department of Psychology, Raleigh, NC 27695. Offers developmental psychology (PhD); ergonomics and experimental psychology (PhD); industrial/organizational psychology (PhD); psychology in the public interest (PhD); school psychology (PhD). *Accreditation:* APA. *Degree requirements:* For doctorate, comprehensive exam, thesis/dissertation. *Entrance requirements:* For doctorate, GRE General Test, GRE Subject Test (industrial/organizational psychology), MAT (recommended), minimum GPA of 3.0 in major. Electronic applications accepted. *Faculty research:* Cognitive and social development (human factors, families, the workplace, community issues and health, aging).

**Northcentral University,** Graduate Studies, San Diego, CA 92106. Offers business (MBA, DBA, PhD, Postbaccalaureate Certificate); education (M Ed, Ed D, PhD, Ed S, Post-Master's Certificate, Postbaccalaureate Certificate); marriage and family therapy (MA, DMFT, PhD, Post-Master's Certificate, Postbaccalaureate Certificate); psychology (MA, PhD, Post-Master's Certificate, Postbaccalaureate Certificate). *Program availability:* Part-time, evening/weekend, online only, 100% online. *Faculty:* 98 full-time (63 women), 385 part-time/adjunct (203 women). *Students:* 5,036 full-time (3,291 women), 5,747 part-time (3,977 women); includes 3,777 minority (2,550 Black or African American, non-Hispanic/Latino; 76 American Indian or Alaska Native, non-Hispanic/Latino; 192 Asian, non-Hispanic/Latino; 603 Hispanic/Latino; 39 Native Hawaiian or other Pacific Islander, non-Hispanic/Latino; 317 Two or more races, non-Hispanic/Latino). Average age 45. In 2016, 799 master's, 399 doctorates, 230 other advanced degrees awarded. *Degree requirements:* For doctorate, comprehensive exam, thesis/dissertation. *Entrance requirements:* For master's, bachelor's degree from regionally- or nationally-accredited institution, current resume or curriculum vitae, statement of intent, interview, and background check (for marriage and family therapy); for doctorate, post-baccalaureate master's degree and/or doctoral degree from nationally- or regionally-accredited academic institution; for other advanced degree, bachelor's-level or higher degree from accredited institution or university (for Post-Baccalaureate Certificate); master's and/or doctoral degree from regionally- or nationally-accredited academic institution (for Post-Master's Certificate). Additional exam requirements/recommendations for international students: Required—TOEFL (minimum score 550 paper-based; 79 iBT), IELTS (minimum score 6.5), PTE (minimum score 53). *Application deadline:* Applications are processed on a rolling basis. Application fee: $0. Electronic applications accepted. *Expenses: Tuition:* Full-time $16,821; part-time $935 per credit hour. One-time fee: $350. Tuition and fees vary according to degree level and program. *Financial support:* Scholarships/grants available. *Faculty research:* Business management, curriculum and instruction, educational leadership, health psychology, organizational behavior. *Unit head:* Dr. David Harpool, Acting Provost, 888-327-2877 Ext. 8181, E-mail: provost@ncu.edu. *Application contact:* Ken Boutelle, Vice President, Enrollment Services, 888-628-4979, E-mail: enrollmentservices@ncu.edu.

**North Dakota State University,** College of Graduate and Interdisciplinary Studies, College of Science and Mathematics, Department of Psychology, Fargo, ND 58102. Offers clinical psychology (MS); health and social psychology (PhD); psychological clinical science (PhD); psychology (MS); visual and cognitive neuroscience (PhD). *Degree requirements:* For master's, thesis; for doctorate, thesis/dissertation. *Entrance requirements:* For master's and doctorate, GRE General Test, GRE Subject Test. Additional exam requirements/recommendations for international students: Required—TOEFL (minimum score 525 paper-based; 71 iBT). Electronic applications accepted. *Faculty research:* Cognition science, neuropsychology, group behavior, applied behavior analysis, behavior therapy.

**Northeastern State University,** College of Education, Department of Psychology and Counseling, Tahlequah, OK 74464-2399. Offers counseling psychology (MS); school counseling (M Ed); substance abuse counseling (MS). *Program availability:* Part-time, evening/weekend. *Faculty:* 16 full-time (7 women), 4 part-time/adjunct (3 women). *Students:* 80 full-time (61 women), 73 part-time (61 women); includes 66 minority (7 Black or African American, non-Hispanic/Latino; 23 American Indian or Alaska Native, non-Hispanic/Latino; 3 Asian, non-Hispanic/Latino; 5 Hispanic/Latino; 28 Two or more races, non-Hispanic/Latino), 1 international. Average age 32. In 2016, 43 master's awarded. *Degree requirements:* For master's, thesis (for some programs), written and oral examinations. *Entrance requirements:* For master's, GRE, minimum GPA of 2.5. Application fee: $25. *Expenses:* Tuition, state resident: full-time $2816; part-time

$216.60 per credit hour. Tuition, nonresident: full-time $6365; part-time $489.60 per credit hour. *Required fees:* $37.40 per credit hour. *Financial support:* Teaching assistantships, career-related internships or fieldwork, and Federal Work-Study available. Financial award application deadline: 3/1. *Unit head:* Dr. Kenny Paris, Department Chair of Psychology and Counseling, 918-444-3021, E-mail: parisk@nsuok.edu. *Application contact:* Josh McCollum, Graduate Coordinator, 918-444-2093, E-mail: mccolluj@nsuok.edu.
Website: https://academics.nsuok.edu/education/EducationHome/COEDepartments/PsychologyCounseling.aspx

**Northeastern University,** College of Science, Boston, MA 02115-5096. Offers applied mathematics (MS); bioinformatics (MS); biology (PhD); biotechnology (MS); chemistry (MS, PhD); ecology, evolution, and marine biology (PhD); marine biology (MS); mathematics (MS, PhD); network science (PhD); operations research (MSOR); physics (MS, PhD); psychology (PhD). *Program availability:* Part-time. *Faculty:* 217 full-time (76 women), 58 part-time/adjunct (20 women). *Students:* 578 full-time (268 women), 63 part-time (27 women). In 2016, 121 master's, 50 doctorates awarded. Terminal master's awarded for partial completion of doctoral program. *Degree requirements:* For master's, comprehensive exam (for some programs), thesis; for doctorate, comprehensive exam (for some programs), thesis/dissertation. *Entrance requirements:* For master's, GRE General Test. *Application deadline:* Applications are processed on a rolling basis. Application fee: $75. Electronic applications accepted. *Expenses:* Contact institution. *Financial support:* Fellowships with tuition reimbursements, research assistantships with tuition reimbursements, teaching assistantships with tuition reimbursements, career-related internships or fieldwork, scholarships/grants, health care benefits, tuition waivers (full and partial), and unspecified assistantships available. Support available to part-time students. Financial award applicants required to submit FAFSA. *Unit head:* Dr. Kenneth Henderson, Dean. *Application contact:* Graduate Student Services, 617-373-4275, E-mail: gradcos@northeastern.edu.
Website: http://www.northeastern.edu/cos/

**Northern Arizona University,** Graduate College, College of Social and Behavioral Sciences, Department of Psychological Sciences, Flagstaff, AZ 86011. Offers clinical health psychology (MA); general psychology (MA); teaching psychology (MA). *Program availability:* Part-time. *Degree requirements:* For master's, comprehensive exam (for some programs), thesis (for some programs), oral defense. *Entrance requirements:* For master's, GRE General Test. Additional exam requirements/recommendations for international students: Required—TOEFL (minimum score 550 paper-based; 80 iBT), IELTS (minimum score 7). Electronic applications accepted. *Expenses:* Tuition, state resident: full-time $8971; part-time $444 per credit hour. Tuition, nonresident: full-time $20,958; part-time $1164 per credit hour. *Required fees:* $1018; $644 per credit hour. Tuition and fees vary according to course load, campus/location and program.

**Northern Illinois University,** Graduate School, College of Liberal Arts and Sciences, Department of Psychology, De Kalb, IL 60115-2854. Offers MA, PhD. *Accreditation:* APA (one or more programs are accredited). *Faculty:* 26 full-time (11 women), 5 part-time/adjunct (1 woman). *Students:* 98 full-time (74 women), 17 part-time (13 women); includes 19 minority (6 Black or African American, non-Hispanic/Latino; 2 Asian, non-Hispanic/Latino; 9 Hispanic/Latino; 2 Two or more races, non-Hispanic/Latino), 6 international. Average age 27. 333 applicants, 13% accepted, 20 enrolled. In 2016, 17 master's, 12 doctorates awarded. *Degree requirements:* For master's, comprehensive exam, thesis optional; for doctorate, thesis/dissertation, candidacy exam, dissertation defense. *Entrance requirements:* For master's, GRE General Test, minimum GPA of 3.0 for last 2 years of undergraduate work; for doctorate, GRE General Test, minimum undergraduate GPA of 2.75, graduate 3.2; master's degree with research thesis. Additional exam requirements/recommendations for international students: Required—TOEFL (minimum score 550 paper-based). *Application deadline:* For fall admission, 3/1 for domestic students, 5/1 for international students; for spring admission, 11/1 for domestic students, 10/1 for international students. Applications are processed on a rolling basis. Application fee: $40. Electronic applications accepted. *Financial support:* In 2016–17, 24 research assistantships with full tuition reimbursements, 64 teaching assistantships with full tuition reimbursements were awarded; fellowships with full tuition reimbursements, career-related internships or fieldwork, Federal Work-Study, scholarships/grants, tuition waivers (full), and staff assistantships also available. Support available to part-time students. Financial award applicants required to submit FAFSA. *Faculty research:* Neglect syndrome, ADHD, workplace discrimination, adolescent suicide, social dilemmas. *Unit head:* Dr. Leslie Matuszewich, Chair, 815-753-7065, E-mail: imatekaitis@niu.edu. *Application contact:* Dr. James V. Corwin, Director, Graduate Studies, 815-753-7088, E-mail: jcorwin@niu.edu.
Website: http://www.niu.edu/psyc/

**Northern Michigan University,** Office of Graduate Education and Research, College of Arts and Sciences, Department of Psychology, Marquette, MI 49855-5301. Offers applied behavior analysis (MS); performance improvement (Graduate Certificate); psychology (MS); training and performance improvement (MS). *Program availability:* Part-time. *Degree requirements:* For master's, thesis (for some programs). *Entrance requirements:* For master's, minimum GPA of 3.0; bachelor's degree preferably in psychology; undergraduate course on introduction to psychology; undergraduate course on statistics; personal statement; 3 letters of recommendation. Additional exam requirements/recommendations for international students: Required—TOEFL (minimum score 550 paper-based; 79 iBT), IELTS (minimum score 6.5). Electronic applications accepted. *Faculty research:* Emotion and cognition, neuropsychopharmacology, sensation and perception, behavior analysis, developmental psychology.

**Northwestern State University of Louisiana,** Graduate Studies and Research, Department of Psychology, Natchitoches, LA 71497. Offers clinical psychology (MS). *Degree requirements:* For master's, comprehensive exam, thesis or alternative. *Entrance requirements:* For master's, GRE General Test, GRE Subject Test, minimum undergraduate GPA of 2.5. Additional exam requirements/recommendations for international students: Required—TOEFL. Electronic applications accepted.

**Northwestern University,** The Graduate School, Judd A. and Marjorie Weinberg College of Arts and Sciences, Department of Psychology, Evanston, IL 60208. Offers brain, behavior and cognition (PhD); clinical psychology (PhD); cognitive psychology (PhD); personality psychology (PhD); social psychology (PhD); JD/PhD. Admissions and degrees offered through The Graduate School. *Accreditation:* APA (one or more programs are accredited). *Program availability:* Part-time. *Degree requirements:* For doctorate, thesis/dissertation. *Entrance requirements:* For doctorate, GRE General Test, GRE Subject Test. Additional exam requirements/recommendations for international students: Required—TOEFL. Electronic applications accepted. *Faculty research:* Memory and higher order cognition, anxiety and depression, effectiveness of psychotherapy, social cognition, molecular basis of memory.

**Northwest University,** College of Social and Behavioral Sciences, Kirkland, WA 98033. Offers counseling psychology (MA, Psy D); international community development (MA). *Program availability:* Evening/weekend. *Entrance requirements:* For master's, 3 character references. Additional exam requirements/recommendations for international students: Required—TOEFL (minimum score 580 paper-based). *Expenses:* Contact institution.

## Psychology—General

**Notre Dame de Namur University,** Division of Academic Affairs, College of Arts and Sciences, Department of Clinical Psychology and Gerontology, Belmont, CA 94002-1908. Offers clinical psychology (MS); clinical psychology: marital and family therapy (MS). *Program availability:* Part-time. *Degree requirements:* For master's, thesis. *Entrance requirements:* For master's, interview, minimum GPA of 2.5. Additional exam requirements/recommendations for international students: Required—TOEFL (minimum score 550 paper-based; 79 iBT). Electronic applications accepted.

**Nova Southeastern University,** College of Psychology, Fort Lauderdale, FL 33314-7796. Offers clinical psychology (PhD, Psy D); counseling (MS); experimental psychology (MS); forensic psychology (MS); general psychology (MS); mental health counseling (MS); school counseling (MS); school psychology (Psy D, Psy S). *Accreditation:* APA (one or more programs are accredited). *Program availability:* 100% online, blended/hybrid learning. *Faculty:* 51 full-time (21 women), 120 part-time/adjunct (70 women). *Students:* 724 full-time (596 women), 918 part-time (792 women); includes 797 minority (276 Black or African American, non-Hispanic/Latino; 1 American Indian or Alaska Native, non-Hispanic/Latino; 44 Asian, non-Hispanic/Latino; 427 Hispanic/Latino; 2 Native Hawaiian or other Pacific Islander, non-Hispanic/Latino; 47 Two or more races, non-Hispanic/Latino), 41 international. Average age 31. 1,349 applicants, 61% accepted, 651 enrolled. In 2016, 377 master's, 177 doctorates, 26 other advanced degrees awarded. Terminal master's awarded for partial completion of doctoral program. *Degree requirements:* For master's, comprehensive exam, 3 practica; for doctorate, thesis/dissertation, clinical internship, competency exam; for Psy S, comprehensive exam, internship. *Entrance requirements:* For doctorate, GRE General Test, GRE Subject Test (recommended), minimum undergraduate GPA of 3.0; for Psy S, GRE General Test. Additional exam requirements/recommendations for international students: Required—TOEFL (minimum score 550 paper-based). *Application deadline:* Applications are processed on a rolling basis. Application fee: $50. Electronic applications accepted. *Expenses:* Contact institution. *Financial support:* In 2016–17, 197 students received support, including 15 research assistantships (averaging $5,600 per year), 68 teaching assistantships (averaging $2,000 per year); career-related internships or fieldwork, Federal Work-Study, institutionally sponsored loans, scholarships/grants, and unspecified assistantships also available. Support available to part-time students. Financial award application deadline: 4/15; financial award applicants required to submit FAFSA. *Faculty research:* Clinical health psychology, multicultural/diversity psychology, clinical neuropsychology, clinical child psychology, family violence. *Unit head:* Dr. Karen Grosby, Dean, 954-262-5712, Fax: 954-262-3859, E-mail: grosby@nova.edu. *Application contact:* Carlos Perez, Senior Manager of Outreach, 954-262-5702, Fax: 954-262-3893, E-mail: gradschool@nova.edu.
Website: http://psychology.nova.edu/

**The Ohio State University,** Graduate School, College of Arts and Sciences, Division of Social and Behavioral Sciences, Department of Psychology, Columbus, OH 43210. Offers behavioral neuroscience (PhD); clinical psychology (PhD); cognitive psychology (PhD); developmental psychology (PhD); intellectual and developmental disabilities psychology (PhD); quantitative psychology (PhD); social psychology (PhD). *Accreditation:* APA. *Faculty:* 57. *Students:* 156 full-time (95 women); includes 23 minority (6 Black or African American, non-Hispanic/Latino; 9 Asian, non-Hispanic/Latino; 8 Hispanic/Latino), 26 international. Average age 26. In 2016, 26 doctorates awarded. *Degree requirements:* For doctorate, thesis/dissertation. *Entrance requirements:* For doctorate, GRE General Test. Additional exam requirements/recommendations for international students: Required—TOEFL (minimum score 600 paper-based; 100 iBT); Recommended—IELTS (minimum score 8). *Application deadline:* For fall admission, 12/1 for domestic and international students. Applications are processed on a rolling basis. Application fee: $60 ($70 for international students). Electronic applications accepted. *Financial support:* Fellowships with tuition reimbursements, research assistantships with tuition reimbursements, and teaching assistantships with tuition reimbursements available. *Unit head:* Dr. John Bruno, Chair, 614-292-3038, E-mail: bruno.1@osu.edu. *Application contact:* Graduate and Professional Admissions, 614-292-9444, Fax: 614-292-3895, E-mail: gpadmissions@osu.edu.
Website: http://www.psy.ohio-state.edu/

**Ohio University,** Graduate College, College of Arts and Sciences, Department of Psychology, Athens, OH 45701-2979. Offers clinical psychology (PhD); experimental psychology (PhD); organizational psychology (PhD). *Accreditation:* APA. *Degree requirements:* For doctorate, one foreign language, comprehensive exam, thesis/dissertation. *Entrance requirements:* For doctorate, GRE General Test, GRE Subject Test. Additional exam requirements/recommendations for international students: Required—TOEFL (minimum score 550 paper-based; 80 iBT) or IELTS (minimum score 6.5). *Application deadline:* For fall admission, 1/1 for domestic and international students. Application fee: $50 ($55 for international students). Electronic applications accepted. *Financial support:* Fellowships with full tuition reimbursements, research assistantships with full tuition reimbursements, teaching assistantships with full tuition reimbursements, career-related internships or fieldwork, Federal Work-Study, institutionally sponsored loans, traineeships, tuition waivers (partial), and unspecified assistantships available. Financial award application deadline: 1/15. *Faculty research:* Health, cognitive, child clinical, and social psychology. *Unit head:* Chantel Weisenmuller, Director, 740-597-1251, E-mail: weisenmu@ohio.edu. *Application contact:* Karyl Jones, Administrative Secretary, 740-593-1090, Fax: 740-593-0579, E-mail: psychology@ohio.edu.
Website: http://www.psych.ohiou.edu/

**Oklahoma State University,** College of Arts and Sciences, Department of Psychology, Stillwater, OK 74078. Offers clinical psychology (PhD); general psychology (MS); lifespan development psychology (PhD). *Accreditation:* APA (one or more programs are accredited). *Faculty:* 31 full-time (19 women), 1 (woman) part-time/adjunct. *Students:* 42 full-time (34 women), 14 part-time (8 women); includes 12 minority (1 Black or African American, non-Hispanic/Latino; 4 American Indian or Alaska Native, non-Hispanic/Latino; 1 Asian, non-Hispanic/Latino; 3 Hispanic/Latino; 1 Native Hawaiian or other Pacific Islander, non-Hispanic/Latino; 2 Two or more races, non-Hispanic/Latino), 2 international. Average age 26. 160 applicants, 6% accepted, 9 enrolled. In 2016, 11 master's, 7 doctorates awarded. *Degree requirements:* For master's, thesis or alternative; for doctorate, comprehensive exam, thesis/dissertation. *Entrance requirements:* For master's and doctorate, GRE General Test. Additional exam requirements/recommendations for international students: Required—TOEFL (minimum score 550 paper-based; 79 iBT). *Application deadline:* For fall admission, 3/1 priority date for international students; for spring admission, 8/1 priority date for international students. Applications are processed on a rolling basis. Application fee: $40 ($75 for international students). Electronic applications accepted. *Expenses:* Tuition, state resident: full-time $3775; part-time $209.70 per credit hour. Tuition, nonresident: full-time $14,851; part-time $825.05 per credit hour. *Required fees:* $2027; $112.60 per credit hour. Tuition and fees vary according to campus/location. *Financial support:* In 2016–17, 15 research assistantships (averaging $13,194 per year), 41 teaching assistantships (averaging $11,532 per year) were awarded; career-related internships or fieldwork, Federal Work-Study, scholarships/grants, health care benefits, tuition waivers (partial), and unspecified assistantships also available. Support available to part-time

students. Financial award application deadline: 3/1; financial award applicants required to submit FAFSA. *Unit head:* Dr. Thad Leffingwell, Department Head, 405-744-7494, Fax: 405-744-8067, E-mail: thad.leffingwell@okstate.edu. *Application contact:* Patricia Alexander, Graduate Advisor, 405-744-7591, Fax: 405-744-8967, E-mail: patricia.alexander@okstate.edu.
Website: http://psychology.okstate.edu

**Old Dominion University,** College of Sciences, Doctoral Program in Psychology, Norfolk, VA 23529. Offers applied psychological sciences (PhD); human factors psychology (PhD); industrial/organizational psychology (PhD). *Faculty:* 28 full-time (12 women), 11 part-time/adjunct (9 women). *Students:* 47 full-time (26 women); includes 4 minority (1 Black or African American, non-Hispanic/Latino; 3 Hispanic/Latino). Average age 25. 74 applicants, 14% accepted, 9 enrolled. In 2016, 3 doctorates awarded. *Degree requirements:* For doctorate, comprehensive exam, thesis/dissertation, candidacy exam. *Entrance requirements:* For doctorate, GRE General Test, GRE Subject Test, 3 recommendation letters. Additional exam requirements/recommendations for international students: Required—TOEFL. *Application deadline:* For winter admission, 1/5 for domestic and international students. Application fee: $50. Electronic applications accepted. *Expenses:* $478 per credit hour in-state; $1,195 per credit hour out-of-state. *Financial support:* In 2016–17, 40 students received support, including 5 research assistantships with full tuition reimbursements available (averaging $15,000 per year), 35 teaching assistantships with full tuition reimbursements available (averaging $15,000 per year). Financial award application deadline: 1/15. *Faculty research:* Human factors, industrial psychology, organizational psychology, applied psychological sciences (health, developmental, community, quantitative). *Total annual research expenditures:* $978,563. *Unit head:* Dr. Debra A. Major, Graduate Program Director, 757-683-4235, Fax: 757-683-5087, E-mail: dmajor@odu.edu. *Application contact:* William Heffelfinger, Director of Graduate Admissions, 757-683-5554, Fax: 757-683-3255, E-mail: gradadmit@odu.edu.
Website: http://www.odu.edu/psychology/

**Old Dominion University,** College of Sciences, Master of Science in Psychology Program, Norfolk, VA 23529. Offers MS. *Program availability:* Part-time. *Faculty:* 27 full-time (13 women), 15 part-time/adjunct (2 women). *Students:* 13 full-time (9 women). Average age 25. 43 applicants, 12% accepted, 4 enrolled. In 2016, 7 master's awarded. Terminal master's awarded for partial completion of doctoral program. *Degree requirements:* For master's, thesis. *Entrance requirements:* For master's, GRE General Test, minimum GPA of 3.0 in major, previous course work in psychology. Additional exam requirements/recommendations for international students: Required—TOEFL. *Application deadline:* For fall admission, 5/15 for domestic and international students. Application fee: $50. Electronic applications accepted. *Expenses:* $478 per credit hour in-state; $1,195 per credit hour out-of-state. *Financial support:* In 2016–17, 2 students received support, including 2 teaching assistantships with full tuition reimbursements available (averaging $12,000 per year). Financial award application deadline: 2/15; financial award applicants required to submit FAFSA. *Faculty research:* Social psychology, developmental psychology, human factors psychology, community psychology, physiopsychology, clinical psychology, industrial/organizational psychology. *Total annual research expenditures:* $978,563. *Unit head:* Dr. James M. Henson, Graduate Program Director, 757-683-5761, Fax: 757-683-5087, E-mail: jhenson@odu.edu. *Application contact:* William Heffelfinger, Director of Graduate Admissions, 757-683-5554, Fax: 757-683-3255, E-mail: gradadmit@odu.edu.

**Oregon State University,** College of Liberal Arts, Program in Psychology, Corvallis, OR 97331. Offers applied cognition (MS, PhD); engineering psychology (MS, PhD); health psychology (MS, PhD). *Faculty:* 11 full-time (7 women), 2 part-time/adjunct (1 woman). *Students:* 3 full-time (2 women). 14 applicants, 21% accepted, 3 enrolled. *Degree requirements:* For doctorate, thesis/dissertation. *Application deadline:* For fall admission, 12/15 for domestic and international students. Application fee: $75 ($85 for international students). *Expenses:* Tuition, state resident: full-time $12,150; part-time $450 per credit. Tuition, nonresident: full-time $21,789; part-time $807 per credit. *Required fees:* $1651; $1507 per credit. One-time fee: $350. Tuition and fees vary according to course load, campus/location and program. *Unit head:* John Edwards, Director. *Application contact:* Aurora Sherman, Associate Professor and Graduate Education Chair, 541-737-1361, E-mail: aurora.sherman@oregonstate.edu.
Website: http://liberalarts.oregonstate.edu/school-psychological-science/psychology/graduate-psychology

**Our Lady of the Lake University,** School of Professional Studies, Program in Psychology, San Antonio, TX 78207-4689. Offers family, couple, and individual psychotherapy (MS); school psychology (MS). *Accreditation:* APA. *Program availability:* Part-time. *Faculty:* 2 full-time (both women), 2 part-time/adjunct (1 woman). *Students:* 27 full-time (25 women), 10 part-time (9 women); includes 31 minority (1 Black or African American, non-Hispanic/Latino; 1 Asian, non-Hispanic/Latino; 29 Hispanic/Latino). Average age 29. 18 applicants, 67% accepted, 10 enrolled. In 2016, 7 master's awarded. *Degree requirements:* For master's, comprehensive exam, practicum. *Entrance requirements:* For master's, GRE General Test or MAT, bachelor's degree with at least 12 undergraduate semester hours in psychology including one course in statistics and minimum cumulative GPA of 3.0; criminal background check; personal statement addressing background in psychology, expectations of the MS program, and professional goals; statement of purpose; 2 letters of recommendation. Additional exam requirements/recommendations for international students: Required—TOEFL. *Application deadline:* For fall admission, 3/1 priority date for domestic and international students. Application fee: $40 ($50 for international students). Electronic applications accepted. Application fee is waived when completed online. *Expenses: Tuition:* Full-time $14,796. Tuition and fees vary according to course load, degree level, campus/location and program. *Financial support:* In 2016–17, 2 students received support. Federal Work-Study, scholarships/grants, unspecified assistantships, and tuition discounts available. Support available to part-time students. Financial award application deadline: 5/1; financial award applicants required to submit FAFSA. *Faculty research:* Providing competent services to diverse client populations. *Unit head:* Psychology Department, 210-431-3914. *Application contact:* Office of Graduate Admissions, 210-431-3995, Fax: 210-431-3945, E-mail: gradadm@lake.ollusa.edu.
Website: http://www.ollusa.edu/s/1190/hybrid/default-hybrid-ollu.aspx?sid-1190&gid-1&pgid-7908

**Pace University,** Dyson College of Arts and Sciences, Department of Psychology, Program in Psychology, New York, NY 10038. Offers MA. *Program availability:* Part-time, evening/weekend. *Students:* 30 full-time (27 women), 8 part-time (7 women); includes 20 minority (7 Black or African American, non-Hispanic/Latino; 3 Asian, non-Hispanic/Latino; 10 Hispanic/Latino), 4 international. Average age 28. In 2016, 12 master's awarded. *Entrance requirements:* For master's, GRE, two letters of recommendation, resume, statement of purpose, all official transcripts, bachelor's degree from accredited institution, at least 9 hours of undergraduate psychology course prerequisites. Additional exam requirements/recommendations for international students: Required—TOEFL (minimum score 88 iBT), IELTS (minimum score 7) or PTE (minimum score 60). *Application deadline:* For fall admission, 8/1 priority date for domestic students, 6/1 for international students; for spring admission, 12/1 for domestic students, 10/1 for international students. Applications are processed on a rolling basis.

Application fee: $70. Electronic applications accepted. *Expenses: Tuition:* Part-time $1195 per credit. *Required fees:* $260 per semester. Tuition and fees vary according to degree level, campus/location and program. *Financial support:* Scholarships/grants available. Financial award application deadline: 2/15; financial award applicants required to submit FAFSA. *Unit head:* Dr. Barbara Mowder, Director of Graduate Psychology Programs, 212-346-1556, E-mail: bmowder@pace.edu. *Application contact:* Susan Ford-Goldschein, Director of Graduate Admissions, 212-346-1531, Fax: 212-346-1585, E-mail: graduateadmission@pace.edu.
Website: http://www.pace.edu/dyson/academic-departments-and-programs/psychology-—-nyc/graduate-programs

**Pacifica Graduate Institute,** Graduate Programs, Carpinteria, CA 93013. Offers clinical psychology (PhD); counseling psychology (MA); depth psychology (MA, PhD); mythological studies (MA, PhD). Terminal master's awarded for partial completion of doctoral program. *Degree requirements:* For master's, thesis (for some programs), practicum; for doctorate, comprehensive exam, thesis/dissertation, internship. *Entrance requirements:* For master's, resume, 3 letters of recommendation, writing sample, interview; for doctorate, resumé, 4 letters of recommendation, writing sample, interview. Additional exam requirements/recommendations for international students: Required—TOEFL. *Faculty research:* Imaginal and archetypal theory; post-Colonial psychoanalytic and Jungian theory; myth literature as it applies to the theory and practice of psychology.

**Pacific University,** School of Professional Psychology, Forest Grove, OR 97116-1797. Offers applied psychological science (MA, MS); clinical psychology (PhD, Psy D). *Accreditation:* APA (one or more programs are accredited). *Program availability:* Part-time. *Degree requirements:* For master's, comprehensive exam (for some programs), thesis (for some programs); for doctorate, comprehensive exam, thesis/dissertation. *Entrance requirements:* For master's, course work in introductory psychology, statistics, and abnormal psychology; minimum GPA of 3.0; for doctorate, GRE General Test, minimum GPA of 3.0, undergraduate course work in psychology, minimum GPA of 3.1 in last 2 years. Additional exam requirements/recommendations for international students: Required—TOEFL (minimum score 600 paper-based). Electronic applications accepted. *Expenses:* Contact institution. *Faculty research:* Neuropsychological assessment, assessment and treatment of anxiety, forensic psychology, cross-cultural psychology, child and adolescent psychopathology.

**Palo Alto University,** MS in Psychology (PhD Prep) Program, Palo Alto, CA 94304. Offers MS. *Program availability:* Part-time, online learning. *Faculty:* 6 full-time (5 women), 4 part-time/adjunct (3 women). *Students:* 9 full-time (6 women), 38 part-time (31 women); includes 19 minority (3 Black or African American, non-Hispanic/Latino; 7 Asian, non-Hispanic/Latino; 8 Hispanic/Latino; 1 Two or more races, non-Hispanic/Latino), 1 international. Average age 31. 46 applicants, 25 enrolled. In 2016, 12 master's awarded. *Degree requirements:* For master's, online program with a 1-week on-campus intensive. *Entrance requirements:* For master's, undergraduate degree in psychology with minimum GPA of 3.3. Additional exam requirements/recommendations for international students: Required—TOEFL. *Application deadline:* For fall admission, 6/30 priority date for domestic and international students. Applications are processed on a rolling basis. Application fee: $40. Electronic applications accepted. *Expenses:* Contact institution. *Financial support:* In 2016–17, 1 student received support. Federal Work-Study and scholarships/grants available. Financial award application deadline: 1/15; financial award applicants required to submit FAFSA. *Unit head:* Dr. Kristel Nazzal, Associate Director, 650-417-2022, E-mail: knazzal@paloaltou.edu. *Application contact:* Deanna Berger, Assistant Director of Admissions, 650-417-2023, E-mail: dberger@paloaltou.edu.
Website: http://www.paloaltou.edu/graduate-programs/masters-degree-programs/ms-psychology-phd-prep

**Palo Alto University,** PhD in Clinical Psychology Program, Palo Alto, CA 94304. Offers PhD, JD/PhD, MBA/PhD. *Accreditation:* APA. *Faculty:* 33 full-time (19 women), 39 part-time/adjunct (25 women). *Students:* 427 full-time (326 women), 9 part-time (all women); includes 132 minority (20 Black or African American, non-Hispanic/Latino; 2 American Indian or Alaska Native, non-Hispanic/Latino; 57 Asian, non-Hispanic/Latino; 41 Hispanic/Latino; 2 Native Hawaiian or other Pacific Islander, non-Hispanic/Latino; 10 Two or more races, non-Hispanic/Latino), 22 international. Average age 32. 251 applicants, 76 enrolled. In 2016, 62 doctorates awarded. *Degree requirements:* For doctorate, comprehensive exam, thesis/dissertation, 2000-hour clinical internship. *Entrance requirements:* For doctorate, GRE General Test, undergraduate or graduate degree in psychology or related area; 4 course prerequisites: biopsychology, abnormal psychology, developmental psychology, and statistics. Additional exam requirements/ recommendations for international students: Required—TOEFL, IELTS. *Application deadline:* For fall admission, 12/2 priority date for domestic and international students. Applications are processed on a rolling basis. Application fee: $50. Electronic applications accepted. *Expenses:* Contact institution. *Financial support:* In 2016–17, 115 students received support, including fellowships (averaging $7,500 per year), research assistantships (averaging $4,000 per year), teaching assistantships (averaging $3,000 per year); Federal Work-Study and scholarships/grants also available. Financial award application deadline: 1/15; financial award applicants required to submit FAFSA. *Faculty research:* Forensic psychology, LGBT psychology, trauma, diversity and community mental health, neuropsychology. *Unit head:* Dr. Rowena Gomez, Director of Clinical Training, 650-433-3823, E-mail: rgomez@paloaltou.edu. *Application contact:* Eirian Williams, Vice President of Enrollment Management, 800-818-6136, E-mail: admissions@paloaltou.edu.
Website: http://www.paloaltou.edu/graduate-programs/phd-programs/phd-clinical-psychology

**Penn State Harrisburg,** Graduate School, School of Behavioral Sciences and Education, Middletown, PA 17057. Offers adult education in the health and medical professions (Certificate); applied behavior analysis (MA); applied clinical psychology (MA); applied psychological research (MA); community psychology and social change (MA); English as a second language (ESL) program specialist and leadership (Certificate); folklore and ethnography (Certificate); health education (M Ed); lifelong learning and adult education (M Ed, D Ed); literacy education (M Ed); literacy leadership (Certificate); psychology: applications in clinical psychology (Certificate); psychology: health psychology (Certificate); teaching and curriculum (M Ed); training and development (M Ed, Certificate). *Program availability:* Part-time, evening/weekend. *Unit head:* Dr. Mukund S. Kulkarni, Chancellor, 717-948-6105, Fax: 717-948-6452. *Application contact:* Robert W. Coffman, Jr., Director of Enrollment Management, Recruitment and Admissions, 717-948-6250, Fax: 717-948-6325, E-mail: hbgadmit@psu.edu.
Website: https://harrisburg.psu.edu/behavioral-sciences-and-education/

**Penn State University Park,** Graduate School, College of the Liberal Arts, Department of Psychology, University Park, PA 16802. Offers psychology (MS, PhD); psychology of leadership at work (MPS). *Accreditation:* APA (one or more programs are accredited). *Unit head:* Dr. Susan Welch, Dean, 814-865-7691, Fax: 814-863-2085. *Application contact:* Lori Hawn, Director, Graduate Student Services, 814-865-1795, Fax: 814-863-4627, E-mail: l-gswww@lists.psu.edu.
Website: http://psych.la.psu.edu/

**Pepperdine University,** Graduate School of Education and Psychology, Division of Psychology, Los Angeles, CA 90045. Offers behavioral psychology (MS); clinical psychology (Psy D); clinical psychology (MA), including marriage and family therapy; clinical psychology with Latinos (MA); psychology (MA). *Program availability:* Part-time, evening/weekend. *Students:* 489 full-time (408 women), 432 part-time (348 women); includes 404 minority (92 Black or African American, non-Hispanic/Latino; 4 American Indian or Alaska Native, non-Hispanic/Latino; 77 Asian, non-Hispanic/Latino; 198 Hispanic/Latino; 5 Native Hawaiian or other Pacific Islander, non-Hispanic/Latino; 28 Two or more races, non-Hispanic/Latino), 46 international. Average age 31. 559 applicants, 77% accepted, 279 enrolled. In 2016, 265 master's, 27 doctorates awarded. *Entrance requirements:* For master's and doctorate, GRE General Test. Additional exam requirements/recommendations for international students: Required—TOEFL. *Application deadline:* For fall admission, 2/1 for domestic students. Applications are processed on a rolling basis. Application fee: $55. *Expenses:* $1,165 per unit (for master's); $1,460 per unit (for doctorate). *Financial support:* Research assistantships, teaching assistantships, career-related internships or fieldwork, and scholarships/grants available. Support available to part-time students. Financial award application deadline: 7/1; financial award applicants required to submit FAFSA. *Unit head:* Dr. Robert A. deMayo, Associate Dean, Psychology Division, 310-568-5747, E-mail: robert.demayo@pepperdine.edu. *Application contact:* Chris Costa, Director of Enrollment, 310-568-2850, E-mail: chris.costa@pepperdine.edu.
Website: http://gsep.pepperdine.edu/masters-psychology/

**Philadelphia College of Osteopathic Medicine,** Graduate and Professional Programs, Department of Psychology, Philadelphia, PA 19131-1694. Offers applied behavior analysis (Certificate); clinical health psychology (Post-Doctoral Certificate); clinical neuropsychology (Post-Doctoral Certificate); clinical psychology (Psy D); mental health counseling (MS); organizational development and leadership (MS); psychology (Certificate); school psychology (MS, Psy D, Ed S). *Accreditation:* APA. *Faculty:* 19 full-time (11 women), 122 part-time/adjunct (58 women). *Students:* 364 (285 women); includes 78 minority (62 Black or African American, non-Hispanic/Latino; 2 American Indian or Alaska Native, non-Hispanic/Latino; 9 Asian, non-Hispanic/Latino; 5 Hispanic/Latino), 2 international. 366 applicants, 51% accepted, 139 enrolled. In 2016, 72 master's, 42 doctorates, 17 other advanced degrees awarded. Terminal master's awarded for partial completion of doctoral program. *Degree requirements:* For master's, comprehensive exam (for some programs), thesis (for some programs); for doctorate, comprehensive exam, thesis/dissertation. *Entrance requirements:* For master's, GRE or MAT, minimum GPA of 3.0; bachelor's degree from regionally-accredited college or university; for doctorate, PRAXIS II (for Psy D in school psychology), minimum undergraduate GPA of 3.0; for other advanced degree, GRE (for Ed S). Additional exam requirements/recommendations for international students: Required—TOEFL (minimum score 79 iBT). *Application deadline:* Applications are processed on a rolling basis. Application fee: $50. Electronic applications accepted. Tuition and fees vary according to course load, degree level and program. *Financial support:* In 2016–17, 28 teaching assistantships were awarded; Federal Work-Study, institutionally sponsored loans, and scholarships/grants also available. Financial award application deadline: 3/15; financial award applicants required to submit FAFSA. *Faculty research:* Adult and childhood anxiety and ADHD; coping with chronic illness; primary care psychology/integrated health care; applied behavior analysis; psychological, educational, and neuropsychological assessment. *Total annual research expenditures:* $533,489. *Unit head:* Dr. Robert DiTomasso, Chairman, 215-871-6442, Fax: 215-871-6458, E-mail: robertd@pcom.edu. *Application contact:* Johnathan Cox, Associate Director of Admissions, 215-871-6700, Fax: 215-871-6719, E-mail: karis@pcom.edu.
**See Display on next page and Close-Up on page 1227.**

**Pittsburg State University,** Graduate School, College of Education, Department of Psychology and Counseling, Program in Psychology, Pittsburg, KS 66762. Offers psychology (MS), including clinical psychology, general psychology. *Students:* 27. In 2016, 10 master's awarded. *Degree requirements:* For master's, thesis or alternative. *Entrance requirements:* For master's, GRE General Test, minimum GPA of 2.8. Additional exam requirements/recommendations for international students: Required—TOEFL (minimum score 550 paper-based; 79 iBT), IELTS (minimum score 6.5), PTE (minimum score 53). *Application deadline:* Applications are processed on a rolling basis. Application fee: $35 ($60 for international students). Electronic applications accepted. *Expenses:* Contact institution. *Financial support:* Teaching assistantships, career-related internships or fieldwork, and Federal Work-Study available. Financial award application deadline: 2/1; financial award applicants required to submit FAFSA. *Unit head:* Dr. David Hurford, Chairperson, 620-235-4521. *Application contact:* Lisa Allen, Assistant Director of Graduate and Continuing Studies, 620-235-4218, Fax: 620-235-4219, E-mail: lallen@pittstate.edu.

**Pontifical Catholic University of Puerto Rico,** College of Graduate Studies in Behavioral Science and Community Affairs, Ponce, PR 00717-0777. Offers clinical psychology (PhD, Psy D); clinical social work (MSW); criminology (MA); industrial psychology (PhD); psychology (PhD); public administration (MSS); rehabilitation counseling (MA). *Program availability:* Part-time, evening/weekend. *Degree requirements:* For master's, thesis; for doctorate, comprehensive exam, thesis/dissertation. *Entrance requirements:* For master's, EXADEP, GRE General Test, 3 letters of recommendation, interview, minimum GPA of 2.75.

**Pontificia Universidad Catolica Madre y Maestra,** Graduate School, Faculty of Social and Administrative Sciences, Santiago, Dominican Republic. Offers business administration (MBA), including business development, finance, international business, management skills (M Mgmt, MBA), marketing, operations, strategic cost management, strategy, tourist destination planning and management; law (LL M), including civil law, corporate business law, criminal law, international relations, real estate law; management (M Mgmt), including higher financial management, insurance program administration, management skills (M Mgmt, MBA); psychology (MA), including clinical child and adolescent psychology, forensic psychology; strategic human resources (EMBA).

**Portland State University,** Graduate Studies, College of Liberal Arts and Sciences, Department of Psychology, Portland, OR 97207-0751. Offers MA, MS, PhD. *Faculty:* 21 full-time (9 women), 18 part-time/adjunct (10 women). *Students:* 47 full-time (36 women), 10 part-time (6 women); includes 12 minority (1 Black or African American, non-Hispanic/Latino; 1 American Indian or Alaska Native, non-Hispanic/Latino; 3 Asian, non-Hispanic/Latino; 4 Hispanic/Latino; 3 Two or more races, non-Hispanic/Latino). Average age 30. 174 applicants, 6% accepted, 11 enrolled. In 2016, 2 master's, 4 doctorates awarded. *Degree requirements:* For master's, variable foreign language requirement, thesis; for doctorate, variable foreign language requirement, comprehensive exam, thesis/dissertation. *Entrance requirements:* Additional exam requirements/recommendations for international students: Required—TOEFL (minimum score 550 paper-based). *Application deadline:* For fall admission, 12/15 for domestic and international students. Application fee: $65. *Expenses:* Contact institution. *Financial support:* In 2016–17, 10 research assistantships with tuition reimbursements (averaging $13,363 per year), 28 teaching assistantships with tuition reimbursements (averaging $10,929 per year) were awarded; career-related internships or fieldwork, Federal Work-

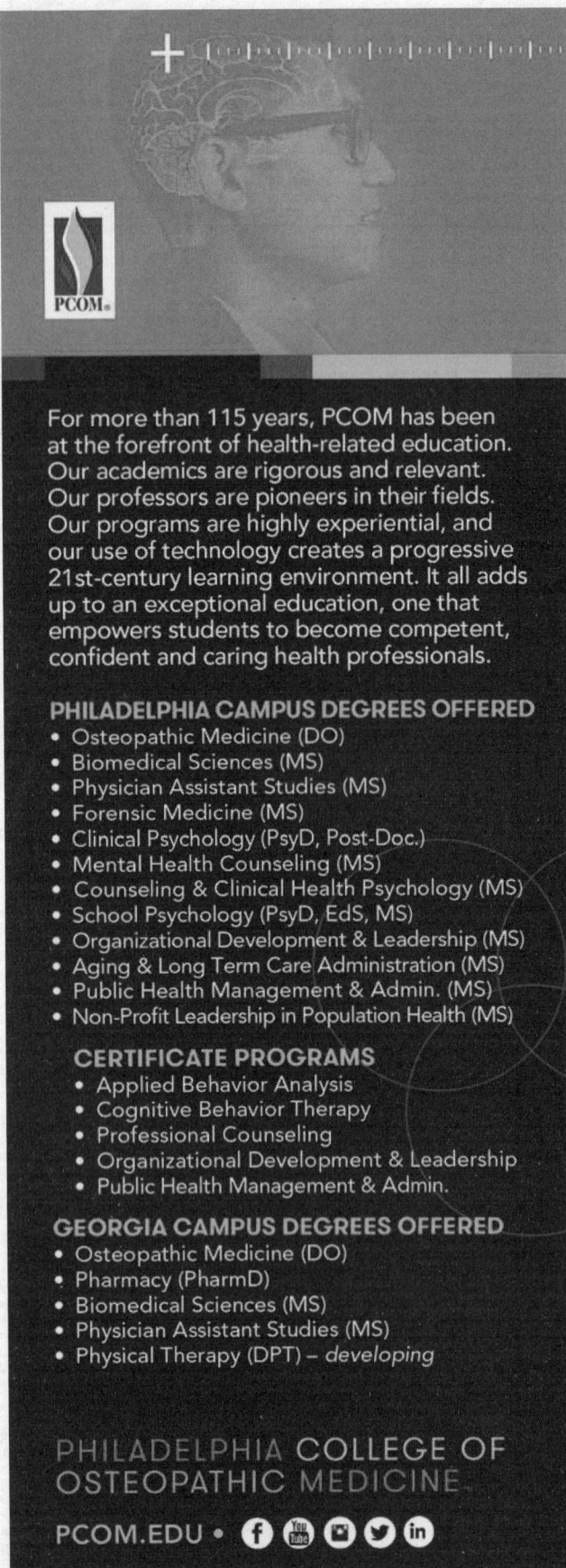

For more than 115 years, PCOM has been at the forefront of health-related education. Our academics are rigorous and relevant. Our professors are pioneers in their fields. Our programs are highly experiential, and our use of technology creates a progressive 21st-century learning environment. It all adds up to an exceptional education, one that empowers students to become competent, confident and caring health professionals.

### PHILADELPHIA CAMPUS DEGREES OFFERED
- Osteopathic Medicine (DO)
- Biomedical Sciences (MS)
- Physician Assistant Studies (MS)
- Forensic Medicine (MS)
- Clinical Psychology (PsyD, Post-Doc.)
- Mental Health Counseling (MS)
- Counseling & Clinical Health Psychology (MS)
- School Psychology (PsyD, EdS, MS)
- Organizational Development & Leadership (MS)
- Aging & Long Term Care Administration (MS)
- Public Health Management & Admin. (MS)
- Non-Profit Leadership in Population Health (MS)

### CERTIFICATE PROGRAMS
- Applied Behavior Analysis
- Cognitive Behavior Therapy
- Professional Counseling
- Organizational Development & Leadership
- Public Health Management & Admin.

### GEORGIA CAMPUS DEGREES OFFERED
- Osteopathic Medicine (DO)
- Pharmacy (PharmD)
- Biomedical Sciences (MS)
- Physician Assistant Studies (MS)
- Physical Therapy (DPT) – *developing*

PHILADELPHIA COLLEGE OF OSTEOPATHIC MEDICINE

PCOM.EDU •

Study, scholarships/grants, tuition waivers (partial), and unspecified assistantships also available. Support available to part-time students. Financial award application deadline: 3/1; financial award applicants required to submit FAFSA. *Faculty research:* Organizational psychology, work and the family, quantitative psychology, decision-making, psychosocial factors affecting health. *Total annual research expenditures:* $2.3 million. *Unit head:* Dr. Ellen Skinner, Chair, 503-725-3966, Fax: 503-725-3904, E-mail: skinnere@pdx.edu. *Application contact:* 503-725-3923, Fax: 503-725-3904. Website: http://www.pdx.edu/psy/

**Portland State University,** Graduate Studies, College of Liberal Arts and Sciences, Systems Science Program, Portland, OR 97207-0751. Offers computational intelligence (Certificate); computer modeling and simulation (Certificate); systems science (MS); systems science/anthropology (PhD); systems science/business administration (PhD); systems science/civil engineering (PhD); systems science/economics (PhD); systems science/engineering management (PhD); systems science/general (PhD); systems science/mathematical sciences (PhD); systems science/mechanical engineering (PhD); systems science/psychology (PhD); systems science/sociology (PhD). *Faculty:* 2 full-time (0 women), 3 part-time/adjunct (1 woman). *Students:* 12 full-time (3 women), 21 part-time (5 women); includes 5 minority (1 Black or African American, non-Hispanic/Latino; 2 Hispanic/Latino; 2 Two or more races, non-Hispanic/Latino). Average age 39. 16 applicants, 69% accepted, 9 enrolled. In 2016, 4 master's, 6 doctorates awarded. *Degree requirements:* For master's, comprehensive exam (for some programs), thesis optional; for doctorate, variable foreign language requirement, comprehensive exam (for some programs), thesis/dissertation. *Entrance requirements:* For master's, GRE/GMAT (recommended), minimum GPA of 3.0 undergraduate or graduate work, 2 letters of recommendation, statement of interest; for doctorate, GMAT, GRE General Test, minimum GPA of 3.0 undergraduate, 3.25 graduate; 2 letters of recommendation; statement of interest. Additional exam requirements/recommendations for international students: Required—TOEFL (minimum score 550 paper-based; 80 iBT). *Application deadline:* For fall admission, 1/15 for domestic and international students; for spring admission, 11/1 for domestic students. Application fee: $65. Electronic applications accepted. *Expenses:* Contact institution. *Financial support:* In 2016–17, 2 research assistantships with tuition reimbursements (averaging $7,830 per year) were awarded; teaching assistantships, career-related internships or fieldwork, Federal Work-Study, scholarships/grants, and unspecified assistantships also available. Support available to part-time students. Financial award application deadline: 3/1; financial award applicants required to submit FAFSA. *Faculty research:* Systems theory and methodology, artificial intelligence neural networks, information theory, nonlinear dynamics/chaos, modeling and simulation. *Unit head:* Dr. Wayne Wakeland, Chair, 503-725-4975, E-mail: wakeland@pdx.edu. Website: http://www.pdx.edu/sysc/

**Princeton University,** Graduate School, Department of Psychology, Princeton, NJ 08544-1019. Offers neuroscience (PhD); psychology (PhD). *Degree requirements:* For doctorate, thesis/dissertation. *Entrance requirements:* For doctorate, GRE General Test, GRE Subject Test. Additional exam requirements/recommendations for international students: Required—TOEFL (minimum score 550 paper-based). Electronic applications accepted.

**Purdue University,** Graduate School, College of Health and Human Sciences, Department of Psychological Sciences, West Lafayette, IN 47907. Offers behavioral neuroscience (PhD); clinical psychology (PhD); cognitive psychology (PhD); industrial/organizational psychology (PhD); mathematical and computational cognitive science (PhD). *Accreditation:* APA. *Faculty:* 46 full-time (18 women), 1 part-time/adjunct. *Students:* 64 full-time (41 women), 4 part-time (3 women); includes 13 minority (1 Black or African American, non-Hispanic/Latino; 4 Asian, non-Hispanic/Latino; 6 Hispanic/Latino; 2 Two or more races, non-Hispanic/Latino), 12 international. Average age 27. 288 applicants, 8% accepted, 16 enrolled. In 2016, 9 doctorates awarded. Terminal master's awarded for partial completion of doctoral program. *Degree requirements:* For doctorate, thesis/dissertation. *Entrance requirements:* For doctorate, GRE General Test, minimum undergraduate GPA of 3.0 or equivalent. Additional exam requirements/recommendations for international students: Required—TOEFL (minimum score 550 paper-based; 77 iBT); Recommended—TWE. *Application deadline:* For fall admission, 12/3 for domestic and international students. Applications are processed on a rolling basis. Application fee: $60 ($75 for international students). Electronic applications accepted. *Financial support:* Fellowships with partial tuition reimbursements, research assistantships with partial tuition reimbursements, teaching assistantships with partial tuition reimbursements, and career-related internships or fieldwork available. Support available to part-time students. Financial award applicants required to submit FAFSA. *Faculty research:* Career development of women in science, development of friendships during childhood and adolescence, social competence, human information processing. *Unit head:* Dr. Christopher R. Agnew, Head, 765-494-6061, Fax: 765-496-1264, E-mail: agnew@psych.purdue.edu. *Application contact:* Nancy A. O'Brien, Graduate Contact, 765-494-6067, Fax: 765-496-1264, E-mail: nobrien@psych.pardue.edu. Website: http://www.psych.purdue.edu/

**Queens College of the City University of New York,** Mathematics and Natural Sciences Division, Department of Psychology, Queens, NY 11367-1597. Offers applied behavior analysis (MA, AC); behavioral neuroscience (MA); psychology (MA). *Program availability:* Part-time. *Faculty:* 29 full-time (17 women), 61 part-time/adjunct (46 women). *Students:* 11 full-time (5 women), 117 part-time (94 women); includes 57 minority (12 Black or African American, non-Hispanic/Latino; 1 American Indian or Alaska Native, non-Hispanic/Latino; 12 Asian, non-Hispanic/Latino; 28 Hispanic/Latino; 4 Two or more races, non-Hispanic/Latino), 4 international. Average age 28. 179 applicants, 64% accepted, 63 enrolled. In 2016, 36 master's, 1 other advanced degree awarded. *Degree requirements:* For master's, comprehensive exam (for some programs), thesis. *Entrance requirements:* For master's, minimum GPA of 3.0. Additional exam requirements/recommendations for international students: Required—TOEFL, IELTS. *Application deadline:* For fall admission, 4/1 for domestic students; for spring admission, 11/1 for domestic students. Applications are processed on a rolling basis. Application fee: $125. Electronic applications accepted. *Expenses:* Tuition, state resident: full-time $5065; part-time $425 per credit. Tuition, nonresident: part-time $780 per credit. *Required fees:* $522; $397 per credit. Part-time tuition and fees vary according to course load and program. *Financial support:* Career-related internships or fieldwork, institutionally sponsored loans, and unspecified assistantships available. Financial award application deadline: 4/1; financial award applicants required to submit FAFSA. *Unit head:* Dr. Jeffery Halperin, Acting Chair, 718-997-3200, E-mail: jeffery.halperin@qc.cuny.edu.

**Queen's University at Kingston,** School of Graduate Studies, Faculty of Arts and Sciences, Department of Psychology, Kingston, ON K7L 3N6, Canada. Offers brain behavior and cognitive science (MA, PhD); clinical psychology (MA, PhD); developmental psychology (MA, PhD); social personality psychology (MA, PhD). *Degree requirements:* For master's, thesis; for doctorate, comprehensive exam, thesis/dissertation. *Entrance requirements:* For master's and doctorate, GRE General Test. Additional exam requirements/recommendations for international students: Required—TOEFL. *Faculty research:* Human development, social, personality, behavioral neuroscience, forensic.

**Rhode Island College,** School of Graduate Studies, Faculty of Arts and Sciences, Department of Psychology, Providence, RI 02908-1991. Offers health psychology (CGS); psychology (MA). *Program availability:* Part-time, evening/weekend. *Faculty:* 4 full-time (2 women). *Students:* 1 full-time (0 women), 5 part-time (all women); includes 1 minority (American Indian or Alaska Native, non-Hispanic/Latino). Average age 25. In 2016, 5 master's awarded. *Degree requirements:* For master's, comprehensive exam. *Entrance requirements:* For master's, GRE, 3 letters of recommendation. Additional exam requirements/recommendations for international students: Recommended—TOEFL (minimum score 550 paper-based; 79 iBT). *Application deadline:* For fall admission, 3/1 for domestic students; for spring admission, 11/1 for domestic students. Applications are processed on a rolling basis. Application fee: $50. Electronic applications accepted. *Expenses:* Tuition, state resident: full-time $8928; part-time $372 per credit. Tuition, nonresident: full-time $17,376; part-time $724 per credit. *Required fees:* $604; $22 per credit. One-time fee: $74. *Financial support:* In 2016–17, 3 teaching assistantships with full tuition reimbursements (averaging $3,500 per year) were awarded; Federal Work-Study, scholarships/grants, health care benefits, and unspecified assistantships also available. Support available to part-time students. Financial award application deadline: 5/15; financial award applicants required to submit FAFSA. *Unit head:* Dr. Randi Kim, Chair, 401-456-8015. *Application contact:* Graduate Studies, 401-456-8700.
Website: http://www.ric.edu/psychology/index.php

**Rice University,** Graduate Programs, School of Humanities, Department of Religious Studies, Houston, TX 77251-1892. Offers African religions (PhD); African-American religions (PhD); contemplative studies (PhD); ghosticism, esotericism, mysticism (PhD); Islam (PhD); Jewish thought and philosophy (PhD); modern Christianity in thought and popular culture (PhD); psychology of religion (PhD); the Bible and beyond (PhD). *Degree requirements:* For doctorate, 2 foreign languages, comprehensive exam, thesis/dissertation. *Entrance requirements:* For doctorate, GRE, letters of recommendation, writing sample. Additional exam requirements/recommendations for international students: Required—TOEFL (minimum score 600 paper-based; 90 iBT). Electronic applications accepted. *Faculty research:* Origins and historical development of Islam, history of Christianity, the study of comparative religion, African-American religion, religion and culture.

**Rice University,** Graduate Programs, School of Social Sciences, Department of Psychology, Houston, TX 77251-1892. Offers cognitive sciences (MA, PhD); industrial-organizational/social psychology (MA, PhD); psychology (MA, PhD). Terminal master's awarded for partial completion of doctoral program. *Degree requirements:* For master's, thesis; for doctorate, thesis/dissertation. *Entrance requirements:* For doctorate, GRE General Test, minimum GPA of 3.0. Additional exam requirements/recommendations for international students: Required—TOEFL. Electronic applications accepted. *Faculty research:* Cognitive, cognitive neuropsychology, human factors, human-computer interaction, industrial-organizational psychology.

**Rivier University,** School of Graduate Studies, Department of Psychology, Nashua, NH 03060. Offers clinical psychology (MS); experimental psychology (MS).

**Roberts Wesleyan College,** Graduate Psychology Programs, Rochester, NY 14624-1997. Offers clinical/school psychology (Psy D); school counseling (MS); school psychology (MS). *Program availability:* Part-time, evening/weekend. *Degree requirements:* For master's, comprehensive exam, PRAXIS II (for school psychology). *Entrance requirements:* For master's, GRE. Electronic applications accepted. Application fee is waived when completed online. *Faculty research:* Counselor supervision, forgiveness, community health psychology, applied research in group process.

**Rochester Institute of Technology,** Graduate Enrollment Services, College of Liberal Arts, Psychology Department, Rochester, NY 14623. Offers engineering psychology (Advanced Certificate); experimental psychology (MS); school psychology (MS, Advanced Certificate). *Program availability:* Part-time. *Students:* 27 full-time (22 women), 8 part-time (4 women); includes 4 minority (2 Black or African American, non-Hispanic/Latino; 1 Asian, non-Hispanic/Latino; 1 Hispanic/Latino). Average age 26. 68 applicants, 32% accepted, 9 enrolled. In 2016, 10 master's, 10 other advanced degrees awarded. *Degree requirements:* For master's, thesis. *Entrance requirements:* For master's, GRE, minimum GPA of 3.0 (recommended). Additional exam requirements/recommendations for international students: Required—PTE (minimum score 58), TOEFL (minimum score 550 paper-based, 79 iBT) or IELTS (minimum score 6.5). *Application deadline:* For fall admission, 2/15 priority date for domestic and international students; for spring admission, 12/15 priority date for domestic and international students. Applications are processed on a rolling basis. Application fee: $60. Electronic applications accepted. *Expenses:* $1,742 per credit hour. *Financial support:* In 2016–17, 22 students received support. Research assistantships with partial tuition reimbursements available, teaching assistantships with partial tuition reimbursements available, career-related internships or fieldwork, scholarships/grants, and unspecified assistantships available. Support available to part-time students. Financial award applicants required to submit FAFSA. *Faculty research:* Human factors, human performance measurement and modeling; cognitive neuroscience, brain and behavior relationships; human development and personality assessment; curriculum-based measurement, multi-tier system of supports; psychophysiological and neuropsychological assessment. *Unit head:* Dr. Andrew Herbert, Graduate Program Director, 585-475-4554, E-mail: amhgss@rit.edu. *Application contact:* Diane Ellison, Associate Vice President, Graduate Enrollment Services, 585-475-2229, Fax: 585-475-7164, E-mail: gradinfo@rit.edu.
Website: http://www.rit.edu/cla/psychology/

**Roosevelt University,** Graduate Division, College of Arts and Sciences, Department of Psychology, Program in Clinical Psychology, Chicago, IL 60605. Offers MA, Psy D.

**Rosalind Franklin University of Medicine and Science,** College of Health Professions, Department of Psychology, North Chicago, IL 60064-3095. Offers clinical psychology (MS, PhD). *Accreditation:* APA. Terminal master's awarded for partial completion of doctoral program. *Degree requirements:* For master's, capstone experience. *Entrance requirements:* For master's, minimum GPA of 3.0, bachelor's degree (preferably in related subject); for doctorate, GRE, minimum GPA of 3.0, bachelor's or master's degree. Additional exam requirements/recommendations for international students: Required—TOEFL. *Faculty research:* Anxiety, pain, psychopathy, epilepsy, neuropsychology.

**Rowan University,** Graduate School, College of Science and Mathematics, Department of Psychology, Glassboro, NJ 08028-1701. Offers MA, CAGS. Electronic applications accepted.

**Rutgers University–Camden,** Graduate School of Arts and Sciences, Program in Psychology, Camden, NJ 08102. Offers MA. *Program availability:* Part-time, evening/weekend. *Degree requirements:* For master's, thesis, 30 credits. *Entrance requirements:* For master's, GRE, 3 letters of recommendation; statement of personal, professional, and academic goals; prerequisite course work in introductory psychology, statistics and experimental psychology. Additional exam requirements/recommendations for international students: Required—TOEFL, IELTS. Electronic applications accepted.

*Faculty research:* Cognitive psychology, sexuality, health psychology, personality psychology, clinical psychology.

**Rutgers University–Newark,** Graduate School, Program in Psychology, Newark, NJ 07102. Offers cognitive neuroscience (PhD); cognitive science (PhD); perception (PhD); psychobiology (PhD); social cognition (PhD). *Degree requirements:* For doctorate, comprehensive exam, thesis/dissertation. *Entrance requirements:* For doctorate, GRE General Test, GRE Subject Test, minimum undergraduate B average. Electronic applications accepted. *Faculty research:* Visual perception (luminance, motion), neuroendocrine mechanisms in behavior (reproduction, pain), attachment theory, connectionist modeling of cognition.

**Rutgers University–New Brunswick,** Graduate School-New Brunswick, Program in Psychology, Piscataway, NJ 08854-8097. Offers behavioral neuroscience (PhD); clinical psychology (PhD); cognitive psychology (PhD); interdisciplinary health psychology (PhD); social psychology (PhD). *Accreditation:* APA. *Degree requirements:* For doctorate, comprehensive exam, thesis/dissertation. *Entrance requirements:* For doctorate, GRE General Test, 3 letters of recommendation. Additional exam requirements/recommendations for international students: Required—TOEFL (minimum score 577 paper-based). Electronic applications accepted. *Faculty research:* Learning and memory, behavioral ecology, hormones and behavior, psychopharmacology, anxiety disorders.

**Sage Graduate School,** School of Health Sciences, Department of Psychology, Troy, NY 12180-4115. Offers MA, Certificate. *Program availability:* Part-time, evening/weekend. *Faculty:* 2 full-time (both women), 3 part-time/adjunct (2 women). *Students:* 3 full-time (all women), 1 (woman) part-time; includes 21 minority (8 Black or African American, non-Hispanic/Latino; 1 American Indian or Alaska Native, non-Hispanic/Latino; 1 Asian, non-Hispanic/Latino; 4 Hispanic/Latino; 7 Two or more races, non-Hispanic/Latino), 1 international. Average age 29. 91 applicants, 45% accepted, 21 enrolled. In 2016, 25 master's awarded. *Degree requirements:* For master's, thesis or alternative. *Entrance requirements:* Additional exam requirements/recommendations for international students: Required—TOEFL (minimum score 550 paper-based). *Application deadline:* Applications are processed on a rolling basis. Application fee: $40. Electronic applications accepted. *Expenses:* Tuition: Full-time $12,240; part-time $680 per credit hour. Tuition and fees vary according to degree level and program. *Financial support:* Fellowships, research assistantships, Federal Work-Study, scholarships/grants, and unspecified assistantships available. Support available to part-time students. Financial award application deadline: 3/1; financial award applicants required to submit FAFSA. *Faculty research:* Effectiveness of arts integration programs in elementary and secondary schools, literacy-based substance abuse program, outcome evaluation of program to increase college entry among urban youth. *Unit head:* Dr. Theresa Hand, Dean, School of Health Sciences, 518-244-2264, Fax: 518-244-4571, E-mail: handt@sage.edu. *Application contact:* Dr. Gayle Morse, Graduate Program Director, 518-292-1819, E-mail: morseg@sage.edu.

**St. Cloud State University,** School of Graduate Studies, School of Education, Department of Educational Leadership and Higher Education, St. Cloud, MN 56301. Offers college counseling and student development (MS); higher education administration (MS, Ed D); rehabilitation counseling (MS); school counseling (MS). *Degree requirements:* For master's, thesis or alternative; for doctorate, comprehensive exam, thesis/dissertation. *Entrance requirements:* For master's, GRE General Test (for some programs), minimum GPA of 2.75; for doctorate, GRE General Test. Additional exam requirements/recommendations for international students: Required—Michigan English Language Assessment Battery; Recommended—TOEFL (minimum score 550 paper-based), IELTS (minimum score 6.5). Electronic applications accepted.

**St. John's University,** St. John's College of Liberal Arts and Sciences, Department of Psychology, Queens, NY 11439. Offers clinical psychology (MA, PhD), including clinical psychology (MA), clinical psychology-child (PhD), clinical psychology-general (PhD); general experimental psychology (MA); school psychology (MS, Psy D). *Accreditation:* APA (one or more programs are accredited). *Program availability:* Part-time, evening/weekend. *Degree requirements:* For master's, comprehensive exam, thesis optional; for doctorate, comprehensive exam, thesis/dissertation, internship. *Entrance requirements:* For master's, GRE, minimum GPA of 3.0, 2 writing samples, transcripts, 3 letters of recommendation, personal essay, 24 credits in psychology or related field, bachelor's degree; for doctorate, GRE General Test, GRE Subject Test, 3 letters of recommendation, 2 writing samples, personal statement. Additional exam requirements/recommendations for international students: Required—TOEFL (minimum score 600 paper-based; 100 iBT), IELTS (minimum score 7). Electronic applications accepted. *Expenses:* Contact institution. *Faculty research:* Clinical psychology, school psychology, developmental psychopathology, risky behaviors and health, cognitive behavior treatments for trauma, assessment and treatment of anger problems, development of mathematical reasoning, personality disorders and depression.

**Saint Joseph's University,** College of Arts and Sciences, Department of Criminal Justice, Philadelphia, PA 19131-1395. Offers behavior analysis (MS, Post-Master's Certificate); behavior management (MS); criminal justice (MS); federal law (MS); intelligence and crime (MS). *Program availability:* Part-time, evening/weekend, 100% online, blended/hybrid learning. *Faculty:* 4 full-time (3 women), 43 part-time/adjunct (18 women). *Students:* 23 full-time (13 women), 380 part-time (269 women); includes 116 minority (91 Black or African American, non-Hispanic/Latino; 2 American Indian or Alaska Native, non-Hispanic/Latino; 5 Asian, non-Hispanic/Latino; 16 Hispanic/Latino; 2 Native Hawaiian or other Pacific Islander, non-Hispanic/Latino), 7 international. Average age 31. 214 applicants, 73% accepted, 110 enrolled. In 2016, 141 master's, 34 other advanced degrees awarded. *Degree requirements:* For master's, thesis. *Entrance requirements:* For master's, 2 letters of recommendation, personal statement, resume, official transcripts, minimum GPA of 3.0. Additional exam requirements/recommendations for international students: Required—TOEFL (minimum score 550 paper-based; 80 iBT). *Application deadline:* For fall admission, 7/15 for international students; for spring admission, 11/1 for international students. Applications are processed on a rolling basis. Application fee: $35. Electronic applications accepted. *Expenses:* $853 per credit. *Financial support:* In 2016–17, 5 students received support. Federal Work-Study and unspecified assistantships available. Financial award application deadline: 5/1; financial award applicants required to submit FAFSA. *Faculty research:* Ethics in policing, multiculturalism, behavior analysis. *Total annual research expenditures:* $17,309. *Unit head:* Sylvia DeSantis, Director, 610-660-3131, E-mail: gradcas@sju.edu. *Application contact:* Graduate Admissions, College of Arts and Sciences, 610-660-3131, E-mail: gradcas@sju.edu.
Website: http://www.sju.edu/majors-programs/graduate-arts-sciences/masters/criminal-justice-ms

**Saint Joseph's University,** College of Arts and Sciences, Department of Psychology, Philadelphia, PA 19131-1395. Offers MS. *Program availability:* Evening/weekend. *Faculty:* 4 full-time (3 women), 2 part-time/adjunct (both women). *Students:* 28 full-time (18 women); includes 3 minority (1 Black or African American, non-Hispanic/Latino; 1 Hispanic/Latino; 1 Two or more races, non-Hispanic/Latino), 1 international. Average age 24. 74 applicants, 36% accepted, 23 enrolled. In 2016, 19 master's awarded. *Entrance requirements:* For master's, GRE General Test, 2 letters of recommendation, official transcripts, personal statement. Additional exam requirements/recommendations

## Psychology—General

for international students: Required—TOEFL (minimum score 550 paper-based; 80 iBT). *Application deadline:* For fall admission, 3/1 priority date for domestic and international students. Electronic applications accepted. *Expenses:* $934 per credit. *Financial support:* In 2016–17, 10 students received support. Teaching assistantships and unspecified assistantships available. Financial award application deadline: 5/1; financial award applicants required to submit FAFSA. *Faculty research:* Causes and consequences of psychological entitlement, neural and hormonal mechanisms of social behavior, risk factors of depression, mild traumatic brain injury, social and moral development in children. *Unit head:* Dr. Jodi Mindell, Director, 610-660-3131, E-mail: gradcas@sju.edu. *Application contact:* Graduate Admissions, College of Arts and Sciences, 610-660-3131, E-mail: gradcas@sju.edu.
Website: http://www.sju.edu/academics/cas/grad/psychology

**Saint Louis University,** Graduate Education, College of Arts and Sciences and Graduate Education, Department of Psychology, St. Louis, MO 63103. Offers clinical psychology (MS-R, PhD); experimental psychology (MS-R, PhD); industrial-organizational psychology (PhD); psychology (PhD). *Accreditation:* APA (one or more programs are accredited). *Program availability:* Part-time. *Degree requirements:* For master's, comprehensive exam, thesis; for doctorate, thesis/dissertation, clinical internship (for clinical psychology PhD). *Entrance requirements:* For master's, GRE General Test, interview, letters of recommendation, resume; for doctorate, GRE General Test, interview, letters of recommendation, resumé, transcripts, goal statement. Additional exam requirements/recommendations for international students: Required—TOEFL (minimum score 550 paper-based). Electronic applications accepted. *Faculty research:* Violence and trauma; neural basis of learning and memory function; eating disorders; body image and health behavior; prejudice, stereotyping, and victimization; memory, cognitive aging and language processing.

**Saint Mary's University,** Faculty of Science, Department of Psychology, Halifax, NS B3H 3C3, Canada. Offers applied psychology (M Sc, PhD), including industrial/organizational psychology (M Sc). *Program availability:* Part-time. *Degree requirements:* For master's, thesis, 500-hour internship; for doctorate, comprehensive exam, thesis/dissertation, research project. *Entrance requirements:* For master's and doctorate, GRE General Test. *Faculty research:* Assessment, health psychology, social psychology, cognition.

**Salem State University,** School of Graduate Studies, Program in Counseling and Psychological Services, Salem, MA 01970-5353. Offers MS, Graduate Certificate. *Program availability:* Part-time, evening/weekend. *Entrance requirements:* For master's, GRE or MAT. Additional exam requirements/recommendations for international students: Required—TOEFL (minimum score 550 paper-based; 80 iBT) or IELTS (minimum score 5.5).

**Sam Houston State University,** College of Humanities and Social Sciences, Department of Psychology and Philosophy, Huntsville, TX 77341. Offers psychology (MA, PhD, SSP), including clinical psychology (MA, PhD), psychology (MA), school psychology (SSP). *Accreditation:* APA. *Program availability:* Part-time. Terminal master's awarded for partial completion of doctoral program. *Degree requirements:* For master's, comprehensive exam, thesis optional; for doctorate, comprehensive exam, thesis/dissertation. *Entrance requirements:* For master's, GRE General Test, personal statement, letters of recommendation; for doctorate, GRE General Test, GRE Subject Test (advanced psychology), personal essay, letters of recommendation, resume. Additional exam requirements/recommendations for international students: Required—TOEFL (minimum score 550 paper-based; 79 iBT), IELTS (minimum score 6.5). Electronic applications accepted.

**San Diego State University,** Graduate and Research Affairs, College of Sciences, Department of Psychology, San Diego, CA 92182. Offers clinical psychology (MS, PhD); industrial and organizational psychology (MS); program evaluation (MS); psychology (MA). PhD offered jointly with University of California, San Diego. *Accreditation:* APA (one or more programs are accredited). Terminal master's awarded for partial completion of doctoral program. *Degree requirements:* For master's, thesis, oral exam; for doctorate, thesis/dissertation. *Entrance requirements:* For master's, GRE General Test, GRE Subject Test, 3 letters of recommendation; for doctorate, GRE General Test, GRE Subject Test, minimum GPA of 3.0, 3 letters of recommendation. Additional exam requirements/recommendations for international students: Required—TOEFL. Electronic applications accepted.

**San Francisco State University,** Division of Graduate Studies, College of Science and Engineering, Department of Psychology, San Francisco, CA 94132-1722. Offers clinical psychology (MA); developmental psychology (MA); industrial/organizational psychology (MS); mind, brain, and behavior (MA); school psychology (MS, Credential); social psychology (MA). *Expenses:* Tuition, state resident: full-time $6738. Tuition, nonresident: full-time $15,666. *Required fees:* $1012. Tuition and fees vary according to degree level and program. *Financial support:* Teaching assistantships available. Financial award application deadline: 3/1. *Unit head:* Dr. Dawn Terrell, Chair, 415-338-7555, Fax: 415-338-2398, E-mail: schen9@sfsu.edu. *Application contact:* Dr. Diane Harris, Graduate Program Coordinator, 415-338-7064, Fax: 415-338-2398, E-mail: dharris@sfsu.edu.
Website: http://psychology.sfsu.edu/graduate/application.html

**San Jose State University,** Graduate Studies and Research, College of Social Sciences, San Jose, CA 95192-0001. Offers applications of technology in planning (Certificate); applied anthropology (MS); communication studies (MS); community design and development (Certificate); economics (MA), including applied economics, social sciences; environmental planning (Certificate); geographic information science (Certificate); geography (MA); global citizenship (Certificate); history (MA), including history education, social sciences; Mexican American studies (MA); psychology (MA, MS), including clinical psychology (MS), industrial/organizational psychology (MS), research and experimental psychology (MA); public administration (MA); real estate development (Certificate); social sciences (MPA, MS); sociology (MA); transportation and land use planning (Certificate). *Program availability:* Part-time, evening/weekend. *Entrance requirements:* For master's, minimum GPA of 3.0. Electronic applications accepted.

**Saybrook University,** LIOS MA Residential Programs, Kirkland, WA 98033. Offers leadership and organization development (MA); psychology counseling (MA). *Degree requirements:* For master's, thesis (for some programs), oral exams. *Entrance requirements:* For master's, bachelor's degree from an accredited university or college. Additional exam requirements/recommendations for international students: Recommended—TOEFL, IELTS, TWE.

**Saybrook University,** School of Psychology and Interdisciplinary Inquiry, San Francisco, CA 94612. Offers human science (MA, PhD), including consciousness and spirituality, humanistic and transpersonal psychology, integrative health studies, organizational systems, social transformation; organizational systems (MA, PhD), including consciousness and spirituality, humanistic and transpersonal psychology, integrative health studies, leadership of sustainable systems (MA), organizational systems, social transformation; psychology (MA, PhD), including consciousness and spirituality, creativity studies (MA), humanistic and transpersonal psychology, integrative health studies, Jungian studies, marriage and family therapy (MA), organizational systems, social transformation. *Program availability:* Online learning. Terminal master's awarded for partial completion of doctoral program. *Degree requirements:* For master's, thesis or alternative; for doctorate, thesis/dissertation. *Entrance requirements:* Additional exam requirements/recommendations for international students: Required—TOEFL (minimum score 580 paper-based; 93 iBT). Electronic applications accepted. *Faculty research:* Humanistic theory, health studies, organizational systems, consciousness and spirituality, social transformation.

**The Seattle School of Theology and Psychology,** Graduate Programs, Seattle, WA 98121. Offers Christian studies (MA); counseling psychology (MA); divinity (M Div). *Program availability:* Part-time. *Entrance requirements:* For master's, MAT.

**Seattle University,** College of Arts and Sciences, Department of Psychology, Seattle, WA 98122-1090. Offers existential and phenomenological therapeutic psychology (MA Psych). *Faculty:* 57 full-time (4 women), 4 part-time/adjunct (3 women). *Students:* 32 full-time (18 women), 2 part-time (both women); includes 8 minority (1 Black or African American, non-Hispanic/Latino; 5 Asian, non-Hispanic/Latino; 1 Hispanic/Latino; 1 Two or more races, non-Hispanic/Latino), 3 international. Average age 30. 58 applicants, 50% accepted, 12 enrolled. In 2016, 26 master's awarded. *Degree requirements:* For master's, thesis optional. *Entrance requirements:* For master's, interview, minimum GPA of 3.0, previous undergraduate course work in psychology, experience (paid or volunteer) in counseling or human services. *Application deadline:* For fall admission, 1/15 for domestic and international students. Application fee: $55. Electronic applications accepted. *Financial support:* In 2016–17, 14 students received support. Career-related internships or fieldwork and Federal Work-Study available. Support available to part-time students. Financial award applicants required to submit FAFSA. *Faculty research:* Interpersonal relations, psychotherapy, qualitative research, trauma, philosophy and psychology. *Unit head:* Dr. Kevin Krycka, Director of Graduate Programs, 206-296-5398, Fax: 206-296-2141, E-mail: krycka@seattleu.edu. *Application contact:* Janet Shandley, Associate Dean of Graduate Admissions, 206-296-5900, Fax: 206-298-5656, E-mail: grad_admissions@seattleu.edu.
Website: http://www.seattleu.edu/artsci/departments/psychology/

**Seton Hall University,** College of Arts and Sciences, Department of Psychology, South Orange, NJ 07079-2697. Offers experimental psychology (MS). *Program availability:* Part-time, evening/weekend. *Degree requirements:* For master's, thesis optional. *Entrance requirements:* For master's, GRE, minimum of 18 credits in psychology with minimum GPA of 3.0. Additional exam requirements/recommendations for international students: Required—TOEFL. Electronic applications accepted. *Faculty research:* Behavioral neuroscience, cognitive psychology, social psychology, perception/motor skills, memory, depression, anxiety.

**Seton Hall University,** College of Education and Human Services, Department of Professional Psychology and Family Therapy, South Orange, NJ 07079-2697. Offers counseling psychology (MA, PhD), including counseling psychology (PhD); school counseling (MA); psychological studies (MA), including individualized, marriage and family therapy, sport and exercise psychology; school psychology (MA). *Accreditation:* APA. *Program availability:* Part-time, evening/weekend, blended/hybrid learning. *Faculty:* 10 full-time (7 women). *Students:* 42 full-time (25 women), 207 part-time (161 women); includes 81 minority (42 Black or African American, non-Hispanic/Latino; 2 American Indian or Alaska Native, non-Hispanic/Latino; 9 Asian, non-Hispanic/Latino; 26 Hispanic/Latino; 2 Two or more races, non-Hispanic/Latino), 7 international. Average age 31. 291 applicants, 42% accepted, 73 enrolled. In 2016, 23 master's, 11 doctorates awarded. Terminal master's awarded for partial completion of doctoral program. *Degree requirements:* For master's, comprehensive exam, case study; for doctorate, comprehensive exam, thesis/dissertation, internship. *Entrance requirements:* For master's, GRE or MAT; for doctorate, GRE, interview. *Application deadline:* For fall admission, 2/15 for domestic students. Applications are processed on a rolling basis. Application fee: $75. *Financial support:* In 2016–17, 4 research assistantships with full tuition reimbursements (averaging $4,500 per year) were awarded; career-related internships or fieldwork also available. Financial award application deadline: 2/1. *Faculty research:* Counseling process, ethics, family systems, child pathology. *Unit head:* Dr. Ben Beitin, Chair, 973-761-9450, E-mail: ben.beitin@shu.edu. *Application contact:* Diana Minakakis, Director of Graduate Admissions, 973-275-2824, Fax: 973-275-2187, E-mail: diana.minakakis@shu.edu.
Website: http://www.shu.edu/academics/education/professional-psychology/

**Shippensburg University of Pennsylvania,** School of Graduate Studies, College of Arts and Sciences, Department of Psychology, Shippensburg, PA 17257-2299. Offers psychological science (MS). *Program availability:* Part-time, evening/weekend. *Faculty:* 7 full-time (4 women), 2 part-time/adjunct (1 woman). *Students:* 19 full-time (7 women), 8 part-time (6 women); includes 3 minority (1 Black or African American, non-Hispanic/Latino; 1 Hispanic/Latino; 1 Two or more races, non-Hispanic/Latino). Average age 25. 39 applicants, 56% accepted, 15 enrolled. In 2016, 9 master's awarded. *Degree requirements:* For master's, comprehensive exam (for some programs), thesis (for some programs), thesis, field experience, or competency exam. *Entrance requirements:* For master's, minimum GPA of 2.75, course in statistics, 9 undergraduate credit hours in psychology, supplemental form with personal goals statement. Additional exam requirements/recommendations for international students: Required—TOEFL (minimum score 550 paper-based, 68 iBT) or IELTS (minimum score 6). *Application deadline:* For fall admission, 3/1 priority date for domestic students, 3/1 for international students; for spring admission, 11/1 priority date for domestic students, 11/1 for international students; for summer admission, 3/1 for domestic students. Applications are processed on a rolling basis. Application fee: $45. Electronic applications accepted. *Expenses:* Tuition, state resident: part-time $483 per credit. Tuition, nonresident: part-time $725 per credit. *Required fees:* $141 per credit. *Financial support:* In 2016–17, 8 students received support. Career-related internships or fieldwork, scholarships/grants, unspecified assistantships, and resident hall director and student payroll positions available. Support available to part-time students. Financial award application deadline: 3/1; financial award applicants required to submit FAFSA. *Unit head:* Dr. Kathryn M. Potoczak, Associate Professor and Program Coordinator, 717-477-1657, Fax: 717-477-4057, E-mail: kmpoto@ship.edu. *Application contact:* Megan N. Luft, Assistant Dean of Graduate Admissions, 717-477-1231, Fax: 717-477-4016, E-mail: mnluft@ship.edu.
Website: http://www.ship.edu/psychology/

**Simon Fraser University,** Office of Graduate Studies and Postdoctoral Fellows, Faculty of Arts and Social Sciences, Department of Psychology, Burnaby, BC V5A 1S6, Canada. Offers MA, PhD. *Faculty:* 36 full-time (11 women). *Students:* 108 full-time (73 women). 171 applicants, 12% accepted, 10 enrolled. In 2016, 10 master's, 7 doctorates awarded. *Degree requirements:* For master's, thesis; for doctorate, comprehensive exam, thesis/dissertation, clinical training (for some programs). *Entrance requirements:* For master's, GRE General Test, GRE Subject Test (psychology), minimum GPA of 3.0 (on scale of 4.33) or 3.33 based on last 60 credits of undergraduate courses; for doctorate, GRE General Test, GRE Subject Test (psychology), minimum GPA of 3.5 (on scale of 4.33). Additional exam requirements/recommendations for international students: Recommended—TOEFL (minimum score 580 paper-based; 93 iBT), IELTS (minimum score 7), TWE (minimum score 5). *Application deadline:* For fall admission, 12/3 for domestic and international students; for spring admission, 1/1 for domestic students. Applications are processed on a rolling basis. Application fee: $90 ($125 for

international students). Electronic applications accepted. *Expenses:* Contact institution. *Financial support:* In 2016–17, 80 students received support, including 40 fellowships (averaging $4,388 per year), teaching assistantships (averaging $5,608 per year); research assistantships, career-related internships or fieldwork, scholarships/grants, and traineeships also available. *Faculty research:* Cognitive and neural sciences; developmental, law and forensic psychology; social history; quantitative and theoretical psychology; clinical sciences. *Unit head:* Dr. Kevin Douglas, Graduate Chair, 778-782-9562, Fax: 778-782-3427, E-mail: psyc-grad-chair@sfu.ca. *Application contact:* Anita Turner, Graduate Secretary, 778-782-4367, Fax: 778-782-3427, E-mail: psyc-grad-sec@sfu.ca.
Website: http://www.psyc.sfu.ca/

**Sofia University,** Hybrid: Face-to-Face/Online Programs, Palo Alto, CA 94303. Offers transpersonal psychology (MA, PhD), including transpersonal psychology (PhD). *Program availability:* Online learning. *Entrance requirements:* For master's, bachelor's degree; for doctorate, bachelor's degree; master's degree. Electronic applications accepted.

**Sofia University,** Residential Programs, Palo Alto, CA 94303. Offers clinical psychology (Psy D); computer science (MS); counseling psychology (MA); transpersonal psychology (MA, PhD). *Program availability:* Part-time, evening/weekend. Terminal master's awarded for partial completion of doctoral program. *Degree requirements:* For doctorate, thesis/dissertation. *Entrance requirements:* For master's, bachelor's degree; for doctorate, bachelor's degree; master's degree (for some programs). Electronic applications accepted.

**Southeastern Baptist Theological Seminary,** Graduate and Professional Programs, Wake Forest, NC 27588-1889. Offers advanced biblical studies (M Div); Christian education (M Div, MACE); Christian ethics (PhD); Christian ministry (M Div); Christian planting (M Div); church music (MACM); counseling (MACO); evangelism (PhD); language (M Div); ministry (D Min); New Testament (PhD); Old Testament (PhD); philosophy (PhD); theology (Th M, PhD); women's studies (M Div). *Accreditation:* ACIPE; ATS (one or more programs are accredited). *Degree requirements:* For master's, thesis (for some programs), oral exam; for doctorate, thesis/dissertation, fieldwork. *Entrance requirements:* For master's, Cooperative English Test, minimum GPA of 2.0, M Div or equivalent (Th M); for doctorate, GRE General Test or MAT, Cooperative English Test, M Div or equivalent, 3 years of professional experience.

**Southeastern Louisiana University,** College of Arts, Humanities and Social Sciences, Department of Psychology, Hammond, LA 70402. Offers industrial/organizational (MA). *Program availability:* Part-time. *Faculty:* 7 full-time (5 women). *Students:* 20 full-time (13 women), 13 part-time (12 women); includes 5 minority (1 Asian, non-Hispanic/Latino; 2 Hispanic/Latino; 2 Two or more races, non-Hispanic/Latino). Average age 26. 38 applicants, 68% accepted, 11 enrolled. In 2016, 11 master's awarded. *Degree requirements:* For master's, comprehensive exam, thesis, 38 hours of psychology course work including core courses in statistics, social psychology, cognition, and physiological psychology. *Entrance requirements:* For master's, GRE (minimum combined score 950). Additional exam requirements/recommendations for international students: Required—TOEFL (minimum score 500 paper-based; 61 iBT). *Application deadline:* For fall admission, 7/15 priority date for domestic students, 6/1 priority date for international students; for spring admission, 12/1 priority date for domestic students, 10/1 priority date for international students. Applications are processed on a rolling basis. Application fee: $20 ($30 for international students). Electronic applications accepted. *Expenses:* Tuition, state resident: full-time $6540; part-time $465 per credit hour. Tuition, nonresident: full-time $19,017; part-time $1158 per credit hour. *Required fees:* $1829. *Financial support:* In 2016–17, 10 students received support, including 10 research assistantships (averaging $9,090 per year); career-related internships or fieldwork, Federal Work-Study, institutionally sponsored loans, scholarships/grants, and traineeships also available. Support available to part-time students. Financial award application deadline: 5/1; financial award applicants required to submit FAFSA. *Faculty research:* Eating disorders, evolutionary psychology, violence exposure effects on children, parental behavior, neurobiology of mental disorders and addiction. *Unit head:* Dr. Susan Coats, Department Head, 985-549-2154, Fax: 985-549-6892, E-mail: scoats@southeastern.edu. *Application contact:* Amanda Harper, Graduate Admissions Analyst, 985-549-5620, Fax: 985-549-5632, E-mail: admissions@southeastern.edu.
Website: http://www.southeastern.edu/acad_research/depts/psyc/index.html

**Southern Adventist University,** School of Education and Psychology, Collegedale, TN 37315-0370. Offers clinical mental health counseling (MS); inclusive education (MS Ed); instructional leadership (MS Ed); literacy education (MS Ed); outdoor teacher education (MS Ed); school counseling (MS). *Accreditation:* NCATE. *Program availability:* Part-time, evening/weekend. *Degree requirements:* For master's, comprehensive exam (for some programs), thesis optional, position paper (MS), portfolio (MS Ed in outdoor teacher education). *Entrance requirements:* For master's, interview (MS); 9 semester hours of upper-division course work in psychology or related field, including 1 course in psychology research or statistics; 9 semester hours of education (MS Ed). Additional exam requirements/recommendations for international students: Required—TOEFL (minimum score 600 paper-based; 100 iBT). Electronic applications accepted.

**Southern California Seminary,** Graduate and Professional Programs, El Cajon, CA 92019. Offers Biblical studies (MABS); counseling psychology (MACP); marriage and family therapy (MAMFT); psychology (Psy D); religious studies (MRS); theology (M Div). *Program availability:* Part-time, evening/weekend, online learning. *Degree requirements:* For master's, thesis (for some programs); for doctorate, thesis/dissertation. *Entrance requirements:* For doctorate, master's degree in psychology. Additional exam requirements/recommendations for international students: Required—TOEFL (minimum score 550 paper-based). Electronic applications accepted.

**Southern Connecticut State University,** School of Graduate Studies, School of Arts and Sciences, Department of Psychology, New Haven, CT 06515-1355. Offers MA. *Program availability:* Part-time, evening/weekend. *Faculty:* 7 full-time (4 women), 1 part-time/adjunct (0 women). *Students:* 23 full-time (17 women), 8 part-time (5 women); includes 11 minority (5 Black or African American, non-Hispanic/Latino; 6 Hispanic/Latino). Average age 27. 63 applicants, 51% accepted, 19 enrolled. In 2016, 12 master's awarded. *Degree requirements:* For master's, thesis or alternative. *Entrance requirements:* For master's, interview, previous course work in psychology. *Application deadline:* For fall admission, 5/15 priority date for domestic students. Applications are processed on a rolling basis. Application fee: $50. Electronic applications accepted. *Expenses:* Tuition, state resident: full-time $6497; part-time $519 per credit hour. Tuition, nonresident: full-time $18,102; part-time $535 per credit hour. *Required fees:* $4722; $55 per semester. Tuition and fees vary according to program. *Financial support:* Career-related internships or fieldwork, scholarships/grants, and unspecified assistantships available. Financial award application deadline: 4/15; financial award applicants required to submit FAFSA. *Unit head:* Dr. Lawrence Brancazio, Chairperson, 203-392-5111, Fax: 203-392-6805, E-mail: brancaziol1@southernct.edu. *Application contact:* Lisa Galvin, Director of Graduate Admissions, 203-392-5240, Fax: 203-392-5235, E-mail: galvinl1@southernct.edu.

**Southern Illinois University Carbondale,** Graduate School, College of Education and Human Services, Program in Behavior Analysis and Therapy, Carbondale, IL 62901-

4701. Offers MS. *Entrance requirements:* Additional exam requirements/recommendations for international students: Required—TOEFL.

**Southern Illinois University Carbondale,** Graduate School, College of Liberal Arts, Department of Psychology, Carbondale, IL 62901-4701. Offers clinical psychology (PhD); counseling psychology (PhD); experimental psychology (MA, MS). *Accreditation:* APA (one or more programs are accredited). *Degree requirements:* For master's, thesis; for doctorate, thesis/dissertation. *Entrance requirements:* For master's, GRE General Test, GRE Subject Test, minimum GPA of 2.7; for doctorate, GRE General Test, GRE Subject Test, minimum GPA of 3.25. Additional exam requirements/recommendations for international students: Required—TOEFL. *Faculty research:* Developmental neuropsychology; smoking, affect, and cognition; personality measurement; vocational psychology; program evaluation.

**Southern Illinois University Edwardsville,** Graduate School, School of Education, Health, and Human Behavior, Department of Psychology, Edwardsville, IL 62026. Offers clinical child and school psychology (MS); clinical psychology (MA); industrial-organizational psychology (MA); school psychology (SD). *Program availability:* Part-time, evening/weekend. *Degree requirements:* For master's, thesis (for some programs), research paper; for SD, thesis. *Entrance requirements:* For master's, GRE. Additional exam requirements/recommendations for international students: Required—TOEFL (minimum score 550 paper-based; 79 iBT), IELTS (minimum score 6.5). Electronic applications accepted.

**Southern Methodist University,** Dedman College of Humanities and Sciences, Department of Psychology, Dallas, TX 75275. Offers clinical psychology (PhD). *Accreditation:* APA. Terminal master's awarded for partial completion of doctoral program. *Degree requirements:* For doctorate, comprehensive exam, thesis/dissertation, oral exam, practicum, research presentation and publication. *Entrance requirements:* For doctorate, GRE General Test, minimum GPA of 3.4. Additional exam requirements/recommendations for international students: Required—TOEFL (minimum score 550 paper-based). Electronic applications accepted. *Faculty research:* Experimental, social, developmental, and cognitive psychology; anger/violence; mood disorders; depression and anxiety; family assessment and development; chronic pain and mental health.

**Southern Nazarene University,** College of Professional and Graduate Studies, Department of Psychology and Counseling, Bethany, OK 73008. Offers counseling psychology (MA, MSCP); marital and family therapy (MA). *Degree requirements:* For master's, thesis optional. *Entrance requirements:* For master's, English proficiency exam, minimum GPA of 3.0 in last 60 hours/major, 2.7 overall.

**Southern New Hampshire University,** School of Arts and Sciences, Manchester, NH 03106-1045. Offers community mental health (Graduate Certificate); community mental health and mental health counseling (MS); fiction and nonfiction (MFA); teaching English as a foreign language (MS). *Program availability:* Part-time, evening/weekend. *Degree requirements:* For master's, one foreign language, thesis. *Entrance requirements:* For master's, minimum GPA of 2.75 (for MS in teaching English as a foreign language), 3.0 (for MFA). Additional exam requirements/recommendations for international students: Required—TOEFL (minimum score 550 paper-based; 79 iBT), IELTS (minimum score 6.5), TWE (minimum score 5). Electronic applications accepted. *Expenses:* Contact institution. *Faculty research:* Action research, state of the art practice in behavioral health services, wraparound approaches to working with youth, learning styles.

**Southern Oregon University,** Graduate Studies, Department of Psychology, Ashland, OR 97520. Offers MHC. *Accreditation:* ACA. *Program availability:* Part-time, online learning. *Faculty:* 10 full-time (5 women), 6 part-time/adjunct (3 women). *Students:* 43 full-time (33 women), 3 part-time (all women); includes 11 minority (4 American Indian or Alaska Native, non-Hispanic/Latino; 5 Hispanic/Latino; 2 Two or more races, non-Hispanic/Latino). Average age 35. 59 applicants, 61% accepted, 22 enrolled. In 2016, 19 master's awarded. *Degree requirements:* For master's, thesis, portfolio, oral defense. *Entrance requirements:* For master's, GRE General Test, minimum cumulative GPA of 3.0 in the last 90 quarter credits (60 semester credits) of undergraduate coursework. Additional exam requirements/recommendations for international students: Required—TOEFL (minimum score 540 paper-based; 76 iBT), IELTS (minimum score 6), ELPT (minimum score 964) or ELS (minimum score 112). *Application deadline:* For fall admission, 7/31 priority date for domestic and international students; for winter admission, 11/15 priority date for domestic and international students; for spring admission, 1/7 priority date for domestic and international students. Applications are processed on a rolling basis. Application fee: $60. Electronic applications accepted. *Expenses:* Tuition, state resident: full-time $10,719; part-time $397 per credit. Tuition, nonresident: full-time $13,419; part-time $497 per credit. *Required fees:* $548. *Financial support:* In 2016–17, 1 student received support, including 1 research assistantship with partial tuition reimbursement available; career-related internships or fieldwork, institutionally sponsored loans, scholarships/grants, and unspecified assistantships also available. *Unit head:* Dr. Josie Wilson, Graduate Program Coordinator, 541-552-6946, E-mail: jwilson@sou.edu. *Application contact:* Lori Courtney, Graduate Coordinator, 541-552-6947, E-mail: courtney@sou.edu.
Website: http://www.sou.edu/psychology/mhc

**Southern University and Agricultural and Mechanical College,** Graduate School, College of Sciences, Department of Psychology, Baton Rouge, LA 70813. Offers rehabilitation counseling (MS). *Degree requirements:* For master's, comprehensive exam, thesis optional. *Entrance requirements:* For master's, GMAT or GRE General Test. Additional exam requirements/recommendations for international students: Required—TOEFL (minimum score 525 paper-based). *Faculty research:* Cultural diversity, professional preparation and participation of minorities, needs and satisfaction of students with disabilities, prediction model for rehabilitation outcome, diabetes.

**Southwestern College,** Program in Psychodrama and Action Methods, Santa Fe, NM 87502-4788. Offers Certificate. *Entrance requirements:* For degree, 3 letters of reference.

**Spalding University,** Graduate Studies, Kosair College of Health and Natural Sciences, School of Professional Psychology, Louisville, KY 40203-2188. Offers clinical psychology (MA, Psy D). *Accreditation:* APA (one or more programs are accredited). *Program availability:* Part-time. *Faculty:* 72 full-time (16 women), 11 part-time/adjunct (8 women). *Students:* 125 full-time (103 women), 58 part-time (50 women); includes 27 minority (13 Black or African American, non-Hispanic/Latino; 4 Asian, non-Hispanic/Latino; 5 Hispanic/Latino; 5 Two or more races, non-Hispanic/Latino), 1 international. Average age 29. 168 applicants, 35% accepted, 34 enrolled. In 2016, 19 master's, 25 doctorates awarded. Terminal master's awarded for partial completion of doctoral program. *Degree requirements:* For master's, comprehensive exam; for doctorate, thesis/dissertation. *Entrance requirements:* For master's and doctorate, GRE General Test, 18 hours of undergraduate course work in psychology, interview, letters of recommendation, writing sample, autobiographical statement. Additional exam requirements/recommendations for international students: Required—TOEFL (minimum score 535 paper-based). *Application deadline:* For fall admission, 1/15 priority date for domestic and international students. Application fee: $30. *Expenses:* Tuition: Full-time $15,300. *Financial support:* In 2016–17, 53 research assistantships (averaging $6,376 per year) were awarded; career-related internships or fieldwork, scholarships/grants,

*Psychology—General*

and unspecified assistantships also available. Financial award applicants required to submit FAFSA. *Faculty research:* Substance abuse, prayer research, end-of-life issues, complementary and alternative medicine, research methodology and statistical inference. *Unit head:* Dr. Steven Katsikas, Chair, 502-873-4459, E-mail: skatsikas@spalding.edu. *Application contact:* Elizabeth A. Simpson, Administrative Assistant, 502-585-7127, E-mail: esimpson@spalding.edu.
Website: https://spalding.edu/academics/psychology/

**Stanford University,** School of Humanities and Sciences, Department of Psychology, Stanford, CA 94305-2004. Offers PhD. *Degree requirements:* For doctorate, thesis/ dissertation, oral exam. *Entrance requirements:* For doctorate, GRE General Test, GRE Subject Test. Additional exam requirements/recommendations for international students: Required—TOEFL. Electronic applications accepted. *Expenses: Tuition:* Full-time $47,331. *Required fees:* $609.

**State University of New York at New Paltz,** Graduate School, School of Liberal Arts and Sciences, Department of Psychology, New Paltz, NY 12561. Offers mental health counseling (MS, AC); psychology (MA); school counseling (MS). *Program availability:* Part-time, evening/weekend. *Students:* 52 full-time (40 women), 19 part-time (12 women); includes 13 minority (1 Black or African American, non-Hispanic/Latino; 1 Asian, non-Hispanic/Latino; 11 Hispanic/Latino), 1 international. 103 applicants, 50% accepted, 33 enrolled. In 2016, 22 master's awarded. *Degree requirements:* For master's, comprehensive exam, thesis. *Entrance requirements:* For master's, GRE General Test, minimum GPA of 3.0. Additional exam requirements/recommendations for international students: Required—TOEFL (minimum score 550 paper-based; 80 iBT), IELTS (minimum score 6.5). *Application deadline:* For fall admission, 2/1 priority date for domestic and international students; for spring admission, 11/15 priority date for domestic and international students. Application fee: $50. Electronic applications accepted. *Financial support:* In 2016–17, 6 teaching assistantships with partial tuition reimbursements (averaging $5,000 per year) were awarded. Financial award application deadline: 8/1. *Faculty research:* Disaster mental health, women's objectification, mate selection, cultural psychology, achievement motivation. *Unit head:* Dr. Glenn Geher, Chair, 845-257-3091, E-mail: geherg@newpaltz.edu. *Application contact:* Dr. Tabitha Holmes, Program Coordinator, 845-257-3955, E-mail: holmest@newpaltz.edu.
Website: http://www.newpaltz.edu/psychology/

**State University of New York at Plattsburgh,** School of Arts and Sciences, Department of Psychology, Plattsburgh, NY 12901-2681. Offers school psychology (MA, CAS). *Program availability:* Part-time. *Entrance requirements:* For master's, GRE General Test, minimum GPA of 3.0. Additional exam requirements/recommendations for international students: Required—TOEFL. *Faculty research:* Alzheimer's disease, adolescent behavior, intellectual assessment, learning disabilities, reading skill acquisition.

**Stephen F. Austin State University,** Graduate School, College of Liberal Arts, Department of Psychology, Nacogdoches, TX 75962. Offers MA. *Degree requirements:* For master's, comprehensive exam, thesis. *Entrance requirements:* For master's, GRE General Test. Additional exam requirements/recommendations for international students: Required—TOEFL.

**Stony Brook University, State University of New York,** Graduate School, College of Arts and Sciences, Department of Psychology, Stony Brook, NY 11794. Offers clinical psychology (PhD); cognitive psychology (PhD); integrative neuroscience (PhD); psychology (MA); social and health psychology (PhD). *Accreditation:* APA (one or more programs are accredited). *Faculty:* 33 full-time (18 women), 2 part-time/adjunct (1 woman). *Students:* 101 full-time (82 women); includes 21 minority (3 Black or African American, non-Hispanic/Latino; 10 Asian, non-Hispanic/Latino; 6 Hispanic/Latino; 2 Two or more races, non-Hispanic/Latino), 11 international. Average age 27. 455 applicants, 5% accepted, 14 enrolled. In 2016, 28 master's, 13 doctorates awarded. *Degree requirements:* For doctorate, thesis/dissertation. *Entrance requirements:* For doctorate, GRE General Test, GRE Subject Test. Additional exam requirements/recommendations for international students: Required—TOEFL (minimum score 90 iBT). *Application deadline:* For fall admission, 1/15 for domestic students; for spring admission, 10/1 for domestic students. Application fee: $100. *Expenses:* Contact institution. *Financial support:* In 2016–17, 15 fellowships, 23 research assistantships, 56 teaching assistantships were awarded; career-related internships or fieldwork also available. *Faculty research:* Clinical psychology, cognitive development or processes, cognitive neuropsychology, developmental psychopathology, emotions. *Total annual research expenditures:* $2.8 million. *Unit head:* Dr. Arthur Samuel, Chair, 631-632-7792, E-mail: arthur.samuel@stonybrook.edu. *Application contact:* Marilynn Wollmuth, Coordinator, 631-632-7855, Fax: 631-632-7876, E-mail: marilyn.wollmuth@stonybrook.edu.
Website: http://www.psychology.sunysb.edu/psychology/

**Suffolk University,** College of Arts and Sciences, Department of Psychology, Boston, MA 02108-2770. Offers clinical psychology (PhD); college admission counseling (Certificate); mental health counseling (MS); school counseling (MS, CAGS). *Accreditation:* APA. *Faculty:* 14 full-time (7 women), 7 part-time/adjunct (6 women). *Students:* 51 full-time (45 women), 42 part-time (38 women); includes 24 minority (3 Black or African American, non-Hispanic/Latino; 8 Asian, non-Hispanic/Latino; 11 Hispanic/Latino; 2 Two or more races, non-Hispanic/Latino), 6 international. Average age 27. 306 applicants, 25% accepted, 38 enrolled. In 2016, 22 master's, 10 doctorates, 14 other advanced degrees awarded. *Degree requirements:* For doctorate, thesis/ dissertation, practicum. *Entrance requirements:* For doctorate, GRE General Test or MAT, 2 letters of recommendation, resume. Additional exam requirements/ recommendations for international students: Required—TOEFL (minimum score 550 paper-based; 80 iBT). *Application deadline:* For fall admission, 12/1 for domestic and international students. Applications are processed on a rolling basis. Application fee: $50. Electronic applications accepted. *Expenses:* Contact institution. *Financial support:* In 2016–17, 54 students received support, including 53 fellowships (averaging $13,943 per year); career-related internships or fieldwork, Federal Work-Study, institutionally sponsored loans, scholarships/grants, and unspecified assistantships also available. Support available to part-time students. Financial award application deadline: 4/1; financial award applicants required to submit FAFSA. *Faculty research:* Assessing exposure in the context of a family-based cognitive behavioral treatment for pediatric OCD, a mindfulness approach to designing and testing the efficacy of a new sexual revictimization prevention program for college women, olfaction and decision-making in substance-dependent individuals, the role of experiential avoidance in Generalized Anxiety Disorder, ego development as a predictor of dogmatism and intolerance in the political right and left. *Unit head:* Dr. Gary Fireman, Chairperson, 617-305-6368, Fax: 617-367-2924, E-mail: gfireman@suffolk.edu. *Application contact:* Mara Marzocchi, Associate Director of Graduate Admissions, 617-573-8302, Fax: 617-305-1733, E-mail: grad.admission@suffolk.edu.
Website: http://www.suffolk.edu/college/graduate/69299.php

**Sul Ross State University,** College of Arts and Sciences, Department of Behavioral and Social Sciences, Program in Psychology, Alpine, TX 79832. Offers MA. *Entrance requirements:* For master's, GRE General Test, minimum GPA of 2.5 in last 60 hours of undergraduate work.

**Teachers College, Columbia University,** Department of Counseling and Clinical Psychology, New York, NY 10027-6696. Offers clinical psychology (PhD); counseling psychology (Ed M, Ed D, PhD); mental health counseling (ME); psychological counseling (ME, ND); psychology in education (MA, ND); school counselor (ME). *Accreditation:* APA (one or more programs are accredited). *Program availability:* Part-time. *Students:* 434 full-time (366 women), 232 part-time (184 women); includes 247 minority (62 Black or African American, non-Hispanic/Latino; 1 American Indian or Alaska Native, non-Hispanic/Latino; 80 Asian, non-Hispanic/Latino; 84 Hispanic/Latino; 20 Two or more races, non-Hispanic/Latino), 134 international. 1,470 applicants, 39% accepted, 253 enrolled. *Expenses: Tuition:* Full-time $36,288; part-time $1512 per credit. *Required fees:* $438 per semester. One-time fee: $510 full-time. Full-time tuition and fees vary according to course load. *Unit head:* Prof. Marie Miville, Head, 212-678-3343, Fax: 212-678-3275, E-mail: miville@tc.columbia.edu. *Application contact:* David Estrella, Director of Admission, 212-678-3305, E-mail: estrella@tc.columbia.edu.

**Temple University,** College of Liberal Arts, Department of Psychology, Philadelphia, PA 19122-6096. Offers MA, MS, PhD. *Accreditation:* APA. *Degree requirements:* For doctorate, thesis/dissertation. *Entrance requirements:* For doctorate, GRE General Test, minimum GPA of 3.0, 2 letters of recommendation. Additional exam requirements/ recommendations for international students: Required—TOEFL (minimum score 620 paper-based; 105 iBT). Electronic applications accepted. *Faculty research:* Behavioral and cognitive neuroscience, cognitive and social development, psychopathology: study and treatment, social cognition and decision-making.

**Tennessee State University,** The School of Graduate Studies and Research, College of Education, Department of Psychology, Nashville, TN 37209-1561. Offers counseling psychology (MS). *Entrance requirements:* For master's, GRE General Test or MAT. Electronic applications accepted.

**Texas A&M International University,** Office of Graduate Studies and Research, College of Arts and Sciences, Department of Psychology and Communication, Laredo, TX 78041-1900. Offers counseling psychology (MACP); psychology (MS). *Degree requirements:* For master's, thesis (for some programs). *Entrance requirements:* For master's, GRE General Test. Additional exam requirements/recommendations for international students: Required—TOEFL (minimum score 550 paper-based; 79 iBT).

**Texas A&M University,** College of Liberal Arts, Department of Psychology, College Station, TX 77843. Offers clinical psychology (PhD); industrial/organizational psychology (PhD); psychology (MS, PhD), including clinical psychology (PhD), industrial/organizational psychology (PhD). *Accreditation:* APA (one or more programs are accredited). *Faculty:* 48. *Students:* 83 full-time (38 women), 14 part-time (10 women); includes 34 minority (7 Black or African American, non-Hispanic/Latino; 4 Asian, non-Hispanic/Latino; 22 Hispanic/Latino; 1 Two or more races, non-Hispanic/ Latino), 13 international. Average age 28. 350 applicants, 9% accepted, 22 enrolled. In 2016, 4 master's, 12 doctorates awarded. *Degree requirements:* For doctorate, comprehensive exam (for some programs), thesis/dissertation. *Entrance requirements:* For doctorate, GRE General Test. Additional exam requirements/recommendations for international students: Required—TOEFL (minimum score 550 paper-based; 80 iBT), IELTS (minimum score 6), PTE (minimum score 53). *Application deadline:* For fall admission, 12/1 for domestic and international students. Application fee: $50 ($90 for international students). Electronic applications accepted. *Expenses:* Contact institution. *Financial support:* In 2016–17, 84 students received support, including 20 fellowships with tuition reimbursements available (averaging $15,749 per year), 31 research assistantships with tuition reimbursements available (averaging $6,408 per year), 55 teaching assistantships with tuition reimbursements available (averaging $10,420 per year); career-related internships or fieldwork, institutionally sponsored loans, scholarships/grants, traineeships, health care benefits, tuition waivers (full and partial), and unspecified assistantships also available. Support available to part-time students. Financial award application deadline: 3/15; financial award applicants required to submit FAFSA. *Unit head:* Dr. Heather Lench, Department Head, 979-845-0377, E-mail: hlench@tamu.edu. *Application contact:* Dr. Charles D. Samuelson, Director of Graduate Studies, 979-845-0880, Fax: 979-845-4727, E-mail: c-samuelson@tamu.edu.
Website: http://psychology.tamu.edu/

**Texas A&M University–Commerce,** College of Education and Human Services, Commerce, TX 75429-3011. Offers counseling (MS); curriculum and instruction (M Ed, MS); early childhood education (M Ed, MS); educational administration (M Ed, Ed D); educational psychology (PhD); educational technology leadership (MS); educational technology library science (MS); health, kinesiology and sports studies (MS); higher education (MS, Ed D); organization, learning, and technology (MS); psychology (MS); reading (M Ed, MS); school psychology (SSP); secondary education (M Ed, MS); social work (MSW); special education (M Ed); supervision, curriculum and instruction-elementary education (Ed D). *Program availability:* Part-time, 100% online, blended/ hybrid learning. *Faculty:* 88 full-time (52 women), 31 part-time/adjunct (24 women). *Students:* 341 full-time (276 women), 1,495 part-time (1,156 women); includes 762 minority (429 Black or African American, non-Hispanic/Latino; 4 American Indian or Alaska Native, non-Hispanic/Latino; 27 Asian, non-Hispanic/Latino; 247 Hispanic/Latino; 1 Native Hawaiian or other Pacific Islander, non-Hispanic/Latino; 54 Two or more races, non-Hispanic/Latino), 18 international. Average age 37. 1,070 applicants, 54% accepted, 452 enrolled. In 2016, 579 master's, 31 doctorates awarded. *Degree requirements:* For master's, one foreign language, comprehensive exam, thesis optional, departmental qualifying exams (for some programs); for doctorate, comprehensive exam, thesis/dissertation, departmental qualifying exam; for SSP, comprehensive exam, thesis optional. *Entrance requirements:* For master's and doctorate, GRE General Test. Additional exam requirements/recommendations for international students: Required—TOEFL (minimum score 550 paper-based; 79 iBT), IELTS (minimum score 6). *Application deadline:* For fall admission, 6/1 priority date for international students; for spring admission, 10/15 priority date for international students; for summer admission, 3/15 priority date for international students. Applications are processed on a rolling basis. Application fee: $50. Electronic applications accepted. *Expenses:* $2,254 resident; $4,744 non-resident. *Financial support:* In 2016–17, 301 students received support, including 39 research assistantships with partial tuition reimbursements available (averaging $9,000 per year), 17 teaching assistantships with partial tuition reimbursements available (averaging $9,000 per year); career-related internships or fieldwork, Federal Work-Study, institutionally sponsored loans, scholarships/grants, health care benefits, and unspecified assistantships also available. Financial award application deadline: 5/1; financial award applicants required to submit FAFSA. *Faculty research:* Cognitive and bilingual education, positive behavioral intervention, literacy, math readiness. *Total annual research expenditures:* $470,963. *Unit head:* Dr. Timothy Letzring, Dean, 903-886-5181, Fax: 903-886-5905, E-mail: tim.letzring@tamuc.edu. *Application contact:* Jennifer Faunce, Graduate Recruiter, 903-886-5030, Fax: 903-886-5905, E-mail: jennifer.faunce@tamuc.edu.
Website: http://www.tamuc.edu/academics/graduateSchool/programs/education/default.aspx

**Texas A&M University–Corpus Christi,** College of Graduate Studies, College of Liberal Arts, Corpus Christi, TX 78412-5503. Offers communication (MA); English (MA); history (MA); psychology (MA), including clinical psychology, general psychology; public administration (MPA); studio art (MFA). *Program availability:* Part-time, evening/

weekend. *Faculty:* 76 full-time (39 women), 9 part-time/adjunct (4 women). *Students:* 81 full-time (49 women), 102 part-time (71 women); includes 90 minority (8 Black or African American, non-Hispanic/Latino; 2 Asian, non-Hispanic/Latino; 76 Hispanic/Latino; 4 Two or more races, non-Hispanic/Latino), 13 international. Average age 32. 134 applicants, 56% accepted, 57 enrolled. In 2016, 48 master's awarded. *Degree requirements:* For master's, comprehensive exam (for some programs), thesis (for some programs). *Entrance requirements:* For master's, portfolio. Additional exam requirements/recommendations for international students: Required—TOEFL (minimum score 550 paper-based; 79 iBT), IELTS (minimum score 6.5). *Application deadline:* For fall admission, 7/15 for domestic students, 5/1 for international students; for spring admission, 11/15 priority date for domestic students, 9/1 priority date for international students. Applications are processed on a rolling basis. Application fee: $50 ($70 for international students). Electronic applications accepted. *Financial support:* Research assistantships, teaching assistantships, career-related internships or fieldwork, Federal Work-Study, institutionally sponsored loans, scholarships/grants, health care benefits, and unspecified assistantships available. Support available to part-time students. Financial award application deadline: 3/15; financial award applicants required to submit FAFSA. *Unit head:* Dr. Mark Hartlaub, Interim Dean, 361-825-2659, Fax: 361-825-5844, E-mail: mark.hartlaub@tamucc.edu. *Application contact:* Graduate Admissions Coordinator, 361-825-2177, Fax: 361-825-2755, E-mail: gradweb@tamucc.edu. Website: http://cla.tamucc.edu/

**Texas A&M University–Kingsville,** College of Graduate Studies, College of Arts and Sciences, Department of Psychology and Sociology, Program in Psychology, Kingsville, TX 78363. Offers MA, MS. *Entrance requirements:* Additional exam requirements/recommendations for international students: Required—TOEFL (minimum score 550 paper-based; 79 iBT); Recommended—IELTS. Electronic applications accepted.

**Texas A&M University–Texarkana,** Graduate Studies and Research, College of Health and Behavioral Sciences, Texarkana, TX 75505-5518. Offers counseling psychology (MS). *Program availability:* Part-time, evening/weekend. *Degree requirements:* For master's, comprehensive exam (for some programs), thesis or alternative. *Entrance requirements:* For master's, minimum GPA of 3.0 in last 60 hours of bachelor's degree. Additional exam requirements/recommendations for international students: Required—TOEFL. Electronic applications accepted.

**Texas Christian University,** College of Science and Engineering, Department of Psychology, Fort Worth, TX 76129. Offers developmental trauma (MS); experimental psychology (PhD), including cognition/developmental, learning, neuroscience, social. *Faculty:* 12 full-time (5 women), 3 part-time/adjunct (2 women). *Students:* 33 full-time (19 women); includes 4 minority (1 Asian, non-Hispanic/Latino; 1 Hispanic/Latino; 2 Two or more races, non-Hispanic/Latino), 2 international. Average age 27. 38 applicants, 32% accepted, 12 enrolled. In 2016, 5 master's, 3 doctorates awarded. Terminal master's awarded for partial completion of doctoral program. *Degree requirements:* For master's, thesis; for doctorate, thesis/dissertation. *Entrance requirements:* For doctorate, GRE General Test. Additional exam requirements/recommendations for international students: Required—TOEFL. *Application deadline:* For fall admission, 2/1 for domestic and international students. Application fee: $60 ($0 for international students). Electronic applications accepted. *Expenses:* Contact institution. *Financial support:* In 2016–17, 23 students received support, including 23 teaching assistantships with full tuition reimbursements available (averaging $19,750 per year); scholarships/grants also available. Financial award application deadline: 2/1; financial award applicants required to submit FAFSA. *Faculty research:* Neuroscience, human and animal learning, cognition, development, experimental social psychology. *Unit head:* Dr. Mauricio R. Papini, Chair, 817-257-7410, Fax: 817-257-7681, E-mail: m.papini@tcu.edu. *Application contact:* Cindy Hayes, Administrative Assistant, 817-257-7410, Fax: 817-257-7681, E-mail: c.hayes@tcu.edu. Website: https://psychology.tcu.edu/current-graduate-students/

**Texas Southern University,** College of Liberal Arts and Behavioral Sciences, Department of Psychology, Houston, TX 77004-4584. Offers MA. Electronic applications accepted.

**Texas State University,** The Graduate College, College of Liberal Arts, Program in Psychological Research, San Marcos, TX 78666. Offers MA. *Program availability:* Part-time. *Faculty:* 19 full-time (10 women), 1 part-time/adjunct (0 women). *Students:* 31 full-time (18 women), 7 part-time (4 women); includes 10 minority (2 Black or African American, non-Hispanic/Latino; 6 Hispanic/Latino; 2 Two or more races, non-Hispanic/Latino), 1 international. Average age 26. 52 applicants, 63% accepted, 18 enrolled. In 2016, 10 master's awarded. *Degree requirements:* For master's, comprehensive exam, thesis optional. *Entrance requirements:* For master's, GRE General Test, baccalaureate degree from regionally-accredited university with minimum GPA of 3.0 on last 60 undergraduate semester hours. Additional exam requirements/recommendations for international students: Required—TOEFL (minimum score 550 paper-based; 78 iBT), IELTS (minimum score 6.5). *Application deadline:* For fall admission, 2/3 priority date for domestic and international students. Applications are processed on a rolling basis. Application fee: $40 ($90 for international students). Electronic applications accepted. *Expenses:* $4,851 per semester. *Financial support:* In 2016–17, 30 students received support, including 1 research assistantship (averaging $6,754 per year), 19 teaching assistantships (averaging $14,073 per year); Federal Work-Study, institutionally sponsored loans, scholarships/grants, health care benefits, and unspecified assistantships also available. Support available to part-time students. Financial award application deadline: 3/1; financial award applicants required to submit FAFSA. *Unit head:* Dr. Ty Schepis, Graduate Advisor, 512-245-2526, Fax: 512-245-3153, E-mail: schepis@txstate.edu. *Application contact:* Dr. Andrea Golato, Dean of Graduate College, 512-245-2581, Fax: 512-245-8365, E-mail: gradcollege@txstate.edu. Website: http://www.psych.txstate.edu/graduate/mapr.html

**Texas Tech University,** Graduate School, College of Arts and Sciences, Department of Psychological Sciences, Lubbock, TX 79409-2051. Offers clinical psychology (PhD); counseling psychology (MA, PhD); general experimental psychology (MA, PhD); psychology (MA). *Accreditation:* APA (one or more programs are accredited). *Faculty:* 32 full-time (14 women), 2 part-time/adjunct (both women). *Students:* 111 full-time (72 women), 12 part-time (6 women); includes 28 minority (3 Black or African American, non-Hispanic/Latino; 1 American Indian or Alaska Native, non-Hispanic/Latino; 8 Asian, non-Hispanic/Latino; 14 Hispanic/Latino; 2 Two or more races, non-Hispanic/Latino), 8 international. Average age 27. 285 applicants, 13% accepted, 29 enrolled. In 2016, 13 master's, 13 doctorates awarded. *Degree requirements:* For doctorate, comprehensive exam, thesis/dissertation, 100 credit hours of organized courses, research credits, and practica. *Entrance requirements:* For master's, GRE General Test, GRE Subject Test, essays, letters of recommendation; for doctorate, GRE General Test, essays, letters of recommendation. Additional exam requirements/recommendations for international students: Required—TOEFL (minimum score 550 paper-based; 79 iBT). *Application deadline:* For fall admission, 6/1 priority date for domestic students, 1/15 priority date for international students; for spring admission, 9/1 priority date for domestic students, 6/15 priority date for international students. Applications are processed on a rolling basis. Application fee: $75. Electronic applications accepted. *Expenses:* $300 per credit hour full-time resident tuition, $708 per credit hour full-time non-resident tuition; $50.50 per credit hour fee plus $608 per term fee. *Financial support:* In 2016–17, 115 students received support, including 113 fellowships (averaging $2,657 per year), 76 research assistantships (averaging $5,066 per year), 95 teaching assistantships (averaging $11,737 per year); Federal Work-Study, institutionally sponsored loans, and unspecified assistantships also available. Financial award application deadline: 4/15; financial award applicants required to submit FAFSA. *Faculty research:* Health psychology, addictive behaviors, depression and suicide risk, sexuality/sexual risk behaviors/HIV, neuroscience/neuroimaging, forensic and correctional psychology. *Total annual research expenditures:* $710,154. *Unit head:* Dr. Robert Morgan, Professor and Chair, 806-834-7117, Fax: 806-742-0818, E-mail: robert.morgan@ttu.edu. *Application contact:* Kay Hill, Admissions Coordinator, 806-742-3711 Ext. 222, Fax: 806-742-0818, E-mail: kay.hill@ttu.edu. Website: http://www.depts.ttu.edu/psy/

**Texas Woman's University,** Graduate School, College of Arts and Sciences, Department of Psychology and Philosophy, Denton, TX 76201. Offers counseling psychology (MA, PhD); school psychology (PhD, SSP). *Accreditation:* APA (one or more programs are accredited). *Students:* 63 full-time (58 women), 43 part-time (39 women); includes 43 minority (11 Black or African American, non-Hispanic/Latino; 10 Asian, non-Hispanic/Latino; 19 Hispanic/Latino; 3 Two or more races, non-Hispanic/Latino). Average age 30. In 2016, 14 master's, 9 doctorates, 5 other advanced degrees awarded. Terminal master's awarded for partial completion of doctoral program. *Degree requirements:* For master's, comprehensive exam (for some programs), thesis (for some programs); for doctorate, comprehensive exam, thesis/dissertation, internship, residency. *Entrance requirements:* For master's, GRE (preferred minimum score 153 [500 old version] Verbal, 144 [500 old version] Quantitative, 4 Analytical), BA/BS or 18 hours in psychology; minimum GPA of 3.0, 3.5 in psychology classes; 3 letters of reference; curriculum vitae; essays; for doctorate, GRE (preferred minimum score 153 [500 old version] Verbal, 144 [500 old version] Quantitative, 4 Analytical), 3 letters of reference, minimum GPA of 3.0 overall and 3.5 in psychology classes, MA in psychology or related discipline with thesis, curriculum vitae, essays. Additional exam requirements/recommendations for international students: Required—TOEFL (minimum score 550 paper-based; 79 iBT). *Application deadline:* For fall admission, 12/15 priority date for domestic students, 12/15 for international students. Applications are processed on a rolling basis. Application fee: $50 ($75 for international students). Electronic applications accepted. *Expenses:* Tuition, state resident: full-time $9046; part-time $251 per credit hour. Tuition, nonresident: full-time $22,922; part-time $614 per credit hour. *International tuition:* $23,046 full-time. *Required fees:* $2690; $1285 per credit hour. One-time fee: $50. Tuition and fees vary according to course level, course load, program and reciprocity agreements. *Financial support:* Research assistantships, teaching assistantships, career-related internships or fieldwork, Federal Work-Study, institutionally sponsored loans, scholarships/grants, traineeships, health care benefits, and unspecified assistantships available. Support available to part-time students. Financial award application deadline: 3/1; financial award applicants required to submit FAFSA. *Faculty research:* Women's anger, school neuropsychological theory and assessment, body image dysfunction, traumatic stress, classical ethics, mental health and behavioral needs of adolescents in alternative education. *Unit head:* Dr. Shannon Scott, Chair, 940-898-2303, Fax: 940-898-2301, E-mail: sscott@twu.edu. *Application contact:* Dr. Samuel Wheeler, Assistant Director of Admissions, 940-898-3188, Fax: 940-898-3081, E-mail: wheelersr@twu.edu. Website: http://www.twu.edu/psychology-philosophy/

**Tiffin University,** Program in Psychology, Tiffin, OH 44883-2161. Offers MS. *Program availability:* Part-time, evening/weekend, online only, 100% online. *Students:* 13 full-time (12 women), 21 part-time (17 women); includes 10 minority (8 Black or African American, non-Hispanic/Latino; 2 Hispanic/Latino). Average age 30. 34 applicants, 82% accepted, 20 enrolled. In 2016, 1 master's awarded. *Entrance requirements:* Additional exam requirements/recommendations for international students: Recommended—TOEFL. *Application deadline:* Applications are processed on a rolling basis. Electronic applications accepted. *Expenses:* Contact institution. *Application contact:* Nikki Hintze, Director of Graduate Admissions and Student Services, 800-968-6446 Ext. 3445, Fax: 419-443-5002, E-mail: hintzenm@tiffin.edu.

**Towson University,** Program in Psychology, Towson, MD 21252-0001. Offers clinical psychology (MA); counseling psychology (MA); experimental psychology (MA); school psychology (MA). *Program availability:* Part-time, evening/weekend. *Students:* 104 full-time (72 women), 27 part-time (23 women); includes 34 minority (12 Black or African American, non-Hispanic/Latino; 7 Asian, non-Hispanic/Latino; 10 Hispanic/Latino; 5 Two or more races, non-Hispanic/Latino). *Degree requirements:* For master's, thesis (for some programs). *Entrance requirements:* For master's, GRE, minimum GPA of 3.0, letters of recommendation. *Application deadline:* For fall admission, 2/1 for domestic and international students. Application fee: $45. Electronic applications accepted. *Expenses:* Tuition, state resident: full-time $7580; part-time $379 per unit. Tuition, nonresident: full-time $15,700; part-time $785 per unit. *Required fees:* $2480. *Financial support:* Application deadline: 4/1. *Unit head:* Dr. Geoffrey Munro, Graduate Program Director, 410-704-2634, E-mail: psyc@towson.edu. *Application contact:* Coverley Beidleman, Assistant Director of Graduate Admissions, 410-704-2113, Fax: 410-704-3030, E-mail: grads@towson.edu. Website: https://www.towson.edu/cla/departments/psychology/grad/

**Tufts University,** Graduate School of Arts and Sciences, Department of Psychology, Medford, MA 02155. Offers cognitive science (PhD); psychology (MS, PhD). *Students:* 40 full-time (30 women); includes 10 minority (2 Black or African American, non-Hispanic/Latino; 5 Asian, non-Hispanic/Latino; 3 Hispanic/Latino), 6 international. Average age 27. 154 applicants, 8% accepted, 7 enrolled. In 2016, 4 master's, 4 doctorates awarded. Terminal master's awarded for partial completion of doctoral program. *Degree requirements:* For master's, thesis; for doctorate, thesis/dissertation. *Entrance requirements:* For master's and doctorate, GRE General Test, GRE Subject Test. Additional exam requirements/recommendations for international students: Required—TOEFL (minimum score 550 paper-based; 80 iBT), IELTS (minimum score 6.5). *Application deadline:* For fall admission, 12/15 for domestic and international students. Applications are processed on a rolling basis. Application fee: $85. Electronic applications accepted. *Expenses:* $29,936 full-time tuition (for PhD). *Financial support:* In 2016–17, 40 students received support. Fellowships, research assistantships, teaching assistantships, Federal Work-Study, scholarships/grants, tuition waivers (full and partial), and unspecified assistantships available. Support available to part-time students. Financial award application deadline: 1/15. *Unit head:* Dr. Ayanna Thomas, Graduate Program Director. *Application contact:* Office of Graduate Admissions, 617-627-3395, E-mail: gradadmissions@tufts.edu. Website: http://ase.tufts.edu/psychology

**Tulane University,** School of Science and Engineering, Department of Psychology, New Orleans, LA 70118-5669. Offers MS, PhD. *Accreditation:* APA (one or more programs are accredited). Terminal master's awarded for partial completion of doctoral program. *Degree requirements:* For master's, variable foreign language requirement, thesis; for doctorate, thesis/dissertation. *Entrance requirements:* For master's, GRE General Test, minimum B average in undergraduate course work; for doctorate, GRE General Test. Additional exam requirements/recommendations for international students: Required—TOEFL. Electronic applications accepted. *Expenses:* Tuition: Full-

## Psychology—General

time \$50,920; part-time \$2829 per credit hour. *Required fees:* \$2040; \$44.50 per credit hour. \$580 per term. Tuition and fees vary according to course load, degree level and program. *Faculty research:* Hormones and behavior, aggression, personnel selection, cognitive development, stereotyping, diabetes.

**Uniformed Services University of the Health Sciences,** F. Edward Hebert School of Medicine, Graduate Programs in the Biomedical Sciences and Public Health, Department of Medical and Clinical Psychology, Bethesda, MD 20814. Offers clinical psychology (PhD); medical psychology (PhD). PhD in clinical psychology available to active duty military only. *Accreditation:* APA. Terminal master's awarded for partial completion of doctoral program. *Degree requirements:* For doctorate, comprehensive exam, thesis/dissertation, qualifying exam. *Entrance requirements:* For doctorate, GRE General Test, minimum GPA of 3.0, U.S. citizenship. Additional exam requirements/recommendations for international students: Required—TOEFL. Electronic applications accepted. *Faculty research:* Addictive and appetitive behavior, psychopharmacology, stress and eating, obesity, health.

**Union College,** Graduate Programs, Department of Psychology, Barbourville, KY 40906-1499. Offers clinical psychology (MA); counseling psychology (MA); school psychology (MA).

**Universidad de las Americas, A.C.,** Program in Psychology, Mexico City, Mexico. Offers family therapy (MA).

**Universidad de las Américas Puebla,** Division of Graduate Studies, School of Social Sciences, Program in Psychology, Puebla, Mexico. Offers MA. *Program availability:* Part-time, evening/weekend. *Degree requirements:* For master's, one foreign language, thesis. *Entrance requirements:* For master's, minimum B+ average. *Faculty research:* Testing, social hemispheric specialization, clinical psychology.

**Université de Montréal,** Faculty of Arts and Sciences, Department of Psychology, Montréal, QC H3C 3J7, Canada. Offers M Sc, PhD. Terminal master's awarded for partial completion of doctoral program. *Degree requirements:* For master's, one foreign language, thesis; for doctorate, one foreign language, thesis/dissertation, general exam. Electronic applications accepted. *Faculty research:* Vision, marital counseling, memory.

**Université de Sherbrooke,** Faculty of Letters and Human Sciences, Department of Psychology, Sherbrooke, QC J1K 2R1, Canada. Offers gerontology (MA). *Degree requirements:* For master's, thesis. *Faculty research:* Human relations.

**Université du Québec à Montréal,** Graduate Programs, Program in Psychology, Montréal, QC H3C 3P8, Canada. Offers D Ps, PhD. Programs offered jointly with Université du Québec à Trois-Rivières. *Program availability:* Part-time. *Degree requirements:* For doctorate, thesis/dissertation. *Entrance requirements:* For doctorate, appropriate master's degree or equivalent, proficiency in French.

**Université du Québec à Trois-Rivières,** Graduate Programs, Program in Psychology, Trois-Rivières, QC G9A 5H7, Canada. Offers PhD, Certificate. *Program availability:* Part-time. *Degree requirements:* For doctorate, thesis/dissertation. *Entrance requirements:* For doctorate, appropriate master's degree, proficiency in French. *Faculty research:* Child and family development, gerontology, mental health.

**Université Laval,** Faculty of Social Sciences, School of Psychology, Programs in Psychology, Québec, QC G1K 7P4, Canada. Offers clinical psychology (PhD); community psychology (PhD); psychology (PhD, Psy D). *Degree requirements:* For doctorate, comprehensive exam, thesis/dissertation. *Entrance requirements:* For doctorate, comprehension of written English, knowledge of French, interview. Electronic applications accepted.

**University at Albany, State University of New York,** College of Arts and Sciences, Department of Psychology, Albany, NY 12222-0001. Offers behavioral neuroscience (PhD); clinical psychology (PhD); cognitive psychology (PhD); industrial/organizational psychology (MA, PhD); social-personality psychology (PhD). *Accreditation:* APA (one or more programs are accredited). *Faculty:* 19 full-time (6 women). *Students:* 68 full-time (42 women), 43 part-time (31 women); includes 26 minority (1 Black or African American, non-Hispanic/Latino; 11 Asian, non-Hispanic/Latino; 9 Hispanic/Latino; 5 Two or more races, non-Hispanic/Latino), 8 international. 304 applicants, 14% accepted, 24 enrolled. In 2016, 7 master's, 11 doctorates awarded. *Degree requirements:* For doctorate, thesis/dissertation. *Entrance requirements:* For doctorate, GRE General Test, GRE Subject Test. Additional exam requirements/recommendations for international students: Required—TOEFL (minimum score 550 paper-based). *Application deadline:* For fall admission, 1/15 for domestic and international students. Application fee: \$75. Electronic applications accepted. *Expenses:* Tuition, state resident: full-time \$10,870; part-time \$453 per credit hour. Tuition, nonresident: full-time \$22,210; part-time \$925 per credit hour. *International tuition:* \$21,550 full-time. *Required fees:* \$1864; \$96 per credit hour. *Financial support:* Fellowships, research assistantships, teaching assistantships, and career-related internships or fieldwork available. Financial award application deadline: 2/1. *Total annual research expenditures:* \$861,900. *Unit head:* James Neely, Chair, 518-442-4820, Fax: 518-442-4867, E-mail: jneely@albany.edu. *Application contact:* Michael DeRensis, Director, Graduate Admissions, 518-442-3980, Fax: 518-442-3922, E-mail: graduate@albany.edu. Website: http://www.albany.edu/psychology/

**University at Buffalo, the State University of New York,** Graduate School, College of Arts and Sciences, Department of Psychology, Buffalo, NY 14260. Offers MA, PhD. *Accreditation:* APA (one or more programs are accredited). *Faculty:* 29 full-time (14 women), 12 part-time/adjunct (6 women). *Students:* 88 full-time (57 women), 3 part-time (0 women); includes 22 minority (1 Black or African American, non-Hispanic/Latino; 11 Asian, non-Hispanic/Latino; 9 Hispanic/Latino; 1 Two or more races, non-Hispanic/Latino), 11 international. Average age 27. 314 applicants, 10% accepted, 16 enrolled. In 2016, 17 master's, 12 doctorates awarded. Terminal master's awarded for partial completion of doctoral program. *Degree requirements:* For master's, project; for doctorate, thesis/dissertation. *Entrance requirements:* For master's and doctorate, GRE General Test. Additional exam requirements/recommendations for international students: Required—TOEFL (minimum score 550 paper-based; 79 iBT). *Application deadline:* For fall admission, 12/1 for domestic and international students. Application fee: \$75. Electronic applications accepted. *Financial support:* In 2016–17, 60 students received support, including 5 fellowships with full tuition reimbursements available (averaging \$14,280 per year), 15 research assistantships with full tuition reimbursements available (averaging \$14,280 per year), 40 teaching assistantships with full tuition reimbursements available (averaging \$14,280 per year); career-related internships or fieldwork, scholarships/grants, health care benefits, tuition waivers (full and partial), and unspecified assistantships also available. Financial award application deadline: 12/1; financial award applicants required to submit FAFSA. *Faculty research:* Neural, endocrine, and molecular bases of behavior; adult mood and anxiety disorders; relationship dysfunction; attention deficit/hyperactivity disorder; psycho-linguistics. *Total annual research expenditures:* \$528,527. *Unit head:* Dr. Stephen T. Tiffany, Chair, 716-645-0244, Fax: 716-645-3801, E-mail: chairpsych@buffalo.edu. *Application contact:* Mary Wlodarczyk, Admissions Officer, 716-645-8617, Fax: 716-645-3801, E-mail: psych@buffalo.edu. Website: http://www.psychology.buffalo.edu/

**The University of Akron,** Graduate School, Buchtel College of Arts and Sciences, Department of Psychology, Akron, OH 44325. Offers adult development and aging (PhD); counseling psychology (MA, PhD); industrial/organizational psychology (MA, PhD); psychology (MA). *Accreditation:* APA (one or more programs are accredited). *Faculty:* 18 full-time (8 women), 6 part-time/adjunct (4 women). *Students:* 69 full-time (44 women), 24 part-time (16 women); includes 21 minority (7 Black or African American, non-Hispanic/Latino; 5 Asian, non-Hispanic/Latino; 6 Hispanic/Latino; 3 Two or more races, non-Hispanic/Latino), 5 international. Average age 27. 184 applicants, 14% accepted, 22 enrolled. In 2016, 24 master's, 5 doctorates awarded. Terminal master's awarded for partial completion of doctoral program. *Degree requirements:* For master's, thesis or specialty exam; for doctorate, one foreign language, comprehensive exam, thesis/dissertation. *Entrance requirements:* For master's, GRE, baccalaureate degree in psychology or extensive background in psychology; minimum cumulative undergraduate GPA of 3.0; three letters of recommendation; for doctorate, GRE, baccalaureate degree in psychology or 30 credits of psychology coursework; minimum cumulative undergraduate GPA of 3.0, 3.25 on all psychology coursework; current vita; declaration of intent; three letters of recommendation. Additional exam requirements/recommendations for international students: Required—TOEFL (minimum score 550 paper-based; 79 iBT), IELTS (minimum score 6.5). *Application deadline:* For fall admission, 12/1 for domestic and international students. Application fee: \$45 (\$70 for international students). Electronic applications accepted. *Expenses:* Tuition, state resident: full-time \$8618; part-time \$359 per credit hour. Tuition, nonresident: full-time \$17,149; part-time \$715 per credit hour. *Required fees:* \$1652. *Financial support:* In 2016–17, 14 research assistantships with full tuition reimbursements, 41 teaching assistantships with full tuition reimbursements were awarded. *Faculty research:* Social cognitive determinants of behavior, the application of psychological principles to the workplace and career planning/development, the psychological processes of aging. *Total annual research expenditures:* \$834,259. *Unit head:* Dr. Paul Levy, Chair, 330-972-8367, E-mail: plevy@uakron.edu. Website: http://www.uakron.edu/psychology/

**The University of Alabama,** Graduate School, College of Arts and Sciences, Department of Psychology, Tuscaloosa, AL 35487. Offers clinical psychology (PhD); experimental psychology (PhD). *Accreditation:* APA. *Faculty:* 27 full-time (14 women), 4 part-time/adjunct (2 women). *Students:* 84 full-time (60 women), 13 part-time (10 women); includes 14 minority (4 Black or African American, non-Hispanic/Latino; 3 Asian, non-Hispanic/Latino; 6 Hispanic/Latino; 1 Two or more races, non-Hispanic/Latino), 8 international. Average age 27. 342 applicants, 7% accepted, 18 enrolled. In 2016, 19 doctorates awarded. *Degree requirements:* For doctorate, thesis/dissertation, internship (for clinical psychology). *Entrance requirements:* For doctorate, GRE. Additional exam requirements/recommendations for international students: Required—TOEFL (minimum score 550 paper-based). *Application deadline:* For fall admission, 12/1 for domestic and international students. Application fee: \$50 (\$60 for international students). Electronic applications accepted. *Expenses:* Tuition, state resident: full-time \$10,470. Tuition, nonresident: full-time \$26,950. *Financial support:* In 2016–17, 73 students received support, including 12 fellowships with full tuition reimbursements available (averaging \$17,000 per year), 40 research assistantships with tuition reimbursements available (averaging \$12,744 per year), 34 teaching assistantships with tuition reimbursements available (averaging \$13,824 per year); career-related internships or fieldwork, institutionally sponsored loans, scholarships/grants, health care benefits, and unspecified assistantships also available. Financial award application deadline: 12/1. *Faculty research:* Cognitive development/disability, child clinical, psychology and law, health/aging, social psychology. *Total annual research expenditures:* \$2.4 million. *Unit head:* Dr. Frances A. Conners, Chair, 205-348-1913, Fax: 205-348-8648, E-mail: fconners@ua.edu. *Application contact:* Mary Beth Hubbard, Information Contact, 205-348-1919, Fax: 205-348-8648, E-mail: mary.b.hubbard@ua.edu. Website: http://www.psychology.ua.edu

**The University of Alabama at Birmingham,** College of Arts and Sciences, Program in Psychology, Birmingham, AL 35294. Offers behavioral neuroscience (PhD); lifespan developmental psychology (PhD); medical/clinical psychology (PhD); psychology (MA). *Accreditation:* APA (one or more programs are accredited). *Entrance requirements:* For master's and doctorate, GRE General Test, letters of recommendation. Electronic applications accepted. Full-time tuition and fees vary according to course load and program. *Faculty research:* Biological basis of behavior structure, function of the nervous system.

**The University of Alabama in Huntsville,** School of Graduate Studies, College of Arts, Humanities, and Social Sciences, Department of Psychology, Huntsville, AL 35899. Offers industrial/organizational psychology (MA); psychology (MA). *Program availability:* Part-time, evening/weekend. *Degree requirements:* For master's, comprehensive exam, thesis or alternative, oral and written exams. *Entrance requirements:* For master's, GRE General Test, 15 hours of course work in psychology, minimum GPA of 3.25, sample of written work. Additional exam requirements/recommendations for international students: Required—TOEFL (minimum score 500 paper-based; 80 iBT), IELTS (minimum score 6.5). Electronic applications accepted. *Expenses:* Tuition, state resident: full-time \$9834; part-time \$600 per credit hour. Tuition, nonresident: full-time \$21,830; part-time \$1325 per credit hour. *Faculty research:* Virtual teams and teamwork, eyewitness identification, aging and memory, psychology of natural disasters and emergency preparedness, pain and pain management research.

**University of Alaska Anchorage,** College of Arts and Sciences, Department of Psychology, Anchorage, AK 99508. Offers clinical psychology (MS); clinical-community psychology with rural-indigenous emphasis (PhD). *Accreditation:* APA. *Program availability:* Part-time. *Degree requirements:* For master's, thesis. *Entrance requirements:* For master's, GRE General Test, GRE Subject Test, interview, references; for doctorate, interview, bachelor's or master's degree in psychology. Additional exam requirements/recommendations for international students: Required—TOEFL (minimum score 550 paper-based). *Faculty research:* Substance abuse, childhood autism, biofeedback, psychological assessment, mental health in Native Alaskans.

**University of Alaska Fairbanks,** College of Liberal Arts, Department of Psychology, Fairbanks, AK 99775-6480. Offers clinical-community psychology (PhD). Program offered jointly with University of Alaska Anchorage. *Accreditation:* APA. *Faculty:* 8 full-time (6 women). *Students:* 6 full-time (3 women), 10 part-time (6 women); includes 8 minority (1 Black or African American, non-Hispanic/Latino; 2 Asian, non-Hispanic/Latino; 2 Hispanic/Latino; 3 Two or more races, non-Hispanic/Latino). Average age 30. In 2016, 1 doctorate awarded. *Degree requirements:* For doctorate, comprehensive exam, thesis/dissertation, oral defense of dissertation. *Entrance requirements:* For doctorate, bachelor's degree from accredited institution with minimum cumulative undergraduate and major GPA of 3.0; criminal background check; interview; course work in abnormal psychology, statistics, and research methods. Additional exam requirements/recommendations for international students: Required—TOEFL (minimum score 550 paper-based; 80 iBT), IELTS (minimum score 6.5). *Application deadline:* For fall admission, 1/15 for domestic and international students. Application fee: \$60. Electronic applications accepted. *Expenses:* Tuition, state resident: full-time \$7992;

part-time $444 per credit. Tuition, nonresident: full-time $16,326; part-time $907 per credit. *Required fees:* $39 per credit. $322 per semester. Tuition and fees vary according to course level, course load, campus/location, program and reciprocity agreements. *Financial support:* In 2016–17, 2 research assistantships with full tuition reimbursements (averaging $13,471 per year), 5 teaching assistantships with full tuition reimbursements (averaging $6,397 per year) were awarded; fellowships with full tuition reimbursements, career-related internships or fieldwork, Federal Work-Study, scholarships/grants, health care benefits, and unspecified assistantships also available. Support available to part-time students. Financial award application deadline: 7/1; financial award applicants required to submit FAFSA. *Faculty research:* Clinical and community psychology; rural, indigenous, and cultural psychology. *Unit head:* Dr. Cecile Lardon, Department Chair, 907-474-7012, Fax: 907-474-5781, E-mail: fypsych@uaf.edu. *Application contact:* Mary Kreta, Director of Admissions, 907-474-7500, Fax: 907-474-7097, E-mail: admissions@uaf.edu.
Website: http://www.uaf.edu/psych/

**University of Alberta,** Faculty of Graduate Studies and Research, Department of Psychology, Edmonton, AB T6G 2E1, Canada. Offers M Sc, MA, PhD. Terminal master's awarded for partial completion of doctoral program. *Degree requirements:* For master's, thesis (for some programs); for doctorate, thesis/dissertation. *Entrance requirements:* For master's and doctorate, GRE. Additional exam requirements/recommendations for international students: Required—TOEFL (minimum score 550 paper-based). Electronic applications accepted. *Faculty research:* Animal behavior processes; cognitive, social and perceptual processes; development and aging; neuroscience.

**The University of Arizona,** College of Science, Department of Psychology, Tucson, AZ 85721. Offers MA, PhD. *Accreditation:* APA (one or more programs are accredited). *Degree requirements:* For doctorate, comprehensive exam, thesis/dissertation. *Entrance requirements:* For master's, GRE General Test, 3 letters of recommendation, statement of purpose; for doctorate, GRE General Test, 3 letters of recommendation. Additional exam requirements/recommendations for international students: Required—TOEFL (minimum score 550 paper-based; 79 iBT). Electronic applications accepted. *Faculty research:* Cognitive neuroscience, aging, law and psychology, psycholinguistics, family psychology.

**University of Arkansas,** Graduate School, J. William Fulbright College of Arts and Sciences, Department of Psychology, Fayetteville, AR 72701. Offers MA, PhD. *Accreditation:* APA (one or more programs are accredited). In 2016, 9 master's, 4 doctorates awarded. *Degree requirements:* For master's, thesis; for doctorate, variable foreign language requirement, thesis/dissertation. *Entrance requirements:* For doctorate, GRE General Test, GRE Subject Test. *Application deadline:* For fall admission, 4/1 for international students; for spring admission, 10/1 for international students. Applications are processed on a rolling basis. Application fee: $40 ($50 for international students). Electronic applications accepted. *Financial support:* In 2016–17, 24 research assistantships, 8 teaching assistantships were awarded; fellowships with tuition reimbursements, career-related internships or fieldwork, Federal Work-Study, and traineeships also available. Support available to part-time students. Financial award application deadline: 4/1; financial award applicants required to submit FAFSA. *Unit head:* Dr. Douglas Behrend, Departmental Chairperson, 479-575-4256, Fax: 479-575-3219, E-mail: psycapp@uark.edu. *Application contact:* Dr. Bill Levine, 479-575-4256, E-mail: psycapp@uark.edu.
Website: http://www.uark.edu/depts/psyc/

**University of Arkansas at Little Rock,** Graduate School, College of Social Sciences and Communication, Department of Psychology, Little Rock, AR 72204-1099. Offers applied psychology (MAP). *Program availability:* Part-time, evening/weekend. *Entrance requirements:* For master's, GRE General Test, minimum GPA of 2.7. *Faculty research:* Psychological methods and theories in business industry, government, and organizations; personnel program evaluation; training; affirmative action; organizational analysis and development.

**The University of British Columbia,** Faculty of Arts and Faculty of Graduate Studies, Department of Psychology, Vancouver, BC V6T 1Z4, Canada. Offers behavioral neuroscience (MA, PhD); clinical psychology (MA, PhD); cognitive science (MA, PhD); developmental psychology (MA, PhD); health psychology (MA, PhD); quantitative methods (MA, PhD); social/personality psychology (MA, PhD). *Accreditation:* APA (one or more programs are accredited). Terminal master's awarded for partial completion of doctoral program. *Degree requirements:* For master's, thesis; for doctorate, comprehensive exam, thesis/dissertation. *Entrance requirements:* For master's and doctorate, GRE General Test. Additional exam requirements/recommendations for international students: Required—TOEFL. *Application deadline:* Applications are processed on a rolling basis. Application fee: $100 Canadian dollars ($162 Canadian dollars for international students). Electronic applications accepted. *Expenses:* $4,802 per year tuition and fees, $8,436 per year international. *Financial support:* Fellowships, research assistantships, teaching assistantships, career-related internships or fieldwork, Federal Work-Study, institutionally sponsored loans, scholarships/grants, health care benefits, tuition waivers (full and partial), and unspecified assistantships available. Financial award application deadline: 1/1. *Faculty research:* Clinical, developmental, social/personality, cognition, behavioral neuroscience. *Application contact:* Jaclyn Shaw, 604-822-5002, Fax: 604-822-6923, E-mail: gradsec@psych.ubc.ca.
Website: http://psych.ubc.ca/

**University of Calgary,** Faculty of Graduate Studies, Faculty of Arts, Department of Psychology, Calgary, AB T2N 1N4, Canada. Offers clinical psychology (M Sc, PhD); psychology (M Sc, PhD). *Degree requirements:* For master's, thesis; for doctorate, thesis/dissertation. *Entrance requirements:* For master's, GRE General Test, bachelor's degree in psychology, minimum GPA of 3.4. Additional exam requirements/recommendations for international students: Required—TOEFL (minimum score 550 paper-based). Electronic applications accepted. *Faculty research:* Cognition and cognitive development, social psychology, theoretical psychology, perception, aging.

**University of California, Berkeley,** Graduate Division, College of Letters and Science, Department of Psychology, Berkeley, CA 94720-1500. Offers PhD. *Accreditation:* APA. *Students:* 102 full-time (66 women); includes 30 minority (9 Black or African American, non-Hispanic/Latino; 11 Asian, non-Hispanic/Latino; 10 Hispanic/Latino), 9 international. Average age 29. 617 applicants, 18 enrolled. In 2016, 9 doctorates awarded. *Degree requirements:* For doctorate, thesis/dissertation, qualifying exam. *Entrance requirements:* For doctorate, GRE General Test, GRE Subject Test, minimum GPA of 3.0, 3 letters of recommendation. *Application deadline:* For fall admission, 11/19 for domestic students. Application fee: $105 ($125 for international students). Electronic applications accepted. *Financial support:* Fellowships, research assistantships, teaching assistantships, institutionally sponsored loans, health care benefits, and unspecified assistantships available. *Unit head:* Prof. Ann Kring, Chair, 510-642-5292, E-mail: psychadmin@berkeley.edu. *Application contact:* Michael Ortt, Graduate Admissions Officer, 510-642-1382, Fax: 510-642-5293, E-mail: psychgradinfo@berkeley.edu.
Website: http://psychology.berkeley.edu/

**University of California, Davis,** Graduate Studies, Program in Psychology, Davis, CA 95616. Offers PhD. *Degree requirements:* For doctorate, thesis/dissertation. *Entrance requirements:* For doctorate, GRE General Test, GRE Subject Test, minimum GPA of 3.0. Additional exam requirements/recommendations for international students: Required—TOEFL (minimum score 550 paper-based). Electronic applications accepted. *Faculty research:* Social personality, perception, cognition, psychobiology.

**University of California, Irvine,** School of Social Ecology, Department of Psychology and Social Behavior, Irvine, CA 92697. Offers PhD. *Students:* 66 full-time (44 women), 2 part-time (0 women); includes 24 minority (1 Black or African American, non-Hispanic/Latino; 8 Asian, non-Hispanic/Latino; 9 Hispanic/Latino; 6 Two or more races, non-Hispanic/Latino), 4 international. Average age 28. 244 applicants, 10% accepted, 16 enrolled. In 2016, 5 doctorates awarded. *Degree requirements:* For doctorate, thesis/dissertation, research project. *Entrance requirements:* For doctorate, GRE General Test, minimum GPA of 3.0. Additional exam requirements/recommendations for international students: Required—TOEFL (minimum score 550 paper-based). *Application deadline:* For fall admission, 12/15 priority date for domestic and international students. Applications are processed on a rolling basis. Application fee: $105 ($125 for international students). Electronic applications accepted. *Financial support:* Fellowships, research assistantships with full tuition reimbursements, teaching assistantships, institutionally sponsored loans, traineeships, health care benefits, and unspecified assistantships available. Financial award application deadline: 3/1; financial award applicants required to submit FAFSA. *Faculty research:* Psychosocial development in children, adolescents, and adults; gerontology; childhood behavior disorders, and developmental psychopathology; sex differences; attitude change; social psychology. *Unit head:* Karen Rooks, Chair, 949-824-7069, Fax: 949-824-3002, E-mail: ksrook@uci.edu. *Application contact:* Roxane C. Silver, Professor, 949-824-2192, Fax: 949-824-3002, E-mail: rsilver@uci.edu.
Website: http://psb.soceco.uci.edu/

**University of California, Irvine,** School of Social Sciences, Department of Cognitive Sciences, Irvine, CA 92697. Offers psychology (PhD). *Students:* 51 full-time (22 women), 2 part-time (1 woman); includes 14 minority (10 Asian, non-Hispanic/Latino; 2 Hispanic/Latino; 2 Two or more races, non-Hispanic/Latino), 3 international. Average age 27. 82 applicants, 20% accepted, 6 enrolled. In 2016, 7 doctorates awarded. *Degree requirements:* For doctorate, thesis/dissertation. *Entrance requirements:* For doctorate, GRE General Test, minimum GPA of 3.0. Additional exam requirements/recommendations for international students: Required—TOEFL (minimum score 550 paper-based). *Application deadline:* For fall admission, 1/15 priority date for domestic and international students. Applications are processed on a rolling basis. Application fee: $105 ($125 for international students). Electronic applications accepted. *Financial support:* Fellowships, research assistantships with full tuition reimbursements, teaching assistantships, institutionally sponsored loans, traineeships, health care benefits, and unspecified assistantships available. Financial award application deadline: 3/1; financial award applicants required to submit FAFSA. *Faculty research:* Mathematical psychology, visual and auditory perception, cognitive development, problem solving, experimental psychology. *Unit head:* Prof. Ramesh Srinivasan, Department Chair, 949-824-2969, E-mail: r.srinivasan@uci.edu. *Application contact:* Emily Grossman, Graduate Director, 949-824-1530, E-mail: grossman@uci.edu.
Website: http://www.cogsci.uci.edu/cs_graduates

**University of California, Los Angeles,** Graduate Division, College of Letters and Science, Department of Psychology, Los Angeles, CA 90034. Offers MA, PhD. *Accreditation:* APA (one or more programs are accredited). Terminal master's awarded for partial completion of doctoral program. *Degree requirements:* For master's, comprehensive exam; for doctorate, thesis/dissertation, oral and written qualifying exams, teaching experience. *Entrance requirements:* For doctorate, GRE General Test, GRE Subject Test (psychology), bachelor's degree; minimum undergraduate GPA of 3.0 (or its equivalent if letter grade system not used); interview. Additional exam requirements/recommendations for international students: Required—TOEFL. Electronic applications accepted.

**University of California, Merced,** Graduate Division, School of Social Sciences, Humanities and Arts, Merced, CA 95343. Offers cognitive and information sciences (PhD); interdisciplinary humanities (MA, PhD); psychological sciences (MA, PhD); social sciences (MA, PhD); sociology (MA, PhD). *Faculty:* 93 full-time (41 women), 3 part-time/adjunct (all women). *Students:* 172 full-time (112 women), 3 part-time (2 women); includes 69 minority (4 Black or African American, non-Hispanic/Latino; 15 Asian, non-Hispanic/Latino; 43 Hispanic/Latino; 7 Two or more races, non-Hispanic/Latino), 25 international. Average age 31. 195 applicants, 50% accepted, 52 enrolled. In 2016, 13 master's, 11 doctorates awarded. Terminal master's awarded for partial completion of doctoral program. *Degree requirements:* For master's, variable foreign language requirement, comprehensive exam, thesis or alternative; for doctorate, variable foreign language requirement, comprehensive exam, thesis/dissertation. *Entrance requirements:* For master's and doctorate, GRE. Additional exam requirements/recommendations for international students: Required—TOEFL (minimum score 550 paper-based; 80 iBT); Recommended—IELTS (minimum score 7). *Application deadline:* For fall admission, 1/15 for domestic and international students. Application fee: $90 ($110 for international students). Electronic applications accepted. *Expenses:* Contact institution. *Financial support:* In 2016–17, 167 students received support, including 12 fellowships with full tuition reimbursements available (averaging $20,237 per year), 12 research assistantships with full tuition reimbursements available (averaging $18,842 per year), 121 teaching assistantships with full tuition reimbursements available (averaging $19,655 per year); scholarships/grants, traineeships, and health care benefits also available. Financial award application deadline: 1/15. *Faculty research:* Social inequality, critical race and ethnic studies, public health and health sciences, cognitive science and language acquisition, political institutions. *Total annual research expenditures:* $1.2 million. *Unit head:* Dr. Jill Robbins, Dean, E-mail: jillrobbins@ucmerced.edu. *Application contact:* Tsu Ya, Director of Admissions and Academic Services, 209-228-4521, Fax: 209-228-6906, E-mail: tya@ucmerced.edu.

**University of California, Riverside,** Graduate Division, Department of Psychology, Riverside, CA 92521-0102. Offers PhD. *Accreditation:* APA. *Degree requirements:* For doctorate, comprehensive exam, thesis/dissertation, 3 quarters of teaching experience, qualifying exams. *Entrance requirements:* For doctorate, GRE General Test, minimum GPA of 3.2. Additional exam requirements/recommendations for international students: Required—TOEFL (minimum score 550 paper-based; 80 iBT). Electronic applications accepted. *Expenses:* Tuition, state resident: full-time $16,666. Tuition, nonresident: full-time $31,768. *Required fees:* $11,055.54 per quarter. $3685.18 per quarter. Tuition and fees vary according to campus/location and program. *Faculty research:* Neuroscience, personality and social psychology, developmental psychology, cognition, health psychology, quantitative psychology.

**University of California, San Diego,** Graduate Division, Department of Psychology, La Jolla, CA 92093. Offers PhD. *Students:* 43 full-time (21 women). 295 applicants, 7% accepted, 6 enrolled. In 2016, 7 doctorates awarded. *Degree requirements:* For doctorate, comprehensive exam, thesis/dissertation, 7 quarters of teaching assistantship. *Entrance requirements:* For doctorate, GRE General Test, minimum GPA of 3.0. Additional exam requirements/recommendations for international students:

## Psychology—General

Required—TOEFL (minimum score 550 paper-based; 80 iBT), IELTS (minimum score 7). *Application deadline:* For fall admission, 12/1 for domestic students. Application fee: $105 ($125 for international students). Electronic applications accepted. *Expenses:* Tuition, state resident: full-time $11,220. Tuition, nonresident: full-time $26,322. *Required fees:* $1864. *Financial support:* Fellowships, research assistantships, teaching assistantships, scholarships/grants, and unspecified assistantships available. Financial award applicants required to submit FAFSA. *Faculty research:* Cognitive and behavioral neuroscience, cognitive psychology, developmental psychology, sensation and perception, social psychology. *Unit head:* Victor Ferreira, Chair, 858-534-6303. *Application contact:* Samantha Llanos, Graduate Coordinator, 858-534-4416, E-mail: psycphdinfo@ucsd.edu.
Website: http://psychology.ucsd.edu/

**University of California, Santa Barbara,** Graduate Division, College of Letters and Sciences, Division of Mathematics, Life, and Physical Sciences, Department of Psychological and Brain Sciences, Santa Barbara, CA 93106-9660. Offers cognitive science (PhD); psychology (PhD); quantitative methods in the social sciences (PhD); technology and society (PhD). Terminal master's awarded for partial completion of doctoral program. *Degree requirements:* For doctorate, comprehensive exam, thesis/dissertation, teaching assistant training, progress report, papers, mini-convention presentation, 1 quarter of student teaching or teaching assistant class with section lab, continued participation in research and weekly area meetings. *Entrance requirements:* For doctorate, GRE General Test. Additional exam requirements/recommendations for international students: Required—TOEFL (minimum score 550 paper-based; 80 iBT) or IELTS (minimum score 7). Electronic applications accepted. *Faculty research:* Social psychology; developmental and evolutionary psychology; neuroscience and behavior; cognition, perception and cognitive neuroscience.

**University of California, Santa Cruz,** Division of Graduate Studies, Division of Social Sciences, Department of Psychology, Santa Cruz, CA 95064. Offers PhD. *Degree requirements:* For doctorate, thesis/dissertation, qualifying exam, seminars. *Entrance requirements:* For doctorate, GRE General Test. Additional exam requirements/recommendations for international students: Required—TOEFL (minimum score 550 paper-based; 83 iBT); Recommended—IELTS (minimum score 8). Electronic applications accepted. *Faculty research:* Cognitive psychology, developmental psychology, social psychology.

**University of Central Arkansas,** Graduate School, College of Health and Behavioral Sciences, Department of Counseling and Psychology, Conway, AR 72035-0001. Offers community counseling (MS); counseling psychology (MS); school psychology (MS, PhD, PMC). *Accreditation:* APA. Terminal master's awarded for partial completion of doctoral program. *Degree requirements:* For master's, comprehensive exam, thesis optional, internship; for doctorate, comprehensive exam, thesis/dissertation, internship. *Entrance requirements:* For master's, GRE General Test, minimum GPA of 2.75; for doctorate, GRE General Test, minimum GPA of 3.25. Additional exam requirements/recommendations for international students: Required—TOEFL (minimum score 550 paper-based). Electronic applications accepted.

**University of Central Florida,** College of Sciences, Department of Psychology, Orlando, FL 32816. Offers applied experimental and human factors psychology (MA, PhD); clinical psychology (MA, PhD); industrial/organizational psychology (MS, PhD). *Accreditation:* APA. *Program availability:* Part-time. *Faculty:* 61 full-time (27 women), 8 part-time/adjunct (3 women). *Students:* 152 full-time (105 women), 6 part-time (4 women); includes 45 minority (5 Black or African American, non-Hispanic/Latino; 14 Asian, non-Hispanic/Latino; 21 Hispanic/Latino; 5 Two or more races, non-Hispanic/Latino), 6 international. Average age 27. 463 applicants, 16% accepted, 41 enrolled. In 2016, 48 master's, 12 doctorates awarded. *Degree requirements:* For doctorate, thesis/dissertation, candidacy exam. *Entrance requirements:* For master's, GRE General Test, minimum GPA of 3.0 in last 60 hours; for doctorate, GRE General Test. Additional exam requirements/recommendations for international students: Required—TOEFL. *Application deadline:* For fall admission, 12/1 for domestic students. Application fee: $30. Electronic applications accepted. *Expenses:* Tuition, state resident: part-time $288.16 per credit hour. Tuition, nonresident: part-time $1071.31 per credit hour. *Financial support:* In 2016–17, 103 students received support, including 52 fellowships with partial tuition reimbursements available (averaging $7,301 per year), 27 research assistantships with partial tuition reimbursements available (averaging $10,188 per year), 69 teaching assistantships with partial tuition reimbursements available (averaging $11,578 per year); career-related internships or fieldwork, Federal Work-Study, institutionally sponsored loans, tuition waivers (partial), and unspecified assistantships also available. Financial award application deadline: 3/1; financial award applicants required to submit FAFSA. *Faculty research:* Professional ethical decision-making, electronic selection systems, psychometrics. *Unit head:* Dr. Jeffrey E. Cassisi, Chair, 407-823-4201, E-mail: jeffrey.cassisi@ucf.edu. *Application contact:* Assistant Director, Graduate Admissions, 407-823-2766, Fax: 407-823-6442, E-mail: gradadmissions@ucf.edu.
Website: http://psychology.cos.ucf.edu/

**University of Central Missouri,** The Graduate School, Warrensburg, MO 64093. Offers accountancy (MA); accounting (MBA); applied mathematics (MS); aviation safety (MA); biology (MS); business administration (MBA); career and technical education leadership (MS); college student personnel administration (MS); communication (MA); computer science (MS); counseling (MS); criminal justice (MS); educational leadership (Ed D); educational technology (MS); elementary and early childhood education (MSE); English (MA); environmental studies (MA); finance (MBA); history (MA); human services/educational technology (Ed S); human services/learning resources (Ed S); human services/professional counseling (Ed S); industrial hygiene (MS); industrial management (MS); information systems (MBA); information technology (MS); kinesiology (MS); library science and information services (MS); literacy education (MSE); marketing (MBA); mathematics (MS); music (MA); occupational safety management (MS); psychology (MS); rural family nursing (MS); school administration (MSE); social gerontology (MS); sociology (MA); special education (MSE); speech language pathology (MS); superintendency (Ed S); teaching (MAT); teaching English as a second language (MA); technology (MS); technology management (PhD); theatre (MA). *Program availability:* Part-time, 100% online, blended/hybrid learning. *Degree requirements:* For master's and Ed S, comprehensive exam (for some programs), thesis (for some programs). *Entrance requirements:* Additional exam requirements/recommendations for international students: Required—TOEFL (minimum score 550 paper-based; 79 iBT). Electronic applications accepted.

**University of Central Oklahoma,** The Jackson College of Graduate Studies, College of Education and Professional Studies, Department of Psychology, Edmond, OK 73034-5209. Offers counseling psychology (MA); experimental psychology (MA); forensic psychology (MA); general psychology (MA); school psychology (MA). *Degree requirements:* For master's, thesis (for some programs). *Entrance requirements:* For master's, GRE. Additional exam requirements/recommendations for international students: Required—TOEFL (minimum score 550 paper-based; 79 iBT), IELTS (minimum score 6.5). Electronic applications accepted. *Faculty research:* Psychopharmacology, computer psychometrics, health psychology research.

**University of Chicago,** Division of the Social Sciences, Department of Psychology, Chicago, IL 60637. Offers PhD. *Students:* 52 full-time (34 women); includes 9 minority (1 Black or African American, non-Hispanic/Latino; 1 American Indian or Alaska Native, non-Hispanic/Latino; 2 Asian, non-Hispanic/Latino; 4 Hispanic/Latino; 1 Two or more races, non-Hispanic/Latino), 12 international. 305 applicants, 6% accepted, 8 enrolled. In 2016, 7 doctorates awarded. *Degree requirements:* For doctorate, one foreign language, thesis/dissertation, exams. *Entrance requirements:* For doctorate, GRE General Test. Additional exam requirements/recommendations for international students: Required—TOEFL (minimum score 104 iBT), IELTS (minimum score 7). *Application deadline:* For fall admission, 12/15 for domestic and international students. Application fee: $90. Electronic applications accepted. *Financial support:* In 2016–17, 8 students received support, including 8 fellowships with full tuition reimbursements available (averaging $23,000 per year); career-related internships or fieldwork, Federal Work-Study, institutionally sponsored loans, scholarships/grants, and health care benefits also available. Financial award application deadline: 12/15. *Unit head:* Prof. Susan C. Levine, Chair, 773-702-8844, Fax: 773-702-0886, E-mail: s-levine@uchicago.edu. *Application contact:* Office of the Dean of Students, 773-702-8415, E-mail: admissions@ssd.uchicago.edu.
Website: http://psychology.uchicago.edu

**University of Cincinnati,** Graduate School, McMicken College of Arts and Sciences, Department of Psychology, Cincinnati, OH 45221. Offers clinical psychology (PhD); experimental psychology (PhD). *Accreditation:* APA. *Degree requirements:* For doctorate, comprehensive exam, thesis/dissertation. *Entrance requirements:* For doctorate, GRE General Test. Additional exam requirements/recommendations for international students: Required—TOEFL. *Expenses: Tuition, area resident:* Full-time $12,790; part-time $389 per credit hour. Tuition, state resident: full-time $13,290; part-time $419 per credit hour. Tuition, nonresident: full-time $24,532; part-time $976 per credit hour. *International tuition:* $24,832 full-time. *Required fees:* $3958; $140 per credit hour. Tuition and fees vary according to course load, degree level, program and reciprocity agreements. *Faculty research:* Neuropsychology, human factors, health.

**University of Colorado Boulder,** Graduate School, College of Arts and Sciences, Department of Psychology and Neuroscience, Boulder, CO 80309. Offers MA, PhD. *Accreditation:* APA (one or more programs are accredited). *Faculty:* 44 full-time (16 women). *Students:* 116 full-time (64 women), 6 part-time (3 women); includes 15 minority (4 Asian, non-Hispanic/Latino; 9 Hispanic/Latino; 2 Two or more races, non-Hispanic/Latino), 3 international. Average age 29. 816 applicants, 2% accepted, 13 enrolled. In 2016, 11 master's, 21 doctorates awarded. Terminal master's awarded for partial completion of doctoral program. *Degree requirements:* For master's, comprehensive exam; for doctorate, thesis/dissertation. *Entrance requirements:* For master's, GRE General Test, minimum undergraduate GPA of 2.75; for doctorate, GRE General Test. *Application deadline:* For fall admission, 12/1 for domestic and international students. Application fee: $60 ($80 for international students). Electronic applications accepted. Application fee is waived when completed online. *Financial support:* In 2016–17, 285 students received support, including 94 fellowships (averaging $6,554 per year), 29 research assistantships with full and partial tuition reimbursements available (averaging $33,456 per year), 61 teaching assistantships with full and partial tuition reimbursements available (averaging $37,320 per year); institutionally sponsored loans, scholarships/grants, health care benefits, and unspecified assistantships also available. Financial award application deadline: 1/1; financial award applicants required to submit FAFSA. *Faculty research:* Psychology, behavioral/experimental psychology, cognitive development/processes, clinical psychology, human learning and memory. *Total annual research expenditures:* $16 million. *Application contact:* E-mail: grad-admissions@psych.colorado.edu.
Website: http://psych.colorado.edu/

**University of Colorado Colorado Springs,** College of Letters, Arts and Sciences, Department of Psychology, Colorado Springs, CO 80918. Offers MA, PhD. *Accreditation:* APA. *Program availability:* Part-time. *Faculty:* 15 full-time (6 women). *Students:* 30 full-time (22 women), 27 part-time (19 women); includes 7 minority (1 Black or African American, non-Hispanic/Latino; 1 Asian, non-Hispanic/Latino; 4 Hispanic/Latino; 1 Two or more races, non-Hispanic/Latino), 2 international. Average age 30. 302 applicants, 14% accepted, 20 enrolled. In 2016, 9 master's, 1 doctorate awarded. *Degree requirements:* For master's, thesis; for doctorate, comprehensive exam, thesis/dissertation. *Entrance requirements:* For master's, GRE, BA in psychology or equivalent background; minimum GPA of 3.0; for doctorate, GRE (minimum score of 1200 cumulative on the Verbal and Quantitative sections, or above the 50th percentile using the new scoring), minimum overall GPA of 3.0 in all undergraduate courses, 3.5 graduate. Additional exam requirements/recommendations for international students: Required—TOEFL (minimum score 550 paper-based; 80 iBT), IELTS (minimum score 6.5). *Application deadline:* For fall admission, 12/1 for domestic and international students. Applications are processed on a rolling basis. Application fee: $60 ($100 for international students). Electronic applications accepted. *Expenses:* Contact institution. *Financial support:* In 2016–17, 44 students received support. Career-related internships or fieldwork, Federal Work-Study, scholarships/grants, and unspecified assistantships available. Support available to part-time students. Financial award application deadline: 3/1; financial award applicants required to submit FAFSA. *Faculty research:* Attention, emotion, neuroscience, adult development, relationship attachment style, attraction, event-related brain potentials, human adaptation from trauma, behavioral genetics, personality disorders, adolescent development, memory and executive function across the life span, early detection of Alzheimer's disease, psychometrics, differential attitudes toward and etiology of sexual abusers, clinical psychology, behavioral gerontology, forensic neuropsychology. *Total annual research expenditures:* $575,295. *Unit head:* Dr. Michael Kisley, Department Chair, 719-255-4177, Fax: 719-255-4166, E-mail: mkisley@uccs.edu. *Application contact:* Dr. David Dubois, Graduate Student Advisor, 719-255-4500, Fax: 719-255-4166, E-mail: ddubois@uccs.edu.
Website: http://www.uccs.edu/~psych/

**University of Connecticut,** Graduate School, College of Liberal Arts and Sciences, Department of Psychology, Storrs, CT 06269. Offers behavioral neuroscience (PhD); biopsychology (PhD); clinical psychology (MA, PhD); cognition and instruction (PhD); developmental psychology (MA, PhD); ecological psychology (PhD); experimental psychology (PhD); general psychology (MA, PhD); industrial/organizational psychology (PhD); language and cognition (PhD); neuroscience (PhD); social psychology (MA, PhD). *Accreditation:* APA. Terminal master's awarded for partial completion of doctoral program. *Degree requirements:* For master's, comprehensive exam; for doctorate, thesis/dissertation. *Entrance requirements:* For master's and doctorate, GRE General Test, GRE Subject Test. Additional exam requirements/recommendations for international students: Required—TOEFL (minimum score 550 paper-based). Electronic applications accepted.

**University of Dallas,** Braniff Graduate School of Liberal Arts, Program in Psychology, Irving, TX 75062-4736. Offers M Psych, MA. *Program availability:* Part-time. *Degree requirements:* For master's, one foreign language, comprehensive exam (for some programs), thesis (for some programs). *Entrance requirements:* Additional exam requirements/recommendations for international students: Required—TOEFL.

**University of Dayton,** Program in General Psychology, Dayton, OH 45469. Offers MA. *Faculty:* 12 full-time (5 women). *Students:* 5 full-time (3 women), 2 part-time (both women); includes 3 minority (2 Black or African American, non-Hispanic/Latino; 1 Hispanic/Latino). Average age 25. 62 applicants, 8% accepted. In 2016, 4 master's awarded. *Degree requirements:* For master's, thesis. *Entrance requirements:* For master's, GRE General Test, GRE Subject Test (recommended), minimum undergraduate GPA of 2.7. Additional exam requirements/recommendations for international students: Required—TOEFL (minimum score 550 paper-based; 80 iBT). *Application deadline:* For fall admission, 3/1 priority date for domestic and international students. Application fee: $0 ($50 for international students). Electronic applications accepted. *Expenses:* $890 per credit hour, $25 registration fee per term. *Financial support:* In 2016–17, 5 students received support, including 5 research assistantships with full tuition reimbursements available (averaging $12,000 per year); teaching assistantships, institutionally sponsored loans, traineeships, and health care benefits also available. Financial award application deadline: 3/1; financial award applicants required to submit FAFSA. *Faculty research:* Biopsychology, cognition and perception, developmental psychology, social psychology and personality. *Unit head:* Dr. R. Matthew Montoya, Graduate Program Director, 937-229-2656, Fax: 937-229-3900, E-mail: mmontoya1@udayton.edu. *Application contact:* 937-229-4411, E-mail: graduateadmission@udayton.edu.
Website: https://www.udayton.edu/artssciences/learn/graduate/psychology-ma.php

**University of Delaware,** College of Arts and Sciences, Department of Psychology, Newark, DE 19716. Offers behavioral neuroscience (PhD); clinical psychology (PhD); cognitive psychology (PhD); social psychology (PhD). *Accreditation:* APA. *Degree requirements:* For doctorate, thesis/dissertation. *Entrance requirements:* For doctorate, GRE General Test. Additional exam requirements/recommendations for international students: Required—TOEFL (minimum score 600 paper-based). Electronic applications accepted. *Faculty research:* Emotion development, neural and cognitive aspects of memory, neural control of feeding, intergroup relations, social cognition and communication.

**University of Denver,** Division of Arts, Humanities and Social Sciences, Department of Psychology, Denver, CO 80208. Offers affect/social psychology (PhD); clinical child psychology (PhD); cognitive psychology (PhD); developmental psychology (PhD). *Accreditation:* APA. *Faculty:* 26 full-time (13 women), 5 part-time/adjunct (3 women). *Students:* 22 full-time (16 women), 2 part-time (both women); includes 5 minority (1 Black or African American, non-Hispanic/Latino; 1 Asian, non-Hispanic/Latino; 3 Hispanic/Latino), 1 international. Average age 28. 294 applicants, 4% accepted, 8 enrolled. In 2016, 8 doctorates awarded. Terminal master's awarded for partial completion of doctoral program. *Degree requirements:* For doctorate, variable foreign language requirement, comprehensive exam (for some programs), thesis/dissertation. *Entrance requirements:* For doctorate, GRE General Test, master's degree, transcripts, biographical statement, three letters of recommendation. Additional exam requirements/recommendations for international students: Required—TOEFL (minimum score 550 paper-based; 80 iBT). *Application deadline:* For fall admission, 12/1 priority date for domestic and international students. Application fee: $65. Electronic applications accepted. *Expenses:* $29,022 per year full-time. *Financial support:* In 2016–17, 24 students received support, including 5 research assistantships with tuition reimbursements available (averaging $16,000 per year), 12 teaching assistantships with tuition reimbursements available (averaging $17,778 per year); Federal Work-Study, institutionally sponsored loans, scholarships/grants, and unspecified assistantships also available. Support available to part-time students. Financial award application deadline: 2/15; financial award applicants required to submit FAFSA. *Faculty research:* Stress and trauma, developmental science, affect science, clinical science, child psychopathology. *Unit head:* Dr. Anne DePrince, Professor and Chair, 303-871-2939, Fax: 303-871-4747, E-mail: adeprinc@du.edu. *Application contact:* Paula Houghtaling, Graduate Program Administrator, 303-871-3803, Fax: 303-871-4747, E-mail: phoughta@du.edu.
Website: http://www.du.edu/ahss/psychology

**University of Denver,** Graduate School of Professional Psychology, Denver, CO 80208. Offers clinical psychology (Psy D); forensic psychology (MA); international disaster psychology (MA); sport and performance psychology (MA); sport coaching (MA). *Accreditation:* APA. *Faculty:* 23 full-time (13 women), 25 part-time/adjunct (14 women). *Students:* 230 full-time (187 women), 72 part-time (46 women); includes 69 minority (16 Black or African American, non-Hispanic/Latino; 1 American Indian or Alaska Native, non-Hispanic/Latino; 9 Asian, non-Hispanic/Latino; 29 Hispanic/Latino; 1 Native Hawaiian or other Pacific Islander, non-Hispanic/Latino; 13 Two or more races, non-Hispanic/Latino), 14 international. Average age 27. 800 applicants, 30% accepted, 129 enrolled. In 2016, 80 master's, 38 doctorates awarded. *Degree requirements:* For master's, comprehensive exam (for some programs); for doctorate, comprehensive exam (for some programs), paper, clinical internship. *Entrance requirements:* For master's and doctorate, GRE General Test, transcripts, resume, two letters of recommendation, essay. Additional exam requirements/recommendations for international students: Required—TOEFL (minimum score 550 paper-based; 80 iBT). *Application deadline:* For fall admission, 1/5 for domestic and international students. Application fee: $65. Electronic applications accepted. *Expenses:* $43,358 per year full-time. *Financial support:* In 2016–17, 124 students received support, including 15 teaching assistantships with tuition reimbursements available (averaging $2,708 per year); career-related internships or fieldwork, Federal Work-Study, institutionally sponsored loans, scholarships/grants, unspecified assistantships, and clinical assistantships also available. Support available to part-time students. Financial award application deadline: 2/15; financial award applicants required to submit FAFSA. *Unit head:* Dr. Shelly Smith-Acuna, Dean, 303-871-3880, Fax: 303-871-4220, E-mail: shelly.smith-acuna@du.edu. *Application contact:* Admissions Counselor, 303-871-3736, Fax: 303-871-4220, E-mail: gsppinfo@du.edu. Website: http://www.du.edu/gspp

**University of Florida,** Graduate School, College of Liberal Arts and Sciences, Department of Psychology, Gainesville, FL 32611. Offers counseling psychology (PhD); psychology (MA, MS, PhD), including psychology (PhD), women's and gender studies (PhD); JD/PhD. *Degree requirements:* For master's, comprehensive exam, thesis or alternative; for doctorate, comprehensive exam, thesis/dissertation. *Entrance requirements:* For master's and doctorate, GRE General Test, minimum GPA of 3.0. Additional exam requirements/recommendations for international students: Required—TOEFL (minimum score 550 paper-based; 80 iBT), IELTS (minimum score 6). Electronic applications accepted. *Faculty research:* Behavior analysis, behavioral and cognitive neuroscience, counseling, developmental psychology, social psychology.

**University of Florida,** Graduate School, College of Public Health and Health Professions, Department of Clinical and Health Psychology, Gainesville, FL 32611. Offers clinical and translational science (PhD); psychology (MS). *Accreditation:* APA (one or more programs are accredited). *Degree requirements:* For doctorate, comprehensive exam, thesis/dissertation, pre-doctoral internship. *Entrance requirements:* For master's and doctorate, GRE General Test, minimum GPA of 3.0. Additional exam requirements/recommendations for international students: Required—TOEFL (minimum score 550 paper-based; 80 iBT), IELTS (minimum score 6). Electronic applications accepted. *Faculty research:* Clinical child and pediatric psychology, medical psychology, neuropsychology, health promotion and aging.

**University of Georgia,** Franklin College of Arts and Sciences, Department of Psychology, Athens, GA 30602. Offers PhD. *Accreditation:* APA. *Degree requirements:* For doctorate, one foreign language, thesis/dissertation. *Entrance requirements:* For doctorate, GRE General Test. Additional exam requirements/recommendations for international students: Required—TOEFL. *Application deadline:* For fall admission, 12/1 for domestic students; for spring admission, 11/15 for domestic students. Application fee: $50. Electronic applications accepted. *Financial support:* Fellowships, research assistantships, teaching assistantships, and unspecified assistantships available. *Unit head:* Dr. W. Keith Campbell, Head, 706-542-2174, Fax: 706-542-3275, E-mail: wkc@uga.edu. *Application contact:* Dr. Billy R. Hammond, Graduate Coordinator, 706-542-4812, Fax: 706-542-3275, E-mail: bhammond@uga.edu.
Website: http://www.uga.edu/psychology/

**University of Guelph,** Graduate Studies, College of Social and Applied Human Sciences, Department of Psychology, Guelph, ON N1G 2W1, Canada. Offers applied social psychology (MA, PhD); clinical psychology: applied development emphasis (PhD); clinical psychology: applied developmental emphasis (MA); industrial/organizational psychology (MA, PhD); neuroscience and applied cognitive science (MA, PhD). *Degree requirements:* For master's, thesis; for doctorate, comprehensive exam, thesis/dissertation. *Entrance requirements:* For master's, GRE General Test, GRE Subject Test, minimum B+ average during previous 2 years of course work; for doctorate, GRE General Test, GRE Subject Test, minimum A- average. Additional exam requirements/recommendations for international students: Required—TOEFL (minimum score 89 iBT). Electronic applications accepted. *Faculty research:* Organizational psychology, reading comprehension and mathematical ability, drug addiction and relapse, gender issues and culture, memory, clinical psychology.

**University of Hartford,** College of Arts and Sciences, Department of Psychology, West Hartford, CT 06117-1599. Offers clinical practices (MA, Psy D), including clinical practices (Psy D), psychology (MA); general experimental psychology (MA); organizational behavior (MS); school psychology (MS). *Accreditation:* APA. *Program availability:* Part-time. *Degree requirements:* For master's, comprehensive exam, thesis (for some programs). *Entrance requirements:* For master's, GRE General Test, GRE Subject Test, minimum GPA of 3.0; for doctorate, GRE General Test, GRE Subject Test. Additional exam requirements/recommendations for international students: Required—TOEFL (minimum score 550 paper-based). Electronic applications accepted. *Expenses:* Contact institution.

**University of Hawaii at Manoa,** Graduate Division, College of Social Sciences, Department of Psychology, Honolulu, HI 96822. Offers clinical psychology (PhD); community and cultural psychology (PhD); community and culture (MA); psychology (MA, PhD, Graduate Certificate). *Accreditation:* APA (one or more programs are accredited). *Program availability:* Part-time. Terminal master's awarded for partial completion of doctoral program. *Degree requirements:* For master's, comprehensive exam, thesis; for doctorate, comprehensive exam, thesis/dissertation. *Entrance requirements:* For master's and doctorate, GRE General Test, GRE Subject Test. Additional exam requirements/recommendations for international students: Required—TOEFL (minimum score 600 paper-based; 100 iBT), IELTS (minimum score 7). *Faculty research:* Cross-cultural psychology, health psychology, marine mammals, child/adult psychopathology.

**University of Houston,** College of Liberal Arts and Social Sciences, Department of Psychology, Houston, TX 77204. Offers clinical psychology (PhD); developmental psychology (PhD); industrial/organizational psychology (PhD); psychology (MA); social psychology (PhD). *Accreditation:* APA (one or more programs are accredited). *Degree requirements:* For master's, comprehensive exam, thesis; for doctorate, comprehensive exam, thesis/dissertation. *Entrance requirements:* For master's, GRE General Test, career statement, 3 letters of recommendation; for doctorate, GRE General Test, 3 letters of recommendation. Additional exam requirements/recommendations for international students: Required—TOEFL (minimum score 550 paper-based; 79 iBT). Electronic applications accepted. *Faculty research:* Health psychology, depression, child/family process, organizational effectiveness, close relationships.

**University of Houston–Clear Lake,** School of Human Sciences and Humanities, Programs in Human Sciences, Houston, TX 77058-1002. Offers behavioral sciences (MA), including criminology, cross cultural studies, general psychology, sociology; clinical psychology (MA); criminology (MA); cross cultural studies (MA); family therapy (MA); fitness and human performance (MA); school psychology (MA). *Accreditation:* AAMFT/COAMFTE. *Program availability:* Part-time, evening/weekend, online learning. *Degree requirements:* For master's, thesis or alternative. *Entrance requirements:* For master's, GRE General Test. Additional exam requirements/recommendations for international students: Required—TOEFL (minimum score 550 paper-based). Electronic applications accepted. *Faculty research:* Smoking cessation, adolescent sexuality, white collar crime, serial murder, human factors/human computer interaction.

**University of Houston–Victoria,** School of Arts and Sciences, Program in Psychology, Victoria, TX 77901-4450. Offers counseling psychology (MA); forensic psychology (MA); school psychology (MA). *Program availability:* Part-time, evening/weekend, online learning. *Degree requirements:* For master's, project or thesis. *Entrance requirements:* For master's, GRE General Test. Additional exam requirements/recommendations for international students: Required—TOEFL (minimum score 550 paper-based). Electronic applications accepted.

**University of Idaho,** College of Graduate Studies, College of Letters, Arts and Social Sciences, Department of Psychology and Communication Studies, Moscow, ID 83844. Offers experimental psychology (PhD); psychology (MS). *Faculty:* 9 full-time, 2 part-time/adjunct. *Students:* 18 full-time, 11 part-time. Average age 31. In 2016, 11 master's awarded. *Entrance requirements:* For master's, GRE, minimum GPA of 3.0. *Application deadline:* For fall admission, 8/1 for domestic students; for spring admission, 12/15 for domestic students. Applications are processed on a rolling basis. Application fee: $60. Electronic applications accepted. *Expenses:* Tuition, state resident: full-time $6460; part-time $414 per credit hour. Tuition, nonresident: full-time $21,268; part-time $1237 per credit hour. *Required fees:* $2070; $60 per credit hour. Full-time tuition and fees vary according to course load and reciprocity agreements. *Financial support:* Fellowships, research assistantships, and teaching assistantships available. Financial award applicants required to submit FAFSA. *Faculty research:* Clinical, experimental, and cognitive psychology. *Unit head:* Dr. Todd Thorsteinson, Chair, 208-885-6324, E-mail: psyc-comm@uidaho.edu. *Application contact:* Sean Scoggin, Graduate Recruitment Coordinator, 208-885-4723, Fax: 208-885-4406, E-mail: graduateadmissions@uidaho.edu. Website: https://www.uidaho.edu/class/psychcomm

**University of Illinois at Chicago,** College of Liberal Arts and Sciences, Department of Psychology, Chicago, IL 60607-7128. Offers MA, PhD. *Accreditation:* APA. *Degree requirements:* For master's, thesis/dissertation, departmental qualifying exam. *Entrance requirements:* For doctorate, GRE General Test, minimum GPA of 2.75. Additional exam requirements/recommendations for international students: Required—TOEFL. Electronic applications accepted. *Expenses:* Contact institution. *Faculty research:* Cognition, behavioral neuroscience, community and prevention research, social and personality.

# SECTION 24: PSYCHOLOGY AND COUNSELING

## Psychology—General

**University of Illinois at Urbana–Champaign,** Graduate College, College of Liberal Arts and Sciences, Department of Psychology, Champaign, IL 61820. Offers MA, MS, PhD. *Accreditation:* APA (one or more programs are accredited).

**University of Indianapolis,** Graduate Programs, School of Psychological Sciences, Indianapolis, IN 46227-3697. Offers clinical psychology (Psy D); clinical psychology/ mental health counseling (MA). *Accreditation:* APA. *Degree requirements:* For master's, practicum; for doctorate, comprehensive exam, thesis/dissertation, 1200 hours of clinical practicum, 2000-hour internship. *Entrance requirements:* For master's, GRE, 3 letters of recommendation; for doctorate, GRE, minimum GPA of 3.0, 18 hours of course work in psychology, 3 letters of recommendation. Additional exam requirements/ recommendations for international students: Required—TOEFL (minimum score 550 paper-based).

**The University of Iowa,** Graduate College, College of Education, Department of Psychological and Quantitative Foundations, Iowa City, IA 52242-1316. Offers counseling psychology (PhD); educational measurement and statistics (MA, PhD); educational psychology (MA, PhD); school psychology (PhD, Ed S). *Accreditation:* APA. *Degree requirements:* For master's, thesis optional, exam; for doctorate, comprehensive exam, thesis/dissertation; for Ed S, exam. *Entrance requirements:* For master's, doctorate, and Ed S, GRE General Test, minimum GPA of 3.0. Additional exam requirements/recommendations for international students: Required—TOEFL (minimum score 550 paper-based; 81 iBT). Electronic applications accepted.

**The University of Iowa,** Graduate College, College of Liberal Arts and Sciences, Department of Psychology, Iowa City, IA 52242-1316. Offers MA, PhD. *Degree requirements:* For master's, thesis optional, exam; for doctorate, comprehensive exam, thesis/dissertation. *Entrance requirements:* For master's and doctorate, GRE General Test, minimum GPA of 3.0. Additional exam requirements/recommendations for international students: Required—TOEFL (minimum score 550 paper-based; 81 iBT) Electronic applications accepted.

**The University of Kansas,** Graduate Studies, College of Liberal Arts and Sciences, Department of Applied Behavioral Science, Lawrence, KS 66045. Offers applied behavioral science (MA); behavioral psychology (PhD); community health and development (Graduate Certificate); PhD/MPH. *Program availability:* Part-time. *Students:* 42 full-time (29 women); includes 40 minority (35 Black or African American, non-Hispanic/Latino; 1 American Indian or Alaska Native, non-Hispanic/Latino; 2 Hispanic/Latino; 2 Native Hawaiian or other Pacific Islander, non-Hispanic/Latino), 2 international. Average age 28. 72 applicants, 14% accepted, 10 enrolled. In 2016, 4 master's, 2 doctorates awarded. Terminal master's awarded for partial completion of doctoral program. *Entrance requirements:* For master's, curriculum vitae; 3 letters of recommendation; personal statement; all academic transcripts; copies of pertinent written work, published or not, as well as presented papers; for doctorate, curriculum vitae; 3 letters of recommendation; personal statement; copies of pertinent written work, published or not, as well as presented papers. Additional exam requirements/ recommendations for international students: Required—TOEFL. *Application deadline:* For fall admission, 12/15 priority date for domestic students, 12/15 for international students. Application fee: $65 ($85 for international students). Electronic applications accepted. *Financial support:* Fellowships, research assistantships, teaching assistantships, career-related internships or fieldwork, traineeships, tuition waivers (full), and unspecified assistantships available. Financial award application deadline: 12/15; financial award applicants required to submit CSS PROFILE or FAFSA. *Faculty research:* Organizational behavioral management, community health and development, early childhood education and intervention, developmental disabilities, behavioral economics of choice. *Unit head:* Dr. Florence D. DiGennaro Reed, Chairperson, 785-864-0521, E-mail: fdreed@ku.edu. *Application contact:* Andrea Noltner, Office Manager, 785-864-0503, E-mail: anoltner@ku.edu.
Website: http://absc.ku.edu

**The University of Kansas,** Graduate Studies, College of Liberal Arts and Sciences, Department of Psychology, Lawrence, KS 66045. Offers clinical psychology (MA, PhD); cognitive and brain sciences (MA, PhD); developmental psychology (MA, PhD); quantitative psychology (PhD); social psychology (MA, PhD). *Accreditation:* APA (one or more programs are accredited). *Program availability:* Part-time. *Students:* 69 full-time (46 women), 1 (woman) part-time; includes 11 minority (5 Black or African American, non-Hispanic/Latino; 3 Asian, non-Hispanic/Latino; 3 Two or more races, non-Hispanic/ Latino), 9 international. Average age 29. 202 applicants, 10% accepted, 14 enrolled. In 2016, 12 master's, 11 doctorates awarded. Terminal master's awarded for partial completion of doctoral program. *Entrance requirements:* For doctorate, GRE General Test, three letters of recommendation, resume/curriculum vitae, statement of purpose/ personal statement, writing sample. Additional exam requirements/recommendations for international students: Required—TOEFL. *Application deadline:* For fall admission, 12/1 for domestic and international students. Application fee: $65 ($85 for international students). Electronic applications accepted. *Financial support:* Fellowships, research assistantships, teaching assistantships, career-related internships or fieldwork, Federal Work-Study, scholarships/grants, health care benefits, and unspecified assistantships available. Financial award application deadline: 12/1; financial award applicants required to submit FAFSA. *Faculty research:* Origins, correlates and treatment of depression; health and emotion; concentration on topics related to prejudice, stereotyping, and intergroup relations; memory, cognitive development, language, perception, attention, aging; psychometric methods, item response theory, structural equation modeling. *Unit head:* Ruth Anne Atchley, Chair, 785-864-4131. *Application contact:* Graduate Officer, 785-864-4195, E-mail: psycgrad@ku.edu.
Website: http://www.psych.ku.edu/

**University of Kentucky,** Graduate School, College of Arts and Sciences, Program in Psychology, Lexington, KY 40506-0032. Offers MA, PhD. *Accreditation:* APA (one or more programs are accredited). *Degree requirements:* For master's, comprehensive exam, thesis; for doctorate, comprehensive exam, thesis/dissertation. *Entrance requirements:* For master's, GRE General Test, minimum undergraduate GPA of 2.75; for doctorate, GRE General Test, minimum graduate GPA of 3.0. Additional exam requirements/recommendations for international students: Required—TOEFL (minimum score 550 paper-based). Electronic applications accepted. *Faculty research:* Psychopharmacology and teratology, behavioral neuroscience, social psychology, cognitive psychology, development and developmental psychobiology.

**University of La Verne,** College of Arts and Sciences, Department of Psychology, La Verne, CA 91750-4443. Offers clinical psychology (Psy D); marriage and family therapy (MS). *Accreditation:* APA (one or more programs are accredited). *Program availability:* Part-time. *Students:* 72 full-time (63 women), 65 part-time (57 women); includes 74 minority (7 Black or African American, non-Hispanic/Latino; 5 Asian, non-Hispanic/ Latino; 60 Hispanic/Latino; 2 Two or more races, non-Hispanic/Latino), 1 international. Average age 29. *Degree requirements:* For master's, thesis, competency exam, fieldwork, culminating project; for doctorate, thesis/dissertation, clinical practica, clinical internship, competency exams, personal psychotherapy. *Entrance requirements:* For master's, minimum undergraduate GPA of 3.0, 5-7-page statement of purpose and autobiography, 3 letters of recommendation, interview, curriculum vitae; for doctorate, GRE, minimum GPA of 3.1, statement of professional goals and aspirations, 3 recommendations, interview, curriculum vitae. Additional exam requirements/

recommendations for international students: Required—TOEFL (minimum score 600 paper-based; 100 iBT); Recommended—IELTS (minimum score 6.5). *Application deadline:* Applications are processed on a rolling basis. *Expenses:* Contact institution. *Financial support:* Career-related internships or fieldwork, scholarships/grants, and unspecified assistantships available. Financial award application deadline: 3/2; financial award applicants required to submit FAFSA. *Unit head:* Dr. Glenn Gamst, Department Chair, 909-448-4176, E-mail: ggamst@laverne.edu. *Application contact:* Christy Ranells, Associate Director of Graduate Admissions, 909-448-4644, Fax: 909-971-2295, E-mail: cranells@laverne.edu.
Website: http://laverne.edu/psychology/

**University of Lethbridge,** School of Graduate Studies, Lethbridge, AB T1K 3M4, Canada. Offers addictions counseling (M Sc); agricultural biotechnology (M Sc); agricultural studies (M Sc, MA); anthropology (MA); archaeology (M Sc, MA); art (MA, MFA); biochemistry (M Sc); biological sciences (M Sc); biomolecular science (PhD); biosystems and biodiversity (PhD); Canadian studies (MA); chemistry (M Sc); computer science (M Sc); computer science and geographical information science (M Sc); counseling (MC); counseling psychology (M Ed); dramatic arts (MA); earth, space, and physical science (PhD); economics (MA); education (MA, PhD); educational leadership (M Ed); English (MA); environmental science (M Sc); evolution and behavior (PhD); exercise science (M Sc); French (MA); French/German (MA); French/Spanish (MA); general education (M Ed); geography (M Sc, MA); German (MA); health sciences (M Sc); individualized multidisciplinary (M Sc, MA); kinesiology (M Sc, MA); management (M Sc), including accounting, finance, human resource management and labor relations, information systems, international management, marketing, policy and strategy; mathematics (M Sc); music (M Mus, MA); Native American studies (MA); neuroscience (M Sc, PhD); new media (M MA, MFA); nursing (M Sc, MN); philosophy (MA); physics (M Sc); political science (MA); psychology (M Sc, MA); religious studies (MA); sociology (MA); theatre and dramatic arts (MFA); theoretical and computational science (PhD); urban and regional studies (MA); women and gender studies (MA). *Program availability:* Part-time, evening/weekend. *Degree requirements:* For master's, thesis (for some programs); for doctorate, comprehensive exam, thesis/dissertation. *Entrance requirements:* For master's, GMAT (for M Sc in management), bachelor's degree in related field, minimum GPA of 3.0 during previous 20 graded semester courses, 2 years' teaching or related experience (M Ed); for doctorate, master's degree, minimum graduate GPA of 3.5. Additional exam requirements/recommendations for international students: Required—TOEFL (minimum score 580 paper-based; 93 iBT). Electronic applications accepted. *Faculty research:* Movement and brain plasticity, gibberellin physiology, photosynthesis, carbon cycling, molecular properties of main-group ring components.

**University of Louisiana at Lafayette,** College of Liberal Arts, Department of Psychology, Program in Psychology, Lafayette, LA 70504. Offers MS. *Degree requirements:* For master's, comprehensive exam, thesis (for some programs). *Entrance requirements:* For master's, GRE General Test. Additional exam requirements/ recommendations for international students: Required—TOEFL (minimum score 550 paper-based).

**University of Louisiana at Monroe,** Graduate School, College of Business and Social Sciences, Department of Psychology, Monroe, LA 71209-0001. Offers forensic psychology (MS); general psychology (MS); psychometrics (MS). *Program availability:* Part-time, evening/weekend, online learning. *Faculty:* 2 full-time (0 women). *Students:* 12 full-time (10 women), 4 part-time (2 women); includes 10 minority (7 Black or African American, non-Hispanic/Latino; 2 Hispanic/Latino; 1 Two or more races, non-Hispanic/ Latino). Average age 26. 109 applicants, 37% accepted, 6 enrolled. In 2016, 4 master's awarded. *Degree requirements:* For master's, comprehensive exam, thesis optional. *Entrance requirements:* For master's, GRE General Test, minimum GPA of 2.75. Additional exam requirements/recommendations for international students: Required— TOEFL (minimum score 500 paper-based; 61 iBT). *Application deadline:* For fall admission, 7/1 for domestic and international students; for winter admission, 12/14 for domestic students; for spring admission, 12/1 for domestic and international students. Applications are processed on a rolling basis. Application fee: $20 ($30 for international students). Electronic applications accepted. *Expenses:* Tuition, state resident: full-time $6489. Tuition, nonresident: full-time $18,589. *Required fees:* $8984. Tuition and fees vary according to course level, course load, degree level and program. *Financial support:* Research assistantships, career-related internships or fieldwork, Federal Work-Study, and unspecified assistantships available. Financial award application deadline: 4/1; financial award applicants required to submit FAFSA. *Application contact:* Dr. Jack Palmer, Graduate Coordinator, 318-342-1345, E-mail: palmer@ulm.edu.
Website: http://www.ulm.edu/psychology

**University of Louisville,** Graduate School, College of Arts and Sciences, Department of Psychological and Brain Sciences, Louisville, KY 40292-0001. Offers clinical psychology (PhD); experimental psychology (PhD), including cognition and development, vision and hearing. *Accreditation:* APA. *Students:* 54 full-time (42 women), 2 part-time (both women); includes 10 minority (3 Black or African American, non-Hispanic/Latino; 2 Asian, non-Hispanic/Latino; 3 Hispanic/Latino; 2 Two or more races, non-Hispanic/Latino), 1 international. Average age 28. 21 applicants, 5% accepted, 2 enrolled. In 2016, 1 doctorate awarded. *Degree requirements:* For doctorate, comprehensive exam, thesis/dissertation, internship (for clinical psychology). *Entrance requirements:* For doctorate, GRE General Test, GRE Subject Test. Additional exam requirements/recommendations for international students: Required—TOEFL. *Application deadline:* For fall and winter admission, 12/1 for domestic and international students. Application fee: $60. *Expenses:* Tuition, state resident: full-time $12,246; part-time $681 per credit hour. Tuition, nonresident: full-time $25,486; part-time $1417 per credit hour. *Required fees:* $196. Tuition and fees vary according to program and reciprocity agreements. *Financial support:* In 2016–17, 6 fellowships with full tuition reimbursements (averaging $22,000 per year), 1 research assistantship with full tuition reimbursement (averaging $22,000 per year), 1 teaching assistantship with full tuition reimbursement (averaging $22,000 per year) were awarded; health care benefits and unspecified assistantships also available. Financial award application deadline: 12/1. *Faculty research:* Cognitive development, hearing/visual science, cognitive neuroscience/imaging, health psychology/mindfulness/stress and trauma, child/adult psychopathology, geropsychology. *Total annual research expenditures:* $1.8 million. *Unit head:* Dr. Suzanne Meeks, Chair, 502-852-6068, Fax: 502-852-8904, E-mail: smeeks@louisville.edu. *Application contact:* Libby Leggett, Director, Graduate Admissions, 502-852-3101, Fax: 502-852-6536, E-mail: gradadm@louisville.edu.
Website: http://louisville.edu/psychology

**University of Maine,** Graduate School, College of Liberal Arts and Sciences, Department of Psychology, Orono, ME 04469. Offers psychological sciences (PhD). *Accreditation:* APA (one or more programs are accredited). *Faculty:* 12 full-time (5 women), 5 part-time/adjunct (3 women). *Students:* 21 full-time (16 women), 4 part-time (1 woman); includes 3 minority (1 American Indian or Alaska Native, non-Hispanic/ Latino; 2 Hispanic/Latino). Average age 27. 121 applicants, 5% accepted, 5 enrolled. In 2016, 8 master's, 6 doctorates awarded. Terminal master's awarded for partial completion of doctoral program. *Degree requirements:* For master's, thesis; for doctorate, comprehensive exam, thesis/dissertation. *Entrance requirements:* For

master's and doctorate, GRE General Test, GRE Subject Test. Additional exam requirements/recommendations for international students: Required—TOEFL. *Application deadline:* For fall admission, 12/1 for domestic and international students. Applications are processed on a rolling basis. *Application fee:* $65. Electronic applications accepted. *Expenses:* Tuition, state resident: full-time $7524; part-time $2508 per credit. Tuition, nonresident: full-time $24,498; part-time $8166 per credit. *Required fees:* $1148; $571 per credit. *Financial support:* In 2016–17, 24 students received support, including 2 fellowships with full tuition reimbursements available (averaging $25,000 per year), 4 research assistantships with full tuition reimbursements available (averaging $14,600 per year), 18 teaching assistantships with full tuition reimbursements available (averaging $14,600 per year); Federal Work-Study, institutionally sponsored loans, and tuition waivers (full and partial) also available. Financial award application deadline: 3/1. *Faculty research:* Social development, hypertension and aging, attitude change, self-confidence in achievement situations, health psychology. *Total annual research expenditures:* $107,015. *Unit head:* Dr. Michael Robbins, Chair, 207-581-2051, Fax: 207-581-6128. *Application contact:* Scott G. Delcourt, Assistant Vice President for Graduate Studies and Senior Associate Dean, 207-581-3291, Fax: 207-581-3232, E-mail: graduate@maine.edu.
Website: http://www.umaine.edu/psychology/

**The University of Manchester,** School of Psychological Sciences, Manchester, United Kingdom. Offers audiology (M Phil, PhD); clinical psychology (M Phil, PhD, Psy D); psychology (M Phil, PhD).

**University of Manitoba,** Faculty of Graduate Studies, Faculty of Arts, Department of Psychology, Winnipeg, MB R3T 2N2, Canada. Offers clinical psychology (PhD); psychology (MA, PhD); school psychology (MA). *Degree requirements:* For master's, thesis; for doctorate, one foreign language, thesis/dissertation. *Entrance requirements:* For master's and doctorate, GRE General Test.

**University of Maryland, Baltimore County,** The Graduate School, College of Arts, Humanities and Social Sciences, Department of Psychology, Baltimore, MD 21250. Offers applied developmental psychology (PhD); human services psychology (MA, PhD), including applied behavioral analysis (MA), human services psychology (PhD); industrial/organizational psychology (MPS). *Accreditation:* APA (one or more programs are accredited). *Faculty:* 25 full-time (14 women), 22 part-time/adjunct (8 women). *Students:* 116 full-time (96 women), 53 part-time (42 women); includes 35 minority (11 Black or African American, non-Hispanic/Latino; 11 Asian, non-Hispanic/Latino; 11 Hispanic/Latino; 2 Two or more races, non-Hispanic/Latino). Average age 25. 160 applicants, 19% accepted, 20 enrolled. In 2016, 18 master's, 12 doctorates awarded. Terminal master's awarded for partial completion of doctoral program. *Degree requirements:* For master's, thesis or alternative; for doctorate, comprehensive exam, thesis/dissertation. *Entrance requirements:* For master's, GRE General Test; for doctorate, GRE General Test, GRE Subject Test, minimum GPA of 3.0. Additional exam requirements/recommendations for international students: Required—TOEFL. *Application deadline:* For fall admission, 12/1 for domestic and international students. *Application fee:* $50. Electronic applications accepted. *Expenses:* Tuition, state resident: full-time $13,294. Tuition, nonresident: full-time $20,286. *Financial support:* In 2016–17, 60 students received support, including 3 fellowships with full tuition reimbursements available (averaging $22,000 per year), 30 research assistantships with full tuition reimbursements available (averaging $20,400 per year), 27 teaching assistantships with full tuition reimbursements available (averaging $17,250 per year); career-related internships or fieldwork, Federal Work-Study, health care benefits, and unspecified assistantships also available. Financial award application deadline: 3/1; financial award applicants required to submit FAFSA. *Faculty research:* Prevention and treatment of behavior problems, early intervention, cultural contexts, applications to education, behavioral medicine. *Unit head:* Dr. Christopher Murphy, Chair, 410-455-2415, Fax: 410-455-1055, E-mail: chmurphy@umbc.edu. *Application contact:* Nicole Mooney, Program Management Specialist, 410-455-2567, Fax: 410-455-1055, E-mail: psycdept@umbc.edu.
Website: http://psychology.umbc.edu/

**University of Maryland, College Park,** Academic Affairs, College of Behavioral and Social Sciences, Department of Psychology, College Park, MD 20742. Offers clinical psychology (PhD); developmental psychology (PhD); experimental psychology (PhD); industrial psychology (MA, MS, PhD); social psychology (PhD). *Accreditation:* APA (one or more programs are accredited). *Degree requirements:* For master's, thesis; for doctorate, variable foreign language requirement, comprehensive exam, thesis/dissertation. *Entrance requirements:* For master's and doctorate, GRE General Test, GRE Subject Test, minimum GPA of 3.5, research and/or work experience, 3 letters of recommendation. Electronic applications accepted. *Faculty research:* Social stereotyping and prejudice, anxiety disorders, auditory neuroethology, counseling and social psychology.

**University of Massachusetts Amherst,** Graduate School, College of Natural Sciences, Department of Psychological and Brain Sciences, Amherst, MA 01003. Offers clinical psychology (MS, PhD); cognitive psychology (MS, PhD); developmental science (MS, PhD); psychology of peace and violence (MS, PhD); social psychology (MS, PhD). *Accreditation:* APA (one or more programs are accredited). Terminal master's awarded for partial completion of doctoral program. *Degree requirements:* For master's, thesis; for doctorate, comprehensive exam, thesis/dissertation. *Entrance requirements:* For master's and doctorate, GRE General Test, 3 letters of recommendation. Additional exam requirements/recommendations for international students: Required—TOEFL (minimum score 550 paper-based; 80 iBT), IELTS (minimum score 6.5). Electronic applications accepted.

**University of Massachusetts Dartmouth,** Graduate School, College of Arts and Sciences, Department of Psychology, North Dartmouth, MA 02747-2300. Offers applied behavioral analysis (MA, Post-Master's Certificate); autism studies (Graduate Certificate); clinical psychology (MA); research psychology (MA). *Program availability:* Part-time, 100% online, blended/hybrid learning. *Faculty:* 19 full-time (12 women), 7 part-time/adjunct (3 women). *Students:* 34 full-time (27 women), 50 part-time (39 women); includes 17 minority (3 Black or African American, non-Hispanic/Latino; 1 Asian, non-Hispanic/Latino; 8 Hispanic/Latino; 5 Two or more races, non-Hispanic/Latino). Average age 29. 99 applicants, 57% accepted, 32 enrolled. In 2016, 25 master's, 2 other advanced degrees awarded. *Degree requirements:* For master's, thesis or comprehensive exam (for clinical psychology); thesis (for research psychology). *Entrance requirements:* For master's, GRE (for research psychology), statement of purpose (minimum of 300 words), resume, 3 letters of recommendation, official transcripts; for other advanced degree, statement of purpose (minimum of 300 words), resume, 3 letters of recommendation, official transcripts. Additional exam requirements/recommendations for international students: Required—TOEFL (minimum score 533 paper-based; 72 iBT). *Application deadline:* For fall admission, 3/1 priority date for domestic students, 2/1 priority date for international students; for spring admission, 12/20 priority date for domestic students, 11/20 priority date for international students. *Application fee:* $60. Electronic applications accepted. *Expenses:* Tuition, state resident: full-time $14,994; part-time $624.75 per credit. Tuition, nonresident: full-time $27,068; part-time $1127.83 per credit. *Required fees:* $405; $25.88 per credit. Tuition and fees vary according to course load and reciprocity agreements. *Financial*

*support:* In 2016–17, 2 fellowships (averaging $7,000 per year) were awarded; institutionally sponsored loans, scholarships/grants, and unspecified assistantships also available. Support available to part-time students. Financial award application deadline: 3/1; financial award applicants required to submit FAFSA. *Faculty research:* Behavioral medicine, learning, social and developmental psychology, child neuropsychology, clinical research, counseling, psychotherapy, nonverbal communication, emotion, cognition, problem solving. *Total annual research expenditures:* $500,000. *Unit head:* Mahzad Hojjat, Graduate Program Director, Research Psychology, 508-999-8951, E-mail: mhojjat@umassd.edu. *Application contact:* Steven Briggs, Director of Marketing and Recruitment for Graduate Studies, 508-999-8604, Fax: 508-999-8183, E-mail: graduate@umassd.edu.
Website: http://www.umassd.edu/cas/psychology/graduateprograms

**University of Massachusetts Lowell,** College of Fine Arts, Humanities and Social Sciences, Department of Psychology, Lowell, MA 01854. Offers community social psychology (MA). *Program availability:* Part-time. *Degree requirements:* For master's, thesis optional. *Entrance requirements:* For master's, GRE General Test or MAT. Electronic applications accepted. *Faculty research:* Domestic violence, youth sports, teen pregnancy, substance abuse, family and work roles.

**University of Memphis,** Graduate School, College of Arts and Sciences, Department of Psychology, Memphis, TN 38152-3230. Offers clinical psychology (PhD); experimental psychology (PhD); general psychology (MS); school psychology (MA, PhD, Ed S). *Accreditation:* APA. *Faculty:* 27 full-time (12 women), 2 part-time/adjunct (0 women). *Students:* 97 full-time (70 women), 17 part-time (11 women); includes 29 minority (16 Black or African American, non-Hispanic/Latino; 5 Asian, non-Hispanic/Latino; 4 Hispanic/Latino; 4 Two or more races, non-Hispanic/Latino), 5 international. Average age 27. 278 applicants, 17% accepted, 35 enrolled. In 2016, 34 master's, 2 doctorates, 9 other advanced degrees awarded. *Degree requirements:* For master's, comprehensive exam (for some programs), thesis (for some programs), 37 credit hours (for MA); 33 credit hours with thesis or 36 with exam (for MS); for doctorate, comprehensive exam, thesis/dissertation, 80 semester hours, major area paper; 1-year placement and 1-year internship (for clinical psychology); internship (for school psychology); for Ed S, 30 credit hours. *Entrance requirements:* For master's, GRE, 3 letters of recommendation, 18 undergraduate hours in psychology; for doctorate, GRE, minimum GPA of 2.75, 18 hours of undergraduate psychology courses, transcripts, personal statement, 3 letters of recommendation, interview; for Ed S, GRE, minimum GPA of 2.75, 18 hours of undergraduate psychology courses, 3 letters of recommendation. Additional exam requirements/recommendations for international students: Required—TOEFL (minimum score 550 paper-based; 79 iBT). *Application deadline:* For fall admission, 12/5 for domestic students. Applications are processed on a rolling basis. *Application fee:* $35 ($60 for international students). Electronic applications accepted. *Expenses:* $5,231.50 per semester full-time in-state, $9,623.50 full-time out-of-state. *Financial support:* In 2016–17, 66 students received support, including 60 research assistantships with full tuition reimbursements available (averaging $17,582 per year), 21 teaching assistantships with full tuition reimbursements available (averaging $6,220 per year); fellowships with full tuition reimbursements available, Federal Work-Study, scholarships/grants, tuition waivers (partial), and unspecified assistantships also available. Financial award application deadline: 2/1; financial award applicants required to submit FAFSA. *Faculty research:* Clinical health; school; child and family psychology; psychotherapy; cognitive and behavioral neuroscience; industrial-organizational psychology. *Unit head:* Dr. Frank Andrasik, Chair, 901-678-2145, Fax: 901-678-2579, E-mail: rcohen@memphis.edu. *Application contact:* Dr. Robert Cohen, Coordinator of Graduate Studies, 901-678-4679, Fax: 901-678-2579, E-mail: rcohen@memphis.edu.
Website: http://www.memphis.edu/psychology

**University of Miami,** Graduate School, College of Arts and Sciences, Department of Psychology, Coral Gables, FL 33124. Offers adult clinical (PhD); behavioral neuroscience (PhD); child clinical (PhD); developmental psychology (PhD); health clinical (PhD); psychology (MS). *Accreditation:* APA (one or more programs are accredited). *Degree requirements:* For doctorate, comprehensive exam, thesis/dissertation. *Entrance requirements:* For doctorate, GRE General Test, minimum GPA of 3.5. Additional exam requirements/recommendations for international students: Required—TOEFL. Electronic applications accepted. *Faculty research:* Behavioral factors in cardiovascular disease and cancer adult psychopathology, developmental disabilities, social and emotional development, mechanisms of coping.

**University of Michigan,** Rackham Graduate School, College of Literature, Science, and the Arts, Department of Psychology, Ann Arbor, MI 48109. Offers biopsychology (PhD); clinical science (PhD); cognition and cognitive neuroscience (PhD); developmental psychology (PhD); personality and social contexts (PhD); social psychology (PhD). *Accreditation:* APA. *Faculty:* 60 full-time (28 women), 30 part-time/adjunct (18 women). *Students:* 147 full-time (111 women); includes 64 minority (15 Black or African American, non-Hispanic/Latino; 1 American Indian or Alaska Native, non-Hispanic/Latino; 14 Asian, non-Hispanic/Latino; 27 Hispanic/Latino; 7 Two or more races, non-Hispanic/Latino), 19 international. Average age 27. 727 applicants, 8% accepted, 34 enrolled. In 2016, 28 doctorates awarded. *Degree requirements:* For doctorate, comprehensive exam, thesis/dissertation, oral defense of dissertation, preliminary exam. *Entrance requirements:* For doctorate, GRE General Test. Additional exam requirements/recommendations for international students: Required—TOEFL. *Application deadline:* For fall admission, 12/1 for domestic and international students. *Application fee:* $75 ($90 for international students). Electronic applications accepted. *Expenses:* Tuition, state resident: full-time $21,466; part-time $1152 per credit hour. Tuition, nonresident: full-time $43,346; part-time $2367 per credit hour. Part-time tuition and fees vary according to course load, degree level and program. *Financial support:* In 2016–17, 104 students received support, including 64 fellowships with full tuition reimbursements available (averaging $19,800 per year), 6 research assistantships with full tuition reimbursements available (averaging $24,243 per year), 71 teaching assistantships with full tuition reimbursements available (averaging $25,136 per year); career-related internships or fieldwork, traineeships, and health care benefits also available. Financial award application deadline: 4/15. *Unit head:* Prof. Patricia Reuter-Lorenz, Department Chair, 734-764-7429. *Application contact:* Sheri M. Circele, Psychology Student Academic Affairs, 734-764-2580, Fax: 734-764-3520, E-mail: psych.saa@umich.edu.
Website: http://www.lsa.umich.edu/psych/

**University of Michigan,** Rackham Graduate School, College of Literature, Science, and the Arts, Department of Women's Studies, Ann Arbor, MI 48109. Offers English and women's studies (PhD); history and women's studies (PhD); LGBTQ studies (Certificate); psychology and women's studies (PhD); women's studies (Certificate). *Degree requirements:* For doctorate, variable foreign language requirement, comprehensive exam (for some programs), thesis/dissertation. *Entrance requirements:* For doctorate, GRE General Test, previous undergraduate coursework in women's studies. Electronic applications accepted. *Expenses:* Tuition, state resident: full-time $21,466; part-time $1152 per credit hour. Tuition, nonresident: full-time $43,346; part-time $2367 per credit hour. Part-time tuition and fees vary according to course load,

## *Psychology—General*

degree level and program. *Faculty research:* LGBTQ studies, sexuality studies, feminist science studies, global feminism, health studies, international studies, cultural studies.

**University of Michigan,** Rackham Graduate School, Combined Program in Education and Psychology, Ann Arbor, MI 48109. Offers PhD. *Accreditation:* TEAC. *Faculty:* 20 part-time/adjunct (11 women). *Students:* 34 full-time (25 women); includes 20 minority (13 Black or African American, non-Hispanic/Latino; 3 Asian, non-Hispanic/Latino; 4 Hispanic/Latino). Average age 27. 110 applicants, 8% accepted, 6 enrolled. In 2016, 9 doctorates awarded. *Degree requirements:* For doctorate, thesis/dissertation, independent research project, preliminary exam, oral defense of dissertation. *Entrance requirements:* For doctorate, GRE General Test with Analytical Writing Test. Additional exam requirements/recommendations for international students: Required—TOEFL (minimum score 600 paper-based; 100 iBT). *Application deadline:* For fall admission, 12/1 for domestic and international students. Application fee: $75. Electronic applications accepted. *Expenses:* Contact institution. *Financial support:* In 2016–17, 34 students received support, including 16 fellowships with full tuition reimbursements available (averaging $29,605 per year), 3 research assistantships with full tuition reimbursements available (averaging $27,737 per year), 15 teaching assistantships with full tuition reimbursements available (averaging $27,737 per year); institutionally sponsored loans, scholarships/grants, health care benefits, and unspecified assistantships also available. Financial award application deadline: 4/15. *Faculty research:* Human development in context of schools, families, communities; cognitive and learning sciences; motivation and self-regulated learning; culture, ethnicity, social and class influences on learning and motivation. *Unit head:* Dr. Stephanie J. Rowley, Chair, 734-647-0626, Fax: 734-615-2164, E-mail: srowley@umich.edu. *Application contact:* Katie Schmitt, Program Coordinator, 734-763-0680, Fax: 734-615-2164, E-mail: cpep@umich.edu.
Website: http://www.soe.umich.edu/academics/doctoral_programs/ep/

**University of Michigan,** School of Social Work, Interdisciplinary PhD Program in Social Work and Social Science, Ann Arbor, MI 48109-1106. Offers social work and anthropology (PhD); social work and economics (PhD); social work and political science (PhD); social work and psychology (PhD); social work and sociology (PhD). Programs offered through the Rackham Graduate School. *Faculty:* 50 full-time (29 women), 62 part-time/adjunct (48 women). *Students:* 59 full-time (42 women); includes 30 minority (14 Black or African American, non-Hispanic/Latino; 9 Asian, non-Hispanic/Latino; 7 Hispanic/Latino). Average age 32. 114 applicants, 7% accepted, 8 enrolled. In 2016, 8 doctorates awarded. *Degree requirements:* For doctorate, thesis/dissertation, oral defense of dissertation, preliminary exam. *Entrance requirements:* For doctorate, GRE General Test. Additional exam requirements/recommendations for international students: Required—TOEFL (minimum score 620 paper-based, 88 iBT) or IELTS. *Application deadline:* For fall admission, 12/1 for domestic and international students. Application fee: $75 ($90 for international students). Electronic applications accepted. *Expenses:* $42,016 fall/winter tuition. *Financial support:* In 2016–17, 59 students received support, including 20 fellowships with full tuition reimbursements available (averaging $15,200 per year), 8 research assistantships with full tuition reimbursements available (averaging $19,737 per year), 17 teaching assistantships with full tuition reimbursements available (averaging $19,737 per year); career-related internships or fieldwork, scholarships/grants, traineeships, health care benefits, tuition waivers (full and partial), and unspecified assistantships also available. Financial award application deadline: 12/1; financial award applicants required to submit FAFSA. *Faculty research:* Children and family, aging, community organization, health and mental health, police and evaluation. *Total annual research expenditures:* $3.8 million. *Unit head:* Dr. Daphne C. Watkins, Director, 734-763-5768, E-mail: daphnew@umich.edu. *Application contact:* Todd Huynh, Graduate Coordinator, 734-647-2554, Fax: 734-615-3192, E-mail: ssw.phd.info@umich.edu.
Website: https://ssw.umich.edu/offices/phd

**University of Minnesota, Twin Cities Campus,** Graduate School, College of Liberal Arts, Department of Psychology, Minneapolis, MN 55455-0213. Offers biological psychopathology (PhD); clinical psychology (PhD); cognitive and biological psychology (PhD); counseling psychology (PhD); industrial/organizational psychology (PhD); personality, individual differences, and behavior genetics (PhD); quantitative/psychometric methods (PhD); school psychology (PhD); social psychology (PhD). *Accreditation:* APA. *Degree requirements:* For doctorate, comprehensive exam, thesis/dissertation. *Entrance requirements:* For doctorate, GRE General Test, GRE Subject Test (recommended), 12 credits of upper-level psychology courses, including a course in statistics or psychological measurement. Additional exam requirements/recommendations for international students: Required—TOEFL (minimum score 79 iBT).

**University of Missouri,** Office of Research and Graduate Studies, College of Arts and Science, Department of Psychological Sciences, Columbia, MO 65211. Offers MA, MS, PhD. *Accreditation:* APA (one or more programs are accredited). *Faculty:* 46 full-time (19 women), 2 part-time/adjunct (1 woman). *Students:* 77 full-time (53 women), 6 part-time (4 women). Terminal master's awarded for partial completion of doctoral program. *Degree requirements:* For doctorate, comprehensive exam, thesis/dissertation. *Entrance requirements:* For master's, GRE General Test, minimum GPA of 3.0; for doctorate, GRE General Test; GRE Subject Test (strongly recommended), minimum GPA of 3.0. Additional exam requirements/recommendations for international students: Required—TOEFL (minimum score 500 paper-based; 61 iBT). *Application deadline:* For fall admission, 12/1 priority date for domestic and international students. Applications are processed on a rolling basis. Application fee: $75 ($90 for international students). Electronic applications accepted. *Expenses:* Tuition, state resident: full-time $6347; part-time $352.60 per credit hour. Tuition, nonresident: full-time $17,379; part-time $965.50 per credit hour. *Required fees:* $1035. Tuition and fees vary according to course load, campus/location and program. *Financial support:* Fellowships with full tuition reimbursements, research assistantships with full tuition reimbursements, teaching assistantships with full tuition reimbursements, career-related internships or fieldwork, institutionally sponsored loans, traineeships, health care benefits, and unspecified assistantships available.
Website: http://psychology.missouri.edu/grad

**University of Missouri–Kansas City,** College of Arts and Sciences, Department of Psychology, Kansas City, MO 64110-2499. Offers community psychology (PhD). PhD (interdisciplinary) offered through the School of Graduate Studies. *Accreditation:* APA. *Faculty:* 12 full-time (8 women). *Students:* 18 full-time (13 women), 13 part-time (9 women); includes 5 minority (1 Black or African American, non-Hispanic/Latino; 3 Hispanic/Latino; 1 Two or more races, non-Hispanic/Latino), 1 international. Average age 30. 85 applicants, 6% accepted, 5 enrolled. In 2016, 4 master's, 3 doctorates awarded. Terminal master's awarded for partial completion of doctoral program. *Degree requirements:* For master's, thesis; for doctorate, comprehensive exam, thesis/dissertation, residency. *Entrance requirements:* For master's, GRE, minimum GPA of 3.5, letter of recommendation; for doctorate, GRE, minimum GPA of 3.25. Additional exam requirements/recommendations for international students: Required—TOEFL (minimum score 550 paper-based; 80 iBT). *Application deadline:* For fall admission, 1/15 for domestic and international students. Applications are processed on a rolling basis. Application fee: $45 ($50 for international students). Electronic applications accepted. *Financial support:* In 2016–17, 1 research assistantship (averaging $12,000 per year), 14 teaching assistantships (averaging $12,684 per year) were awarded; career-related internships or fieldwork, Federal Work-Study, and institutionally sponsored loans also available. Support available to part-time students. Financial award application deadline: 3/1; financial award applicants required to submit FAFSA. *Faculty research:* HIV/AIDS research group, psycho-oncology, sensory and cognitive neuroscience, cognitive psychophysiology, obesity and related metabolic disorders. *Unit head:* Dr. Jennifer Lundgren, Department Chair, 816-235-5384, Fax: 816-235-1062, E-mail: lundgrenj@umkc.edu. *Application contact:* Dr. Cathy Rawlings, Director, Graduate Programs, 816-235-1318, Fax: 816-235-1062, E-mail: psychology@umkc.edu.
Website: http://cas.umkc.edu/psyc

**University of Missouri–St. Louis,** College of Arts and Sciences, Department of Psychological Sciences, St. Louis, MO 63121. Offers behavioral neuroscience (MA, PhD); clinical psychology (PhD); clinical psychology respecialization (Certificate); industrial/organizational psychology (MA, PhD); trauma studies (Certificate). *Accreditation:* APA (one or more programs are accredited). *Program availability:* Evening/weekend. *Faculty:* 1 full-time (0 women). *Students:* 73 full-time (54 women), 13 part-time (9 women); includes 13 minority (4 Black or African American, non-Hispanic/Latino; 2 Asian, non-Hispanic/Latino; 6 Hispanic/Latino; 1 Two or more races, non-Hispanic/Latino), 3 international. Average age 27. 235 applicants, 8% accepted, 18 enrolled. Terminal master's awarded for partial completion of doctoral program. *Degree requirements:* For master's, thesis; for doctorate, thesis/dissertation. *Entrance requirements:* For master's, GRE General Test, 3 letters of recommendation; for doctorate, GRE General Test, GRE Subject Test, 3 letters of recommendation. Additional exam requirements/recommendations for international students: Required—TOEFL (minimum score 550 paper-based; 79 iBT), IELTS (minimum score 6.5). *Application deadline:* For fall admission, 12/15 for domestic and international students. Application fee: $50 ($40 for international students). Electronic applications accepted. *Financial support:* Fellowships with full tuition reimbursements, research assistantships with tuition reimbursements, teaching assistantships with tuition reimbursements, and scholarships/grants available. Financial award applicants required to submit FAFSA. *Faculty research:* Bereavement and loss, neuroscience, post-traumatic stress disorder, conflict and negotiation, social psychology. *Unit head:* Michael G. Griffin, Chair, 314-516-5391, Fax: 314-516-5392, E-mail: michael_griffin@umsl.edu. *Application contact:* 314-516-5458, Fax: 314-516-6996, E-mail: gradadm@umsl.edu.
Website: http://www.umsl.edu/divisions/artscience/psychology/

**University of Montana,** Graduate School, College of Humanities and Sciences, Department of Psychology, Missoula, MT 59812-0002. Offers clinical psychology (PhD); experimental psychology (PhD), including animal behavior psychology, developmental psychology; school psychology (MA, PhD, Ed S). *Accreditation:* APA (one or more programs are accredited). Terminal master's awarded for partial completion of doctoral program. *Degree requirements:* For master's, thesis; for doctorate, thesis/dissertation. *Entrance requirements:* For master's, doctorate, and Ed S, GRE General Test. Additional exam requirements/recommendations for international students: Required—TOEFL.

**University of Nebraska at Omaha,** Graduate Studies, College of Arts and Sciences, Department of Psychology, Omaha, NE 68182. Offers applied behavior analysis (Certificate); human resources and training (Certificate); industrial/organizational psychology (MS); psychology (MA, PhD); school psychology (MS, Ed S). *Program availability:* Part-time. *Faculty:* 10 full-time (1 woman). *Students:* 70 full-time (52 women), 49 part-time (33 women); includes 9 minority (2 Asian, non-Hispanic/Latino; 5 Hispanic/Latino; 2 Two or more races, non-Hispanic/Latino), 1 international. Average age 27. 157 applicants, 25% accepted, 38 enrolled. In 2016, 32 master's, 6 doctorates, 10 other advanced degrees awarded. *Degree requirements:* For master's, comprehensive exam, thesis (for some programs); for doctorate, comprehensive exam, thesis/dissertation. *Entrance requirements:* For master's and doctorate, GRE, minimum GPA of 3.0, official transcripts, 3 letters of recommendation, statement of purpose, writing sample, resume. Additional exam requirements/recommendations for international students: Required—TOEFL, IELTS, PTE. *Application deadline:* For fall admission, 1/5 priority date for domestic and international students. Application fee: $45. Electronic applications accepted. *Financial support:* In 2016–17, 50 students received support, including 23 research assistantships with tuition reimbursements available, 27 teaching assistantships with tuition reimbursements available; fellowships with tuition reimbursements available, career-related internships or fieldwork, Federal Work-Study, institutionally sponsored loans, scholarships/grants, health care benefits, tuition waivers (partial), and unspecified assistantships also available. Financial award application deadline: 3/1; financial award applicants required to submit FAFSA. *Unit head:* Dr. Brigette Ryalls, Chairperson, 402-554-2341, E-mail: graduate@unomaha.edu. *Application contact:* Dr. Joseph Brown, Graduate Program Chair, 402-554-2341, E-mail: graduate@unomaha.edu.

**University of Nebraska–Lincoln,** Graduate College, College of Arts and Sciences, Department of Psychology, Lincoln, NE 68588. Offers biopsychology (PhD); clinical psychology (PhD); cognitive psychology (PhD); developmental psychology (PhD); psychology (MA); social/personality psychology (PhD); JD/MA; JD/PhD. *Accreditation:* APA (one or more programs are accredited). *Degree requirements:* For master's, thesis optional; for doctorate, comprehensive exam, thesis/dissertation. *Entrance requirements:* For master's and doctorate, GRE General Test. Additional exam requirements/recommendations for international students: Required—TOEFL (minimum score 550 paper-based). Electronic applications accepted. *Faculty research:* Law and psychology, rural mental health, chronic mental illness, neuropsychology, child clinical psychology.

**University of Nevada, Las Vegas,** Graduate College, College of Liberal Arts, Department of Psychology, Las Vegas, NV 89154-5030. Offers MA, PhD, Certificate. *Program availability:* Part-time. *Faculty:* 14 full-time (4 women), 3 part-time/adjunct (2 women). *Students:* 64 full-time (47 women), 11 part-time (10 women); includes 13 minority (1 Asian, non-Hispanic/Latino; 9 Hispanic/Latino; 3 Two or more races, non-Hispanic/Latino), 5 international. Average age 29. 109 applicants, 18% accepted, 16 enrolled. In 2016, 11 master's, 6 doctorates awarded. *Degree requirements:* For doctorate, comprehensive exam, thesis/dissertation, oral defense of dissertation. *Entrance requirements:* For doctorate, GRE General and Subject Tests, bachelor's degree with minimum GPA of 3.2 or master's degree with minimum GPA of 3.5; 3 recommendation letters; statement of purpose; interview. Additional exam requirements/recommendations for international students: Required—TOEFL (minimum score 550 paper-based; 80 iBT), IELTS (minimum score 7). *Application deadline:* For fall admission, 12/1 for domestic students. Application fee: $60 ($95 for international students). Electronic applications accepted. *Expenses:* $269.25 per credit, $792 per 3-credit course; $9,634 per year resident; $23,274 per year non-resident; $7,094 fees non-resident (7 credits or more); $1,307 annual health insurance fee. *Financial support:* In 2016–17, 3 fellowships with partial tuition reimbursements (averaging $18,333 per year), 32 research assistantships with partial tuition reimbursements (averaging $16,000 per year), 28 teaching assistantships with partial tuition reimbursements (averaging $15,500 per year) were awarded; institutionally sponsored loans, scholarships/grants, health care benefits, and unspecified assistantships also available. Financial award application deadline: 3/15. *Faculty research:* School absenteeism and selective autism,

schizophrenia and bipolar disorders, biomarkers for dementia and mental disorders, infant cognition and development, affective and cognitive neuroscience. *Total annual research expenditures:* $832,307. *Unit head:* Dr. Christopher Kearney, Chair/Professor, 702-895-0183, Fax: 702-895-0195, E-mail: chris.kearney@unlv.edu. *Application contact:* Dr. Jennifer Rennels, Graduate Coordinator, 702-895-0648, Fax: 702-895-0195, E-mail: jennifer.rennels@unlv.edu.
Website: http://psychology.unlv.edu/

**University of Nevada, Reno,** Graduate School, College of Liberal Arts, Department of Psychology, Reno, NV 89557. Offers behavior analysis (MA, PhD); clinical psychology (MA, PhD); cognitive brain science (MA, PhD). *Accreditation:* APA (one or more programs are accredited). Terminal master's awarded for partial completion of doctoral program. *Degree requirements:* For master's, thesis optional; for doctorate, thesis/dissertation. *Entrance requirements:* For master's, GRE General Test, GRE Subject Test, minimum GPA of 2.75; for doctorate, GRE General Test, GRE Subject Test, minimum GPA of 3.0. Additional exam requirements/recommendations for international students: Required—TOEFL (minimum score 500 paper-based; 61 iBT), IELTS (minimum score 6). Electronic applications accepted. *Faculty research:* Cognitive psychology, social psychological theory, animal and human intelligence, psychotherapy outcome, perception.

**University of New Brunswick Fredericton,** School of Graduate Studies, Faculty of Arts, Department of Psychology, Fredericton, NB E3B 5A3, Canada. Offers MA, PhD. *Program availability:* Part-time. *Degree requirements:* For doctorate, comprehensive exam, thesis/dissertation. *Entrance requirements:* For master's, BA (honors) in psychology or equivalent research experience; for doctorate, minimum GPA of 3.7. Additional exam requirements/recommendations for international students: Required—TOEFL (minimum score 600 paper-based). Electronic applications accepted. *Faculty research:* Brain-behavior relationships, cognitive science, social psychology, marginalized groups, human sexuality, sport and exercise psychology, child and adolescent development, health psychology.

**University of New Brunswick Saint John,** Department of Psychology, Saint John, NB E2L 4L5, Canada. Offers clinical psychology (PhD); experimental psychology (MA, PhD). *Program availability:* Part-time. *Degree requirements:* For master's, thesis. *Entrance requirements:* For master's, GRE General and Subject Tests, honors thesis; minimum GPA of 3.7. Additional exam requirements/recommendations for international students: Required—TOEFL (minimum score 550 paper-based), TWE. Electronic applications accepted. *Faculty research:* Forensic psychology, peer relationships and social skills, polygraph techniques, addictions, attachment and social adjustment, neuroscience, optical illusions, graphical perception, associative learning in animals, bio-psychology.

**University of New Hampshire,** Graduate School, College of Liberal Arts, Department of Psychology, Durham, NH 03824. Offers PhD. *Degree requirements:* For doctorate, thesis/dissertation. *Entrance requirements:* For doctorate, GRE General Test, GRE Subject Test. Additional exam requirements/recommendations for international students: Required—TOEFL (minimum score 550 paper-based; 80 iBT). Electronic applications accepted. *Faculty research:* History of psychology; cognition and perception; learning, developmental, physiological, and social psychology.

**University of New Mexico,** Graduate Studies, College of Arts and Sciences, Program in Psychology, Albuquerque, NM 87131-2039. Offers behavioral neuroscience (PhD); clinical psychology (PhD); cognitive neuroimaging (PhD); developmental psychology (PhD); evolution (PhD); health psychology (PhD); quantitative methodology (PhD). *Accreditation:* APA. *Faculty:* 23 full-time (8 women), 1 part-time/adjunct (0 women). *Students:* 60 full-time (36 women), 16 part-time (10 women); includes 22 minority (2 Black or African American, non-Hispanic/Latino; 2 American Indian or Alaska Native, non-Hispanic/Latino; 3 Asian, non-Hispanic/Latino; 12 Hispanic/Latino; 3 Two or more races, non-Hispanic/Latino), 2 international. Average age 30. 227 applicants, 11% accepted, 16 enrolled. In 2016, 10 doctorates awarded. *Degree requirements:* For doctorate, comprehensive exam, thesis/dissertation. *Entrance requirements:* For doctorate, GRE General Test, GRE Subject Test (psychology), minimum GPA of 3.0. Additional exam requirements/recommendations for international students: Required—TOEFL (minimum score 550 paper-based; 79 iBT), IELTS (minimum score 6.5). *Application deadline:* For fall admission, 12/15 priority date for domestic and international students. Applications are processed on a rolling basis. Application fee: $50. Electronic applications accepted. *Financial support:* Fellowships, research assistantships with tuition reimbursements, teaching assistantships with tuition reimbursements, career-related internships or fieldwork, Federal Work-Study, institutionally sponsored loans, scholarships/grants, health care benefits, tuition waivers (partial), and unspecified assistantships available. Financial award application deadline: 3/1; financial award applicants required to submit FAFSA. *Faculty research:* Addiction, cognition, brain and behavior, developmental, evolutionary, functioning neuroimaging, health psychology, learning and memory, neuroscience. *Total annual research expenditures:* $727,970. *Unit head:* Dr. Jane Ellen Smith, Department Chair, 505-277-4121, Fax: 505-277-1394. *Application contact:* Rikk Murphy, Graduate Program Coordinator, 505-277-5009, Fax: 505-277-1394, E-mail: advising@unm.edu.
Website: http://psych.unm.edu

**University of New Orleans,** Graduate School, College of Sciences, Department of Psychology, New Orleans, LA 70148. Offers MS, PhD. *Degree requirements:* For doctorate, thesis/dissertation. *Entrance requirements:* For doctorate, GRE General Test, minimum GPA of 3.0, 21 hours of course work in psychology. Additional exam requirements/recommendations for international students: Required—TOEFL (minimum score 550 paper-based; 79 iBT), IELTS. Electronic applications accepted. *Faculty research:* Biofeedback, visual and auditory perception, psychopharmacology, neuropeptides.

**The University of North Carolina at Chapel Hill,** Graduate School, College of Arts and Sciences, Department of Psychology, Chapel Hill, NC 27599-3270. Offers behavioral neuroscience psychology (PhD); clinical psychology (PhD); cognitive psychology (PhD); developmental psychology (PhD); quantitative psychology (PhD); social psychology (PhD). *Accreditation:* APA. *Degree requirements:* For doctorate, comprehensive exam, thesis/dissertation. *Entrance requirements:* For doctorate, GRE General Test, minimum GPA of 3.0. Additional exam requirements/recommendations for international students: Required—TOEFL (minimum score 550 paper-based; 79 iBT), IELTS (minimum score 7). Electronic applications accepted. *Faculty research:* Expressed emotion, cognitive development, social cognitive neuroscience, human memory personality.

**The University of North Carolina at Charlotte,** College of Liberal Arts and Sciences, Department of Psychology, Charlotte, NC 28223-0001. Offers cognitive science (Graduate Certificate); health psychology (PhD); industrial/organizational psychology (MA); psychology (MA). *Accreditation:* APA. *Program availability:* Part-time. *Faculty:* 32 full-time (21 women), 1 (woman) part-time/adjunct. *Students:* 37 full-time (32 women), 38 part-time (26 women); includes 19 minority (7 Black or African American, non-Hispanic/Latino; 1 Asian, non-Hispanic/Latino; 8 Hispanic/Latino; 3 Two or more races, non-Hispanic/Latino). Average age 28. 331 applicants, 16% accepted, 28 enrolled. In 2016, 13 master's, 5 doctorates, 3 other advanced degrees awarded. *Degree requirements:* For master's, thesis (for some programs); for doctorate, comprehensive

exam, thesis/dissertation, internship (clinical health students only). *Entrance requirements:* For master's, GRE, GMAT, MAT; for doctorate, GRE, at least 18 hours of coursework in psychology including introductory psychology and research methods, undergraduate course in statistics, transcripts of all academic work attempted since high school including evidence of the completion of a bachelor's degree, at least three references, personal statement, resume or curriculum vitae; for Graduate Certificate, enrolled and in good standing in a graduate degree program at UNC Charlotte, or have minimum GPA of 3.0 for undergraduate courses. Additional exam requirements/recommendations for international students: Required—TOEFL (minimum score 523 paper-based, 70 iBT) or IELTS (6.5). *Application deadline:* For fall admission, 11/15 for domestic and international students. Applications are processed on a rolling basis. Application fee: $75. Electronic applications accepted. *Expenses:* Contact institution. *Financial support:* In 2016–17, 30 students received support, including 1 fellowship (averaging $42,000 per year), 11 research assistantships (averaging $15,622 per year), 18 teaching assistantships (averaging $14,000 per year); career-related internships or fieldwork, Federal Work-Study, institutionally sponsored loans, scholarships/grants, and unspecified assistantships also available. Support available to part-time students. Financial award application deadline: 3/1; financial award applicants required to submit FAFSA. *Total annual research expenditures:* $218,743. *Unit head:* Dr. Fary Cachelin, Chair, 704-687-1315, E-mail: fcacheli@uncc.edu. *Application contact:* Kathy B. Giddings, Director of Graduate Admissions, 704-687-5503, Fax: 704-687-1668, E-mail: gradadm@uncc.edu.
Website: http://psych.uncc.edu

**The University of North Carolina at Greensboro,** Graduate School, College of Arts and Sciences, Department of Psychology, Greensboro, NC 27412-5001. Offers clinical psychology (MA, PhD); cognitive psychology (MA, PhD); developmental psychology (MA, PhD); social psychology (MA, PhD). *Accreditation:* APA (one or more programs are accredited). Terminal master's awarded for partial completion of doctoral program. *Degree requirements:* For master's, comprehensive, thesis; for doctorate, one foreign language, thesis/dissertation, preliminary exam. *Entrance requirements:* For master's and doctorate, GRE General Test. Additional exam requirements/recommendations for international students: Required—TOEFL. Electronic applications accepted. *Faculty research:* Sensory and perceptual determinants; evoked potential: disorders, deafness, and development.

**The University of North Carolina Wilmington,** College of Arts and Sciences, Department of Psychology, Wilmington, NC 28403-3297. Offers psychology (MA), including applied behavior analysis. *Program availability:* Part-time. *Faculty:* 28 full-time (17 women). *Students:* 32 full-time (26 women), 41 part-time (29 women); includes 6 minority (2 Asian, non-Hispanic/Latino; 4 Hispanic/Latino). Average age 25. 122 applicants, 25% accepted, 24 enrolled. In 2016, 17 master's awarded. *Degree requirements:* For master's, comprehensive exam, thesis. *Entrance requirements:* For master's, GRE General Test, GRE Subject Test, minimum B average in undergraduate work, 3 letters of recommendation, statement of interest, resume. Additional exam requirements/recommendations for international students: Required—TOEFL (minimum score 79 iBT), IELTS (minimum score 6.5). *Application deadline:* For fall admission, 1/15 for domestic students. Applications are processed on a rolling basis. Application fee: $60. Electronic applications accepted. *Expenses:* Contact institution. *Financial support:* Research assistantships, teaching assistantships, Federal Work-Study, unspecified assistantships, and out-of-state tuition remission available. Financial award application deadline: 3/15; financial award applicants required to submit FAFSA. *Unit head:* Dr. Julian Keith, Chair, 910-962-3378, Fax: 910-962-7010, E-mail: keithj@uncw.edu. *Application contact:* Dr. Christine Hughes, Graduate Coordinator, 910-962-7795, Fax: 910-962-7010, E-mail: hughesc@uncw.edu.
Website: http://www.uncw.edu/psy/grad/

**University of North Dakota,** Graduate School, College of Arts and Sciences, Department of Psychology, Grand Forks, ND 58202. Offers clinical psychology (PhD); forensic psychology (MA, MS). *Accreditation:* APA (one or more programs are accredited). *Degree requirements:* For master's, thesis, final exam; for doctorate, comprehensive exam, thesis/dissertation, internship, final exam. *Entrance requirements:* For master's, GRE General Test, GRE Subject Test, minimum GPA of 3.0; for doctorate, GRE General Test, GRE Subject Test, minimum GPA of 3.5. Additional exam requirements/recommendations for international students: Required—TOEFL (minimum score 550 paper-based; 79 iBT), IELTS (minimum score 6.5). *Application deadline:* For fall admission, 1/15 for domestic and international students. Application fee: $35. Electronic applications accepted. *Financial support:* Fellowships with full and partial tuition reimbursements, research assistantships with full and partial tuition reimbursements, teaching assistantships with full and partial tuition reimbursements, career-related internships or fieldwork, Federal Work-Study, institutionally sponsored loans, scholarships/grants, health care benefits, tuition waivers (full and partial), and unspecified assistantships available. Support available to part-time students. Financial award application deadline: 3/15; financial award applicants required to submit FAFSA. *Faculty research:* Developmental psychology, clinical social psychology, educational psychology, personality disorders. *Unit head:* Dr. Mark Grabe, Chairperson, 701-777-3451, E-mail: mark.grabe@und.nodak.edu. *Application contact:* Matt Anderson, Admissions Specialist, 701-777-2947, Fax: 701-777-3619, E-mail: matthew.anderson@gradschool.und.edu.
Website: http://arts-sciences.und.edu/psychology/

**University of Northern British Columbia,** Office of Graduate Studies, Prince George, BC V2N 4Z9, Canada. Offers business administration (Diploma); community health science (M Sc); disability management (MA); education (M Ed); first nations studies (MA); gender studies (MA); history (MA); interdisciplinary studies (MA); international studies (MA); mathematical, computer and physical sciences (M Sc); natural resources and environmental studies (M Sc, MA, MNRES, PhD); political science (MA); psychology (M Sc, PhD); social work (MSW). *Program availability:* Part-time, evening/weekend, online learning. *Degree requirements:* For master's, thesis; for doctorate, thesis/dissertation. *Entrance requirements:* For master's, GRE, minimum B average in undergraduate course work; for doctorate, candidacy exam, minimum A average in graduate course work.

**University of Northern Colorado,** Graduate School, College of Education and Behavioral Sciences, School of Psychological Sciences, Greeley, CO 80639. Offers MA, PhD. *Program availability:* Part-time. *Degree requirements:* For master's, comprehensive exam, thesis or alternative; for doctorate, comprehensive exam, thesis/dissertation. *Entrance requirements:* For master's and doctorate, GRE General Test, letters of recommendation. *Application deadline:* Applications are processed on a rolling basis. Application fee: $50 ($60 for international students). Electronic applications accepted. *Financial support:* Fellowships, research assistantships, teaching assistantships, and unspecified assistantships available. Financial award application deadline: 3/1; financial award applicants required to submit FAFSA. *Unit head:* Dr. Mark Alcorn, Director, 970-351-2957, Fax: 970-351-1103. *Application contact:* Linda Sisson, Graduate Student Admission Coordinator, 970-351-1807, Fax: 970-351-2371, E-mail: linda.sisson@unco.edu.
Website: http://www.unco.edu/cebs/psychsci

*Psychology—General*

**University of Northern Iowa,** Graduate College, College of Social and Behavioral Sciences, Department of Psychology, Cedar Falls, IA 50614. Offers MA. *Program availability:* Part-time. *Degree requirements:* For master's, comprehensive exam, thesis. *Entrance requirements:* For master's, GRE, minimum GPA of 3.0, 3 letters of recommendation. Additional exam requirements/recommendations for international students: Required—TOEFL (minimum score 500 paper-based; 61 iBT). Electronic applications accepted.

**University of North Florida,** College of Arts and Sciences, Department of Psychology, Jacksonville, FL 32224. Offers counseling psychology (MAC); general psychology (MA). *Program availability:* Part-time, evening/weekend. *Faculty:* 18 full-time (12 women), 1 part-time/adjunct (0 women). *Students:* 34 full-time (19 women), 4 part-time (3 women); includes 6 minority (1 Black or African American, non-Hispanic/Latino; 4 Hispanic/Latino; 1 Two or more races, non-Hispanic/Latino), 1 international. Average age 27. 72 applicants, 42% accepted, 17 enrolled. *Degree requirements:* For master's, comprehensive exam, thesis optional, practicum. *Entrance requirements:* For master's, GRE General Test, 2 letters of recommendation, minimum GPA of 3.0 in last 60 hours of course work. Additional exam requirements/recommendations for international students: Required—TOEFL (minimum score 500 paper-based; 61 iBT). *Application deadline:* For fall admission, 6/1 priority date for domestic students, 4/1 for international students. Application fee: $30. Electronic applications accepted. Tuition and fees vary according to course load, campus/location and program. *Financial support:* In 2016–17, 17 students received support, including 1 research assistantship (averaging $6,400 per year), 5 teaching assistantships (averaging $3,920 per year); Federal Work-Study, scholarships/grants, and tuition waivers (partial) also available. Financial award application deadline: 4/1; financial award applicants required to submit FAFSA. *Faculty research:* Sensory perception, social cognition, sexual behavior, evolutionary psychology, psychology and law. *Total annual research expenditures:* $145,456. *Unit head:* Dr. Lori Lange, Chair, 904-620-1638, E-mail: llange@unf.edu. *Application contact:* Dr. Amanda Pascale, Director, The Graduate School, 904-620-1360, Fax: 904-620-1362, E-mail: graduateschool@unf.edu. Website: http://www.unf.edu/coas/psychology/

**University of North Texas,** Robert B. Toulouse School of Graduate Studies, Denton, TX 76203-5459. Offers accounting (MS); applied anthropology (MA, MS); applied behavior analysis (Certificate); applied geography (MA); applied technology and performance improvement (M Ed, MS); art education (MA); art history (MA); art museum education (Certificate); arts leadership (Certificate); audiology (Au D); behavior analysis (MS); behavioral science (PhD); biochemistry and molecular biology (MA, MS); biology (MA, MS); biomedical engineering (MS); business analysis (MS); chemistry (MS); clinical health psychology (PhD); communication studies (MA, MS); computer engineering (MS); computer science (MS); counseling (M Ed, MS), including clinical mental health counseling (MS), college and university counseling, elementary school counseling, secondary school counseling; creative writing (MA); criminal justice (MS); curriculum and instruction (M Ed); decision sciences (MBA); design (MA, MFA), including fashion design (MFA), innovation studies, interior design (MFA); early childhood studies (MS); economics (MS); educational leadership (M Ed, Ed D); educational psychology (MS, PhD), including family studies (MS), gifted and talented (MS), human development (MS), learning and cognition (MS), research, measurement and evaluation (MS); electrical engineering (MS); emergency management (MPA); engineering technology (MS); English (MA); English as a second language (MA); environmental science (MS); finance (MBA, MS); financial management (MPA); French (MA); health services management (MBA); higher education (M Ed, Ed D); history (MA, MS); hospitality management (MS); human resources management (MPA); information science (MS); information systems (PhD); information technologies (MBA); interdisciplinary studies (MA, MS); international studies (MA); international sustainable tourism (MS); jazz studies (MM); journalism (MA, MJ, Graduate Certificate), including interactive and virtual digital communication (Graduate Certificate), narrative journalism (Graduate Certificate), public relations (Graduate Certificate); kinesiology (MS); linguistics (MA); local government management (MPA); logistics (PhD); logistics and supply chain management (MBA); long-term care, senior housing, and aging services (MA); management (PhD); marketing (MBA); mathematics (MS); mechanical and energy engineering (MS, PhD); music (MA), including ethnomusicology, music theory, musicology, performance; music composition (PhD); music education (MM Ed, PhD); nonprofit management (MPA); operations and supply chain management (MBA); performance (MM, DMA); philosophy (MA); political science (MA); professional and technical communication (MA); radio, television and film (MA, MFA); rehabilitation counseling (Certificate); sociology (MA); Spanish (MA); special education (M Ed); speech-language pathology (MA); strategic management (MBA); studio art (MFA); teaching (M Ed); MBA/MS. *Program availability:* Part-time, evening/weekend, online learning. Terminal master's awarded for partial completion of doctoral program. *Degree requirements:* For master's, variable foreign language requirement, comprehensive exam (for some programs), thesis (for some programs); for doctorate, variable foreign language requirement, comprehensive exam (for some programs), thesis/dissertation; for other advanced degree, variable foreign language requirement, comprehensive exam (for some programs). *Entrance requirements:* For master's and doctorate, GRE, GMAT. Additional exam requirements/recommendations for international students: Required—TOEFL (minimum score 550 paper-based; 79 iBT). Electronic applications accepted.

**University of Notre Dame,** Graduate School, College of Arts and Letters, Division of Social Science, Department of Psychology, Notre Dame, IN 46556. Offers cognitive psychology (PhD); counseling psychology (PhD); developmental psychology (PhD); quantitative psychology (PhD). *Accreditation:* APA. *Degree requirements:* For doctorate, comprehensive exam, thesis/dissertation, candidacy exam. *Entrance requirements:* For doctorate, GRE General Test, GRE Subject Test (strongly recommended). Additional exam requirements/recommendations for international students: Required—TOEFL (minimum score 600 paper-based; 80 iBT). Electronic applications accepted. *Faculty research:* Cognitive and socio-emotional development, statistical methods and quantitative models applicable to psychology, interpersonal relations, life span development and developmental delay, childhood depression, structural equation and dynamical systems.

**University of Oklahoma,** College of Arts and Sciences, Department of Psychology, Norman, OK 73019. Offers organizational dynamics (MA, Graduate Certificate), including human resource management, project management; psychology (MS, PhD), including general psychology (MS), industrial-organizational psychology, psychology (PhD). *Faculty:* 24 full-time (11 women). *Students:* 65 full-time (39 women), 32 part-time (20 women); includes 20 minority (2 Black or African American, non-Hispanic/Latino; 4 American Indian or Alaska Native, non-Hispanic/Latino; 5 Asian, non-Hispanic/Latino; 6 Hispanic/Latino; 3 Two or more races, non-Hispanic/Latino), 6 international. Average age 29. 123 applicants, 15% accepted, 18 enrolled. In 2016, 14 master's, 13 doctorates awarded. Terminal master's awarded for partial completion of doctoral program. *Degree requirements:* For master's, comprehensive exam, thesis; for doctorate, comprehensive exam, thesis/dissertation. *Entrance requirements:* For master's and doctorate, GRE. Additional exam requirements/recommendations for international students: Required—TOEFL (minimum score 79 iBT) or IELTS (minimum score 6.5). *Application deadline:* For fall admission, 1/1 for domestic and international students. Application fee: $50 ($100 for international students). Electronic applications accepted. *Expenses:* Tuition,

state resident: full-time $4886; part-time $203.60 per credit hour. Tuition, nonresident: full-time $18,989; part-time $791.20 per credit hour. *Required fees:* $3283; $126.25 per credit hour. $126.50 per semester. *Financial support:* In 2016–17, 70 students received support, including 15 fellowships with full tuition reimbursements available (averaging $2,089 per year), 7 research assistantships with full tuition reimbursements available (averaging $15,610 per year), 43 teaching assistantships with full tuition reimbursements available (averaging $14,777 per year); scholarships/grants, health care benefits, and unspecified assistantships also available. Financial award application deadline: 6/1; financial award applicants required to submit FAFSA. *Faculty research:* Decision making and ethical behavior; behavioral statistics; leadership development; exploratory data analysis; genetic influences on brain activity. *Total annual research expenditures:* $492,410. *Unit head:* Dr. Eric Day, Chair, 405-325-4511, Fax: 405-325-4737, E-mail: eday@ou.edu. *Application contact:* Kathryn Paine, Graduate Student Coordinator, 405-325-4512, Fax: 405-325-4737, E-mail: kpaine@ou.edu. Website: http://www.ou.edu/cas/psychology

**University of Oregon,** Graduate School, College of Arts and Sciences, Department of Psychology, Eugene, OR 97403. Offers clinical psychology (PhD); cognitive psychology (MA, MS, PhD); developmental psychology (MA, MS, PhD); physiological psychology (MA, MS, PhD); psychology (MA, MS, PhD); social/personality psychology (MA, MS, PhD). *Accreditation:* APA (one or more programs are accredited). Terminal master's awarded for partial completion of doctoral program. *Degree requirements:* For doctorate, thesis/dissertation. *Entrance requirements:* For master's, GRE General Test, minimum GPA of 3.0; for doctorate, GRE General Test. Additional exam requirements/recommendations for international students: Required—TOEFL.

**University of Ottawa,** Faculty of Graduate and Postdoctoral Studies, Faculty of Social Sciences, School of Psychology, Ottawa, ON K1N 6N5, Canada. Offers PhD. *Degree requirements:* For doctorate, thesis/dissertation. *Entrance requirements:* For doctorate, minimum B+ average. Electronic applications accepted. *Faculty research:* Behavioral neuroscience, social psychology, developmental psychology, cognition.

**University of Pennsylvania,** School of Arts and Sciences, Graduate Group in Psychology, Philadelphia, PA 19104. Offers PhD. *Accreditation:* APA. *Faculty:* 51 full-time (18 women), 16 part-time/adjunct (4 women). *Students:* 60 full-time (38 women); includes 9 minority (3 Asian, non-Hispanic/Latino; 3 Hispanic/Latino; 3 Two or more races, non-Hispanic/Latino), 12 international. Average age 28. 601 applicants, 3% accepted, 9 enrolled. In 2016, 7 doctorates awarded. *Expenses:* Tuition: Full-time $31,068; part-time $5762 per course. *Required fees:* $3200; $336 per course. Full-time tuition and fees vary according to degree level, program and student level. Part-time tuition and fees vary according to course load, degree level and program. Website: http://psychology.sas.upenn.edu/graduate-program

**University of Philosophical Research,** Master's in Transformational Psychology Program, Los Angeles, CA 90027. Offers MA. *Degree requirements:* For master's, thesis. Electronic applications accepted.

**University of Phoenix–Jersey City Campus,** College of Social Services, Jersey City, NJ 07310. Offers psychology (MS). *Program availability:* Online learning.

**University of Phoenix–Online Campus,** College of Social Science, Phoenix, AZ 85034-7209. Offers mediation (Certificate); psychology (MS), including behavioral health, industrial-organizational, psychology. *Program availability:* Evening/weekend, online learning. *Entrance requirements:* Additional exam requirements/recommendations for international students: Required—TOEFL, TOEIC (Test of English as an International Communication), Berlitz Online English Proficiency Exam, PTE, or IELTS. Electronic applications accepted. *Expenses:* Contact institution.

**University of Phoenix–Phoenix Campus,** College of Social Sciences, Tempe, AZ 85282-2371. Offers counseling (MS), including clinical mental health counseling, community counseling, counseling, marriage, family and child therapy; psychology (MS). *Program availability:* Evening/weekend, online learning. *Entrance requirements:* Additional exam requirements/recommendations for international students: Required—TOEFL, TOEIC (Test of English as an International Communication), Berlitz Online English Proficiency Exam, PTE, or IELTS. Electronic applications accepted. *Expenses:* Contact institution.

**University of Phoenix–Southern Arizona Campus,** College of Social Sciences, Tucson, AZ 85711. Offers psychology (MS). *Program availability:* Evening/weekend. *Degree requirements:* For master's, thesis (for some programs). *Entrance requirements:* For master's, minimum undergraduate GPA of 2.5, 3 years of work experience, RN license. Additional exam requirements/recommendations for international students: Required—TOEFL (minimum score 550 paper-based; 79 iBT). Electronic applications accepted.

**University of Phoenix–Southern California Campus,** College of Social Sciences, Costa Mesa, CA 92626. Offers counseling (MS), including counseling, marriage, family and child therapy; psychology (MS), including behavioral health. *Program availability:* Evening/weekend, online learning. *Entrance requirements:* Additional exam requirements/recommendations for international students: Required—TOEFL, TOEIC (Test of English as an International Communication), Berlitz Online English Proficiency Exam, PTE, or IELTS. Electronic applications accepted. *Expenses:* Contact institution.

**University of Phoenix–Washington D.C. Campus,** College of Social Sciences, Washington, DC 20001. Offers industrial/organizational psychology (PhD); psychology (MS).

**University of Pittsburgh,** Dietrich School of Arts and Sciences, Department of Psychology, Pittsburgh, PA 15260. Offers clinical psychology (PhD); psychology (PhD). *Accreditation:* APA. *Faculty:* 56 full-time (25 women), 9 part-time/adjunct (2 women). *Students:* 84 full-time (69 women); includes 28 minority (6 Black or African American, non-Hispanic/Latino; 1 American Indian or Alaska Native, non-Hispanic/Latino; 13 Asian, non-Hispanic/Latino; 8 Hispanic/Latino), 9 international. Average age 26. 546 applicants, 5% accepted, 11 enrolled. In 2016, 9 doctorates awarded. Terminal master's awarded for partial completion of doctoral program. *Degree requirements:* For doctorate, comprehensive exam, thesis/dissertation. *Entrance requirements:* For doctorate, GRE General Test, minimum GPA of 3.0. Additional exam requirements/recommendations for international students: Required—TOEFL (minimum score 90 iBT) or IELTS (minimum score 7). *Application deadline:* For fall admission, 12/1 for domestic and international students. Application fee: $50. Electronic applications accepted. Tuition and fees vary according to program. *Financial support:* In 2016–17, 76 students received support, including 19 fellowships with full tuition reimbursements available (averaging $21,692 per year), 25 research assistantships with full tuition reimbursements available (averaging $18,250 per year), 32 teaching assistantships with full tuition reimbursements available (averaging $18,620 per year); scholarships/grants, traineeships, and health care benefits also available. Financial award application deadline: 12/1. *Faculty research:* Developmental psychopathology; smoking cessation; autism spectrum disorder; cardiovascular medicine; STEM research. *Total annual research expenditures:* $20 million. *Unit head:* Dr. Julie Fiez, Chair, 412-624-4500, E-mail: fiez@pitt.edu. *Application contact:* Stacy McLinden, Graduate Administrator, 412-624-4502, E-mail: psygrad@pitt.edu. Website: http://www.psychology.pitt.edu/

**University of Pittsburgh,** Dietrich School of Arts and Sciences, Program in Computational Modeling and Simulation, Pittsburgh, PA 15260. Offers biological science (PhD); chemistry (PhD); computer science (PhD); economics (PhD); geology and environmental sciences (PhD); mathematics (PhD); physics and astronomy (PhD); psychology (PhD); statistics (PhD). *Program availability:* Part-time. *Faculty:* 4 full-time (1 woman). *Students:* 3 full-time (1 woman), 1 part-time (0 women); includes 1 minority (Asian, non-Hispanic/Latino). Average age 23. 7 applicants, 43% accepted, 2 enrolled. *Degree requirements:* For doctorate, comprehensive exam, thesis/dissertation, preliminary exam. *Entrance requirements:* For doctorate, GRE, statement of purpose, transcripts for all college-level institutions attended, three letters of reference. Additional exam requirements/recommendations for international students: Required—TOEFL (minimum score 90 iBT), IELTS (minimum score 7). *Application deadline:* For fall admission, 1/15 for domestic and international students. Applications are processed on a rolling basis. Application fee: $0 ($50 for international students). *Expenses:* Contact institution. *Financial support:* In 2016–17, 3 students received support, including 2 fellowships with full tuition reimbursements available (averaging $28,500 per year), 2 research assistantships with full tuition reimbursements available (averaging $23,000 per year); tuition waivers (full) also available. Financial award application deadline: 4/15. *Faculty research:* Econometric modeling, developing reduced-scaling first principles approaches for expedited predictions of molecular and materials properties, developing computational models to quantitatively describe origins of reactivity and selectivity in organ catalytic reactions, image retrieval, human-machine communication. *Unit head:* Dr. Holger Hoock, Associate Dean, 412-624-3939, Fax: 412-624-6855. *Application contact:* Wendy G. Janocha, Graduate Administrator, 412-648-7251, E-mail: wgj1@pitt.edu.
Website: http://cmsp.pitt.edu/

**University of Puerto Rico, Río Piedras Campus,** College of Social Sciences, Department of Psychology, San Juan, PR 00931-3300. Offers clinical psychology (MA); industrial organizational psychology (MA); investigative academic psychology (MA); psychology (PhD); social-community psychology (MA). *Program availability:* Part-time. *Degree requirements:* For master's, comprehensive exam, thesis; for doctorate, comprehensive exam, thesis/dissertation, internship. *Entrance requirements:* For master's, GRE or PAEG, interview, minimum GPA of 3.0; for doctorate, GRE or PAEG, interview, master's degree, minimum GPA of 3.0. *Faculty research:* Intervention on depressed Latino youth, biosychosocial training.

**University of Regina,** Faculty of Graduate Studies and Research, Faculty of Arts, Department of Psychology, Regina, SK S4S 0A2, Canada. Offers clinical psychology (MA, PhD); experimental and applied psychology (MA, PhD). *Faculty:* 20 full-time (9 women), 8 part-time/adjunct (0 women). *Students:* 26 full-time (23 women). 28 applicants, 21% accepted. In 2016, 9 master's, 5 doctorates awarded. *Degree requirements:* For master's, thesis; for doctorate, comprehensive exam, thesis/dissertation. *Entrance requirements:* For master's, GRE General Test; for doctorate, GRE General Test and GRE Subject Test (optional for those with a master's degree from a Canadian university). Additional exam requirements/recommendations for international students: Required—TOEFL (minimum score 580 paper-based; 80 iBT), IELTS (minimum score 6.5), PTE (minimum score 59). *Application deadline:* For fall admission, 1/15 for domestic and international students. Application fee: $100. Electronic applications accepted. *Financial support:* In 2016–17, 7 fellowships (averaging $6,714 per year), 17 teaching assistantships (averaging $2,566 per year) were awarded; career-related internships or fieldwork and scholarships/grants also available. Financial award application deadline: 6/15. *Faculty research:* Clinical, experimental, cognitive, and applied psychology; post-traumatic stress disorder, anxiety, and panic disorder; traumatic brain injury; chronic pain; perception and memory. *Unit head:* Dr. Richard MacLennan, Department Head, 306-585-4458, Fax: 306-585-5429, E-mail: richard.maclennan@uregina.ca.
Website: http://www.uregina.ca/arts/psychology

**University of Rhode Island,** Graduate School, College of Health Sciences, Department of Psychology, Kingston, RI 02881. Offers behavioral science (PhD); clinical psychology (PhD); school psychology (MS, PhD). *Accreditation:* APA (one or more programs are accredited). *Program availability:* Part-time. *Faculty:* 24 full-time (14 women), 2 part-time/adjunct (1 woman). *Students:* 81 full-time (62 women), 29 part-time (23 women); includes 19 minority (12 Black or African American, non-Hispanic/Latino; 2 American Indian or Alaska Native, non-Hispanic/Latino; 3 Asian, non-Hispanic/Latino; 2 Hispanic/Latino), 6 international. In 2016, 13 master's, 17 doctorates awarded. *Degree requirements:* For master's, comprehensive exam, thesis optional; for doctorate, thesis/dissertation. *Entrance requirements:* For master's and doctorate, GRE, 3 letters of recommendation. Additional exam requirements/recommendations for international students: Required—TOEFL. *Application deadline:* For fall admission, 12/1 for domestic and international students. Application fee: $65. Electronic applications accepted. *Expenses:* Tuition, state resident: full-time $11,796; part-time $655 per credit. Tuition, nonresident: full-time $24,206; part-time $1345 per credit. *Required fees:* $1546; $44 per credit. One-time fee: $155 full-time; $35 part-time. *Financial support:* In 2016–17, 8 research assistantships with tuition reimbursements (averaging $15,685 per year), 24 teaching assistantships with tuition reimbursements (averaging $14,504 per year) were awarded. Financial award application deadline: 12/1; financial award applicants required to submit FAFSA. *Unit head:* Dr. Mark Robbins, Chair, 401-874-5082, E-mail: markrobb@uri.edu. *Application contact:* Graduate Admission, 401-874-2872, E-mail: gradadm@etal.uri.edu.
Website: http://www.uri.edu/artsci/psy/

**University of Rochester,** School of Arts and Sciences, Department of Clinical and Social Sciences in Psychology, Rochester, NY 14627. Offers clinical psychology (PhD); developmental psychology (PhD); social-personality psychology (PhD). *Accreditation:* APA. *Faculty:* 13 full-time (6 women). *Students:* 47 full-time (41 women); includes 10 minority (1 Black or African American, non-Hispanic/Latino; 3 Asian, non-Hispanic/Latino; 5 Hispanic/Latino; 1 Two or more races, non-Hispanic/Latino), 4 international. Average age 27. 257 applicants, 5% accepted, 7 enrolled. In 2016, 6 doctorates awarded. Terminal master's awarded for partial completion of doctoral program. *Degree requirements:* For doctorate, thesis/dissertation, qualifying exam. *Entrance requirements:* For doctorate, GRE General Test; GRE Subject Test (for clinical psychology, recommended for others). Additional exam requirements/recommendations for international students: Required—TOEFL. *Application deadline:* For fall admission, 4/15 for domestic and international students. Application fee: $60. Electronic applications accepted. *Expenses:* $1,538 per credit. *Financial support:* In 2016–17, 43 students received support, including 4 fellowships with full tuition reimbursements available (averaging $24,000 per year), 19 research assistantships with full tuition reimbursements available (averaging $21,000 per year), 20 teaching assistantships with full tuition reimbursements available (averaging $21,000 per year); career-related internships or fieldwork, scholarships/grants, traineeships, health care benefits, tuition waivers (full), and unspecified assistantships also available. Financial award application deadline: 2/1. *Faculty research:* Clinical psychology, social-personality psychology, developmental psychology, human motivation. *Unit head:* Loisa Bennetto, Chair, 585-275-8712, E-mail: loisa.bennetto@rochester.edu. *Application contact:* April Engram, Academic Coordinator/Analyst, 585-275-8704, E-mail: april.engram@rochester.edu.
Website: http://www.psych.rochester.edu/csp/

**University of Saint Mary,** Graduate Programs, Program in Psychology, Leavenworth, KS 66048-5082. Offers MA. *Program availability:* Part-time, evening/weekend. *Students:* 2 full-time (1 woman); includes 1 minority (Black or African American, non-Hispanic/Latino). Average age 34. In 2016, 3 master's awarded. *Degree requirements:* For master's, thesis. *Entrance requirements:* For master's, minimum undergraduate GPA of 2.75. *Application deadline:* Applications are processed on a rolling basis. Application fee: $25. Electronic applications accepted. *Expenses:* $598 per hour. *Unit head:* Dr. David Strohm, Director of Undergraduate and Graduate Psychology Programs, 913-319-3015.
Website: http://www.stmary.edu/success/Grad-Program/Master-of-Arts-Psychology.aspx

**University of St. Thomas,** Graduate Studies, College of Education, Leadership and Counseling, Graduate School of Professional Psychology, St. Paul, MN 55105-1096. Offers counseling psychology (MA, Psy D). *Accreditation:* APA. *Program availability:* Part-time, evening/weekend. *Degree requirements:* For master's, comprehensive exam, practicum; for doctorate, comprehensive exam, thesis/dissertation, qualifying exam, practicum, internship. *Entrance requirements:* For master's, GRE, minimum GPA of 2.75, letters of recommendation, personal statement; for doctorate, GRE, minimum GPA of 3.2, letters of recommendation, personal statement. Additional exam requirements/recommendations for international students: Required—TOEFL (minimum score 550 paper-based; 80 iBT). *Application deadline:* For fall admission, 2/5 priority date for domestic students; for winter admission, 1/5 priority date for domestic students; for spring admission, 10/15 priority date for domestic students, 3/1 for international students. Electronic applications accepted. *Expenses:* Contact institution. *Financial support:* Fellowships with partial tuition reimbursements, research assistantships, teaching assistantships, institutionally sponsored loans, and scholarships/grants available. Support available to part-time students. Financial award application deadline: 8/1; financial award applicants required to submit FAFSA. *Faculty research:* Elderly, neuropsychology, anxiety, family, therapist expertise, business of practice, religion and psychology, early attachment, relationship of science and practice in psychotherapy. *Unit head:* Dr. Christopher S. Vye, Chair, 651-962-4666, E-mail: csvye@stthomas.edu. *Application contact:* Melissa Anderson, Program Manager, 651-962-4669, Fax: 651-962-4651, E-mail: msanderson@stthomas.edu.

**University of Saskatchewan,** College of Graduate Studies and Research, College of Arts and Science, Department of Psychology, Saskatoon, SK S7N 5A2, Canada. Offers MA, PhD. *Degree requirements:* For master's, thesis; for doctorate, comprehensive exam (for some programs), thesis/dissertation. *Entrance requirements:* Additional exam requirements/recommendations for international students: Required—TOEFL (minimum score 80 iBT); Recommended—IELTS (minimum score 6.5). Electronic applications accepted.

**University of South Africa,** College of Human Sciences, Pretoria, South Africa. Offers adult education (M Ed); African languages (MA, PhD); African politics (MA, PhD); Afrikaans (MA, PhD); ancient history (MA, PhD); ancient Near Eastern studies (MA, PhD); anthropology (MA, PhD); applied linguistics (MA); Arabic (MA, PhD); archaeology (MA); art history (MA); Biblical archaeology (MA); Biblical studies (M Th, D Th, PhD); Christian spirituality (M Th, D Th); church history (M Th, D Th); classical studies (MA, PhD); clinical psychology (MA); communication (MA, PhD); comparative education (M Ed, Ed D); consulting psychology (D Admin, D Com, PhD); curriculum studies (M Ed, Ed D); development studies (M Admin, MA, D Admin, PhD); didactics (M Ed, Ed D); education (M Tech); education management (M Ed, Ed D); educational psychology (M Ed); English (MA); environmental education (M Ed); French (MA, PhD); German (MA, PhD); Greek (MA); guidance and counseling (M Ed); health studies (MA, PhD), including health sciences education (MA), health services management (MA), medical and surgical nursing science (critical care general) (MA), midwifery and neonatal nursing science (MA), trauma and emergency care (MA); history (MA, PhD); history of education (Ed D); inclusive education (M Ed, Ed D); information and communications technology policy and regulation (MA); information science (MA, MIS, PhD); international politics (MA, PhD); Islamic studies (MA, PhD); Italian (MA, PhD); Judaica (MA, PhD); linguistics (MA, PhD); mathematical education (M Ed); mathematics education (MA); missiology (M Th, D Th); modern Hebrew (MA, PhD); musicology (MA, MMus, D Mus, PhD); natural science education (M Ed); New Testament (M Th, D Th); Old Testament (D Th); pastoral therapy (M Th, D Th); philosophy (MA); philosophy of education (M Ed, Ed D); politics (MA, PhD); Portuguese (MA, PhD); practical theology (M Th, D Th); psychology (MA, MS, PhD); psychology of education (M Ed, Ed D); public health (MA); religious studies (MA, D Th, PhD); Romance languages (MA); Russian (MA, PhD); Semitic languages (MA, PhD); social behavior studies in HIV/AIDS (MA); social science (mental health) (MA); social science in development studies (MA); social science in psychology (MA); social science in social work (MA); social science in sociology (MA); social work (MSW, DSW, PhD); socio-education (M Ed, Ed D); sociolinguistics (MA); sociology (MA, PhD); Spanish (MA, PhD); systematic theology (M Th, D Th); TESOL (teaching English to speakers of other languages) (MA); theological ethics (M Th, D Th); theory of literature (MA, PhD); urban ministries (D Th); urban ministry (M Th).

**University of South Alabama,** College of Arts and Sciences, Department of Psychology, Mobile, AL 36688. Offers MS. *Accreditation:* APA. *Program availability:* Part-time, evening/weekend. *Faculty:* 11 full-time (3 women). *Students:* 12 full-time (4 women); includes 13 minority (1 Black or African American, non-Hispanic/Latino; 12 American Indian or Alaska Native, non-Hispanic/Latino). Average age 29. 16 applicants, 50% accepted, 5 enrolled. In 2016, 7 master's awarded. *Degree requirements:* For master's, comprehensive exam, thesis optional. *Entrance requirements:* For master's, GRE General Test, GRE Subject Test (recommended), minimum GPA of 3.0, major in psychology or equivalent. Additional exam requirements/recommendations for international students: Required—TOEFL. *Application deadline:* For fall admission, 7/15 for domestic students, 6/15 for international students. Application fee: $35. Electronic applications accepted. *Expenses:* Tuition, state resident: full-time $9768; part-time $407 per credit hour. Tuition, nonresident: full-time $19,536; part-time $814 per credit hour. *Financial support:* Fellowships, research assistantships, teaching assistantships, career-related internships or fieldwork, Federal Work-Study, institutionally sponsored loans, scholarships/grants, and unspecified assistantships available. Support available to part-time students. Financial award application deadline: 12/15; financial award applicants required to submit FAFSA. *Faculty research:* Language acquisition and development, mechanics of sound production. *Unit head:* Dr. Elise E. Labbe-Coldsmith, Chair, Psychology, 251-460-6371, Fax: 251-460-6320, E-mail: elabbe@southalabama.edu. *Application contact:* Dr. Charles Brown, Graduate Coordinator, 251-460-6372, E-mail: cbrown@southalabama.edu.
Website: http://www.southalabama.edu/colleges/artsandsci/psychology/index.html

**University of South Carolina,** The Graduate School, College of Arts and Sciences, Department of Psychology, Columbia, SC 29208. Offers clinical/community psychology (MA, PhD), including clinical/community psychology (PhD), general psychology (MA); experimental psychology (MA, PhD); school psychology (PhD). *Accreditation:* APA (one or more programs are accredited). Terminal master's awarded for partial completion of doctoral program. *Degree requirements:* For master's, thesis; for doctorate, comprehensive exam, thesis/dissertation. *Entrance requirements:* For master's and doctorate, GRE General Test. Additional exam requirements/recommendations for

*Psychology—General*

international students: Required—TOEFL. Electronic applications accepted. *Faculty research:* Developmental cognitive neuroscience, alcohol and drug addictions, reading and language processing, child and family, prevention.

**The University of South Dakota,** Graduate School, College of Arts and Sciences, Department of Psychology, Vermillion, SD 57069. Offers clinical psychology (MA, PhD); human factors (MA, PhD). *Accreditation:* APA (one or more programs are accredited). *Degree requirements:* For master's, comprehensive exam, thesis; for doctorate, comprehensive exam, thesis/dissertation. *Entrance requirements:* For master's, GRE, minimum GPA of 3.0; for doctorate, GRE General Test, GRE Subject Test, minimum GPA of 3.0. Additional exam requirements/recommendations for international students: Required—TOEFL (minimum score 550 paper-based; 79 iBT). Electronic applications accepted. *Faculty research:* Human-computer interactions, perceptual-cognitive processing, medical psychology, depression, moral psychology.

**University of Southern California,** Graduate School, Dana and David Dornsife College of Letters, Arts and Sciences, Department of Psychology, Los Angeles, CA 90089. Offers brain and cognitive science (PhD); clinical science (PhD); developmental psychology (PhD); human behavior (MHB); quantitative methods (PhD); social psychology (PhD). *Accreditation:* APA. *Degree requirements:* For doctorate, comprehensive exam, thesis/dissertation, one-year internship (for clinical science students). *Entrance requirements:* For doctorate, GRE. Additional exam requirements/recommendations for international students: Recommended—TOEFL (minimum score 600 paper-based; 100 iBT). Electronic applications accepted. *Faculty research:* Affective neuroscience; children and families; vision, culture and ethnicity; intergroup relations; aggression and violence; language and reading development; substance abuse.

**University of Southern Mississippi,** Graduate School, College of Education and Psychology, Department of Psychology, Hattiesburg, MS 39406. Offers applied behavior analysis (MS); clinical psychology (PhD); counseling psychology (MS, PhD); school psychology (PhD). *Accreditation:* APA (one or more programs are accredited). Terminal master's awarded for partial completion of doctoral program. *Degree requirements:* For master's, comprehensive exam, thesis; for doctorate, comprehensive exam, thesis/dissertation. *Entrance requirements:* For master's, GRE General Test, minimum GPA of 3.0; for doctorate, GRE General Test, interview, minimum GPA of 3.5. Additional exam requirements/recommendations for international students: Required—TOEFL, IELTS. *Application deadline:* Applications are processed on a rolling basis. *Application fee:* $60. *Expenses: Tuition, area resident:* Full-time $15,708; part-time $437 per credit hour. *Financial support:* Research assistantships with full tuition reimbursements, teaching assistantships with full tuition reimbursements, career-related internships or fieldwork, Federal Work-Study, institutionally sponsored loans, scholarships/grants, health care benefits, and unspecified assistantships available. Financial award application deadline: 3/15; financial award applicants required to submit FAFSA. *Faculty research:* Psychopathology, alcohol and drug abuse, child clinical psychology, parenting, suicide, career/vocational, marine mammal, cognition, psychological psychology, behavioral interventions, positive psychology, anger/aggression, diversity issues. *Unit head:* Dr. Joe Olmi, Chair, 601-266-5693, Fax: 601-266-5580, E-mail: d.olmi@usm.edu. *Application contact:* Angela Pam, Administrative Assistant, 601-266-4592, Fax: 601-266-5580.
Website: https://www.usm.edu/psychology

**University of South Florida,** College of Arts and Sciences, Department of Psychology, Tampa, FL 33620-9951. Offers psychology (PhD), including clinical psychology, cognition, neuroscience and social psychology, industrial-organizational psychology. *Accreditation:* APA. *Faculty:* 34 full-time (14 women). *Students:* 83 full-time (57 women), 19 part-time (13 women); includes 16 minority (1 Black or African American, non-Hispanic/Latino; 5 Asian, non-Hispanic/Latino; 7 Hispanic/Latino; 3 Two or more races, non-Hispanic/Latino), 9 international. Average age 28. 467 applicants, 3% accepted, 14 enrolled. In 2016, 12 doctorates awarded. *Degree requirements:* For doctorate, comprehensive exam, thesis/dissertation, internship. *Entrance requirements:* For doctorate, GRE General Test, minimum upper-division GPA of 3.4, three letters of recommendation, personal goals statement. Additional exam requirements/recommendations for international students: Required—TOEFL (minimum score 550 paper-based; 79 iBT) or IELTS (minimum score 6.5). *Application deadline:* For fall admission, 12/1 for domestic and international students. *Application fee:* $30. Electronic applications accepted. *Expenses:* Contact institution. *Financial support:* In 2016–17, 48 students received support, including 18 research assistantships with tuition reimbursements available (averaging $14,727 per year), 57 teaching assistantships with tuition reimbursements available (averaging $14,543 per year); tuition waivers (partial) and unspecified assistantships also available. Financial award applicants required to submit FAFSA. *Faculty research:* Clinical, cognitive, neuroscience, social, and industrial/organizational. *Total annual research expenditures:* $2.1 million. *Unit head:* Dr. Toru Shimizu, Chairperson, 813-974-0352, Fax: 813-974-4617, E-mail: shimizu@usf.edu. *Application contact:* Dr. Joseph Vandello, Associate Professor and Graduate Program Director, 813-974-0362, Fax: 813-974-4617, E-mail: vandello@usf.edu.
Website: http://psychology.usf.edu/

**University of South Florida,** College of Education, Department of Educational and Psychological Studies, Tampa, FL 33620-9951. Offers college student affairs (M Ed); counselor education (MA, Ed S); interdisciplinary (PhD, Ed S); school psychology (PhD, Ed S). *Faculty:* 25 full-time (12 women). *Students:* 97 full-time (66 women), 94 part-time (62 women); includes 52 minority (22 Black or African American, non-Hispanic/Latino; 8 Asian, non-Hispanic/Latino; 19 Hispanic/Latino; 3 Two or more races, non-Hispanic/Latino), 25 international. Average age 34. 132 applicants, 45% accepted, 46 enrolled. In 2016, 94 master's, 7 doctorates, 8 other advanced degrees awarded. *Application fee:* $30. *Expenses:* Tuition, state resident: full-time $7766; part-time $431.43 per credit hour. Tuition, nonresident: full-time $15,789; part-time $877.17 per credit hour. *Required fees:* $37 per term. *Faculty research:* College student affairs, counselor education, educational psychology, school psychology, social foundations. *Total annual research expenditures:* $11.1 million. *Unit head:* Dr. Barabara Shircliff, Chair, 813-974-4001, E-mail: shirclif@usf.edu.
Website: http://www.coedu.usf.edu/main/departments/psf/psf.html

**University of South Florida, St. Petersburg,** College of Arts and Sciences, St. Petersburg, FL 33701. Offers digital journalism and design (MA); environmental science and policy (MA, MS); Florida studies (MLA); journalism and media studies (MA); liberal studies (MLA); psychology (MA). *Program availability:* Part-time, online learning. *Degree requirements:* For master's, comprehensive exam, thesis or project. *Entrance requirements:* For master's, GRE, LSAT, MCAT (varies by program), letter of intent, 3 letters of recommendation, writing samples, bachelor's degree from regionally-accredited institution with minimum GPA of 3.0 overall or in upper two years. Additional exam requirements/recommendations for international students: Required—TOEFL (minimum score 550 paper-based; 79 iBT); Recommended—IELTS. Electronic applications accepted.

**The University of Tennessee,** Graduate School, College of Arts and Sciences, Department of Psychology, Knoxville, TN 37996. Offers clinical psychology (PhD); experimental psychology (MA, PhD); psychology (MA). *Accreditation:* APA (one or more programs are accredited). Terminal master's awarded for partial completion of doctoral program. *Degree requirements:* For master's, thesis; for doctorate, thesis/dissertation.

*Entrance requirements:* For master's and doctorate, GRE General Test, GRE Subject Test, minimum GPA of 2.7. Additional exam requirements/recommendations for international students: Required—TOEFL. Electronic applications accepted.

**The University of Tennessee at Chattanooga,** Program in Psychology, Chattanooga, TN 37403. Offers industrial/organizational psychology (MS); research psychology (MS). *Program availability:* Part-time. *Faculty:* 13 full-time (6 women), 1 part-time/adjunct (0 women). *Students:* 41 full-time (25 women), 7 part-time (3 women); includes 5 minority (2 Black or African American, non-Hispanic/Latino; 1 Hispanic/Latino; 2 Two or more races, non-Hispanic/Latino). Average age 26. 99 applicants, 29% accepted, 25 enrolled. In 2016, 21 master's awarded. *Degree requirements:* For master's, comprehensive exam (for some programs), thesis (for some programs), practicum (industrial/organizational psychology). *Entrance requirements:* For master's, GRE General Test, minimum GPA of 2.5 on all undergraduate coursework or 3.0 in senior year. Additional exam requirements/recommendations for international students: Required—TOEFL (minimum score 550 paper-based; 79 iBT), IELTS (minimum score 6). *Application deadline:* For fall admission, 6/15 priority date for domestic students, 7/1 for international students; for spring admission, 11/1 priority date for domestic students, 11/1 for international students. Applications are processed on a rolling basis. *Application fee:* $35 ($40 for international students). Electronic applications accepted. *Expenses:* $9,876 full-time in-state; $25,994 full-time out-of-state; $450 per credit part-time in-state; $1,345 per credit part-time out-of-state. *Financial support:* In 2016–17, 23 research assistantships, 1 teaching assistantship were awarded; career-related internships or fieldwork, scholarships/grants, and unspecified assistantships also available. Support available to part-time students. Financial award application deadline: 7/1; financial award applicants required to submit FAFSA. *Faculty research:* Decision processes, philosophical psychology, memory, social cognition, employee selection. *Total annual research expenditures:* $8,500. *Unit head:* Dr. Brian O'Leary, Department Head, 423-425-4283, Fax: 423-425-4284, E-mail: brian-o'leary@utc.edu. *Application contact:* Dr. Joanne Romagni, Dean of the Graduate School, 423-425-4478, Fax: 423-425-5223, E-mail: joanne-romagni@utc.edu.
Website: http://www.utc.edu/psychology/

**The University of Texas at Arlington,** Graduate School, College of Science, Department of Psychology, Arlington, TX 76019. Offers experimental health psychology (PhD); experimental psychology (MS, PhD); health/neuroscience psychology (MS, PhD); industrial and organizational psychology (MS). *Program availability:* Part-time. Terminal master's awarded for partial completion of doctoral program. *Degree requirements:* For master's, comprehensive exam or thesis; for doctorate, thesis/dissertation (for some programs). *Entrance requirements:* For master's and doctorate, GRE General Test, minimum GPA of 3.0 in last 60 hours of course work. Additional exam requirements/recommendations for international students: Required—TOEFL (minimum score 550 paper-based). *Application deadline:* For fall admission, 6/15 for domestic students. Applications are processed on a rolling basis. *Application fee:* $50. *Financial support:* Fellowships, research assistantships with partial tuition reimbursements, teaching assistantships with partial tuition reimbursements, career-related internships or fieldwork, Federal Work-Study, institutionally sponsored loans, scholarships/grants, traineeships, and unspecified assistantships available. Financial award application deadline: 6/1; financial award applicants required to submit FAFSA. *Unit head:* Dr. Robert Gatchel, Professor/Chair, 817-272-2281, Fax: 817-272-2364, E-mail: gatchel@uta.edu. *Application contact:* Dr. Jared Kenworthy, Graduate Advisor, Psychological Sciences, 817-272-2281, Fax: 817-272-2364, E-mail: kenworthy@uta.edu.
Website: http://www.uta.edu/psychology/

**The University of Texas at Austin,** Graduate School, College of Liberal Arts, Department of Psychology, Austin, TX 78712-1111. Offers behavioral neuroscience (PhD); clinical psychology (PhD); cognitive systems (PhD); developmental psychology (PhD); individual differences and evolutionary psychology (PhD); perceptual systems (PhD); social psychology (PhD). *Accreditation:* APA. *Degree requirements:* For doctorate, thesis/dissertation. *Entrance requirements:* For doctorate, GRE General Test. Electronic applications accepted. *Faculty research:* Behavioral neuroscience, sensory neuroscience, evolutionary psychology, cognitive processes in psychopathology, cognitive processes and their development.

**The University of Texas at Dallas,** School of Behavioral and Brain Sciences, Program in Psychological Sciences, Richardson, TX 75080. Offers early childhood disorders (MS); psychological sciences (MS, PhD). *Program availability:* Part-time, evening/weekend. *Faculty:* 16 full-time (11 women), 4 part-time/adjunct (all women). *Students:* 66 full-time (54 women), 14 part-time (10 women); includes 32 minority (6 Black or African American, non-Hispanic/Latino; 8 Asian, non-Hispanic/Latino; 16 Hispanic/Latino; 2 Two or more races, non-Hispanic/Latino), 4 international. Average age 27. 148 applicants, 36% accepted, 36 enrolled. In 2016, 23 master's, 2 doctorates awarded. *Degree requirements:* For master's, directed project or internship; for doctorate, thesis/dissertation. *Entrance requirements:* For master's and doctorate, GRE General Test, minimum GPA of 3.0 in upper-level course work. Additional exam requirements/recommendations for international students: Required—TOEFL (minimum score 550 paper-based). *Application deadline:* For fall admission, 7/15 for domestic students, 5/1 priority date for international students; for spring admission, 11/15 for domestic students, 9/1 priority date for international students. Applications are processed on a rolling basis. *Application fee:* $50 ($100 for international students). Electronic applications accepted. *Expenses:* Tuition, state resident: full-time $12,418; part-time $690 per semester hour. Tuition, nonresident: full-time $24,150; part-time $1342 per semester hour. Tuition and fees vary according to course load. *Financial support:* In 2016–17, 64 students received support, including 6 research assistantships with partial tuition reimbursements available (averaging $25,546 per year), 21 teaching assistantships with partial tuition reimbursements available (averaging $17,091 per year); fellowships, career-related internships or fieldwork, Federal Work-Study, scholarships/grants, and unspecified assistantships also available. Support available to part-time students. Financial award application deadline: 4/30; financial award applicants required to submit FAFSA. *Faculty research:* Neurocognitive development in young adulthood, infant learning, infant and toddler eye tracking, social aggression. *Unit head:* Dr. Shayla Holub, Program Head, Psychological Sciences, 972-883-4475, Fax: 972-883-2491, E-mail: sholub@utdallas.edu. *Application contact:* Jasmin Stubblefield, Program Coordinator, 972-883-2697, Fax: 972-883-2491, E-mail: psysciencesphd@utdallas.edu.
Website: http://www.utdallas.edu/bbs/degrees/psy-degrees/

**The University of Texas at El Paso,** Graduate School, College of Liberal Arts, Department of Psychology, El Paso, TX 79968-0001. Offers clinical psychology (MA); experimental psychology (MA); psychology (PhD). *Program availability:* Part-time, evening/weekend. *Degree requirements:* For master's, thesis; for doctorate, thesis/dissertation. *Entrance requirements:* For master's, GRE, letters of recommendation; for doctorate, GRE, statement of purpose, letters of recommendation. Additional exam requirements/recommendations for international students: Required—TOEFL; Recommended—IELTS. Electronic applications accepted.

**The University of Texas at San Antonio,** College of Liberal and Fine Arts, Department of Psychology, San Antonio, TX 78249-0617. Offers MS, PhD. *Program availability:* Part-time. *Faculty:* 13 full-time (4 women). *Students:* 37 full-time (24 women), 12 part-

time (7 women); includes 23 minority (2 Black or African American, non-Hispanic/Latino; 2 Asian, non-Hispanic/Latino; 17 Hispanic/Latino; 1 Native Hawaiian or other Pacific Islander, non-Hispanic/Latino; 1 Two or more races, non-Hispanic/Latino), 1 international. Average age 28. 39 applicants, 46% accepted, 14 enrolled. In 2016, 15 master's, 3 doctorates awarded. *Degree requirements:* For master's, comprehensive exam, thesis or alternative; for doctorate, comprehensive exam, thesis/dissertation. *Entrance requirements:* For master's, GRE, minimum GPA 3.2 in last 60 hours and in all psychology courses; 18 hours of psychology courses including inferential statistics and research methods; two letters of recommendation; statement of purpose; for doctorate, GRE, master's degree with minimum GPA of 3.5, three letters of recommendation, statement of purpose. Additional exam requirements/recommendations for international students: Required—TOEFL (minimum score 550 paper-based; 79 iBT), IELTS (minimum score 6.5). *Application deadline:* For fall admission, 6/1 for domestic students, 4/1 for international students; for spring admission, 11/1 for domestic students, 9/1 for international students. Application fee: $45 ($80 for international students). Electronic applications accepted. *Expenses:* Contact institution. *Financial support:* In 2016–17, 11 students received support, including 6 research assistantships with full tuition reimbursements available (averaging $25,000 per year), 5 teaching assistantships (averaging $9,200 per year); tuition waivers (partial) also available. *Faculty research:* Social psychology, cognitive psychology, developmental psychology, industrial/organizational psychology, biopsychology. *Total annual research expenditures:* $361,033. *Unit head:* Dr. Robert Fuhrman, Department Chair, 210-458-7352, Fax: 210-458-5728, E-mail: robert.fuhrman@utsa.edu. *Application contact:* Dr. Rebecca Weston, Graduate Advisor of Record, 210-458-6432, Fax: 210-458-5728, E-mail: rebecca.weston@utsa.edu.
Website: http://colfa.utsa.edu/psychology

**The University of Texas at Tyler,** College of Education and Psychology, Department of Psychology and Counseling, Tyler, TX 75799-0001. Offers clinical psychology (MS), including neuropsychology, school psychology; counseling psychology (MA), including general, marriage and family; interdisciplinary studies (MSIS); school counseling (MA). *Program availability:* Part-time, evening/weekend. *Degree requirements:* For master's, comprehensive exam, thesis optional. *Entrance requirements:* For master's, GRE General Test, minimum GPA of 3.0. Additional exam requirements/recommendations for international students: Required—TOEFL. Electronic applications accepted. *Faculty research:* Neuropsychology, child abuse, psychometric properties of psychological instruments, maternal behavior, clinical practice issues, victimization of women, post-traumatic stress disorder.

**The University of Texas of the Permian Basin,** Office of Graduate Studies, College of Arts and Sciences, Department of Psychology, Odessa, TX 79762-0001. Offers applied research psychology (MA); clinical psychology (MA). *Program availability:* Part-time, evening/weekend. *Degree requirements:* For master's, comprehensive exam, thesis, practicum. *Entrance requirements:* For master's, GRE General Test, 3 letters of recommendation. Additional exam requirements/recommendations for international students: Required—TOEFL (minimum score 550 paper-based).

**The University of Texas Rio Grande Valley,** College of Liberal Arts, Department of Psychological Science, Edinburg, TX 78539. Offers psychology (MA), including clinical psychology, experimental psychology. *Program availability:* Part-time, evening/weekend. *Degree requirements:* For master's, comprehensive exam, thesis optional, internship. *Entrance requirements:* For master's, GRE, letters of recommendation. Additional exam requirements/recommendations for international students: Required—TOEFL. Electronic applications accepted. Tuition and fees vary according to course load and program. *Faculty research:* Biofeedback, acculturation, health, stress/trauma, neuropsychological assessment, false memories, children's theory of mind.

**University of the Pacific,** College of the Pacific, Department of Psychology, Stockton, CA 95211-0197. Offers MA. *Faculty:* 7 full-time (3 women). *Students:* 12 part-time (11 women); includes 6 minority (3 Asian, non-Hispanic/Latino; 2 Hispanic/Latino; 1 Two or more races, non-Hispanic/Latino). Average age 25. 23 applicants, 35% accepted, 6 enrolled. In 2016, 7 master's awarded. *Degree requirements:* For master's, thesis. *Entrance requirements:* For master's, GRE General Test. Additional exam requirements/recommendations for international students: Required—TOEFL. *Application deadline:* For fall admission, 3/1 priority date for domestic students. Applications are processed on a rolling basis. Application fee: $75. *Financial support:* Teaching assistantships and institutionally sponsored loans available. Support available to part-time students. Financial award application deadline: 3/1; financial award applicants required to submit FAFSA. *Unit head:* Dr. Scott Jensen, Chairperson, 209-946-7320, E-mail: sjensen@pacific.edu. *Application contact:* Information Contact, 209-946-2133.

**University of the Rockies,** Graduate Programs, Colorado Springs, CO 80903. Offers MA, Psy D.

**University of the West,** Department of Psychology, Rosemead, CA 91770. Offers Buddhist psychology (MA); multicultural counseling (MA). *Program availability:* Part-time, evening/weekend. *Degree requirements:* For master's, fieldwork; comprehensive exam or thesis. *Application deadline:* For fall admission, 3/15 for domestic and international students; for winter admission, 4/1 for domestic and international students; for spring admission, 11/15 for domestic and international students. Applications are processed on a rolling basis. Application fee: $50 ($100 for international students). *Expenses: Tuition:* Full-time $9324; part-time $4662 per year. *Required fees:* $900; $640 per unit. $320 per semester. Tuition and fees vary according to program. *Financial support:* Applicants required to submit FAFSA. *Unit head:* Dr. Hiroshi Sasaki, Chair, 626-571-8811 Ext. 113, Fax: 626-571-1413, E-mail: hiroshis@uwest.edu. *Application contact:* Rica Toribio, Director of Enrollment Services, 626-571-8811 Ext. 311, Fax: 626-571-1413, E-mail: ricat@uwest.edu.

**The University of Toledo,** College of Graduate Studies, College of Languages, Literature and Social Sciences, Department of Psychology, Toledo, OH 43606-3390. Offers clinical psychology (MA, PhD); experimental psychology (MA, PhD). *Accreditation:* APA. *Degree requirements:* For master's, comprehensive exam, thesis; for doctorate, comprehensive exam, thesis/dissertation. *Entrance requirements:* For master's and doctorate, GRE General Test, GRE Subject Test, minimum cumulative point-hour ratio of 2.7 for all previous academic work, three letters of recommendation, statement of purpose, transcripts from all prior institutions attended. Additional exam requirements/recommendations for international students: Required—TOEFL (minimum score 550 paper-based; 80 iBT). Electronic applications accepted. *Faculty research:* Neural taste response.

**University of Toronto,** School of Graduate Studies, Faculty of Arts and Science, Department of Psychology, Toronto, ON M5S 1A1, Canada. Offers MA, PhD. *Degree requirements:* For master's, thesis; for doctorate, thesis/dissertation, oral exam. *Entrance requirements:* For master's, minimum A- average in last two years, 6 full courses in psychology, laboratory experience; for doctorate, minimum A- average, research experience. Additional exam requirements/recommendations for international students: Required—TOEFL (minimum score 580 paper-based; 93 iBT), TWE (minimum score 5). Electronic applications accepted.

**The University of Tulsa,** Graduate School, Kendall College of Arts and Sciences, Department of Psychology, Tulsa, OK 74104-3189. Offers clinical psychology (MA,

PhD); industrial/organizational psychology (MA, PhD); JD/MA. *Accreditation:* APA (one or more programs are accredited). *Program availability:* Part-time. *Faculty:* 13 full-time (5 women). *Students:* 49 full-time (33 women), 4 part-time (3 women); includes 18 minority (3 American Indian or Alaska Native, non-Hispanic/Latino; 9 Asian, non-Hispanic/Latino; 5 Hispanic/Latino; 1 Two or more races, non-Hispanic/Latino), 1 international. Average age 26. 159 applicants, 15% accepted, 12 enrolled. In 2016, 17 master's, 6 doctorates awarded. Terminal master's awarded for partial completion of doctoral program. *Degree requirements:* For doctorate, comprehensive exam, thesis/dissertation. *Entrance requirements:* For master's and doctorate, GRE General Test. Additional exam requirements/recommendations for international students: Required—TOEFL (minimum score 577 paper-based; 91 iBT), IELTS (minimum score 6.5). Application fee: $55. Electronic applications accepted. *Expenses: Tuition:* Full-time $22,230; part-time $1235 per credit hour. *Required fees:* $990 per semester. Tuition and fees vary according to course load. *Financial support:* In 2016–17, 58 students received support, including 10 fellowships with full tuition reimbursements available (averaging $13,605 per year), 17 research assistantships with full tuition reimbursements available (averaging $14,346 per year), 15 teaching assistantships with full tuition reimbursements available (averaging $13,767 per year); career-related internships or fieldwork, Federal Work-Study, scholarships/grants, health care benefits, tuition waivers (full and partial), and unspecified assistantships also available. Support available to part-time students. Financial award application deadline: 2/1; financial award applicants required to submit FAFSA. *Faculty research:* Traumatic stress studies, randomized control trials of exposure treatments, pain modulation, neuropsychological assessment of health/mental health, psychological assessment, psychometrics, ethics, longitudinal assessment of child development, trauma and journalism, MMPI studies, personnel testing and selection, training, performance appraisal, organizational development, job attitudes and motivation, leadership. *Total annual research expenditures:* $763,451. *Unit head:* Dr. John McNulty, Chairperson, 918-631-2835, Fax: 918-631-2833, E-mail: john-mcnulty@utulsa.edu. *Application contact:* Graduate School, 918-631-2336, Fax: 918-631-2156, E-mail: grad@utulsa.edu.
Website: http://artsandsciences.utulsa.edu/academics/departments-schools/psychology/

**University of Utah,** Graduate School, College of Social and Behavioral Science, Department of Psychology, Salt Lake City, UT 84112. Offers clinical psychology (PhD); psychology (PhD). *Accreditation:* APA. *Faculty:* 26 full-time (13 women), 12 part-time/adjunct (5 women). *Students:* 55 full-time (35 women), 10 part-time (8 women); includes 11 minority (2 Black or African American, non-Hispanic/Latino; 3 Asian, non-Hispanic/Latino; 4 Hispanic/Latino; 2 Two or more races, non-Hispanic/Latino), 3 international. Average age 28. 295 applicants, 8% accepted, 13 enrolled. In 2016, 5 doctorates awarded. *Degree requirements:* For doctorate, thesis/dissertation. *Entrance requirements:* For doctorate, GRE General Test. Additional exam requirements/recommendations for international students: Required—TOEFL (minimum score 500 paper-based). *Application deadline:* For fall admission, 12/15 for domestic and international students. Application fee: $55 ($65 for international students). Electronic applications accepted. *Expenses:* Tuition, state resident: full-time $7011; part-time $3918.24 per credit hour. Tuition, nonresident: full-time $22,154; part-time $11,665.42 per credit hour. *Financial support:* In 2016–17, 56 students received support, including 2 fellowships with full tuition reimbursements available (averaging $17,000 per year), 19 research assistantships with full tuition reimbursements available (averaging $16,800 per year), 34 teaching assistantships with full tuition reimbursements available (averaging $16,800 per year); career-related internships or fieldwork, health care benefits, and unspecified assistantships also available. Financial award applicants required to submit FAFSA. *Faculty research:* Cognitive neuroscience, health, social cognition, psychopathology, cognitive and social development. *Total annual research expenditures:* $1.9 million. *Unit head:* Dr. Lisa G. Aspinwall, Chair, 801-581-8925, Fax: 801-581-5841, E-mail: lisa.aspinwall@utah.edu. *Application contact:* Nancy Seegmiller, Program Manager, 801-581-8925, Fax: 801-581-5841, E-mail: nancy.seegmiller@psych.utah.edu.
Website: http://www.psych.utah.edu/

**University of Vermont,** Graduate College, College of Arts and Sciences, Department of Psychology, Burlington, VT 05405. Offers clinical psychology (PhD); psychology (PhD). *Accreditation:* APA. *Degree requirements:* For doctorate, thesis/dissertation. *Entrance requirements:* For doctorate, GRE General Test, writing sample (for clinical psychology). Additional exam requirements/recommendations for international students: Required—TOEFL (minimum score 550 paper-based; 80 iBT). Electronic applications accepted. *Expenses:* Tuition, state resident: full-time $5814. Tuition, nonresident: full-time $14,670.

**University of Victoria,** Faculty of Graduate Studies, Faculty of Social Sciences, Department of Psychology, Victoria, BC V8W 2Y2, Canada. Offers clinical psychology (PhD); clinical psychology (neuropsychology) (M Sc); cognition and brain science (M Sc, PhD); experimental neuropsychology (M Sc, PhD); individualized study (M Sc, PhD); life span development psychology (PhD); life span developmental psychology (M Sc); social psychology (M Sc, PhD). *Degree requirements:* For master's, thesis; for doctorate, thesis/dissertation, candidacy exam. *Entrance requirements:* For master's and doctorate, GRE General Test. Additional exam requirements/recommendations for international students: Required—TOEFL (minimum score 600 paper-based). Electronic applications accepted. *Faculty research:* Life span development psychology and aging, behavioral neuroscience, cognitive psychology, behavioral psychology, environmental psychology.

**University of Virginia,** College and Graduate School of Arts and Sciences, Department of Psychology, Charlottesville, VA 22903. Offers MA, PhD. *Accreditation:* APA (one or more programs are accredited). *Faculty:* 30 full-time (10 women), 2 part-time/adjunct (0 women). *Students:* 70 full-time (45 women), 1 (woman) part-time; includes 14 minority (3 Black or African American, non-Hispanic/Latino; 4 Asian, non-Hispanic/Latino; 6 Hispanic/Latino; 1 Two or more races, non-Hispanic/Latino), 9 international. Average age 27. 487 applicants, 6% accepted, 15 enrolled. In 2016, 11 master's, 16 doctorates awarded. *Degree requirements:* For master's, pre-dissertation research project; for doctorate, comprehensive exam, thesis/dissertation. *Entrance requirements:* For master's and doctorate, GRE General Test, 3 or more letters of recommendation. Additional exam requirements/recommendations for international students: Required—TOEFL (minimum score 600 paper-based; 90 iBT), IELTS (minimum score 7). *Application deadline:* For fall admission, 12/1 for domestic and international students. Applications are processed on a rolling basis. Application fee: $60. Electronic applications accepted. *Expenses:* Tuition, state resident: full-time $15,026; part-time $834 per credit hour. Tuition, nonresident: full-time $25,168; part-time $1378 per credit hour. *Required fees:* $2654. *Financial support:* Fellowships, research assistantships, and teaching assistantships available. Financial award applicants required to submit FAFSA. *Unit head:* Alev Erisir, Chair, 434-982-4750, Fax: 434-982-4766, E-mail: psy-dept@virginia.edu. *Application contact:* Daniel Willingham Emery, Director of Graduate Studies, 434-982-4750, Fax: 434-982-4766, E-mail: psy-dept@virginia.edu.
Website: http://cacsprd.web.virginia.edu/Psych/Graduates

**University of Washington,** Graduate School, College of Arts and Sciences, Department of Psychology, Seattle, WA 98195. Offers animal behavior (PhD); child psychology (PhD); clinical psychology (PhD); cognition and perception (PhD); developmental psychology (PhD); quantitative psychology (PhD); social psychology and personality (PhD). *Accreditation:* APA. *Degree requirements:* For doctorate, thesis/dissertation. *Entrance requirements:* For doctorate, GRE General Test, minimum GPA of 3.0. Electronic applications accepted. *Faculty research:* Addictive behaviors, artificial intelligence, child psychopathology, mechanisms and development of vision, physiology of ingestive behaviors.

**University of Waterloo,** Graduate Studies, Faculty of Arts, Department of Psychology, Waterloo, ON N2L 3G1, Canada. Offers MA, MA Sc, PhD. Terminal master's awarded for partial completion of doctoral program. *Degree requirements:* For master's, thesis (for some programs); for doctorate, thesis/dissertation. *Entrance requirements:* For master's, GRE, honors degree in psychology, minimum B average; for doctorate, GRE, master's degree in psychology, minimum B average. Additional exam requirements/recommendations for international students: Required—TOEFL, IELTS, PTE. Electronic applications accepted. *Faculty research:* Memory and attention, attitudes and behavior in the workplace, object recognition, judgment and decision making, communication and knowledge in toddlers.

**The University of Western Ontario,** Faculty of Graduate Studies, Biosciences Division, Department of Psychology, London, ON N6A 5B8, Canada. Offers MA, PhD. *Degree requirements:* For master's, thesis; for doctorate, thesis/dissertation. *Entrance requirements:* For master's, minimum B average during last 2 years; for doctorate, MA in psychology. Additional exam requirements/recommendations for international students: Required—TOEFL. *Faculty research:* Clinical, applied and social/personality psychology; psychobiology; cognitive processes.

**University of West Florida,** College of Arts, Social Sciences, and Humanities, Department of Psychology, Pensacola, FL 32514-5750. Offers applied experimental (MA); counseling (MA); industrial-organizational (MA). *Program availability:* Part-time. *Degree requirements:* For master's, thesis (for some programs). *Entrance requirements:* For master's, GRE, official transcripts; minimum GPA of 3.0; writing sample; three letters of reference; field experience or skill sets; oral interview (for counseling specialization). Additional exam requirements/recommendations for international students: Required—TOEFL (minimum score 550 paper-based). *Application deadline:* For fall admission, 6/1 for domestic and international students; for spring admission, 10/1 for domestic and international students. Applications are processed on a rolling basis. Application fee: $30. *Expenses:* Tuition, state resident: full-time $5316.12. Tuition, nonresident: full-time $11,308. *Required fees:* $583.92. Tuition and fees vary according to course load and program. *Financial support:* Fellowships with partial tuition reimbursements, research assistantships with partial tuition reimbursements, teaching assistantships with partial tuition reimbursements, career-related internships or fieldwork, and unspecified assistantships available. Financial award application deadline: 4/15; financial award applicants required to submit FAFSA. *Faculty research:* Prose recall, brain imaging, peak performance, biofeedback and pain control, comparable worth. *Unit head:* Dr. Robert Belter, Interim Department Chair, 850-474-2791, E-mail: rbelter@uwf.edu. *Application contact:* Dr. Robert Belter, Interim Department Chair, 850-474-2791, E-mail: rbelter@uwf.edu.
Website: http://www.uwf.edu/psychology/

**University of West Georgia,** College of Social Sciences, Carrollton, GA 30118. Offers criminology (MA); data analysis and evaluation methods (Postbaccalaureate Certificate); European Union studies (Postbaccalaureate Certificate); integrative health systems (Postbaccalaureate Certificate); nonprofit management and community development (Postbaccalaureate Certificate); psychology (MA, PhD), including consciousness and society (PhD); public administration (MPA); public management (Postbaccalaureate Certificate); sociology (MA). *Program availability:* Part-time, evening/weekend, 100% online, blended/hybrid learning. *Faculty:* 45 full-time (21 women). *Students:* 107 full-time (67 women), 73 part-time (46 women); includes 47 minority (39 Black or African American, non-Hispanic/Latino; 4 Asian, non-Hispanic/Latino; 4 Hispanic/Latino), 10 international. Average age 31. 83 applicants, 88% accepted, 60 enrolled. In 2016, 56 master's, 7 doctorates, 5 other advanced degrees awarded. *Entrance requirements:* Additional exam requirements/recommendations for international students: Required—TOEFL (minimum score 523 paper-based; 69 iBT); Recommended—IELTS (minimum score 6.5). *Application deadline:* For fall admission, 7/15 for domestic students, 6/1 for international students; for spring admission, 11/30 for domestic students, 10/15 for international students; for summer admission, 5/15 for domestic students, 3/30 for international students. Applications are processed on a rolling basis. Application fee: $40. Electronic applications accepted. *Expenses:* Tuition, state resident: full-time $5316; part-time $222 per semester hour. Tuition, nonresident: full-time $20,658; part-time $861 per semester hour. *Required fees:* $1962. Tuition and fees vary according to course load, degree level and program. *Financial support:* Fellowships, research assistantships, teaching assistantships, career-related internships or fieldwork, Federal Work-Study, institutionally sponsored loans, scholarships/grants, and unspecified assistantships available. Support available to part-time students. Financial award application deadline: 4/1; financial award applicants required to submit FAFSA. *Unit head:* Dr. N. Jane McCandless, Dean of Social Sciences, 678-839-5170, Fax: 678-839-5171, E-mail: jmccandl@westga.edu. *Application contact:* Dr. Toby Ziglar, Assistant Dean of the Graduate School, 678-839-1394, Fax: 678-839-1395, E-mail: graduate@westga.edu.
Website: https://www.westga.edu/coss

**University of Windsor,** Faculty of Graduate Studies, Faculty of Arts and Social Sciences, Department of Psychology, Windsor, ON N9B 3P4, Canada. Offers adult clinical (MA, PhD); applied social psychology (MA, PhD); child clinical (MA, PhD); clinical neuropsychology (MA, PhD). *Degree requirements:* For master's, thesis; for doctorate, comprehensive exam, thesis/dissertation. *Entrance requirements:* For master's, GRE General Test, GRE Subject Test in psychology, minimum B average; for doctorate, GRE General Test, GRE Subject Test in psychology, master's degree. Additional exam requirements/recommendations for international students: Required—TOEFL (minimum score 600 paper-based). Electronic applications accepted. *Faculty research:* Gambling, suicidology, emotional competence, psychotherapy and trauma.

**University of Wisconsin–Eau Claire,** College of Arts and Sciences, Department of Psychology, Eau Claire, WI 54702-4004. Offers school psychology (MSE, Ed S). *Program availability:* Part-time. *Degree requirements:* For master's, comprehensive exam, thesis, National Certified School Psychologist Professional Exam, written exam, externship. *Entrance requirements:* For master's, GRE, minimum undergraduate GPA of 3.0; courses in exceptional children and youth, statistics, psychopathology, and theories of counseling. Additional exam requirements/recommendations for international students: Required—TOEFL (minimum score 79 iBT).

**University of Wisconsin–La Crosse,** College of Liberal Studies, Department of Psychology, La Crosse, WI 54601-3742. Offers school psychology (MS Ed, Ed S). *Faculty:* 5 full-time (2 women), 1 (woman) part-time/adjunct. *Students:* 24 full-time (21 women), 11 part-time (10 women); includes 1 minority (Hispanic/Latino). Average age 24. 40 applicants, 48% accepted, 12 enrolled. In 2016, 12 master's, 11 Ed Ss awarded. *Degree requirements:* For master's, thesis, seminar, or comprehensive exams. *Entrance requirements:* For master's and Ed S, GRE. Additional exam requirements/recommendations for international students: Required—TOEFL (minimum score 550

paper-based; 79 iBT). *Application deadline:* For fall admission, 1/31 for domestic and international students. Electronic applications accepted. *Financial support:* Research assistantships, Federal Work-Study, scholarships/grants, and health care benefits available. Support available to part-time students. *Unit head:* Dr. Robert Dixon, Director of the School Psychology Program, 608-785-6893, E-mail: rdixon@uwlax.edu. *Application contact:* Brandon Schaller, Senior Graduate Student Status Examiner, 608-785-8941, E-mail: admissions@uwlax.edu.
Website: https://www.uwlax.edu/Psychology/Graduate-program/

**University of Wisconsin–Madison,** Graduate School, College of Letters and Science, Department of Psychology, Madison, WI 53706-1380. Offers biology of brain and behavior (PhD); clinical psychology (PhD); cognitive neurosciences (PhD); developmental psychology (PhD); perception (PhD); psychology (PhD); social and personality psychology (PhD). *Accreditation:* APA. *Degree requirements:* For doctorate, comprehensive exam, thesis/dissertation. *Entrance requirements:* For doctorate, GRE General Test, minimum undergraduate GPA of 3.0. Additional exam requirements/recommendations for international students: Required—TOEFL. Electronic applications accepted.

**University of Wisconsin–Milwaukee,** Graduate School, College of Letters and Science, Department of Psychology, Milwaukee, WI 53201-0413. Offers experimental psychology (MS, PhD), including behavior analysis, health and social psychology (PhD), health psychology (MS), neuroscience (PhD); psychology (PhD), including clinical psychology. *Accreditation:* APA (one or more programs are accredited). *Students:* 67 full-time (46 women), 19 part-time (11 women); includes 8 minority (2 Asian, non-Hispanic/Latino; 1 Hispanic/Latino; 5 Two or more races, non-Hispanic/Latino), 9 international. Average age 28. 254 applicants, 7% accepted, 16 enrolled. In 2016, 15 master's, 10 doctorates awarded. *Degree requirements:* For master's, thesis; for doctorate, variable foreign language requirement, thesis/dissertation. *Entrance requirements:* For master's and doctorate, GRE General Test, GRE Subject Test. Additional exam requirements/recommendations for international students: Required—TOEFL (minimum score 550 paper-based; 79 iBT), IELTS (minimum score 6.5). *Application deadline:* For fall admission, 1/1 priority date for domestic students; for spring admission, 9/1 for domestic students. Applications are processed on a rolling basis. Application fee: $56 ($96 for international students). Electronic applications accepted. *Financial support:* In 2016–17, 8 fellowships, 6 research assistantships, 46 teaching assistantships were awarded; career-related internships or fieldwork, unspecified assistantships, and project assistantships also available. Support available to part-time students. Financial award application deadline: 4/15; financial award applicants required to submit FAFSA. *Unit head:* Douglas Woods, Department Chair, 414-229-6636, E-mail: dwoods@uwm.edu. *Application contact:* General Information Contact, 414-229-4982, Fax: 414-229-6967, E-mail: gradschool@uwm.edu.
Website: http://www.uwm.edu/dept/psychology/

**University of Wisconsin–Oshkosh,** Graduate Studies, College of Letters and Science, Department of Psychology, Oshkosh, WI 54901. Offers experimental psychology (MS); industrial/organizational psychology (MS). *Degree requirements:* For master's, thesis. *Entrance requirements:* For master's, GRE, 10 semester hours of undergraduate course work in psychology. Additional exam requirements/recommendations for international students: Required—TOEFL (minimum score 550 paper-based; 79 iBT). Electronic applications accepted. *Faculty research:* Performance evaluation, training, biological bases of behavior, tactile perception, aging.

**University of Wisconsin–Whitewater,** School of Graduate Studies, College of Letters and Sciences, Department of Psychology, Whitewater, WI 53190-1790. Offers school psychology (MSE, Ed S). *Program availability:* Part-time, evening/weekend, online learning. *Degree requirements:* For master's, comprehensive exam or thesis. *Entrance requirements:* For master's, MAT or GRE, interview, minimum GPA of 3.0, 3 letters of recommendation. Additional exam requirements/recommendations for international students: Required—TOEFL (minimum score 550 paper-based; 80 iBT), IELTS (minimum score 6). Electronic applications accepted. *Faculty research:* School violence/youth violence; anger/aggression interventions; women's mental health; pedagogy of empathy, social psychology, and personality.

**University of Wyoming,** College of Arts and Sciences, Department of Psychology, Laramie, WY 82071. Offers MA, MS, PhD. *Accreditation:* APA (one or more programs are accredited). Terminal master's awarded for partial completion of doctoral program. *Degree requirements:* For master's, thesis; for doctorate, comprehensive exam, thesis/dissertation. *Entrance requirements:* For master's and doctorate, GRE General Test, GRE Subject Test, minimum GPA of 3.0. Additional exam requirements/recommendations for international students: Required—TOEFL. *Faculty research:* Child development, health psychology, psychology and law, social psychology, mood/anxiety disorders.

**Utah State University,** School of Graduate Studies, Emma Eccles Jones College of Education and Human Services, Department of Psychology, Logan, UT 84322. Offers clinical/counseling/school psychology (PhD); research and evaluation methodology (PhD); school counseling (MS); school psychology (MS). *Accreditation:* APA (one or more programs are accredited). *Program availability:* Part-time, evening/weekend, online learning. Terminal master's awarded for partial completion of doctoral program. *Degree requirements:* For master's, thesis (for some programs); for doctorate, thesis/dissertation. *Entrance requirements:* For master's, GRE General Test (school psychology), MAT (school counseling), minimum GPA of 3.5; for doctorate, GRE General Test, minimum GPA of 3.5. Additional exam requirements/recommendations for international students: Required—TOEFL. *Faculty research:* Hearing loss detection in infancy, ADHD, eating disorders, domestic violence, neuropsychology, bilingual/Spanish speaking students/parents.

**Valdosta State University,** Department of Psychology, Counseling, and Family Therapy, Valdosta, GA 31698. Offers school counseling (M Ed, Ed S). *Accreditation:* AAMFT/COAMFTE. *Program availability:* Part-time, evening/weekend, 100% online, blended/hybrid learning. *Degree requirements:* For master's, thesis or alternative, comprehensive written and/or oral exams; for Ed S, thesis. *Entrance requirements:* For master's, GRE General Test or MAT, GACE; for Ed S, GRE General Test or MAT. Additional exam requirements/recommendations for international students: Required—TOEFL (minimum score 523 paper-based); Recommended—IELTS. Electronic applications accepted. *Expenses:* Contact institution.

**Valparaiso University,** Graduate School and Continuing Education, Department of Psychology, Valparaiso, IN 46383. Offers clinical mental health counseling (MA); JD/MA. *Program availability:* Part-time, evening/weekend. *Degree requirements:* For master's, thesis or alternative, internship. *Entrance requirements:* For master's, minimum GPA of 3.0; 15 credits in the social/behavioral sciences (psychology, sociology, human development, etc.) with minimum GPA of 3.0; course in introductory psychology; recent statistics course with minimum B average. Additional exam requirements/recommendations for international students: Required—TOEFL (minimum score 550 paper-based; 80 iBT), IELTS (minimum score 6). Electronic applications accepted. *Expenses: Tuition:* Full-time $11,070; part-time $615 per credit hour. *Required fees:* $116 per semester. Tuition and fees vary according to course load, degree level and program. *Faculty research:* Environmental psychology, human sexuality, developmental psychopathology, social psychology.

**Vanderbilt University,** Program in Psychological Sciences, Nashville, TN 37240-1001. Offers PhD. *Accreditation:* APA. *Faculty:* 54 full-time (25 women), 1 (woman) part-time/adjunct. *Students:* 77 full-time (52 women), 1 (woman) part-time; includes 8 minority (3 Black or African American, non-Hispanic/Latino; 3 Asian, non-Hispanic/Latino; 2 Hispanic/Latino), 9 international. Average age 27. 583 applicants, 4% accepted, 12 enrolled. In 2016, 22 degrees awarded. *Degree requirements:* For doctorate, comprehensive exam, thesis/dissertation, final and qualifying exams. *Entrance requirements:* For doctorate, GRE General Test, GRE Subject Test. Additional exam requirements/recommendations for international students: Required—TOEFL (minimum score 570 paper-based; 88 iBT). *Application deadline:* For fall admission, 12/1 for domestic and international students. Application fee: $0. Electronic applications accepted. *Expenses:* Contact institution. *Financial support:* Fellowships with full tuition reimbursements, research assistantships with full tuition reimbursements, teaching assistantships with full tuition reimbursements, career-related internships or fieldwork, Federal Work-Study, institutionally sponsored loans, scholarships/grants, traineeships, and health care benefits available. Financial award application deadline: 1/15; financial award applicants required to submit CSS PROFILE or FAFSA. *Faculty research:* Clinical, cognitive, developmental, and social psychology; neuroscience; vision; behavior. *Unit head:* Dr. Daniel T. Levin, Director of Graduate Studies for the Psychology of Human Development in Peabody College, 615-322-1518, Fax: 615-343-9494, E-mail: daniel.t.levin@vanderbilt.edu. *Application contact:* Dr. Rene Marois, Director of Graduate Studies for Psychological Studies in the College of Arts and Science, 615-322-1779, Fax: 615-343-5027, E-mail: r.marois@vanderbilt.edu.
Website: http://peabody.vanderbilt.edu/departments/psych/

**Villanova University,** Graduate School of Liberal Arts and Sciences, Department of Psychology, Villanova, PA 19085-1699. Offers MA, MS. *Program availability:* Part-time, evening/weekend. *Faculty:* 12. *Students:* 55 full-time (36 women); includes 11 minority (2 Black or African American, non-Hispanic/Latino; 2 Asian, non-Hispanic/Latino; 5 Hispanic/Latino; 2 Two or more races, non-Hispanic/Latino). Average age 25. 85 applicants, 36% accepted, 21 enrolled. In 2016, 16 master's awarded. *Degree requirements:* For master's, thesis. *Entrance requirements:* For master's, GRE General Test, minimum GPA of 3.0, statement of goals. Additional exam requirements/recommendations for international students: Required—TOEFL. *Application deadline:* For fall admission, 3/1 for domestic students, 5/1 priority date for international students; for spring admission, 11/15 for domestic students, 10/15 priority date for international students; for summer admission, 5/1 for domestic students. Applications are processed on a rolling basis. Application fee: $50. Electronic applications accepted. *Financial support:* Research assistantships, scholarships/grants, and unspecified assistantships available. Financial award applicants required to submit FAFSA. *Unit head:* Dr. Michael Brown, Director, 610-519-4720.
Website: http://www1.villanova.edu/villanova/artsci/psychology/graduate.html

**Virginia Polytechnic Institute and State University,** Graduate School, College of Science, Blacksburg, VA 24061. Offers biological sciences (MS, PhD); biomedical technology development and management (MS); chemistry (MS, PhD); data analysis and applied statistics (MA); economics (MA, PhD); geosciences (MS, PhD); mathematics (MS, PhD); physics (MS, PhD); psychology (MS, PhD); statistics (MS, PhD). *Faculty:* 299 full-time (92 women), 1 part-time/adjunct (0 women). *Students:* 567 full-time (222 women), 47 part-time (19 women); includes 66 minority (14 Black or African American, non-Hispanic/Latino; 12 Asian, non-Hispanic/Latino; 29 Hispanic/Latino; 11 Two or more races, non-Hispanic/Latino), 247 international. Average age 27. 956 applicants, 17% accepted, 118 enrolled. In 2016, 75 master's, 71 doctorates awarded. *Degree requirements:* For master's, comprehensive exam (for some programs), thesis (for some programs); for doctorate, comprehensive exam (for some programs), thesis/dissertation (for some programs). *Entrance requirements:* For master's and doctorate, GRE/GMAT. Additional exam requirements/recommendations for international students: Required—TOEFL (minimum score 80 iBT). *Application deadline:* For fall admission, 8/1 for domestic students, 4/1 for international students; for spring admission, 1/1 for domestic students, 9/1 for international students. Applications are processed on a rolling basis. Application fee: $75. Electronic applications accepted. *Expenses:* Tuition, state resident: full-time $12,467; part-time $692.50 per credit hour. Tuition, nonresident: full-time $25,095; part-time $1394.25 per credit hour. *Required fees:* $2669; $491.50 per semester. Tuition and fees vary according to course load, campus/location and program. *Financial support:* In 2016–17, 156 research assistantships with full tuition reimbursements (averaging $21,863 per year), 379 teaching assistantships with full tuition reimbursements (averaging $18,980 per year) were awarded. Financial award application deadline: 3/1; financial award applicants required to submit FAFSA. *Total annual research expenditures:* $22.3 million. *Unit head:* Dr. Sally C. Morton, Dean, 540-231-5422, Fax: 540-231-3380, E-mail: scmorton@vt.edu. *Application contact:* Teresa Price, Executive Assistant to the Dean and Grants Specialist, 540-231-6394, Fax: 540-231-3380, E-mail: tfprice@vt.edu.
Website: http://www.science.vt.edu/

**Virginia State University,** College of Graduate Studies, College of Natural and Health Sciences, Department of Psychology, Petersburg, VA 23806-0001. Offers behavioral and community health sciences (PhD); clinical health psychology (PhD); clinical psychology (MS); general psychology (MS). *Degree requirements:* For master's, one foreign language, thesis. *Entrance requirements:* For master's, GRE General Test.

**Wake Forest University,** Graduate School of Arts and Sciences, Department of Psychology, Winston-Salem, NC 27106. Offers MA. *Degree requirements:* For master's, one foreign language, comprehensive exam, thesis. *Entrance requirements:* For master's, GRE General Test. Additional exam requirements/recommendations for international students: Required—TOEFL (minimum score 79 iBT). Electronic applications accepted. *Faculty research:* Developmental, social, personality, experimental, and physiological psychology.

**Walden University,** Graduate Programs, School of Psychology, Minneapolis, MN 55401. Offers clinical psychology (MS), including counseling, general program; forensic psychology (MS), including forensic psychology in the community, general program, mental health applications, program planning and evaluation in forensic settings, psychology and legal systems; industrial organizational (MS, PhD), including consulting psychology, forensic (MS), forensic psychology (PhD), general practice, leadership development and coaching (MS), organizational diversity and social change, research evaluation (PhD); online teaching in psychology (Post-Master's Certificate); organizational psychology and development (Postbaccalaureate Certificate); psychology (MS, PhD), including applied psychology (MS), clinical psychology (PhD), crisis management and response (MS), educational psychology, forensic psychology (PhD), general psychology (MS), general psychology research (PhD), general psychology teaching (PhD), health psychology, leadership development and coaching (MS), psychology of culture (MS), psychology, public administration, and social change (MS), social psychology, terrorism and security (MS); psychology respecialization (Post-Doctoral Certificate). *Program availability:* Part-time, evening/weekend, online only, 100% online. Terminal master's awarded for partial completion of doctoral program. *Degree requirements:* For master's, thesis optional; for doctorate, thesis/dissertation,

residency. *Entrance requirements:* For master's, bachelor's degree or higher; minimum GPA of 2.5; official transcripts; goal statement (for some programs); access to computer and Internet; for doctorate, master's degree or higher; three years of related professional or academic experience (preferred); minimum GPA of 3.0; goal statement and current resume (for select programs); official transcripts; access to computer and Internet; for other advanced degree, relevant work experience; access to computer and Internet. Additional exam requirements/recommendations for international students: Required—TOEFL (minimum score 550 paper-based, 79 iBT), IELTS (minimum score 6.5), Michigan English Language Assessment Battery (minimum score 82), or PTE (minimum score 53). Electronic applications accepted.

**Washburn University,** College of Arts and Sciences, Department of Psychology, Topeka, KS 66621. Offers clinical psychology (MA). *Program availability:* Part-time. *Degree requirements:* For master's, comprehensive exam (for some programs), thesis or alternative. *Entrance requirements:* For master's, GRE General Test, 15 hours of undergraduate course work in psychology. Additional exam requirements/recommendations for international students: Required—TOEFL (minimum score 80 iBT). Electronic applications accepted. *Faculty research:* Metacognition, anxiety disorders, auditory perception, sports performance psychology, ADHD.

**Washington State University,** College of Arts and Sciences, Department of Psychology, Pullman, WA 99164. Offers clinical psychology (PhD); experimental psychology (PhD). Program applications must be made through the Pullman campus. *Accreditation:* APA (one or more programs are accredited). *Degree requirements:* For doctorate, comprehensive exam, thesis/dissertation, oral exam, written exam. *Entrance requirements:* For doctorate, GRE General Test, three letters of reference; summary data form; at least 18 credits of study in psychology; at least one course in statistics and research methodology; official transcripts; minimum cumulative undergraduate GPA of 3.0 or master's degree in psychology. Additional exam requirements/recommendations for international students: Required—TOEFL, IELTS. Electronic applications accepted. *Faculty research:* Adult psychopathology and therapy, child psychopathology, neuropsychology, health psychology.

**Washington University in St. Louis,** The Graduate School, Department of Philosophy, Program in Philosophy-Neuroscience-Psychology, St. Louis, MO 63130-4899. Offers PhD. *Degree requirements:* For doctorate, thesis/dissertation. *Entrance requirements:* For doctorate, GRE General Test, sample of written work. Additional exam requirements/recommendations for international students: Required—TOEFL. Electronic applications accepted. *Faculty research:* Philosophy of mind and language with a special emphasis on the philosophical dimensions of psychology, neuroscience, and linguistics.

**Washington University in St. Louis,** The Graduate School, Department of Psychological and Brain Sciences, St. Louis, MO 63130-4899. Offers aging and development (PhD). Terminal master's awarded for partial completion of doctoral program. *Degree requirements:* For doctorate, thesis/dissertation. *Entrance requirements:* For doctorate, GRE General Test. Additional exam requirements/recommendations for international students: Required—TOEFL. Electronic applications accepted. *Faculty research:* Behavior/brain/cognition; clinical; aging/development; social/personality.

**Wayne State University,** College of Liberal Arts and Sciences, Department of Psychology, Detroit, MI 48202. Offers behavioral and cognitive neuroscience (PhD); clinical psychology (PhD); cognitive, developmental and social psychology (PhD); industrial/organizational psychology (MA, PhD). Doctoral program admits for fall only. *Accreditation:* APA (one or more programs are accredited). *Faculty:* 36. *Students:* 98 full-time (65 women), 31 part-time (16 women); includes 19 minority (4 Black or African American, non-Hispanic/Latino; 2 Asian, non-Hispanic/Latino; 8 Hispanic/Latino; 5 Two or more races, non-Hispanic/Latino), 14 international. Average age 28. 478 applicants, 13% accepted, 33 enrolled. In 2016, 16 master's, 13 doctorates awarded. Terminal master's awarded for partial completion of doctoral program. *Degree requirements:* For master's, thesis (for some programs); for doctorate, thesis/dissertation, training assignments. *Entrance requirements:* For master's, GRE General Test, minimum undergraduate upper-division cumulative GPA of 3.0, courses in introductory psychology and statistics, two letters of recommendation, professional statement; for doctorate, GRE General Test, bachelor's, master's, or other advanced degree; at least twelve credits in psychology with minimum GPA of 3.0; courses in laboratory psychology and statistical methods in psychology; at least three letters of recommendation; statement of purpose. Additional exam requirements/recommendations for international students: Required—TOEFL (minimum score 550 paper-based; 79 iBT), TWE (minimum score 5.5), Michigan English Language Assessment Battery (minimum score 85); Recommended—IELTS (minimum score 6.5). Application fee: $50. Electronic applications accepted. *Expenses:* $16,503 per year resident tuition and fees, $33,697 per year non-resident tuition and fees. *Financial support:* In 2016–17, 90 students received support, including 12 fellowships with tuition reimbursements available (averaging $15,719 per year), 6 research assistantships with tuition reimbursements available (averaging $19,341 per year), 50 teaching assistantships with tuition reimbursements available (averaging $17,994 per year); scholarships/grants, health care benefits, and unspecified assistantships also available. Financial award applicants required to submit FAFSA. *Faculty research:* Behavioral neuroscience, cognitive/neuroscience of development and aging research, children, adolescents, and family research, cognition research, emotion research, health psychology research, homelessness and poverty research, memory research, neuropsychology research, personality/cognition, relationships research, substance use and abuse research, workplace adaptation, well-being and evaluation research. *Total annual research expenditures:* $1.4 million. *Unit head:* Boris Baltes, PhD, Chair/Professor, 313-577-2803, E-mail: b.baltes@wayne.edu. *Application contact:* Alia Allen, Academic Services Officer, 313-577-2823, E-mail: aallen@wayne.edu.
Website: http://clas.wayne.edu/psychology/

**Webster University,** College of Arts and Sciences, Department of Psychology, St. Louis, MO 63119-3194. Offers counseling psychology (MS); gerontology (MS). *Program availability:* Part-time. *Entrance requirements:* Additional exam requirements/recommendations for international students: Required—TOEFL. *Application deadline:* Applications are processed on a rolling basis. Application fee: $35 ($50 for international students). *Expenses: Tuition:* Full-time $21,900; part-time $730 per credit hour. Tuition and fees vary according to campus/location and program. *Financial support:* Federal Work-Study available. Support available to part-time students. Financial award application deadline: 4/1; financial award applicants required to submit FAFSA. *Application contact:* Debi Aholt, Department Manager, 314-246-6970, Fax: 314-246-6094, E-mail: aholtda@webster.edu.

**West Chester University of Pennsylvania,** College of the Sciences and Mathematics, Department of Psychology, West Chester, PA 19383. Offers clinical psychology (Psy D); industrial/organizational psychology (Certificate); psychology (MA), including general psychology, industrial/organizational psychology. *Program availability:* Part-time, evening/weekend. *Faculty:* 13 full-time (11 women), 6 part-time/adjunct (5 women). *Students:* 76 full-time (55 women), 20 part-time (14 women); includes 21 minority (10 Black or African American, non-Hispanic/Latino; 1 Asian, non-Hispanic/Latino; 5 Hispanic/Latino; 5 Two or more races, non-Hispanic/Latino), 1 international. Average

## Psychology—General

age 28. 122 applicants, 58% accepted, 35 enrolled. In 2016, 33 master's awarded. *Degree requirements:* For master's, comprehensive exam, thesis (for some programs). *Entrance requirements:* For master's, GRE General Test, minimum GPA of 3.0 overall, psychology 3.25; three letters of reference; for doctorate, GRE General Test, minimum GPA of 3.0 overall, psychology 3.25; three letters of reference; successful completion of psychology courses at the undergraduate and graduate level in abnormal/clinical psychology, research methods, and statistics; personal goals statement. Additional exam requirements/recommendations for international students: Required—TOEFL or IELTS. *Application deadline:* For fall admission, 5/15 for international students; for spring admission, 10/15 for international students. Applications are processed on a rolling basis. Application fee: $50. Electronic applications accepted. *Expenses:* Tuition, state resident: full-time $8694; part-time $483 per credit. Tuition, nonresident: full-time $13,050; part-time $725 per credit. *Required fees:* $2399; $119.05 per credit. Tuition and fees vary according to campus/location and program. *Financial support:* Scholarships/grants and unspecified assistantships available. Financial award application deadline: 2/15; financial award applicants required to submit FAFSA. *Faculty research:* Stress, coping, and resilience; preventative interventions; workplace stress; organizational leadership; eating disorders; schizophrenia; several other areas including diversity, cognition, and animal behavior. *Unit head:* Dr. Sandra Kerr, Interim Chairperson, 610-436-2945, E-mail: skerr@wcupa.edu. *Application contact:* Dr. Angela Clarke, Graduate Coordinator, 610-436-3136, E-mail: aclarke@wcupa.edu. Website: http://www.wcupa.edu/sciences-mathematics/psychology/

**Western Carolina University,** Graduate School, College of Education and Allied Professions, Department of Psychology, Cullowhee, NC 28723. Offers general psychology (MA). *Program availability:* Part-time. *Degree requirements:* For master's, comprehensive exam, thesis. *Entrance requirements:* For master's, GRE General Test, appropriate undergraduate degree, interview, 3 letters of recommendation. Additional exam requirements/recommendations for international students: Required—TOEFL (minimum score 550 paper-based; 79 iBT). *Expenses:* Tuition, state resident: full-time $2174. Tuition, nonresident: full-time $7377. *Required fees:* $1442. Part-time tuition and fees vary according to course load. *Faculty research:* Five-factor model of personality, evolutionary psychology, stress and worry, body image and physical attractiveness, moral decision-making, memory, learning styles.

**Western Illinois University,** School of Graduate Studies, College of Arts and Sciences, Department of Psychology, Macomb, IL 61455-1390. Offers clinical/community mental health (MS); general experimental psychology (MS); school psychology (SSP). *Program availability:* Part-time. *Students:* 37 full-time (22 women), 15 part-time (13 women); includes 6 minority (1 Black or African American, non-Hispanic/Latino; 2 Hispanic/Latino; 3 Two or more races, non-Hispanic/Latino), 2 international. Average age 25. 66 applicants, 52% accepted, 14 enrolled. In 2016, 11 master's, 7 other advanced degrees awarded. *Degree requirements:* For master's, comprehensive exam (for some programs), thesis or alternative. *Entrance requirements:* For master's and SSP, GRE General Test. Additional exam requirements/recommendations for international students: Required—TOEFL (minimum score 550 paper-based; 80 iBT). *Application fee:* $30. Electronic applications accepted. *Financial support:* In 2016–17, 34 students received support, including 6 research assistantships with full tuition reimbursements available (averaging $7,544 per year); unspecified assistantships also available. Financial award applicants required to submit FAFSA. *Unit head:* Dr. Karen Sears, Chairperson, 309-298-1593. *Application contact:* Dr. Nancy Parsons, Associate Provost and Director of Graduate Studies, 309-298-1806, Fax: 309-298-2345, E-mail: gradoffice@wiu.edu.
Website: http://wiu.edu/psychology

**Western Kentucky University,** Graduate Studies, College of Education and Behavioral Sciences, Department of Psychology, Bowling Green, KY 42101. Offers clinical psychology (MA); experimental psychology (MA); general psychology (MA); industrial/organizational psychology (MA); school psychology (Ed S). *Degree requirements:* For master's, comprehensive exam, thesis (for some programs); for Ed S, thesis, oral exam. *Entrance requirements:* For master's, GRE General Test; for Ed S, GRE General Test, minimum GPA of 3.5. Additional exam requirements/recommendations for international students: Required—TOEFL (minimum score 555 paper-based; 79 iBT). *Faculty research:* Neural regeneration, enhancing mobility in the elderly, improvement in visual processing in older adults, lifespan development.

**Western Michigan University,** Graduate College, College of Arts and Sciences, Department of Psychology, Kalamazoo, MI 49008. Offers behavior analysis (MA, PhD); clinical psychology (PhD); industrial/organizational behavior management (MA). *Accreditation:* APA (one or more programs are accredited). *Degree requirements:* For master's, variable foreign language requirement, thesis; for doctorate, 2 foreign languages, comprehensive exam, thesis/dissertation.

**Western Washington University,** Graduate School, College of Humanities and Social Sciences, Department of Psychology, Bellingham, WA 98225-5996. Offers experimental psychology (MS); mental health counseling (MS); school counseling (M Ed). *Accreditation:* ACA (one or more programs are accredited). *Degree requirements:* For master's, comprehensive exam, thesis (for some programs). *Entrance requirements:* For master's, GRE General Test, minimum GPA of 3.0 in last 60 semester hours or last 90 quarter hours. Additional exam requirements/recommendations for international students: Required—TOEFL (minimum score 567 paper-based). *Faculty research:* Social, cognitive, behavioral neuroscience, counseling/clinical, developmental.

**Westfield State University,** College of Graduate and Continuing Education, Department of Psychology, Westfield, MA 01086. Offers applied behavior analysis (MA); counseling (MA), including forensic mental health counseling, mental health counseling, school adjustment counseling, school guidance counseling. *Program availability:* Part-time, evening/weekend. *Faculty:* 9 full-time (4 women), 6 part-time/adjunct (2 women). *Students:* 57 full-time (45 women), 23 part-time (14 women); includes 12 minority (1 Asian, non-Hispanic/Latino; 9 Hispanic/Latino; 2 Two or more races, non-Hispanic/Latino). Average age 25. 68 applicants, 65% accepted, 33 enrolled. In 2016, 44 master's awarded. *Degree requirements:* For master's, comprehensive exam, practicum. *Entrance requirements:* For master's, GRE General Test, MAT, minimum undergraduate GPA of 3.0. Additional exam requirements/recommendations for international students: Recommended—TOEFL (minimum score 550 paper-based; 79 iBT). *Application deadline:* For fall admission, 2/1 for domestic students. Applications are processed on a rolling basis. Application fee: $50. *Expenses:* Tuition, state resident: part-time $318 per semester hour. Tuition, nonresident: part-time $318 per semester hour. *Required fees:* $75 per semester. Tuition and fees vary according to course load and program. *Financial support:* Unspecified assistantships available. Financial award application deadline: 3/1; financial award applicants required to submit FAFSA. *Unit head:* Dr. Ricki Kantrowitz, Director, 413-572-5378. *Application contact:* Shelly Henrichon, Coordinator of DGCE Admissions, 413-572-8022, Fax: 413-572-5227, E-mail: mhenrichon@westfield.ma.edu.

**West Texas A&M University,** College of Education and Social Sciences, Department of Psychology, Sociology and Social Work, Canyon, TX 79016-0001. Offers psychology (MA); social work (MS). *Program availability:* Part-time, evening/weekend. *Degree requirements:* For master's, comprehensive exam, thesis optional. *Entrance requirements:* For master's, GRE General Test, 3 letters of recommendation; interview;

minimum GPA of 3.25 in psychology, 3.0 overall. Additional exam requirements/recommendations for international students: Required—TOEFL. *Application deadline:* For fall admission, 8/1 for domestic students, 6/1 for international students; for spring admission, 12/1 for domestic students, 11/1 for international students; for summer admission, 5/1 for domestic students. Applications are processed on a rolling basis. Application fee: $40 ($75 for international students). Electronic applications accepted. *Financial support:* Application deadline: 2/1; applicants required to submit FAFSA. *Unit head:* Dr. Keith Price, Department Head, 806-651-2418.

**West Virginia University,** Eberly College of Arts and Sciences, Department of Psychology, Morgantown, WV 26506. Offers behavior analysis (PhD); clinical psychology (MA, PhD); development psychology (PhD); psychology (MS). *Accreditation:* APA (one or more programs are accredited). *Program availability:* Part-time. Terminal master's awarded for partial completion of doctoral program. *Degree requirements:* For master's, thesis optional; for doctorate, comprehensive exam, thesis/dissertation. *Entrance requirements:* For master's and doctorate, GRE General Test, minimum GPA of 3.0. Additional exam requirements/recommendations for international students: Required—TOEFL. *Faculty research:* Adult and child clinical psychology, behavioral assessment and therapy, child and adolescent behavior, life span development, experimental and applied behavior analysis.

**Wheaton College,** Graduate School, Department of Psychology, Wheaton, IL 60187-5593. Offers clinical mental health counseling (MA); clinical psychology (Psy D); counseling ministries (MA); marriage and family therapy (MA). *Accreditation:* APA (one or more programs are accredited). *Faculty:* 14 full-time (7 women), 9 part-time/adjunct (5 women). *Students:* 130 full-time (97 women), 17 part-time (13 women); includes 38 minority (13 Black or African American, non-Hispanic/Latino; 1 American Indian or Alaska Native, non-Hispanic/Latino; 9 Asian, non-Hispanic/Latino; 8 Hispanic/Latino; 7 Two or more races, non-Hispanic/Latino), 17 international. Average age 28. 115 applicants, 80% accepted, 58 enrolled. In 2016, 70 master's, 9 doctorates awarded. Terminal master's awarded for partial completion of doctoral program. *Degree requirements:* For master's, thesis or alternative; for doctorate, thesis/dissertation, internship. *Entrance requirements:* For master's, GRE General Test, 18 hours of course work in psychology; for doctorate, GRE General Test. Additional exam requirements/recommendations for international students: Required—TOEFL (minimum score 550 paper-based; 80 iBT), IELTS (minimum score 6.5), TOEFL (minimum score 600 paper-based; 90 iBT) or IELTS (minimum score 7.5) for PsyD. *Application deadline:* For fall admission, 3/1 priority date for domestic students, 1/1 for international students. Applications are processed on a rolling basis. Application fee: $30. *Expenses: Tuition:* Full-time $19,080; part-time $795 per credit hour. Tuition and fees vary according to degree level and program. *Financial support:* In 2016–17, 3 research assistantships (averaging $4,800 per year) were awarded; career-related internships or fieldwork, Federal Work-Study, scholarships/grants, and unspecified assistantships also available. Financial award application deadline: 3/1; financial award applicants required to submit FAFSA. *Unit head:* Dr. Terri Watson, Associate Dean of Psychology, 630-752-5104, E-mail: psychology@wheaton.edu. *Application contact:* Dusty Di Santo, Director of Graduate Admissions, 630-752-5195, Fax: 630-752-7047, E-mail: graduate.admissions@wheaton.edu.
Website: http://www.wheaton.edu/academics/departments/psychology

**Wichita State University,** Graduate School, Fairmount College of Liberal Arts and Sciences, Department of Psychology, Wichita, KS 67260. Offers clinical (PhD); community (PhD); human factors (PhD). *Accreditation:* APA. *Program availability:* Part-time. *Application deadline:* For fall admission, 12/1 for domestic and international students. Application fee: $50 ($65 for international students). *Unit head:* Dr. Rhonda K. Lewis, Chair, 316-978-3170, Fax: 316-978-3006, E-mail: rhonda.lewis@wichita.edu. *Application contact:* Jordan Oleson, Admissions Coordinator, 316-978-3095, Fax: 316-978-3253, E-mail: jordan.oleson@wichita.edu.
Website: http://www.wichita.edu/psychology

**Widener University,** School of Human Service Professions, Institute for Graduate Clinical Psychology, Law-Psychology Program, Chester, PA 19013-5792. Offers JD/Psy D. *Faculty:* 15 full-time (6 women), 18 part-time/adjunct (10 women). *Students:* 1 full-time (0 women), 1 (woman) part-time. Average age 23. 21 applicants, 19% accepted. *Application deadline:* For fall admission, 2/1 for domestic students. Applications are processed on a rolling basis. Application fee: $60. Electronic applications accepted. Tuition and fees vary according to degree level and program. *Financial support:* Research assistantships, career-related internships or fieldwork, Federal Work-Study, institutionally sponsored loans, and scholarships/grants available. Financial award application deadline: 5/31. *Unit head:* Dr. Amiram Elwork, Director, 610-499-1206, Fax: 610-499-4625, E-mail: amiram.elwork@widener.edu. *Application contact:* Maureen A. Brennan, Admissions Coordinator, 610-499-1206, Fax: 610-499-4625, E-mail: maureen.a.brennan@widener.edu.

**Wilfrid Laurier University,** Faculty of Graduate and Postdoctoral Studies, Faculty of Science, Department of Psychology, Waterloo, ON N2L 3C5, Canada. Offers behavioral neuroscience (M Sc, PhD); cognitive neuroscience (M Sc, PhD); community psychology (MA, PhD); social and developmental psychology (MA, PhD). *Program availability:* Part-time. *Degree requirements:* For master's, thesis; for doctorate, thesis/dissertation. *Entrance requirements:* For master's, GRE General Test, honors BA or the equivalent in psychology, minimum B average in undergraduate course work; for doctorate, GRE General Test, master's degree, minimum A- average. Additional exam requirements/recommendations for international students: Required—TOEFL (minimum score 89 iBT). Electronic applications accepted. *Faculty research:* Brain and cognition, community psychology, social and developmental psychology.

**William Carey University,** Department of Psychology and Graduate Counseling, Hattiesburg, MS 39401-5499. Offers counseling psychology (MS). *Program availability:* Part-time. *Entrance requirements:* For master's, GRE, PRAXIS, MAT, minimum GPA of 2.5. Additional exam requirements/recommendations for international students: Required—TOEFL (minimum score 550 paper-based). *Expenses:* Contact institution. *Faculty research:* Addiction prevention, psychometric measurement, crisis counseling, gerontology.

**William James College,** Graduate Programs, Newton, MA 02459. Offers applied psychology in higher education student personnel administration (MA); clinical psychology (Psy D); counseling psychology (MA); counseling psychology and community mental health (MA); counseling psychology and global mental health (MA); executive coaching (Graduate Certificate); forensic and counseling psychology (MA); leadership psychology (Psy D); organizational psychology (MA); primary care psychology (MA); respecialization in clinical psychology (Certificate); school psychology (Psy D); MA/CAGS. *Accreditation:* APA. *Degree requirements:* For master's, comprehensive exam (for some programs); for doctorate, thesis/dissertation (for some programs). Electronic applications accepted.

**Winthrop University,** College of Arts and Sciences, Department of Psychology, Rock Hill, SC 29733. Offers MS, SSP. *Degree requirements:* For master's, comprehensive exam; for SSP, thesis or alternative, portfolio. *Entrance requirements:* For master's, GRE General Test, interview, minimum GPA of 3.0, 3 letters of recommendation, 15 hours of psychology courses in specified subject areas. Additional exam requirements/

recommendations for international students: Required—TOEFL (minimum score 550 paper-based; 79 iBT), IELTS (minimum score 6). Electronic applications accepted. *Expenses:* Tuition, state resident: full-time $14,312; part-time $599 per credit hour. Tuition, nonresident: full-time $27,570; part-time $1153 per credit hour.

**Wisconsin School of Professional Psychology,** Program in Clinical Psychology, Milwaukee, WI 53225-4960. Offers MA, Psy D. *Accreditation:* APA. *Program availability:* Part-time, evening/weekend. Terminal master's awarded for partial completion of doctoral program. *Degree requirements:* For master's, candidacy exam, 500 hours of supervised clinical practica; for doctorate, thesis/dissertation, 1 year clinical intern and practicum experience (2000 hrs), candidacy and clinical exams. *Entrance requirements:* For master's, GRE General Test, GRE Subject Test, bachelor's degree in psychology, writing sample; for doctorate, GRE General Test, GRE Subject Test, master's degree in clinical psychology or equivalent, writing sample. *Faculty research:* Violence prevention, psychology of women, forensic psychology, custody evaluation, aging, harm reduction in AODA.

**Wright Institute,** Doctoral Program in Clinical Psychology, Berkeley, CA 94704. Offers Psy D. *Accreditation:* APA. *Degree requirements:* For doctorate, comprehensive exam, thesis/dissertation. *Entrance requirements:* For doctorate, GRE General Test, statistics, human development, theories of personality and/or abnormal psychology. Additional exam requirements/recommendations for international students: Required—TOEFL (minimum score 600 paper-based). *Application deadline:* For fall admission, 1/5 priority date for domestic and international students. Application fee: $50. Electronic applications accepted. *Financial support:* Research assistantships, teaching assistantships, career-related internships or fieldwork, Federal Work-Study, and scholarships/grants available. Financial award applicants required to submit FAFSA. *Unit head:* Dr. Gilbert Newman, Dean, 510-841-9230 Ext. 110, E-mail: gnewman@wi.edu. *Application contact:* John Pitts, Director of Admissions, 510-841-9230 Ext. 171, E-mail: jpitts@wi.edu.
Website: https://www.wi.edu/psyd-program

**Wright State University,** Graduate School, College of Science and Mathematics, Department of Psychology, Dayton, OH 45435. Offers human factors and industrial/organizational psychology (MS, PhD). *Degree requirements:* For master's, thesis; for doctorate, thesis/dissertation. *Entrance requirements:* For master's, GRE General Test. Additional exam requirements/recommendations for international students: Required—TOEFL. Application fee: $25. *Expenses:* Tuition, state resident: full-time $9952; part-time $622 per credit hour. Tuition, nonresident: full-time $16,960; part-time $1060 per credit hour. *Financial support:* Fellowships, research assistantships, and teaching assistantships available. Support available to part-time students. Financial award applicants required to submit FAFSA. *Unit head:* Dr. John Flach, Chair, 937-775-2391, Fax: 937-775-3347, E-mail: john.flach@wright.edu. *Application contact:* Dr. Dan Weber, Director, 937-775-2391, Fax: 937-775-3347, E-mail: dan.weber@wright.edu.

**Wright State University,** School of Professional Psychology, Dayton, OH 45435. Offers clinical psychology (Psy D). *Accreditation:* APA. *Degree requirements:* For doctorate, thesis/dissertation. *Entrance requirements:* For doctorate, GRE General Test, GRE Subject Test. Additional exam requirements/recommendations for international

students: Required—TOEFL. *Application deadline:* For fall admission, 12/15 for domestic students. Application fee: $30. *Expenses:* Contact institution. *Financial support:* Fellowships, teaching assistantships, career-related internships or fieldwork, Federal Work-Study, institutionally sponsored loans, and unspecified assistantships available. Financial award application deadline: 4/15; financial award applicants required to submit FAFSA. *Unit head:* Dr. John R. Rudisill, Dean, 937-775-3490, Fax: 937-775-3434, E-mail: john.rudisill@wright.edu. *Application contact:* Leona L. Gray, Director, Student Services and Admissions, 937-775-3492, Fax: 937-775-3493, E-mail: leona.gray@wright.edu.
Website: http://www.wright.edu/sopp/

**Xavier University,** College of Social Sciences, Health and Education, Department of Psychology, Cincinnati, OH 45207. Offers clinical psychology (Psy D); industrial-organizational psychology (MA). *Accreditation:* APA (one or more programs are accredited). *Degree requirements:* For master's, one foreign language, comprehensive exam, thesis, internship; for doctorate, one foreign language, comprehensive exam, thesis/dissertation, internship. *Entrance requirements:* For master's, GRE, official transcript; 3 letters of recommendation; for doctorate, GRE General Test; GRE Subject Test in psychology (if no undergraduate degree in psychology), bachelor's or master's degree; 18 semester hours of psychology coursework; minimum GPA of 3.0; work and research experience; official transcript; 3 letters of recommendation; statement of purpose. Additional exam requirements/recommendations for international students: Required—TOEFL (minimum score 550 paper-based; 79 iBT), IELTS (minimum score 6.5). Electronic applications accepted. *Expenses:* Contact institution. *Faculty research:* Older adults, clinical child and adolescent issues, personnel selection and employee behavior, at-risk youth, sexual abuse.

**Yale University,** Graduate School of Arts and Sciences, Department of Psychology, New Haven, CT 06520. Offers behavioral neuroscience (PhD); clinical psychology (PhD); cognitive psychology (PhD); developmental psychology (PhD); social/personality psychology (PhD). *Accreditation:* APA. *Degree requirements:* For doctorate, thesis/dissertation. *Entrance requirements:* For doctorate, GRE General Test.

**Yeshiva University,** Ferkauf Graduate School of Psychology, New York, NY 10033-3201. Offers MA, PhD, Psy D. *Accreditation:* APA (one or more programs are accredited). *Program availability:* Part-time. *Degree requirements:* For doctorate, comprehensive exam, thesis/dissertation. *Entrance requirements:* For master's and doctorate, GRE General Test.

**York University,** Faculty of Graduate Studies, Faculty of Health, Program in Psychology, Toronto, ON M3J 1P3, Canada. Offers MA, PhD. *Program availability:* Part-time. *Degree requirements:* For master's, thesis, practicum; for doctorate, thesis/dissertation, practicum. *Entrance requirements:* For master's, GRE. Electronic applications accepted.

**Youngstown State University,** Graduate School, College of Liberal Arts and Social Sciences, Department of Psychology, Youngstown, OH 44555-0001. Offers applied behavior analysis (MS).

# Addictions/Substance Abuse Counseling

**Adler Graduate School,** Program in Adlerian Counseling and Psychotherapy, Richfield, MN 55423. Offers Adlerian studies (MA); art therapy (MA); clinical mental health counseling (MA); co-occurring mental health and substance abuse disorders (MA); marriage and family therapy (MA); school counseling (MA). *Program availability:* Part-time, evening/weekend. *Faculty:* 71 part-time/adjunct (55 women). *Students:* 298 part-time (225 women); includes 51 minority (40 Black or African American, non-Hispanic/Latino; 6 American Indian or Alaska Native, non-Hispanic/Latino; 5 Hispanic/Latino). *Degree requirements:* For master's, thesis or alternative, 500-700 hour internship (depending on license choice). *Entrance requirements:* For master's, interview, official transcripts, minimum cumulative GPA of 3.0. *Application deadline:* Applications are processed on a rolling basis. Application fee: $50. Electronic applications accepted. *Financial support:* Career-related internships or fieldwork and tuition waivers available. Support available to part-time students. Financial award applicants required to submit FAFSA. *Unit head:* Dr. Dan Haugen, President, 612-767-7048, Fax: 612-861-7559, E-mail: haugen@alfredadler.edu. *Application contact:* Evelyn B. Haas, Director of Admissions, 612-767-7044, Fax: 612-861-7559, E-mail: ev@alfredadler.edu.

**Adler University,** Programs in Psychology, Chicago, IL 60602. Offers advanced Adlerian psychotherapy (Certificate); art therapy (MA); clinical mental health counseling (MA); clinical neuropsychology (Certificate); clinical psychology (Psy D); community psychology (MA); counseling and organizational psychology (MA); counseling psychology (MA); counselor education and supervision (PhD); couple and family therapy (DCFT); criminology (MA); emergency management leadership (MA); forensic psychology (MA); marriage and family counseling (MA); marriage and family therapy (Certificate); military psychology (MA); nonprofit management (MA); organizational psychology (MA); police psychology (MA); public policy and administration (MA); rehabilitation counseling (MA); sport and health psychology (MA); substance abuse counseling (Certificate); Psy D/Certificate; Psy D/MACAT; Psy D/MACP; Psy D/MAMFC; Psy D/MASAC. *Accreditation:* APA. *Program availability:* Part-time, evening/weekend, online learning. Terminal master's awarded for partial completion of doctoral program. *Degree requirements:* For master's, thesis or alternative, oral exam, practicum; for doctorate, thesis/dissertation, clinical exam, internship, oral exam, practicum, written qualifying exam. *Entrance requirements:* For master's, 12 semester hours in psychology, minimum GPA of 3.0; for doctorate, 18 semester hours in psychology, minimum GPA of 3.25; for Certificate, appropriate master's or doctoral degree. Additional exam requirements/recommendations for international students: Required—TOEFL (minimum score 550 paper-based; 79 iBT). Electronic applications accepted.

**See Display on page 982 and Close-Up on page 1225.**

**Alliant International University–Los Angeles,** California School of Professional Psychology, Program in Couple and Family Therapy, Alhambra, CA 91803. Offers chemical dependency (MA); gerontology (MA); Latin American family therapy (MA). *Accreditation:* AAMFT/COAMFTE. *Program availability:* Part-time, evening/weekend. Terminal master's awarded for partial completion of doctoral program. *Degree requirements:* For master's, comprehensive exam, 50 hours of professional development activities. *Entrance requirements:* Additional exam requirements/recommendations for international students: Required—TOEFL (minimum score 550

paper-based). Electronic applications accepted. *Faculty research:* Foster care, therapy with minority couples, parenting, marriage, trauma.

**Antioch University New England,** Graduate School, Department of Applied Psychology, Program in Clinical Mental Health Counseling, Keene, NH 03431-3552. Offers clinical mental health counseling (MA); substance abuse counseling (MA). *Accreditation:* ACA. *Degree requirements:* For master's, internship, practicum. *Entrance requirements:* For master's, previous course work and work experience in psychology. Additional exam requirements/recommendations for international students: Required—TOEFL (minimum score 550 paper-based). Electronic applications accepted. *Expenses:* Contact institution. *Faculty research:* Multicultural issues in field supervision.

**Argosy University, Hawai`i,** Hawai'i School of Professional Psychology, Program in Substance Abuse Counseling, Honolulu, HI 96813. Offers Certificate.

**Arkansas State University,** Graduate School, College of Nursing and Health Professions, Department of Social Work, State University, AR 72467. Offers addiction studies (Graduate Certificate); social work (MSW). *Accreditation:* CSWE. *Program availability:* Part-time. *Degree requirements:* For master's and Graduate Certificate, comprehensive exam, thesis (for some programs). *Entrance requirements:* For master's and Graduate Certificate, GRE or MAT, appropriate bachelor's degree, letters of reference, personal statement, resume, official transcript, immunization records. Additional exam requirements/recommendations for international students: Required—TOEFL (minimum score 550 paper-based; 79 iBT), IELTS (minimum score 6), PTE (minimum score 56). Electronic applications accepted. *Expenses:* Contact institution.

**Assumption College,** Addiction Counseling Program, Worcester, MA 01609-1296. Offers CGS. *Program availability:* Part-time, evening/weekend. *Entrance requirements:* For degree, bachelor's degree, 3 letters of recommendation, official transcripts, personal statement, current resume. Additional exam requirements/recommendations for international students: Required—TOEFL (minimum score 540 paper-based; 76 iBT), IELTS (minimum score 6). *Application deadline:* Applications are processed on a rolling basis. Application fee: $30. Electronic applications accepted. *Expenses:* Tuition: Full-time $11,610; part-time $645 per credit. *Required fees:* $70 per term. Tuition and fees vary according to course load and program. *Unit head:* Dr. Leonard A. Doerfler, Director, 508-767-7549, Fax: 508-767-7263, E-mail: doerfler@assumption.edu. *Application contact:* Karen Stoyanoff, Director of Recruitment for Graduate Enrollment, 508-767-7442, Fax: 508-799-4412, E-mail: graduate@assumption.edu.
Website: http://graduate.assumption.edu/addiction-counseling/addiction-counseling

**Bay Path University,** Program in Clinical Mental Health Counseling, Longmeadow, MA 01106-2292. Offers clinical mental health counseling (MS), including alcohol and drug abuse counseling, early intervention. Program also offered in Sturbridge and Burlington, MA. *Program availability:* Part-time, blended/hybrid learning. *Students:* 85 full-time (78 women), 83 part-time (76 women); includes 43 minority (19 Black or African American, non-Hispanic/Latino; 1 Asian, non-Hispanic/Latino; 17 Hispanic/Latino; 6 Two or more races, non-Hispanic/Latino), 16 international. Average age 31. 75 applicants, 72% accepted, 40 enrolled. In 2016, 21 master's awarded. *Degree requirements:* For master's, 48 course credits plus 12 credit practicum, internship. *Application deadline:* Applications are processed on a rolling basis. Application fee: $45. Electronic applications accepted. Application fee is waived when completed online. *Expenses:* $21,465. *Financial support:* Unspecified assistantships available. Financial award

## Addictions/Substance Abuse Counseling

applicants required to submit FAFSA. *Unit head:* Dr. Mark Benander, Director, 413-565-1332, E-mail: mbenander@baypath.edu. *Application contact:* Diane Ranaldi, Dean of Graduate Admissions, 413-565-1332, Fax: 413-565-1250, E-mail: dranaldi@baypath.edu.
Website: http://graduate.baypath.edu/graduate-programs/programs-on-campus/ms-programs/clinical-mental-health

**Cambridge College,** School of Psychology and Counseling, Cambridge, MA 02138-5304. Offers addiction counseling (M Ed); alcohol and drug counseling (Certificate); counseling psychology (M Ed, CAGS); counseling psychology: forensic counseling (M Ed); marriage and family therapy (M Ed); mental health and addiction counseling (M Ed); mental health counseling (M Ed); mental health counseling for school guidance counselors (Post Master's Certificate); psychological studies (M Ed); school adjustment and mental health counseling (M Ed); school adjustment, mental health and addiction counseling (M Ed); school guidance counselor (M Ed); trauma studies (Certificate). *Program availability:* Part-time, evening/weekend. *Degree requirements:* For master's and other advanced degree, thesis, practicum/internship. *Entrance requirements:* For master's, resume, 2 professional references; for other advanced degree, official transcripts, documents for transfer credit evaluation, resume, written personal statement/essay, 2 professional references, health insurance, immunizations form. Additional exam requirements/recommendations for international students: Required—TOEFL (minimum score 550 paper-based; 79 iBT), Michigan English Language Assessment Battery (minimum score 85); Recommended—IELTS (minimum score 6). Electronic applications accepted. *Expenses:* Contact institution. *Faculty research:* Trauma, drug and alcohol counseling, cross-cultural issues, school counseling, trauma in schools.

**Capella University,** Harold Abel School of Social and Behavioral Science, Doctoral Programs in Psychology, Minneapolis, MN 55402. Offers addiction psychology (PhD); clinical psychology (Psy D); educational psychology (PhD); general advanced studies in human behavior (PhD); general psychology (PhD); industrial/organizational psychology (PhD); school psychology (Psy D).

**Capella University,** Harold Abel School of Social and Behavioral Science, Master's Programs in Counseling, Minneapolis, MN 55402. Offers child and adolescent development (MS); general addiction counseling (MS); general marriage and family counseling/therapy (MS); general mental health counseling (MS); general school counseling (MS).

**Carlow University,** College of Leadership and Social Change, Program in Professional Counseling, Pittsburgh, PA 15213-3165. Offers addictions (MS); adult/generalist (MS); child and family (MS); professional counseling (Certificate); trauma-informed (MS). *Program availability:* Part-time, evening/weekend. *Students:* 127 full-time (111 women), 23 part-time (19 women); includes 46 minority (34 Black or African American, non-Hispanic/Latino; 1 American Indian or Alaska Native, non-Hispanic/Latino; 2 Asian, non-Hispanic/Latino; 5 Hispanic/Latino; 4 Two or more races, non-Hispanic/Latino), 1 international. Average age 30. 49 applicants, 86% accepted, 26 enrolled. In 2016, 41 master's, 1 other advanced degree awarded. *Entrance requirements:* For master's, personal essay; resume or curriculum vitae; three recommendations; official transcripts; interview; minimum undergraduate GPA of 3.0. Additional exam requirements/recommendations for international students: Required—TOEFL (minimum score 550 paper-based). *Application deadline:* Applications are processed on a rolling basis. Electronic applications accepted. *Expenses: Tuition:* Full-time $11,855; part-time $801 per credit. *Required fees:* $182; $13 per credit. Tuition and fees vary according to course load, degree level and program. *Financial support:* Application deadline: 4/1; applicants required to submit FAFSA. *Unit head:* Dr. Travis W. Schermer, Director, 412-575-6650, Fax: 412-575-6357, E-mail: twschermer@carlow.edu.
Website: http://www.carlow.edu/Master_of_Science_in_Professional_Counseling.aspx

**The College of New Jersey,** Office of Graduate and Advancing Education, School of Education, Department of Counselor Education, Program in Community Counseling: Substance Abuse and Addiction Specialization, Ewing, NJ 08628. Offers MA, Certificate. *Program availability:* Part-time. *Degree requirements:* For master's, comprehensive exam. *Entrance requirements:* For master's, GRE, minimum GPA of 3.0 in field or 2.75 overall; for Certificate, previous master's degree or higher. Additional exam requirements/recommendations for international students: Required—TOEFL. Electronic applications accepted.

**College of St. Joseph,** Graduate Programs, Division of Psychology and Human Services, Program in Alcohol and Substance Abuse Counseling, Rutland, VT 05701-3899. Offers MS. *Program availability:* Part-time. *Degree requirements:* For master's, comprehensive exam. *Entrance requirements:* For master's, official college transcripts; 2 letters of reference. Additional exam requirements/recommendations for international students: Required—TOEFL (minimum score 550 paper-based). *Application deadline:* Applications are processed on a rolling basis. Application fee: $35. Electronic applications accepted. *Expenses: Tuition,* area resident: Full-time $13,800; part-time $560 per credit. *Required fees:* $75 per semester. Full-time tuition and fees vary according to course load. *Financial support:* Application deadline: 3/1. *Unit head:* Dr. Craig Knapp, Chair, 802-773-5900 Ext. 3219, Fax: 802-776-5258, E-mail: cknapp@csj.edu. *Application contact:* Alan Young, Dean of Admissions, 802-773-5900 Ext. 3227, Fax: 802-776-5310, E-mail: alanyoung@csj.edu.

**The College of William and Mary,** School of Education, Program in Counselor Education, Williamsburg, VA 23187-8795. Offers addictions counseling (M Ed); community counseling (M Ed); counselor education (PhD); family counseling (M Ed); school counseling (M Ed). *Accreditation:* ACA; NCATE. *Faculty:* 9 full-time (2 women), 6 part-time/adjunct (5 women). *Students:* 69 full-time (47 women), 4 part-time (3 women); includes 15 minority (4 Black or African American, non-Hispanic/Latino; 1 Asian, non-Hispanic/Latino; 6 Hispanic/Latino; 4 Two or more races, non-Hispanic/Latino), 5 international. Average age 27. 116 applicants, 48% accepted, 28 enrolled. In 2016, 24 master's, 6 doctorates awarded. *Degree requirements:* For doctorate, comprehensive exam, thesis/dissertation. *Entrance requirements:* For master's, GRE, minimum GPA of 3.0; for doctorate, GRE, minimum GPA of 3.5. Additional exam requirements/recommendations for international students: Required—TOEFL (minimum score 100 iBT), IELTS (minimum score 7). *Application deadline:* For fall admission, 1/15 for domestic and international students. Application fee: $50. Electronic applications accepted. *Expenses:* $14,258 per year in-state full-time, $275 per credit in-state part-time; $30,500 per year out-of-state full-time, $1,200 per credit out-of-state part-time. *Financial support:* In 2016–17, 37 students received support, including 29 research assistantships (averaging $17,725 per year); career-related internships or fieldwork, scholarships/grants, and unspecified assistantships also available. Financial award application deadline: 1/15; financial award applicants required to submit FAFSA. *Faculty research:* Sexuality, multicultural education, addiction counseling, transpersonal psychology, measurement and evaluation in counseling. *Unit head:* Dr. Charles F. Gressard, Department Chair, 757-221-2352, E-mail: cfgres@wm.edu. *Application contact:* Dorothy Smith Osborne, Assistant Dean for Academic Programs and Student Services, 757-221-2317, E-mail: dsosbo@wm.edu.
Website: http://education.wm.edu

**Coppin State University,** Division of Graduate Studies, Division of Arts and Sciences, Department of Applied Psychology and Rehabilitation Counseling, Program in Alcohol and Substance Abuse Counseling, Baltimore, MD 21216-3698. Offers MS. *Program availability:* Part-time. *Degree requirements:* For master's, comprehensive exam (for some programs), thesis optional, internship, clinical requirement. *Entrance requirements:* For master's, GRE General Test, interview, minimum GPA of 3.0.

**East Carolina University,** Graduate School, College of Allied Health Sciences, Department of Addictions and Rehabilitation Studies, Greenville, NC 27858-4353. Offers military and trauma counseling (Certificate); rehabilitation and career counseling (MS); rehabilitation counseling (Certificate); rehabilitation counseling and administration (PhD); substance abuse and clinical counseling (MS); substance abuse counseling (Certificate); vocational evaluation (Certificate). *Accreditation:* CORE. *Program availability:* Part-time, evening/weekend. *Students:* 86 full-time (73 women), 44 part-time (38 women); includes 39 minority (34 Black or African American, non-Hispanic/Latino; 1 American Indian or Alaska Native, non-Hispanic/Latino; 2 Asian, non-Hispanic/Latino; 2 Hispanic/Latino). Average age 32. 80 applicants, 85% accepted, 50 enrolled. In 2016, 22 master's, 2 doctorates awarded. *Degree requirements:* For master's, comprehensive exam, thesis or alternative, internship. *Entrance requirements:* For master's, GRE General Test or MAT. Additional exam requirements/recommendations for international students: Required—TOEFL. *Application deadline:* For fall admission, 3/1 priority date for domestic students; for spring admission, 10/1 priority date for domestic students. Applications are processed on a rolling basis. Application fee: $50. *Financial support:* Research assistantships with partial tuition reimbursements, teaching assistantships with partial tuition reimbursements, Federal Work-Study, and scholarships/grants available. Support available to part-time students. Financial award application deadline: 3/1. *Unit head:* Dr. Paul Toriello, Chair, 252-744-6292, E-mail: toriellop@ecu.edu. Website: http://www.ecu.edu/rehb/

**East Carolina University,** Graduate School, College of Health and Human Performance, School of Social Work, Greenville, NC 27858-4353. Offers gerontology (Certificate); social work (MSW); substance abuse (Certificate). *Accreditation:* CSWE. *Program availability:* Online learning. *Students:* 99 full-time (90 women), 38 part-time (32 women); includes 63 minority (51 Black or African American, non-Hispanic/Latino; 3 Asian, non-Hispanic/Latino; 7 Hispanic/Latino; 2 Two or more races, non-Hispanic/Latino). Average age 31. 129 applicants, 77% accepted, 66 enrolled. In 2016, 82 master's awarded. *Degree requirements:* For master's, comprehensive exam. *Entrance requirements:* For master's, GRE or MAT. Additional exam requirements/recommendations for international students: Required—TOEFL. *Application deadline:* For fall admission, 2/1 priority date for domestic and international students. Application fee: $50. *Financial support:* Fellowships and research assistantships available. Financial award application deadline: 6/1. *Faculty research:* Social research, gerontology, women's issues, social services in schools, human behavior. *Unit head:* Dr. Shelia Bunch, Director, 252-328-4202, E-mail: bunchs@ecu.edu. *Application contact:* Dean of Graduate School, 252-328-6012, Fax: 252-328-6071, E-mail: gradschool@ecu.edu.
Website: http://www.ecu.edu/cs-hhp/socw/

**Fairfield University,** Graduate School of Education and Allied Professions, Fairfield, CT 06824. Offers applied behavior analysis (ATC); applied psychology (MA); clinical mental health counseling (MA, CAS); educational technology (MA); elementary education (MA, CAS); family studies (MA); integration of spirituality and religion in counseling (ATC); marriage and family therapy (MA); reading and language development (Sixth Year Certificate); school counseling (MA, CAS); school psychology (MA, CAS); school-based marriage and family therapy (ATC); secondary education (MA); special education (MA, CAS); substance abuse counseling (ATC); teaching (Certificate); teaching and foundations (MA, CAS); TESOL, world languages, and bilingual education (MA, CAS). *Accreditation:* NCATE. *Program availability:* Part-time, evening/weekend. *Faculty:* 19 full-time (15 women), 38 part-time/adjunct (26 women). *Students:* 153 full-time (132 women), 302 part-time (252 women); includes 97 minority (24 Black or African American, non-Hispanic/Latino; 12 Asian, non-Hispanic/Latino; 55 Hispanic/Latino; 6 Two or more races, non-Hispanic/Latino), 6 international. Average age 32. 283 applicants, 61% accepted, 97 enrolled. In 2016, 130 master's awarded. *Degree requirements:* For master's, comprehensive exam. *Entrance requirements:* For master's, minimum GPA of 3.0, 2 recommendations, resume. Additional exam requirements/recommendations for international students: Required—TOEFL (minimum score 550 paper-based; 84 iBT) or IELTS (minimum score 7.5). *Application deadline:* For fall admission, 2/15 for international students; for spring admission, 10/1 for international students. Application fee: $60. Electronic applications accepted. *Expenses:* $725 per credit hour. *Financial support:* In 2016–17, 42 students received support. Career-related internships or fieldwork and unspecified assistantships available. Support available to part-time students. Financial award applicants required to submit FAFSA. *Faculty research:* Reading and literacy, writing, social justice and inequality in education, addictions and mental health issues, therapeutic relationships and clinical supervision. *Unit head:* Dr. Robert D. Hannafin, Dean, 203-254-4250, Fax: 203-254-4241, E-mail: rhannafin@fairfield.edu. *Application contact:* Marianne Gumpper, Director of Graduate Admission, 203-254-4184, Fax: 203-254-4073, E-mail: gradadmis@fairfield.edu.
Website: http://www.fairfield.edu/gseap

**The George Washington University,** Graduate School of Education and Human Development, Department of Counseling and Human Development, Program in Rehabilitation Counseling, Washington, DC 20052. Offers autism spectrum disorder (MA Ed/HD); substance abuse and psychiatric disabilities (MA Ed/HD); traumatic brain injury (MA Ed/HD). *Accreditation:* CORE. *Program availability:* Online learning. *Students:* 29 full-time (18 women), 24 part-time (20 women); includes 18 minority (11 Black or African American, non-Hispanic/Latino; 1 Asian, non-Hispanic/Latino; 5 Hispanic/Latino; 1 Two or more races, non-Hispanic/Latino), 5 international. Average age 34. 45 applicants, 76% accepted, 18 enrolled. In 2016, 8 master's awarded. *Entrance requirements:* For master's, GRE or MAT, two letters of recommendation, 1- to 2-page statement of purpose, official transcripts from all instiutions attended, resume. Additional exam requirements/recommendations for international students: Required—TOEFL or IELTS. Electronic applications accepted. *Unit head:* Dr. Kenneth C. Hergenrather, Director, 202-994-1334, E-mail: hergenkc@gwu.edu. *Application contact:* Sarah Lang, Director of Graduate Admissions, 202-994-1447, Fax: 202-994-7207, E-mail: slang@gwu.edu.
Website: http://gsehd.gwu.edu/rehabilitation-counseling-masters

**Governors State University,** College of Health and Human Services, Program in Addiction Studies and Behavioral Health, University Park, IL 60484. Offers MHS. *Program availability:* Part-time. *Faculty:* 51 full-time (45 women), 60 part-time/adjunct (43 women). *Students:* 32 full-time (21 women), 108 part-time (91 women); includes 94 minority (83 Black or African American, non-Hispanic/Latino; 5 Hispanic/Latino; 6 Two or more races, non-Hispanic/Latino), 1 international. Average age 41. 112 applicants, 79% accepted, 68 enrolled. In 2016, 36 master's awarded. *Entrance requirements:* Additional exam requirements/recommendations for international students: Required—TOEFL (minimum score 550 paper-based; 80 iBT), IELTS. *Application deadline:* For fall admission, 4/1 for domestic students. Application fee: $50. Electronic applications accepted. *Expenses:* $307 per credit hour; $38 per term or $76 per credit hour fees. *Financial support:* Application deadline: 5/1; applicants required to submit FAFSA. *Unit head:* Cheryl Mejta, Chair, Department of Addictions Studies and Behavioral Health, 708-534-4911, E-mail: cmejta@govst.edu. *Application contact:* Yakeea Daniels, Assistant Vice President for Enrollment Services/Director of Admissions, 708-534-4510, E-mail: ydaniels@govst.edu.

**Hazelden Graduate School of Addiction Studies,** Graduate Programs, Center City, MN 55012. Offers addiction counseling (MA, Certificate). *Program availability:* Part-time. *Entrance requirements:* Additional exam requirements/recommendations for international students: Required—TOEFL.

**Hofstra University,** School of Health Professions and Human Services, Programs in Counseling, Hempstead, NY 11549. Offers counseling (MS Ed, PD); creative arts therapy (MA); interdisciplinary transition specialist (Advanced Certificate); marriage and family therapy (MA); mental health counseling (MA, Advanced Certificate), including alcohol and substance abuse (Advanced Certificate); rehabilitation administration (PD); rehabilitation counseling (MS Ed, Advanced Certificate); rehabilitation counseling in mental health (MS Ed, Advanced Certificate); school counselor bilingual extension (Advanced Certificate). *Accreditation:* ACA. *Program availability:* Part-time, evening/weekend. *Students:* 116 full-time (100 women), 66 part-time (59 women); includes 48 minority (18 Black or African American, non-Hispanic/Latino; 11 Asian, non-Hispanic/Latino; 17 Hispanic/Latino; 2 Two or more races, non-Hispanic/Latino), 5 international. Average age 29. 166 applicants, 81% accepted, 66 enrolled. In 2016, 71 master's, 7 other advanced degrees awarded. *Degree requirements:* For master's, comprehensive exam (for some programs), thesis (for some programs), internship, practicum, student teaching, seminars, minimum GPA of 3.0. *Entrance requirements:* For master's, GRE, interview, letters of recommendation, portfolio, essay, professional experience, certification; for other advanced degree, GRE, interview, letters of recommendation, essay, professional experience, resume, master's degree. Additional exam requirements/recommendations for international students: Required—TOEFL (minimum score 550 paper-based; 80 iBT). *Application deadline:* Applications are processed on a rolling basis. Application fee: $75. Electronic applications accepted. *Expenses:* Tuition: Full-time $1240. *Required fees:* $970. Tuition and fees vary according to program. *Financial support:* In 2016–17, 76 students received support, including 40 fellowships with full and partial tuition reimbursements available (averaging $3,465 per year), 5 research assistantships with full and partial tuition reimbursements available (averaging $6,939 per year); career-related internships or fieldwork, Federal Work-Study, institutionally sponsored loans, scholarships/grants, traineeships, tuition waivers (full and partial), and unspecified assistantships also available. Support available to part-time students. Financial award applicants required to submit FAFSA. *Faculty research:* The constructs of hope and grit; the efficacy of support groups in treating eating disorders; attitudes of primary care physicians related to providing integrated care with mental health counselors; expanding the counselor identity through disability cultural competence; vocational evaluation and assessment collaboration; disability cultural competence. *Unit head:* Dr. Jamie Mitus, Chairperson, 516-463-5759, E-mail: jamie.s.mitus@hofstra.edu. *Application contact:* Sunil Samuel, Assistant Vice President of Admissions, 516-463-4723, Fax: 516-463-4664, E-mail: graduateadmission@hofstra.edu.
Website: http://www.hofstra.edu/academics/colleges/healthscienceshumanservices/

**Indiana University Northwest,** College of Arts and Sciences, Gary, IN 46408. Offers clinical counseling (MS), including drug and alcohol counseling; community development/urban studies (Graduate Certificate); computer information systems (Graduate Certificate); liberal studies (MLS); race-ethnic studies (Graduate Certificate); women's and gender studies (Graduate Certificate). *Program availability:* Part-time, evening/weekend. *Students:* 4 full-time (all women), 18 part-time (10 women); includes 10 minority (9 Black or African American, non-Hispanic/Latino; 1 Hispanic/Latino). Average age 39. 22 applicants, 77% accepted, 13 enrolled. In 2016, 6 master's awarded. *Entrance requirements:* For master's, GRE (recommended for MS), minimum undergraduate GPA of 3.0, bachelor's degree from accredited university (for MS). *Application deadline:* For fall admission, 7/1 priority date for domestic and international students; for spring admission, 12/1 priority date for domestic and international students. Application fee: $40 ($60 for international students). Electronic applications accepted. *Expenses:* $276.98 per credit hour in-state; $652.54 per credit hour out-of-state. *Financial support:* Applicants required to submit FAFSA. *Unit head:* Mark Hoyert, Dean, E-mail: mhoyert@iun.edu.
Website: http://www.iun.edu/coas/

**Indiana University Northwest,** School of Social Work, Gary, IN 46408-1197. Offers health (MSW); mental health and addictions (MSW). *Program availability:* Part-time, evening/weekend. *Faculty:* 3 full-time (all women), 4 part-time/adjunct (3 women). *Students:* 26 full-time (24 women), 64 part-time (56 women); includes 36 minority (21 Black or African American, non-Hispanic/Latino; 13 Hispanic/Latino; 2 Two or more races, non-Hispanic/Latino). Average age 33. 65 applicants, 52% accepted, 24 enrolled. In 2016, 27 master's awarded. *Degree requirements:* For master's, practicum. *Entrance requirements:* For master's, minimum GPA of 3.0; bachelor's degree from accredited university including the successful completion of 6 courses in social or behavioral sciences and 1 course in statistics; 3 professional references. *Application deadline:* For fall admission, 7/14 for domestic students; for spring admission, 2/1 priority date for domestic students. Application fee: $40 ($60 for international students). Electronic applications accepted. *Expenses:* $395.98 per credit hour in-state; $942.42 per credit hour out-of-state. *Financial support:* Career-related internships or fieldwork, Federal Work-Study, and tuition waivers (partial) available. Support available to part-time students. Financial award application deadline: 6/1; financial award applicants required to submit FAFSA. *Faculty research:* Educational outcomes, generalist practice, homelessness. *Unit head:* Dr. Darlene Lynch, Director, 219-980-7111, E-mail: darlynch@iun.edu. *Application contact:* Elena Mrozinske, Clinical Assistant Professor, 219-980-6727, E-mail: emrozins@iun.edu.
Website: http://www.iun.edu/social-work/msw-dgree/index.htm

**Indiana University–Purdue University Indianapolis,** School of Science, Department of Psychology, Indianapolis, IN 46202-3275. Offers clinical psychology (MS); industrial/organizational psychology (MS); psychobiology of addictions (PhD). *Accreditation:* APA (one or more programs are accredited). Terminal master's awarded for partial completion of doctoral program. *Degree requirements:* For master's, thesis; for doctorate, thesis/dissertation. *Entrance requirements:* For master's, GRE General Test, minimum undergraduate GPA of 3.0; for doctorate, GRE General Test, GRE Subject Test (clinical psychology), minimum undergraduate GPA of 3.2. Additional exam requirements/recommendations for international students: Required—TOEFL (minimum score 567 paper-based; 86 iBT), IELTS (minimum score 6.5). Electronic applications accepted. *Faculty research:* Severe mental illness, health psychology, neurological research, alcoholism and psychopathology, functional activities within organizations.

**Indiana University South Bend,** School of Education, South Bend, IN 46634-7111. Offers addiction counseling (MS Ed); alcohol and drug counseling (Graduate Certificate); clinical mental health counseling (MS Ed); educational leadership (MS Ed); elementary education (MS Ed); marriage, couple, and family counseling (MS Ed); school counseling (MS Ed); secondary education (MS Ed); special education (MAT, MS Ed);

including intense intervention (MS Ed), mild intervention (MS Ed). *Accreditation:* NCATE. *Program availability:* Part-time, evening/weekend. *Faculty:* 21 full-time (11 women), 9 part-time/adjunct (3 women). *Students:* 26 full-time (19 women), 104 part-time (80 women); includes 22 minority (13 Black or African American, non-Hispanic/Latino; 5 Hispanic/Latino; 4 Two or more races, non-Hispanic/Latino). Average age 35. 51 applicants, 69% accepted, 22 enrolled. In 2016, 31 master's, 2 other advanced degrees awarded. *Degree requirements:* For master's, thesis or alternative, exit project. *Entrance requirements:* For master's, letters of recommendation, GRE or minimum GPA of 3.0. Additional exam requirements/recommendations for international students: Required—TOEFL. *Application deadline:* For fall admission, 7/1 for domestic students; for spring admission, 11/1 for domestic students. Applications are processed on a rolling basis. Application fee: $40 ($60 for international students). Electronic applications accepted. *Expenses:* $276.98 per credit hour in-state; $652.54 per credit hour out-of-state. *Financial support:* Career-related internships or fieldwork available. Support available to part-time students. Financial award application deadline: 3/1; financial award applicants required to submit FAFSA. *Faculty research:* Professional dispositions, early childhood literacy, online learning, program assessments, problem-based learning. *Unit head:* Dr. Marvin Lynn, Dean, 574-520-4339, E-mail: lynnm@iusb.edu. *Application contact:* Yvonne Walker, Student Services Representative, 574-520-4185, E-mail: ydwalker@iusb.edu.
Website: https://www.iusb.edu/education/index.php

**Indiana Wesleyan University,** Graduate School, College of Arts and Sciences, Marion, IN 46953. Offers addictions counseling (MS); clinical mental health counseling (MS); community counseling (MS); marriage and family therapy (MS); school counseling (MS); student development counseling and administration (MS). *Accreditation:* ACA. *Program availability:* Part-time. *Degree requirements:* For master's, thesis or alternative. *Entrance requirements:* For master's, GRE General Test. Additional exam requirements/recommendations for international students: Required—TOEFL. Electronic applications accepted. *Expenses:* Contact institution. *Faculty research:* Community counseling, multicultural counseling, addictions.

**Johns Hopkins University,** Bloomberg School of Public Health, Department of Mental Health, Baltimore, MD 21218. Offers children's mental health services (PhD); drug dependence epidemiology (PhD); mental health (MHS, Dr PH); psychiatric epidemiology (PhD). *Degree requirements:* For master's, thesis (for some programs); for doctorate, thesis/dissertation, 1-year full-time residency, oral and written exams. *Entrance requirements:* For master's, GRE General Test, MCAT, 3 letters of recommendation, curriculum vitae; for doctorate, GRE General Test, MCAT or GMAT, 3 letters of recommendation, curriculum vitae. Additional exam requirements/recommendations for international students: Required—TOEFL (minimum score 600 paper-based; 100 iBT). Electronic applications accepted. *Faculty research:* Etiology, development and prevention of aggressive and antisocial behavior; epidemiology of mental disorders; genetic epidemiology of mental disorders; brain and behavior.

**Johnson & Wales University,** Graduate Studies, MS Program in Counseling, Providence, RI 02903-3703. Offers addictions counseling (MS); mental health counseling (MS).

**Johnson State College,** Program in Counseling, Johnson, VT 05656. Offers addictions counseling (MA); clinical mental health counseling (MA); general counseling (MA); school counseling (MA). *Program availability:* Part-time. *Degree requirements:* For master's, comprehensive exam. *Entrance requirements:* For master's, interview. Additional exam requirements/recommendations for international students: Required—TOEFL. *Application deadline:* For fall admission, 7/1 for domestic students, 2/1 for international students; for spring admission, 11/1 for domestic students, 7/1 for international students; for summer admission, 4/1 for domestic students. Applications are processed on a rolling basis. Electronic applications accepted. Application fee is waived when completed online. *Expenses:* Tuition, state resident: part-time $555 per credit. Tuition, nonresident: part-time $800 per credit. *Financial support:* Career-related internships or fieldwork and unspecified assistantships available. Support available to part-time students. Financial award application deadline: 3/1; financial award applicants required to submit FAFSA. *Unit head:* Dr. David Fink, Coordinator, 802-635-1383, Fax: 802-635-1465, E-mail: david.fink@jsc.edu. *Application contact:* Catherine H. Higley, Administrative Assistant, 800-635-2356 Ext. 1244, Fax: 802-635-1248, E-mail: catherine.higley@jsc.edu.

**Kean University,** Nathan Weiss Graduate College, Program in Counselor Education, Union, NJ 07083. Offers alcohol and drug abuse counseling (MA); clinical mental health counseling (MA); school counseling (MA). *Accreditation:* ACA; NCATE. *Program availability:* Part-time. *Faculty:* 8 full-time (5 women). *Students:* 130 full-time (105 women), 149 part-time (114 women); includes 114 minority (54 Black or African American, non-Hispanic/Latino; 1 American Indian or Alaska Native, non-Hispanic/Latino; 5 Asian, non-Hispanic/Latino; 49 Hispanic/Latino; 5 Two or more races, non-Hispanic/Latino), 3 international. Average age 32. 258 applicants, 30% accepted, 68 enrolled. In 2016, 71 master's awarded. *Degree requirements:* For master's, practicum, internship, portfolio. *Entrance requirements:* For master's, minimum GPA of 3.0, 2 letters of recommendation, personal statement, resume. Additional exam requirements/recommendations for international students: Required—TOEFL (minimum score 550 paper-based; 79 iBT), IELTS. *Application deadline:* For fall admission, 3/2 for domestic and international students; for spring admission, 10/31 for domestic and international students. Applications are processed on a rolling basis. Application fee: $75. Electronic applications accepted. *Expenses:* Tuition, state resident: full-time $13,156; part-time $640 per credit. Tuition, nonresident: full-time $17,831; part-time $785 per credit. *Required fees:* $3316; $151 per credit. Tuition and fees vary according to course level, course load, degree level and program. *Financial support:* Scholarships/grants and unspecified assistantships available. Financial award applicants required to submit FAFSA. *Unit head:* Dr. J. Barry Mascari, Program Coordinator, 908-737-5954, E-mail: jmascari@kean.edu. *Application contact:* Pedro Lopes, Admissions Counselor, 908-737-7100, E-mail: grad-adm@kean.edu.
Website: http://grad.kean.edu/counseling

**Lenoir-Rhyne University,** Graduate Programs, School of Education, Program in Human Services, Hickory, NC 28601. Offers management (MA); substance abuse (MA); vocational strategies (MA). *Program availability:* Part-time, online only, 100% online. *Degree requirements:* For master's, comprehensive exam. *Entrance requirements:* For master's, GRE General Test or MAT, essay; minimum GPA of 2.7 undergraduate, 3.0 graduate. Additional exam requirements/recommendations for international students: Required—TOEFL (minimum score 600 paper-based). Electronic applications accepted. *Expenses:* Contact institution.

**Lewis & Clark College,** Graduate School of Education and Counseling, Department of Counseling Psychology, Program in Professional Mental Health Counseling - Addictions, Portland, OR 97219-7899. Offers MA, MS. *Program availability:* Part-time, evening/weekend. *Degree requirements:* For master's, thesis (MS). *Entrance requirements:* For master's, GRE General Test, minimum undergraduate GPA of 2.75. Additional exam requirements/recommendations for international students: Required—TOEFL (minimum score 575 paper-based). *Application deadline:* For fall admission, 2/1 priority date for domestic and international students; for spring admission, 10/1 priority date for domestic and international students. Application fee: $50. Electronic

## Addictions/Substance Abuse Counseling

applications accepted. *Financial support:* Career-related internships or fieldwork, Federal Work-Study, institutionally sponsored loans, scholarships/grants, health care benefits, and tuition waivers (partial) available. Support available to part-time students. Financial award applicants required to submit FAFSA. *Unit head:* Rick Berman, Director, 503-768-6060, Fax: 503-768-6065, E-mail: cpsy@lclark.edu. *Application contact:* Becky Haas, Director of Admissions, 503-768-6200, Fax: 503-768-6205, E-mail: gseadmit@lclark.edu.
Website: http://graduate.lclark.edu/departments/counseling_psychology/addiction_studies/

**Liberty University,** School of Behavioral Sciences, Lynchburg, VA 24515. Offers clinical mental health counseling (MA); counselor education and supervision (PhD); human services counseling (MA), including addictions and recovery, business, child and family law, Christian ministries, criminal justice, crisis response and trauma, executive leadership, health and wellness, life coaching, marriage and family, military resilience; marriage and family therapy (MA); military resilience (Certificate); professional counseling (MA). *Program availability:* Part-time, online learning. *Students:* 2,041 full-time (1,612 women), 4,970 part-time (3,875 women); includes 1,991 minority (1,678 Black or African American, non-Hispanic/Latino; 33 American Indian or Alaska Native, non-Hispanic/Latino; 48 Asian, non-Hispanic/Latino; 80 Hispanic/Latino; 8 Native Hawaiian or other Pacific Islander, non-Hispanic/Latino; 144 Two or more races, non-Hispanic/Latino), 127 international. Average age 39. 5,496 applicants, 41% accepted, 1257 enrolled. In 2016, 2,813 master's, 11 doctorates, 20 other advanced degrees awarded. *Application deadline:* Applications are processed on a rolling basis. Application fee: $50. Electronic applications accepted. *Financial support:* Applicants required to submit FAFSA. *Unit head:* Dr. Ronald Hawkins, Founding Dean, School of Behavioral Sciences. *Application contact:* Jay Bridge, Director of Admissions, 800-424-9595, Fax: 800-628-7977, E-mail: gradadmissions@liberty.edu.

**Liberty University,** School of Divinity, Lynchburg, VA 24515. Offers Biblical studies (M Div); church history (MAR, Th M); discipleship and church ministry (M Div, MAR, MCM); evangelism and church planting (M Div, MAR, MCM); global studies (M Div, MCM, MGS); homiletics (M Div, MAR, Th M, D Min); leadership (M Div, D Min); marketplace chaplaincy (M Div, MCM); ministry (D Min); pastoral counseling (M Div, MA, MAR, D Min), including addictions and recovery (MA), crisis response and trauma (MA), discipleship and church ministries (MA), leadership (MA), life coaching (MA), marketplace chaplaincy (MA), marriage and family (MA), military resilience (MA); pastoral ministries (M Div, MCM); religious education (MRE); theology (M Div, MAR, MTS); theology and apologetics (PhD); worship (M Div, MAR, MCM, D Min). *Program availability:* Part-time, online learning. *Students:* 2,140 full-time (615 women), 3,020 part-time (906 women); includes 1,312 minority (1,016 Black or African American, non-Hispanic/Latino; 9 American Indian or Alaska Native, non-Hispanic/Latino; 100 Asian, non-Hispanic/Latino; 90 Hispanic/Latino; 7 Native Hawaiian or other Pacific Islander, non-Hispanic/Latino; 90 Two or more races, non-Hispanic/Latino), 158 international. Average age 42. 3,651 applicants, 37% accepted, 909 enrolled. In 2016, 1,551 master's, 39 doctorates, 168 other advanced degrees awarded. *Degree requirements:* For master's, 2 foreign languages, thesis (for some programs); for doctorate, 2 foreign languages, thesis/dissertation. *Entrance requirements:* For master's, minimum undergraduate GPA of 2.0; for doctorate, GRE General Test or MAT, minimum graduate GPA of 3.0. Additional exam requirements/recommendations for international students: Required—TOEFL (minimum score 600 paper-based; 100 iBT). *Application deadline:* For fall admission, 6/1 for domestic students; for spring admission, 11/1 for domestic students. Applications are processed on a rolling basis. Application fee: $50. Electronic applications accepted. *Expenses:* Contact institution. *Financial support:* Teaching assistantships with tuition reimbursements, career-related internships or fieldwork, and Federal Work-Study available. Financial award applicants required to submit FAFSA. *Unit head:* Dr. Ed Hindson, Dean, 434-592-4140, Fax: 434-522-0415, E-mail: ehindson@liberty.edu. *Application contact:* Jay Bridge, Director of Graduate Admissions, 800-424-9595, Fax: 800-628-7977, E-mail: gradadmissions@liberty.edu.
Website: https://www.liberty.edu/divinity/

**Loma Linda University,** School of Behavioral Health, Department of Counseling and Family Sciences, Loma Linda, CA 92350. Offers child life specialist (MS); clinical mediation (Certificate); counseling (MS); drug and alcohol counseling (Certificate); family life education (Certificate); marital and family therapy (DMFT); school counseling (Certificate). *Degree requirements:* For master's, comprehensive exam, thesis optional; for doctorate, comprehensive exam, thesis/dissertation (for some programs). *Entrance requirements:* For master's, minimum GPA of 3.0; for doctorate, GRE. Additional exam requirements/recommendations for international students: Required—TOEFL (minimum score 550 paper-based). Electronic applications accepted.

**Long Island University–Hudson,** Graduate School, Purchase, NY 10577. Offers autism (Advanced Certificate); childhood education (MS Ed); early childhood education (MS Ed); educational leadership (MS Ed); finance (MBA); health administration (MPA); healthcare sector management (MBA); literacy (MS Ed); management (MBA); marriage and family therapy (MS); mental health counseling (MS), including credentialed alcoholism and substance abuse counselor; middle childhood and adolescence education (MS Ed); pharmaceutics (MS), including cosmetic science, industrial pharmacy; public administration (MPA); school counseling (MS Ed, Advanced Certificate); school psychology (MS Ed); special education (MS Ed); TESOL (all grades) (Advanced Certificate); TESOL and bilingual education (MS Ed); the business of pharmaceutics and biotechnology (MBA). *Program availability:* Part-time, evening/weekend, online learning. *Faculty:* 7 full-time (5 women), 42 part-time/adjunct (25 women). *Students:* 55 full-time (41 women), 158 part-time (123 women); includes 40 minority (8 Black or African American, non-Hispanic/Latino; 1 Asian, non-Hispanic/Latino; 31 Hispanic/Latino). Average age 35. *Entrance requirements:* Additional exam requirements/recommendations for international students: Required—TOEFL (minimum score 550 paper-based; 79 iBT). *Application deadline:* Applications are processed on a rolling basis. Application fee: $50. Electronic applications accepted. *Expenses:* Contact institution. *Unit head:* Dr. Sylvia Blake, Dean and Chief Operating Officer, 914-831-2700, E-mail: westchester@liu.edu. *Application contact:* Cindy Pagnotta, Director of Marketing and Enrollment, 914-831-2701, Fax: 914-251-5959, E-mail: cindy.pagnotta@liu.edu.

**Maryville University of Saint Louis,** Walker College of Health Professions, Program in Rehabilitation Counseling, St. Louis, MO 63141-7299. Offers marriage and family therapy (MARC); music therapy (MARC); substance abuse (MARC). *Accreditation:* CORE. *Program availability:* Part-time, evening/weekend. *Faculty:* 2 full-time (0 women), 6 part-time/adjunct (5 women). *Students:* 25 full-time (20 women), 16 part-time (15 women); includes 11 minority (8 Black or African American, non-Hispanic/Latino; 2 Hispanic/Latino; 1 Two or more races, non-Hispanic/Latino), 2 international. Average age 32. In 2016, 10 master's awarded. *Degree requirements:* For master's, internship, seminar. *Entrance requirements:* For master's, minimum cumulative GPA of 3.0, 2 letters of recommendation, interview, essay, transcripts, resume. Additional exam requirements/recommendations for international students: Required—TOEFL (minimum score 563 paper-based). *Application deadline:* For fall admission, 1/15 for domestic students; for spring admission, 10/1 for domestic students. Applications are processed on a rolling basis. Electronic applications accepted. *Expenses:* $650 per credit hour.

*Financial support:* Career-related internships or fieldwork, Federal Work-Study, and campus employment available. Financial award application deadline: 3/1; financial award applicants required to submit FAFSA. *Unit head:* Dr. Michael Kiener, Director, 314-529-9443, Fax: 314-529-9495, E-mail: mkiener@maryville.edu. *Application contact:* Jeannie DeLuca, Director, Admissions and Advising, 314-529-9355, Fax: 314-529-9927, E-mail: jdeluca@maryville.edu.
Website: http://www.maryville.edu/hp/rehabilitation-counseling/

**McNeese State University,** Doré School of Graduate Studies, Burton College of Education, Department of Psychology, Lake Charles, LA 70609. Offers addiction treatment (MA); applied behavior analysis (MA); counseling psychology (MA); general/experimental psychology (MA). *Program availability:* Evening/weekend. *Entrance requirements:* For master's, GRE.

**Monmouth University,** Graduate Studies, Department of Psychological Counseling, West Long Branch, NJ 07764-1898. Offers professional counseling (MS, PMC); psychological counseling (MA), including addiction studies, psychological counseling. *Accreditation:* ACA. *Program availability:* Part-time, evening/weekend. *Degree requirements:* For master's, comprehensive exam (for some programs), thesis optional, fieldwork. *Entrance requirements:* For master's, GRE, minimum GPA of 3.0 overall, 12 credits in psychology or closely-related field, two Monmouth University psychological counseling recommendation forms, narrative essay; for PMC, degree or current enrollment in CACREP-accredited master's program in counseling with minimum cumulative GPA of 3.0. Additional exam requirements/recommendations for international students: Required—TOEFL (minimum score 550 paper-based; 79 iBT), IELTS (minimum score 5), Michigan English Language Assessment Battery (minimum score 77) or Certificate of Advanced English (minimum score B2). Electronic applications accepted. *Faculty research:* Violent crime, single parenting, the African-American male, counseling older women, successful behavior for under-achieving youth.

**Montclair State University,** The Graduate School, College of Education and Human Services, Certified Alcohol and Drug Counselor Certificate Program, Montclair, NJ 07043-1624. Offers Certificate. *Expenses:* Tuition, state resident: part-time $553 per credit. Tuition, nonresident: part-time $854 per credit. *Required fees:* $91 per credit. Tuition and fees vary according to program.

**Northeastern State University,** College of Education, Department of Psychology and Counseling, Tahlequah, OK 74464-2399. Offers counseling psychology (MS); school counseling (M Ed); substance abuse counseling (MS). *Program availability:* Part-time, evening/weekend. *Faculty:* 16 full-time (7 women), 4 part-time/adjunct (3 women). *Students:* 80 full-time (61 women), 73 part-time (61 women); includes 66 minority (7 Black or African American, non-Hispanic/Latino; 23 American Indian or Alaska Native, non-Hispanic/Latino; 3 Asian, non-Hispanic/Latino; 5 Hispanic/Latino; 28 Two or more races, non-Hispanic/Latino), 1 international. Average age 32. In 2016, 43 master's awarded. *Degree requirements:* For master's, thesis (for some programs), written and oral examinations. *Entrance requirements:* For master's, GRE, minimum GPA of 2.5. Application fee: $25. *Expenses:* Tuition, state resident: full-time $2816; part-time $216.60 per credit hour. Tuition, nonresident: full-time $6365; part-time $489.60 per credit hour. *Required fees:* $37.40 per credit hour. *Financial support:* Teaching assistantships, career-related internships or fieldwork, and Federal Work-Study available. Financial award application deadline: 3/1. *Unit head:* Dr. Kenny Paris, Department Chair of Psychology and Counseling, 918-444-3021, E-mail: parisk@nsuok.edu. *Application contact:* Josh McCollum, Graduate Coordinator, 918-444-2093, E-mail: mccolluj@nsuok.edu.
Website: https://academics.nsuok.edu/education/EducationHome/COEDepartments/PsychologyCounseling.aspx

**Northwest Nazarene University,** Program in Social Work, Nampa, ID 83686. Offers clinical mental health and addictions practice (MSW). *Accreditation:* CSWE. *Program availability:* Part-time-only, evening/weekend. *Faculty:* 7 full-time (4 women), 9 part-time/adjunct (5 women). *Students:* 123 full-time (85 women), 24 part-time (13 women); includes 23 minority (3 Black or African American, non-Hispanic/Latino; 1 American Indian or Alaska Native, non-Hispanic/Latino; 12 Hispanic/Latino; 7 Two or more races, non-Hispanic/Latino). Average age 27. 152 applicants, 54% accepted, 73 enrolled. In 2016, 54 master's awarded. *Degree requirements:* For master's, comprehensive exam, thesis or alternative. *Entrance requirements:* For master's, interview, letters of reference, degree from regionally-accredited college/university, written personal statement. *Application deadline:* Applications are processed on a rolling basis. Application fee: $50. Electronic applications accepted. *Expenses: Tuition:* Full-time $9315; part-time $4658 per credit hour. *Required fees:* $120. *Faculty research:* Test anxiety, trauma, statistics. *Unit head:* Dr. Lawanna Lancaster, Director/Department Chair, 208-467-8372, Fax: 208-467-8879, E-mail: mswinfo@nnu.edu. *Application contact:* Jodie Rodriguez-Engel, Program Coordinator, 208-467-8679, Fax: 208-467-8879, E-mail: jrodriguez-engel@nnu.edu.
Website: http://msw.nnu.edu

**Pace University,** Dyson College of Arts and Sciences, Department of Psychology, Program in Mental Health Counseling, New York, NY 10038. Offers grief and loss (MS); mental health counseling (MS, PhD); substance abuse (MS). Program offered at Pleasantville, NY location only. *Program availability:* Part-time, evening/weekend. *Students:* 75 full-time (58 women), 66 part-time (60 women); includes 62 minority (17 Black or African American, non-Hispanic/Latino; 1 American Indian or Alaska Native, non-Hispanic/Latino; 10 Asian, non-Hispanic/Latino; 28 Hispanic/Latino; 6 Two or more races, non-Hispanic/Latino), 4 international. Average age 30. In 2016, 47 master's awarded. Terminal master's awarded for partial completion of doctoral program. *Degree requirements:* For master's, comprehensive exam, qualifying exams, internship; for doctorate, comprehensive exam, thesis/dissertation, internships. *Entrance requirements:* For master's, GRE, resume, personal statement, two letters of reference, official transcripts, interview; for doctorate, three letters of recommendation (two of which are academic in nature); personal statement; official transcripts; internship(s); interview; master's degree in mental health counseling or program with curriculum equivalent to that of Pace's graduate program in mental health counseling. Additional exam requirements/recommendations for international students: Required—TOEFL (minimum score 88 iBT), IELTS (minimum score 7) or PTE (minimum score 60). *Application deadline:* For fall admission, 8/1 priority date for domestic students, 6/1 for international students; for spring admission, 12/1 priority date for domestic students, 10/1 for international students. Applications are processed on a rolling basis. Application fee: $70. Electronic applications accepted. *Expenses: Tuition:* Part-time $1195 per credit. *Required fees:* $260 per semester. Tuition and fees vary according to degree level, campus/location and program. *Financial support:* Research assistantships, teaching assistantships, career-related internships or fieldwork, Federal Work-Study, and tuition waivers (partial) available. Financial award application deadline: 2/15; financial award applicants required to submit FAFSA. *Unit head:* Dr. Ross Robak, Psychology Department Chair/Director, Graduate Program in Counseling, 914-773-3786, E-mail: rrobak@pace.edu. *Application contact:* Susan Ford-Goldschein, Director of Graduate Admissions, 914-422-4283, Fax: 212-346-1585, E-mail: graduateadmission@pace.edu.

Website: http://www.pace.edu/academics/graduate-students/degrees/mental-health-counseling-ms

**Palm Beach Atlantic University,** School of Education and Behavioral Studies, West Palm Beach, FL 33416-4708. Offers counseling psychology (MS), including addictions/mental health, general counseling, marriage and family therapy, mental health counseling, school guidance counseling. *Program availability:* Part-time, evening/weekend. *Faculty:* 8 full-time (2 women), 17 part-time/adjunct (13 women). *Students:* 243 full-time (206 women), 29 part-time (24 women); includes 147 minority (67 Black or African American, non-Hispanic/Latino; 4 Asian, non-Hispanic/Latino; 60 Hispanic/Latino; 1 Native Hawaiian or other Pacific Islander, non-Hispanic/Latino; 15 Two or more races, non-Hispanic/Latino), 6 international. Average age 35. 81 applicants, 89% accepted, 53 enrolled. In 2016, 122 master's awarded. *Entrance requirements:* For master's, GRE or MAT, minimum GPA of 3.0; essay. Additional exam requirements/recommendations for international students: Required—TOEFL (minimum score 550 paper-based; 79 iBT). *Application deadline:* Applications are processed on a rolling basis. Application fee: $50. Electronic applications accepted. *Expenses: Tuition:* Full-time $6600; part-time $550 per credit hour. Full-time tuition and fees vary according to degree level, campus/location and program. *Financial support:* In 2016–17, 11 students received support. Career-related internships or fieldwork, scholarships/grants, and employee education grants available. Financial award application deadline: 5/1; financial award applicants required to submit FAFSA. *Faculty research:* Group dynamics, phenomenology, spirituality, multicultural psychology. *Unit head:* Dr. Gene Sale, Program Director, 561-803-2352. *Application contact:* Graduate Admissions, 888-468-6722, E-mail: grad@pba.edu.
Website: http://www.pba.edu/graduate-counseling-program

**Post University,** Program in Human Services, Waterbury, CT 06723-2540. Offers human services (MS); human services/alcohol and drug counseling (MS); human services/clinical counseling (MS); human services/non-profit management (MS). *Program availability:* Part-time, evening/weekend, online learning.

**Saint Mary's University of Minnesota,** Schools of Graduate and Professional Programs, Graduate School of Health and Human Services, Counseling and Psychological Services Program, Winona, MN 55987-1399. Offers addiction studies (Certificate); counseling and psychological services (MA). Tuition and fees vary according to degree level and program. *Unit head:* Dr. Mary Louise Wise, Associate Program Director, 612-728-5104, Fax: 612-728-5121, E-mail: mlwise@smumn.edu. *Application contact:* James Callinan, Director of Admissions for Graduate and Professional Programs, 612-728-5185, Fax: 612-728-5121, E-mail: jcallina@smumn.edu.
Website: http://www.smumn.edu/graduate-home/areas-of-study/graduate-school-of-health-human-services/ma-in-counseling-psychological-services

**Salve Regina University,** Holistic Graduate Programs, Newport, RI 02840-4192. Offers expressive and creative arts (CAGS, CGS); holistic counseling (MA); holistic leadership (MA, CAGS, CGS); holistic leadership and change management (CAGS); holistic studies (CGS); substance abuse and treatment (CAGS); substance abuse foundations in holistic studies (CGS). *Program availability:* Part-time, evening/weekend. *Degree requirements:* For master's, internship, project. *Entrance requirements:* For master's, GMAT, GRE General Test, or MAT. Additional exam requirements/recommendations for international students: Required—TOEFL (minimum score 600 paper-based; 100 iBT) or IELTS. Electronic applications accepted.

**Salve Regina University,** Program in Rehabilitation Counseling, Newport, RI 02840-4192. Offers mental health (CAGS), including rehabilitation counseling; rehabilitation counseling (MA); substance abuse (CGS), including foundations in rehabilitation counseling. *Accreditation:* CORE. *Program availability:* Part-time, evening/weekend. *Entrance requirements:* For master's, GMAT, GRE General Test or MAT. Additional exam requirements/recommendations for international students: Required—TOEFL (minimum score 600 paper-based; 100 iBT) or IELTS. Electronic applications accepted.

**Springfield College,** Graduate Programs, Programs in Rehabilitation Counseling and Services, Springfield, MA 01109-3797. Offers alcohol and substance abuse services (M Ed); psychiatric rehabilitation and substance abuse counseling (M Ed). *Accreditation:* CORE (one or more programs are accredited). *Program availability:* Part-time. *Degree requirements:* For master's, comprehensive exam. *Entrance requirements:* Additional exam requirements/recommendations for international students: Required—TOEFL (minimum score 550 paper-based); Recommended—IELTS (minimum score 6). Electronic applications accepted. *Expenses: Tuition:* Full-time $29,640; part-time $988 per credit. *Required fees:* $195.

**Stephens College,** Division of Graduate and Continuing Studies, Columbia, MO 65215-0002. Offers counseling (M Ed), including addictions counseling, clinical mental health counseling, school counseling; health information administration (Postbaccalaureate Certificate); physician assistant studies (MPAS); TV and screenwriting (MFA). *Program availability:* Part-time, evening/weekend, online learning. *Faculty:* 14 full-time (9 women), 30 part-time/adjunct (19 women). *Students:* 117 full-time (101 women), 107 part-time (96 women); includes 25 minority (2 Black or African American, non-Hispanic/Latino; 2 American Indian or Alaska Native, non-Hispanic/Latino; 1 Asian, non-Hispanic/Latino; 2 Hispanic/Latino; 1 Native Hawaiian or other Pacific Islander, non-Hispanic/Latino; 17 Two or more races, non-Hispanic/Latino), 1 international. Average age 35. 226 applicants, 43% accepted, 87 enrolled. In 2016, 44 master's awarded. *Entrance requirements:* For master's, minimum GPA of 3.0 in last 60 hours. Additional exam requirements/recommendations for international students: Required—TOEFL (minimum score 79 iBT). *Application deadline:* For fall admission, 8/15 priority date for domestic and international students; for winter admission, 1/9 priority date for domestic and international students; for spring admission, 6/5 priority date for domestic and international students. Applications are processed on a rolling basis. Application fee: $50. Electronic applications accepted. *Expenses: Tuition:* Full-time $3564; part-time $396 per credit hour. *Required fees:* $45 per credit hour. *Financial support:* In 2016–17, 5 fellowships with full tuition reimbursements (averaging $7,673 per year) were awarded; unspecified assistantships also available. Financial award applicants required to submit FAFSA. *Faculty research:* Educational psychology, outcomes assessment. *Unit head:* Dr. Brian Sajko, Vice President of Strategic Enrollment Management, 800-388-7579, Fax: 573-876-7237, E-mail: online@stephens.edu. *Application contact:* Lindsey Boudinot, Director of Graduate and Online Admissions, 800-388-7579, E-mail: online@stephens.edu.

**Stony Brook University, State University of New York,** Stony Brook Medicine, School of Medicine, Program in Public Health, Stony Brook, NY 11794. Offers community health (MPH); evaluation sciences (MPH); family violence (MPH); health communication (Certificate); health economics (MPH); population health (MPH); substance abuse (MPH). *Accreditation:* CEPH. *Program availability:* Part-time, evening/weekend. *Students:* 32 full-time (28 women), 19 part-time (16 women); includes 20 minority (7 Black or African American, non-Hispanic/Latino; 7 Asian, non-Hispanic/Latino; 5 Hispanic/Latino; 1 Two or more races, non-Hispanic/Latino), 2 international. Average age 29. 148 applicants, 68% accepted, 37 enrolled. In 2016, 25 master's, 2 other advanced degrees awarded. *Entrance requirements:* For master's, GRE, 3 references, bachelor's degree from accredited college or university with minimum GPA of 3.0,

essays, interview. Additional exam requirements/recommendations for international students: Required—TOEFL (minimum score 90 iBT). *Application deadline:* For fall admission, 6/1 for domestic students, 3/15 for international students. Application fee: $100. Electronic applications accepted. *Expenses:* Contact institution. *Financial support:* Fellowships available. *Faculty research:* Abnormal psychology, academic achievement, broadcast media, communications, communications systems, public health. *Total annual research expenditures:* $252,529. *Unit head:* Dr. Lisa A. Benz Scott, Director, 631-444-8811, E-mail: lisa.benzscott@stonybrook.edu. *Application contact:* Joanie Maniaci, Senior Academic Coordinator, 631-444-2074, Fax: 631-444-6035, E-mail: joanmarie.maniaci@stonybrook.edu.
Website: http://publichealth.stonybrookmedicine.edu/

**Syracuse University,** David B. Falk College of Sport and Human Dynamics, Programs in Addiction Studies, Syracuse, NY 13244. Offers MA, CAS. *Program availability:* Part-time. In 2016, 10 other advanced degrees awarded. *Entrance requirements:* For master's, GRE, personal statement, official transcripts, three letters of recommendation, resume; for CAS, personal statement, official transcripts, three letters of recommendation, resume. Additional exam requirements/recommendations for international students: Required—TOEFL (minimum score 100 iBT). *Application deadline:* For fall admission, 2/15 priority date for domestic and international students; for spring admission, 11/15 priority date for domestic and international students. Application fee: $75. Electronic applications accepted. *Expenses: Tuition:* Full-time $25,974; part-time $1443 per credit hour. *Required fees:* $802; $50 per course. Tuition and fees vary according to course load and program. *Financial support:* Fellowships, research assistantships, teaching assistantships, and scholarships/grants available. Financial award application deadline: 1/1. *Faculty research:* Alcohol, other drugs and behavioral (process) addictions, public health perspective of substance use and addictive behaviors, prevention and counseling. *Unit head:* Dr. Brooks Gump, Graduate Program Director, 315-443-2208, E-mail: bbgump@syr.edu. *Application contact:* Felicia Otero, Director of College Admissions, 315-443-5555, Fax: 315-443-2562, E-mail: falk@syr.edu.
Website: http://falk.syr.edu/HealthWellness/Addiction_CAS.aspx

**United States International University–Africa,** School of Arts and Sciences, Nairobi, Kenya. Offers counseling psychology (MA), including chemical dependency, health psychology; international relations (MA), including development studies, diplomacy and foreign policy, peace and conflict studies. *Program availability:* Part-time, evening/weekend. *Degree requirements:* For master's, thesis, practicum. *Entrance requirements:* For master's, GRE General Test, 2 letters of recommendation, resume. Additional exam requirements/recommendations for international students: Required—TOEFL. *Faculty research:* Trauma in children, African intellectualism, psychological assessment tools.

**Universidad Central del Caribe,** Program in Substance Abuse Counseling, Bayamón, PR 00960-6032. Offers MHS.

**University of California, Berkeley,** UC Berkeley Extension, Certificate Programs in Behavioral and Health Sciences, Berkeley, CA 94720-1500. Offers alcohol and drug abuse studies (Certificate). *Accreditation:* APA.

**University of Central Oklahoma,** The Jackson College of Graduate Studies, College of Liberal Arts, Department of Sociology, Gerontology, and Substance Abuse Studies, Edmond, OK 73034-5209. Offers gerontology (MA); sociology (MA), including substance abuse studies. *Program availability:* Part-time. *Degree requirements:* For master's, variable foreign language requirement, comprehensive exam (for some programs), thesis (for some programs). *Entrance requirements:* For master's, GRE. Additional exam requirements/recommendations for international students: Required—TOEFL (minimum score 550 paper-based; 79 iBT), IELTS (minimum score 6.5). Electronic applications accepted.

**University of Cincinnati,** Graduate School, College of Education, Criminal Justice, and Human Services, School of Human Services, Counseling Program, Cincinnati, OH 45221. Offers counselor education (Ed D); mental health (MA); school counseling (M Ed); substance abuse prevention (Graduate Certificate). *Accreditation:* ACA (one or more programs are accredited); NCATE. *Program availability:* Part-time. Terminal master's awarded for partial completion of doctoral program. *Degree requirements:* For master's, comprehensive exam, thesis or alternative; for doctorate, comprehensive exam, thesis/dissertation. *Entrance requirements:* For master's and doctorate, GRE General Test, interview. Additional exam requirements/recommendations for international students: Required—TOEFL (minimum score 620 paper-based). *Application deadline:* For fall admission, 1/31 for domestic students. Application fee: $65 ($70 for international students). Electronic applications accepted. *Expenses: Tuition, area resident:* Full-time $12,790; part-time $389 per credit hour. Tuition, state resident: full-time $13,290; part-time $419 per credit hour. Tuition, nonresident: full-time $24,532; part-time $976 per credit hour. *International tuition:* $24,832 full-time. *Required fees:* $3958; $140 per credit hour. Tuition and fees vary according to course load, degree level, program and reciprocity agreements. *Financial support:* Teaching assistantships with full tuition reimbursements, career-related internships or fieldwork, scholarships/grants, tuition waivers (full), and unspecified assistantships available. Support available to part-time students. *Faculty research:* Group work, career development, ecology, prevention, multicultural. *Unit head:* Dr. Michael Brubaker, Program Director, 513-556-9196, Fax: 513-556-3898, E-mail: michael.brubaker@uc.edu. *Application contact:* Amanda Carlisle, Program Coordinator, 513-556-3335, Fax: 513-556-3898, E-mail: amanda.carlisle@uc.edu.
Website: http://cech.uc.edu/human-services/graduate-programs/counselor-ed-phd/about.html

**University of Detroit Mercy,** College of Liberal Arts and Education, Detroit, MI 48221. Offers addiction counseling (MA); addiction studies (Certificate); clinical mental health counseling (MA); clinical psychology (MA, PhD); computer and information systems (MS); criminal justice (MA); curriculum and instruction (MA); economics (MA); educational administration (MA); financial economics (MA); industrial/organizational psychology (MA); information assurance (MS); intelligence analysis (MA); liberal studies (MALS); religious studies (MA); school counseling (MA, Certificate); school psychology (Spec); security administration (MS); special education: emotionally impaired/behaviorally disordered (MA); special education: learning disabilities (MA). *Program availability:* Part-time, evening/weekend. *Degree requirements:* For doctorate, departmental qualifying exam. *Faculty research:* Psychology of aging, history of technology, Renaissance humanism, U.S. and Japanese economic relations.

**University of Illinois at Springfield,** Graduate Programs, College of Education and Human Services, Program in Human Services, Springfield, IL 62703-5407. Offers alcohol and substance abuse (Graduate Certificate); alcoholism and substance abuse (MA); child and family services (MA); gerontology (MA); social services administration (MA). *Program availability:* Part-time, evening/weekend, 100% online, blended/hybrid learning. *Faculty:* 4 full-time (all women), 2 part-time/adjunct (1 woman). *Students:* 10 full-time (8 women), 62 part-time (53 women); includes 28 minority (23 Black or African American, non-Hispanic/Latino; 3 Hispanic/Latino; 2 Two or more races, non-Hispanic/Latino). Average age 34. 37 applicants, 46% accepted, 16 enrolled. In 2016, 32 master's, 3 other advanced degrees awarded. *Degree requirements:* For master's, internship; capstone project or thesis. *Entrance requirements:* For master's, minimum undergraduate GPA of 3.0, 2 letters of recommendation from professional or academic sources, statement of intent, interview. Additional exam requirements/recommendations for international students: Required—TOEFL (minimum score 500 paper-based; 61 iBT). *Application deadline:* Applications are processed on a rolling basis. Application fee: $60 ($75 for international students). Electronic applications accepted. *Expenses:* Tuition, state resident: part-time $329 per credit hour. Tuition, nonresident: part-time $675 per credit hour. *Financial support:* In 2016–17, fellowships with full tuition reimbursements (averaging $9,900 per year), research assistantships with full tuition reimbursements (averaging $9,991 per year), teaching assistantships with full tuition reimbursements (averaging $10,059 per year) were awarded; career-related internships or fieldwork, Federal Work-Study, scholarships/grants, health care benefits, and unspecified assistantships also available. Support available to part-time students. Financial award application deadline: 11/15; financial award applicants required to submit FAFSA. *Unit head:* Dr. Carolyn Peck, Program Administrator, 217-206-7577, Fax: 217-206-6775, E-mail: peck.carolyn@uis.edu. *Application contact:* Dr. Cecelia Cornell, Associate Vice Chancellor for Graduate Education, 217-206-7230, E-mail: ccorn1@uis.edu. Website: http://www.uis.edu/humanservices

**University of Lethbridge,** School of Graduate Studies, Lethbridge, AB T1K 3M4, Canada. Offers addictions counseling (M Sc); agricultural biotechnology (M Sc); agricultural studies (M Sc, MA); anthropology (MA); archaeology (M Sc, MA); art (MA, MFA); biochemistry (M Sc); biological sciences (M Sc); biomolecular science (PhD); biosystems and biodiversity (PhD); Canadian studies (MA); chemistry (PhD); computer science (M Sc); computer science and geographical information science (M Sc); counseling (MC); counseling psychology (M Ed); dramatic arts (MA); earth, space, and physical science (PhD); economics (MA); education (MA, PhD); educational leadership (M Ed); English (MA); environmental science (M Sc); evolution and behavior (PhD); exercise science (M Sc); French (MA); French/German (MA); French/Spanish (MA); general education (M Ed); geography (M Sc, MA); German (MA); health sciences (M Sc); individualized multidisciplinary (M Sc, MA); kinesiology (M Sc, MA); management (M Sc), including accounting, finance, human resource management and labor relations, information systems, international management, marketing, policy and strategy; mathematics (M Sc); music (M Mus, MA); Native American studies (MA); neuroscience (M Sc, PhD); new media (MA, MFA); nursing (M Sc, MN); philosophy (MA); physics (M Sc); political science (MA); psychology (M Sc, MA); religious studies (MA); sociology (MA); theatre and dramatic arts (MFA); theoretical and computational science (PhD); urban and regional studies (MA); women and gender studies (MA). *Program availability:* Part-time, evening/weekend. *Degree requirements:* For master's, thesis (for some programs); for doctorate, comprehensive exam, thesis/dissertation. *Entrance requirements:* For master's, GMAT (for M Sc in management), bachelor's degree in related field, minimum GPA of 3.0 during previous 20 graded semester courses, 2 years' teaching or related experience (M Ed); for doctorate, master's degree, minimum graduate GPA of 3.5. Additional exam requirements/recommendations for international students: Required—TOEFL (minimum score 580 paper-based; 93 iBT). Electronic applications accepted. *Faculty research:* Movement and brain plasticity, gibberellin physiology, photosynthesis, carbon cycling, molecular properties of main-group ring components.

**University of Louisville,** Graduate School, Raymond A. Kent School of Social Work, Louisville, KY 40292-0001. Offers marriage and family therapy (PMC), including mental health; social work (MSSW, PhD), including alcohol and drug counseling (MSSW), gerontology (MSSW), marriage and family (PhD), school social work (MSSW). *Accreditation:* AAMFT/COAMFTE; CSWE (one or more programs are accredited). *Program availability:* Part-time, evening/weekend, 100% online, blended/hybrid learning. *Faculty:* 29 full-time (19 women), 51 part-time/adjunct (42 women). *Students:* 384 full-time (324 women), 81 part-time (65 women); includes 116 minority (65 Black or African American, non-Hispanic/Latino; 7 Asian, non-Hispanic/Latino; 18 Hispanic/Latino; 1 Native Hawaiian or other Pacific Islander, non-Hispanic/Latino; 25 Two or more races, non-Hispanic/Latino), 7 international. Average age 31. 419 applicants, 63% accepted, 184 enrolled. In 2016, 191 master's, 2 doctorates awarded. *Degree requirements:* For doctorate, comprehensive exam, thesis/dissertation. *Entrance requirements:* For master's, GRE or minimum GPA of 2.75; for doctorate, GRE General Test, interview, writing sample. Additional exam requirements/recommendations for international students: Required—TOEFL (minimum score 550 paper-based; 79 iBT), IELTS (minimum score 6.5). *Application deadline:* For fall admission, 5/30 for domestic and international students; for spring admission, 9/30 for domestic and international students; for summer admission, 2/28 for domestic and international students. Applications are processed on a rolling basis. Application fee: $60. Electronic applications accepted. *Expenses:* Contact institution. *Financial support:* In 2016–17, 12 research assistantships with full tuition reimbursements (averaging $21,500 per year) were awarded; health care benefits and unspecified assistantships also available. Financial award application deadline: 5/15; financial award applicants required to submit FAFSA. *Faculty research:* Equipping young children with skills, assisting abused or neglected children, helping juveniles with sexual behavioral problems, illuminating the contributions that men and women make to their families, managing chronic conditions, enhance trauma-informed services, address social and health issues of older adults, palliative and end-of-life care. *Total annual research expenditures:* $4.8 million. *Unit head:* Dr. David Jenkins, Dean, 502-852-3944, Fax: 502-852-0422, E-mail: dajenk03@exchange.louisville.edu. *Application contact:* Misty Kupka, Program Manager for Admissions and Recruitment, 502-852-0414, Fax: 502-852-0422, E-mail: misty.kupka@louisville.edu.
Website: http://www.louisville.edu/kent

**University of Nevada, Las Vegas,** Graduate College, College of Education, Department of Educational and Clinical Studies, Las Vegas, NV 89154-3066. Offers addiction studies (Advanced Certificate); counselor education (M Ed, MS), including clinical mental health (MS), school counseling (M Ed); early childhood education (M Ed); early childhood special education (Certificate), including infancy, preschool; English language learning (M Ed); mental health counseling (Advanced Certificate); special education (M Ed, PhD); PhD/JD. *Program availability:* Part-time, evening/weekend. *Faculty:* 17 full-time (8 women), 28 part-time/adjunct (20 women). *Students:* 269 full-time (219 women), 174 part-time (138 women); includes 181 minority (51 Black or African American, non-Hispanic/Latino; 2 American Indian or Alaska Native, non-Hispanic/Latino; 15 Asian, non-Hispanic/Latino; 81 Hispanic/Latino; 3 Native Hawaiian or other Pacific Islander, non-Hispanic/Latino; 29 Two or more races, non-Hispanic/Latino), 23 international. Average age 34. 256 applicants, 72% accepted, 145 enrolled. In 2016, 178 master's, 3 doctorates awarded. *Degree requirements:* For master's, comprehensive exam (for some programs); for doctorate, comprehensive exam, thesis/dissertation; for other advanced degree, final project. *Entrance requirements:* For master's, bachelor's degree; letter of recommendation; statement of purpose; for doctorate, GRE General Test, statement of purpose; writing sample; 3 letters of recommendation. Additional exam requirements/recommendations for international students: Required—TOEFL (minimum score 550 paper-based; 80 iBT), IELTS (minimum score 7). *Application deadline:* For fall admission, 7/15 for domestic students, 5/1 for international students; for spring admission, 11/15 for domestic students, 10/1 for international students; for summer admission, 4/15 for domestic students. Application fee: $60 ($95 for

international students). Electronic applications accepted. *Expenses:* $269.25 per credit, $792 per 3-credit course; $9,634 per year resident; $23,274 per year non-resident; $7,094 fees non-resident (7 credits or more); $1,307 annual health insurance fee. *Financial support:* In 2016–17, 12 research assistantships with partial tuition reimbursements (averaging $12,569 per year), 27 teaching assistantships with partial tuition reimbursements (averaging $13,759 per year) were awarded; institutionally sponsored loans, scholarships/grants, health care benefits, and unspecified assistantships also available. Financial award application deadline: 3/15. *Faculty research:* Multicultural issues in counseling, academic interventions for students with disabilities, establishment of pro-social skills in young children with severe disabilities, inclusive strategies for students with disabilities, language and literacy for English language learners. *Total annual research expenditures:* $768,906. *Unit head:* Dr. Monica Brown, Interim Department Chair/Professor, 702-895-3167, Fax: 702-895-3205, E-mail: monica.brown@unlv.edu. *Application contact:* Dr. Cori More, Graduate Coordinator, 702-895-3271, Fax: 702-895-3205, E-mail: cori.more@unlv.edu. Website: http://education.unlv.edu/ecs/

**University of New Hampshire,** Graduate School Manchester Campus, Manchester, NH 03101. Offers business administration (MBA); educational administration and supervision (Ed S); educational studies (M Ed); elementary teacher education (M Ed); information technology (MS); public administration (MPA); public health (MPH, Certificate); secondary teacher education (M Ed, MAT); social work (MSW); substance use disorders (Certificate). *Program availability:* Part-time, evening/weekend. *Degree requirements:* For master's, thesis or alternative. *Entrance requirements:* Additional exam requirements/recommendations for international students: Required—TOEFL (minimum score 550 paper-based; 80 iBT). Electronic applications accepted.

**The University of North Carolina at Charlotte,** Cato College of Education, Department of Counseling, Charlotte, NC 28223-0001. Offers counseling (MA); counselor education and supervision (PhD); play therapy (Postbaccalaureate Certificate); school counseling (Post-Master's Certificate); substance abuse counseling (Postbaccalaureate Certificate). *Accreditation:* ACA. *Program availability:* Part-time, evening/weekend. *Faculty:* 12 full-time (7 women), 5 part-time/adjunct (2 women). *Students:* 144 full-time (117 women), 94 part-time (76 women); includes 69 minority (49 Black or African American, non-Hispanic/Latino; 3 Asian, non-Hispanic/Latino; 15 Hispanic/Latino; 2 Two or more races, non-Hispanic/Latino), 3 international. Average age 31. 221 applicants, 63% accepted, 101 enrolled. In 2016, 45 master's, 3 doctorates, 22 other advanced degrees awarded. Terminal master's awarded for partial completion of doctoral program. *Degree requirements:* For master's, thesis or alternative, practicum, internship; for doctorate, thesis/dissertation; for other advanced degree, internship. *Entrance requirements:* For master's, GRE or MAT, bachelor's degree from regionally-accredited university, minimum overall GPA of 3.0, brief statement of purpose, professional references, official transcripts; for doctorate, GRE or MAT, master's degree in counseling from a CACREP-accredited program with minimum cumulative GPA of 3.5; one year of experience as a professional counselor (preferred); letters of reference; essay; interview; for other advanced degree, statement of purpose, three reference letters. Additional exam requirements/recommendations for international students: Required—TOEFL (minimum score 523 paper-based, 70 iBT) or IELTS (6.5). *Application deadline:* For fall admission, 12/1 for domestic and international students; for summer admission, 12/1 for domestic and international students. Applications are processed on a rolling basis. Application fee: $75. Electronic applications accepted. *Expenses:* Tuition, state resident: full-time $4252. Tuition, nonresident: full-time $17,423. *Required fees:* $3026. Tuition and fees vary according to course load and program. *Financial support:* In 2016–17, 9 students received support, including 2 research assistantships (averaging $11,800 per year), 7 teaching assistantships (averaging $6,357 per year); career-related internships or fieldwork, institutionally sponsored loans, scholarships/grants, and unspecified assistantships also available. Support available to part-time students. Financial award application deadline: 3/1; financial award applicants required to submit FAFSA. *Total annual research expenditures:* $28,946. *Unit head:* Dr. Henry L. Harris, Chair, 704-687-8960, E-mail: hharris2@uncc.edu. *Application contact:* Kathy B. Giddings, Director of Graduate Admissions, 704-687-5503, Fax: 704-687-1668, E-mail: gradadm@uncc.edu. Website: http://counseling.uncc.edu/

**University of Oklahoma,** Jeannine Rainbolt College of Education, Department of Educational Psychology, Program in Professional Counseling, Norman, OK 73019. Offers professional counseling (M Ed), including drug and alcohol counseling, Oklahoma licensed professional counseling, research, school counseling. *Students:* 35 full-time (26 women), 4 part-time (1 woman); includes 16 minority (3 Black or African American, non-Hispanic/Latino; 2 American Indian or Alaska Native, non-Hispanic/Latino; 1 Asian, non-Hispanic/Latino; 4 Hispanic/Latino; 6 Two or more races, non-Hispanic/Latino), 1 international. Average age 28. 29 applicants, 83% accepted, 17 enrolled. In 2016, 17 master's awarded. *Degree requirements:* For master's, comprehensive exam, internship. *Entrance requirements:* For master's, GRE. Additional exam requirements/recommendations for international students: Required—TOEFL (minimum score 79 iBT) or IELTS (minimum score 6.5). *Application deadline:* For fall admission, 1/10 for domestic and international students. Application fee: $50 ($100 for international students). Electronic applications accepted. *Expenses:* Tuition, state resident: full-time $4886; part-time $203.60 per credit hour. Tuition, nonresident: full-time $18,989; part-time $791.20 per credit hour. *Required fees:* $3283; $126.25 per credit hour. $126.50 per semester. *Financial support:* In 2016–17, 29 students received support. Research assistantships with full and partial tuition reimbursements available and scholarships/grants available. Financial award application deadline: 6/1; financial award applicants required to submit FAFSA. *Faculty research:* Group therapy interventions; multi and inter disciplinary collaboration; treatment of students in boarding school settings; diversity issues in counseling; applied behavior analysis. *Unit head:* Dr. Nancy E. Marchand-Martella, Chair, Department of Educational Psychology, 405-325-0624, Fax: 405-325-6655, E-mail: nmarchand-martella@ou.edu. *Application contact:* Anna Steele, Graduate Programs Specialist, 405-325-4525, Fax: 405-325-7390, E-mail: jrcoe_gps@ou.edu.
Website: http://www.ou.edu/education/edpy

**The University of South Dakota,** Graduate School, College of Arts and Sciences, Program in Administrative Studies, Vermillion, SD 57069. Offers addiction studies (MSA); criminal justice studies (MSA); health services administration (MSA); human resources (MSA); interdisciplinary studies (MSA); long term care administration (MSA); organizational leadership (MSA). *Program availability:* Part-time, evening/weekend, online learning. *Degree requirements:* For master's, thesis or alternative. *Entrance requirements:* For master's, 3 years of work or experience, minimum GPA of 2.7, resume. Additional exam requirements/recommendations for international students: Required—TOEFL (minimum score 550 paper-based; 79 iBT). Electronic applications accepted.

**University of Southern Maine,** College of Management and Human Service, School of Education and Human Development, Program in Counselor Education, Portland, ME 04103. Offers clinical mental health counseling (MS); counseling (CAS); culturally responsive practices in education and human development (CGS); mental health rehabilitation technician/community (CGS); rehabilitation counseling (MS); school counseling (MS); substance abuse counseling (CGS). *Accreditation:* ACA (one or more programs are accredited); CORE; TEAC. *Program availability:* Part-time, evening/weekend. *Degree requirements:* For master's, comprehensive exam, thesis or alternative; for other advanced degree, thesis or alternative. *Entrance requirements:* For master's, GRE General Test or MAT, interview; for other advanced degree, master's degree. Additional exam requirements/recommendations for international students: Required—TOEFL (minimum score 550 paper-based; 79 iBT). Electronic applications accepted. *Faculty research:* Counselor licensure, group dynamics, counseling theories, healthy adaptation, counselor educator well-being.

**University of South Florida,** College of Behavioral and Community Sciences, Department of Child and Family Studies, Tampa, FL 33620-9951. Offers applied behavior analysis (MA, MS, PhD); behavioral and community sciences (PhD); child and adolescent behavioral health (MS), including developmental disabilities, leadership in child and adolescent health, translational research and evaluation, youth and behavioral health; rehabilitation and mental health counseling (MA), including addictions and substance abuse counseling, marriage and family therapy. *Accreditation:* ACA. *Faculty:* 15 full-time (10 women), 1 (woman) part-time/adjunct. *Students:* 146 full-time (127 women), 90 part-time (74 women); includes 92 minority (22 Black or African American, non-Hispanic/Latino; 12 Asian, non-Hispanic/Latino; 49 Hispanic/Latino; 9 Two or more races, non-Hispanic/Latino), 3 international. Average age 28. 267 applicants, 51% accepted, 93 enrolled. In 2016, 63 master's awarded. *Degree requirements:* For master's, comprehensive exam, thesis (for some programs); for doctorate, comprehensive exam, thesis/dissertation, Behavior Analyst Board Certification Exam. *Entrance requirements:* For master's, GRE General Test, minimum GPA of 3.0 in last 60 hours of coursework; letters of recommendation; one-page narrative describing experience, interest, and career goals in applied behavior analysis; resume or curriculum vitae (varies by program); for doctorate, GRE General Test, master's degree in behavioral analysis or closely-related field; minimum GPA of 3.5 in graduate course work; three letters of recommendation; campus visit with faculty interview; personal statement; curriculum vitae; evidence of research experiences and expertise. Additional exam requirements/recommendations for international students: Required—TOEFL (minimum score 550 paper-based; 79 iBT) or IELTS (minimum score 6.5). *Application deadline:* For fall admission, 12/5 for domestic and international students. Application fee: $30. *Expenses:* Tuition, state resident: full-time $7766; part-time $431.43 per credit hour. Tuition, nonresident: full-time $15,789; part-time $877.17 per credit hour. *Required fees:* $37 per term. *Financial support:* In 2016–17, 50 students received support. Unspecified assistantships available. *Faculty research:* Applied behavior analysis, autism, behavior management, behavioral intervention, children, developmental disabilities, experimental analysis of behavior, functional assessment, positive behavior support. *Total annual research expenditures:* $16.4 million. *Application contact:* Dr. Raymond G. Miltenberger, Professor/Director of Master's Program, 813-974-5079, Fax: 813-974-6115, E-mail: miltenbe@usf.edu.
Website: http://cfs.cbcs.usf.edu/

**The University of Tennessee at Martin,** Graduate Programs, College of Education, Health and Behavioral Sciences, Program in Counseling, Martin, TN 38238. Offers addictions counseling (MS Ed); community counseling (MS Ed); school counseling (MS Ed); student affairs and college counseling (MS Ed). *Accreditation:* NCATE. *Program availability:* Part-time, online only, 100% online. *Students:* 14 full-time (12 women), 62 part-time (59 women); includes 10 minority (6 Black or African American, non-Hispanic/Latino; 3 Hispanic/Latino; 1 Two or more races, non-Hispanic/Latino). Average age 35. 40 applicants, 48% accepted, 18 enrolled. In 2016, 17 master's awarded. *Degree requirements:* For master's, comprehensive exam. *Entrance requirements:* For master's, GRE General Test, minimum GPA of 2.5, resume, letters of reference. Additional exam requirements/recommendations for international students: Required—TOEFL (minimum score 525 paper-based; 71 iBT). *Application deadline:* For fall admission, 7/27 priority date for domestic and international students; for spring admission, 12/17 priority date for domestic and international students; for summer admission, 5/10 priority date for domestic and international students. Applications are processed on a rolling basis. Application fee: $30 ($130 for international students). Electronic applications accepted. *Expenses:* Tuition, state resident: full-time $8254; part-time $459 per credit hour. Tuition, nonresident: full-time $22,198; part-time $1234 per credit hour. *Required fees:* $79 per credit hour. Part-time tuition and fees vary according to course load and campus/location. *Financial support:* Scholarships/grants and unspecified assistantships available. Financial award application deadline: 2/1; financial award applicants required to submit FAFSA. *Unit head:* Cynthia West, Dean, 731-881-7125, Fax: 731-881-7975, E-mail: cwest@utm.edu. *Application contact:* Jolene L. Cunningham, Student Services Specialist, 731-881-7012, Fax: 731-881-7499, E-mail: jcunningham@utm.edu.

**Viterbo University,** Master of Science in Mental Health Counseling Program, La Crosse, WI 54601-4797. Offers addiction counseling (MS); child and adolescent counseling (MS); complementary health and wellness counseling (MS). *Accreditation:* ACA. *Program availability:* Part-time, evening/weekend. *Degree requirements:* For master's, comprehensive exam, thesis, exam, 54 credits of core program courses; 6 elective credits; minimum GPA of 3.0; action research project; practicum/internship experience. *Entrance requirements:* For master's, MAT, BS in a human service or social science discipline; prerequisite coursework in general psychology, behavior disorders/abnormal

psychology, and research methods/statistics; minimum undergraduate cumulative GPA of 3.0; background check; personal statement; undergraduate transcripts; interview. Additional exam requirements/recommendations for international students: Required—TOEFL (minimum score 525 paper-based). Electronic applications accepted. Application fee is waived when completed online. *Expenses:* Contact institution. *Faculty research:* Supervision, recovery substance abuse, culture, counseling theory, health and wellness.

**Walden University,** Graduate Programs, School of Counseling, Minneapolis, MN 55401. Offers addiction counseling (MS), including addictions and public health, child and adolescent counseling, family studies and interventions, forensic counseling, general program, military families and culture, trauma and crisis counseling; clinical mental health counseling (MS), including addiction counseling, forensic counseling, military families and culture, trauma and crisis counseling; counselor education and supervision (PhD), including consultation, counseling and social change, forensic mental health counseling, leadership and program evaluation, trauma and crisis; marriage, couple, and family counseling (MS), including addiction counseling, career counseling, forensic counseling, military families and culture, trauma and crisis counseling; school counseling (MS), including addiction counseling, career counseling, crisis and trauma, military families and culture. *Accreditation:* ACA. *Program availability:* Part-time, evening/weekend, online only, 100% online. *Degree requirements:* For master's, residency, field experience, professional development plan, licensure plan; for doctorate, thesis/dissertation, residency, practicum, internship. *Entrance requirements:* For master's, bachelor's degree or higher; minimum GPA of 2.5; official transcripts; goal statement (for some programs); access to computer and Internet; for doctorate, master's degree or higher; three years of related professional or academic experience (preferred); minimum GPA of 3.0; goal statement and current resume (for select programs); official transcripts; access to computer and Internet. Additional exam requirements/recommendations for international students: Required—TOEFL (minimum score 550 paper-based, 79 iBT), IELTS (minimum score 6.5), Michigan English Language Assessment Battery (minimum score 82), or PTE (minimum score 53). Electronic applications accepted.

**Walden University,** Graduate Programs, School of Social Work and Human Services, Minneapolis, MN 55401. Offers addictions and social work (DSW); advanced clinical practice (MSW); clinical expertise (DSW); criminal justice (DSW); disaster, crisis, and intervention (DSW); family studies and interventions (DSW); human and social services (PhD), including advanced research, community and social services, community intervention and leadership, conflict management, criminal justice, disaster crisis and intervention, family studies and intervention, gerontology, global social services, higher education, human services and nonprofit administration, mental health facilitation; medical social work (DSW); military social work (MSW); policy practice (DSW); social work (PhD), including addictions and social work, clinical expertise, criminal justice, disaster, crisis and intervention, family studies and interventions, medical social work, policy practice, social work administration; social work administration (DSW); social work in healthcare (MSW); social work with children and families (MSW). *Accreditation:* CSWE. *Program availability:* Part-time, evening/weekend, online only, 100% online. *Degree requirements:* For master's, residency (for some programs); for doctorate, thesis/dissertation, residency. *Entrance requirements:* For master's, bachelor's degree or higher; minimum GPA of 2.5; official transcripts; goal statement (for some programs); access to computer and Internet; for doctorate, master's degree or higher; three years of related professional or academic experience (preferred); minimum GPA of 3.0; goal statement and current resume (for select programs); official transcripts; access to computer and Internet. Additional exam requirements/recommendations for international students: Required—TOEFL (minimum score 550 paper-based, 79 iBT), IELTS (minimum score 6.5), Michigan English Language Assessment Battery (minimum score 82), or PTE (minimum score 53). Electronic applications accepted.

**Washburn University,** School of Applied Studies, Department of Human Services, Topeka, KS 66621. Offers addiction counseling (MA). *Program availability:* Evening/weekend. *Entrance requirements:* For master's, minimum GPA of 3.0 in last 60 hours of coursework. Additional exam requirements/recommendations for international students: Required—TOEFL (minimum score 80 iBT). *Faculty research:* Professional identity development in students, expressive therapeutic writing, prevention, community mental health, agency professional development, behavioral analysis, group living among the elderly, ethical identity development, higher education pedagogy, Morita therapy/anxiety disorders, ecological/contextual healing, post-trauma.

**Waynesburg University,** Graduate and Professional Studies, Canonsburg, PA 15370. Offers business (MBA), including energy management, finance, health systems, human resources, leadership, market development; counseling (MA), including addictions counseling, clinical mental health; counselor education and supervision (PhD); criminal investigation (MA); education (M Ed), including autism, curriculum and instruction, educational leadership, online teaching; nursing (MSN), including administration, education, informatics; nursing practice (DNP); special education (M Ed); technology (M Ed); MSN/MBA. *Accreditation:* AACN. *Program availability:* Part-time, evening/weekend. *Degree requirements:* For doctorate, thesis/dissertation. *Entrance requirements:* Additional exam requirements/recommendations for international students: Required—TOEFL. Electronic applications accepted.

# Applied Behavior Analysis

**Antioch University New England,** Graduate School, Department of Applied Psychology, Program in Autism Spectrum Disorders, Keene, NH 03431-3552. Offers applied behavior analysis (Certificate); applied behavior analysis internship (Certificate); autism spectrum disorders (Certificate). *Entrance requirements:* Additional exam requirements/recommendations for international students: Required—TOEFL (minimum score 550 paper-based).

**Antioch University New England,** Graduate School, Department of Education, Experienced Educators Program, Keene, NH 03431-3552. Offers foundations of education (M Ed), including applied behavioral analysis, autism spectrum disorders, educating for sustainability, next-generation learning using technology, problem-based learning using critical skills, teacher leadership; principal certification (PMC). *Degree requirements:* For master's, thesis, practicum. *Entrance requirements:* For master's, previous course work and work experience in education. Additional exam requirements/recommendations for international students: Required—TOEFL (minimum score 550 paper-based). Electronic applications accepted. *Expenses:* Contact institution. *Faculty research:* Classroom action research, school restructuring, problem-based learning, brain-based learning.

**Arcadia University,** College of Arts and Sciences, Department of Psychology, Glenside, PA 19038-3295. Offers applied behavior analysis (MAC); autism (MAC); child/family therapy (MAC); community public health (MAC); counseling/international peace and conflict resolution dual degree (MAC); mental health counseling (MAC); trauma (MAC). *Program availability:* Part-time. *Faculty:* 14 full-time (9 women), 10 part-time/adjunct (9 women). *Students:* 33 full-time (27 women), 39 part-time (30 women); includes 22 minority (13 Black or African American, non-Hispanic/Latino; 2 Asian, non-Hispanic/Latino; 1 Hispanic/Latino; 6 Two or more races, non-Hispanic/Latino), 1 international. Average age 30. 61 applicants, 64% accepted, 24 enrolled. In 2016, 41 master's awarded. *Degree requirements:* For master's, practicum. *Entrance requirements:* For master's, GRE General Test or MAT. *Application deadline:* For fall admission, 1/15 for domestic students; for spring admission, 9/15 for domestic students. Applications are processed on a rolling basis. Application fee: $50. *Expenses:* Contact institution. *Financial support:* Research assistantships, career-related internships or fieldwork, and unspecified assistantships available. Support available to part-time students. Financial award application deadline: 8/15. *Unit head:* Dr. Steven Robbins, Chair, 215-572-2987. *Application contact:* 215-572-2925, Fax: 215-572-2126, E-mail: grad@arcadia.edu.

*Applied Behavior Analysis*

**Arizona State University at the Tempe campus,** College of Liberal Arts and Sciences, Department of Psychology, Tempe, AZ 85287-1104. Offers applied behavior analysis (MS); behavioral neuroscience (PhD); clinical psychology (PhD); cognitive science (PhD); developmental psychology (PhD); quantitative psychology (PhD); social psychology (PhD). *Accreditation:* APA. *Degree requirements:* For doctorate, comprehensive exam, thesis/dissertation, interactive Program of Study (iPOS) submitted before completing 50 percent of required credit hours. *Entrance requirements:* For doctorate, GRE General Test, GRE Subject Test, minimum GPA of 3.0 or equivalent in last 2 years of work leading to bachelor's degree. Additional exam requirements/recommendations for international students: Required—TOEFL, IELTS, or PTE. Electronic applications accepted.

**Assumption College,** Applied Behavior Analysis Program, Worcester, MA 01609-1296. Offers MA, CAGS. *Program availability:* Part-time, evening/weekend. *Faculty:* 1 (woman) full-time. *Students:* 1 part-time. 9 applicants, 44% accepted, 1 enrolled. *Degree requirements:* For master's, thesis optional, practicum; for CAGS, practicum. *Entrance requirements:* For master's, BA with minimum GPA of 3.0, three letters of recommendation, official transcripts, personal statement, current resume; for CAGS, MA/MS in related field, three letters of recommendation, official transcripts, personal statement, current resume. Additional exam requirements/recommendations for international students: Required—TOEFL (minimum score 540 paper-based; 76 iBT), IELTS (minimum score 6). *Application deadline:* For fall admission, 7/1 for domestic and international students. Application fee: $30. Electronic applications accepted. *Expenses: Tuition:* Full-time $11,610; part-time $645 per credit. *Required fees:* $70 per term. Tuition and fees vary according to course load and program. *Financial support:* Tuition waivers (full and partial) and institutional discounts available. Financial award applicants required to submit FAFSA. *Unit head:* Dr. Karen Lionello-DeNolf, Director, 508-767-7498, E-mail: k.lionellodenolf@assumption.edu. *Application contact:* Karen Stoyanoff, Director of Recruitment for Graduate Enrollment, 508-767-7442, Fax: 508-799-4412, E-mail: graduate@assumption.edu.
Website: http://graduate.assumption.edu/applied-behavior/applied-behavior-analysis

**Aurora University,** School of Nursing and Allied Health, Aurora, IL 60506-4892. Offers applied behavior analysis (MS); nursing (MSN). *Accreditation:* AACN. *Program availability:* Part-time, evening/weekend. *Faculty:* 5 full-time (4 women), 10 part-time/adjunct (9 women). *Students:* 18 full-time (all women), 62 part-time (59 women); includes 18 minority (3 Black or African American, non-Hispanic/Latino; 2 Asian, non-Hispanic/Latino; 11 Hispanic/Latino; 2 Two or more races, non-Hispanic/Latino). Average age 34. 37 applicants, 81% accepted, 25 enrolled. In 2016, 31 master's awarded. *Entrance requirements:* Additional exam requirements/recommendations for international students: Required—TOEFL (minimum score 550 paper-based; 79 iBT). *Application deadline:* For fall admission, 6/1 for international students; for spring admission, 10/1 for international students. Applications are processed on a rolling basis. Application fee: $0. Electronic applications accepted. *Expenses:* Contact institution. *Financial support:* In 2016–17, 25 students received support. Federal Work-Study, scholarships/grants, and unspecified assistantships available. Support available to part-time students. Financial award applicants required to submit FAFSA. *Unit head:* Dr. Carmella Moran, Interim Executive Director for the School of Nursing and Allied Health, 630-844-5132, E-mail: cmoran@aurora.edu. *Application contact:* Judson Curry, Dean of Adult and Graduate Studies, 630-947-8946, E-mail: jcurry@aurora.edu.
Website: http://www.aurora.edu/academics/colleges-schools/nursing/

**Ball State University,** Graduate School, Teachers College, Department of Special Education, Program in Applied Behavior Analysis, Muncie, IN 47306. Offers applied behavior analysis (MA), including autism. *Program availability:* Part-time, online only, 100% online. *Entrance requirements:* For master's, minimum baccalaureate GPA of 2.75 or 3.0 in latter half of baccalauareate. Additional exam requirements/recommendations for international students: Required—TOEFL (minimum score 550 paper-based; 79 iBT), IELTS (minimum score 6.5). Electronic applications accepted.

**Baylor University,** Graduate School, School of Education, Department of Educational Psychology, Waco, TX 76798. Offers applied behavior analysis (MS Ed); educational psychology (MA, MS Ed, PhD); exceptionalities (PhD); gifted and talented studies (MS Ed); learning and development (PhD); measurement (PhD); quantitative methods (MA); school psychology (Ed S). *Accreditation:* NCATE. *Faculty:* 11 full-time (6 women). *Students:* 48 full-time (42 women), 17 part-time (15 women); includes 15 minority (4 Black or African American, non-Hispanic/Latino; 2 Asian, non-Hispanic/Latino; 8 Hispanic/Latino; 1 Two or more races, non-Hispanic/Latino), 2 international. Average age 29. 90 applicants, 33% accepted, 30 enrolled. In 2016, 13 master's, 4 doctorates, 7 other advanced degrees awarded. Terminal master's awarded for partial completion of doctoral program. *Degree requirements:* For master's, thesis optional; for doctorate, comprehensive exam, thesis/dissertation; for Ed S, comprehensive exam, thesis or alternative. *Entrance requirements:* For master's, GRE, minimum GPA of 3.0; for doctorate, GRE General Test, master's degree; for Ed S, GRE General Test. Additional exam requirements/recommendations for international students: Required—TOEFL (minimum score 550 paper-based; 80 iBT), IELTS (minimum score 6.5). *Application deadline:* For fall admission, 2/1 priority date for domestic and international students. Application fee: $80. Electronic applications accepted. *Expenses: Tuition:* Full-time $28,494; part-time $1583 per credit hour. *Required fees:* $167 per credit hour. Tuition and fees vary according to course load and program. *Financial support:* In 2016–17, 42 students received support, including 20 fellowships with full and partial tuition reimbursements available, 22 research assistantships with full and partial tuition reimbursements available; career-related internships or fieldwork, Federal Work-Study, institutionally sponsored loans, scholarships/grants, health care benefits, tuition waivers (full and partial), unspecified assistantships, and stipends also available. Financial award application deadline: 2/1; financial award applicants required to submit FAFSA. *Faculty research:* Individual differences, quantitative methods, gifted and talented, special education, school psychology, autism, applied behavior analysis, learning, human development. *Total annual research expenditures:* $300,000. *Unit head:* Dr. Terrill F. Saxon, Professor and Chairman, 254-710-6101, E-mail: terrill_saxon@baylor.edu. *Application contact:* Heather Tindle, Office Manager, 254-710-3112, E-mail: heather_tindle@baylor.edu.
Website: http://www.baylor.edu/soe/EDP/

**Bay Path University,** Program in Applied Behavior Analysis, Longmeadow, MA 01106-2292. Offers applied behavior analysis (MS); autism spectrum disorders (MS). *Program availability:* Part-time, online learning. *Students:* 115 part-time (103 women); includes 11 minority (3 Black or African American, non-Hispanic/Latino; 2 Asian, non-Hispanic/Latino; 4 Hispanic/Latino; 2 Two or more races, non-Hispanic/Latino), 1 international. Average age 30. 85 applicants, 75% accepted, 57 enrolled. In 2016, 18 master's awarded. *Application deadline:* Applications are processed on a rolling basis. Application fee: $45. Electronic applications accepted. Application fee is waived when completed online. *Expenses:* $17,820. *Financial support:* Unspecified assistantships available. Financial award applicants required to submit FAFSA. *Unit head:* Susan Ainsleigh, Director, E-mail: sainsleigh@baypath.edu. *Application contact:* Diane Ranaldi, Dean of Graduate Admissions, 413-565-1332, Fax: 413-565-1250, E-mail: dranaldi@baypath.edu.

**Cairn University,** School of Education, Langhorne, PA 19047-2990. Offers applied behavior analysis (MS Sp Ed, Certificate); educational leadership and administration (MS El); instruction (MS Sp Ed); teacher education (MS Ed). *Program availability:* Part-time, evening/weekend, 100% online, blended/hybrid learning. *Faculty:* 2 full-time (both women), 4 part-time/adjunct (3 women). *Students:* 3 full-time (2 women), 89 part-time (62 women); includes 18 minority (10 Black or African American, non-Hispanic/Latino; 6 Asian, non-Hispanic/Latino; 2 Hispanic/Latino), 21 international. Average age 38. 35 applicants, 100% accepted, 25 enrolled. In 2016, 17 master's awarded. *Entrance requirements:* Additional exam requirements/recommendations for international students: Required—TOEFL (minimum score 550 paper-based). *Application deadline:* Applications are processed on a rolling basis. Application fee: $25. Electronic applications accepted. Application fee is waived when completed online. *Expenses:* $655 per semester credit. *Financial support:* Scholarships/grants available. Support available to part-time students. Financial award applicants required to submit FAFSA. *Unit head:* Joseph Beeson, Interim Dean, 215-702-4498, E-mail: teacher.ed@cairn.edu. *Application contact:* Abigail Simon, Enrollment Counselor, Graduate Education, 800-572-2472, Fax: 215-702-4248, E-mail: asimon@cairn.edu.
Website: http://www.cairn.edu/academics/education

**Caldwell University,** Graduate Studies, Division of Applied Behavior Analysis, Caldwell, NJ 07006-6195. Offers MA, PhD, Post-Master's Certificate. *Program availability:* Part-time. Terminal master's awarded for partial completion of doctoral program. *Degree requirements:* For master's, comprehensive exam; for doctorate, comprehensive exam, thesis/dissertation. *Entrance requirements:* For master's, GRE, MAT; for doctorate, GRE, MAT, ABA Certification. Additional exam requirements/recommendations for international students: Required—TOEFL (minimum score 580 paper-based). Electronic applications accepted. *Faculty research:* Autism research.

**California State University, Fresno,** Division of Research and Graduate Studies, College of Science and Mathematics, Department of Psychology, Fresno, CA 93740-8027. Offers applied behavior analysis (MA); general/experimental psychology (MA); school psychology (Ed S). *Degree requirements:* For master's, thesis. *Entrance requirements:* For master's, GRE General Test, GRE Subject Test, minimum GPA of 3.0. Additional exam requirements/recommendations for international students: Required—TOEFL. *Application deadline:* For fall admission, 5/1 for domestic and international students; for spring admission, 10/1 for domestic and international students. Applications are processed on a rolling basis. Application fee: $55. Electronic applications accepted. *Financial support:* Teaching assistantships, career-related internships or fieldwork, Federal Work-Study, scholarships/grants, and unspecified assistantships available. Support available to part-time students. Financial award application deadline: 3/1; financial award applicants required to submit FAFSA. *Faculty research:* Oncology prediction, parenting stress, wellness, aging and memory, retrieval inhibition, anger, minority mental health. *Unit head:* Dr. Constance Jones, Chair, 559-278-2691, Fax: 559-278-7910, E-mail: conniej@csufresno.edu. *Application contact:* Dr. Marilyn Wilson, Ed S Program Coordinator, 559-278-5129, Fax: 559-278-7910, E-mail: marilynw@csufresno.edu.
Website: http://www.fresnostate.edu/csm/psych/

**California State University, Sacramento,** Office of Graduate Studies, College of Social Sciences and Interdisciplinary Studies, Department of Psychology, Sacramento, CA 95819. Offers applied behavior analysis (MA); counseling psychology (MA); industrial/organizational psychology (MA). *Program availability:* Part-time. *Students:* 13 full-time (9 women), 11 part-time (9 women); includes 6 minority (3 Asian, non-Hispanic/Latino; 3 Hispanic/Latino). Average age 27. 74 applicants, 16% accepted, 11 enrolled. In 2016, 7 master's awarded. *Degree requirements:* For master's, thesis, writing proficiency exam. *Entrance requirements:* For master's, GRE, minimum GPA of 3.0 during previous 2 years. Additional exam requirements/recommendations for international students: Required—TOEFL (minimum score 550 paper-based; 80 iBT). *Application deadline:* For fall admission, 3/1 for domestic and international students; for spring admission, 9/30 for international students. Applications are processed on a rolling basis. Application fee: $55. Electronic applications accepted. *Expenses:* $4,302 full-time tuition and fees per semester, $2,796 part-time. *Financial support:* Career-related internships or fieldwork and Federal Work-Study available. Support available to part-time students. Financial award application deadline: 2/1; financial award applicants required to submit FAFSA. *Unit head:* Dr. Rebecca Cameron, Interim Department Chair, 916-278-6254, E-mail: cameron@csus.edu. *Application contact:* Jose Martinez, Graduate Admissions Supervisor, 916-278-7871, E-mail: martinj@skymail.csus.edu.
Website: http://www.csus.edu/psyc

**California State University, Stanislaus,** College of Human and Health Sciences, Program in Psychology (MA/MS), Turlock, CA 95382. Offers behavior analysis (MS); counseling psychology (MS); psychology (MA). *Program availability:* Part-time. *Degree requirements:* For master's, thesis. *Entrance requirements:* For master's, GRE, minimum GPA of 3.0, 3 letters of reference, 16 psychology prerequisites, personal statement. Additional exam requirements/recommendations for international students: Required—TOEFL (minimum score 550 paper-based). Electronic applications accepted. *Faculty research:* Hedonic tone judgment, syntax and autism, early literacy assessment and native and non-native languages.

**Capella University,** Harold Abel School of Social and Behavioral Science, Master's Programs in Psychology, Minneapolis, MN 55402. Offers applied behavior analysis (MS); clinical psychology (MS); counseling psychology (MS); educational psychology (MS); evaluation, research, and measurement (MS); general advanced studies in human behavior (MS); general psychology (MS); industrial/organizational psychology (MS); leadership coaching psychology (MS); school psychology (MS); sport psychology (MS).

**The Chicago School of Professional Psychology,** Program in Applied Behavior Analysis, Chicago, IL 60610. Offers MS, PhD. *Degree requirements:* For master's, thesis, practicum; for doctorate, thesis/dissertation, practicum. *Entrance requirements:* For doctorate, GRE. Additional exam requirements/recommendations for international students: Required—TOEFL.

**The Chicago School of Professional Psychology at Downtown Los Angeles,** Program in Applied Behavior Analysis, Los Angeles, CA 90017. Offers Psy D.

**The Chicago School of Professional Psychology at Downtown Los Angeles,** Program in Clinical Psychology, Los Angeles, CA 90017. Offers applied behavior analysis (MA); clinical psychology (Psy D); marital and family therapy (MA).

**Drexel University,** Goodwin College of Professional Studies, School of Education, Philadelphia, PA 19104-2875. Offers applied behavior analysis (MS); creativity and innovation (MS); education improvement and transformation (MS); educational administration (MS); educational leadership and management (Ed D); educational leadership development and learning technologies (PhD); global and international education (MS); higher education (MS); human resources development (MS); learning technologies (MS); mathematics, learning and teaching (MS); special education (MS); teaching, learning and curriculum (MS). *Program availability:* Part-time, evening/weekend, online learning. *Degree requirements:* For doctorate, thesis/dissertation. *Entrance requirements:* For doctorate, GRE or GMAT. Additional exam requirements/recommendations for international students: Required—TOEFL, IELTS. Electronic applications accepted. Application fee is waived when completed online. *Expenses:* Contact institution. *Faculty research:* Leadership development, mathematics education, literacy, autism, educational technology.

**Eastern University,** Department of Counseling Psychology, St. Davids, PA 19087-3696. Offers applied behavior analysis (MA, Certificate); counseling (MA); professional counseling (Certificate); school counseling (MA, Certificate); school psychology (MS, Certificate). *Program availability:* Part-time. *Students:* 104 full-time (92 women), 88 part-time (75 women); includes 83 minority (61 Black or African American, non-Hispanic/Latino; 1 American Indian or Alaska Native, non-Hispanic/Latino; 4 Asian, non-Hispanic/Latino; 13 Hispanic/Latino; 4 Two or more races, non-Hispanic/Latino), 3 international. Average age 29. In 2016, 46 master's awarded. *Degree requirements:* For master's, internship. *Entrance requirements:* Additional exam requirements/recommendations for international students: Required—TOEFL (minimum score 550 paper-based; 79 iBT). *Application deadline:* Applications are processed on a rolling basis. Application fee: $35. Electronic applications accepted. Application fee is waived when completed online. *Expenses:* $690 per credit. *Financial support:* Application deadline: 3/15. *Unit head:* Michael Dziedziak, Executive Director of Enrollment, 800-452-0996, E-mail: gpsadmissions@eastern.edu. Website: http://www.eastern.edu/academics/programs/graduate-counseling-and-psychology-department

**Endicott College,** Van Loan School of Graduate and Professional Studies, Program in Autism and Applied Behavior Analysis, Beverly, MA 01915-2096. Offers M Ed, PhD. *Program availability:* Part-time, evening/weekend, 100% online, blended/hybrid learning. *Faculty:* 4 full-time (2 women), 22 part-time/adjunct (19 women). *Students:* 17 full-time (15 women), 126 part-time (112 women); includes 24 minority (5 Black or African American, non-Hispanic/Latino; 4 Asian, non-Hispanic/Latino; 15 Hispanic/Latino). Average age 31. 55 applicants, 96% accepted, 43 enrolled. In 2016, 37 master's awarded. *Degree requirements:* For master's, thesis; for doctorate, thesis/dissertation, qualifying examination. *Entrance requirements:* For master's, MAT or GRE, undergraduate transcript, two recommendations, personal statement. Additional exam requirements/recommendations for international students: Required—TOEFL. *Application deadline:* Applications are processed on a rolling basis. Application fee: $50. Electronic applications accepted. *Expenses:* Contact institution. *Financial support:* Applicants required to submit FAFSA. *Faculty research:* ABA intervention for autism, behavioral assessment, evidence-based treatments. *Unit head:* Dr. Mary Jane Weiss, Director of Autism and Applied Behavior Analysis, 978-232-2199, E-mail: mweiss@endicott.edu. *Application contact:* Ian Menchini, Director, Graduate Enrollment and Advising, 978-232-5292, Fax: 978-232-3000, E-mail: imenchin@endicott.edu. Website: http://www.endicott.edu/VanLoan/Institute-Behavioral-Studies/Degree-Programs/Master-Ed-Autism-ABA.aspx

**Fairfield University,** Graduate School of Education and Allied Professions, Fairfield, CT 06824. Offers applied behavior analysis (ATC); applied psychology (MA); clinical mental health counseling (MA, CAS); educational technology (MA); elementary education (MA, CAS); family studies (MA); integration of spirituality and religion in counseling (ATC); marriage and family therapy (MA); reading and language development (Sixth Year Certificate); school counseling (MA, CAS); school psychology (MA, CAS); school-based marriage and family therapy (ATC); secondary education (MA); special education (MA, CAS); substance abuse counseling (ATC); teaching (Certificate); teaching and foundations (MA, CAS); TESOL, world languages, and bilingual education (MA, CAS). *Accreditation:* NCATE. *Program availability:* Part-time, evening/weekend. *Faculty:* 19 full-time (15 women), 38 part-time/adjunct (26 women). *Students:* 153 full-time (132 women), 302 part-time (252 women); includes 97 minority (24 Black or African American, non-Hispanic/Latino; 12 Asian, non-Hispanic/Latino; 55 Hispanic/Latino; 6 Two or more races, non-Hispanic/Latino), 6 international. Average age 32. 283 applicants, 61% accepted, 97 enrolled. In 2016, 130 master's awarded. *Degree requirements:* For master's, comprehensive exam. *Entrance requirements:* For master's, minimum GPA of 3.0, 2 recommendations, resume. Additional exam requirements/recommendations for international students: Required—TOEFL (minimum score 550 paper-based; 84 iBT) or IELTS (minimum score 7.5). *Application deadline:* For fall admission, 2/15 for international students; for spring admission, 10/1 for international students. Application fee: $60. Electronic applications accepted. *Expenses:* $725 per credit hour. *Financial support:* In 2016–17, 42 students received support. Career-related internships or fieldwork and unspecified assistantships available. Support available to part-time students. Financial award applicants required to submit FAFSA. *Faculty research:* Reading and literacy, writing, social justice and inequality in education, addictions and mental health issues, therapeutic relationships and clinical supervision. *Unit head:* Dr. Robert D. Hannafin, Dean, 203-254-4250, Fax: 203-254-4241, E-mail: rhannafin@fairfield.edu. *Application contact:* Marianne Gumpper, Director of Graduate Admission, 203-254-4184, Fax: 203-254-4073, E-mail: gradadmis@fairfield.edu. Website: http://www.fairfield.edu/gseap

**Florida Institute of Technology,** College of Psychology and Liberal Arts, Program in Applied Behavior Analysis, Melbourne, FL 32901-6975. Offers MS. *Program availability:* Part-time. *Students:* 32 full-time (25 women), 13 part-time (11 women); includes 10 minority (4 Black or African American, non-Hispanic/Latino; 3 Asian, non-Hispanic/Latino; 2 Hispanic/Latino; 1 Two or more races, non-Hispanic/Latino), 6 international. Average age 30. 146 applicants, 36% accepted, 27 enrolled. In 2016, 19 master's awarded. *Degree requirements:* For master's, comprehensive exam, thesis optional, minimum of 44 credit hours, all courses at least grade of B or better. *Entrance requirements:* For master's, GRE General Test, minimum GPA of 3.0, 3 letters of recommendation, resume, statement of objectives. Additional exam requirements/recommendations for international students: Required—TOEFL (minimum score 550 paper-based; 79 iBT). *Application deadline:* Applications are processed on a rolling basis. Application fee: $50. Electronic applications accepted. *Expenses: Tuition:* Full-time $22,338; part-time $1241 per credit hour. *Required fees:* $250. Tuition and fees vary according to degree level, campus/location and program. *Financial support:* Research assistantships with partial tuition reimbursements, teaching assistantships with partial tuition reimbursements, career-related internships or fieldwork, and tuition waivers (partial) available. *Faculty research:* In-home behavioral programs for children, teaching language to autistic children, anticipated strategies in behavioral changes. *Unit head:* Dr. David Wilder, Program Chair, 321-674-7516, E-mail: dawilder@fit.edu. *Application contact:* Cheryl A. Brown, Associate Director of Graduate Admissions, 321-674-7581, Fax: 321-723-9468, E-mail: cbrown@fit.edu. Website: http://cpla.fit.edu/aba/

**Florida Institute of Technology,** College of Psychology and Liberal Arts, Program in Applied Behavior Analysis and Organizational Behavior Management, Melbourne, FL 32901-6975. Offers MS. *Program availability:* Part-time. *Students:* 22 full-time (18 women), 2 part-time (1 woman); includes 9 minority (3 Asian, non-Hispanic/Latino; 4 Hispanic/Latino; 2 Two or more races, non-Hispanic/Latino). Average age 25. 36 applicants, 39% accepted, 7 enrolled. In 2016, 5 master's awarded. *Degree requirements:* For master's, comprehensive exam, thesis or alternative, minimum of 50 credits, all course grades of B or higher. *Entrance requirements:* For master's, GRE General Test, 3 letters of recommendation, resume, statement of objectives. Additional

exam requirements/recommendations for international students: Required—TOEFL (minimum score 550 paper-based; 79 iBT). *Application deadline:* Applications are processed on a rolling basis. Electronic applications accepted. *Expenses: Tuition:* Full-time $22,338; part-time $1241 per credit hour. *Required fees:* $250. Tuition and fees vary according to degree level, campus/location and program. *Unit head:* Dr. David Wilder, Program Chair, 321-674-7516, E-mail: dawilder@fit.edu. *Application contact:* Cheryl A. Brown, Associate Director of Graduate Admissions, 321-674-7581, Fax: 321-723-9468, E-mail: cbrown@fit.edu. Website: http://cpla.fit.edu/programs.php

**Florida Institute of Technology,** College of Psychology and Liberal Arts, Program in Behavior Analysis, Melbourne, FL 32901-6975. Offers PhD. *Program availability:* Evening/weekend. *Students:* 12 full-time (9 women), 2 part-time (1 woman); includes 1 minority (Hispanic/Latino). Average age 30. 12 applicants, 33% accepted, 4 enrolled. In 2016, 2 doctorates awarded. *Degree requirements:* For doctorate, comprehensive exam, thesis/dissertation, minimum of 87 credit hours beyond bachelor's degree (44 credit hours at Florida Tech), all course grades of B or higher. *Entrance requirements:* For doctorate, GRE General Test, 3 letters of recommendation, resume, statement of objectives, minimum graduate GPA of 3.6, minimum undergraduate GPA of 3.0, interviews. Additional exam requirements/recommendations for international students: Required—TOEFL (minimum score 550 paper-based; 79 iBT). *Expenses: Tuition:* Full-time $22,338; part-time $1241 per credit hour. *Required fees:* $250. Tuition and fees vary according to degree level, campus/location and program. *Unit head:* Dr. Jose Martinez-Diaz, Associate Dean, 321-674-8360, E-mail: jmartine@fit.edu. *Application contact:* Cheryl A. Brown, Associate Director of Graduate Admissions, 321-674-7581, Fax: 321-723-9468, E-mail: cbrown@fit.edu. Website: http://www.fit.edu/programs/

**Florida Institute of Technology,** College of Psychology and Liberal Arts, Program in Professional Behavior Analysis, Melbourne, FL 32901-6975. Offers MA. *Accreditation:* APA. *Program availability:* Part-time, 100% online. *Students:* 117 full-time (99 women), 8 part-time (6 women); includes 37 minority (2 Black or African American, non-Hispanic/Latino; 4 Asian, non-Hispanic/Latino; 24 Hispanic/Latino; 7 Two or more races, non-Hispanic/Latino), 4 international. Average age 30. 122 applicants, 74% accepted, 57 enrolled. In 2016, 85 master's awarded. Terminal master's awarded for partial completion of doctoral program. *Degree requirements:* For master's, comprehensive exam, minimum of 45 credit hours. *Entrance requirements:* For master's, resume; statement of objectives; minimum undergraduate GPA of 3.0, 3.5 after taking 12-credit hours at graduate-level institution in behavior analysis; transcripts; 3 letters of recommendation. Additional exam requirements/recommendations for international students: Required—TOEFL (minimum score 550 paper-based; 79 iBT). *Application deadline:* For fall admission, 4/1 for international students; for spring admission, 9/30 for international students. Applications are processed on a rolling basis. Application fee: $0. Electronic applications accepted. *Expenses: Tuition:* Full-time $22,338; part-time $1241 per credit hour. *Required fees:* $250. Tuition and fees vary according to degree level, campus/location and program. *Financial support:* Career-related internships or fieldwork, institutionally sponsored loans, tuition waivers (partial), unspecified assistantships, and tuition remissions available. Support available to part-time students. Financial award application deadline: 3/1; financial award applicants required to submit FAFSA. *Faculty research:* Addictions, neuropsychology, child abuse, assessment, psychological trauma. *Unit head:* Dr. Jose Martinez-Diaz, Head of School of Behavioral Analysis, 321-674-8359, Fax: 321-674-7105, E-mail: jmartine@fit.edu. *Application contact:* Cheryl A. Brown, Associate Director of Graduate Admissions, 321-674-7581, Fax: 321-723-9468, E-mail: cbrown@fit.edu. Website: http://www.fit.edu/programs/

**Florida International University,** College of Arts, Sciences, and Education, Department of Psychology, Miami, FL 33199. Offers behavioral analysis (MS); clinical science (PhD); cognitive neuroscience (PhD); counseling psychology (MS); developmental science (MS, PhD); legal psychology (MS, PhD); organizational psychology (MS, PhD). Program has fall admissions only. *Accreditation:* APA. *Program availability:* Part-time, evening/weekend. *Faculty:* 44 full-time (27 women), 41 part-time/adjunct (30 women). *Students:* 150 full-time (115 women), 17 part-time (10 women); includes 89 minority (8 Black or African American, non-Hispanic/Latino; 5 Asian, non-Hispanic/Latino; 75 Hispanic/Latino; 1 Two or more races, non-Hispanic/Latino), 10 international. Average age 27. 287 applicants, 24% accepted, 57 enrolled. In 2016, 35 master's, 11 doctorates awarded. Terminal master's awarded for partial completion of doctoral program. *Degree requirements:* For master's, thesis; for doctorate, comprehensive exam, thesis/dissertation. *Entrance requirements:* For master's, GRE General Test, minimum GPA of 3.0, resume, 3 letters of recommendation; for doctorate, GRE General Test, 3 letters of recommendation, resume, letter of intent, two writing samples, minimum GPA of 3.0. Additional exam requirements/recommendations for international students: Required—TOEFL (minimum score 550 paper-based; 80 iBT). *Application deadline:* For fall admission, 12/15 for domestic and international students. Application fee: $30. Electronic applications accepted. *Expenses:* Tuition, state resident: full-time $8912; part-time $446 per credit hour. Tuition, nonresident: full-time $21,393; part-time $992 per credit hour. *Required fees:* $2185; $195 per semester. Tuition and fees vary according to program. *Financial support:* Institutionally sponsored loans and scholarships/grants available. Financial award application deadline: 3/1. *Faculty research:* Legal psychology, organizational and industrial psychology, child behavior psychology. *Unit head:* Dr. William Pelham, Chair, 305-348-3002, Fax: 305-348-3646, E-mail: wpelham@fiu.edu. *Application contact:* Nanett Rojas, Assistant Director, Graduate Admissions, 305-348-7464, Fax: 305-348-7441, E-mail: gradadm@fiu.edu.

**Florida State University,** The Graduate School, College of Arts and Sciences, Department of Psychology, Program in Applied Behavior Analysis, Tallahassee, FL 32306. Offers MS. *Faculty:* 3 full-time (1 woman). *Students:* 38 full-time (36 women); includes 7 minority (5 Hispanic/Latino; 2 Two or more races, non-Hispanic/Latino). Average age 25. 78 applicants, 40% accepted, 22 enrolled. In 2016, 16 master's awarded. *Degree requirements:* For master's, comprehensive exam. *Entrance requirements:* For master's, GRE General Test, minimum GPA of 3.0. *Application deadline:* For fall admission, 1/16 for domestic and international students. Application fee: $30. Electronic applications accepted. *Expenses:* Tuition, state resident: full-time $7263; part-time $403.51 per credit hour. Tuition, nonresident: full-time $18,087; part-time $1004.85 per credit hour. *Required fees:* $1365; $75.81 per credit hour. $20 per semester. Tuition and fees vary according to campus/location. *Financial support:* In 2016–17, 38 students received support, including 38 teaching assistantships with full tuition reimbursements available (averaging $17,000 per year); career-related internships or fieldwork and health care benefits also available. Financial award application deadline: 1/16; financial award applicants required to submit FAFSA. *Unit head:* Dr. Jon Bailey, Head, 850-644-1877, Fax: 850-645-7518, E-mail: bailey@psy.fsu.edu. *Application contact:* Lynda L. Gibson, Graduate Program Associate, 850-644-2499, Fax: 850-644-7739, E-mail: grad-info@psy.fsu.edu. Website: http://www.psy.fsu.edu

**Georgian Court University,** School of Arts and Sciences, Lakewood, NJ 08701-2697. Offers applied behavior analysis (MA); clinical mental health counseling (MA); holistic

## Applied Behavior Analysis

health studies (MA, Certificate); homeland security (MS, Certificate); mercy spirituality (Certificate); parish business management (Certificate); professional counselor (Certificate); school psychology (MA, Certificate); theology (MA, Certificate). *Program availability:* Part-time, evening/weekend. *Faculty:* 19 full-time (11 women), 6 part-time/adjunct (3 women). *Students:* 90 full-time (75 women), 107 part-time (79 women); includes 34 minority (9 Black or African American, non-Hispanic/Latino; 20 Hispanic/Latino; 5 Two or more races, non-Hispanic/Latino; 1 international. Average age 34. 187 applicants, 49% accepted, 60 enrolled. In 2016, 66 master's, 17 other advanced degrees awarded. *Degree requirements:* For master's, comprehensive exam (for some programs), thesis (for some programs). *Entrance requirements:* For master's, GRE, GMAT, or NTE/PRAXIS, 3 letters of recommendation. Additional exam requirements/recommendations for international students: Required—TOEFL (minimum score 550 paper-based). *Application deadline:* For fall admission, 8/15 for domestic students, 5/1 for international students; for spring admission, 1/15 for domestic students, 10/1 for international students. Applications are processed on a rolling basis. Application fee: $40. Electronic applications accepted. *Expenses: Tuition:* Full-time $15,079; part-time $839 per credit. *Required fees:* $968; $496 per credit. Tuition and fees vary according to campus/location and program. *Financial support:* Scholarships/grants, health care benefits, and unspecified assistantships available. Financial award application deadline: 4/15; financial award applicants required to submit FAFSA. *Unit head:* Dr. Mary Chinery, Dean, 732-987-2493, Fax: 732-987-2007, E-mail: mchinery@georgian.edu. *Application contact:* Patrick Givens, Director of Graduate and Professional Studies Admissions, 732-987-2736, Fax: 732-987-2000, E-mail: gps@georgian.edu.
Website: http://georgian.edu/academics/school-of-arts-sciences/

**Hofstra University,** School of Education, Specialized Programs in Education, Hempstead, NY 11549. Offers applied behavior analysis (Advanced Certificate); early childhood special education (MS Ed, Advanced Certificate); educational and policy leadership (Ed D); educational leadership (Advanced Certificate), including school building leader/school district business leader; educational leadership and policy studies (MS Ed), including K-12; gifted education (Advanced Certificate); school building leader/school district business leader; health education PK-12 teaching certification (MS); inclusive early childhood special education (MS Ed); inclusive elementary special education (MS Ed); inclusive secondary special education (MS Ed); literacy studies (MS Ed, Ed D, PhD, Advanced Certificate), including birth-grade 6 (MS Ed, Advanced Certificate), birth-grade 6 and special education (birth-grade2) (MS Ed), grades 5-12 (MS Ed, Advanced Certificate); physical education (MS); secondary education generalist (MS Ed), including students with disabilities 7-12; special education (MS Ed, Advanced Certificate); special education assessment and diagnosis (Advanced Certificate); special education generalist (MS Ed), including extension in secondary education; sport science (MS), including strength and conditioning; teaching students with severe or multiple disabilities (Advanced Certificate). *Program availability:* Part-time, evening/weekend, 100% online, blended/hybrid learning. *Students:* 149 full-time (115 women), 258 part-time (187 women); includes 97 minority (50 Black or African American, non-Hispanic/Latino; 1 American Indian or Alaska Native, non-Hispanic/Latino; 11 Asian, non-Hispanic/Latino; 34 Hispanic/Latino; 1 Native Hawaiian or other Pacific Islander, non-Hispanic/Latino; 5 international. Average age 32. 250 applicants, 88% accepted, 146 enrolled. In 2016, 85 master's, 13 doctorates, 35 other advanced degrees awarded. *Degree requirements:* For master's, one foreign language, comprehensive exam (for some programs), thesis (for some programs), electronic portfolio, capstone course, internship, practicum, student teaching, seminars, minimum GPA of 3.0; for doctorate, one foreign language, comprehensive exam, thesis/dissertation, qualifying hearing. *Entrance requirements:* For master's, GRE, interview, letters of recommendation, portfolio, essay, certification; for doctorate, GRE or MAT, interview, resume, essay, master's degree, 3 letters of recommendation, writing sample; for Advanced Certificate, GRE, interview, letters of recommendation, essay, professional experience, resume, master's degree. Additional exam requirements/recommendations for international students: Required—TOEFL (minimum score 550 paper-based; 80 iBT). *Application deadline:* Applications are processed on a rolling basis. Application fee: $75. Electronic applications accepted. *Expenses: Tuition:* Full-time $1240. *Required fees:* $970. Tuition and fees vary according to program. *Financial support:* In 2016–17, 244 students received support, including 117 fellowships with full and partial tuition reimbursements available (averaging $3,705 per year), 12 research assistantships with full and partial tuition reimbursements available (averaging $6,490 per year); career-related internships or fieldwork, Federal Work-Study, institutionally sponsored loans, scholarships/grants, traineeships, tuition waivers (full and partial), and unspecified assistantships also available. Support available to part-time students. Financial award applicants required to submit FAFSA. *Faculty research:* Collaborative teaching and learning; language and culture; new media literacies; applied behavior analysis; K-12 leadership development. *Unit head:* Dr. Elfreda Blue, Chairperson, 516-463-5762, Fax: 516-463-6184, E-mail: elfreda.blue@hofstra.edu. *Application contact:* Sunil Samuel, Assistant Vice President of Admissions, 516-463-4723, Fax: 516-463-4664, E-mail: graduateadmission@hofstra.edu.
Website: http://www.hofstra.edu/education

**James Madison University,** The Graduate School, College of Health and Behavioral Sciences, Program in Psychological Sciences, Harrisonburg, VA 22807. Offers applied research (MA); behavior analysis (MA); experimental psychology (MA); quantitative psychology (MA). *Program availability:* Part-time, evening/weekend. *Students:* 21 full-time (10 women), 3 part-time (2 women); includes 3 minority (1 American Indian or Alaska Native, non-Hispanic/Latino; 1 Native Hawaiian or other Pacific Islander, non-Hispanic/Latino; 1 Two or more races, non-Hispanic/Latino). Average age 30. 58 applicants, 31% accepted, 14 enrolled. In 2016, 14 master's awarded. Application fee: $55. Electronic applications accepted. *Financial support:* In 2016–17, 2 teaching assistantships with full tuition reimbursements (averaging $9,284 per year) were awarded; career-related internships or fieldwork, Federal Work-Study, and 19 assistantships (averaging $7911) also available. Financial award application deadline: 3/1; financial award applicants required to submit FAFSA. *Unit head:* Dr. Jeff S. Dyche, Graduate Program Director, 540-568-4965, E-mail: dychejs@jmu.edu. *Application contact:* Lynette D. Michael, Director of Graduate Admissions, 540-568-6131 Ext. 6395, Fax: 540-568-7860, E-mail: michaeld@jmu.edu.
Website: http://www.psyc.jmu.edu/psycsciences/

**Johns Hopkins University,** School of Education, Certificate Programs in Education, Baltimore, MD 21218. Offers advanced methods for differentiated instruction and inclusive education (Graduate Certificate); applied behavior analysis (Post-Master's Certificate); clinical mental health counseling (Post-Master's Certificate); counseling (Advanced Certificate); data-based decision making and organizational improvement (Graduate Certificate); early intervention/preschool special education specialist (Graduate Certificate); education of students with autism and other pervasive developmental disorders (Graduate Certificate); educational leadership for independent schools (Graduate Certificate); evidence-based teaching in the health professions (Post-Master's Certificate); gifted education (Graduate Certificate); leadership in technology integration (Graduate Certificate); mind, brain and teaching (Graduate Certificate); school administration and supervision (Graduate Certificate); urban education (Graduate Certificate). *Program availability:* Part-time-only, evening/weekend, 100%

online, blended/hybrid learning. *Students:* 5 full-time (all women), 194 part-time (164 women); includes 46 minority (29 Black or African American, non-Hispanic/Latino; 2 American Indian or Alaska Native, non-Hispanic/Latino; 3 Asian, non-Hispanic/Latino; 8 Hispanic/Latino; 4 Two or more races, non-Hispanic/Latino), 7 international. Average age 37. 240 applicants, 75% accepted, 143 enrolled. In 2016, 167 Advanced Certificates awarded. *Entrance requirements:* For degree, minimum of bachelor's degree from regionally- or nationally-accredited institution (master's degree for some programs); minimum GPA of 3.0 in all previous programs of study; official transcripts from all post-secondary institutions attended; essay; curriculum vitae/resume; two letters of recommendation; dispositions survey. *Application deadline:* For fall admission, 4/1 priority date for domestic students; for spring admission, 10/1 priority date for domestic students; for summer admission, 2/1 priority date for domestic students. Applications are processed on a rolling basis. Application fee: $80. Electronic applications accepted. *Expenses:* Contact institution. *Financial support:* Application deadline: 4/1; applicants required to submit FAFSA. *Unit head:* Dr. Christopher C. Morphew, Dean. *Application contact:* Elisabeth Woodward, Director of Admissions, 410-516-9796, Fax: 410-516-9817, E-mail: soe.info@jhu.edu.
Website: http://education.jhu.edu

**Johnson State College,** Program in Education, Johnson, VT 05656. Offers applied behavior analysis (MA Ed); curriculum and instruction (MA Ed); foundations of education (MA Ed); special education (MA Ed). *Program availability:* Part-time. *Degree requirements:* For master's, thesis or alternative, exit interview. *Entrance requirements:* For master's, interview. Additional exam requirements/recommendations for international students: Required—TOEFL. *Application deadline:* For fall admission, 5/1 for domestic students, 2/1 for international students. Applications are processed on a rolling basis. Electronic applications accepted. *Expenses:* Tuition, state resident: part-time $555 per credit. Tuition, nonresident: part-time $800 per credit. *Financial support:* Scholarships/grants and unspecified assistantships available. Financial award application deadline: 3/1; financial award applicants required to submit FAFSA. *Unit head:* Dr. Kathleen Brinegar, Chair, Department of Education, 802-635-1472, Fax: 802-635-1465, E-mail: kathleen.brinegar@jsc.edu. *Application contact:* Catherine H. Higley, Administrative Assistant, 800-635-2356 Ext. 1244, Fax: 802-635-1248, E-mail: catherine.higley@jsc.edu.
Website: http://www.jsc.edu/academics/education/majors-and-minors/master-of-arts-in-education/

**Lipscomb University,** College of Education, Nashville, TN 37204-3951. Offers applied behavior analysis (MS, Certificate); educational leadership (M Ed, Ed S); English language learning (M Ed, Ed S); instructional coaching (M Ed, Certificate, Ed S); instructional practice (M Ed); learning organizations and strategic change (Ed D); literacy coaching (Certificate); reading specialty (M Ed, Ed S); special education (M Ed); teaching, learning, and leading (M Ed); technology integration (M Ed, Ed S); technology integration specialist (Certificate). *Accreditation:* NCATE. *Program availability:* Part-time, evening/weekend, 100% online. *Faculty:* 21 full-time (15 women), 38 part-time/adjunct (26 women). *Students:* 111 full-time (80 women), 345 part-time (292 women); includes 104 minority (70 Black or African American, non-Hispanic/Latino; 1 American Indian or Alaska Native, non-Hispanic/Latino; 3 Asian, non-Hispanic/Latino; 20 Hispanic/Latino; 10 Two or more races, non-Hispanic/Latino), 1 international. Average age 33. In 2016, 201 master's, 36 doctorates, 86 other advanced degrees awarded. *Degree requirements:* For master's, comprehensive exam, portfolio, research project and presentation; for doctorate, practical capstone project in experiential setting. *Entrance requirements:* For master's, MAT (minimum score 31) or GRE General Test (minimum score 294), 2 reference letters, goals statement, writing sample, interview; for doctorate, MAT or GRE General Test, 3 reference letters, artifact of demonstrated academic excellence, written personal statements, interview. Additional exam requirements/recommendations for international students: Required—TOEFL (minimum score 570 paper-based; 80 iBT). *Application deadline:* For fall admission, 8/29 priority date for domestic students; for spring admission, 1/15 priority date for domestic students. Applications are processed on a rolling basis. Application fee: $50 ($75 for international students). Electronic applications accepted. *Expenses:* Tuition: $934 per hour; $570 per hour (Teach for America). *Financial support:* Scholarships/grants, unspecified assistantships, and partnerships with local school districts available. Financial award applicants required to submit FAFSA. *Faculty research:* Facilitative learning styles, leadership, student assessment, interactive multimedia inclusion, learning organizations and strategic change. *Unit head:* Dr. Deborah Boyd, Director of Graduate Studies, 615-966-6263, E-mail: deborah.boyd@lipscomb.edu. *Application contact:* Amanda Logsdon, Director of Enrollment and Outreach, 615-966-7199, E-mail: amanda.logsdon@lipscomb.edu.
Website: http://www.lipscomb.edu/education/graduate-programs

**Long Island University–LIU Brooklyn,** School of Education, Brooklyn, NY 11201-8423. Offers adolescence urban education (MS Ed); applied behavior analysis (Advanced Certificate); bilingual education (Advanced Certificate); bilingual school counselor (MS Ed, Advanced Certificate); childhood urban education (MS Ed); childhood/early childhood urban education (MS Ed); early childhood urban education (MS Ed, Advanced Certificate); educational leadership (Advanced Certificate); marriage and family therapy (MS, Advanced Certificate); mental health counseling (MS, Advanced Certificate); school building district leader (Advanced Certificate); school counselor (MS Ed, Advanced Certificate); school psychologist (MS Ed); teaching urban children/adolescents with disabilities (MS Ed); TESOL (MS Ed). *Accreditation:* TEAC. *Program availability:* Part-time, evening/weekend. *Faculty:* 23 full-time (17 women), 44 part-time/adjunct (32 women). *Students:* 161 full-time (144 women), 594 part-time (461 women); includes 493 minority (229 Black or African American, non-Hispanic/Latino; 1 American Indian or Alaska Native, non-Hispanic/Latino; 30 Asian, non-Hispanic/Latino; 218 Hispanic/Latino; 2 Native Hawaiian or other Pacific Islander, non-Hispanic/Latino; 13 Two or more races, non-Hispanic/Latino), 9 international. 513 applicants, 73% accepted, 272 enrolled. In 2016, 262 master's, 18 other advanced degrees awarded. *Degree requirements:* For master's, thesis optional, electronic portfolio. *Entrance requirements:* For master's, GRE (for MS Ed). Additional exam requirements/recommendations for international students: Required—TOEFL (minimum score 527 paper-based; 75 iBT). *Application deadline:* Applications are processed on a rolling basis. Application fee: $50. Electronic applications accepted. *Expenses:* Tuition: Full-time $28,272; part-time $1178 per credit. *Required fees:* $451 per term. Tuition and fees vary according to degree level, program and student level. *Financial support:* In 2016–17, 81 students received support. Career-related internships or fieldwork, Federal Work-Study, institutionally sponsored loans, scholarships/grants, and unspecified assistantships available. Support available to part-time students. Financial award application deadline: 2/15; financial award applicants required to submit FAFSA. *Faculty research:* Technology in education, teaching civics and sustainability, biliteracy and dual language instruction, diversity in organizations and leadership, counseling diverse couples and families. *Unit head:* Dr. Amy Ginsberg, Dean, 718-246-6308, E-mail: amy.ginsberg@liu.edu. *Application contact:* Gabrielle Gannon, Director of Graduate Admissions, 718-488-1011, Fax: 718-780-6110, E-mail: bkln-admissions@liu.edu.
Website: http://www.liu.edu/Brooklyn/Academics/School-of-Education

**Long Island University–LIU Post,** College of Liberal Arts and Sciences, Brookville, NY 11548-1300. Offers applied mathematics (MS); behavior analysis (MA); biology (MS);

criminal justice (MS); earth science (MS); English (MA); environmental sustainability (MS); genetic counseling (MS); history (MA); interdisciplinary studies (MA, MS); mathematics for secondary school teachers (MS); mobile GIS application development (Advanced Certificate); political science (MA); psychology (MA). *Program availability:* Part-time, evening/weekend, blended/hybrid learning. *Faculty:* 68 full-time (30 women), 20 part-time/adjunct (13 women). *Students:* 155 full-time (117 women), 125 part-time (82 women); includes 65 minority (17 Black or African American, non-Hispanic/Latino; 14 Asian, non-Hispanic/Latino; 27 Hispanic/Latino; 7 Two or more races, non-Hispanic/Latino), 19 international. 485 applicants, 36% accepted, 77 enrolled. In 2016, 91 master's, 15 other advanced degrees awarded. *Degree requirements:* For master's, comprehensive exam (for some programs), thesis (for some programs). *Entrance requirements:* Additional exam requirements/recommendations for international students: Required—PTE, TOEFL (minimum score 550 paper-based, 75 iBT) or IELTS (6.5). *Application deadline:* Applications are processed on a rolling basis. Application fee: $50. Electronic applications accepted. *Expenses: Tuition:* Full-time $28,272; part-time $1178 per credit. *Required fees:* $451 per term. Tuition and fees vary according to degree level and program. *Financial support:* In 2016–17, 24 teaching assistantships with partial tuition reimbursements (averaging $410 per year) were awarded; fellowships, research assistantships, career-related internships or fieldwork, Federal Work-Study, institutionally sponsored loans, scholarships/grants, tuition waivers (partial), and unspecified assistantships also available. Support available to part-time students. Financial award application deadline: 2/15; financial award applicants required to submit FAFSA. *Faculty research:* Biology, criminal justice, environmental sustainability, mathematics, psychology. *Total annual research expenditures:* $218,000. *Unit head:* Dr. Jeffrey Belnap, Acting Dean, 516-299-2233, Fax: 516-299-4140, E-mail: jeffrey.belnap@liu.edu. *Application contact:* Carol Zerah, Director of Graduate Admissions, 516-299-2900, Fax: 516-299-2137, E-mail: post-enroll@liu.edu. Website: http://liu.edu/CWPost/Academics/Schools/CLAS

**McNeese State University,** Doré School of Graduate Studies, Burton College of Education, Department of Psychology, Lake Charles, LA 70609. Offers addiction treatment (MA); applied behavior analysis (MA); counseling psychology (MA); general/experimental psychology (MA). *Program availability:* Evening/weekend. *Entrance requirements:* For master's, GRE.

**Mercyhurst University,** Graduate Studies, Program in Applied Behavior Analysis, Erie, PA 16546. Offers MABA. *Degree requirements:* For master's, thesis, project.

**Mercyhurst University,** Graduate Studies, Program in Special Education, Erie, PA 16546. Offers applied behavior analysis (MS); autism (MS); generalist (MS); higher education leadership and disabilities (MS). *Program availability:* Part-time, evening/weekend. *Degree requirements:* For master's, thesis optional. *Entrance requirements:* For master's, GRE or PRAXIS I, interview, resume, essay, three professional references, transcripts. Additional exam requirements/recommendations for international students: Required—TOEFL. Electronic applications accepted. *Faculty research:* College-age learning disabled program, teacher preparation/collaboration, applied behavior analysis, special education policy issues.

**Missouri State University,** Graduate College, College of Health and Human Services, Department of Psychology, Springfield, MO 65897. Offers applied behavior analysis (MS); clinical psychology (MS); experimental psychology (MS); forensic child psychology (Certificate); industrial/organizational psychology (MS). *Faculty:* 25 full-time (11 women), 4 part-time/adjunct (0 women). *Students:* 65 full-time (49 women), 7 part-time (5 women); includes 12 minority (1 Black or African American, non-Hispanic/Latino; 3 American Indian or Alaska Native, non-Hispanic/Latino; 3 Asian, non-Hispanic/Latino; 2 Hispanic/Latino; 3 Two or more races, non-Hispanic/Latino), 6 international. Average age 25. 159 applicants, 25% accepted, 31 enrolled. In 2016, 22 master's awarded. *Degree requirements:* For master's, comprehensive exam, thesis. *Entrance requirements:* For master's, GRE General Test, GRE Subject Test, minimum GPA of 3.25 in major, 3.0 overall; 20 hours of course work in psychology. Additional exam requirements/recommendations for international students: Required—TOEFL (minimum score 550 paper-based; 79 iBT), IELTS (minimum score 6). *Application deadline:* For fall admission, 2/15 priority date for domestic and international students. Application fee: $35 ($50 for international students). Electronic applications accepted. *Expenses:* Tuition, state resident: full-time $5830. Tuition, nonresident: full-time $10,708. *Required fees:* $1130. Tuition and fees vary according to class time, course level, course load and program. *Financial support:* In 2016–17, 9 research assistantships with full tuition reimbursements (averaging $8,772 per year), 8 teaching assistantships with full tuition reimbursements (averaging $8,772 per year) were awarded; career-related internships or fieldwork, Federal Work-Study, institutionally sponsored loans, scholarships/grants, and unspecified assistantships also available. Financial award application deadline: 3/31; financial award applicants required to submit FAFSA. *Faculty research:* Work-family conflict, child forensic psychology, sports psychology, body image assessment, visual learning. *Unit head:* Dr. Paul Deal, Department Head, 417-836-5797, Fax: 417-836-8330, E-mail: psychology@missouristate.edu. *Application contact:* Michael Edwards, Coordinator of Graduate Admissions, 417-836-5330, Fax: 417-836-6200, E-mail: michaeledwards@missouristate.edu. Website: http://psychology.missouristate.edu/

**Monmouth University,** Graduate Studies, School of Education, West Long Branch, NJ 07764-1898. Offers applied behavioral analysis (Certificate); autism (Certificate); director of school counseling services (Post-Master's Certificate); initial certification (MAT), including elementary level, K-12, secondary level; learning disabilities teacher-consultant (Post-Master's Certificate); principal/school administrator (MS Ed); principal/supervisor (MS Ed); school counseling (MS Ed); special education (MS Ed), including autism, learning disabilities teacher-consultant, teaching in inclusive settings; speech-language pathology (MS Ed); student affairs and college counseling (MS Ed); supervisor (Post-Master's Certificate); teaching English to speakers of other languages (TESOL) (Certificate). *Accreditation:* NCATE. *Program availability:* Part-time, evening/weekend, 100% online, blended/hybrid learning. *Entrance requirements:* For master's, GRE taken within last 5 years (for MS Ed in speech-language pathology); SAT (minimum combined score of 1660 in 3 sections), ACT (23), GRE (minimum score of 4.0 on analytical writing section and minimum combined score of 310 on quantitative and verbal sections), or passing scores on 3 parts of Core Academic Skills Educators, minimum GPA of 3.0 in major; 2 letters of recommendation (for some programs); resume, personal statement or essay (depending on program). Additional exam requirements/recommendations for international students: Required—TOEFL (minimum score 550 paper-based; 79 iBT), IELTS (minimum score 6), Michigan English Language Assessment Battery (minimum score 77) or Certificate of Advanced English (minimum score B2). Electronic applications accepted. *Faculty research:* Multicultural literacy, science and mathematics teaching strategies, teacher as reflective practitioner, children with disabilities.

**Montana State University Billings,** College of Education, Department of Educational Theory and Practice, Program in Special Education, Billings, MT 59101. Offers advanced studies (MS Sp Ed); applied behavior analysis (MS Sp Ed); generalist (MS Sp Ed). *Accreditation:* NCATE. *Program availability:* Part-time. *Faculty:* 2 full-time (both women). *Students:* 42. *Degree requirements:* For master's, thesis or professional paper and/or field experience. *Entrance requirements:* For master's, GRE General Test or MAT, minimum GPA of 3.0. Additional exam requirements/recommendations for

international students: Required—TOEFL (minimum score 79 iBT), IELTS (minimum score 6.5). *Application deadline:* Applications are processed on a rolling basis. Application fee: $40. Electronic applications accepted. *Expenses:* Tuition, state resident: full-time $5265; part-time $3436 per year. Tuition, nonresident: full-time $14,030; part-time $9280 per year. *International tuition:* $19,295 full-time. Tuition and fees vary according to degree level, campus/location and program. *Financial support:* Research assistantships with partial tuition reimbursements, teaching assistantships with partial tuition reimbursements, career-related internships or fieldwork, Federal Work-Study, institutionally sponsored loans, scholarships/grants, tuition waivers (partial), and unspecified assistantships available. Support available to part-time students. Financial award application deadline: 5/1; financial award applicants required to submit FAFSA. *Unit head:* Dr. Ken Miller, Chair, 406-657-2034, E-mail: kmiller@msubillings.edu. *Application contact:* David M. Sullivan, Graduate Studies Counselor, 406-657-2053, Fax: 406-657-2299, E-mail: dsullivan@msubillings.edu.

**Northeastern University,** Bouvé College of Health Sciences, Boston, MA 02115-5096. Offers applied behavior analysis (MS); audiology (Au D); counseling psychology (MS, PhD, CAGS); exercise science (MS); nursing (MS, PhD, CAGS), including administration (MS), adult-gerontology acute care nurse practitioner (MS, CAGS), adult-gerontology primary care nurse practitioner (MS, CAGS), anesthesia (MS), family nurse practitioner (MS, CAGS), neonatal nurse practitioner (MS, CAGS), pediatric nurse practitioner (MS, CAGS), psychiatric mental health nurse practitioner (MS, CAGS); nursing practice (DNP); pharmaceutical sciences (MS, PhD), including interdisciplinary concentration, pharmaceutics and drug delivery systems; pharmacology (MS); pharmacy (Pharm D); school psychology (PhD); urban health (MPH); MS/MBA. *Accreditation:* ACPE (one or more programs are accredited). *Program availability:* Part-time, evening/weekend, online learning. *Faculty:* 192 full-time (119 women), 194 part-time/adjunct (156 women). *Students:* 1,371 full-time (1,009 women), 262 part-time (219 women). In 2016, 352 master's, 312 doctorates, 25 other advanced degrees awarded. *Degree requirements:* For doctorate, thesis/dissertation (for some programs); for CAGS, comprehensive exam. Application fee: $75. Electronic applications accepted. *Expenses:* Contact institution. *Financial support:* Fellowships, research assistantships, teaching assistantships, career-related internships or fieldwork, scholarships/grants, health care benefits, tuition waivers, and unspecified assistantships available. Support available to part-time students. Financial award applicants required to submit FAFSA. *Unit head:* Susan L. Parish, Dean, Bouve College of Health Sciences, 617-373-3323, Fax: 617-373-3030. *Application contact:* E-mail: bouvegrad@northeastern.edu. Website: http://www.northeastern.edu/bouve/

**Northern Michigan University,** Office of Graduate Education and Research, College of Arts and Sciences, Department of Psychology, Marquette, MI 49855-5301. Offers applied behavior analysis (MS); performance improvement (Graduate Certificate); psychology (MS); training and performance improvement (MS). *Program availability:* Part-time. *Degree requirements:* For master's, thesis (for some programs). *Entrance requirements:* For master's, minimum GPA of 3.0; bachelor's degree preferably in psychology; undergraduate course on introduction to psychology; undergraduate course on statistics; personal statement; 3 letters of recommendation. Additional exam requirements/recommendations for international students: Required—TOEFL (minimum score 550 paper-based; 79 iBT), IELTS (minimum score 6.5). Electronic applications accepted. *Faculty research:* Emotion and cognition, neuropsychopharmacology, sensation and perception, behavior analysis, developmental psychology.

**Oakland University,** Graduate Study and Lifelong Learning, School of Education and Human Services, Department of Human Development and Child Studies, Program in Special Education, Rochester, MI 48309-4401. Offers applied behavior analysis (Graduate Certificate); autism spectrum disorder (Graduate Certificate); emotional impairment (Graduate Certificate); special education (M Ed), including applied behavior analysis, autism spectrum disorder, emotional impairment, specific learning disabilities; specific learning disabilities (Graduate Certificate). *Accreditation:* TEAC. *Entrance requirements:* For master's, minimum GPA of 3.0, interview. Additional exam requirements/recommendations for international students: Required—TOEFL (minimum score 550 paper-based). Electronic applications accepted.

**Oklahoma City University,** Petree College of Arts and Sciences, Oklahoma City, OK 73106-1402. Offers applied behavioral studies (M Ed); applied sociology: nonprofit leadership (MA); creative writing (MFA); criminology (MS); early childhood education (M Ed); elementary education (M Ed); general studies (MLA); leadership/management (MLA); moving image arts (MFA); professional counseling (M Ed); teaching (MA); teaching English to speakers of other languages (MA). *Program availability:* Part-time, evening/weekend. *Faculty:* 11 full-time (5 women), 15 part-time/adjunct (6 women). *Students:* 77 full-time (55 women), 46 part-time (30 women); includes 32 minority (13 Black or African American, non-Hispanic/Latino; 1 American Indian or Alaska Native, non-Hispanic/Latino; 2 Asian, non-Hispanic/Latino; 12 Hispanic/Latino; 4 Two or more races, non-Hispanic/Latino), 37 international. Average age 34. 92 applicants, 74% accepted, 46 enrolled. In 2016, 72 master's awarded. *Degree requirements:* For master's, capstone/practicum. *Entrance requirements:* For master's, bachelor's degree from accredited institution with minimum GPA of 3.0, essay, recommendation letters. Additional exam requirements/recommendations for international students: Required—TOEFL (minimum score 550 paper-based; 80 iBT). *Application deadline:* Applications are processed on a rolling basis. Application fee: $50. Electronic applications accepted. *Expenses:* Contact institution. *Financial support:* In 2016–17, 16 students received support. Federal Work-Study, institutionally sponsored loans, scholarships/grants, and tuition waivers (full and partial) available. Support available to part-time students. Financial award application deadline: 6/1; financial award applicants required to submit FAFSA. *Unit head:* Dr. Amy Cataldi, Dean, 405-208-5446, Fax: 405-208-5447, E-mail: acataldi@okcu.edu. *Application contact:* Michael Harrington, Director of Graduate Admissions, 800-633-7242, Fax: 405-208-5356, E-mail: gadmissions@okcu.edu. Website: http://www.okcu.edu/petree/

**Oklahoma State University,** College of Education, School of Applied Health and Educational Psychology, Stillwater, OK 74078. Offers applied behavioral studies (Ed D); applied health and educational psychology (MS, PhD, Ed S). *Accreditation:* APA (one or more programs are accredited). *Program availability:* Part-time. *Faculty:* 38 full-time (22 women), 11 part-time/adjunct (6 women). *Students:* 168 full-time (122 women), 140 part-time (80 women); includes 86 minority (21 Black or African American, non-Hispanic/Latino; 10 American Indian or Alaska Native, non-Hispanic/Latino; 3 Asian, non-Hispanic/Latino; 24 Hispanic/Latino; 28 Two or more races, non-Hispanic/Latino), 13 international. Average age 30. 157 applicants, 51% accepted, 73 enrolled. In 2016, 73 master's, 21 doctorates awarded. *Degree requirements:* For master's, thesis (for some programs); for doctorate, comprehensive exam, thesis/dissertation. *Entrance requirements:* For master's and doctorate, GRE or GMAT. Additional exam requirements/recommendations for international students: Required—TOEFL (minimum score 550 paper-based; 79 iBT). *Application deadline:* For fall admission, 3/1 priority date for international students; for spring admission, 8/1 priority date for international students. Applications are processed on a rolling basis. Application fee: $40 ($75 for international students). Electronic applications accepted. *Expenses:* Tuition, state resident: full-time $3775; part-time $209.70 per credit hour. Tuition, nonresident: full-time $14,851; part-time $825.05 per credit hour. *Required fees:* $2027; $112.60 per

## Applied Behavior Analysis

credit hour. Tuition and fees vary according to campus/location. *Financial support:* In 2016–17, 31 research assistantships (averaging $9,791 per year), 64 teaching assistantships (averaging $11,347 per year) were awarded; career-related internships or fieldwork, Federal Work-Study, scholarships/grants, health care benefits, tuition waivers (partial), and unspecified assistantships also available. Support available to part-time students. Financial award application deadline: 3/1; financial award applicants required to submit FAFSA. *Unit head:* Dr. Aric Warren, Head, 405-744-6040, Fax: 405-744-6779, E-mail: aric.warren@okstate.edu. *Website:* http://education.okstate.edu/sahep

**Penn State Harrisburg,** Graduate School, School of Behavioral Sciences and Education, Middletown, PA 17057. Offers adult education in the health and medical professions (Certificate); applied behavior analysis (MA); applied clinical psychology (MA); applied psychological research (MA); community psychology and social change (MA); English as a second language (ESL) program specialist and leadership (Certificate); folklore and ethnography (Certificate); health education (M Ed); lifelong learning and adult education (M Ed, D Ed); literacy education (M Ed); literacy leadership (Certificate); psychology: applications in clinical psychology (Certificate); psychology: health psychology (Certificate); teaching and curriculum (M Ed); training and development (M Ed, Certificate). *Program availability:* Part-time, evening/weekend. *Unit head:* Dr. Mukund S. Kulkarni, Chancellor, 717-948-6105, Fax: 717-948-6452. *Application contact:* Robert W. Coffman, Jr., Director of Enrollment Management, Recruitment and Admissions, 717-948-6250, Fax: 717-948-6325, E-mail: hbgadmit@psu.edu.
Website: https://harrisburg.psu.edu/behavioral-sciences-and-education/

**Philadelphia College of Osteopathic Medicine,** Graduate and Professional Programs, Department of Psychology, Philadelphia, PA 19131-1694. Offers applied behavior analysis (Certificate); clinical health psychology (Post-Doctoral Certificate); clinical neuropsychology (Post-Doctoral Certificate); clinical psychology (Psy D); mental health counseling (MS); organizational development and leadership (MS); psychology (Certificate); school psychology (MS, Psy D, Ed S). *Accreditation:* APA. *Faculty:* 19 full-time (11 women), 122 part-time/adjunct (58 women). *Students:* 364 (285 women); includes 78 minority (62 Black or African American, non-Hispanic/Latino; 2 American Indian or Alaska Native, non-Hispanic/Latino; 9 Asian, non-Hispanic/Latino; 5 Hispanic/Latino), 2 international. 366 applicants, 51% accepted, 139 enrolled. In 2016, 72 master's, 42 doctorates, 17 other advanced degrees awarded. Terminal master's awarded for partial completion of doctoral program. *Degree requirements:* For master's, comprehensive exam (for some programs), thesis (for some programs); for doctorate, comprehensive exam, thesis/dissertation. *Entrance requirements:* For master's, GRE or MAT, minimum GPA of 3.0; bachelor's degree from regionally-accredited college or university; for doctorate, PRAXIS II (for Psy D in school psychology), minimum undergraduate GPA of 3.0; for other advanced degree, GRE (for Ed S). Additional exam requirements/recommendations for international students: Required—TOEFL (minimum score 79 iBT). *Application deadline:* Applications are processed on a rolling basis. Application fee: $50. Electronic applications accepted. Tuition and fees vary according to course load, degree level and program. *Financial support:* In 2016–17, 28 teaching assistantships were awarded; Federal Work-Study, institutionally sponsored loans, and scholarships/grants also available. Financial award application deadline: 3/15; financial award applicants required to submit FAFSA. *Faculty research:* Adult and childhood anxiety and ADHD; coping with chronic illness; primary care psychology/integrated health care; applied behavior analysis; psychological, educational, and neuropsychological assessment. *Total annual research expenditures:* $533,489. *Unit head:* Dr. Robert DiTomasso, Chairman, 215-871-6442, Fax: 215-871-6458, E-mail: robertd@pcom.edu. *Application contact:* Johnathan Cox, Associate Director of Admissions, 215-871-6700, Fax: 215-871-6719, E-mail: karis@pcom.edu.

**See Display on page 1004 and Close-Up on page 1227.**

**Queens College of the City University of New York,** Mathematics and Natural Sciences Division, Department of Psychology, Queens, NY 11367-1597. Offers applied behavior analysis (MA, AC); behavioral neuroscience (MA); psychology (MA). *Program availability:* Part-time. *Faculty:* 29 full-time (17 women), 61 part-time/adjunct (46 women). *Students:* 11 full-time (5 women), 117 part-time (94 women); includes 57 minority (12 Black or African American, non-Hispanic/Latino; 1 American Indian or Alaska Native, non-Hispanic/Latino; 12 Asian, non-Hispanic/Latino; 28 Hispanic/Latino; 4 Two or more races, non-Hispanic/Latino), 4 international. Average age 28. 179 applicants, 64% accepted, 63 enrolled. In 2016, 36 master's, 1 other advanced degree awarded. *Degree requirements:* For master's, comprehensive exam (for some programs), thesis. *Entrance requirements:* For master's, minimum GPA of 3.0. Additional exam requirements/recommendations for international students: Required—TOEFL, IELTS. *Application deadline:* For fall admission, 4/1 for domestic students; for spring admission, 11/1 for domestic students. Applications are processed on a rolling basis. Application fee: $125. Electronic applications accepted. *Expenses:* Tuition, state resident: full-time $5065; part-time $425 per credit. Tuition, nonresident: part-time $780 per credit. *Required fees:* $522; $397 per credit. Part-time tuition and fees vary according to course load and program. *Financial support:* Career-related internships or fieldwork, institutionally sponsored loans, and unspecified assistantships available. Financial award application deadline: 4/1; financial award applicants required to submit FAFSA. *Unit head:* Dr. Jeffery Halperin, Acting Chair, 718-997-3200, E-mail: jeffery.halperin@qc.cuny.edu.

**Regis College,** School of Nursing and Health Sciences, Weston, MA 02493. Offers applied behavior analysis (MS); counseling psychology (MA); health administration (MS); nurse practitioner (Certificate); nursing (MS, DNP); nursing education (Certificate); occupational therapy (MS). *Accreditation:* ACEN. *Program availability:* Part-time, evening/weekend, 100% online, blended/hybrid learning. *Degree requirements:* For doctorate, thesis/dissertation. *Entrance requirements:* For master's, GRE General Test or MAT, minimum GPA of 3.0; for doctorate, MAT or GRE if GPA from master's lower than 3.5. Additional exam requirements/recommendations for international students: Required—TOEFL; Recommended—IELTS. *Application deadline:* Applications are processed on a rolling basis. Application fee: $75. Electronic applications accepted. *Financial support:* Federal Work-Study, scholarships/grants, traineeships, and unspecified assistantships available. Support available to part-time students. Financial award applicants required to submit FAFSA. *Faculty research:* Health policy, education, aging, job satisfaction, psychiatric nursing, critical thinking. *Application contact:* Catherine Hamilton, Senior Assistant Director, Graduate Admission, 781-768-7101, E-mail: catherine.hamilton@regiscollege.edu.

**Rollins College,** Hamilton Holt School, Master of Arts in Applied Behavior Analysis and Clinical Science Program, Winter Park, FL 32789-4499. Offers MA. *Program availability:* Part-time, evening/weekend. *Faculty:* 3 full-time (all women). *Students:* 24 full-time (22 women), 3 part-time (2 women); includes 8 minority (1 Black or African American, non-Hispanic/Latino; 2 Asian, non-Hispanic/Latino; 4 Hispanic/Latino; 1 Two or more races, non-Hispanic/Latino). Average age 29. 31 applicants, 68% accepted, 19 enrolled. *Degree requirements:* For master's, thesis, Board Certified Behavior Analyst Examination; intensive practicum. *Entrance requirements:* For master's, GRE, official transcripts, three letters of recommendation, essay, resume. Additional exam requirements/recommendations for international students: Required—TOEFL (minimum score 550 paper-based). *Application deadline:* For fall admission, 3/1 priority date for

domestic students. Applications are processed on a rolling basis. Application fee: $50. Electronic applications accepted. *Expenses:* $597 per credit hour. *Financial support:* In 2016–17, 1 student received support. Federal Work-Study, scholarships/grants, and unspecified assistantships available. Support available to part-time students. Financial award applicants required to submit FAFSA. *Unit head:* Dr. Michele Williams, Director, Health Professions, 407-646-2036, E-mail: amwilliams2@rollins.edu. *Application contact:* Graduate Program Admission, 407-646-2232, Fax: 407-646-1551.

**Rowan University,** Graduate School, College of Science and Mathematics, Program in Applied Behavioral Analysis, Glassboro, NJ 08028-1701. Offers MA, CAGS. *Entrance requirements:* For master's, GRE General Test. Additional exam requirements/recommendations for international students: Required—TOEFL.

**Sage Graduate School,** Esteves School of Education, Program in Applied Behavior Analysis and Autism, Troy, NY 12180-4115. Offers MS, Post Master's Certificate. *Program availability:* Part-time, evening/weekend, online only, 100% online. *Faculty:* 6 full-time (5 women), 8 part-time/adjunct (all women). *Students:* 55 full-time (48 women), 141 part-time (115 women); includes 44 minority (11 Black or African American, non-Hispanic/Latino; 1 American Indian or Alaska Native, non-Hispanic/Latino; 10 Asian, non-Hispanic/Latino; 16 Hispanic/Latino; 6 Two or more races, non-Hispanic/Latino). Average age 28. 276 applicants, 43% accepted, 81 enrolled. In 2016, 67 master's, 12 other advanced degrees awarded. *Entrance requirements:* For master's, undergraduate degree with minimum GPA of 2.75. Additional exam requirements/recommendations for international students: Required—TOEFL (minimum score 550 paper-based). *Application deadline:* Applications are processed on a rolling basis. Application fee: $40. Electronic applications accepted. *Expenses: Tuition:* Full-time $12,240; part-time $680 per credit hour. Tuition and fees vary according to degree level and program. *Financial support:* Federal Work-Study, scholarships/grants, tuition waivers (partial), and unspecified assistantships available. Support available to part-time students. Financial award applicants required to submit FAFSA. *Unit head:* Dr. John Pelizza, Interim Dean, Esteves School of Education, 518-244-2051, Fax: 518-244-2334, E-mail: pelizj@sage.edu. *Application contact:* Dr. Lori Finn, Department Chair, Center for Applied Behavior Analysis, 518-244-6873, Fax: 518-244-6880, E-mail: caba@sage.edu. Website: http://www.sage.edu/academics/education/programs/aba_autism

**St. Cloud State University,** School of Graduate Studies, School of Health and Human Services, Department of Counseling and Community Psychology, Program in Applied Behavior Analysis, St. Cloud, MN 56301-4498. Offers MS. *Program availability:* Part-time, online learning. *Degree requirements:* For master's, comprehensive exam (for some programs), thesis or alternative. *Entrance requirements:* For master's, GRE General Test, minimum GPA of 2.75. Additional exam requirements/recommendations for international students: Required—Michigan English Language Assessment Battery; Recommended—TOEFL (minimum score 550 paper-based), IELTS (minimum score 6.5).

**Saint Peter's University,** Graduate Programs in Education, Jersey City, NJ 07306-5997. Offers director of school counseling services (Certificate); educational leadership (MA Ed, Ed D); higher education (Ed D); middle school mathematics (Certificate); professional/associate counselor (Certificate); reading (MA Ed); school business administrator (Certificate); school counseling (MA, Certificate); special education (MA Ed, Certificate), including applied behavioral analysis (MA Ed), literacy (MA Ed), teacher of students with disabilities (Certificate); teaching (MA Ed, Certificate), including 6-8 middle school education, K-12 secondary education, K-5 elementary education. *Accreditation:* TEAC. *Program availability:* Part-time, evening/weekend. *Degree requirements:* For master's, comprehensive exam; for doctorate, comprehensive exam, thesis/dissertation. *Entrance requirements:* For master's and doctorate, GRE or MAT. Additional exam requirements/recommendations for international students: Required—TOEFL. Electronic applications accepted.

**Shenandoah University,** College of Arts and Sciences, Winchester, VA 22601-5195. Offers applied behavior analysis (MS). *Program availability:* Part-time, evening/weekend. *Faculty:* 1 full-time (0 women), 3 part-time/adjunct (all women). *Students:* 14 full-time (13 women), 2 part-time (both women); includes 1 minority (Black or African American, non-Hispanic/Latino). Average age 28. 19 applicants, 84% accepted, 7 enrolled. In 2016, 9 master's awarded. *Degree requirements:* For master's, thesis or alternative, minimum of 37 credit hours, including 21 in coursework, 12 of supervised practical experience, and 4 for capstone project. *Entrance requirements:* For master's, minimum GPA of 3.0 in undergraduate work with bachelor's degree preferably in psychology, education, special education, social work, speech pathology or a similar discipline; essay or writing sample. Additional exam requirements/recommendations for international students: Required—TOEFL (minimum score 550 paper-based; 79 iBT), IELTS (minimum score 6.5). *Application deadline:* For fall admission, 7/15 for domestic and international students. Application fee: $30. Electronic applications accepted. *Expenses:* Contact institution. *Financial support:* In 2016–17, 1 student received support. Scholarships/grants and unspecified assistantships available. Financial award applicants required to submit FAFSA. *Faculty research:* Psychology, applied behavioral analysis. *Unit head:* Jeff W. Coker, PhD, Dean, 540-665-4587, Fax: 540-665-4644, E-mail: jcoker2@su.edu. *Application contact:* Andrew Woodall, Executive Director of Recruitment and Admissions, 540-665-4581, Fax: 540-665-4627, E-mail: admit@su.edu.

**Simmons College,** School of Social Work, Boston, MA 02115. Offers behavior analysis (MS, PhD, Ed S); education (MS Ed); social work (MSW, PhD); special education (MS Ed), including moderate and severe disabilities; teaching (MAT), including elementary education; MSW/MBA. *Accreditation:* CSWE (one or more programs are accredited). *Program availability:* Part-time, 100% online. *Faculty:* 37 full-time (28 women), 62 part-time/adjunct (44 women). *Students:* 797 full-time (705 women), 951 part-time (829 women); includes 420 minority (200 Black or African American, non-Hispanic/Latino; 5 American Indian or Alaska Native, non-Hispanic/Latino; 46 Asian, non-Hispanic/Latino; 122 Hispanic/Latino; 4 Native Hawaiian or other Pacific Islander, non-Hispanic/Latino; 43 Two or more races, non-Hispanic/Latino), 13 international. Average age 31. 1,356 applicants, 78% accepted, 592 enrolled. In 2016, 342 master's, 2 doctorates, 1 other advanced degree awarded. Terminal master's awarded for partial completion of doctoral program. *Degree requirements:* For master's, thesis (for some programs); for doctorate, comprehensive exam (for some programs), thesis/dissertation (for some programs). *Entrance requirements:* For master's, GRE, MAT, Massachusetts Tests for Education Licensure (for different programs); for doctorate, GRE, BCBA Analyst Exam. Additional exam requirements/recommendations for international students: Required—TOEFL (minimum score 600 paper-based; 100 iBT). *Application deadline:* For fall admission, 8/1 for domestic students; for spring admission, 12/15 for domestic students; for summer admission, 5/1 for domestic students. Applications are processed on a rolling basis. Application fee: $35. Electronic applications accepted. *Expenses:* $1,010 per credit; $52 activity fee per semester. *Financial support:* In 2016–17, 12 fellowships with partial tuition reimbursements were awarded; scholarships/grants and unspecified assistantships also available. Support available to part-time students. *Unit head:* Dr. Cheryl Parks, Dean, 617-521-3293, E-mail: cheryl.parks@simmons.edu. *Application contact:* Carlos D. Frontado, Director of Admissions, 617-521-3920, Fax: 617-521-3980, E-mail: ssw@simmons.edu. Website: http://www.simmons.edu/ssw/

**Teachers College, Columbia University,** Department of Health and Behavior Studies, New York, NY 10027-6696. Offers applied behavior analysis (MA, PhD); applied educational psychology: school psychology (Ed M, PhD); behavioral nutrition (PhD), including nutrition (Ed D, PhD); community health education (MS); community nutrition education (Ed M), including community nutrition education; education of deaf and hard of hearing (MA, PhD); health education (MA, Ed D); hearing impairment (Ed D); intellectual disability/autism (MA, Ed D, PhD); nursing education (Ed D, Advanced Certificate); nutrition and education (MS); nutrition and exercise physiology (MS); nutrition and public health (MS); nutrition education (Ed D), including nutrition (Ed D, PhD); physical disabilities (Ed D); reading specialist (MA); severe or multiple disabilities (MA); special education (Ed M, MA, Ed D); teaching of sign language (MA). *Program availability:* Part-time, evening/weekend. *Students:* 282 full-time (262 women), 262 part-time (222 women); includes 180 minority (54 Black or African American, non-Hispanic/Latino; 1 American Indian or Alaska Native, non-Hispanic/Latino; 56 Asian, non-Hispanic/Latino; 56 Hispanic/Latino; 1 Native Hawaiian or other Pacific Islander, non-Hispanic/Latino; 12 Two or more races, non-Hispanic/Latino), 55 international. 503 applicants, 57% accepted, 146 enrolled. Terminal master's awarded for partial completion of doctoral program. *Expenses:* Tuition: Full-time $36,288; part-time $1512 per credit. *Required fees:* $438 per semester. One-time fee: $510 full-time. Full-time tuition and fees vary according to course load. *Unit head:* Prof. Stephen T. Peverly, Chair, 212-678-3964, Fax: 212-678-8259, E-mail: stp4@columbia.edu. *Application contact:* David Estrella, Director of Admission, 212-678-3305, E-mail: estrella@tc.columbia.edu.
Website: http://www.tc.columbia.edu/health-and-behavior-studies/

**Tennessee Technological University,** College of Graduate Studies, College of Education, Department of Curriculum and Instruction, Program in Exceptional Learning, Cookeville, TN 38505. Offers applied behavior analysis (PhD); literacy (PhD); program planning and evaluation (PhD); STEM education (PhD). *Program availability:* Part-time, evening/weekend. *Students:* 10 full-time (6 women), 28 part-time (21 women); includes 2 minority (1 Black or African American, non-Hispanic/Latino; 1 Two or more races, non-Hispanic/Latino), 2 international. 15 applicants, 67% accepted, 7 enrolled. In 2016, 5 doctorates awarded. *Degree requirements:* For doctorate, comprehensive exam, thesis/dissertation. *Entrance requirements:* For doctorate, GRE, minimum GPA of 3.0. Additional exam requirements/recommendations for international students: Required—TOEFL (minimum score 550 paper-based; 79 iBT), IELTS (minimum score 5.5), PTE (minimum score 53), or TOEIC (Test of English as an International Communication). *Application deadline:* For fall admission, 8/1 for domestic students, 5/1 for international students; for spring admission, 12/1 for domestic students, 10/1 for international students; for summer admission, 5/1 for domestic students, 2/1 for international students. Applications are processed on a rolling basis. Application fee: $35 ($40 for international students). Electronic applications accepted. *Expenses:* Tuition, state resident: full-time $9375; part-time $534 per credit hour. Tuition, nonresident: full-time $22,443; part-time $1260 per credit hour. *Financial support:* In 2016–17, 4 fellowships (averaging $8,000 per year), 9 research assistantships (averaging $12,000 per year), 2 teaching assistantships (averaging $12,000 per year) were awarded. Financial award application deadline: 4/1. *Unit head:* Dr. Lisa Zagumny, Director, 931-372-3078, Fax: 931-372-3517, E-mail: lzagumny@tntech.edu. *Application contact:* Shelia K. Kendrick, Coordinator of Graduate Studies, 931-372-3808, Fax: 931-372-3497, E-mail: skendrick@tntech.edu.
Website: https://www.tntech.edu/education/elphd/

**The University of Kansas,** Graduate Studies, College of Liberal Arts and Sciences, Department of Applied Behavioral Science, Lawrence, KS 66045. Offers applied behavioral science (MA); behavioral psychology (PhD); community health and development (Graduate Certificate); PhD/MPH. *Program availability:* Part-time. *Students:* 42 full-time (29 women); includes 40 minority (35 Black or African American, non-Hispanic/Latino; 1 American Indian or Alaska Native, non-Hispanic/Latino; 2 Hispanic/Latino; 2 Native Hawaiian or other Pacific Islander, non-Hispanic/Latino), 2 international. Average age 28. 72 applicants, 14% accepted, 10 enrolled. In 2016, 4 master's, 2 doctorates awarded. Terminal master's awarded for partial completion of doctoral program. *Entrance requirements:* For master's, curriculum vitae; 3 letters of recommendation; personal statement; all academic transcripts; copies of pertinent written work, published or not, as well as presented papers; for doctorate, curriculum vitae; 3 letters of recommendation; personal statement; copies of pertinent written work, published or not, as well as presented papers. Additional exam requirements/recommendations for international students: Required—TOEFL. *Application deadline:* For fall admission, 12/15 priority date for domestic students, 12/15 for international students. Application fee: $65 ($85 for international students). Electronic applications accepted. *Financial support:* Fellowships, research assistantships, teaching assistantships, career-related internships or fieldwork, traineeships, tuition waivers (full), and unspecified assistantships available. Financial award application deadline: 12/15; financial award applicants required to submit CSS PROFILE or FAFSA. *Faculty research:* Organizational behavioral management, community health and development, early childhood education and intervention, developmental disabilities, behavioral economics of choice. *Unit head:* Dr. Florence D. DiGennaro Reed, Chairperson, 785-864-0521, E-mail: fdreed@ku.edu. *Application contact:* Andrea Noltner, Office Manager, 785-864-0503, E-mail: anoltner@ku.edu.
Website: http://absc.ku.edu

**University of Louisville,** Graduate School, College of Education and Human Development, Department of Teaching and Learning, Louisville, KY 40292-0001. Offers art education (MAT); autism and applied behavior analysis (Certificate); curriculum and instruction (PhD); early elementary education (MAT); exercise physiology (MS); health and physical education (MAT); health professions education (Certificate); higher education (MA); human resources and organization development (MS); instructional technology (M Ed); interdisciplinary early childhood education (MAT); middle school education (MAT); music education (MAT); secondary education (MAT); special education (MAT); sport administration (MS); teacher leadership (M Ed). *Program availability:* Part-time, evening/weekend. *Students:* 116 full-time (68 women), 158 part-time (112 women); includes 46 minority (24 Black or African American, non-Hispanic/Latino; 8 Asian, non-Hispanic/Latino; 5 Hispanic/Latino; 9 Two or more races, non-Hispanic/Latino), 6 international. Average age 30. 114 applicants, 71% accepted, 57 enrolled. In 2016, 59 master's, 3 doctorates awarded. *Application deadline:* For spring admission, 1/1 priority date for international students. Application fee: $60. *Expenses:* Tuition, state resident: full-time $12,246; part-time $681 per credit hour. Tuition, nonresident: full-time $25,486; part-time $1417 per credit hour. *Required fees:* $196. Tuition and fees vary according to program and reciprocity agreements. *Financial support:* Application deadline: 6/1; applicants required to submit FAFSA. *Faculty research:* STEM teaching and learning; content literacy for English language learners; social justice in teacher education; adolescent literacy; mathematics teacher development. *Total annual research expenditures:* $1.7 million. *Unit head:* Dr. Ann E. Larson, Dean, College of Education and Human Development, 502-852-6411, Fax: 502-852-1464, E-mail: ann@louisville.edu. *Application contact:* Betty Hampton, Director of Graduate Student Services, 502-852-5597, Fax: 502-852-1465, E-mail: edadvise@louisville.edu.
Website: http://louisville.edu/delphi

**University of Massachusetts Dartmouth,** Graduate School, College of Arts and Sciences, Department of Psychology, North Dartmouth, MA 02747-2300. Offers applied behavioral analysis (MA, Post-Master's Certificate); autism studies (Graduate Certificate); clinical psychology (MA); research psychology (MA). *Program availability:* Part-time, 100% online, blended/hybrid learning. *Faculty:* 19 full-time (12 women), 7 part-time/adjunct (3 women). *Students:* 34 full-time (27 women), 50 part-time (39 women); includes 17 minority (3 Black or African American, non-Hispanic/Latino; 1 Asian, non-Hispanic/Latino; 8 Hispanic/Latino; 5 Two or more races, non-Hispanic/Latino). Average age 29. 99 applicants, 57% accepted, 32 enrolled. In 2016, 25 master's, 2 other advanced degrees awarded. *Degree requirements:* For master's, thesis or comprehensive exam (for clinical psychology); thesis (for research psychology). *Entrance requirements:* For master's, GRE (for research psychology), statement of purpose (minimum of 300 words), resume, 3 letters of recommendation, official transcripts; for other advanced degree, statement of purpose (minimum of 300 words), resume, 3 letters of recommendation, official transcripts. Additional exam requirements/recommendations for international students: Required—TOEFL (minimum score 533 paper-based; 72 iBT). *Application deadline:* For fall admission, 3/1 priority date for domestic students, 2/1 priority date for international students; for spring admission, 12/20 priority date for domestic students, 11/20 priority date for international students. Application fee: $60. Electronic applications accepted. *Expenses:* Tuition, state resident: full-time $14,994; part-time $624.75 per credit. Tuition, nonresident: full-time $27,068; part-time $1127.83 per credit. *Required fees:* $405; $25.88 per credit. Tuition and fees vary according to course load and reciprocity agreements. *Financial support:* In 2016–17, 2 fellowships (averaging $7,000 per year) were awarded; institutionally sponsored loans, scholarships/grants, and unspecified assistantships also available. Support available to part-time students. Financial award application deadline: 3/1; financial award applicants required to submit FAFSA. *Faculty research:* Behavioral medicine, learning, social and developmental psychology, child neuropsychology, clinical research, counseling, psychotherapy, nonverbal communication, emotion, cognition, problem solving. *Total annual research expenditures:* $500,000. *Unit head:* Mahzad Hojjat, Graduate Program Director, Research Psychology, 508-999-8951, E-mail: mhojjat@umassd.edu. *Application contact:* Steven Briggs, Director of Marketing and Recruitment for Graduate Studies, 508-999-8604, Fax: 508-999-8183, E-mail: graduate@umassd.edu.
Website: http://www.umassd.edu/cas/psychology/graduateprograms

**University of Memphis,** Graduate School, College of Education, Department of Instruction and Curriculum Leadership, Memphis, TN 38152. Offers advanced studies in teaching and learning (M Ed); applied behavior analysis (Graduate Certificate); autism studies (Graduate Certificate); early childhood education (MAT, MS, Ed D); elementary education (MAT); instruction and curriculum (MS, Ed D); instruction design and technology (MS, Ed D); instructional design and technology (Graduate Certificate); literacy, leadership, and coaching (Graduate Certificate); reading (MS, Ed D); school library information specialist (Graduate Certificate); secondary education (MAT); special education (MAT, MS, Ed D); STEM teacher leadership (Graduate Certificate); urban education (Graduate Certificate). *Accreditation:* NCATE (one or more programs are accredited). *Program availability:* Part-time. *Faculty:* 24 full-time (14 women), 17 part-time/adjunct (12 women). *Students:* 66 full-time (52 women), 315 part-time (243 women); includes 163 minority (132 Black or African American, non-Hispanic/Latino; 1 American Indian or Alaska Native, non-Hispanic/Latino; 6 Asian, non-Hispanic/Latino; 13 Hispanic/Latino; 1 Native Hawaiian or other Pacific Islander, non-Hispanic/Latino; 10 Two or more races, non-Hispanic/Latino), 4 international. Average age 35. 215 applicants, 78% accepted, 120 enrolled. In 2016, 111 master's, 21 doctorates, 8 other advanced degrees awarded. Terminal master's awarded for partial completion of doctoral program. *Degree requirements:* For master's, comprehensive exam, thesis or alternative; for doctorate, comprehensive exam, thesis/dissertation. *Entrance requirements:* For master's, GRE General Test, PRAXIS, minimum GPA of 2.5, letters of reference; for doctorate, GRE General Test, GRE Subject Test, 2 years of teaching experience, letters of reference, statement of purpose, interview. Additional exam requirements/recommendations for international students: Required—TOEFL (minimum score 550 paper-based; 79 iBT). *Application deadline:* For fall admission, 4/1 priority date for domestic students; for spring admission, 10/1 priority date for domestic students; for summer admission, 2/1 priority date for domestic students. Applications are processed on a rolling basis. Application fee: $35 ($60 for international students). Electronic applications accepted. *Expenses:* $5,231.50 per semester full-time in-state, $9,623.50 full-time out-of-state. *Financial support:* In 2016–17, 2 research assistantships with full tuition reimbursements (averaging $10,000 per year), 3 teaching assistantships with full tuition reimbursements (averaging $10,666 per year) were awarded; career-related internships or fieldwork, Federal Work-Study, institutionally sponsored loans, scholarships/grants, traineeships, and unspecified assistantships also available. Support available to part-time students. Financial award application deadline: 2/1; financial award applicants required to submit FAFSA. *Faculty research:* Effective urban teachers, preparation and retention of urban teachers, technology utilization in schools, field-based teacher preparation programs, effective use of online instruction. *Unit head:* Dr. Angiline Powell, Interim Chair, 901-678-3310, E-mail: apowell3@memphis.edu. *Application contact:* Dr. James Meindl, Coordinator of Graduate Studies, 901-678-3310, E-mail: jnmeindl@memphis.edu.
Website: http://www.memphis.edu/icl/

**University of Nebraska at Omaha,** Graduate Studies, College of Arts and Sciences, Department of Psychology, Omaha, NE 68182. Offers applied behavior analysis (Certificate); human resources and training (Certificate); industrial/organizational psychology (MS); psychology (MA, PhD); school psychology (MS, Ed S). *Program availability:* Part-time. *Faculty:* 10 full-time (1 woman). *Students:* 70 full-time (52 women), 49 part-time (33 women); includes 9 minority (2 Asian, non-Hispanic/Latino; 5 Hispanic/Latino; 2 Two or more races, non-Hispanic/Latino), 1 international. Average age 27. 157 applicants, 25% accepted, 38 enrolled. In 2016, 32 master's, 6 doctorates, 10 other advanced degrees awarded. *Degree requirements:* For master's, comprehensive exam, thesis (for some programs); for doctorate, comprehensive exam, thesis/dissertation. *Entrance requirements:* For master's and doctorate, GRE, minimum GPA of 3.0, official transcripts, 3 letters of recommendation, statement of purpose, writing sample, resume. Additional exam requirements/recommendations for international students: Required—TOEFL, IELTS, PTE. *Application deadline:* For fall admission, 1/5 priority date for domestic and international students. Application fee: $45. Electronic applications accepted. *Financial support:* In 2016–17, 50 students received support, including 23 research assistantships with tuition reimbursements available, 27 teaching assistantships with tuition reimbursements available; fellowships with tuition reimbursements available, career-related internships or fieldwork, Federal Work-Study, institutionally sponsored loans, scholarships/grants, health care benefits, tuition waivers (partial), and unspecified assistantships also available. Financial award application deadline: 3/1; financial award applicants required to submit FAFSA. *Unit head:* Dr. Brigette Ryalls, Chairperson, 402-554-2341, E-mail: graduate@unomaha.edu. *Application contact:* Dr. Joseph Brown, Graduate Program Chair, 402-554-2341, E-mail: graduate@unomaha.edu.

**University of Nebraska Medical Center,** Medical Sciences Interdepartmental Area, Omaha, NE 68198-4000. Offers applied behavior analysis (PhD); clinical translational

## Applied Behavior Analysis

research (MS, PhD); cytotechnology (MS); family medicine (MS, PhD); genetics, cell biology and anatomy (MS, PhD); internal medicine (MS); medical nutrition (MS, PhD); obstetrics and gynecology (MS, PhD); ophthalmology and visual sciences (MS, PhD); oral biology (MS, PhD); orthopedic surgery (MS, PhD); pathology and microbiology (MS, PhD); pediatrics (MS, PhD); pharmacology and experimental neuroscience (MS). *Program availability:* Part-time. *Faculty:* 170 full-time, 20 part-time/adjunct. *Students:* 44 full-time (27 women), 57 part-time (38 women); includes 13 minority (1 Black or African American, non-Hispanic/Latino; 11 Asian, non-Hispanic/Latino; 1 Hispanic/Latino), 20 international. Average age 32. 82 applicants, 59% accepted, 32 enrolled. In 2016, 16 master's, 9 doctorates awarded. Terminal master's awarded for partial completion of doctoral program. *Degree requirements:* For master's, comprehensive exam, thesis; for doctorate, comprehensive exam, thesis/dissertation. *Entrance requirements:* For master's, GRE General Test; for doctorate, GRE General Test, MCAT, DAT, LSAT. Additional exam requirements/recommendations for international students: Required—TOEFL (minimum score 550 paper-based; 80 iBT). *Application deadline:* For fall admission, 6/1 for domestic students, 4/1 for international students; for spring admission, 10/1 for domestic students, 9/1 for international students. Applications are processed on a rolling basis. Application fee: $60. Electronic applications accepted. *Expenses:* $297.25 resident tuition per credit, $850.50 non-resident tuition per credit; $140 fees per semester. *Financial support:* In 2016–17, 85 students received support, including 1 fellowship with full tuition reimbursement available (averaging $23,400 per year), 37 research assistantships with full tuition reimbursements available (averaging $23,400 per year), 2 teaching assistantships with full tuition reimbursements available (averaging $23,400 per year); scholarships/grants and health care benefits also available. Support available to part-time students. Financial award application deadline: 2/15; financial award applicants required to submit FAFSA. *Faculty research:* Molecular genetics, oral biology, veterinary pathology, newborn medicine, immunology, clinical research. *Unit head:* Dr. Laura Bilek, Graduate Committee Chair, 402-559-6923, E-mail: lbilek@unmc.edu. *Application contact:* Rhonda Sheibal-Carver, Interdisciplinary Programs Coordinator, 402-559-5141, E-mail: rhonda.sheibalcarver@unmc.edu. Website: https://www.unmc.edu/msia/index.html

**The University of North Carolina Wilmington,** College of Arts and Sciences, Department of Psychology, Wilmington, NC 28403-3297. Offers psychology (MA), including applied behavior analysis. *Program availability:* Part-time. *Faculty:* 28 full-time (17 women). *Students:* 32 full-time (26 women), 41 part-time (29 women); includes 6 minority (2 Asian, non-Hispanic/Latino; 4 Hispanic/Latino). Average age 25. 122 applicants, 25% accepted, 24 enrolled. In 2016, 17 master's awarded. *Degree requirements:* For master's, comprehensive exam, thesis. *Entrance requirements:* For master's, GRE General Test, GRE Subject Test, minimum B average in undergraduate work, 3 letters of recommendation, statement of interest, resume. Additional exam requirements/recommendations for international students: Required—TOEFL (minimum score 79 iBT), IELTS (minimum score 6.5). *Application deadline:* For fall admission, 1/15 for domestic students. Applications are processed on a rolling basis. Application fee: $60. Electronic applications accepted. *Expenses:* Contact institution. *Financial support:* Research assistantships, teaching assistantships, Federal Work-Study, unspecified assistantships, and out-of-state tuition remission available. Financial award application deadline: 3/15; financial award applicants required to submit FAFSA. *Unit head:* Dr. Julian Keith, Chair, 910-962-3378, Fax: 910-962-7010, E-mail: keithj@uncw.edu. *Application contact:* Dr. Christine Hughes, Graduate Coordinator, 910-962-7795, Fax: 910-962-7010, E-mail: hughesc@uncw.edu.
Website: http://www.uncw.edu/psy/grad/

**University of North Florida,** College of Education and Human Services, Department of Exceptional, Deaf, and Interpreter Education, Jacksonville, FL 32224. Offers American Sign Language (MS); American Sign Language/English interpreting (M Ed); applied behavior analysis (M Ed); autism (M Ed); deaf education (M Ed); disability services (M Ed); exceptional student education (M Ed). *Accreditation:* NCATE. *Program availability:* Part-time, evening/weekend. *Faculty:* 11 full-time (9 women), 6 part-time/adjunct (all women). *Students:* 32 full-time (29 women), 50 part-time (40 women); includes 14 minority (5 Black or African American, non-Hispanic/Latino; 2 Asian, non-Hispanic/Latino; 5 Hispanic/Latino; 2 Two or more races, non-Hispanic/Latino), 4 international. Average age 33. 28 applicants, 46% accepted, 7 enrolled. In 2016, 42 master's awarded. *Entrance requirements:* For master's, GRE General Test, minimum GPA of 3.0 in last 60 hours, interview, 3 letters of recommendation. Additional exam requirements/recommendations for international students: Required—TOEFL (minimum score 500 paper-based). *Application deadline:* For fall admission, 3/31 priority date for domestic students, 5/1 for international students; for spring admission, 12/1 priority date for domestic students, 10/1 for international students; for summer admission, 3/31 priority date for domestic students, 2/1 for international students. Application fee: $30. Electronic applications accepted. Tuition and fees vary according to course load, campus/location and program. *Financial support:* In 2016–17, 7 students received support, including 2 research assistantships (averaging $2,639 per year); teaching assistantships, career-related internships or fieldwork, Federal Work-Study, scholarships/grants, tuition waivers (partial), and unspecified assistantships also available. Support available to part-time students. Financial award application deadline: 4/1; financial award applicants required to submit FAFSA. *Faculty research:* Transportation, energy, communications, healthcare, nano-science and engineering, unmanned aircraft systems, biomedical applications. *Total annual research expenditures:* $706,370. *Unit head:* Dr. Janice Seabrooks-Blackmore, Chair, 904-620-2930, Fax: 904-620-3895, E-mail: janice.seabrooks-blackmore@unf.edu. *Application contact:* Dr. Amanda Pascale, Director, The Graduate School, 904-620-1360, Fax: 904-620-1362, E-mail: graduateschool@unf.edu.
Website: http://www.unf.edu/coehs/edie/

**University of North Texas,** Robert B. Toulouse School of Graduate Studies, Denton, TX 76203-5459. Offers accounting (MS); applied anthropology (MA, MS); applied behavior analysis (Certificate); applied geography (MA); applied technology and performance improvement (M Ed, MS); art education (MA); art history (MA); art museum education (Certificate); arts leadership (Certificate); audiology (Au D); behavior analysis (MS); behavioral science (PhD); biochemistry and molecular biology (MS); biology (MA, MS); biomedical engineering (MS); business analysis (MS); chemistry (MS); clinical health psychology (PhD); communication studies (MA, MS); computer engineering (MS); computer science (MS); counseling (M Ed, MS), including clinical mental health counseling (MS), college and university counseling, elementary school counseling, secondary school counseling; creative writing (MA); criminal justice (MS); curriculum and instruction (M Ed); decision sciences (MBA); design (MA, MFA), including fashion design (MFA), innovation studies, interior design (MFA); early childhood studies (MS); economics (MS); educational leadership (M Ed, Ed D); educational psychology (MS, PhD), including family studies (MS), gifted and talented (MS), human development (MS), learning and cognition (MS), research, measurement and evaluation (MS); electrical engineering (MS); emergency management (MPA); engineering technology (MS); English (MA); English as a second language (MA); environmental science (MS); finance (MBA, MS); financial management (MPA); French (MA); health services management (MBA); higher education (M Ed, Ed D); history (MA, MS); hospitality management (MS); human resources management (MPA); information science (MS); information systems (PhD); information technologies (MBA); interdisciplinary studies (MA, MS); international

studies (MA); international sustainable tourism (MS); jazz studies (MM); journalism (MA, MJ, Graduate Certificate), including interactive and virtual digital communication (Graduate Certificate), narrative journalism (Graduate Certificate), public relations (Graduate Certificate); kinesiology (MS); linguistics (MA); local government management (MPA); logistics (PhD); logistics and supply chain management (MBA); long-term care, senior housing, and aging services (MS); management (PhD); marketing (MBA); mathematics (MA, MS); mechanical and energy engineering (MS, PhD); music (MA), including ethnomusicology, music theory, musicology, performance; music composition (PhD); music education (MM Ed, PhD); nonprofit management (MPA); operations and supply chain management (MBA); performance (MM, DMA); philosophy (MA); political science (MA); professional and technical communication (MA); radio, television and film (MA, MFA); rehabilitation counseling (Certificate); sociology (MA); Spanish (MA); special education (M Ed); speech-language pathology (MA); strategic management (MBA); studio art (MFA); teaching (M Ed); MBA/MS. *Program availability:* Part-time, evening/weekend, online learning. Terminal master's awarded for partial completion of doctoral program. *Degree requirements:* For master's, variable foreign language requirement, comprehensive exam (for some programs), thesis (for some programs); for doctorate, variable foreign language requirement, comprehensive exam (for some programs), thesis/dissertation; for other advanced degree, variable foreign language requirement, comprehensive exam (for some programs). *Entrance requirements:* For master's and doctorate, GRE, GMAT. Additional exam requirements/recommendations for international students: Required—TOEFL (minimum score 550 paper-based; 79 iBT). Electronic applications accepted.

**University of Oklahoma,** Jeannine Rainbolt College of Education, Department of Educational Psychology, Program in Special Education, Norman, OK 73019. Offers applied behavior analysis (M Ed); higher education and community support (PhD); higher education professor (PhD); school instruction and leadership (PhD); secondary transition education (M Ed). *Accreditation:* NCATE. *Program availability:* Part-time, 100% online, blended/hybrid learning. *Students:* 23 full-time (18 women), 57 part-time (49 women); includes 23 minority (6 Black or African American, non-Hispanic/Latino; 5 American Indian or Alaska Native, non-Hispanic/Latino; 1 Asian, non-Hispanic/Latino; 6 Hispanic/Latino; 5 Two or more races, non-Hispanic/Latino), 4 international. Average age 39. 74 applicants, 42% accepted, 21 enrolled. In 2016, 20 master's, 1 doctorate awarded. Terminal master's awarded for partial completion of doctoral program. *Degree requirements:* For master's, thesis optional; for doctorate, comprehensive exam, thesis/dissertation. *Entrance requirements:* For doctorate, GRE. Additional exam requirements/recommendations for international students: Required—TOEFL (minimum score 79 iBT) or IELTS (minimum score 6.5). *Application deadline:* For fall admission, 2/1 for domestic and international students. Application fee: $50 ($100 for international students). Electronic applications accepted. *Expenses:* Tuition, state resident: full-time $4886; part-time $203.60 per credit hour. Tuition, nonresident: full-time $18,989; part-time $791.20 per credit hour. *Required fees:* $3283; $126.25 per credit hour. $126.50 per semester. *Financial support:* In 2016–17, 44 students received support. Teaching assistantships with full and partial tuition reimbursements available and scholarships/grants available. Financial award application deadline: 6/1; financial award applicants required to submit FAFSA. *Faculty research:* Attitudes toward students with cultural and linguistic diversity; grandparents of students with disabilities; K-12 literacy instruction for struggling readers; behavior management; disability awareness and self-advocacy. *Unit head:* Dr. Nancy E. Marchand-Martella, Chair, Department of Educational Psychology, 405-325-0624, Fax: 405-325-6655, E-mail: nmarchand-martella@ou.edu. *Application contact:* Anna Steele, Graduate Programs Specialist, 405-325-4525, Fax: 405-325-7390, E-mail: jrcoe_gps@ou.edu.
Website: http://www.ou.edu/education/edpy

**University of Pittsburgh,** School of Education, Department of Instruction and Learning, Program in Special Education, Pittsburgh, PA 15260. Offers applied behavior analysis (M Ed); early intervention (M Ed, PhD); general special education (M Ed, Ed D); special education teacher preparation (M Ed); vision studies (M Ed, PhD). *Program availability:* Part-time, evening/weekend. *Degree requirements:* For master's, thesis; for doctorate, thesis/dissertation. *Entrance requirements:* For master's, PRAXIS I; for doctorate, GRE General Test. Additional exam requirements/recommendations for international students: Required—TOEFL. Tuition and fees vary according to program.

**University of Saint Joseph,** Department of Counseling and Applied Behavioral Studies, West Hartford, CT 06117-2700. Offers applied behavioral analysis (Graduate Certificate); clinical mental health counseling (MA); school counseling (MA). *Accreditation:* ACA. *Program availability:* Part-time, evening/weekend. *Degree requirements:* For master's, comprehensive exam, thesis optional. *Entrance requirements:* For master's, 2 letters of recommendation. Electronic applications accepted. Application fee is waived when completed online. *Expenses:* Tuition: Full-time $14,580; part-time $729 per credit hour. *Required fees:* $920; $46 per credit hour. Tuition and fees vary according to course load, degree level and program.

**University of Saint Joseph,** Department of Special Education, West Hartford, CT 06117-2700. Offers autism and applied behavior analysis (MS); special education (MA). *Program availability:* Part-time, evening/weekend. *Degree requirements:* For master's, thesis. Electronic applications accepted. Application fee is waived when completed online. *Expenses:* Tuition: Full-time $14,580; part-time $729 per credit hour. *Required fees:* $920; $46 per credit hour. Tuition and fees vary according to course load, degree level and program.

**University of San Francisco,** School of Nursing and Health Professions, Program in Behavioral Health, San Francisco, CA 94117-1080. Offers MS. *Faculty:* 2 full-time (both women), 2 part-time/adjunct (1 woman). *Students:* 17 full-time (16 women); includes 12 minority (3 Black or African American, non-Hispanic/Latino; 1 Asian, non-Hispanic/Latino; 7 Hispanic/Latino; 1 Two or more races, non-Hispanic/Latino), 3 international. Average age 27. 20 applicants, 100% accepted, 9 enrolled. In 2016, 9 master's awarded. *Application deadline:* For fall admission, 4/1 for domestic students. *Expenses:* Tuition: Full-time $23,310; part-time $1295 per credit. Tuition and fees vary according to course load, degree level, campus/location and program. *Financial support:* In 2016–17, 9 students received support. *Unit head:* Dr. Margaret Baker, Dean, 415-422-6681, Fax: 415-422-6877, E-mail: nursing@usfca.edu. *Application contact:* Ingrid McVanner, Information Contact, 415-422-2746, Fax: 415-422-2217.
Website: http://www.usfca.edu/nursing/programs/masters/behavioral-health

**University of Southern Maine,** College of Management and Human Service, School of Education and Human Development, Program in Educational Psychology, Portland, ME 04103. Offers applied behavior analysis (MS, CGS). *Program availability:* Part-time, evening/weekend. *Entrance requirements:* For master's, GRE or MAT. Additional exam requirements/recommendations for international students: Required—TOEFL (minimum score 550 paper-based; 79 iBT). Electronic applications accepted. *Faculty research:* Applied behavior analysis, functional behavioral analysis, positive behavioral interventions and supports.

**University of Southern Mississippi,** Graduate School, College of Education and Psychology, Department of Psychology, Hattiesburg, MS 39406. Offers applied behavior analysis (MS); clinical psychology (PhD); counseling psychology (MS, PhD); school psychology (PhD). *Accreditation:* APA (one or more programs are accredited). Terminal master's awarded for partial completion of doctoral program. *Degree requirements:* For

master's, comprehensive exam, thesis; for doctorate, comprehensive exam, thesis/dissertation. *Entrance requirements:* For master's, GRE General Test, minimum GPA of 3.0; for doctorate, GRE General Test, interview, minimum GPA of 3.5. Additional exam requirements/recommendations for international students: Required—TOEFL, IELTS. *Application deadline:* Applications are processed on a rolling basis. Application fee: $60. *Expenses: Tuition, area resident:* Full-time $15,708; part-time $437 per credit hour. *Financial support:* Research assistantships with full tuition reimbursements, teaching assistantships with full tuition reimbursements, career-related internships or fieldwork, Federal Work-Study, institutionally sponsored loans, scholarships/grants, health care benefits, and unspecified assistantships available. Financial award application deadline: 3/15; financial award applicants required to submit FAFSA. *Faculty research:* Psychopathology, alcohol and drug abuse, child clinical psychology, parenting, suicide, career/vocational, marine mammal, cognition, psychological psychology, behavioral interventions, positive psychology, anger/aggression, diversity issues. *Unit head:* Dr. Joe Olmi, Chair, 601-266-5693, Fax: 601-266-5580, E-mail: d.olmi@usm.edu. *Application contact:* Angela Pam, Administrative Assistant, 601-266-4592, Fax: 601-266-5580.
Website: https://www.usm.edu/psychology

**University of South Florida,** College of Behavioral and Community Sciences, Department of Child and Family Studies, Tampa, FL 33620-9951. Offers applied behavior analysis (MA, MS, PhD); behavioral and community sciences (PhD); child and adolescent behavioral health (MS), including developmental disabilities, leadership in child and adolescent health, translational research and evaluation, youth and behavioral health; rehabilitation and mental health counseling (MA), including addictions and substance abuse counseling, marriage and family therapy. *Accreditation:* ACA. *Faculty:* 15 full-time (10 women), 1 (woman) part-time/adjunct. *Students:* 146 full-time (127 women), 90 part-time (74 women); includes 92 minority (22 Black or African American, non-Hispanic/Latino; 12 Asian, non-Hispanic/Latino; 49 Hispanic/Latino; 9 Two or more races, non-Hispanic/Latino), 3 international. Average age 28. 267 applicants, 51% accepted, 93 enrolled. In 2016, 63 master's awarded. *Degree requirements:* For master's, comprehensive exam, thesis (for some programs); for doctorate, comprehensive exam, thesis/dissertation, Behavior Analyst Board Certification Exam. *Entrance requirements:* For master's, GRE General Test, minimum GPA of 3.0 in last 60 hours of coursework; letters of recommendation; one-page narrative describing experience, interest, and career goals in applied behavior analysis; resume or curriculum vitae (varies by program); for doctorate, GRE General Test, master's degree in behavioral analysis or closely-related field; minimum GPA of 3.5 in graduate course work; three letters of recommendation; campus visit with faculty interview; personal statement; curriculum vitae; evidence of research experiences and expertise. Additional exam requirements/recommendations for international students: Required—TOEFL (minimum score 550 paper-based; 79 iBT) or IELTS (minimum score 6.5). *Application deadline:* For fall admission, 12/5 for domestic and international students. Application fee: $30. *Expenses:* Tuition, state resident: full-time $7766; part-time $431.43 per credit hour. Tuition, nonresident: full-time $15,789; part-time $877.17 per credit hour. *Required fees:* $37 per term. *Financial support:* In 2016–17, 50 students received support. Unspecified assistantships available. *Faculty research:* Applied behavior analysis, autism, behavior management, behavioral intervention, children, developmental disabilities, experimental analysis of behavior, functional assessment, positive behavior support. *Total annual research expenditures:* $16.4 million. *Application contact:* Dr. Raymond G. Miltenberger, Professor/Director of Master's Program, 813-974-5079, Fax: 813-974-6115, E-mail: miltenbe@usf.edu.
Website: http://cfs.cbcs.usf.edu/

**The University of Texas at San Antonio,** College of Education and Human Development, Department of Educational Psychology, San Antonio, TX 78207. Offers applied behavioral analysis (Certificate); digital learning design (Certificate); language acquisition and bilingual psychoeducational assessment (Certificate); school psychology (MA). *Program availability:* Part-time. *Faculty:* 11 full-time (6 women), 1 (woman) part-time/adjunct. *Students:* 38 full-time (31 women), 29 part-time (25 women); includes 43 minority (4 Black or African American, non-Hispanic/Latino; 1 Asian, non-Hispanic/Latino; 35 Hispanic/Latino; 3 Two or more races, non-Hispanic/Latino). Average age 28. 23 applicants, 78% accepted, 13 enrolled. In 2016, 16 master's, 16 other advanced degrees awarded. *Degree requirements:* For master's, comprehensive exam, thesis (for some programs). *Entrance requirements:* For master's, GRE, bachelor's degree with 18 credit hours in field of study or in another appropriate field of study, two letters of recommendation, statement of purpose; for Certificate, 18 hours in psychology, sociology, education, or anything related (for applied behavioral analysis); minimum GPA of 2.7 in last 30 hours (for language acquisition and bilingual psychoeducational assessment). Additional exam requirements/recommendations for international students: Required—TOEFL (minimum score 550 paper-based; 79 iBT), IELTS (minimum score 6.5). *Application deadline:* For fall admission, 7/1 for domestic students, 4/1 for international students; for spring admission, 11/1 for domestic students, 9/1 for international students; for summer admission, 3/1 for international students. Applications are processed on a rolling basis. Application fee: $45 ($80 for international students). Electronic applications accepted. *Financial support:* In 2016–17, 9 research assistantships (averaging $2,829 per year) were awarded. Financial award application deadline: 3/5; financial award applicants required to submit FAFSA. *Faculty research:* Teacher consultation and culturally responsive school psychology practices, youth mentoring, cross-age peer mentoring, adolescent connectedness, pair counseling. *Total annual research expenditures:* $91,630. *Unit head:* Dr. Jeremy Sullivan, Department Chair, 210-458-2378, Fax: 210-458-2019, E-mail: jeremy.sullivan@utsa.edu. *Application contact:* Dr. John Pruiett, Development Specialist, 210-458-2721, Fax: 210-458-2019, E-mail: johnny.pruiett@utsa.edu.
Website: http://education.utsa.edu/educational_psychology

**University of West Florida,** College of Education and Professional Studies, Department of Teacher Education and Educational Leadership, Program in Exceptional Student Education, Pensacola, FL 32514-5750. Offers applied behavior analysis (MA); special and alternative education (MA). *Accreditation:* NCATE. *Program availability:* Part-time, evening/weekend, online learning. *Entrance requirements:* For master's, GRE (minimum score 450 verbal) or MAT (minimum score 396) if bachelor's GPA less than 3.0, state teaching certification; letter of intent; two professional references. Additional exam requirements/recommendations for international students: Required—TOEFL (minimum score 550 paper-based). *Application deadline:* For fall admission, 6/1 for domestic and international students; for spring admission, 10/1 for domestic and international students. Applications are processed on a rolling basis. Application fee: $30. *Expenses:* Tuition, state resident: full-time $5316.12. Tuition, nonresident: full-time $11,308. *Required fees:* $583.92. Tuition and fees vary according to course load and program. *Financial support:* Unspecified assistantships available. Financial award application deadline: 4/15; financial award applicants required to submit FAFSA. *Faculty research:* Memory, semantic structure, remedial programming. *Unit head:* Dr. William H. Evans, Acting Director, 850-474-2892, Fax: 850-474-2844, E-mail: wevans@uwf.edu. *Application contact:* Terry McCray, Assistant Director of Graduate Admissions, 850-473-7718, Fax: 850-473-7714, E-mail: gradadmissions@uwf.edu.

**University of Wisconsin–Milwaukee,** Graduate School, College of Letters and Science, Department of Psychology, Milwaukee, WI 53201-0413. Offers experimental psychology (MS, PhD), including behavior analysis, health and social psychology (PhD), health psychology (MS), neuroscience (PhD); psychology (PhD), including clinical psychology. *Accreditation:* APA (one or more programs are accredited). *Students:* 67 full-time (46 women), 19 part-time (11 women); includes 8 minority (2 Asian, non-Hispanic/Latino; 1 Hispanic/Latino; 5 Two or more races, non-Hispanic/Latino), 9 international. Average age 28. 254 applicants, 7% accepted, 16 enrolled. In 2016, 15 master's, 10 doctorates awarded. *Degree requirements:* For master's, thesis; for doctorate, variable foreign language requirement, thesis/dissertation. *Entrance requirements:* For master's and doctorate, GRE General Test, GRE Subject Test. Additional exam requirements/recommendations for international students: Required—TOEFL (minimum score 550 paper-based; 79 iBT), IELTS (minimum score 6.5). *Application deadline:* For fall admission, 1/1 priority date for domestic students; for spring admission, 9/1 for domestic students. Applications are processed on a rolling basis. Application fee: $56 ($96 for international students). Electronic applications accepted. *Financial support:* In 2016–17, 8 fellowships, 6 research assistantships, 46 teaching assistantships were awarded; career-related internships or fieldwork, unspecified assistantships, and project assistantships also available. Support available to part-time students. Financial award application deadline: 4/15; financial award applicants required to submit FAFSA. *Unit head:* Douglas Woods, Department Chair, 414-229-6636, E-mail: dwoods@uwm.edu. *Application contact:* General Information Contact, 414-229-4982, Fax: 414-229-6967, E-mail: gradschool@uwm.edu.
Website: http://www.uwm.edu/dept/psychology/

**Wayne State University,** College of Education, Division of Theoretical and Behavioral Foundations, Detroit, MI 48202. Offers applied behavior analysis (Certificate); counseling (M Ed, MA, Ed D, PhD, Ed S); counseling psychology (MA); education evaluation and research (M Ed, Ed D, PhD); educational psychology (M Ed, PhD), including learning and instruction sciences (PhD); rehabilitation counseling and community inclusion (MA); school and community psychology (MA); school psychology (Certificate). *Accreditation:* ACA (one or more programs are accredited); CORE (one or more programs are accredited). *Program availability:* Evening/weekend. *Faculty:* 12. *Students:* 211 full-time (179 women), 237 part-time (196 women); includes 167 minority (119 Black or African American, non-Hispanic/Latino; 1 American Indian or Alaska Native, non-Hispanic/Latino; 10 Asian, non-Hispanic/Latino; 17 Hispanic/Latino; 20 Two or more races, non-Hispanic/Latino), 24 international. Average age 32. 294 applicants, 34% accepted, 72 enrolled. In 2016, 87 master's, 12 doctorates, 14 other advanced degrees awarded. *Degree requirements:* For master's, thesis (for some programs); for doctorate, thesis/dissertation. *Entrance requirements:* For master's, GRE, interview, personal statement, portfolio (art therapy); for doctorate, GRE, department-written exam, interview, curriculum vitae, references, master's degree in closely-related field with minimum GPA of 3.5, demonstration of counseling skills (counseling); for other advanced degree, master's degree in counseling and counseling license (for Ed S); good standing in school and community psychology MA program (for Certificate). Additional exam requirements/recommendations for international students: Required—TOEFL (minimum score 550 paper-based; 79 iBT), Michigan English Language Assessment Battery (minimum score 85); Recommended—IELTS (minimum score 6.5), TWE (minimum score 5.5). *Application deadline:* For fall admission, 6/1 priority date for domestic students, 5/1 priority date for international students; for winter admission, 10/1 priority date for domestic students, 9/1 priority date for international students; for spring admission, 2/1 priority date for domestic students, 1/1 priority date for international students. Applications are processed on a rolling basis. Application fee: $50. Electronic applications accepted. *Expenses:* $16,503 per year resident tuition and fees, $33,697 per year non-resident tuition and fees. *Financial support:* In 2016–17, 92 students received support, including 2 research assistantships with tuition reimbursements available (averaging $17,994 per year); fellowships with tuition reimbursements available, teaching assistantships with tuition reimbursements available, Federal Work-Study, scholarships/grants, health care benefits, and unspecified assistantships also available. Support available to part-time students. Financial award applicants required to submit FAFSA. *Faculty research:* Adolescents at risk, supervision of counseling. *Unit head:* Dr. Cheryl Somers, Assistant Dean, 313-577-1670, E-mail: c.somers@wayne.edu. *Application contact:* Janice Green, Assistant Dean, 313-577-1605, E-mail: jwgreen@wayne.edu.
Website: http://coe.wayne.edu/tbf/index.php

**Western New England University,** College of Arts and Sciences, Program in Behavior Analysis, Springfield, MA 01119. Offers applied behavior analysis (MS); behavior analysis (PhD). *Program availability:* Part-time, evening/weekend. *Faculty:* 16 full-time (8 women). *Students:* 160 part-time (134 women); includes 23 minority (6 Black or African American, non-Hispanic/Latino; 1 American Indian or Alaska Native, non-Hispanic/Latino; 9 Asian, non-Hispanic/Latino; 6 Hispanic/Latino; 1 Two or more races, non-Hispanic/Latino), 12 international. Average age 28. 118 applicants, 40% accepted, 44 enrolled. In 2016, 25 master's, 4 doctorates awarded. *Degree requirements:* For doctorate, thesis/dissertation. *Entrance requirements:* For master's, GRE, official transcript, personal statement, resume, three letters of recommendation; for doctorate, GRE, master's degree in behavior analysis with minimum GPA of 3.6, official transcript, personal statement, resume, three letters of recommendation. Additional exam requirements/recommendations for international students: Required—TOEFL (minimum score 79 iBT). *Application deadline:* For fall admission, 1/15 for domestic and international students. Application fee: $30. Electronic applications accepted. *Expenses:* $36,900 (for MS); $69,120 (for PhD). *Financial support:* In 2016–17, 6 fellowships with tuition reimbursements were awarded. Support available to part-time students. Financial award application deadline: 4/15; financial award applicants required to submit FAFSA. *Unit head:* Dr. Gregory Hanley, Director of the PhD Program in Behavioral Analysis/Professor, 413-796-2367, E-mail: ghanley@wne.edu. *Application contact:* Matthew Fox, Director of Admissions for Graduate Students and Adult Learners, 413-782-1410, Fax: 413-782-1777, E-mail: study@wne.edu.
Website: http://www1.wne.edu/academics/graduate/index.cfm#?category=1

**Westfield State University,** College of Graduate and Continuing Education, Department of Psychology, Program in Applied Behavior Analysis, Westfield, MA 01086. Offers MA. *Program availability:* Part-time, evening/weekend. *Faculty:* 4 full-time (1 woman), 2 part-time/adjunct (1 woman). *Students:* 23 full-time (18 women), 5 part-time (1 woman); includes 4 minority (all Hispanic/Latino). Average age 26. 23 applicants, 70% accepted, 13 enrolled. In 2016, 14 master's awarded. *Degree requirements:* For master's, comprehensive exam, thesis (for some programs). *Entrance requirements:* For master's, GRE General Test or MAT, minimum undergraduate GPA of 2.8. Additional exam requirements/recommendations for international students: Recommended—TOEFL (minimum score 550 paper-based; 79 iBT). *Application deadline:* For fall admission, 2/1 for domestic students. Applications are processed on a rolling basis. Application fee: $50. *Expenses:* Tuition, state resident: part-time $318 per semester hour. Tuition, nonresident: part-time $318 per semester hour. *Required fees:* $75 per semester. Tuition and fees vary according to course load and program. *Financial support:* Unspecified assistantships available. Financial award application deadline: 3/1; financial award applicants required to submit FAFSA. *Unit head:* Dr. Jorge Reyes, Advisor, 413-572-8902. *Application contact:* Shelly Henrichon, Admissions Coordinator, 413-572-8022, Fax: 413-572-5227, E-mail: mhenrichon@westfield.ma.edu.

*Applied Behavior Analysis*

**Wright State University,** Graduate School, College of Liberal Arts, Program in Applied Behavioral Science, Criminal Justice and Social Problems, Dayton, OH 45435. Offers criminal justice and social problems (MA). *Degree requirements:* For master's, thesis optional. *Entrance requirements:* Additional exam requirements/recommendations for international students: Required—TOEFL. Application fee: $25. *Expenses:* Tuition, state resident: full-time $9952; part-time $622 per credit hour. Tuition, nonresident: full-time $16,960; part-time $1060 per credit hour. *Financial support:* Fellowships, research assistantships, and unspecified assistantships available. Support available to part-time students. Financial award applicants required to submit FAFSA. *Faculty research:*

Training and development, criminal justice and social problems, community systems, human factors, industrial/organizational psychology. *Unit head:* Dr. David M. Orenstein, Director, 937-775-2667, Fax: 937-775-4228, E-mail: david.orenstein@wright.edu. *Application contact:* John Kimble, Associate Director of Graduate Admissions and Records, 937-775-2957, Fax: 937-775-2453, E-mail: john.kimble@wright.edu.

**Youngstown State University,** Graduate School, College of Liberal Arts and Social Sciences, Department of Psychology, Youngstown, OH 44555-0001. Offers applied behavior analysis (MS).

# Applied Psychology

**Angelo State University,** College of Graduate Studies and Research, Archer College of Health and Human Services, Department of Psychology, Sociology and Social Work, San Angelo, TX 76909. Offers applied psychology (MS); counseling psychology (MS); industrial-organizational psychology (MS). *Program availability:* Part-time, evening/weekend. *Students:* 73 full-time (53 women), 33 part-time (22 women); includes 36 minority (5 Black or African American, non-Hispanic/Latino; 31 Hispanic/Latino), 5 international. Average age 32. *Degree requirements:* For master's, comprehensive exam, thesis optional. *Entrance requirements:* For master's, GRE General Test (for industrial and organizational psychology only), essay, letters of recommendation (for industrial and organizational psychology only). Additional exam requirements/recommendations for international students: Required—TOEFL or IELTS. *Application deadline:* For fall admission, 7/15 priority date for domestic students, 6/10 for international students; for spring admission, 12/1 priority date for domestic students, 11/1 for international students. Applications are processed on a rolling basis. Application fee: $40 ($50 for international students). Electronic applications accepted. *Expenses:* Tuition, state resident: full-time $3726; part-time $2484 per year. Tuition, nonresident: full-time $10,746; part-time $7164 per year. *Required fees:* $2538; $1702 per unit. *Financial support:* Teaching assistantships, career-related internships or fieldwork, Federal Work-Study, scholarships/grants, and unspecified assistantships available. Support available to part-time students. Financial award application deadline: 3/1; financial award applicants required to submit FAFSA. *Unit head:* Dr. James N. Forbes, Chair, 325-486-6120, Fax: 325-942-2290, E-mail: james.forbes@angelo.edu. *Application contact:* Dr. James N. Forbes, Chair, 325-486-6120, Fax: 325-942-2290, E-mail: james.forbes@angelo.edu.
Website: http://www.angelo.edu/dept/psychology_sociology/

**Antioch University Midwest,** Graduate Programs, Individualized Interdisciplinary Studies and Social Sciences Program, Yellow Springs, OH 45387-1609. Offers applied psychology (MA); conflict studies (MA); health and human development (MA); integral studies (MA); peace studies (MA); systems and organizations (MA). *Program availability:* Part-time, evening/weekend, online learning. *Degree requirements:* For master's, thesis or alternative. *Entrance requirements:* For master's, resume, goal statement, interview. *Application deadline:* For fall admission, 8/1 for domestic students; for winter admission, 12/1 for domestic students; for spring admission, 3/10 for domestic students. Applications are processed on a rolling basis. Application fee: $50. Electronic applications accepted. *Expenses:* $799 per credit hour. *Financial support:* Federal Work-Study available. Financial award applicants required to submit FAFSA. *Application contact:* Deena Kent-Hummel, Director of Admissions, 937-769-1800, Fax: 937-769-1804, E-mail: dkent@antioch.edu.
Website: https://www.antioch.edu/midwest/degrees-programs/business-management-leadership/individualized-master-of-arts-ma/interdisciplinary-studies-and-social-

**Antioch University New England,** Graduate School, Department of Applied Psychology, Keene, NH 03431-3552. Offers autism spectrum disorders (Certificate), including applied behavioral analysis internship, autism spectrum disorders; clinical mental health counseling (MA), including clinical mental health counseling, substance abuse counseling; dance/movement therapy and counseling (M Ed, MA, PMC); marriage and family therapy (MA, PhD, Certificate). *Degree requirements:* For master's, internship, practicum. *Entrance requirements:* For master's, previous course work and work experience in psychology. Additional exam requirements/recommendations for international students: Required—TOEFL (minimum score 550 paper-based). Electronic applications accepted. *Expenses:* Contact institution. *Faculty research:* Diversity, descendents of survivors of the Holocaust and American slavery.

**Arizona State University at the Tempe campus,** Ira A. Fulton Schools of Engineering, The Polytechnic School, Applied Psychology Program, Mesa, AZ 85212. Offers MS. *Program availability:* Part-time. Terminal master's awarded for partial completion of doctoral program. *Degree requirements:* For master's, thesis or applied project with oral defense and exam; interactive Program of Study (iPOS) submitted before completing 50 percent of required credit hours. *Entrance requirements:* For master's, GRE, minimum GPA of 3.0 or equivalent in last 2 years of work leading to bachelor's degree. Additional exam requirements/recommendations for international students: Required—TOEFL, IELTS, or PTE. Electronic applications accepted.

**Athabasca University,** Program in Counseling, Athabasca, AB T9S 3A3, Canada. Offers applied psychology (Post Master's Certificate); art therapy (MC); career counseling (MC); counseling (Advanced Certificate); counseling psychology (MC); school counseling (MC).

**Boston College,** Lynch School of Education, Program in Applied Developmental and Educational Psychology, Chestnut Hill, MA 02467-3800. Offers MA, PhD. *Program availability:* Part-time, evening/weekend. *Faculty:* 11 full-time (8 women). *Students:* 19 full-time (18 women), 21 part-time (20 women); includes 8 minority (2 Black or African American, non-Hispanic/Latino; 2 Asian, non-Hispanic/Latino; 3 Hispanic/Latino; 1 Two or more races, non-Hispanic/Latino), 8 international. Average age 27. 97 applicants, 48% accepted, 14 enrolled. In 2016, 15 master's, 2 doctorates awarded. Terminal master's awarded for partial completion of doctoral program. *Degree requirements:* For master's, comprehensive exam; for doctorate, comprehensive exam, thesis/dissertation. *Entrance requirements:* For master's and doctorate, GRE General Test. Additional exam requirements/recommendations for international students: Required—TOEFL (minimum score 100 iBT). *Application deadline:* For fall admission, 12/1 priority date for domestic and international students; for spring admission, 11/1 for domestic and international students. Application fee: $65. Electronic applications accepted. Tuition and fees vary according to program. *Financial support:* Fellowships with tuition reimbursements, research assistantships with tuition reimbursements, teaching assistantships with tuition reimbursements, career-related internships or fieldwork, Federal Work-Study, scholarships/grants, traineeships, health care benefits, tuition waivers (full and partial), and unspecified assistantships available. Support available to part-time students. Financial award applicants required to submit FAFSA. *Faculty research:* Cognitive

learning and culture, effects of social policy reform on children and families, psychosocial trauma, human rights and international justice, positive youth development, children and adolescents living in poverty. *Unit head:* Dr. Penny Hauser-Cram, Chairperson, 617-552-4214, Fax: 617-552-4710. *Application contact:* Kimberly Rose, Graduate Admission Assistant, 617-552-4214, Fax: 617-552-0398, E-mail: roseki@bc.edu.
Website: http://www.bc.edu/schools/lsoe/academics/departments/cdep/adep/madevelop.html

**Brigham Young University,** Graduate Studies, College of Family, Home, and Social Sciences, Department of Psychology, Provo, UT 84602. Offers applied social psychology (PhD); clinical psychology (PhD); cognitive and behavioral neuroscience (PhD); developmental psychology (PhD). *Accreditation:* APA. *Faculty:* 29 full-time (7 women), 8 part-time/adjunct (2 women). *Students:* 59 full-time (34 women); includes 9 minority (2 Black or African American, non-Hispanic/Latino; 4 Asian, non-Hispanic/Latino; 2 Hispanic/Latino; 1 Native Hawaiian or other Pacific Islander, non-Hispanic/Latino). Average age 29. 49 applicants, 33% accepted, 11 enrolled. In 2016, 12 doctorates awarded. *Degree requirements:* For doctorate, comprehensive exam (for some programs), thesis/dissertation, publishable paper. *Entrance requirements:* For doctorate, GRE General Test, minimum GPA of 3.0. Additional exam requirements/recommendations for international students: Required—TOEFL (minimum score 580 paper-based; 85 iBT). *Application deadline:* For fall admission, 12/1 for domestic and international students. Application fee: $50. Electronic applications accepted. *Expenses:* Contact institution. *Financial support:* In 2016–17, 41 students received support, including 32 research assistantships with partial tuition reimbursements available (averaging $12,000 per year), 5 teaching assistantships with partial tuition reimbursements available (averaging $12,000 per year); career-related internships or fieldwork, scholarships/grants, tuition waivers (partial), and unspecified assistantships also available. Financial award application deadline: 5/31. *Faculty research:* Psychotherapy process, Alzheimer's disease/dementia, psychology and law, health, psychology, developmental. *Total annual research expenditures:* $73,281. *Unit head:* Dr. Dawson Hedges, Chair, 801-422-6357, Fax: 801-422-0602, E-mail: dawson_hedges@byu.edu. *Application contact:* Leesa D. Scott, Coordinator of Student Programs, 801-422-4560, Fax: 801-422-0602, E-mail: leesa_scott@byu.edu.
Website: http://psychology.byu.edu/

**California State University, Chico,** Office of Graduate Studies, College of Behavioral and Social Sciences, Department of Psychology, Program in Applied/School Psychology, Chico, CA 95929-0722. Offers MA. *Students:* 20 full-time (14 women); includes 9 minority (2 Black or African American, non-Hispanic/Latino; 1 Asian, non-Hispanic/Latino; 4 Hispanic/Latino; 2 Two or more races, non-Hispanic/Latino). 43 applicants, 49% accepted, 8 enrolled. *Degree requirements:* For master's, thesis or comprehensive exam. *Entrance requirements:* For master's, GRE General Test or MAT, 3 letters of recommendation, statement of purpose. Additional exam requirements/recommendations for international students: Required—TOEFL (minimum score 550 paper-based; 80 iBT), IELTS (minimum score 6.5), PTE. *Application deadline:* For fall admission, 3/1 for domestic and international students. Application fee: $55. Electronic applications accepted. *Financial support:* Application deadline: 3/1; applicants required to submit FAFSA. *Unit head:* Dr. Brian Oppy, Chair, 530-898-4609, Fax: 530-898-4740, E-mail: psy@csuchico.edu. *Application contact:* Judy L. Morris, Graduate Admissions Coordinator, 530-898-5416, Fax: 530-898-3342, E-mail: jlmorris@csuchico.edu.
Website: http://www.csuchico.edu/psy/graduate/appliedPsy.shtml

**The Catholic University of America,** School of Arts and Sciences, Department of Psychology, Washington, DC 20064. Offers applied experimental psychology (PhD); clinical psychology (PhD); general psychology (MA); human development psychology (PhD); human factors (MA); MA/JD. MA/JD offered jointly with Columbus School of Law. *Accreditation:* APA (one or more programs are accredited). *Program availability:* Part-time. *Faculty:* 11 full-time (6 women), 5 part-time/adjunct (2 women). *Students:* 40 full-time (26 women), 36 part-time (29 women); includes 19 minority (3 Black or African American, non-Hispanic/Latino; 5 Asian, non-Hispanic/Latino; 4 Hispanic/Latino; 7 Two or more races, non-Hispanic/Latino), 8 international. Average age 28. 230 applicants, 27% accepted, 23 enrolled. In 2016, 15 master's, 6 doctorates awarded. *Degree requirements:* For master's, comprehensive exam, thesis (for some programs); for doctorate, comprehensive exam, thesis/dissertation. *Entrance requirements:* For master's, GRE General Test, statement of purpose, official copies of academic transcripts, three letters of recommendation; for doctorate, GRE General Test, GRE Subject Test, statement of purpose, official copies of academic transcripts, three letters of recommendation. Additional exam requirements/recommendations for international students: Required—TOEFL (minimum score 550 paper-based; 80 iBT). *Application deadline:* For fall admission, 7/15 priority date for domestic students, 7/1 for international students; for spring admission, 11/15 priority date for domestic students, 11/1 for international students. Applications are processed on a rolling basis. Application fee: $55. Electronic applications accepted. *Expenses:* $42,850 per year; $1,170 per credit; $200 per semester part-time fees. *Financial support:* Fellowships, research assistantships, teaching assistantships, Federal Work-Study, scholarships/grants, tuition waivers (full and partial), and unspecified assistantships available. Financial award application deadline: 2/1; financial award applicants required to submit FAFSA. *Faculty research:* Clinical psychology, applied cognitive science, psychopathology, cognitive neuroscience, psychotherapy. *Total annual research expenditures:* $936,581. *Unit head:* Dr. Marc M. Sebrechts, Chair, 202-319-5750, Fax: 202-319-6263, E-mail: sebrechts@cua.edu. *Application contact:* Director of Graduate Admissions, 202-319-5057, Fax: 202-319-6533, E-mail: cua-admissions@cua.edu.
Website: http://psychology.cua.edu/

**Central Michigan University,** College of Graduate Studies, College of Humanities and Social and Behavioral Sciences, Department of Psychology, Program in Experimental Psychology, Mount Pleasant, MI 48859. Offers applied experimental psychology (PhD);

experimental psychology (MS). *Program availability:* Part-time. *Degree requirements:* For master's, thesis or alternative; for doctorate, thesis/dissertation. Electronic applications accepted. *Faculty research:* Behavioral neuroscience, human development, perception and cognition, social/personal problem solving, psychophysiology.

**The Chicago School of Professional Psychology: Online,** Program in Applied Industrial and Organizational Psychology, Chicago, IL 60654. Offers MA, Certificate.

**Clayton State University,** School of Graduate Studies, College of Arts and Sciences, Program in Psychology, Morrow, GA 30260-0285. Offers applied developmental psychology (MS); clinical/counseling psychology (MS). *Entrance requirements:* For master's, GRE, 2 official transcripts; 3 letters of recommendation; statement of purpose; on-campus interview; background check. Additional exam requirements/recommendations for international students: Required—TOEFL (minimum score 550 paper-based). Electronic applications accepted. *Expenses:* Tuition, state resident: full-time $3528; part-time $196 per credit hour. Tuition, nonresident: full-time $13,176; part-time $732 per credit hour. *Required fees:* $1454; $1454 per credit hour. $727 per semester. Tuition and fees vary according to campus/location and program.

**Clemson University,** Graduate School, College of Behavioral, Social and Health Sciences, Department of Psychology, Program in Applied Psychology, Clemson, SC 29634. Offers MS. *Faculty:* 28 full-time (11 women), 1 (woman) part-time/adjunct. *Students:* 3 full-time (2 women). Average age 25. 63 applicants, 5% accepted, 3 enrolled. In 2016, 6 master's awarded. *Degree requirements:* For master's, thesis. *Entrance requirements:* For master's, GRE General Test, unofficial transcripts, letters of recommendation, statement of intent. Additional exam requirements/recommendations for international students: Required—TOEFL (minimum score 80 iBT), IELTS (minimum score 6.5). *Application deadline:* For fall admission, 1/15 priority date for domestic and international students. Application fee: $80 ($90 for international students). Electronic applications accepted. *Expenses:* $5,617 per semester full-time resident, $11,194 per semester full-time non-resident, $697 per credit hour part-time resident, $1,392 per credit hour part-time non-resident. *Financial support:* In 2016–17, 1 student received support, including 1 research assistantship with partial tuition reimbursement available (averaging $12,000 per year), 1 teaching assistantship with partial tuition reimbursement available (averaging $12,000 per year); career-related internships or fieldwork also available. Financial award application deadline: 1/15. *Faculty research:* Personnel selection and evaluation, occupational health, motivation and decision-making, human factors, transportation safety. *Unit head:* Dr. Patrick Raymark, Department Chair, 864-656-4715, Fax: 864-656-0358, E-mail: praymar@clemson.edu. *Application contact:* Dr. Robert Sinclair, Graduate Program Coordinator, 864-656-3931, E-mail: rsincla@clemson.edu.
Website: http://www.clemson.edu/cbshs/departments/psychology/graduate/msappsy.html

**DEREE - The American College of Greece,** Graduate Programs, Athens, Greece. Offers applied psychology (MS); communication (MA); leadership (MS); marketing (MS).

**Eastern Washington University,** Graduate Studies, College of Social Sciences, Department of Psychology, Program in Mental Health Counseling, Cheney, WA 99004-2431. Offers applied psychology (MS); mental health counseling (MS). *Students:* 13 full-time (10 women); includes 1 minority (Hispanic/Latino). Average age 28. 56 applicants, 20% accepted, 10 enrolled. In 2016, 9 master's awarded. *Degree requirements:* For master's, comprehensive exam, thesis. *Entrance requirements:* For master's, GRE, minimum GPA of 3.0. Additional exam requirements/recommendations for international students: Required—TOEFL (minimum score 580 paper-based; 92 iBT), IELTS (minimum score 7), PTE (minimum score 63). Application fee: $75. Electronic applications accepted. *Expenses:* Tuition, state resident: full-time $11,000; part-time $5500 per credit. Tuition, nonresident: full-time $24,000; part-time $12,000 per credit. *Required fees:* $1300. One-time fee: $50 full-time. Part-time tuition and fees vary according to course load, campus/location and program. *Financial support:* Application deadline: 2/1; applicants required to submit FAFSA. *Unit head:* Dr. Keely Hope, Associate Professor/Director, Counselor Education, 509-359-2439, E-mail: khope@ewu.edu. *Application contact:* Kathy White, Advisor/Recruiter for Graduate Studies, 509-359-6297, Fax: 509-359-6044, E-mail: gradprograms@ewu.edu.

**Eastern Washington University,** Graduate Studies, College of Social Sciences, Department of Psychology, Program in School Counseling, Cheney, WA 99004-2431. Offers applied psychology (MS); school counseling (MS). *Accreditation:* ACA. *Students:* 13 full-time (6 women), 1 (woman) part-time; includes 6 minority (4 Asian, non-Hispanic/Latino; 2 Hispanic/Latino). Average age 26. 33 applicants, 42% accepted, 11 enrolled. In 2016, 2 master's awarded. *Degree requirements:* For master's, comprehensive exam, thesis or alternative. *Entrance requirements:* For master's, GRE General Test, minimum GPA of 3.0. Additional exam requirements/recommendations for international students: Required—TOEFL (minimum score 580 paper-based; 92 iBT), IELTS (minimum score 7), PTE (minimum score 63). *Application deadline:* For fall admission, 2/1 for domestic students. Applications are processed on a rolling basis. Application fee: $75. Electronic applications accepted. *Expenses:* Tuition, state resident: full-time $11,000; part-time $5500 per credit. Tuition, nonresident: full-time $24,000; part-time $12,000 per credit. *Required fees:* $1300. One-time fee: $50 full-time. Part-time tuition and fees vary according to course load, campus/location and program. *Financial support:* In 2016–17, teaching assistantships with partial tuition reimbursements (averaging $10,000 per year) were awarded; career-related internships or fieldwork, Federal Work-Study, institutionally sponsored loans, scholarships/grants, health care benefits, tuition waivers (partial), and unspecified assistantships also available. Support available to part-time students. Financial award application deadline: 2/1; financial award applicants required to submit FAFSA. *Unit head:* Dr. Keely Hope, Associate Professor/Director, Counselor Education, 509-359-2439, E-mail: khope@ewu.edu. *Application contact:* Kathy White, Advisor/Recruiter for Graduate Studies, 509-359-6656, E-mail: gradprograms@ewu.edu.
Website: http://www.ewu.edu/grad/programs/applied-psychology—school-counseling.xml

**Fairfield University,** Graduate School of Education and Allied Professions, Fairfield, CT 06824. Offers applied behavior analysis (ATC); applied psychology (MA); clinical mental health counseling (MA, CAS); educational technology (MA); elementary education (MA, CAS); family studies (MA); integration of spirituality and religion in counseling (ATC); marriage and family therapy (MA); reading and language development (Sixth Year Certificate); school counseling (MA, CAS); school psychology (MA, CAS); school-based marriage and family therapy (ATC); secondary education (MA); special education (MA, CAS); substance abuse counseling (ATC); teaching (Certificate); teaching and foundations (MA, CAS); TESOL, world languages, and bilingual education (MA, CAS). *Accreditation:* NCATE. *Program availability:* Part-time, evening/weekend. *Faculty:* 19 full-time (15 women), 38 part-time/adjunct (26 women). *Students:* 153 full-time (132 women), 302 part-time (252 women); includes 97 minority (24 Black or African American, non-Hispanic/Latino; 12 Asian, non-Hispanic/Latino; 55 Hispanic/Latino; 6 Two or more races, non-Hispanic/Latino), 6 international. Average age 32. 283 applicants, 61% accepted, 97 enrolled. In 2016, 130 master's awarded. *Degree requirements:* For master's, comprehensive exam. *Entrance requirements:* For master's, minimum GPA of 3.0, 2 recommendations, resume. Additional exam requirements/recommendations for international students: Required—TOEFL (minimum

score 550 paper-based; 84 iBT) or IELTS (minimum score 7.5). *Application deadline:* For fall admission, 2/15 for international students; for spring admission, 10/1 for international students. Application fee: $60. Electronic applications accepted. *Expenses:* $725 per credit hour. *Financial support:* In 2016–17, 42 students received support. Career-related internships or fieldwork and unspecified assistantships available. Support available to part-time students. Financial award applicants required to submit FAFSA. *Faculty research:* Reading and literacy, writing, social justice and inequality in education, addictions and mental health issues, therapeutic relationships and clinical supervision. *Unit head:* Dr. Robert D. Hannafin, Dean, 203-254-4250, Fax: 203-254-4241, E-mail: rhannafin@fairfield.edu. *Application contact:* Marianne Gumpper, Director of Graduate Admission, 203-254-4184, Fax: 203-254-4073, E-mail: gradadmis@fairfield.edu.
Website: http://www.fairfield.edu/gseap

**Fordham University,** Graduate School of Arts and Sciences, Department of Psychology, Program in Applied Developmental Psychology, New York, NY 10458. Offers PhD. *Accreditation:* APA. *Students:* 17 full-time (15 women), 5 part-time (4 women); includes 3 minority (1 Black or African American, non-Hispanic/Latino; 2 Asian, non-Hispanic/Latino), 7 international. Average age 31. 65 applicants, 15% accepted, 2 enrolled. In 2016, 5 doctorates awarded. *Degree requirements:* For doctorate, comprehensive exam, thesis/dissertation. *Entrance requirements:* For doctorate, GRE General Test, GRE Subject Test. Additional exam requirements/recommendations for international students: Required—TOEFL (minimum score 600 paper-based). *Application deadline:* For fall admission, 12/14 for domestic students. Application fee: $70. Electronic applications accepted. *Financial support:* In 2016–17, 15 students received support, including 4 fellowships with tuition reimbursements available (averaging $26,065 per year), 2 research assistantships with tuition reimbursements available (averaging $17,529 per year), 2 teaching assistantships with tuition reimbursements available (averaging $10,600 per year); career-related internships or fieldwork, institutionally sponsored loans, tuition waivers (full and partial), and unspecified assistantships also available. Financial award application deadline: 12/14. *Faculty research:* Development of citizenship, impact of participation in community service, impact of poverty on children, development of moral reasoning and behavior. *Unit head:* Dr. Tiffany Yip, Program Director, 718-817-3797, Fax: 718-817-3785, E-mail: tyip@fordham.edu. *Application contact:* Bernadette Valentino-Morrison, Director of Graduate Admissions, 718-817-4419, Fax: 718-817-3566, E-mail: valentinomor@fordham.edu.

**Fordham University,** Graduate School of Arts and Sciences, Department of Psychology, Program in Applied Psychological Methods, New York, NY 10458. Offers MS. *Students:* 1 (woman) full-time, 7 part-time (4 women), 3 international. Average age 27. 69 applicants, 28% accepted, 2 enrolled. In 2016, 5 master's awarded. *Degree requirements:* For master's, three-credit one-semester internship. *Entrance requirements:* For master's, GRE General Test. Additional exam requirements/recommendations for international students: Required—TOEFL. *Application deadline:* For fall admission, 1/4 priority date for domestic students, 1/4 for international students; for spring admission, 10/31 for domestic and international students. Application fee: $70. *Unit head:* Dr. Andrew Rasmussen, Program Director, 718-817-3775, E-mail: arasmussen@fordham.edu. *Application contact:* Bernadette Valentino-Morrison, Director of Graduate Admissions, 718-817-4419, Fax: 718-817-3566, E-mail: valentinomor@fordham.edu.

**Francis Marion University,** Graduate Programs, Department of Psychology, Florence, SC 29502-0547. Offers applied psychology (MS), including clinical/counseling psychology, school psychology; school psychology (SSP). *Program availability:* Part-time, evening/weekend. *Degree requirements:* For master's, internship. *Entrance requirements:* For master's, GRE General Test, official transcripts, two letters of recommendation. Additional exam requirements/recommendations for international students: Required—TOEFL (minimum score 550 paper-based; 79 iBT). *Expenses:* Tuition, state resident: full-time $10,100; part-time $505 per credit hour. Tuition, nonresident: full-time $20,196; part-time $1009.80 per credit hour. *Required fees:* $14.80 per credit hour. $73 per semester. Tuition and fees vary according to course load and program. *Faculty research:* Parenting and family relationships, child development, applied behavioral analysis, post-traumatic stress disorder, clinical psychology in adults.

**George Mason University,** College of Humanities and Social Sciences, Department of Psychology, Fairfax, VA 22030. Offers applied developmental psychology (Certificate); cognitive and behavioral neuroscience (MA); industrial/organizational psychology (PhD). *Accreditation:* APA. *Faculty:* 42 full-time (24 women), 13 part-time/adjunct (11 women). *Students:* 160 full-time (105 women), 57 part-time (30 women); includes 36 minority (9 Black or African American, non-Hispanic/Latino; 8 Asian, non-Hispanic/Latino; 12 Hispanic/Latino; 1 Native Hawaiian or other Pacific Islander, non-Hispanic/Latino; 6 Two or more races, non-Hispanic/Latino), 14 international. Average age 26. 742 applicants, 15% accepted, 57 enrolled. In 2016, 59 master's, 21 doctorates, 7 other advanced degrees awarded. *Degree requirements:* For master's, comprehensive exam, thesis (for biopsychology); for doctorate, comprehensive exam, thesis/dissertation, 2nd-year project. *Entrance requirements:* For master's, GRE, 2 official transcripts; goals statement; 15 undergraduate credits in concentration for which the applicant is applying; for doctorate, GRE, 3 letters of recommendation; resume; goals statement; minimum GPA of 3.0 overall for last 60 undergraduate credits, 3.25 in psychology courses; 15 undergraduate credits in concentration for which the applicant is applying; 2 official transcripts; for Certificate, GRE, 2 official transcripts; expanded goals statement; 3 letters of recommendation. Additional exam requirements/recommendations for international students: Required—TOEFL (minimum score 575 paper-based; 88 iBT), IELTS (minimum score 6.5), PTE (minimum score 59). Application fee: $75 ($80 for international students). Electronic applications accepted. *Expenses:* Tuition, state resident: full-time $10,628; part-time $443 per credit. Tuition, nonresident: full-time $29,306; part-time $1221 per credit. *Required fees:* $3096; $129 per credit. Tuition and fees vary according to program. *Financial support:* In 2016–17, 116 students received support, including 7 fellowships (averaging $11,348 per year), 42 research assistantships with tuition reimbursements available (averaging $14,292 per year), 88 teaching assistantships with tuition reimbursements available (averaging $13,815 per year); career-related internships or fieldwork, Federal Work-Study, scholarships/grants, tuition waivers (partial), unspecified assistantships, and health care benefits (for full-time research or teaching assistantship recipients) also available. Support available to part-time students. Financial award application deadline: 3/1; financial award applicants required to submit FAFSA. *Faculty research:* Applied developmental psychology, biopsychology, clinical psychology, human factors/applied cognition psychology, industrial/organizational psychology, school psychology. *Total annual research expenditures:* $5.6 million. *Unit head:* Reeshad Dalal, Department Chair, 703-993-9487, Fax: 703-993-1359, E-mail: rdalal@gmu.edu. *Application contact:* Michael Hock, Graduate Program Coordinator, 703-993-1548, Fax: 703-993-1359, E-mail: mhock2@gmu.edu.
Website: http://psychology.gmu.edu

**The George Washington University,** Columbian College of Arts and Sciences, Department of Psychology, Washington, DC 20052. Offers applied social psychology (PhD); clinical psychology (PhD); cognitive neuroscience (PhD). *Accreditation:* APA.

## Applied Psychology

*Program availability:* Part-time, evening/weekend. *Faculty:* 25 full-time (14 women). *Students:* 39 full-time (28 women), 30 part-time (21 women); includes 21 minority (9 Black or African American, non-Hispanic/Latino; 4 Asian, non-Hispanic/Latino; 6 Hispanic/Latino; 2 Two or more races, non-Hispanic/Latino), 7 international. Average age 28. 442 applicants, 5% accepted, 12 enrolled. In 2016, 12 doctorates awarded. *Degree requirements:* For doctorate, thesis/dissertation or alternative, general exam. *Entrance requirements:* For doctorate, GRE General Test, minimum GPA of 3.0. Additional exam requirements/recommendations for international students: Required—TOEFL (minimum score 550 paper-based; 80 iBT). *Application deadline:* For fall admission, 1/15 for domestic and international students. Application fee: $75. *Financial support:* In 2016–17, 62 students received support. Fellowships with tuition reimbursements available, teaching assistantships with tuition reimbursements available, career-related internships or fieldwork, Federal Work-Study, and tuition waivers available. *Unit head:* Dr. Paul Poppen, Chair, 202-994-6324, E-mail: pjp@gwu.edu. *Application contact:* Information Contact, 202-994-6320, Fax: 202-994-1602, E-mail: psydept@gwu.edu.
Website: http://psychology.columbian.gwu.edu/

**Laurentian University,** School of Graduate Studies and Research, Programme in Psychology, Sudbury, ON P3E 2C6, Canada. Offers applied psychology (MA); experimental (MA).

**London Metropolitan University,** Graduate Programs, London, United Kingdom. Offers applied psychology (M Sc); architecture (MA); biomedical science (M Sc); blood science (M Sc); cancer pharmacology (M Sc); computer networking and cyber security (M Sc); computing and information systems (M Sc); conference interpreting (MA); counter-terrorism studies (M Sc); creative, digital and professional writing (MA); crime, violence and prevention (M Sc); criminology (M Sc); curating contemporary art (MA); data analytics (M Sc); digital media (MA); early childhood studies (MA); education (MA, Ed D); financial services law, regulation and compliance (LL M); food science (M Sc); forensic psychology (M Sc); health and social care management and policy (M Sc); human nutrition (M Sc); human resource management (MA); human rights and international conflict (MA); information technology (M Sc); intelligence and security studies (M Sc); international oil, gas and energy law (LL M); international relations (MA); interpreting (MA); learning and teaching in higher education (MA); legal practice (LL M); media and entertainment law (LL M); organizational and consumer psychology (M Sc); psychological therapy (M Sc); psychology of mental health (M Sc); public health (M Sc); public policy and management (MPA); security studies (M Sc); social work (M Sc); spatial planning and urban design (MA); sports therapy (M Sc); supporting older children and young people with dyslexia (MA); teaching languages (MA), including Arabic, English; translation (MA); woman and child abuse (MA).

**Loras College,** Graduate Division, Program in Applied Psychology, Dubuque, IA 52004-0178. Offers MA. *Program availability:* Part-time, evening/weekend. *Degree requirements:* For master's, comprehensive exam, thesis (for some programs). *Entrance requirements:* For master's, Ohio State University Psychological Test or GRE General Test, minimum undergraduate GPA of 2.75.

**Lynn University,** College of Arts and Sciences, Boca Raton, FL 33431. Offers administration (MS), including criminal justice; applied psychology (MS); mental health counseling (MS). *Program availability:* Part-time, evening/weekend, blended/hybrid learning. *Faculty:* 52 full-time (22 women), 19 part-time/adjunct (11 women). *Students:* 74 full-time (57 women), 39 part-time (28 women); includes 32 minority (20 Black or African American, non-Hispanic/Latino; 2 Asian, non-Hispanic/Latino; 9 Hispanic/Latino; 1 Native Hawaiian or other Pacific Islander, non-Hispanic/Latino), 10 international. Average age 29. 77 applicants, 77% accepted, 39 enrolled. In 2016, 65 master's awarded. *Degree requirements:* For master's, comprehensive exam (for some programs), thesis (for some programs). *Entrance requirements:* For master's, bachelor's degree from accredited institution, resume, letter of recommendation, essay of professional goals, official transcripts. Additional exam requirements/recommendations for international students: Required—TOEFL (minimum score 550 paper-based; 80 iBT), IELTS (minimum score 6.5). *Application deadline:* For fall admission, 8/18 for domestic students, 8/4 for international students; for spring admission, 12/15 for domestic students, 12/1 for international students; for summer admission, 4/17 for domestic students, 4/3 for international students. Applications are processed on a rolling basis. Application fee: $45. Electronic applications accepted. *Expenses:* $725 per credit. *Financial support:* In 2016–17, 25 students received support. Career-related internships or fieldwork, Federal Work-Study, scholarships/grants, tuition waivers (full and partial), and unspecified assistantships available. Support available to part-time students. Financial award application deadline: 3/1; financial award applicants required to submit FAFSA. *Faculty research:* Personality and social media, learning strategies, personal health behaviors and compliance, using drums in substance abuse groups, interpersonal behaviors with individuals with autism, case conceptualization, teaching case conceptualization across the curriculum. *Unit head:* Dr. Katrina Carter-Tellison, Dean, 561-237-7412, E-mail: kcartertellison@lynn.edu. *Application contact:* Steven Pruitt, Director of Graduate Admission, 561-237-7834, Fax: 561-237-7100, E-mail: admissionpm@lynn.edu.
Website: https://www.lynn.edu/academics/colleges-schools/arts-and-sciences

**New York University,** Steinhardt School of Culture, Education, and Human Development, Department of Applied Psychology, New York, NY 10003. Offers counseling (MA, PhD, Advanced Certificate), including counseling and guidance (MA, Advanced Certificate), counseling for mental health and wellness (MA), counseling psychology (PhD), LGBT health, education, and social services (Advanced Certificate); educational and developmental psychology (MA, PhD), including developmental psychology (PhD), human development and social intervention (MA), psychology and social intervention (PhD); Advanced Certificate/MPH; MA/Advanced Certificate. *Accreditation:* APA (one or more programs are accredited). *Program availability:* Part-time. Terminal master's awarded for partial completion of doctoral program. *Degree requirements:* For master's, thesis (for some programs); for doctorate, thesis/dissertation. *Entrance requirements:* For doctorate, GRE General Test, interview. Additional exam requirements/recommendations for international students: Required—TOEFL (minimum score 100 iBT). Electronic applications accepted. *Faculty research:* Applied measurement and research methods, health and human development, social and emotional development, cultural contexts and immigration.

**Oklahoma State University,** College of Education, School of Applied Health and Educational Psychology, Stillwater, OK 74078. Offers applied behavioral studies (Ed D); applied health and educational psychology (MS, PhD, Ed S). *Accreditation:* APA (one or more programs are accredited). *Program availability:* Part-time. *Faculty:* 38 full-time (22 women), 11 part-time/adjunct (6 women). *Students:* 168 full-time (122 women), 140 part-time (80 women); includes 86 minority (21 Black or African American, non-Hispanic/Latino; 10 American Indian or Alaska Native, non-Hispanic/Latino; 3 Asian, non-Hispanic/Latino; 24 Hispanic/Latino; 28 Two or more races, non-Hispanic/Latino), 3 international. Average age 30. 157 applicants, 51% accepted, 73 enrolled. In 2016, 73 master's, 21 doctorates awarded. *Degree requirements:* For master's, thesis (for some programs); for doctorate, comprehensive exam, thesis/dissertation. *Entrance requirements:* For master's and doctorate, GRE or GMAT. Additional exam requirements/recommendations for international students: Required—TOEFL (minimum

score 550 paper-based; 79 iBT). *Application deadline:* For fall admission, 3/1 priority date for international students; for spring admission, 8/1 priority date for international students. Applications are processed on a rolling basis. Application fee: $40 ($75 for international students). Electronic applications accepted. *Expenses:* Tuition, state resident: full-time $3775; part-time $209.70 per credit hour. Tuition, nonresident: full-time $14,851; part-time $825.05 per credit hour. *Required fees:* $2027; $112.60 per credit hour. Tuition and fees vary according to campus/location. *Financial support:* In 2016–17, 31 research assistantships (averaging $9,791 per year), 64 teaching assistantships (averaging $11,347 per year) were awarded; career-related internships or fieldwork, Federal Work-Study, scholarships/grants, health care benefits, tuition waivers (partial), and unspecified assistantships also available. Support available to part-time students. Financial award application deadline: 3/1; financial award applicants required to submit FAFSA. *Unit head:* Dr. Aric Warren, Head, 405-744-6040, Fax: 405-744-6779, E-mail: aric.warren@okstate.edu.
Website: http://education.okstate.edu/sahep

**Old Dominion University,** College of Sciences, Doctoral Program in Psychology, Norfolk, VA 23529. Offers applied psychological sciences (PhD); human factors psychology (PhD); industrial/organizational psychology (PhD). *Faculty:* 28 full-time (12 women), 12 part-time/adjunct (9 women). *Students:* 47 full-time (26 women); includes 4 minority (1 Black or African American, non-Hispanic/Latino; 3 Hispanic/Latino). Average age 25. 74 applicants, 14% accepted, 9 enrolled. In 2016, 3 doctorates awarded. *Degree requirements:* For doctorate, comprehensive exam, thesis/dissertation, candidacy exam. *Entrance requirements:* For doctorate, GRE General Test, GRE Subject Test, 3 recommendation letters. Additional exam requirements/recommendations for international students: Required—TOEFL. *Application deadline:* For winter admission, 1/5 for domestic and international students. Application fee: $50. Electronic applications accepted. *Expenses:* $478 per credit hour in-state; $1,195 per credit hour out-of-state. *Financial support:* In 2016–17, 40 students received support, including 5 research assistantships with full tuition reimbursements available (averaging $15,000 per year), 35 teaching assistantships with full tuition reimbursements available (averaging $15,000 per year). Financial award application deadline: 1/15. *Faculty research:* Human factors, industrial psychology, organizational psychology, applied psychological sciences (health, developmental, community, quantitative). *Total annual research expenditures:* $978,563. *Unit head:* Dr. Debra A. Major, Graduate Program Director, 757-683-4235, Fax: 757-683-5087, E-mail: dmajor@odu.edu. *Application contact:* William Heffelfinger, Director of Graduate Admissions, 757-683-5554, Fax: 757-683-3255, E-mail: gradadmit@odu.edu.
Website: http://www.odu.edu/psychology

**Penn State Harrisburg,** Graduate School, School of Behavioral Sciences and Education, Middletown, PA 17057. Offers adult education in the health and medical professions (Certificate); applied behavior analysis (MA); applied clinical psychology (MA); applied psychological research (MA); community psychology and social change (MA); English as a second language (ESL) program specialist and leadership (Certificate); folklore and ethnography (Certificate); health education (M Ed); lifelong learning and adult education (M Ed, D Ed); literacy education (M Ed); literacy leadership (Certificate); psychology: applications in clinical psychology (Certificate); psychology: health psychology (Certificate); teaching and curriculum (M Ed); training and development (M Ed, Certificate). *Program availability:* Part-time, evening/weekend. *Unit head:* Dr. Mukund S. Kulkarni, Chancellor, 717-948-6105, Fax: 717-948-6452. *Application contact:* Robert W. Coffman, Jr., Director of Enrollment Management, Recruitment and Admissions, 717-948-6250, Fax: 717-948-6325, E-mail: hbgadmit@psu.edu.
Website: https://harrisburg.psu.edu/behavioral-sciences-and-education/

**Rider University,** College of Liberal Arts, Education, and Sciences, Lawrenceville, NJ 08648-3001. Offers applied psychology (MA); business communication (MA). *Program availability:* Part-time, evening/weekend. *Entrance requirements:* For master's, official transcripts, current resume, two professional letters of recommendation, statement of aims and objectives, personal interview by invitation of faculty. Additional exam requirements/recommendations for international students: Required—TOEFL (minimum score 550 paper-based). Electronic applications accepted.

**Rutgers University–New Brunswick,** Graduate School of Applied and Professional Psychology, Piscataway, NJ 08854. Offers Psy M, Psy D. *Accreditation:* APA (one or more programs are accredited). *Degree requirements:* For doctorate, comprehensive exam, thesis/dissertation, 1 year internship. *Entrance requirements:* For doctorate, GRE General Test, GRE Subject Test, bachelor's degree in psychology or equivalent. Additional exam requirements/recommendations for international students: Required—TOEFL. Electronic applications accepted. *Expenses:* Contact institution. *Faculty research:* Organizational psychology, behavior modification, long- and short-term dynamic therapy, school psychology, addictive behaviors.

**Sacred Heart University,** Graduate Programs, College of Arts and Sciences, Department of Psychology, Fairfield, CT 06825. Offers applied psychology (MS), including community psychology, general applied psychology, industrial-organizational psychology. *Program availability:* Part-time, evening/weekend, online learning. *Faculty:* 8 full-time (7 women). *Students:* 18 full-time (12 women), 94 part-time (75 women); includes 34 minority (19 Black or African American, non-Hispanic/Latino; 1 Asian, non-Hispanic/Latino; 12 Hispanic/Latino; 2 Two or more races, non-Hispanic/Latino), 2 international. Average age 33. 55 applicants, 65% accepted, 16 enrolled. In 2016, 50 master's awarded. *Degree requirements:* For master's, comprehensive exam, thesis optional. *Entrance requirements:* For master's, minimum overall GPA of 3.0, bachelor's degree from accredited college or university. Additional exam requirements/recommendations for international students: Required—TOEFL (minimum score 570 paper-based, 80 iBT), TWE, or IELTS (6.5); Recommended—TSE. *Application deadline:* Applications are processed on a rolling basis. Application fee: $75. Electronic applications accepted. *Expenses:* $850 per credit. *Financial support:* Unspecified assistantships available. Financial award applicants required to submit FAFSA. *Unit head:* Rachel Bowman, Interim Chair/Associate Professor, 203-396-8243, E-mail: bowman@sacredheart.edu. *Application contact:* William Sweeney, Director of Graduate Admissions Operations, 203-365-7916, Fax: 203-365-4732, E-mail: gradstudies@sacredheart.edu.
Website: http://www.sacredheart.edu/academics/collegeofartssciences/academicdepartments/psychology/mastersinappliedpsychology/

**Saint Mary's University,** Faculty of Science, Department of Psychology, Halifax, NS B3H 3C3, Canada. Offers applied psychology (M Sc, PhD), including industrial/organizational psychology (M Sc). *Program availability:* Part-time. *Degree requirements:* For master's, thesis, 500-hour internship; for doctorate, comprehensive exam, thesis/dissertation, research project. *Entrance requirements:* For master's and doctorate, GRE General Test. *Faculty research:* Assessment, health psychology, social psychology, cognition.

**Tarleton State University,** College of Graduate Studies, College of Education, Department of Psychological Sciences, Stephenville, TX 76402. Offers applied psychology (MS). *Program availability:* Part-time, evening/weekend. *Faculty:* 2 full-time (1 woman), 2 part-time/adjunct (1 woman). *Students:* 2 full-time (1 woman), 8 part-time (6 women); includes 2 minority (1 Black or African American, non-Hispanic/Latino; 1

Hispanic/Latino), 1 international. 11 applicants, 100% accepted, 8 enrolled. *Degree requirements:* For master's, comprehensive exam, thesis optional. *Entrance requirements:* For master's, GRE General Test, minimum GPA of 3.0. Additional exam requirements/recommendations for international students: Required—TOEFL (minimum score 550 paper-based; 80 iBT). *Application deadline:* For fall admission, 8/15 priority date for domestic students; for spring admission, 1/7 for domestic students. Applications are processed on a rolling basis. Application fee: $45 ($145 for international students). Electronic applications accepted. *Expenses:* $3,672 tuition; $2,437 fees. *Financial support:* Research assistantships, teaching assistantships, career-related internships or fieldwork, Federal Work-Study, institutionally sponsored loans, and tuition waivers (partial) available. Support available to part-time students. Financial award application deadline: 5/1; financial award applicants required to submit FAFSA. *Unit head:* Dr. Kimberly Rynearson, Department Head, 254-968-9916, E-mail: rynearson@tarleton.edu. *Application contact:* Information Contact, 254-968-9104, Fax: 254-968-9670, E-mail: gradoffice@tarleton.edu.

**Teachers College, Columbia University,** Department of Human Development, New York, NY 10027-6696. Offers applied statistics (MS); cognitive studies in education (MA, Ed D, PhD); developmental psychology (MA, Ed D, PhD); educational psychology-human cognition and learning (Ed M, MA, Ed D, PhD); learning analytics (MS); measurement and evaluation (ME, Ed D, PhD); measurement, evaluation, and statistics (MA, MS, Ed D, PhD). *Program availability:* Part-time. *Students:* 217 full-time (168 women), 131 part-time (93 women); includes 83 minority (30 Black or African American, non-Hispanic/Latino; 31 Asian, non-Hispanic/Latino; 18 Hispanic/Latino; 4 Two or more races, non-Hispanic/Latino), 182 international. 450 applicants, 69% accepted, 132 enrolled. *Expenses: Tuition:* Full-time $36,288; part-time $1512 per credit. *Required fees:* $438 per semester. One-time fee: $510 full-time. Full-time tuition and fees vary according to course load. *Unit head:* Prof. Matthew S. Johnson, Chair, 212-678-3882, Fax: 212-678-3837, E-mail: johnson@tc.columbia.edu. *Application contact:* David Estrella, Director of Admission, 212-678-3305, E-mail: estrella@tc.columbia.edu. Website: http://www.tc.columbia.edu/human-development/

**University of Arkansas at Little Rock,** Graduate School, College of Social Sciences and Communication, Department of Psychology, Little Rock, AR 72204-1099. Offers applied psychology (MAP). *Program availability:* Part-time, evening/weekend. *Entrance requirements:* For master's, GRE General Test, minimum GPA of 2.7. *Faculty research:* Psychological methods and theories in business industry, government, and organizations; personnel program evaluation; training; affirmative action; organizational analysis and development.

**University of Baltimore,** Graduate School, Yale Gordon College of Arts and Sciences, Program in Applied Psychology, Baltimore, MD 21201-5779. Offers counseling psychology (MS). *Program availability:* Part-time, evening/weekend. *Degree requirements:* For master's, thesis optional. *Entrance requirements:* For master's, GRE, minimum GPA of 3.0. Additional exam requirements/recommendations for international students: Required—TOEFL (minimum score 550 paper-based). Electronic applications accepted. *Expenses:* Contact institution. *Faculty research:* Participatory decision-making, counter-productive workplace behavior, organizational consulting, substance abuse treatment, cognitive functioning in head injured.

**University of Calgary,** Faculty of Graduate Studies, Werklund School of Education, Division of Applied Psychology, Calgary, AB T2N 1N4, Canada. Offers counseling psychology (M Sc, MC, PhD); school and applied child psychology (M Ed, M Sc, PhD). *Program availability:* Part-time. *Degree requirements:* For master's, thesis (for some programs), final oral exam; for doctorate, thesis/dissertation, candidacy exam, final oral exam. *Entrance requirements:* For master's, minimum GPA of 3.0, 3 letters of reference; for doctorate, minimum GPA of 3.5, 3 letters of reference. *Faculty research:* Counselor education, family life studies, learning and cognition.

**University of Central Florida,** College of Sciences, Department of Psychology, Program in Applied Experimental and Human Factors Psychology, Orlando, FL 32816. Offers MA, PhD. *Students:* 37 full-time (26 women), 2 part-time (1 woman); includes 8 minority (2 Asian, non-Hispanic/Latino; 6 Hispanic/Latino), 1 international. Average age 28. 46 applicants, 20% accepted, 5 enrolled. In 2016, 9 master's, 9 doctorates awarded. *Degree requirements:* For doctorate, thesis/dissertation, departmental candidacy exam. *Entrance requirements:* For doctorate, GRE General Test, minimum GPA of 3.2 in last 60 hours or master's qualifying exam. Additional exam requirements/recommendations for international students: Required—TOEFL. *Application deadline:* For fall admission, 12/15 for domestic students. Application fee: $30. Electronic applications accepted. *Expenses:* Tuition, state resident: part-time $288.16 per credit hour. Tuition, nonresident: part-time $1071.31 per credit hour. *Financial support:* In 2016–17, 35 students received support, including 27 fellowships with partial tuition reimbursements available (averaging $7,038 per year), 11 research assistantships with partial tuition reimbursements available (averaging $10,497 per year), 22 teaching assistantships with partial tuition reimbursements available (averaging $11,486 per year); career-related internships or fieldwork, Federal Work-Study, institutionally sponsored loans, tuition waivers (partial), and unspecified assistantships also available. Financial award application deadline: 3/1; financial award applicants required to submit FAFSA. *Faculty research:* Categorization and decision, team training, transportation and safety, applied cognition and aging, emerging technology. *Unit head:* Dr. Mustapha Mouloua, Program Director, 407-823-2910, E-mail: mustapha.mouloua@ucf.edu. *Application contact:* Assistant Director, Graduate Admissions, 407-823-2766, Fax: 407-823-6442, E-mail: gradadmissions@ucf.edu.
Website: http://psychology.cos.ucf.edu/graduate/

**University of Guelph,** Graduate Studies, College of Social and Applied Human Sciences, Department of Psychology, Guelph, ON N1G 2W1, Canada. Offers applied social psychology (MA, PhD); clinical psychology: applied development emphasis (PhD); clinical psychology: applied developmental emphasis (MA); industrial/organizational psychology (MA, PhD); neuroscience and applied cognitive science (MA, PhD). *Degree requirements:* For master's, thesis; for doctorate, comprehensive exam, thesis/dissertation. *Entrance requirements:* For master's, GRE General Test, GRE Subject Test, minimum B+ average during previous 2 years of course work; for doctorate, GRE General Test, GRE Subject Test, minimum A- average. Additional exam requirements/recommendations for international students: Required—TOEFL (minimum score 89 iBT). Electronic applications accepted. *Faculty research:* Organizational psychology, reading comprehension and mathematical ability, drug addiction and relapse, gender issues and culture, memory, clinical psychology.

**University of Maryland, Baltimore County,** The Graduate School, College of Arts, Humanities and Social Sciences, Department of Psychology, Program in Applied Developmental Psychology, Baltimore, MD 21250. Offers PhD. *Faculty:* 8 full-time (6 women), 11 part-time/adjunct (4 women). *Students:* 22 full-time (21 women); includes 6 minority (1 Black or African American, non-Hispanic/Latino; 3 Asian, non-Hispanic/Latino; 2 Hispanic/Latino), 2 international. Average age 25. 24 applicants, 8% accepted, 1 enrolled. In 2016, 3 doctorates awarded. *Degree requirements:* For doctorate, comprehensive exam, thesis/dissertation. *Entrance requirements:* For doctorate, GRE General Test, minimum GPA of 3.0. Additional exam requirements/recommendations for international students: Required—TOEFL. *Application deadline:* For fall admission, 1/9 for domestic and international students. Application fee: $50. Electronic applications

accepted. *Expenses:* Tuition, state resident: full-time $13,294. Tuition, nonresident: full-time $20,286. *Financial support:* In 2016–17, 16 students received support, including 1 fellowship with partial tuition reimbursement available (averaging $17,250 per year), 3 research assistantships with full tuition reimbursements available (averaging $20,400 per year), 12 teaching assistantships with full tuition reimbursements available (averaging $17,250 per year); career-related internships or fieldwork, Federal Work-Study, health care benefits, and unspecified assistantships also available. Financial award application deadline: 3/1; financial award applicants required to submit FAFSA. *Faculty research:* Early intervention and development, schooling and development, cultural aspects of development, development in high risk children, social-emotional development. *Unit head:* Dr. Susan Sonnenschein, Director, 410-455-2361, Fax: 410-455-1055, E-mail: sonnenschein@umbc.edu. *Application contact:* Nicole Mooney, Program Management Specialist, 410-455-2567, Fax: 410-455-1055, E-mail: psycdept@umbc.edu.
Website: http://psychology.umbc.edu/

**University of Pennsylvania,** School of Arts and Sciences, College of Liberal and Professional Studies, Philadelphia, PA 19104. Offers applied geosciences (MSAG); applied positive psychology (MAP); chemical sciences (MCS); environmental studies (MES); individualized study (MLA); liberal arts (M Phil); medical physics (MMP); organization dynamics (M Phil). *Students:* 143 full-time (75 women), 337 part-time (189 women); includes 90 minority (28 Black or African American, non-Hispanic/Latino; 2 American Indian or Alaska Native, non-Hispanic/Latino; 22 Asian, non-Hispanic/Latino; 26 Hispanic/Latino; 12 Two or more races, non-Hispanic/Latino), 66 international. Average age 35. 618 applicants, 51% accepted, 231 enrolled. In 2016, 161 master's awarded. *Expenses: Tuition:* Full-time $31,068; part-time $5762 per course. *Required fees:* $3200; $336 per course. Full-time tuition and fees vary according to degree level, program and student level. Part-time tuition and fees vary according to course load, degree level and program. *Unit head:* Nora Lewis, Vice Dean, Professional and Liberal Education, 215-898-7326, E-mail: nlewis@sas.upenn.edu.
Website: http://www.sas.upenn.edu/lps/graduate

**University of Pittsburgh,** School of Education, Department of Psychology in Education, Program in Applied Developmental Psychology, Pittsburgh, PA 15260. Offers M Ed, MS, PhD. *Program availability:* Part-time, evening/weekend. *Degree requirements:* For master's, thesis. *Entrance requirements:* For doctorate, GRE. Additional exam requirements/recommendations for international students: Required—TOEFL. Electronic applications accepted. Tuition and fees vary according to program.

**University of Regina,** Faculty of Graduate Studies and Research, Faculty of Arts, Department of Psychology, Regina, SK S4S 0A2, Canada. Offers clinical psychology (MA, PhD); experimental and applied psychology (MA, PhD). *Faculty:* 20 full-time (9 women), 8 part-time/adjunct (0 women). *Students:* 26 full-time (23 women). 28 applicants, 21% accepted. In 2016, 9 master's, 5 doctorates awarded. *Degree requirements:* For master's, thesis; for doctorate, comprehensive exam, thesis/dissertation. *Entrance requirements:* For master's, GRE General Test; for doctorate, GRE General Test and GRE Subject Test (optional for those with a master's degree from a Canadian university). Additional exam requirements/recommendations for international students: Required—TOEFL (minimum score 580 paper-based; 80 iBT), IELTS (minimum score 6.5), PTE (minimum score 59). *Application deadline:* For fall admission, 1/15 for domestic and international students. Application fee: $100. Electronic applications accepted. *Financial support:* In 2016–17, 7 fellowships (averaging $6,714 per year), 17 teaching assistantships (averaging $2,566 per year) were awarded; career-related internships or fieldwork and scholarships/grants also available. Financial award application deadline: 6/15. *Faculty research:* Clinical, experimental, cognitive, and applied psychology; post-traumatic stress disorder, anxiety, and panic disorder; traumatic brain injury; chronic pain; perception and memory. *Unit head:* Dr. Richard MacLennan, Department Head, 306-585-4458, Fax: 306-585-5429, E-mail: richard.maclennan@uregina.ca.
Website: http://www.uregina.ca/arts/psychology

**University of South Carolina Aiken,** Program in Applied Clinical Psychology, Aiken, SC 29801. Offers MS. *Program availability:* Part-time. *Faculty:* 9 full-time (7 women). *Students:* 19 full-time (16 women), 11 part-time (9 women); includes 5 minority (3 Black or African American, non-Hispanic/Latino; 1 Native Hawaiian or other Pacific Islander, non-Hispanic/Latino; 1 Two or more races, non-Hispanic/Latino). Average age 26. 53 applicants, 34% accepted, 12 enrolled. In 2016, 7 master's awarded. *Degree requirements:* For master's, thesis. *Entrance requirements:* For master's, GRE. Additional exam requirements/recommendations for international students: Required—TOEFL (minimum score 550 paper-based; 80 iBT). *Application deadline:* For fall admission, 5/15 priority date for domestic and international students. Applications are processed on a rolling basis. Application fee: $45. Electronic applications accepted. *Expenses:* Tuition, state resident: full-time $12,798; part-time $533 per credit hour. Tuition, nonresident: full-time $27,408; part-time $1142 per credit hour. *Required fees:* $11 per credit hour. $25 per semester. Full-time tuition and fees vary according to course load. *Financial support:* In 2016–17, 23 students received support, including 16 research assistantships with partial tuition reimbursements available (averaging $3,594 per year), 4 teaching assistantships with partial tuition reimbursements available (averaging $3,438 per year); career-related internships or fieldwork, Federal Work-Study, scholarships/grants, tuition waivers (partial), and unspecified assistantships also available. Financial award application deadline: 3/15; financial award applicants required to submit FAFSA. *Faculty research:* Addictive behaviors, interpersonal attraction, impression formation in zero-acquaintance situations, the influence of emotions on visual perception, executive function, cognitive control, inhibitory control, working memory, episodic memory, emotion regulation, anxiety, stress, cognitive functioning and development, social and personality psychology, ADHD, development of cognition and academic skills, teen pregnancy/parenting. *Unit head:* Dr. Jane Stafford, Director, 803-641-3358, Fax: 803-641-3720, E-mail: jstafford@usca.edu. *Application contact:* Dan Robb, Associate Vice Chancellor for Enrollment Management, 803-641-3487, Fax: 803-641-3727, E-mail: danr@usca.edu.
Website: http://web.usca.edu/psychology/academics/ms-psychology/

**The University of Tennessee,** Graduate School, College of Education, Health and Human Sciences, Department of Educational Psychology and Counseling, Knoxville, TN 37996. Offers adult education (MS); applied educational psychology (MS); collaborative learning (Ed D); college student personnel (MS); mental health counseling (MS); rehabilitation counseling (MS); school counseling (MS). *Accreditation:* ACA (one or more programs are accredited); CORE (one or more programs are accredited); NCATE. *Program availability:* Part-time, evening/weekend. *Degree requirements:* For master's, thesis optional. *Entrance requirements:* For master's, GRE General Test, minimum GPA of 2.7. Additional exam requirements/recommendations for international students: Required—TOEFL. Electronic applications accepted.

**The University of Texas at El Paso,** Graduate School, College of Liberal Arts, Department of Sociology and Anthropology, El Paso, TX 79968-0001. Offers applied anthropology (Certificate); applied social sciences (Certificate); sociology (MA). *Program availability:* Part-time, evening/weekend. *Degree requirements:* For master's, thesis. *Entrance requirements:* For master's, GRE General Test, minimum GPA of 3.0. Additional exam requirements/recommendations for international students: Required—

*Applied Psychology*

TOEFL. Electronic applications accepted. *Faculty research:* U.S.-Mexico border, social inequality, immigration, Chicano culture, Mexico.

**The University of Texas of the Permian Basin,** Office of Graduate Studies, College of Arts and Sciences, Department of Psychology, Odessa, TX 79762-0001. Offers applied research psychology (MA); clinical psychology (MA). *Program availability:* Part-time, evening/weekend. *Degree requirements:* For master's, comprehensive exam, thesis, practicum. *Entrance requirements:* For master's, GRE General Test, 3 letters of recommendation. Additional exam requirements/recommendations for international students: Required—TOEFL (minimum score 550 paper-based).

**University of West Florida,** College of Arts, Social Sciences, and Humanities, Department of Psychology, Pensacola, FL 32514-5750. Offers applied experimental (MA); counseling (MA); industrial-organizational (MA). *Program availability:* Part-time. *Degree requirements:* For master's, thesis (for some programs). *Entrance requirements:* For master's, GRE, official transcripts; minimum GPA of 3.0; writing sample; three letters of reference; field experience or skill sets; oral interview (for counseling specialization). Additional exam requirements/recommendations for international students: Required—TOEFL (minimum score 550 paper-based). *Application deadline:* For fall admission, 6/1 for domestic and international students; for spring admission, 10/1 for domestic and international students. Applications are processed on a rolling basis. Application fee: $30. *Expenses:* Tuition, state resident: full-time $5316.12. Tuition, nonresident: full-time $11,308. *Required fees:* $583.92. Tuition and fees vary according to course load and program. *Financial support:* Fellowships with partial tuition reimbursements, research assistantships with partial tuition reimbursements, teaching assistantships with partial tuition reimbursements, career-related internships or fieldwork, and unspecified assistantships available. Financial award application deadline: 4/15; financial award applicants required to submit FAFSA. *Faculty research:* Prose recall, brain imaging, peak performance, biofeedback and pain control, comparable worth. *Unit head:* Dr. Robert Belter, Interim Department Chair, 850-474-2791, E-mail: rbelter@uwf.edu. *Application contact:* Dr. Robert Belter, Interim Department Chair, 850-474-2791, E-mail: rbelter@uwf.edu.
Website: http://www.uwf.edu/psychology/

**University of Windsor,** Faculty of Graduate Studies, Faculty of Arts and Social Sciences, Department of Psychology, Windsor, ON N9B 3P4, Canada. Offers adult clinical (MA, PhD); applied social psychology (MA, PhD); child clinical (MA, PhD); clinical neuropsychology (MA, PhD). *Degree requirements:* For master's, thesis; for doctorate, comprehensive exam, thesis/dissertation. *Entrance requirements:* For master's, GRE General Test, GRE Subject Test in psychology, minimum B average; for doctorate, GRE General Test, GRE Subject Test in psychology, master's degree. Additional exam requirements/recommendations for international students: Required—TOEFL (minimum score 600 paper-based). Electronic applications accepted. *Faculty research:* Gambling, suicidology, emotional competence, psychotherapy and trauma.

**University of Wisconsin–Stout,** Graduate School, College of Education, Health and Human Sciences, Program in Applied Psychology, Menomonie, WI 54751. Offers MS. *Program availability:* Part-time. *Degree requirements:* For master's, thesis. *Entrance*

*requirements:* For master's, GRE General Test, GRE Subject Test, minimum GPA of 3.0, 15 semester credits of undergraduate course work in psychology, 8 semester credits in research methods and statistics. Additional exam requirements/recommendations for international students: Required—TOEFL (minimum score 500 paper-based; 61 iBT). Electronic applications accepted. *Faculty research:* Health complementary therapies, motivation, group dynamics, social reasoning, stress.

**Walden University,** Graduate Programs, School of Psychology, Minneapolis, MN 55401. Offers clinical psychology (MS), including counseling, general program; forensic psychology (MS), including forensic psychology in the community, general program, mental health applications, program planning and evaluation in forensic settings, psychology and legal systems; industrial organizational (MS, PhD), including consulting psychology, forensic (MS), forensic psychology (PhD), general practice, leadership development and coaching (MS), organizational diversity and social change, research evaluation (PhD); online teaching in psychology (Post-Master's Certificate); organizational psychology and development (Postbaccalaureate Certificate); psychology (MS, PhD), including applied psychology (MS), clinical psychology (PhD), crisis management and response (MS), educational psychology, forensic psychology (PhD), general psychology (MS), general psychology research (PhD), general psychology teaching (PhD), health psychology, leadership development and coaching (MS), psychology of culture (MS), psychology, public administration, and social change (MS), social psychology, terrorism and security (MS); psychology respecialization (Post-Doctoral Certificate). *Program availability:* Part-time, evening/weekend, online only, 100% online. Terminal master's awarded for partial completion of doctoral program. *Degree requirements:* For master's, thesis optional; for doctorate, thesis/dissertation, residency. *Entrance requirements:* For master's, bachelor's degree or higher; minimum GPA of 2.5; official transcripts; goal statement (for some programs); access to computer and Internet; for doctorate, master's degree or higher; three years of related professional or academic experience (preferred); minimum GPA of 3.0; goal statement and current resume (for select programs); official transcripts; access to computer and Internet; for other advanced degree, relevant work experience; access to computer and Internet. Additional exam requirements/recommendations for international students: Required—TOEFL (minimum score 550 paper-based, 79 iBT), IELTS (minimum score 6.5), Michigan English Language Assessment Battery (minimum score 82), or PTE (minimum score 53). Electronic applications accepted.

**William James College,** Graduate Programs, Newton, MA 02459. Offers applied psychology in higher education student personnel administration (MA); clinical psychology (Psy D); counseling psychology (MA); counseling psychology and community mental health (MA); counseling psychology and global mental health (MA); executive coaching (Graduate Certificate); forensic and counseling psychology (MA); leadership psychology (Psy D); organizational psychology (MA); primary care psychology (MA); respecialization in clinical psychology (Certificate); school psychology (Psy D); MA/CAGS. *Accreditation:* APA. *Degree requirements:* For master's, comprehensive exam (for some programs); for doctorate, thesis/dissertation (for some programs). Electronic applications accepted.

# Clinical Psychology

**Abilene Christian University,** Graduate Programs, College of Arts and Sciences, Department of Psychology, Program in Clinical Psychology, Abilene, TX 79699. Offers MS. *Program availability:* Part-time. *Students:* 9 full-time (6 women); includes 3 minority (1 Black or African American, non-Hispanic/Latino; 2 Hispanic/Latino), 1 international. 26 applicants, 31% accepted, 5 enrolled. In 2016, 6 master's awarded. *Degree requirements:* For master's, thesis, practicum. *Entrance requirements:* Additional exam requirements/recommendations for international students: Required—TOEFL (minimum score 80 iBT), IELTS (minimum score 6), PTE. *Application deadline:* For fall admission, 3/30 priority date for domestic students; for spring admission, 11/1 for domestic students. Applications are processed on a rolling basis. Application fee: $50. Electronic applications accepted. *Expenses: Tuition:* Full-time $19,890; part-time $1105 per credit hour. Tuition and fees vary according to course load and program. *Financial support:* In 2016–17, 8 students received support. Career-related internships or fieldwork, Federal Work-Study, scholarships/grants, and unspecified assistantships available. Support available to part-time students. Financial award application deadline: 4/1; financial award applicants required to submit FAFSA. *Unit head:* Dr. Cherisse Flanagan, Graduate Director, 325-674-4826, Fax: 325-674-6968, E-mail: cherisse.flanagan@acu.edu. *Application contact:* Corey Patterson, Director of Graduate Admission and Recruiting, 325-674-6566, Fax: 325-674-6717, E-mail: gradinfo@acu.edu.
Website: http://www.acu.edu/graduate/academics/clinical-psychology.html

**Acadia University,** Faculty of Pure and Applied Science, Department of Psychology, Wolfville, NS B4P 2R6, Canada. Offers clinical psychology (M Sc). *Degree requirements:* For master's, thesis. *Entrance requirements:* For master's, GRE General Test, GRE Subject Test, honors degree or equivalent. Additional exam requirements/recommendations for international students: Required—TOEFL (minimum score 580 paper-based; 93 iBT), IELTS (minimum score 6.5). *Faculty research:* Social psychology, job stress, psychotherapy, cognition perception, development.

**Adelphi University,** Gordon F. Derner School of Psychology, Program in Clinical Psychology, Garden City, NY 11530-0701. Offers PhD. *Students:* 77 full-time (58 women), 23 part-time (17 women); includes 29 minority (4 Black or African American, non-Hispanic/Latino; 8 Asian, non-Hispanic/Latino; 11 Hispanic/Latino; 4 Two or more races, non-Hispanic/Latino), 7 international. Average age 30. 220 applicants, 33% accepted, 20 enrolled. In 2016, 14 doctorates awarded. *Degree requirements:* For doctorate, thesis/dissertation, research component (second-year), 1-year internship. *Entrance requirements:* For doctorate, GRE General Test, GRE Subject Test, interview; resume; undergraduate course work in psychology, experimental psychology, statistics, developmental psychology, and abnormal psychology. Additional exam requirements/recommendations for international students: Required—TOEFL (minimum score 550 paper-based; 80 iBT), IELTS (minimum score 6.5). *Application deadline:* For fall admission, 1/15 priority date for domestic and international students. Application fee: $50. Electronic applications accepted. *Expenses:* Contact institution. *Financial support:* Research assistantships with full and partial tuition reimbursements, teaching assistantships, career-related internships or fieldwork, institutionally sponsored loans, scholarships/grants, traineeships, and unspecified assistantships available. Support available to part-time students. Financial award application deadline: 2/15; financial award applicants required to submit FAFSA. *Unit head:* Dr. J. Christopher Muran, Associate Dean, 516-877-4803, E-mail: jcmuran@adelphi.edu. *Application contact:* Christine Murphy, Director of Admissions, 516-877-3050, Fax: 516-877-3039, E-mail:

graduateadmissions@adelphi.edu.
Website: http://derner.adelphi.edu/psychology/doctoral-program/

**Adler Graduate School,** Program in Adlerian Counseling and Psychotherapy, Richfield, MN 55423. Offers Adlerian studies (MA); art therapy (MA); clinical mental health counseling (MA); co-occurring mental health and substance abuse disorders (MA); marriage and family therapy (MA); school counseling (MA). *Program availability:* Part-time, evening/weekend. *Faculty:* 71 part-time/adjunct (55 women). *Students:* 298 part-time (225 women); includes 51 minority (40 Black or African American, non-Hispanic/Latino; 6 American Indian or Alaska Native, non-Hispanic/Latino; 5 Hispanic/Latino). *Degree requirements:* For master's, thesis or alternative, 500-700 hour internship (depending on license choice). *Entrance requirements:* For master's, interview, official transcripts, minimum cumulative GPA of 3.0. *Application deadline:* Applications are processed on a rolling basis. Application fee: $50. Electronic applications accepted. *Financial support:* Career-related internships or fieldwork and tuition waivers available. Support available to part-time students. Financial award applicants required to submit FAFSA. *Unit head:* Dr. Dan Haugen, President, 612-767-7048, Fax: 612-861-7559, E-mail: haugen@alfredadler.edu. *Application contact:* Evelyn B. Haas, Director of Admissions, 612-767-7044, Fax: 612-861-7559, E-mail: ev@alfredadler.edu.

**Adler University,** Programs in Psychology, Chicago, IL 60602. Offers advanced Adlerian psychotherapy (Certificate); art therapy (MA); clinical mental health counseling (MA); clinical neuropsychology (Certificate); clinical psychology (Psy D); community psychology (MA); counseling and organizational psychology (MA); counseling psychology (MA); counselor education and supervision (PhD); couple and family therapy (DCFT); criminology (MA); emergency management leadership (MA); forensic psychology (MA); marriage and family counseling (MA); marriage and family therapy (Certificate); military psychology (MA); nonprofit management (MA); organizational psychology (MA); police psychology (MA); public policy and administration (MA); rehabilitation counseling (MA); sport and health psychology (MA); substance abuse counseling (Certificate); Psy D/Certificate; Psy D/MACAT; Psy D/MACP; Psy D/MAMFC; Psy D/MASAC. *Accreditation:* APA. *Program availability:* Part-time, evening/weekend, online learning. Terminal master's awarded for partial completion of doctoral program. *Degree requirements:* For master's, thesis or alternative, oral exam, practicum; for doctorate, thesis/dissertation, clinical exam, internship, oral exam, practicum, written qualifying exam. *Entrance requirements:* For master's, 12 semester hours in psychology, minimum GPA of 3.0; for doctorate, 18 semester hours in psychology, minimum GPA of 3.25; for Certificate, appropriate master's or doctoral degree. Additional exam requirements/recommendations for international students: Required—TOEFL (minimum score 550 paper-based; 79 iBT). Electronic applications accepted.

**See Display on page 982 and Close-Up on page 1225.**

**Alabama Agricultural and Mechanical University,** School of Graduate Studies, College of Education, Humanities, and Behavioral Sciences, Department of Social Work, Psychology and Counseling, Huntsville, AL 35811. Offers psychology and counseling (MS, Ed S), including clinical psychology (MS), counseling psychology (MS), guidance and counseling, rehabilitation counseling (MS), school counseling (MS), school psychology (MS), school psychometry (MS); social work (MSW). *Accreditation:* CORE; NCATE. *Program availability:* Part-time, evening/weekend. *Degree requirements:* For master's, comprehensive exam. *Entrance requirements:* For master's, GRE General Test. Additional exam requirements/recommendations for international students: Required—TOEFL (minimum score 500 paper-based; 61 iBT). *Application deadline:* For fall admission, 5/1 for domestic students. Application fee: $15 ($20 for international students). *Expenses:* Tuition, nonresident: part-time $826 per credit hour. Full-time tuition and fees vary according to course load and program. *Financial support:* Career-related internships or fieldwork available. Support available to part-time students. Financial award application deadline: 4/1. *Faculty research:* Increasing number of minorities in special education and speech-language pathology. *Unit head:* Dr. Shirley King, Chair, 256-372-5520, Fax: 256-372-5526.

**Alliant International University–Fresno,** California School of Professional Psychology, PhD Program in Clinical Psychology, Fresno, CA 93727. Offers PhD. *Degree requirements:* For doctorate, comprehensive exam, thesis/dissertation. *Entrance requirements:* For doctorate, minimum GPA of 3.0 in both psychology and overall, letters of recommendation, interview. Additional exam requirements/recommendations for international students: Required—TOEFL (minimum score 550 paper-based; 80 iBT), TWE (minimum score 5). Electronic applications accepted. *Faculty research:* Teaching of psychology, ecosystemic child psychology, cultural competence, neuro-cognitive processes.

**Alliant International University–Fresno,** California School of Professional Psychology, Psy D Program in Clinical Psychology, Fresno, CA 93727. Offers Psy D. *Accreditation:* APA. *Degree requirements:* For doctorate, comprehensive exam, thesis/dissertation. *Entrance requirements:* For doctorate, minimum GPA of 3.0 in both psychology and overall, letters of recommendation, interview. Additional exam requirements/ recommendations for international students: Required—TOEFL (minimum score 550 paper-based; 80 iBT), TWE (minimum score 5). Electronic applications accepted. *Faculty research:* Psychodynamic correlates of self-care behavior, women's health and development, gay and lesbian issues, child development and abuse, trauma.

**Alliant International University–Los Angeles,** California School of Professional Psychology, PhD Program in Clinical Psychology, Alhambra, CA 91803. Offers PhD. *Accreditation:* APA. *Degree requirements:* For doctorate, comprehensive exam, thesis/ dissertation. *Entrance requirements:* For doctorate, interview, minimum GPA of 3.0 in both psychology and overall. Additional exam requirements/recommendations for international students: Required—TOEFL (minimum score 600 paper-based), TWE (minimum score 5). Electronic applications accepted. *Faculty research:* Multicultural and community clinical psychology, health and chronic disease, individual and family psychology, pediatric neuropsychology.

**Alliant International University–Los Angeles,** California School of Professional Psychology, Psy D Program in Clinical Psychology, Alhambra, CA 91803. Offers clinical health psychology (Psy D); family/child and couple clinical psychology (Psy D); multi-interest option (Psy D); multicultural community-clinical psychology (Psy D). *Accreditation:* APA. *Degree requirements:* For doctorate, comprehensive exam, thesis/ dissertation. *Entrance requirements:* For doctorate, interview, minimum GPA of 3.0 in both psychology and overall. Additional exam requirements/recommendations for international students: Required—TOEFL (minimum score 600 paper-based), TWE. Electronic applications accepted. *Faculty research:* Child and family psychology, multicultural and community psychology, acculturation, lesbian and gay issues, women's health.

**Alliant International University–Sacramento,** California School of Professional Psychology, Program in Clinical Psychology, Sacramento, CA 95833. Offers Psy D. *Degree requirements:* For doctorate, comprehensive exam, thesis/dissertation, internship. *Entrance requirements:* For doctorate, minimum GPA of 3.0, letters of recommendation, interview. Additional exam requirements/recommendations for international students: Required—TOEFL (minimum score 600 paper-based; 80 iBT), TWE (minimum score 5). Electronic applications accepted. *Faculty research:* Creating and testing evidence-based interventions for underserved minority populations with cardiovascular disease and cancer, substance abuse treatment and relapse prediction, cultural diversity, personality disorders, trauma.

**Alliant International University–San Diego,** California School of Professional Psychology, Organizational Psychology Division, San Diego, CA 92131. Offers clinical/ industrial organizational psychology (PhD); consulting psychology (PhD); industrial/ organizational psychology (MA, MS, PhD); leadership (PhD). *Program availability:* Part-time, evening/weekend. Terminal master's awarded for partial completion of doctoral program. *Degree requirements:* For doctorate, comprehensive exam, thesis/ dissertation, internship/practicum. *Entrance requirements:* For master's and doctorate, minimum GPA of 3.0, recommendations, essay, interview. Additional exam requirements/recommendations for international students: Required—TOEFL (minimum score 550 paper-based; 80 iBT), TWE (minimum score 5). Electronic applications accepted. *Faculty research:* Cultural diversity in the workplace, work motivation, personnel and performance management, organizational diagnosis.

**Alliant International University–San Diego,** California School of Professional Psychology, PhD Program in Clinical Psychology, San Diego, CA 92131. Offers PhD. *Accreditation:* APA. *Degree requirements:* For doctorate, comprehensive exam, thesis/ dissertation, internship. *Entrance requirements:* For doctorate, interview, minimum GPA of 3.0, recommendations, essay, interview. Additional exam requirements/ recommendations for international students: Required—TOEFL (minimum score 600 paper-based; 80 iBT), TWE (minimum score 5). Electronic applications accepted. *Faculty research:* Pediatric child clinical psychology, neuro-psychological assessment, ADHD, effect of alcohol and abstinence on the central nervous system.

**Alliant International University–San Diego,** California School of Professional Psychology, Psy D Program in Clinical Psychology, San Diego, CA 92131. Offers Psy D. *Accreditation:* APA. *Degree requirements:* For doctorate, comprehensive exam, thesis/ dissertation, internship. *Entrance requirements:* For doctorate, minimum GPA of 3.0, recommendations, essay, interview. Additional exam requirements/recommendations for international students: Required—TOEFL (minimum score 550 paper-based; 80 iBT), TWE (minimum score 5). Electronic applications accepted. *Faculty research:* Forensic psychology, health psychology, family and child psychology, cultural competency in mental health services, women's health.

**Alliant International University–San Francisco,** California School of Forensic Studies, San Francisco, CA 94133. Offers applied criminology (MS), including victimology; clinical forensic psychology (PhD, Psy D). *Degree requirements:* For doctorate, comprehensive exam, thesis/dissertation, internship. *Entrance requirements:* For master's, minimum GPA of 3.0, recommendations, essay; for doctorate, minimum GPA of 3.0, recommendations, essay, interview. Additional exam requirements/ recommendations for international students: Required—TOEFL (minimum score 550 paper-based; 80 iBT), TWE (minimum score 5). *Faculty research:* Post-traumatic stress disorder, correctional mental health.

**Alliant International University–San Francisco,** California School of Professional Psychology, PhD Program in Clinical Psychology, San Francisco, CA 94133. Offers PhD. *Degree requirements:* For doctorate, comprehensive exam, thesis/dissertation, internship. *Entrance requirements:* For doctorate, minimum GPA of 3.0, recommendations, essay, interview. Additional exam requirements/recommendations for international students: Required—TOEFL (minimum score 550 paper-based; 80 iBT),

TWE (minimum score 5). Electronic applications accepted. *Faculty research:* Social model of disability, feminist models of clinical training, post-traumatic stress disorder, gay and lesbian parents and their children, psychology of women.

**Alliant International University–San Francisco,** California School of Professional Psychology, Psy D Program in Clinical Psychology, San Francisco, CA 94133. Offers Psy D, Certificate. *Accreditation:* APA (one or more programs are accredited). *Degree requirements:* For doctorate, comprehensive exam, thesis/dissertation, internship. *Entrance requirements:* For doctorate, minimum GPA of 3.0, recommendations, essay, interview. Additional exam requirements/recommendations for international students: Required—TOEFL (minimum score 550 paper-based; 80 iBT), TWE (minimum score 5). Electronic applications accepted. *Faculty research:* Health psychology, family and child psychology, social justice, multicultural and community psychology, gender issues.

**American International College,** Low Residency Programs, Springfield, MA 01109-3189. Offers counseling psychology (MA); educational leadership and supervision (Ed D); individual and institutional development (Ed D); professional counseling and supervision (Ed D); psychology (Ed D); teaching and learning (Ed D). *Expenses:* Tuition: Full-time $7902; part-time $750 per semester hour. *Required fees:* $60; $60 per semester hour. $30 per semester. One-time fee: $100. Tuition and fees vary according to course load, degree level, campus/location and program. *Application contact:* Kerry Barnes, Director of Graduate Admissions, 413-205-3703, Fax: 413-205-3051, E-mail: kerry.barnes@aic.edu.

**American International College,** School of Business, Arts and Sciences, Springfield, MA 01109-3189. Offers accounting and taxation (MS); business administration (MBA); clinical psychology (MA); educational psychology (Ed D); forensic psychology (MS); general psychology (MA, CAGS); management (CAGS); resort and casino management (MBA, CAGS). *Program availability:* Part-time, evening/weekend. *Degree requirements:* For master's, comprehensive exam (for some programs), thesis (for some programs), practicum; for doctorate, comprehensive exam (for some programs), thesis/dissertation; for CAGS, comprehensive exam (for some programs), thesis (for some programs). *Entrance requirements:* For master's, BS or BA; for doctorate, interview. Additional exam requirements/recommendations for international students: Required—TOEFL (minimum score 550 paper-based; 80 iBT). *Expenses:* Tuition: Full-time $7902; part-time $750 per semester hour. *Required fees:* $60; $60 per semester hour. $30 per semester. One-time fee: $100. Tuition and fees vary according to course load, degree level, campus/location and program.

**American University,** College of Arts and Sciences, Department of Psychology, Washington, DC 22016-8062. Offers addiction and addictive behavior (Certificate); behavior, cognition, and neuroscience (PhD); clinical psychology (PhD); psychobiology of healing (Certificate); psychology (MA). *Accreditation:* APA. *Program availability:* Part-time. *Faculty:* 22 full-time (9 women), 11 part-time/adjunct (3 women). *Students:* 86 full-time (72 women), 12 part-time (9 women); includes 15 minority (5 Black or African American, non-Hispanic/Latino; 4 Asian, non-Hispanic/Latino; 4 Hispanic/Latino; 2 Two or more races, non-Hispanic/Latino), 6 international. Average age 28. 479 applicants, 12% accepted, 34 enrolled. In 2016, 27 master's, 13 doctorates awarded. *Degree requirements:* For master's, comprehensive exam, thesis or alternative; for doctorate, comprehensive exam, thesis/dissertation. *Entrance requirements:* For master's, GRE General Test, GRE Subject Test, statement of purpose, transcripts, 2 letters of recommendation; for doctorate, GRE General Test, GRE Subject Test, 3 letters of recommendation, statement of purpose, transcripts, resume. Additional exam requirements/recommendations for international students: Required—TOEFL (minimum score 100 iBT), IELTS (minimum score 7), PTE (minimum score 68). Application fee: $55. *Expenses:* $1,579 per credit tuition; $690 mandatory fees. *Financial support:* Research assistantships, teaching assistantships, institutionally sponsored loans, scholarships/grants, and unspecified assistantships available. Financial award application deadline: 2/1; financial award applicants required to submit FAFSA. *Unit head:* Dr. David Haaga, Department Chair, 202-885-1718, Fax: 202-885-1023, E-mail: ahrens@american.edu. *Application contact:* Kathleen Clowery, Associate Director, Graduate Admission, 202-885-3620, Fax: 202-885-1344, E-mail: clowery@american.edu.
Website: http://www.american.edu/CAS/Psychology/

**American University of Beirut,** Graduate Programs, Faculty of Arts and Sciences, Beirut, Lebanon. Offers anthropology (MA); Arab and Middle Eastern history (PhD); Arabic language and literature (MA, PhD); archaeology (MA); art history and curating (MA); biology (MS); cell and molecular biology (PhD); chemistry (MS); clinical psychology (MA); computational sciences (MS); computer science (MS); economics (MA); education (MA); English language (MA); English literature (MA); environmental policy planning (MS); financial economics (MAFE); geology (MS); history (MA); Islamic studies (MA); mathematics (MS); media studies (MA); Middle Eastern studies (MA); physics (MS); political studies (MA); psychology (MA); public administration (MA); public policy and international affairs (MA); sociology (MA); statistics (MA, MS); theoretical physics (PhD); transnational American studies (MA). *Program availability:* Part-time. *Faculty:* 133 full-time (42 women), 6 part-time/adjunct (2 women). *Students:* 240 full-time (172 women), 227 part-time (166 women). Average age 27. 286 applicants, 67% accepted, 108 enrolled. In 2016, 60 master's, 3 doctorates awarded. Terminal master's awarded for partial completion of doctoral program. *Degree requirements:* For master's, one foreign language, comprehensive exam, thesis (for some programs); for doctorate, one foreign language, comprehensive exam, thesis/dissertation. *Entrance requirements:* For master's, GRE (for some MA, MS programs), letters of recommendation; for doctorate, GRE, letters of recommendation. Additional exam requirements/ recommendations for international students: Required—TOEFL (minimum score 600 paper-based; 97 iBT), IELTS (minimum score 7). *Application deadline:* For fall admission, 4/3 for domestic students; for winter admission, 11/3 for domestic students. Application fee: $50. Electronic applications accepted. *Expenses:* Contact institution. *Financial support:* In 2016–17, 4 fellowships (averaging $11,200 per year), 18 research assistantships (averaging $5,400 per year) were awarded; teaching assistantships, career-related internships or fieldwork, Federal Work-Study, institutionally sponsored loans, scholarships/grants, traineeships, health care benefits, tuition waivers (full), and unspecified assistantships also available. Support available to part-time students. *Faculty research:* Development economics, spatial econometrics, health economics, labor economics, energy economics, hydrogeology, geophysics, petrophysics, structural geology, mineralogy, petrology, geochemistry, multilingualism, comparative/world literature, translation studies, book histories/ cultures, biocatalysis, molecular recognition, photocatalysis, photophysical and biophysical chemistry, probe chemistry, machine learning, data science. *Unit head:* Dr. Nadia Maria El Cheikh, Dean, Faculty of Arts and Sciences, 961-1374374 Ext. 3800, Fax: 961-1744461, E-mail: nmcheikh@aub.edu.lb. *Application contact:* Dr. Salim Kanaan, Director, Admissions Office, 961-1350000 Ext. 2590, Fax: 961-1750775, E-mail: sk00@aub.edu.lb.
Website: http://www.aub.edu.lb/fas/

**Andrews University,** School of Graduate Studies, School of Education, Department of Graduate Psychology and Counseling, Program in Community Counseling, Berrien Springs, MI 49104. Offers clinical mental health counseling (MA); community counseling (MA). *Students:* 14 full-time (8 women), 6 part-time (4 women); includes 8 minority (5 Black or African American, non-Hispanic/Latino; 3 Hispanic/Latino), 4 international.

## Clinical Psychology

Average age 31. In 2016, 9 master's awarded. *Degree requirements:* For master's, thesis optional. *Entrance requirements:* For master's, GRE. Additional exam requirements/recommendations for international students: Required—TOEFL (minimum score 550 paper-based). Application fee: $40. *Unit head:* Dr. Nancy Carbonell, Coordinator, 269-471-3472. *Application contact:* Justina Clayburn, Supervisor of Graduate Admission, 800-253-2874, Fax: 269-471-6321, E-mail: graduate@andrews.edu.

**Antioch University Los Angeles,** Graduate Programs, Program in Psychology, Culver City, CA 90230. Offers clinical psychology (MA); psychology (MA). *Program availability:* Part-time. *Degree requirements:* For master's, thesis (for some programs), internship. *Entrance requirements:* For master's, interview. Additional exam requirements/recommendations for international students: Required—TOEFL. *Faculty research:* Creativity and humor, ethnic humor, adult development, Jungian theory, psychoanalytic theory.

**Antioch University New England,** Graduate School, Department of Applied Psychology, Program in Clinical Mental Health Counseling, Keene, NH 03431-3552. Offers clinical mental health counseling (MA); substance abuse counseling (MA). *Accreditation:* ACA. *Degree requirements:* For master's, internship, practicum. *Entrance requirements:* For master's, previous course work and work experience in psychology. Additional exam requirements/recommendations for international students: Required—TOEFL (minimum score 550 paper-based). Electronic applications accepted. *Expenses:* Contact institution. *Faculty research:* Multicultural issues in field supervision.

**Antioch University New England,** Graduate School, Department of Clinical Psychology, Keene, NH 03431-3552. Offers Psy D. *Accreditation:* APA. *Degree requirements:* For doctorate, thesis/dissertation, internship, practicum. *Entrance requirements:* For doctorate, GRE General Test, GRE Subject Test, previous course work in psychology, work sample. Additional exam requirements/recommendations for international students: Required—TOEFL (minimum score 550 paper-based). *Expenses:* Contact institution. *Faculty research:* Psychotherapy outcome and process in private practice, neuropsychiatric evaluations, effects of trauma on adults, supervision, clinical training evaluation.

**Antioch University Santa Barbara,** Program in Clinical Psychology, Santa Barbara, CA 93101-1581. Offers MA, Psy D. *Entrance requirements:* Additional exam requirements/recommendations for international students: Required—TOEFL (minimum score 550 paper-based). Electronic applications accepted.

**Appalachian State University,** Cratis D. Williams Graduate School, Department of Human Development and Psychological Counseling, Boone, NC 28608. Offers clinical mental health counseling (MA); college student development (MA); marriage and family therapy (MA); school counseling (MA). *Accreditation:* AAMFT/COAMFTE; ACA; NCATE. *Program availability:* Part-time. *Degree requirements:* For master's, comprehensive exam (for some programs), thesis optional, internships. *Entrance requirements:* For master's, GRE General Test, 3 letters of recommendation. Additional exam requirements/recommendations for international students: Required—TOEFL (minimum score 570 paper-based; 79 iBT), IELTS (minimum score 6.5). *Application deadline:* For fall admission, 2/1 priority date for domestic students, 2/1 for international students; for spring admission, 2/1 for international students. Applications are processed on a rolling basis. Application fee: $55. Electronic applications accepted. *Expenses:* Tuition, state resident: full-time $4744. Tuition, nonresident: full-time $17,913. Full-time tuition and fees vary according to program. *Financial support:* Fellowships, research assistantships, teaching assistantships, career-related internships or fieldwork, Federal Work-Study, scholarships/grants, and unspecified assistantships available. Financial award application deadline: 4/1; financial award applicants required to submit FAFSA. *Faculty research:* Multicultural counseling, addictions counseling, play therapy, expressive arts, child and adolescent therapy, sexual abuse counseling. *Unit head:* Dr. Lee Baruth, Chairman, 828-262-2055, E-mail: baruthlg@appstate.edu. *Application contact:* Dr. Mark Schwarze, Program Director, 828-262-6046, E-mail: asucmhc@appstate.edu.
Website: http://www.ced.appstate.edu/departments/hpc

**Appalachian State University,** Cratis D. Williams Graduate School, Department of Psychology, Boone, NC 28608. Offers clinical health psychology (MA). *Program availability:* Part-time. *Degree requirements:* For master's, comprehensive exam, thesis optional, exit exam. *Entrance requirements:* For master's, GRE General Test, 3 letters of recommendation. Additional exam requirements/recommendations for international students: Required—TOEFL (minimum score 550 paper-based; 79 iBT) or IELTS (minimum score 6.5). *Application deadline:* For fall admission, 2/15 for domestic students, 2/1 for international students. Applications are processed on a rolling basis. Application fee: $55. Electronic applications accepted. *Expenses:* Tuition, state resident: full-time $4744. Tuition, nonresident: full-time $17,913. Full-time tuition and fees vary according to program. *Financial support:* Fellowships, research assistantships, teaching assistantships, career-related internships or fieldwork, Federal Work-Study, scholarships/grants, and unspecified assistantships available. Financial award application deadline: 4/1; financial award applicants required to submit FAFSA. *Faculty research:* Eating disorders, school-based consultations, organizational behavior management, brain mechanisms of sound localization, parenting styles. *Unit head:* Dr. James Denniston, Chair, 828-262-2272, Fax: 828-262-2272, E-mail: dennistonjc@appstate.edu. *Application contact:* Dr. Twila Wingrove, Program Director, 828-262-2272 Ext. 440, E-mail: wingroveta@appstate.edu.
Website: http://www.psych.appstate.edu/

**Argosy University, Atlanta,** Georgia School of Professional Psychology, Atlanta, GA 30328. Offers clinical psychology (MA, Psy D, Postdoctoral Respecialization Certificate), including child and family psychology (Psy D), general adult clinical (Psy D), health psychology (Psy D), neuropsychology/geropsychology (Psy D); community counseling (MA), including marriage and family therapy; counselor education and supervision (Ed D); forensic psychology (MA); industrial organizational psychology (MA); marriage and family therapy (Certificate); sport-exercise psychology (MA). *Accreditation:* APA.

**Argosy University, Chicago,** Illinois School of Professional Psychology, Doctoral Program in Clinical Psychology, Chicago, IL 60601. Offers child and adolescent psychology (Psy D); client-centered and experiential psychotherapies (Psy D); diversity and multicultural psychology (Psy D); family psychology (Psy D); forensic psychology (Psy D); health psychology (Psy D); neuropsychology (Psy D); organizational consulting (Psy D); psychoanalytic psychology (Psy D); psychology and spirituality (Psy D). *Accreditation:* APA.

**Argosy University, Chicago,** Illinois School of Professional Psychology, Master's Program in Clinical Psychology, Chicago, IL 60601. Offers MA.

**Argosy University, Dallas,** College of Psychology and Behavioral Sciences, Program in Clinical Psychology, Farmers Branch, TX 75244. Offers MA, Psy D.

**Argosy University, Denver,** College of Psychology and Behavioral Sciences, Denver, CO 80231. Offers clinical mental health counseling (MA); clinical psychology (MA, Psy D); counseling psychology (Ed D); counselor education and supervision (Ed D); forensic psychology (MA); industrial organizational psychology (MA); marriage and family therapy (MA, DMFT).

**Argosy University, Hawai`i,** Hawai'i School of Professional Psychology, Program in Clinical Psychology, Honolulu, HI 96813. Offers clinical psychology (MA, Psy D, Postdoctoral Respecialization Certificate), including child and family clinical practice (Psy D), diversity in clinical practice (Psy D). *Accreditation:* APA.

**Argosy University, Inland Empire,** College of Psychology and Behavioral Sciences, Ontario, CA 91761. Offers clinical psychology/marriage and family therapy (MA); counseling psychology (Ed D); counseling psychology/marriage and family therapy (MA); forensic psychology (MA); industrial organizational psychology (MA); sport-exercise psychology (MA).

**Argosy University, Los Angeles,** College of Psychology and Behavioral Sciences, Santa Monica, CA 90045. Offers clinical psychology/marriage and family therapy (MA); counseling psychology (Ed D); counseling psychology/marriage and family therapy (MA); forensic psychology (MA).

**Argosy University, Northern Virginia,** American School of Professional Psychology, Arlington, VA 22209. Offers clinical psychology (MA, Psy D), including child and family psychology (Psy D), diversity and multicultural psychology (Psy D), forensic psychology (Psy D), health and neuropsychology (Psy D); community counseling (MA); counseling psychology (Ed D), including counselor education and supervision; counselor education and supervision (Ed D); forensic psychology (MA).

**Argosy University, Orange County,** American School of Professional Psychology, Program in Clinical Psychology, Orange, CA 92868. Offers child and adolescent psychology (Psy D); forensic psychology (Psy D); marriage and family therapy (MA).

**Argosy University, Phoenix,** Arizona School of Professional Psychology, Program in Clinical Psychology, Phoenix, AZ 85021. Offers clinical psychology (MA); neuropsychology (Psy D); sports-exercise psychology (Psy D).

**Argosy University, San Diego,** College of Psychology and Behavioral Sciences, San Diego, CA 92108. Offers clinical psychology/marriage and family therapy (MA); counseling psychology (Ed D); counseling psychology/marriage and family therapy (MA); forensic psychology (MA).

**Argosy University, San Francisco Bay Area,** American School of Professional Psychology, Alameda, CA 94501. Offers clinical psychology (MA, Psy D); counseling psychology (MA, Ed D); forensic psychology (MA); sport-exercise psychology (MA). *Accreditation:* APA (one or more programs are accredited).

**Argosy University, Schaumburg,** Illinois School of Professional Psychology, Schaumburg, IL 60173-5403. Offers clinical psychology (MA, Psy D).

**Argosy University, Seattle,** College of Psychology and Behavioral Sciences, Program in Clinical Psychology, Seattle, WA 98121. Offers MA, Psy D, Postdoctoral Respecialization Certificate.

**Argosy University, Tampa,** Florida School of Professional Psychology, Program in Clinical Psychology, Tampa, FL 33607. Offers clinical psychology (MA, Psy D), including child and adolescent psychology (Psy D), geropsychology (Psy D), marriage/couples and family therapy (Psy D), neuropsychology (Psy D). *Accreditation:* APA.

**Argosy University, Twin Cities,** Minnesota School of Professional Psychology, Eagan, MN 55121. Offers clinical psychology (MA, Psy D), including child and family psychology (Psy D), forensic psychology (Psy D), health and neuropsychology (Psy D), trauma (Psy D); forensic counseling (Post-Graduate Certificate); forensic psychology (MA); industrial organizational psychology (MA); marriage and family therapy (MA, DMFT), including forensic counseling (MA). *Accreditation:* AAMFT; AAMFT/COAMFTE; APA.

**Arizona State University at the Tempe campus,** College of Liberal Arts and Sciences, Department of Psychology, Tempe, AZ 85287-1104. Offers applied behavior analysis (MS); behavioral neuroscience (PhD); clinical psychology (PhD); cognitive science (PhD); developmental psychology (PhD); quantitative psychology (PhD); social psychology (PhD). *Accreditation:* APA. *Degree requirements:* For doctorate, comprehensive exam, thesis/dissertation, interactive Program of Study (iPOS) submitted before completing 50 percent of required credit hours. *Entrance requirements:* For doctorate, GRE General Test, GRE Subject Test, minimum GPA of 3.0 or equivalent in last 2 years of work leading to bachelor's degree. Additional exam requirements/recommendations for international students: Required—TOEFL, IELTS, or PTE. Electronic applications accepted.

**Arkansas State University,** Graduate School, College of Education and Behavioral Science, Department of Psychology and Counseling, State University, AR 72467. Offers clinical mental health counseling (Graduate Certificate); college student personnel services (MS); dyslexia therapy (Graduate Certificate); psychological science (MS); psychology and counseling (Ed S); rehabilitation counseling (MRC); school counseling (MSE); student affairs (Graduate Certificate). *Accreditation:* ACA (one or more programs are accredited); CORE (one or more programs are accredited); NCATE. *Program availability:* Part-time. *Degree requirements:* For master's and other advanced degree, comprehensive exam, thesis or alternative. *Entrance requirements:* For master's, GRE General Test or MAT (for MSE), appropriate bachelor's degree, interview, letters of reference, official transcripts, immunization records, written statement, 2-3 page autobiography; for other advanced degree, GRE General Test, interview, master's degree, letters of reference, official transcript, personal statement, immunization records. Additional exam requirements/recommendations for international students: Required—TOEFL (minimum score 550 paper-based; 79 iBT), IELTS (minimum score 6), PTE (minimum score 56). Electronic applications accepted.

**Ashland Theological Seminary,** Graduate Programs, Ashland, OH 44805. Offers Biblical studies (MA); Christian ministries (MACM), including Black church studies (MACM, D Min), general Christian ministries, leadership, spiritual formation (MACM, D Min); clinical mental health counseling (MA); counseling (MAC); historical and theological studies (MA), including Anabaptism and Pietism, Christian theology, church history, New Testament, Old Testament; ministry (D Min), including Black church studies (MACM, D Min), chaplaincy (M Div, D Min), independent design, spiritual formation (MACM, D Min), transformational leadership; pastoral ministry (M Div), including chaplaincy (M Div, D Min), general ministry. MAC program offered in Detroit, MI. *Accreditation:* ATS. *Program availability:* Part-time. *Degree requirements:* For master's, 2 foreign languages, comprehensive exam (for some programs), thesis (for some programs); for doctorate, thesis/dissertation. *Entrance requirements:* For master's, bachelor's degree from accredited institution with a minimum undergraduate GPA of 2.75; for doctorate, M Div, minimum undergraduate GPA of 3.0. Additional exam requirements/recommendations for international students: Required—TOEFL (minimum score 500 paper-based; 65 iBT). *Application deadline:* For fall admission, 8/30 for domestic students. Applications are processed on a rolling basis. Application fee: $35. Electronic applications accepted. *Expenses: Tuition:* Full-time $15,120; part-time $630 per semester hour. Tuition and fees vary according to program. *Financial support:* Research assistantships, teaching assistantships, career-related internships or fieldwork, institutionally sponsored loans, scholarships/grants, and unspecified assistantships available. Support available to part-time students. Financial award application deadline: 5/15; financial award applicants required to submit FAFSA. *Faculty research:* Semitic languages and linguistics, rhetorical and social-scientific criticism, Anabaptist studies, inner spiritual healing, African-American clergy in film and literature.

*Unit head:* Dr. Mark Harden, President, 419-289-5160, Fax: 419-289-5969, E-mail: mharden@ashland.edu. *Application contact:* Dr. Mark Harden, President, 419-289-5160, Fax: 419-289-5969, E-mail: mharden@ashland.edu.

**Auburn University at Montgomery,** College of Arts and Sciences, Department of Psychology, Montgomery, AL 36124-4023. Offers clinical psychology (MS). *Program availability:* Part-time, evening/weekend. *Degree requirements:* For master's, comprehensive exam, thesis optional. *Entrance requirements:* For master's, GRE General Test or MAT. Electronic applications accepted. *Faculty research:* Community service, diagnosis, behavior modification.

**Austin Peay State University,** College of Graduate Studies, College of Behavioral and Health Sciences, Department of Psychology, Clarksville, TN 37044. Offers industrial-organizational psychology (MS); mental health counseling (MS), including clinical mental health, school counseling; school counseling (MS). *Program availability:* Part-time, online learning. *Faculty:* 9 full-time (6 women), 2 part-time/adjunct (1 woman). *Students:* 49 full-time (41 women), 18 part-time (12 women); includes 17 minority (13 Black or African American, non-Hispanic/Latino; 2 Hispanic/Latino; 2 Two or more races, non-Hispanic/Latino), 1 international. Average age 30. 59 applicants, 59% accepted, 21 enrolled. In 2016, 25 master's awarded. *Degree requirements:* For master's, comprehensive exam, thesis (for some programs). *Entrance requirements:* For master's, GRE General Test, minimum undergraduate GPA of 2.5, 3 letters of recommendation, bachelor's degree. Additional exam requirements/recommendations for international students: Required—TOEFL (minimum score 500 paper-based). *Application deadline:* For fall admission, 8/9 priority date for domestic students. Applications are processed on a rolling basis. Application fee: $45 ($50 for international students). Electronic applications accepted. *Expenses:* Tuition, state resident: full-time $8300; part-time $415 per credit hour. Tuition, nonresident: full-time $22,280; part-time $1114 per credit hour. *Required fees:* $1473; $73.65 per credit hour. *Financial support:* Research assistantships with full tuition reimbursements, career-related internships or fieldwork, Federal Work-Study, institutionally sponsored loans, scholarships/grants, and unspecified assistantships available. Support available to part-time students. Financial award application deadline: 4/1; financial award applicants required to submit FAFSA. *Unit head:* Dr. Nicole Knickmeyer, Chair, 931-221-7232, Fax: 931-221-6267, E-mail: knickmeyer@apsu.edu. *Application contact:* Brad Averitt, Coordinator of Graduate Admissions, 800-859-4723, Fax: 931-221-7641, E-mail: gradadmissions@apsu.edu. Website: http://www.apsu.edu/psychology

**Azusa Pacific University,** School of Behavioral and Applied Sciences, Department of Graduate Psychology, Azusa, CA 91702-7000. Offers clinical psychology (MA, Psy D), including family therapy (MA). *Accreditation:* APA (one or more programs are accredited). *Program availability:* Part-time, evening/weekend. *Degree requirements:* For master's, comprehensive exam, 250 hours of clinical experience, individual and group therapy. *Entrance requirements:* For master's, interview, minimum GPA of 3.0, Minnesota Multiphasic Personality Inventory. Additional exam requirements/recommendations for international students: Required—TOEFL (minimum score 600 paper-based).

**Ball State University,** Graduate School, College of Sciences and Humanities, Department of Psychological Science, Program in Clinical Psychology, Muncie, IN 47306. Offers MA. *Entrance requirements:* For master's, GRE General Test, minimum baccalaureate GPA of 2.75 or 3.0 in latter half of baccalaureate, goals statements, curriculum vitae, letters of recommendation. Additional exam requirements/recommendations for international students: Required—TOEFL (minimum score 550 paper-based; 79 iBT), IELTS (minimum score 6.5). Electronic applications accepted.

**Ball State University,** Graduate School, Teachers College, Department of Counseling Psychology and Guidance Services, Program in Counseling Psychology, Muncie, IN 47306. Offers counseling (MA), including clinical mental health counseling, mental health counseling, rehabilitation counseling, school counseling; counseling psychology (PhD). *Accreditation:* ACA; APA. *Program availability:* Part-time. *Degree requirements:* For doctorate, thesis/dissertation. *Entrance requirements:* For master's, GRE General Test (minimum scores 144 quantitative, 153 verbal), minimum baccalaureate GPA of 2.75 or 3.0 in latter half of baccalauareate, minimum GPA of 3.0 in psychology coursework, three letters of recommendation; for doctorate, GRE General Test, interview, minimum graduate GPA of 3.2, resume. Additional exam requirements/recommendations for international students: Required—TOEFL (minimum score 550 paper-based; 79 iBT), IELTS (minimum score 6.5). Electronic applications accepted.

**Ball State University,** Graduate School, Teachers College, Department of Counseling Psychology and Guidance Services, Program in Social Psychology, Muncie, IN 47306. Offers social psychology (MA); social psychology and clinical mental health counseling (MA). *Entrance requirements:* For master's, GRE General Test (minimum scores 144 quantitative, 153 verbal), minimum baccalaureate GPA of 2.75 or 3.0 in latter half of baccalauareate, minimum GPA of 3.0 in psychology coursework, three letters of recommendation. Additional exam requirements/recommendations for international students: Required—TOEFL (minimum score 550 paper-based; 79 iBT), IELTS (minimum score 6.5). Electronic applications accepted.

**Barry University,** College of Arts and Sciences, Department of Psychology, Miami Shores, FL 33161-6695. Offers clinical psychology (MS); school psychology (MS, SSP). *Program availability:* Part-time, evening/weekend. *Degree requirements:* For master's, thesis, practicum. *Entrance requirements:* For master's, GRE General Test, minimum GPA of 3.0, course work in psychology. Electronic applications accepted. *Faculty research:* Closed head injury, memory and aging, infant/mother interaction, evolutionary aspects of behavior, gender roles.

**Baylor University,** Graduate School, College of Arts and Sciences, Department of Psychology and Neuroscience, Program in Clinical Psychology, Waco, TX 76798. Offers Psy D. *Accreditation:* APA. *Faculty:* 13 full-time (4 women), 5 part-time/adjunct (2 women). *Students:* 34 full-time (30 women); includes 7 minority (2 Asian, non-Hispanic/Latino; 1 Hispanic/Latino; 4 Two or more races, non-Hispanic/Latino), 1 international. 251 applicants, 3% accepted, 7 enrolled. In 2016, 3 doctorates awarded. *Degree requirements:* For doctorate, comprehensive exam, thesis/dissertation, year-long internship at APA-accredited internship site. *Entrance requirements:* For doctorate, GRE General Test, in-person interview. Additional exam requirements/recommendations for international students: Required—TOEFL. *Application deadline:* For fall admission, 12/1 for domestic and international students. Application fee: $50. Electronic applications accepted. *Expenses: Tuition:* Full-time $28,494; part-time $1583 per credit hour. *Required fees:* $167 per credit hour. Tuition and fees vary according to course load and program. *Financial support:* In 2016–17, 32 students received support, including 6 research assistantships with full tuition reimbursements available (averaging $19,000 per year); career-related internships or fieldwork, institutionally sponsored loans, tuition waivers (full), and practicum stipends also available. Financial award application deadline: 12/1; financial award applicants required to submit FAFSA. *Faculty research:* Hypnosis/behavioral medicine, drug and alcohol, pediatric psychology, marital communication, religion and mental health. *Total annual research expenditures:* $700,000. *Unit head:* Dr. Sara Dolan, Graduate Program Director, 254-710-2573, Fax: 254-710-3033, E-mail: sara_dolan@baylor.edu. *Application contact:* Laura Sumrall, Graduate Studies Coordinator, 254-710-2961, Fax: 254-710-3033, E-mail: laura_sumrall@baylor.edu.
Website: http://www.baylor.edu/psychologyneuroscience/index.php?id-72649

**Bay Path University,** Program in Clinical Mental Health Counseling, Longmeadow, MA 01106-2292. Offers clinical mental health counseling (MS), including alcohol and drug abuse counseling, early intervention. Program also offered in Sturbridge and Burlington, MA. *Program availability:* Part-time, blended/hybrid learning. *Students:* 85 full-time (78 women), 83 part-time (76 women); includes 43 minority (19 Black or African American, non-Hispanic/Latino; 1 Asian, non-Hispanic/Latino; 17 Hispanic/Latino; 6 Two or more races, non-Hispanic/Latino), 16 international. Average age 31. 75 applicants, 72% accepted, 40 enrolled. In 2016, 21 master's awarded. *Degree requirements:* For master's, 48 course credits plus 12 credit practicum, internship. *Application deadline:* Applications are processed on a rolling basis. Application fee: $45. Electronic applications accepted. Application fee is waived when completed online. *Expenses:* $21,465. *Financial support:* Unspecified assistantships available. Financial award applicants required to submit FAFSA. *Unit head:* Dr. Mark Benander, Director, 413-565-1332, E-mail: mbenander@baypath.edu. *Application contact:* Diane Ranaldi, Dean of Graduate Admissions, 413-565-1332, Fax: 413-565-1250, E-mail: dranaldi@baypath.edu.
Website: http://graduate.baypath.edu/graduate-programs/programs-on-campus/ms-programs/clinical-mental-health

**Benedictine University,** Graduate Programs, Program in Clinical Psychology, Lisle, IL 60532. Offers MS. *Program availability:* Part-time. *Students:* 31. 47 applicants, 53% accepted, 18 enrolled. In 2016, 14 master's awarded. *Degree requirements:* For master's, comprehensive exam, internship. *Entrance requirements:* For master's, MAT. Additional exam requirements/recommendations for international students: Required—TOEFL (minimum score 550 paper-based). *Application deadline:* For fall admission, 9/1 for domestic students; for winter admission, 12/1 for domestic students; for spring admission, 2/15 for domestic students. Applications are processed on a rolling basis. Application fee: $40. Electronic applications accepted. *Expenses: Tuition:* Full-time $15,600; part-time $650 per hour. *Required fees:* $300. One-time fee: $125 part-time. Tuition and fees vary according to class time, course load, campus/location and program. *Financial support:* Career-related internships or fieldwork and health care benefits available. Support available to part-time students. *Unit head:* Dr. James Crissmon, Director, 630-829-6490, E-mail: jcrissmon@ben.edu. *Application contact:* Kari Gibbons, Associate Vice President, Enrollment Center, 630-829-6200, Fax: 630-829-6584, E-mail: kgibbons@ben.edu.

**Bethel Seminary,** Graduate and Professional Programs, St. Paul, MN 55112-6998. Offers Anglican studies (Certificate); children's and family ministry (MA); Christian studies (Certificate); Christian thought (MA); church planting (Certificate); Greek and Hebrew language (M Div); Greek language (M Div); Hebrew language (M Div); marriage and family therapy (MA, Certificate); mental health counseling (MA); ministry (MA, D Min); ministry practice (Certificate); theological studies (MA, Certificate); transformational leadership (MA); young life youth ministry (Certificate). *Accreditation:* ACIPE. *Program availability:* Part-time, evening/weekend, blended/hybrid learning. *Faculty:* 14 full-time (4 women), 37 part-time/adjunct (17 women). *Students:* 369 full-time (165 women), 147 part-time (43 women); includes 138 minority (48 Black or African American, non-Hispanic/Latino; 45 Asian, non-Hispanic/Latino; 28 Hispanic/Latino; 2 Native Hawaiian or other Pacific Islander, non-Hispanic/Latino; 15 Two or more races, non-Hispanic/Latino), 15 international. 322 applicants, 75% accepted, 174 enrolled. In 2016, 168 master's, 24 doctorates, 6 other advanced degrees awarded. *Degree requirements:* For master's, variable foreign language requirement, thesis (for some programs); for doctorate, thesis/dissertation. *Entrance requirements:* For master's, letters of reference, transcripts, personal statement; for doctorate, M Div, letters of reference, organizational support; for Certificate, letters of reference, family essay, personal statement, and family of origin paper (for marriage and family therapy). Additional exam requirements/recommendations for international students: Required—TOEFL (minimum score 550 paper-based; 87 iBT). *Application deadline:* For fall admission, 8/1 priority date for domestic students, 8/1 for international students; for winter admission, 12/1 priority date for domestic students; for spring admission, 1/1 priority date for domestic students. Applications are processed on a rolling basis. Application fee: $0. Electronic applications accepted. *Expenses:* Contact institution. *Financial support:* In 2016–17, 404 students received support. Teaching assistantships, career-related internships or fieldwork, Federal Work-Study, and scholarships/grants available. Financial award applicants required to submit FAFSA. *Faculty research:* Nature of theology, ethics, Biblical commentaries, nature of God, science and theology. *Unit head:* Dr. David Clark, Vice-President and Dean, 651-638-6659, E-mail: d-clark@bethel.edu. *Application contact:* Jen Niska, Director of Admissions, 651-638-6288, Fax: 651-638-6002, E-mail: seminary-admissions@bethel.edu.
Website: https://www.bethel.edu/seminary

**Binghamton University, State University of New York,** Graduate School, Harpur College of Arts and Sciences, Department of Psychology, Specialization in Clinical Psychology, Binghamton, NY 13902-6000. Offers PhD. *Accreditation:* APA. *Program availability:* Part-time. *Students:* 17 full-time (13 women), 20 part-time (13 women); includes 3 minority (1 Black or African American, non-Hispanic/Latino; 1 Asian, non-Hispanic/Latino; 1 Hispanic/Latino), 1 international. Average age 28. 116 applicants, 9% accepted, 6 enrolled. In 2016, 5 master's awarded. Terminal master's awarded for partial completion of doctoral program. *Degree requirements:* For doctorate, comprehensive exam, thesis/dissertation. *Entrance requirements:* For doctorate, GRE General Test. Additional exam requirements/recommendations for international students: Required—TOEFL (minimum score 550 paper-based; 80 iBT). *Application deadline:* For fall admission, 12/1 priority date for domestic and international students. Application fee: $75. Electronic applications accepted. *Financial support:* In 2016–17, 23 students received support, including 9 research assistantships with full tuition reimbursements available (averaging $17,500 per year), 13 teaching assistantships with full tuition reimbursements available (averaging $17,500 per year); career-related internships or fieldwork, Federal Work-Study, institutionally sponsored loans, scholarships/grants, traineeships, health care benefits, tuition waivers (full and partial), and unspecified assistantships also available. Financial award applicants required to submit FAFSA. *Unit head:* Dr. Brandon E. Gibb, Program Coordinator, 607-777-2511, E-mail: bgibb@binghamton.edu. *Application contact:* Ben Balkaya, Assistant Dean and Director, 607-777-2151, Fax: 607-777-2501, E-mail: balkaya@binghamton.edu.

**Biola University,** Rosemead School of Psychology, La Mirada, CA 90639-0001. Offers clinical psychology (PhD, Psy D). *Accreditation:* APA. *Degree requirements:* For doctorate, comprehensive exam, thesis/dissertation. *Entrance requirements:* For doctorate, GRE General Test, interview, 30 undergraduate semester hours of credits in psychology, minimum GPA of 3.0. Additional exam requirements/recommendations for international students: Required—TOEFL (minimum score 600 paper-based; 100 iBT). Electronic applications accepted. *Expenses:* Contact institution. *Faculty research:* Integration of psychology and theology, psychology of child/adolescent, psychology of marriage, psychology of gender, psychology of trauma, psychology of forensics, multicultural studies and mental health.

**Bowling Green State University,** Graduate College, College of Arts and Sciences, Department of Psychology, Bowling Green, OH 43403. Offers clinical psychology (MA,

## Clinical Psychology

PhD); developmental psychology (MA, PhD); experimental psychology (MA, PhD); industrial/organizational psychology (MA, PhD); quantitative psychology (MA, PhD). *Accreditation:* APA (one or more programs are accredited). *Degree requirements:* For doctorate, thesis/dissertation. *Entrance requirements:* For doctorate, GRE General Test, GRE Subject Test. Additional exam requirements/recommendations for international students: Required—TOEFL. *Application deadline:* For fall admission, 1/1 for domestic students. Application fee: $30. Electronic applications accepted. *Financial support:* Fellowships with full tuition reimbursements, research assistantships with full tuition reimbursements, teaching assistantships with full tuition reimbursements, career-related internships or fieldwork, Federal Work-Study, institutionally sponsored loans, tuition waivers (full), and unspecified assistantships available. Financial award applicants required to submit FAFSA. *Faculty research:* Personnel psychology, developmental-mathematical models, behavioral medication, brain process, child/adolescent social cognition. *Unit head:* Dr. Mike Zickar, Chair, 419-372-2301, E-mail: mzickar@bgsu.edu. *Application contact:* Dr. Terry L. Lawrence, Assistant Dean for Graduate Admissions and Studies, 419-372-7713, Fax: 419-372-8569, E-mail: tlawren@bgnet.bgsu.edu.

**Bowling Green State University,** Graduate College, College of Education and Human Development, School of Intervention Services, Program in Clinical Mental Health Counseling, Bowling Green, OH 43403. Offers clinical mental health counseling (MA); school counseling (M Ed). *Accreditation:* ACA; NCATE. *Program availability:* Part-time. *Students:* 37 full-time (30 women), 24 part-time (18 women); includes 11 minority (7 Black or African American, non-Hispanic/Latino; 4 Hispanic/Latino), 1 international. Average age 30. 44 applicants, 64% accepted, 14 enrolled. In 2016, 34 degrees awarded. *Degree requirements:* For master's, thesis or alternative. *Entrance requirements:* For master's, GRE General Test. Additional exam requirements/recommendations for international students: Required—TOEFL. *Application deadline:* For fall admission, 3/1 priority date for domestic students. Applications are processed on a rolling basis. Application fee: $30. Electronic applications accepted. *Financial support:* In 2016–17, 15 research assistantships with full tuition reimbursements (averaging $5,323 per year) were awarded; teaching assistantships with full tuition reimbursements, career-related internships or fieldwork, and unspecified assistantships also available. Financial award applicants required to submit FAFSA. *Faculty research:* Perfectionism, multicultural counseling, suicide, ethics and legal issues related to counseling, play therapy. *Application contact:* Dr. Greg Garske, Graduate Coordinator, 415-372-7319.

**Bradley University,** The Graduate School, College of Education and Health Sciences, Department of Leadership in Education, Nonprofits and Counseling, Peoria, IL 61625-0002. Offers counseling (MA), including clinical mental health counseling, professional school counseling; leadership in educational administration (MA); nonprofit leadership (MA). *Accreditation:* ACA; NCATE. *Program availability:* Part-time, evening/weekend. *Degree requirements:* For master's, comprehensive exam, thesis optional. *Entrance requirements:* For master's, GRE General Test or MAT, interview, 3 letters of recommendation. Additional exam requirements/recommendations for international students: Required—TOEFL (minimum score 550 paper-based; 79 iBT), IELTS (minimum score 6.5). *Application deadline:* For fall admission, 5/15 priority date for domestic and international students; for spring admission, 10/15 priority date for domestic and international students. Applications are processed on a rolling basis. Application fee: $40 ($50 for international students). Electronic applications accepted. *Expenses:* Tuition: Full-time $7650; part-time $850 per credit. *Required fees:* $50 per credit. One-time fee: $100 full-time. *Financial support:* Research assistantships with full and partial tuition reimbursements, career-related internships or fieldwork, scholarships/grants, tuition waivers (partial), and unspecified assistantships available. Support available to part-time students. Financial award application deadline: 4/1. *Unit head:* Jenny Tripses, Interim Chair, 309-677-3593, E-mail: jtripses@bradley.edu. *Application contact:* Kayla Carroll, Director of International Admissions and Student Services, 309-677-2375, E-mail: klcarroll@fsmail.bradley.edu.
Website: http://www.bradley.edu/academic/departments/lenc/

**Brigham Young University,** Graduate Studies, College of Family, Home, and Social Sciences, Department of Psychology, Provo, UT 84602. Offers applied social psychology (PhD); clinical psychology (PhD); cognitive and behavioral neuroscience (PhD); developmental psychology (PhD). *Accreditation:* APA. *Faculty:* 29 full-time (7 women), 8 part-time/adjunct (2 women). *Students:* 59 full-time (34 women); includes 9 minority (2 Black or African American, non-Hispanic/Latino; 4 Asian, non-Hispanic/Latino; 2 Hispanic/Latino; 1 Native Hawaiian or other Pacific Islander, non-Hispanic/Latino). Average age 29. 49 applicants, 33% accepted, 11 enrolled. In 2016, 12 doctorates awarded. *Degree requirements:* For doctorate, comprehensive exam (for some programs), thesis/dissertation, publishable paper. *Entrance requirements:* For doctorate, GRE General Test, minimum GPA of 3.0. Additional exam requirements/recommendations for international students: Required—TOEFL (minimum score 580 paper-based; 85 iBT). *Application deadline:* For fall admission, 12/1 for domestic and international students. Application fee: $50. Electronic applications accepted. *Expenses:* Contact institution. *Financial support:* In 2016–17, 41 students received support, including 32 research assistantships with partial tuition reimbursements available (averaging $12,000 per year), 5 teaching assistantships with partial tuition reimbursements available (averaging $12,000 per year); career-related internships or fieldwork, scholarships/grants, tuition waivers (partial), and unspecified assistantships also available. Financial award application deadline: 5/31. *Faculty research:* Psychotherapy process, Alzheimer's disease/dementia, psychology and law, health, psychology, developmental. *Total annual research expenditures:* $73,281. *Unit head:* Dr. Dawson Hedges, Chair, 801-422-6357, Fax: 801-422-0602, E-mail: dawson_hedges@byu.edu. *Application contact:* Leesa D. Scott, Coordinator of Student Programs, 801-422-4560, Fax: 801-422-0602, E-mail: leesa_scott@byu.edu.
Website: http://psychology.byu.edu/

**Butler University,** College of Education, Indianapolis, IN 46208-3485. Offers alternative special education licensure (Certificate); educational administration (MS); effective teaching and leadership (MS); international baccalaureate teaching and learning (Certificate); licensed mental health counselor (Certificate); school counseling (MS); teachers of the visually impaired (Certificate). *Accreditation:* ACA; NCATE. *Program availability:* Part-time. *Faculty:* 13 full-time (10 women), 5 part-time/adjunct (4 women). *Students:* 9 full-time (7 women), 119 part-time (85 women); includes 14 minority (10 Black or African American, non-Hispanic/Latino; 1 Asian, non-Hispanic/Latino; 2 Hispanic/Latino; 1 Two or more races, non-Hispanic/Latino). Average age 32. 79 applicants, 76% accepted, 63 enrolled. In 2016, 42 master's, 30 other advanced degrees awarded. *Entrance requirements:* For master's, GRE (minimum score 291) or MAT (minimum score 396) unless undergraduate GPA is a 3.0 or higher, two letters of recommendation, transcripts, interview, professional resume. Additional exam requirements/recommendations for international students: Required—TOEFL (minimum score 550 paper-based; 79 iBT), IELTS (minimum score 6). *Application deadline:* For fall admission, 2/1 for domestic and international students; for spring admission, 11/1 for domestic and international students; for summer admission, 4/1 for domestic and international students. Applications are processed on a rolling basis. Application fee: $0. Electronic applications accepted. *Expenses:* Contact institution. *Financial support:* In 2016–17, 60 students received support. Scholarships/grants and unspecified assistantships available. Financial award application deadline: 7/15; financial award applicants required to submit FAFSA. *Faculty research:* Principals role in school

improvement, leadership and school climate, retention of teachers in special education, the neuro-diversity brain, school counseling intervention. *Unit head:* Dr. Ena Shelley, Dean, 317-940-9752, Fax: 317-940-6481. *Application contact:* Diane Dubord, Graduate Student Services Specialist, 317-940-8100, Fax: 317-940-8250, E-mail: ddubord@butler.edu.
Website: https://www.butler.edu/coe/graduate-programs

**California Institute of Integral Studies,** School of Professional Psychology and Health, San Francisco, CA 94103. Offers clinical psychology (Psy D); community mental health (MA); drama therapy (MA); expressive arts therapy (MA); human sexuality (PhD); integral counseling psychology (MA); integrative health studies (MA); psychological studies (MA); somatic psychology (MA). *Program availability:* Part-time, evening/weekend, 100% online, blended/hybrid learning. *Students:* 526 full-time (408 women), 113 part-time (96 women); includes 173 minority (34 Black or African American, non-Hispanic/Latino; 5 American Indian or Alaska Native, non-Hispanic/Latino; 31 Asian, non-Hispanic/Latino; 58 Hispanic/Latino; 1 Native Hawaiian or other Pacific Islander, non-Hispanic/Latino; 44 Two or more races, non-Hispanic/Latino), 52 international. Average age 38. 319 applicants, 85% accepted, 164 enrolled. In 2016, 157 master's, 21 doctorates awarded. *Degree requirements:* For doctorate, comprehensive exam, thesis/dissertation. *Entrance requirements:* For master's, minimum GPA of 3.0, letters of recommendation, writing sample; for doctorate, GRE, MA in psychology or social work with appropriate practical experience for advanced standing, or BA with a minimum GPA of 3.1; letters of recommendation; writing sample. Additional exam requirements/recommendations for international students: Required—TOEFL. *Application deadline:* For fall admission, 2/1 priority date for domestic and international students; for spring admission, 10/15 priority date for domestic and international students. Applications are processed on a rolling basis. Application fee: $65. Electronic applications accepted. *Expenses:* Tuition: Full-time $19,728; part-time $1098 per semester hour. *Required fees:* $320; $320 per semester hour. *Financial support:* Research assistantships with tuition reimbursements, teaching assistantships with tuition reimbursements, career-related internships or fieldwork, Federal Work-Study, and scholarships/grants available. Support available to part-time students. Financial award application deadline: 4/15; financial award applicants required to submit FAFSA. *Faculty research:* Transpersonal psychology, somatic psychology, expressive arts therapy, drama therapy, community mental health, ecopsychology, integrative health, human sexuality. *Application contact:* Ellen Durst, Director of Admissions, 415-575-6100, Fax: 415-575-1268, E-mail: admissions@ciis.edu.

**California Lutheran University,** Graduate Studies, Department of Psychology, Thousand Oaks, CA 91360-2787. Offers clinical psychology (MS, Psy D); marital and family therapy (MS). *Accreditation:* APA. *Program availability:* Part-time. *Faculty:* 11 full-time (6 women), 15 part-time/adjunct (13 women). *Students:* 133 full-time (109 women), 37 part-time (32 women); includes 63 minority (2 Black or African American, non-Hispanic/Latino; 2 American Indian or Alaska Native, non-Hispanic/Latino; 4 Asian, non-Hispanic/Latino; 30 Hispanic/Latino; 25 Two or more races, non-Hispanic/Latino), 9 international. Average age 30. 234 applicants, 50% accepted, 73 enrolled. In 2016, 60 master's, 7 doctorates awarded. *Degree requirements:* For master's, thesis or comprehensive exams; for doctorate, thesis/dissertation, internship. *Entrance requirements:* For master's, GRE General Test, interview, minimum GPA of 3.0; for doctorate, GRE General Test. *Application deadline:* For fall admission, 12/1 priority date for domestic and international students. Applications are processed on a rolling basis. Application fee: $50. Electronic applications accepted. *Unit head:* Dr. Richard Holigrock, Dean, 805-493-3723. *Application contact:* 805-493-3325, Fax: 805-493-3861, E-mail: clugrad@callutheran.edu.

**California State University, Dominguez Hills,** College of Natural and Behavioral Sciences, Department of Psychology, Carson, CA 90747-0001. Offers clinical psychology (MA); health psychology (MA). *Program availability:* Part-time, evening/weekend. Terminal master's awarded for partial completion of doctoral program. *Degree requirements:* For master's, comprehensive exam, thesis optional. *Entrance requirements:* For master's, GRE General Test or MAT, interview, minimum GPA of 3.0, prerequisite psychology courses. Additional exam requirements/recommendations for international students: Required—TOEFL (minimum score 550 paper-based). Electronic applications accepted. *Faculty research:* Culture and health, neuropsychology and HIV, psychohistory of the Holocaust, community and adolescents, malingering.

**California State University, Fullerton,** Graduate Studies, College of Humanities and Social Sciences, Department of Psychology, Fullerton, CA 92834-9480. Offers clinical psychology (MS); psychology (MA). *Program availability:* Part-time. *Degree requirements:* For master's, thesis. *Entrance requirements:* For master's, GRE General Test, GRE Subject Test, undergraduate major in psychology or related field. Application fee: $55. *Expenses:* Tuition, state resident: full-time $3369; part-time $1953 per unit. Tuition, nonresident: full-time $3915; part-time $2499 per unit. Tuition and fees vary according to course load, degree level and program. *Financial support:* Career-related internships or fieldwork, Federal Work-Study, institutionally sponsored loans, and scholarships/grants available. Support available to part-time students. Financial award application deadline: 3/1; financial award applicants required to submit FAFSA. *Unit head:* Eriko Self, Chair, 657-278-3514, Fax: 657-278-7134. *Application contact:* Admissions/Applications, 657-278-2371.

**California State University, Northridge,** Graduate Studies, College of Social and Behavioral Sciences, Department of Psychology, Northridge, CA 91330. Offers clinical psychology (MA); general experimental psychology (MA). *Faculty:* 27 full-time (9 women), 32 part-time/adjunct (13 women). *Students:* 52 full-time (37 women), 6 part-time (4 women); includes 33 minority (2 Black or African American, non-Hispanic/Latino; 6 Asian, non-Hispanic/Latino; 24 Hispanic/Latino; 1 Two or more races, non-Hispanic/Latino), 2 international. Average age 25. 275 applicants, 23% accepted, 27 enrolled. *Degree requirements:* For master's, thesis. *Entrance requirements:* For master's, GRE General Test, GRE Subject Test, minimum GPA of 3.0, letters of recommendation. Additional exam requirements/recommendations for international students: Required—TOEFL. *Application deadline:* For fall admission, 11/30 for domestic students. Application fee: $55. *Expenses:* Tuition, state resident: full-time $4152. *Financial support:* Application deadline: 3/1. *Unit head:* Jill Razani, Chair, 818-677-3506.
Website: http://www.csun.edu/csbs/departments/psychology/index.html

**California State University, San Bernardino,** Graduate Studies, College of Social and Behavioral Sciences, Department of Psychology, San Bernardino, CA 92407. Offers child development (MA); clinical/counseling psychology (MS); general/experimental psychology (MA); industrial/organizational psychology (MS). *Faculty:* 21 full-time (11 women). *Students:* 59 full-time (43 women), 15 part-time (9 women); includes 47 minority (2 Black or African American, non-Hispanic/Latino; 3 Asian, non-Hispanic/Latino; 33 Hispanic/Latino; 9 Two or more races, non-Hispanic/Latino), 3 international. 217 applicants, 18% accepted, 32 enrolled. In 2016, 38 master's awarded. *Degree requirements:* For master's, comprehensive exam, thesis (for some programs). *Entrance requirements:* Additional exam requirements/recommendations for international students: Required—TOEFL. Application fee: $55. *Expenses:* Tuition, state resident: full-time $7843; part-time $5011.20 per year. Tuition and fees vary according to course load, degree level, program and reciprocity agreements. *Financial support:* Fellowships, research assistantships, and teaching assistantships available. *Faculty research:*

Perceptual development, human memory, psychopharmacology, psychology of women, language acquisition. *Unit head:* Dr. Robert Ricco, Chair, 909-537-5485, Fax: 909-537-7003, E-mail: rricco@csusb.edu. *Application contact:* Dr. Francisca Beer, Dean of Graduate Studies, 909-537-5058, E-mail: fbeer@csusb.edu. Website: http://psychology.csusb.edu/

**California University of Pennsylvania,** School of Graduate Studies and Research, College of Education and Human Services, Department of Counselor Education, California, PA 15419-1394. Offers clinical mental health counseling (MS); school counseling (M Ed). *Accreditation:* ACA; NCATE. *Program availability:* Part-time, evening/weekend. *Degree requirements:* For master's, comprehensive exam, thesis optional. *Entrance requirements:* For master's, MAT, minimum GPA of 3.0, resume, letters of reference. Additional exam requirements/recommendations for international students: Required—TOEFL (minimum score 550 paper-based; 80 iBT). Electronic applications accepted. *Expenses:* Tuition, state resident: full-time $11,592; part-time $483 per credit. Tuition, nonresident: full-time $17,400; part-time $725 per credit. *Required fees:* $3916. Tuition and fees vary according to course load, degree level, campus/location and reciprocity agreements. *Faculty research:* Mind-body theories and practice, grief issues, career development, supervision, sports counseling.

**Capella University,** Harold Abel School of Social and Behavioral Science, Doctoral Programs in Psychology, Minneapolis, MN 55402. Offers addiction psychology (PhD); clinical psychology (PhD); educational psychology (PhD); general advanced studies in human behavior (PhD); general psychology (PhD); industrial/organizational psychology (PhD); school psychology (Psy D).

**Capella University,** Harold Abel School of Social and Behavioral Science, Master's Programs in Psychology, Minneapolis, MN 55402. Offers applied behavior analysis (MS); clinical psychology (MS); counseling psychology (MS); educational psychology (MS); evaluation, research, and measurement (MS); general advanced studies in human behavior (MS); general psychology (MS); industrial/organizational psychology (MS); leadership coaching psychology (MS); school psychology (MS); sport psychology (MS).

**Cardinal Stritch University,** College of Arts and Sciences, Department of Psychology, Milwaukee, WI 53217-3985. Offers clinical psychology (MA). *Program availability:* Part-time, evening/weekend. *Faculty:* 5. *Students:* 11 full-time (8 women), 17 part-time (12 women); includes 6 minority (2 Black or African American, non-Hispanic/Latino; 3 Hispanic/Latino; 1 Two or more races, non-Hispanic/Latino), 5 international. Average age 27. 54 applicants, 87% accepted, 11 enrolled. In 2016, 25 master's awarded. *Degree requirements:* For master's, thesis, portfolio, clinical practicum. *Entrance requirements:* For master's, interview, minimum GPA of 3.0, 3 letters of recommendation. Additional exam requirements/recommendations for international students: Required—TOEFL (minimum score 79 iBT), IELTS (minimum score 6.5). *Application deadline:* For fall admission, 7/15 priority date for domestic students; for spring admission, 12/15 priority date for domestic students. Applications are processed on a rolling basis. Electronic applications accepted. *Expenses: Tuition:* Full-time $11,890; part-time $765 per credit hour. Tuition and fees vary according to class time, course load, degree level, program and student's religious affiliation. *Financial support:* Research assistantships with partial tuition reimbursements, career-related internships or fieldwork, Federal Work-Study, and scholarships/grants available. Financial award applicants required to submit FAFSA. *Unit head:* Dr. Trevor Hyde, Chair, 414-410-4489, E-mail: tfhyde@stritch.edu. *Application contact:* Graduate Admissions, 800-347-8822 Ext. 4042, E-mail: admissions@stritch.edu.

**Carlos Albizu University,** Graduate Programs, San Juan, PR 00901. Offers clinical psychology (MS, PhD, Psy D); general psychology (PhD); industrial/organizational psychology (MS, PhD); speech and language pathology (MS). *Accreditation:* APA (one or more programs are accredited). *Program availability:* Part-time, evening/weekend. Terminal master's awarded for partial completion of doctoral program. *Degree requirements:* For master's, one foreign language, comprehensive exam, thesis; for doctorate, one foreign language, comprehensive exam, thesis/dissertation, written qualifying exams. *Entrance requirements:* For master's, GRE General Test or EXADEP, interview; minimum GPA of 2.8 (industrial/organizational psychology); for doctorate, GRE General Test or EXADEP, interview; minimum GPA of 3.0 (PhD in industrial/organizational psychology and clinical psychology), 3.25 (Psy D). *Faculty research:* Psychotherapeutic techniques for Hispanics, psychology of the aged, school dropouts, stress, violence.

**Carlos Albizu University, Miami Campus,** Graduate Programs, Miami, FL 33172-2209. Offers clinical psychology (PhD, Psy D); entrepreneurship (MBA); exceptional student education (MS); human services (PhD); industrial/organizational psychology (MS); marriage and family therapy (MS); mental health counseling (MS); nonprofit management (MBA); organizational management (MBA); psychology (MS); school counseling (MS); speech and language pathology (MS); teaching English for speakers of other languages (MS). *Accreditation:* APA. *Program availability:* Part-time, evening/weekend, 100% online. *Faculty:* 28 full-time (22 women), 31 part-time/adjunct (19 women). *Students:* 475 full-time (396 women), 191 part-time (161 women); includes 560 minority (56 Black or African American, non-Hispanic/Latino; 1 American Indian or Alaska Native, non-Hispanic/Latino; 4 Asian, non-Hispanic/Latino; 494 Hispanic/Latino; 5 Two or more races, non-Hispanic/Latino), 15 international. Average age 34. 335 applicants, 46% accepted, 122 enrolled. In 2016, 143 master's, 48 doctorates awarded. Terminal master's awarded for partial completion of doctoral program. *Degree requirements:* For master's, comprehensive exam, integrative project (for MBA); research project (for exceptional student education, teaching English as a second language); for doctorate, comprehensive exam, thesis/dissertation, internship, project. *Entrance requirements:* For master's, 3 letters of recommendation, interview, minimum GPA of 3.0, resume, statement of purpose, official transcripts; for doctorate, 3 letters of recommendation, minimum GPA of 3.0, resume, interview, statement of purpose, official transcripts. Additional exam requirements/recommendations for international students: Required—Michigan Test of English Language Proficiency. *Application deadline:* For fall admission, 4/1 priority date for domestic students, 5/1 priority date for international students; for spring admission, 11/1 priority date for domestic students, 9/1 priority date for international students. Applications are processed on a rolling basis. Application fee: $50. Electronic applications accepted. *Expenses:* Contact institution. *Financial support:* In 2016–17, 131 students received support. Federal Work-Study, scholarships/grants, unspecified assistantships, and tuition discounts available. Financial award application deadline: 6/1; financial award applicants required to submit FAFSA. *Faculty research:* Psychotherapy, forensic psychology, neuropsychology, marketing strategy, entrepreneurship, special education, speech-language pathology. *Unit head:* Dr. Etiony Aldarondo, Provost, 305-593-1223 Ext. 3138, Fax: 305-592-7930, E-mail: ealdarondo@albizu.edu. *Application contact:* Sonia Feliciano, Institutional Director of Student Recruitment, 305-593-1223 Ext. 3108, Fax: 305-477-8983, E-mail: sfeliciano@albizu.edu.

**Case Western Reserve University,** School of Graduate Studies, Psychological Sciences Department, Program in Clinical Psychology, Cleveland, OH 44106. Offers PhD. *Accreditation:* APA. *Program availability:* Part-time. *Faculty:* 7 full-time (4 women). *Students:* 29 full-time (21 women); includes 3 minority (1 Black or African American,

non-Hispanic/Latino; 2 Hispanic/Latino). Average age 27. 165 applicants, 4% accepted, 5 enrolled. In 2016, 5 doctorates awarded. *Degree requirements:* For doctorate, thesis/dissertation, internship. *Entrance requirements:* For doctorate, GRE General Test, GRE Subject Test, personal statement; curriculum vitae; three letters of recommendation. Additional exam requirements/recommendations for international students: Required—TOEFL (minimum score 577 paper-based; 90 iBT); Recommended—IELTS (minimum score 7). *Application deadline:* For fall admission, 12/1 priority date for domestic students. Application fee: $50. Electronic applications accepted. *Expenses: Tuition:* Full-time $42,576; part-time $1774 per credit hour. *Required fees:* $34. Tuition and fees vary according to course load and program. *Financial support:* Fellowships, research assistantships, and teaching assistantships available. Financial award application deadline: 12/1; financial award applicants required to submit FAFSA. *Faculty research:* Pediatric psychology, family functioning, depression, geriatric psychopathology, creativity and play. *Unit head:* Dr. Lee Thompson, Professor and Chair, 216-368-6477, E-mail: lee.thompson@case.edu. *Application contact:* Dr. Norah Feeny, Director of Clinical Training, 216-368-2695, Fax: 216-368-4891, E-mail: cwrupsych@gmail.com. Website: http://psychsciences.case.edu/graduate/

**The Catholic University of America,** School of Arts and Sciences, Department of Psychology, Washington, DC 20064. Offers applied experimental psychology (PhD); clinical psychology (PhD); general psychology (MA); human development psychology (PhD); human factors (MA); MA/JD. MA/JD offered jointly with Columbus School of Law. *Accreditation:* APA (one or more programs are accredited). *Program availability:* Part-time. *Faculty:* 11 full-time (6 women), 5 part-time/adjunct (2 women). *Students:* 40 full-time (26 women), 36 part-time (29 women); includes 19 minority (3 Black or African American, non-Hispanic/Latino; 5 Asian, non-Hispanic/Latino; 4 Hispanic/Latino; 7 Two or more races, non-Hispanic/Latino), 8 international. Average age 28. 230 applicants, 27% accepted, 23 enrolled. In 2016, 15 master's, 6 doctorates awarded. *Degree requirements:* For master's, comprehensive exam, thesis (for some programs); for doctorate, comprehensive exam, thesis/dissertation. *Entrance requirements:* For master's, GRE General Test, statement of purpose, official copies of academic transcripts, three letters of recommendation; for doctorate, GRE General Test, GRE Subject Test, statement of purpose, official copies of academic transcripts, three letters of recommendation. Additional exam requirements/recommendations for international students: Required—TOEFL (minimum score 550 paper-based; 80 iBT). *Application deadline:* For fall admission, 7/15 priority date for domestic students, 7/1 for international students; for spring admission, 11/15 priority date for domestic students, 11/1 for international students. Applications are processed on a rolling basis. Application fee: $55. Electronic applications accepted. *Expenses:* $42,850 per year; $1,170 per credit; $200 per semester part-time fees. *Financial support:* Fellowships, research assistantships, teaching assistantships, Federal Work-Study, scholarships/grants, tuition waivers (full and partial), and unspecified assistantships available. Financial award application deadline: 2/1; financial award applicants required to submit FAFSA. *Faculty research:* Clinical psychology, applied cognitive science, psychopathology, cognitive neuroscience, psychotherapy. *Total annual research expenditures:* $936,581. *Unit head:* Dr. Marc M. Sebrechts, Chair, 202-319-5750, Fax: 202-319-6263, E-mail: sebrechts@cua.edu. *Application contact:* Director of Graduate Admissions, 202-319-5057, Fax: 202-319-6533, E-mail: cua-admissions@cua.edu. Website: http://psychology.cua.edu/

**Central Michigan University,** College of Graduate Studies, College of Humanities and Social and Behavioral Sciences, Department of Psychology, Program in Clinical Psychology, Mount Pleasant, MI 48859. Offers PhD. *Accreditation:* APA. *Degree requirements:* For doctorate, thesis/dissertation. *Entrance requirements:* For doctorate, GRE. Electronic applications accepted. *Faculty research:* Applied youth development; emotional processes, personality disorders, and assessment; influence of affective variables on cognitive performance; post-traumatic stress disorder and panic disorder; validation of clinical inferences from psychological tests.

**Chestnut Hill College,** School of Graduate Studies, Division of Psychology, Program in Clinical and Counseling Psychology, Philadelphia, PA 19118-2693. Offers clinical and counseling psychology (MS, CAS), including child and adolescent therapy, child and adolescent therapy with autism spectrum disorders, co-occurring disorders, couple and family therapy, diverse and underserved communities, generalist (MS), trauma studies. *Program availability:* Part-time, evening/weekend. *Degree requirements:* For master's, thesis optional, practica. *Entrance requirements:* For master's, GRE General Test, writing sample, letters of recommendation. Additional exam requirements/recommendations for international students: Required—TOEFL (minimum score 500 paper-based), IELTS (minimum score 6.0), or TWE (minimum score 22). Electronic applications accepted. *Expenses:* Contact institution. *Faculty research:* Play therapy, eating disorders, addictions, group psychology and group therapy, health psychology.

**Chestnut Hill College,** School of Graduate Studies, Division of Psychology, Program in Clinical Psychology, Philadelphia, PA 19118-2693. Offers clinical psychology (Psy D), including clinical psychology, couple and family therapy, psychological assessment. *Accreditation:* APA. *Program availability:* Part-time, evening/weekend. *Degree requirements:* For doctorate, comprehensive exam, thesis/dissertation, internship, practica, clinical competency exam. *Entrance requirements:* For doctorate, GRE General Test, letters of recommendation, writing sample, master's degree in clinical/counseling psychology or closely-related field. Additional exam requirements/recommendations for international students: Required—TOEFL (minimum score 500 paper-based), IELTS (minimum score 6.0), or TWE (minimum score 22). Electronic applications accepted. *Expenses:* Contact institution. *Faculty research:* Psychological testing and assessment, LGBT issues, autism and developmental disorders, stepfamilies, gender issues.

**The Chicago School of Professional Psychology,** Program in Clinical Forensic Psychology, Chicago, IL 60610. Offers Psy D. *Degree requirements:* For doctorate, thesis/dissertation. *Entrance requirements:* For doctorate, GRE. Additional exam requirements/recommendations for international students: Required—TOEFL, IELTS.

**The Chicago School of Professional Psychology,** Program in Clinical Mental Health Counseling, Chicago, IL 60610. Offers MA. *Program availability:* Part-time.

**The Chicago School of Professional Psychology,** Program in Clinical Psychology, Chicago, IL 60610. Offers Psy D. *Accreditation:* APA. *Degree requirements:* For doctorate, comprehensive exam, thesis/dissertation. *Entrance requirements:* For doctorate, GRE, 18 hours of psychology credit (including courses in statistics, normal psychology and human development); minimum GPA of 3.2. Additional exam requirements/recommendations for international students: Required—TOEFL. Electronic applications accepted.

**The Chicago School of Professional Psychology at Downtown Los Angeles,** Program in Clinical Forensic Psychology, Los Angeles, CA 90017. Offers Psy D.

**The Chicago School of Professional Psychology at Downtown Los Angeles,** Program in Clinical Psychology, Los Angeles, CA 90017. Offers applied behavior analysis (MA); clinical psychology (Psy D); marital and family therapy (MA).

**The Chicago School of Professional Psychology at Irvine,** Program in Clinical Forensic Psychology, Irvine, CA 92612. Offers Psy D.

## Clinical Psychology

**City College of the City University of New York,** Graduate School, Colin Powell School for Civic and Global Leadership, Department of Psychology, New York, NY 10031-9198. Offers clinical psychology (PhD); general psychology (MA); mental health counseling (MA). PhD program offered jointly with Graduate School and University Center of the City University of New York. *Accreditation:* APA (one or more programs are accredited). *Program availability:* Part-time. *Degree requirements:* For master's, one foreign language, comprehensive exam, thesis. *Entrance requirements:* For master's, GRE. Additional exam requirements/recommendations for international students: Required—TOEFL (minimum score 550 paper-based; 79 iBT). Electronic applications accepted. Tuition and fees vary according to course load, degree level and program. *Faculty research:* Social/personality psychology, physiological psychology, cognition and development.

**Clarion University of Pennsylvania,** Office of Transfer, Adult and Graduate Admissions, Online Master of Science Programs, Clarion, PA 16214. Offers accounting (MS); applied data analytics (MS); clinical mental health counseling (MS); library science (MSLS); mass media arts and journalism (MS). *Program availability:* Part-time, 100% online. *Faculty:* 15 full-time (7 women), 3 part-time/adjunct (2 women). *Students:* 84 full-time (69 women), 304 part-time (246 women); includes 36 minority (19 Black or African American, non-Hispanic/Latino; 3 Asian, non-Hispanic/Latino; 10 Hispanic/Latino; 4 Two or more races, non-Hispanic/Latino), 1 international. Average age 34. 179 applicants, 93% accepted, 131 enrolled. In 2016, 146 master's awarded. *Degree requirements:* For master's, comprehensive exam, thesis or alternative. *Entrance requirements:* For master's, minimum QPA of 3.0. Additional exam requirements/recommendations for international students: Required—TOEFL (minimum score 600 paper-based; 100 iBT), IELTS (minimum score 7.5). *Application deadline:* For fall admission, 8/1 priority date for domestic students, 4/15 priority date for international students; for spring admission, 12/1 priority date for domestic students, 9/15 priority date for international students. Applications are processed on a rolling basis. Application fee: $40. Electronic applications accepted. *Expenses:* $632.35 per credit. *Financial support:* Career-related internships or fieldwork, Federal Work-Study, scholarships/grants, and unspecified assistantships available. Support available to part-time students. Financial award application deadline: 3/1. *Application contact:* Dana Bearer, Associate Director, Transfer, Adult, and Graduate Programs, 814-393-2337, Fax: 814-393-2772, E-mail: gradstudies@clarion.edu.
Website: http://www.clarion.edu/admissions/graduate/index.html

**Clark University,** Graduate School, Hiatt School of Psychology, Program in Clinical Psychology, Worcester, MA 01610-1477. Offers PhD. *Accreditation:* APA. *Students:* 22 full-time (20 women), 3 part-time (1 woman); includes 6 minority (1 Black or African American, non-Hispanic/Latino; 1 American Indian or Alaska Native, non-Hispanic/Latino; 1 Asian, non-Hispanic/Latino; 3 Hispanic/Latino). Average age 29. In 2016, 6 doctorates awarded. *Degree requirements:* For doctorate, thesis/dissertation. *Entrance requirements:* For doctorate, GRE General Test. Additional exam requirements/recommendations for international students: Required—TOEFL. *Application deadline:* For fall admission, 12/15 priority date for domestic and international students. Applications are processed on a rolling basis. Application fee: $75. *Expenses: Tuition:* Full-time $44,050. *Required fees:* $80. Tuition and fees vary according to course load and program. *Financial support:* In 2016–17, fellowships with full tuition reimbursements (averaging $17,325 per year), research assistantships with full tuition reimbursements (averaging $17,325 per year), teaching assistantships with full tuition reimbursements (averaging $17,325 per year) were awarded; tuition waivers (full) also available. *Faculty research:* Marital relations and interventions, adult emotional development, Latino men and depression, violence prevention. *Unit head:* Dr. James Cordova, Chair, 508-793-7268, E-mail: ecardemil@clarku.edu. *Application contact:* Kelly Boulay, Departmental Administrator, 508-793-7274, Fax: 508-793-7265, E-mail: psychology@clarku.edu.
Website: http://www.clarku.edu/departments/psychology/grad/clinical/index.cfm

**Clayton State University,** School of Graduate Studies, College of Arts and Sciences, Program in Psychology, Morrow, GA 30260-0285. Offers applied developmental psychology (MS); clinical/counseling psychology (MS). *Entrance requirements:* For master's, GRE, 2 official transcripts; 3 letters of recommendation; statement of purpose; on-campus interview; background check. Additional exam requirements/recommendations for international students: Required—TOEFL (minimum score 550 paper-based). Electronic applications accepted. *Expenses:* Tuition, state resident: full-time $3528; part-time $196 per credit hour. Tuition, nonresident: full-time $13,176; part-time $732 per credit hour. *Required fees:* $1454; $1454 per credit hour. $727 per semester. Tuition and fees vary according to campus/location and program.

**College of St. Joseph,** Graduate Programs, Division of Psychology and Human Services, Program in Clinical Mental Health Counseling, Rutland, VT 05701-3899. Offers MS. *Program availability:* Part-time. *Degree requirements:* For master's, comprehensive exam. *Entrance requirements:* For master's, official college transcripts; 2 letters of reference. Additional exam requirements/recommendations for international students: Required—TOEFL (minimum score 550 paper-based). *Application deadline:* Applications are processed on a rolling basis. Application fee: $35. Electronic applications accepted. *Expenses: Tuition,* area resident: Full-time $13,800; part-time $560 per credit. *Required fees:* $75 per semester. Full-time tuition and fees vary according to course load. *Financial support:* Career-related internships or fieldwork, Federal Work-Study, and unspecified assistantships available. Support available to part-time students. Financial award application deadline: 3/1. *Unit head:* Dr. Craig Knapp, Chair, 802-773-5900 Ext. 3219, Fax: 802-776-5258, E-mail: cknapp@csj.edu. *Application contact:* Alan Young, Dean of Admissions, 802-773-5900 Ext. 3227, Fax: 802-776-5310, E-mail: alanyoung@csj.edu.

**College of St. Joseph,** Graduate Programs, Division of Psychology and Human Services, Program in Clinical Psychology, Rutland, VT 05701-3899. Offers MS. *Program availability:* Part-time, evening/weekend. *Degree requirements:* For master's, comprehensive exam, thesis optional. *Entrance requirements:* For master's, official college transcripts; 2 letters of reference. Additional exam requirements/recommendations for international students: Required—TOEFL (minimum score 550 paper-based). *Application deadline:* Applications are processed on a rolling basis. Application fee: $35. Electronic applications accepted. *Expenses: Tuition,* area resident: Full-time $13,800; part-time $560 per credit. *Required fees:* $75 per semester. Full-time tuition and fees vary according to course load. *Financial support:* Teaching assistantships with tuition reimbursements and unspecified assistantships available. Financial award application deadline: 3/1. *Unit head:* Dr. Craig Knapp, Chair, 802-773-5900 Ext. 3219, Fax: 802-776-5258, E-mail: cknapp@csj.edu. *Application contact:* Alan Young, Dean of Admissions, 802-773-5900 Ext. 3227, Fax: 802-776-5310, E-mail: alanyoung@csj.edu.

**College of Staten Island of the City University of New York,** Graduate Programs, Division of Humanities and Social Sciences, Program in Mental Health Counseling, Staten Island, NY 10314-6600. Offers MA. *Faculty:* 6 full-time, 5 part-time/adjunct. *Students:* 57 full-time, 1 part-time. Average age 27. 80 applicants, 28% accepted, 22 enrolled. In 2016, 21 master's awarded. *Degree requirements:* For master's, 16 required courses, practicum, three internship courses. *Entrance requirements:* For master's, BA/BS with minimum GPA of 3.0 and 15-19 credits in certain areas of psychology; 2 letters of recommendation; 1-2 page statement of experience and interest in the field.

Additional exam requirements/recommendations for international students: Required—TOEFL (minimum score 600 paper-based; 100 iBT), IELTS (minimum score 7). *Application deadline:* For fall admission, 3/10 for domestic and international students. Applications are processed on a rolling basis. Application fee: $125. Electronic applications accepted. *Expenses:* Tuition, state resident: full-time $10,130; part-time $425 per credit. Tuition, nonresident: full-time $18,720; part-time $780 per credit. *Required fees:* $181.10 per semester. Tuition and fees vary according to program. *Faculty research:* Child psychopathology, HIV/AIDS counseling, elder care and cognition, psychosocial burn rehabilitation, autism spectrum disorders. *Unit head:* Dr. Frances Melendez, Graduate Program Coordinator, 718-982-3960, E-mail: frances.melendez@csi.cuny.edu. *Application contact:* Sasha Spence, Associate Director for Graduate Admissions, 718-982-2019, Fax: 718-982-2500, E-mail: sasha.spence@csi.cuny.edu.
Website: http://csivc.csi.cuny.edu/psy/files/MHC.html

**Columbus State University,** Graduate Studies, College of Education and Health Professions, Department of Counseling, Foundations, and Leadership, Columbus, GA 31907-5645. Offers clinical mental health counseling (MS); curriculum and leadership (Ed D), including curriculum, educational leadership, higher education (M Ed, Ed D); educational leadership (M Ed, Ed S), including higher education (M Ed, Ed D); school counseling (M Ed, Ed S). *Accreditation:* ACA; NCATE. *Program availability:* Part-time, evening/weekend, 100% online, blended/hybrid learning. *Faculty:* 14 full-time (4 women), 25 part-time/adjunct (14 women). *Students:* 226 full-time (159 women), 294 part-time (219 women); includes 298 minority (270 Black or African American, non-Hispanic/Latino; 1 American Indian or Alaska Native, non-Hispanic/Latino; 5 Asian, non-Hispanic/Latino; 13 Hispanic/Latino; 9 Two or more races, non-Hispanic/Latino), 1 international. Average age 39. 367 applicants, 57% accepted, 162 enrolled. In 2016, 20 master's, 7 doctorates, 121 other advanced degrees awarded. *Degree requirements:* For master's, thesis, exit exam; for doctorate, comprehensive exam, thesis/dissertation; for Ed S, thesis or alternative. *Entrance requirements:* For master's, GRE General Test, minimum undergraduate GPA of 2.75; for doctorate, GRE General Test, minimum graduate GPA of 3.5, four years of professional service; for Ed S, GRE General Test, minimum undergraduate GPA of 2.75, graduate 3.0. Additional exam requirements/recommendations for international students: Required—TOEFL (minimum score 550 paper-based; 79 iBT). *Application deadline:* For fall admission, 6/30 for domestic and international students; for spring admission, 11/1 for domestic and international students; for summer admission, 3/1 for domestic and international students. Applications are processed on a rolling basis. Application fee: $50. Electronic applications accepted. *Expenses:* Tuition, state resident: full-time $4804; part-time $2412 per semester hour. Tuition, nonresident: full-time $19,218; part-time $9612 per semester hour. *Required fees:* $1850; $1850 per semester hour. Tuition and fees vary according to program. *Financial support:* In 2016–17, 43 students received support, including 9 research assistantships with partial tuition reimbursements available (averaging $3,000 per year); career-related internships or fieldwork, Federal Work-Study, institutionally sponsored loans, scholarships/grants, tuition waivers (partial), and unspecified assistantships also available. Support available to part-time students. Financial award application deadline: 5/1; financial award applicants required to submit FAFSA. *Unit head:* Dr. Tom Hackett, Department Chair, 706-507-8968, Fax: 706-569-3134, E-mail: hackett_paul@columbusstate.edu. *Application contact:* Kristin Williams, Director of International and Graduate Recruitment, 706-507-8848, Fax: 706-568-5091, E-mail: williams_kristin@columbusstate.edu.
Website: http://cfl.columbusstate.edu/

**Concordia University,** School of Graduate Studies, Faculty of Arts and Science, Department of Psychology, PhD Program in Psychology, Montréal, QC H3G 1M8, Canada. Offers PhD, Certificate. *Degree requirements:* For doctorate, comprehensive exam, thesis/dissertation. *Entrance requirements:* For doctorate, master's degree in psychology. *Faculty research:* Developmental-clinical psychology, sensory deficits, sexual dysfunction.

**Dalhousie University,** Faculty of Science, Department of Psychology, Halifax, NS B3H 4R2, Canada. Offers clinical psychology (PhD); psychology (M Sc, PhD); psychology/neuroscience (M Sc, PhD). *Degree requirements:* For master's, thesis; for doctorate, thesis/dissertation. *Entrance requirements:* For doctorate, GRE General Test. Additional exam requirements/recommendations for international students: Required—TOEFL, IELTS, CANTEST, CAEL, or Michigan English Language Assessment Battery. Electronic applications accepted. *Faculty research:* Physiological psychology, psychology of learning, learning and behavior, forensic clinical health psychology, development perception and cognition.

**DePaul University,** College of Education, Chicago, IL 60614. Offers bilingual bicultural education (M Ed, MA); counseling (M Ed, MA), including clinical mental health counseling, college student development, school counseling; curriculum studies (M Ed, MA, Ed D); early childhood education (M Ed, MA, Ed D); educating adults (MA); educational leadership (M Ed, MA, Ed D), including administration and supervision (M Ed, MA), principal preparation (M Ed, MA); elementary education (MA); mathematics education (MA); mathematics for teaching (MS); middle school mathematics education (MS); reading specialist (M Ed, MA); secondary education (M Ed); social and cultural foundations in education (MA); special education (M Ed, MA); world languages education (M Ed, MA). *Program availability:* Part-time, evening/weekend, online learning. *Degree requirements:* For doctorate, thesis/dissertation. Electronic applications accepted.

**Drexel University,** College of Arts and Sciences, Department of Psychology, Clinical Psychology Program, Philadelphia, PA 19104-2875. Offers clinical psychology (PhD); forensic psychology (PhD); health psychology (PhD); neuropsychology (PhD). *Accreditation:* APA. *Faculty:* 26 full-time (16 women), 8 part-time/adjunct (7 women). *Students:* 79 full-time (66 women), 8 part-time (5 women); includes 16 minority (4 Black or African American, non-Hispanic/Latino; 5 Asian, non-Hispanic/Latino; 3 Hispanic/Latino; 4 Two or more races, non-Hispanic/Latino), 4 international. Average age 27. In 2016, 10 doctorates awarded. Terminal master's awarded for partial completion of doctoral program. *Degree requirements:* For doctorate, thesis/dissertation, qualifying exam. *Entrance requirements:* For doctorate, GRE General Test, GRE Subject Test, minimum GPA of 3.0. *Application deadline:* For spring admission, 1/15 for domestic students. Application fee: $30. Electronic applications accepted. *Expenses:* Contact institution. *Financial support:* Fellowships, research assistantships, teaching assistantships, career-related internships or fieldwork, Federal Work-Study, institutionally sponsored loans, and tuition waivers (partial) available. Support available to part-time students. Financial award application deadline: 5/1; financial award applicants required to submit FAFSA. *Faculty research:* Cognitive behavioral therapy, stress and coping, eating disorders, substance abuse, developmental disabilities. *Total annual research expenditures:* $3.9 million. *Unit head:* Dr. Maria Schultheis, Head, 215-895-6105. *Application contact:* Director of Graduate Admissions, 215-895-6700, Fax: 215-895-5939, E-mail: enroll@drexel.edu.

**Drexel University,** College of Arts and Sciences, Department of Psychology, Program in Law-Psychology, Philadelphia, PA 19104-2875. Offers JD/PhD. *Students:* 22 full-time (16 women), 9 part-time (8 women); includes 4 minority (2 Black or African American, non-Hispanic/Latino; 2 Hispanic/Latino), 1 international. Average age 27. 11 applicants,

27% accepted, 3 enrolled. *Application deadline:* For fall admission, 2/15 for domestic students. Application fee: $50. Electronic applications accepted. *Expenses:* Contact institution. *Financial support:* Fellowships, research assistantships, teaching assistantships, career-related internships or fieldwork, Federal Work-Study, and institutionally sponsored loans available. Support available to part-time students. Financial award application deadline: 5/1; financial award applicants required to submit FAFSA. *Faculty research:* Mental health law issues, professional ethics, social science applications to law. *Unit head:* Dr. Kirk Heilbrun, Head, 215-895-2402, Fax: 215-895-1333. *Application contact:* Director of Graduate Admissions, 215-895-6700, Fax: 215-895-5939, E-mail: enroll@drexel.edu.

**Duke University,** Graduate School, Department of Psychology and Neuroscience, Durham, NC 27708. Offers biological psychology (PhD); clinical psychology (PhD); cognitive psychology (PhD); developmental psychology (PhD); experimental psychology (PhD); health psychology (PhD); human social development (PhD); JD/MA. *Accreditation:* APA (one or more programs are accredited). *Degree requirements:* For doctorate, thesis/dissertation. *Entrance requirements:* For doctorate, GRE General Test. Additional exam requirements/recommendations for international students: Required—TOEFL (minimum score 577 paper-based; 90 iBT) or IELTS (minimum score 7). Electronic applications accepted.

**Duquesne University,** Graduate School of Liberal Arts, Department of Psychology, Pittsburgh, PA 15282-0001. Offers clinical psychology (PhD). *Accreditation:* APA. *Faculty:* 13 full-time (7 women). *Students:* 45 full-time (29 women); includes 7 minority (2 Black or African American, non-Hispanic/Latino; 1 Asian, non-Hispanic/Latino; 4 Hispanic/Latino), 6 international. Average age 31. 94 applicants, 7% accepted, 7 enrolled. In 2016, 5 doctorates awarded. *Degree requirements:* For doctorate, comprehensive exam, thesis/dissertation. *Entrance requirements:* For doctorate, GRE General Test, MA in psychology. Additional exam requirements/recommendations for international students: Required—TOEFL. *Application deadline:* For fall admission, 12/15 for domestic and international students. Application fee: $0. Electronic applications accepted. *Expenses: Tuition:* Full-time $22,212; part-time $1234 per credit. Tuition and fees vary according to program. *Financial support:* In 2016—17, 38 students received support, including 28 teaching assistantships with full tuition reimbursements available (averaging $17,000 per year); career-related internships or fieldwork, scholarships/grants, tuition waivers (partial), and unspecified assistantships also available. Financial award application deadline: 5/1. *Faculty research:* Emotion, language motivation, imagination, development. *Unit head:* Dr. Leswin Laubscher, Chair, 412-396-1843, E-mail: laubscherl@duq.edu. *Application contact:* Linda Rendulic, Assistant to the Dean, 412-396-6400, Fax: 412-396-5265, E-mail: rendulic@duq.edu.
Website: http://www.duq.edu/academics/schools/liberal-arts/graduate-school/programs/clinical-psychology

**Duquesne University,** School of Education, Department of Counseling, Psychology, and Special Education, Program in Counselor Education, Pittsburgh, PA 15282-0001. Offers clinical mental health counseling (MS Ed, Post-Master's Certificate); counselor education and supervision (Ed D); counselor licensure (Post-Master's Certificate); marriage and family counseling (MS Ed); school counseling (MS Ed). *Accreditation:* ACA (one or more programs are accredited). *Program availability:* Part-time, evening/weekend. *Faculty:* 8 full-time (3 women). *Students:* 188 full-time (139 women), 5 part-time (4 women); includes 39 minority (20 Black or African American, non-Hispanic/Latino; 5 Asian, non-Hispanic/Latino; 5 Hispanic/Latino; 9 Two or more races, non-Hispanic/Latino), 8 international. Average age 29. 152 applicants, 73% accepted, 69 enrolled. In 2016, 34 master's, 9 doctorates awarded. *Degree requirements:* For master's, thesis optional; for doctorate, thesis/dissertation. *Entrance requirements:* For master's, letters of recommendation, essay, interview, bachelor's degree; for doctorate, GRE, letters of recommendation, essay, interview, master's degree; for Post-Master's Certificate, GRE, letters of recommendation, essay, interview, bachelor's/master's degree. Additional exam requirements/recommendations for international students: Required—TOEFL (minimum score 550 paper-based), IELTS (minimum score 7). *Application deadline:* For fall admission, 3/1 for domestic students; for spring admission, 9/1 for domestic students. Applications are processed on a rolling basis. Application fee: $0. Electronic applications accepted. *Expenses: Tuition:* Full-time $22,212; part-time $1234 per credit. Tuition and fees vary according to program. *Financial support:* Research assistantships, teaching assistantships, and Federal Work-Study available. Support available to part-time students. *Unit head:* Dr. Jered Kolbert, Professor/Director, 412-396-4471, Fax: 412-396-1340, E-mail: kolbertj@duq.edu. *Application contact:* Michael Dolinger, Director of Student and Academic Services, 412-396-6647, Fax: 412-396-5585, E-mail: dolingerm@duq.edu.

**East Carolina University,** Graduate School, Thomas Harriot College of Arts and Sciences, Department of Psychology, Greenville, NC 27858-4353. Offers health psychology (PhD), including clinical health psychology, occupational health psychology, pediatric school psychology; industrial and organizational psychology (MA); MA/CAS. *Program availability:* Part-time, evening/weekend. *Students:* 83 full-time (60 women), 23 part-time (16 women); includes 16 minority (8 Black or African American, non-Hispanic/Latino; 1 Asian, non-Hispanic/Latino; 5 Hispanic/Latino; 2 Two or more races, non-Hispanic/Latino). Average age 26. 248 applicants, 19% accepted, 31 enrolled. In 2016, 11 master's, 1 doctorate awarded. *Degree requirements:* For master's, one foreign language, comprehensive exam, thesis. *Entrance requirements:* For master's, GRE General Test, GRE Subject Test. Additional exam requirements/recommendations for international students: Required—TOEFL. *Application deadline:* Applications are processed on a rolling basis. Application fee: $50. *Financial support:* Research assistantships with partial tuition reimbursements, teaching assistantships with partial tuition reimbursements, Federal Work-Study, and traineeships available. Support available to part-time students. Financial award application deadline: 6/1. *Unit head:* Dr. Susan L. McCammon, Chair, 252-328-6357, E-mail: mccammons@ecu.edu. *Application contact:* Dean of Graduate School, 252-328-6012, Fax: 252-328-6071, E-mail: gradschool@ecu.edu.
Website: http://www.ecu.edu/psyc/

**Eastern Illinois University,** Graduate School, College of Sciences, Department of Psychology, Charleston, IL 61920. Offers clinical psychology (MA); school psychology (SSP). *Program availability:* Part-time, evening/weekend. *Degree requirements:* For master's, comprehensive exam, thesis; for SSP, thesis. *Entrance requirements:* For master's and SSP, GMAT or GRE. Additional exam requirements/recommendations for international students: Required—TOEFL (minimum score 500 paper-based; 61 iBT), IELTS (minimum score 6). Electronic applications accepted.

**Eastern Kentucky University,** The Graduate School, College of Arts and Sciences, Department of Psychology, Richmond, KY 40475-3102. Offers clinical psychology (MS); industrial/organizational psychology (MS); school psychology (Psy S). *Program availability:* Part-time. *Entrance requirements:* For master's and Psy S, GRE General Test, minimum GPA of 2.5. *Faculty research:* Autism, social psychology, parenting, assessment of depression/anxiety, reading.

**Eastern Michigan University,** Graduate School, College of Arts and Sciences, Department of Psychology, Ypsilanti, MI 48197. Offers clinical behavioral psychology (MS); clinical psychology (PhD); general clinical psychology (MS); general experimental psychology (MS). *Accreditation:* APA. *Faculty:* 25 full-time (15 women). *Students:* 39

full-time (34 women), 49 part-time (38 women); includes 20 minority (3 Black or African American, non-Hispanic/Latino; 1 American Indian or Alaska Native, non-Hispanic/Latino; 5 Asian, non-Hispanic/Latino; 5 Hispanic/Latino; 6 Two or more races, non-Hispanic/Latino), 1 international. Average age 27. 273 applicants, 14% accepted, 31 enrolled. In 2016, 29 master's, 10 doctorates awarded. *Degree requirements:* For master's, 600-hour practicum; for doctorate, 1500-hour practicum; 2000-hour internship. *Entrance requirements:* For master's and doctorate, GRE. *Application deadline:* For fall admission, 2/15 for domestic students. Application fee: $45. *Financial support:* Fellowships available. *Unit head:* Dr. Carol Freedman-Doan, Department Head, 734-487-1155, Fax: 734-487-6553, E-mail: cfreedman@emich.edu.

**Eastern Virginia Medical School,** The Virginia Consortium Program in Clinical Psychology, Norfolk, VA 23501-1980. Offers Psy D. Program offered jointly with The College of William and Mary, Norfolk State University, and Old Dominion University. *Entrance requirements:* For doctorate, GRE, BS in behavioral sciences or equivalent. Additional exam requirements/recommendations for international students: Required—TOEFL. *Expenses:* Contact institution.

**Eastern Washington University,** Graduate Studies, College of Social Sciences, Department of Psychology, Program in Clinical Psychology, Cheney, WA 99004-2431. Offers MS. *Students:* 17 full-time (13 women); includes 1 minority (Hispanic/Latino). Average age 29. 50 applicants, 18% accepted, 9 enrolled. In 2016, 8 master's awarded. *Degree requirements:* For master's, comprehensive exam (for some programs), thesis or research report; practicum. *Entrance requirements:* For master's, GRE General Test, minimum GPA of 3.0 in last 90 quarter or 60 semester graded credits; curriculum vitae; three letters of recommendation; bachelor's degree in psychology or its equivalent; background check. Additional exam requirements/recommendations for international students: Required—TOEFL (minimum score 580 paper-based; 92 iBT), IELTS (minimum score 7), PTE (minimum score 63). *Application deadline:* For fall admission, 1/15 priority date for domestic students. Application fee: $75. Electronic applications accepted. *Expenses:* Tuition, state resident: full-time $11,000; part-time $5500 per credit. Tuition, nonresident: full-time $24,000; part-time $12,000 per credit. *Required fees:* $1300. One-time fee: $50 full-time. Part-time tuition and fees vary according to course load, campus/location and program. *Financial support:* Application deadline: 2/15; applicants required to submit FAFSA. *Unit head:* Dennis Anderson, Director, 509-359-2087, E-mail: danderson2@ewu.edu. *Application contact:* Kathy White, Advisor/Recruiter for Graduate Studies, 509-359-2491, Fax: 509-359-6044, E-mail: gradprograms@ewu.edu.

**Edinboro University of Pennsylvania,** Department of Counseling, School Psychology and Special Education, Edinboro, PA 16444. Offers counseling (MA), including art therapy, clinical mental health counseling, college counseling, rehabilitation counseling, school counseling; educational psychology (M Ed); school psychology (Ed S); special education (M Ed), including autism, behavior management. *Accreditation:* ACA. *Program availability:* Part-time, evening/weekend. *Degree requirements:* For master's, thesis or alternative, competency exam; for Ed S, thesis or alternative. *Entrance requirements:* For master's and Ed S, GRE or MAT, minimum QPA of 2.5. Electronic applications accepted.

**Emory University,** Laney Graduate School, Department of Psychology, Atlanta, GA 30322-1100. Offers clinical psychology (PhD); cognition and development (PhD); neuroscience and animal behavior (PhD). *Accreditation:* APA. *Degree requirements:* For doctorate, comprehensive exam, thesis/dissertation. *Entrance requirements:* For doctorate, GRE General Test, minimum GPA of 3.25. Additional exam requirements/recommendations for international students: Required—TOEFL. Electronic applications accepted. *Faculty research:* Neuroscience and animal behavior; adult and child psychopathology, cognition development assessment.

**Emporia State University,** Program in Clinical Psychology, Emporia, KS 66801-5415. Offers MS. *Program availability:* Part-time. *Faculty:* 8 full-time (4 women). *Students:* 24 full-time (19 women), 5 part-time (4 women); includes 2 minority (both Hispanic/Latino), 2 international. 37 applicants, 89% accepted, 7 enrolled. In 2016, 7 master's awarded. *Degree requirements:* For master's, comprehensive exam, clinical internship. *Entrance requirements:* For master's, GRE or MAT, 24 hours of course work in undergraduate psychology, 3 letters of recommendation. Additional exam requirements/recommendations for international students: Required—TOEFL (minimum score 520 paper-based; 68 iBT). *Application deadline:* For fall admission, 8/15 for domestic students. Applications are processed on a rolling basis. Application fee: $30 ($75 for international students). Electronic applications accepted. *Expenses:* Tuition, state resident: full-time $5922; part-time $246.75 per credit hour. Tuition, nonresident: full-time $18,414; part-time $767.25 per credit hour. *Required fees:* $1884; $78.50 per credit hour. *Financial support:* In 2016–17, 3 research assistantships with full tuition reimbursements, 7 teaching assistantships with full tuition reimbursements were awarded; career-related internships or fieldwork, Federal Work-Study, institutionally sponsored loans, health care benefits, and unspecified assistantships also available. Support available to part-time students. Financial award application deadline: 3/15; financial award applicants required to submit FAFSA. *Unit head:* Dr. Jim Persinger, Chair, 620-341-5317, E-mail: jpersing@emporia.edu. *Application contact:* Mary Sewell, Admissions Coordinator, 800-950-GRAD, Fax: 620-341-5909, E-mail: msewell@emporia.edu.

**Evangel University,** Department of Behavioral Sciences, Springfield, MO 65802. Offers clinical mental health counseling (MS). *Program availability:* Part-time. *Faculty:* 6 full-time (5 women), 5 part-time/adjunct (all women). *Students:* 35 full-time (26 women), 10 part-time (7 women); includes 5 minority (2 Black or African American, non-Hispanic/Latino; 2 Hispanic/Latino; 1 Two or more races, non-Hispanic/Latino). Average age 33. 27 applicants, 85% accepted, 20 enrolled. In 2016, 34 master's awarded. *Degree requirements:* For master's, comprehensive exam, thesis optional. *Entrance requirements:* For master's, GRE General Test, minimum undergraduate GPA of 3.0. Additional exam requirements/recommendations for international students: Required—TOEFL (minimum score 550 paper-based). *Application deadline:* For fall admission, 7/15 priority date for domestic students, 8/1 for international students; for spring admission, 11/15 priority date for domestic students, 12/1 for international students. Applications are processed on a rolling basis. Application fee: $25. Electronic applications accepted. Application fee is waived when completed online. *Expenses: Tuition:* Part-time $400 per credit hour. *Required fees:* $148 per trimester. One-time fee: $25. Tuition and fees vary according to course load, degree level and program. *Financial support:* In 2016–17, 6 students received support. Unspecified assistantships available. Financial award application deadline: 4/1; financial award applicants required to submit FAFSA. *Unit head:* Christine Arnzen, Program Coordinator, 417-865-2815 Ext. 8618, E-mail: arnzenc@evangel.edu. *Application contact:* Matt Petry, Admissions Representative, Graduate Studies, 417-865-2815 Ext. 7416, Fax: 417-575-5484, E-mail: benitezk@evangel.edu.
Website: https://www.evangel.edu/departments/behavioral-social-sciences/about-the-department/

**Fairfield University,** Graduate School of Education and Allied Professions, Fairfield, CT 06824. Offers applied behavior analysis (ATC); applied psychology (MA); clinical mental health counseling (MA, CAS); educational technology (MA); elementary education (MA, CAS); family studies (MA); integration of spirituality and religion in counseling (ATC);

marriage and family therapy (MA); reading and language development (Sixth Year Certificate); school counseling (MA, CAS); school psychology (MA, CAS); school-based marriage and family therapy (ATC); secondary education (MA); special education (MA, CAS); substance abuse counseling (ATC); teaching (Certificate); teaching and foundations (MA, CAS); TESOL, world languages, and bilingual education (MA, CAS). *Accreditation:* NCATE. *Program availability:* Part-time, evening/weekend. *Faculty:* 19 full-time (15 women), 38 part-time/adjunct (26 women). *Students:* 153 full-time (132 women), 302 part-time (252 women); includes 97 minority (24 Black or African American, non-Hispanic/Latino; 12 Asian, non-Hispanic/Latino; 55 Hispanic/Latino; 6 Two or more races, non-Hispanic/Latino), 6 international. Average age 32. 283 applicants, 61% accepted, 97 enrolled. In 2016, 130 master's awarded. *Degree requirements:* For master's, comprehensive exam. *Entrance requirements:* For master's, minimum GPA of 3.0, 2 recommendations, resume. Additional exam requirements/recommendations for international students: Required—TOEFL (minimum score 550 paper-based; 84 iBT) or IELTS (minimum score 7.5). *Application deadline:* For fall admission, 2/15 for international students; for spring admission, 10/1 for international students. Application fee: $60. Electronic applications accepted. *Expenses:* $725 per credit hour. *Financial support:* In 2016–17, 42 students received support. Career-related internships or fieldwork and unspecified assistantships available. Support available to part-time students. Financial award applicants required to submit FAFSA. *Faculty research:* Reading and literacy, writing, social justice and inequality in education, addictions and mental health issues, therapeutic relationships and clinical supervision. *Unit head:* Dr. Robert D. Hannafin, Dean, 203-254-4250, Fax: 203-254-4241, E-mail: rhannafin@fairfield.edu. *Application contact:* Marianne Gumpper, Director of Graduate Admission, 203-254-4184, Fax: 203-254-4073, E-mail: gradadmis@fairfield.edu.
Website: http://www.fairfield.edu/gseap

**Fairleigh Dickinson University, College at Florham,** Maxwell Becton College of Arts and Sciences, Department of Psychology, Program in Clinical Mental Health Counseling, Madison, NJ 07940-1099. Offers MA. *Accreditation:* ACA.

**Fairleigh Dickinson University, Metropolitan Campus,** University College: Arts, Sciences, and Professional Studies, School of Psychology, Program in Clinical Psychology, Teaneck, NJ 07666-1914. Offers MA, PhD. *Accreditation:* APA.

**Fairleigh Dickinson University, Metropolitan Campus,** University College: Arts, Sciences, and Professional Studies, School of Psychology, Program in Clinical Psychopharmacology, Teaneck, NJ 07666-1914. Offers MA.

**Fielding Graduate University,** Graduate Programs, School of Psychology, Programs in Clinical Psychology, Santa Barbara, CA 93105-3814. Offers clinical psychology (Postbaccalaureate Certificate); forensic psychology (PhD); health psychology (PhD); neuropsychology (PhD); parent-infant mental health (PhD); respecialization in clinical psychology (Post-Doctoral Certificate); violence prevention and control (PhD). *Program availability:* 100% online, blended/hybrid learning. *Faculty:* 28 full-time (19 women), 22 part-time/adjunct (11 women). *Students:* 408 full-time (321 women), 12 part-time (10 women); includes 156 minority (69 Black or African American, non-Hispanic/Latino; 2 American Indian or Alaska Native, non-Hispanic/Latino; 14 Asian, non-Hispanic/Latino; 53 Hispanic/Latino; 18 Two or more races, non-Hispanic/Latino), 5 international. Average age 40. 268 applicants, 39% accepted, 77 enrolled. In 2016, 36 doctorates, 31 other advanced degrees awarded. *Degree requirements:* For doctorate, thesis/dissertation. *Entrance requirements:* For doctorate, bachelor's degree, minimum GPA of 3.0, curriculum vitae, statement of purpose, critical thinking writing sample, 3 letters of recommendation, official transcript; for other advanced degree, bachelor's degree (for post baccalaureate certificate), doctoral degree in psychology (for post doctoral certificate); minimum GPA of 3.0, curriculum vitae, statement of purpose, 3 letters of recommendation, official transcript. *Application deadline:* For fall admission, 2/4 for domestic students, 2/1 for international students; for spring admission, 11/1 for domestic and international students; for summer admission, 3/1 for domestic and international students. Application fee: $75. Electronic applications accepted. *Expenses:* $9,060 per term (for PhD); $8,665 per term (for Post Doctoral Certificate); $720 per credit (for Post Baccalaureate Certificate). *Financial support:* In 2016–17, 28 students received support, including 1 research assistantship (averaging $238 per year), 17 teaching assistantships (averaging $1,973 per year); scholarships/grants also available. Financial award applicants required to submit FAFSA. *Unit head:* Dr. Marilyn Freimuth, Director. *Application contact:* Enrollment Coordinator, 800-340-1099 Ext. 4098, Fax: 805-687-9793, E-mail: psyadmission@fielding.edu.
Website: http://www.fielding.edu/our-programs/school-of-psychology/

**Fisk University,** Division of Graduate Studies, Department of Psychology, Nashville, TN 37208-3051. Offers clinical psychology (MA); psychology (MA). *Degree requirements:* For master's, thesis. *Entrance requirements:* For master's, GRE General Test, GRE Subject Test, minimum GPA of 3.0. Electronic applications accepted. *Faculty research:* Ethnic and gender identity, development, female adolescent development, juvenile delinquency prevention.

**Florida Institute of Technology,** College of Psychology and Liberal Arts, Program in Clinical Psychology, Melbourne, FL 32901-6975. Offers Psy D. *Accreditation:* APA. *Program availability:* Part-time. *Students:* 104 full-time (86 women), 1 (woman) part-time; includes 22 minority (5 Black or African American, non-Hispanic/Latino; 1 American Indian or Alaska Native, non-Hispanic/Latino; 3 Asian, non-Hispanic/Latino; 7 Hispanic/Latino; 6 Two or more races, non-Hispanic/Latino), 3 international. Average age 27. 175 applicants, 26% accepted, 21 enrolled. In 2016, 22 doctorates awarded. *Degree requirements:* For doctorate, comprehensive exam, thesis/dissertation or alternative, minimum of 4 years residency on campus (full-time status), minimum 124 credit hours beyond bachelor's degree, CPE exam, 2nd-year student review, minimum GPA of 3.2, research project, accredited internship of at least 2,000 hours. *Entrance requirements:* For doctorate, GRE General Test, GRE Subject Test (psychology), resume, 3 letters of recommendation, statement of objectives, 18 hours of psychology coursework (statistics, personality theory, abnormal psychology, learning, physiological psychology, and social psychology). Additional exam requirements/recommendations for international students: Required—TOEFL (minimum score 550 paper-based; 79 iBT). *Application deadline:* For fall admission, 3/15 for domestic students, 4/1 for international students; for spring admission, 9/30 for international students. Applications are processed on a rolling basis. Electronic applications accepted. *Expenses: Tuition:* Full-time $22,338; part-time $1241 per credit hour. *Required fees:* $250. Tuition and fees vary according to degree level, campus/location and program. *Financial support:* Fellowships with tuition reimbursements, research assistantships with tuition reimbursements, teaching assistantships with tuition reimbursements, career-related internships or fieldwork, institutionally sponsored loans, tuition waivers (partial), unspecified assistantships, and tuition remissions available. Support available to part-time students. Financial award application deadline: 3/1; financial award applicants required to submit FAFSA. *Faculty research:* Addictions, neuropsychology, child abuse, gender issues, personality assessment, eating disorders, psychological trauma. *Unit head:* Dr. Linda Garcia-Shelton, Program Chair, 321-674-7121, Fax: 321-674-7105, E-mail: lgarciashelton@fit.edu. *Application contact:* Cheryl A. Brown, Associate Director of Graduate Admissions, 321-674-7581, Fax: 321-723-9468, E-mail: cbrown@fit.edu.
Website: http://cpla.fit.edu/clinical/

**Florida International University,** College of Arts, Sciences, and Education, Department of Leadership and Professional Studies, Miami, FL 33199. Offers adult education and human resource development (MS, Ed D); counseling (MS), including rehabilitation counseling, school counseling; counselor education (MS), including clinical mental health counseling; educational administration and supervision (Ed D); educational leadership (MS, Certificate, Ed S); higher education (Ed D); higher education administration (MS); international and comparative education (MS); recreation and sport management (MS), including recreation and sport management, recreational therapy; school psychology (Ed S); urban education (MS), including instruction in urban settings, learning technologies, multicultural/bilingual, multicultural/TESOL, urban education. *Program availability:* Part-time, evening/weekend. *Faculty:* 27 full-time (19 women), 38 part-time/adjunct (25 women). *Students:* 253 full-time (191 women), 306 part-time (241 women); includes 444 minority (129 Black or African American, non-Hispanic/Latino; 3 Asian, non-Hispanic/Latino; 304 Hispanic/Latino; 8 Two or more races, non-Hispanic/Latino), 18 international. Average age 31. 366 applicants, 60% accepted, 115 enrolled. In 2016, 193 master's, 8 doctorates awarded. *Degree requirements:* For doctorate, thesis/dissertation. *Entrance requirements:* For master's, minimum GPA of 3.0; for doctorate and other advanced degree, GRE General Test. Additional exam requirements/recommendations for international students: Required—TOEFL (minimum score 550 paper-based; 80 iBT), IELTS (minimum score 6.3). *Application deadline:* For fall admission, 6/1 priority date for domestic students, 4/1 for international students; for winter admission, 10/1 priority date for domestic students, 9/1 for international students; for spring admission, 3/1 priority date for domestic students, 2/1 for international students. Applications are processed on a rolling basis. Application fee: $30. Electronic applications accepted. *Expenses:* Tuition, state resident: full-time $8912; part-time $446 per credit hour. Tuition, nonresident: full-time $21,393; part-time $992 per credit hour. *Required fees:* $2185; $195 per semester. Tuition and fees vary according to program. *Financial support:* Fellowships, research assistantships with tuition reimbursements, teaching assistantships with tuition reimbursements, Federal Work-Study, and tuition waivers (full and partial) available. Support available to part-time students. Financial award applicants required to submit FAFSA. *Unit head:* Dr. Benjamin Baez, Chair, 305-348-3214, Fax: 305-348-1515, E-mail: benjamin.baez@fiu.edu. *Application contact:* Nanett Rojas, Assistant Director, Graduate Admissions, 305-348-7464, Fax: 305-348-7441, E-mail: gradadm@fiu.edu.
Website: http://education.fiu.edu

**Florida International University,** College of Arts, Sciences, and Education, Department of Psychology, Miami, FL 33199. Offers behavioral analysis (MS); clinical science (PhD); cognitive neuroscience (PhD); counseling psychology (MS); developmental science (MS, PhD); legal psychology (MS, PhD); organizational psychology (MS, PhD). Program has fall admissions only. *Accreditation:* APA. *Program availability:* Part-time, evening/weekend. *Faculty:* 44 full-time (27 women), 41 part-time/adjunct (30 women). *Students:* 150 full-time (115 women), 17 part-time (10 women); includes 89 minority (8 Black or African American, non-Hispanic/Latino; 5 Asian, non-Hispanic/Latino; 75 Hispanic/Latino; 1 Two or more races, non-Hispanic/Latino), 10 international. Average age 27. 287 applicants, 24% accepted, 57 enrolled. In 2016, 35 master's, 11 doctorates awarded. Terminal master's awarded for partial completion of doctoral program. *Degree requirements:* For master's, thesis; for doctorate, comprehensive exam, thesis/dissertation. *Entrance requirements:* For master's, GRE General Test, minimum GPA of 3.0, resume, 3 letters of recommendation; for doctorate, GRE General Test, 3 letters of recommendation, resume, letter of intent, two writing samples, minimum GPA of 3.0. Additional exam requirements/recommendations for international students: Required—TOEFL (minimum score 550 paper-based; 80 iBT). *Application deadline:* For fall admission, 12/15 for domestic and international students. Application fee: $30. Electronic applications accepted. *Expenses:* Tuition, state resident: full-time $8912; part-time $446 per credit hour. Tuition, nonresident: full-time $21,393; part-time $992 per credit hour. *Required fees:* $2185; $195 per semester. Tuition and fees vary according to program. *Financial support:* Institutionally sponsored loans and scholarships/grants available. Financial award application deadline: 3/1. *Faculty research:* Legal psychology, organizational and industrial psychology, child behavior psychology. *Unit head:* Dr. William Pelham, Chair, 305-348-3002, Fax: 305-348-3646, E-mail: wpelham@fiu.edu. *Application contact:* Nanett Rojas, Assistant Director, Graduate Admissions, 305-348-7464, Fax: 305-348-7441, E-mail: gradadm@fiu.edu.

**Florida State University,** The Graduate School, College of Arts and Sciences, Department of Psychology, Program in Clinical Psychology, Tallahassee, FL 32306. Offers PhD. *Accreditation:* APA. *Faculty:* 15 full-time (8 women). *Students:* 53 full-time (40 women), 7 part-time (4 women); includes 11 minority (1 Black or African American, non-Hispanic/Latino; 2 Asian, non-Hispanic/Latino; 5 Hispanic/Latino; 3 Two or more races, non-Hispanic/Latino), 1 international. Average age 30. 230 applicants, 7% accepted, 8 enrolled. In 2016, 9 doctorates awarded. Terminal master's awarded for partial completion of doctoral program. *Degree requirements:* For doctorate, comprehensive exam, thesis/dissertation. *Entrance requirements:* For doctorate, GRE General Test, minimum GPA of 3.3, research experience, letters of recommendation. Additional exam requirements/recommendations for international students: Required—TOEFL (minimum score 80 iBT). *Application deadline:* For fall admission, 12/1 for domestic and international students. Application fee: $30. Electronic applications accepted. *Expenses:* Tuition, state resident: full-time $7263; part-time $403.51 per credit hour. Tuition, nonresident: full-time $18,087; part-time $1004.85 per credit hour. *Required fees:* $1365; $75.81 per credit hour. $20 per semester. Tuition and fees vary according to campus/location. *Financial support:* In 2016–17, 49 students received support, including 3 fellowships with full tuition reimbursements available (averaging $22,815 per year), 22 research assistantships with full tuition reimbursements available (averaging $23,815 per year), 24 teaching assistantships with full tuition reimbursements available (averaging $18,315 per year); career-related internships or fieldwork and health care benefits also available. Financial award application deadline: 12/1; financial award applicants required to submit FAFSA. *Faculty research:* Antisocial behavior, depression, addictive behavior, developmental psychopathology, anxiety. *Total annual research expenditures:* $7.2 million. *Unit head:* Dr. Jesse Cougle, Director, 850-645-8729, Fax: 850-644-7739, E-mail: cougle@psy.fsu.edu. *Application contact:* Lynda L. Gibson, Graduate Program Associate, 850-644-2499, Fax: 850-644-7739, E-mail: grad-info@psy.fsu.edu.
Website: http://www.psy.fsu.edu/

**Fordham University,** Graduate School of Arts and Sciences, Department of Psychology, Program in Clinical Psychology, New York, NY 10458. Offers PhD. *Students:* 58 full-time (44 women), 6 part-time (4 women); includes 15 minority (7 Black or African American, non-Hispanic/Latino; 1 American Indian or Alaska Native, non-Hispanic/Latino; 7 Asian, non-Hispanic/Latino), 2 international. Average age 30. 796 applicants, 2% accepted, 17 enrolled. In 2016, 8 doctorates awarded. Terminal master's awarded for partial completion of doctoral program. *Degree requirements:* For doctorate, comprehensive exam, thesis/dissertation, clinical internship. *Entrance requirements:* For doctorate, GRE General Test, GRE Subject Test. Additional exam requirements/recommendations for international students: Required—TOEFL (minimum score 600 paper-based). *Application deadline:* For fall admission, 12/14 for domestic students. Application fee: $70. Electronic applications accepted. *Financial support:* In 2016–17,

55 students received support, including 8 fellowships with tuition reimbursements available (averaging $26,390 per year), 10 research assistantships with tuition reimbursements available (averaging $12,285 per year), 7 teaching assistantships with tuition reimbursements available (averaging $12,871 per year); career-related internships or fieldwork, institutionally sponsored loans, tuition waivers (full and partial), and unspecified assistantships also available. Financial award application deadline: 12/14. *Total annual research expenditures:* $1.9 million. *Unit head:* Dr. Monica Rivera-Mindt, Program Director, 212-636-7453, E-mail: riveramindt@fordham.edu. *Application contact:* Bernadette Valentino-Morrison, Director of Graduate Admissions, 718-817-4419, Fax: 718-817-3566, E-mail: valentinomor@fordham.edu.

**Franciscan University of Steubenville,** Graduate Programs, Department of Clinical Mental Health Counseling, Steubenville, OH 43952-1763. Offers MA. *Accreditation:* ACA. *Program availability:* Part-time. *Degree requirements:* For master's, case presentation, integrative paper. *Entrance requirements:* For master's, GRE General Test or MAT for those with a GPA below 3.0, minimum undergraduate GPA of 2.5. Additional exam requirements/recommendations for international students: Required—TOEFL. Electronic applications accepted. Application fee is waived when completed online.

**Francis Marion University,** Graduate Programs, Department of Psychology, Florence, SC 29502-0547. Offers applied psychology (MS), including clinical/counseling psychology, school psychology; school psychology (SSP). *Program availability:* Part-time, evening/weekend. *Degree requirements:* For master's, internship. *Entrance requirements:* For master's, GRE General Test, official transcripts, two letters of recommendation. Additional exam requirements/recommendations for international students: Required—TOEFL (minimum score 550 paper-based; 79 iBT). *Expenses:* Tuition, state resident: full-time $10,100; part-time $505 per credit hour. Tuition, nonresident: full-time $20,196; part-time $1009.80 per credit hour. *Required fees:* $14.80 per credit hour. $73 per semester. Tuition and fees vary according to course load and program. *Faculty research:* Parenting and family relationships, child development, applied behavioral analysis, post-traumatic stress disorder, clinical psychology in adults.

**Fuller Theological Seminary,** Graduate Programs, Pasadena, CA 91182. Offers Christian leadership (MACL); clinical psychology (PhD, Psy D); family studies (MA); global leadership (MA); global ministries (D Min); global ministries (Korean language) (D Min); intercultural studies (MA, Th M, PhD); intercultural studies (Korean language) (MA); marital and family therapy (MS); marriage and family enrichment (Certificate); ministry (M Div, D Min); missiology (D Miss); missiology (Korean language) (Th M); theology (MA, Th M, PhD), including evangelism (MA), family life education (MA), pastoral ministry (MA), recovery ministry (MA), worship music ministry (MA), worship, theology, and the arts (MA); youth, family, and culture (MA); theology and ministry (MA).

**Gallaudet University,** The Graduate School, Washington, DC 20002-3625. Offers American Sign Language/English bilingual early childhood deaf education: birth to 5 (Certificate); audiology (Au D); clinical psychology (PhD); deaf and hard of hearing infants, toddlers, and their families (Certificate); deaf education (MA, Ed S); deaf history (Certificate); deaf studies (Certificate); educating deaf students with disabilities (Certificate); education: teacher preparation (MA), including deaf education, early childhood education and deaf education, elementary education and deaf education, secondary education and deaf education; educational neuroscience (PhD); hearing, speech and language sciences (MS, PhD); international development (MA); interpretation (MA, PhD), including combined interpreting practice and research (MA), interpreting research (MA); linguistics (MA, PhD); mental health counseling (MA); peer mentoring (Certificate); public administration (MPA); school counseling (MA); school psychology (Psy S); sign language teaching (MA); social work (MSW); speech-language pathology (MS). *Program availability:* Part-time. *Students:* 297 full-time (231 women), 129 part-time (97 women); includes 105 minority (35 Black or African American, non-Hispanic/Latino; 20 Asian, non-Hispanic/Latino; 39 Hispanic/Latino; 11 Two or more races, non-Hispanic/Latino), 22 international. Average age 30. 471 applicants, 52% accepted, 147 enrolled. In 2016, 138 master's, 25 doctorates, 14 other advanced degrees awarded. Terminal master's awarded for partial completion of doctoral program. *Degree requirements:* For master's, comprehensive exam (for some programs), thesis optional; for doctorate, comprehensive exam, thesis/dissertation. *Entrance requirements:* For master's and doctorate, GRE General Test or MAT, letters of recommendation, interviews, goals statement, American Sign Language proficiency interview, written English competency. Additional exam requirements/recommendations for international students: Required—TOEFL. *Application deadline:* For fall admission, 2/15 for domestic students. Applications are processed on a rolling basis. Application fee: $75. Electronic applications accepted. *Expenses: Tuition:* Full-time $17,100; part-time $950 per credit hour. *Required fees:* $3725; $276 per semester. *Financial support:* Fellowships, research assistantships, teaching assistantships, career-related internships or fieldwork, Federal Work-Study, scholarships/grants, tuition waivers (partial), and unspecified assistantships available. Support available to part-time students. Financial award application deadline: 7/1; financial award applicants required to submit FAFSA. *Faculty research:* Signing math dictionaries, telecommunications access, cancer genetics, linguistics, visual language and visual learning, integrated quantum materials, deaf legal discourse, advance recruitment and retention in geosciences. *Unit head:* Dr. Gaurav Mathur, Dean, Graduate School and Continuing Studies, 202-250-2380, Fax: 202-651-5027, E-mail: gaurav.mathur@gallaudet.edu. *Application contact:* Wednesday Luria, Coordinator of Prospective Graduate Student Services, 202-651-5400, Fax: 202-651-5295, E-mail: graduate.school@gallaudet.edu.

**Gannon University,** School of Graduate Studies, College of Humanities, Education, and Social Sciences, School of Humanities, Program in Clinical Mental Health Counseling, Erie, PA 16541-0001. Offers MS. *Accreditation:* ACA. *Program availability:* Part-time, evening/weekend. *Students:* 25 full-time (20 women), 9 part-time (8 women); includes 1 minority (Black or African American, non-Hispanic/Latino), 2 international. Average age 27. 36 applicants, 50% accepted, 11 enrolled. In 2016, 12 master's awarded. *Degree requirements:* For master's, thesis, internship. *Entrance requirements:* For master's, bachelor's degree from approved institution, resume, 3 letters of recommendation, essay, interview, minimum GPA of 2.8, PA child abuse clearances and PA State Police criminal record check dated within a year of application. Additional exam requirements/recommendations for international students: Required—TOEFL (minimum score 79 iBT). *Application deadline:* Applications are processed on a rolling basis. Application fee: $25. Electronic applications accepted. Application fee is waived when completed online. *Expenses: Tuition:* Full-time $17,370. *Required fees:* $550. Tuition and fees vary according to course load and program. *Financial support:* Federal Work-Study and unspecified assistantships available. Financial award application deadline: 7/1; financial award applicants required to submit FAFSA. *Unit head:* Dr. Timothy Coppock, Director, 814-871-5793, E-mail: coppock001@gannon.edu. *Application contact:* Bridget Philip, Director of Graduate Admissions, 814-871-7412, E-mail: graduate@gannon.edu.

**Geneva College,** Master of Arts in Counseling Program, Beaver Falls, PA 15010-3599. Offers clinical mental health counseling (MA); marriage and family counseling (MA); school counseling (MA). *Accreditation:* ACA. *Program availability:* Part-time, evening/weekend. *Faculty:* 6 full-time (3 women), 3 part-time/adjunct (2 women). *Students:* 35 full-time (28 women), 32 part-time (23 women); includes 11 minority (9 Black or African American, non-Hispanic/Latino; 2 Hispanic/Latino). Average age 34. 42 applicants, 71%

accepted, 21 enrolled. In 2016, 24 master's awarded. *Degree requirements:* For master's, comprehensive exam, 50-60 credits (depending on program), practicum, internship. *Entrance requirements:* For master's, minimum GPA of 3.0 (preferred), 3 letters of recommendation, essay on career goals, resume of educational and professional experiences. Additional exam requirements/recommendations for international students: Required—TOEFL. *Application deadline:* For fall admission, 9/1 for domestic students; for spring admission, 1/10 for domestic students. Applications are processed on a rolling basis. Electronic applications accepted. *Expenses:* $670 per credit. *Financial support:* In 2016–17, 3 students received support. Research assistantships, teaching assistantships, career-related internships or fieldwork, and unspecified assistantships available. Financial award application deadline: 8/1; financial award applicants required to submit FAFSA. *Faculty research:* Blended family counseling; premarital and newlywed couples; religion in clinical supervision; conceptual mapping in research, supervision, and clinical work. *Unit head:* Dr. Shannan Shiderly, Program Director, 724-847-6649, Fax: 724-847-6101, E-mail: slshider@geneva.edu. *Application contact:* Marina Frazier, Graduate Program Manager, 724-847-6697, E-mail: counseling@geneva.edu.
Website: http://www.geneva.edu/page/grad_counseling

**George Fox University,** College of Education, Graduate Department of Counseling, Newberg, OR 97132-2697. Offers clinical mental health counseling (MA); marriage, couple and family counseling (MA, Certificate); school counseling (MA, Certificate); school psychology (Ed S). *Program availability:* Part-time. *Degree requirements:* For master's, clinical project. *Entrance requirements:* For master's, MAT or GRE, bachelor's degree from regionally-accredited college or university, minimum cumulative GPA of 3.0, 1 professional and 1 academic reference, resume, on-campus interview, official transcripts. Additional exam requirements/recommendations for international students: Required—TOEFL (minimum score 577 paper-based; 90 iBT), IELTS (minimum score 7). Electronic applications accepted. *Expenses:* Contact institution.

**George Fox University,** Program in Clinical Psychology, Newberg, OR 97132-2697. Offers Psy D. *Accreditation:* APA. *Degree requirements:* For doctorate, thesis/dissertation, internship. *Entrance requirements:* For doctorate, GRE General Test, bachelor's degree from regionally-accredited university or college, minimum undergraduate GPA of 3.0 during previous 2 years, interview, official transcripts. Additional exam requirements/recommendations for international students: Required—TOEFL (minimum score 80 iBT), IELTS (minimum score 6.5). Electronic applications accepted. *Expenses:* Contact institution. *Faculty research:* Psychological assessment, impact of psychological services on medical outcome, spirituality and wellness, effectiveness of clinical training and supervision, shame.

**The George Washington University,** Columbian College of Arts and Sciences, Department of Psychology, Washington, DC 20052. Offers applied social psychology (PhD); clinical psychology (PhD); cognitive neuroscience (PhD). *Accreditation:* APA. *Program availability:* Part-time, evening/weekend. *Faculty:* 25 full-time (14 women). *Students:* 39 full-time (28 women), 30 part-time (21 women); includes 21 minority (9 Black or African American, non-Hispanic/Latino; 4 Asian, non-Hispanic/Latino; 6 Hispanic/Latino; 2 Two or more races, non-Hispanic/Latino), 7 international. Average age 28. 442 applicants, 5% accepted, 12 enrolled. In 2016, 12 doctorates awarded. *Degree requirements:* For doctorate, thesis/dissertation or alternative, general exam. *Entrance requirements:* For doctorate, GRE General Test, minimum GPA of 3.0. Additional exam requirements/recommendations for international students: Required—TOEFL (minimum score 550 paper-based; 80 iBT). *Application deadline:* For fall admission, 1/15 for domestic and international students. Application fee: $75. *Financial support:* In 2016–17, 62 students received support. Fellowships with tuition reimbursements available, teaching assistantships with tuition reimbursements available, career-related internships or fieldwork, Federal Work-Study, and tuition waivers available. *Unit head:* Dr. Paul Poppen, Chair, 202-994-6324, E-mail: pjp@gwu.edu. *Application contact:* Information Contact, 202-994-6320, Fax: 202-994-1602, E-mail: psydept@gwu.edu.
Website: http://psychology.columbian.gwu.edu/

**The George Washington University,** Graduate School of Education and Human Development, Department of Counseling and Human Development, Program in Clinical Mental Health Counseling, Washington, DC 20052. Offers MA. *Students:* 26 full-time (22 women), 6 part-time (all women); includes 13 minority (5 Black or African American, non-Hispanic/Latino; 4 Asian, non-Hispanic/Latino; 4 Hispanic/Latino), 1 international. Average age 28. 157 applicants, 34% accepted, 15 enrolled. In 2016, 18 master's awarded. *Degree requirements:* For master's, internship. *Entrance requirements:* For master's, GRE or MAT, two letters of recommendation, 1- to 2-page statement of purpose, official transcripts from all institutions attended, resume. Additional exam requirements/recommendations for international students: Required—TOEFL or IELTS. *Financial support:* Fellowships available. *Unit head:* Dr. Kenneth C. Hergenrather, Chair, 202-994-1334, E-mail: hergenkc@gwu.edu. *Application contact:* Sarah Lang, Director of Graduate Admissions, 202-994-1447, Fax: 202-994-7207, E-mail: slang@gwu.edu.
Website: http://gsehd.gwu.edu/clinical-mental-health-counseling-masters

**Georgian Court University,** School of Arts and Sciences, Lakewood, NJ 08701-2697. Offers applied behavior analysis (MA); clinical mental health counseling (MA); holistic health studies (MA, Certificate); homeland security (MS, Certificate); mercy spirituality (Certificate); parish business management (Certificate); professional counselor (Certificate); school psychology (MA, Certificate); theology (MA, Certificate). *Program availability:* Part-time, evening/weekend. *Faculty:* 19 full-time (11 women), 6 part-time/adjunct (3 women). *Students:* 90 full-time (75 women), 107 part-time (79 women); includes 34 minority (9 Black or African American, non-Hispanic/Latino; 20 Hispanic/Latino; 5 Two or more races, non-Hispanic/Latino), 1 international. Average age 34. 187 applicants, 49% accepted, 60 enrolled. In 2016, 66 master's, 17 other advanced degrees awarded. *Degree requirements:* For master's, comprehensive exam (for some programs), thesis (for some programs). *Entrance requirements:* For master's, GRE, GMAT, or NTE/PRAXIS, 3 letters of recommendation. Additional exam requirements/recommendations for international students: Required—TOEFL (minimum score 550 paper-based). *Application deadline:* For fall admission, 8/15 for domestic students, 5/1 for international students; for spring admission, 1/15 for domestic students, 10/1 for international students. Applications are processed on a rolling basis. Application fee: $40. Electronic applications accepted. *Expenses: Tuition:* Full-time $15,079; part-time $839 per credit. *Required fees:* $968; $496 per credit. Tuition and fees vary according to campus/location and program. *Financial support:* Scholarships/grants, health care benefits, and unspecified assistantships available. Financial award application deadline: 4/15; financial award applicants required to submit FAFSA. *Unit head:* Dr. Mary Chinery, Dean, 732-987-2493, Fax: 732-987-2007, E-mail: mchinery@georgian.edu. *Application contact:* Patrick Givens, Director of Graduate and Professional Studies Admissions, 732-987-2736, Fax: 732-987-2000, E-mail: gps@georgian.edu.
Website: http://georgian.edu/academics/school-of-arts-sciences/

**Georgia Southern University,** Jack N. Averitt College of Graduate Studies, College of Liberal Arts and Social Sciences, Program in Psychology, Statesboro, GA 30460. Offers clinical psychology (Psy D); psychology (MS). *Students:* 53 full-time (35 women), 15 part-time (10 women); includes 14 minority (3 Black or African American, non-Hispanic/

## Clinical Psychology

Latino; 3 Asian, non-Hispanic/Latino; 5 Hispanic/Latino; 3 Two or more races, non-Hispanic/Latino), 1 international. Average age 27. 118 applicants, 27% accepted, 18 enrolled. In 2016, 11 master's, 3 doctorates awarded. Terminal master's awarded for partial completion of doctoral program. *Degree requirements:* For master's, comprehensive exam, thesis (for some programs), terminal exam; for doctorate, comprehensive exam, thesis/dissertation, clinical qualifying exam, practicum, internship. *Entrance requirements:* For master's, GRE General Test, minimum GPA of 3.0, introductory courses in psychology and statistics, letters of recommendation; for doctorate, GRE General Test; GRE Subject Test (if no undergraduate degree in psychology), minimum undergraduate GPA of 3.25; 3 letters of reference; statement of purpose. Additional exam requirements/recommendations for international students: Required—TOEFL (minimum score 550 paper-based; 80 iBT), IELTS (minimum score 6). *Application deadline:* For fall admission, 1/15 priority date for domestic students, 1/15 for international students. Application fee: $50. Electronic applications accepted. *Expenses:* Tuition, state resident: full-time $7236; part-time $277 per semester hour. Tuition, nonresident: full-time $27,118; part-time $1105 per semester hour. *Required fees:* $2092. *Financial support:* In 2016–17, 39 students received support, including 4 fellowships with full tuition reimbursements available (averaging $7,750 per year), 6 research assistantships with full tuition reimbursements available (averaging $7,750 per year), 17 teaching assistantships with full tuition reimbursements available (averaging $7,750 per year); career-related internships or fieldwork, Federal Work-Study, scholarships/grants, tuition waivers (full), and unspecified assistantships also available. Support available to part-time students. Financial award application deadline: 4/15; financial award applicants required to submit FAFSA. *Faculty research:* Clinical psychology, cognitive psychology, social psychology, developmental psychology, teaching and research, social judgment and behavior, psychology of religion. *Unit head:* Dr. Michael Nielsen, Graduate Director, 912-478-5539, Fax: 912-478-0751, E-mail: mnielsen@georgiasouthern.edu.
Website: http://class.georgiasouthern.edu/psychology/

**Georgia State University,** College of Arts and Sciences, Department of Psychology, Atlanta, GA 30302-3083. Offers clinical (PhD); cognitive sciences (PhD); community (PhD); developmental (PhD); neuropsychology and behavioral neuroscience (PhD). *Accreditation:* APA. *Faculty:* 40 full-time (26 women). *Students:* 101 full-time (80 women), 2 part-time (both women); includes 25 minority (8 Black or African American, non-Hispanic/Latino; 9 Asian, non-Hispanic/Latino; 3 Hispanic/Latino; 5 Two or more races, non-Hispanic/Latino), 7 international. Average age 28. 517 applicants, 6% accepted, 17 enrolled. In 2016, 19 doctorates awarded. *Degree requirements:* For doctorate, comprehensive exam, thesis/dissertation, residency year (for clinical only). *Entrance requirements:* For doctorate, GRE. Additional exam requirements/recommendations for international students: Required—TOEFL (minimum score 550 paper-based; 80 iBT). *Application deadline:* For fall admission, 12/1 for domestic and international students. Application fee: $50. Electronic applications accepted. *Expenses:* Tuition, state resident: full-time $6876; part-time $382 per credit hour. Tuition, nonresident: full-time $22,374; part-time $1243 per credit hour. *Required fees:* $2128; $1064 per term. Part-time tuition and fees vary according to course load and program. *Financial support:* In 2016–17, fellowships with full tuition reimbursements (averaging $19,282 per year), research assistantships with full tuition reimbursements (averaging $5,173 per year), teaching assistantships with full tuition reimbursements (averaging $6,389 per year) were awarded; scholarships/grants, traineeships, health care benefits, and unspecified assistantships also available. Financial award applicants required to submit FAFSA. *Faculty research:* Clinical psychology, developmental psychology, community psychology, neuropsychology and behavioral neuroscience, cognitive sciences. *Unit head:* Dr. Lisa Armistead, Chair, 404-413-6205, Fax: 404-413-6207, E-mail: lparmistead@gsu.edu. *Application contact:* Dr. Lindsey Cohen, Director of Graduate Studies, 404-413-6263, Fax: 404-413-6207, E-mail: llcohen@gsu.edu.

**Goddard College,** Graduate Division, Master of Arts in Clinical Mental Health Counseling Program, Plainfield, VT 05667-9432. Offers MA.

**Grace College,** Department of Graduate Counseling, Winona Lake, IN 46590-1294. Offers clinical mental health counseling (MA). *Accreditation:* ACA. *Program availability:* Part-time. *Degree requirements:* For master's, comprehensive exam, portfolio, internships. *Entrance requirements:* For master's, GRE, references, background check, interview, minimum GPA of 3.0. Additional exam requirements/recommendations for international students: Required—TOEFL. Electronic applications accepted. Application fee is waived when completed online. *Faculty research:* Trauma and sexual abuse.

**The Graduate Center, City University of New York,** Graduate Studies, Program in Psychology, New York, NY 10016-4039. Offers basic applied neurocognition (PhD); biopsychology (PhD); clinical psychology (PhD); developmental psychology (PhD); environmental psychology (PhD); experimental psychology (PhD); industrial psychology (PhD); learning processes (PhD); neuropsychology (PhD); psychology (PhD); social personality (PhD). *Degree requirements:* For doctorate, one foreign language, thesis/dissertation. *Entrance requirements:* For doctorate, GRE General Test. Additional exam requirements/recommendations for international students: Required—TOEFL. Electronic applications accepted.

**Hawai`i Pacific University,** College of Liberal Arts, Program in Clinical Mental Health Counseling, Honolulu, HI 96813. Offers MA. *Program availability:* Part-time, evening/weekend. *Faculty:* 5 full-time (3 women), 5 part-time/adjunct (3 women). *Students:* 23 full-time (17 women), 7 part-time (5 women); includes 16 minority (4 Asian, non-Hispanic/Latino; 4 Hispanic/Latino; 8 Two or more races, non-Hispanic/Latino), 1 international. Average age 28. 26 applicants, 77% accepted, 10 enrolled. In 2016, 16 master's awarded. *Entrance requirements:* For master's, GRE, minimum cumulative undergraduate GPA of 3.0; minimum of 15 credit hours of work in psychology, including at least one course each in statistics and research methods. Additional exam requirements/recommendations for international students: Recommended—TOEFL (minimum score 550 paper-based; 80 iBT), IELTS (minimum score 6), TWE (minimum score 5). *Application deadline:* For fall admission, 2/15 priority date for domestic students. Applications are processed on a rolling basis. Application fee: $50. Electronic applications accepted. *Expenses: Tuition:* Full-time $17,190; part-time $955 per credit. *Required fees:* $150; $26 per credit. Tuition and fees vary according to course load and program. *Financial support:* In 2016–17, 6 students received support. Career-related internships or fieldwork, Federal Work-Study, scholarships/grants, tuition waivers, and unspecified assistantships available. Financial award application deadline: 3/1; financial award applicants required to submit FAFSA. *Unit head:* Dr. Michael Erickson, Department Chair, 808-356-5211, E-mail: merickson@hpu.edu. *Application contact:* Danny Lam, Assistant Director of Graduate Admissions, 808-544-1135, E-mail: graduate@hpu.edu.
Website: http://www.hpu.edu/CHSS/Psychology/MA_CHMC/index.html

**Heidelberg University,** Master of Arts in Counseling Program, Tiffin, OH 44883-2462. Offers clinical mental health counseling (MA); school counseling (MA). *Accreditation:* ACA. *Program availability:* Part-time, evening/weekend. *Students:* 15 full-time (11 women), 31 part-time (26 women). In 2016, 12 master's awarded. *Degree requirements:* For master's, thesis or alternative, counseling practicum, internship. *Entrance requirements:* For master's, bachelor's degree, minimum GPA of 2.9, 12 hours of course work in behavioral sciences, 3 letters of reference, 2-3 page goal statement, background check, interview. Additional exam requirements/recommendations for international students: Required—TOEFL (minimum score 550 paper-based, 79 iBT) or IELTS (minimum score 6.5). *Application deadline:* Applications are processed on a rolling basis. Electronic applications accepted. *Expenses:* $510 per semester hour. *Financial support:* Applicants required to submit FAFSA. *Unit head:* Dr. Jo-Ann Lipford Sanders, Associate Dean and Director of Master of Arts in Counseling, 419-448-2312, E-mail: jsanders@heidelberg.edu. *Application contact:* Katie Slosser, Graduate Admissions Coordinator, 419-448-2602, Fax: 419-448-2565, E-mail: kslosser@heidelberg.edu. Website: https://www.heidelberg.edu/academics/programs/master-of-counseling

**Hodges University,** Graduate Programs, Naples, FL 34119. Offers accounting (M Acc); business administration (MBA); clinical mental health counseling (MS); health services administration (MS); information systems management (MIS); legal studies (MS); management (MSM). *Program availability:* Part-time, evening/weekend, 100% online, blended/hybrid learning. *Degree requirements:* For master's, comprehensive exam (for some programs), thesis (for some programs). *Entrance requirements:* For master's, essay. Additional exam requirements/recommendations for international students: Recommended—TOEFL. Electronic applications accepted.

**Hofstra University,** College of Liberal Arts and Sciences, Programs in Psychology, Hempstead, NY 11549. Offers applied organizational psychology (PhD); clinical psychology (PhD); industrial/organizational psychology (MA); school-community psychology (Psy D). *Accreditation:* APA. *Program availability:* Part-time, evening/weekend. *Students:* 195 full-time (130 women), 32 part-time (18 women); includes 43 minority (9 Black or African American, non-Hispanic/Latino; 2 American Indian or Alaska Native, non-Hispanic/Latino; 8 Asian, non-Hispanic/Latino; 21 Hispanic/Latino; 2 Native Hawaiian or other Pacific Islander, non-Hispanic/Latino; 1 Two or more races, non-Hispanic/Latino), 21 international. Average age 27. 299 applicants, 40% accepted, 54 enrolled. In 2016, 51 master's, 36 doctorates awarded. *Degree requirements:* For master's, comprehensive exam, thesis optional, internship, minimum GPA of 3.0; for doctorate, comprehensive exam, thesis/dissertation, 1st year qualifying examination, 2nd year research project, successful practicum/externship placements, written presentation and successful oral defense of dissertation, completion of full-time internship. *Entrance requirements:* For master's, GRE General Test, minimum GPA of 3.0, essay, interview; for doctorate, GRE General Test, GRE Subject Test (psychology), 3 letters of recommendation, interview, essay, curriculum vitae. Additional exam requirements/recommendations for international students: Required—TOEFL (minimum score 550 paper-based; 80 iBT). *Application deadline:* For fall admission, 12/31 for domestic and international students. Application fee: $75. Electronic applications accepted. *Expenses: Tuition:* Full-time $1240. *Required fees:* $970. Tuition and fees vary according to program. *Financial support:* In 2016–17, 119 students received support, including 112 fellowships with full and partial tuition reimbursements available (averaging $8,418 per year), 4 research assistantships with full and partial tuition reimbursements available (averaging $5,940 per year); career-related internships or fieldwork, Federal Work-Study, institutionally sponsored loans, scholarships/grants, traineeships, tuition waivers (full and partial), and unspecified assistantships also available. Support available to part-time students. Financial award applicants required to submit FAFSA. *Faculty research:* PTSD, secondary trauma, childhood adjustment problems, the impact of exercise on emotional states treatment of anxiety disorders and depression, cognitive appraisal and emotion, evolutionary psychology - implications for clinical psychology (evolutionary psychopathology, theory of human nature), treatment of phobic and post-traumatic stress disorders with exposure therapies, self-help and motivational interviewing. *Unit head:* Dr. Craig Johnson, Chairperson, 516-463-5636, E-mail: craig.a.johnson@hofstra.edu. *Application contact:* Sunil Samuel, Assistant Vice President of Admissions, 516-463-4723, Fax: 516-463-4664, E-mail: graduateadmission@hofstra.edu.
Website: http://www.hofstra.edu/hclas

**Hood College,** Graduate School, Program in Counseling, Frederick, MD 21701-8575. Offers clinical mental health counseling (MS); school counseling (MS). *Program availability:* Part-time, evening/weekend. *Faculty:* 5 full-time, 2 part-time/adjunct. *Students:* 28 full-time (24 women), 15 part-time (all women); includes 5 minority (3 Black or African American, non-Hispanic/Latino; 2 Hispanic/Latino), 2 international. Average age 30. 41 applicants, 83% accepted, 24 enrolled. *Degree requirements:* For master's, practicum, internship. *Entrance requirements:* For master's, minimum GPA of 3.0, personal statement, resume, two letters of recommendation. Additional exam requirements/recommendations for international students: Required—TOEFL (minimum score 575 paper-based; 89 iBT), IELTS (minimum score 6.5). *Application deadline:* For fall admission, 6/15 for domestic and international students; for winter admission, 11/15 for domestic and international students. Application fee: $35. Electronic applications accepted. *Expenses:* $620 per credit hour; $110 comprehensive fee per semester. *Financial support:* Research assistantships with full tuition reimbursements, tuition waivers (partial), and unspecified assistantships available. Financial award applicants required to submit FAFSA. *Unit head:* April Boulton, Interim Dean of the Graduate School, 301-696-3600, E-mail: gofurther@hood.edu. *Application contact:* Jan Marcus, Assistant Director of Graduate Admissions, 301-696-3600, E-mail: gofurther@hood.edu.

**Howard University,** Graduate School, Department of Psychology, Washington, DC 20059-0002. Offers clinical psychology (PhD); developmental psychology (PhD); experimental psychology (PhD); neuropsychology (PhD); personality psychology (PhD); psychology (MS); social psychology (PhD). *Accreditation:* APA (one or more programs are accredited). *Program availability:* Part-time. *Degree requirements:* For master's, thesis; for doctorate, comprehensive exam, thesis/dissertation, qualifying exam. *Entrance requirements:* For master's, GRE General Test, minimum GPA of 2.5, bachelor's degree in psychology or related field; for doctorate, GRE General Test, minimum GPA of 3.0. *Faculty research:* Personality and psychophysiology, educational and social development of African-American children, child and adult psychopathology.

**Husson University,** Graduate Programs in Counseling and Human Relations, Bangor, ME 04401-2999. Offers clinical mental health counseling (MS); human relations (MS); school counseling (MS). *Accreditation:* ACA. *Program availability:* Part-time, evening/weekend. *Faculty:* 3 full-time (2 women), 5 part-time/adjunct (all women). *Students:* 17 full-time (15 women), 55 part-time (48 women); includes 1 minority (Black or African American, non-Hispanic/Latino), 2 international. Average age 32. 50 applicants, 52% accepted, 20 enrolled. In 2016, 16 master's awarded. *Degree requirements:* For master's, comprehensive exam (for some programs), thesis optional. *Entrance requirements:* For master's, BS with minimum GPA of 3.0, letters of recommendation, interview. Additional exam requirements/recommendations for international students: Required—TOEFL (minimum score 550 paper-based; 80 iBT), IELTS (minimum score 6.5). *Application deadline:* For fall admission, 2/1 for domestic students. Application fee: $50. Electronic applications accepted. *Expenses:* $560 per credit tuition; $450 full-time fees; $220 part-time (6-9 credits); $110 part-time (less than 6 credits per year). *Financial support:* Federal Work-Study, scholarships/grants, and unspecified assistantships available. Financial award application deadline: 4/15; financial award applicants required to submit FAFSA. *Faculty research:* Challenges and rewards of counseling practice in rural, small town and neighborhood settings. *Unit head:* Dr. Deborah Drew, Director, Graduate Counseling Programs, 207-992-4912, Fax: 207-992-4952, E-mail: drewd@husson.edu. *Application contact:* Kristen Card, Director of Graduate

Admissions, 207-404-5660, Fax: 207-941-7935, E-mail: cardk@husson.edu. Website: http://www.husson.edu/college-of-health-and-education/school-of-education/graduate-programs/

**Idaho State University,** Office of Graduate Studies, College of Arts and Letters, Department of Psychology, Program in Clinical Psychology, Pocatello, ID 83209-8112. Offers PhD. *Degree requirements:* For doctorate, comprehensive exam, thesis/dissertation, 1 year full-time clinical internship. *Entrance requirements:* For doctorate, GRE General Test, GRE Subject Test, MS in psychology. Additional exam requirements/recommendations for international students: Required—TOEFL (minimum score 550 paper-based; 80 iBT). Electronic applications accepted. *Faculty research:* Pre-adolescent behavior, substance abuse training, trauma related problems.

**Illinois Institute of Technology,** Graduate College, Lewis College of Human Sciences, Department of Psychology, Chicago, IL 60616. Offers clinical psychology (PhD); industrial and organizational psychology (PhD); personnel and human resource development (MS); rehabilitation and mental health counseling (MS); rehabilitation counseling education (PhD). *Accreditation:* APA (one or more programs are accredited); CORE. *Program availability:* Part-time, evening/weekend. Terminal master's awarded for partial completion of doctoral program. *Degree requirements:* For master's, thesis (for some programs); for doctorate, comprehensive exam, thesis/dissertation, minimum of 107 credit hours, 1-year full-time internship. *Entrance requirements:* For master's, GRE General Test (minimum score 298 Quantitative and Verbal, 3.0 Analytical Writing), minimum GPA of 3.0; 3 letters of recommendation; bachelor's degree from accredited institution (for personnel and human resource development); for doctorate, GRE General Test (minimum score 298 Quantitative and Verbal, 3.0 Analytical Writing), bachelor's or master's degree from accredited institution, recommendations. Additional exam requirements/recommendations for international students: Required—TOEFL (minimum score 550 paper-based; 80 iBT). Electronic applications accepted. *Faculty research:* Clinical psychology, rehabilitation and mental health counseling, industrial organizational psychology.

**Illinois State University,** Graduate School, College of Arts and Sciences, Department of Psychology, Normal, IL 61790-2200. Offers psychology (MA, MS), including clinical-counseling psychology, cognitive and behavioral sciences, developmental psychology, industrial/organizational-social psychology; school psychology (PhD, SSP). *Accreditation:* APA. *Degree requirements:* For master's, thesis or alternative; for doctorate, variable foreign language requirement, thesis/dissertation, 2 terms of residency, internship, practicum. *Entrance requirements:* For master's, GRE General Test, GRE Subject Test, minimum GPA of 3.0 in last 60 hours of course work; for doctorate, GRE General Test. *Faculty research:* Comprehensive evaluation system for the central region professional development grant, Illinois school psychology internship consortium, for children's sake.

**Immaculata University,** College of Graduate Studies, Department of Psychology, Immaculata, PA 19345. Offers clinical mental health counseling (MA); clinical psychology (Psy D); forensic psychology (Graduate Certificate); integrative psychotherapy (Graduate Certificate); neuropsychology (Graduate Certificate); psychodynamic psychotherapy (Graduate Certificate); psychological testing (Graduate Certificate); school counseling (MA, Graduate Certificate); school psychology (MA). *Accreditation:* APA. *Program availability:* Part-time, evening/weekend. Terminal master's awarded for partial completion of doctoral program. *Degree requirements:* For master's, comprehensive exam, thesis optional; for doctorate, comprehensive exam, thesis/dissertation. *Entrance requirements:* For master's, GRE General Test or MAT, minimum GPA of 3.0; for doctorate, GRE General Test or MAT, minimum GPA of 3.5. Additional exam requirements/recommendations for international students: Required—TOEFL, IELTS. Electronic applications accepted. *Faculty research:* Supervision ethics, psychology of teaching, gender.

**Indiana State University,** College of Graduate and Professional Studies, Bayh College of Education, Department of Communication Disorders and Counseling, School, and Educational Psychology, Terre Haute, IN 47809. Offers clinical mental health counseling (MS); communication disorders (MS); school counseling (M Ed); school psychology (PhD, Ed S); MA/MS. *Accreditation:* ACA; ASHA; NCATE. *Program availability:* Part-time, evening/weekend. *Degree requirements:* For master's, thesis optional; for doctorate, thesis/dissertation, research tools proficiency tests. *Entrance requirements:* For master's, GRE General Test or MAT, minimum undergraduate GPA of 2.75; for doctorate, GRE General Test, master's degree, minimum undergraduate GPA of 3.5. Electronic applications accepted. *Faculty research:* Vocational development supervision.

**Indiana State University,** College of Graduate and Professional Studies, College of Arts and Sciences, Department of Psychology, Terre Haute, IN 47809. Offers clinical psychology (Psy D); general psychology (MA, MS). *Accreditation:* APA (one or more programs are accredited). Terminal master's awarded for partial completion of doctoral program. *Degree requirements:* For master's, thesis (for some programs); for doctorate, comprehensive exam, thesis/dissertation, internship, professional research project. *Entrance requirements:* For master's, GRE General Test, 12 semester hours of course work in psychology, minimum GPA of 2.75; for doctorate, GRE General Test, minimum GPA of 3.0. Additional exam requirements/recommendations for international students: Required—TOEFL (minimum score 550 paper-based). Electronic applications accepted.

**Indiana University of Pennsylvania,** School of Graduate Studies and Research, College of Education and Educational Technology, Department of Counseling, Program in Clinical Mental Health Counseling, Indiana, PA 15705. Offers MA. *Program availability:* Part-time, evening/weekend. *Faculty:* 12 full-time (10 women), 5 part-time/adjunct (all women). *Students:* 70 full-time (58 women), 33 part-time (27 women); includes 10 minority (6 Black or African American, non-Hispanic/Latino; 2 Hispanic/Latino; 2 Two or more races, non-Hispanic/Latino), 1 international. Average age 30. 112 applicants, 46% accepted, 40 enrolled. In 2016, 43 master's awarded. *Entrance requirements:* For master's, minimum undergraduate GPA of 2.8. Additional exam requirements/recommendations for international students: Required—TOEFL (minimum score 540 paper-based). *Application deadline:* For fall admission, 3/17 priority date for domestic students. Electronic applications accepted. *Expenses:* Tuition, state resident: full-time $8694; part-time $483 per credit. Tuition, nonresident: full-time $13,050; part-time $725 per credit. *Required fees:* $157 per credit. $50 per term. Tuition and fees vary according to course load and program. *Financial support:* In 2016–17, 13 research assistantships with tuition reimbursements (averaging $2,609 per year) were awarded; fellowships with full tuition reimbursements, career-related internships or fieldwork, Federal Work-Study, scholarships/grants, and unspecified assistantships also available. Financial award application deadline: 4/15; financial award applicants required to submit FAFSA. *Unit head:* Dr. Robert Witchel, Program Coordinator, 724-357-2306, E-mail: bwitchel@iup.edu. *Application contact:* Claire Dandeneau, Program Coordinator, 724-357-4534, E-mail: cdanden@iup.edu.

**Indiana University of Pennsylvania,** School of Graduate Studies and Research, College of Natural Sciences and Mathematics, Department of Psychology, Program in Clinical Psychology, Indiana, PA 15705. Offers Psy D. *Accreditation:* APA. *Program availability:* Part-time. *Faculty:* 13 full-time (7 women). *Students:* 43 full-time (29 women), 22 part-time (15 women); includes 9 minority (3 Asian, non-Hispanic/Latino; 5

Hispanic/Latino; 1 Two or more races, non-Hispanic/Latino), 2 international. Average age 26. 227 applicants, 13% accepted, 15 enrolled. In 2016, 10 doctorates awarded. *Degree requirements:* For doctorate, comprehensive exam, thesis/dissertation, internship, practicum. *Entrance requirements:* For doctorate, GRE General Test, minimum GPA of 3.0, 3 letters of recommendation, interview. Additional exam requirements/recommendations for international students: Required—TOEFL (minimum score 540 paper-based). *Application deadline:* For fall admission, 12/15 priority date for domestic students. Application fee: $50. Electronic applications accepted. *Expenses:* Contact institution. *Financial support:* In 2016–17, 13 fellowships with full tuition reimbursements (averaging $522 per year), 44 research assistantships with tuition reimbursements (averaging $2,611 per year), 2 teaching assistantships with partial tuition reimbursements (averaging $23,305 per year) were awarded; career-related internships or fieldwork, Federal Work-Study, scholarships/grants, and unspecified assistantships also available. Financial award application deadline: 4/15; financial award applicants required to submit FAFSA. *Unit head:* Dr. David LaPorte, Graduate Coordinator, 724-357-2426, E-mail: laporte@iup.edu. Website: http://www.iup.edu/psychology/grad/clinical-psychology-psyd/default.aspx

**Indiana University–Purdue University Indianapolis,** School of Science, Department of Psychology, Indianapolis, IN 46202-3275. Offers clinical psychology (MS); industrial/organizational psychology (MS); psychobiology of addictions (PhD). *Accreditation:* APA (one or more programs are accredited). Terminal master's awarded for partial completion of doctoral program. *Degree requirements:* For master's, thesis; for doctorate, thesis/dissertation. *Entrance requirements:* For master's, GRE General Test, minimum undergraduate GPA of 3.0; for doctorate, GRE General Test, GRE Subject Test (clinical psychology), minimum undergraduate GPA of 3.2. Additional exam requirements/recommendations for international students: Required—TOEFL (minimum score 567 paper-based; 86 iBT), IELTS (minimum score 6.5). Electronic applications accepted. *Faculty research:* Severe mental illness, health psychology, neurological research, alcoholism and psychopathology, functional activities within organizations.

**Indiana University South Bend,** School of Education, South Bend, IN 46634-7111. Offers addiction counseling (MS Ed); alcohol and drug counseling (Graduate Certificate); clinical mental health counseling (MS Ed); educational leadership (MS Ed); elementary education (MS Ed); marriage, couple, and family counseling (MS Ed); school counseling (MS Ed); secondary education (MS Ed); special education (MAT, MS Ed), including intense intervention (MS Ed), mild intervention (MS Ed). *Accreditation:* NCATE. *Program availability:* Part-time, evening/weekend. *Faculty:* 21 full-time (11 women), 9 part-time/adjunct (3 women). *Students:* 26 full-time (19 women), 104 part-time (80 women); includes 22 minority (13 Black or African American, non-Hispanic/Latino; 5 Hispanic/Latino; 4 Two or more races, non-Hispanic/Latino). Average age 35. 51 applicants, 69% accepted, 22 enrolled. In 2016, 31 master's, 2 other advanced degrees awarded. *Degree requirements:* For master's, thesis or alternative, exit project. *Entrance requirements:* For master's, letters of recommendation, GRE or minimum GPA of 3.0. Additional exam requirements/recommendations for international students: Required—TOEFL. *Application deadline:* For fall admission, 7/1 for domestic students; for spring admission, 11/1 for domestic students. Applications are processed on a rolling basis. Application fee: $40 ($60 for international students). Electronic applications accepted. *Expenses:* $276.98 per credit hour in-state; $652.54 per credit hour out-of-state. *Financial support:* Career-related internships or fieldwork available. Support available to part-time students. Financial award application deadline: 3/1; financial award applicants required to submit FAFSA. *Faculty research:* Professional dispositions, early childhood literacy, online learning, program assessments, problem-based learning. *Unit head:* Dr. Marvin Lynn, Dean, 574-520-4339, E-mail: lynnm@iusb.edu. *Application contact:* Yvonne Walker, Student Services Representative, 574-520-4185, E-mail: ydwalker@iusb.edu. Website: https://www.iusb.edu/education/index.php

**The Institute for the Psychological Sciences,** Program in Clinical Psychology, Arlington, VA 30327. Offers MS, Psy D. *Program availability:* Part-time. *Degree requirements:* For master's, comprehensive exam; for doctorate, comprehensive exam, thesis/dissertation. *Entrance requirements:* For master's and doctorate, GRE. Additional exam requirements/recommendations for international students: Required—TOEFL.

**Jackson State University,** Graduate School, College of Education and Human Development, Department of Counseling, Rehabilitation and Psychometric Services, Jackson, MS 39217. Offers clinical mental health (MS); rehabilitation counseling (MS); school counseling (MS Ed). *Accreditation:* ACA; CORE (one or more programs are accredited); NCATE. *Program availability:* Part-time, evening/weekend, 100% online, blended/hybrid learning. *Faculty:* 9 full-time (6 women), 1 part-time/adjunct (0 women). *Students:* 48 full-time (7 women), 82 part-time (74 women); includes 121 minority (118 Black or African American, non-Hispanic/Latino; 1 American Indian or Alaska Native, non-Hispanic/Latino; 1 Hispanic/Latino; 1 Two or more races, non-Hispanic/Latino). Average age 37. 106 applicants, 64% accepted, 47 enrolled. In 2016, 26 master's awarded. *Degree requirements:* For master's, comprehensive exam, thesis. *Entrance requirements:* For master's, GRE General Test. Additional exam requirements/recommendations for international students: Required—TOEFL (minimum score 520 paper-based; 67 iBT). *Application deadline:* For fall admission, 3/1 priority date for domestic students, 2/1 for international students; for spring admission, 10/1 for domestic and international students. Applications are processed on a rolling basis. Application fee: $25. Electronic applications accepted. *Expenses:* Contact institution. *Financial support:* Career-related internships or fieldwork, Federal Work-Study, scholarships/grants, and unspecified assistantships available. Support available to part-time students. Financial award application deadline: 3/1; financial award applicants required to submit FAFSA. *Unit head:* Dr. Dion Porter, Chair, 601-979-3364, Fax: 601-979-2213, E-mail: dion.porter@jsums.edu. *Application contact:* Dr. Dion Porter, Chair, 601-979-3364, Fax: 601-979-2213, E-mail: dion.porter@jsums.edu. Website: http://www.jsums.edu/commcounseling/

**Jackson State University,** Graduate School, College of Liberal Arts, Department of Psychology, Jackson, MS 39217. Offers clinical psychology (PhD). *Accreditation:* APA. *Degree requirements:* For doctorate, comprehensive exam, thesis/dissertation. *Entrance requirements:* For doctorate, MAT, GRE. Additional exam requirements/recommendations for international students: Required—TOEFL (minimum score 520 paper-based; 67 iBT). *Application deadline:* For fall admission, 1/15 for domestic and international students. Application fee: $25. *Expenses:* Tuition, state resident: full-time $7141. Tuition, nonresident: full-time $17,494. *Required fees:* $1080. Tuition and fees vary according to class time, course level, course load, degree level, campus/location, program and student level. *Financial support:* Fellowships, research assistantships, teaching assistantships, career-related internships or fieldwork, Federal Work-Study, scholarships/grants, tuition waivers (full), and unspecified assistantships available. Support available to part-time students. Financial award application deadline: 3/1; financial award applicants required to submit FAFSA. *Unit head:* Dr. Pamela G. Banks, Chair, 601-979-3378, Fax: 601-979-3947, E-mail: pbanks@jsums.edu. *Application contact:* Fatoumatta Sisay, Manager of Graduate Admissions, 601-979-0342, Fax: 601-977-4325, E-mail: fatoumatta.sisay@jsums.edu. Website: http://www.jsums.edu/psychology/

*Clinical Psychology*

**James Madison University,** The Graduate School, College of Health and Behavioral Sciences, Clinical Mental Health Counseling Program, Harrisonburg, VA 22807. Offers MA/Ed S. *Accreditation:* ACA. *Program availability:* Part-time, evening/weekend. *Students:* 67 full-time (52 women), 19 part-time (13 women); includes 17 minority (10 Black or African American, non-Hispanic/Latino; 1 Asian, non-Hispanic/Latino; 5 Hispanic/Latino; 1 Two or more races, non-Hispanic/Latino), 1 international. Average age 30. *Financial support:* Career-related internships or fieldwork, Federal Work-Study, and 53 assistantships (averaging $7911) available. Financial award application deadline: 3/1; financial award applicants required to submit FAFSA.

**James Madison University,** The Graduate School, College of Health and Behavioral Sciences, Program in Combined-Integrated Clinical and School Psychology, Harrisonburg, VA 22807. Offers Psy D. *Program availability:* Part-time, evening/ weekend. *Students:* 23 full-time (17 women), 1 (woman) part-time; includes 2 minority (1 Black or African American, non-Hispanic/Latino; 1 Hispanic/Latino), 3 international. Average age 30. 32 applicants, 19% accepted, 6 enrolled. In 2016, 5 doctorates awarded. Application fee: $55. Electronic applications accepted. *Financial support:* In 2016–17, 1 fellowship was awarded; teaching assistantships, Federal Work-Study, unspecified assistantships, and 17 doctoral assistantships (stipend varies) also available. Financial award application deadline: 3/1; financial award applicants required to submit FAFSA. *Unit head:* Dr. Gregg R. Henriques, Graduate Program Director, 540-568-7857, E-mail: henrigg@jmu.edu. *Application contact:* Lynette D. Michael, Director of Graduate Admissions, 540-568-6131 Ext. 6395, Fax: 540-568-7860, E-mail: michaeld@jmu.edu.
Website: http://www.psyc.jmu.edu/cipsyd/

**John Brown University,** Graduate Counseling Programs, Siloam Springs, AR 72761-2121. Offers clinical mental health counseling (MS); marriage and family therapy (MS); play therapy (Graduate Certificate); school counseling (MS). *Accreditation:* NCATE. *Program availability:* Part-time, evening/weekend. *Faculty:* 9 full-time (2 women), 18 part-time/adjunct (6 women). *Students:* 157 full-time (124 women), 153 part-time (124 women); includes 94 minority (50 Black or African American, non-Hispanic/Latino; 7 American Indian or Alaska Native, non-Hispanic/Latino; 3 Asian, non-Hispanic/Latino; 21 Hispanic/Latino; 13 Two or more races, non-Hispanic/Latino), 1 international. Average age 32. 129 applicants, 74% accepted, 83 enrolled. In 2016, 68 master's awarded. *Degree requirements:* For master's, practica or internships. *Entrance requirements:* For master's, GRE (minimum score of 300), recommendation forms from three people, 200-word essay describing professional plans and reason for seeking acceptance. Additional exam requirements/recommendations for international students: Required—TOEFL (minimum score 550 paper-based; 79 iBT). *Application deadline:* Applications are processed on a rolling basis. Application fee: $35 ($100 for international students). Electronic applications accepted. *Expenses:* Contact institution. *Financial support:* Fellowships, institutionally sponsored loans, scholarships/grants, and unspecified assistantships available. Financial award applicants required to submit FAFSA. *Unit head:* Dr. John V. Carmack, Program Director, 479-524-8630, E-mail: jcarmack@jbu.edu. *Application contact:* Mark Bjornsen, Graduate Counseling Representative, 479-631-4665, E-mail: mbjornsen@jbu.edu.
Website: http://www.jbu.edu/

**Johns Hopkins University,** Bloomberg School of Public Health, Department of Mental Health, Baltimore, MD 21218. Offers children's mental health services (PhD); drug dependence epidemiology (PhD); mental health (MHS, Dr PH); psychiatric epidemiology (PhD). *Degree requirements:* For master's, thesis (for some programs); for doctorate, thesis/dissertation, 1-year full-time residency, oral and written exams. *Entrance requirements:* For master's, GRE General Test, MCAT, 3 letters of recommendation, curriculum vitae; for doctorate, GRE General Test, MCAT or GMAT, 3 letters of recommendation, curriculum vitae. Additional exam requirements/recommendations for international students: Required—TOEFL (minimum score 600 paper-based; 100 iBT). Electronic applications accepted. *Faculty research:* Etiology, development and prevention of aggressive and antisocial behavior; epidemiology of mental disorders; genetic epidemiology of mental disorders; brain and behavior.

**Johnson & Wales University,** Graduate Studies, MS Program in Counseling, Providence, RI 02903-3703. Offers addictions counseling (MS); mental health counseling (MS).

**Johnson University,** Graduate and Professional Programs, Knoxville, TN 37998-1001. Offers biblical interpretation (Graduate Certificate); business administration (MBA); Christian ministries (Graduate Certificate); clinical mental health counseling (MA); educational technology (MA); intercultural studies (MA); leadership (MBA); leadership studies (PhD); New Testament (MA); nonprofit management (MBA); school counseling (MA); spiritual formation and leadership (Graduate Certificate); strategic ministry (MA); teacher education (MA). *Program availability:* Part-time, evening/weekend, 100% online, blended/hybrid learning. *Faculty:* 26 full-time (10 women), 32 part-time/adjunct (9 women). *Students:* 126 full-time (46 women), 170 part-time (65 women); includes 33 minority (13 Black or African American, non-Hispanic/Latino; 1 American Indian or Alaska Native, non-Hispanic/Latino; 4 Asian, non-Hispanic/Latino; 8 Hispanic/Latino; 7 Two or more races, non-Hispanic/Latino), 21 international. Average age 35. In 2016, 106 master's, 3 doctorates awarded. *Degree requirements:* For master's, variable foreign language requirement, comprehensive exam, thesis (for some programs), internships; for doctorate, variable foreign language requirement, comprehensive exam, thesis/dissertation, internships. *Entrance requirements:* For master's, PRAXIS (for MA in teacher education); MAT (for counseling); GRE or GMAT (for MBA), interview, 3 references, transcripts, essay, minimum GPA of 2.5 or 3.0 (depending on program); for doctorate, GRE or MAT (taken not less than 5 years prior), interview, 3 references, transcripts, essay, minimum GPA of 3.0; for Graduate Certificate, interview, 3 references, transcripts, essay, minimum GPA of 3.0. Additional exam requirements/recommendations for international students: Required—TOEFL (minimum score 527 paper-based; 71 iBT). *Application deadline:* For fall admission, 7/1 for domestic students; for spring admission, 11/1 for domestic students; for summer admission, 4/1 for domestic students. Application fee: $50. Electronic applications accepted. *Expenses:* Contact institution. *Financial support:* Scholarships/grants available. Financial award application deadline: 4/15; financial award applicants required to submit FAFSA. *Unit head:* Richard Clark, Vice President for External Relations, 865-251-2327, E-mail: rclark@johnsonu.edu. *Application contact:* Lisa Tarwater, Director of Graduate Admissions, 865-251-3400, E-mail: ltarwater@johnsonu.edu.

**Judson University,** Master of Arts in Clinical Mental Health Counseling Program, Elgin, IL 60123-1498. Offers MA. *Program availability:* Evening/weekend. *Faculty:* 1 (woman) full-time. *Application deadline:* Applications are processed on a rolling basis. Electronic applications accepted. *Unit head:* Dr. Susan Wesner, Chair, Professional Studies, 847-628-1544, E-mail: susan.wesner@judsonu.edu. *Application contact:* Maria Aguirre, Student Academic Advisor, 847-628-1160, E-mail: maguirre@judsonu.edu.

**Kean University,** Nathan Weiss Graduate College, Program in Combined School and Clinical Psychology, Union, NJ 07083. Offers Psy D. *Program availability:* Part-time. *Faculty:* 6 full-time (3 women). *Students:* 35 full-time (28 women), 15 part-time (11 women); includes 16 minority (3 Black or African American, non-Hispanic/Latino; 3 Asian, non-Hispanic/Latino; 9 Hispanic/Latino; 1 Two or more races, non-Hispanic/Latino). Average age 27. 50 applicants, 22% accepted, 10 enrolled. In 2016, 8

doctorates awarded. *Degree requirements:* For doctorate, comprehensive exam, thesis/dissertation, externship. *Entrance requirements:* For doctorate, GRE General Test, GRE Subject Test in psychology (taken within last 5 years ), minimum undergraduate GPA of 3.3, graduate 3.5; 3 letters of recommendation; personal interview; prerequisite coursework in theories of personality, abnormal psychology, tests and measurements, statistics, and experimental psychology; personal statement. Additional exam requirements/recommendations for international students: Required—TOEFL (minimum score 550 paper-based; 79 iBT), IELTS (minimum score 6.5). *Application deadline:* For fall admission, 2/2 for domestic and international students. Applications are processed on a rolling basis. Application fee: $75. Electronic applications accepted. *Expenses:* Contact institution. *Financial support:* Scholarships/grants and unspecified assistantships available. Financial award applicants required to submit FAFSA. *Unit head:* Dr. Jennifer Block-Lerner, Program Coordinator, 908-737-5864, E-mail: jlerner@kean.edu. *Application contact:* Pedro Lopes, Admissions Counselor, 908-737-7100, E-mail: grad-adm@kean.edu.
Website: http://grad.kean.edu/doctoral-programs/combined-school-and-clinical-psychology

**Kean University,** Nathan Weiss Graduate College, Program in Counselor Education, Union, NJ 07083. Offers alcohol and drug abuse counseling (MA); clinical mental health counseling (MA); school counseling (MA). *Accreditation:* ACA; NCATE. *Program availability:* Part-time. *Faculty:* 8 full-time (5 women). *Students:* 130 full-time (105 women), 149 part-time (114 women); includes 114 minority (54 Black or African American, non-Hispanic/Latino; 1 American Indian or Alaska Native, non-Hispanic/Latino; 5 Asian, non-Hispanic/Latino; 49 Hispanic/Latino; 5 Two or more races, non-Hispanic/Latino), 3 international. Average age 32. 258 applicants, 30% accepted, 68 enrolled. In 2016, 71 master's awarded. *Degree requirements:* For master's, practicum, internship, portfolio. *Entrance requirements:* For master's, minimum GPA of 3.0, 2 letters of recommendation, personal statement, resume. Additional exam requirements/recommendations for international students: Required—TOEFL (minimum score 550 paper-based; 79 iBT), IELTS. *Application deadline:* For fall admission, 3/2 for domestic and international students; for spring admission, 10/31 for domestic and international students. Applications are processed on a rolling basis. Application fee: $75. Electronic applications accepted. *Expenses:* Tuition, state resident: full-time $13,156; part-time $640 per credit. Tuition, nonresident: full-time $17,831; part-time $785 per credit. *Required fees:* $3316; $151 per credit. Tuition and fees vary according to course level, course load, degree level and program. *Financial support:* Scholarships/grants and unspecified assistantships available. Financial award applicants required to submit FAFSA. *Unit head:* Dr. J. Barry Mascari, Program Coordinator, 908-737-5954, E-mail: jmascari@kean.edu. *Application contact:* Pedro Lopes, Admissions Counselor, 908-737-7100, E-mail: grad-adm@kean.edu.
Website: http://grad.kean.edu/counseling

**Kent State University,** College of Arts and Sciences, Department of Psychological Sciences, Kent, OH 44242-0001. Offers clinical psychology (MA, PhD), including gerontology (MA), psychological sciences (MA); experimental psychology (MA, PhD), including gerontology (MA), psychological sciences (MA). *Accreditation:* APA (one or more programs are accredited). *Program availability:* Part-time. *Faculty:* 29 full-time (15 women). *Students:* 29 full-time (24 women); includes 9 minority (4 Black or African American, non-Hispanic/Latino; 2 Asian, non-Hispanic/Latino; 2 Hispanic/Latino; 1 Two or more races, non-Hispanic/Latino), 1 international. Average age 31. 323 applicants, 5% accepted, 17 enrolled. Terminal master's awarded for partial completion of doctoral program. *Degree requirements:* For master's, thesis; for doctorate, thesis/dissertation. *Entrance requirements:* For master's and doctorate, GRE General Test, personal statement, transcripts, 3 letters of recommendation. Additional exam requirements/recommendations for international students: Required—TOEFL (minimum score of 525 paper-based, 71 iBT), IELTS (minimum score of 6), Michigan English Language Assessment Battery (minimum score of 75), or PTE (minimum score of 48). *Application deadline:* For fall admission, 12/1 for domestic and international students. Applications are processed on a rolling basis. Application fee: $45 ($70 for international students). Electronic applications accepted. *Expenses:* Tuition, state resident: full-time $10,864; part-time $495 per credit hour. Tuition, nonresident: full-time $18,380; part-time $837 per credit hour. *Financial support:* Unspecified assistantships available. Financial award application deadline: 12/1. *Unit head:* Dr. Maria S. Zaragoza, Professor and Chair, 330-672-2166, E-mail: mzaragoz@kent.edu. *Application contact:* Dr. John A. Updegraff, Professor and Graduate Coordinator, 330-672-2166, E-mail: jupdegr1@kent.edu.
Website: http://www.kent.edu/psychology/graduate-programs

**Kutztown University of Pennsylvania,** College of Education, Program in Counseling Psychology, Kutztown, PA 19530-0730. Offers clinical mental health counseling (MA); marriage, couple and family counseling (MA). *Program availability:* Part-time, evening/ weekend. *Faculty:* 5 full-time (2 women). *Students:* 75 full-time (69 women), 51 part-time (43 women); includes 23 minority (8 Black or African American, non-Hispanic/Latino; 2 Asian, non-Hispanic/Latino; 11 Hispanic/Latino; 2 Two or more races, non-Hispanic/ Latino), 1 international. Average age 29. 72 applicants, 71% accepted, 24 enrolled. In 2016, 38 master's awarded. *Degree requirements:* For master's, comprehensive exam, thesis optional. *Entrance requirements:* For master's, GRE General Test, 3 letters of recommendation, minimum undergraduate GPA of 3.0, psychobiographical statement, resume. Additional exam requirements/recommendations for international students: Required—TOEFL (minimum score 550 paper-based, 79 iBT) or IELTS (minimum score 6.5). *Application deadline:* For fall admission, 3/1 for domestic and international students; for spring admission, 10/1 for domestic and international students. Application fee: $35. Electronic applications accepted. *Expenses:* Tuition, state resident: full-time $4347; part-time $483 per credit. Tuition, nonresident: full-time $6525; part-time $725 per credit. *Required fees:* $88 per credit. One-time fee: $50 full-time. *Financial support:* Career-related internships or fieldwork, Federal Work-Study, scholarships/grants, and unspecified assistantships available. Financial award application deadline: 3/1; financial award applicants required to submit FAFSA. *Faculty research:* Family addictions. *Unit head:* Dr. Helen S Hamlet, Department Chair, 610-683-4204, Fax: 610-683-1585, E-mail: hamlet@kutztown.edu.
Website: https://www.kutztown.edu/academics/graduate-programs/counseling.htm

**LaGrange College,** Graduate Programs, Program in Clinical Mental Health Counseling, LaGrange, GA 30240-2999. Offers MS. *Entrance requirements:* For master's, GRE or MAT, bachelor's degree, 3 letters of reference, essay, background check.

**Lakehead University,** Graduate Studies, Department of Psychology, Thunder Bay, ON P7B 5E1, Canada. Offers clinical psychology (PhD); experimental psychology (MA). *Program availability:* Part-time, evening/weekend. *Degree requirements:* For master's, thesis optional; for doctorate, thesis/dissertation, 2 comprehensive exams, internship. *Entrance requirements:* For master's, GRE, honors degree in psychology, advanced course work in statistics, minimum B average; for doctorate, GRE, minimum B average. Additional exam requirements/recommendations for international students: Required—TOEFL. *Faculty research:* Chaos theory, health psychology, counseling psychology, gerontology, women's studies.

**Lamar University,** College of Graduate Studies, College of Arts and Sciences, Department of Psychology, Beaumont, TX 77710. Offers clinical psychology (MS); industrial/organizational psychology (MS). *Program availability:* Part-time. *Faculty:* 6 full-

time (4 women). *Students:* 8 full-time (6 women), 8 part-time (6 women); includes 5 minority (1 Black or African American, non-Hispanic/Latino; 3 Hispanic/Latino; 1 Two or more races, non-Hispanic/Latino), 1 international. Average age 28. 15 applicants, 100% accepted, 3 enrolled. In 2016, 6 master's awarded. *Degree requirements:* For master's, thesis, practicum. *Entrance requirements:* For master's, GRE General Test, minimum GPA of 2.75 in last 60 hours of undergraduate course work. Additional exam requirements/recommendations for international students: Required—TOEFL (minimum score 550 paper-based; 79 iBT), IELTS (minimum score 6.5). *Application deadline:* For fall admission, 8/10 for domestic students, 7/1 for international students; for spring admission, 1/5 for domestic students, 12/1 for international students. Application fee: $25 ($50 for international students). *Expenses:* $8,134 in-state full-time, $5,574 in-state part-time; $15,604 out-of-state full-time, $10,554 out-of-state part-time per year. *Financial support:* In 2016–17, 12 students received support. Fellowships, research assistantships, teaching assistantships, career-related internships or fieldwork, Federal Work-Study, scholarships/grants, and tuition waivers (partial) available. Support available to part-time students. Financial award application deadline: 4/1. *Faculty research:* Group think, health psychology, school psychology, behavioral neuroscience. *Unit head:* Dr. Edythe E. Kirk, Chair, 409-880-8285, Fax: 409-880-1710. *Application contact:* Deidre Mayer, Interim Director, Admissions and Academic Services, 409-880-8888, Fax: 409-880-7419, E-mail: gradmissions@lamar.edu.
Website: http://artssciences.lamar.edu/psychology

**Lamar University,** College of Graduate Studies, College of Education and Human Development, Department of Counseling and Special Populations, Beaumont, TX 77710. Offers clinical mental health counseling (M Ed); school counseling (M Ed); special education (M Ed), including special education. *Accreditation:* ACA. *Faculty:* 6 full-time (3 women), 29 part-time/adjunct (11 women). *Students:* 16 full-time (9 women), 1,586 part-time (1,424 women); includes 758 minority (373 Black or African American, non-Hispanic/Latino; 6 American Indian or Alaska Native, non-Hispanic/Latino; 20 Asian, non-Hispanic/Latino; 337 Hispanic/Latino; 2 Native Hawaiian or other Pacific Islander, non-Hispanic/Latino; 20 Two or more races, non-Hispanic/Latino), 5 international. Average age 37. 840 applicants, 96% accepted, 393 enrolled. In 2016, 703 master's awarded. *Entrance requirements:* Additional exam requirements/recommendations for international students: Required—TOEFL (minimum score 550 paper-based; 79 iBT), IELTS (minimum score 6.5). *Application deadline:* For fall admission, 8/10 for domestic students, 7/1 for international students; for spring admission, 1/5 for domestic students, 12/1 for international students. Applications are processed on a rolling basis. Application fee: $25 ($50 for international students). Electronic applications accepted. *Expenses:* $8,134 in-state full-time, $5,574 in-state part-time; $15,604 out-of-state full-time, $10,554 out-of-state part-time per year. *Financial support:* Applicants required to submit FAFSA. *Unit head:* Dr. Rebecca Weinbaum, Interim Chair, 409-880-8978, Fax: 409-880-2263. *Application contact:* Deidre Mayer, Interim Director, Admissions and Academic Services, 409-880-8888, Fax: 409-880-7419, E-mail: gradmissions@lamar.edu.
Website: http://education.lamar.edu/counseling-and-special-populations

**La Salle University,** School of Arts and Sciences, Program in Clinical Psychology, Philadelphia, PA 19141-1199. Offers child clinical psychology (Psy D); clinical health psychology (Psy D); clinical psychology (MA); general practice psychology (Psy D). *Accreditation:* AAMFT/COAMFTE. *Program availability:* Part-time, evening/weekend. *Faculty:* 9 full-time (7 women), 6 part-time/adjunct (3 women). *Students:* 77 full-time (62 women), 37 part-time (28 women); includes 15 minority (2 Black or African American, non-Hispanic/Latino; 6 Asian, non-Hispanic/Latino; 4 Hispanic/Latino; 3 Two or more races, non-Hispanic/Latino), 4 international. Average age 27. 301 applicants, 22% accepted, 17 enrolled. In 2016, 20 master's, 17 doctorates awarded. Terminal master's awarded for partial completion of doctoral program. *Degree requirements:* For doctorate, comprehensive exam, thesis/dissertation. *Entrance requirements:* For doctorate, GRE (minimum scores of 148 on both the Verbal Reasoning and Quantitative Reasoning sections strongly recommended); GRE Subject Test in psychology (for those entering with bachelor's degree), baccalaureate degree from accredited institution with major in psychology or related discipline; minimum undergraduate GPA of 3.0, 3.2 graduate; three letters of recommendation; statement of interest and intent; curriculum vitae or resume; personal interview. Additional exam requirements/recommendations for international students: Required—TOEFL. *Application deadline:* For fall admission, 1/15 for domestic students, 1/1 for international students. Application fee: $35. Electronic applications accepted. Application fee is waived when completed online. *Expenses:* Contact institution. *Financial support:* In 2016–17, 26 students received support. Scholarships/grants and unspecified assistantships available. Financial award application deadline: 8/31; financial award applicants required to submit FAFSA. *Unit head:* Dr. Randy Fingerhut, Director, 215-951-1284, Fax: 215-951-5140, E-mail: psyd@lasalle.edu. *Application contact:* Elizabeth Heenan, Director, Graduate and Adult Enrollment, 215-951-1100, Fax: 215-951-1462, E-mail: heenan@lasalle.edu.
Website: http://www.lasalle.edu/doctor-of-psychology/

**La Salle University,** School of Arts and Sciences, Program in Counseling and Family Therapy, Philadelphia, PA 19141-1199. Offers industrial/organizational management and human resources (MA); marriage and family therapy (MA); pastoral counseling (MA); professional clinical counseling (MA). *Accreditation:* ACA; APA. *Program availability:* Part-time, evening/weekend. *Faculty:* 8 full-time (3 women), 20 part-time/adjunct (13 women). *Students:* 77 full-time (55 women), 180 part-time (147 women); includes 84 minority (44 Black or African American, non-Hispanic/Latino; 5 Asian, non-Hispanic/Latino; 31 Hispanic/Latino; 4 Two or more races, non-Hispanic/Latino), 5 international. Average age 30. 156 applicants, 76% accepted, 48 enrolled. In 2016, 106 master's awarded. *Degree requirements:* For master's, comprehensive exam. *Entrance requirements:* For master's, GRE or MAT (waived for applicants that already possess a master's degree in any field or for applicants that have a cumulative GPA of 3.5 or higher), minimum of 15 hours in psychology, counseling, or marriage and family studies; minimum GPA of 3.0; three letters of recommendation; personal statement; work experience (paid or volunteer). Additional exam requirements/recommendations for international students: Required—TOEFL. *Application deadline:* For fall admission, 8/15 priority date for domestic students, 7/15 for international students; for spring admission, 12/15 priority date for domestic students, 11/15 for international students; for summer admission, 4/15 priority date for domestic students, 3/15 for international students. Applications are processed on a rolling basis. Application fee: $35. Electronic applications accepted. Application fee is waived when completed online. *Expenses:* Contact institution. *Financial support:* In 2016–17, 37 students received support. Scholarships/grants and unspecified assistantships available. Support available to part-time students. Financial award application deadline: 8/31; financial award applicants required to submit FAFSA. *Faculty research:* Cognitive therapy, attribution theory, work habits, single parent families, treatment of addictions. *Unit head:* Dr. Donna A. Tonrey, Director, 215-951-1767, Fax: 215-951-1843, E-mail: psyma@lasalle.edu. *Application contact:* Elizabeth Heenan, Director, Graduate and Adult Enrollment, 215-951-1100, Fax: 215-951-1462, E-mail: heenan@lasalle.edu.
Website: http://www.lasalle.edu/counseling-family-therapy/

**Lenoir-Rhyne University,** Graduate Programs, School of Counseling and Human Services, Program in Clinical Mental Health Counseling, Hickory, NC 28601. Offers MA. *Accreditation:* ACA. *Program availability:* Part-time, evening/weekend. *Degree requirements:* For master's, comprehensive exam, thesis optional. *Entrance requirements:* For master's, GRE General Test or MAT, writing sample; minimum undergraduate GPA of 2.7, graduate 3.0. Additional exam requirements/recommendations for international students: Required—TOEFL (minimum score 600 paper-based). Electronic applications accepted. *Expenses:* Contact institution.

**Lesley University,** Graduate School of Arts and Social Sciences, Cambridge, MA 02138-2790. Offers clinical mental health counseling (MA), including holistic counseling, school and community counseling, trauma studies; counseling psychology (MA, CAGS), including professional counseling (MA), school counseling (MA); creative writing (MFA); expressive therapies (MA, PhD, CAGS), including art (MA), clinical mental health counseling (MA), dance (MA), expressive therapies (MA), music (MA); independent studies (CAGS); independent study (MA); intercultural relations (MA, CAGS); interdisciplinary studies (MA), including individualized studies, integrative holistic health, mindfulness studies, peace and conflict transformation, trauma sensitive assessment, intervention, and consultation, women's studies; urban environmental leadership (MA). *Program availability:* Part-time, online learning. *Degree requirements:* For master's, internship, practicum, thesis (for expressive therapies); for doctorate, thesis/dissertation, arts apprenticeship, field placement; for CAGS, thesis, internship (for counseling psychology, expressive therapies). *Entrance requirements:* For master's, MAT (counseling psychology), interview, writing samples, art portfolio; for doctorate, GRE or MAT, interview, master's degree; for CAGS, interview, master's degree. Additional exam requirements/recommendations for international students: Required—TOEFL (minimum score 550 paper-based; 80 iBT). Electronic applications accepted. *Faculty research:* Psychotherapy and culture; psychotherapy and psychological trauma; women's issues in art, teaching and psychotherapy; community-based art, psycho-spiritual inquiry.

**Lewis University,** College of Arts and Sciences, Program in Clinical Mental Health Counseling, Romeoville, IL 60446. Offers child and adolescent counseling (MA); mental health counseling (MA). *Program availability:* Part-time, evening/weekend. *Students:* 52 full-time (42 women), 65 part-time (55 women); includes 29 minority (9 Black or African American, non-Hispanic/Latino; 1 Asian, non-Hispanic/Latino; 16 Hispanic/Latino; 1 Native Hawaiian or other Pacific Islander, non-Hispanic/Latino; 2 Two or more races, non-Hispanic/Latino). Average age 27. In 2016, 27 master's awarded. *Degree requirements:* For master's, comprehensive exam, thesis optional, practicum, internship. *Entrance requirements:* For master's, 15 hours of psychology, including statistics or research; 2 letters of recommendation; minimum GPA of 3.0 in last 60 hours; interview. Additional exam requirements/recommendations for international students: Required—TOEFL (minimum score 550 paper-based; 80 iBT). *Application deadline:* For fall admission, 5/1 priority date for international students; for spring admission, 11/15 priority date for international students. Applications are processed on a rolling basis. Application fee: $40. Electronic applications accepted. *Expenses: Tuition:* Full-time $13,860; part-time $770 per credit hour. *Required fees:* $75 per semester. Tuition and fees vary according to degree level and program. *Financial support:* Federal Work-Study, scholarships/grants, tuition waivers, and unspecified assistantships available. Financial award application deadline: 5/1; financial award applicants required to submit FAFSA. *Faculty research:* Cognitive development, attitude formation, juvenile delinquency, gender issues, work-family conflict. *Unit head:* Dr. Katherine Helm-Lewis, Director, 815-838-0500 Ext. 5604, Fax: 815-836-5032, E-mail: helmka@lewisu.edu. *Application contact:* Nancy Hanley, Information Contact, 815-838-0500 Ext. 5604, E-mail: hanleyna@lewisu.edu.
Website: http://www.lewisu.edu/academics/grad.htm/

**Liberty University,** School of Behavioral Sciences, Lynchburg, VA 24515. Offers clinical mental health counseling (MA); counselor education and supervision (PhD); human services counseling (MA), including addictions and recovery, business, child and family law, Christian ministries, criminal justice, crisis response and trauma, executive leadership, health and wellness, life coaching, marriage and family, military resilience; marriage and family therapy (MA); military resilience (Certificate); professional counseling (MA). *Program availability:* Part-time, online learning. *Students:* 2,041 full-time (1,612 women), 4,970 part-time (3,875 women); includes 1,991 minority (1,678 Black or African American, non-Hispanic/Latino; 33 American Indian or Alaska Native, non-Hispanic/Latino; 48 Asian, non-Hispanic/Latino; 80 Hispanic/Latino; 8 Native Hawaiian or other Pacific Islander, non-Hispanic/Latino; 144 Two or more races, non-Hispanic/Latino), 127 international. Average age 39. 5,496 applicants, 41% accepted, 1257 enrolled. In 2016, 2,813 master's, 11 doctorates, 20 other advanced degrees awarded. *Application deadline:* Applications are processed on a rolling basis. Application fee: $50. Electronic applications accepted. *Financial support:* Applicants required to submit FAFSA. *Unit head:* Dr. Ronald Hawkins, Founding Dean, School of Behavioral Sciences. *Application contact:* Jay Bridge, Director of Admissions, 800-424-9595, Fax: 800-628-7977, E-mail: gradadmissions@liberty.edu.

**Lipscomb University,** Department of Graduate Psychology and Counseling, Nashville, TN 37204-3951. Offers clinical mental health counseling (MS); counseling psychology (Certificate); marriage and family therapy (MMFT); psychology (MS). *Program availability:* Part-time, evening/weekend. *Faculty:* 13 full-time (5 women), 10 part-time/adjunct (6 women). *Students:* 120 full-time (92 women), 30 part-time (27 women); includes 38 minority (22 Black or African American, non-Hispanic/Latino; 1 American Indian or Alaska Native, non-Hispanic/Latino; 1 Asian, non-Hispanic/Latino; 11 Hispanic/Latino; 3 Two or more races, non-Hispanic/Latino), 2 international. Average age 28. In 2016, 44 master's, 1 other advanced degree awarded. *Degree requirements:* For master's, thesis (for some programs), practicum, internship, capstone. *Entrance requirements:* For master's, GRE, resume, 3 reference letters, transcripts, goals statement. Additional exam requirements/recommendations for international students: Required—TOEFL (minimum score 570 paper-based; 80 iBT). *Application deadline:* For fall admission, 7/1 for domestic students; for spring admission, 11/1 for domestic students. Applications are processed on a rolling basis. Application fee: $50 ($75 for international students). Electronic applications accepted. *Expenses:* $898 per hour. *Financial support:* Scholarships/grants and unspecified assistantships available. Financial award applicants required to submit FAFSA. *Faculty research:* Cognitive psychology, neuroscience, health psychology, grief issues. *Unit head:* Dr. Shanna Ray, Director/Professor of Psychology, 615-966-5833, E-mail: shanna.ray@lipscomb.edu. *Application contact:* Kathi Johnson, Recruiting and Marketing Coordinator, 615-966-5237, E-mail: kathi.johnson@lipscomb.edu.
Website: http://www.lipscomb.edu/psychology/graduate-programs

**Lock Haven University of Pennsylvania,** The Stephen Poorman College of Business, Information Systems, and Human Services, Lock Haven, PA 17745-2390. Offers clinical mental health counseling (MS); sport science (MS). *Program availability:* Online learning. *Degree requirements:* For master's, thesis. *Entrance requirements:* For master's, minimum undergraduate GPA of 3.0. Additional exam requirements/recommendations for international students: Required—TOEFL. Electronic applications accepted.

**Loma Linda University,** School of Behavioral Health, Department of Psychology, Loma Linda, CA 92350. Offers clinical psychology (PhD, Psy D). *Accreditation:* APA. *Degree requirements:* For doctorate, comprehensive exam, thesis/dissertation. *Entrance requirements:* For doctorate, GRE General Test, three letters of recommendation.

## Clinical Psychology

Additional exam requirements/recommendations for international students: Required—TOEFL (minimum score 550 paper-based; 80 iBT). Electronic applications accepted.

**London Metropolitan University,** Graduate Programs, London, United Kingdom. Offers applied psychology (M Sc); architecture (MA); biomedical science (M Sc); blood science (M Sc); cancer pharmacology (M Sc); computer networking and cyber security (M Sc); computing and information systems (M Sc); conference interpreting (MA); counter-terrorism studies (M Sc); creative, digital and professional writing (MA); crime, violence and prevention (M Sc); criminology (M Sc); curating contemporary art (MA); data analytics (M Sc); digital media (MA); early childhood studies (MA); education (MA, Ed D); financial services law, regulation and compliance (LL M); food science (M Sc); forensic psychology (M Sc); health and social care management and policy (M Sc); human nutrition (M Sc); human resource management (MA); human rights and international conflict (M Sc); information technology (M Sc); intelligence and security studies (M Sc); international oil, gas and energy law (LL M); international relations (MA); interpreting (MA); learning and teaching in higher education (MA); legal practice (LL M); media and entertainment law (LL M); organizational and consumer psychology (M Sc); psychological therapy (M Sc); psychology of mental health (M Sc); public health (M Sc); public policy and management (MPA); security studies (M Sc); social work (M Sc); spatial planning and urban design (MA); sports therapy (M Sc); supporting older children and young people with dyslexia (MA); teaching languages (MA), including Arabic, English; translation (MA); woman and child abuse (MA).

**Long Island University–Brentwood Campus,** Graduate Programs, Brentwood, NY 11717. Offers childhood education (grades 1-6) (MS), including grades 1-6; childhood education/literacy (grades 1-6) (MS); childhood education/special education (grades 1-6) (MS); clinical mental health counseling (MS, Advanced Certificate); early childhood education (B-2) (MS); literacy (B-6) (MS Ed); school counselor (MS); special education (grades 1-6) (MS Ed); students with disabilities generalist (grades 7-12) (Advanced Certificate). *Program availability:* Part-time. *Faculty:* 54 part-time/adjunct (30 women). *Students:* 98 full-time (80 women), 57 part-time (47 women); includes 28 minority (7 Black or African American, non-Hispanic/Latino; 1 Asian, non-Hispanic/Latino; 20 Hispanic/Latino). 85 applicants, 89% accepted, 43 enrolled. In 2016, 99 master's, 11 other advanced degrees awarded. *Degree requirements:* For master's, comprehensive exam (for some programs), thesis optional. *Entrance requirements:* For master's and Advanced Certificate, GRE. Additional exam requirements/recommendations for international students: Required—TOEFL or IELTS. *Application deadline:* Applications are processed on a rolling basis. Application fee: $50. Electronic applications accepted. Application fee is waived when completed online. *Expenses: Tuition:* Full-time $28,272; part-time $1178 per credit. *Required fees:* $451 per term. *Financial support:* Scholarships/grants and unspecified assistantships available. Support available to part-time students. Financial award applicants required to submit FAFSA. *Unit head:* Donna Di Donato, Dean and Chief Operating Officer, 631-287-8010, Fax: 631-287-8575, E-mail: donna.didonato@liu.edu. *Application contact:* Scott Aug, Associate Director of Enrollment Management, 631-287-8500, Fax: 631-287-8575, E-mail: scott.aug@liu.edu. Website: http://liu.edu/brentwood

**Long Island University–LIU Brooklyn,** Richard L. Conolly College of Liberal Arts and Sciences, Brooklyn, NY 11201-8423. Offers biology (MS); chemistry (MS); clinical psychology (PhD); communication sciences and disorders (MS); creative writing (MFA); English (MA); media arts (MA, MFA); political science (MA); psychology (MA); social science (MS); sociology (MA); speech-language pathology (MS); United Nations (Advanced Certificate); urban studies (MA); writing and production for television (MFA). *Program availability:* Part-time, evening/weekend. *Faculty:* 90 full-time (35 women), 125 part-time/adjunct (67 women). *Students:* 355 full-time (276 women), 220 part-time (161 women); includes 245 minority (119 Black or African American, non-Hispanic/Latino; 32 Asian, non-Hispanic/Latino; 80 Hispanic/Latino; 1 Native Hawaiian or other Pacific Islander, non-Hispanic/Latino; 13 Two or more races, non-Hispanic/Latino), 85 international. 792 applicants, 41% accepted, 141 enrolled. In 2016, 154 master's, 18 doctorates, 4 other advanced degrees awarded. *Degree requirements:* For master's, comprehensive exam (for some programs), thesis (for some programs); for doctorate, comprehensive exam (for some programs), thesis/dissertation (for some programs). *Entrance requirements:* For master's and doctorate, GRE. Additional exam requirements/recommendations for international students: Recommended—TOEFL (minimum score 550 paper-based; 79 iBT). *Application deadline:* Applications are processed on a rolling basis. Application fee: $50. Electronic applications accepted. *Expenses: Tuition:* Full-time $28,272; part-time $1178 per credit. *Required fees:* $451 per term. Tuition and fees vary according to degree level, program and student level. *Financial support:* In 2016–17, 120 fellowships with full and partial tuition reimbursements (averaging $915 per year), 5 research assistantships with full and partial tuition reimbursements (averaging $2,300 per year), 136 teaching assistantships with full and partial tuition reimbursements (averaging $2,300 per year) were awarded; career-related internships or fieldwork, Federal Work-Study, institutionally sponsored loans, scholarships/grants, tuition waivers (full and partial), and unspecified assistantships also available. Support available to part-time students. Financial award application deadline: 2/15; financial award applicants required to submit FAFSA. *Faculty research:* Nanocrystal polymerization of cellulose using electron microscopy. *Unit head:* Dr. Kevin Lauth, Acting Dean, 718-488-1347, E-mail: kevin.lauth@liu.edu. *Application contact:* Gabrielle Gannon, Director of Graduate Admissions, 718-488-1011, Fax: 718-780-6110, E-mail: bkln-admissions@liu.edu.

**Long Island University–LIU Post,** College of Education, Information and Technology, Brookville, NY 11548-1300. Offers adolescence education (MS); adolescence education 7-12 (MS); archives and records management (AC); art education (MS); childhood education (MS); childhood teaching literacy B-6 (MS); childhood/special education (MS); clinical mental health counseling (MS, AC); early childhood education (MS); early childhood education/childhood education (MS); educational leadership (AC); educational technology (MS); information studies (PhD); interdisciplinary educational studies (Ed D); middle childhood education (MS); music education (MS); school counselor education (MS); special education (MS Ed); speech-language pathology (MA); students with disabilities, 7-12 generalist (AC); TESOL (MS). *Accreditation:* TEAC. *Program availability:* Part-time, 100% online, blended/hybrid learning. *Faculty:* 55 full-time (35 women), 104 part-time/adjunct (57 women). *Students:* 464 full-time (390 women), 740 part-time (580 women); includes 265 minority (99 Black or African American, non-Hispanic/Latino; 45 Asian, non-Hispanic/Latino; 113 Hispanic/Latino; 1 Native Hawaiian or other Pacific Islander, non-Hispanic/Latino; 7 Two or more races, non-Hispanic/Latino), 33 international. 928 applicants, 76% accepted, 406 enrolled. In 2016, 334 master's, 10 doctorates, 137 other advanced degrees awarded. Terminal master's awarded for partial completion of doctoral program. *Degree requirements:* For master's, variable foreign language requirement, comprehensive exam (for some programs), thesis optional; for doctorate, comprehensive exam, thesis/dissertation. *Entrance requirements:* For master's and AC, GRE. Additional exam requirements/recommendations for international students: Required—PTE, TOEFL (minimum score 550 paper-based, 75 iBT) or IELTS. *Application deadline:* Applications are processed on a rolling basis. Application fee: $50. Electronic applications accepted. *Expenses: Tuition:* Full-time $28,272; part-time $1178 per credit. *Required fees:* $451 per term. Tuition and fees vary according to degree level and program. *Financial support:* Career-related internships or fieldwork, Federal Work-Study, institutionally sponsored loans,

scholarships/grants, tuition waivers (partial), and unspecified assistantships available. Support available to part-time students. Financial award application deadline: 2/15; financial award applicants required to submit FAFSA. *Faculty research:* English language learners, early childhood literacy development through play, sleep, social justice through education, using a structured protocol for discussing bad news. *Total annual research expenditures:* $575,000. *Unit head:* Dr. Albert Inserra, Dean, 516-299-2210, E-mail: albert.inserra@liu.edu. *Application contact:* Carol Zerah, Director of Graduate Admissions, 516-299-2900, Fax: 516-299-2137, E-mail: post-enroll@liu.edu. Website: http://liu.edu/CWPost/Academics/College-of-Education-Information-and-Technology

**Louisiana State University and Agricultural & Mechanical College,** Graduate School, College of Humanities and Social Sciences, Department of Psychology, Baton Rouge, LA 70803. Offers biological psychology (MA, PhD); clinical psychology (MA, PhD); cognitive psychology (MA, PhD); developmental psychology (MA, PhD); school psychology (MA, PhD). *Accreditation:* APA (one or more programs are accredited).

**Loyola University Chicago,** Graduate School, Program in Clinical Psychology, Chicago, IL 60660. Offers MA, PhD. *Accreditation:* APA. *Faculty:* 9 full-time (7 women). *Students:* 34 full-time (30 women); includes 8 minority (4 Black or African American, non-Hispanic/Latino; 2 Asian, non-Hispanic/Latino; 2 Hispanic/Latino). Average age 26. 199 applicants, 3% accepted, 5 enrolled. In 2016, 8 master's, 6 doctorates awarded. Terminal master's awarded for partial completion of doctoral program. *Degree requirements:* For master's, thesis; for doctorate, comprehensive exam, thesis/dissertation, clinical internship. *Entrance requirements:* For doctorate, GRE General Test, GRE Subject Test, letters of recommendation, personal statement, curriculum vitae, transcript. Additional exam requirements/recommendations for international students: Recommended—TOEFL. *Application deadline:* For fall admission, 12/1 for domestic students. Application fee: $0. Electronic applications accepted. *Expenses: Tuition:* Full-time $18,594. *Required fees:* $848. Part-time tuition and fees vary according to course load, degree level and program. *Financial support:* In 2016–17, 22 students received support, including 7 fellowships with full tuition reimbursements available (averaging $18,000 per year), 11 research assistantships with full tuition reimbursements available (averaging $18,000 per year), 5 teaching assistantships with full tuition reimbursements available (averaging $18,000 per year); career-related internships or fieldwork, scholarships/grants, and unspecified assistantships also available. Financial award application deadline: 12/1. *Faculty research:* Child and family, AIDS, ethics and professional practice, psychotherapy, stress and coping, positive youth development, pediatric psychology, adolescence, inner city youth, emerging adulthood, mental health services, exposure to violence, obesity, spina bifida, asthma, neuroscience of depression. *Unit head:* Dr. Grayson Holmbeck, Director of Clinical Training, 773-508-2967, Fax: 773-508-8713, E-mail: gholmbe@luc.edu. *Application contact:* Jacquie Hamilton, Senior Secretary, 773-508-2974, Fax: 773-508-8713, E-mail: jhamilt@luc.edu. Website: http://www.luc.edu/psychology/clinical.shtml

**Loyola University Maryland,** Graduate Programs, Loyola College of Arts and Sciences, Department of Psychology, Program in Clinical Psychology, Baltimore, MD 21210-2699. Offers MS, Psy D, CAS. *Accreditation:* APA. *Program availability:* Part-time, evening/weekend. *Faculty:* 65 full-time (40 women), 26 part-time/adjunct (18 women). *Students:* 25 full-time (24 women), 14 part-time (12 women); includes 9 minority (1 Black or African American, non-Hispanic/Latino; 1 Asian, non-Hispanic/Latino; 4 Hispanic/Latino; 3 Two or more races, non-Hispanic/Latino). Average age 26. 480 applicants, 26% accepted, 55 enrolled. In 2016, 36 master's, 12 doctorates awarded. *Degree requirements:* For master's, thesis; for doctorate, thesis/dissertation. *Entrance requirements:* For master's, doctorate, and CAS, GRE General Test, GRE Subject Test (recommended), transcripts, essay, 3 letters of recommendation. Additional exam requirements/recommendations for international students: Required—TOEFL (minimum score 550 paper-based), IELTS (minimum score 7). *Application deadline:* For fall admission, 3/1 for domestic and international students. Application fee: $60. Electronic applications accepted. *Expenses:* Contact institution. *Financial support:* In 2016–17, 2 students received support. Scholarships/grants and unspecified assistantships available. Financial award application deadline: 4/15; financial award applicants required to submit FAFSA. *Unit head:* Dr. Matthew W. Kirkhart, Chair, 410-617-5498, E-mail: mkirkhart@loyola.edu. *Application contact:* Maureen Faux, Executive Director, Graduate Admissions, 410-617-5020, Fax: 410-617-2002, E-mail: graduate@loyola.edu.

**Loyola University New Orleans,** Department of Counseling, New Orleans, LA 70118-6195. Offers clinical mental health counseling (MS). *Program availability:* Part-time, evening/weekend. *Faculty:* 5 full-time (2 women), 2 part-time/adjunct (1 woman). *Students:* 44 full-time (42 women), 17 part-time (15 women); includes 9 minority (5 Black or African American, non-Hispanic/Latino; 1 Asian, non-Hispanic/Latino; 3 Hispanic/Latino). Average age 28. 26 applicants, 58% accepted, 13 enrolled. In 2016, 23 master's awarded. *Degree requirements:* For master's, comprehensive exam, minimum GPA of 3.0 in counseling coursework. *Entrance requirements:* For master's, GRE, resume, transcripts, letters of recommendation, statement of objectives, degree from regionally-accredited institution, interview, writing sample. Additional exam requirements/recommendations for international students: Required—TOEFL (minimum score 550 paper-based; 79 iBT). *Application deadline:* For fall admission, 12/1 priority date for domestic and international students. Applications are processed on a rolling basis. Application fee: $0. Electronic applications accepted. *Expenses:* $818 per credit hour full-time tuition, $883 fees; $409 per credit hour part-time tuition, $527 fees; $275 graduation fee. *Financial support:* Research assistantships, career-related internships or fieldwork, and tuition waivers (partial) available. Support available to part-time students. Financial award application deadline: 5/1; financial award applicants required to submit FAFSA. *Faculty research:* Counseling theory, spirituality issues, group counseling, multicultural applications. *Unit head:* Dr. Thomas Foster, Chair, 504-864-7867, Fax: 504-864-7844, E-mail: counselingdept@loyno.edu. *Application contact:* Dianna Whitfield, Department Assistant, 504-864-7848, Fax: 504-864-7844, E-mail: counselingdept@loyno.edu. Website: http://css.loyno.edu/counseling

**Lynchburg College,** Graduate Studies, M Ed Program in Clinical Mental Health Counseling, Lynchburg, VA 24501-3199. Offers M Ed. *Accreditation:* ACA. *Program availability:* Part-time, evening/weekend. *Students:* 26 full-time (24 women), 15 part-time (13 women); includes 3 minority (1 Black or African American, non-Hispanic/Latino; 1 Asian, non-Hispanic/Latino; 1 Hispanic/Latino). In 2016, 15 master's awarded. *Degree requirements:* For master's, counseling internship. *Entrance requirements:* For master's, GRE, minimum GPA of 3.0 (preferred), official transcripts (bachelor's, others as relevant), three letters of recommendation, career goals statement. Additional exam requirements/recommendations for international students: Required—TOEFL (minimum score 550 paper-based; 79 iBT), IELTS (minimum score 6.5). *Application deadline:* For fall admission, 7/31 for domestic students, 6/1 for international students; for spring admission, 11/30 for domestic students, 10/15 for international students. Applications are processed on a rolling basis. Application fee: $30. Electronic applications accepted. Application fee is waived when completed online. *Expenses:* Contact institution. *Financial support:* Federal Work-Study, scholarships/grants, health care benefits, and unspecified assistantships available. Support available to part-time students. Financial award application deadline: 7/31; financial award applicants required to submit FAFSA. *Unit head:* Dr. Karena Heyward, Assistant Professor and Program Director, 434-544-8067, E-mail: heyward.k@lynchburg.edu. Website: http://www.lynchburg.edu/graduate/master-of-education-in-counselor-education/clinical-mental-health-counseling.

**Madonna University,** Department of Psychology, Livonia, MI 48150-1173. Offers clinical psychology (MSCP). *Program availability:* Part-time, evening/weekend. *Degree requirements:* For master's, thesis or alternative. *Entrance requirements:* Additional exam requirements/recommendations for international students: Required—TOEFL. Electronic applications accepted.

**Marquette University,** Graduate School, College of Education, Department of Counselor Education and Counseling Psychology, Milwaukee, WI 53201-1881. Offers clinical mental health counseling (MS); community counseling (MA); counseling psychology (PhD); school counseling (MA). *Accreditation:* ACA. *Program availability:* Part-time. *Faculty:* 6 full-time (3 women), 5 part-time/adjunct (3 women). *Students:* 69 full-time (53 women), 13 part-time (10 women); includes 18 minority (6 Black or African American, non-Hispanic/Latino; 3 Asian, non-Hispanic/Latino; 7 Hispanic/Latino; 2 Two or more races, non-Hispanic/Latino), 3 international. Average age 26. 122 applicants, 47% accepted, 32 enrolled. In 2016, 24 master's, 2 doctorates awarded. Terminal master's awarded for partial completion of doctoral program. *Degree requirements:* For master's, comprehensive exam, thesis (for some programs); for doctorate, thesis/dissertation, qualifying exam. *Entrance requirements:* For master's, GRE General Test or MAT, official transcripts from all current and previous colleges/universities except Marquette, three letters of recommendation, statement of purpose; for doctorate, GRE General Test, MAT, sample of written work, official transcripts from all current and previous colleges/universities except Marquette, three letters of recommendation, statement of purpose, resume/curriculum vitae. Additional exam requirements/recommendations for international students: Required—TOEFL (minimum score 530 paper-based). *Application deadline:* For fall admission, 1/15 for domestic and international students. Application fee: $50. *Financial support:* Fellowships, research assistantships, scholarships/grants, health care benefits, tuition waivers (partial), and unspecified assistantships available. Support available to part-time students. Financial award application deadline: 2/15. *Faculty research:* Ethical and legal issues in education, anxiety disorders, multicultural counseling, child psychopathology, group counseling and dynamics. *Unit head:* Dr. Alan Burkard, Chair, 414-288-3434, E-mail: alan.burkard@marquette.edu. *Application contact:* Dr. Alan Burkard.

**Marshall University,** Academic Affairs Division, College of Liberal Arts, Department of Psychology, Huntington, WV 25755. Offers clinical psychology (Certificate); psychology (MA, Psy D). *Accreditation:* APA. *Degree requirements:* For master's, thesis optional. *Entrance requirements:* For master's, GRE General Test or MAT.

**Marymount University,** School of Education and Human Services, Program in Counseling, Arlington, VA 22207-4299. Offers clinical mental health counseling (MA); pastoral counseling (MA); school counseling (MA). *Accreditation:* ACA. *Program availability:* Part-time, evening/weekend. *Faculty:* 29 full-time (21 women), 7 part-time/adjunct (all women). *Students:* 84 full-time (74 women), 57 part-time (51 women); includes 55 minority (28 Black or African American, non-Hispanic/Latino; 2 American Indian or Alaska Native, non-Hispanic/Latino; 3 Asian, non-Hispanic/Latino; 17 Hispanic/Latino; 5 Two or more races, non-Hispanic/Latino), 2 international. Average age 30. 83 applicants, 77% accepted, 45 enrolled. In 2016, 39 master's awarded. *Degree requirements:* For master's, thesis or alternative, capstone/internship. *Entrance requirements:* For master's, GRE, 2 letters of recommendation, interview, resume, personal statement. Additional exam requirements/recommendations for international students: Required—TOEFL (minimum score 600 paper-based; 96 iBT), IELTS (minimum score 6.5). *Application deadline:* For fall admission, 1/15 priority date for domestic and international students; for spring admission, 10/5 for domestic and international students. Applications are processed on a rolling basis. Application fee: $40. Electronic applications accepted. *Expenses: Tuition:* Full-time $8460; part-time $940 per credit hour. *Required fees:* $10 per credit hour. One-time fee: $240 part-time. Tuition and fees vary according to program. *Financial support:* In 2016–17, 15 students received support, including 8 research assistantships with tuition reimbursements available, 4 teaching assistantships with tuition reimbursements available; career-related internships or fieldwork, Federal Work-Study, scholarships/grants, and unspecified assistantships also available. Support available to part-time students. Financial award applicants required to submit FAFSA. *Unit head:* Dr. Lisa Jackson-Cherry, Chair, Counseling, 703-284-1633, Fax: 703-284-5708, E-mail: lisa.jacksoncherry@marymount.edu. *Application contact:* Francesca Reed, Director, Graduate Admissions, 703-284-5901, Fax: 703-527-3815, E-mail: grad.admissions@marymount.edu. Website: http://www.marymount.edu/Academics/School-of-Education-Human-Services/Graduate-Programs/Counseling-(M-A-)

**Marywood University,** Academic Affairs, Reap College of Education and Human Development, Department of Psychology and Counseling, Program in Clinical Psychology, Scranton, PA 18509-1598. Offers Psy D. *Accreditation:* APA. *Program availability:* Part-time. Electronic applications accepted. *Expenses:* Contact institution.

**Marywood University,** Academic Affairs, Reap College of Education and Human Development, Department of Psychology and Counseling, Program in Psychology, Scranton, PA 18509-1598. Offers clinical services (MA); general theoretical psychology (MA). *Program availability:* Part-time. Electronic applications accepted.

**McGill University,** Faculty of Graduate and Postdoctoral Studies, Faculty of Science, Department of Psychology, Montréal, QC H3A 2T5, Canada. Offers clinical psychology (PhD); experimental psychology (M Sc, MA, PhD).

**McKendree University,** Graduate Programs, Master of Arts Program in Clinical Mental Health Counseling, Lebanon, IL 62254-1299. Offers MA. *Program availability:* Part-time, evening/weekend. *Degree requirements:* For master's, comprehensive exam, internship. *Entrance requirements:* For master's, official transcripts from each college or university attended, minimum undergraduate GPA of 3.0, three letters of recommendation, personal statement, completion of six undergraduate credit hours in a behavior science, curriculum vitae or resume. Electronic applications accepted.

**Medaille College,** Programs in Psychology, Buffalo, NY 14214-2695. Offers clinical psychology (Psy D); marriage and family therapy (MA); mental health counseling (MA); psychology (MA). *Accreditation:* ACA. *Program availability:* Part-time, evening/weekend. *Degree requirements:* For master's, comprehensive exam (for some programs), thesis (for some programs). *Entrance requirements:* For master's, GRE General Test (psychology), minimum GPA of 2.75 (psychology). Additional exam requirements/recommendations for international students: Required—TOEFL (minimum score 550 paper-based). Electronic applications accepted. *Faculty research:* Schizophrenia, Parkinson's Disease, eyewitness testimony, methodology.

**Memorial University of Newfoundland,** School of Graduate Studies, Department of Psychology, St. John's, NL A1C 5S7, Canada. Offers applied psychological sciences (MAPS); clinical psychology (Psy D); experimental psychology (M Sc, PhD). *Program availability:* Part-time. *Degree requirements:* For master's, workterms (MASP), thesis

(M Sc); for doctorate, comprehensive exam, thesis/dissertation, oral thesis defense. *Entrance requirements:* For master's, GRE, honors bachelor's degree of high second class standing or equivalent; for doctorate, GRE, master's or honors degree. Electronic applications accepted. *Faculty research:* Behavioral neuroscience, cognition, theory and research on abnormal behavior.

**Mercer University,** Graduate Studies, Cecil B. Day Campus, Penfield College, Atlanta, GA 30341. Offers certified rehabilitation counseling (MS); clinical mental health (MS); counselor education and supervision (PhD); criminal justice and public safety leadership (MS); health informatics (MS); human services (MS), including child and adolescent services, gerontology services; organizational leadership (MS); school counseling (MS). *Program availability:* Part-time, evening/weekend, 100% online, blended/hybrid learning. *Faculty:* 15 full-time (8 women), 22 part-time/adjunct (18 women). *Students:* 168 full-time (136 women), 242 part-time (201 women); includes 231 minority (192 Black or African American, non-Hispanic/Latino; 1 American Indian or Alaska Native, non-Hispanic/Latino; 15 Asian, non-Hispanic/Latino; 19 Hispanic/Latino; 1 Native Hawaiian or other Pacific Islander, non-Hispanic/Latino; 3 Two or more races, non-Hispanic/Latino), 2 international. Average age 32. 300 applicants, 45% accepted, 114 enrolled. In 2016, 92 master's, 8 doctorates awarded. *Degree requirements:* For master's, comprehensive exam (for some programs), thesis (for some programs); for doctorate, thesis/dissertation. *Entrance requirements:* For master's, GRE or MAT, Georgia Professional Standards Commission (GPSC) Certification at the SC-5 level; for doctorate, GRE or MAT. Additional exam requirements/recommendations for international students: Recommended—TOEFL (minimum score 550 paper-based; 80 iBT), IELTS (minimum score 6.5). *Application deadline:* For fall admission, 7/1 priority date for domestic and international students; for spring admission, 11/1 priority date for domestic and international students; for summer admission, 4/1 priority date for domestic and international students. Application fee: $35. Electronic applications accepted. Application fee is waived when completed online. *Expenses:* $588 per credit hour. *Financial support:* In 2016–17, 32 students received support. Federal Work-Study, scholarships/grants, and unspecified assistantships available. Financial award applicants required to submit FAFSA. *Faculty research:* Marriage and families issues, leadership and ethics, cyber-bullying, trauma, narrative counseling and theory. *Total annual research expenditures:* $85,000. *Unit head:* Dr. Priscilla R. Danheiser, Dean, 678-547-6028, Fax: 678-547-6008, E-mail: danheiser_p@mercer.edu. Website: http://penfield.mercer.edu/programs/graduate-professional/

**Merrimack College,** School of Liberal Arts, North Andover, MA 01845-5800. Offers clinical mental health counseling (MS); public affairs (MPA). *Program availability:* Part-time, evening/weekend. *Faculty:* 6 full-time, 4 part-time/adjunct. *Students:* 22 full-time (16 women), 2 part-time (0 women); includes 3 minority (2 Black or African American, non-Hispanic/Latino; 1 Hispanic/Latino), 1 international. Average age 32. 22 applicants, 95% accepted, 16 enrolled. *Degree requirements:* For master's, internship/strategic capstone. *Entrance requirements:* For master's, official college transcripts, resume, personal statement, 2 recommendations. Additional exam requirements/recommendations for international students: Required—TOEFL (minimum score 84 iBT), IELTS (minimum score 6.5), PTE (minimum score 56). *Application deadline:* For fall admission, 8/14 for domestic students, 7/14 for international students; for spring admission, 1/10 for domestic students, 12/10 for international students; for summer admission, 5/10 for domestic students, 4/10 for international students. Applications are processed on a rolling basis. Electronic applications accepted. *Expenses:* Contact institution. *Financial support:* Career-related internships or fieldwork, scholarships/grants, and health care benefits available. Support available to part-time students. Financial award application deadline: 5/1; financial award applicants required to submit FAFSA. *Faculty research:* Resilience, bereavement and grief, cultural competency training in counseling, government spending and taxation, applied ethics. *Application contact:* Jennifer Greenwood, Graduate Admissions Counselor, 978-837-3563, E-mail: greenwoodjl@merrimack.edu.

**Messiah College,** Program in Counseling, Mechanicsburg, PA 17055. Offers clinical mental health counseling (MAC); counseling (CAGS); marriage, couple and family counseling (MAC); school counseling (MAC). *Accreditation:* ACA. *Program availability:* Part-time, online learning. *Entrance requirements:* For master's, minimum undergraduate cumulative GPA of 3.0, 2 recommendations, resume or curriculum vitae, interview; for CAGS, bachelor's degree, minimum undergraduate cumulative GPA of 3.0, essay, two recommendations, resume or curriculum vitae, interview. Electronic applications accepted.

**Michigan School of Professional Psychology,** MA and Psy D Programs in Clinical Psychology, Farmington Hills, MI 48334. Offers MA, Psy D. *Accreditation:* APA. *Program availability:* Part-time. *Faculty:* 8 full-time (4 women), 13 part-time/adjunct (11 women). *Students:* 84 full-time (66 women), 56 part-time (46 women); includes 42 minority (29 Black or African American, non-Hispanic/Latino; 2 Asian, non-Hispanic/Latino; 5 Hispanic/Latino; 6 Two or more races, non-Hispanic/Latino), 1 international. Average age 34. 155 applicants, 54% accepted, 61 enrolled. In 2016, 42 master's, 17 doctorates awarded. *Degree requirements:* For master's, practicum; for doctorate, comprehensive exam, thesis/dissertation, internship, practicum. *Entrance requirements:* For master's, undergraduate degree from accredited institution with minimum GPA of 2.5; major in psychology, social work, or counseling; for doctorate, GRE General Test, undergraduate degree from accredited institution with minimum GPA of 2.5; graduate degree in psychology, social work, or counseling from accredited institution with minimum GPA of 3.25; graduate-level practicum. Additional exam requirements/recommendations for international students: Required—TOEFL (minimum score 550 paper-based; 79 iBT). *Application deadline:* For fall admission, 8/15 for domestic students; for winter admission, 12/1 for domestic students; for spring admission, 4/3 for domestic students. Applications are processed on a rolling basis. Application fee: $75. Electronic applications accepted. *Expenses:* Contact institution. *Financial support:* In 2016–17, 6 students received support, including 1 research assistantship, 5 teaching assistantships (averaging $14,436 per year); institutionally sponsored loans, scholarships/grants, and unspecified assistantships also available. Financial award application deadline: 8/30; financial award applicants required to submit FAFSA. *Faculty research:* Health psychology, trauma. *Unit head:* Dr. Frances Brown, Program Director, 248-476-1122, Fax: 248-476-1125. *Application contact:* Carrie Hauser, Coordinator of Admissions and Student Engagement, 248-476-1122 Ext. 117, Fax: 248-476-1125, E-mail: chauser@mispp.edu. Website: http://www.mispp.edu

**MidAmerica Nazarene University,** School of Behavioral Sciences and Counseling, Olathe, KS 66062-1899. Offers counseling (MA), including clinical mental health, marriage, couple and family, school counseling, spiritual formation in counseling. *Accreditation:* ACA. *Program availability:* Evening/weekend. *Faculty:* 10 full-time (4 women), 13 part-time/adjunct (9 women). *Students:* 109 full-time (92 women), 100 part-time (87 women); includes 39 minority (21 Black or African American, non-Hispanic/Latino; 3 Asian, non-Hispanic/Latino; 5 Hispanic/Latino; 1 Native Hawaiian or other Pacific Islander, non-Hispanic/Latino; 9 Two or more races, non-Hispanic/Latino). 97 applicants, 79% accepted, 61 enrolled. In 2016, 55 master's awarded. *Degree requirements:* For master's, comprehensive exam. *Entrance requirements:* For master's, on-site writing assessment, official transcript, three recommendations, personal interview. Additional exam requirements/recommendations for international students: Required—TOEFL (minimum score 81 iBT). *Application deadline:* For winter admission, 2/15 for domestic and international students; for spring admission, 4/1 for domestic and international students. Electronic applications accepted. *Expenses:* $34,620 tuition, $250 lab fee, $1,200 technology fee. *Financial support:* Applicants required to submit FAFSA. *Faculty research:* Technology and intimacy, play therapy, interpersonal neurobiology, sexual addiction. *Unit head:* Dr. Todd Frye, Dean, School of Behavioral Sciences and Counseling, 913-971-3449, Fax: 913-971-3402, E-mail: tmfrye@mnu.edu. *Application contact:* Jean Blades, Administrative Assistant, 913-971-3730, E-mail: jmblades@mnu.edu.

**Middle Tennessee State University,** College of Graduate Studies, College of Behavioral and Health Sciences, Department of Psychology, Murfreesboro, TN 37132. Offers clinical psychology (MA); experimental psychology (MA); industrial/organizational psychology (MA); psychology (MA, Ed S); quantitative psychology (MA); school psychology (MA). *Program availability:* Part-time, evening/weekend, online learning. *Degree requirements:* For master's, comprehensive exam, thesis. *Entrance requirements:* For master's, GRE. Additional exam requirements/recommendations for international students: Required—TOEFL (minimum score 525 paper-based; 71 iBT) or IELTS (minimum score 6). Electronic applications accepted. *Faculty research:* Health psychology, industrial/organizational psychology, experimental psychology.

**Midwestern State University,** Billie Doris McAda Graduate School, Prothro-Yeager College of Humanities and Social Sciences, Department of Psychology, Wichita Falls, TX 76308. Offers clinical/counseling psychology (MA). *Program availability:* Part-time, evening/weekend. *Degree requirements:* For master's, one foreign language, comprehensive exam, thesis optional. *Entrance requirements:* For master's, GRE General Test, 3 recommendation forms. Additional exam requirements/recommendations for international students: Required—TOEFL (minimum score 550 paper-based). Electronic applications accepted. *Faculty research:* Child assessment and treatment outcomes, Christianity as it relates to psychology, treatment of behavioral/emotional problems in childhood, people struggling with HIV/AIDS, educational psychology.

**Midwestern University, Downers Grove Campus,** College of Health Sciences, Illinois Campus, Program in Clinical Psychology, Downers Grove, IL 60515-1235. Offers MA, Psy D. *Accreditation:* APA. *Degree requirements:* For doctorate, thesis/dissertation, qualifying examination. *Entrance requirements:* For master's and doctorate, GRE, minimum overall GPA of 2.75, 3 letters of recommendation. Additional exam requirements/recommendations for international students: Required—TOEFL.

**Midwestern University, Glendale Campus,** College of Health Sciences, Arizona Campus, Program in Clinical Psychology, Glendale, AZ 85308. Offers Psy D. *Accreditation:* APA.

**Millersville University of Pennsylvania,** College of Graduate Studies and Adult Learning, College of Education and Human Services, Department of Psychology, Program in Clinical Psychology, Millersville, PA 17551-0302. Offers MA. *Program availability:* Part-time, evening/weekend. *Faculty:* 19 full-time (13 women). *Students:* 30 full-time (23 women), 24 part-time (21 women); includes 7 minority (2 Black or African American, non-Hispanic/Latino; 1 American Indian or Alaska Native, non-Hispanic/Latino; 1 Asian, non-Hispanic/Latino; 3 Hispanic/Latino), 1 international. Average age 26. 42 applicants, 67% accepted, 15 enrolled. In 2016, 16 master's awarded. *Degree requirements:* For master's, comprehensive exam, thesis optional, internship. *Entrance requirements:* For master's, GRE or MAT (if cumulative GPA is lower than 3.0), at least 1 academic reference; interview; 18 undergraduate credits in psychology. Additional exam requirements/recommendations for international students: Required—TOEFL (minimum score 600 paper-based), IELTS (minimum score 6). *Application deadline:* For fall admission, 1/15 for domestic and international students; for spring admission, 10/1 for domestic and international students. Application fee: $40. Electronic applications accepted. *Expenses:* $483 per credit resident tuition; $725 per credit non-resident tuition. *Financial support:* In 2016–17, 20 students received support. Unspecified assistantships available. Financial award application deadline: 3/15; financial award applicants required to submit FAFSA. *Faculty research:* Cognitive behavioral treatments, child social-emotional development, empirically supported treatments and evidence-based practices, humanistic/existential therapy, animal assisted therapy. *Unit head:* Dr. Claudia J. Haferkamp, Coordinator, 717-871-7273, Fax: 717-871-7946, E-mail: claudia.haferkamp@millersville.edu. *Application contact:* Dr. Victor S. DeSantis, Dean of College of Graduate Studies and Adult Learning/Associate Provost for Civic and Community Engagement, 717-871-7619, Fax: 717-871-7954, E-mail: victor.desantis@millersville.edu.
Website: http://www.millersville.edu/psychology/graduate/clinical-psychology/index.php

**Milligan College,** Area of Social Learning, Milligan College, TN 37682. Offers clinical mental health counseling (MSC); counseling ministry (Graduate Certificate); school counseling (MSC). *Program availability:* Part-time. *Faculty:* 3 full-time (all women), 2 part-time/adjunct (0 women). *Students:* 25 full-time (22 women), 3 part-time (2 women); includes 2 minority (1 Black or African American, non-Hispanic/Latino; 1 Two or more races, non-Hispanic/Latino), 1 international. Average age 31. 29 applicants, 72% accepted, 14 enrolled. In 2016, 15 master's awarded. *Degree requirements:* For master's, thesis or alternative. *Entrance requirements:* For master's, GRE General Test if undergraduate degree is less than 3.0, undergraduate degree and supporting transcripts, essay/personal statement, professional recommendations, interview. Additional exam requirements/recommendations for international students: Required—TOEFL (minimum score 550 paper-based, 79 iBT) or IELTS (6.5). *Application deadline:* For fall admission, 8/1 for domestic students, 6/1 for international students. Applications are processed on a rolling basis. Application fee: $30. Electronic applications accepted. *Expenses:* $430 per hour tuition; $325 per semester tech/activity fees. *Financial support:* Scholarships/grants available. Financial award application deadline: 12/1; financial award applicants required to submit FAFSA. *Faculty research:* Parent-child interaction therapy/autism; childhood sexual abuse/trauma; poverty and homelessness; social justice advocacy and competence; school-based mental health. *Unit head:* Dr. Christine Browning, Director of Master of Science in Counseling Program, 423-461-3513, Fax: 423-461-8777, E-mail: cmbrowning@milligan.edu. *Application contact:* Jenni Duran, Graduate Admissions Recruiter, Healthcare Programs, 423-461-8424, Fax: 423-461-8789, E-mail: jduran@milligan.edu.
Website: http://www.Milligan.edu/GPS

**Minnesota State University Mankato,** College of Graduate Studies and Research, College of Social and Behavioral Sciences, Department of Psychology, Mankato, MN 56001. Offers clinical psychology (MA); industrial/organizational psychology (MA); school psychology (Psy D). *Program availability:* Part-time. *Students:* 51 full-time (34 women), 12 part-time (11 women). *Degree requirements:* For master's, one foreign language, comprehensive exam, thesis (for some programs). *Entrance requirements:* For master's, GRE General Test, GRE Subject Test (clinical psychology), minimum GPA of 3.0 during previous 2 years, 3 letters of reference. Additional exam requirements/recommendations for international students: Required—TOEFL. *Application deadline:* For fall admission, 1/1 priority date for domestic students. Applications are processed on a rolling basis. Application fee: $40. Electronic applications accepted. *Financial support:* Research assistantships, teaching assistantships with full tuition reimbursements,

career-related internships or fieldwork, Federal Work-Study, institutionally sponsored loans, and unspecified assistantships available. Support available to part-time students. Financial award application deadline: 3/15; financial award applicants required to submit FAFSA.
Website: http://sbs.mnsu.edu/psych/

**Mississippi State University,** College of Arts and Sciences, Department of Psychology, Mississippi State, MS 39762. Offers applied cognitive science (PhD); clinical psychology (PhD), including clinical psychology; psychology (MS). *Accreditation:* APA. *Faculty:* 21 full-time (9 women), 2 part-time/adjunct (1 woman). *Students:* 33 full-time (21 women), 6 part-time (5 women); includes 6 minority (3 Black or African American, non-Hispanic/Latino; 2 Asian, non-Hispanic/Latino; 1 Two or more races, non-Hispanic/Latino), 2 international. Average age 27. 53 applicants, 23% accepted, 8 enrolled. In 2016, 1 master's, 3 doctorates awarded. Terminal master's awarded for partial completion of doctoral program. *Degree requirements:* For master's, comprehensive exam, thesis; for doctorate, thesis/dissertation, qualifying exam, comprehensive written and oral exam. *Entrance requirements:* For master's, GRE General Test, minimum GPA of 2.75 on last two years of undergraduate courses; for doctorate, GRE General Test, proficiency in at least 1 computer language, minimum GPA of 3.0. Additional exam requirements/recommendations for international students: Required—TOEFL (minimum score 477 paper-based; 53 iBT); Recommended—IELTS (minimum score 4.5). *Application deadline:* For fall admission, 1/15 priority date for domestic students, 5/1 for international students; for spring admission, 11/1 priority date for domestic students, 9/1 for international students. Applications are processed on a rolling basis. Application fee: $60. Electronic applications accepted. *Expenses:* Tuition, state resident: $7670; part-time $852.50 per credit hour. Tuition, nonresident: full-time $20,790; part-time $2310.50 per credit hour. Part-time tuition and fees vary according to course load. *Financial support:* In 2016–17, 5 research assistantships with full tuition reimbursements (averaging $13,441 per year), 21 teaching assistantships with full tuition reimbursements (averaging $10,291 per year) were awarded; career-related internships or fieldwork, Federal Work-Study, institutionally sponsored loans, scholarships/grants, and unspecified assistantships also available. Financial award application deadline: 4/1; financial award applicants required to submit FAFSA. *Faculty research:* Personality type, alcoholism, blindness and low vision, mental retardation, language comprehension. *Total annual research expenditures:* $1.7 million. *Unit head:* Dr. Mitchell E. Berman, Department Head, 662-325-3202, Fax: 662-325-7212, E-mail: mberman@psychology.msstate.edu. *Application contact:* Lakan Drinker, Admissions and Enrollment Assistant, 662-325-8951, E-mail: ldrinker@grad.msstate.edu.
Website: http://www.psychology.msstate.edu/

**Mississippi State University,** College of Education, Department of Counseling, Educational Psychology, and Foundations, Mississippi State, MS 39762. Offers clinical mental health (MS); college counseling (MS); college/post secondary student counseling and personnel services (PhD); counselor education (Ed S); counselor education/student counseling and guidance services (PhD); general educational psychology (MS); psychometry (MS); rehabilitation (MS); school counseling (MS); school psychology (PhD, Ed S); student affairs (MS). *Accreditation:* ACA (one or more programs are accredited); APA; CORE (one or more programs are accredited); NCATE. *Program availability:* Part-time, blended/hybrid learning. *Faculty:* 21 full-time (14 women), 2 part-time/adjunct (both women). *Students:* 125 full-time (94 women), 70 part-time (60 women); includes 63 minority (48 Black or African American, non-Hispanic/Latino; 1 American Indian or Alaska Native, non-Hispanic/Latino; 4 Asian, non-Hispanic/Latino; 5 Hispanic/Latino; 5 Two or more races, non-Hispanic/Latino), 6 international. Average age 30. 151 applicants, 64% accepted, 70 enrolled. In 2016, 49 master's, 3 doctorates, 4 other advanced degrees awarded. Terminal master's awarded for partial completion of doctoral program. *Degree requirements:* For master's, comprehensive exam, thesis optional; for doctorate, thesis/dissertation, comprehensive oral and written exam. *Entrance requirements:* For master's, GRE (taken within the last five years), BS with minimum GPA of 2.75 on last 60 hours; for doctorate, GRE, MS from CACREP- or CORE-accredited program in counseling; for Ed S, GRE, MS in counseling or related field, minimum GPA of 3.3 on all graduate work. Additional exam requirements/recommendations for international students: Required—TOEFL (minimum score 550 paper-based; 79 iBT); Recommended—IELTS (minimum score 6.5). *Application deadline:* For fall admission, 2/1 priority date for domestic and international students. Applications are processed on a rolling basis. Application fee: $60. Electronic applications accepted. *Expenses:* Tuition, state resident: full-time $7670; part-time $852.50 per credit hour. Tuition, nonresident: full-time $20,790; part-time $2310.50 per credit hour. Part-time tuition and fees vary according to course load. *Financial support:* In 2016–17, 9 teaching assistantships with full tuition reimbursements (averaging $8,401 per year) were awarded; career-related internships or fieldwork, Federal Work-Study, institutionally sponsored loans, and unspecified assistantships also available. Financial award application deadline: 2/1; financial award applicants required to submit FAFSA. *Faculty research:* HIV/AIDS in college population, substance abuse in youth and college students, ADHD and conduct disorders in youth, assessment and identification of early childhood disabilities, assessment and vocational transition of the disabled. *Unit head:* Dr. David Morse, Professor and Head, 662-325-3426, Fax: 662-325-3263, E-mail: dmorse@colled.msstate.edu. *Application contact:* Linda Bonner, Senior Admissions Assistant, 662-325-3363, E-mail: lbonner@grad.msstate.edu.
Website: http://www.cep.msstate.edu/

**Missouri State University,** Graduate College, College of Health and Human Services, Department of Psychology, Springfield, MO 65897. Offers applied behavior analysis (MS); clinical psychology (MS); experimental psychology (MS); forensic child psychology (Certificate); industrial/organizational psychology (MS). *Faculty:* 25 full-time (11 women), 4 part-time/adjunct (0 women). *Students:* 65 full-time (49 women), 7 part-time (5 women); includes 12 minority (1 Black or African American, non-Hispanic/Latino; 3 American Indian or Alaska Native, non-Hispanic/Latino; 3 Asian, non-Hispanic/Latino; 2 Hispanic/Latino; 3 Two or more races, non-Hispanic/Latino), 6 international. Average age 25. 159 applicants, 25% accepted, 31 enrolled. In 2016, 22 master's awarded. *Degree requirements:* For master's, comprehensive exam, thesis. *Entrance requirements:* For master's, GRE General Test, GRE Subject Test, minimum GPA of 3.25 in major, 3.0 overall; 20 hours of course work in psychology. Additional exam requirements/recommendations for international students: Required—TOEFL (minimum score 550 paper-based; 79 iBT), IELTS (minimum score 6). *Application deadline:* For fall admission, 2/15 priority date for domestic and international students. Application fee: $35 ($50 for international students). Electronic applications accepted. *Expenses:* Tuition, state resident: full-time $5830. Tuition, nonresident: full-time $10,708. *Required fees:* $1130. Tuition and fees vary according to class time, course level, course load and program. *Financial support:* In 2016–17, 9 research assistantships with full tuition reimbursements (averaging $8,772 per year), 8 teaching assistantships with full tuition reimbursements (averaging $8,772 per year) were awarded; career-related internships or fieldwork, Federal Work-Study, institutionally sponsored loans, scholarships/grants, and unspecified assistantships also available. Financial award application deadline: 3/31; financial award applicants required to submit FAFSA. *Faculty research:* Work-family conflict, child forensic psychology, sports psychology, body image assessment, visual learning. *Unit head:* Dr. Paul Deal, Department Head, 417-836-5797, Fax: 417-836-8330, E-mail: psychology@missouristate.edu. *Application contact:* Michael Edwards,

Coordinator of Graduate Admissions, 417-836-5330, Fax: 417-836-6200, E-mail: michaeledwards@missouristate.edu. Website: http://psychology.missouristate.edu/

**Molloy College,** Program in Clinical Mental Health Counseling, Rockville Centre, NY 11571-5002. Offers MS. *Program availability:* Part-time-only, evening/weekend. *Faculty:* 2 full-time (both women), 1 part-time/adjunct (0 women). *Students:* 27 part-time (24 women); includes 8 minority (3 Black or African American, non-Hispanic/Latino; 1 American Indian or Alaska Native, non-Hispanic/Latino; 3 Hispanic/Latino; 1 Two or more races, non-Hispanic/Latino). Average age 37. 35 applicants, 54% accepted, 12 enrolled. *Degree requirements:* For master's, comprehensive exam. *Entrance requirements:* Additional exam requirements/recommendations for international students: Required—TOEFL (minimum score 550 paper-based; 79 iBT). *Application deadline:* Applications are processed on a rolling basis. Application fee: $60. Electronic applications accepted. *Expenses: Tuition:* Full-time $19,170; part-time $1065 per credit. *Required fees:* $950; $790 per credit. Tuition and fees vary according to course load. *Financial support:* Applicants required to submit FAFSA. *Faculty research:* Intervention of group therapy for decreasing parenting stress in parents with children with disabilities; mindfulness for counseling students and mental health professionals; the use of therapeutic theater and group counseling to support clients in early eating disorder recovery; the lived experience of mothers who have children with autism; the use of music to support master's counseling students in learning existential counseling concepts. *Unit head:* Dr. Laura B. Kestemberg, Associate Dean and Director for Department of Clinical Mental Health Counseling, 516-323-3842, E-mail: lkestemberg@molloy.edu. *Application contact:* Jaclyn Machowicz, Assistant Director for Admissions, 516-323-4010, E-mail: jmachowicz@molloy.edu.

**Montclair State University,** The Graduate School, College of Humanities and Social Sciences, Program in Clinical Psychology, Montclair, NJ 07043-1624. Offers MA. *Program availability:* Part-time, evening/weekend. *Entrance requirements:* For master's, GRE General Test, 2 letters of recommendation, essay. Additional exam requirements/recommendations for international students: Required—TOEFL (minimum score 83 iBT), IELTS (minimum score 6.5). Electronic applications accepted. *Expenses:* Tuition, state resident: part-time $553 per credit. Tuition, nonresident: part-time $854 per credit. *Required fees:* $91 per credit. Tuition and fees vary according to program. *Faculty research:* Community psychology, infant cognitive development.

**Morehead State University,** Graduate Programs, College of Science and Technology, Department of Psychology, Morehead, KY 40351. Offers clinical/counseling psychology (MS); general/experimental psychology (MS). *Program availability:* Part-time, evening/ weekend. *Degree requirements:* For master's, comprehensive exam, thesis optional. *Entrance requirements:* For master's, GRE General Test, 18 undergraduate hours in psychology, minimum GPA of 3.0, 3 letters of recommendation. Additional exam requirements/recommendations for international students: Required—TOEFL (minimum score 500 paper-based). Electronic applications accepted. *Faculty research:* Mood induction effects, serotonin receptor activity, stress, perceptual processes.

**Mount Mary University,** Graduate Programs, Program in Counseling, Milwaukee, WI 53222-4597. Offers clinical mental health counseling (MS, Certificate); clinical rehabilitation counseling (MS, Certificate); school counseling (MS, Certificate); vocational rehabilitation counseling (MS, Certificate). *Accreditation:* ACA. *Program availability:* Part-time, evening/weekend. *Faculty:* 6 full-time (all women), 12 part-time/ adjunct (10 women). *Students:* 91 full-time (84 women), 17 part-time (14 women); includes 25 minority (12 Black or African American, non-Hispanic/Latino; 1 Asian, non-Hispanic/Latino; 8 Hispanic/Latino; 1 Native Hawaiian or other Pacific Islander, non-Hispanic/Latino; 3 Two or more races, non-Hispanic/Latino). Average age 31. 68 applicants, 59% accepted, 29 enrolled. In 2016, 42 master's, 1 other advanced degree awarded. *Degree requirements:* For master's, comprehensive exam, thesis or alternative. *Entrance requirements:* For master's, minimum GPA of 3.0. Additional exam requirements/recommendations for international students: Required—TOEFL (minimum score 550 paper-based; 80 iBT); Recommended—IELTS (minimum score 6.5). *Application deadline:* For fall admission, 5/1 for domestic and international students; for spring admission, 10/1 for domestic and international students; for summer admission, 4/15 for domestic and international students. Applications are processed on a rolling basis. Application fee: $45. Electronic applications accepted. *Expenses:* Contact institution. *Financial support:* Career-related internships or fieldwork, Federal Work-Study, and unspecified assistantships available. Support available to part-time students. Financial award application deadline: 5/1; financial award applicants required to submit FAFSA. *Faculty research:* Cognitive behavioral interventions for depression, eating disorders and compliance, trauma-informed care. *Unit head:* Dr. Carrie King, Graduate Program Director, 414-258-4810 Ext. 318, E-mail: kingc@mtmary.edu. *Application contact:* Kirk Heller de Messer, Director, Graduate Admissions, 414-930-3221, E-mail: hellerk@mtmary.edu. Website: http://www.mtmary.edu/majors-programs/graduate/counseling/index.html

**Murray State University,** College of Humanities and Fine Arts, Program in Psychology, Murray, KY 42071. Offers clinical psychology (MA, MS); psychology (MA, MS). *Program availability:* Part-time. *Degree requirements:* For master's, one foreign language, comprehensive exam (for some programs), thesis. *Entrance requirements:* For master's, GRE General Test. Additional exam requirements/recommendations for international students: Required—TOEFL.

**National University,** Academic Affairs, College of Letters and Sciences, La Jolla, CA 92037-1011. Offers biology (MS); counseling psychology (MA), including licensed professional clinical counseling; creative writing (MFA). *Program availability:* Part-time, evening/weekend, 100% online, blended/hybrid learning. *Faculty:* 68 full-time (33 women), 70 part-time/adjunct (34 women). *Students:* 566 full-time (408 women), 287 part-time (197 women); includes 394 minority (101 Black or African American, non-Hispanic/Latino; 3 American Indian or Alaska Native, non-Hispanic/Latino; 47 Asian, non-Hispanic/Latino; 185 Hispanic/Latino; 8 Native Hawaiian or other Pacific Islander, non-Hispanic/Latino; 50 Two or more races, non-Hispanic/Latino), 3 international. Average age 34. In 2016, 450 master's awarded. *Degree requirements:* For master's, thesis (for some programs). *Entrance requirements:* For master's, interview, minimum GPA of 2.5. Additional exam requirements/recommendations for international students: Required—TOEFL (minimum score 550 paper-based; 79 iBT), IELTS (minimum score 6). *Application deadline:* Applications are processed on a rolling basis. Application fee: $60 ($65 for international students). Electronic applications accepted. *Financial support:* Career-related internships or fieldwork, institutionally sponsored loans, scholarships/ grants, and tuition waivers (partial) available. Support available to part-time students. Financial award application deadline: 6/30; financial award applicants required to submit FAFSA. *Unit head:* College of Letters and Sciences, 800-628-8648, E-mail: cols@nu.edu. *Application contact:* Brandon Jouganatos, Interim Vice President for Enrollment Services, 800-628-8648, E-mail: advisor@nu.edu. Website: http://www.nu.edu/OurPrograms/CollegeOfLettersAndSciences.html

**Neumann University,** Program in Pastoral Clinical Mental Health Counseling, Aston, PA 19014-1298. Offers pastoral care specialist (Certificate); pastoral clinical mental health counseling (MS); pastoral clinical mental health counseling certificate of advanced study (Certificate); pastoral counseling (PhD); spiritual formation and direction (CSD); spiritual formation and direction supervision certificate of advanced study (Certificate). *Program availability:* Part-time, evening/weekend. *Faculty:* 7 full-time (5 women), 3 part-time/adjunct (2 women). *Students:* 15 full-time (14 women), 90 part-time (64 women); includes 15 minority (10 Black or African American, non-Hispanic/Latino; 1 Asian, non-Hispanic/Latino; 2 Hispanic/Latino; 2 Two or more races, non-Hispanic/ Latino). Average age 47. 61 applicants, 52% accepted, 27 enrolled. In 2016, 22 master's, 1 doctorate awarded. *Degree requirements:* For doctorate, comprehensive exam, thesis/dissertation. *Entrance requirements:* For master's and other advanced degree, official transcripts from all institutions attended, letter of intent, three official letters of recommendation; for doctorate, MAT, master's degree, official transcripts from all institutions attended, resume or curriculum vitae, letter of intent, two official letters of recommendation. Additional exam requirements/recommendations for international students: Required—TOEFL (minimum score 70 iBT). *Application deadline:* For fall admission, 8/1 for domestic students; for spring admission, 12/1 for domestic students. Applications are processed on a rolling basis. Application fee: $0. Electronic applications accepted. *Expenses:* $670 per credit tuition (for master's and Certificate); $830 per credit (for PhD in pastoral counseling). *Financial support:* Scholarships/grants and health care benefits available. Support available to part-time students. Financial award application deadline: 3/15; financial award applicants required to submit FAFSA. *Unit head:* Sr. Suzanne Mayer, Director of Pastoral Clinical Mental Health Counseling Program, 610-361-2292, Fax: 610-358-4525, E-mail: mayers@neumann.edu. *Application contact:* Dr. Erika Davis, Director of Adult and Graduate Admissions, 800-9-NEUMANN Ext. 5208, Fax: 610-361-2548, E-mail: GradAdultAdmiss@neumann.edu.

**New Mexico Highlands University,** Graduate Studies, College of Arts and Sciences, Department of Social and Behavioral Sciences, Las Vegas, NM 87701. Offers psychology (MS), including clinical psychology/counseling, general psychology; public affairs (MA), including applied sociology; Southwest studies (MA), including anthropology. *Program availability:* Part-time. *Degree requirements:* For master's, comprehensive exam, thesis or alternative. *Entrance requirements:* For master's, minimum undergraduate GPA of 3.0. Additional exam requirements/recommendations for international students: Required—TOEFL (minimum score 540 paper-based). *Faculty research:* Southwest Native American resettlement development, community-level interventions, neurochemistry of personality, comparative criminal justice, social theory and activism.

**The New School,** The New School for Social Research, Department of Psychology, New York, NY 10003. Offers clinical psychology (PhD); cognitive, social, and developmental psychology (PhD); psychology (MA). *Accreditation:* APA (one or more programs are accredited). *Program availability:* Part-time. *Faculty:* 16 full-time (6 women), 12 part-time/adjunct (4 women). *Students:* 115 full-time (85 women), 99 part-time (77 women); includes 36 minority (9 Black or African American, non-Hispanic/ Latino; 1 American Indian or Alaska Native, non-Hispanic/Latino; 11 Asian, non-Hispanic/Latino; 12 Hispanic/Latino; 3 Two or more races, non-Hispanic/Latino), 32 international. Average age 29. 247 applicants, 84% accepted, 60 enrolled. In 2016, 57 master's, 19 doctorates awarded. Terminal master's awarded for partial completion of doctoral program. *Degree requirements:* For master's, comprehensive exam, thesis (for some programs); for doctorate, comprehensive exam, thesis/dissertation. *Entrance requirements:* For master's, GRE, letters of recommendation, writing sample, essays, unofficial transcripts; for doctorate, letters of recommendation, writing sample, essays, unofficial transcripts. Additional exam requirements/recommendations for international students: Required—TOEFL (minimum score 100 iBT), IELTS (minimum score 7), PTE (minimum score 68). *Application deadline:* For fall admission, 8/1 priority date for domestic and international students; for spring admission, 10/15 priority date for domestic and international students. Applications are processed on a rolling basis. Application fee: $50. Electronic applications accepted. *Expenses:* Contact institution. *Financial support:* Fellowships, research assistantships, teaching assistantships, career-related internships or fieldwork, Federal Work-Study, scholarships/grants, and tuition waivers (full and partial) available. Support available to part-time students. Financial award application deadline: 2/1; financial award applicants required to submit FAFSA. *Faculty research:* Cognitive, social, and developmental psychology; clinical psychology; mental health and substance abuse counseling. *Unit head:* Dr. William Milberg, Dean, The New School for Social Research, 212-229-5777, E-mail: milbergw@newschool.edu. *Application contact:* Dana Messinger, Director of Graduate Admission, 212-229-5150 Ext. 2300, E-mail: socialresearchadmit@newschool.edu.

**Nicholls State University,** Graduate Studies, College of Education, Department of Psychology, Counseling and Family Studies, Thibodaux, LA 70310. Offers clinical mental health counseling (MA); school counseling (M Ed); school psychology (SSP). *Accreditation:* NCATE. *Program availability:* Part-time, evening/weekend. *Degree requirements:* For master's, comprehensive exam; for SSP, comprehensive exam, internship. *Entrance requirements:* For master's, GRE General Test. Electronic applications accepted.

**Norfolk State University,** School of Graduate Studies, School of Liberal Arts, Department of Psychology, Program in Community/Clinical Psychology, Norfolk, VA 23504. Offers MA. *Degree requirements:* For master's, comprehensive exam, thesis or alternative. *Entrance requirements:* For master's, minimum GPA of 2.7.

**North Dakota State University,** College of Graduate and Interdisciplinary Studies, College of Science and Mathematics, Department of Psychology, Fargo, ND 58102. Offers clinical psychology (MS); health and social psychology (PhD); psychological clinical science (PhD); psychology (MS); visual and cognitive neuroscience (PhD). *Degree requirements:* For master's, thesis; for doctorate, thesis/dissertation. *Entrance requirements:* For master's and doctorate, GRE General Test, GRE Subject Test. Additional exam requirements/recommendations for international students: Required— TOEFL (minimum score 525 paper-based; 71 iBT). Electronic applications accepted. *Faculty research:* Cognition science, neuropsychology, group behavior, applied behavior analysis, behavior therapy.

**Northern Arizona University,** Graduate College, College of Social and Behavioral Sciences, Department of Psychological Sciences, Flagstaff, AZ 86011. Offers clinical health psychology (MA); general psychology (MA); teaching psychology (MA). *Program availability:* Part-time. *Degree requirements:* For master's, comprehensive exam (for some programs), thesis (for some programs), oral defense. *Entrance requirements:* For master's, GRE General Test. Additional exam requirements/recommendations for international students: Required—TOEFL (minimum score 550 paper-based; 80 iBT), IELTS (minimum score 7). Electronic applications accepted. *Expenses:* Tuition, state resident: full-time $8971; part-time $444 per credit hour. Tuition, nonresident: full-time $20,958; part-time $1164 per credit hour. *Required fees:* $1018; $644 per credit hour. Tuition and fees vary according to course load, campus/location and program.

**Northern Kentucky University,** Office of Graduate Programs, College of Education and Human Services, Clinical Mental Health Counseling Program, Highland Heights, KY 41099. Offers MS. *Accreditation:* ACA. *Program availability:* Part-time, evening/ weekend. *Degree requirements:* For master's, comprehensive exam. *Entrance requirements:* For master's, GRE or MAT. Additional exam requirements/ recommendations for international students: Required—TOEFL (minimum score 550 paper-based; 79 iBT); Recommended—IELTS (minimum score 6.5). Electronic applications accepted. *Faculty research:* Preferences for college counseling,

## Clinical Psychology

accreditation, partner violence prevention, data-based school counseling, creativity in counseling.

**Northern State University,** MS Ed Program in Counseling, Aberdeen, SD 57401-7198. Offers clinical mental health counseling (MS Ed); school counseling (MS Ed). *Accreditation:* NCATE. *Program availability:* Part-time, online learning. *Degree requirements:* For master's, comprehensive exam, thesis optional. *Entrance requirements:* For master's, minimum GPA of 2.75. Additional exam requirements/recommendations for international students: Required—TOEFL (minimum score 550 paper-based; 78 iBT), IELTS (minimum score 6). Electronic applications accepted.

**Northwestern State University of Louisiana,** Graduate Studies and Research, Department of Psychology, Natchitoches, LA 71497. Offers clinical psychology (MS). *Degree requirements:* For master's, comprehensive exam, thesis or alternative. *Entrance requirements:* For master's, GRE General Test, GRE Subject Test, minimum undergraduate GPA of 2.5. Additional exam requirements/recommendations for international students: Required—TOEFL. Electronic applications accepted.

**Northwestern University,** The Graduate School, Judd A. and Marjorie Weinberg College of Arts and Sciences, Department of Psychology, Evanston, IL 60208. Offers brain, behavior and cognition (PhD); clinical psychology (PhD); cognitive psychology (PhD); personality psychology (PhD); social psychology (PhD); JD/PhD. Admissions and degrees offered through The Graduate School. *Accreditation:* APA (one or more programs are accredited). *Program availability:* Part-time. *Degree requirements:* For doctorate, thesis/dissertation. *Entrance requirements:* For doctorate, GRE General Test, GRE Subject Test. Additional exam requirements/recommendations for international students: Required—TOEFL. Electronic applications accepted. *Faculty research:* Memory and higher order cognition, anxiety and depression, effectiveness of psychotherapy, social cognition, molecular basis of memory.

**Northwestern University,** The Graduate School and Feinberg School of Medicine, Program in Clinical Psychology, Evanston, IL 60208. Offers clinical psychology (PhD), including clinical neuropsychology. Admissions and degree offered through The Graduate School. *Accreditation:* APA. *Degree requirements:* For doctorate, thesis/dissertation, clinical internship. *Entrance requirements:* For doctorate, GRE General Test, GRE Subject Test, minimum GPA of 3.2, course work in psychology. Additional exam requirements/recommendations for international students: Required—TOEFL. *Faculty research:* Cancer and cardiovascular risk reduction, evaluation of mental health services and policy, neuropsychological assessment, outcome of psychotherapy, cognitive therapy, pediatric and clinical child psychology.

**Northwest Nazarene University,** Program in Social Work, Nampa, ID 83686. Offers clinical mental health and addictions practice (MSW). *Accreditation:* CSWE. *Program availability:* Part-time-only, evening/weekend. *Faculty:* 7 full-time (4 women), 9 part-time/adjunct (5 women). *Students:* 123 full-time (85 women), 24 part-time (13 women); includes 23 minority (3 Black or African American, non-Hispanic/Latino; 1 American Indian or Alaska Native, non-Hispanic/Latino; 12 Hispanic/Latino; 7 Two or more races, non-Hispanic/Latino). Average age 27. 152 applicants, 54% accepted, 73 enrolled. In 2016, 54 master's awarded. *Degree requirements:* For master's, comprehensive exam, thesis or alternative. *Entrance requirements:* For master's, interview, letters of reference, degree from regionally-accredited college/university, written personal statement. *Application deadline:* Applications are processed on a rolling basis. Application fee: $50. Electronic applications accepted. *Expenses: Tuition:* Full-time $9315; part-time $4658 per credit hour. *Required fees:* $120. *Faculty research:* Test anxiety, trauma, statistics. *Unit head:* Dr. Lawanna Lancaster, Director/Department Chair, 208-467-8372, Fax: 208-467-8879, E-mail: mswinfo@nnu.edu. *Application contact:* Jodie Rodriguez-Engel, Program Coordinator, 208-467-8679, Fax: 208-467-8879, E-mail: jrodriguez-engel@nnu.edu.
Website: http://msw.nnu.edu

**Notre Dame de Namur University,** Division of Academic Affairs, College of Arts and Sciences, Department of Clinical Psychology and Gerontology, Program in Clinical Psychology, Belmont, CA 94002-1908. Offers MS. *Program availability:* Part-time. *Degree requirements:* For master's, thesis. *Entrance requirements:* Additional exam requirements/recommendations for international students: Required—TOEFL (minimum score 550 paper-based; 79 iBT). Electronic applications accepted.

**Nova Southeastern University,** College of Psychology, Fort Lauderdale, FL 33314-7796. Offers clinical psychology (PhD, Psy D); counseling (MS); experimental psychology (MS); forensic psychology (MS); general psychology (MS); mental health counseling (MS); school counseling (MS); school psychology (Psy D, Psy S). *Accreditation:* APA (one or more programs are accredited). *Program availability:* 100% online, blended/hybrid learning. *Faculty:* 51 full-time (21 women), 120 part-time/adjunct (70 women). *Students:* 724 full-time (596 women), 918 part-time (792 women); includes 797 minority (276 Black or African American, non-Hispanic/Latino; 1 American Indian or Alaska Native, non-Hispanic/Latino; 44 Asian, non-Hispanic/Latino; 427 Hispanic/Latino; 2 Native Hawaiian or other Pacific Islander, non-Hispanic/Latino; 47 Two or more races, non-Hispanic/Latino), 41 international. Average age 31. 1,349 applicants, 61% accepted, 651 enrolled. In 2016, 377 master's, 177 doctorates, 26 other advanced degrees awarded. Terminal master's awarded for partial completion of doctoral program. *Degree requirements:* For master's, comprehensive exam, 3 practica; for doctorate, thesis/dissertation, clinical internship, competency exam; for Psy S, comprehensive exam, internship. *Entrance requirements:* For doctorate, GRE General Test, GRE Subject Test (recommended), minimum undergraduate GPA of 3.0; for Psy S, GRE General Test. Additional exam requirements/recommendations for international students: Required—TOEFL (minimum score 550 paper-based). *Application deadline:* Applications are processed on a rolling basis. Application fee: $50. Electronic applications accepted. *Expenses:* Contact institution. *Financial support:* In 2016–17, 197 students received support, including 15 research assistantships (averaging $5,600 per year), 68 teaching assistantships (averaging $2,000 per year); career-related internships or fieldwork, Federal Work-Study, institutionally sponsored loans, scholarships/grants, and unspecified assistantships also available. Financial award application deadline: 4/15; financial award applicants required to submit FAFSA. *Faculty research:* Clinical health psychology, multicultural/diversity psychology, clinical neuropsychology, clinical child psychology, family violence. *Unit head:* Dr. Karen Grosby, Dean, 954-262-5712, Fax: 954-262-3859, E-mail: grosby@nova.edu. *Application contact:* Carlos Perez, Senior Manager of Outreach, 954-262-5702, Fax: 954-262-3893, E-mail: gradschool@nova.edu.
Website: http://psychology.nova.edu/

**The Ohio State University,** Graduate School, College of Arts and Sciences, Division of Social and Behavioral Sciences, Department of Psychology, Columbus, OH 43210. Offers behavioral neuroscience (PhD); clinical psychology (PhD); cognitive psychology (PhD); developmental psychology (PhD); intellectual and developmental disabilities psychology (PhD); quantitative psychology (PhD); social psychology (PhD). *Accreditation:* APA. *Faculty:* 57. *Students:* 156 full-time (95 women); includes 23 minority (6 Black or African American, non-Hispanic/Latino; 9 Asian, non-Hispanic/Latino; 8 Hispanic/Latino), 26 international. Average age 26. In 2016, 26 doctorates awarded. *Degree requirements:* For doctorate, thesis/dissertation. *Entrance*

*requirements:* For doctorate, GRE General Test. Additional exam requirements/recommendations for international students: Required—TOEFL (minimum score 600 paper-based; 100 iBT); Recommended—IELTS (minimum score 8). *Application deadline:* For fall admission, 12/1 for domestic and international students. Applications are processed on a rolling basis. Application fee: $60 ($70 for international students). Electronic applications accepted. *Financial support:* Fellowships with tuition reimbursements, research assistantships with tuition reimbursements, and teaching assistantships with tuition reimbursements available. *Unit head:* Dr. John Bruno, Chair, 614-292-3038, E-mail: bruno.1@osu.edu. *Application contact:* Graduate and Professional Admissions, 614-292-9444, Fax: 614-292-3895, E-mail: gpadmissions@osu.edu.
Website: http://www.psy.ohio-state.edu/

**Ohio University,** Graduate College, College of Arts and Sciences, Department of Psychology, Program in Clinical Psychology, Athens, OH 45701-2979. Offers PhD. *Accreditation:* APA. *Degree requirements:* For doctorate, one foreign language, comprehensive exam, thesis/dissertation. *Entrance requirements:* For doctorate, GRE General Test, GRE Subject Test, minimum graduate GPA of 3.4. Additional exam requirements/recommendations for international students: Required—TOEFL. *Application deadline:* For fall admission, 1/1 for domestic students. Application fee: $50 ($55 for international students). *Financial support:* Fellowships with full tuition reimbursements, research assistantships with full tuition reimbursements, teaching assistantships with full tuition reimbursements, career-related internships or fieldwork, Federal Work-Study, institutionally sponsored loans, traineeships, tuition waivers (full), and unspecified assistantships available. Financial award application deadline: 1/15. *Faculty research:* Health psychology, child clinical psychology, psychotherapy outcomes. *Unit head:* Chantel Weisenmuller, Director, 740-597-1251, E-mail: weisenmu@ohio.edu. *Application contact:* Karyl Jones, Administrative Secretary, 740-593-1090, Fax: 740-593-0579, E-mail: psychology@ohio.edu.
Website: http://www.psych.ohiou.edu/

**Oklahoma State University,** College of Arts and Sciences, Department of Psychology, Stillwater, OK 74078. Offers clinical psychology (PhD); general psychology (MS); lifespan development psychology (PhD). *Accreditation:* APA (one or more programs are accredited). *Faculty:* 31 full-time (19 women), 1 (woman) part-time/adjunct. *Students:* 42 full-time (34 women), 14 part-time (8 women); includes 10 minority (1 Black or African American, non-Hispanic/Latino; 4 American Indian or Alaska Native, non-Hispanic/Latino; 1 Asian, non-Hispanic/Latino; 3 Hispanic/Latino; 1 Native Hawaiian or other Pacific Islander, non-Hispanic/Latino; 2 Two or more races, non-Hispanic/Latino), 2 international. Average age 26. 160 applicants, 6% accepted, 9 enrolled. In 2016, 11 master's, 7 doctorates awarded. *Degree requirements:* For master's, thesis or alternative; for doctorate, comprehensive exam, thesis/dissertation. *Entrance requirements:* For master's and doctorate, GRE General Test. Additional exam requirements/recommendations for international students: Required—TOEFL (minimum score 550 paper-based; 79 iBT). *Application deadline:* For fall admission, 3/1 priority date for international students; for spring admission, 8/1 priority date for international students. Applications are processed on a rolling basis. Application fee: $40 ($75 for international students). Electronic applications accepted. *Expenses:* Tuition: state resident: full-time $3775; part-time $209.70 per credit hour. Tuition, nonresident: full-time $14,851; part-time $825.05 per credit hour. *Required fees:* $2027; $112.60 per credit hour. Tuition and fees vary according to campus/location. *Financial support:* In 2016–17, 15 research assistantships (averaging $13,194 per year), 41 teaching assistantships (averaging $11,532 per year) were awarded; career-related internships or fieldwork, Federal Work-Study, scholarships/grants, health care benefits, tuition waivers (partial), and unspecified assistantships also available. Support available to part-time students. Financial award application deadline: 3/1; financial award applicants required to submit FAFSA. *Unit head:* Dr. Thad Leffingwell, Department Head, 405-744-7494, Fax: 405-744-8067, E-mail: thad.leffingwell@okstate.edu. *Application contact:* Patricia Alexander, Graduate Advisor, 405-744-7591, Fax: 405-744-8967, E-mail: patricia.alexander@okstate.edu.
Website: http://psychology.okstate.edu

**Old Dominion University,** College of Sciences, Virginia Consortium Program in Clinical Psychology, Norfolk, VA 23529. Offers PhD. Program offered jointly with Eastern Virginia Medical School and Norfolk State University. *Faculty:* 29 full-time (15 women). *Students:* 10 full-time (7 women), 17 part-time (12 women); includes 10 minority (7 Black or African American, non-Hispanic/Latino; 1 Asian, non-Hispanic/Latino; 2 Two or more races, non-Hispanic/Latino). Average age 27. 77 applicants, 12% accepted, 6 enrolled. In 2016, 5 doctorates awarded. *Degree requirements:* For doctorate, comprehensive exam, thesis/dissertation, internship. *Entrance requirements:* For doctorate, GRE General Test. Additional exam requirements/recommendations for international students: Required—TOEFL. *Application deadline:* For fall admission, 12/1 for domestic and international students. Application fee: $65. Electronic applications accepted. *Expenses:* Contact institution. *Financial support:* In 2016–17, 24 students received support, including 2 research assistantships with partial tuition reimbursements available (averaging $9,000 per year), 11 teaching assistantships with partial tuition reimbursements available (averaging $15,000 per year); scholarships/grants, traineeships, health care benefits, and unspecified assistantships also available. Financial award application deadline: 12/1; financial award applicants required to submit FAFSA. *Faculty research:* Health psychology, minority and women's issues, neuropsychology, assessment, substance abuse. *Unit head:* Dr. Robin Lewis, Director of Clinical Training, 757-451-7733, Fax: 757-823-8919, E-mail: rlewis@odu.edu. *Application contact:* Elaine Ross, Administrator, 757-451-7733, Fax: 757-823-8919, E-mail: emross@odu.edu.
Website: http://odu.edu/vcpcp/

**Oregon State University,** College of Education, Program in Counseling, Corvallis, OR 97331. Offers clinical mental health (M Coun); counseling (MS, PhD); school counseling (M Coun). *Accreditation:* ACA (one or more programs are accredited); NCATE. *Program availability:* Part-time, blended/hybrid learning. *Faculty:* 9 full-time (3 women), 13 part-time/adjunct (11 women). *Students:* 73 full-time (60 women), 105 part-time (80 women); includes 40 minority (6 Black or African American, non-Hispanic/Latino; 7 Asian, non-Hispanic/Latino; 17 Hispanic/Latino; 1 Native Hawaiian or other Pacific Islander, non-Hispanic/Latino; 9 Two or more races, non-Hispanic/Latino), 1 international. Average age 36. 177 applicants, 51% accepted, 66 enrolled. In 2016, 31 master's, 5 doctorates awarded. *Degree requirements:* For master's, thesis or alternative; for doctorate, one foreign language, thesis/dissertation. *Entrance requirements:* For master's, minimum GPA of 3.0 in last 90 hours; for doctorate, GRE or MAT, master's degree, minimum GPA of 3.0 in last 90 hours of course work, 2 years of teaching experience. Additional exam requirements/recommendations for international students: Required—TOEFL (minimum score 575 paper-based). *Application deadline:* For fall admission, 1/31 for domestic students. Application fee: $75 ($85 for international students). *Expenses:* Tuition, state resident: full-time $12,150; part-time $450 per credit. Tuition, nonresident: full-time $21,789; part-time $807 per credit. *Required fees:* $1651; $1507 per credit. One-time fee: $350. Tuition and fees vary according to course load, campus/location and program. *Financial support:* Teaching assistantships, career-related internships or fieldwork, Federal Work-Study, and institutionally sponsored loans available. Support available to part-time students. Financial award application deadline: 3/1. *Faculty*

*research:* Counseling and guidance improvement in social services agencies, elementary and secondary schools. *Unit head:* Dr. Larry Flick, Dean. *Application contact:* Mary Aguilera, Advisor, 541-737-2232, E-mail: mary.aguilera@oregonstate.edu.
Website: http://education.oregonstate.edu/counseling

**Pace University,** Dyson College of Arts and Sciences, Department of Psychology, Program in School-Clinical Child Psychology, New York, NY 10038. Offers school psychology (MS Ed); school-clinical child psychology (Psy D). *Accreditation:* APA (one or more programs are accredited). *Students:* 62 full-time (51 women), 28 part-time (22 women); includes 18 minority (2 Black or African American, non-Hispanic/Latino; 7 Asian, non-Hispanic/Latino; 5 Hispanic/Latino; 1 Native Hawaiian or other Pacific Islander, non-Hispanic/Latino; 3 Two or more races, non-Hispanic/Latino), 3 international. Average age 27. In 2016, 21 master's, 23 doctorates awarded. Terminal master's awarded for partial completion of doctoral program. *Degree requirements:* For master's, qualifying exams, internship; for doctorate, comprehensive exam, thesis/dissertation, qualifying exams, externship, internship. *Entrance requirements:* For master's, GRE General Test, GRE Subject Test in psychology (recommended), interview, 3 letters of recommendation, resume, personal statement; for doctorate, GRE General Test, GRE Subject Test in psychology (recommended), interview, transcripts, 3 letters of recommendation. Additional exam requirements/recommendations for international students: Required—TOEFL (minimum score 88 iBT), IELTS (minimum score 7) or PTE (minimum score 60). *Application deadline:* For fall admission, 1/15 priority date for domestic students. Application fee: $70. Electronic applications accepted. *Expenses: Tuition:* Part-time $1195 per credit. *Required fees:* $260 per semester. Tuition and fees vary according to degree level, campus/location and program. *Financial support:* Scholarships/grants and unspecified assistantships available. Financial award application deadline: 1/15; financial award applicants required to submit FAFSA. *Unit head:* Dr. Barbara Mowder, Director of Graduate Psychology Programs, 212-346-1556, E-mail: bmowder@pace.edu. *Application contact:* Susan Ford-Goldschein, Director of Graduate Admissions, 212-346-1531, Fax: 212-346-1585, E-mail: graduateadmission@pace.edu.
Website: http://www.pace.edu/dyson/academic-departments-and-programs/psychology—-nyc/graduate-programs

**Pacifica Graduate Institute,** Graduate Programs, Carpinteria, CA 93013. Offers clinical psychology (PhD); counseling psychology (MA); depth psychology (MA, PhD); mythological studies (MA, PhD). Terminal master's awarded for partial completion of doctoral program. *Degree requirements:* For master's, thesis (for some programs), practicum; for doctorate, comprehensive exam, thesis/dissertation, internship. *Entrance requirements:* For master's, resume, 3 letters of recommendation, writing sample, interview; for doctorate, resumé, 4 letters of recommendation, writing sample, interview. Additional exam requirements/recommendations for international students: Required—TOEFL. *Faculty research:* Imaginal and archetypal theory; post-Colonial psychoanalytic and Jungian theory; myth literature as it applies to the theory and practice of psychology.

**Pacific University,** School of Professional Psychology, Forest Grove, OR 97116-1797. Offers applied psychological science (MA, MS); clinical psychology (PhD, Psy D). *Accreditation:* APA (one or more programs are accredited). *Program availability:* Part-time. *Degree requirements:* For master's, comprehensive exam (for some programs), thesis (for some programs); for doctorate, comprehensive exam, thesis/dissertation. *Entrance requirements:* For master's, course work in introductory psychology, statistics, and abnormal psychology; minimum GPA of 3.0; for doctorate, GRE General Test, minimum GPA of 3.0, undergraduate course work in psychology, minimum GPA of 3.1 in last 2 years. Additional exam requirements/recommendations for international students: Required—TOEFL (minimum score 600 paper-based). Electronic applications accepted. *Expenses:* Contact institution. *Faculty research:* Neuropsychological assessment, assessment and treatment of anxiety, forensic psychology, cross-cultural psychology, child and adolescent psychopathology.

**Palo Alto University,** MA in Counseling Program, Palo Alto, CA 94304. Offers clinical mental health (MA); marriage, family and child (MA). *Program availability:* Part-time, 100% online, blended/hybrid learning. *Faculty:* 6 full-time (4 women), 5 part-time/adjunct (4 women). *Students:* 38 full-time (34 women), 28 part-time (22 women); includes 29 minority (3 Black or African American, non-Hispanic/Latino; 9 Asian, non-Hispanic/Latino; 14 Hispanic/Latino; 3 Two or more races, non-Hispanic/Latino), 1 international. Average age 32. 111 applicants, 91% accepted, 89 enrolled. In 2016, 91 master's awarded. *Degree requirements:* For master's, capstone project. *Entrance requirements:* For master's, undergraduate degree in psychology with minimum GPA of 3.3. Additional exam requirements/recommendations for international students: Required—TOEFL. *Application deadline:* For fall admission, 6/30 priority date for domestic and international students; for spring admission, 3/21 for domestic and international students. Applications are processed on a rolling basis. Application fee: $40. Electronic applications accepted. *Expenses:* Contact institution. *Financial support:* In 2016–17, 12 students received support. Federal Work-Study and scholarships/grants available. Financial award application deadline: 1/15; financial award applicants required to submit FAFSA. *Unit head:* Dr. William Snow, Director of Counseling, 831-246-2440, E-mail: wsnow@paloaltou.edu. *Application contact:* Deanna Berger, Assistant Director of Admissions, 650-417-2023, E-mail: dberger@paloaltou.edu.
Website: http://www.paloaltou.edu/graduate-programs/masters-programs/ma-counseling

**Palo Alto University,** PGSP-Stanford Psy D Consortium Program, Palo Alto, CA 94304. Offers Psy D. Program offered jointly with Stanford University. *Accreditation:* APA. *Faculty:* 16 full-time (12 women), 31 part-time/adjunct (22 women). *Students:* 155 full-time (129 women), 4 part-time (all women); includes 47 minority (5 Black or African American, non-Hispanic/Latino; 25 Asian, non-Hispanic/Latino; 14 Hispanic/Latino; 3 Two or more races, non-Hispanic/Latino), 3 international. Average age 29. 339 applicants, 17% accepted, 32 enrolled. In 2016, 29 doctorates awarded. *Degree requirements:* For doctorate, comprehensive exam, thesis/dissertation, 2000-hour clinical internship. *Entrance requirements:* For doctorate, GRE General Test (minimum overall score 1200); GRE Subject Test in psychology (highly recommended), undergraduate degree in psychology or related area with minimum GPA of 3.3. Additional exam requirements/recommendations for international students: Required—TOEFL, IELTS. *Application deadline:* For fall admission, 12/2 priority date for domestic and international students. Applications are processed on a rolling basis. Application fee: $50. Electronic applications accepted. *Expenses:* Contact institution. *Financial support:* In 2016–17, 48 students received support, including fellowships (averaging $4,000 per year), research assistantships (averaging $1,000 per year), teaching assistantships (averaging $3,000 per year); Federal Work-Study and scholarships/grants also available. Financial award application deadline: 1/15; financial award applicants required to submit FAFSA. *Unit head:* Dr. Steve Smith, Co-Director of Clinical Training, PGSP-Stanford Psy D Consortium, E-mail: stevesmith@paloaltou.edu. *Application contact:* Dr. Kimberly Hill, Co-Director of Clinical Training, PGSP-Stanford Psy D Consortium, 650-725-5582, E-mail: khill@paloaltou.edu.
Website: http://www.paloaltou.edu/graduate-programs/pgsp-psyd-stanford-consortium

**Palo Alto University,** PhD in Clinical Psychology Program, Palo Alto, CA 94304. Offers PhD, JD/PhD, MBA/PhD. *Accreditation:* APA. *Faculty:* 33 full-time (19 women), 39 part-

time/adjunct (25 women). *Students:* 427 full-time (326 women), 9 part-time (all women); includes 132 minority (20 Black or African American, non-Hispanic/Latino; 2 American Indian or Alaska Native, non-Hispanic/Latino; 57 Asian, non-Hispanic/Latino; 41 Hispanic/Latino; 2 Native Hawaiian or other Pacific Islander, non-Hispanic/Latino; 10 Two or more races, non-Hispanic/Latino), 22 international. Average age 32. 251 applicants, 76 enrolled. In 2016, 62 doctorates awarded. *Degree requirements:* For doctorate, comprehensive exam, thesis/dissertation, 2000-hour clinical internship. *Entrance requirements:* For doctorate, GRE General Test, undergraduate or graduate degree in psychology or related area; 4 course prerequisites: biopsychology, abnormal psychology, developmental psychology, and statistics. Additional exam requirements/recommendations for international students: Required—TOEFL, IELTS. *Application deadline:* For fall admission, 12/2 priority date for domestic and international students. Applications are processed on a rolling basis. Application fee: $50. Electronic applications accepted. *Expenses:* Contact institution. *Financial support:* In 2016–17, 115 students received support, including fellowships (averaging $7,500 per year), research assistantships (averaging $4,000 per year), teaching assistantships (averaging $3,000 per year); Federal Work-Study and scholarships/grants also available. Financial award application deadline: 1/15; financial award applicants required to submit FAFSA. *Faculty research:* Forensic psychology, LGBT psychology, trauma, diversity and community mental health, neuropsychology. *Unit head:* Dr. Rowena Gomez, Director of Clinical Training, 650-433-3823, E-mail: rgomez@paloaltou.edu. *Application contact:* Eirian Williams, Vice President of Enrollment Management, 800-818-6136, E-mail: admissions@paloaltou.edu.
Website: http://www.paloaltou.edu/graduate-programs/phd-programs/phd-clinical-psychology

**Penn State Harrisburg,** Graduate School, School of Behavioral Sciences and Education, Middletown, PA 17057. Offers adult education in the health and medical professions (Certificate); applied behavior analysis (MA); applied clinical psychology (MA); applied psychological research (MA); community psychology and social change (MA); English as a second language (ESL) program specialist and leadership (Certificate); folklore and ethnography (Certificate); health education (M Ed); lifelong learning and adult education (M Ed, D Ed); literacy education (M Ed); literacy leadership (Certificate); psychology: applications in clinical psychology (Certificate); psychology: health psychology (Certificate); teaching and curriculum (M Ed); training and development (M Ed, Certificate). *Program availability:* Part-time, evening/weekend. *Unit head:* Dr. Mukund S. Kulkarni, Chancellor, 717-948-6105, Fax: 717-948-6452. *Application contact:* Robert W. Coffman, Jr., Director of Enrollment Management, Recruitment and Admissions, 717-948-6250, Fax: 717-948-6325, E-mail: hbgadmit@psu.edu.
Website: https://harrisburg.psu.edu/behavioral-sciences-and-education/

**Pepperdine University,** Graduate School of Education and Psychology, Division of Psychology, Los Angeles, CA 90045. Offers behavioral psychology (MS); clinical psychology (Psy D); clinical psychology (MA), including marriage and family therapy; clinical psychology with Latinos (MA); psychology (MA). *Program availability:* Part-time, evening/weekend. *Students:* 489 full-time (408 women), 432 part-time (348 women); includes 404 minority (92 Black or African American, non-Hispanic/Latino; 4 American Indian or Alaska Native, non-Hispanic/Latino; 77 Asian, non-Hispanic/Latino; 198 Hispanic/Latino; 5 Native Hawaiian or other Pacific Islander, non-Hispanic/Latino; 28 Two or more races, non-Hispanic/Latino), 46 international. Average age 31. 559 applicants, 77% accepted, 279 enrolled. In 2016, 265 master's, 27 doctorates awarded. *Entrance requirements:* For master's and doctorate, GRE General Test. Additional exam requirements/recommendations for international students: Required—TOEFL. *Application deadline:* For fall admission, 2/1 for domestic students. Applications are processed on a rolling basis. Application fee: $55. *Expenses:* $1,165 per unit (for master's); $1,460 per unit (for doctorate). *Financial support:* Research assistantships, teaching assistantships, career-related internships or fieldwork, and scholarships/grants available. Support available to part-time students. Financial award application deadline: 7/1; financial award applicants required to submit FAFSA. *Unit head:* Dr. Robert A. deMayo, Associate Dean, Psychology Division, 310-568-5747, E-mail: robert.demayo@pepperdine.edu. *Application contact:* Chris Costa, Director of Enrollment, 310-568-2850, E-mail: chris.costa@pepperdine.edu.
Website: http://gsep.pepperdine.edu/masters-psychology/

**Philadelphia College of Osteopathic Medicine,** Graduate and Professional Programs, Department of Psychology, Philadelphia, PA 19131-1694. Offers applied behavior analysis (Certificate); clinical health psychology (Post-Doctoral Certificate); clinical neuropsychology (Post-Doctoral Certificate); clinical psychology (Psy D); mental health counseling (MS); organizational development and leadership (MS); psychology (Certificate); school psychology (MS, Psy D, Ed S). *Accreditation:* APA. *Faculty:* 19 full-time (11 women), 122 part-time/adjunct (58 women). *Students:* 364 (285 women); includes 78 minority (62 Black or African American, non-Hispanic/Latino; 2 American Indian or Alaska Native, non-Hispanic/Latino; 9 Asian, non-Hispanic/Latino; 5 Hispanic/Latino), 2 international. 366 applicants, 51% accepted, 139 enrolled. In 2016, 72 master's, 42 doctorates, 17 other advanced degrees awarded. Terminal master's awarded for partial completion of doctoral program. *Degree requirements:* For master's, comprehensive exam (for some programs), thesis (for some programs); for doctorate, comprehensive exam, thesis/dissertation. *Entrance requirements:* For master's, GRE or MAT, minimum GPA of 3.0; bachelor's degree from regionally-accredited college or university; for doctorate, PRAXIS II (for Psy D in school psychology), minimum undergraduate GPA of 3.0; for other advanced degree, GRE (for Ed S). Additional exam requirements/recommendations for international students: Required—TOEFL (minimum score 79 iBT). *Application deadline:* Applications are processed on a rolling basis. Application fee: $50. Electronic applications accepted. Tuition and fees vary according to course load, degree level and program. *Financial support:* In 2016–17, 28 teaching assistantships were awarded; Federal Work-Study, institutionally sponsored loans, and scholarships/grants also available. Financial award application deadline: 3/15; financial award applicants required to submit FAFSA. *Faculty research:* Adult and childhood anxiety and ADHD; coping with chronic illness; primary care psychology/integrated health care; applied behavior analysis; psychological, educational, and neuropsychological assessment. *Total annual research expenditures:* $533,489. *Unit head:* Dr. Robert DiTomasso, Chairman, 215-871-6442, Fax: 215-871-6458, E-mail: robertd@pcom.edu. *Application contact:* Johnathan Cox, Associate Director of Admissions, 215-871-6700, Fax: 215-871-6719, E-mail: karis@pcom.edu.
**See Display on page 1004 and Close-Up on page 1227.**

**Pittsburg State University,** Graduate School, College of Education, Department of Psychology and Counseling, Program in Psychology, Pittsburg, KS 66762. Offers psychology (MS), including clinical psychology, general psychology. *Students:* 27. In 2016, 10 master's awarded. *Degree requirements:* For master's, thesis or alternative. *Entrance requirements:* For master's, GRE General Test, minimum GPA of 2.8. Additional exam requirements/recommendations for international students: Required—TOEFL (minimum score 550 paper-based; 79 iBT), IELTS (minimum score 6.5), PTE (minimum score 53). *Application deadline:* Applications are processed on a rolling basis. Application fee: $35 ($60 for international students). Electronic applications accepted. *Expenses:* Contact institution. *Financial support:* Teaching assistantships, career-related internships or fieldwork, and Federal Work-Study available. Financial award application deadline: 2/1; financial award applicants required to submit FAFSA. *Unit head:* Dr. David Hurford, Chairperson, 620-235-4521. *Application contact:* Lisa Allen, Assistant Director of Graduate and Continuing Studies, 620-235-4218, Fax: 620-235-4219, E-mail: lallen@pittstate.edu.

**Plymouth State University,** College of Graduate Studies, Graduate Studies in Education, Certificate of Advanced Graduate Studies Programs, Plymouth, NH 03264-1595. Offers clinical mental health counseling (CAGS); educational leadership (CAGS); higher education (CAGS); school psychology (CAGS). *Program availability:* Part-time, evening/weekend.

**Plymouth State University,** College of Graduate Studies, Graduate Studies in Education, Program in Science, Plymouth, NH 03264-1595. Offers applied meteorology (MS); biology (MS); clinical mental health counseling (MS); environmental science and policy (MS); science education (MS).

**Point Loma Nazarene University,** Program in Clinical Counseling, San Diego, CA 92106-2899. Offers MA. *Faculty:* 1 full-time, 1 part-time/adjunct. *Students:* 10 full-time (8 women), 7 part-time (4 women); includes 8 minority (1 Asian, non-Hispanic/Latino; 6 Hispanic/Latino; 1 Native Hawaiian or other Pacific Islander, non-Hispanic/Latino). Average age 27. 21 applicants, 86% accepted, 17 enrolled. *Expenses:* $750 per credit. *Financial support:* Scholarships/grants available. Financial award applicants required to submit FAFSA. *Unit head:* Dan Jenkins, 619-849-2282, E-mail: danieljenkins@pointloma.edu. *Application contact:* Claire Buckley, Director of Graduate Admissions, 866-692-4723, E-mail: gradinfo@pointloma.edu. Website: http://gps.pointloma.edu/ma-clinical-counseling

**Point Park University,** School of Arts and Sciences, Department of Humanities and Human Sciences, Pittsburgh, PA 15222-1984. Offers clinical-community psychology (MA).

**Ponce Health Sciences University,** Program in Clinical Psychology, Ponce, PR 00732-7004. Offers PhD, Psy D. *Accreditation:* APA. *Degree requirements:* For doctorate, one foreign language, comprehensive exam, thesis/dissertation, internship. *Entrance requirements:* For doctorate, GRE General Test or EXADEP, proficiency in Spanish and English; 2 letters of recommendation; minimum undergraduate GPA of 2.7, graduate 3.0; criminal background check.

**Pontifical Catholic University of Puerto Rico,** College of Graduate Studies in Behavioral Science and Community Affairs, Program in Clinical Psychology, Ponce, PR 00717-0777. Offers PhD, Psy D. *Program availability:* Part-time, evening/weekend. *Degree requirements:* For doctorate, comprehensive exam, thesis/dissertation. *Entrance requirements:* For doctorate, EXADEP, minimum GPA of 2.75.

**Pontificia Universidad Catolica Madre y Maestra,** Graduate School, Faculty of Social and Administrative Sciences, Santiago, Dominican Republic. Offers business administration (MBA), including business development, finance, international business, management skills (M Mgmt, MBA), marketing, operations, strategic cost management, strategy, tourist destination planning and management; law (LL M), including civil law, corporate business law, criminal law, international relations, real estate law; management (M Mgmt), including higher financial management, insurance program administration, management skills (M Mgmt, MBA); psychology (MA), including clinical child and adolescent psychology, forensic psychology; strategic human resources (EMBA).

**Prairie View A&M University,** College of Juvenile Justice and Psychology, Prairie View, TX 77446. Offers clinical adolescent psychology (PhD); juvenile forensic psychology (MSJFP); juvenile justice (MSJJ, PhD). *Program availability:* Part-time, evening/weekend, online only, 100% online. *Faculty:* 6 full-time (2 women), 6 part-time/adjunct (3 women). *Students:* 29 full-time (24 women), 31 part-time (22 women); includes 53 minority (49 Black or African American, non-Hispanic/Latino; 3 Hispanic/Latino; 1 Two or more races, non-Hispanic/Latino), 5 international. Average age 30. 37 applicants, 92% accepted, 25 enrolled. In 2016, 16 master's, 2 doctorates awarded. *Degree requirements:* For master's, comprehensive exam; for doctorate, thesis/dissertation. *Entrance requirements:* For master's, GRE, minimum GPA of 2.75; for doctorate, GRE, previous course work in clinical adolescent psychology, minimum GPA of 3.5. Additional exam requirements/recommendations for international students: Required—TOEFL (minimum score 550 paper-based; 79 iBT). *Application deadline:* For fall admission, 5/1 priority date for domestic and international students; for spring admission, 10/1 priority date for domestic students, 9/1 priority date for international students; for summer admission, 3/1 priority date for domestic students, 2/1 priority date for international students. Applications are processed on a rolling basis. Application fee: $50. Electronic applications accepted. *Expenses:* Tuition, state resident: full-time $4362; part-time $273.48 per credit hour. Tuition, nonresident: full-time $12,390; part-time $534.10 per credit hour. *Required fees:* $2782; $178.26 per credit hour. *Financial support:* In 2016–17, 20 students received support, including 20 research assistantships; teaching assistantships, scholarships/grants, and unspecified assistantships also available. Financial award application deadline: 4/1; financial award applicants required to submit FAFSA. *Faculty research:* Juvenile justice, community policing, adolescent substance use, reducing mental illness stigma and promoting positive psychological well-being in diverse communities, promoting prosocial behavior among at-risk youth. *Unit head:* Dr. Tamara L. Brown, Dean, 936-261-5206, Fax: 936-261-5253, E-mail: tlbrown@pvamu.edu. *Application contact:* Pauline Walker, Executive Secretary, Graduate Program, 936-261-3521, Fax: 936-261-3529, E-mail: gradadmissions@pvamu.edu.

**Purdue University,** Graduate School, College of Health and Human Sciences, Department of Psychological Sciences, West Lafayette, IN 47907. Offers behavioral neuroscience (PhD); clinical psychology (PhD); cognitive psychology (PhD); industrial/organizational psychology (PhD); mathematical and computational cognitive science (PhD). *Accreditation:* APA. *Faculty:* 46 full-time (18 women), 1 part-time/adjunct. *Students:* 64 full-time (41 women), 4 part-time (3 women); includes 13 minority (1 Black or African American, non-Hispanic/Latino; 4 Asian, non-Hispanic/Latino; 6 Hispanic/Latino; 2 Two or more races, non-Hispanic/Latino), 12 international. Average age 27. 288 applicants, 8% accepted, 16 enrolled. In 2016, 9 doctorates awarded. Terminal master's awarded for partial completion of doctoral program. *Degree requirements:* For doctorate, thesis/dissertation. *Entrance requirements:* For doctorate, GRE General Test, minimum undergraduate GPA of 3.0 or equivalent. Additional exam requirements/recommendations for international students: Required—TOEFL (minimum score 550 paper-based; 77 iBT); Recommended—TWE. *Application deadline:* For fall admission, 12/3 for domestic and international students. Applications are processed on a rolling basis. Application fee: $60 ($75 for international students). Electronic applications accepted. *Financial support:* Fellowships with partial tuition reimbursements, research assistantships with partial tuition reimbursements, teaching assistantships with partial tuition reimbursements, and career-related internships or fieldwork available. Support available to part-time students. Financial award applicants required to submit FAFSA. *Faculty research:* Career development of women in science, development of friendships during childhood and adolescence, social competence, human information processing. *Unit head:* Dr. Christopher R. Agnew, Head, 765-494-6061, Fax: 765-496-1264, E-mail: agnew@psych.purdue.edu. *Application contact:* Nancy A. O'Brien, Graduate Contact,

765-494-6067, Fax: 765-496-1264, E-mail: nobrien@psych.purdue.edu. Website: http://www.psych.purdue.edu/

**Queen's University at Kingston,** School of Graduate Studies, Faculty of Arts and Sciences, Department of Psychology, Kingston, ON K7L 3N6, Canada. Offers brain behavior and cognitive science (MA, PhD); clinical psychology (MA, PhD); developmental psychology (MA, PhD); social personality psychology (MA, PhD). *Degree requirements:* For master's, thesis; for doctorate, comprehensive exam, thesis/dissertation. *Entrance requirements:* For master's and doctorate, GRE General Test. Additional exam requirements/recommendations for international students: Required—TOEFL. *Faculty research:* Human development, social, personality, behavioral neuroscience, forensic.

**Regent University,** Graduate School, School of Psychology and Counseling, Virginia Beach, VA 23464-9800. Offers clinical mental health counseling (MA); clinical psychology (Psy D); counseling and psychological studies (PhD); counseling studies (CAGS); counselor education and supervision (PhD); general psychology (MS); marriage, couple, and family counseling (MA); pastoral counseling (MA); school counseling (MA); M Div/MA; M Ed/MA; MBA/MA. *Accreditation:* ACA; APA (one or more programs are accredited). *Program availability:* Part-time, evening/weekend, 100% online, blended/hybrid learning. *Faculty:* 28 full-time (17 women), 45 part-time/adjunct (26 women). *Students:* 295 full-time (240 women), 331 part-time (252 women); includes 244 minority (186 Black or African American, non-Hispanic/Latino; 4 American Indian or Alaska Native, non-Hispanic/Latino; 11 Asian, non-Hispanic/Latino; 29 Hispanic/Latino; 14 Two or more races, non-Hispanic/Latino), 10 international. Average age 36. 1,192 applicants, 29% accepted, 235 enrolled. In 2016, 156 master's, 41 doctorates, 1 other advanced degree awarded. *Degree requirements:* For master's, thesis or alternative, internship, practicum, written competency exam; for doctorate, thesis/dissertation or alternative. *Entrance requirements:* For master's, GRE General Test (including writing exam) or MAT, minimum undergraduate GPA of 3.0, resume, transcripts, writing sample, personal goals statement; for doctorate, GRE General Test (including writing exam), minimum undergraduate GPA of 3.0, graduate 3.5; writing sample; 3 recommendations; resume; college transcripts; personal goals statement. Additional exam requirements/recommendations for international students: Required—TOEFL (minimum score 577 paper-based). *Application deadline:* For fall admission, 4/1 priority date for domestic students; for spring admission, 11/1 priority date for domestic students. Applications are processed on a rolling basis. Application fee: $50. Electronic applications accepted. *Expenses:* Contact institution. *Financial support:* In 2016–17, 446 students received support, including 5 fellowships (averaging $4,000 per year), 10 research assistantships (averaging $3,200 per year); career-related internships or fieldwork, scholarships/grants, and unspecified assistantships also available. Support available to part-time students. *Faculty research:* Marriage enrichment, clinical psychology, troubled youth, faith and learning, trauma. *Unit head:* Dr. William Hathaway, Dean, 757-352-4294, Fax: 757-352-4282, E-mail: willhat@regent.edu. *Application contact:* Heidi Cece, Assistant Vice President of Enrollment Management, 800-373-5504, Fax: 757-352-4381, E-mail: admissions@regent.edu. Website: http://www.regent.edu/spc/

**Richmont Graduate University,** School of Counseling, Atlanta, GA 30339. Offers clinical mental health counseling (MA); marriage and family therapy (MA). *Accreditation:* ACA. *Program availability:* Part-time, evening/weekend. *Degree requirements:* For master's, comprehensive exam, thesis optional. *Entrance requirements:* For master's, GRE or MAT. *Application deadline:* Applications are processed on a rolling basis. Application fee: $50. Electronic applications accepted. *Expenses:* Tuition: Part-time $665 per credit hour. *Required fees:* $200 per semester. One-time fee: $250. *Financial support:* Career-related internships or fieldwork, scholarships/grants, and unspecified assistantships available. Financial award application deadline: 5/1. *Unit head:* Dr. Stephen P. Bradshaw, Dean, E-mail: sbradshaw@richmont.edu. *Application contact:* Admissions, 888-924-6774, Fax: 866-363-4323, E-mail: admissions@richmont.edu. Website: http://richmont.edu/academics/school-of-counseling/

**Rivier University,** School of Graduate Studies, Department of Psychology, Nashua, NH 03060. Offers clinical psychology (MS); experimental psychology (MS).

**Roberts Wesleyan College,** Graduate Psychology Programs, Rochester, NY 14624-1997. Offers clinical/school psychology (Psy D); school counseling (MS); school psychology (MS). *Program availability:* Part-time, evening/weekend. *Degree requirements:* For master's, comprehensive exam, PRAXIS II (for school psychology). *Entrance requirements:* For master's, GRE. Electronic applications accepted. Application fee is waived when completed online. *Faculty research:* Counselor supervision, forgiveness, community health psychology, applied research in group process.

**Roger Williams University,** Feinstein College of Arts and Sciences, Forensic Mental Health Counseling, Bristol, RI 02809. Offers clinical psychology (MA). *Expenses:* Contact institution.

**Roosevelt University,** Graduate Division, College of Arts and Sciences, Department of Psychology, Program in Clinical Professional Psychology, Chicago, IL 60605. Offers MA. *Accreditation:* APA.

**Rosalind Franklin University of Medicine and Science,** College of Health Professions, Department of Psychology, North Chicago, IL 60064-3095. Offers clinical psychology (MS, PhD). *Accreditation:* APA. Terminal master's awarded for partial completion of doctoral program. *Degree requirements:* For master's, capstone experience. *Entrance requirements:* For master's, minimum GPA of 3.0, bachelor's degree (preferably in related subject); for doctorate, GRE, minimum GPA of 3.0, bachelor's or master's degree. Additional exam requirements/recommendations for international students: Required—TOEFL. *Faculty research:* Anxiety, pain, psychopathy, epilepsy, neuropsychology.

**Rowan University,** Graduate School, College of Science and Mathematics, Program in Clinical Mental Health Counseling, Glassboro, NJ 08028-1701. Offers MA, CAGS. *Program availability:* Part-time, evening/weekend. *Entrance requirements:* For master's, GRE General Test. Additional exam requirements/recommendations for international students: Required—TOEFL.

**Rutgers University–New Brunswick,** Graduate School-New Brunswick, Program in Psychology, Piscataway, NJ 08854-8097. Offers behavioral neuroscience (PhD); clinical psychology (PhD); cognitive psychology (PhD); interdisciplinary health psychology (PhD); social psychology (PhD). *Accreditation:* APA. *Degree requirements:* For doctorate, comprehensive exam, thesis/dissertation. *Entrance requirements:* For doctorate, GRE General Test, 3 letters of recommendation. Additional exam requirements/recommendations for international students: Required—TOEFL (minimum score 577 paper-based). Electronic applications accepted. *Faculty research:* Learning and memory, behavioral ecology, hormones and behavior, psychopharmacology, anxiety disorders.

**Rutgers University–New Brunswick,** Graduate School of Applied and Professional Psychology, Department of Clinical Psychology, Piscataway, NJ 08854-8097. Offers Psy M, Psy D. *Accreditation:* APA (one or more programs are accredited). *Degree requirements:* For doctorate, comprehensive exam, thesis/dissertation, 1 year internship. *Entrance requirements:* For doctorate, GRE General Test, GRE Subject Test, bachelor's degree in psychology or equivalent. Additional exam requirements/recommendations for international students: Required—TOEFL. Electronic applications accepted. *Expenses:* Contact institution. *Faculty research:* Long- and short-term dynamic therapy, community psychology, cognitive-behavioral therapy: anxiety and depressive disorders, addictive behaviors: eating disorders and alcoholism.

**St. John's University,** St. John's College of Liberal Arts and Sciences, Department of Psychology, Program in Clinical Psychology, Queens, NY 11439. Offers clinical psychology-child (PhD); clinical psychology-general (PhD). *Accreditation:* APA. *Degree requirements:* For doctorate, comprehensive exam, thesis/dissertation, internship, practicum. *Entrance requirements:* For doctorate, GRE General Test, GRE Subject Test, 24 credits of undergraduate course work in psychology, 2 writing samples, 3 letters of recommendation, personal statement, bachelor's degree, transcript. Additional exam requirements/recommendations for international students: Required—TOEFL (minimum score 600 paper-based; 100 iBT), IELTS (minimum score 7). Electronic applications accepted. *Expenses:* Contact institution. *Faculty research:* Cognitive-behavioral therapy, sucking cessation pedagogical research and implicit attitudes.

**St. John's University,** The School of Education, Department of Counselor Education, Program in Clinical Mental Health Counseling, Queens, NY 11439. Offers MS Ed, Adv C. *Program availability:* Part-time, evening/weekend. *Degree requirements:* For master's, internship, state examination. *Entrance requirements:* For master's, bachelor's degree from an accredited college or university, minimum GPA of 3.0, 2 letters of recommendation, interview, 18 credits in behavioral and social science. Additional exam requirements/recommendations for international students: Required—TOEFL (minimum score 600 paper-based; 100 iBT), IELTS (minimum score 7). Electronic applications accepted.

**St. John's University,** The School of Education, Department of Education Specialties, Queens, NY 11439. Offers clinical mental health counseling (MS Ed, Adv C); literacy (MS Ed, PhD, Adv C), including literacy (PhD), teaching literacy (Adv C), teaching literacy 5-12 (MS Ed), teaching literacy B-12 (MS Ed), teaching literacy B-6 (MS Ed), teaching literacy B-6 and children with disabilities (MS Ed); school counseling (MS Ed, Adv C); school counseling with bilingual extension (MS Ed); teaching children with disabilities in childhood education (MS Ed, Adv C); teaching English to speakers of other languages and bilingual education (MS Ed, Adv C). *Program availability:* Part-time, evening/weekend, online learning. *Degree requirements:* For master's, one foreign language, comprehensive exam, thesis, internship; for doctorate, one foreign language, comprehensive exam, thesis/dissertation. *Entrance requirements:* For master's, minimum GPA of 3.0, 2 letters of recommendation, interview, minimum of 18 credits in behavioral science, bachelor's degree; for doctorate, MAT, GRE General Test (analytical), official transcript showing conferral of degree with minimum GPA of 3.2, 2 letters of recommendation, statement of goals, resume, evidence of teaching experience, interview; for Adv C, statement of goals, official transcript showing conferral of degree with minimum GPA of 3.0, 2 letters of recommendation, interview. Additional exam requirements/recommendations for international students: Required—TOEFL (minimum score 600 paper-based; 100 iBT), IELTS (minimum score 7). Electronic applications accepted. *Faculty research:* Assisting troubled children and teens with substance abuse, truancy, and coping skills; literacy development for ESL learners; investigating Caribbean and Creole language and culture.

**Saint Louis University,** Graduate Education, College of Arts and Sciences and Graduate Education, Department of Psychology, St. Louis, MO 63103. Offers clinical psychology (MS-R, PhD); experimental psychology (MS-R, PhD); industrial-organizational psychology (PhD); psychology (PhD). *Accreditation:* APA (one or more programs are accredited). *Program availability:* Part-time. *Degree requirements:* For master's, comprehensive exam, thesis; for doctorate, thesis/dissertation, clinical internship (for clinical psychology PhD). *Entrance requirements:* For master's, GRE General Test, interview, letters of recommendation, resume; for doctorate, GRE General Test, interview, letters of recommendation, resumé, transcripts, goal statement. Additional exam requirements/recommendations for international students: Required—TOEFL (minimum score 550 paper-based). Electronic applications accepted. *Faculty research:* Violence and trauma; neural basis of learning and memory function; eating disorders; body image and health behavior; prejudice, stereotyping, and victimization; memory, cognitive aging and language processing.

**Saint Michael's College,** Graduate Programs, Program in Clinical Psychology, Colchester, VT 05439. Offers MA. *Program availability:* Part-time, evening/weekend. *Faculty:* 5 full-time (3 women), 11 part-time/adjunct (9 women). *Students:* 17 full-time (16 women), 20 part-time (13 women); includes 4 minority (1 Black or African American, non-Hispanic/Latino; 2 Asian, non-Hispanic/Latino; 1 Two or more races, non-Hispanic/Latino), 2 international. Average age 28. 19 applicants, 74% accepted, 14 enrolled. In 2016, 13 master's awarded. *Degree requirements:* For master's, thesis or alternative, internship, practicum, research seminar. *Entrance requirements:* For master's, GRE General Test, GRE Subject Test, undergraduate major in psychology or related area, minimum 12 credits in psychology, minimum GPA of 3.0, official transcripts, 2 references, resume. Additional exam requirements/recommendations for international students: Required—TOEFL (minimum score 79 iBT). *Application deadline:* For fall admission, 6/1 priority date for domestic students. Applications are processed on a rolling basis. Application fee: $50. Electronic applications accepted. *Expenses: Tuition:* Full-time $10,620; part-time $590 per credit. Part-time tuition and fees vary according to course load and program. *Financial support:* Teaching assistantships with partial tuition reimbursements, career-related internships or fieldwork, Federal Work-Study, scholarships/grants, tuition waivers (partial), and unspecified assistantships available. Financial award application deadline: 5/1; financial award applicants required to submit FAFSA. *Faculty research:* Psychodynamic psychotherapy, family therapy, philosophical foundations of clinical psychology. *Unit head:* Dr. Ronald B. Miller, Director, 802-654-2206, Fax: 802-654-2664, E-mail: rmiller@smcvt.edu. *Application contact:* Lindsay A. Damici, Marketing Communications Manager, 802-654-2556, Fax: 802-654-2732. Website: http://www.smcvt.edu/graduate-programs/academic-programs/clinical-psychology.aspx

**Sam Houston State University,** College of Humanities and Social Sciences, Department of Psychology and Philosophy, Huntsville, TX 77341. Offers psychology (MA, PhD, SSP), including clinical psychology (MA, PhD), psychology (MA), school psychology (SSP). *Accreditation:* APA. *Program availability:* Part-time. Terminal master's awarded for partial completion of doctoral program. *Degree requirements:* For master's, comprehensive exam, thesis optional; for doctorate, comprehensive exam, thesis/dissertation. *Entrance requirements:* For master's, GRE General Test, personal statement, letters of recommendation; for doctorate, GRE General Test, GRE Subject Test (advanced psychology), personal essay, letters of recommendation, resume. Additional exam requirements/recommendations for international students: Required—TOEFL (minimum score 550 paper-based; 79 iBT), IELTS (minimum score 6.5). Electronic applications accepted.

**San Diego State University,** Graduate and Research Affairs, College of Sciences, Department of Psychology, San Diego, CA 92182. Offers clinical psychology (MS, PhD); industrial and organizational psychology (MS); program evaluation (MS); psychology (MA). PhD offered jointly with University of California, San Diego. *Accreditation:* APA

(one or more programs are accredited). Terminal master's awarded for partial completion of doctoral program. *Degree requirements:* For master's, thesis, oral exam; for doctorate, thesis/dissertation. *Entrance requirements:* For master's, GRE General Test, GRE Subject Test, 3 letters of recommendation; for doctorate, GRE General Test, GRE Subject Test, minimum GPA of 3.0, 3 letters of recommendation. Additional exam requirements/recommendations for international students: Required—TOEFL. Electronic applications accepted.

**San Francisco State University,** Division of Graduate Studies, College of Science and Engineering, Department of Psychology, San Francisco, CA 94132-1722. Offers clinical psychology (MS); developmental psychology (MA); industrial/organizational psychology (MS); mind, brain, and behavior (MA); school psychology (MS, Credential); social psychology (MA). *Expenses:* Tuition, state resident: full-time $6738. Tuition, nonresident: full-time $15,666. *Required fees:* $1012. Tuition and fees vary according to degree level and program. *Financial support:* Teaching assistantships available. Financial award application deadline: 3/1. *Unit head:* Dr. Dawn Terrell, Chair, 415-338-7555, Fax: 415-338-2398, E-mail: schen9@sfsu.edu. *Application contact:* Dr. Diane Harris, Graduate Program Coordinator, 415-338-7064, Fax: 415-338-2398, E-mail: dharris@sfsu.edu.
Website: http://psychology.sfsu.edu/graduate/application.html

**San Jose State University,** Graduate Studies and Research, College of Social Sciences, San Jose, CA 95192-0001. Offers applications of technology in planning (Certificate); applied anthropology (MA); communication studies (MS); community design and development (Certificate); economics (MA), including applied economics, social sciences; environmental planning (Certificate); geographic information science (Certificate); geography (MA); global citizenship (Certificate); history (MA), including history education, social sciences; Mexican American studies (MA); psychology (MA, MS), including clinical psychology (MS), industrial/organizational psychology (MS), research and experimental psychology (MA); public administration (MA); real estate development (Certificate); social sciences (MPA, MS); sociology (MA); transportation and land use planning (Certificate). *Program availability:* Part-time, evening/weekend. *Entrance requirements:* For master's, minimum GPA of 3.0. Electronic applications accepted.

**Saybrook University,** School of Clinical Psychology, San Francisco, CA 94612. Offers MA. Program offered jointly with Bastyr University. *Degree requirements:* For master's, thesis (for some programs), oral exams. *Entrance requirements:* For master's, bachelor's degree from an accredited university or college. *Faculty research:* Family systems theory, marriage and family therapy, systems consultation, family and culture of origin, personal authority.

**Seattle Pacific University,** PhD in Clinical Psychology Program, Seattle, WA 98119-1997. Offers PhD. *Accreditation:* APA. *Degree requirements:* For doctorate, thesis/dissertation, clinical internship, practicum. *Entrance requirements:* For doctorate, GRE (preferred minimum score 1100 verbal and quantitative, taken within the last five years), BA, personal statement. Additional exam requirements/recommendations for international students: Required—TOEFL (minimum score 600 paper-based). Electronic applications accepted. *Expenses:* Contact institution. *Faculty research:* Social network support, attachment, integration of faith and family psychology, developmental psychology.

**Shippensburg University of Pennsylvania,** School of Graduate Studies, College of Education and Human Services, Department of Counseling, Shippensburg, PA 17257-2299. Offers clinical mental health (MS); college counseling (MS); college student personnel (MS); counselor education and supervision (Ed D); couple and family counseling (Certificate); school counseling (M Ed). *Accreditation:* ACA (one or more programs are accredited); NCATE. *Program availability:* Part-time, evening/weekend, blended/hybrid learning. *Faculty:* 8 full-time (3 women), 6 part-time/adjunct (4 women). *Students:* 90 full-time (76 women), 57 part-time (45 women); includes 35 minority (21 Black or African American, non-Hispanic/Latino; 1 Asian, non-Hispanic/Latino; 10 Hispanic/Latino; 3 Two or more races, non-Hispanic/Latino), 5 international. Average age 28. 115 applicants, 44% accepted, 34 enrolled. In 2016, 51 master's awarded. *Degree requirements:* For master's, fieldwork, research project, internship, candidacy; for doctorate, thesis/dissertation, practicum, internship. *Entrance requirements:* For master's, GRE or MAT (for MS if GPA is less than 2.75), minimum GPA of 2.75 (3.0 for M Ed), resume, 3 letter of recommendation forms, one year of relevant work experience, on-campus interview, autobiographical statement; for doctorate, master's degree in counseling or related discipline; resume; three recommendation letters (1 from employer; 1 from clinical supervisor, 1 from prior graduate school faculty member); personal essay; interview with department chair. Additional exam requirements/recommendations for international students: Required—TOEFL (minimum score 550 paper-based, 68 iBT) or IELTS (minimum score 6). *Application deadline:* Applications are processed on a rolling basis. Application fee: $45. Electronic applications accepted. *Expenses:* Tuition, state resident: part-time $483 per credit. Tuition, nonresident: part-time $725 per credit. *Required fees:* $141 per credit. *Financial support:* In 2016–17, 62 students received support. Career-related internships or fieldwork, scholarships/grants, unspecified assistantships, and resident hall director and student payroll positions available. Support available to part-time students. Financial award application deadline: 3/1; financial award applicants required to submit FAFSA. *Unit head:* Dr. Kurt L. Kraus, Departmental Chair and Program Coordinator, 717-477-1603, Fax: 717-477-4016, E-mail: klkrau@ship.edu. *Application contact:* Megan N. Luft, Assistant Dean of Graduate Admissions, 717-477-1231, Fax: 717-477-4016, E-mail: mnluft@ship.edu. Website: http://www.ship.edu/counsel/

**Siena Heights University,** Graduate College, Adrian, MI 49221-1796. Offers clinical mental health counseling (MA); educational leadership (Specialist); leadership (MA), including health care leadership, organizational leadership; teacher education (MA), including early childhood education, early childhood education: Montessori, education leadership: principal, elementary education: reading K-12, leadership: higher education, secondary education: reading K-12, special education: cognitive impairment, special education: learning disabilities. *Program availability:* Part-time, evening/weekend. *Degree requirements:* For master's, thesis, presentation. *Entrance requirements:* For master's, minimum GPA of 3.0, current resume, essay, all post-secondary transcripts, 3 letters of reference, conviction disclosure form; copy of teaching certificate (for some education programs); for Specialist, master's degree, minimum GPA of 3.0, current resume, essay, all post-secondary transcripts, 3 letters of reference, conviction disclosure form; copy of teaching certificate (for some education programs). Electronic applications accepted.

**Slippery Rock University of Pennsylvania,** Graduate Studies (Recruitment), College of Education, Department of Counseling and Development, Slippery Rock, PA 16057-1383. Offers clinical mental health (MA); school counseling (M Ed); student affairs in higher education (MA); student affairs in higher education with college counseling (MA). *Accreditation:* ACA (one or more programs are accredited); NCATE. *Program availability:* Part-time, evening/weekend. *Faculty:* 7 full-time (5 women), 1 (woman) part-time/adjunct. *Students:* 86 full-time (55 women), 23 part-time (18 women); includes 13 minority (7 Black or African American, non-Hispanic/Latino; 4 Hispanic/Latino; 2 Two or more races, non-Hispanic/Latino), 1 international. Average age 28. 107 applicants, 57% accepted, 42 enrolled. In 2016, 39 master's awarded. *Degree requirements:* For

*Clinical Psychology*

master's, comprehensive exam, thesis (for some programs). *Entrance requirements:* For master's, GRE General Test or MAT, official transcripts, personal statement, three letters of recommendation, interview. Additional exam requirements/recommendations for international students: Required—TOEFL (minimum score 550 paper-based; 80 iBT). *Application deadline:* For fall admission, 1/15 priority date for domestic and international students. Applications are processed on a rolling basis. Application fee: $25 ($30 for international students). Electronic applications accepted. *Expenses:* $646.50 per credit in-state, $936.80 per credit out-of-state; $581.45 per online credit in-state, $648.65 per online credit out-of-state. *Financial support:* In 2016–17, 58 students received support. Career-related internships or fieldwork, Federal Work-Study, institutionally sponsored loans, scholarships/grants, tuition waivers (partial), and unspecified assistantships available. Support available to part-time students. Financial award application deadline: 5/1; financial award applicants required to submit FAFSA. *Unit head:* Dr. Stacy Jacob, Graduate Coordinator, 724-738-2758, Fax: 724-738-4859, E-mail: stacy.jacob@sru.edu. *Application contact:* Brandi Weber-Mortimer, Director of Graduate Admissions, 724-738-2051, Fax: 724-738-2146, E-mail: graduate.admissions@sru.edu. Website: http://www.sru.edu/academics/colleges-and-departments/coe/departments/counseling-and-development

**Sofia University,** Residential Programs, Palo Alto, CA 94303. Offers clinical psychology (Psy D); computer science (MS); counseling psychology (MA); transpersonal psychology (MA, PhD). *Program availability:* Part-time, evening/weekend. Terminal master's awarded for partial completion of doctoral program. *Degree requirements:* For doctorate, thesis/dissertation. *Entrance requirements:* For master's, bachelor's degree; for doctorate, bachelor's degree; master's degree (for some programs). Electronic applications accepted.

**Sonoma State University,** School of Social Sciences, Department of Counseling, Rohnert Park, CA 94928-3609. Offers clinical mental health counseling (MA); school counseling (MA). *Accreditation:* ACA. *Program availability:* Part-time. *Degree requirements:* For master's, internship. *Entrance requirements:* For master's, minimum GPA of 3.0. Additional exam requirements/recommendations for international students: Required—TOEFL (minimum score 500 paper-based). *Application deadline:* For fall admission, 11/30 for domestic students. Application fee: $55. *Expenses:* Tuition, state resident: full-time $6738; part-time $3906 per unit. *Required fees:* $1916; $1916 per year. Tuition and fees vary according to course load, degree level and program. *Financial support:* Fellowships and career-related internships or fieldwork available. Financial award application deadline: 3/2; financial award applicants required to submit FAFSA. *Unit head:* Dr. Adam Zagelbaum, Chair, 707-664-2544, E-mail: adam.zagelbaum@sonoma.edu. Website: http://www.sonoma.edu/counseling

**Southeastern Oklahoma State University,** School of Behavioral Sciences, Durant, OK 74701-0609. Offers clinical mental health counseling (MS). *Accreditation:* ACA. *Program availability:* Part-time, evening/weekend. *Degree requirements:* For master's, comprehensive exam, thesis optional. *Entrance requirements:* For master's, GRE General Test, minimum GPA of 3.0 in last 60 hours or 2.75 overall. Additional exam requirements/recommendations for international students: Required—TOEFL (minimum score 550 paper-based; 79 iBT). Electronic applications accepted.

**Southern Illinois University Carbondale,** Graduate School, College of Liberal Arts, Department of Psychology, Carbondale, IL 62901-4701. Offers clinical psychology (PhD); counseling psychology (PhD); experimental psychology (MA, MS). *Accreditation:* APA (one or more programs are accredited). *Degree requirements:* For master's, thesis; for doctorate, thesis/dissertation. *Entrance requirements:* For master's, GRE General Test, GRE Subject Test, minimum GPA of 2.7; for doctorate, GRE General Test, GRE Subject Test, minimum GPA of 3.25. Additional exam requirements/recommendations for international students: Required—TOEFL. *Faculty research:* Developmental neuropsychology; smoking, affect, and cognition; personality measurement; vocational psychology; program evaluation.

**Southern Illinois University Edwardsville,** Graduate School, School of Education, Health, and Human Behavior, Department of Psychology, Program in Clinical Child and School Psychology, Edwardsville, IL 62026-0001. Offers MS. *Program availability:* Part-time. *Degree requirements:* For master's, thesis (for some programs), research project. *Entrance requirements:* For master's, GRE. Additional exam requirements/recommendations for international students: Required—TOEFL (minimum score 550 paper-based, 79 iBT), IELTS (minimum score 6.5), Michigan Test of English Language Proficiency or PTE. Electronic applications accepted.

**Southern Illinois University Edwardsville,** Graduate School, School of Education, Health, and Human Behavior, Department of Psychology, Program in Clinical Psychology, Edwardsville, IL 62026-0001. Offers MA. *Program availability:* Part-time, evening/weekend. *Degree requirements:* For master's, comprehensive exam (for some programs), thesis (for some programs). *Entrance requirements:* For master's, GRE. Additional exam requirements/recommendations for international students: Required—TOEFL (minimum score 550 paper-based; 79 iBT), IELTS (minimum score 6.5). Electronic applications accepted.

**Southern Methodist University,** Dedman College of Humanities and Sciences, Department of Psychology, Program in Clinical Psychology, Dallas, TX 75275. Offers PhD. *Accreditation:* APA. *Degree requirements:* For doctorate, comprehensive exam, thesis/dissertation, research presentation and publication. *Entrance requirements:* For doctorate, GRE General Test, minimum GPA of 3.0, 3 letters of recommendation. Additional exam requirements/recommendations for international students: Required—TOEFL (minimum score 550 paper-based). Electronic applications accepted. *Faculty research:* Family violence, family assessment, anxiety disorders, personality disorders.

**South University,** Program in Clinical Mental Health Counseling, Cleveland, OH 44128. Offers MA.

**Spalding University,** Graduate Studies, Kosair College of Health and Natural Sciences, School of Professional Psychology, Louisville, KY 40203-2188. Offers clinical psychology (MA, Psy D). *Accreditation:* APA (one or more programs are accredited). *Program availability:* Part-time. *Faculty:* 27 full-time (16 women), 11 part-time/adjunct (8 women). *Students:* 125 full-time (103 women), 58 part-time (50 women); includes 27 minority (13 Black or African American, non-Hispanic/Latino; 4 Asian, non-Hispanic/Latino; 5 Hispanic/Latino; 5 Two or more races, non-Hispanic/Latino), 1 international. Average age 29. 168 applicants, 35% accepted, 34 enrolled. In 2016, 19 master's, 25 doctorates awarded. Terminal master's awarded for partial completion of doctoral program. *Degree requirements:* For master's, comprehensive exam; for doctorate, thesis/dissertation. *Entrance requirements:* For master's and doctorate, GRE General Test, 18 hours of undergraduate course work in psychology, interview, letters of recommendation, writing sample, autobiographical statement. Additional exam requirements/recommendations for international students: Required—TOEFL (minimum score 535 paper-based). *Application deadline:* For fall admission, 1/15 priority date for domestic and international students. Application fee: $30. *Expenses:* Tuition: Full-time $15,300. *Financial support:* In 2016–17, 53 research assistantships (averaging $6,376 per year) were awarded; career-related internships or fieldwork, scholarships/grants, and unspecified assistantships also available. Financial award applicants required to submit FAFSA. *Faculty research:* Substance abuse, prayer research, end-of-life issues,

complementary and alternative medicine, research methodology and statistical inference. *Unit head:* Dr. Steven Katsikas, Chair, 502-873-4459, E-mail: skatsikas@spalding.edu. *Application contact:* Elizabeth A. Simpson, Administrative Assistant, 502-585-7127, E-mail: esimpson@spalding.edu. Website: https://spalding.edu/academics/psychology/

**Springfield College,** Graduate Programs, Programs in Psychology, Springfield, MA 01109-3797. Offers athletic counseling (MS, CAGS); clinical mental health counseling (M Ed, CAGS); counseling psychology (Psy D); industrial and organizational psychology (M Ed, CAGS); school guidance counseling (M Ed, CAGS); student personnel administration in higher education (M Ed). *Accreditation:* APA. *Program availability:* Part-time. *Degree requirements:* For master's, research project, portfolio; for doctorate, dissertation project, 1500 hours of counseling psychology practicum, full-year internship. *Entrance requirements:* Additional exam requirements/recommendations for international students: Required—TOEFL (minimum score 550 paper-based). Electronic applications accepted. *Expenses:* Tuition: Full-time $29,640; part-time $988 per credit. *Required fees:* $195.

**State University of New York at Plattsburgh,** School of Education, Health, and Human Services, Department of Counselor Education, Plattsburgh, NY 12901-2681. Offers clinical mental health counseling (MS, Advanced Certificate); school counselor (MS Ed, CAS); student affairs counseling (MS). *Accreditation:* ACA (one or more programs are accredited); TEAC. *Program availability:* Part-time. *Entrance requirements:* For master's, GRE General Test or MAT, minimum GPA of 2.8. Additional exam requirements/recommendations for international students: Required—TOEFL. *Faculty research:* Campus violence, program accreditation, substance abuse, vocational assessment, group counseling, divorce.

**Stephens College,** Division of Graduate and Continuing Studies, Columbia, MO 65215-0002. Offers counseling (M Ed), including addictions counseling, clinical mental health counseling, school counseling; health information administration (Postbaccalaureate Certificate); physician assistant studies (MPAS); TV and screenwriting (MFA). *Program availability:* Part-time, evening/weekend, online learning. *Faculty:* 14 full-time (9 women), 30 part-time/adjunct (19 women). *Students:* 117 full-time (101 women), 107 part-time (96 women); includes 25 minority (2 Black or African American, non-Hispanic/Latino; 2 American Indian or Alaska Native, non-Hispanic/Latino; 1 Asian, non-Hispanic/Latino; 2 Hispanic/Latino; 1 Native Hawaiian or other Pacific Islander, non-Hispanic/Latino; 17 Two or more races, non-Hispanic/Latino), 1 international. Average age 35. 226 applicants, 43% accepted, 87 enrolled. In 2016, 44 master's awarded. *Entrance requirements:* For master's, minimum GPA of 3.0 in last 60 hours. Additional exam requirements/recommendations for international students: Required—TOEFL (minimum score 79 iBT). *Application deadline:* For fall admission, 8/15 priority date for domestic and international students; for winter admission, 1/9 priority date for domestic and international students; for spring admission, 6/5 priority date for domestic and international students. Applications are processed on a rolling basis. Application fee: $50. Electronic applications accepted. *Expenses:* Tuition: Full-time $3564; part-time $396 per credit hour. *Required fees:* $45 per credit hour. *Financial support:* In 2016–17, 5 fellowships with full tuition reimbursements (averaging $7,673 per year) were awarded; unspecified assistantships also available. Financial award applicants required to submit FAFSA. *Faculty research:* Educational psychology, outcomes assessment. *Unit head:* Dr. Brian Sajko, Vice President of Strategic Enrollment Management, 800-388-7579, Fax: 573-876-7237, E-mail: online@stephens.edu. *Application contact:* Lindsey Boudinot, Director of Graduate and Online Admissions, 800-388-7579, E-mail: online@stephens.edu.

**Stony Brook University, State University of New York,** Graduate School, College of Arts and Sciences, Department of Psychology, Program in Clinical Psychology, Stony Brook, NY 11794. Offers PhD. *Accreditation:* APA. *Students:* 32 full-time (28 women); includes 7 minority (1 Black or African American, non-Hispanic/Latino; 2 Asian, non-Hispanic/Latino; 4 Hispanic/Latino), 5 international. Average age 27. 342 applicants, 3% accepted, 6 enrolled. In 2016, 6 doctorates awarded. *Degree requirements:* For doctorate, thesis/dissertation. *Entrance requirements:* For doctorate, GRE General Test, GRE Subject Test. Additional exam requirements/recommendations for international students: Required—TOEFL (minimum score 90 iBT). *Application deadline:* For fall admission, 1/15 for domestic students; for spring admission, 10/1 for domestic students. Application fee: $100. *Expenses:* Contact institution. *Financial support:* In 2016–17, 5 fellowships, 8 research assistantships, 15 teaching assistantships were awarded. *Unit head:* Dr. Arthur Samuel, Chair, 631-632-7792, E-mail: arthur.samuel@stonybrook.edu. *Application contact:* Marilynn Wollmuth, Coordinator, 631-632-7855, Fax: 631-632-7876, E-mail: marilyn.wollmuth@stonybrook.edu.

**Suffolk University,** College of Arts and Sciences, Department of Psychology, Boston, MA 02108-2770. Offers clinical psychology (PhD); college admission counseling (Certificate); mental health counseling (MS); school counseling (MS, CAGS). *Accreditation:* APA. *Faculty:* 14 full-time (7 women), 7 part-time/adjunct (6 women). *Students:* 51 full-time (45 women), 42 part-time (38 women); includes 24 minority (3 Black or African American, non-Hispanic/Latino; 8 Asian, non-Hispanic/Latino; 11 Hispanic/Latino; 2 Two or more races, non-Hispanic/Latino), 6 international. Average age 27. 306 applicants, 25% accepted, 38 enrolled. In 2016, 22 master's, 10 doctorates, 14 other advanced degrees awarded. *Degree requirements:* For doctorate, thesis/dissertation, practicum. *Entrance requirements:* For doctorate, GRE General Test or MAT, 2 letters of recommendation, resume. Additional exam requirements/recommendations for international students: Required—TOEFL (minimum score 550 paper-based; 80 iBT). *Application deadline:* For fall admission, 12/1 for domestic and international students. Applications are processed on a rolling basis. Application fee: $50. Electronic applications accepted. *Expenses:* Contact institution. *Financial support:* In 2016–17, 54 students received support, including 53 fellowships (averaging $13,943 per year); career-related internships or fieldwork, Federal Work-Study, institutionally sponsored loans, scholarships/grants, and unspecified assistantships also available. Support available to part-time students. Financial award application deadline: 4/1; financial award applicants required to submit FAFSA. *Faculty research:* Assessing exposure in the context of a family-based cognitive behavioral treatment for pediatric OCD, a mindfulness approach to designing and testing the efficacy of a new sexual revictimization prevention program for college women, olfaction and decision-making in substance-dependent individuals, the role of experiential avoidance in Generalized Anxiety Disorder, ego development and intolerance in the political right and left. *Unit head:* Dr. Gary Fireman, Chairperson, 617-305-6368, Fax: 617-367-2924, E-mail: gfireman@suffolk.edu. *Application contact:* Mara Marzocchi, Associate Director of Graduate Admissions, 617-573-8302, Fax: 617-305-1733, E-mail: grad.admission@suffolk.edu. Website: http://www.suffolk.edu/college/graduate/69299.php

**Syracuse University,** College of Arts and Sciences, Programs in Psychology, Syracuse, NY 13244. Offers clinical psychology (PhD); cognition, brain, and behavior (PhD); school psychology (PhD); social psychology (PhD). *Accreditation:* APA. In 2016, 1 doctorate awarded. Terminal master's awarded for partial completion of doctoral program. *Degree requirements:* For doctorate, comprehensive exam, thesis/dissertation. *Entrance requirements:* For doctorate, GRE General Test, GRE Subject Test, resume, personal statement, three letters of recommendation. Additional exam

requirements/recommendations for international students: Required—TOEFL (minimum score 100 iBT). *Application deadline:* For fall admission, 12/1 priority date for domestic and international students. Application fee: $75. Electronic applications accepted. *Expenses: Tuition:* Full-time $25,974; part-time $1443 per credit hour. *Required fees:* $802; $50 per course. Tuition and fees vary according to course load and program. *Financial support:* Fellowships with full tuition reimbursements, research assistantships with tuition reimbursements, teaching assistantships with tuition reimbursements, and scholarships/grants available. Financial award application deadline: 1/1. *Faculty research:* Clinical psychology; cognition, brain, and behavior; school psychology; social psychology. *Unit head:* Dr. Larry Lewandowski, Professor of Psychology/Interim Chair, 315-443-1015, E-mail: ljlewand@syr.edu. *Application contact:* Alecia Zema, Curriculum Coordinator, 315-443-2760, E-mail: azema@syr.edu.
Website: http://psychology.syr.edu/graduate/Clinical.html

**Syracuse University,** School of Education, MS Program in Clinical Mental Health Counseling, Syracuse, NY 13244. Offers MS. *Program availability:* Part-time. *Entrance requirements:* For master's, GRE or MAT, baccalaureate degree from regionally-accredited college/university, relevant work experience, three letters of recommendation, personal statement, interview, transcripts. Additional exam requirements/recommendations for international students: Required—TOEFL (minimum score 100 iBT). *Application deadline:* For fall admission, 1/15 priority date for domestic and international students; for spring admission, 10/1 priority date for domestic and international students; for summer admission, 1/15 priority date for domestic and international students. Applications are processed on a rolling basis. Application fee: $75. Electronic applications accepted. *Expenses: Tuition:* Full-time $25,974; part-time $1443 per credit hour. *Required fees:* $802; $50 per course. Tuition and fees vary according to course load and program. *Financial support:* Fellowships with full tuition reimbursements, research assistantships, teaching assistantships, career-related internships or fieldwork, and scholarships/grants available. Financial award application deadline: 1/15. *Faculty research:* Community mental health counseling, counseling people with disabilities, substance abuse services, counseling with youth, crisis counseling. *Unit head:* Dr. Nicole Hill, Chair, 315-443-2266, E-mail: nrhill@syr.edu. *Application contact:* Speranza Migliore, Graduate Admissions Recruiter, 315-443-2505, E-mail: gradrcrt@syr.edu.
Website: http://soeweb.syr.edu/academic/counseling_and_human_services/graduate/masters/clinical_mental_health_counseling/default.aspx

**Teachers College, Columbia University,** Department of Counseling and Clinical Psychology, New York, NY 10027-6696. Offers clinical psychology (PhD); counseling psychology (Ed M, Ed D, PhD); mental health counseling (ME); psychological counseling (ME, ND); psychology in education (MA, ND); school counselor (ME). *Accreditation:* APA (one or more programs are accredited). *Program availability:* Part-time. *Students:* 434 full-time (366 women), 232 part-time (184 women); includes 247 minority (62 Black or African American, non-Hispanic/Latino; 1 American Indian or Alaska Native, non-Hispanic/Latino; 80 Asian, non-Hispanic/Latino; 84 Hispanic/Latino; 20 Two or more races, non-Hispanic/Latino), 134 international. 1,470 applicants, 39% accepted, 253 enrolled. *Expenses: Tuition:* Full-time $36,288; part-time $1512 per credit. *Required fees:* $438 per semester. One-time fee: $510 full-time. Full-time tuition and fees vary according to course load. *Unit head:* Prof. Marie Miville, Head, 212-678-3343, Fax: 212-678-3275, E-mail: miville@tc.columbia.edu. *Application contact:* David Estrella, Director of Admission, 212-678-3305, E-mail: estrella@tc.columbia.edu.

**Texas A&M University,** College of Liberal Arts, Department of Psychology, College Station, TX 77843. Offers clinical psychology (PhD); industrial/organizational psychology (PhD); psychology (MS, PhD), including clinical psychology (PhD), industrial/organizational psychology (PhD). *Accreditation:* APA (one or more programs are accredited). *Faculty:* 48. *Students:* 83 full-time (38 women), 14 part-time (10 women); includes 34 minority (7 Black or African American, non-Hispanic/Latino; 4 Asian, non-Hispanic/Latino; 22 Hispanic/Latino; 1 Two or more races, non-Hispanic/Latino), 13 international. Average age 28. 350 applicants, 9% accepted, 22 enrolled. In 2016, 4 master's, 12 doctorates awarded. *Degree requirements:* For doctorate, comprehensive exam (for some programs), thesis/dissertation. *Entrance requirements:* For doctorate, GRE General Test. Additional exam requirements/recommendations for international students: Required—TOEFL (minimum score 550 paper-based; 80 iBT), IELTS (minimum score 6), PTE (minimum score 53). *Application deadline:* For fall admission, 12/1 for domestic and international students. Application fee: $50 ($90 for international students). Electronic applications accepted. *Expenses:* Contact institution. *Financial support:* In 2016–17, 84 students received support, including 20 fellowships with tuition reimbursements available (averaging $15,749 per year), 31 research assistantships with tuition reimbursements available (averaging $6,408 per year), 55 teaching assistantships with tuition reimbursements available (averaging $10,420 per year); career-related internships or fieldwork, institutionally sponsored loans, scholarships/grants, traineeships, health care benefits, tuition waivers (full and partial), and unspecified assistantships also available. Support available to part-time students. Financial award application deadline: 3/15; financial award applicants required to submit FAFSA. *Unit head:* Dr. Heather Lench, Department Head, 979-845-0377, E-mail: hlench@tamu.edu. *Application contact:* Dr. Charles D. Samuelson, Director of Graduate Studies, 979-845-0880, Fax: 979-845-4727, E-mail: c-samuelson@tamu.edu.
Website: http://psychology.tamu.edu/

**Texas A&M University–Central Texas,** Graduate Studies and Research, Killeen, TX 76549. Offers accounting (MS); business administration (MBA); clinical mental health counseling (MS); criminal justice (MCJ); curriculum and instruction (M Ed); educational administration (M Ed); educational psychology - experimental psychology (MS); history (MA); human resource management (MS); information systems (MS); liberal studies (MS); management and leadership (MS); marriage and family therapy (MS); mathematics (MS); political science (MA); school counseling (M Ed); school psychology (Ed S).

**Texas A&M University–Corpus Christi,** College of Graduate Studies, College of Liberal Arts, Program in Psychology, Corpus Christi, TX 78412-5503. Offers clinical psychology (MA); general psychology (MA). *Program availability:* Part-time, evening/weekend. *Students:* 27 full-time (21 women), 5 part-time (3 women); includes 15 minority (14 Hispanic/Latino; 1 Two or more races, non-Hispanic/Latino), 2 international. Average age 27. 50 applicants, 32% accepted, 15 enrolled. In 2016, 8 master's awarded. *Degree requirements:* For master's, comprehensive exam, thesis (for some programs). *Entrance requirements:* For master's, GRE (taken within 5 years); waived if candidate already has master's degree), minimum GPA of 3.0 in last 60 hours, essay (500-1000 words), 2 letters of recommendation. Additional exam requirements/recommendations for international students: Required—TOEFL (minimum score 550 paper-based; 79 iBT), IELTS (minimum score 6.5). *Application deadline:* For fall admission, 3/15 priority date for domestic and international students. Applications are processed on a rolling basis. Application fee: $50 ($70 for international students). Electronic applications accepted. *Financial support:* Research assistantships, teaching assistantships, career-related internships or fieldwork, Federal Work-Study, institutionally sponsored loans, scholarships/grants, health care benefits, and unspecified assistantships available. Support available to part-time students. Financial award application deadline: 3/15; financial award applicants required to submit FAFSA.

*Unit head:* Dr. Amy Houlihan, Chair, 361-825-2971, E-mail: amy.houlihan@tamucc.edu. *Application contact:* Graduate Admissions Coordinator, 361-825-2177, Fax: 361-825-2755, E-mail: gradweb@tamucc.edu.
Website: http://cla.tamucc.edu/psychology/pages/graduate.html

**Texas Tech University,** Graduate School, College of Arts and Sciences, Department of Psychological Sciences, Lubbock, TX 79409-2051. Offers clinical psychology (PhD); counseling psychology (MA, PhD); general experimental psychology (MA, PhD); psychology (MA). *Accreditation:* APA (one or more programs are accredited). *Faculty:* 32 full-time (14 women), 2 part-time/adjunct (both women). *Students:* 111 full-time (72 women), 12 part-time (6 women); includes 28 minority (3 Black or African American, non-Hispanic/Latino; 1 American Indian or Alaska Native, non-Hispanic/Latino; 8 Asian, non-Hispanic/Latino; 14 Hispanic/Latino; 2 Two or more races, non-Hispanic/Latino), 8 international. Average age 27. 285 applicants, 13% accepted, 23 enrolled. In 2016, 13 master's, 13 doctorates awarded. *Degree requirements:* For doctorate, comprehensive exam, thesis/dissertation, 100 credit hours of organized courses, research credits, and practica. *Entrance requirements:* For master's, GRE General Test, GRE Subject Test, essays, letters of recommendation; for doctorate, GRE General Test, essays, letters of recommendation. Additional exam requirements/recommendations for international students: Required—TOEFL (minimum score 550 paper-based; 79 iBT). *Application deadline:* For fall admission, 6/1 priority date for domestic students, 1/15 priority date for international students; for spring admission, 9/1 priority date for domestic students, 6/15 priority date for international students. Applications are processed on a rolling basis. Application fee: $75. Electronic applications accepted. *Expenses:* $300 per credit hour full-time resident tuition, $708 per credit hour full-time non-resident tuition; $50.50 per credit hour fee plus $608 per term fee. *Financial support:* In 2016–17, 115 students received support, including 113 fellowships (averaging $2,657 per year), 76 research assistantships (averaging $5,066 per year), 95 teaching assistantships (averaging $11,737 per year); Federal Work-Study, institutionally sponsored loans, and unspecified assistantships also available. Financial award application deadline: 4/15; financial award applicants required to submit FAFSA. *Faculty research:* Health psychology, addictive behaviors, depression and suicide risk, sexuality/sexual risk behaviors/HIV, neuroscience/neuroimaging, forensic and correctional psychology. *Total annual research expenditures:* $710,154. *Unit head:* Dr. Robert Morgan, Professor and Chair, 806-834-7117, Fax: 806-742-0818, E-mail: robert.morgan@ttu.edu. *Application contact:* Kay Hill, Admissions Coordinator, 806-742-3711 Ext. 222, Fax: 806-742-0818, E-mail: kay.hill@ttu.edu.
Website: http://www.depts.ttu.edu/psy/

**Trinity Washington University,** School of Education, Washington, DC 20017-1094. Offers clinical mental health counseling (MA); early childhood education (MAT); educating for change (M Ed); educational administration (MSA); elementary education (MAT); reading (M Ed); school counseling (MA); secondary education (MAT), including English, social studies; special education (MAT). *Accreditation:* NCATE. *Program availability:* Part-time, evening/weekend. *Degree requirements:* For master's, thesis (for some programs), capstone project(s). *Entrance requirements:* For master's, PRAXIS I, minimum GPA of 2.8. Additional exam requirements/recommendations for international students: Required—TOEFL (minimum score 550 paper-based). *Faculty research:* Technology, literacy, special education, organizations, inclusion models.

**Uniformed Services University of the Health Sciences,** F. Edward Hebert School of Medicine, Graduate Programs in the Biomedical Sciences and Public Health, Department of Medical and Clinical Psychology, Bethesda, MD 20814. Offers clinical psychology (PhD); medical psychology (PhD). PhD in clinical psychology available to active duty military only. *Accreditation:* APA. Terminal master's awarded for partial completion of doctoral program. *Degree requirements:* For doctorate, comprehensive exam, thesis/dissertation, qualifying exam. *Entrance requirements:* For doctorate, GRE General Test, minimum GPA of 3.0, U.S. citizenship. Additional exam requirements/recommendations for international students: Required—TOEFL. Electronic applications accepted. *Faculty research:* Addictive and appetitive behavior, psychopharmacology, stress and eating, obesity, health.

**Union College,** Graduate Programs, Department of Psychology, Barbourville, KY 40906-1499. Offers clinical psychology (MA); counseling psychology (MA); school psychology (MA).

**Union Institute & University,** Master of Arts Program in Clinical Mental Health Counseling, Cincinnati, OH 45206-1925. Offers MA. *Program availability:* Online only, blended/hybrid learning. *Faculty:* 4 full-time (2 women), 6 part-time/adjunct (4 women). *Students:* 34 full-time (29 women), 29 part-time (20 women); includes 11 minority (7 Black or African American, non-Hispanic/Latino; 1 Asian, non-Hispanic/Latino; 2 Hispanic/Latino; 1 Two or more races, non-Hispanic/Latino). Average age 40. In 2016, 12 master's awarded. Terminal master's awarded for partial completion of doctoral program. *Degree requirements:* For master's, thesis, internship. *Entrance requirements:* For master's, transcripts, letters of recommendation, essay. Additional exam requirements/recommendations for international students: Recommended—TOEFL. *Application deadline:* Applications are processed on a rolling basis. Application fee: $50. Electronic applications accepted. *Expenses:* Contact institution. *Financial support:* Federal Work-Study available. Financial award applicants required to submit FAFSA. *Unit head:* Dr. Bill Lax, Dean, 802-254-0152, E-mail: bill.lax@myunion.edu. *Application contact:* Director of Admissions, 888-828-8575.

**Universidad de Iberoamerica,** Graduate School, San Jose, Costa Rica. Offers clinical neuropsychology (PhD); clinical psychology (M Psych); educational psychology (M Psych); forensic psychology (M Psych); hospital management (MHA); intensive care nursing (MN); medicine (MD).

**Université Laval,** Faculty of Social Sciences, School of Psychology, Programs in Psychology, Québec, QC G1K 7P4, Canada. Offers clinical psychology (PhD); community psychology (PhD); psychology (PhD, Psy D). *Degree requirements:* For doctorate, comprehensive exam, thesis/dissertation. *Entrance requirements:* For doctorate, comprehension of written English, knowledge of French, interview. Electronic applications accepted.

**University at Albany, State University of New York,** College of Arts and Sciences, Department of Psychology, Albany, NY 12222-0001. Offers behavioral neuroscience (PhD); clinical psychology (PhD); cognitive psychology (PhD); industrial/organizational psychology (MA, PhD); social-personality psychology (PhD). *Accreditation:* APA (one or more programs are accredited). *Faculty:* 19 full-time (6 women). *Students:* 68 full-time (42 women), 43 part-time (31 women); includes 26 minority (1 Black or African American, non-Hispanic/Latino; 11 Asian, non-Hispanic/Latino; 9 Hispanic/Latino; 5 Two or more races, non-Hispanic/Latino), 8 international. 304 applicants, 14% accepted, 24 enrolled. In 2016, 7 master's, 11 doctorates awarded. *Degree requirements:* For doctorate, thesis/dissertation. *Entrance requirements:* For doctorate, GRE General Test, GRE Subject Test. Additional exam requirements/recommendations for international students: Required—TOEFL (minimum score 550 paper-based). *Application deadline:* For fall admission, 1/15 for domestic and international students. Application fee: $75. Electronic applications accepted. *Expenses:* Tuition, state resident: full-time $10,870; part-time $453 per credit hour. Tuition, nonresident: full-time $22,210; part-time $925 per credit hour. *International tuition:* $21,550 full-time. *Required fees:* $1864; $96 per

credit hour. *Financial support:* Fellowships, research assistantships, teaching assistantships, and career-related internships or fieldwork available. Financial award application deadline: 2/1. *Total annual research expenditures:* $861,900. *Unit head:* James Neely, Chair, 518-442-4820, Fax: 518-442-4867, E-mail: jneely@albany.edu. *Application contact:* Michael DeRensis, Director, Graduate Admissions, 518-442-3980, Fax: 518-442-3922, E-mail: graduate@albany.edu.
Website: http://www.albany.edu/psychology/

**The University of Akron,** Graduate School, College of Health Professions, School of Counseling, Program in Clinical Mental Health Counseling, Akron, OH 44325. Offers MA. *Accreditation:* ACA; NCATE. *Students:* 44 full-time (37 women), 30 part-time (25 women); includes 16 minority (9 Black or African American, non-Hispanic/Latino; 2 Asian, non-Hispanic/Latino; 5 Hispanic/Latino). Average age 29. 51 applicants, 51% accepted, 15 enrolled. In 2016, 26 master's awarded. *Degree requirements:* For master's, comprehensive exam. *Entrance requirements:* For master's, minimum GPA of 2.75, letters of recommendation, interview. Additional exam requirements/ recommendations for international students: Required—TOEFL (minimum score 550 paper-based; 79 iBT), IELTS (minimum score 6.5). *Application deadline:* Applications are processed on a rolling basis. Application fee: $45 ($70 for international students). Electronic applications accepted. *Expenses:* Tuition, state resident: full-time $8618; part-time $359 per credit hour. Tuition, nonresident: full-time $17,149; part-time $715 per credit hour. *Required fees:* $1652. *Application contact:* Dr. Robert Schwartz, Program Coordinator, 330-972-8155, E-mail: rcs@uakron.edu.
Website: https://www.uakron.edu/soc/masters/cmhc

**The University of Alabama,** Graduate School, College of Arts and Sciences, Department of Psychology, Tuscaloosa, AL 35487. Offers clinical psychology (PhD); experimental psychology (PhD). *Accreditation:* APA. *Faculty:* 27 full-time (14 women), 4 part-time/adjunct (2 women). *Students:* 84 full-time (60 women), 13 part-time (10 women); includes 14 minority (4 Black or African American, non-Hispanic/Latino; 3 Asian, non-Hispanic/Latino; 6 Hispanic/Latino; 1 Two or more races, non-Hispanic/ Latino), 8 international. Average age 27. 342 applicants, 7% accepted, 18 enrolled. In 2016, 19 doctorates awarded. *Degree requirements:* For doctorate, thesis/dissertation, internship (for clinical psychology). *Entrance requirements:* For doctorate, GRE. Additional exam requirements/recommendations for international students: Required— TOEFL (minimum score 550 paper-based). *Application deadline:* For fall admission, 12/ 1 for domestic and international students. Application fee: $50 ($60 for international students). Electronic applications accepted. *Expenses:* Tuition, state resident: full-time $10,470. Tuition, nonresident: full-time $26,950. *Financial support:* In 2016–17, 73 students received support, including 12 fellowships with full tuition reimbursements available (averaging $17,000 per year), 40 research assistantships with tuition reimbursements available (averaging $12,744 per year), 34 teaching assistantships with tuition reimbursements available (averaging $13,824 per year); career-related internships or fieldwork, institutionally sponsored loans, scholarships/grants, health care benefits, and unspecified assistantships also available. Financial award application deadline: 12/1. *Faculty research:* Cognitive development/disability, child clinical, psychology and law, health/aging, social psychology. *Total annual research expenditures:* $2.4 million. *Unit head:* Dr. Frances A. Conners, Chair, 205-348-1913, Fax: 205-348-8648, E-mail: fconners@ua.edu. *Application contact:* Mary Beth Hubbard, Information Contact, 205-348-1919, Fax: 205-348-8648, E-mail: mary.b.hubbard@ua.edu.
Website: http://www.psychology.ua.edu

**The University of Alabama at Birmingham,** College of Arts and Sciences, Program in Psychology, Birmingham, AL 35294. Offers behavioral neuroscience (PhD); lifespan developmental psychology (PhD); medical/clinical psychology (PhD); psychology (MA). *Accreditation:* APA (one or more programs are accredited). *Entrance requirements:* For master's and doctorate, GRE General Test, letters of recommendation. Electronic applications accepted. Full-time tuition and fees vary according to course load and program. *Faculty research:* Biological basis of behavior structure, function of the nervous system.

**University of Alaska Anchorage,** College of Arts and Sciences, Department of Psychology, Anchorage, AK 99508. Offers clinical psychology (MS); clinical-community psychology with rural-indigenous emphasis (PhD). *Accreditation:* APA. *Program availability:* Part-time. *Degree requirements:* For master's, thesis. *Entrance requirements:* For master's, GRE General Test, GRE Subject Test, interview, references; for doctorate, interview, bachelor's or master's degree in psychology. Additional exam requirements/recommendations for international students: Required— TOEFL (minimum score 550 paper-based). *Faculty research:* Substance abuse, childhood autism, biofeedback, psychological assessment, mental health in Native Alaskans.

**University of Alaska Fairbanks,** College of Liberal Arts, Department of Psychology, Fairbanks, AK 99775-6480. Offers clinical-community psychology (PhD). Program offered jointly with University of Alaska Anchorage. *Accreditation:* APA. *Faculty:* 8 full-time (6 women). *Students:* 6 full-time (3 women), 10 part-time (6 women); includes 8 minority (1 Black or African American, non-Hispanic/Latino; 2 Asian, non-Hispanic/ Latino; 2 Hispanic/Latino; 3 Two or more races, non-Hispanic/Latino). Average age 30. In 2016, 1 doctorate awarded. *Degree requirements:* For doctorate, comprehensive exam, thesis/dissertation, oral defense of dissertation. *Entrance requirements:* For doctorate, bachelor's degree from accredited institution with minimum cumulative undergraduate and major GPA of 3.0; criminal background check; interview; course work in abnormal psychology, statistics, and research methods. Additional exam requirements/recommendations for international students: Required—TOEFL (minimum score 550 paper-based; 80 iBT), IELTS (minimum score 6.5). *Application deadline:* For fall admission, 1/15 for domestic and international students. Application fee: $60. Electronic applications accepted. *Expenses:* Tuition, state resident: full-time $7992; part-time $444 per credit. Tuition, nonresident: full-time $16,326; part-time $907 per credit. *Required fees:* $39 per credit. $322 per semester. Tuition and fees vary according to course level, course load, campus/location, program and reciprocity agreements. *Financial support:* In 2016–17, 2 research assistantships with full tuition reimbursements (averaging $13,471 per year), 5 teaching assistantships with full tuition reimbursements (averaging $6,397 per year) were awarded; fellowships with full tuition reimbursements, career-related internships or fieldwork, Federal Work-Study, scholarships/grants, health care benefits, and unspecified assistantships also available. Support available to part-time students. Financial award application deadline: 7/1; financial award applicants required to submit FAFSA. *Faculty research:* Clinical and community psychology; rural, indigenous, and cultural psychology. *Unit head:* Dr. Cecile Lardon, Department Chair, 907-474-7012, Fax: 907-474-5781, E-mail: fypsych@uaf.edu. *Application contact:* Mary Kreta, Director of Admissions, 907-474-7500, Fax: 907-474-7097, E-mail: admissions@uaf.edu.
Website: http://www.uaf.edu/psych/

**University of Bridgeport,** School of Arts and Sciences, Department of Counseling, Bridgeport, CT 06604. Offers clinical mental health counseling (MS); college student personnel (MS); community counseling (MS); human resource development (MS); human service (MS). *Program availability:* Part-time, evening/weekend. *Degree requirements:* For master's, thesis, project. *Entrance requirements:* Additional exam

requirements/recommendations for international students: Recommended—TOEFL (minimum score 550 paper-based; 80 iBT), IELTS (minimum score 6.5). Electronic applications accepted. *Expenses:* Contact institution.

**The University of British Columbia,** Faculty of Arts and Faculty of Graduate Studies, Department of Psychology, Vancouver, BC V6T 1Z4, Canada. Offers behavioral neuroscience (MA, PhD); clinical psychology (MA, PhD); cognitive science (MA, PhD); developmental psychology (MA, PhD); health psychology (MA, PhD); quantitative methods (MA, PhD); social/personality psychology (MA, PhD). *Accreditation:* APA (one or more programs are accredited). Terminal master's awarded for partial completion of doctoral program. *Degree requirements:* For master's, thesis; for doctorate, comprehensive exam, thesis/dissertation. *Entrance requirements:* For master's and doctorate, GRE General Test. Additional exam requirements/recommendations for international students: Required—TOEFL. *Application deadline:* Applications are processed on a rolling basis. Application fee: $100 Canadian dollars ($162 Canadian dollars for international students). Electronic applications accepted. *Expenses:* $4,802 per year tuition and fees, $8,436 per year international. *Financial support:* Fellowships, research assistantships, teaching assistantships, career-related internships or fieldwork, Federal Work-Study, institutionally sponsored loans, scholarships/grants, health care benefits, tuition waivers (full and partial), and unspecified assistantships available. Financial award application deadline: 1/1. *Faculty research:* Clinical, developmental, social/personality, cognition, behavioral neuroscience. *Application contact:* Jaclyn Shaw, 604-822-5002, Fax: 604-822-6923, E-mail: gradsec@psych.ubc.ca.
Website: http://psych.ubc.ca/

**University of Calgary,** Faculty of Graduate Studies, Faculty of Arts, Department of Psychology, Calgary, AB T2N 1N4, Canada. Offers clinical psychology (M Sc, PhD); psychology (M Sc, PhD). *Degree requirements:* For master's, thesis; for doctorate, thesis/dissertation. *Entrance requirements:* For master's, GRE General Test, bachelor's degree in psychology, minimum GPA of 3.4. Additional exam requirements/ recommendations for international students: Required—TOEFL (minimum score 550 paper-based). Electronic applications accepted. *Faculty research:* Cognition and cognitive development, social psychology, theoretical psychology, perception, aging.

**University of California, San Diego,** Graduate Division, Program in Clinical Psychology, San Diego, CA 92120. Offers PhD. Program offered jointly with San Diego State University. *Accreditation:* APA. *Students:* 60 part-time (56 women). In 2016, 12 doctorates awarded. *Degree requirements:* For doctorate, comprehensive exam, thesis/ dissertation, 1-year full-time internship. *Entrance requirements:* For doctorate, GRE General Test, GRE Subject Test, minimum GPA of 3.25. Additional exam requirements/ recommendations for international students: Required—TOEFL (minimum score 550 paper-based; 80 iBT), IELTS (minimum score 7). Electronic applications accepted. *Expenses:* Tuition, state resident: full-time $11,220. Tuition, nonresident: full-time $26,322. *Required fees:* $1864. *Financial support:* Fellowships, research assistantships, teaching assistantships, scholarships/grants, and unspecified assistantships available. Financial award applicants required to submit FAFSA. *Faculty research:* Behavioral medicine, experimental psychopathology, neuropsychology. *Unit head:* Robert Heaton, Director, 858-534-4044, E-mail: rheaton@ucsd.edu. *Application contact:* Kristin Deveraux, Program Coordinator, 858-534-7653, E-mail: kdeveraux@ucsd.edu.
Website: http://clinpsyc.sdsu.edu/

**University of California, Santa Barbara,** Graduate Division, Gevirtz Graduate School of Education, Santa Barbara, CA 93106-9490. Offers counseling, clinical and school psychology (MA, PhD, Credential), including clinical psychology (PhD), counseling psychology (MA, PhD), pupil personnel services (Credential), school psychology (PhD); education (MA, PhD); teacher education (M Ed, Credential), including multiple subject teaching (Credential), single subject teaching (Credential), special education (Credential), teaching (M Ed); MA/PhD. *Accreditation:* APA (one or more programs are accredited). Terminal master's awarded for partial completion of doctoral program. *Degree requirements:* For master's, comprehensive exam (for some programs), thesis (for some programs); for doctorate, comprehensive exam (for some programs), thesis/ dissertation. *Entrance requirements:* For master's and doctorate, GRE; for Credential, GRE or MAT, CSET, CBEST. Additional exam requirements/recommendations for international students: Required—TOEFL (minimum score 550 paper-based; 80 iBT), IELTS (minimum score 7). Electronic applications accepted. *Faculty research:* Needs of diverse students, school accountability and leadership, school violence, language learning and literacy, science/math education.

**University of Central Florida,** College of Sciences, Department of Psychology, Program in Clinical Psychology, Orlando, FL 32816. Offers MA, PhD. *Accreditation:* APA. *Students:* 63 full-time (46 women), 3 part-time (2 women); includes 24 minority (2 Black or African American, non-Hispanic/Latino; 6 Asian, non-Hispanic/Latino; 11 Hispanic/Latino; 5 Two or more races, non-Hispanic/Latino), 1 international. Average age 27. 260 applicants, 14% accepted, 22 enrolled. In 2016, 23 master's, 3 doctorates awarded. *Degree requirements:* For master's, thesis or alternative, clinical internship; for doctorate, thesis/dissertation, candidacy exam, internship. *Entrance requirements:* For master's and doctorate, GRE General Test, minimum GPA of 3.0 in last 60 hours, resume. Additional exam requirements/recommendations for international students: Required—TOEFL. *Application deadline:* For fall admission, 1/1 for domestic students. Application fee: $30. Electronic applications accepted. *Expenses:* Tuition, state resident: part-time $288.16 per credit hour. Tuition, nonresident: part-time $1071.31 per credit hour. *Financial support:* In 2016–17, 36 students received support, including 16 fellowships with partial tuition reimbursements available (averaging $5,688 per year), 9 research assistantships with partial tuition reimbursements available (averaging $11,278 per year), 25 teaching assistantships with partial tuition reimbursements available (averaging $11,996 per year); career-related internships or fieldwork, Federal Work-Study, institutionally sponsored loans, tuition waivers (partial), and unspecified assistantships also available. Financial award application deadline: 3/1; financial award applicants required to submit FAFSA. *Faculty research:* Professional ethical decision-making, computer experience and anxiety, effects of expert testimony on decision-making in a rape trial, religiosity, relationship beliefs and marital adjustment. *Unit head:* Dr. Bernard Jensen, Program Director, 407-823-0862, E-mail: bernard.jensen@ucf.edu. *Application contact:* Assistant Director, Graduate Admissions, 407-823-2766, Fax: 407-823-6442, E-mail: gradadmissions@ucf.edu.
Website: http://psychology.cos.ucf.edu/graduate/

**University of Cincinnati,** Graduate School, McMicken College of Arts and Sciences, Department of Psychology, Cincinnati, OH 45221. Offers clinical psychology (PhD); experimental psychology (PhD). *Accreditation:* APA. *Degree requirements:* For doctorate, comprehensive exam, thesis/dissertation. *Entrance requirements:* For doctorate, GRE General Test. Additional exam requirements/recommendations for international students: Required—TOEFL. *Expenses: Tuition, area resident:* Full-time $12,790; part-time $389 per credit hour. Tuition, state resident: full-time $13,290; part-time $419 per credit hour. Tuition, nonresident: full-time $24,532; part-time $976 per credit hour. *International tuition:* $24,832 full-time. *Required fees:* $3958; $140 per credit hour. Tuition and fees vary according to course load, degree level, program and reciprocity agreements. *Faculty research:* Neuropsychology, human factors, health.

**University of Colorado Denver,** College of Liberal Arts and Sciences, Department of Psychology, Denver, CO 80217. Offers clinical health (PhD); psychology (MA). *Program availability:* Part-time, evening/weekend. *Faculty:* 20 full-time (8 women), 1 (woman) part-time/adjunct. *Students:* 15 full-time (13 women), 13 part-time (8 women); includes 3 minority (1 Asian, non-Hispanic/Latino; 2 Hispanic/Latino). Average age 29. 173 applicants, 3% accepted, 6 enrolled. In 2016, 8 master's, 4 doctorates awarded. *Degree requirements:* For master's, 31-33 semester hours, thesis or internship, minimum GPA of 3.0; for doctorate, comprehensive exam, thesis/dissertation, 69 credits of coursework, minimum of 12 clinical practicum hours, 30 dissertation hours, three credits of pre-doctoral internship. *Entrance requirements:* For master's, GRE General Test; GRE Subject Test (recommended), undergraduate courses in psychological statistics, abnormal psychology and introductory psychology; minimum GPA of 3.0; three letters of recommendation; personal statement; resume; for doctorate, GRE General Test; GRE Subject Test (recommended), minimum GPA of 3.5; undergraduate courses in introductory psychology, psychological statistics, research methods and abnormal psychology; letters of recommendation; personal statement; resume. Additional exam requirements/recommendations for international students: Required—TOEFL (minimum score 537 paper-based; 75 iBT); Recommended—IELTS (minimum score 6.5). *Application deadline:* For fall admission, 12/15 for domestic students, 12/1 for international students. Application fee: $50 ($75 for international students). Electronic applications accepted. *Expenses:* Tuition, state resident: full-time $11,006; part-time $474 per credit. Tuition, nonresident: full-time $28,212; part-time $1264 per credit hour. *Required fees:* $256 per semester. One-time fee: $94.32. Tuition and fees vary according to campus/location and program. *Financial support:* In 2016–17, 32 students received support. Fellowships, research assistantships, teaching assistantships, career-related internships or fieldwork, Federal Work-Study, institutionally sponsored loans, scholarships/grants, and traineeships available. Financial award application deadline: 4/1; financial award applicants required to submit FAFSA. *Faculty research:* Organizational behavior, body image perception, professional ethics, infant perception and cognition, charismatic leadership. *Unit head:* Dr. Kevin S. Masters, Clinical Health Psychology Program Director, 303-352-3961, Fax: 303-556-3520, E-mail: kevin.masters@ucdenver.edu. *Application contact:* Anne Beard, Program Assistant, 303-556-2192, Fax: 303-556-3520, E-mail: anne.beard@ucdenver.edu. Website: http://www.ucdenver.edu/academics/colleges/CLAS/Departments/psychology/Pages/Psychology.aspx

**University of Colorado Denver,** School of Education and Human Development, Program in Counseling Psychology and Counselor Education, Denver, CO 80217. Offers counseling (MA), including clinical mental health counseling, couple and family counseling, multicultural counseling, school counseling; school counseling (MA). *Accreditation:* ACA; NCATE. *Program availability:* Part-time, evening/weekend. *Students:* 179 full-time (139 women), 42 part-time (32 women); includes 45 minority (10 Black or African American, non-Hispanic/Latino; 5 Asian, non-Hispanic/Latino; 25 Hispanic/Latino; 5 Two or more races, non-Hispanic/Latino), 1 international. Average age 30. 227 applicants, 28% accepted, 26 enrolled. In 2016, 61 master's awarded. *Degree requirements:* For master's, comprehensive exam (for some programs), thesis or alternative, 63-66 hours. *Entrance requirements:* For master's, GRE or MAT (unless applicant already holds a graduate degree), letters of recommendation, interview, resume, transcripts from all colleges/universities attended. Additional exam requirements/recommendations for international students: Required—TOEFL (minimum score 525 paper-based; 71 iBT); Recommended—IELTS (minimum score 6.3). *Application deadline:* For fall admission, 1/15 for domestic students, 1/1 for international students; for spring admission, 9/15 for domestic students, 9/1 for international students. Application fee: $50 ($75 for international students). Electronic applications accepted. *Expenses:* Contact institution. *Financial support:* In 2016–17, 16 students received support. Research assistantships, Federal Work-Study, institutionally sponsored loans, scholarships/grants, and traineeships available. Financial award application deadline: 4/1; financial award applicants required to submit FAFSA. *Faculty research:* Spiritual issues in counseling, multicultural and diversity issues in counseling, adolescent suicide, career development. *Unit head:* Farah Ibrahim, Counseling Professor, 303-315-6329, E-mail: farah.ibrahim@ucdenver.edu. *Application contact:* Student Services Coordinator, 303-315-6300, Fax: 303-315-6311, E-mail: education@ucdenver.edu. Website: http://www.ucdenver.edu/academics/colleges/SchoolOfEducation/Academics/MASTERS/counseling/Pages/default.aspx

**University of Connecticut,** Graduate School, College of Liberal Arts and Sciences, Department of Psychology, Storrs, CT 06269. Offers behavioral neuroscience (PhD); biopsychology (PhD); clinical psychology (MA, PhD); cognition and instruction (PhD); developmental psychology (MA, PhD); ecological psychology (PhD); experimental psychology (PhD); general psychology (MA, PhD); industrial/organizational psychology (PhD); language and cognition (PhD); neuroscience (PhD); social psychology (MA, PhD). *Accreditation:* APA. Terminal master's awarded for partial completion of doctoral program. *Degree requirements:* For master's, comprehensive exam; for doctorate, thesis/dissertation. *Entrance requirements:* For master's and doctorate, GRE General Test, GRE Subject Test. Additional exam requirements/recommendations for international students: Required—TOEFL (minimum score 550 paper-based). Electronic applications accepted.

**University of Dayton,** Department of Counselor Education and Human Services, Dayton, OH 45469. Offers clinical mental health counseling (MS Ed); college student personnel (MS Ed); higher education administration (MS Ed); human services (MS Ed); school counseling (MS Ed); school psychology (MS Ed, Ed S). *Accreditation:* ACA; NCATE. *Program availability:* Part-time, evening/weekend. *Faculty:* 10 full-time (6 women), 24 part-time/adjunct (15 women). *Students:* 198 full-time (155 women), 95 part-time (75 women); includes 15 minority (8 Black or African American, non-Hispanic/Latino; 2 Asian, non-Hispanic/Latino; 2 Hispanic/Latino; 3 Two or more races, non-Hispanic/Latino), 3 international. Average age 36. 426 applicants, 28% accepted. In 2016, 115 master's, 9 Ed Ss awarded. *Entrance requirements:* For master's, MAT or GRE (if GPA less than 2.75), essays (for some programs). Additional exam requirements/recommendations for international students: Required—TOEFL (minimum score 550 paper-based; 80 iBT); Recommended—IELTS. *Application deadline:* For fall admission, 3/10 priority date for domestic and international students; for spring admission, 9/10 priority date for domestic and international students; for summer admission, 12/1 priority date for domestic and international students. Application fee: $0 ($50 for international students). Electronic applications accepted. *Expenses:* $620 per credit hour (master's degree programs); $740 per credit hour (for Ed S). *Financial support:* In 2016–17, 7 research assistantships with partial tuition reimbursements (averaging $8,038 per year), 4 teaching assistantships with partial tuition reimbursements (averaging $9,390 per year) were awarded; career-related internships or fieldwork, institutionally sponsored loans, health care benefits, and unspecified assistantships also available. Financial award application deadline: 1/9; financial award applicants required to submit FAFSA. *Faculty research:* School bonding, traumatic brain injuries, second-year student experience, impact of physical space on learning, integrative health and mental health care. *Total annual research expenditures:* $1,500. *Unit head:* Dr. Alan Demmitt, Chair, 937-229-3644, Fax: 937-229-1055, E-mail: ademmitt1@udayton.edu. *Application contact:* Kathleen Brown, Administrative Assistant, 937-229-3644, Fax: 937-229-1055, E-mail: kbrown1@udayton.edu. Website: https://www.udayton.edu/education/departments_and_programs/edc/

**University of Dayton,** Program in Clinical Psychology, Dayton, OH 45469. Offers MA. *Faculty:* 6 full-time (2 women). *Students:* 11 full-time (8 women). Average age 23. 84 applicants, 7% accepted. In 2016, 7 master's awarded. *Degree requirements:* For master's, thesis, clinical practicum. *Entrance requirements:* For master's, GRE General Test, GRE Subject Test (recommended), minimum undergraduate GPA of 3.0, 3.3 during final 2 years of course work. Additional exam requirements/recommendations for international students: Required—TOEFL (minimum score 550 paper-based; 80 iBT). *Application deadline:* For fall admission, 2/15 priority date for domestic and international students. Application fee: $0 ($50 for international students). Electronic applications accepted. *Expenses:* $890 per credit hour, $25 registration fee per term. *Financial support:* In 2016–17, 5 research assistantships with full tuition reimbursements (averaging $11,500 per year) were awarded; teaching assistantships, institutionally sponsored loans, traineeships, and health care benefits also available. Financial award application deadline: 3/1; financial award applicants required to submit FAFSA. *Faculty research:* Family relationship issues, conduct disorders, trauma/victimization, homelessness stigma, obesity stigma. *Unit head:* Dr. Catherine L. Zois, Director, 937-229-2164, Fax: 937-229-3900, E-mail: czois1@udayton.edu. *Application contact:* 937-229-4411, E-mail: graduateadmission@udayton.edu. Website: https://www.udayton.edu/artssciences/academics/psychology/grad/clinical_psych/index.php

**University of Delaware,** College of Arts and Sciences, Department of Psychology, Newark, DE 19716. Offers behavioral neuroscience (PhD); clinical psychology (PhD); cognitive psychology (PhD); social psychology (PhD). *Accreditation:* APA. *Degree requirements:* For doctorate, thesis/dissertation. *Entrance requirements:* For doctorate, GRE General Test. Additional exam requirements/recommendations for international students: Required—TOEFL (minimum score 600 paper-based). Electronic applications accepted. *Faculty research:* Emotion development, neural and cognitive aspects of memory, neural control of feeding, intergroup relations, social cognition and communication.

**University of Denver,** Division of Arts, Humanities and Social Sciences, Department of Psychology, Denver, CO 80208. Offers affect/social psychology (PhD); clinical child psychology (PhD); cognitive psychology (PhD); developmental psychology (PhD). *Accreditation:* APA. *Faculty:* 26 full-time (13 women), 5 part-time/adjunct (3 women). *Students:* 22 full-time (16 women), 2 part-time (both women); includes 5 minority (1 Black or African American, non-Hispanic/Latino; 1 Asian, non-Hispanic/Latino; 3 Hispanic/Latino), 1 international. Average age 28. 294 applicants, 4% accepted, 8 enrolled. In 2016, 8 doctorates awarded. Terminal master's awarded for partial completion of doctoral program. *Degree requirements:* For doctorate, variable foreign language requirement, comprehensive exam (for some programs), thesis/dissertation. *Entrance requirements:* For doctorate, GRE General Test, master's degree, transcripts, biographical statement, three letters of recommendation. Additional exam requirements/recommendations for international students: Required—TOEFL (minimum score 550 paper-based; 80 iBT). *Application deadline:* For fall admission, 12/1 priority date for domestic and international students. Application fee: $65. Electronic applications accepted. *Expenses:* $29,022 per year full-time. *Financial support:* In 2016–17, 24 students received support, including 5 research assistantships with tuition reimbursements available (averaging $16,000 per year), 12 teaching assistantships with tuition reimbursements available (averaging $17,778 per year); Federal Work-Study, institutionally sponsored loans, scholarships/grants, and unspecified assistantships also available. Support available to part-time students. Financial award application deadline: 2/15; financial award applicants required to submit FAFSA. *Faculty research:* Stress and trauma, developmental science, affect science, clinical science, child psychopathology. *Unit head:* Dr. Anne DePrince, Professor and Chair, 303-871-2939, Fax: 303-871-4747, E-mail: adeprinc@du.edu. *Application contact:* Paula Houghtaling, Graduate Program Administrator, 303-871-3803, Fax: 303-871-4747, E-mail: phoughta@du.edu. Website: http://www.du.edu/ahss/psychology

**University of Denver,** Graduate School of Professional Psychology, Denver, CO 80208. Offers clinical psychology (Psy D); forensic psychology (MA); international disaster psychology (MA); sport and performance psychology (MA); sport coaching (MA). *Accreditation:* APA. *Faculty:* 23 full-time (13 women), 25 part-time/adjunct (14 women). *Students:* 230 full-time (187 women), 72 part-time (46 women); includes 69 minority (16 Black or African American, non-Hispanic/Latino; 1 American Indian or Alaska Native, non-Hispanic/Latino; 9 Asian, non-Hispanic/Latino; 29 Hispanic/Latino; 1 Native Hawaiian or other Pacific Islander, non-Hispanic/Latino; 13 Two or more races, non-Hispanic/Latino), 14 international. Average age 27. 800 applicants, 30% accepted, 129 enrolled. In 2016, 80 master's, 38 doctorates awarded. *Degree requirements:* For master's, comprehensive exam (for some programs); for doctorate, comprehensive exam (for some programs), paper, clinical internship. *Entrance requirements:* For master's and doctorate, GRE General Test, transcripts, resume, two letters of recommendation, essay. Additional exam requirements/recommendations for international students: Required—TOEFL (minimum score 550 paper-based; 80 iBT). *Application deadline:* For fall admission, 1/5 for domestic and international students. Application fee: $65. Electronic applications accepted. *Expenses:* $43,358 per year full-time. *Financial support:* In 2016–17, 124 students received support, including 15 teaching assistantships with tuition reimbursements available (averaging $2,708 per year); career-related internships or fieldwork, Federal Work-Study, institutionally sponsored loans, scholarships/grants, unspecified assistantships, and clinical assistantships also available. Support available to part-time students. Financial award application deadline: 2/15; financial award applicants required to submit FAFSA. *Unit head:* Dr. Shelly Smith-Acuna, Dean, 303-871-3880, Fax: 303-871-4220, E-mail: shelly.smith-acuna@du.edu. *Application contact:* Admissions Counselor, 303-871-3736, Fax: 303-871-4220, E-mail: gsppinfo@du.edu. Website: http://www.du.edu/gspp

**University of Detroit Mercy,** College of Liberal Arts and Education, Detroit, MI 48221. Offers addiction counseling (MA); addiction studies (Certificate); clinical mental health counseling (MA); clinical psychology (MA, PhD); computer and information systems (MS); criminal justice (MA); curriculum and instruction (MA); economics (MA); educational administration (MA); financial economics (MA); industrial/organizational psychology (MA); information assurance (MS); intelligence analysis (MA); liberal studies (MALS); religious studies (MA); school counseling (MA, Certificate); school psychology (Spec); security administration (MS); special education: emotionally impaired/behaviorally disordered (MA); special education: learning disabilities (MA). *Program availability:* Part-time, evening/weekend. *Degree requirements:* For doctorate, departmental qualifying exam. *Faculty research:* Psychology of aging, history of technology, Renaissance humanism, U.S. and Japanese economic relations.

**University of Florida,** Graduate School, College of Public Health and Health Professions, Department of Clinical and Health Psychology, Gainesville, FL 32611. Offers clinical and translational science (PhD); psychology (MS). *Accreditation:* APA (one or more programs are accredited). *Degree requirements:* For doctorate, comprehensive exam, thesis/dissertation, pre-doctoral internship. *Entrance requirements:* For master's and doctorate, GRE General Test, minimum GPA of 3.0.

## Clinical Psychology

Additional exam requirements/recommendations for international students: Required—TOEFL (minimum score 550 paper-based; 80 iBT), IELTS (minimum score 6). Electronic applications accepted. *Faculty research:* Clinical child and pediatric psychology, medical psychology, neuropsychology, health promotion and aging.

**University of Guelph,** Graduate Studies, College of Social and Applied Human Sciences, Department of Psychology, Guelph, ON N1G 2W1, Canada. Offers applied social psychology (MA, PhD); clinical psychology: applied development emphasis (PhD); clinical psychology: applied developmental emphasis (MA); industrial/organizational psychology (MA, PhD); neuroscience and applied cognitive science (MA, PhD). *Degree requirements:* For master's, thesis; for doctorate, comprehensive exam, thesis/dissertation. *Entrance requirements:* For master's, GRE General Test, GRE Subject Test, minimum B+ average during previous 2 years of course work; for doctorate, GRE General Test, GRE Subject Test, minimum A- average. Additional exam requirements/recommendations for international students: Required—TOEFL (minimum score 89 iBT). Electronic applications accepted. *Faculty research:* Organizational psychology, reading comprehension and mathematical ability, drug addiction and relapse, gender issues and culture, memory, clinical psychology.

**University of Hartford,** College of Arts and Sciences, Department of Psychology, Program in Clinical Practices, West Hartford, CT 06117-1599. Offers clinical practices (Psy D); psychology (MA). *Accreditation:* APA. *Degree requirements:* For master's, comprehensive exam, thesis optional. *Entrance requirements:* For master's, GRE General Test, GRE Subject Test, minimum GPA of 3.0, 3 letters of recommendation. Additional exam requirements/recommendations for international students: Required—TOEFL (minimum score 550 paper-based). Electronic applications accepted. *Faculty research:* Attachment issues, child abuse prevention, master's psychologist issues, neuropsychology.

**University of Hawaii at Manoa,** Graduate Division, College of Social Sciences, Department of Psychology, Honolulu, HI 96822. Offers clinical psychology (PhD); community and cultural psychology (PhD); community and culture (MA); psychology (MA, PhD, Graduate Certificate). *Accreditation:* APA (one or more programs are accredited). *Program availability:* Part-time. Terminal master's awarded for partial completion of doctoral program. *Degree requirements:* For master's, comprehensive exam, thesis; for doctorate, comprehensive exam, thesis/dissertation. *Entrance requirements:* For master's and doctorate, GRE General Test, GRE Subject Test. Additional exam requirements/recommendations for international students: Required—TOEFL (minimum score 600 paper-based; 100 iBT), IELTS (minimum score 7). *Faculty research:* Cross-cultural psychology, health psychology, marine mammals, child/adult psychopathology.

**University of Houston,** College of Liberal Arts and Social Sciences, Department of Psychology, Houston, TX 77204. Offers clinical psychology (PhD); developmental psychology (PhD); industrial/organizational psychology (PhD); psychology (MA); social psychology (PhD). *Accreditation:* APA (one or more programs are accredited). *Degree requirements:* For master's, comprehensive exam, thesis; for doctorate, comprehensive exam, thesis/dissertation. *Entrance requirements:* For master's, GRE General Test, career statement, 3 letters of recommendation; for doctorate, GRE General Test, 3 letters of recommendation. Additional exam requirements/recommendations for international students: Required—TOEFL (minimum score 550 paper-based; 79 iBT). Electronic applications accepted. *Faculty research:* Health psychology, depression, child/family process, organizational effectiveness, close relationships.

**University of Houston–Clear Lake,** School of Human Sciences and Humanities, Programs in Human Sciences, Houston, TX 77058-1002. Offers behavioral sciences (MA), including criminology, cross cultural studies, general psychology, sociology; clinical psychology (MA); criminology (MA); cross cultural studies (MA); family therapy (MA); fitness and human performance (MA); school psychology (MA). *Accreditation:* AAMFT/COAMFTE. *Program availability:* Part-time, evening/weekend, online learning. *Degree requirements:* For master's, thesis or alternative. *Entrance requirements:* For master's, GRE General Test. Additional exam requirements/recommendations for international students: Required—TOEFL (minimum score 550 paper-based). Electronic applications accepted. *Faculty research:* Smoking cessation, adolescent sexuality, white collar crime, serial murder, human factors/human computer interaction.

**University of Indianapolis,** Graduate Programs, School of Psychological Sciences, Indianapolis, IN 46227-3697. Offers clinical psychology (Psy D); clinical psychology/mental health counseling (MA). *Accreditation:* APA. *Degree requirements:* For master's, practicum; for doctorate, comprehensive exam, thesis/dissertation, 1200 hours of clinical practicum, 2000-hour internship. *Entrance requirements:* For master's, GRE, 3 letters of recommendation; for doctorate, GRE, minimum GPA of 3.0, 18 hours of course work in psychology, 3 letters of recommendation. Additional exam requirements/recommendations for international students: Required—TOEFL (minimum score 550 paper-based).

**The University of Kansas,** Graduate Studies, College of Liberal Arts and Sciences, Department of Psychology, Lawrence, KS 66045. Offers clinical psychology (MA, PhD); cognitive and brain sciences (MA, PhD); developmental psychology (MA, PhD); quantitative psychology (PhD); social psychology (MA, PhD). *Accreditation:* APA (one or more programs are accredited). *Program availability:* Part-time. *Students:* 69 full-time (46 women), 1 (woman) part-time; includes 11 minority (5 Black or African American, non-Hispanic/Latino; 3 Asian, non-Hispanic/Latino; 3 Two or more races, non-Hispanic/Latino), 9 international. Average age 29. 202 applicants, 10% accepted, 14 enrolled. In 2016, 12 master's, 11 doctorates awarded. Terminal master's awarded for partial completion of doctoral program. *Entrance requirements:* For doctorate, GRE General Test, three letters of recommendation, resume/curriculum vitae, statement of purpose/personal statement, writing sample. Additional exam requirements/recommendations for international students: Required—TOEFL. *Application deadline:* For fall admission, 12/1 for domestic and international students. Application fee: $65 ($85 for international students). Electronic applications accepted. *Financial support:* Fellowships, research assistantships, teaching assistantships, career-related internships or fieldwork, Federal Work-Study, scholarships/grants, health care benefits, and unspecified assistantships available. Financial award application deadline: 12/1; financial award applicants required to submit FAFSA. *Faculty research:* Origins, correlates and treatment of depression; health and emotion; concentration on topics related to prejudice, stereotyping, and intergroup relations; memory, cognitive development, language, perception, attention, aging; psychometric methods, item response theory, structural equation modeling. *Unit head:* Ruth Anne Atchley, Chair, 785-864-4131. *Application contact:* Graduate Officer, 785-864-4195, E-mail: psycgrad@ku.edu. Website: http://www.psych.ku.edu/

**University of La Verne,** College of Arts and Sciences, Department of Psychology, Program in Clinical Psychology, La Verne, CA 91750-4443. Offers Psy D. *Students:* 33 full-time (27 women), 37 part-time (33 women); includes 27 minority (4 Black or African American, non-Hispanic/Latino; 3 Asian, non-Hispanic/Latino; 19 Hispanic/Latino; 1 Two or more races, non-Hispanic/Latino), 1 international. Average age 28. *Degree requirements:* For doctorate, thesis/dissertation, clinical practica, clinical internship, competency exams, personal psychotherapy. *Entrance requirements:* For doctorate, GRE, minimum undergraduate GPA of 3.1, statement of professional goals and aspirations, 3 recommendations, interview, curriculum vitae. Additional exam requirements/recommendations for international students: Required—TOEFL (minimum score 600 paper-based; 100 iBT), IELTS (minimum score 6.5). *Application deadline:* For fall admission, 12/15 for domestic and international students. Application fee: $75. Electronic applications accepted. *Expenses:* Contact institution. *Financial support:* Career-related internships or fieldwork, institutionally sponsored loans, scholarships/grants, and unspecified assistantships available. Financial award application deadline: 3/2; financial award applicants required to submit FAFSA. *Unit head:* Dr. Jerry Kernes, Program Chairperson, 909-448-4414, E-mail: jkernes@laverne.edu. *Application contact:* Christy Ranells, Associate Director of Graduate Admissions, 909-448-4644, Fax: 909-971-2295, E-mail: cranells@laverne.edu. Website: http://www.laverne.edu/psychology/psyd-program/

**University of Louisiana at Monroe,** Graduate School, College of Health and Pharmaceutical Sciences, Programs in Counseling Studies, Monroe, LA 71209-0001. Offers clinical mental health counseling (MS); school counseling (MS). *Accreditation:* ACA; NCATE. *Program availability:* Part-time, evening/weekend, online learning. *Faculty:* 4 full-time (3 women), 2 part-time/adjunct (1 woman). *Students:* 35 full-time (22 women), 16 part-time (7 women); includes 21 minority (20 Black or African American, non-Hispanic/Latino; 1 Asian, non-Hispanic/Latino), 1 international. Average age 30. 167 applicants, 13% accepted, 8 enrolled. In 2016, 13 master's awarded. *Degree requirements:* For master's, comprehensive exam, thesis. *Entrance requirements:* For master's, GRE General Test, minimum GPA of 2.8 in last 60 hours. Additional exam requirements/recommendations for international students: Required—TOEFL (minimum score 500 paper-based; 61 iBT). *Application deadline:* For fall admission, 8/24 priority date for domestic students, 7/1 for international students; for winter admission, 12/14 priority date for domestic students; for spring admission, 1/19 for domestic students, 11/1 for international students. Applications are processed on a rolling basis. Application fee: $20 ($30 for international students). Electronic applications accepted. *Expenses:* Tuition, state resident: full-time $6489. Tuition, nonresident: full-time $18,589. *Required fees:* $8984. Tuition and fees vary according to course level, course load, degree level and program. *Financial support:* Career-related internships or fieldwork, Federal Work-Study, and unspecified assistantships available. Financial award application deadline: 4/1; financial award applicants required to submit FAFSA. *Unit head:* Dr. Jana Sutton, Director, 318-342-1246, E-mail: sutton@ulm.edu. Website: http://www.ulm.edu/counseling/

**University of Louisville,** Graduate School, College of Arts and Sciences, Department of Psychological and Brain Sciences, Louisville, KY 40292-0001. Offers clinical psychology (PhD); experimental psychology (PhD), including cognition and development, vision and hearing. *Accreditation:* APA. *Students:* 44 full-time (42 women), 2 part-time (both women); includes 10 minority (3 Black or African American, non-Hispanic/Latino; 2 Asian, non-Hispanic/Latino; 3 Hispanic/Latino; 2 Two or more races, non-Hispanic/Latino), 1 international. Average age 28. 21 applicants, 5% accepted, 2 enrolled. In 2016, 1 doctorate awarded. *Degree requirements:* For doctorate, comprehensive exam, thesis/dissertation, internship (for clinical psychology). *Entrance requirements:* For doctorate, GRE General Test, GRE Subject Test. Additional exam requirements/recommendations for international students: Required—TOEFL. *Application deadline:* For fall and winter admission, 12/1 for domestic and international students. Application fee: $60. *Expenses:* Tuition, state resident: full-time $12,246; part-time $681 per credit hour. Tuition, nonresident: full-time $25,486; part-time $1417 per credit hour. *Required fees:* $196. Tuition and fees vary according to program and reciprocity agreements. *Financial support:* In 2016–17, 6 fellowships with full tuition reimbursements (averaging $22,000 per year), 1 research assistantship with full tuition reimbursement (averaging $22,000 per year), 1 teaching assistantship with full tuition reimbursement (averaging $22,000 per year) were awarded; health care benefits and unspecified assistantships also available. Financial award application deadline: 12/1. *Faculty research:* Cognitive development, hearing/visual science, cognitive neuroscience/imaging, health psychology/mindfulness/stress and trauma, child/adult psychopathology, geropsychology. *Total annual research expenditures:* $1.8 million. *Unit head:* Dr. Suzanne Meeks, Chair, 502-852-6068, Fax: 502-852-8904, E-mail: smeeks@louisville.edu. *Application contact:* Libby Leggett, Director, Graduate Admissions, 502-852-3101, Fax: 502-852-6536, E-mail: gradadm@louisville.edu. Website: http://louisville.edu/psychology

**The University of Manchester,** School of Psychological Sciences, Manchester, United Kingdom. Offers audiology (M Phil; PhD); clinical psychology (M Phil, PhD, Psy D); psychology (M Phil, PhD).

**University of Manitoba,** Faculty of Graduate Studies, Faculty of Arts, Department of Psychology, Winnipeg, MB R3T 2N2, Canada. Offers clinical psychology (PhD); psychology (MA, PhD); school psychology (MA). *Degree requirements:* For master's, thesis; for doctorate, one foreign language, thesis/dissertation. *Entrance requirements:* For master's and doctorate, GRE General Test.

**University of Mary Hardin-Baylor,** Graduate Studies in Counseling, Belton, TX 76513. Offers clinical and mental health counseling (MA); marriage, family and child counseling (MA); non-clinical professional studies (MA). *Accreditation:* ACA. *Program availability:* Part-time, evening/weekend. *Faculty:* 13 full-time (8 women), 8 part-time/adjunct (3 women). *Students:* 49 full-time (39 women), 22 part-time (16 women); includes 30 minority (17 Black or African American, non-Hispanic/Latino; 12 Hispanic/Latino; 1 Two or more races, non-Hispanic/Latino). Average age 32. 51 applicants, 71% accepted, 23 enrolled. In 2016, 25 master's awarded. *Degree requirements:* For master's, comprehensive exam. *Entrance requirements:* For master's, GRE General Test with minimum cumulative score of 300 on verbal and quantitative portions and minimum score of 3.0 on analytical section (if overall undergraduate GPA is below a 3.0), minimum cumulative undergraduate GPA of 2.75 or 3.0 on last 60 hours of course work; three letters of recommendation; interview with departmental graduate admissions committee. Additional exam requirements/recommendations for international students: Required—TOEFL (minimum score 60 iBT), IELTS (minimum score 4.5). *Application deadline:* For fall admission, 6/1 for domestic students, 4/30 priority date for international students; for spring admission, 11/1 for domestic students, 9/30 priority date for international students. Applications are processed on a rolling basis. Application fee: $35 ($135 for international students). Electronic applications accepted. *Expenses:* Tuition: Full-time $14,940; part-time $830 per credit hour. *Required fees:* $1350; $75 per credit hour. $50 per term. Tuition and fees vary according to course load and degree level. *Financial support:* In 2016–17, 41 students received support. Federal Work-Study, unspecified assistantships, and scholarships for some active duty military personnel available. Support available to part-time students. Financial award applicants required to submit FAFSA. *Faculty research:* Teaching mindfulness skills as part of an interdisciplinary training protocol for doctor of physical therapy students; using symbolic art cards and oracle cards in supervision as a method for teaching appropriate self-disclosure, clinical reflection and counselor development reflection; understanding integral breath therapy. *Unit head:* Dr. Dan Williamson, Director, Graduate Counseling, 254-295-5018, E-mail: dwilliamson@umhb.edu. *Application contact:* Sharon Aguilera, Assistant Director, Graduate Admissions, 254-295-4835, Fax: 254-295-5038, E-mail: saguilera@umhb.edu. Website: http://graduate.umhb.edu/counseling/

**University of Maryland, Baltimore County,** The Graduate School, College of Arts, Humanities and Social Sciences, Department of Psychology, Program in Human Services Psychology, Baltimore, MD 21250. Offers applied behavioral analysis (MA); human services psychology (PhD), including behavioral medicine, clinical psychology, community psychology. *Faculty:* 17 full-time (9 women), 11 part-time/adjunct (4 women). *Students:* 82 full-time (65 women), 1 (woman) part-time; includes 26 minority (10 Black or African American, non-Hispanic/Latino; 6 Asian, non-Hispanic/Latino; 9 Hispanic/Latino; 1 Two or more races, non-Hispanic/Latino). Average age 25. 136 applicants, 21% accepted, 18 enrolled. In 2016, 25 master's, 7 doctorates awarded. *Degree requirements:* For master's, thesis; for doctorate, comprehensive exam, thesis/dissertation. *Entrance requirements:* For master's, GRE General Test, minimum GPA of 3.0; for doctorate, GRE General Test, GRE Subject Test, minimum GPA of 3.0. Additional exam requirements/recommendations for international students: Required—TOEFL. *Application deadline:* For fall admission, 12/1 for domestic and international students. Application fee: $50. Electronic applications accepted. *Expenses:* Tuition, state resident: full-time $13,294. Tuition, nonresident: full-time $20,286. *Financial support:* In 2016–17, 43 students received support, including 3 fellowships with full tuition reimbursements available (averaging $26,000 per year), 26 research assistantships with full tuition reimbursements available (averaging $20,400 per year), 9 teaching assistantships with full tuition reimbursements available (averaging $17,250 per year); career-related internships or fieldwork, Federal Work-Study, scholarships/grants, health care benefits, tuition waivers, and unspecified assistantships also available. Financial award application deadline: 3/1; financial award applicants required to submit FAFSA. *Faculty research:* Addictive behaviors, cardiovascular and cerebrovascular disease, family violence, pediatric psychology, community prevention. *Unit head:* Dr. Lynnda Dahlquist, Director, 410-455-2567, Fax: 410-455-1055, E-mail: dahlquis@umbc.edu. *Application contact:* Nicole Mooney, Program Management Specialist, 410-455-2567, Fax: 410-455-1055, E-mail: psycdept@umbc.edu. Website: http://psychology.umbc.edu/

**University of Maryland, College Park,** Academic Affairs, College of Behavioral and Social Sciences, Department of Psychology, College Park, MD 20742. Offers clinical psychology (PhD); developmental psychology (PhD); experimental psychology (PhD); industrial psychology (MA, MS, PhD); social psychology (PhD). *Accreditation:* APA (one or more programs are accredited). *Degree requirements:* For master's, thesis; for doctorate, variable foreign language requirement, comprehensive exam, thesis/dissertation. *Entrance requirements:* For master's and doctorate, GRE General Test, GRE Subject Test, minimum GPA of 3.5, research and/or work experience, 3 letters of recommendation. Electronic applications accepted. *Faculty research:* Social stereotyping and prejudice, anxiety disorders, auditory neuroethology, counseling and social psychology.

**University of Massachusetts Amherst,** Graduate School, College of Natural Sciences, Department of Psychological and Brain Sciences, Amherst, MA 01003. Offers clinical psychology (MS, PhD); cognitive psychology (MS, PhD); developmental science (MS, PhD); psychology of peace and violence (MS, PhD); social psychology (MS, PhD). *Accreditation:* APA (one or more programs are accredited). Terminal master's awarded for partial completion of doctoral program. *Degree requirements:* For master's, thesis; for doctorate, comprehensive exam, thesis/dissertation. *Entrance requirements:* For master's and doctorate, GRE General Test, 3 letters of recommendation. Additional exam requirements/recommendations for international students: Required—TOEFL (minimum score 550 paper-based; 80 iBT), IELTS (minimum score 6.5). Electronic applications accepted.

**University of Massachusetts Boston,** College of Liberal Arts, Program in Clinical Psychology, Boston, MA 02125-3393. Offers PhD. *Accreditation:* APA. *Faculty:* 31 full-time (23 women), 21 part-time/adjunct (14 women). *Students:* 42 full-time (38 women), 11 part-time (9 women); includes 27 minority (5 Black or African American, non-Hispanic/Latino; 7 Asian, non-Hispanic/Latino; 9 Hispanic/Latino; 6 Two or more races, non-Hispanic/Latino). Average age 29. 287 applicants, 5% accepted, 8 enrolled. In 2016, 6 doctorates awarded. *Degree requirements:* For doctorate, thesis/dissertation, practicum, qualifying exam, internship. *Entrance requirements:* For doctorate, GRE General Test, GRE Subject Test, minimum GPA of 2.75. *Application deadline:* For fall admission, 1/2 for domestic students. *Expenses:* Tuition, state resident: full-time $16,863. Tuition, nonresident: full-time $32,913. *Required fees:* $177. *Financial support:* Research assistantships with full tuition reimbursements, teaching assistantships with full tuition reimbursements, career-related internships or fieldwork, Federal Work-Study, and unspecified assistantships available. Support available to part-time students. Financial award application deadline: 3/1; financial award applicants required to submit FAFSA. *Faculty research:* Community psychology, psychology, racism and mental health, gender and culture, post-traumatic stress disorder. *Unit head:* Dr. Jane Adams. *Application contact:* Peggy Roldan Patel, Graduate Admissions Coordinator, 617-287-6400, Fax: 617-287-6236, E-mail: bos.gadm@dpc.umassp.edu.

**University of Massachusetts Dartmouth,** Graduate School, College of Arts and Sciences, Department of Psychology, North Dartmouth, MA 02747-2300. Offers applied behavioral analysis (MA, Post-Master's Certificate); autism studies (Graduate Certificate); clinical psychology (MA); research psychology (MA). *Program availability:* Part-time, 100% online, blended/hybrid learning. *Faculty:* 19 full-time (12 women), 7 part-time/adjunct (3 women). *Students:* 34 full-time (27 women), 50 part-time (39 women); includes 17 minority (3 Black or African American, non-Hispanic/Latino; 1 Asian, non-Hispanic/Latino; 8 Hispanic/Latino; 5 Two or more races, non-Hispanic/Latino). Average age 29. 99 applicants, 57% accepted, 32 enrolled. In 2016, 25 master's, 2 other advanced degrees awarded. *Degree requirements:* For master's, thesis or comprehensive exam (for clinical psychology); thesis (for research psychology). *Entrance requirements:* For master's, GRE (for research psychology), statement of purpose (minimum of 300 words), resume, 3 letters of recommendation, official transcripts; for other advanced degree, statement of purpose (minimum of 300 words), resume, 3 letters of recommendation, official transcripts. Additional exam requirements/recommendations for international students: Required—TOEFL (minimum score 533 paper-based; 72 iBT). *Application deadline:* For fall admission, 3/1 priority date for domestic students, 2/1 priority date for international students; for spring admission, 12/20 priority date for domestic students, 11/20 priority date for international students. Application fee: $60. Electronic applications accepted. *Expenses:* Tuition, state resident: full-time $14,994; part-time $624.75 per credit. Tuition, nonresident: full-time $27,068; part-time $1127.83 per credit. *Required fees:* $405; $25.88 per credit. Tuition and fees vary according to course load and reciprocity agreements. *Financial support:* In 2016–17, 2 fellowships (averaging $7,000 per year) were awarded; institutionally sponsored loans, scholarships/grants, and unspecified assistantships also available. Support available to part-time students. Financial award application deadline: 3/1; financial award applicants required to submit FAFSA. *Faculty research:* Behavioral medicine, learning, social and developmental psychology, child neuropsychology, clinical research, counseling, psychotherapy, nonverbal communication, emotion, cognition, problem solving. *Total annual research expenditures:* $500,000. *Unit head:* Mahzad Hojjat, Graduate Program Director, Research Psychology, 508-999-8951, E-mail: mhojjat@umassd.edu. *Application contact:* Steven Briggs, Director of Marketing and Recruitment for Graduate Studies, 508-999-8604, Fax: 508-999-8183, E-mail: graduate@umassd.edu. Website: http://www.umassd.edu/cas/psychology/graduateprograms

**University of Memphis,** Graduate School, College of Arts and Sciences, Department of Psychology, Memphis, TN 38152-3230. Offers clinical psychology (PhD); experimental psychology (PhD); general psychology (MS); school psychology (MA, PhD, Ed S). *Accreditation:* APA. *Faculty:* 27 full-time (12 women), 2 part-time/adjunct (0 women). *Students:* 97 full-time (70 women), 17 part-time (11 women); includes 29 minority (16 Black or African American, non-Hispanic/Latino; 5 Asian, non-Hispanic/Latino; 4 Hispanic/Latino; 4 Two or more races, non-Hispanic/Latino), 5 international. Average age 27. 278 applicants, 17% accepted, 35 enrolled. In 2016, 34 master's, 2 doctorates, 9 other advanced degrees awarded. *Degree requirements:* For master's, comprehensive exam (for some programs), thesis (for some programs), 37 credit hours (for MA); 33 credit hours with thesis or 36 with exam (for MS); for doctorate, comprehensive exam, thesis/dissertation, 80 semester hours, major area paper; 1-year placement and 1-year internship (for clinical psychology); internship (for school psychology); for Ed S, 30 credit hours. *Entrance requirements:* For master's, GRE, 3 letters of recommendation, 18 undergraduate hours in psychology; for doctorate, GRE, minimum GPA of 2.75, 18 hours of undergraduate psychology courses, transcripts, personal statement, 3 letters of recommendation, interview; for Ed S, GRE, minimum GPA of 2.75, 18 hours of undergraduate psychology courses, 3 letters of recommendation. Additional exam requirements/recommendations for international students: Required—TOEFL (minimum score 550 paper-based; 79 iBT). *Application deadline:* For fall admission, 12/5 for domestic students. Applications are processed on a rolling basis. Application fee: $35 ($60 for international students). Electronic applications accepted. *Expenses:* $5,231.50 per semester full-time in-state, $9,623.50 full-time out-of-state. *Financial support:* In 2016–17, 66 students received support, including 60 research assistantships with full tuition reimbursements available (averaging $17,582 per year), 21 teaching assistantships with full tuition reimbursements available (averaging $6,220 per year); fellowships with full tuition reimbursements available, Federal Work-Study, scholarships/grants, tuition waivers (partial), and unspecified assistantships also available. Financial award application deadline: 2/1; financial award applicants required to submit FAFSA. *Faculty research:* Clinical health; school, child and family psychology; psychotherapy; cognitive and behavioral neuroscience; industrial-organizational psychology. *Unit head:* Dr. Frank Andrasik, Chair, 901-678-2145, Fax: 901-678-2579, E-mail: rcohen@memphis.edu. *Application contact:* Dr. Robert Cohen, Coordinator of Graduate Studies, 901-678-4679, Fax: 901-678-2579, E-mail: rcohen@memphis.edu. Website: http://www.memphis.edu/psychology

**University of Memphis,** Graduate School, College of Education, Department of Counseling, Educational Psychology and Research, Memphis, TN 38152. Offers counseling (MS, Ed D), including clinical mental health counseling (MS), clinical rehabilitation counseling (MS), rehabilitation counseling (MS), school counseling (MS); counseling psychology (PhD); educational psychology and research (MS, PhD), including educational psychology, educational research. *Accreditation:* ACA (one or more programs are accredited); APA (one or more programs are accredited); CORE (one or more programs are accredited); NCATE. *Program availability:* Blended/hybrid learning. *Faculty:* 26 full-time (18 women), 10 part-time/adjunct (7 women). *Students:* 124 full-time (99 women), 79 part-time (60 women); includes 64 minority (48 Black or African American, non-Hispanic/Latino; 3 Asian, non-Hispanic/Latino; 6 Hispanic/Latino; 7 Two or more races, non-Hispanic/Latino), 7 international. Average age 32. 82 applicants, 68% accepted, 39 enrolled. In 2016, 65 master's, 8 doctorates awarded. *Degree requirements:* For master's, comprehensive exam, thesis or alternative, internship; for doctorate, comprehensive exam, thesis/dissertation, practicum, internship, residency, scholarly work. *Entrance requirements:* For master's, GRE General Test or MAT, minimum GPA of 2.5, letters of reference, interview; for doctorate, GRE General Test, master's degree or equivalent, letters of reference, interview, curriculum vitae, personal statement. Additional exam requirements/recommendations for international students: Required—TOEFL (minimum score 550 paper-based; 79 iBT). *Application deadline:* For fall admission, 10/1 priority date for domestic students; for spring admission, 4/1 priority date for domestic students. Applications are processed on a rolling basis. Application fee: $35 ($60 for international students). Electronic applications accepted. *Expenses:* $5,231.50 per semester full-time in-state, $9,623.50 full-time out-of-state. *Financial support:* In 2016–17, 130 students received support, including 13 research assistantships with full tuition reimbursements available (averaging $14,820 per year), 11 teaching assistantships with full tuition reimbursements available (averaging $15,600 per year); fellowships with full tuition reimbursements available, career-related internships or fieldwork, Federal Work-Study, scholarships/grants, and unspecified assistantships also available. Financial award application deadline: 2/1; financial award applicants required to submit FAFSA. *Faculty research:* Anger management, aging and disability, supervision, multicultural counseling. *Unit head:* Dr. Steve West, Chair, 901-678-2841, Fax: 901-678-5114, E-mail: slwest@memphis.edu. *Application contact:* Dr. Suzanne Lease, Interim Assistant Dean of Education and Graduate Programs, 901-678-4476, Fax: 901-678-4778, E-mail: slease@memphis.edu. Website: http://www.memphis.edu/cepr/

**University of Miami,** Graduate School, College of Arts and Sciences, Department of Psychology, Coral Gables, FL 33124. Offers adult clinical (PhD); behavioral neuroscience (PhD); child clinical (PhD); developmental psychology (PhD); health clinical (PhD); psychology (MS). *Accreditation:* APA (one or more programs are accredited). *Degree requirements:* For doctorate, comprehensive exam, thesis/dissertation. *Entrance requirements:* For doctorate, GRE General Test, minimum GPA of 3.5. Additional exam requirements/recommendations for international students: Required—TOEFL. Electronic applications accepted. *Faculty research:* Behavioral factors in cardiovascular disease and cancer adult psychopathology, developmental disabilities, social and emotional development, mechanisms of coping.

**University of Michigan,** Rackham Graduate School, College of Literature, Science, and the Arts, Department of Psychology, Ann Arbor, MI 48109. Offers biopsychology (PhD); clinical science (PhD); cognition and cognitive neuroscience (PhD); developmental psychology (PhD); personality and social contexts (PhD); social psychology (PhD). *Accreditation:* APA. *Faculty:* 60 full-time (28 women), 30 part-time/adjunct (18 women). *Students:* 147 full-time (111 women); includes 64 minority (15 Black or African American, non-Hispanic/Latino; 1 American Indian or Alaska Native, non-Hispanic/Latino; 14 Asian, non-Hispanic/Latino; 27 Hispanic/Latino; 7 Two or more races, non-Hispanic/Latino), 19 international. Average age 27. 727 applicants, 8% accepted, 34 enrolled. In 2016, 28 doctorates awarded. *Degree requirements:* For doctorate, comprehensive exam, thesis/dissertation, oral defense of dissertation, preliminary exam. *Entrance requirements:* For doctorate, GRE General Test. Additional exam requirements/recommendations for international students: Required—TOEFL. *Application deadline:* For fall admission, 12/1 for domestic and international students. Application fee: $75 ($90 for international students). Electronic applications accepted. *Expenses:* Tuition, state resident: full-time $21,466; part-time $1152 per credit hour. Tuition, nonresident: full-time $43,346; part-time $2367 per credit hour. Part-time tuition and fees vary according to course load, degree level and program. *Financial support:* In 2016–17, 104 students received support, including 64 fellowships with full tuition

reimbursements available (averaging $19,800 per year), 6 research assistantships with full tuition reimbursements available (averaging $24,243 per year), 71 teaching assistantships with full tuition reimbursements available (averaging $25,136 per year); career-related internships or fieldwork, traineeships, and health care benefits also available. Financial award application deadline: 4/15. *Unit head:* Prof. Patricia Reuter-Lorenz, Department Chair, 734-764-7429. *Application contact:* Sheri M. Circele, Psychology Student Academic Affairs, 734-764-2580, Fax: 734-764-3520, E-mail: psych.saa@umich.edu.
Website: http://www.lsa.umich.edu/psych/

**University of Michigan–Dearborn,** College of Arts, Sciences, and Letters, Master of Science in Psychology Program, Dearborn, MI 48128. Offers clinical health psychology (MS); health psychology (MS). *Program availability:* Part-time. *Faculty:* 17 full-time (9 women). *Students:* 23 full-time (18 women), 7 part-time (6 women); includes 4 minority (1 Black or African American, non-Hispanic/Latino; 1 Asian, non-Hispanic/Latino; 2 Hispanic/Latino), 3 international. Average age 28. 57 applicants, 49% accepted, 11 enrolled. In 2016, 10 master's awarded. *Degree requirements:* For master's, thesis optional. *Entrance requirements:* For master's, GRE, 3 letters of recommendation. Additional exam requirements/recommendations for international students: Required—TOEFL (minimum score 560 paper-based; 84 iBT), IELTS (minimum score 6.5). *Application deadline:* For fall admission, 3/15 for domestic and international students. Application fee: $60. Electronic applications accepted. *Expenses:* Contact institution. *Financial support:* In 2016–17, 11 students received support. Career-related internships or fieldwork, scholarships/grants, and non-resident tuition scholarships available. Financial award application deadline: 3/1; financial award applicants required to submit FAFSA. *Faculty research:* Cardiovascular reactivity; chronic pain; gender and couples health; personality and multicultural assessment; neuropsychology and cognition. *Unit head:* Dr. Nancy Wrobel, Program Director, 313-593-5088, E-mail: nwrobel@umich.edu. *Application contact:* Carol Ligienza, Coordinator, CASL Graduate Programs, 313-593-1183, Fax: 313-583-6700, E-mail: caslgrad@umich.edu.
Website: http://umdearborn.edu/casl/psychology/

**University of Minnesota, Twin Cities Campus,** Graduate School, College of Liberal Arts, Department of Psychology, Program in Clinical Psychology, Minneapolis, MN 55455-0213. Offers PhD. *Accreditation:* APA. *Degree requirements:* For doctorate, comprehensive exam, thesis/dissertation, internship. *Entrance requirements:* For doctorate, GRE General Test, minimum GPA of 3.5; 12 credits of upper-level psychology courses, including statistics or psychological measurement; previous course work in abnormal psychology. Additional exam requirements/recommendations for international students: Required—TOEFL (minimum score 550 paper-based; 79 iBT).

**University of Missouri–St. Louis,** College of Arts and Sciences, Department of Psychological Sciences, St. Louis, MO 63121. Offers behavioral neuroscience (MA, PhD); clinical psychology (PhD); clinical psychology respecialization (Certificate); industrial/organizational psychology (MA, PhD); trauma studies (Certificate). *Accreditation:* APA (one or more programs are accredited). *Program availability:* Evening/weekend. *Faculty:* 1 full-time (0 women). *Students:* 73 full-time (54 women), 13 part-time (9 women); includes 13 minority (4 Black or African American, non-Hispanic/Latino; 2 Asian, non-Hispanic/Latino; 6 Hispanic/Latino; 1 Two or more races, non-Hispanic/Latino), 3 international. Average age 27. 235 applicants, 8% accepted, 18 enrolled. Terminal master's awarded for partial completion of doctoral program. *Degree requirements:* For master's, thesis; for doctorate, thesis/dissertation. *Entrance requirements:* For master's, GRE General Test, 3 letters of recommendation; for doctorate, GRE General Test, GRE Subject Test, 3 letters of recommendation. Additional exam requirements/recommendations for international students: Required—TOEFL (minimum score 550 paper-based; 79 iBT), IELTS (minimum score 6.5). *Application deadline:* For fall admission, 12/15 for domestic and international students. Application fee: $50 ($40 for international students). Electronic applications accepted. *Financial support:* Fellowships with full tuition reimbursements, research assistantships with tuition reimbursements, teaching assistantships with tuition reimbursements, and scholarships/grants available. Financial award applicants required to submit FAFSA. *Faculty research:* Bereavement and loss, neuroscience, post-traumatic stress disorder, conflict and negotiation, social psychology. *Unit head:* Michael G. Griffin, Chair, 314-516-5391, Fax: 314-516-5392, E-mail: michael_griffin@umsl.edu. *Application contact:* 314-516-5458, Fax: 314-516-6996, E-mail: gradadm@umsl.edu.
Website: http://www.umsl.edu/divisions/artscience/psychology/

**University of Missouri–St. Louis,** College of Education, Department of Counseling and Family Therapy, St. Louis, MO 63121. Offers clinical mental health counseling (M Ed); counseling (PhD); elementary school counseling (M Ed); secondary school counseling (M Ed). *Accreditation:* ACA; NCATE. *Program availability:* Part-time, evening/weekend. *Faculty:* 8 full-time (4 women), 7 part-time/adjunct (6 women). *Students:* 58 full-time (48 women), 164 part-time (129 women); includes 61 minority (48 Black or African American, non-Hispanic/Latino; 2 American Indian or Alaska Native, non-Hispanic/Latino; 3 Asian, non-Hispanic/Latino; 4 Hispanic/Latino; 4 Two or more races, non-Hispanic/Latino), 4 international. Average age 32. 74 applicants, 72% accepted, 44 enrolled. *Degree requirements:* For master's, comprehensive exam. *Entrance requirements:* For master's, 3 letters of recommendation; for doctorate, GRE General Test, 3 letters of recommendation. Additional exam requirements/recommendations for international students: Recommended—TOEFL (minimum score 550 paper-based; 79 iBT), IELTS (minimum score 6.5). *Application deadline:* For fall admission, 5/1 for domestic and international students; for spring admission, 10/1 for domestic and international students. Application fee: $50 ($40 for international students). Electronic applications accepted. *Financial support:* Teaching assistantships with tuition reimbursements available. Financial award application deadline: 4/1; financial award applicants required to submit FAFSA. *Faculty research:* Vocational interests, self-concept, decision-making factors, developmental differences. *Unit head:* Dr. Mark Pope, Chair, 314-516-5782. *Application contact:* 314-516-5458, Fax: 314-516-6996, E-mail: gradadm@umsl.edu.

**University of Montana,** Graduate School, College of Humanities and Sciences, Department of Psychology, Missoula, MT 59812-0002. Offers clinical psychology (PhD); experimental psychology (PhD), including animal behavior psychology, developmental psychology; school psychology (MA, PhD, Ed S). *Accreditation:* APA (one or more programs are accredited). Terminal master's awarded for partial completion of doctoral program. *Degree requirements:* For master's, thesis; for doctorate, thesis/dissertation. *Entrance requirements:* For master's, doctorate, and Ed S, GRE General Test. Additional exam requirements/recommendations for international students: Required—TOEFL.

**University of Montana,** Graduate School, Phyllis J. Washington College of Education and Human Sciences, Department of Counselor Education, Missoula, MT 59812-0002. Offers clinical mental health counseling (MA); counseling and supervision (Ed D); counselor education (Ed S); intercultural youth and family development (MA); school counseling (MA). *Accreditation:* ACA. *Degree requirements:* For doctorate, thesis/dissertation. *Entrance requirements:* For master's, doctorate, and Ed S, GRE General Test. Additional exam requirements/recommendations for international students: Required—TOEFL.

**University of Nebraska–Lincoln,** Graduate College, College of Arts and Sciences, Department of Psychology, Lincoln, NE 68588. Offers biopsychology (PhD); clinical psychology (PhD); cognitive psychology (PhD); developmental psychology (PhD); psychology (MA); social/personality psychology (PhD); JD/MA; JD/PhD. *Accreditation:* APA (one or more programs are accredited). *Degree requirements:* For master's, thesis optional; for doctorate, comprehensive exam, thesis/dissertation. *Entrance requirements:* For master's and doctorate, GRE General Test. Additional exam requirements/recommendations for international students: Required—TOEFL (minimum score 550 paper-based). Electronic applications accepted. *Faculty research:* Law and psychology, rural mental health, chronic mental illness, neuropsychology, child clinical psychology.

**University of Nevada, Las Vegas,** Graduate College, College of Education, Department of Educational and Clinical Studies, Las Vegas, NV 89154-3066. Offers addiction studies (Advanced Certificate); counselor education (M Ed, MS), including clinical mental health (MS), school counseling (M Ed); early childhood education (M Ed); early childhood special education (Certificate), including infancy, preschool; English language learning (M Ed); mental health counseling (Advanced Certificate); special education (M Ed, PhD); PhD/JD. *Program availability:* Part-time, evening/weekend. *Faculty:* 17 full-time (8 women), 28 part-time/adjunct (20 women). *Students:* 269 full-time (219 women), 174 part-time (138 women); includes 181 minority (51 Black or African American, non-Hispanic/Latino; 2 American Indian or Alaska Native, non-Hispanic/Latino; 15 Asian, non-Hispanic/Latino; 81 Hispanic/Latino; 3 Native Hawaiian or other Pacific Islander, non-Hispanic/Latino; 29 Two or more races, non-Hispanic/Latino), 23 international. Average age 34. 256 applicants, 72% accepted, 145 enrolled. In 2016, 178 master's, 3 doctorates awarded. *Degree requirements:* For master's, comprehensive exam (for some programs); for doctorate, comprehensive exam, thesis/dissertation; for other advanced degree, final project. *Entrance requirements:* For master's, bachelor's degree; letter of recommendation; statement of purpose; for doctorate, GRE General Test, statement of purpose; writing sample; 3 letters of recommendation. Additional exam requirements/recommendations for international students: Required—TOEFL (minimum score 550 paper-based; 80 iBT), IELTS (minimum score 7). *Application deadline:* For fall admission, 7/15 for domestic students, 5/1 for international students; for spring admission, 11/15 for domestic students, 10/1 for international students; for summer admission, 4/15 for domestic students. Application fee: $60 ($95 for international students). Electronic applications accepted. *Expenses:* $269.25 per credit, $792 per 3-credit course; $9,634 per year resident; $23,274 per year non-resident; $7,094 fees non-resident (7 credits or more); $1,307 annual health insurance fee. *Financial support:* In 2016–17, 12 research assistantships with partial tuition reimbursements (averaging $12,569 per year), 27 teaching assistantships with partial tuition reimbursements (averaging $13,759 per year) were awarded; institutionally sponsored loans, scholarships/grants, health care benefits, and unspecified assistantships also available. Financial award application deadline: 3/15. *Faculty research:* Multicultural issues in counseling, academic interventions for students with disabilities, establishment of pro-social skills in young children with severe disabilities, inclusive strategies for students with disabilities, language and literacy for English language learners. *Total annual research expenditures:* $768,906. *Unit head:* Dr. Monica Brown, Interim Department Chair/Professor, 702-895-3167, Fax: 702-895-3205, E-mail: monica.brown@unlv.edu. *Application contact:* Dr. Cori More, Graduate Coordinator, 702-895-3271, Fax: 702-895-3205, E-mail: cori.more@unlv.edu.
Website: http://education.unlv.edu/ecs/

**University of Nevada, Reno,** Graduate School, College of Liberal Arts, Department of Psychology, Program in Clinical Psychology, Reno, NV 89557. Offers PhD. Terminal master's awarded for partial completion of doctoral program. *Degree requirements:* For doctorate, comprehensive exam, thesis/dissertation. *Entrance requirements:* For doctorate, GRE Subject Test (psychology), minimum GPA of 3.0. Additional exam requirements/recommendations for international students: Required—TOEFL (minimum score 500 paper-based; 61 iBT), IELTS (minimum score 6). Electronic applications accepted. *Faculty research:* Health behavior, domestic violence, verbal relations, anxiety.

**University of New Brunswick Saint John,** Department of Psychology, Saint John, NB E2L 4L5, Canada. Offers clinical psychology (PhD); experimental psychology (MA, PhD). *Program availability:* Part-time. *Degree requirements:* For master's, thesis. *Entrance requirements:* For master's, GRE General and Subject Tests, honors thesis; minimum GPA of 3.7. Additional exam requirements/recommendations for international students: Required—TOEFL (minimum score 550 paper-based), TWE. Electronic applications accepted. *Faculty research:* Forensic psychology, peer relationships and social skills, polygraph techniques, addictions, attachment and social adjustment, neuroscience, optical illusions, graphical perception, associative learning in animals, bio-psychology.

**University of New Mexico,** Graduate Studies, College of Arts and Sciences, Program in Psychology, Albuquerque, NM 87131-2039. Offers behavioral neuroscience (PhD); clinical psychology (PhD); cognitive neuroimaging (PhD); developmental psychology (PhD); evolution (PhD); health psychology (PhD); quantitative methodology (PhD). *Accreditation:* APA. *Faculty:* 23 full-time (8 women), 1 part-time/adjunct (0 women). *Students:* 60 full-time (36 women), 16 part-time (10 women); includes 22 minority (2 Black or African American, non-Hispanic/Latino; 2 American Indian or Alaska Native, non-Hispanic/Latino; 3 Asian, non-Hispanic/Latino; 12 Hispanic/Latino; 3 Two or more races, non-Hispanic/Latino), 2 international. Average age 30. 227 applicants, 11% accepted, 16 enrolled. In 2016, 10 doctorates awarded. *Degree requirements:* For doctorate, comprehensive exam, thesis/dissertation. *Entrance requirements:* For doctorate, GRE General Test, GRE Subject Test (psychology), minimum GPA of 3.0. Additional exam requirements/recommendations for international students: Required—TOEFL (minimum score 550 paper-based; 79 iBT), IELTS (minimum score 6.5). *Application deadline:* For fall admission, 12/15 priority date for domestic and international students. Applications are processed on a rolling basis. Application fee: $50. Electronic applications accepted. *Financial support:* Fellowships, research assistantships with tuition reimbursements, teaching assistantships with tuition reimbursements, career-related internships or fieldwork, Federal Work-Study, institutionally sponsored loans, scholarships/grants, health care benefits, tuition waivers (partial), and unspecified assistantships available. Financial award application deadline: 3/1; financial award applicants required to submit FAFSA. *Faculty research:* Addiction, cognition, brain and behavior, developmental, evolutionary, functioning neuroimaging, health psychology, learning and memory, neuroscience. *Total annual research expenditures:* $727,970. *Unit head:* Dr. Jane Ellen Smith, Department Chair, 505-277-4121, Fax: 505-277-1394. *Application contact:* Rikk Murphy, Graduate Program Coordinator, 505-277-5009, Fax: 505-277-1394, E-mail: advising@unm.edu.
Website: http://psych.unm.edu

**University of North Alabama,** College of Education, Department of Counselor Education, Florence, AL 35632-0001. Offers clinical mental health counseling (MA); counseling (MA Ed). *Accreditation:* ACA; NCATE. *Program availability:* Part-time. *Faculty:* 4 full-time (all women), 1 part-time/adjunct (0 women). *Students:* 14 full-time (11 women), 32 part-time (24 women); includes 7 minority (3 Black or African American, non-Hispanic/Latino; 1 Hispanic/Latino; 3 Two or more races, non-Hispanic/Latino).

Average age 35. 25 applicants, 64% accepted, 12 enrolled. In 2016, 15 master's awarded. *Degree requirements:* For master's, comprehensive exam. *Entrance requirements:* For master's, GRE, MAT, or NTE, minimum GPA of 2.5, Alabama Class B Certificate or equivalent, teaching experience. Additional exam requirements/recommendations for international students: Required—TOEFL (minimum score 79 iBT), IELTS (minimum score 6), PTE (minimum score 54). *Application deadline:* Applications are processed on a rolling basis. Application fee: $50 ($100 for international students). Electronic applications accepted. *Expenses:* Tuition, state resident: full-time $2799; part-time $1866 per semester. Tuition, nonresident: full-time $5598; part-time $3732 per semester. *Required fees:* $915; $642 per semester. Tuition and fees vary according to course load. *Financial support:* In 2016–17, 1 student received support. Scholarships/grants available. Financial award application deadline: 2/1; financial award applicants required to submit FAFSA. *Unit head:* Dr. Sandra Loew, Chair, 256-765-4763, Fax: 256-765-4159, E-mail: saloew@una.edu. *Application contact:* Hillary N. Coats, Graduate Admissions Coordinator, 256-765-4447, E-mail: graduate@una.edu. Website: http://www.una.edu/education/departments/counselor-education.html

**The University of North Carolina at Chapel Hill,** Graduate School, College of Arts and Sciences, Department of Psychology, Chapel Hill, NC 27599-3270. Offers behavioral neuroscience psychology (PhD); clinical psychology (PhD); cognitive psychology (PhD); developmental psychology (PhD); quantitative psychology (PhD); social psychology (PhD). *Accreditation:* APA. *Degree requirements:* For doctorate, comprehensive exam, thesis/dissertation. *Entrance requirements:* For doctorate, GRE General Test, minimum GPA of 3.0. Additional exam requirements/recommendations for international students: Required—TOEFL (minimum score 550 paper-based; 79 iBT), IELTS (minimum score 7). Electronic applications accepted. *Faculty research:* Expressed emotion, cognitive development, social cognitive neuroscience, human memory personality.

**The University of North Carolina at Greensboro,** Graduate School, College of Arts and Sciences, Department of Psychology, Greensboro, NC 27412-5001. Offers clinical psychology (MA, PhD); cognitive psychology (MA, PhD); developmental psychology (MA, PhD); social psychology (MA, PhD). *Accreditation:* APA (one or more programs are accredited). Terminal master's awarded for partial completion of doctoral program. *Degree requirements:* For master's, comprehensive exam, thesis; for doctorate, one foreign language, thesis/dissertation, preliminary exam. *Entrance requirements:* For master's and doctorate, GRE General Test. Additional exam requirements/recommendations for international students: Required—TOEFL. Electronic applications accepted. *Faculty research:* Sensory and perceptual determinants; evoked potential: disorders, deafness, and development.

**University of North Dakota,** Graduate School, College of Arts and Sciences, Department of Psychology, Grand Forks, ND 58202. Offers clinical psychology (PhD); forensic psychology (MA, MS). *Accreditation:* APA (one or more programs are accredited). *Degree requirements:* For master's, thesis, final exam; for doctorate, comprehensive exam, thesis/dissertation, internship, final exam. *Entrance requirements:* For master's, GRE General Test, GRE Subject Test, minimum GPA of 3.0; for doctorate, GRE General Test, GRE Subject Test, minimum GPA of 3.5. Additional exam requirements/recommendations for international students: Required—TOEFL (minimum score 550 paper-based; 79 iBT), IELTS (minimum score 6.5). *Application deadline:* For fall admission, 1/15 for domestic and international students. Application fee: $35. Electronic applications accepted. *Financial support:* Fellowships with full and partial tuition reimbursements, research assistantships with full and partial tuition reimbursements, teaching assistantships with full and partial tuition reimbursements, career-related internships or fieldwork, Federal Work-Study, institutionally sponsored loans, scholarships/grants, health care benefits, tuition waivers (full and partial), and unspecified assistantships available. Support available to part-time students. Financial award application deadline: 3/15; financial award applicants required to submit FAFSA. *Faculty research:* Developmental psychology, clinical social psychology, educational psychology, personality disorders. *Unit head:* Dr. Mark Grabe, Chairperson, 701-777-3451, E-mail: mark.grabe@und.nodak.edu. *Application contact:* Matt Anderson, Admissions Specialist, 701-777-2947, Fax: 701-777-3619, E-mail: matthew.anderson@gradschool.und.edu. Website: http://arts-sciences.und.edu/psychology/

**University of North Georgia,** Department of Clinical Mental Health Counseling, Dahlonega, GA 30597. Offers MS. *Program availability:* Part-time. *Faculty:* 3 full-time (1 woman). *Students:* 25 full-time (21 women), 23 part-time (17 women); includes 9 minority (3 Black or African American, non-Hispanic/Latino; 1 Asian, non-Hispanic/Latino; 4 Hispanic/Latino; 1 Two or more races, non-Hispanic/Latino). Average age 29. 53 applicants, 43% accepted, 22 enrolled. In 2016, 8 master's awarded. *Degree requirements:* For master's, internship, counseling practicum. *Entrance requirements:* For master's, GRE, official transcripts, personal statement, 3 UNG recommendations, resume, immunization. Additional exam requirements/recommendations for international students: Required—TOEFL (minimum score 550 paper-based; 79 iBT), IELTS (minimum score 6.5). *Application deadline:* For fall admission, 3/1 for domestic students. Application fee: $40. Electronic applications accepted. *Expenses:* Contact institution. *Financial support:* Fellowships, research assistantships, teaching assistantships, and career-related internships or fieldwork available. Financial award application deadline: 3/17; financial award applicants required to submit FAFSA. *Unit head:* Dr. P. Clay Rowell, Department Head, 706-867-2791, E-mail: clay.rowell@ung.edu. *Application contact:* Melinda Maxwell, Director of Graduate Admissions, 706-864-1543, E-mail: melinda.maxwell@ung.edu. Website: http://ung.edu/clinical-mental-health-counseling/

**University of North Texas,** Robert B. Toulouse School of Graduate Studies, Denton, TX 76203-5459. Offers accounting (MS); applied anthropology (MA, MS); applied behavior analysis (Certificate); applied geography (MA); applied technology and performance improvement (M Ed, MS); art education (MA); art history (MA); art museum education (Certificate); arts leadership (Certificate); audiology (Au D); behavior analysis (MS); behavioral science (PhD); biochemistry and molecular biology (MS); biology (MA, MS); biomedical engineering (MS); business analysis (MS); chemistry (MS); clinical health psychology (PhD); communication studies (MA, MS); computer engineering (MS); computer science (MS); counseling (M Ed, MS), including clinical mental health counseling (MS), college and university counseling, elementary school counseling, secondary school counseling; creative writing (MA); criminal justice (MS); curriculum and instruction (M Ed); decision sciences (MBA); design (MA, MFA), including fashion design (MFA), innovation studies, interior design (MFA); early childhood studies (MS); economics (MS); educational leadership (M Ed, Ed D); educational psychology (MS, PhD), including family studies (MS), gifted and talented (MS), human development (MS), learning and cognition (MS), research, measurement and evaluation (MS); electrical engineering (MS); emergency management (MPA); engineering technology (MS); English (MA); English as a second language (MA); environmental science (MS); finance (MBA, MS); financial management (MPA); French (MA); health services management (MBA); higher education (M Ed, Ed D); history (MA, MS); hospitality management (MS); human resources management (MPA); information science (MS); information systems (PhD); information technologies (MBA); interdisciplinary studies (MA, MS); international studies (MA); international sustainable tourism (MS); jazz studies (MM); journalism (MA, MJ, Graduate Certificate), including interactive and virtual digital communication

(Graduate Certificate), narrative journalism (Graduate Certificate), public relations (Graduate Certificate); kinesiology (MS); linguistics (MA); local government management (MPA); logistics (PhD); logistics and supply chain management (MBA); long-term care, senior housing, and aging services (MA); management (PhD); marketing (MBA); mathematics (MA, MS); mechanical and energy engineering (MS, PhD); music (MA), including ethnomusicology, music theory, musicology, performance; music composition (PhD); music education (MM Ed, PhD); nonprofit management (MPA); operations and supply chain management (MBA); performance (MM, DMA); philosophy (MA); political science (MA); professional and technical communication (MA); radio, television and film (MA, MFA); rehabilitation counseling (Certificate); sociology (MA); Spanish (MA); special education (M Ed); speech-language pathology (MA); strategic management (MBA); studio art (MFA); teaching (M Ed); MBA/MS. *Program availability:* Part-time, evening/weekend, online learning. Terminal master's awarded for partial completion of doctoral program. *Degree requirements:* For master's, variable foreign language requirement, comprehensive exam (for some programs), thesis (for some programs); for doctorate, variable foreign language requirement, comprehensive exam (for some programs), thesis/dissertation; for other advanced degree, variable foreign language requirement, comprehensive exam (for some programs). *Entrance requirements:* For master's and doctorate, GRE, GMAT. Additional exam requirements/recommendations for international students: Required—TOEFL (minimum score 550 paper-based; 79 iBT). Electronic applications accepted.

**University of North Texas at Dallas,** Graduate School, Dallas, TX 75241. Offers accounting (MBA); counseling (M Ed, MS); criminal justice (MS); curriculum and instruction (M Ed); educational administration (M Ed); human resources and organizational behavior (MBA); public leadership (MS); strategic management (MBA).

**University of Oklahoma,** College of Arts and Sciences, Department of Human Relations, Norman, OK 73019. Offers clinical mental health (MHR); helping skills in human relations (Graduate Certificate); human relations (MHR); human resource diversity and development (Graduate Certificate); human resources (MHR); licensed professional counselor (MHR). *Program availability:* Part-time, evening/weekend. *Faculty:* 24 full-time (16 women), 6 part-time/adjunct (3 women). *Students:* 262 full-time (190 women), 397 part-time (260 women); includes 331 minority (161 Black or African American, non-Hispanic/Latino; 23 American Indian or Alaska Native, non-Hispanic/Latino; 25 Asian, non-Hispanic/Latino; 74 Hispanic/Latino; 2 Native Hawaiian or other Pacific Islander, non-Hispanic/Latino; 46 Two or more races, non-Hispanic/Latino), 15 international. Average age 35. 135 applicants, 93% accepted, 89 enrolled. In 2016, 289 master's, 113 other advanced degrees awarded. *Degree requirements:* For master's, comprehensive exam (for some programs), thesis (for some programs), comprehensive exam or thesis; 15 hours in human relations classroom courses. *Entrance requirements:* For degree, minimum GPA of 3.0. Additional exam requirements/recommendations for international students: Required—TOEFL (minimum score 79 iBT) or IELTS (minimum score 6.5). *Application deadline:* For fall admission, 8/21 for domestic and international students; for spring admission, 1/23 for domestic and international students; for summer admission, 6/5 for domestic and international students. Application fee: $50 ($100 for international students). Electronic applications accepted. *Expenses:* Tuition, state resident: full-time $4886; part-time $203.60 per credit hour. Tuition, nonresident: full-time $18,989; part-time $791.20 per credit hour. *Required fees:* $3283; $126.25 per credit hour. $126.50 per semester. *Financial support:* In 2016–17, 148 students received support, including 8 research assistantships with full tuition reimbursements available (averaging $11,124 per year), 5 teaching assistantships with full tuition reimbursements available (averaging $12,199 per year); scholarships/grants also available. Financial award application deadline: 6/1; financial award applicants required to submit FAFSA. *Faculty research:* At-risk youth, strength model, women's health, adolescent addiction and recovery, group psychotherapy. *Unit head:* Dr. Wesley Long, Chair of Department of Human Relations, 405-325-1756, Fax: 405-325-4402, E-mail: wlong@ou.edu. *Application contact:* Lawana Miller, Admissions Coordinator, 405-325-1756, Fax: 405-325-4402, E-mail: lmiller@ou.edu. Website: http://humanrelations.ou.edu

**University of Oregon,** Graduate School, College of Arts and Sciences, Department of Psychology, Program in Clinical Psychology, Eugene, OR 97403. Offers PhD. *Accreditation:* APA. *Degree requirements:* For doctorate, thesis/dissertation. *Entrance requirements:* For doctorate, GRE General Test. Additional exam requirements/recommendations for international students: Required—TOEFL.

**University of Phoenix–Phoenix Campus,** College of Social Sciences, Tempe, AZ 85282-2371. Offers counseling (MS), including clinical mental health counseling, community counseling, counseling, marriage, family and child therapy; psychology (MS). *Program availability:* Evening/weekend, online learning. *Entrance requirements:* Additional exam requirements/recommendations for international students: Required—TOEFL, TOEIC (Test of English as an International Communication), Berlitz Online English Proficiency Exam, PTE, or IELTS. Electronic applications accepted. *Expenses:* Contact institution.

**University of Pittsburgh,** Dietrich School of Arts and Sciences, Department of Psychology, Pittsburgh, PA 15260. Offers clinical psychology (PhD); psychology (PhD). *Accreditation:* APA. *Faculty:* 56 full-time (25 women), 9 part-time/adjunct (2 women). *Students:* 84 full-time (69 women); includes 28 minority (6 Black or African American, non-Hispanic/Latino; 1 American Indian or Alaska Native, non-Hispanic/Latino; 13 Asian, non-Hispanic/Latino; 8 Hispanic/Latino), 9 international. Average age 26. 546 applicants, 5% accepted, 11 enrolled. In 2016, 9 doctorates awarded. Terminal master's awarded for partial completion of doctoral program. *Degree requirements:* For doctorate, comprehensive exam, thesis/dissertation. *Entrance requirements:* For doctorate, GRE General Test, minimum GPA of 3.0. Additional exam requirements/recommendations for international students: Required—TOEFL (minimum score 90 iBT) or IELTS (minimum score 7). *Application deadline:* For fall admission, 12/1 for domestic and international students. Application fee: $50. Electronic applications accepted. Tuition and fees vary according to program. *Financial support:* In 2016–17, 76 students received support, including 19 fellowships with full tuition reimbursements available (averaging $21,692 per year), 25 research assistantships with full tuition reimbursements available (averaging $18,250 per year), 32 teaching assistantships with full tuition reimbursements available (averaging $18,620 per year); scholarships/grants, traineeships, and health care benefits also available. Financial award application deadline: 12/1. *Faculty research:* Developmental psychopathology; smoking cessation; autism spectrum disorder; cardiovascular medicine; STEM research. *Total annual research expenditures:* $20 million. *Unit head:* Dr. Julie Fiez, Chair, 412-624-4500, E-mail: fiez@pitt.edu. *Application contact:* Stacy McLinden, Graduate Administrator, 412-624-4502, E-mail: psygrad@pitt.edu. Website: http://www.psychology.pitt.edu/

**University of Puerto Rico, Río Piedras Campus,** College of Social Sciences, Department of Psychology, San Juan, PR 00931-3300. Offers clinical psychology (MA); industrial organizational psychology (MA); investigative academic psychology (MA); psychology (PhD); social-community psychology (MA). *Program availability:* Part-time. *Degree requirements:* For master's, comprehensive exam, thesis; for doctorate, comprehensive exam, thesis/dissertation, internship. *Entrance requirements:* For master's, GRE or PAEG, interview, minimum GPA of 3.0; for doctorate, GRE or PAEG,

## Clinical Psychology

interview, master's degree, minimum GPA of 3.0. *Faculty research:* Intervention on depressed Latino youth, biosychosocial training.

**University of Regina,** Faculty of Graduate Studies and Research, Faculty of Arts, Department of Psychology, Regina, SK S4S 0A2, Canada. Offers clinical psychology (MA, PhD); experimental and applied psychology (MA, PhD). *Faculty:* 20 full-time (9 women), 8 part-time/adjunct (0 women). *Students:* 26 full-time (23 women). 28 applicants, 21% accepted. In 2016, 9 master's, 5 doctorates awarded. *Degree requirements:* For master's, thesis; for doctorate, comprehensive exam, thesis/dissertation. *Entrance requirements:* For master's, GRE General Test; for doctorate, GRE General Test and GRE Subject Test (optional for those with a master's degree from a Canadian university). Additional exam requirements/recommendations for international students: Required—TOEFL (minimum score 580 paper-based; 80 iBT), IELTS (minimum score 6.5), PTE (minimum score 59). *Application deadline:* For fall admission, 1/15 for domestic and international students. Application fee: $100. Electronic applications accepted. *Financial support:* In 2016–17, 7 fellowships (averaging $6,714 per year), 17 teaching assistantships (averaging $2,566 per year) were awarded; career-related internships or fieldwork and scholarships/grants also available. Financial award application deadline: 6/15. *Faculty research:* Clinical, experimental, cognitive, and applied psychology; post-traumatic stress disorder, anxiety, and panic disorder; traumatic brain injury; chronic pain; perception and memory. *Unit head:* Dr. Richard MacLennan, Department Head, 306-585-4458, Fax: 306-585-5429, E-mail: richard.maclennan@uregina.ca.
Website: http://www.uregina.ca/arts/psychology

**University of Rhode Island,** Graduate School, College of Health Sciences, Department of Psychology, Kingston, RI 02881. Offers behavioral science (PhD); clinical psychology (PhD); school psychology (MS, PhD). *Accreditation:* APA (one or more programs are accredited). *Program availability:* Part-time. *Faculty:* 24 full-time (14 women), 2 part-time/adjunct (1 woman). *Students:* 81 full-time (62 women), 29 part-time (23 women); includes 19 minority (12 Black or African American, non-Hispanic/Latino; 2 American Indian or Alaska Native, non-Hispanic/Latino; 3 Asian, non-Hispanic/Latino; 2 Hispanic/Latino), 6 international. In 2016, 13 master's, 17 doctorates awarded. *Degree requirements:* For master's, comprehensive exam, thesis optional; for doctorate, thesis/dissertation. *Entrance requirements:* For master's and doctorate, GRE, 3 letters of recommendation. Additional exam requirements/recommendations for international students: Required—TOEFL. *Application deadline:* For fall admission, 12/1 for domestic and international students. Application fee: $65. Electronic applications accepted. *Expenses:* Tuition, state resident: full-time $11,796; part-time $655 per credit. Tuition, nonresident: full-time $24,206; part-time $1345 per credit. *Required fees:* $1546; $44 per credit. One-time fee: $155 full-time; $35 part-time. *Financial support:* In 2016–17, 8 research assistantships with tuition reimbursements (averaging $15,685 per year), 24 teaching assistantships with tuition reimbursements (averaging $14,504 per year) were awarded. Financial award application deadline: 12/1; financial award applicants required to submit FAFSA. *Unit head:* Dr. Mark Robbins, Chair, 401-874-5082, E-mail: markrobb@uri.edu. *Application contact:* Graduate Admission, 401-874-2872, E-mail: gradadm@etal.uri.edu.
Website: http://www.uri.edu/artsci/psy/

**University of Rochester,** School of Arts and Sciences, Department of Clinical and Social Sciences in Psychology, Rochester, NY 14627. Offers clinical psychology (PhD); developmental psychology (PhD); social-personality psychology (PhD). *Accreditation:* APA. *Faculty:* 13 full-time (6 women). *Students:* 47 full-time (41 women); includes 10 minority (1 Black or African American, non-Hispanic/Latino; 3 Asian, non-Hispanic/Latino; 5 Hispanic/Latino; 1 Two or more races, non-Hispanic/Latino), 4 international. Average age 27. 257 applicants, 5% accepted, 7 enrolled. In 2016, 6 doctorates awarded. Terminal master's awarded for partial completion of doctoral program. *Degree requirements:* For doctorate, thesis/dissertation, qualifying exam. *Entrance requirements:* For doctorate, GRE General Test; GRE Subject Test (for clinical psychology, recommended for others). Additional exam requirements/recommendations for international students: Required—TOEFL. *Application deadline:* For fall admission, 4/15 for domestic and international students. Application fee: $60. Electronic applications accepted. *Expenses:* $1,538 per credit. *Financial support:* In 2016–17, 43 students received support, including 4 fellowships with full tuition reimbursements available (averaging $24,000 per year), 19 research assistantships with full tuition reimbursements available (averaging $21,000 per year), 20 teaching assistantships with full tuition reimbursements available (averaging $21,000 per year); career-related internships or fieldwork, scholarships/grants, traineeships, health care benefits, tuition waivers (full), and unspecified assistantships also available. Financial award application deadline: 2/1. *Faculty research:* Clinical psychology, social-personality psychology, developmental psychology, human motivation. *Unit head:* Loisa Bennetto, Chair, 585-275-8712, E-mail: loisa.bennetto@rochester.edu. *Application contact:* April Engram, Academic Coordinator/Analyst, 585-275-8704, E-mail: april.engram@rochester.edu.
Website: http://www.psych.rochester.edu/csp/

**University of Saint Francis,** Graduate School, Department of Behavioral and Social Sciences, Fort Wayne, IN 46808-3994. Offers clinical mental health counseling (MS, Post Master's Certificate); psychology (MS); school counseling (MS Ed). *Program availability:* Part-time, evening/weekend. *Faculty:* 3 full-time (1 woman). *Students:* 25 full-time (22 women), 10 part-time (6 women); includes 7 minority (6 Black or African American, non-Hispanic/Latino; 1 Hispanic/Latino), 2 international. Average age 31. 21 applicants, 95% accepted, 13 enrolled. In 2016, 19 master's awarded. *Entrance requirements:* For master's, GRE/MAT if undergraduate GPA is below 3.0 (or MS Ed), minimum undergraduate GPA of 3.0 (2.8 for MS Ed); undergraduate coursework in psychology; statement of professional goals (for MS); 2 professional recommendations; interview (for mental health counseling and school counseling). Additional exam requirements/recommendations for international students: Required—TOEFL (minimum score 550 paper-based) or IELTS (minimum score 6.5). *Application deadline:* Applications are processed on a rolling basis. Application fee: $0. Electronic applications accepted. *Expenses: Tuition:* Full-time $16,290; part-time $905 per credit hour. *Required fees:* $25 per credit hour. $140 per semester. Tuition and fees vary according to campus/location and program. *Financial support:* In 2016–17, 5 students received support. Federal Work-Study, scholarships/grants, and unspecified assistantships available. Support available to part-time students. Financial award application deadline: 3/10; financial award applicants required to submit FAFSA. *Unit head:* Dr. John Brinkman, Chair of Department of Behavioral and Social Sciences, 260-399-7700 Ext. 8425, Fax: 260-399-8170, E-mail: jbrinkman@sf.edu. *Application contact:* Kyle Richardson, Enrollment Services Specialist, 260-399-7700 Ext. 6310, Fax: 260-399-8152, E-mail: krichardson@sf.edu.
Website: http://bhvscience.sf.edu/

**University of Saint Joseph,** Department of Counseling and Applied Behavioral Studies, West Hartford, CT 06117-2700. Offers applied behavioral analysis (Graduate Certificate); clinical mental health counseling (MA); school counseling (MA). *Accreditation:* ACA. *Program availability:* Part-time, evening/weekend. *Degree requirements:* For master's, comprehensive exam, thesis optional. *Entrance requirements:* For master's, 2 letters of recommendation. Electronic applications accepted. Application fee is waived when completed online. *Expenses: Tuition:* Full-time

$14,580; part-time $729 per credit hour. *Required fees:* $920; $46 per credit hour. Tuition and fees vary according to course load, degree level and program.

**University of San Francisco,** School of Nursing and Health Professions, Program in Clinical Psychology, San Francisco, CA 94117-1080. Offers Psy D. *Faculty:* 7 full-time (4 women), 1 (woman) part-time/adjunct. *Students:* 36 full-time (25 women), 14 part-time (12 women); includes 18 minority (5 Black or African American, non-Hispanic/Latino; 8 Asian, non-Hispanic/Latino; 5 Two or more races, non-Hispanic/Latino), 9 international. Average age 30. 48 applicants, 52% accepted, 13 enrolled. *Entrance requirements:* For doctorate, GRE General Test and GRE Subject Test in psychology (taken within five years of application), bachelor's degree from accredited institution; official transcripts; personal statement of interest; professional resume or curriculum vitae; three letters of recommendation; minimum undergraduate GPA of 3.0 in major and overall. Additional exam requirements/recommendations for international students: Required—TOEFL or IELTS. *Application deadline:* For fall admission, 1/2 for domestic students. *Expenses: Tuition:* Full-time $23,310; part-time $1295 per credit. Tuition and fees vary according to course load, degree level, campus/location and program. *Financial support:* In 2016–17, 12 students received support. *Unit head:* Dr. Michelle Montagno, Director, 415-422-6681, E-mail: mjmontagno@usfca.edu. *Application contact:* Information Contact, 415-422-4723, Fax: 415-422-2217.
Website: http://www.usfca.edu/nursing/psyd/

**The University of Scranton,** Panuska College of Professional Studies, Department of Counseling and Human Services, Program in Clinical Mental Health Counseling, Scranton, PA 18510. Offers MS. *Accreditation:* ACA. *Program availability:* Part-time, evening/weekend. *Degree requirements:* For master's, comprehensive exam (for some programs), thesis (for some programs), capstone experience. *Entrance requirements:* For master's, minimum GPA of 3.0, three letters of reference. Additional exam requirements/recommendations for international students: Required—TOEFL (minimum score 500 paper-based; 80 iBT), IELTS (minimum score 6.5). Electronic applications accepted. *Faculty research:* Play therapy, expressive arts, identity development, counseling supervision.

**University of South Africa,** College of Human Sciences, Pretoria, South Africa. Offers adult education (M Ed); African languages (MA, PhD); African politics (MA, PhD); Afrikaans (MA, PhD); ancient history (MA, PhD); ancient Near Eastern studies (MA, PhD); anthropology (MA, PhD); applied linguistics (MA); Arabic (MA, PhD); archaeology (MA); art history (MA); Biblical archaeology (MA); Biblical studies (M Th, D Th, PhD); Christian spirituality (M Th, D Th); church history (M Th, D Th); classical studies (MA, PhD); clinical psychology (MA); communication (MA, PhD); comparative education (M Ed, Ed D); consulting psychology (D Admin, D Com, PhD); curriculum studies (M Ed, Ed D); development studies (M Admin, MA, D Admin, PhD); didactics (M Ed, Ed D); education (M Tech); education management (M Ed, Ed D); educational psychology (M Ed); English (MA); environmental education (M Ed); French (MA, PhD); German (MA, PhD); Greek (MA); guidance and counseling (M Ed); health studies (MA, PhD), including health sciences education (MA), health services management (MA), medical and surgical nursing science (critical care general) (MA), midwifery and neonatal nursing science (MA), trauma and emergency care (MA); history (MA, PhD); history of education (Ed D); inclusive education (M Ed, Ed D); information and communications technology policy and regulation (MA); information science (MA, MIS, PhD); international politics (MA, PhD); Islamic studies (MA, PhD); Italian (MA, PhD); Judaica (MA, PhD); linguistics (MA, PhD); mathematical education (M Ed); mathematics education (MA); missiology (M Th, D Th); modern Hebrew (MA, PhD); musicology (MA, MMus, D Mus, PhD); natural science education (M Ed); New Testament (M Th, D Th); Old Testament (D Th); pastoral therapy (M Th, D Th); philosophy (MA); philosophy of education (M Ed, Ed D); politics (MA, PhD); Portuguese (MA, PhD); practical theology (M Th, D Th); psychology (MA, MS, PhD); psychology of education (M Ed, Ed D); public health (MA); religious studies (MA, D Th, PhD); Romance languages (MA); Russian (MA, PhD); Semitic languages (MA, PhD); social behavior studies in HIV/AIDS (MA); social science (mental health) (MA); social science in development studies (MA); social science in psychology (MA); social science in social work (MA); social science in sociology (MA); social work (MSW, DSW, PhD); socio-education (M Ed, Ed D); sociolinguistics (MA); sociology (MA, PhD); Spanish (MA, PhD); systematic theology (M Th, D Th); TESOL (teaching English to speakers of other languages) (MA); theological ethics (M Th, D Th); theory of literature (MA, PhD); urban ministries (D Th); urban ministry (M Th).

**University of South Alabama,** College of Education and Professional Studies, Department of Counseling and Instructional Sciences, Mobile, AL 36688. Offers clinical mental health counseling (MS); educational media (M Ed, MS); instructional design and development (MS, PhD); school counseling (M Ed). *Accreditation:* NCATE. *Program availability:* Part-time. *Faculty:* 12 full-time (8 women), 6 part-time/adjunct (5 women). *Students:* 104 full-time (83 women), 67 part-time (56 women); includes 49 minority (35 Black or African American, non-Hispanic/Latino; 2 American Indian or Alaska Native, non-Hispanic/Latino; 2 Asian, non-Hispanic/Latino; 8 Hispanic/Latino; 1 Native Hawaiian or other Pacific Islander, non-Hispanic/Latino; 1 Two or more races, non-Hispanic/Latino), 4 international. Average age 35. 59 applicants, 51% accepted, 26 enrolled. In 2016, 28 master's, 8 doctorates awarded. *Degree requirements:* For master's, comprehensive exam; for doctorate, comprehensive exam, thesis/dissertation. *Entrance requirements:* For master's, GRE General Test or MAT, minimum GPA of 3.0, two letters of recommendation; for doctorate, GRE, three letters of recommendation, master's degree in field or completion of prerequisites, resume. Additional exam requirements/recommendations for international students: Required—TOEFL (minimum score 525 paper-based; 71 iBT). *Application deadline:* For fall admission, 6/15 for domestic students, 5/15 for international students; for spring admission, 12/1 for domestic students, 11/1 for international students; for summer admission, 4/1 for domestic students. Applications are processed on a rolling basis. Application fee: $35. Electronic applications accepted. *Expenses:* Tuition, state resident: full-time $9768; part-time $407 per credit hour. Tuition, nonresident: full-time $19,536; part-time $814 per credit hour. *Financial support:* Fellowships, research assistantships, teaching assistantships, career-related internships or fieldwork, Federal Work-Study, institutionally sponsored loans, scholarships/grants, and unspecified assistantships available. Support available to part-time students. Financial award application deadline: 5/31; financial award applicants required to submit FAFSA. *Faculty research:* Agency counseling, rehabilitation counseling, school psychometry. *Unit head:* Dr. Tres Stefurak, Department Chair, 251-380-2734, Fax: 251-380-2713, E-mail: jstefurak@southalabama.edu. *Application contact:* Dr. Susan Santoli, Director of Graduate Studies, 251-380-2836, Fax: 251-380-2758, E-mail: ssantoli@southalabama.edu.
Website: http://www.southalabama.edu/colleges/ceps/cins/

**University of South Alabama,** Graduate School, Program in Clinical and Counseling Psychology, Mobile, AL 36688. Offers PhD. *Accreditation:* ACA. *Faculty:* 4 full-time (2 women). *Students:* 28 full-time (18 women), 6 part-time (5 women); includes 5 minority (3 Black or African American, non-Hispanic/Latino; 1 American Indian or Alaska Native, non-Hispanic/Latino; 1 Two or more races, non-Hispanic/Latino). Average age 27. 112 applicants, 10% accepted, 11 enrolled. In 2016, 5 doctorates awarded. *Degree requirements:* For doctorate, thesis/dissertation, capstone internship. *Entrance requirements:* For doctorate, GRE, three letters of recommendation, statement of purpose, curriculum vitae. Additional exam requirements/recommendations for international students: Required—TOEFL (minimum score 525 paper-based; 71 iBT). *Application deadline:* For fall admission, 12/15 for domestic students. Application fee: $35. Electronic applications accepted. *Expenses:* Tuition, state resident: full-time $9768; part-time $407 per credit hour. Tuition, nonresident: full-time $19,536; part-time $814 per credit hour. *Financial support:* Fellowships, research assistantships, teaching assistantships, career-related internships or fieldwork, institutionally sponsored loans, scholarships/grants, and unspecified assistantships available. Support available to part-time students. Financial award application deadline: 5/31; financial award applicants required to submit FAFSA. *Faculty research:* Suicidal behaviors, healthy youth and families. *Unit head:* Dr. Julio Turrens, Interim Dean of the Graduate School, 251-460-6310, E-mail: jturrens@southalabama.edu. *Application contact:* Dr. Joe Currier, Director of Clinical Training, 251-460-6622, E-mail: jcurrier@southalabama.edu. Website: http://www.southalabama.edu/ccp/

**University of South Carolina,** The Graduate School, College of Arts and Sciences, Department of Psychology, Program in Clinical/Community Psychology, Columbia, SC 29208. Offers clinical/community psychology (PhD); general psychology (MA). *Accreditation:* APA. *Degree requirements:* For master's, comprehensive exam, thesis; for doctorate, comprehensive exam, thesis/dissertation. *Entrance requirements:* For doctorate, GRE General Test, minimum GPA of 3.2. Additional exam requirements/recommendations for international students: Required—TOEFL. Electronic applications accepted. *Faculty research:* Developmental psychopathology, health disparities, community-level interventions for psychological well being.

**University of South Carolina Aiken,** Program in Applied Clinical Psychology, Aiken, SC 29801. Offers MS. *Program availability:* Part-time. *Faculty:* 9 full-time (7 women). *Students:* 19 full-time (16 women), 11 part-time (9 women); includes 5 minority (3 Black or African American, non-Hispanic/Latino; 1 Native Hawaiian or other Pacific Islander, non-Hispanic/Latino; 1 Two or more races, non-Hispanic/Latino). Average age 26. 53 applicants, 34% accepted, 12 enrolled. In 2016, 7 master's awarded. *Degree requirements:* For master's, thesis. *Entrance requirements:* For master's, GRE. Additional exam requirements/recommendations for international students: Required—TOEFL (minimum score 550 paper-based; 80 iBT). *Application deadline:* For fall admission, 5/15 priority date for domestic and international students. Applications are processed on a rolling basis. Application fee: $45. Electronic applications accepted. *Expenses:* Tuition, state resident: full-time $12,798; part-time $533 per credit hour. Tuition, nonresident: full-time $27,408; part-time $1142 per credit hour. *Required fees:* $11 per credit hour. $25 per semester. Full-time tuition and fees vary according to course load. *Financial support:* In 2016–17, 23 students received support, including 16 research assistantships with partial tuition reimbursements available (averaging $3,594 per year), 4 teaching assistantships with partial tuition reimbursements available (averaging $3,438 per year); career-related internships or fieldwork, Federal Work-Study, scholarships/grants, tuition waivers (partial), and unspecified assistantships also available. Financial award application deadline: 3/15; financial award applicants required to submit FAFSA. *Faculty research:* Addictive behaviors, interpersonal attraction, impression formation in zero-acquaintance situations, the influence of emotions on visual perception, executive function, cognitive control, inhibitory control, working memory, episodic memory, emotion regulation, anxiety, stress, cognitive functioning and development, social and personality psychology, ADHD, development of cognition and academic skills, teen pregnancy/parenting. *Unit head:* Dr. Jane Stafford, Director, 803-641-3358, Fax: 803-641-3720, E-mail: jstafford@usca.edu. *Application contact:* Dan Robb, Associate Vice Chancellor for Enrollment Management, 803-641-3487, Fax: 803-641-3727, E-mail: danr@usca.edu. Website: http://web.usca.edu/psychology/academics/ms-psychology/

**The University of South Dakota,** Graduate School, College of Arts and Sciences, Department of Psychology, Vermillion, SD 57069. Offers clinical psychology (MA, PhD); human factors (MA, PhD). *Accreditation:* APA (one or more programs are accredited). *Degree requirements:* For master's, comprehensive exam, thesis; for doctorate, comprehensive exam, thesis/dissertation. *Entrance requirements:* For master's, GRE, minimum GPA of 3.0; for doctorate, GRE General Test, GRE Subject Test, minimum GPA of 3.0. Additional exam requirements/recommendations for international students: Required—TOEFL (minimum score 550 paper-based; 79 iBT). Electronic applications accepted. *Faculty research:* Human-computer interactions, perceptual-cognitive processing, medical psychology, depression, moral psychology.

**University of Southern California,** Graduate School, Dana and David Dornsife College of Letters, Arts and Sciences, Department of Psychology, Los Angeles, CA 90089. Offers brain and cognitive science (PhD); clinical science (PhD); developmental psychology (PhD); human behavior (MHB); quantitative methods (PhD); social psychology (PhD). *Accreditation:* APA. *Degree requirements:* For doctorate, comprehensive exam, thesis/dissertation, one-year internship (for clinical science students). *Entrance requirements:* For doctorate, GRE. Additional exam requirements/recommendations for international students: Recommended—TOEFL (minimum score 600 paper-based; 100 iBT). Electronic applications accepted. *Faculty research:* Affective neuroscience; children and families; vision, culture and ethnicity; intergroup relations; aggression and violence; language and reading development; substance abuse.

**University of Southern Mississippi,** Graduate School, College of Education and Psychology, Department of Psychology, Hattiesburg, MS 39406. Offers applied behavior analysis (MS); clinical psychology (PhD); counseling psychology (MS, PhD); school psychology (PhD). *Accreditation:* APA (one or more programs are accredited). Terminal master's awarded for partial completion of doctoral program. *Degree requirements:* For master's, comprehensive exam, thesis; for doctorate, comprehensive exam, thesis/dissertation. *Entrance requirements:* For master's, GRE General Test, minimum GPA of 3.0; for doctorate, GRE General Test, interview, minimum GPA of 3.5. Additional exam requirements/recommendations for international students: Required—TOEFL, IELTS. *Application deadline:* Applications are processed on a rolling basis. Application fee: $60. *Expenses:* Tuition, area resident: Full-time $15,708; part-time $437 per credit hour. *Financial support:* Research assistantships with full tuition reimbursements, teaching assistantships with full tuition reimbursements, career-related internships or fieldwork, Federal Work-Study, institutionally sponsored loans, scholarships/grants, health care benefits, and unspecified assistantships available. Financial award application deadline: 3/15; financial award applicants required to submit FAFSA. *Faculty research:* Psychopathology, alcohol and drug abuse, child clinical psychology, parenting, suicide, career/vocational, marine mammal, cognition, psychological psychology, behavioral interventions, positive psychology, anger/aggression, diversity issues. *Unit head:* Dr. Joe Olmi, Chair, 601-266-5693, Fax: 601-266-5580, E-mail: d.olmi@usm.edu. *Application contact:* Angela Pam, Administrative Assistant, 601-266-4592, Fax: 601-266-5580. Website: https://www.usm.edu/psychology

**University of South Florida,** College of Arts and Sciences, Department of Psychology, Tampa, FL 33620-9951. Offers psychology (PhD), including clinical psychology, cognition, neuroscience and social psychology, industrial-organizational psychology. *Accreditation:* APA. *Faculty:* 34 full-time (14 women). *Students:* 83 full-time (57 women), 19 part-time (13 women); includes 16 minority (1 Black or African American, non-Hispanic/Latino; 5 Asian, non-Hispanic/Latino; 7 Hispanic/Latino; 3 Two or more races, non-Hispanic/Latino), 9 international. Average age 28. 467 applicants, 3% accepted, 14

enrolled. In 2016, 12 doctorates awarded. *Degree requirements:* For doctorate, comprehensive exam, thesis/dissertation, internship. *Entrance requirements:* For doctorate, GRE General Test, minimum upper-division GPA of 3.4, three letters of recommendation, personal goals statement. Additional exam requirements/recommendations for international students: Required—TOEFL (minimum score 550 paper-based; 79 iBT) or IELTS (minimum score 6.5). *Application deadline:* For fall admission, 12/1 for domestic and international students. Application fee: $30. Electronic applications accepted. *Expenses:* Contact institution. *Financial support:* In 2016–17, 48 students received support, including 18 research assistantships with tuition reimbursements available (averaging $14,727 per year), 57 teaching assistantships with tuition reimbursements available (averaging $14,543 per year); tuition waivers (partial) and unspecified assistantships also available. Financial award applicants required to submit FAFSA. *Faculty research:* Clinical, cognitive, neuroscience, social, and industrial/organizational. Total annual research expenditures: $2.1 million. *Unit head:* Dr. Toru Shimizu, Chairperson, 813-974-0352, Fax: 813-974-4617, E-mail: shimizu@usf.edu. *Application contact:* Dr. Joseph Vandello, Associate Professor and Graduate Program Director, 813-974-0362, Fax: 813-974-4617, E-mail: vandello@usf.edu. Website: http://psychology.usf.edu/

**The University of Tennessee,** Graduate School, College of Arts and Sciences, Department of Psychology, Knoxville, TN 37996. Offers clinical psychology (PhD); experimental psychology (MA, PhD); psychology (MA). *Accreditation:* APA (one or more programs are accredited). Terminal master's awarded for partial completion of doctoral program. *Degree requirements:* For master's, thesis; for doctorate, thesis/dissertation. *Entrance requirements:* For master's and doctorate, GRE General Test, GRE Subject Test, minimum GPA of 2.7. Additional exam requirements/recommendations for international students: Required—TOEFL. Electronic applications accepted.

**The University of Texas at Austin,** Graduate School, College of Liberal Arts, Department of Psychology, Austin, TX 78712-1111. Offers behavioral neuroscience (PhD); clinical psychology (PhD); cognitive systems (PhD); developmental psychology (PhD); individual differences and evolutionary psychology (PhD); perceptual systems (PhD); social psychology (PhD). *Accreditation:* APA. *Degree requirements:* For doctorate, thesis/dissertation. *Entrance requirements:* For doctorate, GRE General Test. Electronic applications accepted. *Faculty research:* Behavioral neuroscience, sensory neuroscience, evolutionary psychology, cognitive processes in psychopathology, cognitive processes and their development.

**The University of Texas at El Paso,** Graduate School, College of Liberal Arts, Department of Psychology, El Paso, TX 79968-0001. Offers clinical psychology (MA); experimental psychology (MA); psychology (PhD). *Program availability:* Part-time, evening/weekend. *Degree requirements:* For master's, thesis; for doctorate, thesis/dissertation. *Entrance requirements:* For master's, GRE, letters of recommendation; for doctorate, GRE, statement of purpose, letters of recommendation. Additional exam requirements/recommendations for international students: Required—TOEFL; Recommended—IELTS. Electronic applications accepted.

**The University of Texas at Tyler,** College of Education and Psychology, Department of Psychology and Counseling, Tyler, TX 75799-0001. Offers clinical psychology (MS), including neuropsychology, school psychology; counseling psychology (MA), including general, marriage and family; interdisciplinary studies (MSIS); school counseling (MA). *Program availability:* Part-time, evening/weekend. *Degree requirements:* For master's, comprehensive exam, thesis optional. *Entrance requirements:* For master's, GRE General Test, minimum GPA of 3.0. Additional exam requirements/recommendations for international students: Required—TOEFL. Electronic applications accepted. *Faculty research:* Neuropsychology, child abuse, psychometric properties of psychological instruments, maternal behavior, clinical practice issues, victimization of women, post-traumatic stress disorder.

**The University of Texas of the Permian Basin,** Office of Graduate Studies, College of Arts and Sciences, Department of Psychology, Odessa, TX 79762-0001. Offers applied research psychology (MA); clinical psychology (MA). *Program availability:* Part-time, evening/weekend. *Degree requirements:* For master's, comprehensive exam, thesis, practicum. *Entrance requirements:* For master's, GRE General Test, 3 letters of recommendation. Additional exam requirements/recommendations for international students: Required—TOEFL (minimum score 550 paper-based).

**The University of Texas Rio Grande Valley,** College of Education and P-16 Integration, Department of Counseling and Guidance, Edinburg, TX 78539. Offers clinical mental health counseling (M Ed); school counseling (M Ed). Tuition and fees vary according to course load and program.

**The University of Texas Rio Grande Valley,** College of Liberal Arts, Department of Psychological Science, Edinburg, TX 78539. Offers psychology (MA), including clinical psychology, experimental psychology. *Program availability:* Part-time, evening/weekend. *Degree requirements:* For master's, comprehensive exam, thesis optional, internship. *Entrance requirements:* For master's, GRE, letters of recommendation. Additional exam requirements/recommendations for international students: Required—TOEFL. Electronic applications accepted. Tuition and fees vary according to course load and program. *Faculty research:* Biofeedback, acculturation, health, stress/trauma, neuropsychological assessment, false memories, children's theory of mind.

**The University of Texas Southwestern Medical Center,** Southwestern Graduate School of Biomedical Sciences, Clinical Psychology Program, Dallas, TX 75390. Offers PhD. *Accreditation:* APA. *Degree requirements:* For doctorate, thesis/dissertation, clinical and qualifying exams. *Entrance requirements:* For doctorate, GRE General Test, minimum undergraduate GPA of 3.0. Electronic applications accepted. *Faculty research:* Health psychology, depression, cross-cultural research, neuropsychology, sequelae children's illness.

**University of the Cumberlands,** Program in Clinical Psychology, Williamsburg, KY 40769-1372. Offers PhD. *Program availability:* Part-time, evening/weekend, online learning.

**The University of Toledo,** College of Graduate Studies, College of Languages, Literature and Social Sciences, Department of Psychology, Toledo, OH 43606-3390. Offers clinical psychology (MA, PhD); experimental psychology (MA, PhD). *Accreditation:* APA. *Degree requirements:* For master's, comprehensive exam, thesis; for doctorate, comprehensive exam, thesis/dissertation. *Entrance requirements:* For master's and doctorate, GRE General Test, GRE Subject Test, minimum cumulative point-hour ratio of 2.7 for all previous academic work, three letters of recommendation, statement of purpose, transcripts from all prior institutions attended. Additional exam requirements/recommendations for international students: Required—TOEFL (minimum score 550 paper-based; 80 iBT). Electronic applications accepted. *Faculty research:* Neural taste response.

**The University of Tulsa,** Graduate School, Kendall College of Arts and Sciences, Department of Psychology, Program in Clinical Psychology, Tulsa, OK 74104-3189. Offers MA, PhD, JD/MA. *Accreditation:* APA (one or more programs are accredited). *Program availability:* Part-time. *Faculty:* 8 full-time (3 women). *Students:* 33 full-time (23 women), 2 part-time (both women); includes 8 minority (5 Asian, non-Hispanic/Latino; 3 Hispanic/Latino). Average age 26. 122 applicants, 10% accepted, 7 enrolled. In 2016, 8

## Clinical Psychology

master's, 6 doctorates awarded. Terminal master's awarded for partial completion of doctoral program. *Degree requirements:* For master's, thesis (for some programs), 6 credit hours of practicum training; for doctorate, comprehensive exam, thesis/dissertation, 1-year pre-doctoral internship. *Entrance requirements:* For master's and doctorate, GRE General Test, interview, resume. Additional exam requirements/recommendations for international students: Required—TOEFL (minimum score 577 paper-based; 91 iBT), IELTS (minimum score 6.5). *Application deadline:* For fall admission, 12/1 for domestic and international students. Application fee: $55. Electronic applications accepted. *Expenses:* Tuition: Full-time $22,230; part-time $1235 per credit hour. *Required fees:* $990 per semester. Tuition and fees vary according to course load. *Financial support:* In 2016–17, 35 students received support, including 5 fellowships with full tuition reimbursements available (averaging $20,566 per year), 17 research assistantships with full tuition reimbursements available (averaging $14,346 per year), 6 teaching assistantships with full tuition reimbursements available (averaging $13,908 per year); career-related internships or fieldwork, Federal Work-Study, health care benefits, tuition waivers (full and partial), and unspecified assistantships also available. Support available to part-time students. Financial award application deadline: 2/1; financial award applicants required to submit FAFSA. *Faculty research:* Traumatic stress studies, randomized control trials of exposure treatments, pain modulation, neuropsychological assessment of health/mental health, psychological assessment, psychometrics, ethics, longitudinal assessment of child development, trauma and journalism, MMPI studies. *Total annual research expenditures:* $706,887. *Unit head:* Dr. Michael Basso, Director, 918-631-3151, Fax: 918-631-2836, E-mail: michael-basso@utulsa.edu. *Application contact:* Information Contact, 800-882-4723, E-mail: grad@utulsa.edu.

**University of Utah,** Graduate School, College of Education, Department of Educational Psychology, Salt Lake City, UT 84111. Offers clinical mental health counseling (M Ed); counseling psychology (PhD); elementary education (M Ed); instructional design and educational technology (M Ed); instructional design and technology (MS); learning and cognition (MS, PhD); reading and literacy (M Ed, PhD); school counseling (M Ed); school psychology (M Ed, PhD, Ed S); statistics (M Stat). *Accreditation:* APA (one or more programs are accredited). *Faculty:* 23 full-time (12 women), 15 part-time/adjunct (10 women). *Students:* 119 full-time (95 women), 106 part-time (74 women); includes 37 minority (2 Black or African American, non-Hispanic/Latino; 6 Asian, non-Hispanic/Latino; 22 Hispanic/Latino; 7 Two or more races, non-Hispanic/Latino), 6 international. Average age 31. 296 applicants, 27% accepted, 73 enrolled. In 2016, 47 master's, 8 doctorates awarded. Terminal master's awarded for partial completion of doctoral program. *Degree requirements:* For master's, variable foreign language requirement, comprehensive exam (for some programs), thesis (for some programs), projects; for doctorate, variable foreign language requirement, comprehensive exam, thesis/dissertation, oral exam. *Entrance requirements:* For master's and doctorate, GRE General Test, minimum GPA of 3.0. Additional exam requirements/recommendations for international students: Required—TOEFL (minimum score 80 iBT). *Application deadline:* For fall admission, 12/15 for domestic and international students; for winter admission, 11/1 for domestic and international students; for spring admission, 3/15 for domestic and international students. Application fee: $55 ($65 for international students). Electronic applications accepted. *Expenses:* Contact institution. *Financial support:* In 2016–17, 84 students received support, including 12 fellowships with full and partial tuition reimbursements available (averaging $18,000 per year), 21 research assistantships with full and partial tuition reimbursements available (averaging $14,500 per year), 57 teaching assistantships with full and partial tuition reimbursements available (averaging $14,500 per year); career-related internships or fieldwork, Federal Work-Study, institutionally sponsored loans, scholarships/grants, traineeships, health care benefits, and unspecified assistantships also available. Financial award application deadline: 4/1; financial award applicants required to submit FAFSA. *Faculty research:* Autism, computer technology and instruction, cognitive behavior, aging, group counseling. *Total annual research expenditures:* $620,935. *Unit head:* Dr. Anne E. Cook, Chair, 801-581-7148, Fax: 801-581-5566, E-mail: anne.cook@utah.edu. *Application contact:* JoLynn N. Yates, Academic Coordinator, 801-581-7148, Fax: 801-581-5566, E-mail: jo.yates@utah.edu.
Website: http://www.ed.utah.edu/edps/

**University of Utah,** Graduate School, College of Social and Behavioral Science, Department of Psychology, Salt Lake City, UT 84112. Offers clinical psychology (PhD); psychology (PhD). *Accreditation:* APA. *Faculty:* 26 full-time (13 women), 12 part-time/adjunct (5 women). *Students:* 55 full-time (35 women), 10 part-time (8 women); includes 11 minority (2 Black or African American, non-Hispanic/Latino; 3 Asian, non-Hispanic/Latino; 4 Hispanic/Latino; 2 Two or more races, non-Hispanic/Latino), 3 international. Average age 28. 295 applicants, 8% accepted, 13 enrolled. In 2016, 5 doctorates awarded. *Degree requirements:* For doctorate, thesis/dissertation. *Entrance requirements:* For doctorate, GRE General Test. Additional exam requirements/recommendations for international students: Required—TOEFL (minimum score 500 paper-based). *Application deadline:* For fall admission, 12/15 for domestic and international students. Application fee: $55 ($65 for international students). Electronic applications accepted. *Expenses:* Tuition, state resident: full-time $7011; part-time $3918.24 per credit hour. Tuition, nonresident: full-time $22,154; part-time $11,665.42 per credit hour. *Financial support:* In 2016–17, 56 students received support, including 2 fellowships with full tuition reimbursements available (averaging $17,000 per year), 19 research assistantships with full tuition reimbursements available (averaging $16,800 per year), 34 teaching assistantships with full tuition reimbursements available (averaging $16,800 per year); career-related internships or fieldwork, health care benefits, and unspecified assistantships also available. Financial award applicants required to submit FAFSA. *Faculty research:* Cognitive neuroscience, health, social cognition, psychopathology, cognitive and social development. *Total annual research expenditures:* $1.9 million. *Unit head:* Dr. Lisa G. Aspinwall, Chair, 801-581-8925, Fax: 801-581-5841, E-mail: lisa.aspinwall@utah.edu. *Application contact:* Nancy Seegmiller, Program Manager, 801-581-8925, Fax: 801-581-5841, E-mail: nancy.seegmiller@psych.utah.edu.
Website: http://www.psych.utah.edu/

**University of Vermont,** Graduate College, College of Arts and Sciences, Department of Psychology, Burlington, VT 05405. Offers clinical psychology (PhD); psychology (PhD). *Accreditation:* APA. *Degree requirements:* For doctorate, thesis/dissertation. *Entrance requirements:* For doctorate, GRE General Test, writing sample (for clinical psychology). Additional exam requirements/recommendations for international students: Required—TOEFL (minimum score 550 paper-based; 80 iBT). Electronic applications accepted. *Expenses:* Tuition, state resident: full-time $5814. Tuition, nonresident: full-time $14,670.

**University of Victoria,** Faculty of Graduate Studies, Faculty of Social Sciences, Department of Psychology, Victoria, BC V8W 2Y2, Canada. Offers clinical psychology (PhD); clinical psychology (neuropsychology) (M Sc); cognition and brain science (M Sc, PhD); experimental neuropsychology (M Sc, PhD); individualized study (M Sc, PhD); life span development psychology (PhD); life span developmental psychology (M Sc); social psychology (M Sc, PhD). *Degree requirements:* For master's, thesis; for doctorate, thesis/dissertation, candidacy exam. *Entrance requirements:* For master's and doctorate, GRE General Test. Additional exam requirements/recommendations for international students: Required—TOEFL (minimum score 600 paper-based). Electronic applications accepted. *Faculty research:* Life span development psychology and aging, behavioral neuroscience, cognitive psychology, behavioral psychology, environmental psychology.

**University of Virginia,** Curry School of Education, Department of Human Services, Program in Clinical and School Psychology, Charlottesville, VA 22903. Offers PhD. *Students:* 20 full-time (19 women), 2 part-time (both women); includes 7 minority (3 Black or African American, non-Hispanic/Latino; 1 Asian, non-Hispanic/Latino; 1 Hispanic/Latino), 4% accepted, 5 enrolled. In 2016, 6 doctorates awarded. *Expenses:* Tuition, state resident: full-time $15,026; part-time $834 per credit hour. Tuition, nonresident: full-time $25,168; part-time $1378 per credit hour. *Required fees:* $2654. *Unit head:* Jason Downer, Program Area Director, 434-924-0792, E-mail: jdowner@virginia.edu. *Application contact:* Eric Molnar, Assistant Director, Admissions and Enrollment Reporting, 434-243-2085, E-mail: eric.molnar@virginia.edu.
Website: http://curry.virginia.edu/academics/areas-of-study/clinical-school-psychology

**University of Washington,** Graduate School, College of Arts and Sciences, Department of Psychology, Seattle, WA 98195. Offers animal behavior (PhD); child psychology (PhD); clinical psychology (PhD); cognition and perception (PhD); developmental psychology (PhD); quantitative psychology (PhD); social psychology and personality (PhD). *Accreditation:* APA. *Degree requirements:* For doctorate, thesis/dissertation. *Entrance requirements:* For doctorate, GRE General Test, minimum GPA of 3.0. Electronic applications accepted. *Faculty research:* Addictive behaviors, artificial intelligence, child psychopathology, mechanisms and development of vision, physiology of ingestive behaviors.

**University of Windsor,** Faculty of Graduate Studies, Faculty of Arts and Social Sciences, Department of Psychology, Windsor, ON N9B 3P4, Canada. Offers adult clinical (MA, PhD); applied social psychology (MA, PhD); child clinical (MA, PhD); clinical neuropsychology (MA, PhD). *Degree requirements:* For master's, thesis; for doctorate, comprehensive exam, thesis/dissertation. *Entrance requirements:* For master's, GRE General Test, GRE Subject Test in psychology, minimum B average; for doctorate, GRE General Test, GRE Subject Test in psychology, master's degree. Additional exam requirements/recommendations for international students: Required—TOEFL (minimum score 600 paper-based). Electronic applications accepted. *Faculty research:* Gambling, suicidology, emotional competence, psychotherapy and trauma.

**University of Wisconsin–Madison,** Graduate School, College of Letters and Science, Department of Psychology, Program in Clinical Psychology, Madison, WI 53706-1380. Offers PhD. *Accreditation:* APA. *Degree requirements:* For doctorate, comprehensive exam, thesis/dissertation. *Entrance requirements:* For doctorate, GRE General Test, minimum undergraduate GPA of 3.0. Additional exam requirements/recommendations for international students: Required—TOEFL. Electronic applications accepted.

**University of Wisconsin–Milwaukee,** Graduate School, College of Letters and Science, Department of Psychology, Milwaukee, WI 53201-0413. Offers experimental psychology (MS, PhD), including behavior analysis, health and social psychology (PhD), health psychology (MS), neuroscience (PhD); psychology (PhD), including clinical psychology. *Accreditation:* APA (one or more programs are accredited). *Students:* 67 full-time (46 women), 19 part-time (11 women); includes 8 minority (2 Asian, non-Hispanic/Latino; 1 Hispanic/Latino; 5 Two or more races, non-Hispanic/Latino), 9 international. Average age 28. 254 applicants, 7% accepted, 16 enrolled. In 2016, 15 master's, 10 doctorates awarded. *Degree requirements:* For master's, thesis; for doctorate, variable foreign language requirement, thesis/dissertation. *Entrance requirements:* For master's and doctorate, GRE General Test, GRE Subject Test. Additional exam requirements/recommendations for international students: Required—TOEFL (minimum score 550 paper-based; 79 iBT), IELTS (minimum score 6.5). *Application deadline:* For fall admission, 1/1 priority date for domestic students; for spring admission, 9/1 for domestic students. Applications are processed on a rolling basis. Application fee: $56 ($96 for international students). Electronic applications accepted. *Financial support:* In 2016–17, 8 fellowships, 6 research assistantships, 46 teaching assistantships were awarded; career-related internships or fieldwork, unspecified assistantships, and project assistantships also available. Support available to part-time students. Financial award application deadline: 4/15; financial award applicants required to submit FAFSA. *Unit head:* Douglas Woods, Department Chair, 414-229-6636, E-mail: dwoods@uwm.edu. *Application contact:* General Information Contact, 414-229-4982, Fax: 414-229-6967, E-mail: gradschool@uwm.edu.
Website: http://www.uwm.edu/dept/psychology/

**University of Wisconsin–Stout,** Graduate School, College of Education, Health and Human Sciences, Program in Clinical Mental Health Counseling, Menomonie, WI 54751. Offers MS. *Accreditation:* ACA. *Program availability:* Part-time. *Degree requirements:* For master's, comprehensive exam or thesis. *Entrance requirements:* For master's, minimum GPA of 2.75. Additional exam requirements/recommendations for international students: Required—TOEFL (minimum score 500 paper-based; 61 iBT). Electronic applications accepted. *Faculty research:* Body image, gender issues, eating disorders, cognitive behavioral therapy.

**Utah State University,** School of Graduate Studies, Emma Eccles Jones College of Education and Human Services, Department of Psychology, Logan, UT 84322. Offers clinical/counseling/school psychology (PhD); research and evaluation methodology (PhD); school counseling (MS); school psychology (MS). *Accreditation:* APA (one or more programs are accredited). *Program availability:* Part-time, evening/weekend, online learning. Terminal master's awarded for partial completion of doctoral program. *Degree requirements:* For master's, thesis (for some programs); for doctorate, thesis/dissertation. *Entrance requirements:* For master's, GRE General Test (school psychology), MAT (school counseling), minimum GPA of 3.5; for doctorate, GRE General Test, minimum GPA of 3.5. Additional exam requirements/recommendations for international students: Required—TOEFL. *Faculty research:* Hearing loss detection in infancy, ADHD, eating disorders, domestic violence, neuropsychology, bilingual/Spanish speaking students/parents.

**Valparaiso University,** Graduate School and Continuing Education, Department of Psychology, Valparaiso, IN 46383. Offers clinical mental health counseling (MA); JD/MA. *Program availability:* Part-time, evening/weekend. *Degree requirements:* For master's, thesis or alternative, internship. *Entrance requirements:* For master's, minimum GPA of 3.0; 15 credits in the social/behavioral sciences (psychology, sociology, human development, etc.) with minimum GPA of 3.0; course in introductory psychology; recent statistics course with minimum B average. Additional exam requirements/recommendations for international students: Required—TOEFL (minimum score 550 paper-based; 80 iBT), IELTS (minimum score 6). Electronic applications accepted. *Expenses:* Tuition: Full-time $11,070; part-time $615 per credit hour. *Required fees:* $116 per semester. Tuition and fees vary according to course load, degree level and program. *Faculty research:* Environmental psychology, human sexuality, developmental psychopathology, social psychology.

**Vanguard University of Southern California,** Graduate Program in Clinical Psychology, Costa Mesa, CA 92626-9601. Offers MS. *Program availability:* Part-time, evening/weekend. *Degree requirements:* For master's, thesis or alternative, completion of personal therapy. *Entrance requirements:* For master's, minimum GPA of 3.0. Additional exam requirements/recommendations for international students: Required—TOEFL (minimum score 550 paper-based; 79 iBT). Electronic applications accepted. *Expenses:* Contact institution.

**Virginia Commonwealth University,** Graduate School, College of Humanities and Sciences, Department of Psychology, Program in Clinical Psychology, Richmond, VA 23284-9005. Offers behavioral medicine (PhD); clinical child psychology (PhD). *Accreditation:* APA. *Degree requirements:* For doctorate, thesis/dissertation. *Entrance requirements:* For doctorate, GRE General Test. Additional exam requirements/recommendations for international students: Required—TOEFL (minimum score 600 paper-based; 100 iBT); Recommended—IELTS (minimum score 6.5). *Application deadline:* For fall admission, 12/1 for domestic students. Application fee: $50. Electronic applications accepted. *Financial support:* Fellowships, research assistantships, teaching assistantships, Federal Work-Study, institutionally sponsored loans, and scholarships/grants available. Support available to part-time students. *Faculty research:* Clinical child/adolescent and behavioral medicine. *Unit head:* Dr. Michael Southam-Gerow, Director of Graduate Studies, 804-827-0585, Fax: 804-828-2237, E-mail: masouthamger@vcu.edu. *Application contact:* Dr. Bruce D. Rybarczyk, Program Director, 804-827-1675, Fax: 804-828-2237, E-mail: bdrybarczyk@vcu.edu. Website: http://www.psychology.vcu.edu/clinical/index.shtml

**Virginia State University,** College of Graduate Studies, College of Natural and Health Sciences, Department of Psychology, Petersburg, VA 23806-0001. Offers behavioral and community health sciences (PhD); clinical health psychology (PhD); clinical psychology (MS); general psychology (MS). *Degree requirements:* For master's, one foreign language, thesis. *Entrance requirements:* For master's, GRE General Test.

**Walden University,** Graduate Programs, School of Psychology, Minneapolis, MN 55401. Offers clinical psychology (MS), including counseling, general program; forensic psychology (MS), including forensic psychology in the community, general program, mental health applications, program planning and evaluation in forensic settings, psychology and legal systems; industrial organizational (MS, PhD), including consulting psychology, forensic (MS), forensic psychology (PhD), general practice, leadership development and coaching (MS), organizational diversity and social change, research evaluation (PhD); online teaching in psychology (Post-Master's Certificate); organizational psychology and development (Postbaccalaureate Certificate); psychology (MS, PhD), including applied psychology (MS), clinical psychology (PhD), crisis management and response (MS), educational psychology, forensic psychology (PhD), general psychology (MS), general psychology research (PhD), general psychology teaching (PhD), health psychology, leadership development and coaching (MS), psychology of culture (MS), psychology, public administration, and social change (MS), social psychology, terrorism and security (MS); psychology respecialization (Post-Doctoral Certificate). *Program availability:* Part-time, evening/weekend, online only, 100% online. Terminal master's awarded for partial completion of doctoral program. *Degree requirements:* For master's, thesis optional; for doctorate, thesis/dissertation, residency. *Entrance requirements:* For master's, bachelor's degree or higher; minimum GPA of 2.5; official transcripts; goal statement (for some programs); access to computer and Internet; for doctorate, master's degree or higher; three years of related professional or academic experience (preferred); minimum GPA of 3.0; goal statement and current resume (for select programs); official transcripts; access to computer and Internet; for other advanced degree, relevant work experience; access to computer and Internet. Additional exam requirements/recommendations for international students: Required—TOEFL (minimum score 550 paper-based, 79 iBT), IELTS (minimum score 6.5), Michigan English Language Assessment Battery (minimum score 82), or PTE (minimum score 53). Electronic applications accepted.

**Washburn University,** College of Arts and Sciences, Department of Psychology, Topeka, KS 66621. Offers clinical psychology (MA). *Program availability:* Part-time. *Degree requirements:* For master's, comprehensive exam (for some programs), thesis or alternative. *Entrance requirements:* For master's, GRE General Test, 15 hours of undergraduate course work in psychology. Additional exam requirements/recommendations for international students: Required—TOEFL (minimum score 80 iBT). Electronic applications accepted. *Faculty research:* Metacognition, anxiety disorders, auditory perception, sports performance psychology, ADHD.

**Washington State University,** College of Arts and Sciences, Department of Psychology, Pullman, WA 99164. Offers clinical psychology (PhD); experimental psychology (PhD). Program applications must be made through the Pullman campus. *Accreditation:* APA (one or more programs are accredited). *Degree requirements:* For doctorate, comprehensive exam, thesis/dissertation, oral exam, written exam. *Entrance requirements:* For doctorate, GRE General Test, three letters of reference; summary data form; at least 18 credits of study in psychology; at least one course in statistics and research methodology; official transcripts; minimum cumulative undergraduate GPA of 3.0 or master's degree in psychology. Additional exam requirements/recommendations for international students: Required—TOEFL, IELTS. Electronic applications accepted. *Faculty research:* Adult psychopathology and therapy, child psychopathology, neuropsychology, health psychology.

**Waynesburg University,** Graduate and Professional Studies, Canonsburg, PA 15370. Offers business (MBA), including energy management, finance, health systems, human resources, leadership, market development; counseling (MA), including addictions counseling, clinical mental health; counselor education and supervision (PhD); criminal investigation (MA); education (M Ed), including autism, curriculum and instruction, educational leadership, online teaching; nursing (MSN), including administration, education, informatics; nursing practice (DNP); special education (M Ed); technology (M Ed); MSN/MBA. *Accreditation:* AACN. *Program availability:* Part-time, evening/weekend. *Degree requirements:* For doctorate, thesis/dissertation. *Entrance requirements:* Additional exam requirements/recommendations for international students: Required—TOEFL. Electronic applications accepted.

**Wayne State University,** College of Liberal Arts and Sciences, Department of Psychology, Detroit, MI 48202. Offers behavioral and cognitive neuroscience (PhD); clinical psychology (PhD); cognitive, developmental and social psychology (PhD); industrial/organizational psychology (MA, PhD). Doctoral program admits for fall only. *Accreditation:* APA (one or more programs are accredited). *Faculty:* 36. *Students:* 98 full-time (65 women), 31 part-time (16 women); includes 19 minority (4 Black or African American, non-Hispanic/Latino; 2 Asian, non-Hispanic/Latino; 8 Hispanic/Latino; 5 Two or more races, non-Hispanic/Latino), 14 international. Average age 28. 478 applicants, 13% accepted, 33 enrolled. In 2016, 16 master's, 13 doctorates awarded. Terminal master's awarded for partial completion of doctoral program. *Degree requirements:* For master's, thesis (for some programs); for doctorate, thesis/dissertation, training assignments. *Entrance requirements:* For master's, GRE General Test, minimum undergraduate upper-division cumulative GPA of 3.0, courses in introductory psychology and statistics, two letters of recommendation, professional statement; for doctorate, GRE General Test, bachelor's, master's, or other advanced degree; at least twelve credits in psychology with minimum GPA of 3.0; courses in laboratory psychology and statistical methods in psychology; at least three letters of recommendation; statement of purpose. Additional exam requirements/recommendations for international students: Required—TOEFL (minimum score 550 paper-based; 79 iBT), TWE (minimum

score 5.5), Michigan English Language Assessment Battery (minimum score 85); Recommended—IELTS (minimum score 6.5). Application fee: $50. Electronic applications accepted. *Expenses:* $16,503 per year resident tuition and fees, $33,697 per year non-resident tuition and fees. *Financial support:* In 2016–17, 90 students received support, including 12 fellowships with tuition reimbursements available (averaging $15,719 per year), 6 research assistantships with tuition reimbursements available (averaging $19,341 per year), 50 teaching assistantships with tuition reimbursements available (averaging $17,994 per year); scholarships/grants, health care benefits, and unspecified assistantships also available. Financial award applicants required to submit FAFSA. *Faculty research:* Behavioral neuroscience, cognitive/neuroscience of development and aging research, children, adolescents, and family research, cognition research, emotion research, health psychology research, homelessness and poverty research, memory research, neuropsychology research, personality/cognition, relationships research, substance use and abuse research, workplace adaptation, well-being and evaluation research. *Total annual research expenditures:* $1.4 million. *Unit head:* Boris Baltes, PhD, Chair/Professor, 313-577-2803, E-mail: b.baltes@wayne.edu. *Application contact:* Alia Allen, Academic Services Officer, 313-577-2823, E-mail: aallen@wayne.edu. Website: http://clas.wayne.edu/psychology/

**West Chester University of Pennsylvania,** College of Education and Social Work, Department of Counselor Education, West Chester, PA 19383. Offers clinical mental health counseling (MS); counseling (Certificate); higher education counseling (Post Master's Certificate); higher education counseling/student affairs (MS, Certificate); school counseling (M Ed). *Accreditation:* ACA; NCATE. *Program availability:* Part-time, evening/weekend. *Faculty:* 10 full-time (6 women), 5 part-time/adjunct (3 women). *Students:* 130 full-time (100 women), 65 part-time (55 women); includes 48 minority (27 Black or African American, non-Hispanic/Latino; 2 Asian, non-Hispanic/Latino; 13 Hispanic/Latino; 6 Two or more races, non-Hispanic/Latino), 1 international. Average age 27. 199 applicants, 56% accepted, 66 enrolled. In 2016, 78 master's, 3 other advanced degrees awarded. *Degree requirements:* For master's, comprehensive exam. *Entrance requirements:* For master's, minimum GPA of 3.0, three letters of reference. Additional exam requirements/recommendations for international students: Required—TOEFL or IELTS. *Application deadline:* For fall admission, 5/15 for international students; for spring admission, 10/15 for international students. Applications are processed on a rolling basis. Application fee: $50. Electronic applications accepted. *Expenses:* Tuition, state resident: full-time $8694; part-time $483 per credit. Tuition, nonresident: full-time $13,050; part-time $725 per credit. *Required fees:* $2399; $119.05 per credit. Tuition and fees vary according to campus/location and program. *Financial support:* Scholarships/grants and unspecified assistantships available. Financial award application deadline: 2/15; financial award applicants required to submit FAFSA. *Faculty research:* Teacher and student cognition, adolescent cognitive development, college counseling, motivational interviewing. *Unit head:* Dr. Eric Owens, Chair, 610-436-2559, Fax: 610-425-7432, E-mail: eowens@wcupa.edu. *Application contact:* Dr. Cheryl Neale-McFall, Graduate Coordinator, 610-436-2559, Fax: 610-425-7432, E-mail: cneale-mcfall@wcupa.edu. Website: http://www.wcupa.edu/education-socialWork/counselorEducation/

**West Chester University of Pennsylvania,** College of the Sciences and Mathematics, Department of Psychology, West Chester, PA 19383. Offers clinical psychology (Psy D); industrial/organizational psychology (Certificate); psychology (MA), including general psychology, industrial/organizational psychology. *Program availability:* Part-time, evening/weekend. *Faculty:* 13 full-time (11 women), 6 part-time/adjunct (5 women). *Students:* 76 full-time (55 women), 20 part-time (14 women); includes 21 minority (10 Black or African American, non-Hispanic/Latino; 1 Asian, non-Hispanic/Latino; 5 Hispanic/Latino; 5 Two or more races, non-Hispanic/Latino), 1 international. Average age 28. 122 applicants, 58% accepted, 35 enrolled. In 2016, 33 master's awarded. *Degree requirements:* For master's, comprehensive exam, thesis (for some programs). *Entrance requirements:* For master's, GRE General Test, minimum GPA of 3.0 overall, psychology 3.25; three letters of reference; for doctorate, GRE General Test, minimum GPA of 3.0 overall, psychology 3.25; three letters of reference; successful completion of psychology courses at the undergraduate and graduate level in abnormal/clinical psychology, research methods, and statistics; personal goals statement. Additional exam requirements/recommendations for international students: Required—TOEFL or IELTS. *Application deadline:* For fall admission, 5/15 for international students; for spring admission, 10/15 for international students. Applications are processed on a rolling basis. Application fee: $50. Electronic applications accepted. *Expenses:* Tuition, state resident: full-time $8694; part-time $483 per credit. Tuition, nonresident: full-time $13,050; part-time $725 per credit. *Required fees:* $2399; $119.05 per credit. Tuition and fees vary according to campus/location and program. *Financial support:* Scholarships/grants and unspecified assistantships available. Financial award application deadline: 2/15; financial award applicants required to submit FAFSA. *Faculty research:* Stress, coping, and resilience; preventative interventions; workplace stress; organizational leadership; eating disorders; schizophrenia; several other areas including diversity, cognition, and animal behavior. *Unit head:* Dr. Sandra Kerr, Interim Chairperson, 610-436-2945, E-mail: skerr@wcupa.edu. *Application contact:* Dr. Angela Clarke, Graduate Coordinator, 610-436-3136, E-mail: aclarke@wcupa.edu. Website: http://www.wcupa.edu/sciences-mathematics/psychology/

**Western Connecticut State University,** Division of Graduate Studies, School of Professional Studies, Department of Education and Educational Psychology, Program in Clinical Mental Health Counseling, Danbury, CT 06810-6885. Offers MS. *Accreditation:* ACA. *Program availability:* Part-time. *Degree requirements:* For master's, practicum, internship, completion of program in 6 years. *Entrance requirements:* For master's, minimum GPA of 2.8, 3 letters of reference, interview, 9 hours of psychology. Additional exam requirements/recommendations for international students: Recommended—TOEFL (minimum score 550 paper-based; 79 iBT), IELTS (minimum score 6).

**Western Illinois University,** School of Graduate Studies, College of Arts and Sciences, Department of Psychology, Macomb, IL 61455-1390. Offers clinical/community mental health (MS); general experimental psychology (MS); school psychology (SSP). *Program availability:* Part-time. *Students:* 37 full-time (22 women), 15 part-time (13 women); includes 6 minority (1 Black or African American, non-Hispanic/Latino; 2 Hispanic/Latino; 3 Two or more races, non-Hispanic/Latino), 2 international. Average age 25. 66 applicants, 52% accepted, 14 enrolled. In 2016, 11 master's, 7 other advanced degrees awarded. *Degree requirements:* For master's, comprehensive exam (for some programs), thesis or alternative. *Entrance requirements:* For master's and SSP, GRE General Test. Additional exam requirements/recommendations for international students: Required—TOEFL (minimum score 550 paper-based; 80 iBT). Application fee: $30. Electronic applications accepted. *Financial support:* In 2016–17, 34 students received support, including 6 research assistantships with full tuition reimbursements available (averaging $7,544 per year); unspecified assistantships also available. Financial award applicants required to submit FAFSA. *Unit head:* Dr. Karen Sears, Chairperson, 309-298-1593. *Application contact:* Dr. Nancy Parsons, Associate Provost and Director of Graduate Studies, 309-298-1806, Fax: 309-298-2345, E-mail: grad-office@wiu.edu. Website: http://wiu.edu/psychology

## Clinical Psychology

**Western Kentucky University,** Graduate Studies, College of Education and Behavioral Sciences, Department of Psychology, Bowling Green, KY 42101. Offers clinical psychology (MA); experimental psychology (MA); general psychology (MA); industrial/organizational psychology (MA); school psychology (Ed S). *Degree requirements:* For master's, comprehensive exam, thesis (for some programs); for Ed S, thesis, oral exam. *Entrance requirements:* For master's, GRE General Test; for Ed S, GRE General Test, minimum GPA of 3.5. Additional exam requirements/recommendations for international students: Required—TOEFL (minimum score 555 paper-based; 79 iBT). *Faculty research:* Neural regeneration, enhancing mobility in the elderly, improvement in visual processing in older adults, lifespan development.

**Western Michigan University,** Graduate College, College of Arts and Sciences, Department of Psychology, Kalamazoo, MI 49008. Offers behavior analysis (MA, PhD); clinical psychology (PhD); industrial/organizational behavior management (MA). *Accreditation:* APA (one or more programs are accredited). *Degree requirements:* For master's, variable foreign language requirement, thesis; for doctorate, 2 foreign languages, comprehensive exam, thesis/dissertation.

**West Virginia University,** Eberly College of Arts and Sciences, Department of Psychology, Morgantown, WV 26506. Offers behavior analysis (PhD); clinical psychology (MA, PhD); development psychology (PhD); psychology (MS). *Accreditation:* APA (one or more programs are accredited). *Program availability:* Part-time. Terminal master's awarded for partial completion of doctoral program. *Degree requirements:* For master's, thesis optional; for doctorate, comprehensive exam, thesis/dissertation. *Entrance requirements:* For master's and doctorate, GRE General Test, minimum GPA of 3.0. Additional exam requirements/recommendations for international students: Required—TOEFL. *Faculty research:* Adult and child clinical psychology, behavioral assessment and therapy, child and adolescent behavior, life span development, experimental and applied behavior analysis.

**Wheaton College,** Graduate School, Department of Psychology, Wheaton, IL 60187-5593. Offers clinical mental health counseling (MA); clinical psychology (Psy D); counseling ministries (MA); marriage and family therapy (MA). *Accreditation:* APA (one or more programs are accredited). *Faculty:* 14 full-time (7 women), 9 part-time/adjunct (5 women). *Students:* 130 full-time (97 women), 17 part-time (13 women); includes 38 minority (13 Black or African American, non-Hispanic/Latino; 1 American Indian or Alaska Native, non-Hispanic/Latino; 9 Asian, non-Hispanic/Latino; 8 Hispanic/Latino; 7 Two or more races, non-Hispanic/Latino), 17 international. Average age 28. 115 applicants, 80% accepted, 58 enrolled. In 2016, 70 master's, 9 doctorates awarded. Terminal master's awarded for partial completion of doctoral program. *Degree requirements:* For master's, thesis or alternative; for doctorate, thesis/dissertation, internship. *Entrance requirements:* For master's, GRE General Test, 18 hours of course work in psychology; for doctorate, GRE General Test. Additional exam requirements/recommendations for international students: Required—TOEFL (minimum score 550 paper-based; 80 iBT), IELTS (minimum score 6.5), TOEFL (minimum score 600 paper-based; 90 iBT) or IELTS (minimum score 7.5) for PsyD. *Application deadline:* For fall admission, 3/1 priority date for domestic students, 1/1 for international students. Applications are processed on a rolling basis. Application fee: $30. *Expenses: Tuition:* Full-time $19,080; part-time $795 per credit hour. Tuition and fees vary according to degree level and program. *Financial support:* In 2016–17, 3 research assistantships (averaging $4,800 per year) were awarded; career-related internships or fieldwork, Federal Work-Study, scholarships/grants, and unspecified assistantships also available. Financial award application deadline: 3/1; financial award applicants required to submit FAFSA. *Unit head:* Dr. Terri Watson, Associate Dean of Psychology, 630-752-5104, E-mail: psychology@wheaton.edu. *Application contact:* Dusty Di Santo, Director of Graduate Admissions, 630-752-5195, Fax: 630-752-7047, E-mail: graduate.admissions@wheaton.edu.
Website: http://www.wheaton.edu/academics/departments/psychology

**Wichita State University,** Graduate School, Fairmount College of Liberal Arts and Sciences, Department of Psychology, Wichita, KS 67260. Offers clinical (PhD); community (PhD); human factors (PhD). *Accreditation:* APA. *Program availability:* Part-time. *Application deadline:* For fall admission, 12/1 for domestic and international students. Application fee: $50 ($65 for international students). *Unit head:* Dr. Rhonda K. Lewis, Chair, 316-978-3170, Fax: 316-978-3006, E-mail: rhonda.lewis@wichita.edu. *Application contact:* Jordan Oleson, Admissions Coordinator, 316-978-3095, Fax: 316-978-3253, E-mail: jordan.oleson@wichita.edu.
Website: http://www.wichita.edu/psychology

**Widener University,** School of Human Service Professions, Institute for Graduate Clinical Psychology, Program in Clinical Psychology, Chester, PA 19013-5792. Offers Psy D, Psy D/M Ed, Psy D/MA, Psy D/MBA, Psy D/MHA, Psy D/MPA. *Accreditation:* APA. *Students:* 159 full-time (122 women), 15 part-time (10 women); includes 42 minority (10 Black or African American, non-Hispanic/Latino; 15 Asian, non-Hispanic/Latino; 13 Hispanic/Latino; 4 Two or more races, non-Hispanic/Latino), 3 international. Average age 24. In 2016, 26 doctorates awarded. *Degree requirements:* For doctorate, thesis/dissertation, final oral and written qualifying exams. *Entrance requirements:* For doctorate, GRE General Test or MAT. *Application deadline:* For fall admission, 12/31 for domestic students. Application fee: $75. Electronic applications accepted. *Expenses:* Contact institution. *Financial support:* Career-related internships or fieldwork, Federal Work-Study, institutionally sponsored loans, scholarships/grants, and stipends available. Financial award application deadline: 4/15. *Faculty research:* Cognitive and personality diagnostic testing, depression, child and adolescent competencies, learning disabilities, family therapy. *Unit head:* Dr. Virginia Brabender, Associate Dean/Director, 610-499-1208, Fax: 610-499-4625, E-mail: graduate.psychology@widener.edu. *Application contact:* Ellen Madison, Admissions Coordinator, 611-499-1206, Fax: 610-499-4625, E-mail: ellen.t.madison@widener.edu.
Website: http://www.widener.edu/academics/schools/shsp/psyd/default.aspx

**Widener University,** School of Human Service Professions, Institute for Graduate Clinical Psychology, Program in Clinical Psychology and Health and Medical Services Administration, Chester, PA 19013-5792. Offers Psy D/MBA, Psy D/MHA. *Accreditation:* APA (one or more programs are accredited); CAHME. *Faculty:* 15 full-time (6 women), 18 part-time/adjunct (10 women). *Students:* 3 full-time (2 women). Average age 28. *Application deadline:* For fall admission, 12/31 for domestic students. Application fee: $75. Electronic applications accepted. Tuition and fees vary according to degree level and program. *Financial support:* Career-related internships or fieldwork, Federal Work-Study, and institutionally sponsored loans available. Financial award application deadline: 5/31. *Faculty research:* Psychosocial competence, family systems, medical care systems and financing. *Unit head:* Dr. Hal Shorey, Director, 610-499-4598, Fax: 610-499-4625.

**William James College,** Graduate Programs, Newton, MA 02459. Offers applied psychology in higher education student personnel administration (MA); clinical psychology (Psy D); counseling psychology (MA); counseling psychology and community mental health (MA); counseling psychology and global mental health (MA); executive coaching (Graduate Certificate); forensic and counseling psychology (MA); leadership psychology (Psy D); organizational psychology (MA); primary care psychology (MA); respecialization in clinical psychology (Certificate); school psychology (Psy D); MA/CAGS. *Accreditation:* APA. *Degree requirements:* For master's,

comprehensive exam (for some programs); for doctorate, thesis/dissertation (for some programs). Electronic applications accepted.

**William Paterson University of New Jersey,** College of Humanities and Social Sciences, Wayne, NJ 07470-8420. Offers applied sociology (MA); clinical and counseling psychology (MA); clinical psychology (Psy D); creative and professional writing (MFA); English (MA); history (MA); political science and public policy (MA); public policy and international affairs (MA). *Program availability:* Part-time, evening/weekend. *Faculty:* 35 full-time (19 women), 8 part-time/adjunct (5 women). *Students:* 58 full-time (38 women), 62 part-time (46 women); includes 40 minority (9 Black or African American, non-Hispanic/Latino; 6 Asian, non-Hispanic/Latino; 21 Hispanic/Latino; 4 Two or more races, non-Hispanic/Latino), 4 international. Average age 32. 160 applicants, 55% accepted, 50 enrolled. In 2016, 56 master's awarded. *Degree requirements:* For master's, thesis (for some programs), internship (for some programs). *Entrance requirements:* For master's, GRE/MAT, minimum GPA of 3.0; 2 letters of recommendation; writing sample/personal statement. Additional exam requirements/recommendations for international students: Required—TOEFL (minimum score 550 paper-based; 79 iBT), IELTS (minimum score 6). *Application deadline:* For fall admission, 8/1 for domestic students, 4/1 for international students; for spring admission, 12/1 for domestic students, 11/1 for international students; for summer admission, 5/1 for domestic students, 2/1 for international students. Applications are processed on a rolling basis. Application fee: $50. Electronic applications accepted. *Expenses:* Tuition, state resident: full-time $12,480; part-time $611 per credit. Tuition, nonresident: full-time $20,263; part-time $992 per credit. *Required fees:* $1573; $77 per credit. Tuition and fees vary according to course load, degree level and program. *Financial support:* Career-related internships or fieldwork, Federal Work-Study, scholarships/grants, and unspecified assistantships available. Support available to part-time students. Financial award applicants required to submit FAFSA. *Faculty research:* Relationship violence among adolescents; autism in young children; game theory; gender, governance and empowerment in India; Chinese development policies concerning Africa. *Total annual research expenditures:* $162,900. *Unit head:* Dr. Kara Rabbitt, Dean, 973-720-2180, Fax: 973-720-2955, E-mail: rabbittk@wpunj.edu. *Application contact:* Tinu Adeniran, Associate Director, Graduate Admissions, 973-720-2764, Fax: 973-720-2035, E-mail: adenirant@wpunj.edu.
Website: http://www.wpunj.edu/cohss

**Wilmington University,** College of Social and Behavioral Sciences, New Castle, DE 19720-6491. Offers administration of human services (MS); administration of justice (MS); clinical mental health counseling (MS); homeland security (MS). *Accreditation:* ACA. *Program availability:* Part-time, evening/weekend. *Faculty:* 8 full-time (5 women), 79 part-time/adjunct (35 women). *Students:* 210 full-time (162 women), 444 part-time (325 women); includes 320 minority (285 Black or African American, non-Hispanic/Latino; 12 American Indian or Alaska Native, non-Hispanic/Latino; 9 Asian, non-Hispanic/Latino; 12 Hispanic/Latino; 1 Native Hawaiian or other Pacific Islander, non-Hispanic/Latino; 1 Two or more races, non-Hispanic/Latino), 4 international. Average age 35. 255 applicants, 100% accepted, 255 enrolled. In 2016, 248 master's awarded. *Entrance requirements:* Additional exam requirements/recommendations for international students: Required—TOEFL (minimum score 500 paper-based). *Application deadline:* Applications are processed on a rolling basis. Application fee: $35. Electronic applications accepted. *Expenses: Tuition:* Full-time $8388; part-time $466 per credit. *Required fees:* $25 per semester. Tuition and fees vary according to degree level. *Financial support:* Applicants required to submit FAFSA. *Unit head:* Dr. Edward L. Guthrie, Dean. *Application contact:* Laura Morris, Director of Admissions, 877-967-5464, E-mail: inquire@wilmcoll.edu.
Website: http://www.wilmu.edu/behavioralscience/

**Wisconsin School of Professional Psychology,** Program in Clinical Psychology, Milwaukee, WI 53225-4960. Offers MA, Psy D. *Accreditation:* APA. *Program availability:* Part-time, evening/weekend. Terminal master's awarded for partial completion of doctoral program. *Degree requirements:* For master's, candidacy exam, 500 hours of supervised clinical practica; for doctorate, thesis/dissertation, 1 year clinical intern and practicum experience (2000 hrs), candidacy and clinical exams. *Entrance requirements:* For master's, GRE General Test, GRE Subject Test, bachelor's degree in psychology, writing sample; for doctorate, GRE General Test, GRE Subject Test, master's degree in clinical psychology or equivalent, writing sample. *Faculty research:* Violence prevention, psychology of women, forensic psychology, custody evaluation, aging, harm reduction in AODA.

**Wright Institute,** Doctoral Program in Clinical Psychology, Berkeley, CA 94704. Offers Psy D. *Accreditation:* APA. *Degree requirements:* For doctorate, comprehensive exam, thesis/dissertation. *Entrance requirements:* For doctorate, GRE General Test, statistics, human development, theories of personality and/or abnormal psychology. Additional exam requirements/recommendations for international students: Required—TOEFL (minimum score 600 paper-based). *Application deadline:* For fall admission, 1/5 priority date for domestic and international students. Application fee: $50. Electronic applications accepted. *Financial support:* Research assistantships, teaching assistantships, career-related internships or fieldwork, Federal Work-Study, and scholarships/grants available. Financial award applicants required to submit FAFSA. *Unit head:* Dr. Gilbert Newman, Dean, 510-841-9230 Ext. 110, E-mail: gnewman@wi.edu. *Application contact:* John Pitts, Director of Admissions, 510-841-9230 Ext. 171, E-mail: jpitts@wi.edu.
Website: https://www.wi.edu/psyd-program

**Wright State University,** School of Professional Psychology, Dayton, OH 45435. Offers clinical psychology (Psy D). *Accreditation:* APA. *Degree requirements:* For doctorate, thesis/dissertation. *Entrance requirements:* For doctorate, GRE General Test, GRE Subject Test. Additional exam requirements/recommendations for international students: Required—TOEFL. *Application deadline:* For fall admission, 12/15 for domestic students. Application fee: $30. *Expenses:* Contact institution. *Financial support:* Fellowships, teaching assistantships, career-related internships or fieldwork, Federal Work-Study, institutionally sponsored loans, and unspecified assistantships available. Financial award application deadline: 4/15; financial award applicants required to submit FAFSA. *Unit head:* Dr. John R. Rudisill, Dean, 937-775-3490, Fax: 937-775-3434, E-mail: john.rudisill@wright.edu. *Application contact:* Leona L. Gray, Director, Student Services and Admissions, 937-775-3492, Fax: 937-775-3493, E-mail: leona.gray@wright.edu.
Website: http://www.wright.edu/sopp/

**Xavier University,** College of Social Sciences, Health and Education, Department of Psychology, Cincinnati, OH 45207. Offers clinical psychology (Psy D); industrial-organizational psychology (MA). *Accreditation:* APA (one or more programs are accredited). *Degree requirements:* For master's, one foreign language, comprehensive exam, thesis, internship; for doctorate, one foreign language, comprehensive exam, thesis/dissertation, internship. *Entrance requirements:* For master's, GRE, official transcript; 3 letters of recommendation; for doctorate, GRE General Test; GRE Subject Test in psychology (if no undergraduate degree in psychology), bachelor's or master's degree; 18 semester hours of psychology coursework; minimum GPA of 3.0; work and research experience; official transcript; 3 letters of recommendation; statement of purpose. Additional exam requirements/recommendations for international students:

Required—TOEFL (minimum score 550 paper-based; 79 iBT), IELTS (minimum score 6.5). Electronic applications accepted. *Expenses:* Contact institution. *Faculty research:* Older adults, clinical child and adolescent issues, personnel selection and employee behavior, at-risk youth, sexual abuse.

**Xavier University,** College of Social Sciences, Health and Education, School of Education, Department of Counseling, Cincinnati, OH 45207. Offers clinical mental health counseling (MA); school counseling (MA). *Program availability:* Part-time, evening/weekend. *Degree requirements:* For master's, internship. *Entrance requirements:* For master's, GRE or MAT, minimum GPA of 3.0; 2 letters of recommendation; resume; official transcript; statement of purpose. Additional exam requirements/recommendations for international students: Required—TOEFL (minimum score 550 paper-based; 79 iBT). Electronic applications accepted. Application fee is waived when completed online. *Expenses:* Contact institution. *Faculty research:* Supervision, ethics, consultation, self-injury, bullying.

**Yale University,** Graduate School of Arts and Sciences, Department of Psychology, New Haven, CT 06520. Offers behavioral neuroscience (PhD); clinical psychology

(PhD); cognitive psychology (PhD); developmental psychology (PhD); social/personality psychology (PhD). *Accreditation:* APA. *Degree requirements:* For doctorate, thesis/dissertation. *Entrance requirements:* For doctorate, GRE General Test.

**Yeshiva University,** Ferkauf Graduate School of Psychology, Program in Clinical Psychology, New York, NY 10033-3201. Offers Psy D. *Accreditation:* APA. *Program availability:* Part-time. *Degree requirements:* For doctorate, comprehensive exam, thesis/dissertation. *Entrance requirements:* For doctorate, GRE General Test. *Faculty research:* Psychotherapy, family therapy, psychoanalysis, cognitive behavior therapy.

**Yeshiva University,** Ferkauf Graduate School of Psychology, Program in School/Clinical-Child Psychology, New York, NY 10033-3201. Offers Psy D. *Accreditation:* APA. *Program availability:* Part-time. *Degree requirements:* For doctorate, comprehensive exam, thesis/dissertation. *Entrance requirements:* For doctorate, GRE General Test. *Faculty research:* Testing, early childhood intervention, child and adolescent psychotherapy, clinical child psychology.

# Cognitive Sciences

**American University,** College of Arts and Sciences, Department of Psychology, Washington, DC 22016-8062. Offers addiction and addictive behavior (Certificate); behavior, cognition, and neuroscience (PhD); clinical psychology (PhD); psychobiology of healing (Certificate); psychology (MA). *Accreditation:* APA. *Program availability:* Part-time. *Faculty:* 22 full-time (9 women), 11 part-time/adjunct (3 women). *Students:* 86 full-time (72 women), 12 part-time (9 women); includes 15 minority (5 Black or African American, non-Hispanic/Latino; 4 Asian, non-Hispanic/Latino; 4 Hispanic/Latino; 2 Two or more races, non-Hispanic/Latino), 6 international. Average age 28. 479 applicants, 12% accepted, 34 enrolled. In 2016, 27 master's, 13 doctorates awarded. *Degree requirements:* For master's, comprehensive exam, thesis or alternative; for doctorate, comprehensive exam, thesis/dissertation. *Entrance requirements:* For master's, GRE General Test, GRE Subject Test, statement of purpose, transcripts, 2 letters of recommendation; for doctorate, GRE General Test, GRE Subject Test, 3 letters of recommendation, statement of purpose, transcripts, resume. Additional exam requirements/recommendations for international students: Required—TOEFL (minimum score 100 iBT), IELTS (minimum score 7), PTE (minimum score 68). Application fee: $55. *Expenses:* $1,579 per credit tuition; $690 mandatory fees. *Financial support:* Research assistantships, teaching assistantships, institutionally sponsored loans, scholarships/grants, and unspecified assistantships available. Financial award application deadline: 2/1; financial award applicants required to submit FAFSA. *Unit head:* Dr. David Haaga, Department Chair, 202-885-1718, Fax: 202-885-1023, E-mail: ahrens@american.edu. *Application contact:* Kathleen Clowery, Associate Director, Graduate Admission, 202-885-3620, Fax: 202-885-1344, E-mail: clowery@american.edu.
Website: http://www.american.edu/CAS/Psychology/

**Arizona State University at the Tempe campus,** College of Liberal Arts and Sciences, Department of Psychology, Tempe, AZ 85287-1104. Offers applied behavior analysis (MS); behavioral neuroscience (PhD); clinical psychology (PhD); cognitive science (PhD); developmental psychology (PhD); quantitative psychology (PhD); social psychology (PhD). *Accreditation:* APA. *Degree requirements:* For doctorate, comprehensive exam, thesis/dissertation, interactive Program of Study (iPOS) submitted before completing 50 percent of required credit hours. *Entrance requirements:* For doctorate, GRE General Test, GRE Subject Test, minimum GPA of 3.0 or equivalent in last 2 years of work leading to bachelor's degree. Additional exam requirements/recommendations for international students: Required—TOEFL, IELTS, or PTE. Electronic applications accepted.

**Arizona State University at the Tempe campus,** Ira A. Fulton Schools of Engineering, The Polytechnic School, Department of Engineering, Mesa, AZ 85212. Offers simulation, modeling, and applied cognitive science (PhD). *Program availability:* Part-time. *Degree requirements:* For doctorate, comprehensive exam, thesis/dissertation, interactive Program of Study (iPOS) submitted before completing 50 percent of required credit hours. *Entrance requirements:* For doctorate, GRE, master's degree in psychology, engineering, cognitive science, or computer science; 3 letters of recommendation; statement of research interests. Additional exam requirements/recommendations for international students: Required—TOEFL, IELTS, or PTE. Electronic applications accepted. *Faculty research:* Software process and automated workflow, software architecture, dotal technologies, relational database systems, embedded systems.

**Ball State University,** Graduate School, College of Sciences and Humanities, Department of Psychological Science, Program in Cognitive and Social Processes, Muncie, IN 47306. Offers MA. *Entrance requirements:* For master's, GRE General Test, minimum baccalaureate GPA of 2.75 or 3.0 in latter half of baccalauareate, goals statements, curriculum vitae, letters of recommendation. Additional exam requirements/recommendations for international students: Required—TOEFL (minimum score 550 paper-based; 79 iBT), IELTS (minimum score 6.5). Electronic applications accepted.

**Binghamton University, State University of New York,** Graduate School, Harpur College of Arts and Sciences, Department of Psychology, Specialization in Cognitive and Behavioral Science, Binghamton, NY 13902-6000. Offers PhD. *Program availability:* Part-time. *Students:* 11 full-time (3 women), 9 part-time (6 women); includes 4 minority (1 Asian, non-Hispanic/Latino; 1 Hispanic/Latino; 2 Two or more races, non-Hispanic/Latino), 1 international. Average age 30. 33 applicants, 21% accepted, 4 enrolled. In 2016, 4 doctorates awarded. Terminal master's awarded for partial completion of doctoral program. *Degree requirements:* For doctorate, thesis/dissertation. *Entrance requirements:* For doctorate, GRE General Test. Additional exam requirements/recommendations for international students: Required—TOEFL (minimum score 550 paper-based; 80 iBT). *Application deadline:* For fall admission, 12/31 priority date for domestic and international students. Application fee: $75. Electronic applications accepted. *Financial support:* In 2016–17, 17 students received support, including 3 research assistantships with full tuition reimbursements available (averaging $16,500 per year), 12 teaching assistantships with full tuition reimbursements available (averaging $16,500 per year); career-related internships or fieldwork, Federal Work-Study, institutionally sponsored loans, scholarships/grants, traineeships, health care benefits, tuition waivers (full and partial), and unspecified assistantships also available. Financial award applicants required to submit FAFSA. *Unit head:* Dr. Sarah Laszlo, Program Coordinator, 607-777-3380, E-mail: slaszlo@binghamton.edu. *Application contact:* Ben Balkaya, Assistant Dean and Director, 607-777-2151, Fax: 607-777-2501, E-mail: balkaya@binghamton.edu.

**Brandeis University,** Graduate School of Arts and Sciences, Department of Psychology, Waltham, MA 02454-9110. Offers brain, body and behavior (PhD); cognitive neuroscience (PhD); general psychology (MA); social/developmental psychology (PhD). *Program availability:* Part-time. *Faculty:* 14 full-time (7 women), 4 part-time/adjunct (3 women). *Students:* 40 full-time (27 women), 1 (woman) part-time; includes 5 minority (1 Black or African American, non-Hispanic/Latino; 2 Asian, non-Hispanic/Latino; 2 Hispanic/Latino), 9 international. 148 applicants, 23% accepted, 15 enrolled. In 2016, 8 master's, 3 doctorates awarded. Terminal master's awarded for partial completion of doctoral program. *Degree requirements:* For master's, thesis or alternative; for doctorate, thesis/dissertation, research reports. *Entrance requirements:* For master's and doctorate, GRE General Test; GRE Subject Test (recommended), 3 letters of recommendation, statement of purpose, transcript(s), resume. Additional exam requirements/recommendations for international students: Required—TOEFL (minimum score 600 paper-based; 100 iBT); Recommended—IELTS (minimum score 7), TSE (minimum score 68). *Application deadline:* For fall admission, 1/15 priority date for domestic and international students. Application fee: $75. Electronic applications accepted. *Financial support:* In 2016–17, 22 students received support, including 22 fellowships with full tuition reimbursements available (averaging $24,000 per year), 34 teaching assistantships with partial tuition reimbursements available (averaging $3,200 per year); Federal Work-Study, scholarships/grants, health care benefits, and tuition waivers (full and partial) also available. Support available to part-time students. Financial award application deadline: 4/15; financial award applicants required to submit FAFSA. *Faculty research:* Brain, body, and behavior across the lifespan; face perception and nonverbal communication; learning and memory; motor control and spatial orientation; neurophysiology of learning and decision making; personality and cognition in adulthood and old age; social, cultural and affective neuroscience; social relations and health physiology; speech comprehension and memory; taste physiology and psychophysics; visual perception. *Unit head:* Prof. Paul DiZio, Department Chair, 781-736-3300, Fax: 781-736-3291, E-mail: dizio@brandeis.edu. *Application contact:* Phil Gnatowski, Department Administrator, 781-736-3302, Fax: 781-736-3291, E-mail: gnat@brandeis.edu.
Website: http://www.brandeis.edu/departments/psych/

**Brigham Young University,** Graduate Studies, College of Family, Home, and Social Sciences, Department of Psychology, Provo, UT 84602. Offers applied social psychology (PhD); clinical psychology (PhD); cognitive and behavioral neuroscience (PhD); developmental psychology (PhD). *Accreditation:* APA. *Faculty:* 29 full-time (7 women), 8 part-time/adjunct (2 women). *Students:* 59 full-time (34 women); includes 9 minority (2 Black or African American, non-Hispanic/Latino; 4 Asian, non-Hispanic/Latino; 2 Hispanic/Latino; 1 Native Hawaiian or other Pacific Islander, non-Hispanic/Latino). Average age 29. 49 applicants, 33% accepted, 11 enrolled. In 2016, 12 doctorates awarded. *Degree requirements:* For doctorate, comprehensive exam (for some programs), thesis/dissertation, publishable paper. *Entrance requirements:* For doctorate, GRE General Test, minimum GPA of 3.0. Additional exam requirements/recommendations for international students: Required—TOEFL (minimum score 580 paper-based; 85 iBT). *Application deadline:* For fall admission, 12/1 for domestic and international students. Application fee: $50. Electronic applications accepted. *Expenses:* Contact institution. *Financial support:* In 2016–17, 41 students received support, including 32 research assistantships with partial tuition reimbursements available (averaging $12,000 per year), 5 teaching assistantships with partial tuition reimbursements available (averaging $12,000 per year); career-related internships or fieldwork, scholarships/grants, tuition waivers (partial), and unspecified assistantships also available. Financial award application deadline: 5/31. *Faculty research:* Psychotherapy process, Alzheimer's disease/dementia, psychology and law, health, psychology, developmental. *Total annual research expenditures:* $73,281. *Unit head:* Dr. Dawson Hedges, Chair, 801-422-6357, Fax: 801-422-0602, E-mail: dawson_hedges@byu.edu. *Application contact:* Leesa D. Scott, Coordinator of Student Programs, 801-422-4560, Fax: 801-422-0602, E-mail: leesa_scott@byu.edu.
Website: http://psychology.byu.edu/

**Brown University,** Graduate School, Department of Cognitive, Linguistic and Psychological Sciences, Providence, RI 02912. Offers cognitive science (Sc M, PhD); linguistics (AM, PhD); psychology (PhD). *Degree requirements:* For master's, one foreign language, thesis or alternative; for doctorate, 2 foreign languages, thesis/dissertation.

**Carleton University,** Faculty of Graduate Studies, Faculty of Arts and Social Sciences, Program in Cognitive Science, Ottawa, ON K1S 5B6, Canada. Offers PhD. *Degree requirements:* For doctorate, thesis/dissertation. *Entrance requirements:* For doctorate, master's degree. *Faculty research:* Language, attention, artificial intelligence, symbol recognition, consciousness.

**Carnegie Mellon University,** Dietrich College of Humanities and Social Sciences, Department of Psychology, Area of Cognitive Neuroscience, Pittsburgh, PA 15213-3891. Offers PhD. *Degree requirements:* For doctorate, comprehensive exam, thesis/dissertation. *Entrance requirements:* For doctorate, GRE General Test. Additional exam requirements/recommendations for international students: Required—TOEFL.

**Carnegie Mellon University,** Dietrich College of Humanities and Social Sciences, Department of Psychology, Area of Cognitive Psychology, Pittsburgh, PA 15213-3891. Offers PhD. *Degree requirements:* For doctorate, comprehensive exam, thesis/

## Cognitive Sciences

dissertation. *Entrance requirements:* For doctorate, GRE General Test. Additional exam requirements/recommendations for international students: Required—TOEFL.

**Case Western Reserve University,** School of Graduate Studies, Department of Cognitive Science, Cleveland, OH 44106. Offers cognitive linguistics (MA). *Program availability:* Part-time. *Faculty:* 4 full-time (2 women), 12 part-time/adjunct (4 women). *Students:* 8 full-time (4 women); includes 1 minority (Asian, non-Hispanic/Latino). Average age 27. 4 applicants, 75% accepted, 1 enrolled. *Degree requirements:* For master's, thesis. *Entrance requirements:* For master's, GRE, statement of purpose, three letters of recommendation, writing sample. Additional exam requirements/recommendations for international students: Required—TOEFL (minimum score 577 paper-based; 90 iBT); Recommended—IELTS (minimum score 7). *Application deadline:* For fall admission, 5/1 priority date for domestic students. Application fee: $50. Electronic applications accepted. *Expenses: Tuition:* Full-time $42,576; part-time $1774 per credit hour. *Required fees:* $34. Tuition and fees vary according to course load and program. *Faculty research:* Workings of the human mind in design, art, and technology; interaction of brain and culture in development and evolution; origins of human higher-order cognition; the role of the body and social interaction in shaping human cognition; operation of systems that human beings have invented to guide their thought and action individually and culturally. *Unit head:* Dr. William Deal, Chair, 216-368-2205, E-mail: william.deal@case.edu.
Website: http://cognitivescience.case.edu/

**Central European University,** Department of Cognitive Science, Budapest, Hungary. Offers PhD. *Faculty:* 26 full-time (12 women), 1 part-time/adjunct (0 women). *Students:* 29 full-time (16 women). Average age 27. 69 applicants, 14% accepted, 5 enrolled. *Degree requirements:* For doctorate, one foreign language, comprehensive exam, thesis/dissertation. *Entrance requirements:* For doctorate, essay, interview. Additional exam requirements/recommendations for international students: Required—TOEFL (minimum score 570 paper-based); Recommended—IELTS (minimum score 6.5). *Application deadline:* For fall admission, 2/4 priority date for domestic and international students. Application fee: $30. Electronic applications accepted. *Expenses: Tuition:* Full-time 13,500 euros. Tuition and fees vary according to degree level, program and student level. *Financial support:* In 2016–17, 6 students received support. Fellowships, career-related internships or fieldwork, scholarships/grants, and health care benefits available. *Faculty research:* Cognitive anthropology, developmental psychology, language and cognition, mathematical modeling of cognition, economics and cognition, social cognition. *Unit head:* Dr. Natalie Sebanz, Head of Department, 36 1 887-5137, E-mail: sebanzn@ceu.edu. *Application contact:* Zsuzsanna Jaszberenyi, Admissions Officer, 361-324-3009, Fax: 367-327-3211, E-mail: admissions@ceu.edu.
Website: http://cognitivescience.ceu.edu/

**Claremont Graduate University,** Graduate Programs, School of Social Science, Policy and Evaluation, Department of Psychology, Claremont, CA 91711-6160. Offers advanced study in evaluation (Certificate); cognitive psychology (MA, PhD); developmental psychology (MA, PhD); evaluation and applied research methods (MA, PhD); health behavior research and evaluation (MA, PhD); human resource development and evaluation (MA); industrial/organizational psychology (MA, PhD); organizational behavior (MA, PhD); organizational psychology (MA, PhD); social psychology (MA, PhD); MBA/PhD. *Program availability:* Part-time. *Faculty:* 19 full-time (9 women), 1 part-time/adjunct (0 women). *Students:* 244 full-time (160 women), 66 part-time (38 women); includes 93 minority (15 Black or African American, non-Hispanic/Latino; 2 American Indian or Alaska Native, non-Hispanic/Latino; 29 Asian, non-Hispanic/Latino; 31 Hispanic/Latino; 2 Native Hawaiian or other Pacific Islander, non-Hispanic/Latino; 14 Two or more races, non-Hispanic/Latino), 41 international. Average age 30. In 2016, 61 master's, 23 doctorates, 5 other advanced degrees awarded. Terminal master's awarded for partial completion of doctoral program. *Entrance requirements:* For master's and doctorate, GRE General Test. Additional exam requirements/recommendations for international students: Required—TOEFL (minimum score 75 iBT). *Application deadline:* For fall admission, 1/15 priority date for domestic and international students. Applications are processed on a rolling basis. Application fee: $80. Electronic applications accepted. *Expenses: Tuition:* Full-time $44,328; part-time $1847 per unit. *Required fees:* $600; $300 per semester. Tuition and fees vary according to course load and program. *Financial support:* Fellowships, research assistantships, teaching assistantships, Federal Work-Study, institutionally sponsored loans, scholarships/grants, and tuition waivers (full and partial) available. Support available to part-time students. Financial award application deadline: 2/15; financial award applicants required to submit FAFSA. *Faculty research:* Social intervention, diversity in organizations, eyewitness memory, aging and cognition, drug policy. *Unit head:* William Crano, Chair, 909-607-3311, E-mail: william.crano@cgu.edu. *Application contact:* Paige Piontkowsky, Senior Assistant Director of Admissions, 909-607-3240, E-mail: paige.piontkowsky@cgu.edu.
Website: https://www.cgu.edu/school/ssspe/programs/?areas_of_study=psychology

**Cornell University,** Graduate School, Graduate Fields of Arts and Sciences, Field of Information Science, Ithaca, NY 14853. Offers cognition (PhD); human computer interaction (PhD); information science (PhD); information systems (PhD); social aspects of information (PhD). *Degree requirements:* For doctorate, comprehensive exam, thesis/dissertation. *Entrance requirements:* For doctorate, GRE General Test, 3 letters of recommendation. Additional exam requirements/recommendations for international students: Required—TOEFL (minimum score 550 paper-based; 77 iBT). Electronic applications accepted. *Faculty research:* Digital libraries, game theory, data mining, human-computer interaction, computational linguistics.

**Dartmouth College,** School of Graduate and Advanced Studies, Department of Psychological and Brain Sciences, Program in Cognitive Neuroscience, Hanover, NH 03755. Offers PhD. *Students:* 6 full-time (3 women); includes 1 minority (Two or more races, non-Hispanic/Latino), 4 international. Average age 27. 7 applicants, 14% accepted, 1 enrolled. In 2016, 3 doctorates awarded. *Entrance requirements:* Additional exam requirements/recommendations for international students: Required—TOEFL. *Application deadline:* For fall admission, 11/30 for domestic students. Application fee: $50. *Unit head:* Dr. Adina Roskies, Chair, 603-646-2112. *Application contact:* Elizabeth Cassell, Department Administrator, 603-646-0470, E-mail: liz.cassell@dartmouth.edu.

**Duke University,** Graduate School, Department of Psychology and Neuroscience, Durham, NC 27708. Offers biological psychology (PhD); clinical psychology (PhD); cognitive psychology (PhD); developmental psychology (PhD); experimental psychology (PhD); health psychology (PhD); human social development (PhD); JD/MA. *Accreditation:* APA (one or more programs are accredited). *Degree requirements:* For doctorate, thesis/dissertation. *Entrance requirements:* For doctorate, GRE General Test. Additional exam requirements/recommendations for international students: Required—TOEFL (minimum score 577 paper-based; 90 iBT) or IELTS (minimum score 7). Electronic applications accepted.

**Emory University,** Laney Graduate School, Department of Psychology, Atlanta, GA 30322-1100. Offers clinical psychology (PhD); cognition and development (PhD); neuroscience and animal behavior (PhD). *Accreditation:* APA. *Degree requirements:* For doctorate, comprehensive exam, thesis/dissertation. *Entrance requirements:* For doctorate, GRE General Test, minimum GPA of 3.25. Additional exam requirements/recommendations for international students: Required—TOEFL. Electronic applications

accepted. *Faculty research:* Neuroscience and animal behavior; adult and child psychopathology, cognition development assessment.

**Florida International University,** College of Arts, Sciences, and Education, Department of Psychology, Miami, FL 33199. Offers behavioral analysis (MS); clinical science (PhD); cognitive neuroscience (PhD); counseling psychology (MS); developmental science (MS, PhD); legal psychology (MS, PhD); organizational psychology (MS, PhD). Program has fall admissions only. *Accreditation:* APA. *Program availability:* Part-time, evening/weekend. *Faculty:* 44 full-time (27 women), 41 part-time/adjunct (30 women). *Students:* 150 full-time (115 women), 17 part-time (10 women); includes 89 minority (8 Black or African American, non-Hispanic/Latino; 5 Asian, non-Hispanic/Latino; 75 Hispanic/Latino; 1 Two or more races, non-Hispanic/Latino), 10 international. Average age 27. 287 applicants, 24% accepted, 57 enrolled. In 2016, 35 master's, 11 doctorates awarded. Terminal master's awarded for partial completion of doctoral program. *Degree requirements:* For master's, thesis; for doctorate, comprehensive exam, thesis/dissertation. *Entrance requirements:* For master's, GRE General Test, minimum GPA of 3.0, resume, 3 letters of recommendation; for doctorate, GRE General Test, 3 letters of recommendation, resume, letter of intent, two writing samples, minimum GPA of 3.0. Additional exam requirements/recommendations for international students: Required—TOEFL (minimum score 550 paper-based; 80 iBT). *Application deadline:* For fall admission, 12/15 for domestic and international students. Application fee: $30. Electronic applications accepted. *Expenses:* Tuition, state resident: full-time $8912; part-time $446 per credit hour. Tuition, nonresident: full-time $21,393; part-time $992 per credit hour. *Required fees:* $2185; $195 per semester. Tuition and fees vary according to program. *Financial support:* Institutionally sponsored loans and scholarships/grants available. Financial award application deadline: 3/1. *Faculty research:* Legal psychology, organizational and industrial psychology, child behavior psychology. *Unit head:* Dr. William Pelham, Chair, 305-348-3002, Fax: 305-348-3646, E-mail: wpelham@fiu.edu. *Application contact:* Nanett Rojas, Assistant Director, Graduate Admissions, 305-348-7464, Fax: 305-348-7441, E-mail: gradadm@fiu.edu.

**Florida State University,** The Graduate School, College of Arts and Sciences, Department of Psychology, Program in Cognitive Psychology, Tallahassee, FL 32306. Offers PhD. *Faculty:* 7 full-time (1 woman). *Students:* 23 full-time (10 women), 2 part-time (0 women); includes 5 minority (1 Black or African American, non-Hispanic/Latino; 1 Asian, non-Hispanic/Latino; 2 Hispanic/Latino; 1 Two or more races, non-Hispanic/Latino), 2 international. Average age 29. 45 applicants, 11% accepted, 5 enrolled. In 2016, 3 doctorates awarded. Terminal master's awarded for partial completion of doctoral program. *Degree requirements:* For doctorate, comprehensive exam, thesis/dissertation. *Entrance requirements:* For doctorate, GRE General Test, minimum GPA of 3.0, research experience, letters of recommendation. Additional exam requirements/recommendations for international students: Required—TOEFL (minimum score 80 iBT). *Application deadline:* For fall admission, 12/16 for domestic and international students. Application fee: $30. Electronic applications accepted. *Expenses:* Tuition, state resident: full-time $7263; part-time $403.51 per credit hour. Tuition, nonresident: full-time $18,087; part-time $1004.85 per credit hour. *Required fees:* $1365; $75.81 per credit hour. $20 per semester. Tuition and fees vary according to campus/location. *Financial support:* In 2016–17, 23 students received support, including 2 fellowships with full tuition reimbursements available (averaging $22,815 per year), 7 research assistantships with full tuition reimbursements available (averaging $23,815 per year), 14 teaching assistantships with full tuition reimbursements available (averaging $18,315 per year); health care benefits also available. Financial award application deadline: 12/16; financial award applicants required to submit FAFSA. *Faculty research:* Memory, learning and reading disabilities; expert performance; aging. *Total annual research expenditures:* $801,549. *Unit head:* Dr. Walter Boot, Director, 850-645-8734, Fax: 850-644-7739, E-mail: boot@psy.fsu.edu. *Application contact:* Lynda L. Gibson, Graduate Program Associate, 850-644-2499, Fax: 850-644-7739, E-mail: grad-info@psy.fsu.edu.
Website: http://www.psy.fsu.edu/

**George Mason University,** College of Humanities and Social Sciences, Department of Psychology, Fairfax, VA 22030. Offers applied developmental psychology (Certificate); cognitive and behavioral neuroscience (MA); industrial/organizational psychology (PhD). *Accreditation:* APA. *Faculty:* 42 full-time (20 women), 13 part-time/adjunct (11 women). *Students:* 160 full-time (105 women), 57 part-time (30 women); includes 36 minority (9 Black or African American, non-Hispanic/Latino; 8 Asian, non-Hispanic/Latino; 12 Hispanic/Latino; 1 Native Hawaiian or other Pacific Islander, non-Hispanic/Latino; 6 Two or more races, non-Hispanic/Latino), 14 international. Average age 26. 742 applicants, 15% accepted, 57 enrolled. In 2016, 59 master's, 21 doctorates, 7 other advanced degrees awarded. *Degree requirements:* For master's, comprehensive exam, thesis (for biopsychology); for doctorate, comprehensive exam, thesis/dissertation, 2nd-year project. *Entrance requirements:* For master's, GRE, 2 official transcripts; goals statement; 15 undergraduate credits in concentration for which the applicant is applying; for doctorate, GRE, 3 letters of recommendation; resume; goals statement; minimum GPA of 3.0 overall for last 60 undergraduate credits, 3.25 in psychology courses; 15 undergraduate credits in concentration for which the applicant is applying; 2 official transcripts; for Certificate, GRE, 2 official transcripts; expanded goals statement; 3 letters of recommendation. Additional exam requirements/recommendations for international students: Required—TOEFL (minimum score 575 paper-based; 88 iBT), IELTS (minimum score 6.5), PTE (minimum score 59). Application fee: $75 ($80 for international students). Electronic applications accepted. *Expenses:* Tuition, state resident: full-time $10,628; part-time $443 per credit. Tuition, nonresident: full-time $29,306; part-time $1221 per credit. *Required fees:* $3096; $129 per credit. Tuition and fees vary according to program. *Financial support:* In 2016–17, 116 students received support, including 7 fellowships (averaging $11,348 per year), 42 research assistantships with tuition reimbursements available (averaging $14,292 per year), 88 teaching assistantships with tuition reimbursements available (averaging $13,815 per year); career-related internships or fieldwork, Federal Work-Study, scholarships/grants, tuition waivers (partial), unspecified assistantships, and health care benefits (for full-time research or teaching assistantship recipients) also available. Support available to part-time students. Financial award application deadline: 3/1; financial award applicants required to submit FAFSA. *Faculty research:* Applied developmental psychology, biopsychology, clinical psychology, human factors/applied cognition psychology, industrial/organizational psychology, school psychology. *Total annual research expenditures:* $5.6 million. *Unit head:* Reeshad Dalal, Department Chair, 703-993-9487, Fax: 703-993-1359, E-mail: rdalal@gmu.edu. *Application contact:* Michael Hock, Graduate Program Coordinator, 703-993-1548, Fax: 703-993-1359, E-mail: mhock2@gmu.edu.
Website: http://psychology.gmu.edu

**The George Washington University,** Columbian College of Arts and Sciences, Department of Psychology, Washington, DC 20052. Offers applied social psychology (PhD); clinical psychology (PhD); cognitive neuroscience (PhD). *Accreditation:* APA. *Program availability:* Part-time, evening/weekend. *Faculty:* 25 full-time (16 women). *Students:* 39 full-time (28 women), 30 part-time (21 women); includes 21 minority (9 Black or African American, non-Hispanic/Latino; 4 Asian, non-Hispanic/Latino; 6 Hispanic/Latino; 2 Two or more races, non-Hispanic/Latino), 7 international. Average age 28. 442 applicants, 5% accepted, 12 enrolled. In 2016, 12 doctorates awarded.

*Degree requirements:* For doctorate, thesis/dissertation or alternative, general exam. *Entrance requirements:* For doctorate, GRE General Test, minimum GPA of 3.0. Additional exam requirements/recommendations for international students: Required—TOEFL (minimum score 550 paper-based; 80 iBT). *Application deadline:* For fall admission, 1/15 for domestic and international students. Application fee: $75. *Financial support:* In 2016–17, 62 students received support. Fellowships with tuition reimbursements available, teaching assistantships with tuition reimbursements available, career-related internships or fieldwork, Federal Work-Study, and tuition waivers available. *Unit head:* Dr. Paul Poppen, Chair, 202-994-6324, E-mail: pjp@gwu.edu. *Application contact:* Information Contact, 202-994-6320, Fax: 202-994-1602, E-mail: psydept@gwu.edu. Website: http://psychology.columbian.gwu.edu/

**Georgia State University,** College of Arts and Sciences, Department of Psychology, Atlanta, GA 30302-3083. Offers clinical (PhD); cognitive sciences (PhD); community (PhD); developmental (PhD); neuropsychology and behavioral neuroscience (PhD). *Accreditation:* APA. *Faculty:* 40 full-time (26 women). *Students:* 101 full-time (80 women), 2 part-time (both women); includes 25 minority (8 Black or African American, non-Hispanic/Latino; 9 Asian, non-Hispanic/Latino; 3 Hispanic/Latino; 5 Two or more races, non-Hispanic/Latino), 7 international. Average age 28. 517 applicants, 6% accepted, 17 enrolled. In 2016, 19 doctorates awarded. *Degree requirements:* For doctorate, comprehensive exam, thesis/dissertation, residency year (for clinical only). *Entrance requirements:* For doctorate, GRE. Additional exam requirements/recommendations for international students: Required—TOEFL (minimum score 550 paper-based; 80 iBT). *Application deadline:* For fall admission, 12/1 for domestic and international students. Application fee: $50. Electronic applications accepted. *Expenses:* Tuition, state resident: full-time $6876; part-time $382 per credit hour. Tuition, nonresident: full-time $22,374; part-time $1243 per credit hour. *Required fees:* $2128; $1064 per term. Part-time tuition and fees vary according to course load and program. *Financial support:* In 2016–17, fellowships with full tuition reimbursements (averaging $19,282 per year), research assistantships with full tuition reimbursements (averaging $5,173 per year), teaching assistantships with full tuition reimbursements (averaging $6,389 per year) were awarded; scholarships/grants, traineeships, health care benefits, and unspecified assistantships also available. Financial award applicants required to submit FAFSA. *Faculty research:* Clinical psychology, developmental psychology, community psychology, neuropsychology and behavioral neuroscience, cognitive sciences. *Unit head:* Dr. Lisa Armistead, Chair, 404-413-6205, Fax: 404-413-6207, E-mail: lparmistead@gsu.edu. *Application contact:* Dr. Lindsey Cohen, Director of Graduate Studies, 404-413-6263, Fax: 404-413-6207, E-mail: llcohen@gsu.edu.

**The Graduate Center, City University of New York,** Graduate Studies, Program in Psychology, New York, NY 10016-4039. Offers basic applied neurocognition (PhD); biopsychology (PhD); clinical psychology (PhD); developmental psychology (PhD); environmental psychology (PhD); experimental psychology (PhD); industrial psychology (PhD); learning processes (PhD); neuropsychology (PhD); psychology (PhD); social personality (PhD). *Degree requirements:* For doctorate, one foreign language, thesis/dissertation. *Entrance requirements:* For doctorate, GRE General Test. Additional exam requirements/recommendations for international students: Required—TOEFL. Electronic applications accepted.

**Grand Canyon University,** College of Doctoral Studies, Phoenix, AZ 85017-1097. Offers data analytics (DBA); general psychology (PhD), including cognition and instruction, industrial and organizational psychology, integrating technology, learning, and psychology, performance psychology; management (DBA); marketing (DBA); organizational leadership (Ed D), including behavioral health, Christian ministry, health care administration, organizational development. *Degree requirements:* For doctorate, comprehensive exam, thesis/dissertation. *Entrance requirements:* For doctorate, minimum GPA of 3.4 on earned advanced degree from regionally-accredited institution; transcripts; goals statement. Application fee: $0. *Unit head:* Michael Berger, Dean, 602-639-7255. *Application contact:* Michael Berger, Dean, 602-639-7255. Website: https://www.gcu.edu/college-of-doctoral-studies.php

**Harvard University,** Graduate School of Arts and Sciences, Department of Psychology, Cambridge, MA 02138. Offers psychology (PhD), including behavior and decision analysis, cognition, developmental psychology, experimental psychology, personality, psychobiology, psychopathology; social psychology (PhD). *Accreditation:* APA. *Degree requirements:* For doctorate, thesis/dissertation, general exams. *Entrance requirements:* For doctorate, GRE General Test. Additional exam requirements/recommendations for international students: Required—TOEFL.

**Harvard University,** Harvard Graduate School of Education, Master's Programs in Education, Cambridge, MA 02138. Offers arts in education (Ed M); education policy and management (Ed M); higher education (Ed M); human development and psychology (Ed M); international education policy (Ed M); language and literacy (Ed M); learning and teaching (Ed M); mind, brain, and education (Ed M); prevention science and practice (Ed M); school leadership (Ed M); special studies (Ed M); teacher education (Ed M); technology, innovation, and education (Ed M). *Program availability:* Part-time. *Entrance requirements:* For master's, GRE General Test, statement of purpose, 3 letters of recommendation, resume, official transcripts. Additional exam requirements/recommendations for international students: Required—TOEFL (minimum score 613 paper-based; 104 iBT), TWE (minimum score 5). Electronic applications accepted. *Faculty research:* Learning and development, educational leadership and organizations, education policy analysis.

**Illinois State University,** Graduate School, College of Arts and Sciences, Department of Psychology, Normal, IL 61790-2200. Offers psychology (MA, MS), including clinical-counseling psychology, cognitive and behavioral sciences, developmental psychology, industrial/organizational-social psychology; school psychology (PhD, SSP). *Accreditation:* APA. *Degree requirements:* For master's, thesis or alternative; for doctorate, variable foreign language requirement, thesis/dissertation, 2 terms of residency, internship, practicum. *Entrance requirements:* For master's, GRE General Test, GRE Subject Test, minimum GPA of 3.0 in last 60 hours of course work; for doctorate, GRE General Test. *Faculty research:* Comprehensive evaluation system for the central region professional development grant, Illinois school psychology internship consortium, for children's sake.

**Indiana University Bloomington,** University Graduate School, College of Arts and Sciences, Cognitive Science Program, Bloomington, IN 47406-7512. Offers PhD. *Faculty:* 78 full-time (19 women). *Students:* 25 full-time (8 women); includes 5 minority (2 Hispanic/Latino; 3 Two or more races, non-Hispanic/Latino), 7 international. Average age 31. 55 applicants, 11% accepted, 4 enrolled. In 2016, 2 doctorates awarded. *Degree requirements:* For doctorate, comprehensive exam, thesis/dissertation, research project; colloquia course. *Entrance requirements:* For doctorate, GRE, 3 letters of reference. Additional exam requirements/recommendations for international students: Required—TOEFL (minimum score 600 paper-based; 94 iBT), IELTS (minimum score 6.5). *Application deadline:* For fall admission, 1/3 for domestic students, 12/1 for international students. Application fee: $55 ($65 for international students). Electronic applications accepted. *Expenses:* $1,142.75 per unit. *Financial support:* In 2016–17, 1 student received support, including 3 fellowships with full tuition reimbursements available (averaging $22,000 per year), 1 research assistantship with full tuition reimbursement available (averaging $10,833 per year), 11 teaching assistantships with full tuition reimbursements available (averaging $21,766 per year); scholarships/grants and traineeships also available. Financial award application deadline: 12/1. *Faculty research:* Learning concepts, neural network models, language, animal cognition, dynamic and robotics systems approaches to behavior and cognition. *Unit head:* Peter Todd, Director, 812-855-3914, E-mail: pmtodd@indiana,edu. *Application contact:* Susan Palmer, Graduate Administrator, 812-855-0031, E-mail: stowle@indiana.edu. Website: http://www.cogs.indiana.edu/

**Indiana University Bloomington,** University Graduate School, College of Arts and Sciences, Department of Psychological and Brain Sciences, Bloomington, IN 47405. Offers clinical science (PhD); cognitive neuroscience (PhD); cognitive psychology (PhD); developmental psychology (PhD); methods of behavior (PhD); molecular systems neuroscience (PhD); social psychology (PhD). *Accreditation:* APA. *Degree requirements:* For doctorate, comprehensive exam, 90 credit hours, 2 advanced statistics/methods courses, 2 written research projects, the teaching of psychology course, teaching 1 semester of undergraduate methods course, qualifying examination, minor or a second major, first-year research seminar course, dissertation defense, written dissertation. *Entrance requirements:* For doctorate, GRE. Additional exam requirements/recommendations for international students: Required—TOEFL (minimum score 550 paper-based; 79 iBT). Electronic applications accepted. *Faculty research:* Clinical science, cognitive neuroscience, cognitive psychology, developmental psychology, mechanisms of behavior, molecular and systems neuroscience, social psychology.

**Iowa State University of Science and Technology,** Department of Psychology, Ames, IA 50011. Offers cognitive psychology (PhD); counseling psychology (PhD); psychology (MS); social psychology (PhD). *Accreditation:* APA (one or more programs are accredited). *Entrance requirements:* For doctorate, GRE General Test, GRE Subject Test (psychology), 3 letters of recommendation. Additional exam requirements/recommendations for international students: Required—TOEFL (minimum score 560 paper-based; 79 iBT), IELTS (minimum score 6.5). *Application deadline:* For fall admission, 1/2 priority date for domestic and international students. Application fee: $60 ($90 for international students). Electronic applications accepted. *Faculty research:* Counseling psychology, cognitive psychology, social psychology, health psychology, psychology and public policy. *Application contact:* Sarah Kallsen, Application Contact, 515-294-1742, Fax: 515-294-6424, E-mail: psychadm@iastate.edu. Website: http://www.psychology.iastate.edu/

**Johns Hopkins University,** Zanvyl Krieger School of Arts and Sciences, Department of Cognitive Science, Baltimore, MD 21218. Offers PhD. Terminal master's awarded for partial completion of doctoral program. *Degree requirements:* For doctorate, thesis/dissertation, 2 research papers. *Entrance requirements:* For doctorate, GRE General Test, 3 letters of recommendation, sample of work, statement of purpose, original transcripts from all previous post-secondary institutions. Additional exam requirements/recommendations for international students: Required—TOEFL (minimum score 600 paper-based; 100 iBT), IELTS (minimum score 7). Electronic applications accepted. *Faculty research:* Acquisition and development, cognitive neuropsychology and neuroscience, computational studies, psycholinguistics and cognitive psychology, theoretical linguistics.

**Louisiana State University and Agricultural & Mechanical College,** Graduate School, College of Humanities and Social Sciences, Department of Psychology, Baton Rouge, LA 70803. Offers biological psychology (MA, PhD); clinical psychology (MA, PhD); cognitive psychology (MA, PhD); developmental psychology (MA, PhD); school psychology (MA, PhD). *Accreditation:* APA (one or more programs are accredited).

**Massachusetts Institute of Technology,** School of Science, Department of Brain and Cognitive Sciences, Cambridge, MA 02139. Offers cognitive science (PhD); neuroscience (PhD). *Faculty:* 36 full-time (13 women). *Students:* 98 full-time (35 women); includes 14 minority (1 Black or African American, non-Hispanic/Latino; 4 Asian, non-Hispanic/Latino; 8 Hispanic/Latino; 1 Two or more races, non-Hispanic/Latino), 34 international. Average age 28. 493 applicants, 10% accepted, 21 enrolled. In 2016, 22 doctorates awarded. *Degree requirements:* For doctorate, comprehensive exam, thesis/dissertation. *Entrance requirements:* For doctorate, GRE General Test. Additional exam requirements/recommendations for international students: Required—TOEFL, IELTS. *Application deadline:* For fall admission, 12/1 for domestic and international students. Application fee: $75. Electronic applications accepted. *Expenses:* Tuition: Full-time $46,400; part-time $725 per credit. One-time fee: $312 full-time. Full-time tuition and fees vary according to course load and program. *Financial support:* In 2016–17, 81 students received support, including 49 fellowships (averaging $42,300 per year), 33 research assistantships (averaging $40,300 per year), 8 teaching assistantships (averaging $38,800 per year); Federal Work-Study, institutionally sponsored loans, scholarships/grants, traineeships, health care benefits, unspecified assistantships, and resident tutors also available. Support available to part-time students. Financial award application deadline: 5/1; financial award applicants required to submit FAFSA. *Faculty research:* Vision, audition, and other perceptual systems: physiology and computation; learning, memory, and executive control: molecular and systems approaches; sensorimotor systems: physiology and computation; neural and cognitive development and plasticity; language and high-level cognition: learning, acquisition, and computation. *Total annual research expenditures:* $41 million. *Unit head:* Prof. James Dicarlo, Head, 617-253-5748, Fax: 617-258-9216, E-mail: bcs-info@mit.edu. *Application contact:* bcs-admissions@mit.edu. Website: http://bcs.mit.edu/

**Michigan Technological University,** Graduate School, College of Sciences and Arts, Department of Cognitive and Learning Sciences, Houghton, MI 49931. Offers applied cognitive science and human factors (MS, PhD); applied science education (MS); post-secondary STEM education (Graduate Certificate). *Program availability:* Part-time, blended/hybrid learning. *Faculty:* 24 full-time (9 women), 11 part-time/adjunct (3 women). *Students:* 12 full-time (8 women), 21 part-time (10 women); includes 2 minority (1 Black or African American, non-Hispanic/Latino; 1 Two or more races, non-Hispanic/Latino), 3 international. Average age 35. 46 applicants, 20% accepted, 5 enrolled. In 2016, 6 master's, 4 doctorates awarded. Terminal master's awarded for partial completion of doctoral program. *Degree requirements:* For master's, comprehensive exam (for some programs), thesis (for some programs); for doctorate, comprehensive exam, thesis/dissertation, applied internship experience. *Entrance requirements:* For master's, GRE (for applied cognitive science and human factors program only), statement of purpose, personal statement, official transcripts, 3 letters of recommendation, resume/curriculum vitae; for doctorate, GRE, statement of purpose, personal statement, official transcripts, 3 letters of recommendation, resume/curriculum vitae. Additional exam requirements/recommendations for international students: Required—TOEFL (recommended minimum score 90 iBT) or IELTS. *Application deadline:* For fall admission, 2/15 priority date for domestic and international students. Applications are processed on a rolling basis. Electronic applications accepted. *Expenses:* Tuition, state resident: full-time $16,290; part-time $905 per credit. Tuition, nonresident: full-time $16,290; part-time $905 per credit. *Required fees:* $248; $124 per term. Tuition and fees vary according to course load and program. *Financial support:* In 2016–17, 14 students received support, including 2 fellowships (averaging $15,242 per

*Cognitive Sciences*

year), 7 research assistantships with tuition reimbursements available (averaging $15,242 per year), teaching assistantships (averaging $15,242 per year); career-related internships or fieldwork, Federal Work-Study, scholarships/grants, health care benefits, unspecified assistantships, and adjunct instructor positions also available. Financial award applicants required to submit FAFSA. *Faculty research:* Physical ergonomics, applied science education, applied cognitive science, human factors, educational technology cognitive modeling. *Total annual research expenditures:* $308,969. *Unit head:* Dr. Susan L. Amato-Henderson, Chair, 906-487-2536, Fax: 906-487-2468, E-mail: slamato@mtu.edu. *Application contact:* Carol T. Wingerson, Senior Staff Assistant, 906-487-2328, Fax: 906-487-2284, E-mail: gradadms@mtu.edu. Website: http://www.mtu.edu/cls/

**Mississippi State University,** College of Arts and Sciences, Department of Psychology, Mississippi State, MS 39762. Offers applied cognitive science (PhD); clinical psychology (PhD), including clinical psychology; psychology (MS). *Accreditation:* APA. *Faculty:* 21 full-time (9 women), 2 part-time/adjunct (1 woman). *Students:* 33 full-time (21 women), 6 part-time (5 women); includes 6 minority (3 Black or African American, non-Hispanic/Latino; 2 Asian, non-Hispanic/Latino; 1 Two or more races, non-Hispanic/Latino), 2 international. Average age 27. 53 applicants, 23% accepted, 8 enrolled. In 2016, 1 master's, 3 doctorates awarded. Terminal master's awarded for partial completion of doctoral program. *Degree requirements:* For master's, comprehensive exam, thesis; for doctorate, thesis/dissertation, qualifying exam, comprehensive written and oral exam. *Entrance requirements:* For master's, GRE General Test, minimum GPA of 2.75 on last two years of undergraduate courses; for doctorate, GRE General Test, proficiency in at least 1 computer language, minimum GPA of 3.0. Additional exam requirements/recommendations for international students: Required—TOEFL (minimum score 477 paper-based; 53 iBT); Recommended—IELTS (minimum score 4.5). *Application deadline:* For fall admission, 1/15 priority date for domestic students, 5/1 for international students; for spring admission, 11/1 priority date for domestic students, 9/1 for international students. Applications are processed on a rolling basis. Application fee: $60. Electronic applications accepted. *Expenses:* Tuition, state resident: full-time $7670; part-time $852.50 per credit hour. Tuition, nonresident: full-time $20,790; part-time $2310.50 per credit hour. Part-time tuition and fees vary according to course load. *Financial support:* In 2016–17, 5 research assistantships with full tuition reimbursements (averaging $13,441 per year), 21 teaching assistantships with full tuition reimbursements (averaging $10,291 per year) were awarded; career-related internships or fieldwork, Federal Work-Study, institutionally sponsored loans, scholarships/grants, and unspecified assistantships also available. Financial award application deadline: 4/1; financial award applicants required to submit FAFSA. *Faculty research:* Personality type, alcoholism, blindness and low vision, mental retardation, language comprehension. *Total annual research expenditures:* $1.7 million. *Unit head:* Dr. Mitchell E. Berman, Department Head, 662-325-3202, Fax: 662-325-7212, E-mail: mberman@psychology.msstate.edu. *Application contact:* Lakan Drinker, Admissions and Enrollment Assistant, 662-325-8951, E-mail: ldrinker@grad.msstate.edu. Website: http://www.psychology.msstate.edu/

**The New School,** The New School for Social Research, Department of Psychology, New York, NY 10003. Offers clinical psychology (PhD); cognitive, social, and developmental psychology (PhD); psychology (MA). *Accreditation:* APA (one or more programs are accredited). *Program availability:* Part-time. *Faculty:* 16 full-time (6 women), 12 part-time/adjunct (4 women). *Students:* 115 full-time (85 women), 99 part-time (77 women); includes 36 minority (9 Black or African American, non-Hispanic/Latino; 1 American Indian or Alaska Native, non-Hispanic/Latino; 11 Asian, non-Hispanic/Latino; 12 Hispanic/Latino; 3 Two or more races, non-Hispanic/Latino), 32 international. Average age 29. 247 applicants, 84% accepted, 60 enrolled. In 2016, 57 master's, 19 doctorates awarded. Terminal master's awarded for partial completion of doctoral program. *Degree requirements:* For master's, comprehensive exam, thesis (for some programs); for doctorate, comprehensive exam, thesis/dissertation. *Entrance requirements:* For master's, GRE, letters of recommendation, writing sample, essays, unofficial transcripts; for doctorate, letters of recommendation, writing sample, essays, unofficial transcripts. Additional exam requirements/recommendations for international students: Required—TOEFL (minimum score 100 iBT), IELTS (minimum score 7), PTE (minimum score 68). *Application deadline:* For fall admission, 8/1 priority date for domestic and international students; for spring admission, 10/15 priority date for domestic and international students. Applications are processed on a rolling basis. Application fee: $50. Electronic applications accepted. *Expenses:* Contact institution. *Financial support:* Fellowships, research assistantships, teaching assistantships, career-related internships or fieldwork, Federal Work-Study, scholarships/grants, and tuition waivers (full and partial) available. Support available to part-time students. Financial award application deadline: 2/1; financial award applicants required to submit FAFSA. *Faculty research:* Cognitive, social, and developmental psychology; clinical psychology; mental health and substance abuse counseling. *Unit head:* Dr. William Milberg, Dean, The New School for Social Research, 212-229-5777, E-mail: milbergw@newschool.edu. *Application contact:* Dana Messinger, Director of Graduate Admission, 212-229-5150 Ext. 2300, E-mail: socialresearchadmit@newschool.edu.

**New York University,** Graduate School of Arts and Science, Department of Psychology, New York, NY 10012-1019. Offers cognition and perception (PhD); community psychology (PhD); general psychology (MA); industrial/organizational psychology (MA); psychotherapy and psychoanalysis (Advanced Certificate); social/personality psychology (PhD). *Program availability:* Part-time. Terminal master's awarded for partial completion of doctoral program. *Degree requirements:* For master's, comprehensive exam, thesis or alternative; for doctorate, thesis/dissertation. *Entrance requirements:* For master's and doctorate, GRE General Test. Additional exam requirements/recommendations for international students: Required—TOEFL. *Faculty research:* Vision, memory, social cognition, social and cognitive development, relationships.

**North Dakota State University,** College of Graduate and Interdisciplinary Studies, College of Science and Mathematics, Department of Psychology, Fargo, ND 58102. Offers clinical psychology (MS); health and social psychology (PhD); psychological clinical science (PhD); psychology (MS); visual and cognitive neuroscience (PhD). *Degree requirements:* For master's, thesis; for doctorate, thesis/dissertation. *Entrance requirements:* For master's and doctorate, GRE General Test, GRE Subject Test. Additional exam requirements/recommendations for international students: Required—TOEFL (minimum score 525 paper-based; 71 iBT). Electronic applications accepted. *Faculty research:* Cognition science, neuropsychology, group behavior, applied behavior analysis, behavior therapy.

**Northwestern University,** The Graduate School, Judd A. and Marjorie Weinberg College of Arts and Sciences, Department of Psychology, Evanston, IL 60208. Offers brain, behavior and cognition (PhD); clinical psychology (PhD); cognitive psychology (PhD); personality psychology (PhD); social psychology (PhD); JD/PhD. Admissions and degrees offered through The Graduate School. *Accreditation:* APA (one or more programs are accredited). *Program availability:* Part-time. *Degree requirements:* For doctorate, thesis/dissertation. *Entrance requirements:* For doctorate, GRE General Test, GRE Subject Test. Additional exam requirements/recommendations for international students: Required—TOEFL. Electronic applications accepted. *Faculty research:*

Memory and higher order cognition, anxiety and depression, effectiveness of psychotherapy, social cognition, molecular basis of memory.

**The Ohio State University,** Graduate School, College of Arts and Sciences, Division of Social and Behavioral Sciences, Department of Psychology, Columbus, OH 43210. Offers behavioral neuroscience (PhD); clinical psychology (PhD); cognitive psychology (PhD); developmental psychology (PhD); intellectual and developmental disabilities psychology (PhD); quantitative psychology (PhD); social psychology (PhD). *Accreditation:* APA. *Faculty:* 57. *Students:* 156 full-time (95 women); includes 23 minority (6 Black or African American, non-Hispanic/Latino; 9 Asian, non-Hispanic/Latino; 8 Hispanic/Latino), 26 international. Average age 26. In 2016, 26 doctorates awarded. *Degree requirements:* For doctorate, thesis/dissertation. *Entrance requirements:* For doctorate, GRE General Test. Additional exam requirements/recommendations for international students: Required—TOEFL (minimum score 600 paper-based; 100 iBT); Recommended—IELTS (minimum score 8). *Application deadline:* For fall admission, 12/1 for domestic and international students. Applications are processed on a rolling basis. Application fee: $60 ($70 for international students). Electronic applications accepted. *Financial support:* Fellowships with tuition reimbursements, research assistantships with tuition reimbursements, and teaching assistantships with tuition reimbursements available. *Unit head:* Dr. John Bruno, Chair, 614-292-3038, E-mail: bruno.1@osu.edu. *Application contact:* Graduate and Professional Admissions, 614-292-9444, Fax: 614-292-3895, E-mail: gpadmissions@osu.edu. Website: http://www.psy.ohio-state.edu/

**Oregon State University,** College of Liberal Arts, Program in Psychology, Corvallis, OR 97331. Offers applied cognition (MS, PhD); engineering psychology (MS, PhD); health psychology (MS, PhD). *Faculty:* 11 full-time (7 women), 2 part-time/adjunct (1 woman). *Students:* 3 full-time (2 women). 14 applicants, 21% accepted, 3 enrolled. *Degree requirements:* For doctorate, thesis/dissertation. *Application deadline:* For fall admission, 12/15 for domestic and international students. Application fee: $75 ($85 for international students). *Expenses:* Tuition, state resident: full-time $12,150; part-time $450 per credit. Tuition, nonresident: full-time $21,789; part-time $807 per credit. *Required fees:* $1651; $1507 per credit. One-time fee: $350. Tuition and fees vary according to course load, campus/location and program. *Unit head:* John Edwards, Director. *Application contact:* Aurora Sherman, Associate Professor and Graduate Education Chair, 541-737-1361, E-mail: aurora.sherman@oregonstate.edu. Website: http://liberalarts.oregonstate.edu/school-psychological-science/psychology/graduate-psychology

**Purdue University,** Graduate School, College of Health and Human Sciences, Department of Psychological Sciences, West Lafayette, IN 47907. Offers behavioral neuroscience (PhD); clinical psychology (PhD); cognitive psychology (PhD); industrial/organizational psychology (PhD); mathematical and computational cognitive science (PhD). *Accreditation:* APA. *Faculty:* 46 full-time (18 women), 1 part-time/adjunct. *Students:* 64 full-time (41 women), 4 part-time (3 women); includes 13 minority (1 Black or African American, non-Hispanic/Latino; 4 Asian, non-Hispanic/Latino; 6 Hispanic/Latino; 2 Two or more races, non-Hispanic/Latino), 12 international. Average age 27. 288 applicants, 8% accepted, 16 enrolled. In 2016, 9 doctorates awarded. Terminal master's awarded for partial completion of doctoral program. *Degree requirements:* For doctorate, thesis/dissertation. *Entrance requirements:* For doctorate, GRE General Test, minimum undergraduate GPA of 3.0 or equivalent. Additional exam requirements/recommendations for international students: Required—TOEFL (minimum score 550 paper-based; 77 iBT); Recommended—TWE. *Application deadline:* For fall admission, 12/3 for domestic and international students. Applications are processed on a rolling basis. Application fee: $60 ($75 for international students). Electronic applications accepted. *Financial support:* Fellowships with partial tuition reimbursements, research assistantships with partial tuition reimbursements, teaching assistantships with partial tuition reimbursements, and career-related internships or fieldwork available. Support available to part-time students. Financial award applicants required to submit FAFSA. *Faculty research:* Career development of women in science, development of friendships during childhood and adolescence, social competence, human information processing. *Unit head:* Dr. Christopher R. Agnew, Head, 765-494-6061, Fax: 765-496-1264, E-mail: agnew@psych.purdue.edu. *Application contact:* Nancy A. O'Brien, Graduate Contact, 765-494-6067, Fax: 765-496-1264, E-mail: nobrien@psych.pardue.edu. Website: http://www.psych.purdue.edu/

**Queen's University at Kingston,** School of Graduate Studies, Faculty of Arts and Sciences, Department of Psychology, Kingston, ON K7L 3N6, Canada. Offers brain behavior and cognitive science (MA, PhD); clinical psychology (MA, PhD); developmental psychology (MA, PhD); social personality psychology (MA, PhD). *Degree requirements:* For master's, thesis; for doctorate, comprehensive exam, thesis/dissertation. *Entrance requirements:* For master's and doctorate, GRE General Test. Additional exam requirements/recommendations for international students: Required—TOEFL. *Faculty research:* Human development, social, personality, behavioral neuroscience, forensic.

**Rensselaer Polytechnic Institute,** Graduate School, School of Humanities, Arts, and Social Sciences, Program in Cognitive Science, Troy, NY 12180-3590. Offers PhD. *Faculty:* 20 full-time (4 women), 1 part-time/adjunct (0 women). *Students:* 10 full-time (2 women), 4 part-time (1 woman). 23 applicants, 13% accepted, 2 enrolled. In 2016, 1 doctorate awarded. *Degree requirements:* For doctorate, thesis/dissertation. *Entrance requirements:* For doctorate, GRE. Additional exam requirements/recommendations for international students: Required—TOEFL (minimum score 600 paper-based; 100 iBT), IELTS (minimum score 7), PTE (minimum score 68). *Application deadline:* For fall admission, 1/1 priority date for domestic and international students. Applications are processed on a rolling basis. Application fee: $75. Electronic applications accepted. *Expenses: Tuition:* Full-time $49,520; part-time $2060 per credit hour. *Required fees:* $2617. *Financial support:* In 2016–17, research assistantships (averaging $22,000 per year), teaching assistantships (averaging $22,000 per year) were awarded; fellowships also available. Financial award application deadline: 1/1. *Faculty research:* Artificial intelligence, cognitive engineering, computational cognitive modeling, computational linguistics, human factors, perception and action, social interaction, social simulation and multi-agent modeling, theoretical neuroscience, vision science. *Unit head:* Dr. Wayne Gray, Graduate Program Director, 518-276-3315, E-mail: grayw@rpi.edu. *Application contact:* Office of Graduate Admissions, 518-276-6216, E-mail: gradadmissions@rpi.edu. Website: http://www.cogsci.rpi.edu/pl/phd-cognitive-science

**Rice University,** Graduate Programs, School of Social Sciences, Department of Psychology, Houston, TX 77251-1892. Offers cognitive sciences (MA, PhD); industrial-organizational/social psychology (MA, PhD); psychology (MA, PhD). Terminal master's awarded for partial completion of doctoral program. *Degree requirements:* For master's, thesis; for doctorate, thesis/dissertation. *Entrance requirements:* For doctorate, GRE General Test, minimum GPA of 3.0. Additional exam requirements/recommendations for international students: Required—TOEFL. Electronic applications accepted. *Faculty research:* Cognitive, cognitive neuropsychology, human factors, human-computer interaction, industrial-organizational psychology.

**Rutgers University–Newark,** Graduate School, Program in Psychology, Newark, NJ 07102. Offers cognitive neuroscience (PhD); cognitive science (PhD); perception (PhD); psychobiology (PhD); social cognition (PhD). *Degree requirements:* For doctorate, comprehensive exam, thesis/dissertation. *Entrance requirements:* For doctorate, GRE General Test, GRE Subject Test, minimum undergraduate B average. Electronic applications accepted. *Faculty research:* Visual perception (luminance, motion), neuroendocrine mechanisms in behavior (reproduction, pain), attachment theory, connectionist modeling of cognition.

**Rutgers University–New Brunswick,** Graduate School-New Brunswick, Program in Psychology, Piscataway, NJ 08854-8097. Offers behavioral neuroscience (PhD); clinical psychology (PhD); cognitive psychology (PhD); interdisciplinary health psychology (PhD); social psychology (PhD). *Accreditation:* APA. *Degree requirements:* For doctorate, comprehensive exam, thesis/dissertation. *Entrance requirements:* For doctorate, GRE General Test, 3 letters of recommendation. Additional exam requirements/recommendations for international students: Required—TOEFL (minimum score 577 paper-based). Electronic applications accepted. *Faculty research:* Learning and memory, behavioral ecology, hormones and behavior, psychopharmacology, anxiety disorders.

**Stony Brook University, State University of New York,** Graduate School, College of Arts and Sciences, Department of Psychology, Program in Cognitive Psychology, Stony Brook, NY 11794. Offers PhD. *Students:* 19 full-time (10 women); includes 3 minority (1 Asian, non-Hispanic/Latino; 1 Hispanic/Latino; 1 Two or more races, non-Hispanic/Latino), 4 international. Average age 28. 40 applicants, 13% accepted, 2 enrolled. In 2016, 2 doctorates awarded. *Degree requirements:* For doctorate, thesis/dissertation. *Entrance requirements:* For doctorate, GRE General Test, GRE Subject Test. Additional exam requirements/recommendations for international students: Required—TOEFL (minimum score 90 iBT). *Application deadline:* For fall admission, 1/15 for domestic students; for spring admission, 10/1 for domestic students. Application fee: $100. Electronic applications accepted. *Expenses:* Contact institution. *Financial support:* In 2016–17, 1 fellowship, 3 research assistantships, 12 teaching assistantships were awarded. *Unit head:* Dr. Arthur Samuel, Chair, 631-632-7792, E-mail: arthur.samuel@stonybrook.edu. *Application contact:* Marilynn Wollmuth, Graduate Director, 631-632-7855, Fax: 631-632-7876, E-mail: marilynn.wollmuth@stonybrook.edu.
Website: http://www.stonybrook.edu/commcms/psychology/cognitive/overview.html

**Syracuse University,** College of Arts and Sciences, Programs in Psychology, Syracuse, NY 13244. Offers clinical psychology (PhD); cognition, brain, and behavior (PhD); school psychology (PhD); social psychology (PhD). *Accreditation:* APA. In 2016, 1 doctorate awarded. Terminal master's awarded for partial completion of doctoral program. *Degree requirements:* For doctorate, comprehensive exam, thesis/dissertation. *Entrance requirements:* For doctorate, GRE General Test, GRE Subject Test, resume, personal statement, 3 letters of recommendation. Additional exam requirements/recommendations for international students: Required—TOEFL (minimum score 100 iBT). *Application deadline:* For fall admission, 12/1 priority date for domestic and international students. Application fee: $75. Electronic applications accepted. *Expenses: Tuition:* Full-time $25,974; part-time $1443 per credit hour. *Required fees:* $802; $50 per course. Tuition and fees vary according to course load and program. *Financial support:* Fellowships with full tuition reimbursements, research assistantships with tuition reimbursements, teaching assistantships with tuition reimbursements, and scholarships/grants available. Financial award application deadline: 1/1. *Faculty research:* Clinical psychology; cognition, brain, and behavior; school psychology; social psychology. *Unit head:* Dr. Larry Lewandowski, Professor of Psychology/Interim Chair, 315-443-1015, E-mail: ljlewand@syr.edu. *Application contact:* Alecia Zema, Curriculum Coordinator, 315-443-2760, E-mail: azema@syr.edu.
Website: http://psychology.syr.edu/graduate/Clinical.html

**Texas Christian University,** College of Science and Engineering, Department of Psychology, Fort Worth, TX 76129. Offers developmental trauma (MS); experimental psychology (PhD), including cognition/developmental, learning, neuroscience, social. *Faculty:* 12 full-time (5 women), 3 part-time/adjunct (2 women). *Students:* 33 full-time (19 women); includes 4 minority (1 Asian, non-Hispanic/Latino; 1 Hispanic/Latino; 2 Two or more races, non-Hispanic/Latino), 2 international. Average age 27. 38 applicants, 32% accepted, 12 enrolled. In 2016, 5 master's, 3 doctorates awarded. Terminal master's awarded for partial completion of doctoral program. *Degree requirements:* For master's, thesis; for doctorate, thesis/dissertation. *Entrance requirements:* For doctorate, GRE General Test. Additional exam requirements/recommendations for international students: Required—TOEFL. *Application deadline:* For fall admission, 2/1 for domestic and international students. Application fee: $60 ($0 for international students). Electronic applications accepted. *Expenses:* Contact institution. *Financial support:* In 2016–17, 23 students received support, including 23 teaching assistantships with full tuition reimbursements available (averaging $19,750 per year); scholarships/grants also available. Financial award application deadline: 2/1; financial award applicants required to submit FAFSA. *Faculty research:* Neuroscience, human and animal learning, cognition, development, experimental social psychology. *Unit head:* Dr. Mauricio R. Papini, Chair, 817-257-7410, Fax: 817-257-7681, E-mail: m.papini@tcu.edu. *Application contact:* Cindy Hayes, Administrative Assistant, 817-257-7410, Fax: 817-257-7681, E-mail: c.hayes@tcu.edu.
Website: https://psychology.tcu.edu/current-graduate-students/

**Tufts University,** Graduate School of Arts and Sciences, Department of Psychology, Medford, MA 02155. Offers cognitive science (PhD); psychology (MS, PhD). *Students:* 40 full-time (30 women); includes 10 minority (2 Black or African American, non-Hispanic/Latino; 5 Asian, non-Hispanic/Latino; 3 Hispanic/Latino), 6 international. Average age 27. 154 applicants, 8% accepted, 7 enrolled. In 2016, 4 master's, 4 doctorates awarded. Terminal master's awarded for partial completion of doctoral program. *Degree requirements:* For master's, thesis; for doctorate, thesis/dissertation. *Entrance requirements:* For master's and doctorate, GRE General Test, GRE Subject Test. Additional exam requirements/recommendations for international students: Required—TOEFL (minimum score 550 paper-based; 80 iBT), IELTS (minimum score 6.5). *Application deadline:* For fall admission, 12/15 for domestic and international students. Applications are processed on a rolling basis. Application fee: $85. Electronic applications accepted. *Expenses:* $29,936 full-time tuition (for PhD). *Financial support:* In 2016–17, 40 students received support. Fellowships, research assistantships, teaching assistantships, Federal Work-Study, scholarships/grants, tuition waivers (full and partial), and unspecified assistantships available. Support available to part-time students. Financial award application deadline: 1/15. *Unit head:* Dr. Ayanna Thomas, Graduate Program Director. *Application contact:* Office of Graduate Admissions, 617-627-3395, E-mail: gradadmissions@tufts.edu.
Website: http://ase.tufts.edu/psychology

**Tufts University,** School of Engineering, Department of Computer Science, Medford, MA 02155. Offers bioengineering (ME, MS), including bioinformatics; cognitive science (PhD); computer science (MS, PhD). *Program availability:* Part-time. Terminal master's awarded for partial completion of doctoral program. *Degree requirements:* For master's, thesis (for some programs); for doctorate, thesis/dissertation. *Entrance requirements:* For master's and doctorate, GRE General Test. Additional exam requirements/

recommendations for international students: Required—TOEFL (minimum score 550 paper-based; 80 iBT), IELTS (minimum score 6.5). Electronic applications accepted. *Expenses: Tuition:* Full-time $49,892; part-time $1248 per credit hour. *Required fees:* $844. Full-time tuition and fees vary according to degree level, program and student level. Part-time tuition and fees vary according to course load. *Faculty research:* Computational biology, computational geometry, and computational systems biology; cognitive sciences, human-computer interaction, and human-robotic interaction; visualization and graphics, educational technologies; machine learning and data mining; programming languages and systems.

**University at Albany, State University of New York,** College of Arts and Sciences, Department of Psychology, Albany, NY 12222-0001. Offers behavioral neuroscience (PhD); clinical psychology (PhD); cognitive psychology (PhD); industrial/organizational psychology (MA, PhD); social-personality psychology (PhD). *Accreditation:* APA (one or more programs are accredited). *Faculty:* 19 full-time (6 women). *Students:* 68 full-time (42 women), 43 part-time (31 women); includes 26 minority (1 Black or African American, non-Hispanic/Latino; 11 Asian, non-Hispanic/Latino; 9 Hispanic/Latino; 5 Two or more races, non-Hispanic/Latino), 8 international. 304 applicants, 14% accepted, 24 enrolled. In 2016, 7 master's, 11 doctorates awarded. *Degree requirements:* For doctorate, thesis/dissertation. *Entrance requirements:* For doctorate, GRE General Test, GRE Subject Test. Additional exam requirements/recommendations for international students: Required—TOEFL (minimum score 550 paper-based). *Application deadline:* For fall admission, 1/15 for domestic and international students. Application fee: $75. Electronic applications accepted. *Expenses:* Tuition, state resident: full-time $10,870; part-time $453 per credit hour. Tuition, nonresident: full-time $22,210; part-time $925 per credit hour. *International tuition:* $21,550 full-time. *Required fees:* $1864; $96 per credit hour. *Financial support:* Fellowships, research assistantships, teaching assistantships, and career-related internships or fieldwork available. Financial award application deadline: 2/1. *Total annual research expenditures:* $861,900. *Unit head:* James Neely, Chair, 518-442-4820, Fax: 518-442-4867, E-mail: jneely@albany.edu. *Application contact:* Michael DeRensis, Director, Graduate Admissions, 518-442-3980, Fax: 518-442-3922, E-mail: graduate@albany.edu.
Website: http://www.albany.edu/psychology/

**The University of British Columbia,** Faculty of Arts and Faculty of Graduate Studies, Department of Psychology, Vancouver, BC V6T 1Z4, Canada. Offers behavioral neuroscience (MA, PhD); clinical psychology (MA, PhD); cognitive science (MA, PhD); health psychology (MA, PhD); quantitative methods (MA, PhD); social/personality psychology (MA, PhD). *Accreditation:* APA (one or more programs are accredited). Terminal master's awarded for partial completion of doctoral program. *Degree requirements:* For master's, thesis; for doctorate, comprehensive exam, thesis/dissertation. *Entrance requirements:* For master's and doctorate, GRE General Test. Additional exam requirements/recommendations for international students: Required—TOEFL. *Application deadline:* Applications are processed on a rolling basis. Application fee: $100 Canadian dollars ($162 Canadian dollars for international students). Electronic applications accepted. *Expenses:* $4,802 per year tuition and fees, $8,436 per year international. *Financial support:* Fellowships, research assistantships, teaching assistantships, career-related internships or fieldwork, Federal Work-Study, institutionally sponsored loans, scholarships/grants, health care benefits, tuition waivers (full and partial), and unspecified assistantships available. Financial award application deadline: 1/1. *Faculty research:* Clinical, developmental, social/personality, cognition, behavioral neuroscience. *Application contact:* Jaclyn Shaw, 604-822-5002, Fax: 604-822-6923, E-mail: gradsec@psych.ubc.ca.
Website: http://psych.ubc.ca/

**University of California, Merced,** Graduate Division, School of Social Sciences, Humanities and Arts, Merced, CA 95343. Offers cognitive and information sciences (PhD); interdisciplinary humanities (MA, PhD); psychological sciences (MA, PhD); social sciences (MA, PhD); sociology (MA, PhD). *Faculty:* 93 full-time (41 women), 3 part-time/adjunct (all women). *Students:* 172 full-time (112 women), 3 part-time (2 women); includes 69 minority (4 Black or African American, non-Hispanic/Latino; 15 Asian, non-Hispanic/Latino; 43 Hispanic/Latino; 7 Two or more races, non-Hispanic/Latino), 25 international. Average age 31. 195 applicants, 50% accepted, 52 enrolled. In 2016, 13 master's, 11 doctorates awarded. Terminal master's awarded for partial completion of doctoral program. *Degree requirements:* For master's, variable foreign language requirement, comprehensive exam, thesis or alternative; for doctorate, variable foreign language requirement, comprehensive exam, thesis/dissertation. *Entrance requirements:* For master's and doctorate, GRE. Additional exam requirements/recommendations for international students: Required—TOEFL (minimum score 550 paper-based; 80 iBT); Recommended—IELTS (minimum score 7). *Application deadline:* For fall admission, 1/15 for domestic and international students. Application fee: $90 ($110 for international students). Electronic applications accepted. *Expenses:* Contact institution. *Financial support:* In 2016–17, 167 students received support, including 12 fellowships with full tuition reimbursements available (averaging $20,237 per year), 12 research assistantships with full tuition reimbursements available (averaging $18,842 per year), 121 teaching assistantships with full tuition reimbursements available (averaging $19,655 per year); scholarships/grants, traineeships, and health care benefits also available. Financial award application deadline: 1/15. *Faculty research:* Social inequality, critical race and ethnic studies, public health and health sciences, cognitive science and language acquisition, political institutions. *Total annual research expenditures:* $1.2 million. *Unit head:* Dr. Jill Robbins, Dean, E-mail: jillrobbins@ucmerced.edu. *Application contact:* Tsu Ya, Director of Admissions and Academic Services, 209-228-4521, Fax: 209-228-6906, E-mail: tya@ucmerced.edu.

**University of California, San Diego,** Graduate Division, Department of Cognitive Science, La Jolla, CA 92093. Offers cognitive science (PhD). *Students:* 40 full-time (17 women), 2 part-time (0 women). 131 applicants, 14% accepted, 9 enrolled. In 2016, 5 doctorates awarded. *Degree requirements:* For doctorate, one foreign language, thesis/dissertation, 1-quarter teaching assistantship for each academic year in residence. *Entrance requirements:* For doctorate, GRE General Test, minimum GPA of 3.0, letters of recommendation, statement of purpose. Additional exam requirements/recommendations for international students: Required—TOEFL (minimum score 550 paper-based; 80 iBT), IELTS (minimum score 7), PTE. *Application deadline:* For fall admission, 2/28 for domestic students. Application fee: $105 ($125 for international students). Electronic applications accepted. *Expenses:* Tuition, state resident: full-time $11,220. Tuition, nonresident: full-time $26,322. *Required fees:* $1864. *Financial support:* Fellowships, research assistantships, teaching assistantships, scholarships/grants, and unspecified assistantships available. Financial award applicants required to submit FAFSA. *Faculty research:* Normal development of spatial analytic processing, flexible problem solving, specific language impairment, empirical analysis of change in scientific culture, co-evolutionary analysis of drug resistance in HIV. *Unit head:* Marta Kutas, Chair, 858-534-7141, E-mail: mkutas@ucsd.edu. *Application contact:* Beverley Walton, Graduate Coordinator, 858-534-7141, E-mail: gradinfo@cogsci.ucsd.edu.
Website: http://www.cogsci.ucsd.edu

**University of California, Santa Barbara,** Graduate Division, College of Engineering, Department of Computer Science, Santa Barbara, CA 93106-5110. Offers computer science (MS, PhD), including cognitive science (PhD), computational science and

## Cognitive Sciences

engineering (PhD), technology and society (PhD). Terminal master's awarded for partial completion of doctoral program. *Degree requirements:* For master's, comprehensive exam (for some programs), thesis (for some programs), project (for some programs); for doctorate, thesis/dissertation. *Entrance requirements:* For master's and doctorate, GRE. Additional exam requirements/recommendations for international students: Required—TOEFL (minimum score 600 paper-based; 100 iBT), IELTS (minimum score 7). Electronic applications accepted. *Faculty research:* Algorithms and theory, computational science and engineering, computer architecture, database and information systems, machine learning and data mining, networking, operating systems and distributed systems, programming languages and software engineering, security and cryptography, social computing, visual computing and interaction.

**University of California, Santa Barbara,** Graduate Division, College of Letters and Sciences, Division of Humanities and Fine Arts, Department of Religious Studies, Santa Barbara, CA 93106-3130. Offers ancient Mediterranean studies (PhD); cognitive science (PhD); European medieval studies (PhD); feminist studies (PhD); global studies (PhD); religious studies (MA, PhD); translation studies (PhD); MA/PhD. Terminal master's awarded for partial completion of doctoral program. *Degree requirements:* For master's, one foreign language, comprehensive exam (for some programs), thesis (for some programs); for doctorate, 2 foreign languages, thesis/dissertation, methodology. *Entrance requirements:* For master's and doctorate, GRE General Test. Additional exam requirements/recommendations for international students: Required—TOEFL (minimum score 550 paper-based; 80 iBT), IELTS (minimum score 7). Electronic applications accepted. *Faculty research:* Area studies; religious traditions; theory and method in the study of religion; religion, culture, and politics; spirituality and religious experience.

**University of California, Santa Barbara,** Graduate Division, College of Letters and Sciences, Division of Mathematics, Life, and Physical Sciences, Department of Geography, Santa Barbara, CA 93106-4060. Offers cognitive science (PhD); geography (MA, PhD); global studies (PhD); quantitative methods in the social sciences (PhD); technology and society (PhD); transportation (PhD); MA/PhD. Terminal master's awarded for partial completion of doctoral program. *Degree requirements:* For master's, comprehensive exam (for some programs), thesis or alternative; for doctorate, comprehensive exam, thesis/dissertation, 1 quarter of teaching assistantship. *Entrance requirements:* For master's and doctorate, GRE (minimum combined verbal and quantitative scores above 1100 in old scoring system or 301 in new scoring system). Additional exam requirements/recommendations for international students: Required—TOEFL (minimum score 550 paper-based; 80 iBT), IELTS (minimum score 7). Electronic applications accepted. *Faculty research:* Earth system science; human environment relations; modeling, measurement, and computation.

**University of California, Santa Barbara,** Graduate Division, College of Letters and Sciences, Division of Mathematics, Life, and Physical Sciences, Department of Psychological and Brain Sciences, Santa Barbara, CA 93106-9660. Offers cognitive science (PhD); psychology (PhD); quantitative methods in the social sciences (PhD); technology and society (PhD). Terminal master's awarded for partial completion of doctoral program. *Degree requirements:* For doctorate, comprehensive exam, thesis/dissertation, teaching assistant training, progress report, papers, mini-convention presentation, 1 quarter of student teaching or teaching assistant class with section lab, continued participation in research and weekly area meetings. *Entrance requirements:* For doctorate, GRE General Test. Additional exam requirements/recommendations for international students: Required—TOEFL (minimum score 550 paper-based; 80 iBT) or IELTS (minimum score 7). Electronic applications accepted. *Faculty research:* Social psychology; developmental and evolutionary psychology; neuroscience and behavior; cognition, perception and cognitive neuroscience.

**University of California, Santa Barbara,** Graduate Division, College of Letters and Sciences, Division of Social Sciences, Department of Communication, Santa Barbara, CA 93106-4020. Offers cognitive science (PhD); communication (PhD); feminist studies (PhD); language, interaction and social organization (PhD); quantitative methods in the social sciences (PhD); society and technology (PhD); MA/PhD. Terminal master's awarded for partial completion of doctoral program. *Degree requirements:* For doctorate, comprehensive exam, thesis/dissertation. *Entrance requirements:* For doctorate, GRE. Additional exam requirements/recommendations for international students: Required—TOEFL (minimum score 80 iBT), IELTS (minimum score 7). Electronic applications accepted. *Faculty research:* Interpersonal, intergroup, intercultural, organizational, health, media.

**University of Connecticut,** Graduate School, College of Liberal Arts and Sciences, Department of Psychology, Storrs, CT 06269. Offers behavioral neuroscience (PhD); biopsychology (PhD); clinical psychology (MA, PhD); cognition and instruction (PhD); developmental psychology (MA, PhD); ecological psychology (PhD); experimental psychology (PhD); general psychology (MA, PhD); industrial/organizational psychology (PhD); language and cognition (PhD); neuroscience (PhD); social psychology (MA, PhD). *Accreditation:* APA. Terminal master's awarded for partial completion of doctoral program. *Degree requirements:* For master's, comprehensive exam; for doctorate, thesis/dissertation. *Entrance requirements:* For master's and doctorate, GRE General Test, GRE Subject Test. Additional exam requirements/recommendations for international students: Required—TOEFL (minimum score 550 paper-based). Electronic applications accepted.

**University of Connecticut,** Graduate School, Neag School of Education, Department of Educational Psychology, Cognition, Instruction, and Learning Technology Program, Storrs, CT 06269. Offers MA, PhD. *Degree requirements:* For master's, comprehensive exam; for doctorate, thesis/dissertation. *Entrance requirements:* For doctorate, GRE General Test. Additional exam requirements/recommendations for international students: Required—TOEFL (minimum score 550 paper-based). Electronic applications accepted.

**University of Delaware,** College of Arts and Sciences, Department of Linguistics and Cognitive Science, Newark, DE 19716. Offers linguistics (PhD); linguistics and cognitive science (MA). *Degree requirements:* For doctorate, one foreign language, comprehensive exam, thesis/dissertation, publishable research papers. *Entrance requirements:* For master's, GRE General Test; for doctorate, GRE General Test, writing sample. Additional exam requirements/recommendations for international students: Required—TOEFL (minimum score 600 paper-based). Electronic applications accepted. *Faculty research:* East Asian, Austronesian and Romance languages, phonology, phonetics, syntax, cognitive science, semantics, psycholinguistics, language acquisition, endangered languages.

**University of Delaware,** College of Arts and Sciences, Department of Psychology, Newark, DE 19716. Offers behavioral neuroscience (PhD); clinical psychology (PhD); cognitive psychology (PhD); social psychology (PhD). *Accreditation:* APA. *Degree requirements:* For doctorate, thesis/dissertation. *Entrance requirements:* For doctorate, GRE General Test. Additional exam requirements/recommendations for international students: Required—TOEFL (minimum score 600 paper-based). Electronic applications accepted. *Faculty research:* Emotion development, neural and cognitive aspects of memory, neural control of feeding, intergroup relations, social cognition and communication.

**University of Denver,** Division of Arts, Humanities and Social Sciences, Department of Psychology, Denver, CO 80208. Offers affect/social psychology (PhD); clinical child psychology (PhD); cognitive psychology (PhD); developmental psychology (PhD). *Accreditation:* APA. *Faculty:* 26 full-time (13 women), 5 part-time/adjunct (3 women). *Students:* 22 full-time (16 women), 2 part-time (both women); includes 5 minority (1 Black or African American, non-Hispanic/Latino; 1 Asian, non-Hispanic/Latino; 3 Hispanic/Latino), 1 international. Average age 28. 294 applicants, 4% accepted, 8 enrolled. In 2016, 8 doctorates awarded. Terminal master's awarded for partial completion of doctoral program. *Degree requirements:* For doctorate, variable foreign language requirement, comprehensive exam (for some programs), thesis/dissertation. *Entrance requirements:* For doctorate, GRE General Test, master's degree, transcripts, biographical statement, three letters of recommendation. Additional exam requirements/recommendations for international students: Required—TOEFL (minimum score 550 paper-based; 80 iBT). *Application deadline:* For fall admission, 12/1 priority date for domestic and international students. Application fee: $65. Electronic applications accepted. *Expenses:* $29,022 per year full-time. *Financial support:* In 2016–17, 24 students received support, including 5 research assistantships with tuition reimbursements available (averaging $16,000 per year), 12 teaching assistantships with tuition reimbursements available (averaging $17,778 per year); Federal Work-Study, institutionally sponsored loans, scholarships/grants, and unspecified assistantships also available. Support available to part-time students. Financial award application deadline: 2/15; financial award applicants required to submit FAFSA. *Faculty research:* Stress and trauma, developmental science, affect science, clinical science, child psychopathology. *Unit head:* Dr. Anne DePrince, Professor and Chair, 303-871-2939, Fax: 303-871-4747, E-mail: adeprinc@du.edu. *Application contact:* Paula Houghtaling, Graduate Program Administrator, 303-871-3803, Fax: 303-871-4747, E-mail: phoughta@du.edu. Website: http://www.du.edu/ahss/psychology

**University of Guelph,** Graduate Studies, College of Social and Applied Human Sciences, Department of Psychology, Guelph, ON N1G 2W1, Canada. Offers applied social psychology (MA, PhD); clinical psychology: applied development emphasis (PhD); clinical psychology: applied developmental emphasis (MA); industrial/organizational psychology (MA, PhD); neuroscience and applied cognitive science (MA, PhD). *Degree requirements:* For master's, thesis; for doctorate, comprehensive exam, thesis/dissertation. *Entrance requirements:* For master's, GRE General Test, GRE Subject Test, minimum B+ average during previous 2 years of course work; for doctorate, GRE General Test, GRE Subject Test, minimum A- average. Additional exam requirements/recommendations for international students: Required—TOEFL (minimum score 89 iBT). Electronic applications accepted. *Faculty research:* Organizational psychology, reading comprehension and mathematical ability, drug addiction and relapse, gender issues and culture, memory, clinical psychology.

**The University of Kansas,** Graduate Studies, College of Liberal Arts and Sciences, Department of Psychology, Lawrence, KS 66045. Offers clinical psychology (MA, PhD); cognitive and brain sciences (MA, PhD); developmental psychology (MA, PhD); quantitative psychology (PhD); social psychology (MA, PhD). *Accreditation:* APA (one or more programs are accredited). *Program availability:* Part-time. *Students:* 69 full-time (46 women), 1 (woman) part-time; includes 11 minority (5 Black or African American, non-Hispanic/Latino; 3 Asian, non-Hispanic/Latino; 3 Two or more races, non-Hispanic/Latino), 9 international. Average age 29. 202 applicants, 10% accepted, 14 enrolled. In 2016, 12 master's, 11 doctorates awarded. Terminal master's awarded for partial completion of doctoral program. *Entrance requirements:* For doctorate, GRE General Test, three letters of recommendation, resume/curriculum vitae, statement of purpose/personal statement, writing sample. Additional exam requirements/recommendations for international students: Required—TOEFL. *Application deadline:* For fall admission, 12/1 for domestic and international students. Application fee: $65 ($85 for international students). Electronic applications accepted. *Financial support:* Fellowships, research assistantships, teaching assistantships, career-related internships or fieldwork, Federal Work-Study, scholarships/grants, health care benefits, and unspecified assistantships available. Financial award application deadline: 12/1; financial award applicants required to submit FAFSA. *Faculty research:* Origins, correlates and treatment of depression; health and emotion; concentration on topics related to prejudice, stereotyping, and intergroup relations; memory, cognitive development, language, perception, attention, aging; psychometric methods, item response theory, structural equation modeling. *Unit head:* Ruth Anne Atchley, Chair, 785-864-4131. *Application contact:* Graduate Officer, 785-864-4195, E-mail: psycgrad@ku.edu. Website: http://www.psych.ku.edu

**University of Louisiana at Lafayette,** College of Sciences, Institute of Cognitive Science, Lafayette, LA 70504. Offers PhD. *Degree requirements:* For doctorate, comprehensive exam, thesis/dissertation. *Entrance requirements:* For doctorate, GRE General Test, minimum GPA of 3.25. Additional exam requirements/recommendations for international students: Required—TOEFL (minimum score 550 paper-based). Electronic applications accepted. *Faculty research:* Computational models of cognition, comparative cognition, cognitive development, computational cognitive neuroscience, memory.

**University of Louisville,** Graduate School, College of Arts and Sciences, Department of Psychological and Brain Sciences, Louisville, KY 40292-0001. Offers clinical psychology (PhD); experimental psychology (PhD), including cognition and development, vision and hearing. *Accreditation:* APA. *Students:* 54 full-time (42 women), 2 part-time (both women); includes 10 minority (3 Black or African American, non-Hispanic/Latino; 2 Asian, non-Hispanic/Latino; 3 Hispanic/Latino; 2 Two or more races, non-Hispanic/Latino), 1 international. Average age 28. 21 applicants, 5% accepted, 2 enrolled. In 2016, 1 doctorate awarded. *Degree requirements:* For doctorate, comprehensive exam, thesis/dissertation, internship (for clinical psychology). *Entrance requirements:* For doctorate, GRE General Test, GRE Subject Test. Additional exam requirements/recommendations for international students: Required—TOEFL. *Application deadline:* For fall and winter admission, 12/1 for domestic and international students. Application fee: $60. *Expenses:* Tuition, state resident: full-time $12,246; part-time $681 per credit hour. Tuition, nonresident: full-time $25,486; part-time $1417 per credit hour. *Required fees:* $196. Tuition and fees vary according to program and reciprocity agreements. *Financial support:* In 2016–17, 6 fellowships with full tuition reimbursements (averaging $22,000 per year), 1 research assistantship with full tuition reimbursement (averaging $22,000 per year), 1 teaching assistantship with full tuition reimbursement (averaging $22,000 per year) were awarded; health care benefits and unspecified assistantships also available. Financial award application deadline: 12/1. *Faculty research:* Cognitive development, hearing/visual science, cognitive neuroscience/imaging, health psychology/mindfulness/stress and trauma, child/adult psychopathology, geropsychology. *Total annual research expenditures:* $1.8 million. *Unit head:* Dr. Suzanne Meeks, Chair, 502-852-6068, Fax: 502-852-8904, E-mail: smeeks@louisville.edu. *Application contact:* Libby Leggett, Director, Graduate Admissions, 502-852-3101, Fax: 502-852-6536, E-mail: gradadm@louisville.edu. Website: http://louisville.edu/psychology

**University of Maryland, Baltimore County,** The Graduate School, College of Natural and Mathematical Sciences, Department of Biological Sciences, Program in Neuroscience and Cognitive Sciences, Baltimore, MD 21250. Offers PhD. *Faculty:* 6 full-time (3 women). *Students:* 3 full-time (2 women); includes 1 minority (Black or African American, non-Hispanic/Latino). Average age 29. 7 applicants, 29% accepted, 2 enrolled. *Degree requirements:* For doctorate, thesis/dissertation. *Entrance requirements:* For doctorate, GRE General Test, minimum GPA of 3.0. Additional exam requirements/recommendations for international students: Required—TOEFL (minimum score 80 iBT). *Application deadline:* For fall admission, 1/1 priority date for domestic and international students. Application fee: $50. Electronic applications accepted. *Expenses:* Tuition, state resident: full-time $13,294. Tuition, nonresident: full-time $20,286. *Financial support:* In 2016–17, 3 students received support, including 1 research assistantship with full tuition reimbursement available (averaging $24,600 per year), 2 teaching assistantships with full tuition reimbursements available (averaging $23,518 per year); health care benefits also available. *Faculty research:* Developmental biology and neural tube defects, vision science, olfactory systems, neurobiological adaptations of animals, conversion of light into a biological signal in vision. *Unit head:* Dr. Michelle Starz-Gaiano, Director, 410-455-2217, Fax: 410-455-3875, E-mail: biograd@umbc.edu. Website: http://biology.umbc.edu

**University of Maryland, College Park,** Academic Affairs, College of Behavioral and Social Sciences, Program in Neurosciences and Cognitive Sciences, College Park, MD 20742. Offers PhD. *Degree requirements:* For doctorate, comprehensive exam, thesis/dissertation. *Entrance requirements:* For doctorate, GRE General Test, 3 letters of recommendation. Additional exam requirements/recommendations for international students: Required—TOEFL. Electronic applications accepted. *Faculty research:* Molecular neurobiology, cognition, neural and behavioral systems language, memory, human development.

**University of Massachusetts Amherst,** Graduate School, College of Natural Sciences, Department of Psychological and Brain Sciences, Amherst, MA 01003. Offers clinical psychology (MS, PhD); cognitive psychology (MS, PhD); developmental science (MS, PhD); psychology of peace and violence (MS, PhD); social psychology (MS, PhD). *Accreditation:* APA (one or more programs are accredited). Terminal master's awarded for partial completion of doctoral program. *Degree requirements:* For master's, thesis; for doctorate, comprehensive exam, thesis/dissertation. *Entrance requirements:* For master's and doctorate, GRE General Test, 3 letters of recommendation. Additional exam requirements/recommendations for international students: Required—TOEFL (minimum score 550 paper-based; 80 iBT), IELTS (minimum score 6.5). Electronic applications accepted.

**University of Massachusetts Amherst,** Graduate School, Interdisciplinary Programs, Program in Neuroscience and Behavior, Amherst, MA 01003. Offers animal behavior and learning (PhD); molecular and cellular neuroscience (PhD); neural and behavioral development (PhD); neuroendocrinology (PhD); neuroscience and behavior (MS); sensorimotor, cognitive, and computational neuroscience (PhD). Terminal master's awarded for partial completion of doctoral program. *Degree requirements:* For master's, thesis or alternative; for doctorate, comprehensive exam, thesis/dissertation. *Entrance requirements:* For master's, GRE General Test; for doctorate, GRE General Test; GRE Subject Test in psychology, biology, or mathematics (recommended). Additional exam requirements/recommendations for international students: Required—TOEFL (minimum score 550 paper-based; 80 iBT), IELTS (minimum score 6.5). Electronic applications accepted.

**University of Massachusetts Boston,** College of Liberal Arts, Program in Developmental and Brain Sciences, Boston, MA 02125-3393. Offers MA. *Students:* 21 full-time (16 women), 1 (woman) part-time; includes 5 minority (1 Black or African American, non-Hispanic/Latino; 1 Hispanic/Latino; 3 Two or more races, non-Hispanic/Latino), 6 international. Average age 27. 28 applicants, 18% accepted, 4 enrolled. *Entrance requirements:* Additional exam requirements/recommendations for international students: Required—TOEFL; Recommended—IELTS. *Expenses:* Tuition, state resident: full-time $16,863. Tuition, nonresident: full-time $32,913. *Required fees:* $177. *Application contact:* Peggy Roldan Patel, Graduate Admissions Coordinator, 617-287-6400, Fax: 617-287-6236, E-mail: bos.gadm@dpc.umassp.edu. Website: http://www.umb.edu/academics/cla/psychology/grad/dbs

**University of Michigan,** Rackham Graduate School, College of Literature, Science, and the Arts, Department of Psychology, Ann Arbor, MI 48109. Offers biopsychology (PhD); clinical science (PhD); cognition and cognitive neuroscience (PhD); developmental psychology (PhD); personality and social contexts (PhD); social psychology (PhD). *Accreditation:* APA. *Faculty:* 60 full-time (28 women), 30 part-time/adjunct (18 women). *Students:* 147 full-time (111 women); includes 64 minority (15 Black or African American, non-Hispanic/Latino; 1 American Indian or Alaska Native, non-Hispanic/Latino; 14 Asian, non-Hispanic/Latino; 27 Hispanic/Latino; 7 Two or more races, non-Hispanic/Latino), 19 international. Average age 27. 727 applicants, 8% accepted, 34 enrolled. In 2016, 28 doctorates awarded. *Degree requirements:* For doctorate, comprehensive exam, thesis/dissertation, oral defense of dissertation, preliminary exam. *Entrance requirements:* For doctorate, GRE General Test. Additional exam requirements/recommendations for international students: Required—TOEFL. *Application deadline:* For fall admission, 12/1 for domestic and international students. Application fee: $75 ($90 for international students). Electronic applications accepted. *Expenses:* Tuition, state resident: full-time $21,466; part-time $1152 per credit hour. Tuition, nonresident: full-time $43,346; part-time $2367 per credit hour. Part-time tuition and fees vary according to course load, degree level and program. *Financial support:* In 2016–17, 104 students received support, including 64 fellowships with full tuition reimbursements available (averaging $19,800 per year), 6 research assistantships with full tuition reimbursements available (averaging $24,243 per year), 71 teaching assistantships with full tuition reimbursements available (averaging $25,136 per year); career-related internships or fieldwork, traineeships, and health care benefits also available. Financial award application deadline: 4/15. *Unit head:* Prof. Patricia Reuter-Lorenz, Department Chair, 734-764-7429. *Application contact:* Sheri M. Circele, Psychology Student Academic Affairs, 734-764-2580, Fax: 734-764-3520, E-mail: psych.saa@umich.edu. Website: http://www.lsa.umich.edu/psych/

**University of Minnesota, Twin Cities Campus,** Graduate School, College of Liberal Arts, Department of Psychology, Program in Cognitive and Biological Psychology, Minneapolis, MN 55455-0213. Offers PhD. *Degree requirements:* For doctorate, comprehensive exam, thesis/dissertation. *Entrance requirements:* For doctorate, GRE General Test, GRE Subject Test (recommended), 12 credits of upper-level psychology courses, including a course in statistics or psychological measurement. Additional exam requirements/recommendations for international students: Required—TOEFL (minimum score 550 paper-based; 79 iBT).

**University of Nebraska–Lincoln,** Graduate College, College of Arts and Sciences, Department of Psychology, Lincoln, NE 68588. Offers biopsychology (PhD); clinical psychology (PhD); cognitive psychology (PhD); developmental psychology (PhD); psychology (MA); social/personality psychology (PhD); JD/MA; JD/PhD. *Accreditation:* APA (one or more programs are accredited). *Degree requirements:* For master's, thesis optional; for doctorate, comprehensive exam, thesis/dissertation. *Entrance requirements:* For master's and doctorate, GRE General Test. Additional exam requirements/recommendations for international students: Required—TOEFL (minimum score 550 paper-based). Electronic applications accepted. *Faculty research:* Law and

psychology, rural mental health, chronic mental illness, neuropsychology, child clinical psychology.

**University of Nebraska–Lincoln,** Graduate College, College of Education and Human Sciences, Department of Educational Psychology, Lincoln, NE 68588. Offers cognition, learning and development (MA); counseling psychology (MA); educational psychology (MA, Ed S); psychological studies in education (PhD), including cognition, learning and development, counseling psychology, quantitative, qualitative, and psychometric methods, school psychology; quantitative, qualitative, and psychometric methods (MA); school psychology (MA, Ed S). *Accreditation:* APA (one or more programs are accredited); NCATE. *Degree requirements:* For master's, thesis optional. *Entrance requirements:* For master's, GRE General Test. Additional exam requirements/recommendations for international students: Required—TOEFL (minimum score 500 paper-based). Electronic applications accepted. *Faculty research:* Measurement and assessment, metacognition, academic skills, child development, multicultural education and counseling.

**University of Nevada, Reno,** Graduate School, College of Liberal Arts, Department of Psychology, Program in Cognitive Brain Science, Reno, NV 89557. Offers MA, PhD. Terminal master's awarded for partial completion of doctoral program. *Degree requirements:* For master's, thesis optional; for doctorate, comprehensive exam, thesis/dissertation. *Entrance requirements:* For master's, GRE General Test, minimum GPA of 2.75; for doctorate, GRE General Test, minimum GPA of 3.0. Additional exam requirements/recommendations for international students: Required—TOEFL (minimum score 500 paper-based; 61 iBT), IELTS (minimum score 6). Electronic applications accepted. *Faculty research:* Comparative psychology, cognition, perception.

**University of New Mexico,** Graduate Studies, College of Arts and Sciences, Program in Psychology, Albuquerque, NM 87131-2039. Offers behavioral neuroscience (PhD); clinical psychology (PhD); cognitive neuroimaging (PhD); developmental psychology (PhD); evolution (PhD); health psychology (PhD); quantitative methodology (PhD). *Accreditation:* APA. *Faculty:* 23 full-time (8 women), 1 part-time/adjunct (0 women). *Students:* 60 full-time (36 women), 16 part-time (10 women); includes 22 minority (2 Black or African American, non-Hispanic/Latino; 2 American Indian or Alaska Native, non-Hispanic/Latino; 3 Asian, non-Hispanic/Latino; 12 Hispanic/Latino; 3 Two or more races, non-Hispanic/Latino), 2 international. Average age 30. 227 applicants, 11% accepted, 16 enrolled. In 2016, 10 doctorates awarded. *Degree requirements:* For doctorate, comprehensive exam, thesis/dissertation. *Entrance requirements:* For doctorate, GRE General Test, GRE Subject Test (psychology), minimum GPA of 3.0. Additional exam requirements/recommendations for international students: Required—TOEFL (minimum score 550 paper-based; 79 iBT), IELTS (minimum score 6.5). *Application deadline:* For fall admission, 12/15 priority date for domestic and international students. Applications are processed on a rolling basis. Application fee: $50. Electronic applications accepted. *Financial support:* Fellowships, research assistantships with tuition reimbursements, teaching assistantships with tuition reimbursements, career-related internships or fieldwork, Federal Work-Study, institutionally sponsored loans, scholarships/grants, health care benefits, tuition waivers (partial), and unspecified assistantships available. Financial award application deadline: 3/1; financial award applicants required to submit FAFSA. *Faculty research:* Addiction, cognition, brain and behavior, developmental, evolutionary, functioning neuroimaging, health psychology, learning and memory, neuroscience. *Total annual research expenditures:* $727,970. *Unit head:* Dr. Jane Ellen Smith, Department Chair, 505-277-4121, Fax: 505-277-1394. *Application contact:* Rikk Murphy, Graduate Program Coordinator, 505-277-5009, Fax: 505-277-1394, E-mail: advising@unm.edu. Website: http://psych.unm.edu

**The University of North Carolina at Chapel Hill,** Graduate School, College of Arts and Sciences, Department of Psychology, Chapel Hill, NC 27599-3270. Offers behavioral neuroscience (PhD); clinical psychology (PhD); cognitive psychology (PhD); developmental psychology (PhD); quantitative psychology (PhD); social psychology (PhD). *Accreditation:* APA. *Degree requirements:* For doctorate, comprehensive exam, thesis/dissertation. *Entrance requirements:* For doctorate, GRE General Test, minimum GPA of 3.0. Additional exam requirements/recommendations for international students: Required—TOEFL (minimum score 550 paper-based; 79 iBT), IELTS (minimum score 7). Electronic applications accepted. *Faculty research:* Expressed emotion, cognitive development, social cognitive neuroscience, human memory personality.

**The University of North Carolina at Charlotte,** College of Liberal Arts and Sciences, Department of Psychology, Charlotte, NC 28223-0001. Offers cognitive science (Graduate Certificate); health psychology (MA); industrial/organizational psychology (MA); psychology (MA). *Accreditation:* APA. *Program availability:* Part-time. *Faculty:* 32 full-time (21 women), 1 (woman) part-time/adjunct. *Students:* 37 full-time (32 women), 38 part-time (26 women); includes 19 minority (7 Black or African American, non-Hispanic/Latino; 1 Asian, non-Hispanic/Latino; 8 Hispanic/Latino; 3 Two or more races, non-Hispanic/Latino). Average age 28. 331 applicants, 16% accepted, 28 enrolled. In 2016, 13 master's, 5 doctorates, 3 other advanced degrees awarded. *Degree requirements:* For master's, thesis (for some programs); for doctorate, comprehensive exam, thesis/dissertation, internship (clinical health students only). *Entrance requirements:* For master's, GRE, GMAT, MAT; for doctorate, GRE, at least 18 hours of coursework in psychology including introductory psychology and research methods, undergraduate course in statistics, transcripts of all academic work attempted since high school including evidence of the completion of a bachelor's degree, at least three references, personal statement, resume or curriculum vitae; for Graduate Certificate, enrolled and in good standing in a graduate degree program at UNC Charlotte, or have minimum GPA of 3.0 for undergraduate courses. Additional exam requirements/recommendations for international students: Required—TOEFL (minimum score 523 paper-based, 70 iBT) or IELTS (6.5). Applications are processed on a rolling basis. Application fee: $75. Electronic applications accepted. *Expenses:* Contact institution. *Financial support:* In 2016–17, 30 students received support, including 1 fellowship (averaging $42,000 per year), 11 research assistantships (averaging $15,622 per year), 18 teaching assistantships (averaging $14,000 per year); career-related internships or fieldwork, Federal Work-Study, institutionally sponsored loans, scholarships/grants, and unspecified assistantships also available. Support available to part-time students. Financial award application deadline: 3/1; financial award applicants required to submit FAFSA. *Total annual research expenditures:* $218,743. *Unit head:* Dr. Fary Cachelin, Chair, 704-687-1315, E-mail: fcacheli@uncc.edu. *Application contact:* Kathy B. Giddings, Director of Graduate Admissions, 704-687-5503, Fax: 704-687-1668, E-mail: gradadm@uncc.edu. Website: http://psych.uncc.edu

**The University of North Carolina at Greensboro,** Graduate School, College of Arts and Sciences, Department of Psychology, Greensboro, NC 27412-5001. Offers clinical psychology (MA, PhD); cognitive psychology (MA, PhD); developmental psychology (MA, PhD); social psychology (MA, PhD). *Accreditation:* APA (one or more programs are accredited). Terminal master's awarded for partial completion of doctoral program. *Degree requirements:* For master's, comprehensive exam, thesis; for doctorate, one foreign language, thesis/dissertation, preliminary exam. *Entrance requirements:* For master's and doctorate, GRE General Test. Additional exam requirements/

recommendations for international students: Required—TOEFL. Electronic applications accepted. *Faculty research:* Sensory and perceptual determinants; evoked potential: disorders, deafness, and development.

**University of Notre Dame,** Graduate School, College of Arts and Letters, Division of Social Science, Department of Psychology, Notre Dame, IN 46556. Offers cognitive psychology (PhD); counseling psychology (PhD); developmental psychology (PhD); quantitative psychology (PhD). *Accreditation:* APA. *Degree requirements:* For doctorate, comprehensive exam, thesis/dissertation, candidacy exam. *Entrance requirements:* For doctorate, GRE General Test, GRE Subject Test (strongly recommended). Additional exam requirements/recommendations for international students: Required—TOEFL (minimum score 600 paper-based; 80 iBT). Electronic applications accepted. *Faculty research:* Cognitive and socio-emotional development, statistical methods and quantitative models applicable to psychology, interpersonal relations, life span development and developmental delay, childhood depression, structural equation and dynamical systems.

**University of Oregon,** Graduate School, College of Arts and Sciences, Department of Psychology, Eugene, OR 97403. Offers clinical psychology (PhD); cognitive psychology (MA, MS, PhD); developmental psychology (MA, MS, PhD); physiological psychology (MA, MS, PhD); psychology (MA, MS, PhD); social/personality psychology (MA, MS, PhD). *Accreditation:* APA (one or more programs are accredited). Terminal master's awarded for partial completion of doctoral program. *Degree requirements:* For doctorate, thesis/dissertation. *Entrance requirements:* For master's, GRE General Test, minimum GPA of 3.0; for doctorate, GRE General Test. Additional exam requirements/recommendations for international students: Required—TOEFL.

**University of Rochester,** School of Arts and Sciences, Department of Brain and Cognitive Sciences, Rochester, NY 14627. Offers PhD. *Faculty:* 16 full-time (4 women). *Students:* 40 full-time (21 women); includes 9 minority (3 Asian, non-Hispanic/Latino; 4 Hispanic/Latino; 2 Two or more races, non-Hispanic/Latino), 12 international. Average age 27. 127 applicants, 10% accepted, 6 enrolled. In 2016, 4 doctorates awarded. Terminal master's awarded for partial completion of doctoral program. *Degree requirements:* For doctorate, thesis/dissertation, qualifying exam. *Entrance requirements:* For doctorate, GRE General Test. Additional exam requirements/recommendations for international students: Required—TOEFL (minimum score 600 paper-based; 100 iBT). *Application deadline:* For fall admission, 12/1 for domestic and international students. Application fee: $60. Electronic applications accepted. *Expenses:* $1,538 per credit hour. *Financial support:* In 2016–17, 39 students received support, including 9 fellowships (averaging $32,000 per year), 30 research assistantships (averaging $27,200 per year); scholarships/grants, health care benefits, and tuition waivers (full) also available. Financial award application deadline: 12/1. *Faculty research:* Perception and action; language processing and acquisition; learning, development and neural plasticity; cognitive neuroscience; computation, cognition and the brain. *Unit head:* Gregory DeAngelis, Chair, 585-275-8677, E-mail: gdeangelis@ur.rochester.edu. *Application contact:* Kathy Corser, Graduate Program Coordinator, 585-275-1844.
Website: http://www.bcs.rochester.edu/graduate/index.html

**University of Southern California,** Graduate School, Dana and David Dornsife College of Letters, Arts and Sciences, Department of Psychology, Los Angeles, CA 90089. Offers brain and cognitive science (PhD); clinical science (PhD); developmental psychology (PhD); human behavior (MHB); quantitative methods (PhD); social psychology (PhD). *Accreditation:* APA. *Degree requirements:* For doctorate, comprehensive exam, thesis/dissertation, one-year internship (for clinical science students). *Entrance requirements:* For doctorate, GRE. Additional exam requirements/recommendations for international students: Recommended—TOEFL (minimum score 600 paper-based; 100 iBT). Electronic applications accepted. *Faculty research:* Affective neuroscience; children and families; vision, culture and ethnicity; intergroup relations; aggression and violence; language and reading development; substance abuse.

**University of South Florida,** College of Arts and Sciences, Department of Psychology, Tampa, FL 33620-9951. Offers psychology (PhD), including clinical psychology, cognition, neuroscience and social psychology, industrial-organizational psychology. *Accreditation:* APA. *Faculty:* 34 full-time (14 women). *Students:* 83 full-time (57 women), 19 part-time (13 women); includes 16 minority (1 Black or African American, non-Hispanic/Latino; 5 Asian, non-Hispanic/Latino; 7 Hispanic/Latino; 3 Two or more races, non-Hispanic/Latino), 9 international. Average age 28. 467 applicants, 3% accepted, 14 enrolled. In 2016, 12 doctorates awarded. *Degree requirements:* For doctorate, comprehensive exam, thesis/dissertation, internship. *Entrance requirements:* For doctorate, GRE General Test, minimum upper-division GPA of 3.4, three letters of recommendation, personal goals statement. Additional exam requirements/recommendations for international students: Required—TOEFL (minimum score 550 paper-based; 79 iBT) or IELTS (minimum score 6.5). *Application deadline:* For fall admission, 12/1 for domestic and international students. Application fee: $30. Electronic applications accepted. *Expenses:* Contact institution. *Financial support:* In 2016–17, 48 students received support, including 18 research assistantships with tuition reimbursements available (averaging $14,727 per year), 57 teaching assistantships with tuition reimbursements available (averaging $14,543 per year); tuition waivers (partial) and unspecified assistantships also available. Financial award applicants required to submit FAFSA. *Faculty research:* Clinical, cognitive, neuroscience, social, and industrial/organizational. *Total annual research expenditures:* $2.1 million. *Unit head:* Dr. Toru Shimizu, Chairperson, 813-974-0352, Fax: 813-974-4617, E-mail: shimizu@usf.edu. *Application contact:* Dr. Joseph Vandello, Associate Professor and Graduate Program Director, 813-974-0362, Fax: 813-974-4617, E-mail: vandello@usf.edu. Website: http://psychology.usf.edu/

**The University of Texas at Dallas,** School of Behavioral and Brain Sciences, Program in Cognition and Neuroscience, Richardson, TX 75080. Offers applied cognition and neuroscience (MS); cognition and neuroscience (PhD). *Program availability:* Part-time, evening/weekend. *Faculty:* 30 full-time (10 women), 3 part-time/adjunct (all women). *Students:* 181 full-time (110 women), 41 part-time (30 women); includes 61 minority (8 Black or African American, non-Hispanic/Latino; 1 American Indian or Alaska Native, non-Hispanic/Latino; 17 Asian, non-Hispanic/Latino; 29 Hispanic/Latino; 6 Two or more races, non-Hispanic/Latino), 50 international. Average age 28. 172 applicants, 51% accepted, 69 enrolled. In 2016, 82 master's, 5 doctorates awarded. *Degree requirements:* For master's, internship; for doctorate, thesis/dissertation. *Entrance requirements:* For master's and doctorate, GRE General Test, minimum GPA of 3.0 in upper-level coursework in field. Additional exam requirements/recommendations for international students: Required—TOEFL (minimum score 550 paper-based).

*Application deadline:* For fall admission, 7/15 for domestic students, 5/1 priority date for international students; for spring admission, 11/15 for domestic students, 9/1 priority date for international students. Applications are processed on a rolling basis. Application fee: $50 ($100 for international students). Electronic applications accepted. *Expenses:* Tuition, state resident: full-time $12,418; part-time $690 per semester hour. Tuition, nonresident: full-time $24,150; part-time $1342 per semester hour. Tuition and fees vary according to course load. *Financial support:* In 2016–17, 142 students received support, including 1 fellowship (averaging $5,000 per year), 24 research assistantships with partial tuition reimbursements available (averaging $29,434 per year), 39 teaching assistantships with partial tuition reimbursements available (averaging $17,842 per year); career-related internships or fieldwork, Federal Work-Study, institutionally sponsored loans, scholarships/grants, and unspecified assistantships also available. Support available to part-time students. Financial award application deadline: 4/30; financial award applicants required to submit FAFSA. *Faculty research:* Neural plasticity, neuroimaging, face recognition, cognitive and neurobiological mechanisms of human memory, treatment interventions for semantic memory retrieval problems. *Unit head:* Dr. Christa McIntyre Rodriguez, Program Head, 972-883-2235, Fax: 972-883-2491, E-mail: christa.mcintyre@utdallas.edu. *Application contact:* 972-883-4311, Fax: 972-883-2491, E-mail: cogneurophd@utdallas.edu.
Website: http://www.utdallas.edu/bbs/degrees/cn-degrees/

**University of Washington,** Graduate School, College of Arts and Sciences, Department of Psychology, Seattle, WA 98195. Offers animal behavior (PhD); child psychology (PhD); clinical psychology (PhD); cognition and perception (PhD); developmental psychology (PhD); quantitative psychology (PhD); social psychology and personality (PhD). *Accreditation:* APA. *Degree requirements:* For doctorate, thesis/dissertation. *Entrance requirements:* For doctorate, GRE General Test, minimum GPA of 3.0. Electronic applications accepted. *Faculty research:* Addictive behaviors, artificial intelligence, child psychopathology, mechanisms and development of vision, physiology of ingestive behaviors.

**University of Wisconsin–Madison,** Graduate School, College of Letters and Science, Department of Psychology, Program in Cognitive Neurosciences, Madison, WI 53706-1380. Offers PhD. *Degree requirements:* For doctorate, comprehensive exam, thesis/dissertation. *Entrance requirements:* For doctorate, GRE General Test, minimum undergraduate GPA of 3.0. Additional exam requirements/recommendations for international students: Required—TOEFL. Electronic applications accepted.

**University of Wisconsin–Madison,** Graduate School, College of Letters and Science, Department of Psychology, Program in Perception, Madison, WI 53706-1380. Offers PhD. *Degree requirements:* For doctorate, comprehensive exam, thesis/dissertation. *Entrance requirements:* For doctorate, GRE General Test, minimum GPA of 3.0. Electronic applications accepted.

**Wayne State University,** College of Liberal Arts and Sciences, Department of Psychology, Detroit, MI 48202. Offers behavioral and cognitive neuroscience (PhD); clinical psychology (PhD); cognitive, developmental and social psychology (PhD); industrial/organizational psychology (MA, PhD). Doctoral program admits for fall only. *Accreditation:* APA (one or more programs are accredited). *Faculty:* 36. *Students:* 98 full-time (65 women), 31 part-time (16 women); includes 19 minority (4 Black or African American, non-Hispanic/Latino; 2 Asian, non-Hispanic/Latino; 8 Hispanic/Latino; 5 Two or more races, non-Hispanic/Latino), 14 international. Average age 28. 478 applicants, 13% accepted, 33 enrolled. In 2016, 16 master's, 13 doctorates awarded. Terminal master's awarded for partial completion of doctoral program. *Degree requirements:* For master's, thesis (for some programs); for doctorate, thesis/dissertation, training assignments. *Entrance requirements:* For master's, GRE General Test, minimum undergraduate upper-division cumulative GPA of 3.0, courses in introductory psychology and statistics, two letters of recommendation, professional statement; for doctorate, GRE General Test, bachelor's, master's, or other advanced degree; at least twelve credits in psychology with minimum GPA of 3.0; courses in laboratory psychology and statistical methods in psychology; at least three letters of recommendation; statement of purpose. Additional exam requirements/recommendations for international students: Required—TOEFL (minimum score 550 paper-based; 79 iBT), TWE (minimum score 5.5), Michigan English Language Assessment Battery (minimum score 85); Recommended—IELTS (minimum score 6.5). Application fee: $50. Electronic applications accepted. *Expenses:* $16,503 per year resident tuition and fees, $33,697 per year non-resident tuition and fees. *Financial support:* In 2016–17, 90 students received support, including 12 fellowships with tuition reimbursements available (averaging $15,719 per year), 6 research assistantships with tuition reimbursements available (averaging $19,341 per year), 50 teaching assistantships with tuition reimbursements available (averaging $17,994 per year); scholarships/grants, health care benefits, and unspecified assistantships also available. Financial award applicants required to submit FAFSA. *Faculty research:* Behavioral neuroscience, cognitive/neuroscience of development and aging research, children, adolescents, and family research, cognition research, emotion research, health psychology research, homelessness and poverty research, memory research, neuropsychology research, personality/cognition, relationships research, substance use and abuse research, workplace adaptation, well-being and evaluation research. *Total annual research expenditures:* $1.4 million. *Unit head:* Boris Baltes, PhD, Chair/Professor, 313-577-2803, E-mail: b.baltes@wayne.edu. *Application contact:* Alia Allen, Academic Services Officer, 313-577-2823, E-mail: aallen@wayne.edu.
Website: http://clas.wayne.edu/psychology/

**Wilfrid Laurier University,** Faculty of Graduate and Postdoctoral Studies, Faculty of Science, Department of Psychology, Waterloo, ON N2L 3C5, Canada. Offers behavioral neuroscience (M Sc, PhD); cognitive neuroscience (M Sc, PhD); community psychology (MA, PhD); social and developmental psychology (MA, PhD). *Program availability:* Part-time. *Degree requirements:* For master's, thesis; for doctorate, thesis/dissertation. *Entrance requirements:* For master's, GRE General Test, honors BA or the equivalent in psychology, minimum B average in undergraduate course work; for doctorate, GRE General Test, master's degree, minimum A- average. Additional exam requirements/recommendations for international students: Required—TOEFL (minimum score 89 iBT). Electronic applications accepted. *Faculty research:* Brain and cognition, community psychology, social and developmental psychology.

**Yale University,** Graduate School of Arts and Sciences, Department of Psychology, New Haven, CT 06520. Offers behavioral neuroscience (PhD); clinical psychology (PhD); cognitive psychology (PhD); developmental psychology (PhD); social/personality psychology (PhD). *Accreditation:* APA. *Degree requirements:* For doctorate, thesis/dissertation. *Entrance requirements:* For doctorate, GRE General Test.

# Counseling Psychology

**Abilene Christian University,** Graduate Programs, College of Arts and Sciences, Department of Psychology, Program in Counseling Psychology, Abilene, TX 79699. Offers MS. *Program availability:* Part-time. *Students:* 6 full-time (4 women), 2 part-time (1 woman); includes 1 minority (Hispanic/Latino), 1 international. 22 applicants, 18% accepted, 2 enrolled. In 2016, 7 master's awarded. *Degree requirements:* For master's, comprehensive exam, thesis, practicum. *Entrance requirements:* Additional exam requirements/recommendations for international students: Required—TOEFL (minimum score 80 iBT), IELTS (minimum score 6), PTE. *Application deadline:* For fall admission, 3/30 priority date for domestic students; for spring admission, 11/1 for domestic students. Applications are processed on a rolling basis. Application fee: $50. Electronic applications accepted. *Expenses: Tuition:* Full-time $19,890; part-time $1105 per credit hour. Tuition and fees vary according to course load and program. *Financial support:* In 2016–17, 4 students received support. Scholarships/grants and unspecified assistantships available. Financial award application deadline: 4/1; financial award applicants required to submit FAFSA. *Unit head:* Dr. Cherisse Flanagan, Graduate Director, 325-674-4826, Fax: 325-674-6968, E-mail: cherisse.flanagan@acu.edu. *Application contact:* Corey Patterson, Director of Graduate Admission and Recruiting, 325-674-6566, Fax: 325-674-6717, E-mail: gradinfo@acu.edu. Website: http://www.acu.edu/graduate/academics/counseling-psychology.html

**Adelphi University,** Gordon F. Derner School of Psychology, Program in Mental Health Counseling, Garden City, NY 11530-0701. Offers MA. *Students:* 36 full-time (28 women); includes 41 minority (11 Black or African American, non-Hispanic/Latino; 8 Asian, non-Hispanic/Latino; 19 Hispanic/Latino; 3 Two or more races, non-Hispanic/Latino), 6 international. Average age 24. 79 applicants, 57% accepted, 19 enrolled. In 2016, 19 master's awarded. *Degree requirements:* For master's, comprehensive exam. *Entrance requirements:* For master's, GRE General Test, GRE Subject Test, minimum cumulative GPA of 3.1; interview; course work in developmental psychology, research methods, and psycho-pathology; 2 letters of recommendation. Additional exam requirements/recommendations for international students: Required—TOEFL (minimum score 550 paper-based; 80 iBT), IELTS (minimum score 6.5). *Application deadline:* For fall admission, 4/1 priority date for domestic students, 5/1 priority date for international students. Application fee: $50. Electronic applications accepted. *Expenses:* Contact institution. *Financial support:* Research assistantships with full and partial tuition reimbursements, teaching assistantships, career-related internships or fieldwork, institutionally sponsored loans, scholarships/grants, traineeships, and unspecified assistantships available. Support available to part-time students. *Unit head:* Dr. Errol Rodriguez, Assistant Dean, 516-237-8572, E-mail: erodriguez@adelphi.edu. *Application contact:* Christine Murphy, Director of Admissions, 516-877-3050, Fax: 516-877-3039, E-mail: graduateadmissions@adelphi.edu. Website: http://derner.adelphi.edu/psychology/graduate/ma-mental-health-counseling/

**Adler Graduate School,** Program in Adlerian Counseling and Psychotherapy, Richfield, MN 55423. Offers Adlerian studies (MA); art therapy (MA); clinical mental health counseling (MA); co-occurring mental health and substance abuse disorders (MA); marriage and family therapy (MA); school counseling (MA). *Program availability:* Part-time, evening/weekend. *Faculty:* 71 part-time/adjunct (55 women). *Students:* 298 part-time (225 women); includes 51 minority (40 Black or African American, non-Hispanic/Latino; 6 American Indian or Alaska Native, non-Hispanic/Latino; 5 Hispanic/Latino). *Degree requirements:* For master's, thesis or alternative, 500-700 hour internship (depending on license choice). *Entrance requirements:* For master's, interview, official transcripts, minimum cumulative GPA of 3.0. *Application deadline:* Applications are processed on a rolling basis. Application fee: $50. Electronic applications accepted. *Financial support:* Career-related internships or fieldwork and tuition waivers available. Support available to part-time students. Financial award applicants required to submit FAFSA. *Unit head:* Dr. Dan Haugen, President, 612-767-7048, Fax: 612-861-7559, E-mail: haugen@alfredadler.edu. *Application contact:* Evelyn B. Haas, Director of Admissions, 612-767-7044, Fax: 612-861-7559, E-mail: ev@alfredadler.edu.

**Adler University,** Programs in Psychology, Chicago, IL 60602. Offers advanced Adlerian psychotherapy (Certificate); art therapy (MA); clinical mental health counseling (MA); clinical neuropsychology (Certificate); clinical psychology (Psy D); community psychology (MA); counseling and organizational psychology (MA); counseling psychology (MA); counselor education and supervision (PhD); couple and family therapy (DCFT); criminology (MA); emergency management leadership (MA); forensic psychology (MA); marriage and family counseling (MA); marriage and family therapy (Certificate); military psychology (MA); nonprofit management (MA); organizational psychology (MA); police psychology (MA); public policy and administration (MA); rehabilitation counseling (MA); sport and health psychology (MA); substance abuse counseling (Psy D/Certificate; Psy D/MACAT; Psy D/MACP; Psy D/MAMFC; Psy D/MASAC. *Accreditation:* APA. *Program availability:* Part-time, evening/weekend, online learning. Terminal master's awarded for partial completion of doctoral program. *Degree requirements:* For master's, thesis or alternative, oral exam, practicum; for doctorate, thesis/dissertation, clinical exam, internship, oral exam, practicum, written qualifying exam. *Entrance requirements:* For master's, 12 semester hours in psychology, minimum GPA of 3.0; for doctorate, 18 semester hours in psychology, minimum GPA of 3.25; for Certificate, appropriate master's or doctoral degree. Additional exam requirements/recommendations for international students: Required—TOEFL (minimum score 550 paper-based; 79 iBT). Electronic applications accepted.

**See Display on page 982 and Close-Up on page 1225.**

**Alabama Agricultural and Mechanical University,** School of Graduate Studies, College of Education, Humanities, and Behavioral Sciences, Department of Social Work, Psychology and Counseling, Huntsville, AL 35811. Offers psychology and counseling (MS, Ed S), including clinical psychology (MS), counseling psychology (MS), guidance and counseling, rehabilitation counseling (MS), school counseling (MS), school psychology (MS), school psychometry (MS); social work (MSW). *Accreditation:* CORE; NCATE. *Program availability:* Part-time, evening/weekend. *Degree requirements:* For master's, comprehensive exam. *Entrance requirements:* For master's, GRE General Test. Additional exam requirements/recommendations for international students: Required—TOEFL (minimum score 500 paper-based; 61 iBT). *Application deadline:* For fall admission, 5/1 for domestic students. Application fee: $15 ($20 for international students). *Expenses:* Tuition, nonresident: part-time $826 per credit hour. Full-time tuition and fees vary according to course load and program. *Financial support:* Career-related internships or fieldwork available. Support available to part-time students. Financial award application deadline: 4/1. *Faculty research:* Increasing numbers of minorities in special education and speech-language pathology. *Unit head:* Dr. Shirley King, Chair, 256-372-5520, Fax: 256-372-5526.

**Alaska Pacific University,** Graduate Programs, Department of Counseling, Psychological Studies, and Human Services, Program in Counseling Psychology, Anchorage, AK 99508-4672. Offers MSCP.

**Alfred University,** Graduate School, Counseling and School Psychology Program, Alfred, NY 14802-1205. Offers mental health counseling (MS Ed); school counseling (MS Ed, CAS); school psychology (MA, Psy D, CAS). *Accreditation:* APA. *Faculty:* 10 full-time (3 women), 4 part-time/adjunct (2 women). *Students:* 43 full-time (35 women), 40 part-time (31 women); includes 11 minority (6 Black or African American, non-Hispanic/Latino; 1 Asian, non-Hispanic/Latino; 4 Hispanic/Latino), 1 international. Average age 25. 40 applicants, 80% accepted, 24 enrolled. In 2016, 85 master's, 8 doctorates, 18 other advanced degrees awarded. *Degree requirements:* For master's, internship; for doctorate, thesis/dissertation, internship. *Entrance requirements:* For master's and doctorate, GRE General Test. Additional exam requirements/recommendations for international students: Required—TOEFL (minimum score 590 paper-based; 90 iBT), IELTS (minimum score 6.5). *Application deadline:* For fall admission, 1/15 priority date for domestic and international students. Application fee: $60. Electronic applications accepted. *Expenses: Tuition:* Full-time $38,020; part-time $810 per credit. *Required fees:* $970; $82 per semester. *Financial support:* Research assistantships with partial tuition reimbursements, career-related internships or fieldwork, and unspecified assistantships available. Financial award application deadline: 8/1; financial award applicants required to submit FAFSA. *Faculty research:* Family processes, alternative assessment approaches, behavior disorders in children, parent involvement, school psychology training issues. *Unit head:* Dr. Nancy Evangelista, Chair, 607-871-2212, E-mail: fevangel@alfred.edu. *Application contact:* Sara Love, Coordinator of Graduate Admissions, 607-871-2115, Fax: 607-871-2198, E-mail: gradinquiry@alfred.edu.

**Amberton University,** Graduate School, Programs in Counseling, Garland, TX 75041-5595. Offers MA. *Entrance requirements:* For master's, minimum GPA of 3.0.

**American International College,** Low Residency Programs, Springfield, MA 01109-3189. Offers counseling psychology (MA); educational leadership and supervision (Ed D); individual and institutional development (Ed D); professional counseling and supervision (Ed D); psychology (Ed D); teaching and learning (Ed D). *Expenses: Tuition:* Full-time $7902; part-time $750 per semester hour. *Required fees:* $60; $60 per semester hour. $30 per semester. One-time fee: $100. Tuition and fees vary according to course load, degree level, campus/location and program. *Application contact:* Kerry Barnes, Director of Graduate Admissions, 413-205-3703, Fax: 413-205-3051, E-mail: kerry.barnes@aic.edu.

**Amridge University,** Graduate and Professional Programs, Montgomery, AL 36117. Offers Biblical studies (MA, PhD); Christian ministry (MS); family therapy (D Min); human services (MS); leadership and management (MS); marriage and family therapy (M Div, MA, PhD); ministerial leadership (M Div, MS); New Testament studies (MA); Old Testament studies (MA); professional counseling (M Div, MA, PhD); theology (M Div, D Min). *Program availability:* Part-time, evening/weekend, online learning. *Faculty:* 22 full-time (3 women), 10 part-time/adjunct (6 women). *Students:* 81 full-time (49 women), 225 part-time (137 women); includes 81 minority (80 Black or African American, non-Hispanic/Latino; 1 Hispanic/Latino). Average age 41. 122 applicants, 100% accepted, 79 enrolled. *Degree requirements:* For master's, one foreign language, comprehensive exam (for some programs), thesis (for some programs); for doctorate, one foreign language, comprehensive exam (for some programs), thesis/dissertation (for some programs). *Entrance requirements:* For master's, official transcript showing an earned 4-year BA or BS from regionally- or nationally-accredited institution; for doctorate, official transcript showing earned graduate degree from regionally- or nationally-accredited institution; writing sample (e.g. career monograph, published journal article, term paper from master's degree or doctoral dissertation); interview. Additional exam requirements/recommendations for international students: Required—TOEFL (minimum score 79 iBT). *Application deadline:* Applications are processed on a rolling basis. Application fee: $50. Electronic applications accepted. *Expenses: Tuition:* Full-time $12,870; part-time $715 per credit hour. *Required fees:* $1300; $650 per semester. *Financial support:* In 2016–17, 45 students received support. Federal Work-Study and scholarships/grants available. Support available to part-time students. Financial award applicants required to submit FAFSA. *Faculty research:* Technology and mental healthcare, resilience in black families, theology and congregational ministry. *Unit head:* Laina Costanza, Vice President, Student Affairs, 888-790-8080 Ext. 1, Fax: 334-387-3878, E-mail: cc@amridgeuniversity.edu. *Application contact:* Brooks Housley, Student Affairs Coordinator, 888-790-8080 Ext. 1, Fax: 334-387-3878, E-mail: admissions@amridgeuniversity.edu.

**Andrews University,** School of Graduate Studies, School of Education, Department of Graduate Psychology and Counseling, Program in Community Counseling, Berrien Springs, MI 49104. Offers clinical mental health counseling (MA); community counseling (MA). *Students:* 14 full-time (8 women), 6 part-time (4 women); includes 8 minority (5 Black or African American, non-Hispanic/Latino; 3 Hispanic/Latino), 4 international. Average age 31. In 2016, 9 master's awarded. *Degree requirements:* For master's, thesis optional. *Entrance requirements:* For master's, GRE. Additional exam requirements/recommendations for international students: Required—TOEFL (minimum score 550 paper-based). Application fee: $40. *Unit head:* Dr. Nancy Carbonell, Coordinator, 269-471-3472. *Application contact:* Justina Clayburn, Supervisor of Graduate Admission, 800-253-2874, Fax: 269-471-6321, E-mail: graduate@andrews.edu.

**Andrews University,** School of Graduate Studies, School of Education, Department of Graduate Psychology and Counseling, Program in Counseling Psychology, Berrien Springs, MI 49104. Offers PhD. *Students:* 27 full-time (21 women), 2 part-time (both women); includes 8 minority (6 Black or African American, non-Hispanic/Latino; 1 Hispanic/Latino; 1 Two or more races, non-Hispanic/Latino), 5 international. Average age 37. In 2016, 2 doctorates awarded. *Degree requirements:* For doctorate, thesis/dissertation. *Entrance requirements:* Additional exam requirements/recommendations for international students: Required—TOEFL (minimum score 550 paper-based). Application fee: $40. *Unit head:* Dr. Carole Woolford, Coordinator, 269-471-6074. *Application contact:* Justina Clayburn, Supervisor of Graduate Admission, 800-253-2874, Fax: 269-471-6321, E-mail: graduate@andrews.edu.

**Angelo State University,** College of Graduate Studies and Research, Archer College of Health and Human Services, Department of Psychology, Sociology and Social Work, San Angelo, TX 76909. Offers applied psychology (MS); counseling psychology (MS); industrial-organizational psychology (MS). *Program availability:* Part-time, evening/weekend. *Students:* 73 full-time (53 women), 33 part-time (22 women); includes 36 minority (5 Black or African American, non-Hispanic/Latino; 31 Hispanic/Latino), 5 international. Average age 32. *Degree requirements:* For master's, comprehensive

exam, thesis optional. *Entrance requirements:* For master's, GRE General Test (for industrial and organizational psychology only), essay, letters of recommendation (for industrial and organizational psychology only). Additional exam requirements/recommendations for international students: Required—TOEFL or IELTS. *Application deadline:* For fall admission, 7/15 priority date for domestic students, 6/10 for international students; for spring admission, 12/1 priority date for domestic students, 11/1 for international students. Applications are processed on a rolling basis. Application fee: $40 ($50 for international students). Electronic applications accepted. *Expenses:* Tuition, state resident: full-time $3726; part-time $2484 per year. Tuition, nonresident: full-time $10,746; part-time $7164 per year. *Required fees:* $2538; $1702 per unit. *Financial support:* Teaching assistantships, career-related internships or fieldwork, Federal Work-Study, scholarships/grants, and unspecified assistantships available. Support available to part-time students. Financial award application deadline: 3/1; financial award applicants required to submit FAFSA. *Unit head:* Dr. James N. Forbes, Chair, 325-486-6120, Fax: 325-942-2290, E-mail: james.forbes@angelo.edu. *Application contact:* Dr. James N. Forbes, Chair, 325-486-6120, Fax: 325-942-2290, E-mail: james.forbes@angelo.edu.
Website: http://www.angelo.edu/dept/psychology_sociology/

**Anna Maria College,** Graduate Division, Program in Counseling Psychology, Paxton, MA 01612. Offers counseling psychology (MA). *Program availability:* Part-time, evening/weekend. *Degree requirements:* For master's, comprehensive exam, practicum. *Entrance requirements:* Additional exam requirements/recommendations for international students: Required—TOEFL (minimum score 500 paper-based). Electronic applications accepted.

**Antioch University New England,** Graduate School, Department of Applied Psychology, Program in Clinical Mental Health Counseling, Keene, NH 03431-3552. Offers clinical mental health counseling (MA); substance abuse counseling (MA). *Accreditation:* ACA. *Degree requirements:* For master's, internship, practicum. *Entrance requirements:* For master's, previous course work and work experience in psychology. Additional exam requirements/recommendations for international students: Required—TOEFL (minimum score 550 paper-based). Electronic applications accepted. *Expenses:* Contact institution. *Faculty research:* Multicultural issues in field supervision.

**Appalachian State University,** Cratis D. Williams Graduate School, Department of Human Development and Psychological Counseling, Boone, NC 28608. Offers clinical mental health counseling (MA); college student development (MA); marriage and family therapy (MA); school counseling (MA). *Accreditation:* AAMFT/COAMFTE; ACA; NCATE. *Program availability:* Part-time. *Degree requirements:* For master's, comprehensive exam (for some programs), thesis optional, internships. *Entrance requirements:* For master's, GRE General Test, 3 letters of recommendation. Additional exam requirements/recommendations for international students: Required—TOEFL (minimum score 570 paper-based; 79 iBT), IELTS (minimum score 6.5). *Application deadline:* For fall admission, 2/1 priority date for domestic students, 2/1 for international students; for spring admission, 2/1 for international students. Applications are processed on a rolling basis. Application fee: $55. Electronic applications accepted. *Expenses:* Tuition, state resident: full-time $4744. Tuition, nonresident: full-time $17,913. Full-time tuition and fees vary according to program. *Financial support:* Fellowships, research assistantships, teaching assistantships, career-related internships or fieldwork, Federal Work-Study, scholarships/grants, and unspecified assistantships available. Financial award application deadline: 4/1; financial award applicants required to submit FAFSA. *Faculty research:* Multicultural counseling, addictions counseling, play therapy, expressive arts, child and adolescent therapy, sexual abuse counseling. *Unit head:* Dr. Lee Baruth, Chairman, 828-262-2055, E-mail: baruthlg@appstate.edu. *Application contact:* Dr. Mark Schwarze, Program Director, 828-262-6046, E-mail: asucmhc@appstate.edu.
Website: http://www.ced.appstate.edu/departments/hpc

**Arcadia University,** College of Arts and Sciences, Department of Psychology, Glenside, PA 19038-3295. Offers applied behavior analysis (MAC); autism (MAC); child/family therapy (MAC); community public health (MAC); counseling/international peace and conflict resolution dual degree (MAC); mental health counseling (MAC); trauma (MAC). *Program availability:* Part-time. *Faculty:* 14 full-time (9 women), 10 part-time/adjunct (9 women). *Students:* 33 full-time (27 women), 39 part-time (30 women); includes 22 minority (13 Black or African American, non-Hispanic/Latino; 2 Asian, non-Hispanic/Latino; 1 Hispanic/Latino; 6 Two or more races, non-Hispanic/Latino), 1 international. Average age 30. 61 applicants, 64% accepted, 24 enrolled. In 2016, 41 master's awarded. *Degree requirements:* For master's, practicum. *Entrance requirements:* For master's, GRE General Test or MAT. *Application deadline:* For fall admission, 1/15 for domestic students; for spring admission, 9/15 for domestic students. Applications are processed on a rolling basis. Application fee: $50. *Expenses:* Contact institution. *Financial support:* Research assistantships, career-related internships or fieldwork, and unspecified assistantships available. Support available to part-time students. Financial award application deadline: 8/15. *Unit head:* Dr. Steven Robbins, Chair, 215-572-2987. *Application contact:* 215-572-2925, Fax: 215-572-2126, E-mail: grad@arcadia.edu.

**Argosy University, Chicago,** Illinois School of Professional Psychology, Doctoral Program in Clinical Psychology, Chicago, IL 60601. Offers child and adolescent psychology (Psy D); client-centered and experiential psychotherapies (Psy D); diversity and multicultural psychology (Psy D); family psychology (Psy D); forensic psychology (Psy D); health psychology (Psy D); neuropsychology (Psy D); organizational consulting (Psy D); psychoanalytic psychology (Psy D); psychology and spirituality (Psy D). *Accreditation:* APA.

**Argosy University, Chicago,** Illinois School of Professional Psychology, Program in Counseling Psychology, Chicago, IL 60601. Offers counselor education and supervision (Ed D). *Accreditation:* ACA. *Program availability:* Online learning.

**Argosy University, Denver,** College of Psychology and Behavioral Sciences, Denver, CO 80231. Offers clinical mental health counseling (MA); clinical psychology (MA, Psy D); counseling psychology (Ed D); counselor education and supervision (Ed D); forensic psychology (MA); industrial organizational psychology (MA); marriage and family therapy (MA, DMFT).

**Argosy University, Hawai'i,** Hawai'i School of Professional Psychology, Program in Counseling Psychology, Honolulu, HI 96813. Offers Ed D.

**Argosy University, Inland Empire,** College of Psychology and Behavioral Sciences, Ontario, CA 91761. Offers clinical psychology/marriage and family therapy (MA); counseling psychology (Ed D); counseling psychology/marriage and family therapy (MA); forensic psychology (MA); industrial organizational psychology (MA); sport-exercise psychology (MA).

**Argosy University, Los Angeles,** College of Psychology and Behavioral Sciences, Santa Monica, CA 90045. Offers clinical psychology/marriage and family therapy (MA); counseling psychology (Ed D); counseling psychology/marriage and family therapy (MA); forensic psychology (MA).

**Argosy University, Nashville,** College of Psychology and Behavioral Sciences, Nashville, TN 37214. Offers counselor education and supervision (Ed D); mental health counseling (MA).

**Argosy University, Northern Virginia,** American School of Professional Psychology, Arlington, VA 22209. Offers clinical psychology (MA, Psy D), including child and family psychology (Psy D), diversity and multicultural psychology (Psy D); forensic psychology (Psy D), health and neuropsychology (Psy D); community counseling (MA); counseling psychology (Ed D), including counselor education and supervision; counselor education and supervision (Ed D); forensic psychology (MA).

**Argosy University, Orange County,** American School of Professional Psychology, Program in Counseling Psychology, Orange, CA 92868. Offers counseling psychology (Ed D); marriage and family therapy (MA).

**Argosy University, Phoenix,** Arizona School of Professional Psychology, Program in Mental Health Counseling, Phoenix, AZ 85021. Offers MA.

**Argosy University, Salt Lake City,** College of Psychology and Behavioral Sciences, Draper, UT 84020. Offers counseling psychology (Ed D); counselor education and supervision (Ed D); forensic psychology (MA); marriage and family therapy (MA, DMFT); mental health counseling (MA).

**Argosy University, San Diego,** College of Psychology and Behavioral Sciences, San Diego, CA 92108. Offers clinical psychology/marriage and family therapy (MA); counseling psychology (Ed D); counseling psychology/marriage and family therapy (MA); forensic psychology (MA).

**Argosy University, San Francisco Bay Area,** American School of Professional Psychology, Program in Counseling Psychology, Alameda, CA 94501. Offers MA, Ed D.

**Argosy University, Sarasota,** College of Psychology and Behavioral Sciences, Sarasota, FL 34235. Offers community counseling (MA); counseling psychology (Ed D); counselor education and supervision (Ed D); forensic psychology (MA); marriage and family therapy (MA); mental health counseling (MA); pastoral community counseling (Ed D).

**Argosy University, Schaumburg,** College of Behavioral Sciences, Schaumburg, IL 60173-5403. Offers clinical mental health counseling (MA); forensic psychology (MA, Post-Graduate Certificate); industrial organizational psychology (MA); sport-exercise psychology (MA). *Accreditation:* ACA; APA.

**Argosy University, Seattle,** College of Psychology and Behavioral Sciences, Program in Counseling Psychology, Seattle, WA 98121. Offers MA, Ed D.

**Argosy University, Tampa,** Florida School of Professional Psychology, Tampa, FL 33607. Offers clinical psychology (MA, Psy D), including clinical psychology; counselor education and supervision (Ed D); industrial organizational psychology (MA); marriage and family therapy (MA); mental health counseling (MA).

**Arizona State University at the Tempe campus,** School of Letters and Sciences, Program in Counseling Psychology, Tempe, AZ 85287-0811. Offers PhD. *Accreditation:* APA. *Degree requirements:* For doctorate, comprehensive exam, thesis/dissertation, internship/practica, interactive Program of Study (iPOS) submitted before completing 50 percent of required credit hours. *Entrance requirements:* For doctorate, GRE, minimum GPA of 3.0 or equivalent in last 2 years of work leading to bachelor's degree, 3 letters of recommendation, personal statement describing history and academic/professional goals, completed Biographical Information form, 7-page sample of expository writing. Additional exam requirements/recommendations for international students: Required—TOEFL, IELTS, or PTE. Electronic applications accepted.

**Assumption College,** Clinical Counseling Psychology Program, Worcester, MA 01609-1296. Offers child and family interventions (MA); clinical counseling (CAGS); cognitive-behavioral therapies (MA). *Program availability:* Part-time, evening/weekend. *Faculty:* 4 full-time (2 women), 7 part-time/adjunct (2 women). *Students:* 40 full-time (31 women), 29 part-time (26 women); includes 11 minority (1 Black or African American, non-Hispanic/Latino; 1 American Indian or Alaska Native, non-Hispanic/Latino; 4 Asian, non-Hispanic/Latino; 5 Hispanic/Latino). Average age 27. 63 applicants, 51% accepted, 20 enrolled. In 2016, 25 master's awarded. *Degree requirements:* For master's, comprehensive exam, internship, practicum; for CAGS, comprehensive exam. *Entrance requirements:* For master's, bachelor's degree and at least 6 psychology courses completed with minimum GPA of 3.0 both overall and in the psychology courses; 3 letters of recommendation; official transcripts; personal statement; current resume; for CAGS, master's degree in clinical counseling psychology or mental health counseling, or baccalaureate degree and at least 6 psychology courses with minimum GPA of 3.0 overall and in psychology courses; 3 letters of recommendation; official transcripts; personal statement; current resume; interview. Additional exam requirements/recommendations for international students: Required—TOEFL (minimum score 540 paper-based; 76 iBT), IELTS (minimum score 6). *Application deadline:* For fall admission, 3/7 priority date for domestic and international students; for spring admission, 10/5 for domestic and international students; for summer admission, 2/8 for domestic and international students. Application fee: $30. Electronic applications accepted. *Expenses: Tuition:* Full-time $11,610; part-time $645 per credit. *Required fees:* $70 per term. Tuition and fees vary according to course load and program. *Financial support:* In 2016–17, 17 students received support, including 12 fellowships with full tuition reimbursements available; tuition waivers (full and partial), unspecified assistantships, and institutional discounts also available. Financial award application deadline: 3/7; financial award applicants required to submit FAFSA. *Faculty research:* Mood disorders, adjustment to life-threatening illness, perception of movement, socioemotional development of young children, discovery versus disclosure. *Unit head:* Dr. Leonard A. Doerfler, Director, 508-767-7549, Fax: 508-767-7263, E-mail: doerfler@assumption.edu. *Application contact:* Karen Stoyanoff, Director of Recruitment for Graduate Enrollment, 508-767-7442, Fax: 508-799-4412, E-mail: graduate@assumption.edu.
Website: http://graduate.assumption.edu/counseling-psychology/ma-clinical-counseling-psychology-overview

**Athabasca University,** Program in Counseling, Athabasca, AB T9S 3A3, Canada. Offers applied psychology (Post Master's Certificate); art therapy (MC); career counseling (MC); counseling (Advanced Certificate); counseling psychology (MC); school counseling (MC).

**Austin Peay State University,** College of Graduate Studies, College of Behavioral and Health Sciences, Department of Psychology, Program in Mental Health Counseling, Clarksville, TN 37044. Offers MS. *Program availability:* Part-time. *Faculty:* 9 full-time (6 women), 2 part-time/adjunct (1 woman). *Students:* 28 full-time (22 women), 9 part-time (6 women); includes 9 minority (6 Black or African American, non-Hispanic/Latino; 2 Hispanic/Latino; 1 Two or more races, non-Hispanic/Latino), 1 international. Average age 30. 33 applicants, 61% accepted, 12 enrolled. In 2016, 20 master's awarded. *Degree requirements:* For master's, comprehensive exam. *Entrance requirements:* For master's, GRE General Test, 3 letters of recommendation, minimum GPA of 3.0. Additional exam requirements/recommendations for international students: Required—TOEFL (minimum score 500 paper-based). *Application deadline:* For fall admission, 8/9 priority date for domestic students. Applications are processed on a rolling basis.

Application fee: $45 ($50 for international students). Electronic applications accepted. *Expenses:* Tuition, state resident: full-time $8300; part-time $415 per credit hour. Tuition, nonresident: full-time $22,280; part-time $1114 per credit hour. *Required fees:* $1473; $73.65 per credit hour. *Financial support:* Research assistantships with full tuition reimbursements, career-related internships or fieldwork, Federal Work-Study, institutionally sponsored loans, scholarships/grants, and unspecified assistantships available. Support available to part-time students. Financial award application deadline: 4/1; financial award applicants required to submit FAFSA. *Unit head:* Dr. Shunda L. Brown, Coordinator, 931-221-7238, E-mail: brownsl@apsu.edu. *Application contact:* Brad Averitt, Coordinator of Graduate Admissions, 800-859-4723, Fax: 931-221-7641, E-mail: gradadmissions@apsu.edu.
Website: http://www.apsu.edu/psychology/mhclass

**Avila University,** Department of Psychology, Kansas City, MO 64145-1698. Offers counseling psychology (MS); psychology (MS). *Program availability:* Part-time. *Faculty:* 7 full-time (6 women), 10 part-time/adjunct (4 women). *Students:* 92 full-time (78 women), 22 part-time (20 women); includes 39 minority (25 Black or African American, non-Hispanic/Latino; 1 American Indian or Alaska Native, non-Hispanic/Latino; 3 Asian, non-Hispanic/Latino; 8 Hispanic/Latino; 2 Two or more races, non-Hispanic/Latino; 1 international. Average age 34. 93 applicants, 43% accepted, 30 enrolled. In 2016, 48 master's awarded. *Degree requirements:* For master's, thesis optional, capstone project. *Entrance requirements:* For master's, bachelor's degree, minimum GPA of 3.0 in all previous undergraduate and graduate coursework, 2 letters of recommendation, letter of intent, resume. Additional exam requirements/recommendations for international students: Required—TOEFL (minimum score 80 iBT). *Application deadline:* Applications are processed on a rolling basis. Application fee: $0. Electronic applications accepted. *Expenses:* $583 per credit hour. *Financial support:* In 2016–17, 15 students received support, including 5 research assistantships with partial tuition reimbursements available; career-related internships or fieldwork, scholarships/grants, and unspecified assistantships also available. Support available to part-time students. Financial award applicants required to submit FAFSA. *Faculty research:* Emotional regulation, embodied cognition, trauma and restorative justice, psychophysiology of public speaking anxiety. *Unit head:* Aaron R. Coffey, Director of Graduate Psychology Enrollment Management, 816-501-0419, Fax: 816-501-2455, E-mail: aaron.coffey@avila.edu. *Application contact:* Tamika Doolin, Graduate Admissions Advisor, 816-501-3661, Fax: 816-501-2455, E-mail: gradpsych@avila.edu.
Website: https://www.avila.edu/psychology/

**Ball State University,** Graduate School, Teachers College, Department of Counseling Psychology and Guidance Services, Program in Counseling Psychology, Muncie, IN 47306. Offers counseling (MA), including clinical mental health counseling, mental health counseling, rehabilitation counseling, school counseling; counseling psychology (PhD). *Accreditation:* ACA; APA. *Program availability:* Part-time. *Degree requirements:* For doctorate, thesis/dissertation. *Entrance requirements:* For master's, GRE General Test (minimum scores 144 quantitative, 153 verbal), minimum baccalaureate GPA of 2.75 or 3.0 in latter half of baccalaureate, minimum GPA of 3.0 in psychology coursework, three letters of recommendation; for doctorate, GRE General Test, interview, minimum graduate GPA of 3.2, resume. Additional exam requirements/recommendations for international students: Required—TOEFL (minimum score 550 paper-based; 79 iBT), IELTS (minimum score 6.5). Electronic applications accepted.

**Baruch College of the City University of New York,** Weissman School of Arts and Sciences, Program in Mental Health Counseling, New York, NY 10010-5585. Offers MA. *Faculty:* 10 full-time (6 women), 2 part-time/adjunct (both women). *Students:* 37; includes 15 minority (7 Black or African American, non-Hispanic/Latino; 3 Asian, non-Hispanic/Latino; 5 Hispanic/Latino), 2 international. 138 applicants, 29% accepted, 18 enrolled. In 2016, 19 master's awarded. *Entrance requirements:* For master's, bachelor's degree from accredited institution, minimum undergraduate GPA of 3.2, relevant professional or volunteer experience, minimum of 15 credits in psychology, personal statement, three letters of recommendation, official transcript. Additional exam requirements/recommendations for international students: Required—TOEFL. *Application deadline:* For fall admission, 2/1 for domestic and international students. Application fee: $125. Electronic applications accepted. *Financial support:* Career-related internships or fieldwork and Federal Work-Study available. Financial award applicants required to submit FAFSA. *Faculty research:* Character analysis; shame and guilt; self-perceptions and moral affect; pedagogical development; self-efficacy and cognitive performance; sleep loss, fatigue and effort; environmental sustainability; cultural competence; behavioral obesity treatment; ADHD. *Unit head:* Dr. Nita Lutwak, Director, 646-312-1000. *Application contact:* Cathy Levkulic, Assistant Director, Graduate Studies, 646-312-4493, Fax: 646-312-3871, E-mail: wsas.graduate.studies@baruch.cuny.edu.
Website: http://www.baruch.cuny.edu/wsas/academics/graduate_studies/mhc/

**Bastyr University,** School of Natural Health Arts and Sciences, Kenmore, WA 98028-4966. Offers counseling psychology (MA); holistic landscape design (Certificate); midwifery (MS); nutrition (MS); nutrition and clinical health psychology (MS). *Accreditation:* AND. *Program availability:* Part-time. *Degree requirements:* For master's, thesis optional. *Entrance requirements:* For master's, 1-2 years' basic sciences course work (depending on program). Additional exam requirements/recommendations for international students: Required—TOEFL (minimum score 550 paper-based; 79 iBT). *Faculty research:* Whole-food nutrition for type 2 diabetes; meditation in end-of-life care; stress management; Qi Gong, Tai Chi and yoga for older adults; Echinacea and immunology.

**Becker College,** Program in Mental Health Counseling, Worcester, MA 01609. Offers community mental health (MA); school consultation (MA). *Entrance requirements:* For master's, GRE, interview, official transcript, three letters of recommendation, essay. Electronic applications accepted.

**Bethel University,** Graduate School, St. Paul, MN 55112-6999. Offers business administration (MBA); classroom management (Certificate); counseling (MA); international baccalaureate teaching and learning (Certificate); K-12 education (MA); leadership (Ed D); leadership foundations (Certificate); nurse educator (MS, Certificate); nurse-midwifery (MS); physician assistant (MS); special education (MA); strategic leadership (MA); teaching (MA). *Program availability:* Part-time, evening/weekend, 100% online, blended/hybrid learning. *Faculty:* 19 full-time (15 women), 57 part-time/adjunct (189 women). *Students:* 674 full-time (466 women), 378 part-time (256 women); includes 188 minority (94 Black or African American, non-Hispanic/Latino; 3 American Indian or Alaska Native, non-Hispanic/Latino; 43 Asian, non-Hispanic/Latino; 31 Hispanic/Latino; 1 Native Hawaiian or other Pacific Islander, non-Hispanic/Latino; 16 Two or more races, non-Hispanic/Latino), 33 international. *Degree requirements:* For master's, comprehensive exam (for some programs), thesis (for some programs); for doctorate, comprehensive exam, thesis/dissertation. *Entrance requirements:* Additional exam requirements/recommendations for international students: Required—TOEFL (minimum score 550 paper-based, 80 iBT) or IELTS. *Application deadline:* Applications are processed on a rolling basis. Application fee: $0. Electronic applications accepted. *Expenses:* Contact institution. *Financial support:* Teaching assistantships, career-related internships or fieldwork, and scholarships/grants available. Support available to part-time students. Financial award applicants required to submit FAFSA. *Unit head:*

Dick Crombie, Vice-President/Dean, 651-635-8000, Fax: 651-635-8004, E-mail: gs@bethel.edu. *Application contact:* Director of Admissions, 651-635-8000, Fax: 651-635-8004, E-mail: gs@bethel.edu.
Website: https://www.bethel.edu/graduate/

**Boston College,** Lynch School of Education, Program in Mental Health Counseling, Chestnut Hill, MA 02467-3800. Offers counseling psychology (PhD); mental health counseling (MA); MA/MA. *Accreditation:* APA (one or more programs are accredited). *Faculty:* 14 full-time (9 women). *Students:* 105 full-time (88 women), 26 part-time (24 women); includes 26 minority (9 Black or African American, non-Hispanic/Latino; 3 Asian, non-Hispanic/Latino; 13 Hispanic/Latino; 1 Two or more races, non-Hispanic/Latino), 23 international. Average age 24. 194 applicants, 79% accepted, 56 enrolled. In 2016, 45 master's awarded. Terminal master's awarded for partial completion of doctoral program. *Degree requirements:* For master's, comprehensive exam; for doctorate, comprehensive exam, thesis/dissertation. *Entrance requirements:* For master's and doctorate, GRE General Test. Additional exam requirements/recommendations for international students: Required—TOEFL (minimum score 550 paper-based; 100 iBT). *Application deadline:* For fall admission, 12/1 priority date for domestic and international students; for spring admission, 11/1 priority date for domestic and international students. Application fee: $65. Electronic applications accepted. Tuition and fees vary according to program. *Financial support:* Fellowships with partial tuition reimbursements, research assistantships with partial tuition reimbursements, Federal Work-Study, tuition waivers (partial), and unspecified assistantships available. Support available to part-time students. *Unit head:* Dr. Penny Hauser-Cram, Chairperson, 617-552-4214, Fax: 617-552-4710. *Application contact:* Kimberly Rose, Graduate Admission Assistant, 617-552-4214, Fax: 617-552-0398, E-mail: roseki@bc.edu.

**Boston Graduate School of Psychoanalysis,** Master's Programs, Brookline, MA 02446-4602. Offers mental health counseling (MA); psychoanalysis (MA); psychoanalysis, society and culture (MA). *Program availability:* Part-time. Terminal master's awarded for partial completion of doctoral program. *Degree requirements:* For master's, thesis. *Entrance requirements:* For master's, interview, BA, personal statement, writing sample, 3 letters of recommendation. Additional exam requirements/recommendations for international students: Required—TOEFL (minimum score 550 paper-based; 79 iBT). *Faculty research:* Qualitative and narrative research methodologies, ethical conflicts and dual loyalties in health professionals, psychodynamics of social processes, treatment approaches for intractable patients, psychoanalytic research methodologies.

**Boston University,** School of Medicine, Division of Graduate Medical Sciences, Program in Mental Health Counseling and Behavioral Medicine, Boston, MA 02215. Offers MA. *Faculty research:* HIV/AIDS, trauma, behavioral medicine (obesity, breast cancer), neurosciences, autism, serious mental illness, sports psychology. *Unit head:* Dr. Stephen Brady, Director, 617-414-2320, Fax: 617-414-2323, E-mail: sbrady@bu.edu. *Application contact:* GMS Admissions Office, 617-638-5255, E-mail: askgms@bu.edu.
Website: http://www.bumc.bu.edu/mhbm/

**Bowie State University,** Graduate Programs, Program in Counseling Psychology, Bowie, MD 20715-9465. Offers MA. *Program availability:* Part-time, evening/weekend. *Degree requirements:* For master's, comprehensive exam, thesis optional, research paper, practicum. *Entrance requirements:* For master's, minimum GPA of 2.5, 3 recommendations. Electronic applications accepted.

**Bowie State University,** Graduate Programs, Program in Mental Health Counseling, Bowie, MD 20715-9465. Offers MA. *Program availability:* Part-time, evening/weekend. *Degree requirements:* For master's, comprehensive exam. *Entrance requirements:* For master's, 3 letters of recommendation, minimum GPA of 3.0, 12 undergraduate credit hours in counseling or psychology. Electronic applications accepted.

**Bradley University,** The Graduate School, College of Education and Health Sciences, Department of Leadership in Education, Nonprofits and Counseling, Peoria, IL 61625-0002. Offers counseling (MA), including clinical mental health counseling, professional school counseling; leadership in educational administration (MA); nonprofit leadership (MA). *Accreditation:* ACA; NCATE. *Program availability:* Part-time, evening/weekend. *Degree requirements:* For master's, comprehensive exam, thesis optional. *Entrance requirements:* For master's, GRE General Test or MAT, interview, 3 letters of recommendation. Additional exam requirements/recommendations for international students: Required—TOEFL (minimum score 550 paper-based; 79 iBT), IELTS (minimum score 6.5). *Application deadline:* For fall admission, 5/15 priority date for domestic and international students; for spring admission, 10/15 priority date for domestic and international students. Applications are processed on a rolling basis. Application fee: $40 ($50 for international students). Electronic applications accepted. *Expenses:* Tuition: Full-time $7650; part-time $850 per credit. *Required fees:* $50 per credit. One-time fee: $100 full-time. *Financial support:* Research assistantships with full and partial tuition reimbursements, career-related internships or fieldwork, scholarships/grants, tuition waivers (partial), and unspecified assistantships available. Support available to part-time students. Financial award application deadline: 4/1. *Unit head:* Jenny Tripses, Interim Chair, 309-677-3593, E-mail: jtripses@bradley.edu. *Application contact:* Kayla Carroll, Director of International Admissions and Student Services, 309-677-2375, E-mail: klcarroll@fsmail.bradley.edu.
Website: http://www.bradley.edu/academic/departments/lenc/

**Brandman University,** School of Arts and Sciences, Irvine, CA 92618. Offers psychology (MA), including counseling, marriage and family therapy, professional clinical counseling. *Expenses:* Tuition: Full-time $14,880; part-time $620 per credit hour. Tuition and fees vary according to degree level and program. *Unit head:* Dr. Jeremy Korr, Dean, 949-341-9831.
Website: https://www.brandman.edu/arts-sciences

**Brigham Young University,** Graduate Studies, David O. McKay School of Education, Department of Counseling Psychology and Special Education, Provo, UT 84602. Offers counseling psychology (PhD); school psychology (Ed S); special education (MS). *Program availability:* Part-time, evening/weekend. *Faculty:* 13 full-time (3 women), 9 part-time/adjunct (3 women). *Students:* 66 full-time (45 women), 15 part-time (14 women); includes 8 minority (1 Black or African American, non-Hispanic/Latino; 2 American Indian or Alaska Native, non-Hispanic/Latino; 4 Hispanic/Latino; 1 Native Hawaiian or other Pacific Islander, non-Hispanic/Latino; 4 international. Average age 29. 73 applicants, 42% accepted, 27 enrolled. In 2016, 2 master's, 7 doctorates, 12 other advanced degrees awarded. *Degree requirements:* For master's and Ed S, comprehensive exam, thesis; for doctorate, comprehensive exam, thesis/dissertation. *Entrance requirements:* For master's, GRE General Test or MAT, minimum cumulative GPA of 3.0 in undergraduate coursework; for doctorate and Ed S, GRE General Test, minimum cumulative GPA of 3.0 in undergraduate coursework. Additional exam requirements/recommendations for international students: Required—TOEFL (minimum score 580 paper-based; 85 iBT), IELTS (minimum score 7). *Application deadline:* For fall admission, 1/15 for domestic and international students. Application fee: $50. Electronic applications accepted. *Expenses:* Contact institution. *Financial support:* In 2016–17, 51 students received support, including 51 research assistantships (averaging $9,000 per

## Counseling Psychology

year); institutionally sponsored loans and tuition waivers (partial) also available. Financial award application deadline: 3/31. *Faculty research:* Autism, religious and spiritual values in counseling, school-based crisis intervention, behavior interventions in MTSS framework, counseling and psychotherapy process and outcomes. *Unit head:* Dr. Lane Fischer, Department Chair, 801-422-3857, E-mail: lane_fischer@byu.edu. *Application contact:* Diane E. Hancock, Executive Secretary, 801-422-3859, E-mail: diane_hancock@byu.edu.
Website: http://education.byu.edu/cpse/

**Brooklyn College of the City University of New York,** School of Natural and Behavioral Sciences, Department of Health and Nutrition Sciences, Brooklyn, NY 11210-2889. Offers community health (MA), including community health education, thanatology; grief counseling (CAS); nutrition (MS); public health (MPH), including general public health, health care policy and administration. *Program availability:* Part-time, evening/weekend. *Degree requirements:* For master's, thesis or alternative. *Entrance requirements:* For master's, GRE, essay, 2 letters of recommendation. Additional exam requirements/recommendations for international students: Required—TOEFL. Electronic applications accepted. *Faculty research:* Medical ethics, relocation stress, risk reduction, disease prevention, history of public health, computer applications.

**Brooklyn College of the City University of New York,** School of Natural and Behavioral Sciences, Department of Psychology, Brooklyn, NY 11210-2889. Offers experimental psychology (MA); industrial and organizational psychology (MA), including human relations, organizational behavior; mental health counseling (MA); psychology (PhD). *Program availability:* Part-time. *Degree requirements:* For master's, comprehensive exam, thesis (for some programs). *Entrance requirements:* For master's, minimum GPA of 3.0, 2 letters of recommendation, essay; for doctorate, GRE. Additional exam requirements/recommendations for international students: Required—TOEFL (minimum score 520 paper-based; 69 iBT). Electronic applications accepted.

**Caldwell University,** Graduate Studies, Department of Psychology, Caldwell, NJ 07006-6195. Offers art therapy (MA); counseling (MA), including art therapy, mental health, school counseling; director of school counseling (Post-Master's Certificate); professional counselor (Post-Master's Certificate); school counselor (Post-Master's Certificate). *Accreditation:* ACA. *Program availability:* Part-time, evening/weekend. *Degree requirements:* For master's, comprehensive exam. *Entrance requirements:* For master's, GRE or MAT, interview. Electronic applications accepted. *Faculty research:* Counseling, school counseling, art therapy.

**California Baptist University,** Program in Counseling Ministry and Counseling Psychology (Dual Master's), Riverside, CA 92504-3206. Offers MA/MS. *Program availability:* Part-time, evening/weekend. *Faculty:* 18 full-time (11 women), 10 part-time/adjunct (7 women). *Students:* 14 full-time (11 women), 2 part-time (1 woman); includes 12 minority (2 Black or African American, non-Hispanic/Latino; 1 Asian, non-Hispanic/Latino; 9 Hispanic/Latino). Average age 31. 11 applicants, 45% accepted, 5 enrolled. *Entrance requirements:* Additional exam requirements/recommendations for international students: Required—TOEFL (minimum score 80 iBT). *Application deadline:* For fall admission, 8/1 priority date for domestic students, 7/1 for international students; for spring admission, 12/1 priority date for domestic students, 11/1 for international students. Applications are processed on a rolling basis. Application fee: $45. Electronic applications accepted. *Expenses:* Contact institution. *Financial support:* In 2016–17, 2 students received support. Federal Work-Study and scholarships/grants available. Financial award applicants required to submit CSS PROFILE or FAFSA. *Faculty research:* Law enforcement psychology, neuroethology, organizational neuroscience, integration of theology and behavioral science, cognitive development/cross-cultural psychology. *Unit head:* Dr. Jacqueline Gustafson, Dean, School of Behavioral Sciences, 951-343-4487, E-mail: jcraig@calbaptist.edu. *Application contact:* Mischa Routon, Director of Counseling Psychology Program, 951-343-4206, Fax: 877-228-8877, E-mail: mrouton@calbaptist.edu.
Website: http://www.calbaptist.edu/mft

**California Baptist University,** Program in Counseling Psychology, Riverside, CA 92504-3206. Offers counseling psychology (MS); forensic psychology (MS); professional clinical counselor (MS). *Program availability:* Part-time, evening/weekend, 100% online, blended/hybrid learning. *Faculty:* 18 full-time (11 women), 10 part-time/adjunct (7 women). *Students:* 258 full-time (211 women), 97 part-time (82 women); includes 238 minority (64 Black or African American, non-Hispanic/Latino; 1 American Indian or Alaska Native, non-Hispanic/Latino; 14 Asian, non-Hispanic/Latino; 146 Hispanic/Latino; 1 Native Hawaiian or other Pacific Islander, non-Hispanic/Latino; 12 Two or more races, non-Hispanic/Latino), 1 international. Average age 31. 98 applicants, 78% accepted, 64 enrolled. In 2016, 106 master's awarded. *Degree requirements:* For master's, comprehensive exam, 24 (individual) or 50 hours (group) of psychotherapy, practicum. *Entrance requirements:* For master's, minimum undergraduate GPA of 2.75; official transcripts; three recommendations; 500-word essay; interview; 3 prerequisite courses completed with minimum C grade. Additional exam requirements/recommendations for international students: Required—TOEFL (minimum score 80 iBT). *Application deadline:* For fall admission, 8/1 priority date for domestic students, 7/1 for international students; for spring admission, 12/1 priority date for domestic students, 11/1 for international students. Applications are processed on a rolling basis. Application fee: $45. Electronic applications accepted. *Expenses:* Contact institution. *Financial support:* In 2016–17, 79 students received support. Federal Work-Study and scholarships/grants available. Financial award applicants required to submit CSS PROFILE or FAFSA. *Faculty research:* Identify formation, faith integration, psychological assessment, child abuse and child welfare, clinical psychology and crisis intervention techniques. *Unit head:* Dr. Jacqueline Gustafson, Dean, School of Behavioral Sciences, 951-343-4487, E-mail: jcraig@calbaptist.edu. *Application contact:* Mischa Routon, Associate Dean of Graduate Programs, 951-343-4206, Fax: 951-343-4569, E-mail: mrouton@calbaptist.edu.
Website: http://www.calbaptist.edu/mft/

**California Institute of Integral Studies,** School of Professional Psychology and Health, San Francisco, CA 94103. Offers clinical psychology (Psy D); community mental health (MA); drama therapy (MA); expressive arts therapy (MA); human sexuality (PhD); integral counseling psychology (MA); integrative health studies (MA); psychological studies (MA); somatic psychology (MA). *Program availability:* Part-time, evening/weekend, 100% online, blended/hybrid learning. *Students:* 526 full-time (408 women), 113 part-time (96 women); includes 173 minority (34 Black or African American, non-Hispanic/Latino; 5 American Indian or Alaska Native, non-Hispanic/Latino; 31 Asian, non-Hispanic/Latino; 58 Hispanic/Latino; 1 Native Hawaiian or other Pacific Islander, non-Hispanic/Latino; 44 Two or more races, non-Hispanic/Latino), 52 international. Average age 38. 319 applicants, 85% accepted, 164 enrolled. In 2016, 157 master's, 21 doctorates awarded. *Degree requirements:* For doctorate, comprehensive exam, thesis/dissertation. *Entrance requirements:* For master's, minimum GPA of 3.0, letters of recommendation, writing sample; for doctorate, GRE, MA in psychology or social work with appropriate practical experience for advanced standing, or BA with a minimum GPA of 3.1; letters of recommendation; writing sample. Additional exam requirements/recommendations for international students: Required—TOEFL. *Application deadline:* For fall admission, 2/1 priority date for domestic and international students; for spring

admission, 10/15 priority date for domestic and international students. Applications are processed on a rolling basis. Application fee: $65. Electronic applications accepted. *Expenses: Tuition:* Full-time $19,728; part-time $1098 per semester hour. *Required fees:* $320; $320 per semester hour. *Financial support:* Research assistantships with tuition reimbursements, teaching assistantships with tuition reimbursements, career-related internships or fieldwork, Federal Work-Study, and scholarships/grants available. Support available to part-time students. Financial award application deadline: 4/15; financial award applicants required to submit FAFSA. *Faculty research:* Transpersonal psychology, somatic psychology, expressive arts therapy, drama therapy, community mental health, ecopsychology, integrative health, human sexuality. *Application contact:* Ellen Durst, Director of Admissions, 415-575-6100, Fax: 415-575-1268, E-mail: admissions@ciis.edu.

**California State University, Bakersfield,** Division of Graduate Studies, School of Social Sciences and Education, Program in Counseling Psychology, Bakersfield, CA 93311. Offers MS. *Students:* 50 full-time (43 women), 6 part-time (5 women); includes 36 minority (2 Black or African American, non-Hispanic/Latino; 1 American Indian or Alaska Native, non-Hispanic/Latino; 4 Asian, non-Hispanic/Latino; 26 Hispanic/Latino; 3 Two or more races, non-Hispanic/Latino), 2 international. Average age 28. 48 applicants, 50% accepted, 20 enrolled. In 2016, 18 master's awarded. *Degree requirements:* For master's, comprehensive exam. Application fee: $55. *Expenses:* Tuition, state resident: full-time $2246; part-time $1302 per semester. *Financial support:* In 2016–17, fellowships (averaging $1,850 per year) were awarded; Federal Work-Study, scholarships/grants, and tuition waivers (full and partial) also available. Financial award application deadline: 3/2; financial award applicants required to submit FAFSA. *Unit head:* Dr. Sarah Appleton, Graduate Coordinator, 661-654-3941, Fax: 661-654-6955, E-mail: sappleton3@csub.edu. *Application contact:* Debbie Blowers, Assistant Director of Admissions and Evaluations, 661-654-3381, E-mail: dblowers@csub.edu. Website: https://www.csub.edu/psychology/mscounselingpsych/index.html

**California State University, Fresno,** Division of Research and Graduate Studies, Kremen School of Education and Human Development, Department of Counselor Education and Rehabilitation, Fresno, CA 93740-8027. Offers clinical rehabilitation and mental health counseling (MS); marriage, family and child counseling (MS); student affairs and college counseling (MS). *Program availability:* Part-time, evening/weekend. *Degree requirements:* For master's, thesis or alternative. *Entrance requirements:* For master's, GRE General Test, MAT, minimum GPA of 2.75. Additional exam requirements/recommendations for international students: Required—TOEFL. *Application deadline:* For fall admission, 5/1 for domestic and international students; for spring admission, 10/1 for domestic and international students. Applications are processed on a rolling basis. Application fee: $55. Electronic applications accepted. *Financial support:* Career-related internships or fieldwork, Federal Work-Study, scholarships/grants, and research awards available. Support available to part-time students. Financial award application deadline: 3/1; financial award applicants required to submit FAFSA. *Faculty research:* Child abuse prevention, aging, career development. *Unit head:* Song Lee, Chair, 559-278-0340, Fax: 559-278-0045, E-mail: malee@csufresno.edu. *Application contact:* April Cardiel, Administrative Support Coordinator, 559-278-0342, Fax: 559-278-4658, E-mail: acardiel@csufresno.edu. Website: http://www.fresnostate.edu/kremen/departments/cer.html

**California State University, Sacramento,** Office of Graduate Studies, College of Social Sciences and Interdisciplinary Studies, Department of Psychology, Sacramento, CA 95819. Offers applied behavior analysis (MA); counseling psychology (MA); industrial/organizational psychology (MA). *Program availability:* Part-time. *Students:* 13 full-time (9 women), 11 part-time (9 women); includes 6 minority (3 Asian, non-Hispanic/Latino; 3 Hispanic/Latino). Average age 27. 74 applicants, 16% accepted, 11 enrolled. In 2016, 7 master's awarded. *Degree requirements:* For master's, thesis, writing proficiency exam. *Entrance requirements:* For master's, GRE, minimum GPA of 3.0 during previous 2 years. Additional exam requirements/recommendations for international students: Required—TOEFL (minimum score 550 paper-based; 80 iBT). *Application deadline:* For fall admission, 3/1 for domestic and international students; for spring admission, 9/30 for international students. Applications are processed on a rolling basis. Application fee: $55. Electronic applications accepted. *Expenses:* $4,302 full-time tuition and fees per semester, $2,796 part-time. *Financial support:* Career-related internships or fieldwork and Federal Work-Study available. Support available to part-time students. Financial award application deadline: 2/1; financial award applicants required to submit FAFSA. *Unit head:* Dr. Rebecca Cameron, Interim Department Chair, 916-278-6254, E-mail: cameron@csus.edu. *Application contact:* Jose Martinez, Graduate Admissions Supervisor, 916-278-7871, E-mail: martinj@skymail.csus.edu. Website: http://www.csus.edu/psyc

**California State University, San Bernardino,** Graduate Studies, College of Social and Behavioral Sciences, Department of Psychology, San Bernardino, CA 92407. Offers child development (MA); clinical/counseling psychology (MS); general/experimental psychology (MA); industrial/organizational psychology (MS). *Faculty:* 21 full-time (11 women). *Students:* 59 full-time (43 women), 15 part-time (9 women); includes 47 minority (2 Black or African American, non-Hispanic/Latino; 3 Asian, non-Hispanic/Latino; 33 Hispanic/Latino; 9 Two or more races, non-Hispanic/Latino), 3 international. 217 applicants, 18% accepted, 32 enrolled. In 2016, 38 master's awarded. *Degree requirements:* For master's, comprehensive exam, thesis (for some programs). *Entrance requirements:* Additional exam requirements/recommendations for international students: Required—TOEFL. Application fee: $55. *Expenses:* Tuition, state resident: full-time $7843; part-time $5011.20 per year. Tuition and fees vary according to course load, degree level, program and reciprocity agreements. *Financial support:* Fellowships, research assistantships, and teaching assistantships available. *Faculty research:* Perceptual development, human memory, psychopharmacology, psychology of women, language acquisition. *Unit head:* Dr. Robert Ricco, Chair, 909-537-5485, Fax: 909-537-7003, E-mail: rricco@csusb.edu. *Application contact:* Dr. Francisca Beer, Dean of Graduate Studies, 909-537-5058, E-mail: fbeer@csusb.edu. Website: http://psychology.csusb.edu/

**California State University, Stanislaus,** College of Human and Health Sciences, Program in Psychology (MA/MS), Turlock, CA 95382. Offers behavior analysis (MS); counseling psychology (MS); psychology (MA). *Program availability:* Part-time. *Degree requirements:* For master's, thesis. *Entrance requirements:* For master's, GRE, minimum GPA of 3.0, 3 letters of reference, 16 psychology prerequisites, personal statement. Additional exam requirements/recommendations for international students: Required—TOEFL (minimum score 550 paper-based). Electronic applications accepted. *Faculty research:* Hedonic tone judgment, syntax and autism, early literacy assessment and native and non-native languages.

**California University of Pennsylvania,** School of Graduate Studies and Research, College of Education and Human Services, Department of Counselor Education, California, PA 15419-1394. Offers clinical mental health counseling (MS); school counseling (M Ed). *Accreditation:* ACA; NCATE. *Program availability:* Part-time, evening/weekend. *Degree requirements:* For master's, comprehensive exam, thesis optional. *Entrance requirements:* For master's, MAT, minimum GPA of 3.0, resume, letters of reference. Additional exam requirements/recommendations for international students: Required—TOEFL (minimum score 550 paper-based; 80 iBT). Electronic applications accepted. *Expenses:* Tuition, state resident: full-time $11,592; part-time $483 per credit. Tuition, nonresident: full-time $17,400; part-time $725 per credit. *Required fees:* $3916. Tuition and fees vary according to course load, degree level, campus/location and reciprocity agreements. *Faculty research:* Mind-body theories and practice, grief issues, career development, supervision, sports counseling.

**Cambridge College,** School of Psychology and Counseling, Cambridge, MA 02138-5304. Offers addiction counseling (M Ed); alcohol and drug counseling (Certificate); counseling psychology (M Ed, CAGS); counseling psychology: forensic counseling (M Ed); marriage and family therapy (M Ed); mental health and addiction counseling (M Ed); mental health counseling (M Ed); mental health counseling for school guidance counselors (Post Master's Certificate); psychological studies (M Ed); school adjustment and mental health counseling (M Ed); school adjustment, mental health and addiction counseling (M Ed); school guidance counselor (M Ed); trauma studies (Certificate). *Program availability:* Part-time, evening/weekend. *Degree requirements:* For master's and other advanced degree, thesis, practicum/internship. *Entrance requirements:* For master's, resume, 2 professional references; for other advanced degree, official transcripts, documents for transfer credit evaluation, resume, written personal statement/essay, 2 professional references, health insurance, immunizations form. Additional exam requirements/recommendations for international students: Required—TOEFL (minimum score 550 paper-based; 79 iBT), Michigan English Language Assessment Battery (minimum score 85); Recommended—IELTS (minimum score 6). Electronic applications accepted. *Expenses:* Contact institution. *Faculty research:* Trauma, drug and alcohol counseling, cross-cultural issues, school counseling, trauma in schools.

**Capella University,** Harold Abel School of Social and Behavioral Science, Master's Programs in Counseling, Minneapolis, MN 55402. Offers child and adolescent development (MS); general addiction counseling (MS); general marriage and family counseling/therapy (MS); general mental health counseling (MS); general school counseling (MS).

**Capella University,** Harold Abel School of Social and Behavioral Science, Master's Programs in Psychology, Minneapolis, MN 55402. Offers applied behavior analysis (MS); clinical psychology (MS); counseling psychology (MS); educational psychology (MS); evaluation, research, and measurement (MS); general advanced studies in human behavior (MS); general psychology (MS); industrial/organizational psychology (MS); leadership coaching psychology (MS); school psychology (MS); sport psychology (MS).

**Carlos Albizu University, Miami Campus,** Graduate Programs, Miami, FL 33172-2209. Offers clinical psychology (PhD, Psy D); entrepreneurship (MBA); exceptional student education (MS); human services (PhD); industrial/organizational psychology (MS); marriage and family therapy (MS); mental health counseling (MS); nonprofit management (MBA); organizational management (MBA); psychology (MS); school counseling (MS); speech and language pathology (MS); teaching English for speakers of other languages (MS). *Accreditation:* APA. *Program availability:* Part-time, evening/weekend, 100% online. *Faculty:* 28 full-time (22 women), 31 part-time/adjunct (19 women). *Students:* 475 full-time (396 women), 191 part-time (161 women); includes 560 minority (56 Black or African American, non-Hispanic/Latino; 1 American Indian or Alaska Native, non-Hispanic/Latino; 4 Asian, non-Hispanic/Latino; 494 Hispanic/Latino; 5 Two or more races, non-Hispanic/Latino), 15 international. Average age 34. 335 applicants, 46% accepted, 122 enrolled. In 2016, 143 master's, 48 doctorates awarded. Terminal master's awarded for partial completion of doctoral program. *Degree requirements:* For master's, comprehensive exam, integrative project (for MBA); research project (for exceptional student education, teaching English as a second language); for doctorate, comprehensive exam, thesis/dissertation, internship, project. *Entrance requirements:* For master's, 3 letters of recommendation, interview, minimum GPA of 3.0, resume, statement of purpose, official transcripts; for doctorate, 3 letters of recommendation, minimum GPA of 3.0, resume, interview, statement of purpose, official transcripts. Additional exam requirements/recommendations for international students: Required—Michigan Test of English Language Proficiency. *Application deadline:* For fall admission, 4/1 priority date for domestic students, 5/1 priority date for international students; for spring admission, 11/1 priority date for domestic students, 9/1 priority date for international students. Applications are processed on a rolling basis. Application fee: $50. Electronic applications accepted. *Expenses:* Contact institution. *Financial support:* In 2016–17, 131 students received support. Federal Work-Study, scholarships/grants, unspecified assistantships, and tuition discounts available. Financial award application deadline: 6/1; financial award applicants required to submit FAFSA. *Faculty research:* Psychotherapy, forensic psychology, neuropsychology, marketing strategy, entrepreneurship, special education, speech-language pathology. *Unit head:* Dr. Etiony Aldarondo, Provost, 305-593-1223 Ext. 3138, Fax: 305-592-7930, E-mail: ealdarondo@albizu.edu. *Application contact:* Sonia Feliciano, Institutional Director of Student Recruitment, 305-593-1223 Ext. 3108, Fax: 305-477-8983, E-mail: sfeliciano@albizu.edu.

**Carlow University,** College of Leadership and Social Change, Program in Counseling Psychology, Pittsburgh, PA 15213-3165. Offers Psy D. *Accreditation:* APA. *Program availability:* Part-time, evening/weekend. *Students:* 22 full-time (17 women), 10 part-time (7 women); includes 3 minority (2 Black or African American, non-Hispanic/Latino; 1 Asian, non-Hispanic/Latino). Average age 30. 19 applicants, 68% accepted, 10 enrolled. In 2016, 12 doctorates awarded. *Degree requirements:* For doctorate, thesis/dissertation, internship. *Entrance requirements:* For doctorate, GRE, resume or curriculum vitae; personal essay; reflective essay; official transcripts from all previous undergraduate and graduate institutions; three letters of recommendation; master's degree in closely-related field; interview. Additional exam requirements/recommendations for international students: Required—TOEFL (minimum score 550 paper-based). *Application deadline:* Applications are processed on a rolling basis. Electronic applications accepted. *Expenses:* Contact institution. *Financial support:* Unspecified assistantships available. Financial award application deadline: 4/1; financial award applicants required to submit FAFSA. *Unit head:* Dr. Joseph M. Roberts, Chair, Psy D Program, 412-575-6331, Fax: 412-578-6357, E-mail: jmroberts@carlow.edu. *Application contact:* 412-578-6059, Fax: 412-578-6321, E-mail: gradstudies@carlow.edu.
Website: http://www.carlow.edu/PsyD_Counseling_Psychology.aspx

**Carlow University,** College of Leadership and Social Change, Program in Professional Counseling, Pittsburgh, PA 15213-3165. Offers addictions (MS); adult/generalist (MS); child and family (MS); professional counseling (Certificate); trauma-informed (MS). *Program availability:* Part-time, evening/weekend. *Students:* 127 full-time (111 women), 23 part-time (19 women); includes 46 minority (34 Black or African American, non-Hispanic/Latino; 1 American Indian or Alaska Native, non-Hispanic/Latino; 2 Asian, non-Hispanic/Latino; 5 Hispanic/Latino; 4 Two or more races, non-Hispanic/Latino), 1 international. Average age 30. 49 applicants, 86% accepted, 26 enrolled. In 2016, 41 master's, 1 other advanced degree awarded. *Entrance requirements:* For master's, personal essay; resume or curriculum vitae; three recommendations; official transcripts; interview; minimum undergraduate GPA of 3.0. Additional exam requirements/recommendations for international students: Required—TOEFL (minimum score 550 paper-based). *Application deadline:* Applications are processed on a rolling basis.

Electronic applications accepted. *Expenses: Tuition:* Full-time $11,855; part-time $801 per credit. *Required fees:* $182; $13 per credit. Tuition and fees vary according to course load, degree level and program. *Financial support:* Application deadline: 4/1; applicants required to submit FAFSA. *Unit head:* Dr. Travis W. Schermer, Director, 412-575-6650, Fax: 412-575-6357, E-mail: twschermer@carlow.edu.
Website: http://www.carlow.edu/Master_of_Science_in_Professional_Counseling.aspx

**Centenary University,** Program in Counseling Psychology, Hackettstown, NJ 07840-2100. Offers counseling (MA); counseling psychology (MA). *Program availability:* Part-time, evening/weekend, online learning. *Degree requirements:* For master's, thesis, fieldwork.

**Central Michigan University,** Central Michigan University Global Campus, Program in Counseling, Mount Pleasant, MI 48859. Offers professional counseling (MA); school counseling (MA). *Accreditation:* TEAC. *Program availability:* Part-time, evening/weekend. *Faculty:* 6 full-time (2 women), 12 part-time/adjunct (10 women). *Students:* 123 (103 women); includes 43 minority (30 Black or African American, non-Hispanic/Latino; 2 Asian, non-Hispanic/Latino; 1 Hispanic/Latino; 10 Two or more races, non-Hispanic/Latino). Average age 38. In 2016, 13 master's awarded. *Entrance requirements:* For master's, MAT, minimum GPA of 2.7. Additional exam requirements/recommendations for international students: Required—TOEFL. *Application deadline:* Applications are processed on a rolling basis. Application fee: $50. Electronic applications accepted. *Financial support:* Scholarships/grants available. Support available to part-time students. *Unit head:* Dr. Twinet Parmer, Chair, 989-774-3776, E-mail: parme1t@cmich.edu. *Application contact:* 877-268-4636, E-mail: cmuglobal@cmich.edu.

**Central Michigan University,** College of Graduate Studies, College of Humanities and Social and Behavioral Sciences, Department of Psychology, Mount Pleasant, MI 48859. Offers clinical psychology (PhD); experimental psychology (MS, PhD), including applied experimental psychology (PhD), experimental psychology (MS); industrial and organizational psychology (MA, PhD), including industrial and organizational psychology, occupational health psychology (PhD); neuroscience (MS, PhD); school psychology (PhD, S Psy S), including psychological services (S Psy S), school psychology (PhD). *Accreditation:* APA (one or more programs are accredited). Terminal master's awarded for partial completion of doctoral program. *Degree requirements:* For master's, thesis or alternative; for doctorate, thesis/dissertation; for S Psy S, thesis. *Entrance requirements:* For doctorate, GRE. Electronic applications accepted. *Faculty research:* Experimental psychology, clinical psychology, industrial/organizational psychology, school psychology, neuroscience.

**Central Washington University,** Graduate Studies and Research, College of the Sciences, Department of Psychology, Program in Mental Health Counseling, Ellensburg, WA 98926. Offers MS. *Accreditation:* ACA. *Degree requirements:* For master's, thesis or alternative, internship. *Entrance requirements:* For master's, GRE General Test, minimum GPA of 3.0. Additional exam requirements/recommendations for international students: Required—TOEFL (minimum score 550 paper-based; 79 iBT). Electronic applications accepted.

**Chaminade University of Honolulu,** Office of Professional and Continuing Education, Program in Counseling Psychology, Honolulu, HI 96816-1578. Offers marriage and family counseling (MSCP); mental health counseling (MSCP); school counseling (MSCP). *Program availability:* Part-time, evening/weekend, blended/hybrid learning. *Faculty:* 7 full-time (2 women), 15 part-time/adjunct (6 women). *Students:* 163 full-time (122 women), 44 part-time (35 women); includes 137 minority (15 Black or African American, non-Hispanic/Latino; 3 American Indian or Alaska Native, non-Hispanic/Latino; 58 Asian, non-Hispanic/Latino; 12 Hispanic/Latino; 48 Native Hawaiian or other Pacific Islander, non-Hispanic/Latino; 1 Two or more races, non-Hispanic/Latino), 2 international. Average age 31. 49 applicants, 98% accepted, 33 enrolled. In 2016, 70 master's awarded. *Degree requirements:* For master's, comprehensive exam, internship/practicum. *Entrance requirements:* For master's, minimum undergraduate GPA of 3.0, 3 letters of recommendation, resume, interview. Additional exam requirements/recommendations for international students: Required—TOEFL (minimum score 550 paper-based; 79 iBT). *Application deadline:* Applications are processed on a rolling basis. Application fee: $40. Electronic applications accepted. *Expenses:* $775 per credit hour plus $93 fee per online course. *Financial support:* Applicants required to submit FAFSA. *Unit head:* Dr. Robert G. Santee, Dean, 808-735-4751, Fax: 808-739-4670, E-mail: mscp@chaminade.edu. *Application contact:* 808-735-4755, E-mail: gradserv@chaminade.edu.
Website: http://www.chaminade.edu/mscp

**Chatham University,** Program in Counseling Psychology, Pittsburgh, PA 15232-2826. Offers child, adolescent and family (MSCP); counseling psychology (Psy D); health and holistic (MSCP); infant mental health (MSCP); organization and supervision (MSCP); sport and exercise (MSCP). *Accreditation:* APA. *Program availability:* Part-time, evening/weekend. *Degree requirements:* For master's, thesis optional, supervised internship; for doctorate, thesis/dissertation, internship. *Entrance requirements:* For master's, minimum GPA of 3.0; 2 letters of recommendation; resume; prerequisite coursework in statistics, biology, and psychology; for doctorate, GRE. Additional exam requirements/recommendations for international students: Required—TOEFL (minimum score 600 paper-based; 100 iBT), IELTS (minimum score 7), TWE. Electronic applications accepted. Application fee is waived when completed online. *Expenses: Tuition:* Full-time $16,254; part-time $903 per credit hour. *Required fees:* $468; $26 per credit hour. *Faculty research:* Trauma and recovery, hypnosis, psychospiritual dimensions of healing, psychotherapy of schizophrenia.

**Chestnut Hill College,** School of Graduate Studies, Division of Psychology, Program in Clinical and Counseling Psychology, Philadelphia, PA 19118-2693. Offers clinical and counseling psychology (MS, CAS), including child and adolescent therapy, child and adolescent therapy with autism spectrum disorders, co-occurring disorders, couple and family therapy, diverse and underserved communities, generalist (MS), trauma studies. *Program availability:* Part-time, evening/weekend. *Degree requirements:* For master's, thesis optional, practica. *Entrance requirements:* For master's, GRE General Test, writing sample, letters of recommendation. Additional exam requirements/recommendations for international students: Required—TOEFL (minimum score 500 paper-based), IELTS (minimum score 6.0), or TWE (minimum score 22). Electronic applications accepted. *Expenses:* Contact institution. *Faculty research:* Play therapy, eating disorders, addictions, group psychology and group therapy, health psychology.

**City University of Seattle,** Graduate Division, Division of Arts and Sciences, Seattle, WA 98121. Offers counseling psychology (MA). *Accreditation:* ACA. *Program availability:* Part-time, evening/weekend, online learning. *Degree requirements:* For master's, comprehensive exam (for some programs), thesis (for some programs). *Entrance requirements:* For master's, baccalaureate degree or equivalent from an accredited or otherwise recognized institution. Additional exam requirements/recommendations for international students: Recommended—TOEFL (minimum score 567 paper-based; 87 iBT), IELTS, TWE. Electronic applications accepted. *Expenses:* Contact institution.

**Clemson University,** Graduate School, College of Education, Department of Education and Human Development, Program in Counselor Education, Clemson, SC 29634.

## Counseling Psychology

Offers counselor education (M Ed, Ed S), including clinical mental health counseling, school counseling. *Accreditation:* ACA; NCATE. *Program availability:* Part-time, evening/weekend. *Faculty:* 2 full-time (both women). *Students:* 142 full-time (114 women), 14 part-time (13 women); includes 39 minority (24 Black or African American, non-Hispanic/Latino; 4 Asian, non-Hispanic/Latino; 7 Hispanic/Latino; 4 Two or more races, non-Hispanic/Latino). Average age 26. 256 applicants, 46% accepted, 57 enrolled. In 2016, 73 master's, 38 Ed Ss awarded. *Degree requirements:* For master's, comprehensive exam. *Entrance requirements:* For master's, GRE General Test, unofficial transcripts, two letters of recommendation, essays. Additional exam requirements/recommendations for international students: Required—TOEFL (minimum score 80 iBT), IELTS (minimum score 6.5). *Application deadline:* For fall admission, 2/1 priority date for domestic and international students; for summer admission, 2/1 priority date for domestic and international students. Application fee: $80 ($90 for international students). Electronic applications accepted. *Expenses:* $4,027 per semester full-time resident, $8,013 per semester full-time non-resident, $437 per credit hour part-time resident, $874 per credit hour part-time non-resident. *Financial support:* Application deadline: 2/1. *Faculty research:* School counseling, disabilities, college readiness, transitions, counselor education. *Unit head:* Dr. Amy Milsom, Program Coordinator, 864-656-0927, E-mail: amilsom@clemson.edu.
Website: http://www.clemson.edu/education/departments/education-human-development/academics/index.html

**Cleveland State University,** College of Graduate Studies, College of Education and Human Services, Department of Counseling, Administration, Supervision and Adult Learning (CASAL), Cleveland, OH 44115. Offers adult learning and development (M Ed); counselor education (PhD); early childhood mental health counseling (Certificate); educational administration and supervision (M Ed). *Accreditation:* ACA (one or more programs are accredited). *Program availability:* Part-time, evening/weekend. *Faculty:* 15 full-time (8 women), 19 part-time/adjunct (10 women). *Students:* 104 full-time (85 women), 259 part-time (197 women); includes 138 minority (115 Black or African American, non-Hispanic/Latino; 1 American Indian or Alaska Native, non-Hispanic/Latino; 3 Asian, non-Hispanic/Latino; 16 Hispanic/Latino; 3 Two or more races, non-Hispanic/Latino), 8 international. Average age 34. 57 applicants, 93% accepted, 51 enrolled. In 2016, 102 master's awarded. *Degree requirements:* For master's, comprehensive exam (for some programs), thesis optional, internship. *Entrance requirements:* For master's, GRE General Test or MAT, letter of recommendation and minimum GPA of 2.75 (for counseling); 2 letters of recommendation and interviews (for organizational leadership). Additional exam requirements/recommendations for international students: Required—TOEFL (minimum score 550 paper-based; 78 iBT), IELTS (minimum score 6). *Application deadline:* For fall admission, 6/21 for domestic students, 5/15 for international students; for spring admission, 8/31 for domestic students, 11/1 for international students. Application fee: $40. Electronic applications accepted. *Expenses:* Tuition, state resident: full-time $9565. Tuition, nonresident: full-time $17,980. Tuition and fees vary according to program. *Financial support:* In 2016–17, 19 students received support, including 10 research assistantships with tuition reimbursements available (averaging $11,882 per year), 5 teaching assistantships with tuition reimbursements available (averaging $11,882 per year); scholarships/grants and unspecified assistantships also available. Support available to part-time students. *Faculty research:* Education law, career development, bullying, psychopharmacology, counseling and spirituality. *Total annual research expenditures:* $225,821. *Unit head:* Dr. Ann L. Bauer, Chairperson, 216-687-4582, Fax: 216-687-5378, E-mail: a.l.bauer@csuohio.edu. *Application contact:* Deborah L. Brown, Interim Assistant Director, Graduate Admissions, 216-523-7572, Fax: 216-687-5400, E-mail: d.l.brown@csuohio.edu.
Website: http://www.csuohio.edu/cehs/departments/CASAL/casal_dept.html

**Cleveland State University,** College of Graduate Studies, College of Education and Human Services, Program in Urban Education, Specialization in Counseling Psychology, Cleveland, OH 44115. Offers PhD. *Faculty:* 5 full-time (3 women), 1 part-time/adjunct (0 women). *Students:* 17 full-time (14 women), 10 part-time (6 women); includes 5 minority (2 Black or African American, non-Hispanic/Latino; 2 Hispanic/Latino; 1 Two or more races, non-Hispanic/Latino), 4 international. Average age 30. 36 applicants, 31% accepted, 3 enrolled. In 2016, 2 doctorates awarded. *Degree requirements:* For doctorate, comprehensive exam, thesis/dissertation, internship. *Entrance requirements:* For doctorate, GRE (Verbal, Quantitative, and Writing), minimum undergraduate GPA of 2.75, graduate 3.0; 3 letters of recommendation; personal statement; curriculum vitae; interview. Additional exam requirements/recommendations for international students: Required—TOEFL (minimum score 550 paper-based; 78 iBT), IELTS (minimum score 6). *Application deadline:* For fall admission, 1/15 for domestic and international students. Application fee: $40. Electronic applications accepted. *Expenses:* Tuition, state resident: full-time $9565. Tuition, nonresident: full-time $17,980. Tuition and fees vary according to program. *Financial support:* In 2016–17, 14 students received support, including 11 research assistantships with partial tuition reimbursements available (averaging $5,900 per year), 3 teaching assistantships with partial tuition reimbursements available (averaging $5,900 per year); tuition waivers (partial) and unspecified assistantships also available. Financial award application deadline: 1/15. *Faculty research:* Vocational psychology, low SES urban youth, women's identity and work, work and family integration, professional issues in psychology, clinical supervision and training, research productivity of psychologists and psychology trainees, leadership training in professional organizations, college students' development and adjustment, diversity issues with a focus on gender and sexual minorities, social constructionism, childhood career development, multicultural issues in mental health. *Unit head:* Dr. Graham Stead, Director of Doctoral Studies, 216-687-4697, Fax: 216-687-5378, E-mail: g.b.stead@csuohio.edu. *Application contact:* Rita M. Grabowski, Administrative Assistant, 216-687-4697, Fax: 216-687-5378, E-mail: r.grabowski@csuohio.edu.
Website: http://www.csuohio.edu/cehs/departments/DOC/cp_doc.html

**The College at Brockport, State University of New York,** School of Education, Health, and Human Services, Department of Counselor Education, Brockport, NY 14420-2997. Offers college counseling (MS Ed, CAS); mental health counseling (MS, CAS); school counseling (MS Ed, CAS); school counselor supervision (CAS). *Accreditation:* ACA (one or more programs are accredited). *Program availability:* Part-time. *Faculty:* 5 full-time (3 women), 6 part-time/adjunct (4 women). *Students:* 26 full-time (20 women), 75 part-time (60 women); includes 22 minority (12 Black or African American, non-Hispanic/Latino; 1 American Indian or Alaska Native, non-Hispanic/Latino; 1 Asian, non-Hispanic/Latino; 3 Hispanic/Latino; 5 Two or more races, non-Hispanic/Latino). 102 applicants, 34% accepted, 26 enrolled. In 2016, 20 master's, 4 other advanced degrees awarded. *Degree requirements:* For master's, thesis, internship. *Entrance requirements:* For master's, group interview, letters of recommendation, written objectives, audio response; for CAS, master's degree, New York state school counselor certificate. Additional exam requirements/recommendations for international students: Required—TOEFL (minimum score 550 paper-based; 79 iBT), IELTS (minimum score 6.5). *Application deadline:* For fall admission, 2/1 priority date for domestic and international students; for spring admission, 9/1 priority date for domestic and international students; for summer admission, 2/1 priority date for domestic and international students. Application fee: $80. Electronic applications accepted. *Expenses:*

Contact institution. *Financial support:* In 2016–17, 1 fellowship with full tuition reimbursement (averaging $7,500 per year), 1 teaching assistantship with full tuition reimbursement (averaging $6,000 per year) were awarded; Federal Work-Study, scholarships/grants, and unspecified assistantships also available. Support available to part-time students. Financial award application deadline: 3/15; financial award applicants required to submit FAFSA. *Faculty research:* Gender and diversity issues; counseling outcomes; spirituality; school, college and mental health counseling; obesity. *Unit head:* Dr. Susan Seem, Chair, 585-395-5492, Fax: 585-395-2366, E-mail: sseem@brockport.edu. *Application contact:* Danielle A. Welch, Graduate Admissions Counselor, 585-395-5465, Fax: 585-395-2515.
Website: http://www.brockport.edu/edc/

**The College of New Rochelle,** Graduate School, Division of Human Services, Program in Guidance and Counseling, New Rochelle, NY 10805-2308. Offers MS, Advanced Certificate. *Program availability:* Part-time. *Degree requirements:* For master's, internship. *Entrance requirements:* For master's, interview.

**The College of New Rochelle,** Graduate School, Division of Human Services, Program in Mental Health Counseling, New Rochelle, NY 10805-2308. Offers mental health counseling (MS); thanatology (Certificate). *Degree requirements:* For Certificate, internship.

**College of Saint Elizabeth,** Department of Psychology, Morristown, NJ 07960-6989. Offers counseling psychology (MA); forensic psychology (MA); mental health counseling (Certificate); psychology (Psy D); student affairs in higher education (Certificate). *Program availability:* Part-time. *Degree requirements:* For master's, thesis or alternative. *Entrance requirements:* For master's, minimum GPA of 3.0, BA in psychology (preferred), 12 credits of course work in psychology; for doctorate, GRE, 3 letters of recommendation from professionals who can comment on the applicant's qualifications for doctoral study; master's degree in counseling psychology, forensic psychology and counseling, or its equivalent. Additional exam requirements/recommendations for international students: Required—TOEFL (minimum score 550 paper-based; 79 iBT), IELTS (minimum score 6.5). Electronic applications accepted. *Expenses:* Contact institution.

**College of St. Joseph,** Graduate Programs, Division of Psychology and Human Services, Program in Clinical Mental Health Counseling, Rutland, VT 05701-3899. Offers MS. *Program availability:* Part-time. *Degree requirements:* For master's, comprehensive exam. *Entrance requirements:* For master's, official college transcripts; 2 letters of reference. Additional exam requirements/recommendations for international students: Required—TOEFL (minimum score 550 paper-based). *Application deadline:* Applications are processed on a rolling basis. Application fee: $35. Electronic applications accepted. *Expenses:* Tuition, area resident: Full-time $13,800; part-time $560 per credit. *Required fees:* $75 per semester. Full-time tuition and fees vary according to course load. *Financial support:* Career-related internships or fieldwork, Federal Work-Study, and unspecified assistantships available. Support available to part-time students. Financial award application deadline: 3/1. *Unit head:* Dr. Craig Knapp, Chair, 802-773-5900 Ext. 3219, Fax: 802-776-5258, E-mail: cknapp@csj.edu. *Application contact:* Alan Young, Dean of Admissions, 802-773-5900 Ext. 3227, Fax: 802-776-5310, E-mail: alanyoung@csj.edu.

**The College of Saint Rose,** Graduate Studies, Thelma P. Lally School of Education, Programs in Clinical Mental Health Counseling, Albany, NY 12203-1419. Offers clinical mental health counseling (Certificate); school counseling (MS Ed, Certificate), including mental health counseling (MS Ed). *Students:* 58 full-time (53 women), 23 part-time (19 women); includes 9 minority (5 Black or African American, non-Hispanic/Latino; 2 Asian, non-Hispanic/Latino; 1 Hispanic/Latino; 1 Two or more races, non-Hispanic/Latino), 1 international. Average age 28. 60 applicants, 78% accepted, 32 enrolled. In 2016, 1 Certificate awarded. *Entrance requirements:* For master's, minimum undergraduate GPA of 3.0. Additional exam requirements/recommendations for international students: Required—TOEFL (minimum score 550 paper-based; 80 iBT), IELTS (minimum score 6), PTE (minimum score 56). *Application deadline:* For fall admission, 4/1 for domestic and international students; for spring admission, 10/15 priority date for domestic and international students; for summer admission, 3/15 for domestic and international students. Applications are processed on a rolling basis. Application fee: $40. Electronic applications accepted. *Expenses:* Tuition: Full-time $14,382; part-time $799 per credit. *Required fees:* $814; $32 per credit. $88 per semester. Tuition and fees vary according to course load. *Financial support:* Career-related internships or fieldwork, scholarships/grants, tuition waivers (partial), and unspecified assistantships available. Support available to part-time students. Financial award application deadline: 4/15. *Unit head:* Dr. Claudia Lingertat-Putnam, Chair, 518-337-4311, E-mail: lingertc@strose.edu. *Application contact:* Cris Murray, Assistant Vice President for Graduate Recruitment and Enrollment, 518-485-3390, Fax: 518-458-5479, E-mail: grad@strose.edu.
Website: https://www.strose.edu/counseling/

**College of Staten Island of the City University of New York,** Graduate Programs, Division of Humanities and Social Sciences, Program in Mental Health Counseling, Staten Island, NY 10314-6600. Offers MA. *Faculty:* 6 full-time, 5 part-time/adjunct. *Students:* 57 full-time, 1 part-time. Average age 27. 80 applicants, 28% accepted, 22 enrolled. In 2016, 21 master's awarded. *Degree requirements:* For master's, 16 required courses, practicum, three internship courses. *Entrance requirements:* For master's, BA/BS with minimum GPA of 3.0 and 15-19 credits in certain areas of psychology; 2 letters of recommendation; 1-2 page statement of experience and interest in the field. Additional exam requirements/recommendations for international students: Required—TOEFL (minimum score 600 paper-based; 100 iBT), IELTS (minimum score 7). *Application deadline:* For fall admission, 3/10 for domestic and international students. Applications are processed on a rolling basis. Application fee: $125. Electronic applications accepted. *Expenses:* Tuition, state resident: full-time $10,130; part-time $425 per credit. Tuition, nonresident: full-time $18,720; part-time $780 per credit. *Required fees:* $181.10 per semester. Tuition and fees vary according to program. *Faculty research:* Child psychopathology, HIV/AIDS counseling, elder care and cognition, psychosocial burn rehabilitation, autism spectrum disorders. *Unit head:* Dr. Frances Melendez, Graduate Program Coordinator, 718-982-3960, E-mail: frances.melendez@csi.cuny.edu. *Application contact:* Sasha Spence, Associate Director for Graduate Admissions, 718-982-2019, Fax: 718-982-2500, E-mail: sasha.spence@csi.cuny.edu.
Website: http://csivc.csi.cuny.edu/psy/files/MHC.html

**Colorado Christian University,** Program in Counseling, Lakewood, CO 80226. Offers MAC. *Accreditation:* ACA. *Program availability:* Part-time, evening/weekend. *Degree requirements:* For master's, thesis optional. *Entrance requirements:* For master's, GRE General Test, 3 letters of recommendation. Additional exam requirements/recommendations for international students: Required—TOEFL. Electronic applications accepted. *Expenses:* Contact institution.

**Concordia University Chicago,** College of Graduate and Innovative Programs, Program in Community Counseling, River Forest, IL 60305-1499. Offers MA. *Accreditation:* ACA. *Degree requirements:* For master's, final project. *Entrance requirements:* For master's, minimum GPA of 2.9. Additional exam requirements/

recommendations for international students: Required—TOEFL (minimum score 550 paper-based). Electronic applications accepted.

**Dallas Baptist University,** College of Humanities and Social Sciences, Professional Counseling Program, Main Campus, Dallas, TX 75211-9299. Offers MA. *Program availability:* Part-time, evening/weekend. *Application deadline:* Applications are processed on a rolling basis. Application fee: $25. Electronic applications accepted. Application fee is waived when completed online. *Expenses:* Tuition: Full-time $15,408; part-time $856 per credit hour. *Required fees:* $400 per semester. Tuition and fees vary according to course load and degree level. *Faculty research:* Therapy effectiveness. *Unit head:* Dr. Mary Becerril, Director, 214-333-5265, E-mail: maryb@dbu.edu. *Application contact:* Bobby Soto, Director of Admissions, 214-333-5242, E-mail: graduate@dbu.edu.
Website: http://www3.dbu.edu/graduate/mapc.asp

**Dallas Baptist University,** College of Humanities and Social Sciences, Professional Counseling Program, North Campus, Dallas, TX 75211-9299. Offers MA. *Program availability:* Part-time, evening/weekend. *Application deadline:* Applications are processed on a rolling basis. Application fee: $25. Electronic applications accepted. Application fee is waived when completed online. *Expenses:* Tuition: Full-time $15,408; part-time $856 per credit hour. *Required fees:* $400 per semester. Tuition and fees vary according to course load and degree level. *Unit head:* Dr. Joseph Cook, Director, 214-333-5787, E-mail: joec@dbu.edu. *Application contact:* Bobby Soto, Director of Admissions, 214-333-5242, E-mail: graduate@dbu.edu.
Website: http://www3.dbu.edu/graduate/mapc.asp

**Delaware Valley University,** Program in Counseling Psychology, Doylestown, PA 18901-2697. Offers child and adolescent therapy (MA); social justice community counseling (MA).

**DePaul University,** College of Education, Chicago, IL 60614. Offers bilingual bicultural education (M Ed, MA); counseling (M Ed, MA), including clinical mental health counseling, college student development, school counseling; curriculum studies (M Ed, MA, Ed D); early childhood education (M Ed, MA, Ed D); educating adults (MA); educational leadership (M Ed, MA, Ed D), including administration and supervision (M Ed, MA), principal preparation (M Ed, MA); elementary education (MA); mathematics education (MA); mathematics for teaching (MS); middle school mathematics education (MS); reading specialist (M Ed, MA); secondary education (M Ed); social and cultural foundations in education (MA); special education (M Ed, MA); world languages education (M Ed, MA). *Program availability:* Part-time, evening/weekend, online learning. *Degree requirements:* For doctorate, thesis/dissertation. Electronic applications accepted.

**Dominican University of California,** School of Education and Counseling Psychology, Counseling Psychology Department, San Rafael, CA 94901-2298. Offers general (MS); marriage and family therapy (MS). *Program availability:* Part-time, evening/weekend. *Degree requirements:* For master's, comprehensive exam (for some programs), thesis (for some programs). *Entrance requirements:* For master's, minimum GPA of 3.0 for last 60 units, autobiography, response to scenario. Additional exam requirements/recommendations for international students: Required—TOEFL (minimum score 550 paper-based; 80 iBT), IELTS (minimum score 6.5). Electronic applications accepted. Application fee is waived when completed online. *Expenses:* Contact institution.

**Duquesne University,** School of Education, Department of Counseling, Psychology, and Special Education, Program in Counselor Education, Pittsburgh, PA 15282-0001. Offers clinical mental health counseling (MS Ed, Post-Master's Certificate); counselor education and supervision (Ed D); counselor licensure (Post-Master's Certificate); marriage and family counseling (MS Ed); school counseling (MS Ed). *Accreditation:* ACA (one or more programs are accredited). *Program availability:* Part-time, evening/weekend. *Faculty:* 8 full-time (3 women). *Students:* 188 full-time (139 women), 5 part-time (4 women); includes 39 minority (20 Black or African American, non-Hispanic/Latino; 5 Asian, non-Hispanic/Latino; 5 Hispanic/Latino; 9 Two or more races, non-Hispanic/Latino), 8 international. Average age 29. 152 applicants, 73% accepted, 69 enrolled. In 2016, 34 master's, 9 doctorates awarded. *Degree requirements:* For master's, thesis optional; for doctorate, thesis/dissertation. *Entrance requirements:* For master's, letters of recommendation, essay, interview, bachelor's degree; for doctorate, GRE, letters of recommendation, essay, interview, master's degree; for Post-Master's Certificate, GRE, letters of recommendation, essay, interview, bachelor's/master's degree. Additional exam requirements/recommendations for international students: Required—TOEFL (minimum score 550 paper-based), IELTS (minimum score 7). *Application deadline:* For fall admission, 3/1 for domestic students; for spring admission, 9/1 for domestic students. Applications are processed on a rolling basis. Application fee: $0. Electronic applications accepted. *Expenses:* Tuition: Full-time $22,212; part-time $1234 per credit. Tuition and fees vary according to program. *Financial support:* Research assistantships, teaching assistantships, and Federal Work-Study available. Support available to part-time students. *Unit head:* Dr. Jered Kolbert, Professor/Director, 412-396-4471, Fax: 412-396-1340, E-mail: kolbertj@duq.edu. *Application contact:* Michael Dolinger, Director of Student and Academic Services, 412-396-6647, Fax: 412-396-5585, E-mail: dolingerm@duq.edu.

**Eastern Nazarene College,** Adult and Graduate Studies, Program in Marriage and Family Therapy, Quincy, MA 02170. Offers MS. *Program availability:* Part-time, evening/weekend. *Entrance requirements:* For master's, 3 letters of recommendation, resume. Additional exam requirements/recommendations for international students: Required—TOEFL (minimum score 550 paper-based).

**Eastern University,** Department of Counseling Psychology, St. Davids, PA 19087-3696. Offers applied behavior analysis (MA, Certificate); counseling (MA); professional counseling (Certificate); school counseling (MA, Certificate); school psychology (MS, Certificate). *Program availability:* Part-time. *Students:* 104 full-time (92 women), 88 part-time (75 women); includes 83 minority (61 Black or African American, non-Hispanic/Latino; 1 American Indian or Alaska Native, non-Hispanic/Latino; 4 Asian, non-Hispanic/Latino; 13 Hispanic/Latino; 4 Two or more races, non-Hispanic/Latino), 3 international. Average age 29. In 2016, 46 master's awarded. *Degree requirements:* For master's, internship. *Entrance requirements:* Additional exam requirements/recommendations for international students: Required—TOEFL (minimum score 550 paper-based; 79 iBT). *Application deadline:* Applications are processed on a rolling basis. Application fee: $35. Electronic applications accepted. Application fee is waived when completed online. *Expenses:* $690 per credit. *Financial support:* Application deadline: 3/15. *Unit head:* Michael Dziedziak, Executive Director of Enrollment, 800-452-0996, E-mail: gpsadmissions@eastern.edu.
Website: http://www.eastern.edu/academics/programs/graduate-counseling-and-psychology-department

**Eastern Washington University,** Graduate Studies, College of Social Sciences, Department of Psychology, Program in Mental Health Counseling, Cheney, WA 99004-2431. Offers applied psychology (MS); mental health counseling (MS). *Students:* 13 full-time (10 women); includes 1 minority (Hispanic/Latino). Average age 28. 56 applicants, 20% accepted, 10 enrolled. In 2016, 9 master's awarded. *Entrance requirements:* For master's, GRE, minimum GPA of 3.0. Additional exam requirements/recommendations for international

students: Required—TOEFL (minimum score 580 paper-based; 92 iBT), IELTS (minimum score 7), PTE (minimum score 63). Application fee: $75. Electronic applications accepted. *Expenses:* Tuition, state resident: full-time $11,000; part-time $5500 per credit. Tuition, nonresident: full-time $24,000; part-time $12,000 per credit. *Required fees:* $1300. One-time fee: $50 full-time. Tuition and fees vary according to course load, campus/location and program. *Financial support:* Application deadline: 2/1; applicants required to submit FAFSA. *Unit head:* Dr. Keely Hope, Associate Professor/Director, Counselor Education, 509-359-2439, E-mail: khope@ewu.edu. *Application contact:* Kathy White, Advisor/Recruiter for Graduate Studies, 509-359-6297, Fax: 509-359-6044, E-mail: gradprograms@ewu.edu.

**East Texas Baptist University,** Master of Arts in Counseling Program, Marshall, TX 75670-1498. Offers MA. *Program availability:* Part-time, evening/weekend. *Faculty:* 4 full-time (3 women), 1 part-time/adjunct (0 women). *Students:* 25 full-time (20 women), 19 part-time (12 women); includes 29 minority (27 Black or African American, non-Hispanic/Latino; 2 Hispanic/Latino). Average age 32. 30 applicants, 60% accepted, 17 enrolled. In 2016, 6 master's awarded. *Entrance requirements:* Additional exam requirements/recommendations for international students: Recommended—TOEFL (minimum score 550 paper-based; 79 iBT). *Application deadline:* For fall admission, 8/17 for domestic students; for spring admission, 1/10 for domestic students; for summer admission, 5/2 for domestic students. Applications are processed on a rolling basis. Application fee: $50. Electronic applications accepted. *Expenses:* $735 per credit hour tuition; $150 per semester fees (6 or more hours enrolled); $75 per semester fees (1-5 hours enrolled). *Financial support:* In 2016–17, 6 students received support. Federal Work-Study, unspecified assistantships, and staff grants available. Financial award applicants required to submit FAFSA. *Unit head:* Dr. David Deel, Director, 903-923-2252, E-mail: macounsel@etbu.edu. *Application contact:* Den Murley, Director of Graduate Admissions, 903-923-2079, Fax: 903-934-8115, E-mail: dmurley@etbu.edu.
Website: https://www.etbu.edu/sciences/master-arts-counseling/

**Edinboro University of Pennsylvania,** Department of Counseling, School Psychology and Special Education, Edinboro, PA 16444. Offers counseling (MA), including art therapy, clinical mental health counseling, college counseling, rehabilitation counseling, school counseling; educational psychology (M Ed); school psychology (Ed S); special education (M Ed), including autism, behavior management. *Accreditation:* ACA. *Program availability:* Part-time, evening/weekend. *Degree requirements:* For master's, thesis or alternative, competency exam; for Ed S, thesis or alternative. *Entrance requirements:* For master's and Ed S, GRE or MAT, minimum QPA of 2.5. Electronic applications accepted.

**Emporia State University,** Program in Clinical Counseling, Emporia, KS 66801-5415. Offers MS. *Accreditation:* ACA. *Program availability:* Part-time. *Faculty:* 11 full-time (7 women), 1 (woman) part-time/adjunct. *Students:* 27 full-time (20 women), 10 part-time (all women); includes 7 minority (5 Black or African American, non-Hispanic/Latino; 2 Asian, non-Hispanic/Latino), 1 international. 38 applicants, 95% accepted, 10 enrolled. In 2016, 16 master's awarded. *Degree requirements:* For master's, comprehensive exam, internship. *Entrance requirements:* For master's, GRE or MAT. Additional exam requirements/recommendations for international students: Required—TOEFL (minimum score 520 paper-based; 68 iBT). *Application deadline:* For fall admission, 8/15 for domestic students. Applications are processed on a rolling basis. Application fee: $30 ($75 for international students). Electronic applications accepted. *Expenses:* Tuition, state resident: full-time $5922; part-time $246.75 per credit hour. Tuition, nonresident: full-time $18,414; part-time $767.25 per credit hour. *Required fees:* $1884; $78.50 per credit hour. *Financial support:* In 2016–17, 9 research assistantships with full tuition reimbursements (averaging $7,344 per year) were awarded; Federal Work-Study, institutionally sponsored loans, health care benefits, and unspecified assistantships also available. Financial award application deadline: 3/15; financial award applicants required to submit FAFSA. *Unit head:* Dr. Katrina Miller, Interim Chair, 620-341-5791, E-mail: kmille12@emporia.edu. *Application contact:* Mary Sewell, Admissions Coordinator, 800-950-GRAD, Fax: 620-341-5909, E-mail: msewell@emporia.edu.

**Evangel University,** Department of Behavioral Sciences, Springfield, MO 65802. Offers clinical mental health counseling (MS). *Program availability:* Part-time. *Faculty:* 6 full-time (5 women), 5 part-time/adjunct (all women). *Students:* 35 full-time (26 women), 10 part-time (7 women); includes 5 minority (2 Black or African American, non-Hispanic/Latino; 2 Hispanic/Latino; 1 Two or more races, non-Hispanic/Latino). Average age 33. 27 applicants, 85% accepted, 20 enrolled. In 2016, 34 master's awarded. *Degree requirements:* For master's, comprehensive exam, thesis optional. *Entrance requirements:* For master's, GRE General Test, minimum undergraduate GPA of 3.0. Additional exam requirements/recommendations for international students: Required—TOEFL (minimum score 550 paper-based). *Application deadline:* For fall admission, 7/15 priority date for domestic students, 8/1 for international students; for spring admission, 11/15 priority date for domestic students, 12/1 for international students. Applications are processed on a rolling basis. Application fee: $25. Electronic applications accepted. Application fee is waived when completed online. *Expenses:* Tuition: Part-time $400 per credit hour. *Required fees:* $148 per trimester. One-time fee: $25. Tuition and fees vary according to course load, degree level and program. *Financial support:* In 2016–17, 6 students received support. Unspecified assistantships available. Financial award application deadline: 4/1; financial award applicants required to submit FAFSA. *Unit head:* Christine Arnzen, Program Coordinator, 417-865-2815 Ext. 8618, E-mail: arnzenc@evangel.edu. *Application contact:* Matt Petry, Admissions Representative, Graduate Studies, 417-865-2815 Ext. 7416, Fax: 417-575-5484, E-mail: benitezk@evangel.edu.
Website: https://www.evangel.edu/departments/behavioral-social-sciences/about-the-department/

**Fairfield University,** Graduate School of Education and Allied Professions, Fairfield, CT 06824. Offers applied behavior analysis (ATC); applied psychology (MA); clinical mental health counseling (MA, CAS); educational technology (MA); elementary education (MA, CAS); family studies (MA); integration of spirituality and religion in counseling (ATC); marriage and family therapy (MA); reading and language development (Sixth Year Certificate); school counseling (MA, CAS); school psychology (MA, CAS); school-based marriage and family therapy (ATC); secondary education (MA); special education (MA, CAS); substance abuse counseling (ATC); teaching (Certificate); teaching and foundations (MA, CAS); TESOL, world languages, and bilingual education (MA, CAS). *Accreditation:* NCATE. *Program availability:* Part-time, evening/weekend. *Faculty:* 19 full-time (15 women), 38 part-time/adjunct (26 women). *Students:* 153 full-time (132 women), 302 part-time (252 women); includes 97 minority (24 Black or African American, non-Hispanic/Latino; 12 Asian, non-Hispanic/Latino; 55 Hispanic/Latino; 6 Two or more races, non-Hispanic/Latino), 6 international. Average age 32. 283 applicants, 61% accepted, 97 enrolled. In 2016, 130 master's awarded. *Degree requirements:* For master's, comprehensive exam. *Entrance requirements:* For master's, minimum GPA of 3.0, 2 recommendations, resume. Additional exam requirements/recommendations for international students: Required—TOEFL (minimum score 550 paper-based; 84 iBT) or IELTS (minimum score 7.5). *Application deadline:* For fall admission, 2/15 for international students; for spring admission, 10/1 for international students. Application fee: $60. Electronic applications accepted. *Expenses:* $725 per credit hour. *Financial support:* In 2016–17, 42 students received support.

*Counseling Psychology*

Career-related internships or fieldwork and unspecified assistantships available. Support available to part-time students. Financial award applicants required to submit FAFSA. *Faculty research:* Reading and literacy, writing, social justice and inequality in education, addictions and mental health issues, therapeutic relationships and clinical supervision. *Unit head:* Dr. Robert D. Hannafin, Dean, 203-254-4250, Fax: 203-254-4241, E-mail: rhannafin@fairfield.edu. *Application contact:* Marianne Gumpper, Director of Graduate Admission, 203-254-4184, Fax: 203-254-4073, E-mail: gradadmis@fairfield.edu.
Website: http://www.fairfield.edu/gseap

**Fairleigh Dickinson University, College at Florham,** Maxwell Becton College of Arts and Sciences, Department of Psychology, Program in Clinical Mental Health Counseling, Madison, NJ 07940-1099. Offers MA. *Accreditation:* ACA.

**Fairleigh Dickinson University, College at Florham,** Maxwell Becton College of Arts and Sciences, Department of Psychology, Program in Counseling, Madison, NJ 07940-1099. Offers MA. *Accreditation:* ACA.

**Felician University,** Program in Counseling Psychology, Lodi, NJ 07644-2117. Offers MA. *Program availability:* Part-time, evening/weekend. *Faculty:* 4 full-time (1 woman), 8 part-time/adjunct (7 women). *Students:* 28 full-time (21 women), 23 part-time (18 women); includes 35 minority (12 Black or African American, non-Hispanic/Latino; 3 Asian, non-Hispanic/Latino; 18 Hispanic/Latino; 1 Native Hawaiian or other Pacific Islander, non-Hispanic/Latino; 1 Two or more races, non-Hispanic/Latino), 1 international. Average age 31. 28 applicants, 71% accepted, 12 enrolled. In 2016, 12 master's awarded. *Degree requirements:* For master's, comprehensive exam, scholarly project. *Entrance requirements:* For master's, two letters of recommendation, interview, resume, personal statement, graduation from accredited baccalaureate program. Additional exam requirements/recommendations for international students: Required—TOEFL (minimum score 650 paper-based; 79 iBT), IELTS (minimum score 6.5). *Application deadline:* Applications are processed on a rolling basis. Application fee: $40. Electronic applications accepted. Application fee is waived when completed online. *Expenses:* $850 per credit, $290 comprehensive fee, $165 mandatory fee per term. *Financial support:* Federal Work-Study and scholarships/grants available. Financial award applicants required to submit FAFSA. *Faculty research:* Evidence-based practice, mindfulness of multi cultures, sports psychology, performance enhancement. *Unit head:* Dr. Daniel Mahoney, Director of the Master's in Counseling Program, 201-559-6161, E-mail: mahoneyd@felician.edu. *Application contact:* Michael Szarek, Assistant Vice-President, Graduate Admissions, 201-559-1450, E-mail: szarekm@felician.edu.

**Fitchburg State University,** Division of Graduate and Continuing Education, Programs in Counseling, Fitchburg, MA 01420-2697. Offers elementary school guidance counseling (MS); mental health counseling (MS); secondary school guidance counseling (MS). *Accreditation:* NCATE. *Program availability:* Part-time, evening/weekend. *Entrance requirements:* Additional exam requirements/recommendations for international students: Required—TOEFL (minimum score 550 paper-based; 79 iBT). Electronic applications accepted. *Expenses:* Tuition, state resident: full-time $2871; part-time $1914 per year. Tuition, nonresident: full-time $2871; part-time $1914 per year. *Required fees:* $3828. Tuition and fees vary according to program.

**Florida International University,** College of Arts, Sciences, and Education, Department of Leadership and Professional Studies, Miami, FL 33199. Offers adult education and human resource development (MS, Ed D); counseling (MS), including rehabilitation counseling, school counseling; counselor education (MS), including clinical mental health counseling; educational administration and supervision (Ed D); educational leadership (MS, Certificate, Ed S); higher education (Ed D); higher education administration (MS); international and comparative education (MS); recreation and sport management (MS), including recreation and sport management, recreational therapy; school psychology (Ed S); urban education (MS), including instruction in urban settings, learning technologies, multicultural/bilingual, multicultural/TESOL, urban education. *Program availability:* Part-time, evening/weekend. *Faculty:* 27 full-time (19 women), 38 part-time/adjunct (25 women). *Students:* 253 full-time (191 women), 306 part-time (241 women); includes 444 minority (129 Black or African American, non-Hispanic/Latino; 3 Asian, non-Hispanic/Latino; 304 Hispanic/Latino; 8 Two or more races, non-Hispanic/Latino), 18 international. Average age 31. 366 applicants, 60% accepted, 115 enrolled. In 2016, 193 master's, 8 doctorates awarded. *Degree requirements:* For doctorate, thesis/dissertation. *Entrance requirements:* For master's, minimum GPA of 3.0; for doctorate and other advanced degree, GRE General Test. Additional exam requirements/recommendations for international students: Required—TOEFL (minimum score 550 paper-based; 80 iBT), IELTS (minimum score 6.3). *Application deadline:* For fall admission, 6/1 priority date for domestic students, 4/1 for international students; for winter admission, 10/1 priority date for domestic students, 9/1 for international students; for spring admission, 3/1 priority date for domestic students, 2/1 for international students. Applications are processed on a rolling basis. Application fee: $30. Electronic applications accepted. *Expenses:* Tuition, state resident: full-time $8912; part-time $446 per credit hour. Tuition, nonresident: full-time $21,393; part-time $992 per credit hour. *Required fees:* $2185; $195 per semester. Tuition and fees vary according to program. *Financial support:* Fellowships, research assistantships with tuition reimbursements, teaching assistantships with tuition reimbursements, Federal Work-Study, and tuition waivers (full and partial) available. Support available to part-time students. Financial award applicants required to submit FAFSA. *Unit head:* Dr. Benjamin Baez, Chair, 305-348-3214, Fax: 305-348-1515, E-mail: benjamin.baez@fiu.edu. *Application contact:* Nanett Rojas, Assistant Director, Graduate Admissions, 305-348-7464, Fax: 305-348-7441, E-mail: gradadm@fiu.edu.
Website: http://education.fiu.edu

**Florida International University,** College of Arts, Sciences, and Education, Department of Psychology, Miami, FL 33199. Offers behavioral analysis (MS); clinical science (PhD); cognitive neuroscience (PhD); counseling psychology (MS); developmental science (MS, PhD); legal psychology (MS, PhD); organizational psychology (MS, PhD). Program has fall admissions only. *Accreditation:* APA. *Program availability:* Part-time, evening/weekend. *Faculty:* 44 full-time (27 women), 41 part-time/adjunct (30 women). *Students:* 150 full-time (115 women), 17 part-time (10 women); includes 89 minority (8 Black or African American, non-Hispanic/Latino; 5 Asian, non-Hispanic/Latino; 75 Hispanic/Latino; 1 Two or more races, non-Hispanic/Latino), 10 international. Average age 27. 287 applicants, 24% accepted, 57 enrolled. In 2016, 35 master's, 11 doctorates awarded. Terminal master's awarded for partial completion of doctoral program. *Degree requirements:* For master's, thesis; for doctorate, comprehensive exam, thesis/dissertation. *Entrance requirements:* For master's, GRE General Test, minimum GPA of 3.0, resume, 3 letters of recommendation; for doctorate, GRE General Test, 3 letters of recommendation, resume, letter of intent, two writing samples, minimum GPA of 3.0. Additional exam requirements/recommendations for international students: Required—TOEFL (minimum score 550 paper-based; 80 iBT). *Application deadline:* For fall admission, 12/15 for domestic and international students. Application fee: $30. Electronic applications accepted. *Expenses:* Tuition, state resident: full-time $8912; part-time $446 per credit hour. Tuition, nonresident: full-time $21,393; part-time $992 per credit hour. *Required fees:* $2185; $195 per semester. Tuition and fees vary according to program. *Financial support:* Institutionally sponsored loans and scholarships/grants available. Financial award application deadline: 3/1.

*Faculty research:* Legal psychology, organizational and industrial psychology, child behavior psychology. *Unit head:* Dr. William Pelham, Chair, 305-348-3002, Fax: 305-348-3646, E-mail: wpelham@fiu.edu. *Application contact:* Nanett Rojas, Assistant Director, Graduate Admissions, 305-348-7464, Fax: 305-348-7441, E-mail: gradadm@fiu.edu.

**Florida State University,** The Graduate School, College of Education, Program in Counseling and Human Systems, Tallahassee, FL 32306. Offers MS/Ed S. *Accreditation:* ACA. Terminal master's awarded for partial completion of doctoral program. *Entrance requirements:* Additional exam requirements/recommendations for international students: Required—TOEFL (minimum score 550 paper-based, 80 iBT), IELTS (minimum score 6.5), Michigan English Language Assessment Battery (minimum score 77), or PTE (minimum score 55). Application fee: $30. Electronic applications accepted. *Expenses:* Tuition, state resident: full-time $7263; part-time $403.51 per credit hour. Tuition, nonresident: full-time $18,087; part-time $1004.85 per credit hour. *Required fees:* $1365; $75.81 per credit hour. $20 per semester. Tuition and fees vary according to campus/location. *Financial support:* Fellowships, research assistantships, teaching assistantships, scholarships/grants, tuition waivers (full and partial), and unspecified assistantships available. Financial award application deadline: 1/15; financial award applicants required to submit FAFSA. *Faculty research:* Vocational behavior and career services; disability issues; trauma and suicide; cognitive, social-emotional, behavioral assessment; multicultural, diversity and social justice. *Unit head:* Dr. Deb Osborn, Associate Professor/Program Coordinator, 850-644-3742, Fax: 850-644-8776, E-mail: dosborn@fsu.edu. *Application contact:* Samantha DeZerga, Academic Program Specialist, 850-644-8046, Fax: 850-644-8776, E-mail: sdezerga@fsu.edu.
Website: http://education.fsu.edu/degrees-and-programs/graduate-programs

**Florida State University,** The Graduate School, College of Education, Program in Counseling Psychology and School Psychology, Tallahassee, FL 32306. Offers PhD. *Degree requirements:* For doctorate, comprehensive exam, thesis/dissertation, diagnostic exam, preliminary exam, prospectus defense, dissertation defense. *Entrance requirements:* For doctorate, GRE General Test, minimum upper-division GPA of 3.0. Additional exam requirements/recommendations for international students: Required—TOEFL (minimum score 550 paper-based, 80 iBT), IELTS (minimum score 6.5), Michigan English Language Assessment Battery (minimum score 77), or PTE (minimum score 55). Application fee: $30. Electronic applications accepted. *Expenses:* Tuition, state resident: full-time $7263; part-time $403.51 per credit hour. Tuition, nonresident: full-time $18,087; part-time $1004.85 per credit hour. *Required fees:* $1365; $75.81 per credit hour. $20 per semester. Tuition and fees vary according to campus/location. *Financial support:* Fellowships, research assistantships, teaching assistantships, scholarships/grants, tuition waivers (full and partial), and unspecified assistantships available. Financial award application deadline: 1/15; financial award applicants required to submit FAFSA. *Faculty research:* Vocational behavior and career services; disability issues; trauma and suicide; cognitive, social-emotional, behavioral assessment; multicultural, diversity and social justice. *Unit head:* Dr. Deb Ebener, Associate Professor/Program Coordinator, 850-644-1789, Fax: 850-644-8776, E-mail: debener@fsu.edu. *Application contact:* Samantha DeZerga, Academic Program Specialist, 850-644-8046, Fax: 850-644-8776, E-mail: sdezerga@fsu.edu.
Website: http://education.fsu.edu/degrees-and-programs/counseling-psychology-and-school-psychology

**Fordham University,** Graduate School of Education, Division of Psychological and Educational Services, New York, NY 10023. Offers counseling and personnel services (MSE); counseling psychology (PhD); school psychology (PhD). *Accreditation:* APA (one or more programs are accredited); NCATE. *Program availability:* Part-time, evening/weekend. Terminal master's awarded for partial completion of doctoral program. *Degree requirements:* For master's, comprehensive exam (for some programs); for doctorate, comprehensive exam (for some programs), thesis/dissertation. *Entrance requirements:* For doctorate, GRE General Test. Additional exam requirements/recommendations for international students: Required—TOEFL (minimum score 577 paper-based; 90 iBT), IELTS (minimum score 7). Electronic applications accepted.

**Fort Valley State University,** College of Graduate Studies and Extended Education, Department of Counseling Psychology, Program in Mental Health Counseling, Fort Valley, GA 31030. Offers MS. *Accreditation:* ACA. *Program availability:* Part-time. *Degree requirements:* For master's, comprehensive exam (for some programs), thesis optional. *Entrance requirements:* For master's, GRE General Test or MAT. Additional exam requirements/recommendations for international students: Recommended—TOEFL.

**Franciscan University of Steubenville,** Graduate Programs, Department of Clinical Mental Health Counseling, Steubenville, OH 43952-1763. Offers MA. *Accreditation:* ACA. *Program availability:* Part-time. *Degree requirements:* For master's, case presentation, integrative paper. *Entrance requirements:* For master's, GRE General Test or MAT for those with a GPA below 3.0, minimum undergraduate GPA of 2.5. Additional exam requirements/recommendations for international students: Required—TOEFL. Electronic applications accepted. Application fee is waived when completed online.

**Francis Marion University,** Graduate Programs, Department of Psychology, Florence, SC 29502-0547. Offers applied psychology (MS), including clinical/counseling psychology, school psychology; school psychology (SSP). *Program availability:* Part-time, evening/weekend. *Degree requirements:* For master's, internship. *Entrance requirements:* For master's, GRE General Test, official transcripts, two letters of recommendation. Additional exam requirements/recommendations for international students: Required—TOEFL (minimum score 550 paper-based; 79 iBT). *Expenses:* Tuition, state resident: full-time $10,100; part-time $505 per credit hour. Tuition, nonresident: full-time $20,196; part-time $1009.80 per credit hour. *Required fees:* $14.80 per credit hour. $73 per semester. Tuition and fees vary according to course load and program. *Faculty research:* Parenting and family relationships, child development, applied behavioral analysis, post-traumatic stress disorder, clinical psychology in adults.

**Frostburg State University,** Graduate School, College of Liberal Arts and Sciences, Department of Psychology, Program in Counseling Psychology, Frostburg, MD 21532-1099. Offers MS. *Program availability:* Part-time, evening/weekend. *Degree requirements:* For master's, internship. *Entrance requirements:* For master's, GRE General Test or MAT, interview, minimum GPA of 3.0, resume. Additional exam requirements/recommendations for international students: Required—TOEFL. Electronic applications accepted.

**Gallaudet University,** The Graduate School, Washington, DC 20002-3625. Offers American Sign Language/English bilingual early childhood deaf education: birth to 5 (Certificate); audiology (Au D); clinical psychology (PhD); deaf and hard of hearing infants, toddlers, and their families (Certificate); deaf education (MA, Ed S); deaf history (Certificate); deaf studies (Certificate); educating deaf students with disabilities (Certificate); education: teacher preparation (MA), including deaf education, early childhood education and deaf education, elementary education and deaf education, secondary education and deaf education; educational neuroscience (PhD); hearing, speech and language sciences (MS, PhD); international development (MA);

interpretation (MA, PhD), including combined interpreting practice and research (MA); interpreting research (MA); linguistics (MA, PhD); mental health counseling (MA); peer mentoring (Certificate); public administration (MPA); school counseling (MA); school psychology (Psy S); sign language teaching (MA); social work (MSW); speech-language pathology (MS). *Program availability:* Part-time. *Students:* 297 full-time (231 women), 129 part-time (97 women); includes 105 minority (35 Black or African American, non-Hispanic/Latino; 20 Asian, non-Hispanic/Latino; 39 Hispanic/Latino; 11 Two or more races, non-Hispanic/Latino), 22 international. Average age 30. 471 applicants, 52% accepted, 147 enrolled. In 2016, 138 master's, 25 doctorates, 14 other advanced degrees awarded. Terminal master's awarded for partial completion of doctoral program. *Degree requirements:* For master's, comprehensive exam (for some programs), thesis optional; for doctorate, comprehensive exam, thesis/dissertation. *Entrance requirements:* For master's and doctorate, GRE General Test or MAT, letters of recommendation, interviews, goals statement, American Sign Language proficiency interview, written English competency. Additional exam requirements/recommendations for international students: Required—TOEFL. *Application deadline:* For fall admission, 2/15 for domestic students. Applications are processed on a rolling basis. Application fee: $75. Electronic applications accepted. *Expenses: Tuition:* Full-time $17,100; part-time $950 per credit hour. *Required fees:* $3725; $276 per semester. *Financial support:* Fellowships, research assistantships, teaching assistantships, career-related internships or fieldwork, Federal Work-Study, scholarships/grants, tuition waivers (partial), and unspecified assistantships available. Support available to part-time students. Financial award application deadline: 7/1; financial award applicants required to submit FAFSA. *Faculty research:* Signing math dictionaries, telecommunications access, cancer genetics, linguistics, visual language and visual learning, integrated quantum materials, deaf legal discourse, advance recruitment and retention in geosciences. *Unit head:* Dr. Gaurav Mathur, Dean, Graduate School and Continuing Studies, 202-250-2380, Fax: 202-651-5027, E-mail: gaurav.mathur@gallaudet.edu. *Application contact:* Wednesday Luria, Coordinator of Prospective Graduate Student Services, 202-651-5400, Fax: 202-651-5295, E-mail: graduate.school@gallaudet.edu.

**Gannon University,** School of Graduate Studies, College of Humanities, Education, and Social Sciences, School of Humanities, Program in Clinical Mental Health Counseling, Erie, PA 16541-0001. Offers MS. *Accreditation:* ACA. *Program availability:* Part-time, evening/weekend. *Students:* 25 full-time (20 women), 9 part-time (8 women); includes 1 minority (Black or African American, non-Hispanic/Latino), 2 international. Average age 27. 36 applicants, 50% accepted, 11 enrolled. In 2016, 12 master's awarded. *Degree requirements:* For master's, thesis, internship. *Entrance requirements:* For master's, bachelor's degree from approved institution, resume, 3 letters of recommendation, essay, interview, minimum GPA of 2.8, PA child abuse clearances and PA State Police criminal record check dated within a year of application. Additional exam requirements/recommendations for international students: Required—TOEFL (minimum score 79 iBT). *Application deadline:* Applications are processed on a rolling basis. Application fee: $25. Electronic applications accepted. Application fee is waived when completed online. *Expenses: Tuition:* Full-time $17,370. *Required fees:* $550. Tuition and fees vary according to course load and program. *Financial support:* Federal Work-Study and unspecified assistantships available. Financial award application deadline: 7/1; financial award applicants required to submit FAFSA. *Unit head:* Dr. Timothy Coppock, Director, 814-871-5793, E-mail: coppock001@gannon.edu. *Application contact:* Bridget Philip, Director of Graduate Admissions, 814-871-7412, E-mail: graduate@gannon.edu.

**Gardner-Webb University,** Graduate School, School of Psychology, Program in Mental Health Counseling, Boiling Springs, NC 28017. Offers MA. *Accreditation:* ACA. *Program availability:* Part-time, evening/weekend. *Faculty:* 5 full-time (4 women), 4 part-time/adjunct (2 women). *Students:* 3 full-time (all women), 47 part-time (38 women); includes 13 minority (11 Black or African American, non-Hispanic/Latino; 2 Hispanic/Latino). Average age 30. 78 applicants, 32% accepted, 25 enrolled. In 2016, 5 master's awarded. *Degree requirements:* For master's, comprehensive exam. *Entrance requirements:* For master's, GRE General Test, MAT, minimum GPA of 2.7. *Application deadline:* For fall admission, 7/1 priority date for domestic students. Applications are processed on a rolling basis. Electronic applications accepted. *Expenses:* Contact institution. *Financial support:* Unspecified assistantships available. *Unit head:* Dr. Angela Shores, Coordinator, 704-406-3965, Fax: 704-406-4329, E-mail: ashores1@gardner-webb.edu. *Application contact:* Office of Graduate Admissions, 877-498-4723, Fax: 704-406-3895, E-mail: gradinfo@gardner-webb.edu.

**Geneva College,** Master of Arts in Counseling Program, Beaver Falls, PA 15010-3599. Offers clinical mental health counseling (MA); marriage and family counseling (MA); school counseling (MA). *Accreditation:* ACA. *Program availability:* Part-time, evening/weekend. *Faculty:* 6 full-time (3 women), 3 part-time/adjunct (2 women). *Students:* 35 full-time (28 women), 32 part-time (23 women); includes 11 minority (9 Black or African American, non-Hispanic/Latino; 2 Hispanic/Latino). Average age 34. 42 applicants, 71% accepted, 21 enrolled. In 2016, 24 master's awarded. *Degree requirements:* For master's, comprehensive exam, 50-60 credits (depending on program), practicum, internship. *Entrance requirements:* For master's, minimum GPA of 3.0 (preferred), 3 letters of recommendation, essay on career goals, resume of educational and professional experiences. Additional exam requirements/recommendations for international students: Required—TOEFL. *Application deadline:* For fall admission, 9/1 for domestic students; for spring admission, 1/10 for domestic students. Applications are processed on a rolling basis. Electronic applications accepted. *Expenses:* $670 per credit. *Financial support:* In 2016–17, 3 students received support. Research assistantships, teaching assistantships, career-related internships or fieldwork, and unspecified assistantships available. Financial award application deadline: 8/1; financial award applicants required to submit FAFSA. *Faculty research:* Blended family counseling; premarital and newlywed couples; religion in clinical supervision; conceptual mapping in research, supervision, and clinical work. *Unit head:* Dr. Shannan Shiderly, Program Director, 724-847-6649, Fax: 724-847-6101, E-mail: slshider@geneva.edu. *Application contact:* Marina Frazier, Graduate Program Manager, 724-847-6697, E-mail: counseling@geneva.edu.
Website: http://www.geneva.edu/page/grad_counseling

**George Fox University,** College of Education, Graduate Department of Counseling, Newberg, OR 97132-2697. Offers clinical mental health counseling (MA); marriage, couple and family counseling (MA, Certificate); school counseling (MA, Certificate); school psychology (Ed S). *Program availability:* Part-time. *Degree requirements:* For master's, clinical project. *Entrance requirements:* For master's, MAT or GRE, bachelor's degree from regionally-accredited college or university, minimum cumulative GPA of 3.0, 1 professional and 1 academic reference, resume, on-campus interview, official transcripts. Additional exam requirements/recommendations for international students: Required—TOEFL (minimum score 577 paper-based; 90 iBT), IELTS (minimum score 7). Electronic applications accepted. *Expenses:* Contact institution.

**Georgian Court University,** School of Arts and Sciences, Lakewood, NJ 08701-2697. Offers applied behavior analysis (MA); clinical mental health counseling (MA); holistic health studies (MA, Certificate); homeland security (MS, Certificate); mercy spirituality (Certificate); parish business management (Certificate); professional counselor (Certificate); school psychology (MA, Certificate); theology (MA, Certificate). *Program*

*availability:* Part-time, evening/weekend. *Faculty:* 19 full-time (11 women), 6 part-time/adjunct (3 women). *Students:* 90 full-time (75 women), 107 part-time (79 women); includes 34 minority (9 Black or African American, non-Hispanic/Latino; 20 Hispanic/Latino; 5 Two or more races, non-Hispanic/Latino), 1 international. Average age 34. 187 applicants, 49% accepted, 60 enrolled. In 2016, 66 master's, 17 other advanced degrees awarded. *Degree requirements:* For master's, comprehensive exam (for some programs), thesis (for some programs). *Entrance requirements:* For master's, GRE, GMAT, or NTE/PRAXIS, 3 letters of recommendation. Additional exam requirements/recommendations for international students: Required—TOEFL (minimum score 550 paper-based). *Application deadline:* For fall admission, 8/15 for domestic students, 5/1 for international students; for spring admission, 1/15 for domestic students, 10/1 for international students. Applications are processed on a rolling basis. Application fee: $40. Electronic applications accepted. *Expenses: Tuition:* Full-time $15,079; part-time $839 per credit. *Required fees:* $968; $496 per credit. Tuition and fees vary according to campus/location and program. *Financial support:* Scholarships/grants, health care benefits, and unspecified assistantships available. Financial award application deadline: 4/15; financial award applicants required to submit FAFSA. *Unit head:* Dr. Mary Chinery, Dean, 732-987-2493, Fax: 732-987-2007, E-mail: mchinery@georgian.edu. *Application contact:* Patrick Givens, Director of Graduate and Professional Studies Admissions, 732-987-2736, Fax: 732-987-2000, E-mail: gps@georgian.edu.
Website: http://georgian.edu/academics/school-of-arts-sciences/

**Georgia State University,** College of Education and Human Development, Department of Counseling and Psychological Services, Program in Mental Health Counseling, Atlanta, GA 30302-3083. Offers MS, Ed S. *Accreditation:* ACA (one or more programs are accredited); APA (one or more programs are accredited). *Degree requirements:* For master's, comprehensive exam. *Entrance requirements:* For master's, GRE, goal statement, resume, 3 letters of recommendation, transcripts. Additional exam requirements/recommendations for international students: Required—TOEFL. *Application deadline:* For fall admission, 2/1 for domestic and international students. Application fee: $50. Electronic applications accepted. *Expenses:* Tuition, state resident: full-time $6876; part-time $382 per credit hour. Tuition, nonresident: full-time $22,374; part-time $1243 per credit hour. *Required fees:* $2128; $1064 per term. Part-time tuition and fees vary according to course load and program. *Financial support:* Research assistantships with tuition reimbursements, teaching assistantships with tuition reimbursements, career-related internships or fieldwork, scholarships/grants, health care benefits, and unspecified assistantships available. Financial award application deadline: 4/1. *Faculty research:* Motivational interviewing, basic counseling skills, group counseling, addictions, spirituality. *Unit head:* Dr. Brian Dew, Chairperson, 404-413-8168, Fax: 404-413-8013, E-mail: bdew@gsu.edu.
Website: http://cps.education.gsu.edu/programs/mental-health-counseling/

**Governors State University,** College of Education, Program in Counseling, University Park, IL 60484. Offers MA. *Accreditation:* ACA. *Program availability:* Part-time. *Faculty:* 47 full-time (31 women), 49 part-time/adjunct (39 women). *Students:* 74 full-time (66 women), 139 part-time (125 women); includes 120 minority (94 Black or African American, non-Hispanic/Latino; 3 Asian, non-Hispanic/Latino; 17 Hispanic/Latino; 6 Two or more races, non-Hispanic/Latino), 2 international. Average age 36. 186 applicants, 45% accepted, 70 enrolled. In 2016, 38 master's awarded. *Entrance requirements:* Additional exam requirements/recommendations for international students: Required—TOEFL (minimum score 550 paper-based; 80 iBT), IELTS. *Application deadline:* For fall admission, 4/1 for domestic students. Application fee: $50. Electronic applications accepted. *Expenses:* $307 per credit hour; $38 per term or $76 per credit hour fees; $415 per credit hour tuition (for counseling education and supervision). *Financial support:* Application deadline: 5/1; applicants required to submit FAFSA. *Unit head:* Shannon Dermer, Chair, Division of Psychology and Counseling, 708-534-3142, E-mail: sdermer@govst.edu. *Application contact:* Yakeea Daniels, Assistant Vice President for Enrollment Services/Director of Admission, 708-534-4510, E-mail: ydaniels@govst.edu.

**Grace University,** College of Graduate Studies, Counseling Program, Omaha, NE 68108. Offers MA. *Entrance requirements:* For master's, minimum undergraduate GPA of 3.0.

**Harding University,** College of Bible and Ministry, Program in Marriage and Family Therapy, Searcy, AR 72149-0001. Offers marriage and family therapy (MS); mental health counseling (MS). *Program availability:* Part-time. *Faculty:* 5 full-time (1 woman). *Students:* 17 full-time (13 women). Average age 27. 9 applicants, 100% accepted, 9 enrolled. In 2016, 12 master's awarded. *Degree requirements:* For master's, comprehensive exam, 15-month practicum. *Entrance requirements:* For master's, GRE General Test, minimum undergraduate GPA of 2.75, graduate 3.0. Additional exam requirements/recommendations for international students: Required—TOEFL (minimum score 550 paper-based; 79 iBT). *Application deadline:* For fall admission, 4/1 priority date for domestic students. Applications are processed on a rolling basis. Application fee: $40. Tuition and fees vary according to degree level and program. *Financial support:* In 2016–17, 5 students received support. Scholarships/grants available. Financial award applicants required to submit FAFSA. *Faculty research:* Forgiveness, substance abuse, post-traumatic stress disorder. *Unit head:* Dr. Lewis L. Moore, Chairman, 501-279-4347, Fax: 501-279-4417, E-mail: lmoore@harding.edu. *Application contact:* Ruth Ann Dawson, Office Manager, 501-279-4347, Fax: 501-279-4417, E-mail: radawson@harding.edu.
Website: http://www.harding.edu/MFT/

**Hardin-Simmons University,** Graduate School, Cynthia Ann Parker College of Liberal Arts, Department of Psychology, Program in Clinical Counseling and Marriage and Family Therapy, Abilene, TX 79698-0001. Offers MA. *Program availability:* Part-time. *Faculty:* 6 full-time (3 women). *Students:* 14 full-time (all women), 2 part-time (both women); includes 5 minority (all Hispanic/Latino). Average age 29. In 2016, 13 master's awarded. *Degree requirements:* For master's, comprehensive exam, clinical experience, project. *Entrance requirements:* For master's, minimum undergraduate GPA of 3.0 in major, 2.7 overall; 21 semester hours of course work in psychology, 18 of those in upper-division classes; writing sample; letters of recommendation. Additional exam requirements/recommendations for international students: Required—TOEFL (minimum score 550 paper-based; 75 iBT). *Application deadline:* For fall admission, 8/15 priority date for domestic students, 4/1 for international students; for spring admission, 1/5 priority date for domestic students, 9/1 for international students. Applications are processed on a rolling basis. Application fee: $50. *Expenses: Tuition:* Full-time $12,510; part-time $695 per credit hour. *Required fees:* $325; $110 per semester. *Financial support:* In 2016–17, 14 students received support, including 8 fellowships (averaging $1,750 per year); career-related internships or fieldwork and scholarships/grants also available. Support available to part-time students. Financial award application deadline: 6/30; financial award applicants required to submit FAFSA. *Faculty research:* Family stress management, spirituality in marriage, intimacy and sexuality in marriage, sex education in the church, role of faith in marital satisfaction. *Unit head:* Dr. Sherry Rosenblad, Program Director, 325-671-2271, Fax: 325-670-1458, E-mail: sherry.rosenblad@hsutx.edu. *Application contact:* Dr. Nancy Kucinski, Dean of Graduate Studies, 325-670-1298, Fax: 325-670-1564, E-mail: gradoff@hsutx.edu.
Website: http://www.hsutx.edu/academics/cap/graduate/ccmf

*Counseling Psychology*

**Heidelberg University,** Master of Arts in Counseling Program, Tiffin, OH 44883-2462. Offers clinical mental health counseling (MA); school counseling (MA). *Accreditation:* ACA. *Program availability:* Part-time, evening/weekend. *Students:* 15 full-time (11 women), 31 part-time (26 women). In 2016, 12 master's awarded. *Degree requirements:* For master's, thesis or alternative, counseling practicum, internship. *Entrance requirements:* For master's, bachelor's degree, minimum GPA of 2.9, 12 hours of course work in behavioral sciences, 3 letters of reference, 2-3 page goal statement, background check, interview. Additional exam requirements/recommendations for international students: Required—TOEFL (minimum score 550 paper-based, 79 iBT) or IELTS (minimum score 6.5). *Application deadline:* Applications are processed on a rolling basis. Electronic applications accepted. *Expenses:* $510 per semester hour. *Financial support:* Applicants required to submit FAFSA. *Unit head:* Dr. Jo-Ann Lipford Sanders, Associate Dean and Director of Master of Arts in Counseling, 419-448-2312, E-mail: jsanders@heidelberg.edu. *Application contact:* Katie Slosser, Graduate Admissions Coordinator, 419-448-2602, Fax: 419-448-2565, E-mail: kslosser@heidelberg.edu. Website: https://www.heidelberg.edu/academics/programs/master-of-counseling

**Henderson State University,** Graduate Studies, Teachers College, Department of Counselor Education, Arkadelphia, AR 71999-0001. Offers clinical mental health counseling (MS); developmental therapy (MS, Graduate Certificate); secondary school counseling (MSE). *Accreditation:* ACA; NCATE. *Program availability:* Part-time. *Faculty:* 6 full-time (2 women). *Students:* 46 full-time (33 women), 84 part-time (74 women); includes 48 minority (40 Black or African American, non-Hispanic/Latino; 1 American Indian or Alaska Native, non-Hispanic/Latino; 4 Hispanic/Latino; 3 Two or more races, non-Hispanic/Latino). Average age 34. 18 applicants, 100% accepted, 18 enrolled. In 2016, 36 master's awarded. *Entrance requirements:* For master's, GRE General Test or MAT, letters of recommendation, minimum GPA of 2.7, teacher certification. Additional exam requirements/recommendations for international students: Required—TOEFL (minimum score 600 paper-based); Recommended—IELTS (minimum score 6.5). *Application deadline:* For fall admission, 8/1 priority date for domestic students, 6/30 priority date for international students; for spring admission, 1/1 priority date for domestic students, 11/30 priority date for international students. Applications are processed on a rolling basis. Application fee: $25 ($75 for international students). *Expenses:* Tuition, state resident: full-time $6288; part-time $3144 per credit hour. Tuition, nonresident: full-time $12,888; part-time $6444 per credit hour. *Required fees:* $1429; $1024 per credit hour. Tuition and fees vary according to course load and student level. *Financial support:* In 2016–17, 1 teaching assistantship with partial tuition reimbursement (averaging $4,000 per year) was awarded; scholarships/grants and unspecified assistantships also available. Financial award application deadline: 4/15; financial award applicants required to submit FAFSA. *Unit head:* Dr. Mike Kelly, Interim Chairperson, 870-230-5216, Fax: 870-230-5459, E-mail: kellym@hsu.edu. *Application contact:* Dr. Ken Taylor, Graduate Dean, 870-230-5126, Fax: 870-230-5479, E-mail: taylorke@hsu.edu. Website: http://www.hsu.edu/counselor-education/

**Hodges University,** Graduate Programs, Naples, FL 34119. Offers accounting (M Acc); business administration (MBA); clinical mental health counseling (MS); health services administration (MS); information systems management (MIS); legal studies (MS); management (MSM). *Program availability:* Part-time, evening/weekend, 100% online, blended/hybrid learning. *Degree requirements:* For master's, comprehensive exam (for some programs), thesis (for some programs). *Entrance requirements:* For master's, essay. Additional exam requirements/recommendations for international students: Recommended—TOEFL. Electronic applications accepted.

**Hofstra University,** School of Health Professions and Human Services, Programs in Counseling, Hempstead, NY 11549. Offers counseling (MS Ed, PD); creative arts therapy (MA); interdisciplinary transition specialist (Advanced Certificate); marriage and family therapy (MA); mental health counseling (MA, Advanced Certificate), including alcohol and substance abuse (Advanced Certificate); rehabilitation administration (PD); rehabilitation counseling (MS Ed, Advanced Certificate); rehabilitation counseling in mental health (MS Ed, Advanced Certificate); school counselor bilingual extension (Advanced Certificate). *Accreditation:* ACA. *Program availability:* Part-time, evening/weekend. *Students:* 116 full-time (100 women), 66 part-time (59 women); includes 48 minority (18 Black or African American, non-Hispanic/Latino; 11 Asian, non-Hispanic/Latino; 17 Hispanic/Latino; 2 Two or more races, non-Hispanic/Latino), 5 international. Average age 29. 166 applicants, 81% accepted, 66 enrolled. In 2016, 71 master's, 7 other advanced degrees awarded. *Degree requirements:* For master's, comprehensive exam (for some programs), thesis (for some programs), internship, practicum, student teaching, seminars, minimum GPA of 3.0. *Entrance requirements:* For master's, GRE, interview, letters of recommendation, portfolio, essay, professional experience, certification; for other advanced degree, GRE, interview, letters of recommendation, essay, professional experience, resume, master's degree. Additional exam requirements/recommendations for international students: Required—TOEFL (minimum score 550 paper-based; 80 iBT). *Application deadline:* Applications are processed on a rolling basis. Application fee: $75. Electronic applications accepted. *Expenses: Tuition:* Full-time $1240. *Required fees:* $970. Tuition and fees vary according to program. *Financial support:* In 2016–17, 76 students received support, including 40 fellowships with full and partial tuition reimbursements available (averaging $3,465 per year), 5 research assistantships with full and partial tuition reimbursements available (averaging $6,939 per year); career-related internships or fieldwork, Federal Work-Study, institutionally sponsored loans, scholarships/grants, traineeships, tuition waivers (full and partial), and unspecified assistantships also available. Support available to part-time students. Financial award applicants required to submit FAFSA. *Faculty research:* The constructs of hope and grit; the efficacy of support groups in treating eating disorders; attitudes of primary care physicians related to providing integrated care with mental health counselors; expanding the counselor identity through disability cultural competence; vocational evaluation and assessment collaboration; disability cultural competence. *Unit head:* Dr. Jamie Mitus, Chairperson, 516-463-5759, E-mail: jamie.s.mitus@hofstra.edu. *Application contact:* Sunil Samuel, Assistant Vice President of Admissions, 516-463-4723, Fax: 516-463-4664, E-mail: graduateadmission@hofstra.edu. Website: http://www.hofstra.edu/academics/colleges/healthscienceshumanservices/

**Holy Family University,** Division of Academic Affairs, Philadelphia, PA 19114. Offers accountancy (MS); business administration (MBA); counseling psychology (MS); criminal justice (MA); education (M Ed); educational leadership (Ed D); nursing (MS). *Accreditation:* ACBSP. *Program availability:* Part-time, evening/weekend. *Faculty:* 28 full-time (19 women), 66 part-time/adjunct (36 women). *Students:* 329 full-time (281 women), 458 part-time (327 women); includes 153 minority (83 Black or African American, non-Hispanic/Latino; 1 American Indian or Alaska Native, non-Hispanic/Latino; 27 Asian, non-Hispanic/Latino; 41 Hispanic/Latino; 1 Native Hawaiian or other Pacific Islander, non-Hispanic/Latino), 4 international. Average age 34. 467 applicants, 69% accepted, 262 enrolled. In 2016, 6 master's, 2 doctorates awarded. *Degree requirements:* For master's, comprehensive exam, thesis or alternative; for doctorate, comprehensive exam, thesis/dissertation. *Entrance requirements:* For master's, minimum GPA of 3.0, interview, essay/professional statement, 2 recommendations, current resume, official transcripts of college or university work. Additional exam requirements/recommendations for international students: Required—TOEFL (minimum

score 550 paper-based; 79 iBT), IELTS (minimum score 6). *Application deadline:* For fall admission, 7/1 priority date for domestic and international students; for spring admission, 11/1 priority date for domestic and international students; for summer admission, 4/1 priority date for domestic and international students. Applications are processed on a rolling basis. Application fee: $25. Electronic applications accepted. *Expenses:* $9,292 per year. *Financial support:* Available to part-time students. Applicants required to submit FAFSA. *Unit head:* Dr. Michael Markowitz, Vice President of Academic Affairs, 267-341-3286, E-mail: mmarkowitz@holyfamily.edu. *Application contact:* Don Reinmold, Director of Graduate Admissions, 267-341-5001 Ext. 3230, Fax: 215-633-0558, E-mail: dreinmold@holyfamily.edu.

**Holy Family University,** Graduate and Professional Programs, School of Arts and Sciences, Program in Counseling Psychology, Philadelphia, PA 19114. Offers MS. *Program availability:* Part-time, evening/weekend. *Students:* 133 full-time, 23 part-time. 82 applicants, 51% accepted, 30 enrolled. In 2016, 46 master's awarded. *Degree requirements:* For master's, comprehensive exam, thesis optional. *Entrance requirements:* For master's, GRE or MAT (if GPA is below 3.0), baccalaureate degree from accredited college or university; minimum undergraduate cumulative GPA of 3.0; 2 letters of recommendation; personal statement; official transcripts; interview. Additional exam requirements/recommendations for international students: Required—TOEFL (minimum score 550 paper-based; 79 iBT), IELTS (minimum score 6), PTE (minimum score 54). *Application deadline:* For fall admission, 7/1 priority date for domestic and international students; for winter admission, 1/1 for domestic students; for spring admission, 10/1 priority date for domestic students, 11/1 priority date for international students; for summer admission, 4/1 priority date for domestic and international students. Applications are processed on a rolling basis. Application fee: $25. Electronic applications accepted. *Expenses: Tuition:* Part-time $751 per hour. *Required fees:* $140 per semester. One-time fee: $165 part-time. Part-time tuition and fees vary according to degree level and program. *Financial support:* Available to part-time students. Application deadline: 5/1; applicants required to submit FAFSA. *Unit head:* Dr. Freda Ginsberg, Director, 267-341-4035. *Application contact:* Donald Reimold, Director of Graduate Admissions, 267-341-5001, Fax: 215-637-1478, E-mail: dreimold@holyfamily.edu. Website: http://www.holyfamily.edu/choosing-holy-family-u/academics/schools-of-study/school-of-arts-sciences/graduate-programs/112-master-of-science-in-counsel

**Holy Names University,** Graduate Division, Department of Counseling Psychology, Oakland, CA 94619-1699. Offers counseling and forensic counseling (MA); counseling psychology (MA); forensic psychology (MA). *Program availability:* Part-time, evening/weekend. *Students:* 37 full-time (all women), 37 part-time (32 women); includes 55 minority (37 Black or African American, non-Hispanic/Latino; 6 Asian, non-Hispanic/Latino; 9 Hispanic/Latino; 2 Native Hawaiian or other Pacific Islander, non-Hispanic/Latino; 1 Two or more races, non-Hispanic/Latino), 3 international. Average age 33. 38 applicants, 82% accepted, 18 enrolled. In 2016, 33 master's awarded. *Degree requirements:* For master's, comprehensive paper, seminars. *Entrance requirements:* For master's, minimum undergraduate GPA of 2.6 overall, 3.0 in major. Additional exam requirements/recommendations for international students: Required—TOEFL (minimum score 550 paper-based; 79 iBT). *Application deadline:* For fall admission, 8/1 priority date for domestic students, 7/15 for international students; for spring admission, 12/1 priority date for domestic students, 12/1 for international students; for summer admission, 5/1 priority date for domestic students, 5/1 for international students. Applications are processed on a rolling basis. Application fee: $65. Electronic applications accepted. Application fee is waived when completed online. *Expenses:* Contact institution. *Financial support:* Career-related internships or fieldwork, Federal Work-Study, scholarships/grants, and unspecified assistantships available. Support available to part-time students. Financial award application deadline: 3/2; financial award applicants required to submit FAFSA. *Faculty research:* Cognitive psychology, anger management, grief and grief counseling, post-modernism and psychotherapy, spirituality and psychology. *Unit head:* Dr. Perri Franskoviak, Program Director, 510-436-1465, E-mail: franskoviak@hnu.edu. *Application contact:* 510-436-1351, Fax: 510-436-1325, E-mail: graduateadmissions@hnu.edu.

**Houston Baptist University,** College of Education and Behavioral Sciences, Program in Counseling, Houston, TX 77074-3298. Offers MAC. *Program availability:* Part-time, evening/weekend. *Students:* 40 full-time (31 women), 79 part-time (70 women); includes 70 minority (25 Black or African American, non-Hispanic/Latino; 1 American Indian or Alaska Native, non-Hispanic/Latino; 10 Asian, non-Hispanic/Latino; 32 Hispanic/Latino; 2 Two or more races, non-Hispanic/Latino), 3 international. Average age 31. 118 applicants, 27% accepted, 22 enrolled. In 2016, 14 master's awarded. *Degree requirements:* For master's, comprehensive exam, practicum. *Entrance requirements:* For master's, GRE (waived if GPA is 3.0 or higher), two academic or professional recommendations, bachelor's degree conferred transcript, resume, interview. Additional exam requirements/recommendations for international students: Required—TOEFL (minimum score 80 iBT), IELTS (minimum score 6.5). *Application deadline:* For fall admission, 8/1 for domestic students, 6/1 for international students; for spring admission, 1/1 for domestic students, 11/1 for international students; for summer admission, 5/1 for domestic students, 3/1 for international students. Applications are processed on a rolling basis. Application fee: $0 ($100 for international students). Electronic applications accepted. Application fee is waived when completed online. *Expenses:* $1,650 per 3-hour course; $1,275 annual general fee; $1,060 annual technology fee. *Financial support:* In 2016–17, 2 students received support. Career-related internships or fieldwork, Federal Work-Study, and scholarships/grants available. Support available to part-time students. Financial award application deadline: 4/1; financial award applicants required to submit FAFSA. *Faculty research:* Multicultural psychology, counseling: technology integration. *Unit head:* Dr. Stephanie Ellis, Director, 281-649-3241, E-mail: sellis@hbu.edu. *Application contact:* Victoria Humphreys, Administrative Assistant to the Dean, 281-649-3131, E-mail: vhumphreys@hbu.edu. Website: http://www.hbu.edu/mac

**Howard University,** School of Education, Department of Human Development and Psychoeducational Studies, Program in Counseling Psychology, Washington, DC 20059-0002. Offers PhD. *Accreditation:* APA. *Program availability:* Part-time. *Degree requirements:* For doctorate, one foreign language, comprehensive exam, thesis/dissertation, expository writing exam, internship. *Entrance requirements:* For doctorate, GRE General Test, minimum GPA of 3.4. Additional exam requirements/recommendations for international students: Required—TOEFL (minimum score 550 paper-based; 79 iBT). Electronic applications accepted. *Faculty research:* Cultural issues in counseling and psychotherapy, counseling theory construction, self-actualization black psychology.

**Humboldt State University,** Academic Programs, College of Professional Studies, Department of Psychology, Arcata, CA 95521-8299. Offers psychology (MA), including biological psychology, counseling, developmental psychopathology, school psychology, social and environmental psychology. *Degree requirements:* For master's, thesis. *Entrance requirements:* For master's, appropriate bachelor's degree, minimum GPA of 2.5. Additional exam requirements/recommendations for international students: Required—TOEFL (minimum score 500 paper-based). *Expenses:* Tuition, state resident: full-time $6738; part-time $1953 per semester. Tuition, nonresident: full-time

$13,434; part-time $3813 per semester. *Required fees:* $1738; $653 per semester. Tuition and fees vary according to program. *Faculty research:* School psychology, counseling, eating disorders, mood induction, depression.

**Husson University,** Graduate Programs in Counseling and Human Relations, Bangor, ME 04401-2999. Offers clinical mental health counseling (MS); human relations (MS); school counseling (MS). *Accreditation:* ACA. *Program availability:* Part-time, evening/weekend. *Faculty:* 3 full-time (2 women), 5 part-time/adjunct (all women). *Students:* 17 full-time (15 women), 55 part-time (48 women); includes 1 minority (Black or African American, non-Hispanic/Latino), 2 international. Average age 32. 50 applicants, 52% accepted, 20 enrolled. In 2016, 16 master's awarded. *Degree requirements:* For master's, comprehensive exam (for some programs), thesis optional. *Entrance requirements:* For master's, BS with minimum GPA of 3.0, letters of recommendation, interview. Additional exam requirements/recommendations for international students: Required—TOEFL (minimum score 550 paper-based), IELTS (minimum score 6.5). *Application deadline:* For fall admission, 2/1 for domestic students. Application fee: $50. Electronic applications accepted. *Expenses:* $560 per credit tuition; $450 full-time fees, $220 part-time (6-9 credits), $110 part-time (less than 6 credits per year). *Financial support:* Federal Work-Study, scholarships/grants, and unspecified assistantships available. Financial award application deadline: 4/15; financial award applicants required to submit FAFSA. *Faculty research:* Challenges and rewards of counseling practice in rural, small town and neighborhood settings. *Unit head:* Dr. Deborah Drew, Director, Graduate Counseling Programs, 207-992-4912, Fax: 207-992-4952, E-mail: drewd@husson.edu. *Application contact:* Kristen Card, Director of Graduate Admissions, 207-404-5660, Fax: 207-941-7935, E-mail: cardk@husson.edu. Website: http://www.husson.edu/college-of-health-and-education/school-of-education/graduate-programs/

**Idaho State University,** Office of Graduate Studies, Kasiska College of Health Professions, Department of Counseling, Pocatello, ID 83209-8120. Offers counseling (M Coun, Ed S), including marriage and family counseling (M Coun), mental health counseling (M Coun), school counseling (M Coun), student affairs and college counseling (M Coun); counselor education and counseling (PhD). *Accreditation:* ACA (one or more programs are accredited). *Program availability:* Part-time. *Degree requirements:* For master's, comprehensive exam, thesis, 4 semesters resident graduate study, practicum/internship; for doctorate, comprehensive exam, thesis/dissertation, 3 semesters internship, 4 consecutive semesters doctoral-level study on campus; for Ed S, comprehensive exam, thesis, case studies, oral exam. *Entrance requirements:* For master's, GRE General Test, MAT, minimum GPA of 3.0, bachelors degree, interview, 3 letters of recommendation; for doctorate, GRE General Test, MAT, minimum graduate GPA of 3.0, resume, interview, counseling license, master's degree; for Ed S, GRE General Test, minimum graduate GPA of 3.0, master's degree in counseling, 3 letters of recommendation, 2 years work experience. Additional exam requirements/recommendations for international students: Required—TOEFL (minimum score 600 paper-based; 80 iBT). Electronic applications accepted. *Faculty research:* Group counseling, multicultural counseling, family counseling, child therapy, supervision.

**Illinois State University,** Graduate School, College of Arts and Sciences, Department of Psychology, Normal, IL 61790-2200. Offers psychology (MA, MS), including clinical-counseling psychology, cognitive and behavioral sciences, developmental psychology, industrial/organizational-social psychology; school psychology (PhD, SSP). *Accreditation:* APA. *Degree requirements:* For master's, thesis or alternative; for doctorate, variable foreign language requirement, thesis/dissertation, 2 terms of residency, internship, practicum. *Entrance requirements:* For master's, GRE General Test, GRE Subject Test, minimum GPA of 3.0 in last 60 hours of course work; for doctorate, GRE General Test. *Faculty research:* Comprehensive evaluation system for the central region professional development grant, Illinois school psychology internship consortium, for children's sake.

**Immaculata University,** College of Graduate Studies, Department of Psychology, Immaculata, PA 19345. Offers clinical mental health counseling (MA); clinical psychology (Psy D); forensic psychology (Graduate Certificate); integrative psychotherapy (Graduate Certificate); neuropsychology (Graduate Certificate); psychodynamic psychotherapy (Graduate Certificate); psychological testing (Graduate Certificate); school counseling (MA, Graduate Certificate); school psychology (MA). *Accreditation:* APA. *Program availability:* Part-time, evening/weekend. Terminal master's awarded for partial completion of doctoral program. *Degree requirements:* For master's, comprehensive exam, thesis optional; for doctorate, comprehensive exam, thesis/dissertation. *Entrance requirements:* For master's, GRE General Test or MAT, minimum GPA of 3.0; for doctorate, GRE General Test or MAT, minimum GPA of 3.5. Additional exam requirements/recommendations for international students: Required—TOEFL, IELTS. Electronic applications accepted. *Faculty research:* Supervision ethics, psychology of teaching, gender.

**Indiana University Northwest,** College of Arts and Sciences, Gary, IN 46408. Offers clinical counseling (MS), including drug and alcohol counseling; community development/urban studies (Graduate Certificate); computer information systems (Graduate Certificate); liberal studies (MLS); race-ethnic studies (Graduate Certificate); women's and gender studies (Graduate Certificate). *Program availability:* Part-time, evening/weekend. *Students:* 4 full-time (all women), 18 part-time (10 women); includes 10 minority (9 Black or African American, non-Hispanic/Latino; 1 Hispanic/Latino). Average age 39. 22 applicants, 77% accepted, 13 enrolled. In 2016, 6 master's awarded. *Entrance requirements:* For master's, GRE (recommended for MS), minimum undergraduate GPA of 3.0, bachelor's degree from accredited university (for MS). *Application deadline:* For fall admission, 7/1 priority date for domestic and international students; for spring admission, 12/1 priority date for domestic and international students. Application fee: $40 ($60 for international students). Electronic applications accepted. *Expenses:* $276.98 per credit hour in-state; $652.54 per credit hour out-of-state. *Financial support:* Applicants required to submit FAFSA. *Unit head:* Mark Hoyert, Dean, E-mail: mhoyert@iun.edu. Website: http://www.iun.edu/coas/

**Indiana University South Bend,** School of Education, South Bend, IN 46634-7111. Offers addiction counseling (MS Ed); alcohol and drug counseling (Graduate Certificate); clinical mental health counseling (MS Ed); educational leadership (MS Ed); elementary education (MS Ed); marriage, couple, and family counseling (MS Ed); school counseling (MS Ed); secondary education (MS Ed); special education (MAT, MS Ed), including intense intervention (MS Ed), mild intervention (MS Ed). *Accreditation:* NCATE. *Program availability:* Part-time, evening/weekend. *Faculty:* 21 full-time (11 women), 9 part-time/adjunct (3 women). *Students:* 26 full-time (19 women), 104 part-time (80 women); includes 22 minority (13 Black or African American, non-Hispanic/Latino; 5 Hispanic/Latino; 4 Two or more races, non-Hispanic/Latino). Average age 35. 51 applicants, 69% accepted, 22 enrolled. In 2016, 31 master's, 2 other advanced degrees awarded. *Degree requirements:* For master's, thesis or alternative, exit project. *Entrance requirements:* For master's, letters of recommendation, GRE or minimum GPA of 3.0. Additional exam requirements/recommendations for international students: Required—TOEFL. *Application deadline:* For fall admission, 7/1 for domestic students; for spring admission, 11/1 for domestic students. Applications are processed on a rolling basis. Application fee: $40 ($60 for international students). Electronic applications accepted. *Expenses:* $276.98 per credit hour in-state; $652.54 per credit hour out-of-state. *Financial support:* Career-related internships or fieldwork available. Support available to part-time students. Financial award application deadline: 3/1; financial award applicants required to submit FAFSA. *Faculty research:* Professional dispositions, early childhood literacy, online learning, program assessments, problem-based learning. *Unit head:* Dr. Marvin Lynn, Dean, 574-520-4339, E-mail: lynnm@iusb.edu. *Application contact:* Yvonne Walker, Student Services Representative, 574-520-4185, E-mail: ydwalker@iusb.edu. Website: https://www.iusb.edu/education/index.php

**Indiana Wesleyan University,** Graduate School, College of Arts and Sciences, Marion, IN 46953. Offers addictions counseling (MS); clinical mental health counseling (MS); community counseling (MS); marriage and family therapy (MS); school counseling (MS); student development counseling and administration (MS). *Accreditation:* ACA. *Program availability:* Part-time. *Degree requirements:* For master's, thesis or alternative. *Entrance requirements:* For master's, GRE General Test. Additional exam requirements/recommendations for international students: Required—TOEFL. Electronic applications accepted. *Expenses:* Contact institution. *Faculty research:* Community counseling, multicultural counseling, addictions.

**Instituto Tecnologico de Santo Domingo,** Graduate School, Area of Humanities and Social Sciences, Santo Domingo, Dominican Republic. Offers accounting (Certificate); adult education (Certificate); applied linguistics (MA); economics (MA); education (M Ed); educational psychology (MA, Certificate); gender and development (MA, Certificate); humanistic studies (MA); international marketing management (Certificate); international relations in the Caribbean basin (Certificate); intervention systems in family therapy (MA); linguistic and literary communication (Certificate); pedagogical support (MA); social science education (M Ed); sustainable human development (MA); terminal illness and death psychology (Certificate); youth and adult education (M Ed).

**Inter American University of Puerto Rico, Aguadilla Campus,** Graduate School, Aguadilla, PR 00605. Offers accounting (MBA); counseling psychology specializing in family (MS); criminal justice (MA); educative management and leadership (MA); elementary education (M Ed); finance (MBA); human resources (MBA); industrial management (MBA); management information systems (MBA); marketing (MBA). *Program availability:* Part-time, evening/weekend. *Degree requirements:* For master's, comprehensive exam. *Entrance requirements:* For master's, EXADEP, 2 letters of recommendation, minimum GPA of 2.5. Electronic applications accepted.

**Inter American University of Puerto Rico, Metropolitan Campus,** Graduate Programs, Program in Psychology, San Juan, PR 00919-1293. Offers counseling psychology (MA, PhD); industrial/organizational psychology (MA, PhD); labor relations (MA); school psychology (MA, PhD). *Degree requirements:* For master's, comprehensive exam. *Entrance requirements:* For master's, GRE or EXADEP, interview. Electronic applications accepted.

**Inter American University of Puerto Rico, San Germán Campus,** Graduate Studies Center, Program in Psychology, San Germán, PR 00683-5008. Offers counseling psychology (MA, PhD); school psychology (MA, PhD). *Program availability:* Part-time, evening/weekend. *Degree requirements:* For master's, comprehensive exam, thesis; for doctorate, comprehensive exam, thesis/dissertation. *Entrance requirements:* For master's, GRE General Test or EXADEP, minimum GPA of 3.0; for doctorate, GRE, EXADEP or MAT, minimum GPA of 3.0.

**Iona College,** School of Arts and Science, Department of Psychology, New Rochelle, NY 10801-1890. Offers general-experimental psychology (MA); human resources (Certificate); industrial-organizational psychology (MA); mental health counseling (MA); organizational behavior (Certificate); psychology (MA); school psychology (MA). *Program availability:* Part-time. *Faculty:* 9 full-time (5 women), 6 part-time/adjunct (5 women). *Students:* 61 full-time (42 women), 32 part-time (23 women); includes 40 minority (8 Black or African American, non-Hispanic/Latino; 3 Asian, non-Hispanic/Latino; 28 Hispanic/Latino; 1 Two or more races, non-Hispanic/Latino), 2 international. Average age 25. 91 applicants, 80% accepted, 37 enrolled. In 2016, 18 master's awarded. *Degree requirements:* For master's, thesis (for some programs), literature review (for some programs). *Entrance requirements:* For master's, BA in psychology including 3 credits each in psychology statistics and experimental research methods, or 9 credits in psychology including 3 credits in psychology statistics, 3 credits in psychology research methods and 3 credits of upper-level coursework. Additional exam requirements/recommendations for international students: Required—TOEFL (minimum score 550 paper-based), IELTS (minimum score 6.5). *Application deadline:* For fall admission, 8/15 for domestic students, 5/1 for international students; for spring admission, 1/15 for domestic students, 9/1 for international students. Applications are processed on a rolling basis. Application fee: $50. Electronic applications accepted. *Expenses: Tuition:* Full-time $19,692; part-time $1094 per credit. *Required fees:* $245 per term. Tuition and fees vary according to program. *Financial support:* In 2016–17, 49 students received support. Research assistantships with partial tuition reimbursements available, tuition waivers (partial), and unspecified assistantships available. Support available to part-time students. Financial award application deadline: 4/15; financial award applicants required to submit FAFSA. *Faculty research:* Non-suicidal self-injury, trauma response, performance appraisal and evaluation, diversity infusion, assessment and treatment of sexual offenders. *Unit head:* Patricia Oswald, PhD, Chair, 914-633-2374, E-mail: poswald@iona.edu. *Application contact:* Katelyn Brunck, Assistant Director, Graduate Admissions, 914-633-2451, Fax: 914-633-2277, E-mail: kbrunck@iona.edu. Website: http://www.iona.edu/Academics/School-of-Arts-Science/Departments/Psychology/Graduate-Programs.aspx

**Iowa State University of Science and Technology,** Department of Psychology, Ames, IA 50011. Offers cognitive psychology (PhD); counseling psychology (PhD); psychology (MS, PhD); social psychology (PhD). *Accreditation:* APA (one or more programs are accredited). *Entrance requirements:* For doctorate, GRE General Test, GRE Subject Test (psychology), 3 letters of recommendation. Additional exam requirements/recommendations for international students: Required—TOEFL (minimum score 560 paper-based; 79 iBT), IELTS (minimum score 6.5). *Application deadline:* For fall admission, 1/2 priority date for domestic and international students. Application fee: $60 ($90 for international students). Electronic applications accepted. *Faculty research:* Counseling psychology, cognitive psychology, social psychology, health psychology, psychology and public policy. *Application contact:* Sarah Kallsen, Application Contact, 515-294-1742, Fax: 515-294-6424, E-mail: psychadm@iastate.edu. Website: http://www.psychology.iastate.edu/

**Jacksonville University,** Brooks Rehabilitation College of Healthcare Sciences, School of Applied Health Sciences, Program in Clinical Mental Health Counseling, Jacksonville, FL 32211. Offers MS. *Degree requirements:* For master's, 1,000-hour community-based clinical field experience. *Expenses: Tuition:* Full-time $13,320. One-time fee: $50 part-time. Tuition and fees vary according to course load, degree level, campus/location and program.

**James Madison University,** The Graduate School, College of Health and Behavioral Sciences, Clinical Mental Health Counseling Program, Harrisonburg, VA 22807. Offers

## Counseling Psychology

MA/Ed S. *Accreditation:* ACA. *Program availability:* Part-time, evening/weekend. *Students:* 67 full-time (52 women), 19 part-time (13 women); includes 17 minority (10 Black or African American, non-Hispanic/Latino; 1 Asian, non-Hispanic/Latino; 5 Hispanic/Latino; 1 Two or more races, non-Hispanic/Latino), 1 international. Average age 30. *Financial support:* Career-related internships or fieldwork, Federal Work-Study, and 53 assistantships (averaging $7911) available. Financial award application deadline: 3/1; financial award applicants required to submit FAFSA.

**James Madison University,** The Graduate School, College of Health and Behavioral Sciences, Program in Counseling and Supervision, Harrisonburg, VA 22807. Offers PhD. *Program availability:* Part-time, evening/weekend. *Students:* 8 full-time (5 women), 6 part-time (4 women); includes 4 minority (3 Black or African American, non-Hispanic/Latino; 1 Hispanic/Latino). Average age 30. 3 applicants. Application fee: $55. Electronic applications accepted. *Financial support:* In 2016–17, 2 students received support. Fellowships, Federal Work-Study, and 4 assistantships (averaging $7911) available. Financial award application deadline: 3/1; financial award applicants required to submit FAFSA. *Unit head:* Dr. Robin Anderson, Department Head, 540-568-3293, E-mail: ander2rd@jmu.edu. *Application contact:* Lynette D. Michael, Director of Graduate Admissions, 540-568-6131 Ext. 6395, Fax: 540-568-7860, E-mail: michaeld@jmu.edu. Website: http://psyc.jmu.edu/counseling/supervision/

**John Brown University,** Graduate Counseling Programs, Siloam Springs, AR 72761-2121. Offers clinical mental health counseling (MS); marriage and family therapy (MS); play therapy (Graduate Certificate); school counseling (MS). *Accreditation:* NCATE. *Program availability:* Part-time, evening/weekend. *Faculty:* 9 full-time (2 women), 18 part-time/adjunct (6 women). *Students:* 157 full-time (124 women), 153 part-time (124 women); includes 94 minority (50 Black or African American, non-Hispanic/Latino; 7 American Indian or Alaska Native, non-Hispanic/Latino; 3 Asian, non-Hispanic/Latino; 21 Hispanic/Latino; 13 Two or more races, non-Hispanic/Latino), 1 international. Average age 32. 129 applicants, 74% accepted, 83 enrolled. In 2016, 68 master's awarded. *Degree requirements:* For master's, practica or internships. *Entrance requirements:* For master's, GRE (minimum score of 300), recommendation forms from three people, 200-word essay describing professional plans and reason for seeking acceptance. Additional exam requirements/recommendations for international students: Required—TOEFL (minimum score 550 paper-based; 79 iBT). *Application deadline:* Applications are processed on a rolling basis. Application fee: $35 ($100 for international students). Electronic applications accepted. *Expenses:* Contact institution. *Financial support:* Fellowships, institutionally sponsored loans, scholarships/grants, and unspecified assistantships available. Financial award applicants required to submit FAFSA. *Unit head:* Dr. John V. Carmack, Program Director, 479-524-8630, E-mail: jcarmack@jbu.edu. *Application contact:* Mark Bjornsen, Graduate Counseling Representative, 479-631-4665, E-mail: mbjornsen@jbu.edu. Website: http://www.jbu.edu/

**John Carroll University,** Graduate Studies, Program in Clinical Mental Health Counseling, University Heights, OH 44118-4581. Offers clinical counseling (Certificate); community counseling (MA). *Accreditation:* ACA. *Program availability:* Part-time, evening/weekend. *Faculty:* 7 full-time (4 women), 15 part-time/adjunct (10 women). *Students:* 36 full-time (33 women), 12 part-time (8 women); includes 4 minority (3 Black or African American, non-Hispanic/Latino; 1 Hispanic/Latino). Average age 32. 53 applicants, 40% accepted, 21 enrolled. In 2016, 22 master's awarded. *Degree requirements:* For master's, comprehensive exam, internship, practicum. *Entrance requirements:* For master's, MAT or GRE, minimum GPA of 2.75, statement of volunteer experience, interview, 12-18 hours of social science course work. Additional exam requirements/recommendations for international students: Required—TOEFL. *Application deadline:* For fall admission, 8/15 priority date for domestic students; for spring admission, 1/3 for domestic students. Applications are processed on a rolling basis. Application fee: $25 ($35 for international students). Electronic applications accepted. *Expenses: Tuition:* Full-time $10,425; part-time $695 per credit hour. One-time fee: $200 full-time. Tuition and fees vary according to course load, campus/location and program. *Financial support:* In 2016–17, 20 students received support, including 1 teaching assistantship with full tuition reimbursement available (averaging $8,000 per year); career-related internships or fieldwork, institutionally sponsored loans, and unspecified assistantships also available. Financial award application deadline: 3/1; financial award applicants required to submit FAFSA. *Faculty research:* Child and adolescent development, HIV, hypnosis, wellness, women's issues. *Unit head:* Dr. Cecile Brennan, Coordinator, 216-397-1987, Fax: 216-397-3045, E-mail: counseladmin@jcu.edu. *Application contact:* Jennifer L. Tucker, Records Management Assistant, 216-397-1925, Fax: 216-397-1835, E-mail: jtucker@jcu.edu.

**John F. Kennedy University,** Graduate School of Holistic Studies, Department of Counseling Psychology, Program in Counseling Psychology, Pleasant Hill, CA 94523-4817. Offers holistic studies (MA); somatic psychology (MA); transpersonal psychology (MA). *Program availability:* Part-time, evening/weekend. *Degree requirements:* For master's, thesis or alternative. *Entrance requirements:* For master's, interview. Additional exam requirements/recommendations for international students: Required—TOEFL.

**John F. Kennedy University,** Graduate School of Professional Psychology, Program in Counseling Psychology, Pleasant Hill, CA 94523-4817. Offers MA. *Program availability:* Part-time, evening/weekend. *Degree requirements:* For master's, thesis or alternative. *Entrance requirements:* For master's, interview. Additional exam requirements/recommendations for international students: Required—TOEFL.

**Johns Hopkins University,** School of Education, Certificate Programs in Education, Baltimore, MD 21218. Offers advanced methods for differentiated instruction and inclusive education (Graduate Certificate); applied behavior analysis (Post-Master's Certificate); clinical mental health counseling (Post-Master's Certificate); counseling (Advanced Certificate); data-based decision making and organizational improvement (Graduate Certificate); early intervention/preschool special education specialist (Graduate Certificate); education of students with autism and other pervasive developmental disorders (Graduate Certificate); educational leadership for independent schools (Graduate Certificate); evidence-based teaching in the health professions (Post-Master's Certificate); gifted education (Graduate Certificate); leadership in technology integration (Graduate Certificate); mind, brain and teaching (Graduate Certificate); school administration and supervision (Graduate Certificate); urban education (Graduate Certificate). *Program availability:* Part-time-only, evening/weekend, 100% online, blended/hybrid learning. *Students:* 5 full-time (all women), 194 part-time (164 women); includes 46 minority (29 Black or African American, non-Hispanic/Latino; 2 American Indian or Alaska Native, non-Hispanic/Latino; 3 Asian, non-Hispanic/Latino; 8 Hispanic/Latino; 4 Two or more races, non-Hispanic/Latino), 7 international. Average age 37. 240 applicants, 75% accepted, 143 enrolled. In 2016, 167 Advanced Certificates awarded. *Entrance requirements:* For degree, minimum of bachelor's degree from regionally- or nationally-accredited institution (master's degree for some programs); minimum GPA of 3.0 in all previous programs of study; official transcripts from all post-secondary institutions attended; essay; curriculum vitae/resume; two letters of recommendation; dispositions survey. *Application deadline:* For fall admission, 4/1 priority date for domestic students; for spring admission, 10/1 priority date for domestic students; for summer admission, 2/1 priority date for domestic students. Applications are

processed on a rolling basis. Application fee: $80. Electronic applications accepted. *Expenses:* Contact institution. *Financial support:* Application deadline: 4/1; applicants required to submit FAFSA. *Unit head:* Dr. Christopher C. Morphew, Dean. *Application contact:* Elisabeth Woodward, Director of Admissions, 410-516-9796, Fax: 410-516-9817, E-mail: soe.info@jhu.edu. Website: http://education.jhu.edu

**Johns Hopkins University,** School of Education, Master's Programs in Education, Baltimore, MD 21218. Offers counseling (MS), including clinical mental health counseling, school counseling; education (MS), including educational studies, gifted education, reading, school administration and supervision, technology for educators; elementary education (MAT); health professions (M Ed); intelligence analysis (MS); organizational leadership (MS); secondary education (MAT), including biology, chemistry, earth/space science, English, physics, social studies; special education (MS), including early childhood special education, general special education studies, mild to moderate disabilities, severe disabilities. *Program availability:* Part-time, evening/weekend, 100% online, blended/hybrid learning. *Students:* 345 full-time (265 women), 1,601 part-time (1,245 women); includes 837 minority (392 Black or African American, non-Hispanic/Latino; 7 American Indian or Alaska Native, non-Hispanic/Latino; 141 Asian, non-Hispanic/Latino; 207 Hispanic/Latino; 7 Native Hawaiian or other Pacific Islander, non-Hispanic/Latino; 2 Two or more races, non-Hispanic/Latino), 55 international. Average age 27. 1,352 applicants, 76% accepted, 819 enrolled. In 2016, 642 master's awarded. *Degree requirements:* For master's, comprehensive exam (for some programs), portfolio, capstone project and/or internship; PRAXIS II (subject area assessments) for initial teacher preparation programs that lead to licensure. *Entrance requirements:* For master's, GRE (for full-time programs only); PRAXIS I/core or state-approved alternative (for initial teacher preparation programs that lead to licensure), minimum of bachelor's degree from regionally- or nationally-accredited institution; minimum GPA of 3.0 in all programs of study; official transcripts from all post-secondary institutions attended; essay; curriculum vitae/resume; letters of recommendation (3 for full-time programs, 2 for part-time programs); dispositions survey. Additional exam requirements/recommendations for international students: Required—TOEFL (minimum score 600 paper-based; 100 iBT), IELTS (minimum score 7). *Application deadline:* For fall admission, 4/1 priority date for domestic students, 4/1 for international students; for spring admission, 10/1 priority date for domestic students, 10/1 for international students; for summer admission, 2/1 priority date for domestic students, 2/1 for international students. Applications are processed on a rolling basis. Application fee: $80. Electronic applications accepted. *Expenses:* Contact institution. *Financial support:* Application deadline: 4/1; applicants required to submit FAFSA. *Unit head:* Dr. Christopher C. Morphew, Dean. *Application contact:* Elisabeth Woodward, Director of Admissions, 410-516-9796, Fax: 410-516-9817, E-mail: soe.info@jhu.edu. Website: http://education.jhu.edu

**Kean University,** College of Liberal Arts, Program in Psychology, Union, NJ 07083. Offers forensic psychology (MA); human behavior and organizational psychology (MA); psychological services (MA). *Program availability:* Part-time. *Faculty:* 18 full-time (14 women). *Students:* 45 full-time (35 women), 39 part-time (25 women); includes 48 minority (21 Black or African American, non-Hispanic/Latino; 8 Asian, non-Hispanic/Latino; 16 Hispanic/Latino; 1 Native Hawaiian or other Pacific Islander, non-Hispanic/Latino; 2 Two or more races, non-Hispanic/Latino), 2 international. Average age 27. 54 applicants, 91% accepted, 44 enrolled. In 2016, 25 master's awarded. *Degree requirements:* For master's, comprehensive exam, research component, two semesters of advanced seminar. *Entrance requirements:* For master's, GRE General Test, minimum GPA of 3.0; official transcripts from all institutions attended; two letters of recommendation; professional resume/curriculum vitae; 12 credits in behavioral sciences on the undergraduate level. Additional exam requirements/recommendations for international students: Required—TOEFL (minimum score 550 paper-based; 79 iBT), IELTS (minimum score 6.5). *Application deadline:* For fall admission, 6/1 for domestic and international students; for spring admission, 12/1 for domestic and international students. Applications are processed on a rolling basis. Application fee: $75. Electronic applications accepted. *Expenses:* Tuition, state resident: full-time $13,156; part-time $640 per credit. Tuition, nonresident: full-time $17,831; part-time $785 per credit. *Required fees:* $3316; $151 per credit. Tuition and fees vary according to course level, course load, degree level and program. *Financial support:* Scholarships/grants and unspecified assistantships available. Financial award applicants required to submit FAFSA. *Unit head:* Dr. Muriel Singer, Program Coordinator, 908-737-5886, E-mail: msinger@kean.edu. *Application contact:* Amy Clark, Program Assistant, 908-737-7100, E-mail: grad-adm@kean.edu. Website: http://grad.kean.edu/masters-programs/psychological-services

**Kean University,** Nathan Weiss Graduate College, Program in Counselor Education, Union, NJ 07083. Offers alcohol and drug abuse counseling (MA); clinical mental health counseling (MA); school counseling (MA). *Accreditation:* ACA; NCATE. *Program availability:* Part-time. *Faculty:* 8 full-time (5 women). *Students:* 130 full-time (105 women), 149 part-time (114 women); includes 114 minority (54 Black or African American, non-Hispanic/Latino; 1 American Indian or Alaska Native, non-Hispanic/Latino; 5 Asian, non-Hispanic/Latino; 49 Hispanic/Latino; 5 Two or more races, non-Hispanic/Latino), 3 international. Average age 32. 258 applicants, 30% accepted, 68 enrolled. In 2016, 71 master's awarded. *Degree requirements:* For master's, practicum, internship, portfolio. *Entrance requirements:* For master's, minimum GPA of 3.0, 2 letters of recommendation, personal statement, resume. Additional exam requirements/recommendations for international students: Required—TOEFL (minimum score 550 paper-based; 79 iBT), IELTS. *Application deadline:* For fall admission, 3/2 for domestic and international students; for spring admission, 10/31 for domestic and international students. Applications are processed on a rolling basis. Application fee: $75. Electronic applications accepted. *Expenses:* Tuition, state resident: full-time $13,156; part-time $640 per credit. Tuition, nonresident: full-time $17,831; part-time $785 per credit. *Required fees:* $3316; $151 per credit. Tuition and fees vary according to course level, course load, degree level and program. *Financial support:* Scholarships/grants and unspecified assistantships available. Financial award applicants required to submit FAFSA. *Unit head:* Dr. J. Barry Mascari, Program Coordinator, 908-737-5954, E-mail: jmascari@kean.edu. *Application contact:* Pedro Lopes, Admissions Counselor, 908-737-7100, E-mail: grad-adm@kean.edu. Website: http://grad.kean.edu/counseling

**Kent State University,** College of Education, Health and Human Services, School of Lifespan Development and Educational Sciences, Program in Clinical Mental Health Counseling, Kent, OH 44242-0001. Offers M Ed. *Accreditation:* ACA; NCATE. *Entrance requirements:* For master's, minimum GPA of 2.75, 2 letters of reference, goals statement, moral character form, interview. Additional exam requirements/recommendations for international students: Required—TOEFL (minimum score 550 paper-based; 80 iBT). Electronic applications accepted. *Expenses:* Tuition, state resident: full-time $10,864; part-time $495 per credit hour. Tuition, nonresident: full-time $18,380; part-time $837 per credit hour. *Faculty research:* Group work, personality assessment, family/child therapy, substance abuse counseling, clinical supervision.

**Kutztown University of Pennsylvania,** College of Education, Program in Counseling Psychology, Kutztown, PA 19530-0730. Offers clinical mental health counseling (MA); marriage, couple and family counseling (MA). *Program availability:* Part-time, evening/

weekend. *Faculty:* 5 full-time (2 women). *Students:* 75 full-time (69 women), 51 part-time (43 women); includes 23 minority (8 Black or African American, non-Hispanic/Latino; 2 Asian, non-Hispanic/Latino; 11 Hispanic/Latino; 2 Two or more races, non-Hispanic/Latino), 1 international. Average age 29. 72 applicants, 71% accepted, 24 enrolled. In 2016, 38 master's awarded. *Degree requirements:* For master's, comprehensive exam, thesis optional. *Entrance requirements:* For master's, GRE General Test, 3 letters of recommendation, minimum undergraduate GPA of 3.0, psychobiographical statement, resume. Additional exam requirements/recommendations for international students: Required—TOEFL (minimum score 550 paper-based, 79 iBT) or IELTS (minimum score 6.5). *Application deadline:* For fall admission, 3/1 for domestic and international students; for spring admission, 10/1 for domestic and international students. Application fee: $35. Electronic applications accepted. *Expenses:* Tuition, state resident: full-time $4347; part-time $483 per credit. Tuition, nonresident: full-time $6525; part-time $725 per credit. *Required fees:* $88 per credit. One-time fee: $50 full-time. *Financial support:* Career-related internships or fieldwork, Federal Work-Study, scholarships/grants, and unspecified assistantships available. Financial award application deadline: 3/1; financial award applicants required to submit FAFSA. *Faculty research:* Family addictions. *Unit head:* Dr. Helen S Hamlet, Department Chair, 610-683-4204, Fax: 610-683-1585, E-mail: hamlet@kutztown.edu.
Website: https://www.kutztown.edu/academics/graduate-programs/counseling.htm

**Lamar University,** College of Graduate Studies, College of Education and Human Development, Department of Counseling and Special Populations, Beaumont, TX 77710. Offers clinical mental health counseling (M Ed); school counseling (M Ed); special education (M Ed), including special education. *Accreditation:* ACA. *Faculty:* 6 full-time (3 women), 29 part-time/adjunct (11 women). *Students:* 16 full-time (9 women), 1,586 part-time (1,424 women); includes 758 minority (373 Black or African American, non-Hispanic/Latino; 6 American Indian or Alaska Native, non-Hispanic/Latino; 20 Asian, non-Hispanic/Latino; 337 Hispanic/Latino; 2 Native Hawaiian or other Pacific Islander, non-Hispanic/Latino; 20 Two or more races, non-Hispanic/Latino), 5 international. Average age 37. 840 applicants, 96% accepted, 393 enrolled. In 2016, 703 master's awarded. *Entrance requirements:* Additional exam requirements/recommendations for international students: Required—TOEFL (minimum score 550 paper-based; 79 iBT), IELTS (minimum score 6.5). *Application deadline:* For fall admission, 8/10 for domestic students, 7/1 for international students; for spring admission, 1/5 for domestic students, 12/1 for international students. Applications are processed on a rolling basis. Application fee: $25 ($50 for international students). Electronic applications accepted. *Expenses:* $8,134 in-state full-time, $5,574 in-state part-time; $15,604 out-of-state full-time, $10,554 out-of-state part-time per year. *Financial support:* Applicants required to submit FAFSA. *Unit head:* Dr. Rebecca Weinbaum, Interim Chair, 409-880-8978, Fax: 409-880-2263. *Application contact:* Deidre Mayer, Interim Director, Admissions and Academic Services, 409-880-8888, Fax: 409-880-7419, E-mail: gradmissions@lamar.edu.
Website: http://education.lamar.edu/counseling-and-special-populations

**Lancaster Bible College,** Graduate School, Lancaster, PA 17601-5036. Offers adult ministries (MA); Bible (MA); children and family ministry (MA); church planting (MA); consulting resource teacher (M Ed); elementary school counseling (M Ed); leadership (PhD); leadership studies (MA); marriage and family counseling (MA); mental health counseling (MA); pastoral studies (MA); secondary school counseling (M Ed); sports ministry (MA); student ministry (MA); town and country ministry (MA). *Program availability:* Part-time, evening/weekend. *Degree requirements:* For master's, comprehensive exam (for some programs), thesis (for some programs). *Entrance requirements:* For master's, bachelor's degree with a minimum of 30 credits of course work in Bible, minimum undergraduate GPA of 3.0, interview. Additional exam requirements/recommendations for international students: Required—TOEFL.

**La Salle University,** School of Arts and Sciences, Program in Counseling and Family Therapy, Philadelphia, PA 19141-1199. Offers industrial/organizational management and human resources (MA); marriage and family therapy (MA); pastoral counseling (MA); professional clinical counseling (MA). *Accreditation:* ACA; APA. *Program availability:* Part-time, evening/weekend. *Faculty:* 8 full-time (3 women), 20 part-time/adjunct (13 women). *Students:* 77 full-time (55 women), 180 part-time (147 women); includes 84 minority (44 Black or African American, non-Hispanic/Latino; 5 Asian, non-Hispanic/Latino; 31 Hispanic/Latino; 4 Two or more races, non-Hispanic/Latino), 5 international. Average age 30. 156 applicants, 76% accepted, 48 enrolled. In 2016, 106 master's awarded. *Degree requirements:* For master's, comprehensive exam. *Entrance requirements:* For master's, GRE or MAT (waived for applicants that already possess a master's degree in any field or for applicants that have a cumulative GPA of 3.5 or higher), minimum of 15 hours in psychology, counseling, or marriage and family studies; minimum GPA of 3.0; three letters of recommendation; personal statement; work experience (paid or volunteer). Additional exam requirements/recommendations for international students: Required—TOEFL. *Application deadline:* For fall admission, 8/15 priority date for domestic students, 7/15 for international students; for spring admission, 12/15 priority date for domestic students, 11/15 for international students; for summer admission, 4/15 priority date for domestic students, 3/15 for international students. Applications are processed on a rolling basis. Application fee: $35. Electronic applications accepted. Application fee is waived when completed online. *Expenses:* Contact institution. *Financial support:* In 2016–17, 37 students received support. Scholarships/grants and unspecified assistantships available. Support available to part-time students. Financial award application deadline: 8/31; financial award applicants required to submit FAFSA. *Faculty research:* Cognitive therapy, attribution theory, work habits, single parent families, treatment of addictions. *Unit head:* Dr. Donna A. Tonrey, Director, 215-951-1767, Fax: 215-951-1843, E-mail: psyma@lasalle.edu. *Application contact:* Elizabeth Heenan, Director, Graduate and Adult Enrollment, 215-951-1100, Fax: 215-951-1462, E-mail: heenan@lasalle.edu.
Website: http://www.lasalle.edu/counseling-family-therapy/

**Lee University,** Graduate Studies in Counseling, Cleveland, TN 37320-3450. Offers holistic child development (MS); marriage and family studies (MS); marriage and family therapy (MS); school counseling (MS). *Program availability:* Part-time, 100% online. *Faculty:* 8 full-time (3 women), 3 part-time/adjunct (0 women). *Students:* 86 full-time (65 women), 27 part-time (18 women); includes 46 minority (9 Black or African American, non-Hispanic/Latino; 1 American Indian or Alaska Native, non-Hispanic/Latino; 1 Asian, non-Hispanic/Latino; 33 Hispanic/Latino; 2 Two or more races, non-Hispanic/Latino), 8 international. Average age 31. 34 applicants, 65% accepted, 18 enrolled. In 2016, 31 master's awarded. *Degree requirements:* For master's, variable foreign language requirement, comprehensive exam (for some programs), thesis (for some programs), internship. *Entrance requirements:* For master's, GRE General Test or MAT (waived if undergraduate GPA is greater than 3.0 or if applicant already has a graduate degree), minimum undergraduate GPA of 3.0, 3 letters of recommendation, interview, official transcripts, essay. Additional exam requirements/recommendations for international students: Required—TOEFL (minimum score 61 iBT). *Application deadline:* For fall admission, 4/1 priority date for domestic and international students; for spring admission, 11/1 priority date for domestic and international students. Applications are processed on a rolling basis. Application fee: $25. Electronic applications accepted. *Expenses:* Tuition: Full-time $11,367; part-time $632 per credit hour. *Required fees:* $35 per term. One-time fee: $25. Tuition and fees vary according to program. *Financial*

*support:* In 2016–17, 25 students received support. Career-related internships or fieldwork, Federal Work-Study, institutionally sponsored loans, scholarships/grants, and unspecified assistantships available. Financial award application deadline: 3/1; financial award applicants required to submit FAFSA. *Unit head:* Dr. Trevor Milliron, Director, 423-614-8126, Fax: 423-614-8124, E-mail: tmilliron@leeuniversity.edu.
Website: http://www.leeuniversity.edu/academics/graduate/counseling/

**Lehigh University,** College of Education, Program in Counseling Psychology, Bethlehem, PA 18015. Offers counseling and human services (M Ed); counseling psychology (PhD); international counseling (M Ed, Certificate); school counseling (M Ed). *Accreditation:* APA (one or more programs are accredited). *Program availability:* Blended/hybrid learning. *Faculty:* 8 full-time (5 women), 6 part-time/adjunct (all women). *Students:* 60 full-time (53 women), 31 part-time (26 women); includes 21 minority (7 Black or African American, non-Hispanic/Latino; 3 Asian, non-Hispanic/Latino; 11 Hispanic/Latino), 15 international. Average age 30. 167 applicants, 31% accepted, 19 enrolled. In 2016, 35 master's, 7 doctorates awarded. *Degree requirements:* For doctorate, comprehensive exam, thesis/dissertation. *Entrance requirements:* For master's, minimum GPA of 3.0, 2 letters of recommendation, essay, transcript; for doctorate, GRE General Test, 2 letters of recommendation, transcript, essay; for Certificate, minimum GPA of 3.0 (undergraduate), 3.5 (graduate). Additional exam requirements/recommendations for international students: Required—TOEFL (minimum score 600 paper-based; 93 iBT). *Application deadline:* For fall admission, 2/1 for domestic and international students. Application fee: $65. Electronic applications accepted. *Expenses:* $565 per credit. *Financial support:* In 2016–17, 23 students received support, including 4 research assistantships with partial tuition reimbursements available (averaging $15,800 per year); fellowships, career-related internships or fieldwork, scholarships/grants, tuition waivers, and unspecified assistantships also available. Financial award application deadline: 2/15; financial award applicants required to submit FAFSA. *Faculty research:* Maternal/infant attachment, multicultural training and counseling, career development and health interventions, intersection of identities, community based participatory research. *Total annual research expenditures:* $729,282. *Unit head:* Dr. Christpher Liang, Director, 610-758-3253, Fax: 610-758-3227, E-mail: ctl212@lehigh.edu. *Application contact:* Lauryn Woodman, Coordinator, Counseling, 610-758-3250, Fax: 610-758-6223, E-mail: laa314@lehigh.edu.
Website: http://coe.lehigh.edu/academics/disciplines/cp

**Lenoir-Rhyne University,** Graduate Programs, School of Counseling and Human Services, Program in Clinical Mental Health Counseling, Hickory, NC 28601. Offers MA. *Accreditation:* ACA. *Program availability:* Part-time, evening/weekend. *Degree requirements:* For master's, comprehensive exam, thesis optional. *Entrance requirements:* For master's, GRE General Test or MAT, writing sample; minimum undergraduate GPA of 2.7, graduate 3.0. Additional exam requirements/recommendations for international students: Required—TOEFL (minimum score 600 paper-based). Electronic applications accepted. *Expenses:* Contact institution.

**Lesley University,** Graduate School of Arts and Social Sciences, Cambridge, MA 02138-2790. Offers clinical mental health counseling (MA), including holistic counseling, school and community counseling, trauma studies; counseling psychology (MA, CAGS), including professional counseling (MA), school counseling (MA); creative writing (MFA); expressive therapies (MA, PhD, CAGS), including art (MA), clinical mental health counseling (MA), dance (MA), expressive therapies (MA), music (MA); independent studies (CAGS); independent study (MA); intercultural relations (MA, CAGS); interdisciplinary studies (MA), including individualized studies, integrative holistic health, mindfulness studies, peace and conflict transformation, trauma sensitive assessment, intervention, and consultation, women's studies; urban environmental leadership (MA). *Program availability:* Part-time, online learning. *Degree requirements:* For master's, internship, practicum, thesis (for expressive therapies); for doctorate, thesis/dissertation, arts apprenticeship, field placement; for CAGS, thesis, internship (for counseling psychology, expressive therapies). *Entrance requirements:* For master's, MAT (counseling psychology), interview, writing samples, art portfolio; for doctorate, GRE or MAT, interview, master's degree; for CAGS, interview, master's degree. Additional exam requirements/recommendations for international students: Required—TOEFL (minimum score 550 paper-based; 80 iBT). Electronic applications accepted. *Faculty research:* Psychotherapy and culture; psychotherapy and psychological trauma; women's issues in art, teaching and psychotherapy; community-based art, psycho-spiritual inquiry.

**LeTourneau University,** Graduate Programs, Longview, TX 75607-7001. Offers business (MBA); counseling (MA), including licensed professional counselor, marriage and family therapy, school counseling; curriculum and instruction (M Ed); educational administration (M Ed); engineering (ME, MS); engineering management (MEM); health care administration (MS); marriage and family therapy (MA); psychology (MA); strategic leadership (MSL); teacher leadership (M Ed); teaching and learning (M Ed). *Program availability:* Part-time, 100% online, blended/hybrid learning. *Faculty:* 24 full-time (7 women), 40 part-time/adjunct (15 women). *Students:* 82 full-time (48 women), 428 part-time (331 women); includes 234 minority (138 Black or African American, non-Hispanic/Latino; 5 American Indian or Alaska Native, non-Hispanic/Latino; 5 Asian, non-Hispanic/Latino; 50 Hispanic/Latino; 36 Two or more races, non-Hispanic/Latino), 15 international. Average age 37. 257 applicants, 60% accepted, 141 enrolled. In 2016, 136 master's awarded. *Degree requirements:* For master's, thesis (for some programs). *Entrance requirements:* Additional exam requirements/recommendations for international students: Required—TOEFL. *Application deadline:* For fall admission, 8/22 for domestic students, 8/29 for international students; for winter admission, 10/10 for domestic students; for spring admission, 1/2 for domestic students, 1/10 for international students; for summer admission, 5/1 for domestic and international students. Applications are processed on a rolling basis. Electronic applications accepted. *Expenses:* $10,890-$18,450 tuition per year (depending on program). *Financial support:* Research assistantships, institutionally sponsored loans, and unspecified assistantships available. Financial award applicants required to submit FAFSA. *Application contact:* Chris Fontaine, Assistant Vice President for Enrollment Services and Global Admissions, 903-233-4312, E-mail: chrisfontaine@letu.edu. Website: http://www.letu.edu

**Lewis & Clark College,** Graduate School of Education and Counseling, Department of Counseling Psychology, Program in Professional Mental Health Counseling, Portland, OR 97219-7899. Offers MA, MS. *Program availability:* Part-time, evening/weekend. *Degree requirements:* For master's, thesis (MS). *Entrance requirements:* For master's, GRE General Test, minimum undergraduate GPA of 2.75. Additional exam requirements/recommendations for international students: Required—TOEFL (minimum score 575 paper-based). *Application deadline:* For fall admission, 2/1 priority date for domestic and international students; for spring admission, 10/1 priority date for domestic and international students. Application fee: $50. Electronic applications accepted. *Financial support:* Career-related internships or fieldwork, Federal Work-Study, institutionally sponsored loans, scholarships/grants, and health care benefits available. Support available to part-time students. Financial award application deadline: 3/1; financial award applicants required to submit FAFSA. *Unit head:* Dr. Amy Rees, Coordinator, 503-768-6060, Fax: 503-768-6065, E-mail: cpsy@lclark.edu. *Application contact:* Becky Haas, Director of Admissions, 503-768-6200, Fax: 503-768-6205, E-mail: gseadmit@lclark.edu.
Website: http://graduate.lclark.edu/departments/counseling_psychology/mental_health/

## Counseling Psychology

**Lewis University,** College of Arts and Sciences, Program in Clinical Mental Health Counseling, Romeoville, IL 60446. Offers child and adolescent counseling (MA); mental health counseling (MA). *Program availability:* Part-time, evening/weekend. *Students:* 52 full-time (42 women), 65 part-time (55 women); includes 29 minority (9 Black or African American, non-Hispanic/Latino; 1 Asian, non-Hispanic/Latino; 16 Hispanic/Latino; 1 Native Hawaiian or other Pacific Islander, non-Hispanic/Latino; 2 Two or more races, non-Hispanic/Latino). Average age 27. In 2016, 27 master's awarded. *Degree requirements:* For master's, comprehensive exam, thesis optional, practicum, internship. *Entrance requirements:* For master's, 15 hours of psychology, including statistics or research; 2 letters of recommendation; minimum GPA of 3.0 in last 60 hours; interview. Additional exam requirements/recommendations for international students: Required— TOEFL (minimum score 550 paper-based; 80 iBT). *Application deadline:* For fall admission, 5/1 priority date for international students; for spring admission, 11/15 priority date for international students. Applications are processed on a rolling basis. Application fee: $40. Electronic applications accepted. *Expenses: Tuition:* Full-time $13,860; part-time $770 per credit hour. *Required fees:* $75 per semester. Tuition and fees vary according to degree level and program. *Financial support:* Federal Work-Study, scholarships/grants, tuition waivers, and unspecified assistantships available. Financial award application deadline: 5/1; financial award applicants required to submit FAFSA. *Faculty research:* Cognitive development, attitude formation, juvenile delinquency, gender issues, work-family conflict. *Unit head:* Dr. Katherine Helm-Lewis, Director, 815-838-0500 Ext. 5604, Fax: 815-836-5032, E-mail: helmka@lewisu.edu. *Application contact:* Nancy Hanley, Information Contact, 815-838-0500 Ext. 5604, E-mail: hanleyna@lewisu.edu.
Website: http://www.lewisu.edu/academics/grad.htm/

**Liberty University,** School of Behavioral Sciences, Lynchburg, VA 24515. Offers clinical mental health counseling (MA); counselor education and supervision (PhD); human services counseling (MA), including addictions and recovery, business, child and family law, Christian ministries, criminal justice, crisis response and trauma, executive leadership, health and wellness, life coaching, marriage and family, military resilience; marriage and family therapy (MA); military resilience (Certificate); professional counseling (MA). *Program availability:* Part-time, online learning. *Students:* 2,041 full-time (1,612 women), 4,970 part-time (3,875 women); includes 1,991 minority (1,678 Black or African American, non-Hispanic/Latino; 33 American Indian or Alaska Native, non-Hispanic/Latino; 48 Asian, non-Hispanic/Latino; 80 Hispanic/Latino; 8 Native Hawaiian or other Pacific Islander, non-Hispanic/Latino; 144 Two or more races, non-Hispanic/Latino), 127 international. Average age 39. 5,496 applicants, 41% accepted, 1257 enrolled. In 2016, 2,813 master's, 11 doctorates, 20 other advanced degrees awarded. *Application deadline:* Applications are processed on a rolling basis. Application fee: $50. Electronic applications accepted. *Financial support:* Applicants required to submit FAFSA. *Unit head:* Dr. Ronald Hawkins, Founding Dean, School of Behavioral Sciences. *Application contact:* Jay Bridge, Director of Admissions, 800-424-9595, Fax: 800-628-7977, E-mail: gradadmissions@liberty.edu.

**Lindenwood University,** Graduate Programs, School of Education, St. Charles, MO 63301-1695. Offers education (MA), including autism spectrum disorders, character education, early intervention in autism and sensory impairment, gifted, technology; educational administration (MA, Ed D, Ed S); English to speakers of other languages (MA); instructional leadership (Ed D, Ed S); library media (MA); professional counseling (MA); school administration (MA, Ed S); school counseling (MA); teaching (MA). *Program availability:* Part-time, evening/weekend, 100% online, blended/hybrid learning. *Faculty:* 39 full-time (27 women), 210 part-time/adjunct (136 women). *Students:* 292 full-time (227 women), 1,580 part-time (1,203 women); includes 404 minority (333 Black or African American, non-Hispanic/Latino; 4 American Indian or Alaska Native, non-Hispanic/Latino; 10 Asian, non-Hispanic/Latino; 36 Hispanic/Latino; 1 Native Hawaiian or other Pacific Islander, non-Hispanic/Latino; 20 Two or more races, non-Hispanic/Latino), 20 international. Average age 36. 558 applicants, 72% accepted, 353 enrolled. In 2016, 491 master's, 72 doctorates, 111 other advanced degrees awarded. *Degree requirements:* For master's, thesis (for some programs), minimum GPA of 3.0; for doctorate, thesis/dissertation, minimum GPA of 3.0; for Ed S, comprehensive exam, project, minimum GPA of 3.0. *Entrance requirements:* For master's, interview, minimum undergraduate cumulative GPA of 3.0, writing sample, letter of recommendation; for doctorate, GRE, minimum graduate GPA of 3.4, resume, interview, writing sample, 4 letters of recommendation; for Ed S, master's degree in education, relevant work experience. Additional exam requirements/recommendations for international students: Required—TOEFL (minimum score 550 paper-based; 80 iBT); Recommended—IELTS (minimum score 6.5). *Application deadline:* For fall admission, 8/28 priority date for domestic and international students; for spring admission, 1/8 priority date for domestic and international students; for summer admission, 6/5 priority date for domestic and international students. Applications are processed on a rolling basis. Application fee: $30 ($100 for international students). Electronic applications accepted. *Expenses: Tuition:* Full-time $15,672; part-time $453 per credit hour. *Required fees:* $205 per semester. Tuition and fees vary according to course level, course load and degree level. *Financial support:* In 2016–17, 334 students received support. Career-related internships or fieldwork, Federal Work-Study, institutionally sponsored loans, scholarships/grants, tuition waivers (partial), and unspecified assistantships available. Financial award application deadline: 6/30; financial award applicants required to submit FAFSA. *Unit head:* Dr. Cynthia Bice, Dean, School of Education, 636-949-4618, Fax: 636-949-4197, E-mail: cbice@lindenwood.edu. *Application contact:* Tyler Kostich, Director, Evening and Graduate Admissions, 636-949-4138, Fax: 636-949-4109, E-mail: adultadmissions@lindenwood.edu.
Website: http://www.lindenwood.edu/academics/academic-schools/school-of-education/

**Lindsey Wilson College,** School of Professional Counseling, Columbia, KY 42728. Offers counseling and human development (M Ed); counselor education and supervision (PhD). *Accreditation:* ACA (one or more programs are accredited). *Program availability:* Part-time, evening/weekend, online learning.

**Lipscomb University,** Department of Graduate Psychology and Counseling, Nashville, TN 37204-3951. Offers clinical mental health counseling (MS); counseling psychology (Certificate); marriage and family therapy (MMFT); psychology (MS). *Program availability:* Part-time, evening/weekend. *Faculty:* 13 full-time (5 women), 10 part-time/adjunct (6 women). *Students:* 120 full-time (92 women), 30 part-time (27 women); includes 38 minority (22 Black or African American, non-Hispanic/Latino; 1 American Indian or Alaska Native, non-Hispanic/Latino; 1 Asian, non-Hispanic/Latino; 11 Hispanic/Latino; 3 Two or more races, non-Hispanic/Latino), 2 international. Average age 28. In 2016, 44 master's, 1 other advanced degree awarded. *Degree requirements:* For master's, thesis (for some programs), practicum, internship, capstone. *Entrance requirements:* For master's, GRE, resume, 3 reference letters, transcripts, goals statement. Additional exam requirements/recommendations for international students: Required—TOEFL (minimum score 570 paper-based; 80 iBT). *Application deadline:* For fall admission, 7/1 for domestic students; for spring admission, 11/1 for domestic students. Applications are processed on a rolling basis. Application fee: $50 ($75 for international students). Electronic applications accepted. *Expenses:* $898 per hour. *Financial support:* Scholarships/grants and unspecified assistantships available. Financial award applicants required to submit FAFSA. *Faculty research:* Cognitive psychology, neuroscience, health psychology, grief issues. *Unit head:* Dr. Shanna Ray,

Director/Professor of Psychology, 615-966-5833, E-mail: shanna.ray@lipscomb.edu. *Application contact:* Kathi Johnson, Recruiting and Marketing Coordinator, 615-966-5237, E-mail: kathi.johnson@lipscomb.edu.
Website: http://www.lipscomb.edu/psychology/graduate-programs

**Lock Haven University of Pennsylvania,** The Stephen Poorman College of Business, Information Systems, and Human Services, Lock Haven, PA 17745-2390. Offers clinical mental health counseling (MS); sport science (MS). *Program availability:* Online learning. *Degree requirements:* For master's, thesis. *Entrance requirements:* For master's, minimum undergraduate GPA of 3.0. Additional exam requirements/recommendations for international students: Required—TOEFL. Electronic applications accepted.

**London Metropolitan University,** Graduate Programs, London, United Kingdom. Offers applied psychology (M Sc); architecture (MA); biomedical science (M Sc); blood science (M Sc); cancer pharmacology (M Sc); computer networking and cyber security (M Sc); computing and information systems (M Sc); conference interpreting (MA); counter-terrorism studies (M Sc); creative, digital and professional writing (MA); crime, violence and prevention (M Sc); criminology (M Sc); curating contemporary art (MA); data analytics (M Sc); digital media (MA); early childhood studies (MA); education (MA, Ed D); financial services law, regulation and compliance (LL M); food science (M Sc); forensic psychology (M Sc); health and social care management and policy (M Sc); human nutrition (M Sc); human resource management (MA); human rights and international conflict (MA); information technology (M Sc); intelligence and security studies (M Sc); international oil, gas and energy law (LL M); international relations (MA); interpreting (MA); learning and teaching in higher education (MA); legal practice (LL M); media and entertainment law (LL M); organizational and consumer psychology (M Sc); psychological therapy (M Sc); psychology of mental health (M Sc); public health (M Sc); public policy and management (MPA); security studies (M Sc); social work (M Sc); spatial planning and urban design (MA); sports therapy (M Sc); supporting older children and young people with dyslexia (MA); teaching languages (MA), including Arabic, English; translation (MA); woman and child abuse (MA).

**Long Island University–Brentwood Campus,** Graduate Programs, Brentwood, NY 11717. Offers childhood education (grades 1-6) (MS), including grades 1-6; childhood education/literacy (grades 1-6) (MS); childhood education/special education (grades 1-6) (MS); clinical mental health counseling (MS, Advanced Certificate); early childhood education (B-2) (MS); literacy (B-6) (MS Ed); school counselor (MS); special education (grades 1-6) (MS Ed); students with disabilities generalist (grades 7-12) (Advanced Certificate). *Program availability:* Part-time. *Faculty:* 54 part-time/adjunct (30 women). *Students:* 98 full-time (80 women), 57 part-time (47 women); includes 28 minority (7 Black or African American, non-Hispanic/Latino; 1 Asian, non-Hispanic/Latino; 20 Hispanic/Latino). 85 applicants, 89% accepted, 43 enrolled. In 2016, 99 master's, 11 other advanced degrees awarded. *Degree requirements:* For master's, comprehensive exam (for some programs), thesis optional. *Entrance requirements:* For master's and Advanced Certificate, GRE. Additional exam requirements/recommendations for international students: Required—TOEFL or IELTS. *Application deadline:* Applications are processed on a rolling basis. Application fee: $50. Electronic applications accepted. Application fee is waived when completed online. *Expenses: Tuition:* Full-time $28,272; part-time $1178 per credit. *Required fees:* $451 per term. *Financial support:* Scholarships/grants and unspecified assistantships available. Support available to part-time students. Financial award applicants required to submit FAFSA. *Unit head:* Donna Di Donato, Dean and Chief Operating Officer, 631-287-8010, Fax: 631-287-8575, E-mail: donna.didonato@liu.edu. *Application contact:* Scott Aug, Associate Director of Enrollment Management, 631-287-8500, Fax: 631-287-8575, E-mail: scott.aug@liu.edu.
Website: http://liu.edu/brentwood

**Long Island University–Hudson,** Graduate School, Purchase, NY 10577. Offers autism (Advanced Certificate); childhood education (MS Ed); early childhood education (MS Ed); educational leadership (MS Ed); finance (MBA); health administration (MPA); healthcare sector management (MBA); literacy (MS Ed); management (MBA); marriage and family therapy (MS); mental health counseling (MS), including credentialed alcoholism and substance abuse counselor; middle childhood and adolescence education (MS Ed); pharmaceutics (MS), including cosmetic science, industrial pharmacy; public administration (MPA); school counseling (MS Ed, Advanced Certificate); school psychology (MS Ed); special education (MS Ed); TESOL (all grades) (Advanced Certificate); TESOL and bilingual education (MS Ed); the business of pharmaceutics and biotechnology (MBA). *Program availability:* Part-time, evening/weekend, online learning. *Faculty:* 7 full-time (5 women), 42 part-time/adjunct (25 women). *Students:* 55 full-time (41 women), 158 part-time (123 women); includes 40 minority (8 Black or African American, non-Hispanic/Latino; 1 Asian, non-Hispanic/Latino; 31 Hispanic/Latino). Average age 35. *Entrance requirements:* Additional exam requirements/recommendations for international students: Required—TOEFL (minimum score 550 paper-based; 79 iBT). *Application deadline:* Applications are processed on a rolling basis. Application fee: $50. Electronic applications accepted. *Expenses:* Contact institution. *Unit head:* Dr. Sylvia Blake, Dean and Chief Operating Officer, 914-831-2700, E-mail: westchester@liu.edu. *Application contact:* Cindy Pagnotta, Director of Marketing and Enrollment, 914-831-2701, Fax: 914-251-5959, E-mail: cindy.pagnotta@liu.edu.

**Long Island University–LIU Brooklyn,** School of Education, Brooklyn, NY 11201-8423. Offers adolescence urban education (MS Ed); applied behavior analysis (Advanced Certificate); bilingual education (Advanced Certificate); bilingual school counselor (MS Ed, Advanced Certificate); childhood urban education (MS Ed); childhood/early childhood urban education (MS Ed); early childhood urban education (MS Ed, Advanced Certificate); educational leadership (Advanced Certificate); marriage and family therapy (MS, Advanced Certificate); mental health counseling (MS, Advanced Certificate); school building district leader (Advanced Certificate); school counselor (MS Ed, Advanced Certificate); school psychologist (MS Ed); teaching urban children/adolescents with disabilities (MS Ed); TESOL (MS Ed). *Accreditation:* TEAC. *Program availability:* Part-time, evening/weekend. *Faculty:* 23 full-time (17 women), 44 part-time/adjunct (32 women). *Students:* 161 full-time (144 women), 594 part-time (461 women); includes 493 minority (229 Black or African American, non-Hispanic/Latino; 1 American Indian or Alaska Native, non-Hispanic/Latino; 30 Asian, non-Hispanic/Latino; 218 Hispanic/Latino; 2 Native Hawaiian or other Pacific Islander, non-Hispanic/Latino; 13 Two or more races, non-Hispanic/Latino), 9 international. 513 applicants, 73% accepted, 272 enrolled. In 2016, 262 master's, 18 other advanced degrees awarded. *Degree requirements:* For master's, thesis optional, electronic portfolio. *Entrance requirements:* For master's, GRE (for MS Ed). Additional exam requirements/recommendations for international students: Required—TOEFL (minimum score 527 paper-based; 75 iBT). *Application deadline:* Applications are processed on a rolling basis. Application fee: $50. Electronic applications accepted. *Expenses: Tuition:* Full-time $28,272; part-time $1178 per credit. *Required fees:* $451 per term. Tuition and fees vary according to degree level, program and student level. *Financial support:* In 2016–17, 81 students received support. Career-related internships or fieldwork, Federal Work-Study, institutionally sponsored loans, scholarships/grants, and unspecified assistantships available. Support available to part-time students. Financial award application deadline: 2/15; financial award applicants required to submit FAFSA. *Faculty research:* Technology in education, teaching civics and sustainability, biliteracy and dual language instruction, diversity in organizations and leadership, counseling diverse couples and families. *Unit head:* Dr. Amy Ginsberg, Dean, 718-246-6308, E-mail: amy.ginsberg@liu.edu. *Application contact:* Gabrielle Gannon, Director of Graduate Admissions, 718-488-1011, Fax: 718-780-6110, E-mail: bkln-admissions@liu.edu. Website: http://www.liu.edu/Brooklyn/Academics/School-of-Education

**Long Island University–LIU Post,** College of Education, Information and Technology, Brookville, NY 11548-1300. Offers adolescence education (MS); adolescence education 7-12 (MS); archives and records management (AC); art education (MS); childhood education (MS); childhood teaching literacy B-6 (MS); childhood/special education (MS); clinical mental health counseling (MS, AC); early childhood education (MS); early childhood education/childhood education (MS); educational leadership (AC); educational technology (MS); information studies (PhD); interdisciplinary educational studies (Ed D); middle childhood education (MS); music education (MS); school counselor (MS); special education (MS Ed); speech-language pathology (MA); students with disabilities, 7-12 generalist (AC); TESOL (MA). *Accreditation:* TEAC. *Program availability:* Part-time, 100% online, blended/hybrid learning. *Faculty:* 55 full-time (35 women), 104 part-time/adjunct (57 women). *Students:* 464 full-time (390 women), 740 part-time (580 women); includes 265 minority (99 Black or African American, non-Hispanic/Latino; 45 Asian, non-Hispanic/Latino; 113 Hispanic/Latino; 1 Native Hawaiian or other Pacific Islander, non-Hispanic/Latino; 7 Two or more races, non-Hispanic/Latino), 33 international. 928 applicants, 76% accepted, 406 enrolled. In 2016, 334 master's, 10 doctorates, 137 other advanced degrees awarded. Terminal master's awarded for partial completion of doctoral program. *Degree requirements:* For master's, variable foreign language requirement, comprehensive exam (for some programs), thesis optional; for doctorate, comprehensive exam, thesis/dissertation. *Entrance requirements:* For master's and AC, GRE. Additional exam requirements/recommendations for international students: Required—PTE, TOEFL (minimum score 550 paper-based, 75 iBT) or IELTS. *Application deadline:* Applications are processed on a rolling basis. Application fee: $50. Electronic applications accepted. *Expenses: Tuition:* Full-time $28,272; part-time $1178 per credit. *Required fees:* $451 per term. Tuition and fees vary according to degree level and program. *Financial support:* Career-related internships or fieldwork, Federal Work-Study, institutionally sponsored loans, scholarships/grants, tuition waivers (partial), and unspecified assistantships available. Support available to part-time students. Financial award application deadline: 2/15; financial award applicants required to submit FAFSA. *Faculty research:* English language learners, early childhood literacy development through play, sleep, social justice through education, using a structured protocol for discussing bad news. *Total annual research expenditures:* $575,000. *Unit head:* Dr. Albert Inserra, Dean, 516-299-2210, E-mail: albert.inserra@liu.edu. *Application contact:* Carol Zerah, Director of Graduate Admissions, 516-299-2900, Fax: 516-299-2137, E-mail: post-enroll@liu.edu. Website: http://liu.edu/CWPost/Academics/College-of-Education-Information-and-Technology

**Louisiana Tech University,** Graduate School, College of Education, Department of Psychology and Behavioral Sciences, Ruston, LA 71272. Offers counseling and guidance (MA); counseling psychology (PhD); industrial and organizational psychology (MA, PhD). *Accreditation:* APA (one or more programs are accredited). *Program availability:* Part-time. *Degree requirements:* For master's, thesis or alternative; for doctorate, thesis/dissertation. *Entrance requirements:* For master's and doctorate, GRE General Test. *Application deadline:* For fall admission, 7/29 for domestic students; for spring admission, 2/3 for domestic students. Application fee: $20 ($30 for international students). *Financial support:* Fellowships, research assistantships, teaching assistantships, and career-related internships or fieldwork available. Financial award application deadline: 2/1. *Unit head:* Dr. Donna Thomas, Chair, 318-257-5066, Fax: 318-257-2379, E-mail: dthomas@latech.edu. *Application contact:* Dr. Cathy Stockton, Associate Dean of Graduate Studies, 318-257-3229, Fax: 318-257-2379, E-mail: cstock@latech.edu.
Website: http://education.latech.edu/departments/psychology/

**Loyola Marymount University,** School of Education, Department of Educational Support Services, Program in Counseling, Los Angeles, CA 90045-2659. Offers MA. *Students:* 70 full-time (59 women), 13 part-time (all women); includes 44 minority (7 Black or African American, non-Hispanic/Latino; 6 Asian, non-Hispanic/Latino; 30 Hispanic/Latino; 1 Two or more races, non-Hispanic/Latino), 4 international. Average age 29. 42 applicants, 79% accepted, 28 enrolled. In 2016, 17 master's awarded. *Entrance requirements:* For master's, CBEST, 2 letters of recommendation, letter of intent. Additional exam requirements/recommendations for international students: Required—TOEFL (minimum score 600 paper-based; 100 iBT). *Application deadline:* For fall admission, 6/15 for domestic students; for spring admission, 11/15 for domestic students. Application fee: $50. Electronic applications accepted. *Financial support:* In 2016–17, 33 students received support. *Unit head:* Dr. Sheri Atwater, Program Director, 310-338-7163, E-mail: satwater@lmu.edu. *Application contact:* Chake H. Kouyoumjian, Associate Dean of Graduate Studies, 310-338-2721, Fax: 310-338-6086, E-mail: ckouyoum@lmu.edu.
Website: http://soe.lmu.edu/academics/counseling/

**Loyola University Chicago,** School of Education, Program in Counseling Psychology, Chicago, IL 60660. Offers PhD. *Accreditation:* APA. *Faculty:* 6 full-time (2 women), 6 part-time/adjunct (4 women). *Students:* 17 full-time (12 women); includes 11 minority (4 Black or African American, non-Hispanic/Latino; 3 Asian, non-Hispanic/Latino; 3 Hispanic/Latino; 1 Two or more races, non-Hispanic/Latino), 2 international. Average age 29. 45 applicants, 7% accepted, 3 enrolled. In 2016, 6 doctorates awarded. *Degree requirements:* For doctorate, comprehensive exam, thesis/dissertation. *Entrance requirements:* For doctorate, GRE General Test, GRE Subject Test, interview; minimum graduate GPA of 3.5, undergraduate 3.0; letters of recommendation. Additional exam requirements/recommendations for international students: Required—TOEFL (minimum score 550 paper-based; 79 iBT). *Application deadline:* For fall admission, 12/1 for domestic and international students. Application fee: $50. Electronic applications accepted. Application fee is waived when completed online. *Expenses:* $949 per hour; $2,847 per course; $8,541-$11,388 per semester plus fees $432 per semester and $225 the first semester. *Financial support:* In 2016–17, 26 students received support, including 9 research assistantships with full tuition reimbursements available (averaging $14,000 per year), 17 teaching assistantships with full tuition reimbursements available (averaging $4,000 per year); career-related internships or fieldwork, institutionally sponsored loans, scholarships/grants, traineeships, health care benefits, and unspecified assistantships also available. Financial award application deadline: 2/1; financial award applicants required to submit FAFSA. *Faculty research:* Career choice and development, multicultural counseling, psychological measurement, prevention and intervention, family therapy. *Unit head:* Dr. Steven Brown, Director, 312-915-6311, E-mail: sbrown@luc.edu. *Application contact:* Thomas Ott, Information Contact, 312-915-6800, E-mail: schleduc@luc.edu.

**Loyola University Maryland,** Graduate Programs, Loyola College of Arts and Sciences, Department of Psychology, Program in Counseling Psychology, Baltimore, MD 21210-2699. Offers MS, CAS. *Program availability:* Part-time, evening/weekend. *Faculty:* 65 full-time (40 women), 26 part-time/adjunct (18 women). *Students:* 25 full-time (24 women), 14 part-time (12 women); includes 9 minority (1 Black or African American,

non-Hispanic/Latino; 1 Asian, non-Hispanic/Latino; 4 Hispanic/Latino; 3 Two or more races, non-Hispanic/Latino). Average age 26. 62 applicants, 48% accepted, 15 enrolled. *Degree requirements:* For master's, thesis. *Entrance requirements:* For master's, GRE General Test, GRE Subject Test (recommended), transcript, essay, 3 letters of recommendation; for CAS, GRE General Test, GRE Subject Test (recommended). Additional exam requirements/recommendations for international students: Required—TOEFL (minimum score 550 paper-based), IELTS (minimum score 7). *Application deadline:* For fall admission, 3/1 for domestic and international students. Application fee: $60. Electronic applications accepted. *Expenses:* Contact institution. *Financial support:* Unspecified assistantships available. Financial award application deadline: 4/15; financial award applicants required to submit FAFSA. *Unit head:* Dr. Matthew W. Kirkhart, Chair, 410-617-5498, E-mail: mkirkhart@loyola.edu. *Application contact:* Maureen Faux, Interim Director, Graduate Admissions, 410-617-5020, Fax: 410-617-2002, E-mail: graduate@loyola.edu.

**Lynchburg College,** Graduate Studies, M Ed Program in Clinical Mental Health Counseling, Lynchburg, VA 24501-3199. Offers M Ed. *Accreditation:* ACA. *Program availability:* Part-time, evening/weekend. *Students:* 26 full-time (24 women), 15 part-time (13 women); includes 3 minority (1 Black or African American, non-Hispanic/Latino; 1 Asian, non-Hispanic/Latino; 1 Hispanic/Latino). In 2016, 15 master's awarded. *Degree requirements:* For master's, counseling internship. *Entrance requirements:* For master's, GRE, minimum GPA of 3.0 (preferred), official transcripts (bachelor's, others as relevant), three letters of recommendation, career goals statement. Additional exam requirements/recommendations for international students: Required—TOEFL (minimum score 550 paper-based; 79 iBT), IELTS (minimum score 6.5). *Application deadline:* For fall admission, 7/31 for domestic students, 6/1 for international students; for spring admission, 11/30 for domestic students, 10/15 for international students. Applications are processed on a rolling basis. Application fee: $30. Electronic applications accepted. Application fee is waived when completed online. *Expenses:* Contact institution. *Financial support:* Federal Work-Study, scholarships/grants, health care benefits, and unspecified assistantships available. Support available to part-time students. Financial award application deadline: 7/31; financial award applicants required to submit FAFSA. *Unit head:* Dr. Karena Heyward, Assistant Professor and Program Director, 434-544-8067, E-mail: heyward.k@lynchburg.edu.
Website: http://www.lynchburg.edu/graduate/master-of-education-in-counselor-education/clinical-mental-health-counseling/

**Lynn University,** College of Arts and Sciences, Boca Raton, FL 33431. Offers administration (MS), including criminal justice; applied psychology (MS); mental health counseling (MS). *Program availability:* Part-time, evening/weekend, blended/hybrid learning. *Faculty:* 52 full-time (22 women), 19 part-time/adjunct (11 women). *Students:* 74 full-time (57 women), 39 part-time (28 women); includes 32 minority (20 Black or African American, non-Hispanic/Latino; 2 Asian, non-Hispanic/Latino; 9 Hispanic/Latino; 1 Native Hawaiian or other Pacific Islander, non-Hispanic/Latino), 10 international. Average age 29. 77 applicants, 77% accepted, 39 enrolled. In 2016, 65 master's awarded. *Degree requirements:* For master's, comprehensive exam (for some programs), thesis (for some programs). *Entrance requirements:* For master's, bachelor's degree from accredited institution, resume, letter of recommendation, essay of professional goals, official transcripts. Additional exam requirements/recommendations for international students: Required—TOEFL (minimum score 550 paper-based; 80 iBT), IELTS (minimum score 6.5). *Application deadline:* For fall admission, 8/18 for domestic students, 8/4 for international students; for spring admission, 12/15 for domestic students, 12/1 for international students; for summer admission, 4/17 for domestic students, 4/3 for international students. Applications are processed on a rolling basis. Application fee: $45. Electronic applications accepted. *Expenses:* $725 per credit. *Financial support:* In 2016–17, 25 students received support. Career-related internships or fieldwork, Federal Work-Study, scholarships/grants, tuition waivers (full and partial), and unspecified assistantships available. Support available to part-time students. Financial award application deadline: 3/1; financial award applicants required to submit FAFSA. *Faculty research:* Personality and social media, learning strategies, personal health behaviors and compliance, using drums in substance abuse groups, interpersonal behaviors with individuals with autism, case conceptualization, teaching case conceptualization across the curriculum. *Unit head:* Dr. Katrina Carter-Tellison, Dean, 561-237-7412, E-mail: kcartertellison@lynn.edu. *Application contact:* Steven Pruitt, Director of Graduate Admission, 561-237-7834, Fax: 561-237-7100, E-mail: admissionpm@lynn.edu.
Website: https://www.lynn.edu/academics/colleges-schools/arts-and-sciences

**Marist College,** Graduate Programs, School of Social and Behavioral Sciences, Poughkeepsie, NY 12601-1387. Offers education (M Ed, MA); mental health counseling (MA); school psychology (MA, Adv C). *Program availability:* Part-time, evening/weekend. *Degree requirements:* For master's, thesis optional. *Entrance requirements:* For master's, GRE General Test, letters of recommendation, minimum undergraduate GPA of 3.0, interview. Additional exam requirements/recommendations for international students: Required—TOEFL (minimum score 550 paper-based; 80 iBT); Recommended—IELTS (minimum score 6.5). Electronic applications accepted. *Faculty research:* AIDS prevention, educational intervention, humanistic counseling research, aging and development, neuroimaging.

**Marquette University,** Graduate School, College of Education, Department of Counselor Education and Counseling Psychology, Milwaukee, WI 53201-1881. Offers clinical mental health counseling (MS); community counseling (MA); counseling psychology (PhD); school counseling (MA). *Accreditation:* ACA. *Program availability:* Part-time. *Faculty:* 6 full-time (3 women), 5 part-time/adjunct (3 women). *Students:* 69 full-time (53 women), 13 part-time (10 women); includes 18 minority (6 Black or African American, non-Hispanic/Latino; 3 Asian, non-Hispanic/Latino; 7 Hispanic/Latino; 2 Two or more races, non-Hispanic/Latino), 3 international. Average age 26. 122 applicants, 47% accepted, 32 enrolled. In 2016, 24 master's, 2 doctorates awarded. Terminal master's awarded for partial completion of doctoral program. *Degree requirements:* For master's, comprehensive exam, thesis (for some programs); for doctorate, thesis/dissertation, qualifying exam. *Entrance requirements:* For master's, GRE General Test or MAT, official transcripts from all current and previous colleges/universities except Marquette, three letters of recommendation, statement of purpose; for doctorate, GRE General Test, MAT, sample of written work, official transcripts from all current and previous colleges/universities except Marquette, three letters of recommendation, statement of purpose, resume/curriculum vitae. Additional exam requirements/recommendations for international students: Required—TOEFL (minimum score 530 paper-based). *Application deadline:* For fall admission, 1/15 for domestic and international students. Application fee: $50. *Financial support:* Fellowships, research assistantships, scholarships/grants, health care benefits, tuition waivers (partial), and unspecified assistantships available. Support available to part-time students. Financial award application deadline: 2/15. *Faculty research:* Ethical and legal issues in education, anxiety disorders, multicultural counseling, child psychopathology, group counseling and dynamics. *Unit head:* Dr. Alan Burkard, Chair, 414-288-3434, E-mail: alan.burkard@marquette.edu. *Application contact:* Dr. Alan Burkard.

**Marymount University,** School of Education and Human Services, Program in Counseling, Arlington, VA 22207-4299. Offers clinical mental health counseling (MA);

pastoral counseling (MA); school counseling (MA). *Accreditation:* ACA. *Program availability:* Part-time, evening/weekend. *Faculty:* 29 full-time (21 women), 7 part-time/adjunct (all women). *Students:* 84 full-time (74 women), 57 part-time (51 women); includes 55 minority (28 Black or African American, non-Hispanic/Latino; 2 American Indian or Alaska Native, non-Hispanic/Latino; 3 Asian, non-Hispanic/Latino; 17 Hispanic/Latino; 5 Two or more races, non-Hispanic/Latino), 2 international. Average age 30. 83 applicants, 77% accepted, 45 enrolled. In 2016, 39 master's awarded. *Degree requirements:* For master's, thesis or alternative, capstone/internship. *Entrance requirements:* For master's, GRE, 2 letters of recommendation, interview, resume, personal statement. Additional exam requirements/recommendations for international students: Required—TOEFL (minimum score 600 paper-based; 96 iBT), IELTS (minimum score 6.5). *Application deadline:* For fall admission, 1/15 priority date for domestic and international students; for spring admission, 10/5 for domestic and international students. Applications are processed on a rolling basis. Application fee: $40. Electronic applications accepted. *Expenses:* Tuition: Full-time $8460; part-time $940 per credit hour. *Required fees:* $10 per credit hour. One-time fee: $240 part-time. Tuition and fees vary according to program. *Financial support:* In 2016–17, 15 students received support, including 8 research assistantships with tuition reimbursements available, 4 teaching assistantships with tuition reimbursements available; career-related internships or fieldwork, Federal Work-Study, scholarships/grants, and unspecified assistantships also available. Support available to part-time students. Financial award applicants required to submit FAFSA. *Unit head:* Dr. Lisa Jackson-Cherry, Chair, Counseling, 703-284-1633, Fax: 703-284-5708, E-mail: lisa.jackson-cherry@marymount.edu. *Application contact:* Francesca Reed, Director, Graduate Admissions, 703-284-5901, Fax: 703-527-3815, E-mail: grad.admissions@marymount.edu. Website: http://www.marymount.edu/Academics/School-of-Education-Human-Services/Graduate-Programs/Counseling-(M-A-)

**Marywood University,** Academic Affairs, Reap College of Education and Human Development, Department of Psychology and Counseling, Program in Mental Health Counseling, Scranton, PA 18509-1598. Offers MA. *Accreditation:* ACA. Electronic applications accepted.

**McGill University,** Faculty of Graduate and Postdoctoral Studies, Faculty of Education, Department of Educational and Counseling Psychology, Montréal, QC H3A 2T5, Canada. Offers counseling psychology (MA, PhD); educational psychology (M Ed, MA, PhD); school/applied child psychology and applied developmental psychology (M Ed, MA, PhD, Diploma), including school psychology. *Accreditation:* APA.

**McKendree University,** Graduate Programs, Master of Arts Program in Clinical Mental Health Counseling, Lebanon, IL 62254-1299. Offers MA. *Program availability:* Part-time, evening/weekend. *Degree requirements:* For master's, comprehensive exam, internship. *Entrance requirements:* For master's, official transcripts from each college or university attended, minimum undergraduate GPA of 3.0, three letters of recommendation, personal statement, completion of six undergraduate credit hours in a behavior science, curriculum vitae or resume. Electronic applications accepted.

**McNeese State University,** Doré School of Graduate Studies, Burton College of Education, Department of Psychology, Lake Charles, LA 70609. Offers addiction treatment (MA); applied behavior analysis (MA); counseling psychology (MA); general/experimental psychology (MA). *Program availability:* Evening/weekend. *Entrance requirements:* For master's, GRE.

**Medaille College,** Programs in Psychology, Buffalo, NY 14214-2695. Offers clinical psychology (Psy D); marriage and family therapy (MA); mental health counseling (MA); psychology (MA). *Accreditation:* ACA. *Program availability:* Part-time, evening/weekend. *Degree requirements:* For master's, comprehensive exam (for some programs), thesis (for some programs). *Entrance requirements:* For master's, GRE General Test (psychology), minimum GPA of 2.75 (psychology). Additional exam requirements/recommendations for international students: Required—TOEFL (minimum score 550 paper-based). Electronic applications accepted. *Faculty research:* Schizophrenia, Parkinson's Disease, eyewitness testimony, methodology.

**Mercy College,** School of Social and Behavioral Sciences, Program in Counseling, Dobbs Ferry, NY 10522-1189. Offers counseling (MS); family counseling (Certificate). *Program availability:* Part-time, evening/weekend, 100% online, blended/hybrid learning. *Students:* 51 full-time (42 women), 107 part-time (91 women); includes 116 minority (41 Black or African American, non-Hispanic/Latino; 4 Asian, non-Hispanic/Latino; 70 Hispanic/Latino; 3 Two or more races, non-Hispanic/Latino). Average age 34. 127 applicants, 60% accepted, 51 enrolled. In 2016, 40 master's, 2 other advanced degrees awarded. *Degree requirements:* For master's, comprehensive exam (for some programs). *Entrance requirements:* For master's, essay, two professional letters of recommendation, resume, undergraduate transcript with minimum GPA of 3.0. Additional exam requirements/recommendations for international students: Required—TOEFL (minimum score 600 paper-based; 100 iBT), IELTS (minimum score 8). *Application deadline:* For fall admission, 8/1 for international students. Applications are processed on a rolling basis. Application fee: $40. Electronic applications accepted. *Expenses:* Tuition: Full-time $15,156; part-time $842 per credit hour. *Required fees:* $620; $155 per term. Tuition and fees vary according to course load and program. *Financial support:* Career-related internships or fieldwork, Federal Work-Study, scholarships/grants, and unspecified assistantships available. Support available to part-time students. Financial award applicants required to submit FAFSA. *Unit head:* Dr. Karol Dean, Dean, School of Social and Behavioral Sciences, 914-674-7517, E-mail: kdean@mercy.edu. *Application contact:* Allison Gurdineer, Senior Director of Admissions, 914-674-2946, Fax: 914-674-7382, E-mail: admissions@mercy.edu. Website: https://www.mercy.edu/degrees-programs/ms-counseling

**Mercy College,** School of Social and Behavioral Sciences, Program in Mental Health Counseling, Dobbs Ferry, NY 10522-1189. Offers MS. *Program availability:* Part-time, evening/weekend. *Students:* 72 full-time (63 women), 79 part-time (77 women); includes 136 minority (81 Black or African American, non-Hispanic/Latino; 3 Asian, non-Hispanic/Latino; 48 Hispanic/Latino; 1 Native Hawaiian or other Pacific Islander, non-Hispanic/Latino; 3 Two or more races, non-Hispanic/Latino), 2 international. Average age 34. 115 applicants, 48% accepted, 37 enrolled. In 2016, 34 master's awarded. *Degree requirements:* For master's, comprehensive exam. *Entrance requirements:* For master's, essay, resume, interview, two letters of recommendation, undergraduate transcript. Additional exam requirements/recommendations for international students: Required—TOEFL (minimum score 600 paper-based; 100 iBT), IELTS (minimum score 8). *Application deadline:* For fall admission, 8/1 for international students. Applications are processed on a rolling basis. Application fee: $40. Electronic applications accepted. *Expenses:* Tuition: Full-time $15,156; part-time $842 per credit hour. *Required fees:* $620; $155 per term. Tuition and fees vary according to course load and program. *Financial support:* Career-related internships or fieldwork, Federal Work-Study, scholarships/grants, and unspecified assistantships available. Support available to part-time students. Financial award applicants required to submit FAFSA. *Unit head:* Dr. Karol Dean, Dean, School of Social and Behavioral Sciences, 914-674-7809. *Application contact:* Allison Gurdineer, Senior Director of Admissions, 877-637-2946, Fax: 914-674-7382, E-mail: admissions@mercy.edu. Website: https://www.mercy.edu/degrees-programs/ms-mental-health-counseling

**Messiah College,** Program in Counseling, Mechanicsburg, PA 17055. Offers clinical mental health counseling (MAC); counseling (CAGS); marriage, couple, and family counseling (MAC); school counseling (MAC). *Accreditation:* ACA. *Program availability:* Part-time, online learning. *Entrance requirements:* For master's, minimum undergraduate cumulative GPA of 3.0, 2 recommendations, resume or curriculum vitae, interview; for CAGS, bachelor's degree, minimum undergraduate cumulative GPA of 3.0, essay, two recommendations, resume or curriculum vitae, interview. Electronic applications accepted.

**Mid-America Christian University,** Program in Counseling, Oklahoma City, OK 73170-4504. Offers marital and family therapy (MS); pastoral/spiritual direction (MS); professional counselor (MS). *Entrance requirements:* For master's, MAT, bachelor's degree from a regionally accredited college or university, minimum overall cumulative GPA of 2.75 of bachelor course work. Additional exam requirements/recommendations for international students: Required—TOEFL (minimum score 550 paper-based).

**Middle Tennessee State University,** College of Graduate Studies, College of Education, Department of Educational Leadership, Program in Professional Counseling, Murfreesboro, TN 37132. Offers mental health counseling (M Ed); school counseling (M Ed). *Accreditation:* ACA; NCATE. *Program availability:* Part-time, evening/weekend, online learning. *Degree requirements:* For master's, comprehensive exam, thesis. *Entrance requirements:* For master's, GRE or MAT. Additional exam requirements/recommendations for international students: Required—TOEFL (minimum score 525 paper-based; 71 iBT) or IELTS (minimum score 6). Electronic applications accepted.

**Midwestern State University,** Billie Doris McAda Graduate School, Prothro-Yeager College of Humanities and Social Sciences, Department of Psychology, Wichita Falls, TX 76308. Offers clinical/counseling psychology (MA). *Program availability:* Part-time, evening/weekend. *Degree requirements:* For master's, one foreign language, comprehensive exam, thesis optional. *Entrance requirements:* For master's, GRE General Test, 3 recommendation forms. Additional exam requirements/recommendations for international students: Required—TOEFL (minimum score 550 paper-based). Electronic applications accepted. *Faculty research:* Child assessment and treatment outcomes, Christianity as it relates to psychology, treatment of behavioral/emotional problems in childhood, people struggling with HIV/AIDS, educational psychology.

**Minnesota State University Mankato,** College of Graduate Studies and Research, College of Education, Department of Counseling and Student Personnel, Mankato, MN 56001. Offers college student affairs (MS); counselor education and supervision (Ed D); mental health counseling (MS); professional school counseling (K-12) (MS). *Accreditation:* ACA (one or more programs are accredited); NCATE. *Students:* 77 full-time (68 women), 38 part-time (26 women). *Degree requirements:* For master's, comprehensive exam, thesis or alternative. *Entrance requirements:* For master's, GRE General Test or MAT (if GPA less than 3.0 for last 2 years), minimum GPA of 3.0 during previous 2 years, 3 letters of reference. Additional exam requirements/recommendations for international students: Required—TOEFL. *Application deadline:* For fall admission, 1/15 priority date for domestic students. Applications are processed on a rolling basis. Application fee: $40. Electronic applications accepted. *Financial support:* Research assistantships with full tuition reimbursements, teaching assistantships with full tuition reimbursements, career-related internships or fieldwork, Federal Work-Study, institutionally sponsored loans, and unspecified assistantships available. Support available to part-time students. Financial award application deadline: 3/15; financial award applicants required to submit FAFSA. *Unit head:* Dr. Jackie Lewis, Chair, E-mail: jacqueline.lewis@mnsu.edu. Website: http://ed.mnsu.edu/csp/

**Mississippi College,** Graduate School, School of Education, Department of Psychology and Counseling, Clinton, MS 39058. Offers counseling (Ed S); marriage and family counseling (MS); mental health counseling (MS); school counseling (M Ed). *Program availability:* Part-time. *Degree requirements:* For master's and Ed S, comprehensive exam, thesis optional. *Entrance requirements:* For master's, GRE or NTE. Additional exam requirements/recommendations for international students: Recommended—TOEFL, IELTS. Electronic applications accepted.

**Missouri State University,** Graduate College, College of Education, Department of Counseling, Leadership, and Special Education, Program in Counseling, Springfield, MO 65897. Offers elementary school counseling (MS); mental health counseling (MS); secondary school counseling (MS). *Accreditation:* ACA. *Program availability:* Part-time, evening/weekend. *Students:* 67 full-time (51 women), 43 part-time (39 women); includes 16 minority (4 Black or African American, non-Hispanic/Latino; 7 Hispanic/Latino; 5 Two or more races, non-Hispanic/Latino), 3 international. Average age 30. 46 applicants, 50% accepted, 18 enrolled. In 2016, 35 master's awarded. *Degree requirements:* For master's, comprehensive exam, thesis or alternative. *Entrance requirements:* For master's, GRE or MAT, minimum GPA of 2.75. Additional exam requirements/recommendations for international students: Required—TOEFL (minimum score 550 paper-based; 79 iBT), IELTS (minimum score 6). *Application deadline:* For fall admission, 2/1 priority date for domestic students, 1/1 priority date for international students; for spring admission, 10/1 priority date for domestic students, 9/1 priority date for international students. Application fee: $35 ($50 for international students). Electronic applications accepted. *Expenses:* Tuition, state resident: full-time $5830. Tuition, nonresident: full-time $10,708. *Required fees:* $1130. Tuition and fees vary according to class time, course level, course load and program. *Financial support:* Federal Work-Study, institutionally sponsored loans, scholarships/grants, and unspecified assistantships available. Financial award application deadline: 3/31; financial award applicants required to submit FAFSA. *Unit head:* Dr. James Satterfield, Department Head, 417-836-5392, Fax: 417-836-4918, E-mail: clse@missouristate.edu. *Application contact:* Michael Edwards, Coordinator of Graduate Admissions, 417-836-5300, Fax: 417-836-6200, E-mail: michaeledwards@missouristate.edu. Website: http://education.missouristate.edu/clse/

**Monmouth University,** Graduate Studies, Department of Psychological Counseling, West Long Branch, NJ 07764-1898. Offers professional counseling (MS, PMC); psychological counseling (MA), including addiction studies, psychological counseling. *Accreditation:* ACA. *Program availability:* Part-time, evening/weekend. *Degree requirements:* For master's, comprehensive exam (for some programs), thesis optional, fieldwork. *Entrance requirements:* For master's, GRE, minimum GPA of 3.0 overall, 12 credits in psychology or closely-related field, two Monmouth University psychological counseling recommendation forms, narrative essay; for PMC, degree or current enrollment in CACREP-accredited master's program in counseling with minimum cumulative GPA of 3.0. Additional exam requirements/recommendations for international students: Required—TOEFL (minimum score 550 paper-based; 79 iBT), IELTS (minimum score 5), Michigan English Language Assessment Battery (minimum score 77) or Certificate of Advanced English (minimum score B2). Electronic applications accepted. *Faculty research:* Violent crime, single parenting, the African-American male, counseling older women, successful behavior for under-achieving youth.

**Montana State University Billings,** College of Allied Health Professions, Program in Clinical Rehabilitation and Mental Health Counseling, Billings, MT 59101. Offers MS.

*Accreditation:* CORE. *Program availability:* Part-time. *Faculty:* 4 full-time (2 women), 1 (woman) part-time/adjunct. *Students:* 33. *Degree requirements:* For master's, thesis or professional paper and/or field experience. *Entrance requirements:* For master's, GRE General Test or MAT, minimum GPA of 3.0, letters of recommendation, letter of intent. Additional exam requirements/recommendations for international students: Required—TOEFL (minimum score 79 iBT), IELTS (minimum score 6.5). *Application deadline:* For fall admission, 7/15 for international students; for spring admission, 12/1 for international students. Applications are processed on a rolling basis. Application fee: $40. Electronic applications accepted. *Expenses:* Tuition, state resident: full-time $5265; part-time $3436 per year. Tuition, nonresident: full-time $14,030; part-time $9280 per year. International tuition: $19,295 full-time. Tuition and fees vary according to degree level, campus/location and program. *Financial support:* Research assistantships with partial tuition reimbursements, teaching assistantships with partial tuition reimbursements, career-related internships or fieldwork, Federal Work-Study, institutionally sponsored loans, scholarships/grants, tuition waivers (partial), and unspecified assistantships available. Support available to part-time students. Financial award application deadline: 5/1; financial award applicants required to submit FAFSA. *Unit head:* Dr. Terry Blackwell, Chair, 406-896-5834, E-mail: tblackwell@msubillings.edu. *Application contact:* David M. Sullivan, Graduate Studies Counselor, 406-657-2053, Fax: 406-657-2299, E-mail: dsullivan@msubillings.edu.

**Moody Theological Seminary–Michigan,** Graduate Programs, Plymouth, MI 48170. Offers Bible (Graduate Certificate); Christian education (MA); counseling psychology (MA); divinity (M Div); theological studies (MA). *Program availability:* Part-time, evening/weekend. *Degree requirements:* For master's, one foreign language, thesis. *Faculty research:* Judaism, cults, world religions.

**Morehead State University,** Graduate Programs, College of Science and Technology, Department of Psychology, Morehead, KY 40351. Offers clinical/counseling psychology (MS); general/experimental psychology (MS). *Program availability:* Part-time, evening/weekend. *Degree requirements:* For master's, comprehensive exam, thesis optional. *Entrance requirements:* For master's, GRE General Test, 18 undergraduate hours in psychology, minimum GPA of 3.0, 3 letters of recommendation. Additional exam requirements/recommendations for international students: Required—TOEFL (minimum score 500 paper-based). Electronic applications accepted. *Faculty research:* Mood induction effects, serotonin receptor activity, stress, perceptual processes.

**Mount Mary University,** Graduate Programs, Program in Counseling, Milwaukee, WI 53222-4597. Offers clinical mental health counseling (MS, Certificate); clinical rehabilitation counseling (MS, Certificate); school counseling (MS, Certificate); vocational rehabilitation counseling (MS, Certificate). *Accreditation:* ACA. *Program availability:* Part-time, evening/weekend. *Faculty:* 6 full-time (all women), 12 part-time/adjunct (10 women). *Students:* 91 full-time (84 women), 17 part-time (14 women); includes 25 minority (12 Black or African American, non-Hispanic/Latino; 1 Asian, non-Hispanic/Latino; 8 Hispanic/Latino; 1 Native Hawaiian or other Pacific Islander, non-Hispanic/Latino; 3 Two or more races, non-Hispanic/Latino). Average age 31. 68 applicants, 59% accepted, 29 enrolled. In 2016, 42 master's, 1 other advanced degree awarded. *Degree requirements:* For master's, comprehensive exam, thesis or alternative. *Entrance requirements:* For master's, minimum GPA of 3.0. Additional exam requirements/recommendations for international students: Required—TOEFL (minimum score 550 paper-based; 80 iBT); Recommended—IELTS (minimum score 6.5). *Application deadline:* For fall admission, 5/1 for domestic and international students; for spring admission, 10/1 for domestic and international students; for summer admission, 4/15 for domestic and international students. Applications are processed on a rolling basis. Application fee: $45. Electronic applications accepted. *Expenses:* Contact institution. *Financial support:* Career-related internships or fieldwork, Federal Work-Study, and unspecified assistantships available. Support available to part-time students. Financial award application deadline: 5/1; financial award applicants required to submit FAFSA. *Faculty research:* Cognitive behavioral interventions for depression, eating disorders and compliance, trauma-informed care. *Unit head:* Dr. Carrie King, Graduate Program Director, 414-258-4810 Ext. 318, E-mail: kingc@mtmary.edu. *Application contact:* Kirk Heller de Messer, Director, Graduate Admissions, 414-930-3221, E-mail: hellerk@mtmary.edu.
Website: http://www.mtmary.edu/majors-programs/graduate/counseling/index.html

**Mount Saint Mary's University,** Graduate Division, Los Angeles, CA 90049. Offers business administration (MBA); counseling psychology (MS); creative writing (MFA); education (MS, Certificate); film and television (MFA); health policy and management (MS); humanities (MA); nursing (MSN, Certificate); physical therapy (DPT); religious studies (MA). *Program availability:* Part-time, evening/weekend. *Faculty:* 50 full-time (35 women), 116 part-time/adjunct (81 women). *Students:* 670 full-time (518 women), 147 part-time (116 women); includes 414 minority (73 Black or African American, non-Hispanic/Latino; 4 American Indian or Alaska Native, non-Hispanic/Latino; 60 Asian, non-Hispanic/Latino; 259 Hispanic/Latino; 7 Native Hawaiian or other Pacific Islander, non-Hispanic/Latino; 11 Two or more races, non-Hispanic/Latino), 4 international. Average age 32. 1,398 applicants, 21% accepted, 242 enrolled. In 2016, 170 master's, 28 doctorates, 35 other advanced degrees awarded. *Entrance requirements:* Additional exam requirements/recommendations for international students: Required—TOEFL. *Application deadline:* For fall admission, 6/30 priority date for domestic and international students; for spring admission, 10/30 priority date for domestic and international students; for summer admission, 3/30 priority date for domestic and international students. Applications are processed on a rolling basis. Application fee: $50. Electronic applications accepted. *Expenses: Tuition:* Full-time $9983; part-time $829 per unit. One-time fee: $135. Tuition and fees vary according to degree level and program. *Financial support:* Career-related internships or fieldwork, Federal Work-Study, institutionally sponsored loans, and tuition waivers (full and partial) available. Support available to part-time students. Financial award application deadline: 3/15; financial award applicants required to submit FAFSA. *Unit head:* Albert Ramos, Director of Graduate Admissions, 213-477-2800, E-mail: gradprograms@msmu.edu. *Application contact:* Shawn Peters, Graduate Admission Counselor, 213-477-2676, E-mail: gradprograms@msmu.edu.
Website: http://www.msmu.edu/graduate-programs/

**Naropa University,** Graduate Programs, Program in Clinical Mental Health Counseling, Boulder, CO 80302-6697. Offers contemplative psychotherapy and Buddhist psychology (MA); mindfulness-based transpersonal counseling (MA); somatic counseling: body psychotherapy (MA); somatic counseling: dance/movement therapy (MA); transpersonal art therapy (MA); transpersonal wilderness therapy (MA). *Program availability:* Online learning. *Faculty:* 17 full-time (10 women), 23 part-time/adjunct (17 women). *Students:* 285 full-time (223 women), 107 part-time (71 women); includes 73 minority (6 Black or African American, non-Hispanic/Latino; 4 American Indian or Alaska Native, non-Hispanic/Latino; 7 Asian, non-Hispanic/Latino; 36 Hispanic/Latino; 1 Native Hawaiian or other Pacific Islander, non-Hispanic/Latino; 19 Two or more races, non-Hispanic/Latino), 9 international. Average age 31. 302 applicants, 79% accepted, 153 enrolled. In 2016, 117 degrees awarded. *Degree requirements:* For master's, internships, counseling practicum, paper. *Entrance requirements:* For master's, interview, 2 letters of recommendation, professional resume, statement of interest essay, supplementary essay; minimum 100 hours of paid or volunteer work in a helping profession (for some

concentrations); wilderness experience (for some concentrations). Additional exam requirements/recommendations for international students: Required—TOEFL (minimum score 550 paper-based; 80 iBT). *Application deadline:* For fall admission, 1/15 priority date for domestic and international students. Applications are processed on a rolling basis. Application fee: $60. Electronic applications accepted. *Expenses:* $25,900 per year. *Financial support:* In 2016–17, 180 students received support, including 8 research assistantships with partial tuition reimbursements available (averaging $2,156 per year), 5 teaching assistantships with partial tuition reimbursements available (averaging $3,000 per year); career-related internships or fieldwork, Federal Work-Study, scholarships/grants, tuition waivers (partial), and unspecified assistantships also available. Support available to part-time students. Financial award application deadline: 3/1; financial award applicants required to submit FAFSA. *Unit head:* Dr. Deborah Bowman, Dean, Graduate School of Counseling and Psychology, 303-546-3559, E-mail: bowman@naropa.edu. *Application contact:* Office of Admissions, 303-546-3572, Fax: 303-546-3583, E-mail: admissions@naropa.edu.

**National University,** Academic Affairs, College of Letters and Sciences, La Jolla, CA 92037-1011. Offers biology (MS); counseling psychology (MA), including licensed professional clinical counseling; creative writing (MFA). *Program availability:* Part-time, evening/weekend, 100% online, blended/hybrid learning. *Faculty:* 68 full-time (33 women), 70 part-time/adjunct (34 women). *Students:* 566 full-time (408 women), 287 part-time (197 women); includes 394 minority (101 Black or African American, non-Hispanic/Latino; 3 American Indian or Alaska Native, non-Hispanic/Latino; 47 Asian, non-Hispanic/Latino; 185 Hispanic/Latino; 8 Native Hawaiian or other Pacific Islander, non-Hispanic/Latino; 50 Two or more races, non-Hispanic/Latino), 3 international. Average age 34. In 2016, 450 master's awarded. *Degree requirements:* For master's, thesis (for some programs). *Entrance requirements:* For master's, interview, minimum GPA of 2.5. Additional exam requirements/recommendations for international students: Required—TOEFL (minimum score 550 paper-based; 79 iBT), IELTS (minimum score 6). *Application deadline:* Applications are processed on a rolling basis. Application fee: $60 ($65 for international students). Electronic applications accepted. *Financial support:* Career-related internships or fieldwork, institutionally sponsored loans, scholarships/grants, and tuition waivers (partial) available. Support available to part-time students. Financial award application deadline: 6/30; financial award applicants required to submit FAFSA. *Unit head:* College of Letters and Sciences, 800-628-8648, E-mail: cols@nu.edu. *Application contact:* Brandon Jouganatos, Interim Vice President for Enrollment Services, 800-628-8648, E-mail: advisor@nu.edu.
Website: http://www.nu.edu/OurPrograms/CollegeOfLettersAndSciences.html

**New England College,** Program in Community Mental Health Counseling, Henniker, NH 03242-3293. Offers human services (MS); mental health counseling (MS). *Program availability:* Part-time, evening/weekend. *Degree requirements:* For master's, internship.

**New Mexico Highlands University,** Graduate Studies, College of Arts and Sciences, Department of Social and Behavioral Sciences, Las Vegas, NM 87701. Offers psychology (MS), including clinical psychology/counseling, general psychology; public affairs (MA), including applied sociology; Southwest studies (MA), including anthropology. *Program availability:* Part-time. *Degree requirements:* For master's, comprehensive exam, thesis or alternative. *Entrance requirements:* For master's, minimum undergraduate GPA of 3.0. Additional exam requirements/recommendations for international students: Required—TOEFL (minimum score 540 paper-based). *Faculty research:* Southwest Native American resettlement development, community-level interventions, neurochemistry of personality, comparative criminal justice, social theory and activism.

**New Mexico State University,** College of Education, Department of Counseling and Educational Psychology, Las Cruces, NM 88003. Offers counseling psychology (PhD); educational diagnostics (MA), including counseling and guidance, educational diagnostics; school psychology (Ed S). *Accreditation:* ACA; APA (one or more programs are accredited); NCATE. *Program availability:* Part-time. *Faculty:* 11 full-time (9 women), 4 part-time/adjunct (2 women). *Students:* 74 full-time (56 women), 12 part-time (9 women); includes 58 minority (2 Black or African American, non-Hispanic/Latino; 1 American Indian or Alaska Native, non-Hispanic/Latino; 6 Asian, non-Hispanic/Latino; 48 Hispanic/Latino; 1 Two or more races, non-Hispanic/Latino), 1 international. Average age 29. 115 applicants, 36% accepted, 26 enrolled. In 2016, 12 master's, 6 doctorates, 9 other advanced degrees awarded. *Degree requirements:* For master's, comprehensive exam, thesis optional, internship; for doctorate, comprehensive exam, thesis/dissertation, internship; for Ed S, comprehensive exam, thesis or alternative, internship. *Entrance requirements:* For master's, doctorate, and Ed S, GRE General Test, minimum GPA of 3.0. Additional exam requirements/recommendations for international students: Required—TOEFL (minimum score 550 paper-based; 79 iBT), IELTS (minimum score 6.5). *Application deadline:* For fall admission, 12/15 for domestic and international students; for spring admission, 2/1 priority date for domestic students, 2/1 for international students. Application fee: $40 ($50 for international students). Electronic applications accepted. *Expenses:* Tuition, state resident: full-time $4086. Tuition, nonresident: full-time $14,254. Required fees: $853. Tuition and fees vary according to course load. *Financial support:* In 2016–17, 69 students received support, including 6 fellowships (averaging $4,088 per year), 5 research assistantships (averaging $12,036 per year), 23 teaching assistantships (averaging $12,358 per year); career-related internships or fieldwork, Federal Work-Study, scholarships/grants, traineeships, health care benefits, and unspecified assistantships also available. Support available to part-time students. Financial award application deadline: 3/1. *Faculty research:* Multicultural counseling and training, school and counseling psychology, social justice, integrated primary care behavioral health training, mental health disparities. *Total annual research expenditures:* $122,042. *Unit head:* Dr. Gladys DeNecochea, Interim Department Head, 575-646-2121, Fax: 575-646-8035, E-mail: gdenecoc@nmsu.edu. *Application contact:* Norma Arrieta, Student Program Coordinator, 575-646-2121, Fax: 575-646-8035, E-mail: cep@nmsu.edu.
Website: http://cep.education.nmsu.edu

**New York University,** Steinhardt School of Culture, Education, and Human Development, Department of Applied Psychology, Programs in Counseling, New York, NY 10003. Offers counseling and guidance (MA, Advanced Certificate), including bilingual school counseling K-12 (MA), school counseling K-12 (MA); counseling for mental health and wellness (MA); counseling psychology (PhD); LGBT health, education, and social services (Advanced Certificate); Advanced Certificate/MPH; MA/Advanced Certificate. *Accreditation:* APA (one or more programs are accredited). *Program availability:* Part-time. *Degree requirements:* For master's, thesis (for some programs); for doctorate, thesis/dissertation. *Entrance requirements:* For doctorate, GRE General Test, interview. Additional exam requirements/recommendations for international students: Required—TOEFL (minimum score 100 iBT). Electronic applications accepted. *Faculty research:* Sexual and gender identities, group dynamics, psychopathy and personality, multicultural assessment, working people's lives.

**Niagara University,** Graduate Division of Education, Niagara University, NY 14109. Offers educational leadership (MS Ed, Certificate), including school building leader (MS Ed), school district business leader (Certificate), school district leader; literacy instruction (MS Ed); mental health counseling (MS, Certificate); school counseling (MS Ed, Certificate); school psychology (MS); teacher education (MS, MS Ed,

## Counseling Psychology

Certificate), including early childhood and childhood education (MS Ed, Certificate), early childhood special education (MS), middle and adolescence education (Certificate), special education (MS Ed), special education (grades 1-6) (Certificate), special education (grades 7-12) (Certificate), teaching English to speakers of other languages (TESOL) (Certificate). *Accreditation:* NCATE (one or more programs are accredited). *Program availability:* Part-time, evening/weekend. *Students:* 239 full-time (195 women), 302 part-time (234 women); includes 53 minority (26 Black or African American, non-Hispanic/Latino; 1 American Indian or Alaska Native, non-Hispanic/Latino; 3 Asian, non-Hispanic/Latino; 15 Hispanic/Latino; 8 Two or more races, non-Hispanic/Latino), 79 international. Average age 31. In 2016, 159 master's, 35 other advanced degrees awarded. *Entrance requirements:* For master's, GRE General Test or MAT. Additional exam requirements/recommendations for international students: Required—TOEFL (minimum score 550 paper-based; 79 iBT), IELTS (minimum score 6). *Application deadline:* For fall admission, 8/1 for domestic students. Applications are processed on a rolling basis. Application fee: $30. *Expenses:* Contact institution. *Financial support:* Research assistantships with tuition reimbursements, teaching assistantships with tuition reimbursements, career-related internships or fieldwork, Federal Work-Study, scholarships/grants, and unspecified assistantships available. Financial award application deadline: 4/15; financial award applicants required to submit FAFSA. *Faculty research:* Instructional supervision, appraisal and evaluation, career opportunities. *Unit head:* Dr. Chandra Foote, Dean, College of Education, 716-286-8549, Fax: 716-286-8561, E-mail: cjf@niagara.edu. *Application contact:* Evan Pierce, Associate Director for Graduate Recruitment, 716-286-8769, Fax: 716-286-8170, E-mail: epierce@niagara.edu.
Website: http://www.niagara.edu/advance/

**North Dakota State University,** College of Graduate and Interdisciplinary Studies, College of Human Development and Education, School of Education, Program in Counselor Education, Fargo, ND 58102. Offers clinical mental health counseling (M Ed, MS); counselor education and supervision (PhD); school counseling (M Ed, MS). *Accreditation:* ACA; NCATE. *Program availability:* Part-time, online learning. *Degree requirements:* For master's, comprehensive exam, thesis or alternative; for doctorate, comprehensive exam, thesis/dissertation. *Entrance requirements:* For master's, GRE, MAT, interview. Additional exam requirements/recommendations for international students: Required—TOEFL. *Faculty research:* Supervision, program assessment, multicultural issues.

**Northeastern State University,** College of Education, Department of Psychology and Counseling, Tahlequah, OK 74464-2399. Offers counseling psychology (MS); school counseling (M Ed); substance abuse counseling (MS). *Program availability:* Part-time, evening/weekend. *Faculty:* 16 full-time (7 women), 4 part-time/adjunct (3 women). *Students:* 80 full-time (61 women), 73 part-time (61 women); includes 66 minority (7 Black or African American, non-Hispanic/Latino; 23 American Indian or Alaska Native, non-Hispanic/Latino; 3 Asian, non-Hispanic/Latino; 5 Hispanic/Latino; 28 Two or more races, non-Hispanic/Latino), 1 international. Average age 32. In 2016, 43 master's awarded. *Degree requirements:* For master's, thesis (for some programs), written and oral examinations. *Entrance requirements:* For master's, GRE, minimum GPA of 2.5. Application fee: $25. *Expenses:* Tuition, state resident: full-time $2816; part-time $216.60 per credit hour. Tuition, nonresident: full-time $6365; part-time $489.60 per credit hour. *Required fees:* $37.40 per credit hour. *Financial support:* Teaching assistantships, career-related internships or fieldwork, and Federal Work-Study available. Financial award application deadline: 3/1. *Unit head:* Dr. Kenny Paris, Department Chair of Psychology and Counseling, 918-444-3021, E-mail: parisk@nsuok.edu. *Application contact:* Josh McCollum, Graduate Coordinator, 918-444-2093, E-mail: mccolluj@nsuok.edu.
Website: https://academics.nsuok.edu/education/EducationHome/COEDepartments/PsychologyCounseling.aspx

**Northeastern University,** Bouvé College of Health Sciences, Boston, MA 02115-5096. Offers applied behavior analysis (MS); audiology (Au D); counseling psychology (MS, PhD, CAGS); exercise science (MS); nursing (MS, PhD, CAGS), including administration (MS), adult-gerontology acute care nurse practitioner (MS, CAGS), adult-gerontology primary care nurse practitioner (MS, CAGS), anesthesia (MS), family nurse practitioner (MS, CAGS), neonatal nurse practitioner (MS, CAGS), pediatric nurse practitioner (MS, CAGS), psychiatric mental health nurse practitioner (MS, CAGS); nursing practice (DNP); pharmaceutical sciences (MS, PhD), including interdisciplinary concentration, pharmaceutics and drug delivery systems; pharmacology (MS); pharmacy (Pharm D); school psychology (PhD); urban health (MPH); MS/MBA. *Accreditation:* ACPE (one or more programs are accredited). *Program availability:* Part-time, evening/weekend, online learning. *Faculty:* 192 full-time (119 women), 194 part-time/adjunct (156 women). *Students:* 1,371 full-time (1,009 women), 262 part-time (219 women). In 2016, 352 master's, 312 doctorates, 25 other advanced degrees awarded. *Degree requirements:* For doctorate, thesis/dissertation (for some programs); for CAGS, comprehensive exam. Application fee: $75. Electronic applications accepted. *Expenses:* Contact institution. *Financial support:* Fellowships, research assistantships, teaching assistantships, career-related internships or fieldwork, scholarships/grants, health care benefits, tuition waivers, and unspecified assistantships available. Support available to part-time students. Financial award applicants required to submit FAFSA. *Unit head:* Susan L. Parish, Dean, Bouve College of Health Sciences, 617-373-3323, Fax: 617-373-3030. *Application contact:* E-mail: bouvegrad@northeastern.edu.
Website: http://www.northeastern.edu/bouve/

**Northern Arizona University,** Graduate College, College of Education, Department of Educational Psychology, Flagstaff, AZ 86011. Offers counseling (MA); educational psychology (PhD), including counseling psychology, school psychology; human relations (M Ed); school counseling (M Ed); school psychology (Ed S); student affairs (M Ed). *Program availability:* Part-time, online learning. Terminal master's awarded for partial completion of doctoral program. *Degree requirements:* For master's, internship (for some programs); for doctorate, comprehensive exam, thesis/dissertation, internship. *Entrance requirements:* Additional exam requirements/recommendations for international students: Required—TOEFL (minimum score 550 paper-based; 80 iBT), IELTS (minimum score 7). Electronic applications accepted. *Expenses:* Tuition, state resident: full-time $8971; part-time $444 per credit hour. Tuition, nonresident: full-time $20,958; part-time $1164 per credit hour. *Required fees:* $1018; $644 per credit hour. Tuition and fees vary according to course load, campus/location and program.

**Northern Kentucky University,** Office of Graduate Programs, College of Education and Human Services, Clinical Mental Health Counseling Program, Highland Heights, KY 41099. Offers MS. *Accreditation:* ACA. *Program availability:* Part-time, evening/weekend. *Degree requirements:* For master's, comprehensive exam. *Entrance requirements:* For master's, GRE or MAT. Additional exam requirements/recommendations for international students: Required—TOEFL (minimum score 550 paper-based; 79 iBT); Recommended—IELTS (minimum score 6.5). Electronic applications accepted. *Faculty research:* Preferences for college counseling, accreditation, partner violence prevention, data-based school counseling, creativity in counseling.

**Northern State University,** MS Ed Program in Counseling, Aberdeen, SD 57401-7198. Offers clinical mental health counseling (MS Ed); school counseling (MS Ed).

*Accreditation:* NCATE. *Program availability:* Part-time, online learning. *Degree requirements:* For master's, comprehensive exam, thesis optional. *Entrance requirements:* For master's, minimum GPA of 2.75. Additional exam requirements/recommendations for international students: Required—TOEFL (minimum score 550 paper-based; 78 iBT), IELTS (minimum score 6). Electronic applications accepted.

**Northwest Christian University,** School of Education and Counseling, Eugene, OR 97401-3745. Offers clinical mental health counseling (MA); elementary teaching (MAT); English for speakers of other languages (ESOL) (MAT); school counseling (MA); secondary teaching (MAT). *Program availability:* Part-time, evening/weekend, online learning. *Faculty:* 9 full-time (5 women), 21 part-time/adjunct (14 women). *Students:* 87 full-time (64 women), 52 part-time (40 women); includes 22 minority (5 Black or African American, non-Hispanic/Latino; 2 American Indian or Alaska Native, non-Hispanic/Latino; 2 Asian, non-Hispanic/Latino; 7 Hispanic/Latino; 2 Native Hawaiian or other Pacific Islander, non-Hispanic/Latino; 4 Two or more races, non-Hispanic/Latino). Average age 36. In 2016, 76 master's awarded. *Degree requirements:* For master's, thesis (for some programs). *Entrance requirements:* For master's, MAT, minimum undergraduate GPA of 3.0, interview, 2-3 page statement of purpose, two letters of recommendation, resume, background check. Additional exam requirements/recommendations for international students: Required—TOEFL (minimum score 550 paper-based; 80 iBT). *Application deadline:* Applications are processed on a rolling basis. Electronic applications accepted. *Expenses:* Contact institution. *Unit head:* Gene James, Dean of Counseling, 541-684-7261, Fax: 541-684-7310, E-mail: gjames@nwcu.edu. *Application contact:* Billy Dorsch, Admission Counselor for Graduate Studies, 541-684-7279, Fax: 541-349-5281, E-mail: wdorsch@nwcu.edu.

**Northwestern Oklahoma State University,** School of Professional Studies, Program in Counseling Psychology, Alva, OK 73717-2799. Offers MCP. *Program availability:* Part-time. *Degree requirements:* For master's, comprehensive exam. *Entrance requirements:* For master's, GRE General Test or MAT, minimum GPA of 2.75.

**Northwest University,** College of Social and Behavioral Sciences, Kirkland, WA 98033. Offers counseling psychology (MA, Psy D); international community development (MA). *Program availability:* Evening/weekend. *Entrance requirements:* For master's, 3 character references. Additional exam requirements/recommendations for international students: Required—TOEFL (minimum score 580 paper-based). *Expenses:* Contact institution.

**Nova Southeastern University,** College of Psychology, Fort Lauderdale, FL 33314-7796. Offers clinical psychology (PhD, Psy D); counseling (MS); experimental psychology (MS); forensic psychology (MS); general psychology (MS); mental health counseling (MS); school counseling (MS); school psychology (Psy D, Psy S). *Accreditation:* APA (one or more programs are accredited). *Program availability:* 100% online, blended/hybrid learning. *Faculty:* 51 full-time (21 women), 120 part-time/adjunct (70 women). *Students:* 724 full-time (596 women), 918 part-time (792 women); includes 797 minority (276 Black or African American, non-Hispanic/Latino; 1 American Indian or Alaska Native, non-Hispanic/Latino; 44 Asian, non-Hispanic/Latino; 427 Hispanic/Latino; 2 Native Hawaiian or other Pacific Islander, non-Hispanic/Latino; 47 Two or more races, non-Hispanic/Latino), 41 international. Average age 31. 1,349 applicants, 61% accepted, 651 enrolled. In 2016, 377 master's, 177 doctorates, 26 other advanced degrees awarded. Terminal master's awarded for partial completion of doctoral program. *Degree requirements:* For master's, comprehensive exam, 3 practica; for doctorate, thesis/dissertation, clinical internship, competency exam; for Psy S, comprehensive exam, internship. *Entrance requirements:* For doctorate, GRE General Test, GRE Subject Test (recommended), minimum undergraduate GPA of 3.0; for Psy S, GRE General Test. Additional exam requirements/recommendations for international students: Required—TOEFL (minimum score 550 paper-based). *Application deadline:* Applications are processed on a rolling basis. Application fee: $50. Electronic applications accepted. *Expenses:* Contact institution. *Financial support:* In 2016–17, 197 students received support, including 15 research assistantships (averaging $5,600 per year), 68 teaching assistantships (averaging $2,000 per year); career-related internships or fieldwork, Federal Work-Study, institutionally sponsored loans, scholarships/grants, and unspecified assistantships also available. Support available to part-time students. Financial award application deadline: 4/15; financial award applicants required to submit FAFSA. *Faculty research:* Clinical health psychology, multicultural/diversity psychology, clinical neuropsychology, clinical child psychology, family violence. *Unit head:* Dr. Karen Grosby, Dean, 954-262-5712, Fax: 954-262-3859, E-mail: grosby@nova.edu. *Application contact:* Carlos Perez, Senior Manager of Outreach, 954-262-5702, Fax: 954-262-3893, E-mail: gradschool@nova.edu.
Website: http://psychology.nova.edu/

**Nyack College,** Alliance Graduate School of Counseling, Nyack, NY 10960. Offers marriage and family therapy (MA); mental health counseling (MA). *Program availability:* Part-time, evening/weekend, 100% online. *Students:* 84 full-time (69 women), 123 part-time (103 women); includes 152 minority (64 Black or African American, non-Hispanic/Latino; 44 Asian, non-Hispanic/Latino; 41 Hispanic/Latino; 3 Two or more races, non-Hispanic/Latino), 9 international. Average age 37. In 2016, 70 master's awarded. *Degree requirements:* For master's, comprehensive exam, counselor-in-training therapy, internship, CPCE exam. *Entrance requirements:* For master's, Millon Clinical Multiaxial Inventory-3, Minnesota Multiphasic Personality Inventory-2, transcripts, statement of Christian life and experience, statement of support systems. Additional exam requirements/recommendations for international students: Required—TOEFL (minimum score 550 paper-based; 80 iBT). *Application deadline:* For fall admission, 8/1 for domestic students, 2/15 for international students; for spring admission, 12/15 for domestic students, 7/15 for international students. Applications are processed on a rolling basis. Application fee: $30. Electronic applications accepted. *Expenses:* $775 per credit. *Financial support:* Career-related internships or fieldwork and scholarships/grants available. Financial award applicants required to submit FAFSA. *Unit head:* Dr. Carol Robles, Associate Dean, 845-770-5735. *Application contact:* Esther Guzman, Admissions Associate, 800-541-6891, E-mail: admissions.grad@nyack.edu.
Website: http://www.nyack.edu/agsc

**Oakland University,** Graduate Study and Lifelong Learning, School of Education and Human Services, Department of Counseling, Rochester, MI 48309-4401. Offers MA, PhD, Certificate. *Accreditation:* ACA (one or more programs are accredited). *Program availability:* Part-time, evening/weekend. *Degree requirements:* For doctorate, thesis/dissertation. *Entrance requirements:* Additional exam requirements/recommendations for international students: Required—TOEFL (minimum score 550 paper-based). Electronic applications accepted.

**Old Dominion University,** Darden College of Education, Counseling Program, Norfolk, VA 23529. Offers clinical mental health counseling (MS Ed); college counseling (MS Ed); counseling (Ed S); counselor education (PhD); school counseling (MS Ed). *Accreditation:* ACA. *Program availability:* Part-time, evening/weekend. *Faculty:* 14 full-time (7 women), 9 part-time/adjunct (7 women). *Students:* 125 full-time (107 women), 58 part-time (43 women); includes 74 minority (44 Black or African American, non-Hispanic/Latino; 1 American Indian or Alaska Native, non-Hispanic/Latino; 5 Asian, non-Hispanic/Latino; 18 Hispanic/Latino; 6 Two or more races, non-Hispanic/Latino), 8 international. Average age 31. 195 applicants, 57% accepted, 79 enrolled. In 2016, 53 master's, 9

doctorates, 3 other advanced degrees awarded. *Degree requirements:* For master's and Ed S, comprehensive exam; for doctorate, comprehensive exam, thesis/dissertation. *Entrance requirements:* For master's and Ed S, GRE General Test, resume, essay, transcripts, recommendations; for doctorate, GRE General Test, resume, interview, essay, transcripts, recommendations. Additional exam requirements/recommendations for international students: Required—TOEFL. *Application deadline:* For fall admission, 3/1 for domestic and international students; for winter admission, 1/10 for domestic students; for spring admission, 10/1 for domestic and international students; for summer admission, 3/1 for domestic students, 2/1 for international students. Application fee: $50. Electronic applications accepted. *Expenses:* Tuition, state resident: full-time $8604; part-time $478 per credit hour. Tuition, nonresident: full-time $21,510; part-time $1195 per credit hour. *Required fees:* $66 per semester. Tuition and fees vary according to campus/location, program and reciprocity agreements. *Financial support:* In 2016–17, 20 students received support, including 2 fellowships with full tuition reimbursements available (averaging $15,000 per year), 13 research assistantships (averaging $9,000 per year), 20 teaching assistantships with full tuition reimbursements available (averaging $20,000 per year); career-related internships or fieldwork, Federal Work-Study, institutionally sponsored loans, scholarships/grants, tuition waivers (partial), and unspecified assistantships also available. Support available to part-time students. Financial award application deadline: 10/1; financial award applicants required to submit FAFSA. *Faculty research:* Group counseling, counselor education, career counseling, spirituality and counseling, school counseling, LGBT counseling, legal and ethical issues. *Total annual research expenditures:* $75,000. *Unit head:* Dr. Jeff Moe, Graduate Program Director, 757-683-6235, Fax: 757-683-5756, E-mail: jmoe@odu.edu. *Application contact:* Jeff Moe, Graduate Program Director, 757-683-6235, Fax: 757-683-5756, E-mail: jmoe@odu.edu.
Website: http://www.odu.edu/chs

**Ottawa University,** Graduate Studies-Arizona, Program in Professional Counseling, Ottawa, KS 66067-3399. Offers Christian counseling (MA); expressive arts therapy (MA); marriage and family therapy (MA); treatment of trauma, abuse and deprivation (MA). Programs offered in Mesa, Phoenix, Tempe and West Valley, AZ. *Program availability:* Part-time, evening/weekend, online learning. *Degree requirements:* For master's, comprehensive exam, thesis or alternative, field experience, practicum. *Entrance requirements:* For master's, minimum undergraduate GPA of 3.0; course work in theories of personality, abnormal psychology, and human growth and development. Additional exam requirements/recommendations for international students: Required—TOEFL (minimum score 550 paper-based).

**Our Lady of the Lake University,** School of Professional Studies, Program in Counseling Psychology, San Antonio, TX 78207-4689. Offers Psy D. *Faculty:* 9 full-time (7 women), 10 part-time/adjunct (6 women). *Students:* 34 full-time (33 women), 3 part-time (2 women); includes 24 minority (5 Black or African American, non-Hispanic/Latino; 19 Hispanic/Latino). Average age 31. 29 applicants, 24% accepted, 7 enrolled. In 2016, 9 doctorates awarded. *Degree requirements:* For doctorate, comprehensive exam, thesis/dissertation, internship, 3-years of residency in San Antonio. *Entrance requirements:* For doctorate, GRE General Test, GRE Subject Test (psychology), master's degree in psychology or closely-related discipline of at least 45 hours from regionally-accredited institution; minimum cumulative GPA of 3.5 in the master's program; criminal background check; 3 letters of recommendation; pertinent professional experience; personal statement. Additional exam requirements/recommendations for international students: Required—TOEFL. *Application deadline:* For fall admission, 1/15 for domestic and international students. Application fee: $40 ($50 for international students). Electronic applications accepted. Application fee is waived when completed online. *Expenses:* Contact institution. *Financial support:* In 2016–17, 8 students received support. Federal Work-Study, scholarships/grants, unspecified assistantships, and tuition discounts available. Support available to part-time students. Financial award application deadline: 5/1; financial award applicants required to submit FAFSA. *Faculty research:* Providing competent services to diverse client populations. *Unit head:* Psychology Department, 210-431-3914. *Application contact:* Office of Graduate Admissions, 210-431-3995, Fax: 210-431-3945, E-mail: gradadm@lake.ollusa.edu.
Website: http://www.ollusa.edu/s/1190/hybrid/default-hybrid-ollu.aspx?sid-1190&gid-1&pgid-7957

**Pace University,** Dyson College of Arts and Sciences, Department of Psychology, Program in Mental Health Counseling, New York, NY 10038. Offers grief and loss (MS); mental health counseling (MS, PhD); substance abuse (MS). Program offered at Pleasantville, NY location only. *Program availability:* Part-time, evening/weekend. *Students:* 75 full-time (58 women), 66 part-time (60 women); includes 62 minority (17 Black or African American, non-Hispanic/Latino; 1 American Indian or Alaska Native, non-Hispanic/Latino; 10 Asian, non-Hispanic/Latino; 28 Hispanic/Latino; 6 Two or more races, non-Hispanic/Latino), 4 international. Average age 30. In 2016, 47 master's awarded. Terminal master's awarded for partial completion of doctoral program. *Degree requirements:* For master's, comprehensive exam, qualifying exams, internship; for doctorate, comprehensive exam, thesis/dissertation, internships. *Entrance requirements:* For master's, GRE, resume, personal statement, two letters of reference, official transcripts, interview; for doctorate, three letters of recommendation (two of which are academic in nature); personal statement; official transcripts; internship(s); interview; master's degree in mental health counseling or program with curriculum equivalent to that of Pace's graduate program in mental health counseling. Additional exam requirements/recommendations for international students: Required—TOEFL (minimum score 88 iBT), IELTS (minimum score 7) or PTE (minimum score 60). *Application deadline:* For fall admission, 8/1 priority date for domestic students, 6/1 for international students; for spring admission, 12/1 priority date for domestic students, 10/1 for international students. Applications are processed on a rolling basis. Application fee: $70. Electronic applications accepted. *Expenses:* Tuition: Part-time $1195 per credit. *Required fees:* $260 per semester. Tuition and fees vary according to degree level, campus/location and program. *Financial support:* Research assistantships, teaching assistantships, career-related internships or fieldwork, Federal Work-Study, and tuition waivers (partial) available. Financial award application deadline: 2/15; financial award applicants required to submit FAFSA. *Unit head:* Dr. Ross Robak, Psychology Department Chair/Director, Graduate Program in Counseling, 914-773-3786, E-mail: rrobak@pace.edu. *Application contact:* Susan Ford-Goldschein, Director of Graduate Admissions, 914-422-4283, Fax: 212-346-1585, E-mail: graduateadmission@pace.edu.
Website: http://www.pace.edu/academics/graduate-students/degrees/mental-health-counseling-ms

**Pacifica Graduate Institute,** Graduate Programs, Carpinteria, CA 93013. Offers clinical psychology (PhD); counseling psychology (MA); depth psychology (MA, PhD); mythological studies (MA, PhD). Terminal master's awarded for partial completion of doctoral program. *Degree requirements:* For master's, thesis (for some programs), practicum; for doctorate, comprehensive exam, thesis/dissertation, internship. *Entrance requirements:* For master's, resume, 3 letters of recommendation, writing sample, interview; for doctorate, resumé, 4 letters of recommendation, writing sample, interview. Additional exam requirements/recommendations for international students: Required—

TOEFL. *Faculty research:* Imaginal and archetypal theory; post-Colonial psychoanalytic and Jungian theory; myth literature as it applies to the theory and practice of psychology.

**Palm Beach Atlantic University,** School of Education and Behavioral Studies, West Palm Beach, FL 33416-4708. Offers counseling psychology (MS), including addictions/mental health, general counseling, marriage and family therapy, mental health counseling, school guidance counseling. *Program availability:* Part-time, evening/weekend. *Faculty:* 8 full-time (2 women), 17 part-time/adjunct (13 women). *Students:* 243 full-time (206 women), 29 part-time (24 women); includes 147 minority (67 Black or African American, non-Hispanic/Latino; 4 Asian, non-Hispanic/Latino; 60 Hispanic/Latino; 1 Native Hawaiian or other Pacific Islander, non-Hispanic/Latino; 15 Two or more races, non-Hispanic/Latino), 6 international. Average age 35. 81 applicants, 89% accepted, 53 enrolled. In 2016, 122 master's awarded. *Entrance requirements:* For master's, GRE or MAT, minimum GPA of 3.0; essay. Additional exam requirements/recommendations for international students: Required—TOEFL (minimum score 550 paper-based; 79 iBT). *Application deadline:* Applications are processed on a rolling basis. Application fee: $50. Electronic applications accepted. *Expenses: Tuition:* Full-time $6600; part-time $550 per credit hour. Full-time tuition and fees vary according to degree level, campus/location and program. *Financial support:* In 2016–17, 11 students received support. Career-related internships or fieldwork, scholarships/grants, and employee education grants available. Financial award application deadline: 5/1; financial award applicants required to submit FAFSA. *Faculty research:* Group dynamics, phenomenology, spirituality, multicultural psychology. *Unit head:* Dr. Gene Sale, Program Director, 561-803-2352. *Application contact:* Graduate Admissions, 888-468-6722, E-mail: grad@pba.edu.
Website: http://www.pba.edu/graduate-counseling-program

**Palo Alto University,** MA in Counseling Program, Palo Alto, CA 94304. Offers clinical mental health (MA); marriage, family and child (MA). *Program availability:* Part-time, 100% online, blended/hybrid learning. *Faculty:* 6 full-time (4 women), 5 part-time/adjunct (4 women). *Students:* 38 full-time (34 women), 28 part-time (22 women); includes 29 minority (3 Black or African American, non-Hispanic/Latino; 9 Asian, non-Hispanic/Latino; 14 Hispanic/Latino; 3 Two or more races, non-Hispanic/Latino), 1 international. Average age 32. 111 applicants, 91% accepted, 89 enrolled. In 2016, 91 master's awarded. *Degree requirements:* For master's, capstone project. *Entrance requirements:* For master's, undergraduate degree in psychology with minimum GPA of 3.3. Additional exam requirements/recommendations for international students: Required—TOEFL. *Application deadline:* For fall admission, 6/30 priority date for domestic and international students; for spring admission, 3/21 for domestic and international students. Applications are processed on a rolling basis. Application fee: $40. Electronic applications accepted. *Expenses:* Contact institution. *Financial support:* In 2016–17, 12 students received support. Federal Work-Study and scholarships/grants available. Financial award application deadline: 1/15; financial award applicants required to submit FAFSA. *Unit head:* Dr. William Snow, Director of Counseling, 831-246-2440, E-mail: wsnow@paloaltou.edu. *Application contact:* Deanna Berger, Assistant Director of Admissions, 650-417-2023, E-mail: dberger@paloaltou.edu.
Website: http://www.paloaltou.edu/graduate-programs/masters-programs/ma-counseling

**Philadelphia College of Osteopathic Medicine,** Graduate and Professional Programs, Department of Psychology, Philadelphia, PA 19131-1694. Offers applied behavior analysis (Certificate); clinical health psychology (Post-Doctoral Certificate); clinical neuropsychology (Post-Doctoral Certificate); clinical psychology (Psy D); mental health counseling (MS); organizational development and leadership (MS); psychology (Certificate); school psychology (MS, Psy D, Ed S). *Accreditation:* APA. *Faculty:* 19 full-time (11 women), 122 part-time/adjunct (58 women). *Students:* 364 (285 women); includes 78 minority (62 Black or African American, non-Hispanic/Latino; 2 American Indian or Alaska Native, non-Hispanic/Latino; 9 Asian, non-Hispanic/Latino; 5 Hispanic/Latino), 2 international. 366 applicants, 51% accepted, 139 enrolled. In 2016, 72 master's, 42 doctorates, 17 other advanced degrees awarded. Terminal master's awarded for partial completion of doctoral program. *Degree requirements:* For master's, comprehensive exam (for some programs), thesis (for some programs); for doctorate, comprehensive exam, thesis/dissertation. *Entrance requirements:* For master's, GRE or MAT, minimum GPA of 3.0; bachelor's degree from regionally-accredited college or university; for doctorate, PRAXIS II (for Psy D in school psychology), minimum undergraduate GPA of 3.0; for other advanced degree, GRE (for Ed S). Additional exam requirements/recommendations for international students: Required—TOEFL (minimum score 79 iBT). *Application deadline:* Applications are processed on a rolling basis. Application fee: $50. Electronic applications accepted. Tuition and fees vary according to course load, degree level and program. *Financial support:* In 2016–17, 28 teaching assistantships were awarded; Federal Work-Study, institutionally sponsored loans, and scholarships/grants also available. Financial award application deadline: 3/15; financial award applicants required to submit FAFSA. *Faculty research:* Adult and childhood anxiety and ADHD; coping with chronic illness; primary care psychology/integrated health care; applied behavior analysis; psychological, educational, and neuropsychological assessment. *Total annual research expenditures:* $533,489. *Unit head:* Dr. Robert DiTomasso, Chairman, 215-871-6442, Fax: 215-871-6458, E-mail: robertd@pcom.edu. *Application contact:* Johnathan Cox, Associate Director of Admissions, 215-871-6700, Fax: 215-871-6719, E-mail: karis@pcom.edu.
**See Display on page 1004 and Close-Up on page 1227.**

**Phoenix Seminary,** Graduate Programs, Phoenix, AZ 85018. Offers Biblical and theological studies (Graduate Diploma); Biblical communication (M Div); Biblical leadership (MA); Christian counseling (Graduate Diploma); counseling and family (M Div); leadership development (M Div); ministry (D Min); professional counseling (MA). *Accreditation:* ATS (one or more programs are accredited). *Program availability:* Part-time, evening/weekend. *Degree requirements:* For master's, 2 foreign languages, comprehensive exam; for doctorate, 2 foreign languages, thesis/dissertation. *Entrance requirements:* For master's, undergraduate degree with minimum GPA of 2.5; for doctorate, M Div (94 hours) with minimum GPA of 3.0. Additional exam requirements/recommendations for international students: Required—TOEFL (minimum score 587 paper-based; 92 iBT), TWE (minimum score 4.5).

**Prescott College,** Graduate Programs, Program in Counseling and Psychology, Prescott, AZ 86301. Offers adventure-based psychotherapy (MA); counseling psychology (MA); ecopsychology (MA); ecotherapy (MA); equine-assisted mental health (MA); expressive arts therapy (MA); somatic psychology (MA); student-directed independent study (MA). *Program availability:* Part-time, online learning. *Faculty:* 4 full-time (2 women), 9 part-time/adjunct (6 women). *Students:* 45 full-time (41 women), 139 part-time (113 women); includes 26 minority (1 Black or African American, non-Hispanic/Latino; 4 American Indian or Alaska Native, non-Hispanic/Latino; 2 Asian, non-Hispanic/Latino; 7 Hispanic/Latino; 1 Native Hawaiian or other Pacific Islander, non-Hispanic/Latino; 11 Two or more races, non-Hispanic/Latino), 7 international. Average age 38. 129 applicants, 84% accepted, 69 enrolled. In 2016, 24 master's awarded. Terminal master's awarded for partial completion of doctoral program. *Degree requirements:* For master's, thesis, fieldwork or internship, practicum. *Entrance requirements:* For master's, 2 letters of recommendation, resume. Additional exam requirements/recommendations for international students: Required—TOEFL (minimum score 500

## Counseling Psychology

paper-based). *Application deadline:* For fall admission, 4/15 priority date for domestic and international students; for spring admission, 9/15 priority date for domestic and international students. Applications are processed on a rolling basis. Application fee: $40. Electronic applications accepted. *Expenses: Tuition:* Full-time $19,680. One-time fee: $260 part-time. *Financial support:* Fellowships, research assistantships, teaching assistantships, career-related internships or fieldwork, Federal Work-Study, institutionally sponsored loans, scholarships/grants, traineeships, health care benefits, tuition waivers, and unspecified assistantships available. Support available to part-time students. Financial award applicants required to submit FAFSA. *Unit head:* Dr. Stacey Carillo, Department Chair for Counseling, E-mail: stacey.carillo@prescott.edu. *Application contact:* Robert Monk, Graduate Admissions Counselor, 928-350-2109, E-mail: robert.monk@prescott.edu.

**Providence University College & Theological Seminary,** Theological Seminary, Otterburne, MB R0A 1G0, Canada. Offers children's ministry (Certificate); Christian studies (MA, Certificate); counseling (MA); cross-cultural discipleship (Certificate); divinity (M Div); educational studies (MA), including counseling psychology, educational ministries, student development, teaching English to speakers of other languages, training teachers of English to speakers of other languages; global studies (MA); lay counseling (Diploma); ministry (D Min); teaching English to speakers of other languages (Certificate); theological studies (MA); training teacher of English to speakers of other languages (Certificate); youth ministry (Certificate). *Accreditation:* ATS. *Program availability:* Part-time. *Degree requirements:* For master's, variable foreign language requirement, thesis (for some programs); for doctorate, thesis/dissertation. *Entrance requirements:* Additional exam requirements/recommendations for international students: Recommended—TOEFL (minimum score 550 paper-based). *Faculty research:* Studies in Isaiah, theology of sin.

**Purdue University Northwest,** Graduate Studies Office, School of Education, Program in Counseling, Hammond, IN 46323-2094. Offers human services (MS Ed); mental health counseling (MS Ed); school counseling (MS Ed). *Accreditation:* ACA. *Entrance requirements:* Additional exam requirements/recommendations for international students: Required—TOEFL.

**Queens College of the City University of New York,** Division of Education, Department of Educational and Community Programs, Queens, NY 11367-1597. Offers bilingual pupil personnel (AC); counselor education (MS Ed); mental health counseling (MS); school building leader (AC); school district leader (AC); school psychologist (MS Ed); special education-childhood education (AC); special education-early childhood (MS Ed); teacher of special education 1-6 (MS Ed); teacher of special education birth-2 (MS Ed); teaching students with disabilities, grades 7-12 (MS Ed, AC). *Program availability:* Part-time. *Faculty:* 20 full-time (14 women), 50 part-time/adjunct (26 women). *Students:* 101 full-time (85 women), 459 part-time (383 women); includes 230 minority (44 Black or African American, non-Hispanic/Latino; 3 American Indian or Alaska Native, non-Hispanic/Latino; 46 Asian, non-Hispanic/Latino; 128 Hispanic/Latino; 1 Native Hawaiian or other Pacific Islander, non-Hispanic/Latino; 8 Two or more races, non-Hispanic/Latino), 3 international. Average age 28. 515 applicants, 57% accepted, 230 enrolled. In 2016, 158 master's, 68 other advanced degrees awarded. *Degree requirements:* For master's, research project; for AC, internship. *Entrance requirements:* For master's, minimum GPA of 3.0. Additional exam requirements/recommendations for international students: Required—TOEFL, IELTS. *Application deadline:* For fall admission, 3/1 for domestic students. Applications are processed on a rolling basis. Application fee: $125. Electronic applications accepted. *Expenses:* Tuition, state resident: full-time $5065; part-time $425 per credit. Tuition, nonresident: part-time $780 per credit. *Required fees:* $522; $397 per credit. Part-time tuition and fees vary according to course load and program. *Financial support:* Career-related internships or fieldwork available. Financial award application deadline: 4/1; financial award applicants required to submit FAFSA. *Unit head:* Dr. Lynn Howell, Chairperson, 718-997-5250, E-mail: lynn.howell@qc.cuny.edu.

**Radford University,** College of Graduate Studies and Research, Program in Counseling Psychology, Radford, VA 24142. Offers Psy D. *Faculty:* 23 full-time (16 women). *Students:* 15 full-time (9 women), 4 part-time (all women); includes 3 minority (1 Black or African American, non-Hispanic/Latino; 1 Asian, non-Hispanic/Latino; 1 Two or more races, non-Hispanic/Latino). Average age 27. 13 applicants, 38% accepted, 5 enrolled. In 2016, 5 doctorates awarded. *Degree requirements:* For doctorate, comprehensive exam, thesis/dissertation. *Entrance requirements:* For doctorate, GRE General Test, master's degree; minimum graduate GPA of 3.5; letter of interest describing professional and/or research experience; curriculum vitae/resume; essay on cultural background and experiences; 3 letters of recommendation; official transcripts. Additional exam requirements/recommendations for international students: Required—TOEFL (minimum score 550 paper-based; 79 iBT), IELTS (minimum score 6.5). *Application deadline:* For fall admission, 12/15 priority date for domestic students, 12/1 for international students. Applications are processed on a rolling basis. Application fee: $50. Electronic applications accepted. *Expenses:* Tuition, state resident: full-time $7868; part-time $328 per credit hour. Tuition, nonresident: full-time $16,394; part-time $683 per credit hour. *Required fees:* $3090; $130 per credit hour. Tuition and fees vary according to course load and program. *Financial support:* In 2016–17, 15 students received support, including 2 research assistantships (averaging $13,800 per year), 5 teaching assistantships (averaging $13,800 per year); career-related internships or fieldwork, scholarships/grants, and unspecified assistantships also available. Support available to part-time students. Financial award application deadline: 3/1; financial award applicants required to submit FAFSA. *Faculty research:* Human sexuality and conflict in close relationships, rural mental health and psychology practice, self-compassion and body image, effectiveness of multicultural training, treatments for post-traumatic stress disorder. *Unit head:* Dr. Valerie Leake, Program Director, 540-831-5361, Fax: 540-831-6113, E-mail: vleake@radford.edu.
Website: http://www.radford.edu/content/chbs/home/psychology/programs/counseling.html

**Regent University,** Graduate School, School of Psychology and Counseling, Virginia Beach, VA 23464-9800. Offers clinical mental health counseling (MA); clinical psychology (Psy D); counseling and psychological studies (PhD); counseling studies (CAGS); counselor education and supervision (PhD); general psychology (MS); marriage, couple, and family counseling (MA); pastoral counseling (MA); school counseling (MA); M Div/MA; M Ed/MA; MBA/MA. *Accreditation:* ACA; APA (one or more programs are accredited). *Program availability:* Part-time, evening/weekend, 100% online, blended/hybrid learning. *Faculty:* 28 full-time (17 women), 45 part-time/adjunct (26 women). *Students:* 295 full-time (240 women), 331 part-time (252 women); includes 244 minority (186 Black or African American, non-Hispanic/Latino; 4 American Indian or Alaska Native, non-Hispanic/Latino; 11 Asian, non-Hispanic/Latino; 29 Hispanic/Latino; 14 Two or more races, non-Hispanic/Latino), 10 international. Average age 36. 1,192 applicants, 29% accepted, 235 enrolled. In 2016, 156 master's, 41 doctorates, 1 other advanced degree awarded. *Degree requirements:* For master's, thesis or alternative, internship, practicum, written competency exam; for doctorate, thesis/dissertation or alternative. *Entrance requirements:* For master's, GRE General Test (including writing exam) or MAT, minimum undergraduate GPA of 3.0, resume, transcripts, writing sample, personal goals statement; for doctorate, GRE General Test (including writing exam), minimum undergraduate GPA of 3.0, graduate 3.5; writing sample; 3 recommendations; resume; college transcripts; personal goals statement. Additional exam requirements/recommendations for international students: Required—TOEFL (minimum score 577 paper-based). *Application deadline:* For fall admission, 4/1 priority date for domestic students; for spring admission, 11/1 priority date for domestic students. Applications are processed on a rolling basis. Application fee: $50. Electronic applications accepted. *Expenses:* Contact institution. *Financial support:* In 2016–17, 446 students received support, including 5 fellowships (averaging $4,000 per year), 10 research assistantships (averaging $3,200 per year); career-related internships or fieldwork, scholarships/grants, and unspecified assistantships also available. Support available to part-time students. *Faculty research:* Marriage enrichment, clinical psychology, troubled youth, faith and learning, trauma. *Unit head:* Dr. William Hathaway, Dean, 757-352-4294, Fax: 757-352-4282, E-mail: willhat@regent.edu. *Application contact:* Heidi Cece, Assistant Vice President of Enrollment Management, 800-373-5504, Fax: 757-352-4381, E-mail: admissions@regent.edu.
Website: http://www.regent.edu/spc/

**Regis College,** School of Nursing and Health Sciences, Weston, MA 02493. Offers applied behavior analysis (MS); counseling psychology (MA); health administration (MS); nurse practitioner (Certificate); nursing (MS, DNP); nursing education (Certificate); occupational therapy (MS). *Accreditation:* ACEN. *Program availability:* Part-time, evening/weekend, 100% online, blended/hybrid learning. *Degree requirements:* For doctorate, thesis/dissertation. *Entrance requirements:* For master's, GRE General Test or MAT, minimum GPA of 3.0; for doctorate, MAT or GRE if GPA from master's lower than 3.5. Additional exam requirements/recommendations for international students: Required—TOEFL; Recommended—IELTS. *Application deadline:* Applications are processed on a rolling basis. Application fee: $75. Electronic applications accepted. *Financial support:* Federal Work-Study, scholarships/grants, traineeships, and unspecified assistantships available. Support available to part-time students. Financial award applicants required to submit FAFSA. *Faculty research:* Health policy, education, aging, job satisfaction, psychiatric nursing, critical thinking. *Application contact:* Catherine Hamilton, Senior Assistant Director, Graduate Admission, 781-768-7101, E-mail: catherine.hamilton@regiscollege.edu.

**Rhode Island College,** School of Graduate Studies, Feinstein School of Education and Human Development, Department of Counseling, Educational Leadership, and School Psychology, Providence, RI 02908-1991. Offers advanced counseling (CGS); agency counseling (MA); clinical mental health counseling (MS); co-occurring disorders (MA, CGS); educational leadership (M Ed); mental health counseling (CAGS); school counseling (MA); school psychology (CAGS); teacher leadership (CGS). *Accreditation:* ACA; NCATE. *Program availability:* Part-time, evening/weekend. *Faculty:* 9 full-time (5 women), 10 part-time/adjunct (all women). *Students:* 34 full-time (28 women), 83 part-time (72 women); includes 16 minority (5 Black or African American, non-Hispanic/Latino; 1 Asian, non-Hispanic/Latino; 10 Hispanic/Latino). Average age 33. In 2016, 50 master's, 34 other advanced degrees awarded. *Degree requirements:* For master's and other advanced degree, comprehensive exam (for some programs), thesis (for some programs). *Entrance requirements:* For master's, GRE General Test or MAT, undergraduate transcripts; minimum undergraduate GPA of 3.0; for other advanced degree, GRE or MAT (for most programs), undergraduate transcripts; minimum undergraduate GPA of 3.0; 3 letters of recommendation; current resume. Additional exam requirements/recommendations for international students: Recommended—TOEFL (minimum score 550 paper-based; 79 iBT). *Application deadline:* For fall admission, 3/1 for domestic students; for spring admission, 11/1 for domestic students. Applications are processed on a rolling basis. Application fee: $50. Electronic applications accepted. *Expenses:* Tuition, state resident: full-time $8928; part-time $372 per credit. Tuition, nonresident: full-time $17,376; part-time $724 per credit. *Required fees:* $604; $22 per credit. One-time fee: $74. *Financial support:* In 2016–17, 3 teaching assistantships with full tuition reimbursements (averaging $2,500 per year) were awarded; career-related internships or fieldwork, Federal Work-Study, scholarships/grants, health care benefits, and unspecified assistantships also available. Support available to part-time students. Financial award application deadline: 5/15; financial award applicants required to submit FAFSA. *Unit head:* Dr. Andrew Snyder, Chair, 401-456-9633. *Application contact:* Graduate Studies, 401-456-8700.
Website: http://www.ric.edu/counselingEducationalLeadershipSchoolPsychology/index.php

**Rivier University,** School of Graduate Studies, Department of Education, Nashua, NH 03060. Offers curriculum and instruction (M Ed); early childhood education (M Ed); educational administration (M Ed); educational studies (M Ed); elementary education (M Ed); elementary education and general special education (M Ed); emotional and behavioral disorders (M Ed); general social education (M Ed); leadership and learning (Ed D, CAGS); learning disabilities (M Ed); learning disabilities and reading (M Ed); mental health counseling (MA); reading (M Ed); school counseling (M Ed). *Program availability:* Part-time, evening/weekend. *Degree requirements:* For master's, comprehensive exam (for some programs), internships. *Entrance requirements:* For master's, GRE General Test or MAT.

**Robert Morris University,** School of Education and Social Sciences, Moon Township, PA 15108-1189. Offers business education (MS); counseling psychology (MS); education (Postbaccalaureate Certificate); higher education (MS); instructional leadership (MS), including education; instructional management and leadership (PhD); literacy (MS); special education (MS). *Accreditation:* TEAC. *Program availability:* Part-time, evening/weekend, online learning. *Faculty:* 17 full-time (9 women), 4 part-time/adjunct (3 women). *Students:* 154 part-time (104 women); includes 18 minority (11 Black or African American, non-Hispanic/Latino; 2 Hispanic/Latino; 5 Two or more races, non-Hispanic/Latino), 1 international. Average age 26. 69 applicants, 26% accepted, 18 enrolled. In 2016, 40 master's, 15 doctorates awarded. *Degree requirements:* For doctorate, thesis/dissertation. *Entrance requirements:* Additional exam requirements/recommendations for international students: Required—TOEFL (minimum score 550 paper-based; 79 iBT). *Application deadline:* For fall admission, 7/1 priority date for domestic and international students; for spring admission, 11/1 priority date for domestic and international students. Applications are processed on a rolling basis. Application fee: $35. Electronic applications accepted. *Expenses:* $840 per credit (for master's degree). *Unit head:* Dr. Mary Ann Rafoth, Dean, 412-397-6020, Fax: 412-397-6044, E-mail: rafoth@rmu.edu.
Website: http://www.rmu.edu/web/cms/schools/sess/

**Rosemont College,** Schools of Graduate and Professional Studies, Counseling Psychology Program, Rosemont, PA 19010-1699. Offers human services (MA); school counseling (MA). *Program availability:* Part-time, evening/weekend. *Degree requirements:* For master's, thesis or alternative, practicum. *Entrance requirements:* For master's, minimum undergraduate GPA of 3.0, 3 letters of recommendation. Additional exam requirements/recommendations for international students: Required—TOEFL. Electronic applications accepted. Application fee is waived when completed online. *Expenses:* Contact institution. *Faculty research:* Addictions counseling.

**Rutgers University–New Brunswick,** Graduate School of Education, Department of Educational Psychology, Programs in School Counseling and Counseling Psychology, Piscataway, NJ 08854-8097. Offers Ed M. *Program availability:* Part-time, evening/

weekend. *Entrance requirements:* For master's, GRE General Test, 3 letters of recommendation. Additional exam requirements/recommendations for international students: Required—TOEFL (minimum score 550 paper-based; 83 iBT). Electronic applications accepted. *Faculty research:* Children and family in cross-cultural context, attachment theory, multicultural counseling, therapy relationship.

**Sage Graduate School,** School of Health Sciences, Department of Psychology, Program in Counseling and Community Psychology, Troy, NY 12180-4115. Offers MA. *Program availability:* Part-time, evening/weekend. *Faculty:* 3 full-time (all women), 1 (woman) part-time/adjunct. *Students:* 24 full-time (22 women), 45 part-time (36 women); includes 18 minority (8 Black or African American, non-Hispanic/Latino; 1 American Indian or Alaska Native, non-Hispanic/Latino; 4 Hispanic/Latino; 5 Two or more races, non-Hispanic/Latino). Average age 29. 85 applicants, 44% accepted, 19 enrolled. In 2016, 23 master's awarded. *Degree requirements:* For master's, externship, internship, thesis or research seminar. *Entrance requirements:* For master's, official transcripts of all previous undergraduate study; 2 letters of reference (academic or professional); undergraduate courses in statistics, history and systems of psychology; 3 other courses in behavioral science; personal prospectus statement; current resume. Additional exam requirements/recommendations for international students: Required—TOEFL (minimum score 550 paper-based). *Application deadline:* Applications are processed on a rolling basis. Application fee: $40. Electronic applications accepted. *Expenses: Tuition:* Full-time $12,240; part-time $680 per credit hour. Tuition and fees vary according to degree level and program. *Financial support:* Fellowships, research assistantships, teaching assistantships, Federal Work-Study, scholarships/grants, and unspecified assistantships available. Support available to part-time students. Financial award applicants required to submit FAFSA. *Unit head:* Dr. Theresa Hand, Dean of School of Health Sciences, 518-244-2264, Fax: 518-244-4571, E-mail: handt@sage.edu. *Application contact:* Dr. Gayle Morse, Graduate Program Director, 518-292-1819, E-mail: morseg@sage.edu.
Website: http://www.sage.edu/academics/psychology/programs/counseling/

**St. Bonaventure University,** School of Graduate Studies, School of Education, Program in Counselor Education, St. Bonaventure, NY 14778-2284. Offers community mental health counseling (MS Ed); rehabilitation counseling (MS Ed); school counseling (MS Ed); school counselor (Adv C). *Accreditation:* ACA. *Program availability:* Part-time, evening/weekend, 100% online. *Faculty:* 5 full-time (1 woman), 8 part-time/adjunct (6 women). *Students:* 53 full-time (40 women), 21 part-time (14 women); includes 6 minority (3 Black or African American, non-Hispanic/Latino; 3 Two or more races, non-Hispanic/Latino), 2 international. Average age 29. 64 applicants, 69% accepted, 29 enrolled. In 2016, 20 master's, 2 Adv Cs awarded. *Degree requirements:* For master's, comprehensive exam, thesis optional, internship, portfolio; for Adv C, internship. *Entrance requirements:* For master's, statement of intent/writing sample; transcripts from all colleges previously attended; two references; interview; minimum undergraduate GPA of 3.0; for Adv C, interview, writing sample, minimum undergraduate GPA of 3.0, two letters of recommendation, master's degree, transcripts from all colleges previously attended. Additional exam requirements/recommendations for international students: Required—TOEFL (minimum score 550 paper-based; 79 iBT). *Application deadline:* For fall admission, 3/15 priority date for domestic students, 2/1 priority date for international students; for spring admission, 11/15 priority date for domestic students, 7/1 priority date for international students. Applications are processed on a rolling basis. Application fee: $0. Electronic applications accepted. *Expenses:* $733 per credit, $100 graduation fee. *Financial support:* Career-related internships or fieldwork, Federal Work-Study, scholarships/grants, health care benefits, and unspecified assistantships available. Support available to part-time students. Financial award application deadline: 4/15; financial award applicants required to submit FAFSA. *Faculty research:* Balance between technology and personal contact in counselor education, special education and cyberbullying, school response to child abuse. *Unit head:* Dr. S. Alan Silliker, Director, 716-375-2368, Fax: 716-375-2360, E-mail: silliker@sbu.edu. *Application contact:* Bruce Campbell, Director of Graduate Admissions, 716-375-2429, Fax: 716-375-4015, E-mail: gradsch@sbu.edu.
Website: http://www.sbu.edu/academics/schools/education

**St. Edward's University,** School of Education, Program in Counseling, Austin, TX 78704. Offers MA. *Program availability:* Part-time, evening/weekend. *Students:* 91 full-time (78 women), 135 part-time (108 women); includes 71 minority (14 Black or African American, non-Hispanic/Latino; 5 Asian, non-Hispanic/Latino; 47 Hispanic/Latino; 5 Two or more races, non-Hispanic/Latino), 1 international. Average age 33. 146 applicants, 57% accepted, 46 enrolled. In 2016, 81 master's awarded. *Degree requirements:* For master's, 54 hours of coursework with minimum cumulative GPA of 3.0. *Entrance requirements:* For master's, GRE, two letters of recommendation; minimum GPA of 3.0 on last 60 semester hours of work or 2.75 on all college-level work. Additional exam requirements/recommendations for international students: Required—TOEFL (minimum score 79 iBT), IELTS (minimum score 6). *Application deadline:* For fall admission, 6/1 priority date for domestic and international students; for spring admission, 10/1 priority date for domestic and international students; for summer admission, 3/1 priority date for domestic and international students. Applications are processed on a rolling basis. Application fee: $50. Electronic applications accepted. *Expenses: Tuition:* Full-time $25,092; part-time $1394 per credit hour. *Required fees:* $75 per trimester. Full-time tuition and fees vary according to course load and program. *Unit head:* Dr. Elizabeth Katz, Program Director, 512-464-8833, Fax: 512-448-8492, E-mail: elizk@stedwards.edu. *Application contact:* Jane Hamann, Graduate Admission Counselor, 512-326-7333, Fax: 512-464-8877, E-mail: jhamann1@stedwards.edu.

**St. John Fisher College,** Wegmans School of Nursing, Program in Mental Health Counseling, Rochester, NY 14618-3597. Offers MS. *Accreditation:* ACA. *Program availability:* Part-time. *Faculty:* 5 full-time (3 women). *Students:* 48 full-time (38 women), 19 part-time (13 women); includes 14 minority (4 Black or African American, non-Hispanic/Latino; 1 Asian, non-Hispanic/Latino; 6 Hispanic/Latino; 3 Two or more races, non-Hispanic/Latino). Average age 28. 75 applicants, 65% accepted, 36 enrolled. In 2016, 33 master's awarded. *Degree requirements:* For master's, practicum experience, internship. *Entrance requirements:* For master's, GRE (if GPA below 3.0), 2 letters of recommendation, personal statement, current resume, interview. Additional exam requirements/recommendations for international students: Required—TOEFL (minimum score 575 paper-based; 80 iBT). *Application deadline:* Applications are processed on a rolling basis. Application fee: $30. Electronic applications accepted. *Expenses:* $885 per credit hour. *Financial support:* Scholarships/grants available. Financial award applicants required to submit FAFSA. *Faculty research:* Social class issues, clinical supervision, counselor education, play therapy. *Unit head:* Dr. Rachel Jordan, Director, 585-899-3858, E-mail: rjordan@sjfc.edu. *Application contact:* Michelle Gosier, Associate Director of Transfer and Graduate Admissions, 585-385-8064, E-mail: mgosier@sjfc.edu.
Website: https://www.sjfc.edu/graduate-programs/ms-in-mental-health-counseling/

**St. John's University,** The School of Education, Department of Counselor Education, Program in Clinical Mental Health Counseling, Queens, NY 11439. Offers MS Ed, Adv C. *Program availability:* Part-time, evening/weekend. *Degree requirements:* For master's, internship, state examination. *Entrance requirements:* For master's, bachelor's degree from an accredited college or university, minimum GPA of 3.0, 2 letters of recommendation, interview, 18 credits in behavioral and social science. Additional exam

requirements/recommendations for international students: Required—TOEFL (minimum score 600 paper-based; 100 iBT), IELTS (minimum score 7). Electronic applications accepted.

**St. John's University,** The School of Education, Department of Education Specialties, Queens, NY 11439. Offers clinical mental health counseling (MS Ed, Adv C); literacy (MS Ed, PhD, Adv C), including literacy (PhD), teaching literacy (Adv C), teaching literacy 5-12 (MS Ed), teaching literacy B-12 (MS Ed), teaching literacy B-6 (MS Ed), teaching literacy B-6 and children with disabilities (MS Ed); school counseling (MS Ed, Adv C); school counseling with bilingual extension (MS Ed); teaching children with disabilities in childhood education (MS Ed, Adv C); teaching English to speakers of other languages and bilingual education (MS Ed, Adv C). *Program availability:* Part-time, evening/weekend, online learning. *Degree requirements:* For master's, one foreign language, comprehensive exam, thesis, internship; for doctorate, one foreign language, comprehensive exam, thesis/dissertation. *Entrance requirements:* For master's, minimum GPA of 3.0, 2 letters of recommendation, interview, minimum of 18 credits in behavioral science, bachelor's degree; for doctorate, MAT, GRE General Test (analytical), official transcript showing conferral of degree with minimum GPA of 3.2, 2 letters of recommendation, statement of goals, resume, evidence of teaching experience, interview; for Adv C, statement of goals, official transcript showing conferral of degree with minimum GPA of 3.0, 2 letters of recommendation, interview. Additional exam requirements/recommendations for international students: Required—TOEFL (minimum score 600 paper-based; 100 iBT), IELTS (minimum score 7). Electronic applications accepted. *Faculty research:* Assisting troubled children and teens with substance abuse, truancy, and coping skills; literacy development for ESL learners; investigating Caribbean and Creole language and culture.

**Saint Martin's University,** Office of Graduate Studies, Program in Counseling Psychology, Lacey, WA 98503. Offers MAC. *Program availability:* Part-time. *Faculty:* 3 full-time (2 women), 2 part-time/adjunct (both women). *Students:* 75 full-time (66 women), 28 part-time (25 women); includes 34 minority (5 Black or African American, non-Hispanic/Latino; 1 American Indian or Alaska Native, non-Hispanic/Latino; 2 Asian, non-Hispanic/Latino; 15 Hispanic/Latino; 2 Native Hawaiian or other Pacific Islander, non-Hispanic/Latino; 9 Two or more races, non-Hispanic/Latino). Average age 35. 36 applicants, 50% accepted, 15 enrolled. In 2016, 30 master's awarded. *Degree requirements:* For master's, clinical experience, interview. *Entrance requirements:* For master's, clinical experience. Additional exam requirements/recommendations for international students: Required—TOEFL (minimum score 550 paper-based; 79 iBT); Recommended—IELTS (minimum score 6.5). *Application deadline:* For fall admission, 4/1 priority date for domestic and international students; for spring admission, 11/1 priority date for domestic and international students. Applications are processed on a rolling basis. Application fee: $50. Electronic applications accepted. *Expenses: Tuition:* Full-time $13,800; part-time $1150 per credit hour. *Required fees:* $720; $60 per credit hour. Tuition and fees vary according to course level and program. *Financial support:* Career-related internships or fieldwork, Federal Work-Study, and institutionally sponsored loans available. Support available to part-time students. Financial award application deadline: 3/1; financial award applicants required to submit FAFSA. *Faculty research:* Alcohol studies, clinical effectiveness, social justice, parent adolescent interaction. *Unit head:* Dr. Godfrey J. Ellis, Director, 360-438-4560, E-mail: gellis@stmartin.edu. *Application contact:* Casey Caronna, Administrative Assistant, 360-412-6128, E-mail: ccaronna@stmartin.edu.
Website: https://www.stmartin.edu

**St. Mary's University,** Graduate Studies, Program in Clinical Mental Health Counseling, San Antonio, TX 78228-8507. Offers MA. *Program availability:* Part-time, evening/weekend. *Students:* 31 full-time (23 women), 13 part-time (10 women); includes 20 minority (1 Black or African American, non-Hispanic/Latino; 1 Asian, non-Hispanic/Latino; 18 Hispanic/Latino), 5 international. Average age 34. 55 applicants, 53% accepted, 10 enrolled. In 2016, 19 master's awarded. *Degree requirements:* For master's, comprehensive exam, 700-hour clinical experience (practicum/internship). *Entrance requirements:* For master's, GRE General Test or MAT, bachelor's degree from accredited college or university; recommendations from past employers and/or from faculty members of previous undergraduate studies; personal statement indicating interest in becoming professional counselor or doing work that requires counseling skills. Additional exam requirements/recommendations for international students: Required—TOEFL (minimum score 550 paper-based; 80 iBT), IELTS (minimum score 6). *Application deadline:* For fall admission, 7/1 for domestic students; for spring admission, 11/15 for domestic students; for summer admission, 4/1 for domestic students. Applications are processed on a rolling basis. Application fee: $0. Electronic applications accepted. *Expenses: Tuition:* Full-time $15,600; part-time $865 per credit hour. *Required fees:* $148 per semester. *Financial support:* Application deadline: 3/31; applicants required to submit FAFSA. *Faculty research:* Relational-cultural theory, aging, human personality, interculturalism. *Unit head:* Dr. Melanie Harper, Program Director, 210-438-6400, E-mail: mharper@stmarytx.edu. *Application contact:* Kim Thornton, Director, Graduate and Adult Enrollment Services, 210-436-3101, E-mail: kthornton@stmarytx.edu.
Website: https://www.stmarytx.edu/academics/graduate/masters/counseling/clinical-mental-health-counseling

**Saint Mary's University of Minnesota,** Schools of Graduate and Professional Programs, Graduate School of Health and Human Services, Counseling and Psychological Services Program, Winona, MN 55987-1399. Offers addiction studies (Certificate); counseling and psychological services (MA). Tuition and fees vary according to degree level and program. *Unit head:* Dr. Mary Louise Wise, Associate Program Director, 612-728-5104, Fax: 612-728-5121, E-mail: mlwise@smumn.edu. *Application contact:* James Callinan, Director of Admissions for Graduate and Professional Programs, 612-728-5185, Fax: 612-728-5121, E-mail: jcallina@smumn.edu.
Website: http://www.smumn.edu/graduate-home/areas-of-study/graduate-school-of-health-human-services/ma-in-counseling-psychological-services

**Saint Mary's University of Minnesota,** Schools of Graduate and Professional Programs, Graduate School of Health and Human Services, Counseling Psychology Program, Winona, MN 55987-1399. Offers Psy D. Tuition and fees vary according to degree level and program. *Unit head:* Dr. Ashley Sovereign, Director, 612-238-4557, E-mail: asoverei@smumn.edu. *Application contact:* James Callinan, Director of Admissions for Graduate and Professional Programs, 612-728-5185, Fax: 612-728-5121, E-mail: jcallina@smumn.edu.
Website: http://www.smumn.edu/graduate-home/areas-of-study/graduate-school-of-health-human-services/doctor-of-psychology-in-counseling-psychology

**Saint Paul University,** Faculty of Human Sciences, Program in Counseling and Spirituality, Ottawa, ON K1S 1C4, Canada. Offers individual or marital/couple counseling (MA); spiritual care (MA). *Program availability:* Part-time. *Degree requirements:* For master's, research project or thesis. *Entrance requirements:* For master's, honors BA in human sciences, minimum B average, 12 theology credits.

**St. Thomas University,** Biscayne College, Department of Social Sciences and Counseling, Program in Mental Health Counseling, Miami Gardens, FL 33054-6459. Offers MS. *Program availability:* Part-time, evening/weekend. *Degree requirements:* For

master's, comprehensive exam. *Entrance requirements:* For master's, interview, minimum GPA of 3.0 or GRE. Additional exam requirements/recommendations for international students: Required—TOEFL (minimum score 550 paper-based; 79 iBT). Electronic applications accepted.

**Salem State University,** School of Graduate Studies, Program in Counseling and Psychological Services, Salem, MA 01970-5353. Offers MS, Graduate Certificate. *Program availability:* Part-time, evening/weekend. *Entrance requirements:* For master's, GRE or MAT. Additional exam requirements/recommendations for international students: Required—TOEFL (minimum score 550 paper-based; 80 iBT) or IELTS (minimum score 5.5).

**Salem State University,** School of Graduate Studies, Program of Advanced Professional Studies in Counseling, Salem, MA 01970-5353. Offers Graduate Certificate. *Program availability:* Part-time, evening/weekend. *Entrance requirements:* Additional exam requirements/recommendations for international students: Required—TOEFL (minimum score 550 paper-based; 80 iBT) or IELTS (minimum score 5.5).

**Salve Regina University,** Holistic Graduate Programs, Newport, RI 02840-4192. Offers expressive and creative arts (CAGS, CGS); holistic counseling (MA); holistic leadership (MA, CAGS, CGS); holistic leadership and change management (CAGS); holistic studies (CGS); substance abuse and treatment (CAGS); substance abuse foundations in holistic studies (CGS). *Program availability:* Part-time, evening/weekend. *Degree requirements:* For master's, internship, project. *Entrance requirements:* For master's, GMAT, GRE General Test, or MAT. Additional exam requirements/recommendations for international students: Required—TOEFL (minimum score 600 paper-based; 100 iBT) or IELTS. Electronic applications accepted.

**Salve Regina University,** Program in Rehabilitation Counseling, Newport, RI 02840-4192. Offers mental health (CAGS), including rehabilitation counseling; rehabilitation counseling (MA); substance abuse (CGS), including foundations in rehabilitation counseling. *Accreditation:* CORE. *Program availability:* Part-time, evening/weekend. *Entrance requirements:* For master's, GMAT, GRE General Test or MAT. Additional exam requirements/recommendations for international students: Required—TOEFL (minimum score 600 paper-based; 100 iBT) or IELTS. Electronic applications accepted.

**San Francisco State University,** Division of Graduate Studies, College of Health and Social Sciences, Department of Counseling, San Francisco, CA 94132-1722. Offers clinical rehabilitation and mental health counseling (MS); counseling (MS); marriage, family, and child counseling (MSC); school counseling (Credential). *Accreditation:* ACA (one or more programs are accredited). *Program availability:* Part-time. *Application deadline:* Applications are processed on a rolling basis. *Expenses:* Tuition, state resident: full-time $6738. Tuition, nonresident: full-time $15,666. *Required fees:* $1012. Tuition and fees vary according to degree level and program. *Unit head:* Dr. Graciela Orozco, Chair, 415-338-2005, Fax: 415-338-0594, E-mail: counsel@sfsu.edu. *Application contact:* Dr. Alison Cerezo, College Counseling Coordinator, 415-338-1064, Fax: 415-338-0594, E-mail: acerezo@sfsu.edu.
Website: http://counseling.sfsu.edu/

**Santa Clara University,** School of Education and Counseling Psychology, Santa Clara, CA 95053. Offers Catholic school teaching (MA); counseling (MA); counseling psychology (MA); educational leadership (MA); interdisciplinary education (MA); teaching multiple subjects (MA); teaching single subjects (MA). *Program availability:* Part-time, evening/weekend. *Faculty:* 32 full-time (22 women), 40 part-time/adjunct (25 women). *Students:* 265 full-time (213 women), 333 part-time (270 women); includes 282 minority (16 Black or African American, non-Hispanic/Latino; 1 American Indian or Alaska Native, non-Hispanic/Latino; 78 Asian, non-Hispanic/Latino; 156 Hispanic/Latino; 31 Two or more races, non-Hispanic/Latino), 46 international. Average age 30. 266 applicants, 74% accepted, 126 enrolled. In 2016, 253 master's awarded. *Entrance requirements:* For master's, transcript, letters of recommendation, statement of purpose, resume. Additional exam requirements/recommendations for international students: Required—TOEFL (minimum score 90 iBT) or IELTS (6.5). *Application deadline:* Applications are processed on a rolling basis. *Application fee:* $50. Electronic applications accepted. *Expenses:* $581 per unit. *Financial support:* Fellowships, research assistantships, teaching assistantships, career-related internships or fieldwork, Federal Work-Study, scholarships/grants, traineeships, health care benefits, and tuition waivers available. Support available to part-time students. Financial award applicants required to submit FAFSA. *Unit head:* Dr. Sabrina Zirkel, Dean, 408-551-3074, Fax: 408-554-4367, E-mail: szirkel@scu.edu. *Application contact:* Victoria Rodriguez, Graduate Admissions Advisor, 408-554-4723, E-mail: v1rodriguez@scu.edu.
Website: http://www.scu.edu/ecp/

**Saybrook University,** LIOS MA Residential Programs, Kirkland, WA 98033. Offers leadership and organization development (MA); psychology counseling (MA). *Degree requirements:* For master's, thesis (for some programs), oral exams. *Entrance requirements:* For master's, bachelor's degree from an accredited university or college. Additional exam requirements/recommendations for international students: Recommended—TOEFL, IELTS, TWE.

**The Seattle School of Theology and Psychology,** Graduate Programs, Seattle, WA 98121. Offers Christian studies (MA); counseling psychology (MA); divinity (M Div). *Program availability:* Part-time. *Entrance requirements:* For master's, MAT.

**Seton Hall University,** College of Education and Human Services, Department of Professional Psychology and Family Therapy, Program in Counseling Psychology, South Orange, NJ 07079-2697. Offers counseling psychology (PhD); school counseling (MA). *Accreditation:* APA. *Faculty:* 10 full-time (7 women). *Students:* 40 full-time (30 women), 203 part-time (170 women). Average age 32. 133 applicants, 39% accepted, 28 enrolled. In 2016, 9 master's, 14 doctorates awarded. *Degree requirements:* For doctorate, comprehensive exam, thesis/dissertation, internship. *Entrance requirements:* For master's and doctorate, GRE, interview. *Application deadline:* For fall admission, 1/15 for domestic students. Application fee: $50. *Financial support:* In 2016–17, 1 research assistantship with full tuition reimbursement (averaging $4,500 per year) was awarded; career-related internships or fieldwork also available. Financial award application deadline: 2/1. *Faculty research:* Vocational indecision, coping skills, cognitive behavioral interventions, vocational development. *Unit head:* Dr. Ben Beitin, Chair, 973-761-9451, E-mail: beitinbe@shu.edu. *Application contact:* Diana Minakakis, Director of Graduate Admissions, 973-275-2824, Fax: 973-275-2181, E-mail: diana.minakakis@shu.edu.
Website: http://www.shu.edu/academics/education/professional-psychology/

**Siena Heights University,** Graduate College, Adrian, MI 49221-1796. Offers clinical mental health counseling (MA); educational leadership (Specialist); leadership (MA), including health care leadership, organizational leadership; teacher education (MA), including early childhood education, early childhood education: Montessori, education leadership: principal, elementary education: reading K-12, leadership: higher education, secondary education: reading K-12, special education: cognitive impairment, special education: learning disabilities. *Program availability:* Part-time, evening/weekend. *Degree requirements:* For master's, thesis, presentation. *Entrance requirements:* For master's, minimum GPA of 3.0, current resume, essay, all post-secondary transcripts, 3 letters of reference, conviction disclosure form; copy of teaching certificate (for some education programs); for Specialist, master's degree, minimum GPA of 3.0, current

resume, essay, all post-secondary transcripts, 3 letters of reference, conviction disclosure form; copy of teaching certificate (for some education programs). Electronic applications accepted.

**Simpson University,** School of Graduate Studies, Redding, CA 96003-8606. Offers counseling psychology (MA); organizational leadership (MA). *Program availability:* Evening/weekend, 100% online, blended/hybrid learning. *Faculty:* 10 part-time/adjunct (8 women). *Students:* 30 full-time (24 women), 9 part-time (7 women); includes 11 minority (1 Black or African American, non-Hispanic/Latino; 2 Asian, non-Hispanic/Latino; 7 Hispanic/Latino; 1 Two or more races, non-Hispanic/Latino), 1 international. Average age 35. In 2016, 17 master's awarded. *Degree requirements:* For master's, thesis optional, portfolio capstone, integrative essay. *Entrance requirements:* For master's, three letters of recommendation, personal statement, resume, transcripts, personal interview, bachelor's degree in psychology or related field with minimum GPA of 3.0 in final 60 credits (for counseling psychology); two references (for organizational leadership). Additional exam requirements/recommendations for international students: Required—TOEFL (minimum score 550 paper-based; 79 iBT). *Application deadline:* For fall admission, 3/1 for domestic and international students; for spring admission, 11/1 for domestic and international students. Application fee: $35. Electronic applications accepted. *Expenses:* $510 per credit. *Financial support:* Applicants required to submit FAFSA. *Faculty research:* Development of executive functioning in young children, cognitive neuropsychology, historical issues in the neurosciences, neurotheology. *Unit head:* Adeline Jackson, Dean, 530-226-4788, E-mail: ajackson@simpsonu.edu. *Application contact:* Stacy Burgess, Director of Admissions for Adult and Graduate Studies, 530-226-4961, E-mail: sburgess@simpsonu.edu.
Website: http://gs.simpsonu.edu/

**Slippery Rock University of Pennsylvania,** Graduate Studies (Recruitment), College of Education, Department of Counseling and Development, Slippery Rock, PA 16057-1383. Offers clinical mental health (MA); school counseling (M Ed); student affairs in higher education (MA); student affairs in higher education with college counseling (MA). *Accreditation:* ACA (one or more programs are accredited); NCATE. *Program availability:* Part-time, evening/weekend. *Faculty:* 7 full-time (5 women), 1 (woman) part-time/adjunct. *Students:* 86 full-time (55 women), 23 part-time (18 women); includes 13 minority (7 Black or African American, non-Hispanic/Latino; 4 Hispanic/Latino; 2 Two or more races, non-Hispanic/Latino), 1 international. Average age 28. 107 applicants, 57% accepted, 42 enrolled. In 2016, 39 master's awarded. *Degree requirements:* For master's, comprehensive exam, thesis (for some programs). *Entrance requirements:* For master's, GRE General Test or MAT, official transcripts, personal statement, three letters of recommendation, interview. Additional exam requirements/recommendations for international students: Required—TOEFL (minimum score 550 paper-based; 80 iBT). *Application deadline:* For fall admission, 1/15 priority date for domestic and international students. Applications are processed on a rolling basis. *Application fee:* $25 ($30 for international students). Electronic applications accepted. *Expenses:* $646.50 per credit in-state, $936.80 per credit out-of-state; $581.45 per online credit in-state, $648.65 per online credit out-of-state. *Financial support:* In 2016–17, 58 students received support. Career-related internships or fieldwork, Federal Work-Study, institutionally sponsored loans, scholarships/grants, tuition waivers (partial), and unspecified assistantships available. Support available to part-time students. Financial award application deadline: 5/1; financial award applicants required to submit FAFSA. *Unit head:* Dr. Stacy Jacob, Graduate Coordinator, 724-738-2758, Fax: 724-738-4859, E-mail: stacy.jacob@sru.edu. *Application contact:* Brandi Weber-Mortimer, Director of Graduate Admissions, 724-738-2051, Fax: 724-738-2146, E-mail: graduate.admissions@sru.edu.
Website: http://www.sru.edu/academics/colleges-and-departments/coe/departments/counseling-and-development

**Sofia University,** Residential Programs, Palo Alto, CA 94303. Offers clinical psychology (Psy D); computer science (MS); counseling psychology (MA); transpersonal psychology (MA, PhD). *Program availability:* Part-time, evening/weekend. Terminal master's awarded for partial completion of doctoral program. *Degree requirements:* For doctorate, thesis/dissertation. *Entrance requirements:* For master's, bachelor's degree; for doctorate, bachelor's degree; master's degree (for some programs). Electronic applications accepted.

**Sonoma State University,** School of Social Sciences, Department of Counseling, Rohnert Park, CA 94928-3609. Offers clinical mental health counseling (MA); school counseling (MA). *Accreditation:* ACA. *Program availability:* Part-time. *Degree requirements:* For master's, internship. *Entrance requirements:* For master's, minimum GPA of 3.0. Additional exam requirements/recommendations for international students: Required—TOEFL (minimum score 500 paper-based). *Application deadline:* For fall admission, 11/30 for domestic students. Application fee: $55. *Expenses:* Tuition, state resident: full-time $6738; part-time $3906 per unit. *Required fees:* $1916; $1916 per year. Tuition and fees vary according to course load, degree level and program. *Financial support:* Fellowships and career-related internships or fieldwork available. Financial award application deadline: 3/2; financial award applicants required to submit FAFSA. *Unit head:* Dr. Adam Zagelbaum, Chair, 707-664-2544, E-mail: adam.zagelbaum@sonoma.edu.
Website: http://www.sonoma.edu/counseling

**Southeastern Oklahoma State University,** School of Behavioral Sciences, Durant, OK 74701-0609. Offers clinical mental health counseling (MS). *Accreditation:* ACA. *Program availability:* Part-time, evening/weekend. *Degree requirements:* For master's, comprehensive exam, thesis optional. *Entrance requirements:* For master's, GRE General Test, minimum GPA of 3.0 in last 60 hours or 2.75 overall. Additional exam requirements/recommendations for international students: Required—TOEFL (minimum score 550 paper-based; 79 iBT). Electronic applications accepted.

**Southeastern University,** College of Behavioral and Social Sciences, Lakeland, FL 33801-6099. Offers human services (MA); international community development (MA); marriage and family counseling (MS); professional counseling (MS); school counseling (MS); social work (MSW). *Program availability:* Evening/weekend. *Expenses:* Tuition: Full-time $9450; part-time $6300 per credit. *Required fees:* $500; $250 per semester. One-time fee: $150. Tuition and fees vary according to degree level, campus/location and program. *Unit head:* Erica H. Sirrine, Dean, 863-667-5341, E-mail: ehsirrine@seu.edu.
Website: http://www.seu.edu/behavior/

**Southeast Missouri State University,** School of Graduate Studies, Department of Educational Leadership and Counseling, Counseling Program, Cape Girardeau, MO 63701-4799. Offers career counseling (MA); mental health counseling (MA); school counseling (MA). *Accreditation:* ACA; NCATE. *Program availability:* Part-time, evening/weekend. *Faculty:* 5 full-time (4 women), 2 part-time/adjunct (both women). *Students:* 33 full-time (24 women), 39 part-time (36 women); includes 6 minority (4 Black or African American, non-Hispanic/Latino; 2 American Indian or Alaska Native, non-Hispanic/Latino), 1 international. Average age 33. 48 applicants, 67% accepted, 31 enrolled. In 2016, 44 master's, 7 other advanced degrees awarded. *Degree requirements:* For master's and Ed S, comprehensive exam, thesis or alternative. *Entrance requirements:* For master's, personal essay, interview, minimum GPA of 3.5; for Ed S, minimum graduate GPA of 3.7. Additional exam requirements/recommendations for international students: Required—TOEFL (minimum score 550 paper-based; 79 iBT), IELTS

(minimum score 6), PTE (minimum score 53). *Application deadline:* For fall admission, 3/1 for domestic and international students; for spring admission, 11/21 for domestic students, 10/1 for international students; for summer admission, 3/1 for domestic students. Applications are processed on a rolling basis. Application fee: $30 ($40 for international students). Electronic applications accepted. *Expenses:* Tuition, state resident: full-time $3130; part-time $260.80 per credit hour. Tuition, nonresident: full-time $5842; part-time $486.80 per credit hour. *Required fees:* $33.70 per credit hour. *Financial support:* In 2016–17, 10 students received support. Career-related internships or fieldwork, Federal Work-Study, scholarships/grants, traineeships, tuition waivers (full), and unspecified assistantships available. Financial award application deadline: 6/30; financial award applicants required to submit FAFSA. *Faculty research:* School counseling, mental health, career and family counseling, social justice and spirituality in counseling. *Unit head:* Dr. C. P. Gause, Department Chair, 573-651-2137, Fax: 573-986-6512, E-mail: cpgause@semo.edu. *Application contact:* Dr. Melissa Odegard-Koester, Associate Professor, 573-651-2420, Fax: 573-986-6512, E-mail: modegard@semo.edu.
Website: http://www.semo.edu/eduleadcounsel/

**Southern Adventist University,** School of Education and Psychology, Collegedale, TN 37315-0370. Offers clinical mental health counseling (MS); inclusive education (MS Ed); instructional leadership (MS Ed); literacy education (MS Ed); outdoor teacher education (MS Ed); school counseling (MS). *Accreditation:* NCATE. *Program availability:* Part-time, evening/weekend. *Degree requirements:* For master's, comprehensive exam (for some programs), thesis optional, position paper (MS), portfolio (MS Ed in outdoor teacher education). *Entrance requirements:* For master's, interview (MS); 9 semester hours of upper-division course work in psychology or related field, including 1 course in psychology research or statistics; 9 semester hours of education (MS Ed). Additional exam requirements/recommendations for international students: Required—TOEFL (minimum score 600 paper-based; 100 iBT). Electronic applications accepted.

**Southern California Seminary,** Graduate and Professional Programs, El Cajon, CA 92019. Offers Biblical studies (MABS); counseling psychology (MACP); marriage and family therapy (MAMFT); psychology (Psy D); religious studies (MRS); theology (M Div). *Program availability:* Part-time, evening/weekend, online learning. *Degree requirements:* For master's, thesis (for some programs); for doctorate, thesis/dissertation. *Entrance requirements:* For doctorate, master's degree in psychology. Additional exam requirements/recommendations for international students: Required—TOEFL (minimum score 550 paper-based). Electronic applications accepted.

**Southern Illinois University Carbondale,** Graduate School, College of Liberal Arts, Department of Psychology, Carbondale, IL 62901-4701. Offers clinical psychology (PhD); counseling psychology (PhD); experimental psychology (MA, MS). *Accreditation:* APA (one or more programs are accredited). *Degree requirements:* For master's, thesis; for doctorate, thesis/dissertation. *Entrance requirements:* For master's, GRE General Test, GRE Subject Test, minimum GPA of 2.7; for doctorate, GRE General Test, GRE Subject Test, minimum GPA of 3.25. Additional exam requirements/recommendations for international students: Required—TOEFL. *Faculty research:* Developmental neuropsychology; smoking, affect, and cognition; personality measurement; vocational psychology; program evaluation.

**Southern Nazarene University,** College of Professional and Graduate Studies, Department of Psychology and Counseling, Bethany, OK 73008. Offers counseling psychology (MA, MSCP); marital and family therapy (MA). *Degree requirements:* For master's, thesis optional. *Entrance requirements:* For master's, English proficiency exam, minimum GPA of 3.0 in last 60 hours/major, 2.7 overall.

**Southern Oregon University,** Graduate Studies, Department of Psychology, Ashland, OR 97520. Offers MHC. *Accreditation:* ACA. *Program availability:* Part-time, online learning. *Faculty:* 10 full-time (5 women), 6 part-time/adjunct (3 women). *Students:* 43 full-time (33 women), 3 part-time (all women); includes 11 minority (4 American Indian or Alaska Native, non-Hispanic/Latino; 5 Hispanic/Latino; 2 Two or more races, non-Hispanic/Latino). Average age 35. 59 applicants, 61% accepted, 22 enrolled. In 2016, 19 master's awarded. *Degree requirements:* For master's, thesis, portfolio, oral defense. *Entrance requirements:* For master's, GRE General Test, minimum cumulative GPA of 3.0 in the last 90 quarter credits (60 semester credits) of undergraduate coursework. Additional exam requirements/recommendations for international students: Required—TOEFL (minimum score 540 paper-based; 76 iBT), IELTS (minimum score 6), ELPT (minimum score 964) or ELS (minimum score 112). *Application deadline:* For fall admission, 7/31 priority date for domestic and international students; for winter admission, 11/15 priority date for domestic and international students; for spring admission, 1/7 priority date for domestic and international students. Applications are processed on a rolling basis. Application fee: $60. Electronic applications accepted. *Expenses:* Tuition, state resident: full-time $10,719; part-time $397 per credit. Tuition, nonresident: full-time $13,419; part-time $497 per credit. *Required fees:* $548. *Financial support:* In 2016–17, 1 student received support, including 1 research assistantship with partial tuition reimbursement available; career-related internships or fieldwork, institutionally sponsored loans, scholarships/grants, and unspecified assistantships also available. *Unit head:* Dr. Josie Wilson, Graduate Program Coordinator, 541-552-6946, E-mail: jwilson@sou.edu. *Application contact:* Lori Courtney, Graduate Coordinator, 541-552-6947, E-mail: courtney@sou.edu.
Website: http://www.sou.edu/psychology/mhc

**South University,** Graduate Programs, College of Arts and Sciences, Program in Clinical Mental Health Counseling, Savannah, GA 31406. Offers MA.

**South University,** Program in Clinical Mental Health Counseling, Montgomery, AL 36116-1120. Offers MA.

**South University,** Program in Clinical Mental Health Counseling, Columbia, SC 29203. Offers MA.

**South University,** Program in Clinical Mental Health Counseling, Royal Palm Beach, FL 33411. Offers MA.

**South University,** Program in Clinical Mental Health Counseling, Glen Allen, VA 23060. Offers MA.

**South University,** Program in Clinical Mental Health Counseling, Virginia Beach, VA 23452. Offers MA.

**South University,** Program in Clinical Mental Health Counseling, Novi, MI 48377. Offers MA.

**South University,** Program in Clinical Mental Health Counseling, High Point, NC 27265. Offers MA.

**South University,** Program in Clinical Mental Health Counseling, Cleveland, OH 44128. Offers MA.

**South University,** Program in Clinical Mental Health Counseling, Round Rock, TX 78681. Offers MA.

**Southwestern Assemblies of God University,** Thomas F. Harrison School of Graduate Studies, Program in Counseling Psychology, Waxahachie, TX 75165-5735. Offers counseling psychology (clinical) (MCP); human services counseling (MS). *Program availability:* Part-time. *Degree requirements:* For master's, comprehensive written and oral exams. *Entrance requirements:* For master's, GRE General Test, minimum GPA of 2.5. Electronic applications accepted.

**Southwestern College,** Program in Art Therapy/Counseling, Santa Fe, NM 87502-4788. Offers MA. *Program availability:* Part-time, evening/weekend. *Degree requirements:* For master's, internship. *Entrance requirements:* For master's, resume, slide portfolio, interview, 3 letters of reference. Additional exam requirements/recommendations for international students: Required—TOEFL.

**Southwestern College,** Program in Counseling, Santa Fe, NM 87502-4788. Offers MA. *Program availability:* Part-time, evening/weekend. *Degree requirements:* For master's, internship. *Entrance requirements:* For master's, resume, 3 letters of reference, interview. Additional exam requirements/recommendations for international students: Required—TOEFL.

**Southwestern College,** Program in Grief, Loss and Trauma Counseling, Santa Fe, NM 87502-4788. Offers MA, Certificate. *Program availability:* Part-time, evening/weekend, online learning. *Entrance requirements:* For master's, interview, references, resume; for Certificate, 3 letters of reference, interview.

**Spring Arbor University,** School of Human Services, Spring Arbor, MI 49283-9799. Offers counseling (MAC); family studies (MAFS); nursing (MSN). *Program availability:* Part-time, evening/weekend, online learning. *Entrance requirements:* For master's, bachelor's degree from regionally-accredited college or university, minimum GPA of 3.0 for at least the last two years of the bachelor's degree, at least two recommendations from professional/academic individuals. Additional exam requirements/recommendations for international students: Required—TOEFL (minimum score 600 paper-based). Electronic applications accepted.

**Springfield College,** Graduate Programs, Programs in Psychology, Springfield, MA 01109-3797. Offers athletic counseling (MS, CAGS); clinical mental health counseling (M Ed, CAGS); counseling psychology (Psy D); industrial and organizational psychology (M Ed, CAGS); school guidance counseling (M Ed, CAGS); student personnel administration in higher education (M Ed). *Accreditation:* APA. *Program availability:* Part-time. *Degree requirements:* For master's, research project, portfolio; for doctorate, dissertation project, 1500 hours of counseling psychology practicum, full-year internship. *Entrance requirements:* Additional exam requirements/recommendations for international students: Required—TOEFL (minimum score 550 paper-based). Electronic applications accepted. *Expenses:* Tuition: Full-time $29,640; part-time $988 per credit. *Required fees:* $195.

**State University of New York at New Paltz,** Graduate School, School of Liberal Arts and Sciences, Department of Psychology, New Paltz, NY 12561. Offers mental health counseling (MS, AC); psychology (MA); school counseling (MS). *Program availability:* Part-time, evening/weekend. *Students:* 52 full-time (40 women), 19 part-time (12 women); includes 13 minority (1 Black or African American, non-Hispanic/Latino; 1 Asian, non-Hispanic/Latino; 11 Hispanic/Latino), 1 international. 103 applicants, 50% accepted, 33 enrolled. In 2016, 22 master's awarded. *Degree requirements:* For master's, comprehensive exam, thesis. *Entrance requirements:* For master's, GRE General Test, minimum GPA of 3.0. Additional exam requirements/recommendations for international students: Required—TOEFL (minimum score 550 paper-based; 80 iBT), IELTS (minimum score 6.5). *Application deadline:* For fall admission, 2/1 priority date for domestic and international students; for spring admission, 11/15 priority date for domestic and international students. Application fee: $50. Electronic applications accepted. *Financial support:* In 2016–17, 6 teaching assistantships with partial tuition reimbursements (averaging $5,000 per year) were awarded. Financial award application deadline: 8/1. *Faculty research:* Disaster mental health, women's objectification, mate selection, cultural psychology, achievement motivation. *Unit head:* Dr. Glenn Geher, Chair, 845-257-3091, E-mail: geherg@newpaltz.edu. *Application contact:* Dr. Tabitha Holmes, Program Coordinator, 845-257-3955, E-mail: holmest@newpaltz.edu.
Website: http://www.newpaltz.edu/psychology/

**State University of New York at Oswego,** Graduate Studies, School of Education, Department of Counseling and Psychological Services, Oswego, NY 13126. Offers mental health counseling (MS); MS/CAS. *Degree requirements:* For master's, comprehensive exam, thesis optional. *Entrance requirements:* For master's, GRE General Test, interview, minimum GPA of 3.0. Additional exam requirements/recommendations for international students: Required—TOEFL (minimum score 560 paper-based). *Faculty research:* Lowenfeld mosaics as predictor validation of preschool screening.

**State University of New York at Plattsburgh,** School of Education, Health, and Human Services, Department of Counselor Education, Plattsburgh, NY 12901-2681. Offers clinical mental health counseling (MS, Advanced Certificate); school counselor (MS Ed, CAS); student affairs counseling (MS). *Accreditation:* ACA (one or more programs are accredited); TEAC. *Program availability:* Part-time. *Entrance requirements:* For master's, GRE General Test or MAT, minimum GPA of 2.8. Additional exam requirements/recommendations for international students: Required—TOEFL. *Faculty research:* Campus violence, program accreditation, substance abuse, vocational assessment, group counseling, divorce.

**State University of New York College at Old Westbury,** Program in Mental Health Counseling, Old Westbury, NY 11568-0210. Offers MS. *Faculty:* 3 full-time (0 women), 2 part-time/adjunct (both women). *Students:* 34 full-time (29 women); includes 11 minority (4 Black or African American, non-Hispanic/Latino; 2 Asian, non-Hispanic/Latino; 5 Hispanic/Latino). Average age 29. 39 applicants, 64% accepted, 21 enrolled. In 2016, 14 master's awarded. *Entrance requirements:* For master's, essay, letters of recommendation. Application fee: $50. *Expenses:* Tuition, state resident: full-time $10,870; part-time $453 per credit. Tuition, nonresident: full-time $22,210; part-time $925 per credit. *Required fees:* $24.35 per credit. $76 per semester. Tuition and fees vary according to course load. *Unit head:* Dr. Fred Millan, 516-876-3315, E-mail: millanf@oldwestbury.edu. *Application contact:* Philip D'Angelo, Graduate Admissions Office, 516-876-3073, E-mail: enroll@oldwestbury.edu.

**Stetson University,** College of Arts and Sciences, Division of Education, Department of Counselor Education, DeLand, FL 32723. Offers marriage, couple and family counseling (MS); mental health counseling (MS); school counseling (MS). *Accreditation:* ACA. *Program availability:* Evening/weekend. *Faculty:* 5 full-time (all women), 7 part-time/adjunct (6 women). *Students:* 114 full-time (102 women), 13 part-time (9 women); includes 36 minority (9 Black or African American, non-Hispanic/Latino; 1 Asian, non-Hispanic/Latino; 21 Hispanic/Latino; 5 Two or more races, non-Hispanic/Latino), 3 international. Average age 29. 61 applicants, 70% accepted, 37 enrolled. In 2016, 16 master's awarded. *Entrance requirements:* For master's, GRE or MAT, transcripts, three letters of recommendation, group interview. Additional exam requirements/recommendations for international students: Required—TOEFL (minimum score 90 iBT), IELTS (minimum score 7). *Application deadline:* For fall admission, 8/1 priority date for domestic students; for spring admission, 1/1 priority date for domestic students; for summer admission, 5/1 priority date for domestic students. Applications are processed on a rolling basis. Application fee: $50. Electronic applications accepted. *Expenses:* $886 per credit hour. *Financial support:* In 2016–17, 45 students received support. Federal Work-Study, scholarships/grants, unspecified assistantships, and tuition waivers for staff and dependents available. Support available to part-time students.

### Counseling Psychology

*Faculty research:* Play therapy, trauma, wellness, infertility, counselor education training, gatekeeping and counselor education. *Unit head:* Dr. Leila Roach, Chair, 386-822-8992. *Application contact:* Jamie Vanderlip, Senior Associate Director of Graduate Admissions, 386-822-7100, Fax: 386-822-7112, E-mail: jlvander@stetson.edu.

**Suffolk University,** College of Arts and Sciences, Department of Psychology, Boston, MA 02108-2770. Offers clinical psychology (PhD); college admission counseling (Certificate); mental health counseling (MS); school counseling (MS, CAGS). *Accreditation:* APA. *Faculty:* 14 full-time (7 women), 7 part-time/adjunct (6 women). *Students:* 51 full-time (45 women), 42 part-time (38 women); includes 24 minority (3 Black or African American, non-Hispanic/Latino; 8 Asian, non-Hispanic/Latino; 11 Hispanic/Latino; 2 Two or more races, non-Hispanic/Latino), 6 international. Average age 27. 306 applicants, 25% accepted, 38 enrolled. In 2016, 22 master's, 10 doctorates, 14 other advanced degrees awarded. *Degree requirements:* For doctorate, thesis/dissertation, practicum. *Entrance requirements:* For doctorate, GRE General Test or MAT, 2 letters of recommendation, resume. Additional exam requirements/recommendations for international students: Required—TOEFL (minimum score 550 paper-based; 80 iBT). *Application deadline:* For fall admission, 12/1 for domestic and international students. Applications are processed on a rolling basis. Application fee: $50. Electronic applications accepted. *Expenses:* Contact institution. *Financial support:* In 2016–17, 54 students received support, including 53 fellowships (averaging $13,943 per year); career-related internships or fieldwork, Federal Work-Study, institutionally sponsored loans, scholarships/grants, and unspecified assistantships also available. Support available to part-time students. Financial award application deadline: 4/1; financial award applicants required to submit FAFSA. *Faculty research:* Assessing exposure in the context of a family-based cognitive behavioral treatment for pediatric OCD, a mindfulness approach to designing and testing the efficacy of a new sexual revictimization prevention program for college women, olfaction and decision-making in substance-dependent individuals, the role of experiential avoidance in Generalized Anxiety Disorder, ego development as a predictor of dogmatism and intolerance in the political right and left. *Unit head:* Dr. Gary Fireman, Chairperson, 617-305-6368, Fax: 617-367-2924, E-mail: gfireman@suffolk.edu. *Application contact:* Mara Marzocchi, Associate Director of Graduate Admissions, 617-573-8302, Fax: 617-305-1733, E-mail: grad.admission@suffolk.edu.
Website: http://www.suffolk.edu/college/graduate/69299.php

**Tarleton State University,** College of Graduate Studies, College of Education, Department of Psychological Sciences, Stephenville, TX 76402. Offers applied psychology (MS). *Program availability:* Part-time, evening/weekend. *Faculty:* 2 full-time (1 woman), 2 part-time/adjunct (1 woman). *Students:* 2 full-time (1 woman), 8 part-time (6 women); includes 2 minority (1 Black or African American, non-Hispanic/Latino; 1 Hispanic/Latino), 1 international. 11 applicants, 100% accepted, 8 enrolled. *Degree requirements:* For master's, comprehensive exam, thesis optional. *Entrance requirements:* For master's, GRE General Test, minimum GPA of 3.0. Additional exam requirements/recommendations for international students: Required—TOEFL (minimum score 550 paper-based; 80 iBT). *Application deadline:* For fall admission, 8/15 priority date for domestic students; for spring admission, 1/7 for domestic students. Applications are processed on a rolling basis. Application fee: $45 ($145 for international students). Electronic applications accepted. *Expenses:* $3,672 tuition; $2,437 fees. *Financial support:* Research assistantships, teaching assistantships, career-related internships or fieldwork, Federal Work-Study, institutionally sponsored loans, and tuition waivers (partial) available. Support available to part-time students. Financial award application deadline: 5/1; financial award applicants required to submit FAFSA. *Unit head:* Dr. Kimberly Rynearson, Department Head, 254-968-9916, E-mail: rynearson@tarleton.edu. *Application contact:* Information Contact, 254-968-9104, Fax: 254-968-9670, E-mail: gradoffice@tarleton.edu.

**Teachers College, Columbia University,** Department of Counseling and Clinical Psychology, New York, NY 10027-6696. Offers clinical psychology (PhD); counseling psychology (Ed M, Ed D, PhD); mental health counseling (ME); psychological counseling (ME, ND); psychology in education (MA, ND); school counselor (ME). *Accreditation:* APA (one or more programs are accredited). *Program availability:* Part-time. *Students:* 434 full-time (366 women), 232 part-time (184 women); includes 247 minority (62 Black or African American, non-Hispanic/Latino; 1 American Indian or Alaska Native, non-Hispanic/Latino; 80 Asian, non-Hispanic/Latino; 84 Hispanic/Latino; 20 Two or more races, non-Hispanic/Latino), 134 international. 1,470 applicants, 39% accepted, 253 enrolled. *Expenses: Tuition:* Full-time $36,288; part-time $1512 per credit. *Required fees:* $438 per semester. One-time fee: $510 full-time. Full-time tuition and fees vary according to course load. *Unit head:* Prof. Marie Miville, Head, 212-678-3343, Fax: 212-678-3275, E-mail: miville@tc.columbia.edu. *Application contact:* David Estrella, Director of Admission, 212-678-3305, E-mail: estrella@tc.columbia.edu.

**Temple University,** College of Education, Department of Psychological Studies in Education, Philadelphia, PA 19122-6096. Offers adult and organizational development (Ed M); counseling psychology (Ed M, PhD), including agency counseling (Ed M), counseling psychology (PhD); school counseling (Ed M); education (PhD); educational leadership (Ed M); educational leadership and policy studies (Ed M, Ed D), including educational leadership; educational psychology (Ed M); school psychology (Ed M, PhD, Ed S); special education (Ed M). *Accreditation:* APA (one or more programs are accredited). *Program availability:* Part-time, evening/weekend. Terminal master's awarded for partial completion of doctoral program. *Degree requirements:* For master's, thesis or alternative; for doctorate, thesis/dissertation. *Entrance requirements:* Additional exam requirements/recommendations for international students: Required—TOEFL (minimum score 550 paper-based; 79 iBT).

**Tennessee State University,** The School of Graduate Studies and Research, College of Education, Department of Psychology, Nashville, TN 37209-1561. Offers counseling psychology (MS). *Entrance requirements:* For master's, GRE General Test or MAT. Electronic applications accepted.

**Texas A&M International University,** Office of Graduate Studies and Research, College of Arts and Sciences, Department of Psychology and Communication, Laredo, TX 78041-1900. Offers counseling psychology (MACP); psychology (MS). *Degree requirements:* For master's, thesis (for some programs). *Entrance requirements:* For master's, GRE General Test. Additional exam requirements/recommendations for international students: Required—TOEFL (minimum score 550 paper-based; 79 iBT).

**Texas A&M University,** College of Education and Human Development, Department of Educational Psychology, College Station, TX 77843. Offers bilingual education (M Ed, MS); counseling psychology (PhD); educational psychology (M Ed, MS, PhD); educational technology (M Ed); school psychology (PhD); special education (M Ed, MS). *Accreditation:* APA (one or more programs are accredited). *Program availability:* Part-time, evening/weekend, blended/hybrid learning. *Faculty:* 42. *Students:* 172 full-time (139 women), 281 part-time (233 women); includes 144 minority (27 Black or African American, non-Hispanic/Latino; 1 American Indian or Alaska Native, non-Hispanic/Latino; 19 Asian, non-Hispanic/Latino; 86 Hispanic/Latino; 1 Native Hawaiian or other Pacific Islander, non-Hispanic/Latino; 10 Two or more races, non-Hispanic/Latino), 48 international. Average age 33. 181 applicants, 44% accepted, 45 enrolled. In 2016, 99 master's, 27 doctorates awarded. *Degree requirements:* For master's, thesis optional; for doctorate, thesis/dissertation. *Entrance requirements:* For master's and doctorate,

GRE General Test. Additional exam requirements/recommendations for international students: Required—TOEFL (minimum score 550 paper-based; 80 iBT), IELTS (minimum score 6), PTE (minimum score 53). *Application deadline:* For fall admission, 12/1 for domestic students; for spring admission, 10/15 for domestic students. Application fee: $50 ($90 for international students). Electronic applications accepted. *Expenses:* Contact institution. *Financial support:* In 2016–17, 231 students received support, including 8 fellowships with tuition reimbursements available (averaging $9,919 per year), 98 research assistantships with tuition reimbursements available (averaging $6,004 per year), 13 teaching assistantships with tuition reimbursements available (averaging $9,368 per year); career-related internships or fieldwork, institutionally sponsored loans, scholarships/grants, traineeships, health care benefits, tuition waivers (full and partial), and unspecified assistantships also available. Support available to part-time students. Financial award application deadline: 3/15; financial award applicants required to submit FAFSA. *Unit head:* Dr. Victor Willson, Department Head, 979-845-1394, E-mail: v-willson@tamu.edu. *Application contact:* Kristie Stramaski, Senior Academic Advisor, 979-845-1833, E-mail: epsyadvisor@tamu.edu.
Website: http://epsy.tamu.edu

**Texas A&M University–Texarkana,** Graduate Studies and Research, College of Health and Behavioral Sciences, Texarkana, TX 75505-5518. Offers counseling psychology (MS). *Program availability:* Part-time, evening/weekend. *Degree requirements:* For master's, comprehensive exam (for some programs), thesis or alternative. *Entrance requirements:* For master's, minimum GPA of 3.0 in last 60 hours of bachelor's degree. Additional exam requirements/recommendations for international students: Required—TOEFL. Electronic applications accepted.

**Texas Tech University,** Graduate School, College of Arts and Sciences, Department of Psychological Sciences, Lubbock, TX 79409-2051. Offers clinical psychology (PhD); counseling psychology (MA, PhD); general experimental psychology (MA, PhD); psychology (MA). *Accreditation:* APA (one or more programs are accredited). *Faculty:* 32 full-time (14 women), 2 part-time/adjunct (both women). *Students:* 111 full-time (72 women), 12 part-time (6 women); includes 28 minority (3 Black or African American, non-Hispanic/Latino; 1 American Indian or Alaska Native, non-Hispanic/Latino; 8 Asian, non-Hispanic/Latino; 14 Hispanic/Latino; 2 Two or more races, non-Hispanic/Latino), 8 international. Average age 27. 285 applicants, 13% accepted, 23 enrolled. In 2016, 13 master's, 13 doctorates awarded. *Degree requirements:* For doctorate, comprehensive exam, thesis/dissertation, 100 credit hours of organized courses, research credits, and practica. *Entrance requirements:* For master's, GRE General Test, GRE Subject Test, essays, letters of recommendation; for doctorate, GRE General Test, essays, letters of recommendation. Additional exam requirements/recommendations for international students: Required—TOEFL (minimum score 550 paper-based; 79 iBT). *Application deadline:* For fall admission, 6/1 priority date for domestic students, 1/15 priority date for international students; for spring admission, 9/1 priority date for domestic students, 6/15 priority date for international students. Applications are processed on a rolling basis. Application fee: $75. Electronic applications accepted. *Expenses:* $300 per credit hour full-time resident tuition; $708 per credit hour full-time non-resident tuition; $50.50 per credit hour fee plus $608 per term fee. *Financial support:* In 2016–17, 115 students received support, including 113 fellowships (averaging $2,657 per year), 76 research assistantships (averaging $5,066 per year), 95 teaching assistantships (averaging $11,737 per year); Federal Work-Study, institutionally sponsored loans, and unspecified assistantships also available. Financial award application deadline: 4/15; financial award applicants required to submit FAFSA. *Faculty research:* Health psychology, addictive behaviors, depression and suicide risk, sexuality/sexual risk behaviors/HIV, neuroscience/neuroimaging, forensic and correctional psychology. *Total annual research expenditures:* $710,154. *Unit head:* Dr. Robert Morgan, Professor and Chair, 806-834-7117, Fax: 806-742-0818, E-mail: robert.morgan@ttu.edu. *Application contact:* Kay Hill, Admissions Coordinator, 806-742-3711 Ext. 222, Fax: 806-742-0818, E-mail: kay.hill@ttu.edu.
Website: http://www.depts.ttu.edu/psy/

**Texas Wesleyan University,** Graduate Programs, Programs in Education, Fort Worth, TX 76105. Offers education (M Ed, Ed D); marriage and family therapy (MSMFT, PhD); professional counseling (MA); school counseling (MS). *Program availability:* Part-time, evening/weekend. *Faculty:* 18 full-time (9 women), 10 part-time/adjunct (5 women). *Students:* 23 full-time (18 women), 217 part-time (190 women); includes 121 minority (61 Black or African American, non-Hispanic/Latino; 3 American Indian or Alaska Native, non-Hispanic/Latino; 2 Asian, non-Hispanic/Latino; 47 Hispanic/Latino; 8 Two or more races, non-Hispanic/Latino), 9 international. Average age 36. 194 applicants, 70% accepted, 118 enrolled. In 2016, 52 master's, 8 doctorates awarded. *Degree requirements:* For master's, comprehensive exam (for some programs); for doctorate, thesis/dissertation. *Entrance requirements:* For master's and doctorate, GRE General Test. Additional exam requirements/recommendations for international students: Required—TOEFL (minimum score 550 paper-based; 79 iBT), IELTS (minimum score 6.5). *Application deadline:* Applications are processed on a rolling basis. Application fee: $64. Electronic applications accepted. *Expenses:* Contact institution. *Financial support:* Career-related internships or fieldwork, Federal Work-Study, scholarships/grants, and tuition waivers (full and partial) available. Support available to part-time students. Financial award application deadline: 3/15; financial award applicants required to submit FAFSA. *Faculty research:* Teacher effectiveness, bilingual education, analytic teaching. *Unit head:* Dr. Carlos Martinez, Dean, School of Education, 817-531-4940, Fax: 817-531-4943. *Application contact:* Amy Orcutt, Interim Director of Graduate Admissions, 817-531-4288, Fax: 817-531-4261, E-mail: arorcutt@txwes.edu.
Website: https://txwes.edu/academics/school-of-education/

**Texas Woman's University,** Graduate School, College of Arts and Sciences, Department of Psychology and Philosophy, Denton, TX 76201. Offers counseling psychology (MA, PhD); school psychology (PhD, SSP). *Accreditation:* APA (one or more programs are accredited). *Students:* 63 full-time (58 women), 43 part-time (39 women); includes 43 minority (11 Black or African American, non-Hispanic/Latino; 10 Asian, non-Hispanic/Latino; 19 Hispanic/Latino; 3 Two or more races, non-Hispanic/Latino). Average age 30. In 2016, 14 master's, 9 doctorates, 5 other advanced degrees awarded. Terminal master's awarded for partial completion of doctoral program. *Degree requirements:* For master's, comprehensive exam (for some programs), thesis (for some programs); for doctorate, comprehensive exam, thesis/dissertation, internship, residency. *Entrance requirements:* For master's, GRE (preferred minimum score 153 [500 old version] Verbal, 144 [500 old version] Quantitative, 4 Analytical), BA/BS or 18 hours in psychology; minimum GPA 3.0, 3.5 in psychology classes; 3 letters of reference; curriculum vitae; essays; for doctorate, GRE (preferred minimum score 153 [500 old version] Verbal, 144 [500 old version] Quantitative, 4 Analytical), 3 letters of reference, minimum GPA of 3.0 overall and 3.5 in psychology classes, MA in psychology or related discipline with thesis, curriculum vitae, essays. Additional exam requirements/recommendations for international students: Required—TOEFL (minimum score 550 paper-based; 79 iBT). *Application deadline:* For fall admission, 12/15 priority date for domestic students, 12/15 for international students. Applications are processed on a rolling basis. Application fee: $50 ($75 for international students). Electronic applications accepted. *Expenses: Tuition,* state resident: full-time $9046; part-time $251 per credit hour. *Tuition,* nonresident: full-time $22,922; part-time $614 per credit hour. *International tuition:* $23,046 full-time. *Required fees:* $2690; $1285 per credit hour.

One-time fee: $50. Tuition and fees vary according to course level, course load, program and reciprocity agreements. *Financial support:* Research assistantships, teaching assistantships, career-related internships or fieldwork, Federal Work-Study, institutionally sponsored loans, scholarships/grants, traineeships, health care benefits, and unspecified assistantships available. Support available to part-time students. Financial award application deadline: 3/1; financial award applicants required to submit FAFSA. *Faculty research:* Women's anger, school neuropsychological theory and assessment, body image dysfunction, traumatic stress, classical ethics, mental health and behavioral needs of adolescents in alternative education. *Unit head:* Dr. Shannon Scott, Chair, 940-898-2303, Fax: 940-898-2301, E-mail: sscott@twu.edu. *Application contact:* Dr. Samuel Wheeler, Assistant Director of Admissions, 940-898-3188, Fax: 940-898-3081, E-mail: wheelersr@twu.edu.
Website: http://www.twu.edu/psychology-philosophy/

**Touro College,** School of Health Sciences, Bay Shore, NY 11706. Offers industrial-organizational psychology (MS); mental health counseling (MS); occupational therapy (MS); physical therapy (DPT); physician assistant (MS); speech-language pathology (MS). *Faculty:* 81 full-time (55 women), 77 part-time/adjunct (46 women). *Students:* 628 full-time (470 women), 113 part-time (73 women); includes 143 minority (31 Black or African American, non-Hispanic/Latino; 1 American Indian or Alaska Native, non-Hispanic/Latino; 61 Asian, non-Hispanic/Latino; 42 Hispanic/Latino; 1 Native Hawaiian or other Pacific Islander, non-Hispanic/Latino; 7 Two or more races, non-Hispanic/Latino; 63 international. Average age 28. *Expenses:* Contact institution. *Financial support:* Fellowships available. *Unit head:* Dr. Louis Primavera, Dean, School of Health Sciences, 516-673-3200, E-mail: louis.primavera@touro.edu. *Application contact:* Brian J. Diele, Director of Student Administrative Services, 631-665-1600 Ext. 6311, E-mail: brian.diele@touro.edu.

**Towson University,** Program in Psychology, Towson, MD 21252-0001. Offers clinical psychology (MA); counseling psychology (MA); experimental psychology (MA); school psychology (MA). *Program availability:* Part-time, evening/weekend. *Students:* 104 full-time (72 women), 27 part-time (23 women); includes 34 minority (12 Black or African American, non-Hispanic/Latino; 7 Asian, non-Hispanic/Latino; 10 Hispanic/Latino; 5 Two or more races, non-Hispanic/Latino). *Degree requirements:* For master's, thesis (for some programs). *Entrance requirements:* For master's, GRE, minimum GPA of 3.0, letters of recommendation. *Application deadline:* For fall admission, 2/1 for domestic and international students. Application fee: $45. Electronic applications accepted. *Expenses:* Tuition, state resident: full-time $7580; part-time $379 per unit. Tuition, nonresident: full-time $15,700; part-time $785 per unit. *Required fees:* $2480. *Financial support:* Application deadline: 4/1. *Unit head:* Dr. Geoffrey Munro, Graduate Program Director, 410-704-2634, E-mail: psyc@towson.edu. *Application contact:* Coverley Beidleman, Assistant Director of Graduate Admissions, 410-704-2113, Fax: 410-704-3030, E-mail: grads@towson.edu.
Website: https://www.towson.edu/cla/departments/psychology/grad/

**Trinity Christian College,** Program in Counseling Psychology, Palos Heights, IL 60463-0929. Offers MA. *Program availability:* Evening/weekend, online learning.

**Trinity International University,** Trinity Evangelical Divinity School, Deerfield, IL 60015-1284. Offers academic ministry (M Div); Biblical and Near Eastern archaeology and languages (MA); chaplaincy and ministry care (MA); Christian studies (Certificate); church and parachurch ministry (M Div); church history (MA, Th M); counseling (Th M); educational ministries (MA); educational ministry (Th M); educational studies (PhD); intercultural studies (MA, PhD); leadership and management (D Min); mental health counseling (MA); military chaplaincy (D Min); ministry (MA); missions (Th M); missions and evangelism (D Min); New Testament (MA, Th M); Old Testament (Th M); Old Testament and Semitic languages (MA); pastoral ministry and care (D Min); pastoral theology (Th M); preaching and teaching (D Min); spiritual formation and education (D Min); systematic theology (MA, Th M); theological studies (MA, PhD); urban ministry (MA). *Program availability:* Part-time, online learning. *Students:* 578 full-time (141 women), 711 part-time (202 women). *Degree requirements:* For master's, comprehensive exam, thesis, fieldwork; for doctorate, comprehensive exam (for some programs), thesis/dissertation; for Certificate, comprehensive exam, integrative papers. *Entrance requirements:* For master's, GRE, MAT, minimum cumulative undergraduate GPA of 3.0; for doctorate, GRE, minimum cumulative graduate GPA of 3.2; for Certificate, GRE, MAT, minimum undergraduate GPA of 2.5. Additional exam requirements/recommendations for international students: Required—TOEFL (minimum score 580 paper-based), TWE (minimum score 4). *Application deadline:* For fall admission, 7/15 priority date for domestic and international students. Applications are processed on a rolling basis. Application fee: $25. Electronic applications accepted. *Expenses:* Tuition, area resident: Full-time $19,898. *Required fees:* $200. *Financial support:* Fellowships with partial tuition reimbursements, teaching assistantships with partial tuition reimbursements, career-related internships or fieldwork, Federal Work-Study, scholarships/grants, and tuition waivers (partial) available. Financial award application deadline: 4/1; financial award applicants required to submit FAFSA. *Unit head:* Dr. Tite Tienou, Academic Dean, 847-317-8086, Fax: 847-317-8014, E-mail: ttienou@teds.edu. *Application contact:* Ron Campbell, Director of Admissions, 800-345-8337, Fax: 847-317-8097, E-mail: rcampbel@tiu.edu.
Website: https://divinity.tiu.edu/

**Trinity International University,** Trinity Graduate School, Deerfield, IL 60015-1284. Offers athletic training (MA); bioethics (MA); counseling psychology (MA); diverse learning (M Ed); leadership (MA); teaching (MA). *Program availability:* Part-time, evening/weekend, online learning. *Degree requirements:* For master's, comprehensive exam. *Entrance requirements:* For master's, GRE General Test or MAT, minimum undergraduate GPA of 3.0. Additional exam requirements/recommendations for international students: Required—TOEFL (minimum score 580 paper-based), TWE (minimum score 4). *Application deadline:* For fall admission, 8/1 priority date for domestic students, 5/1 for international students; for spring admission, 12/1 priority date for domestic students, 12/1 for international students. Applications are processed on a rolling basis. Application fee: $25. Electronic applications accepted. *Expenses:* Tuition, area resident: Full-time $19,898. *Required fees:* $200. *Financial support:* Career-related internships or fieldwork, Federal Work-Study, institutionally sponsored loans, and tuition waivers (partial) available. Support available to part-time students. Financial award application deadline: 4/1; financial award applicants required to submit FAFSA. *Unit head:* Dr. Thomas Cornman, Dean, 847-317-7001, Fax: 847-317-4786. *Application contact:* Blaise Brankatelli, Director of Graduate Admissions, 847-317-8000, Fax: 847-317-8097, E-mail: gradadmissions@tiu.edu.
Website: https://graduate.tiu.edu/

**Trinity International University Florida,** Graduate School, Davie, FL 33324. Offers MA.

**Trinity Washington University,** School of Education, Washington, DC 20017-1094. Offers clinical mental health counseling (MA); early childhood education (MAT); educating for change (M Ed); educational administration (MSA); elementary education (MAT); reading (M Ed); school counseling (MA); secondary education (MAT), including English, social studies; special education (MAT). *Accreditation:* NCATE. *Program availability:* Part-time, evening/weekend. *Degree requirements:* For master's, thesis (for some programs), capstone project(s). *Entrance requirements:* For master's, PRAXIS I,

minimum GPA of 2.8. Additional exam requirements/recommendations for international students: Required—TOEFL (minimum score 550 paper-based). *Faculty research:* Technology, literacy, special education, organizations, inclusion models.

**Trinity Western University,** School of Graduate Studies, Program in Counseling Psychology, Langley, BC V2Y 1Y1, Canada. Offers MA. *Accreditation:* ACA. *Program availability:* Part-time. *Degree requirements:* For master's, comprehensive exam, thesis. *Entrance requirements:* For master's, GRE (if out of school for 5 years prior to applying), BA in honors psychology, minimum GPA of 3.0 for 3rd and 4th year of BA. Additional exam requirements/recommendations for international students: Required—TOEFL (minimum score 600 paper-based). *Faculty research:* Meaning, group counseling, trauma, counseling supervision.

**Union College,** Graduate Programs, Department of Psychology, Barbourville, KY 40906-1499. Offers clinical psychology (MA); counseling psychology (MA); school psychology (MA).

**United States International University–Africa,** School of Arts and Sciences, Nairobi, Kenya. Offers counseling psychology (MA), including chemical dependency, health psychology; international relations (MA), including development studies, diplomacy and foreign policy, peace and conflict studies. *Program availability:* Part-time, evening/weekend. *Degree requirements:* For master's, thesis, practicum. *Entrance requirements:* For master's, GRE General Test, 2 letters of recommendation, resume. Additional exam requirements/recommendations for international students: Required—TOEFL. *Faculty research:* Trauma in children, African intellectualism, psychological assessment tools.

**Universidad del Turabo,** Graduate Programs, School of Social Sciences and Humanities, Programs in Psychology, Program in Counseling Psychology, Gurabo, PR 00778-3030. Offers M Psych, Psy D, Certificate. *Students:* 124 full-time (94 women), 107 part-time (73 women); all minorities (all Hispanic/Latino). Average age 31. 176 applicants, 52% accepted, 67 enrolled. In 2016, 31 master's, 10 doctorates, 1 Certificate awarded. *Entrance requirements:* For master's, GRE, GMAT, or EXADEP, interview, essay, official transcript, recommendation letters. *Application deadline:* Applications are processed on a rolling basis. Application fee: $25. Electronic applications accepted. *Financial support:* Institutionally sponsored loans available. Financial award applicants required to submit FAFSA. *Unit head:* Maria del Carmen Santos, Dean, 787-743-7979 Ext. 4232. *Application contact:* Diriee Rodriguez, Admissions Director, 787-743-7979 Ext. 4453, E-mail: admisiones-ut@suagm.edu.
Website: http://ut.suagm.edu/es/sociales

**Universidad Metropolitana,** School of Social Sciences, Humanities and Communications, Program in Counseling Psychology, San Juan, PR 00928-1150. Offers MA.

**University at Albany, State University of New York,** School of Education, Division of Counseling Psychology, Albany, NY 12222-0001. Offers counseling psychology (PhD); mental health counseling (MS). *Program availability:* Evening/weekend. *Entrance requirements:* For master's, GRE General Test. Additional exam requirements/recommendations for international students: Required—TOEFL (minimum score 550 paper-based). *Application deadline:* For fall admission, 2/15 for domestic and international students. Application fee: $75. Electronic applications accepted. *Expenses:* Tuition, state resident: full-time $10,870; part-time $453 per credit hour. Tuition, nonresident: full-time $22,210; part-time $925 per credit hour. *International tuition:* $21,550 full-time. *Required fees:* $1864; $96 per credit hour. *Financial support:* Career-related internships or fieldwork available. *Unit head:* Micki Friedlander, Director, 518-442-5049, E-mail: mfriedlander@albany.edu.
Website: http://www.albany.edu/counseling_psych/

**University at Buffalo, the State University of New York,** Graduate School, Graduate School of Education, Department of Counseling, School, and Educational Psychology, Buffalo, NY 14260. Offers applied statistical analysis (Advanced Certificate); counseling/school psychology (PhD); counselor education (Ed M); education studies (Ed M); educational psychology (MA, PhD); mental health counseling (MS, Certificate); mindful counseling for wellness and engagement (Advanced Certificate); rehabilitation counseling (MS, Advanced Certificate); school counseling (Ed M, Certificate). *Accreditation:* CORE (one or more programs are accredited). *Program availability:* Part-time, 100% online. *Faculty:* 27 full-time (11 women), 52 part-time/adjunct (45 women). *Students:* 161 full-time (131 women), 140 part-time (109 women); includes 30 minority (22 Black or African American, non-Hispanic/Latino; 2 American Indian or Alaska Native, non-Hispanic/Latino; 3 Asian, non-Hispanic/Latino; 3 Hispanic/Latino; 20 international. Average age 32. 321 applicants, 56% accepted, 113 enrolled. In 2016, 62 master's, 10 doctorates, 47 other advanced degrees awarded. *Degree requirements:* For master's, comprehensive exam (for some programs), thesis (for some programs); for doctorate, comprehensive exam, thesis/dissertation. *Entrance requirements:* For master's, GRE General Test, interview, letters of reference; for doctorate, GRE General Test, interview, letters of reference, writing sample. Additional exam requirements/recommendations for international students: Required—TOEFL (minimum score 79 iBT). *Application deadline:* For fall admission, 2/1 priority date for domestic and international students. Application fee: $50. Electronic applications accepted. *Financial support:* In 2016–17, 20 fellowships (averaging $8,477 per year), 33 research assistantships with tuition reimbursements (averaging $10,419 per year) were awarded; teaching assistantships, career-related internships or fieldwork, Federal Work-Study, institutionally sponsored loans, scholarships/grants, tuition waivers (full and partial), and unspecified assistantships also available. Financial award application deadline: 2/1; financial award applicants required to submit FAFSA. *Faculty research:* Multicultural counseling, class size effects, good work in counseling, eating disorders, outcome assessment, change agents and therapeutic factors in group counseling. *Total annual research expenditures:* $1.3 million. *Unit head:* Dr. Jeremy Finn, Chair, 716-645-1126, Fax: 716-645-6616, E-mail: finn@buffalo.edu. *Application contact:* Joanne Laska, Admissions Assistant, 716-645-2110, Fax: 716-645-7937, E-mail: jlaska@buffalo.edu.
Website: http://gse.buffalo.edu/csep

**The University of Akron,** Graduate School, Buchtel College of Arts and Sciences, Department of Psychology, Program in Counseling Psychology, Akron, OH 44325. Offers MA, PhD. *Accreditation:* APA (one or more programs are accredited). *Students:* 25 full-time (19 women), 8 part-time (5 women); includes 10 minority (6 Black or African American, non-Hispanic/Latino; 4 Hispanic/Latino), 2 international. Average age 27. 60 applicants, 8% accepted, 4 enrolled. In 2016, 6 master's, 2 doctorates awarded. *Degree requirements:* For doctorate, one foreign language, comprehensive exam, thesis/dissertation. *Entrance requirements:* For doctorate, GRE, bachelor's degree in psychology or 30 credits of psychology coursework; current curriculum vitae; declaration of intent outlining goals and interests; three letters of recommendation. Additional exam requirements/recommendations for international students: Required—TOEFL (minimum score 550 paper-based; 79 iBT), IELTS (minimum score 6.5). *Application deadline:* For fall admission, 12/1 for domestic and international students. Application fee: $45 ($70 for international students). Electronic applications accepted. *Expenses:* Tuition, state resident: full-time $8618; part-time $359 per credit hour. Tuition, nonresident: full-time $17,149; part-time $715 per credit hour. *Required fees:* $1652. *Faculty research:* Counseling process and outcome, suicide, diversity issues and counseling psychology

## Counseling Psychology

(e.g., gender, race, ethnicity, sexual orientation) vocational psychology, assessment. *Unit head:* Dr. Paul Levy, Chair, 330-972-8639, E-mail: pelevy@uakron.edu. Website: http://www.uakron.edu/psychology/academics/cpcp/

**The University of Akron,** Graduate School, College of Health Professions, School of Counseling, Program in Clinical Mental Health Counseling, Akron, OH 44325. Offers MA. *Accreditation:* ACA; NCATE. *Students:* 44 full-time (37 women), 30 part-time (25 women); includes 16 minority (9 Black or African American, non-Hispanic/Latino; 2 Asian, non-Hispanic/Latino; 5 Hispanic/Latino). Average age 29. 51 applicants, 51% accepted, 15 enrolled. In 2016, 26 master's awarded. *Degree requirements:* For master's, comprehensive exam. *Entrance requirements:* For master's, minimum GPA of 2.75, letters of recommendation, interview. Additional exam requirements/recommendations for international students: Required—TOEFL (minimum score 550 paper-based; 79 iBT), IELTS (minimum score 6.5). *Application deadline:* Applications are processed on a rolling basis. Application fee: $45 ($70 for international students). Electronic applications accepted. *Expenses:* Tuition, state resident: full-time $8618; part-time $359 per credit hour. Tuition, nonresident: full-time $17,149; part-time $715 per credit hour. *Required fees:* $1652. *Application contact:* Dr. Robert Schwartz, Program Coordinator, 330-972-8155, E-mail: rcs@uakron.edu. Website: https://www.uakron.edu/soc/masters/cmhc/

**The University of Akron,** Graduate School, College of Health Professions, School of Counseling, Program in Counseling Psychology, Akron, OH 44325. Offers PhD. *Accreditation:* APA. *Students:* 9 full-time (8 women), 15 part-time (11 women); includes 7 minority (all Black or African American, non-Hispanic/Latino). Average age 32. 35 applicants, 17% accepted, 2 enrolled. In 2016, 3 doctorates awarded. *Degree requirements:* For doctorate, one foreign language, comprehensive exam, thesis/dissertation, written and oral exams. *Entrance requirements:* For doctorate, GRE, minimum GPA of 2.75 on all undergraduate coursework, 3.25 graduate; three letters of recommendation; declaration of intent outlining occupational goals, interests, and commitment to program; current curriculum vitae. Additional exam requirements/recommendations for international students: Required—TOEFL (minimum score 550 paper-based), IELTS (minimum score 6.5). *Application deadline:* For fall admission, 12/1 for domestic and international students. Application fee: $45 ($70 for international students). Electronic applications accepted. *Expenses:* Tuition, state resident: full-time $8618; part-time $359 per credit hour. Tuition, nonresident: full-time $17,149; part-time $715 per credit hour. *Required fees:* $1652. *Application contact:* Dr. John Queener, Co-Director, 330-972-6149, E-mail: jqueener@uakron.edu. Website: https://www.uakron.edu/psychology/academics/cpcp/index.dot

**University of Alberta,** Faculty of Graduate Studies and Research, Department of Educational Psychology, Edmonton, AB T6G 2E1, Canada. Offers counseling psychology (M Ed, PhD); educational psychology (M Ed, PhD); instructional technology (M Ed); school counseling (M Ed); school psychology (M Ed, PhD); special education (M Ed, PhD); special education-deafness studies (M Ed); teaching English as a second language (M Ed). *Program availability:* Part-time. *Degree requirements:* For master's, thesis optional; for doctorate, comprehensive exam, thesis/dissertation. *Entrance requirements:* For master's and doctorate, minimum GPA of 3.0. Additional exam requirements/recommendations for international students: Required—TOEFL. *Faculty research:* Human learning, development and assessment.

**The University of Arizona,** College of Education, Department of Disability and Psychoeducational Studies, Program in Counseling and Mental Health, Tucson, AZ 85721. Offers rehabilitation counseling (MA); school counseling (MA). *Accreditation:* ACA. *Entrance requirements:* Additional exam requirements/recommendations for international students: Required—TOEFL (minimum score 550 paper-based; 80 iBT). *Faculty research:* Further knowledge and understanding of abilities, disabilities, adaptations, interventions, and support systems; preparing professionals to educate and facilitate the development of individuals with disabilities and special abilities; providing leadership at the local, state, national, and international levels.

**University of Baltimore,** Graduate School, Yale Gordon College of Arts and Sciences, Program in Applied Psychology, Baltimore, MD 21201-5779. Offers counseling psychology (MS). *Program availability:* Part-time, evening/weekend. *Degree requirements:* For master's, thesis optional. *Entrance requirements:* For master's, GRE, minimum GPA of 3.0. Additional exam requirements/recommendations for international students: Required—TOEFL (minimum score 550 paper-based). Electronic applications accepted. *Expenses:* Contact institution. *Faculty research:* Participatory decision-making, counter-productive workplace behavior, organizational consulting, substance abuse treatment, cognitive functioning in head injured.

**University of Bridgeport,** School of Arts and Sciences, Department of Counseling, Bridgeport, CT 06604. Offers clinical mental health counseling (MS); college student personnel (MS); community counseling (MS); human resource development (MS); human service (MS). *Program availability:* Part-time, evening/weekend. *Degree requirements:* For master's, thesis, project. *Entrance requirements:* Additional exam requirements/recommendations for international students: Recommended—TOEFL (minimum score 550 paper-based; 80 iBT), IELTS (minimum score 6.5). Electronic applications accepted. *Expenses:* Contact institution.

**The University of British Columbia,** Faculty of Education, Department of Educational and Counseling Psychology, and Special Education, Vancouver, BC V6T 1Z4, Canada. Offers counseling psychology (M Ed, MA, PhD); guidance studies (Diploma); human development, learning and culture (M Ed, MA, PhD); measurement, evaluation, and research methodology (M Ed, MA, PhD); school psychology (M Ed, MA, PhD); special education (M Ed, MA, PhD, Diploma). *Program availability:* Part-time. *Degree requirements:* For master's, thesis (for some programs); for doctorate, comprehensive exam, thesis/dissertation. *Entrance requirements:* For master's, GRE General Test (counseling psychology MA); for doctorate, GRE General Test. Additional exam requirements/recommendations for international students: Required—TOEFL. Application fee: $102 Canadian dollars ($165 Canadian dollars for international students). Electronic applications accepted. *Expenses:* $6,865 per year tuition, $10,938 per year international (for MA, M Ed); $4,802 per year tuition, $8,436 per year international (for PhD). *Financial support:* Fellowships, research assistantships, teaching assistantships, career-related internships or fieldwork, Federal Work-Study, institutionally sponsored loans, scholarships/grants, health care benefits, tuition waivers (full and partial), and unspecified assistantships available. *Faculty research:* Women, family, social problems, career transition, stress and coping problems. *Application contact:* Karen Yan, Graduate Program Assistant, 604-822-6371, Fax: 604-822-3302, E-mail: karen.yan@ubc.ca. Website: http://ecps.educ.ubc.ca/

**University of Calgary,** Faculty of Graduate Studies, Werklund School of Education, Division of Applied Psychology, Calgary, AB T2N 1N4, Canada. Offers counseling psychology (M Sc, MC, PhD); school and applied child psychology (M Ed, M Sc, PhD). *Program availability:* Part-time. *Degree requirements:* For master's, thesis (for some programs), final oral exam; for doctorate, thesis/dissertation, candidacy exam, final oral exam. *Entrance requirements:* For master's, minimum GPA of 3.0, 3 letters of reference; for doctorate, minimum GPA of 3.5, 3 letters of reference. *Faculty research:* Counselor education, family life studies, learning and cognition.

**University of California, Berkeley,** UC Berkeley Extension, Certificate Programs in Behavioral and Health Sciences, Berkeley, CA 94720-1500. Offers alcohol and drug abuse studies (Certificate). *Accreditation:* APA.

**University of California, Santa Barbara,** Graduate Division, Gevirtz Graduate School of Education, Santa Barbara, CA 93106-9490. Offers counseling, clinical and school psychology (MA, PhD, Credential), including clinical psychology (PhD), counseling psychology (MA, PhD), pupil personnel services (Credential), school psychology (PhD); education (MA, PhD); teacher education (M Ed, Credential), including multiple subject teaching (Credential), single subject teaching (Credential), special education (Credential), teaching (M Ed); MA/PhD. *Accreditation:* APA (one or more programs are accredited). Terminal master's awarded for partial completion of doctoral program. *Degree requirements:* For master's, comprehensive exam (for some programs), thesis (for some programs); for doctorate, comprehensive exam (for some programs), thesis/dissertation. *Entrance requirements:* For master's and doctorate, GRE; for Credential, GRE or MAT, CSET, CBEST. Additional exam requirements/recommendations for international students: Required—TOEFL (minimum score 550 paper-based; 80 iBT), IELTS (minimum score 7). Electronic applications accepted. *Faculty research:* Needs of diverse students, school accountability and leadership, school violence, language learning and literacy, science/math education.

**University of Central Arkansas,** Graduate School, College of Health and Behavioral Sciences, Department of Counseling and Psychology, Program in Counseling Psychology, Conway, AR 72035-0001. Offers MS. *Degree requirements:* For master's, comprehensive exam, thesis optional. *Entrance requirements:* For master's, GRE General Test, minimum GPA of 2.7. Additional exam requirements/recommendations for international students: Required—TOEFL (minimum score 550 paper-based). Electronic applications accepted.

**University of Central Missouri,** The Graduate School, Warrensburg, MO 64093. Offers accountancy (MA); accounting (MBA); applied mathematics (MS); aviation safety (MA); biology (MS); business administration (MBA); career and technical education leadership (MS); college student personnel administration (MS); communication (MA); computer science (MS); counseling (MS); criminal justice (MS); educational leadership (Ed D); educational technology (MS); elementary and early childhood education (MSE); English (MA); environmental studies (MA); finance (MBA); history (MA); human services/educational technology (Ed S); human services/learning resources (Ed S); human services/professional counseling (Ed S); industrial hygiene (MS); industrial management (MS); information systems (MBA); information technology (MS); kinesiology (MS); library science and information services (MS); literacy education (MSE); marketing (MBA); mathematics (MS); music (MA); occupational safety management (MS); psychology (MS); rural family nursing (MS); school administration (MS); social gerontology (MS); sociology (MA); special education (MSE); speech language pathology (MS); superintendency (Ed S); teaching (MAT); teaching English as a second language (MA); technology (MS); technology management (PhD); theatre (MA). *Program availability:* Part-time, 100% online, blended/hybrid learning. *Degree requirements:* For master's and Ed S, comprehensive exam (for some programs), thesis (for some programs). *Entrance requirements:* Additional exam requirements/recommendations for international students: Required—TOEFL (minimum score 550 paper-based; 79 iBT). Electronic applications accepted.

**University of Central Oklahoma,** The Jackson College of Graduate Studies, College of Education and Professional Studies, Department of Psychology, Edmond, OK 73034-5209. Offers counseling psychology (MA); experimental psychology (MA); forensic psychology (MA); general psychology (MA); school psychology (MA). *Degree requirements:* For master's, thesis (for some programs). *Entrance requirements:* For master's, GRE. Additional exam requirements/recommendations for international students: Required—TOEFL (minimum score 550 paper-based; 79 iBT), IELTS (minimum score 6.5). Electronic applications accepted. *Faculty research:* Psychopharmacology, computer psychometrics, health psychology research.

**University of Colorado Denver,** School of Education and Human Development, Program in Counseling Psychology and Counselor Education, Denver, CO 80217. Offers counseling (MA), including clinical mental health counseling, couple and family counseling, multicultural counseling, school counseling; school counseling (MA). *Accreditation:* ACA; NCATE. *Program availability:* Part-time, evening/weekend. *Students:* 179 full-time (139 women), 42 part-time (32 women); includes 45 minority (10 Black or African American, non-Hispanic/Latino; 5 Asian, non-Hispanic/Latino; 25 Hispanic/Latino; 5 Two or more races, non-Hispanic/Latino), 1 international. Average age 30. 227 applicants, 28% accepted, 26 enrolled. In 2016, 61 master's awarded. *Degree requirements:* For master's, comprehensive exam (for some programs), thesis or alternative, 63-66 hours. *Entrance requirements:* For master's, GRE or MAT (unless applicant already holds a graduate degree), letters of recommendation, interview, resume, transcripts from all colleges/universities attended. Additional exam requirements/recommendations for international students: Required—TOEFL (minimum score 525 paper-based; 71 iBT); Recommended—IELTS (minimum score 6.3). *Application deadline:* For fall admission, 1/15 for domestic students, 1/1 for international students; for spring admission, 9/15 for domestic students, 9/1 for international students. Application fee: $50 ($75 for international students). Electronic applications accepted. *Expenses:* Contact institution. *Financial support:* In 2016–17, 16 students received support. Research assistantships, Federal Work-Study, institutionally sponsored loans, scholarships/grants, and traineeships available. Financial award application deadline: 4/1; financial award applicants required to submit FAFSA. *Faculty research:* Spiritual issues in counseling, multicultural and diversity issues in counseling, adolescent suicide, career development. *Unit head:* Farah Ibrahim, Counseling Professor, 303-315-6329, E-mail: farah.ibrahim@ucdenver.edu. *Application contact:* Student Services Coordinator, 303-315-6300, Fax: 303-315-6311, E-mail: education@ucdenver.edu. Website: http://www.ucdenver.edu/academics/colleges/SchoolOfEducation/Academics/MASTERS/counseling/Pages/default.aspx

**University of Connecticut,** Graduate School, Neag School of Education, Department of Educational Psychology, Program in Counseling Psychology, Storrs, CT 06269. Offers counseling psychology (PhD); school counseling (MA). *Accreditation:* ACA. Terminal master's awarded for partial completion of doctoral program. *Degree requirements:* For master's, comprehensive exam, thesis or alternative; for doctorate, thesis/dissertation. *Entrance requirements:* For doctorate, GRE General Test. Additional exam requirements/recommendations for international students: Required—TOEFL (minimum score 550 paper-based). Electronic applications accepted.

**University of Dayton,** Department of Counselor Education and Human Services, Dayton, OH 45469. Offers clinical mental health counseling (MS Ed); college student personnel (MS Ed); higher education administration (MS Ed); human services (MS Ed); school counseling (MS Ed); school psychology (MS Ed, Ed S). *Accreditation:* ACA; NCATE. *Program availability:* Part-time, evening/weekend. *Faculty:* 10 full-time (6 women), 24 part-time/adjunct (15 women). *Students:* 198 full-time (155 women), 95 part-time (75 women); includes 15 minority (8 Black or African American, non-Hispanic/Latino; 2 Asian, non-Hispanic/Latino; 2 Hispanic/Latino; 3 Two or more races, non-Hispanic/Latino), 3 international. Average age 36. 426 applicants, 28% accepted. In 2016, 115 master's, 9 Ed Ss awarded. *Degree requirements:* For Ed S, thesis. *Entrance requirements:* For master's, MAT or GRE (if GPA less than 2.75), essays (for some

programs). Additional exam requirements/recommendations for international students: Required—TOEFL (minimum score 550 paper-based; 80 iBT); Recommended—IELTS. *Application deadline:* For fall admission, 3/10 priority date for domestic and international students; for spring admission, 9/10 priority date for domestic and international students; for summer admission, 12/1 priority date for domestic and international students. Application fee: $0 ($50 for international students). Electronic applications accepted. *Expenses:* $620 per credit hour (for master's degree programs); $740 per credit hour (for Ed S). *Financial support:* In 2016–17, 7 research assistantships with partial tuition reimbursements (averaging $8,038 per year), 4 teaching assistantships with partial tuition reimbursements (averaging $9,390 per year) were awarded; career-related internships or fieldwork, institutionally sponsored loans, health care benefits, and unspecified assistantships also available. Financial award application deadline: 1/9; financial award applicants required to submit FAFSA. *Faculty research:* School bonding, traumatic brain injuries, second-year student experience, impact of physical space on learning, integrative health and mental health care. *Total annual research expenditures:* $1,500. *Unit head:* Dr. Alan Demmitt, Chair, 937-229-3644, Fax: 937-229-1055, E-mail: ademmitt1@udayton.edu. *Application contact:* Kathleen Brown, Administrative Assistant, 937-229-3644, Fax: 937-229-1055, E-mail: kbrown1@udayton.edu. Website: https://www.udayton.edu/education/departments_and_programs/edc/

**University of Denver,** Morgridge College of Education, Denver, CO 80208. Offers child, family and school psychology (MA, PhD, Ed S); counseling psychology (MA, PhD); curriculum and instruction (MA, Ed D, PhD); curriculum instruction and teaching (Certificate); early childhood special education (MA, Certificate); educational leadership and policy studies (MA, Ed D, PhD, Certificate); higher education (Ed D, PhD); library and information science (MLIS); research methods and statistics (MA, PhD). *Accreditation:* ALA; APA (one or more programs are accredited). *Program availability:* Part-time, evening/weekend, online learning. *Faculty:* 39 full-time (29 women), 60 part-time/adjunct (42 women). *Students:* 498 full-time (392 women), 362 part-time (282 women); includes 223 minority (63 Black or African American, non-Hispanic/Latino; 6 American Indian or Alaska Native, non-Hispanic/Latino; 20 Asian, non-Hispanic/Latino; 102 Hispanic/Latino; 1 Native Hawaiian or other Pacific Islander, non-Hispanic/Latino; 31 Two or more races, non-Hispanic/Latino), 40 international. Average age 32. 1,027 applicants, 69% accepted, 386 enrolled. In 2016, 252 master's, 36 doctorates, 141 other advanced degrees awarded. Terminal master's awarded for partial completion of doctoral program. *Degree requirements:* For master's, comprehensive exam; for doctorate, 2 foreign languages, comprehensive exam, thesis/dissertation. *Entrance requirements:* For master's and doctorate, GRE General Test or GMAT. Additional exam requirements/recommendations for international students: Required—TOEFL (minimum score 550 paper-based; 80 iBT). *Application deadline:* Applications are processed on a rolling basis. Application fee: $65. Electronic applications accepted. *Expenses:* $29,022 per year full-time. *Financial support:* In 2016–17, 697 students received support, including 37 research assistantships with tuition reimbursements available (averaging $11,209 per year), 66 teaching assistantships with tuition reimbursements available (averaging $3,742 per year); career-related internships or fieldwork, Federal Work-Study, institutionally sponsored loans, scholarships/grants, and unspecified assistantships also available. Support available to part-time students. Financial award application deadline: 2/15; financial award applicants required to submit FAFSA. *Faculty research:* Early childhood education, access and equity, educational leadership, family and school partnerships, neurodevelopmental disorders. *Total annual research expenditures:* $3.3 million. *Unit head:* Dr. Karen Riley, Dean, 303-871-3665, Fax: 303-871-4456, E-mail: karen.riley@du.edu. *Application contact:* Jodi Dye, Director of Admissions, 303-871-2510, Fax: 303-871-4456, E-mail: jodi.dye@du.edu. Website: http://morgridge.du.edu

**University of Florida,** Graduate School, College of Liberal Arts and Sciences, Department of Psychology, Gainesville, FL 32611. Offers counseling psychology (PhD); psychology (MA, MS, PhD), including psychology (PhD), women's and gender studies (PhD); JD/PhD. *Degree requirements:* For master's, comprehensive exam, thesis or alternative; for doctorate, comprehensive exam, thesis/dissertation. *Entrance requirements:* For master's and doctorate, GRE General Test, minimum GPA of 3.0. Additional exam requirements/recommendations for international students: Required—TOEFL (minimum score 550 paper-based; 80 iBT), IELTS (minimum score 6). Electronic applications accepted. *Faculty research:* Behavior analysis, behavioral and cognitive neuroscience, counseling, developmental psychology, social psychology.

**University of Great Falls,** Graduate Studies, Program in Counseling, Great Falls, MT 59405. Offers MSC. *Program availability:* Part-time, evening/weekend. *Degree requirements:* For master's, thesis optional, internship. *Entrance requirements:* For master's, GRE General Test, 3 letters of recommendation. Additional exam requirements/recommendations for international students: Required—TOEFL (minimum score 500 paper-based). *Application deadline:* For fall admission, 8/15 priority date for domestic students, 6/15 priority date for international students; for spring admission, 12/15 priority date for domestic students, 10/15 priority date for international students. Applications are processed on a rolling basis. Application fee: $50. Electronic applications accepted. *Expenses:* Tuition: Full-time $14,256; part-time $9504 per semester. *Financial support:* Career-related internships or fieldwork, Federal Work-Study, institutionally sponsored loans, and scholarships/grants available. Support available to part-time students. Financial award application deadline: 6/1. *Faculty research:* Self concept and adolescent offenders, juvenile delinquency, community mental health counseling. *Unit head:* Sylvia Lindinger-Sternart, Coordinator, 406-791-5353, Fax: 406-791-5990. *Application contact:* Melanie Houge, Director of Admissions, 406-791-5210, Fax: 406-791-5209, E-mail: melanie.houge@ugf.edu.

**University of Hawaii at Hilo,** Program in Counseling Psychology, Hilo, HI 96720-4091. Offers MA. *Entrance requirements:* Additional exam requirements/recommendations for international students: Required—TOEFL, IELTS.

**University of Houston,** College of Education, Department of Educational Psychology, Houston, TX 77204. Offers administration and supervision - higher education (M Ed); counseling (M Ed); counseling psychology (PhD); educational psychology (M Ed); school psychology (PhD); school psychology and individual differences (PhD); special education (M Ed). *Accreditation:* NCATE. *Program availability:* Part-time, evening/weekend, online learning. *Degree requirements:* For master's, comprehensive exam or thesis; for doctorate, comprehensive exam, thesis/dissertation. *Entrance requirements:* For master's, GRE, transcripts, 3 letters of recommendation, curriculum vita, goal statement; for doctorate, GRE, transcripts, 3 letters of recommendation, curriculum vita, goal statement, writing sample, interview. Additional exam requirements/recommendations for international students: Required—TOEFL (minimum score 550 paper-based; 79 iBT), IELTS (minimum score 6.5). Electronic applications accepted. *Faculty research:* Evidence-based assessment and intervention, multicultural issues in psychology, social and cultural context of learning, systemic barriers to college, motivational aspects of self-regulated learning.

**University of Houston–Victoria,** School of Arts and Sciences, Program in Psychology, Victoria, TX 77901-4450. Offers counseling psychology (MA); forensic psychology (MA); school psychology (MA). *Program availability:* Part-time, evening/weekend, online learning. *Degree requirements:* For master's, project or thesis. *Entrance requirements:* For master's, GRE General Test. Additional exam requirements/recommendations for

international students: Required—TOEFL (minimum score 550 paper-based). Electronic applications accepted.

**University of Indianapolis,** Graduate Programs, School of Psychological Sciences, Indianapolis, IN 46227-3697. Offers clinical psychology (Psy D); clinical psychology/mental health counseling (MA). *Accreditation:* APA. *Degree requirements:* For master's, practicum; for doctorate, comprehensive exam, thesis/dissertation, 1200 hours of clinical practicum, 2000-hour internship. *Entrance requirements:* For master's, GRE, 3 letters of recommendation; for doctorate, GRE, minimum GPA of 3.0, 18 hours of course work in psychology, 3 letters of recommendation. Additional exam requirements/recommendations for international students: Required—TOEFL (minimum score 550 paper-based).

**The University of Iowa,** Graduate College, College of Education, Department of Psychological and Quantitative Foundations, Iowa City, IA 52242-1316. Offers counseling psychology (PhD); educational measurement and statistics (MA, PhD); educational psychology (MA, PhD); school psychology (PhD, Ed S). *Accreditation:* APA. *Degree requirements:* For master's, thesis optional, exam; for doctorate, comprehensive exam, thesis/dissertation; for Ed S, exam. *Entrance requirements:* For master's, doctorate, and Ed S, GRE General Test, minimum GPA of 3.0. Additional exam requirements/recommendations for international students: Required—TOEFL (minimum score 550 paper-based; 81 iBT). Electronic applications accepted.

**The University of Iowa,** Graduate College, College of Education, Department of Rehabilitation and Counselor Education, Iowa City, IA 52242-1316. Offers counselor education and supervision (PhD); couple and family therapy (PhD); rehabilitation and mental health counseling (MA); rehabilitation counselor education (PhD); school counseling (MA). *Accreditation:* ACA (one or more programs are accredited); CORE (one or more programs are accredited). *Degree requirements:* For master's, thesis optional, exam; for doctorate, comprehensive exam, thesis/dissertation. *Entrance requirements:* For master's and doctorate, GRE General Test, minimum GPA of 3.0. Additional exam requirements/recommendations for international students: Required—TOEFL (minimum score 550 paper-based; 81 iBT). Electronic applications accepted.

**The University of Kansas,** Graduate Studies, School of Education, Department of Educational Psychology, Program in Counseling Psychology, Lawrence, KS 66045. Offers MS, PhD. *Accreditation:* APA (one or more programs are accredited). *Program availability:* Part-time. *Students:* 65 full-time (47 women); includes 12 minority (4 Black or African American, non-Hispanic/Latino; 1 Asian, non-Hispanic/Latino; 2 Hispanic/Latino; 5 Two or more races, non-Hispanic/Latino), 6 international. Average age 28. 117 applicants, 28% accepted, 18 enrolled. In 2016, 14 master's, 2 doctorates awarded. *Entrance requirements:* For master's and doctorate, GRE General Test, minimum GPA of 3.0, resume, statement of purpose, official transcript, three letters of recommendation. Additional exam requirements/recommendations for international students: Required—TOEFL or IELTS. *Application deadline:* For fall admission, 12/1 priority date for domestic and international students. Application fee: $65 ($85 for international students). Electronic applications accepted. *Financial support:* Fellowships, research assistantships, teaching assistantships, career-related internships or fieldwork, scholarships/grants, and unspecified assistantships available. Financial award application deadline: 12/1. *Faculty research:* Career development, assessment and intervention, multi-cultural counseling, counselor training, positive psychology. *Unit head:* Dr. Changming Duan, Director of Counseling Psychology, 785-864-2426, E-mail: duanc@ku.edu. *Application contact:* Penny Fritts, Graduate Admissions Contact, 785-864-9645, E-mail: fritts@ku.edu. Website: http://pre.soe.ku.edu/academics/cpsy/masters

**University of Kentucky,** Graduate School, College of Education, Program in Educational and Counseling Psychology, Lexington, KY 40506-0032. Offers counseling psychology (MS, PhD, Ed S); educational psychology (MS, PhD); school psychology (PhD, Ed S). *Accreditation:* APA (one or more programs are accredited); NCATE. *Degree requirements:* For doctorate, comprehensive exam, thesis/dissertation; for Ed S, comprehensive exam. *Entrance requirements:* For doctorate, GRE General Test, minimum graduate GPA of 3.0; for Ed S, GRE General Test. Additional exam requirements/recommendations for international students: Required—TOEFL (minimum score 550 paper-based). Electronic applications accepted.

**University of Lethbridge,** School of Graduate Studies, Lethbridge, AB T1K 3M4, Canada. Offers addictions counseling (M Sc); agricultural biotechnology (M Sc); agricultural studies (M Sc, MA); anthropology (MA); archaeology (M Sc, MA); art (MA, MFA); biochemistry (M Sc); biological sciences (M Sc); biomolecular science (PhD); biosystems and biodiversity (PhD); Canadian studies (MA); chemistry (M Sc); computer science (M Sc); computer science and geographical information science (M Sc); counseling (MC); counseling psychology (M Ed); dramatic arts (MA); earth, space, and physical science (PhD); economics (MA); education (MA, PhD); educational leadership (M Ed); English (MA); environmental science (M Sc); evolution and behavior (PhD); exercise science (M Sc); French (MA); French/German (MA); French/Spanish (MA); general education (M Ed); geography (M Sc, MA); German (MA); health sciences (M Sc); individualized multidisciplinary (M Sc, MA); kinesiology (M Sc, MA); management (M Sc), including accounting, finance, human resource management and labor relations, information systems, international management, marketing, policy and strategy; mathematics (M Sc); music (M Mus, MA); Native American studies (MA); neuroscience (M Sc, PhD); new media (MA, MFA); nursing (M Sc, MN); philosophy (MA); physics (M Sc); political science (MA); psychology (M Sc, MA); religious studies (MA); sociology (MA); theatre and dramatic arts (MFA); theoretical and computational science (PhD); urban and regional studies (MA); women and gender studies (MA). *Program availability:* Part-time, evening/weekend. *Degree requirements:* For master's, thesis (for some programs); for doctorate, comprehensive exam, thesis/dissertation. *Entrance requirements:* For master's, GMAT (for M Sc in management), bachelor's degree in related field, minimum GPA of 3.0 during previous 20 graded semester courses, 2 years' teaching or related experience (M Ed); for doctorate, master's degree, minimum graduate GPA of 3.5. Additional exam requirements/recommendations for international students: Required—TOEFL (minimum score 580 paper-based; 93 iBT). Electronic applications accepted. *Faculty research:* Movement and brain plasticity, gibberellin physiology, photosynthesis, carbon cycling, molecular properties of main-group ring components.

**University of Louisiana at Monroe,** Graduate School, College of Health and Pharmaceutical Sciences, Programs in Counseling Studies, Monroe, LA 71209-0001. Offers clinical mental health counseling (MS); school counseling (MS). *Accreditation:* ACA; NCATE. *Program availability:* Part-time, evening/weekend, online learning. *Faculty:* 4 full-time (3 women), 2 part-time/adjunct (1 woman). *Students:* 35 full-time (22 women), 16 part-time (7 women); includes 21 minority (20 Black or African American, non-Hispanic/Latino; 1 Asian, non-Hispanic/Latino), 1 international. Average age 30. 167 applicants, 13% accepted, 8 enrolled. In 2016, 13 master's awarded. *Degree requirements:* For master's, comprehensive exam, thesis. *Entrance requirements:* For master's, GRE General Test, minimum GPA of 2.8 in last 60 hours. Additional exam requirements/recommendations for international students: Required—TOEFL (minimum score 500 paper-based; 61 iBT). *Application deadline:* For fall admission, 8/24 priority date for domestic students, 7/1 for international students; for winter admission, 12/14 priority date for domestic students; for spring admission, 1/19 for domestic students, 11/

## Counseling Psychology

1 for international students. Applications are processed on a rolling basis. Application fee: $20 ($30 for international students). Electronic applications accepted. *Expenses:* Tuition, state resident: full-time $6489. Tuition, nonresident: full-time $18,589. *Required fees:* $8984. Tuition and fees vary according to course level, course load, degree level and program. *Financial support:* Career-related internships or fieldwork, Federal Work-Study, and unspecified assistantships available. Financial award application deadline: 4/1; financial award applicants required to submit FAFSA. *Unit head:* Dr. Jana Sutton, Director, 318-342-1246, E-mail: sutton@ulm.edu.
Website: http://www.ulm.edu/counseling/

**University of Louisville,** Graduate School, College of Education and Human Development, Department of Counseling and Human Development, Louisville, KY 40292-0001. Offers counseling and personnel services (M Ed, PhD), including art therapy (M Ed), clinical mental health counseling (M Ed), college student personnel, counseling psychology, counselor education and supervision (PhD), educational psychology, measurement, and evaluation (PhD), school counseling (M Ed). *Accreditation:* APA; NCATE. *Program availability:* Part-time, evening/weekend. *Students:* 148 full-time (115 women), 58 part-time (42 women); includes 52 minority (36 Black or African American, non-Hispanic/Latino; 1 American Indian or Alaska Native, non-Hispanic/Latino; 4 Asian, non-Hispanic/Latino; 7 Hispanic/Latino; 4 Two or more races, non-Hispanic/Latino), 2 international. Average age 28. 206 applicants, 56% accepted, 73 enrolled. In 2016, 38 master's, 1 doctorate awarded. *Degree requirements:* For doctorate, comprehensive exam, thesis/dissertation. *Entrance requirements:* For master's and doctorate, GRE General Test. Application fee: $60. *Expenses:* Tuition, state resident: full-time $12,246; part-time $681 per credit hour. Tuition, nonresident: full-time $25,486; part-time $1417 per credit hour. *Required fees:* $196. Tuition and fees vary according to program and reciprocity agreements. *Financial support:* Fellowships, research assistantships, teaching assistantships, career-related internships or fieldwork, Federal Work-Study, scholarships/grants, health care benefits, and unspecified assistantships available. Financial award application deadline: 6/1; financial award applicants required to submit FAFSA. *Faculty research:* Mental health services and under-served populations; health disparities and outcomes; well-being identity development; measurement and evaluation. *Total annual research expenditures:* $295,684. *Unit head:* Dr. Mark M. Leach, Interim Chair/Professor, 502-852-0588, Fax: 502-852-0629, E-mail: m.leach@louisville.edu. *Application contact:* Betty Hampton, Director of Graduate Student Services, 502-852-5597, Fax: 502-852-1465, E-mail: edadvise@louisville.edu.
Website: http://www.louisville.edu/education/departments/ecpy

**The University of Manchester,** School of Education, Manchester, United Kingdom. Offers counseling (D Couns); counseling psychology (D Couns); education (M Phil, Ed D, PhD); educational and child psychology (Ed D); educational psychology (Ed D).

**University of Mary Hardin-Baylor,** Graduate Studies in Counseling, Belton, TX 76513. Offers clinical and mental health counseling (MA); marriage, family and child counseling (MA); non-clinical professional studies (MA). *Accreditation:* ACA. *Program availability:* Part-time, evening/weekend. *Faculty:* 13 full-time (8 women), 8 part-time/adjunct (3 women). *Students:* 49 full-time (39 women), 22 part-time (16 women); includes 30 minority (17 Black or African American, non-Hispanic/Latino; 12 Hispanic/Latino; 1 Two or more races, non-Hispanic/Latino). Average age 32. 51 applicants, 71% accepted, 23 enrolled. In 2016, 25 master's awarded. *Degree requirements:* For master's, comprehensive exam. *Entrance requirements:* For master's, GRE General Test with minimum cumulative score of 300 on verbal and quantitative portions and minimum score of 3.0 on analytical section (if overall undergraduate GPA is below a 3.0), minimum cumulative undergraduate GPA of 2.75 or 3.0 on last 60 hours of course work; three letters of recommendation; interview with departmental graduate admissions committee. Additional exam requirements/recommendations for international students: Required—TOEFL (minimum score 60 iBT), IELTS (minimum score 4.5). *Application deadline:* For fall admission, 6/1 for domestic students, 4/30 priority date for international students; for spring admission, 11/1 for domestic students, 9/30 priority date for international students. Applications are processed on a rolling basis. Application fee: $35 ($135 for international students). Electronic applications accepted. *Expenses:* Tuition: Full-time $14,940; part-time $830 per credit hour. *Required fees:* $1350; $75 per credit hour. $50 per term. Tuition and fees vary according to course load and degree level. *Financial support:* In 2016–17, 41 students received support. Federal Work-Study, unspecified assistantships, and scholarships for some active duty military personnel available. Support available to part-time students. Financial award applicants required to submit FAFSA. *Faculty research:* Teaching mindfulness skills as part of an interdisciplinary training protocol for doctor of physical therapy students; using symbolic art cards and oracle cards in supervision as a method for teaching appropriate self-disclosure, clinical reflection and counselor development reflection; understanding integral breath therapy. *Unit head:* Dr. Dan Williamson, Director, Graduate Counseling, 254-295-5018, E-mail: dwilliamson@umhb.edu. *Application contact:* Sharon Aguilera, Assistant Director, Graduate Admissions, 254-295-4835, Fax: 254-295-5038, E-mail: saguilera@umhb.edu.
Website: http://graduate.umhb.edu/counseling/

**University of Maryland, College Park,** Academic Affairs, College of Education, Department of Counseling, Higher Education and Special Education, College Park, MD 20742. Offers college student personnel (M Ed, MA); college student personnel administration (PhD); community counseling (CAGS); community/career counseling (M Ed, MA); counseling and personnel services (M Ed, MA, PhD), including art therapy (M Ed), college student personnel (M Ed), counseling and personnel services (PhD), counseling psychology (M Ed), mental health counseling (M Ed), school counseling (M Ed); counseling psychology (PhD); counselor education (PhD); rehabilitation counseling (M Ed, MA, AGSC); school counseling (M Ed, MA); school psychology (M Ed, MA, PhD). *Accreditation:* ACA (one or more programs are accredited); APA (one or more programs are accredited); NCATE. *Program availability:* Part-time, evening/weekend, online learning. *Degree requirements:* For master's, thesis (for some programs); for doctorate, thesis/dissertation. *Entrance requirements:* For master's, GRE General Test or MAT, minimum GPA of 3.0, 3 letters of recommendation; for doctorate, GRE General Test or MAT, minimum GPA of 3.5, 3 letters of recommendation. Additional exam requirements/recommendations for international students: Required—TOEFL. Electronic applications accepted. *Faculty research:* Educational psychology, counseling, health.

**University of Massachusetts Boston,** College of Education and Human Development, Program in Counseling and School Psychology, Boston, MA 02125-3393. Offers PhD. *Accreditation:* ACA; CORE. *Program availability:* Part-time, evening/weekend. *Faculty:* 16 full-time (11 women), 17 part-time/adjunct (9 women). *Students:* 36 full-time (31 women), 3 part-time (all women); includes 8 minority (2 Black or African American, non-Hispanic/Latino; 4 Hispanic/Latino; 2 Two or more races, non-Hispanic/Latino), 4 international. Average age 30. 52 applicants, 27% accepted, 9 enrolled. *Application deadline:* For fall admission, 12/1 for domestic students. *Expenses:* Tuition, state resident: full-time $16,863. Tuition, nonresident: full-time $32,913. *Required fees:* $177. *Financial support:* Research assistantships with full tuition reimbursements, teaching assistantships with full tuition reimbursements, career-related internships or fieldwork, Federal Work-Study, and unspecified assistantships available. Support available to part-

time students. Financial award application deadline: 3/1; financial award applicants required to submit FAFSA. *Faculty research:* Persuasion and power in the counseling process, self-efficacy for counselors and clients, career and biracial issues in family therapy. *Unit head:* Dr. Takuya Minami, Chair of the Department. *Application contact:* Peggy Roldan Patel, Graduate Admissions Coordinator, 617-287-6400, Fax: 617-287-6236, E-mail: bos.gadm@dpc.umassp.edu.

**University of Massachusetts Boston,** College of Education and Human Development, Program in Mental Health Counseling, Boston, MA 02125-3393. Offers MS. *Students:* 65 full-time (55 women), 25 part-time (18 women); includes 20 minority (5 Black or African American, non-Hispanic/Latino; 5 Asian, non-Hispanic/Latino; 8 Hispanic/Latino; 2 Two or more races, non-Hispanic/Latino), 6 international. Average age 34. 98 applicants, 66% accepted, 41 enrolled. In 2016, 41 master's awarded. *Expenses:* Tuition, state resident: full-time $16,863. Tuition, nonresident: full-time $32,913. *Required fees:* $177. *Financial support:* Research assistantships available. *Unit head:* Dr. Boaz Levy, Director. *Application contact:* Peggy Roldan Patel, Graduate Admissions Coordinator, 617-287-6400, Fax: 617-287-6236, E-mail: bos.gadm@dpc.umassp.edu.

**University of Memphis,** Graduate School, College of Education, Department of Counseling, Educational Psychology and Research, Memphis, TN 38152. Offers counseling (MS, Ed D), including clinical mental health counseling (MS), clinical rehabilitation counseling (MS), rehabilitation counseling (MS), school counseling (MS); counseling psychology (PhD); educational psychology and research (MS, PhD), including educational psychology, educational research. *Accreditation:* ACA (one or more programs are accredited); APA (one or more programs are accredited); CORE (one or more programs are accredited); NCATE. *Program availability:* Blended/hybrid learning. *Faculty:* 26 full-time (18 women), 10 part-time/adjunct (7 women). *Students:* 124 full-time (99 women), 79 part-time (60 women); includes 64 minority (48 Black or African American, non-Hispanic/Latino; 3 Asian, non-Hispanic/Latino; 6 Hispanic/Latino; 7 Two or more races, non-Hispanic/Latino), 7 international. Average age 32. 82 applicants, 68% accepted, 39 enrolled. In 2016, 65 master's, 8 doctorates awarded. *Degree requirements:* For master's, comprehensive exam, thesis or alternative, internship; for doctorate, comprehensive exam, thesis/dissertation, practicum, internship, residency, scholarly work. *Entrance requirements:* For master's, GRE General Test or MAT, minimum GPA of 2.5, letters of reference, interview; for doctorate, GRE General Test, master's degree or equivalent, letters of reference, interview, curriculum vitae, personal statement. Additional exam requirements/recommendations for international students: Required—TOEFL (minimum score 550 paper-based; 79 iBT). *Application deadline:* For fall admission, 10/1 priority date for domestic students; for spring admission, 4/1 priority date for domestic students. Applications are processed on a rolling basis. Application fee: $35 ($60 for international students). Electronic applications accepted. *Expenses:* $5,231.50 per semester full-time in-state, $9,623.50 full-time out-of-state. *Financial support:* In 2016–17, 130 students received support, including 13 research assistantships with full tuition reimbursements available (averaging $14,820 per year), 11 teaching assistantships with full tuition reimbursements available (averaging $15,600 per year); fellowships with full tuition reimbursements available, career-related internships or fieldwork, Federal Work-Study, scholarships/grants, and unspecified assistantships also available. Financial award application deadline: 2/1; financial award applicants required to submit FAFSA. *Faculty research:* Anger management, aging and disability, supervision, multicultural counseling. *Unit head:* Dr. Steve West, Chair, 901-678-2841, Fax: 901-678-5114, E-mail: slwest@memphis.edu. *Application contact:* Dr. Suzanne Lease, Interim Assistant Dean of Education and Graduate Programs, 901-678-4476, Fax: 901-678-4778, E-mail: slease@memphis.edu.
Website: http://www.memphis.edu/cepr/

**University of Miami,** Graduate School, School of Education and Human Development, Department of Educational and Psychological Studies, Program in Counseling Psychology, Coral Gables, FL 33124. Offers PhD. *Accreditation:* APA. *Faculty:* 6 full-time (3 women), 13 part-time/adjunct (8 women). *Students:* 31 full-time (22 women); includes 14 minority (3 Black or African American, non-Hispanic/Latino; 2 Asian, non-Hispanic/Latino; 7 Hispanic/Latino; 2 Two or more races, non-Hispanic/Latino). Average age 29. 112 applicants, 17% accepted, 4 enrolled. In 2016, 7 doctorates awarded. *Degree requirements:* For doctorate, thesis/dissertation, qualifying exam. *Entrance requirements:* For doctorate, GRE General Test. Additional exam requirements/recommendations for international students: Required—TOEFL (minimum score 550 paper-based; 80 iBT); Recommended—IELTS (minimum score 6.5). *Application deadline:* For fall admission, 12/10 for domestic students, 11/1 for international students. Application fee: $65. Electronic applications accepted. *Financial support:* In 2016–17, 19 students received support. Fellowships, research assistantships, teaching assistantships, career-related internships or fieldwork, institutionally sponsored loans, scholarships/grants, health care benefits, tuition waivers (full and partial), and unspecified assistantships available. Financial award application deadline: 3/1; financial award applicants required to submit FAFSA. *Faculty research:* Cocaine recidivism, family systems, behavior and health, nontraditional families, stress and coping. *Unit head:* Dr. Lydia Buki, Associate Professor and Director of Training, 305-284-2230, Fax: 305-284-3003, E-mail: l.buki@miami.edu. *Application contact:* Lois Heffernan, Graduate Admissions Coordinator, 305-284-2167, Fax: 305-284-9395, E-mail: lheffernan@miami.edu.
Website: http://www.education.miami.edu/program/Programs.asp?Program_ID-47rc-Graduate

**University of Minnesota, Twin Cities Campus,** Graduate School, College of Liberal Arts, Department of Psychology, Program in Counseling Psychology, Minneapolis, MN 55455-0213. Offers PhD. *Accreditation:* APA. *Degree requirements:* For doctorate, comprehensive exam, thesis/dissertation, internship. *Entrance requirements:* For doctorate, GRE General Test, GRE Subject Test (recommended), 12 credits of upper-level psychology courses, including a course in statistics or psychological measurement. Additional exam requirements/recommendations for international students: Required—TOEFL (minimum score 550 paper-based; 79 iBT).

**University of Missouri,** Office of Research and Graduate Studies, College of Education, Department of Educational, School, and Counseling Psychology, Columbia, MO 65211. Offers counseling psychology (M Ed, MA, PhD, Ed S); educational psychology (M Ed, MA, PhD, Ed S); learning and instruction (M Ed); school psychology (M Ed, MA, PhD, Ed S). *Accreditation:* APA (one or more programs are accredited). *Program availability:* Part-time. *Faculty:* 29 full-time (12 women), 1 part-time/adjunct (0 women). *Students:* 177 full-time (106 women), 204 part-time (102 women). *Degree requirements:* For doctorate, thesis/dissertation. *Entrance requirements:* For master's, doctorate, and Ed S, GRE General Test, minimum GPA of 3.0. Additional exam requirements/recommendations for international students: Required—TOEFL (minimum score 580 paper-based; 92 iBT). *Application deadline:* For fall admission, 12/1 priority date for domestic and international students. Applications are processed on a rolling basis. Application fee: $75 ($90 for international students). Electronic applications accepted. *Expenses:* Tuition, state resident: full-time $6347; part-time $352.60 per credit hour. Tuition, nonresident: full-time $17,379; part-time $965.50 per credit hour. *Required fees:* $1035. Tuition and fees vary according to course load, campus/location and program. *Financial support:* Fellowships, research assistantships, teaching

assistantships, institutionally sponsored loans, traineeships, health care benefits, and unspecified assistantships available. Support available to part-time students. Website: http://education.missouri.edu/ESCP/

**University of Missouri–Kansas City,** School of Education, Kansas City, MO 64110-2499. Offers administration (Ed D); counseling and guidance (MA, Ed S), including mental health counseling (Ed S); school counseling (Ed S); counseling psychology (PhD); curriculum and instruction (MA, Ed S), including language and literacy (Ed S); education (PhD), including higher education administration, PK-12 education administration; educational administration (MA, Ed S), including advanced principal (Ed S), beginning principal (Ed S), district-level administration (Ed S); reading education (MA); special education (MA). PhD in education offered through the School of Graduate Studies. *Accreditation:* NCATE. *Program availability:* Part-time, evening/weekend. *Faculty:* 33 full-time (26 women), 51 part-time/adjunct (39 women). *Students:* 136 full-time (103 women), 275 part-time (194 women); includes 110 minority (71 Black or African American, non-Hispanic/Latino; 3 American Indian or Alaska Native, non-Hispanic/Latino; 8 Asian, non-Hispanic/Latino; 22 Hispanic/Latino; 6 Two or more races, non-Hispanic/Latino), 20 international. Average age 32. 324 applicants, 45% accepted, 108 enrolled. In 2016, 152 master's, 13 doctorates, 50 other advanced degrees awarded. *Degree requirements:* For doctorate, thesis/dissertation, internship, practicum. *Entrance requirements:* For master's, GRE, minimum GPA of 2.75, 2 letters of reference, written statement of purpose; for doctorate, GRE, minimum GPA of 3.0; for Ed S, minimum GPA of 3.0. Additional exam requirements/recommendations for international students: Required—TOEFL (minimum score 550 paper-based; 80 iBT). *Application deadline:* For fall admission, 4/1 priority date for domestic and international students; for spring admission, 11/1 priority date for domestic and international students. Applications are processed on a rolling basis. Application fee: $45 ($50 for international students). *Financial support:* In 2016–17, 12 research assistantships with partial tuition reimbursements (averaging $12,476 per year) were awarded; career-related internships or fieldwork, Federal Work-Study, institutionally sponsored loans, and tuition waivers (full and partial) also available. Support available to part-time students. Financial award application deadline: 3/1; financial award applicants required to submit FAFSA. *Faculty research:* Urban education, inquiry-based field study, theories of counseling and psychotherapy, school literacy, educational technology. *Unit head:* Justin Perry, Dean, 816-235-5663, Fax: 816-235-5270, E-mail: education@umkc.edu. Website: http://education.umkc.edu

**University of Missouri–St. Louis,** College of Education, Department of Counseling and Family Therapy, St. Louis, MO 63121. Offers clinical mental health counseling (M Ed); counseling (PhD); elementary school counseling (M Ed); secondary school counseling (M Ed). *Accreditation:* ACA; NCATE. *Program availability:* Part-time, evening/weekend. *Faculty:* 8 full-time (4 women), 7 part-time/adjunct (6 women). *Students:* 58 full-time (48 women), 164 part-time (129 women); includes 61 minority (48 Black or African American, non-Hispanic/Latino; 2 American Indian or Alaska Native, non-Hispanic/Latino; 3 Asian, non-Hispanic/Latino; 4 Hispanic/Latino; 4 Two or more races, non-Hispanic/Latino), 4 international. Average age 32. 74 applicants, 72% accepted, 44 enrolled. *Degree requirements:* For master's, comprehensive exam. *Entrance requirements:* For master's, 3 letters of recommendation; for doctorate, GRE General Test, 3 letters of recommendation. Additional exam requirements/recommendations for international students: Recommended—TOEFL (minimum score 550 paper-based; 79 iBT), IELTS (minimum score 6.5). *Application deadline:* For fall admission, 5/1 for domestic and international students; for spring admission, 10/1 for domestic and international students. Application fee: $50 ($40 for international students). Electronic applications accepted. *Financial support:* Teaching assistantships with tuition reimbursements available. Financial award application deadline: 4/1; financial award applicants required to submit FAFSA. *Faculty research:* Vocational interests, self-concept, decision-making factors, developmental differences. *Unit head:* Dr. Mark Pope, Chair, 314-516-5782. *Application contact:* 314-516-5458, Fax: 314-516-6996, E-mail: gradadm@umsl.edu.

**University of Montana,** Graduate School, Phyllis J. Washington College of Education and Human Sciences, Department of Counselor Education, Missoula, MT 59812-0002. Offers clinical mental health counseling (MA); counseling and supervision (Ed D); counselor education (Ed S); intercultural youth and family development (MA); school counseling (MA). *Accreditation:* ACA. *Degree requirements:* For doctorate, thesis/dissertation. *Entrance requirements:* For master's, doctorate, and Ed S, GRE General Test. Additional exam requirements/recommendations for international students: Required—TOEFL.

**University of Nebraska at Kearney,** College of Education, Department of Counseling and School Psychology, Kearney, NE 68849-0001. Offers clinical mental health counseling (MS Ed); school counseling (MS Ed), including elementary, secondary; school psychology (Ed S); student affairs (MS Ed). *Accreditation:* ACA; NCATE. *Program availability:* Part-time, evening/weekend, 100% online. *Faculty:* 7 full-time (3 women). *Students:* 69 full-time (56 women), 102 part-time (81 women); includes 21 minority (2 Black or African American, non-Hispanic/Latino; 2 Asian, non-Hispanic/Latino; 12 Hispanic/Latino; 5 Two or more races, non-Hispanic/Latino), 4 international. Average age 30. 43 applicants, 100% accepted, 37 enrolled. In 2016, 24 master's, 13 Ed Ss awarded. *Degree requirements:* For master's, comprehensive exam, thesis optional; for Ed S, thesis. *Entrance requirements:* For master's and Ed S, personal statement, recommendations, resume, interview. Additional exam requirements/recommendations for international students: Recommended—TOEFL (minimum score 550 paper-based; 79 iBT), IELTS (minimum score 6.5). *Application deadline:* For fall admission, 6/15 for domestic and international students; for spring admission, 10/15 for domestic and international students; for summer admission, 3/15 for domestic and international students. Application fee: $45. Electronic applications accepted. *Expenses:* Tuition, state resident: full-time $4064; part-time $225.75 per credit hour. Tuition, nonresident: full-time $8915; part-time $495.25 per credit hour. *Required fees:* $772; $23 per credit hour. Part-time tuition and fees vary according to course load, campus/location, program and reciprocity agreements. *Financial support:* In 2016–17, 7 students received support, including 7 research assistantships with full tuition reimbursements available (averaging $10,500 per year); fellowships, career-related internships or fieldwork, scholarships/grants, health care benefits, and unspecified assistantships also available. Support available to part-time students. Financial award application deadline: 2/28; financial award applicants required to submit FAFSA. *Faculty research:* Multicultural counseling and diversity issues, team decision-making, adult development, women's issues, brief therapy. *Unit head:* Dr. Grace Mims, Chair, Counseling and School Psychology, 308-865-8508, E-mail: mimsga@unk.edu. *Application contact:* Linda Johnson, Director, Graduate Admissions and Programs, 800-717-7881, Fax: 308-865-8837, E-mail: gradstudies@unk.edu. Website: http://www.unk.edu/academics/csp/

**University of Nebraska–Lincoln,** Graduate College, College of Education and Human Sciences, Department of Educational Psychology, Lincoln, NE 68588. Offers cognition, learning and development (MA); counseling psychology (MA); educational psychology (MA, Ed S); psychological studies in education (PhD), including cognition, learning and development, counseling psychology, quantitative, qualitative, and psychometric methods, school psychology; quantitative, qualitative, and psychometric methods (MA);

school psychology (MA, Ed S). *Accreditation:* APA (one or more programs are accredited); NCATE. *Degree requirements:* For master's, thesis optional. *Entrance requirements:* For master's, GRE General Test. Additional exam requirements/recommendations for international students: Required—TOEFL (minimum score 500 paper-based). Electronic applications accepted. *Faculty research:* Measurement and assessment, metacognition, academic skills, child development, multicultural education and counseling.

**University of Nevada, Las Vegas,** Graduate College, College of Education, Department of Educational and Clinical Studies, Las Vegas, NV 89154-3066. Offers addiction studies (Advanced Certificate); counselor education (M Ed, MS), including clinical mental health (MS), school counseling (M Ed); early childhood education (M Ed); early childhood special education (Certificate), including infancy, preschool; English language learning (M Ed); mental health counseling (Advanced Certificate); special education (M Ed, PhD); PhD/JD. *Program availability:* Part-time, evening/weekend. *Faculty:* 17 full-time (8 women), 28 part-time/adjunct (20 women). *Students:* 269 full-time (219 women), 174 part-time (138 women); includes 181 minority (51 Black or African American, non-Hispanic/Latino; 2 American Indian or Alaska Native, non-Hispanic/Latino; 15 Asian, non-Hispanic/Latino; 81 Hispanic/Latino; 3 Native Hawaiian or other Pacific Islander, non-Hispanic/Latino; 29 Two or more races, non-Hispanic/Latino), 23 international. Average age 34. 256 applicants, 72% accepted, 145 enrolled. In 2016, 178 master's, 3 doctorates awarded. *Degree requirements:* For master's, comprehensive exam (for some programs); for doctorate, comprehensive exam, thesis/dissertation; for other advanced degree, final project. *Entrance requirements:* For master's, bachelor's degree; letter of recommendation; statement of purpose; for doctorate, GRE General Test, statement of purpose; writing sample; 3 letters of recommendation. Additional exam requirements/recommendations for international students: Required—TOEFL (minimum score 550 paper-based; 80 iBT), IELTS (minimum score 7). *Application deadline:* For fall admission, 7/15 for domestic students, 5/1 for international students; for spring admission, 11/15 for domestic students, 10/1 for international students; for summer admission, 4/15 for domestic students. Application fee: $60 ($95 for international students). Electronic applications accepted. *Expenses:* $269.25 per credit, $792 per 3-credit course; $9,634 per year resident; $23,274 per year non-resident; $7,094 fees non-resident (7 credits or more); $1,307 annual health insurance fee. *Financial support:* In 2016–17, 12 research assistantships with partial tuition reimbursements (averaging $12,569 per year), 27 teaching assistantships with partial tuition reimbursements (averaging $13,759 per year) were awarded; institutionally sponsored loans, scholarships/grants, health care benefits, and unspecified assistantships also available. Financial award application deadline: 3/15. *Faculty research:* Multicultural issues in counseling, academic interventions for students with disabilities, establishment of pro-social skills in young children with severe disabilities, inclusive strategies for students with disabilities, language and literacy for English language learners. *Total annual research expenditures:* $768,906. *Unit head:* Dr. Monica Brown, Interim Department Chair/Professor, 702-895-3167, Fax: 702-895-3205, E-mail: monica.brown@unlv.edu. *Application contact:* Dr. Cori More, Graduate Coordinator, 702-895-3271, Fax: 702-895-3205, E-mail: cori.more@unlv.edu. Website: http://education.unlv.edu/ecs/

**The University of North Carolina at Greensboro,** Graduate School, School of Education, Department of Counseling and Educational Development, Greensboro, NC 27412-5001. Offers advanced school counseling (PMC); counseling and counselor education (PhD); counseling and educational development (MS); couple and family counseling (PMC); school counseling (PMC); MS/Ed S. *Accreditation:* ACA (one or more programs are accredited); NCATE. *Degree requirements:* For master's, comprehensive exam, practicum, internship; for doctorate, comprehensive exam, thesis/dissertation. *Entrance requirements:* For master's, doctorate, and PMC, GRE General Test. Additional exam requirements/recommendations for international students: Required—TOEFL. Electronic applications accepted. *Faculty research:* Gerontology, invitational theory, career development, marriage and family therapy, drug and alcohol abuse prevention.

**The University of North Carolina at Pembroke,** The Graduate School, School of Education, Programs in Counseling, Pembroke, NC 28372-1510. Offers clinical mental health counseling (MA Ed); professional school counseling (MA Ed). *Accreditation:* NCATE. *Program availability:* Part-time, evening/weekend. *Degree requirements:* For master's, comprehensive exam, thesis optional. *Entrance requirements:* For master's, GRE General Test or MAT, minimum GPA of 3.0 in major, 2.5 overall. Additional exam requirements/recommendations for international students: Required—TOEFL.

**University of North Dakota,** Graduate School, College of Education and Human Development, Department of Counseling Psychology and Community Services, Grand Forks, ND 58202. Offers counseling (MA); counseling psychology (PhD). *Degree requirements:* For master's, comprehensive exam, thesis or alternative; for doctorate, comprehensive exam, thesis/dissertation, final examination. *Entrance requirements:* For master's, GRE General Test or MAT, minimum GPA of 3.0; for doctorate, GRE General Test, minimum GPA of 3.0. Additional exam requirements/recommendations for international students: Required—TOEFL (minimum score 550 paper-based; 79 iBT), IELTS (minimum score 6.5). *Application deadline:* For fall admission, 3/21 for domestic and international students. Application fee: $35. Electronic applications accepted. *Financial support:* Fellowships with full and partial tuition reimbursements, research assistantships with full tuition reimbursements, teaching assistantships with full tuition reimbursements, career-related internships or fieldwork, Federal Work-Study, institutionally sponsored loans, scholarships/grants, tuition waivers (full and partial), and unspecified assistantships available. Support available to part-time students. Financial award application deadline: 3/15; financial award applicants required to submit FAFSA. *Faculty research:* Group dynamics, addictive behavior, item response theory, geopsychology, women's health. *Unit head:* Dr. Dorlene Walker, Graduate Director, 701-777-3737, Fax: 701-777-3184, E-mail: dorlene.walker@und.edu. *Application contact:* Staci Wells, Admissions Associate, 701-777-2945, Fax: 701-777-3619, E-mail: staci.wells@gradschool.und.edu. Website: http://www.und.edu/dept/grad/depts/coun/

**University of Northern Iowa,** Graduate College, College of Social and Behavioral Sciences, School of Applied Human Sciences, MA Program in Counseling, Cedar Falls, IA 50614. Offers mental health counseling (MA); school counseling (MA). *Accreditation:* ACA. *Program availability:* Part-time, evening/weekend. *Degree requirements:* For master's, comprehensive exam, thesis or alternative. *Entrance requirements:* For master's, minimum GPA of 3.0. Additional exam requirements/recommendations for international students: Required—TOEFL (minimum score 500 paper-based; 61 iBT). Electronic applications accepted.

**University of North Florida,** College of Arts and Sciences, Department of Psychology, Jacksonville, FL 32224. Offers counseling psychology (MAC); general psychology (MA). *Program availability:* Part-time, evening/weekend. *Faculty:* 18 full-time (12 women), 1 part-time/adjunct (0 women). *Students:* 34 full-time (19 women), 4 part-time (3 women); includes 6 minority (1 Black or African American, non-Hispanic/Latino; 4 Hispanic/Latino; 1 Two or more races, non-Hispanic/Latino), 1 international. Average age 27. 72 applicants, 42% accepted, 17 enrolled. *Degree requirements:* For master's, comprehensive exam, thesis optional, practicum. *Entrance requirements:* For master's,

*Counseling Psychology*

GRE General Test, 2 letters of recommendation, minimum GPA of 3.0 in last 60 hours of course work. Additional exam requirements/recommendations for international students: Required—TOEFL (minimum score 500 paper-based; 61 iBT). *Application deadline:* For fall admission, 6/1 priority date for domestic students, 4/1 for international students. Application fee: $30. Electronic applications accepted. Tuition and fees vary according to course load, campus/location and program. *Financial support:* In 2016–17, 17 students received support, including 1 research assistantship (averaging $6,400 per year), 5 teaching assistantships (averaging $3,920 per year); Federal Work-Study, scholarships/grants, and tuition waivers (partial) also available. Financial award application deadline: 4/1; financial award applicants required to submit FAFSA. *Faculty research:* Sensory perception, social cognition, sexual behavior, evolutionary psychology, psychology and law. *Total annual research expenditures:* $145,456. *Unit head:* Dr. Lori Lange, Chair, 904-620-1638, E-mail: llange@unf.edu. *Application contact:* Dr. Amanda Pascale, Director, The Graduate School, 904-620-1360, Fax: 904-620-1362, E-mail: graduateschool@unf.edu.
Website: http://www.unf.edu/coas/psychology/

**University of North Texas,** Robert B. Toulouse School of Graduate Studies, Denton, TX 76203-5459. Offers accounting (MS); applied anthropology (MA, MS); applied behavior analysis (Certificate); applied geography (MA); applied technology and performance improvement (M Ed, MS); art education (MA); art history (MA); art museum education (Certificate); arts leadership (Certificate); audiology (Au D); behavior analysis (MS); behavioral science (PhD); biochemistry and molecular biology (MS); biology (MA, MS); biomedical engineering (MS); business analysis (MS); chemistry (MS); clinical health psychology (PhD); communication studies (MA, MS); computer engineering (MS); computer science (MS); counseling (M Ed, MS), including clinical mental health counseling (MS), college and university counseling, elementary school counseling, secondary school counseling; creative writing (MA); criminal justice (MS); curriculum and instruction (M Ed); decision sciences (MBA); design (MA, MFA), including fashion design (MFA), innovation studies, interior design (MFA); early childhood studies (MS); economics (MS); educational leadership (M Ed, Ed D); educational psychology (MS, PhD), including family studies (MS), gifted and talented (MS), human development (MS), learning and cognition (MS), research, measurement and evaluation (MS); electrical engineering (MS); emergency management (MPA); engineering technology (MS); English (MA); English as a second language (MA); environmental science (MS); finance (MBA, MS); financial management (MPA); French (MA); health services management (MBA); higher education (M Ed, Ed D); history (MA, MS); hospitality management (MS); human resources management (MPA); information science (MS); information systems (PhD); information technologies (MBA); interdisciplinary studies (MA, MS); international studies (MA); international sustainable tourism (MS); jazz studies (MM); journalism (MA, MJ, Graduate Certificate), including interactive and virtual digital communication (Graduate Certificate), narrative journalism (Graduate Certificate), public relations (Graduate Certificate); kinesiology (MS); linguistics (MA); local government management (MPA); logistics (PhD); logistics and supply chain management (MBA); long-term care, senior housing, and aging services (MA); management (PhD); marketing (MBA); mathematics (MA, MS); mechanical and energy engineering (MS, PhD); music (MA), including ethnomusicology, music theory, musicology, performance; music composition (PhD); music education (MM Ed, PhD); nonprofit management (MPA); operations and supply chain management (MBA); performance (MM, DMA); philosophy (MA); political science (MA); professional and technical communication (MA); radio, television and film (MA, MFA); rehabilitation counseling (Certificate); sociology (MA); Spanish (MA); special education (M Ed); speech-language pathology (MA); strategic management (MBA); studio art (MFA); teaching (M Ed); MBA/MS. *Program availability:* Part-time, evening/weekend, online learning. Terminal master's awarded for partial completion of doctoral program. *Degree requirements:* For master's, variable foreign language requirement, comprehensive exam (for some programs), thesis (for some programs); for doctorate, variable foreign language requirement, comprehensive exam (for some programs), thesis/dissertation; for other advanced degree, variable foreign language requirement, comprehensive exam (for some programs). *Entrance requirements:* For master's and doctorate, GRE, GMAT. Additional exam requirements/recommendations for international students: Required—TOEFL (minimum score 550 paper-based; 79 iBT). Electronic applications accepted.

**University of Notre Dame,** Graduate School, College of Arts and Letters, Division of Social Science, Department of Psychology, Notre Dame, IN 46556. Offers cognitive psychology (PhD); counseling psychology (PhD); developmental psychology (PhD); quantitative psychology (PhD). *Accreditation:* APA. *Degree requirements:* For doctorate, comprehensive exam, thesis/dissertation, candidacy exam. *Entrance requirements:* For doctorate, GRE General Test, GRE Subject Test (strongly recommended). Additional exam requirements/recommendations for international students: Required—TOEFL (minimum score 600 paper-based; 80 iBT). Electronic applications accepted. *Faculty research:* Cognitive and socio-emotional development, statistical methods and quantitative models applicable to psychology, interpersonal relations, life span development and developmental delay, childhood depression, structural equation and dynamical systems.

**University of Oklahoma,** Jeannine Rainbolt College of Education, Department of Educational Psychology, Program in Counseling Psychology, Norman, OK 73019. Offers PhD. *Accreditation:* APA. *Students:* 11 full-time (7 women), 10 part-time (8 women); includes 10 minority (2 Black or African American, non-Hispanic/Latino; 1 American Indian or Alaska Native, non-Hispanic/Latino; 1 Asian, non-Hispanic/Latino; 2 Hispanic/Latino; 4 Two or more races, non-Hispanic/Latino), 1 international. Average age 31. 39 applicants, 13% accepted, 4 enrolled. In 2016, 9 doctorates awarded. *Degree requirements:* For doctorate, comprehensive exam, thesis/dissertation. *Entrance requirements:* For doctorate, GRE. Additional exam requirements/recommendations for international students: Required—TOEFL (minimum score 79 iBT) or IELTS (minimum score 6.5). *Application deadline:* For fall admission, 12/7 for domestic and international students. Application fee: $50 ($100 for international students). Electronic applications accepted. *Expenses:* Tuition, state resident: full-time $4886; part-time $203.60 per credit hour. Tuition, nonresident: full-time $18,989; part-time $791.20 per credit hour. *Required fees:* $3283; $126.25 per credit hour. $126.50 per semester. *Financial support:* In 2016–17, 15 students received support. Fellowships with full tuition reimbursements available, research assistantships with full tuition reimbursements available, teaching assistantships with full tuition reimbursements available, health care benefits, and unspecified assistantships available. Financial award application deadline: 6/1; financial award applicants required to submit FAFSA. *Faculty research:* Working with survivors of trauma and members of oppressed groups; sexual violence; gender roles, relational quality, and relational cultural theory; diversity and social justice; supervision provision and training. *Unit head:* Dr. Nancy E. Marchand-Martella, Chair, Department of Educational Psychology, 405-325-0624, Fax: 405-325-6655, E-mail: nmarchand-martella@ou.edu. *Application contact:* Anna Steele, Graduate Programs Specialist, 405-325-4525, Fax: 405-325-7390, E-mail: jrcoe_gps@ou.edu.
Website: http://www.ou.edu/content/education/edpy/counseling-psychology-degrees-and-programs.html

**University of Oklahoma,** Jeannine Rainbolt College of Education, Department of Educational Psychology, Program in Professional Counseling, Norman, OK 73019. Offers professional counseling (M Ed), including drug and alcohol counseling, Oklahoma

licensed professional counseling, research, school counseling. *Students:* 35 full-time (26 women), 4 part-time (1 woman); includes 16 minority (3 Black or African American, non-Hispanic/Latino; 2 American Indian or Alaska Native, non-Hispanic/Latino; 1 Asian, non-Hispanic/Latino; 4 Hispanic/Latino; 6 Two or more races, non-Hispanic/Latino), 1 international. Average age 28. 29 applicants, 83% accepted, 17 enrolled. In 2016, 17 master's awarded. *Degree requirements:* For master's, comprehensive exam, internship. *Entrance requirements:* For master's, GRE. Additional exam requirements/recommendations for international students: Required—TOEFL (minimum score 79 iBT) or IELTS (minimum score 6.5). *Application deadline:* For fall admission, 1/10 for domestic and international students. Application fee: $50 ($100 for international students). Electronic applications accepted. *Expenses:* Tuition, state resident: full-time $4886; part-time $203.60 per credit hour. Tuition, nonresident: full-time $18,989; part-time $791.20 per credit hour. *Required fees:* $3283; $126.25 per credit hour. $126.50 per semester. *Financial support:* In 2016–17, 29 students received support. Research assistantships with full and partial tuition reimbursements available and scholarships/grants available. Financial award application deadline: 6/1; financial award applicants required to submit FAFSA. *Faculty research:* Group therapy interventions; multi and inter disciplinary collaboration; treatment of students in boarding school settings; diversity issues in counseling; applied behavior analysis. *Unit head:* Dr. Nancy E. Marchand-Martella, Chair, Department of Educational Psychology, 405-325-0624, Fax: 405-325-6655, E-mail: nmarchand-martella@ou.edu. *Application contact:* Anna Steele, Graduate Programs Specialist, 405-325-4525, Fax: 405-325-7390, E-mail: jrcoe_gps@ou.edu.
Website: http://www.ou.edu/education/edpy

**University of Pennsylvania,** Graduate School of Education, Division of Human Development and Quantitative Methods, Program in Counseling and Mental Health Services, Philadelphia, PA 19104. Offers M Phil, MS Ed. *Students:* 76 full-time (61 women), 1 (woman) part-time; includes 21 minority (5 Black or African American, non-Hispanic/Latino; 7 Asian, non-Hispanic/Latino; 6 Hispanic/Latino; 3 Two or more races, non-Hispanic/Latino), 26 international. Average age 25. 202 applicants, 64% accepted, 91 enrolled. In 2016, 69 master's awarded. *Expenses: Tuition:* Full-time $31,068; part-time $5762 per course. *Required fees:* $3200; $336 per course. Full-time tuition and fees vary according to degree level, program and student level. Part-time tuition and fees vary according to course load, degree level and program.
Website: http://www.gse.upenn.edu/aphd/cmhs/msed

**University of Phoenix–Las Vegas Campus,** College of Human Services, Las Vegas, NV 89135. Offers marriage, family, and child therapy (MSC); mental health counseling (MSC); school counseling (MSC). *Program availability:* Online learning. *Entrance requirements:* For master's, minimum undergraduate GPA of 2.5, 3 years of work experience. Additional exam requirements/recommendations for international students: Required—TOEFL (minimum score 550 paper-based; 79 iBT). Electronic applications accepted.

**University of Phoenix–Phoenix Campus,** College of Social Sciences, Tempe, AZ 85282-2371. Offers counseling (MS), including clinical mental health counseling, community counseling, counseling, marriage, family and child therapy; psychology (MS). *Program availability:* Evening/weekend, online learning. *Entrance requirements:* Additional exam requirements/recommendations for international students: Required—TOEFL, TOEIC (Test of English as an International Communication), Berlitz Online English Proficiency Exam, PTE, or IELTS. Electronic applications accepted. *Expenses:* Contact institution.

**University of Puget Sound,** School of Education, Program in Counseling, Tacoma, WA 98416. Offers mental health counseling (M Ed); school counseling (M Ed). *Program availability:* Part-time. *Faculty:* 2 full-time (both women), 1 (woman) part-time/adjunct. *Students:* 27 part-time (25 women); includes 5 minority (1 Asian, non-Hispanic/Latino; 2 Hispanic/Latino; 2 Two or more races, non-Hispanic/Latino). Average age 31. 33 applicants, 61% accepted, 17 enrolled. In 2016, 9 master's awarded. *Degree requirements:* For master's, capstone course. *Entrance requirements:* For master's, GRE General Test, interview. Additional exam requirements/recommendations for international students: Required—TOEFL (minimum score 550 paper-based; 90 iBT). *Application deadline:* For fall admission, 3/1 priority date for domestic and international students. Applications are processed on a rolling basis. Application fee: $60. Electronic applications accepted. *Expenses:* Contact institution. *Financial support:* In 2016–17, 1 student received support. Scholarships/grants available. Financial award application deadline: 3/31; financial award applicants required to submit FAFSA. *Faculty research:* Suicide prevention. *Unit head:* Dr. Grace Kirchner, Director, 253-879-3785, Fax: 253-879-3926, E-mail: kirchner@pugetsound.edu. *Application contact:* Karen Stump, Certification Officer/Admission Coordinator, 253-879-3382, Fax: 253-879-3926, E-mail: kstump@pugetsound.edu.
Website: http://www.pugetsound.edu/academics/departments-and-programs/graduate/school-of-education/med/

**University of Rhode Island,** Graduate School, College of Health Sciences, Department of Human Development and Family Studies, Kingston, RI 02881. Offers college student personnel (MS); human development and family studies (MS); marriage and family therapy (MS). *Accreditation:* AAMFT/COAMFTE. *Program availability:* Part-time. *Faculty:* 15 full-time (10 women). *Students:* 43 full-time (28 women), 14 part-time (10 women); includes 11 minority (7 Black or African American, non-Hispanic/Latino; 1 Asian, non-Hispanic/Latino; 1 Hispanic/Latino; 2 Two or more races, non-Hispanic/Latino). In 2016, 26 master's awarded. *Degree requirements:* For master's, comprehensive exam (for some programs), thesis optional. *Entrance requirements:* For master's, GRE or MAT, 2 letters of recommendation; resume (for college student personnel specialization). Additional exam requirements/recommendations for international students: Required—TOEFL. *Application deadline:* For fall admission, 1/15 for domestic and international students. Application fee: $65. Electronic applications accepted. *Expenses:* Tuition, state resident: full-time $11,796; part-time $655 per credit. Tuition, nonresident: full-time $24,206; part-time $1345 per credit. *Required fees:* $1546; $44 per credit. One-time fee: $155 full-time; $35 part-time. *Financial support:* In 2016–17, 2 research assistantships (averaging $8,592 per year), 4 teaching assistantships (averaging $11,456 per year) were awarded. Financial award application deadline: 1/15; financial award applicants required to submit FAFSA. *Unit head:* Dr. Karen McCurdy, Chair, 401-874-5960, Fax: 401-874-4020, E-mail: kmccurdy@uri.edu. *Application contact:* Graduate Admissions, 401-874-2872, E-mail: gradadm@etal.uri.edu.
Website: http://www.uri.edu/hss/hdf/

**University of Saint Francis,** Graduate School, Department of Behavioral and Social Sciences, Fort Wayne, IN 46808-3994. Offers clinical mental health counseling (MS, Post Master's Certificate); psychology (MS); school counseling (MS Ed). *Program availability:* Part-time, evening/weekend. *Faculty:* 3 full-time (1 woman). *Students:* 25 full-time (22 women), 10 part-time (6 women); includes 7 minority (6 Black or African American, non-Hispanic/Latino; 1 Hispanic/Latino), 2 international. Average age 31. 21 applicants, 95% accepted, 13 enrolled. In 2016, 19 master's awarded. *Entrance requirements:* For master's, GRE/MAT if undergraduate GPA is below 3.0 (for MS Ed), minimum undergraduate GPA of 3.0 (2.8 for MS Ed); undergraduate coursework in psychology; statement of professional goals (for MS); 2 professional recommendations;

interview (for mental health counseling and school counseling). Additional exam requirements/recommendations for international students: Required—TOEFL (minimum score 550 paper-based) or IELTS (minimum score 6.5). *Application deadline:* Applications are processed on a rolling basis. Application fee: $0. Electronic applications accepted. *Expenses: Tuition:* Full-time $16,290; part-time $905 per credit hour. *Required fees:* $25 per credit hour. $140 per semester. Tuition and fees vary according to campus/location and program. *Financial support:* In 2016–17, 5 students received support. Federal Work-Study, scholarships/grants, and unspecified assistantships available. Support available to part-time students. Financial award application deadline: 3/10; financial award applicants required to submit FAFSA. *Unit head:* Dr. John Brinkman, Chair of Department of Behavioral and Social Sciences, 260-399-7700 Ext. 8425, Fax: 260-399-8170, E-mail: jbrinkman@sf.edu. *Application contact:* Kyle Richardson, Enrollment Services Specialist, 260-399-7700 Ext. 6310, Fax: 260-399-8152, E-mail: krichardson@sf.edu.
Website: http://bhvscience.sf.edu/

**University of Saint Joseph,** Department of Counseling and Applied Behavioral Studies, West Hartford, CT 06117-2700. Offers applied behavioral analysis (Graduate Certificate); clinical mental health counseling (MA); school counseling (MA). *Accreditation:* ACA. *Program availability:* Part-time, evening/weekend. *Degree requirements:* For master's, comprehensive exam, thesis optional. *Entrance requirements:* For master's, 2 letters of recommendation. Electronic applications accepted. Application fee is waived when completed online. *Expenses: Tuition:* Full-time $14,580; part-time $729 per credit hour. *Required fees:* $920; $46 per credit hour. Tuition and fees vary according to course load, degree level and program.

**University of Saint Mary,** Graduate Programs, Program in Counseling Psychology, Leavenworth, KS 66048-5082. Offers MA. *Program availability:* Part-time, evening/weekend. *Students:* 37 full-time (28 women), 3 part-time (all women); includes 3 minority (all Black or African American, non-Hispanic/Latino), 1 international. Average age 35. In 2016, 5 master's awarded. *Entrance requirements:* For master's, bachelor's degree in psychology from accredited college, official transcripts, minimum GPA of 2.75, three professional recommendations, essay. Application fee: $25. Electronic applications accepted. *Expenses: Tuition:* Full-time $22,140; part-time $615 per credit hour. Tuition and fees vary according to campus/location and program. *Unit head:* Dr. David Strohm, Director of Undergraduate and Graduate Psychology Programs, 913-319-3012, E-mail: strohm57@stmary.edu.
Website: http://www.stmary.edu/success/Grad-Program/Master-of-Arts-in-Counseling-Psychology.aspx

**University of San Diego,** School of Leadership and Education Sciences, Department of Counseling and Marital and Family Therapy, San Diego, CA 92110-2492. Offers clinical mental health counseling (MA); marital and family therapy (MA). *Accreditation:* ACA. *Program availability:* Part-time, evening/weekend. *Faculty:* 11 full-time (5 women), 28 part-time/adjunct (18 women). *Students:* 144 full-time (129 women), 41 part-time (38 women); includes 80 minority (10 Black or African American, non-Hispanic/Latino; 1 American Indian or Alaska Native, non-Hispanic/Latino; 12 Asian, non-Hispanic/Latino; 50 Hispanic/Latino; 7 Two or more races, non-Hispanic/Latino), 2 international. Average age 27. 387 applicants, 43% accepted, 83 enrolled. In 2016, 72 master's awarded. *Degree requirements:* For master's, comprehensive exam, international experience. *Entrance requirements:* For master's, minimum GPA of 3.0, interview with faculty member. Additional exam requirements/recommendations for international students: Required—TOEFL (minimum score 580 paper-based; 83 iBT), TWE. *Application deadline:* For fall admission, 1/13 priority date for domestic and international students. Applications are processed on a rolling basis. Application fee: $45. Electronic applications accepted. *Financial support:* In 2016–17, 151 students received support. Career-related internships or fieldwork, Federal Work-Study, institutionally sponsored loans, unspecified assistantships, and stipends available. Support available to part-time students. Financial award application deadline: 4/1; financial award applicants required to submit FAFSA. *Faculty research:* Action research, collaboration between family therapists and medical professionals, family therapy training and supervision, multicultural counseling, school counseling. *Unit head:* Dr. Ann Garland, Director, 619-260-7879, E-mail: agarland@sandiego.edu. *Application contact:* Monica Mahon, Director of Admissions and Enrollment, 619-260-4524, Fax: 619-260-4158, E-mail: grads@sandiego.edu.
Website: http://www.sandiego.edu/soles/departments/school-family-mental-health-professions/

**University of San Francisco,** School of Education, Department of Counseling Psychology, San Francisco, CA 94117-1080. Offers counseling (MA), including educational counseling, life transitions counseling, marital and family therapy. *Program availability:* Part-time. *Faculty:* 9 full-time (7 women), 43 part-time/adjunct (23 women). *Students:* 240 full-time (204 women), 72 part-time (59 women); includes 181 minority (18 Black or African American, non-Hispanic/Latino; 46 Asian, non-Hispanic/Latino; 96 Hispanic/Latino; 3 Native Hawaiian or other Pacific Islander, non-Hispanic/Latino; 18 Two or more races, non-Hispanic/Latino), 6 international. Average age 29. 270 applicants, 69% accepted, 108 enrolled. In 2016, 94 master's awarded. *Entrance requirements:* Additional exam requirements/recommendations for international students: Required—TOEFL, IELTS, PTE. *Application deadline:* For fall admission, 3/1 priority date for domestic students, 3/1 for international students; for spring admission, 10/15 priority date for domestic students, 10/15 for international students. Applications are processed on a rolling basis. Application fee: $55 ($65 for international students). Electronic applications accepted. *Expenses: Tuition:* Full-time $23,310; part-time $1295 per credit. Tuition and fees vary according to course load, degree level, campus/location and program. *Financial support:* In 2016–17, 34 students received support. Fellowships, research assistantships, and teaching assistantships available. Financial award application deadline: 3/2; financial award applicants required to submit FAFSA. *Unit head:* Dr. Christine Yeh, Chair, 415-422-6868. *Application contact:* Peter Cole, Admission Coordinator, 415-422-5467, E-mail: schoolofeducation@usfca.edu.

**The University of Scranton,** Panuska College of Professional Studies, Department of Counseling and Human Services, Program in Clinical Mental Health Counseling, Scranton, PA 18510. Offers MS. *Accreditation:* ACA. *Program availability:* Part-time, evening/weekend. *Degree requirements:* For master's, comprehensive exam (for some programs), thesis (for some programs), capstone experience. *Entrance requirements:* For master's, minimum GPA of 3.0, three letters of reference. Additional exam requirements/recommendations for international students: Required—TOEFL (minimum score 500 paper-based; 80 iBT), IELTS (minimum score 6.5). Electronic applications accepted. *Faculty research:* Play therapy, expressive arts, identity development, counseling supervision.

**University of South Africa,** College of Human Sciences, Pretoria, South Africa. Offers adult education (M Ed); African languages (MA, PhD); African politics (MA, PhD); Afrikaans (MA, PhD); ancient history (MA, PhD); ancient Near Eastern studies (MA, PhD); anthropology (MA, PhD); applied linguistics (MA); Arabic (MA, PhD); archaeology (MA); art history (MA); Biblical archaeology (MA); Biblical studies (M Th, D Th, PhD); Christian spirituality (M Th, D Th); church history (M Th, D Th); classical studies (MA, PhD); clinical psychology (MA); communication (MA, PhD); comparative education (M Ed, Ed D); consulting psychology (D Admin, D Com, PhD); curriculum studies (M Ed,

Ed D); development studies (M Admin, MA, D Admin, PhD); didactics (M Ed, Ed D); education (M Tech); education management (M Ed, Ed D); educational psychology (M Ed); English (MA); environmental education (M Ed); French (MA, PhD); German (MA, PhD); Greek (MA); guidance and counseling (M Ed); health studies (MA, PhD), including health sciences education (MA), health services management (MA), medical and surgical nursing science (critical care general) (MA), midwifery and neonatal nursing science (MA), trauma and emergency care (MA); history (MA, PhD); history of education (Ed D); inclusive education (M Ed, Ed D); information and communications technology policy and regulation (MA); information science (MA, MIS, PhD); international politics (MA, PhD); Islamic studies (MA, PhD); Italian (MA, PhD); Judaica (MA, PhD); linguistics (MA, PhD); mathematical education (M Ed); mathematics education (MA); missiology (M Th, D Th); modern Hebrew (MA, PhD); musicology (MA, MMus, D Mus, PhD); natural science education (M Ed); New Testament (M Th, D Th); Old Testament (D Th); pastoral therapy (M Th, D Th); philosophy (MA); philosophy of education (M Ed, Ed D); politics (MA, PhD); Portuguese (MA, PhD); practical theology (M Th, D Th); psychology (MA, MS, PhD); psychology of education (M Ed, Ed D); public health (MA); religious studies (MA, D Th, PhD); Romance languages (MA); Russian (MA, PhD); Semitic languages (MA, PhD); social behavior studies in HIV/AIDS (MA); social science (mental health) (MA); social science in development studies (MA); social science in psychology (MA); social science in social work (MA); social science in sociology (MA); social work (MSW, DSW, PhD); socio-education (M Ed, Ed D); sociolinguistics (MA); sociology (MA, PhD); Spanish (MA, PhD); systematic theology (M Th, D Th); TESOL (teaching English to speakers of other languages) (MA); theological ethics (M Th, D Th); theory of literature (MA, PhD); urban ministries (D Th); urban ministry (M Th).

**University of South Alabama,** College of Education and Professional Studies, Department of Counseling and Instructional Sciences, Mobile, AL 36688. Offers clinical mental health counseling (MS); educational media (M Ed, MS); instructional design and development (MS, PhD); school counseling (M Ed). *Accreditation:* NCATE. *Program availability:* Part-time. *Faculty:* 12 full-time (8 women), 6 part-time/adjunct (5 women). *Students:* 104 full-time (83 women), 67 part-time (56 women); includes 49 minority (35 Black or African American, non-Hispanic/Latino; 2 American Indian or Alaska Native, non-Hispanic/Latino; 2 Asian, non-Hispanic/Latino; 8 Hispanic/Latino; 1 Native Hawaiian or other Pacific Islander, non-Hispanic/Latino; 1 Two or more races, non-Hispanic/Latino), 4 international. Average age 35. 59 applicants, 51% accepted, 26 enrolled. In 2016, 28 master's, 8 doctorates awarded. *Degree requirements:* For master's, comprehensive exam; for doctorate, comprehensive exam, thesis/dissertation. *Entrance requirements:* For master's, GRE General Test or MAT, minimum GPA of 3.0, two letters of recommendation; for doctorate, GRE, three letters of recommendation, master's degree in field or completion of prerequisites, resume. Additional exam requirements/recommendations for international students: Required—TOEFL (minimum score 525 paper-based; 71 iBT). *Application deadline:* For fall admission, 6/15 for domestic students, 5/15 for international students; for spring admission, 12/1 for domestic students, 11/1 for international students; for summer admission, 4/1 for domestic students. Applications are processed on a rolling basis. Application fee: $35. Electronic applications accepted. *Expenses:* Tuition, state resident: full-time $9768; part-time $407 per credit hour. Tuition, nonresident: full-time $19,536; part-time $814 per credit hour. *Financial support:* Fellowships, research assistantships, teaching assistantships, career-related internships or fieldwork, Federal Work-Study, institutionally sponsored loans, scholarships/grants, and unspecified assistantships available. Support available to part-time students. Financial award application deadline: 5/31; financial award applicants required to submit FAFSA. *Faculty research:* Agency counseling, rehabilitation counseling, school psychometry. *Unit head:* Dr. Tres Stefurak, Department Chair, 251-380-2734, Fax: 251-380-2713, E-mail: jstefurak@southalabama.edu. *Application contact:* Dr. Susan Santoli, Director of Graduate Studies, 251-380-2836, Fax: 251-380-2758, E-mail: ssantoli@southalabama.edu.
Website: http://www.southalabama.edu/colleges/ceps/cins/

**University of South Alabama,** Graduate School, Program in Clinical and Counseling Psychology, Mobile, AL 36688. Offers PhD. *Accreditation:* ACA. *Faculty:* 4 full-time (2 women). *Students:* 28 full-time (18 women), 6 part-time (5 women); includes 5 minority (3 Black or African American, non-Hispanic/Latino; 1 American Indian or Alaska Native, non-Hispanic/Latino; 1 Two or more races, non-Hispanic/Latino). Average age 27. 112 applicants, 10% accepted, 11 enrolled. In 2016, 5 doctorates awarded. *Degree requirements:* For doctorate, thesis/dissertation, capstone internship. *Entrance requirements:* For doctorate, GRE, three letters of recommendation, statement of purpose, curriculum vitae. Additional exam requirements/recommendations for international students: Required—TOEFL (minimum score 525 paper-based; 71 iBT). *Application deadline:* For fall admission, 12/15 for domestic students. Application fee: $35. Electronic applications accepted. *Expenses:* Tuition, state resident: full-time $9768; part-time $407 per credit hour. Tuition, nonresident: full-time $19,536; part-time $814 per credit hour. *Financial support:* Fellowships, research assistantships, teaching assistantships, career-related internships or fieldwork, institutionally sponsored loans, scholarships/grants, and unspecified assistantships available. Support available to part-time students. Financial award application deadline: 5/31; financial award applicants required to submit FAFSA. *Faculty research:* Suicidal behaviors, healthy youth and families. *Unit head:* Dr. Julio Turrens, Interim Dean of the Graduate School, 251-460-6310, E-mail: jturrens@southalabama.edu. *Application contact:* Dr. Joe Currier, Director of Clinical Training, 251-460-6622, E-mail: jcurrier@southalabama.edu.
Website: http://www.southalabama.edu/ccp/

**University of Southern Maine,** College of Management and Human Service, School of Education and Human Development, Program in Counselor Education, Portland, ME 04103. Offers clinical mental health counseling (MS); counseling (CAS); culturally responsive practices in education and human development (CGS); mental health rehabilitation technician/community (CGS); rehabilitation counseling (MS); school counseling (MS); substance abuse counseling (CGS). *Accreditation:* ACA (one or more programs are accredited); CORE; TEAC. *Program availability:* Part-time, evening/weekend. *Degree requirements:* For master's, comprehensive exam, thesis or alternative; for other advanced degree, thesis or alternative. *Entrance requirements:* For master's, GRE General Test or MAT, interview; for other advanced degree, master's degree. Additional exam requirements/recommendations for international students: Required—TOEFL (minimum score 550 paper-based; 79 iBT). Electronic applications accepted. *Faculty research:* Counselor licensure, group dynamics, counseling theories, healthy adaptation, counselor educator well-being.

**University of Southern Mississippi,** Graduate School, College of Education and Psychology, Department of Psychology, Hattiesburg, MS 39406. Offers applied behavior analysis (MS); clinical psychology (PhD); counseling psychology (MS, PhD); school psychology (PhD). *Accreditation:* APA (one or more programs are accredited). Terminal master's awarded for partial completion of doctoral program. *Degree requirements:* For master's, comprehensive exam, thesis; for doctorate, comprehensive exam, thesis/dissertation. *Entrance requirements:* For master's, GRE General Test, minimum GPA of 3.0; for doctorate, GRE General Test, interview, minimum GPA of 3.5. Additional exam requirements/recommendations for international students: Required—TOEFL, IELTS. *Application deadline:* Applications are processed on a rolling basis. Application fee: $60. *Expenses: Tuition, area resident:* Full-time $15,708; part-time $437 per credit hour. *Financial support:* Research assistantships with full tuition reimbursements, teaching

## Counseling Psychology

assistantships with full tuition reimbursements, career-related internships or fieldwork, Federal Work-Study, institutionally sponsored loans, scholarships/grants, health care benefits, and unspecified assistantships available. Financial award application deadline: 3/15; financial award applicants required to submit FAFSA. *Faculty research:* Psychopathology, alcohol and drug abuse, child clinical psychology, parenting, suicide, career/vocational, marine mammal, cognition, psychological psychology, behavioral interventions, positive psychology, anger/aggression, diversity issues. *Unit head:* Dr. Joe Olmi, Chair, 601-266-5693, Fax: 601-266-5580, E-mail: d.olmi@usm.edu. *Application contact:* Angela Pam, Administrative Assistant, 601-266-4592, Fax: 601-266-5580.
Website: https://www.usm.edu/psychology

**University of South Florida,** College of Behavioral and Community Sciences, Department of Child and Family Studies, Tampa, FL 33620-9951. Offers applied behavior analysis (MA, MS, PhD); behavioral and community sciences (PhD); child and adolescent behavioral health (MS), including developmental disabilities, leadership in child and adolescent health, translational research and evaluation, youth and behavioral health; rehabilitation and mental health counseling (MA), including addictions and substance abuse counseling, marriage and family therapy. *Accreditation:* ACA. *Faculty:* 15 full-time (10 women), 1 (woman) part-time/adjunct. *Students:* 146 full-time (127 women), 90 part-time (74 women); includes 92 minority (22 Black or African American, non-Hispanic/Latino; 12 Asian, non-Hispanic/Latino; 49 Hispanic/Latino; 9 Two or more races, non-Hispanic/Latino), 3 international. Average age 28. 267 applicants, 51% accepted, 93 enrolled. In 2016, 63 master's awarded. *Degree requirements:* For master's, comprehensive exam, thesis (for some programs); for doctorate, comprehensive exam, thesis/dissertation, Behavior Analyst Board Certification Exam. *Entrance requirements:* For master's, GRE General Test, minimum GPA of 3.0 in last 60 hours of coursework; letters of recommendation; one-page narrative describing experience, interest, and career goals in applied behavior analysis; resume or curriculum vitae (varies by program); for doctorate, GRE General Test, master's degree in behavioral analysis or closely-related field; minimum GPA of 3.5 in graduate course work; three letters of recommendation; campus visit with faculty interview; personal statement; curriculum vitae; evidence of research experiences and expertise. Additional exam requirements/recommendations for international students: Required—TOEFL (minimum score 550 paper-based; 79 iBT) or IELTS (minimum score 6.5). *Application deadline:* For fall admission, 12/5 for domestic and international students. Application fee: $30. *Expenses:* Tuition, state resident: full-time $7766; part-time $431.43 per credit hour. Tuition, nonresident: full-time $15,789; part-time $877.17 per credit hour. *Required fees:* $37 per term. *Financial support:* In 2016–17, 50 students received support. Unspecified assistantships available. *Faculty research:* Applied behavior analysis, autism, behavior management, behavioral intervention, children, developmental disabilities, experimental analysis of behavior, functional assessment, positive behavior support. *Total annual research expenditures:* $16.4 million. *Application contact:* Dr. Raymond G. Miltenberger, Professor/Director of Master's Program, 813-974-5079, Fax: 813-974-6115, E-mail: miltenbe@usf.edu.
Website: http://cfs.cbcs.usf.edu/

**University of South Florida,** Innovative Education, Tampa, FL 33620-9951. Offers adult, career and higher education (Graduate Certificate), including college teaching, leadership in developing human resources, leadership in higher education; Africana studies (Graduate Certificate), including diasporas and health disparities, genocide and human rights; aging studies (Graduate Certificate), including gerontology; art research (Graduate Certificate), including museum studies; business foundations (Graduate Certificate); chemical and biomedical engineering (Graduate Certificate), including materials science and engineering, water, health and sustainability; child and family studies (Graduate Certificate), including positive behavior support; civil and industrial engineering (Graduate Certificate), including transportation systems analysis; community and family health (Graduate Certificate), including maternal and child health, social marketing and public health, violence and injury: prevention and intervention, women's health; criminology (Graduate Certificate), including criminal justice administration; educational measurement and research (Graduate Certificate), including evaluation; English (Graduate Certificate), including comparative literary studies, creative writing, professional and technical communication; entrepreneurship (Graduate Certificate); environmental health (Graduate Certificate), including safety management; epidemiology and biostatistics (Graduate Certificate), including applied biostatistics, biostatistics, concepts and tools of epidemiology, epidemiology, epidemiology of infectious diseases; geography, environment and planning (Graduate Certificate), including community development, environmental policy and management, geographical information systems; geology (Graduate Certificate), including hydrogeology; global health (Graduate Certificate), including disaster management, global health and Latin American and Caribbean studies, global health practice, humanitarian assistance, infection control; government and international affairs (Graduate Certificate), including Cuban studies, globalization studies; health policy and management (Graduate Certificate), including health management and leadership, public health policy and programs; hearing specialist: early intervention (Graduate Certificate); industrial and management systems engineering (Graduate Certificate), including systems engineering, technology management; information studies (Graduate Certificate), including school library media specialist; information systems/decision sciences (Graduate Certificate), including analytics and business intelligence; instructional technology (Graduate Certificate), including distance education, Florida digital/virtual educator, instructional design, multimedia design, Web design; internal medicine, bioethics and medical humanities (Graduate Certificate), including biomedical ethics; Latin American and Caribbean studies (Graduate Certificate); mass communications (Graduate Certificate), including multimedia journalism; mathematics and statistics (Graduate Certificate), including mathematics; medicine (Graduate Certificate), including aging and neuroscience, bioinformatics, biotechnology, brain fitness and memory management, clinical investigation, health informatics, health sciences, integrative weight management, intellectual property, medicine and gender, metabolic and nutritional medicine, metabolic cardiology, pharmacy sciences; national and competitive intelligence (Graduate Certificate); psychological and social foundations (Graduate Certificate), including career counseling, college teaching, diversity in education, mental health counseling, school counseling; public affairs (Graduate Certificate), including nonprofit management, public management, research administration; public health (Graduate Certificate), including environmental health, health equity, public health generalist, translational research in adolescent behavioral health; public health practices (Graduate Certificate), including planning for healthy communities; rehabilitation and mental health counseling (Graduate Certificate), including integrative mental health care, marriage and family therapy, rehabilitation technology; secondary education (Graduate Certificate), including ESOL, foreign language education: culture and content, foreign language education: professional; social work (Graduate Certificate), including geriatric social work/clinical gerontology; special education (Graduate Certificate), including autism spectrum disorder, disabilities education: severe/profound; world languages (Graduate Certificate), including teaching English as a second language (TESL) or foreign language. *Expenses:* Tuition, state resident: full-time $7766; part-time $431.43 per credit hour. Tuition, nonresident: full-time $15,789; part-time $877.17 per credit hour. *Required fees:* $37 per term. *Unit head:*

Kathy Barnes, Interdisciplinary Programs Coordinator, 813-974-8031, Fax: 813-974-7061, E-mail: barnesk@usf.edu. *Application contact:* Karen Tylinski, Metro Initiatives, 813-974-9943, Fax: 813-974-7061, E-mail: ktylinsk@usf.edu.
Website: http://www.usf.edu/innovative-education/

**The University of Tennessee,** Graduate School, College of Education, Health and Human Sciences, Department of Educational Psychology and Counseling, Knoxville, TN 37996. Offers adult education (MS); applied educational psychology (MS); collaborative learning (Ed D); college student personnel (MS); mental health counseling (MS); rehabilitation counseling (MS); school counseling (MS). *Accreditation:* ACA (one or more programs are accredited); CORE (one or more programs are accredited); NCATE. *Program availability:* Part-time, evening/weekend. *Degree requirements:* For master's, thesis optional. *Entrance requirements:* For master's, GRE General Test, minimum GPA of 2.7. Additional exam requirements/recommendations for international students: Required—TOEFL. Electronic applications accepted.

**The University of Texas at Austin,** Graduate School, College of Education, Department of Educational Psychology, Austin, TX 78712-1111. Offers academic educational psychology (M Ed, MA); counseling psychology (PhD); counselor education (M Ed); human development, culture and learning sciences (PhD); program evaluation (MA); quantitative methods (M Ed, MA, PhD); school psychology (MA, PhD). *Accreditation:* APA (one or more programs are accredited). *Degree requirements:* For master's, thesis optional; for doctorate, thesis/dissertation. *Entrance requirements:* For master's and doctorate, GRE General Test, 3 letters of recommendation. Additional exam requirements/recommendations for international students: Required—TOEFL.

**The University of Texas at Tyler,** College of Education and Psychology, Department of Psychology and Counseling, Tyler, TX 75799-0001. Offers clinical psychology (MS), including neuropsychology, school psychology; counseling psychology (MA), including general, marriage and family; interdisciplinary studies (MSIS); school counseling (MA). *Program availability:* Part-time, evening/weekend. *Degree requirements:* For master's, comprehensive exam, thesis optional. *Entrance requirements:* For master's, GRE General Test, minimum GPA of 3.0. Additional exam requirements/recommendations for international students: Required—TOEFL. Electronic applications accepted. *Faculty research:* Neuropsychology, child abuse, psychometric properties of psychological instruments, maternal behavior, clinical practice issues, victimization of women, post-traumatic stress disorder.

**University of the Cumberlands,** Program in Professional Counseling, Williamsburg, KY 40769-1372. Offers MA. Program also offered in San Francisco. *Accreditation:* ACA. *Program availability:* Part-time, evening/weekend, online learning. Electronic applications accepted.

**University of the District of Columbia,** College of Arts and Sciences, Program in Counseling, Washington, DC 20008-1175. Offers MS. *Accreditation:* ACA.

**University of the Southwest,** Graduate Programs, Hobbs, NM 88240-9129. Offers business administration (MBA); curriculum and instruction (MSE); curriculum and instruction: bilingual (MSE); curriculum and instruction: TESOL (MSE); early childhood education (MSE); educational administration (MSE); mental health counseling (MSE); school counseling (MSE); special education (MSE); sports management (MBA). *Program availability:* Part-time, evening/weekend, online learning. *Degree requirements:* For master's, comprehensive exam, thesis (for some programs). *Entrance requirements:* Additional exam requirements/recommendations for international students: Recommended—TOEFL. Electronic applications accepted.

**University of Utah,** Graduate School, College of Education, Department of Educational Psychology, Salt Lake City, UT 84112. Offers clinical mental health counseling (M Ed); counseling psychology (PhD); elementary education (M Ed); instructional design and educational technology (M Ed); instructional design and technology (MS); learning and cognition (MS, PhD); reading and literacy (M Ed, PhD); school counseling (M Ed); school psychology (M Ed, PhD, Ed S); statistics (M Stat). *Accreditation:* APA (one or more programs are accredited). *Faculty:* 23 full-time (12 women), 15 part-time/adjunct (10 women). *Students:* 119 full-time (95 women), 106 part-time (74 women); includes 37 minority (2 Black or African American, non-Hispanic/Latino; 6 Asian, non-Hispanic/Latino; 22 Hispanic/Latino; 7 Two or more races, non-Hispanic/Latino), 6 international. Average age 31. 296 applicants, 27% accepted, 73 enrolled. In 2016, 47 master's, 8 doctorates awarded. Terminal master's awarded for partial completion of doctoral program. *Degree requirements:* For master's, variable foreign language requirement, comprehensive exam (for some programs), thesis (for some programs), projects; for doctorate, variable foreign language requirement, comprehensive exam, thesis/dissertation, oral exam. *Entrance requirements:* For master's and doctorate, GRE General Test, minimum GPA of 3.0. Additional exam requirements/recommendations for international students: Required—TOEFL (minimum score 80 iBT). *Application deadline:* For fall admission, 12/15 for domestic and international students; for winter admission, 11/1 for domestic and international students; for spring admission, 3/15 for domestic and international students. Application fee: $55 ($65 for international students). Electronic applications accepted. *Expenses:* Contact institution. *Financial support:* In 2016–17, 84 students received support, including 12 fellowships with full and partial tuition reimbursements available (averaging $18,000 per year), 21 research assistantships with full and partial tuition reimbursements available (averaging $14,500 per year), 57 teaching assistantships with full and partial tuition reimbursements available (averaging $14,500 per year); career-related internships or fieldwork, Federal Work-Study, institutionally sponsored loans, scholarships/grants, traineeships, health care benefits, and unspecified assistantships also available. Financial award application deadline: 4/1; financial award applicants required to submit FAFSA. *Faculty research:* Autism, computer technology and instruction, cognitive behavior, aging, group counseling. *Total annual research expenditures:* $620,935. *Unit head:* Dr. Anne E. Cook, Chair, 801-581-7148, Fax: 801-581-5566, E-mail: anne.cook@utah.edu. *Application contact:* JoLynn N. Yates, Academic Coordinator, 801-581-7148, Fax: 801-581-5566, E-mail: jo.yates@utah.edu.
Website: http://www.ed.utah.edu/edps/

**University of Vermont,** Graduate College, College of Education and Social Services, Department of Leadership and Developmental Sciences, Counseling Program, Burlington, VT 05405. Offers MS. *Accreditation:* ACA; NCATE. *Entrance requirements:* For master's, GRE General Test, resume. Additional exam requirements/recommendations for international students: Required—TOEFL (minimum score 550 paper-based; 80 iBT). Electronic applications accepted. *Expenses:* Tuition, state resident: full-time $5814. Tuition, nonresident: full-time $14,670. *Faculty research:* Women and tenure, counseling children and adolescents.

**University of Victoria,** Faculty of Graduate Studies, Faculty of Education, Department of Educational Psychology and Leadership Studies, Victoria, BC V8W 2Y2, Canada. Offers aboriginal communities counseling (M Ed); counseling (M Ed, MA); educational psychology (M Ed, MA, PhD), including counseling psychology (M Ed, MA), leadership studies (PhD), learning and development (MA, PhD), measurement and evaluation, special education (M Ed, MA); leadership studies (M Ed, MA). *Program availability:* Part-time. *Degree requirements:* For master's, thesis (for some programs), comprehensive exam (M Ed); for doctorate, comprehensive exam, thesis/dissertation, candidacy exam. *Entrance requirements:* For master's, 2 years of work experience in a relevant field; for

doctorate, GRE, 2 years of work experience in a relevant field, minimum B average. Additional exam requirements/recommendations for international students: Required—TOEFL (minimum score 575 paper-based), IELTS (minimum score 7). *Faculty research:* Learning and development (child, adolescent and adult), special education and exceptional children.

**The University of Western Ontario,** Faculty of Graduate Studies, Social Sciences Division, Faculty of Education, Program in Counseling Psychology, London, ON N6A 5B8, Canada. Offers M Ed. *Program availability:* Part-time. *Entrance requirements:* For master's, minimum B average, 3 years' experience in helping profession. *Faculty research:* Women's issues in counseling, causes for sexual harassment in the workplace, counselor memory and confidence in clinical judgements.

**University of West Florida,** College of Arts, Social Sciences, and Humanities, Department of Psychology, Pensacola, FL 32514-5750. Offers applied experimental (MA); counseling (MA); industrial-organizational (MA). *Program availability:* Part-time. *Degree requirements:* For master's, thesis (for some programs). *Entrance requirements:* For master's, GRE, official transcripts; minimum GPA of 3.0; writing sample; three letters of reference; field experience or skill sets; oral interview (for counseling specialization). Additional exam requirements/recommendations for international students: Required—TOEFL (minimum score 550 paper-based). *Application deadline:* For fall admission, 6/1 for domestic and international students; for spring admission, 10/1 for domestic and international students. Applications are processed on a rolling basis. Application fee: $30. *Expenses:* Tuition, state resident: full-time $5316.12. Tuition, nonresident: full-time $11,308. *Required fees:* $583.92. Tuition and fees vary according to course load and program. *Financial support:* Fellowships with partial tuition reimbursements, research assistantships with partial tuition reimbursements, teaching assistantships with partial tuition reimbursements, career-related internships or fieldwork, and unspecified assistantships available. Financial award application deadline: 4/15; financial award applicants required to submit FAFSA. *Faculty research:* Prose recall, brain imaging, peak performance, biofeedback and pain control, comparable worth. *Unit head:* Dr. Robert Belter, Interim Department Chair, 850-474-2791, E-mail: rbelter@uwf.edu. *Application contact:* Dr. Robert Belter, Interim Department Chair, 850-474-2791, E-mail: rbelter@uwf.edu.
Website: http://www.uwf.edu/psychology/

**University of Wisconsin–Madison,** Graduate School, School of Education, Department of Counseling Psychology, Program in Counseling Psychology, Madison, WI 53706-1380. Offers PhD. *Accreditation:* APA. *Degree requirements:* For doctorate, thesis/dissertation.

**University of Wisconsin–Milwaukee,** Graduate School, School of Education, Department of Educational Psychology, Milwaukee, WI 53201-0413. Offers children's mental health for school professionals (Graduate Certificate); community counseling (MS); counseling psychology (PhD); educational statistics and measurement (MS, PhD); learning and development (MS, PhD); multicultural knowledge of mental health practices (Graduate Certificate); school counseling (MS); school counseling (Graduate Certificate); school psychology (MS, PhD, Ed S). *Accreditation:* APA. *Program availability:* Part-time. *Students:* 161 full-time (121 women), 53 part-time (39 women); includes 47 minority (12 Black or African American, non-Hispanic/Latino; 1 American Indian or Alaska Native, non-Hispanic/Latino; 5 Asian, non-Hispanic/Latino; 8 Hispanic/Latino; 1 Native Hawaiian or other Pacific Islander, non-Hispanic/Latino; 20 Two or more races, non-Hispanic/Latino), 6 international. Average age 30. 266 applicants, 45% accepted, 71 enrolled. In 2016, 73 master's, 9 doctorates, 18 other advanced degrees awarded. *Degree requirements:* For master's, comprehensive exam, thesis; for doctorate, thesis/dissertation. *Entrance requirements:* For master's, minimum GPA of 3.0; for doctorate, GRE General Test, minimum GPA of 3.0. Additional exam requirements/recommendations for international students: Required—TOEFL (minimum score 550 paper-based; 79 iBT), IELTS (minimum score 6.5). *Application deadline:* For fall admission, 1/1 priority date for domestic students; for spring admission, 9/1 for domestic students. Applications are processed on a rolling basis. Application fee: $56 ($96 for international students). Electronic applications accepted. *Financial support:* In 2016–17, 14 fellowships, 1 research assistantship, 8 teaching assistantships were awarded; career-related internships or fieldwork, health care benefits, unspecified assistantships, and project assistantships also available. Support available to part-time students. Financial award application deadline: 4/15; financial award applicants required to submit FAFSA. *Application contact:* General Information Contact, 414-229-4721, E-mail: soeinfo@uwm.edu.
Website: http://uwm.edu/education/academics/educational-psychology-department/

**University of Wisconsin–Stout,** Graduate School, College of Education, Health and Human Sciences, School of Education, Program in School Counseling, Menomonie, WI 54751. Offers MS. *Accreditation:* ACA. *Program availability:* Part-time. *Degree requirements:* For master's, thesis. *Entrance requirements:* For master's, minimum GPA of 2.75. Additional exam requirements/recommendations for international students: Required—TOEFL (minimum score 500 paper-based; 61 iBT). Electronic applications accepted. *Faculty research:* Adventure-based learning, body image, domestic violence, resilience, school climate.

**Utah State University,** School of Graduate Studies, Emma Eccles Jones College of Education and Human Services, Department of Psychology, Logan, UT 84322. Offers clinical/counseling/school psychology (PhD); research and evaluation methodology (PhD); school counseling (MS); school psychology (MS). *Accreditation:* APA (one or more programs are accredited). *Program availability:* Part-time, evening/weekend, online learning. Terminal master's awarded for partial completion of doctoral program. *Degree requirements:* For master's, thesis (for some programs); for doctorate, thesis/dissertation. *Entrance requirements:* For master's, GRE General Test (school psychology), MAT (school counseling), minimum GPA of 3.5; for doctorate, GRE General Test, minimum GPA of 3.5. Additional exam requirements/recommendations for international students: Required—TOEFL. *Faculty research:* Hearing loss detection in infancy, ADHD, eating disorders, domestic violence, neuropsychology, bilingual/Spanish speaking students/parents.

**Virginia Commonwealth University,** Graduate School, College of Humanities and Sciences, Department of Psychology, Program in Counseling Psychology, Richmond, VA 23284-9005. Offers PhD. *Accreditation:* ACA; APA. *Degree requirements:* For doctorate, thesis/dissertation. *Entrance requirements:* For doctorate, GRE General Test, GRE Subject Test. Additional exam requirements/recommendations for international students: Required—TOEFL (minimum score 600 paper-based; 100 iBT); Recommended—IELTS (minimum score 6.5). *Application deadline:* For fall admission, 12/1 for domestic students. Application fee: $50. Electronic applications accepted. *Financial support:* Fellowships, research assistantships, teaching assistantships, Federal Work-Study, institutionally sponsored loans, and scholarships/grants available. Support available to part-time students. *Unit head:* Dr. Michael Southam-Gerow, Director, Graduate Programs in Psychology, 804-827-0585, Fax: 804-828-2237, E-mail: masouthamger@vcu.edu. *Application contact:* Dr. Marilyn Stern, Co-Director, Counseling Psychology Training Program, 804-827-0400, Fax: 804-828-2237, E-mail: mstern@vcu.edu.
Website: http://www.psychology.vcu.edu/counseling/

**Virginia Commonwealth University,** Graduate School, School of Allied Health Professions, Program in Patient Counseling, Richmond, VA 23284-9005. Offers MS. *Accreditation:* ACA. *Entrance requirements:* For master's, GRE General Test. Additional exam requirements/recommendations for international students: Required—TOEFL (minimum score 600 paper-based; 100 iBT). *Application deadline:* For fall admission, 2/1 for domestic students. Applications are processed on a rolling basis. Application fee: $50. Electronic applications accepted. *Financial support:* Application deadline: 3/1; applicants required to submit FAFSA. *Unit head:* Dr. D. Mark Cooper, Chair, 804-828-0540, Fax: 804-828-0542, E-mail: dmcooper@vcu.edu. *Application contact:* Angela H. Flack, Graduate Program Director, 804-828-0540, E-mail: aflack@vcu.edu.
Website: http://www.sahp.vcu.edu/ptc/

**Viterbo University,** Master of Science in Mental Health Counseling Program, La Crosse, WI 54601-4797. Offers addiction counseling (MS); child and adolescent counseling (MS); complementary health and wellness counseling (MS). *Accreditation:* ACA. *Program availability:* Part-time, evening/weekend. *Degree requirements:* For master's, comprehensive exam, thesis, 54 credits of core program courses; 6 elective credits; minimum GPA of 3.0; action research project; practicum/internship experience. *Entrance requirements:* For master's, MAT, BS in a human service or social science discipline; prerequisite coursework in general psychology, behavior disorders/abnormal psychology, and research methods/statistics; minimum undergraduate cumulative GPA of 3.0; background check; personal statement; undergraduate transcripts; interview. Additional exam requirements/recommendations for international students: Required—TOEFL (minimum score 525 paper-based). Electronic applications accepted. Application fee is waived when completed online. *Expenses:* Contact institution. *Faculty research:* Supervision, recovery substance abuse, culture, counseling theory, health and wellness.

**Walden University,** Graduate Programs, School of Counseling, Minneapolis, MN 55401. Offers addiction counseling (MS), including addictions and public health, child and adolescent counseling, family studies and interventions, forensic counseling, general program, military families and culture, trauma and crisis counseling; clinical mental health counseling (MS), including addiction counseling, forensic counseling, military families and culture, trauma and crisis counseling; counselor education and supervision (PhD), including consultation, counseling and social change, forensic mental health counseling, leadership and program evaluation, trauma and crisis; marriage, couple, and family counseling (MS), including addiction counseling, career counseling, forensic counseling, military families and culture, trauma and crisis counseling; school counseling (MS), including addiction counseling, career counseling, crisis and trauma, military families and culture. *Accreditation:* ACA. *Program availability:* Part-time, evening/weekend, online only, 100% online. *Degree requirements:* For master's, residency, field experience, professional development plan, licensure plan; for doctorate, thesis/dissertation, residency, practicum, internship. *Entrance requirements:* For master's, bachelor's degree or higher; minimum GPA of 2.5; official transcripts; goal statement (for some programs); access to computer and Internet; for doctorate, master's degree or higher; three years of related professional or academic experience (preferred); minimum GPA of 3.0; goal statement and current resume (for select programs); official transcripts; access to computer and Internet. Additional exam requirements/recommendations for international students: Required—TOEFL (minimum score 550 paper-based, 79 iBT), IELTS (minimum score 6.5), Michigan English Language Assessment Battery (minimum score 82), or PTE (minimum score 53). Electronic applications accepted.

**Walden University,** Graduate Programs, School of Psychology, Minneapolis, MN 55401. Offers clinical psychology (MS), including counseling, general program; forensic psychology (MS), including forensic psychology in the community, general program, mental health applications, program planning and evaluation in forensic settings, psychology and legal systems; industrial organizational (MS, PhD), including consulting psychology, forensic (MS), forensic psychology (PhD), general practice, leadership development and coaching (MS), organizational diversity and social change, research evaluation (PhD); online teaching in psychology (Post-Master's Certificate); organizational psychology and development (Postbaccalaureate Certificate); psychology (MS, PhD), including applied psychology (MS), clinical psychology (PhD), crisis management and response (MS), educational psychology, forensic psychology (PhD), general psychology (MS), general psychology research (PhD), general psychology teaching (PhD), health psychology, leadership development and coaching (MS), psychology of culture (MS), psychology, public administration, and social change (MS), social psychology, terrorism and security (MS); psychology respecialization (Post-Doctoral Certificate). *Program availability:* Part-time, evening/weekend, online only, 100% online. Terminal master's awarded for partial completion of doctoral program. *Degree requirements:* For master's, thesis optional; for doctorate, thesis/dissertation, residency. *Entrance requirements:* For master's, bachelor's degree or higher; minimum GPA of 2.5; official transcripts; goal statement (for some programs); access to computer and Internet; for doctorate, master's degree or higher; three years of related professional or academic experience (preferred); minimum GPA of 3.0; goal statement and current resume (for select programs); official transcripts; access to computer and Internet; for other advanced degree, relevant work experience; access to computer and Internet. Additional exam requirements/recommendations for international students: Required—TOEFL (minimum score 550 paper-based, 79 iBT), IELTS (minimum score 6.5), Michigan English Language Assessment Battery (minimum score 82), or PTE (minimum score 53). Electronic applications accepted.

**Walden University,** Graduate Programs, School of Social Work and Human Services, Minneapolis, MN 55401. Offers addictions and social work (DSW); advanced clinical practice (MSW); clinical expertise (DSW); criminal justice (DSW); disaster, crisis, and intervention (DSW); family studies and interventions (DSW); human and social services (PhD), including advanced research, community and social services, community intervention and leadership, conflict management, criminal justice, disaster crisis and intervention, family studies and intervention, gerontology, global social services, higher education, human services and nonprofit administration, mental health facilitation; medical social work (DSW); military social work (MSW); policy practice (DSW); social work (PhD), including addictions and social work, clinical expertise, criminal justice, disaster, crisis and intervention, family studies and interventions, medical social work, policy practice, social work administration; social work administration (DSW); social work in healthcare (MSW); social work with children and families (MSW). *Accreditation:* CSWE. *Program availability:* Part-time, evening/weekend, online only, 100% online. *Degree requirements:* For master's, residency (for some programs); for doctorate, thesis/dissertation, residency. *Entrance requirements:* For master's, bachelor's degree or higher; minimum GPA of 2.5; official transcripts; goal statement (for some programs); access to computer and Internet; for doctorate, master's degree or higher; three years of related professional or academic experience (preferred); minimum GPA of 3.0; goal statement and current resume (for select programs); official transcripts; access to computer and Internet. Additional exam requirements/recommendations for international students: Required—TOEFL (minimum score 550 paper-based, 79 iBT), IELTS (minimum score 6.5), Michigan English Language Assessment Battery (minimum score 82), or PTE (minimum score 53). Electronic applications accepted.

## Counseling Psychology

**Walsh University,** Graduate Programs, Program in Counseling and Human Development, North Canton, OH 44720-3396. Offers clinical mental health counseling (MA); school counseling (MA); student affairs in higher education (MA). *Accreditation:* ACA. *Program availability:* Part-time, evening/weekend. *Faculty:* 5 full-time (4 women), 10 part-time/adjunct (8 women). *Students:* 34 full-time (24 women), 66 part-time (51 women); includes 11 minority (6 Black or African American, non-Hispanic/Latino; 2 American Indian or Alaska Native, non-Hispanic/Latino; 2 Hispanic/Latino; 1 Two or more races, non-Hispanic/Latino), 1 international. Average age 30. 58 applicants, 69% accepted, 27 enrolled. In 2016, 24 master's awarded. *Degree requirements:* For master's, comprehensive exam, internship, practicum. *Entrance requirements:* For master's, GRE (minimum score of 145 verbal and 146 quantitative) or MAT (minimum score of 397), interview, minimum GPA of 3.0, writing sample, reference forms, notarized affidavit of good moral conduct. Additional exam requirements/recommendations for international students: Required—TOEFL (minimum score 500 paper-based; 61 iBT). *Application deadline:* For fall admission, 7/15 priority date for domestic students. Applications are processed on a rolling basis. Application fee: $25. Electronic applications accepted. Application fee is waived when completed online. *Expenses:* $665 per credit hour. *Financial support:* In 2016–17, 11 students received support, including 11 research assistantships with partial tuition reimbursements available (averaging $8,442 per year). Financial award application deadline: 12/31. *Faculty research:* Supervision of clinical mental health, clinical mental health practice/issues, clinical mental health skills development, advocacy, teaching and professional development, career development, refugee development in US, supervision in student affairs, offender treatment, domestic violence issues, alcohol and drug treatment issues, Professional identity and advocacy in school counseling, Efficacy in counseling clinic. *Unit head:* Dr. Ruthann Anderson, Program Director, 330-490-7338, Fax: 330-490-7323, E-mail: randerson@walsh.edu. *Application contact:* Audra Dice, Graduate and Transfer Admissions Counselor, 330-490-7181, Fax: 330-244-4925, E-mail: adice@walsh.edu. Website: http://www.walsh.edu/counseling-graduate-program

**Washington Adventist University,** Program in Counseling Psychology, Takoma Park, MD 20912. Offers MA. *Program availability:* Part-time. *Entrance requirements:* Additional exam requirements/recommendations for international students: Required—TOEFL (minimum score 550 paper-based), IELTS (minimum score 5).

**Washington Adventist University,** Program in Professional Counseling Psychology, Takoma Park, MD 20912. Offers MA. *Program availability:* Part-time. *Entrance requirements:* Additional exam requirements/recommendations for international students: Required—TOEFL (minimum score 550 paper-based), IELTS (minimum score 5).

**Washington State University,** College of Education, Department of Educational Leadership, Sports Studies, and Educational/Counseling Psychology, Pullman, WA 99164-2136. Offers counseling psychology (PhD); educational leadership (Ed M, MA, Ed D, PhD); educational psychology (MA, PhD); sport management (MA). Programs also offered at the Spokane, Tri-Cities, Vancouver and Global (online) campuses. *Program availability:* Part-time, online learning. *Degree requirements:* For master's, comprehensive exam (for some programs), thesis (for some programs), oral or written exam; for doctorate, comprehensive exam, thesis/dissertation, oral and written exam, internship. *Entrance requirements:* For master's and doctorate, GRE General Test, minimum GPA of 3.0, 3 letters of recommendation, transcripts showing all college or university course work, statement of professional objectives, current curriculum vitae/resume. Additional exam requirements/recommendations for international students: Required—TOEFL (minimum score 550 paper-based; 80 iBT). Electronic applications accepted. *Faculty research:* Multicultural counseling and career development, educational and psychological measurement issues, business decision-making process and power relationships, leadership practices and processes as suffused with and constituted by emotion work.

**Wayland Baptist University,** Graduate Programs, Programs in Behavioral and Social Sciences, Plainview, TX 79072-6998. Offers counseling (MA); criminal justice (MACJ); government administration (MPA); history (MA); homeland security (MPA); humanities (MAH); justice administration (MPA). *Program availability:* Part-time, evening/weekend, online learning. *Degree requirements:* For master's, comprehensive exam. *Entrance requirements:* For master's, GRE, MAT. Additional exam requirements/recommendations for international students: Required—TOEFL (minimum score 500 paper-based; 61 iBT). Electronic applications accepted.

**Waynesburg University,** Graduate and Professional Studies, Canonsburg, PA 15370. Offers business (MBA), including energy management, finance, health systems, human resources, leadership, market development; counseling (MA), including addictions counseling, clinical mental health; counselor education and supervision (PhD); criminal investigation (MA); education (M Ed), including autism, curriculum and instruction, educational leadership, online teaching; nursing (MSN), including administration, education, informatics; nursing practice (DNP); special education (M Ed); technology (M Ed); MSN/MBA. *Accreditation:* AACN. *Program availability:* Part-time, evening/weekend. *Degree requirements:* For doctorate, thesis/dissertation. *Entrance requirements:* Additional exam requirements/recommendations for international students: Required—TOEFL. Electronic applications accepted.

**Wayne State University,** College of Education, Division of Theoretical and Behavioral Foundations, Detroit, MI 48202. Offers applied behavior analysis (Certificate); counseling (M Ed, MA, Ed D, PhD, Ed S); counseling psychology (MA); education evaluation and research (M Ed, Ed D, PhD); educational psychology (M Ed, PhD), including learning and instruction sciences (PhD); rehabilitation counseling and community inclusion (MA); school and community psychology (MA); school psychology (Certificate). *Accreditation:* ACA (one or more programs are accredited); CORE (one or more programs are accredited). *Program availability:* Evening/weekend. *Faculty:* 12. *Students:* 211 full-time (179 women), 237 part-time (196 women); includes 167 minority (119 Black or African American, non-Hispanic/Latino; 1 American Indian or Alaska Native, non-Hispanic/Latino; 10 Asian, non-Hispanic/Latino; 17 Hispanic/Latino; 20 Two or more races, non-Hispanic/Latino), 24 international. Average age 32. 294 applicants, 34% accepted, 72 enrolled. In 2016, 87 master's, 12 doctorates, 14 other advanced degrees awarded. *Degree requirements:* For master's, thesis (for some programs); for doctorate, thesis/dissertation. *Entrance requirements:* For master's, GRE, interview, personal statement, portfolio (art therapy); for doctorate, GRE, department-written exam, interview, curriculum vitae, references, master's degree in closely-related field with minimum GPA of 3.5, demonstration of counseling skills (counseling); for other advanced degree, master's degree in counseling and counseling license (for Ed S); good standing in school and community psychology MA program (for Certificate). Additional exam requirements/recommendations for international students: Required—TOEFL (minimum score 550 paper-based; 79 iBT), Michigan English Language Assessment Battery (minimum score 85); Recommended—IELTS (minimum score 6.5), TWE (minimum score 5.5). *Application deadline:* For fall admission, 6/1 priority date for domestic students, 5/1 priority date for international students; for winter admission, 10/1 priority date for domestic students, 9/1 priority date for international students; for spring admission, 2/1 priority date for domestic students, 1/1 priority date for international students. Applications are processed on a rolling basis. Application fee: $50. Electronic applications accepted. *Expenses:* $16,503 per year resident tuition and fees, $33,697

per year non-resident tuition and fees. *Financial support:* In 2016–17, 92 students received support, including 2 research assistantships with tuition reimbursements available (averaging $17,994 per year); fellowships with tuition reimbursements available, teaching assistantships with tuition reimbursements available, Federal Work-Study, scholarships/grants, health care benefits, and unspecified assistantships also available. Support available to part-time students. Financial award applicants required to submit FAFSA. *Faculty research:* Adolescents at risk, supervision of counseling. *Unit head:* Dr. Cheryl Somers, Assistant Dean, 313-577-1670, E-mail: c.somers@wayne.edu. *Application contact:* Janice Green, Assistant Dean, 313-577-1605, E-mail: jwgreen@wayne.edu. Website: http://coe.wayne.edu/tbf/index.php

**Webster University,** College of Arts and Sciences, Department of Professional Counseling, St. Louis, MO 63119-3194. Offers counseling (MA). *Accreditation:* ACA. *Program availability:* Part-time. *Entrance requirements:* Additional exam requirements/recommendations for international students: Required—TOEFL. *Application deadline:* Applications are processed on a rolling basis. Application fee: $35 ($50 for international students). *Expenses: Tuition:* Full-time $21,900; part-time $730 per credit hour. Tuition and fees vary according to campus/location and program. *Financial support:* Federal Work-Study available. Support available to part-time students. Financial award application deadline: 4/1; financial award applicants required to submit FAFSA. *Application contact:* Mary Claire Sorensen, Department Associate, 314-246-7795, Fax: 314-246-6094, E-mail: marysorensen60@webster.edu.

**Webster University,** College of Arts and Sciences, Department of Psychology, St. Louis, MO 63119-3194. Offers counseling psychology (MS); gerontology (MS). *Program availability:* Part-time. *Entrance requirements:* Additional exam requirements/recommendations for international students: Required—TOEFL. *Application deadline:* Applications are processed on a rolling basis. Application fee: $35 ($50 for international students). *Expenses: Tuition:* Full-time $21,900; part-time $730 per credit hour. Tuition and fees vary according to campus/location and program. *Financial support:* Federal Work-Study available. Support available to part-time students. Financial award application deadline: 4/1; financial award applicants required to submit FAFSA. *Application contact:* Debi Aholt, Department Manager, 314-246-6970, Fax: 314-246-6094, E-mail: aholtda@webster.edu.

**Western Kentucky University,** Graduate Studies, College of Education and Behavioral Sciences, Department of Counseling and Student Affairs, Bowling Green, KY 42101. Offers counseling (MA Ed), including marriage and family therapy, mental health counseling; school counseling (P-12) (MA Ed); student affairs in higher education (MA Ed). *Accreditation:* ACA; NCATE. *Program availability:* Part-time, evening/weekend. *Degree requirements:* For master's, comprehensive exam, thesis optional. *Entrance requirements:* For master's, GRE General Test. Additional exam requirements/recommendations for international students: Required—TOEFL (minimum score 555 paper-based; 79 iBT). *Faculty research:* Counselor education, research for residential workers.

**Western Michigan University,** Graduate College, College of Education and Human Development, Department of Counselor Education and Counseling Psychology, Kalamazoo, MI 49008. Offers counseling psychology (MA, PhD); counselor education (MA, PhD), including counselor education (MA). *Accreditation:* ACA (one or more programs are accredited); APA (one or more programs are accredited); CORE; NCATE. *Degree requirements:* For doctorate, thesis/dissertation.

**Western Washington University,** Graduate School, College of Humanities and Social Sciences, Department of Psychology, Program in Mental Health Counseling, Bellingham, WA 98225-5996. Offers MS. *Accreditation:* ACA. *Degree requirements:* For master's, thesis optional. *Entrance requirements:* For master's, GRE General Test, minimum GPA of 3.0 in last 60 semester hours or last 90 quarter hours. Additional exam requirements/recommendations for international students: Required—TOEFL (minimum score 567 paper-based). Electronic applications accepted.

**Westfield State University,** College of Graduate and Continuing Education, Department of Psychology, Program in Counseling, Westfield, MA 01086. Offers forensic mental health counseling (MA); mental health counseling (MA); school adjustment counseling (MA); school guidance counseling (MA). *Program availability:* Part-time, evening/weekend. *Degree requirements:* For master's, comprehensive exam, practicum. *Entrance requirements:* For master's, GRE General Test, MAT, minimum undergraduate GPA of 3.0. Additional exam requirements/recommendations for international students: Recommended—TOEFL (minimum score 550 paper-based; 79 iBT). *Expenses:* Tuition, state resident: part-time $318 per semester hour. Tuition, nonresident: part-time $318 per semester hour. *Required fees:* $75 per semester. Tuition and fees vary according to course load and program.

**Westminster College,** Master of Science in Mental Health Counseling Program, Salt Lake City, UT 84105-3697. Offers MSMHC. *Program availability:* Part-time, evening/weekend. *Faculty:* 4 full-time (all women), 1 (woman) part-time/adjunct. *Students:* 19 full-time (18 women), 11 part-time (8 women); includes 3 minority (1 Asian, non-Hispanic/Latino; 1 Hispanic/Latino; 1 Two or more races, non-Hispanic/Latino). Average age 31. 23 applicants, 70% accepted, 10 enrolled. In 2016, 17 master's awarded. *Degree requirements:* For master's, comprehensive exam, thesis, internship. *Entrance requirements:* For master's, GRE (taken within the past 5 years), baccalaureate degree from regionally-accredited college or university or a recognized international college or university; official copies of transcripts sent by the registrar of each college or university attended; three letters of recommendation; proof of clear state and federal background checks. Additional exam requirements/recommendations for international students: Required—TOEFL (minimum score 600 paper-based; 100 iBT), IELTS (minimum score 7.5). *Application deadline:* For fall admission, 2/1 priority date for domestic and international students. Applications are processed on a rolling basis. Application fee: $50. Electronic applications accepted. *Expenses:* $735 per credit hour tuition, $13 per credit hour student fee (Fall and Spring semesters only). *Financial support:* In 2016–17, 2 students received support. Career-related internships or fieldwork, scholarships/grants, unspecified assistantships, and tuition reimbursements, tuition remission available. Support available to part-time students. Financial award applicants required to submit FAFSA. *Faculty research:* Mental health issues, trauma, eating disorder, anxiety, depression, interpersonal relationships. *Unit head:* Colleen Sandor, Director, 801-832-2422, E-mail: csandor@westminstercollege.edu. *Application contact:* Ashley Williams, Director of Graduate Admissions, 801-832-2213, Fax: 801-832-3101, E-mail: awilliams@westminstercollege.edu. Website: http://www.westminstercollege.edu/mspc/

**West Virginia University,** College of Education and Human Services, Department of Counseling, Rehabilitation Counseling, and Counseling Psychology, Program in Counseling Psychology, Morgantown, WV 26506. Offers PhD. *Accreditation:* ACA; APA. *Degree requirements:* For doctorate, comprehensive exam, thesis/dissertation, APA-approved 1 year internship. *Entrance requirements:* For doctorate, GRE General Test, interview. Additional exam requirements/recommendations for international students: Required—TOEFL (minimum score 550 paper-based; 65 iBT). Electronic applications accepted.

**Wheaton College,** Graduate School, Department of Psychology, Wheaton, IL 60187-5593. Offers clinical mental health counseling (MA); clinical psychology (Psy D); counseling ministries (MA); marriage and family therapy (MA). *Accreditation:* APA (one or more programs are accredited). *Faculty:* 14 full-time (7 women), 9 part-time/adjunct (5 women). *Students:* 130 full-time (97 women), 17 part-time (13 women); includes 38 minority (13 Black or African American, non-Hispanic/Latino; 1 American Indian or Alaska Native, non-Hispanic/Latino; 9 Asian, non-Hispanic/Latino; 8 Hispanic/Latino; 7 Two or more races, non-Hispanic/Latino; 17 international. Average age 28. 115 applicants, 80% accepted, 58 enrolled. In 2016, 70 master's, 9 doctorates awarded. Terminal master's awarded for partial completion of doctoral program. *Degree requirements:* For master's, thesis or alternative; for doctorate, thesis/dissertation, internship. *Entrance requirements:* For master's, GRE General Test, 18 hours of course work in psychology; for doctorate, GRE General Test. Additional exam requirements/recommendations for international students: Required—TOEFL (minimum score 550 paper-based; 80 iBT), IELTS (minimum score 6.5), TOEFL (minimum score 600 paper-based; 90 iBT) or IELTS (minimum score 7.5) for PsyD. *Application deadline:* For fall admission, 3/1 priority date for domestic students, 1/1 for international students. Applications are processed on a rolling basis. Application fee: $30. *Expenses: Tuition:* Full-time $19,080; part-time $795 per credit hour. Tuition and fees vary according to degree level and program. *Financial support:* In 2016–17, 3 research assistantships (averaging $4,800 per year) were awarded; career-related internships or fieldwork, Federal Work-Study, scholarships/grants, and unspecified assistantships also available. Financial award application deadline: 3/1; financial award applicants required to submit FAFSA. *Unit head:* Dr. Terri Watson, Associate Dean of Psychology, 630-752-5104, E-mail: psychology@wheaton.edu. *Application contact:* Dusty Di Santo, Director of Graduate Admissions, 630-752-5195, Fax: 630-752-7047, E-mail: graduate.admissions@wheaton.edu.
Website: http://www.wheaton.edu/academics/departments/psychology

**William Carey University,** Department of Psychology and Graduate Counseling, Hattiesburg, MS 39401-5499. Offers counseling psychology (MS). *Program availability:* Part-time. *Entrance requirements:* For master's, GRE, PRAXIS, MAT, minimum GPA of 2.5. Additional exam requirements/recommendations for international students: Required—TOEFL (minimum score 550 paper-based). *Expenses:* Contact institution. *Faculty research:* Addiction prevention, psychometric measurement, crisis counseling, gerontology.

**William James College,** Graduate Programs, Newton, MA 02459. Offers applied psychology in higher education student personnel administration (MA); clinical psychology (Psy D); counseling psychology (MA); counseling psychology and community mental health (MA); counseling psychology and global mental health (MA); executive coaching (Graduate Certificate); forensic and counseling psychology (MA); leadership psychology (Psy D); organizational psychology (MA); primary care psychology (MA); respecialization in clinical psychology (Certificate); school psychology (Psy D); MA/CAGS. *Accreditation:* APA. *Degree requirements:* For master's, comprehensive exam (for some programs); for doctorate, thesis/dissertation (for some programs). Electronic applications accepted.

**William Paterson University of New Jersey,** College of Humanities and Social Sciences, Wayne, NJ 07470-8420. Offers applied sociology (MA); clinical and counseling psychology (MA); clinical psychology (Psy D); creative and professional writing (MFA); English (MA); history (MA); political science and public policy (MA); public policy and international affairs (MA). *Program availability:* Part-time, evening/weekend. *Faculty:* 35 full-time (19 women), 8 part-time/adjunct (5 women). *Students:* 58 full-time (38 women), 62 part-time (46 women); includes 40 minority (9 Black or African American, non-Hispanic/Latino; 6 Asian, non-Hispanic/Latino; 21 Hispanic/Latino; 4 Two or more races, non-Hispanic/Latino), 4 international. Average age 32. 160 applicants, 55% accepted, 50 enrolled. In 2016, 56 master's awarded. *Degree requirements:* For master's, thesis (for some programs), internship (for some programs). *Entrance requirements:* For master's, GRE/MAT, minimum GPA of 3.0; 2 letters of recommendation; writing sample/personal statement. Additional exam requirements/recommendations for international students: Required—TOEFL (minimum score 500 paper-based; 79 iBT), IELTS (minimum score 6). *Application deadline:* For fall admission, 8/1 for domestic students, 4/1 for international students; for spring admission, 12/1 for domestic students, 11/1 for international students; for summer admission, 5/1 for domestic students, 2/1 for international students. Applications are processed on a rolling basis. Application fee: $50. Electronic applications accepted. *Expenses:* Tuition, state resident: full-time $12,480; part-time $611 per credit. Tuition, nonresident: full-time $20,263; part-time $992 per credit. *Required fees:* $1573; $77 per credit. Tuition and fees vary according to course load, degree level and program. *Financial support:* Career-related internships or fieldwork, Federal Work-Study, scholarships/grants, and unspecified assistantships available. Support available to part-time students. Financial award applicants required to submit FAFSA. *Faculty research:* Relationship violence among adolescents; autism in young children; game theory; gender, governance and empowerment in India; Chinese development policies concerning Africa. *Total annual research expenditures:* $162,900. *Unit head:* Dr. Kara Rabbitt, Dean, 973-720-2180, Fax: 973-720-2955, E-mail: rabbittk@wpunj.edu. *Application contact:* Tinu Adeniran, Associate Director, Graduate Admissions, 973-720-2764, Fax: 973-720-2035, E-mail: adenirant@wpunj.edu.
Website: http://www.wpunj.edu/cohss

**Wilmington University,** College of Social and Behavioral Sciences, New Castle, DE 19720-6491. Offers administration of human services (MS); administration of justice (MS); clinical mental health counseling (MS); homeland security (MS). *Accreditation:*

ACA. *Program availability:* Part-time, evening/weekend. *Faculty:* 8 full-time (5 women), 79 part-time/adjunct (35 women). *Students:* 210 full-time (162 women), 444 part-time (325 women); includes 320 minority (285 Black or African American, non-Hispanic/Latino; 12 American Indian or Alaska Native, non-Hispanic/Latino; 9 Asian, non-Hispanic/Latino; 12 Hispanic/Latino; 1 Native Hawaiian or other Pacific Islander, non-Hispanic/Latino; 1 Two or more races, non-Hispanic/Latino), 4 international. Average age 35. 255 applicants, 100% accepted, 255 enrolled. In 2016, 248 master's awarded. *Entrance requirements:* Additional exam requirements/recommendations for international students: Required—TOEFL (minimum score 500 paper-based). *Application deadline:* Applications are processed on a rolling basis. Application fee: $35. Electronic applications accepted. *Expenses: Tuition:* Full-time $8388; part-time $466 per credit. *Required fees:* $25 per semester. Tuition and fees vary according to degree level. *Financial support:* Applicants required to submit FAFSA. *Unit head:* Dr. Edward L. Guthrie, Dean. *Application contact:* Laura Morris, Director of Admissions, 877-967-5464, E-mail: inquire@wilmcoll.edu. Website: http://www.wilmu.edu/behavioralscience/

**Winebrenner Theological Seminary,** Graduate Programs, Findlay, OH 45840. Offers clinical counseling (MA); family ministry (MA); practical theology (MA); theological and ministerial studies (M Div, D Min); theological studies (MA). *Accreditation:* ATS (one or more programs are accredited). *Program availability:* Part-time, 100% online, blended/hybrid learning. *Faculty:* 7 full-time (2 women), 22 part-time/adjunct (8 women). *Students:* 16 full-time (10 women), 50 part-time (23 women); includes 12 minority (8 Black or African American, non-Hispanic/Latino; 2 Asian, non-Hispanic/Latino; 2 Two or more races, non-Hispanic/Latino), 2 international. Average age 41. 25 applicants, 76% accepted, 12 enrolled. In 2016, 8 master's, 2 doctorates awarded. *Degree requirements:* For master's, variable foreign language requirement, thesis (for some programs); for doctorate, thesis/dissertation. *Entrance requirements:* For doctorate, 3 years of post-M Div full-time ministry. Additional exam requirements/recommendations for international students: Required—TOEFL (minimum score 550 paper-based; 80 iBT). *Application deadline:* For fall admission, 8/15 priority date for domestic students, 7/15 priority date for international students; for winter admission, 12/15 priority date for domestic students, 11/15 priority date for international students; for spring admission, 4/15 priority date for domestic students, 3/15 priority date for international students. Applications are processed on a rolling basis. Application fee: $30. Electronic applications accepted. *Expenses: Tuition:* Full-time $14,175; part-time $525 per credit hour. *Required fees:* $450; $150 per trimester. Tuition and fees vary according to degree level. *Financial support:* In 2016–17, 32 students received support, including 3 teaching assistantships with partial tuition reimbursements available (averaging $1,575 per year); research assistantships, institutionally sponsored loans, scholarships/grants, unspecified assistantships, and denominational discounts, spousal discounts also available. Financial award application deadline: 7/1; financial award applicants required to submit FAFSA. *Faculty research:* Inductive biblical language grammar; review of Tobias Hagerland's "Jesus and the Scriptures"; Teleios profile of student wholeness; Puritanism; theological aesthetics. *Unit head:* Dr. Joel W. Cocklin, Academic Dean, 419-434-4250, Fax: 419-434-4267, E-mail: jcocklin@winebrenner.edu. *Application contact:* Jim Smarkel, Director of Enrollment Management, 419-434-4220, Fax: 419-434-4267, E-mail: admissions@winebrenner.edu.
Website: http://www.winebrenner.edu

**Wright Institute,** Master of Arts in Counseling Psychology Program, Berkeley, CA 94704-1796. Offers MA. *Program availability:* Part-time, evening/weekend. *Degree requirements:* For master's, comprehensive exam. *Entrance requirements:* Additional exam requirements/recommendations for international students: Required—TOEFL. *Application deadline:* Applications are processed on a rolling basis. Application fee: $50. Electronic applications accepted. *Financial support:* Career-related internships or fieldwork, Federal Work-Study, and scholarships/grants available. Financial award applicants required to submit FAFSA. *Unit head:* Dr. Milena Esherick, Program Director, 510-841-9230 Ext. 144. *Application contact:* John Pitts, Director of Admissions, 510-841-9230 Ext. 171, E-mail: jpitts@wi.edu.
Website: https://www.wi.edu/ma-program

**Xavier University,** College of Social Sciences, Health and Education, School of Education, Department of Counseling, Cincinnati, OH 45207. Offers clinical mental health counseling (MA); school counseling (MA). *Program availability:* Part-time, evening/weekend. *Degree requirements:* For master's, internship. *Entrance requirements:* For master's, GRE or MAT, minimum GPA of 3.0; 2 letters of recommendation; resume; official transcript; statement of purpose. Additional exam requirements/recommendations for international students: Required—TOEFL (minimum score 550 paper-based; 79 iBT). Electronic applications accepted. Application fee is waived when completed online. *Expenses:* Contact institution. *Faculty research:* Supervision, ethics, consultation, self-injury, bullying.

**Yeshiva University,** Ferkauf Graduate School of Psychology, Program in Mental Health Counseling Psychology, New York, NY 10033-3201. Offers MA. *Program availability:* Part-time. *Entrance requirements:* For master's, GRE General Test. *Faculty research:* Substance abuse treatment, group therapy.

**Youngstown State University,** Graduate School, Beeghly College of Education, Department of Counseling, Youngstown, OH 44555-0001. Offers community counseling (MS Ed); school counseling (MS Ed). *Accreditation:* ACA; NCATE. *Program availability:* Part-time, evening/weekend. *Degree requirements:* For master's, comprehensive exam. *Entrance requirements:* For master's, MAT, interview, minimum GPA of 2.7. Additional exam requirements/recommendations for international students: Required—TOEFL. *Faculty research:* Suicide, euthanasia, ethical issues, marriage and family.

# Developmental Psychology

**Andrews University,** School of Graduate Studies, School of Education, Department of Graduate Psychology and Counseling, Program in Educational and Developmental Psychology, Berrien Springs, MI 49104. Offers educational and developmental psychology (MA); educational psychology (Ed D, PhD). *Students:* 17 full-time (12 women), 3 part-time (2 women); includes 9 minority (6 Black or African American, non-Hispanic/Latino; 3 Hispanic/Latino), 5 international. Average age 37. In 2016, 9 master's, 1 doctorate awarded. *Degree requirements:* For master's, thesis optional. *Entrance requirements:* For master's, GRE. Additional exam requirements/recommendations for international students: Required—TOEFL (minimum score 550 paper-based). *Application deadline:* Applications are processed on a rolling basis. Application fee: $40. *Unit head:* Dr. Jimmy Kijai, Coordinator, 269-471-6240. *Application contact:* Justina Clayburn, Supervisor of Graduate Admission, 800-253-2874, Fax: 269-471-6321, E-mail: graduate@andrews.edu.

**Arizona State University at the Tempe campus,** College of Liberal Arts and Sciences, Department of Psychology, Tempe, AZ 85287-1104. Offers applied behavior analysis (MS); behavioral neuroscience (PhD); clinical psychology (PhD); cognitive science (PhD); developmental psychology (PhD); quantitative psychology (PhD); social psychology (PhD). *Accreditation:* APA. *Degree requirements:* For doctorate, comprehensive exam, thesis/dissertation, interactive Program of Study (iPOS) submitted before completing 50 percent of required credit hours. *Entrance requirements:* For doctorate, GRE General Test, GRE Subject Test, minimum GPA of 3.0 or equivalent in last 2 years of work leading to bachelor's degree. Additional exam requirements/recommendations for international students: Required—TOEFL, IELTS, or PTE. Electronic applications accepted.

**Bay Path University,** Program in Developmental Psychology, Longmeadow, MA 01106-2292. Offers developmental psychology (MS). *Program availability:* Part-time, 100%

## Developmental Psychology

online. *Students:* 4 full-time (3 women), 15 part-time (14 women); includes 8 minority (3 Black or African American, non-Hispanic/Latino; 4 Hispanic/Latino; 1 Two or more races, non-Hispanic/Latino). Average age 38. 24 applicants, 54% accepted, 8 enrolled. In 2016, 7 master's awarded. *Degree requirements:* For master's, nine core courses (27 credits) and three elective courses (9 credits); 160 hours of community-based field work. *Entrance requirements:* For master's, bachelor's degree in psychology or related field; minimum cumulative GPA of 3.0; working knowledge of statistics, research methods, abnormal psychology, personality, and developmental psychology (strongly recommended). *Application deadline:* Applications are processed on a rolling basis. Application fee: $45. Electronic applications accepted. Application fee is waived when completed online. *Expenses:* $21,465. *Financial support:* Unspecified assistantships available. Financial award applicants required to submit FAFSA. *Unit head:* Dr. Mark Benander, Program Director, 413-565-1332, E-mail: mbenander@baypath.edu. *Application contact:* Diane Ranaldi, Dean of Graduate Admissions, 413-565-1332, Fax: 413-565-1250, E-mail: dranaldi@baypath.edu. Website: http://www.baypath.edu/academics/graduate-programs/developmental-psychology-ms/

**Boston College,** Lynch School of Education, Program in Applied Developmental and Educational Psychology, Chestnut Hill, MA 02467-3800. Offers MA, PhD. *Program availability:* Part-time, evening/weekend. *Faculty:* 11 full-time (8 women). *Students:* 19 full-time (18 women), 21 part-time (20 women); includes 8 minority (2 Black or African American, non-Hispanic/Latino; 2 Asian, non-Hispanic/Latino; 3 Hispanic/Latino; 1 Two or more races, non-Hispanic/Latino), 8 international. Average age 27. 97 applicants, 48% accepted, 14 enrolled. In 2016, 15 master's, 2 doctorates awarded. Terminal master's awarded for partial completion of doctoral program. *Degree requirements:* For master's, comprehensive exam; for doctorate, comprehensive exam, thesis/dissertation. *Entrance requirements:* For master's and doctorate, GRE General Test. Additional exam requirements/recommendations for international students: Required—TOEFL (minimum score 100 iBT). *Application deadline:* For fall admission, 12/1 priority date for domestic and international students; for spring admission, 11/1 for domestic and international students. Application fee: $65. Electronic applications accepted. Tuition and fees vary according to program. *Financial support:* Fellowships with tuition reimbursements, research assistantships with tuition reimbursements, teaching assistantships with tuition reimbursements, career-related internships or fieldwork, Federal Work-Study, scholarships/grants, traineeships, health care benefits, tuition waivers (full and partial), and unspecified assistantships available. Support available to part-time students. Financial award applicants required to submit FAFSA. *Faculty research:* Cognitive learning and culture, effects of social policy reform on children and families, psychosocial trauma, human rights and international justice, positive youth development, children and adolescents living in poverty. *Unit head:* Dr. Penny Hauser-Cram, Chairperson, 617-552-4214, Fax: 617-552-4710. *Application contact:* Kimberly Rose, Graduate Admission Assistant, 617-552-4214, Fax: 617-552-0398, E-mail: roseki@bc.edu.
Website: http://www.bc.edu/schools/lsoe/academics/departments/cdep/adep/madevelop.html

**Boston Graduate School of Psychoanalysis,** CAGS and Certificate Programs, Brookline, MA 02446-4602. Offers child and adolescent intervention (CAGS); psychoanalysis (Certificate); psychoanalytic psychotherapy (CAGS). *Program availability:* Part-time. *Degree requirements:* For other advanced degree, thesis. *Entrance requirements:* For degree, interview, BA, writing sample, 3 letters of reference, transcripts. Additional exam requirements/recommendations for international students: Required—TOEFL (minimum score 500 paper-based; 79 iBT). *Faculty research:* Treatment approaches for intractable patients, unconscious symbolic processes, female adolescent development, evaluation of school mental health interventions, development of symbolic processes in early childhood.

**Bowling Green State University,** Graduate College, College of Arts and Sciences, Department of Psychology, Bowling Green, OH 43403. Offers clinical psychology (MA, PhD); developmental psychology (MA, PhD); experimental psychology (MA, PhD); industrial/organizational psychology (MA, PhD); quantitative psychology (MA, PhD). *Accreditation:* APA (one or more programs are accredited). *Degree requirements:* For doctorate, thesis/dissertation. *Entrance requirements:* For doctorate, GRE General Test, GRE Subject Test. Additional exam requirements/recommendations for international students: Required—TOEFL. *Application deadline:* For fall admission, 1/1 for domestic students. Application fee: $30. Electronic applications accepted. *Financial support:* Fellowships with full tuition reimbursements, research assistantships with full tuition reimbursements, teaching assistantships with full tuition reimbursements, career-related internships or fieldwork, Federal Work-Study, institutionally sponsored loans, tuition waivers (full), and unspecified assistantships available. Financial award applicants required to submit FAFSA. *Faculty research:* Personnel psychology, developmental-mathematical models, behavioral medication, brain process, child/adolescent social cognition. *Unit head:* Dr. Mike Zickar, Chair, 419-372-2301, E-mail: mzickar@bgsu.edu. *Application contact:* Dr. Terry L. Lawrence, Assistant Dean for Graduate Admissions and Studies, 419-372-7713, Fax: 419-372-8569, E-mail: tlawren@bgnet.bgsu.edu.

**Brandeis University,** Graduate School of Arts and Sciences, Department of Psychology, Waltham, MA 02454-9110. Offers brain, body and behavior (PhD); cognitive neuroscience (PhD); general psychology (MA); social/developmental psychology (PhD). *Program availability:* Part-time. *Faculty:* 14 full-time (7 women), 4 part-time/adjunct (3 women). *Students:* 40 full-time (27 women), 1 (woman) part-time; includes 5 minority (1 Black or African American, non-Hispanic/Latino; 2 Asian, non-Hispanic/Latino; 2 Hispanic/Latino), 9 international. 148 applicants, 23% accepted, 15 enrolled. In 2016, 8 master's, 3 doctorates awarded. Terminal master's awarded for partial completion of doctoral program. *Degree requirements:* For master's, thesis or alternative; for doctorate, thesis/dissertation, research reports. *Entrance requirements:* For master's and doctorate, GRE General Test; GRE Subject Test (recommended), 3 letters of recommendation, statement of purpose, transcript(s), resume. Additional exam requirements/recommendations for international students: Required—TOEFL (minimum score 600 paper-based; 100 iBT); Recommended—IELTS (minimum score 7), TSE (minimum score 68). *Application deadline:* For fall admission, 1/15 priority date for domestic and international students. Application fee: $75. Electronic applications accepted. *Financial support:* In 2016–17, 22 students received support, including 22 fellowships with full tuition reimbursements available (averaging $24,000 per year), 34 teaching assistantships with partial tuition reimbursements available (averaging $3,200 per year); Federal Work-Study, scholarships/grants, health care benefits, and tuition waivers (full and partial) also available. Support available to part-time students. Financial award application deadline: 4/15; financial award applicants required to submit FAFSA. *Faculty research:* Brain, body, and behavior across the lifespan; face perception and nonverbal communication; learning and memory; motor control and spatial orientation; neurophysiology of learning and decision making; personality and cognition in adulthood and old age; social, cultural and affective neuroscience; social relations and health physiology; speech comprehension and memory; taste physiology and psychophysics; visual perception. *Unit head:* Prof. Paul DiZio, Department Chair, 781-736-3300, Fax: 781-736-3291, E-mail: dizio@brandeis.edu. *Application contact:* Phil Gnatowski, Department Administrator, 781-736-3302, Fax: 781-736-3291, E-mail: gnat@brandeis.edu.
Website: http://www.brandeis.edu/departments/psych/

**Brigham Young University,** Graduate Studies, College of Family, Home, and Social Sciences, Department of Psychology, Provo, UT 84602. Offers applied social psychology (PhD); clinical psychology (PhD); cognitive and behavioral neuroscience (PhD); developmental psychology (PhD). *Accreditation:* APA. *Faculty:* 29 full-time (7 women), 8 part-time/adjunct (2 women). *Students:* 59 full-time (34 women); includes 9 minority (2 Black or African American, non-Hispanic/Latino; 4 Asian, non-Hispanic/Latino; 2 Hispanic/Latino; 1 Native Hawaiian or other Pacific Islander, non-Hispanic/Latino). Average age 29. 49 applicants, 33% accepted, 11 enrolled. In 2016, 12 doctorates awarded. *Degree requirements:* For doctorate, comprehensive exam (for some programs), thesis/dissertation, publishable paper. *Entrance requirements:* For doctorate, GRE General Test, minimum GPA of 3.0. Additional exam requirements/recommendations for international students: Required—TOEFL (minimum score 580 paper-based; 85 iBT). *Application deadline:* For fall admission, 12/1 for domestic and international students. Application fee: $50. Electronic applications accepted. *Expenses:* Contact institution. *Financial support:* In 2016–17, 41 students received support, including 32 research assistantships with partial tuition reimbursements available (averaging $12,000 per year), 5 teaching assistantships with partial tuition reimbursements available (averaging $12,000 per year); career-related internships or fieldwork, scholarships/grants, tuition waivers (partial), and unspecified assistantships also available. Financial award application deadline: 5/31. *Faculty research:* Psychotherapy process, Alzheimer's disease/dementia, psychology and law, health, psychology, developmental. *Total annual research expenditures:* $73,281. *Unit head:* Dr. Dawson Hedges, Chair, 801-422-6357, Fax: 801-422-0602, E-mail: dawson_hedges@byu.edu. *Application contact:* Leesa D. Scott, Coordinator of Student Programs, 801-422-4560, Fax: 801-422-0602, E-mail: leesa_scott@byu.edu.
Website: http://psychology.byu.edu/

**Capella University,** Harold Abel School of Social and Behavioral Science, Master's Programs in Counseling, Minneapolis, MN 55402. Offers child and adolescent development (MS); general addiction counseling (MS); general marriage and family counseling/therapy (MS); general mental health counseling (MS); general school counseling (MS).

**Carnegie Mellon University,** Dietrich College of Humanities and Social Sciences, Department of Psychology, Area of Developmental Psychology, Pittsburgh, PA 15213-3891. Offers PhD. *Degree requirements:* For doctorate, comprehensive exam, thesis/dissertation. *Entrance requirements:* For doctorate, GRE General Test. Additional exam requirements/recommendations for international students: Required—TOEFL. *Faculty research:* Cognitive development, language acquisition.

**Chatham University,** Program in Counseling Psychology, Pittsburgh, PA 15232-2826. Offers child, adolescent and family (MSCP); counseling psychology (Psy D); health and holistic (MSCP); infant mental health (MSCP); organization and supervision (MSCP); sport and exercise (MSCP). *Accreditation:* APA. *Program availability:* Part-time, evening/weekend. *Degree requirements:* For master's, thesis optional, supervised internship; for doctorate, thesis/dissertation, internship. *Entrance requirements:* For master's, minimum GPA of 3.0; 2 letters of recommendation; resume; prerequisite coursework in statistics, biology, and psychology; for doctorate, GRE. Additional exam requirements/recommendations for international students: Required—TOEFL (minimum score 600 paper-based; 100 iBT), IELTS (minimum score 7), TWE. Electronic applications accepted. Application fee is waived when completed online. *Expenses:* Tuition: Full-time $16,254; part-time $903 per credit hour. *Required fees:* $468; $26 per credit hour. *Faculty research:* Trauma and recovery, hypnosis, psychospiritual dimensions of healing, psychotherapy of schizophrenia.

**Claremont Graduate University,** Graduate Programs, School of Social Science, Policy and Evaluation, Department of Psychology, Claremont, CA 91711-6160. Offers advanced study in evaluation (Certificate); cognitive psychology (MA, PhD); developmental psychology (MA, PhD); evaluation and applied research methods (MA, PhD); health behavior research and evaluation (MA, PhD); human resource development and evaluation (MA); industrial/organizational psychology (MA, PhD); organizational behavior (MA, PhD); organizational psychology (MA, PhD); social psychology (MA, PhD); MBA/PhD. *Program availability:* Part-time. *Faculty:* 19 full-time (9 women), 1 part-time/adjunct (0 women). *Students:* 244 full-time (160 women), 66 part-time (38 women); includes 93 minority (15 Black or African American, non-Hispanic/Latino; 2 American Indian or Alaska Native, non-Hispanic/Latino; 29 Asian, non-Hispanic/Latino; 31 Hispanic/Latino; 2 Native Hawaiian or other Pacific Islander, non-Hispanic/Latino; 14 Two or more races, non-Hispanic/Latino), 41 international. Average age 30. In 2016, 61 master's, 23 doctorates, 5 other advanced degrees awarded. Terminal master's awarded for partial completion of doctoral program. *Entrance requirements:* For master's and doctorate, GRE General Test. Additional exam requirements/recommendations for international students: Required—TOEFL (minimum score 75 iBT). *Application deadline:* For fall admission, 1/15 priority date for domestic and international students. Applications are processed on a rolling basis. Application fee: $80. Electronic applications accepted. *Expenses:* Tuition: Full-time $44,328; part-time $1847 per unit. *Required fees:* $600; $300 per semester. Tuition and fees vary according to course load and program. *Financial support:* Fellowships, research assistantships, teaching assistantships, Federal Work-Study, institutionally sponsored loans, scholarships/grants, and tuition waivers (full and partial) available. Support available to part-time students. Financial award application deadline: 2/15; financial award applicants required to submit FAFSA. *Faculty research:* Social intervention, diversity in organizations, eyewitness memory, aging and cognition, drug policy. *Unit head:* William Crano, Chair, 909-607-3311, E-mail: william.crano@cgu.edu. *Application contact:* Paige Piontkowsky, Senior Assistant Director of Admissions, 909-607-3240, E-mail: paige.piontkowsky@cgu.edu.
Website: https://www.cgu.edu/school/ssspe/programs/?areas_of_study=psychology

**Clark University,** Graduate School, Hiatt School of Psychology, Program in Developmental Psychology, Worcester, MA 01610-1477. Offers PhD. *Students:* 7 full-time (6 women), 2 international. Average age 27. In 2016, 3 doctorates awarded. *Degree requirements:* For doctorate, thesis/dissertation. *Entrance requirements:* For doctorate, GRE General Test. Additional exam requirements/recommendations for international students: Required—TOEFL. *Application deadline:* For fall admission, 12/15 priority date for domestic students, 12/15 for international students. Applications are processed on a rolling basis. Application fee: $75. *Expenses:* Tuition: Full-time $44,050. *Required fees:* $80. Tuition and fees vary according to course load and program. *Financial support:* In 2016–17, fellowships with full tuition reimbursements (averaging $17,325 per year), research assistantships with full tuition reimbursements (averaging $17,325 per year), teaching assistantships with full tuition reimbursements (averaging $17,325 per year) were awarded; tuition waivers (full) also available. *Faculty research:* Development of psychological processes in sociocultural context, conceptualizing and reasoning, symbolization, parental structure in families of adolescents, transition to kindergarten. *Unit head:* Dr. Michael Bamberg, Chair, 508-793-7135, E-mail: ljensen@clarku.edu. *Application contact:* Kelly Boulay, Departmental Administrator, 508-793-7274, Fax: 508-793-7265, E-mail: psychology@clarku.edu.
Website: http://www.clarku.edu/departments/psychology/grad/developmental/index.cfm

**Clayton State University,** School of Graduate Studies, College of Arts and Sciences, Program in Psychology, Morrow, GA 30260-0285. Offers applied developmental

psychology (MS); clinical/counseling psychology (MS). *Entrance requirements:* For master's, GRE, 2 official transcripts; 3 letters of recommendation; statement of purpose; on-campus interview; background check. Additional exam requirements/recommendations for international students: Required—TOEFL (minimum score 550 paper-based). Electronic applications accepted. *Expenses:* Tuition, state resident: full-time $3528; part-time $196 per credit hour. Tuition, nonresident: full-time $13,176; part-time $732 per credit hour. *Required fees:* $1454; $1454 per credit hour. $727 per semester. Tuition and fees vary according to campus/location and program.

**Cornell University,** Graduate School, Graduate Fields of Human Ecology, Field of Human Development, Ithaca, NY 14853. Offers developmental psychology (MA, PhD), including cognitive development, developmental psychopathology, ecology of human development, social and personality development; human development and family studies (MA, PhD), including ecology of human development, family studies and the life course. *Degree requirements:* For doctorate, comprehensive exam, thesis/dissertation, pre-doctoral research project, teaching experience. *Entrance requirements:* For doctorate, GRE General Test, 2 letters of recommendation. Additional exam requirements/recommendations for international students: Required—TOEFL (minimum score 550 paper-based; 77 iBT). Electronic applications accepted. *Faculty research:* Cognitive development, developmental psychopathology, ecology of human development, family studies and the life course, social and personality development.

**Delaware Valley University,** Program in Counseling Psychology, Doylestown, PA 18901-2697. Offers child and adolescent therapy (MA); social justice community counseling (MA).

**Duke University,** Graduate School, Department of Psychology and Neuroscience, Durham, NC 27708. Offers biological psychology (PhD); clinical psychology (PhD); cognitive psychology (PhD); developmental psychology (PhD); experimental psychology (PhD); health psychology (PhD); human social development (PhD); JD/MA. *Accreditation:* APA (one or more programs are accredited). *Degree requirements:* For doctorate, thesis/dissertation. *Entrance requirements:* For doctorate, GRE General Test. Additional exam requirements/recommendations for international students: Required—TOEFL (minimum score 577 paper-based; 90 iBT) or IELTS (minimum score 7). Electronic applications accepted.

**Emory University,** Laney Graduate School, Department of Psychology, Atlanta, GA 30322-1100. Offers clinical psychology (PhD); cognition and development (PhD); neuroscience and animal behavior (PhD). *Accreditation:* APA. *Degree requirements:* For doctorate, comprehensive exam, thesis/dissertation. *Entrance requirements:* For doctorate, GRE General Test, minimum GPA of 3.25. Additional exam requirements/recommendations for international students: Required—TOEFL. Electronic applications accepted. *Faculty research:* Neuroscience and animal behavior; adult and child psychopathology, cognition development assessment.

**Erikson Institute,** Academic Programs, Chicago, IL 60654. Offers administration (Certificate); bilingual/ESL (Certificate); child development (MS); early childhood education (MS); infant mental health (Certificate); infant studies (Certificate); MS/MSW. MS/MSW offered jointly with Loyola University Chicago. *Program availability:* Part-time, evening/weekend. *Degree requirements:* For master's, comprehensive exam, internship; for Certificate, internship. *Entrance requirements:* For master's and Certificate, minimum GPA of 2.75. Additional exam requirements/recommendations for international students: Required—TOEFL. *Faculty research:* Assessment strategies from early childhood through elementary years; language, literacy, and the arts in children's development; inclusive special education; parent-child relationships; cognitive development.

**Florida International University,** College of Arts, Sciences, and Education, Department of Psychology, Miami, FL 33199. Offers behavioral analysis (MS); clinical science (PhD); cognitive neuroscience (PhD); counseling psychology (MS); developmental science (MS, PhD); legal psychology (MS, PhD); organizational psychology (MS, PhD). Program has fall admissions only. *Accreditation:* APA. *Program availability:* Part-time, evening/weekend. *Faculty:* 44 full-time (27 women), 41 part-time/adjunct (30 women). *Students:* 150 full-time (115 women), 17 part-time (10 women); includes 89 minority (8 Black or African American, non-Hispanic/Latino; 5 Asian, non-Hispanic/Latino; 75 Hispanic/Latino; 1 Two or more races, non-Hispanic/Latino), 10 international. Average age 27. 287 applicants, 24% accepted, 57 enrolled. In 2016, 35 master's, 11 doctorates awarded. Terminal master's awarded for partial completion of doctoral program. *Degree requirements:* For master's, thesis; for doctorate, comprehensive exam, thesis/dissertation. *Entrance requirements:* For master's, GRE General Test, minimum GPA of 3.0, resume, 3 letters of recommendation; for doctorate, GRE General Test, 3 letters of recommendation, resume, letter of intent, two writing samples, minimum GPA of 3.0. Additional exam requirements/recommendations for international students: Required—TOEFL (minimum score 550 paper-based; 80 iBT). *Application deadline:* For fall admission, 12/15 for domestic and international students. Application fee: $30. Electronic applications accepted. *Expenses:* Tuition, state resident: full-time $8912; part-time $446 per credit hour. Tuition, nonresident: full-time $21,393; part-time $992 per credit hour. *Required fees:* $2185; $195 per semester. Tuition and fees vary according to program. *Financial support:* Institutionally sponsored loans and scholarships/grants available. Financial award application deadline: 3/1. *Faculty research:* Legal psychology, organizational and industrial psychology, child behavior psychology. *Unit head:* Dr. William Pelham, Chair, 305-348-3002, Fax: 305-348-3646, E-mail: wpelham@fiu.edu. *Application contact:* Nanett Rojas, Assistant Director, Graduate Admissions, 305-348-7464, Fax: 305-348-7441, E-mail: gradadm@fiu.edu.

**Florida State University,** The Graduate School, College of Arts and Sciences, Department of Psychology, Program in Developmental Psychology, Tallahassee, FL 32306. Offers PhD. *Faculty:* 6 full-time (3 women). *Students:* 7 full-time (all women), 1 (woman) part-time; includes 4 minority (2 Black or African American, non-Hispanic/Latino; 1 Hispanic/Latino; 1 Two or more races, non-Hispanic/Latino). Average age 29. 18 applicants, 17% accepted, 3 enrolled. In 2016, 2 doctorates awarded. Terminal master's awarded for partial completion of doctoral program. *Degree requirements:* For doctorate, comprehensive exam, thesis/dissertation. *Entrance requirements:* For doctorate, GRE General Test, minimum GPA of 3.0, research experience, letters of recommendation. Additional exam requirements/recommendations for international students: Required—TOEFL (minimum score 80 iBT). *Application deadline:* For fall admission, 12/15 for domestic and international students. Application fee: $30. Electronic applications accepted. *Expenses:* Tuition, state resident: full-time $7263; part-time $403.51 per credit hour. Tuition, nonresident: full-time $18,087; part-time $1004.85 per credit hour. *Required fees:* $1365; $75.81 per credit hour. $20 per semester. Tuition and fees vary according to campus/location. *Financial support:* In 2016–17, 8 students received support, including 2 fellowships with full tuition reimbursements available (averaging $22,815 per year), 3 research assistantships with full tuition reimbursements available (averaging $23,815 per year), 3 teaching assistantships with full tuition reimbursements available (averaging $18,315 per year); health care benefits also available. Financial award application deadline: 12/15; financial award applicants required to submit FAFSA. *Faculty research:* Learning disabilities, phonological processing, psychology of reading, emergent literacy, aging. *Total annual research expenditures:* $2.7 million. *Unit head:* Dr. Sara Hart, Director, 850-645-9693,

Fax: 850-644-7739, E-mail: shart@fcrr.org. *Application contact:* Lynda L. Gibson, Graduate Program Associate, 850-644-2499, Fax: 850-644-7739, E-mail: grad-info@psy.fsu.edu. Website: http://www.psy.fsu.edu

**Fordham University,** Graduate School of Arts and Sciences, Department of Psychology, Program in Applied Developmental Psychology, New York, NY 10458. Offers PhD. *Accreditation:* APA. *Students:* 17 full-time (15 women), 5 part-time (4 women); includes 3 minority (1 Black or African American, non-Hispanic/Latino; 2 Asian, non-Hispanic/Latino), 7 international. Average age 31. 65 applicants, 15% accepted, 2 enrolled. In 2016, 5 doctorates awarded. *Degree requirements:* For doctorate, comprehensive exam, thesis/dissertation. *Entrance requirements:* For doctorate, GRE General Test, GRE Subject Test. Additional exam requirements/recommendations for international students: Required—TOEFL (minimum score 600 paper-based). *Application deadline:* For fall admission, 12/14 for domestic students. Application fee: $70. Electronic applications accepted. *Financial support:* In 2016–17, 15 students received support, including 4 fellowships with tuition reimbursements available (averaging $26,065 per year), 2 research assistantships with tuition reimbursements available (averaging $17,529 per year), 2 teaching assistantships with tuition reimbursements available (averaging $10,600 per year); career-related internships or fieldwork, institutionally sponsored loans, tuition waivers (full and partial), and unspecified assistantships also available. Financial award application deadline: 12/14. *Faculty research:* Development of citizenship, impact of participation in community service, impact of poverty on children, development of moral reasoning and behavior. *Unit head:* Dr. Tiffany Yip, Program Director, 718-817-3797, Fax: 718-817-3785, E-mail: tyip@fordham.edu. *Application contact:* Bernadette Valentino-Morrison, Director of Graduate Admissions, 718-817-4419, Fax: 718-817-3566, E-mail: valentinomor@fordham.edu.

**George Mason University,** College of Humanities and Social Sciences, Department of Psychology, Fairfax, VA 22030. Offers applied developmental psychology (Certificate); cognitive and behavioral neuroscience (MA); industrial/organizational psychology (PhD). *Accreditation:* APA. *Faculty:* 42 full-time (20 women), 13 part-time/adjunct (11 women). *Students:* 160 full-time (105 women), 57 part-time (30 women); includes 36 minority (9 Black or African American, non-Hispanic/Latino; 8 Asian, non-Hispanic/Latino; 12 Hispanic/Latino; 1 Native Hawaiian or other Pacific Islander, non-Hispanic/Latino; 6 Two or more races, non-Hispanic/Latino), 14 international. Average age 26. 742 applicants, 15% accepted, 57 enrolled. In 2016, 59 master's, 21 doctorates, 7 other advanced degrees awarded. *Degree requirements:* For master's, comprehensive exam, thesis (for biopsychology); for doctorate, comprehensive exam, thesis/dissertation, 2nd-year project. *Entrance requirements:* For master's, GRE, 2 official transcripts; goals statement; 15 undergraduate credits in concentration for which the applicant is applying; for doctorate, GRE, 3 letters of recommendation; resume; goals statement; minimum GPA of 3.0 overall for last 60 undergraduate credits, 3.25 in psychology courses; 15 undergraduate credits in concentration for which the applicant is applying; 2 official transcripts; for Certificate, GRE, 2 official transcripts; expanded goals statement; 3 letters of recommendation. Additional exam requirements/recommendations for international students: Required—TOEFL (minimum score 575 paper-based; 88 iBT), IELTS (minimum score 6.5), PTE (minimum score 59). Application fee: $75 ($80 for international students). Electronic applications accepted. *Expenses:* Tuition, state resident: full-time $10,628; part-time $443 per credit. Tuition, nonresident: full-time $29,306; part-time $1221 per credit. *Required fees:* $3096; $129 per credit. Tuition and fees vary according to program. *Financial support:* In 2016–17, 116 students received support, including 7 fellowships (averaging $11,348 per year), 42 research assistantships with tuition reimbursements available (averaging $14,292 per year), 88 teaching assistantships with tuition reimbursements available (averaging $13,815 per year); career-related internships or fieldwork, Federal Work-Study, scholarships/grants, tuition waivers (partial), unspecified assistantships, and health care benefits (for full-time research or teaching assistantship recipients) also available. Support available to part-time students. Financial award application deadline: 3/1; financial award applicants required to submit FAFSA. *Faculty research:* Applied developmental psychology, biopsychology, clinical psychology, human factors/applied cognition psychology, industrial/organizational psychology, school psychology. *Total annual research expenditures:* $5.6 million. *Unit head:* Reeshad Dalal, Department Chair, 703-993-9487, Fax: 703-993-1359, E-mail: rdalal@gmu.edu. *Application contact:* Michael Hock, Graduate Program Coordinator, 703-993-1548, Fax: 703-993-1359, E-mail: mhock2@gmu.edu. Website: http://psychology.gmu.edu

**Georgia State University,** College of Arts and Sciences, Department of Psychology, Atlanta, GA 30302-3083. Offers clinical (PhD); cognitive sciences (PhD); community (PhD); developmental (PhD); neuropsychology and behavioral neuroscience (PhD). *Accreditation:* APA. *Faculty:* 40 full-time (26 women). *Students:* 101 full-time (80 women), 2 part-time (both women); includes 25 minority (8 Black or African American, non-Hispanic/Latino; 9 Asian, non-Hispanic/Latino; 3 Hispanic/Latino; 5 Two or more races, non-Hispanic/Latino), 7 international. Average age 28. 517 applicants, 6% accepted, 17 enrolled. In 2016, 19 doctorates awarded. *Degree requirements:* For doctorate, comprehensive exam, thesis/dissertation, residency year (for clinical only). *Entrance requirements:* For doctorate, GRE. Additional exam requirements/recommendations for international students: Required—TOEFL (minimum score 550 paper-based; 80 iBT). *Application deadline:* For fall admission, 12/1 for domestic and international students. Application fee: $50. Electronic applications accepted. *Expenses:* Tuition, state resident: full-time $6876; part-time $382 per credit hour. Tuition, nonresident: full-time $22,374; part-time $1243 per credit hour. *Required fees:* $2128; $1064 per term. Part-time tuition and fees vary according to course load and program. *Financial support:* In 2016–17, fellowships with full tuition reimbursements (averaging $19,282 per year), research assistantships with full tuition reimbursements (averaging $5,173 per year), teaching assistantships with full tuition reimbursements (averaging $6,389 per year) were awarded; scholarships/grants, traineeships, health care benefits, and unspecified assistantships also available. Financial award applicants required to submit FAFSA. *Faculty research:* Clinical psychology, developmental psychology, community psychology, neuropsychology and behavioral neuroscience, cognitive sciences. *Unit head:* Dr. Lisa Armistead, Chair, 404-413-6205, Fax: 404-413-6207, E-mail: lparmistead@gsu.edu. *Application contact:* Dr. Lindsey Cohen, Director of Graduate Studies, 404-413-6263, Fax: 404-413-6207, E-mail: llcohen@gsu.edu.

**The Graduate Center, City University of New York,** Graduate Studies, Program in Psychology, New York, NY 10016-4039. Offers basic applied neurocognition (PhD); biopsychology (PhD); clinical psychology (PhD); developmental psychology (PhD); environmental psychology (PhD); experimental psychology (PhD); industrial psychology (PhD); learning processes (PhD); neuropsychology (PhD); psychology (PhD); social personality (PhD). *Degree requirements:* For doctorate, one foreign language, thesis/dissertation. *Entrance requirements:* For doctorate, GRE General Test. Additional exam requirements/recommendations for international students: Required—TOEFL. Electronic applications accepted.

**Harvard University,** Graduate School of Arts and Sciences, Department of Psychology, Cambridge, MA 02138. Offers psychology (PhD), including behavior and decision analysis, cognition, developmental psychology, experimental psychology, personality,

## Developmental Psychology

psychobiology, psychopathology; social psychology (PhD). *Accreditation:* APA. *Degree requirements:* For doctorate, thesis/dissertation, general exams. *Entrance requirements:* For doctorate, GRE General Test. Additional exam requirements/recommendations for international students: Required—TOEFL.

**Howard University,** Graduate School, Department of Psychology, Washington, DC 20059-0002. Offers clinical psychology (PhD); developmental psychology (PhD); experimental psychology (PhD); neuropsychology (PhD); personality psychology (PhD); psychology (MS); social psychology (PhD). *Accreditation:* APA (one or more programs are accredited). *Program availability:* Part-time. *Degree requirements:* For master's, thesis; for doctorate, comprehensive exam, thesis/dissertation, qualifying exam. *Entrance requirements:* For master's, GRE General Test, minimum GPA of 2.5, bachelor's degree in psychology or related field; for doctorate, GRE General Test, minimum GPA of 3.0. *Faculty research:* Personality and psychophysiology, educational and social development of African-American children, child and adult psychopathology.

**Humboldt State University,** Academic Programs, College of Professional Studies, Department of Psychology, Arcata, CA 95521-8299. Offers psychology (MA), including biological psychology, counseling, developmental psychopathology, school psychology, social and environmental psychology. *Degree requirements:* For master's, thesis. *Entrance requirements:* For master's, appropriate bachelor's degree, minimum GPA of 2.5. Additional exam requirements/recommendations for international students: Required—TOEFL (minimum score 500 paper-based). *Expenses:* Tuition, state resident: full-time $6738; part-time $1953 per semester. Tuition, nonresident: full-time $13,434; part-time $3813 per semester. *Required fees:* $1738; $653 per semester. Tuition and fees vary according to program. *Faculty research:* School psychology, counseling, eating disorders, mood induction, depression.

**Illinois State University,** Graduate School, College of Arts and Sciences, Department of Psychology, Normal, IL 61790-2200. Offers psychology (MA, MS), including clinical-counseling psychology, cognitive and behavioral sciences, developmental psychology, industrial/organizational-social psychology; school psychology (PhD, SSP). *Accreditation:* APA. *Degree requirements:* For master's, thesis or alternative; for doctorate, variable foreign language requirement, thesis/dissertation, 2 terms of residency, internship, practicum. *Entrance requirements:* For master's, GRE General Test, GRE Subject Test, minimum GPA of 3.0 in last 60 hours of course work; for doctorate, GRE General Test. *Faculty research:* Comprehensive evaluation system for the central region professional development grant, Illinois school psychology internship consortium, for children's sake.

**Indiana University Bloomington,** University Graduate School, College of Arts and Sciences, Department of Psychological and Brain Sciences, Bloomington, IN 47405. Offers clinical science (PhD); cognitive neuroscience (PhD); cognitive psychology (PhD); developmental psychology (PhD); methods of behavior (PhD); molecular systems neuroscience (PhD); social psychology (PhD). *Accreditation:* APA. *Degree requirements:* For doctorate, comprehensive exam, 90 credit hours, 2 advanced statistics/methods courses, 2 written research projects, the teaching of psychology course, teaching 1 semester of undergraduate methods course, qualifying examination, minor or a second major, first-year research seminar course, dissertation defense, written dissertation. *Entrance requirements:* For doctorate, GRE. Additional exam requirements/recommendations for international students: Required—TOEFL (minimum score 550 paper-based; 79 iBT). Electronic applications accepted. *Faculty research:* Clinical science, cognitive neuroscience, cognitive psychology, developmental psychology, mechanisms of behavior, molecular and systems neuroscience, social psychology.

**La Salle University,** School of Arts and Sciences, Program in Clinical Psychology, Philadelphia, PA 19141-1199. Offers child clinical psychology (Psy D); clinical health psychology (Psy D); clinical psychology (MA); general practice psychology (Psy D). *Accreditation:* AAMFT/COAMFTE. *Program availability:* Part-time, evening/weekend. *Faculty:* 9 full-time (7 women), 6 part-time/adjunct (3 women). *Students:* 77 full-time (62 women), 37 part-time (28 women); includes 15 minority (2 Black or African American, non-Hispanic/Latino; 6 Asian, non-Hispanic/Latino; 4 Hispanic/Latino; 3 Two or more races, non-Hispanic/Latino), 4 international. Average age 27. 301 applicants, 22% accepted, 17 enrolled. In 2016, 20 master's, 17 doctorates awarded. Terminal master's awarded for partial completion of doctoral program. *Degree requirements:* For doctorate, comprehensive exam, thesis/dissertation. *Entrance requirements:* For doctorate, GRE (minimum scores of 148 on both the Verbal Reasoning and Quantitative Reasoning sections strongly recommended); GRE Subject Test in psychology (for those entering with bachelor's degree), baccalaureate degree from accredited institution with major in psychology or related discipline; minimum undergraduate GPA of 3.0, 3.2 graduate; three letters of recommendation; statement of interest and intent; curriculum vitae or resume; personal interview. Additional exam requirements/recommendations for international students: Required—TOEFL. *Application deadline:* For fall admission, 1/15 for domestic students, 1/1 for international students. Application fee: $35. Electronic applications accepted. Application fee is waived when completed online. *Expenses:* Contact institution. *Financial support:* In 2016–17, 26 students received support. Scholarships/grants and unspecified assistantships available. Financial award application deadline: 8/31; financial award applicants required to submit FAFSA. *Unit head:* Dr. Randy Fingerhut, Director, 215-951-1284, Fax: 215-951-5140, E-mail: psyd@lasalle.edu. *Application contact:* Elizabeth Heenan, Director, Graduate and Adult Enrollment, 215-951-1100, Fax: 215-951-1462, E-mail: heenan@lasalle.edu. Website: http://www.lasalle.edu/doctor-of-psychology/

**Louisiana State University and Agricultural & Mechanical College,** Graduate School, College of Humanities and Social Sciences, Department of Psychology, Baton Rouge, LA 70803. Offers biological psychology (MA, PhD); clinical psychology (MA, PhD); cognitive psychology (MA, PhD); developmental psychology (MA, PhD); school psychology (MA, PhD). *Accreditation:* APA (one or more programs are accredited).

**Loyola University Chicago,** Graduate School, Programs in Non-Clinical Psychology, Chicago, IL 60660. Offers developmental psychology (PhD). *Faculty:* 7 full-time (2 women), 1 (woman) part-time/adjunct. *Students:* 40 full-time (31 women), 5 part-time (all women); includes 14 minority (6 Black or African American, non-Hispanic/Latino; 4 Hispanic/Latino; 4 Two or more races, non-Hispanic/Latino), 2 international. Average age 29. 92 applicants, 17% accepted, 14 enrolled. In 2016, 9 master's, 9 doctorates awarded. Terminal master's awarded for partial completion of doctoral program. *Degree requirements:* For master's, thesis; for doctorate, comprehensive exam, thesis/dissertation, internship. *Entrance requirements:* For master's and doctorate, GRE General Test, sample of written work. Additional exam requirements/recommendations for international students: Required—TOEFL. *Application deadline:* For fall admission, 1/15 for domestic and international students. Application fee: $50. Electronic applications accepted. Application fee is waived when completed online. *Expenses: Tuition:* Full-time $18,594. *Required fees:* $848. Part-time tuition and fees vary according to course load, degree level and program. *Financial support:* In 2016–17, 1 fellowship with tuition reimbursement (averaging $16,000 per year), 5 research assistantships with tuition reimbursements (averaging $16,000 per year), 1 teaching assistantship with tuition reimbursement (averaging $16,000 per year) were awarded; career-related internships or fieldwork, Federal Work-Study, and scholarships/grants also available. Financial award application deadline: 12/15; financial award applicants required to submit FAFSA.

*Faculty research:* Program evaluation, attitudes and prejudice, psychological well-being, self esteem and relationships, groups and organizations. *Total annual research expenditures:* $150,000. *Unit head:* Dr. Christine Li-Grine, Graduate Department Head, 773-508-8225, Fax: 773-508-8713, E-mail: cligrining@luc.edu. *Application contact:* Ron Martin, Assistant Director of Enrollment Management, 312-915-8950, Fax: 312-915-8905, E-mail: gradapp@luc.edu.

**McGill University,** Faculty of Graduate and Postdoctoral Studies, Faculty of Education, Department of Educational and Counseling Psychology, Montréal, QC H3A 2T5, Canada. Offers counseling psychology (MA, PhD); educational psychology (M Ed, MA, PhD); school/applied child psychology and applied developmental psychology (M Ed, MA, PhD, Diploma), including school psychology. *Accreditation:* APA.

**New York University,** Steinhardt School of Culture, Education, and Human Development, Department of Applied Psychology, Programs in Educational and Developmental Psychology, New York, NY 10003. Offers developmental psychology (PhD); human development and social intervention (MA); psychology and social intervention (PhD). *Accreditation:* APA (one or more programs are accredited). *Program availability:* Part-time. *Degree requirements:* For master's, thesis (for some programs); for doctorate, thesis/dissertation. *Entrance requirements:* For doctorate, GRE General Test, interview. Additional exam requirements/recommendations for international students: Required—TOEFL. Electronic applications accepted. *Faculty research:* Schools and communities, self-regulation and academic achievement, intervention and social change, trauma and resilience, cognition.

**North Carolina State University,** Graduate School, College of Humanities and Social Sciences, Department of Psychology, Raleigh, NC 27695. Offers developmental psychology (PhD); ergonomics and experimental psychology (PhD); industrial/organizational psychology (PhD); psychology in the public interest (PhD); school psychology (PhD). *Accreditation:* APA. *Degree requirements:* For doctorate, comprehensive exam, thesis/dissertation. *Entrance requirements:* For doctorate, GRE General Test, GRE Subject Test (industrial/organizational psychology), MAT (recommended), minimum GPA of 3.0 in major. Electronic applications accepted. *Faculty research:* Cognitive and social development (human factors, families, the workplace, community issues and health, aging).

**North Dakota State University,** College of Graduate and Interdisciplinary Studies, College of Human Development and Education, Department of Human Development and Family Science, Program in Developmental Science, Fargo, ND 58102. Offers PhD. Electronic applications accepted.

**The Ohio State University,** Graduate School, College of Arts and Sciences, Division of Social and Behavioral Sciences, Department of Psychology, Columbus, OH 43210. Offers behavioral neuroscience (PhD); clinical psychology (PhD); cognitive psychology (PhD); developmental psychology (PhD); intellectual and developmental disabilities psychology (PhD); quantitative psychology (PhD); social psychology (PhD). *Accreditation:* APA. *Faculty:* 57. *Students:* 156 full-time (95 women); includes 23 minority (6 Black or African American, non-Hispanic/Latino; 9 Asian, non-Hispanic/Latino; 8 Hispanic/Latino), 26 international. Average age 26. In 2016, 26 doctorates awarded. *Degree requirements:* For doctorate, thesis/dissertation. *Entrance requirements:* For doctorate, GRE General Test. Additional exam requirements/recommendations for international students: Required—TOEFL (minimum score 600 paper-based; 100 iBT); Recommended—IELTS (minimum score 8). *Application deadline:* For fall admission, 12/1 for domestic and international students. Applications are processed on a rolling basis. Application fee: $60 ($70 for international students). Electronic applications accepted. *Financial support:* Fellowships with tuition reimbursements, research assistantships with tuition reimbursements, and teaching assistantships with tuition reimbursements available. *Unit head:* Dr. John Bruno, Chair, 614-292-3038, E-mail: bruno.1@osu.edu. *Application contact:* Graduate and Professional Admissions, 614-292-9444, Fax: 614-292-3895, E-mail: gpadmissions@osu.edu. Website: http://www.psy.ohio-state.edu/

**Pace University,** Dyson College of Arts and Sciences, Department of Psychology, Program in School-Clinical Child Psychology, New York, NY 10038. Offers school psychology (MS Ed); school-clinical child psychology (Psy D). *Accreditation:* APA (one or more programs are accredited). *Students:* 62 full-time (51 women), 28 part-time (22 women); includes 18 minority (2 Black or African American, non-Hispanic/Latino; 7 Asian, non-Hispanic/Latino; 5 Hispanic/Latino; 1 Native Hawaiian or other Pacific Islander, non-Hispanic/Latino; 3 Two or more races, non-Hispanic/Latino), 3 international. Average age 27. In 2016, 21 master's, 23 doctorates awarded. Terminal master's awarded for partial completion of doctoral program. *Degree requirements:* For master's, qualifying exams, internship; for doctorate, comprehensive exam, thesis/dissertation, qualifying exams, externship, internship. *Entrance requirements:* For master's, GRE General Test, GRE Subject Test in psychology (recommended), interview, 3 letters of recommendation, resume, personal statement; for doctorate, GRE General Test, GRE Subject Test in psychology (recommended), interview, transcripts, 3 letters of recommendation. Additional exam requirements/recommendations for international students: Required—TOEFL (minimum score 88 iBT), IELTS (minimum score 7) or PTE (minimum score 60). *Application deadline:* For fall admission, 1/15 priority date for domestic students. Application fee: $70. Electronic applications accepted. *Expenses: Tuition:* Part-time $1195 per credit. *Required fees:* $260 per semester. Tuition and fees vary according to degree level, campus/location and program. *Financial support:* Scholarships/grants and unspecified assistantships available. Financial award application deadline: 1/15; financial award applicants required to submit FAFSA. *Unit head:* Dr. Barbara Mowder, Director of Graduate Psychology Programs, 212-346-1556, E-mail: bmowder@pace.edu. *Application contact:* Susan Ford-Goldschein, Director of Graduate Admissions, 212-346-1531, Fax: 212-346-1585, E-mail: graduateadmission@pace.edu. Website: http://www.pace.edu/dyson/academic-departments-and-programs/psychology—-nyc/graduate-programs

**Pontificia Universidad Catolica Madre y Maestra,** Graduate School, Faculty of Social and Administrative Sciences, Santiago, Dominican Republic. Offers business administration (MBA), including business development, finance, international business, management skills (M Mgmt, MBA), marketing, operations, strategic cost management, strategy, tourist destination planning and management; law (LL M), including civil law, corporate business law, criminal law, international relations, real estate law; management (M Mgmt), including higher financial management, insurance program administration, management skills (M Mgmt, MBA); psychology (MA), including clinical child and adolescent psychology, forensic psychology; strategic human resources (EMBA).

**Queens College of the City University of New York,** Division of Education, Department of Elementary and Early Childhood Education, Queens, NY 11367-1597. Offers bilingual education (MS Ed); child development psychology (AC); childhood education (MAT, MS Ed); childhood education and special education (MAT); childhood education-bilingual education (MAT, MS Ed, AC); children's literacy (AC); early childhood education (MAT); early childhood education birth-2 (MS Ed, AC); elementary education (MS Ed); literacy birth-grade 6 (AC); literacy technology birth-grade 6

(MS Ed); social studies education grades 1-6 (AC). *Program availability:* Part-time, evening/weekend. *Faculty:* 25 full-time (19 women), 33 part-time/adjunct (28 women). *Students:* 134 full-time (119 women), 374 part-time (349 women); includes 251 minority (55 Black or African American, non-Hispanic/Latino; 1 American Indian or Alaska Native, non-Hispanic/Latino; 82 Asian, non-Hispanic/Latino; 103 Hispanic/Latino; 10 Two or more races, non-Hispanic/Latino), 12 international. Average age 29. 364 applicants, 72% accepted, 224 enrolled. In 2016, 184 master's, 62 other advanced degrees awarded. *Degree requirements:* For master's, research project. *Entrance requirements:* For master's, minimum GPA of 3.0. Additional exam requirements/recommendations for international students: Required—TOEFL, IELTS. *Application deadline:* For fall admission, 4/1 for domestic students. Applications are processed on a rolling basis. Application fee: $125. Electronic applications accepted. *Expenses:* Tuition, state resident: full-time $5065; part-time $425 per credit. Tuition, nonresident: part-time $780 per credit. *Required fees:* $522; $397 per credit. Part-time tuition and fees vary according to course load and program. *Financial support:* Career-related internships or fieldwork available. Financial award application deadline: 4/1; financial award applicants required to submit FAFSA. *Unit head:* Dr. Mary Bushnell Greiner, Chairperson, 718-997-5328, E-mail: mary.greiner@qc.cuny.edu.

**Queen's University at Kingston,** School of Graduate Studies, Faculty of Arts and Sciences, Department of Psychology, Kingston, ON K7L 3N6, Canada. Offers brain behavior and cognitive science (MA, PhD); clinical psychology (MA, PhD); developmental psychology (MA, PhD); social personality psychology (MA, PhD). *Degree requirements:* For master's, thesis; for doctorate, comprehensive exam, thesis/dissertation. *Entrance requirements:* For master's and doctorate, GRE General Test. Additional exam requirements/recommendations for international students: Required—TOEFL. *Faculty research:* Human development, social, personality, behavioral neuroscience, forensic.

**Regis University,** Rueckert-Hartman College for Health Professions, Denver, CO 80221-1099. Offers advanced practice nurse (DNP); counseling (MA); counseling children and adolescents (Post-Graduate Certificate); counseling military families (Post-Graduate Certificate); depth psychotherapy (Post-Graduate Certificate); fellowship in orthopedic manual physical therapy (Certificate); health care business management (Certificate); health care quality and patient safety (Certificate); health industry leadership (MBA); health services administration (MS); marriage and family therapy (MA, Post-Graduate Certificate); neonatal nurse practitioner (MSN); nursing education (MSN); nursing leadership (MSN); occupational therapy (OTD); pharmacy (Pharm D); physical therapy (DPT). *Program availability:* Part-time, evening/weekend, 100% online, blended/hybrid learning. *Faculty:* 66 full-time (44 women), 33 part-time/adjunct (25 women). *Students:* 1,088 full-time (788 women), 316 part-time (253 women); includes 403 minority (59 Black or African American, non-Hispanic/Latino; 5 American Indian or Alaska Native, non-Hispanic/Latino; 101 Asian, non-Hispanic/Latino; 187 Hispanic/Latino; 51 Two or more races, non-Hispanic/Latino), 11 international. Average age 33. 2,199 applicants, 25% accepted, 277 enrolled. In 2016, 428 master's, 160 doctorates awarded. *Degree requirements:* For master's, thesis (for some programs), internship. *Entrance requirements:* For master's, official transcript reflecting baccalaureate degree awarded from regionally-accredited college or university. Additional exam requirements/recommendations for international students: Required—TOEFL (minimum score 550 paper-based; 82 iBT). *Application deadline:* For fall admission, 8/15 priority date for domestic students; for spring admission, 1/10 priority date for domestic students; for summer admission, 5/1 priority date for domestic students. Applications are processed on a rolling basis. Application fee: $75. Electronic applications accepted. *Expenses:* Contact institution. *Financial support:* In 2016–17, 102 students received support. Federal Work-Study and scholarships/grants available. Financial award application deadline: 4/15; financial award applicants required to submit FAFSA. *Faculty research:* Normal and pathological balance and gait research, normal/pathological upper limb motor control/biomechanics, exercise energy/metabolism research, optical treatment protocols for therapeutic modalities. *Unit head:* Dr. Janet Houser, Academic Dean. *Application contact:* Cate Clark, Director of Admissions, 303-458-4900, Fax: 303-964-5534, E-mail: ruadmissions@regis.edu.
Website: http://www.regis.edu/RHCHP.aspx

**San Francisco State University,** Division of Graduate Studies, College of Science and Engineering, Department of Psychology, San Francisco, CA 94132-1722. Offers clinical psychology (MS); developmental psychology (MA); industrial/organizational psychology (MS); mind, brain, and behavior (MA); school psychology (MS, Credential); social psychology (MA). *Expenses:* Tuition, state resident: full-time $6738. Tuition, nonresident: full-time $15,666. *Required fees:* $1012. Tuition and fees vary according to degree level and program. *Financial support:* Teaching assistantships available. Financial award application deadline: 3/1. *Unit head:* Dr. Dawn Terrell, Chair, 415-338-7555, Fax: 415-338-2398, E-mail: schen9@sfsu.edu. *Application contact:* Dr. Diane Harris, Graduate Program Coordinator, 415-338-7064, Fax: 415-338-2398, E-mail: dharris@sfsu.edu.
Website: http://psychology.sfsu.edu/graduate/application.html

**Teachers College, Columbia University,** Department of Human Development, New York, NY 10027-6696. Offers applied statistics (MS); cognitive studies in education (MA, Ed D, PhD); developmental psychology (MA, Ed D, PhD); educational psychology-human cognition and learning (Ed M, MA, Ed D, PhD); learning analytics (MS); measurement and evaluation (ME, Ed D, PhD); measurement, evaluation, and statistics (MA, MS, Ed D, PhD). *Program availability:* Part-time. *Students:* 217 full-time (168 women), 131 part-time (93 women); includes 83 minority (30 Black or African American, non-Hispanic/Latino; 31 Asian, non-Hispanic/Latino; 18 Hispanic/Latino; 4 Two or more races, non-Hispanic/Latino), 182 international. 450 applicants, 69% accepted, 132 enrolled. *Expenses: Tuition:* Full-time $36,288; part-time $1512 per credit. *Required fees:* $438 per semester. One-time fee: $510 full-time. Full-time tuition and fees vary according to course load. *Unit head:* Prof. Matthew S. Johnson, Chair, 212-678-3882, Fax: 212-678-3837, E-mail: johnson@tc.columbia.edu. *Application contact:* David Estrella, Director of Admission, 212-678-3305, E-mail: estrella@tc.columbia.edu.
Website: http://www.tc.columbia.edu/human-development/

**Texas Christian University,** College of Science and Engineering, Department of Psychology, Fort Worth, TX 76129. Offers developmental trauma (MS); experimental psychology (PhD), including cognition/developmental, learning, neuroscience, social. *Faculty:* 12 full-time (5 women), 3 part-time/adjunct (2 women). *Students:* 33 full-time (19 women); includes 4 minority (1 Asian, non-Hispanic/Latino; 1 Hispanic/Latino; 2 Two or more races, non-Hispanic/Latino), 2 international. Average age 27. 38 applicants, 32% accepted, 12 enrolled. In 2016, 5 master's, 3 doctorates awarded. Terminal master's awarded for partial completion of doctoral program. *Degree requirements:* For master's, thesis; for doctorate, thesis/dissertation. *Entrance requirements:* For doctorate, GRE General Test. Additional exam requirements/recommendations for international students: Required—TOEFL. *Application deadline:* For fall admission, 2/1 for domestic and international students. Application fee: $60 ($0 for international students). Electronic applications accepted. *Expenses:* Contact institution. *Financial support:* In 2016–17, 23 students received support, including 23 teaching assistantships with full tuition reimbursements available (averaging $19,750 per year); scholarships/grants also available. Financial award application deadline: 2/1; financial award

applicants required to submit FAFSA. *Faculty research:* Neuroscience, human and animal learning, cognition, development, experimental social psychology. *Unit head:* Dr. Mauricio R. Papini, Chair, 817-257-7410, Fax: 817-257-7681, E-mail: m.papini@tcu.edu. *Application contact:* Cindy Hayes, Administrative Assistant, 817-257-7410, Fax: 817-257-7681, E-mail: c.hayes@tcu.edu.
Website: https://psychology.tcu.edu/current-graduate-students/

**Université de Montréal,** Faculty of Arts and Sciences, School of Psychoeducation, Montréal, QC H3C 3J7, Canada. Offers M Sc, PhD. *Program availability:* Part-time. *Degree requirements:* For master's, one foreign language, thesis. Electronic applications accepted. *Faculty research:* Child maladjustment, family, prevention, treatment, antisocial behavior.

**The University of Alabama at Birmingham,** College of Arts and Sciences, Program in Psychology, Birmingham, AL 35294. Offers behavioral neuroscience (PhD); lifespan developmental psychology (PhD); medical/clinical psychology (PhD); psychology (MA). *Accreditation:* APA (one or more programs are accredited). *Entrance requirements:* For master's and doctorate, GRE General Test, letters of recommendation. Electronic applications accepted. Full-time tuition and fees vary according to course load and program. *Faculty research:* Biological basis of behavior structure, function of the nervous system.

**The University of British Columbia,** Faculty of Arts and Faculty of Graduate Studies, Department of Psychology, Vancouver, BC V6T 1Z4, Canada. Offers behavioral neuroscience (MA, PhD); clinical psychology (MA, PhD); cognitive science (MA, PhD); developmental psychology (MA, PhD); health psychology (MA, PhD); quantitative methods (MA, PhD); social/personality psychology (MA, PhD). *Accreditation:* APA (one or more programs are accredited). Terminal master's awarded for partial completion of doctoral program. *Degree requirements:* For master's, thesis; for doctorate, comprehensive exam, thesis/dissertation. *Entrance requirements:* For master's and doctorate, GRE General Test. Additional exam requirements/recommendations for international students: Required—TOEFL. *Application deadline:* Applications are processed on a rolling basis. Application fee: $100 Canadian dollars ($162 Canadian dollars for international students). Electronic applications accepted. *Expenses:* $4,802 per year tuition and fees, $8,436 per year international. *Financial support:* Fellowships, research assistantships, teaching assistantships, career-related internships or fieldwork, Federal Work-Study, institutionally sponsored loans, scholarships/grants, health care benefits, tuition waivers (full and partial), and unspecified assistantships available. Financial award application deadline: 1/1. *Faculty research:* Clinical, developmental, social/personality, cognition, behavioral neuroscience. *Application contact:* Jaclyn Shaw, 604-822-5002, Fax: 604-822-6923, E-mail: gradsec@psych.ubc.ca.
Website: http://psych.ubc.ca/

**University of Connecticut,** Graduate School, College of Liberal Arts and Sciences, Department of Psychology, Storrs, CT 06269. Offers behavioral neuroscience (PhD); biopsychology (PhD); clinical psychology (MA, PhD); cognition and instruction (PhD); developmental psychology (MA, PhD); ecological psychology (PhD); experimental psychology (PhD); general psychology (MA, PhD); industrial/organizational psychology (PhD); language and cognition (PhD); neuroscience (PhD); social psychology (MA, PhD). *Accreditation:* APA. Terminal master's awarded for partial completion of doctoral program. *Degree requirements:* For master's, comprehensive exam; for doctorate, thesis/dissertation. *Entrance requirements:* For master's and doctorate, GRE General Test, GRE Subject Test. Additional exam requirements/recommendations for international students: Required—TOEFL (minimum score 550 paper-based). Electronic applications accepted.

**University of Denver,** Division of Arts, Humanities and Social Sciences, Department of Psychology, Denver, CO 80208. Offers affect/social psychology (PhD); clinical child psychology (PhD); cognitive psychology (PhD); developmental psychology (PhD). *Accreditation:* APA. *Faculty:* 26 full-time (13 women), 5 part-time/adjunct (3 women). *Students:* 22 full-time (16 women), 2 part-time (both women); includes 5 minority (1 Black or African American, non-Hispanic/Latino; 1 Asian, non-Hispanic/Latino; 3 Hispanic/Latino), 1 international. Average age 28. 294 applicants, 4% accepted, 8 enrolled. In 2016, 8 doctorates awarded. Terminal master's awarded for partial completion of doctoral program. *Degree requirements:* For doctorate, variable foreign language requirement, comprehensive exam (for some programs), thesis/dissertation. *Entrance requirements:* For doctorate, GRE General Test, master's degree, transcripts, biographical statement, three letters of recommendation. Additional exam requirements/recommendations for international students: Required—TOEFL (minimum score 550 paper-based; 80 iBT). *Application deadline:* For fall admission, 12/1 priority date for domestic and international students. Application fee: $65. Electronic applications accepted. *Expenses:* $29,022 per year full-time. *Financial support:* In 2016–17, 24 students received support, including 5 research assistantships with tuition reimbursements available (averaging $16,000 per year), 12 teaching assistantships with tuition reimbursements available (averaging $17,778 per year); Federal Work-Study, institutionally sponsored loans, scholarships/grants, and unspecified assistantships also available. Support available to part-time students. Financial award application deadline: 2/15; financial award applicants required to submit FAFSA. *Faculty research:* Stress and trauma, developmental, affect science, clinical science, child psychopathology. *Unit head:* Dr. Anne DePrince, Professor and Chair, 303-871-2939, Fax: 303-871-4747, E-mail: adeprinc@du.edu. *Application contact:* Paula Houghtaling, Graduate Program Administrator, 303-871-3803, Fax: 303-871-4747, E-mail: phoughta@du.edu.
Website: http://www.du.edu/ahss/psychology

**University of Houston,** College of Liberal Arts and Social Sciences, Department of Psychology, Houston, TX 77204. Offers clinical psychology (PhD); developmental psychology (PhD); industrial/organizational psychology (PhD); psychology (MA); social psychology (PhD). *Accreditation:* APA (one or more programs are accredited). *Degree requirements:* For master's, comprehensive exam, thesis; for doctorate, comprehensive exam, thesis/dissertation. *Entrance requirements:* For master's, GRE General Test, career statement, 3 letters of recommendation; for doctorate, GRE General Test, 3 letters of recommendation. Additional exam requirements/recommendations for international students: Required—TOEFL (minimum score 550 paper-based; 79 iBT). Electronic applications accepted. *Faculty research:* Health psychology, depression, child/family process, organizational effectiveness, close relationships.

**University of Illinois at Chicago,** College of Education, Department of Educational Psychology, Chicago, IL 60607-7128. Offers early childhood education (M Ed); educational psychology (PhD); measurement, evaluation, statistics, and assessment (M Ed); youth development (M Ed). *Program availability:* Part-time, online learning. *Faculty research:* Children's construction of morality, development of resilience in the face of enduring economical difficulties, cognition and cognitive development, test fairness.

**The University of Kansas,** Graduate Studies, College of Liberal Arts and Sciences, Department of Psychology, Lawrence, KS 66045. Offers clinical psychology (MA, PhD); cognitive and brain sciences (MA, PhD); developmental psychology (MA, PhD); quantitative psychology (PhD); social psychology (MA, PhD). *Accreditation:* APA (one or more programs are accredited). *Program availability:* Part-time. *Students:* 69 full-time (46 women), 1 (woman) part-time; includes 11 minority (5 Black or African American,

## Developmental Psychology

non-Hispanic/Latino; 3 Asian, non-Hispanic/Latino; 3 Two or more races, non-Hispanic/Latino), 9 international. Average age 29. 202 applicants, 10% accepted, 14 enrolled. In 2016, 12 master's, 11 doctorates awarded. Terminal master's awarded for partial completion of doctoral program. *Entrance requirements:* For doctorate, GRE General Test, three letters of recommendation, resume/curriculum vitae, statement of purpose/personal statement, writing sample. Additional exam requirements/recommendations for international students: Required—TOEFL. *Application deadline:* For fall admission, 12/1 for domestic and international students. Application fee: $65 ($85 for international students). Electronic applications accepted. *Financial support:* Fellowships, research assistantships, teaching assistantships, career-related internships or fieldwork, Federal Work-Study, scholarships/grants, health care benefits, and unspecified assistantships available. Financial award application deadline: 12/1; financial award applicants required to submit FAFSA. *Faculty research:* Origins, correlates and treatment of depression; health and emotion; concentration on topics related to prejudice, stereotyping, and intergroup relations; memory, cognitive development, language, perception, attention, aging; psychometric methods, item response theory, structural equation modeling. *Unit head:* Ruth Anne Atchley, Chair, 785-864-4131. *Application contact:* Graduate Officer, 785-864-4195, E-mail: psycgrad@ku.edu.
Website: http://www.psych.ku.edu/

**The University of Kansas,** Graduate Studies, College of Liberal Arts and Sciences, Program in Child Language, Lawrence, KS 66045. Offers MA, PhD. *Students:* 5 full-time (all women); includes 1 minority (Asian, non-Hispanic/Latino). Average age 28. 4 applicants, 50% accepted, 1 enrolled. *Entrance requirements:* For master's and doctorate, GRE, official transcripts, three letters of recommendation, personal statement, curriculum vitae. Additional exam requirements/recommendations for international students: Required—TOEFL. *Application deadline:* For fall admission, 1/15 for domestic and international students. Application fee: $65 ($85 for international students). Electronic applications accepted. *Financial support:* Fellowships, research assistantships, teaching assistantships, career-related internships or fieldwork, traineeships, and unspecified assistantships available. Financial award application deadline: 1/15. *Faculty research:* Language impairments in children, specific language impairment, genetics of language acquisition, brain processing of language, language of aging. *Unit head:* Mabel L. Rice, Director, 785-864-4570, E-mail: mabel@ku.edu. *Application contact:* Linda Mann, Graduate Admissions Contact, 785-864-4804, E-mail: childlang@ku.edu.
Website: http://cldp.ku.edu/

**University of Louisville,** Graduate School, College of Arts and Sciences, Department of Psychological and Brain Sciences, Louisville, KY 40292-0001. Offers clinical psychology (PhD); experimental psychology (PhD), including cognition and development, vision and hearing. *Accreditation:* APA. *Students:* 54 full-time (42 women), 2 part-time (both women); includes 10 minority (3 Black or African American, non-Hispanic/Latino; 2 Asian, non-Hispanic/Latino; 3 Hispanic/Latino; 2 Two or more races, non-Hispanic/Latino), 1 international. Average age 28. 21 applicants, 5% accepted, 2 enrolled. In 2016, 1 doctorate awarded. *Degree requirements:* For doctorate, comprehensive exam, thesis/dissertation, internship (for clinical psychology). *Entrance requirements:* For doctorate, GRE General Test, GRE Subject Test. Additional exam requirements/recommendations for international students: Required—TOEFL. *Application deadline:* For fall and winter admission, 12/1 for domestic and international students. Application fee: $60. *Expenses:* Tuition, state resident: full-time $12,246; part-time $681 per credit hour. Tuition, nonresident: full-time $25,486; part-time $1417 per credit hour. *Required fees:* $196. Tuition and fees vary according to program and reciprocity agreements. *Financial support:* In 2016–17, 6 fellowships with full tuition reimbursements (averaging $22,000 per year), 1 research assistantship with full tuition reimbursement (averaging $22,000 per year), 1 teaching assistantship with full tuition reimbursement (averaging $22,000 per year) were awarded; health care benefits and unspecified assistantships also available. Financial award application deadline: 12/1. *Faculty research:* Cognitive development, hearing/visual science, cognitive neuroscience/imaging, health psychology/mindfulness/stress and trauma, child/adult psychopathology, geropsychology. *Total annual research expenditures:* $1.8 million. *Unit head:* Dr. Suzanne Meeks, Chair, 502-852-6068, Fax: 502-852-8904, E-mail: smeeks@louisville.edu. *Application contact:* Libby Leggett, Director, Graduate Admissions, 502-852-3101, Fax: 502-852-6536, E-mail: gradadm@louisville.edu.
Website: http://louisville.edu/psychology

**The University of Manchester,** School of Education, Manchester, United Kingdom. Offers counseling (D Couns); counseling psychology (D Couns); education (M Phil, Ed D, PhD); educational and child psychology (Ed D); educational psychology (Ed D).

**University of Maryland, Baltimore County,** The Graduate School, College of Arts, Humanities and Social Sciences, Department of Psychology, Program in Applied Developmental Psychology, Baltimore, MD 21250. Offers PhD. *Faculty:* 8 full-time (6 women), 11 part-time/adjunct (4 women). *Students:* 22 full-time (21 women); includes 6 minority (1 Black or African American, non-Hispanic/Latino; 3 Asian, non-Hispanic/Latino; 2 Hispanic/Latino), 2 international. Average age 25. 24 applicants, 8% accepted, 1 enrolled. In 2016, 3 doctorates awarded. *Degree requirements:* For doctorate, comprehensive exam, thesis/dissertation. *Entrance requirements:* For doctorate, GRE General Test, minimum GPA of 3.0. Additional exam requirements/recommendations for international students: Required—TOEFL. *Application deadline:* For fall admission, 1/9 for domestic and international students. Application fee: $50. Electronic applications accepted. *Expenses:* Tuition, state resident: full-time $13,294. Tuition, nonresident: full-time $20,286. *Financial support:* In 2016–17, 16 students received support, including 1 fellowship with partial tuition reimbursement available (averaging $17,250 per year), 3 research assistantships with full tuition reimbursements available (averaging $20,400 per year), 12 teaching assistantships with full tuition reimbursements available (averaging $17,250 per year); career-related internships or fieldwork, Federal Work-Study, health care benefits, and unspecified assistantships also available. Financial award application deadline: 3/1; financial award applicants required to submit FAFSA. *Faculty research:* Early intervention and development, schooling and development, cultural aspects of development, development in high risk children, social-emotional development. *Unit head:* Dr. Susan Sonnenschein, Director, 410-455-2361, Fax: 410-455-1055, E-mail: sonnenschein@umbc.edu. *Application contact:* Nicole Mooney, Program Management Specialist, 410-455-2567, Fax: 410-455-1055, E-mail: psycdept@umbc.edu.
Website: http://psychology.umbc.edu/

**University of Maryland, College Park,** Academic Affairs, College of Behavioral and Social Sciences, Department of Psychology, College Park, MD 20742. Offers clinical psychology (PhD); developmental psychology (PhD); experimental psychology (PhD); industrial psychology (MA, MS, PhD); social psychology (PhD). *Accreditation:* APA (one or more programs are accredited). *Degree requirements:* For master's, thesis; for doctorate, variable foreign language requirement, comprehensive exam, thesis/dissertation. *Entrance requirements:* For master's and doctorate, GRE General Test, GRE Subject Test, minimum GPA of 3.5, research and/or work experience, 3 letters of recommendation. Electronic applications accepted. *Faculty research:* Social stereotyping and prejudice, anxiety disorders, auditory neuroethology, counseling and social psychology.

**University of Massachusetts Amherst,** Graduate School, College of Natural Sciences, Department of Psychological and Brain Sciences, Amherst, MA 01003. Offers clinical psychology (MS, PhD); cognitive psychology (MS, PhD); developmental science (MS, PhD); psychology of peace and violence (MS, PhD); social psychology (MS, PhD). *Accreditation:* APA (one or more programs are accredited). Terminal master's awarded for partial completion of doctoral program. *Degree requirements:* For master's, thesis; for doctorate, comprehensive exam, thesis/dissertation. *Entrance requirements:* For master's and doctorate, GRE General Test, 3 letters of recommendation. Additional exam requirements/recommendations for international students: Required—TOEFL (minimum score 550 paper-based; 80 iBT), IELTS (minimum score 6.5). Electronic applications accepted.

**University of Miami,** Graduate School, College of Arts and Sciences, Department of Psychology, Coral Gables, FL 33124. Offers adult clinical (PhD); behavioral neuroscience (PhD); child clinical (PhD); developmental psychology (PhD); health clinical (PhD); psychology (MS). *Accreditation:* APA (one or more programs are accredited). *Degree requirements:* For doctorate, comprehensive exam, thesis/dissertation. *Entrance requirements:* For doctorate, GRE General Test, minimum GPA of 3.5. Additional exam requirements/recommendations for international students: Required—TOEFL. Electronic applications accepted. *Faculty research:* Behavioral factors in cardiovascular disease and cancer adult psychopathology, developmental disabilities, social and emotional development, mechanisms of coping.

**University of Michigan,** Rackham Graduate School, College of Literature, Science, and the Arts, Department of Psychology, Ann Arbor, MI 48109. Offers biopsychology (PhD); clinical science (PhD); cognition and cognitive neuroscience (PhD); developmental psychology (PhD); personality and social contexts (PhD); social psychology (PhD). *Accreditation:* APA. *Faculty:* 60 full-time (28 women), 30 part-time/adjunct (18 women). *Students:* 147 full-time (111 women); includes 64 minority (15 Black or African American, non-Hispanic/Latino; 1 American Indian or Alaska Native, non-Hispanic/Latino; 14 Asian, non-Hispanic/Latino; 27 Hispanic/Latino; 7 Two or more races, non-Hispanic/Latino), 19 international. Average age 27. 727 applicants, 8% accepted, 34 enrolled. In 2016, 28 doctorates awarded. *Degree requirements:* For doctorate, comprehensive exam, thesis/dissertation, oral defense of dissertation, preliminary exam. *Entrance requirements:* For doctorate, GRE General Test. Additional exam requirements/recommendations for international students: Required—TOEFL. *Application deadline:* For fall admission, 12/1 for domestic and international students. Application fee: $75 ($90 for international students). Electronic applications accepted. *Expenses:* Tuition, state resident: full-time $21,466; part-time $1152 per credit hour. Tuition, nonresident: full-time $43,346; part-time $2367 per credit hour. Part-time tuition and fees vary according to course load, degree level and program. *Financial support:* In 2016–17, 104 students received support, including 64 fellowships with full tuition reimbursements available (averaging $19,800 per year), 6 research assistantships with full tuition reimbursements available (averaging $24,243 per year), 71 teaching assistantships with full tuition reimbursements available (averaging $25,136 per year); career-related internships or fieldwork, traineeships, and health care benefits also available. Financial award application deadline: 4/15. *Unit head:* Prof. Patricia Reuter-Lorenz, Department Chair, 734-764-7429. *Application contact:* Sheri M. Circele, Psychology Student Academic Affairs, 734-764-2580, Fax: 734-764-3520, E-mail: psych.saa@umich.edu.
Website: http://www.lsa.umich.edu/psych/

**University of Montana,** Graduate School, College of Humanities and Sciences, Department of Psychology, Missoula, MT 59812-0002. Offers clinical psychology (PhD); experimental psychology (PhD), including animal behavior psychology, developmental psychology; school psychology (MA, PhD, Ed S). *Accreditation:* APA (one or more programs are accredited). Terminal master's awarded for partial completion of doctoral program. *Degree requirements:* For master's, thesis; for doctorate, thesis/dissertation. *Entrance requirements:* For master's, doctorate, and Ed S, GRE General Test. Additional exam requirements/recommendations for international students: Required—TOEFL.

**University of Nebraska–Lincoln,** Graduate College, College of Arts and Sciences, Department of Psychology, Lincoln, NE 68588. Offers biopsychology (PhD); clinical psychology (PhD); cognitive psychology (PhD); developmental psychology (PhD); psychology (MA); social/personality psychology (PhD); JD/MA; JD/PhD. *Accreditation:* APA (one or more programs are accredited). *Degree requirements:* For master's, thesis optional; for doctorate, comprehensive exam, thesis/dissertation. *Entrance requirements:* For master's and doctorate, GRE General Test. Additional exam requirements/recommendations for international students: Required—TOEFL (minimum score 550 paper-based). Electronic applications accepted. *Faculty research:* Law and psychology, rural mental health, chronic mental illness, neuropsychology, child clinical psychology.

**University of Nebraska–Lincoln,** Graduate College, College of Education and Human Sciences, Department of Educational Psychology, Lincoln, NE 68588. Offers cognition, learning and development (MA); counseling psychology (MA); educational psychology (MA, Ed S); psychological studies in education (PhD), including cognition, learning and development, counseling psychology, quantitative, qualitative, and psychometric methods, school psychology; quantitative, qualitative, and psychometric methods (MA); school psychology (MA, Ed S). *Accreditation:* APA (one or more programs are accredited); NCATE. *Degree requirements:* For master's, thesis optional. *Entrance requirements:* For master's, GRE General Test. Additional exam requirements/recommendations for international students: Required—TOEFL (minimum score 500 paper-based). Electronic applications accepted. *Faculty research:* Measurement and assessment, metacognition, academic skills, child development, multicultural education and counseling.

**University of New Mexico,** Graduate Studies, College of Arts and Sciences, Program in Psychology, Albuquerque, NM 87131-2039. Offers behavioral neuroscience (PhD); clinical psychology (PhD); cognitive neuroimaging (PhD); developmental psychology (PhD); evolution (PhD); health psychology (PhD); quantitative methodology (PhD). *Accreditation:* APA. *Faculty:* 23 full-time (8 women), 1 part-time/adjunct (0 women). *Students:* 60 full-time (36 women), 16 part-time (10 women); includes 22 minority (2 Black or African American, non-Hispanic/Latino; 2 American Indian or Alaska Native, non-Hispanic/Latino; 3 Asian, non-Hispanic/Latino; 12 Hispanic/Latino; 3 Two or more races, non-Hispanic/Latino), 2 international. Average age 30. 227 applicants, 11% accepted, 16 enrolled. In 2016, 10 doctorates awarded. *Degree requirements:* For doctorate, comprehensive exam, thesis/dissertation. *Entrance requirements:* For doctorate, GRE General Test, GRE Subject Test (psychology), minimum GPA of 3.0. Additional exam requirements/recommendations for international students: Required—TOEFL (minimum score 550 paper-based; 79 iBT), IELTS (minimum score 6.5). *Application deadline:* For fall admission, 12/15 priority date for domestic and international students. Applications are processed on a rolling basis. Application fee: $50. Electronic applications accepted. *Financial support:* Fellowships, research assistantships with tuition reimbursements, teaching assistantships with tuition reimbursements, career-related internships or fieldwork, Federal Work-Study, institutionally sponsored loans, scholarships/grants, health care benefits, tuition waivers (partial), and unspecified assistantships available. Financial award application deadline:

3/1; financial award applicants required to submit FAFSA. *Faculty research:* Addiction, cognition, brain and behavior, developmental, evolutionary, functioning neuroimaging, health psychology, learning and memory, neuroscience. *Total annual research expenditures:* $727,970. *Unit head:* Dr. Jane Ellen Smith, Department Chair, 505-277-4121, Fax: 505-277-1394. *Application contact:* Rikk Murphy, Graduate Program Coordinator, 505-277-5009, Fax: 505-277-1394, E-mail: advising@unm.edu. Website: http://psych.unm.edu

**The University of North Carolina at Chapel Hill,** Graduate School, College of Arts and Sciences, Department of Psychology, Chapel Hill, NC 27599-3270. Offers behavioral neuroscience psychology (PhD); clinical psychology (PhD); cognitive psychology (PhD); developmental psychology (PhD); quantitative psychology (PhD); social psychology (PhD). *Accreditation:* APA. *Degree requirements:* For doctorate, comprehensive exam, thesis/dissertation. *Entrance requirements:* For doctorate, GRE General Test, minimum GPA of 3.0. Additional exam requirements/recommendations for international students: Required—TOEFL (minimum score 550 paper-based; 79 iBT), IELTS (minimum score 7). Electronic applications accepted. *Faculty research:* Expressed emotion, cognitive development, social cognitive neuroscience, human memory personality.

**The University of North Carolina at Greensboro,** Graduate School, College of Arts and Sciences, Department of Psychology, Greensboro, NC 27412-5001. Offers clinical psychology (MA, PhD); cognitive psychology (MA, PhD); developmental psychology (MA, PhD); social psychology (MA, PhD). *Accreditation:* APA (one or more programs are accredited). Terminal master's awarded for partial completion of doctoral program. *Degree requirements:* For master's, comprehensive exam, thesis; for doctorate, one foreign language, thesis/dissertation, preliminary exam. *Entrance requirements:* For master's and doctorate, GRE General Test. Additional exam requirements/ recommendations for international students: Required—TOEFL. Electronic applications accepted. *Faculty research:* Sensory and perceptual determinants; evoked potential: disorders, deafness, and development.

**University of Notre Dame,** Graduate School, College of Arts and Letters, Division of Social Science, Department of Psychology, Notre Dame, IN 46556. Offers cognitive psychology (PhD); counseling psychology (PhD); developmental psychology (PhD); quantitative psychology (PhD). *Accreditation:* APA. *Degree requirements:* For doctorate, comprehensive exam, thesis/dissertation, candidacy exam. *Entrance requirements:* For doctorate, GRE General Test, GRE Subject Test (strongly recommended). Additional exam requirements/recommendations for international students: Required—TOEFL (minimum score 600 paper-based; 80 iBT). Electronic applications accepted. *Faculty research:* Cognitive and socio-emotional development, statistical methods and quantitative models applicable to psychology, interpersonal relations, life span development and developmental delay, childhood depression, structural equation and dynamical systems.

**University of Oregon,** Graduate School, College of Arts and Sciences, Department of Psychology, Eugene, OR 97403. Offers clinical psychology (PhD); cognitive psychology (MA, MS, PhD); developmental psychology (MA, MS, PhD); physiological psychology (MA, MS, PhD); psychology (MA, MS, PhD); social/personality psychology (MA, MS, PhD). *Accreditation:* APA (one or more programs are accredited). Terminal master's awarded for partial completion of doctoral program. *Degree requirements:* For doctorate, thesis/dissertation. *Entrance requirements:* For master's, GRE General Test, minimum GPA of 3.0; for doctorate, GRE General Test. Additional exam requirements/ recommendations for international students: Required—TOEFL.

**University of Pittsburgh,** School of Education, Department of Psychology in Education, Program in Applied Developmental Psychology, Pittsburgh, PA 15260. Offers M Ed, MS, PhD. *Program availability:* Part-time, evening/weekend. *Degree requirements:* For master's, thesis. *Entrance requirements:* For doctorate, GRE. Additional exam requirements/recommendations for international students: Required—TOEFL. Electronic applications accepted. Tuition and fees vary according to program.

**University of Rochester,** School of Arts and Sciences, Department of Clinical and Social Sciences in Psychology, Rochester, NY 14627. Offers clinical psychology (PhD); developmental psychology (PhD); social-personality psychology (PhD). *Accreditation:* APA. *Faculty:* 13 full-time (6 women). *Students:* 47 full-time (41 women); includes 10 minority (1 Black or African American, non-Hispanic/Latino; 3 Asian, non-Hispanic/Latino; 5 Hispanic/Latino; 1 Two or more races, non-Hispanic/Latino), 4 international. Average age 27. 257 applicants, 5% accepted, 7 enrolled. In 2016, 6 doctorates awarded. Terminal master's awarded for partial completion of doctoral program. *Degree requirements:* For doctorate, thesis/dissertation, qualifying exam. *Entrance requirements:* For doctorate, GRE General Test; GRE Subject Test (for clinical psychology, recommended for others). Additional exam requirements/recommendations for international students: Required—TOEFL. *Application deadline:* For fall admission, 4/15 for domestic and international students. Application fee: $60. Electronic applications accepted. *Expenses:* $1,538 per credit. *Financial support:* In 2016–17, 43 students received support, including 4 fellowships with full tuition reimbursements available (averaging $24,000 per year), 19 research assistantships with full tuition reimbursements available (averaging $21,000 per year), 20 teaching assistantships with full tuition reimbursements available (averaging $21,000 per year); career-related internships or fieldwork, scholarships/grants, traineeships, health care benefits, tuition waivers (full), and unspecified assistantships also available. Financial award application deadline: 2/1. *Faculty research:* Clinical psychology, social-personality psychology, developmental psychology, human motivation. *Unit head:* Loisa Bennetto, Chair, 585-275-8712, E-mail: loisa.bennetto@rochester.edu. *Application contact:* April Engram, Academic Coordinator/Analyst, 585-275-8704, E-mail: april.engram@rochester.edu. Website: http://www.psych.rochester.edu/csp/

**University of Southern California,** Graduate School, Dana and David Dornsife College of Letters, Arts and Sciences, Department of Psychology, Los Angeles, CA 90089. Offers brain and cognitive science (PhD); clinical science (PhD); developmental psychology (PhD); human behavior (MHB); quantitative methods (PhD); social psychology (PhD). *Accreditation:* APA. *Degree requirements:* For doctorate, comprehensive exam, thesis/dissertation, one-year internship (for clinical science students). *Entrance requirements:* For doctorate, GRE. Additional exam requirements/ recommendations for international students: Recommended—TOEFL (minimum score 600 paper-based; 100 iBT). Electronic applications accepted. *Faculty research:* Affective neuroscience; children and families; vision, culture and ethnicity; intergroup relations; aggression and violence; language and reading development; substance abuse.

**The University of Texas at Austin,** Graduate School, College of Liberal Arts, Department of Psychology, Austin, TX 78712-1111. Offers behavioral neuroscience (PhD); clinical psychology (PhD); cognitive systems (PhD); developmental psychology (PhD); individual differences and evolutionary psychology (PhD); perceptual systems (PhD); social psychology (PhD). *Accreditation:* APA. *Degree requirements:* For doctorate, thesis/dissertation. *Entrance requirements:* For doctorate, GRE General Test. Electronic applications accepted. *Faculty research:* Behavioral neuroscience, sensory neuroscience, evolutionary psychology, cognitive processes in psychopathology, cognitive processes and their development.

**University of Victoria,** Faculty of Graduate Studies, Faculty of Social Sciences, Department of Psychology, Victoria, BC V8W 2Y2, Canada. Offers clinical psychology (PhD); clinical psychology (neuropsychology) (M Sc); cognition and brain science (M Sc, PhD); experimental neuropsychology (M Sc, PhD); individualized study (M Sc, PhD); life span development psychology (PhD); life span developmental psychology (M Sc); social psychology (M Sc, PhD). *Degree requirements:* For master's, thesis; for doctorate, thesis/dissertation, candidacy exam. *Entrance requirements:* For master's and doctorate, GRE General Test. Additional exam requirements/recommendations for international students: Required—TOEFL (minimum score 600 paper-based). Electronic applications accepted. *Faculty research:* Life span development psychology and aging, behavioral neuroscience, cognitive psychology, behavioral psychology, environmental psychology.

**University of Washington,** Graduate School, College of Arts and Sciences, Department of Psychology, Seattle, WA 98195. Offers animal behavior (PhD); child psychology (PhD); clinical psychology (PhD); cognition and perception (PhD); developmental psychology (PhD); quantitative psychology (PhD); social psychology and personality (PhD). *Accreditation:* APA. *Degree requirements:* For doctorate, thesis/ dissertation. *Entrance requirements:* For doctorate, GRE General Test, minimum GPA of 3.0. Electronic applications accepted. *Faculty research:* Addictive behaviors, artificial intelligence, child psychopathology, mechanisms and development of vision, physiology of ingestive behaviors.

**University of Wisconsin–Madison,** Graduate School, College of Letters and Science, Department of Psychology, Program in Developmental Psychology, Madison, WI 53706-1380. Offers PhD. *Degree requirements:* For doctorate, comprehensive exam, thesis/ dissertation. *Entrance requirements:* For doctorate, GRE General Test, minimum undergraduate GPA of 3.0. Additional exam requirements/recommendations for international students: Required—TOEFL. Electronic applications accepted.

**University of Wisconsin–Milwaukee,** Graduate School, School of Education, Department of Educational Psychology, Milwaukee, WI 53201-0413. Offers children's mental health for school professionals (Graduate Certificate); community counseling (MS); counseling psychology (PhD); educational statistics and measurement (MS, PhD); learning and development (MS, PhD); multicultural knowledge of mental health practices (Graduate Certificate); school counseling (MS); school counseling (Graduate Certificate); school psychology (MS, PhD, Ed S). *Accreditation:* APA. *Program availability:* Part-time. *Students:* 161 full-time (121 women), 53 part-time (39 women); includes 47 minority (12 Black or African American, non-Hispanic/Latino; 1 American Indian or Alaska Native, non-Hispanic/Latino; 5 Asian, non-Hispanic/Latino; 8 Hispanic/ Latino; 1 Native Hawaiian or other Pacific Islander, non-Hispanic/Latino; 20 Two or more races, non-Hispanic/Latino), 6 international. Average age 30. 266 applicants, 45% accepted, 71 enrolled. In 2016, 73 master's, 9 doctorates, 18 other advanced degrees awarded. *Degree requirements:* For master's, comprehensive exam, thesis; for doctorate, thesis/dissertation. *Entrance requirements:* For master's, minimum GPA of 3.0; for doctorate, GRE General Test, minimum GPA of 3.0. Additional exam requirements/recommendations for international students: Required—TOEFL (minimum score 550 paper-based; 79 iBT), IELTS (minimum score 6.5). *Application deadline:* For fall admission, 1/1 priority date for domestic students; for spring admission, 9/1 for domestic students. Applications are processed on a rolling basis. Application fee: $56 ($96 for international students). Electronic applications accepted. *Financial support:* In 2016–17, 14 fellowships, 1 research assistantship, 8 teaching assistantships were awarded; career-related internships or fieldwork, health care benefits, unspecified assistantships, and project assistantships also available. Support available to part-time students. Financial award application deadline: 4/15; financial award applicants required to submit FAFSA. *Application contact:* General Information Contact, 414-229-4721, E-mail: soeinfo@uwm.edu.
Website: http://uwm.edu/education/academics/educational-psychology-department/

**Viterbo University,** Master of Science in Mental Health Counseling Program, La Crosse, WI 54601-4797. Offers addiction counseling (MS); child and adolescent counseling (MS); complementary health and wellness counseling (MS). *Accreditation:* ACA. *Program availability:* Part-time, evening/weekend. *Degree requirements:* For master's, comprehensive exam, thesis, 54 credits of core program courses; 6 elective credits; minimum GPA of 3.0; action research project; practicum/internship experience. *Entrance requirements:* For master's, MAT, BS in a human service or social science discipline; prerequisite coursework in general psychology, behavior disorders/abnormal psychology, and research methods/statistics; minimum undergraduate cumulative GPA of 3.0; background check; personal statement; undergraduate transcripts; interview. Additional exam requirements/recommendations for international students: Required—TOEFL (minimum score 525 paper-based). Electronic applications accepted. Application fee is waived when completed online. *Expenses:* Contact institution. *Faculty research:* Supervision, recovery substance abuse, culture, counseling theory, health and wellness.

**Washington University in St. Louis,** The Graduate School, Department of Psychological and Brain Sciences, St. Louis, MO 63130-4899. Offers aging and development (PhD). Terminal master's awarded for partial completion of doctoral program. *Degree requirements:* For doctorate, thesis/dissertation. *Entrance requirements:* For doctorate, GRE General Test. Additional exam requirements/ recommendations for international students: Required—TOEFL. Electronic applications accepted. *Faculty research:* Behavior/brain/cognition; clinical; aging/development; social/personality.

**Wayne State University,** College of Liberal Arts and Sciences, Department of Psychology, Detroit, MI 48202. Offers behavioral and cognitive neuroscience (PhD); clinical psychology (PhD); cognitive, developmental and social psychology (PhD); industrial/organizational psychology (MA, PhD). Doctoral program admits for fall only. *Accreditation:* APA (one or more programs are accredited). *Faculty:* 36. *Students:* 98 full-time (65 women), 31 part-time (16 women); includes 19 minority (4 Black or African American, non-Hispanic/Latino; 2 Asian, non-Hispanic/Latino; 8 Hispanic/Latino; 5 Two or more races, non-Hispanic/Latino), 14 international. Average age 28. 478 applicants, 13% accepted, 33 enrolled. In 2016, 16 master's, 13 doctorates awarded. Terminal master's awarded for partial completion of doctoral program. *Degree requirements:* For master's, thesis (for some programs); for doctorate, thesis/dissertation, training assignments. *Entrance requirements:* For master's, GRE General Test, minimum undergraduate upper-division cumulative GPA of 3.0, courses in introductory psychology and statistics, two letters of recommendation, professional statement; for doctorate, GRE General Test, bachelor's, master's, or other advanced degree; at least twelve credits in psychology with minimum GPA of 3.0; courses in laboratory psychology and statistical methods in psychology; at least three letters of recommendation; statement of purpose. Additional exam requirements/recommendations for international students: Required—TOEFL (minimum score 550 paper-based; 79 iBT), TWE (minimum score 5.5), Michigan English Language Assessment Battery (minimum score 85); Recommended—IELTS (minimum score 6.5). Application fee: $50. Electronic applications accepted. *Expenses:* $16,503 per year resident tuition and fees, $33,697 per year non-resident tuition and fees. *Financial support:* In 2016–17, 90 students received support, including 12 fellowships with tuition reimbursements available (averaging $15,719 per year), 6 research assistantships with tuition reimbursements available (averaging $19,341 per year), 50 teaching assistantships with tuition reimbursements available (averaging $17,994 per year); scholarships/grants, health

care benefits, and unspecified assistantships also available. Financial award applicants required to submit FAFSA. *Faculty research:* Behavioral neuroscience, cognitive/neuroscience of development and aging research, children, adolescents, and family research, cognition research, emotion research, health psychology research, homelessness and poverty research, memory research, neuropsychology research, personality/cognition, relationships research, substance use and abuse research, workplace adaptation, well-being and evaluation research. *Total annual research expenditures:* $1.4 million. *Unit head:* Boris Baltes, PhD, Chair/Professor, 313-577-2803, E-mail: b.baltes@wayne.edu. *Application contact:* Alia Allen, Academic Services Officer, 313-577-2823, E-mail: aallen@wayne.edu.
Website: http://clas.wayne.edu/psychology/

**West Virginia University,** Eberly College of Arts and Sciences, Department of Psychology, Morgantown, WV 26506. Offers behavior analysis (PhD); clinical psychology (MA, PhD); development psychology (PhD); psychology (MS). *Accreditation:* APA (one or more programs are accredited). *Program availability:* Part-time. Terminal master's awarded for partial completion of doctoral program. *Degree requirements:* For master's, thesis optional; for doctorate, comprehensive exam, thesis/dissertation. *Entrance requirements:* For master's and doctorate, GRE General Test, minimum GPA of 3.0. Additional exam requirements/recommendations for international students: Required—TOEFL. *Faculty research:* Adult and child clinical psychology, behavioral

assessment and therapy, child and adolescent behavior, life span development, experimental and applied behavior analysis.

**Wilfrid Laurier University,** Faculty of Graduate and Postdoctoral Studies, Faculty of Science, Department of Psychology, Waterloo, ON N2L 3C5, Canada. Offers behavioral neuroscience (M Sc, PhD); cognitive neuroscience (M Sc, PhD); community psychology (MA, PhD); social and developmental psychology (MA, PhD). *Program availability:* Part-time. *Degree requirements:* For master's, thesis; for doctorate, thesis/dissertation. *Entrance requirements:* For master's, GRE General Test, honors BA or the equivalent in psychology, minimum B average in undergraduate course work; for doctorate, GRE General Test, master's degree, minimum A- average. Additional exam requirements/recommendations for international students: Required—TOEFL (minimum score 89 iBT). Electronic applications accepted. *Faculty research:* Brain and cognition, community psychology, social and developmental psychology.

**Yale University,** Graduate School of Arts and Sciences, Department of Psychology, New Haven, CT 06520. Offers behavioral neuroscience (PhD); clinical psychology (PhD); cognitive psychology (PhD); developmental psychology (PhD); social/personality psychology (PhD). *Accreditation:* APA. *Degree requirements:* For doctorate, thesis/dissertation. *Entrance requirements:* For doctorate, GRE General Test.

# Experimental Psychology

**Bowling Green State University,** Graduate College, College of Arts and Sciences, Department of Psychology, Bowling Green, OH 43403. Offers clinical psychology (MA, PhD); developmental psychology (MA, PhD); experimental psychology (MA, PhD); industrial/organizational psychology (MA, PhD); quantitative psychology (MA, PhD). *Accreditation:* APA (one or more programs are accredited). *Degree requirements:* For doctorate, thesis/dissertation. *Entrance requirements:* For doctorate, GRE General Test, GRE Subject Test. Additional exam requirements/recommendations for international students: Required—TOEFL. *Application deadline:* For fall admission, 1/1 for domestic students. Application fee: $30. Electronic applications accepted. *Financial support:* Fellowships with full tuition reimbursements, research assistantships with full tuition reimbursements, teaching assistantships with full tuition reimbursements, career-related internships or fieldwork, Federal Work-Study, institutionally sponsored loans, tuition waivers (full), and unspecified assistantships available. Financial award applicants required to submit FAFSA. *Faculty research:* Personnel psychology, developmental-mathematical models, behavioral medication, brain process, child/adolescent social cognition. *Unit head:* Dr. Mike Zickar, Chair, 419-372-2301, E-mail: mzickar@bgsu.edu. *Application contact:* Dr. Terry L. Lawrence, Assistant Dean for Graduate Admissions and Studies, 419-372-7713, Fax: 419-372-8569, E-mail: tlawren@bgnet.bgsu.edu.

**Brooklyn College of the City University of New York,** School of Natural and Behavioral Sciences, Department of Psychology, Brooklyn, NY 11210-2889. Offers experimental psychology (MA); industrial and organizational psychology (MA), including human relations, organizational behavior; mental health counseling (MA); psychology (PhD). *Program availability:* Part-time. *Degree requirements:* For master's, comprehensive exam, thesis (for some programs). *Entrance requirements:* For master's, minimum GPA of 3.0, 2 letters of recommendation, essay; for doctorate, GRE. Additional exam requirements/recommendations for international students: Required—TOEFL (minimum score 520 paper-based; 69 iBT). Electronic applications accepted.

**California State University, Fresno,** Division of Research and Graduate Studies, College of Science and Mathematics, Department of Psychology, Fresno, CA 93740-8027. Offers applied behavior analysis (MA); general/experimental psychology (MA); school psychology (Ed S). *Degree requirements:* For master's, thesis. *Entrance requirements:* For master's, GRE General Test, GRE Subject Test, minimum GPA of 3.0. Additional exam requirements/recommendations for international students: Required—TOEFL. *Application deadline:* For fall admission, 5/1 for domestic and international students; for spring admission, 10/1 for domestic and international students. Applications are processed on a rolling basis. Application fee: $55. Electronic applications accepted. *Financial support:* Teaching assistantships, career-related internships or fieldwork, Federal Work-Study, scholarships/grants, and unspecified assistantships available. Support available to part-time students. Financial award application deadline: 3/1; financial award applicants required to submit FAFSA. *Faculty research:* Oncology prediction, parenting stress, wellness, aging and memory, retrieval inhibition, anger, minority mental health. *Unit head:* Dr. Constance Jones, Chair, 559-278-2691, Fax: 559-278-7910, E-mail: conniej@csufresno.edu. *Application contact:* Dr. Marilyn Wilson, Ed S Program Coordinator, 559-278-5129, Fax: 559-278-7910, E-mail: marilynw@csufresno.edu.
Website: http://www.fresnostate.edu/csm/psych/

**California State University, Northridge,** Graduate Studies, College of Social and Behavioral Sciences, Department of Psychology, Northridge, CA 91330. Offers clinical psychology (MA); general experimental psychology (MA). *Faculty:* 27 full-time (9 women), 32 part-time/adjunct (13 women). *Students:* 52 full-time (37 women), 6 part-time (4 women); includes 33 minority (2 Black or African American, non-Hispanic/Latino; 6 Asian, non-Hispanic/Latino; 24 Hispanic/Latino; 1 Two or more races, non-Hispanic/Latino), 2 international. Average age 25. 275 applicants, 23% accepted, 27 enrolled. *Degree requirements:* For master's, thesis. *Entrance requirements:* For master's, GRE General Test, GRE Subject Test, minimum GPA of 3.0, letters of recommendation. Additional exam requirements/recommendations for international students: Required—TOEFL. *Application deadline:* For fall admission, 11/30 for domestic students. Application fee: $55. *Expenses:* Tuition, state resident: full-time $4152. *Financial support:* Application deadline: 3/1. *Unit head:* Jill Razani, Chair, 818-677-3506.
Website: http://www.csun.edu/csbs/departments/psychology/index.html

**California State University, San Bernardino,** Graduate Studies, College of Social and Behavioral Sciences, Department of Psychology, San Bernardino, CA 92407. Offers child development (MA); clinical/counseling psychology (MS); general/experimental psychology (MA); industrial/organizational psychology (MS). *Faculty:* 21 full-time (11 women). *Students:* 59 full-time (43 women), 15 part-time (9 women); includes 47 minority (2 Black or African American, non-Hispanic/Latino; 3 Asian, non-Hispanic/Latino; 33 Hispanic/Latino; 9 Two or more races, non-Hispanic/Latino), 3 international. 217 applicants, 18% accepted, 32 enrolled. In 2016, 38 master's awarded. *Degree requirements:* For master's, comprehensive exam, thesis (for some programs). *Entrance requirements:* Additional exam requirements/recommendations for international students: Required—TOEFL. Application fee: $55. *Expenses:* Tuition, state resident: full-time $7843; part-time $5011.20 per year. Tuition and fees vary according to course load, degree level, program and reciprocity agreements. *Financial support:* Fellowships,

research assistantships, and teaching assistantships available. *Faculty research:* Perceptual development, human memory, psychopharmacology, psychology of women, language acquisition. *Unit head:* Dr. Robert Ricco, Chair, 909-537-5485, Fax: 909-537-7003, E-mail: rricco@csusb.edu. *Application contact:* Dr. Francisca Beer, Dean of Graduate Studies, 909-537-5058, E-mail: fbeer@csusb.edu.
Website: http://psychology.csusb.edu/

**Case Western Reserve University,** School of Graduate Studies, Psychological Sciences Department, Program in Experimental Psychology, Cleveland, OH 44106. Offers PhD. *Faculty:* 10 full-time (5 women). *Students:* 8 full-time (4 women); includes 1 minority (Asian, non-Hispanic/Latino). Average age 27. 165 applicants, 4% accepted, 3 enrolled. In 2016, 4 doctorates awarded. *Degree requirements:* For doctorate, thesis/dissertation, internship. *Entrance requirements:* For doctorate, GRE General Test, GRE Subject Test, personal statement, three letters of recommendation, curriculum vitae. Additional exam requirements/recommendations for international students: Required—TOEFL (minimum score 577 paper-based; 90 iBT); Recommended—IELTS (minimum score 7). *Application deadline:* For fall admission, 1/15 priority date for domestic students. Application fee: $50. Electronic applications accepted. *Expenses: Tuition:* Full-time $42,576; part-time $1774 per credit hour. *Required fees:* $34. Tuition and fees vary according to course load and program. *Financial support:* Research assistantships and teaching assistantships available. Financial award application deadline: 1/15; financial award applicants required to submit FAFSA. *Faculty research:* Development and evaluation of cognitive behavioral treatments for anxiety and mood disorders, evaluating treatments for post-traumatic stress disorder (PTSD), depression and bipolar disorder in youth, family relations and emotional expressions. *Unit head:* Dr. Lee Thompson, Professor and Chair, 216-368-6477, Fax: 216-368-4891, E-mail: cwrupsych@gmail.com. *Application contact:* Dr. Elizabeth J. Short, Director of Experimental Training, 216-368-2815, Fax: 216-368-4891, E-mail: cwrupsych@gmail.com.
Website: http://psychsciences.case.edu/graduate/

**The Catholic University of America,** School of Arts and Sciences, Department of Psychology, Washington, DC 20064. Offers applied experimental psychology (PhD); clinical psychology (PhD); general psychology (MA); human development psychology (PhD); human factors (MA); MA/JD. MA/JD offered jointly with Columbus School of Law. *Accreditation:* APA (one or more programs are accredited). *Program availability:* Part-time. *Faculty:* 11 full-time (6 women), 5 part-time/adjunct (2 women). *Students:* 40 full-time (26 women), 36 part-time (29 women); includes 19 minority (3 Black or African American, non-Hispanic/Latino; 5 Asian, non-Hispanic/Latino; 4 Hispanic/Latino; 7 Two or more races, non-Hispanic/Latino), 8 international. Average age 28. 230 applicants, 27% accepted, 23 enrolled. In 2016, 15 master's, 6 doctorates awarded. *Degree requirements:* For master's, comprehensive exam, thesis (for some programs); for doctorate, comprehensive exam, thesis/dissertation. *Entrance requirements:* For master's, GRE General Test, statement of purpose, official copies of academic transcripts, three letters of recommendation; for doctorate, GRE General Test, GRE Subject Test, statement of purpose, official copies of academic transcripts, three letters of recommendation. Additional exam requirements/recommendations for international students: Required—TOEFL (minimum score 550 paper-based; 80 iBT). *Application deadline:* For fall admission, 7/15 priority date for domestic students, 7/1 for international students; for spring admission, 11/15 priority date for domestic students, 11/1 for international students. Applications are processed on a rolling basis. Application fee: $55. Electronic applications accepted. *Expenses:* $42,850 per year; $1,170 per credit; $200 per semester part-time fees. *Financial support:* Fellowships, research assistantships, teaching assistantships, Federal Work-Study, scholarships/grants, tuition waivers (full and partial), and unspecified assistantships available. Financial award application deadline: 2/1; financial award applicants required to submit FAFSA. *Faculty research:* Clinical psychology, applied cognitive science, psychopathology, cognitive neuroscience, psychotherapy. *Total annual research expenditures:* $936,581. *Unit head:* Dr. Marc M. Sebrechts, Chair, 202-319-5750, Fax: 202-319-6263, E-mail: sebrechts@cua.edu. *Application contact:* Director of Graduate Admissions, 202-319-5057, Fax: 202-319-6533, E-mail: cua-admissions@cua.edu.
Website: http://psychology.cua.edu/

**Central Michigan University,** College of Graduate Studies, College of Humanities and Social and Behavioral Sciences, Department of Psychology, Program in Experimental Psychology, Mount Pleasant, MI 48859. Offers applied experimental psychology (PhD); experimental psychology (MS). *Program availability:* Part-time. *Degree requirements:* For master's, thesis or alternative; for doctorate, thesis/dissertation. Electronic applications accepted. *Faculty research:* Behavioral neuroscience, human development, perception and cognition, social/personal problem solving, psychophysiology.

**Central Washington University,** Graduate Studies and Research, College of the Sciences, Department of Psychology, Program in Experimental Psychology, Ellensburg, WA 98926. Offers MS. *Degree requirements:* For master's, thesis or alternative. *Entrance requirements:* For master's, GRE General Test, minimum GPA of 3.0. Additional exam requirements/recommendations for international students: Required—TOEFL (minimum score 550 paper-based; 79 iBT). Electronic applications accepted.

**Cornell University,** Graduate School, Graduate Fields of Arts and Sciences, Field of Psychology, Ithaca, NY 14853. Offers biopsychology (PhD); human experimental psychology (PhD); personality and social psychology (PhD). *Degree requirements:* For doctorate, comprehensive exam, thesis/dissertation, 2 semesters of teaching experience. *Entrance requirements:* For doctorate, GRE General Test, 3 letters of recommendation. Additional exam requirements/recommendations for international students: Required—TOEFL (minimum score 550 paper-based; 77 iBT). Electronic applications accepted. *Faculty research:* Sensory and perceptual systems, social cognition, cognitive development, quantitative and computational modeling, behavioral neuroscience.

**Duke University,** Graduate School, Department of Psychology and Neuroscience, Durham, NC 27708. Offers biological psychology (PhD); clinical psychology (PhD); cognitive psychology (PhD); developmental psychology (PhD); experimental psychology (PhD); health psychology (PhD); human social development (PhD); JD/MA. *Accreditation:* APA (one or more programs are accredited). *Degree requirements:* For doctorate, thesis/dissertation. *Entrance requirements:* For doctorate, GRE General Test. Additional exam requirements/recommendations for international students: Required—TOEFL (minimum score 577 paper-based; 90 iBT) or IELTS (minimum score 7). Electronic applications accepted.

**Eastern Washington University,** Graduate Studies, College of Social Sciences, Department of Psychology, Program in Experimental Psychology, Cheney, WA 99004-2431. Offers MS. *Students:* 5 full-time (3 women), 2 part-time (1 woman); includes 2 minority (1 Asian, non-Hispanic/Latino; 1 Hispanic/Latino). Average age 29. 15 applicants, 20% accepted, 3 enrolled. In 2016, 1 master's awarded. *Degree requirements:* For master's, comprehensive exam (for some programs), thesis or research report; practicum. *Entrance requirements:* For master's, GRE, minimum GPA of 3.0 in last 90 quarter or 60 semester graded credits; official transcripts; curriculum vitae; three letters of recommendation. Additional exam requirements/recommendations for international students: Required—TOEFL (minimum score 580 paper-based; 92 iBT), IELTS (minimum score 7), PTE (minimum score 63). *Application deadline:* For fall admission, 3/1 for domestic students. Application fee: $75. Electronic applications accepted. *Expenses:* Tuition, state resident: full-time $11,000; part-time $5500 per credit. Tuition, nonresident: full-time $24,000; part-time $12,000 per credit. *Required fees:* $1300. One-time fee: $50 full-time. Part-time tuition and fees vary according to course load, campus/location and program. *Financial support:* Application deadline: 2/15; applicants required to submit FAFSA. *Unit head:* Dennis Anderson, Director, 509-359-2087, E-mail: danderson2@ewu.edu. *Application contact:* Kathy White, Advisor/Recruiter for Graduate Studies, 509-359-2491, Fax: 509-359-6044, E-mail: gradprograms@ewu.edu.

**Fairleigh Dickinson University, Metropolitan Campus,** University College: Arts, Sciences, and Professional Studies, School of Psychology, Program in General-Theoretical Psychology, Teaneck, NJ 07666-1914. Offers MA, Certificate.

**The Graduate Center, City University of New York,** Graduate Studies, Program in Psychology, New York, NY 10016-4039. Offers basic applied neurocognition (PhD); biopsychology (PhD); clinical psychology (PhD); developmental psychology (PhD); environmental psychology (PhD); experimental psychology (PhD); industrial psychology (PhD); learning processes (PhD); neuropsychology (PhD); psychology (PhD); social personality (PhD). *Degree requirements:* For doctorate, one foreign language, thesis/dissertation. *Entrance requirements:* For doctorate, GRE General Test. Additional exam requirements/recommendations for international students: Required—TOEFL. Electronic applications accepted.

**Harvard University,** Graduate School of Arts and Sciences, Department of Psychology, Cambridge, MA 02138. Offers psychology (PhD), including behavior and decision analysis, cognition, developmental psychology, experimental psychology, personality, psychobiology, psychopathology; social psychology (PhD). *Accreditation:* APA. *Degree requirements:* For doctorate, thesis/dissertation, general exams. *Entrance requirements:* For doctorate, GRE General Test. Additional exam requirements/recommendations for international students: Required—TOEFL.

**Howard University,** Graduate School, Department of Psychology, Washington, DC 20059-0002. Offers clinical psychology (PhD); developmental psychology (PhD); experimental psychology (PhD); neuropsychology (PhD); personality psychology (PhD); psychology (MS); social psychology (PhD). *Accreditation:* APA (one or more programs are accredited). *Program availability:* Part-time. *Degree requirements:* For master's, thesis; for doctorate, comprehensive exam, thesis/dissertation, qualifying exam. *Entrance requirements:* For master's, GRE General Test, minimum GPA of 2.5, bachelor's degree in psychology or related field; for doctorate, GRE General Test, minimum GPA of 3.0. *Faculty research:* Personality and psychophysiology, educational and social development of African-American children, child and adult psychopathology.

**Idaho State University,** Office of Graduate Studies, College of Arts and Letters, Department of Psychology, Program in Experimental Psychology, Pocatello, ID 83209. Offers PhD. *Entrance requirements:* For doctorate, GRE, BA/BS in psychology or the equivalent, minimum undergraduate GPA of 3.0 for the last two years.

**Iona College,** School of Arts and Science, Department of Psychology, New Rochelle, NY 10801-1890. Offers general-experimental psychology (MA); human resources (Certificate); industrial-organizational psychology (MA); mental health counseling (MA); organizational behavior (Certificate); psychology (MA); school psychology (MA). *Program availability:* Part-time. *Faculty:* 9 full-time (5 women), 6 part-time/adjunct (5 women). *Students:* 61 full-time (42 women), 32 part-time (23 women); includes 40 minority (8 Black or African American, non-Hispanic/Latino; 3 Asian, non-Hispanic/Latino; 28 Hispanic/Latino; 1 Two or more races, non-Hispanic/Latino), 2 international. Average age 25. 91 applicants, 80% accepted, 37 enrolled. In 2016, 18 master's awarded. *Degree requirements:* For master's, thesis (for some programs), literature review (for some programs). *Entrance requirements:* For master's, BA in psychology including 3 credits each in psychology statistics and experimental research methods, or 9 credits in psychology including 3 credits in psychology statistics, 3 credits in psychology research methods and 3 credits of upper-level coursework. Additional exam requirements/recommendations for international students: Required—TOEFL (minimum score 550 paper-based), IELTS (minimum score 6.5). *Application deadline:* For fall admission, 8/15 for domestic students, 5/1 for international students; for spring admission, 1/15 for domestic students, 9/1 for international students. Applications are processed on a rolling basis. Application fee: $50. Electronic applications accepted. *Expenses:* Tuition: Full-time $19,692; part-time $1094 per credit. *Required fees:* $245 per term. Tuition and fees vary according to program. *Financial support:* In 2016–17, 49 students received support. Research assistantships with partial tuition reimbursements available, tuition waivers (partial), and unspecified assistantships available. Support available to part-time students. Financial award application deadline: 4/15; financial award applicants required to submit FAFSA. *Faculty research:* Non-suicidal self-injury, trauma response, performance appraisal and evaluation, diversity infusion, assessment and treatment of sexual offenders. *Unit head:* Patricia Oswald, PhD, Chair, 914-633-2374, E-mail: poswald@iona.edu. *Application contact:* Katelyn Brunck, Assistant Director, Graduate Admissions, 914-633-2451, Fax: 914-633-2277, E-mail: kbrunck@iona.edu.

Website: http://www.iona.edu/Academics/School-of-Arts-Science/Departments/Psychology/Graduate-Programs.aspx

**James Madison University,** The Graduate School, College of Health and Behavioral Sciences, Program in Psychological Sciences, Harrisonburg, VA 22807. Offers applied research (MA); behavior analysis (MA); experimental psychology (MA); quantitative psychology (MA). *Program availability:* Part-time, evening/weekend. *Students:* 21 full-time (10 women), 3 part-time (2 women); includes 3 minority (1 American Indian or Alaska Native, non-Hispanic/Latino; 1 Native Hawaiian or other Pacific Islander, non-Hispanic/Latino; 1 Two or more races, non-Hispanic/Latino). Average age 30. 58 applicants, 31% accepted, 14 enrolled. In 2016, 14 master's awarded. Application fee: $55. Electronic applications accepted. *Financial support:* In 2016–17, 2 teaching assistantships with full tuition reimbursements (averaging $9,284 per year) were awarded; career-related internships or fieldwork, Federal Work-Study, and 19 assistantships (averaging $7911) also available. Financial award application deadline: 3/1; financial award applicants required to submit FAFSA. *Unit head:* Dr. Jeff S. Dyche, Graduate Program Director, 540-568-4965, E-mail: dychejs@jmu.edu. *Application contact:* Lynette D. Michael, Director of Graduate Admissions, 540-568-6131 Ext. 6395, Fax: 540-568-7860, E-mail: michaeld@jmu.edu. Website: http://www.psyc.jmu.edu/psycsciences/

**Kent State University,** College of Arts and Sciences, Department of Psychological Sciences, Kent, OH 44242-0001. Offers clinical psychology (MA, PhD), including gerontology (MA), psychological sciences (MA); experimental psychology (MA, PhD), including gerontology (MA), psychological sciences (MA). *Accreditation:* APA (one or more programs are accredited). *Program availability:* Part-time. *Faculty:* 29 full-time (15 women). *Students:* 29 full-time (24 women); includes 9 minority (4 Black or African American, non-Hispanic/Latino; 2 Asian, non-Hispanic/Latino; 2 Hispanic/Latino; 1 Two or more races, non-Hispanic/Latino), 1 international. Average age 31. 323 applicants, 5% accepted, 17 enrolled. Terminal master's awarded for partial completion of doctoral program. *Degree requirements:* For master's, thesis; for doctorate, thesis/dissertation. *Entrance requirements:* For master's and doctorate, GRE General Test, personal statement, transcripts, 3 letters of recommendation. Additional exam requirements/recommendations for international students: Required—TOEFL (minimum score of 525 paper-based, 71 iBT), IELTS (minimum score of 6), Michigan English Language Assessment Battery (minimum score of 75), or PTE (minimum score of 48). *Application deadline:* For fall admission, 12/1 for domestic and international students. Applications are processed on a rolling basis. Application fee: $45 ($70 for international students). Electronic applications accepted. *Expenses:* Tuition, state resident: full-time $10,864; part-time $495 per credit hour. Tuition, nonresident: full-time $18,380; part-time $837 per credit hour. *Financial support:* Unspecified assistantships available. Financial award application deadline: 12/1. *Unit head:* Dr. Maria S. Zaragoza, Professor and Chair, 330-672-2166, E-mail: mzaragoz@kent.edu. *Application contact:* Dr. John A. Updegraff, Professor and Graduate Coordinator, 330-672-2166, E-mail: jupdegr1@kent.edu. Website: http://www.kent.edu/psychology/graduate-programs

**Lakehead University,** Graduate Studies, Department of Psychology, Thunder Bay, ON P7B 5E1, Canada. Offers clinical psychology (PhD); experimental psychology (MA). *Program availability:* Part-time, evening/weekend. *Degree requirements:* For master's, thesis optional; for doctorate, thesis/dissertation, 2 comprehensive exams, internship. *Entrance requirements:* For master's, GRE, honors degree in psychology, advanced course work in statistics, minimum B average; for doctorate, GRE, minimum B average. Additional exam requirements/recommendations for international students: Required—TOEFL. *Faculty research:* Chaos theory, health psychology, counseling psychology, gerontology, women's studies.

**Laurentian University,** School of Graduate Studies and Research, Programme in Psychology, Sudbury, ON P3E 2C6, Canada. Offers applied psychology (MA); experimental psychology (MA).

**McGill University,** Faculty of Graduate and Postdoctoral Studies, Faculty of Science, Department of Psychology, Montréal, QC H3A 2T5, Canada. Offers clinical psychology (PhD); experimental psychology (M Sc, MA, PhD).

**McNeese State University,** Doré School of Graduate Studies, Burton College of Education, Department of Psychology, Lake Charles, LA 70609. Offers addiction treatment (MA); applied behavior analysis (MA); counseling psychology (MA); general/experimental psychology (MA). *Program availability:* Evening/weekend. *Entrance requirements:* For master's, GRE.

**Memorial University of Newfoundland,** School of Graduate Studies, Department of Psychology, St. John's, NL A1C 5S7, Canada. Offers applied psychological sciences (MAPS); clinical psychology (Psy D); experimental psychology (M Sc, PhD). *Program availability:* Part-time. *Degree requirements:* For master's, workterms (MASP), thesis (M Sc); for doctorate, comprehensive exam, thesis/dissertation, oral thesis defense. *Entrance requirements:* For master's, GRE, honors bachelor's degree of high second class standing or equivalent; for doctorate, GRE, master's or honors degree. Electronic applications accepted. *Faculty research:* Behavioral neuroscience, cognition, theory and research on abnormal behavior.

**Middle Tennessee State University,** College of Graduate Studies, College of Behavioral and Health Sciences, Department of Psychology, Murfreesboro, TN 37132. Offers clinical psychology (MA); experimental psychology (MA); industrial/organizational psychology (MA); psychology (MA, Ed S); quantitative psychology (MA); school psychology (MA). *Program availability:* Part-time, evening/weekend, online learning. *Degree requirements:* For master's, comprehensive exam, thesis. *Entrance requirements:* For master's, GRE. Additional exam requirements/recommendations for international students: Required—TOEFL (minimum score 525 paper-based; 71 iBT) or IELTS (minimum score 6). Electronic applications accepted. *Faculty research:* Health psychology, industrial/organizational psychology, experimental psychology.

**Missouri State University,** Graduate College, College of Health and Human Services, Department of Psychology, Springfield, MO 65897. Offers applied behavior analysis (MS); clinical psychology (MS); experimental psychology (MS); forensic child psychology (Certificate); industrial/organizational psychology (MS). *Faculty:* 25 full-time (11 women), 4 part-time/adjunct (0 women). *Students:* 65 full-time (49 women), 7 part-time (5 women); includes 12 minority (1 Black or African American, non-Hispanic/Latino; 3 American Indian or Alaska Native, non-Hispanic/Latino; 3 Asian, non-Hispanic/Latino; 2 Hispanic/Latino; 3 Two or more races, non-Hispanic/Latino), 6 international. Average age 25. 159 applicants, 25% accepted, 31 enrolled. In 2016, 22 master's awarded. *Degree requirements:* For master's, comprehensive exam, thesis. *Entrance requirements:* For master's, GRE General Test, GRE Subject Test, minimum GPA of 3.25 in major, 3.0 overall; 20 hours of course work in psychology. Additional exam requirements/recommendations for international students: Required—TOEFL (minimum score 550 paper-based; 79 iBT), IELTS (minimum score 6). *Application deadline:* For fall admission, 2/15 priority date for domestic and international students. Application fee: $35 ($50 for international students). Electronic applications accepted. *Expenses:* Tuition, state resident: full-time $5830. Tuition, nonresident: full-time $10,708. *Required fees:* $1130. Tuition and fees vary according to class time, course level, course load and program. *Financial support:* In 2016–17, 9 research assistantships with full tuition reimbursements (averaging $8,772 per year), 8 teaching assistantships with full tuition

reimbursements (averaging $8,772 per year) were awarded; career-related internships or fieldwork, Federal Work-Study, institutionally sponsored loans, scholarships/grants, and unspecified assistantships also available. Financial award application deadline: 3/31; financial award applicants required to submit FAFSA. *Faculty research:* Work-family conflict, child forensic psychology, sports psychology, body image assessment, visual learning. *Unit head:* Dr. Paul Deal, Department Head, 417-836-5797, Fax: 417-836-8330, E-mail: psychology@missouristate.edu. *Application contact:* Michael Edwards, Coordinator of Graduate Admissions, 417-836-5330, Fax: 417-836-6200, E-mail: michaeledwards@missouristate.edu.
Website: http://psychology.missouristate.edu/

**Morehead State University,** Graduate Programs, College of Science and Technology, Department of Psychology, Morehead, KY 40351. Offers clinical/counseling psychology (MS); general/experimental psychology (MS). *Program availability:* Part-time, evening/weekend. *Degree requirements:* For master's, comprehensive exam, thesis optional. *Entrance requirements:* For master's, GRE General Test, 18 undergraduate hours in psychology, minimum GPA of 3.0, 3 letters of recommendation. Additional exam requirements/recommendations for international students: Required—TOEFL (minimum score 500 paper-based). Electronic applications accepted. *Faculty research:* Mood induction effects, serotonin receptor activity, stress, perceptual processes.

**North Carolina State University,** Graduate School, College of Humanities and Social Sciences, Department of Psychology, Raleigh, NC 27695. Offers developmental psychology (PhD); ergonomics and experimental psychology (PhD); industrial/organizational psychology (PhD); psychology in the public interest (PhD); school psychology (PhD). *Accreditation:* APA. *Degree requirements:* For doctorate, comprehensive exam, thesis/dissertation. *Entrance requirements:* For doctorate, GRE General Test, GRE Subject Test (industrial/organizational psychology), MAT (recommended), minimum GPA of 3.0 in major. Electronic applications accepted. *Faculty research:* Cognitive and social development (human factors, families, the workplace, community issues and health, aging).

**Nova Southeastern University,** College of Psychology, Fort Lauderdale, FL 33314-7796. Offers clinical psychology (PhD, Psy D); counseling (MS); experimental psychology (MS); forensic psychology (MS); general psychology (MS); mental health counseling (MS); school counseling (MS); school psychology (Psy D, Psy S). *Accreditation:* APA (one or more programs are accredited). *Program availability:* 100% online, blended/hybrid learning. *Faculty:* 51 full-time (21 women), 120 part-time/adjunct (70 women). *Students:* 724 full-time (596 women), 918 part-time (792 women); includes 797 minority (276 Black or African American, non-Hispanic/Latino; 1 American Indian or Alaska Native, non-Hispanic/Latino; 44 Asian, non-Hispanic/Latino; 427 Hispanic/Latino; 2 Native Hawaiian or other Pacific Islander, non-Hispanic/Latino; 47 Two or more races, non-Hispanic/Latino), 41 international. Average age 31. 1,349 applicants, 61% accepted, 651 enrolled. In 2016, 377 master's, 177 doctorates, 26 other advanced degrees awarded. Terminal master's awarded for partial completion of doctoral program. *Degree requirements:* For master's, comprehensive exam, 3 practica; for doctorate, thesis/dissertation, clinical internship, competency exam; for Psy S, comprehensive exam, internship. *Entrance requirements:* For doctorate, GRE General Test, GRE Subject Test (recommended), minimum undergraduate GPA of 3.0; for Psy S, GRE General Test. Additional exam requirements/recommendations for international students: Required—TOEFL (minimum score 550 paper-based). *Application deadline:* Applications are processed on a rolling basis. Application fee: $50. Electronic applications accepted. *Expenses:* Contact institution. *Financial support:* In 2016–17, 197 students received support, including 15 research assistantships (averaging $5,600 per year), 68 teaching assistantships (averaging $2,000 per year); career-related internships or fieldwork, Federal Work-Study, institutionally sponsored loans, scholarships/grants, and unspecified assistantships also available. Support available to part-time students. Financial award application deadline: 4/15; financial award applicants required to submit FAFSA. *Faculty research:* Clinical health psychology, multicultural/diversity psychology, clinical neuropsychology, clinical child psychology, family violence. *Unit head:* Dr. Karen Grosby, Dean, 954-262-5712, Fax: 954-262-3859, E-mail: grosby@nova.edu. *Application contact:* Carlos Perez, Senior Manager of Outreach, 954-262-5702, Fax: 954-262-3893, E-mail: gradschool@nova.edu.
Website: http://psychology.nova.edu/

**Ohio University,** Graduate College, College of Arts and Sciences, Department of Psychology, Program in Experimental Psychology, Athens, OH 45701-2979. Offers PhD. *Degree requirements:* For doctorate, one foreign language, comprehensive exam, thesis/dissertation. *Entrance requirements:* For doctorate, GRE General Test, GRE Subject Test, minimum graduate GPA of 3.4. Additional exam requirements/recommendations for international students: Required—TOEFL. *Application deadline:* For fall admission, 1/1 for domestic students. Application fee: $50 ($55 for international students). *Financial support:* Fellowships with full tuition reimbursements, research assistantships with full tuition reimbursements, teaching assistantships with full tuition reimbursements, Federal Work-Study, institutionally sponsored loans, tuition waivers (full), and unspecified assistantships available. Financial award application deadline: 1/15. *Faculty research:* Cognitive psychology, quantitative psychology, social psychology, judgment and decision-making, health psychology. *Unit head:* Chantel Weisenmuller, Director, 740-597-1251, E-mail: weisenmu@ohio.edu. *Application contact:* Karyl Jones, Administrative Assistant, 740-593-1090, Fax: 740-593-0579, E-mail: psychology@ohio.edu. Website: http://www.psych.ohiou.edu/

**Rivier University,** School of Graduate Studies, Department of Psychology, Nashua, NH 03060. Offers clinical psychology (MS); experimental psychology (MS).

**Rochester Institute of Technology,** Graduate Enrollment Services, College of Liberal Arts, Psychology Department, MS Program in Experimental Psychology, Rochester, NY 14623. Offers MS. *Program availability:* Part-time. *Students:* 8 full-time (6 women), 5 part-time (2 women); includes 2 minority (1 Black or African American, non-Hispanic/Latino; 1 Hispanic/Latino). Average age 27. 28 applicants, 25% accepted, 3 enrolled. In 2016, 3 master's awarded. *Degree requirements:* For master's, thesis. *Entrance requirements:* For master's, GRE, minimum GPA of 3.0 (recommended). Additional exam requirements/recommendations for international students: Required—TOEFL (minimum score 550 paper-based; 79 iBT), IELTS (minimum score 6.5), PTE (minimum score 58). *Application deadline:* For fall admission, 2/15 priority date for domestic and international students; for spring admission, 12/15 priority date for domestic and international students. Applications are processed on a rolling basis. Application fee: $60. Electronic applications accepted. *Expenses:* $1,742 per credit hour. *Financial support:* In 2016–17, 9 students received support. Research assistantships with partial tuition reimbursements available, teaching assistantships with partial tuition reimbursements available, career-related internships or fieldwork, scholarships/grants, and unspecified assistantships available. Support available to part-time students. Financial award applicants required to submit FAFSA. *Faculty research:* Human factors in complex systems, human performance measurement and modeling, mental workload, decision-making, human error and reliability, perception, cognitive neuroscience, brain and behavior relationships, human development. *Unit head:* Dr. Suzanne Bamonto, Graduate Program Director, 585-475-2765, E-mail: sbggsp@rit.edu. *Application contact:* Diane Ellison, Associate Vice President, Graduate Enrollment Services, 585-475-2229,

Fax: 585-475-7164, E-mail: gradinfo@rit.edu.
Website: http://www.rit.edu/cla/psychology/graduate/ms-experimental-psych/overview

**St. John's University,** St. John's College of Liberal Arts and Sciences, Department of Psychology, Program in General Experimental Psychology, Queens, NY 11439. Offers MA. *Program availability:* Part-time, evening/weekend. *Degree requirements:* For master's, comprehensive exam, thesis optional. *Entrance requirements:* For master's, minimum GPA of 3.0, 2 writing samples, bachelor's degree, minimum of 24 undergraduate credits in psychology, personal statement, transcript. Additional exam requirements/recommendations for international students: Required—TOEFL (minimum score 600 paper-based; 100 iBT), IELTS (minimum score 7). Electronic applications accepted. *Faculty research:* Learning and memory neuropsychology, perception, social psychology, developmental psychology.

**Saint Louis University,** Graduate Education, College of Arts and Sciences and Graduate Education, Department of Psychology, St. Louis, MO 63103. Offers clinical psychology (MS-R, PhD); experimental psychology (MS-R, PhD); industrial-organizational psychology (PhD); psychology (PhD). *Accreditation:* APA (one or more programs are accredited). *Program availability:* Part-time. *Degree requirements:* For master's, comprehensive exam, thesis; for doctorate, thesis/dissertation, clinical internship (for clinical psychology PhD). *Entrance requirements:* For master's, GRE General Test, interview, letters of recommendation, resume; for doctorate, GRE General Test, interview, letters of recommendation, resumé, transcripts, goal statement. Additional exam requirements/recommendations for international students: Required—TOEFL (minimum score 550 paper-based). Electronic applications accepted. *Faculty research:* Violence and trauma; neural basis of learning and memory function; eating disorders; body image and health behavior; prejudice, stereotyping, and victimization; memory, cognitive aging and language processing.

**San Jose State University,** Graduate Studies and Research, College of Social Sciences, San Jose, CA 95192-0001. Offers applications of technology in planning (Certificate); applied anthropology (MA); communication studies (MS); community design and development (Certificate); economics (MA), including applied economics, social sciences; environmental planning (Certificate); geographic information science (Certificate); geography (MA); global citizenship (Certificate); history (MA), including history education, social sciences; Mexican American studies (MA); psychology (MA, MS), including clinical psychology (MS), industrial/organizational psychology (MS), research and experimental psychology (MA); public administration (MA); real estate development (Certificate); social sciences (MPA, MS); sociology (MA); transportation and land use planning (Certificate). *Program availability:* Part-time, evening/weekend. *Entrance requirements:* For master's, minimum GPA of 3.0. Electronic applications accepted.

**Seton Hall University,** College of Arts and Sciences, Department of Psychology, South Orange, NJ 07079-2697. Offers experimental psychology (MS). *Program availability:* Part-time, evening/weekend. *Degree requirements:* For master's, thesis optional. *Entrance requirements:* For master's, GRE, minimum of 18 credits in psychology with minimum GPA of 3.0. Additional exam requirements/recommendations for international students: Required—TOEFL. Electronic applications accepted. *Faculty research:* Behavioral neuroscience, cognitive psychology, social psychology, perception/motor skills, memory, depression, anxiety.

**Southern Illinois University Carbondale,** Graduate School, College of Liberal Arts, Department of Psychology, Carbondale, IL 62901-4701. Offers clinical psychology (PhD); counseling psychology (PhD); experimental psychology (MA, MS). *Accreditation:* APA (one or more programs are accredited). *Degree requirements:* For master's, thesis; for doctorate, thesis/dissertation. *Entrance requirements:* For master's, GRE General Test, GRE Subject Test, minimum GPA of 2.7; for doctorate, GRE General Test, GRE Subject Test, minimum GPA of 3.25. Additional exam requirements/recommendations for international students: Required—TOEFL. *Faculty research:* Developmental neuropsychology; smoking, affect, and cognition; personality measurement; vocational psychology; program evaluation.

**Southern Methodist University,** Bobby B. Lyle School of Engineering, Department of Environmental and Civil Engineering, Dallas, TX 75275-0340. Offers air pollution control and atmospheric sciences (PhD); civil engineering (MS); environmental engineering (MS); environmental science (MS); structural engineering (PhD); sustainability and development (MA); water and wastewater engineering (PhD). *Program availability:* Part-time, evening/weekend, online learning. Terminal master's awarded for partial completion of doctoral program. *Degree requirements:* For master's, thesis optional; for doctorate, thesis/dissertation, oral and written qualifying exams. *Entrance requirements:* For master's, GRE General Test, minimum GPA of 3.0 in last 2 years; bachelor's degree in engineering, mathematics, or sciences; for doctorate, GRE, BS and MS in related field, minimum GPA of 3.3. Additional exam requirements/recommendations for international students: Required—TOEFL. Electronic applications accepted. *Faculty research:* Human and environmental health effects of endocrine disrupters, development of air pollution control systems for diesel engines, structural analysis and design, modeling and design of waste treatment systems.

**Texas A&M University–Central Texas,** Graduate Studies and Research, Killeen, TX 76549. Offers accounting (MS); business administration (MBA); clinical mental health counseling (MS); criminal justice (MCJ); curriculum and instruction (M Ed); educational administration (M Ed); educational psychology - experimental psychology (MS); history (MA); human resource management (MS); information systems (MS); liberal studies (MS); management and leadership (MS); marriage and family therapy (MS); mathematics (MS); political science (MA); school counseling (M Ed); school psychology (Ed S).

**Texas Christian University,** College of Science and Engineering, Department of Psychology, Fort Worth, TX 76129. Offers developmental trauma (MS); experimental psychology (PhD), including cognition/developmental, learning, neuroscience, social. *Faculty:* 12 full-time (5 women), 3 part-time/adjunct (2 women). *Students:* 33 full-time (19 women); includes 4 minority (1 Asian, non-Hispanic/Latino; 1 Hispanic/Latino; 2 Two or more races, non-Hispanic/Latino), 2 international. Average age 27. 38 applicants, 32% accepted, 12 enrolled. In 2016, 5 master's, 3 doctorates awarded. Terminal master's awarded for partial completion of doctoral program. *Degree requirements:* For master's, thesis; for doctorate, thesis/dissertation. *Entrance requirements:* For doctorate, GRE General Test. Additional exam requirements/recommendations for international students: Required—TOEFL. *Application deadline:* For fall admission, 2/1 for domestic and international students. Application fee: $60 ($0 for international students). Electronic applications accepted. *Expenses:* Contact institution. *Financial support:* In 2016–17, 23 students received support, including 23 teaching assistantships with full tuition reimbursements available (averaging $19,750 per year); scholarships/grants also available. Financial award application deadline: 2/1; financial award applicants required to submit FAFSA. *Faculty research:* Neuroscience, human and animal learning, cognition, development, experimental social psychology. *Unit head:* Dr. Mauricio R. Papini, Chair, 817-257-7410, Fax: 817-257-7681, E-mail: m.papini@tcu.edu. *Application contact:* Cindy Hayes, Administrative Assistant, 817-257-7410, Fax: 817-257-7681, E-mail: c.hayes@tcu.edu.
Website: https://psychology.tcu.edu/current-graduate-students/

**Texas Tech University,** Graduate School, College of Arts and Sciences, Department of Psychological Sciences, Lubbock, TX 79409-2051. Offers clinical psychology (PhD); counseling psychology (MA, PhD); general experimental psychology (MA, PhD); psychology (MA). *Accreditation:* APA (one or more programs are accredited). *Faculty:* 32 full-time (14 women), 2 part-time/adjunct (both women). *Students:* 111 full-time (72 women), 12 part-time (6 women); includes 28 minority (3 Black or African American, non-Hispanic/Latino; 1 American Indian or Alaska Native, non-Hispanic/Latino; 8 Asian, non-Hispanic/Latino; 14 Hispanic/Latino; 2 Two or more races, non-Hispanic/Latino), 8 international. Average age 27. 285 applicants, 13% accepted, 23 enrolled. In 2016, 13 master's, 13 doctorates awarded. *Degree requirements:* For doctorate, comprehensive exam, thesis/dissertation, 100 credit hours of organized courses, research credits, and practica. *Entrance requirements:* For master's, GRE General Test, GRE Subject Test, essays, letters of recommendation; for doctorate, GRE General Test, essays, letters of recommendation. Additional exam requirements/recommendations for international students: Required—TOEFL (minimum score 550 paper-based; 79 iBT). *Application deadline:* For fall admission, 6/1 priority date for domestic students, 1/15 priority date for international students; for spring admission, 9/1 priority date for domestic students, 6/15 priority date for international students. Applications are processed on a rolling basis. Application fee: $75. Electronic applications accepted. *Expenses:* $300 per credit hour full-time resident tuition, $708 per credit hour full-time non-resident tuition; $50.50 per credit hour fee plus $608 per term fee. *Financial support:* In 2016–17, 115 students received support, including 113 fellowships (averaging $2,657 per year), 76 research assistantships (averaging $5,066 per year), 95 teaching assistantships (averaging $11,737 per year); Federal Work-Study, institutionally sponsored loans, and unspecified assistantships also available. Financial award application deadline: 4/15; financial award applicants required to submit FAFSA. *Faculty research:* Health psychology, addictive behaviors, depression and suicide risk, sexuality/sexual risk behaviors/HIV, neuroscience/neuroimaging, forensic and correctional psychology. *Total annual research expenditures:* $710,154. *Unit head:* Dr. Robert Morgan, Professor and Chair, 806-834-7117, Fax: 806-742-0818, E-mail: robert.morgan@ttu.edu. *Application contact:* Kay Hill, Admissions Coordinator, 806-742-3711 Ext. 222, Fax: 806-742-0818, E-mail: kay.hill@ttu.edu.
Website: http://www.depts.ttu.edu/psy/

**Towson University,** Program in Psychology, Towson, MD 21252-0001. Offers clinical psychology (MA); counseling psychology (MA); experimental psychology (MA); school psychology (MA). *Program availability:* Part-time, evening/weekend. *Students:* 104 full-time (72 women), 27 part-time (23 women); includes 34 minority (12 Black or African American, non-Hispanic/Latino; 7 Asian, non-Hispanic/Latino; 10 Hispanic/Latino; 5 Two or more races, non-Hispanic/Latino). *Degree requirements:* For master's, thesis (for some programs). *Entrance requirements:* For master's, GRE, minimum GPA of 3.0, letters of recommendation. *Application deadline:* For fall admission, 2/1 for domestic and international students. Application fee: $45. Electronic applications accepted. *Expenses:* Tuition, state resident: full-time $7580; part-time $379 per unit. Tuition, nonresident: full-time $15,700; part-time $785 per unit. *Required fees:* $2480. *Financial support:* Application deadline: 4/1. *Unit head:* Dr. Geoffrey Munro, Graduate Program Director, 410-704-2634, E-mail: psyc@towson.edu. *Application contact:* Coverley Beidleman, Assistant Director of Graduate Admissions, 410-704-2113, Fax: 410-704-3030, E-mail: grads@towson.edu.
Website: https://www.towson.edu/cla/departments/psychology/grad/

**The University of Alabama,** Graduate School, College of Arts and Sciences, Department of Psychology, Tuscaloosa, AL 35487. Offers clinical psychology (PhD); experimental psychology (PhD). *Accreditation:* APA. *Faculty:* 27 full-time (14 women), 4 part-time/adjunct (2 women). *Students:* 84 full-time (60 women), 13 part-time (10 women); includes 14 minority (4 Black or African American, non-Hispanic/Latino; 3 Asian, non-Hispanic/Latino; 6 Hispanic/Latino; 1 Two or more races, non-Hispanic/Latino), 8 international. Average age 27. 342 applicants, 7% accepted, 18 enrolled. In 2016, 19 doctorates awarded. *Degree requirements:* For doctorate, thesis/dissertation, internship (for clinical psychology). *Entrance requirements:* For doctorate, GRE. Additional exam requirements/recommendations for international students: Required—TOEFL (minimum score 550 paper-based). *Application deadline:* For fall admission, 12/1 for domestic and international students. Application fee: $50 ($60 for international students). Electronic applications accepted. *Expenses:* Tuition, state resident: full-time $10,470. Tuition, nonresident: full-time $26,950. *Financial support:* In 2016–17, 73 students received support, including 12 fellowships with full tuition reimbursements available (averaging $17,000 per year), 40 research assistantships with tuition reimbursements available (averaging $12,744 per year), 34 teaching assistantships with tuition reimbursements available (averaging $13,824 per year); career-related internships or fieldwork, institutionally sponsored loans, scholarships/grants, health care benefits, and unspecified assistantships also available. Financial award application deadline: 12/1. *Faculty research:* Cognitive development/disability, child clinical, psychology and law, health/aging, social psychology. *Total annual research expenditures:* $2.4 million. *Unit head:* Dr. Frances A. Conners, Chair, 205-348-1913, Fax: 205-348-8648, E-mail: fconners@ua.edu. *Application contact:* Mary Beth Hubbard, Information Contact, 205-348-1919, Fax: 205-348-8648, E-mail: mary.b.hubbard@ua.edu.
Website: http://www.psychology.ua.edu

**University of Central Florida,** College of Sciences, Department of Psychology, Program in Applied Experimental and Human Factors Psychology, Orlando, FL 32816. Offers MA, PhD. *Students:* 37 full-time (26 women), 2 part-time (1 woman); includes 8 minority (2 Asian, non-Hispanic/Latino; 6 Hispanic/Latino), 1 international. Average age 28. 46 applicants, 20% accepted, 5 enrolled. In 2016, 9 master's, 9 doctorates awarded. *Degree requirements:* For doctorate, thesis/dissertation, departmental candidacy exam. *Entrance requirements:* For doctorate, GRE General Test, minimum GPA of 3.2 in last 60 hours or master's qualifying exam. Additional exam requirements/recommendations for international students: Required—TOEFL. *Application deadline:* For fall admission, 12/15 for domestic students. Application fee: $30. Electronic applications accepted. *Expenses:* Tuition, state resident: part-time $288.16 per credit hour. Tuition, nonresident: part-time $1071.31 per credit hour. *Financial support:* In 2016–17, 35 students received support, including 27 fellowships with partial tuition reimbursements available (averaging $7,038 per year), 11 research assistantships with partial tuition reimbursements available (averaging $10,497 per year), 22 teaching assistantships with partial tuition reimbursements available (averaging $11,486 per year); career-related internships or fieldwork, Federal Work-Study, institutionally sponsored loans, tuition waivers (partial), and unspecified assistantships also available. Financial award application deadline: 3/1; financial award applicants required to submit FAFSA. *Faculty research:* Categorization and decision, team training, transportation and safety, applied cognition and aging, emerging technology. *Unit head:* Dr. Mustapha Mouloua, Program Director, 407-823-2910, E-mail: mustapha.mouloua@ucf.edu. *Application contact:* Assistant Director, Graduate Admissions, 407-823-2766, Fax: 407-823-6442, E-mail: gradadmissions@ucf.edu.
Website: http://psychology.cos.ucf.edu/graduate/

**University of Central Oklahoma,** The Jackson College of Graduate Studies, College of Education and Professional Studies, Department of Psychology, Edmond, OK 73034-5209. Offers counseling psychology (MA); experimental psychology (MA); forensic

psychology (MA); general psychology (MA); school psychology (MA). *Degree requirements:* For master's, thesis (for some programs). *Entrance requirements:* For master's, GRE. Additional exam requirements/recommendations for international students: Required—TOEFL (minimum score 550 paper-based; 79 iBT), IELTS (minimum score 6.5). Electronic applications accepted. *Faculty research:* Psychopharmacology, computer psychometrics, health psychology research.

**University of Cincinnati,** Graduate School, McMicken College of Arts and Sciences, Department of Psychology, Cincinnati, OH 45221. Offers clinical psychology (PhD); experimental psychology (PhD). *Accreditation:* APA. *Degree requirements:* For doctorate, comprehensive exam, thesis/dissertation. *Entrance requirements:* For doctorate, GRE General Test. Additional exam requirements/recommendations for international students: Required—TOEFL. *Expenses: Tuition, area resident:* Full-time $12,790; part-time $389 per credit hour. Tuition, state resident: full-time $13,290; part-time $419 per credit hour. Tuition, nonresident: full-time $24,532; part-time $976 per credit hour. *International tuition:* $24,832 full-time. *Required fees:* $3958; $140 per credit hour. Tuition and fees vary according to course load, degree level, program and reciprocity agreements. *Faculty research:* Neuropsychology, human factors, health.

**University of Connecticut,** Graduate School, College of Liberal Arts and Sciences, Department of Psychology, Storrs, CT 06269. Offers behavioral neuroscience (PhD); biopsychology (PhD); clinical psychology (MA, PhD); cognition and instruction (PhD); developmental psychology (MA, PhD); ecological psychology (PhD); experimental psychology (PhD); general psychology (MA, PhD); industrial/organizational psychology (PhD); language and cognition (PhD); neuroscience (PhD); social psychology (MA, PhD). *Accreditation:* APA. Terminal master's awarded for partial completion of doctoral program. *Degree requirements:* For master's, comprehensive exam; for doctorate, thesis/dissertation. *Entrance requirements:* For master's and doctorate, GRE General Test, GRE Subject Test. Additional exam requirements/recommendations for international students: Required—TOEFL (minimum score 550 paper-based). Electronic applications accepted.

**University of Hartford,** College of Arts and Sciences, Department of Psychology, Program in General Experimental Psychology, West Hartford, CT 06117-1599. Offers MA. *Program availability:* Part-time. *Degree requirements:* For master's, comprehensive exam, thesis or alternative. *Entrance requirements:* For master's, GRE General Test, GRE Subject Test, minimum GPA of 3.0, 3 letters of recommendation. Additional exam requirements/recommendations for international students: Required—TOEFL (minimum score 550 paper-based). Electronic applications accepted. *Faculty research:* Decision making, social judgment and stereotyping, stress and health.

**University of Idaho,** College of Graduate Studies, College of Letters, Arts and Social Sciences, Department of Psychology and Communication Studies, Moscow, ID 83844. Offers experimental psychology (PhD); psychology (MS). *Faculty:* 9 full-time, 2 part-time/adjunct. *Students:* 18 full-time, 11 part-time. Average age 31. In 2016, 11 master's awarded. *Entrance requirements:* For master's, GRE, minimum GPA of 3.0. *Application deadline:* For fall admission, 8/1 for domestic students; for spring admission, 12/15 for domestic students. Applications are processed on a rolling basis. Application fee: $60. Electronic applications accepted. *Expenses:* Tuition, state resident: full-time $6460; part-time $414 per credit hour. Tuition, nonresident: full-time $21,268; part-time $1237 per credit hour. *Required fees:* $2070; $60 per credit hour. Full-time tuition and fees vary according to course load and reciprocity agreements. *Financial support:* Fellowships, research assistantships, and teaching assistantships available. Financial award applicants required to submit FAFSA. *Faculty research:* Clinical, experimental, and cognitive psychology. *Unit head:* Dr. Todd Thorsteinson, Chair, 208-885-6324, E-mail: psyc-comm@uidaho.edu. *Application contact:* Sean Scoggin, Graduate Recruitment Coordinator, 208-885-4723, Fax: 208-885-4406, E-mail: graduateadmissions@uidaho.edu.
Website: https://www.uidaho.edu/class/psychcomm

**University of Louisville,** Graduate School, College of Arts and Sciences, Department of Psychological and Brain Sciences, Louisville, KY 40292-0001. Offers clinical psychology (PhD); experimental psychology (PhD), including cognition and development, vision and hearing. *Accreditation:* APA. *Students:* 54 full-time (42 women), 2 part-time (both women); includes 10 minority (3 Black or African American, non-Hispanic/Latino; 2 Asian, non-Hispanic/Latino; 3 Hispanic/Latino; 2 Two or more races, non-Hispanic/Latino), 1 international. Average age 28. 21 applicants, 5% accepted, 2 enrolled. In 2016, 1 doctorate awarded. *Degree requirements:* For doctorate, comprehensive exam, thesis/dissertation, internship (for clinical psychology). *Entrance requirements:* For doctorate, GRE General Test, GRE Subject Test. Additional exam requirements/recommendations for international students: Required—TOEFL. *Application deadline:* For fall and winter admission, 12/1 for domestic and international students. Application fee: $60. *Expenses:* Tuition, state resident: full-time $12,246; part-time $681 per credit hour. Tuition, nonresident: full-time $25,486; part-time $1417 per credit hour. *Required fees:* $196. Tuition and fees vary according to program and reciprocity agreements. *Financial support:* In 2016–17, 6 fellowships with full tuition reimbursements (averaging $22,000 per year), 1 research assistantship with full tuition reimbursement (averaging $22,000 per year), 1 teaching assistantship with full tuition reimbursement (averaging $22,000 per year) were awarded; health care benefits and unspecified assistantships also available. Financial award application deadline: 12/1. *Faculty research:* Cognitive development, hearing/visual science, cognitive neuroscience/imaging, health psychology/mindfulness/stress and trauma, child/adult psychopathology, geropsychology. *Total annual research expenditures:* $1.8 million. *Unit head:* Dr. Suzanne Meeks, Chair, 502-852-6068, Fax: 502-852-8904, E-mail: smeeks@louisville.edu. *Application contact:* Libby Leggett, Director, Graduate Admissions, 502-852-3101, Fax: 502-852-6536, E-mail: gradadm@louisville.edu.
Website: http://louisville.edu/psychology

**University of Maryland, College Park,** Academic Affairs, College of Behavioral and Social Sciences, Department of Psychology, College Park, MD 20742. Offers clinical psychology (PhD); developmental psychology (PhD); experimental psychology (PhD); industrial psychology (MA, MS, PhD); social psychology (PhD). *Accreditation:* APA (one or more programs are accredited). *Degree requirements:* For master's, thesis; for doctorate, variable foreign language requirement, comprehensive exam, thesis/dissertation. *Entrance requirements:* For master's and doctorate, GRE General Test, GRE Subject Test, minimum GPA of 3.5, research and/or work experience, 3 letters of recommendation. Electronic applications accepted. *Faculty research:* Social stereotyping and prejudice, anxiety disorders, auditory neuroethology, counseling and social psychology.

**University of Massachusetts Dartmouth,** Graduate School, College of Arts and Sciences, Department of Psychology, North Dartmouth, MA 02747-2300. Offers applied behavioral analysis (MA, Post-Master's Certificate); autism studies (Graduate Certificate); clinical psychology (MA); research psychology (MA). *Program availability:* Part-time, 100% online, blended/hybrid learning. *Faculty:* 19 full-time (12 women), 7 part-time/adjunct (3 women). *Students:* 34 full-time (27 women), 50 part-time (39 women); includes 17 minority (3 Black or African American, non-Hispanic/Latino; 1 Asian, non-Hispanic/Latino; 8 Hispanic/Latino; 5 Two or more races, non-Hispanic/Latino). Average age 29. 99 applicants, 57% accepted, 32 enrolled. In 2016, 25 master's, 2 other advanced degrees awarded. *Degree requirements:* For master's,

## Experimental Psychology

thesis or comprehensive exam (for clinical psychology); thesis (for research psychology). *Entrance requirements:* For master's, GRE (for research psychology), statement of purpose (minimum of 300 words), resume, 3 letters of recommendation, official transcripts; for other advanced degree, statement of purpose (minimum of 300 words), resume, 3 letters of recommendation, official transcripts. Additional exam requirements/recommendations for international students: Required—TOEFL (minimum score 533 paper-based; 72 iBT). *Application deadline:* For fall admission, 3/1 priority date for domestic students, 2/1 priority date for international students; for spring admission, 12/20 priority date for domestic students, 11/20 priority date for international students. Application fee: $60. Electronic applications accepted. *Expenses:* Tuition, state resident: full-time $14,994; part-time $624.75 per credit. Tuition, nonresident: full-time $27,068; part-time $1127.83 per credit. *Required fees:* $405; $25.88 per credit. Tuition and fees vary according to course load and reciprocity agreements. *Financial support:* In 2016–17, 2 fellowships (averaging $7,000 per year) were awarded; institutionally sponsored loans, scholarships/grants, and unspecified assistantships also available. Support available to part-time students. Financial award application deadline: 3/1; financial award applicants required to submit FAFSA. *Faculty research:* Behavioral medicine, learning, social and developmental psychology, child neuropsychology, clinical research, counseling, psychotherapy, nonverbal communication, emotion, cognition, problem solving. *Total annual research expenditures:* $500,000. *Unit head:* Mahzad Hojjat, Graduate Program Director, Research Psychology, 508-999-8951, E-mail: mhojjat@umassd.edu. *Application contact:* Steven Briggs, Director of Marketing and Recruitment for Graduate Studies, 508-999-8604, Fax: 508-999-8183, E-mail: graduate@umassd.edu.
Website: http://www.umassd.edu/cas/psychology/graduateprograms

**University of Memphis,** Graduate School, College of Arts and Sciences, Department of Psychology, Memphis, TN 38152-3230. Offers clinical psychology (PhD); experimental psychology (PhD); general psychology (MS); school psychology (MA, PhD, Ed S). *Accreditation:* APA. *Faculty:* 27 full-time (12 women), 2 part-time/adjunct (0 women). *Students:* 97 full-time (70 women), 17 part-time (11 women); includes 29 minority (16 Black or African American, non-Hispanic/Latino; 5 Asian, non-Hispanic/Latino; 4 Hispanic/Latino; 4 Two or more races, non-Hispanic/Latino), 5 international. Average age 27. 278 applicants, 17% accepted, 35 enrolled. In 2016, 34 master's, 2 doctorates, 9 other advanced degrees awarded. *Degree requirements:* For master's, comprehensive exam (for some programs), thesis (for some programs), 37 credit hours (for MA); 33 credit hours with thesis or 36 with exam (for MS); for doctorate, comprehensive exam, thesis/dissertation, 80 semester hours, major area paper; 1-year placement and 1-year internship (for clinical psychology); internship (for school psychology); for Ed S, 30 credit hours. *Entrance requirements:* For master's, GRE, 3 letters of recommendation, 18 undergraduate hours in psychology; for doctorate, GRE, minimum GPA of 2.75, 18 hours of undergraduate psychology courses, transcripts, personal statement, 3 letters of recommendation, interview; for Ed S, GRE, minimum GPA of 2.75, 18 hours of undergraduate psychology courses, 3 letters of recommendation. Additional exam requirements/recommendations for international students: Required—TOEFL (minimum score 550 paper-based; 79 iBT). *Application deadline:* For fall admission, 12/5 for domestic students. Applications are processed on a rolling basis. Application fee: $35 ($60 for international students). Electronic applications accepted. *Expenses:* $5,231.50 per semester full-time in-state, $9,623.50 full-time out-of-state. *Financial support:* In 2016–17, 66 students received support, including 60 research assistantships with full tuition reimbursements available (averaging $17,582 per year), 21 teaching assistantships with full tuition reimbursements available (averaging $6,220 per year); fellowships with full tuition reimbursements available, Federal Work-Study, scholarships/grants, tuition waivers (partial), and unspecified assistantships also available. Financial award application deadline: 2/1; financial award applicants required to submit FAFSA. *Faculty research:* Clinical health; school, child and family psychology; psychotherapy; cognitive and behavioral neuroscience; industrial-organizational psychology. *Unit head:* Dr. Frank Andrasik, Chair, 901-678-2145, Fax: 901-678-2579, E-mail: rcohen@memphis.edu. *Application contact:* Dr. Robert Cohen, Coordinator of Graduate Studies, 901-678-4679, Fax: 901-678-2579, E-mail: rcohen@memphis.edu.
Website: http://www.memphis.edu/psychology

**University of Mississippi,** Graduate School, College of Liberal Arts, University, MS 38677. Offers anthropology (MA); biology (MS, PhD); chemistry (MS, PhD); economics (MA, PhD); English (MA, PhD); experimental psychology (PhD); history (MA, PhD); mathematics (MS, PhD); modern languages (MA); music (MM); philosophy (MA); physics (MA, MS, PhD); political science (MA, PhD); studio art (MFA). *Program availability:* Part-time. *Faculty:* 472 full-time (263 women), 75 part-time/adjunct (35 women). *Students:* 415 full-time (210 women), 57 part-time (20 women); includes 70 minority (35 Black or African American, non-Hispanic/Latino; 13 Asian, non-Hispanic/Latino; 14 Hispanic/Latino; 8 Two or more races, non-Hispanic/Latino), 102 international. Average age 27. *Degree requirements:* For doctorate, thesis/dissertation. *Entrance requirements:* For master's, GRE General Test, minimum GPA of 3.0; for doctorate, GRE General Test. Additional exam requirements/recommendations for international students: Required—TOEFL. *Application deadline:* For fall admission, 4/1 for domestic students; for spring admission, 10/1 for domestic students. Applications are processed on a rolling basis. Application fee: $40. Electronic applications accepted. *Financial support:* Fellowships, research assistantships, teaching assistantships, career-related internships or fieldwork, Federal Work-Study, institutionally sponsored loans, scholarships/grants, and unspecified assistantships available. Financial award application deadline: 3/1; financial award applicants required to submit FAFSA. *Unit head:* Dr. Lee Michael Cohen, Dean, 662-915-7177, Fax: 662-915-5792, E-mail: libarts@olemiss.edu. *Application contact:* Dr. Christy M. Wyandt, Associate Dean of Graduate School, 662-915-7474, Fax: 662-915-7577, E-mail: cwyandt@olemiss.edu.
Website: https://www.olemiss.edu

**University of Montana,** Graduate School, College of Humanities and Sciences, Department of Psychology, Missoula, MT 59812-0002. Offers clinical psychology (PhD); experimental psychology (PhD), including animal behavior psychology, developmental psychology; school psychology (MA, PhD, Ed S). *Accreditation:* APA (one or more programs are accredited). Terminal master's awarded for partial completion of doctoral program. *Degree requirements:* For master's, thesis; for doctorate, thesis/dissertation. *Entrance requirements:* For master's, doctorate, and Ed S, GRE General Test. Additional exam requirements/recommendations for international students: Required—TOEFL.

**University of New Brunswick Saint John,** Department of Psychology, Saint John, NB E2L 4L5, Canada. Offers clinical psychology (PhD); experimental psychology (MA, PhD). *Program availability:* Part-time. *Degree requirements:* For master's, thesis. *Entrance requirements:* For master's, GRE General and Subject Tests, honors thesis; minimum GPA of 3.7. Additional exam requirements/recommendations for international students: Required—TOEFL (minimum score 550 paper-based), TWE. Electronic applications accepted. *Faculty research:* Forensic psychology, peer relationships and social skills, polygraph techniques, addictions, attachment and social adjustment, neuroscience, optical illusions, graphical perception, associative learning in animals, bio-psychology.

**University of Regina,** Faculty of Graduate Studies and Research, Faculty of Arts, Department of Psychology, Regina, SK S4S 0A2, Canada. Offers clinical psychology (MA, PhD); experimental and applied psychology (MA, PhD). *Faculty:* 20 full-time (9 women), 8 part-time/adjunct (0 women). *Students:* 26 full-time (23 women). 28 applicants, 21% accepted. In 2016, 9 master's, 5 doctorates awarded. *Degree requirements:* For master's, thesis; for doctorate, comprehensive exam, thesis/ dissertation. *Entrance requirements:* For master's, GRE General Test; for doctorate, GRE General Test and GRE Subject Test (optional for those with a master's degree from a Canadian university). Additional exam requirements/recommendations for international students: Required—TOEFL (minimum score 580 paper-based; 80 iBT), IELTS (minimum score 6.5), PTE (minimum score 59). *Application deadline:* For fall admission, 1/15 for domestic and international students. Application fee: $100. Electronic applications accepted. *Financial support:* In 2016–17, 7 fellowships (averaging $6,714 per year), 17 teaching assistantships (averaging $2,566 per year) were awarded; career-related internships or fieldwork and scholarships/grants also available. Financial award application deadline: 6/15. *Faculty research:* Clinical, experimental, cognitive, and applied psychology; post-traumatic stress disorder, anxiety, and panic disorder; traumatic brain injury; chronic pain; perception and memory. *Unit head:* Dr. Richard MacLennan, Department Head, 306-585-4458, Fax: 306-585-5429, E-mail: richard.maclennan@uregina.ca.
Website: http://www.uregina.ca/arts/psychology

**University of South Carolina,** The Graduate School, College of Arts and Sciences, Department of Psychology, Program in Experimental Psychology, Columbia, SC 29208. Offers MA, PhD. Terminal master's awarded for partial completion of doctoral program. *Degree requirements:* For master's, comprehensive exam, thesis; for doctorate, comprehensive exam, thesis/dissertation. *Entrance requirements:* For master's and doctorate, GRE General Test. Additional exam requirements/recommendations for international students: Required—TOEFL. Electronic applications accepted. *Faculty research:* Cognition, development, neuroscience.

**The University of Tennessee,** Graduate School, College of Arts and Sciences, Department of Psychology, Knoxville, TN 37996. Offers clinical psychology (PhD); experimental psychology (MA, PhD); psychology (MA). *Accreditation:* APA (one or more programs are accredited). Terminal master's awarded for partial completion of doctoral program. *Degree requirements:* For master's, thesis; for doctorate, thesis/dissertation. *Entrance requirements:* For master's and doctorate, GRE General Test, GRE Subject Test, minimum GPA of 2.7. Additional exam requirements/recommendations for international students: Required—TOEFL. Electronic applications accepted.

**The University of Tennessee at Chattanooga,** Program in Psychology, Chattanooga, TN 37403. Offers industrial/organizational psychology (MS); research psychology (MS). *Program availability:* Part-time. *Faculty:* 13 full-time (6 women), 1 part-time/adjunct (0 women). *Students:* 41 full-time (25 women), 7 part-time (3 women); includes 5 minority (2 Black or African American, non-Hispanic/Latino; 1 Hispanic/Latino; 2 Two or more races, non-Hispanic/Latino). Average age 26. 99 applicants, 29% accepted, 25 enrolled. In 2016, 21 master's awarded. *Degree requirements:* For master's, comprehensive exam (for some programs), thesis (for some programs), practicum (industrial/ organizational psychology). *Entrance requirements:* For master's, GRE General Test, minimum GPA of 2.5 on all undergraduate coursework or 3.0 in senior year. Additional exam requirements/recommendations for international students: Required—TOEFL (minimum score 550 paper-based; 79 iBT), IELTS (minimum score 6). *Application deadline:* For fall admission, 6/15 priority date for domestic students, 7/1 for international students; for spring admission, 11/1 priority date for domestic students, 11/1 for international students. Applications are processed on a rolling basis. Application fee: $35 ($40 for international students). Electronic applications accepted. *Expenses:* $9,876 full-time in-state; $25,994 full-time out-of-state; $450 per credit part-time in-state; $1,345 per credit part-time out-of-state. *Financial support:* In 2016–17, 23 research assistantships, 1 teaching assistantship were awarded; career-related internships or fieldwork, scholarships/grants, and unspecified assistantships also available. Support available to part-time students. Financial award application deadline: 7/1; financial award applicants required to submit FAFSA. *Faculty research:* Decision processes, philosophical psychology, memory, social cognition, employee selection. *Total annual research expenditures:* $8,500. *Unit head:* Dr. Brian O'Leary, Department Head, 423-425-4283, Fax: 423-425-4284, E-mail: brian-o'leary@utc.edu. *Application contact:* Dr. Joanne Romagni, Dean of the Graduate School, 423-425-4478, Fax: 423-425-5223, E-mail: joanne-romagni@utc.edu.
Website: http://www.utc.edu/psychology/

**The University of Texas at Arlington,** Graduate School, College of Science, Department of Psychology, Arlington, TX 76019. Offers experimental health psychology (PhD); experimental psychology (MS, PhD); health/neuroscience psychology (MS, PhD); industrial and organizational psychology (MS). *Program availability:* Part-time. Terminal master's awarded for partial completion of doctoral program. *Degree requirements:* For master's, comprehensive exam or thesis; for doctorate, thesis/ dissertation (for some programs). *Entrance requirements:* For master's and doctorate, GRE General Test, minimum GPA of 3.0 in last 60 hours of course work. Additional exam requirements/recommendations for international students: Required—TOEFL (minimum score 550 paper-based). *Application deadline:* For fall admission, 6/15 for domestic students. Applications are processed on a rolling basis. Application fee: $50. *Financial support:* Fellowships, research assistantships with partial tuition reimbursements, teaching assistantships with partial tuition reimbursements, career-related internships or fieldwork, Federal Work-Study, institutionally sponsored loans, scholarships/grants, traineeships, and unspecified assistantships available. Financial award application deadline: 6/1; financial award applicants required to submit FAFSA. *Unit head:* Dr. Robert Gatchel, Professor/Chair, 817-272-2281, Fax: 817-272-2364, E-mail: gatchel@uta.edu. *Application contact:* Dr. Jared Kenworthy, Graduate Advisor, Psychological Sciences, 817-272-2281, Fax: 817-272-2364, E-mail: kenworthy@uta.edu.
Website: http://www.uta.edu/psychology/

**The University of Texas at El Paso,** Graduate School, College of Liberal Arts, Department of Psychology, El Paso, TX 79968-0001. Offers clinical psychology (MA); experimental psychology (MA); psychology (PhD). *Program availability:* Part-time, evening/weekend. *Degree requirements:* For master's, thesis; for doctorate, thesis/ dissertation. *Entrance requirements:* For master's, GRE, letters of recommendation; for doctorate, GRE, statement of purpose, letters of recommendation. Additional exam requirements/recommendations for international students: Required—TOEFL; Recommended—IELTS. Electronic applications accepted.

**The University of Texas of the Permian Basin,** Office of Graduate Studies, College of Arts and Sciences, Department of Psychology, Odessa, TX 79762-0001. Offers applied research psychology (MA); clinical psychology (MA). *Program availability:* Part-time, evening/weekend. *Degree requirements:* For master's, comprehensive exam, thesis, practicum. *Entrance requirements:* For master's, GRE General Test, 3 letters of recommendation. Additional exam requirements/recommendations for international students: Required—TOEFL (minimum score 550 paper-based).

**The University of Texas Rio Grande Valley,** College of Liberal Arts, Department of Psychological Science, Edinburg, TX 78539. Offers psychology (MA), including clinical psychology, experimental psychology. *Program availability:* Part-time, evening/weekend. *Degree requirements:* For master's, comprehensive exam, thesis optional, internship. *Entrance requirements:* For master's, GRE, letters of recommendation. Additional exam requirements/recommendations for international students: Required—TOEFL. Electronic applications accepted. Tuition and fees vary according to course load and program. *Faculty research:* Biofeedback, acculturation, health, stress/trauma, neuropsychological assessment, false memories, children's theory of mind.

**The University of Toledo,** College of Graduate Studies, College of Languages, Literature and Social Sciences, Department of Psychology, Toledo, OH 43606-3390. Offers clinical psychology (MA, PhD); experimental psychology (MA, PhD). *Accreditation:* APA. *Degree requirements:* For master's, comprehensive exam, thesis; for doctorate, comprehensive exam, thesis/dissertation. *Entrance requirements:* For master's and doctorate, GRE General Test, GRE Subject Test, minimum cumulative point-hour ratio of 2.7 for all previous academic work, three letters of recommendation, statement of purpose, transcripts from all prior institutions attended. Additional exam requirements/recommendations for international students: Required—TOEFL (minimum score 550 paper-based; 80 iBT). Electronic applications accepted. *Faculty research:* Neural taste response.

**University of Victoria,** Faculty of Graduate Studies, Faculty of Social Sciences, Department of Psychology, Victoria, BC V8W 2Y2, Canada. Offers clinical psychology (PhD); clinical psychology (neuropsychology) (M Sc); cognition and brain science (M Sc, PhD); experimental neuropsychology (M Sc, PhD); individualized study (M Sc, PhD); life span development psychology (PhD); life span developmental psychology (M Sc); social psychology (M Sc, PhD). *Degree requirements:* For master's, thesis; for doctorate, thesis/dissertation, candidacy exam. *Entrance requirements:* For master's and doctorate, GRE General Test. Additional exam requirements/recommendations for international students: Required—TOEFL (minimum score 600 paper-based). Electronic applications accepted. *Faculty research:* Life span development psychology and aging, behavioral neuroscience, cognitive psychology, behavioral psychology, environmental psychology.

**The University of West Alabama,** School of Graduate Studies, College of Liberal Arts, Livingston, AL 35470. Offers experimental psychology (MS). *Program availability:* Part-time, evening/weekend, 100% online. *Faculty:* 3 full-time (1 woman), 7 part-time/adjunct (4 women). *Students:* 11 (9 women); includes 3 minority (all Black or African American, non-Hispanic/Latino). Average age 28. 9 applicants, 56% accepted, 5 enrolled. In 2016, 1 master's awarded. *Degree requirements:* For master's, thesis. *Entrance requirements:* For master's, GRE General Test, minimum GPA of 3.0. Additional exam requirements/recommendations for international students: Required—TOEFL (minimum score 500 paper-based; 61 iBT). *Application deadline:* Applications are processed on a rolling basis. Application fee: $40. Electronic applications accepted. *Expenses:* Tuition, state resident: part-time $355 per credit hour. Tuition, nonresident: part-time $710 per credit hour. *Required fees:* $130 per semester. *Financial support:* Teaching assistantships, Federal Work-Study, scholarships/grants, and unspecified assistantships available. Support available to part-time students. Financial award application deadline: 3/1; financial award applicants required to submit FAFSA. *Unit head:* Dr. Mark Davis, Dean, 205-652-3570, Fax: 205-652-3717, E-mail: mdavis@uwa.edu.
Website: http://www.uwa.edu/cola/

**University of West Florida,** College of Arts, Social Sciences, and Humanities, Department of Psychology, Pensacola, FL 32514-5750. Offers applied experimental (MA); counseling (MA); industrial-organizational (MA). *Program availability:* Part-time. *Degree requirements:* For master's, thesis (for some programs). *Entrance requirements:* For master's, GRE, official transcripts; minimum GPA of 3.0; writing sample; three letters of reference; field experience or skill sets; oral interview (for counseling specialization). Additional exam requirements/recommendations for international students: Required—TOEFL (minimum score 550 paper-based). *Application deadline:* For fall admission, 6/1 for domestic and international students; for spring admission, 10/1 for domestic and international students. Applications are processed on a rolling basis. Application fee: $30. *Expenses:* Tuition, state resident: full-time $5316.12. Tuition, nonresident: full-time $11,308. *Required fees:* $583.92. Tuition and fees vary according to course load and program. *Financial support:* Fellowships with partial tuition reimbursements, research assistantships with partial tuition reimbursements, teaching assistantships with partial tuition reimbursements, career-related internships or fieldwork, and unspecified assistantships available. Financial award application deadline: 4/15; financial award applicants required to submit FAFSA. *Faculty research:* Prose recall, brain imaging, peak performance, biofeedback and pain control, comparable worth. *Unit head:* Dr. Robert Belter, Interim Department Chair, 850-474-2791, E-mail: rbelter@uwf.edu. *Application contact:* Dr. Robert Belter, Interim Department Chair, 850-474-2791, E-mail: rbelter@uwf.edu.
Website: http://www.uwf.edu/psychology/

**University of Wisconsin–Milwaukee,** Graduate School, College of Letters and Science, Department of Psychology, Milwaukee, WI 53201-0413. Offers experimental psychology (MS, PhD), including behavior analysis, health and social psychology (PhD), health psychology (MS), neuroscience (PhD); psychology (PhD), including clinical psychology. *Accreditation:* APA (one or more programs are accredited). *Students:* 67 full-time (46 women), 19 part-time (11 women); includes 8 minority (2 Asian, non-

Hispanic/Latino; 1 Hispanic/Latino; 5 Two or more races, non-Hispanic/Latino), 9 international. Average age 28. 254 applicants, 7% accepted, 16 enrolled. In 2016, 15 master's, 10 doctorates awarded. *Degree requirements:* For master's, thesis; for doctorate, variable foreign language requirement, thesis/dissertation. *Entrance requirements:* For master's and doctorate, GRE General Test, GRE Subject Test. Additional exam requirements/recommendations for international students: Required—TOEFL (minimum score 550 paper-based; 79 iBT), IELTS (minimum score 6.5). *Application deadline:* For fall admission, 1/1 priority date for domestic students; for spring admission, 9/1 for domestic students. Applications are processed on a rolling basis. Application fee: $56 ($96 for international students). Electronic applications accepted. *Financial support:* In 2016–17, 8 fellowships, 6 research assistantships, 46 teaching assistantships were awarded; career-related internships or fieldwork, unspecified assistantships, and project assistantships also available. Support available to part-time students. Financial award application deadline: 4/15; financial award applicants required to submit FAFSA. *Unit head:* Douglas Woods, Department Chair, 414-229-6636, E-mail: dwoods@uwm.edu. *Application contact:* General Information Contact, 414-229-4982, Fax: 414-229-6967, E-mail: gradschool@uwm.edu.
Website: http://www.uwm.edu/dept/psychology/

**University of Wisconsin–Oshkosh,** Graduate Studies, College of Letters and Science, Department of Psychology, Oshkosh, WI 54901. Offers experimental psychology (MS); industrial/organizational psychology (MS). *Degree requirements:* For master's, thesis. *Entrance requirements:* For master's, GRE, 10 semester hours of undergraduate course work in psychology. Additional exam requirements/recommendations for international students: Required—TOEFL (minimum score 550 paper-based; 79 iBT). Electronic applications accepted. *Faculty research:* Performance evaluation, training, biological bases of behavior, tactile perception, aging.

**Washington State University,** College of Arts and Sciences, Department of Psychology, Pullman, WA 99164. Offers clinical psychology (PhD); experimental psychology (PhD). Program applications must be made through the Pullman campus. *Accreditation:* APA (one or more programs are accredited). *Degree requirements:* For doctorate, comprehensive exam, thesis/dissertation, oral exam, written exam. *Entrance requirements:* For doctorate, GRE General Test, three letters of reference; summary data form; at least 18 credits of study in psychology; at least one course in statistics and research methodology; official transcripts; minimum cumulative undergraduate GPA of 3.0 or master's degree in psychology. Additional exam requirements/recommendations for international students: Required—TOEFL, IELTS. Electronic applications accepted. *Faculty research:* Adult psychopathology and therapy, child psychopathology, neuropsychology, health psychology.

**Western Illinois University,** School of Graduate Studies, College of Arts and Sciences, Department of Psychology, Macomb, IL 61455-1390. Offers clinical/community mental health (MS); general experimental psychology (MS); school psychology (SSP). *Program availability:* Part-time. *Students:* 37 full-time (22 women), 15 part-time (13 women); includes 6 minority (1 Black or African American, non-Hispanic/Latino; 2 Hispanic/Latino; 3 Two or more races, non-Hispanic/Latino), 2 international. Average age 25. 66 applicants, 52% accepted, 14 enrolled. In 2016, 11 master's, 7 other advanced degrees awarded. *Degree requirements:* For master's, comprehensive exam (for some programs), thesis or alternative. *Entrance requirements:* For master's and SSP, GRE General Test. Additional exam requirements/recommendations for international students: Required—TOEFL (minimum score 550 paper-based; 80 iBT). Application fee: $30. Electronic applications accepted. *Financial support:* In 2016–17, 34 students received support, including 6 research assistantships with full tuition reimbursements available (averaging $7,544 per year); unspecified assistantships also available. Financial award applicants required to submit FAFSA. *Unit head:* Dr. Karen Sears, Chairperson, 309-298-1593. *Application contact:* Dr. Nancy Parsons, Associate Provost and Director of Graduate Studies, 309-298-1806, Fax: 309-298-2345, E-mail: grad-office@wiu.edu.
Website: http://wiu.edu/psychology

**Western Kentucky University,** Graduate Studies, College of Education and Behavioral Sciences, Department of Psychology, Bowling Green, KY 42101. Offers clinical psychology (MA); experimental psychology (MA); general psychology (MA); industrial/organizational psychology (MA); school psychology (Ed S). *Degree requirements:* For master's, comprehensive exam, thesis (for some programs); for Ed S, thesis, oral exam. *Entrance requirements:* For master's, GRE General Test; for Ed S, GRE General Test, minimum GPA of 3.5. Additional exam requirements/recommendations for international students: Required—TOEFL (minimum score 555 paper-based; 79 iBT). *Faculty research:* Neural regeneration, enhancing mobility in the elderly, improvement in visual processing in older adults, lifespan development.

**Western Washington University,** Graduate School, College of Humanities and Social Sciences, Department of Psychology, Program in Experimental Psychology, Bellingham, WA 98225-5996. Offers MS. *Degree requirements:* For master's, thesis. *Entrance requirements:* For master's, GRE General Test, minimum GPA of 3.0 in last 60 semester hours or last 90 quarter hours. Additional exam requirements/recommendations for international students: Required—TOEFL (minimum score 567 paper-based). Electronic applications accepted.

# Forensic Psychology

**Adler University,** Programs in Psychology, Chicago, IL 60602. Offers advanced Adlerian psychotherapy (Certificate); art therapy (MA); clinical mental health counseling (MA); clinical neuropsychology (Certificate); clinical psychology (Psy D); community psychology (MA); counseling and organizational psychology (MA); counseling psychology (MA); counselor education and supervision (PhD); couple and family therapy (DCFT); criminology (MA); emergency management leadership (MA); forensic psychology (MA); marriage and family counseling (MA); marriage and family therapy (Certificate); military psychology (MA); nonprofit management (MA); organizational psychology (MA); police psychology (MA); public policy and administration (MA); rehabilitation counseling (MA); sport and health psychology (MA); substance abuse counseling (Certificate); Psy D/Certificate; Psy D/MACAT; Psy D/MACP; Psy D/MAMFC; Psy D/MASAC. *Accreditation:* APA. *Program availability:* Part-time, evening/weekend, online learning. Terminal master's awarded for partial completion of doctoral program. *Degree requirements:* For master's, thesis or alternative, oral exam, practicum; for doctorate, thesis/dissertation, clinical exam, internship, oral exam, practicum, written qualifying exam. *Entrance requirements:* For master's, 12 semester hours in psychology, minimum GPA of 3.0; for doctorate, 18 semester hours in psychology, minimum GPA of 3.25; for Certificate, appropriate master's or doctoral

degree. Additional exam requirements/recommendations for international students: Required—TOEFL (minimum score 550 paper-based; 79 iBT). Electronic applications accepted.

**See Display on page 982 and Close-Up on page 1225.**

**Alliant International University–Fresno,** California School of Forensic Studies, PhD Program in Clinical Forensic Psychology, Fresno, CA 93727. Offers PhD. *Degree requirements:* For doctorate, comprehensive exam, thesis/dissertation, research internship. *Entrance requirements:* For doctorate, minimum GPA of 3.0, letters of recommendation, essay, interview. Additional exam requirements/recommendations for international students: Required—TOEFL (minimum score 550 paper-based), TWE (minimum score 5). *Faculty research:* Effects of stress in law enforcement officers, treatment for mentally ill offenders, psychotic disorders and violence, behavioral threat assessment/risk analysis, juvenile delinquency.

**Alliant International University–Fresno,** California School of Forensic Studies, PsyD Program in Clinical Forensic Psychology, Fresno, CA 93727. Offers victimology (Psy D). *Degree requirements:* For doctorate, comprehensive exam, thesis/dissertation, internship. *Entrance requirements:* For doctorate, minimum GPA of 3.0,

*Forensic Psychology*

recommendations, essay, interview. Additional exam requirements/recommendations for international students: Required—TOEFL (minimum score 550 paper-based), TWE (minimum score 5). Electronic applications accepted. *Faculty research:* Correctional psychology, psychopathology, police psychology, substance abuse and ADHD, investigative psychology.

**Alliant International University–Irvine,** California School of Forensic Studies, Irvine, CA 92606. Offers Psy D. *Degree requirements:* For doctorate, comprehensive exam, thesis/dissertation, internship. *Entrance requirements:* For doctorate, minimum GPA of 3.0, recommendations, essay. Additional exam requirements/recommendations for international students: Required—TOEFL (minimum score 80 iBT), TWE (minimum score 5). Electronic applications accepted. *Faculty research:* Detecting deception, psychological safety of undercover police officers, domestic violence, risk assessment, competency evaluations.

**Alliant International University–Los Angeles,** California School of Forensic Studies, Alhambra, CA 91803. Offers forensic psychology (Psy D). *Degree requirements:* For doctorate, comprehensive exam, thesis/dissertation. *Entrance requirements:* For doctorate, interview; master's degree in psychology, forensic psychology, criminology, criminal justice, social work or law; minimum GPA of 3.0 in psychology and overall. Additional exam requirements/recommendations for international students: Required— TOEFL (minimum score 600 paper-based), TWE (minimum score 5). *Faculty research:* Court testimony, juvenile offenders, violence risk assessment, Miranda rights, police psychology.

**Alliant International University–Sacramento,** California School of Forensic Studies, Program in Clinical Forensic Psychology, Sacramento, CA 95833. Offers Psy D. *Degree requirements:* For doctorate, comprehensive exam, thesis/dissertation. *Entrance requirements:* For doctorate, minimum GPA of 3.0, recommendations, essay. Additional exam requirements/recommendations for international students: Required—TOEFL (minimum score 550 paper-based; 80 iBT), TWE (minimum score 5). Electronic applications accepted. *Faculty research:* Correctional mental health treatment, psychopathy, child maltreatment, interventions for delinquent youth, malingering.

**Alliant International University–San Diego,** California School of Forensic Studies, Psy D Program in Clinical Forensic Psychology, San Diego, CA 92131. Offers Psy D. *Degree requirements:* For doctorate, comprehensive exam, internship. *Entrance requirements:* Additional exam requirements/recommendations for international students: Required—TOEFL (minimum score 550 paper-based; 80 iBT), TWE (minimum score 5).

**Alliant International University–San Francisco,** California School of Forensic Studies, San Francisco, CA 94133. Offers applied criminology (MS), including victimology; clinical forensic psychology (PhD, Psy D). *Degree requirements:* For doctorate, comprehensive exam, thesis/dissertation, internship. *Entrance requirements:* For master's, minimum GPA of 3.0, recommendations, essay; for doctorate, minimum GPA of 3.0, recommendations, essay, interview. Additional exam requirements/ recommendations for international students: Required—TOEFL (minimum score 550 paper-based; 80 iBT), TWE (minimum score 5). *Faculty research:* Post-traumatic stress disorder, correctional mental health.

**American International College,** School of Business, Arts and Sciences, Springfield, MA 01109-3189. Offers accounting and taxation (MS); business administration (MBA); clinical psychology (MA); educational psychology (Ed D); forensic psychology (MS); general psychology (MA, CAGS); management (CAGS); resort and casino management (MBA, CAGS). *Program availability:* Part-time, evening/weekend. *Degree requirements:* For master's, comprehensive exam (for some programs), thesis (for some programs), practicum; for doctorate, comprehensive exam (for some programs), thesis/dissertation; for CAGS, comprehensive exam (for some programs), thesis (for some programs). *Entrance requirements:* For master's, BS or BA; for doctorate, interview. Additional exam requirements/recommendations for international students: Required—TOEFL (minimum score 550 paper-based; 80 iBT). *Expenses: Tuition:* Full-time $7902; part-time $750 per semester hour. *Required fees:* $60; $60 per semester hour. $30 per semester. One-time fee: $100. Tuition and fees vary according to course load, degree level, campus/location and program.

**Argosy University, Atlanta,** Georgia School of Professional Psychology, Atlanta, GA 30328. Offers clinical psychology (MA, Psy D, Postdoctoral Respecialization Certificate), including child and family psychology (Psy D), general adult clinical (Psy D), health psychology (Psy D), neuropsychology/geropsychology (Psy D); community counseling (MA), including marriage and family therapy; counselor education and supervision (Ed D); forensic psychology (MA); industrial organizational psychology (MA); marriage and family therapy (Certificate); sport-exercise psychology (MA). *Accreditation:* APA.

**Argosy University, Chicago,** Illinois School of Professional Psychology, Doctoral Program in Clinical Psychology, Chicago, IL 60601. Offers child and adolescent psychology (Psy D); client-centered and experiential psychotherapies (Psy D); diversity and multicultural psychology (Psy D); family psychology (Psy D); forensic psychology (Psy D); health psychology (Psy D); neuropsychology (Psy D); organizational consulting (Psy D); psychoanalytic psychology (Psy D); psychology and spirituality (Psy D). *Accreditation:* APA.

**Argosy University, Dallas,** College of Psychology and Behavioral Sciences, Program in Forensic Psychology, Farmers Branch, TX 75244. Offers MA.

**Argosy University, Denver,** College of Psychology and Behavioral Sciences, Denver, CO 80231. Offers clinical mental health counseling (MA); clinical psychology (MA, Psy D); counseling psychology (Ed D); counselor education and supervision (Ed D); forensic psychology (MA); industrial organizational psychology (MA); marriage and family therapy (MA, DMFT).

**Argosy University, Hawai`i,** Hawai'i School of Professional Psychology, Program in Forensic Psychology, Honolulu, HI 96813. Offers MA.

**Argosy University, Inland Empire,** College of Psychology and Behavioral Sciences, Ontario, CA 91761. Offers clinical psychology/marriage and family therapy (MA); counseling psychology (Ed D); counseling psychology/marriage and family therapy (MA); forensic psychology (MA); industrial organizational psychology (MA); sport-exercise psychology (MA).

**Argosy University, Los Angeles,** College of Psychology and Behavioral Sciences, Santa Monica, CA 90045. Offers clinical psychology/marriage and family therapy (MA); counseling psychology (Ed D); counseling psychology/marriage and family therapy (MA); forensic psychology (MA).

**Argosy University, Northern Virginia,** American School of Professional Psychology, Arlington, VA 22209. Offers clinical psychology (MA, Psy D), including child and family psychology (Psy D), diversity and multicultural psychology (Psy D), forensic psychology (Psy D), health and neuropsychology (Psy D); community counseling (MA); counseling psychology (Ed D), including counselor education and supervision; counselor education and supervision (Ed D); forensic psychology (MA).

**Argosy University, Orange County,** American School of Professional Psychology, Program in Forensic Psychology, Orange, CA 92868. Offers MA.

**Argosy University, Phoenix,** Arizona School of Professional Psychology, Program in Forensic Psychology, Phoenix, AZ 85021. Offers MA.

**Argosy University, Salt Lake City,** College of Psychology and Behavioral Sciences, Draper, UT 84020. Offers counseling psychology (Ed D); counselor education and supervision (Ed D); forensic psychology (MA); marriage and family therapy (MA, DMFT); mental health counseling (MA).

**Argosy University, San Diego,** College of Psychology and Behavioral Sciences, San Diego, CA 92108. Offers clinical psychology/marriage and family therapy (MA); counseling psychology (Ed D); counseling psychology/marriage and family therapy (MA); forensic psychology (MA).

**Argosy University, San Francisco Bay Area,** American School of Professional Psychology, Program in Forensic Psychology, Alameda, CA 94501. Offers MA.

**Argosy University, Sarasota,** College of Psychology and Behavioral Sciences, Sarasota, FL 34235. Offers community counseling (MA); counseling psychology (Ed D); counselor education and supervision (Ed D); forensic psychology (MA); marriage and family therapy (MA); mental health counseling (MA); pastoral community counseling (Ed D).

**Argosy University, Schaumburg,** College of Behavioral Sciences, Schaumburg, IL 60173-5403. Offers clinical mental health counseling (MA); forensic psychology (MA, Post-Graduate Certificate); industrial organizational psychology (MA); sport-exercise psychology (MA). *Accreditation:* ACA; APA.

**Argosy University, Twin Cities,** Minnesota School of Professional Psychology, Eagan, MN 55121. Offers clinical psychology (MA, Psy D), including child and family psychology (Psy D), forensic psychology (Psy D), health and neuropsychology (Psy D), trauma (Psy D); forensic counseling (Post-Graduate Certificate); forensic psychology (MA); industrial organizational psychology (MA); marriage and family therapy (MA, DMFT), including forensic counseling (MA). *Accreditation:* AAMFT; AAMFT/COAMFTE; APA.

**California Baptist University,** Program in Counseling Psychology, Riverside, CA 92504-3206. Offers counseling psychology (MS); forensic psychology (MS); professional clinical counselor (MS). *Program availability:* Part-time, evening/weekend, 100% online, blended/hybrid learning. *Faculty:* 18 full-time (11 women), 10 part-time/ adjunct (7 women). *Students:* 258 full-time (211 women), 97 part-time (82 women); includes 238 minority (64 Black or African American, non-Hispanic/Latino; 1 American Indian or Alaska Native, non-Hispanic/Latino; 14 Asian, non-Hispanic/Latino; 146 Hispanic/Latino; 1 Native Hawaiian or other Pacific Islander, non-Hispanic/Latino; 12 Two or more races, non-Hispanic/Latino), 1 international. Average age 31. 98 applicants, 78% accepted, 64 enrolled. In 2016, 106 master's awarded. *Degree requirements:* For master's, comprehensive exam, 24 (individual) or 50 hours (group) of psychotherapy, practicum. *Entrance requirements:* For master's, minimum undergraduate GPA of 2.75; official transcripts; three recommendations; 500-word essay; interview; 3 prerequisite courses completed with minimum C grade. Additional exam requirements/recommendations for international students: Required—TOEFL (minimum score 80 iBT). *Application deadline:* For fall admission, 8/1 priority date for domestic students, 7/1 for international students; for spring admission, 12/1 priority date for domestic students, 11/1 for international students. Applications are processed on a rolling basis. Application fee: $45. Electronic applications accepted. *Expenses:* Contact institution. *Financial support:* In 2016–17, 79 students received support. Federal Work-Study and scholarships/grants available. Financial award applicants required to submit CSS PROFILE or FAFSA. *Faculty research:* Identify formation, faith integration, psychological assessment, child abuse and child welfare, clinical psychology and crisis intervention techniques. *Unit head:* Dr. Jacqueline Gustafson, Dean, School of Behavioral Sciences, 951-343-4487, E-mail: jcraig@calbaptist.edu. *Application contact:* Mischa Routon, Associate Dean of Graduate Programs, 951-343-4206, Fax: 951-343-4569, E-mail: mrouton@calbaptist.edu. Website: http://www.calbaptist.edu/mft/

**California Baptist University,** Program in Forensic Psychology, Riverside, CA 92504-3206. Offers MA. *Program availability:* Part-time, evening/weekend. *Faculty:* 4 full-time (3 women), 1 (woman) part-time/adjunct. *Students:* 68 full-time (55 women), 9 part-time (7 women); includes 44 minority (11 Black or African American, non-Hispanic/Latino; 31 Hispanic/Latino; 2 Two or more races, non-Hispanic/Latino), 1 international. Average age 26. 48 applicants, 75% accepted, 32 enrolled. In 2016, 20 master's awarded. *Degree requirements:* For master's, comprehensive exam, thesis or alternative, 9-month practicum. *Entrance requirements:* For master's, minimum undergraduate GPA of 2.75; three recommendations; 500-word essay; interview; four prerequisite courses completed with minimum C grade. Additional exam requirements/recommendations for international students: Required—TOEFL (minimum score 80 iBT). *Application deadline:* For fall admission, 8/1 priority date for domestic students, 7/1 for international students; for spring admission, 12/1 priority date for domestic students, 11/1 for international students. Applications are processed on a rolling basis. Application fee: $45. Electronic applications accepted. *Expenses:* Contact institution. *Financial support:* In 2016–17, 12 students received support. Federal Work-Study and scholarships/grants available. Financial award applicants required to submit CSS PROFILE or FAFSA. *Faculty research:* Criminal profiling, police psychology, post-traumatic stress disorder in law enforcement, religiosity as a protective factor in the incarcerated, media influence on perception of police. *Unit head:* Dr. Jacqueline Gustafson, Dean, School of Behavioral Sciences, 951-343-4487, E-mail: jcraig@calbaptist.edu. *Application contact:* Dr. Anne-Marie Larsen, Director, Graduate Program in Forensic Psychology, 951-343-4761, E-mail: alarsen@calbaptist.edu. Website: http://www.calbaptist.edu/for_psych/

**Cambridge College,** School of Psychology and Counseling, Cambridge, MA 02138-5304. Offers addiction counseling (M Ed); alcohol and drug counseling (Certificate); counseling psychology (M Ed, CAGS); counseling psychology: forensic counseling (M Ed); marriage and family therapy (M Ed); mental health and addiction counseling (M Ed); mental health counseling (M Ed); mental health counseling for school guidance counselors (Post Master's Certificate); psychological studies (M Ed); school adjustment and mental health counseling (M Ed); school adjustment, mental health and addiction counseling (M Ed); school guidance counselor (M Ed); trauma studies (Certificate). *Program availability:* Part-time, evening/weekend. *Degree requirements:* For master's and other advanced degree, thesis, practicum/internship. *Entrance requirements:* For master's, resume, 2 professional references; for other advanced degree, official transcripts, documents for transfer credit evaluation, resume, written personal statement/essay, 2 professional references, health insurance, immunizations form. Additional exam requirements/recommendations for international students: Required— TOEFL (minimum score 550 paper-based; 79 iBT), Michigan English Language Assessment Battery (minimum score 85); Recommended—IELTS (minimum score 6). Electronic applications accepted. *Expenses:* Contact institution. *Faculty research:* Trauma, drug and alcohol counseling, cross-cultural issues, school counseling, trauma in schools.

**Castleton University,** Division of Graduate Studies, Department of Psychology, Castleton, VT 05735. Offers forensic psychology (MA). *Degree requirements:* For master's, thesis. *Entrance requirements:* For master's, GRE General Test, minimum undergraduate GPA of 3.5, previous course work in research methodology and statistics. Additional exam requirements/recommendations for international students: Required—TOEFL. *Faculty research:* Psychology and law, juvenile delinquency, criminal psychology, correctional psychology, police psychology.

**The Chicago School of Professional Psychology,** Program in Clinical Forensic Psychology, Chicago, IL 60610. Offers Psy D. *Degree requirements:* For doctorate, thesis/dissertation. *Entrance requirements:* For doctorate, GRE. Additional exam requirements/recommendations for international students: Required—TOEFL, IELTS.

**The Chicago School of Professional Psychology,** Program in Forensic Psychology, Chicago, IL 60610. Offers MA. *Degree requirements:* For master's, thesis optional. *Entrance requirements:* For master's, GRE (highly recommended), 1 course each in research methods, statistics, and psychology. Additional exam requirements/ recommendations for international students: Required—TOEFL (minimum score 550 paper-based; 79 iBT).

**The Chicago School of Professional Psychology at Downtown Los Angeles,** Program in Clinical Forensic Psychology, Los Angeles, CA 90017. Offers Psy D.

**The Chicago School of Professional Psychology at Irvine,** Program in Clinical Forensic Psychology, Irvine, CA 92612. Offers Psy D.

**The Chicago School of Professional Psychology: Online,** Program in Forensic Psychology, Chicago, IL 60654. Offers MA, Certificate.

**College of Saint Elizabeth,** Department of Psychology, Morristown, NJ 07960-6989. Offers counseling psychology (MA); forensic psychology (MA); mental health counseling (Certificate); psychology (Psy D); student affairs in higher education (Certificate). *Program availability:* Part-time. *Degree requirements:* For master's, thesis or alternative. *Entrance requirements:* For master's, minimum GPA of 3.0, BA in psychology (preferred), 12 credits of course work in psychology; for doctorate, GRE, 3 letters of recommendation from professionals who can comment on the applicant's qualifications for doctoral study; master's degree in counseling psychology, forensic psychology and counseling, or its equivalent. Additional exam requirements/recommendations for international students: Required—TOEFL (minimum score 550 paper-based; 79 iBT), IELTS (minimum score 6.5). Electronic applications accepted. *Expenses:* Contact institution.

**Drexel University,** College of Arts and Sciences, Department of Psychology, Clinical Psychology Program, Philadelphia, PA 19104-2875. Offers clinical psychology (PhD); forensic psychology (PhD); health psychology (PhD); neuropsychology (PhD). *Accreditation:* APA. *Faculty:* 26 full-time (16 women), 8 part-time/adjunct (7 women). *Students:* 79 full-time (66 women), 8 part-time (5 women); includes 16 minority (4 Black or African American, non-Hispanic/Latino; 5 Asian, non-Hispanic/Latino; 3 Hispanic/Latino; 4 Two or more races, non-Hispanic/Latino), 4 international. Average age 27. In 2016, 10 doctorates awarded. Terminal master's awarded for partial completion of doctoral program. *Degree requirements:* For doctorate, thesis/dissertation, qualifying exam. *Entrance requirements:* For doctorate, GRE General Test, GRE Subject Test, minimum GPA of 3.0. *Application deadline:* For spring admission, 1/15 for domestic students. Application fee: $30. Electronic applications accepted. *Expenses:* Contact institution. *Financial support:* Fellowships, research assistantships, teaching assistantships, career-related internships or fieldwork, Federal Work-Study, institutionally sponsored loans, and tuition waivers (partial) available. Support available to part-time students. Financial award application deadline: 5/1; financial award applicants required to submit FAFSA. *Faculty research:* Cognitive behavioral therapy, stress and coping, eating disorders, substance abuse, developmental disabilities. *Total annual research expenditures:* $3.9 million. *Unit head:* Dr. Maria Schultheis, Head, 215-895-6105. *Application contact:* Director of Graduate Admissions, 215-895-6700, Fax: 215-895-5939, E-mail: enroll@drexel.edu.

**Fairleigh Dickinson University, Metropolitan Campus,** University College: Arts, Sciences, and Professional Studies, School of Psychology, Program in Forensic Psychology, Teaneck, NJ 07666-1914. Offers MA.

**Fielding Graduate University,** Graduate Programs, School of Psychology, Programs in Clinical Psychology, Santa Barbara, CA 93105-3814. Offers clinical psychology (Postbaccalaureate Certificate); forensic psychology (PhD); health psychology (PhD); neuropsychology (PhD); parent-infant mental health (PhD); respecialization in clinical psychology (Post-Doctoral Certificate); violence prevention and control (PhD). *Program availability:* 100% online, blended/hybrid learning. *Faculty:* 28 full-time (19 women), 22 part-time/adjunct (11 women). *Students:* 408 full-time (321 women), 12 part-time (10 women); includes 156 minority (69 Black or African American, non-Hispanic/Latino; 2 American Indian or Alaska Native, non-Hispanic/Latino; 14 Asian, non-Hispanic/Latino; 53 Hispanic/Latino; 18 Two or more races, non-Hispanic/Latino), 5 international. Average age 40. 268 applicants, 39% accepted, 77 enrolled. In 2016, 36 doctorates, 31 other advanced degrees awarded. *Degree requirements:* For doctorate, thesis/ dissertation. *Entrance requirements:* For doctorate, bachelor's degree, minimum GPA of 3.0, curriculum vitae, statement of purpose, critical thinking writing sample, 3 letters of recommendation, official transcript; for other advanced degree, bachelor's degree (for post baccalaureate certificate), doctoral degree in psychology (for post doctoral certificate); minimum GPA of 3.0, curriculum vitae, statement of purpose, 3 letters of recommendation, official transcript. *Application deadline:* For fall admission, 2/4 for domestic students, 2/1 for international students; for spring admission, 11/1 for domestic and international students; for summer admission, 3/1 for domestic and international students. Application fee: $75. Electronic applications accepted. *Expenses:* $9,060 per term (for PhD); $8,665 per term (for Post Doctoral Certificate); $720 per credit (for Post Baccalaureate Certificate). *Financial support:* In 2016–17, 28 students received support, including 1 research assistantship (averaging $238 per year), 17 teaching assistantships (averaging $1,973 per year); scholarships/grants also available. Financial award applicants required to submit FAFSA. *Unit head:* Dr. Marilyn Freimuth, Director. *Application contact:* Enrollment Coordinator, 800-340-1099 Ext. 4098, Fax: 805-687-9793, E-mail: psyadmission@fielding.edu.
Website: http://www.fielding.edu/our-programs/school-of-psychology/

**The George Washington University,** Graduate School of Education and Human Development, Department of Counseling and Human Development, Program in Forensic Rehabilitation Counseling, Washington, DC 20052. Offers Graduate Certificate. *Unit head:* Dr. Kenneth C. Hergenrather, Chair, 202-994-1334, E-mail: hergenkc@gwu.edu. *Application contact:* Sarah Lang, Director of Graduate Admissions, 202-994-1447, Fax: 202-994-7207, E-mail: slang@gwu.edu.
Website: http://gsehd.gwu.edu/

**Holy Names University,** Graduate Division, Department of Counseling Psychology, Oakland, CA 94619-1699. Offers counseling and forensic counseling (MA); counseling psychology (MA); forensic psychology (MA). *Program availability:* Part-time, evening/weekend. *Students:* 37 full-time (all women), 37 part-time (32 women); includes 55 minority (37 Black or African American, non-Hispanic/Latino; 6 Asian, non-Hispanic/Latino; 9 Hispanic/Latino; 2 Native Hawaiian or other Pacific Islander, non-Hispanic/Latino; 1 Two or more races, non-Hispanic/Latino), 3 international. Average age 33. 28 applicants, 82% accepted, 18 enrolled. In 2016, 33 master's awarded. *Degree requirements:* For master's, comprehensive paper, seminars. *Entrance requirements:* For master's, minimum undergraduate GPA of 2.6 overall, 3.0 in major. Additional exam

requirements/recommendations for international students: Required—TOEFL (minimum score 550 paper-based; 79 iBT). *Application deadline:* For fall admission, 8/1 priority date for domestic students, 7/15 for international students; for spring admission, 12/1 priority date for domestic students, 12/1 for international students; for summer admission, 5/1 priority date for domestic students, 5/1 for international students. Applications are processed on a rolling basis. Application fee: $65. Electronic applications accepted. Application fee is waived when completed online. *Expenses:* Contact institution. *Financial support:* Career-related internships or fieldwork, Federal Work-Study, scholarships/grants, and unspecified assistantships available. Support available to part-time students. Financial award application deadline: 3/2; financial award applicants required to submit FAFSA. *Faculty research:* Cognitive psychology, anger management, grief and grief counseling, post-modernism and psychotherapy, spirituality and psychology. *Unit head:* Dr. Perri Franskoviak, Program Director, 510-436-1465, E-mail: franskoviak@hnu.edu. *Application contact:* 510-436-1351, Fax: 510-436-1325, E-mail: graduateadmissions@hnu.edu.

**Immaculata University,** College of Graduate Studies, Department of Psychology, Immaculata, PA 19345. Offers clinical mental health counseling (MA); clinical psychology (Psy D); forensic psychology (Graduate Certificate); integrative psychotherapy (Graduate Certificate); neuropsychology (Graduate Certificate); psychodynamic psychotherapy (Graduate Certificate); psychological testing (Graduate Certificate); school counseling (MA, Graduate Certificate); school psychology (MA). *Accreditation:* APA. *Program availability:* Part-time, evening/weekend. Terminal master's awarded for partial completion of doctoral program. *Degree requirements:* For master's, comprehensive exam, thesis optional; for doctorate, comprehensive exam, thesis/dissertation. *Entrance requirements:* For master's, GRE General Test or MAT, minimum GPA of 3.0; for doctorate, GRE General Test or MAT, minimum GPA of 3.5. Additional exam requirements/recommendations for international students: Required—TOEFL, IELTS. Electronic applications accepted. *Faculty research:* Supervision ethics, psychology of teaching, gender.

**John Jay College of Criminal Justice of the City University of New York,** Graduate Studies, Program in Forensic Psychology, New York, NY 10019. Offers MA, PhD, MA/ JD. MA/JD offered with New York Law School. *Accreditation:* APA. *Program availability:* Part-time, evening/weekend. *Degree requirements:* For master's, thesis or alternative, externship. *Entrance requirements:* For master's, GRE General Test, minimum B average in major. Additional exam requirements/recommendations for international students: Required—TOEFL (minimum score 500 paper-based).

**John Jay College of Criminal Justice of the City University of New York,** Graduate Studies, Programs in Criminal Justice, New York, NY 10019. Offers criminal justice (MA, PhD); criminology and deviance (PhD); forensic psychology (PhD); forensic science (PhD); international crime and justice (MA); law and philosophy (PhD); organizational behavior (PhD); public policy (PhD). *Program availability:* Part-time, evening/weekend. Terminal master's awarded for partial completion of doctoral program. *Degree requirements:* For master's, thesis or alternative; for doctorate, one foreign language, thesis/dissertation. *Entrance requirements:* For master's, GRE General Test, minimum B average; for doctorate, GRE General Test. Additional exam requirements/ recommendations for international students: Required—TOEFL (minimum score 500 paper-based).

**Kean University,** College of Liberal Arts, Program in Forensic Psychology, Union, NJ 07083. Offers MA. *Faculty:* 18 full-time (14 women). *Students:* 4 full-time (3 women), 5 part-time (all women); includes 3 minority (1 Black or African American, non-Hispanic/Latino; 2 Hispanic/Latino). Average age 24. 10 applicants, 80% accepted, 9 enrolled. *Degree requirements:* For master's, project. *Entrance requirements:* For master's, baccalaureate degree from accredited college or university in psychology or related field; minimum cumulative GPA of 3.0; official transcripts; two letters of recommendation; professional resume/curriculum vitae; personal statement. Additional exam requirements/recommendations for international students: Required—TOEFL (minimum score 550 paper-based, 79 iBT) or IELTS (6.5). *Application deadline:* For fall admission, 6/1 for domestic students; for spring admission, 12/1 for domestic students. Application fee: $75. Electronic applications accepted. *Expenses:* Tuition, state resident: full-time $13,156; part-time $640 per credit. Tuition, nonresident: full-time $17,831; part-time $785 per credit. *Required fees:* $3316; $151 per credit. Tuition and fees vary according to course level, course load, degree level and program. *Financial support:* Scholarships/grants and unspecified assistantships available. Financial award applicants required to submit FAFSA. *Unit head:* Dr. Richard Conti, Director, 908-737-5883, E-mail: rconti@kean.edu. *Application contact:* Amy Clark, Program Assistant, 908-737-7100, E-mail: grad-adm@kean.edu.
Website: http://grad.kean.edu/masters-programs/forensic-psychology

**Kean University,** College of Liberal Arts, Program in Psychology, Union, NJ 07083. Offers forensic psychology (MA); human behavior and organizational psychology (MA); psychological services (MA). *Program availability:* Part-time. *Faculty:* 18 full-time (14 women). *Students:* 45 full-time (35 women), 39 part-time (25 women); includes 48 minority (21 Black or African American, non-Hispanic/Latino; 8 Asian, non-Hispanic/Latino; 16 Hispanic/Latino; 1 Native Hawaiian or other Pacific Islander, non-Hispanic/Latino; 2 Two or more races, non-Hispanic/Latino), 2 international. Average age 27. 54 applicants, 91% accepted, 44 enrolled. In 2016, 25 master's awarded. *Degree requirements:* For master's, comprehensive exam, research component, two semesters of advanced seminar. *Entrance requirements:* For master's, GRE General Test, minimum GPA of 3.0; official transcripts from all institutions attended; two letters of recommendation; professional resume/curriculum vitae; 12 credits in behavioral sciences on the undergraduate level. Additional exam requirements/recommendations for international students: Required—TOEFL (minimum score 550 paper-based; 79 iBT), IELTS (minimum score 6.5). *Application deadline:* For fall admission, 6/1 for domestic and international students; for spring admission, 12/1 for domestic and international students. Applications are processed on a rolling basis. Application fee: $75. Electronic applications accepted. *Expenses:* Tuition, state resident: full-time $13,156; part-time $640 per credit. Tuition, nonresident: full-time $17,831; part-time $785 per credit. *Required fees:* $3316; $151 per credit. Tuition and fees vary according to course level, course load, degree level and program. *Financial support:* Scholarships/grants and unspecified assistantships available. Financial award applicants required to submit FAFSA. *Unit head:* Dr. Muriel Singer, Program Coordinator, 908-737-5886, E-mail: msinger@kean.edu. *Application contact:* Amy Clark, Program Assistant, 908-737-7100, E-mail: grad-adm@kean.edu.
Website: http://grad.kean.edu/masters-programs/psychological-services

**London Metropolitan University,** Graduate Programs, London, United Kingdom. Offers applied psychology (M Sc); architecture (MA); biomedical science (M Sc); blood science (M Sc); cancer pharmacology (M Sc); computer networking and cyber security (M Sc); computing and information systems (M Sc); conference interpreting (MA); counter-terrorism studies (M Sc); creative, digital and professional writing (MA); crime, violence and prevention (M Sc); criminology (M Sc); curating contemporary art (MA); data analytics (M Sc); digital media (MA); early childhood studies (MA); education (MA, Ed D); financial services law, regulation and compliance (LL M); food science (M Sc); forensic psychology (M Sc); health and social care management and policy (M Sc); human nutrition (M Sc); human resource management (MA); human rights and

## Forensic Psychology

international conflict (MA); information technology (M Sc); intelligence and security studies (M Sc); international oil, gas and energy law (LL M); international relations (MA); interpreting (MA); learning and teaching in higher education (MA); legal practice (LL M); media and entertainment law (LL M); organizational and consumer psychology (M Sc); psychological therapy (M Sc); psychology of mental health (M Sc); public health (M Sc); public policy and management (MPA); security studies (M Sc); social work (M Sc); spatial planning and urban design (MA); sports therapy (M Sc); supporting older children and young people with dyslexia (MA); teaching languages (MA), including Arabic, English; translation (MA); woman and child abuse (MA).

**Marymount University,** School of Education and Human Services, Program in Forensic and Legal Psychology, Arlington, VA 22207-4299. Offers forensic and legal psychology (MA); intelligence studies (MA); MA/MA. *Program availability:* Part-time, evening/weekend. *Faculty:* 17 full-time (9 women), 12 part-time/adjunct (10 women). *Students:* 125 full-time (114 women), 34 part-time (29 women); includes 39 minority (11 Black or African American, non-Hispanic/Latino; 1 American Indian or Alaska Native, non-Hispanic/Latino; 2 Asian, non-Hispanic/Latino; 16 Hispanic/Latino; 9 Two or more races, non-Hispanic/Latino), 2 international. Average age 25. 138 applicants, 83% accepted, 69 enrolled. In 2016, 78 master's awarded. *Degree requirements:* For master's, thesis or alternative, capstone/internship. *Entrance requirements:* For master's, GRE, 2 letters of recommendation, resume, personal statement. Additional exam requirements/recommendations for international students: Required—TOEFL (minimum score 600 paper-based; 96 iBT), IELTS (minimum score 6.5). *Application deadline:* For fall admission, 2/17 for domestic and international students. Application fee: $40. Electronic applications accepted. *Expenses: Tuition:* Full-time $8460; part-time $940 per credit hour. *Required fees:* $10 per credit hour. One-time fee: $240 part-time. Tuition and fees vary according to program. *Financial support:* In 2016–17, 12 students received support, including 7 research assistantships with tuition reimbursements available, 5 teaching assistantships with tuition reimbursements available; career-related internships or fieldwork, Federal Work-Study, scholarships/grants, and unspecified assistantships also available. Support available to part-time students. Financial award applicants required to submit FAFSA. *Unit head:* Dr. Mary Lindahl, Chair, Forensic and Legal Psychology, 703-526-6821, Fax: 703-284-5708, E-mail: mary.lindahl@marymount.edu. *Application contact:* Francesca Reed, Director, Graduate Admissions, 703-284-5901, Fax: 703-527-3815, E-mail: grad.admissions@marymount.edu.
Website: http://www.marymount.edu/Academics/School-of-Education-Human-Services/Graduate-Programs/Forensic-Legal-Psychology-(M-A-)

**Montclair State University,** The Graduate School, College of Humanities and Social Sciences, Family/Civil Forensic Psychology Certificate Program, Montclair, NJ 07043-1624. Offers Certificate. *Expenses:* Tuition, state resident: part-time $553 per credit. Tuition, nonresident: part-time $854 per credit. *Required fees:* $91 per credit. Tuition and fees vary according to program.

**Montclair State University,** The Graduate School, College of Humanities and Social Sciences, Forensic Psychology Certificate Program, Montclair, NJ 07043-1624. Offers Certificate. *Program availability:* Part-time, evening/weekend. *Entrance requirements:* For degree, 2 letters of recommendation, essay. Additional exam requirements/recommendations for international students: Required—TOEFL (minimum score 83 iBT), IELTS (minimum score 6.5). Electronic applications accepted. *Expenses:* Tuition, state resident: part-time $553 per credit. Tuition, nonresident: part-time $854 per credit. *Required fees:* $91 per credit. Tuition and fees vary according to program. *Faculty research:* Forensic interviewing, child abuse.

**Nova Southeastern University,** College of Psychology, Fort Lauderdale, FL 33314-7796. Offers clinical psychology (PhD, Psy D); counseling (MS); experimental psychology (MS); forensic psychology (MS); general psychology (MS); mental health counseling (MS); school counseling (MS); school psychology (Psy D, Psy S). *Accreditation:* APA (one or more programs are accredited). *Program availability:* 100% online, blended/hybrid learning. *Faculty:* 51 full-time (21 women), 120 part-time/adjunct (70 women). *Students:* 724 full-time (596 women), 918 part-time (792 women); includes 797 minority (276 Black or African American, non-Hispanic/Latino; 1 American Indian or Alaska Native, non-Hispanic/Latino; 44 Asian, non-Hispanic/Latino; 427 Hispanic/Latino; 2 Native Hawaiian or other Pacific Islander, non-Hispanic/Latino; 47 Two or more races, non-Hispanic/Latino), 41 international. Average age 31. 1,349 applicants, 61% accepted, 651 enrolled. In 2016, 377 master's, 177 doctorates, 26 other advanced degrees awarded. Terminal master's awarded for partial completion of doctoral program. *Degree requirements:* For master's, comprehensive exam, 3 practica; for doctorate, thesis/dissertation, clinical internship, competency exam; for Psy S, comprehensive exam, internship. *Entrance requirements:* For doctorate, GRE General Test, GRE Subject Test (recommended), minimum undergraduate GPA of 3.0; for Psy S, GRE General Test. Additional exam requirements/recommendations for international students: Required—TOEFL (minimum score 550 paper-based). *Application deadline:* Applications are processed on a rolling basis. Application fee: $50. Electronic applications accepted. *Expenses:* Contact institution. *Financial support:* In 2016–17, 197 students received support, including 15 research assistantships (averaging $5,600 per year), 68 teaching assistantships (averaging $2,000 per year); career-related internships or fieldwork, Federal Work-Study, institutionally sponsored loans, scholarships/grants, and unspecified assistantships also available. Support available to part-time students. Financial award application deadline: 4/15; financial award applicants required to submit FAFSA. *Faculty research:* Clinical health psychology, multicultural/diversity psychology, clinical neuropsychology, clinical child psychology, family violence. *Unit head:* Dr. Karen Grosby, Dean, 954-262-5712, Fax: 954-262-3859, E-mail: grosby@nova.edu. *Application contact:* Carlos Perez, Senior Manager of Outreach, 954-262-5702, Fax: 954-262-3893, E-mail: gradschool@nova.edu.
Website: http://psychology.nova.edu/

**Pontificia Universidad Catolica Madre y Maestra,** Graduate School, Faculty of Social and Administrative Sciences, Santiago, Dominican Republic. Offers business administration (MBA), including business development, finance, international business, management skills (M Mgmt, MBA), marketing, operations, strategic cost management, strategy, tourist destination planning and management; law (LL M), including civil law, corporate business law, criminal law, international relations, real estate law; management (M Mgmt), including higher financial management, insurance program administration, management skills (M Mgmt, MBA); psychology (MA), including clinical child and adolescent psychology, forensic psychology; strategic human resources (EMBA).

**Prairie View A&M University,** College of Juvenile Justice and Psychology, Prairie View, TX 77446. Offers clinical adolescent psychology (PhD); juvenile forensic psychology (MSJFP); juvenile justice (MSJJ, PhD). *Program availability:* Part-time, evening/weekend, online only, 100% online. *Faculty:* 6 full-time (2 women), 6 part-time/adjunct (3 women). *Students:* 29 full-time (24 women), 31 part-time (22 women); includes 53 minority (49 Black or African American, non-Hispanic/Latino; 3 Hispanic/Latino; 1 Two or more races, non-Hispanic/Latino), 5 international. Average age 30. 37 applicants, 92% accepted, 25 enrolled. In 2016, 16 master's, 2 doctorates awarded. *Degree requirements:* For master's, comprehensive exam; for doctorate, thesis/dissertation. *Entrance requirements:* For master's, GRE, minimum GPA of 2.75; for

doctorate, GRE, previous course work in clinical adolescent psychology, minimum GPA of 3.5. Additional exam requirements/recommendations for international students: Required—TOEFL (minimum score 550 paper-based; 79 iBT). *Application deadline:* For fall admission, 5/1 priority date for domestic and international students; for spring admission, 10/1 priority date for domestic students, 9/1 priority date for international students; for summer admission, 3/1 priority date for domestic students, 2/1 priority date for international students. Applications are processed on a rolling basis. Application fee: $50. Electronic applications accepted. *Expenses:* Tuition, state resident: full-time $4362; part-time $273.48 per credit hour. Tuition, nonresident: full-time $12,390; part-time $534.10 per credit hour. *Required fees:* $2782; $178.26 per credit hour. *Financial support:* In 2016–17, 20 students received support, including 20 research assistantships; teaching assistantships, scholarships/grants, and unspecified assistantships also available. Financial award application deadline: 4/1; financial award applicants required to submit FAFSA. *Faculty research:* Juvenile justice, community policing, adolescent substance use, reducing mental illness stigma and promoting positive psychological well-being in diverse communities, promoting prosocial behavior among at-risk youth. *Unit head:* Dr. Tamara L. Brown, Dean, 936-261-5206, Fax: 936-261-5253, E-mail: tlbrown@pvamu.edu. *Application contact:* Pauline Walker, Executive Secretary, Graduate Program, 936-261-3521, Fax: 936-261-3529, E-mail: gradadmissions@pvamu.edu.

**Roger Williams University,** Feinstein College of Arts and Sciences, Forensic and Legal Psychology, Bristol, RI 02809. Offers forensic psychology (MA). *Expenses:* Contact institution.

**Sage Graduate School,** School of Health Sciences, Program in Forensic Mental Health, Troy, NY 12180-4115. Offers MS, Certificate. *Program availability:* Part-time, evening/weekend. *Faculty:* 6 part-time/adjunct (5 women). *Students:* 18 full-time (16 women), 17 part-time (16 women); includes 13 minority (5 Black or African American, non-Hispanic/Latino; 1 Asian, non-Hispanic/Latino; 4 Hispanic/Latino; 3 Two or more races, non-Hispanic/Latino). Average age 29. 35 applicants, 46% accepted, 9 enrolled. In 2016, 12 master's, 3 other advanced degrees awarded. *Entrance requirements:* Additional exam requirements/recommendations for international students: Required—TOEFL (minimum score 550 paper-based). *Application deadline:* Applications are processed on a rolling basis. Application fee: $40. Electronic applications accepted. *Expenses:* Tuition: Full-time $12,240; part-time $680 per credit hour. Tuition and fees vary according to degree level and program. *Financial support:* Fellowships, research assistantships, Federal Work-Study, scholarships/grants, and unspecified assistantships available. Support available to part-time students. Financial award applicants required to submit FAFSA. *Unit head:* Dr. Maureen McLeod, Coordinator, Forensic Mental Health, 518-244-2211, E-mail: mcleom@sage.edu. *Application contact:* Wendy D. Diefendorf, Director of Graduate and Adult Admission, 518-244-2443, Fax: 518-244-6880, E-mail: diefew@sage.edu.

**Tiffin University,** Program in Criminal Justice, Tiffin, OH 44883-2161. Offers criminal justice (MS), including crime analysis, criminal behavior, forensic psychology, homeland security administration, justice administration. *Program availability:* Part-time, evening/weekend, 100% online, blended/hybrid learning. *Students:* 83 full-time (61 women), 191 part-time (109 women); includes 85 minority (71 Black or African American, non-Hispanic/Latino; 6 Hispanic/Latino; 1 Native Hawaiian or other Pacific Islander, non-Hispanic/Latino; 7 Two or more races, non-Hispanic/Latino), 6 international. Average age 31. In 2016, 59 master's awarded. *Degree requirements:* For master's, thesis optional. *Entrance requirements:* For master's, minimum undergraduate GPA of 2.5, work experience. Additional exam requirements/recommendations for international students: Required—TOEFL (minimum score 550 paper-based; 79 iBT). *Application deadline:* For fall admission, 9/3 for domestic students, 8/1 for international students; for spring admission, 1/9 priority date for domestic students, 12/1 for international students. Applications are processed on a rolling basis. Application fee: $50. Electronic applications accepted. *Expenses:* Contact institution. *Financial support:* Available to part-time students. Application deadline: 7/31; applicants required to submit FAFSA. *Faculty research:* Terrorism, intelligence, homeland security, guns and crime. *Unit head:* Dr. Kevin Cashen, Dean of Criminal Justice and Security Studies, 419-448-3322, Fax: 419-443-5002, E-mail: cashenk@tiffin.edu. *Application contact:* Nikki Hintze, Director of Graduate and Distance Education Academic Advising, 800-968-6446 Ext. 3596, Fax: 419-443-5002, E-mail: hintzenm@tiffin.edu.
Website: http://www.tiffin.edu

**Trine University,** Program in Criminal Justice, Angola, IN 46703-1764. Offers emergency management (MS); forensic psychology (MS); law (MS); public administration (MS). *Program availability:* Part-time, evening/weekend. *Entrance requirements:* Additional exam requirements/recommendations for international students: Required—TOEFL. *Expenses:* Tuition: Full-time $13,320. *Required fees:* $460. Tuition and fees vary according to degree level, campus/location, program and student level. *Application deadline:* Application deadline: 3/1; applicants required to submit FAFSA. *Unit head:* Craig Laker, Dean, College of Graduate and Professional Studies/Associate Professor, 260-665-4862, E-mail: lakerc@trine.edu.
Website: http://www.trine.edu/academics/majors-and-minors/graduate/criminal-justice/index.aspx

**Universidad de Iberoamerica,** Graduate School, San Jose, Costa Rica. Offers clinical neuropsychology (PhD); clinical psychology (M Psych); educational psychology (M Psych); forensic psychology (M Psych); hospital management (MHA); intensive care nursing (MN); medicine (MD).

**Universidad del Turabo,** Graduate Programs, School of Social Sciences and Humanities, Programs in Psychology, Gurabo, PR 00778-3030. Offers counseling psychology (M Psych, Psy D, Certificate); forensic psychology (Certificate); psychology (M Psych). *Students:* 124 full-time (94 women), 116 part-time (80 women); all minorities (all Hispanic/Latino). Average age 36. 181 applicants, 51% accepted, 69 enrolled. In 2016, 37 master's, 10 doctorates, 1 Certificate awarded. *Entrance requirements:* For master's, GRE, GMAT or EXADEP, interview, essay, official transcript, recommendation letters; for doctorate, GRE, GMAT or EXADEP, interview, essay, official transcript, recommendation letters, curriculum vitae. Electronic applications accepted. *Financial support:* Institutionally sponsored loans available. Financial award applicants required to submit FAFSA. *Unit head:* Maria del Carmen Santos, Dean, 787-743-7979 Ext. 4232. *Application contact:* Diriee Rodriguez, Admissions Director, 787-743-7979 Ext. 4453, E-mail: admisiones-ut@suagm.edu.
Website: http://ut.suagm.edu/es/sociales

**University of Central Oklahoma,** The Jackson College of Graduate Studies, College of Education and Professional Studies, Department of Psychology, Edmond, OK 73034-5209. Offers counseling psychology (MA); experimental psychology (MA); forensic psychology (MA); general psychology (MA); school psychology (MA). *Degree requirements:* For master's, thesis (for some programs). *Entrance requirements:* For master's, GRE. Additional exam requirements/recommendations for international students: Required—TOEFL (minimum score 550 paper-based; 79 iBT), IELTS (minimum score 6.5). Electronic applications accepted. *Faculty research:* Psychopharmacology, computer psychometrics, health psychology research.

**University of Denver,** Graduate School of Professional Psychology, Denver, CO 80208. Offers clinical psychology (Psy D); forensic psychology (MA); international disaster psychology (MA); sport and performance psychology (MA); sport coaching (MA). *Accreditation:* APA. *Faculty:* 23 full-time (13 women), 25 part-time/adjunct (14 women). *Students:* 230 full-time (187 women), 72 part-time (46 women); includes 69 minority (16 Black or African American, non-Hispanic/Latino; 1 American Indian or Alaska Native, non-Hispanic/Latino; 9 Asian, non-Hispanic/Latino; 29 Hispanic/Latino; 1 Native Hawaiian or other Pacific Islander, non-Hispanic/Latino; 13 Two or more races, non-Hispanic/Latino), 14 international. Average age 27. 800 applicants, 30% accepted, 129 enrolled. In 2016, 80 master's, 38 doctorates awarded. *Degree requirements:* For master's, comprehensive exam (for some programs); for doctorate, comprehensive exam (for some programs), paper, clinical internship. *Entrance requirements:* For master's and doctorate, GRE General Test, transcripts, resume, two letters of recommendation, essay. Additional exam requirements/recommendations for international students: Required—TOEFL (minimum score 550 paper-based; 80 iBT). *Application deadline:* For fall admission, 1/5 for domestic and international students. Application fee: $65. Electronic applications accepted. *Expenses:* $43,358 per year full-time. *Financial support:* In 2016–17, 124 students received support, including 15 teaching assistantships with tuition reimbursements available (averaging $2,708 per year); career-related internships or fieldwork, Federal Work-Study, institutionally sponsored loans, scholarships/grants, unspecified assistantships, and clinical assistantships also available. Support available to part-time students. Financial award application deadline: 2/15; financial award applicants required to submit FAFSA. *Unit head:* Dr. Shelly Smith-Acuna, Dean, 303-871-3880, Fax: 303-871-4220, E-mail: shelly.smith-acuna@du.edu. *Application contact:* Admissions Counselor, 303-871-3736, Fax: 303-871-4220, E-mail: gsppinfo@du.edu.
Website: http://www.du.edu/gspp

**University of Houston–Victoria,** School of Arts and Sciences, Program in Psychology, Victoria, TX 77901-4450. Offers counseling psychology (MA); forensic psychology (MA); school psychology (MA). *Program availability:* Part-time, evening/weekend, online learning. *Degree requirements:* For master's, project or thesis. *Entrance requirements:* For master's, GRE General Test. Additional exam requirements/recommendations for international students: Required—TOEFL (minimum score 550 paper-based). Electronic applications accepted.

**University of Louisiana at Monroe,** Graduate School, College of Business and Social Sciences, Department of Psychology, Monroe, LA 71209-0001. Offers forensic psychology (MS); general psychology (MS); psychometrics (MS). *Program availability:* Part-time, evening/weekend, online learning. *Faculty:* 2 full-time (0 women). *Students:* 12 full-time (10 women), 4 part-time (2 women); includes 10 minority (7 Black or African American, non-Hispanic/Latino; 2 Hispanic/Latino; 1 Two or more races, non-Hispanic/Latino). Average age 26. 109 applicants, 37% accepted, 6 enrolled. In 2016, 4 master's awarded. *Degree requirements:* For master's, comprehensive exam, thesis optional. *Entrance requirements:* For master's, GRE General Test, minimum GPA of 2.75. Additional exam requirements/recommendations for international students: Required—TOEFL (minimum score 500 paper-based; 61 iBT). *Application deadline:* For fall admission, 7/1 for domestic and international students; for winter admission, 12/14 for domestic students; for spring admission, 12/1 for domestic and international students. Applications are processed on a rolling basis. Application fee: $20 ($30 for international students). Electronic applications accepted. *Expenses:* Tuition, state resident: full-time $6489. Tuition, nonresident: full-time $18,589. *Required fees:* $8984. Tuition and fees vary according to course level, course load, degree level and program. *Financial support:* Research assistantships, career-related internships or fieldwork, Federal Work-Study, and unspecified assistantships available. Financial award application deadline: 4/1; financial award applicants required to submit FAFSA. *Application contact:* Dr. Jack Palmer, Graduate Coordinator, 318-342-1345, E-mail: palmer@ulm.edu.
Website: http://www.ulm.edu/psychology

**University of New Haven,** Graduate School, College of Arts and Sciences, Program in Community Psychology, West Haven, CT 06516. Offers applications of psychology (Graduate Certificate); community clinical services (MA); community psychology (MA); forensic psychology (MA); program development (MA). *Program availability:* Part-time, evening/weekend. *Students:* 37 full-time (36 women), 6 part-time (4 women); includes 13 minority (6 Black or African American, non-Hispanic/Latino; 1 American Indian or Alaska Native, non-Hispanic/Latino; 3 Hispanic/Latino; 3 Two or more races, non-Hispanic/Latino). Average age 25. 48 applicants, 81% accepted, 21 enrolled. In 2016, 26 master's awarded. *Degree requirements:* For master's, thesis or alternative, fieldwork. *Entrance requirements:* Additional exam requirements/recommendations for international students: Required—TOEFL (minimum score 80 iBT), IELTS, PTE. *Application deadline:* Applications are processed on a rolling basis. Application fee: $50. Electronic applications accepted. Application fee is waived when completed online. *Expenses:* Tuition: Full-time $15,660; part-time $870 per credit hour. *Required fees:* $200; $85 per term. Tuition and fees vary according to program. *Financial support:* Research assistantships with partial tuition reimbursements, teaching assistantships with partial tuition reimbursements, career-related internships or fieldwork, Federal Work-Study, scholarships/grants, and unspecified assistantships available. Support available to part-time students. Financial award application deadline: 5/1; financial award applicants required to submit FAFSA. *Unit head:* Dr. Michael Morris, Coordinator, 203-932-7289, E-mail: mmorris@newhaven.edu.
Website: http://www.newhaven.edu/4725/

**University of New Haven,** Graduate School, Henry C. Lee College of Criminal Justice and Forensic Sciences, Program in Criminal Justice, West Haven, CT 06516. Offers crime analysis (MS); criminal justice (MS, PhD); criminal justice management (MS, Graduate Certificate); forensic computer investigation (MS); forensic psychology (MS); information protection and security (Graduate Certificate); victim advocacy and services management (Graduate Certificate); victimology (MS). *Program availability:* Part-time, evening/weekend, online learning. *Students:* 120 full-time (83 women), 121 part-time (69 women); includes 84 minority (49 Black or African American, non-Hispanic/Latino; 10 Asian, non-Hispanic/Latino; 14 Hispanic/Latino; 1 Native Hawaiian or other Pacific Islander, non-Hispanic/Latino; 10 Two or more races, non-Hispanic/Latino), 10 international. Average age 29. 128 applicants, 90% accepted, 73 enrolled. In 2016, 52 master's, 2 doctorates, 8 other advanced degrees awarded. *Degree requirements:* For master's, thesis or alternative. *Entrance requirements:* Additional exam requirements/recommendations for international students: Required—TOEFL (minimum score 80 iBT), IELTS, PTE (minimum score 53). *Application deadline:* Applications are processed on a rolling basis. Application fee: $50. Electronic applications accepted. Application fee is waived when completed online. *Expenses:* Tuition: Full-time $15,660; part-time $870 per credit hour. *Required fees:* $200; $85 per term. Tuition and fees vary according to program. *Financial support:* Research assistantships with partial tuition reimbursements, teaching assistantships with partial tuition reimbursements, career-related internships or fieldwork, Federal Work-Study, scholarships/grants, and unspecified assistantships available. Support available to part-time students. Financial award applicants required to submit FAFSA. *Application contact:* Michelle Mason, Director of Graduate Enrollment, 203-932-7067, E-mail: mmason@newhaven.edu.
Website: http://www.newhaven.edu/5921/

**University of New Haven,** Graduate School, Henry C. Lee College of Criminal Justice and Forensic Sciences, Program in Forensic Science, West Haven, CT 06516. Offers advanced investigation (MS); criminalistics (MS); fire science administration (MS); forensic computer investigation (Graduate Certificate); forensic psychology (Graduate Certificate); forensic science (MS); forensic science/fire science (Graduate Certificate). *Program availability:* Part-time, evening/weekend. *Students:* 68 full-time (52 women), 7 part-time (4 women); includes 16 minority (5 Black or African American, non-Hispanic/Latino; 1 Asian, non-Hispanic/Latino; 9 Hispanic/Latino; 1 Two or more races, non-Hispanic/Latino), 5 international. Average age 25. 101 applicants, 69% accepted, 39 enrolled. In 2016, 31 master's, 3 other advanced degrees awarded. *Degree requirements:* For master's, thesis or alternative, research project or internship. *Entrance requirements:* For master's, GRE. Additional exam requirements/recommendations for international students: Required—TOEFL (minimum score 80 iBT), IELTS, PTE (minimum score 53). *Application deadline:* Applications are processed on a rolling basis. Application fee: $50. Electronic applications accepted. Application fee is waived when completed online. *Expenses:* Tuition: Full-time $15,660; part-time $870 per credit hour. *Required fees:* $200; $85 per term. Tuition and fees vary according to program. *Financial support:* Research assistantships with partial tuition reimbursements, teaching assistantships with partial tuition reimbursements, career-related internships or fieldwork, Federal Work-Study, scholarships/grants, and unspecified assistantships available. Support available to part-time students. Financial award applicants required to submit FAFSA. *Unit head:* Dr. Virginia Maxwell, E-mail: vmaxwell@newhaven.edu. *Application contact:* Michelle Mason, Director of Graduate Enrollment, 203-932-7067, E-mail: mmason@newhaven.edu.
Website: http://www.newhaven.edu/5923/

**University of North Dakota,** Graduate School, College of Arts and Sciences, Department of Psychology, Grand Forks, ND 58202. Offers clinical psychology (PhD); forensic psychology (MA, MS). *Accreditation:* APA (one or more programs are accredited). *Degree requirements:* For master's, thesis, final exam; for doctorate, comprehensive exam, thesis/dissertation, internship, final exam. *Entrance requirements:* For master's, GRE General Test, GRE Subject Test, minimum GPA of 3.0; for doctorate, GRE General Test, GRE Subject Test, minimum GPA of 3.5. Additional exam requirements/recommendations for international students: Required—TOEFL (minimum score 550 paper-based; 79 iBT), IELTS (minimum score 6.5). *Application deadline:* For fall admission, 1/15 for domestic and international students. Application fee: $35. Electronic applications accepted. *Financial support:* Fellowships with full and partial tuition reimbursements, research assistantships with full and partial tuition reimbursements, teaching assistantships with full and partial tuition reimbursements, career-related internships or fieldwork, Federal Work-Study, institutionally sponsored loans, scholarships/grants, health care benefits, tuition waivers (full and partial), and unspecified assistantships available. Support available to part-time students. Financial award application deadline: 3/15; financial award applicants required to submit FAFSA. *Faculty research:* Developmental psychology, clinical social psychology, educational psychology, personality disorders. *Unit head:* Dr. Mark Grabe, Chairperson, 701-777-3451, E-mail: mark.grabe@und.nodak.edu. *Application contact:* Matt Anderson, Admissions Specialist, 701-777-2947, Fax: 701-777-3619, E-mail: matthew.anderson@gradschool.und.edu.
Website: http://arts-sciences.und.edu/psychology/

**Walden University,** Graduate Programs, School of Counseling, Minneapolis, MN 55401. Offers addiction counseling (MS), including addictions and public health, child and adolescent counseling, family studies and interventions, forensic counseling, general program, military families and culture, trauma and crisis counseling; clinical mental health counseling (MS), including addiction counseling, forensic counseling, military families and culture, trauma and crisis counseling; counselor education and supervision (PhD), including consultation, counseling and social change, forensic mental health counseling, leadership and program evaluation, trauma and crisis; marriage, couple, and family counseling (MS), including addiction counseling, career counseling, forensic counseling, military families and culture, trauma and crisis counseling; school counseling (MS), including addiction counseling, career counseling, crisis and trauma, military families and culture. *Accreditation:* ACA. *Program availability:* Part-time, evening/weekend, online only, 100% online. *Degree requirements:* For master's, residency, field experience, professional development plan, licensure plan; for doctorate, thesis/dissertation, residency, practicum, internship. *Entrance requirements:* For master's, bachelor's degree or higher; minimum GPA of 2.5; official transcripts; goal statement (for some programs); access to computer and Internet; for doctorate, master's degree or higher; three years of related professional or academic experience (preferred); minimum GPA of 3.0; goal statement and current resume (for select programs); official transcripts; access to computer and Internet. Additional exam requirements/recommendations for international students: Required—TOEFL (minimum score 550 paper-based, 79 iBT), IELTS (minimum score 6.5), Michigan English Language Assessment Battery (minimum score 82), or PTE (minimum score 53). Electronic applications accepted.

**Walden University,** Graduate Programs, School of Psychology, Minneapolis, MN 55401. Offers clinical psychology (MS), including counseling, general program; forensic psychology (MS), including forensic psychology in the community, general program, mental health applications, program planning and evaluation in forensic settings, psychology and legal systems; industrial organizational (MS, PhD), including consulting psychology, forensic (MS), forensic psychology (PhD), general practice, leadership development and coaching (MS), organizational diversity and social change, research evaluation (PhD); online teaching in psychology (Post-Master's Certificate); organizational psychology and development (Postbaccalaureate Certificate); psychology (MS, PhD), including applied psychology (MS), clinical psychology (PhD), crisis management and response (MS), educational psychology, forensic psychology (PhD), general psychology (MS), general psychology research (PhD), general psychology teaching (PhD), health psychology, leadership development and coaching (MS), psychology of culture (MS), psychology, public administration, and social change (MS), social psychology, terrorism and security (MS); psychology respecialization (Post-Doctoral Certificate). *Program availability:* Part-time, evening/weekend, online only, 100% online. Terminal master's awarded for partial completion of doctoral program. *Degree requirements:* For master's, thesis optional; for doctorate, thesis/dissertation, residency. *Entrance requirements:* For master's, bachelor's degree or higher; minimum GPA of 2.5; official transcripts; goal statement (for some programs); access to computer and Internet; for doctorate, master's degree or higher; three years of related professional or academic experience (preferred); minimum GPA of 3.0; goal statement and current resume (for select programs); official transcripts; access to computer and Internet; for other advanced degree, relevant work experience; access to computer and Internet. Additional exam requirements/recommendations for international students: Required—TOEFL (minimum score 550 paper-based, 79 iBT), IELTS (minimum score 6.5), Michigan English Language Assessment Battery (minimum score 82), or PTE (minimum score 53). Electronic applications accepted.

**Westfield State University,** College of Graduate and Continuing Education, Department of Psychology, Program in Counseling, Westfield, MA 01086. Offers forensic mental health counseling (MA); mental health counseling (MA); school adjustment counseling (MA); school guidance counseling (MA). *Program availability:*

Part-time, evening/weekend. *Degree requirements:* For master's, comprehensive exam, practicum. *Entrance requirements:* For master's, GRE General Test, MAT, minimum undergraduate GPA of 3.0. Additional exam requirements/recommendations for international students: Recommended—TOEFL (minimum score 550 paper-based; 79 iBT). *Expenses:* Tuition, state resident: part-time $318 per semester hour. Tuition, nonresident: part-time $318 per semester hour. *Required fees:* $75 per semester. Tuition and fees vary according to course load and program.

**William James College,** Graduate Programs, Newton, MA 02459. Offers applied psychology in higher education student personnel administration (MA); clinical psychology (Psy D); counseling psychology (MA); counseling psychology and community mental health (MA); counseling psychology and global mental health (MA); executive coaching (Graduate Certificate); forensic and counseling psychology (MA); leadership psychology (Psy D); organizational psychology (MA); primary care psychology (MA); respecialization in clinical psychology (Certificate); school psychology (Psy D); MA/CAGS. *Accreditation:* APA. *Degree requirements:* For master's, comprehensive exam (for some programs); for doctorate, thesis/dissertation (for some programs). Electronic applications accepted.

# Genetic Counseling

**Arcadia University,** College of Health Sciences, Department of Genetic Counseling, Glenside, PA 19038-3295. Offers MSGC. *Faculty:* 3 full-time (all women), 18 part-time/adjunct (16 women). *Students:* 31 full-time (22 women); includes 3 minority (1 Black or African American, non-Hispanic/Latino; 1 Asian, non-Hispanic/Latino; 1 Hispanic/Latino), 2 international. Average age 25. 115 applicants, 34% accepted, 16 enrolled. In 2016, 14 master's awarded. *Degree requirements:* For master's, thesis. *Entrance requirements:* For master's, GRE. Additional exam requirements/recommendations for international students: Required—TOEFL or IELTS. *Application deadline:* For fall admission, 3/1 for domestic students. Application fee: $50. *Expenses:* Contact institution. *Financial support:* Tuition waivers (partial) and unspecified assistantships available. *Unit head:* Kathleen Valverde, Chair, 215-572-4058. *Application contact:* 215-572-2910, Fax: 215-572-4049, E-mail: admiss@arcadia.edu.

**Boston University,** School of Medicine, Division of Graduate Medical Sciences, Program in Genetic Counseling, Boston, MA 02215. Offers MS. *Application deadline:* For fall admission, 2/1 for domestic students. *Financial support:* In 2016–17, 15 students received support. Institutionally sponsored loans and unspecified assistantships available. Financial award application deadline: 1/1; financial award applicants required to submit FAFSA. *Unit head:* Maureen Flynn, Assistant Director, 617-638-5980, E-mail: maflynn@bu.edu. *Application contact:* GMS Admissions Office, 617-638-5255, E-mail: askgms@bu.edu.
Website: http://www.bumc.bu.edu/gms/m-s-genetic-counseling-program/

**Brandeis University,** Graduate School of Arts and Sciences, Program in Genetic Counseling, Waltham, MA 02454-9110. Offers MS. *Faculty:* 8 part-time/adjunct (all women). *Students:* 20 full-time (19 women); includes 1 minority (Asian, non-Hispanic/Latino), 6 international. 128 applicants, 22% accepted, 10 enrolled. In 2016, 10 master's awarded. *Degree requirements:* For master's, thesis, proseminar, journal club, research project, internship/fieldwork. *Entrance requirements:* For master's, GRE General Test, resume, 3 letters of recommendation, statement of purpose, transcript(s). Additional exam requirements/recommendations for international students: Required—TOEFL (minimum score 600 paper-based; 100 iBT); Recommended—IELTS (minimum score 7), TSE (minimum score 68). *Application deadline:* For fall admission, 1/15 for domestic and international students. Application fee: $75. Electronic applications accepted. *Expenses:* Contact institution. *Financial support:* Federal Work-Study, scholarships/grants, and tuition waivers (partial) available. Financial award application deadline: 4/15; financial award applicants required to submit FAFSA. *Faculty research:* Genetics, genetic counseling, DNA sequencing, medical genetics. *Unit head:* Dr. Gretchen Schneider, Co-Director, 781-736-3108, Fax: 781-736-3107, E-mail: gcinfo@brandeis.edu. *Application contact:* Missy Goldberg, Department Administrator, 781-736-3179, Fax: 781-736-3107, E-mail: goldberg@brandeis.edu.
Website: http://www.brandeis.edu/gsas

**California State University, Stanislaus,** College of Natural Sciences, Program in Genetic Counseling (MS), Turlock, CA 95382. Offers MS. *Degree requirements:* For master's, thesis. *Entrance requirements:* For master's, GRE, minimum GPA of 3.0, 3 letters of reference, personal statement. Additional exam requirements/recommendations for international students: Required—TOEFL (minimum score 550 paper-based). Electronic applications accepted. *Expenses:* Contact institution.

**Case Western Reserve University,** School of Medicine and School of Graduate Studies, Graduate Programs in Medicine, Department of Genetics and Genome Sciences, Program in Genetic Counseling, Cleveland, OH 44106. Offers MS. *Degree requirements:* For master's, comprehensive exam, thesis. *Entrance requirements:* For master's, GRE General Test. Additional exam requirements/recommendations for international students: Required—TOEFL. *Expenses:* Tuition: Full-time $42,576; part-time $1774 per credit hour. *Required fees:* $34. Tuition and fees vary according to course load and program. *Faculty research:* Genetic testing, ethical issues in genetics, cancer genetics, reproductive genetics, prenatal diagnosis.

**Emory University,** School of Medicine, Programs in Allied Health Professions, Genetic Counseling Training Program, Atlanta, GA 30322. Offers MM Sc. *Degree requirements:* For master's, thesis, capstone project. *Entrance requirements:* For master's, GRE General Test, minimum GPA of 3.0; prerequisites: genetics, statistics, psychology, and biochemistry. Additional exam requirements/recommendations for international students: Required—TOEFL. *Faculty research:* Cancer genetics, lysosomal storage disease, carrier screening, public health genomics, genetic counseling, psychology, molecular genetics.

**Icahn School of Medicine at Mount Sinai,** Graduate School of Biomedical Sciences, New York, NY 10029-6504. Offers biomedical sciences (MS, PhD); clinical research education (MS, PhD); community medicine (MPH); genetic counseling (MS); neurosciences (PhD); MD/PhD. Terminal master's awarded for partial completion of doctoral program. *Degree requirements:* For master's, thesis; for doctorate, comprehensive exam, thesis/dissertation. *Entrance requirements:* For master's, GRE General Test; for doctorate, GRE General Test, GRE Subject Test, 3 years of college pre-med course work. Additional exam requirements/recommendations for international students: Required—TOEFL. Electronic applications accepted. *Faculty research:* Cancer, genetics and genomics, immunology, neuroscience, developmental and stem cell biology, translational research.

**Johns Hopkins University,** Bloomberg School of Public Health, Department of Health, Behavior and Society, Baltimore, MD 21218. Offers genetic counseling (Sc M); health education and health communication (MSPH); social and behavioral sciences (Dr PH, PhD); social factors in health (MHS). *Degree requirements:* For master's, comprehensive exam (for some programs), thesis (for some programs); for doctorate, comprehensive exam, thesis/dissertation. *Entrance requirements:* For master's, GRE, curriculum vitae, 3 letters of recommendation; for doctorate, GRE, transcripts, curriculum vitae, 3 recommendation letters. Additional exam requirements/recommendations for international students: Required—TOEFL (minimum score 600 paper-based; 100 iBT). Electronic applications accepted. *Faculty research:* Social determinants of health and structural and community-level inventions to improve health, communication and health education, behavioral and social aspects of genetic counseling.

**Long Island University–LIU Post,** College of Liberal Arts and Sciences, Brookville, NY 11548-1300. Offers applied mathematics (MS); behavior analysis (MA); biology (MS); criminal justice (MS); earth science (MS); English (MA); environmental sustainability (MS); genetic counseling (MS); history (MA); interdisciplinary studies (MA, MS); mathematics for secondary school teachers (MS); mobile GIS application development (Advanced Certificate); political science (MA); psychology (MA). *Program availability:* Part-time, evening/weekend, blended/hybrid learning. *Faculty:* 68 full-time (30 women), 20 part-time/adjunct (13 women). *Students:* 155 full-time (117 women), 125 part-time (82 women); includes 65 minority (17 Black or African American, non-Hispanic/Latino; 14 Asian, non-Hispanic/Latino; 27 Hispanic/Latino; 7 Two or more races, non-Hispanic/Latino), 19 international. 485 applicants, 36% accepted, 77 enrolled. In 2016, 91 master's, 15 other advanced degrees awarded. *Degree requirements:* For master's, comprehensive exam (for some programs), thesis (for some programs). *Entrance requirements:* Additional exam requirements/recommendations for international students: Required—PTE, TOEFL (minimum score 550 paper-based, 75 iBT) or IELTS (6.5). *Application deadline:* Applications are processed on a rolling basis. Application fee: $50. Electronic applications accepted. *Expenses: Tuition:* Full-time $28,272; part-time $1178 per credit. *Required fees:* $451 per term. Tuition and fees vary according to degree level and program. *Financial support:* In 2016–17, 24 teaching assistantships with partial tuition reimbursements (averaging $410 per year) were awarded; fellowships, research assistantships, career-related internships or fieldwork, Federal Work-Study, institutionally sponsored loans, scholarships/grants, tuition waivers (partial), and unspecified assistantships also available. Support available to part-time students. Financial award application deadline: 2/15; financial award applicants required to submit FAFSA. *Faculty research:* Biology, criminal justice, environmental sustainability, mathematics, psychology. *Total annual research expenditures:* $218,000. *Unit head:* Dr. Jeffrey Belnap, Acting Dean, 516-299-2233, Fax: 516-299-4140, E-mail: jeffrey.belnap@liu.edu. *Application contact:* Carol Zerah, Director of Graduate Admissions, 516-299-2900, Fax: 516-299-2137, E-mail: post-enroll@liu.edu.
Website: http://liu.edu/CWPost/Academics/Schools/CLAS

**McGill University,** Faculty of Graduate and Postdoctoral Studies, Faculty of Medicine, Department of Human Genetics, Montréal, QC H3A 2T5, Canada. Offers genetic counseling (M Sc); human genetics (M Sc, PhD).

**Northwestern University,** The Graduate School, Program in Genetic Counseling, Evanston, IL 60208. Offers MS. *Degree requirements:* For master's, thesis. *Entrance requirements:* For master's, GRE General Test, interview. Additional exam requirements/recommendations for international students: Required—TOEFL. *Faculty research:* Preimplantation genetic diagnosis, gene expression in preimplantation embryos, fetal cells in maternal blood: first trimester prenatal screening for Down's Syndrome, genetic counseling efficacy and counseling issues in prenatal diagnosis.

**Sarah Lawrence College,** Graduate Studies, Joan H. Marks Graduate Program in Human Genetics, Bronxville, NY 10708-5999. Offers MS. *Program availability:* Part-time. *Degree requirements:* For master's, thesis, fieldwork. *Entrance requirements:* For master's, previous course work in biology, chemistry, developmental biology, genetics, probability and statistics. Additional exam requirements/recommendations for international students: Required—TOEFL (minimum score 600 paper-based). Electronic applications accepted. *Expenses:* Contact institution.

**Thomas Jefferson University,** Jefferson College of Biomedical Sciences, MS Program in Human Genetics and Genetic Counseling, Philadelphia, PA 19107. Offers MS. *Entrance requirements:* For master's, BA, personal statement, official transcripts, recommendation letters. Additional exam requirements/recommendations for international students: Required—TOEFL, IELTS (minimum score 7). *Application deadline:* For fall admission, 3/15 for domestic students. Applications are processed on a rolling basis. Application fee: $50. *Financial support:* Federal Work-Study and institutionally sponsored loans available. Support available to part-time students. Financial award application deadline: 5/1; financial award applicants required to submit FAFSA. *Unit head:* Dr. Rachael Brandt, Program Director, E-mail: rachael.brandt@jefferson.edu. *Application contact:* Marc E. Stearns, Director of Admissions, 215-503-0155, Fax: 215-503-3433, E-mail: jgsbs-info@jefferson.edu.

**Université de Montréal,** Faculty of Medicine, Program in Genetic Counseling, Montréal, QC H3C 3J7, Canada. Offers DESS.

**The University of Alabama at Birmingham,** School of Health Professions, Program in Genetic Counseling, Birmingham, AL 35294. Offers MS. *Entrance requirements:* For master's, GRE, minimum undergraduate GPA of 3.0, letters of recommendation, paid or volunteer experience, personal statement. Additional exam requirements/recommendations for international students: Required—TOEFL, TWE. Electronic applications accepted. Full-time tuition and fees vary according to course load and program.

**University of Arkansas for Medical Sciences,** College of Health Professions, Little Rock, AR 72205-7199. Offers audiology (Au D); communication sciences and disorders (MS, PhD); genetic counseling (MS); nuclear medicine advanced associate (MIS); physician assistant studies (MPAS); radiologist assistant (MIS). PhD offered through consortium with University of Arkansas at Little Rock and University of Central Arkansas. *Program availability:* Part-time, online learning. *Degree requirements:* For master's, thesis (for some programs); for doctorate, comprehensive exam (for some programs), thesis/dissertation (for some programs). *Entrance requirements:* For master's, GRE. Additional exam requirements/recommendations for international students: Required—TOEFL (minimum score 550 paper-based; 79 iBT). Electronic applications accepted. *Expenses:* Contact institution. *Faculty research:* Auditory-based intervention, soy diet, nutrition and cancer.

**The University of British Columbia,** Faculty of Medicine, Department of Medical Genetics, M Sc Program in Genetic Counselling, Vancouver, BC V6H 3N1, Canada. Offers M Sc. Electronic applications accepted. *Expenses:* Contact institution. *Financial support:* In 2016–17, 2 students received support. Scholarships/grants available. *Application contact:* Courtnae Cameron, Graduate Program Staff, 604-875-3486, Fax: 604-875-3490, E-mail: ubcgctp@cw.bc.ca. Website: http://medgen.med.ubc.ca/graduate-program/

**University of California, Irvine,** School of Medicine, Program in Genetic Counseling, Irvine, CA 92697. Offers MS. *Students:* 13 full-time (12 women), 2 part-time (both women); includes 2 minority (both Hispanic/Latino), 4 international. Average age 27. 137 applicants, 11% accepted, 7 enrolled. In 2016, 7 master's awarded. *Degree requirements:* For master's, thesis. *Entrance requirements:* For master's, GRE General Test, minimum GPA of 3.0. Additional exam requirements/recommendations for international students: Required—TOEFL (minimum score 550 paper-based). *Application deadline:* For fall admission, 1/15 priority date for domestic students, 1/15 for international students. Applications are processed on a rolling basis. Application fee: $105 ($125 for international students). Electronic applications accepted. *Financial support:* In 2016–17, 3 students received support. Research assistantships with full tuition reimbursements available, teaching assistantships, career-related internships or fieldwork, institutionally sponsored loans, traineeships, health care benefits, and unspecified assistantships available. Financial award application deadline: 3/1; financial award applicants required to submit FAFSA. *Faculty research:* Gene mapping and linkage analysis, delineation of new malformation and chromosomal syndromes, ethical and counseling issues in genetics. *Unit head:* Pamela Flodman, Director, 714-456-8470, E-mail: pflodman@uci.edu. Website: http://www.pediatrics.uci.edu/masters-genetic-counseling.asp

**University of Cincinnati,** Graduate School, College of Allied Health Sciences, Program in Genetic Counseling, Cincinnati, OH 45221. Offers medical genetics (MS). *Program availability:* Part-time. *Degree requirements:* For master's, thesis. *Entrance requirements:* For master's, GRE General Test. Additional exam requirements/recommendations for international students: Required—TOEFL. Electronic applications accepted. *Expenses: Tuition,* area resident: Full-time $12,790; part-time $389 per credit hour. Tuition, state resident: full-time $13,290; part-time $419 per credit hour. Tuition, nonresident: full-time $24,532; part-time $976 per credit hour. *International tuition:* $24,832 full-time. *Required fees:* $3958; $140 per credit hour. Tuition and fees vary according to course load, degree level, program and reciprocity agreements. *Faculty research:* Lysosomal disease, Tourette's syndrome, epidemiology of Down syndrome, genetic counseling, genetic disease treatment.

**University of Colorado Denver,** School of Medicine, Graduate Program in Genetic Counseling, Aurora, CO 80045. Offers biophysics and genetics (MS, PhD). *Students:* 11 full-time (10 women). Average age 27. 135 applicants, 4% accepted, 6 enrolled. In 2016, 9 master's awarded. *Degree requirements:* For master's, 44 core semester hours, project or thesis; for doctorate, comprehensive exam, thesis/dissertation, 30 hours each of didactic course work and research credits. *Entrance requirements:* For master's, GRE, minimum undergraduate GPA of 3.0; 4 letters of recommendation; prerequisite coursework in biology, general chemistry, general biochemistry, general genetics, general psychology; experience in counseling and laboratory settings and strong understanding of genetic counseling field (highly recommended); for doctorate, GRE, three letters of recommendation, laboratory research experience and solid undergraduate foundation in mathematics and biological sciences. Additional exam requirements/recommendations for international students: Required—TOEFL (minimum score 570 paper-based; 89 iBT). *Application deadline:* For fall admission, 1/1 for domestic students, 12/1 for international students. Application fee: $50 ($75 for international students). Electronic applications accepted. *Expenses:* Contact institution. *Financial support:* In 2016–17, 8 students received support. Fellowships, research assistantships, teaching assistantships, career-related internships or fieldwork, Federal Work-Study, institutionally sponsored loans, scholarships/grants, traineeships, and unspecified assistantships available. Financial award application deadline: 4/1; financial award applicants required to submit FAFSA. *Faculty research:* Psychosocial aspects of genetic counseling, clinical cytogenetics and molecular genetics, human inborn errors of metabolism, congenital malformations and disorders of the newborn, cancer genetics and genetic counseling. *Application contact:* Kenton Owsley, Program Administrator, 303-724-3468, E-mail: somadmin@ucdenver.edu. Website: http://www.ucdenver.edu/academics/colleges/Graduate-School/academic-programs/genetic-counseling/Pages/default.aspx

**University of Maryland, Baltimore,** School of Medicine, Genetic Counseling Training Program, Baltimore, MD 21201. Offers MGC. *Students:* 16 full-time (15 women); includes 2 minority (1 Asian, non-Hispanic/Latino; 1 Hispanic/Latino). Average age 25. 120 applicants, 7% accepted, 8 enrolled. In 2016, 7 master's awarded. *Expenses:* Contact institution. *Unit head:* Shannan DeLany Dixon, Director, 410-706-4713, Fax: 410-706-1644, E-mail: sdelany@som.umaryland.edu.

**University of Michigan,** Rackham Graduate School, Program in Biomedical Sciences (PIBS), Department of Human Genetics, Ann Arbor, MI 48109-5618. Offers genetic counseling (MS); human genetics (MS, PhD). Terminal master's awarded for partial completion of doctoral program. *Degree requirements:* For master's, research project; for doctorate, thesis/dissertation, oral preliminary exam, oral defense of dissertation. *Entrance requirements:* For master's, GRE General Test, bachelor's degree; 3 letters of recommendation; advocacy experience (for the MS in genetic counseling); for doctorate, GRE General Test, bachelor's degree; 3 letters of recommendation. Additional exam requirements/recommendations for international students: Required—TOEFL (minimum score 84 iBT). Electronic applications accepted. *Expenses:* Contact institution. *Faculty research:* Molecular and developmental genetics, genetics of Mendelian and complex human disease, genome biology, statistical and population genetics, epigenetics.

**University of Minnesota, Twin Cities Campus,** Graduate School, Program in Molecular, Cellular, Developmental Biology and Genetics, Minneapolis, MN 55455-0213. Offers genetic counseling (MS); molecular, cellular, developmental biology and genetics (PhD). Terminal master's awarded for partial completion of doctoral program. *Degree requirements:* For master's, thesis optional; for doctorate, thesis/dissertation. *Entrance requirements:* For master's and doctorate, GRE General Test. Additional exam requirements/recommendations for international students: Required—TOEFL (minimum score 625 paper-based; 80 iBT). Electronic applications accepted. *Faculty research:* Membrane receptors and membrane transport, cell interactions, cytoskeleton and cell mobility, regulation of gene expression, plant cell and molecular biology.

**The University of North Carolina at Greensboro,** Graduate School, School of Health and Human Sciences, Program in Genetic Counseling, Greensboro, NC 27412-5001. Offers MS. Electronic applications accepted.

**University of Oklahoma Health Sciences Center,** College of Medicine and Graduate College, Department of Genetic Counseling, Oklahoma City, OK 73190. Offers MS. *Entrance requirements:* For master's, GRE General Test, 3 letters of recommendation.

**University of Pittsburgh,** Graduate School of Public Health, Department of Human Genetics, Pittsburgh, PA 15261. Offers genetic counseling (MS); human genetics (MS, PhD); public health genetics (MPH, Certificate); MD/PhD; MS/MPH. *Faculty:* 17 full-time (8 women), 42 part-time/adjunct (36 women). *Students:* 53 full-time (39 women), 27 part-time (20 women); includes 13 minority (3 Black or African American, non-Hispanic/Latino; 4 Asian, non-Hispanic/Latino; 4 Hispanic/Latino; 2 Two or more races, non-Hispanic/Latino), 11 international. Average age 27. 157 applicants, 46% accepted, 26 enrolled. In 2016, 16 master's, 9 doctorates awarded. *Degree requirements:* For master's, comprehensive exam, thesis; for doctorate, comprehensive exam, thesis/dissertation, qualifying examination. *Entrance requirements:* For master's and doctorate, GRE General Test (above the 70th percentile for the verbal and quantitative tests), previous course work in biochemistry and behavioral or social sciences (recommended); bachelor's degree in a discipline related to the biological or behavioral sciences from accredited college or university with minimum GPA of 3.0, introductory courses in genetics and calculus. Additional exam requirements/recommendations for international students: Required—TOEFL (minimum score 550 paper-based, 80 iBT) or IELTS (minimum score 6.5); GRE. *Application deadline:* For fall admission, 1/15 priority date for domestic and international students; for spring admission, 10/15 priority date for domestic students, 8/1 priority date for international students. Applications are processed on a rolling basis. Application fee: $120. Electronic applications accepted. *Expenses:* $12,750 full-time in-state per term, $21,065 full-time out-of-state per term, $415 full-time fees; $1,039 part-time in-state per credit, $1,726 part-time out-of-state per credit, $265 part-time fees. *Financial support:* In 2016–17, 19 students received support, including 19 research assistantships (averaging $17,186 per year); scholarships/grants, traineeships, and health care benefits also available. Financial award application deadline: 4/15; financial award applicants required to submit CSS PROFILE or FAFSA. *Faculty research:* Atherosclerotic cardiovascular disease, Alzheimer's disease, statistical genetics, chromosomal instability, gene mapping. *Total annual research expenditures:* $3.1 million. *Unit head:* Dr. Dietrich A. Stephan, Chair, 412-648-3353, Fax: 412-624-3020, E-mail: dstephan@pitt.edu. *Application contact:* Noel C. Harrie, Student Services Coordinator, 412-624-3066, Fax: 412-624-3020, E-mail: nce1@pitt.edu. Website: http://www.publichealth.pitt.edu/human-genetics

**University of South Carolina,** School of Medicine and The Graduate School, Graduate Programs in Medicine, Program in Genetic Counseling, Columbia, SC 29203. Offers MS. *Degree requirements:* For master's, comprehensive exam, internship, practicum. *Entrance requirements:* For master's, GRE General Test. Electronic applications accepted. *Expenses:* Contact institution. *Faculty research:* Genetic counseling, international, transition, prenatal diagnosis.

**The University of Texas Health Science Center at Houston,** MD Anderson UTHealth Graduate School, Houston, TX 77225-0036. Offers biochemistry and cell biology (PhD); biomedical sciences (MS); cancer biology (PhD); genetic counseling (MS); genetics and epigenetics (PhD); immunology (PhD); medical physics (MS, PhD); microbiology and infectious diseases (PhD); neuroscience (PhD); quantitative sciences (PhD); therapeutics and pharmacology (PhD); MD/PhD. Terminal master's awarded for partial completion of doctoral program. *Degree requirements:* For master's, thesis; for doctorate, thesis/dissertation. *Entrance requirements:* For master's and doctorate, GRE General Test. Additional exam requirements/recommendations for international students: Required—TOEFL. Electronic applications accepted. *Faculty research:* Biomedical sciences.

**University of Toronto,** Faculty of Medicine, Department of Molecular Genetics, Toronto, ON M5S 1A1, Canada. Offers genetic counseling (M Sc); molecular genetics (M Sc, PhD). *Degree requirements:* For master's, thesis; for doctorate, thesis/dissertation. *Entrance requirements:* For master's, B Sc or equivalent; for doctorate, M Sc or equivalent, minimum B+ average. Additional exam requirements/recommendations for international students: Required—TOEFL, IELTS (minimum score 7), Michigan English Language Assessment Battery (minimum score 85), or COPE (minimum score 4). Electronic applications accepted. *Faculty research:* Structural biology, developmental genetics, molecular medicine, genetic counseling.

**University of Wisconsin–Madison,** Graduate School, College of Agricultural and Life Sciences and Graduate Programs in Medicine, Department of Genetics, Madison, WI 53706-1380. Offers genetic counseling (MS); genetics (PhD). *Degree requirements:* For doctorate, thesis/dissertation.

**University of Wisconsin–Madison,** School of Medicine and Public Health, Master of Genetic Counselor Studies Program, Madison, WI 53706. Offers MGCS. *Students:* 12 full-time. *Entrance requirements:* Additional exam requirements/recommendations for international students: Required—TOEFL. Electronic applications accepted. *Unit head:* Catherine Ann Reiser, Associate Professor, E-mail: reiser@pediatrics.wisc.edu. *Application contact:* April Meiller, Graduate Coordinator, 608-262-9674, E-mail: ameiller@wisc.edu. Website: http://www.med.wisc.edu/education/graduate-programs/genetic-counseling/main/26910

**Wayne State University,** School of Medicine, Office of Biomedical Graduate Programs, Detroit, MI 48202. Offers anatomy and cell biology (MS, PhD); basic medical sciences (MS); biochemistry and molecular biology (MS, PhD); cancer biology (MS, PhD); clinical and translational science (Graduate Certificate); family medicine and public health sciences (MPH, Graduate Certificate), including public health practice; genetic counseling (MS); immunology and microbiology (MS, PhD); medical physics (MS, PhD, Graduate Certificate); medical research (MS); molecular medicine and genomics (MS, PhD), including molecular genetics and genomics; pathology (PhD); pharmacology (MS, PhD); physiology (MS, PhD), including physiology, reproductive sciences (PhD); psychiatry and behavioral neurosciences (PhD), including translational neuroscience; MD/MPH; MD/PhD; MPH/MA; MSW/MPH. *Program availability:* Part-time, evening/weekend. *Students:* 301 full-time (150 women), 112 part-time (56 women); includes 114 minority (19 Black or African American, non-Hispanic/Latino; 1 American Indian or Alaska Native, non-Hispanic/Latino; 65 Asian, non-Hispanic/Latino; 12 Hispanic/Latino; 17 Two or more races, non-Hispanic/Latino), 62 international. Average age 27. 1,009 applicants, 22% accepted, 161 enrolled. In 2016, 65 master's, 22 doctorates, 8 other advanced degrees awarded. Terminal master's awarded for partial completion of doctoral program. *Degree requirements:* For master's, thesis (for some programs); for doctorate, thesis/dissertation. *Entrance requirements:* For master's, doctorate, and Graduate Certificate, GRE. Additional exam requirements/recommendations for international students: Required—TOEFL (minimum score 550 paper-based; 100 iBT), Michigan English Language Assessment Battery (minimum score 85); Recommended—IELTS (minimum score 6.5), TWE (minimum score 5.5). *Application deadline:* For fall admission, 2/1 for domestic and international students. Applications are processed on a rolling basis. Application fee: $50. Electronic applications accepted. *Expenses:* $20,126 per year resident tuition and fees, $36,434 per year non-resident tuition and fees. *Financial support:* In 2016–17, 197 students received support, including 67 fellowships with full tuition reimbursements available (averaging $24,294 per year), 94 research assistantships with full tuition reimbursements available (averaging $26,850 per year); scholarships/grants, traineeships, and health care benefits also available. *Faculty research:* Cancer biology, neurosciences, vision sciences, molecular biology, pathology,

physiology, pharmacology, public health, medical physics. *Unit head:* Dr. Daniel A. Walz, Associate Dean for Biomedical Graduate Programs, 313-577-1455, Fax: 313-577-8796, E-mail: gradprogs@med.wayne.edu.
Website: https://www.med.wayne.edu/biomedical-graduate-programs/

# Health Psychology

**Adler University,** Programs in Psychology, Chicago, IL 60602. Offers advanced Adlerian psychotherapy (Certificate); art therapy (MA); clinical mental health counseling (MA); clinical neuropsychology (Certificate); clinical psychology (Psy D); community psychology (MA); counseling and organizational psychology (MA); counseling psychology (MA); counselor education and supervision (PhD); couple and family therapy (DCFT); criminology (MA); emergency management leadership (MA); forensic psychology (MA); marriage and family counseling (MA); marriage and family therapy (Certificate); military psychology (MA); nonprofit management (MA); organizational psychology (MA); police psychology (MA); public policy and administration (MA); rehabilitation counseling (MA); sport and health psychology (MA); substance abuse counseling (Certificate); Psy D/Certificate; Psy D/MACAT; Psy D/MACP; Psy D/MAMFC; Psy D/MASAC. *Accreditation:* APA. *Program availability:* Part-time, evening/weekend, online learning. Terminal master's awarded for partial completion of doctoral program. *Degree requirements:* For master's, thesis or alternative, oral exam, practicum; for doctorate, thesis/dissertation, clinical exam, internship, oral exam, practicum, written qualifying exam. *Entrance requirements:* For master's, 12 semester hours in psychology, minimum GPA of 3.0; for doctorate, 18 semester hours in psychology, minimum GPA of 3.25; for Certificate, appropriate master's or doctoral degree. Additional exam requirements/recommendations for international students: Required—TOEFL (minimum score 550 paper-based; 79 iBT). Electronic applications accepted.

**See Display on page 982 and Close-Up on page 1225.**

**Alliant International University–Los Angeles,** California School of Professional Psychology, Psy D Program in Clinical Psychology, Alhambra, CA 91803. Offers clinical health psychology (Psy D); family/child and couple clinical psychology (Psy D); multi-interest option (Psy D); multicultural community-clinical psychology (Psy D). *Accreditation:* APA. *Degree requirements:* For doctorate, comprehensive exam, thesis/dissertation. *Entrance requirements:* For doctorate, interview, minimum GPA of 3.0 in both psychology and overall. Additional exam requirements/recommendations for international students: Required—TOEFL (minimum score 600 paper-based), TWE. Electronic applications accepted. *Faculty research:* Child and family psychology, multicultural and community psychology, acculturation, lesbian and gay issues, women's health.

**Appalachian State University,** Cratis D. Williams Graduate School, Department of Psychology, Boone, NC 28608. Offers clinical health psychology (MA). *Program availability:* Part-time. *Degree requirements:* For master's, comprehensive exam, thesis optional, exit exam. *Entrance requirements:* For master's, GRE General Test, 3 letters of recommendation. Additional exam requirements/recommendations for international students: Required—TOEFL (minimum score 550 paper-based; 79 iBT) or IELTS (minimum score 6.5). *Application deadline:* For fall admission, 2/15 for domestic students, 2/1 for international students. Applications are processed on a rolling basis. Application fee: $55. Electronic applications accepted. *Expenses:* Tuition, state resident: full-time $4744. Tuition, nonresident: full-time $17,913. Full-time tuition and fees vary according to program. *Financial support:* Fellowships, research assistantships, teaching assistantships, career-related internships or fieldwork, Federal Work-Study, scholarships/grants, and unspecified assistantships available. Financial award application deadline: 4/1; financial award applicants required to submit FAFSA. *Faculty research:* Eating disorders, school-based consultations, organizational behavior management, brain mechanisms of sound localization, parenting styles. *Unit head:* Dr. James Denniston, Chair, 828-262-2272, Fax: 828-262-2272, E-mail: dennistonjc@appstate.edu. *Application contact:* Dr. Twila Wingrove, Program Director, 828-262-2272 Ext. 440, E-mail: wingroveta@appstate.edu.
Website: http://www.psych.appstate.edu/

**Argosy University, Atlanta,** Georgia School of Professional Psychology, Atlanta, GA 30328. Offers clinical psychology (MA, Psy D, Postdoctoral Respecialization Certificate), including child and family psychology (Psy D), general adult clinical (Psy D), health psychology (Psy D), neuropsychology/geropsychology (Psy D); community counseling (MA), including marriage and family therapy; counselor education and supervision (Ed D); forensic psychology (MA); industrial organizational psychology (MA); marriage and family therapy (Certificate); sport-exercise psychology (MA). *Accreditation:* APA.

**Argosy University, Chicago,** Illinois School of Professional Psychology, Doctoral Program in Clinical Psychology, Chicago, IL 60601. Offers child and adolescent psychology (Psy D); client-centered and experiential psychotherapies (Psy D); diversity and multicultural psychology (Psy D); family psychology (Psy D); forensic psychology (Psy D); health psychology (Psy D); neuropsychology (Psy D); organizational consulting (Psy D); psychoanalytic psychology (Psy D); psychology and spirituality (Psy D). *Accreditation:* APA.

**Argosy University, Northern Virginia,** American School of Professional Psychology, Arlington, VA 22209. Offers clinical psychology (MA, Psy D), including child and family psychology (Psy D), diversity and multicultural psychology (Psy D), forensic psychology (Psy D), health and neuropsychology (Psy D); community counseling (MA); counseling psychology (Ed D), including counselor education and supervision; counselor education and supervision (Ed D); forensic psychology (MA).

**Argosy University, Twin Cities,** Minnesota School of Professional Psychology, Eagan, MN 55121. Offers clinical psychology (MA, Psy D), including child and family psychology (Psy D), forensic psychology (Psy D), health and neuropsychology (Psy D), trauma (Psy D); forensic counseling (Post-Graduate Certificate); forensic psychology (MA); industrial organizational psychology (MA); marriage and family therapy (MA, DMFT), including forensic counseling (MA). *Accreditation:* AAMFT; AAMFT/COAMFTE; APA.

**Bastyr University,** School of Natural Health Arts and Sciences, Kenmore, WA 98028-4966. Offers counseling psychology (MA); holistic landscape design (Certificate); midwifery (MS); nutrition (MS); nutrition and clinical health psychology (MS). *Accreditation:* AND. *Program availability:* Part-time. *Degree requirements:* For master's, thesis optional. *Entrance requirements:* For master's, 1-2 years' basic sciences course work (depending on program). Additional exam requirements/recommendations for international students: Required—TOEFL (minimum score 550 paper-based; 79 iBT). *Faculty research:* Whole-food nutrition for type 2 diabetes; meditation in end-of-life care; stress management; Qi Gong, Tai Chi and yoga for older adults; Echinacea and immunology.

**California Institute of Integral Studies,** School of Professional Psychology and Health, San Francisco, CA 94103. Offers clinical psychology (Psy D); community mental health (MA); drama therapy (MA); expressive arts therapy (MA); human sexuality (PhD); integral counseling psychology (MA); integrative health studies (MA); psychological studies (MA); somatic psychology (MA). *Program availability:* Part-time, evening/weekend, 100% online, blended/hybrid learning. *Students:* 526 full-time (408 women), 113 part-time (96 women); includes 173 minority (34 Black or African American, non-Hispanic/Latino; 5 American Indian or Alaska Native, non-Hispanic/Latino; 31 Asian, non-Hispanic/Latino; 58 Hispanic/Latino; 1 Native Hawaiian or other Pacific Islander, non-Hispanic/Latino; 44 Two or more races, non-Hispanic/Latino), 52 international. Average age 38. 319 applicants, 85% accepted, 164 enrolled. In 2016, 157 master's, 21 doctorates awarded. *Degree requirements:* For doctorate, comprehensive exam, thesis/dissertation. *Entrance requirements:* For master's, minimum GPA of 3.0, letters of recommendation, writing sample; for doctorate, GRE, MA in psychology or social work with appropriate practical experience for advanced standing, or BA with a minimum GPA of 3.1; letters of recommendation; writing sample. Additional exam requirements/recommendations for international students: Required—TOEFL. *Application deadline:* For fall admission, 2/1 priority date for domestic and international students; for spring admission, 10/15 priority date for domestic and international students. Applications are processed on a rolling basis. Application fee: $65. Electronic applications accepted. *Expenses:* Tuition: Full-time $19,728; part-time $1098 per semester hour. *Required fees:* $320; $320 per semester hour. *Financial support:* Research assistantships with tuition reimbursements, teaching assistantships with tuition reimbursements, career-related internships or fieldwork, Federal Work-Study, and scholarships/grants available. Support available to part-time students. Financial award application deadline: 4/15; financial award applicants required to submit FAFSA. *Faculty research:* Transpersonal psychology, somatic psychology, expressive arts therapy, drama therapy, community mental health, ecopsychology, integrative health, human sexuality. *Application contact:* Ellen Durst, Director of Admissions, 415-575-6100, Fax: 415-575-1268, E-mail: admissions@ciis.edu.

**California State University, Dominguez Hills,** College of Natural and Behavioral Sciences, Department of Psychology, Carson, CA 90747-0001. Offers clinical psychology (MA); health psychology (MA). *Program availability:* Part-time, evening/weekend. Terminal master's awarded for partial completion of doctoral program. *Degree requirements:* For master's, comprehensive exam, thesis optional. *Entrance requirements:* For master's, GRE General Test or MAT, interview, minimum GPA of 3.0, prerequisite psychology courses. Additional exam requirements/recommendations for international students: Required—TOEFL (minimum score 550 paper-based). Electronic applications accepted. *Faculty research:* Culture and health, neuropsychology and HIV, psychohistory of the Holocaust, community and adolescents, malingering.

**Central Michigan University,** College of Graduate Studies, College of Humanities and Social and Behavioral Sciences, Department of Psychology, Program in Industrial and Organizational Psychology, Mount Pleasant, MI 48859. Offers industrial and organizational psychology (MA, PhD); occupational health psychology (PhD). *Degree requirements:* For master's, thesis; for doctorate, comprehensive exam, thesis/dissertation. *Entrance requirements:* For master's and doctorate, GRE. Electronic applications accepted. *Faculty research:* Job stress, retirement, leadership, and careers; personality in the workplace, personnel selection, and structural equation modeling in industrial/organizational psychology; personnel psychology, evolutionary psychology, and influences on HRM utilization; occupational health psychology and job stress; work attitudes, psychological ownership in work, and performance appraisal.

**Chatham University,** Program in Counseling Psychology, Pittsburgh, PA 15232-2826. Offers child, adolescent and family (MSCP); counseling psychology (Psy D); health and holistic (MSCP); infant mental health (MSCP); organization and supervision (MSCP); sport and exercise (MSCP). *Accreditation:* APA. *Program availability:* Part-time, evening/weekend. *Degree requirements:* For master's, thesis optional, supervised internship; for doctorate, thesis/dissertation, internship. *Entrance requirements:* For master's, minimum GPA of 3.0; 2 letters of recommendation; resume; prerequisite coursework in statistics, biology, and psychology; for doctorate, GRE. Additional exam requirements/recommendations for international students: Required—TOEFL (minimum score 600 paper-based; 100 iBT), IELTS (minimum score 7), TWE. Electronic applications accepted. Application fee is waived when completed online. *Expenses:* Tuition: Full-time $16,254; part-time $903 per credit hour. *Required fees:* $468; $26 per credit hour. *Faculty research:* Trauma and recovery, hypnosis, psychospiritual dimensions of healing, psychotherapy of schizophrenia.

**Claremont Graduate University,** Graduate Programs, School of Social Science, Policy and Evaluation, Department of Psychology, Claremont, CA 91711-6160. Offers advanced study in evaluation (Certificate); cognitive psychology (MA, PhD); developmental psychology (MA, PhD); evaluation and applied research methods (MA, PhD); health behavior research and evaluation (MA, PhD); human resource development and evaluation (MA); industrial/organizational psychology (MA, PhD); organizational behavior (MA, PhD); organizational psychology (MA, PhD); social psychology (MA, PhD); MBA/PhD. *Program availability:* Part-time. *Faculty:* 19 full-time (9 women), 1 part-time/adjunct (0 women). *Students:* 244 full-time (160 women), 66 part-time (38 women); includes 93 minority (15 Black or African American, non-Hispanic/Latino; 2 American Indian or Alaska Native, non-Hispanic/Latino; 29 Asian, non-Hispanic/Latino; 31 Hispanic/Latino; 2 Native Hawaiian or other Pacific Islander, non-Hispanic/Latino; 14 Two or more races, non-Hispanic/Latino), 41 international. Average age 30. In 2016, 61 master's, 23 doctorates, 5 other advanced degrees awarded. Terminal master's awarded for partial completion of doctoral program. *Entrance requirements:* For master's and doctorate, GRE General Test. Additional exam requirements/recommendations for international students: Required—TOEFL (minimum score 75 iBT). *Application deadline:* For fall admission, 1/15 priority date for domestic and international students. Applications are processed on a rolling basis. Application fee: $80. Electronic applications accepted. *Expenses:* Tuition: Full-time $44,328; part-time $1847 per unit. *Required fees:* $600; $300 per semester. Tuition and fees vary according to course load and program. *Financial support:* Fellowships, research assistantships, teaching assistantships, Federal Work-Study, institutionally sponsored loans, scholarships/grants, and tuition waivers (full and partial) available. Support available to part-time students. Financial award application deadline: 2/15; financial award applicants required to submit FAFSA. *Faculty research:* Social intervention,

diversity in organizations, eyewitness memory, aging and cognition, drug policy. *Unit head:* William Crano, Chair, 909-607-3311, E-mail: william.crano@cgu.edu. *Application contact:* Paige Piontkowsky, Senior Assistant Director of Admissions, 909-607-3240, E-mail: paige.piontkowsky@cgu.edu.
Website: https://www.cgu.edu/school/ssspe/programs/?areas_of_study=psychology

**Drexel University,** College of Arts and Sciences, Department of Psychology, Clinical Psychology Program, Philadelphia, PA 19104-2875. Offers clinical psychology (PhD); forensic psychology (PhD); health psychology (PhD); neuropsychology (PhD). *Accreditation:* APA. *Faculty:* 26 full-time (16 women), 8 part-time/adjunct (7 women). *Students:* 79 full-time (66 women), 8 part-time (5 women); includes 16 minority (4 Black or African American, non-Hispanic/Latino; 5 Asian, non-Hispanic/Latino; 3 Hispanic/Latino; 4 Two or more races, non-Hispanic/Latino), 4 international. Average age 27. In 2016, 10 doctorates awarded. Terminal master's awarded for partial completion of doctoral program. *Degree requirements:* For doctorate, thesis/dissertation, qualifying exam. *Entrance requirements:* For doctorate, GRE General Test, GRE Subject Test, minimum GPA of 3.0. *Application deadline:* For spring admission, 1/15 for domestic students. Application fee: $30. Electronic applications accepted. *Expenses:* Contact institution. *Financial support:* Fellowships, research assistantships, teaching assistantships, career-related internships or fieldwork, Federal Work-Study, institutionally sponsored loans, and tuition waivers (partial) available. Support available to part-time students. Financial award application deadline: 5/1; financial award applicants required to submit FAFSA. *Faculty research:* Cognitive behavioral therapy, stress and coping, eating disorders, substance abuse, developmental disabilities. *Total annual research expenditures:* $3.9 million. *Unit head:* Dr. Maria Schultheis, Head, 215-895-6105. *Application contact:* Director of Graduate Admissions, 215-895-6700, Fax: 215-895-5939, E-mail: enroll@drexel.edu.

**Drexel University,** College of Arts and Sciences, Department of Psychology, Program in Law-Psychology, Philadelphia, PA 19104-2875. Offers JD/PhD. *Students:* 22 full-time (16 women), 9 part-time (8 women); includes 4 minority (2 Black or African American, non-Hispanic/Latino; 2 Hispanic/Latino), 1 international. Average age 27. 11 applicants, 27% accepted, 3 enrolled. *Application deadline:* For fall admission, 2/15 for domestic students. Application fee: $50. Electronic applications accepted. *Expenses:* Contact institution. *Financial support:* Fellowships, research assistantships, teaching assistantships, career-related internships or fieldwork, Federal Work-Study, and institutionally sponsored loans available. Support available to part-time students. Financial award application deadline: 5/1; financial award applicants required to submit FAFSA. *Faculty research:* Mental health law issues, professional ethics, social science applications to law. *Unit head:* Dr. Kirk Heilbrun, Head, 215-895-2402, Fax: 215-895-1333. *Application contact:* Director of Graduate Admissions, 215-895-6700, Fax: 215-895-5939, E-mail: enroll@drexel.edu.

**Duke University,** Graduate School, Department of Psychology and Neuroscience, Durham, NC 27708. Offers biological psychology (PhD); clinical psychology (PhD); cognitive psychology (PhD); developmental psychology (PhD); experimental psychology (PhD); health psychology (PhD); human social development (PhD); JD/MA. *Accreditation:* APA (one or more programs are accredited). *Degree requirements:* For doctorate, thesis/dissertation. *Entrance requirements:* For doctorate, GRE General Test. Additional exam requirements/recommendations for international students: Required—TOEFL (minimum score 577 paper-based; 90 iBT) or IELTS (minimum score 7). Electronic applications accepted.

**East Carolina University,** Graduate School, Thomas Harriot College of Arts and Sciences, Department of Psychology, Greenville, NC 27858-4353. Offers health psychology (PhD), including clinical health psychology, occupational health psychology, pediatric school psychology; industrial and organizational psychology (MA); MA/CAS. *Program availability:* Part-time, evening/weekend. *Students:* 83 full-time (60 women), 23 part-time (16 women); includes 16 minority (8 Black or African American, non-Hispanic/Latino; 1 Asian, non-Hispanic/Latino; 5 Hispanic/Latino; 2 Two or more races, non-Hispanic/Latino). Average age 26. 248 applicants, 19% accepted, 31 enrolled. In 2016, 11 master's, 1 doctorate awarded. *Degree requirements:* For master's, one foreign language, comprehensive exam, thesis. *Entrance requirements:* For master's, GRE General Test, GRE Subject Test. Additional exam requirements/recommendations for international students: Required—TOEFL. *Application deadline:* Applications are processed on a rolling basis. Application fee: $50. *Financial support:* Research assistantships with partial tuition reimbursements, teaching assistantships with partial tuition reimbursements, Federal Work-Study, and traineeships available. Support available to part-time students. Financial award application deadline: 6/1. *Unit head:* Dr. Susan L. McCammon, Chair, 252-328-6357, Fax: 252-328-6357, E-mail: mccammons@ecu.edu. *Application contact:* Dean of Graduate School, 252-328-6012, Fax: 252-328-6071, E-mail: gradschool@ecu.edu.
Website: http://www.ecu.edu/psyc/

**Fielding Graduate University,** Graduate Programs, School of Psychology, Programs in Clinical Psychology, Santa Barbara, CA 93105-3814. Offers clinical psychology (Postbaccalaureate Certificate); forensic psychology (PhD); health psychology (PhD); neuropsychology (PhD); parent-infant mental health (PhD); respecialization in clinical psychology (Post-Doctoral Certificate); violence prevention and control (PhD). *Program availability:* 100% online, blended/hybrid learning. *Faculty:* 28 full-time (19 women), 22 part-time/adjunct (11 women). *Students:* 408 full-time (321 women), 12 part-time (10 women); includes 156 minority (69 Black or African American, non-Hispanic/Latino; 2 American Indian or Alaska Native, non-Hispanic/Latino; 14 Asian, non-Hispanic/Latino; 53 Hispanic/Latino; 18 Two or more races, non-Hispanic/Latino), 5 international. Average age 40. 268 applicants, 39% accepted, 77 enrolled. In 2016, 36 doctorates, 31 other advanced degrees awarded. *Degree requirements:* For doctorate, thesis/dissertation. *Entrance requirements:* For doctorate, bachelor's degree, minimum GPA of 3.0, curriculum vitae, statement of purpose, critical thinking writing sample, 3 letters of recommendation, official transcript; for other advanced degree, bachelor's degree (for post baccalaureate certificate), doctoral degree in psychology (for post doctoral certificate); minimum GPA of 3.0, curriculum vitae, statement of purpose, 3 letters of recommendation, official transcript. *Application deadline:* For fall admission, 2/4 for domestic students, 2/1 for international students; for spring admission, 11/1 for domestic and international students; for summer admission, 3/1 for domestic and international students. Application fee: $75. Electronic applications accepted. *Expenses:* $9,060 per term (for PhD); $8,665 per term (for Post Doctoral Certificate); $720 per credit (for Post Baccalaureate Certificate). *Financial support:* In 2016–17, 28 students received support, including 1 research assistantship (averaging $238 per year), 17 teaching assistantships (averaging $1,973 per year); scholarships/grants also available. Financial award applicants required to submit FAFSA. *Unit head:* Dr. Marilyn Freimuth, Director. *Application contact:* Enrollment Coordinator, 800-340-1099 Ext. 4098, Fax: 805-687-9793, E-mail: psyadmission@fielding.edu.
Website: http://www.fielding.edu/our-programs/school-of-psychology/

**Georgian Court University,** School of Arts and Sciences, Lakewood, NJ 08701-2697. Offers applied behavior analysis (MA); clinical mental health counseling (MA); holistic health studies (MA, Certificate); homeland security (MS, Certificate); mercy spirituality (Certificate); parish business management (Certificate); professional counselor (Certificate); school psychology (MA, Certificate); theology (MA, Certificate). *Program*

*availability:* Part-time, evening/weekend. *Faculty:* 19 full-time (11 women), 6 part-time/adjunct (3 women). *Students:* 90 full-time (75 women), 107 part-time (79 women); includes 34 minority (9 Black or African American, non-Hispanic/Latino; 20 Hispanic/Latino; 5 Two or more races, non-Hispanic/Latino), 1 international. Average age 34. 187 applicants, 49% accepted, 60 enrolled. In 2016, 66 master's, 17 other advanced degrees awarded. *Degree requirements:* For master's, comprehensive exam (for some programs), thesis (for some programs). *Entrance requirements:* For master's, GRE, GMAT, or NTE/PRAXIS, 3 letters of recommendation. Additional exam requirements/recommendations for international students: Required—TOEFL (minimum score 550 paper-based). *Application deadline:* For fall admission, 8/15 for domestic students, 5/1 for international students; for spring admission, 1/15 for domestic students, 10/1 for international students. Applications are processed on a rolling basis. Application fee: $40. Electronic applications accepted. *Expenses: Tuition:* Full-time $15,079; part-time $839 per credit. *Required fees:* $968; $496 per credit. Tuition and fees vary according to campus/location and program. *Financial support:* Scholarships/grants, health care benefits, and unspecified assistantships available. Financial award application deadline: 4/15; financial award applicants required to submit FAFSA. *Unit head:* Dr. Mary Chinery, Dean, 732-987-2493, Fax: 732-987-2007, E-mail: mchinery@georgian.edu. *Application contact:* Patrick Givens, Director of Graduate and Professional Studies Admissions, 732-987-2736, Fax: 732-987-2000, E-mail: gps@georgian.edu.
Website: http://georgian.edu/academics/school-of-arts-sciences/

**John F. Kennedy University,** Graduate School of Holistic Studies, Department of Counseling Psychology, Program in Counseling Psychology, Pleasant Hill, CA 94523-4817. Offers holistic studies (MA); somatic psychology (MA); transpersonal psychology (MA). *Program availability:* Part-time, evening/weekend. *Degree requirements:* For master's, thesis or alternative. *Entrance requirements:* For master's, interview. Additional exam requirements/recommendations for international students: Required—TOEFL.

**La Salle University,** School of Arts and Sciences, Program in Clinical Psychology, Philadelphia, PA 19141-1199. Offers child clinical psychology (Psy D); clinical health psychology (Psy D); clinical psychology (MA); general practice psychology (Psy D). *Accreditation:* AAMFT/COAMFTE. *Program availability:* Part-time, evening/weekend. *Faculty:* 9 full-time (7 women), 6 part-time/adjunct (3 women). *Students:* 77 full-time (62 women), 37 part-time (28 women); includes 15 minority (2 Black or African American, non-Hispanic/Latino; 6 Asian, non-Hispanic/Latino; 4 Hispanic/Latino; 3 Two or more races, non-Hispanic/Latino), 4 international. Average age 27. 301 applicants, 22% accepted, 17 enrolled. In 2016, 20 master's, 17 doctorates awarded. Terminal master's awarded for partial completion of doctoral program. *Degree requirements:* For doctorate, comprehensive exam, thesis/dissertation. *Entrance requirements:* For doctorate, GRE (minimum scores of 148 on both the Verbal Reasoning and Quantitative Reasoning sections strongly recommended); GRE Subject Test in psychology (for those entering with bachelor's degree), baccalaureate degree from accredited institution with major in psychology or related discipline; minimum undergraduate GPA of 3.0, 3.2 graduate; three letters of recommendation; statement of interest and intent; curriculum vitae or resume; personal interview. Additional exam requirements/recommendations for international students: Required—TOEFL. *Application deadline:* For fall admission, 1/15 for domestic students, 1/1 for international students. Application fee: $35. Electronic applications accepted. Application fee is waived when completed online. *Expenses:* Contact institution. *Financial support:* In 2016–17, 26 students received support. Scholarships/grants and unspecified assistantships available. Financial award application deadline: 8/31; financial award applicants required to submit FAFSA. *Unit head:* Dr. Randy Fingerhut, Director, 215-951-1284, Fax: 215-951-5140, E-mail: psyd@lasalle.edu. *Application contact:* Elizabeth Heenan, Director, Graduate and Adult Enrollment, 215-951-1100, Fax: 215-951-1462, E-mail: heenan@lasalle.edu.
Website: http://www.lasalle.edu/doctor-of-psychology/

**Lesley University,** Graduate School of Arts and Social Sciences, Cambridge, MA 02138-2790. Offers clinical mental health counseling (MA), including holistic counseling, school and community counseling, trauma studies; counseling psychology (MA, CAGS), including professional counseling (MA); school counseling (MA); creative writing (MFA); expressive therapies (MA, PhD, CAGS), including art (MA), clinical mental health counseling (MA), dance (MA), expressive therapies (MA), music (MA); independent studies (CAGS); independent study (MA); intercultural relations (MA, CAGS); interdisciplinary studies (MA), including individualized studies, integrative holistic health, mindfulness studies, peace and conflict transformation, trauma sensitive assessment, intervention, and consultation, women's studies; urban environmental leadership (MA). *Program availability:* Part-time, online learning. *Degree requirements:* For master's, internship, practicum, thesis (for expressive therapies); for doctorate, thesis/dissertation, arts apprenticeship, field placement; for CAGS, thesis, internship (for counseling psychology, expressive therapies). *Entrance requirements:* For master's, MAT (counseling psychology), interview, writing samples, art portfolio; for doctorate, GRE or MAT, interview, master's degree; for CAGS, interview, master's degree. Additional exam requirements/recommendations for international students: Required—TOEFL (minimum score 550 paper-based; 80 iBT). Electronic applications accepted. *Faculty research:* Psychotherapy and culture; psychotherapy and psychological trauma; women's issues in art, teaching and psychotherapy; community-based art, psycho-spiritual inquiry.

**North Dakota State University,** College of Graduate and Interdisciplinary Studies, College of Science and Mathematics, Department of Psychology, Fargo, ND 58102. Offers clinical psychology (PhD); health and social psychology (PhD); psychological clinical science (PhD); psychology (MS); visual and cognitive neuroscience (PhD). *Degree requirements:* For master's, thesis; for doctorate, thesis/dissertation. *Entrance requirements:* For master's and doctorate, GRE General Test, GRE Subject Test. Additional exam requirements/recommendations for international students: Required—TOEFL (minimum score 525 paper-based; 71 iBT). Electronic applications accepted. *Faculty research:* Cognition science, neuropsychology, group behavior, applied behavior analysis, behavior therapy.

**Northern Kentucky University,** Office of Graduate Programs, College of Arts and Sciences, Program in Industrial-Organizational Psychology, Highland Heights, KY 41099. Offers industrial psychology (Certificate); industrial-organizational psychology (MS); occupational health psychology (Certificate); organizational psychology (Certificate). *Program availability:* Part-time, evening/weekend. *Degree requirements:* For master's, thesis optional, capstone. *Entrance requirements:* For master's, GRE General Test (minimum scores of 141 verbal, 144 quantitative, and 3.5 writing), bachelor's degree with minimum GPA of 3.0, nine semester hours of psychology coursework, at least one undergraduate course in statistics with minimum B grade, official transcripts, current resume or vita, statement of personal interest, three letters of recommendation; for Certificate, official transcripts, bachelor's degree, minimum undergraduate GPA of 3.0, no grade lower than B on all graduate coursework previously taken that may apply. Additional exam requirements/recommendations for international students: Required—TOEFL (minimum score 79 iBT); Recommended—IELTS (minimum score 6.5). Electronic applications accepted. *Faculty research:* Workplace bullying and abuse, assessment and situational judgment tasks, human factors and work design, racial and social stereotyping in employment, social conflict.

## Health Psychology

**Oklahoma State University,** College of Education, School of Applied Health and Educational Psychology, Stillwater, OK 74078. Offers applied behavioral studies (Ed D); applied health and educational psychology (MS, PhD, Ed S). *Accreditation:* APA (one or more programs are accredited). *Program availability:* Part-time. *Faculty:* 38 full-time (22 women), 11 part-time/adjunct (6 women). *Students:* 168 full-time (122 women), 140 part-time (80 women); includes 86 minority (21 Black or African American, non-Hispanic/Latino; 10 American Indian or Alaska Native, non-Hispanic/Latino; 3 Asian, non-Hispanic/Latino; 24 Hispanic/Latino; 28 Two or more races, non-Hispanic/Latino), 13 international. Average age 30. 157 applicants, 51% accepted, 73 enrolled. In 2016, 73 master's, 21 doctorates awarded. *Degree requirements:* For master's, thesis (for some programs); for doctorate, comprehensive exam, thesis/dissertation. *Entrance requirements:* For master's and doctorate, GRE or GMAT. Additional exam requirements/recommendations for international students: Required—TOEFL (minimum score 550 paper-based; 79 iBT). *Application deadline:* For fall admission, 3/1 priority date for international students; for spring admission, 8/1 priority date for international students. Applications are processed on a rolling basis. Application fee: $40 ($75 for international students). Electronic applications accepted. *Expenses:* Tuition, state resident: full-time $3775; part-time $209.70 per credit hour. Tuition, nonresident: full-time $14,851; part-time $825.05 per credit hour. *Required fees:* $2027; $112.60 per credit hour. Tuition and fees vary according to campus/location. *Financial support:* In 2016–17, 31 research assistantships (averaging $9,791 per year), 64 teaching assistantships (averaging $11,347 per year) were awarded; career-related internships or fieldwork, Federal Work-Study, scholarships/grants, health care benefits, tuition waivers (partial), and unspecified assistantships also available. Support available to part-time students. Financial award application deadline: 3/1; financial award applicants required to submit FAFSA. *Unit head:* Dr. Aric Warren, Head, 405-744-6040, Fax: 405-744-6779, E-mail: aric.warren@okstate.edu.
Website: http://education.okstate.edu/sahep

**Oregon State University,** College of Liberal Arts, Program in Psychology, Corvallis, OR 97331. Offers applied cognition (MS, PhD); engineering psychology (MS, PhD); health psychology (MS, PhD). *Faculty:* 11 full-time (7 women), 2 part-time/adjunct (1 woman). *Students:* 3 full-time (2 women). 14 applicants, 21% accepted, 3 enrolled. *Degree requirements:* For doctorate, thesis/dissertation. *Application deadline:* For fall admission, 12/15 for domestic and international students. Application fee: $75 ($85 for international students). *Expenses:* Tuition, state resident: full-time $12,150; part-time $450 per credit. Tuition, nonresident: full-time $21,789; part-time $807 per credit. *Required fees:* $1651; $1507 per credit. One-time fee: $350. Tuition and fees vary according to course load, campus/location and program. *Unit head:* John Edwards, Director. *Application contact:* Aurora Sherman, Associate Professor and Graduate Education Chair, 541-737-1361, E-mail: aurora.sherman@oregonstate.edu.
Website: http://liberalarts.oregonstate.edu/school-psychological-science/psychology/graduate-psychology

**Penn State Harrisburg,** Graduate School, School of Behavioral Sciences and Education, Middletown, PA 17057. Offers adult education in the health and medical professions (Certificate); applied behavior analysis (MA); applied clinical psychology (MA); applied psychological research (MA); community psychology and social change (MA); English as a second language (ESL) program specialist and leadership (Certificate); folklore and ethnography (Certificate); health education (M Ed); lifelong learning and adult education (M Ed, D Ed); literacy education (M Ed); literacy leadership (Certificate); psychology: applications in clinical psychology (Certificate); psychology: health psychology (Certificate); teaching and curriculum (M Ed); training and development (M Ed, Certificate). *Program availability:* Part-time, evening/weekend. *Unit head:* Dr. Mukund S. Kulkarni, Chancellor, 717-948-6105, Fax: 717-948-6452. *Application contact:* Robert W. Coffman, Jr., Director of Enrollment Management, Recruitment and Admissions, 717-948-6250, Fax: 717-948-6325, E-mail: hbgadmit@psu.edu.
Website: https://harrisburg.psu.edu/behavioral-sciences-and-education/

**Prescott College,** Graduate Programs, Program in Counseling and Psychology, Prescott, AZ 86301. Offers adventure-based psychotherapy (MA); counseling psychology (MA); ecopsychology (MA); ecotherapy (MA); equine-assisted mental health (MA); expressive arts therapy (MA); somatic psychology (MA); student-directed independent study (MA). *Program availability:* Part-time, online learning. *Faculty:* 4 full-time (2 women), 9 part-time/adjunct (6 women). *Students:* 45 full-time (41 women), 139 part-time (113 women); includes 26 minority (1 Black or African American, non-Hispanic/Latino; 4 American Indian or Alaska Native, non-Hispanic/Latino; 2 Asian, non-Hispanic/Latino; 7 Hispanic/Latino; 1 Native Hawaiian or other Pacific Islander, non-Hispanic/Latino; 11 Two or more races, non-Hispanic/Latino), 7 international. Average age 38. 129 applicants, 84% accepted, 69 enrolled. In 2016, 24 master's awarded. Terminal master's awarded for partial completion of doctoral program. *Degree requirements:* For master's, thesis, fieldwork or internship, practicum. *Entrance requirements:* For master's, 2 letters of recommendation, resume. Additional exam requirements/recommendations for international students: Required—TOEFL (minimum score 500 paper-based). *Application deadline:* For fall admission, 4/15 priority date for domestic and international students; for spring admission, 9/15 priority date for domestic and international students. Applications are processed on a rolling basis. Application fee: $40. Electronic applications accepted. *Expenses: Tuition:* Full-time $19,680. One-time fee: $260 part-time. *Financial support:* Fellowships, research assistantships, teaching assistantships, career-related internships or fieldwork, Federal Work-Study, institutionally sponsored loans, scholarships/grants, traineeships, health care benefits, tuition waivers, and unspecified assistantships available. Support available to part-time students. Financial award applicants required to submit FAFSA. *Unit head:* Dr. Stacey Carillo, Department Chair for Counseling, E-mail: stacey.carillo@prescott.edu. *Application contact:* Robert Monk, Graduate Admissions Counselor, 928-350-2109, E-mail: robert.monk@prescott.edu.

**Rhode Island College,** School of Graduate Studies, Faculty of Arts and Sciences, Department of Psychology, Providence, RI 02908-1991. Offers health psychology (CGS); psychology (MA). *Program availability:* Part-time, evening/weekend. *Faculty:* 4 full-time (2 women). *Students:* 1 full-time (0 women), 5 part-time (all women); includes 1 minority (American Indian or Alaska Native, non-Hispanic/Latino). Average age 25. In 2016, 5 master's awarded. *Degree requirements:* For master's, comprehensive exam. *Entrance requirements:* For master's, GRE, 3 letters of recommendation. Additional exam requirements/recommendations for international students: Recommended—TOEFL (minimum score 550 paper-based; 79 iBT). *Application deadline:* For fall admission, 3/1 for domestic students; for spring admission, 11/1 for domestic students. Applications are processed on a rolling basis. Application fee: $50. Electronic applications accepted. *Expenses:* Tuition, state resident: full-time $8928; part-time $372 per credit. Tuition, nonresident: full-time $17,376; part-time $724 per credit. *Required fees:* $604; $22 per credit. One-time fee: $74. *Financial support:* In 2016–17, 3 teaching assistantships with full tuition reimbursements (averaging $3,500 per year) were awarded; Federal Work-Study, scholarships/grants, health care benefits, and unspecified assistantships also available. Support available to part-time students. Financial award application deadline: 5/15; financial award applicants required to submit FAFSA. *Unit head:* Dr. Randi Kim, Chair, 401-456-8015. *Application contact:* Graduate

Studies, 401-456-8700.
Website: http://www.ric.edu/psychology/index.php

**Rutgers University–New Brunswick,** Graduate School-New Brunswick, Program in Psychology, Piscataway, NJ 08854-8097. Offers behavioral neuroscience (PhD); clinical psychology (PhD); cognitive psychology (PhD); interdisciplinary health psychology (PhD); social psychology (PhD). *Accreditation:* APA. *Degree requirements:* For doctorate, comprehensive exam, thesis/dissertation. *Entrance requirements:* For doctorate, GRE General Test, 3 letters of recommendation. Additional exam requirements/recommendations for international students: Required—TOEFL (minimum score 577 paper-based). Electronic applications accepted. *Faculty research:* Learning and memory, behavioral ecology, hormones and behavior, psychopharmacology, anxiety disorders.

**San Diego State University,** Graduate and Research Affairs, College of Health and Human Services, Graduate School of Public Health, San Diego, CA 92182. Offers environmental health (MPH, PhD); epidemiology (MPH, PhD), including biostatistics (MPH); global emergency preparedness and response (MS); global health (PhD); health behavior (PhD); health promotion (MPH); health services administration (MPH); toxicology (MS); MPH/MA; MSW/MPH. *Accreditation:* CAHME (one or more programs are accredited); CEPH (one or more programs are accredited). *Program availability:* Part-time. *Degree requirements:* For master's, comprehensive exam (for some programs), thesis (for some programs); for doctorate, thesis/dissertation. *Entrance requirements:* For master's, GMAT (MPH in health services administration), GRE General Test; for doctorate, GRE General Test. Additional exam requirements/recommendations for international students: Required—TOEFL. *Faculty research:* Evaluation of tobacco, AIDS prevalence and prevention, mammography, infant death project, Alzheimer's in elderly Chinese.

**Saybrook University,** School of Psychology and Interdisciplinary Inquiry, San Francisco, CA 94612. Offers human science (MA, PhD), including consciousness and spirituality, humanistic and transpersonal psychology, integrative health studies, organizational systems, social transformation; organizational systems (MA, PhD), including consciousness and spirituality, humanistic and transpersonal psychology, integrative health studies, leadership of sustainable systems (MA), organizational systems, social transformation; psychology (MA, PhD), including consciousness and spirituality, creativity studies (MA), humanistic and transpersonal psychology, integrative health studies, Jungian studies, marriage and family therapy (MA), organizational systems, social transformation. *Program availability:* Online learning. Terminal master's awarded for partial completion of doctoral program. *Degree requirements:* For master's, thesis or alternative; for doctorate, thesis/dissertation. *Entrance requirements:* Additional exam requirements/recommendations for international students: Required—TOEFL (minimum score 580 paper-based; 93 iBT). Electronic applications accepted. *Faculty research:* Humanistic theory, health studies, organizational systems, consciousness and spirituality, social transformation.

**Southwestern College,** Program in Integral Somatic Psychology, Santa Fe, NM 87502-4788. Offers Certificate.

**Stony Brook University, State University of New York,** Graduate School, College of Arts and Sciences, Department of Psychology, Program in Social and Health Psychology, Stony Brook, NY 11794. Offers PhD. *Students:* 21 full-time (all women); includes 6 minority (1 Black or African American, non-Hispanic/Latino; 4 Asian, non-Hispanic/Latino; 1 Two or more races, non-Hispanic/Latino). Average age 28. 57 applicants, 9% accepted, 5 enrolled. In 2016, 3 doctorates awarded. *Degree requirements:* For doctorate, thesis/dissertation. *Entrance requirements:* For doctorate, GRE General Test, GRE Subject Test. Additional exam requirements/recommendations for international students: Required—TOEFL (minimum score 90 iBT). *Application deadline:* For fall admission, 1/15 for domestic students; for spring admission, 10/1 for domestic students. Application fee: $100. Electronic applications accepted. *Expenses:* Contact institution. *Financial support:* In 2016–17, 1 fellowship, 1 research assistantship, 14 teaching assistantships were awarded. *Unit head:* Dr. Arthur Samuel, Chair, 631-632-7792, E-mail: arthur.samuel@stonybrook.edu. *Application contact:* Marilynn Wollmuth, Coordinator, 631-632-7855, Fax: 631-632-7876, E-mail: marilyn.wollmuth@stonybrook.edu.
Website: http://www.stonybrook.edu/commcms/psychology/social_health/overview.html

**United States International University–Africa,** School of Arts and Sciences, Nairobi, Kenya. Offers counseling psychology (MA), including chemical dependency, health psychology; international relations (MA), including development studies, diplomacy and foreign policy, peace and conflict studies. *Program availability:* Part-time, evening/weekend. *Degree requirements:* For master's, thesis, practicum. *Entrance requirements:* For master's, GRE General Test, 2 letters of recommendation, resume. Additional exam requirements/recommendations for international students: Required—TOEFL. *Faculty research:* Trauma in children, African intellectualism, psychological assessment tools.

**The University of Alabama at Birmingham,** School of Public Health, Program in Public Health, Birmingham, AL 35294. Offers applied epidemiology and pharmacoepidemiology (MSPH); biostatistics (MPH); clinical and translational science (MSPH); environmental health (MPH); environmental health and toxicology (MSPH); epidemiology (MPH); general theory and practice (MPH); health behavior (MPH); health care organization (MPH); health policy quantitative policy analysis (MPH); industrial hygiene (MPH, MSPH); maternal and child health policy (Dr PH); maternal and child health policy and leadership (MPH); occupational health and safety (MPH); outcomes research (MSPH, Dr PH); public health (PhD); public health management (Dr PH); public health preparedness management (MPH). *Accreditation:* CEPH. *Program availability:* Part-time, online learning. *Degree requirements:* For doctorate, comprehensive exam, thesis/dissertation. *Entrance requirements:* For master's and doctorate, GRE. Additional exam requirements/recommendations for international students: Recommended—TOEFL (minimum score 550 paper-based; 79 iBT), IELTS (minimum score 6.5). Electronic applications accepted. Full-time tuition and fees vary according to course load and program.

**The University of British Columbia,** Faculty of Arts and Faculty of Graduate Studies, Department of Psychology, Vancouver, BC V6T 1Z4, Canada. Offers behavioral neuroscience (MA, PhD); clinical psychology (MA, PhD); cognitive science (MA, PhD); developmental psychology (MA, PhD); health psychology (MA, PhD); quantitative methods (MA, PhD); social/personality psychology (MA, PhD). *Accreditation:* APA (one or more programs are accredited). Terminal master's awarded for partial completion of doctoral program. *Degree requirements:* For master's, thesis; for doctorate, comprehensive exam, thesis/dissertation. *Entrance requirements:* For master's and doctorate, GRE General Test. Additional exam requirements/recommendations for international students: Required—TOEFL. *Application deadline:* Applications are processed on a rolling basis. Application fee: $100 Canadian dollars ($162 Canadian dollars for international students). Electronic applications accepted. *Expenses:* $4,802 per year tuition and fees, $8,436 per year international. *Financial support:* Fellowships, research assistantships, teaching assistantships, career-related internships or fieldwork, Federal Work-Study, institutionally sponsored loans, scholarships/grants, health care benefits, tuition waivers (full and partial), and unspecified assistantships available.

Financial award application deadline: 1/1. *Faculty research:* Clinical, developmental, social/personality, cognition, behavioral neuroscience. *Application contact:* Jaclyn Shaw, 604-822-5002, Fax: 604-822-6923, E-mail: gradsec@psych.ubc.ca. Website: http://psych.ubc.ca/

**University of Colorado Denver,** College of Liberal Arts and Sciences, Department of Psychology, Denver, CO 80217. Offers clinical health (PhD); psychology (MA). *Program availability:* Part-time, evening/weekend. *Faculty:* 20 full-time (8 women), 1 (woman) part-time/adjunct. *Students:* 15 full-time (13 women), 13 part-time (8 women); includes 3 minority (1 Asian, non-Hispanic/Latino; 2 Hispanic/Latino). Average age 29. 173 applicants, 3% accepted, 6 enrolled. In 2016, 8 master's, 4 doctorates awarded. *Degree requirements:* For master's, 31-33 semester hours, thesis or internship, minimum GPA of 3.0; for doctorate, comprehensive exam, thesis/dissertation, 69 credits of coursework, minimum of 12 clinical practicum hours, 30 dissertation hours, three credits of pre-doctoral internship. *Entrance requirements:* For master's, GRE General Test; GRE Subject Test (recommended), undergraduate courses in psychological statistics, abnormal psychology and introductory psychology; minimum GPA of 3.0; three letters of recommendation; personal statement; resume; for doctorate, GRE General Test; GRE Subject Test (recommended), minimum GPA of 3.5; undergraduate courses in introductory psychology, psychological statistics, research methods and abnormal psychology; letters of recommendation; personal statement; resume. Additional exam requirements/recommendations for international students: Required—TOEFL (minimum score 537 paper-based; 75 iBT); Recommended—IELTS (minimum score 6.5). *Application deadline:* For fall admission, 12/15 for domestic students, 12/1 for international students. Application fee: $50 ($75 for international students). Electronic applications accepted. *Expenses:* Tuition, state resident: full-time $11,006; part-time $474 per credit. Tuition, nonresident: full-time $28,212; part-time $1264 per credit hour. *Required fees:* $256 per semester. One-time fee: $94.32. Tuition and fees vary according to campus/location and program. *Financial support:* In 2016–17, 32 students received support. Fellowships, research assistantships, teaching assistantships, career-related internships or fieldwork, Federal Work-Study, institutionally sponsored loans, scholarships/grants, and traineeships available. Financial award application deadline: 4/1; financial award applicants required to submit FAFSA. *Faculty research:* Organizational behavior, body image perception, professional ethics, infant perception and cognition, charismatic leadership. *Unit head:* Dr. Kevin S. Masters, Clinical Health Psychology Program Director, 303-352-3961, Fax: 303-556-3520, E-mail: kevin.masters@ucdenver.edu. *Application contact:* Anne Beard, Program Assistant, 303-556-2192, Fax: 303-556-3520, E-mail: anne.beard@ucdenver.edu. Website: http://www.ucdenver.edu/academics/colleges/CLAS/Departments/psychology/Pages/Psychology.aspx

**University of Florida,** Graduate School, College of Public Health and Health Professions, Department of Clinical and Health Psychology, Gainesville, FL 32611. Offers clinical and translational science (PhD); psychology (MS). *Accreditation:* APA (one or more programs are accredited). *Degree requirements:* For doctorate, comprehensive exam, thesis/dissertation, pre-doctoral internship. *Entrance requirements:* For master's and doctorate, GRE General Test, minimum GPA of 3.0. Additional exam requirements/recommendations for international students: Required—TOEFL (minimum score 550 paper-based; 80 iBT), IELTS (minimum score 6). Electronic applications accepted. *Faculty research:* Clinical child and pediatric psychology, medical psychology, neuropsychology, health promotion and aging.

**University of Michigan–Dearborn,** College of Arts, Sciences, and Letters, Master of Science in Psychology Program, Dearborn, MI 48128. Offers clinical health psychology (MS); health psychology (MS). *Program availability:* Part-time. *Faculty:* 17 full-time (9 women). *Students:* 23 full-time (18 women), 7 part-time (6 women); includes 4 minority (1 Black or African American, non-Hispanic/Latino; 1 Asian, non-Hispanic/Latino; 2 Hispanic/Latino), 3 international. Average age 28. 57 applicants, 49% accepted, 11 enrolled. In 2016, 10 master's awarded. *Degree requirements:* For master's, thesis optional. *Entrance requirements:* For master's, GRE, 3 letters of recommendation. Additional exam requirements/recommendations for international students: Required—TOEFL (minimum score 560 paper-based; 84 iBT), IELTS (minimum score 6.5). *Application deadline:* For fall admission, 3/15 for domestic and international students. Application fee: $60. Electronic applications accepted. *Expenses:* Contact institution. *Financial support:* In 2016–17, 11 students received support. Career-related internships or fieldwork, scholarships/grants, and non-resident tuition scholarships available. Financial award application deadline: 3/1; financial award applicants required to submit FAFSA. *Faculty research:* Cardiovascular reactivity; chronic pain; gender and couples health; personality and multicultural assessment; neuropsychology and cognition. *Unit head:* Dr. Nancy Wrobel, Program Director, 313-593-5088, E-mail: nwrobel@umich.edu. *Application contact:* Carol Ligienza, Coordinator, CASL Graduate Programs, 313-593-1183, Fax: 313-583-6700, E-mail: caslgrad@umich.edu. Website: http://umdearborn.edu/casl/psychology/

**University of New Mexico,** Graduate Studies, College of Arts and Sciences, Program in Psychology, Albuquerque, NM 87131-2039. Offers behavioral neuroscience (PhD); clinical psychology (PhD); cognitive neuroimaging (PhD); developmental psychology (PhD); evolution (PhD); health psychology (PhD); quantitative methodology (PhD). *Accreditation:* APA. *Faculty:* 23 full-time (8 women), 1 part-time/adjunct (0 women). *Students:* 60 full-time (36 women), 16 part-time (10 women); includes 22 minority (2 Black or African American, non-Hispanic/Latino; 2 American Indian or Alaska Native, non-Hispanic/Latino; 3 Asian, non-Hispanic/Latino; 12 Hispanic/Latino; 3 Two or more races, non-Hispanic/Latino), 2 international. Average age 30. 227 applicants, 11% accepted, 16 enrolled. In 2016, 10 doctorates awarded. *Degree requirements:* For doctorate, comprehensive exam, thesis/dissertation. *Entrance requirements:* For doctorate, GRE General Test, GRE Subject Test (psychology), minimum GPA of 3.0. Additional exam requirements/recommendations for international students: Required—TOEFL (minimum score 550 paper-based; 79 iBT), IELTS (minimum score 6.5). *Application deadline:* For fall admission, 12/15 priority date for domestic and international students. Applications are processed on a rolling basis. Application fee: $50. Electronic applications accepted. *Financial support:* Fellowships, research assistantships with tuition reimbursements, teaching assistantships with tuition reimbursements, career-related internships or fieldwork, Federal Work-Study, institutionally sponsored loans, scholarships/grants, health care benefits, tuition waivers (partial), and unspecified assistantships available. Financial award application deadline: 3/1; financial award applicants required to submit FAFSA. *Faculty research:* Addiction, cognition, brain and behavior, developmental, evolutionary, functioning neuroimaging, health psychology, learning and memory, neuroscience. *Total annual research expenditures:* $727,970. *Unit head:* Dr. Jane Ellen Smith, Department Chair, 505-277-4121, Fax: 505-277-1394. *Application contact:* Rikki Murphy, Graduate Program Coordinator, 505-277-5009, Fax: 505-277-1394, E-mail: advising@unm.edu. Website: http://psych.unm.edu

**The University of North Carolina at Chapel Hill,** Graduate School, Gillings School of Global Public Health, Department of Health Behavior, Chapel Hill, NC 27599. Offers MPH, PhD, MPH/MCRP, MSPH/PhD. *Accreditation:* CEPH (one or more programs are accredited). *Faculty:* 32 full-time (26 women), 45 part-time/adjunct (33 women). *Students:* 132 full-time (117 women), 3 part-time (2 women); includes 54 minority (15

Black or African American, non-Hispanic/Latino; 18 Asian, non-Hispanic/Latino; 12 Hispanic/Latino; 9 Two or more races, non-Hispanic/Latino), 5 international. Average age 27. 351 applicants, 44% accepted, 53 enrolled. In 2016, 49 master's, 7 doctorates awarded. *Degree requirements:* For master's, comprehensive exam, thesis or alternative, major paper, capstone, practicum; for doctorate, comprehensive exam, thesis/dissertation, practicum. *Entrance requirements:* For master's, GRE General Test or MCAT, three letters of recommendation (academic and/or professional); for doctorate, GRE General Test, master's degree, three letters of recommendation (academic and/or professional). Additional exam requirements/recommendations for international students: Required—TOEFL (minimum score 90 iBT), IELTS (minimum score 7). *Application deadline:* For fall admission, 12/1 for domestic and international students. Applications are processed on a rolling basis. Application fee: $85. Electronic applications accepted. *Financial support:* Fellowships with tuition reimbursements, research assistantships with tuition reimbursements, teaching assistantships with tuition reimbursements, career-related internships or fieldwork, Federal Work-Study, institutionally sponsored loans, scholarships/grants, traineeships, health care benefits, and unspecified assistantships available. Financial award application deadline: 12/10; financial award applicants required to submit FAFSA. *Faculty research:* Cancer prevention and control, aging health promotion and disease prevention, adolescent health, nutrition intervention. *Unit head:* Dr. Leslie A. Lytle, Chair, 919-843-8171, E-mail: llytle@email.unc.edu. *Application contact:* Da'esha McPhaul, Student Services Manager, 919-966-5771, E-mail: daesha09@email.unc.edu. Website: http://www2.sph.unc.edu/hbhe/

**The University of North Carolina at Charlotte,** College of Liberal Arts and Sciences, Department of Psychology, Charlotte, NC 28223-0001. Offers cognitive science (Graduate Certificate); health psychology (PhD); industrial/organizational psychology (MA); psychology (MA). *Accreditation:* APA. *Program availability:* Part-time. *Faculty:* 32 full-time (21 women), 1 (woman) part-time/adjunct. *Students:* 37 full-time (32 women), 38 part-time (26 women); includes 19 minority (7 Black or African American, non-Hispanic/Latino; 1 Asian, non-Hispanic/Latino; 8 Hispanic/Latino; 3 Two or more races, non-Hispanic/Latino). Average age 28. 331 applicants, 16% accepted, 28 enrolled. In 2016, 13 master's, 5 doctorates, 3 other advanced degrees awarded. *Degree requirements:* For master's, thesis (for some programs); for doctorate, comprehensive exam, thesis/dissertation, internship (clinical health students only). *Entrance requirements:* For master's, GRE, GMAT, MAT; for doctorate, GRE, at least 18 hours of coursework in psychology including introductory psychology and research methods, undergraduate course in statistics, transcripts of all academic work attempted since high school including evidence of the completion of a bachelor's degree, at least three references, personal statement, resume or curriculum vitae; for Graduate Certificate, enrolled and in good standing in a graduate degree program at UNC Charlotte, or have minimum GPA of 3.0 for undergraduate courses. Additional exam requirements/recommendations for international students: Required—TOEFL (minimum score 523 paper-based, 70 iBT) or IELTS (6.5). *Application deadline:* For fall admission, 11/15 for domestic and international students. Applications are processed on a rolling basis. Application fee: $75. Electronic applications accepted. *Expenses:* Contact institution. *Financial support:* In 2016–17, 30 students received support, including 1 fellowship (averaging $42,000 per year), 11 research assistantships (averaging $15,622 per year), 18 teaching assistantships (averaging $14,000 per year); career-related internships or fieldwork, Federal Work-Study, institutionally sponsored loans, scholarships/grants, and unspecified assistantships also available. Support available to part-time students. Financial award application deadline: 3/1; financial award applicants required to submit FAFSA. *Total annual research expenditures:* $218,743. *Unit head:* Dr. Fary Cachelin, Chair, 704-687-1315, E-mail: fcacheli@uncc.edu. *Application contact:* Kathy B. Giddings, Director of Graduate Admissions, 704-687-5503, Fax: 704-687-1668, E-mail: gradadm@uncc.edu. Website: http://psych.uncc.edu

**The University of Texas at Arlington,** Graduate School, College of Science, Department of Psychology, Arlington, TX 76019. Offers experimental health psychology (PhD); experimental psychology (MS, PhD); health/neuroscience psychology (MS, PhD); industrial and organizational psychology (MS). *Program availability:* Part-time. Terminal master's awarded for partial completion of doctoral program. *Degree requirements:* For master's, comprehensive exam or thesis; for doctorate, thesis/dissertation (for some programs). *Entrance requirements:* For master's and doctorate, GRE General Test, minimum GPA of 3.0 in last 60 hours of course work. Additional exam requirements/recommendations for international students: Required—TOEFL (minimum score 550 paper-based). *Application deadline:* For fall admission, 6/15 for domestic students. Applications are processed on a rolling basis. Application fee: $50. *Financial support:* Fellowships, research assistantships with partial tuition reimbursements, teaching assistantships with partial tuition reimbursements, career-related internships or fieldwork, Federal Work-Study, institutionally sponsored loans, scholarships/grants, traineeships, and unspecified assistantships available. Financial award application deadline: 6/1; financial award applicants required to submit FAFSA. *Unit head:* Dr. Robert Gatchel, Professor/Chair, 817-272-2281, Fax: 817-272-2364, E-mail: gatchel@uta.edu. *Application contact:* Dr. Jared Kenworthy, Graduate Advisor, Psychological Sciences, 817-272-2281, Fax: 817-272-2364, E-mail: kenworthy@uta.edu. Website: http://www.uta.edu/psychology/

**University of the Sciences,** Program in Health Psychology, Philadelphia, PA 19104-4495. Offers MS. *Entrance requirements:* For master's, bachelor's degree in related field, minimum GPA of 3.0 in major. Additional exam requirements/recommendations for international students: Required—TOEFL, TWE. *Expenses:* Contact institution. *Faculty research:* Stress and immune system, women's health and breast cancer, memory, health care policy.

**University of Wisconsin–Milwaukee,** Graduate School, College of Letters and Science, Department of Psychology, Milwaukee, WI 53201-0413. Offers experimental psychology (MS, PhD), including behavior analysis, health and social psychology (PhD), health psychology (MS), neuroscience (PhD); psychology (PhD), including clinical psychology. *Accreditation:* APA (one or more programs are accredited). *Students:* 67 full-time (46 women), 19 part-time (11 women); includes 8 minority (2 Asian, non-Hispanic/Latino; 1 Hispanic/Latino; 5 Two or more races, non-Hispanic/Latino), 9 international. Average age 28. 254 applicants, 7% accepted, 16 enrolled. In 2016, 15 master's, 10 doctorates awarded. *Degree requirements:* For master's, thesis; for doctorate, variable foreign language requirement, thesis/dissertation. *Entrance requirements:* For master's and doctorate, GRE General Test, GRE Subject Test. Additional exam requirements/recommendations for international students: Required—TOEFL (minimum score 550 paper-based; 79 iBT), IELTS (minimum score 6.5). *Application deadline:* For fall admission, 1/1 priority date for domestic students; for spring admission, 9/1 for domestic students. Applications are processed on a rolling basis. Application fee: $56 ($96 for international students). Electronic applications accepted. *Financial support:* In 2016–17, 8 fellowships, 6 research assistantships, 46 teaching assistantships were awarded; career-related internships or fieldwork, unspecified assistantships, and project assistantships also available. Support available to part-time students. Financial award application deadline: 4/15; financial award applicants required to submit FAFSA. *Unit head:* Douglas Woods, Department Chair,

414-229-6636, E-mail: dwoods@uwm.edu. *Application contact:* General Information Contact, 414-229-4982, Fax: 414-229-6967, E-mail: gradschool@uwm.edu. Website: http://www.uwm.edu/dept/psychology/

**Virginia Commonwealth University,** Graduate School, College of Humanities and Sciences, Department of Psychology, Richmond, VA 23284-9005. Offers clinical psychology (PhD), including behavioral medicine, clinical child psychology; counseling psychology (PhD); health psychology (PhD). *Accreditation:* APA. *Degree requirements:* For doctorate, thesis/dissertation. *Entrance requirements:* For doctorate, GRE General Test. Additional exam requirements/recommendations for international students: Required—TOEFL (minimum score 600 paper-based; 100 iBT); Recommended—IELTS (minimum score 6.5). *Application deadline:* For fall admission, 12/1 for domestic students. Application fee: $50. Electronic applications accepted. *Financial support:* Fellowships, research assistantships, teaching assistantships, Federal Work-Study, institutionally sponsored loans, and scholarships/grants available. Support available to part-time students. *Faculty research:* Biopsychology, clinical psychology, counseling psychology, developmental psychology, health psychology, social psychology. *Unit head:* Dr. Wendy Kliewer, Chair, 804-828-1193, Fax: 804-828-2237, E-mail: kliewer@vcu.edu. *Application contact:* Dr. Michael Southam-Gerow, Director of Graduate Studies, 804-828-1193, Fax: 804-828-2237, E-mail: masouthamger@vcu.edu. Website: http://www.psychology.vcu.edu/

**Virginia State University,** College of Graduate Studies, College of Natural and Health Sciences, Department of Psychology, Petersburg, VA 23806-0001. Offers behavioral and community health sciences (PhD); clinical health psychology (PhD); clinical psychology (MS); general psychology (MS). *Degree requirements:* For master's, one foreign language, thesis. *Entrance requirements:* For master's, GRE General Test.

**Viterbo University,** Master of Science in Mental Health Counseling Program, La Crosse, WI 54601-4797. Offers addiction counseling (MS); child and adolescent counseling (MS); complementary health and wellness counseling (MS). *Accreditation:* ACA. *Program availability:* Part-time, evening/weekend. *Degree requirements:* For master's, comprehensive exam, thesis, 54 credits of core program courses; 6 elective credits; minimum GPA of 3.0; action research project; practicum/internship experience. *Entrance requirements:* For master's, MAT, BS in a human service or social science discipline; prerequisite coursework in general psychology, behavior disorders/abnormal psychology, and research methods/statistics; minimum undergraduate cumulative GPA of 3.0; background check; personal statement; undergraduate transcripts; interview. Additional exam requirements/recommendations for international students: Required—TOEFL (minimum score 525 paper-based). Electronic applications accepted.

Application fee is waived when completed online. *Expenses:* Contact institution. *Faculty research:* Supervision, recovery substance abuse, culture, counseling theory, health and wellness.

**Walden University,** Graduate Programs, School of Psychology, Minneapolis, MN 55401. Offers clinical psychology (MS), including counseling, general program; forensic psychology (MS), including forensic psychology in the community, general program, mental health applications, program planning and evaluation in forensic settings, psychology and legal systems; industrial organizational (MS, PhD), including consulting psychology, forensic (MS), forensic psychology (PhD), general practice, leadership development and coaching (MS), organizational diversity and social change, research evaluation (PhD); online teaching in psychology (Post-Master's Certificate); organizational psychology and development (Postbaccalaureate Certificate); psychology (MS, PhD), including applied psychology (MS), clinical psychology (PhD), crisis management and response (MS), educational psychology, forensic psychology (PhD), general psychology (MS), general psychology research (PhD), general psychology teaching (PhD), health psychology, leadership development and coaching (MS), psychology of culture (MS), psychology, public administration, and social change (MS), social psychology, terrorism and security (MS); psychology respecialization (Post-Doctoral Certificate). *Program availability:* Part-time, evening/weekend, online only, 100% online. Terminal master's awarded for partial completion of doctoral program. *Degree requirements:* For master's, thesis optional; for doctorate, thesis/dissertation, residency. *Entrance requirements:* For master's, bachelor's degree or higher; minimum GPA of 2.5; official transcripts; goal statement (for some programs); access to computer and Internet; for doctorate, master's degree or higher; three years of related professional or academic experience (preferred); minimum GPA of 3.0; goal statement and current resume (for select programs); official transcripts; access to computer and Internet; for other advanced degree, relevant work experience; access to computer and Internet. Additional exam requirements/recommendations for international students: Required—TOEFL (minimum score 550 paper-based, 79 iBT), IELTS (minimum score 6.5), Michigan English Language Assessment Battery (minimum score 82), or PTE (minimum score 53). Electronic applications accepted.

**Yeshiva University,** Ferkauf Graduate School of Psychology, Program in Clinical Health Psychology, New York, NY 10033-3201. Offers PhD. *Accreditation:* APA. *Program availability:* Part-time. *Degree requirements:* For doctorate, comprehensive exam, thesis/dissertation. *Entrance requirements:* For doctorate, GRE General Test. *Faculty research:* Dieting, substance abuse, adolescent depression and suicide, cancer research, MS research.

# Human Development

**Alabama Agricultural and Mechanical University,** School of Graduate Studies, College of Agricultural, Life and Natural Sciences, Department of Family and Consumer Sciences, Huntsville, AL 35811. Offers apparel, merchandising and design (MS); family and consumer sciences (MS); human development and family studies (MS); nutrition and hospitality management (MS). *Program availability:* Part-time, evening/weekend. *Degree requirements:* For master's, comprehensive exam, thesis optional. *Entrance requirements:* For master's, GRE General Test. Additional exam requirements/recommendations for international students: Required—TOEFL (minimum score 500 paper-based; 61 iBT). *Application deadline:* For fall admission, 5/1 for domestic students. Applications are processed on a rolling basis. Application fee: $25. Electronic applications accepted. *Expenses:* Tuition, nonresident: part-time $826 per credit hour. Full-time tuition and fees vary according to course load and program. *Financial support:* Research assistantships with tuition reimbursements, teaching assistantships with tuition reimbursements, career-related internships or fieldwork, Federal Work-Study, and traineeships available. Financial award application deadline: 4/1. *Faculty research:* Food biotechnology, nutrition, food microbiology, food engineering, food chemistry. *Unit head:* Dr. Cynthia Smith, Chair, 256-372-4172, Fax: 256-372-5433, E-mail: cynthia.smith@aamu.edu. Website: http://www.aamu.edu/academics/alns/consumersciences/

**Argosy University, Chicago,** Illinois School of Professional Psychology, Doctoral Program in Clinical Psychology, Chicago, IL 60601. Offers child and adolescent psychology (Psy D); client-centered and experiential psychotherapies (Psy D); diversity and multicultural psychology (Psy D); family psychology (Psy D); forensic psychology (Psy D); health psychology (Psy D); neuropsychology (Psy D); organizational consulting (Psy D); psychoanalytic psychology (Psy D); psychology and spirituality (Psy D). *Accreditation:* APA.

**Arizona State University at the Tempe campus,** College of Liberal Arts and Sciences, School of Social and Family Dynamics, Tempe, AZ 85287-3701. Offers family and human development (MS, PhD); infant-family practice (MAS); marriage and family therapy (MAS); sociology (MA, PhD). Terminal master's awarded for partial completion of doctoral program. *Degree requirements:* For master's, thesis or alternative, interactive Program of Study (iPOS) submitted before completing 50 percent of required credit hours; for doctorate, thesis/dissertation, interactive Program of Study (iPOS) submitted before completing 50 percent of required credit hours. *Entrance requirements:* For master's and doctorate, GRE, minimum GPA of 3.0 or equivalent in last 2 years of work leading to bachelor's degree. Additional exam requirements/recommendations for international students: Required—TOEFL, IELTS, or PTE. Electronic applications accepted. *Expenses:* Contact institution.

**Auburn University,** Graduate School, College of Human Sciences, Department of Human Development and Family Studies, Auburn University, AL 36849. Offers MS, PhD. *Accreditation:* AAMFT/COAMFTE (one or more programs are accredited). *Program availability:* Part-time. *Faculty:* 24 full-time (15 women). *Students:* 22 full-time (18 women), 11 part-time (9 women); includes 9 minority (6 Black or African American, non-Hispanic/Latino; 1 Asian, non-Hispanic/Latino; 2 Hispanic/Latino). Average age 26. 52 applicants, 27% accepted, 11 enrolled. In 2016, 8 master's, 6 doctorates awarded. *Degree requirements:* For master's, thesis, oral exam; for doctorate, thesis/dissertation. *Entrance requirements:* For master's, GRE General Test; for doctorate, GRE General Test, master's degree. *Application deadline:* Applications are processed on a rolling basis. Application fee: $50 ($60 for international students). *Expenses:* Tuition, state resident: full-time $9072; part-time $504 per credit hour. Tuition, nonresident: full-time $27,216; part-time $1512 per credit hour. *Required fees:* $812 per semester. Tuition and fees vary according to degree level and program. *Financial support:* Research assistantships, teaching assistantships, and Federal Work-Study available. Support available to part-time students. Financial award application deadline: 3/15; financial award applicants required to submit FAFSA. *Faculty research:* Family influences on personality and social development, parent-child relations, infancy, day care, parent

education. *Unit head:* Dr. Joe F. Pittman, Jr., Head, 334-844-3242, E-mail: mbradbar@humsci.auburn.edu. *Application contact:* Dr. George Flowers, Dean of the Graduate School, 334-844-2125. Website: http://www.humsci.auburn.edu/hdfs/

**Ball State University,** Graduate School, Teachers College, Department of Educational Psychology, Muncie, IN 47306. Offers educational psychology (MA, MS), including educational psychology (MA, MS, PhD); educational psychology (PhD), including educational psychology (MA, MS, PhD); gifted and talented education (Certificate); human development and learning (Certificate); instructional design and assessment (Certificate); neuropsychology (Certificate); quantitative psychology (MS); response to intervention (Certificate); school psychology (MA, PhD), including school psychology (MA, PhD, Ed S); school psychology (Ed S), including school psychology (MA, PhD, Ed S). *Program availability:* 100% online. *Degree requirements:* For doctorate, thesis/dissertation; for other advanced degree, thesis. *Entrance requirements:* For master's, GRE General Test, minimum baccalaureate GPA of 2.75 or 3.0 in latter half of baccalauareate, professional goals and self-assessment; for doctorate, GRE General Test, minimum graduate GPA of 3.2; for other advanced degree, GRE General Test. Additional exam requirements/recommendations for international students: Required—TOEFL (minimum score 550 paper-based; 79 iBT), IELTS (minimum score 6.5). Electronic applications accepted.

**Bradley University,** The Graduate School, College of Education and Health Sciences, Department of Leadership in Education, Nonprofits and Counseling, Peoria, IL 61625-0002. Offers counseling (MA), including clinical mental health counseling, professional school counseling; leadership in educational administration (MA); nonprofit leadership (MA). *Accreditation:* ACA; NCATE. *Program availability:* Part-time, evening/weekend. *Degree requirements:* For master's, comprehensive exam, thesis optional. *Entrance requirements:* For master's, GRE General Test or MAT, interview, 3 letters of recommendation. Additional exam requirements/recommendations for international students: Required—TOEFL (minimum score 550 paper-based; 79 iBT), IELTS (minimum score 6.5). *Application deadline:* For fall admission, 5/15 priority date for domestic and international students; for spring admission, 10/15 priority date for domestic and international students. Applications are processed on a rolling basis. Application fee: $40 ($50 for international students). Electronic applications accepted. *Expenses:* Tuition: Full-time $7650; part-time $850 per credit. *Required fees:* $50 per credit. One-time fee: $100 full-time. *Financial support:* Research assistantships with full and partial tuition reimbursements, career-related internships or fieldwork, scholarships/grants, tuition waivers (partial), and unspecified assistantships available. Support available to part-time students. Financial award application deadline: 4/1. *Unit head:* Jenny Tripses, Interim Chair, 309-677-3593, E-mail: jtripses@bradley.edu. *Application contact:* Kayla Carroll, Director of International Admissions and Student Services, 309-677-2375, E-mail: klcarroll@fsmail.bradley.edu. Website: http://www.bradley.edu/academic/departments/lenc/

**Brigham Young University,** Graduate Studies, College of Family, Home, and Social Sciences, Program in Marriage, Family and Human Development, Provo, UT 84602. Offers MS, PhD. *Accreditation:* AAMFT/COAMFTE. *Faculty:* 24 full-time (5 women). *Students:* 27 full-time (15 women); includes 4 minority (1 American Indian or Alaska Native, non-Hispanic/Latino; 2 Asian, non-Hispanic/Latino; 1 Native Hawaiian or other Pacific Islander, non-Hispanic/Latino), 3 international. Average age 27. 24 applicants, 54% accepted, 11 enrolled. In 2016, 5 master's, 4 doctorates awarded. *Degree requirements:* For master's, thesis; for doctorate, comprehensive exam, thesis/dissertation. *Entrance requirements:* For master's and doctorate, GRE General Test, minimum GPA of 3.0 in last 60 semester hours, letters of recommendation. Additional exam requirements/recommendations for international students: Required—TOEFL (minimum score 580 paper-based; 85 iBT), IELTS (minimum score 7). *Application deadline:* For fall admission, 1/10 for domestic and international students. Application fee: $50. Electronic applications accepted. *Expenses:* Tuition: Full-time $6680; part-time

$393 per credit. Tuition and fees vary according to course load, program and student's religious affiliation. *Financial support:* In 2016–17, 23 students received support, including 23 research assistantships with full and partial tuition reimbursements available (averaging $8,560 per year), 1 teaching assistantship with tuition reimbursement available (averaging $2,800 per year); scholarships/grants and unspecified assistantships also available. Financial award application deadline: 3/25. *Faculty research:* Family studies and family process, marriage, adolescence and emerging adulthood, adult development and aging, child development. *Unit head:* Dr. Dean M. Busby, Director, School of Life, 801-422-2069, Fax: 801-422-0230, E-mail: dean_busby@byu.edu. *Application contact:* Graduate Secretary, 801-422-2060, E-mail: mfhdgrad@byu.edu.
Website: http://mfhd.byu.edu

**Brock University,** Faculty of Graduate Studies, Faculty of Social Sciences, Program in Psychology, St. Catharines, ON L2S 3A1, Canada. Offers behavioral neuroscience (MA, PhD); life span development (MA, PhD); social personality (MA, PhD). *Program availability:* Part-time. *Degree requirements:* For master's, thesis; for doctorate, thesis/dissertation. *Entrance requirements:* For master's, GRE, honors degree; for doctorate, GRE, master's degree. Additional exam requirements/recommendations for international students: Required—TOEFL (minimum score 550 paper-based; 80 iBT), IELTS (minimum score 6.5), TWE (minimum score 4). Electronic applications accepted. *Faculty research:* Social personality, behavioral neuroscience, life-span development.

**California State University, Fresno,** Division of Research and Graduate Studies, Kremen School of Education and Human Development, Fresno, CA 93740-8027. Offers MA, MS, Ed D. *Accreditation:* NCATE. *Program availability:* Part-time, evening/weekend. *Degree requirements:* For master's, thesis or alternative; for doctorate, thesis/dissertation. *Entrance requirements:* For master's, GRE General Test, MAT; for doctorate, GRE or MAT, minimum GPA of 3.2, master's degree. Additional exam requirements/recommendations for international students: Required—TOEFL. *Application deadline:* For fall admission, 5/1 for domestic and international students; for spring admission, 10/1 for domestic and international students. Applications are processed on a rolling basis. Application fee: $55. Electronic applications accepted. *Financial support:* Career-related internships or fieldwork, Federal Work-Study, scholarships/grants, and research awards available. Support available to part-time students. Financial award application deadline: 3/1; financial award applicants required to submit FAFSA. *Faculty research:* Adult community education, parenting, gifted and talented curriculum and instruction, peer mediation and conflict resolution. *Unit head:* Dr. Paul Beare, Dean, 559-278-0210, Fax: 559-278-0113, E-mail: pbeare@csufresno.edu. *Application contact:* Administrative Assistant, 559-278-2448, Fax: 559-278-4658.
Website: http://www.fresnostate.edu/kremen/

**Central Michigan University,** College of Graduate Studies, College of Education and Human Services, Department of Human Environmental Studies, Mount Pleasant, MI 48859. Offers apparel product development and merchandising technology (MS); gerontology (Graduate Certificate); human development and family studies (MA); nutrition and dietetics (MS). *Program availability:* Part-time, evening/weekend. *Degree requirements:* For master's, thesis or alternative. Electronic applications accepted. *Faculty research:* Human growth and development, family studies and human sexuality, human nutrition and dietetics, apparel and textile retailing, computer-aided design for apparel.

**Claremont Graduate University,** Graduate Programs, School of Educational Studies, Claremont, CA 91711-6160. Offers Africana education (Certificate); education and policy (MA, PhD); higher education/student affairs (MA, PhD); human development (MA, PhD); public school administration (MA, PhD); quantitative evaluation (MA, PhD); special education (MA, PhD); teacher education (MA); teaching and learning (MA, PhD); urban leadership (PhD); MBA/PhD. PhD program offered jointly with San Diego State University. *Program availability:* Part-time. *Faculty:* 14 full-time (9 women), 1 part-time/adjunct (0 women). *Students:* 195 full-time (143 women), 196 part-time (137 women); includes 217 minority (43 Black or African American, non-Hispanic/Latino; 4 American Indian or Alaska Native, non-Hispanic/Latino; 32 Asian, non-Hispanic/Latino; 117 Hispanic/Latino; 2 Native Hawaiian or other Pacific Islander, non-Hispanic/Latino; 19 Two or more races, non-Hispanic/Latino), 14 international. Average age 38. In 2016, 48 master's, 39 doctorates, 7 other advanced degrees awarded. Terminal master's awarded for partial completion of doctoral program. *Entrance requirements:* For master's and doctorate, GRE General Test. Additional exam requirements/recommendations for international students: Required—TOEFL (minimum score 75 iBT). *Application deadline:* For fall admission, 3/1 priority date for domestic and international students. Applications are processed on a rolling basis. Application fee: $80. Electronic applications accepted. *Expenses:* Tuition: Full-time $44,328; part-time $1847 per unit. *Required fees:* $600; $300 per semester. Tuition and fees vary according to course load and program. *Financial support:* Fellowships, research assistantships, Federal Work-Study, institutionally sponsored loans, and scholarships/grants available. Support available to part-time students. Financial award application deadline: 2/15; financial award applicants required to submit FAFSA. *Faculty research:* Education administration, K-12 and higher education, multicultural education, education policy, diversity in higher education, faculty issues. *Unit head:* Allen Omoto, Dean, 909-607-3786, E-mail: allen.omoto@cgu.edu. *Application contact:* Rachel Camacho, Senior Assistant Director of Admission, 909-607-9418, E-mail: camacho@cgu.edu.
Website: https://www.cgu.edu/school/school-of-educational-studies/

**Clemson University,** Graduate School, College of Behavioral, Social and Health Sciences, Department of Parks, Recreation, and Tourism Management, Program in Youth Development Leadership, Clemson, SC 29634. Offers MS, Certificate. *Program availability:* Part-time, evening/weekend, online only, 100% online. *Faculty:* 3 full-time (0 women). *Students:* 32 part-time (23 women); includes 11 minority (8 Black or African American, non-Hispanic/Latino; 2 Asian, non-Hispanic/Latino; 1 Two or more races, non-Hispanic/Latino). Average age 29. 17 applicants, 76% accepted, 11 enrolled. In 2016, 32 other advanced degrees awarded. *Entrance requirements:* For master's, GRE General Test, unofficial transcripts, letter of intent, letters of recommendation; for Certificate, GRE General Test, unofficial transcripts, letters of recommendation. Additional exam requirements/recommendations for international students: Required—TOEFL (minimum score 80 iBT), IELTS (minimum score 6.5). *Application deadline:* For fall admission, 4/15 for international students; for spring admission, 10/15 for international students. Applications are processed on a rolling basis. Application fee: $80 ($90 for international students). Electronic applications accepted. *Expenses:* $4,027 per semester full-time resident, $8,013 per semester full-time non-resident, $437 per credit hour part-time resident, $874 per credit hour part-time non-resident. *Total annual research expenditures:* $43,160. *Unit head:* Dr. James McDonell, Interim Department Chair, 864-656-6746, E-mail: jmcdnll@clemson.edu. *Application contact:* Dr. William Quinn, Graduate Program Coordinator, 864-656-1501, E-mail: wquinn@clemson.edu.
Website: http://www.clemson.edu/hehd/departments/youthdevelopment/

**Colorado State University,** College of Health and Human Sciences, Department of Human Development and Family Studies, Fort Collins, CO 80523-1570. Offers applied developmental science (PhD); family and developmental studies (MS); marriage and family therapy (MS). *Accreditation:* AAMFT/COAMFTE. *Faculty:* 18 full-time (15 women), 3 part-time/adjunct (0 women). *Students:* 34 full-time (30 women), 4 part-time

(3 women); includes 6 minority (2 Asian, non-Hispanic/Latino; 4 Hispanic/Latino), 1 international. Average age 27. 64 applicants, 38% accepted, 14 enrolled. In 2016, 6 master's, 3 doctorates awarded. Terminal master's awarded for partial completion of doctoral program. *Degree requirements:* For master's, thesis; for doctorate, comprehensive exam, thesis/dissertation. *Entrance requirements:* For master's and doctorate, GRE General Test, 3 letters of recommendation; minimum GPA of 3.0. Additional exam requirements/recommendations for international students: Required—TOEFL (minimum score 550 paper-based; 80 iBT), IELTS (minimum score 6.5), PTE (minimum score 58). *Application deadline:* For fall admission, 1/2 priority date for domestic and international students. Application fee: $60 ($70 for international students). Electronic applications accepted. *Expenses:* Tuition, state resident: full-time $9628. Tuition, nonresident: full-time $23,603. *Required fees:* $2253; $528.14 per credit hour. $264.07 per semester. Tuition and fees vary according to course load and program. *Financial support:* In 2016–17, 35 students received support, including 14 research assistantships with full and partial tuition reimbursements available (averaging $10,449 per year), 13 teaching assistantships with full and partial tuition reimbursements available (averaging $8,038 per year); fellowships with full and partial tuition reimbursements available, Federal Work-Study, scholarships/grants, health care benefits, and unspecified assistantships also available. Financial award application deadline: 1/2; financial award applicants required to submit FAFSA. *Faculty research:* Risk, resilience, and developmental psychopathology; treatment, intervention, and prevention science; emotion, regulation, and relational processes; adult development and aging; cultural context and diversity. *Total annual research expenditures:* $1.2 million. *Unit head:* Dr. Lise Youngblade, Department Head, 970-491-3581, Fax: 970-491-7975, E-mail: lise.youngblade@colostate.edu. *Application contact:* Mary Daughtrey, Administrative Assistant III, 970-491-2872, Fax: 970-491-7975, E-mail: mary.daughtrey@colostate.edu.
Website: http://www.hdfs.chhs.colostate.edu/

**Cornell University,** Graduate School, Graduate Fields of Human Ecology, Field of Human Development, Ithaca, NY 14853. Offers developmental psychology (MA, PhD), including cognitive development, developmental psychopathology, ecology of human development, social and personality development; human development and family studies (MA, PhD), including ecology of human development, family studies and the life course. *Degree requirements:* For doctorate, comprehensive exam, thesis/dissertation, pre-doctoral research project, teaching experience. *Entrance requirements:* For doctorate, GRE General Test, 2 letters of recommendation. Additional exam requirements/recommendations for international students: Required—TOEFL (minimum score 550 paper-based; 77 iBT). Electronic applications accepted. *Faculty research:* Cognitive development, developmental psychopathology, ecology of human development, family studies and the life course, social and personality development.

**Duke University,** Graduate School, Department of Psychology and Neuroscience, Durham, NC 27708. Offers biological psychology (PhD); clinical psychology (PhD); cognitive psychology (PhD); developmental psychology (PhD); experimental psychology (PhD); health psychology (PhD); human social development (PhD); JD/MA. *Accreditation:* APA (one or more programs are accredited). *Degree requirements:* For doctorate, thesis/dissertation. *Entrance requirements:* For doctorate, GRE General Test. Additional exam requirements/recommendations for international students: Required—TOEFL (minimum score 577 paper-based; 90 iBT) or IELTS (minimum score 7). Electronic applications accepted.

**East Tennessee State University,** School of Graduate Studies, College of Education, Department of Counseling and Human Services, Johnson City, TN 37614. Offers MA. *Accreditation:* ACA; NCATE. *Program availability:* Part-time. Terminal master's awarded for partial completion of doctoral program. *Degree requirements:* For master's, comprehensive exam, thesis optional, internship, student teaching, culminating experience. *Entrance requirements:* For master's, GRE General Test, minimum GPA of 3.0, three letters of recommendation, interview. Additional exam requirements/recommendations for international students: Required—TOEFL (minimum score 550 paper-based; 79 iBT). Electronic applications accepted. *Faculty research:* Intervention and assistance with at-risk and under-served youth and high conflict families; service and social justice; women and girls' issues in counseling; counseling competence with LGBTQ individuals; counselor education and supervision.

**Erikson Institute,** Academic Programs, Chicago, IL 60654. Offers administration (Certificate); bilingual/ESL (Certificate); child development (MS); early childhood education (MS); infant mental health (Certificate); infant studies (Certificate); MS/MSW. MS/MSW offered jointly with Loyola University Chicago. *Program availability:* Part-time, evening/weekend. *Degree requirements:* For master's, comprehensive exam, internship; for Certificate, internship. *Entrance requirements:* For master's and Certificate, minimum GPA of 2.75. Additional exam requirements/recommendations for international students: Required—TOEFL. *Faculty research:* Assessment strategies from early childhood through elementary years; language, literacy, and the arts in children's development; inclusive special education; parent-child relationships; cognitive development.

**Fielding Graduate University,** Graduate Programs, School of Leadership Studies, Programs in Human and Organizational Development, Santa Barbara, CA 93105-3814. Offers human development (PhD); nonprofit leadership (Certificate); organizational consulting (Certificate); organizational development and change (PhD); organizational development and leadership (MA, Certificate). *Program availability:* Part-time, 100% online, blended/hybrid learning. *Faculty:* 14 full-time (7 women), 33 part-time/adjunct (19 women). *Students:* 221 full-time (163 women), 53 part-time (41 women); includes 75 minority (29 Black or African American, non-Hispanic/Latino; 4 American Indian or Alaska Native, non-Hispanic/Latino; 16 Asian, non-Hispanic/Latino; 17 Hispanic/Latino; 1 Native Hawaiian or other Pacific Islander, non-Hispanic/Latino; 8 Two or more races, non-Hispanic/Latino), 3 international. Average age 49. 66 applicants, 91% accepted, 46 enrolled. In 2016, 30 master's, 39 doctorates, 3 other advanced degrees awarded. *Entrance requirements:* For master's and Certificate, bachelor's or master's degree, resume, statement of purpose, official transcript; for doctorate, bachelor's or master's degree, resume, statement of purpose, reflexive essay, official transcript. *Application deadline:* For fall admission, 7/16 for domestic and international students; for spring admission, 11/1 for domestic and international students; for summer admission, 3/1 for domestic and international students. Application fee: $75. Electronic applications accepted. *Expenses:* Contact institution. *Financial support:* In 2016–17, 10 students received support, including 2 research assistantships (averaging $1,350 per year); scholarships/grants also available. Financial award applicants required to submit FAFSA. *Unit head:* Dr. Dorothy Agger-Gupta, Program Director, E-mail: dotagger@fielding.edu. *Application contact:* Enrollment Coordinator, 800-340-1099 Ext. 4098, Fax: 805-687-9793, E-mail: hodadmission@fielding.edu.
Website: http://www.fielding.edu/our-programs/school-of-leadership-studies/

**Georgetown University,** Graduate School of Arts and Sciences, Walsh School of Foreign Service, Program in Global Human Development, Washington, DC 20057. Offers MA.

**The George Washington University,** Graduate School of Education and Human Development, Department of Educational Leadership, Individualized Master's Program, Washington, DC 20052. Offers MA Ed. *Students:* 19 part-time (17 women); includes 7

## Human Development

minority (4 Black or African American, non-Hispanic/Latino; 1 Asian, non-Hispanic/Latino; 2 Hispanic/Latino). Average age 43. 3 applicants, 33% accepted. In 2016, 14 master's awarded. *Degree requirements:* For master's, comprehensive exam. *Entrance requirements:* For master's, GRE General Test or MAT, minimum GPA of 2.75. *Application deadline:* For fall admission, 3/1 priority date for domestic students; for spring admission, 10/1 for domestic students. Applications are processed on a rolling basis. Application fee: $75. *Financial support:* Application deadline: 1/15; applicants required to submit FAFSA. *Unit head:* Michael Feuer, Dean, 202-994-6161, Fax: 202-994-7207, E-mail: mjfeuer@gwu.edu. *Application contact:* Sarah Lang, Director of Graduate Admissions, 202-994-1447, Fax: 202-994-7207, E-mail: slang@gwu.edu.

**Georgia State University,** College of Education and Human Development, Atlanta, GA 30302-3083. Offers M Ed, MAT, MS, Ed D, PhD, Ed S. *Accreditation:* NCATE. *Program availability:* Part-time, evening/weekend, online learning. *Faculty:* 148 full-time (98 women). *Students:* 785 full-time (573 women), 395 part-time (270 women); includes 521 minority (371 Black or African American, non-Hispanic/Latino; 1 American Indian or Alaska Native, non-Hispanic/Latino; 39 Asian, non-Hispanic/Latino; 74 Hispanic/Latino; 36 Two or more races, non-Hispanic/Latino), 44 international. Average age 32. 1,113 applicants, 34% accepted, 280 enrolled. In 2016, 366 master's, 65 doctorates, 28 other advanced degrees awarded. Terminal master's awarded for partial completion of doctoral program. *Degree requirements:* For master's, comprehensive exam (for some programs), thesis (for some programs), minimum GPA of 3.0; for doctorate, comprehensive exam, thesis/dissertation, minimum GPA of 3.5; for Ed S, thesis or alternative, minimum GPA of 3.0. *Entrance requirements:* For master's, GRE, MAT (for some programs), minimum GPA of 2.5 on all undergraduate work attempted in which letter grades were awarded; for doctorate, GRE, MAT (for some programs), minimum GPA of 3.3 on all graduate coursework for which letter grades were awarded (for PhD); for Ed S, GRE, MAT (for some programs), graduate degree from regionally-accredited college or university unless specified otherwise by the program with minimum GPA of 3.25 on all graduate coursework for which letter grades were awarded. Additional exam requirements/recommendations for international students: Required—TOEFL (minimum score 550 paper-based; 79 iBT) or IELTS (minimum score 6.5). Application fee: $50. Electronic applications accepted. *Expenses:* Tuition, state resident: full-time $6876; part-time $382 per credit hour. Tuition, nonresident: full-time $22,374; part-time $1243 per credit hour. *Required fees:* $2128; $1064 per term. Part-time tuition and fees vary according to course load and program. *Financial support:* In 2016–17, fellowships with full tuition reimbursements (averaging $25,000 per year), research assistantships with tuition reimbursements (averaging $4,867 per year), teaching assistantships with tuition reimbursements (averaging $4,683 per year) were awarded; career-related internships or fieldwork, Federal Work-Study, scholarships/grants, tuition waivers (partial), and unspecified assistantships also available. Support available to part-time students. Financial award applicants required to submit FAFSA. *Faculty research:* Literacy: early, middle-secondary, adult and deaf/hard of hearing; teacher professional development, evaluation and urban education; STEM teacher education; health, physical activity and exercise science; school safety and counseling. *Unit head:* Dr. Paul A. Alberto, Interim Dean, 404-413-8100, Fax: 404-413-8103, E-mail: palberto@gsu.edu. *Application contact:* Nancy Keita, Director, Office of Academic Assistance and Graduate Admissions, 404-413-8001, E-mail: nkeita@gsu.edu.
Website: http://education.gsu.edu/main/

**Harvard University,** Harvard Graduate School of Education, Master's Programs in Education, Cambridge, MA 02138. Offers arts in education (Ed M); education policy and management (Ed M); higher education (Ed M); human development and psychology (Ed M); international education policy (Ed M); language and literacy (Ed M); learning and teaching (Ed M); mind, brain, and education (Ed M); prevention science and practice (Ed M); school leadership (Ed M); special studies (Ed M); teacher education (Ed M); technology, innovation, and education (Ed M). *Program availability:* Part-time. *Entrance requirements:* For master's, GRE General Test, statement of purpose, 3 letters of recommendation, resume, official transcripts. Additional exam requirements/recommendations for international students: Required—TOEFL (minimum score 613 paper-based; 104 iBT), TWE (minimum score 5). Electronic applications accepted. *Faculty research:* Learning and development, educational leadership and organizations, education policy analysis.

**Hofstra University,** School of Education, Programs in Teacher Education, Hempstead, NY 11549. Offers bilingual education (MA, Advanced Certificate); bilingual extension (Advanced Certificate), including education/speech language pathology; business education (MS Ed); early childhood and childhood education (MS Ed); early childhood education (MA, MS Ed); education technology (Advanced Certificate); elementary education (MA, MS Ed), including science, technology, engineering, and mathematics (STEM) (MA); English education (MS Ed); family and consumer science (MS Ed); fine arts and music education (Advanced Certificate); fine arts education (MS Ed); foreign language and TESOL (MS Ed); foreign language education (MS Ed), including French, German, Russian, Spanish; learning and teaching (Ed D), including applied linguistics, art education, arts and humanities, early childhood education, English education, human development, math education, math, science, and technology, multicultural education, physical education, science education, social studies education, special education; mathematics education (MA, MS Ed); middle school extension (Advanced Certificate), including grades 5-6, grades 7-9; music education (MA, MS Ed); science education (MA, MS Ed), including biology, chemistry, earth science, geology, physics; secondary education (Advanced Certificate); social studies education (MA, MS Ed); teaching languages other than English and TESOL (MS Ed); TESOL (MS Ed, Advanced Certificate). *Program availability:* Part-time, evening/weekend, blended/hybrid learning. *Students:* 139 full-time (97 women), 145 part-time (106 women); includes 60 minority (15 Black or African American, non-Hispanic/Latino; 1 American Indian or Alaska Native, non-Hispanic/Latino; 12 Asian, non-Hispanic/Latino; 31 Hispanic/Latino; 1 Two or more races, non-Hispanic/Latino), 21 international. Average age 29. 255 applicants, 86% accepted, 122 enrolled. In 2016, 101 master's, 4 doctorates, 43 other advanced degrees awarded. *Degree requirements:* For master's, comprehensive exam, thesis (for some programs), exit project, student teaching, fieldwork, electronic portfolio, curriculum project, minimum GPA of 3.0; for doctorate, thesis/dissertation; for Advanced Certificate, 3 foreign languages, comprehensive exam (for some programs), thesis project. *Entrance requirements:* For master's, GRE, MAT, 2 letters of recommendation, portfolio, teacher certification (MA), interview, essay; for doctorate, GMAT, GRE, LSAT, or MAT; for Advanced Certificate, 2 letters of recommendation, essay, interview and/or portfolio, teaching certificate. Additional exam requirements/recommendations for international students: Required—TOEFL (minimum score 550 paper-based; 80 iBT). *Application deadline:* Applications are processed on a rolling basis. Application fee: $75. Electronic applications accepted. *Expenses: Tuition:* Full-time $1240. *Required fees:* $970. Tuition and fees vary according to program. *Financial support:* In 2016–17, 149 students received support, including 58 fellowships with full and partial tuition reimbursements available (averaging $5,309 per year), 5 research assistantships with full and partial tuition reimbursements available (averaging $7,073 per year); career-related internships or fieldwork, Federal Work-Study, institutionally sponsored loans, scholarships/grants, traineeships, tuition waivers (full and partial), and unspecified assistantships also available. Support available to part-time students. Financial award applicants required to submit FAFSA. *Faculty research:* Educational interventions that foster critical-thinking

skills; teachers' attitudes about professional development; threats to teacher quality. *Unit head:* Dr. Eustace Thompson, Chairperson, 516-463-5749, Fax: 516-463-6275, E-mail: eustace.g.thompson@hofstra.edu. *Application contact:* Sunil Samuel, Assistant Vice President of Admissions, 516-463-4723, Fax: 516-463-4664, E-mail: graduateadmission@hofstra.edu.
Website: http://www.hofstra.edu/education/

**Hood College,** Graduate School, Programs in Human Sciences, Frederick, MD 21701-8575. Offers human sciences (MA), including psychology. *Program availability:* Part-time, evening/weekend. *Faculty:* 5 full-time, 3 part-time/adjunct. *Students:* 11 full-time (8 women), 25 part-time (18 women); includes 6 minority (3 Black or African American, non-Hispanic/Latino; 1 Asian, non-Hispanic/Latino; 2 Two or more races, non-Hispanic/Latino), 1 international. Average age 38. 20 applicants, 95% accepted, 16 enrolled. In 2016, 29 master's awarded. *Degree requirements:* For master's, comprehensive exam, thesis optional, capstone/research project. *Entrance requirements:* For master's, minimum GPA of 2.75, essay. Additional exam requirements/recommendations for international students: Required—TOEFL (minimum score 575 paper-based; 89 iBT), IELTS (minimum score 6.5). *Application deadline:* For fall admission, 8/15 priority date for domestic students, 8/5 for international students; for spring admission, 12/1 priority date for domestic students, 12/1 for international students; for summer admission, 5/1 priority date for domestic students, 4/15 for international students. Applications are processed on a rolling basis. Application fee: $35. Electronic applications accepted. *Expenses:* $450 per credit hour; $105 comprehensive fee per semester. *Financial support:* Research assistantships with full tuition reimbursements, tuition waivers (partial), and unspecified assistantships available. Financial award applicants required to submit FAFSA. *Faculty research:* Mind-body medicine and multicultural healing, the New Orleans jazz funeral, death practices in African-American culture, bereavement theories and gender differences, Piaget's theory of cognitive development as a formal mathematical model. *Unit head:* April Boulton, Interim Dean of the Graduate School, 301-696-3600, E-mail: gofurther@hood.edu. *Application contact:* Jan Marcus, Assistant Director of Graduate Admissions, 301-696-3600, E-mail: gofurther@hood.ed.
Website: http://www.hood.edu/graduate

**Iowa State University of Science and Technology,** Department of Human Development and Family Studies, Ames, IA 50011. Offers human development and family studies (MFCS, MS, PhD). *Degree requirements:* For master's, thesis; for doctorate, thesis/dissertation. *Entrance requirements:* For master's and doctorate, GRE General Test. Additional exam requirements/recommendations for international students: Required—TOEFL (minimum score 550 paper-based; 79 iBT), IELTS (minimum score 6.5). *Application deadline:* For fall admission, 1/15 priority date for domestic and international students. Application fee: $60 ($90 for international students). Electronic applications accepted. *Faculty research:* Child development, early childhood education, family resource management and housing, life span studies. *Application contact:* Brenda Nelson, Application Contact, 515-294-6321, Fax: 515-294-2502, E-mail: hdfs-grad-adm@iastate.edu.
Website: http://www.hdfs.hs.iastate.edu/graduate/

**Kansas State University,** Graduate School, College of Human Ecology, Doctorate in Human Ecology Program, Manhattan, KS 66506-1407. Offers apparel and textiles (PhD); applied family sciences (PhD); couple and family therapy (PhD); hospitality administration (PhD); kinesiology (PhD); life-span human development (PhD). *Program availability:* Part-time. *Faculty:* 36 full-time (23 women). *Students:* 44 full-time (26 women), 16 part-time (10 women); includes 9 minority (3 Black or African American, non-Hispanic/Latino; 2 Asian, non-Hispanic/Latino; 2 Hispanic/Latino; 2 Two or more races, non-Hispanic/Latino), 18 international. Average age 30. 43 applicants, 35% accepted, 8 enrolled. In 2016, 13 doctorates awarded. *Degree requirements:* For doctorate, thesis/dissertation. *Entrance requirements:* Additional exam requirements/recommendations for international students: Required—TOEFL. *Application deadline:* For fall admission, 2/1 priority date for domestic and international students; for spring admission, 8/1 priority date for domestic and international students. Applications are processed on a rolling basis. Application fee: $50 ($75 for international students). Electronic applications accepted. *Expenses:* Tuition, state resident: full-time $9670. Tuition, nonresident: full-time $21,828. *Required fees:* $862. *Financial support:* In 2016–17, research assistantships with partial tuition reimbursements (averaging $12,000 per year), teaching assistantships with partial tuition reimbursements (averaging $12,000 per year) were awarded. Financial award application deadline: 3/1. *Total annual research expenditures:* $1.8 million. *Unit head:* Dr. John Buckwalter, Dean, 785-532-5500, Fax: 785-532-5504, E-mail: jbb3@ksu.edu. *Application contact:* Dr. Bronwyn Fees, Associate Dean for Academic Affairs, 785-532-5500, Fax: 785-532-5504, E-mail: fees@ksu.edu.

**Kansas State University,** Graduate School, College of Human Ecology, School of Family Studies and Human Services, Manhattan, KS 66506-1403. Offers applied family sciences (MS); communication sciences and disorders (MS); conflict resolution (Graduate Certificate); couple and family therapy (MS); early childhood education (MS); family and community service (MS); life-span human development (MS); personal financial planning (MS, PhD, Graduate Certificate); youth development (MS, Graduate Certificate). *Accreditation:* AAMFT/COAMFTE; ASHA. *Program availability:* Part-time, online learning. *Faculty:* 43 full-time (30 women), 4 part-time/adjunct (3 women). *Students:* 55 full-time (45 women), 87 part-time (73 women); includes 30 minority (9 Black or African American, non-Hispanic/Latino; 1 American Indian or Alaska Native, non-Hispanic/Latino; 1 Asian, non-Hispanic/Latino; 14 Hispanic/Latino; 1 Native Hawaiian or other Pacific Islander, non-Hispanic/Latino; 4 Two or more races, non-Hispanic/Latino), 6 international. Average age 29. 182 applicants, 29% accepted, 38 enrolled. In 2016, 39 master's, 17 other advanced degrees awarded. *Degree requirements:* For master's, comprehensive exam (for some programs), thesis optional. *Entrance requirements:* For master's, GRE, minimum GPA of 3.0 in last 2 years (60 semester hours) of undergraduate study; for doctorate, GRE. Additional exam requirements/recommendations for international students: Required—TOEFL (minimum score 600 paper-based). *Application deadline:* For fall admission, 2/1 priority date for domestic students, 1/1 priority date for international students; for spring admission, 10/1 priority date for domestic students, 8/1 priority date for international students; for summer admission, 2/1 priority date for domestic students, 12/1 priority date for international students. Applications are processed on a rolling basis. Application fee: $50 ($75 for international students). Electronic applications accepted. *Expenses:* Tuition, state resident: full-time $9670. Tuition, nonresident: full-time $21,828. *Required fees:* $862. *Financial support:* In 2016–17, 35 students received support, including 25 research assistantships (averaging $10,000 per year), 9 teaching assistantships with full tuition reimbursements available (averaging $10,000 per year); unspecified assistantships also available. Financial award application deadline: 3/1. *Faculty research:* Health and security of military families, training in and evaluation of professional human services (marriage and couple therapy, family life education, treatment of speech and swallowing disorders, financial therapy), disorders of communication and swallowing, family and relationship development and health, financial decision-making. *Total annual research expenditures:* $8.4 million. *Unit head:* Dr. Dottie Durband, Director, 785-532-5510, Fax: 785-532-5505, E-mail: dottie@ksu.edu. *Application contact:* Kristi Hageman, Administrative Specialist, 785-

532-5510, Fax: 785-532-5505, E-mail: klsmith@ksu.edu.
Website: http://www.he.k-state.edu/fshs/

**Kent State University,** College of Education, Health and Human Services, School of Lifespan Development and Educational Sciences, Program in Counseling and Human Development Services, Kent, OH 44242-0001. Offers PhD. *Accreditation:* ACA; NCATE. *Degree requirements:* For doctorate, comprehensive exam, thesis/dissertation. *Entrance requirements:* For doctorate, GRE General Test, preliminary written exam, 2 letters of reference, resume, interview. Additional exam requirements/recommendations for international students: Required—TOEFL (minimum score 550 paper-based; 80 iBT). Electronic applications accepted. *Expenses:* Tuition, state resident: full-time $10,864; part-time $495 per credit hour. Tuition, nonresident: full-time $18,380; part-time $837 per credit hour. *Faculty research:* Family/child therapy, clinical supervision, group work, experiential training methods.

**Kent State University,** College of Education, Health and Human Services, School of Lifespan Development and Educational Sciences, Program in Human Development and Family Studies, Kent, OH 44242-0001. Offers MA. *Degree requirements:* For master's, thesis optional. *Entrance requirements:* For master's, minimum undergraduate GPA of 3.0, 3 letters of reference, goals statement. Additional exam requirements/recommendations for international students: Required—TOEFL (minimum score 550 paper-based; 80 iBT). *Expenses:* Tuition, state resident: full-time $10,864; part-time $495 per credit hour. Tuition, nonresident: full-time $18,380; part-time $837 per credit hour.

**Laurentian University,** School of Graduate Studies and Research, Programme in Human Development, Sudbury, ON P3E 2C6, Canada. Offers M Sc, MA. Interdisciplinary program consisting of the Departments of Psychology, Sociology, and Human Movement. *Program availability:* Part-time. *Degree requirements:* For master's, thesis or alternative. *Entrance requirements:* For master's, honors degree with second class or better. *Faculty research:* Aging and well-being, physical, social and cognitive development of children, social cognition and social relationships including peers and family, education and schooling.

**Lindsey Wilson College,** School of Professional Counseling, Columbia, KY 42728. Offers counseling and human development (M Ed); counselor education and supervision (PhD). *Accreditation:* ACA (one or more programs are accredited). *Program availability:* Part-time, evening/weekend, online learning.

**Marywood University,** Academic Affairs, Center for Interdisciplinary Studies, Scranton, PA 18509-1598. Offers human development (PhD), including educational administration, health promotion, higher education administration, instructional leadership, social work. *Program availability:* Part-time. Electronic applications accepted. *Expenses:* Contact institution.

**Mississippi State University,** College of Agriculture and Life Sciences, School of Human Sciences, Mississippi State, MS 39762. Offers agriculture and extension education (MS, PhD), including agriculture and extension education (PhD), leadership (MS), teaching (MS); human development and family studies (MS, PhD). *Accreditation:* NCATE (one or more programs are accredited). *Program availability:* Part-time. *Faculty:* 23 full-time (13 women), 1 part-time/adjunct (0 women). *Students:* 35 full-time (25 women), 61 part-time (45 women); includes 19 minority (15 Black or African American, non-Hispanic/Latino; 2 Hispanic/Latino; 2 Two or more races, non-Hispanic/Latino), 5 international. Average age 35. 22 applicants, 73% accepted, 12 enrolled. In 2016, 8 master's, 4 doctorates awarded. *Degree requirements:* For master's, thesis optional, comprehensive oral or written exam. *Entrance requirements:* For master's, GRE, minimum GPA of 2.75 in last 4 semesters of course work; for doctorate, minimum GPA of 3.0 on prior graduate work. Additional exam requirements/recommendations for international students: Required—TOEFL (minimum score 477 paper-based; 53 iBT); Recommended—IELTS (minimum score 4.5). *Application deadline:* For fall admission, 7/1 for domestic students, 5/1 for international students; for spring admission, 11/1 for domestic students, 9/1 for international students. Applications are processed on a rolling basis. Application fee: $60. Electronic applications accepted. *Expenses:* Tuition, state resident: full-time $7670; part-time $852.50 per credit hour. Tuition, nonresident: full-time $20,790; part-time $2310.50 per credit hour. Part-time tuition and fees vary according to course load. *Financial support:* Federal Work-Study, institutionally sponsored loans, and unspecified assistantships available. Financial award application deadline: 4/1; financial award applicants required to submit FAFSA. *Faculty research:* Animal welfare, agro science, information technology, learning styles, problem solving. *Unit head:* Dr. Michael Newman, Director and Professor, 662-325-2950, E-mail: mnewman@humansci.msstate.edu. *Application contact:* Marina Hunt, Admissions and Enrollment Assistant, 662-325-5188, E-mail: mhunt@grad.msstate.edu.
Website: http://www.humansci.msstate.edu

**Montana State University,** The Graduate School, College of Education, Health, and Human Development, Department of Health and Human Development, Bozeman, MT 59717. Offers family and consumer sciences (MS). *Accreditation:* ACA. *Program availability:* Part-time, online learning. *Degree requirements:* For master's, comprehensive exam. *Entrance requirements:* For master's, GRE (minimum scores: verbal 480; quantitative 480). Additional exam requirements/recommendations for international students: Required—TOEFL (minimum score 550 paper-based). Electronic applications accepted. *Faculty research:* Community food systems, ethic of care for teachers and coaches, influence of public policy on families and communities, cost effectiveness of early childhood education, exercise metabolism, winter sport performance enhancement, assessment of physical activity.

**National Louis University,** National College of Education, Chicago, IL 60603. Offers administration and supervision (M Ed, Ed D, CAS, Ed S); curriculum and instruction (M Ed, MS Ed, CAS); early childhood administration (M Ed, CAS); early childhood education (M Ed, MAT, MS Ed, CAS); education (Ed D); educational psychology/human learning and development (M Ed, MS Ed, CAS, Ed S); elementary education (MAT); interdisciplinary curriculum and instruction (M Ed); mathematics education (M Ed, MS Ed, CAS); middle grades education (MAT); reading and language (M Ed, MS Ed, CAS); school psychology (M Ed, Ed S); science education (M Ed, MS Ed, CAS); secondary education (MAT); special education (M Ed, MAT, CAS); technology in education (M Ed, CAS). *Accreditation:* NCATE. *Program availability:* Part-time, evening/weekend. *Degree requirements:* For doctorate, comprehensive exam, thesis/dissertation. *Entrance requirements:* For master's, MAT or GRE, minimum GPA of 3.0; for doctorate, GRE General Test, minimum GPA of 3.25, interview, resume, writing sample, 4 recommendations. Additional exam requirements/recommendations for international students: Required—TOEFL (minimum score 550 paper-based; 79 iBT).

**New York University,** Steinhardt School of Culture, Education, and Human Development, New York, NY 10003. Offers MA, MFA, MM, MPH, MS, DPS, DPT, Ed D, PhD, Advanced Certificate, Post Master's Certificate, Postbaccalaureate Certificate, Advanced Certificate/MPH, MA/Advanced Certificate, MA/MA, MA/MS, MLIS/MA. *Accreditation:* TEAC. *Program availability:* Part-time. *Degree requirements:* For master's, thesis (for some programs); for doctorate, comprehensive exam (for some programs), thesis/dissertation. *Entrance requirements:* For doctorate, GRE General Test, interview. Additional exam requirements/recommendations for international students: Required—TOEFL (minimum score 100 iBT). Electronic applications

accepted. *Expenses:* Contact institution. *Faculty research:* Equity, urban adolescents, arts in education, globalization, multivariate analysis, psychometrics.

**New York University,** Steinhardt School of Culture, Education, and Human Development, Department of Applied Psychology, Programs in Educational and Developmental Psychology, New York, NY 10003. Offers developmental psychology (PhD); human development and social intervention (MA); psychology and social intervention (PhD). *Accreditation:* APA (one or more programs are accredited). *Program availability:* Part-time. *Degree requirements:* For master's, thesis (for some programs); for doctorate, thesis/dissertation. *Entrance requirements:* For doctorate, GRE General Test, interview. Additional exam requirements/recommendations for international students: Required—TOEFL. Electronic applications accepted. *Faculty research:* Schools and communities, self-regulation and academic achievement, intervention and social change, trauma and resilience, cognition.

**Northern Arizona University,** Graduate College, College of Social and Behavioral Sciences, Institute for Human Development, Flagstaff, AZ 86011. Offers assistive technology (Certificate); disability policy and practice (Certificate). *Program availability:* Part-time. *Entrance requirements:* Additional exam requirements/recommendations for international students: Required—TOEFL (minimum score 550 paper-based; 80 iBT), IELTS (minimum score 7). Electronic applications accepted. *Expenses:* Tuition, state resident: full-time $8971; part-time $444 per credit hour. Tuition, nonresident: full-time $20,958; part-time $1164 per credit hour. *Required fees:* $1018; $644 per credit hour. Tuition and fees vary according to course load, campus/location and program.

**Northwestern University,** The Graduate School, School of Education and Social Policy, Program in Human Development and Social Policy, Evanston, IL 60208. Offers PhD. Admissions and degrees offered through The Graduate School. *Degree requirements:* For doctorate, comprehensive exam, thesis/dissertation. *Entrance requirements:* For doctorate, GRE General Test. Additional exam requirements/recommendations for international students: Required—TOEFL (minimum score 600 paper-based; 100 iBT). Electronic applications accepted. *Faculty research:* Individual development and the personal narrative; the life course and culture; development, intervention and culture; the life course and policy; analysis of policy effects on lives.

**The Ohio State University,** Graduate School, College of Education and Human Ecology, Department of Human Sciences, Columbus, OH 43210. Offers consumer sciences (MS, PhD); human development and family science (PhD); human nutrition (MS, PhD); kinesiology (MA, PhD). *Program availability:* Part-time. *Faculty:* 54. *Students:* 128 full-time (77 women), 8 part-time (6 women); includes 21 minority (7 Black or African American, non-Hispanic/Latino; 8 Hispanic/Latino; 6 Two or more races, non-Hispanic/Latino), 30 international. Average age 27. In 2016, 27 master's, 17 doctorates awarded. *Degree requirements:* For master's, thesis optional; for doctorate, thesis/dissertation. *Entrance requirements:* For master's and doctorate, GRE. Additional exam requirements/recommendations for international students: Required—TOEFL (minimum score 550 paper-based; 79 iBT), Michigan English Language Assessment Battery (minimum score 82); Recommended—IELTS (minimum score 7). *Application deadline:* For fall admission, 12/1 priority date for domestic and international students. Applications are processed on a rolling basis. Application fee: $60 ($70 for international students). Electronic applications accepted. *Financial support:* Fellowships with tuition reimbursements, research assistantships with tuition reimbursements, teaching assistantships with tuition reimbursements, Federal Work-Study, and institutionally sponsored loans available. Support available to part-time students. *Unit head:* Dr. Joe Wheaton, Interim Chair, E-mail: wheaton.3@osu.edu. *Application contact:* Graduate and Professional Admissions, 614-292-9444, Fax: 614-292-3895, E-mail: gpadmissions@osu.edu.
Website: http://ehe.osu.edu/human-sciences/

**Oklahoma State University,** College of Arts and Sciences, Department of Psychology, Stillwater, OK 74078. Offers clinical psychology (PhD); general psychology (MS); lifespan development psychology (PhD). *Accreditation:* APA (one or more programs are accredited). *Faculty:* 31 full-time (19 women), 1 (woman) part-time/adjunct. *Students:* 42 full-time (34 women), 14 part-time (8 women); includes 12 minority (1 Black or African American, non-Hispanic/Latino; 4 American Indian or Alaska Native, non-Hispanic/Latino; 1 Asian, non-Hispanic/Latino; 3 Hispanic/Latino; 1 Native Hawaiian or other Pacific Islander, non-Hispanic/Latino; 2 Two or more races, non-Hispanic/Latino), 2 international. Average age 26. 160 applicants, 6% accepted, 9 enrolled. In 2016, 11 master's, 7 doctorates awarded. *Degree requirements:* For master's, thesis or alternative; for doctorate, comprehensive exam, thesis/dissertation. *Entrance requirements:* For master's and doctorate, GRE General Test. Additional exam requirements/recommendations for international students: Required—TOEFL (minimum score 550 paper-based; 79 iBT). *Application deadline:* For fall admission, 3/1 priority date for international students; for spring admission, 8/1 priority date for international students. Applications are processed on a rolling basis. Application fee: $40 ($75 for international students). Electronic applications accepted. *Expenses:* Tuition, state resident: full-time $3775; part-time $209.70 per credit hour. Tuition, nonresident: full-time $14,851; part-time $825.05 per credit hour. *Required fees:* $2027; $112.60 per credit hour. Tuition and fees vary according to campus/location. *Financial support:* In 2016–17, 15 research assistantships (averaging $13,194 per year), 41 teaching assistantships (averaging $11,532 per year) were awarded; career-related internships or fieldwork, Federal Work-Study, scholarships/grants, health care benefits, tuition waivers (partial), and unspecified assistantships also available. Support available to part-time students. Financial award application deadline: 3/1; financial award applicants required to submit FAFSA. *Unit head:* Dr. Thad Leffingwell, Department Head, 405-744-7494, Fax: 405-744-8067, E-mail: thad.leffingwell@okstate.edu. *Application contact:* Patricia Alexander, Graduate Advisor, 405-744-7591, Fax: 405-744-8967, E-mail: patricia.alexander@okstate.edu.
Website: http://psychology.okstate.edu

**Oregon State University,** College of Public Health and Human Sciences, Program in Human Development and Family Studies, Corvallis, OR 97331. Offers MS, PhD. *Faculty:* 15 full-time (13 women), 2 part-time/adjunct (both women). *Students:* 29 full-time (24 women), 4 part-time (3 women); includes 8 minority (1 Black or African American, non-Hispanic/Latino; 2 American Indian or Alaska Native, non-Hispanic/Latino; 2 Asian, non-Hispanic/Latino; 2 Hispanic/Latino; 1 Two or more races, non-Hispanic/Latino), 2 international. Average age 32. 20 applicants, 40% accepted, 6 enrolled. In 2016, 2 master's, 7 doctorates awarded. *Entrance requirements:* For master's, GRE; for doctorate, GRE, master's degree (including thesis). Additional exam requirements/recommendations for international students: Required—TOEFL (minimum score 80 iBT), IELTS (minimum score 6.5). *Application deadline:* For fall admission, 4/15 for domestic and international students. *Expenses:* Tuition, state resident: full-time $12,150; part-time $450 per credit. Tuition, nonresident: full-time $21,789; part-time $807 per credit. *Required fees:* $1651; $1507 per credit. One-time fee: $350. Tuition and fees vary according to course load, campus/location and program. *Financial support:* Fellowships, research assistantships, and teaching assistantships available. Financial award application deadline: 1/2. *Unit head:* Dr. Robert Stawski, Associate Professor. *Application contact:* Megan Ferris, Doctoral Programs Manager, E-mail: megan.ferris@oregonstate.edu.
Website: http://health.oregonstate.edu/degrees/graduate/hdfs

## Human Development

**Pacific Oaks College,** Graduate School, Program in Human Development, Pasadena, CA 91103. Offers MA. *Program availability:* Part-time, evening/weekend, online learning. *Degree requirements:* For master's, thesis. *Entrance requirements:* Additional exam requirements/recommendations for international students: Required—TOEFL (minimum score 550 paper-based). *Faculty research:* Bicultural development, teaching adults, art education, literacy development, adolescent development.

**Penn State University Park,** Graduate School, College of Health and Human Development, Department of Human Development and Family Studies, University Park, PA 16802. Offers MS, PhD. *Unit head:* Dr. Ann C. Crouter, Dean, 814-865-1420, Fax: 814-865-3282. *Application contact:* Lori Hawn, Director, Graduate Student Services, 814-865-1795, Fax: 814-863-4627, E-mail: l-gswww@lists.psu.edu.
Website: http://hhd.psu.edu/hdfs/

**Purdue University,** Graduate School, College of Health and Human Sciences, Department of Child Development and Family Studies, West Lafayette, IN 47907. Offers developmental studies (MS, PhD); family studies (MS, PhD); marriage and family therapy (MS, PhD). *Accreditation:* AAMFT/COAMFTE (one or more programs are accredited). *Program availability:* Part-time. *Faculty:* 19 full-time (11 women), 1 (woman) part-time/adjunct. *Students:* 22 full-time (21 women), 1 (woman) part-time; includes 3 minority (1 Black or African American, non-Hispanic/Latino; 1 Hispanic/Latino; 1 Two or more races, non-Hispanic/Latino), 5 international. Average age 26. 41 applicants, 29% accepted, 8 enrolled. In 2016, 4 master's, 3 doctorates awarded. Terminal master's awarded for partial completion of doctoral program. *Degree requirements:* For master's, thesis; for doctorate, thesis/dissertation. *Entrance requirements:* For master's and doctorate, GRE General Test (minimum score 1000 combined verbal and quantitative), minimum undergraduate GPA of 3.0 or equivalent. Additional exam requirements/recommendations for international students: Required—TOEFL (minimum score 600 paper-based; 90 iBT), TWE (minimum score 4). *Application deadline:* For fall admission, 1/4 for domestic and international students. Applications are processed on a rolling basis. Application fee: $60 ($75 for international students). Electronic applications accepted. *Financial support:* Fellowships with full tuition reimbursements, research assistantships with full tuition reimbursements, teaching assistantships with full tuition reimbursements, and career-related internships or fieldwork available. Support available to part-time students. Financial award application deadline: 1/15; financial award applicants required to submit FAFSA. *Faculty research:* Inclusion of children with special needs, families as learning environments, relationships in child care, work-family relations, AIDS prevention. *Unit head:* Dr. Doran C. French, Head, 765-494-9511, E-mail: dcfrench@purdue.edu. *Application contact:* Tina Putz, Graduate Contact, 765-496-3816, E-mail: tputz@purdue.edu.
Website: http://www.purdue.edu/hhs/hdfs/

**St. Lawrence University,** Department of Education, Program in Counseling and Human Development, Canton, NY 13617. Offers mental health counseling (MS); school counseling (M Ed, CAS). *Program availability:* Part-time, evening/weekend. *Entrance requirements:* For master's, GRE General Test. *Faculty research:* Defense mechanisms and mediation.

**Saint Louis University,** Graduate Education, College of Education and Public Service and Graduate Education, Department of Counseling and Family Therapy, St. Louis, MO 63103. Offers counseling and family therapy (PhD); human development counseling (MA); marriage and family therapy (Certificate); school counseling (MA, MA-R). *Accreditation:* AAMFT/COAMFTE; NCATE. *Program availability:* Part-time. *Degree requirements:* For master's, comprehensive exam, thesis (for some programs); for doctorate, comprehensive exam, thesis/dissertation, preliminary oral and written exams. *Entrance requirements:* For master's, GRE General Test, letters of recommendation, resume; for doctorate, GRE General Test, letters of recommendation, resumé, transcripts, goal statement. Additional exam requirements/recommendations for international students: Required—TOEFL (minimum score 550 paper-based). Electronic applications accepted. *Faculty research:* Medical family therapy/collaborative health care multicultural counseling, mental health needs of diverse, minority, or Immigrant/refugee populations, divorce, aging families.

**Saint Mary's University of Minnesota,** Schools of Graduate and Professional Programs, Graduate School of Business and Technology, Human Development Program, Winona, MN 55987-1399. Offers MA. Tuition and fees vary according to degree level and program. *Unit head:* Dr. Jim Ollhoff, Director, 651-295-2454, Fax: 612-728-5121, E-mail: jollhoff@smumn.edu. *Application contact:* James Callinan, Director of Admissions for Graduate and Professional Programs, 612-728-5185, Fax: 612-728-5121, E-mail: jcallina@smumn.edu.
Website: http://www.smumn.edu/graduate-home/areas-of-study/graduate-school-of-business-technology/ma-in-human-development

**Texas Tech University,** Graduate School, College of Human Sciences, Department of Human Development and Family Studies, Lubbock, TX 79409-1230. Offers human development and family studies (MS, PhD), including gerontology (MS). *Accreditation:* AAMFT/COAMFTE (one or more programs are accredited). *Faculty:* 24 full-time (21 women), 7 part-time/adjunct (all women). *Students:* 28 full-time (23 women), 20 part-time (14 women); includes 12 minority (3 Black or African American, non-Hispanic/Latino; 1 American Indian or Alaska Native, non-Hispanic/Latino; 7 Hispanic/Latino; 1 Two or more races, non-Hispanic/Latino), 12 international. Average age 33. 34 applicants, 44% accepted, 4 enrolled. In 2016, 5 master's, 4 doctorates awarded. *Degree requirements:* For master's, thesis; for doctorate, comprehensive exam, thesis/dissertation. *Entrance requirements:* For master's and doctorate, GRE General Test. Additional exam requirements/recommendations for international students: Required—TOEFL (minimum score 550 paper-based; 79 iBT). *Application deadline:* For fall admission, 6/1 priority date for domestic students, 1/15 priority date for international students; for spring admission, 9/1 priority date for domestic students, 6/15 priority date for international students. Applications are processed on a rolling basis. Application fee: $75. Electronic applications accepted. *Expenses:* $315 per credit hour full-time resident tuition, $723 per credit hour full-time non-resident tuition; $50.50 per credit hour fee plus $608 per term fee. *Financial support:* In 2016–17, 38 students received support, including 35 fellowships (averaging $4,579 per year), 24 research assistantships (averaging $8,526 per year), 23 teaching assistantships (averaging $9,522 per year); scholarships/grants and unspecified assistantships also available. Financial award application deadline: 4/15; financial award applicants required to submit FAFSA. *Faculty research:* 34226. *Total annual research expenditures:* $64,339. *Unit head:* Dr. Ann M. Mastergeorge, Chairperson, 806-834-7162, Fax: 806-742-3042, E-mail: ann.mastergeorge@ttu.edu. *Application contact:* Dr. Malinda Colwell, Graduate Program Director, 806-742-3000 Ext. 250, Fax: 806-742-0285, E-mail: malinda.colwell@ttu.edu.
Website: http://www.depts.ttu.edu/hdfs

**Tufts University,** Graduate School of Arts and Sciences, Eliot-Pearson Department of Child Study and Human Development, Medford, MA 02155. Offers child study and human development (MA, PhD); early childhood education (MAT). *Program availability:* Part-time. *Faculty:* 21 full-time (16 women), 15 part-time/adjunct (13 women). *Students:* 81 full-time (70 women), 6 part-time (5 women); includes 19 minority (6 Black or African American, non-Hispanic/Latino; 7 Asian, non-Hispanic/Latino; 3 Hispanic/Latino; 3 Two or more races, non-Hispanic/Latino), 16 international. Average age 27. 129 applicants,

59% accepted, 37 enrolled. In 2016, 19 master's, 5 doctorates awarded. *Degree requirements:* For master's, thesis (for some programs); for doctorate, comprehensive exam, thesis/dissertation. *Entrance requirements:* For master's and doctorate, GRE General Test. Additional exam requirements/recommendations for international students: Required—TOEFL (minimum score 550 paper-based; 80 iBT), IELTS (minimum score 6.5). *Application deadline:* For fall admission, 12/1 priority date for domestic and international students. Applications are processed on a rolling basis. Application fee: $85. Electronic applications accepted. *Expenses:* $49,982 full-time tuition (for MA); $29,936 full-time tuition (for PhD). *Financial support:* In 2016–17, 78 students received support. Fellowships, research assistantships, teaching assistantships, Federal Work-Study, scholarships/grants, tuition waivers (full and partial), and unspecified assistantships available. Support available to part-time students. Financial award application deadline: 1/15. *Faculty research:* Reading and language, developmental technologies, cognitive and social development, policy and program evaluation. *Unit head:* Dr. David Henry Feldman, Graduate Program Director. *Application contact:* Office of Graduate Admissions, 617-627-3395, E-mail: gradadmissions@tufts.edu.
Website: http://ase.tufts.edu/epcd

**The University of Alabama,** Graduate School, College of Human Environmental Sciences, Department of Human Development and Family Studies, Tuscaloosa, AL 35487. Offers human development and family studies (MSHES); marriage and family therapy (MSHES); parent and family life education (MSHES). *Faculty:* 10 full-time (8 women). *Students:* 23 full-time (22 women), 6 part-time (all women); includes 6 minority (5 Black or African American, non-Hispanic/Latino; 1 Two or more races, non-Hispanic/Latino). Average age 25. 25 applicants, 72% accepted, 10 enrolled. In 2016, 10 master's awarded. Terminal master's awarded for partial completion of doctoral program. *Degree requirements:* For master's, comprehensive exam (for some programs), thesis (for some programs). *Entrance requirements:* For master's, GRE General Test or MAT, minimum GPA of 3.0. Additional exam requirements/recommendations for international students: Required—TOEFL (minimum score 79 iBT), IELTS (minimum score 6.5). *Application deadline:* For fall admission, 12/15 priority date for domestic and international students. Applications are processed on a rolling basis. Application fee: $50 ($60 for international students). Electronic applications accepted. *Expenses:* Tuition, state resident: full-time $10,470. Tuition, nonresident: full-time $26,950. *Financial support:* In 2016–17, 8 students received support, including 3 research assistantships with full tuition reimbursements available (averaging $13,140 per year), 5 teaching assistantships (averaging $13,140 per year); fellowships, career-related internships or fieldwork, Federal Work-Study, scholarships/grants, health care benefits, and unspecified assistantships also available. Financial award application deadline: 3/15. *Faculty research:* Parent/child relationships, preschool curricula and quality measures for child care programs, family strengths and adolescent behaviors, depression in mothers and infants, word association and word learning in young children, bullying behaviors in children, attachment parenting, medical play therapy, socialization of young children, impact of daily experiences on relationship quality, re-entry of service members into civilian roles. *Total annual research expenditures:* $1,650. *Unit head:* Dr. Carroll M. Tingle, Chair, 205-348-6158, Fax: 205-348-8153, E-mail: ctingle@ches.ua.edu. *Application contact:* Dr. Maria Hernandez-Reif, Professor, 205-348-5894, Fax: 205-348-8153, E-mail: mhernandez-reif@ches.ua.edu.
Website: http://www.hdfs.ches.ua.edu/

**The University of Arizona,** College of Education, Department of Disability and Psychoeducational Studies, Tucson, AZ 85721. Offers counseling and mental health (MA), including rehabilitation counseling, school counseling; family studies and human development (M Ed); rehabilitation counseling (PhD); school counseling (MA); school psychology (PhD, Ed S); special education (MA, PhD), including cross-categorical special education (MA), deaf and hard of hearing (MA), learning disabilities (MA), severe and multiple disabilities (MA), special education (PhD), visual impairment (MA). *Accreditation:* CORE. *Program availability:* Part-time. Terminal master's awarded for partial completion of doctoral program. *Degree requirements:* For master's, comprehensive exam, thesis optional; for doctorate, comprehensive exam, thesis/dissertation. *Entrance requirements:* For master's, statement of purpose; for doctorate, GRE General Test (minimum score 1100) or MAT, 3 letters of recommendation. Additional exam requirements/recommendations for international students: Required—TOEFL (minimum score 550 paper-based; 79 iBT).

**The University of British Columbia,** Faculty of Education, Department of Educational and Counseling Psychology, and Special Education, Vancouver, BC V6T 1Z4, Canada. Offers counseling psychology (M Ed, MA, PhD); guidance studies (Diploma); human development, learning and culture (M Ed, MA, PhD); measurement, evaluation, and research methodology (M Ed, MA, PhD); school psychology (M Ed, MA, PhD); special education (M Ed, MA, PhD, Diploma). *Program availability:* Part-time. *Degree requirements:* For master's, thesis (for some programs); for doctorate, comprehensive exam, thesis/dissertation. *Entrance requirements:* For master's, GRE General Test (counseling psychology MA); for doctorate, GRE General Test. Additional exam requirements/recommendations for international students: Required—TOEFL. Application fee: $102 Canadian dollars ($165 Canadian dollars for international students). Electronic applications accepted. *Expenses:* $6,865 per year tuition, $10,938 per year international (for MA, M Ed); $4,802 per year tuition, $8,436 per year international (for PhD). *Financial support:* Fellowships, research assistantships, teaching assistantships, career-related internships or fieldwork, Federal Work-Study, institutionally sponsored loans, scholarships/grants, health care benefits, tuition waivers (full and partial), and unspecified assistantships available. *Faculty research:* Women, family, social problems, career transition, stress and coping problems. *Application contact:* Karen Yan, Graduate Program Assistant, 604-822-6371, Fax: 604-822-3302, E-mail: karen.yan@ubc.ca.
Website: http://ecps.educ.ubc.ca/

**University of California, Berkeley,** Graduate Division, School of Education, Programs in Education, Berkeley, CA 94720-1500. Offers development in mathematics and science (MA); education in mathematics, science, and technology (MA, PhD); human development and education (MA, PhD); leadership education (MA); special education (PhD); teacher education (MA); MA/Credential; PhD/Credential; PhD/MA. *Students:* 286 full-time (207 women); includes 133 minority (31 Black or African American, non-Hispanic/Latino; 2 American Indian or Alaska Native, non-Hispanic/Latino; 44 Asian, non-Hispanic/Latino; 56 Hispanic/Latino), 29 international. Average age 33. 643 applicants, 84 enrolled. In 2016, 105 master's, 31 doctorates awarded. Terminal master's awarded for partial completion of doctoral program. *Degree requirements:* For master's, exam or thesis; for doctorate, thesis/dissertation, oral qualifying exam. *Entrance requirements:* For master's and doctorate, GRE General Test, minimum GPA of 3.0 during last 2 years of undergraduate course work. *Application deadline:* For fall admission, 12/16 for domestic students. Application fee: $105 ($125 for international students). Electronic applications accepted. *Financial support:* Fellowships, research assistantships, teaching assistantships, institutionally sponsored loans, health care benefits, and unspecified assistantships available. *Faculty research:* Human development, social and moral educational psychology, developmental teacher preparation. *Unit head:* Prof. Prudence L. Carter, Dean, 510-642-3726, E-mail:

gsedeansoffice@lists.berkeley.edu.
Website: https://gse.berkeley.edu

**University of California, Davis,** Graduate Studies, Graduate Group in Human Development, Davis, CA 95616. Offers PhD. *Degree requirements:* For doctorate, thesis/dissertation. *Entrance requirements:* For doctorate, GRE General Test, GRE Subject Test, minimum GPA of 3.0. Additional exam requirements/recommendations for international students: Required—TOEFL (minimum score 550 paper-based). Electronic applications accepted. *Faculty research:* Life span socioemotional and cognitive development, individual differences, relationship between biological and behavioral development, cross-cultural and cross-generational development.

**University of Central Oklahoma,** The Jackson College of Graduate Studies, College of Education and Professional Studies, Department of Human Environmental Sciences, Edmond, OK 73034-5209. Offers family and child studies (MS), including family life education, infant/child specialist, marriage and family therapy; nutrition-food management (MS). *Program availability:* Part-time. *Degree requirements:* For master's, comprehensive exam (for some programs), thesis (for some programs). *Entrance requirements:* For master's, GRE, essay, physical, CPR and First Aid training. Additional exam requirements/recommendations for international students: Required—TOEFL (minimum score 550 paper-based; 79 iBT), IELTS (minimum score 6.5). Electronic applications accepted.

**University of Chicago,** Division of the Social Sciences, Department of Comparative Human Development, Chicago, IL 60637. Offers PhD. *Students:* 52 full-time (36 women); includes 12 minority (6 Black or African American, non-Hispanic/Latino; 1 American Indian or Alaska Native, non-Hispanic/Latino; 2 Asian, non-Hispanic/Latino; 2 Hispanic/Latino; 1 Two or more races, non-Hispanic/Latino), 8 international. 51 applicants, 12% accepted, 5 enrolled. In 2016, 5 doctorates awarded. *Degree requirements:* For doctorate, one foreign language, thesis/dissertation, trial research project. *Entrance requirements:* For doctorate, GRE General Test. Additional exam requirements/recommendations for international students: Required—TOEFL (minimum score 104 iBT), IELTS (minimum score 7). *Application deadline:* For fall admission, 12/15 for domestic and international students. Application fee: $90. Electronic applications accepted. *Financial support:* In 2016–17, 5 students received support, including 5 fellowships with full tuition reimbursements available (averaging $23,000 per year); career-related internships or fieldwork, Federal Work-Study, institutionally sponsored loans, scholarships/grants, and health care benefits also available. Financial award application deadline: 12/15. *Unit head:* Margaret Beale Spencer, Chair. *Application contact:* Office of the Dean of Students, 773-702-8415, E-mail: admissions@ssd.uchicago.edu.
Website: http://humdev.uchicago.edu

**University of Colorado Denver,** School of Education and Human Development, Programs in Educational and School Psychology, Denver, CO 80217. Offers educational psychology (MA), including educational assessment, educational psychology, human development, human learning, research and evaluation; school psychology (Psy D, Ed S). MA program also offered in partnership with Boulder Journey School, Friends? School and Stanley British Primary School. *Program availability:* Part-time, evening/weekend. *Students:* 210 full-time (171 women), 79 part-time (71 women); includes 47 minority (5 Black or African American, non-Hispanic/Latino; 2 American Indian or Alaska Native, non-Hispanic/Latino; 5 Asian, non-Hispanic/Latino; 28 Hispanic/Latino; 7 Two or more races, non-Hispanic/Latino), 6 international. Average age 30. 179 applicants, 94% accepted, 126 enrolled. In 2016, 166 master's, 7 doctorates, 11 other advanced degrees awarded. *Degree requirements:* For master's, comprehensive exam, 9 hours of core courses, embedded within a minimum of 36 to 38 hours of relevant coursework, including an educational psychology practicum, independent study project or thesis (recommended); for Ed S, comprehensive exam, minimum of 75 semester hours (61 hours of coursework, 6 of 500-hour practicum in field, and 8 of 1200-hour internship); PRAXIS II. *Entrance requirements:* For master's, GRE if undergraduate GPA below 2.75, resume, three letters of recommendation, transcripts; for Ed S, GRE, resume, letters of recommendation, transcripts. Additional exam requirements/recommendations for international students: Required—TOEFL (minimum score 537 paper-based; 75 iBT); Recommended—IELTS (minimum score 6.5). *Application deadline:* For fall admission, 4/15 for domestic students, 4/1 for international students; for spring admission, 9/15 for domestic students, 9/1 for international students. Application fee: $50 ($75 for international students). Electronic applications accepted. *Expenses:* Contact institution. *Financial support:* In 2016–17, 90 students received support. Research assistantships, Federal Work-Study, institutionally sponsored loans, scholarships/grants, and traineeships available. Financial award application deadline: 4/1; financial award applicants required to submit FAFSA. *Faculty research:* Crisis response and intervention, school violence prevention, immigrant experience, educational environments for English language learners, culturally competent assessment and intervention, child and youth suicide. *Unit head:* Francie Crepeau-Hobson, Associate Professor and Program Director, 303-315-6315, E-mail: franci.creapeau-hobson@ucdenver.edu. *Application contact:* 303-315-6300, E-mail: education@ucdenver.edu.
Website: http://www.ucdenver.edu/academics/colleges/SchoolOfEducation/Academics/MASTERS/EPSY/Pages/default.aspx

**University of Connecticut,** Graduate School, College of Liberal Arts and Sciences, Department of Human Development and Family Studies, Storrs, CT 06269. Offers MA, PhD. *Accreditation:* AAMFT/COAMFTE (one or more programs are accredited). Terminal master's awarded for partial completion of doctoral program. *Degree requirements:* For master's, comprehensive exam; for doctorate, thesis/dissertation. *Entrance requirements:* For doctorate, GRE General Test. Additional exam requirements/recommendations for international students: Required—TOEFL (minimum score 550 paper-based). Electronic applications accepted.

**University of Dayton,** Department of Counselor Education and Human Services, Dayton, OH 45469. Offers clinical mental health counseling (MS Ed); college student personnel (MS Ed); higher education administration (MS Ed); human services (MS Ed); school counseling (MS Ed); school psychology (MS Ed, Ed S). *Accreditation:* ACA; NCATE. *Program availability:* Part-time, evening/weekend. *Faculty:* 10 full-time (6 women), 24 part-time/adjunct (15 women). *Students:* 198 full-time (155 women), 95 part-time (75 women); includes 15 minority (8 Black or African American, non-Hispanic/Latino; 2 Asian, non-Hispanic/Latino; 2 Hispanic/Latino; 3 Two or more races, non-Hispanic/Latino), 3 international. Average age 36. 426 applicants, 28% accepted. In 2016, 115 master's, 9 Ed Ss awarded. *Degree requirements:* For Ed S, thesis. *Entrance requirements:* For master's, MAT or GRE (if GPA less than 2.75), essays (for some programs). Additional exam requirements/recommendations for international students: Required—TOEFL (minimum score 550 paper-based; 80 iBT); Recommended—IELTS. *Application deadline:* For fall admission, 3/10 priority date for domestic and international students; for spring admission, 9/10 priority date for domestic and international students; for summer admission, 12/1 priority date for domestic and international students. Application fee: $0 ($50 for international students). Electronic applications accepted. *Expenses:* $620 per credit hour (for master's degree programs); $740 per credit hour (for Ed S). *Financial support:* In 2016–17, 7 research assistantships with partial tuition reimbursements (averaging $8,038 per year), 4 teaching assistantships with partial

tuition reimbursements (averaging $9,390 per year) were awarded; career-related internships or fieldwork, institutionally sponsored loans, health care benefits, and unspecified assistantships also available. Financial award application deadline: 1/9; financial award applicants required to submit FAFSA. *Faculty research:* School bonding, traumatic brain injuries, second-year student experience, impact of physical space on learning, integrative health and mental health care. *Total annual research expenditures:* $1,500. *Unit head:* Dr. Alan Demmitt, Chair, 937-229-3644, Fax: 937-229-1055, E-mail: ademmitt1@udayton.edu. *Application contact:* Kathleen Brown, Administrative Assistant, 937-229-3644, Fax: 937-229-1055, E-mail: kbrown1@udayton.edu.
Website: https://www.udayton.edu/education/departments_and_programs/edc/

**University of Delaware,** College of Education and Human Development, Department of Human Development and Family Studies, Newark, DE 19716. Offers MS, PhD. *Program availability:* Part-time. Terminal master's awarded for partial completion of doctoral program. *Degree requirements:* For master's, thesis or alternative; for doctorate, comprehensive exam, thesis/dissertation. *Entrance requirements:* For master's and doctorate, GRE General Test, 3 letters of recommendation. Additional exam requirements/recommendations for international students: Required—TOEFL. Electronic applications accepted. *Faculty research:* Early childhood inclusive education, relationships, family risk and resilience, disability issues, program development and evaluation.

**University of Guelph,** Graduate Studies, College of Social and Applied Human Sciences, Department of Family Relations and Applied Nutrition, Guelph, ON N1G 2W1, Canada. Offers applied nutrition (MAN); family relations and human development (M Sc, PhD), including applied human nutrition, couple and family therapy (M Sc), family relations and human development. *Accreditation:* AAMFT/COAMFTE (one or more programs are accredited). *Program availability:* Part-time. *Degree requirements:* For master's, thesis (for some programs); for doctorate, comprehensive exam, thesis/dissertation. *Entrance requirements:* For master's, minimum B+ average; for doctorate, master's degree in family relations and human development or related field with a minimum B+ average or master's degree in applied human nutrition. Additional exam requirements/recommendations for international students: Required—TOEFL (minimum score 600 paper-based). Electronic applications accepted. *Faculty research:* Child and adolescent development, social gerontology, family roles and relations, couple and family therapy, applied human nutrition.

**University of Illinois at Chicago,** College of Applied Health Sciences, Department of Disability and Human Development, Chicago, IL 60607-7128. Offers MS, PhD. *Accreditation:* AOTA. *Program availability:* Part-time. *Degree requirements:* For master's, thesis optional; for doctorate, thesis/dissertation. *Entrance requirements:* For master's and doctorate, GRE General Test. Additional exam requirements/recommendations for international students: Required—TOEFL. Electronic applications accepted. *Faculty research:* Emerging trends in disability, demography and financial structure of disability services, aging and disability, empowerment of people with disabilities, health promotion in disabilities.

**University of Illinois at Springfield,** Graduate Programs, College of Education and Human Services, Program in Human Development Counseling, Springfield, IL 62703-5407. Offers MA. *Accreditation:* ACA. *Program availability:* Part-time, evening/weekend. *Faculty:* 6 full-time (4 women), 2 part-time/adjunct (1 woman). *Students:* 58 full-time (52 women), 36 part-time (27 women); includes 10 minority (6 Black or African American, non-Hispanic/Latino; 3 Hispanic/Latino; 1 Two or more races, non-Hispanic/Latino), 2 international. Average age 30. 59 applicants, 47% accepted, 21 enrolled. In 2016, 27 master's awarded. *Degree requirements:* For master's, comprehensive exam, project or thesis. *Entrance requirements:* For master's, minimum undergraduate GPA of 3.0 in last 60 hours of coursework or cumulative; essay; personal references; interview. Additional exam requirements/recommendations for international students: Required—TOEFL (minimum score 500 paper-based; 61 iBT). *Application deadline:* Applications are processed on a rolling basis. Application fee: $60 ($75 for international students). Electronic applications accepted. *Expenses:* Tuition, state resident: part-time $329 per credit hour. Tuition, nonresident: part-time $675 per credit hour. *Financial support:* In 2016–17, fellowships with full tuition reimbursements (averaging $9,900 per year), research assistantships with full tuition reimbursements (averaging $9,991 per year), teaching assistantships with full tuition reimbursements (averaging $10,059 per year) were awarded; career-related internships or fieldwork, Federal Work-Study, scholarships/grants, health care benefits, and unspecified assistantships also available. Support available to part-time students. Financial award application deadline: 11/15; financial award applicants required to submit FAFSA. *Unit head:* Dr. William Abler, Program Administrator, 217-206-7567, Fax: 217-206-6775, E-mail: abler.bill@uis.edu. *Application contact:* Dr. Cecelia Cornell, Associate Vice Chancellor for Graduate Education, 217-206-7230, E-mail: ccorn1@uis.edu.
Website: http://www.uis.edu/hdc

**University of Illinois at Urbana–Champaign,** Graduate College, College of Agricultural, Consumer and Environmental Sciences, Department of Human and Community Development, Champaign, IL 61820. Offers MS, PhD.

**University of Maine,** Graduate School, College of Education and Human Development, School of Educational Leadership, Higher Education, and Human Development, Orono, ME 04469. Offers educational leadership (M Ed, CAS); higher education (CAS); human development (MS). *Program availability:* Part-time. *Students:* 48 full-time (32 women), 84 part-time (62 women); includes 10 minority (3 Black or African American, non-Hispanic/Latino; 2 American Indian or Alaska Native, non-Hispanic/Latino; 3 Hispanic/Latino; 2 Two or more races, non-Hispanic/Latino), 2 international. Average age 38. 85 applicants, 93% accepted, 61 enrolled. In 2016, 28 master's, 2 doctorates, 10 other advanced degrees awarded. *Degree requirements:* For master's, thesis (for some programs); for doctorate, comprehensive exam, thesis/dissertation. *Entrance requirements:* For master's, GRE General Test, MAT; for doctorate, GRE. Additional exam requirements/recommendations for international students: Required—TOEFL. *Application deadline:* For fall admission, 2/1 priority date for domestic students. Applications are processed on a rolling basis. Application fee: $65. Electronic applications accepted. *Expenses:* Tuition, state resident: full-time $7524; part-time $2508 per credit. Tuition, nonresident: full-time $24,498; part-time $8166 per credit. *Required fees:* $1148; $571 per credit. *Financial support:* In 2016–17, 22 students received support, including 4 teaching assistantships (averaging $14,600 per year); career-related internships or fieldwork, Federal Work-Study, institutionally sponsored loans, tuition waivers (full and partial), and unspecified assistantships also available. Financial award application deadline: 3/1. *Faculty research:* Leadership formation, school organization, collective efficacy and collaborative climate of high schools, change process in high schools, principalship; equity policy; gender and education; doctoral student development, retention, and attrition; faculty development and socialization; sexuality education and curriculum development; family/domestic violence; friendship/kin relationships; early childhood education; support for families with members with disabilities. *Unit head:* Dr. Jim Artesani, Associate Dean of Accreditation and Graduate Affairs, 207-581-4061, Fax: 207-581-3120. *Application contact:* Scott G. Delcourt, Senior Associate Dean of the Graduate School, 207-581-3291, Fax: 207-581-3232, E-mail: graduate@maine.edu.
Website: http://www.umaine.edu/edhd/

**University of Maryland, College Park,** Academic Affairs, College of Education, Department of Human Development and Quantitative Methodology, College Park, MD 20742. Offers MA, Ed D, PhD. *Entrance requirements:* Additional exam requirements/recommendations for international students: Required—TOEFL.

**University of Missouri,** Office of Research and Graduate Studies, College of Human Environmental Sciences, Department of Human Development and Family Studies, Columbia, MO 65211. Offers MA, MS, PhD. *Entrance requirements:* For master's, GRE General Test, minimum GPA of 3.0. Additional exam requirements/recommendations for international students: Required—TOEFL (minimum score 550 paper-based; 80 iBT). Electronic applications accepted. *Expenses:* Tuition, state resident: full-time $6347; part-time $352.60 per credit hour. Tuition, nonresident: full-time $17,379; part-time $965.50 per credit hour. *Required fees:* $1035. Tuition and fees vary according to course load, campus/location and program.

**University of Nebraska–Lincoln,** Graduate College, College of Education and Human Sciences, Department of Child, Youth and Family Studies, Lincoln, NE 68588. Offers child development/early childhood education (MS, PhD); child, youth and family studies (MS); family and consumer sciences education (MS, PhD); family financial planning (MS); family science (MS, PhD); gerontology (PhD); human sciences (PhD), including child, youth and family studies, gerontology, medical family therapy; marriage and family therapy (MS); medical family therapy (PhD); youth development (MS). *Accreditation:* AAMFT/COAMFTE (one or more programs are accredited). *Program availability:* Online learning. *Degree requirements:* For master's, thesis optional. *Entrance requirements:* For master's, GRE. Additional exam requirements/recommendations for international students: Required—TOEFL (minimum score 550 paper-based). Electronic applications accepted. *Faculty research:* Marriage and family therapy, child development/early childhood education, family financial management.

**University of Nebraska–Lincoln,** Graduate College, College of Education and Human Sciences, Department of Special Education and Communication Disorders, Lincoln, NE 68588. Offers audiology research (PhD); clinical audiology (Au D); educational studies (PhD); human sciences (PhD), including communication disorders; special education (M Ed, MA, Ed S), including special education (M Ed, MA), special education and communication disorders (Ed S); speech-language pathology and audiology (MS, Au D), including audiology and hearing science (Au D), speech-language pathology (Au D), speech-language pathology and audiology (MS). *Accreditation:* ASHA (one or more programs are accredited); NCATE. *Degree requirements:* For master's, thesis optional. *Entrance requirements:* For master's, GRE General Test. Additional exam requirements/recommendations for international students: Required—TOEFL. Electronic applications accepted. *Faculty research:* Curriculum-based assessment, paraprofessional and parent training, behavior management for special needs individuals, augmentative communication, speech/language disorders.

**University of Nebraska–Lincoln,** Graduate College, College of Education and Human Sciences, Department of Textiles, Clothing and Design, Lincoln, NE 68588. Offers human sciences (PhD), including textiles, clothing and design (MS, PhD); merchandising (MS); textile history/quilt studies (MA); textile science (MS); textile-apparel (MA); textiles, clothing and design (MA, MS), including textiles, clothing and design (MS, PhD). *Program availability:* Part-time, online learning. *Degree requirements:* For master's, thesis optional. *Entrance requirements:* For master's, GRE General Test. Additional exam requirements/recommendations for international students: Required—TOEFL (minimum score 550 paper-based). Electronic applications accepted. *Faculty research:* Merchandising, textile science, fiber arts, textile history, quilt studies.

**University of Nevada, Reno,** Graduate School, College of Education, Department of Human Development and Family Studies, Reno, NV 89557. Offers MS. *Degree requirements:* For master's, thesis optional. *Entrance requirements:* For master's, GRE General Test, minimum GPA of 2.75. Additional exam requirements/recommendations for international students: Required—TOEFL (minimum score 500 paper-based; 61 iBT), IELTS (minimum score 6). Electronic applications accepted. *Faculty research:* Early childhood/adolescent development, family studies.

**University of New Mexico,** Graduate Studies, College of Education, Program in Family Studies, Albuquerque, NM 87131-2039. Offers family life education (MA); family relations (MA); family studies (PhD); human development in families (MA). *Program availability:* Part-time, evening/weekend. *Faculty:* 4 full-time (1 woman). *Students:* 18 full-time (15 women), 14 part-time (12 women); includes 19 minority (2 Black or African American, non-Hispanic/Latino; 1 American Indian or Alaska Native, non-Hispanic/Latino; 16 Hispanic/Latino), 4 international. Average age 38. 11 applicants, 91% accepted, 10 enrolled. In 2016, 2 master's, 1 doctorate awarded. *Degree requirements:* For master's, comprehensive exam, thesis (for some programs); for doctorate, comprehensive exam, thesis/dissertation. *Entrance requirements:* For master's, written paper, 3 letters of recommendation, personal statement; for doctorate, GRE General Test, written paper, 3 letters of recommendation, personal statement, interview. Additional exam requirements/recommendations for international students: Required—TOEFL (minimum score 550 paper-based). *Application deadline:* For fall admission, 3/15 priority date for domestic and international students; for spring admission, 10/15 priority date for domestic and international students. Applications are processed on a rolling basis. Application fee: $50. Electronic applications accepted. *Financial support:* Fellowships, teaching assistantships with tuition reimbursements, and unspecified assistantships available. Financial award application deadline: 3/1; financial award applicants required to submit FAFSA. *Faculty research:* Home, community and school relations; multicultural issues; parent-child interactions; grandparents as primary caretakers for grandchildren; fathering; early childhood evaluation; early childhood development; globalization and indigenous cultures. *Unit head:* Dr. Ziarat Hossain, Program Coordinator, 505-277-4162, Fax: 505-277-8361, E-mail: zhossain@unm.edu. *Application contact:* Cynthia Salas, Department Administrator, 505-277-4535, Fax: 505-277-8361, E-mail: divbse@unm.edu.
Website: https://coe.unm.edu/departments-programs/ifce/family-studies/

**The University of North Carolina at Greensboro,** Graduate School, School of Health and Human Sciences, Department of Human Development and Family Studies, Greensboro, NC 27412-5001. Offers M Ed, MS, PhD. *Degree requirements:* For master's, one foreign language; for doctorate, one foreign language, thesis/dissertation. *Entrance requirements:* For master's and doctorate, GRE General Test. Additional exam requirements/recommendations for international students: Required—TOEFL. Electronic applications accepted. *Expenses:* Contact institution. *Faculty research:* Adolescent mothers, multi-handicapped, older adults.

**University of North Texas,** Robert B. Toulouse School of Graduate Studies, Denton, TX 76203-5459. Offers accounting (MS); applied anthropology (MA, MS); applied behavior analysis (Certificate); applied geography (MA); applied technology and performance improvement (M Ed, MS); art education (MA); art history (MA); art museum education (Certificate); arts leadership (Certificate); audiology (Au D); behavior analysis (MS); behavioral science (PhD); biochemistry and molecular biology (MS); biology (MA, MS); biomedical engineering (MS); business analysis (MS); chemistry (MS); clinical health psychology (PhD); communication studies (MA, MS); computer engineering (MS); computer science (MS); counseling (M Ed, MS), including clinical mental health counseling (MS), college and university counseling, elementary school counseling,

secondary school counseling; creative writing (MA); criminal justice (MS); curriculum and instruction (M Ed); decision sciences (MBA); design (MA, MFA), including fashion design (MFA), innovation studies, interior design (MFA); early childhood studies (MS); economics (MS); educational leadership (M Ed, Ed D); educational psychology (MS, PhD), including family studies (MS), gifted and talented (MS), human development (MS); learning and cognition (MS), research, measurement and evaluation (MS); electrical engineering (MS); emergency management (MPA); engineering technology (MS); English (MA); English as a second language (MA); environmental science (MS); finance (MBA, MS); financial management (MPA); French (MA); health services management (MBA); higher education (M Ed, Ed D); history (MA, MS); hospitality management (MS); human resources management (MPA); information science (MS); information systems (PhD); information technologies (MBA); interdisciplinary studies (MA, MS); international studies (MA); international sustainable tourism (MS); jazz studies (MM); journalism (MA, MJ, Graduate Certificate), including interactive and virtual digital communication (Graduate Certificate), narrative journalism (Graduate Certificate), public relations (Graduate Certificate); kinesiology (MS); linguistics (MA); local government management (MPA); logistics (PhD); logistics and supply chain management (MBA); long-term care, senior housing, and aging services (MA); management (PhD); marketing (MBA); mathematics (MA, MS); mechanical and energy engineering (MS, PhD); music (MA), including ethnomusicology, music theory, musicology, performance; music composition (PhD); music education (MM Ed, PhD); nonprofit management (MPA); operations and supply chain management (MBA); performance (MM, DMA); philosophy (MA); political science (MA); professional and technical communication (MA); radio, television and film (MA, MFA); rehabilitation counseling (Certificate); sociology (MA); Spanish (MA); special education (M Ed); speech-language pathology (MA); strategic management (MBA); studio art (MFA); teaching (M Ed); MBA/MS. *Program availability:* Part-time, evening/weekend, online learning. Terminal master's awarded for partial completion of doctoral program. *Degree requirements:* For master's, variable foreign language requirement, comprehensive exam (for some programs), thesis (for some programs); for doctorate, variable foreign language requirement, comprehensive exam (for some programs), thesis/dissertation; for other advanced degree, variable foreign language requirement, comprehensive exam (for some programs). *Entrance requirements:* For master's and doctorate, GRE, GMAT. Additional exam requirements/recommendations for international students: Required—TOEFL (minimum score 550 paper-based; 79 iBT). Electronic applications accepted.

**University of Pennsylvania,** Graduate School of Education, Division of Human Development and Quantitative Methods, Program in Interdisciplinary Studies in Human Development, Philadelphia, PA 19104. Offers MS Ed, PhD. *Program availability:* Part-time. *Students:* 48 full-time (41 women), 7 part-time (all women); includes 10 minority (3 Black or African American, non-Hispanic/Latino; 5 Asian, non-Hispanic/Latino; 2 Hispanic/Latino), 31 international. Average age 28. 135 applicants, 50% accepted, 28 enrolled. In 2016, 15 master's awarded. Terminal master's awarded for partial completion of doctoral program. *Expenses:* Tuition: Full-time $31,068; part-time $5762 per course. *Required fees:* $3200; $336 per course. Full-time tuition and fees vary according to degree level, program and student level. Part-time tuition and fees vary according to course load, degree level and program.
Website: http://www.gse.upenn.edu/aphd/ishd/msed

**University of Rhode Island,** Graduate School, College of Health Sciences, Department of Human Development and Family Studies, Kingston, RI 02881. Offers college student personnel (MS); human development and family studies (MS); marriage and family therapy (MS). *Accreditation:* AAMFT/COAMFTE. *Program availability:* Part-time. *Faculty:* 15 full-time (10 women). *Students:* 43 full-time (28 women), 14 part-time (10 women); includes 11 minority (7 Black or African American, non-Hispanic/Latino; 1 Asian, non-Hispanic/Latino; 1 Hispanic/Latino; 2 Two or more races, non-Hispanic/Latino). In 2016, 26 master's awarded. *Degree requirements:* For master's, comprehensive exam (for some programs), thesis optional. *Entrance requirements:* For master's, GRE or MAT, 2 letters of recommendation; resume (for college student personnel specialization). Additional exam requirements/recommendations for international students: Required—TOEFL. *Application deadline:* For fall admission, 1/15 for domestic and international students. Application fee: $65. Electronic applications accepted. *Expenses:* Tuition, state resident: full-time $11,796; part-time $655 per credit. Tuition, nonresident: full-time $24,206; part-time $1345 per credit. *Required fees:* $1546; $44 per credit. One-time fee: $155 full-time; $35 part-time. *Financial support:* In 2016–17, 2 research assistantships (averaging $8,592 per year), 4 teaching assistantships (averaging $11,456 per year) were awarded. Financial award application deadline: 1/15; financial award applicants required to submit FAFSA. *Unit head:* Dr. Karen McCurdy, Chair, 401-874-5960, Fax: 401-874-4020, E-mail: kmccurdy@uri.edu. *Application contact:* Graduate Admissions, 401-874-2872, E-mail: gradadm@etal.uri.edu.
Website: http://www.uri.edu/hss/hdf/

**University of Rochester,** Margaret Warner Graduate School of Education and Human Development, Doctoral Programs in Education, Rochester, NY 14627. Offers counseling (Ed D); educational administration (Ed D); educational policy and theory (PhD); higher education (PhD); human development in educational context (PhD); teaching, curriculum, and change (PhD). *Expenses:* Tuition: Full-time $47,450; part-time $1482 per credit hour. *Required fees:* $528. Tuition and fees vary according to program.

**University of Rochester,** Margaret Warner Graduate School of Education and Human Development, Master's Program in Human Development, Rochester, NY 14627. Offers MS. *Expenses:* Tuition: Full-time $47,450; part-time $1482 per credit hour. *Required fees:* $528. Tuition and fees vary according to program.

**University of St. Thomas,** Graduate Studies, College of Education, Leadership and Counseling, Department of Organization Learning and Development, St. Paul, MN 55105-1096. Offers organization development and change (MA, Ed D); public safety and law enforcement leadership (MA). *Program availability:* Part-time, evening/weekend. *Degree requirements:* For master's, practicum; for doctorate, comprehensive exam, thesis/dissertation. *Entrance requirements:* For master's, minimum GPA of 3.0, 2 letters of reference, personal statement, 2-5 years of organization experience; for doctorate, minimum GPA of 3.5, interview, 5-7 years of organization development or leadership experience. Additional exam requirements/recommendations for international students: Required—TOEFL (minimum score 550 paper-based). *Application deadline:* For fall admission, 7/15 priority date for domestic and international students; for spring admission, 12/9 priority date for domestic and international students; for summer admission, 4/3 priority date for domestic students, 4/3 for international students. Applications are processed on a rolling basis. Electronic applications accepted. *Expenses:* Contact institution. *Financial support:* Fellowships, research assistantships, institutionally sponsored loans, and scholarships/grants available. Support available to part-time students. Financial award application deadline: 8/1; financial award applicants required to submit FAFSA. *Faculty research:* Workplace conflict, physician leaders, virtual teams, technology use in schools/workplace, developing masterful practitioners. *Unit head:* Jean Davidson, Chair, 651-962-4387, Fax: 651-962-4169, E-mail: jmdavidson@stthomas.edu. *Application contact:* Liz G. Knight, Program Manager, 651-962-4459, Fax: 651-962-4169, E-mail: egknight@stthomas.edu.

**University of South Africa,** College of Human Sciences, Pretoria, South Africa. Offers adult education (M Ed); African languages (MA, PhD); African politics (MA, PhD); Afrikaans (MA, PhD); ancient history (MA, PhD); ancient Near Eastern studies (MA, PhD); anthropology (MA, PhD); applied linguistics (MA); Arabic (MA, PhD); archaeology (MA); art history (MA); Biblical archaeology (MA); Biblical studies (M Th, D Th, PhD); Christian spirituality (M Th, D Th); church history (M Th, D Th); classical studies (MA, PhD); clinical psychology (MA); communication (MA, PhD); comparative education (M Ed, Ed D); consulting psychology (D Admin, D Com, PhD); curriculum studies (M Ed, Ed D); development studies (M Admin, MA, D Admin, PhD); didactics (M Ed, Ed D); education (M Tech); education management (M Ed, Ed D); educational psychology (M Ed); English (MA); environmental education (M Ed); French (MA, PhD); German (MA, PhD); Greek (MA); guidance and counseling (M Ed); health studies (MA, PhD), including health sciences education (MA), health services management (MA), medical and surgical nursing science (critical care general) (MA), midwifery and neonatal nursing science (MA), trauma and emergency care (MA); history (MA, PhD); history of education (Ed D); inclusive education (M Ed, Ed D); information and communications technology policy and regulation (MA); information science (MA, MIS, PhD); international politics (MA, PhD); Islamic studies (MA, PhD); Italian (MA, PhD); Judaica (MA, PhD); linguistics (MA, PhD); mathematical education (M Ed); mathematics education (MA); missiology (M Th, D Th); modern Hebrew (MA, PhD); musicology (MA, MMus, D Mus, PhD); natural science education (M Ed); New Testament (M Th, D Th); Old Testament (D Th); pastoral therapy (M Th, D Th); philosophy (MA); philosophy of education (M Ed, Ed D); politics (MA, PhD); Portuguese (MA, PhD); practical theology (M Th, D Th); psychology (MA, MS, PhD); psychology of education (M Ed, Ed D); public health (MA); religious studies (MA, D Th, PhD); Romance languages (MA); Russian (MA, PhD); Semitic languages (MA, PhD); social behavior studies in HIV/AIDS (MA); social science (mental health) (MA); social science in development studies (MA); social science in psychology (MA); social science in social work (MA); social science in sociology (MA); social work (MSW, DSW, PhD); socio-education (M Ed, Ed D); sociolinguistics (MA); sociology (MA, PhD); Spanish (MA, PhD); systematic theology (M Th, D Th); TESOL (teaching English to speakers of other languages) (MA); theological ethics (M Th, D Th); theory of literature (MA, PhD); urban ministries (D Th); urban ministry (M Th).

**The University of South Dakota,** Graduate School, School of Education, Division of Counseling and Psychology in Education, Vermillion, SD 57069. Offers counseling (MA, PhD, Ed S); human development and educational psychology (MA, PhD, Ed S); school psychology (PhD, Ed S). *Accreditation:* ACA (one or more programs are accredited); NCATE. *Program availability:* Part-time. *Degree requirements:* For master's and Ed S, comprehensive exam, thesis or alternative; for doctorate, comprehensive exam, thesis/dissertation. *Entrance requirements:* For master's and doctorate, GRE General Test, minimum GPA of 3.0. Additional exam requirements/recommendations for international students: Required—TOEFL (minimum score 550 paper-based; 79 iBT). Electronic applications accepted.

**The University of Texas at Austin,** Graduate School, College of Education, Department of Educational Psychology, Austin, TX 78712-1111. Offers academic educational psychology (M Ed, MA); counseling psychology (PhD); counselor education (M Ed); human development, culture and learning sciences (PhD); program evaluation (MA); quantitative methods (M Ed, MA, PhD); school psychology (MA, PhD). *Accreditation:* APA (one or more programs are accredited). *Degree requirements:* For master's, thesis optional; for doctorate, thesis/dissertation. *Entrance requirements:* For master's and doctorate, GRE General Test, 3 letters of recommendation. Additional exam requirements/recommendations for international students: Required—TOEFL.

**The University of Texas at Austin,** Graduate School, College of Fine Arts, Sarah and Ernest Butler School of Music, Austin, TX 78712-1111. Offers band and wind conducting (M Music, DMA); brass/woodwind/percussion (MM, DMA); chamber music (MM); choral conducting (MM, DMA); collaborative piano (MM, DMA); composition (MM, DMA), including composition, jazz, jazz (DMA); ethnomusicology (MM, PhD); literature and pedagogy (MM); music and human learning (MM, PhD); music and human learning (DMA), including jazz (MM, DMA), piano pedagogy; musicology (MM, PhD); opera performance (MM, DMA); orchestral conducting (MM, DMA); organ (MM), including sacred music; organ performance (MM, DMA); performance (MM), including jazz (MM, DMA); performance (DMA), including jazz (MM, DMA); piano (DMA), including jazz (MM, DMA); piano literature and pedagogy (MM); piano performance (MM, DMA); string performance (MM, DMA); theory (MM, PhD); vocal performance (MM, DMA); voice (DMA), including opera; voice performance pedagogy (DMA); woodwind, brass, percussion performance (MM). *Accreditation:* NASM. *Program availability:* Part-time. *Degree requirements:* For master's, one foreign language, comprehensive exam, thesis (for some programs), recital (performance or composition majors); for doctorate, one foreign language, comprehensive exam, thesis/dissertation (for some programs), recital (for performance or composition majors). *Entrance requirements:* For master's and doctorate, GRE General Test (except for performance or composition majors), audition (performance majors). Electronic applications accepted.

**University of Utah,** Graduate School, College of Social and Behavioral Science, Department of Family and Consumer Studies, Salt Lake City, UT 84112-0080. Offers human development and social policy (MS). *Program availability:* Part-time. *Faculty:* 15 full-time (7 women), 5 part-time/adjunct (all women). *Students:* 8 full-time (all women), 2 part-time (both women). Average age 25. 12 applicants, 67% accepted, 7 enrolled. In 2016, 7 master's awarded. *Degree requirements:* For master's, comprehensive exam (for some programs), thesis (for some programs), thesis or project. *Entrance requirements:* For master's, GRE General Test, minimum undergraduate GPA of 3.0, courses in research methods and statistics. Additional exam requirements/recommendations for international students: Required—TOEFL (minimum score 550 paper-based). *Application deadline:* For fall admission, 2/1 priority date for domestic and international students. Applications are processed on a rolling basis. Application fee: $55 ($65 for international students). Electronic applications accepted. *Expenses:* Contact institution. *Financial support:* In 2016–17, 6 students received support, including 1 research assistantship with full tuition reimbursement available (averaging $14,000 per year), 4 teaching assistantships with full tuition reimbursements available (averaging $14,000 per year). Financial award application deadline: 5/1. *Faculty research:* Social, physical, educational and economic contexts of individuals, families and communities. *Unit head:* Prof. Lori Kowaleski-Jones, PhD, Chair, 801-585-0074, Fax: 801-581-5156, E-mail: lk2700@fcs.utah.edu. *Application contact:* Prof. Sonia Salari, PhD, Graduate Director, 801-581-5725, E-mail: sonia.salari@fcs.utah.edu. Website: http://fcs.utah.edu/

**University of Victoria,** Faculty of Graduate Studies, Faculty of Education, Department of Educational Psychology and Leadership Studies, Victoria, BC V8W 2Y2, Canada. Offers aboriginal communities counseling (M Ed); counseling (M Ed, MA); educational psychology (M Ed, MA, PhD), including counseling psychology (M Ed, MA), leadership studies (PhD), learning and development (MA, PhD), measurement and evaluation, special education (M Ed, MA); leadership studies (M Ed, MA). *Program availability:* Part-time. *Degree requirements:* For master's, thesis (for some programs), comprehensive exam (M Ed); for doctorate, comprehensive exam, thesis/dissertation, candidacy exam. *Entrance requirements:* For master's, 2 years of work experience in a relevant field; for doctorate, GRE, 2 years of work experience in a relevant field, minimum B average.

Additional exam requirements/recommendations for international students: Required—TOEFL (minimum score 575 paper-based), IELTS (minimum score 7). *Faculty research:* Learning and development (child, adolescent and adult), special education and exceptional children.

**University of Victoria,** Faculty of Graduate Studies, Faculty of Human and Social Development, Studies in Policy and Practice Program, Victoria, BC V8W 2Y2, Canada. Offers MA. *Program availability:* Part-time. *Degree requirements:* For master's, thesis. *Entrance requirements:* For master's, resume. Additional exam requirements/recommendations for international students: Required—TOEFL (minimum score 575 paper-based), IELTS (minimum score 7). Electronic applications accepted. *Faculty research:* Women's issues, public policy formation and implementation, health promotion and education, children, youth and families.

**University of Washington,** Graduate School, College of Education, Program in Educational Psychology, Seattle, WA 98195. Offers educational psychology (PhD); human development and cognition (M Ed); learning sciences (M Ed, PhD); measurement, statistics and research design (M Ed); school psychology (M Ed). *Accreditation:* APA. *Degree requirements:* For master's, thesis optional; for doctorate, thesis/dissertation. *Entrance requirements:* For master's and doctorate, GRE General Test, minimum GPA of 3.0. Additional exam requirements/recommendations for international students: Required—TOEFL.

**University of Wisconsin–Madison,** Graduate School, School of Human Ecology, Program in Human Development and Family Studies, Madison, WI 53706-1380. Offers MS, PhD. *Program availability:* Part-time. Terminal master's awarded for partial completion of doctoral program. *Degree requirements:* For master's, thesis; for doctorate, comprehensive exam, thesis/dissertation. *Entrance requirements:* For master's, GRE General Test, 3 letters of recommendation; for doctorate, GRE General Test, MS or MA, 3 letters of recommendation. Additional exam requirements/recommendations for international students: Required—TOEFL (minimum score 580 paper-based; 92 iBT). Electronic applications accepted. *Faculty research:* Human development, adolescence, adulthood, prevention, intervention.

**University of Wisconsin–Stevens Point,** College of Professional Studies, School of Health Promotion and Human Development, Stevens Point, WI 54481-3897. Offers human and community resources (MS); nutritional sciences (MS). *Program availability:* Part-time. *Degree requirements:* For master's, thesis or alternative. *Entrance requirements:* For master's, minimum GPA of 2.75.

**Utah State University,** School of Graduate Studies, Emma Eccles Jones College of Education and Human Services, Department of Family, Consumer, and Human Development, Logan, UT 84322. Offers family and human development (MFHD); family, consumer, and human development (MS, PhD), including adolescence/youth (MS), adult development/aging (MS), consumer science (MS), infancy/childhood (MS), marriage and family relations (MS), marriage and family therapy (MS). *Accreditation:* AAMFT/COAMFTE (one or more programs are accredited). *Program availability:* Part-time, evening/weekend, online learning. *Degree requirements:* For master's, thesis; for doctorate, comprehensive exam, thesis/dissertation, competencies. *Entrance requirements:* For master's, GRE General Test or MAT, minimum GPA of 3.0, 3 letters of recommendation; for doctorate, GRE, minimum GPA of 3.0, 3 letters of recommendation. Additional exam requirements/recommendations for international students: Required—TOEFL. Electronic applications accepted. *Faculty research:* Marriage and family relations, adolescent problem behavior, family financial management, early literacy, mental health in the elderly, parent child attachment.

**Vanderbilt University,** Peabody College, Department of Human and Organizational Development, Nashville, TN 37240-1001. Offers community development and action (M Ed); human development counseling (M Ed). *Accreditation:* ACA; NCATE. *Program availability:* Part-time. *Faculty:* 30 full-time (18 women), 38 part-time/adjunct (26 women). *Students:* 113 full-time (94 women), 12 part-time (10 women); includes 19 minority (7 Black or African American, non-Hispanic/Latino; 2 Asian, non-Hispanic/Latino; 6 Hispanic/Latino; 4 Two or more races, non-Hispanic/Latino), 5 international. Average age 25. 217 applicants, 48% accepted, 53 enrolled. In 2016, 60 master's awarded. *Degree requirements:* For master's, comprehensive exam, thesis optional. *Entrance requirements:* For master's, GRE General Test, MAT. Additional exam requirements/recommendations for international students: Required—TOEFL (minimum score 550 paper-based; 80 iBT). *Application deadline:* For fall admission, 12/31 priority date for domestic and international students; for spring admission, 11/1 priority date for domestic and international students. Applications are processed on a rolling basis. Application fee: $0. Electronic applications accepted. *Expenses:* Tuition: Part-time $1854 per credit hour. *Financial support:* Fellowships with partial tuition reimbursements, research assistantships with partial tuition reimbursements, teaching assistantships with partial tuition reimbursements, Federal Work-Study, institutionally sponsored loans, scholarships/grants, tuition waivers (partial), and unspecified assistantships available. Support available to part-time students. Financial award application deadline: 1/15; financial award applicants required to submit FAFSA. *Faculty research:* Community psychology and community development; counseling and mental health services, prevention and positive youth development; organizational and community change; youth physical and behavioral health in schools and communities. *Unit head:* Dr. Paul Speer, Chair, 615-322-6881, Fax: 615-322-1141, E-mail: paul.w.speer@vanderbilt.edu. *Application contact:* Sherrie Lane, Educational Coordinator, 615-322-8484, Fax: 615-322-1141, E-mail: sherrie.a.lane@vanderbilt.edu.

**Virginia Polytechnic Institute and State University,** Graduate School, College of Liberal Arts and Human Sciences, Blacksburg, VA 24061. Offers career and technical education (MS Ed, Ed D, PhD, Ed S); communication (MA); counselor education (MA Ed, Ed D, PhD, Ed S); creative writing (MFA); curriculum and instruction (MA Ed, Ed D, PhD, Ed S); educational leadership and policy studies (MA Ed, Ed D, PhD, Ed S); educational research and evaluation (PhD); English (MA); foreign languages, cultures, and literatures (MA); higher education (PhD); higher education and student affairs (MA Ed); history (MA); human development (MS, PhD); material culture and public humanities (MA); philosophy (MA); political science (MA); rhetoric and writing (PhD); science and technology studies (MS, PhD); social, political, ethical, and cultural thought (PhD); sociology (MS, PhD); theater arts (MFA). *Faculty:* 408 full-time (204 women), 3 part-time/adjunct (2 women). *Students:* 657 full-time (446 women), 457 part-time (292 women); includes 213 minority (114 Black or African American, non-Hispanic/Latino; 3 American Indian or Alaska Native, non-Hispanic/Latino; 29 Asian, non-Hispanic/Latino; 44 Hispanic/Latino; 23 Two or more races, non-Hispanic/Latino), 93 international. Average age 33. 805 applicants, 55% accepted, 328 enrolled. In 2016, 270 master's, 91 doctorates awarded. *Degree requirements:* For master's, comprehensive exam (for some programs), thesis (for some programs); for doctorate, comprehensive exam (for some programs), thesis/dissertation (for some programs). *Entrance requirements:* For master's and doctorate, GRE/GMAT. Additional exam requirements/recommendations for international students: Required—TOEFL (minimum score 80 iBT). *Application deadline:* For fall admission, 8/1 for domestic students, 4/1 for international students; for spring admission, 1/1 for domestic students, 9/1 for international students. Applications are processed on a rolling basis. Application fee: $75. Electronic applications accepted. *Expenses:* Tuition, state resident: full-time $12,467; part-time $692.50 per credit hour. Tuition, nonresident: full-time $25,095; part-time $1394.25 per credit hour. *Required*

*Human Development*

fees: $2669; $491.50 per semester. Tuition and fees vary according to course load, campus/location and program. *Financial support:* In 2016–17, 21 research assistantships with full tuition reimbursements (averaging $19,817 per year), 237 teaching assistantships with full tuition reimbursements (averaging $15,497 per year) were awarded. Financial award application deadline: 3/1; financial award applicants required to submit FAFSA. *Total annual research expenditures:* $6.6 million. *Unit head:* Rosemary Blieszner, Interim Dean, 540-231-6779, Fax: 540-231-7157, E-mail: liberalartsdean@vt.edu. *Application contact:* Chelsea Blanchet, Executive Assistant, 540-231-6779, Fax: 540-231-7157, E-mail: bchels1@vt.edu.
Website: http://www.liberalarts.vt.edu/

**Washington State University,** College of Agricultural, Human, and Natural Resource Sciences, Department of Human Development, Pullman, WA 99164-4852. Offers prevention science (PhD). Program also offered at the Spokane campus. *Program availability:* Part-time. *Degree requirements:* For doctorate, comprehensive exam, thesis/dissertation. *Entrance requirements:* For doctorate, GRE General Test, bachelor's or master's degree in prevention science related field (e.g., communication, educational psychology, human development, nursing, psychology, sociology); written statement specifying qualifications, educational goals, and career objectives; official copies of all college transcripts; three letters of reference. Additional exam requirements/recommendations for international students: Required—TOEFL, IELTS. Electronic applications accepted. *Faculty research:* Prevention science, program implementation

and dissemination, drug and alcohol prevention, health communication, equine assisted interventions, obesity prevention, health promotion in emerging adulthood, family processes, disenfranchised youth, rural poverty, adolescent sexuality, cultural competency, community collaborations, parent-child relationships, healthy aging.

**West Virginia University,** Davis College of Agriculture, Forestry and Consumer Sciences, Division of Resource Management and Sustainable Development, Morgantown, WV 26506. Offers agricultural and extension education (MS, PhD), including agricultural and extension education, teaching vocational-agriculture (MS); agricultural and resource economics (MS); human and community development (PhD); natural resource economics (PhD); resource management (PhD); resource management and sustainable development (PhD). *Program availability:* Part-time. *Degree requirements:* For master's, thesis; for doctorate, comprehensive exam, thesis/dissertation. *Entrance requirements:* For master's, GRE General Test. Additional exam requirements/recommendations for international students: Required—TOEFL. *Faculty research:* Environmental economics, energy economics, agriculture.

**Wheelock College,** Graduate Programs, Division of Arts and Sciences, Boston, MA 02215. Offers human development (MS). *Entrance requirements:* Additional exam requirements/recommendations for international students: Required—TOEFL. Electronic applications accepted.

# Industrial and Organizational Psychology

**Adler University,** Programs in Psychology, Chicago, IL 60602. Offers advanced Adlerian psychotherapy (Certificate); art therapy (MA); clinical mental health counseling (MA); clinical neuropsychology (Certificate); clinical psychology (Psy D); community psychology (MA); counseling and organizational psychology (MA); counseling psychology (MA); counselor education and supervision (PhD); couple and family therapy (DCFT); criminology (MA); emergency management leadership (MA); forensic psychology (MA); marriage and family counseling (MA); marriage and family therapy (Certificate); military psychology (MA); nonprofit management (MA); organizational psychology (MA); police psychology (MA); public policy and administration (MA); rehabilitation counseling (MA); sport and health psychology (MA); substance abuse counseling (Certificate); Psy D/Certificate; Psy D/MACAT; Psy D/MACP; Psy D/MAMFC; Psy D/MASAC. *Accreditation:* APA. *Program availability:* Part-time, evening/weekend, online learning. Terminal master's awarded for partial completion of doctoral program. *Degree requirements:* For master's, thesis or alternative, oral exam, practicum; for doctorate, thesis/dissertation, clinical exam, internship, oral exam, practicum, written qualifying exam. *Entrance requirements:* For master's, 12 semester hours in psychology, minimum GPA of 3.0; for doctorate, 18 semester hours in psychology, minimum GPA of 3.25; for Certificate, appropriate master's or doctoral degree. Additional exam requirements/recommendations for international students: Required—TOEFL (minimum score 550 paper-based; 79 iBT). Electronic applications accepted.

**See Display on page 982 and Close-Up on page 1225.**

**Alliant International University–Fresno,** California School of Professional Psychology, Organizational Psychology Programs, Fresno, CA 93727. Offers organizational behavior (MA); organizational development (Psy D); MA/PhD; Psy D/MA. *Program availability:* Part-time, evening/weekend. *Degree requirements:* For doctorate, thesis/dissertation. *Entrance requirements:* For doctorate, interview, minimum GPA of 3.0. Additional exam requirements/recommendations for international students: Required—TOEFL (minimum score 550 paper-based; 80 iBT), TWE (minimum score 5). Electronic applications accepted. *Faculty research:* Team development, international organizational development, mergers and acquisitions, strategic change, information technology implementations.

**Alliant International University–Los Angeles,** California School of Professional Psychology, Organizational Psychology Division, Alhambra, CA 91803. Offers MA, PhD. *Accreditation:* APA. *Program availability:* Part-time. Terminal master's awarded for partial completion of doctoral program. *Degree requirements:* For doctorate, comprehensive exam, thesis/dissertation. *Entrance requirements:* For master's and doctorate, interview, minimum GPA of 3.0 in both psychology and overall. Additional exam requirements/recommendations for international students: Required—TOEFL (minimum score 600 paper-based), TWE (minimum score 5). Electronic applications accepted. *Faculty research:* Organizational transitions, productivity, workforce demographics, management technology, comparative and international research.

**Alliant International University–San Diego,** California School of Professional Psychology, Organizational Psychology Division, San Diego, CA 92131. Offers clinical/industrial organizational psychology (PhD); consulting psychology (PhD); industrial/organizational psychology (MA, MS, PhD); leadership (PhD). *Program availability:* Part-time, evening/weekend. Terminal master's awarded for partial completion of doctoral program. *Degree requirements:* For doctorate, comprehensive exam, thesis/dissertation, internship/practicum. *Entrance requirements:* For master's and doctorate, minimum GPA of 3.0, recommendations, essay, interview. Additional exam requirements/recommendations for international students: Required—TOEFL (minimum score 550 paper-based; 80 iBT), TWE (minimum score 5). Electronic applications accepted. *Faculty research:* Cultural diversity in the workplace, work motivation, personnel and performance management, organizational diagnosis.

**Alliant International University–San Francisco,** California School of Professional Psychology, Organizational Psychology Division, San Francisco, CA 94133. Offers MA, PhD. *Accreditation:* APA. *Program availability:* Part-time, evening/weekend. Terminal master's awarded for partial completion of doctoral program. *Degree requirements:* For doctorate, comprehensive exam, thesis/dissertation, field placement. *Entrance requirements:* For master's and doctorate, minimum GPA of 3.0, interview. Additional exam requirements/recommendations for international students: Required—TOEFL (minimum score 550 paper-based; 80 iBT), TWE (minimum score 5). Electronic applications accepted. *Faculty research:* Leadership, ethics and management, career development, organizational behavior, strategic change.

**American InterContinental University Online,** Program in Business Administration, Schaumburg, IL 60173. Offers accounting and finance (MBA); finance (MBA); healthcare management (MBA); human resource management (MBA); international business (MBA); management (MBA); marketing (MBA); operations management (MBA); organizational psychology and development (MBA); project management (MBA). *Accreditation:* ACBSP. *Program availability:* Evening/weekend, online learning. *Entrance requirements:* Additional exam requirements/recommendations for

international students: Required—TOEFL (minimum score 550 paper-based). Electronic applications accepted.

**Angelo State University,** College of Graduate Studies and Research, Archer College of Health and Human Services, Department of Psychology, Sociology and Social Work, San Angelo, TX 76909. Offers applied psychology (MS); counseling psychology (MS); industrial-organizational psychology (MS). *Program availability:* Part-time, evening/weekend. *Students:* 73 full-time (53 women), 33 part-time (22 women); includes 36 minority (5 Black or African American, non-Hispanic/Latino; 31 Hispanic/Latino), 5 international. Average age 32. *Degree requirements:* For master's, comprehensive exam, thesis optional. *Entrance requirements:* For master's, GRE General Test (for industrial and organizational psychology only), essay, letters of recommendation (for industrial and organizational psychology only). Additional exam requirements/recommendations for international students: Required—TOEFL or IELTS. *Application deadline:* For fall admission, 7/15 priority date for domestic students, 6/10 for international students; for spring admission, 12/1 priority date for domestic students, 11/1 for international students. Applications are processed on a rolling basis. Application fee: $40 ($50 for international students). Electronic applications accepted. *Expenses:* Tuition, state resident: full-time $3726; part-time $2484 per year. Tuition, nonresident: full-time $10,746; part-time $7164 per year. *Required fees:* $2538; $1702 per unit. *Financial support:* Teaching assistantships, career-related internships or fieldwork, Federal Work-Study, scholarships/grants, and unspecified assistantships available. Support available to part-time students. Financial award application deadline: 3/1; financial award applicants required to submit FAFSA. *Unit head:* Dr. James N. Forbes, Chair, 325-486-6120, Fax: 325-942-2290, E-mail: james.forbes@angelo.edu. *Application contact:* Dr. James N. Forbes, Chair, 325-486-6120, Fax: 325-942-2290, E-mail: james.forbes@angelo.edu.
Website: http://www.angelo.edu/dept/psychology_sociology/

**Anna Maria College,** Graduate Division, Program in Industrial/Organizational Psychology, Paxton, MA 01612. Offers MS.

**Argosy University, Atlanta,** Georgia School of Professional Psychology, Atlanta, GA 30328. Offers clinical psychology (MA, Psy D, Postdoctoral Respecialization Certificate), including child and family psychology (Psy D), general adult clinical (Psy D), health psychology (Psy D), neuropsychology/geropsychology (Psy D); community counseling (MA), including marriage and family therapy; counselor education and supervision (Ed D); forensic psychology (MA); industrial organizational psychology (MA); marriage and family therapy (Certificate); sport-exercise psychology (MA). *Accreditation:* APA.

**Argosy University, Chicago,** Illinois School of Professional Psychology, Chicago, IL 60601. Offers clinical psychology (MA, Psy D), including child and adolescent psychology (Psy D), client-centered and experiential psychotherapies (Psy D), diversity and multicultural psychology (Psy D), family psychology (Psy D), forensic psychology (Psy D), health psychology (Psy D), neuropsychology (Psy D), organizational consulting (Psy D), psychoanalytic psychology (Psy D), psychology and spirituality (Psy D); community counseling (MA); counseling psychology (Ed D), including counselor education and supervision; counselor education and supervision (Ed D); industrial organizational psychology (MA). *Accreditation:* APA (one or more programs are accredited). *Program availability:* Online learning.

**Argosy University, Dallas,** College of Psychology and Behavioral Sciences, Program in Industrial Organizational Psychology, Farmers Branch, TX 75244. Offers MA.

**Argosy University, Denver,** College of Psychology and Behavioral Sciences, Denver, CO 80231. Offers clinical mental health counseling (MA); clinical psychology (MA, Psy D); counseling psychology (Ed D); counselor education and supervision (Ed D); forensic psychology (MA); industrial organizational psychology (MA); marriage and family therapy (MA, DMFT).

**Argosy University, Inland Empire,** College of Psychology and Behavioral Sciences, Ontario, CA 91761. Offers clinical psychology/marriage and family therapy (MA); counseling psychology (Ed D); counseling psychology/marriage and family therapy (MA); forensic psychology (MA); industrial organizational psychology (MA); sport-exercise psychology (MA).

**Argosy University, Phoenix,** Arizona School of Professional Psychology, Program in Industrial Organizational Psychology, Phoenix, AZ 85021. Offers MA.

**Argosy University, Schaumburg,** College of Behavioral Sciences, Schaumburg, IL 60173-5403. Offers clinical mental health counseling (MA); forensic psychology (MA, Post-Graduate Certificate); industrial organizational psychology (MA); sport-exercise psychology (MA). *Accreditation:* ACA; APA.

**Argosy University, Tampa,** Florida School of Professional Psychology, Tampa, FL 33607. Offers clinical psychology (MA, Psy D), including clinical psychology; counselor education and supervision (Ed D); industrial organizational psychology (MA); marriage and family therapy (MA); mental health counseling (MA).

**Argosy University, Twin Cities,** Minnesota School of Professional Psychology, Eagan, MN 55121. Offers clinical psychology (MA, Psy D), including child and family psychology

(Psy D), forensic psychology (Psy D), health and neuropsychology (Psy D), trauma (Psy D); forensic counseling (Post-Graduate Certificate); forensic psychology (MA); industrial organizational psychology (MA); marriage and family therapy (MA, DMFT), including forensic counseling (MA). *Accreditation:* AAMFT; AAMFT/COAMFTE; APA.

**Austin Peay State University,** College of Graduate Studies, College of Behavioral and Health Sciences, Department of Psychology, Program in Industrial-Organizational Psychology, Clarksville, TN 37044. Offers MS. *Program availability:* Part-time, online learning. *Faculty:* 9 full-time (6 women), 2 part-time/adjunct (1 woman). *Students:* 21 full-time (19 women), 9 part-time (9 women); includes 8 minority (7 Black or African American, non-Hispanic/Latino; 1 Two or more races, non-Hispanic/Latino). Average age 29. 26 applicants, 58% accepted, 9 enrolled. In 2016, 11 degrees awarded. *Degree requirements:* For master's, comprehensive exam. *Entrance requirements:* For master's, GRE, 3 letters of recommendation, minimum GPA of 2.5. Additional exam requirements/recommendations for international students: Required—TOEFL (minimum score 500 paper-based). *Application deadline:* For fall admission, 8/9 for domestic students. Applications are processed on a rolling basis. Application fee: $45 ($50 for international students). Electronic applications accepted. *Expenses:* Tuition, state resident: full-time $8300; part-time $415 per credit hour. Tuition, nonresident: full-time $22,280; part-time $1114 per credit hour. *Required fees:* $1473; $73.65 per credit hour. *Financial support:* In 2016–17, research assistantships with full tuition reimbursements (averaging $5,184 per year) were awarded; career-related internships or fieldwork, Federal Work-Study, institutionally sponsored loans, scholarships/grants, and unspecified assistantships also available. Support available to part-time students. Financial award application deadline: 3/1; financial award applicants required to submit FAFSA. *Unit head:* Dr. Uma J. Iyer, Coordinator, 931-221-6331, Fax: 931-221-6267, E-mail: iyeru@apsu.edu. *Application contact:* Brad Averitt, Graduate Coordinator, 800-859-4723, Fax: 931-221-7641, E-mail: gradadmissions@apsu.edu.
Website: http://www.apsu.edu/ioprogram

**Baruch College of the City University of New York,** Weissman School of Arts and Sciences, Program in Industrial/Organizational Psychology, New York, NY 10010-5585. Offers MS. *Program availability:* Part-time, evening/weekend. *Faculty:* 4 full-time (0 women), 6 part-time/adjunct (4 women). *Students:* 132. 147 applicants, 48% accepted, 39 enrolled. In 2016, 43 master's awarded. Terminal master's awarded for partial completion of doctoral program. *Degree requirements:* For master's, thesis or alternative. *Entrance requirements:* For master's, GRE, 2 letters of recommendation, personal essay, resume. Additional exam requirements/recommendations for international students: Required—TOEFL. *Application deadline:* For fall admission, 3/15 for domestic and international students; for spring admission, 11/1 for domestic and international students. Application fee: $125. Electronic applications accepted. *Financial support:* Career-related internships or fieldwork and Federal Work-Study available. Financial award applicants required to submit FAFSA. *Faculty research:* Examining possible explanations for race-based differences on intelligence and cognitive ability tests; developing alternative formats and types of intelligence tests as well as examining the role of previous experience, test taking skills, and test characteristics on performance on these types of tests; identified employee surveys; personnel staffing and equal employment opportunity issues; leadership development; organizational culture. *Unit head:* Dr. Harold Goldstein, Director, 646-312-3820. *Application contact:* Cathy Levkulic, Assistant Director, Graduate Studies, 646-312-4493, Fax: 646-312-4491, E-mail: wsas.graduate.studies@baruch.cuny.edu.
Website: http://www.baruch.cuny.edu/wsas/academics/graduate_studies/Grad_MS_IOPsych.htm

**Baruch College of the City University of New York,** Zicklin School of Business, Program in Industrial and Organizational Psychology, New York, NY 10010-5585. Offers MBA, MS, PhD. PhD offered jointly with Graduate School and University Center of the City University of New York. *Program availability:* Part-time, evening/weekend. *Degree requirements:* For master's, thesis or alternative; for doctorate, comprehensive exam, thesis/dissertation. *Entrance requirements:* For master's, GMAT or GRE General Test, 2 letters of recommendation, resumé, 2 years of work experience; for doctorate, GMAT or GRE General Test. Additional exam requirements/recommendations for international students: Required—TOEFL (minimum score 590 paper-based), TWE. *Faculty research:* Job attitudes, power and leadership in organizations, measurement issues in organizational behavior, work motivation, fair employment practices.

**Bayamón Central University,** Graduate Programs, Program in Organizational Psychology, Bayamón, PR 00960-1725. Offers MA. *Program availability:* Part-time, evening/weekend. *Degree requirements:* For master's, comprehensive exam. *Entrance requirements:* For master's, EXADEP, bachelor's degree in psychology or related field.

**Bowling Green State University,** Graduate College, College of Arts and Sciences, Department of Psychology, Bowling Green, OH 43403. Offers clinical psychology (MA, PhD); developmental psychology (MA, PhD); experimental psychology (MA, PhD); industrial/organizational psychology (MA, PhD); quantitative psychology (MA, PhD). *Accreditation:* APA (one or more programs are accredited). *Degree requirements:* For doctorate, thesis/dissertation. *Entrance requirements:* For doctorate, GRE General Test, GRE Subject Test. Additional exam requirements/recommendations for international students: Required—TOEFL. *Application deadline:* For fall admission, 1/1 for domestic students. Application fee: $30. Electronic applications accepted. *Financial support:* Fellowships with full tuition reimbursements, research assistantships with full tuition reimbursements, teaching assistantships with full tuition reimbursements, career-related internships or fieldwork, Federal Work-Study, institutionally sponsored loans, tuition waivers (full), and unspecified assistantships available. Financial award applicants required to submit FAFSA. *Faculty research:* Personnel psychology, developmental-mathematical models, behavioral medication, brain process, child/adolescent social cognition. *Unit head:* Dr. Mike Zickar, Chair, 419-372-2301, E-mail: mzickar@bgsu.edu. *Application contact:* Dr. Terry L. Lawrence, Assistant Dean for Graduate Admissions and Studies, 419-372-7713, Fax: 419-372-8569, E-mail: tlawren@bgnet.bgsu.edu.

**Brooklyn College of the City University of New York,** School of Natural and Behavioral Sciences, Department of Psychology, Brooklyn, NY 11210-2889. Offers experimental psychology (MA); industrial and organizational psychology (MA), including human relations, organizational behavior; mental health counseling (MA); psychology (PhD). *Program availability:* Part-time. *Degree requirements:* For master's, comprehensive exam, thesis (for some programs). *Entrance requirements:* For master's, minimum GPA of 3.0, 2 letters of recommendation, essay; for doctorate, GRE. Additional exam requirements/recommendations for international students: Required—TOEFL (minimum score 520 paper-based; 69 iBT). Electronic applications accepted.

**California State University, Long Beach,** Graduate Studies, College of Liberal Arts, Department of Psychology, Long Beach, CA 90840. Offers human factors (MS); industrial/organizational psychology (MS); psychology (MA). *Program availability:* Part-time, evening/weekend. *Degree requirements:* For master's, comprehensive exam, thesis. *Entrance requirements:* For master's, GRE General Test, GRE Subject Test. *Application deadline:* For fall admission, 3/1 for domestic students. Applications are processed on a rolling basis. Application fee: $55. Electronic applications accepted. *Financial support:* Federal Work-Study, institutionally sponsored loans, and scholarships/grants available. Financial award application deadline: 3/2. *Faculty research:* Physiological psychology, social and personality psychology, community-

clinical psychology, industrial-organizational psychology, developmental psychology. *Unit head:* David J. Whitney, Chair, 562-985-5001, Fax: 562-985-8004. *Application contact:* Dr. Mark Wiley, Associate Dean, 562-985-5381, Fax: 562-985-2463, E-mail: mwiley@csulb.edu.

**California State University, Sacramento,** Office of Graduate Studies, College of Social Sciences and Interdisciplinary Studies, Department of Psychology, Sacramento, CA 95819. Offers applied behavior analysis (MA); counseling psychology (MA); industrial/organizational psychology (MA). *Program availability:* Part-time. *Students:* 13 full-time (9 women), 11 part-time (9 women); includes 6 minority (3 Asian, non-Hispanic/Latino; 3 Hispanic/Latino). Average age 27. 74 applicants, 16% accepted, 11 enrolled. In 2016, 7 master's awarded. *Degree requirements:* For master's, thesis, writing proficiency exam. *Entrance requirements:* For master's, GRE, minimum GPA of 3.0 during previous 2 years. Additional exam requirements/recommendations for international students: Required—TOEFL (minimum score 550 paper-based; 80 iBT). *Application deadline:* For fall admission, 3/1 for domestic and international students; for spring admission, 9/30 for international students. Applications are processed on a rolling basis. Application fee: $55. Electronic applications accepted. *Expenses:* $4,302 full-time tuition and fees per semester, $2,796 part-time. *Financial support:* Career-related internships or fieldwork and Federal Work-Study available. Support available to part-time students. Financial award application deadline: 2/1; financial award applicants required to submit FAFSA. *Unit head:* Dr. Rebecca Cameron, Interim Department Chair, 916-278-6254, E-mail: cameron@csus.edu. *Application contact:* Jose Martinez, Graduate Admissions Supervisor, 916-278-7871, E-mail: martinj@skymail.csus.edu.
Website: http://www.csus.edu/psyc

**California State University, San Bernardino,** Graduate Studies, College of Social and Behavioral Sciences, Department of Psychology, San Bernardino, CA 92407. Offers child development (MA); clinical/counseling psychology (MS); general/experimental psychology (MA); industrial/organizational psychology (MS). *Faculty:* 21 full-time (11 women). *Students:* 59 full-time (43 women), 15 part-time (9 women); includes 47 minority (2 Black or African American, non-Hispanic/Latino; 3 Asian, non-Hispanic/Latino; 33 Hispanic/Latino; 9 Two or more races, non-Hispanic/Latino), 3 international. 217 applicants, 18% accepted, 32 enrolled. In 2016, 38 master's awarded. *Degree requirements:* For master's, comprehensive exam, thesis (for some programs). *Entrance requirements:* Additional exam requirements/recommendations for international students: Required—TOEFL. Application fee: $55. *Expenses:* Tuition, state resident: full-time $7843; part-time $5011.20 per year. Tuition and fees vary according to course load, degree level, program and reciprocity agreements. *Financial support:* Fellowships, research assistantships, and teaching assistantships available. *Faculty research:* Perceptual development, human memory, psychopharmacology, psychology of women, language acquisition. *Unit head:* Dr. Robert Ricco, Chair, 909-537-5485, Fax: 909-537-7003, E-mail: rricco@csusb.edu. *Application contact:* Dr. Francisca Beer, Dean of Graduate Studies, 909-537-5058, E-mail: fbeer@csusb.edu.
Website: http://psychology.csusb.edu/

**Capella University,** Harold Abel School of Social and Behavioral Science, Doctoral Programs in Psychology, Minneapolis, MN 55402. Offers addiction psychology (PhD); clinical psychology (Psy D); educational psychology (PhD); general advanced studies in human behavior (PhD); general psychology (PhD); industrial/organizational psychology (PhD); school psychology (Psy D).

**Capella University,** Harold Abel School of Social and Behavioral Science, Master's Programs in Psychology, Minneapolis, MN 55402. Offers applied behavior analysis (MS); clinical psychology (MS); counseling psychology (MS); educational psychology (MS); evaluation, research, and measurement (MS); general advanced studies in human behavior (MS); general psychology (MS); industrial/organizational psychology (MS); leadership coaching psychology (MS); school psychology (MS); sport psychology (MS).

**Carlos Albizu University,** Graduate Programs, San Juan, PR 00901. Offers clinical psychology (MS, PhD, Psy D); general psychology (PhD); industrial/organizational psychology (MS, PhD); speech and language pathology (MS). *Accreditation:* APA (one or more programs are accredited). *Program availability:* Part-time, evening/weekend. Terminal master's awarded for partial completion of doctoral program. *Degree requirements:* For master's, one foreign language, comprehensive exam, thesis; for doctorate, one foreign language, comprehensive exam, thesis/dissertation, written qualifying exams. *Entrance requirements:* For master's, GRE General Test or EXADEP, interview; minimum GPA of 2.8 (industrial/organizational psychology); for doctorate, GRE General Test or EXADEP, interview; minimum GPA of 3.0 (PhD in industrial/organizational psychology and clinical psychology), 3.25 (Psy D). *Faculty research:* Psychotherapeutic techniques for Hispanics, psychology of the aged, school dropouts, stress, violence.

**Carlos Albizu University, Miami Campus,** Graduate Programs, Miami, FL 33172-2209. Offers clinical psychology (PhD, Psy D); entrepreneurship (MBA); exceptional student education (MS); human services (PhD); industrial/organizational psychology (MS); marriage and family therapy (MS); mental health counseling (MS); nonprofit management (MBA); organizational management (MBA); psychology (MS); school counseling (MS); speech and language pathology (MS); teaching English for speakers of other languages (MS). *Accreditation:* APA. *Program availability:* Part-time, evening/weekend, 100% online. *Faculty:* 28 full-time (22 women), 31 part-time/adjunct (19 women). *Students:* 475 full-time (396 women), 191 part-time (161 women); includes 560 minority (56 Black or African American, non-Hispanic/Latino; 1 American Indian or Alaska Native, non-Hispanic/Latino; 4 Asian, non-Hispanic/Latino; 494 Hispanic/Latino; 5 Two or more races, non-Hispanic/Latino), 15 international. Average age 34. 335 applicants, 46% accepted, 122 enrolled. In 2016, 143 master's, 48 doctorates awarded. Terminal master's awarded for partial completion of doctoral program. *Degree requirements:* For master's, comprehensive exam, integrative project (for MBA); research project (for exceptional student education, teaching English as a second language); for doctorate, comprehensive exam, thesis/dissertation, internship, project. *Entrance requirements:* For master's, 3 letters of recommendation, interview, minimum GPA of 3.0, resume, statement of purpose, official transcripts; for doctorate, 3 letters of recommendation, minimum GPA of 3.0, resume, interview, statement of purpose, official transcripts. Additional exam requirements/recommendations for international students: Required—Michigan Test of English Language Proficiency. *Application deadline:* For fall admission, 4/1 priority date for domestic students, 5/1 priority date for international students; for spring admission, 11/1 priority date for domestic students, 9/1 priority date for international students. Applications are processed on a rolling basis. Application fee: $50. Electronic applications accepted. *Expenses:* Contact institution. *Financial support:* In 2016–17, 131 students received support. Federal Work-Study, scholarships/grants, unspecified assistantships, and tuition discounts available. Financial award application deadline: 6/1; financial award applicants required to submit FAFSA. *Faculty research:* Psychotherapy, forensic psychology, neuropsychology, marketing strategy, entrepreneurship, special education, speech-language pathology. *Unit head:* Dr. Etiony Aldarondo, Provost, 305-593-1223 Ext. 3138, Fax: 305-592-7930, E-mail: ealdarondo@albizu.edu. *Application contact:* Sonia Feliciano, Institutional Director of Student Recruitment, 305-593-1223 Ext. 3108, Fax: 305-477-8983, E-mail: sfeliciano@albizu.edu.

## Industrial and Organizational Psychology

**Central Michigan University,** College of Graduate Studies, College of Humanities and Social and Behavioral Sciences, Department of Psychology, Program in Industrial and Organizational Psychology, Mount Pleasant, MI 48859. Offers industrial and organizational psychology (MA, PhD); occupational health psychology (PhD). *Degree requirements:* For master's, thesis; for doctorate, comprehensive exam, thesis/dissertation. *Entrance requirements:* For master's and doctorate, GRE. Electronic applications accepted. *Faculty research:* Job stress, retirement, leadership, and careers; personality in the workplace, personnel selection, and structural equation modeling in industrial/organizational psychology; personnel psychology, evolutionary psychology, and influences on HRM utilization; occupational health psychology and job stress; work attitudes, psychological ownership in work, and performance appraisal.

**Chatham University,** Program in Counseling Psychology, Pittsburgh, PA 15232-2826. Offers child, adolescent and family (MSCP); counseling psychology (Psy D); health and holistic (MSCP); infant mental health (MSCP); organization and supervision (MSCP); sport and exercise (MSCP). *Accreditation:* APA. *Program availability:* Part-time, evening/weekend. *Degree requirements:* For master's, thesis optional, supervised internship; for doctorate, thesis/dissertation, internship. *Entrance requirements:* For master's, minimum GPA of 3.0; 2 letters of recommendation; resume; prerequisite coursework in statistics, biology, and psychology; for doctorate, GRE. Additional exam requirements/recommendations for international students: Required—TOEFL (minimum score 600 paper-based; 100 iBT), IELTS (minimum score 7), TWE. Electronic applications accepted. Application fee is waived when completed online. *Expenses: Tuition:* Full-time $16,254; part-time $903 per credit hour. *Required fees:* $468; $26 per credit hour. *Faculty research:* Trauma and recovery, hypnosis, psychospiritual dimensions of healing, psychotherapy of schizophrenia.

**The Chicago School of Professional Psychology,** Program in Business Psychology, Chicago, IL 60610. Offers business psychology (PhD); industrial and organizational business psychology (Psy D); industrial and organizational psychology (MA); organizational leadership (MA, PhD). *Degree requirements:* For doctorate, thesis/dissertation optional. *Entrance requirements:* For doctorate, GRE. Additional exam requirements/recommendations for international students: Required—TOEFL.

**The Chicago School of Professional Psychology,** Program in Industrial and Organizational Psychology, Chicago, IL 60610. Offers business psychology (Psy D); industrial and organizational psychology (MA) *Program availability:* Part-time, evening/weekend. *Degree requirements:* For master's, internship; for doctorate, thesis/dissertation, internship. *Entrance requirements:* For master's, 1 course each in psychology, statistics, and research methods. Additional exam requirements/recommendations for international students: Required—TOEFL (minimum score 550 paper-based; 79 iBT).

**The Chicago School of Professional Psychology at Downtown Los Angeles,** Program in Industrial and Organizational Psychology, Los Angeles, CA 90017. Offers MA.

**The Chicago School of Professional Psychology: Online,** PhD Program in Organizational Leadership, Chicago, IL 60654. Offers PhD.

**The Chicago School of Professional Psychology: Online,** Program in Applied Industrial and Organizational Psychology, Chicago, IL 60654. Offers MA, Certificate.

**Claremont Graduate University,** Graduate Programs, School of Social Science, Policy and Evaluation, Department of Psychology, Claremont, CA 91711-6160. Offers advanced study in evaluation (Certificate); cognitive psychology (MA, PhD); developmental psychology (MA, PhD); evaluation and applied research methods (MA, PhD); health behavior research and evaluation (MA, PhD); human resource development and evaluation (MA); industrial/organizational psychology (MA, PhD); organizational behavior (MA, PhD); organizational psychology (MA, PhD); social psychology (MA, PhD); MBA/PhD. *Program availability:* Part-time. *Faculty:* 19 full-time (9 women), 1 part-time/adjunct (0 women). *Students:* 244 full-time (160 women), 66 part-time (38 women); includes 93 minority (15 Black or African American, non-Hispanic/Latino; 2 American Indian or Alaska Native, non-Hispanic/Latino; 29 Asian, non-Hispanic/Latino; 31 Hispanic/Latino; 2 Native Hawaiian or other Pacific Islander, non-Hispanic/Latino; 14 Two or more races, non-Hispanic/Latino), 41 international. Average age 30. In 2016, 61 master's, 23 doctorates, 5 other advanced degrees awarded. Terminal master's awarded for partial completion of doctoral program. *Entrance requirements:* For master's and doctorate, GRE General Test. Additional exam requirements/recommendations for international students: Required—TOEFL (minimum score 75 iBT). *Application deadline:* For fall admission, 1/15 priority date for domestic and international students. Applications are processed on a rolling basis. Application fee: $80. Electronic applications accepted. *Expenses: Tuition:* Full-time $44,328; part-time $1847 per unit. *Required fees:* $600; $300 per semester. Tuition and fees vary according to course load and program. *Financial support:* Fellowships, research assistantships, teaching assistantships, Federal Work-Study, institutionally sponsored loans, scholarships/grants, and tuition waivers (full and partial) available. Support available to part-time students. Financial award application deadline: 2/15; financial award applicants required to submit FAFSA. *Faculty research:* Social intervention, diversity in organizations, eyewitness memory, aging and cognition, drug policy. *Unit head:* William Crano, Chair, 909-607-3311, E-mail: william.crano@cgu.edu. *Application contact:* Paige Piontkowsky, Senior Assistant Director of Admissions, 909-607-3240, E-mail: paige.piontkowsky@cgu.edu.
Website: https://www.cgu.edu/school/ssspe/programs/?areas_of_study=psychology

**Clemson University,** Graduate School, College of Behavioral, Social and Health Sciences, Department of Psychology, Program in Industrial-Organizational Psychology, Clemson, SC 29634. Offers PhD. *Faculty:* 29 full-time (11 women), 1 (woman) part-time/adjunct. *Students:* 17 full-time (11 women), 4 part-time (all women); includes 1 minority (Hispanic/Latino). Average age 27. 119 applicants, 5% accepted, 4 enrolled. In 2016, 10 doctorates awarded. *Degree requirements:* For doctorate, comprehensive exam, thesis/dissertation. *Entrance requirements:* For doctorate, GRE General Test, unofficial transcripts, letters of recommendation, statement of intent. Additional exam requirements/recommendations for international students: Required—TOEFL (minimum score 80 iBT), IELTS (minimum score 6.5). *Application deadline:* For fall admission, 1/15 priority date for domestic and international students. Application fee: $80 ($90 for international students). Electronic applications accepted. *Expenses:* $5,617 per semester full-time resident, $11,194 per semester full-time non-resident, $697 per credit hour part-time resident, $1,392 per credit hour part-time non-resident. *Financial support:* In 2016–17, 18 students received support, including 15 teaching assistantships with partial tuition reimbursements available (averaging $14,667 per year); career-related internships or fieldwork and unspecified assistantships also available. Financial award application deadline: 1/15. *Faculty research:* Personnel selection; occupational health; judgment and decision-making; organizational psychology; aging, retirement, and return to work. *Unit head:* Dr. Patrick Raymark, Chair, 864-656-4715, Fax: 864-656-0358, E-mail: praymar@clemson.edu. *Application contact:* Dr. Robert Sinclair, Graduate Program Coordinator, 864-656-3931.
Website: http://www.clemson.edu/cbshs/departments/psychology/graduate/iophd.html

**East Carolina University,** Graduate School, Thomas Harriot College of Arts and Sciences, Department of Psychology, Greenville, NC 27858-4353. Offers health

psychology (PhD), including clinical health psychology, occupational health psychology, pediatric school psychology; industrial and organizational psychology (MA); MA/CAS. *Program availability:* Part-time, evening/weekend. *Students:* 83 full-time (60 women), 23 part-time (16 women); includes 16 minority (8 Black or African American, non-Hispanic/Latino; 1 Asian, non-Hispanic/Latino; 5 Hispanic/Latino; 2 Two or more races, non-Hispanic/Latino). Average age 26. 248 applicants, 19% accepted, 31 enrolled. In 2016, 11 master's, 1 doctorate awarded. *Degree requirements:* For master's, one foreign language, comprehensive exam, thesis. *Entrance requirements:* For master's, GRE General Test, GRE Subject Test. Additional exam requirements/recommendations for international students: Required—TOEFL. *Application deadline:* Applications are processed on a rolling basis. Application fee: $50. *Financial support:* Research assistantships with partial tuition reimbursements, teaching assistantships with partial tuition reimbursements, Federal Work-Study, and traineeships available. Support available to part-time students. Financial award application deadline: 6/1. *Unit head:* Dr. Susan L. McCammon, Chair, 252-328-6357, E-mail: mccammons@ecu.edu. *Application contact:* Dean of Graduate School, 252-328-6012, Fax: 252-328-6071, E-mail: gradschool@ecu.edu.
Website: http://www.ecu.edu/psyc/

**Eastern Kentucky University,** The Graduate School, College of Arts and Sciences, Department of Psychology, Richmond, KY 40475-3102. Offers clinical psychology (MS); industrial/organizational psychology (MS); school psychology (Psy S). *Program availability:* Part-time. *Entrance requirements:* For master's and Psy S, GRE General Test, minimum GPA of 2.5. *Faculty research:* Autism, social psychology, parenting, assessment of depression/anxiety, reading.

**Elmhurst College,** Graduate Programs, Program in Industrial/Organizational Psychology, Elmhurst, IL 60126-3296. Offers MA. *Program availability:* Part-time, evening/weekend. *Faculty:* 2 full-time (1 woman), 4 part-time/adjunct (1 woman). *Students:* 15 full-time (11 women), 49 part-time (30 women); includes 8 minority (3 Black or African American, non-Hispanic/Latino; 2 Asian, non-Hispanic/Latino; 2 Hispanic/Latino; 1 Two or more races, non-Hispanic/Latino). Average age 25. 71 applicants, 48% accepted, 32 enrolled. In 2016, 12 master's awarded. *Degree requirements:* For master's, thesis optional. *Entrance requirements:* For master's, GRE General Test, 3 recommendations, resume, statement of purpose. Additional exam requirements/recommendations for international students: Required—TOEFL (minimum score 550 paper-based; 79 iBT). *Application deadline:* Applications are processed on a rolling basis. Application fee: $0. Electronic applications accepted. *Expenses:* $775 per semester hour. *Financial support:* In 2016–17, 46 students received support. Scholarships/grants available. Support available to part-time students. Financial award application deadline: 3/1; financial award applicants required to submit FAFSA. *Unit head:* Carrie Hewitt. *Application contact:* Timothy J. Panfil, Director of Enrollment Management, School for Professional and Continuing Education, 630-617-3300 Ext. 3256, Fax: 630-617-6471, E-mail: panfilt@elmhurst.edu.
Website: http://www.elmhurst.edu/iop

**Emporia State University,** Program in Psychology, Emporia, KS 66801-5415. Offers general psychology (MS); industrial/organizational psychology (MS). *Program availability:* Part-time. *Faculty:* 8 full-time (4 women). *Students:* 10 full-time (7 women), 9 part-time (6 women); includes 2 minority (both Black or African American, non-Hispanic/Latino), 2 international. 16 applicants, 94% accepted, 4 enrolled. In 2016, 8 master's awarded. *Degree requirements:* For master's, comprehensive exam or thesis, internship. *Entrance requirements:* For master's, GRE General Test or MAT, essay exam, appropriate bachelor's degree, letters of recommendation. Additional exam requirements/recommendations for international students: Required—TOEFL (minimum score 520 paper-based; 68 iBT). *Application deadline:* For fall admission, 6/1 priority date for domestic students; for spring admission, 10/1 for domestic students. Applications are processed on a rolling basis. Application fee: $30 ($75 for international students). Electronic applications accepted. *Expenses:* Tuition, state resident: full-time $5922; part-time $246.75 per credit hour. Tuition, nonresident: full-time $18,414; part-time $767.25 per credit hour. *Required fees:* $1884; $78.50 per credit hour. *Financial support:* In 2016–17, 8 research assistantships with full tuition reimbursements (averaging $7,353 per year), 4 teaching assistantships with full tuition reimbursements (averaging $7,344 per year) were awarded; career-related internships or fieldwork, Federal Work-Study, institutionally sponsored loans, health care benefits, and unspecified assistantships also available. Financial award application deadline: 3/15; financial award applicants required to submit FAFSA. *Faculty research:* Driving under the influence (DUI) personality, lifestyles and imposter phenomenon. *Unit head:* Dr. Jim Persinger, Chair, 620-341-5317, E-mail: jpersing@emporia.edu. *Application contact:* Mary Sewell, Admissions Coordinator, 800-950-GRAD, Fax: 620-341-5909, E-mail: msewell@emporia.edu.

**Fairleigh Dickinson University, College at Florham,** Maxwell Becton College of Arts and Sciences, Department of Psychology, Program in Industrial/Organizational Psychology, Madison, NJ 07940-1099. Offers MA, MA/MBA. *Entrance requirements:* For master's, GRE General Test.

**Florida Institute of Technology,** College of Psychology and Liberal Arts, Program in Industrial/Organizational Psychology, Melbourne, FL 32901-6975. Offers MS, PhD. *Program availability:* Part-time. *Students:* 48 full-time (30 women), 4 part-time (all women); includes 7 minority (2 Black or African American, non-Hispanic/Latino; 1 Asian, non-Hispanic/Latino; 3 Hispanic/Latino; 1 Two or more races, non-Hispanic/Latino), 11 international. Average age 30. 187 applicants, 21% accepted, 17 enrolled. In 2016, 8 master's, 4 doctorates awarded. *Degree requirements:* For master's, comprehensive exam (for some programs), thesis (for some programs), minimum of 45 credit hours; for doctorate, thesis/dissertation, minimum of 90 credit hours beyond bachelor's degree. *Entrance requirements:* For master's, GRE General Test, minimum GPA of 3.0, 3 letters of recommendation, resume, statement of objectives, bachelor's degree in psychology; for doctorate, GRE General Test, minimum GPA of 3.2, 3 letters of recommendation, statement of objectives, resume. Additional exam requirements/recommendations for international students: Required—TOEFL (minimum score 550 paper-based; 79 iBT). *Application deadline:* For fall admission, 3/15 for domestic students. Applications are processed on a rolling basis. Electronic applications accepted. *Expenses: Tuition:* Full-time $22,338; part-time $1241 per credit hour. *Required fees:* $250. Tuition and fees vary according to degree level, campus/location and program. *Financial support:* Fellowships, research assistantships with tuition reimbursements, teaching assistantships with tuition reimbursements, career-related internships or fieldwork, and tuition waivers (partial) available. Financial award application deadline: 3/1; financial award applicants required to submit FAFSA. *Faculty research:* Faking, personality measures, team performance, behavioral change, strategies for programming, analysis of verbal behavior. *Unit head:* Dr. Lisa Steelman, Chair of Industrial and Organizational Psychology Programs, 321-674-7316, E-mail: lsteelma@fit.edu. *Application contact:* Cheryl A. Brown, Associate Director of Graduate Admissions, 321-674-7581, Fax: 321-674-9468, E-mail: cbrown@fit.edu.
Website: http://cpla.fit.edu/programs.php

**Florida International University,** College of Arts, Sciences, and Education, Department of Psychology, Miami, FL 33199. Offers behavioral analysis (MS); clinical science (PhD); cognitive neuroscience (PhD); counseling psychology (MS);

developmental science (MS, PhD); legal psychology (MS, PhD); organizational psychology (MS, PhD). Program has fall admissions only. *Accreditation:* APA. *Program availability:* Part-time, evening/weekend. *Faculty:* 44 full-time (27 women), 41 part-time/adjunct (30 women). *Students:* 150 full-time (115 women), 17 part-time (10 women); includes 89 minority (8 Black or African American, non-Hispanic/Latino; 5 Asian, non-Hispanic/Latino; 75 Hispanic/Latino; 1 Two or more races, non-Hispanic/Latino), 10 international. Average age 27. 287 applicants, 24% accepted, 57 enrolled. In 2016, 35 master's, 11 doctorates awarded. Terminal master's awarded for partial completion of doctoral program. *Degree requirements:* For master's, thesis; for doctorate, comprehensive exam, thesis/dissertation. *Entrance requirements:* For master's, GRE General Test, minimum GPA of 3.0, resume, 3 letters of recommendation; for doctorate, GRE General Test, 3 letters of recommendation, resume, letter of intent, two writing samples, minimum GPA of 3.0. Additional exam requirements/recommendations for international students: Required—TOEFL (minimum score 550 paper-based; 80 iBT). *Application deadline:* For fall admission, 12/15 for domestic and international students. *Application fee:* $30. Electronic applications accepted. *Expenses:* Tuition, state resident: full-time $8912; part-time $446 per credit hour. Tuition, nonresident: full-time $21,393; part-time $992 per credit hour. *Required fees:* $2185; $195 per semester. Tuition and fees vary according to program. *Financial support:* Institutionally sponsored loans and scholarships/grants available. Financial award application deadline: 3/1. *Faculty research:* Legal psychology, organizational and industrial psychology, child behavior psychology. *Unit head:* Dr. William Pelham, Chair, 305-348-3002, Fax: 305-348-3646, E-mail: wpelham@fiu.edu. *Application contact:* Nanett Rojas, Assistant Director, Graduate Admissions, 305-348-7464, Fax: 305-348-7441, E-mail: gradadm@fiu.edu.

**George Mason University,** College of Humanities and Social Sciences, Department of Psychology, Fairfax, VA 22030. Offers applied developmental psychology (Certificate); cognitive and behavioral neuroscience (MA); industrial/organizational psychology (PhD). *Accreditation:* APA. *Faculty:* 42 full-time (20 women), 13 part-time/adjunct (11 women). *Students:* 160 full-time (105 women), 57 part-time (30 women); includes 36 minority (9 Black or African American, non-Hispanic/Latino; 8 Asian, non-Hispanic/Latino; 12 Hispanic/Latino; 1 Native Hawaiian or other Pacific Islander, non-Hispanic/Latino; 6 Two or more races, non-Hispanic/Latino), 14 international. Average age 26. 742 applicants, 15% accepted, 57 enrolled. In 2016, 59 master's, 21 doctorates, 7 other advanced degrees awarded. *Degree requirements:* For master's, comprehensive exam, thesis (for biopsychology); for doctorate, comprehensive exam, thesis/dissertation, 2nd-year project. *Entrance requirements:* For master's, GRE, 2 official transcripts; goals statement; 15 undergraduate credits in concentration for which the applicant is applying; for doctorate, GRE, 3 letters of recommendation; resume; goals statement; minimum GPA of 3.0 overall for last 60 undergraduate credits, 3.25 in psychology courses; 15 undergraduate credits in concentration for which the applicant is applying; 2 official transcripts; for Certificate, GRE, 2 official transcripts; expanded goals statement; 3 letters of recommendation. Additional exam requirements/recommendations for international students: Required—TOEFL (minimum score 575 paper-based; 88 iBT), IELTS (minimum score 6.5), PTE (minimum score 59). Application fee: $75 ($80 for international students). Electronic applications accepted. *Expenses:* Tuition, state resident: full-time $10,628; part-time $443 per credit. Tuition, nonresident: full-time $29,306; part-time $1221 per credit. *Required fees:* $3096; $129 per credit. Tuition and fees vary according to program. *Financial support:* In 2016–17, 116 students received support, including 7 fellowships (averaging $11,348 per year), 42 research assistantships with tuition reimbursements available (averaging $14,292 per year), 88 teaching assistantships with tuition reimbursements available (averaging $13,815 per year); career-related internships or fieldwork, Federal Work-Study, scholarships/grants, tuition waivers (partial), unspecified assistantships, and health care benefits (for full-time research or teaching assistantship recipients) also available. Support available to part-time students. Financial award application deadline: 3/1; financial award applicants required to submit FAFSA. *Faculty research:* Applied developmental psychology, biopsychology, clinical psychology, human factors/applied cognition psychology, industrial/organizational psychology, school psychology. *Total annual research expenditures:* $5.6 million. *Unit head:* Reeshad Dalal, Department Chair, 703-993-9487, Fax: 703-993-1359, E-mail: rdalal@gmu.edu. *Application contact:* Michael Hock, Graduate Program Coordinator, 703-993-1548, Fax: 703-993-1359, E-mail: mhock2@gmu.edu.
Website: http://psychology.gmu.edu

**The Graduate Center, City University of New York,** Graduate Studies, Program in Psychology, New York, NY 10016-4039. Offers basic applied neurocognition (PhD); biopsychology (PhD); clinical psychology (PhD); developmental psychology (PhD); environmental psychology (PhD); experimental psychology (PhD); industrial psychology (PhD); learning processes (PhD); neuropsychology (PhD); psychology (PhD); social personality (PhD). *Degree requirements:* For doctorate, one foreign language, thesis/dissertation. *Entrance requirements:* For doctorate, GRE General Test. Additional exam requirements/recommendations for international students: Required—TOEFL. Electronic applications accepted.

**Grand Canyon University,** College of Doctoral Studies, Phoenix, AZ 85017-1097. Offers data analytics (DBA); general psychology (PhD), including cognition and instruction, industrial and organizational psychology, integrating technology, learning, and psychology, performance psychology; management (DBA); marketing (DBA); organizational leadership (Ed D), including behavioral health, Christian ministry, health care administration, organizational development. *Degree requirements:* For doctorate, comprehensive exam, thesis/dissertation. *Entrance requirements:* For doctorate, minimum GPA of 3.4 on earned advanced degree from regionally-accredited institution; transcripts; goals statement. Application fee: $0. *Unit head:* Michael Berger, Dean, 602-639-7255. *Application contact:* Michael Berger, Dean, 602-639-7255.
Website: https://www.gcu.edu/college-of-doctoral-studies.php

**Hofstra University,** College of Liberal Arts and Sciences, Programs in Psychology, Hempstead, NY 11549. Offers applied organizational psychology (PhD); clinical psychology (PhD); industrial/organizational psychology (MA); school-community psychology (Psy D). *Accreditation:* APA. *Program availability:* Part-time, evening/weekend. *Students:* 195 full-time (130 women), 32 part-time (18 women); includes 43 minority (9 Black or African American, non-Hispanic/Latino; 2 American Indian or Alaska Native, non-Hispanic/Latino; 8 Asian, non-Hispanic/Latino; 21 Hispanic/Latino; 2 Native Hawaiian or other Pacific Islander, non-Hispanic/Latino; 1 Two or more races, non-Hispanic/Latino), 21 international. Average age 27. 299 applicants, 40% accepted, 54 enrolled. In 2016, 51 master's, 36 doctorates awarded. *Degree requirements:* For master's, comprehensive exam, thesis optional, internship, minimum GPA of 3.0; for doctorate, comprehensive exam, thesis/dissertation, 1st year qualifying examination, 2nd year research project, successful practicum/externship placements, written presentation and successful oral defense of dissertation, completion of full-time internship. *Entrance requirements:* For master's, GRE General Test, minimum GPA of 3.0, essay, interview; for doctorate, GRE General Test, GRE Subject Test (psychology), 3 letters of recommendation, interview, essay, curriculum vitae. Additional exam requirements/recommendations for international students: Required—TOEFL (minimum score 550 paper-based; 80 iBT). *Application deadline:* For fall admission, 12/31 for domestic and international students. Application fee: $75. Electronic applications

accepted. *Expenses: Tuition:* Full-time $1240. *Required fees:* $970. Tuition and fees vary according to program. *Financial support:* In 2016–17, 119 students received support, including 112 fellowships with full and partial tuition reimbursements available (averaging $8,418 per year), 4 research assistantships with full and partial tuition reimbursements available (averaging $5,940 per year); career-related internships or fieldwork, Federal Work-Study, institutionally sponsored loans, scholarships/grants, traineeships, tuition waivers (full and partial), and unspecified assistantships also available. Support available to part-time students. Financial award applicants required to submit FAFSA. *Faculty research:* PTSD, secondary trauma, childhood adjustment problems, the impact of exercise on emotional states treatment of anxiety disorders and depression, cognitive appraisal and emotion, evolutionary psychology - implications for clinical psychology (evolutionary psychopathology, theory of human nature), treatment of phobic and post-traumatic stress disorders with exposure therapies, self-help and motivational interviewing. *Unit head:* Dr. Craig Johnson, Chairperson, 516-463-5636, E-mail: craig.a.johnson@hofstra.edu. *Application contact:* Sunil Samuel, Assistant Vice President of Admissions, 516-463-4723, Fax: 516-463-4664, E-mail: graduateadmission@hofstra.edu.
Website: http://www.hofstra.edu/hclas

**Illinois Institute of Technology,** Graduate College, Lewis College of Human Sciences, Department of Psychology, Chicago, IL 60616. Offers clinical psychology (PhD); industrial and organizational psychology (PhD); personnel and human resource development (MS); rehabilitation and mental health counseling (MS); rehabilitation counseling education (PhD). *Accreditation:* APA (one or more programs are accredited); CORE. *Program availability:* Part-time, evening/weekend. Terminal master's awarded for partial completion of doctoral program. *Degree requirements:* For master's, thesis (for some programs); for doctorate, comprehensive exam, thesis/dissertation, minimum of 107 credit hours, 1-year full-time internship. *Entrance requirements:* For master's, GRE General Test (minimum score 298 Quantitative and Verbal, 3.0 Analytical Writing, minimum GPA of 3.0; 3 letters of recommendation; bachelor's degree from accredited institution (for personnel and human resource development); for doctorate, GRE General Test (minimum score 298 Quantitative and Verbal, 3.0 Analytical Writing), bachelor's or master's degree from accredited institution, recommendations. Additional exam requirements/recommendations for international students: Required—TOEFL (minimum score 550 paper-based; 80 iBT). Electronic applications accepted. *Faculty research:* Clinical psychology, rehabilitation and mental health counseling, industrial organizational psychology.

**Illinois State University,** Graduate School, College of Arts and Sciences, Department of Psychology, Normal, IL 61790-2200. Offers psychology (MA, MS), including clinical-counseling psychology, cognitive and behavioral sciences, developmental psychology, industrial/organizational-social psychology; school psychology (PhD, SSP). *Accreditation:* APA. *Degree requirements:* For master's, thesis or alternative; for doctorate, variable foreign language requirement, thesis/dissertation, 2 terms of residency, internship, practicum. *Entrance requirements:* For master's, GRE General Test, GRE Subject Test, minimum GPA of 3.0 in last 60 hours of course work; for doctorate, GRE General Test. *Faculty research:* Comprehensive evaluation system for the central region professional development grant, Illinois school psychology internship consortium, for children's sake.

**Indiana University–Purdue University Indianapolis,** School of Science, Department of Psychology, Indianapolis, IN 46202-3275. Offers clinical psychology (MS); industrial/organizational psychology (MS); psychobiology of addictions (PhD). *Accreditation:* APA (one or more programs are accredited). Terminal master's awarded for partial completion of doctoral program. *Degree requirements:* For master's, thesis; for doctorate, thesis/dissertation. *Entrance requirements:* For master's, GRE General Test, minimum undergraduate GPA of 3.0; for doctorate, GRE General Test, GRE Subject Test (clinical psychology), minimum undergraduate GPA of 3.2. Additional exam requirements/recommendations for international students: Required—TOEFL (minimum score 567 paper-based; 86 iBT), IELTS (minimum score 6.5). Electronic applications accepted. *Faculty research:* Severe mental illness, health psychology, neurological research, alcoholism and psychopathology, functional activities within organizations.

**Inter American University of Puerto Rico, Metropolitan Campus,** Graduate Programs, Program in Psychology, San Juan, PR 00919-1293. Offers counseling psychology (MA, PhD); industrial/organizational psychology (MA, PhD); labor relations (MA); school psychology (MA, PhD). *Degree requirements:* For master's, comprehensive exam. *Entrance requirements:* For master's, GRE or EXADEP, interview. Electronic applications accepted.

**Iona College,** School of Arts and Science, Department of Psychology, New Rochelle, NY 10801-1890. Offers general-experimental psychology (MA); human resources (Certificate); industrial-organizational psychology (MA); mental health counseling (MA); organizational behavior (Certificate); psychology (MA); school psychology (MA). *Program availability:* Part-time. *Faculty:* 9 full-time (5 women), 6 part-time/adjunct (5 women). *Students:* 61 full-time (42 women), 32 part-time (23 women); includes 40 minority (8 Black or African American, non-Hispanic/Latino; 3 Asian, non-Hispanic/Latino; 28 Hispanic/Latino; 1 Two or more races, non-Hispanic/Latino), 2 international. Average age 25. 91 applicants, 80% accepted, 37 enrolled. In 2016, 18 master's awarded. *Degree requirements:* For master's, thesis (for some programs), literature review (for some programs). *Entrance requirements:* For master's, BA in psychology including 3 credits each in psychology statistics and experimental research methods, or 9 credits in psychology including 3 credits in psychology statistics, 3 credits in psychology research methods and 3 credits of upper-level coursework. Additional exam requirements/recommendations for international students: Required—TOEFL (minimum score 550 paper-based), IELTS (minimum score 6.5). *Application deadline:* For fall admission, 8/15 for domestic students, 5/1 for international students; for spring admission, 1/15 for domestic students, 9/1 for international students. Applications are processed on a rolling basis. Application fee: $50. Electronic applications accepted. *Expenses: Tuition:* Full-time $19,692; part-time $1094 per credit. *Required fees:* $245 per term. Tuition and fees vary according to program. *Financial support:* In 2016–17, 49 students received support. Research assistantships with partial tuition reimbursements available, tuition waivers (partial), and unspecified assistantships available. Support available to part-time students. Financial award application deadline: 4/15; financial award applicants required to submit FAFSA. *Faculty research:* Non-suicidal self-injury, trauma response, performance appraisal and evaluation, diversity infusion, assessment and treatment of sexual offenders. *Unit head:* Patricia Oswald, PhD, Chair, 914-633-2374, E-mail: poswald@iona.edu. *Application contact:* Katelyn Brunck, Assistant Director, Graduate Admissions, 914-633-2451, Fax: 914-633-2277, E-mail: kbrunck@iona.edu.
Website: http://www.iona.edu/Academics/School-of-Arts-Science/Departments/Psychology/Graduate-Programs.aspx

**John F. Kennedy University,** Graduate School of Professional Psychology, Program in Organizational Psychology, Pleasant Hill, CA 94523-4817. Offers MA, Certificate. *Program availability:* Part-time, evening/weekend. *Degree requirements:* For master's, thesis or alternative. *Entrance requirements:* For master's, interview. Additional exam requirements/recommendations for international students: Required—TOEFL.

## Industrial and Organizational Psychology

**Kean University,** College of Liberal Arts, Program in Psychology, Union, NJ 07083. Offers forensic psychology (MA); human behavior and organizational psychology (MA); psychological services (MA). *Program availability:* Part-time. *Faculty:* 18 full-time (14 women). *Students:* 45 full-time (35 women), 39 part-time (25 women); includes 48 minority (21 Black or African American, non-Hispanic/Latino; 8 Asian, non-Hispanic/Latino; 16 Hispanic/Latino; 1 Native Hawaiian or other Pacific Islander, non-Hispanic/Latino; 2 Two or more races, non-Hispanic/Latino), 2 international. Average age 27. 54 applicants, 91% accepted, 44 enrolled. In 2016, 25 master's awarded. *Degree requirements:* For master's, comprehensive exam, research component, two semesters of advanced seminar. *Entrance requirements:* For master's, GRE General Test, minimum GPA of 3.0; official transcripts from all institutions attended; two letters of recommendation; professional resume/curriculum vitae; 12 credits in behavioral sciences on the undergraduate level. Additional exam requirements/recommendations for international students: Required—TOEFL (minimum score 550 paper-based; 79 iBT), IELTS (minimum score 6.5). *Application deadline:* For fall admission, 6/1 for domestic and international students; for spring admission, 12/1 for domestic and international students. Applications are processed on a rolling basis. Application fee: $75. Electronic applications accepted. *Expenses:* Tuition, state resident: full-time $13,156; part-time $640 per credit. Tuition, nonresident: full-time $17,831; part-time $785 per credit. *Required fees:* $3316; $151 per credit. Tuition and fees vary according to course level, course load, degree level and program. *Financial support:* Scholarships/grants and unspecified assistantships available. Financial award applicants required to submit FAFSA. *Unit head:* Dr. Muriel Singer, Program Coordinator, 908-737-5886, E-mail: msinger@kean.edu. *Application contact:* Amy Clark, Program Assistant, 908-737-7100, E-mail: grad-adm@kean.edu.
Website: http://grad.kean.edu/masters-programs/psychological-services

**Keiser University,** MS in Organizational Psychology Program, Ft. Lauderdale, FL 33309. Offers MS. *Degree requirements:* For master's, thesis.

**Keiser University,** PhD in Industrial and Organizational Psychology Program, Ft. Lauderdale, FL 33309. Offers PhD.

**Lamar University,** College of Graduate Studies, College of Arts and Sciences, Department of Psychology, Beaumont, TX 77710. Offers clinical psychology (MS); industrial/organizational psychology (MS). *Program availability:* Part-time. *Faculty:* 6 full-time (4 women). *Students:* 8 full-time (6 women), 8 part-time (6 women); includes 5 minority (1 Black or African American, non-Hispanic/Latino; 3 Hispanic/Latino; 1 Two or more races, non-Hispanic/Latino), 1 international. Average age 28. 15 applicants, 100% accepted, 3 enrolled. In 2016, 6 master's awarded. *Degree requirements:* For master's, thesis, practicum. *Entrance requirements:* For master's, GRE General Test, minimum GPA of 2.75 in last 60 hours of undergraduate course work. Additional exam requirements/recommendations for international students: Required—TOEFL (minimum score 550 paper-based; 79 iBT), IELTS (minimum score 6.5). *Application deadline:* For fall admission, 8/10 for domestic students, 7/1 for international students; for spring admission, 1/5 for domestic students, 12/1 for international students. Application fee: $25 ($50 for international students). *Expenses:* $8,134 in-state full-time, $5,574 in-state part-time; $15,604 out-of-state full-time, $10,554 out-of-state part-time per year. *Financial support:* In 2016–17, 12 students received support. Fellowships, research assistantships, teaching assistantships, career-related internships or fieldwork, Federal Work-Study, scholarships/grants, and tuition waivers (partial) available. Support available to part-time students. Financial award application deadline: 4/1. *Faculty research:* Group think, health psychology, school psychology, behavioral neuroscience. *Unit head:* Dr. Edythe E. Kirk, Chair, 409-880-8285, Fax: 409-880-1710. *Application contact:* Deidre Mayer, Interim Director, Admissions and Academic Services, 409-880-8888, Fax: 409-880-7419, E-mail: gradmissions@lamar.edu.
Website: http://artssciences.lamar.edu/psychology

**London Metropolitan University,** Graduate Programs, London, United Kingdom. Offers applied psychology (M Sc); architecture (MA); biomedical science (M Sc); blood science (M Sc); cancer pharmacology (M Sc); computer networking and cyber security (M Sc); computing and information systems (M Sc); conference interpreting (MA); counter-terrorism studies (M Sc); creative, digital and professional writing (MA); crime, violence and prevention (M Sc); criminology (M Sc); curating contemporary art (MA); data analytics (M Sc); digital media (MA); early childhood studies (MA); education (MA, Ed D); financial services law, regulation and compliance (LL M); food science (M Sc); forensic psychology (M Sc); health and social care management and policy (M Sc); human nutrition (M Sc); human resource management (MA); human rights and international conflict (MA); information technology (M Sc); intelligence and security studies (M Sc); international oil, gas and energy law (LL M); international relations (MA); interpreting (MA); learning and teaching in higher education (MA); legal practice (LL M); media and entertainment law (LL M); organizational and consumer psychology (M Sc); psychological therapy (M Sc); psychology of mental health (M Sc); public health (M Sc); public policy and management (MPA); security studies (M Sc); social work (M Sc); spatial planning and urban design (MA); sports therapy (M Sc); supporting older children and young people with dyslexia (MA); teaching languages (MA), including Arabic, English; translation (MA); woman and child abuse (MA).

**Louisiana Tech University,** Graduate School, College of Education, Department of Psychology and Behavioral Sciences, Ruston, LA 71272. Offers counseling and guidance (MA); counseling psychology (PhD); industrial and organizational psychology (MA, PhD). *Accreditation:* APA (one or more programs are accredited). *Program availability:* Part-time. *Degree requirements:* For master's, thesis or alternative; for doctorate, thesis/dissertation. *Entrance requirements:* For master's and doctorate, GRE General Test. *Application deadline:* For fall admission, 7/29 for domestic students; for spring admission, 2/3 for domestic students. Application fee: $20 ($30 for international students). *Financial support:* Fellowships, research assistantships, teaching assistantships, and career-related internships or fieldwork available. Financial award application deadline: 2/1. *Unit head:* Dr. Donna Thomas, Chair, 318-257-5066, Fax: 318-257-2379, E-mail: dthomas@latech.edu. *Application contact:* Dr. Cathy Stockton, Associate Dean of Graduate Studies, 318-257-3229, Fax: 318-257-2379, E-mail: cstock@latech.edu.
Website: http://education.latech.edu/departments/psychology/

**Middle Tennessee State University,** College of Graduate Studies, College of Behavioral and Health Sciences, Department of Psychology, Murfreesboro, TN 37132. Offers clinical psychology (MA); experimental psychology (MA); industrial/organizational psychology (MA); psychology (MA, Ed S); quantitative psychology (MA); school psychology (MA). *Program availability:* Part-time, evening/weekend, online learning. *Degree requirements:* For master's, comprehensive exam, thesis. *Entrance requirements:* For master's, GRE. Additional exam requirements/recommendations for international students: Required—TOEFL (minimum score 525 paper-based; 71 iBT) or IELTS (minimum score 6). Electronic applications accepted. *Faculty research:* Health psychology, industrial/organizational psychology, experimental psychology.

**Minnesota State University Mankato,** College of Graduate Studies and Research, College of Social and Behavioral Sciences, Department of Psychology, Mankato, MN 56001. Offers clinical psychology (MA); industrial/organizational psychology (MA); school psychology (Psy D). *Program availability:* Part-time. *Students:* 51 full-time (34 women), 12 part-time (11 women). *Degree requirements:* For master's, one foreign language, comprehensive exam, thesis (for some programs). *Entrance requirements:* For master's, GRE General Test, GRE Subject Test (clinical psychology), minimum GPA of 3.0 during previous 2 years, 3 letters of reference. Additional exam requirements/recommendations for international students: Required—TOEFL. *Application deadline:* For fall admission, 1/1 priority date for domestic students. Applications are processed on a rolling basis. Application fee: $40. Electronic applications accepted. *Financial support:* Research assistantships, teaching assistantships with full tuition reimbursements, career-related internships or fieldwork, Federal Work-Study, institutionally sponsored loans, and unspecified assistantships available. Support available to part-time students. Financial award application deadline: 3/15; financial award applicants required to submit FAFSA.
Website: http://sbs.mnsu.edu/psych/

**Missouri State University,** Graduate College, College of Health and Human Services, Department of Psychology, Springfield, MO 65897. Offers applied behavior analysis (MS); clinical psychology (MS); experimental psychology (MS); forensic child psychology (Certificate); industrial/organizational psychology (MS). *Faculty:* 25 full-time (11 women), 4 part-time/adjunct (0 women). *Students:* 65 full-time (49 women), 7 part-time (5 women); includes 12 minority (1 Black or African American, non-Hispanic/Latino; 3 American Indian or Alaska Native, non-Hispanic/Latino; 3 Asian, non-Hispanic/Latino; 2 Hispanic/Latino; 3 Two or more races, non-Hispanic/Latino), 6 international. Average age 25. 159 applicants, 25% accepted, 31 enrolled. In 2016, 22 master's awarded. *Degree requirements:* For master's, comprehensive exam, thesis. *Entrance requirements:* For master's, GRE General Test, GRE Subject Test, minimum GPA of 3.25 in major, 3.0 overall; 20 hours of course work in psychology. Additional exam requirements/recommendations for international students: Required—TOEFL (minimum score 550 paper-based; 79 iBT), IELTS (minimum score 6). *Application deadline:* For fall admission, 2/15 priority date for domestic and international students. Application fee: $35 ($50 for international students). Electronic applications accepted. *Expenses:* Tuition, state resident: full-time $5830. Tuition, nonresident: full-time $10,708. *Required fees:* $1130. Tuition and fees vary according to class time, course level, course load and program. *Financial support:* In 2016–17, 9 research assistantships with full tuition reimbursements (averaging $8,772 per year), 8 teaching assistantships with full tuition reimbursements (averaging $8,772 per year) were awarded; career-related internships or fieldwork, Federal Work-Study, institutionally sponsored loans, scholarships/grants, and unspecified assistantships also available. Financial award application deadline: 3/31; financial award applicants required to submit FAFSA. *Faculty research:* Work-family conflict, child forensic psychology, sports psychology, body image assessment, visual learning. *Unit head:* Dr. Paul Deal, Department Head, 417-836-5797, Fax: 417-836-8330, E-mail: psychology@missouristate.edu. *Application contact:* Michael Edwards, Coordinator of Graduate Admissions, 417-836-5330, Fax: 417-836-6200, E-mail: michaeledwards@missouristate.edu.
Website: http://psychology.missouristate.edu/

**Montclair State University,** The Graduate School, College of Humanities and Social Sciences, Program in Industrial and Organizational Psychology, Montclair, NJ 07043-1624. Offers MA. *Program availability:* Part-time, evening/weekend. *Degree requirements:* For master's, thesis. *Entrance requirements:* For master's, GRE General Test, 2 letters of recommendation, essay. Additional exam requirements/recommendations for international students: Required—TOEFL (minimum score 83 iBT), IELTS (minimum score 6.5). Electronic applications accepted. *Expenses:* Tuition, state resident: part-time $553 per credit. Tuition, nonresident: part-time $854 per credit. *Required fees:* $91 per credit. Tuition and fees vary according to program. *Faculty research:* Study of behavior in the work place; job satisfaction, organizational commitment and how to select individuals for given positions in an organization.

**New York University,** Graduate School of Arts and Science, Department of Psychology, New York, NY 10012-1019. Offers cognition and perception (PhD); community psychology (PhD); general psychology (MA); industrial/organizational psychology (MA); psychotherapy and psychoanalysis (Advanced Certificate); social/personality psychology (PhD). *Program availability:* Part-time. Terminal master's awarded for partial completion of doctoral program. *Degree requirements:* For master's, comprehensive exam, thesis or alternative; for doctorate, thesis/dissertation. *Entrance requirements:* For master's and doctorate, GRE General Test. Additional exam requirements/recommendations for international students: Required—TOEFL. *Faculty research:* Vision, memory, social cognition, social and cognitive development, relationships.

**North Carolina State University,** Graduate School, College of Humanities and Social Sciences, Department of Psychology, Raleigh, NC 27695. Offers developmental psychology (PhD); ergonomics and experimental psychology (PhD); industrial/organizational psychology (PhD); psychology in the public interest (PhD); school psychology (PhD). *Accreditation:* APA. *Degree requirements:* For doctorate, comprehensive exam, thesis/dissertation. *Entrance requirements:* For doctorate, GRE General Test, GRE Subject Test (industrial/organizational psychology), MAT (recommended), minimum GPA of 3.0 in major. Electronic applications accepted. *Faculty research:* Cognitive and social development (human factors, families, the workplace, community issues and health, aging).

**Northern Kentucky University,** Office of Graduate Programs, College of Arts and Sciences, Program in Industrial-Organizational Psychology, Highland Heights, KY 41099. Offers industrial psychology (Certificate); industrial/organizational psychology (MS); occupational health psychology (Certificate); organizational psychology (Certificate). *Program availability:* Part-time, evening/weekend. *Degree requirements:* For master's, thesis optional, capstone. *Entrance requirements:* For master's, GRE General Test (minimum scores of 141 verbal, 144 quantitative, and 3.5 writing), bachelor's degree with minimum GPA of 3.0, nine semester hours of psychology coursework, at least one undergraduate course in statistics with minimum B grade, official transcripts, current resume or vita, statement of personal interest, three letters of recommendation; for Certificate, official transcripts, bachelor's degree, minimum undergraduate GPA of 3.0, no grade lower than B on all graduate coursework previously taken that may apply. Additional exam requirements/recommendations for international students: Required—TOEFL (minimum score 79 iBT); Recommended—IELTS (minimum score 6.5). Electronic applications accepted. *Faculty research:* Workplace bullying and abuse, assessment and situational judgment tasks, human factors and work design, racial and social stereotyping in employment, social conflict.

**Ohio University,** Graduate College, College of Arts and Sciences, Department of Psychology, Program in Organizational Psychology, Athens, OH 45701-2979. Offers PhD. *Degree requirements:* For doctorate, one foreign language, comprehensive exam, thesis/dissertation. *Entrance requirements:* For doctorate, GRE General Test, GRE Subject Test. Additional exam requirements/recommendations for international students: Required—TOEFL. *Application deadline:* For fall admission, 1/1 for domestic students. Application fee: $50 ($55 for international students). *Financial support:* Fellowships with full tuition reimbursements, research assistantships with full tuition reimbursements, teaching assistantships with full tuition reimbursements, career-related internships or fieldwork, Federal Work-Study, institutionally sponsored loans, tuition waivers (full), and unspecified assistantships available. Financial award application deadline: 1/15. *Faculty research:* Performance appraisal, job satisfaction, organizational entry, sexual harassment. *Unit head:* Chantel Weisenmuller, Director, 740-597-1251, E-mail: weisenmu@ohio.edu. *Application contact:* Karyl Jones, Administrative Assistant, 740-593-1090, Fax: 740-593-0579, E-mail: psychology@ohio.edu. Website: http://www.psych.ohiou.edu/

**Old Dominion University,** College of Sciences, Doctoral Program in Psychology, Norfolk, VA 23529. Offers applied psychological sciences (PhD); human factors psychology (PhD); industrial/organizational psychology (PhD). *Faculty:* 28 full-time (12 women), 11 part-time/adjunct (9 women). *Students:* 47 full-time (26 women); includes 4 minority (1 Black or African American, non-Hispanic/Latino; 3 Hispanic/Latino). Average age 25. 74 applicants, 14% accepted, 9 enrolled. In 2016, 3 doctorates awarded. *Degree requirements:* For doctorate, comprehensive exam, thesis/dissertation, candidacy exam. *Entrance requirements:* For doctorate, GRE General Test, GRE Subject Test, 3 recommendation letters. Additional exam requirements/recommendations for international students: Required—TOEFL. *Application deadline:* For winter admission, 1/5 for domestic and international students. Application fee: $50. Electronic applications accepted. *Expenses:* $478 per credit hour in-state; $1,195 per credit hour out-of-state. *Financial support:* In 2016–17, 40 students received support, including 5 research assistantships with full tuition reimbursements available (averaging $15,000 per year), 35 teaching assistantships with full tuition reimbursements available (averaging $15,000 per year). Financial award application deadline: 1/15. *Faculty research:* Human factors, industrial psychology, organizational psychology, applied psychological sciences (health, developmental, community, quantitative). *Total annual research expenditures:* $978,563. *Unit head:* Dr. Debra A. Major, Graduate Program Director, 757-683-4235, Fax: 757-683-5087, E-mail: dmajor@odu.edu. *Application contact:* William Heffelfinger, Director of Graduate Admissions, 757-683-5554, Fax: 757-683-3255, E-mail: gradadmit@odu.edu. Website: http://www.odu.edu/psychology/

**Philadelphia College of Osteopathic Medicine,** Graduate and Professional Programs, Department of Psychology, Philadelphia, PA 19131-1694. Offers applied behavior analysis (Certificate); clinical health psychology (Post-Doctoral Certificate); clinical neuropsychology (Post-Doctoral Certificate); clinical psychology (Psy D); mental health counseling (MS); organizational development and leadership (MS); psychology (Certificate); school psychology (MS, Psy D, Ed S). *Accreditation:* APA. *Faculty:* 19 full-time (11 women), 122 part-time/adjunct (58 women). *Students:* 364 (285 women); includes 78 minority (62 Black or African American, non-Hispanic/Latino; 2 American Indian or Alaska Native, non-Hispanic/Latino; 9 Asian, non-Hispanic/Latino; 5 Hispanic/Latino), 2 international. 366 applicants, 51% accepted, 139 enrolled. In 2016, 72 master's, 42 doctorates, 17 other advanced degrees awarded. Terminal master's awarded for partial completion of doctoral program. *Degree requirements:* For master's, comprehensive exam (for some programs), thesis (for some programs); for doctorate, comprehensive exam, thesis/dissertation. *Entrance requirements:* For master's, GRE or MAT, minimum GPA of 3.0; bachelor's degree from regionally-accredited college or university; for doctorate, PRAXIS II (for Psy D in school psychology), minimum undergraduate GPA of 3.0; for other advanced degree, GRE (for Ed S). Additional exam requirements/recommendations for international students: Required—TOEFL (minimum score 79 iBT). *Application deadline:* Applications are processed on a rolling basis. Application fee: $50. Electronic applications accepted. Tuition and fees vary according to course load, degree level and program. *Financial support:* In 2016–17, 28 teaching assistantships were awarded; Federal Work-Study, institutionally sponsored loans, and scholarships/grants also available. Financial award application deadline: 3/15; financial award applicants required to submit FAFSA. *Faculty research:* Adult and childhood anxiety and ADHD; coping with chronic illness; primary care psychology/integrated health care; applied behavior analysis; psychological, educational, and neuropsychological assessment. *Total annual research expenditures:* $533,489. *Unit head:* Dr. Robert DiTomasso, Chairman, 215-871-6442, Fax: 215-871-6458, E-mail: robertd@pcom.edu. *Application contact:* Johnathan Cox, Associate Director of Admissions, 215-871-6700, Fax: 215-871-6719, E-mail: karis@pcom.edu.

**See Display on page 1004 and Close-Up on page 1227.**

**Pontifical Catholic University of Puerto Rico,** College of Graduate Studies in Behavioral Science and Community Affairs, Program in Industrial Psychology (Doctorate), Ponce, PR 00717-0777. Offers PhD. *Program availability:* Part-time, evening/weekend. *Entrance requirements:* For doctorate, EXADEP, minimum GPA of 2.75.

**Purdue University,** Graduate School, College of Health and Human Sciences, Department of Psychological Sciences, West Lafayette, IN 47907. Offers behavioral neuroscience (PhD); clinical psychology (PhD); cognitive psychology (PhD); industrial/organizational psychology (PhD); mathematical and computational cognitive science (PhD). *Accreditation:* APA. *Faculty:* 46 full-time (18 women), 1 part-time/adjunct. *Students:* 64 full-time (41 women), 4 part-time (3 women); includes 13 minority (1 Black or African American, non-Hispanic/Latino; 4 Asian, non-Hispanic/Latino; 6 Hispanic/Latino; 2 Two or more races, non-Hispanic/Latino), 12 international. Average age 27. 288 applicants, 8% accepted, 16 enrolled. In 2016, 9 doctorates awarded. Terminal master's awarded for partial completion of doctoral program. *Degree requirements:* For doctorate, thesis/dissertation. *Entrance requirements:* For doctorate, GRE General Test, minimum undergraduate GPA of 3.0 or equivalent. Additional exam requirements/recommendations for international students: Required—TOEFL (minimum score 550 paper-based; 77 iBT); Recommended—TWE. *Application deadline:* For fall admission, 12/3 for domestic and international students. Applications are processed on a rolling basis. Application fee: $60 ($75 for international students). Electronic applications accepted. *Financial support:* Fellowships with partial tuition reimbursements, research assistantships with partial tuition reimbursements, teaching assistantships with partial tuition reimbursements, and career-related internships or fieldwork available. Support available to part-time students. Financial award applicants required to submit FAFSA. *Faculty research:* Career development of women in science, development of friendships during childhood and adolescence, social competence, human information processing. *Unit head:* Dr. Christopher R. Agnew, Head, 765-494-6061, Fax: 765-496-1264, E-mail: agnew@psych.purdue.edu. *Application contact:* Nancy A. O'Brien, Graduate Contact, 765-494-6067, Fax: 765-496-1264, E-mail: nobrien@psych.pardue.edu. Website: http://www.psych.purdue.edu/

**Rice University,** Graduate Programs, School of Social Sciences, Department of Psychology, Houston, TX 77251-1892. Offers cognitive sciences (MA, PhD); industrial-organizational/social psychology (MA, PhD); psychology (MA, PhD). Terminal master's awarded for partial completion of doctoral program. *Degree requirements:* For master's, thesis; for doctorate, thesis/dissertation. *Entrance requirements:* For doctorate, GRE General Test, minimum GPA of 3.0. Additional exam requirements/recommendations for international students: Required—TOEFL. Electronic applications accepted. *Faculty research:* Cognitive, cognitive neuropsychology, human factors, human-computer interaction, industrial-organizational psychology.

**Roosevelt University,** Graduate Division, College of Arts and Sciences, Department of Psychology, Program in Industrial/Organizational Psychology, Chicago, IL 60605. Offers MA, PhD.

**Sacred Heart University,** Graduate Programs, College of Arts and Sciences, Department of Psychology, Fairfield, CT 06825. Offers applied psychology (MS), including community psychology, general applied psychology, industrial-organizational psychology. *Program availability:* Part-time, evening/weekend, online learning. *Faculty:* 8 full-time (7 women). *Students:* 18 full-time (12 women), 94 part-time (75 women); includes 34 minority (19 Black or African American, non-Hispanic/Latino; 1 Asian, non-Hispanic/Latino; 12 Hispanic/Latino; 2 Two or more races, non-Hispanic/Latino), 2 international. Average age 33. 55 applicants, 65% accepted, 16 enrolled. In 2016, 50 master's awarded. *Degree requirements:* For master's, comprehensive exam, thesis optional. *Entrance requirements:* For master's, minimum overall GPA of 3.0, bachelor's degree from accredited college or university. Additional exam requirements/recommendations for international students: Required—TOEFL (minimum score 570 paper-based, 80 iBT), TWE, or IELTS (6.5); Recommended—TSE. *Application deadline:* Applications are processed on a rolling basis. Application fee: $75. Electronic applications accepted. *Expenses:* $850 per credit. *Financial support:* Unspecified assistantships available. Financial award applicants required to submit FAFSA. *Unit head:* Rachel Bowman, Interim Chair/Associate Professor, 203-396-8243, E-mail: bowmanr@sacredheart.edu. *Application contact:* William Sweeney, Director of Graduate Admissions Operations, 203-365-7916, Fax: 203-365-4732, E-mail: gradstudies@sacredheart.edu.
Website: http://www.sacredheart.edu/academics/collegeofartssciences/academicdepartments/psychology/mastersinappliedpsychology/

**St. Cloud State University,** School of Graduate Studies, College of Liberal Arts, Program in Industrial-Organizational Psychology, St. Cloud, MN 56301-4498. Offers MS. *Degree requirements:* For master's, thesis or portfolio. *Entrance requirements:* For master's, GRE General Test, minimum GPA of 2.75. Additional exam requirements/recommendations for international students: Required—TOEFL (minimum score 550 paper-based) or IELTS (minimum score 6.5). Electronic applications accepted.

**Saint Louis University,** Graduate Education, College of Arts and Sciences and Graduate Education, Department of Psychology, St. Louis, MO 63103. Offers clinical psychology (MS-R, PhD); experimental psychology (MS-R, PhD); industrial-organizational psychology (PhD); psychology (PhD). *Accreditation:* APA (one or more programs are accredited). *Program availability:* Part-time. *Degree requirements:* For master's, comprehensive exam, thesis; for doctorate, thesis/dissertation, clinical internship (for clinical psychology PhD). *Entrance requirements:* For master's, GRE General Test, interview, letters of recommendation, resume; for doctorate, GRE General Test, interview, letters of recommendation, resumé, transcripts, goal statement. Additional exam requirements/recommendations for international students: Required—TOEFL (minimum score 550 paper-based). Electronic applications accepted. *Faculty research:* Violence and trauma; neural basis of learning and memory function; eating disorders; body image and health behavior; prejudice, stereotyping, and victimization; memory, cognitive aging and language processing.

**Saint Mary's University,** Faculty of Science, Department of Psychology, Halifax, NS B3H 3C3, Canada. Offers applied psychology (M Sc, PhD), including industrial/organizational psychology (M Sc). *Program availability:* Part-time. *Degree requirements:* For master's, thesis, 500-hour internship; for doctorate, comprehensive exam, thesis/dissertation, research project. *Entrance requirements:* For master's and doctorate, GRE General Test. *Faculty research:* Assessment, health psychology, social psychology, cognition.

**St. Mary's University,** Graduate Studies, Program in Industrial/Organizational Psychology, San Antonio, TX 78228-8507. Offers MA, MS. *Program availability:* Part-time, evening/weekend. *Faculty:* 3 full-time (1 woman), 4 part-time/adjunct (1 woman). *Students:* 15 full-time (10 women), 5 part-time (all women); includes 12 minority (1 Black or African American, non-Hispanic/Latino; 1 Asian, non-Hispanic/Latino; 10 Hispanic/Latino). Average age 26. 42 applicants, 60% accepted, 16 enrolled. In 2016, 7 master's awarded. *Degree requirements:* For master's, comprehensive exam, thesis optional. *Entrance requirements:* For master's, GRE (minimum combined score on verbal and quantitative sections of 294; no less than 146 on the verbal section or 140 on the quantitative section), bachelor's degree from accredited institution; satisfactory completion of the following prerequisite courses or their equivalent (12 credit hours): general psychology, introductory statistics, research methods or experimental psychology, or upper-level psychology course. Additional exam requirements/recommendations for international students: Required—TOEFL (minimum score 550 paper-based; 80 iBT), IELTS (minimum score 6). *Application deadline:* For fall admission, 3/1 priority date for domestic students. Application fee: $0. Electronic applications accepted. *Expenses:* Tuition: Full-time $15,600; part-time $865 per credit hour. *Required fees:* $148 per semester. *Financial support:* Fellowships, research assistantships, career-related internships or fieldwork, Federal Work-Study, institutionally sponsored loans, scholarships/grants, health care benefits, and unspecified assistantships available. Financial award application deadline: 3/31; financial award applicants required to submit FAFSA. *Faculty research:* Social undermining in the workplace, majority and minority influence, multivariate statistics, development, social influence. *Unit head:* Dr. Gregory Pool, Graduate Program Director, 210-436-3314, E-mail: gpool@stmarytx.edu. *Application contact:* Kim Thornton, Director, Graduate and Adult Enrollment Services, 210-436-3101, E-mail: kthornton@stmarytx.edu.
Website: http://catalog.stmarytx.edu/graduate/humanities-social-science/industrial-organizational-psychology/

**San Diego State University,** Graduate and Research Affairs, College of Sciences, Department of Psychology, San Diego, CA 92182. Offers clinical psychology (MS, PhD); industrial and organizational psychology (MS); program evaluation (MS); psychology (MA). PhD offered jointly with University of California, San Diego. *Accreditation:* APA (one or more programs are accredited). Terminal master's awarded for partial completion of doctoral program. *Degree requirements:* For master's, thesis, oral exam; for doctorate, thesis/dissertation. *Entrance requirements:* For master's, GRE General Test, GRE Subject Test, 3 letters of recommendation; for doctorate, GRE General Test, GRE Subject Test, minimum GPA of 3.0, 3 letters of recommendation. Additional exam requirements/recommendations for international students: Required—TOEFL. Electronic applications accepted.

**San Francisco State University,** Division of Graduate Studies, College of Science and Engineering, Department of Psychology, San Francisco, CA 94132-1722. Offers clinical psychology (MS); developmental psychology (MA); industrial/organizational psychology (MS); mind, brain, and behavior (MA); school psychology (MS, Credential); social psychology (MA). *Expenses:* Tuition, state resident: full-time $6738. Tuition, nonresident: full-time $15,666. *Required fees:* $1012. Tuition and fees vary according to degree level and program. *Financial support:* Teaching assistantships available. Financial award application deadline: 3/1. *Unit head:* Dr. Dawn Terrell, Chair, 415-338-7555, Fax: 415-338-2398, E-mail: schen9@sfsu.edu. *Application contact:* Dr. Diane Harris, Graduate Program Coordinator, 415-338-7064, Fax: 415-338-2398, E-mail: dharris@sfsu.edu.
Website: http://psychology.sfsu.edu/graduate/application.html

**San Jose State University,** Graduate Studies and Research, College of Social Sciences, San Jose, CA 95192-0001. Offers applications of technology in planning

# SECTION 24: PSYCHOLOGY AND COUNSELING

## Industrial and Organizational Psychology

(Certificate); applied anthropology (MA); communication studies (MS); community design and development (Certificate); economics (MA), including applied economics, social sciences; environmental planning (Certificate); geographic information science (Certificate); geography (MA); global citizenship (Certificate); history (MA), including history education, social sciences; Mexican American studies (MA); psychology (MA, MS), including clinical psychology (MS), industrial/organizational psychology (MS), research and experimental psychology (MA); public administration (MA); real estate development (Certificate); social sciences (MPA, MS); sociology (MA); transportation and land use planning (Certificate). *Program availability:* Part-time, evening/weekend. *Entrance requirements:* For master's, minimum GPA of 3.0. Electronic applications accepted.

**Seattle Pacific University,** Industrial Organizational Psychology Program, Seattle, WA 98119-1997. Offers MA, PhD. *Degree requirements:* For master's, research project; for doctorate, thesis/dissertation, field placement. *Entrance requirements:* For master's, GRE (administered within five years of application to program, with minimum combined score of 950/295 new scoring on verbal and quantitative sections preferred), personal statement; recommendations; language competency; statement of financial support; for doctorate, GRE (administered within five years of application to program, with minimum combined score of 1100/300 new scoring on verbal and quantitative sections preferred), personal statement; recommendations; language competency; statement of financial support. Additional exam requirements/recommendations for international students: Required—TOEFL (minimum score 550 paper-based). Electronic applications accepted.

**South Dakota State University,** Graduate School, College of Arts and Science, Department of Psychology, Brookings, SD 57007. Offers industrial/organizational psychology (MS). *Degree requirements:* For master's, thesis, internship.

**Southeastern Louisiana University,** College of Arts, Humanities and Social Sciences, Department of Psychology, Hammond, LA 70402. Offers industrial/organizational. *Program availability:* Part-time. *Faculty:* 7 full-time (5 women). *Students:* 20 full-time (13 women), 13 part-time (12 women); includes 5 minority (1 Asian, non-Hispanic/Latino; 2 Two or more races, non-Hispanic/Latino). Average age 26. 38 applicants, 68% accepted, 11 enrolled. In 2016, 11 master's awarded. *Degree requirements:* For master's, comprehensive exam, thesis, 38 hours of psychology course work including core courses in statistics, social psychology, cognition, and physiological psychology. *Entrance requirements:* For master's, GRE (minimum combined score 950). Additional exam requirements/recommendations for international students: Required—TOEFL (minimum score 500 paper-based; 61 iBT). *Application deadline:* For fall admission, 7/15 priority date for domestic students, 6/1 priority date for international students; for spring admission, 12/1 priority date for domestic students, 10/1 priority date for international students. Applications are processed on a rolling basis. Application fee: $20 ($30 for international students). Electronic applications accepted. *Expenses:* Tuition, state resident: full-time $6540; part-time $465 per credit hour. Tuition, nonresident: full-time $19,017; part-time $1158 per credit hour. *Required fees:* $1829. *Financial support:* In 2016–17, 10 students received support, including 10 research assistantships (averaging $9,090 per year); career-related internships or fieldwork, Federal Work-Study, institutionally sponsored loans, scholarships/grants, and traineeships also available. Support available to part-time students. Financial award application deadline: 5/1; financial award applicants required to submit FAFSA. *Faculty research:* Eating disorders, evolutionary psychology, violence exposure effects on children, parental behavior, neurobiology of mental disorders and addiction. *Unit head:* Dr. Susan Coats, Department Head, 985-549-2154, Fax: 985-549-6892, E-mail: scoats@southeastern.edu. *Application contact:* Amanda Harper, Graduate Admissions Analyst, 985-549-5620, Fax: 985-549-5632, E-mail: admissions@southeastern.edu. Website: http://www.southeastern.edu/acad_research/depts/psyc/index.html

**Southern Illinois University Edwardsville,** Graduate School, School of Education, Health, and Human Behavior, Department of Psychology, Program in Industrial-Organizational Psychology, Edwardsville, IL 62026. Offers MA. *Program availability:* Part-time. *Degree requirements:* For master's, thesis. *Entrance requirements:* For master's, GRE. Additional exam requirements/recommendations for international students: Required—TOEFL (minimum score 550 paper-based, 79 iBT), IELTS (minimum score 6.5), Michigan Test of English Language Proficiency or PTE. Electronic applications accepted.

**Springfield College,** Graduate Programs, Programs in Psychology, Springfield, MA 01109-3797. Offers athletic counseling (MS, CAGS); clinical mental health counseling (M Ed, CAGS); counseling psychology (Psy D); industrial and organizational psychology (M Ed, CAGS); school guidance counseling (M Ed, CAGS); student personnel administration in higher education (M Ed). *Accreditation:* APA. *Program availability:* Part-time. *Degree requirements:* For master's, research project, portfolio; for doctorate, dissertation project, 1500 hours of counseling psychology practicum, full-year internship. *Entrance requirements:* Additional exam requirements/recommendations for international students: Required—TOEFL (minimum score 550 paper-based). Electronic applications accepted. *Expenses:* Tuition: Full-time $29,640; part-time $988 per credit. *Required fees:* $195.

**Teachers College, Columbia University,** Department of Organization and Leadership, New York, NY 10027-6696. Offers adult education guided intensive study (Ed D); adult learning and leadership (Ed M, MA, Ed D); educational leadership (Ed D); higher and postsecondary education (MA, Ed D); leadership, policy and politics (Ed D); nurse executive (MA, Ed D), including administration studies (MA), professional studies (MA); private school leadership (Ed M, MA); public school building leadership (Ed M, MA); social and organizational psychology (MA); urban education leaders (Ed D); MA/MBA. *Program availability:* Part-time, evening/weekend. *Students:* 310 full-time (214 women), 390 part-time (250 women); includes 276 minority (116 Black or African American, non-Hispanic/Latino; 3 American Indian or Alaska Native, non-Hispanic/Latino; 61 Asian, non-Hispanic/Latino; 79 Hispanic/Latino; 17 Two or more races, non-Hispanic/Latino); 93 international. 624 applicants, 57% accepted, 172 enrolled. *Degree requirements:* For doctorate, thesis/dissertation. *Expenses:* Tuition: Full-time $36,288; part-time $1512 per credit. *Required fees:* $438 per semester. One-time fee: $510 full-time. Full-time tuition and fees vary according to course load. *Unit head:* Prof. Anna Neumann, Chair, 212-678-3272, Fax: 212-678-3036, E-mail: neumann@tc.columbia.edu. *Application contact:* David Estrella, Director of Admission, 212-678-3305, E-mail: estrella@tc.columbia.edu.

**Temple University,** College of Education, Department of Psychological Studies in Education, Philadelphia, PA 19122-6096. Offers adult and organizational development (Ed M); counseling psychology (Ed M, PhD), including agency counseling (Ed M), counseling psychology (PhD), school counseling (Ed M); education (PhD); educational leadership (Ed M); educational leadership and policy studies (Ed M, Ed D), including educational leadership; educational psychology (Ed M); school psychology (Ed M, PhD, Ed S); special education (Ed M). *Accreditation:* APA (one or more programs are accredited). *Program availability:* Part-time, evening/weekend. Terminal master's awarded for partial completion of doctoral program. *Degree requirements:* For master's, thesis or alternative; for doctorate, thesis/dissertation. *Entrance requirements:* Additional exam requirements/recommendations for international students: Required—TOEFL (minimum score 550 paper-based; 79 iBT).

**Texas A&M University,** College of Liberal Arts, Department of Psychology, College Station, TX 77843. Offers clinical psychology (PhD); industrial/organizational psychology (PhD); psychology (MS, PhD), including clinical psychology (PhD), industrial/organizational psychology (PhD). *Accreditation:* APA (one or more programs are accredited). *Faculty:* 48. *Students:* 83 full-time (38 women), 14 part-time (10 women); includes 34 minority (7 Black or African American, non-Hispanic/Latino; 4 Asian, non-Hispanic/Latino; 22 Hispanic/Latino; 1 Two or more races, non-Hispanic/Latino), 13 international. Average age 28. 350 applicants, 9% accepted, 22 enrolled. In 2016, 4 master's, 12 doctorates awarded. *Degree requirements:* For doctorate, comprehensive exam (for some programs), thesis/dissertation. *Entrance requirements:* For doctorate, GRE General Test. Additional exam requirements/recommendations for international students: Required—TOEFL (minimum score 550 paper-based; 80 iBT), IELTS (minimum score 6), PTE (minimum score 53). *Application deadline:* For fall admission, 12/1 for domestic and international students. Application fee: $50 ($90 for international students). Electronic applications accepted. *Expenses:* Contact institution. *Financial support:* In 2016–17, 84 students received support, including 20 fellowships with tuition reimbursements available (averaging $15,749 per year), 31 research assistantships with tuition reimbursements available (averaging $6,408 per year), 55 teaching assistantships with tuition reimbursements available (averaging $10,420 per year); career-related internships or fieldwork, institutionally sponsored loans, scholarships/grants, traineeships, health care benefits, tuition waivers (full and partial), and unspecified assistantships also available. Support available to part-time students. Financial award application deadline: 3/15; financial award applicants required to submit FAFSA. *Unit head:* Dr. Heather Lench, Department Head, 979-845-0377, E-mail: hlench@tamu.edu. *Application contact:* Dr. Charles D. Samuelson, Director of Graduate Studies, 979-845-0880, Fax: 979-845-4727, E-mail: c-samuelson@tamu.edu. Website: http://psychology.tamu.edu/

**Touro College,** School of Health Sciences, Bay Shore, NY 11706. Offers industrial-organizational psychology (MS); mental health counseling (MS); occupational therapy (MS); physical therapy (DPT); physician assistant (MS); speech-language pathology (MS). *Faculty:* 81 full-time (55 women), 77 part-time/adjunct (46 women). *Students:* 628 full-time (470 women), 113 part-time (73 women); includes 143 minority (31 Black or African American, non-Hispanic/Latino; 1 American Indian or Alaska Native, non-Hispanic/Latino; 61 Asian, non-Hispanic/Latino; 42 Hispanic/Latino; 1 Native Hawaiian or other Pacific Islander, non-Hispanic/Latino; 7 Two or more races, non-Hispanic/Latino), 63 international. Average age 28. *Expenses:* Contact institution. *Financial support:* Fellowships available. *Unit head:* Dr. Louis Primavera, Dean, School of Health Sciences, 516-673-3200, E-mail: louis.primavera@touro.edu. *Application contact:* Brian J. Diele, Director of Student Administrative Services, 631-665-1600 Ext. 6311, E-mail: brian.diele@touro.edu.

**University at Albany, State University of New York,** College of Arts and Sciences, Department of Psychology, Albany, NY 12222-0001. Offers behavioral neuroscience (PhD); clinical psychology (PhD); cognitive psychology (PhD); industrial/organizational psychology (MA, PhD); social-personality psychology (PhD). *Accreditation:* APA (one or more programs are accredited). *Faculty:* 19 full-time (6 women). *Students:* 68 full-time (42 women), 43 part-time (31 women); includes 26 minority (1 Black or African American, non-Hispanic/Latino; 11 Asian, non-Hispanic/Latino; 9 Hispanic/Latino; 5 Two or more races, non-Hispanic/Latino), 8 international. 304 applicants, 14% accepted, 24 enrolled. In 2016, 7 master's, 11 doctorates awarded. *Degree requirements:* For doctorate, thesis/dissertation. *Entrance requirements:* For doctorate, GRE General Test, GRE Subject Test. Additional exam requirements/recommendations for international students: Required—TOEFL (minimum score 550 paper-based). *Application deadline:* For fall admission, 1/15 for domestic and international students. Application fee: $75. Electronic applications accepted. *Expenses:* Tuition, state resident: full-time $10,870; part-time $453 per credit hour. Tuition, nonresident: full-time $22,210; part-time $925 per credit hour. *International tuition:* $21,550 full-time. *Required fees:* $1864; $96 per credit hour. *Financial support:* Fellowships, research assistantships, teaching assistantships, and career-related internships or fieldwork available. Financial award application deadline: 2/1. *Total annual research expenditures:* $861,900. *Unit head:* James Neely, Chair, 518-442-4820, Fax: 518-442-4867, E-mail: jneely@albany.edu. *Application contact:* Michael DeRensis, Director, Graduate Admissions, 518-442-3980, Fax: 518-442-3922, E-mail: graduate@albany.edu. Website: http://www.albany.edu/psychology/

**The University of Akron,** Graduate School, Buchtel College of Arts and Sciences, Department of Psychology, Program in Industrial/Organizational Psychology, Akron, OH 44325. Offers MA, PhD. *Students:* 34 full-time (17 women), 15 part-time (11 women); includes 10 minority (1 Black or African American, non-Hispanic/Latino; 5 Asian, non-Hispanic/Latino; 2 Hispanic/Latino; 2 Two or more races, non-Hispanic/Latino), 2 international. Average age 26. 107 applicants, 16% accepted, 14 enrolled. In 2016, 17 master's, 3 doctorates awarded. Terminal master's awarded for partial completion of doctoral program. *Degree requirements:* For master's, thesis or specialty exam; for doctorate, one foreign language, comprehensive exam, thesis/dissertation. *Entrance requirements:* For master's, GRE General Test, minimum GPA of 2.75, three letters of recommendation, personal statement, curriculum vitae; for doctorate, GRE General Test, minimum graduate GPA of 3.25, three letters of recommendation, personal statement, curriculum vitae. Additional exam requirements/recommendations for international students: Required—TOEFL (minimum score 550 paper-based; 79 iBT), IELTS (minimum score 6.5). *Application deadline:* For fall admission, 1/15 for domestic and international students. Application fee: $45 ($70 for international students). Electronic applications accepted. *Expenses:* Tuition, state resident: full-time $8618; part-time $359 per credit hour. Tuition, nonresident: full-time $17,149; part-time $715 per credit hour. *Required fees:* $1652. *Faculty research:* Personnel selection, performance management, leadership, self-regulation, affect. *Unit head:* Dr. Paul Levy, Chair, 330-972-8369, E-mail: pelevy@uakron.edu. Website: http://www.uakron.edu/psychology/academics/industrial-organizational-psychology/index.dot

**The University of Alabama in Huntsville,** School of Graduate Studies, College of Arts, Humanities, and Social Sciences, Department of Psychology, Huntsville, AL 35899. Offers industrial/organizational psychology (MA); psychology (MA). *Program availability:* Part-time, evening/weekend. *Degree requirements:* For master's, comprehensive exam, thesis or alternative, oral and written exams. *Entrance requirements:* For master's, GRE General Test, 15 hours of course work in psychology, minimum GPA of 3.25, sample of written work. Additional exam requirements/recommendations for international students: Required—TOEFL (minimum score 500 paper-based; 80 iBT), IELTS (minimum score 6.5). Electronic applications accepted. *Expenses:* Tuition, state resident: full-time $9834; part-time $600 per credit hour. Tuition, nonresident: full-time $21,830; part-time $1325 per credit hour. *Faculty research:* Virtual teams and teamwork, eyewitness identification, aging and memory, psychology of natural disasters and emergency preparedness, pain and pain management research.

**University of Central Florida,** College of Sciences, Department of Psychology, Program in Industrial/Organizational Psychology, Orlando, FL 32816. Offers MS, PhD. *Students:* 52 full-time (33 women), 1 (woman) part-time; includes 13 minority (3 Black or African American, non-Hispanic/Latino; 6 Asian, non-Hispanic/Latino; 4 Hispanic/

Latino), 4 international. Average age 25. 157 applicants, 17% accepted, 14 enrolled. In 2016, 16 master's awarded. *Degree requirements:* For master's, comprehensive exam, thesis, practicum; for doctorate, thesis/dissertation, candidacy examination. *Entrance requirements:* For master's, GRE General Test, minimum GPA of 3.0 in last 60 hours, resume; for doctorate, GRE General Test. Additional exam requirements/recommendations for international students: Required—TOEFL. *Application deadline:* For fall admission, 12/15 for domestic students. Application fee: $30. Electronic applications accepted. *Expenses:* Tuition, state resident: part-time $288.16 per credit hour. Tuition, nonresident: part-time $1071.31 per credit hour. *Financial support:* In 2016–17, 32 students received support, including 9 fellowships (averaging $10,959 per year), 7 research assistantships with partial tuition reimbursements available (averaging $8,299 per year), 22 teaching assistantships with partial tuition reimbursements available (averaging $11,194 per year); career-related internships or fieldwork, Federal Work-Study, institutionally sponsored loans, tuition waivers (partial), and unspecified assistantships also available. Financial award application deadline: 3/1; financial award applicants required to submit FAFSA. *Faculty research:* Sports psychology, electronic selection systems, team training, stress effects, psychometrics. *Unit head:* Dr. Mindy Shoss, Program Director, 407-823-2560, E-mail: mindy.shoss@ucf.edu. *Application contact:* Assistant Director, Graduate Admissions, 407-823-2766, Fax: 407-823-6442, E-mail: gradadmissions@ucf.edu.
Website: http://psychology.cos.ucf.edu/graduate/

**University of Connecticut,** Graduate School, College of Liberal Arts and Sciences, Department of Psychology, Storrs, CT 06269. Offers behavioral neuroscience (PhD); biopsychology (PhD); clinical psychology (MA, PhD); cognition and instruction (PhD); developmental psychology (MA, PhD); ecological psychology (PhD); experimental psychology (PhD); general psychology (MA, PhD); industrial/organizational psychology (PhD); language and cognition (PhD); neuroscience (PhD); social psychology (MA, PhD). *Accreditation:* APA. Terminal master's awarded for partial completion of doctoral program. *Degree requirements:* For master's, comprehensive exam; for doctorate, thesis/dissertation. *Entrance requirements:* For master's and doctorate, GRE General Test, GRE Subject Test. Additional exam requirements/recommendations for international students: Required—TOEFL (minimum score 550 paper-based). Electronic applications accepted.

**University of Detroit Mercy,** College of Liberal Arts and Education, Detroit, MI 48221. Offers addiction counseling (MA); addiction studies (Certificate); clinical mental health counseling (MA); clinical psychology (MA, PhD); computer and information systems (MS); criminal justice (MA); curriculum and instruction (MA); economics (MA); educational administration (MA); financial economics (MA); industrial/organizational psychology (MA); information assurance (MS); intelligence analysis (MA); liberal studies (MALS); religious studies (MA); school counseling (MA, Certificate); school psychology (Spec); security administration (MS); special education: emotionally impaired/behaviorally disordered (MA); special education: learning disabilities (MA). *Program availability:* Part-time, evening/weekend. *Degree requirements:* For doctorate, departmental qualifying exam. *Faculty research:* Psychology of aging, history of technology, Renaissance humanism, U.S. and Japanese economic relations.

**University of Guelph,** Graduate Studies, College of Social and Applied Human Sciences, Department of Psychology, Guelph, ON N1G 2W1, Canada. Offers applied social psychology (MA, PhD); clinical psychology: applied development emphasis (PhD); clinical psychology: applied developmental emphasis (MA); industrial/organizational psychology (MA, PhD); neuroscience and applied cognitive science (MA, PhD). *Degree requirements:* For master's, thesis; for doctorate, comprehensive exam, thesis/dissertation. *Entrance requirements:* For master's, GRE General Test, GRE Subject Test, minimum B+ average during previous 2 years of course work; for doctorate, GRE General Test, GRE Subject Test, minimum A- average. Additional exam requirements/recommendations for international students: Required—TOEFL (minimum score 89 iBT). Electronic applications accepted. *Faculty research:* Organizational psychology, reading comprehension and mathematical ability, drug addiction and relapse, gender issues and culture, memory, clinical psychology.

**University of Houston,** College of Liberal Arts and Social Sciences, Department of Psychology, Houston, TX 77204. Offers clinical psychology (PhD); developmental psychology (PhD); industrial/organizational psychology (PhD); psychology (MA); social psychology (PhD). *Accreditation:* APA (one or more programs are accredited). *Degree requirements:* For master's, comprehensive exam, thesis; for doctorate, comprehensive exam, thesis/dissertation. *Entrance requirements:* For master's, GRE General Test, career statement, 3 letters of recommendation; for doctorate, GRE General Test, 3 letters of recommendation. Additional exam requirements/recommendations for international students: Required—TOEFL (minimum score 550 paper-based; 79 iBT). Electronic applications accepted. *Faculty research:* Health psychology, depression, child/family process, organizational effectiveness, close relationships.

**The University of Manchester,** Alliance Manchester Business School, M15 6PB, United Kingdom. Offers accounting and finance (M Sc); business (M Ent); business analysis and strategic management (M Sc); business analytics: operational research and risk analysis (M Sc); business psychology (M Sc); corporate communications and reputation management (M Sc); finance (M Sc); finance and business economics (M Sc); human resource management and industrial relations (M Sc); innovation management and entrepreneurship (M Sc); international business and management (M Sc); international human resource management and comparative industrial relations (M Sc); management (M Sc); marketing (M Sc); operations, project and supply chain management (M Sc); organizational psychology (M Sc); quantitative finance (M Sc). *Entrance requirements:* For master's, UK 2:1 honours degree or overseas equivalent. Additional exam requirements/recommendations for international students: Required—TOEFL (minimum score 100 iBT), IELTS (minimum score 7), PTE. Electronic applications accepted. *Faculty research:* Accounting and finance, management sciences and marketing, people management and organization, innovation management and policy, decision sciences.

**University of Maryland, Baltimore County,** The Graduate School, College of Arts, Humanities and Social Sciences, Department of Psychology, Program in Industrial/Organizational Psychology, Rockville, MD 20850. Offers MPS. *Program availability:* Part-time, evening/weekend. *Faculty:* 1 full-time (0 women), 15 part-time/adjunct (5 women). *Students:* 18 full-time (15 women), 64 part-time (45 women); includes 36 minority (15 Black or African American, non-Hispanic/Latino; 6 Asian, non-Hispanic/Latino; 7 Hispanic/Latino; 2 Native Hawaiian or other Pacific Islander, non-Hispanic/Latino; 6 Two or more races, non-Hispanic/Latino), 2 international. Average age 28. 132 applicants, 45% accepted, 30 enrolled. In 2016, 34 master's awarded. *Entrance requirements:* Additional exam requirements/recommendations for international students: Required—TOEFL (minimum score 80 iBT), IELTS (minimum score 6.5). *Application deadline:* For fall admission, 3/1 for domestic students, 1/1 for international students. Applications are processed on a rolling basis. Application fee: $50. Electronic applications accepted. *Expenses:* Contact institution. *Financial support:* In 2016–17, 1 teaching assistantship with full tuition reimbursement (averaging $14,000 per year) was awarded. *Faculty research:* Organizations, human factors, group dynamics, change management. *Unit head:* Dr. Elliot Lasson, Program Director, 301-738-6171, E-mail: elasson@umbc.edu. *Application contact:* Rickeysha Jones, Program Coordinator, 301-

738-6285, E-mail: rcjones@umbc.edu.
Website: http://www.umbc.edu/shadygrove/io/

**University of Maryland, College Park,** Academic Affairs, College of Behavioral and Social Sciences, Department of Psychology, College Park, MD 20742. Offers clinical psychology (PhD); developmental psychology (PhD); experimental psychology (PhD); industrial psychology (MA, MS, PhD); social psychology (PhD). *Accreditation:* APA (one or more programs are accredited). *Degree requirements:* For master's, thesis; for doctorate, variable foreign language requirement, comprehensive exam, thesis/dissertation. *Entrance requirements:* For master's and doctorate, GRE General Test, GRE Subject Test, minimum GPA of 3.5, research and/or work experience, 3 letters of recommendation. Electronic applications accepted. *Faculty research:* Social stereotyping and prejudice, anxiety disorders, auditory neuroethology, counseling and social psychology.

**University of Minnesota, Twin Cities Campus,** Graduate School, College of Liberal Arts, Department of Psychology, Program in Industrial/Organizational Psychology, Minneapolis, MN 55455-0213. Offers PhD. *Degree requirements:* For doctorate, comprehensive exam, thesis/dissertation. *Entrance requirements:* For doctorate, GRE General Test, GRE Subject Test (recommended), 12 credits of upper-level psychology courses, including a course in statistics or psychological measurement. Additional exam requirements/recommendations for international students: Required—TOEFL (minimum score 550 paper-based; 79 iBT).

**University of Missouri–St. Louis,** College of Arts and Sciences, Department of Psychological Sciences, St. Louis, MO 63121. Offers behavioral neuroscience (MA, PhD); clinical psychology (PhD); clinical psychology respecialization (Certificate); industrial/organizational psychology (MA, PhD); trauma studies (Certificate). *Accreditation:* APA (one or more programs are accredited). *Program availability:* Evening/weekend. *Faculty:* 1 full-time (0 women). *Students:* 73 full-time (54 women), 13 part-time (9 women); includes 13 minority (4 Black or African American, non-Hispanic/Latino; 2 Asian, non-Hispanic/Latino; 6 Hispanic/Latino; 1 Two or more races, non-Hispanic/Latino), 3 international. Average age 27. 235 applicants, 8% accepted, 18 enrolled. Terminal master's awarded for partial completion of doctoral program. *Degree requirements:* For master's, thesis; for doctorate, thesis/dissertation. *Entrance requirements:* For master's, GRE General Test, 3 letters of recommendation; for doctorate, GRE General Test, GRE Subject Test, 3 letters of recommendation. Additional exam requirements/recommendations for international students: Required—TOEFL (minimum score 550 paper-based; 79 iBT), IELTS (minimum score 6.5). *Application deadline:* For fall admission, 12/15 for domestic and international students. Application fee: $50 ($40 for international students). Electronic applications accepted. *Financial support:* Fellowships with full tuition reimbursements, research assistantships with tuition reimbursements, teaching assistantships with tuition reimbursements, and scholarships/grants available. Financial award applicants required to submit FAFSA. *Faculty research:* Bereavement and loss, neuroscience, post-traumatic stress disorder, conflict and negotiation, social psychology. *Unit head:* Michael G. Griffin, Chair, 314-516-5391, Fax: 314-516-5392, E-mail: michael_griffin@umsl.edu. *Application contact:* 314-516-5458, Fax: 314-516-6996, E-mail: gradadm@umsl.edu.
Website: http://www.umsl.edu/divisions/artscience/psychology/

**University of Nebraska at Omaha,** Graduate Studies, College of Arts and Sciences, Department of Psychology, Omaha, NE 68182. Offers applied behavior analysis (Certificate); human resources and training (Certificate); industrial/organizational psychology (MS); psychology (MA, PhD); school psychology (MS, Ed S). *Program availability:* Part-time. *Faculty:* 10 full-time (1 woman). *Students:* 70 full-time (52 women), 49 part-time (33 women); includes 9 minority (2 Asian, non-Hispanic/Latino; 5 Hispanic/Latino; 2 Two or more races, non-Hispanic/Latino), 1 international. Average age 27. 157 applicants, 25% accepted, 38 enrolled. In 2016, 32 master's, 6 doctorates, 10 other advanced degrees awarded. *Degree requirements:* For master's, comprehensive exam, thesis (for some programs); for doctorate, comprehensive exam, thesis/dissertation. *Entrance requirements:* For master's and doctorate, GRE, minimum GPA of 3.0, official transcripts, 3 letters of recommendation, statement of purpose, writing sample, resume. Additional exam requirements/recommendations for international students: Required—TOEFL, IELTS, PTE. *Application deadline:* For fall admission, 1/5 priority date for domestic and international students. Application fee: $45. Electronic applications accepted. *Financial support:* In 2016–17, 50 students received support, including 23 research assistantships with tuition reimbursements available, 27 teaching assistantships with tuition reimbursements available; fellowships with tuition reimbursements available, career-related internships or fieldwork, Federal Work-Study, institutionally sponsored loans, scholarships/grants, health care benefits, tuition waivers (partial), and unspecified assistantships also available. Financial award application deadline: 3/1; financial award applicants required to submit FAFSA. *Unit head:* Dr. Brigette Ryalls, Chairperson, 402-554-2341, E-mail: graduate@unomaha.edu. *Application contact:* Dr. Joseph Brown, Graduate Program Chair, 402-554-2341, E-mail: graduate@unomaha.edu.

**University of New Haven,** Graduate School, College of Arts and Sciences, Program in Industrial and Organizational Psychology, West Haven, CT 06516. Offers conflict management (MA); industrial organizational psychology (MA); industrial-human resources psychology (MA); organizational development and consultation (MA); psychology of conflict management (Graduate Certificate). *Program availability:* Part-time, evening/weekend. *Students:* 72 full-time (49 women), 18 part-time (12 women); includes 20 minority (10 Black or African American, non-Hispanic/Latino; 1 American Indian or Alaska Native, non-Hispanic/Latino; 6 Asian, non-Hispanic/Latino; 2 Hispanic/Latino; 1 Two or more races, non-Hispanic/Latino), 4 international. Average age 26. 117 applicants, 84% accepted, 34 enrolled. In 2016, 59 master's awarded. *Degree requirements:* For master's, thesis or alternative, internship or practicum. *Entrance requirements:* Additional exam requirements/recommendations for international students: Required—TOEFL (minimum score 80 iBT), IELTS, PTE. *Application deadline:* Applications are processed on a rolling basis. Application fee: $50. Electronic applications accepted. Application fee is waived when completed online. *Expenses:* Contact institution. *Financial support:* Research assistantships with partial tuition reimbursements, teaching assistantships with partial tuition reimbursements, career-related internships or fieldwork, Federal Work-Study, scholarships/grants, and unspecified assistantships available. Support available to part-time students. Financial award applicants required to submit FAFSA. *Unit head:* Dr. Eric Marcus, Coordinator, 203-932-1242, E-mail: emarcus@newhaven.edu. *Application contact:* Michelle Mason, Director of Graduate Enrollment, 203-932-7067.
Website: http://www.newhaven.edu/4730/

**The University of North Carolina at Charlotte,** College of Liberal Arts and Sciences, Department of Psychology, Charlotte, NC 28223-0001. Offers cognitive science (Graduate Certificate); health psychology (PhD); industrial/organizational psychology (MA); psychology (MA). *Accreditation:* APA. *Program availability:* Part-time. *Faculty:* 32 full-time (21 women), 1 (woman) part-time/adjunct. *Students:* 37 full-time (32 women), 38 part-time (26 women); includes 19 minority (7 Black or African American, non-Hispanic/Latino; 1 Asian, non-Hispanic/Latino; 8 Hispanic/Latino; 3 Two or more races, non-Hispanic/Latino). Average age 28. 331 applicants, 16% accepted, 28 enrolled. In 2016, 13 master's, 5 doctorates, 3 other advanced degrees awarded. *Degree*

## Industrial and Organizational Psychology

*requirements:* For master's, thesis (for some programs); for doctorate, comprehensive exam, thesis/dissertation, internship (clinical health students only). *Entrance requirements:* For master's, GRE, GMAT, MAT; for doctorate, GRE, at least 18 hours of coursework in psychology including introductory psychology and research methods, undergraduate course in statistics, transcripts of all academic work attempted since high school including evidence of the completion of a bachelor's degree, at least three references, personal statement, resume or curriculum vitae; for Graduate Certificate, enrolled and in good standing in a graduate degree program at UNC Charlotte, or have minimum GPA of 3.0 for undergraduate courses. Additional exam requirements/recommendations for international students: Required—TOEFL (minimum score 523 paper-based, 70 iBT) or IELTS (6.5). *Application deadline:* For fall admission, 11/15 for domestic and international students. Applications are processed on a rolling basis. Application fee: $75. Electronic applications accepted. *Expenses:* Contact institution. *Financial support:* In 2016–17, 30 students received support, including 1 fellowship (averaging $42,000 per year), 11 research assistantships (averaging $15,622 per year), 18 teaching assistantships (averaging $14,000 per year); career-related internships or fieldwork, Federal Work-Study, institutionally sponsored loans, scholarships/grants, and unspecified assistantships also available. Support available to part-time students. Financial award application deadline: 3/1; financial award applicants required to submit FAFSA. *Total annual research expenditures:* $218,743. *Unit head:* Dr. Fary Cachelin, Chair, 704-687-1315, E-mail: fcacheli@uncc.edu. *Application contact:* Kathy B. Giddings, Director of Graduate Admissions, 704-687-5503, Fax: 704-687-1668, E-mail: gradadm@uncc.edu.
Website: http://psych.uncc.edu

**University of Oklahoma,** College of Arts and Sciences, Department of Psychology, Program in Psychology, Norman, OK 73019. Offers industrial organizational psychology (MS, PhD); psychology (MS, PhD). *Students:* 79 full-time (43 women), 8 part-time (6 women); includes 19 minority (1 Black or African American, non-Hispanic/Latino; 2 American Indian or Alaska Native, non-Hispanic/Latino; 7 Asian, non-Hispanic/Latino; 5 Hispanic/Latino; 4 Two or more races, non-Hispanic/Latino), 4 international. Average age 26. 110 applicants, 10% accepted, 13 enrolled. In 2016, 8 master's, 13 doctorates awarded. Terminal master's awarded for partial completion of doctoral program. *Degree requirements:* For master's, comprehensive exam, thesis; for doctorate, comprehensive exam, thesis/dissertation. *Entrance requirements:* For master's and doctorate, GRE. Additional exam requirements/recommendations for international students: Required—TOEFL (minimum score 79 iBT) or IELTS (minimum score 6.5). *Application deadline:* For fall admission, 1/1 for domestic and international students. Application fee: $50 ($100 for international students). Electronic applications accepted. *Expenses:* Tuition, state resident: full-time $4886; part-time $203.60 per credit hour. Tuition, nonresident: full-time $18,989; part-time $791.20 per credit hour. *Required fees:* $3283; $126.25 per credit hour. $126.50 per semester. *Financial support:* In 2016–17, 58 students received support. Fellowships, research assistantships with full tuition reimbursements available, teaching assistantships with full tuition reimbursements available, and health care benefits available. Financial award application deadline: 6/1; financial award applicants required to submit FAFSA. *Faculty research:* Ethics in organizations, creativity in the workplace, organizational design and development, complex skill acquisition, performance feedback. *Unit head:* Dr. Eric Day, Chair, 405-325-4511, Fax: 405-325-4737, E-mail: eday@ou.edu. *Application contact:* Kathryn Paine, Graduate Student Coordinator, 405-325-4512, Fax: 405-325-4737, E-mail: kpaine@ou.edu.
Website: http://www.ou.edu/psychology

**University of Phoenix–Online Campus,** College of Social Science, Phoenix, AZ 85034-7209. Offers mediation (Certificate); psychology (MS), including behavioral health, industrial-organizational, psychology. *Program availability:* Evening/weekend, online learning. *Entrance requirements:* Additional exam requirements/recommendations for international students: Required—TOEFL, TOEIC (Test of English as an International Communication), Berlitz Online English Proficiency Exam, PTE, or IELTS. Electronic applications accepted. *Expenses:* Contact institution.

**University of Phoenix–Online Campus,** School of Advanced Studies, Phoenix, AZ 85034-7209. Offers business administration (DBA); education (Ed S); educational leadership (Ed D), including curriculum and instruction, education technology, educational leadership; health administration (DHA); higher education administration (PhD); industrial/organizational psychology (PhD); nursing (PhD); organizational leadership (DM), including information systems and technology, organizational leadership. *Program availability:* Evening/weekend, online learning. *Degree requirements:* For doctorate, thesis/dissertation. *Entrance requirements:* Additional exam requirements/recommendations for international students: Required—TOEFL, TOEIC (Test of English as an International Communication), Berlitz Online English Proficiency Exam, PTE, or IELTS. Electronic applications accepted. *Expenses:* Contact institution.

**University of Phoenix–Washington D.C. Campus,** College of Social Sciences, Washington, DC 20001. Offers industrial/organizational psychology (PhD); psychology (MS).

**University of Puerto Rico, Río Piedras Campus,** College of Social Sciences, Department of Psychology, San Juan, PR 00931-3300. Offers clinical psychology (MA); industrial organizational psychology (MA); investigative academic psychology (MA); psychology (PhD); social-community psychology (MA). *Program availability:* Part-time. *Degree requirements:* For master's, comprehensive exam, thesis; for doctorate, comprehensive exam, thesis/dissertation, internship. *Entrance requirements:* For master's, GRE or PAEG, interview, minimum GPA of 3.0; for doctorate, GRE or PAEG, interview, master's degree, minimum GPA of 3.0. *Faculty research:* Intervention on depressed Latino youth, biopsychosocial training.

**University of South Africa,** College of Economic and Management Sciences, Pretoria, South Africa. Offers accounting (D Admin, D Com); accounting science (DA); auditing (D Admin, D Com); business administration (M Tech); business economics (D Admin); business leadership (DBL); business management (D Admin, D Com); economic management analysis (M Tech); economics (D Admin, D Com, PhD); human resource development (M Tech); industrial psychology (D Admin, D Com, PhD); logistics (D Com); marketing (M Tech); public administration (D Admin, D Com, DPA, PhD); public management (M Tech); quantitative management (D Admin, D Com); real estate (M Tech); statistics (D Admin, PhD); tourism management (D Admin, D Com); transport economics (D Admin, D Com).

**University of South Africa,** College of Human Sciences, Pretoria, South Africa. Offers adult education (M Ed); African languages (MA, PhD); African politics (MA, PhD); Afrikaans (MA, PhD); ancient history (MA, PhD); ancient Near Eastern studies (MA, PhD); anthropology (MA, PhD); applied linguistics (MA); Arabic (MA, PhD); archaeology (MA); art history (MA); Biblical archaeology (MA); Biblical studies (M Th, D Th, PhD); Christian spirituality (M Th, D Th); church history (M Th, D Th); classical studies (MA, PhD); clinical psychology (MA); communication (MA, PhD); comparative education (M Ed, Ed D); consulting psychology (D Admin, D Com, PhD); curriculum studies (M Ed, Ed D); development studies (M Admin, MA, D Admin, PhD); didactics (M Ed, Ed D); education (M Tech); education management (M Ed, Ed D); educational psychology (M Ed); English (MA); environmental education (M Ed); French (MA, PhD); German (MA, PhD); Greek (MA); guidance and counseling (M Ed); health studies (MA, PhD);

including health sciences education (MA), health services management (MA), medical and surgical nursing science (critical care general) (MA), midwifery and neonatal nursing science (MA), trauma and emergency care (MA); history (MA, PhD); history of education (Ed D); inclusive education (M Ed, Ed D); information and communications technology policy and regulation (MA); information science (MA, MIS, PhD); international politics (MA, PhD); Islamic studies (MA, PhD); Italian (MA, PhD); Judaica (MA, PhD); linguistics (MA, PhD); mathematical education (M Ed); mathematics education (MA); missiology (M Th, D Th); modern Hebrew (MA, PhD); musicology (MA, MMus, D Mus, PhD); natural science education (M Ed); New Testament (M Th, D Th); Old Testament (D Th); pastoral therapy (M Th, D Th); philosophy (MA); philosophy of education (M Ed, Ed D); politics (MA, PhD); Portuguese (MA, PhD); practical theology (M Th, D Th); psychology (MA, MS, PhD); psychology of education (M Ed, Ed D); public health (MA); religious studies (MA, D Th, PhD); Romance languages (MA); Russian (MA, PhD); Semitic languages (MA, PhD); social behavior studies in HIV/AIDS (MA); social science (mental health) (MA); social science in development studies (MA); social science in psychology (MA); social science in social work (MA); social science in sociology (MA); social work (MSW, DSW, PhD); socio-education (M Ed, Ed D); sociolinguistics (MA); sociology (MA, PhD); Spanish (MA, PhD); systematic theology (M Th, D Th); TESOL (teaching English to speakers of other languages) (MA); theological ethics (M Th, D Th); theory of literature (MA, PhD); urban ministries (D Th); urban ministry (M Th).

**University of South Florida,** College of Arts and Sciences, Department of Psychology, Tampa, FL 33620-9951. Offers psychology (PhD), including clinical psychology, cognition, neuroscience and social psychology, industrial-organizational psychology. *Accreditation:* APA. *Faculty:* 34 full-time (14 women). *Students:* 83 full-time (57 women), 19 part-time (13 women); includes 16 minority (1 Black or African American, non-Hispanic/Latino; 5 Asian, non-Hispanic/Latino; 7 Hispanic/Latino; 3 Two or more races, non-Hispanic/Latino), 9 international. Average age 28. 467 applicants, 3% accepted, 14 enrolled. In 2016, 12 doctorates awarded. *Degree requirements:* For doctorate, comprehensive exam, thesis/dissertation, internship. *Entrance requirements:* For doctorate, GRE General Test, minimum upper-division GPA of 3.4, three letters of recommendation, personal goals statement. Additional exam requirements/recommendations for international students: Required—TOEFL (minimum score 550 paper-based; 79 iBT) or IELTS (minimum score 6.5). *Application deadline:* For fall admission, 12/1 for domestic and international students. Application fee: $30. Electronic applications accepted. *Expenses:* Contact institution. *Financial support:* In 2016–17, 48 students received support, including 18 research assistantships with tuition reimbursements available (averaging $14,727 per year), 57 teaching assistantships with tuition reimbursements available (averaging $14,543 per year); tuition waivers (partial) and unspecified assistantships also available. Financial award applicants required to submit FAFSA. *Faculty research:* Clinical, cognitive, neuroscience, social, and industrial/organizational. *Total annual research expenditures:* $2.1 million. *Unit head:* Dr. Toru Shimizu, Chairperson, 813-974-0352, Fax: 813-974-4617, E-mail: shimizu@usf.edu. *Application contact:* Dr. Joseph Vandello, Associate Professor and Graduate Program Director, 813-974-0362, Fax: 813-974-4617, E-mail: vandello@usf.edu.
Website: http://psychology.usf.edu/

**The University of Tennessee,** Graduate School, College of Business Administration, Program in Industrial and Organizational Psychology, Knoxville, TN 37996. Offers PhD. *Degree requirements:* For doctorate, thesis/dissertation. *Entrance requirements:* For doctorate, GRE General Test, minimum GPA of 2.7. Additional exam requirements/recommendations for international students: Required—TOEFL. Electronic applications accepted.

**The University of Tennessee at Chattanooga,** Program in Psychology, Chattanooga, TN 37403. Offers industrial/organizational psychology (MS); research psychology (MS). *Program availability:* Part-time. *Faculty:* 13 full-time (6 women), 1 part-time/adjunct (0 women). *Students:* 41 full-time (25 women), 7 part-time (3 women); includes 5 minority (2 Black or African American, non-Hispanic/Latino; 1 Hispanic/Latino; 2 Two or more races, non-Hispanic/Latino). Average age 26. 99 applicants, 29% accepted, 25 enrolled. In 2016, 21 master's awarded. *Degree requirements:* For master's, comprehensive exam (for some programs), thesis (for some programs), practicum (industrial/organizational psychology). *Entrance requirements:* For master's, GRE General Test, minimum GPA of 2.5 on all undergraduate coursework or 3.0 in senior year. Additional exam requirements/recommendations for international students: Required—TOEFL (minimum score 550 paper-based; 79 iBT), IELTS (minimum score 6). *Application deadline:* For fall admission, 6/15 priority date for domestic students, 7/1 for international students; for spring admission, 11/1 priority date for domestic students, 11/1 for international students. Applications are processed on a rolling basis. Application fee: $35 ($40 for international students). Electronic applications accepted. *Expenses:* $9,876 full-time in-state; $25,994 full-time out-of-state; $450 per credit part-time in-state; $1,345 per credit part-time out-of-state. *Financial support:* In 2016–17, 23 research assistantships, 1 teaching assistantship were awarded; career-related internships or fieldwork, scholarships/grants, and unspecified assistantships also available. Support available to part-time students. Financial award application deadline: 7/1; financial award applicants required to submit FAFSA. *Faculty research:* Decision processes, philosophical psychology, memory, social cognition, employee selection. *Total annual research expenditures:* $8,500. *Unit head:* Dr. Brian O'Leary, Department Head, 423-425-4283, Fax: 423-425-4284, E-mail: brian-o'leary@utc.edu. *Application contact:* Dr. Joanne Romagni, Dean of the Graduate School, 423-425-4478, Fax: 423-425-5223, E-mail: joanne-romagni@utc.edu.
Website: http://www.utc.edu/psychology/

**The University of Texas at Arlington,** Graduate School, College of Science, Department of Psychology, Arlington, TX 76019. Offers experimental health psychology (PhD); experimental psychology (MS, PhD); health/neuroscience psychology (MS, PhD); industrial and organizational psychology (MS). *Program availability:* Part-time. Terminal master's awarded for partial completion of doctoral program. *Degree requirements:* For master's, comprehensive exam or thesis; for doctorate, thesis/dissertation (for some programs). *Entrance requirements:* For master's and doctorate, GRE General Test, minimum GPA of 3.0 in last 60 hours of course work. Additional exam requirements/recommendations for international students: Required—TOEFL (minimum score 550 paper-based). *Application deadline:* For fall admission, 6/15 for domestic students. Applications are processed on a rolling basis. Application fee: $50. *Financial support:* Fellowships, research assistantships with partial tuition reimbursements, teaching assistantships with partial tuition reimbursements, career-related internships or fieldwork, Federal Work-Study, institutionally sponsored loans, scholarships/grants, traineeships, and unspecified assistantships available. Financial award application deadline: 6/1; financial award applicants required to submit FAFSA. *Unit head:* Dr. Robert Gatchel, Professor/Chair, 817-272-2281, Fax: 817-272-2364, E-mail: gatchel@uta.edu. *Application contact:* Dr. Jared Kenworthy, Graduate Advisor, Psychological Sciences, 817-272-2281, Fax: 817-272-2364, E-mail: kenworthy@uta.edu.
Website: http://www.uta.edu/psychology/

**The University of Tulsa,** Graduate School, Kendall College of Arts and Sciences, Department of Psychology, Program in Industrial/Organizational Psychology, Tulsa, OK 74104-3189. Offers MA, PhD, JD/MA. *Program availability:* Part-time. *Faculty:* 5 full-time

(2 women). *Students:* 16 full-time (10 women), 2 part-time (1 woman); includes 7 minority (4 Asian, non-Hispanic/Latino; 2 Hispanic/Latino; 1 Two or more races, non-Hispanic/Latino), 1 international. Average age 25. 37 applicants, 32% accepted, 5 enrolled. In 2016, 7 master's, 2 doctorates awarded. Terminal master's awarded for partial completion of doctoral program. *Degree requirements:* For master's, comprehensive exam, thesis (for some programs), 200-hour internship; for doctorate, comprehensive exam, thesis/dissertation. *Entrance requirements:* For master's and doctorate, GRE General Test. Additional exam requirements/recommendations for international students: Required—TOEFL (minimum score 577 paper-based; 91 iBT), IELTS (minimum score 6.5). *Application deadline:* For fall admission, 12/15 for domestic and international students. Application fee: $55. Electronic applications accepted. *Expenses:* Tuition: Full-time $22,230; part-time $1235 per credit hour. *Required fees:* $990 per semester. Tuition and fees vary according to course load. *Financial support:* In 2016–17, 23 students received support, including 5 fellowships with full tuition reimbursements available (averaging $6,644 per year), 9 teaching assistantships with full tuition reimbursements available (averaging $13,627 per year); research assistantships with full tuition reimbursements available, career-related internships or fieldwork, Federal Work-Study, scholarships/grants, health care benefits, tuition waivers (full and partial), and unspecified assistantships also available. Support available to part-time students. Financial award application deadline: 2/1; financial award applicants required to submit FAFSA. *Faculty research:* Personnel testing and selection, training, performance appraisal, organizational development, job attitudes and motivation, leadership. *Unit head:* Dr. Robert Tett, Director, 918-631-2737, Fax: 918-631-2833, E-mail: robert-tett@utulsa.edu. *Application contact:* Information Contact, 800-882-4723, E-mail: grad@utulsa.edu.

**University of West Florida,** College of Arts, Social Sciences, and Humanities, Department of Psychology, Pensacola, FL 32514-5750. Offers applied experimental (MA); counseling (MA); industrial-organizational (MA). *Program availability:* Part-time. *Degree requirements:* For master's, thesis (for some programs). *Entrance requirements:* For master's, GRE, official transcripts; minimum GPA of 3.0; writing sample; three letters of reference; field experience or skill sets; oral interview (for counseling specialization). Additional exam requirements/recommendations for international students: Required—TOEFL (minimum score 550 paper-based). *Application deadline:* For fall admission, 6/1 for domestic and international students; for spring admission, 10/1 for domestic and international students. Applications are processed on a rolling basis. Application fee: $30. *Expenses:* Tuition, state resident: full-time $5316.12. Tuition, nonresident: full-time $11,308. *Required fees:* $583.92. Tuition and fees vary according to course load and program. *Financial support:* Fellowships with partial tuition reimbursements, research assistantships with partial tuition reimbursements, teaching assistantships with partial tuition reimbursements, career-related internships or fieldwork, and unspecified assistantships available. Financial award application deadline: 4/15; financial award applicants required to submit FAFSA. *Faculty research:* Prose recall, brain imaging, peak performance, biofeedback and pain control, comparable worth. *Unit head:* Dr. Robert Belter, Interim Department Chair, 850-474-2791, E-mail: rbelter@uwf.edu. *Application contact:* Dr. Robert Belter, Interim Department Chair, 850-474-2791, E-mail: rbelter@uwf.edu.
Website: http://www.uwf.edu/psychology/

**University of Wisconsin–Oshkosh,** Graduate Studies, College of Letters and Science, Department of Psychology, Oshkosh, WI 54901. Offers experimental psychology (MS); industrial/organizational psychology (MS). *Degree requirements:* For master's, thesis. *Entrance requirements:* For master's, GRE, 10 semester hours of undergraduate course work in psychology. Additional exam requirements/recommendations for international students: Required—TOEFL (minimum score 550 paper-based; 79 iBT). Electronic applications accepted. *Faculty research:* Performance evaluation, training, biological bases of behavior, tactile perception, aging.

**Walden University,** Graduate Programs, School of Psychology, Minneapolis, MN 55401. Offers clinical psychology (MS), including counseling, general program; forensic psychology (MS), including forensic psychology in the community, general program, mental health applications, program planning and evaluation in forensic settings, psychology and legal systems; industrial organizational (MS, PhD), including consulting psychology, forensic (MS), forensic psychology (PhD), general practice, leadership development and coaching (MS), organizational diversity and social change, research evaluation (PhD); online teaching in psychology (Post-Master's Certificate); organizational psychology and development (Postbaccalaureate Certificate); psychology (MS, PhD), including applied psychology (MS), clinical psychology (PhD), crisis management and response (MS), educational psychology, forensic psychology (PhD), general psychology (MS), general psychology research (PhD), general psychology teaching (PhD), health psychology, leadership development and coaching (MS), psychology of culture (MS), psychology, public administration, and social change (MS), social psychology, terrorism and security (MS); psychology respecialization (Post-Doctoral Certificate). *Program availability:* Part-time, evening/weekend, online only, 100% online. Terminal master's awarded for partial completion of doctoral program. *Degree requirements:* For master's, thesis optional; for doctorate, thesis/dissertation, residency. *Entrance requirements:* For master's, bachelor's degree or higher; minimum GPA of 2.5; official transcripts; goal statement (for some programs); access to computer and Internet; for doctorate, master's degree or higher; three years of related professional or academic experience (preferred); minimum GPA of 3.0; goal statement and current resume (for select programs); official transcripts; access to computer and Internet; for other advanced degree, relevant work experience; access to computer and Internet. Additional exam requirements/recommendations for international students: Required—TOEFL (minimum score 550 paper-based, 79 iBT), IELTS (minimum score 6.5), Michigan English Language Assessment Battery (minimum score 82), or PTE (minimum score 53). Electronic applications accepted.

**Wayne State University,** College of Liberal Arts and Sciences, Department of Psychology, Detroit, MI 48202. Offers behavioral and cognitive neuroscience (PhD); clinical psychology (PhD); cognitive, developmental and social psychology (PhD); industrial/organizational psychology (MA, PhD). Doctoral program admits for fall only. *Accreditation:* APA (one or more programs are accredited). *Faculty:* 36. *Students:* 98 full-time (65 women), 31 part-time (16 women); includes 19 minority (4 Black or African American, non-Hispanic/Latino; 2 Asian, non-Hispanic/Latino; 8 Hispanic/Latino; 5 Two or more races, non-Hispanic/Latino), 14 international. Average age 28. 478 applicants, 13% accepted, 33 enrolled. In 2016, 16 master's, 13 doctorates awarded. Terminal master's awarded for partial completion of doctoral program. *Degree requirements:* For master's, thesis (for some programs); for doctorate, thesis/dissertation, training assignments. *Entrance requirements:* For master's, GRE General Test, minimum undergraduate upper-division cumulative GPA of 3.0, courses in introductory psychology and statistics, two letters of recommendation, professional statement; for doctorate, GRE General Test, bachelor's, master's, or other advanced degree; at least twelve credits in psychology with minimum GPA of 3.0; courses in laboratory psychology and statistical methods in psychology; at least three letters of recommendation; statement of purpose. Additional exam requirements/recommendations for international

students: Required—TOEFL (minimum score 550 paper-based; 79 iBT), TWE (minimum score 5.5), Michigan English Language Assessment Battery (minimum score 85); Recommended—IELTS (minimum score 6.5). Application fee: $50. Electronic applications accepted. *Expenses:* $16,503 per year resident tuition and fees, $33,697 per year non-resident tuition and fees. *Financial support:* In 2016–17, 90 students received support, including 12 fellowships with tuition reimbursements available (averaging $15,719 per year), 6 research assistantships with tuition reimbursements available (averaging $19,341 per year), 50 teaching assistantships with tuition reimbursements available (averaging $17,994 per year); scholarships/grants, health care benefits, and unspecified assistantships also available. Financial award applicants required to submit FAFSA. *Faculty research:* Behavioral neuroscience, cognitive/neuroscience of development and aging research, children, adolescents, and family research, cognition research, emotion research, health psychology research, homelessness and poverty research, memory research, neuropsychology research, personality/cognition, relationships research, substance use and abuse research, workplace adaptation, well-being and evaluation research. *Total annual research expenditures:* $1.4 million. *Unit head:* Boris Baltes, PhD, Chair/Professor, 313-577-2803, E-mail: b.baltes@wayne.edu. *Application contact:* Alia Allen, Academic Services Officer, 313-577-2823, E-mail: aallen@wayne.edu.
Website: http://clas.wayne.edu/psychology/

**West Chester University of Pennsylvania,** College of the Sciences and Mathematics, Department of Psychology, West Chester, PA 19383. Offers clinical psychology (Psy D); industrial/organizational psychology (Certificate); psychology (MA), including general psychology, industrial/organizational psychology. *Program availability:* Part-time, evening/weekend. *Faculty:* 13 full-time (11 women), 6 part-time/adjunct (5 women). *Students:* 76 full-time (55 women), 20 part-time (14 women); includes 21 minority (10 Black or African American, non-Hispanic/Latino; 1 Asian, non-Hispanic/Latino; 5 Hispanic/Latino; 5 Two or more races, non-Hispanic/Latino), 1 international. Average age 28. 122 applicants, 58% accepted, 35 enrolled. In 2016, 33 master's awarded. *Degree requirements:* For master's, comprehensive exam, thesis (for some programs). *Entrance requirements:* For master's, GRE General Test, minimum GPA of 3.0 overall, psychology 3.25; three letters of reference; for doctorate, GRE General Test, minimum GPA of 3.0 overall, psychology 3.25; three letters of reference; successful completion of psychology courses at the undergraduate and graduate level in abnormal/clinical psychology, research methods, and statistics; personal goals statement. Additional exam requirements/recommendations for international students: Required—TOEFL or IELTS. *Application deadline:* For fall admission, 5/15 for international students; for spring admission, 10/15 for international students. Applications are processed on a rolling basis. Application fee: $50. Electronic applications accepted. *Expenses:* Tuition, state resident: full-time $8694; part-time $483 per credit. Tuition, nonresident: full-time $13,050; part-time $725 per credit. *Required fees:* $2399; $119.05 per credit. Tuition and fees vary according to campus/location and program. *Financial support:* Scholarships/grants and unspecified assistantships available. Financial award application deadline: 2/15; financial award applicants required to submit FAFSA. *Faculty research:* Stress, coping, and resilience; preventative interventions; workplace stress; organizational leadership; eating disorders; schizophrenia; several other areas including diversity, cognition, and animal behavior. *Unit head:* Dr. Sandra Kerr, Interim Chairperson, 610-436-2945, E-mail: skerr@wcupa.edu. *Application contact:* Dr. Angela Clarke, Graduate Coordinator, 610-436-3136, E-mail: aclarke@wcupa.edu.
Website: http://www.wcupa.edu/sciences-mathematics/psychology/

**Western Kentucky University,** Graduate Studies, College of Education and Behavioral Sciences, Department of Psychology, Bowling Green, KY 42101. Offers clinical psychology (MA); experimental psychology (MA); general psychology (MA); industrial/organizational psychology (MA); school psychology (Ed S). *Degree requirements:* For master's, comprehensive exam, thesis (for some programs); for Ed S, thesis, oral exam. *Entrance requirements:* For master's, GRE General Test; for Ed S, GRE General Test, minimum GPA of 3.5. Additional exam requirements/recommendations for international students: Required—TOEFL (minimum score 555 paper-based; 79 iBT). *Faculty research:* Neural regeneration, enhancing mobility in the elderly, improvement in visual processing in older adults, lifespan development.

**Western Michigan University,** Graduate College, College of Arts and Sciences, Department of Psychology, Kalamazoo, MI 49008. Offers behavior analysis (MA, PhD); clinical psychology (PhD); industrial/organizational behavior management (MA). *Accreditation:* APA (one or more programs are accredited). *Degree requirements:* For master's, variable foreign language requirement, thesis; for doctorate, 2 foreign languages, comprehensive exam, thesis/dissertation.

**William James College,** Graduate Programs, Newton, MA 02459. Offers applied psychology in higher education student personnel administration (MA); clinical psychology (Psy D); counseling psychology (MA); counseling psychology and community mental health (MA); counseling psychology and global mental health (MA); executive coaching (Graduate Certificate); forensic and counseling psychology (MA); leadership psychology (Psy D); organizational psychology (MA); primary care psychology (MA); respecialization in clinical psychology (Certificate); school psychology (Psy D); MA/CAGS. *Accreditation:* APA. *Degree requirements:* For master's, comprehensive exam (for some programs); for doctorate, thesis/dissertation (for some programs). Electronic applications accepted.

**Wright State University,** Graduate School, College of Science and Mathematics, Department of Psychology, Program in Human Factors and Industrial/Organizational Psychology, Dayton, OH 45435. Offers MS, PhD. *Degree requirements:* For master's, thesis; for doctorate, thesis/dissertation. *Expenses:* Tuition, state resident: full-time $9952; part-time $622 per credit hour. Tuition, nonresident: full-time $16,960; part-time $1060 per credit hour. *Unit head:* Dr. Dan Weber, Director, 937-775-2391, Fax: 937-775-3347, E-mail: dan.weber@wright.edu. *Application contact:* Dr. Dan Weber, Director, 937-775-2391, Fax: 937-775-3347, E-mail: dan.weber@wright.edu.

**Xavier University,** College of Social Sciences, Health and Education, Department of Psychology, Cincinnati, OH 45207. Offers clinical psychology (Psy D); industrial-organizational psychology (MA). *Accreditation:* APA (one or more programs are accredited). *Degree requirements:* For master's, one foreign language, comprehensive exam, thesis, internship; for doctorate, one foreign language, comprehensive exam, thesis/dissertation, internship. *Entrance requirements:* For master's, GRE, official transcript; 3 letters of recommendation; for doctorate, GRE General Test; GRE Subject Test in psychology (if no undergraduate degree in psychology), bachelor's or master's degree; 18 semester hours of psychology coursework; minimum GPA of 3.0; work and research experience; official transcript; 3 letters of recommendation; statement of purpose. Additional exam requirements/recommendations for international students: Required—TOEFL (minimum score 550 paper-based; 79 iBT), IELTS (minimum score 6.5). Electronic applications accepted. *Expenses:* Contact institution. *Faculty research:* Older adults, clinical child and adolescent issues, personnel selection and employee behavior, at-risk youth, sexual abuse.

# Marriage and Family Therapy

**Abilene Christian University,** College of Graduate and Professional Studies, Online Program in Marriage and Family Therapy, Abilene, TX 79699. Offers child and adolescent therapy (MMFT); medical family therapy (MMFT); therapy with military families (MMFT); treatment of trauma (MMFT). *Program availability:* Part-time, online only. *Students:* 80 full-time (67 women), 39 part-time (34 women); includes 59 minority (35 Black or African American, non-Hispanic/Latino; 2 Asian, non-Hispanic/Latino; 20 Hispanic/Latino; 2 Two or more races, non-Hispanic/Latino), 1 international. 92 applicants, 97% accepted, 77 enrolled. *Entrance requirements:* For master's, statement of purpose, three letters of recommendation. Additional exam requirements/recommendations for international students: Required—TOEFL (minimum score 80 iBT), IELTS (minimum score 6). *Application deadline:* For fall admission, 8/15 for domestic students; for winter admission, 10/1 for domestic students; for spring admission, 12/15 for domestic students; for summer admission, 4/15 for domestic students. Applications are processed on a rolling basis. Application fee: $50. *Expenses:* $800 per credit hour. *Financial support:* Application deadline: 4/1; applicants required to submit FAFSA. *Unit head:* Dr. Sara Salkil, Program Director, 325-674-2333, Fax: 325-674-6717, E-mail: seb04b@acu.edu. *Application contact:* Graduate Admissions, 855-219-7000, E-mail: gradonline@acu.edu.
Website: http://www.acu.edu/online/academics/marriage-and-family-therapy.html

**Abilene Christian University,** Graduate Programs, College of Biblical Studies, Program in Marriage and Family Therapy, Abilene, TX 79699. Offers MMFT. *Accreditation:* AAMFT/COAMFTE. *Faculty:* 2 full-time (0 women), 6 part-time/adjunct (2 women). *Students:* 34 full-time (22 women), 3 part-time (2 women); includes 11 minority (5 Black or African American, non-Hispanic/Latino; 5 Hispanic/Latino; 1 Two or more races, non-Hispanic/Latino), 1 international. 44 applicants, 57% accepted, 16 enrolled. In 2016, 22 master's awarded. *Degree requirements:* For master's, comprehensive exam, internship. *Entrance requirements:* For master's, GRE General Test, interview, writing sample. Additional exam requirements/recommendations for international students: Required—TOEFL (minimum score 80 iBT), IELTS (minimum score 6), PTE. *Application deadline:* For fall admission, 2/15 for domestic students. Applications are processed on a rolling basis. Application fee: $50. Electronic applications accepted. *Expenses:* $1,040 per credit hour. *Financial support:* In 2016–17, 11 students received support. Research assistantships, career-related internships or fieldwork, and scholarships/grants available. Support available to part-time students. Financial award application deadline: 4/1; financial award applicants required to submit FAFSA. *Faculty research:* Overeating variables, family systems, intervention strategies. *Unit head:* Dr. Dale Bertram, Program Director, 325-674-3780, Fax: 325-674-3779, E-mail: deb12a@acu.edu. *Application contact:* Corey Patterson, Director of Graduate Admission and Recruiting, 325-674-6566, Fax: 325-674-6717, E-mail: gradinfo@acu.edu.
Website: http://www.acu.edu/graduate/academics/marriage-and-family-therapy.html

**Adler Graduate School,** Program in Adlerian Counseling and Psychotherapy, Richfield, MN 55423. Offers Adlerian studies (MA); art therapy (MA); clinical mental health counseling (MA); co-occurring mental health and substance disorders (MA); marriage and family therapy (MA); school counseling (MA). *Program availability:* Part-time, evening/weekend. *Faculty:* 71 part-time/adjunct (55 women). *Students:* 298 part-time (225 women); includes 51 minority (40 Black or African American, non-Hispanic/Latino; 6 American Indian or Alaska Native, non-Hispanic/Latino; 5 Hispanic/Latino). *Degree requirements:* For master's, thesis or alternative, 500-700 hour internship (depending on license choice). *Entrance requirements:* For master's, interview, official transcripts, minimum cumulative GPA of 3.0. *Application deadline:* Applications are processed on a rolling basis. Application fee: $50. Electronic applications accepted. *Financial support:* Career-related internships or fieldwork and tuition waivers available. Support available to part-time students. Financial award applicants required to submit FAFSA. *Unit head:* Dr. Dan Haugen, President, 612-767-7048, Fax: 612-861-7559, E-mail: haugen@alfredadler.edu. *Application contact:* Evelyn B. Haas, Director of Admissions, 612-767-7044, Fax: 612-861-7559, E-mail: ev@alfredadler.edu.

**Adler University,** Programs in Psychology, Chicago, IL 60602. Offers advanced Adlerian psychotherapy (Certificate); art therapy (MA); clinical mental health counseling (MA); clinical neuropsychology (Certificate); clinical psychology (Psy D); community psychology (MA); counseling and organizational psychology (MA); counseling psychology (MA); counselor education and supervision (PhD); couple and family therapy (DCFT); criminology (MA); emergency management leadership (MA); forensic psychology (MA); marriage and family counseling (MA); marriage and family therapy (Certificate); military psychology (MA); nonprofit management (MA); organizational psychology (MA); police psychology (MA); public policy and administration (MA); rehabilitation counseling (MA); sport and health psychology (MA); substance abuse counseling (Certificate); Psy D/Certificate; Psy D/MACAT; Psy D/MACP; Psy D/MAMFC; Psy D/MASAC. *Accreditation:* APA. *Program availability:* Part-time, evening/weekend, online learning. Terminal master's awarded for partial completion of doctoral program. *Degree requirements:* For master's, thesis or alternative, oral exam, practicum; for doctorate, thesis/dissertation, clinical exam, internship, oral exam, practicum, written qualifying exam. *Entrance requirements:* For master's, 12 semester hours in psychology, minimum GPA of 3.0; for doctorate, 18 semester hours in psychology, minimum GPA of 3.25; for Certificate, appropriate master's or doctoral degree. Additional exam requirements/recommendations for international students: Required—TOEFL (minimum score 550 paper-based; 79 iBT). Electronic applications accepted.

**See Display on page 982 and Close-Up on page 1225.**

**Alliant International University–Irvine,** California School of Professional Psychology, Program in Couple and Family Therapy, Irvine, CA 92606. Offers MA, Psy D. *Accreditation:* AAMFT/COAMFTE. *Program availability:* Part-time. *Degree requirements:* For doctorate, thesis/dissertation. *Entrance requirements:* For master's, minimum GPA of 3.0, letters of recommendation, interview; for doctorate, letters of recommendation, minimum GPA of 3.0, interview. Additional exam requirements/recommendations for international students: Required—TOEFL (minimum score 550 paper-based; 80 iBT), TWE (minimum score 5). Electronic applications accepted. *Faculty research:* Chemical dependency, gender issues in couples relationships, multicultural competence in therapy, contextual family therapy, relationship quality and stability.

**Alliant International University–Los Angeles,** California School of Professional Psychology, Program in Couple and Family Therapy, Alhambra, CA 91803. Offers chemical dependency (MA); gerontology (MA); Latin American family therapy (MA). *Accreditation:* AAMFT/COAMFTE. *Program availability:* Part-time, evening/weekend. *Degree requirements:* For master's, comprehensive exam, 50 hours of professional development activities. *Entrance requirements:* Additional exam requirements/recommendations for international students: Required—TOEFL (minimum score 550 paper-based). Electronic applications accepted. *Faculty research:* Foster care, therapy with minority couples, parenting, marriage, trauma.

**Alliant International University–Los Angeles,** California School of Professional Psychology, Psy D Program in Clinical Psychology, Alhambra, CA 91803. Offers clinical health psychology (Psy D); family/child and couple clinical psychology (Psy D); multi-interest option (Psy D); multicultural community-clinical psychology (Psy D). *Accreditation:* APA. *Degree requirements:* For doctorate, comprehensive exam, thesis/dissertation. *Entrance requirements:* For doctorate, interview, minimum GPA of 3.0 in both psychology and overall. Additional exam requirements/recommendations for international students: Required—TOEFL (minimum score 600 paper-based), TWE. Electronic applications accepted. *Faculty research:* Child and family psychology, multicultural and community psychology, acculturation, lesbian and gay issues, women's health.

**Alliant International University–Sacramento,** California School of Professional Psychology, Program in Couple and Family Therapy, Sacramento, CA 95833. Offers MA, Psy D. *Accreditation:* AAMFT/COAMFTE. *Degree requirements:* For master's, practicum; for doctorate, thesis/dissertation, practicum. *Entrance requirements:* For master's and doctorate, minimum GPA of 3.0, letters of recommendation, interview. Additional exam requirements/recommendations for international students: Required—TOEFL (minimum score 600 paper-based), TWE (minimum score 5). Electronic applications accepted. *Faculty research:* Adolescent risky behaviors including substance abuse, family therapy process, cultural issues, therapy with the LGBT community, commonalities of healthy and distressed couples.

**Alliant International University–San Diego,** California School of Professional Psychology, Program in Couple and Family Therapy, San Diego, CA 92131. Offers marital and family therapy (MA, Psy D). *Accreditation:* AAMFT/COAMFTE. *Program availability:* Part-time. *Degree requirements:* For doctorate, thesis/dissertation. *Entrance requirements:* For master's and doctorate, minimum GPA of 3.0, letters of recommendation, interview. Additional exam requirements/recommendations for international students: Required—TOEFL (minimum score 550 paper-based; 80 iBT), TWE (minimum score 5). Electronic applications accepted. *Faculty research:* Chemical dependency, women's issues, emotionally-focused therapy, couple relationships, work/family/parenting.

**Amridge University,** Graduate and Professional Programs, Montgomery, AL 36117. Offers Biblical studies (MA, PhD); Christian ministry (MS); family therapy (D Min); human services (MS); leadership and management (MS); marriage and family therapy (M Div, MA, PhD); ministerial leadership (M Div, MS); New Testament studies (MA); Old Testament studies (MA); professional counseling (M Div, MA, PhD); theology (M Div, D Min). *Program availability:* Part-time, evening/weekend, online learning. *Faculty:* 22 full-time (3 women), 10 part-time/adjunct (6 women). *Students:* 81 full-time (49 women), 225 part-time (137 women); includes 81 minority (80 Black or African American, non-Hispanic/Latino; 1 Hispanic/Latino). Average age 41. 122 applicants, 100% accepted, 79 enrolled. *Degree requirements:* For master's, one foreign language, comprehensive exam (for some programs), thesis (for some programs); for doctorate, one foreign language, comprehensive exam (for some programs), thesis/dissertation (for some programs). *Entrance requirements:* For master's, official transcript showing an earned 4-year BA or BS from regionally- or nationally-accredited institution; for doctorate, official transcript showing earned graduate degree from regionally- or nationally-accredited institution; writing sample (e.g. career monograph, published journal article, term paper from master's degree or doctoral dissertation); interview. Additional exam requirements/recommendations for international students: Required—TOEFL (minimum score 79 iBT). *Application deadline:* Applications are processed on a rolling basis. Application fee: $50. Electronic applications accepted. *Expenses: Tuition:* Full-time $12,870; part-time $715 per credit hour. *Required fees:* $1300; $650 per semester. *Financial support:* In 2016–17, 45 students received support. Federal Work-Study and scholarships/grants available. Support available to part-time students. Financial award applicants required to submit FAFSA. *Faculty research:* Technology and mental healthcare, resilience in black families, theology and congregational ministry. *Unit head:* Laina Costanza, Vice President, Student Affairs, 888-790-8080 Ext. 1, Fax: 334-387-3878, E-mail: cc@amridgeuniversity.edu. *Application contact:* Brooks Housley, Student Affairs Coordinator, 888-790-8080 Ext. 1, Fax: 334-387-3878, E-mail: admissions@amridgeuniversity.edu.

**Antioch University New England,** Graduate School, Department of Applied Psychology, Program in Marriage and Family Therapy, Keene, NH 03431-3552. Offers MA, PhD, Certificate. *Accreditation:* AAMFT/COAMFTE. *Degree requirements:* For master's, internship, practicum. *Entrance requirements:* For master's, previous course work and work experience in psychology; resume; 3 letters of recommendation. Additional exam requirements/recommendations for international students: Required—TOEFL (minimum score 550 paper-based). Electronic applications accepted. *Expenses:* Contact institution. *Faculty research:* Use of reflective team model in case teaching and in organizational consulting, executive mentoring and coaching.

**Appalachian State University,** Cratis D. Williams Graduate School, Department of Human Development and Psychological Counseling, Boone, NC 28608. Offers clinical mental health counseling (MA); college student development (MA); marriage and family therapy (MA); school counseling (MA). *Accreditation:* AAMFT/COAMFTE; ACA; NCATE. *Program availability:* Part-time. *Degree requirements:* For master's, comprehensive exam (for some programs), thesis optional, internships. *Entrance requirements:* For master's, GRE General Test, 3 letters of recommendation. Additional exam requirements/recommendations for international students: Required—TOEFL (minimum score 570 paper-based; 79 iBT), IELTS (minimum score 6.5). *Application deadline:* For fall admission, 2/1 priority date for domestic students, 2/1 for international students; for spring admission, 2/1 for international students. Applications are processed on a rolling basis. Application fee: $55. Electronic applications accepted. *Expenses: Tuition,* state resident: full-time $4744. Tuition, nonresident: full-time $17,913. Full-time tuition and fees vary according to program. *Financial support:* Fellowships, research assistantships, teaching assistantships, career-related internships or fieldwork, Federal Work-Study, scholarships/grants, and unspecified assistantships available. Financial award application deadline: 4/1; financial award applicants required to submit FAFSA. *Faculty research:* Multicultural counseling, addictions counseling, play therapy, expressive arts, child and adolescent therapy, sexual abuse counseling. *Unit head:* Dr. Lee Baruth, Chairman, 828-262-2055, E-mail: baruthlg@appstate.edu. *Application contact:* Dr. Mark Schwarze, Program Director, 828-262-6046, E-mail: asucmhc@appstate.edu.
Website: http://www.ced.appstate.edu/departments/hpc

**Arcadia University,** College of Arts and Sciences, Department of Psychology, Glenside, PA 19038-3295. Offers applied behavior analysis (MAC); autism (MAC); child/family therapy (MAC); community public health (MAC); counseling/international peace and conflict resolution dual degree (MAC); mental health counseling (MAC); trauma (MAC). *Program availability:* Part-time. *Faculty:* 14 full-time (9 women), 10 part-time/adjunct (9 women). *Students:* 33 full-time (27 women), 39 part-time (30 women); includes 22 minority (13 Black or African American, non-Hispanic/Latino; 2 Asian, non-Hispanic/Latino; 1 Hispanic/Latino; 6 Two or more races, non-Hispanic/Latino), 1 international. Average age 30. 61 applicants, 64% accepted, 24 enrolled. In 2016, 41 master's awarded. *Degree requirements:* For master's, practicum. *Entrance requirements:* For master's, GRE General Test or MAT. *Application deadline:* For fall admission, 1/15 for domestic students; for spring admission, 9/15 for domestic students. Applications are processed on a rolling basis. Application fee: $50. *Expenses:* Contact institution. *Financial support:* Research assistantships, career-related internships or fieldwork, and unspecified assistantships available. Support available to part-time students. Financial award application deadline: 8/15. *Unit head:* Dr. Steven Robbins, Chair, 215-572-2987. *Application contact:* 215-572-2925, Fax: 215-572-2126, E-mail: grad@arcadia.edu.

**Argosy University, Atlanta,** Georgia School of Professional Psychology, Atlanta, GA 30328. Offers clinical psychology (MA, Psy D, Postdoctoral Respecialization Certificate), including child and family psychology (Psy D), general adult clinical (Psy D), health psychology (Psy D), neuropsychology/geropsychology (Psy D); community counseling (MA), including marriage and family therapy; counselor education and supervision (Ed D); forensic psychology (MA); industrial organizational psychology (MA); marriage and family therapy (Certificate); sport-exercise psychology (MA). *Accreditation:* APA.

**Argosy University, Chicago,** Illinois School of Professional Psychology, Doctoral Program in Clinical Psychology, Chicago, IL 60601. Offers child and adolescent psychology (Psy D); client-centered and experiential psychotherapies (Psy D); diversity and multicultural psychology (Psy D); family psychology (Psy D); forensic psychology (Psy D); health psychology (Psy D); neuropsychology (Psy D); organizational consulting (Psy D); psychoanalytic psychology (Psy D); psychology and spirituality (Psy D). *Accreditation:* APA.

**Argosy University, Denver,** College of Psychology and Behavioral Sciences, Denver, CO 80231. Offers clinical mental health counseling (MA); clinical psychology (MA, Psy D); counseling psychology (Ed D); counselor education and supervision (Ed D); forensic psychology (MA); industrial organizational psychology (MA); marriage and family therapy (MA, DMFT).

**Argosy University, Hawai`i,** Hawai'i School of Professional Psychology, Program in Marriage and Family Therapy, Honolulu, HI 96813. Offers MA.

**Argosy University, Inland Empire,** College of Psychology and Behavioral Sciences, Ontario, CA 91761. Offers clinical psychology/marriage and family therapy (MA); counseling psychology (Ed D); counseling psychology/marriage and family therapy (MA); forensic psychology (MA); industrial organizational psychology (MA); sport-exercise psychology (MA).

**Argosy University, Los Angeles,** College of Psychology and Behavioral Sciences, Santa Monica, CA 90045. Offers clinical psychology/marriage and family therapy (MA); counseling psychology (Ed D); counseling psychology/marriage and family therapy (MA); forensic psychology (MA).

**Argosy University, Northern Virginia,** American School of Professional Psychology, Arlington, VA 22209. Offers clinical psychology (MA, Psy D), including child and family psychology (Psy D), diversity and multicultural psychology (Psy D); forensic psychology (Psy D), health and neuropsychology (Psy D); community counseling (MA); counseling psychology (Ed D), including counselor education and supervision; counselor education and supervision (Ed D); forensic psychology (MA).

**Argosy University, Orange County,** American School of Professional Psychology, Program in Clinical Psychology, Orange, CA 92868. Offers child and adolescent psychology (Psy D); forensic psychology (Psy D); marriage and family therapy (MA).

**Argosy University, Orange County,** American School of Professional Psychology, Program in Counseling Psychology, Orange, CA 92868. Offers counseling psychology (Ed D); marriage and family therapy (MA).

**Argosy University, Salt Lake City,** College of Psychology and Behavioral Sciences, Draper, UT 84020. Offers counseling psychology (Ed D); counselor education and supervision (Ed D); forensic psychology (MA); marriage and family therapy (MA, DMFT); mental health counseling (MA).

**Argosy University, San Diego,** College of Psychology and Behavioral Sciences, San Diego, CA 92108. Offers clinical psychology/marriage and family therapy (MA); counseling psychology (Ed D); counseling psychology/marriage and family therapy (MA); forensic psychology (MA).

**Argosy University, Sarasota,** College of Psychology and Behavioral Sciences, Sarasota, FL 34235. Offers community counseling (MA); counseling psychology (Ed D); counselor education and supervision (Ed D); forensic psychology (MA); marriage and family therapy (MA); mental health counseling (MA); pastoral community counseling (Ed D).

**Argosy University, Tampa,** Florida School of Professional Psychology, Program in Clinical Psychology, Tampa, FL 33607. Offers clinical psychology (MA, Psy D), including child and adolescent psychology (Psy D), geropsychology (Psy D), marriage/couples and family therapy (Psy D), neuropsychology (Psy D). *Accreditation:* APA.

**Argosy University, Twin Cities,** Minnesota School of Professional Psychology, Eagan, MN 55121. Offers clinical psychology (MA, Psy D), including child and family psychology (Psy D), forensic psychology (Psy D), health and neuropsychology (Psy D), trauma (Psy D); forensic counseling (Post-Graduate Certificate); forensic psychology (MA); industrial organizational psychology (MA); marriage and family therapy (MA, DMFT), including forensic counseling (MA). *Accreditation:* AAMFT; AAMFT/COAMFTE; APA.

**Arizona State University at the Tempe campus,** College of Liberal Arts and Sciences, School of Social and Family Dynamics, Tempe, AZ 85287-3701. Offers family and human development (MS, PhD); infant-family practice (MAS); marriage and family therapy (MAS); sociology (MA, PhD). Terminal master's awarded for partial completion of doctoral program. *Degree requirements:* For master's, thesis or alternative, interactive Program of Study (iPOS) submitted before completing 50 percent of required credit hours; for doctorate, thesis/dissertation, interactive Program of Study (iPOS) submitted before completing 50 percent of required credit hours. *Entrance requirements:* For master's and doctorate, GRE, minimum GPA of 3.0 or equivalent in last 2 years of work leading to bachelor's degree. Additional exam requirements/recommendations for international students: Required—TOEFL, IELTS, or PTE. Electronic applications accepted. *Expenses:* Contact institution.

**Azusa Pacific University,** School of Behavioral and Applied Sciences, Department of Graduate Psychology, Azusa, CA 91702-7000. Offers clinical psychology (MA, Psy D), including family therapy (MA). *Accreditation:* APA (one or more programs are accredited). *Program availability:* Part-time, evening/weekend. *Degree requirements:* For master's, comprehensive exam, 250 hours of clinical experience, individual and group therapy. *Entrance requirements:* For master's, interview, minimum GPA of 3.0, Minnesota Multiphasic Personality Inventory. Additional exam requirements/recommendations for international students: Required—TOEFL (minimum score 600 paper-based).

**Barry University,** School of Education, Program in Marital, Couple and Family Counseling/Therapy, Miami Shores, FL 33161-6695. Offers MS, Ed S. *Program availability:* Part-time, evening/weekend. *Degree requirements:* For master's, comprehensive exam, scholarly paper; for Ed S, comprehensive exam. *Entrance requirements:* For master's, GRE General Test or MAT, minimum GPA of 3.0; for Ed S, GRE General Test, minimum GPA of 3.0. Electronic applications accepted.

**Bayamón Central University,** Graduate Programs, Program in Education, Bayamón, PR 00960-1725. Offers administration and supervision (MA Ed); commercial education (MA Ed); elementary education (K–3) (MA Ed); family counseling (Graduate Certificate); guidance and counseling (MA Ed); pre-elementary teacher (MA Ed); rehabilitation counseling (MA Ed); special education (MA Ed), including attention deficit disorder, education of the autistic, learning disabilities. *Program availability:* Part-time, evening/weekend. *Degree requirements:* For master's, comprehensive exam. *Entrance requirements:* For master's, EXADEP, bachelor's degree in education or related field.

**Bethel Seminary,** Graduate and Professional Programs, St. Paul, MN 55112-6998. Offers Anglican studies (Certificate); children's and family ministry (MA); Christian studies (Certificate); Christian thought (MA); church planting (Certificate); Greek and Hebrew language (M Div); Greek language (M Div); Hebrew language (M Div); marriage and family therapy (MA, Certificate); mental health counseling (MA); ministry (MA, D Min); ministry practice (Certificate); theological studies (MA, Certificate); transformational leadership (MA); young life youth ministry (Certificate). *Accreditation:* ACIPE. *Program availability:* Part-time, evening/weekend, blended/hybrid learning. *Faculty:* 14 full-time (4 women), 37 part-time/adjunct (17 women). *Students:* 369 full-time (165 women), 147 part-time (43 women); includes 138 minority (48 Black or African American, non-Hispanic/Latino; 45 Asian, non-Hispanic/Latino; 28 Hispanic/Latino; 2 Native Hawaiian or other Pacific Islander, non-Hispanic/Latino; 15 Two or more races, non-Hispanic/Latino), 15 international. 322 applicants, 75% accepted, 174 enrolled. In 2016, 168 master's, 24 doctorates, 6 other advanced degrees awarded. *Degree requirements:* For master's, variable foreign language requirement, thesis (for some programs); for doctorate, thesis/dissertation. *Entrance requirements:* For master's, letters of reference, transcripts, personal statement; for doctorate, M Div, letters of reference, organizational support; for Certificate, letters of reference, family essay, personal statement, and family of origin paper (for marriage and family therapy). Additional exam requirements/recommendations for international students: Required—TOEFL (minimum score 550 paper-based; 87 iBT). *Application deadline:* For fall admission, 8/1 priority date for domestic students, 8/1 for international students; for winter admission, 12/1 priority date for domestic students; for spring admission, 1/1 priority date for domestic students. Applications are processed on a rolling basis. Application fee: $0. Electronic applications accepted. *Expenses:* Contact institution. *Financial support:* In 2016–17, 404 students received support. Teaching assistantships, career-related internships or fieldwork, Federal Work-Study, and scholarships/grants available. Financial award applicants required to submit FAFSA. *Faculty research:* Nature of theology, ethics, Biblical commentaries, nature of God, science and theology. *Unit head:* Dr. David Clark, Vice-President and Dean, 651-638-6659, E-mail: d-clark@bethel.edu. *Application contact:* Jen Niska, Director of Admissions, 651-638-6288, Fax: 651-638-6002, E-mail: seminary-admissions@bethel.edu. Website: https://www.bethel.edu/seminary

**Brandman University,** School of Arts and Sciences, Irvine, CA 92618. Offers psychology (MA), including counseling, marriage and family therapy, professional clinical counseling. *Expenses: Tuition:* Full-time $14,880; part-time $620 per credit hour. Tuition and fees vary according to degree level and program. *Unit head:* Dr. Jeremy Korr, Dean, 949-341-9831.
Website: https://www.brandman.edu/arts-sciences

**Briercrest Seminary,** Graduate Programs, Program in Christian Ministries, Caronport, SK S0H 0S0, Canada. Offers leadership (MA); marriage and family counseling (MA); missions (MA); pastoral counseling (MA); worship (MA); youth and family ministry (MA). *Program availability:* Part-time. *Degree requirements:* For master's, comprehensive exam, thesis optional. *Entrance requirements:* Additional exam requirements/recommendations for international students: Required—TOEFL (minimum score 550 paper-based).

**Brigham Young University,** Graduate Studies, College of Family, Home, and Social Sciences, Marriage and Family Therapy Program, Provo, UT 84602. Offers MS, PhD. *Accreditation:* AAMFT/COAMFTE. *Faculty:* 8 full-time (2 women), 4 part-time/adjunct (2 women). *Students:* 31 full-time (23 women); includes 6 minority (1 Black or African American, non-Hispanic/Latino; 4 Asian, non-Hispanic/Latino; 1 Native Hawaiian or other Pacific Islander, non-Hispanic/Latino), 3 international. Average age 29. 78 applicants, 18% accepted, 12 enrolled. In 2016, 10 master's, 3 doctorates awarded. *Degree requirements:* For master's, thesis, 500 clinical hours; for doctorate, comprehensive exam, thesis/dissertation, 500 clinical hours, portfolio. *Entrance requirements:* For master's and doctorate, GRE General Test, minimum GPA of 3.0 in last 60 hours of course work. Additional exam requirements/recommendations for international students: Required—TOEFL (minimum score 85 iBT). *Application deadline:* For fall admission, 12/1 for domestic and international students. Application fee: $50. Electronic applications accepted. *Expenses: Tuition:* Full-time $6680; part-time $393 per credit. Tuition and fees vary according to course load, program and student's religious affiliation. *Financial support:* In 2016–17, 28 students received support, including 28 research assistantships with tuition reimbursements available (averaging $31,239 per year); teaching assistantships, career-related internships or fieldwork, scholarships/grants, and tuition waivers (full and partial) also available. *Faculty research:* Therapy processes and outcomes, family relationships across the life cycle, adjustment to medical illnesses, health family processes. *Unit head:* Jonathan Sandberg, Program Director, 801-422-5680, Fax: 801-422-0163, E-mail: roy_bean@byu.edu. *Application contact:* Dr. Lauren A. Barnes, Director of Clinical Training, 801-422-3889, Fax: 801-422-0163, E-mail: lauren_barnes@byu.edu.
Website: http://mft.byu.edu

**California Lutheran University,** Graduate Studies, Department of Psychology, Thousand Oaks, CA 91360-2787. Offers clinical psychology (MS, Psy D); marital and family therapy (MS). *Accreditation:* APA. *Program availability:* Part-time. *Faculty:* 11 full-time (6 women), 15 part-time/adjunct (13 women). *Students:* 133 full-time (109 women), 37 part-time (32 women); includes 63 minority (2 Black or African American, non-Hispanic/Latino; 2 American Indian or Alaska Native, non-Hispanic/Latino; 4 Asian, non-Hispanic/Latino; 30 Hispanic/Latino; 25 Two or more races, non-Hispanic/Latino), 9 international. Average age 30. 234 applicants, 50% accepted, 73 enrolled. In 2016, 60 master's, 7 doctorates awarded. *Degree requirements:* For master's, thesis or comprehensive exams; for doctorate, thesis/dissertation, internship. *Entrance requirements:* For master's, GRE General Test, interview, minimum GPA of 3.0; for doctorate, GRE General Test. *Application deadline:* For fall admission, 12/1 priority date for domestic and international students. Applications are processed on a rolling basis. Application fee: $50. Electronic applications accepted. *Unit head:* Dr. Richard Holigrock,

Dean, 805-493-3723. *Application contact:* 805-493-3325, Fax: 805-493-3861, E-mail: clugrad@callutheran.edu.

**California State University, Chico,** Office of Graduate Studies, College of Behavioral and Social Sciences, Department of Psychology, Program in Marriage and Family Therapy, Chico, CA 95929-0722. Offers MS. *Students:* 49 full-time (40 women), 5 part-time (all women); includes 11 minority (1 Asian, non-Hispanic/Latino; 4 Hispanic/Latino; 6 Two or more races, non-Hispanic/Latino). 51 applicants, 55% accepted, 20 enrolled. *Degree requirements:* For master's, oral exam and thesis or analytical review and written exam. *Entrance requirements:* For master's, GRE General Test or MAT, 3 letters of recommendation, statement of purpose. Additional exam requirements/recommendations for international students: Required—TOEFL (minimum score 550 paper-based; 80 iBT), IELTS (minimum score 6.5), PTE. *Application deadline:* For fall admission, 3/1 for domestic and international students. Application fee: $55. Electronic applications accepted. *Financial support:* Research assistantships available. Financial award application deadline: 3/1; financial award applicants required to submit FAFSA. *Unit head:* Dr. Brian Oppy, Chair, 530-898-4609, Fax: 530-898-4740, E-mail: psy@csuchico.edu. *Application contact:* Judy L. Morris, Graduate Admissions Coordinator, 530-898-5416, Fax: 530-898-3342, E-mail: jlmorris@csuchico.edu. Website: http://www.csuchico.edu/psy/graduate/marriageFamily.shtml

**California State University, Dominguez Hills,** College of Health, Human Services and Nursing, Program in Marital and Family Therapy, Carson, CA 90747-0001. Offers MS. *Program availability:* Part-time, evening/weekend. *Degree requirements:* For master's, comprehensive exam. *Entrance requirements:* For master's, minimum GPA of 3.0. Additional exam requirements/recommendations for international students: Required—TOEFL (minimum score 550 paper-based). Electronic applications accepted. *Faculty research:* Sociology of the family, clinical psychology theory, employee assistance programs, race and sport, secondary trauma.

**California State University, East Bay,** Office of Graduate Studies, College of Education and Allied Studies, Department of Educational Psychology, Counseling Program, Hayward, CA 94542-3000. Offers marriage and family therapy (MS); school counseling (MS); school psychology (MS). *Accreditation:* NCATE. *Students:* 104 full-time (85 women), 2 part-time (both women); includes 54 minority (3 Black or African American, non-Hispanic/Latino; 15 Asian, non-Hispanic/Latino; 26 Hispanic/Latino; 10 Two or more races, non-Hispanic/Latino), 1 international. Average age 29. 178 applicants, 34% accepted, 50 enrolled. In 2016, 42 master's awarded. *Degree requirements:* For master's, comprehensive exam, project or thesis. *Entrance requirements:* For master's, GRE or MAT, interview, minimum GPA of 2.5 during previous 2 years of course work. Additional exam requirements/recommendations for international students: Required—TOEFL (minimum score 550 paper-based). *Application deadline:* For fall admission, 6/30 for domestic and international students. Application fee: $55. Electronic applications accepted. *Financial support:* Career-related internships or fieldwork, Federal Work-Study, and institutionally sponsored loans available. Support available to part-time students. Financial award application deadline: 3/2; financial award applicants required to submit FAFSA. *Unit head:* Dr. Jack Davis, Chair, Educational Psychology, 510-885-3011, Fax: 510-885-4642, E-mail: jack.davis@csueastbay.edu. *Application contact:* Prof. Greg Jennings, Graduate Coordinator, 510-885-2296, Fax: 510-885-4642, E-mail: greg.jennings@csueastbay.edu. Website: http://www20.csueastbay.edu/ceas/departments/epsy/

**California State University, Fresno,** Division of Research and Graduate Studies, Kremen School of Education and Human Development, Department of Counselor Education and Rehabilitation, Program in Marriage, Family and Child Counseling, Fresno, CA 93740-8027. Offers MS. *Accreditation:* ACA. *Program availability:* Part-time, evening/weekend. *Degree requirements:* For master's, thesis or alternative. *Entrance requirements:* For master's, GRE General Test, MAT, minimum GPA of 3.0. Additional exam requirements/recommendations for international students: Required—TOEFL. *Application deadline:* For fall admission, 5/1 for domestic and international students; for spring admission, 10/1 for domestic and international students. Applications are processed on a rolling basis. Application fee: $55. Electronic applications accepted. *Financial support:* Career-related internships or fieldwork, Federal Work-Study, scholarships/grants, and research awards available. Support available to part-time students. Financial award application deadline: 3/1; financial award applicants required to submit FAFSA. *Faculty research:* Child abuse prevention, early childhood education.

**California State University, Long Beach,** Graduate Studies, College of Education, Department of Advanced Studies in Education and Counseling, Long Beach, CA 90840. Offers counseling (MS), including marriage and family therapy, school counseling, student development in higher education; education (MA, Ed D); educational administration (MA, Ed D); educational psychology (MA); special education (MS). *Program availability:* Part-time, evening/weekend. *Entrance requirements:* For master's, GRE General Test, minimum GPA of 2.75. *Application deadline:* For fall admission, 3/1 for domestic students. Applications are processed on a rolling basis. Application fee: $55. Electronic applications accepted. *Financial support:* Federal Work-Study, institutionally sponsored loans, and scholarships/grants available. Financial award application deadline: 3/2. *Unit head:* Dr. Hiromi Masunaga, Chair, 562-985-4517, E-mail: asec@csulb.edu.

**California State University, Northridge,** Graduate Studies, Michael D. Eisner College of Education, Department of Educational Psychology and Counseling, Northridge, CA 91330. Offers counseling (MS), including career counseling, college counseling and student services, marriage and family therapy, school counseling, school psychology; educational psychology (MA Ed), including development, learning and instruction, early childhood education. *Accreditation:* ACA (one or more programs are accredited); NCATE. *Program availability:* Part-time, evening/weekend. *Faculty:* 17 full-time (4 women), 46 part-time/adjunct (15 women). *Students:* 283 full-time (235 women), 79 part-time (72 women); includes 180 minority (8 Black or African American, non-Hispanic/Latino; 22 Asian, non-Hispanic/Latino; 132 Hispanic/Latino; 18 Two or more races, non-Hispanic/Latino), 13 international. Average age 29. 411 applicants, 36% accepted, 129 enrolled. *Entrance requirements:* For master's, GRE General Test or minimum GPA of 3.0. Additional exam requirements/recommendations for international students: Required—TOEFL. *Application deadline:* For fall admission, 11/30 for domestic students. Application fee: $55. *Expenses:* Tuition, state resident: full-time $4152. *Financial support:* Scholarships/grants available. Support available to part-time students. Financial award application deadline: 3/1. *Unit head:* Dr. Shari Tarver-Behring, Chair, 818-677-2599. *Application contact:* 818-677-3755. Website: http://www.csun.edu/eisner-education/educational-psychology-counseling

**Cambridge College,** School of Psychology and Counseling, Cambridge, MA 02138-5304. Offers addiction counseling (M Ed); alcohol and drug counseling (Certificate); counseling psychology (M Ed, CAGS); counseling psychology: forensic counseling (M Ed); marriage and family therapy (M Ed); mental health and addiction counseling (M Ed); mental health counseling (M Ed); mental health counseling for school guidance counselors (Post Master's Certificate); psychological studies (M Ed); school adjustment and mental health counseling (M Ed); school adjustment, mental health and addiction counseling (M Ed); school guidance counselor (M Ed); trauma studies (Certificate). *Program availability:* Part-time, evening/weekend. *Degree requirements:* For master's

and other advanced degree, thesis, practicum/internship. *Entrance requirements:* For master's, resume, 2 professional references; for other advanced degree, official transcripts, documents for transfer credit evaluation, resume, written personal statement/essay, 2 professional references, health insurance, immunizations form. Additional exam requirements/recommendations for international students: Required—TOEFL (minimum score 550 paper-based; 79 iBT), Michigan English Language Assessment Battery (minimum score 85); Recommended—IELTS (minimum score 6). Electronic applications accepted. *Expenses:* Contact institution. *Faculty research:* Trauma, drug and alcohol counseling, cross-cultural issues, school counseling, trauma in schools.

**Campbellsville University,** School of Theology, Campbellsville, KY 42718-2799. Offers marriage and family therapy (MMFT); theology (M Th). *Program availability:* Part-time, evening/weekend, 100% online, blended/hybrid learning. *Faculty:* 12 full-time (2 women), 5 part-time/adjunct (1 woman). *Students:* 5 full-time (2 women), 83 part-time (41 women); includes 33 minority (27 Black or African American, non-Hispanic/Latino; 1 American Indian or Alaska Native, non-Hispanic/Latino; 4 Hispanic/Latino; 1 Two or more races, non-Hispanic/Latino), 1 international. Average age 43. 60 applicants, 62% accepted, 30 enrolled. In 2016, 31 master's awarded. *Degree requirements:* For master's, comprehensive exam, thesis optional. *Entrance requirements:* For master's, GRE General Test, minimum GPA of 3.0 in major, 2.75 overall; 18 hours of undergraduate coursework in Christian studies; college transcripts; letters of recommendation. Additional exam requirements/recommendations for international students: Recommended—TOEFL (minimum score 550 paper-based; 79 iBT), IELTS (minimum score 6). *Application deadline:* Applications are processed on a rolling basis. Application fee: $25. Electronic applications accepted. Application fee is waived when completed online. *Expenses:* $399 per credit hour. *Financial support:* Application deadline: 6/1; applicants required to submit FAFSA. *Faculty research:* Clergy needing graduate theology education, trinity and Christian faith, Old Testament David narratives, leadership principles on Christian university integration of Christian principles in counseling process, church history. *Unit head:* Dr. John E. Hurtgen, Dean, 270-789-5077, Fax: 270-789-5050, E-mail: jehurtgen@campbellsville.edu. *Application contact:* Monica Bamwine, Assistant Director of Graduate Admissions, 270-789-5221, Fax: 270-789-5071, E-mail: mkbamwine@campbellsville.edu. Website: http://www.campbellsville.edu/

**Capella University,** Harold Abel School of Social and Behavioral Science, Master's Programs in Counseling, Minneapolis, MN 55402. Offers child and adolescent development (MS); general addiction counseling (MS); general marriage and family counseling/therapy (MS); general mental health counseling (MS); general school counseling (MS).

**Carlos Albizu University, Miami Campus,** Graduate Programs, Miami, FL 33172-2209. Offers clinical psychology (PhD, Psy D); entrepreneurship (MBA); exceptional student education (MS); human services (PhD); industrial/organizational psychology (MS); marriage and family therapy (MS); mental health counseling (MS); nonprofit management (MBA); organizational management (MBA); psychology (MS); school counseling (MS); speech and language pathology (MS); teaching English for speakers of other languages (MS). *Accreditation:* APA. *Program availability:* Part-time, evening/weekend, 100% online. *Faculty:* 28 full-time (22 women), 31 part-time/adjunct (19 women). *Students:* 475 full-time (396 women), 191 part-time (161 women); includes 560 minority (56 Black or African American, non-Hispanic/Latino; 1 American Indian or Alaska Native, non-Hispanic/Latino; 4 Asian, non-Hispanic/Latino; 494 Hispanic/Latino; 5 Two or more races, non-Hispanic/Latino), 15 international. Average age 34. 335 applicants, 46% accepted, 122 enrolled. In 2016, 143 master's, 48 doctorates awarded. Terminal master's awarded for partial completion of doctoral program. *Degree requirements:* For master's, comprehensive exam, integrative project (for MBA); research project (for exceptional student education, teaching English as a second language); for doctorate, comprehensive exam, thesis/dissertation, internship, project. *Entrance requirements:* For master's, 3 letters of recommendation, interview, minimum GPA of 3.0, resume, statement of purpose, official transcripts; for doctorate, 3 letters of recommendation, minimum GPA of 3.0, resume, interview, statement of purpose, official transcripts. Additional exam requirements/recommendations for international students: Required—Michigan Test of English Language Proficiency. *Application deadline:* For fall admission, 4/1 priority date for domestic students, 5/1 priority date for international students; for spring admission, 11/1 priority date for domestic students, 9/1 priority date for international students. Applications are processed on a rolling basis. Application fee: $50. Electronic applications accepted. *Expenses:* Contact institution. *Financial support:* In 2016–17, 131 students received support. Federal Work-Study, scholarships/grants, unspecified assistantships, and tuition discounts available. Financial award application deadline: 6/1; financial award applicants required to submit FAFSA. *Faculty research:* Psychotherapy, forensic psychology, neuropsychology, marketing strategy, entrepreneurship, special education, speech-language pathology. *Unit head:* Dr. Etiony Aldarondo, Provost, 305-593-1223 Ext. 3138, Fax: 305-592-7930, E-mail: ealdarondo@albizu.edu. *Application contact:* Sonia Feliciano, Institutional Director of Student Recruitment, 305-593-1223 Ext. 3108, Fax: 305-477-8983, E-mail: sfeliciano@albizu.edu.

**Central Connecticut State University,** School of Graduate Studies, School of Education and Professional Studies, Department of Counselor Education and Family Therapy, New Britain, CT 06050-4010. Offers marriage and family therapy (MS); professional counseling (MS, AC, Certificate); school counseling (MS); student development in higher education (MS). *Accreditation:* AAMFT/COAMFTE; ACA. *Program availability:* Part-time, evening/weekend. *Faculty:* 10 full-time (5 women), 23 part-time/adjunct (21 women). *Students:* 157 full-time (120 women), 193 part-time (151 women); includes 99 minority (41 Black or African American, non-Hispanic/Latino; 3 Asian, non-Hispanic/Latino; 46 Hispanic/Latino; 9 Two or more races, non-Hispanic/Latino). Average age 39. 201 applicants, 64% accepted, 95 enrolled. In 2016, 96 master's, 7 other advanced degrees awarded. *Degree requirements:* For master's, comprehensive exam, thesis or alternative; for other advanced degree, qualifying exam. *Entrance requirements:* For master's, minimum undergraduate GPA of 2.7, essay, interview, letters of recommendation. Additional exam requirements/recommendations for international students: Required—TOEFL (minimum score 550 paper-based; 79 iBT). *Application deadline:* For fall admission, 3/1 for domestic and international students; for spring admission, 11/1 for domestic and international students. Applications are processed on a rolling basis. Application fee: $50. Electronic applications accepted. *Expenses: Tuition, area resident:* Full-time $6497; part-time $606 per credit. *Tuition, state resident:* full-time $9748; part-time $622 per credit. *Tuition, nonresident:* full-time $18,102; part-time $622 per credit. *Required fees:* $4459; $246 per credit. *Financial support:* In 2016–17, 46 students received support. Career-related internships or fieldwork, Federal Work-Study, scholarships/grants, and unspecified assistantships available. Support available to part-time students. Financial award application deadline: 3/1; financial award applicants required to submit FAFSA. *Faculty research:* Elementary and secondary school counseling, marriage and family therapy, rehabilitation counseling, counseling in higher educational settings. *Unit head:* Dr. Connie Tait, Chair, 860-832-2154, E-mail: taitc@ccsu.edu. *Application contact:* Patricia Gardner, Associate Director of Graduate Studies, 860-832-2350, Fax: 860-832-2362. Website: http://www.ccsu.edu/ceft/

**Chaminade University of Honolulu,** Office of Professional and Continuing Education, Program in Counseling Psychology, Honolulu, HI 96816-1578. Offers marriage and family counseling (MSCP); mental health counseling (MSCP); school counseling (MSCP). *Program availability:* Part-time, evening/weekend, blended/hybrid learning. *Faculty:* 7 full-time (2 women), 15 part-time/adjunct (6 women). *Students:* 163 full-time (122 women), 44 part-time (35 women); includes 137 minority (15 Black or African American, non-Hispanic/Latino; 3 American Indian or Alaska Native, non-Hispanic/Latino; 58 Asian, non-Hispanic/Latino; 12 Hispanic/Latino; 48 Native Hawaiian or other Pacific Islander, non-Hispanic/Latino; 1 Two or more races, non-Hispanic/Latino), 2 international. Average age 31. 49 applicants, 98% accepted, 33 enrolled. In 2016, 70 master's awarded. *Degree requirements:* For master's, comprehensive exam, internship/practicum. *Entrance requirements:* For master's, minimum undergraduate GPA of 3.0, 3 letters of recommendation, resume, interview. *Additional exam requirements/recommendations for international students:* Required—TOEFL (minimum score 550 paper-based; 79 iBT). *Application deadline:* Applications are processed on a rolling basis. Application fee: $40. Electronic applications accepted. *Expenses:* $775 per credit hour plus $93 fee per online course. *Financial support:* Applicants required to submit FAFSA. *Unit head:* Dr. Robert G. Santee, Dean, 808-735-4751, Fax: 808-739-4670, E-mail: mscp@chaminade.edu. *Application contact:* 808-735-4755, E-mail: gradserv@chaminade.edu.
Website: http://www.chaminade.edu/mscp

**Chapman University,** Crean College of Health and Behavioral Sciences, Marriage and Family Therapy Program, Orange, CA 92866. Offers MA. *Accreditation:* AAMFT/COAMFTE. *Program availability:* Part-time, evening/weekend. *Faculty:* 3 full-time (1 woman), 8 part-time/adjunct (6 women). *Students:* 34 full-time (30 women), 34 part-time (28 women); includes 27 minority (2 Black or African American, non-Hispanic/Latino; 1 American Indian or Alaska Native, non-Hispanic/Latino; 3 Asian, non-Hispanic/Latino; 19 Hispanic/Latino; 2 Two or more races, non-Hispanic/Latino), 1 international. Average age 27. 99 applicants, 37% accepted, 18 enrolled. In 2016, 25 master's awarded. *Degree requirements:* For master's, comprehensive exam, thesis optional. *Entrance requirements:* For master's, GRE (if undergraduate GPA less than 3.3). *Additional exam requirements/recommendations for international students:* Required—TOEFL (minimum score 550 paper-based, 80 iBT), IELTS (6.5), PTE Academic (53), or CAE. *Application deadline:* For fall admission, 2/1 for domestic students. Applications are processed on a rolling basis. Application fee: $60. Electronic applications accepted. *Expenses:* Contact institution. *Financial support:* Fellowships, Federal Work-Study, and scholarships/grants available. Financial award applicants required to submit FAFSA. *Unit head:* Dr. Naveen Jonathan, Director, 714-997-6932, E-mail: jonathan@chapman.edu. *Application contact:* Monica Chen, Graduate Admission Counselor, 714-289-3590, E-mail: mchen@chapman.edu.

**Chatham University,** Program in Counseling Psychology, Pittsburgh, PA 15232-2826. Offers child, adolescent and family (MSCP); counseling psychology (Psy D); health and holistic (MSCP); infant mental health (MSCP); organization and supervision (MSCP); sport and exercise (MSCP). *Accreditation:* APA. *Program availability:* Part-time, evening/weekend. *Degree requirements:* For master's, thesis optional, supervised internship; for doctorate, thesis/dissertation, internship. *Entrance requirements:* For master's, minimum GPA of 3.0; 2 letters of recommendation; resume; prerequisite coursework in statistics, biology, and psychology; for doctorate, GRE. *Additional exam requirements/recommendations for international students:* Required—TOEFL (minimum score 600 paper-based; 100 iBT), IELTS (minimum score 7), TWE. Electronic applications accepted. Application fee is waived when completed online. *Expenses: Tuition:* Full-time $16,254; part-time $903 per credit hour. *Required fees:* $468; $26 per credit hour. *Faculty research:* Trauma and recovery, hypnosis, psychospiritual dimensions of healing, psychotherapy of schizophrenia.

**Chestnut Hill College,** School of Graduate Studies, Division of Psychology, Program in Clinical and Counseling Psychology, Philadelphia, PA 19118-2693. Offers clinical and counseling psychology (MS, CAS), including child and adolescent therapy, child and adolescent therapy with autism spectrum disorders, co-occurring disorders, couple and family therapy, diverse and underserved communities, generalist (MS), trauma studies. *Program availability:* Part-time, evening/weekend. *Degree requirements:* For master's, thesis optional, practica. *Entrance requirements:* For master's, GRE General Test, writing sample, letters of recommendation. *Additional exam requirements/recommendations for international students:* Required—TOEFL (minimum score 500 paper-based), IELTS (minimum score 6.0), or TWE (minimum score 22). Electronic applications accepted. *Expenses:* Contact institution. *Faculty research:* Play therapy, eating disorders, addictions, group psychology and group therapy, health psychology.

**Chestnut Hill College,** School of Graduate Studies, Division of Psychology, Program in Clinical Psychology, Philadelphia, PA 19118-2693. Offers clinical psychology (Psy D), including clinical psychology, couple and family therapy, psychological assessment. *Accreditation:* APA. *Program availability:* Part-time, evening/weekend. *Degree requirements:* For doctorate, comprehensive exam, thesis/dissertation, internship, practica, clinical competency exam. *Entrance requirements:* For doctorate, GRE General Test, letters of recommendation, writing sample, master's degree in clinical/counseling psychology or closely-related field. *Additional exam requirements/recommendations for international students:* Required—TOEFL (minimum score 500 paper-based), IELTS (minimum score 6.0), or TWE (minimum score 22). Electronic applications accepted. *Expenses:* Contact institution. *Faculty research:* Psychological testing and assessment, LGBT issues, autism and developmental disorders, stepfamilies, gender issues.

**The Chicago School of Professional Psychology at Downtown Los Angeles,** Program in Clinical Psychology, Los Angeles, CA 90017. Offers applied behavior analysis (MA); clinical psychology (Psy D); marital and family therapy (MA).

**The Chicago School of Professional Psychology at Irvine,** Program in Marital and Family Therapy, Irvine, CA 92612. Offers clinical psychology (MA), including marital and family therapy; management practice (Psy D); psychodynamic psychotherapy (Psy D).

**Christian Theological Seminary,** Graduate and Professional Programs, Indianapolis, IN 46208-3301. Offers educational and arts ministries (MA); marriage and family therapy (MA); pastoral care and counseling (D Min); psychotherapy and faith (MA); theological studies (MTS); theology (M Div). *Accreditation:* AAMFT/COAMFTE (one or more programs are accredited); ACIPE; ATS. *Program availability:* Part-time. Terminal master's awarded for partial completion of doctoral program. *Degree requirements:* For master's, comprehensive exam (for some programs), thesis (for some programs), missionary and cross-cultural experience (for M Div); for doctorate, comprehensive exam, thesis/dissertation. *Entrance requirements:* For doctorate, M Div. *Additional exam requirements/recommendations for international students:* Recommended—TOEFL. Electronic applications accepted. *Faculty research:* Faith formation, peer learning post graduation.

**The College of New Jersey,** Office of Graduate and Advancing Education, School of Education, Department of Counselor Education, Program in Marriage and Family Therapy, Ewing, NJ 08628. Offers Ed S. *Program availability:* Part-time. *Entrance requirements:* For master's, previous master's degree or higher. *Additional exam requirements/recommendations for international students:* Required—TOEFL.

**The College of New Rochelle,** Graduate School, Division of Human Services, Program in Marriage and Family Therapy, New Rochelle, NY 10805-2308. Offers MMFT. *Degree requirements:* For master's, practica. *Entrance requirements:* For master's, minimum GPA of 3.0 in baccalaureate or other graduate-level work (overall and major field); undergraduate major in psychology, social work, or related field; personal statement; two letters of recommendation; official transcripts from all colleges/universities attended; proof of immunizations.

**The College of William and Mary,** School of Education, Program in Counselor Education, Williamsburg, VA 23187-8795. Offers addictions counseling (M Ed); community counseling (M Ed); counselor education (PhD); family counseling (M Ed); school counseling (M Ed). *Accreditation:* ACA; NCATE. *Faculty:* 9 full-time (2 women), 6 part-time/adjunct (5 women). *Students:* 69 full-time (47 women), 4 part-time (3 women); includes 15 minority (4 Black or African American, non-Hispanic/Latino; 1 Asian, non-Hispanic/Latino; 6 Hispanic/Latino; 4 Two or more races, non-Hispanic/Latino), 5 international. Average age 27. 116 applicants, 48% accepted, 28 enrolled. In 2016, 24 master's, 6 doctorates awarded. *Degree requirements:* For doctorate, comprehensive exam, thesis/dissertation. *Entrance requirements:* For master's, GRE, minimum GPA of 3.0; for doctorate, GRE, minimum GPA of 3.5. *Additional exam requirements/recommendations for international students:* Required—TOEFL (minimum score 100 iBT), IELTS (minimum score 7). *Application deadline:* For fall admission, 1/15 for domestic and international students. Application fee: $50. Electronic applications accepted. *Expenses:* $14,258 per year in-state full-time, $275 per credit in-state part-time; $30,500 per year out-of-state full-time, $1,200 per credit out-of-state part-time. *Financial support:* In 2016–17, 37 students received support, including 29 research assistantships (averaging $17,725 per year); career-related internships or fieldwork, scholarships/grants, and unspecified assistantships also available. Financial award application deadline: 1/15; financial award applicants required to submit FAFSA. *Faculty research:* Sexuality, multicultural education, addiction counseling, transpersonal psychology, measurement and evaluation in counseling. *Unit head:* Dr. Charles F. Gressard, Department Chair, 757-221-2352, E-mail: cfgres@wm.edu. *Application contact:* Dorothy Smith Osborne, Assistant Dean for Academic Programs and Student Services, 757-221-2317, E-mail: dsosbo@wm.edu.
Website: http://education.wm.edu

**Colorado State University,** College of Health and Human Sciences, Department of Human Development and Family Studies, Fort Collins, CO 80523-1570. Offers applied developmental science (PhD); family and developmental studies (MS); marriage and family therapy (MS). *Accreditation:* AAMFT/COAMFTE. *Faculty:* 18 full-time (15 women), 3 part-time/adjunct (0 women). *Students:* 34 full-time (30 women), 4 part-time (3 women); includes 6 minority (2 Asian, non-Hispanic/Latino; 4 Hispanic/Latino), 1 international. Average age 27. 64 applicants, 38% accepted, 14 enrolled. In 2016, 6 master's, 3 doctorates awarded. Terminal master's awarded for partial completion of doctoral program. *Degree requirements:* For master's, thesis; for doctorate, comprehensive exam, thesis/dissertation. *Entrance requirements:* For master's and doctorate, GRE General Test, 3 letters of recommendation; minimum GPA of 3.0. *Additional exam requirements/recommendations for international students:* Required—TOEFL (minimum score 550 paper-based; 80 iBT), IELTS (minimum score 6.5), PTE (minimum score 58). *Application deadline:* For fall admission, 1/2 priority date for domestic and international students. Application fee: $60 ($70 for international students). Electronic applications accepted. *Expenses: Tuition,* state resident: full-time $9628. Tuition, nonresident: full-time $23,603. *Required fees:* $2253; $528.14 per credit hour. $264.07 per semester. Tuition and fees vary according to course load and program. *Financial support:* In 2016–17, 35 students received support, including 14 research assistantships with full and partial tuition reimbursements available (averaging $10,449 per year), 13 teaching assistantships with full and partial tuition reimbursements available (averaging $8,038 per year); fellowships with full and partial tuition reimbursements available, Federal Work-Study, scholarships/grants, health care benefits, and unspecified assistantships also available. Financial award application deadline: 1/2; financial award applicants required to submit FAFSA. *Faculty research:* Risk, resilience, and developmental psychopathology; treatment, intervention, and prevention science; emotion, regulation, and relational processes; adult development and aging; cultural context and diversity. *Total annual research expenditures:* $1.2 million. *Unit head:* Dr. Lise Youngblade, Department Head, 970-491-3581, Fax: 970-491-7975, E-mail: lise.youngblade@colostate.edu. *Application contact:* Mary Daughtrey, Administrative Assistant III, 970-491-2872, Fax: 970-491-7975, E-mail: mary.daughtrey@colostate.edu.
Website: http://www.hdfs.chhs.colostate.edu/

**Converse College,** School of Education and Graduate Studies, Program in Marriage and Family Therapy, Spartanburg, SC 29302. Offers MMFT. *Accreditation:* AAMFT/COAMFTE. *Expenses: Tuition:* Full-time $3600; part-time $400 per credit hour. *Required fees:* $70 per term. *Application contact:* 864-596-9404, E-mail: graduate@converse.edu.

**Denver Seminary,** Graduate and Professional Programs, Littleton, CO 80120. Offers apologetics (Certificate); biblical studies (MA); Christian formation and soul care (MA, Certificate); Christian studies (MA, Certificate); church and parachurch leadership (D Min); counseling licensure (MA); counseling ministry (MA); intercultural ministry (Certificate); leadership (MA, Certificate); marriage and family counseling (D Min); pastoral ministry (D Min); philosophy of religion (MA); spiritual guidance (Certificate); theology (M Div, Certificate); worship (Certificate); youth and family ministry (MA). *Accreditation:* ACA; ACIPE; ATS (one or more programs are accredited). *Program availability:* Part-time, evening/weekend, online learning. *Degree requirements:* For master's, 2 foreign languages, thesis (for some programs); for doctorate, 2 foreign languages, thesis/dissertation. *Entrance requirements:* For doctorate, M Div, 3 years of ministry experience. *Additional exam requirements/recommendations for international students:* Required—TOEFL (minimum score 575 paper-based; 90 iBT). Electronic applications accepted.

**Dominican University of California,** School of Education and Counseling Psychology, Counseling Psychology Department, San Rafael, CA 94901-2298. Offers general (MS); marriage and family therapy (MS). *Program availability:* Part-time, evening/weekend. *Degree requirements:* For master's, comprehensive exam (for some programs), thesis (for some programs). *Entrance requirements:* For master's, minimum GPA of 3.0 for last 60 units, autobiography, response to scenario. *Additional exam requirements/recommendations for international students:* Required—TOEFL (minimum score 550 paper-based; 80 iBT), IELTS (minimum score 6.5). Electronic applications accepted. Application fee is waived when completed online. *Expenses:* Contact institution.

**Drexel University,** College of Nursing and Health Professions, Department of Couple and Family Therapy, Philadelphia, PA 19104-2875. Offers MFT, PhD. *Accreditation:* AAMFT/COAMFTE (one or more programs are accredited). *Program availability:* Part-time. *Faculty:* 7 full-time (4 women), 13 part-time/adjunct (7 women). *Students:* 47 full-time (42 women), 17 part-time (all women); includes 25 minority (13 Black or African American, non-Hispanic/Latino; 5 Asian, non-Hispanic/Latino; 3 Hispanic/Latino; 4 Two or more races, non-Hispanic/Latino), 5 international. Average age 29. In 2016, 16 master's, 2 doctorates awarded. Terminal master's awarded for partial completion of doctoral program. *Degree requirements:* For master's, comprehensive exam, thesis; for

doctorate, thesis/dissertation, qualifying exam. *Entrance requirements:* For master's, GRE General Test or MAT, minimum GPA of 2.75; for doctorate, GRE General Test, minimum GPA of 3.0. *Application deadline:* For fall admission, 3/1 for domestic students. Applications are processed on a rolling basis. Application fee: $50. Electronic applications accepted. *Expenses: Tuition:* Full-time $32,184; part-time $1192 per credit hour. *Required fees:* $280. Tuition and fees vary according to campus/location and program. *Financial support:* Career-related internships or fieldwork, Federal Work-Study, and institutionally sponsored loans available. Support available to part-time students. Financial award application deadline: 5/1; financial award applicants required to submit FAFSA. *Faculty research:* Family assessment, gender issues, chronic illness, early intervention. *Unit head:* Dr. Marlene Watson, Director, 215-762-6782, E-mail: marlene.f.watson@drexel.edu. *Application contact:* Director of Graduate Admissions, 215-895-6700, Fax: 215-895-5939, E-mail: enroll@drexel.edu.
Website: http://drexel.edu/familyTherapy/

**Duquesne University,** School of Education, Department of Counseling, Psychology, and Special Education, Program in Counselor Education, Pittsburgh, PA 15282-0001. Offers clinical mental health counseling (MS Ed, Post-Master's Certificate); counselor education and supervision (Ed D); counselor licensure (Post-Master's Certificate); marriage and family counseling (MS Ed); school counseling (MS Ed). *Accreditation:* ACA (one or more programs are accredited). *Program availability:* Part-time, evening/weekend. *Faculty:* 8 full-time (3 women). *Students:* 188 full-time (139 women), 5 part-time (4 women); includes 39 minority (20 Black or African American, non-Hispanic/Latino; 5 Asian, non-Hispanic/Latino; 5 Hispanic/Latino; 9 Two or more races, non-Hispanic/Latino), 8 international. Average age 29. 152 applicants, 73% accepted, 69 enrolled. In 2016, 34 master's, 9 doctorates awarded. *Degree requirements:* For master's, thesis optional; for doctorate, thesis/dissertation. *Entrance requirements:* For master's, letters of recommendation, essay, interview, bachelor's degree; for doctorate, GRE, letters of recommendation, essay, interview, master's degree; for Post-Master's Certificate, GRE, letters of recommendation, essay, interview, bachelor's/master's degree. Additional exam requirements/recommendations for international students: Required—TOEFL (minimum score 550 paper-based), IELTS (minimum score 7). *Application deadline:* For fall admission, 3/1 for domestic students; for spring admission, 9/1 for domestic students. Applications are processed on a rolling basis. Application fee: $0. Electronic applications accepted. *Expenses: Tuition:* Full-time $22,212; part-time $1234 per credit. Tuition and fees vary according to program. *Financial support:* Research assistantships, teaching assistantships, and Federal Work-Study available. Support available to part-time students. *Unit head:* Dr. Jered Kolbert, Professor/Director, 412-396-4471, Fax: 412-396-1340, E-mail: kolbertj@duq.edu. *Application contact:* Michael Dolinger, Director of Student and Academic Services, 412-396-6647, Fax: 412-396-5585, E-mail: dolingerm@duq.edu.

**East Carolina University,** Graduate School, College of Health and Human Performance, Department of Human Development and Family Science, Greenville, NC 27858-4353. Offers birth through kindergarten education (MA Ed); child development and family relations (MS); marriage and family therapy (MS); medical family therapy (PhD). *Accreditation:* AAMFT/COAMFTE. *Program availability:* Part-time. *Students:* 67 full-time (62 women), 25 part-time (23 women); includes 22 minority (13 Black or African American, non-Hispanic/Latino; 2 American Indian or Alaska Native, non-Hispanic/Latino; 1 Asian, non-Hispanic/Latino; 3 Hispanic/Latino; 1 Native Hawaiian or other Pacific Islander, non-Hispanic/Latino; 2 Two or more races, non-Hispanic/Latino), 1 international. Average age 29. 126 applicants, 49% accepted, 43 enrolled. In 2016, 24 master's, 4 doctorates awarded. *Degree requirements:* For master's, comprehensive exam, thesis optional. *Application deadline:* For fall admission, 1/15 for domestic students; for spring admission, 10/15 for domestic students. Applications are processed on a rolling basis. Application fee: $50. *Financial support:* Research assistantships, teaching assistantships, career-related internships or fieldwork, Federal Work-Study, institutionally sponsored loans, and scholarships/grants available. Support available to part-time students. Financial award application deadline: 6/1. *Faculty research:* Child care quality, mental health delivery systems for children, family violence. *Unit head:* Dr. Sharon Ballard, Interim Chair, 252-328-1356, E-mail: ballards@ecu.edu. *Application contact:* Dean of Graduate School, 252-328-6012, Fax: 252-328-6071, E-mail: gradschool@ecu.edu.
Website: http://www.ecu.edu/cs-hhp/hdfs/

**Eastern Nazarene College,** Adult and Graduate Studies, Program in Marriage and Family Therapy, Quincy, MA 02170. Offers MS. *Program availability:* Part-time, evening/weekend. *Entrance requirements:* For master's, 3 letters of recommendation, resume. Additional exam requirements/recommendations for international students: Required—TOEFL (minimum score 550 paper-based).

**Eastern University,** Program in Marriage and Family Therapy Studies, St. Davids, PA 19087-3696. Offers marriage and family studies (DA); marriage and family therapy (PhD). *Program availability:* Evening/weekend, online learning. *Students:* 60 full-time (43 women); includes 41 minority (37 Black or African American, non-Hispanic/Latino; 1 Asian, non-Hispanic/Latino; 2 Hispanic/Latino; 1 Two or more races, non-Hispanic/Latino), 1 international. Average age 43. In 2016, 8 doctorates awarded. *Degree requirements:* For doctorate, thesis/dissertation. *Entrance requirements:* Additional exam requirements/recommendations for international students: Required—TOEFL (minimum score 550 paper-based; 79 iBT). *Application deadline:* Applications are processed on a rolling basis. Application fee: $75. Electronic applications accepted. Application fee is waived when completed online. *Expenses:* $785 per credit. *Unit head:* Michael Dziedziak, Executive Director of Enrollment, 800-452-0996, E-mail: gpsadmissions@eastern.edu.
Website: http://www.eastern.edu/academics/programs/da-marriage-and-family/da-marriage-and-family

**Edgewood College,** Program in Marriage and Family Therapy, Madison, WI 53711. Offers MS. *Accreditation:* AAMFT/COAMFTE. *Program availability:* Part-time, evening/weekend. *Faculty:* 2 full-time (both women), 8 part-time/adjunct (5 women). *Students:* 23 full-time (20 women), 24 part-time (21 women); includes 5 minority (4 Black or African American, non-Hispanic/Latino; 1 Hispanic/Latino), 2 international. Average age 32. 34 applicants, 44% accepted, 12 enrolled. In 2016, 32 master's awarded. *Degree requirements:* For master's, research project. *Entrance requirements:* For master's, minimum GPA of 3.0, 2 letters of reference, interviews. Additional exam requirements/recommendations for international students: Required—TOEFL. *Application deadline:* For fall admission, 2/1 for domestic students; for spring admission, 10/1 for domestic students. Application fee: $30. Electronic applications accepted. *Expenses: Tuition:* Part-time $898 per credit. Tuition and fees vary according to course load. *Faculty research:* Self-compassion. *Unit head:* Dr. William Hutter, Associate Dean, 608-663-3211, Fax: 608-663-3291, E-mail: whutter@edgewood.edu. *Application contact:* Jenna Alsteen, Admissions Counselor, 608-663-3250, Fax: 608-663-2214, E-mail: gps@edgewood.edu.
Website: http://www.edgewood.edu/academics/graduate/MFT/default.aspx

**Evangelical Seminary,** Graduate and Professional Programs, Myerstown, PA 17067-1212. Offers Biblical studies (MAR); congregational ministry (M Div); global and contextual studies (M Div, MAR); historical and theological studies (MAR); interdisciplinary studies (MAR); marriage and family counseling (M Div); marriage and family therapy (MA); New Testament (MAR); Old Testament (MAR); spiritual formation (MAR); teaching ministry (M Div); youth ministry (M Div). *Accreditation:* ATS (one or more programs are accredited). *Program availability:* Part-time, online learning. *Degree requirements:* For master's, 2 foreign languages. *Entrance requirements:* For master's, minimum GPA of 2.5. Additional exam requirements/recommendations for international students: Required—TOEFL (minimum score 550 paper-based). *Faculty research:* Literary form and structure within the Hebrew and Greek scriptures, Wesley studies, esoteric biblical languages, the Mosaic law and the Christian, ethics.

**Fairfield University,** Graduate School of Education and Allied Professions, Fairfield, CT 06824. Offers applied behavior analysis (ATC); applied psychology (MA); clinical mental health counseling (MA, CAS); educational technology (MA); elementary education (MA, CAS); family studies (MA); integration of spirituality and religion in counseling (ATC); marriage and family therapy (MA); reading and language development (Sixth Year Certificate); school counseling (MA, CAS); school psychology (MA, CAS); school-based marriage and family therapy (ATC); secondary education (MA); special education (MA, CAS); substance abuse counseling (ATC); teaching (Certificate); teaching and foundations (MA, CAS); TESOL, world languages, and bilingual education (MA, CAS). *Accreditation:* NCATE. *Program availability:* Part-time, evening/weekend. *Faculty:* 19 full-time (15 women), 38 part-time/adjunct (26 women). *Students:* 153 full-time (132 women), 302 part-time (252 women); includes 97 minority (24 Black or African American, non-Hispanic/Latino; 12 Asian, non-Hispanic/Latino; 55 Hispanic/Latino; 6 Two or more races, non-Hispanic/Latino), 6 international. Average age 32. 283 applicants, 61% accepted, 97 enrolled. In 2016, 130 master's awarded. *Degree requirements:* For master's, comprehensive exam. *Entrance requirements:* For master's, minimum GPA of 3.0, 2 recommendations, resume. Additional exam requirements/recommendations for international students: Required—TOEFL (minimum score 550 paper-based; 84 iBT) or IELTS (minimum score 7.5). *Application deadline:* For fall admission, 2/15 for international students; for spring admission, 10/1 for international students. Application fee: $60. Electronic applications accepted. *Expenses:* $725 per credit hour. *Financial support:* In 2016–17, 42 students received support. Career-related internships or fieldwork and unspecified assistantships available. Support available to part-time students. Financial award applicants required to submit FAFSA. *Faculty research:* Reading and literacy, writing, social justice and inequality in education, addictions and mental health issues, therapeutic relationships and clinical supervision. *Unit head:* Dr. Robert D. Hannafin, Dean, 203-254-4250, Fax: 203-254-4241, E-mail: rhannafin@fairfield.edu. *Application contact:* Marianne Gumpper, Director of Graduate Admission, 203-254-4184, Fax: 203-254-4073, E-mail: gradadmis@fairfield.edu.
Website: http://www.fairfield.edu/gseap

**Florida State University,** The Graduate School, College of Human Sciences, Department of Family and Child Sciences, Tallahassee, FL 32306. Offers family and child sciences (MS); family relations (PhD); marriage and family therapy (PhD). *Accreditation:* AAMFT/COAMFTE. *Program availability:* Part-time. *Faculty:* 14 full-time (9 women). *Students:* 30 full-time (20 women), 3 part-time (all women); includes 13 minority (7 Black or African American, non-Hispanic/Latino; 1 Asian, non-Hispanic/Latino; 2 Hispanic/Latino; 1 Native Hawaiian or other Pacific Islander, non-Hispanic/Latino; 2 Two or more races, non-Hispanic/Latino), 1 international. 38 applicants, 37% accepted, 10 enrolled. In 2016, 6 master's, 4 doctorates awarded. Terminal master's awarded for partial completion of doctoral program. *Degree requirements:* For master's, thesis optional; for doctorate, thesis/dissertation, preliminary examination; clinical examination (for marriage and family therapy). *Entrance requirements:* For master's and doctorate, GRE General Test, writing assessment, minimum GPA of 3.0. Additional exam requirements/recommendations for international students: Required—TOEFL (minimum score 550 paper-based; 80 iBT). *Application deadline:* For fall admission, 12/1 for domestic and international students. Applications are processed on a rolling basis. Application fee: $30. Electronic applications accepted. *Expenses:* Tuition, state resident: full-time $7263; part-time $403.51 per credit hour. Tuition, nonresident: full-time $18,087; part-time $1004.85 per credit hour. *Required fees:* $1365; $75.81 per credit hour. $20 per semester. Tuition and fees vary according to campus/location. *Financial support:* In 2016–17, 31 students received support, including 8 research assistantships with full tuition reimbursements available (averaging $11,647 per year), 23 teaching assistantships with full tuition reimbursements available (averaging $10,594 per year); fellowships with partial tuition reimbursements available, career-related internships or fieldwork, Federal Work-Study, institutionally sponsored loans, scholarships/grants, health care benefits, and unspecified assistantships also available. Financial award application deadline: 1/5; financial award applicants required to submit FAFSA. *Faculty research:* Family therapy, parent-child relations, distressed families and foster care, marital processes, relational interventions, family structural complexity. *Total annual research expenditures:* $889,003. *Unit head:* Dr. Joseph Grzywacz, Department Chair, 850-644-3217, Fax: 850-644-3439, E-mail: jgrzywacz@fsu.edu. *Application contact:* Donna Romano, Office Administrator, 850-644-3217, Fax: 850-644-3439, E-mail: dromano@fsu.edu.
Website: http://www.chs.fsu.edu/Departments/Family-Child-Sciences

**Fresno Pacific University,** Biblical Seminary, Program in Marriage and Family Therapy, Fresno, CA 93702-4709. Offers MA. *Degree requirements:* For master's, thesis or alternative. *Entrance requirements:* For master's, minimum GPA of 3.0. Additional exam requirements/recommendations for international students: Required—TOEFL (minimum score 550 paper-based). *Expenses:* Contact institution.

**Friends University,** Graduate School, Wichita, KS 67213. Offers family therapy (MSFT); global business administration (MBA), including accounting, business law, change management, health care leadership, management information systems, supply chain management and logistics; health care leadership (MHCL); management information systems (MMIS); professional business administration (MBA), including accounting, business law, change management, health care leadership, management information systems, supply chain management and logistics. *Program availability:* Part-time, evening/weekend, online learning. *Degree requirements:* For master's, research project. *Entrance requirements:* For master's, bachelor's degree from accredited institution, official transcripts, interview with program director, letter(s) of recommendation. Additional exam requirements/recommendations for international students: Required—TOEFL (minimum score 560 paper-based). Electronic applications accepted.

**Fuller Theological Seminary,** Graduate Programs, Pasadena, CA 91182. Offers Christian leadership (MACL); clinical psychology (PhD, Psy D); family studies (MA); global leadership (MA); global ministries (D Min); global ministries (Korean language) (D Min); intercultural studies (MA, Th M, PhD); intercultural studies (Korean language) (MA); marital and family therapy (MS); marriage and family enrichment (Certificate); ministry (M Div, D Min); missiology (D Miss); missiology (Korean language) (Th M); theology (MA, Th M, PhD), including evangelism (MA), family life education (MA), pastoral ministry (MA), recovery ministry (MA), worship music ministry (MA), worship, theology, and the arts (MA), youth, family, and culture (MA); theology and ministry (MA).

**Geneva College,** Master of Arts in Counseling Program, Beaver Falls, PA 15010-3599. Offers clinical mental health counseling (MA); marriage and family counseling (MA); school counseling (MA). *Accreditation:* ACA. *Program availability:* Part-time, evening/

weekend. *Faculty:* 6 full-time (3 women), 3 part-time/adjunct (2 women). *Students:* 35 full-time (28 women), 32 part-time (23 women); includes 11 minority (9 Black or African American, non-Hispanic/Latino; 2 Hispanic/Latino). Average age 34. 42 applicants, 71% accepted, 21 enrolled. In 2016, 24 master's awarded. *Degree requirements:* For master's, comprehensive exam, 50-60 credits (depending on program), practicum, internship. *Entrance requirements:* For master's, minimum GPA of 3.0 (preferred), 3 letters of recommendation, essay on career goals, resume of educational and professional experiences. Additional exam requirements/recommendations for international students: Required—TOEFL. *Application deadline:* For fall admission, 9/1 for domestic students; for spring admission, 1/10 for domestic students. Applications are processed on a rolling basis. Electronic applications accepted. *Expenses:* $670 per credit. *Financial support:* In 2016–17, 3 students received support. Research assistantships, teaching assistantships, career-related internships or fieldwork, and unspecified assistantships available. Financial award application deadline: 8/1; financial award applicants required to submit FAFSA. *Faculty research:* Blended family counseling; premarital and newlywed couples; religion in clinical supervision; conceptual mapping in research, supervision, and clinical work. *Unit head:* Dr. Shannan Shiderly, Program Director, 724-847-6649, Fax: 724-847-6101, E-mail: slshider@geneva.edu. *Application contact:* Marina Frazier, Graduate Program Manager, 724-847-6697, E-mail: counseling@geneva.edu.

**George Fox University,** College of Education, Graduate Department of Counseling, Newberg, OR 97132-2697. Offers clinical mental health counseling (MA); marriage, couple and family counseling (MA, Certificate); school counseling (MA, Certificate); school psychology (Ed S). *Program availability:* Part-time. *Degree requirements:* For master's, clinical project. *Entrance requirements:* For master's, MAT or GRE, bachelor's degree from regionally-accredited college or university, minimum cumulative GPA of 3.0, 1 professional and 1 academic reference, resume, on-campus interview, official transcripts. Additional exam requirements/recommendations for international students: Required—TOEFL (minimum score 577 paper-based; 90 iBT), IELTS (minimum score 7). Electronic applications accepted. *Expenses:* Contact institution.

**Gonzaga University,** School of Education, Spokane, WA 99258. Offers clinical mental health counseling (MA); elementary education (MIT); leadership and administration (MA); marriage and family counseling (MA); school counseling (MA); secondary education (MIT); special education (M Ed, MIT); sport and athletic administration (MA). *Accreditation:* NCATE. *Program availability:* Part-time, evening/weekend, 100% online. *Faculty:* 22 full-time (17 women), 38 part-time/adjunct (22 women). *Students:* 104 full-time (73 women), 275 part-time (184 women); includes 31 minority (5 Black or African American, non-Hispanic/Latino; 1 American Indian or Alaska Native, non-Hispanic/Latino; 3 Asian, non-Hispanic/Latino; 18 Hispanic/Latino; 4 Two or more races, non-Hispanic/Latino), 163 international. Average age 32. 419 applicants, 67% accepted, 165 enrolled. In 2016, 39 master's awarded. *Degree requirements:* For master's, comprehensive exam. *Entrance requirements:* For master's, GRE, MAT, and/or Washington Educators Skills Test-Basic (WEST-B), official transcripts from all colleges or universities attended, interview, two letters of recommendation, resume, essay, minimum GPA of 3.0. Additional exam requirements/recommendations for international students: Required—TOEFL (minimum score 580 paper-based, 88 iBT) or IELTS (minimum score 6.5). *Application deadline:* Applications are processed on a rolling basis. Application fee: $50. Electronic applications accepted. *Expenses:* Contact institution. *Financial support:* In 2016–17, 28 students received support. Scholarships/grants and tuition waivers available. Support available to part-time students. Financial award applicants required to submit FAFSA. *Unit head:* Dr. Vincent Alfonso, Dean, 509-313-3594, Fax: 509-313-5821, E-mail: alfonso@gonzaga.edu. *Application contact:* Luke Cairney, Graduate Admissions Program Specialist, 509-313-3821, E-mail: cairney@gonzaga.edu.
Website: http://www.gonzaga.edu/Academics/Colleges-and-Schools/School-of-Education

**Harding University,** College of Bible and Ministry, Program in Marriage and Family Therapy, Searcy, AR 72149-0001. Offers marriage and family therapy (MS); mental health counseling (MS). *Program availability:* Part-time. *Faculty:* 5 full-time (1 woman). *Students:* 17 full-time (13 women). Average age 27. 9 applicants, 100% accepted, 9 enrolled. In 2016, 12 master's awarded. *Degree requirements:* For master's, comprehensive exam, 15-month practicum. *Entrance requirements:* For master's, GRE General Test, minimum undergraduate GPA of 2.75, graduate 3.0. Additional exam requirements/recommendations for international students: Required—TOEFL (minimum score 550 paper-based; 79 iBT). *Application deadline:* For fall admission, 4/1 priority date for domestic students. Applications are processed on a rolling basis. Application fee: $40. Tuition and fees vary according to degree level and program. *Financial support:* In 2016–17, 5 students received support. Scholarships/grants available. Financial award applicants required to submit FAFSA. *Faculty research:* Forgiveness, substance abuse, post-traumatic stress disorder. *Unit head:* Dr. Lewis L. Moore, Chairman, 501-279-4347, Fax: 501-279-4417, E-mail: lmoore@harding.edu. *Application contact:* Ruth Ann Dawson, Office Manager, 501-279-4347, Fax: 501-279-4417, E-mail: radawson@harding.edu.
Website: http://www.harding.edu/MFT/

**Hardin-Simmons University,** Graduate School, Cynthia Ann Parker College of Liberal Arts, Department of Psychology, Program in Clinical Counseling and Marriage and Family Therapy, Abilene, TX 79698-0001. Offers MA. *Program availability:* Part-time. *Faculty:* 6 full-time (3 women). *Students:* 14 full-time (all women), 2 part-time (both women); includes 5 minority (all Hispanic/Latino). Average age 29. In 2016, 13 master's awarded. *Degree requirements:* For master's, comprehensive exam, clinical experience, project. *Entrance requirements:* For master's, minimum undergraduate GPA of 3.0 in major, 2.7 overall; 21 semester hours of course work in psychology, 18 of those in upper-division classes; writing sample; letters of recommendation. Additional exam requirements/recommendations for international students: Required—TOEFL (minimum score 550 paper-based; 75 iBT). *Application deadline:* For fall admission, 8/15 priority date for domestic students, 4/1 for international students; for spring admission, 1/5 priority date for domestic students, 9/1 for international students. Applications are processed on a rolling basis. Application fee: $50. *Expenses: Tuition:* Full-time $12,510; part-time $695 per credit hour. *Required fees:* $325; $110 per semester. *Financial support:* In 2016–17, 14 students received support, including 8 fellowships (averaging $1,750 per year); career-related internships or fieldwork and scholarships/grants also available. Support available to part-time students. Financial award application deadline: 6/30; financial award applicants required to submit FAFSA. *Faculty research:* Family stress management, spirituality in marriage, intimacy and sexuality in marriage, sex education in the church, role of faith in marital satisfaction. *Unit head:* Dr. Sherry Rosenblad, Program Director, 325-671-2271, Fax: 325-670-1458, E-mail: sherry.rosenblad@hsutx.edu. *Application contact:* Dr. Nancy Kucinski, Dean of Graduate Studies, 325-670-1298, Fax: 325-670-1564, E-mail: gradoff@hsutx.edu.
Website: http://www.hsutx.edu/academics/cap/graduate/ccmf

**Hofstra University,** School of Health Professions and Human Services, Programs in Counseling, Hempstead, NY 11549. Offers counseling (MS Ed, PD); creative arts therapy (MA); interdisciplinary transition specialist (Advanced Certificate); marriage and family therapy (MA); mental health counseling (MA, Advanced Certificate), including alcohol and substance abuse (Advanced Certificate); rehabilitation administration (PD); rehabilitation counseling (MS Ed, Advanced Certificate); rehabilitation counseling in mental health (MS Ed, Advanced Certificate); school counselor bilingual extension (Advanced Certificate). *Accreditation:* ACA. *Program availability:* Part-time, evening/weekend. *Students:* 116 full-time (100 women), 66 part-time (59 women); includes 48 minority (18 Black or African American, non-Hispanic/Latino; 11 Asian, non-Hispanic/Latino; 17 Hispanic/Latino; 2 Two or more races, non-Hispanic/Latino), 5 international. Average age 29. 166 applicants, 81% accepted, 66 enrolled. In 2016, 71 master's, 7 other advanced degrees awarded. *Degree requirements:* For master's, comprehensive exam (for some programs), thesis (for some programs), internship, practicum, student teaching, seminars, minimum GPA of 3.0. *Entrance requirements:* For master's, GRE, interview, letters of recommendation, portfolio, essay, professional experience, certification; for other advanced degree, GRE, interview, letters of recommendation, essay, professional experience, resume, master's degree. Additional exam requirements/recommendations for international students: Required—TOEFL (minimum score 550 paper-based; 80 iBT). *Application deadline:* Applications are processed on a rolling basis. Application fee: $75. Electronic applications accepted. *Expenses: Tuition:* Full-time $1240. *Required fees:* $970. Tuition and fees vary according to program. *Financial support:* In 2016–17, 76 students received support, including 40 fellowships with full and partial tuition reimbursements available (averaging $3,465 per year), 5 research assistantships with full and partial tuition reimbursements available (averaging $6,939 per year); career-related internships or fieldwork, Federal Work-Study, institutionally sponsored loans, scholarships/grants, traineeships, tuition waivers (full and partial), and unspecified assistantships also available. Support available to part-time students. Financial award applicants required to submit FAFSA. *Faculty research:* The constructs of hope and grit; the efficacy of support groups in treating eating disorders; attitudes of primary care physicians related to providing integrated care with mental health counselors; expanding the counselor identity through disability cultural competence; vocational evaluation and assessment collaboration; disability cultural competence. *Unit head:* Dr. Jamie Mitus, Chairperson, 516-463-5759, E-mail: jamie.s.mitus@hofstra.edu. *Application contact:* Sunil Samuel, Assistant Vice President of Admissions, 516-463-4723, Fax: 516-463-4664, E-mail: graduateadmission@hofstra.edu.
Website: http://www.hofstra.edu/academics/colleges/healthscienceshumanservices/

**Hope International University,** School of Graduate and Professional Studies, Program in Marriage and Family Therapy, Fullerton, CA 92831-3138. Offers MA, MFT. *Accreditation:* AAMFT/COAMFTE. *Degree requirements:* For master's, comprehensive exam, thesis (for some programs), final exam, practicum. *Entrance requirements:* For master's, minimum GPA of 3.0, interview, bachelor's degree, 2 references. Additional exam requirements/recommendations for international students: Required—TOEFL (minimum score 550 paper-based; 86 iBT); Recommended—IELTS (minimum score 6.5). Electronic applications accepted. *Expenses:* Contact institution.

**Idaho State University,** Office of Graduate Studies, Kasiska College of Health Professions, Department of Counseling, Pocatello, ID 83209-8120. Offers counseling (M Coun, Ed S), including marriage and family counseling (M Coun), mental health counseling (M Coun), school counseling (M Coun), student affairs and college counseling (M Coun); counselor education and counseling (PhD). *Accreditation:* ACA (one or more programs are accredited). *Program availability:* Part-time. *Degree requirements:* For master's, comprehensive exam, thesis, 4 semesters resident graduate study, practicum/internship; for doctorate, comprehensive exam, thesis/dissertation, 3 semesters internship, 4 consecutive semesters doctoral-level study on campus; for Ed S, comprehensive exam, thesis, case studies, oral exam. *Entrance requirements:* For master's, GRE General Test, MAT, minimum GPA of 3.0, bachelors degree, interview, 3 letters of recommendation; for doctorate, GRE General Test, MAT, minimum graduate GPA of 3.0, resume, interview, counseling license, master's degree; for Ed S, GRE General Test, minimum graduate GPA of 3.0, master's degree in counseling, 3 letters of recommendation, 2 years work experience. Additional exam requirements/recommendations for international students: Required—TOEFL (minimum score 600 paper-based; 80 iBT). Electronic applications accepted. *Faculty research:* Group counseling, multicultural counseling, family counseling, child therapy, supervision.

**Indiana University–Purdue University Fort Wayne,** College of Education and Public Policy, Department of Professional Studies, Fort Wayne, IN 46805-1499. Offers couple and family counseling (MS Ed); educational leadership (MS Ed); school counseling (MS Ed); special education (MS Ed, Certificate). *Program availability:* Part-time. *Degree requirements:* For master's, comprehensive exam, practicum, internship, portfolio. *Entrance requirements:* For master's, minimum GPA of 2.5, three professional letters of recommendation. Additional exam requirements/recommendations for international students: Required—TOEFL (minimum score 550 paper-based; 79 iBT). *Faculty research:* Learning opportunities with deafness and the hearing impaired, adolescent emotion, student evaluation of teaching.

**Indiana University South Bend,** School of Education, South Bend, IN 46634-7111. Offers addiction counseling (MS Ed); alcohol and drug counseling (Graduate Certificate); clinical mental health counseling (MS Ed); educational leadership (MS Ed); elementary education (MS Ed); marriage, couple, and family counseling (MS Ed); school counseling (MS Ed); secondary education (MS Ed); special education (MAT, MS Ed), including intense intervention (MS Ed), mild intervention (MS Ed). *Accreditation:* NCATE. *Program availability:* Part-time, evening/weekend. *Faculty:* 21 full-time (11 women), 9 part-time/adjunct (3 women). *Students:* 26 full-time (19 women), 104 part-time (80 women); includes 22 minority (13 Black or African American, non-Hispanic/Latino; 5 Hispanic/Latino; 4 Two or more races, non-Hispanic/Latino). Average age 35. 51 applicants, 69% accepted, 22 enrolled. In 2016, 31 master's, 2 other advanced degrees awarded. *Degree requirements:* For master's, thesis or alternative, exit project. *Entrance requirements:* For master's, letters of recommendation, GRE or minimum GPA of 3.0. Additional exam requirements/recommendations for international students: Required—TOEFL. *Application deadline:* For fall admission, 7/1 for domestic students; for spring admission, 11/1 for domestic students. Applications are processed on a rolling basis. Application fee: $40 ($60 for international students). Electronic applications accepted. *Expenses:* $276.98 per credit hour in-state; $652.54 per credit hour out-of-state. *Financial support:* Career-related internships or fieldwork available. Support available to part-time students. Financial award application deadline: 3/1; financial award applicants required to submit FAFSA. *Faculty research:* Professional dispositions, early childhood literacy, online learning, program assessments, problem-based learning. *Unit head:* Dr. Marvin Lynn, Dean, 574-520-4339, E-mail: lynnm@iusb.edu. *Application contact:* Yvonne Walker, Student Services Representative, 574-520-4185, E-mail: ydwalker@iusb.edu.
Website: https://www.iusb.edu/education/index.php

**Indiana Wesleyan University,** Graduate School, College of Arts and Sciences, Marion, IN 46953. Offers addictions counseling (MS); clinical mental health counseling (MS); community counseling (MS); marriage and family therapy (MS); school counseling (MS); student development counseling and administration (MS). *Accreditation:* ACA. *Program availability:* Part-time. *Degree requirements:* For master's, thesis or alternative. *Entrance*

## Marriage and Family Therapy

*requirements:* For master's, GRE General Test. Additional exam requirements/recommendations for international students: Required—TOEFL. Electronic applications accepted. *Expenses:* Contact institution. *Faculty research:* Community counseling, multicultural counseling, addictions.

**Instituto Tecnologico de Santo Domingo,** Graduate School, Area of Humanities and Social Sciences, Santo Domingo, Dominican Republic. Offers accounting (Certificate); adult education (Certificate); applied linguistics (MA); economics (MA); education (M Ed); educational psychology (MA, Certificate); gender and development (MA, Certificate); humanistic studies (MA); international marketing management (Certificate); international relations in the Caribbean basin (Certificate); intervention systems in family therapy (MA); linguistic and literary communication (Certificate); pedagogical support (MA); social science education (M Ed); sustainable human development (MA); terminal illness and death psychology (Certificate); youth and adult education (M Ed).

**Iona College,** School of Arts and Science, Marriage and Family Therapy Program, New Rochelle, NY 10801-1890. Offers MS. *Accreditation:* AAMFT/COAMFTE. *Program availability:* Part-time. *Faculty:* 4 full-time (1 woman), 2 part-time/adjunct (both women). *Students:* 37 full-time (32 women), 4 part-time (all women); includes 14 minority (11 Black or African American, non-Hispanic/Latino; 1 Asian, non-Hispanic/Latino; 9 Hispanic/Latino), 2 international. Average age 34. 16 applicants, 100% accepted, 10 enrolled. In 2016, 14 master's awarded. *Degree requirements:* For master's, thesis, project. *Entrance requirements:* For master's, interview, minimum GPA of 3.0. *Application deadline:* For fall admission, 8/1 priority date for domestic students, 7/1 for international students. Applications are processed on a rolling basis. Application fee: $50. Electronic applications accepted. *Expenses:* Contact institution. *Financial support:* In 2016–17, 12 students received support. Career-related internships or fieldwork, tuition waivers (partial), and unspecified assistantships available. Support available to part-time students. Financial award application deadline: 4/15; financial award applicants required to submit FAFSA. *Unit head:* Robert Burns, PhD, Program Director, 914-633-2418, E-mail: rburns@iona.edu. *Application contact:* Katelyn Brunck, Assistant Director of Graduate Admissions, 914-633-2451, Fax: 914-633-2277, E-mail: kbrunck@iona.edu.
Website: http://www.iona.edu/Academics/School-of-Arts-Science/Departments/Marriage-and-Family-Therapy/Graduate-Programs.aspx

**John Brown University,** Graduate Counseling Programs, Siloam Springs, AR 72761-2121. Offers clinical mental health counseling (MS); marriage and family therapy (MS); play therapy (Graduate Certificate); school counseling (MS). *Accreditation:* NCATE. *Program availability:* Part-time, evening/weekend. *Faculty:* 9 full-time (2 women), 18 part-time/adjunct (6 women). *Students:* 157 full-time (124 women), 153 part-time (124 women); includes 94 minority (50 Black or African American, non-Hispanic/Latino; 7 American Indian or Alaska Native, non-Hispanic/Latino; 3 Asian, non-Hispanic/Latino; 21 Hispanic/Latino; 13 Two or more races, non-Hispanic/Latino), 1 international. Average age 32. 129 applicants, 74% accepted, 83 enrolled. In 2016, 68 master's awarded. *Degree requirements:* For master's, practica or internships. *Entrance requirements:* For master's, GRE (minimum score of 300), recommendation forms from three people, 200-word essay describing professional plans and reason for seeking acceptance. Additional exam requirements/recommendations for international students: Required—TOEFL (minimum score 550 paper-based; 79 iBT). *Application deadline:* Applications are processed on a rolling basis. Application fee: $35 ($100 for international students). Electronic applications accepted. *Expenses:* Contact institution. *Financial support:* Fellowships, institutionally sponsored loans, scholarships/grants, and unspecified assistantships available. Financial award applicants required to submit FAFSA. *Unit head:* Dr. John V. Carmack, Program Director, 479-524-8630, E-mail: jcarmack@jbu.edu. *Application contact:* Mark Bjornsen, Graduate Counseling Representative, 479-631-4665, E-mail: mbjornsen@jbu.edu.
Website: http://www.jbu.edu/

**Kansas State University,** Graduate School, College of Human Ecology, Doctorate in Human Ecology Program, Manhattan, KS 66506-1407. Offers apparel and textiles (PhD); applied family sciences (PhD); couple and family therapy (PhD); hospitality administration (PhD); kinesiology (PhD); life-span human development (PhD). *Program availability:* Part-time. *Faculty:* 36 full-time (23 women). *Students:* 44 full-time (26 women), 16 part-time (10 women); includes 9 minority (3 Black or African American, non-Hispanic/Latino; 2 Asian, non-Hispanic/Latino; 2 Hispanic/Latino; 2 Two or more races, non-Hispanic/Latino), 18 international. Average age 30. 43 applicants, 35% accepted, 8 enrolled. In 2016, 13 doctorates awarded. *Degree requirements:* For doctorate, thesis/dissertation. *Entrance requirements:* Additional exam requirements/recommendations for international students: Required—TOEFL. *Application deadline:* For fall admission, 2/1 priority date for domestic and international students; for spring admission, 8/1 priority date for domestic and international students. Applications are processed on a rolling basis. Application fee: $50 ($75 for international students). Electronic applications accepted. *Expenses:* Tuition, state resident: full-time $9670. Tuition, nonresident: full-time $21,828. *Required fees:* $862. *Financial support:* In 2016–17, research assistantships with partial tuition reimbursements (averaging $12,000 per year), teaching assistantships with partial tuition reimbursements (averaging $12,000 per year) were awarded. Financial award application deadline: 3/1. *Total annual research expenditures:* $1.8 million. *Unit head:* Dr. John Buckwalter, Dean, 785-532-5500, Fax: 785-532-5504, E-mail: jbb3@ksu.edu. *Application contact:* Dr. Bronwyn Fees, Associate Dean for Academic Affairs, 785-532-5500, Fax: 785-532-5504, E-mail: fees@ksu.edu.

**Kansas State University,** Graduate School, College of Human Ecology, School of Family Studies and Human Services, Manhattan, KS 66506-1403. Offers applied family sciences (MS); communication sciences and disorders (MS); conflict resolution (Graduate Certificate); couple and family therapy (MS); early childhood education (MS); family and community service (MS); life-span human development (MS); personal financial planning (MS, PhD, Graduate Certificate); youth development (MS, Graduate Certificate). *Accreditation:* AAMFT/COAMFTE; ASHA. *Program availability:* Part-time, online learning. *Faculty:* 43 full-time (30 women), 4 part-time/adjunct (3 women). *Students:* 55 full-time (45 women), 87 part-time (73 women); includes 30 minority (9 Black or African American, non-Hispanic/Latino; 1 American Indian or Alaska Native, non-Hispanic/Latino; 1 Asian, non-Hispanic/Latino; 14 Hispanic/Latino; 1 Native Hawaiian or other Pacific Islander, non-Hispanic/Latino; 4 Two or more races, non-Hispanic/Latino), 6 international. Average age 29. 182 applicants, 29% accepted, 38 enrolled. In 2016, 39 master's, 17 other advanced degrees awarded. *Degree requirements:* For master's, comprehensive exam (for some programs), thesis optional. *Entrance requirements:* For master's, GRE, minimum GPA of 3.0 in last 2 years (60 semester hours) of undergraduate study; for doctorate, GRE. Additional exam requirements/recommendations for international students: Required—TOEFL (minimum score 600 paper-based). *Application deadline:* For fall admission, 2/1 priority date for domestic students, 1/1 priority date for international students; for spring admission, 10/1 priority date for domestic students, 8/1 priority date for international students; for summer admission, 2/1 priority date for domestic students, 12/1 priority date for international students. Applications are processed on a rolling basis. Application fee: $50 ($75 for international students). Electronic applications accepted. *Expenses:* Tuition, state resident: full-time $9670. Tuition, nonresident: full-time $21,828. *Required*

*fees:* $862. *Financial support:* In 2016–17, 35 students received support, including 25 research assistantships (averaging $10,000 per year), 9 teaching assistantships with full tuition reimbursements available (averaging $10,000 per year); unspecified assistantships also available. Financial award application deadline: 3/1. *Faculty research:* Health and security of military families, training in and evaluation of professional human services (marriage and couple therapy, family life education, treatment of speech and swallowing disorders, financial therapy), disorders of communication and swallowing, family and relationship development and health, financial decision-making. *Total annual research expenditures:* $8.4 million. *Unit head:* Dr. Dottie Durband, Director, 785-532-5510, Fax: 785-532-5505, E-mail: dottie@ksu.edu. *Application contact:* Kristi Hageman, Administrative Specialist, 785-532-5510, Fax: 785-532-5505, E-mail: klsmith@ksu.edu.
Website: http://www.he.k-state.edu/fshs/

**Kean University,** College of Liberal Arts, Program in Marriage and Family Therapy, Union, NJ 07083. Offers MA, Diploma. *Program availability:* Part-time. *Faculty:* 18 full-time (14 women). *Students:* 28 full-time (27 women), 8 part-time (6 women); includes 21 minority (13 Black or African American, non-Hispanic/Latino; 8 Hispanic/Latino). Average age 31. 11 applicants, 45% accepted, 5 enrolled. In 2016, 16 master's, 9 other advanced degrees awarded. *Degree requirements:* For Diploma, comprehensive exam, thesis, practicum in individual, marital and family therapy; internship. *Entrance requirements:* For degree, GRE General Test, minimum GPA of 3.0; official transcripts from all institutions attended; three letters of recommendation written by faculty and/or person(s) in professionally-related area; professional resume/curriculum vitae; interview; personal statement. Additional exam requirements/recommendations for international students: Required—TOEFL (minimum score 550 paper-based; 79 iBT), IELTS (minimum score 6.5). *Application deadline:* For fall admission, 6/1 for domestic and international students; for spring admission, 12/1 for domestic and international students. Applications are processed on a rolling basis. Application fee: $75. Electronic applications accepted. *Expenses:* Tuition, state resident: full-time $13,156; part-time $640 per credit. Tuition, nonresident: full-time $17,831; part-time $785 per credit. *Required fees:* $3316; $151 per credit. Tuition and fees vary according to course level, course load, degree level and program. *Financial support:* Scholarships/grants and unspecified assistantships available. Financial award applicants required to submit FAFSA. *Unit head:* Dr. Muriel Singer, Program Coordinator, 908-737-5886, E-mail: msinger@kean.edu. *Application contact:* Amy Clark, Program Assistant, 908-737-7100, E-mail: grad-adm@kean.edu.
Website: http://grad.kean.edu/professional-diploma-programs/marriage-family-therapy

**Kutztown University of Pennsylvania,** College of Education, Program in Counseling Psychology, Kutztown, PA 19530-0730. Offers clinical mental health counseling (MA); marriage, couple and family counseling (MA). *Program availability:* Part-time, evening/weekend. *Faculty:* 5 full-time (2 women). *Students:* 75 full-time (69 women), 51 part-time (43 women); includes 23 minority (8 Black or African American, non-Hispanic/Latino; 2 Asian, non-Hispanic/Latino; 11 Hispanic/Latino; 2 Two or more races, non-Hispanic/Latino), 1 international. Average age 29. 72 applicants, 71% accepted, 24 enrolled. In 2016, 38 master's awarded. *Degree requirements:* For master's, comprehensive exam, thesis optional. *Entrance requirements:* For master's, GRE General Test, 3 letters of recommendation, minimum undergraduate GPA of 3.0, psychobiographical statement, resume. Additional exam requirements/recommendations for international students: Required—TOEFL (minimum score 550 paper-based, 79 iBT) or IELTS (minimum score 6.5). *Application deadline:* For fall admission, 3/1 for domestic and international students; for spring admission, 10/1 for domestic and international students. Application fee: $35. Electronic applications accepted. *Expenses:* Tuition, state resident: full-time $4347; part-time $483 per credit. Tuition, nonresident: full-time $6525; part-time $725 per credit. *Required fees:* $88 per credit. One-time fee: $50 full-time. *Financial support:* Career-related internships or fieldwork, Federal Work-Study, scholarships/grants, and unspecified assistantships available. Financial award application deadline: 3/1; financial award applicants required to submit FAFSA. *Faculty research:* Family addictions. *Unit head:* Dr. Helen S Hamlet, Department Chair, 610-683-4204, Fax: 610-683-1585, E-mail: hamlet@kutztown.edu.
Website: https://www.kutztown.edu/academics/graduate-programs/counseling.htm

**Lancaster Bible College,** Graduate School, Lancaster, PA 17601-5036. Offers adult ministries (MA); Bible (MA); children and family ministry (MA); church planting (MA); consulting resource teacher (M Ed); elementary school counseling (M Ed); leadership (PhD); leadership studies (MA); marriage and family counseling (MA); mental health counseling (MA); pastoral studies (MA); secondary school counseling (M Ed); sports ministry (MA); student ministry (MA); town and country ministry (MA). *Program availability:* Part-time, evening/weekend. *Degree requirements:* For master's, comprehensive exam (for some programs), thesis (for some programs). *Entrance requirements:* For master's, bachelor's degree with a minimum of 30 credits of course work in Bible, minimum undergraduate GPA of 3.0, interview. Additional exam requirements/recommendations for international students: Required—TOEFL.

**La Salle University,** School of Arts and Sciences, Program in Counseling and Family Therapy, Philadelphia, PA 19141-1199. Offers industrial/organizational management and human resources (MA); marriage and family therapy (MA); pastoral counseling (MA); professional clinical counseling (MA). *Accreditation:* ACA; APA. *Program availability:* Part-time, evening/weekend. *Faculty:* 8 full-time (3 women), 20 part-time/adjunct (13 women). *Students:* 77 full-time (55 women), 180 part-time (147 women); includes 84 minority (44 Black or African American, non-Hispanic/Latino; 5 Asian, non-Hispanic/Latino; 31 Hispanic/Latino; 4 Two or more races, non-Hispanic/Latino), 5 international. Average age 30. 156 applicants, 76% accepted, 48 enrolled. In 2016, 106 master's awarded. *Degree requirements:* For master's, comprehensive exam. *Entrance requirements:* For master's, GRE or MAT (waived for applicants that already possess a master's degree in any field or for applicants that have a cumulative GPA of 3.5 or higher), minimum of 15 hours in psychology, counseling, or marriage and family studies; minimum GPA of 3.0; three letters of recommendation; personal statement; work experience (paid or volunteer). Additional exam requirements/recommendations for international students: Required—TOEFL. *Application deadline:* For fall admission, 8/15 priority date for domestic students, 7/15 for international students; for spring admission, 12/15 priority date for domestic students, 11/15 for international students; for summer admission, 4/15 priority date for domestic students, 3/15 for international students. Applications are processed on a rolling basis. Application fee: $35. Electronic applications accepted. Application fee is waived when completed online. *Expenses:* Contact institution. *Financial support:* In 2016–17, 37 students received support. Scholarships/grants and unspecified assistantships available. Support available to part-time students. Financial award application deadline: 8/31; financial award applicants required to submit FAFSA. *Faculty research:* Cognitive therapy, attribution theory, work habits, single parent families, treatment of addictions. *Unit head:* Dr. Donna A. Tonrey, Director, 215-951-1767, Fax: 215-951-1843, E-mail: psyma@lasalle.edu. *Application contact:* Elizabeth Heenan, Director, Graduate and Adult Enrollment, 215-951-1100, Fax: 215-951-1462, E-mail: heenan@lasalle.edu.
Website: http://www.lasalle.edu/counseling-family-therapy/

**Lee University,** Graduate Studies in Counseling, Cleveland, TN 37320-3450. Offers holistic child development (MS); marriage and family studies (MS); marriage and family therapy (MS); school counseling (MS). *Program availability:* Part-time, 100% online. *Faculty:* 8 full-time (3 women), 3 part-time/adjunct (0 women). *Students:* 86 full-time (65 women), 27 part-time (18 women); includes 46 minority (9 Black or African American, non-Hispanic/Latino; 1 American Indian or Alaska Native, non-Hispanic/Latino; 1 Asian, non-Hispanic/Latino; 33 Hispanic/Latino; 2 Two or more races, non-Hispanic/Latino), 8 international. Average age 31. 34 applicants, 65% accepted, 18 enrolled. In 2016, 31 master's awarded. *Degree requirements:* For master's, variable foreign language requirement, comprehensive exam (for some programs), thesis (for some programs), internship. *Entrance requirements:* For master's, GRE General Test or MAT (waived if undergraduate GPA is greater than 3.0 or if applicant already has a graduate degree), minimum undergraduate GPA of 3.0, 3 letters of recommendation, interview, official transcripts, essay. Additional exam requirements/recommendations for international students: Required—TOEFL (minimum score 61 iBT). *Application deadline:* For fall admission, 4/1 priority date for domestic and international students; for spring admission, 11/1 priority date for domestic and international students. Applications are processed on a rolling basis. Application fee: $25. Electronic applications accepted. *Expenses:* Tuition: Full-time $11,367; part-time $632 per credit hour. *Required fees:* $35 per term. One-time fee: $25. Tuition and fees vary according to program. *Financial support:* In 2016–17, 25 students received support. Career-related internships or fieldwork, Federal Work-Study, institutionally sponsored loans, scholarships/grants, and unspecified assistantships available. Financial award application deadline: 3/1; financial award applicants required to submit FAFSA. *Unit head:* Dr. Trevor Milliron, Director, 423-614-8126, Fax: 423-614-8124, E-mail: tmilliron@leeuniversity.edu. Website: http://www.leeuniversity.edu/academics/graduate/counseling.

**LeTourneau University,** Graduate Programs, Longview, TX 75607-7001. Offers business (MBA); counseling (MA), including licensed professional counselor, marriage and family therapy, school counseling; curriculum and instruction (M Ed); educational administration (M Ed); engineering (ME, MS); engineering management (MEM); health care administration (MS); marriage and family therapy (MA); psychology (MA); strategic leadership (MSL); teacher leadership (M Ed); teaching and learning (M Ed). *Program availability:* Part-time, 100% online, blended/hybrid learning. *Faculty:* 24 full-time (7 women), 40 part-time/adjunct (15 women). *Students:* 82 full-time (48 women), 428 part-time (331 women); includes 234 minority (138 Black or African American, non-Hispanic/Latino; 5 American Indian or Alaska Native, non-Hispanic/Latino; 5 Asian, non-Hispanic/Latino; 50 Hispanic/Latino; 36 Two or more races, non-Hispanic/Latino), 15 international. Average age 37. 257 applicants, 60% accepted, 141 enrolled. In 2016, 136 master's awarded. *Degree requirements:* For master's, thesis (for some programs). *Entrance requirements:* Additional exam requirements/recommendations for international students: Required—TOEFL. *Application deadline:* For fall admission, 8/22 for domestic students, 8/29 for international students; for winter admission, 10/10 for domestic students; for spring admission, 1/2 for domestic students, 1/10 for international students; for summer admission, 5/1 for domestic and international students. Applications are processed on a rolling basis. Electronic applications accepted. *Expenses:* $10,890-$18,450 tuition per year (depending on program). *Financial support:* Research assistantships, institutionally sponsored loans, and unspecified assistantships available. Financial award applicants required to submit FAFSA. *Application contact:* Chris Fontaine, Assistant Vice President for Enrollment Services and Global Admissions, 903-233-4312, E-mail: chrisfontaine@letu.edu. Website: http://www.letu.edu

**Lewis & Clark College,** Graduate School of Education and Counseling, Department of Counseling Psychology, Program in Marriage, Couple, and Family Therapy, Portland, OR 97219-7899. Offers MA, MS. *Accreditation:* AAMFT/COAMFTE. *Program availability:* Part-time, evening/weekend. *Degree requirements:* For master's, thesis (MS). *Entrance requirements:* For master's, GRE General Test, minimum undergraduate GPA of 2.75. Additional exam requirements/recommendations for international students: Required—TOEFL (minimum score 575 paper-based). *Application deadline:* For fall admission, 2/1 priority date for domestic and international students. Application fee: $50. Electronic applications accepted. *Financial support:* Career-related internships or fieldwork, Federal Work-Study, institutionally sponsored loans, scholarships/grants, health care benefits, and tuition waivers (partial) available. Support available to part-time students. Financial award application deadline: 3/1; financial award applicants required to submit FAFSA. *Unit head:* Dr. Teresa McDowell, Chair, 503-768-6060, Fax: 503-768-6065, E-mail: teresamc@lclark.edu. *Application contact:* Becky Haas, Director of Admissions, 503-768-6200, Fax: 503-768-6205, E-mail: gseadmit@lclark.edu. Website: http://graduate.lclark.edu/departments/counseling_psychology/marriage_couple_and_family_therapy/

**Liberty University,** School of Behavioral Sciences, Lynchburg, VA 24515. Offers clinical mental health counseling (MA); counselor education and supervision (PhD); human services counseling (MA), including addictions and recovery, business, child and family law, Christian ministries, criminal justice, crisis response and trauma, executive leadership, health and wellness, life coaching, marriage and family, military resilience; marriage and family therapy (MA); military resilience (Certificate); professional counseling (MA). *Program availability:* Part-time, online learning. *Students:* 2,041 full-time (1,612 women), 4,970 part-time (3,875 women); includes 1,991 minority (1,678 Black or African American, non-Hispanic/Latino; 33 American Indian or Alaska Native, non-Hispanic/Latino; 48 Asian, non-Hispanic/Latino; 80 Hispanic/Latino; 8 Native Hawaiian or other Pacific Islander, non-Hispanic/Latino; 144 Two or more races, non-Hispanic/Latino), 127 international. Average age 39. 5,496 applicants, 41% accepted, 1257 enrolled. In 2016, 2,813 master's, 11 doctorates, 20 other advanced degrees awarded. *Application deadline:* Applications are processed on a rolling basis. Application fee: $50. Electronic applications accepted. *Financial support:* Applicants required to submit FAFSA. *Unit head:* Dr. Ronald Hawkins, Founding Dean, School of Behavioral Sciences. *Application contact:* Jay Bridge, Director of Admissions, 800-424-9595, Fax: 800-628-7977, E-mail: gradadmissions@liberty.edu.

**Liberty University,** School of Divinity, Lynchburg, VA 24515. Offers Biblical studies (M Div); church history (MAR, Th M); discipleship and church ministry (M Div, MAR, MCM); evangelism and church planting (M Div, MAR, MCM); global studies (M Div, MCM, MGS); homiletics (M Div, MAR, Th M, D Min); leadership (M Div, D Min); marketplace chaplaincy (M Div, MCM); ministry (D Min); pastoral counseling (M Div, MA, MAR, D Min), including addictions and recovery (MA), crisis response and trauma (MA), discipleship and church ministries (MA), leadership (MA), life coaching (MA), marketplace chaplaincy (MA), marriage and family (MA), military resilience (MA), pastoral counseling (MA); pastoral ministries (M Div, MCM); religious education (MRE); theology (M Div, MAR, MTS); theology and apologetics (PhD); worship (M Div, MAR, MCM, D Min). *Program availability:* Part-time, online learning. *Students:* 2,140 full-time (615 women), 3,020 part-time (906 women); includes 1,312 minority (1,016 Black or African American, non-Hispanic/Latino; 9 American Indian or Alaska Native, non-Hispanic/Latino; 100 Asian, non-Hispanic/Latino; 90 Hispanic/Latino; 7 Native Hawaiian or other Pacific Islander, non-Hispanic/Latino; 90 Two or more races, non-Hispanic/Latino), 158 international. Average age 42. 3,651 applicants, 37% accepted, 909 enrolled. In 2016, 1,551 master's, 39 doctorates, 168 other advanced degrees awarded. *Degree requirements:* For master's, 2 foreign languages, thesis (for some programs); for doctorate, 2 foreign languages, thesis/dissertation. *Entrance requirements:* For

master's, minimum undergraduate GPA of 2.0; for doctorate, GRE General Test or MAT, minimum graduate GPA of 3.0. Additional exam requirements/recommendations for international students: Required—TOEFL (minimum score 600 paper-based; 100 iBT). *Application deadline:* For fall admission, 6/1 for domestic students; for spring admission, 11/1 for domestic students. Applications are processed on a rolling basis. Application fee: $50. Electronic applications accepted. *Expenses:* Contact institution. *Financial support:* Teaching assistantships with tuition reimbursements, career-related internships or fieldwork, and Federal Work-Study available. Financial award applicants required to submit FAFSA. *Unit head:* Dr. Ed Hindson, Dean, 434-592-4140, Fax: 434-522-0415, E-mail: ehindson@liberty.edu. *Application contact:* Jay Bridge, Director of Graduate Admissions, 800-424-9595, Fax: 800-628-7977, E-mail: gradadmissions@liberty.edu.
Website: https://www.liberty.edu/divinity/

**Lipscomb University,** Department of Graduate Psychology and Counseling, Nashville, TN 37204-3951. Offers clinical mental health counseling (MS); counseling psychology (Certificate); marriage and family therapy (MMFT); psychology (MS). *Program availability:* Part-time, evening/weekend. *Faculty:* 13 full-time (5 women), 10 part-time/adjunct (6 women). *Students:* 120 full-time (92 women), 30 part-time (27 women); includes 38 minority (22 Black or African American, non-Hispanic/Latino; 1 American Indian or Alaska Native, non-Hispanic/Latino; 1 Asian, non-Hispanic/Latino; 11 Hispanic/Latino; 3 Two or more races, non-Hispanic/Latino), 2 international. Average age 28. In 2016, 44 master's, 1 other advanced degree awarded. *Degree requirements:* For master's, thesis (for some programs), practicum, internship, capstone. *Entrance requirements:* For master's, GRE, resume, 3 reference letters, transcripts, goals statement. Additional exam requirements/recommendations for international students: Required—TOEFL (minimum score 570 paper-based; 80 iBT). *Application deadline:* For fall admission, 7/1 for domestic students; for spring admission, 11/1 for domestic students. Applications are processed on a rolling basis. Application fee: $50 ($75 for international students). Electronic applications accepted. *Expenses:* $898 per hour. *Financial support:* Scholarships/grants and unspecified assistantships available. Financial award applicants required to submit FAFSA. *Faculty research:* Cognitive psychology, neuroscience, health psychology, grief issues. *Unit head:* Dr. Shanna Ray, Director/Professor of Psychology, 615-966-5833, E-mail: shanna.ray@lipscomb.edu. *Application contact:* Kathi Johnson, Recruiting and Marketing Coordinator, 615-966-5237, E-mail: kathi.johnson@lipscomb.edu.
Website: http://www.lipscomb.edu/psychology/graduate-programs

**Loma Linda University,** School of Behavioral Health, Department of Counseling and Family Sciences, Loma Linda, CA 92350. Offers child life specialist (MS); clinical mediation (Certificate); counseling (MS); drug and alcohol counseling (Certificate); family life education (Certificate); marital and family therapy (DMFT); school counseling (Certificate). *Degree requirements:* For master's, comprehensive exam, thesis optional; for doctorate, comprehensive exam, thesis/dissertation (for some programs). *Entrance requirements:* For master's, minimum GPA of 3.0; for doctorate, GRE. Additional exam requirements/recommendations for international students: Required—TOEFL (minimum score 550 paper-based). Electronic applications accepted.

**Long Island University–Hudson,** Graduate School, Purchase, NY 10577. Offers autism (Advanced Certificate); childhood education (MS Ed); early childhood education (MS Ed); educational leadership (MS Ed); finance (MBA); health administration (MPA); healthcare sector management (MBA); literacy (MS Ed); management (MBA); marriage and family therapy (MS); mental health counseling (MS), including credentialed alcoholism and substance abuse counselor; middle childhood and adolescence education (MS Ed); pharmaceutics (MS), including cosmetic science, industrial pharmacy; public administration (MPA); school counseling (MS Ed, Advanced Certificate); school psychology (MS Ed); special education (MS Ed); TESOL (all grades) (Advanced Certificate); TESOL and bilingual education (MS Ed); the business of pharmaceutics and biotechnology (MBA). *Program availability:* Part-time, evening/weekend, online learning. *Faculty:* 7 full-time (5 women), 42 part-time/adjunct (25 women). *Students:* 55 full-time (41 women), 158 part-time (123 women); includes 40 minority (8 Black or African American, non-Hispanic/Latino; 1 Asian, non-Hispanic/Latino; 31 Hispanic/Latino). Average age 35. *Entrance requirements:* Additional exam requirements/recommendations for international students: Required—TOEFL (minimum score 550 paper-based; 79 iBT). *Application deadline:* Applications are processed on a rolling basis. Application fee: $50. Electronic applications accepted. *Expenses:* Contact institution. *Unit head:* Dr. Sylvia Blake, Dean and Chief Operating Officer, 914-831-2700, E-mail: westchester@liu.edu. *Application contact:* Cindy Pagnotta, Director of Marketing and Enrollment, 914-831-2701, Fax: 914-251-5959, E-mail: cindy.pagnotta@liu.edu.

**Long Island University–LIU Brooklyn,** School of Education, Brooklyn, NY 11201-8423. Offers adolescence urban education (MS Ed); applied behavior analysis (Advanced Certificate); bilingual education (Advanced Certificate); bilingual school counselor (MS Ed, Advanced Certificate); childhood urban education (MS Ed); childhood/early childhood urban education (MS Ed); early childhood urban education (MS Ed, Advanced Certificate); educational leadership (Advanced Certificate); marriage and family therapy (MS, Advanced Certificate); mental health counseling (MS, Advanced Certificate); school building district leader (Advanced Certificate); school counselor (MS Ed, Advanced Certificate); school psychologist (MS Ed); teaching urban children/adolescents with disabilities (MS Ed); TESOL (MS Ed). *Accreditation:* TEAC. *Program availability:* Part-time, evening/weekend. *Faculty:* 23 full-time (17 women), 44 part-time/adjunct (32 women). *Students:* 161 full-time (144 women), 594 part-time (461 women); includes 493 minority (229 Black or African American, non-Hispanic/Latino; 1 American Indian or Alaska Native, non-Hispanic/Latino; 30 Asian, non-Hispanic/Latino; 218 Hispanic/Latino; 2 Native Hawaiian or other Pacific Islander, non-Hispanic/Latino; 13 Two or more races, non-Hispanic/Latino), 9 international. 513 applicants, 73% accepted, 272 enrolled. In 2016, 262 master's, 18 other advanced degrees awarded. *Degree requirements:* For master's, thesis optional, electronic portfolio. *Entrance requirements:* For master's, GRE (for MS Ed). Additional exam requirements/recommendations for international students: Required—TOEFL (minimum score 527 paper-based; 75 iBT). *Application deadline:* Applications are processed on a rolling basis. Application fee: $50. Electronic applications accepted. *Expenses:* Tuition: Full-time $28,272; part-time $1178 per credit. *Required fees:* $451 per term. Tuition and fees vary according to degree level, program and student level. *Financial support:* In 2016–17, 81 students received support. Career-related internships or fieldwork, Federal Work-Study, institutionally sponsored loans, scholarships/grants, and unspecified assistantships available. Support available to part-time students. Financial award application deadline: 2/15; financial award applicants required to submit FAFSA. *Faculty research:* Technology in education, teaching civics and sustainability, biliteracy and dual language instruction, diversity in organizations and leadership, counseling diverse couples and families. *Unit head:* Dr. Amy Ginsberg, Dean, 718-246-6308, E-mail: amy.ginsberg@liu.edu. *Application contact:* Gabrielle Gannon, Director of Graduate Admissions, 718-488-1011, Fax: 718-780-6110, E-mail: bkln-admissions@liu.edu.
Website: http://www.liu.edu/Brooklyn/Academics/School-of-Education

**Loyola Marymount University,** College of Fine Arts, Department of Marital and Family Therapy, Program in Marital and Family Therapy, Los Angeles, CA 90045-2659. Offers MA. *Students:* 50 full-time (49 women); includes 24 minority (1 Black or African

## Marriage and Family Therapy

American, non-Hispanic/Latino; 5 Asian, non-Hispanic/Latino; 14 Hispanic/Latino; 4 Two or more races, non-Hispanic/Latino). Average age 29. 48 applicants, 56% accepted, 22 enrolled. In 2016, 21 master's awarded. *Degree requirements:* For master's, thesis, 840-hour internship. *Entrance requirements:* For master's, GRE or MAT (minimum score of 396), all art and psychology prerequisites and bachelor's degree documented on transcripts, autobiography, portfolio with thumbnail list and statement, letters of recommendation, online video interview. Additional exam requirements/recommendations for international students: Required—TOEFL (minimum score 600 paper-based; 100 iBT). *Application deadline:* For fall admission, 12/1 for domestic students. Application fee: $50. Electronic applications accepted. *Expenses:* Contact institution. *Financial support:* In 2016–17, 46 students received support, including 3 research assistantships; career-related internships or fieldwork, institutionally sponsored loans, scholarships/grants, and unspecified assistantships also available. Financial award application deadline: 6/30; financial award applicants required to submit FAFSA. *Unit head:* Dr. Debra B. Linesch, Chair, 310-338-7674, E-mail: dlinesch@lmu.edu. *Application contact:* Chake H. Kouyoumjian, Associate Dean of Graduate Studies, 310-338-2721, E-mail: ckouyoum@lmu.edu.
Website: http://cfa.lmu.edu/programs/mft/

**Maryville University of Saint Louis,** Walker College of Health Professions, Program in Rehabilitation Counseling, St. Louis, MO 63141-7299. Offers marriage and family therapy (MARC); music therapy (MARC); substance abuse (MARC). *Accreditation:* CORE. *Program availability:* Part-time, evening/weekend. *Faculty:* 2 full-time (0 women), 6 part-time/adjunct (5 women). *Students:* 25 full-time (20 women), 16 part-time (15 women); includes 11 minority (8 Black or African American, non-Hispanic/Latino; 2 Hispanic/Latino; 1 Two or more races, non-Hispanic/Latino), 2 international. Average age 32. In 2016, 10 master's awarded. *Degree requirements:* For master's, internship, seminar. *Entrance requirements:* For master's, minimum cumulative GPA of 3.0, 2 letters of recommendation, interview, essay, transcripts, resume. Additional exam requirements/recommendations for international students: Required—TOEFL (minimum score 563 paper-based). *Application deadline:* For fall admission, 1/15 for domestic students; for spring admission, 10/1 for domestic students. Applications are processed on a rolling basis. Electronic applications accepted. *Expenses:* $650 per credit hour. *Financial support:* Career-related internships or fieldwork, Federal Work-Study, and campus employment available. Financial award application deadline: 3/1; financial award applicants required to submit FAFSA. *Unit head:* Dr. Michael Kiener, Director, 314-529-9443, Fax: 314-529-9495, E-mail: mkiener@maryville.edu. *Application contact:* Jeannie DeLuca, Director, Admissions and Advising, 314-529-9355, Fax: 314-529-9927, E-mail: jdeluca@maryville.edu.
Website: http://www.maryville.edu/hp/rehabilitation-counseling/

**Medaille College,** Programs in Psychology, Buffalo, NY 14214-2695. Offers clinical psychology (Psy D); marriage and family therapy (MA); mental health counseling (MA); psychology (MA). *Accreditation:* ACA. *Program availability:* Part-time, evening/weekend. *Degree requirements:* For master's, comprehensive exam (for some programs), thesis (for some programs). *Entrance requirements:* For master's, GRE General Test (psychology), minimum GPA of 2.75 (psychology). Additional exam requirements/recommendations for international students: Required—TOEFL (minimum score 550 paper-based). Electronic applications accepted. *Faculty research:* Schizophrenia, Parkinson's Disease, eyewitness testimony, methodology.

**Mercy College,** School of Social and Behavioral Sciences, Program in Counseling, Dobbs Ferry, NY 10522-1189. Offers counseling (MS); family counseling (Certificate). *Program availability:* Part-time, evening/weekend, 100% online, blended/hybrid learning. *Students:* 51 full-time (42 women), 107 part-time (91 women); includes 118 minority (41 Black or African American, non-Hispanic/Latino; 4 Asian, non-Hispanic/Latino; 70 Hispanic/Latino; 3 Two or more races, non-Hispanic/Latino). Average age 34. 127 applicants, 60% accepted, 51 enrolled. In 2016, 40 master's, 2 other advanced degrees awarded. *Degree requirements:* For master's, comprehensive exam (for some programs). *Entrance requirements:* For master's, essay, two professional letters of recommendation, resume, undergraduate transcript with minimum GPA of 3.0. Additional exam requirements/recommendations for international students: Required—TOEFL (minimum score 600 paper-based; 100 iBT), IELTS (minimum score 8). *Application deadline:* For fall admission, 8/1 for international students. Applications are processed on a rolling basis. Application fee: $40. Electronic applications accepted. *Expenses:* Tuition: Full-time $15,156; part-time $842 per credit hour. *Required fees:* $620; $155 per term. Tuition and fees vary according to course load and program. *Financial support:* Career-related internships or fieldwork, Federal Work-Study, scholarships/grants, and unspecified assistantships available. Support available to part-time students. Financial award applicants required to submit FAFSA. *Unit head:* Dr. Karol Dean, Dean, School of Social and Behavioral Sciences, 914-674-7517, E-mail: kdean@mercy.edu. *Application contact:* Allison Gurdineer, Senior Director of Admissions, 914-637-2946, Fax: 914-674-7382, E-mail: admissions@mercy.edu.
Website: https://www.mercy.edu/degrees-programs/ms-counseling

**Mercy College,** School of Social and Behavioral Sciences, Program in Marriage and Family Therapy, Dobbs Ferry, NY 10522-1189. Offers MS. *Program availability:* Part-time, evening/weekend. *Students:* 15 full-time (14 women), 19 part-time (17 women); includes 21 minority (6 Black or African American, non-Hispanic/Latino; 2 Asian, non-Hispanic/Latino; 13 Hispanic/Latino), 2 international. Average age 34. 29 applicants, 55% accepted, 12 enrolled. In 2016, 23 master's awarded. *Degree requirements:* For master's, thesis (for some programs), practicum, research project. *Entrance requirements:* For master's, essay, resume, interview, two letters of recommendation, undergraduate transcript. Additional exam requirements/recommendations for international students: Required—TOEFL (minimum score 600 paper-based; 100 iBT), IELTS (minimum score 8). *Application deadline:* For fall admission, 8/1 for international students. Applications are processed on a rolling basis. Application fee: $40. Electronic applications accepted. *Expenses:* Tuition: Full-time $15,156; part-time $842 per credit hour. *Required fees:* $620; $155 per term. Tuition and fees vary according to course load and program. *Financial support:* Career-related internships or fieldwork, Federal Work-Study, scholarships/grants, and unspecified assistantships available. Support available to part-time students. Financial award applicants required to submit FAFSA. *Unit head:* Dr. Karol Dean, Dean, School of Social and Behavioral Sciences, 914-674-7517, E-mail: kdean@mercy.edu. *Application contact:* Allison Gurdineer, Senior Director of Admissions, 877-637-2946, Fax: 914-674-7382, E-mail: admissions@mercy.edu.
Website: https://www.mercy.edu/degrees-programs/ms-marriage-and-family-therapy

**Messiah College,** Program in Counseling, Mechanicsburg, PA 17055. Offers clinical mental health counseling (MAC); counseling (CAGS); marriage, couple, and family counseling (MAC); school counseling (MAC). *Accreditation:* ACA. *Program availability:* Part-time, online learning. *Entrance requirements:* For master's, minimum undergraduate cumulative GPA of 3.0, 2 recommendations, resume or curriculum vitae, interview; for CAGS, bachelor's degree, minimum undergraduate cumulative GPA of 3.0, essay, two recommendations, resume or curriculum vitae, interview. Electronic applications accepted.

**Michigan State University,** The Graduate School, College of Social Science, Department of Family and Child Ecology, East Lansing, MI 48824. Offers child development (MA); community services (MS); family and child ecology (PhD); family

studies (MA); marriage and family therapy (MA); youth development (MA). *Accreditation:* AAMFT/COAMFTE (one or more programs are accredited). *Entrance requirements:* For master's, GRE General Test, minimum GPA of 3.0 in last 2 years of undergraduate course work, 3 letters of recommendation; for doctorate, GRE General Test, minimum GPA of 3.0, 3 letters of recommendation, background in behavioral sciences. Additional exam requirements/recommendations for international students: Required—TOEFL. Electronic applications accepted.

**Mid-America Christian University,** Program in Counseling, Oklahoma City, OK 73170-4504. Offers marital and family therapy (MS); pastoral/spiritual direction (MS); professional counselor (MS). *Entrance requirements:* For master's, MAT, bachelor's degree from a regionally accredited college or university, minimum overall cumulative GPA of 2.75 of bachelor course work. Additional exam requirements/recommendations for international students: Required—TOEFL (minimum score 550 paper-based).

**MidAmerica Nazarene University,** School of Behavioral Sciences and Counseling, Olathe, KS 66062-1899. Offers counseling (MA), including clinical mental health, marriage, couple and family, school counseling, spiritual formation in counseling. *Accreditation:* ACA. *Program availability:* Evening/weekend. *Faculty:* 10 full-time (4 women), 13 part-time/adjunct (9 women). *Students:* 109 full-time (92 women), 100 part-time (87 women); includes 39 minority (21 Black or African American, non-Hispanic/Latino; 3 Asian, non-Hispanic/Latino; 5 Hispanic/Latino; 1 Native Hawaiian or other Pacific Islander, non-Hispanic/Latino; 9 Two or more races, non-Hispanic/Latino). 97 applicants, 79% accepted, 61 enrolled. In 2016, 55 master's awarded. *Degree requirements:* For master's, comprehensive exam. *Entrance requirements:* For master's, on-site writing assessment, official transcript, three recommendations, personal interview. Additional exam requirements/recommendations for international students: Required—TOEFL (minimum score 81 iBT). *Application deadline:* For winter admission, 2/15 for domestic and international students; for spring admission, 4/1 for domestic and international students. Electronic applications accepted. *Expenses:* $34,620 tuition, $250 lab fee, $1,200 technology fee. *Financial support:* Applicants required to submit FAFSA. *Faculty research:* Technology and intimacy, play therapy, interpersonal neurobiology, sexual addiction. *Unit head:* Dr. Todd Frye, Dean, School of Behavioral Sciences and Counseling, 913-971-3449, Fax: 913-971-3402, E-mail: tmfrye@mnu.edu. *Application contact:* Jean Blades, Administrative Assistant, 913-971-3730, E-mail: jmblades@mnu.edu.

**Mississippi College,** Graduate School, School of Education, Department of Psychology and Counseling, Clinton, MS 39058. Offers counseling (Ed S); marriage and family counseling (MS); mental health counseling (MS); school counseling (M Ed). *Program availability:* Part-time. *Degree requirements:* For master's and Ed S, comprehensive exam, thesis optional. *Entrance requirements:* For master's, GRE or NTE. Additional exam requirements/recommendations for international students: Recommended—TOEFL, IELTS. Electronic applications accepted.

**Mount Mercy University,** Program in Marriage and Family Therapy, Cedar Rapids, IA 52402-4797. Offers MA. *Accreditation:* AAMFT/COAMFTE. *Program availability:* Evening/weekend.

**Northcentral University,** Graduate Studies, San Diego, CA 92106. Offers business (MBA, DBA, PhD, Postbaccalaureate Certificate); education (M Ed, Ed D, PhD, Ed S, Post-Master's Certificate, Postbaccalaureate Certificate); marriage and family therapy (MA, DMFT, PhD, Post-Master's Certificate, Postbaccalaureate Certificate); psychology (MA, PhD, Post-Master's Certificate, Postbaccalaureate Certificate). *Program availability:* Part-time, evening/weekend, online only, 100% online. *Faculty:* 98 full-time (63 women), 385 part-time/adjunct (203 women). *Students:* 5,036 full-time (3,291 women), 5,747 part-time (3,977 women); includes 3,777 minority (2,550 Black or African American, non-Hispanic/Latino; 76 American Indian or Alaska Native, non-Hispanic/Latino; 192 Asian, non-Hispanic/Latino; 603 Hispanic/Latino; 39 Native Hawaiian or other Pacific Islander, non-Hispanic/Latino; 317 Two or more races, non-Hispanic/Latino). Average age 45. In 2016, 799 master's, 399 doctorates, 230 other advanced degrees awarded. *Degree requirements:* For doctorate, comprehensive exam, thesis/dissertation. *Entrance requirements:* For master's, bachelor's degree from regionally- or nationally-accredited institution, current resume or curriculum vitae, statement of intent, interview, and background check (for marriage and family therapy); for doctorate, post-baccalaureate master's degree and/or doctoral degree from nationally- or regionally-accredited academic institution; for other advanced degree, bachelor's-level or higher degree from accredited institution or university (for Post-Baccalaureate Certificate); master's and/or doctoral degree from regionally- or nationally-accredited academic institution (for Post-Master's Certificate). Additional exam requirements/recommendations for international students: Required—TOEFL (minimum score 550 paper-based; 79 iBT), IELTS (minimum score 6.5), PTE (minimum score 53). *Application deadline:* Applications are processed on a rolling basis. Application fee: $0. Electronic applications accepted. *Expenses:* Tuition: Full-time $16,821; part-time $935 per credit hour. One-time fee: $350. Tuition and fees vary according to degree level and program. *Financial support:* Scholarships/grants available. *Faculty research:* Business management, curriculum and instruction, educational leadership, health psychology, organizational behavior. *Unit head:* Dr. David Harpool, Acting Provost, 888-327-2877 Ext. 8181, E-mail: provost@ncu.edu. *Application contact:* Ken Boutelle, Vice President, Enrollment Services, 888-628-4979, E-mail: enrollmentservices@ncu.edu.

**North Dakota State University,** College of Graduate and Interdisciplinary Studies, College of Human Development and Education, Department of Human Development and Family Science, Program in Couple and Family Therapy, Fargo, ND 58102. Offers PhD. *Degree requirements:* For doctorate, thesis/dissertation, 180 hours of supervisory experience; one year of research, teaching, or clinical internship experience; scholarly portfolio; oral examination.

**Northeastern Illinois University,** College of Graduate Studies and Research, College of Education, Program in Family Counseling, Chicago, IL 60625-4699. Offers MA.

**Northern Kentucky University,** Office of Graduate Programs, College of Informatics, Program in Communication, Highland Heights, KY 41099. Offers communication (MA); communication teaching (Certificate); documentary studies (Certificate); public relations (Certificate); relationships (Certificate). *Program availability:* Part-time, evening/weekend. Terminal master's awarded for partial completion of doctoral program. *Degree requirements:* For master's, comprehensive exams, thesis or applied capstone project. *Entrance requirements:* For master's, GRE, minimum GPA of 3.0, 3 letters of recommendation, letter of intent. Additional exam requirements/recommendations for international students: Required—TOEFL (minimum score 79 iBT); Recommended—IELTS (minimum score 6.5). Electronic applications accepted. *Faculty research:* Mediating effect of health communication, organizational communication, quantitative and qualitative research methods, family and interpersonal communication.

**Northwestern University,** The Graduate School, Program in Marital and Family Therapy, Evanston, IL 60208. Offers MS. *Entrance requirements:* For master's, GRE General Test. *Faculty research:* Marital and family therapy training, gender, psychotherapy outcome, adolescents and pre-school children at risk, families.

**Northwest Nazarene University,** Program in Counselor Education, Nampa, ID 83686-5897. Offers clinical counseling (MS); marriage and family counseling (MS); school counseling (MS). *Program availability:* Part-time. *Faculty:* 6 full-time (4 women), 10 part-time/adjunct (6 women). *Students:* 92 full-time (74 women), 26 part-time (19 women); includes 10 minority (2 Black or African American, non-Hispanic/Latino; 6 Hispanic/Latino; 2 Two or more races, non-Hispanic/Latino), 1 international. Average age 35. 47 applicants, 66% accepted, 25 enrolled. In 2016, 33 master's awarded. *Degree requirements:* For master's, comprehensive exam. *Entrance requirements:* For master's, minimum GPA of 3.0, BA. Additional exam requirements/recommendations for international students: Required—TOEFL. *Application deadline:* For fall admission, 2/15 for domestic and international students; for spring admission, 9/15 for domestic and international students. Application fee: $50. Electronic applications accepted. *Expenses:* Tuition: Full-time $9315; part-time $4658 per credit hour. *Required fees:* $120. *Unit head:* Dr. Michael Pitts, Chair, 208-467-8040, Fax: 208-467-8339. *Application contact:* Lynette Kingsmore, Graduate Admissions Counselor, 208-467-8107, E-mail: lkingsmore@nnu.edu.

**Notre Dame de Namur University,** Division of Academic Affairs, College of Arts and Sciences, Department of Clinical Psychology and Gerontology, Program in Clinical Psychology: Marital and Family Therapy, Belmont, CA 94002-1908. Offers MS. *Program availability:* Part-time. *Degree requirements:* For master's, thesis. *Entrance requirements:* Additional exam requirements/recommendations for international students: Required—TOEFL (minimum score 550 paper-based; 79 iBT). Electronic applications accepted.

**Nova Southeastern University,** College of Arts, Humanities, and Social Sciences, Fort Lauderdale, FL 33314-7796. Offers advanced conflict resolution practice (Graduate Certificate); college student affairs (MS); conflict analysis and resolution (MS, PhD); cross-disciplinary studies (MA); family studies (Graduate Certificate); family systems health care (Graduate Certificate); family therapy (MS, PhD); marriage and family therapy (DMFT); peace studies (Graduate Certificate); qualitative research (Graduate Certificate); solution focused coaching (Graduate Certificate). *Accreditation:* AAMFT/COAMFTE (one or more programs are accredited). *Program availability:* Part-time, evening/weekend, 100% online, blended/hybrid learning. *Faculty:* 29 full-time (18 women), 27 part-time/adjunct (21 women). *Students:* 306 full-time (242 women), 889 part-time (683 women); includes 677 minority (403 Black or African American, non-Hispanic/Latino; 2 American Indian or Alaska Native, non-Hispanic/Latino; 20 Asian, non-Hispanic/Latino; 224 Hispanic/Latino; 1 Native Hawaiian or other Pacific Islander, non-Hispanic/Latino; 27 Two or more races, non-Hispanic/Latino), 53 international. Average age 37. 624 applicants, 61% accepted, 285 enrolled. In 2016, 303 master's, 71 doctorates, 34 other advanced degrees awarded. *Degree requirements:* For master's, thesis optional, comprehensive exams, portfolios (for some programs), table-top exams (for some programs); for doctorate, comprehensive exam, thesis/dissertation, qualifying exams, portfolios (for some programs). *Entrance requirements:* For master's, interview, minimum GPA of 3.0, writing sample; for doctorate, interview, minimum GPA of 3.5, master's degree in related field, writing sample; for Graduate Certificate, minimum GPA of 3.0. Additional exam requirements/recommendations for international students: Required—TOEFL. *Application deadline:* For fall admission, 5/17 priority date for domestic and international students; for winter admission, 12/1 priority date for domestic and international students; for spring admission, 4/1 priority date for domestic and international students. Applications are processed on a rolling basis. Application fee: $50. Electronic applications accepted. *Expenses:* $1,005. *Financial support:* In 2016–17, 170 students received support. Career-related internships or fieldwork, Federal Work-Study, scholarships/grants, and unspecified assistantships available. Financial award application deadline: 4/1; financial award applicants required to submit CSS PROFILE. *Faculty research:* Conflict resolution, family therapy, peace research, international conflict, multi-disciplinary studies, college student affairs, national security affairs, health care conflict resolution, family systems health care, advanced family systems, qualitative research, solution-focused coaching. *Unit head:* Dr. Honggang Yang, Dean, 954-262-3016, Fax: 954-262-3968, E-mail: yangh@nova.edu. *Application contact:* Marcia Arango, Student Recruitment Coordinator, 954-262-3006, Fax: 954-262-3968, E-mail: marango@nsu.nova.edu.
Website: http://cahss.nova.edu/

**Nyack College,** Alliance Graduate School of Counseling, Nyack, NY 10960. Offers marriage and family therapy (MA); mental health counseling (MA). *Program availability:* Part-time, evening/weekend, 100% online. *Students:* 84 full-time (69 women), 123 part-time (103 women); includes 152 minority (64 Black or African American, non-Hispanic/Latino; 44 Asian, non-Hispanic/Latino; 41 Hispanic/Latino; 3 Two or more races, non-Hispanic/Latino), 9 international. Average age 37. In 2016, 70 master's awarded. *Degree requirements:* For master's, comprehensive exam, counselor-in-training therapy, internship, CPCE exam. *Entrance requirements:* For master's, Millon Clinical Multiaxial Inventory-3, Minnesota Multiphasic Personality Inventory-2, transcripts, statement of Christian life and experience, statement of support systems. Additional exam requirements/recommendations for international students: Required—TOEFL (minimum score 550 paper-based; 80 iBT). *Application deadline:* For fall admission, 8/1 for domestic students, 2/15 for international students; for spring admission, 12/15 for domestic students, 7/15 for international students. Applications are processed on a rolling basis. Application fee: $30. Electronic applications accepted. *Expenses:* $775 per credit. *Financial support:* Career-related internships or fieldwork and scholarships/grants available. Financial award applicants required to submit FAFSA. *Unit head:* Dr. Carol Robles, Associate Dean, 845-770-5735. *Application contact:* Esther Guzman, Admissions Associate, 800-541-6891, E-mail: admissions.grad@nyack.edu.
Website: http://www.nyack.edu/agsc

**Oklahoma Baptist University,** Program in Marriage and Family Therapy, Shawnee, OK 74804. Offers MS. *Program availability:* Part-time, evening/weekend. *Degree requirements:* For master's, thesis optional, practicum. *Entrance requirements:* For master's, GRE General Test. Additional exam requirements/recommendations for international students: Required—TOEFL. Electronic applications accepted. *Faculty research:* Marriage and family therapy supervision, intimate partner violence in migrant populations, medical family therapy, violence and aggression, protective factors and adolescent delinquency.

**Oklahoma State University,** College of Human Sciences, Department of Human Development and Family Science, Stillwater, OK 74078. Offers human development and family science (MS, PhD), including family financial planning (MS), human environmental sciences; marriage and family therapy (MS). *Accreditation:* AAMFT/COAMFTE (one or more programs are accredited). *Program availability:* Online learning. *Faculty:* 31 full-time (22 women), 11 part-time/adjunct (9 women). *Students:* 26 full-time (23 women), 35 part-time (30 women); includes 16 minority (7 Black or African American, non-Hispanic/Latino; 1 American Indian or Alaska Native, non-Hispanic/Latino; 5 Hispanic/Latino; 3 Two or more races, non-Hispanic/Latino), 1 international. Average age 30. 47 applicants, 55% accepted, 22 enrolled. In 2016, 27 master's, 2 doctorates awarded. *Degree requirements:* For master's, thesis (for some programs); for doctorate, comprehensive exam, thesis/dissertation. *Entrance requirements:* For master's and doctorate, GRE or GMAT. Additional exam requirements/recommendations for international students: Required—TOEFL (minimum score 550 paper-based; 79 iBT). *Application deadline:* For fall admission, 3/1 priority date for international students; for spring admission, 8/1 priority date for international students. Applications are processed on a rolling basis. Application fee: $40 ($75 for international

students). Electronic applications accepted. *Expenses:* Tuition, state resident: full-time $3775; part-time $209.70 per credit hour. Tuition, nonresident: full-time $14,851; part-time $825.05 per credit hour. *Required fees:* $2027; $112.60 per credit hour. Tuition and fees vary according to campus/location. *Financial support:* In 2016–17, 37 research assistantships (averaging $4,670 per year), 31 teaching assistantships (averaging $4,921 per year) were awarded; career-related internships or fieldwork, Federal Work-Study, scholarships/grants, health care benefits, tuition waivers (partial), and unspecified assistantships also available. Support available to part-time students. Financial award application deadline: 3/1; financial award applicants required to submit FAFSA. *Faculty research:* Family relations and child development, consequences of adolescent parenting, family stress and coping, impacts of sexual abuse on families, children's social cognition and self-competence, gerontology and health care. *Unit head:* Dr. Sissy Osteen, Department Head, 405-744-4741, Fax: 405-744-6344, E-mail: sissy.osteen@okstate.edu. *Application contact:* Dr. Michael Criss, Graduate Coordinator, 405-744-5057, Fax: 405-744-6344, E-mail: michael.criss@okstate.edu.
Website: http://humansciences.okstate.edu/hdfs/

**Oral Roberts University,** School of Theology and Missions, Tulsa, OK 74171. Offers biblical literature (MA), including advanced languages, Judaic-Christian studies; Christian counseling (MA), including marriage and family therapy; divinity (M Div); missions (MA); practical theology (MA); theological/historical studies (MA); theology (D Min). *Accreditation:* ATS. *Program availability:* Part-time, online learning. *Degree requirements:* For master's, thesis (for some programs), practicum/internship; for doctorate, thesis/dissertation, applied research project. *Entrance requirements:* For master's, GRE General Test or MAT, minimum GPA of 2.5; for doctorate, M Div, minimum GPA of 3.0, 3 years of full-time ministry experience. Additional exam requirements/recommendations for international students: Required—TOEFL (minimum score 550 paper-based; 79 iBT). Electronic applications accepted.

**Ottawa University,** Graduate Studies-Arizona, Program in Professional Counseling, Ottawa, KS 66067-3399. Offers Christian counseling (MA); expressive arts therapy (MA); marriage and family therapy (MA); treatment of trauma, abuse and deprivation (MA). Programs offered in Mesa, Phoenix, Tempe and West Valley, AZ. *Program availability:* Part-time, evening/weekend, online learning. *Degree requirements:* For master's, comprehensive exam, thesis or alternative, field experience, practicum. *Entrance requirements:* For master's, minimum undergraduate GPA of 3.0; course work in theories of personality, abnormal psychology, and human growth and development. Additional exam requirements/recommendations for international students: Required—TOEFL (minimum score 550 paper-based).

**Pacific Lutheran University,** Division of Social Sciences, Program in Marriage and Family Therapy, Tacoma, WA 98447. Offers MA. *Accreditation:* AAMFT/COAMFTE. *Program availability:* Part-time. *Degree requirements:* For master's, thesis optional, clinical competency. *Entrance requirements:* Additional exam requirements/recommendations for international students: Required—TOEFL (minimum score 550 paper-based; 88 iBT). Electronic applications accepted.

**Pacific Oaks College,** Graduate School, Program in Marriage and Family Therapy, Pasadena, CA 91103. Offers marriage, family and child counseling (MA). *Program availability:* Part-time, evening/weekend. *Degree requirements:* For master's, thesis. *Entrance requirements:* For master's, interview. Additional exam requirements/recommendations for international students: Required—TOEFL (minimum score 550 paper-based). *Faculty research:* Family systems, cross-cultural development, therapeutic intervention and Latino families, battered women.

**Palm Beach Atlantic University,** School of Education and Behavioral Studies, West Palm Beach, FL 33416-4708. Offers counseling psychology (MS), including addictions/mental health, general counseling, marriage and family therapy, mental health counseling, school guidance counseling. *Program availability:* Part-time, evening/weekend. *Faculty:* 8 full-time (2 women), 17 part-time/adjunct (13 women). *Students:* 243 full-time (206 women), 29 part-time (24 women); includes 147 minority (67 Black or African American, non-Hispanic/Latino; 4 Asian, non-Hispanic/Latino; 60 Hispanic/Latino; 1 Native Hawaiian or other Pacific Islander, non-Hispanic/Latino; 15 Two or more races, non-Hispanic/Latino), 6 international. Average age 35. 81 applicants, 89% accepted, 53 enrolled. In 2016, 122 master's awarded. *Entrance requirements:* For master's, GRE or MAT, minimum GPA of 3.0; essay. Additional exam requirements/recommendations for international students: Required—TOEFL (minimum score 550 paper-based; 79 iBT). *Application deadline:* Applications are processed on a rolling basis. Application fee: $50. Electronic applications accepted. *Expenses: Tuition:* Full-time $6600; part-time $550 per credit hour. Full-time tuition and fees vary according to degree level, campus/location and program. *Financial support:* In 2016–17, 11 students received support. Career-related internships or fieldwork, scholarships/grants, and employee education grants available. Financial award application deadline: 5/1; financial award applicants required to submit FAFSA. *Faculty research:* Group dynamics, phenomenology, spirituality, multicultural psychology. *Unit head:* Dr. Gene Sale, Program Director, 561-803-2352. *Application contact:* Graduate Admissions, 888-468-6722, E-mail: grad@pba.edu.
Website: http://www.pba.edu/graduate-counseling-program

**Palo Alto University,** MA in Counseling Program, Palo Alto, CA 94304. Offers clinical mental health (MA); marriage, family and child (MA). *Program availability:* Part-time, 100% online, blended/hybrid learning. *Faculty:* 6 full-time (4 women), 5 part-time/adjunct (4 women). *Students:* 38 full-time (34 women), 28 part-time (22 women); includes 29 minority (3 Black or African American, non-Hispanic/Latino; 9 Asian, non-Hispanic/Latino; 14 Hispanic/Latino; 3 Two or more races, non-Hispanic/Latino), 1 international. Average age 32. 111 applicants, 91% accepted, 89 enrolled. In 2016, 91 master's awarded. *Degree requirements:* For master's, capstone project. *Entrance requirements:* For master's, undergraduate degree in psychology with minimum GPA of 3.3. Additional exam requirements/recommendations for international students: Required—TOEFL. *Application deadline:* For fall admission, 6/30 priority date for domestic and international students; for spring admission, 3/21 for domestic and international students. Applications are processed on a rolling basis. Application fee: $40. Electronic applications accepted. *Expenses:* Contact institution. *Financial support:* In 2016–17, 12 students received support. Federal Work-Study and scholarships/grants available. Financial award application deadline: 1/15; financial award applicants required to submit FAFSA. *Unit head:* Dr. William Snow, Director of Counseling, 831-246-2440, E-mail: wsnow@paloaltou.edu. *Application contact:* Deanna Berger, Assistant Director of Admissions, 650-417-2023, E-mail: dberger@paloaltou.edu.
Website: http://www.paloaltou.edu/graduate-programs/masters-programs/ma-counseling

**Pepperdine University,** Graduate School of Education and Psychology, Division of Psychology, Los Angeles, CA 90045. Offers behavioral psychology (MS); clinical psychology (Psy D); clinical psychology (MA), including marriage and family therapy; clinical psychology with Latinos (MA); psychology (MA). *Program availability:* Part-time, evening/weekend. *Students:* 489 full-time (408 women), 432 part-time (348 women); includes 404 minority (92 Black or African American, non-Hispanic/Latino; 4 American Indian or Alaska Native, non-Hispanic/Latino; 77 Asian, non-Hispanic/Latino; 198 Hispanic/Latino; 5 Native Hawaiian or other Pacific Islander, non-Hispanic/Latino; 28 Two or more races, non-Hispanic/Latino), 46 international. Average age 31. 559

## Marriage and Family Therapy

applicants, 77% accepted, 279 enrolled. In 2016, 265 master's, 27 doctorates awarded. *Entrance requirements:* For master's and doctorate, GRE General Test. Additional exam requirements/recommendations for international students: Required—TOEFL. *Application deadline:* For fall admission, 2/1 for domestic students. Applications are processed on a rolling basis. Application fee: $55. *Expenses:* $1,165 per unit (for master's); $1,460 per unit (for doctorate). *Financial support:* Research assistantships, teaching assistantships, career-related internships or fieldwork, and scholarships/grants available. Support available to part-time students. Financial award application deadline: 7/1; financial award applicants required to submit FAFSA. *Unit head:* Dr. Robert A. deMayo, Associate Dean, Psychology Division, 310-568-5747, E-mail: robert.demayo@pepperdine.edu. *Application contact:* Chris Costa, Director of Enrollment, 310-568-2850, E-mail: chris.costa@pepperdine.edu. Website: http://gsep.pepperdine.edu/masters-psychology/

**Phillips Graduate University,** Programs in Marriage and Family Therapy and School Counseling, Chatsworth, CA 91311. Offers art therapy (MA); marriage and family therapy (MA); school counseling (MA). *Program availability:* Evening/weekend. *Degree requirements:* For master's, comprehensive exam, thesis. *Entrance requirements:* For master's, minimum GPA of 2.5. Electronic applications accepted. *Faculty research:* Integration of interpersonal psychological theory, systems approach, firsthand experiential learning.

**Pontifical John Paul II Institute for Studies on Marriage and Family,** Graduate Programs, Washington, DC 20064. Offers biotechnology and ethics (MTS); marriage and family (MTS, STD, STL); theology (PhD).

**Purdue University,** Graduate School, College of Health and Human Sciences, Department of Child Development and Family Studies, West Lafayette, IN 47907. Offers developmental studies (MS, PhD); family studies (MS, PhD); marriage and family therapy (MS, PhD). *Accreditation:* AAMFT/COAMFTE (one or more programs are accredited). *Program availability:* Part-time. *Faculty:* 19 full-time (11 women), 1 (woman) part-time/adjunct. *Students:* 22 full-time (21 women), 1 (woman) part-time; includes 3 minority (1 Black or African American, non-Hispanic/Latino; 1 Hispanic/Latino; 1 Two or more races, non-Hispanic/Latino), 5 international. Average age 26. 41 applicants, 29% accepted, 8 enrolled. In 2016, 4 master's, 3 doctorates awarded. Terminal master's awarded for partial completion of doctoral program. *Degree requirements:* For master's, thesis; for doctorate, thesis/dissertation. *Entrance requirements:* For master's and doctorate, GRE General Test (minimum score 1000 combined verbal and quantitative), minimum undergraduate GPA of 3.0 or equivalent. Additional exam requirements/recommendations for international students: Required—TOEFL (minimum score 600 paper-based; 90 iBT), TWE (minimum score 4). *Application deadline:* For fall admission, 1/4 for domestic and international students. Applications are processed on a rolling basis. Application fee: $60 ($75 for international students). Electronic applications accepted. *Financial support:* Fellowships with full tuition reimbursements, research assistantships with full tuition reimbursements, teaching assistantships with full tuition reimbursements, and career-related internships or fieldwork available. Support available to part-time students. Financial award application deadline: 1/15; financial award applicants required to submit FAFSA. *Faculty research:* Inclusion of children with special needs, families as learning environments, relationships in child care, work-family relations, AIDS prevention. *Unit head:* Dr. Doran C. French, Head, 765-494-9511, E-mail: dcfrench@purdue.edu. *Application contact:* Tina Putz, Graduate Contact, 765-496-3816, E-mail: tputz@purdue.edu.
Website: http://www.purdue.edu/hhs/hdfs/

**Purdue University Northwest,** Graduate Studies Office, School of Liberal Arts and Social Sciences, Department of Behavioral Sciences, Hammond, IN 46323-2094. Offers child development and family studies (MS); marriage and family therapy (MS). *Accreditation:* AAMFT/COAMFTE. *Program availability:* Part-time. *Degree requirements:* For master's, thesis. *Entrance requirements:* For master's, GRE, interview. Additional exam requirements/recommendations for international students: Required—TOEFL. *Faculty research:* Substance abuse, sexual abuse, couple therapy, professional issues, adolescent therapy.

**Reformed Theological Seminary–Jackson Campus,** Graduate and Professional Programs, Jackson, MS 39209-3004. Offers Bible, theology, and missions (Certificate); Biblical exegesis (M Div); biblical studies (MA); Christian education (MA); counseling (M Div); marriage and family therapy (MA); ministry (D Min); missions (M Div, MA, D Min); theological studies (MA). *Accreditation:* AAMFT/COAMFTE (one or more programs are accredited); ATS (one or more programs are accredited). *Degree requirements:* For master's, thesis (for some programs), fieldwork; for doctorate, 2 foreign languages, thesis/dissertation. *Entrance requirements:* For master's, minimum GPA of 2.6; for doctorate, minimum GPA of 3.0. Additional exam requirements/recommendations for international students: Required—TOEFL.

**Regent University,** Graduate School, School of Psychology and Counseling, Virginia Beach, VA 23464-9800. Offers clinical mental health counseling (MA); clinical psychology (Psy D); counseling and psychological studies (PhD); counseling studies (CAGS); counselor education and supervision (PhD); general psychology (MS); marriage, couple, and family counseling (MA); pastoral counseling (MA); school counseling (MA); M Div/MA; M Ed/MA; MBA/MA. *Accreditation:* ACA; APA (one or more programs are accredited). *Program availability:* Part-time, evening/weekend, 100% online, blended/hybrid learning. *Faculty:* 28 full-time (17 women), 45 part-time/adjunct (26 women). *Students:* 295 full-time (240 women), 331 part-time (252 women); includes 244 minority (186 Black or African American, non-Hispanic/Latino; 4 American Indian or Alaska Native, non-Hispanic/Latino; 11 Asian, non-Hispanic/Latino; 29 Hispanic/Latino; 14 Two or more races, non-Hispanic/Latino), 10 international. Average age 36. 1,192 applicants, 29% accepted, 235 enrolled. In 2016, 156 master's, 41 doctorates, 1 other advanced degree awarded. *Degree requirements:* For master's, thesis or alternative, internship, practicum, written competency exam; for doctorate, thesis/dissertation or alternative. *Entrance requirements:* For master's, GRE General Test (including writing exam) or MAT, minimum undergraduate GPA of 3.0, resume, transcripts, writing sample, personal goals statement; for doctorate, GRE General Test (including writing exam), minimum undergraduate GPA of 3.0, graduate 3.5; writing sample; 3 recommendations; resume; college transcripts; personal goals statement. Additional exam requirements/recommendations for international students: Required—TOEFL (minimum score 577 paper-based). *Application deadline:* For fall admission, 4/1 priority date for domestic students; for spring admission, 11/1 priority date for domestic students. Applications are processed on a rolling basis. Application fee: $50. Electronic applications accepted. *Expenses:* Contact institution. *Financial support:* In 2016–17, 446 students received support, including 5 fellowships (averaging $4,000 per year), 10 research assistantships (averaging $3,200 per year); career-related internships or fieldwork, scholarships/grants, and unspecified assistantships also available. Support available to part-time students. *Faculty research:* Marriage enrichment, clinical psychology, troubled youth, faith and learning, trauma. *Unit head:* Dr. William Hathaway, Dean, 757-352-4294, Fax: 757-352-4282, E-mail: willhat@regent.edu. *Application contact:* Heidi Cece, Assistant Vice President of Enrollment Management, 800-373-5504, Fax: 757-352-4381, E-mail: admissions@regent.edu.
Website: http://www.regent.edu/spc/

**Regis University,** Rueckert-Hartman College for Health Professions, Denver, CO 80221-1099. Offers advanced practice nurse (DNP); counseling (MA); counseling children and adolescents (Post-Graduate Certificate); counseling military families (Post-Graduate Certificate); depth psychotherapy (Post-Graduate Certificate); fellowship in orthopedic manual physical therapy (Certificate); health care business management (Certificate); health care quality and patient safety (Certificate); health industry leadership (MBA); health services administration (MS); marriage and family therapy (MA, Post-Graduate Certificate); neonatal nurse practitioner (MSN); nursing education (MSN); nursing leadership (MSN); occupational therapy (OTD); pharmacy (Pharm D); physical therapy (DPT). *Program availability:* Part-time, evening/weekend, 100% online, blended/hybrid learning. *Faculty:* 66 full-time (44 women), 33 part-time/adjunct (25 women). *Students:* 1,088 full-time (788 women), 316 part-time (253 women); includes 403 minority (59 Black or African American, non-Hispanic/Latino; 5 American Indian or Alaska Native, non-Hispanic/Latino; 101 Asian, non-Hispanic/Latino; 187 Hispanic/Latino; 51 Two or more races, non-Hispanic/Latino), 11 international. Average age 33. 2,199 applicants, 25% accepted, 277 enrolled. In 2016, 428 master's, 160 doctorates awarded. *Degree requirements:* For master's, thesis (for some programs), internship. *Entrance requirements:* For master's, official transcript reflecting baccalaureate degree awarded from regionally-accredited college or university. Additional exam requirements/recommendations for international students: Required—TOEFL (minimum score 550 paper-based; 82 iBT). *Application deadline:* For fall admission, 8/15 priority date for domestic students; for spring admission, 1/10 priority date for domestic students; for summer admission, 5/1 priority date for domestic students. Applications are processed on a rolling basis. Application fee: $75. Electronic applications accepted. *Expenses:* Contact institution. *Financial support:* In 2016–17, 102 students received support. Federal Work-Study and scholarships/grants available. Financial award application deadline: 4/15; financial award applicants required to submit FAFSA. *Faculty research:* Normal and pathological balance and gait research, normal/pathological upper limb motor control/biomechanics, exercise energy/metabolism research, optical treatment protocols for therapeutic modalities. *Unit head:* Dr. Janet Houser, Academic Dean. *Application contact:* Cate Clark, Director of Admissions, 303-458-4900, Fax: 303-964-5534, E-mail: ruadmissions@regis.edu.
Website: http://www.regis.edu/RHCHP.aspx

**Richmont Graduate University,** School of Counseling, Atlanta, GA 30339. Offers clinical mental health counseling (MA); marriage and family therapy (MA). *Accreditation:* ACA. *Program availability:* Part-time, evening/weekend. *Degree requirements:* For master's, comprehensive exam, thesis optional. *Entrance requirements:* For master's, GRE or MAT. *Application deadline:* Applications are processed on a rolling basis. Application fee: $50. Electronic applications accepted. *Expenses: Tuition:* Part-time $665 per credit hour. *Required fees:* $200 per semester. One-time fee: $250. *Financial support:* Career-related internships or fieldwork, scholarships/grants, and unspecified assistantships available. Financial award application deadline: 5/1. *Unit head:* Dr. Stephen P. Bradshaw, Dean, E-mail: sbradshaw@richmont.edu. *Application contact:* Admissions, 888-924-6774, Fax: 866-363-4323, E-mail: admissions@richmont.edu. Website: http://richmont.edu/academics/school-of-counseling/

**St. Cloud State University,** School of Graduate Studies, School of Health and Human Services, Department of Counseling and Community Psychology, Program in Marriage and Family Therapy, St. Cloud, MN 56301-4498. Offers MS. *Accreditation:* AAMFT/COAMFTE. *Entrance requirements:* Additional exam requirements/recommendations for international students: Required—Michigan English Language Assessment Battery; Recommended—TOEFL (minimum score 550 paper-based), IELTS (minimum score 6.5). Electronic applications accepted.

**Saint Louis University,** Graduate Education, College of Education and Public Service and Graduate Education, Department of Counseling and Family Therapy, St. Louis, MO 63103. Offers counseling and family therapy (PhD); human development counseling (MA); marriage and family therapy (Certificate); school counseling (MA, MA-R). *Accreditation:* AAMFT/COAMFTE; NCATE. *Program availability:* Part-time. *Degree requirements:* For master's, comprehensive exam, thesis (for some programs); for doctorate, comprehensive exam, thesis/dissertation, preliminary oral and written exams. *Entrance requirements:* For master's, GRE General Test, letters of recommendation, resume; for doctorate, GRE General Test, letters of recommendation, resumé, transcripts, goal statement. Additional exam requirements/recommendations for international students: Required—TOEFL (minimum score 550 paper-based). Electronic applications accepted. *Faculty research:* Medical family therapy/collaborative health care multicultural counseling, mental health needs of diverse, minority, or Immigrant/refugee populations, divorce, aging families.

**Saint Mary's College of California,** Kalmanovitz School of Education, Program in Counseling, Moraga, CA 94575. Offers career counseling (MA); college student services (Credential); general counseling (MA); marriage and family therapy (MA); pupil personnel services (Credential), including school counseling, school psychology; school counseling (MA); school psychology (MA). *Program availability:* Part-time, evening/weekend. *Degree requirements:* For master's, thesis or alternative. *Entrance requirements:* For master's, interview, minimum GPA of 3.0. *Faculty research:* Counselor training effectiveness, multicultural development, empathy, the interface of spirituality and psychotherapy, gender issues.

**St. Mary's University,** Graduate Studies, Program in Marriage and Family Therapy, San Antonio, TX 78228-8507. Offers MA, PhD. *Accreditation:* AAMFT/COAMFTE. *Program availability:* Part-time, evening/weekend. *Faculty:* 3 full-time (1 woman), 8 part-time/adjunct (5 women). *Students:* 34 full-time (25 women), 35 part-time (28 women); includes 30 minority (3 Black or African American, non-Hispanic/Latino; 3 Asian, non-Hispanic/Latino; 24 Hispanic/Latino), 8 international. Average age 33. 25 applicants, 28% accepted. In 2016, 12 master's, 5 doctorates awarded. *Degree requirements:* For master's, comprehensive exam, thesis optional, internship; for doctorate, comprehensive exam, thesis/dissertation, internship. *Entrance requirements:* For master's, GRE, MAT; for doctorate, GRE, bachelor's degree or master's degree in marriage and family therapy from accredited college or university; three recommendations from faculties of previous undergraduate/graduate studies and/or past employers relating to professional mental health experience. Additional exam requirements/recommendations for international students: Required—TOEFL (minimum score 550 paper-based; 80 iBT), IELTS (minimum score 6). *Application deadline:* For fall admission, 7/1 for domestic students; for spring admission, 11/15 for domestic students; for summer admission, 4/1 for domestic students. Applications are processed on a rolling basis. Application fee: $0. Electronic applications accepted. *Expenses: Tuition:* Full-time $15,600; part-time $865 per credit hour. *Required fees:* $148 per semester. *Financial support:* Fellowships, research assistantships, career-related internships or fieldwork, Federal Work-Study, institutionally sponsored loans, scholarships/grants, health care benefits, and unspecified assistantships available. Financial award application deadline: 3/31; financial award applicants required to submit FAFSA. *Faculty research:* Crime rate in aging population, therapeutic humor in counseling, identity formation in mixed-ethnicity individuals families. *Unit head:* Dr. Jason Northrup, Program Director, 210-438-6400, E-mail: jnorthrup1@stmarytx.edu. *Application contact:* Kim Thornton, Director, Graduate and Adult Enrollment Services, 210-436-3101, E-mail:

kthornton@stmarytx.edu.
Website: https://www.stmarytx.edu/snippets/marriage-family-therapy-ph-d/

**Saint Mary's University of Minnesota,** Schools of Graduate and Professional Programs, Graduate School of Health and Human Services, Marriage and Family Therapy Program, Winona, MN 55987-1399. Offers MA. Tuition and fees vary according to degree level and program. *Unit head:* Dr. Samantha Zaid, Program Director, 612-728-5140, Fax: 612-728-5121, E-mail: szaid@smumn.edu. *Application contact:* James Callinan, Director of Admissions for Graduate and Professional Programs, 612-728-5185, Fax: 612-728-5121, E-mail: jcallina@smumn.edu.
Website: http://www.smumn.edu/graduate-home/areas-of-study/graduate-school-of-health-human-services/ma-in-marriage-family-therapy

**Saint Paul University,** Faculty of Human Sciences, Program in Counseling and Spirituality, Ottawa, ON K1S 1C4, Canada. Offers individual or marital/couple counseling (MA); spiritual care (MA). *Program availability:* Part-time. *Degree requirements:* For master's, research project or thesis. *Entrance requirements:* For master's, honors BA in human sciences, minimum B average, 12 theology credits.

**St. Thomas University,** Biscayne College, Department of Social Sciences and Counseling, Program in Marriage and Family Therapy, Miami Gardens, FL 33054-6459. Offers MS, Post-Master's Certificate. *Program availability:* Part-time, evening/weekend. *Degree requirements:* For master's, comprehensive exam. *Entrance requirements:* For master's, interview, minimum GPA of 3.0 or GRE. Additional exam requirements/recommendations for international students: Required—TOEFL. Electronic applications accepted.

**San Francisco State University,** Division of Graduate Studies, College of Health and Social Sciences, Department of Counseling, San Francisco, CA 94132-1722. Offers clinical rehabilitation and mental health counseling (MS); counseling (MS); marriage, family, and child counseling (MSC); school counseling (Credential). *Accreditation:* ACA (one or more programs are accredited). *Program availability:* Part-time. *Application deadline:* Applications are processed on a rolling basis. *Expenses:* Tuition, state resident: full-time $6738. Tuition, nonresident: full-time $15,666. *Required fees:* $1012. Tuition and fees vary according to degree level and program. *Unit head:* Dr. Graciela Orozco, Chair, 415-338-2005, Fax: 415-338-0594, E-mail: counsel@sfsu.edu. *Application contact:* Dr. Alison Cerezo, College Counseling Coordinator, 415-338-1064, Fax: 415-338-0594, E-mail: acerezo@sfsu.edu.
Website: http://counseling.sfsu.edu

**Saybrook University,** School of Psychology and Interdisciplinary Inquiry, San Francisco, CA 94612. Offers human science (MA, PhD), including consciousness and spirituality, humanistic and transpersonal psychology, integrative health studies, organizational systems, social transformation; organizational systems (MA, PhD), including consciousness and spirituality, humanistic and transpersonal psychology, integrative health studies, leadership of sustainable systems (MA), organizational systems, social transformation; psychology (MA, PhD), including consciousness and spirituality, creativity studies (MA), humanistic and transpersonal psychology, integrative health studies, Jungian studies, marriage and family therapy (MA), organizational systems, social transformation. *Program availability:* Online learning. Terminal master's awarded for partial completion of doctoral program. *Degree requirements:* For master's, thesis or alternative; for doctorate, thesis/dissertation. *Entrance requirements:* Additional exam requirements/recommendations for international students: Required—TOEFL (minimum score 580 paper-based; 93 iBT). Electronic applications accepted. *Faculty research:* Humanistic theory, health studies, organizational systems, consciousness and spirituality, social transformation.

**Seattle Pacific University,** MS in Marriage and Family Therapy Program, Seattle, WA 98119-1997. Offers marriage and family therapy (MS); medical family therapy (Certificate). *Accreditation:* AAMFT/COAMFTE. *Program availability:* Part-time. *Degree requirements:* For master's, thesis optional, internship, clinical portfolio. *Entrance requirements:* For master's, GRE General Test or MAT, interview. Additional exam requirements/recommendations for international students: Required—TOEFL (minimum score 550 paper-based). Electronic applications accepted. *Expenses:* Contact institution. *Faculty research:* Roles of therapists, models of collaboration, medical and mental health theories of marriage and family therapy.

**Seattle University,** School of Theology and Ministry, Program in Couples and Family Therapy, Seattle, WA 98122-1090. Offers MA. *Program availability:* Part-time, evening/weekend. *Faculty:* 11 full-time (6 women), 14 part-time/adjunct (6 women). *Students:* 18 full-time (15 women), 19 part-time (17 women); includes 12 minority (2 Black or African American, non-Hispanic/Latino; 5 Asian, non-Hispanic/Latino; 4 Hispanic/Latino; 1 Two or more races, non-Hispanic/Latino). Average age 36. 21 applicants, 62% accepted, 8 enrolled. In 2016, 13 master's awarded. *Entrance requirements:* For master's, minimum GPA of 2.75 (3.0 for international students); two years of experience in some form of education, ministry, or service as a profession or volunteer; recommendations; interview with admissions committee. *Application deadline:* For fall admission, 7/1 for domestic students. *Expenses:* Contact institution. *Financial support:* In 2016–17, 30 students received support. Scholarships/grants available. *Unit head:* Rev. Clinton McNair, Director, 206-296-6968. *Application contact:* Catherine Kehoe Fallon, Admissions Coordinator, 206-296-5333, Fax: 206-296-5329, E-mail: fallon@seattleu.edu.
Website: https://www.seattleu.edu/stm/degrees/macft/

**Seton Hall University,** College of Education and Human Services, Department of Professional Psychology and Family Therapy, Program in Psychological Studies, South Orange, NJ 07079-2697. Offers individualized (MA); marriage and family therapy (MA); sport and exercise psychology (MA). *Program availability:* Part-time, evening/weekend. *Faculty:* 5 full-time (3 women). *Students:* 19 full-time (18 women), 17 part-time (14 women); includes 13 minority (4 Black or African American, non-Hispanic/Latino; 3 Asian, non-Hispanic/Latino; 6 Hispanic/Latino), 3 international. Average age 29. 35 applicants, 66% accepted, 9 enrolled. In 2016, 7 master's awarded. *Degree requirements:* For master's, comprehensive exam. *Entrance requirements:* For master's, GRE or MAT. *Application deadline:* Applications are processed on a rolling basis. Application fee: $75. *Financial support:* Application deadline: 2/1. *Faculty research:* Cognitive style, self-esteem anxiety in preadolescence, object relation, bonding. *Unit head:* Dr. Sandra Lee, Director, 973-275-2734, E-mail: sandra.lee@shu.edu. *Application contact:* Diana Minakakis, Director of Graduate Admissions, 973-275-2824, Fax: 973-275-2187, E-mail: diana.minakakis@shu.edu.

**Seton Hill University,** Program in Marriage and Family Therapy, Greensburg, PA 15601. Offers MA. *Accreditation:* AAMFT/COAMFTE. *Program availability:* Part-time, evening/weekend. *Entrance requirements:* For master's, 3 letters of recommendation, interview, resume, letter of intent, transcripts. Additional exam requirements/recommendations for international students: Required—TOEFL (minimum score 650 paper-based; 114 iBT), IELTS (minimum score 7). Electronic applications accepted.

**Shippensburg University of Pennsylvania,** School of Graduate Studies, College of Education and Human Services, Department of Counseling, Shippensburg, PA 17257-2299. Offers clinical mental health (MS); college counseling (MS); college student personnel (MS); counselor education and supervision (Ed D); couple and family counseling (Certificate); school counseling (M Ed). *Accreditation:* ACA (one or more programs are accredited); NCATE. *Program availability:* Part-time, evening/weekend,

blended/hybrid learning. *Faculty:* 8 full-time (3 women), 6 part-time/adjunct (4 women). *Students:* 90 full-time (76 women), 57 part-time (45 women); includes 35 minority (21 Black or African American, non-Hispanic/Latino; 1 Asian, non-Hispanic/Latino; 10 Hispanic/Latino; 3 Two or more races, non-Hispanic/Latino), 5 international. Average age 28. 115 applicants, 44% accepted, 34 enrolled. In 2016, 51 master's awarded. *Degree requirements:* For master's, fieldwork, research project, internship, candidacy; for doctorate, thesis/dissertation, practicum, internship. *Entrance requirements:* For master's, GRE or MAT (for MS if GPA is less than 2.75), minimum GPA of 2.75 (3.0 for M Ed), resume, 3 letter of recommendation forms, one year of relevant work experience, on-campus interview, autobiographical statement; for doctorate, master's degree in counseling or related discipline; resume; three recommendation letters (1 from employer; 1 from clinical supervisor, 1 from prior graduate school faculty member); personal essay; interview with department chair. Additional exam requirements/recommendations for international students: Required—TOEFL (minimum score 550 paper-based, 68 iBT) or IELTS (minimum score 6). *Application deadline:* Applications are processed on a rolling basis. Application fee: $45. Electronic applications accepted. *Expenses:* Tuition, state resident: part-time $483 per credit. Tuition, nonresident: part-time $725 per credit. *Required fees:* $141 per credit. *Financial support:* In 2016–17, 62 students received support. Career-related internships or fieldwork, scholarships/grants, unspecified assistantships, and resident hall director and student payroll positions available. Support available to part-time students. Financial award application deadline: 3/1; financial award applicants required to submit FAFSA. *Unit head:* Dr. Kurt L. Kraus, Departmental Chair and Program Coordinator, 717-477-1603, Fax: 717-477-4016, E-mail: klkrau@ship.edu. *Application contact:* Megan N. Luft, Assistant Dean of Graduate Admissions, 717-477-1231, Fax: 717-477-4016, E-mail: mnluft@ship.edu.
Website: http://www.ship.edu/counsel/

**Sioux Falls Seminary,** Graduate and Professional Programs, Master of Divinity Program, Sioux Falls, SD 57105-1599. Offers marriage and family therapy (M Div); pastoral care and counseling (M Div). Program also offered in Omaha, NE. *Accreditation:* ACIPE. *Program availability:* Part-time, online learning. *Application deadline:* For fall admission, 8/1 priority date for domestic students; for spring admission, 1/1 priority date for domestic students. Applications are processed on a rolling basis. Application fee: $25. *Financial support:* Career-related internships or fieldwork and scholarships/grants available. Support available to part-time students. *Unit head:* Larry Caldwell, Chief Academic Officer/Dean, 605-336-6588, Fax: 605-335-9090, E-mail: lcaldwell@sfseminary.edu. *Application contact:* Dustin Brouwer, Director of Enrollment Management, 605-336-6588, Fax: 605-335-9090, E-mail: dbrouwer@sfseminary.edu.
Website: http://sfseminary.edu/prospective-students/programs/master-of-divinity/

**Southeastern University,** College of Behavioral and Social Sciences, Lakeland, FL 33801-6099. Offers human services (MA); international community development (MA); marriage and family counseling (MS); professional counseling (MS); school counseling (MS); social work (MSW). *Program availability:* Evening/weekend. *Expenses:* Tuition: Full-time $9450; part-time $6300 per credit. *Required fees:* $500; $250 per semester. One-time fee: $150. Tuition and fees vary according to degree level, campus/location and program. *Unit head:* Erica H. Sirrine, Dean, 863-667-5341, E-mail: ehsirrine@seu.edu.
Website: http://www.seu.edu/behavior/

**Southern California Seminary,** Graduate and Professional Programs, El Cajon, CA 92019. Offers Biblical studies (MABS); counseling psychology (MACP); marriage and family therapy (MAMFT); psychology (Psy D); religious studies (MRS); theology (M Div). *Program availability:* Part-time, evening/weekend, online learning. *Degree requirements:* For master's, thesis (for some programs); for doctorate, thesis/dissertation. *Entrance requirements:* For doctorate, master's degree in psychology. Additional exam requirements/recommendations for international students: Required—TOEFL (minimum score 550 paper-based). Electronic applications accepted.

**Southern Nazarene University,** College of Professional and Graduate Studies, Department of Psychology and Counseling, Bethany, OK 73008. Offers counseling psychology (MA, MSCP); marital and family therapy (MA). *Degree requirements:* For master's, thesis optional. *Entrance requirements:* For master's, English proficiency exam, minimum GPA of 3.0 in last 60 hours/major, 2.7 overall.

**Stetson University,** College of Arts and Sciences, Division of Education, Department of Counselor Education, DeLand, FL 32723. Offers marriage, couple and family counseling (MS); mental health counseling (MS); school counseling (MS). *Accreditation:* ACA. *Program availability:* Evening/weekend. *Faculty:* 5 full-time (all women), 7 part-time/adjunct (6 women). *Students:* 114 full-time (102 women), 13 part-time (9 women); includes 36 minority (9 Black or African American, non-Hispanic/Latino; 1 Asian, non-Hispanic/Latino; 21 Hispanic/Latino; 5 Two or more races, non-Hispanic/Latino), 3 international. Average age 29. 61 applicants, 70% accepted, 37 enrolled. In 2016, 16 master's awarded. *Entrance requirements:* For master's, GRE or MAT, transcripts, three letters of recommendation, group interview. Additional exam requirements/recommendations for international students: Required—TOEFL (minimum score 90 iBT), IELTS (minimum score 7). *Application deadline:* For fall admission, 8/1 priority date for domestic students; for spring admission, 1/1 priority date for domestic students; for summer admission, 5/1 priority date for domestic students. Applications are processed on a rolling basis. Application fee: $50. Electronic applications accepted. *Expenses:* $886 per credit hour. *Financial support:* In 2016–17, 45 students received support. Federal Work-Study, scholarships/grants, unspecified assistantships, and tuition waivers for staff and dependents available. Support available to part-time students. *Faculty research:* Play therapy, trauma, wellness, infertility, counselor education training, gatekeeping and counselor education. *Unit head:* Dr. Leila Roach, Chair, 386-822-8992. *Application contact:* Jamie Vanderlip, Senior Associate Director of Graduate Admissions, 386-822-7100, Fax: 386-822-7112, E-mail: jlvander@stetson.edu.

**Syracuse University,** David B. Falk College of Sport and Human Dynamics, Dual Master's Program in Social Work and Marriage and Family Therapy (MSW/MA), Syracuse, NY 13244. Offers MSW/MA. *Accreditation:* AAMFT/COAMFTE. *Entrance requirements:* Additional exam requirements/recommendations for international students: Required—TOEFL or IELTS. *Application deadline:* For fall admission, 2/15 priority date for domestic and international students; for summer admission, 1/15 priority date for domestic students, 1/15 for international students. Application fee: $75. Electronic applications accepted. *Expenses:* Tuition: Full-time $25,974; part-time $1443 per credit hour. *Required fees:* $802; $50 per course. Tuition and fees vary according to course load and program. *Financial support:* Fellowships, research assistantships, teaching assistantships, career-related internships or fieldwork, and scholarships/grants available. Financial award application deadline: 1/1. *Faculty research:* Human diversity in social context, foundations of social work practice, policy and services in child welfare, child and family policy, social welfare policy and services. *Unit head:* Prof. Keith Alford, Director, School of Social Work, 315-443-5562, Fax: 315-443-2562, E-mail: kalford@syr.edu. *Application contact:* Felicia Otero, Director of College Admissions, 315-443-5555, Fax: 315-443-2562, E-mail: falk@syr.edu.

**Syracuse University,** David B. Falk College of Sport and Human Dynamics, Programs in Marriage and Family Therapy, Syracuse, NY 13244. Offers MA, PhD. *Accreditation:* AAMFT/COAMFTE. *Program availability:* Part-time. *Degree requirements:* For master's,

## Marriage and Family Therapy

thesis or alternative, internship; for doctorate, comprehensive exam, thesis/dissertation. *Entrance requirements:* For master's and doctorate, GRE, personal statement, three letters of recommendation, official transcripts, resume. Additional exam requirements/recommendations for international students: Required—TOEFL (minimum score 100 iBT). *Application deadline:* For fall admission, 2/15 priority date for domestic and international students; for spring admission, 11/1 priority date for domestic students, 11/15 priority date for international students. Application fee: $75. Electronic applications accepted. *Expenses: Tuition:* Full-time $25,974; part-time $1443 per credit hour. *Required fees:* $802; $50 per course. Tuition and fees vary according to course load and program. *Financial support:* Fellowships with full tuition reimbursements, research assistantships with tuition reimbursements, teaching assistantships with tuition reimbursements, career-related internships or fieldwork, and tuition waivers available. Financial award application deadline: 1/1; financial award applicants required to submit FAFSA. *Faculty research:* Marriage and family therapy theory and techniques. *Unit head:* Dr. Thom deLara, Chair, 315-443-9830, E-mail: tdelara@syr.edu. *Application contact:* Felicia Otero, Director of Graduate Admissions, 315-443-5555, E-mail: falk@syr.edu.
Website: http://falk.syr.edu/MarriageFamilyTherapy/Default.aspx

**Texas A&M University–Central Texas,** Graduate Studies and Research, Killeen, TX 76549. Offers accounting (MS); business administration (MBA); clinical mental health counseling (MS); criminal justice (MCJ); curriculum and instruction (M Ed); educational administration (M Ed); educational psychology - experimental psychology (MS); history (MA); human resource management (MS); information systems (MS); liberal studies (MS); management and leadership (MS); marriage and family therapy (MS); mathematics (MS); political science (MA); school counseling (M Ed); school psychology (Ed S).

**Texas State University,** The Graduate College, College of Education, Program in Professional Counseling, San Marcos, TX 78666. Offers community counseling (MA); marital, couple and family counseling (MA); school counseling (MA). *Accreditation:* ACA. *Program availability:* Part-time. *Faculty:* 13 full-time (11 women), 6 part-time/adjunct (all women). *Students:* 94 full-time (77 women), 107 part-time (89 women); includes 53 minority (4 Black or African American, non-Hispanic/Latino; 7 Asian, non-Hispanic/Latino; 34 Hispanic/Latino; 8 Two or more races, non-Hispanic/Latino), 2 international. Average age 32. 114 applicants, 52% accepted, 29 enrolled. In 2016, 54 master's awarded. *Degree requirements:* For master's, comprehensive exam, thesis optional, internship. *Entrance requirements:* For master's, GRE General Test (minimum preferred score of 291 [150 verbal, 141 quantitative]), baccalaureate degree from regionally-accredited institution with minimum GPA of 3.0 in last 60 hours of undergraduate work; resume; statement of purpose addressing professional goals, reasoning for specified emphasis (i.e., community, school, marital), strengths and weaknesses, and perspective on diversity; 3 references. Additional exam requirements/recommendations for international students: Required—TOEFL (minimum score 550 paper-based; 78 iBT), IELTS (minimum score 6.5). *Application deadline:* For fall admission, 2/15 for domestic and international students; for spring admission, 10/1 for domestic and international students; for summer admission, 2/15 for domestic and international students. Applications are processed on a rolling basis. Application fee: $40 ($90 for international students). Electronic applications accepted. *Expenses:* $4,851 per semester. *Financial support:* In 2016–17, 105 students received support, including 8 research assistantships (averaging $8,504 per year); teaching assistantships, Federal Work-Study, institutionally sponsored loans, and scholarships/grants also available. Support available to part-time students. Financial award application deadline: 3/1; financial award applicants required to submit FAFSA. *Unit head:* Dr. Kevin Fall, Graduate Advisor, 512-245-2081, Fax: 512-245-8872, E-mail: kf22@txstate.edu. *Application contact:* Dr. Andrea Golato, Dean of Graduate School, 512-245-2581, Fax: 512-245-8365, E-mail: gradcollege@txstate.edu.

**Texas Tech University,** Graduate School, College of Human Sciences, Department of Community, Family, and Addiction Sciences, Lubbock, TX 79409-1250. Offers marriage and family therapy (MS, PhD). *Accreditation:* AAMFT/COAMFTE. *Faculty:* 16 full-time (8 women), 1 part-time/adjunct (0 women). *Students:* 52 full-time (38 women), 10 part-time (1 woman); includes 15 minority (3 Black or African American, non-Hispanic/Latino; 8 Hispanic/Latino; 4 Two or more races, non-Hispanic/Latino), 5 international. Average age 28. 75 applicants, 27% accepted, 20 enrolled. In 2016, 9 master's, 6 doctorates awarded. *Degree requirements:* For master's, comprehensive exam, thesis optional; for doctorate, thesis/dissertation. *Entrance requirements:* For master's and doctorate, GRE. Additional exam requirements/recommendations for international students: Required—TOEFL (minimum score 550 paper-based; 79 iBT). *Application deadline:* For fall admission, 6/1 priority date for domestic students, 1/15 priority date for international students; for spring admission, 9/1 priority date for domestic students, 6/15 priority date for international students. Applications are processed on a rolling basis. Application fee: $75. Electronic applications accepted. *Expenses:* $315 per credit hour full-time resident tuition, $723 per credit hour full-time non-resident tuition; $50.50 per credit hour fee plus $608 per term fee. *Financial support:* In 2016–17, 52 students received support, including 47 fellowships (averaging $4,528 per year), 16 research assistantships (averaging $12,286 per year), 24 teaching assistantships (averaging $13,120 per year); career-related internships or fieldwork, Federal Work-Study, scholarships/grants, health care benefits, and unspecified assistantships also available. Financial award application deadline: 2/1; financial award applicants required to submit FAFSA. *Faculty research:* Medical family therapy, systemic intervention for intimate partner violence, neuroscience of addiction and the brain, long-term recovery from addictive disorders, co-parenting and parent-child relationships in diverse settings. *Total annual research expenditures:* $719,121. *Unit head:* Dr. Sterling T. Shumway, Department Chair, 806-742-3060, Fax: 806-742-0053, E-mail: sterling.shumway@ttu.edu. *Application contact:* Lori Minner, Senior Business Assistant, 806-742-3060, Fax: 806-742-0053, E-mail: lori.minner@ttu.edu.
Website: http://www.depts.ttu.edu/hs/cfas

**Texas Wesleyan University,** Graduate Programs, Programs in Education, Fort Worth, TX 76105. Offers education (M Ed, Ed D); marriage and family therapy (MSMFT, PhD); professional counseling (MA); school counseling (MS). *Program availability:* Part-time, evening/weekend. *Faculty:* 18 full-time (9 women), 10 part-time/adjunct (5 women). *Students:* 23 full-time (18 women), 217 part-time (190 women); includes 121 minority (61 Black or African American, non-Hispanic/Latino; 3 American Indian or Alaska Native, non-Hispanic/Latino; 2 Asian, non-Hispanic/Latino; 47 Hispanic/Latino; 8 Two or more races, non-Hispanic/Latino), 9 international. Average age 36. 194 applicants, 70% accepted, 118 enrolled. In 2016, 52 master's, 8 doctorates awarded. *Degree requirements:* For master's, comprehensive exam (for some programs); for doctorate, thesis/dissertation. *Entrance requirements:* For master's and doctorate, GRE General Test. Additional exam requirements/recommendations for international students: Required—TOEFL (minimum score 550 paper-based; 79 iBT), IELTS (minimum score 6.5). *Application deadline:* Applications are processed on a rolling basis. Application fee: $64. Electronic applications accepted. *Expenses:* Contact institution. *Financial support:* Career-related internships or fieldwork, Federal Work-Study, scholarships/grants, and tuition waivers (full and partial) available. Support available to part-time students. Financial award application deadline: 3/15; financial award applicants required to submit FAFSA. *Faculty research:* Teacher effectiveness, bilingual education, analytic teaching.

*Unit head:* Dr. Carlos Martinez, Dean, School of Education, 817-531-4940, Fax: 817-531-4943. *Application contact:* Amy Orcutt, Interim Director of Graduate Admissions, 817-531-4288, Fax: 817-531-4261, E-mail: arorcutt@txwes.edu.
Website: https://txwes.edu/academics/school-of-education/

**Texas Woman's University,** Graduate School, College of Professional Education, Department of Family Sciences, Denton, TX 76204-5769. Offers child development (MS); counseling and development (MS); early childhood development and education (PhD); early childhood education (M Ed); early studies (MS, PhD); family therapy (MS, PhD). *Accreditation:* ACA (one or more programs are accredited). *Program availability:* Part-time, evening/weekend. *Students:* Average age 34. In 2016, 99 master's, 9 doctorates awarded. Terminal master's awarded for partial completion of doctoral program. *Degree requirements:* For master's, comprehensive exam (for some programs), thesis (for some programs); for doctorate, comprehensive exam, thesis/dissertation. *Entrance requirements:* Additional exam requirements/recommendations for international students: Required—TOEFL (minimum score 550 paper-based; 79 iBT). *Application deadline:* For fall admission, 7/1 priority date for domestic students, 2/15 for international students; for spring admission, 9/15 priority date for domestic students, 7/1 for international students. Applications are processed on a rolling basis. Application fee: $50 ($75 for international students). Electronic applications accepted. *Expenses:* Tuition, state resident: full-time $9046; part-time $251 per credit hour. Tuition, nonresident: full-time $22,922; part-time $614 per credit hour. *International tuition:* $23,046 full-time. *Required fees:* $2690; $1285 per credit hour. One-time fee: $50. Tuition and fees vary according to course level, course load, program and reciprocity agreements. *Financial support:* Research assistantships, teaching assistantships, career-related internships or fieldwork, Federal Work-Study, institutionally sponsored loans, scholarships/grants, traineeships, health care benefits, and unspecified assistantships available. Support available to part-time students. Financial award application deadline: 3/1; financial award applicants required to submit FAFSA. *Faculty research:* Parenting/parent education, military families, play therapy, family sexuality, diversity, healthy relationships/healthy marriages, childhood obesity, male communication. *Unit head:* Dr. Karen Petty, Chair, 940-898-2685, Fax: 940-898-2676, E-mail: famsci@twu.edu. *Application contact:* Dr. Samuel Wheeler, Assistant Director of Admissions, 940-898-3188, Fax: 940-898-3081, E-mail: wheelersr@twu.edu.
Website: http://www.twu.edu/family-sciences/

**Thomas Jefferson University,** Jefferson College of Health Professions, Department of Couple and Family Therapy, Philadelphia, PA 19107. Offers MFT. *Accreditation:* AAMFT/COAMFTE. *Faculty:* 10 full-time (6 women). *Students:* 43 full-time (36 women); includes 8 minority (7 Black or African American, non-Hispanic/Latino; 1 Hispanic/Latino), 1 international. Average age 26. 44 applicants, 66% accepted, 21 enrolled. In 2016, 22 master's awarded. *Entrance requirements:* Additional exam requirements/recommendations for international students: Required—TOEFL (minimum score 87 iBT). *Application deadline:* For fall admission, 8/1 for domestic students, 5/15 for international students. Applications are processed on a rolling basis. Application fee: $50. Electronic applications accepted. *Financial support:* In 2016–17, 30 students received support. Federal Work-Study, institutionally sponsored loans, scholarships/grants, and unspecified assistantships available. Financial award application deadline: 4/1; financial award applicants required to submit FAFSA. *Faculty research:* Developing multicultural therapy competence: exploring the impact of a clinical practicum with marginalized clients in non-traditional settings. *Unit head:* Dr. Kenneth Covelman, Dean, 215-955-6000. *Application contact:* Donald Sharples, Director of Graduate Admissions, 215-503-1040, Fax: 215-503-7241, E-mail: donald.sharples@jefferson.edu.
Website: http://www.jefferson.edu/health_professions/departments/couple-family-therapy

**Trevecca Nazarene University,** Graduate Counseling Program, Nashville, TN 37210-2877. Offers clinical counseling: teaching and supervision (PhD); clinical mental health counseling (MA); marriage and family counseling/therapy (MMFC/T). *Accreditation:* ACA. *Program availability:* Part-time, evening/weekend. *Faculty:* 5 full-time (1 woman), 10 part-time/adjunct (6 women). *Students:* 135 full-time (94 women), 76 part-time (63 women); includes 49 minority (40 Black or African American, non-Hispanic/Latino; 1 American Indian or Alaska Native, non-Hispanic/Latino; 2 Hispanic/Latino; 6 Two or more races, non-Hispanic/Latino). Average age 34. In 2016, 55 master's, 5 doctorates awarded. *Degree requirements:* For master's, comprehensive exam; for doctorate, comprehensive exam, thesis/dissertation. *Entrance requirements:* For master's, MAT (minimum score of 380) or GRE (minimum score of 290 combined verbal and quantitative), minimum GPA of 2.7, official transcript from regionally accredited institution, 2 reference assessment forms; for doctorate, GRE (minimum scores: 300 combined verbal and quantitative, 3.5 analytical writing), minimum GPA of 3.25, official transcript of master's degree from regionally-accredited institution, 3 recommendation forms, 400-word letter of intent, professional vita, interview. Additional exam requirements/recommendations for international students: Required—TOEFL (minimum score 600 paper-based). *Application deadline:* Applications are processed on a rolling basis. Application fee: $0. Electronic applications accepted. *Expenses:* $636 per credit hour (for MA and MMFC/T); $799 per credit hour (for PhD). *Financial support:* Applicants required to submit FAFSA. *Unit head:* Dr. Peter Wilson, Director, 615-248-1384, Fax: 615-248-1662, E-mail: admissions_gradcouns@trevecca.edu. *Application contact:* 615-248-1384, Fax: 615-248-1662, E-mail: admissions_gradcouns@trevecca.edu.
Website: http://trevecca.edu/gradcounseling

**Universidad de las Americas, A.C.,** Program in Psychology, Mexico City, Mexico. Offers family therapy (MA).

**The University of Akron,** Graduate School, College of Health Professions, School of Counseling, Program in Marriage and Family Counseling/Therapy, Akron, OH 44325. Offers MA, MS. *Accreditation:* AAMFT/COAMFTE; ACA. *Students:* 58 full-time (48 women), 57 part-time (46 women); includes 31 minority (16 Black or African American, non-Hispanic/Latino; 1 American Indian or Alaska Native, non-Hispanic/Latino; 3 Asian, non-Hispanic/Latino; 3 Hispanic/Latino; 8 Two or more races, non-Hispanic/Latino), 1 international. Average age 30. 51 applicants, 55% accepted, 24 enrolled. In 2016, 30 master's awarded. *Degree requirements:* For master's, comprehensive exam. *Entrance requirements:* For master's, minimum GPA of 2.75, three letters of recommendation. Additional exam requirements/recommendations for international students: Required—TOEFL (minimum score 550 paper-based; 79 iBT), IELTS (minimum score 6.5). *Application deadline:* For fall admission, 3/15 for domestic and international students; for spring admission, 10/1 for domestic and international students. Application fee: $45 ($70 for international students). Electronic applications accepted. *Expenses:* Tuition, state resident: full-time $8618; part-time $359 per credit hour. Tuition, nonresident: full-time $17,149; part-time $715 per credit hour. *Required fees:* $1652. *Application contact:* Heather Katafiasz, Program Director, 330-972-6637, E-mail: hkatafiasz@uakron.edu.
Website: https://www.uakron.edu/soc/masters/mft-masters/index.dot

**The University of Alabama,** Graduate School, College of Human Environmental Sciences, Department of Human Development and Family Studies, Tuscaloosa, AL 35487. Offers human development and family studies (MSHES); marriage and family therapy (MSHES); parent and family life education (MSHES). *Faculty:* 10 full-time (8 women). *Students:* 23 full-time (22 women), 6 part-time (all women); includes 6 minority

(5 Black or African American, non-Hispanic/Latino; 1 Two or more races, non-Hispanic/Latino). Average age 25. 25 applicants, 72% accepted, 10 enrolled. In 2016, 10 master's awarded. Terminal master's awarded for partial completion of doctoral program. *Degree requirements:* For master's, comprehensive exam (for some programs), thesis (for some programs). *Entrance requirements:* For master's, GRE General Test or MAT, minimum GPA of 3.0. Additional exam requirements/recommendations for international students: Required—TOEFL (minimum score 79 iBT), IELTS (minimum score 6.5). *Application deadline:* For fall admission, 12/15 priority date for domestic and international students. Applications are processed on a rolling basis. Application fee: $50 ($60 for international students). Electronic applications accepted. *Expenses:* Tuition, state resident: full-time $10,470. Tuition, nonresident: full-time $26,950. *Financial support:* In 2016–17, 8 students received support, including 3 research assistantships with full tuition reimbursements available (averaging $13,140 per year), 5 teaching assistantships (averaging $13,140 per year); fellowships, career-related internships or fieldwork, Federal Work-Study, scholarships/grants, health care benefits, and unspecified assistantships also available. Financial award application deadline: 3/15. *Faculty research:* Parent/child relationships, preschool curricula and quality measures for child care programs, family strengths and adolescent behaviors, depression in mothers and infants, word association and word learning in young children, bullying behaviors in children, attachment parenting, medical play therapy, socialization of young children, impact of daily experiences on relationship quality, re-entry of service members into civilian roles. *Total annual research expenditures:* $1,650. *Unit head:* Dr. Carroll M. Tingle, Chair, 205-348-6158, Fax: 205-348-8153, E-mail: ctingle@ches.ua.edu. *Application contact:* Dr. Maria Hernandez-Reif, Professor, 205-348-5894, Fax: 205-348-8153, E-mail: mhernandez-reif@ches.ua.edu.
Website: http://www.hdfs.ches.ua.edu/

**University of Central Florida,** College of Education and Human Performance, Department of Educational and Human Sciences, Program in Marriage, Couple, and Family Therapy, Orlando, FL 32816. Offers MA, Certificate. *Students:* 42 full-time (36 women), 13 part-time (all women); includes 18 minority (6 Black or African American, non-Hispanic/Latino; 2 Asian, non-Hispanic/Latino; 8 Hispanic/Latino; 2 Two or more races, non-Hispanic/Latino; 1 international. Average age 29. 41 applicants, 41% accepted, 12 enrolled. In 2016, 23 master's, 30 other advanced degrees awarded. *Degree requirements:* For master's, thesis or alternative. *Entrance requirements:* For master's, GRE. Additional exam requirements/recommendations for international students: Required—TOEFL. *Application deadline:* For fall admission, 2/15 for domestic students; for spring admission, 9/15 for domestic students. Application fee: $30. Electronic applications accepted. *Expenses:* Tuition, state resident: part-time $288.16 per credit hour. Tuition, nonresident: part-time $1071.31 per credit hour. *Financial support:* In 2016–17, 8 students received support, including 3 fellowships (averaging $1,600 per year), 5 research assistantships with partial tuition reimbursements available (averaging $9,441 per year); tuition waivers also available. Financial award application deadline: 3/1; financial award applicants required to submit FAFSA. *Unit head:* Dr. Sejal Barden, Program Coordinator, 407-823-6106, E-mail: sejal.barden@ucf.edu. *Application contact:* Assistant Director, Graduate Admissions, 407-823-2766, Fax: 407-823-6442, E-mail: gradadmissions@ucf.edu.
Website: http://education.ucf.edu/programs.cfm?pid=g&cat=2

**University of Central Oklahoma,** The Jackson College of Graduate Studies, College of Education and Professional Studies, Department of Human Environmental Sciences, Edmond, OK 73034-5209. Offers family and child studies (MS), including family life education, infant/child specialist, marriage and family therapy; nutrition-food management (MS). *Program availability:* Part-time. *Degree requirements:* For master's, comprehensive exam (for some programs), thesis (for some programs). *Entrance requirements:* For master's, GRE, essay, physical, CPR and First Aid training. Additional exam requirements/recommendations for international students: Required—TOEFL (minimum score 550 paper-based; 79 iBT), IELTS (minimum score 6.5). Electronic applications accepted.

**University of Colorado Denver,** School of Education and Human Development, Program in Counseling Psychology and Counselor Education, Denver, CO 80217. Offers counseling (MA), including clinical mental health counseling, couple and family counseling, multicultural counseling, school counseling; school counseling (MA). *Accreditation:* ACA; NCATE. *Program availability:* Part-time, evening/weekend. *Students:* 179 full-time (139 women), 42 part-time (32 women); includes 45 minority (10 Black or African American, non-Hispanic/Latino; 5 Asian, non-Hispanic/Latino; 25 Hispanic/Latino; 5 Two or more races, non-Hispanic/Latino), 1 international. Average age 30. 227 applicants, 28% accepted, 26 enrolled. In 2016, 61 master's awarded. *Degree requirements:* For master's, comprehensive exam (for some programs), thesis or alternative, 63-66 hours. *Entrance requirements:* For master's, GRE or MAT (unless applicant already holds a graduate degree), letters of recommendation, interview, resume, transcripts from all colleges/universities attended. Additional exam requirements/recommendations for international students: Required—TOEFL (minimum score 525 paper-based; 71 iBT); Recommended—IELTS (minimum score 6.3). *Application deadline:* For fall admission, 1/15 for domestic students, 1/1 for international students; for spring admission, 9/15 for domestic students, 9/1 for international students. Application fee: $50 ($75 for international students). Electronic applications accepted. *Expenses:* Contact institution. *Financial support:* In 2016–17, 16 students received support. Research assistantships, Federal Work-Study, institutionally sponsored loans, scholarships/grants, and traineeships available. Financial award application deadline: 4/1; financial award applicants required to submit FAFSA. *Faculty research:* Spiritual issues in counseling, multicultural and diversity issues in counseling, adolescent suicide, career development. *Unit head:* Farah Ibrahim, Counseling Professor, 303-315-6329, E-mail: farah.ibrahim@ucdenver.edu. *Application contact:* Student Services Coordinator, 303-315-6300, Fax: 303-315-6311, E-mail: education@ucdenver.edu.
Website: http://www.ucdenver.edu/academics/colleges/SchoolOfEducation/Academics/MASTERS/counseling/Pages/default.aspx

**University of Denver,** Graduate School of Social Work, Denver, CO 80208. Offers animal-assisted social work (Certificate); couples and family therapy (Certificate); social work (MSW, PhD); social work with Latinos/as (Certificate). *Accreditation:* CSWE (one or more programs are accredited). *Program availability:* Part-time, evening/weekend. *Faculty:* 40 full-time (27 women), 103 part-time/adjunct (88 women). *Students:* 483 full-time (428 women), 13 part-time (11 women); includes 110 minority (16 Black or African American, non-Hispanic/Latino; 5 American Indian or Alaska Native, non-Hispanic/Latino; 9 Asian, non-Hispanic/Latino; 56 Hispanic/Latino; 24 Two or more races, non-Hispanic/Latino), 2 international. Average age 28. 848 applicants, 78% accepted, 277 enrolled. In 2016, 265 master's, 6 doctorates, 70 other advanced degrees awarded. *Degree requirements:* For doctorate, comprehensive exam, thesis/dissertation. *Entrance requirements:* For master's, 20 undergraduate semester hours in the arts and humanities, social/behavioral sciences, and biological sciences; for doctorate, master's degree in social work or in one of the social sciences with substantial professional experience in the social work field; two years of post-master's practice experience (preferred). Additional exam requirements/recommendations for international students: Required—TOEFL (minimum score 587 paper-based; 95 iBT). *Application deadline:* For fall admission, 1/15 priority date for domestic and international students. Applications are processed on a rolling basis. Application fee: $65. Electronic applications accepted.

*Expenses:* $43,458 per year full-time. *Financial support:* In 2016–17, 462 students received support, including 8 teaching assistantships with tuition reimbursements available (averaging $12,559 per year); Federal Work-Study, scholarships/grants, and unspecified assistantships also available. Support available to part-time students. Financial award application deadline: 2/15; financial award applicants required to submit FAFSA. *Faculty research:* Aging, youth, community, mental health, families. *Unit head:* Dr. Amanda Moore McBride, Dean, 303-871-2203, Fax: 303-871-2845. *Application contact:* Colin Schneider, Director of Enrollment Management, 303-871-3634, Fax: 303-871-2845, E-mail: gssw-admission@du.edu.
Website: http://www.du.edu/socialwork

**University of Florida,** Graduate School, College of Education, School of Human Development and Organizational Studies in Education, Gainesville, FL 32611. Offers counseling and counselor education (Ed D, PhD), including counseling and counselor education, marriage and family counseling, mental health counseling, school counseling and guidance; educational leadership (M Ed, MAE, Ed D, PhD, Ed S), including educational leadership (Ed D, PhD), educational policy (Ed D, PhD); higher education administration (Ed D, PhD), including education policy (Ed D), educational policy, higher education administration; marriage and family counseling (M Ed, MAE, Ed D, PhD, Ed S); mental health counseling (M Ed, MAE, Ed D, PhD, Ed S); research and evaluation methodology (M Ed, MAE, Ed D, PhD); school counseling and guidance (M Ed, MAE, Ed D, PhD, Ed S); student personnel in higher education (M Ed, MAE). *Accreditation:* ACA (one or more programs are accredited); NCATE. *Program availability:* Part-time, online learning. Terminal master's awarded for partial completion of doctoral program. *Degree requirements:* For master's, thesis optional; for doctorate, comprehensive exam, thesis/dissertation. *Entrance requirements:* For master's and doctorate, GRE General Test, minimum GPA of 3.0 (undergraduate), 3.5 (graduate); for Ed S, GRE General Test. Additional exam requirements/recommendations for international students: Required—TOEFL (minimum score 550 paper-based; 80 iBT), IELTS (minimum score 6). Electronic applications accepted.

**University of Guelph,** Graduate Studies, College of Social and Applied Human Sciences, Department of Family Relations and Applied Nutrition, Guelph, ON N1G 2W1, Canada. Offers applied nutrition (MAN); family relations and human development (M Sc, PhD), including applied human nutrition, couple and family therapy (M Sc), family relations and human development. *Accreditation:* AAMFT/COAMFTE (one or more programs are accredited). *Program availability:* Part-time. *Degree requirements:* For master's, thesis (for some programs); for doctorate, comprehensive exam, thesis/dissertation. *Entrance requirements:* For master's, minimum B+ average; for doctorate, master's degree in family relations and human development or related field with a minimum B+ average or master's degree in applied human nutrition. Additional exam requirements/recommendations for international students: Required—TOEFL (minimum score 600 paper-based). Electronic applications accepted. *Faculty research:* Child and adolescent development, social gerontology, family roles and relations, couple and family therapy, applied human nutrition.

**University of Holy Cross,** Program in Education and Counseling, New Orleans, LA 70131-7399. Offers administration and supervision (M Ed); curriculum and instruction (M Ed); marriage and family counseling (MA); school counseling (M Ed, MA). *Accreditation:* ACA; NCATE. *Program availability:* Part-time, evening/weekend. *Degree requirements:* For master's, thesis. *Entrance requirements:* For master's, GRE General Test, minimum GPA of 2.7.

**University of Houston–Clear Lake,** School of Human Sciences and Humanities, Programs in Human Sciences, Houston, TX 77058-1002. Offers behavioral sciences (MA), including criminology, cross cultural studies, general psychology, sociology; clinical psychology (MA); criminology (MA); cross cultural studies (MA); family therapy (MA); fitness and human performance (MA); school psychology (MA). *Accreditation:* AAMFT/COAMFTE. *Program availability:* Part-time, evening/weekend, online learning. *Degree requirements:* For master's, thesis or alternative. *Entrance requirements:* For master's, GRE General Test. Additional exam requirements/recommendations for international students: Required—TOEFL (minimum score 550 paper-based). Electronic applications accepted. *Faculty research:* Smoking cessation, adolescent sexuality, white collar crime, serial murder, human factors/human computer interaction.

**The University of Iowa,** Graduate College, College of Education, Department of Rehabilitation and Counselor Education, Iowa City, IA 52242-1316. Offers counselor education and supervision (PhD); couple and family therapy (PhD); rehabilitation and mental health counseling (MA); rehabilitation counselor education (PhD); school counseling (MA). *Accreditation:* ACA (one or more programs are accredited); CORE (one or more programs are accredited). *Degree requirements:* For master's, thesis optional, exam; for doctorate, comprehensive exam, thesis/dissertation. *Entrance requirements:* For master's and doctorate, GRE General Test, minimum GPA of 3.0. Additional exam requirements/recommendations for international students: Required—TOEFL (minimum score 550 paper-based; 81 iBT). Electronic applications accepted.

**University of La Verne,** College of Arts and Sciences, Department of Psychology, Program in Marriage and Family Therapy, La Verne, CA 91750-4443. Offers MS. *Program availability:* Part-time. *Students:* 39 full-time (36 women), 28 part-time (24 women); includes 53 minority (3 Black or African American, non-Hispanic/Latino; 2 Asian, non-Hispanic/Latino; 47 Hispanic/Latino; 1 Two or more races, non-Hispanic/Latino). Average age 29. *Degree requirements:* For master's, thesis, competency exam, fieldwork, culminating project. *Entrance requirements:* For master's, minimum undergraduate GPA of 3.0, 5-7-page statement of purpose and autobiography, 3 letters of recommendation, interview, curriculum vitae. Additional exam requirements/recommendations for international students: Required—TOEFL (minimum score 600 paper-based; 100 iBT), IELTS (minimum score 6.5). *Application deadline:* For fall admission, 3/15 for domestic and international students. Application fee: $50. *Expenses:* Contact institution. *Financial support:* Career-related internships or fieldwork, institutionally sponsored loans, scholarships/grants, and unspecified assistantships available. Financial award application deadline: 3/2; financial award applicants required to submit FAFSA. *Unit head:* Dr. Amy Demyan, Department Chair, 909-448-4181, E-mail: ademyan@laverne.edu. *Application contact:* Christy Ranells, Associate Director of Graduate Admissions, 909-448-4644, Fax: 909-392-2744, E-mail: cranells@laverne.edu.
Website: http://sites.laverne.edu/psychology/mft_program/

**University of Louisiana at Monroe,** Graduate School, College of Health and Pharmaceutical Sciences, Program in Marriage and Family Therapy, Monroe, LA 71209-0001. Offers MA, PhD. *Accreditation:* AAMFT/COAMFTE (one or more programs are accredited); ACA. *Program availability:* Part-time, evening/weekend. *Faculty:* 6 full-time (4 women), 3 part-time/adjunct (2 women). *Students:* 35 full-time (22 women), 16 part-time (7 women); includes 21 minority (20 Black or African American, non-Hispanic/Latino; 1 Asian, non-Hispanic/Latino), 1 international. Average age 30. 132 applicants, 43% accepted, 13 enrolled. In 2016, 8 master's, 6 doctorates awarded. *Degree requirements:* For master's, thesis optional; for doctorate, comprehensive exam, thesis/dissertation, clinical experience. *Entrance requirements:* For master's, GRE General Test, minimum GPA of 2.8; for doctorate, GRE General Test, minimum GPA of 3.5. Additional exam requirements/recommendations for international students: Required—TOEFL (minimum score 500 paper-based; 61 iBT). *Application deadline:* For fall

## Marriage and Family Therapy

admission, 8/24 priority date for domestic students, 7/1 for international students; for winter admission, 12/14 priority date for domestic students; for spring admission, 1/19 for domestic students, 11/1 for international students. Applications are processed on a rolling basis. Application fee: $20 ($30 for international students). Electronic applications accepted. *Expenses:* Tuition, state resident: full-time $6489. Tuition, nonresident: full-time $18,589. *Required fees:* $8984. Tuition and fees vary according to course level, course load, degree level and program. *Financial support:* Career-related internships or fieldwork, Federal Work-Study, and unspecified assistantships available. Financial award application deadline: 4/1; financial award applicants required to submit FAFSA. *Faculty research:* Family systems, substance abuse. *Unit head:* Dr. David Hale, Director, 318-342-1246, E-mail: dhale@ulm.edu.
Website: http://www.ulm.edu/mft/

**University of Louisville,** Graduate School, Raymond A. Kent School of Social Work, Louisville, KY 40292-0001. Offers marriage and family therapy (PMC), including mental health; social work (MSSW, PhD), including alcohol and drug counseling (MSSW), gerontology (MSSW), marriage and family (PhD), school social work (MSSW). *Accreditation:* AAMFT/COAMFTE; CSWE (one or more programs are accredited). *Program availability:* Part-time, evening/weekend, 100% online, blended/hybrid learning. *Faculty:* 29 full-time (19 women), 51 part-time/adjunct (42 women). *Students:* 384 full-time (324 women), 81 part-time (65 women); includes 116 minority (65 Black or African American, non-Hispanic/Latino; 7 Asian, non-Hispanic/Latino; 18 Hispanic/Latino; 1 Native Hawaiian or other Pacific Islander, non-Hispanic/Latino; 25 Two or more races, non-Hispanic/Latino), 7 international. Average age 31. 419 applicants, 63% accepted, 184 enrolled. In 2016, 191 master's, 2 doctorates awarded. *Degree requirements:* For doctorate, comprehensive exam, thesis/dissertation. *Entrance requirements:* For master's, GRE or minimum GPA of 2.75; for doctorate, GRE General Test, interview, writing sample. Additional exam requirements/recommendations for international students: Required—TOEFL (minimum score 550 paper-based; 79 iBT), IELTS (minimum score 6.5). *Application deadline:* For fall admission, 5/30 for domestic and international students; for spring admission, 9/30 for domestic and international students; for summer admission, 2/28 for domestic and international students. Applications are processed on a rolling basis. Application fee: $60. Electronic applications accepted. *Expenses:* Contact institution. *Financial support:* In 2016–17, 12 research assistantships with full tuition reimbursements (averaging $21,500 per year) were awarded; health care benefits and unspecified assistantships also available. Financial award application deadline: 5/15; financial award applicants required to submit FAFSA. *Faculty research:* Equipping young children with skills, assisting abused or neglected children, helping juveniles with sexual behavioral problems, illuminating the contributions that men and women make to their families, managing chronic conditions, enhance trauma-informed services, address social and health issues of older adults, palliative and end-of-life care. *Total annual research expenditures:* $4.8 million. *Unit head:* Dr. David Jenkins, Dean, 502-852-3944, Fax: 502-852-0422, E-mail: dajenk03@exchange.louisville.edu. *Application contact:* Misty Kupka, Program Manager for Admissions and Recruitment, 502-852-0414, Fax: 502-852-0422, E-mail: misty.kupka@louisville.edu.
Website: http://www.louisville.edu/kent

**University of Mary Hardin-Baylor,** Graduate Studies in Counseling, Belton, TX 76513. Offers clinical and mental health counseling (MA); marriage, family and child counseling (MA); non-clinical professional studies (MA). *Accreditation:* ACA. *Program availability:* Part-time, evening/weekend. *Faculty:* 13 full-time (8 women), 8 part-time/adjunct (3 women). *Students:* 49 full-time (39 women), 22 part-time (16 women); includes 30 minority (17 Black or African American, non-Hispanic/Latino; 12 Hispanic/Latino; 1 Two or more races, non-Hispanic/Latino). Average age 32. 51 applicants, 71% accepted, 23 enrolled. In 2016, 25 master's awarded. *Degree requirements:* For master's, comprehensive exam. *Entrance requirements:* For master's, GRE General Test with minimum cumulative score of 300 on verbal and quantitative portions and minimum score of 3.0 on analytical section (if overall undergraduate GPA is below a 3.0), minimum cumulative undergraduate GPA of 2.75 or 3.0 on last 60 hours of course work; three letters of recommendation; interview with departmental graduate admissions committee. Additional exam requirements/recommendations for international students: Required—TOEFL (minimum score 60 iBT), IELTS (minimum score 4.5). *Application deadline:* For fall admission, 6/1 for domestic students, 4/30 priority date for international students; for spring admission, 11/1 for domestic students, 9/30 priority date for international students. Applications are processed on a rolling basis. Application fee: $35 ($135 for international students). Electronic applications accepted. *Expenses:* Tuition: Full-time $14,940; part-time $830 per credit hour. *Required fees:* $1350; $75 per credit hour. $50 per term. Tuition and fees vary according to course load and degree level. *Financial support:* In 2016–17, 41 students received support. Federal Work-Study, unspecified assistantships, and scholarships for some active duty military personnel available. Support available to part-time students. Financial award applicants required to submit FAFSA. *Faculty research:* Teaching mindfulness skills as part of an interdisciplinary training protocol for doctor of physical therapy students; using symbolic art cards and oracle cards in supervision as a method for teaching appropriate self-disclosure, clinical reflection and counselor development reflection; understanding integral breath therapy. *Unit head:* Dr. Dan Williamson, Director, Graduate Counseling, 254-295-5018, E-mail: dwilliamson@umhb.edu. *Application contact:* Sharon Aguilera, Assistant Director, Graduate Admissions, 254-295-4835, Fax: 254-295-5038, E-mail: saguilera@umhb.edu.
Website: http://graduate.umhb.edu/counseling/

**University of Maryland, College Park,** Academic Affairs, School of Public Health, Department of Family Science, College Park, MD 20742. Offers family studies (PhD); marriage and family therapy (MS); maternal and child health (PhD). *Accreditation:* AAMFT/COAMFTE. *Program availability:* Part-time, evening/weekend. *Degree requirements:* For master's, thesis or alternative; for doctorate, comprehensive exam, thesis/dissertation, oral defense. *Entrance requirements:* For master's, GRE General Test, minimum GPA of 3.0, 3 letters of recommendation; for doctorate, GRE General Test, minimum GPA of 3.0, 3 letters of recommendation, research sample. Electronic applications accepted. *Faculty research:* Family life quality, interracial couples, child support, homeless families, family and child well-being.

**University of Massachusetts Boston,** College of Education and Human Development, Program in Family Therapy, Boston, MA 02125-3393. Offers MS. *Students:* 3 full-time (all women), 7 part-time (all women); includes 3 minority (2 Black or African American, non-Hispanic/Latino; 1 Asian, non-Hispanic/Latino), 1 international. Average age 33. 4 applicants, 75% accepted. In 2016, 19 master's awarded. *Expenses:* Tuition, state resident: full-time $16,863. Tuition, nonresident: full-time $32,913. *Required fees:* $177. *Financial support:* Research assistantships available. *Unit head:* Dr. Gonzalo Bacigalupe, Director, 617-287-7631, E-mail: gonzalo.bacigalupe@umb.edu. *Application contact:* Peggy Roldan Patel, Graduate Admissions Coordinator, 617-287-6400, Fax: 617-287-6236, E-mail: bos.gadm@dpc.umassp.edu.

**University of Miami,** Graduate School, School of Education and Human Development, Department of Educational and Psychological Studies, Program in Counseling, Coral Gables, FL 33124. Offers counseling and research (MS Ed); Latino mental health (Certificate); marriage and family therapy (MS Ed); mental health counseling (MS Ed).

*Program availability:* Part-time, evening/weekend. *Faculty:* 6 full-time (2 women). *Students:* 36 full-time (30 women), 8 part-time (all women); includes 28 minority (6 Black or African American, non-Hispanic/Latino; 22 Hispanic/Latino; 2 international. Average age 30. 60 applicants, 38% accepted, 17 enrolled. In 2016, 14 master's awarded. *Degree requirements:* For master's, comprehensive exam, personal growth experience. *Entrance requirements:* For master's, GRE General Test. Additional exam requirements/recommendations for international students: Required—TOEFL (minimum score 550 paper-based; 80 iBT); Recommended—IELTS (minimum score 6.5). *Application deadline:* For fall admission, 2/1 for domestic students. Application fee: $65. Electronic applications accepted. *Financial support:* Career-related internships or fieldwork and institutionally sponsored loans available. Support available to part-time students. Financial award application deadline: 3/1; financial award applicants required to submit FAFSA. *Faculty research:* Cocaine recidivism, HIV, non-traditional families, health psychology, diversity. *Unit head:* Dr. Anabel Bejarano, Assistant Professor of Professional Practice/Program Director, 305-284-4829, Fax: 305-284-3003, E-mail: bejarano@miami.edu. *Application contact:* Lois Heffernan, Graduate Admissions Coordinator, 305-284-2167, Fax: 305-284-9395, E-mail: lheffernan@miami.edu.
Website: http://www.education.miami.edu

**University of Minnesota, Twin Cities Campus,** Graduate School, College of Education and Human Development, Department of Family Social Science, Minneapolis, MN 55455-0213. Offers family education (M Ed); marriage and family therapy (MA, PhD); prevention science (MA). *Accreditation:* AAMFT/COAMFTE (one or more programs are accredited). *Faculty:* 19 full-time (13 women). *Students:* 54 full-time (44 women), 34 part-time (32 women); includes 19 minority (4 Black or African American, non-Hispanic/Latino; 8 Asian, non-Hispanic/Latino; 5 Hispanic/Latino; 2 Two or more races, non-Hispanic/Latino), 8 international. Average age 34. 31 applicants, 42% accepted, 13 enrolled. In 2016, 46 master's, 12 doctorates awarded. *Degree requirements:* For master's, thesis; for doctorate, thesis/dissertation. *Entrance requirements:* For master's and doctorate, GRE General Test, minimum undergraduate GPA of 3.0 (preferred). Additional exam requirements/recommendations for international students: Required—TOEFL. *Application deadline:* For fall admission, 12/15 for domestic students. Application fee: $75 ($95 for international students). *Financial support:* In 2016–17, 5 fellowships, 27 research assistantships (averaging $10,744 per year), 16 teaching assistantships (averaging $8,454 per year) were awarded; career-related internships or fieldwork, Federal Work-Study, institutionally sponsored loans, and tuition waivers (partial) also available. Financial award application deadline: 6/30; financial award applicants required to submit FAFSA. *Faculty research:* Ethnicity, culture and diverse families in social context; family stress, loss, and trauma; family finances; parenting; family transitions, and child adjustment in a family context. *Total annual research expenditures:* $2.2 million. *Unit head:* Dr. Lynne Borden, Head, 612-625-1900, Fax: 612-625-4227, E-mail: lmborden@umn.edu. *Application contact:* Dr. Jodi Dworkin, Director of Graduate Studies, 612-624-3732, Fax: 612-625-4227, E-mail: jdworkin@umn.edu.
Website: http://www.cehd.umn.edu/fsos/

**University of Missouri–St. Louis,** College of Education, Department of Counseling and Family Therapy, St. Louis, MO 63121. Offers clinical mental health counseling (M Ed); counseling (PhD); elementary school counseling (M Ed); secondary school counseling (M Ed). *Accreditation:* ACA; NCATE. *Program availability:* Part-time, evening/weekend. *Faculty:* 8 full-time (4 women), 7 part-time/adjunct (6 women). *Students:* 58 full-time (48 women), 164 part-time (129 women); includes 61 minority (48 Black or African American, non-Hispanic/Latino; 2 American Indian or Alaska Native, non-Hispanic/Latino; 3 Asian, non-Hispanic/Latino; 4 Hispanic/Latino; 4 Two or more races, non-Hispanic/Latino), 4 international. Average age 32. 74 applicants, 72% accepted, 44 enrolled. *Degree requirements:* For master's, comprehensive exam. *Entrance requirements:* For master's, 3 letters of recommendation; for doctorate, GRE General Test, 3 letters of recommendation. Additional exam requirements/recommendations for international students: Recommended—TOEFL (minimum score 550 paper-based; 79 iBT), IELTS (minimum score 6.5). *Application deadline:* For fall admission, 5/1 for domestic and international students; for spring admission, 10/1 for domestic and international students. Application fee: $50 ($40 for international students). Electronic applications accepted. *Financial support:* Teaching assistantships with tuition reimbursements available. Financial award application deadline: 4/1; financial award applicants required to submit FAFSA. *Faculty research:* Vocational interests, self-concept, decision-making factors, developmental differences. *Unit head:* Dr. Mark Pope, Chair, 314-516-5782. *Application contact:* 314-516-5458, Fax: 314-516-6996, E-mail: gradadm@umsl.edu.

**University of Mobile,** Graduate Studies, Program in Marriage and Family Counseling, Mobile, AL 36613. Offers MA. *Program availability:* Part-time, evening/weekend. *Degree requirements:* For master's, comprehensive exam, thesis optional. *Entrance requirements:* For master's, GRE. Additional exam requirements/recommendations for international students: Required—TOEFL (minimum score 550 paper-based; 80 iBT). Electronic applications accepted.

**University of Nebraska–Lincoln,** Graduate College, College of Education and Human Sciences, Department of Child, Youth and Family Studies, Lincoln, NE 68588. Offers child development/early childhood education (MS, PhD); child, youth and family studies (MS); family and consumer sciences education (MS, PhD); family financial planning (MS); family science (MS, PhD); gerontology (PhD); human sciences (PhD), including child, youth and family studies, gerontology, medical family therapy; marriage and family therapy (MS); medical family therapy (PhD); youth development (MS). *Accreditation:* AAMFT/COAMFTE (one or more programs are accredited). *Program availability:* Online learning. *Degree requirements:* For master's, thesis optional. *Entrance requirements:* For master's, GRE. Additional exam requirements/recommendations for international students: Required—TOEFL (minimum score 550 paper-based). Electronic applications accepted. *Faculty research:* Marriage and family therapy, child development/early childhood education, family financial management.

**University of Nevada, Las Vegas,** Graduate College, Greenspun College of Urban Affairs, Marriage and Family Therapy Program, Las Vegas, NV 89154-3045. Offers MS. *Accreditation:* AAMFT/COAMFTE; ACA. *Faculty:* 4 full-time (4 women), 6 part-time/adjunct (4 women). *Students:* 63 full-time (51 women), 17 part-time (13 women); includes 25 minority (5 Black or African American, non-Hispanic/Latino; 1 Asian, non-Hispanic/Latino; 13 Hispanic/Latino; 1 Native Hawaiian or other Pacific Islander, non-Hispanic/Latino; 5 Two or more races, non-Hispanic/Latino), 2 international. Average age 31. 64 applicants, 56% accepted, 28 enrolled. In 2016, 28 master's awarded. *Degree requirements:* For master's, thesis optional. *Entrance requirements:* For master's, GRE General Test, bachelor's degree; 3 letters of recommendation; 2 writing samples. Additional exam requirements/recommendations for international students: Required—TOEFL (minimum score 550 paper-based; 80 iBT), IELTS (minimum score 7). *Application deadline:* For fall admission, 1/15 for domestic students. Application fee: $60 ($95 for international students). Electronic applications accepted. *Expenses:* $269.25 per credit, $792 per 3-credit course; $9,634 per year resident; $23,274 per year non-resident; $7,094 fees non-resident (7 credits or more); $1,307 annual health insurance fee. *Financial support:* In 2016–17, 9 research assistantships with partial tuition reimbursements (averaging $10,278 per year), 12 teaching assistantships with partial tuition reimbursements (averaging $10,250 per year) were awarded; institutionally sponsored loans, scholarships/grants, health care benefits, and unspecified assistantships also available. Financial award application deadline: 3/15. *Faculty research:* Forgiveness, couple change processes, sex therapy, infidelity, technology in couples and families. *Unit head:* Dr. Katherine Hertlein, Director, 702-895-3210, Fax: 702-895-1869, E-mail: katherine.hertlein@unlv.edu. Website: http://mft.unlv.edu/grad.html

**University of New Hampshire,** Graduate School, College of Health and Human Services, Department of Human Development and Family Studies, Durham, NH 03824. Offers adolescent development (Postbaccalaureate Certificate); human development and family studies (MS); marriage and family therapy (MS). Program offered in fall only. *Accreditation:* AAMFT/COAMFTE. *Program availability:* Part-time. *Degree requirements:* For master's, thesis or alternative. *Entrance requirements:* For master's, GRE General Test. Additional exam requirements/recommendations for international students: Required—TOEFL (minimum score 550 paper-based; 80 iBT). Electronic applications accepted.

**The University of North Carolina at Greensboro,** Graduate School, School of Education, Department of Counseling and Educational Development, Greensboro, NC 27412-5001. Offers advanced school counseling (PMC); counseling and counselor education (PhD); counseling and educational development (MS); couple and family counseling (PMC); school counseling (PMC); MS/Ed S. *Accreditation:* ACA (one or more programs are accredited); NCATE. *Degree requirements:* For master's, comprehensive exam, practicum, internship; for doctorate, comprehensive exam, thesis/dissertation. *Entrance requirements:* For master's, doctorate, and PMC, GRE General Test. Additional exam requirements/recommendations for international students: Required—TOEFL. Electronic applications accepted. *Faculty research:* Gerontology, invitational theory, career development, marriage and family therapy, drug and alcohol abuse prevention.

**University of Phoenix–Bay Area Campus,** College of Social Sciences, San Jose, CA 95134-1805. Offers marriage, family, and child therapy (MSC). *Program availability:* Evening/weekend. *Degree requirements:* For master's, thesis or alternative. *Entrance requirements:* For master's, Comprehensive Cognitive Assessment, minimum undergraduate GPA of 2.5, 3 years of work experience.

**University of Phoenix–Central Valley Campus,** College of Human Services, Fresno, CA 93720-1552. Offers marriage, family and child therapy (MSC).

**University of Phoenix–Las Vegas Campus,** College of Human Services, Las Vegas, NV 89135. Offers marriage, family, and child therapy (MSC); mental health counseling (MSC); school counseling (MSC). *Program availability:* Online learning. *Entrance requirements:* For master's, minimum undergraduate GPA of 2.5, 3 years of work experience. Additional exam requirements/recommendations for international students: Required—TOEFL (minimum score 550 paper-based; 79 iBT). Electronic applications accepted.

**University of Phoenix–Phoenix Campus,** College of Social Sciences, Tempe, AZ 85282-2371. Offers counseling (MS), including clinical mental health counseling, community counseling, counseling, marriage, family and child therapy; psychology (MS). *Program availability:* Evening/weekend, online learning. *Entrance requirements:* Additional exam requirements/recommendations for international students: Required—TOEFL, TOEIC (Test of English as an International Communication), Berlitz Online English Proficiency Exam, PTE, or IELTS. Electronic applications accepted. *Expenses:* Contact institution.

**University of Phoenix–Southern California Campus,** College of Social Sciences, Costa Mesa, CA 92626. Offers counseling (MS), including counseling, marriage, family and child therapy; psychology (MS), including behavioral health. *Program availability:* Evening/weekend, online learning. *Entrance requirements:* Additional exam requirements/recommendations for international students: Required—TOEFL, TOEIC (Test of English as an International Communication), Berlitz Online English Proficiency Exam, PTE, or IELTS. Electronic applications accepted. *Expenses:* Contact institution.

**University of Rhode Island,** Graduate School, College of Health Sciences, Department of Human Development and Family Studies, Kingston, RI 02881. Offers college student personnel (MS); human development and family studies (MS); marriage and family therapy (MS). *Accreditation:* AAMFT/COAMFTE. *Program availability:* Part-time. *Faculty:* 15 full-time (10 women). *Students:* 43 full-time (28 women), 14 part-time (10 women); includes 11 minority (7 Black or African American, non-Hispanic/Latino; 1 Asian, non-Hispanic/Latino; 1 Hispanic/Latino; 2 Two or more races, non-Hispanic/Latino). In 2016, 26 master's awarded. *Degree requirements:* For master's, comprehensive exam (for some programs), thesis optional. *Entrance requirements:* For master's, GRE or MAT, 2 letters of recommendation; resume (for college student personnel specialization). Additional exam requirements/recommendations for international students: Required—TOEFL. *Application deadline:* For fall admission, 1/15 for domestic and international students. Application fee: $65. Electronic applications accepted. *Expenses:* Tuition, state resident: full-time $11,796; part-time $655 per credit. Tuition, nonresident: full-time $24,206; part-time $1345 per credit. *Required fees:* $1546; $44 per credit. One-time fee: $155 full-time; $35 part-time. *Financial support:* In 2016–17, 2 research assistantships (averaging $8,592 per year), 4 teaching assistantships (averaging $11,456 per year) were awarded. Financial award application deadline: 1/15; financial award applicants required to submit FAFSA. *Unit head:* Dr. Karen McCurdy, Chair, 401-874-5960, Fax: 401-874-4020, E-mail: kmccurdy@uri.edu. *Application contact:* Graduate Admissions, 401-874-2872, E-mail: gradadm@etal.uri.edu. Website: http://www.uri.edu/hss/hdf/

**University of Rochester,** School of Medicine and Dentistry, Graduate Programs in Medicine and Dentistry, Department of Psychiatry, Rochester, NY 14627. Offers marriage and family therapy (MS). *Accreditation:* AAMFT/COAMFTE. *Program availability:* Part-time. *Degree requirements:* For master's, projects. *Entrance requirements:* For master's, GRE General Test. *Expenses:* Tuition: Full-time $47,450; part-time $1482 per credit hour. *Required fees:* $528. Tuition and fees vary according to program.

**University of Saint Joseph,** Program in Marriage and Family Therapy, West Hartford, CT 06117-2700. Offers MA. *Accreditation:* AAMFT/COAMFTE. *Program availability:* Part-time, evening/weekend. *Degree requirements:* For master's, comprehensive exam, thesis or alternative, practicum, internship. *Entrance requirements:* For master's, 2 letters of recommendation. Electronic applications accepted. Application fee is waived when completed online. *Expenses:* Tuition: Full-time $14,580; part-time $729 per credit hour. *Required fees:* $920; $46 per credit hour. Tuition and fees vary according to course load, degree level and program.

**University of San Diego,** School of Leadership and Education Sciences, Department of Counseling and Marital and Family Therapy, San Diego, CA 92110-2492. Offers clinical mental health counseling (MA); marital and family therapy (MA). *Accreditation:* ACA. *Program availability:* Part-time, evening/weekend. *Faculty:* 11 full-time (5 women), 18 part-time/adjunct (18 women). *Students:* 144 full-time (129 women), 41 part-time (38 women); includes 80 minority (10 Black or African American, non-Hispanic/Latino; 1

American Indian or Alaska Native, non-Hispanic/Latino; 12 Asian, non-Hispanic/Latino; 50 Hispanic/Latino; 7 Two or more races, non-Hispanic/Latino), 2 international. Average age 27. 387 applicants, 43% accepted, 83 enrolled. In 2016, 72 master's awarded. *Degree requirements:* For master's, comprehensive exam, international experience. *Entrance requirements:* For master's, minimum GPA of 3.0, interview with faculty member. Additional exam requirements/recommendations for international students: Required—TOEFL (minimum score 580 paper-based; 83 iBT), TWE. *Application deadline:* For fall admission, 1/13 priority date for domestic and international students. Applications are processed on a rolling basis. Application fee: $45. Electronic applications accepted. *Financial support:* In 2016–17, 151 students received support. Career-related internships or fieldwork, Federal Work-Study, institutionally sponsored loans, unspecified assistantships, and stipends available. Support available to part-time students. Financial award application deadline: 4/1; financial award applicants required to submit FAFSA. *Faculty research:* Action research, collaboration between family therapists and medical professionals, family therapy training and supervision, multicultural counseling, school counseling. *Unit head:* Dr. Ann Garland, Director, 619-260-7879, E-mail: agarland@sandiego.edu. *Application contact:* Monica Mahon, Director of Admissions and Enrollment, 619-260-4524, Fax: 619-260-4158, E-mail: grads@sandiego.edu. Website: http://www.sandiego.edu/soles/departments/school-family-mental-health-professions/

**University of San Francisco,** School of Education, Department of Counseling Psychology, San Francisco, CA 94117-1080. Offers counseling (MA), including educational counseling, life transitions counseling, marital and family therapy. *Program availability:* Part-time. *Faculty:* 9 full-time (7 women), 43 part-time/adjunct (23 women). *Students:* 240 full-time (204 women), 72 part-time (59 women); includes 181 minority (18 Black or African American, non-Hispanic/Latino; 46 Asian, non-Hispanic/Latino; 96 Hispanic/Latino; 3 Native Hawaiian or other Pacific Islander, non-Hispanic/Latino; 18 Two or more races, non-Hispanic/Latino), 6 international. Average age 29. 270 applicants, 69% accepted, 108 enrolled. In 2016, 94 master's awarded. *Entrance requirements:* Additional exam requirements/recommendations for international students: Required—TOEFL, IELTS, PTE. *Application deadline:* For fall admission, 3/1 priority date for domestic students, 3/1 for international students; for spring admission, 10/15 priority date for domestic students, 10/15 for international students. Applications are processed on a rolling basis. Application fee: $55 ($65 for international students). Electronic applications accepted. *Expenses: Tuition:* Full-time $23,310; part-time $1295 per credit. Tuition and fees vary according to course load, degree level, campus/location and program. *Financial support:* In 2016–17, 34 students received support. Fellowships, research assistantships, and teaching assistantships available. Financial award application deadline: 3/2; financial award applicants required to submit FAFSA. *Unit head:* Dr. Christine Yeh, Chair, 415-422-6868. *Application contact:* Peter Cole, Admission Coordinator, 415-422-5467, E-mail: schoolofeducation@usfca.edu.

**University of Southern California,** Graduate School, Rossier School of Education, Master's Programs in Education, Los Angeles, CA 90089-4038. Offers educational counseling (ME); marriage, family and child counseling (MMFT); postsecondary administration and student affairs [PASA] (ME); school counseling (ME); teaching (online) (MAT); teaching and teaching credential (MAT); teaching English to speakers of other languages (MAT). *Program availability:* Part-time, evening/weekend, online learning. *Degree requirements:* For master's, thesis optional. *Entrance requirements:* For master's, GRE (for all programs except MAT). Additional exam requirements/recommendations for international students: Required—TOEFL (minimum score 100 iBT). Electronic applications accepted. *Faculty research:* College access and equity, preparing teachers for culturally diverse populations, sociocultural basis of learning as mediated by instruction with focus on reading and literacy in English learners, social and political aspects of teaching and learning English, school counselor development and training.

**University of Southern Mississippi,** Graduate School, College of Education and Psychology, Department of Child and Family Studies, Hattiesburg, MS 39406. Offers child and family studies (MS); marriage and family therapy (MS); school counseling (M Ed). *Accreditation:* AAMFT/COAMFTE (one or more programs are accredited). *Program availability:* Part-time, online learning. *Degree requirements:* For master's, comprehensive exam, thesis optional. *Entrance requirements:* For master's, GRE General Test, minimum GPA of 2.75 on last 60 hours. Additional exam requirements/recommendations for international students: Required—TOEFL. *Application deadline:* For fall admission, 3/1 priority date for domestic students, 3/1 for international students; for spring admission, 1/1 priority date for domestic and international students. Applications are processed on a rolling basis. Application fee: $60. Electronic applications accepted. *Expenses: Tuition,* area resident: Full-time $15,708; part-time $437 per credit hour. *Financial support:* Fellowships, research assistantships with full tuition reimbursements, career-related internships or fieldwork, Federal Work-Study, institutionally sponsored loans, scholarships/grants, health care benefits, and unspecified assistantships available. Financial award application deadline: 3/15; financial award applicants required to submit FAFSA. *Faculty research:* School food service, teen pregnancy, diet and cholesterol metabolism. *Unit head:* Pat Sims, Chair, 601-266-6990, Fax: 601-266-4680. *Application contact:* Shonna Breland, Manager of Graduate Admissions, 601-266-6563, Fax: 601-266-5138. Website: https://www.usm.edu/family-studies-child-development

**University of South Florida,** College of Behavioral and Community Sciences, Department of Child and Family Studies, Tampa, FL 33620-9951. Offers applied behavior analysis (MA, MS, PhD); behavioral and community sciences (PhD); child and adolescent behavioral health (MS), including developmental disabilities, leadership in child and adolescent health, translational research and evaluation, youth and behavioral health; rehabilitation and mental health counseling (MA), including addictions and substance abuse counseling, marriage and family therapy. *Accreditation:* ACA. *Faculty:* 15 full-time (10 women), 1 (woman) part-time/adjunct. *Students:* 146 full-time (127 women), 90 part-time (74 women); includes 92 minority (22 Black or African American, non-Hispanic/Latino; 12 Asian, non-Hispanic/Latino; 49 Hispanic/Latino; 9 Two or more races, non-Hispanic/Latino), 3 international. Average age 28. 267 applicants, 51% accepted, 93 enrolled. In 2016, 63 master's awarded. *Degree requirements:* For master's, comprehensive exam, thesis (for some programs); for doctorate, comprehensive exam, thesis/dissertation, Behavior Analyst Board Certification Exam. *Entrance requirements:* For master's, GRE General Test, minimum GPA of 3.0 in last 60 hours of coursework; letters of recommendation; one-page narrative describing experience, interest, and career goals in applied behavior analysis; resume or curriculum vitae (varies by program); for doctorate, GRE General Test, master's degree in behavioral analysis or closely-related field; minimum GPA of 3.5 in graduate course work; three letters of recommendation; campus visit with faculty interview; personal statement; curriculum vitae; evidence of research experiences and expertise. Additional exam requirements/recommendations for international students: Required—TOEFL (minimum score 550 paper-based; 79 iBT) or IELTS (minimum score 6.5). *Application deadline:* For fall admission, 12/5 for domestic and international students. Application fee: $30. *Expenses: Tuition,* state resident: full-time $7766; part-time $431.43 per credit hour. Tuition, nonresident: full-time $15,789; part-time $877.17 per credit hour. *Required fees:* $37 per term. *Financial support:* In 2016–17, 50 students received

## Marriage and Family Therapy

support. Unspecified assistantships available. *Faculty research:* Applied behavior analysis, autism, behavior management, behavioral intervention, children, developmental disabilities, experimental analysis of behavior, functional assessment, positive behavior support. *Total annual research expenditures:* $16.4 million. *Application contact:* Dr. Raymond G. Miltenberger, Professor/Director of Master's Program, 813-974-5079, Fax: 813-974-6115, E-mail: miltenbe@usf.edu. Website: http://cfs.cbcs.usf.edu/

**University of South Florida,** Innovative Education, Tampa, FL 33620-9951. Offers adult, career and higher education (Graduate Certificate), including college teaching, leadership in developing human resources, leadership in higher education; Africana studies (Graduate Certificate), including diasporas and health disparities, genocide and human rights; aging studies (Graduate Certificate), including gerontology; art research (Graduate Certificate), including museum studies; business foundations (Graduate Certificate); chemical and biomedical engineering (Graduate Certificate), including materials science and engineering, water, health and sustainability; child and family studies (Graduate Certificate), including positive behavior support; civil and industrial engineering (Graduate Certificate), including transportation systems analysis; community and family health (Graduate Certificate), including maternal and child health, social marketing and public health, violence and injury: prevention and intervention, women's health; criminology (Graduate Certificate), including criminal justice administration; educational measurement and research (Graduate Certificate), including evaluation; English (Graduate Certificate), including comparative literary studies, creative writing, professional and technical communication; entrepreneurship (Graduate Certificate); environmental health (Graduate Certificate), including safety management; epidemiology and biostatistics (Graduate Certificate), including applied biostatistics, biostatistics, concepts and tools of epidemiology, epidemiology, epidemiology of infectious diseases; geography, environment and planning (Graduate Certificate), including community development, environmental policy and management, geographical information systems; geology (Graduate Certificate), including hydrogeology; global health (Graduate Certificate), including disaster management, global health and Latin American and Caribbean studies, global health practice, humanitarian assistance, infection control; government and international affairs (Graduate Certificate), including Cuban studies, globalization studies; health policy and management (Graduate Certificate), including health management and leadership, public health policy and programs; hearing specialist: early intervention (Graduate Certificate); industrial and management systems engineering (Graduate Certificate), including systems engineering, technology management; information studies (Graduate Certificate), including school library media specialist; information systems/decision sciences (Graduate Certificate), including analytics and business intelligence; instructional technology (Graduate Certificate), including distance education, Florida digital/virtual educator, instructional design, multimedia design, Web design; internal medicine, bioethics and medical humanities (Graduate Certificate), including biomedical ethics; Latin American and Caribbean studies (Graduate Certificate); mass communications (Graduate Certificate), including multimedia journalism; mathematics and statistics (Graduate Certificate), including mathematics; medicine (Graduate Certificate), including aging and neuroscience, bioinformatics, biotechnology, brain fitness and memory management, clinical investigation, health informatics, health sciences, integrative weight management, intellectual property, medicine and gender, metabolic and nutritional medicine, metabolic cardiology, pharmacy sciences; national and competitive intelligence (Graduate Certificate); psychological and social foundations (Graduate Certificate), including career counseling, college teaching, diversity in education, mental health counseling, school counseling; public affairs (Graduate Certificate), including nonprofit management, public management, research administration; public health (Graduate Certificate), including environmental health, health equity, public health generalist, translational research in adolescent behavioral health; public health practices (Graduate Certificate), including planning for healthy communities; rehabilitation and mental health counseling (Graduate Certificate), including integrative mental health care, marriage and family therapy, rehabilitation technology; secondary education (Graduate Certificate), including ESOL, foreign language education: culture and content, foreign language education: professional; social work (Graduate Certificate), including geriatric social work/clinical gerontology; special education (Graduate Certificate), including autism spectrum disorder, disabilities education: severe/profound; world languages (Graduate Certificate), including teaching English as a second language (TESL) or foreign language. *Expenses:* Tuition, state resident: full-time $7766; part-time $431.43 per credit hour. Tuition, nonresident: full-time $15,789; part-time $877.17 per credit hour. *Required fees:* $37 per term. *Unit head:* Kathy Barnes, Interdisciplinary Programs Coordinator, 813-974-8031, Fax: 813-974-7061, E-mail: barnesk@usf.edu. *Application contact:* Karen Tylinski, Metro Initiatives, 813-974-9943, Fax: 813-974-7061, E-mail: ktylinsk@usf.edu. Website: http://www.usf.edu/innovative-education/

**The University of Texas at Tyler,** College of Education and Psychology, Department of Psychology and Counseling, Tyler, TX 75799-0001. Offers clinical psychology (MS), including neuropsychology, school psychology; counseling psychology (MA), including general, marriage and family; interdisciplinary studies (MSIS); school counseling (MA). *Program availability:* Part-time, evening/weekend. *Degree requirements:* For master's, comprehensive exam, thesis optional. *Entrance requirements:* For master's, GRE General Test, minimum GPA of 3.0. Additional exam requirements/recommendations for international students: Required—TOEFL. Electronic applications accepted. *Faculty research:* Neuropsychology, child abuse, psychometric properties of psychological instruments, maternal behavior, clinical practice issues, victimization of women, post-traumatic stress disorder.

**The University of West Alabama,** School of Graduate Studies, College of Education, Departments of Instructional Leadership and Support/Curriculum and Instruction, Program in Continuing Education, Livingston, AL 35470. Offers counseling and psychology (MSCE); family counseling (MSCE); general (MSCE); guidance and counseling (MSCE); library media (MSCE); student affairs in higher education (MSCE). *Accreditation:* NCATE. *Program availability:* Part-time, evening/weekend, 100% online. *Faculty:* 14 full-time (11 women), 45 part-time/adjunct (31 women). *Students:* 352 (295 women); includes 247 minority (234 Black or African American, non-Hispanic/Latino; 3 American Indian or Alaska Native, non-Hispanic/Latino; 1 Asian, non-Hispanic/Latino; 3 Hispanic/Latino; 1 Native Hawaiian or other Pacific Islander, non-Hispanic/Latino; 5 Two or more races, non-Hispanic/Latino). Average age 34. 92 applicants, 90% accepted, 72 enrolled. In 2016, 117 master's awarded. *Degree requirements:* For master's, comprehensive exam, thesis optional. *Entrance requirements:* For master's, GRE General Test, MAT, minimum GPA of 2.75. Additional exam requirements/recommendations for international students: Required—TOEFL (minimum score 500 paper-based; 61 iBT). *Application deadline:* Applications are processed on a rolling basis. Application fee: $40. Electronic applications accepted. *Expenses:* Tuition, state resident: part-time $355 per credit hour. Tuition, nonresident: part-time $710 per credit hour. *Required fees:* $130 per semester. *Financial support:* Teaching assistantships, Federal Work-Study, scholarships/grants, and unspecified assistantships available. Support available for part-time students. Financial award applicants required to submit FAFSA. *Unit head:* Dr. Reenay Rogers, Chair of Instructional Leadership and Support, 205-652-5423, Fax: 205-652-3706, E-mail: rrogers@uwa.edu. *Application contact:* Dr.

B. J. Kimbrough, Dean of Graduate Studies, 205-652-3647, Fax: 205-652-3670, E-mail: bkimbrough@uwa.edu.

**The University of Winnipeg,** Faculty of Theology, Winnipeg, MB R3B 2E9, Canada. Offers marriage and family therapy (MMFT, Certificate); sacred theology (STM); theology (M Div). *Accreditation:* AAMFT/COAMFTE; ATS. *Program availability:* Part-time.

**University of Wisconsin–Milwaukee,** Graduate School, Helen Bader School of Social Welfare, Department of Social Work, Milwaukee, WI 53201-0413. Offers applied gerontology (Certificate); marriage and family therapy (Certificate); non-profit management (Certificate); social welfare (PhD); social work (MSW, PhD). *Accreditation:* CSWE. *Program availability:* Part-time. *Students:* 232 full-time (194 women), 84 part-time (69 women); includes 79 minority (43 Black or African American, non-Hispanic/Latino; 1 American Indian or Alaska Native, non-Hispanic/Latino; 6 Asian, non-Hispanic/Latino; 2 Hispanic/Latino; 27 Two or more races, non-Hispanic/Latino), 2 international. Average age 30. 383 applicants, 57% accepted, 129 enrolled. In 2016, 126 master's, 2 doctorates, 6 other advanced degrees awarded. *Degree requirements:* For master's, thesis or alternative. *Entrance requirements:* For doctorate, GRE, bachelor's degree. Additional exam requirements/recommendations for international students: Required—TOEFL (minimum score 550 paper-based; 79 iBT), IELTS (minimum score 6.5). *Application deadline:* For fall admission, 1/1 priority date for domestic students; for spring admission, 9/1 for domestic students. Applications are processed on a rolling basis. Application fee: $56 ($96 for international students). Electronic applications accepted. *Financial support:* Fellowships, research assistantships, teaching assistantships, career-related internships or fieldwork, health care benefits, unspecified assistantships, and project assistantships available. Support available to part-time students. Financial award application deadline: 4/15; financial award applicants required to submit FAFSA. *Application contact:* Deb Padgett, Associate Professor, Social Work, 414-229-6452, E-mail: dpadgett@uwm.edu. Website: http://uwm.edu/socialwelfare/academics/

**University of Wisconsin–Stout,** Graduate School, College of Education, Health and Human Sciences, Program in Marriage and Family Therapy, Menomonie, WI 54751. Offers MS. *Accreditation:* AAMFT/COAMFTE. *Program availability:* Part-time. *Degree requirements:* For master's, thesis or alternative. *Entrance requirements:* For master's, minimum GPA of 2.75. Additional exam requirements/recommendations for international students: Required—TOEFL (minimum score 500 paper-based; 61 iBT). Electronic applications accepted. *Faculty research:* Abuse, addiction, resilience, diversity, narrative therapy.

**Utah State University,** School of Graduate Studies, Emma Eccles Jones College of Education and Human Services, Department of Family, Consumer, and Human Development, Logan, UT 84322. Offers family and human development (MFHD); family, consumer, and human development (MS, PhD), including adolescence/youth (MS), adult development/aging (MS), consumer science (MS), infancy/childhood (MS), marriage and family relations (MS), marriage and family therapy (MS). *Accreditation:* AAMFT/COAMFTE (one or more programs are accredited). *Program availability:* Part-time, evening/weekend, online learning. *Degree requirements:* For master's, thesis; for doctorate, comprehensive exam, thesis/dissertation, competencies. *Entrance requirements:* For master's, GRE General Test or MAT, minimum GPA of 3.0, 3 letters of recommendation; for doctorate, GRE, minimum GPA of 3.0, 3 letters of recommendation. Additional exam requirements/recommendations for international students: Required—TOEFL. Electronic applications accepted. *Faculty research:* Marriage and family relations, adolescent problem behavior, family financial management, early literacy, mental health in the elderly, parent child attachment.

**Valdosta State University,** Department of Psychology, Counseling, and Family Therapy, Valdosta, GA 31698. Offers school counseling (M Ed, Ed S). *Accreditation:* AAMFT/COAMFTE. *Program availability:* Part-time, evening/weekend, 100% online, blended/hybrid learning. *Degree requirements:* For master's, thesis or alternative, comprehensive written and/or oral exams; for Ed S, thesis. *Entrance requirements:* For master's, GRE General Test or MAT, GACE; for Ed S, GRE General Test or MAT. Additional exam requirements/recommendations for international students: Required—TOEFL (minimum score 523 paper-based); Recommended—IELTS. Electronic applications accepted. *Expenses:* Contact institution.

**Walden University,** Graduate Programs, School of Counseling, Minneapolis, MN 55401. Offers addiction counseling (MS), including addictions and public health, child and adolescent counseling, family studies and interventions, forensic counseling, general program, military families and culture, trauma and crisis counseling; clinical mental health counseling (MS), including addiction counseling, forensic counseling, military families and culture, trauma and crisis counseling; counselor education and supervision (PhD), including consultation, counseling and social change, forensic mental health counseling, leadership and program evaluation, trauma and crisis; marriage, couple, and family counseling (MS), including addiction counseling, career counseling, forensic counseling, military families and culture, trauma and crisis counseling; school counseling (MS), including addiction counseling, career counseling, crisis and trauma, military families and culture. *Accreditation:* ACA. *Program availability:* Part-time, evening/weekend, online only, 100% online. *Degree requirements:* For master's, residency, field experience, professional development plan, licensure plan; for doctorate, thesis/dissertation, residency, practicum, internship. *Entrance requirements:* For master's, bachelor's degree or higher; minimum GPA of 2.5; official transcripts; goal statement (for some programs); access to computer and Internet; for doctorate, master's degree or higher; three years of related professional or academic experience (preferred); minimum GPA of 3.0; goal statement and current resume (for select programs); official transcripts; access to computer and Internet. Additional exam requirements/recommendations for international students: Required—TOEFL (minimum score 550 paper-based, 79 iBT), IELTS (minimum score 6.5), Michigan English Language Assessment Battery (minimum score 82), or PTE (minimum score 53). Electronic applications accepted.

**Western Kentucky University,** Graduate Studies, College of Education and Behavioral Sciences, Department of Counseling and Student Affairs, Bowling Green, KY 42101. Offers counseling (MA Ed), including marriage and family therapy, mental health counseling; school counseling (P-12) (MA Ed); student affairs in higher education (MA Ed). *Accreditation:* ACA; NCATE. *Program availability:* Part-time, evening/weekend. *Degree requirements:* For master's, comprehensive exam, thesis optional. *Entrance requirements:* For master's, GRE General Test. Additional exam requirements/recommendations for international students: Required—TOEFL (minimum score 555 paper-based; 79 iBT). *Faculty research:* Counselor education, research for residential workers.

**Western Seminary–Sacramento Campus,** Program in Marital and Family Therapy, Sacramento, CA 95821. Offers MA. *Entrance requirements:* For master's, essays, undergraduate transcripts, 4 recommendations. Additional exam requirements/recommendations for international students: Required—TOEFL.

**Western Seminary–San Jose Campus,** Graduate Programs, Los Gatos, CA 95032-4520. Offers Bible and theology (Graduate Diploma); Bible, camp and conference ministry (CGS); Biblical and theological studies (MA), including exegetical track, theological track; coaching (CGS); expositional ministry (M Div); marital and family therapy (MA); ministry (Graduate Diploma); ministry and leadership (MA), including camp and conference ministry, coaching, pastoral care to women, youth ministry; pastoral care to women (CGS, Graduate Diploma); pastoral ministry (M Div); theology (CGS); youth and family (CGS). *Program availability:* Part-time, evening/weekend, online learning. *Entrance requirements:* For master's, minimum GPA of 3.0. Electronic applications accepted.

**Wheaton College,** Graduate School, Department of Psychology, Wheaton, IL 60187-5593. Offers clinical mental health counseling (MA); clinical psychology (Psy D); counseling ministries (MA); marriage and family therapy (MA). *Accreditation:* APA (one or more programs are accredited). *Faculty:* 14 full-time (7 women), 9 part-time/adjunct (5 women). *Students:* 130 full-time (97 women), 17 part-time (13 women); includes 38 minority (13 Black or African American, non-Hispanic/Latino; 1 American Indian or Alaska Native, non-Hispanic/Latino; 9 Asian, non-Hispanic/Latino; 8 Hispanic/Latino; 7 Two or more races, non-Hispanic/Latino), 17 international. Average age 28. 115 applicants, 80% accepted, 58 enrolled. In 2016, 70 master's, 9 doctorates awarded. Terminal master's awarded for partial completion of doctoral program. *Degree requirements:* For master's, thesis or alternative; for doctorate, thesis/dissertation,

internship. *Entrance requirements:* For master's, GRE General Test, 18 hours of course work in psychology; for doctorate, GRE General Test. Additional exam requirements/recommendations for international students: Required—TOEFL (minimum score 550 paper-based; 80 iBT), IELTS (minimum score 6.5), TOEFL (minimum score 600 paper-based; 90 iBT) or IELTS (minimum score 7.5) for PsyD. *Application deadline:* For fall admission, 3/1 priority date for domestic students, 1/1 for international students. Applications are processed on a rolling basis. Application fee: $30. *Expenses:* Tuition: Full-time $19,080; part-time $795 per credit hour. Tuition and fees vary according to degree level and program. *Financial support:* In 2016–17, 3 research assistantships (averaging $4,800 per year) were awarded; career-related internships or fieldwork, Federal Work-Study, scholarships/grants, and unspecified assistantships also available. Financial award application deadline: 3/1; financial award applicants required to submit FAFSA. *Unit head:* Dr. Terri Watson, Associate Dean of Psychology, 630-752-5104, E-mail: psychology@wheaton.edu. *Application contact:* Dusty Di Santo, Director of Graduate Admissions, 630-752-5195, Fax: 630-752-7047, E-mail: graduate.admissions@wheaton.edu.
Website: http://www.wheaton.edu/academics/departments/psychology

# Psychoanalysis and Psychotherapy

**Adler Graduate School,** Program in Adlerian Counseling and Psychotherapy, Richfield, MN 55423. Offers Adlerian studies (MA); art therapy (MA); clinical mental health counseling (MA); co-occurring mental health and substance abuse disorders (MA); marriage and family therapy (MA); school counseling (MA). *Program availability:* Part-time, evening/weekend. *Faculty:* 71 part-time/adjunct (55 women). *Students:* 298 part-time (225 women); includes 51 minority (40 Black or African American, non-Hispanic/Latino; 6 American Indian or Alaska Native, non-Hispanic/Latino; 5 Hispanic/Latino). *Degree requirements:* For master's, thesis or alternative, 500-700 hour internship (depending on license choice). *Entrance requirements:* For master's, interview, official transcripts, minimum cumulative GPA of 3.0. *Application deadline:* Applications are processed on a rolling basis. Application fee: $50. Electronic applications accepted. *Financial support:* Career-related internships or fieldwork and tuition waivers available. Support available to part-time students. Financial award applicants required to submit FAFSA. *Unit head:* Dr. Dan Haugen, President, 612-767-7048, Fax: 612-861-7559, E-mail: haugen@alfredadler.edu. *Application contact:* Evelyn B. Haas, Director of Admissions, 612-767-7044, Fax: 612-861-7559, E-mail: ev@alfredadler.edu.

**Adler University,** Programs in Psychology, Chicago, IL 60602. Offers advanced Adlerian psychotherapy (Certificate); art therapy (MA); clinical mental health counseling (MA); clinical neuropsychology (Certificate); clinical psychology (Psy D); community psychology (MA); counseling and organizational psychology (MA); counseling psychology (MA); counselor education and supervision (PhD); couple and family therapy (DCFT); criminology (MA); emergency management leadership (MA); forensic psychology (MA); marriage and family counseling (MA); marriage and family therapy (Certificate); military psychology (MA); nonprofit management (MA); organizational psychology (MA); police psychology (MA); public policy and administration (MA); rehabilitation counseling (MA); sport and health psychology (MA); substance abuse counseling (Certificate); Psy D/Certificate; Psy D/MACAT; Psy D/MACP; Psy D/MAMFC; Psy D/MASAC. *Accreditation:* APA. *Program availability:* Part-time, evening/weekend, online learning. Terminal master's awarded for partial completion of doctoral program. *Degree requirements:* For master's, thesis or alternative, oral exam, practicum; for doctorate, thesis/dissertation, clinical exam, internship, oral exam, practicum, written qualifying exam. *Entrance requirements:* For master's, 12 semester hours in psychology, minimum GPA of 3.0; for doctorate, 18 semester hours in psychology, minimum GPA of 3.25; for Certificate, appropriate master's or doctoral degree. Additional exam requirements/recommendations for international students: Required—TOEFL (minimum score 550 paper-based; 79 iBT). Electronic applications accepted.

See Display on page 982 and Close-Up on page 1225.

**Argosy University, Chicago,** Illinois School of Professional Psychology, Doctoral Program in Clinical Psychology, Chicago, IL 60601. Offers child and adolescent psychology (Psy D); client-centered and experiential psychotherapies (Psy D); diversity and multicultural psychology (Psy D); family psychology (Psy D); forensic psychology (Psy D); health psychology (Psy D); neuropsychology (Psy D); organizational consulting (Psy D); psychoanalytic psychology (Psy D); psychology and spirituality (Psy D). *Accreditation:* APA.

**Atlantic University,** Program in Integrated Imagery: Regression Hypnosis, Virginia Beach, VA 23451-2061. Offers Graduate Certificate. *Program availability:* Blended/hybrid learning. *Entrance requirements:* For degree, bachelor's degree, minimum undergraduate GPA of 3.0, official transcripts, 1000-word essay. *Application deadline:* For fall admission, 8/13 for domestic students; for spring admission, 11/13 for domestic students; for summer admission, 4/9 for domestic students. Application fee: $50. *Expenses:* $360 tuition per credit. *Application contact:* Rachel Alvidrez, Educational Services Manager, 757-631-8101, Fax: 757-631-8096, E-mail: info@atlanticuniv.edu. Website: http://www.atlanticuniv.edu/integratedimagery.html

**Boston Graduate School of Psychoanalysis,** BGSP-New Jersey, Brookline, MA 02446-4602. Offers psychoanalysis (MA); psychoanalytic counseling (MA). Programs offered in conjunction with Academic of Clinical and Applied Psychoanalysis in Livingston, NJ.

**Boston Graduate School of Psychoanalysis,** CAGS and Certificate Programs, Brookline, MA 02446-4602. Offers child and adolescent intervention (CAGS); psychoanalysis (Certificate); psychoanalytic psychotherapy (CAGS). *Program availability:* Part-time. *Degree requirements:* For other advanced degree, thesis. *Entrance requirements:* For degree, interview, BA, writing sample, 3 letters of reference, transcripts. Additional exam requirements/recommendations for international students: Required—TOEFL (minimum score 550 paper-based; 79 iBT). *Faculty research:* Treatment approaches for intractable patients, unconscious symbolic processes, female adolescent development, evaluation of school mental health interventions, development of symbolic processes in early childhood.

**Boston Graduate School of Psychoanalysis,** Doctoral Programs, Brookline, MA 02446-4602. Offers psychoanalysis (Psya D); psychoanalysis, society and culture (Psya D). *Program availability:* Part-time. *Degree requirements:* For doctorate, thesis/dissertation. *Entrance requirements:* For doctorate, interview, BA, personal statement, writing sample, 3 letters of recommendation. Additional exam requirements/recommendations for international students: Required—TOEFL (minimum score 550

paper-based; 79 iBT). *Faculty research:* Unconscious symbolic processes, female adolescent development, psychodynamics of social processes, dreams and other symbolic processes, cultural expressions of psychopathology.

**Boston Graduate School of Psychoanalysis,** Master's Programs, Brookline, MA 02446-4602. Offers mental health counseling (MA); psychoanalysis (MA); psychoanalysis, society and culture (MA). *Program availability:* Part-time. Terminal master's awarded for partial completion of doctoral program. *Degree requirements:* For master's, thesis. *Entrance requirements:* For master's, interview, BA, personal statement, writing sample, 3 letters of recommendation. Additional exam requirements/recommendations for international students: Required—TOEFL (minimum score 550 paper-based; 79 iBT). *Faculty research:* Qualitative and narrative research methodologies, ethical conflicts and dual loyalties in health professionals, psychodynamics of social processes, treatment approaches for intractable patients, psychoanalytic research methodologies.

**Boston Graduate School of Psychoanalysis,** New York Graduate School of Psychoanalysis, New York, NY 10011. Offers MA. *Program availability:* Part-time. *Degree requirements:* For master's, thesis. *Entrance requirements:* For master's, interview, BA, writing sample, letters of recommendation. Additional exam requirements/recommendations for international students: Required—TOEFL.

**Immaculata University,** College of Graduate Studies, Department of Psychology, Immaculata, PA 19345. Offers clinical mental health counseling (MA); clinical psychology (Psy D); forensic psychology (Graduate Certificate); integrative psychotherapy (Graduate Certificate); neuropsychology (Graduate Certificate); psychodynamic psychotherapy (Graduate Certificate); psychological testing (Graduate Certificate); school counseling (MA, Graduate Certificate); school psychology (MA). *Accreditation:* APA. *Program availability:* Part-time, evening/weekend. Terminal master's awarded for partial completion of doctoral program. *Degree requirements:* For master's, comprehensive exam, thesis optional; for doctorate, comprehensive exam, thesis/dissertation. *Entrance requirements:* For master's, GRE General Test or MAT, minimum GPA of 3.0; for doctorate, GRE General Test or MAT, minimum GPA of 3.5. Additional exam requirements/recommendations for international students: Required—TOEFL, IELTS. Electronic applications accepted. *Faculty research:* Supervision ethics, psychology of teaching, gender.

**Naropa University,** Graduate Programs, Program in Clinical Mental Health Counseling, Concentration in Contemplative Psychotherapy and Buddhist Psychology, Boulder, CO 80302-6697. Offers MA. *Faculty:* 3 full-time (0 women), 5 part-time/adjunct (all women). *Students:* 58 full-time (32 women), 35 part-time (22 women); includes 18 minority (1 Black or African American, non-Hispanic/Latino; 1 American Indian or Alaska Native, non-Hispanic/Latino; 1 Asian, non-Hispanic/Latino; 11 Hispanic/Latino; 1 Native Hawaiian or other Pacific Islander, non-Hispanic/Latino; 3 Two or more races, non-Hispanic/Latino), 3 international. Average age 33. 60 applicants, 77% accepted, 32 enrolled. In 2016, 18 master's awarded. *Degree requirements:* For master's, thesis, internship. *Entrance requirements:* For master's, interview, curriculum vitae/resume with pertinent academic, employment and volunteer activities; 2 letters of recommendation; statement of interest essay; transcripts; paid or volunteer experience in a clinical setting (recommended). Additional exam requirements/recommendations for international students: Required—TOEFL (minimum score 550 paper-based; 80 iBT). *Application deadline:* For fall admission, 1/15 priority date for domestic and international students. Applications are processed on a rolling basis. Application fee: $60. Electronic applications accepted. *Expenses:* $28,471 for first year in program. *Financial support:* In 2016–17, 41 students received support, including 3 research assistantships with partial tuition reimbursements available (averaging $2,000 per year), 2 teaching assistantships with partial tuition reimbursements available (averaging $3,000 per year); career-related internships or fieldwork, Federal Work-Study, scholarships/grants, tuition waivers (partial), and unspecified assistantships also available. Support available to part-time students. Financial award application deadline: 3/1; financial award applicants required to submit FAFSA. *Unit head:* Dr. Deborah Bowman, Dean, Graduate School of Counseling and Psychology, 303-546-3559, E-mail: bowman@naropa.edu. *Application contact:* Office of Admissions, 303-546-3572, Fax: 303-546-3583.
Website: http://www.naropa.edu/academics/masters/clinical-mental-health-counseling/contemplative-psychotherapy-buddhist-psychology/index.php

**Naropa University,** Graduate Programs, Program in Clinical Mental Health Counseling, Concentration in Somatic Counseling: Body Psychotherapy, Boulder, CO 80302-6697. Offers MA. *Faculty:* 3 full-time (2 women), 8 part-time/adjunct (all women). *Students:* 20 full-time (17 women), 12 part-time (10 women); includes 7 minority (1 American Indian or Alaska Native, non-Hispanic/Latino; 2 Asian, non-Hispanic/Latino; 2 Hispanic/Latino; 2 Two or more races, non-Hispanic/Latino), 1 international. Average age 33. 32 applicants, 69% accepted, 12 enrolled. In 2016, 9 master's awarded. *Degree requirements:* For master's, thesis, internship, clinical practicum. *Entrance requirements:* For master's, BA (preferably in field related to the helping professions); minimum of 100 hours of paid or volunteer experience in mental health field or community facility/service organization; interview; state of interest essay; supplemental essays; 2 letters of recommendation; transcripts. Additional exam requirements/recommendations for international students: Required—TOEFL (minimum score 550 paper-based; 80 iBT). *Application deadline:* For fall admission, 1/15 priority date for

*Psychoanalysis and Psychotherapy*

domestic and international students. Applications are processed on a rolling basis. Application fee: $60. Electronic applications accepted. *Expenses:* $25,545 for first year. *Financial support:* In 2016–17, 19 students received support, including 1 research assistantship with partial tuition reimbursement available (averaging $1,500 per year), 1 teaching assistantship with partial tuition reimbursement available (averaging $3,000 per year); career-related internships or fieldwork, Federal Work-Study, scholarships/grants, tuition waivers (partial), and unspecified assistantships also available. Support available to part-time students. Financial award application deadline: 3/1; financial award applicants required to submit FAFSA. *Unit head:* Dr. Deborah Bowman, Dean, Graduate School of Counseling and Psychology, 303-546-3559, E-mail: bowman@naropa.edu. *Application contact:* Office of Admissions, 303-546-3572, Fax: 303-546-3583, E-mail: admissions@naropa.edu.
Website: http://www.naropa.edu/academics/masters/clinical-mental-health-counseling/somatic-counseling/body-psychotherapy/index.php

**The New School,** The New School for Social Research, Department of Philosophy, New York, NY 10003. Offers philosophy (M Phil, MA); psychoanalysis (PhD). *Program availability:* Part-time. *Faculty:* 5 full-time (1 woman), 12 part-time/adjunct (4 women). *Students:* 132 full-time (42 women), 25 part-time (5 women); includes 25 minority (2 Black or African American, non-Hispanic/Latino; 1 Asian, non-Hispanic/Latino; 15 Hispanic/Latino; 7 Two or more races, non-Hispanic/Latino), 42 international. Average age 32. 167 applicants, 70% accepted, 27 enrolled. In 2016, 31 master's, 12 doctorates awarded. Terminal master's awarded for partial completion of doctoral program. *Degree requirements:* For master's, one foreign language, comprehensive exam, thesis; for doctorate, one foreign language, comprehensive exam, thesis/dissertation. *Entrance requirements:* For master's, GRE, letters of recommendation, writing sample, essays, unofficial transcript; for doctorate, letters of recommendation, writing sample, essays, unofficial transcript. Additional exam requirements/recommendations for international students: Required—TOEFL (minimum score 100 iBT), IELTS (minimum score 7), PTE (minimum score 68). *Application deadline:* For fall admission, 8/1 priority date for domestic and international students; for spring admission, 10/15 priority date for domestic and international students. Applications are processed on a rolling basis. Application fee: $50. Electronic applications accepted. *Expenses:* Contact institution. *Financial support:* Fellowships, research assistantships, teaching assistantships, Federal Work-Study, and scholarships/grants available. Support available to part-time students. Financial award application deadline: 2/1; financial award applicants required to submit FAFSA. *Faculty research:* History of Western philosophical thought and the European philosophical tradition, particularly contemporary Continental philosophy. *Total annual research expenditures:* $60,000. *Unit head:* Dr. William Milberg, Dean, The New School for Social Research, 212-229-5777, E-mail: milbergw@newschool.edu. *Application contact:* Dana Messinger, Director of Graduate Admission, 212-229-5150 Ext. 2300, E-mail: socialresearchadmit@newschool.edu.
Website: http://www.newschool.edu/nssr/philosophy/

**New York University,** Graduate School of Arts and Science, Department of Psychology, New York, NY 10012-1019. Offers cognition and perception (PhD); community psychology (PhD); general psychology (MA); industrial/organizational psychology (MA); psychotherapy and psychoanalysis (Advanced Certificate); social/personality psychology (PhD). *Program availability:* Part-time. Terminal master's awarded for partial completion of doctoral program. *Degree requirements:* For master's, comprehensive exam, thesis or alternative; for doctorate, thesis/dissertation. *Entrance requirements:* For master's and doctorate, GRE General Test. Additional exam requirements/recommendations for international students: Required—TOEFL. *Faculty research:* Vision, memory, social cognition, social and cognitive development, relationships.

**Prescott College,** Graduate Programs, Program in Counseling and Psychology, Prescott, AZ 86301. Offers adventure-based psychotherapy (MA); counseling psychology (MA); ecopsychology (MA); ecotherapy (MA); equine-assisted mental health

(MA); expressive arts therapy (MA); somatic psychology (MA); student-directed independent study (MA). *Program availability:* Part-time, online learning. *Faculty:* 4 full-time (2 women), 9 part-time/adjunct (6 women). *Students:* 45 full-time (41 women), 139 part-time (113 women); includes 26 minority (1 Black or African American, non-Hispanic/Latino; 4 American Indian or Alaska Native, non-Hispanic/Latino; 2 Asian, non-Hispanic/Latino; 7 Hispanic/Latino; 1 Native Hawaiian or other Pacific Islander, non-Hispanic/Latino; 11 Two or more races, non-Hispanic/Latino), 7 international. Average age 38. 129 applicants, 84% accepted, 69 enrolled. In 2016, 24 master's awarded. Terminal master's awarded for partial completion of doctoral program. *Degree requirements:* For master's, thesis, fieldwork or internship, practicum. *Entrance requirements:* For master's, 2 letters of recommendation, resume. Additional exam requirements/recommendations for international students: Required—TOEFL (minimum score 500 paper-based). *Application deadline:* For fall admission, 4/15 priority date for domestic and international students; for spring admission, 9/15 priority date for domestic and international students. Applications are processed on a rolling basis. Application fee: $40. Electronic applications accepted. *Expenses: Tuition:* Full-time $19,680. One-time fee: $260 part-time. *Financial support:* Fellowships, research assistantships, teaching assistantships, career-related internships or fieldwork, Federal Work-Study, institutionally sponsored loans, scholarships/grants, traineeships, health care benefits, tuition waivers, and unspecified assistantships available. Support available to part-time students. Financial award applicants required to submit FAFSA. *Unit head:* Dr. Stacey Carillo, Department Chair for Counseling, E-mail: stacey.carillo@prescott.edu. *Application contact:* Robert Monk, Graduate Admissions Counselor, 928-350-2109, E-mail: robert.monk@prescott.edu.

**Regent University,** Graduate School, School of Communication and the Arts, Virginia Beach, VA 23464-9800. Offers communication (MA, PhD), including media and arts management and promotion (MA), political communication (MA), strategic communication (MA); directing for cinema/television (MFA); film and TV (MA), including producing, production, script writing; journalism (MA); producing for cinema/television (MFA); script and screenwriting (MFA); theatre (MA). *Program availability:* Part-time, 100% online, blended/hybrid learning. *Faculty:* 19 full-time (3 women), 51 part-time/adjunct (17 women). *Students:* 92 full-time (52 women), 344 part-time (225 women); includes 163 minority (116 Black or African American, non-Hispanic/Latino; 6 American Indian or Alaska Native, non-Hispanic/Latino; 7 Asian, non-Hispanic/Latino; 25 Hispanic/Latino; 1 Native Hawaiian or other Pacific Islander, non-Hispanic/Latino; 8 Two or more races, non-Hispanic/Latino), 8 international. Average age 37. 368 applicants, 52% accepted, 124 enrolled. In 2016, 91 master's, 7 doctorates awarded. *Degree requirements:* For master's, thesis or alternative; for doctorate, thesis/dissertation. *Entrance requirements:* For master's, transcripts, writing sample, resume, audition (for MFA programs); for doctorate, GRE General Test, resume, writing sample, recommendations, interview, transcripts, personal goals statement. Additional exam requirements/recommendations for international students: Required—TOEFL (minimum score 577 paper-based). *Application deadline:* For fall admission, 3/1 priority date for domestic students; for spring admission, 10/1 priority date for domestic students. Applications are processed on a rolling basis. Application fee: $50. Electronic applications accepted. *Expenses:* $685 per credit (for MA); $895 per credit (for MFA in acting); $885 per credit (for PhD); $250 per semester technology fee. *Financial support:* In 2016–17, 178 students received support, including 2 fellowships (averaging $10,000 per year); career-related internships or fieldwork, scholarships/grants, and unspecified assistantships also available. Support available to part-time students. *Faculty research:* Screenwriting, digital media production, communication, acting, directing. *Unit head:* Dr. Mitch Land, Dean, 757-352-4916, Fax: 757-352-4291, E-mail: mland@regent.edu. *Application contact:* Heidi Cece, Assistant Vice President of Enrollment Management, 800-373-5504, Fax: 757-352-4381, E-mail: admissions@regent.edu.
Website: http://www.regent.edu/sca

# Rehabilitation Counseling

**Adler University,** Programs in Psychology, Chicago, IL 60602. Offers advanced Adlerian psychotherapy (Certificate); art therapy (MA); clinical mental health counseling (MA); clinical neuropsychology (Certificate); clinical psychology (Psy D); community psychology (MA); counseling and organizational psychology (MA); counseling psychology (MA); counselor education and supervision (PhD); couple and family therapy (DCFT); criminology (MA); emergency management leadership (MA); forensic psychology (MA); marriage and family counseling (MA); marriage and family therapy (Certificate); military psychology (MA); nonprofit management (MA); organizational psychology (MA); police psychology (MA); public policy and administration (MA); rehabilitation counseling (MA); sport and health psychology (MA); substance abuse counseling (Certificate); Psy D/Certificate; Psy D/MACAT; Psy D/MACP; Psy D/MAMFC; Psy D/MASAC. *Accreditation:* APA. *Program availability:* Part-time, evening/weekend, online learning. Terminal master's awarded for partial completion of doctoral program. *Degree requirements:* For master's, thesis or alternative, oral exam, practicum; for doctorate, thesis/dissertation, clinical exam, internship, oral exam, practicum, written qualifying exam. *Entrance requirements:* For master's, 12 semester hours in psychology, minimum GPA of 3.0; for doctorate, 18 semester hours in psychology, minimum GPA of 3.25; for Certificate, appropriate master's or doctoral degree. Additional exam requirements/recommendations for international students: Required—TOEFL (minimum score 550 paper-based; 79 iBT). Electronic applications accepted.

**See Display on page 982 and Close-Up on page 1225.**

**Alabama Agricultural and Mechanical University,** School of Graduate Studies, College of Education, Humanities, and Behavioral Sciences, Department of Social Work, Psychology and Counseling, Huntsville, AL 35811. Offers psychology and counseling (MS, Ed S), including clinical psychology (MS), counseling psychology (MS), guidance and counseling, rehabilitation counseling (MS), school counseling (MS), school psychology (MS), school psychometry (MS); social work (MSW). *Accreditation:* CORE; NCATE. *Program availability:* Part-time, evening/weekend. *Degree requirements:* For master's, comprehensive exam. *Entrance requirements:* For master's, GRE General Test. Additional exam requirements/recommendations for international students: Required—TOEFL (minimum score 500 paper-based; 61 iBT). *Application deadline:* For fall admission, 5/1 for domestic students. Application fee: $15 ($20 for international students). *Expenses:* Tuition, nonresident: part-time $826 per credit hour. Full-time tuition and fees vary according to course load and program. *Financial support:* Career-related internships or fieldwork available. Support available to part-time students. Financial award application deadline: 4/1. *Faculty research:*

Increasing numbers of minorities in special education and speech-language pathology. *Unit head:* Dr. Shirley King, Chair, 256-372-5520, Fax: 256-372-5526.

**Alabama State University,** College of Health Sciences, Department of Rehabilitation Studies, Montgomery, AL 36101-0271. Offers rehabilitation counseling (MRC). *Accreditation:* CORE. *Faculty:* 5 full-time (3 women). *Students:* 26 full-time (18 women), 4 part-time (all women); includes 26 minority (all Black or African American, non-Hispanic/Latino), 2 international. Average age 25. 32 applicants, 63% accepted, 11 enrolled. In 2016, 15 master's awarded. *Degree requirements:* For master's, comprehensive exam. *Entrance requirements:* Additional exam requirements/recommendations for international students: Required—TOEFL (minimum score 500 paper-based). *Application deadline:* For fall admission, 4/15 priority date for domestic students, 4/15 for international students; for spring admission, 11/15 for domestic and international students; for summer admission, 3/15 for domestic and international students. Application fee: $25. Electronic applications accepted. *Expenses:* Tuition, state resident: full-time $3087; part-time $2744 per credit. Tuition, nonresident: full-time $6174; part-time $5488 per credit. *Required fees:* $2284; $1142 per credit. $571 per semester. Tuition and fees vary according to class time, course level, course load, degree level, program and student level. *Financial support:* Research assistantships available. Financial award application deadline: 6/30; financial award applicants required to submit FAFSA. *Unit head:* Dr. Naoko Y. Yasui, Interim Chair/Program Coordinator, 334-229-8776, E-mail: nyasui@alasu.edu. *Application contact:* Dr. William Person, Dean of Graduate Studies, 334-229-4274, Fax: 334-229-4928, E-mail: wperson@alasu.edu.
Website: http://www.alasu.edu/academics/colleges—departments/health-sciences/rehabilitation-studies/master-of-rehabilitation-counseling/index.aspx

**Arkansas State University,** Graduate School, College of Education and Behavioral Science, Department of Psychology and Counseling, State University, AR 72467. Offers clinical mental health counseling (Graduate Certificate); college student personnel services (MS); dyslexia therapy (Graduate Certificate); psychological science (MS); psychology and counseling (Ed S); rehabilitation counseling (MRC); school counseling (MSE); student affairs (Graduate Certificate). *Accreditation:* ACA (one or more programs are accredited); CORE (one or more programs are accredited); NCATE. *Program availability:* Part-time. *Degree requirements:* For master's and other advanced degree, comprehensive exam, thesis or alternative. *Entrance requirements:* For master's, GRE General Test or MAT (for MSE), appropriate bachelor's degree, interview, letters of reference, official transcripts, immunization records, written statement, 2-3 page autobiography; for other advanced degree, GRE General Test, interview, master's degree, letters of reference, official transcript, personal statement, immunization records. Additional exam requirements/recommendations for international students: Required—TOEFL (minimum score 550 paper-based; 79 iBT), IELTS (minimum score 6), PTE (minimum score 56). Electronic applications accepted.

**Assumption College,** Rehabilitation Counseling Program, Worcester, MA 01609-1296. Offers MA, CAGS. *Accreditation:* CORE. *Program availability:* Part-time, evening/weekend, blended/hybrid learning. *Faculty:* 1 full-time, 14 part-time/adjunct (6 women). *Students:* 31 full-time (25 women), 45 part-time (33 women); includes 19 minority (11 Black or African American, non-Hispanic/Latino; 1 Asian, non-Hispanic/Latino; 6 Hispanic/Latino; 1 Two or more races, non-Hispanic/Latino). Average age 34. 25 applicants, 68% accepted, 16 enrolled. In 2016, 22 master's, 1 other advanced degree awarded. *Degree requirements:* For master's, comprehensive exam, internship, practicum. *Entrance requirements:* For master's, bachelor's degree with at least 15 semester hours of undergraduate course work in the behavioral and social sciences and minimum GPA of 2.75; 3 letters of recommendation; official transcripts; personal statement; current resume; interview; for CAGS, master's degree in human service, counseling, education, social work or related field; 3 letters of recommendation; official transcripts; personal statement; current resume; interview. Additional exam requirements/recommendations for international students: Required—TOEFL (minimum score 540 paper-based; 76 iBT), IELTS (minimum score 6). *Application deadline:* For fall admission, 7/1 for domestic and international students; for spring admission, 12/1 for domestic and international students; for summer admission, 4/15 for domestic and international students. Application fee: $30. Electronic applications accepted. *Expenses:* Tuition: Full-time $11,610; part-time $645 per credit. *Required fees:* $70 per term. Tuition and fees vary according to course load and program. *Financial support:* In 2016–17, 21 students received support. Scholarships/grants, tuition waivers (full and partial), unspecified assistantships, and institutional discounts available. Financial award application deadline: 4/15; financial award applicants required to submit FAFSA. *Faculty research:* Job placement for severe disabilities, vocational counseling, conflict resolution, health issues in mental illness. *Unit head:* Dr. Nicholas Cioe, Director, 508-767-7370, Fax: 508-798-2872, E-mail: nj.cioe@assumption.edu. *Application contact:* Karen Stoyanoff, Director of Recruitment for Graduate Enrollment, 508-767-7442, Fax: 508-799-4915, E-mail: graduate@assumption.edu. Website: http://graduate.assumption.edu/rehabilitation-counseling/masterofarts

**Ball State University,** Graduate School, Teachers College, Department of Counseling Psychology and Guidance Services, Program in Counseling Psychology, Muncie, IN 47306. Offers counseling (MA), including clinical mental health counseling, mental health counseling, rehabilitation counseling, school counseling; counseling psychology (PhD). *Accreditation:* ACA; APA. *Program availability:* Part-time. *Degree requirements:* For doctorate, thesis/dissertation. *Entrance requirements:* For master's, GRE General Test (minimum scores 144 quantitative, 153 verbal), minimum baccalaureate GPA of 2.75 or 3.0 in latter half of baccalaureate, minimum GPA of 3.0 in psychology coursework, three letters of recommendation; for doctorate, GRE General Test, interview, minimum graduate GPA of 3.2, resume. Additional exam requirements/recommendations for international students: Required—TOEFL (minimum score 550 paper-based; 79 iBT), IELTS (minimum score 6.5). Electronic applications accepted.

**Barry University,** School of Education, Program in Rehabilitation Counseling, Miami Shores, FL 33161-6695. Offers MS, Ed S. *Program availability:* Part-time, evening/weekend. *Degree requirements:* For master's, comprehensive exam, scholarly paper; for Ed S, comprehensive exam. *Entrance requirements:* For master's, GRE General Test or MAT, minimum GPA of 3.0; for Ed S, GRE General Test, minimum GPA of 3.0. Electronic applications accepted.

**Bayamón Central University,** Graduate Programs, Program in Education, Bayamón, PR 00960-1725. Offers administration and supervision (MA Ed); commercial education (MA Ed); elementary education (K–3) (MA Ed); family counseling (Graduate Certificate); guidance and counseling (MA Ed); pre-elementary teacher (MA Ed); rehabilitation counseling (MA Ed); special education (MA Ed), including attention deficit disorder, education of the autistic, learning disabilities. *Program availability:* Part-time, evening/weekend. *Degree requirements:* For master's, comprehensive exam. *Entrance requirements:* For master's, EXADEP, bachelor's degree in education or related field.

**California State University, Fresno,** Division of Research and Graduate Studies, Kremen School of Education and Human Development, Department of Counselor Education and Rehabilitation, Program in Clinical Rehabilitation and Mental Health Counseling, Fresno, CA 93740-8027. Offers MS. *Accreditation:* CORE. *Program availability:* Part-time, evening/weekend. *Degree requirements:* For master's, internship; project, thesis, or comprehensive exam. *Entrance requirements:* For master's, GRE General Test, MAT, minimum GPA of 3.0, official transcripts. Additional exam requirements/recommendations for international students: Required—TOEFL. *Application deadline:* For fall admission, 5/1 for domestic and international students; for spring admission, 10/1 for domestic and international students. Applications are processed on a rolling basis. Application fee: $55. Electronic applications accepted. *Financial support:* Career-related internships or fieldwork, Federal Work-Study, scholarships/grants, and research awards available. Support available to part-time students. Financial award application deadline: 3/1; financial award applicants required to submit FAFSA. *Faculty research:* Aging, career development, job retention, rehabilitation administration. *Unit head:* Dr. Steve Koobatian, Coordinator, 559-278-0316, Fax: 559-278-0045, E-mail: skoobatian@csufresno.edu. Website: http://www.fresnostate.edu/kremen/graduate-counseling/ms-rehab-coun.html

**California State University, Los Angeles,** Graduate Studies, Charter College of Education, Division of Special Education and Counseling, Los Angeles, CA 90032-8530. Offers counseling (MS), including applied behavior analysis, community college counseling, rehabilitation counseling, school counseling, school psychology; special education (MA, PhD). *Accreditation:* ACA. *Program availability:* Part-time, evening/weekend. *Entrance requirements:* For master's, minimum GPA of 2.75 in last 90 units of course work, teaching certificate. Additional exam requirements/recommendations for international students: Required—TOEFL (minimum score 500 paper-based). Electronic applications accepted.

**California State University, San Bernardino,** Graduate Studies, College of Education, Program in Counseling and Guidance, San Bernardino, CA 92407. Offers counseling and guidance (MS); rehabilitation counseling (MA). *Accreditation:* NCATE. *Program availability:* Part-time, evening/weekend. *Students:* 124 full-time (101 women), 15 part-time (10 women); includes 93 minority (6 Black or African American, non-Hispanic/Latino; 4 Asian, non-Hispanic/Latino; 81 Hispanic/Latino; 2 Two or more races, non-Hispanic/Latino), 3 international. 95 applicants, 62% accepted, 46 enrolled. In 2016, 39 master's awarded. *Degree requirements:* For master's, comprehensive exam, thesis or alternative. *Entrance requirements:* Additional exam requirements/recommendations for international students: Required—TOEFL. *Application deadline:* For fall admission, 7/16 for domestic students. Application fee: $55. *Expenses:* Tuition, state resident: full-time $7843; part-time $5011.20 per year. Tuition and fees vary according to course load, degree level, program and reciprocity agreements. *Unit head:* Dr. Judith Sylva, Chair, 909-537-5606, E-mail: jsylva@csusb.edu. *Application contact:* Dr. Francisca Beer, Dean of Graduate Studies, 909-537-5058, E-mail: fbeer@csusb.edu.

**California State University, San Bernardino,** Graduate Studies, College of Education, Program in Rehabilitation Counseling, San Bernardino, CA 92407. Offers MA. *Accreditation:* CORE; NCATE. *Program availability:* Part-time, evening/weekend. *Students:* 4 full-time (all women), 51 part-time (38 women); includes 36 minority (10 Black or African American, non-Hispanic/Latino; 3 Asian, non-Hispanic/Latino; 21 Hispanic/Latino; 2 Two or more races, non-Hispanic/Latino). 32 applicants, 88% accepted, 23 enrolled. In 2016, 10 master's awarded. *Degree requirements:* For master's, thesis or alternative. *Entrance requirements:* Additional exam requirements/recommendations for international students: Required—TOEFL. *Application deadline:* For fall admission, 7/16 for domestic students. Application fee: $55. *Expenses:* Tuition, state resident: full-time $7843; part-time $5011.20 per year. Tuition and fees vary according to course load, degree level, program and reciprocity agreements. *Financial support:* Career-related internships or fieldwork and Federal Work-Study available. Support available to part-time students. *Unit head:* Dr. Judith Sylva, Chair, 909-537-5606, E-mail: jsylva@csusb.edu. *Application contact:* Dr. Francisca Beer, Dean of Graduate Studies, 909-537-5058, E-mail: fbeer@csusb.edu.

**Central Connecticut State University,** School of Graduate Studies, School of Education and Professional Studies, Department of Counselor Education and Family Therapy, New Britain, CT 06050-4010. Offers marriage and family therapy (MS); professional counseling (MS, AC, Certificate); school counseling (MS); student development in higher education (MS). *Accreditation:* AAMFT/COAMFTE; ACA. *Program availability:* Part-time, evening/weekend. *Faculty:* 10 full-time (5 women), 23 part-time/adjunct (21 women). *Students:* 157 full-time (120 women), 193 part-time (151 women); includes 99 minority (41 Black or African American, non-Hispanic/Latino; 3 Asian, non-Hispanic/Latino; 46 Hispanic/Latino; 9 Two or more races, non-Hispanic/Latino). Average age 39. 201 applicants, 64% accepted, 95 enrolled. In 2016, 96 master's, 7 other advanced degrees awarded. *Degree requirements:* For master's, comprehensive exam, thesis or alternative; for other advanced degree, qualifying exam. *Entrance requirements:* For master's, minimum undergraduate GPA of 2.7, essay, interview, letters of recommendation. Additional exam requirements/recommendations for international students: Required—TOEFL (minimum score 550 paper-based; 79 iBT). *Application deadline:* For fall admission, 3/1 for domestic and international students; for spring admission, 11/1 for domestic and international students. Applications are processed on a rolling basis. Application fee: $50. Electronic applications accepted. *Expenses:* Tuition, area resident: Part-time $6497; part-time $606 per credit. Tuition, state resident: full-time $9748; part-time $622 per credit. Tuition, nonresident: full-time $18,102; part-time $622 per credit. *Required fees:* $4459; $246 per credit. *Financial support:* In 2016–17, 46 students received support. Career-related internships or fieldwork, Federal Work-Study, scholarships/grants, and unspecified assistantships available. Support available to part-time students. Financial award application deadline: 3/1; financial award applicants required to submit FAFSA. *Faculty research:* Elementary and secondary school counseling, marriage and family therapy, rehabilitation counseling, counseling in higher educational settings. *Unit head:* Dr. Connie Tait, Chair, 860-832-2154, E-mail: taitc@ccsu.edu. *Application contact:* Patricia Gardner, Associate Director of Graduate Studies, 860-832-2350, Fax: 860-832-2362. Website: http://www.ccsu.edu/ceft/

**Coppin State University,** Division of Graduate Studies, Division of Arts and Sciences, Department of Applied Psychology and Rehabilitation Counseling, Program in Rehabilitation Counseling, Baltimore, MD 21216-3698. Offers M Ed. *Accreditation:* CORE. *Program availability:* Part-time. *Degree requirements:* For master's, comprehensive exam (for some programs), thesis optional, internship, clinical requirements. *Entrance requirements:* For master's, GRE General Test, interview, minimum GPA of 3.0.

**East Carolina University,** Graduate School, College of Allied Health Sciences, Department of Addictions and Rehabilitation Studies, Greenville, NC 27858-4353. Offers military and trauma counseling (Certificate); rehabilitation and career counseling (MS); rehabilitation counseling (Certificate); rehabilitation counseling and administration (PhD); substance abuse and clinical counseling (MS); substance abuse counseling (Certificate); vocational evaluation (Certificate). *Accreditation:* CORE. *Program availability:* Part-time, evening/weekend. *Students:* 86 full-time (73 women), 44 part-time (38 women); includes 39 minority (34 Black or African American, non-Hispanic/Latino; 1 American Indian or Alaska Native, non-Hispanic/Latino; 2 Asian, non-Hispanic/Latino; 2 Hispanic/Latino). Average age 32. 80 applicants, 85% accepted, 50 enrolled. In 2016, 22 master's, 2 doctorates awarded. *Degree requirements:* For master's, comprehensive exam, thesis or alternative, internship. *Entrance requirements:* For master's, GRE General Test or MAT. Additional exam requirements/recommendations for international students: Required—TOEFL. *Application deadline:* For fall admission, 3/1 priority date for domestic students; for spring admission, 10/1 priority date for domestic students. Applications are processed on a rolling basis. Application fee: $50. *Financial support:* Research assistantships with partial tuition reimbursements, teaching assistantships with partial tuition reimbursements, Federal Work-Study, and scholarships/grants available. Support available to part-time students. Financial award application deadline: 3/1. *Unit head:* Dr. Paul Toriello, Chair, 252-744-6292, E-mail: toriellop@ecu.edu. Website: http://www.ecu.edu/rehb/

**East Central University,** School of Graduate Studies, Department of Human Resources, Ada, OK 74820. Offers administration (MSHR); counseling (MSHR); criminal justice (MSHR); human services (MSHR); rehabilitation counseling (MSHR). *Accreditation:* CORE. *Program availability:* Part-time, evening/weekend. *Degree requirements:* For master's, thesis optional. *Entrance requirements:* For master's, GRE General Test, MAT, minimum GPA of 2.5. Electronic applications accepted.

**Edinboro University of Pennsylvania,** Department of Counseling, School Psychology and Special Education, Edinboro, PA 16444. Offers counseling (MA), including art therapy, clinical mental health counseling, college counseling, rehabilitation counseling, school counseling; educational psychology (M Ed); school psychology (Ed S); special education (M Ed), including autism, behavior management. *Accreditation:* ACA. *Program availability:* Part-time, evening/weekend. *Degree requirements:* For master's, thesis or alternative, competency exam; for Ed S, thesis or alternative. *Entrance requirements:* For master's and Ed S, GRE or MAT, minimum QPA of 2.5. Electronic applications accepted.

**Emporia State University,** Program in Rehabilitation Counseling, Emporia, KS 66801-5415. Offers MS. *Accreditation:* CORE. *Program availability:* Part-time. *Faculty:* 11 full-time (7 women). *Students:* 17 full-time (all women), 7 part-time (5 women); includes 3 minority (1 Black or African American, non-Hispanic/Latino; 1 American Indian or Alaska Native, non-Hispanic/Latino; 1 Asian, non-Hispanic/Latino). 3 applicants, 100% accepted, 1 enrolled. In 2016, 3 master's awarded. *Degree requirements:* For master's, comprehensive exam or thesis, practicum. *Entrance requirements:* For master's, GRE or MAT, essay exam, appropriate bachelor's degree, interview, letters of recommendation. *Application deadline:* For fall admission, 8/15 priority date for domestic students. Applications are processed on a rolling basis. Application fee: $30 ($75 for international students). Electronic applications accepted. *Expenses:* Tuition, state resident: full-time $5922; part-time $246.75 per credit hour. Tuition, nonresident: full-time $18,414; part-time $767.25 per credit hour. *Required fees:* $1884; $78.50 per credit hour. *Financial support:* Career-related internships or fieldwork, Federal Work-Study,

## Rehabilitation Counseling

institutionally sponsored loans, health care benefits, and unspecified assistantships available. Financial award application deadline: 3/15; financial award applicants required to submit FAFSA. *Unit head:* Dr. Katrina Miller, Chair/Graduate Co-Coordinator, 620-341-5791, E-mail: kmille12@emporia.edu. *Application contact:* Mary Sewell, Admissions Coordinator, 800-950-GRAD, Fax: 620-341-5909, E-mail: msewell@emporia.edu.

**Florida International University,** College of Arts, Sciences, and Education, Department of Leadership and Professional Studies, Miami, FL 33199. Offers adult education and human resource development (MS, Ed D); counseling (MS), including rehabilitation counseling, school counseling; counselor education (MS), including clinical mental health counseling; educational administration and supervision (Ed D); educational leadership (MS, Certificate, Ed S); higher education (Ed D); higher education administration (MS); international and comparative education (MS); recreation and sport management (MS), including recreation and sport management, recreational therapy; school psychology (Ed S); urban education (MS), including instruction in urban settings, learning technologies, multicultural/bilingual, multicultural/TESOL, urban education. *Program availability:* Part-time, evening/weekend. *Faculty:* 27 full-time (19 women), 38 part-time/adjunct (25 women). *Students:* 253 full-time (191 women), 306 part-time (241 women); includes 444 minority (129 Black or African American, non-Hispanic/Latino; 3 Asian, non-Hispanic/Latino; 304 Hispanic/Latino; 8 Two or more races, non-Hispanic/Latino), 18 international. Average age 31. 366 applicants, 60% accepted, 115 enrolled. In 2016, 193 master's, 8 doctorates awarded. *Degree requirements:* For doctorate, thesis/dissertation. *Entrance requirements:* For master's, minimum GPA of 3.0; for doctorate and other advanced degree, GRE General Test. Additional exam requirements/recommendations for international students: Required—TOEFL (minimum score 550 paper-based; 80 iBT), IELTS (minimum score 6.3). *Application deadline:* For fall admission, 6/1 priority date for domestic students, 4/1 for international students; for winter admission, 10/1 priority date for domestic students, 9/1 for international students; for spring admission, 3/1 priority date for domestic students, 2/1 for international students. Applications are processed on a rolling basis. Application fee: $30. Electronic applications accepted. *Expenses:* Tuition, state resident: full-time $8912; part-time $446 per credit hour. Tuition, nonresident: full-time $21,393; part-time $992 per credit hour. *Required fees:* $2185; $195 per semester. Tuition and fees vary according to program. *Financial support:* Fellowships, research assistantships with tuition reimbursements, teaching assistantships with tuition reimbursements, Federal Work-Study, and tuition waivers (full and partial) available. Support available to part-time students. Financial award applicants required to submit FAFSA. *Unit head:* Dr. Benjamin Baez, Chair, 305-348-3214, Fax: 305-348-1515, E-mail: benjamin.baez@fiu.edu. *Application contact:* Nanett Rojas, Assistant Director, Graduate Admissions, 305-348-7464, Fax: 305-348-7441, E-mail: gradadm@fiu.edu.
Website: http://education.fiu.edu

**Fort Valley State University,** College of Graduate Studies and Extended Education, Department of Counseling Psychology, Program in Rehabilitation Counseling, Fort Valley, GA 31030. Offers MS. *Accreditation:* CORE. *Program availability:* Part-time. *Degree requirements:* For master's, comprehensive exam (for some programs), thesis optional. *Entrance requirements:* For master's, GRE General Test or MAT. Additional exam requirements/recommendations for international students: Recommended—TOEFL.

**The George Washington University,** Graduate School of Education and Human Development, Department of Counseling and Human Development, Program in Rehabilitation Counseling, Washington, DC 20052. Offers autism spectrum disorder (MA Ed/HD); substance abuse and psychiatric disabilities (MA Ed/HD); traumatic brain injury (MA Ed/HD). *Accreditation:* CORE. *Program availability:* Online learning. *Students:* 29 full-time (18 women), 24 part-time (20 women); includes 18 minority (11 Black or African American, non-Hispanic/Latino; 1 Asian, non-Hispanic/Latino; 5 Hispanic/Latino; 1 Two or more races, non-Hispanic/Latino), 8 international. Average age 34. 45 applicants, 76% accepted, 18 enrolled. In 2016, 8 master's awarded. *Entrance requirements:* For master's, GRE or MAT, two letters of recommendation, 1- to 2-page statement of purpose, official transcripts from all instiutions attended, resume. Additional exam requirements/recommendations for international students: Required—TOEFL or IELTS. Electronic applications accepted. *Unit head:* Dr. Kenneth C. Hergenrather, Director, 202-994-1334, E-mail: hergenkc@gwu.edu. *Application contact:* Sarah Lang, Director of Graduate Admissions, 202-994-1447, Fax: 202-994-7207, E-mail: slang@gwu.edu.
Website: http://gsehd.gwu.edu/rehabilitation-counseling-masters

**Georgia State University,** College of Education and Human Development, Department of Counseling and Psychological Services, Program in Rehabilitation Counseling, Atlanta, GA 30302-3083. Offers MS. *Accreditation:* CORE. *Program availability:* Online learning. *Degree requirements:* For master's, comprehensive exam. *Entrance requirements:* For master's, GRE, goal statement, resume, 3 letters of recommendation, transcripts. Additional exam requirements/recommendations for international students: Required—TOEFL. *Application deadline:* For fall admission, 2/1 for domestic and international students. Application fee: $50. Electronic applications accepted. *Expenses:* Tuition, state resident: full-time $6876; part-time $382 per credit hour. Tuition, nonresident: full-time $22,374; part-time $1243 per credit hour. *Required fees:* $2128; $1064 per term. Part-time tuition and fees vary according to course load and program. *Financial support:* In 2016–17, research assistantships with tuition reimbursements (averaging $13,000 per year), teaching assistantships with partial tuition reimbursements (averaging $1,000 per year) were awarded; career-related internships or fieldwork, institutionally sponsored loans, scholarships/grants, health care benefits, tuition waivers, and unspecified assistantships also available. Financial award application deadline: 4/1. *Faculty research:* Career counseling; sexual and gender minority issues; trauma, stress and coping; disability services; disability employment. *Unit head:* Dr. Brian Dew, Department Chair, 404-413-8168, Fax: 404-413-8013, E-mail: bdew@gsu.edu. *Application contact:* CPS Admissions Office, 404-413-8200.
Website: http://cps.education.gsu.edu/programs/clinical-rehabilitation-counseling/

**Hofstra University,** School of Health Professions and Human Services, Programs in Counseling, Hempstead, NY 11549. Offers counseling (MS Ed, PD); creative arts therapy (MA); interdisciplinary transition specialist (Advanced Certificate); marriage and family therapy (MA); mental health counseling (MA, Advanced Certificate), including alcohol and substance abuse (Advanced Certificate); rehabilitation administration (PD); rehabilitation counseling (MS Ed, Advanced Certificate); rehabilitation counseling in mental health (MS Ed, Advanced Certificate); school counselor bilingual extension (Advanced Certificate). *Accreditation:* ACA. *Program availability:* Part-time, evening/weekend. *Students:* 116 full-time (100 women), 66 part-time (59 women); includes 48 minority (18 Black or African American, non-Hispanic/Latino; 11 Asian, non-Hispanic/Latino; 17 Hispanic/Latino; 2 Two or more races, non-Hispanic/Latino), 5 international. Average age 29. 166 applicants, 81% accepted, 66 enrolled. In 2016, 71 master's, 7 other advanced degrees awarded. *Degree requirements:* For master's, comprehensive exam (for some programs), thesis (for some programs), internship, practicum, student teaching, seminars, minimum GPA of 3.0. *Entrance requirements:* For master's, GRE, interview, letters of recommendation, portfolio, essay, professional experience, certification; for other advanced degree, GRE, interview, letters of recommendation, essay, professional experience, resume, master's degree. Additional exam

requirements/recommendations for international students: Required—TOEFL (minimum score 550 paper-based; 80 iBT). *Application deadline:* Applications are processed on a rolling basis. Application fee: $75. Electronic applications accepted. *Expenses: Tuition:* Full-time $1240. *Required fees:* $970. Tuition and fees vary according to program. *Financial support:* In 2016–17, 76 students received support, including 40 fellowships with full and partial tuition reimbursements available (averaging $3,465 per year), 5 research assistantships with full and partial tuition reimbursements available (averaging $6,939 per year); career-related internships or fieldwork, Federal Work-Study, institutionally sponsored loans, scholarships/grants, traineeships, tuition waivers (full and partial), and unspecified assistantships also available. Support available to part-time students. Financial award applicants required to submit FAFSA. *Faculty research:* The constructs of hope and grit; the efficacy of support groups in treating eating disorders; attitudes of primary care physicians related to providing integrated care with mental health counselors; expanding the counselor identity through disability cultural competence; vocational evaluation and assessment collaboration; disability cultural competence. *Unit head:* Dr. Jamie Mitus, Chairperson, 516-463-5759, E-mail: jamie.s.mitus@hofstra.edu. *Application contact:* Sunil Samuel, Assistant Vice President of Admissions, 516-463-4723, Fax: 516-463-4664, E-mail: graduateadmission@hofstra.edu.
Website: http://www.hofstra.edu/academics/colleges/healthscienceshumanservices/

**Hunter College of the City University of New York,** Graduate School, School of Education, Department of Educational Foundations and Counseling, Program in Rehabilitation Counseling, New York, NY 10065-5085. Offers MS Ed. *Accreditation:* CORE. *Degree requirements:* For master's, thesis, seminar. *Entrance requirements:* For master's, interview, minimum GPA of 2.7, recommendations. Additional exam requirements/recommendations for international students: Required—TOEFL, TWE. *Application deadline:* For fall admission, 4/1 for domestic students, 2/1 for international students; for spring admission, 11/1 for domestic students, 9/1 for international students. Applications are processed on a rolling basis. *Financial support:* Federal Work-Study and tuition waivers (partial) available. Support available to part-time students. *Unit head:* Dr. Arnold Wolf, Coordinator, 212-772-4616, E-mail: awo@hunter.cuny.edu. *Application contact:* Milena Solo, Director for Graduate Admissions, 212-772-4482, E-mail: admissions@hunter.cuny.edu.

**Illinois Institute of Technology,** Graduate College, Lewis College of Human Sciences, Department of Psychology, Chicago, IL 60616. Offers clinical psychology (PhD); industrial and organizational psychology (PhD); personnel and human resource development (MS); rehabilitation and mental health counseling (MS); rehabilitation counseling education (PhD). *Accreditation:* APA (one or more programs are accredited); CORE. *Program availability:* Part-time, evening/weekend. Terminal master's awarded for partial completion of doctoral program. *Degree requirements:* For master's, thesis (for some programs); for doctorate, comprehensive exam, thesis/dissertation, minimum of 107 credit hours, 1-year full-time internship. *Entrance requirements:* For master's, GRE General Test (minimum score 298 Quantitative and Verbal, 3.0 Analytical Writing), minimum GPA of 3.0; 3 letters of recommendation; bachelor's degree from accredited institution (for personnel and human resource development); for doctorate, GRE General Test (minimum score 298 Quantitative and Verbal, 3.0 Analytical Writing), bachelor's or master's degree from accredited institution, recommendations. Additional exam requirements/recommendations for international students: Required—TOEFL (minimum score 550 paper-based; 80 iBT). Electronic applications accepted. *Faculty research:* Clinical psychology, rehabilitation and mental health counseling, industrial organizational psychology.

**Kent State University,** College of Education, Health and Human Services, School of Lifespan Development and Educational Sciences, Program in Rehabilitation Counseling, Kent, OH 44242-0001. Offers M Ed. *Accreditation:* CORE. *Entrance requirements:* For master's, 2 letters of reference, goals statement, minimum undergraduate GPA of 2.75, interview. Additional exam requirements/recommendations for international students: Required—TOEFL (minimum score 550 paper-based; 80 iBT). Electronic applications accepted. *Expenses:* Tuition, state resident: full-time $10,864; part-time $495 per credit hour. Tuition, nonresident: full-time $18,380; part-time $837 per credit hour.

**Langston University,** School of Education and Behavioral Sciences, Langston, OK 73050. Offers bilingual/multicultural (M Ed); elementary education (M Ed); English as a second language (M Sc); rehabilitation counseling (M Sc); urban education (M Ed). *Accreditation:* CORE; NCATE (one or more programs are accredited). *Program availability:* Part-time. *Degree requirements:* For master's, comprehensive exam, thesis optional. *Entrance requirements:* For master's, GRE, writing skills test, minimum GPA of 2.5, 3 letters of recommendation. Additional exam requirements/recommendations for international students: Required—TOEFL, TWE. *Faculty research:* Bilingual/multicultural education, financing post-secondary education.

**Louisiana State University Health Sciences Center,** School of Allied Health Professions, Department of Clinical Rehabilitation and Counseling, New Orleans, LA 70112-2262. Offers MHS. *Accreditation:* CORE. *Faculty:* 5 full-time (4 women). *Students:* 26 full-time (22 women); includes 11 minority (8 Black or African American, non-Hispanic/Latino; 2 Hispanic/Latino; 1 Two or more races, non-Hispanic/Latino). Average age 25. 13 applicants, 85% accepted, 11 enrolled. In 2016, 9 master's awarded. *Degree requirements:* For master's, clinical internship. *Entrance requirements:* For master's, GRE General Test, minimum GPA of 2.5, 2 letters of recommendation. Additional exam requirements/recommendations for international students: Required—TOEFL (minimum score 550 paper-based; 79 iBT). *Application deadline:* For fall admission, 4/15 priority date for domestic students. Applications are processed on a rolling basis. Application fee: $50. *Expenses:* Contact institution. *Financial support:* In 2016–17, 14 students received support. Traineeships available. Financial award application deadline: 4/15; financial award applicants required to submit FAFSA. *Faculty research:* Job placement, clinical judgment, counseling process, consumer satisfaction, vocational assessment. *Total annual research expenditures:* $10,000. *Unit head:* Dr. Erin M. Dugan, Interim Head, 504-556-3403, Fax: 504-556-7540, E-mail: emart3@lsuhsc.edu. *Application contact:* Yudialys Delgado Cazanas, Student Affairs Director, 504-568-4253, Fax: 504-568-3185, E-mail: ydelga@lsuhsc.edu.
Website: http://alliedhealth.lsuhsc.edu/crc/default.aspx

**Maryville University of Saint Louis,** Walker College of Health Professions, Program in Rehabilitation Counseling, St. Louis, MO 63141-7299. Offers marriage and family therapy (MARC); music therapy (MARC); substance abuse (MARC). *Accreditation:* CORE. *Program availability:* Part-time, evening/weekend. *Faculty:* 2 full-time (0 women), 6 part-time/adjunct (5 women). *Students:* 25 full-time (20 women), 16 part-time (15 women); includes 11 minority (8 Black or African American, non-Hispanic/Latino; 2 Hispanic/Latino; 1 Two or more races, non-Hispanic/Latino), 2 international. Average age 32. In 2016, 10 master's awarded. *Degree requirements:* For master's, internship, seminar. *Entrance requirements:* For master's, minimum cumulative GPA of 3.0, 2 letters of recommendation, interview, essay, transcripts, resume. Additional exam requirements/recommendations for international students: Required—TOEFL (minimum score 563 paper-based). *Application deadline:* For fall admission, 1/15 for domestic students; for spring admission, 10/1 for domestic students. Applications are processed on a rolling basis. Electronic applications accepted. *Expenses:* $650 per credit hour.

*Financial support:* Career-related internships or fieldwork, Federal Work-Study, and campus employment available. Financial award application deadline: 3/1; financial award applicants required to submit FAFSA. *Unit head:* Dr. Michael Kiener, Director, 314-529-9443, Fax: 314-529-9495, E-mail: mkiener@maryville.edu. *Application contact:* Jeannie DeLuca, Director, Admissions and Advising, 314-529-9355, Fax: 314-529-9927, E-mail: jdeluca@maryville.edu.
Website: http://www.maryville.edu/hp/rehabilitation-counseling/

**Mercer University,** Graduate Studies, Cecil B. Day Campus, Penfield College, Atlanta, GA 30341. Offers certified rehabilitation counseling (MS); clinical mental health (MS); counselor education and supervision (PhD); criminal justice and public safety leadership (MS); health informatics (MS); human services (MS), including child and adolescent services, gerontology services; organizational leadership (MS); school counseling (MS). *Program availability:* Part-time, evening/weekend, 100% online, blended/hybrid learning. *Faculty:* 15 full-time (8 women), 22 part-time/adjunct (18 women). *Students:* 168 full-time (136 women), 242 part-time (201 women); includes 231 minority (192 Black or African American, non-Hispanic/Latino; 1 American Indian or Alaska Native, non-Hispanic/Latino; 15 Asian, non-Hispanic/Latino; 19 Hispanic/Latino; 1 Native Hawaiian or other Pacific Islander, non-Hispanic/Latino; 3 Two or more races, non-Hispanic/Latino), 2 international. Average age 32. 300 applicants, 45% accepted, 114 enrolled. In 2016, 92 master's, 8 doctorates awarded. *Degree requirements:* For master's, comprehensive exam (for some programs), thesis (for some programs); for doctorate, thesis/ dissertation. *Entrance requirements:* For master's, GRE or MAT, Georgia Professional Standards Commission (GPSC) Certification at the SC-5 level; for doctorate, GRE or MAT. Additional exam requirements/recommendations for international students: Recommended—TOEFL (minimum score 550 paper-based; 80 iBT), IELTS (minimum score 6.5). *Application deadline:* For fall admission, 7/1 priority date for domestic and international students; for spring admission, 11/1 priority date for domestic and international students; for summer admission, 4/1 priority date for domestic and international students. Application fee: $35. Electronic applications accepted. Application fee is waived when completed online. *Expenses:* $588 per credit hour. *Financial support:* In 2016–17, 32 students received support. Federal Work-Study, scholarships/grants, and unspecified assistantships available. Financial award applicants required to submit FAFSA. *Faculty research:* Marriage and families issues, leadership and ethics, cyber-bullying, trauma, narrative counseling and theory. *Total annual research expenditures:* $85,000. *Unit head:* Dr. Priscilla R. Danheiser, Dean, 678-547-6028, Fax: 678-547-6008, E-mail: danheiser_p@mercer.edu.
Website: http://penfield.mercer.edu/programs/graduate-professional/

**Michigan State University,** The Graduate School, College of Education, Department of Counseling, Educational Psychology and Special Education, East Lansing, MI 48824. Offers counseling (MA); educational psychology and educational technology (PhD); educational technology (MA); measurement and quantitative methods (PhD); rehabilitation counseling (MA); rehabilitation counselor education (PhD); school psychology (MA, PhD, Ed S); special education (MA, PhD). *Accreditation:* APA (one or more programs are accredited); CORE (one or more programs are accredited). *Program availability:* Part-time. *Entrance requirements:* Additional exam requirements/ recommendations for international students: Required—TOEFL. Electronic applications accepted.

**Minnesota State University Mankato,** College of Graduate Studies and Research, College of Allied Health and Nursing, Program in Rehabilitation Counseling, Mankato, MN 56001. Offers MS. *Accreditation:* CORE. *Students:* 6 full-time (5 women), 2 part-time (both women). *Degree requirements:* For master's, comprehensive exam. *Entrance requirements:* For master's, GRE General Test, minimum GPA of 3.0 during previous 2 years, references. *Application deadline:* For fall admission, 3/1 priority date for domestic students. Applications are processed on a rolling basis. Application fee: $40. *Financial support:* Research assistantships with full tuition reimbursements and teaching assistantships with full tuition reimbursements available. Financial award application deadline: 3/15; financial award applicants required to submit FAFSA. *Unit head:* Bruce Poburka, Coordinator, 507-389-5843, E-mail: bruce.poburka@mnsu.edu.
Website: http://ahn.mnsu.edu/rehabilitation/

**Mississippi State University,** College of Education, Department of Counseling, Educational Psychology, and Foundations, Mississippi State, MS 39762. Offers clinical mental health (MS); college counseling (MS); college/post secondary student counseling and personnel services (PhD); counselor education (Ed S); counselor education/student counseling and guidance services (PhD); general educational psychology (MS); psychometry (MS); rehabilitation (MS); school counseling (MS); school psychology (PhD, Ed S); student affairs (MS). *Accreditation:* ACA (one or more programs are accredited); APA; CORE (one or more programs are accredited); NCATE. *Program availability:* Part-time, blended/hybrid learning. *Faculty:* 21 full-time (14 women), 2 part-time/adjunct (both women). *Students:* 125 full-time (94 women), 70 part-time (60 women); includes 63 minority (48 Black or African American, non-Hispanic/Latino; 1 American Indian or Alaska Native, non-Hispanic/Latino; 4 Asian, non-Hispanic/Latino; 5 Hispanic/Latino; 5 Two or more races, non-Hispanic/Latino), 6 international. Average age 30. 151 applicants, 64% accepted, 70 enrolled. In 2016, 49 master's, 3 doctorates, 4 other advanced degrees awarded. Terminal master's awarded for partial completion of doctoral program. *Degree requirements:* For master's, comprehensive exam, thesis optional; for doctorate, thesis/dissertation, comprehensive oral and written exam. *Entrance requirements:* For master's, GRE (taken within the last five years), BS with minimum GPA of 2.75 on last 60 hours; for doctorate, GRE, MS from CACREP- or CORE-accredited program in counseling; for Ed S, GRE, MS in counseling or related field, minimum GPA of 3.3 on all graduate work. Additional exam requirements/ recommendations for international students: Required—TOEFL (minimum score 550 paper-based; 79 iBT); Recommended—IELTS (minimum score 6.5). *Application deadline:* For fall admission, 2/1 priority date for domestic and international students. Applications are processed on a rolling basis. Application fee: $60. Electronic applications accepted. *Expenses:* Tuition, state resident: full-time $7670; part-time $852.50 per credit hour. Tuition, nonresident: full-time $20,790; part-time $2310.50 per credit hour. Part-time tuition and fees vary according to course load. *Financial support:* In 2016–17, 9 teaching assistantships with full tuition reimbursements (averaging $8,401 per year) were awarded; career-related internships or fieldwork, Federal Work-Study, institutionally sponsored loans, and unspecified assistantships also available. Financial award application deadline: 2/1; financial award applicants required to submit FAFSA. *Faculty research:* HIV/AIDS in college population, substance abuse in youth and college students, ADHD and conduct disorders in youth, assessment and identification of early childhood disabilities, assessment and vocational transition of the disabled. *Unit head:* Dr. David Morse, Professor and Head, 662-325-3426, Fax: 662-325-3263, E-mail: dmorse@colled.msstate.edu. *Application contact:* Linda Bonner, Senior Admissions Assistant, 662-325-3363, E-mail: lbonner@grad.msstate.edu.
Website: http://www.cep.msstate.edu

**Montana State University Billings,** College of Allied Health Professions, Program in Clinical Rehabilitation and Mental Health Counseling, Billings, MT 59101. Offers MS. *Accreditation:* CORE. *Program availability:* Part-time. *Faculty:* 4 full-time (2 women), 1 (woman) part-time/adjunct. *Students:* 33. *Degree requirements:* For master's, thesis or professional paper and/or field experience. *Entrance requirements:* For master's, GRE

General Test or MAT, minimum GPA of 3.0, letters of recommendation, letter of intent. Additional exam requirements/recommendations for international students: Required— TOEFL (minimum score 79 iBT), IELTS (minimum score 6.5). *Application deadline:* For fall admission, 7/15 for international students; for spring admission, 12/1 for international students. Applications are processed on a rolling basis. Application fee: $40. Electronic applications accepted. *Expenses:* Tuition, state resident: full-time $5265; part-time $3436 per year. Tuition, nonresident: full-time $14,030; part-time $9280 per year. *International tuition:* $19,295 full-time. Tuition and fees vary according to degree level, campus/location and program. *Financial support:* Research assistantships with partial tuition reimbursements, teaching assistantships with partial tuition reimbursements, career-related internships or fieldwork, Federal Work-Study, institutionally sponsored loans, scholarships/grants, tuition waivers (partial), and unspecified assistantships available. Support available to part-time students. Financial award application deadline: 5/1; financial award applicants required to submit FAFSA. *Unit head:* Dr. Terry Blackwell, Chair, 406-896-5834, E-mail: tblackwell@msubillings.edu. *Application contact:* David M. Sullivan, Graduate Studies Counselor, 406-657-2053, Fax: 406-657-2299, E-mail: dsullivan@msubillings.edu.

**Mount Mary University,** Graduate Programs, Program in Counseling, Milwaukee, WI 53222-4597. Offers clinical mental health counseling (MS, Certificate); clinical rehabilitation counseling (MS, Certificate); school counseling (MS, Certificate); vocational rehabilitation counseling (MS, Certificate). *Accreditation:* ACA. *Program availability:* Part-time, evening/weekend. *Faculty:* 6 full-time (all women), 12 part-time/ adjunct (10 women). *Students:* 91 full-time (84 women), 17 part-time (14 women); includes 25 minority (12 Black or African American, non-Hispanic/Latino; 1 Asian, non-Hispanic/Latino; 8 Hispanic/Latino; 1 Native Hawaiian or other Pacific Islander, non-Hispanic/Latino; 3 Two or more races, non-Hispanic/Latino). Average age 31. 68 applicants, 59% accepted, 29 enrolled. In 2016, 42 master's, 1 other advanced degree awarded. *Degree requirements:* For master's, comprehensive exam, thesis or alternative. *Entrance requirements:* For master's, minimum GPA of 3.0. Additional exam requirements/recommendations for international students: Required—TOEFL (minimum score 550 paper-based; 80 iBT); Recommended—IELTS (minimum score 6.5). *Application deadline:* For fall admission, 5/1 for domestic and international students; for spring admission, 10/1 for domestic and international students; for summer admission, 4/15 for domestic and international students. Applications are processed on a rolling basis. Application fee: $45. Electronic applications accepted. *Expenses:* Contact institution. *Financial support:* Career-related internships or fieldwork, Federal Work-Study, and unspecified assistantships available. Support available to part-time students. Financial award application deadline: 5/1; financial award applicants required to submit FAFSA. *Faculty research:* Cognitive behavioral interventions for depression, eating disorders and compliance, trauma-informed care. *Unit head:* Dr. Carrie King, Graduate Program Director, 414-258-4810 Ext. 318, E-mail: kingc@mtmary.edu. *Application contact:* Kirk Heller de Messer, Director, Graduate Admissions, 414-930-3221, E-mail: hellerk@mtmary.edu.
Website: http://www.mtmary.edu/majors-programs/graduate/counseling/index.html

**Northeastern Illinois University,** College of Graduate Studies and Research, College of Education, Program in Rehabilitation Counseling, Chicago, IL 60625-4699. Offers MA. *Accreditation:* CORE.

**Ohio University,** Graduate College, Gladys W. and David H. Patton College of Education and Human Services, Department of Counseling and Higher Education, Athens, OH 45701-2979. Offers college student personnel (M Ed); community/agency counseling (M Ed); counselor education (PhD); higher education (PhD); rehabilitation counseling (M Ed); school counseling (M Ed). *Accreditation:* ACA; CORE. *Program availability:* Part-time, evening/weekend. *Degree requirements:* For master's, comprehensive exam (for some programs), thesis or alternative; for doctorate, comprehensive exam, thesis/dissertation. *Entrance requirements:* For master's, GRE General Test or MAT (if GPA less than 2.9), 3 letters of reference; for doctorate, GRE General Test, work experience, minimum GPA of 3.4. Additional exam requirements/ recommendations for international students: Required—TOEFL (minimum score 550 paper-based; 80 iBT) or IELTS (minimum score 6.5). *Application deadline:* For fall admission, 1/15 for domestic and international students. Application fee: $50 ($55 for international students). Electronic applications accepted. *Financial support:* Research assistantships with full tuition reimbursements, teaching assistantships with full tuition reimbursements, Federal Work-Study, institutionally sponsored loans, tuition waivers (partial), and unspecified assistantships available. Financial award application deadline: 1/15. *Faculty research:* Youth violence, gender studies, student affairs, chemical dependency, disabilities issues. *Unit head:* Dr. Tracy Leinbaugh, Chair, 740-593-0846, Fax: 740-593-0477, E-mail: leinbaug@ohio.edu. *Application contact:* Floyd J. Doney, Director of Student Affairs, 740-593-4400, Fax: 740-593-9310, E-mail: doney@ohio.edu.
Website: http://www.cehs.ohio.edu/academics/che/

**Pontifical Catholic University of Puerto Rico,** College of Graduate Studies in Behavioral Science and Community Affairs, Program in Rehabilitation Counseling, Ponce, PR 00717-0777. Offers MA. *Accreditation:* CORE. *Program availability:* Part-time. *Degree requirements:* For master's, thesis. *Entrance requirements:* For master's, EXADEP, GRE General Test, 3 letters of recommendation, interview, minimum GPA of 2.75.

**Rutgers University–Newark,** School of Health Related Professions, Department of Psychiatric Rehabilitation and Counseling Professions, Program in Psychiatric Rehabilitation, Newark, NJ 07102. Offers MS, PhD. *Accreditation:* CORE. *Program availability:* Part-time, evening/weekend, online learning. *Degree requirements:* For doctorate, comprehensive exam, thesis/dissertation. *Entrance requirements:* For master's, all transcripts, interview, statement of interest, bachelor's degree, 2 reference letters; for doctorate, GRE General Test, all transcripts, bachelor's degree, personal statement, 3 reference letters. Additional exam requirements/recommendations for international students: Required—TOEFL (minimum score 500 paper-based; 79 iBT). Electronic applications accepted.

**Rutgers University–Newark,** School of Health Related Professions, Department of Psychiatric Rehabilitation and Counseling Professions, Program in Rehabilitation Counseling, Newark, NJ 07102. Offers community counseling (MS). Programs offered at Scotch Plains and Stratford campuses. *Accreditation:* CORE. *Program availability:* Part-time, evening/weekend. *Degree requirements:* For master's, internship, practicum. *Entrance requirements:* For master's, bachelor's degree with transcript, interview, personal goals statement, 2 reference letters. Additional exam requirements/ recommendations for international students: Required—TOEFL (minimum score 500 paper-based; 79 iBT). Electronic applications accepted.

**St. Bonaventure University,** School of Graduate Studies, School of Education, Program in Counselor Education, St. Bonaventure, NY 14778-2284. Offers community mental health counseling (MS Ed); rehabilitation counseling (MS Ed); school counseling (MS Ed); school counselor (Adv C). *Accreditation:* ACA. *Program availability:* Part-time, evening/weekend, 100% online. *Faculty:* 5 full-time (1 woman), 8 part-time/adjunct (6 women). *Students:* 53 full-time (40 women), 21 part-time (14 women); includes 6 minority (3 Black or African American, non-Hispanic/Latino; 3 Two or more races, non-Hispanic/Latino), 2 international. Average age 29. 64 applicants, 69% accepted, 29 enrolled. In 2016, 20 master's, 2 Adv Cs awarded. *Degree requirements:* For master's,

## Rehabilitation Counseling

comprehensive exam, thesis optional, internship, portfolio; for Adv C, internship. *Entrance requirements:* For master's, statement of intent/writing sample; transcripts from all colleges previously attended; two references; interview; minimum undergraduate GPA of 3.0; for Adv C, interview, writing sample, minimum undergraduate GPA of 3.0, two letters of recommendation, master's degree, transcripts from all colleges previously attended. Additional exam requirements/recommendations for international students: Required—TOEFL (minimum score 550 paper-based; 79 iBT). *Application deadline:* For fall admission, 3/15 priority date for domestic students, 2/1 priority date for international students; for spring admission, 11/15 priority date for domestic students, 7/1 priority date for international students. Applications are processed on a rolling basis. Application fee: $0. Electronic applications accepted. *Expenses:* $733 per credit, $100 graduation fee. *Financial support:* Career-related internships or fieldwork, Federal Work-Study, scholarships/grants, health care benefits, and unspecified assistantships available. Support available to part-time students. Financial award application deadline: 4/15; financial award applicants required to submit FAFSA. *Faculty research:* Balance between technology and personal contact in counselor education, special education and cyberbullying, school response to child abuse. *Unit head:* Dr. S. Alan Silliker, Director, 716-375-2368, Fax: 716-375-2360, E-mail: silliker@sbu.edu. *Application contact:* Bruce Campbell, Director of Graduate Admissions, 716-375-2429, Fax: 716-375-4015, E-mail: gradsch@sbu.edu. Website: http://www.sbu.edu/academics/schools/education

**St. Cloud State University,** School of Graduate Studies, School of Education, Department of Educational Leadership and Higher Education, Program in Rehabilitation Counseling, St. Cloud, MN 56301-4498. Offers MS. *Accreditation:* CORE. *Degree requirements:* For master's, comprehensive exam (for some programs), thesis or alternative. *Entrance requirements:* For master's, GRE General Test, minimum GPA of 2.75. Additional exam requirements/recommendations for international students: Required—Michigan English Language Assessment Battery; Recommended—TOEFL (minimum score 550 paper-based), IELTS (minimum score 6.5). Electronic applications accepted.

**Salve Regina University,** Program in Rehabilitation Counseling, Newport, RI 02840-4192. Offers mental health (CAGS), including rehabilitation counseling; rehabilitation counseling (MA); substance abuse (CGS), including foundations in rehabilitation counseling. *Accreditation:* CORE. *Program availability:* Part-time, evening/weekend. *Entrance requirements:* For master's, GMAT, GRE General Test or MAT. Additional exam requirements/recommendations for international students: Required—TOEFL (minimum score 600 paper-based; 100 iBT) or IELTS. Electronic applications accepted.

**San Diego State University,** Graduate and Research Affairs, College of Education, Department of Administration, Rehabilitation and Post-Secondary Education, San Diego, CA 92182. Offers educational leadership in post-secondary education (MA); rehabilitation counseling (MS), including deafness. *Program availability:* Evening/weekend, online learning. *Degree requirements:* For master's, comprehensive exam (for some programs), thesis (for some programs). *Entrance requirements:* For master's, GRE General Test, letters of reference. Additional exam requirements/recommendations for international students: Required—TOEFL. Electronic applications accepted. *Faculty research:* Rehabilitation in cultural diversity, distance learning technology.

**San Francisco State University,** Division of Graduate Studies, College of Health and Social Sciences, Department of Counseling, San Francisco, CA 94132-1722. Offers clinical rehabilitation and mental health counseling (MS); counseling (MS); marriage, family, and child counseling (MSC); school counseling (Credential). *Accreditation:* ACA (one or more programs are accredited). *Program availability:* Part-time. *Application deadline:* Applications are processed on a rolling basis. *Expenses:* Tuition, state resident: full-time $6738. Tuition, nonresident: full-time $15,666. *Required fees:* $1012. Tuition and fees vary according to degree level and program. *Unit head:* Dr. Graciela Orozco, Chair, 415-338-2005, Fax: 415-338-0594, E-mail: counsel@sfsu.edu. *Application contact:* Dr. Alison Cerezo, College Counseling Coordinator, 415-338-1064, Fax: 415-338-0594, E-mail: acerezo@sfsu.edu. Website: http://counseling.sfsu.edu

**South Carolina State University,** College of Graduate and Professional Studies, Department of Human Services, Orangeburg, SC 29117-0001. Offers counselor education (M Ed); rehabilitation counseling (MA). *Accreditation:* CORE. *Program availability:* Part-time, evening/weekend. *Faculty:* 8 full-time (6 women), 1 (woman) part-time/adjunct. *Students:* 81 full-time (65 women), 21 part-time (16 women); includes 97 minority (all Black or African American, non-Hispanic/Latino). Average age 33. 40 applicants, 85% accepted, 32 enrolled. In 2016, 54 master's awarded. *Degree requirements:* For master's, comprehensive exam (for some programs), departmental qualifying exam, internship. *Entrance requirements:* For master's, GRE, MAT, minimum GPA of 2.7. *Application deadline:* For fall admission, 6/15 priority date for domestic students, 6/15 for international students; for spring admission, 11/1 for domestic and international students. Application fee: $25. Electronic applications accepted. *Expenses:* Tuition, state resident: full-time $8938; part-time $579 per credit hour. Tuition, nonresident: full-time $19,018; part-time $1139 per credit hour. *Required fees:* $1482; $82 per credit hour. *Financial support:* Fellowships, career-related internships or fieldwork, scholarships/grants, and unspecified assistantships available. Financial award application deadline: 6/1. *Unit head:* Dr. Michelle Maultsby-Priester, Interim Chair, Department of Human Services, 803-536-7075, Fax: 803-533-3636, E-mail: mmaultsb@scsu.edu. *Application contact:* Curtis Foskey, Coordinator of Graduate Admissions, 803-536-8419, Fax: 803-536-8812, E-mail: cfoskey@scsu.edu.

**Southern University and Agricultural and Mechanical College,** Graduate School, College of Sciences, Department of Psychology, Program in Rehabilitation Counseling, Baton Rouge, LA 70813. Offers MS. *Accreditation:* CORE. *Degree requirements:* For master's, comprehensive exam, thesis optional. *Entrance requirements:* For master's, GMAT or GRE General Test. Additional exam requirements/recommendations for international students: Required—TOEFL. *Faculty research:* Cultural diversity, professional preparation and participation of minorities, needs and satisfaction of students with disabilities, prediction model for rehabilitation outcome, diabetes.

**Springfield College,** Graduate Programs, Programs in Rehabilitation Counseling and Services, Springfield, MA 01109-3797. Offers alcohol and substance abuse services (M Ed); psychiatric rehabilitation and substance abuse counseling (M Ed). *Accreditation:* CORE (one or more programs are accredited). *Program availability:* Part-time. *Degree requirements:* For master's, comprehensive exam. *Entrance requirements:* Additional exam requirements/recommendations for international students: Required—TOEFL (minimum score 550 paper-based); Recommended—IELTS (minimum score 6). Electronic applications accepted. *Expenses: Tuition:* Full-time $29,640; part-time $988 per credit. *Required fees:* $195.

**Texas Tech University Health Sciences Center,** School of Health Professions, Program in Rehabilitation Counseling, Lubbock, TX 79430. Offers MRC. *Accreditation:* CORE. *Program availability:* Part-time, online only. *Faculty:* 5 full-time (2 women). *Students:* 23 full-time (15 women), 50 part-time (40 women); includes 29 minority (11 Black or African American, non-Hispanic/Latino; 16 Hispanic/Latino; 1 Native Hawaiian or other Pacific Islander, non-Hispanic/Latino; 1 Two or more races, non-Hispanic/ Latino). Average age 37. 70 applicants, 54% accepted, 38 enrolled. In 2016, 29 master's awarded. *Entrance requirements:* Additional exam requirements/recommendations for international students: Required—TOEFL (minimum score 550 paper-based; 79 iBT), IELTS. *Application deadline:* For fall admission, 6/1 for domestic students; for spring admission, 11/1 for domestic students. Applications are processed on a rolling basis. Application fee: $40. Electronic applications accepted. *Expenses:* Contact institution. *Financial support:* Career-related internships or fieldwork and institutionally sponsored loans available. Financial award application deadline: 9/1; financial award applicants required to submit FAFSA. *Unit head:* Dr. Evans Spears, Program Director, 806-743-2590, Fax: 806-743-3244, E-mail: evans.spears@ttuhsc.edu. *Application contact:* Lindsay Johnson, Associate Dean for Admissions and Student Affairs, 806-743-3220, Fax: 806-743-2994, E-mail: lindsay.johnson@ttuhsc.edu. Website: http://www.ttuhsc.edu/health-professions/master-rehabilitation-counseling/

**Thomas University,** Department of Human Services, Thomasville, GA 31792-7499. Offers community counseling (MSCC); rehabilitation counseling (MRC). *Accreditation:* CORE. *Program availability:* Part-time. *Entrance requirements:* For master's, resume, 3 academic/professional references. Additional exam requirements/recommendations for international students: Required—TOEFL (minimum score 600 paper-based). Electronic applications accepted.

**University at Buffalo, the State University of New York,** Graduate School, Graduate School of Education, Department of Counseling, School, and Educational Psychology, Buffalo, NY 14260. Offers applied statistical analysis (Advanced Certificate); counseling/school psychology (PhD); counselor education (PhD); education studies (Ed M); educational psychology (MA, PhD); mental health counseling (MS, Certificate); mindful counseling for wellness and engagement (Advanced Certificate); rehabilitation counseling (MS, Advanced Certificate); school counseling (Ed M, Certificate). *Accreditation:* CORE (one or more programs are accredited). *Program availability:* Part-time, 100% online. *Faculty:* 27 full-time (11 women), 52 part-time/adjunct (45 women). *Students:* 161 full-time (131 women), 140 part-time (109 women); includes 30 minority (22 Black or African American, non-Hispanic/Latino; 2 American Indian or Alaska Native, non-Hispanic/Latino; 3 Asian, non-Hispanic/Latino; 3 Hispanic/Latino), 20 international. Average age 32. 321 applicants, 56% accepted, 113 enrolled. In 2016, 62 master's, 10 doctorates, 47 other advanced degrees awarded. *Degree requirements:* For master's, comprehensive exam (for some programs), thesis (for some programs); for doctorate, comprehensive exam, thesis/dissertation. *Entrance requirements:* For master's, GRE General Test, interview, letters of reference; for doctorate, GRE General Test, interview, letters of reference, writing sample. Additional exam requirements/recommendations for international students: Required—TOEFL (minimum score 79 iBT). *Application deadline:* For fall admission, 2/1 priority date for domestic and international students. Application fee: $50. Electronic applications accepted. *Financial support:* In 2016–17, 20 fellowships (averaging $8,477 per year), 33 research assistantships with tuition reimbursements (averaging $10,419 per year) were awarded; teaching assistantships, career-related internships or fieldwork, Federal Work-Study, institutionally sponsored loans, scholarships/grants, tuition waivers (full and partial), and unspecified assistantships also available. Financial award application deadline: 2/1; financial award applicants required to submit FAFSA. *Faculty research:* Multicultural counseling, class size effects, good work in counseling, eating disorders, outcome assessment, change agents and therapeutic factors in group counseling. *Total annual research expenditures:* $1.3 million. *Unit head:* Dr. Jeremy Finn, Chair, 716-645-1126, Fax: 716-645-6616, E-mail: finn@buffalo.edu. *Application contact:* Joanne Laska, Admissions Assistant, 716-645-2110, Fax: 716-645-7937, E-mail: jlaska@buffalo.edu. Website: http://gse.buffalo.edu/csep

**The University of Arizona,** College of Education, Department of Disability and Psychoeducational Studies, Program in Counseling and Mental Health, Tucson, AZ 85721. Offers rehabilitation counseling (MA); school counseling (MA). *Accreditation:* ACA. *Entrance requirements:* Additional exam requirements/recommendations for international students: Required—TOEFL (minimum score 550 paper-based; 80 iBT). *Faculty research:* Further knowledge and understanding of abilities, disabilities, adaptations, interventions, and support systems; preparing professionals to educate and facilitate the development of individuals with disabilities and special abilities; providing leadership at the local, state, national, and international levels.

**The University of Arizona,** College of Education, Department of Disability and Psychoeducational Studies, Program in Rehabilitation Counseling, Tucson, AZ 85721. Offers PhD. *Accreditation:* CORE. *Entrance requirements:* For doctorate, GMAT, 3 letters of recommendation. Additional exam requirements/recommendations for international students: Required—TOEFL (minimum score 550 paper-based; 79 iBT). Electronic applications accepted.

**University of Arkansas,** Graduate School, College of Education and Health Professions, Department of Rehabilitation, Human Resources and Communication Disorders, Program in Rehabilitation, Fayetteville, AR 72701. Offers MS, PhD. *Accreditation:* CORE (one or more programs are accredited). *Program availability:* Part-time. In 2016, 12 master's, 3 doctorates awarded. *Degree requirements:* For doctorate, thesis/dissertation. *Entrance requirements:* For doctorate, GRE General Test. *Application deadline:* For fall admission, 4/1 for international students; for spring admission, 10/1 for international students. Applications are processed on a rolling basis. Application fee: $40 ($50 for international students). Electronic applications accepted. *Financial support:* In 2016–17, 6 research assistantships were awarded; fellowships with tuition reimbursements, teaching assistantships, career-related internships or fieldwork, and Federal Work-Study also available. Support available to part-time students. Financial award application deadline: 4/1; financial award applicants required to submit FAFSA. *Unit head:* Dr. Kate Mamiseishvili, Department Chairperson, 479-575-4758, Fax: 479-575-3319, E-mail: kmamisei@uark.edu. *Application contact:* Dr. Brent Williams, Graduate Coordinator, 479-575-4758, E-mail: btwilli@uark.edu. Website: http://rhrc.uark.edu

**University of Arkansas at Little Rock,** Graduate School, College of Education and Health Professions, Department of Counseling, Adult and Rehabilitation Education, Little Rock, AR 72204-1099. Offers adult education (M Ed); counselor education (M Ed); rehabilitation counseling (MA, Graduate Certificate); rehabilitation for the blind: orientation and mobility (MA). *Accreditation:* CORE; NCATE. *Program availability:* Part-time. *Entrance requirements:* For master's, interview, minimum GPA of 2.75. *Faculty research:* Low vision, orientation and mobility instruction.

**University of Idaho,** College of Graduate Studies, College of Education, Department of Leadership and Counseling, Boise, ID 83702. Offers adult/organizational learning and leadership (MS, Ed S); educational leadership (M Ed, Ed S); rehabilitation counseling and human services (M Ed, MS); school counseling (M Ed, MS); special education (M Ed). *Faculty:* 14 full-time, 7 part-time/adjunct. *Students:* 37 full-time (26 women), 154 part-time (84 women). Average age 39. In 2016, 75 master's, 21 other advanced degrees awarded. *Entrance requirements:* For master's, minimum GPA of 3.0. Additional exam requirements/recommendations for international students: Required—TOEFL. *Application deadline:* Applications are processed on a rolling basis. Application fee: $60. Electronic applications accepted. *Expenses:* Tuition, state resident: full-time $6460; part-time $414 per credit hour. Tuition, nonresident: full-time $21,268; part-time $1237 per credit hour. *Required fees:* $2070; $60 per credit hour. Full-time tuition and

fees vary according to course load and reciprocity agreements. *Financial support:* Applicants required to submit FAFSA. *Unit head:* Dr. Kathy Canfield-Davis, Chair, 208-364-4047, E-mail: lead@uidaho.edu. *Application contact:* Sean Scoggin, Graduate Recruitment Coordinator, 208-885-4723, Fax: 208-885-4406, E-mail: graduateadmissions@uidaho.edu. Website: https://www.uidaho.edu/ed/lc

**The University of Iowa,** Graduate College, College of Education, Department of Rehabilitation and Counselor Education, Iowa City, IA 52242-1316. Offers counselor education and supervision (PhD); couple and family therapy (PhD); rehabilitation and mental health counseling (MA); rehabilitation counselor education (PhD); school counseling (MA). *Accreditation:* ACA (one or more programs are accredited); CORE (one or more programs are accredited). *Degree requirements:* For master's, thesis optional, exam; for doctorate, comprehensive exam, thesis/dissertation. *Entrance requirements:* For master's and doctorate, GRE General Test, minimum GPA of 3.0. Additional exam requirements/recommendations for international students: Required— TOEFL (minimum score 550 paper-based; 81 iBT). Electronic applications accepted.

**University of Kentucky,** Graduate School, College of Education, Program in Special Education, Lexington, KY 40506-0032. Offers early childhood (MS Ed); rehabilitation counseling (MRC, PhD); special education (MS Ed, PhD). *Accreditation:* CORE; NCATE. Terminal master's awarded for partial completion of doctoral program. *Degree requirements:* For master's, comprehensive exam, thesis optional; for doctorate, comprehensive exam, thesis/dissertation. *Entrance requirements:* For master's, GRE General Test, minimum undergraduate GPA of 2.75; for doctorate, GRE General Test, minimum graduate GPA of 3.0. Additional exam requirements/recommendations for international students: Required—TOEFL (minimum score 550 paper-based). Electronic applications accepted. *Faculty research:* Applied behavior analysis applications in special education, single subject research design in classroom settings, transition research across life span, rural special education personnel.

**University of Louisiana at Lafayette,** College of Liberal Arts, Department of Psychology, Program in Rehabilitation Counseling, Lafayette, LA 70504. Offers MS. *Entrance requirements:* For master's, GRE General Test, minimum GPA of 3.0. Additional exam requirements/recommendations for international students: Required— TOEFL (minimum score 550 paper-based). Electronic applications accepted. *Faculty research:* Vocational assessment, psychology.

**University of Maryland, College Park,** Academic Affairs, College of Education, Department of Counseling, Higher Education and Special Education, College Park, MD 20742. Offers college student personnel (M Ed, MA); college student personnel administration (PhD); community counseling (CAGS); community/career counseling (M Ed, MA); counseling and personnel services (M Ed, MA, PhD), including art therapy (M Ed); college student personnel (M Ed), counseling and personnel services (PhD), counseling psychology (M Ed), mental health counseling (M Ed), school counseling (M Ed); counseling psychology (PhD); counselor education (PhD); rehabilitation counseling (M Ed, MA, AGSC); school counseling (M Ed, MA); school psychology (M Ed, MA, PhD). *Accreditation:* ACA (one or more programs are accredited); APA (one or more programs are accredited); NCATE. *Program availability:* Part-time, evening/weekend, online learning. *Degree requirements:* For master's, thesis (for some programs); for doctorate, thesis/dissertation. *Entrance requirements:* For master's, GRE General Test or MAT, minimum GPA of 3.0, 3 letters of recommendation; for doctorate, GRE General Test or MAT, minimum GPA of 3.5, 3 letters of recommendation. Additional exam requirements/recommendations for international students: Required— TOEFL. Electronic applications accepted. *Faculty research:* Educational psychology, counseling, health.

**University of Maryland Eastern Shore,** Graduate Programs, Department of Rehabilitation Services, Princess Anne, MD 21853-1299. Offers rehabilitation counseling (MS). *Accreditation:* CORE. *Program availability:* Part-time, evening/weekend. *Degree requirements:* For master's, internship. *Entrance requirements:* For master's, interview. Additional exam requirements/recommendations for international students: Required—TOEFL (minimum score 80 iBT). Electronic applications accepted. *Faculty research:* Long-term rehabilitation training.

**University of Massachusetts Boston,** Graduate School of Global Inclusion and Social Development, Program in Rehabilitation Counseling, Boston, MA 02125-3393. Offers MS. *Accreditation:* CORE. *Students:* 16 full-time (10 women), 14 part-time (10 women); includes 8 minority (1 Black or African American, non-Hispanic/Latino; 3 Asian, non-Hispanic/Latino; 4 Hispanic/Latino); 1 international. Average age 40. 17 applicants, 76% accepted, 7 enrolled. In 2016, 8 master's awarded. *Expenses:* Tuition, state resident: full-time $16,863. Tuition, nonresident: full-time $32,913. *Required fees:* $177. *Unit head:* Dr. Kristy Alster, Associate Provost, 617-287-5700, Fax: 617-287-5699, E-mail: kristine.alster@umb.edu. *Application contact:* Peggy Roldan Patel, Graduate Admissions Coordinator, 617-287-6400, Fax: 617-287-6236, E-mail: bos.gadm@dpc.umassp.edu.

**University of Memphis,** Graduate School, College of Education, Department of Counseling, Educational Psychology and Research, Memphis, TN 38152. Offers counseling (MS, Ed D), including clinical mental health counseling (MS), clinical rehabilitation counseling (MS), rehabilitation counseling (MS), school counseling (MS); counseling psychology (PhD); educational psychology and research (MS, PhD), including educational psychology, educational research. *Accreditation:* ACA (one or more programs are accredited); APA (one or more programs are accredited); CORE (one or more programs are accredited); NCATE. *Program availability:* Blended/hybrid learning. *Faculty:* 26 full-time (18 women), 10 part-time/adjunct (7 women). *Students:* 124 full-time (99 women), 79 part-time (60 women); includes 64 minority (48 Black or African American, non-Hispanic/Latino; 3 Asian, non-Hispanic/Latino; 6 Hispanic/Latino; 7 Two or more races, non-Hispanic/Latino), 7 international. Average age 32. 82 applicants, 68% accepted, 39 enrolled. In 2016, 65 master's, 8 doctorates awarded. *Degree requirements:* For master's, comprehensive exam, thesis or alternative, internship; for doctorate, comprehensive exam, thesis/dissertation, practicum, internship, residency, scholarly work. *Entrance requirements:* For master's, GRE General Test or MAT, minimum GPA of 2.5, letters of reference, interview; for doctorate, GRE General Test, master's degree or equivalent, letters of reference, interview, curriculum vitae, personal statement. Additional exam requirements/recommendations for international students: Required—TOEFL (minimum score 550 paper-based; 79 iBT). *Application deadline:* For fall admission, 10/1 priority date for domestic students; for spring admission, 4/1 priority date for domestic students. Applications are processed on a rolling basis. Application fee: $35 ($60 for international students). Electronic applications accepted. *Expenses:* $5,231.50 per semester full-time in-state, $9,623.50 full-time out-of-state. *Financial support:* In 2016–17, 130 students received support, including 13 research assistantships with full tuition reimbursements available (averaging $14,820 per year), 11 teaching assistantships with full tuition reimbursements available (averaging $15,600 per year); fellowships with full tuition reimbursements available, career-related internships or fieldwork, Federal Work-Study, scholarships/grants, and unspecified assistantships also available. Financial award application deadline: 2/1; financial award applicants required to submit FAFSA. *Faculty research:* Anger management, aging and disability, supervision, multicultural counseling. *Unit head:* Dr. Steve West, Chair, 901-678-2841, Fax: 901-678-5114,

E-mail: slwest@memphis.edu. *Application contact:* Dr. Suzanne Lease, Interim Assistant Dean of Education and Graduate Programs, 901-678-4476, Fax: 901-678-4778, E-mail: slease@memphis.edu. Website: http://www.memphis.edu/cepr/

**The University of North Carolina at Chapel Hill,** School of Medicine and Graduate School, Graduate Programs in Medicine, Chapel Hill, NC 27599. Offers allied health sciences (MPT, MS, Au D, DPT, PhD), including human movement science (MS, PhD), occupational science (MS, PhD), physical therapy (MPT, MS, DPT), rehabilitation counseling and psychology (MS), speech and hearing sciences (MS, Au D, PhD); biochemistry and biophysics (MS, PhD); bioinformatics and computational biology (PhD); biomedical engineering (MS, PhD); cell and developmental biology (PhD); cell and molecular physiology (PhD); genetics and molecular biology (PhD); microbiology and immunology (MS, PhD), including immunology, microbiology; neurobiology (PhD); pathology and laboratory medicine (PhD), including experimental pathology; pharmacology (PhD); MD/PhD. *Program availability:* Online learning. Terminal master's awarded for partial completion of doctoral program. *Degree requirements:* For master's, comprehensive exam; for doctorate, thesis/dissertation. Electronic applications accepted. *Expenses:* Contact institution.

**The University of North Carolina at Chapel Hill,** School of Medicine and Graduate School, Graduate Programs in Medicine, Department of Allied Health Sciences, Division of Clinical Rehabilitation and Mental Health Counseling, Chapel Hill, NC 27599. Offers MS. *Accreditation:* CORE. *Degree requirements:* For master's, comprehensive exam, thesis or alternative, internship. *Entrance requirements:* For master's, GRE. Additional exam requirements/recommendations for international students: Required—TOEFL (minimum score 550 paper-based). *Faculty research:* Motor development, motor control; treatment of sports/orthopedic patient problems; movement in older adults; postural control across the lifespan; research in clinical practice; fetal, preterm, and infant movement; functional assessment across the lifespan.

**University of Northern Colorado,** Graduate School, College of Natural and Health Sciences, School of Human Sciences, Program in Rehabilitation, Greeley, CO 80639. Offers rehabilitation counseling (MA); rehabilitation sciences (PhD). *Accreditation:* CORE (one or more programs are accredited). *Program availability:* Part-time. *Degree requirements:* For master's, comprehensive exam, thesis or alternative; for doctorate, comprehensive exam, thesis/dissertation. *Entrance requirements:* For master's, GRE General Test or MAT, 2 letters of recommendation; for doctorate, GRE General Test, 2 letters of recommendation. *Application deadline:* Applications are processed on a rolling basis. Application fee: $50 ($60 for international students). Electronic applications accepted. *Financial support:* Fellowships, research assistantships, teaching assistantships, and unspecified assistantships available. Financial award application deadline: 3/1; financial award applicants required to submit FAFSA. *Unit head:* Dr. Joe Ososkie, Program Coordinator, 970-351-2403. *Application contact:* Linda Sisson, Graduate Student Admission Coordinator, 970-351-1807, Fax: 970-351-2371, E-mail: linda.sisson@unco.edu. Website: http://www.unco.edu/nhs/rehabilitation/

**University of North Texas,** Robert B. Toulouse School of Graduate Studies, Denton, TX 76203-5459. Offers accounting (MS); applied anthropology (MA, MS); applied behavior analysis (Certificate); applied geography (MA); applied technology and performance improvement (M Ed, MS); art education (MA); art history; art museum education (Certificate); arts leadership (Certificate); audiology (Au D); behavior analysis (MS); behavioral science (PhD); biochemistry and molecular biology (MS); biology (MA, MS); biomedical engineering (MS); business analysis (MS); chemistry (MS); clinical health psychology (PhD); communication studies (MA, MS); computer engineering (MS); computer science (MS); counseling (M Ed, MS), including clinical mental health counseling (MS), college and university counseling, elementary school counseling, secondary school counseling; creative writing (MA); criminal justice (MS); curriculum and instruction (M Ed); decision sciences (MBA); design (MA, MFA), including fashion design (MFA), innovation studies, interior design (MFA); early childhood studies (MS); economics (MS); educational leadership (M Ed, Ed D); educational psychology (MS, PhD), including family studies (MS), gifted and talented (MS), human development (MS), learning and cognition (MS), research, measurement and evaluation (MS); electrical engineering (MS); emergency management (MPA); engineering technology (MS); English (MA); English as a second language (MA); environmental science (MS); finance (MBA, MS); financial management (MPA); French (MA); health services management (MBA); higher education (M Ed, Ed D); history (MA, MS); hospitality management (MS); human resources management (MPA); information science (MS); information systems (PhD); information technologies (MBA); interdisciplinary studies (MA, MS); international studies (MA); international sustainable tourism (MS); jazz studies (MM); journalism (MA, MJ, Graduate Certificate), including interactive and virtual digital communication (Graduate Certificate), narrative journalism (Graduate Certificate), public relations (Graduate Certificate); kinesiology (MS); linguistics (MA); local government management (MPA); logistics (PhD); logistics and supply chain management (MBA); long-term care, senior housing, and aging services (MA); management (PhD); marketing (MBA); mathematics (MA, MS); mechanical and energy engineering (MS, PhD); music (MA), including ethnomusicology, music theory, musicology, performance; music composition (PhD); music education (MM Ed, PhD); nonprofit management (MPA); operations and supply chain management (MBA); performance (MM, DMA); philosophy (MA); political science (MA); professional and technical communication (MA); radio, television and film (MA, MFA); rehabilitation counseling (Certificate); sociology (MA); Spanish (MA); special education (M Ed); speech-language pathology (MA); strategic management (MBA); studio art (MFA); teaching (M Ed); MBA/MS. *Program availability:* Part-time, evening/weekend, online learning. Terminal master's awarded for partial completion of doctoral program. *Degree requirements:* For master's, variable foreign language requirement, comprehensive exam (for some programs), thesis (for some programs); for doctorate, variable foreign language requirement, comprehensive exam (for some programs), thesis/dissertation; for other advanced degree, variable foreign language requirement, comprehensive exam (for some programs). *Entrance requirements:* For master's and doctorate, GRE, GMAT. Additional exam requirements/recommendations for international students: Required—TOEFL (minimum score 550 paper-based; 79 iBT). Electronic applications accepted.

**University of Puerto Rico, Río Piedras Campus,** College of Social Sciences, Graduate School of Rehabilitation Counseling, San Juan, PR 00931-3300. Offers MRC. *Accreditation:* CORE. *Program availability:* Part-time. *Degree requirements:* For master's, comprehensive exam, thesis, internship. *Entrance requirements:* For master's, GRE or PAEG, interview, minimum GPA of 3.0, letter of recommendation.

**The University of Scranton,** Panuska College of Professional Studies, Department of Counseling and Human Services, Program in Rehabilitation Counseling, Scranton, PA 18510. Offers MS. *Accreditation:* CORE. *Program availability:* Part-time, evening/weekend. *Degree requirements:* For master's, comprehensive exam (for some programs), thesis (for some programs), capstone experience. *Entrance requirements:* For master's, minimum GPA of 3.0, three letters of reference. Additional exam requirements/recommendations for international students: Required—TOEFL (minimum score 500 paper-based; 80 iBT), IELTS (minimum score 6.5). Electronic applications accepted.

## Rehabilitation Counseling

**University of South Carolina,** School of Medicine and The Graduate School, Graduate Programs in Medicine, Program in Rehabilitation Counseling, Columbia, SC 29208. Offers psychiatric rehabilitation (Certificate); rehabilitation counseling (MRC). *Accreditation:* CORE. *Program availability:* Part-time, evening/weekend. *Degree requirements:* For master's, comprehensive exam, internship, practicum. *Entrance requirements:* For master's and Certificate, GRE General Test or GMAT. Electronic applications accepted. *Expenses:* Contact institution. *Faculty research:* Quality of life, alcohol dependency, technology for disabled, psychiatric rehabilitation, women with disabilities.

**University of Southern Maine,** College of Management and Human Service, School of Education and Human Development, Program in Counselor Education, Portland, ME 04103. Offers clinical mental health counseling (MS); counseling (CAS); culturally responsive practices in education and human development (CGS); mental health rehabilitation technician/community (CGS); rehabilitation counseling (MS); school counseling (MS); substance abuse counseling (CGS). *Accreditation:* ACA (one or more programs are accredited); CORE; TEAC. *Program availability:* Part-time, evening/weekend. *Degree requirements:* For master's, comprehensive exam, thesis or alternative; for other advanced degree, thesis or alternative. *Entrance requirements:* For master's, GRE General Test or MAT, interview; for other advanced degree, master's degree. Additional exam requirements/recommendations for international students: Required—TOEFL (minimum score 550 paper-based; 79 iBT). Electronic applications accepted. *Faculty research:* Counselor licensure, group dynamics, counseling theories, healthy adaptation, counselor educator well-being.

**University of South Florida,** College of Behavioral and Community Sciences, Department of Child and Family Studies, Tampa, FL 33620-9951. Offers applied behavior analysis (MA, MS, PhD); behavioral and community sciences (PhD); child and adolescent behavioral health (MS), including developmental disabilities, leadership in child and adolescent health, translational research and evaluation, youth and behavioral health; rehabilitation and mental health counseling (MA), including addictions and substance abuse counseling, marriage and family therapy. *Accreditation:* ACA. *Faculty:* 15 full-time (10 women), 1 (woman) part-time/adjunct. *Students:* 146 full-time (127 women), 90 part-time (74 women); includes 92 minority (22 Black or African American, non-Hispanic/Latino; 12 Asian, non-Hispanic/Latino; 49 Hispanic/Latino; 9 Two or more races, non-Hispanic/Latino), 3 international. Average age 28. 267 applicants, 51% accepted, 93 enrolled. In 2016, 63 master's awarded. *Degree requirements:* For master's, comprehensive exam, thesis (for some programs); for doctorate, comprehensive exam, thesis/dissertation, Behavior Analyst Board Certification Exam. *Entrance requirements:* For master's, GRE General Test, minimum GPA of 3.0 in last 60 hours of coursework; letters of recommendation; one-page narrative describing experience, interest, and career goals in applied behavior analysis; resume or curriculum vitae (varies by program); for doctorate, GRE General Test, master's degree in behavioral analysis or closely-related field; minimum GPA of 3.5 in graduate course work; three letters of recommendation; campus visit with faculty interview; personal statement; curriculum vitae; evidence of research experiences and expertise. Additional exam requirements/recommendations for international students: Required—TOEFL (minimum score 550 paper-based; 79 iBT) or IELTS (minimum score 6.5). *Application deadline:* For fall admission, 12/5 for domestic and international students. Application fee: $30. *Expenses:* Tuition, state resident: full-time $7766; part-time $431.43 per credit hour. Tuition, nonresident: full-time $15,789; part-time $877.17 per credit hour. *Required fees:* $37 per term. *Financial support:* In 2016–17, 50 students received support. Unspecified assistantships available. *Faculty research:* Applied behavior analysis, autism, behavior management, behavioral intervention, children, developmental disabilities, experimental analysis of behavior, functional assessment, positive behavior support. *Total annual research expenditures:* $16.4 million. *Application contact:* Dr. Raymond G. Miltenberger, Professor/Director of Master's Program, 813-974-5079, Fax: 813-974-6115, E-mail: miltenbe@usf.edu.
Website: http://cfs.cbcs.usf.edu/

**University of South Florida,** Innovative Education, Tampa, FL 33620-9951. Offers adult, career and higher education (Graduate Certificate), including college teaching, leadership in developing human resources, leadership in higher education; Africana studies (Graduate Certificate), including diasporas and health disparities, genocide and human rights; aging studies (Graduate Certificate), including gerontology; art research (Graduate Certificate), including museum studies; business foundations (Graduate Certificate); chemical and biomedical engineering (Graduate Certificate), including materials science and engineering, water, health and sustainability; child and family studies (Graduate Certificate), including positive behavior support; civil and industrial engineering (Graduate Certificate), including transportation systems analysis; community and family health (Graduate Certificate), including maternal and child health, social marketing and public health, violence and injury: prevention and intervention, women's health; criminology (Graduate Certificate), including criminal justice administration; educational measurement and research (Graduate Certificate), including evaluation; English (Graduate Certificate), including comparative literary studies, creative writing, professional and technical communication; entrepreneurship (Graduate Certificate); environmental health (Graduate Certificate), including safety management; epidemiology and biostatistics (Graduate Certificate), including applied biostatistics, biostatistics, concepts and tools of epidemiology, epidemiology, epidemiology of infectious diseases; geography, environment and planning (Graduate Certificate), including community development, environmental policy and management, geographical information systems; geology (Graduate Certificate), including hydrogeology; global health (Graduate Certificate), including disaster management, global health and Latin American and Caribbean studies, global health practice, humanitarian assistance, infection control; government and international affairs (Graduate Certificate), including Cuban studies, globalization studies; health policy and management (Graduate Certificate), including health management and leadership, public health policy and programs; hearing specialist: early intervention (Graduate Certificate); industrial and management systems engineering (Graduate Certificate), including systems engineering, technology management; information studies (Graduate Certificate), including school library media specialist; information systems/decision sciences (Graduate Certificate), including analytics and business intelligence; instructional technology (Graduate Certificate), including distance education, Florida digital/virtual educator, instructional design, multimedia design, Web design; internal medicine, bioethics and medical humanities (Graduate Certificate), including biomedical ethics; Latin American and Caribbean studies (Graduate Certificate); mass communications (Graduate Certificate), including multimedia journalism; mathematics and statistics (Graduate Certificate), including mathematics; medicine (Graduate Certificate), including aging and neuroscience, bioinformatics, biotechnology, brain fitness and memory management, clinical investigation, health informatics, health sciences, integrative weight management, intellectual property, medicine and gender, metabolic and nutritional medicine, metabolic cardiology, pharmacy sciences; national and competitive intelligence (Graduate Certificate); psychological and social foundations (Graduate Certificate), including career counseling, college teaching, diversity in education, mental health counseling, school counseling; public affairs (Graduate Certificate), including nonprofit management, public management, research administration; public health (Graduate Certificate), including environmental health,

health equity, public health generalist, translational research in adolescent behavioral health; public health practices (Graduate Certificate), including planning for healthy communities; rehabilitation and mental health counseling (Graduate Certificate), including integrative mental health care, marriage and family therapy, rehabilitation technology; secondary education (Graduate Certificate), including ESOL, foreign language education: culture and content, foreign language education: professional; social work (Graduate Certificate), including geriatric social work/clinical gerontology; special education (Graduate Certificate), including autism spectrum disorder, disabilities education: severe/profound; world languages (Graduate Certificate), including teaching English as a second language (TESL) or foreign language. *Expenses:* Tuition, state resident: full-time $7766; part-time $431.43 per credit hour. Tuition, nonresident: full-time $15,789; part-time $877.17 per credit hour. *Required fees:* $37 per term. *Unit head:* Kathy Barnes, Interdisciplinary Programs Coordinator, 813-974-8031, Fax: 813-974-7061, E-mail: barnesk@usf.edu. *Application contact:* Karen Tylinski, Metro Initiatives, 813-974-9943, Fax: 813-974-7061, E-mail: ktylinsk@usf.edu.
Website: http://www.usf.edu/innovative-education/

**The University of Tennessee,** Graduate School, College of Education, Health and Human Sciences, Department of Educational Psychology and Counseling, Knoxville, TN 37996. Offers adult education (MS); applied educational psychology (MS); collaborative learning (Ed D); college student personnel (MS); mental health counseling (MS); rehabilitation counseling (MS); school counseling (MS). *Accreditation:* ACA (one or more programs are accredited); CORE (one or more programs are accredited); NCATE. *Program availability:* Part-time, evening/weekend. *Degree requirements:* For master's, thesis optional. *Entrance requirements:* For master's, GRE General Test, minimum GPA of 2.7. Additional exam requirements/recommendations for international students: Required—TOEFL. Electronic applications accepted.

**The University of Texas at Austin,** Graduate School, College of Education, Department of Special Education, Austin, TX 78712-1111. Offers autism and developmental disabilities (Ed D, PhD); autism and developmental disability (M Ed, MA); early childhood special education (M Ed, MA, Ed D, PhD); learning disabilities (Ed D, PhD); learning disabilities/behavior disorders (M Ed, MA); multicultural special education (M Ed, MA, Ed D, PhD); rehabilitation counselor (M Ed); rehabilitation counselor education (Ed D, PhD); special education administration (Ed D, PhD). *Accreditation:* CORE. *Program availability:* Part-time, evening/weekend, online learning. *Degree requirements:* For master's, thesis or alternative; for doctorate, thesis/dissertation. *Entrance requirements:* For master's and doctorate, GRE General Test. *Faculty research:* Anchored instruction, reading disabilities, multicultural/bilingual.

**The University of Texas at El Paso,** Graduate School, College of Health Sciences, Rehabilitation Counseling Program, El Paso, TX 79968-0001. Offers MRC. *Accreditation:* CORE. *Program availability:* Part-time, evening/weekend. *Degree requirements:* For master's, comprehensive exam, thesis optional. *Entrance requirements:* For master's, GRE, minimum GPA of 3.0, statement of professional goals, letters of recommendation. Additional exam requirements/recommendations for international students: Required—TOEFL; Recommended—IELTS. Electronic applications accepted. *Faculty research:* Psychosocial adjustment to disability, attribution regarding disability, self-regulation, professional issues in rehabilitation counseling, rehabilitation education.

**The University of Texas Rio Grande Valley,** College of Health Affairs, School of Rehabilitation Services and Counseling, Edinburg, TX 78539. Offers MS, PhD. *Accreditation:* CORE. *Program availability:* Part-time, evening/weekend. *Degree requirements:* For master's, comprehensive exam, thesis optional. *Entrance requirements:* For master's, minimum GPA of 3.0. Tuition and fees vary according to course load and program. *Faculty research:* Attitudes and disability, substance abuse, multicultural counseling, Hispanics and disability, Social Security beneficiary characteristics.

**The University of Texas Southwestern Medical Center,** Southwestern School of Health Professions, Rehabilitation Counseling Psychology Program, Dallas, TX 75390. Offers MRC. *Accreditation:* CORE. *Degree requirements:* For master's, thesis. *Entrance requirements:* For master's, GRE General Test, minimum GPA of 3.0. Electronic applications accepted. *Faculty research:* Psychophysiology of stress and emotion, psychosocial rehabilitation, assessment of learning disabilities.

**University of the District of Columbia,** College of Arts and Sciences, Program in Rehabilitation Counseling, Washington, DC 20008-1175. Offers MA.

**University of Wisconsin–Madison,** Graduate School, School of Education, Department of Rehabilitation Psychology and Special Education, Program in Rehabilitation Psychology, Madison, WI 53706-1380. Offers MA, MS, PhD. *Accreditation:* CORE (one or more programs are accredited). *Degree requirements:* For doctorate, thesis/dissertation.

**University of Wisconsin–Stout,** Graduate School, College of Education, Health and Human Sciences, Program in Vocational Rehabilitation, Menomonie, WI 54751. Offers MS. *Accreditation:* CORE. *Program availability:* Part-time, online learning. *Degree requirements:* For master's, comprehensive exam or thesis. *Entrance requirements:* For master's, minimum GPA of 2.75. Additional exam requirements/recommendations for international students: Required—TOEFL (minimum score 500 paper-based; 61 iBT). Electronic applications accepted. *Faculty research:* Aging/gerontology, athletics, neuropsychology, recreation, transition to work.

**Utah State University,** School of Graduate Studies, Emma Eccles Jones College of Education and Human Services, Department of Special Education and Rehabilitation, Program in Rehabilitation Counselor Education, Logan, UT 84322. Offers MRC. *Accreditation:* CORE. *Program availability:* Part-time, online learning. *Degree requirements:* For master's, internship. *Entrance requirements:* For master's, GRE General Test, minimum GPA of 3.0. Additional exam requirements/recommendations for international students: Required—TOEFL (minimum score 550 paper-based). Electronic applications accepted. *Expenses:* Contact institution. *Faculty research:* Distance education, Hispanic rehabilitation, transition from school to work.

**Virginia Commonwealth University,** Graduate School, School of Allied Health Professions, Department of Rehabilitation Counseling, Richmond, VA 23284-9005. Offers MS. *Accreditation:* CORE. *Entrance requirements:* For master's, GRE General Test or MAT. Additional exam requirements/recommendations for international students: Required—TOEFL (minimum score 600 paper-based; 100 iBT). *Application deadline:* For fall admission, 6/1 for domestic students; for spring admission, 10/1 for domestic students. Applications are processed on a rolling basis. Application fee: $50. Electronic applications accepted. *Financial support:* Fellowships, research assistantships, teaching assistantships, career-related internships or fieldwork, and tuition waivers (full and partial) available. Financial award application deadline: 3/1; financial award applicants required to submit FAFSA. *Faculty research:* Substance abuse/addictions, lifelong disabilities, consumer empowerment, counseling models, adjustment to disability. *Unit head:* Dr. Allen N. Lewis, Chair, 804-828-1132, Fax: 801-828-1321, E-mail: anlewis@vcu.edu. *Application contact:* Dr. Amy J. Armstrong, Vice Chair, 804-828-0913, Fax: 804-828-1321, E-mail: ajarmstr@vcu.edu.
Website: http://www.sahp.vcu.edu/rehab/

**Wayne State University,** College of Education, Division of Theoretical and Behavioral Foundations, Detroit, MI 48202. Offers applied behavior analysis (Certificate); counseling (M Ed, MA, Ed D, PhD, Ed S); counseling psychology (MA); education evaluation and research (M Ed, Ed D, PhD); educational psychology (M Ed, PhD), including learning and instruction sciences (PhD); rehabilitation counseling and community inclusion (MA); school and community psychology (MA); school psychology (Certificate). *Accreditation:* ACA (one or more programs are accredited); CORE (one or more programs are accredited). *Program availability:* Evening/weekend. *Faculty:* 12. *Students:* 211 full-time (179 women); 237 part-time (196 women); includes 167 minority (119 Black or African American, non-Hispanic/Latino; 1 American Indian or Alaska Native, non-Hispanic/Latino; 10 Asian, non-Hispanic/Latino; 17 Hispanic/Latino; 20 Two or more races, non-Hispanic/Latino), 24 international. Average age 32. 294 applicants, 34% accepted, 72 enrolled. In 2016, 87 master's, 12 doctorates, 14 other advanced degrees awarded. *Degree requirements:* For master's, thesis (for some programs); for doctorate, thesis/dissertation. *Entrance requirements:* For master's, GRE, interview, personal statement, portfolio (art therapy); for doctorate, GRE, department-written exam, interview, curriculum vitae, references, master's degree in closely-related field with minimum GPA of 3.5, demonstration of counseling skills (counseling); for other advanced degree, master's degree in counseling and counseling license (for Ed S); good standing in school and community psychology MA program (for Certificate). Additional exam requirements/recommendations for international students: Required—TOEFL (minimum score 550 paper-based; 79 iBT), Michigan English Language Assessment Battery (minimum score 85); Recommended—IELTS (minimum score 6.5), TWE (minimum score 5.5). *Application deadline:* For fall admission, 6/1 priority date for domestic students, 5/1 priority date for international students; for winter admission, 10/1 priority date for domestic students, 9/1 priority date for international students; for spring admission, 2/1 priority date for domestic students, 1/1 priority date for international students. Applications are processed on a rolling basis. Application fee: $50. Electronic applications accepted. *Expenses:* $16,503 per year resident tuition and fees, $33,697 per year non-resident tuition and fees. *Financial support:* In 2016–17, 92 students received support, including 2 research assistantships with tuition reimbursements available (averaging $17,994 per year); fellowships with tuition reimbursements available, teaching assistantships with tuition reimbursements available, Federal Work-Study, scholarships/grants, health care benefits, and unspecified assistantships also available. Support available to part-time students. Financial award applicants required to submit FAFSA. *Faculty research:* Adolescents at risk, supervision of counseling. *Unit head:* Dr. Cheryl Somers, Assistant Dean, 313-577-1670, E-mail: c.somers@wayne.edu. *Application contact:* Janice Green, Assistant Dean, 313-577-1605, E-mail: jwgreen@wayne.edu.
Website: http://coe.wayne.edu/tbf/index.php

**Western Michigan University,** Graduate College, College of Health and Human Services, Department of Blindness and Low Vision Studies, Kalamazoo, MI 49008. Offers orientation and mobility (MA); orientation and mobility of children (MA); vision rehabilitation therapy (MA). *Accreditation:* CORE.

**Western Oregon University,** Graduate Programs, College of Education, Division of Special Education, Program in Rehabilitation Counseling, Monmouth, OR 97361. Offers MS. *Accreditation:* CORE. *Degree requirements:* For master's, thesis optional, oral exam, portfolio. *Entrance requirements:* For master's, interview, minimum GPA of 3.0. Additional exam requirements/recommendations for international students: Required—TOEFL (minimum score 550 paper-based; 79 iBT), IELTS (minimum score 6.5). *Faculty research:* Deafness, rehabilitation counseling.

**Western Washington University,** Graduate School, Woodring College of Education, Program in Rehabilitation Counseling, Bellingham, WA 98225-5996. Offers MA. *Accreditation:* CORE. *Program availability:* Part-time, evening/weekend, online learning. *Degree requirements:* For master's, research project. *Entrance requirements:* For master's, GRE General Test or MAT, minimum GPA of 3.0 in last 60 semester hours or last 90 quarter hours of course work. Additional exam requirements/recommendations for international students: Required—TOEFL (minimum score 567 paper-based). Electronic applications accepted. *Faculty research:* Employment issues for individuals with significant disabilities, research and statistics techniques, rehabilitation counselor education.

**West Virginia University,** College of Education and Human Services, Department of Counseling, Rehabilitation Counseling, and Counseling Psychology, Program in Rehabilitation Counseling, Morgantown, WV 26506. Offers MS. *Accreditation:* CORE. *Program availability:* Part-time, online learning. *Degree requirements:* For master's, content exams. *Entrance requirements:* For master's, GRE General Test, minimum GPA of 2.5, interview. Additional exam requirements/recommendations for international students: Required—TOEFL (minimum score 550 paper-based; 65 iBT). Electronic applications accepted. *Faculty research:* Work adjustment, job modification for the handicapped, computer resource networks, vocational evaluation.

**Wilberforce University,** Program in Rehabilitation Counseling, Wilberforce, OH 45384. Offers MS. *Entrance requirements:* For master's, bachelor's degree, 3 letters of recommendation, interview. Additional exam requirements/recommendations for international students: Required—TOEFL.

**Winston-Salem State University,** Program in Rehabilitation Counseling, Winston-Salem, NC 27110-0003. Offers MRC. *Program availability:* Part-time, online learning. *Degree requirements:* For master's, thesis optional. *Entrance requirements:* For master's, GRE, 3 letters of recommendation. Electronic applications accepted. *Faculty research:* Drug addiction, recovery, HIV/AIDS interventions.

**Wright State University,** Graduate School, College of Education and Human Services, Department of Human Services, Program in Rehabilitation Counseling, Dayton, OH 45435. Offers chemical dependency (MRC). *Accreditation:* CORE. *Degree requirements:* For master's, comprehensive exam. *Entrance requirements:* For master's, GRE General Test, MAT, interview. Additional exam requirements/recommendations for international students: Required—TOEFL. Application fee: $25. *Expenses:* Tuition, state resident: full-time $9952; part-time $622 per credit hour. Tuition, nonresident: full-time $16,960; part-time $1060 per credit hour. *Financial support:* Career-related internships or fieldwork, institutionally sponsored loans, and tuition waivers (full and partial) available. Support available to part-time students. Financial award applicants required to submit FAFSA. *Unit head:* Dr. Jan La Forge, Director, 937-775-2075, Fax: 937-775-2042, E-mail: jan.laforge@wright.edu. *Application contact:* John Kimble, Associate Director of Graduate Admissions and Records, 937-775-2957, Fax: 937-775-2453, E-mail: john.kimble@wright.edu.

# School Psychology

**Abilene Christian University,** Graduate Programs, College of Arts and Sciences, Department of Psychology, Specialist in School Psychology Program, Abilene, TX 79699. Offers Specialist. *Students:* 12 full-time (8 women), 3 part-time (all women); includes 6 minority (2 Black or African American, non-Hispanic/Latino; 3 Hispanic/Latino; 1 Two or more races, non-Hispanic/Latino), 1 international. 17 applicants, 65% accepted, 5 enrolled. *Entrance requirements:* Additional exam requirements/recommendations for international students: Required—TOEFL (minimum score 80 iBT), IELTS (minimum score 6), PTE. *Application deadline:* For fall admission, 3/30 priority date for domestic students; for spring admission, 11/1 for domestic students. Applications are processed on a rolling basis. Application fee: $50. Electronic applications accepted. *Expenses: Tuition:* Full-time $19,890; part-time $1105 per credit hour. Tuition and fees vary according to course load and program. *Financial support:* In 2016–17, 10 students received support. Federal Work-Study and scholarships/grants available. Support available to part-time students. Financial award application deadline: 4/1; financial award applicants required to submit FAFSA. *Unit head:* Dr. Rachel Team, Graduate Program Director, 325-674-2285, Fax: 325-674-6968, E-mail: rmg97j@acu.edu. *Application contact:* Corey Patterson, Director of Graduate Admission and Recruiting, 325-674-6566, Fax: 325-674-6717, E-mail: gradinfo@acu.edu.
Website: http://www.acu.edu/graduate/academics/school-psychology.html

**Adelphi University,** Gordon F. Derner School of Psychology, Program in School Psychology, Garden City, NY 11530-0701. Offers MA. *Program availability:* Part-time. *Students:* 35 full-time (32 women), 15 part-time (12 women); includes 26 minority (12 Black or African American, non-Hispanic/Latino; 2 Asian, non-Hispanic/Latino; 10 Hispanic/Latino; 2 Two or more races, non-Hispanic/Latino). Average age 25. 38 applicants, 49% accepted, 18 enrolled. In 2016, 24 master's awarded. *Degree requirements:* For master's, comprehensive exam. *Entrance requirements:* For master's, minimum GPA of 3.0; 15 credits of course work in psychology including general psychology, developmental child or adolescent psychology, abnormal personality in school psychology, tests and measurements, statistics; 3 letters of recommendation. Additional exam requirements/recommendations for international students: Required—TOEFL (minimum score 550 paper-based; 80 iBT), IELTS (minimum score 6.5). *Application deadline:* For fall admission, 5/1 for domestic students, 4/1 for international students. Application fee: $50. Electronic applications accepted. *Expenses:* Contact institution. *Financial support:* Research assistantships with full and partial tuition reimbursements, teaching assistantships, career-related internships or fieldwork, institutionally sponsored loans, scholarships/grants, traineeships, and unspecified assistantships available. Support available to part-time students. *Unit head:* Dr. Ionas Sapountzis, Director, 516-877-4743, E-mail: isapountzis@adelphi.edu. *Application contact:* Christine Murphy, Director of Admissions, 516-877-3050, Fax: 516-877-3039, E-mail: graduateadmissions@adelphi.edu.
Website: http://derner.adelphi.edu/psychology/graduate/ma-in-school-psychology/

**Alabama Agricultural and Mechanical University,** School of Graduate Studies, College of Education, Humanities, and Behavioral Sciences, Department of Social Work, Psychology and Counseling, Huntsville, AL 35811. Offers psychology and counseling (MS, Ed S), including clinical psychology (MS), counseling psychology (MS), guidance and counseling, rehabilitation counseling (MS), school counseling (MS), school psychology (MS), school psychometry (MS); social work (MSW). *Accreditation:* CORE; NCATE. *Program availability:* Part-time, evening/weekend. *Degree requirements:* For master's, comprehensive exam. *Entrance requirements:* For master's, GRE General Test. Additional exam requirements/recommendations for international students: Required—TOEFL (minimum score 500 paper-based; 61 iBT). *Application deadline:* For fall admission, 5/1 for domestic students. Application fee: $15 ($20 for international students). *Expenses: Tuition,* nonresident: part-time $826 per credit hour. Full-time tuition and fees vary according to course load and program. *Financial support:* Career-related internships or fieldwork available. Support available to part-time students. Financial award application deadline: 4/1. *Faculty research:* Increasing numbers of minorities in special education and speech-language pathology. *Unit head:* Dr. Shirley King, Chair, 256-372-5520, Fax: 256-372-5526.

**Alfred University,** Graduate School, Counseling and School Psychology Program, Alfred, NY 14802-1205. Offers mental health counseling (MS Ed); school counseling (MS Ed, CAS); school psychology (MA, Psy D, CAS). *Accreditation:* APA. *Faculty:* 10 full-time (3 women), 4 part-time/adjunct (2 women). *Students:* 43 full-time (35 women), 40 part-time (31 women); includes 11 minority (6 Black or African American, non-Hispanic/Latino; 1 Asian, non-Hispanic/Latino; 4 Hispanic/Latino), 1 international. Average age 25. 40 applicants, 80% accepted, 24 enrolled. In 2016, 85 master's, 8 doctorates, 18 other advanced degrees awarded. *Degree requirements:* For master's, internship; for doctorate, thesis/dissertation, internship. *Entrance requirements:* For master's and doctorate, GRE General Test. Additional exam requirements/recommendations for international students: Required—TOEFL (minimum score 590 paper-based; 90 iBT), IELTS (minimum score 6.5). *Application deadline:* For fall admission, 1/15 priority date for domestic and international students. Application fee: $60. Electronic applications accepted. *Expenses: Tuition:* Full-time $38,020; part-time $810 per credit. *Required fees:* $970; $82 per semester. *Financial support:* Research assistantships with partial tuition reimbursements, career-related internships or fieldwork, and unspecified assistantships available. Financial award application deadline: 8/1; financial award applicants required to submit FAFSA. *Faculty research:* Family processes, alternative assessment approaches, behavior disorders in children, parent involvement, school psychology training issues. *Unit head:* Dr. Nancy Evangelista, Chair, 607-871-2212, E-mail: fevangel@alfred.edu. *Application contact:* Sara Love, Coordinator of Graduate Admissions, 607-871-2115, Fax: 607-871-2198, E-mail: gradinquiry@alfred.edu.

**Alliant International University–Irvine,** Shirley M. Hufstedler School of Education, Educational Psychology Programs, Irvine, CA 92606. Offers educational psychology (Psy D); pupil personnel services (Credential); school psychology (MA). *Program availability:* Part-time. *Degree requirements:* For doctorate, thesis/dissertation. *Entrance requirements:* For master's, minimum GPA of 2.5, letters of recommendation; for doctorate, interview, minimum GPA of 3.0, letters of recommendation. Additional exam requirements/recommendations for international students: Required—TOEFL (minimum score 550 paper-based; 80 iBT), TWE (minimum score 5). *Faculty research:* School-based mental health.

**Alliant International University–Los Angeles,** Shirley M. Hufstedler School of Education, Educational Psychology Programs, Alhambra, CA 91803. Offers educational

## School Psychology

psychology (Psy D); pupil personnel services (Credential); school psychology (MA). *Program availability:* Part-time. *Degree requirements:* For doctorate, comprehensive exam, thesis/dissertation. *Entrance requirements:* For master's, minimum GPA of 2.5, letters of recommendation; for doctorate, interview, minimum GPA of 3.0, letters of recommendation. Additional exam requirements/recommendations for international students: Required—TOEFL (minimum score 550 paper-based), TWE (minimum score 5). Electronic applications accepted. *Faculty research:* Early identification and intervention with high-risk preschoolers, pediatric neuropsychology, interpersonal violence, ADHD, learning theories.

**Alliant International University–San Diego,** Shirley M. Hufstedler School of Education, Educational Psychology Programs, San Diego, CA 92131. Offers educational psychology (Psy D); pupil personnel services (Credential); school neuropsychology (Certificate); school psychology (MA); school-based mental health (Certificate). *Program availability:* Part-time. *Degree requirements:* For doctorate, comprehensive exam, thesis/dissertation, internship. *Entrance requirements:* For master's, minimum GPA of 2.5, letters of recommendation; for doctorate, minimum GPA of 3.0, letters of recommendation. Additional exam requirements/recommendations for international students: Required—TOEFL (minimum score 550 paper-based; 80 iBT), TWE (minimum score 5). Electronic applications accepted. *Faculty research:* School-based mental health, pupil personnel services, childhood mood, school-based assessment.

**Alliant International University–San Francisco,** Shirley M. Hufstedler School of Education, Educational Psychology Programs, San Francisco, CA 94133. Offers educational psychology (Psy D); pupil personnel services (Credential); school psychology (MA). *Program availability:* Part-time. Terminal master's awarded for partial completion of doctoral program. *Degree requirements:* For doctorate, thesis/dissertation. *Entrance requirements:* For master's, minimum GPA of 3.0, letters of recommendation; for doctorate, interview, minimum GPA of 3.0, letters of recommendation. Additional exam requirements/recommendations for international students: Required—TOEFL (minimum score 550 paper-based), TWE (minimum score 5). Electronic applications accepted. *Faculty research:* Social skills, ADHD, cognitive functioning and learning, innovative teaching methods.

**Andrews University,** School of Graduate Studies, School of Education, Department of Graduate Psychology and Counseling, Program in School Counseling, Berrien Springs, MI 49104. Offers MA. *Students:* 2 full-time (both women). Average age 38. In 2016, 6 master's awarded. *Degree requirements:* For master's, thesis optional. *Entrance requirements:* For master's, GRE. Additional exam requirements/recommendations for international students: Required—TOEFL (minimum score 550 paper-based). Application fee: $40. *Unit head:* Dr. Rudolph N. Bailey, Coordinator, 269-471-3466. *Application contact:* Justina Clayburn, Supervisor of Graduate Admission, 800-253-2874, Fax: 269-471-6321, E-mail: graduate@andrews.edu.

**Andrews University,** School of Graduate Studies, School of Education, Department of Graduate Psychology and Counseling, Program in School Psychology, Berrien Springs, MI 49104. Offers Ed S. *Program availability:* Part-time. *Students:* 7 full-time (6 women), 1 (woman) part-time; includes 1 minority (Black or African American, non-Hispanic/Latino), 3 international. Average age 32. In 2016, 2 Ed Ss awarded. *Entrance requirements:* Additional exam requirements/recommendations for international students: Required—TOEFL (minimum score 550 paper-based). *Application deadline:* Applications are processed on a rolling basis. Application fee: $40. *Unit head:* Dr. Elizabeth Lundy, Coordinator, 269-471-6251. *Application contact:* Justina Clayburn, Supervisor of Graduate Admission, 800-253-2874, Fax: 269-471-6321, E-mail: graduate@andrews.edu.

**Appalachian State University,** Cratis D. Williams Graduate School, Department of Human Development and Psychological Counseling, Boone, NC 28608. Offers clinical mental health counseling (MA); college student development (MA); marriage and family therapy (MA); school counseling (MA). *Accreditation:* AAMFT/COAMFTE; ACA; NCATE. *Program availability:* Part-time. *Degree requirements:* For master's, comprehensive exam (for some programs), thesis optional, internships. *Entrance requirements:* For master's, GRE General Test, 3 letters of recommendation. Additional exam requirements/recommendations for international students: Required—TOEFL (minimum score 570 paper-based; 79 iBT), IELTS (minimum score 6.5). *Application deadline:* For fall admission, 2/1 priority date for domestic students, 2/1 for international students; for spring admission, 2/1 for international students. Applications are processed on a rolling basis. Application fee: $55. Electronic applications accepted. *Expenses:* Tuition, state resident: full-time $4744. Tuition, nonresident: full-time $17,913. Full-time tuition and fees vary according to program. *Financial support:* Fellowships, research assistantships, teaching assistantships, career-related internships or fieldwork, Federal Work-Study, scholarships/grants, and unspecified assistantships available. Financial award application deadline: 4/1; financial award applicants required to submit FAFSA. *Faculty research:* Multicultural counseling, addictions counseling, play therapy, expressive arts, child and adolescent therapy, sexual abuse counseling. *Unit head:* Dr. Lee Baruth, Chairman, 828-262-2055, E-mail: baruthlg@appstate.edu. *Application contact:* Dr. Mark Schwarze, Program Director, 828-262-6046, E-mail: asucmhc@appstate.edu.
Website: http://www.ced.appstate.edu/departments/hpc

**Argosy University, Dallas,** College of Education, Farmers Branch, TX 75244. Offers educational administration (MA Ed); educational leadership (Ed D); higher and postsecondary education (MA Ed); instructional leadership (MA Ed); school psychology (MA).

**Argosy University, Hawai`i,** College of Education, Program in School Psychology, Honolulu, HI 96813. Offers MA.

**Argosy University, Phoenix,** College of Education, Program in School Psychology, Phoenix, AZ 85021. Offers MA, Psy D.

**Argosy University, Sarasota,** College of Education, Sarasota, FL 34235. Offers community college executive leadership (Ed D); educational leadership (MA Ed, Ed D, Ed S), including higher education administration (Ed D), K-12 education (Ed D); school counseling (MA, Ed S); school psychology (MA); teaching and learning (MA Ed, Ed D, Ed S), including education technology (Ed D), higher education (Ed D), K-12 education (Ed D).

**Arkansas State University,** Graduate School, College of Education and Behavioral Science, Department of Psychology and Counseling, State University, AR 72467. Offers clinical mental health counseling (Graduate Certificate); college student personnel services (MS); dyslexia therapy (Graduate Certificate); psychological science (MS); psychology and counseling (Ed S); rehabilitation counseling (MRC); school counseling (MSE); student affairs (Graduate Certificate). *Accreditation:* ACA (one or more programs are accredited); CORE (one or more programs are accredited); NCATE. *Program availability:* Part-time. *Degree requirements:* For master's and other advanced degree, comprehensive exam, thesis or alternative. *Entrance requirements:* For master's, GRE General Test or MAT (for MSE), appropriate bachelor's degree, interview, letters of reference, official transcripts, immunization records, written statement, 2-3 page autobiography; for other advanced degree, GRE General Test, interview, master's degree, letters of reference, official transcript, personal statement, immunization

records. Additional exam requirements/recommendations for international students: Required—TOEFL (minimum score 550 paper-based; 79 iBT), IELTS (minimum score 6), PTE (minimum score 56). Electronic applications accepted.

**Assumption College,** School Counseling Program, Worcester, MA 01609-1296. Offers resiliency (CAGS); school counseling (MA, CAGS). *Program availability:* Part-time, evening/weekend. *Faculty:* 3 full-time (1 woman), 7 part-time/adjunct (4 women). *Students:* 43 full-time (36 women), 24 part-time (22 women); includes 7 minority (6 Hispanic/Latino; 1 Two or more races, non-Hispanic/Latino). Average age 27. 44 applicants, 66% accepted, 16 enrolled. In 2016, 22 master's, 6 other advanced degrees awarded. *Degree requirements:* For master's, comprehensive exam, internship, practicum; for CAGS, comprehensive exam, practicum. *Entrance requirements:* For master's, bachelor's degree with minimum GPA of 3.0, 3 letters of recommendation, official transcripts, personal statement, current resume, interview; for CAGS, master's degree in counseling or closely-related field, 3 letters of recommendation, official transcripts, personal statement, current resume, interview. Additional exam requirements/recommendations for international students: Required—TOEFL (minimum score 540 paper-based; 76 iBT), IELTS (minimum score 6). *Application deadline:* Applications are processed on a rolling basis. Application fee: $30. Electronic applications accepted. *Expenses: Tuition:* Full-time $11,610; part-time $645 per credit. *Required fees:* $70 per term. Tuition and fees vary according to course load and program. *Financial support:* In 2016-17, 8 students received support. Tuition waivers (full and partial), unspecified assistantships, and institutional discounts available. Financial award applicants required to submit FAFSA. *Faculty research:* Low dose stress reduction interventions for elementary school teachers. *Unit head:* Dr. Susan Scully-Hill, Interim Director, 508-767-7319, Fax: 508-798-2872, E-mail: sscully@assumption.edu. *Application contact:* Karen Stoyanoff, Director of Recruitment for Graduate Enrollment, 508-767-7442, Fax: 508-799-4915, E-mail: graduate@assumption.edu.
Website: http://graduate.assumption.edu/school-counseling/masterofarts

**Azusa Pacific University,** School of Education, Department of School Counseling and School Psychology, Program in Educational Psychology, Azusa, CA 91702-7000. Offers MA. *Accreditation:* APA.

**Ball State University,** Graduate School, Teachers College, Department of Educational Psychology, Program in School Psychology, Muncie, IN 47306. Offers MA, PhD, Ed S. *Accreditation:* APA (one or more programs are accredited); NCATE. *Program availability:* Part-time. *Degree requirements:* For doctorate, thesis/dissertation; for Ed S, thesis. *Entrance requirements:* For doctorate, GRE General Test, interview, minimum graduate GPA of 3.2; for Ed S, GRE General Test. Additional exam requirements/recommendations for international students: Required—TOEFL (minimum score 550 paper-based; 79 iBT), IELTS (minimum score 6.5). Electronic applications accepted.

**Barry University,** College of Arts and Sciences, Department of Psychology, Miami Shores, FL 33161-6695. Offers clinical psychology (MS); school psychology (MS, SSP). *Program availability:* Part-time, evening/weekend. *Degree requirements:* For master's, thesis, practicum. *Entrance requirements:* For master's, GRE General Test, minimum GPA of 3.0, course work in psychology. Electronic applications accepted. *Faculty research:* Closed head injury, memory and aging, infant/mother interaction, evolutionary aspects of behavior, gender roles.

**Baylor University,** Graduate School, School of Education, Department of Educational Psychology, Waco, TX 76798. Offers applied behavior analysis (MS Ed); educational psychology (MA, MS Ed, PhD); exceptionalities (PhD); gifted and talented studies (MS Ed); learning and development (PhD); measurement (PhD); quantitative methods (MA); school psychology (Ed S). *Accreditation:* NCATE. *Faculty:* 11 full-time (6 women). *Students:* 48 full-time (42 women), 17 part-time (15 women); includes 15 minority (4 Black or African American, non-Hispanic/Latino; 2 Asian, non-Hispanic/Latino; 8 Hispanic/Latino; 1 Two or more races, non-Hispanic/Latino), 2 international. Average age 29. 90 applicants, 33% accepted, 30 enrolled. In 2016, 13 master's, 4 doctorates, 7 other advanced degrees awarded. Terminal master's awarded for partial completion of doctoral program. *Degree requirements:* For master's, thesis optional; for doctorate, comprehensive exam, thesis/dissertation; for Ed S, comprehensive exam, thesis or alternative. *Entrance requirements:* For master's, GRE, minimum GPA of 3.0; for doctorate, GRE General Test, master's degree; for Ed S, GRE General Test. Additional exam requirements/recommendations for international students: Required—TOEFL (minimum score 550 paper-based; 80 iBT), IELTS (minimum score 6.5). *Application deadline:* For fall admission, 2/1 priority date for domestic and international students. Application fee: $80. Electronic applications accepted. *Expenses: Tuition:* Full-time $28,494; part-time $1583 per credit hour. *Required fees:* $167 per credit hour. Tuition and fees vary according to course load and program. *Financial support:* In 2016-17, 42 students received support, including 20 fellowships with full and partial tuition reimbursements available, 22 research assistantships with full and partial tuition reimbursements available; career-related internships or fieldwork, Federal Work-Study, institutionally sponsored loans, scholarships/grants, health care benefits, tuition waivers (full and partial), unspecified assistantships, and stipends also available. Financial award application deadline: 2/1; financial award applicants required to submit FAFSA. *Faculty research:* Individual differences, quantitative methods, gifted and talented, special education, school psychology, autism, applied behavior analysis, learning, human development. *Total annual research expenditures:* $300,000. *Unit head:* Dr. Terrill F. Saxon, Professor and Chairman, 254-710-6101, E-mail: terrill_saxon@baylor.edu. *Application contact:* Heather Tindle, Office Manager, 254-710-3112, E-mail: heather_tindle@baylor.edu.
Website: http://www.baylor.edu/soe/EDP/

**Bloomsburg University of Pennsylvania,** School of Graduate Studies, College of Education, Department of Teaching and Learning, Program in Educational Leadership, Bloomsburg, PA 17815-1301. Offers college student affairs (M Ed); PreK-12 curriculum and instruction (M Ed); PreK-12 school counseling (M Ed); PreK-12 school principal (M Ed). *Faculty:* 6 full-time (2 women), 1 (woman) part-time/adjunct. *Students:* 64 full-time (42 women), 39 part-time (26 women); includes 18 minority (8 Black or African American, non-Hispanic/Latino; 4 Asian, non-Hispanic/Latino; 3 Hispanic/Latino; 1 Native Hawaiian or other Pacific Islander, non-Hispanic/Latino; 2 Two or more races, non-Hispanic/Latino), 1 international. Average age 27. 87 applicants, 60% accepted, 43 enrolled. In 2016, 39 master's awarded. *Degree requirements:* For master's, practicum. *Entrance requirements:* For master's, 3 letters of recommendation, resume, minimum QPA of 3.0, personal statement, interview. Additional exam requirements/recommendations for international students: Required—TOEFL, IELTS. Application fee: $35 ($60 for international students). Electronic applications accepted. *Expenses:* Tuition, state resident: full-time $9660; part-time $483 per credit. Tuition, nonresident: full-time $14,500; part-time $725 per credit. *Required fees:* $2410; $107 per credit. $75 per term. Tuition and fees vary according to course load, degree level and program. *Financial support:* Federal Work-Study and unspecified assistantships available. Financial award applicants required to submit FAFSA. *Unit head:* Dr. Ingrid Everett, Program Coordinator, 570-389-5120, Fax: 570-389-3030, E-mail: ieverett@bloomu.edu. *Application contact:* Jennifer Kessler, Administrative Assistant, 570-389-4015, Fax: 570-389-3054, E-mail: jkessler@bloomu.edu.

**Brigham Young University,** Graduate Studies, David O. McKay School of Education, Department of Counseling Psychology and Special Education, Provo, UT 84602. Offers counseling psychology (PhD); school psychology (Ed S); special education (MS). *Program availability:* Part-time, evening/weekend. *Faculty:* 13 full-time (3 women), 9 part-time/adjunct (3 women). *Students:* 66 full-time (45 women), 15 part-time (14 women); includes 8 minority (1 Black or African American, non-Hispanic/Latino; 2 American Indian or Alaska Native, non-Hispanic/Latino; 4 Hispanic/Latino; 1 Native Hawaiian or other Pacific Islander, non-Hispanic/Latino), 4 international. Average age 29. 73 applicants, 42% accepted, 27 enrolled. In 2016, 2 master's, 7 doctorates, 12 other advanced degrees awarded. *Degree requirements:* For master's and Ed S, comprehensive exam, thesis; for doctorate, comprehensive exam, thesis/dissertation. *Entrance requirements:* For master's, GRE General Test or MAT, minimum cumulative GPA of 3.0 in undergraduate coursework; for doctorate and Ed S, GRE General Test, minimum cumulative GPA of 3.0 in undergraduate coursework. Additional exam requirements/recommendations for international students: Required—TOEFL (minimum score 580 paper-based; 85 iBT), IELTS (minimum score 7). *Application deadline:* For fall admission, 1/15 for domestic and international students. Application fee: $50. Electronic applications accepted. *Expenses:* Contact institution. *Financial support:* In 2016–17, 51 students received support, including 51 research assistantships (averaging $9,000 per year); institutionally sponsored loans and tuition waivers (partial) also available. Financial award application deadline: 3/31. *Faculty research:* Autism, religious and spiritual values in counseling, school-based crisis intervention, behavior interventions in MTSS framework, counseling and psychotherapy process and outcomes. *Unit head:* Dr. Lane Fischer, Department Chair, 801-422-3857, E-mail: lane_fischer@byu.edu. *Application contact:* Diane E. Hancock, Executive Secretary, 801-422-3859, E-mail: diane_hancock@byu.edu.
Website: http://education.byu.edu/cpse/

**Brooklyn College of the City University of New York,** School of Education, Program in School Psychologist, Brooklyn, NY 11210-2889. Offers play therapy (AC); school psychologist (MS Ed). *Program availability:* Part-time, evening/weekend. *Degree requirements:* For master's, internship. *Entrance requirements:* For master's, interview, previous course work in education and psychology, teaching certificate, resume, 2 letters of recommendation. Additional exam requirements/recommendations for international students: Required—TOEFL (minimum score 500 paper-based; 61 iBT). Electronic applications accepted.

**Caldwell University,** Graduate Studies, Department of Psychology, Caldwell, NJ 07006-6195. Offers art therapy (MA); counseling (MA), including art therapy, mental health, school counseling; director of school counseling (Post-Master's Certificate); professional counselor (Post-Master's Certificate); school counselor (Post-Master's Certificate). *Accreditation:* ACA. *Program availability:* Part-time, evening/weekend. *Degree requirements:* For master's, comprehensive exam. *Entrance requirements:* For master's, GRE or MAT, interview. Electronic applications accepted. *Faculty research:* Counseling, school counseling, art therapy.

**California Baptist University,** Program in School Psychology, Riverside, CA 92504-3206. Offers MS. *Program availability:* Part-time, evening/weekend. *Faculty:* 2 full-time (both women), 5 part-time/adjunct (3 women). *Students:* 23 full-time (all women), 23 part-time (21 women); includes 23 minority (3 Black or African American, non-Hispanic/Latino; 3 Asian, non-Hispanic/Latino; 17 Hispanic/Latino). Average age 31. 43 applicants, 67% accepted, 26 enrolled. In 2016, 9 master's awarded. *Degree requirements:* For master's, 450 hours of introductory fieldwork, 1200 hours of field experience/internship, PRAXIS. *Entrance requirements:* For master's, CBEST, minimum GPA of 3.0, completion of prerequisites with minimum C grade, three letters of recommendation, 500-word essay. Additional exam requirements/recommendations for international students: Required—TOEFL (minimum score 80 iBT). *Application deadline:* For fall admission, 7/1 priority date for domestic and international students; for spring admission, 12/1 priority date for domestic students, 11/1 priority date for international students. Applications are processed on a rolling basis. Application fee: $45. Electronic applications accepted. *Expenses:* Contact institution. *Financial support:* In 2016–17, 16 students received support. Federal Work-Study and scholarships/grants available. Financial award applicants required to submit CSS PROFILE or FAFSA. *Faculty research:* Cultural competence, learning handicapped, cognitive development, school neuropsychology, behavioral assessment. *Unit head:* Dr. John Shoup, Dean, School of Education, 951-343-4205, E-mail: jshoup@calbaptist.edu. *Application contact:* Dr. Jane McGuire, Program Coordinator, School Psychology, 951-343-4707, E-mail: jmcguire@calbaptiat.edu.
Website: http://www.calbaptist.edu/academics/schools-colleges/school-education/programs/graduate/master-science-school-psychology/

**California State University, Chico,** Office of Graduate Studies, College of Behavioral and Social Sciences, Department of Psychology, Program in Applied/School Psychology, Chico, CA 95929-0722. Offers MA. *Students:* 20 full-time (14 women); includes 9 minority (2 Black or African American, non-Hispanic/Latino; 1 Asian, non-Hispanic/Latino; 4 Hispanic/Latino; 2 Two or more races, non-Hispanic/Latino). 43 applicants, 49% accepted, 8 enrolled. *Degree requirements:* For master's, thesis or comprehensive exam. *Entrance requirements:* For master's, GRE General Test or MAT, 3 letters of recommendation, statement of purpose. Additional exam requirements/recommendations for international students: Required—TOEFL (minimum score 550 paper-based; 80 iBT), IELTS (minimum score 6.5), PTE. *Application deadline:* For fall admission, 3/1 for domestic and international students. Application fee: $55. Electronic applications accepted. *Financial support:* Application deadline: 3/1; applicants required to submit FAFSA. *Unit head:* Dr. Brian Oppy, Chair, 530-898-4609, Fax: 530-898-4740, E-mail: psy@csuchico.edu. *Application contact:* Judy L. Morris, Graduate Admissions Coordinator, 530-898-5416, Fax: 530-898-3342, E-mail: jlmorris@csuchico.edu.
Website: http://www.csuchico.edu/psy/graduate/appliedPsy.shtml

**California State University, Dominguez Hills,** College of Education, Division of Graduate Education, Program in Counseling, Carson, CA 90747-0001. Offers college counseling (MS); school counseling (MS). *Program availability:* Part-time, evening/weekend. *Degree requirements:* For master's, comprehensive exam. *Entrance requirements:* For master's, minimum GPA of 3.0. Additional exam requirements/recommendations for international students: Required—TOEFL. *Faculty research:* Social development.

**California State University, East Bay,** Office of Graduate Studies, College of Education and Allied Studies, Department of Educational Psychology, Counseling Program, Hayward, CA 94542-3000. Offers marriage and family therapy (MS); school counseling (MS); school psychology (MS). *Accreditation:* NCATE. *Students:* 104 full-time (85 women), 2 part-time (both women); includes 54 minority (3 Black or African American, non-Hispanic/Latino; 15 Asian, non-Hispanic/Latino; 26 Hispanic/Latino; 10 Two or more races, non-Hispanic/Latino), 1 international. Average age 29. 178 applicants, 34% accepted, 50 enrolled. In 2016, 42 master's awarded. *Degree requirements:* For master's, comprehensive exam, project or thesis. *Entrance requirements:* For master's, GRE or MAT, interview, minimum GPA of 2.5 during previous 2 years of course work. Additional exam requirements/recommendations for international students: Required—TOEFL (minimum score 550 paper-based). *Application deadline:* For fall admission, 6/30 for domestic and international students.

Application fee: $55. Electronic applications accepted. *Financial support:* Career-related internships or fieldwork, Federal Work-Study, and institutionally sponsored loans available. Support available to part-time students. Financial award application deadline: 3/2; financial award applicants required to submit FAFSA. *Unit head:* Dr. Jack Davis, Chair, Educational Psychology, 510-885-3011, Fax: 510-885-4642, E-mail: jack.davis@csueastbay.edu. *Application contact:* Prof. Greg Jennings, Graduate Coordinator, 510-885-2296, Fax: 510-885-4642, E-mail: greg.jennings@csueastbay.edu.
Website: http://www20.csueastbay.edu/ceas/departments/epsy/

**California State University, Fresno,** Division of Research and Graduate Studies, College of Science and Mathematics, Department of Psychology, Fresno, CA 93740-8027. Offers applied behavior analysis (MA); general/experimental psychology (MA); school psychology (Ed S). *Degree requirements:* For master's, thesis. *Entrance requirements:* For master's, GRE General Test, GRE Subject Test, minimum GPA of 3.0. Additional exam requirements/recommendations for international students: Required—TOEFL. *Application deadline:* For fall admission, 5/1 for domestic and international students; for spring admission, 10/1 for domestic and international students. Applications are processed on a rolling basis. Application fee: $55. Electronic applications accepted. *Financial support:* Teaching assistantships, career-related internships or fieldwork, Federal Work-Study, scholarships/grants, and unspecified assistantships available. Support available to part-time students. Financial award application deadline: 3/1; financial award applicants required to submit FAFSA. *Faculty research:* Oncology prediction, parenting stress, wellness, aging and memory, retrieval inhibition, anger, minority mental health. *Unit head:* Dr. Constance Jones, Chair, 559-278-2691, Fax: 559-278-7910, E-mail: conniej@csufresno.edu. *Application contact:* Dr. Marilyn Wilson, Ed S Program Coordinator, 559-278-5129, Fax: 559-278-7910, E-mail: marilynw@csufresno.edu.
Website: http://www.fresnostate.edu/csm/psych/

**California State University, Los Angeles,** Graduate Studies, Charter College of Education, Division of Special Education and Counseling, Los Angeles, CA 90032-8530. Offers counseling (MS), including applied behavior analysis, community college counseling, rehabilitation counseling, school counseling, school psychology; special education (MA, PhD). *Accreditation:* ACA. *Program availability:* Part-time, evening/weekend. *Entrance requirements:* For master's, minimum GPA of 2.75 in last 90 units of course work, teaching certificate. Additional exam requirements/recommendations for international students: Required—TOEFL (minimum score 500 paper-based). Electronic applications accepted.

**California State University, Northridge,** Graduate Studies, Michael D. Eisner College of Education, Department of Educational Psychology and Counseling, Northridge, CA 91330. Offers counseling (MS), including career counseling, college counseling and student services, marriage and family therapy, school counseling, school psychology; educational psychology (MA Ed), including development, learning, and instruction, early childhood education. *Accreditation:* ACA (one or more programs are accredited); NCATE. *Program availability:* Part-time, evening/weekend. *Faculty:* 17 full-time (4 women), 46 part-time/adjunct (15 women). *Students:* 283 full-time (235 women), 79 part-time (72 women); includes 180 minority (8 Black or African American, non-Hispanic/Latino; 22 Asian, non-Hispanic/Latino; 132 Hispanic/Latino; 18 Two or more races, non-Hispanic/Latino), 13 international. Average age 29. 411 applicants, 36% accepted, 129 enrolled. *Entrance requirements:* For master's, GRE General Test or minimum GPA of 3.0. Additional exam requirements/recommendations for international students: Required—TOEFL. *Application deadline:* For fall admission, 11/30 for domestic students. Application fee: $55. *Expenses:* Tuition, state resident: full-time $4152. *Financial support:* Scholarships/grants available. Support available to part-time students. Financial award application deadline: 3/1. *Unit head:* Dr. Shari Tarver-Behring, Chair, 818-677-2599. *Application contact:* 818-677-3755.
Website: http://www.csun.edu/eisner-education/educational-psychology-counseling

**California State University, Sacramento,** Office of Graduate Studies, College of Education, Department of Graduate and Professional Studies in Education, Sacramento, CA 95819. Offers child development (MA); counseling (MS); curriculum and instruction (MA); education (Ed D); education leadership and policy studies (MA), including higher education, PreK-12; educational technology (MA); gender equity (MA); language and literacy (MA); multicultural education (MA); school psychology (MA); special education (MA); workforce development advocacy (MA). *Program availability:* Part-time. *Students:* 446 full-time (335 women), 125 part-time (97 women); includes 298 minority (39 Black or African American, non-Hispanic/Latino; 3 American Indian or Alaska Native, non-Hispanic/Latino; 97 Asian, non-Hispanic/Latino; 153 Hispanic/Latino; 6 Native Hawaiian or other Pacific Islander, non-Hispanic/Latino). Average age 32. 540 applicants, 76% accepted, 250 enrolled. In 2016, 107 master's, 7 doctorates awarded. *Degree requirements:* For master's, thesis or project; writing proficiency exam. *Entrance requirements:* For master's, minimum GPA of 2.5, 3.0 in last 60 units. Additional exam requirements/recommendations for international students: Required—TOEFL (minimum score 550 paper-based; 80 iBT). *Application deadline:* For fall admission, 2/15 for domestic students, 1/15 for international students. Applications are processed on a rolling basis. Application fee: $55. Electronic applications accepted. *Expenses:* $4,302 full-time tuition and fees per semester, $2,796 part-time. *Financial support:* Career-related internships or fieldwork and Federal Work-Study available. Support available to part-time students. Financial award application deadline: 3/1; financial award applicants required to submit FAFSA. *Unit head:* Dr. Susan Heredia, Chair, 916-278-5942, E-mail: coe@csus.edu. *Application contact:* Jose Martinez, Graduate Admissions Supervisor, 916-278-7871, E-mail: martinj@skymail.csus.edu.
Website: http://www.csus.edu/coe/academics/graduate/index.html

**California University of Pennsylvania,** School of Graduate Studies and Research, College of Liberal Arts, Program in School Psychology, California, PA 15419-1394. Offers MS. *Accreditation:* NCATE. *Program availability:* Part-time, evening/weekend. *Degree requirements:* For master's, comprehensive exam, thesis optional, internship. *Entrance requirements:* For master's, MAT or GRE, minimum GPA of 3.0, work experience in psychology, letters of reference. Additional exam requirements/recommendations for international students: Required—TOEFL (minimum score 550 paper-based; 80 iBT). Electronic applications accepted. *Expenses:* Tuition, state resident: full-time $11,592; part-time $483 per credit. Tuition, nonresident: full-time $17,400; part-time $725 per credit. *Required fees:* $3916. Tuition and fees vary according to course load, degree level, campus/location and reciprocity agreements.

**Cambridge College,** School of Education, Cambridge, MA 02138-5304. Offers autism specialist (M Ed); autism/behavior analyst (M Ed); behavior analyst (Post-Master's Certificate); behavioral management (M Ed); early childhood teacher (M Ed); education specialist in curriculum and instruction (CAGS); educational leadership (Ed D); elementary teacher (M Ed); English as a second language (M Ed, Certificate); general science (M Ed); health education (Post-Master's Certificate); health/family and consumer sciences (M Ed); history (M Ed); individualized (M Ed); information technology literacy (M Ed); instructional technology (M Ed); interdisciplinary studies (M Ed); library teacher (M Ed); literacy education (M Ed); mathematics (M Ed); mathematics specialist (Certificate); middle school mathematics and science (M Ed); school administration (M Ed, CAGS); school guidance counselor (M Ed); school nurse

*School Psychology*

education (M Ed); school social worker/school adjustment counselor (M Ed); special education administrator (CAGS); special education/moderate disabilities (M Ed); teaching skills and methodologies (M Ed). *Program availability:* Part-time, evening/weekend, online learning. *Degree requirements:* For master's, thesis, internship/practicum (licensure program only); for doctorate, thesis/dissertation; for other advanced degree, thesis. *Entrance requirements:* For master's, interview, resume, documentation of licensure, 2 professional references; for doctorate, official transcripts, interview, resume, documentation of licensure (if any), written personal statement/essay, portfolio of scholarly and professional work, qualifying assessment, 2 professional references, health insurance, immunizations form; for other advanced degree, official transcripts, interview, resume, documentation of licensure (if any), written personal statement/essay, 2 professional references, health insurance, immunizations form. Additional exam requirements/recommendations for international students: Required—TOEFL (minimum score 550 paper-based; 79 iBT), Michigan English Language Assessment Battery (minimum score 85); Recommended—IELTS (minimum score 6). Electronic applications accepted. *Expenses:* Contact institution. *Faculty research:* Adult education, accelerated learning, mathematics education, brain compatible learning, special education and law.

**Cambridge College,** School of Psychology and Counseling, Cambridge, MA 02138-5304. Offers addiction counseling (M Ed); alcohol and drug counseling (Certificate); counseling psychology (M Ed, CAGS); counseling psychology: forensic counseling (M Ed); marriage and family therapy (M Ed); mental health and addiction counseling (M Ed); mental health counseling (M Ed); mental health counseling for school guidance counselors (Post Master's Certificate); psychological studies (M Ed); school adjustment and mental health counseling (M Ed); school adjustment, mental health and addiction counseling (M Ed); school guidance counselor (M Ed); trauma studies (Certificate). *Program availability:* Part-time, evening/weekend. *Degree requirements:* For master's and other advanced degree, thesis, practicum/internship. *Entrance requirements:* For master's, resume, 2 professional references; for other advanced degree, official transcripts, documents for transfer credit evaluation, resume, written personal statement/essay, 2 professional references, health insurance, immunizations form. Additional exam requirements/recommendations for international students: Required—TOEFL (minimum score 550 paper-based; 79 iBT), Michigan English Language Assessment Battery (minimum score 85); Recommended—IELTS (minimum score 6). Electronic applications accepted. *Expenses:* Contact institution. *Faculty research:* Trauma, drug and alcohol counseling, cross-cultural issues, school counseling, trauma in schools.

**Canisius College,** Graduate Division, School of Education and Human Services, Programs in Counseling and Human Services, Buffalo, NY 14208-1098. Offers community mental health counseling (MS); counseling and human services (MS); school agency counseling (MS). *Accreditation:* ACA. *Program availability:* Part-time, evening/weekend. *Faculty:* 6 full-time (3 women), 10 part-time/adjunct (7 women). *Students:* 83 full-time (67 women), 39 part-time (33 women); includes 25 minority (13 Black or African American, non-Hispanic/Latino; 1 Asian, non-Hispanic/Latino; 6 Hispanic/Latino; 5 Two or more races, non-Hispanic/Latino), 5 international. Average age 26. 109 applicants, 86% accepted, 37 enrolled. In 2016, 48 master's awarded. *Degree requirements:* For master's, thesis, research project. *Entrance requirements:* For master's, GRE (if cumulative GPA less than 2.7), transcripts, two letters of recommendation, interview, BA. Additional exam requirements/recommendations for international students: Required—TOEFL (minimum score 550 paper-based, 79 iBT), IELTS (minimum score 6.5), or CAEL (minimum score 70). *Application deadline:* Applications are processed on a rolling basis. Application fee: $25. Electronic applications accepted. Application fee is waived when completed online. *Expenses: Tuition:* Full-time $14,742. *Required fees:* $724. *Financial support:* Career-related internships or fieldwork, Federal Work-Study, scholarships/grants, tuition waivers (partial), and unspecified assistantships available. Support available to part-time students. Financial award application deadline: 4/30; financial award applicants required to submit FAFSA. *Faculty research:* Impact of trauma on adults, long term psych-social impact on police officers. *Unit head:* Dr. Christine Moll, Chair, 716-888-3287, E-mail: moll@canisius.edu. *Application contact:* Kathleen B. Davis, Vice President of Enrollment Management, 716-888-2500, Fax: 716-888-3195, E-mail: daviskb@canisius.edu.
Website: http://www.canisius.edu/masters-counseling/

**Capella University,** Harold Abel School of Social and Behavioral Science, Doctoral Programs in Psychology, Minneapolis, MN 55402. Offers addiction psychology (PhD); clinical psychology (Psy D); educational psychology (PhD); general advanced studies in human behavior (PhD); general psychology (PhD); industrial/organizational psychology (PhD); school psychology (Psy D).

**Capella University,** Harold Abel School of Social and Behavioral Science, Master's Programs in Psychology, Minneapolis, MN 55402. Offers applied behavior analysis (MS); clinical psychology (MS); counseling psychology (MS); educational psychology (MS); evaluation, research, and measurement (MS); general advanced studies in human behavior (MS); general psychology (MS); industrial/organizational psychology (MS); leadership coaching psychology (MS); school psychology (MS); sport psychology (MS).

**Carlos Albizu University, Miami Campus,** Graduate Programs, Miami, FL 33172-2209. Offers clinical psychology (PhD, Psy D); entrepreneurship (MBA); exceptional student education (MS); human services (PhD); industrial/organizational psychology (MS); marriage and family therapy (MS); mental health counseling (MS); nonprofit management (MBA); organizational management (MBA); psychology (MS); school counseling (MS); speech and language pathology (MS); teaching English for speakers of other languages (MS). *Accreditation:* APA. *Program availability:* Part-time, evening/weekend, 100% online. *Faculty:* 28 full-time (22 women), 31 part-time/adjunct (19 women). *Students:* 475 full-time (396 women), 191 part-time (161 women); includes 560 minority (56 Black or African American, non-Hispanic/Latino; 1 American Indian or Alaska Native, non-Hispanic/Latino; 4 Asian, non-Hispanic/Latino; 494 Hispanic/Latino; 5 Two or more races, non-Hispanic/Latino), 15 international. Average age 34. 335 applicants, 46% accepted, 122 enrolled. In 2016, 143 master's, 48 doctorates awarded. Terminal master's awarded for partial completion of doctoral program. *Degree requirements:* For master's, comprehensive exam, integrative project (for MBA); research project (for exceptional student education, teaching English as a second language); for doctorate, comprehensive exam, thesis/dissertation, internship, project. *Entrance requirements:* For master's, 3 letters of recommendation, interview, minimum GPA of 3.0, resume, statement of purpose, official transcripts; for doctorate, 3 letters of recommendation, minimum GPA of 3.0, resume, interview, statement of purpose, official transcripts. Additional exam requirements/recommendations for international students: Required—Michigan Test of English Language Proficiency. *Application deadline:* For fall admission, 4/1 priority date for domestic students, 5/1 priority date for international students; for spring admission, 11/1 priority date for domestic students, 9/1 priority date for international students. Applications are processed on a rolling basis. Application fee: $50. Electronic applications accepted. *Expenses:* Contact institution. *Financial support:* In 2016–17, 131 students received support. Federal Work-Study, scholarships/grants, unspecified assistantships, and tuition discounts available. Financial award application deadline: 6/1; financial award applicants required to submit FAFSA. *Faculty research:*

Psychotherapy, forensic psychology, neuropsychology, marketing strategy, entrepreneurship, special education, speech-language pathology. *Unit head:* Dr. Etiony Aldarondo, Provost, 305-593-1223 Ext. 3138, Fax: 305-592-7930, E-mail: ealdarondo@albizu.edu. *Application contact:* Sonia Feliciano, Institutional Director of Student Recruitment, 305-593-1223 Ext. 3108, Fax: 305-477-8983, E-mail: sfeliciano@albizu.edu.

**Central Connecticut State University,** School of Graduate Studies, School of Education and Professional Studies, Department of Counselor Education and Family Therapy, New Britain, CT 06050-4010. Offers marriage and family therapy (MS); professional counseling (MS, AC, Certificate); school counseling (MS); student development in higher education (MS). *Accreditation:* AAMFT/COAMFTE; ACA. *Program availability:* Part-time, evening/weekend. *Faculty:* 10 full-time (5 women), 23 part-time/adjunct (21 women). *Students:* 157 full-time (120 women), 193 part-time (151 women); includes 99 minority (41 Black or African American, non-Hispanic/Latino; 3 Asian, non-Hispanic/Latino; 46 Hispanic/Latino; 9 Two or more races, non-Hispanic/Latino). Average age 39. 201 applicants, 64% accepted, 95 enrolled. In 2016, 96 master's, 7 other advanced degrees awarded. *Degree requirements:* For master's, comprehensive exam, thesis or alternative; for other advanced degree, qualifying exam. *Entrance requirements:* For master's, minimum undergraduate GPA of 2.7, essay, interview, letters of recommendation. Additional exam requirements/recommendations for international students: Required—TOEFL (minimum score 550 paper-based; 79 iBT). *Application deadline:* For fall admission, 3/1 for domestic and international students; for spring admission, 11/1 for domestic and international students. Applications are processed on a rolling basis. Application fee: $50. Electronic applications accepted. *Expenses: Tuition, area resident:* Full-time $6497; part-time $606 per credit. Tuition, state resident: full-time $9748; part-time $622 per credit. Tuition, nonresident: full-time $18,102; part-time $622 per credit. *Required fees:* $4459; $246 per credit. *Financial support:* In 2016–17, 46 students received support. Career-related internships or fieldwork, Federal Work-Study, scholarships/grants, and unspecified assistantships available. Support available to part-time students. Financial award application deadline: 3/1; financial award applicants required to submit FAFSA. *Faculty research:* Elementary and secondary school counseling, marriage and family therapy, rehabilitation counseling, counseling in higher educational settings. *Unit head:* Dr. Connie Tait, Chair, 860-832-2154, E-mail: taitc@ccsu.edu. *Application contact:* Patricia Gardner, Associate Director of Graduate Studies, 860-832-2350, Fax: 860-832-2362.
Website: http://www.ccsu.edu/ceft

**Central Michigan University,** College of Graduate Studies, College of Humanities and Social and Behavioral Sciences, Department of Psychology, Program in School Psychology, Mount Pleasant, MI 48859. Offers PhD; S Psy S. *Accreditation:* APA. *Degree requirements:* For doctorate, thesis/dissertation; for S Psy S, thesis. *Entrance requirements:* For doctorate, GRE. Electronic applications accepted. *Faculty research:* Psychology and education foundations, psychology and education assessment, intervention strategies.

**Central Washington University,** Graduate Studies and Research, College of the Sciences, Department of Psychology, Program in School Psychology, Ellensburg, WA 98926. Offers M Ed. *Degree requirements:* For master's, thesis or alternative, internship. *Entrance requirements:* For master's, GRE General Test, minimum GPA of 3.0. Additional exam requirements/recommendations for international students: Required—TOEFL (minimum score 550 paper-based; 79 iBT). Electronic applications accepted.

**Chaminade University of Honolulu,** Office of Professional and Continuing Education, Program in Counseling Psychology, Honolulu, HI 96816-1578. Offers marriage and family counseling (MSCP); mental health counseling (MSCP); school counseling (MSCP). *Program availability:* Part-time, evening/weekend, blended/hybrid learning. *Faculty:* 7 full-time (2 women), 15 part-time/adjunct (6 women). *Students:* 163 full-time (122 women), 44 part-time (35 women); includes 137 minority (15 Black or African American, non-Hispanic/Latino; 3 American Indian or Alaska Native, non-Hispanic/Latino; 58 Asian, non-Hispanic/Latino; 12 Hispanic/Latino; 48 Native Hawaiian or other Pacific Islander, non-Hispanic/Latino; 1 Two or more races, non-Hispanic/Latino), 2 international. Average age 31. 49 applicants, 98% accepted, 33 enrolled. In 2016, 70 master's awarded. *Degree requirements:* For master's, comprehensive exam, internship/practicum. *Entrance requirements:* For master's, minimum undergraduate GPA of 3.0, 3 letters of recommendation, resume, interview. Additional exam requirements/recommendations for international students: Required—TOEFL (minimum score 550 paper-based; 79 iBT). *Application deadline:* Applications are processed on a rolling basis. Application fee: $40. Electronic applications accepted. *Expenses:* $775 per credit hour plus $93 fee per online course. *Financial support:* Applications required to submit FAFSA. *Unit head:* Dr. Robert G. Santee, Dean, 808-735-4751, Fax: 808-739-4670, E-mail: mscp@chaminade.edu. *Application contact:* 808-735-4755, E-mail: gradserv@chaminade.edu.
Website: http://www.chaminade.edu/mscp

**Chapman University,** College of Educational Studies, Orange, CA 92866. Offers counseling (MA), including school counseling (MA, Credential); education (PhD), including cultural and curricular studies, disability studies, leadership studies, school psychology (PhD, Credential); educational psychology (MA); leadership development (MA); multiple subjects (Credential), including Spanish/English bilingual; pupil personnel services (Credential), including school counseling (MA, Credential), school psychology (PhD, Credential); school psychology (Ed S); single subject (Credential); special education (MA, Credential), including mild/moderate (Credential), moderate/severe (Credential); teaching (MA), including elementary education, secondary education, secondary music education. *Accreditation:* TEAC. *Program availability:* Part-time, evening/weekend. *Faculty:* 29 full-time (14 women), 36 part-time/adjunct (28 women). *Students:* 186 full-time (148 women), 186 part-time (134 women); includes 144 minority (9 Black or African American, non-Hispanic/Latino; 39 Asian, non-Hispanic/Latino; 78 Hispanic/Latino; 2 Native Hawaiian or other Pacific Islander, non-Hispanic/Latino; 16 Two or more races, non-Hispanic/Latino), 8 international. Average age 29. 143 applicants, 63% accepted, 64 enrolled. In 2016, 111 master's, 24 doctorates awarded. *Degree requirements:* For doctorate, thesis/dissertation. *Entrance requirements:* Additional exam requirements/recommendations for international students: Required—TOEFL (minimum score 550 paper-based, 80 iBT), IELTS (6.5), PTE Academic (53), or CAE. *Application deadline:* Applications are processed on a rolling basis. Application fee: $60. Electronic applications accepted. *Expenses:* Contact institution. *Financial support:* Fellowships and scholarships/grants available. Financial award application deadline: 3/2; financial award applicants required to submit FAFSA. *Unit head:* Dr. Margaret Grogan, Dean, 714-516-5968, E-mail: grogan@chapman.edu. *Application contact:* Sara Simon, Graduate Admission Counselor, 714-997-6770, E-mail: simon@chapman.edu.
Website: http://www.chapman.edu/CES/

**The Chicago School of Professional Psychology,** Program in School Psychology, Chicago, IL 60610. Offers Ed D, Ed S. *Program availability:* Part-time. *Entrance requirements:* For degree, GRE (recommended), minimum GPA of 3.2 (recommended); completion of one course in statistics or research methods and one course in psychology. Additional exam requirements/recommendations for international students: Required—TOEFL (minimum score 550 paper-based; 79 iBT).

**The Citadel, The Military College of South Carolina,** Citadel Graduate College, School of Humanities and Social Sciences, Department of Psychology, Charleston, SC 29409. Offers psychology (MA), including clinical counseling; school psychology (Ed S). *Program availability:* Part-time, evening/weekend. *Faculty:* 4 full-time (1 woman), 4 part-time/adjunct (3 women). *Students:* 50 full-time (41 women), 50 part-time (45 women); includes 14 minority (6 Black or African American, non-Hispanic/Latino; 5 Hispanic/Latino; 1 Native Hawaiian or other Pacific Islander, non-Hispanic/Latino; 2 Two or more races, non-Hispanic/Latino). In 2016, 20 master's, 9 other advanced degrees awarded. *Degree requirements:* For master's, comprehensive exam, practicum; internship (written and oral presentation of a case study as part of internship); for Ed S, comprehensive exam, thesis (for some programs), practicum, internship. *Entrance requirements:* For master's, GRE (minimum combined score of 297, 150 on verbal reasoning and 141 on quantitative reasoning) or MAT (minimum score of 410), minimum undergraduate GPA of 3.0; 12 credit hours in psychology or minimum score on GRE Subject Test in psychology of 600; 2 letters of recommendation; for Ed S, GRE (minimum combined score of 297, 150 on verbal reasoning and 147 on quantitative reasoning) or MAT (minimum score of 410), minimum undergraduate or graduate GPA of 3.0; 2 letters of recommendation. Additional exam requirements/recommendations for international students: Required—TOEFL (minimum score 550 paper-based; 79 iBT). *Application deadline:* Applications are processed on a rolling basis. Application fee: $40. Electronic applications accepted. *Expenses:* Tuition, state resident: full-time $5121; part-time $569 per credit hour. Tuition, nonresident: full-time $8613; part-time $957 per credit hour. *Required fees:* $90 per term. *Financial support:* Fellowships and unspecified assistantships available. Support available to part-time students. Financial award application deadline: 7/1; financial award applicants required to submit FAFSA. *Unit head:* Dr. Steve A. Nida, Department Head, 843-953-5320, E-mail: steve.nida@citadel.edu. *Application contact:* Dr. Genelle K. Sawyer, Director of the MA in Clinical Counseling Program, 843-953-5427, E-mail: genelle.sawyer@citadel.edu. Website: http://www.citadel.edu/root/psychology-graduateprograms

**The Citadel, The Military College of South Carolina,** Citadel Graduate College, Zucker Family School of Education, Charleston, SC 29409. Offers elementary/secondary school administration and supervision (M Ed); elementary/secondary school counseling (M Ed); interdisciplinary STEM education (M Ed); literacy education (M Ed, Graduate Certificate); middle grades (MAT), including English, mathematics, science, social studies; physical education (grades K-12) (MAT); school superintendency (Ed S); secondary education (MAT), including biology, English, mathematics, social studies; student affairs (Graduate Certificate); student affairs and college counseling (M Ed). *Accreditation:* NCATE. *Program availability:* Part-time, evening/weekend, 100% online, blended/hybrid learning. *Faculty:* 9 full-time (4 women), 9 part-time/adjunct (5 women). *Students:* 70 full-time (58 women), 249 part-time (200 women); includes 87 minority (70 Black or African American, non-Hispanic/Latino; 1 Asian, non-Hispanic/Latino; 9 Hispanic/Latino; 7 Two or more races, non-Hispanic/Latino), 2 international. 146 applicants, 98% accepted, 105 enrolled. In 2016, 85 master's, 7 other advanced degrees awarded. *Degree requirements:* For master's, comprehensive exam (for some programs). *Entrance requirements:* For master's, GRE (minimum combined verbal and quantitative score of 290) or MAT (minimum score 396). Additional exam requirements/recommendations for international students: Required—TOEFL (minimum score 550 paper-based; 79 iBT). *Application deadline:* Applications are processed on a rolling basis. Application fee: $40. Electronic applications accepted. *Expenses:* Tuition, state resident: full-time $5121; part-time $569 per credit hour. Tuition, nonresident: full-time $8613; part-time $957 per credit hour. *Required fees:* $90 per term. *Financial support:* Fellowships and unspecified assistantships available. Support available to part-time students. Financial award application deadline: 7/1; financial award applicants required to submit FAFSA. *Unit head:* Dr. Larry G. Daniel, Dean, 843-953-5097, E-mail: ldaniel@citadel.edu. *Application contact:* Dr. Tammy J. Graham, Associate Professor, 843-953-6854, E-mail: tammy.graham@citadel.edu. Website: http://www.citadel.edu/root/education-graduate-programs

**Clemson University,** Graduate School, College of Education, Department of Education and Human Development, Program in Counselor Education, Clemson, SC 29634. Offers counselor education (M Ed, Ed S), including clinical mental health counseling, school counseling. *Accreditation:* ACA; NCATE. *Program availability:* Part-time, evening/weekend. *Faculty:* 2 full-time (both women). *Students:* 142 full-time (114 women), 14 part-time (13 women); includes 39 minority (24 Black or African American, non-Hispanic/Latino; 4 Asian, non-Hispanic/Latino; 7 Hispanic/Latino; 4 Two or more races, non-Hispanic/Latino). Average age 26. 256 applicants, 46% accepted, 57 enrolled. In 2016, 73 master's, 38 Ed Ss awarded. *Degree requirements:* For master's, comprehensive exam. *Entrance requirements:* For master's, GRE General Test, unofficial transcripts, two letters of recommendation, essays. Additional exam requirements/recommendations for international students: Required—TOEFL (minimum score 80 iBT), IELTS (minimum score 6.5). *Application deadline:* For fall admission, 2/1 priority date for domestic and international students; for summer admission, 2/1 priority date for domestic and international students. Application fee: $80 ($90 for international students). Electronic applications accepted. *Expenses:* $4,027 per semester full-time resident, $8,013 per semester full-time non-resident, $437 per credit hour part-time resident, $874 per credit hour part-time non-resident. *Financial support:* Application deadline: 2/1. *Faculty research:* School counseling, disabilities, college readiness, transitions, counselor education. *Unit head:* Dr. Amy Milsom, Program Coordinator, 864-656-0927, E-mail: amilsom@clemson.edu. Website: http://www.clemson.edu/education/departments/education-human-development/academics/index.html

**The College of New Rochelle,** Graduate School, Division of Human Services, Program in School Psychology, New Rochelle, NY 10805-2308. Offers MS. *Degree requirements:* For master's, comprehensive exam, clinical fieldwork journal. *Entrance requirements:* For master's, interview, minimum GPA of 3.0, course work in psychology, sample of written work.

**College of St. Joseph,** Graduate Programs, Division of Psychology and Human Services, Program in School Guidance Counseling, Rutland, VT 05701-3899. Offers MS. *Program availability:* Part-time, evening/weekend. *Degree requirements:* For master's, comprehensive exam, thesis optional. *Entrance requirements:* For master's, PRAXIS I, official college transcripts; 2 letters of reference. Additional exam requirements/recommendations for international students: Required—TOEFL (minimum score 550 paper-based). *Application deadline:* Applications are processed on a rolling basis. Application fee: $35. Electronic applications accepted. *Expenses:* Tuition, area resident: Full-time $13,800; part-time $560 per credit. *Required fees:* $75 per semester. Full-time tuition and fees vary according to course load. *Financial support:* Unspecified assistantships available. Financial award application deadline: 3/1. *Unit head:* Dr. Craig Knapp, Chair, 802-773-5900 Ext. 3219, Fax: 802-776-5258, E-mail: cknapp@csj.edu. *Application contact:* Alan Young, Dean of Admissions, 802-773-5900 Ext. 3227, Fax: 802-776-5310, E-mail: alanyoung@csj.edu.

**The College of Saint Rose,** Grad Studies, Thelma P. Lally School of Education, Educational and School Psychology Programs, Albany, NY 12203-1419. Offers educational psychology (MS Ed, Certificate); school psychology (MS Ed). *Students:* 37 full-time (32 women), 9 part-time (6 women); includes 7 minority (1 Black or African American, non-Hispanic/Latino; 1 American Indian or Alaska Native, non-Hispanic/Latino; 1 Asian, non-Hispanic/Latino; 3 Hispanic/Latino; 1 Two or more races, non-Hispanic/Latino), 4 international. Average age 33. 47 applicants, 77% accepted, 21 enrolled. In 2016, 23 master's awarded. *Entrance requirements:* For master's, minimum undergraduate GPA of 3.0. Additional exam requirements/recommendations for international students: Required—TOEFL (minimum score 550 paper-based; 80 iBT), IELTS (minimum score 6), PTE (minimum score 56). *Application deadline:* For fall admission, 2/15 priority date for domestic and international students. Applications are processed on a rolling basis. Application fee: $40. Electronic applications accepted. *Expenses:* Tuition: Full-time $14,382; part-time $799 per credit. *Required fees:* $814; $32 per credit. $88 per semester. Tuition and fees vary according to course load. *Financial support:* Career-related internships or fieldwork, scholarships/grants, tuition waivers (partial), and unspecified assistantships available. Support available to part-time students. Financial award application deadline: 4/15. *Unit head:* Dr. Andrew Shanock, Chair, 518-337-5694, E-mail: shanocka@strose.edu. *Application contact:* Cris Murray, Assistant Vice President for Graduate Recruitment and Enrollment, 518-485-3390, Fax: 518-458-5479, E-mail: grad@strose.edu. Website: https://www.strose.edu/school-psychology/

**The College of William and Mary,** School of Education, Program in School Psychology, Williamsburg, VA 23187-8795. Offers M Ed, Ed S. *Accreditation:* NCATE. *Faculty:* 2 full-time (1 woman), 7 part-time/adjunct (6 women). *Students:* 9 full-time (8 women), 6 part-time (all women). Average age 26. 60 applicants, 43% accepted, 8 enrolled. In 2016, 9 Ed Ss awarded. *Degree requirements:* For Ed S, internship. *Entrance requirements:* For master's and Ed S, GRE, minimum GPA of 3.5. Additional exam requirements/recommendations for international students: Required—TOEFL (minimum score 100 iBT), IELTS (minimum score 7). *Application deadline:* For fall admission, 1/15 for domestic and international students. Application fee: $50. Electronic applications accepted. *Expenses:* $14,258 per year in-state full-time, $275 per credit in-state part-time; $30,500 per year out-of-state full-time, $1,200 per credit out-of-state part-time. *Financial support:* In 2016-17, 7 students received support, including 9 research assistantships (averaging $9,350 per year); scholarships/grants and unspecified assistantships also available. Financial award application deadline: 1/15; financial award applicants required to submit FAFSA. *Faculty research:* Assessment, diagnostic decision making, quantitative methods, multi-tiered interventions, behavioral interventions. *Unit head:* Dr. Ryan McGill, Assistant Professor, 757-221-6072, E-mail: rmcgill@wm.edu. *Application contact:* Dorothy Smith Osborne, Assistant Dean for Academic Programs and Student Services, 757-221-2317, E-mail: dsosbo@wm.edu. Website: http://education.wm.edu

**Creighton University,** Graduate School, College of Arts and Sciences, Department of Education, Program in School Counseling and Preventive Mental Health, Omaha, NE 68178-0001. Offers elementary school guidance (MS); secondary school guidance (MS). *Program availability:* Part-time, online only, 100% online, blended/hybrid learning. *Faculty:* 3 full-time (1 woman). *Students:* 12 full-time (10 women), 37 part-time (32 women); includes 1 minority (Asian, non-Hispanic/Latino). Average age 35. In 2016, 10 master's awarded. *Degree requirements:* For master's, comprehensive exam. *Entrance requirements:* For master's, resume, 3 letters of recommendation, personal statement, background check. Additional exam requirements/recommendations for international students: Required—TOEFL (minimum score 90 iBT). *Application deadline:* For fall admission, 7/1 for domestic students, 3/1 for international students; for winter admission, 10/1 for domestic students, 7/1 for international students; for spring admission, 3/1 for domestic students, 9/1 for international students; for summer admission, 3/1 for domestic and international students. Application fee: $50. Electronic applications accepted. *Expenses:* Tuition: Full-time $14,400; part-time $800 per credit hour. *Required fees:* $158 per semester. Tuition and fees vary according to course load, campus/location, program, reciprocity agreements and student's religious affiliation. *Financial support:* Scholarships/grants available. Support available to part-time students. Financial award applicants required to submit FAFSA. *Unit head:* Dr. Timothy Dickel, Professor of Education, 402-280-2230, E-mail: ctdickel@creighton.edu. *Application contact:* Lindsay Johnson, Director of Graduate and Adult Recruitment, 402-280-2703, Fax: 402-280-2423, E-mail: gradschool@creighton.edu.

**DePaul University,** College of Education, Chicago, IL 60614. Offers bilingual bicultural education (M Ed, MA); counseling (M Ed, MA), including clinical mental health counseling, college student development, school counseling; curriculum studies (M Ed, MA, Ed D); early childhood education (M Ed, MA, Ed D); educating adults (MA); educational leadership (M Ed, MA, Ed D), including administration and supervision (M Ed, MA), principal preparation (M Ed, MA); elementary education (MA); mathematics education (MA); mathematics for teaching (MS); middle school mathematics education (MS); reading specialist (M Ed, MA); secondary education (M Ed); social and cultural foundations in education (MA); special education (M Ed, MA); world languages education (M Ed, MA). *Program availability:* Part-time, evening/weekend, online learning. *Degree requirements:* For doctorate, thesis/dissertation. Electronic applications accepted.

**Duquesne University,** School of Education, Department of Counseling, Psychology, and Special Education, Program in School Psychology, Pittsburgh, PA 15282-0001. Offers child psychology (MS Ed). *Program availability:* Part-time, evening/weekend. *Faculty:* 8 full-time (5 women). *Students:* 87 full-time (75 women), 4 part-time (3 women); includes 5 minority (3 Black or African American, non-Hispanic/Latino; 1 Hispanic/Latino; 1 Two or more races, non-Hispanic/Latino), 2 international. Average age 27. 73 applicants, 78% accepted, 23 enrolled. In 2016, 22 master's, 14 doctorates awarded. *Degree requirements:* For master's, thesis optional; for doctorate, thesis/dissertation. *Entrance requirements:* For master's, bachelor's degree; for doctorate, GRE, letters of reference, letter of intent, interview, master's degree. Additional exam requirements/recommendations for international students: Required—TOEFL (minimum score 550 paper-based), IELTS (minimum score 7). *Application deadline:* For fall admission, 3/1 for domestic students; for spring admission, 9/1 for domestic students. Applications are processed on a rolling basis. Application fee: $0. Electronic applications accepted. *Expenses:* Tuition: Full-time $22,212; part-time $1234 per credit. Tuition and fees vary according to program. *Financial support:* Research assistantships and Federal Work-Study available. Support available to part-time students. *Unit head:* Dr. Ara Schmitt, Associate Professor, 412-396-1057, Fax: 412-396-1340, E-mail: schmitta2106@duq.edu. *Application contact:* Michael Dolinger, Director of Student and Academic Services, 412-396-6647, Fax: 412-396-5585, E-mail: dolingerm@duq.edu.

**Eastern Illinois University,** Graduate School, College of Sciences, Department of Psychology, Charleston, IL 61920. Offers clinical psychology (MA); school psychology (SSP). *Program availability:* Part-time, evening/weekend. *Degree requirements:* For master's, comprehensive exam, thesis; for SSP, thesis. *Entrance requirements:* For master's and SSP, GMAT or GRE. Additional exam requirements/recommendations for international students: Required—TOEFL (minimum score 500 paper-based; 61 iBT), IELTS (minimum score 6). Electronic applications accepted.

**Eastern Kentucky University,** The Graduate School, College of Arts and Sciences, Department of Psychology, Richmond, KY 40475-3102. Offers clinical psychology (MS);

industrial/organizational psychology (MS); school psychology (Psy S). *Program availability:* Part-time. *Entrance requirements:* For master's and Psy S, GRE General Test, minimum GPA of 2.5. *Faculty research:* Autism, social psychology, parenting, assessment of depression/anxiety, reading.

**Eastern University,** Department of Counseling Psychology, St. Davids, PA 19087-3696. Offers applied behavior analysis (MA, Certificate); counseling (MA); professional counseling (Certificate); school counseling (MA, Certificate); school psychology (MS, Certificate). *Program availability:* Part-time. *Students:* 104 full-time (92 women), 88 part-time (75 women); includes 83 minority (61 Black or African American, non-Hispanic/Latino; 1 American Indian or Alaska Native, non-Hispanic/Latino; 4 Asian, non-Hispanic/Latino; 13 Hispanic/Latino; 4 Two or more races, non-Hispanic/Latino), 3 international. Average age 29. In 2016, 46 master's awarded. *Degree requirements:* For master's, internship. *Entrance requirements:* Additional exam requirements/recommendations for international students: Required—TOEFL (minimum score 550 paper-based; 79 iBT). *Application deadline:* Applications are processed on a rolling basis. Application fee: $35. Electronic applications accepted. Application fee is waived when completed online. *Expenses:* $690 per credit. *Financial support:* Application deadline: 3/15. *Unit head:* Michael Dziedziak, Executive Director of Enrollment, 800-452-0996, E-mail: gpsadmissions@eastern.edu. Website: http://www.eastern.edu/academics/programs/graduate-counseling-and-psychology-department

**Eastern Washington University,** Graduate Studies, College of Social Sciences, Department of Psychology, Program in School Psychology, Cheney, WA 99004-2431. Offers Ed S. *Students:* 38 full-time (30 women), 25 part-time (18 women); includes 8 minority (4 Black or African American, non-Hispanic/Latino; 1 American Indian or Alaska Native, non-Hispanic/Latino; 1 Asian, non-Hispanic/Latino; 2 Hispanic/Latino), 2 international. Average age 34. 35 applicants, 46% accepted, 13 enrolled. *Entrance requirements:* Additional exam requirements/recommendations for international students: Required—TOEFL (minimum score 580 paper-based; 92 iBT), IELTS (minimum score 7), PTE (minimum score 63). *Application deadline:* Applications are processed on a rolling basis. Application fee: $75. Electronic applications accepted. *Expenses:* Tuition, state resident: full-time $11,000; part-time $5500 per credit. Tuition, nonresident: full-time $24,000; part-time $12,000 per credit. *Required fees:* $1300. One-time fee: $50 full-time. Part-time tuition and fees vary according to course load, campus/location and program. *Financial support:* In 2016–17, teaching assistantships with partial tuition reimbursements (averaging $10,000 per year) were awarded; career-related internships or fieldwork, Federal Work-Study, institutionally sponsored loans, scholarships/grants, tuition waivers (partial), and unspecified assistantships also available. Support available to part-time students. Financial award application deadline: 2/1; financial award applicants required to submit FAFSA. *Unit head:* Dr. Susan Ruby, Associate Professor/Director of School Psychology Program, 509-359-6050, Fax: 509-359-6325. *Application contact:* Kathy White, Advisor/Recruiter for Graduate Studies, 509-359-6297, Fax: 509-359-6044, E-mail: gradprograms@ewu.edu.

**Edinboro University of Pennsylvania,** Department of Counseling, School Psychology and Special Education, Edinboro, PA 16444. Offers counseling (MA), including art therapy, clinical mental health counseling, college counseling, rehabilitation counseling, school counseling; educational psychology (M Ed); school psychology (Ed S); special education (M Ed), including autism, behavior management. *Accreditation:* ACA. *Program availability:* Part-time, evening/weekend. *Degree requirements:* For master's, thesis or alternative, competency exam; for Ed S, thesis or alternative. *Entrance requirements:* For master's and Ed S, GRE or MAT, minimum QPA of 2.5. Electronic applications accepted.

**Emporia State University,** Program in School Psychology, Emporia, KS 66801-5415. Offers MS, Ed S. *Accreditation:* NCATE. *Program availability:* Part-time. *Faculty:* 8 full-time (4 women). *Students:* 22 full-time (18 women), 5 part-time (all women); includes 2 minority (1 Black or African American, non-Hispanic/Latino; 1 Two or more races, non-Hispanic/Latino), 1 international. 17 applicants, 100% accepted, 6 enrolled. In 2016, 5 master's, 4 other advanced degrees awarded. *Degree requirements:* For master's, comprehensive exam or thesis, internship; for Ed S, comprehensive exam, thesis or alternative, internship. *Entrance requirements:* For master's, GRE General Test or MAT, essay exam, appropriate bachelor's degree, teacher certification, letters of recommendation; for Ed S, GRE, essay exam, letters of recommendation, teacher certification. Additional exam requirements/recommendations for international students: Required—TOEFL (minimum score 520 paper-based; 68 iBT). *Application deadline:* For fall admission, 8/15 priority date for domestic students. Applications are processed on a rolling basis. Application fee: $30 ($75 for international students). Electronic applications accepted. *Expenses:* Tuition, state resident: full-time $5922; part-time $246.75 per credit hour. Tuition, nonresident: full-time $18,414; part-time $767.25 per credit hour. *Required fees:* $1884; $78.50 per credit hour. *Financial support:* In 2016–17, 4 teaching assistantships with full tuition reimbursements (averaging $7,335 per year) were awarded; career-related internships or fieldwork, Federal Work-Study, institutionally sponsored loans, health care benefits, and unspecified assistantships also available. Financial award application deadline: 3/15; financial award applicants required to submit FAFSA. *Unit head:* Dr. Jim Persinger, Chair, 620-341-5317, E-mail: jpersing@emporia.edu. *Application contact:* Mary Sewell, Admissions Coordinator, 800-950-GRAD, Fax: 620-341-5909, E-mail: msewell@emporia.edu.

**Evangel University,** School Counseling Program, Springfield, MO 65802. Offers MS. *Program availability:* Part-time, evening/weekend. *Faculty:* 4 full-time (3 women), 4 part-time/adjunct (all women). *Students:* 25 full-time (22 women), 20 part-time (15 women); includes 2 minority (both Black or African American, non-Hispanic/Latino). Average age 31. 12 applicants, 100% accepted, 12 enrolled. In 2016, 20 master's awarded. *Degree requirements:* For master's, comprehensive exam. *Entrance requirements:* For master's, MAT (preferred) or GRE. Additional exam requirements/recommendations for international students: Required—TOEFL (minimum score 550 paper-based). *Application deadline:* For fall admission, 7/15 priority date for domestic students, 7/1 for international students; for spring admission, 11/15 priority date for domestic students, 12/1 for international students. Applications are processed on a rolling basis. Application fee: $25. Electronic applications accepted. *Expenses:* Tuition: Part-time $400 per credit hour. *Required fees:* $148 per trimester. One-time fee: $25. Tuition and fees vary according to course load, degree level and program. *Financial support:* In 2016–17, 2 students received support. Unspecified assistantships available. Financial award application deadline: 4/1; financial award applicants required to submit FAFSA. *Unit head:* Christine Arnzen, Program Coordinator, 417-865-2815 Ext. 8678, Fax: 417-575-5484, E-mail: arnzenc@evangel.edu. *Application contact:* Karen Benitez, Admissions Representative, Graduate Studies, 417-865-2815 Ext. 7416, Fax: 417-575-5484, E-mail: benitezk@evangel.edu. Website: http://www.evangel.edu/academics/graduate-studies/graduate-programs

**Fairfield University,** Graduate School of Education and Allied Professions, Fairfield, CT 06824. Offers applied behavior analysis (ATC); applied psychology (MA); clinical mental health counseling (MA, CAS); educational technology (MA); elementary education (MA, CAS); family studies (MA); integration of spirituality and religion in counseling (ATC); marriage and family therapy (MA); reading and language development (Sixth Year Certificate); school counseling (MA, CAS); school psychology (MA, CAS); school-based marriage and family therapy (ATC); secondary education (MA); special education (MA, CAS); substance abuse counseling (ATC); teaching (Certificate); teaching and foundations (MA, CAS); TESOL, world languages, and bilingual education (MA, CAS). *Accreditation:* NCATE. *Program availability:* Part-time, evening/weekend. *Faculty:* 19 full-time (15 women), 38 part-time/adjunct (26 women). *Students:* 153 full-time (132 women), 302 part-time (252 women); includes 97 minority (24 Black or African American, non-Hispanic/Latino; 12 Asian, non-Hispanic/Latino; 55 Hispanic/Latino; 6 Two or more races, non-Hispanic/Latino), 6 international. Average age 32. 283 applicants, 61% accepted, 97 enrolled. In 2016, 130 master's awarded. *Degree requirements:* For master's, comprehensive exam. *Entrance requirements:* For master's, minimum GPA of 3.0, 2 recommendations, resume. Additional exam requirements/recommendations for international students: Required—TOEFL (minimum score 550 paper-based; 84 iBT) or IELTS (minimum score 7.5). *Application deadline:* For fall admission, 2/15 for international students; for spring admission, 10/1 for international students. Application fee: $60. Electronic applications accepted. *Expenses:* $725 per credit. *Financial support:* In 2016–17, 42 students received support. Career-related internships or fieldwork and unspecified assistantships available. Support available to part-time students. Financial award applicants required to submit FAFSA. *Faculty research:* Reading and literacy, writing, social justice and inequality in education, addictions and mental health issues, therapeutic relationships and clinical supervision. *Unit head:* Dr. Robert D. Hannafin, Dean, 203-254-4250, Fax: 203-254-4241, E-mail: rhannafin@fairfield.edu. *Application contact:* Marianne Gumpper, Director of Graduate Admission, 203-254-4184, Fax: 203-254-4073, E-mail: gradadmis@fairfield.edu. Website: http://www.fairfield.edu/gseap

**Fairleigh Dickinson University, Metropolitan Campus,** University College: Arts, Sciences, and Professional Studies, School of Psychology, Program in School Psychology, Teaneck, NJ 07666-1914. Offers MA, Psy D.

**Florida International University,** College of Arts, Sciences, and Education, Department of Leadership and Professional Studies, Miami, FL 33199. Offers adult education and human resource development (MS, Ed D); counseling (MS), including rehabilitation counseling, school counseling; counselor education (MS), including clinical mental health counseling; educational administration and supervision (Ed D); educational leadership (MS, Certificate, Ed S); higher education (Ed D); higher education administration (MS); international and comparative education (MS); recreation and sport management (MS), including recreation and sport management, recreational therapy; school psychology (Ed S); urban education (MS), including instruction in urban settings, learning technologies, multicultural/bilingual, multicultural/TESOL, urban education. *Program availability:* Part-time, evening/weekend. *Faculty:* 51 full-time (19 women), 38 part-time/adjunct (25 women). *Students:* 253 full-time (191 women), 306 part-time (241 women); includes 444 minority (129 Black or African American, non-Hispanic/Latino; 3 Asian, non-Hispanic/Latino; 304 Hispanic/Latino; 8 Two or more races, non-Hispanic/Latino), 18 international. Average age 31. 366 applicants, 60% accepted, 115 enrolled. In 2016, 193 master's, 8 doctorates awarded. *Degree requirements:* For doctorate, thesis/dissertation. *Entrance requirements:* For master's, minimum GPA of 3.0; for doctorate and other advanced degree, GRE General Test. Additional exam requirements/recommendations for international students: Required—TOEFL (minimum score 550 paper-based; 80 iBT), IELTS (minimum score 6.3). *Application deadline:* For fall admission, 6/1 priority date for domestic students, 4/1 for international students; for winter admission, 10/1 priority date for domestic students, 9/1 for international students; for spring admission, 3/1 priority date for domestic students, 2/1 for international students. Applications are processed on a rolling basis. Application fee: $30. Electronic applications accepted. *Expenses:* Tuition, state resident: full-time $8912; part-time $446 per credit hour. Tuition, nonresident: full-time $21,393; part-time $992 per credit hour. *Required fees:* $2185; $195 per semester. Tuition and fees vary according to program. *Financial support:* Fellowships, research assistantships with tuition reimbursements, teaching assistantships with tuition reimbursements, Federal Work-Study, and tuition waivers (full and partial) available. Support available to part-time students. Financial award applicants required to submit FAFSA. *Unit head:* Dr. Benjamin Baez, Chair, 305-348-3214, Fax: 305-348-1515, E-mail: benjamin.baez@fiu.edu. *Application contact:* Nanett Rojas, Assistant Director, Graduate Admissions, 305-348-7464, Fax: 305-348-7441, E-mail: gradadm@fiu.edu. Website: http://education.fiu.edu

**Florida State University,** The Graduate School, College of Education, Program in Counseling Psychology and School Psychology, Tallahassee, FL 32306. Offers PhD. *Degree requirements:* For doctorate, comprehensive exam, thesis/dissertation, diagnostic exam, preliminary exam, prospectus defense, dissertation defense. *Entrance requirements:* For doctorate, GRE General Test, minimum upper-division GPA of 3.0. Additional exam requirements/recommendations for international students: Required—TOEFL (minimum score 550 paper-based, 80 iBT), IELTS (minimum score 6.5), Michigan English Language Assessment Battery (minimum score 77), or PTE (minimum score 55). Application fee: $30. Electronic applications accepted. *Expenses:* Tuition, state resident: full-time $7263; part-time $403.51 per credit hour. Tuition, nonresident: full-time $18,087; part-time $1004.85 per credit hour. *Required fees:* $1365; $75.81 per credit hour. $20 per semester. Tuition and fees vary according to campus/location. *Financial support:* Fellowships, research assistantships, teaching assistantships, scholarships/grants, tuition waivers (full and partial), and unspecified assistantships available. Financial award application deadline: 1/15; financial award applicants required to submit FAFSA. *Faculty research:* Vocational behavior and career services; disability issues; trauma and suicide; cognitive, social-emotional, behavioral assessment; multicultural, diversity and social justice. *Unit head:* Dr. Deb Ebener, Associate Professor/Program Coordinator, 850-644-1789, Fax: 850-644-8776, E-mail: debener@fsu.edu. *Application contact:* Samantha DeZerga, Academic Program Specialist, 850-644-8046, Fax: 850-644-8776, E-mail: sdezerga@fsu.edu. Website: http://education.fsu.edu/degrees-and-programs/counseling-psychology-and-school-psychology

**Fordham University,** Graduate School of Education, Division of Psychological and Educational Services, New York, NY 10023. Offers counseling and personnel services (MSE); counseling psychology (PhD); school psychology (PhD). *Accreditation:* APA (one or more programs are accredited); NCATE. *Program availability:* Part-time, evening/weekend. Terminal master's awarded for partial completion of doctoral program. *Degree requirements:* For master's, comprehensive exam (for some programs); for doctorate, comprehensive exam (for some programs), thesis/dissertation. *Entrance requirements:* For doctorate, GRE General Test. Additional exam requirements/recommendations for international students: Required—TOEFL (minimum score 577 paper-based; 90 iBT), IELTS (minimum score 7). Electronic applications accepted.

**Fort Hays State University,** Graduate School, College of Arts and Sciences, Department of Psychology, Program in School Psychology, Hays, KS 67601-4099. Offers Ed S. *Accreditation:* NCATE. *Degree requirements:* For Ed S, comprehensive exam, thesis. *Entrance requirements:* Additional exam requirements/recommendations for international students: Required—TOEFL (minimum score 550 paper-based). Electronic applications accepted.

**Francis Marion University,** Graduate Programs, Department of Psychology, Florence, SC 29502-0547. Offers applied psychology (MS), including clinical/counseling psychology, school psychology; school psychology (SSP). *Program availability:* Part-time, evening/weekend. *Degree requirements:* For master's, internship. *Entrance requirements:* For master's, GRE General Test, official transcripts, two letters of recommendation. Additional exam requirements/recommendations for international students: Required—TOEFL (minimum score 550 paper-based; 79 iBT). *Expenses:* Tuition, state resident: full-time $10,100; part-time $505 per credit hour. Tuition, nonresident: full-time $20,196; part-time $1009.80 per credit hour. *Required fees:* $14.80 per credit hour. $73 per semester. Tuition and fees vary according to course load and program. *Faculty research:* Parenting and family relationships, child development, applied behavioral analysis, post-traumatic stress disorder, clinical psychology in adults.

**Fresno Pacific University,** Graduate Programs, School of Education, Division of Pupil Personnel Services, Program in School Psychology, Fresno, CA 93702-4709. Offers MA. *Program availability:* Part-time, evening/weekend. *Degree requirements:* For master's, thesis or alternative. *Entrance requirements:* Additional exam requirements/recommendations for international students: Required—TOEFL (minimum score 550 paper-based). *Expenses:* Contact institution.

**Gallaudet University,** The Graduate School, Washington, DC 20002-3625. Offers American Sign Language/English bilingual early childhood deaf education: birth to 5 (Certificate); audiology (Au D); clinical psychology (PhD); deaf and hard of hearing infants, toddlers, and their families (Certificate); deaf education (MA, Ed S); deaf history (Certificate); deaf studies (Certificate); educating deaf students with disabilities (Certificate); education: teacher preparation (MA), including deaf education, early childhood education and deaf education, elementary education and deaf education, secondary education and deaf education; educational neuroscience (PhD); hearing, speech and language sciences (MS, PhD); international development (MA); interpretation (MA, PhD), including combined interpreting practice and research (MA), interpreting research (MA); linguistics (MA, PhD); mental health counseling (MA); peer mentoring (Certificate); public administration (MPA); school counseling (MA); school psychology (Psy S); sign language teaching (MA); social work (MSW); speech-language pathology (MS). *Program availability:* Part-time. *Students:* 297 full-time (231 women), 129 part-time (97 women); includes 105 minority (35 Black or African American, non-Hispanic/Latino; 20 Asian, non-Hispanic/Latino; 39 Hispanic/Latino; 11 Two or more races, non-Hispanic/Latino), 22 international. Average age 30. 471 applicants, 52% accepted, 147 enrolled. In 2016, 138 master's, 25 doctorates, 14 other advanced degrees awarded. Terminal master's awarded for partial completion of doctoral program. *Degree requirements:* For master's, comprehensive exam (for some programs), thesis optional; for doctorate, comprehensive exam, thesis/dissertation. *Entrance requirements:* For master's and doctorate, GRE General Test or MAT, letters of recommendation, interviews, goals statement, American Sign Language proficiency interview, written English competency. Additional exam requirements/recommendations for international students: Required—TOEFL. *Application deadline:* For fall admission, 2/15 for domestic students. Applications are processed on a rolling basis. Application fee: $75. Electronic applications accepted. *Expenses: Tuition:* Full-time $17,100; part-time $950 per credit hour. *Required fees:* $3725; $276 per semester. *Financial support:* Fellowships, research assistantships, teaching assistantships, career-related internships or fieldwork, Federal Work-Study, scholarships/grants, tuition waivers (partial), and unspecified assistantships available. Support available to part-time students. Financial award application deadline: 7/1; financial award applicants required to submit FAFSA. *Faculty research:* Signing math dictionaries, telecommunications access, cancer genetics, linguistics, visual language and visual learning, integrated quantum materials, deaf legal discourse, advance recruitment and retention in geosciences. *Unit head:* Dr. Gaurav Mathur, Dean, Graduate School and Continuing Studies, 202-250-2380, Fax: 202-651-5027, E-mail: gaurav.mathur@gallaudet.edu. *Application contact:* Wednesday Luria, Coordinator of Prospective Graduate Student Services, 202-651-5400, Fax: 202-651-5295, E-mail: graduate.school@gallaudet.edu.

**Gardner-Webb University,** Graduate School, School of Psychology, Program in School Counseling, Boiling Springs, NC 28017. Offers MA. *Accreditation:* NCATE. *Program availability:* Part-time, evening/weekend. *Faculty:* 5 full-time (4 women), 4 part-time/adjunct (2 women). *Students:* 21 part-time (19 women); includes 3 minority (2 Black or African American, non-Hispanic/Latino; 1 Hispanic/Latino). Average age 27. 36 applicants, 31% accepted, 11 enrolled. In 2016, 2 master's awarded. *Degree requirements:* For master's, comprehensive exam. *Entrance requirements:* For master's, GRE General Test, MAT, minimum GPA of 2.7. *Application deadline:* For fall admission, 7/1 priority date for domestic students. Applications are processed on a rolling basis. Electronic applications accepted. *Expenses:* Contact institution. *Financial support:* Unspecified assistantships available. *Unit head:* Dr. David Carscaddon, Coordinator, 704-406-4437, Fax: 704-406-4329, E-mail: ppartin@gardner-webb.edu. *Application contact:* Office of Graduate Admissions, 877-498-4723, Fax: 704-406-3895, E-mail: gradinfo@gardner-webb.edu.

**George Fox University,** College of Education, Graduate Department of Counseling, Newberg, OR 97132-2697. Offers clinical mental health counseling (MA); marriage, couple and family counseling (MA, Certificate); school counseling (MA, Certificate); school psychology (Ed S). *Program availability:* Part-time. *Degree requirements:* For master's, clinical project. *Entrance requirements:* For master's, MAT or GRE, bachelor's degree from regionally-accredited college or university, minimum cumulative GPA of 3.0, 1 professional and 1 academic reference, resume, on-campus interview, official transcripts. Additional exam requirements/recommendations for international students: Required—TOEFL (minimum score 577 paper-based; 90 iBT), IELTS (minimum score 7). Electronic applications accepted. *Expenses:* Contact institution.

**Georgian Court University,** School of Arts and Sciences, Lakewood, NJ 08701-2697. Offers applied behavior analysis (MA); clinical mental health counseling (MA); holistic health studies (MA, Certificate); homeland security (MS, Certificate); mercy spirituality (Certificate); parish business management (Certificate); professional counselor (Certificate); school psychology (MA, Certificate); theology (MA, Certificate). *Program availability:* Part-time, evening/weekend. *Faculty:* 19 full-time (11 women), 6 part-time/adjunct (3 women). *Students:* 90 full-time (75 women), 107 part-time (79 women); includes 34 minority (9 Black or African American, non-Hispanic/Latino; 20 Hispanic/Latino; 5 Two or more races, non-Hispanic/Latino), 1 international. Average age 34. 187 applicants, 49% accepted, 60 enrolled. In 2016, 66 master's, 17 other advanced degrees awarded. *Degree requirements:* For master's, comprehensive exam (for some programs), thesis (for some programs). *Entrance requirements:* For master's, GRE, GMAT, or NTE/PRAXIS, 3 letters of recommendation. Additional exam requirements/recommendations for international students: Required—TOEFL (minimum score 550 paper-based). *Application deadline:* For fall admission, 8/15 for domestic students, 5/1 for international students; for spring admission, 1/15 for domestic students, 10/1 for international students. Applications are processed on a rolling basis. Application fee: $40. Electronic applications accepted. *Expenses: Tuition:* Full-time $15,079; part-time $839 per credit. *Required fees:* $968; $496 per credit. Tuition and fees vary according to campus/location and program. *Financial support:* Scholarships/grants, health care benefits, and unspecified assistantships available. Financial award application deadline: 4/15; financial award applicants required to submit FAFSA. *Unit head:* Dr. Mary Chinery,

Dean, 732-987-2493, Fax: 732-987-2007, E-mail: mchinery@georgian.edu. *Application contact:* Patrick Givens, Director of Graduate and Professional Studies Admissions, 732-987-2736, Fax: 732-987-2000, E-mail: gps@georgian.edu. Website: http://georgian.edu/academics/school-of-arts-sciences/

**Georgia Southern University,** Jack N. Averitt College of Graduate Studies, College of Education, Department of Leadership, Technology, and Human Development, Program in School Psychology, Statesboro, GA 30460. Offers M Ed, Ed S. *Accreditation:* NCATE. *Program availability:* Part-time, evening/weekend. *Students:* 40 full-time (38 women), 9 part-time (8 women); includes 16 minority (15 Black or African American, non-Hispanic/Latino; 1 Hispanic/Latino). Average age 26. 27 applicants, 74% accepted, 13 enrolled. In 2016, 7 master's, 3 Ed Ss awarded. *Degree requirements:* For Ed S, comprehensive exam. *Entrance requirements:* For degree, GRE General Test or MAT, minimum graduate GPA of 3.25, letters of reference, interview. Additional exam requirements/recommendations for international students: Required—TOEFL (minimum score 550 paper-based; 80 iBT), IELTS (minimum score 6). *Application deadline:* For fall admission, 4/10 for domestic students, 3/1 priority date for international students; for spring admission, 11/10 for domestic students, 10/1 for international students. Application fee: $50. Electronic applications accepted. *Expenses:* Tuition, state resident: full-time $7236; part-time $277 per semester hour. Tuition, nonresident: full-time $27,118; part-time $1105 per semester hour. *Required fees:* $2092. *Financial support:* In 2016–17, 12 students received support, including 3 fellowships with full tuition reimbursements available (averaging $7,750 per year); research assistantships with partial tuition reimbursements available, teaching assistantships with partial tuition reimbursements available, career-related internships or fieldwork, Federal Work-Study, scholarships/grants, tuition waivers (full), and unspecified assistantships also available. Support available to part-time students. Financial award application deadline: 4/15; financial award applicants required to submit FAFSA. *Faculty research:* K-12 online learning as it applies to school psychology, supervision, training in school psychology, cyber bullying. *Unit head:* Dr. Dawn Tysinger, Coordinator, 912-478-5792, Fax: 912-478-7104, E-mail: dtysinger@georgiasouthern.edu. *Application contact:* Lydia Cross, Coordinator for Graduate Student Recruitment, 912-478-8664, E-mail: lcross@georgiasouthern.edu. Website: http://coe.georgiasouthern.edu/espy/

**Georgia State University,** College of Education and Human Development, Department of Counseling and Psychological Services, Program in School Psychology, Atlanta, GA 30302-3083. Offers M Ed, PhD, Ed S. *Accreditation:* APA (one or more programs are accredited); NCATE. Terminal master's awarded for partial completion of doctoral program. *Degree requirements:* For master's and Ed S, comprehensive exam; for doctorate, comprehensive exam, thesis/dissertation. *Entrance requirements:* For master's and doctorate, GRE, writing sample, resume, 3 letters of recommendation, goal statement, transcripts. Additional exam requirements/recommendations for international students: Required—TOEFL. *Application deadline:* For fall admission, 12/1 for domestic and international students. Application fee: $50. Electronic applications accepted. *Expenses:* Tuition, state resident: full-time $6876; part-time $382 per credit hour. Tuition, nonresident: full-time $22,374; part-time $1243 per credit hour. *Required fees:* $2128; $1064 per term. Part-time tuition and fees vary according to course load and program. *Financial support:* Fellowships with full tuition reimbursements, research assistantships with tuition reimbursements, teaching assistantships with tuition reimbursements, career-related internships or fieldwork, institutionally sponsored loans, scholarships/grants, health care benefits, and unspecified assistantships available. Financial award application deadline: 4/1. *Faculty research:* School safety, school climate, and classroom management; alternative schools; children with disabilities; prevention of bullying, cyberbullying, and the commercial sexual exploitation of children; school psychology professional diversity. *Unit head:* Dr. Brian Dew, Chairperson, 404-413-8168, Fax: 404-413-8013, E-mail: bdew@gsu.edu. *Application contact:* Nancy Keita, Director, Office of Academic Assistance and Graduate Admissions, 404-413-8001, E-mail: nkeita@gsu.edu. Website: http://education.gsu.edu/CPS/4514.html

**Grand Valley State University,** College of Education, Program in School Counseling, Allendale, MI 49401-9403. Offers M Ed. *Program availability:* Part-time. *Students:* 14 full-time (11 women), 20 part-time (12 women); includes 3 minority (1 American Indian or Alaska Native, non-Hispanic/Latino; 1 Asian, non-Hispanic/Latino; 1 Hispanic/Latino), 1 international. Average age 31. 27 applicants, 89% accepted, 8 enrolled. In 2016, 13 master's awarded. *Degree requirements:* For master's, project or thesis. *Entrance requirements:* For master's, GRE General Test or minimum GPA of 3.0; last 60 credits from regionally-accredited college/university; 3 letters of recommendation. Additional exam requirements/recommendations for international students: Required—TOEFL (minimum score 550 paper-based, 80 iBT), IELTS (6.5), or Michigan English Language Assessment Battery. *Application deadline:* Applications are processed on a rolling basis. Application fee: $30. Electronic applications accepted. *Expenses:* $628 per credit hour. *Financial support:* In 2016–17, 4 students received support. Career-related internships or fieldwork and unspecified assistantships available. *Faculty research:* Multicultural issues in counselor education, use of technology in counseling programs. *Unit head:* Dr. Shawn Bultsma, Program Director, 616-331-6648, E-mail: bultsmas@gvsu.edu. *Application contact:* Thomas Owens, Director, Student Information and Services Center, 616-331-6282, Fax: 616-331-6217, E-mail: owenst@gvsu.edu.

**Grand Valley State University,** College of Liberal Arts and Sciences, Program in School Psychology, Allendale, MI 49401-9403. Offers MS, Psy S. *Program availability:* Part-time. *Faculty:* 3 full-time (all women). *Students:* 22 full-time (20 women), 18 part-time (14 women); includes 3 minority (2 Black or African American, non-Hispanic/Latino; 1 Two or more races, non-Hispanic/Latino). Average age 27. 55 applicants, 44% accepted, 16 enrolled. In 2016, 11 master's awarded. *Degree requirements:* For master's, project, internship. *Entrance requirements:* For master's, GRE, bachelor's degree in psychology, special education, or related field with minimum GPA of 3.0; completion of prerequisite courses in child development, statistics, and research methods; professional vitae or resume; 3 letters of recommendation; personal statement. Additional exam requirements/recommendations for international students: Required—TOEFL (minimum score 550 paper-based, 80 iBT), IELTS (6.5), or Michigan English Language Assessment Battery. *Application deadline:* For fall admission, 12/15 for domestic and international students. Applications are processed on a rolling basis. Application fee: $30. Electronic applications accepted. *Expenses:* $628 per credit hour. *Financial support:* In 2016–17, 8 students received support, including 1 fellowship, 8 research assistantships with full and partial tuition reimbursements available (averaging $8,000 per year); unspecified assistantships also available. *Unit head:* Dr. Robert Hendersen, Director, 616-331-2195, E-mail: hendersr@gvsu.edu. *Application contact:* Dr. Amy Campbell, Associate Director for Graduate Recruitment, 616-331-2409, Fax: 616-331-2480, E-mail: campbeam@gvsu.edu. Website: http://www.gvsu.edu/grad/schoolpsy

**Heidelberg University,** Master of Arts in Counseling Program, Tiffin, OH 44883-2462. Offers clinical mental health counseling (MA); school counseling (MA). *Accreditation:* ACA. *Program availability:* Part-time, evening/weekend. *Students:* 15 full-time (11 women), 31 part-time (26 women). In 2016, 12 master's awarded. *Degree requirements:* For master's, thesis or alternative, counseling practicum, internship. *Entrance*

## School Psychology

*requirements:* For master's, bachelor's degree, minimum GPA of 2.9, 12 hours of course work in behavioral sciences, 3 letters of reference, 2-3 page goal statement, background check, interview. Additional exam requirements/recommendations for international students: Required—TOEFL (minimum score 550 paper-based, 79 iBT) or IELTS (minimum score 6.5). *Application deadline:* Applications are processed on a rolling basis. Electronic applications accepted. *Expenses:* $510 per semester hour. *Financial support:* Applicants required to submit FAFSA. *Unit head:* Dr. Jo-Ann Lipford Sanders, Associate Dean and Director of Master of Arts in Counseling, 419-448-2312, E-mail: jsanders@heidelberg.edu. *Application contact:* Katie Slosser, Graduate Admissions Coordinator, 419-448-2602, Fax: 419-448-2565, E-mail: kslosser@heidelberg.edu. Website: https://www.heidelberg.edu/academics/programs/master-of-counseling

**Hofstra University,** College of Liberal Arts and Sciences, Programs in Psychology, Hempstead, NY 11549. Offers applied organizational psychology (PhD); clinical psychology (PhD); industrial/organizational psychology (MA); school-community psychology (Psy D). *Accreditation:* APA. *Program availability:* Part-time, evening/weekend. *Students:* 195 full-time (130 women), 32 part-time (18 women); includes 43 minority (9 Black or African American, non-Hispanic/Latino; 2 American Indian or Alaska Native, non-Hispanic/Latino; 8 Asian, non-Hispanic/Latino; 21 Hispanic/Latino; 2 Native Hawaiian or other Pacific Islander, non-Hispanic/Latino; 1 Two or more races, non-Hispanic/Latino), 21 international. Average age 27. 299 applicants, 40% accepted, 54 enrolled. In 2016, 51 master's, 36 doctorates awarded. *Degree requirements:* For master's, comprehensive exam, thesis optional, internship, minimum GPA of 3.0; for doctorate, comprehensive exam, thesis/dissertation, 1st year qualifying examination, 2nd year research project, successful practicum/externship placements, written presentation and successful oral defense of dissertation, completion of full-time internship. *Entrance requirements:* For master's, GRE General Test, minimum GPA of 3.0, essay, interview; for doctorate, GRE General Test, GRE Subject Test (psychology), 3 letters of recommendation, interview, essay, curriculum vitae. Additional exam requirements/recommendations for international students: Required—TOEFL (minimum score 550 paper-based; 80 iBT). *Application deadline:* For fall admission, 12/31 for domestic and international students. Application fee: $75. Electronic applications accepted. *Expenses: Tuition:* Full-time $1240. *Required fees:* $970. Tuition and fees vary according to program. *Financial support:* In 2016–17, 119 students received support, including 112 fellowships with full and partial tuition reimbursements available (averaging $8,418 per year), 4 research assistantships with full and partial tuition reimbursements available (averaging $5,940 per year); career-related internships or fieldwork, Federal Work-Study, institutionally sponsored loans, scholarships/grants, traineeships, tuition waivers (full and partial), and unspecified assistantships also available. Support available to part-time students. Financial award applicants required to submit FAFSA. *Faculty research:* PTSD, secondary trauma, childhood adjustment problems, the impact of exercise on emotional states treatment of anxiety disorders and depression, cognitive appraisal and emotion, evolutionary psychology - implications for clinical psychology (evolutionary psychopathology, theory of human nature), treatment of phobic and post-traumatic stress disorders with exposure therapies, self-help and motivational interviewing. *Unit head:* Dr. Craig Johnson, Chairperson, 516-463-5636, E-mail: craig.a.johnson@hofstra.edu. *Application contact:* Sunil Samuel, Assistant Vice President of Admissions, 516-463-4723, Fax: 516-463-4664, E-mail: graduateadmission@hofstra.edu.
Website: http://www.hofstra.edu/hclas

**Hood College,** Graduate School, Program in Counseling, Frederick, MD 21701-8575. Offers clinical mental health counseling (MS); school counseling (MS). *Program availability:* Part-time, evening/weekend. *Faculty:* 5 full-time, 2 part-time/adjunct. *Students:* 28 full-time (24 women), 15 part-time (all women); includes 5 minority (3 Black or African American, non-Hispanic/Latino; 2 Hispanic/Latino), 2 international. Average age 30. 41 applicants, 83% accepted, 24 enrolled. *Degree requirements:* For master's, practicum, internship. *Entrance requirements:* For master's, minimum GPA of 3.0, personal statement, resume, two letters of recommendation. Additional exam requirements/recommendations for international students: Required—TOEFL (minimum score 575 paper-based; 89 iBT), IELTS (minimum score 6.5). *Application deadline:* For fall admission, 6/15 for domestic and international students; for winter admission, 11/15 for domestic and international students. Application fee: $35. Electronic applications accepted. *Expenses:* $620 per credit hour; $110 comprehensive fee per semester. *Financial support:* Research assistantships with full tuition reimbursements, tuition waivers (partial), and unspecified assistantships available. Financial award applicants required to submit FAFSA. *Unit head:* April Boulton, Interim Dean of the Graduate School, 301-696-3600, E-mail: gofurther@hood.edu. *Application contact:* Jan Marcus, Assistant Director of Graduate Admissions, 301-696-3600, E-mail: gofurther@hood.edu.

**Houston Baptist University,** College of Education and Behavioral Sciences, Program in Psychology, Houston, TX 77074-3298. Offers school psychology (MAP). *Program availability:* Part-time, evening/weekend. *Students:* 42 full-time (38 women), 61 part-time (53 women); includes 67 minority (38 Black or African American, non-Hispanic/Latino; 8 Asian, non-Hispanic/Latino; 20 Hispanic/Latino; 1 Two or more races, non-Hispanic/Latino) 3 international. Average age 30. 162 applicants, 33% accepted, 26 enrolled. In 2016, 27 master's awarded. *Degree requirements:* For master's, comprehensive exam, thesis. *Entrance requirements:* For master's, GRE (waived with a cumulative GPA of 3.0 or higher), minimum GPA of 2.5, two recommendations, resume, bachelor's degree conferred transcript. Additional exam requirements/recommendations for international students: Required—TOEFL (minimum score 80 iBT), IELTS (minimum score 6.5). *Application deadline:* For fall admission, 8/1 for domestic students, 6/1 for international students; for spring admission, 1/1 for domestic students, 11/1 for international students; for summer admission, 5/1 for domestic students, 3/1 for international students. Applications are processed on a rolling basis. Application fee: $0 ($100 for international students). Electronic applications accepted. Application fee is waived when completed online. *Expenses:* $1,650 per 3-hour course; $1,275 annual general fee; $1,060 annual technology fee. *Financial support:* In 2016–17, 2 students received support. Federal Work-Study and scholarships/grants available. Support available to part-time students. Financial award application deadline: 4/1; financial award applicants required to submit FAFSA. *Faculty research:* Drug and alcohol abuse in relation to delinquency, mental health and school factors, chronic stress, coping strategies. *Unit head:* Dr. Renata Nero, Chair, 281-649-3171, Fax: 281-649-3361, E-mail: rnero@hbu.edu. *Application contact:* Victoria Humphreys, Administrative Assistant to the Dean, 281-649-3131, E-mail: vhumphreys@hbu.edu.
Website: http://www.hbu.edu/MAP

**Howard University,** School of Education, Department of Human Development and Psychoeducational Studies, Program in School Psychology, Washington, DC 20059-0002. Offers M Ed, PhD. *Accreditation:* NCATE. *Degree requirements:* For doctorate, one foreign language, comprehensive exam, thesis/dissertation, expository writing exam, internship. *Entrance requirements:* For doctorate, GRE General Test, minimum GPA of 3.4. Additional exam requirements/recommendations for international students: Required—TOEFL (minimum score 550 paper-based; 79 iBT). Electronic applications accepted. *Faculty research:* Psychopathology, maltreatment abuse and neglect, children exposed to political unrest, family conflict and community violence.

**Humboldt State University,** Academic Programs, College of Professional Studies, Department of Psychology, Arcata, CA 95521-8299. Offers psychology (MA), including biological psychology, counseling, developmental psychopathology, school psychology, social and environmental psychology. *Degree requirements:* For master's, thesis. *Entrance requirements:* For master's, appropriate bachelor's degree, minimum GPA of 2.5. Additional exam requirements/recommendations for international students: Required—TOEFL (minimum score 500 paper-based). *Expenses:* Tuition, state resident: full-time $6738; part-time $1953 per semester. Tuition, nonresident: full-time $13,434; part-time $3813 per semester. *Required fees:* $1738; $653 per semester. Tuition and fees vary according to program. *Faculty research:* School psychology, counseling, eating disorders, mood induction, depression.

**Husson University,** Graduate Programs in Counseling and Human Relations, Bangor, ME 04401-2999. Offers clinical mental health counseling (MS); human relations (MS); school counseling (MS). *Accreditation:* ACA. *Program availability:* Part-time, evening/weekend. *Faculty:* 3 full-time (2 women), 5 part-time/adjunct (all women). *Students:* 17 full-time (15 women), 55 part-time (48 women); includes 1 minority (Black or African American, non-Hispanic/Latino), 2 international. Average age 32. 50 applicants, 52% accepted, 20 enrolled. In 2016, 16 master's awarded. *Degree requirements:* For master's, comprehensive exam (for some programs), thesis optional. *Entrance requirements:* For master's, BS with minimum GPA of 3.0, letters of recommendation, interview. Additional exam requirements/recommendations for international students: Required—TOEFL (minimum score 550 paper-based; 80 iBT), IELTS (minimum score 6.5). *Application deadline:* For fall admission, 2/1 for domestic students. Application fee: $50. Electronic applications accepted. *Expenses:* $560 per credit tuition; $450 full-time fees, $220 part-time (6-9 credits), $110 part-time (less than 6 credits per year). *Financial support:* Federal Work-Study, scholarships/grants, and unspecified assistantships available. Financial award application deadline: 4/15; financial award applicants required to submit FAFSA. *Faculty research:* Challenges and rewards of counseling practice in rural, small town and neighborhood settings. *Unit head:* Dr. Deborah Drew, Director, Graduate Counseling Programs, 207-992-4912, Fax: 207-992-4952, E-mail: drewd@husson.edu. *Application contact:* Kristen Card, Director of Graduate Admissions, 207-404-5660, Fax: 207-941-7935, E-mail: cardk@husson.edu.
Website: http://www.husson.edu/college-of-health-and-education/school-of-education/graduate-programs/

**Idaho State University,** Office of Graduate Studies, College of Education, Department of School Psychology, Literacy, and Special Education, Pocatello, ID 83209-8059. Offers deaf education (M Ed); human exceptionality (M Ed); literacy (M Ed); school psychology (Ed S); special education (Ed S). *Program availability:* Part-time. *Degree requirements:* For master's, comprehensive exam, thesis (for some programs), oral thesis defense or written comprehensive exam and oral exam; for Ed S, comprehensive exam, thesis (for some programs), oral exam, specialist paper or portfolio. *Entrance requirements:* For master's, GRE or MAT, minimum undergraduate GPA of 3.0, bachelor's degree, professional experience in an educational context; for Ed S, GRE or MAT, master's degree in related field. Additional exam requirements/recommendations for international students: Required—TOEFL (minimum score 550 paper-based; 80 iBT). Electronic applications accepted. *Faculty research:* Literacy, school psychology, special education.

**Idaho State University,** Office of Graduate Studies, Kasiska College of Health Professions, Department of Counseling, Pocatello, ID 83209-8120. Offers counseling (M Coun, Ed S), including marriage and family counseling (M Coun), mental health counseling (M Coun), school counseling (M Coun), student affairs and college counseling (M Coun); counselor education and counseling (PhD). *Accreditation:* ACA (one or more programs are accredited). *Program availability:* Part-time. *Degree requirements:* For master's, comprehensive exam, thesis, 4 semesters resident graduate study, practicum/internship; for doctorate, comprehensive exam, thesis/dissertation, 3 semesters internship, 4 consecutive semesters doctoral-level study on campus; for Ed S, comprehensive exam, thesis, case studies, oral exam. *Entrance requirements:* For master's, GRE General Test, MAT, minimum GPA of 3.0, bachelors degree, interview, 3 letters of recommendation; for doctorate, GRE General Test, MAT, minimum graduate GPA of 3.0, resume, interview, counseling license, master's degree; for Ed S, GRE General Test, minimum graduate GPA of 3.0, master's degree in counseling, 3 letters of recommendation, 2 years work experience. Additional exam requirements/recommendations for international students: Required—TOEFL (minimum score 600 paper-based; 80 iBT). Electronic applications accepted. *Faculty research:* Group counseling, multicultural counseling, family counseling, child therapy, supervision.

**Illinois State University,** Graduate School, College of Arts and Sciences, Department of Psychology, Program in School Psychology, Normal, IL 61790-2200. Offers PhD, SSP. *Accreditation:* APA (one or more programs are accredited); NCATE (one or more programs are accredited). *Degree requirements:* For doctorate, variable foreign language requirement, thesis/dissertation, 2 terms of residency, internship, practicum. *Entrance requirements:* For doctorate, GRE General Test.

**Immaculata University,** College of Graduate Studies, Department of Psychology, Immaculata, PA 19345. Offers clinical mental health counseling (MA); clinical psychology (Psy D); forensic psychology (Graduate Certificate); integrative psychotherapy (Graduate Certificate); neuropsychology (Graduate Certificate); psychodynamic psychotherapy (Graduate Certificate); psychological testing (Graduate Certificate); school counseling (MA, Graduate Certificate); school psychology (MA). *Accreditation:* APA. *Program availability:* Part-time, evening/weekend. Terminal master's awarded for partial completion of doctoral program. *Degree requirements:* For master's, comprehensive exam, thesis optional; for doctorate, comprehensive exam, thesis/dissertation. *Entrance requirements:* For master's, GRE General Test or MAT, minimum GPA of 3.0; for doctorate, GRE General Test or MAT, minimum GPA of 3.5. Additional exam requirements/recommendations for international students: Required—TOEFL, IELTS. Electronic applications accepted. *Faculty research:* Supervision ethics, psychology of teaching, gender.

**Indiana State University,** College of Graduate and Professional Studies, Bayh College of Education, Department of Communication Disorders and Counseling, School, and Educational Psychology, Terre Haute, IN 47809. Offers clinical mental health counseling (MS); communication disorders (MS); school counseling (M Ed); school psychology (PhD, Ed S); MA/MS. *Accreditation:* ACA; ASHA; NCATE. *Program availability:* Part-time, evening/weekend. *Degree requirements:* For master's, thesis optional; for doctorate, thesis/dissertation, research tools proficiency tests. *Entrance requirements:* For master's, GRE General Test or MAT, minimum undergraduate GPA of 2.75; for doctorate, GRE General Test, master's degree, minimum undergraduate GPA of 3.5. Electronic applications accepted. *Faculty research:* Vocational development supervision.

**Indiana University Bloomington,** School of Education, Department of Counseling and Educational Psychology, Bloomington, IN 47405-1006. Offers counseling (MS, PhD, Ed S); counselor education (MS, Ed S); educational psychology (MS, PhD); inquiry methodology (PhD); learning and developmental sciences (MS, PhD); school psychology (PhD, Ed S). *Accreditation:* ACA (one or more programs are accredited); APA (one or more programs are accredited); NCATE. Terminal master's awarded for partial completion of doctoral program. *Degree requirements:* For master's, thesis optional; for doctorate, thesis/dissertation; for Ed S, comprehensive exam or project. *Entrance requirements:* For master's, doctorate, and Ed S, GRE General Test. Additional exam requirements/recommendations for international students: Required—TOEFL. Electronic applications accepted. *Faculty research:* Counseling psychology, inquiry methodology, school psychology, learning sciences, human development, educational psychology.

**Indiana University of Pennsylvania,** School of Graduate Studies and Research, College of Education and Educational Technology, Department of Educational and School Psychology, Program in School Psychology, Indiana, PA 15705. Offers D Ed, Certificate. *Accreditation:* NCATE. *Program availability:* Part-time, evening/weekend. *Faculty:* 8 full-time (3 women). *Students:* 13 full-time (9 women), 45 part-time (36 women); includes 5 minority (3 Black or African American, non-Hispanic/Latino; 1 Hispanic/Latino; 1 Two or more races, non-Hispanic/Latino). Average age 30. 36 applicants, 75% accepted, 18 enrolled. In 2016, 6 doctorates, 10 Certificates awarded. *Degree requirements:* For doctorate, comprehensive exam, thesis/dissertation. *Entrance requirements:* For doctorate, GRE General Test, PRAXIS II School Psychology Exam, 2 letters of recommendation. Additional exam requirements/recommendations for international students: Required—TOEFL (minimum score 540 paper-based). *Application deadline:* For fall admission, 2/1 priority date for domestic students. Applications are processed on a rolling basis. Application fee: $50. Electronic applications accepted. *Expenses:* Tuition, state resident: full-time $8694; part-time $483 per credit. Tuition, nonresident: full-time $13,050; part-time $725 per credit. *Required fees:* $157 per credit. $50 per term. Tuition and fees vary according to course load and program. *Financial support:* In 2016–17, 7 fellowships with full tuition reimbursements (averaging $607 per year), 3 teaching assistantships with partial tuition reimbursements (averaging $11,652 per year) were awarded; research assistantships with tuition reimbursements, career-related internships or fieldwork, Federal Work-Study, scholarships/grants, and unspecified assistantships also available. Support available to part-time students. Financial award application deadline: 4/15; financial award applicants required to submit FAFSA. *Unit head:* Dr. Joseph Kovaleski, Graduate Coordinator, 724-357-2316, E-mail: jkov@iup.edu.
Website: http://www.iup.edu/schoolpsychology/grad/school-psychology-ded/default.aspx

**Indiana University South Bend,** School of Education, South Bend, IN 46634-7111. Offers addiction counseling (MS Ed); alcohol and drug counseling (Graduate Certificate); clinical mental health counseling (MS Ed); educational leadership (MS Ed); elementary education (MS Ed); marriage, couple, and family counseling (MS Ed); school counseling (MS Ed); secondary education (MS Ed); special education (MAT, MS Ed), including intense intervention (MS Ed), mild intervention (MS Ed). *Accreditation:* NCATE. *Program availability:* Part-time, evening/weekend. *Faculty:* 21 full-time (11 women), 9 part-time/adjunct (3 women). *Students:* 26 full-time (19 women), 104 part-time (80 women); includes 22 minority (13 Black or African American, non-Hispanic/Latino; 5 Hispanic/Latino; 4 Two or more races, non-Hispanic/Latino). Average age 35. 51 applicants, 69% accepted, 22 enrolled. In 2016, 31 master's, 2 other advanced degrees awarded. *Degree requirements:* For master's, thesis or alternative, exit project. *Entrance requirements:* For master's, letters of recommendation, GRE or minimum GPA of 3.0. Additional exam requirements/recommendations for international students: Required—TOEFL. *Application deadline:* For fall admission, 7/1 for domestic students; for spring admission, 11/1 for domestic students. Applications are processed on a rolling basis. Application fee: $40 ($60 for international students). Electronic applications accepted. *Expenses:* $276.98 per credit hour in-state; $652.54 per credit hour out-of-state. *Financial support:* Career-related internships or fieldwork available. Support available to part-time students. Financial award application deadline: 3/1; financial award applicants required to submit FAFSA. *Faculty research:* Professional dispositions, early childhood literacy, online learning, program assessments, problem-based learning. *Unit head:* Dr. Marvin Lynn, Dean, 574-520-4339, E-mail: lynnm@iusb.edu. *Application contact:* Yvonne Walker, Student Services Representative, 574-520-4185, E-mail: ydwalker@iusb.edu.
Website: https://www.iusb.edu/education/index.php

**Inter American University of Puerto Rico, Metropolitan Campus,** Graduate Programs, Program in Psychology, San Juan, PR 00919-1293. Offers counseling psychology (MA, PhD); industrial/organizational psychology (MA, PhD); labor relations (MA); school psychology (MA, PhD). *Degree requirements:* For master's, comprehensive exam. *Entrance requirements:* For master's, GRE or EXADEP, interview. Electronic applications accepted.

**Inter American University of Puerto Rico, San Germán Campus,** Graduate Studies Center, Program in Psychology, San Germán, PR 00683-5008. Offers counseling psychology (MA, PhD); school psychology (MA, PhD). *Program availability:* Part-time, evening/weekend. *Degree requirements:* For master's, comprehensive exam, thesis; for doctorate, comprehensive exam, thesis/dissertation. *Entrance requirements:* For master's, GRE General Test or EXADEP, minimum GPA of 3.0; for doctorate, GRE, EXADEP or MAT, minimum GPA of 3.0.

**Iona College,** School of Arts and Science, Department of Psychology, New Rochelle, NY 10801-1890. Offers general-experimental psychology (MA); human resources (Certificate); industrial-organizational psychology (MA); mental health counseling (MA); organizational behavior (Certificate); psychology (MA); school psychology (MA). *Program availability:* Part-time. *Faculty:* 9 full-time (5 women), 6 part-time/adjunct (5 women). *Students:* 61 full-time (42 women), 32 part-time (23 women); includes 40 minority (8 Black or African American, non-Hispanic/Latino; 3 Asian, non-Hispanic/Latino; 28 Hispanic/Latino; 1 Two or more races, non-Hispanic/Latino), 2 international. Average age 25. 91 applicants, 80% accepted, 37 enrolled. In 2016, 18 master's awarded. *Degree requirements:* For master's, thesis (for some programs), literature review (for some programs). *Entrance requirements:* For master's, BA in psychology including 3 credits each in psychology statistics and experimental research methods, or 9 credits in psychology including 3 credits in psychology statistics, 3 credits in psychology research methods and 3 credits of upper-level coursework. Additional exam requirements/recommendations for international students: Required—TOEFL (minimum score 550 paper-based), IELTS (minimum score 6.5). *Application deadline:* For fall admission, 8/15 for domestic students, 5/1 for international students; for spring admission, 1/15 for domestic students, 9/1 for international students. Applications are processed on a rolling basis. Application fee: $50. Electronic applications accepted. *Expenses: Tuition:* Full-time $19,692; part-time $1094 per credit. *Required fees:* $245 per term. Tuition and fees vary according to program. *Financial support:* In 2016–17, 49 students received support. Research assistantships with partial tuition reimbursements available, tuition waivers (partial), and unspecified assistantships available. Support available to part-time students. Financial award application deadline: 4/15; financial award applicants required to submit FAFSA. *Faculty research:* Non-suicidal self-injury, trauma response, performance appraisal and evaluation, diversity infusion, assessment and treatment of sexual offenders. *Unit head:* Patricia Oswald, PhD, Chair, 914-633-2374, E-mail: poswald@iona.edu. *Application contact:* Katelyn Brunck, Assistant Director, Graduate Admissions, 914-633-2451, Fax: 914-633-2277, E-mail: kbrunck@iona.edu.

Website: http://www.iona.edu/Academics/School-of-Arts-Science/Departments/Psychology/Graduate-Programs.aspx

**Jackson State University,** Graduate School, College of Education and Human Development, Department of Counseling, Rehabilitation and Psychometric Services, Jackson, MS 39217. Offers clinical mental health (MS); rehabilitation counseling (MS); school counseling (MS Ed). *Accreditation:* ACA; CORE (one or more programs are accredited); NCATE. *Program availability:* Part-time, evening/weekend, 100% online, blended/hybrid learning. *Faculty:* 9 full-time (6 women), 1 part-time/adjunct (0 women). *Students:* 48 full-time (7 women), 82 part-time (74 women); includes 121 minority (118 Black or African American, non-Hispanic/Latino; 1 American Indian or Alaska Native, non-Hispanic/Latino; 1 Hispanic/Latino; 1 Two or more races, non-Hispanic/Latino). Average age 37. 106 applicants, 64% accepted, 47 enrolled. In 2016, 26 master's awarded. *Degree requirements:* For master's, comprehensive exam, thesis. *Entrance requirements:* For master's, GRE General Test. Additional exam requirements/recommendations for international students: Required—TOEFL (minimum score 520 paper-based; 67 iBT). *Application deadline:* For fall admission, 3/1 priority date for domestic students, 2/1 for international students; for spring admission, 10/1 for domestic and international students. Applications are processed on a rolling basis. Application fee: $25. Electronic applications accepted. *Expenses:* Contact institution. *Financial support:* Career-related internships or fieldwork, Federal Work-Study, scholarships/grants, and unspecified assistantships available. Support available to part-time students. Financial award application deadline: 3/1; financial award applicants required to submit FAFSA. *Unit head:* Dr. Dion Porter, Chair, 601-979-3364, Fax: 601-979-2213, E-mail: dion.porter@jsums.edu. *Application contact:* Dr. Dion Porter, Chair, 601-979-3364, Fax: 601-979-2213, E-mail: dion.porter@jsums.edu.
Website: http://www.jsums.edu/commcounseling/

**James Madison University,** The Graduate School, College of Health and Behavioral Sciences, Program in Combined-Integrated Clinical and School Psychology, Harrisonburg, VA 22807. Offers Psy D. *Program availability:* Part-time, evening/weekend. *Students:* 23 full-time (17 women), 1 (woman) part-time; includes 2 minority (1 Black or African American, non-Hispanic/Latino; 1 Hispanic/Latino), 3 international. Average age 30. 32 applicants, 19% accepted, 6 enrolled. In 2016, 5 doctorates awarded. Application fee: $55. Electronic applications accepted. *Financial support:* In 2016–17, 1 fellowship was awarded; teaching assistantships, Federal Work-Study, unspecified assistantships, and 17 doctoral assistantships (stipend varies) also available. Financial award application deadline: 3/1; financial award applicants required to submit FAFSA. *Unit head:* Dr. Gregg R. Henriques, Graduate Program Director, 540-568-7857, E-mail: henrigg@jmu.edu. *Application contact:* Lynette D. Michael, Director of Graduate Admissions, 540-568-6131 Ext. 6395, Fax: 540-568-7860, E-mail: michaeld@jmu.edu.
Website: http://www.psyc.jmu.edu/cipsyd/

**James Madison University,** The Graduate School, College of Health and Behavioral Sciences, Program in School Psychology, Harrisonburg, VA 22807. Offers MA, Ed S. *Accreditation:* APA (one or more programs are accredited); NCATE (one or more programs are accredited). *Program availability:* Part-time, evening/weekend. *Students:* 17 full-time (13 women), 8 part-time (5 women); includes 6 minority (4 Black or African American, non-Hispanic/Latino; 1 Hispanic/Latino; 1 Two or more races, non-Hispanic/Latino), 1 international. Average age 30. 68 applicants, 25% accepted, 10 enrolled. In 2016, 8 master's, 9 other advanced degrees awarded. Application fee: $55. Electronic applications accepted. *Financial support:* In 2016–17, 2 fellowships, 1 teaching assistantship with full tuition reimbursement (averaging $9,284 per year) were awarded; career-related internships or fieldwork, Federal Work-Study, and 15 assistantships (averaging $7911) also available. Financial award application deadline: 3/1; financial award applicants required to submit FAFSA. *Unit head:* Dr. Tammy D. Gilligan, Graduate Program Director, 540-568-6564, E-mail: gilligtd@jmu.edu. *Application contact:* Lynette D. Michael, Director of Graduate Admissions, 540-568-6131 Ext. 6395, Fax: 540-568-7860, E-mail: michaeld@jmu.edu.
Website: http://psyc.jmu.edu/school/

**Johnson State College,** Program in Counseling, Johnson, VT 05656. Offers addictions counseling (MA); clinical mental health counseling (MA); general counseling (MA); school counseling (MA). *Program availability:* Part-time. *Degree requirements:* For master's, comprehensive exam. *Entrance requirements:* For master's, interview. Additional exam requirements/recommendations for international students: Required—TOEFL. *Application deadline:* For fall admission, 7/1 for domestic students, 2/1 for international students; for spring admission, 11/1 for domestic students, 7/1 for international students; for summer admission, 4/1 for domestic students. Applications are processed on a rolling basis. Electronic applications accepted. Application fee is waived when completed online. *Expenses: Tuition,* state resident: part-time $555 per credit. Tuition, nonresident: part-time $800 per credit. *Financial support:* Career-related internships or fieldwork and unspecified assistantships available. Support available to part-time students. Financial award application deadline: 3/1; financial award applicants required to submit FAFSA. *Unit head:* Dr. David Fink, Coordinator, 802-635-1383, Fax: 802-635-1465, E-mail: david.fink@jsc.edu. *Application contact:* Catherine H. Higley, Administrative Assistant, 800-635-2356 Ext. 1244, Fax: 802-635-1248, E-mail: catherine.higley@jsc.edu.

**Kean University,** Nathan Weiss Graduate College, Program in Combined School and Clinical Psychology, Union, NJ 07083. Offers Psy D. *Program availability:* Part-time. *Faculty:* 6 full-time (3 women). *Students:* 35 full-time (28 women), 15 part-time (11 women); includes 16 minority (3 Black or African American, non-Hispanic/Latino; 3 Asian, non-Hispanic/Latino; 9 Hispanic/Latino; 1 Two or more races, non-Hispanic/Latino). Average age 27. 50 applicants, 22% accepted, 10 enrolled. In 2016, 8 doctorates awarded. *Degree requirements:* For doctorate, comprehensive exam, thesis/dissertation, externship. *Entrance requirements:* For doctorate, GRE General Test, GRE Subject Test in psychology (taken within last 5 years ), minimum undergraduate GPA of 3.3, graduate 3.5; 3 letters of recommendation; personal interview; prerequisite coursework in theories of personality, abnormal psychology, tests and measurements, statistics, and experimental psychology; personal statement. Additional exam requirements/recommendations for international students: Required—TOEFL (minimum score 550 paper-based; 79 iBT), IELTS (minimum score 6.5). *Application deadline:* For fall admission, 2/2 for domestic and international students. Applications are processed on a rolling basis. Application fee: $75. Electronic applications accepted. *Expenses:* Contact institution. *Financial support:* Scholarships/grants and unspecified assistantships available. Financial award applicants required to submit FAFSA. *Unit head:* Dr. Jennifer Block-Lerner, Program Coordinator, 908-737-5864, E-mail: jlerner@kean.edu. *Application contact:* Pedro Lopes, Admissions Counselor, 908-737-7100, E-mail: grad-adm@kean.edu.
Website: http://grad.kean.edu/doctoral-programs/combined-school-and-clinical-psychology

**Kean University,** Nathan Weiss Graduate College, Program in School Psychology, Union, NJ 07083. Offers Diploma. *Accreditation:* APA. *Program availability:* Part-time. *Faculty:* 6 full-time (4 women). *Students:* 23 full-time (20 women), 15 part-time (14 women); includes 10 minority (1 Asian, non-Hispanic/Latino; 9 Hispanic/Latino). Average age 24. In 2016, 9 Diplomas awarded. *Degree requirements:* For Diploma,

comprehensive exam, practicum, externship. *Entrance requirements:* For degree, GRE General Test, minimum GPA of 3.0, interview, 3 letters of recommendation, prerequisites in psychology, official transcripts from all institutions attended, resume. Additional exam requirements/recommendations for international students: Required—TOEFL (minimum score 550 paper-based; 79 iBT), IELTS. *Application deadline:* For fall admission, 3/2 for domestic and international students. Application fee: $75. Electronic applications accepted. *Expenses:* Tuition, state resident: full-time $13,156; part-time $640 per credit. Tuition, nonresident: full-time $17,831; part-time $785 per credit. *Required fees:* $3316; $151 per credit. Tuition and fees vary according to course level, course load, degree level and program. *Financial support:* Scholarships/grants and unspecified assistantships available. Financial award applicants required to submit FAFSA. *Unit head:* Dr. Adrienne Garro, Program Coordinator, 908-737-5863, E-mail: agarro@kean.edu. *Application contact:* Pedro Lopes, Admissions Counselor, 908-737-7100, E-mail: grad-adm@kean.edu.
Website: http://grad.kean.edu/professional-diploma-programs/school-psychology

**Keene State College,** School of Professional and Graduate Studies, Keene, NH 03435. Offers curriculum and instruction (M Ed); education leadership (PMC); educational leadership (M Ed); safety and occupational health applied science (MS); school counselor (M Ed, PMC); special education (M Ed). *Accreditation:* NCATE. *Program availability:* Part-time, evening/weekend. *Faculty:* 9 full-time (4 women), 8 part-time/adjunct (3 women). *Students:* 24 full-time (17 women), 66 part-time (38 women); includes 3 minority (1 Black or African American, non-Hispanic/Latino; 1 Hispanic/Latino; 1 Two or more races, non-Hispanic/Latino), 1 international. Average age 33. 24 applicants, 100% accepted, 24 enrolled. In 2016, 26 master's, 1 other advanced degree awarded. *Degree requirements:* For master's, thesis (for some programs). *Entrance requirements:* For master's, PRAXIS I, 3 references; official transcripts; minimum GPA of 2.5; interview; essay; teacher/educator certificate; work/internship experience. Additional exam requirements/recommendations for international students: Required—TOEFL (minimum score 550 paper-based; 61 iBT). *Application deadline:* For fall admission, 4/1 for domestic and international students; for spring admission, 11/1 for domestic and international students; for summer admission, 3/1 for domestic and international students. Applications are processed on a rolling basis. Application fee: $50. Electronic applications accepted. *Expenses:* Tuition, state resident: full-time $9180; part-time $510 per credit. Tuition, nonresident: full-time $10,080; part-time $560 per credit. *Required fees:* $1908; $510 per credit. Tuition and fees vary according to course load. *Financial support:* In 2016–17, 27 students received support. Career-related internships or fieldwork, Federal Work-Study, institutionally sponsored loans, scholarships/grants, and unspecified assistantships available. Support available to part-time students. Financial award application deadline: 3/1; financial award applicants required to submit FAFSA. *Unit head:* Dr. Karrie Kalich, Dean of Professional and Graduate Studies, 603-358-2885, E-mail: kkalich@keene.edu. *Application contact:* Peter Tandy, Assistant Director for Graduate Studies, 603-358-2332, E-mail: kscgraduatestudies@keene.edu.
Website: http://www.keene.edu/academics/graduate/

**Kent State University,** College of Education, Health and Human Services, School of Lifespan Development and Educational Sciences, Program in School Psychology, Kent, OH 44242-0001. Offers M Ed, PhD, Ed S. *Accreditation:* APA; NCATE. *Degree requirements:* For doctorate, comprehensive exam, thesis/dissertation. *Entrance requirements:* For master's, doctorate, and Ed S, GRE General Test, 2 letters of reference, goals statement, moral character form, sample of written work, resume, interview. Additional exam requirements/recommendations for international students: Required—TOEFL (minimum score 550 paper-based; 80 iBT). Electronic applications accepted. *Expenses:* Tuition, state resident: full-time $10,864; part-time $495 per credit hour. Tuition, nonresident: full-time $18,380; part-time $837 per credit hour. *Faculty research:* Special education policy and practice, treatment fidelity, school-based consultation.

**La Sierra University,** School of Education, Department of School Psychology and Counseling, Riverside, CA 92515. Offers counseling (MA); educational psychology (Ed S); school psychology (Ed S). *Program availability:* Part-time, evening/weekend. *Degree requirements:* For master's, thesis optional; for Ed S, practicum (educational psychology). *Entrance requirements:* For master's, California Basic Educational Skills Test, NTE, minimum GPA of 3.0; for Ed S, minimum GPA of 3.3. *Faculty research:* Equivalent score scales, self perception.

**Lehigh University,** College of Education, Program in School Psychology, Bethlehem, PA 18015. Offers PhD, Ed S. *Accreditation:* APA (one or more programs are accredited). *Program availability:* Part-time. *Faculty:* 6 full-time (5 women), 2 part-time/adjunct (0 women). *Students:* 29 full-time (27 women), 9 part-time (8 women); includes 1 minority (Black or African American, non-Hispanic/Latino). Average age 26. 58 applicants, 40% accepted, 8 enrolled. In 2016, 9 doctorates awarded. *Degree requirements:* For doctorate, comprehensive exam, thesis/dissertation, internship, research qualifying exam; for Ed S, comprehensive exam, internship. *Entrance requirements:* For doctorate and Ed S, GRE General Test, minimum GPA of 3.0, 2 letters of recommendation (at least one academic), transcripts, vitae. Additional exam requirements/recommendations for international students: Required—TOEFL (minimum score 93 iBT). *Application deadline:* For fall admission, 1/1 for domestic and international students. Application fee: $65. Electronic applications accepted. *Expenses:* $565 per credit. *Financial support:* In 2016–17, 6 research assistantships (averaging $8,576 per year) were awarded; fellowships, scholarships/grants, traineeships, and unspecified assistantships also available. Financial award application deadline: 1/31. *Faculty research:* Applied behavior analysis, developmental disabilities, at-risk students, learning and behavior problems, pediatric psychology, ADHD, school readiness. *Total annual research expenditures:* $5,135. *Unit head:* Dr. Robin Hojnoski, Program Director/Associate Professor, 610-758-3268, Fax: 610-758-6223, E-mail: roh206@lehigh.edu. *Application contact:* Sharon Y. Warden, Coordinator, 610-758-3256, Fax: 610-758-6223, E-mail: sy00@lehigh.edu.
Website: http://ed.lehigh.edu

**Lesley University,** Graduate School of Arts and Social Sciences, Cambridge, MA 02138-2790. Offers clinical mental health counseling (MA), including holistic counseling, school and community counseling, trauma studies; counseling psychology (MA, CAGS), including professional counseling (MA), school counseling (MA); creative writing (MFA); expressive therapies (MA, PhD, CAGS), including art (MA), clinical mental health counseling (MA), dance (MA), expressive therapies (MA), music (MA); independent studies (CAGS); independent study (MA); intercultural relations (MA, CAGS); interdisciplinary studies (MA), including individualized studies, integrative holistic health, mindfulness studies, peace and conflict transformation, trauma sensitive assessment, intervention, and consultation, women's studies; urban environmental leadership (MA). *Program availability:* Part-time, online learning. *Degree requirements:* For master's, internship, practicum, thesis (for expressive therapies); for doctorate, thesis/dissertation, arts apprenticeship, field placement; for CAGS, thesis, internship (for counseling psychology, expressive therapies). *Entrance requirements:* For master's, MAT (counseling psychology), interview, writing samples, art portfolio; for doctorate, GRE or MAT, interview, master's degree; for CAGS, interview, master's degree. Additional exam requirements/recommendations for international students: Required—TOEFL (minimum

score 550 paper-based; 80 iBT). Electronic applications accepted. *Faculty research:* Psychotherapy and culture; psychotherapy and psychological trauma; women's issues in art, teaching and psychotherapy; community-based art, psycho-spiritual inquiry.

**LeTourneau University,** Graduate Programs, Longview, TX 75607-7001. Offers business (MBA); counseling (MA), including licensed professional counselor, marriage and family therapy, school counseling; curriculum and instruction (M Ed); educational administration (M Ed); engineering (ME, MS); engineering management (MEM); health care administration (MS); marriage and family therapy (MA); psychology (MA); strategic leadership (MSL); teacher leadership (M Ed); teaching and learning (M Ed). *Program availability:* Part-time, 100% online, blended/hybrid learning. *Faculty:* 24 full-time (7 women), 40 part-time/adjunct (15 women). *Students:* 82 full-time (48 women), 428 part-time (331 women); includes 234 minority (138 Black or African American, non-Hispanic/Latino; 5 American Indian or Alaska Native, non-Hispanic/Latino; 5 Asian, non-Hispanic/Latino; 50 Hispanic/Latino; 36 Two or more races, non-Hispanic/Latino), 15 international. Average age 37. 257 applicants, 60% accepted, 141 enrolled. In 2016, 136 master's awarded. *Degree requirements:* For master's, thesis (for some programs). *Entrance requirements:* Additional exam requirements/recommendations for international students: Required—TOEFL. *Application deadline:* For fall admission, 8/22 for domestic students, 8/29 for international students; for winter admission, 10/10 for domestic students; for spring admission, 1/2 for domestic students, 1/10 for international students; for summer admission, 5/1 for domestic and international students. Applications are processed on a rolling basis. Electronic applications accepted. *Expenses:* $10,890-$18,450 tuition per year (depending on program). *Financial support:* Research assistantships, institutionally sponsored loans, and unspecified assistantships available. Financial award applicants required to submit FAFSA. *Application contact:* Chris Fontaine, Assistant Vice President for Enrollment Services and Global Admissions, 903-233-4312, E-mail: chrisfontaine@letu.edu.
Website: http://www.letu.edu

**Lewis & Clark College,** Graduate School of Education and Counseling, Department of Counseling Psychology, Program in School Psychology, Portland, OR 97219-7899. Offers Ed S. *Program availability:* Part-time, evening/weekend. *Entrance requirements:* Additional exam requirements/recommendations for international students: Required—TOEFL (minimum score 575 paper-based). *Application deadline:* For fall admission, 2/1 for domestic and international students. Application fee: $50. Electronic applications accepted. *Financial support:* Career-related internships or fieldwork, Federal Work-Study, institutionally sponsored loans, scholarships/grants, health care benefits, and tuition waivers (partial) available. Support available to part-time students. Financial award application deadline: 3/1; financial award applicants required to submit FAFSA. *Unit head:* Dr. Peter Mortola, Director, 503-768-6072, Fax: 503-768-6065, E-mail: cpsy@lclark.edu. *Application contact:* Becky Haas, Director of Admissions, 503-768-6200, Fax: 503-768-6205, E-mail: gseadmit@lclark.edu.
Website: http://graduate.lclark.edu/departments/counseling_psychology/school_psychology/

**Lewis & Clark College,** Graduate School of Education and Counseling, Department of Educational Leadership, Program in School Counseling, Portland, OR 97219-7899. Offers M Ed. *Program availability:* Part-time, evening/weekend. *Entrance requirements:* For master's, minimum undergraduate GPA of 2.75. Additional exam requirements/recommendations for international students: Required—TOEFL (minimum score 575 paper-based). *Application deadline:* For fall admission, 2/1 for domestic and international students. Application fee: $50. Electronic applications accepted. *Financial support:* Career-related internships or fieldwork, Federal Work-Study, institutionally sponsored loans, scholarships/grants, health care benefits, and tuition waivers (partial) available. Support available to part-time students. Financial award application deadline: 3/1; financial award applicants required to submit FAFSA. *Unit head:* Dr. Danielle Torres, Coordinator, 503-768-6140, Fax: 503-768-6085, E-mail: schcoun@lclark.edu. *Application contact:* Becky Haas, Director of Admissions, 503-768-6200, Fax: 503-768-6205, E-mail: gseadmit@lclark.edu.
Website: http://graduate.lclark.edu/departments/educational_leadership/school_counseling/

**Lindenwood University,** Graduate Programs, School of Education, St. Charles, MO 63301-1695. Offers education (MA), including autism spectrum disorders, character education, early intervention in autism and sensory impairment, gifted, technology; educational administration (MA, Ed D, Ed S); English to speakers of other languages (MA); instructional leadership (Ed D, Ed S); library media (MA); professional counseling (MA); school administration (MA, Ed S); school counseling (MA); teaching (MA). *Program availability:* Part-time, evening/weekend, 100% online, blended/hybrid learning. *Faculty:* 39 full-time (27 women), 210 part-time/adjunct (136 women). *Students:* 292 full-time (227 women), 1,580 part-time (1,203 women); includes 404 minority (333 Black or African American, non-Hispanic/Latino; 4 American Indian or Alaska Native, non-Hispanic/Latino; 10 Asian, non-Hispanic/Latino; 36 Hispanic/Latino; 1 Native Hawaiian or other Pacific Islander, non-Hispanic/Latino; 20 Two or more races, non-Hispanic/Latino), 20 international. Average age 36. 558 applicants, 72% accepted, 353 enrolled. In 2016, 491 master's, 72 doctorates, 111 other advanced degrees awarded. *Degree requirements:* For master's, thesis (for some programs), minimum GPA of 3.0; for doctorate, thesis/dissertation, minimum GPA of 3.0; for Ed S, comprehensive exam, project, minimum GPA of 3.0. *Entrance requirements:* For master's, interview, minimum undergraduate cumulative GPA of 3.0, writing sample, letter of recommendation; for doctorate, GRE, minimum graduate GPA of 3.4, resume, interview, writing sample, 4 letters of recommendation; for Ed S, master's degree in education, relevant work experience. Additional exam requirements/recommendations for international students: Required—TOEFL (minimum score 550 paper-based; 80 iBT); Recommended—IELTS (minimum score 6.5). *Application deadline:* For fall admission, 8/28 priority date for domestic and international students; for spring admission, 1/8 priority date for domestic and international students; for summer admission, 6/5 priority date for domestic and international students. Applications are processed on a rolling basis. Application fee: $30 ($100 for international students). Electronic applications accepted. *Expenses:* Tuition: Full-time $15,672; part-time $453 per credit hour. *Required fees:* $205 per semester. Tuition and fees vary according to course level, course load and degree level. *Financial support:* In 2016–17, 334 students received support. Career-related internships or fieldwork, Federal Work-Study, institutionally sponsored loans, scholarships/grants, tuition waivers (partial), and unspecified assistantships available. Financial award application deadline: 6/30; financial award applicants required to submit FAFSA. *Unit head:* Dr. Cynthia Bice, Dean, School of Education, 636-949-4618, Fax: 636-949-4197, E-mail: cbice@lindenwood.edu. *Application contact:* Tyler Kostich, Director, Evening and Graduate Admissions, 636-949-4138, Fax: 636-949-4109, E-mail: adultadmissions@lindenwood.edu.
Website: http://www.lindenwood.edu/academics/academic-schools/school-of-education/

**Long Island University–Hudson,** Graduate School, Purchase, NY 10577. Offers autism (Advanced Certificate); childhood education (MS Ed); early childhood education (MS Ed); educational leadership (MS Ed); finance (MBA); health administration (MPA); healthcare sector management (MBA); literacy (MS Ed); management (MBA); marriage and family therapy (MS); mental health counseling (MS), including credentialed alcoholism and substance abuse counselor; middle childhood and adolescence education (MS Ed); pharmaceutics (MS), including cosmetic science, industrial pharmacy; public administration (MPA); school counseling (MS Ed, Advanced Certificate); school psychology (MS Ed); special education (MS Ed); TESOL (all grades) (Advanced Certificate); TESOL and bilingual education (MS Ed); the business of pharmaceutics and biotechnology (MBA). *Program availability:* Part-time, evening/weekend, online learning. *Faculty:* 7 full-time (5 women), 42 part-time/adjunct (25 women). *Students:* 55 full-time (41 women), 158 part-time (123 women); includes 40 minority (8 Black or African American, non-Hispanic/Latino; 1 Asian, non-Hispanic/Latino; 31 Hispanic/Latino). Average age 35. *Entrance requirements:* Additional exam requirements/recommendations for international students: Required—TOEFL (minimum score 550 paper-based; 79 iBT). *Application deadline:* Applications are processed on a rolling basis. Application fee: $50. Electronic applications accepted. *Expenses:* Contact institution. *Unit head:* Dr. Sylvia Blake, Dean and Chief Operating Officer, 914-831-2700, E-mail: westchester@liu.edu. *Application contact:* Cindy Pagnotta, Director of Marketing and Enrollment, 914-831-2701, Fax: 914-251-5959, E-mail: cindy.pagnotta@liu.edu.

**Long Island University–LIU Post,** College of Education, Information and Technology, Brookville, NY 11548-1300. Offers adolescence education (MS); adolescence education 7-12 (MS); archives and records management (AC); art education (MS); childhood education (MS); childhood teaching literacy B-6 (MS); childhood/special education (MS); clinical mental health counseling (MS, AC); early childhood education (MS); early childhood education/childhood education (MS); educational leadership (AC); educational technology (MS); information studies (PhD); interdisciplinary educational studies (Ed D); middle childhood education (MS); music education (MS); school counselor education (MS); special education (MS Ed); speech-language pathology (MA); students with disabilities, 7-12 generalist (AC); TESOL (MA). *Accreditation:* TEAC. *Program availability:* Part-time, 100% online, blended/hybrid learning. *Faculty:* 55 full-time (35 women), 104 part-time/adjunct (57 women). *Students:* 464 full-time (390 women), 740 part-time (580 women); includes 265 minority (99 Black or African American, non-Hispanic/Latino; 45 Asian, non-Hispanic/Latino; 113 Hispanic/Latino; 1 Native Hawaiian or other Pacific Islander, non-Hispanic/Latino; 7 Two or more races, non-Hispanic/Latino), 33 international. 928 applicants, 76% accepted, 406 enrolled. In 2016, 334 master's, 10 doctorates, 137 other advanced degrees awarded. Terminal master's awarded for partial completion of doctoral program. *Degree requirements:* For master's, variable foreign language requirement, comprehensive exam (for some programs), thesis optional; for doctorate, comprehensive exam, thesis/dissertation. *Entrance requirements:* For master's and AC, GRE. Additional exam requirements/recommendations for international students: Required—PTE, TOEFL (minimum score 550 paper-based, 75 iBT) or IELTS. *Application deadline:* Applications are processed on a rolling basis. Application fee: $50. Electronic applications accepted. *Expenses: Tuition:* Full-time $28,272; part-time $1178 per credit. *Required fees:* $451 per term. Tuition and fees vary according to degree level and program. *Financial support:* Career-related internships or fieldwork, Federal Work-Study, institutionally sponsored loans, scholarships/grants, tuition waivers (partial), and unspecified assistantships available. Support available to part-time students. Financial award application deadline: 2/15; financial award applicants required to submit FAFSA. *Faculty research:* English language learners, early childhood literacy development through play, sleep, social justice through education, using a structured protocol for discussing bad news. *Total annual research expenditures:* $575,000. *Unit head:* Dr. Albert Inserra, Dean, 516-299-2210, E-mail: albert.inserra@liu.edu. *Application contact:* Carol Zerah, Director of Graduate Admissions, 516-299-2900, Fax: 516-299-2137, E-mail: post-enroll@liu.edu. Website: http://liu.edu/CWPost/Academics/College-of-Education-Information-and-Technology

**Louisiana State University and Agricultural & Mechanical College,** Graduate School, College of Humanities and Social Sciences, Department of Psychology, Baton Rouge, LA 70803. Offers biological psychology (MA, PhD); clinical psychology (MA, PhD); cognitive psychology (MA, PhD); developmental psychology (MA, PhD); school psychology (MA, PhD). *Accreditation:* APA (one or more programs are accredited).

**Louisiana State University in Shreveport,** College of Business, Education, and Human Development, Program in School Psychology, Shreveport, LA 71115-2399. Offers SSP. *Students:* 14 full-time (13 women), 6 part-time (5 women); includes 5 minority (1 Black or African American, non-Hispanic/Latino; 4 Two or more races, non-Hispanic/Latino). Average age 25. 23 applicants, 100% accepted, 9 enrolled. In 2016, 2 SSPs awarded. *Entrance requirements:* For degree, GRE General Test, minimum GPA of 2.75, references, letter of intent, interview. Additional exam requirements/recommendations for international students: Required—TOEFL (minimum score 550 paper-based; 61 iBT). *Application deadline:* For fall admission, 6/30 for domestic and international students; for spring admission, 11/30 for domestic and international students; for summer admission, 4/30 for domestic and international students. Applications are processed on a rolling basis. Application fee: $20 ($30 for international students). Electronic applications accepted. *Expenses:* Tuition, state resident: full-time $5163; part-time $350 per credit hour. Tuition, nonresident: full-time $15,578; part-time $1038 per credit hour. *Required fees:* $63 per credit hour. Tuition and fees vary according to course load and program. *Financial support:* Unspecified assistantships available. Financial award applicants required to submit FAFSA. *Unit head:* Dr. Kevin Jones, Program Director, 318-797-5050, Fax: 318-798-4171, E-mail: ssp@lsus.edu. *Application contact:* Mary Catherine Harvison, Director of Admissions, 318-797-2400, Fax: 318-797-5286, E-mail: mary.harvison@lsus.edu.

**Loyola Marymount University,** School of Education, Department of Educational Support Services, Program in School Psychology, Los Angeles, CA 90045-2659. Offers MA. *Program availability:* Part-time, evening/weekend. *Students:* 55 full-time (51 women), 1 (woman) part-time; includes 30 minority (2 Black or African American, non-Hispanic/Latino; 7 Asian, non-Hispanic/Latino; 19 Hispanic/Latino; 2 Two or more races, non-Hispanic/Latino). Average age 25. 47 applicants, 68% accepted, 22 enrolled. In 2016, 16 master's awarded. *Entrance requirements:* For master's, GRE, CBEST, 3 letters of recommendation. Additional exam requirements/recommendations for international students: Required—TOEFL (minimum score 600 paper-based; 100 iBT). *Application deadline:* For summer admission, 4/15 for domestic students. Application fee: $50. Electronic applications accepted. *Financial support:* In 2016–17, 47 students received support, including 3 research assistantships, 1 teaching assistantship; scholarships/grants and unspecified assistantships also available. Support available to part-time students. Financial award application deadline: 6/30; financial award applicants required to submit FAFSA. *Unit head:* Dr. Brian P. Leung, Director, 310-338-1707, E-mail: bleung@lmu.edu. *Application contact:* Chake H. Kouyoumjian, Associate Dean of Graduate Studies, 310-338-2721, E-mail: ckouyoum@lmu.edu. Website: http://soe.lmu.edu/academics/schoolpsychology

**Loyola University Chicago,** School of Education, Program in School Psychology, Chicago, IL 60660. Offers Ed D, PhD, Ed S. PhD offered through the Graduate School. *Program availability:* Blended/hybrid learning. *Faculty:* 6 full-time (5 women), 3 part-time/adjunct (1 woman). *Students:* 81 full-time (71 women), 16 part-time (14 women); includes 35 minority (15 Black or African American, non-Hispanic/Latino; 4 Asian, non-Hispanic/Latino; 13 Hispanic/Latino; 3 Two or more races, non-Hispanic/Latino), 2 international. Average age 29. 118 applicants, 59% accepted, 33 enrolled. In 2016, 15 doctorates awarded. Terminal master's awarded for partial completion of doctoral

program. *Degree requirements:* For doctorate, comprehensive exam, thesis/dissertation; for Ed S, comprehensive exam. *Entrance requirements:* For doctorate, GRE, interview, letters of recommendation, minimum GPA of 3.0. Additional exam requirements/recommendations for international students: Required—TOEFL (minimum score 550 paper-based; 79 iBT). *Application deadline:* For fall admission, 12/1 for domestic and international students. Application fee: $50. Electronic applications accepted. Application fee is waived when completed online. *Expenses:* $949 per hour; $2,847 per course; $8,541-$11,388 per semester plus fees $432 per semester and $225 the first semester. *Financial support:* In 2016–17, 61 students received support, including 27 fellowships with partial tuition reimbursements available, 15 research assistantships with full tuition reimbursements available (averaging $14,000 per year), 19 teaching assistantships (averaging $4,000 per year); career-related internships or fieldwork, institutionally sponsored loans, scholarships/grants, health care benefits, and unspecified assistantships also available. Support available to part-time students. Financial award application deadline: 2/1. *Faculty research:* Learning theory and teaching, school reform, instructional intervention, violence prevention, mental health programming in schools and communities. *Unit head:* Dr. Gina Coffee, Program Chair, 312-915-6854, E-mail: gcoffee@luc.edu. *Application contact:* Thomas Ott, Information Contact, 312-915-8907, E-mail: tott@luc.edu.

**Lynchburg College,** Graduate Studies, M Ed Program in School Counseling, Lynchburg, VA 24501-3199. Offers M Ed. *Accreditation:* ACA. *Program availability:* Part-time, evening/weekend. *Students:* 9 full-time (8 women), 15 part-time (13 women); includes 6 minority (5 Black or African American, non-Hispanic/Latino; 1 Hispanic/Latino). In 2016, 10 master's awarded. *Degree requirements:* For master's, counseling internship. *Entrance requirements:* For master's, GRE, minimum GPA of 3.0 (preferred), official transcripts (bachelor's, others as relevant), three letters of recommendation, career goals statement. Additional exam requirements/recommendations for international students: Required—TOEFL (minimum score 550 paper-based; 79 iBT), IELTS (minimum score 6.5). *Application deadline:* For fall admission, 7/31 for domestic students, 6/1 for international students; for spring admission, 11/30 for domestic students, 10/15 for international students. Applications are processed on a rolling basis. Application fee: $30. Electronic applications accepted. Application fee is waived when completed online. *Expenses:* Contact institution. *Financial support:* Federal Work-Study, scholarships/grants, health care benefits, and unspecified assistantships available. Support available to part-time students. Financial award application deadline: 7/31; financial award applicants required to submit FAFSA. *Unit head:* Dr. Jeanne Booth, Associate Professor/Coordinator of M Ed in School Counseling, 434-544-8551, E-mail: booth@lynchburg.edu. Website: http://www.lynchburg.edu/graduate/master-of-education-in-counselor-education/school-counseling/

**Marist College,** Graduate Programs, School of Social and Behavioral Sciences, Poughkeepsie, NY 12601-1387. Offers education (M Ed, MA); mental health counseling (MA); school psychology (MA, Adv C). *Program availability:* Part-time, evening/weekend. *Degree requirements:* For master's, thesis optional. *Entrance requirements:* For master's, GRE General Test, letters of recommendation, minimum undergraduate GPA of 3.0, interview. Additional exam requirements/recommendations for international students: Required—TOEFL (minimum score 550 paper-based; 80 iBT); Recommended—IELTS (minimum score 6.5). Electronic applications accepted. *Faculty research:* AIDS prevention, educational intervention, humanistic counseling research, aging and development, neuroimaging.

**Marshall University,** Academic Affairs Division, College of Education and Professional Development, Program in School Psychology, Huntington, WV 25755. Offers Ed S. *Accreditation:* NCATE. *Program availability:* Part-time, evening/weekend. *Entrance requirements:* For degree, master's degree in psychology.

**McGill University,** Faculty of Graduate and Postdoctoral Studies, Faculty of Education, Department of Educational and Counseling Psychology, Montréal, QC H3A 2T5, Canada. Offers counseling psychology (MA, PhD); educational psychology (M Ed, MA, PhD); school/applied child psychology and applied developmental psychology (M Ed, MA, PhD, Diploma), including school psychology. *Accreditation:* APA.

**McNeese State University,** Doré School of Graduate Studies, Burton College of Education, Office of Graduate Education Programs, Program in School Counseling, Lake Charles, LA 70609. Offers M Ed. *Accreditation:* NCATE. *Program availability:* Evening/weekend. *Entrance requirements:* For master's, GRE, 18 hours in professional education.

**Mercer University,** Graduate Studies, Cecil B. Day Campus, Penfield College, Atlanta, GA 30341. Offers certified rehabilitation counseling (MS); clinical mental health (MS); counselor education and supervision (PhD); criminal justice and public safety leadership (MS); health informatics (MS); human services (MS), including child and adolescent services, gerontology services; organizational leadership (MS); school counseling (MS). *Program availability:* Part-time, evening/weekend, 100% online, blended/hybrid learning. *Faculty:* 15 full-time (8 women), 22 part-time/adjunct (18 women). *Students:* 168 full-time (136 women), 242 part-time (201 women); includes 231 minority (192 Black or African American, non-Hispanic/Latino; 1 American Indian or Alaska Native, non-Hispanic/Latino; 15 Asian, non-Hispanic/Latino; 19 Hispanic/Latino; 1 Native Hawaiian or other Pacific Islander, non-Hispanic/Latino; 3 Two or more races, non-Hispanic/Latino), 2 international. Average age 32. 300 applicants, 45% accepted, 114 enrolled. In 2016, 92 master's, 8 doctorates awarded. *Degree requirements:* For master's, comprehensive exam (for some programs), thesis (for some programs); for doctorate, thesis/dissertation. *Entrance requirements:* For master's, GRE or MAT, Georgia Professional Standards Commission (GPSC) Certification at the SC-5 level; for doctorate, GRE or MAT. Additional exam requirements/recommendations for international students: Recommended—TOEFL (minimum score 550 paper-based; 80 iBT), IELTS (minimum score 6.5). *Application deadline:* For fall admission, 7/1 priority date for domestic and international students; for spring admission, 11/1 priority date for domestic and international students; for summer admission, 4/1 priority date for domestic and international students. Application fee: $35. Electronic applications accepted. Application fee is waived when completed online. *Expenses:* $588 per credit hour. *Financial support:* In 2016–17, 32 students received support. Federal Work-Study, scholarships/grants, and unspecified assistantships available. Financial award applicants required to submit FAFSA. *Faculty research:* Marriage and families issues, leadership and ethics, cyber-bullying, trauma, narrative counseling and theory. *Total annual research expenditures:* $85,000. *Unit head:* Dr. Priscilla R. Danheiser, Dean, 678-547-6028, Fax: 678-547-6008, E-mail: danheiser_p@mercer.edu. Website: http://penfield.mercer.edu/programs/graduate-professional/

**Mercy College,** School of Social and Behavioral Sciences, Program in School Psychology, Dobbs Ferry, NY 10522-1189. Offers MS. *Program availability:* Part-time, evening/weekend. *Students:* 27 full-time (25 women), 15 part-time (14 women); includes 21 minority (5 Black or African American, non-Hispanic/Latino; 16 Hispanic/Latino). Average age 34. 68 applicants, 37% accepted, 19 enrolled. In 2016, 10 master's awarded. *Degree requirements:* For master's, thesis (for some programs), practicum, fieldwork, internship, integrative project. *Entrance requirements:* For master's, interview, 3 letters of recommendation, undergraduate transcript. Additional exam requirements/recommendations for international students: Required—TOEFL (minimum score 600

*School Psychology*

paper-based; 100 iBT), IELTS (minimum score 8). *Application deadline:* For fall admission, 8/1 for international students. Applications are processed on a rolling basis. Application fee: $40. Electronic applications accepted. *Expenses: Tuition:* Full-time $15,156; part-time $842 per credit hour. *Required fees:* $620; $155 per term. Tuition and fees vary according to course load and program. *Financial support:* Career-related internships or fieldwork, Federal Work-Study, scholarships/grants, and unspecified assistantships available. Support available to part-time students. Financial award applicants required to submit FAFSA. *Unit head:* Dr. Karol Dean, Dean, School of Social and Behavioral Sciences, 914-674-7517, E-mail: kdean@mercy.edu. *Application contact:* Allison Gurdineer, Senior Director of Admissions, 877-637-2946, Fax: 914-674-7382, E-mail: admissions@mercy.edu.
Website: https://www.mercy.edu/degrees-programs/ms-school-psychology

**Merrimack College,** School of Education and Social Policy, North Andover, MA 01845-5800. Offers community engagement (M Ed), including community organizations, higher education, K–12 education; criminology and criminal justice (MS); curriculum and instruction (M Ed); early childhood education (M Ed); educational leadership (CAGS), including instructional leadership; elementary education (M Ed); English as a second language (PreK–6) (M Ed); high school education (M Ed); higher education (M Ed), including leadership and organizational development, student affairs; middle school education (M Ed); moderate disabilities (PreK–8) (M Ed); school counseling (M Ed). *Program availability:* Part-time, evening/weekend, 100% online courses with immersion events and in-classroom practicum close to home. *Faculty:* 17 full-time, 34 part-time/adjunct. *Students:* 204 full-time (172 women), 83 part-time (67 women); includes 32 minority (4 Black or African American, non-Hispanic/Latino; 2 Asian, non-Hispanic/Latino; 23 Hispanic/Latino; 3 Two or more races, non-Hispanic/Latino), 1 international. Average age 27. 261 applicants, 89% accepted, 200 enrolled. In 2016, 153 master's, 2 other advanced degrees awarded. *Degree requirements:* For master's, practicum, portfolio, and state test (for licensure track); capstone (for higher education, curriculum and instruction, and community engagement tracks). *Entrance requirements:* For master's, Massachusetts Teacher Education Licensure (MTEL), official transcripts from other colleges, resume, personal statement, 2 letters of recommendation. Additional exam requirements/recommendations for international students: Required—TOEFL (minimum score 84 iBT), IELTS (minimum score 6.5), PTE (minimum score 56). *Application deadline:* For fall admission, 8/14 for domestic students, 7/14 for international students; for spring admission, 1/10 for domestic students, 12/10 for international students; for summer admission, 5/10 for domestic students, 4/10 for international students. Applications are processed on a rolling basis. Application fee: $0. Electronic applications accepted. *Expenses:* Contact institution. *Financial support:* Fellowships with full tuition reimbursements, career-related internships or fieldwork, scholarships/grants, and health care benefits available. Support available to part-time students. Financial award application deadline: 5/1; financial award applicants required to submit FAFSA. *Faculty research:* Feminist praxis in higher education, transgender student agency and belonging, campus sexual violence prevention, the scholarship of engagement; community engagement; service learning; diversity education; community-university partnerships, college going behaviors and indicators of success for inner city youth, strategies to increase students pursuit and success in STEM higher education, effective workforce development for displaced or under employed individuals, police reform, e.g. surveillance. *Application contact:* Alyssa Frey, Graduate Admissions Counselor, 978-837-3563, E-mail: freya@merrimack.edu.
Website: http://www.merrimack.edu/academics/graduate/education/

**Michigan State University,** The Graduate School, College of Education, Department of Counseling, Educational Psychology and Special Education, East Lansing, MI 48824. Offers counseling (MA); educational psychology and educational technology (PhD); educational technology (MA); measurement and quantitative methods (PhD); rehabilitation counseling (MA); rehabilitation counselor education (PhD); school psychology (MA, PhD, Ed S); special education (MA, PhD). *Accreditation:* APA (one or more programs are accredited); CORE (one or more programs are accredited). *Program availability:* Part-time. *Entrance requirements:* Additional exam requirements/recommendations for international students: Required—TOEFL. Electronic applications accepted.

**MidAmerica Nazarene University,** School of Behavioral Sciences and Counseling, Olathe, KS 66062-1899. Offers counseling (MA), including clinical mental health, marriage, couple and family, school counseling, spiritual formation in counseling. *Accreditation:* ACA. *Program availability:* Evening/weekend. *Faculty:* 10 full-time (4 women), 13 part-time/adjunct (9 women). *Students:* 109 full-time (92 women), 100 part-time (87 women); includes 39 minority (21 Black or African American, non-Hispanic/Latino; 3 Asian, non-Hispanic/Latino; 5 Hispanic/Latino; 1 Native Hawaiian or other Pacific Islander, non-Hispanic/Latino; 9 Two or more races, non-Hispanic/Latino). 97 applicants, 79% accepted, 61 enrolled. In 2016, 55 master's awarded. *Degree requirements:* For master's, comprehensive exam. *Entrance requirements:* For master's, on-site writing assessment, official transcript, three recommendations, personal interview. Additional exam requirements/recommendations for international students: Required—TOEFL (minimum score 81 iBT). *Application deadline:* For winter admission, 2/15 for domestic and international students; for spring admission, 4/1 for domestic and international students. Electronic applications accepted. *Expenses:* $34,620 tuition, $250 lab fee, $1,200 technology fee. *Financial support:* Applicants required to submit FAFSA. *Faculty research:* Technology and intimacy, play therapy, interpersonal neurobiology, sexual addiction. *Unit head:* Dr. Todd Frye, Dean, School of Behavioral Sciences and Counseling, 913-971-3449, Fax: 913-971-3402, E-mail: tmfrye@mnu.edu. *Application contact:* Jean Blades, Administrative Assistant, 913-971-3730, E-mail: jmblades@mnu.edu.

**Middle Tennessee State University,** College of Graduate Studies, College of Behavioral and Health Sciences, Department of Psychology, Murfreesboro, TN 37132. Offers clinical psychology (MA); experimental psychology (MA); industrial/organizational psychology (MA); psychology (MA, Ed S); quantitative psychology (MA); school psychology (MA). *Program availability:* Part-time, evening/weekend, online learning. *Degree requirements:* For master's, comprehensive exam, thesis. *Entrance requirements:* For master's, GRE. Additional exam requirements/recommendations for international students: Required—TOEFL (minimum score 525 paper-based; 71 iBT) or IELTS (minimum score 6). Electronic applications accepted. *Faculty research:* Health psychology, industrial/organizational psychology, experimental psychology.

**Millersville University of Pennsylvania,** College of Graduate Studies and Adult Learning, College of Education and Human Services, Department of Psychology, Program in School Counseling, Millersville, PA 17551-0302. Offers M Ed. *Accreditation:* NCATE. *Program availability:* Part-time, evening/weekend. *Faculty:* 19 full-time (13 women). *Students:* 7 full-time (6 women), 24 part-time (23 women); includes 3 minority (1 Black or African American, non-Hispanic/Latino; 1 Hispanic/Latino; 1 Two or more races, non-Hispanic/Latino). Average age 29. 13 applicants, 100% accepted, 9 enrolled. In 2016, 8 master's awarded. *Degree requirements:* For master's, thesis optional, portfolio, practicum, internship. *Entrance requirements:* For master's, GRE or MAT (if cumulative GPA is lower than 3.0), at least 1 academic reference; interview; 6 undergraduate credits in psychology. Additional exam requirements/recommendations for international students: Required—TOEFL (minimum score 600 paper-based), IELTS

(minimum score 6). *Application deadline:* For fall admission, 1/15 for domestic and international students; for spring admission, 10/1 for domestic and international students. Application fee: $40. Electronic applications accepted. *Expenses:* $483 per credit resident tuition; $725 per credit non-resident tuition. *Financial support:* In 2016–17, 6 students received support. Unspecified assistantships available. Financial award application deadline: 3/15; financial award applicants required to submit FAFSA. *Faculty research:* Solution-focused counseling, the psychological and social impact of urban gardening with children, comprehensive developmental school counseling programs, sustainability education and research, national model implementation. *Unit head:* Dr. Jason B. Baker, Director, 717-871-7267, Fax: 717-871-7946, E-mail: jason.baker@millersville.edu. *Application contact:* Dr. Victor S. DeSantis, Dean of College of Graduate Studies and Adult Learning/Associate Provost for Civic and Community Engagement, 717-871-7619, Fax: 717-871-7954, E-mail: victor.desantis@millersville.edu.
Website: http://www.millersville.edu/psychology/graduate/school-counseling/index.php

**Millersville University of Pennsylvania,** College of Graduate Studies and Adult Learning, College of Education and Human Services, Department of Psychology, Program in School Psychology, Millersville, PA 17551-0302. Offers MS. *Program availability:* Part-time, evening/weekend. *Faculty:* 19 full-time (13 women). *Students:* 17 full-time (16 women), 9 part-time (8 women); includes 5 minority (1 Black or African American, non-Hispanic/Latino; 3 Hispanic/Latino; 1 Two or more races, non-Hispanic/Latino). Average age 25. 23 applicants, 87% accepted, 12 enrolled. In 2016, 9 master's awarded. *Degree requirements:* For master's, comprehensive exam, thesis optional, portfolio, practicum, internship. *Entrance requirements:* For master's, GRE or MAT (if cumulative GPA is lower than 3.0), at least 1 academic reference; interview; 18 undergraduate credits in psychology. Additional exam requirements/recommendations for international students: Required—TOEFL (minimum score 600 paper-based), IELTS (minimum score 6). *Application deadline:* For fall admission, 1/15 for domestic and international students; for spring admission, 10/1 for domestic and international students. Application fee: $40. Electronic applications accepted. *Expenses:* $483 per credit resident tuition; $725 per credit non-resident tuition. *Financial support:* In 2016–17, 11 students received support. Unspecified assistantships available. Financial award application deadline: 3/15; financial award applicants required to submit FAFSA. *Faculty research:* Modification of ELL reading and writing instruction based on CALP, parent participation in ELL education, assessment tools for diverse children. *Unit head:* Dr. Helena Tuleya-Payne, Coordinator, 717-871-4420, Fax: 717-871-7946, E-mail: helena.tuleya-payne@millersville.edu. *Application contact:* Dr. Victor S. DeSantis, Dean of College of Graduate Studies and Adult Learning/Associate Provost for Civic and Community Engagement, 717-871-7619, Fax: 717-871-7954, E-mail: victor.desantis@millersville.edu.
Website: http://www.millersville.edu/psychology/graduate/school-psychology/

**Minnesota State University Mankato,** College of Graduate Studies and Research, College of Social and Behavioral Sciences, Department of Psychology, Mankato, MN 56001. Offers clinical psychology (MA); industrial/organizational psychology (MA); school psychology (Psy D). *Program availability:* Part-time. *Students:* 51 full-time (34 women), 12 part-time (11 women). *Degree requirements:* For master's, one foreign language, comprehensive exam, thesis (for some programs). *Entrance requirements:* For master's, GRE General Test, GRE Subject Test (clinical psychology), minimum GPA of 3.0 during previous 2 years, 3 letters of reference. Additional exam requirements/recommendations for international students: Required—TOEFL. *Application deadline:* For fall admission, 1/1 priority date for domestic students. Applications are processed on a rolling basis. Application fee: $40. Electronic applications accepted. *Financial support:* Research assistantships, teaching assistantships with full tuition reimbursements, career-related internships or fieldwork, Federal Work-Study, institutionally sponsored loans, and unspecified assistantships available. Support available to part-time students. Financial award application deadline: 3/15; financial award applicants required to submit FAFSA.
Website: http://sbs.mnsu.edu/psych/

**Minnesota State University Moorhead,** Graduate Studies, College of Science, Health and the Environment, Moorhead, MN 56563. Offers healthcare administration (MHA); nursing (MS); school psychology (MS, Psy S). *Program availability:* Part-time. *Students:* 34 full-time (29 women), 88 part-time (76 women). Average age 33. 85 applicants, 51% accepted. In 2016, 29 master's awarded. *Degree requirements:* For master's, comprehensive exam (for some programs), thesis. *Entrance requirements:* For master's, GRE (for school psychology program), minimum GPA of 3.0, essay, letters of reference. Additional exam requirements/recommendations for international students: Required—TOEFL (minimum score 550 paper-based). *Application deadline:* For fall admission, 4/15 for domestic students; for spring admission, 11/15 for domestic students. Applications are processed on a rolling basis. Application fee: $20. Electronic applications accepted. *Expenses:* Tuition, state resident: full-time $9000; part-time $4500 per credit. Tuition, nonresident: full-time $18,000; part-time $9000 per credit. *Required fees:* $942; $39.25 per credit. One-time fee: $90 full-time. Full-time tuition and fees vary according to course load, degree level, program and reciprocity agreements. *Financial support:* Federal Work-Study and unspecified assistantships available. Financial award application deadline: 10/1; financial award applicants required to submit FAFSA. *Unit head:* Dr. Jeffrey Bodwin, Dean, 218-477-5892, E-mail: jeffrey.bodwin@mnstate.edu. *Application contact:* Karla Wenger, Graduate Studies Office Manager, 218-477-2344, Fax: 218-477-2482, E-mail: wengerk@mnstate.edu.
Website: http://www.mnstate.edu/cshe/

**Minot State University,** Graduate School, Program in School Psychology, Minot, ND 58707-0002. Offers Ed Sp. *Degree requirements:* For Ed Sp, comprehensive exam, thesis optional. *Entrance requirements:* For degree, GRE General Test, minimum GPA of 3.0. Additional exam requirements/recommendations for international students: Required—TOEFL (minimum score 79 iBT), IELTS (minimum score 6).

**Mississippi State University,** College of Education, Department of Counseling, Educational Psychology, and Foundations, Mississippi State, MS 39762. Offers clinical mental health (MS); college counseling (MS); college/post secondary student counseling and personnel services (PhD); counselor education (Ed S); counselor education/student counseling and guidance services (PhD); general educational psychology (MS); psychometry (MS); rehabilitation (MS); school counseling (MS); school psychology (PhD, Ed S); student affairs (MS). *Accreditation:* ACA (one or more programs are accredited); APA; CORE (one or more programs are accredited); NCATE. *Program availability:* Part-time, blended/hybrid learning. *Faculty:* 21 full-time (14 women), 2 part-time/adjunct (both women). *Students:* 125 full-time (94 women), 70 part-time (60 women); includes 63 minority (48 Black or African American, non-Hispanic/Latino; 1 American Indian or Alaska Native, non-Hispanic/Latino; 4 Asian, non-Hispanic/Latino; 5 Hispanic/Latino; 5 Two or more races, non-Hispanic/Latino), 6 international. Average age 30. 151 applicants, 64% accepted, 70 enrolled. In 2016, 49 master's, 3 doctorates, 4 other advanced degrees awarded. Terminal master's awarded for partial completion of doctoral program. *Degree requirements:* For master's, comprehensive exam, thesis optional; for doctorate, thesis/dissertation, comprehensive oral and written exam. *Entrance requirements:* For master's, GRE (taken within the last five years), BS with minimum GPA of 2.75 on last 60 hours; for doctorate, GRE, MS from CACREP- or

CORE-accredited program in counseling; for Ed S, GRE, MS in counseling or related field, minimum GPA of 3.3 on all graduate work. Additional exam requirements/recommendations for international students: Required—TOEFL (minimum score 550 paper-based; 79 iBT); Recommended—IELTS (minimum score 6.5). *Application deadline:* For fall admission, 2/1 priority date for domestic and international students. Applications are processed on a rolling basis. Application fee: $60. Electronic applications accepted. *Expenses:* Tuition, state resident: full-time $7670; part-time $852.50 per credit hour. Tuition, nonresident: full-time $20,790; part-time $2310.50 per credit hour. Part-time tuition and fees vary according to course load. *Financial support:* In 2016–17, 9 teaching assistantships with full tuition reimbursements (averaging $8,401 per year) were awarded; career-related internships or fieldwork, Federal Work-Study, institutionally sponsored loans, and unspecified assistantships also available. Financial award application deadline: 2/1; financial award applicants required to submit FAFSA. *Faculty research:* HIV/AIDS in college population, substance abuse in youth and college students, ADHD and conduct disorders in youth, assessment and identification of early childhood disabilities, assessment and vocational transition of the disabled. *Unit head:* Dr. David Morse, Professor and Head, 662-325-3426, Fax: 662-325-3263, E-mail: dmorse@colled.msstate.edu. *Application contact:* Linda Bonner, Senior Admissions Assistant, 662-325-3363, E-mail: lbonner@grad.msstate.edu. Website: http://www.cep.msstate.edu/

**Monmouth University,** Graduate Studies, School of Education, West Long Branch, NJ 07764-1898. Offers applied behavioral analysis (Certificate); autism (Certificate); director of school counseling services (Post-Master's Certificate); initial certification (MAT), including elementary level, K-12, secondary level; learning disabilities teacher-consultant (Post-Master's Certificate); principal/school administrator (MS Ed); principal/supervisor (MS Ed); school counseling (MS Ed); special education (MS Ed), including autism, learning disabilities teacher-consultant, teaching in inclusive settings; speech-language pathology (MS Ed); student affairs and college counseling (MS Ed); supervisor (Post-Master's Certificate); teaching English to speakers of other languages (TESOL) (Certificate). *Accreditation:* NCATE. *Program availability:* Part-time, evening/weekend, 100% online, blended/hybrid learning. *Entrance requirements:* For master's, GRE taken within last 5 years (for MS Ed in speech-language pathology); SAT (minimum combined score of 1660 in 3 sections), ACT (23), GRE (minimum score of 4.0 on analytical writing section and minimum combined score of 310 on quantitative and verbal sections), or passing scores on 3 parts of Core Academic Skills Educators, minimum GPA of 3.0 in major; 2 letters of recommendation (for some programs); resume, personal statement or essay (depending on program). Additional exam requirements/recommendations for international students: Required—TOEFL (minimum score 550 paper-based; 79 iBT), IELTS (minimum score 6), Michigan English Language Assessment Battery (minimum score 77) or Certificate of Advanced English (minimum score B2). Electronic applications accepted. *Faculty research:* Multicultural literacy, science and mathematics teaching strategies, teacher as reflective practitioner, children with disabilities.

**Montana State University,** The Graduate School, College of Education, Health, and Human Development, Department of Education, Bozeman, MT 59717. Offers adult and higher education (Ed D); curriculum and instruction (M Ed, Ed D), including professional educator (M Ed), technology education (M Ed); education (M Ed), including adult and higher education, educational leadership, school counseling; educational leadership (Ed D, Ed S). *Accreditation:* TEAC. *Program availability:* Part-time, online learning. *Degree requirements:* For master's, comprehensive exam; for doctorate, comprehensive exam, thesis/dissertation. *Entrance requirements:* For master's, GRE, 3 letters of reference, essays, BA transcripts; for doctorate, GRE, MAT, 3 letters of reference, essay, BA and M Ed transcripts; for Ed S, PRAXIS. Additional exam requirements/recommendations for international students: Required—TOEFL (minimum score 550 paper-based). Electronic applications accepted. *Faculty research:* Critical literacy; standards-based education; school Improvement, organizational change, leadership in rural education, leadership in Indian education; student Learning; multicultural/culturally responsive education for social justice Native American indigenous education, community-centered education teacher preparation.

**Mount Saint Vincent University,** Graduate Programs, Faculty of Education, Program in School Psychology, Halifax, NS B3M 2J6, Canada. Offers MASP. *Degree requirements:* For master's, thesis, 500 hour practicum. *Entrance requirements:* For master's, bachelor's degree in psychology or equivalent, related work experience. Electronic applications accepted. *Faculty research:* Relationship between cognitive and emotional development, expression of emotions, cognitive-behavioral constituents of racism.

**National Louis University,** National College of Education, Chicago, IL 60603. Offers administration and supervision (M Ed, Ed D, CAS, Ed S); curriculum and instruction (M Ed, MS Ed, CAS); early childhood administration (M Ed, CAS); early childhood education (M Ed, MAT, MS Ed, CAS); education (Ed D); educational psychology/human learning and development (M Ed, MS Ed, CAS, Ed S); elementary education (MAT); interdisciplinary curriculum and instruction (M Ed); mathematics education (M Ed, MS Ed, CAS); middle grades education (MAT); reading and language (M Ed, MS Ed, CAS); school psychology (M Ed, Ed S); science education (M Ed, MS Ed, CAS); secondary education (MAT); special education (M Ed, MAT, CAS); technology in education (M Ed, CAS). *Accreditation:* NCATE. *Program availability:* Part-time, evening/weekend. *Degree requirements:* For doctorate, comprehensive exam, thesis/dissertation. *Entrance requirements:* For master's, MAT or GRE, minimum GPA of 3.0; for doctorate, GRE General Test, minimum GPA of 3.25, interview, resume, writing sample, 4 recommendations. Additional exam requirements/recommendations for international students: Required—TOEFL (minimum score 550 paper-based; 79 iBT).

**New Mexico State University,** College of Education, Department of Counseling and Educational Psychology, Las Cruces, NM 88003. Offers counseling psychology (PhD); educational diagnostics (MA), including counseling and guidance, educational diagnostics; school psychology (Ed S). *Accreditation:* ACA; APA (one or more programs are accredited); NCATE. *Program availability:* Part-time. *Faculty:* 11 full-time (9 women), 4 part-time/adjunct (2 women). *Students:* 74 full-time (56 women), 12 part-time (9 women); includes 58 minority (2 Black or African American, non-Hispanic/Latino; 1 American Indian or Alaska Native, non-Hispanic/Latino; 6 Asian, non-Hispanic/Latino; 48 Hispanic/Latino; 1 Two or more races, non-Hispanic/Latino), 1 international. Average age 29. 115 applicants, 36% accepted, 26 enrolled. In 2016, 12 master's, 6 doctorates, 9 other advanced degrees awarded. *Degree requirements:* For master's, comprehensive exam, thesis optional, internship; for doctorate, comprehensive exam, thesis/dissertation, internship; for Ed S, comprehensive exam, thesis or alternative, internship. *Entrance requirements:* For master's, doctorate, and Ed S, GRE General Test, minimum GPA of 3.0. Additional exam requirements/recommendations for international students: Required—TOEFL (minimum score 550 paper-based; 79 iBT), IELTS (minimum score 6.5). *Application deadline:* For fall admission, 12/15 for domestic and international students; for spring admission, 2/1 priority date for domestic students, 2/1 for international students. Application fee: $40 ($50 for international students). Electronic applications accepted. *Expenses:* Tuition, state resident: full-time $4086. Tuition, nonresident: full-time $14,254. *Required fees:* $853. Tuition and fees vary according to course load. *Financial support:* In 2016–17, 69 students received support, including 6 fellowships (averaging $4,088 per year), 5 research assistantships

(averaging $12,036 per year), 23 teaching assistantships (averaging $12,358 per year); career-related internships or fieldwork, Federal Work-Study, scholarships/grants, traineeships, health care benefits, and unspecified assistantships also available. Support available to part-time students. Financial award application deadline: 3/1. *Faculty research:* Multicultural counseling and training, school and counseling psychology, social justice, integrated primary care behavioral health training, mental health disparities. *Total annual research expenditures:* $122,042. *Unit head:* Dr. Gladys DeNecochea, Interim Department Head, 575-646-2121, Fax: 575-646-8035, E-mail: gdenecoc@nmsu.edu. *Application contact:* Norma Arrieta, Student Program Coordinator, 575-646-2121, Fax: 575-646-8035, E-mail: cep@nmsu.edu. Website: http://cep.education.nmsu.edu

**Niagara University,** Graduate Division of Education, Concentration in School Psychology, Niagara University, NY 14109. Offers MS. *Program availability:* Part-time. *Students:* 18 full-time (15 women), 15 part-time (14 women); includes 4 minority (1 Black or African American, non-Hispanic/Latino; 2 Hispanic/Latino; 1 Two or more races, non-Hispanic/Latino), 3 international. Average age 26. In 2016, 7 master's awarded. *Entrance requirements:* For master's, GRE. Additional exam requirements/recommendations for international students: Required—TOEFL (minimum score 550 paper-based; 79 iBT), IELTS (minimum score 6). *Application deadline:* For fall admission, 8/1 for domestic students. Application fee: $30. *Expenses:* Contact institution. *Financial support:* Research assistantships with tuition reimbursements, teaching assistantships with tuition reimbursements, career-related internships or fieldwork, Federal Work-Study, scholarships/grants, and unspecified assistantships available. Financial award application deadline: 4/15; financial award applicants required to submit FAFSA. *Unit head:* Dr. Kristine Augustyniak, Chair, 716-286-8548, E-mail: kma@niagara.edu. *Application contact:* Evan Pierce, Associate Director, Graduate Studies, 716-286-8769, Fax: 716-286-8170, E-mail: epierce@niagara.edu. Website: http://www.niagara.edu/school-psychology

**Nicholls State University,** Graduate Studies, College of Education, Department of Psychology, Counseling and Family Studies, Thibodaux, LA 70310. Offers clinical mental health counseling (MA); school counseling (M Ed); school psychology (SSP). *Accreditation:* NCATE. *Program availability:* Part-time, evening/weekend. *Degree requirements:* For master's, comprehensive exam; for SSP, comprehensive exam, internship. *Entrance requirements:* For master's, GRE General Test. Electronic applications accepted.

**North Carolina State University,** Graduate School, College of Humanities and Social Sciences, Department of Psychology, Raleigh, NC 27695. Offers developmental psychology (PhD); ergonomics and experimental psychology (PhD); industrial/organizational psychology (PhD); psychology in the public interest (PhD); school psychology (PhD). *Accreditation:* APA. *Degree requirements:* For doctorate, comprehensive exam, thesis/dissertation. *Entrance requirements:* For doctorate, GRE General Test, GRE Subject Test (industrial/organizational psychology), MAT (recommended), minimum GPA of 3.0 in major. Electronic applications accepted. *Faculty research:* Cognitive and social development (human factors, families, the workplace, community issues and health, aging).

**North Dakota State University,** College of Graduate and Interdisciplinary Studies, College of Human Development and Education, School of Education, Program in Counselor Education, Fargo, ND 58102. Offers clinical mental health counseling (M Ed, MS); counselor education and supervision (PhD); school counseling (M Ed, MS). *Accreditation:* ACA; NCATE. *Program availability:* Part-time, online learning. *Degree requirements:* For master's, comprehensive exam, thesis or alternative; for doctorate, comprehensive exam, thesis/dissertation. *Entrance requirements:* For master's, GRE, MAT, interview. Additional exam requirements/recommendations for international students: Required—TOEFL. *Faculty research:* Supervision, program assessment, multicultural issues.

**Northeastern University,** Bouvé College of Health Sciences, Boston, MA 02115-5096. Offers applied behavior analysis (MS); audiology (Au D); counseling psychology (MS, PhD, CAGS); exercise science (MS); nursing (MS, PhD, CAGS), including administration (MS), adult-gerontology acute care nurse practitioner (MS, CAGS), adult-gerontology primary care nurse practitioner (MS, CAGS), anesthesia (MS), family nurse practitioner (MS, CAGS), neonatal nurse practitioner (MS, CAGS), pediatric nurse practitioner (MS, CAGS), psychiatric mental health nurse practitioner (MS, CAGS); nursing practice (DNP); pharmaceutical sciences (MS, PhD), including interdisciplinary concentration, pharmaceutics and drug delivery systems; pharmacology (MS); pharmacy (Pharm D); school psychology (PhD); urban health (MPH); MS/MBA. *Accreditation:* ACPE (one or more programs are accredited). *Program availability:* Part-time, evening/weekend, online learning. *Faculty:* 192 full-time (119 women), 194 part-time/adjunct (156 women). *Students:* 1,371 full-time (1,009 women), 262 part-time (219 women). In 2016, 352 master's, 312 doctorates, 25 other advanced degrees awarded. *Degree requirements:* For doctorate, thesis/dissertation (for some programs); for CAGS, comprehensive exam. Application fee: $75. Electronic applications accepted. *Expenses:* Contact institution. *Financial support:* Fellowships, research assistantships, teaching assistantships, career-related internships or fieldwork, scholarships/grants, health care benefits, tuition waivers, and unspecified assistantships available. Support available to part-time students. Financial award applicants required to submit FAFSA. *Unit head:* Susan L. Parish, Dean, Bouve College of Health Sciences, 617-373-3323, Fax: 617-373-3030. *Application contact:* E-mail: bouvegrad@northeastern.edu. Website: http://www.northeastern.edu/bouve

**Northern Arizona University,** Graduate College, College of Education, Department of Educational Psychology, Flagstaff, AZ 86011. Offers counseling (MA); educational psychology (PhD), including counseling psychology, school psychology; human relations (M Ed); school counseling (M Ed); school psychology (Ed S); student affairs (M Ed). *Program availability:* Part-time, online learning. Terminal master's awarded for partial completion of doctoral program. *Degree requirements:* For master's, internship (for some programs); for doctorate, comprehensive exam, thesis/dissertation, internship. *Entrance requirements:* Additional exam requirements/recommendations for international students: Required—TOEFL (minimum score 550 paper-based; 80 iBT), IELTS (minimum score 7). Electronic applications accepted. *Expenses:* Tuition, state resident: full-time $8971; part-time $444 per credit hour. Tuition, nonresident: full-time $20,958; part-time $1164 per credit hour. *Required fees:* $1018; $644 per credit hour. Tuition and fees vary according to course load, campus/location and program.

**Northwest Nazarene University,** Program in Counselor Education, Nampa, ID 83686-5897. Offers clinical counseling (MS); marriage and family counseling (MS); school counseling (MS). *Program availability:* Part-time. *Faculty:* 6 full-time (4 women), 10 part-time/adjunct (6 women). *Students:* 92 full-time (74 women), 26 part-time (19 women); includes 10 minority (2 Black or African American, non-Hispanic/Latino; 6 Hispanic/Latino; 2 Two or more races, non-Hispanic/Latino), 1 international. Average age 35. 47 applicants, 66% accepted, 25 enrolled. In 2016, 33 master's awarded. *Degree requirements:* For master's, comprehensive exam. *Entrance requirements:* For master's, minimum GPA of 3.0, BA. Additional exam requirements/recommendations for international students: Required—TOEFL. *Application deadline:* For fall admission, 2/15 for domestic and international students; for spring admission, 9/15 for domestic and international students. Application fee: $50. Electronic applications accepted. *Expenses:*

*Tuition:* Full-time $9315; part-time $4658 per credit hour. *Required fees:* $120. *Unit head:* Dr. Michael Pitts, Chair, 208-467-8040, Fax: 208-467-8339. *Application contact:* Lynette Kingsmore, Graduate Admissions Counselor, 208-467-8107, E-mail: lkingsmore@nnu.edu.

**Nova Southeastern University,** College of Psychology, Fort Lauderdale, FL 33314-7796. Offers clinical psychology (PhD, Psy D); counseling (MS); experimental psychology (MS); forensic psychology (MS); general psychology (MS); mental health counseling (MS); school counseling (MS); school psychology (Psy D, Psy S). *Accreditation:* APA (one or more programs are accredited). *Program availability:* 100% online, blended/hybrid learning. *Faculty:* 51 full-time (21 women), 120 part-time/adjunct (70 women). *Students:* 724 full-time (596 women), 918 part-time (792 women); includes 797 minority (276 Black or African American, non-Hispanic/Latino; 1 American Indian or Alaska Native, non-Hispanic/Latino; 44 Asian, non-Hispanic/Latino; 427 Hispanic/Latino; 2 Native Hawaiian or other Pacific Islander, non-Hispanic/Latino; 47 Two or more races, non-Hispanic/Latino), 41 international. Average age 31. 1,349 applicants, 61% accepted, 651 enrolled. In 2016, 377 master's, 177 doctorates, 26 other advanced degrees awarded. Terminal master's awarded for partial completion of doctoral program. *Degree requirements:* For master's, comprehensive exam, 3 practica; for doctorate, thesis/dissertation, clinical internship, competency exam; for Psy S, comprehensive exam, internship. *Entrance requirements:* For doctorate, GRE General Test, GRE Subject Test (recommended), minimum undergraduate GPA of 3.0; for Psy S, GRE General Test. Additional exam requirements/recommendations for international students: Required—TOEFL (minimum score 550 paper-based). *Application deadline:* Applications are processed on a rolling basis. Application fee: $50. Electronic applications accepted. *Expenses:* Contact institution. *Financial support:* In 2016–17, 197 students received support, including 15 research assistantships (averaging $5,600 per year), 68 teaching assistantships (averaging $2,000 per year); career-related internships or fieldwork, Federal Work-Study, institutionally sponsored loans, scholarships/grants, and unspecified assistantships also available. Support available to part-time students. Financial award application deadline: 4/15; financial award applicants required to submit FAFSA. *Faculty research:* Clinical health psychology, multicultural/diversity psychology, clinical neuropsychology, clinical child psychology, family violence. *Unit head:* Dr. Karen Grosby, Dean, 954-262-5712, Fax: 954-262-3859, E-mail: grosby@nova.edu. *Application contact:* Carlos Perez, Senior Manager of Outreach, 954-262-5702, Fax: 954-262-3893, E-mail: gradschool@nova.edu. Website: http://psychology.nova.edu/

**Old Dominion University,** Darden College of Education, Counseling Program, Norfolk, VA 23529. Offers clinical mental health counseling (MS Ed); college counseling (MS Ed); counseling (Ed S); counselor education (PhD); school counseling (MS Ed). *Accreditation:* ACA. *Program availability:* Part-time, evening/weekend. *Faculty:* 14 full-time (7 women), 9 part-time/adjunct (7 women). *Students:* 125 full-time (107 women), 58 part-time (43 women); includes 74 minority (44 Black or African American, non-Hispanic/Latino; 1 American Indian or Alaska Native, non-Hispanic/Latino; 5 Asian, non-Hispanic/Latino; 18 Hispanic/Latino; 6 Two or more races, non-Hispanic/Latino), 8 international. Average age 31. 195 applicants, 57% accepted, 79 enrolled. In 2016, 53 master's, 9 doctorates, 3 other advanced degrees awarded. *Degree requirements:* For master's and Ed S, comprehensive exam; for doctorate, comprehensive exam, thesis/dissertation. *Entrance requirements:* For master's and Ed S, GRE General Test, resume, essay, transcripts, recommendations; for doctorate, GRE General Test, resume, interview, essay, transcripts, recommendations. Additional exam requirements/recommendations for international students: Required—TOEFL. *Application deadline:* For fall admission, 3/1 for domestic and international students; for winter admission, 1/10 for domestic students; for spring admission, 10/1 for domestic and international students; for summer admission, 3/1 for domestic students, 2/1 for international students. Application fee: $50. Electronic applications accepted. *Expenses:* Tuition, state resident: full-time $8604; part-time $478 per credit hour. Tuition, nonresident: full-time $21,510; part-time $1195 per credit hour. *Required fees:* $66 per semester. Tuition and fees vary according to campus/location, program and reciprocity agreements. *Financial support:* In 2016–17, 20 students received support, including 2 fellowships with full tuition reimbursements available (averaging $15,000 per year), 13 research assistantships (averaging $9,000 per year), 20 teaching assistantships with full tuition reimbursements available (averaging $20,000 per year); career-related internships or fieldwork, Federal Work-Study, institutionally sponsored loans, scholarships/grants, tuition waivers (partial), and unspecified assistantships also available. Support available to part-time students. Financial award application deadline: 10/1; financial award applicants required to submit FAFSA. *Faculty research:* Group counseling, counselor education, career counseling, spirituality and counseling, school counseling, LGBT counseling, legal and ethical issues. *Total annual research expenditures:* $75,000. *Unit head:* Dr. Jeff Moe, Graduate Program Director, 757-683-6235, Fax: 757-683-5756, E-mail: jmoe@odu.edu. *Application contact:* Jeff Moe, Graduate Program Director, 757-683-6235, Fax: 757-683-5756, E-mail: jmoe@odu.edu. Website: http://www.odu.edu/chs

**Oregon State University,** College of Education, Program in Counseling, Corvallis, OR 97331. Offers clinical mental health counseling (M Coun); counseling (MS, PhD); school counseling (M Coun). *Accreditation:* ACA (one or more programs are accredited); NCATE. *Program availability:* Part-time, blended/hybrid learning. *Faculty:* 9 full-time (3 women), 13 part-time/adjunct (11 women). *Students:* 73 full-time (60 women), 105 part-time (80 women); includes 40 minority (6 Black or African American, non-Hispanic/Latino; 7 Asian, non-Hispanic/Latino; 17 Hispanic/Latino; 1 Native Hawaiian or other Pacific Islander, non-Hispanic/Latino; 9 Two or more races, non-Hispanic/Latino), 1 international. Average age 36. 177 applicants, 51% accepted, 66 enrolled. In 2016, 31 master's, 5 doctorates awarded. *Degree requirements:* For master's, thesis or alternative; for doctorate, one foreign language, thesis/dissertation. *Entrance requirements:* For master's, minimum GPA of 3.0 in last 90 hours; for doctorate, GRE or MAT, master's degree, minimum GPA of 3.0 in last 90 hours of course work, 2 years of teaching experience. Additional exam requirements/recommendations for international students: Required—TOEFL (minimum score 575 paper-based). *Application deadline:* For fall admission, 1/31 for domestic students. Application fee: $75 ($85 for international students). *Expenses:* Tuition, state resident: full-time $12,150; part-time $450 per credit. Tuition, nonresident: full-time $21,789; part-time $807 per credit. *Required fees:* $1651; $1507 per credit. One-time fee: $350. Tuition and fees vary according to course load, campus/location and program. *Financial support:* Teaching assistantships, career-related internships or fieldwork, Federal Work-Study, and institutionally sponsored loans available. Support available to part-time students. Financial award application deadline: 3/1. *Faculty research:* Counseling and guidance improvement in social services agencies, elementary and secondary schools. *Unit head:* Dr. Larry Flick, Dean. *Application contact:* Mary Aguilera, Advisor, 541-737-2232, E-mail: mary.aguilera@oregonstate.edu. Website: http://education.oregonstate.edu/counseling

**Oregon State University–Cascades,** Program in Counseling, Bend, OR 97701. Offers community counseling (MS); school counseling (MS).

**Ottawa University,** Graduate Studies-Arizona, Program in Education, Ottawa, KS 66067-3399. Offers community college counseling (MA); curriculum and instruction (MA); early childhood (MA); education intervention (MA); education leadership (MA);

education technology (MA); Montessori early childhood education (MA); Montessori elementary education (MA); professional development (MA); school guidance counseling (MA); special education - cross categorical (MA). Programs offered in Mesa, Phoenix, Tempe and West Valley, AZ. *Accreditation:* NCATE. *Program availability:* Part-time. *Degree requirements:* For master's, thesis or alternative. *Entrance requirements:* For master's, minimum undergraduate GPA of 3.0, copy of current state certification or teaching license. Additional exam requirements/recommendations for international students: Required—TOEFL (minimum score 550 paper-based). Electronic applications accepted. *Expenses:* Contact institution.

**Our Lady of the Lake University,** School of Professional Studies, Program in Psychology, San Antonio, TX 78207-4689. Offers family, couple, and individual psychotherapy (MS); school psychology (MS). *Accreditation:* APA. *Program availability:* Part-time. *Faculty:* 2 full-time (both women), 2 part-time/adjunct (1 woman). *Students:* 27 full-time (25 women), 10 part-time (9 women); includes 31 minority (1 Black or African American, non-Hispanic/Latino; 1 Asian, non-Hispanic/Latino; 29 Hispanic/Latino). Average age 29. 18 applicants, 67% accepted, 10 enrolled. In 2016, 7 master's awarded. *Degree requirements:* For master's, comprehensive exam, practicum. *Entrance requirements:* For master's, GRE General Test or MAT, bachelor's degree with at least 12 undergraduate semester hours in psychology including one course in statistics and minimum cumulative GPA of 3.0; criminal background check; personal statement addressing background in psychology, expectations of the MS program, and professional goals; statement of purpose; 2 letters of recommendation. Additional exam requirements/recommendations for international students: Required—TOEFL. *Application deadline:* For fall admission, 3/1 priority date for domestic and international students. Application fee: $40 ($50 for international students). Electronic applications accepted. Application fee is waived when completed online. *Expenses: Tuition:* Full-time $14,796. Tuition and fees vary according to course load, degree level, campus/location and program. *Financial support:* In 2016–17, 2 students received support. Federal Work-Study, scholarships/grants, unspecified assistantships, and tuition discounts available. Support available to part-time students. Financial award application deadline: 5/1; financial award applicants required to submit FAFSA. *Faculty research:* Providing competent services to diverse client populations. *Unit head:* Psychology Department, 210-431-3914. *Application contact:* Office of Graduate Admissions, 210-431-3995, Fax: 210-431-3945, E-mail: gradadm@lake.ollusa.edu. Website: http://www.ollusa.edu/s/1190/hybrid/default-hybrid-ollu.aspx?sid-1190&gid-1&pgid-7908

**Pace University,** Dyson College of Arts and Sciences, Department of Psychology, Program in School-Clinical Child Psychology, New York, NY 10038. Offers school psychology (MS Ed); school-clinical child psychology (Psy D). *Accreditation:* APA (one or more programs are accredited). *Students:* 62 full-time (51 women), 28 part-time (22 women); includes 18 minority (2 Black or African American, non-Hispanic/Latino; 7 Asian, non-Hispanic/Latino; 5 Hispanic/Latino; 1 Native Hawaiian or other Pacific Islander, non-Hispanic/Latino; 3 Two or more races, non-Hispanic/Latino), 3 international. Average age 27. In 2016, 21 master's, 23 doctorates awarded. Terminal master's awarded for partial completion of doctoral program. *Degree requirements:* For master's, qualifying exams, internship; for doctorate, comprehensive exam, thesis/dissertation, qualifying exams, externship, internship. *Entrance requirements:* For master's, GRE General Test, GRE Subject Test in psychology (recommended), interview, 3 letters of recommendation, resume, personal statement; for doctorate, GRE General Test, GRE Subject Test in psychology (recommended), interview, transcripts, 3 letters of recommendation. Additional exam requirements/recommendations for international students: Required—TOEFL (minimum score 88 iBT), IELTS (minimum score 7) or PTE (minimum score 60). *Application deadline:* For fall admission, 1/15 priority date for domestic students. Application fee: $70. Electronic applications accepted. *Expenses: Tuition:* Part-time $1195 per credit. *Required fees:* $260 per semester. Tuition and fees vary according to degree level, campus/location and program. *Financial support:* Scholarships/grants and unspecified assistantships available. Financial award application deadline: 1/15; financial award applicants required to submit FAFSA. *Unit head:* Dr. Barbara Mowder, Director of Graduate Psychology Programs, 212-346-1556, E-mail: bmowder@pace.edu. *Application contact:* Susan Ford-Goldschein, Director of Graduate Admissions, 212-346-1531, Fax: 212-346-1585, E-mail: graduateadmission@pace.edu. Website: http://www.pace.edu/dyson/academic-departments-and-programs/psychology---nyc/graduate-programs

**Penn State University Park,** Graduate School, College of Education, Department of Educational Psychology, Counseling, and Special Education, University Park, PA 16802. Offers counselor education (M Ed, D Ed, PhD, Certificate); educational psychology (MS, PhD, Certificate); school psychology (M Ed, MS, PhD, Certificate); special education (M Ed, MS, PhD, Certificate). *Unit head:* Dr. David H. Monk, Dean, 814-865-2523, Fax: 814-865-0555. *Application contact:* Lori Hawn, Director, Graduate Student Services, 814-865-1795, Fax: 814-863-4627, E-mail: l-gswww@lists.psu.edu. Website: http://ed.psu.edu/epcse

**Philadelphia College of Osteopathic Medicine,** Graduate and Professional Programs, Department of Psychology, Philadelphia, PA 19131-1694. Offers applied behavior analysis (Certificate); clinical health psychology (Post-Doctoral Certificate); clinical neuropsychology (Post-Doctoral Certificate); clinical psychology (Psy D); mental health counseling (MS); organizational development and leadership (MS); psychology (Certificate); school psychology (MS, Psy D, Ed S). *Accreditation:* APA. *Faculty:* 19 full-time (11 women), 122 part-time/adjunct (58 women). *Students:* 364 (285 women); includes 78 minority (62 Black or African American, non-Hispanic/Latino; 2 American Indian or Alaska Native, non-Hispanic/Latino; 9 Asian, non-Hispanic/Latino; 5 Hispanic/Latino), 2 international. 366 applicants, 51% accepted, 139 enrolled. In 2016, 72 master's, 42 doctorates, 17 other advanced degrees awarded. Terminal master's awarded for partial completion of doctoral program. *Degree requirements:* For master's, comprehensive exam (for some programs), thesis (for some programs); for doctorate, comprehensive exam, thesis/dissertation. *Entrance requirements:* For master's, GRE or MAT, minimum GPA of 3.0; bachelor's degree from regionally-accredited college or university; for doctorate, PRAXIS II (for Psy D in school psychology), minimum undergraduate GPA of 3.0; for other advanced degree, GRE (for Ed S). Additional exam requirements/recommendations for international students: Required—TOEFL (minimum score 79 iBT). *Application deadline:* Applications are processed on a rolling basis. Application fee: $50. Electronic applications accepted. Tuition and fees vary according to course load, degree level and program. *Financial support:* In 2016–17, 28 teaching assistantships were awarded; Federal Work-Study, institutionally sponsored loans, and scholarships/grants also available. Financial award application deadline: 3/15; financial award applicants required to submit FAFSA. *Faculty research:* Adult and childhood anxiety and ADHD; coping with chronic illness; primary care psychology/integrated health care; applied behavior analysis; psychological, educational, and neuropsychological assessment. *Total annual research expenditures:* $533,489. *Unit head:* Dr. Robert DiTomasso, Chairman, 215-871-6442, Fax: 215-871-6458, E-mail: robertd@pcom.edu. *Application contact:* Johnathan Cox, Associate Director of Admissions, 215-871-6700, Fax: 215-871-6719, E-mail: karis@pcom.edu.

**See Display on page 1004 and Close-Up on page 1227.**

**Pittsburg State University,** Graduate School, College of Education, Department of Psychology and Counseling, Program in School Psychology, Pittsburg, KS 66762. Offers Ed S. *Accreditation:* NCATE. *Program availability:* Part-time. *Students:* 2. In 2016, 2 Ed Ss awarded. *Degree requirements:* For Ed S, thesis or alternative. *Entrance requirements:* For degree, GRE General Test, minimum GPA of 3.0. Additional exam requirements/recommendations for international students: Required—TOEFL (minimum score 550 paper-based; 79 iBT), IELTS (minimum score 6.5), PTE (minimum score 53). *Application deadline:* Applications are processed on a rolling basis. Application fee: $35 ($60 for international students). Electronic applications accepted. *Expenses:* Contact institution. *Financial support:* Teaching assistantships, career-related internships or fieldwork, and Federal Work-Study available. Financial award application deadline: 2/1; financial award applicants required to submit FAFSA. *Unit head:* Dr. David Hurford, Chairperson, 620-235-4521. *Application contact:* Lisa Allen, Assistant Director of Graduate and Continuing Studies, 620-235-4218, Fax: 620-235-4219, E-mail: lallen@pittstate.edu.

**Plymouth State University,** College of Graduate Studies, Graduate Studies in Education, Certificate of Advanced Graduate Studies Programs, Plymouth, NH 03264-1595. Offers clinical mental health counseling (CAGS); educational leadership (CAGS); higher education (CAGS); school psychology (CAGS). *Program availability:* Part-time, evening/weekend.

**Plymouth State University,** College of Graduate Studies, Graduate Studies in Education, Programs in Counseling, Plymouth, NH 03264-1595. Offers human relations (M Ed); school counseling (M Ed); school psychology (M Ed). *Accreditation:* ACA; NCATE. *Program availability:* Part-time, evening/weekend. *Degree requirements:* For master's, PRAXIS I. *Entrance requirements:* For master's, MAT, minimum GPA of 3.0.

**Purdue University Northwest,** Graduate Studies Office, School of Education, Program in Counseling, Hammond, IN 46323-2094. Offers human services (MS Ed); mental health counseling (MS Ed); school counseling (MS Ed). *Accreditation:* ACA. *Entrance requirements:* Additional exam requirements/recommendations for international students: Required—TOEFL.

**Queens College of the City University of New York,** Division of Education, Department of Educational and Community Programs, Queens, NY 11367-1597. Offers bilingual pupil personnel (AC); counselor education (MS Ed); mental health counseling (MS); school building leader (AC); school district leader (AC); school psychologist (MS Ed); special education-childhood education (AC); special education-early childhood (MS Ed); teacher of special education 1-6 (MS Ed); teacher of special education birth-2 (MS Ed); teaching students with disabilities, grades 7-12 (MS Ed, AC). *Program availability:* Part-time. *Faculty:* 20 full-time (14 women), 50 part-time/adjunct (26 women). *Students:* 101 full-time (85 women), 459 part-time (383 women); includes 230 minority (44 Black or African American, non-Hispanic/Latino; 3 American Indian or Alaska Native, non-Hispanic/Latino; 46 Asian, non-Hispanic/Latino; 128 Hispanic/Latino; 1 Native Hawaiian or other Pacific Islander, non-Hispanic/Latino; 8 Two or more races, non-Hispanic/Latino), 3 international. Average age 28. 515 applicants, 57% accepted, 230 enrolled. In 2016, 158 master's, 68 other advanced degrees awarded. *Degree requirements:* For master's, research project; for AC, internship. *Entrance requirements:* For master's, minimum GPA of 3.0. Additional exam requirements/recommendations for international students: Required—TOEFL, IELTS. *Application deadline:* For fall admission, 3/1 for domestic students. Applications are processed on a rolling basis. Application fee: $125. Electronic applications accepted. *Expenses:* Tuition, state resident: full-time $5065; part-time $425 per credit. Tuition, nonresident: part-time $780 per credit. *Required fees:* $522; $397 per credit. Part-time tuition and fees vary according to course load and program. *Financial support:* Career-related internships or fieldwork available. Financial award application deadline: 4/1; financial award applicants required to submit FAFSA. *Unit head:* Dr. Lynn Howell, Chairperson, 718-997-5250, E-mail: lynn.howell@qc.cuny.edu.

**Quincy University,** Master of Science in Education Counseling Program, Quincy, IL 62301-2699. Offers college personnel (MS Ed); counseling (MS Ed); school counseling (MS Ed). *Program availability:* Part-time, evening/weekend. *Degree requirements:* For master's, comprehensive exam, practicum, internship. *Entrance requirements:* For master's, MAT or GRE. Additional exam requirements/recommendations for international students: Required—TOEFL (minimum score 550 paper-based; 79 iBT). Electronic applications accepted.

**Radford University,** College of Graduate Studies and Research, Program in School Psychology, Radford, VA 24142. Offers Ed S. *Accreditation:* NCATE. *Faculty:* 23 full-time (16 women). *Students:* 18 full-time (16 women), 7 part-time (6 women); includes 3 minority (1 Black or African American, non-Hispanic/Latino; 1 Asian, non-Hispanic/Latino; 1 Hispanic/Latino), 1 international. Average age 25. 31 applicants, 77% accepted, 9 enrolled. In 2016, 3 Ed Ss awarded. *Degree requirements:* For Ed S, comprehensive exam. *Entrance requirements:* For degree, GRE, minimum GPA of 3.0, 2 letters of reference, essay, resume, official transcripts. Additional exam requirements/recommendations for international students: Required—TOEFL (minimum score 550 paper-based; 79 iBT), IELTS (minimum score 6.5). *Application deadline:* For fall admission, 2/15 priority date for domestic students, 12/1 for international students; for spring admission, 7/1 for international students. Applications are processed on a rolling basis. Application fee: $50. Electronic applications accepted. *Expenses:* Tuition, state resident: full-time $7868; part-time $328 per credit. Tuition, nonresident: full-time $16,394; part-time $683 per credit hour. *Required fees:* $3090; $130 per credit hour. Tuition and fees vary according to course load and program. *Financial support:* In 2016–17, 13 students received support, including 2 teaching assistantships (averaging $7,500 per year); career-related internships or fieldwork, scholarships/grants, and unspecified assistantships also available. Support available to part-time students. Financial award application deadline: 3/1; financial award applicants required to submit FAFSA. *Faculty research:* Civility in the classroom, intellectual assessment and identification of learning difficulties, behaviorally-based academic interventions in students experiencing learning difficulties, pediatric neuropsychology. *Unit head:* Dr. Eric Mesmer, Coordinator, 540-831-5361, Fax: 540-831-6113, E-mail: emesmer@radford.edu.
Website: http://www.radford.edu/content/chbs/home/psychology/programs/school.html

**Rhode Island College,** School of Graduate Studies, Feinstein School of Education and Human Development, Department of Counseling, Educational Leadership, and School Psychology, Providence, RI 02908-1991. Offers advanced counseling (CGS); agency counseling (MA); clinical mental health counseling (MS); co-occurring disorders (MA, CGS); educational leadership (M Ed); mental health counseling (CAGS); school counseling (MA); school psychology (CAGS); teacher leadership (CGS). *Accreditation:* ACA; NCATE. *Program availability:* Part-time, evening/weekend. *Faculty:* 9 full-time (5 women), 10 part-time/adjunct (all women). *Students:* 34 full-time (28 women), 83 part-time (72 women); includes 16 minority (5 Black or African American, non-Hispanic/Latino; 1 Asian, non-Hispanic/Latino; 10 Hispanic/Latino). Average age 33. In 2016, 50 master's, 34 other advanced degrees awarded. *Degree requirements:* For master's and other advanced degree, comprehensive exam (for some programs), thesis (for some programs). *Entrance requirements:* For master's, GRE General Test or MAT, undergraduate transcripts; minimum undergraduate GPA of 3.0; for other advanced degree, GRE or MAT (for most programs), undergraduate transcripts; minimum

undergraduate GPA of 3.0; 3 letters of recommendation; current resume. Additional exam requirements/recommendations for international students: Recommended—TOEFL (minimum score 550 paper-based; 79 iBT). *Application deadline:* For fall admission, 3/1 for domestic students; for spring admission, 11/1 for domestic students. Applications are processed on a rolling basis. Application fee: $50. Electronic applications accepted. *Expenses:* Tuition, state resident: full-time $8928; part-time $372 per credit. Tuition, nonresident: full-time $17,376; part-time $724 per credit. *Required fees:* $604; $22 per credit. One-time fee: $74. *Financial support:* In 2016–17, 3 teaching assistantships with full tuition reimbursements (averaging $2,500 per year) were awarded; career-related internships or fieldwork, Federal Work-Study, scholarships/grants, health care benefits, and unspecified assistantships also available. Support available to part-time students. Financial award application deadline: 5/15; financial award applicants required to submit FAFSA. *Unit head:* Dr. Andrew Snyder, Chair, 401-456-9633. *Application contact:* Graduate Studies, 401-456-8700.
Website: http://www.ric.edu/counselingEducationalLeadershipSchoolPsychology/index.php

**Rider University,** Department of Graduate Education, Leadership and Counseling, Program in School Psychology, Lawrenceville, NJ 08648-3001. Offers Certificate, Ed S. *Entrance requirements:* For degree, GRE or MAT, resume, 2 professional references, interview, 1 year of counseling experience. Additional exam requirements/recommendations for international students: Required—TOEFL (minimum score 550 paper-based). *Faculty research:* Prenatal factors on child development, child abuse developmental assessments.

**Roberts Wesleyan College,** Graduate Psychology Programs, Rochester, NY 14624-1997. Offers clinical/school psychology (Psy D); school counseling (MS); school psychology (MS). *Program availability:* Part-time, evening/weekend. *Degree requirements:* For master's, comprehensive exam, PRAXIS II (for school psychology). *Entrance requirements:* For master's, GRE. Electronic applications accepted. Application fee is waived when completed online. *Faculty research:* Counselor supervision, forgiveness, community health psychology, applied research in group process.

**Rochester Institute of Technology,** Graduate Enrollment Services, College of Liberal Arts, Psychology Department, Advanced Certificate Program in School Psychology, Rochester, NY 14623. Offers Advanced Certificate. *Program availability:* Part-time. *Students:* 2 full-time (1 woman). 3 applicants. In 2016, 6 Advanced Certificates awarded. *Entrance requirements:* For degree, minimum GPA of 3.0 (recommended). Additional exam requirements/recommendations for international students: Required—TOEFL (minimum score 600 paper-based; 100 iBT), IELTS (minimum score 7), PTE (minimum score 68). *Application deadline:* For fall admission, 2/15 priority date for domestic and international students; for spring admission, 12/15 priority date for domestic students, 11/15 priority date for international students. Applications are processed on a rolling basis. Application fee: $60. Electronic applications accepted. *Expenses:* $1,742 per credit hour. *Financial support:* In 2016–17, 1 student received support. Scholarships/grants available. Support available to part-time students. Financial award applicants required to submit FAFSA. *Unit head:* Dr. Suzanne Bamonto, Graduate Program Director, 585-475-2765, E-mail: sbggsp@rit.edu. *Application contact:* Diane Ellison, Associate Vice President, Graduate Enrollment Services, 585-475-2229, Fax: 585-475-7164, E-mail: gradinfo@rit.edu.
Website: http://www.rit.edu/cla/psychology/advanced-certificates/school-psychology

**Rochester Institute of Technology,** Graduate Enrollment Services, College of Liberal Arts, Psychology Department, MS Program in School Psychology, Rochester, NY 14623. Offers MS. *Program availability:* Part-time. *Students:* 17 full-time (15 women), 1 (woman) part-time; includes 1 minority (Black or African American, non-Hispanic/Latino). Average age 25. 34 applicants, 41% accepted, 5 enrolled. In 2016, 6 master's awarded. *Degree requirements:* For master's, internship, portfolio. *Entrance requirements:* For master's, GRE, minimum GPA of 3.0 (recommended). Additional exam requirements/recommendations for international students: Required—TOEFL (minimum score 600 paper-based; 100 iBT), IELTS (minimum score 7), PTE (minimum score 68). *Application deadline:* For fall admission, 2/15 priority date for domestic and international students; for spring admission, 12/15 priority date for domestic and international students. Applications are processed on a rolling basis. Application fee: $60. Electronic applications accepted. *Expenses:* $1,742 per credit hour. *Financial support:* In 2016–17, 12 students received support. Teaching assistantships with partial tuition reimbursements available, career-related internships or fieldwork, scholarships/grants, and unspecified assistantships available. Support available to part-time students. Financial award applicants required to submit FAFSA. *Faculty research:* Personality assessment, autism spectrum disorders, developmental disabilities, psychometrics, curriculum-based measurement, multi-tier system of supports, psychophysiological and neuropsychological assessment, impulsivity, aggression, attention. *Unit head:* Dr. Suzanne Bamonto, Graduate Program Director, 585-475-2765, E-mail: sbggsp@rit.edu. *Application contact:* Diane Ellison, Associate Vice President, Graduate Enrollment Services, 585-475-2229, Fax: 585-475-7164, E-mail: gradinfo@rit.edu.
Website: http://www.rit.edu/cla/psychology/graduate/ms-school-psych/overview

**Rowan University,** Graduate School, College of Education, Department of Educational Services and Leadership, Ed S in School Psychology Program, Glassboro, NJ 08028-1701. Offers Ed S. *Degree requirements:* For Ed S, practicum, internship. *Entrance requirements:* For degree, master's degree, official transcripts, current professional resume, statement of professional objectives, two letters of recommendation, interview. Electronic applications accepted.

**Rowan University,** Graduate School, College of Education, Department of Educational Services and Leadership, MA in School Psychology Program, Glassboro, NJ 08028-1701. Offers MA. *Accreditation:* NCATE. *Program availability:* Part-time, evening/weekend. *Degree requirements:* For master's, comprehensive exam, thesis. *Entrance requirements:* For master's, GRE General Test, GRE Subject Test, interview, minimum GPA of 3.0. Additional exam requirements/recommendations for international students: Required—TOEFL.

**Rutgers University–New Brunswick,** Graduate School of Applied and Professional Psychology, Program in School Psychology, Piscataway, NJ 08854-8097. Offers Psy M, Psy D. *Accreditation:* APA (one or more programs are accredited). *Degree requirements:* For doctorate, comprehensive exam, thesis/dissertation, 1 year internship. *Entrance requirements:* For doctorate, GRE General Test, GRE Subject Test, bachelor's degree in psychology or equivalent. Additional exam requirements/recommendations for international students: Required—TOEFL. Electronic applications accepted. *Expenses:* Contact institution. *Faculty research:* Consultation, program evaluation, applied educational psychology, exceptional children, crisis intervention.

**St. John's University,** St. John's College of Liberal Arts and Sciences, Department of Psychology, Program in School Psychology, Queens, NY 11439. Offers MS, Psy D. *Program availability:* Part-time. *Degree requirements:* For master's, comprehensive exam, thesis optional; for doctorate, comprehensive exam, thesis/dissertation, internship, practicum. *Entrance requirements:* For master's, GRE General Test, GRE Subject Test, minimum GPA of 3.0, 2 writing samples, 3 letters of recommendation, minimum of 24 undergraduate credits in psychology, personal statement, transcript,

## School Psychology

bachelor's degree; for doctorate, GRE General Test, GRE Subject Test, minimum GPA of 3.0, 2 writing samples, 3 letters of recommendation, minimum of 24 undergraduate credits in psychology, personal statement. Additional exam requirements/recommendations for international students: Required—TOEFL (minimum score 600 paper-based; 100 iBT), IELTS (minimum score 7). Electronic applications accepted. *Expenses:* Contact institution. *Faculty research:* Therapeutic alliance, intelligence testing, multicultural assessment, neuropsychological assessment, adolescent suicide.

**Saint Mary's College of California,** Kalmanovitz School of Education, Program in Counseling, Moraga, CA 94575. Offers career counseling (MA); college student services (Credential); general counseling (MA); marriage and family therapy (MA); pupil personnel services (Credential), including school counseling, school psychology; school counseling (MA); school psychology (MA). *Program availability:* Part-time, evening/weekend. *Degree requirements:* For master's, thesis or alternative. *Entrance requirements:* For master's, interview, minimum GPA of 3.0. *Faculty research:* Counselor training effectiveness, multicultural development, empathy, the interface of spirituality and psychotherapy, gender issues.

**Sam Houston State University,** College of Humanities and Social Sciences, Department of Psychology and Philosophy, Huntsville, TX 77341. Offers psychology (MA, PhD, SSP), including clinical psychology (MA, PhD), psychology (MA), school psychology (SSP). *Accreditation:* APA. *Program availability:* Part-time. Terminal master's awarded for partial completion of doctoral program. *Degree requirements:* For master's, comprehensive exam, thesis optional; for doctorate, comprehensive exam, thesis/dissertation. *Entrance requirements:* For master's, GRE General Test, personal statement, letters of recommendation; for doctorate, GRE General Test, GRE Subject Test (advanced psychology), personal essay, letters of recommendation, resume. Additional exam requirements/recommendations for international students: Required—TOEFL (minimum score 550 paper-based; 79 iBT), IELTS (minimum score 6.5). Electronic applications accepted.

**San Diego State University,** Graduate and Research Affairs, College of Education, Department of Counseling and School Psychology, San Diego, CA 92182. Offers MS. *Accreditation:* NCATE. *Program availability:* Evening/weekend. *Degree requirements:* For master's, comprehensive exam (for some programs), thesis (for some programs). *Entrance requirements:* For master's, GRE General Test, interview, letters of reference. Additional exam requirements/recommendations for international students: Required—TOEFL. Electronic applications accepted. *Faculty research:* Multicultural and cross-cultural counseling and training, AIDS counseling.

**San Francisco State University,** Division of Graduate Studies, College of Science and Engineering, Department of Psychology, San Francisco, CA 94132-1722. Offers clinical psychology (MS); developmental psychology (MA); industrial/organizational psychology (MS); mind, brain, and behavior (MA); school psychology (MS, Credential); social psychology (MA). *Expenses:* Tuition, state resident: full-time $6738. Tuition, nonresident: full-time $15,666. *Required fees:* $1012. Tuition and fees vary according to degree level and program. *Financial support:* Teaching assistantships available. Financial award application deadline: 3/1. *Unit head:* Dr. Dawn Terrell, Chair, 415-338-7555, Fax: 415-338-2398, E-mail: schen9@sfsu.edu. *Application contact:* Dr. Diane Harris, Graduate Program Coordinator, 415-338-7064, Fax: 415-338-2398, E-mail: dharris@sfsu.edu.
Website: http://psychology.sfsu.edu/graduate/application.html

**San Jose State University,** Graduate Studies and Research, Connie L. Lurie College of Education, San Jose, CA 95192-0001. Offers child and adolescent development (MA); common core mathematics (K-8) (Certificate, Credential); education (MA, Credential), including counseling and student personnel (MA); speech pathology (MA); educational leadership (MA, Ed D, Credential), including administration and supervision (MA), higher education (MA), preliminary administrative services (Credential), professional administrative services (Credential); elementary education (MA), including curriculum and instruction; K-12 school counseling (Credential); K-12 school counseling internship (Credential); school child welfare attendance (Credential); single subject (Credential). *Accreditation:* NCATE. *Program availability:* Evening/weekend. Electronic applications accepted.

**Seattle University,** College of Education, Program in Counseling and School Psychology, Seattle, WA 98122-1090. Offers MA, Certificate, Ed S. *Accreditation:* ACA; NCATE. *Program availability:* Part-time, evening/weekend. *Faculty:* 11 full-time (6 women), 3 part-time/adjunct (2 women). *Students:* 75 full-time (65 women), 142 part-time (119 women); includes 73 minority (13 Black or African American, non-Hispanic/Latino; 3 American Indian or Alaska Native, non-Hispanic/Latino; 15 Asian, non-Hispanic/Latino; 30 Hispanic/Latino; 12 Two or more races, non-Hispanic/Latino), 4 international. Average age 30. 207 applicants, 43% accepted, 52 enrolled. In 2016, 36 master's, 20 other advanced degrees awarded. *Degree requirements:* For master's, comprehensive exam. *Entrance requirements:* For master's, interview; GRE, MAT, or minimum GPA of 3.0; related work experience. Additional exam requirements/recommendations for international students: Required—TOEFL. *Application deadline:* For fall admission, 7/1 for domestic students; for winter admission, 10/20 for domestic students; for spring admission, 1/20 for domestic students. Application fee: $55. *Financial support:* In 2016–17, 20 students received support. *Unit head:* Hutch Haney, Director, 206-296-5750, E-mail: schpsy@seattleu.edu. *Application contact:* Janet Shandley, Associate Dean of Graduate Admissions, 206-296-5900, Fax: 206-298-5656, E-mail: grad_admissions@seattleu.edu.

**Seton Hall University,** College of Education and Human Services, Department of Professional Psychology and Family Therapy, Program in School Psychology, South Orange, NJ 07079-2697. Offers MA. *Faculty:* 2 full-time (1 woman), 8 part-time/adjunct (2 women). *Students:* 1 (woman) full-time, 19 part-time (17 women); includes 6 minority (4 Black or African American, non-Hispanic/Latino; 2 Asian, non-Hispanic/Latino). Average age 27. 10 applicants, 100% accepted, 5 enrolled. In 2016, 11 master's awarded. *Degree requirements:* For master's, comprehensive exam, thesis, internship. *Entrance requirements:* For master's, GRE or MAT, interview. *Application deadline:* For fall admission, 2/1 priority date for domestic and international students. Applications are processed on a rolling basis. Application fee: $75. *Financial support:* In 2016–17, 5 students received support, including 3 research assistantships with full tuition reimbursements available (averaging $4,500 per year). Financial award application deadline: 2/1; financial award applicants required to submit CSS PROFILE. *Faculty research:* Family systems, ethical behavior, childhood depression. *Unit head:* Dr. Thomas Massarelli, Director, 973-313-6129, Fax: 973-275-2188, E-mail: massarth@shu.edu. *Application contact:* Diana Minakakis, Director of Graduate Admissions, 973-275-2824.
Website: http://www.shu.edu/academics/ma-eds-school-psychology.cfm

**Slippery Rock University of Pennsylvania,** Graduate Studies (Recruitment), College of Education, Department of Counseling and Development, Slippery Rock, PA 16057-1383. Offers clinical mental health (MA); school counseling (M Ed); student affairs in higher education (MA); student affairs in higher education with college counseling (MA). *Accreditation:* ACA (one or more programs are accredited); NCATE. *Program availability:* Part-time, evening/weekend. *Faculty:* 7 full-time (5 women), 1 (woman) part-time/adjunct. *Students:* 86 full-time (55 women), 23 part-time (18 women); includes 13

minority (7 Black or African American, non-Hispanic/Latino; 4 Hispanic/Latino; 2 Two or more races, non-Hispanic/Latino), 1 international. Average age 28. 107 applicants, 57% accepted, 42 enrolled. In 2016, 39 master's awarded. *Degree requirements:* For master's, comprehensive exam, thesis (for some programs). *Entrance requirements:* For master's, GRE General Test or MAT, official transcripts, personal statement, three letters of recommendation, interview. Additional exam requirements/recommendations for international students: Required—TOEFL (minimum score 550 paper-based; 80 iBT). *Application deadline:* For fall admission, 1/15 priority date for domestic and international students. Applications are processed on a rolling basis. Application fee: $25 ($30 for international students). Electronic applications accepted. *Expenses:* $646.50 per credit in-state, $936.80 per credit out-of-state; $581.45 per online credit in-state, $648.65 per online credit out-of-state. *Financial support:* In 2016–17, 58 students received support. Career-related internships or fieldwork, Federal Work-Study, institutionally sponsored loans, scholarships/grants, tuition waivers (partial), and unspecified assistantships available. Support available to part-time students. Financial award application deadline: 5/1; financial award applicants required to submit FAFSA. *Unit head:* Dr. Stacy Jacob, Graduate Coordinator, 724-738-2758, Fax: 724-738-4859, E-mail: stacy.jacob@sru.edu. *Application contact:* Brandi Weber-Mortimer, Director of Graduate Admissions, 724-738-2051, Fax: 724-738-2146, E-mail: graduate.admissions@sru.edu. Website: http://www.sru.edu/academics/colleges-and-departments/coe/departments/counseling-and-development

**Sonoma State University,** School of Social Sciences, Department of Counseling, Rohnert Park, CA 94928-3609. Offers clinical mental health counseling (MA); school counseling (MA). *Accreditation:* ACA. *Program availability:* Part-time. *Degree requirements:* For master's, internship. *Entrance requirements:* For master's, minimum GPA of 3.0. Additional exam requirements/recommendations for international students: Required—TOEFL (minimum score 500 paper-based). *Application deadline:* For fall admission, 11/30 for domestic students. Application fee: $55. *Expenses:* Tuition, state resident: full-time $6738; part-time $3906 per unit. *Required fees:* $1916; $1916 per year. Tuition and fees vary according to course load, degree level and program. *Financial support:* Fellowships and career-related internships or fieldwork available. Financial award application deadline: 3/2; financial award applicants required to submit FAFSA. *Unit head:* Dr. Adam Zagelbaum, Chair, 707-664-2544, E-mail: adam.zagelbaum@sonoma.edu.
Website: http://www.sonoma.edu/counseling

**Southern Connecticut State University,** School of Graduate Studies, School of Education, Department of Counseling and School Psychology, New Haven, CT 06515-1355. Offers community counseling (MS); counseling (Diploma); school counseling (MS); school psychology (MS, Diploma). *Accreditation:* ACA (one or more programs are accredited); NCATE. *Program availability:* Part-time, evening/weekend. *Faculty:* 10 full-time (8 women). *Students:* 71 full-time (62 women), 58 part-time (46 women); includes 27 minority (18 Black or African American, non-Hispanic/Latino; 8 Hispanic/Latino; 1 Two or more races, non-Hispanic/Latino). Average age 29. 202 applicants, 44% accepted, 54 enrolled. In 2016, 42 master's, 13 other advanced degrees awarded. *Degree requirements:* For master's, comprehensive exam. *Entrance requirements:* For master's, interview, previous course work in behavioral sciences, minimum QPA of 2.7. *Application deadline:* For fall admission, 1/15 for domestic students; for spring admission, 10/15 for domestic students. Application fee: $50. Electronic applications accepted. *Expenses:* Tuition, state resident: full-time $6497; part-time $519 per credit hour. Tuition, nonresident: full-time $18,102; part-time $535 per credit hour. *Required fees:* $4722; $55 per semester. Tuition and fees vary according to program. *Financial support:* Career-related internships or fieldwork, scholarships/grants, and unspecified assistantships available. Financial award application deadline: 4/15; financial award applicants required to submit FAFSA. *Unit head:* Dr. Margaret Generali, Chairperson, 203-392-5175, Fax: 203-392-5910, E-mail: generalim1@southernct.edu. *Application contact:* Lisa Galvin, Director of Graduate Admissions, 203-392-5240, Fax: 203-392-5235, E-mail: galvinl1@southernct.edu.

**Southern Illinois University Edwardsville,** Graduate School, School of Education, Health, and Human Behavior, Department of Psychology, Program in School Psychology, Edwardsville, IL 62026. Offers SD. *Accreditation:* NCATE. *Program availability:* Part-time, evening/weekend. *Degree requirements:* For SD, thesis. *Entrance requirements:* For degree, GRE. Additional exam requirements/recommendations for international students: Required—TOEFL (minimum score 550 paper-based; 79 iBT), IELTS (minimum score 6.5). Electronic applications accepted.

**Southwestern Oklahoma State University,** College of Professional and Graduate Studies, School of Behavioral Sciences and Education, Specialization in School Psychology, Weatherford, OK 73096-3098. Offers MS.

**State University of New York at Plattsburgh,** School of Arts and Sciences, Department of Psychology, Plattsburgh, NY 12901-2681. Offers school psychology (MA, CAS). *Program availability:* Part-time. *Entrance requirements:* For master's, GRE General Test, minimum GPA of 3.0. Additional exam requirements/recommendations for international students: Required—TOEFL. *Faculty research:* Alzheimer's disease, adolescent behavior, intellectual assessment, learning disabilities, reading skill acquisition.

**Stephen F. Austin State University,** Graduate School, College of Education, Department of Human Services, Nacogdoches, TX 75962. Offers counseling (MA); school psychology (MA); special education (M Ed); speech pathology (MS). *Accreditation:* ACA (one or more programs are accredited); ASHA (one or more programs are accredited); CORE; NCATE. *Degree requirements:* For master's, comprehensive exam, thesis (for some programs). *Entrance requirements:* For master's, GRE General Test, minimum GPA of 2.8. Additional exam requirements/recommendations for international students: Required—TOEFL.

**Suffolk University,** College of Arts and Sciences, Department of Psychology, Boston, MA 02108-2770. Offers clinical psychology (PhD); college admission counseling (Certificate); mental health counseling (MS); school counseling (MS, CAGS). *Accreditation:* APA. *Faculty:* 14 full-time (7 women), 7 part-time/adjunct (6 women). *Students:* 51 full-time (45 women), 42 part-time (38 women); includes 24 minority (3 Black or African American, non-Hispanic/Latino; 8 Asian, non-Hispanic/Latino; 11 Hispanic/Latino; 2 Two or more races, non-Hispanic/Latino), 6 international. Average age 27. 306 applicants, 25% accepted, 38 enrolled. In 2016, 22 master's, 10 doctorates, 14 other advanced degrees awarded. *Degree requirements:* For doctorate, thesis/dissertation, practicum. *Entrance requirements:* For doctorate, GRE General Test or MAT, 2 letters of recommendation, resume. Additional exam requirements/recommendations for international students: Required—TOEFL (minimum score 550 paper-based; 80 iBT). *Application deadline:* For fall admission, 12/1 for domestic and international students. Applications are processed on a rolling basis. Application fee: $50. Electronic applications accepted. *Expenses:* Contact institution. *Financial support:* In 2016–17, 54 students received support, including 53 fellowships (averaging $13,943 per year); career-related internships or fieldwork, Federal Work-Study, institutionally sponsored loans, scholarships/grants, and unspecified assistantships also available. Support available to part-time students. Financial award application deadline: 4/1; financial award applicants required to submit FAFSA. *Faculty research:* Assessing exposure in the context of a family-based cognitive behavioral treatment for pediatric

OCD, a mindfulness approach to designing and testing the efficacy of a new sexual revictimization prevention program for college women, olfaction and decision-making in substance-dependent individuals, the role of experiential avoidance in Generalized Anxiety Disorder, ego development as a predictor of dogmatism and intolerance in the political right and left. *Unit head:* Dr. Gary Fireman, Chairperson, 617-305-6368, Fax: 617-367-2924, E-mail: gfireman@suffolk.edu. *Application contact:* Mara Marzocchi, Associate Director of Graduate Admissions, 617-573-8302, Fax: 617-305-1733, E-mail: grad.admission@suffolk.edu.
Website: http://www.suffolk.edu/college/graduate/69299.php

**Syracuse University,** College of Arts and Sciences, Programs in Psychology, Syracuse, NY 13244. Offers clinical psychology (PhD); cognition, brain, and behavior (PhD); school psychology (PhD); social psychology (PhD). *Accreditation:* APA. In 2016, 1 doctorate awarded. Terminal master's awarded for partial completion of doctoral program. *Degree requirements:* For doctorate, comprehensive exam, thesis/ dissertation. *Entrance requirements:* For doctorate, GRE General Test, GRE Subject Test, resume, personal statement, three letters of recommendation. Additional exam requirements/recommendations for international students: Required—TOEFL (minimum score 100 iBT). *Application deadline:* For fall admission, 12/1 priority date for domestic and international students. Application fee: $75. Electronic applications accepted. *Expenses:* Tuition: Full-time $25,974; part-time $1443 per credit hour. *Required fees:* $802; $50 per course. Tuition and fees vary according to course load and program. *Financial support:* Fellowships with full tuition reimbursements, research assistantships with tuition reimbursements, teaching assistantships with tuition reimbursements, and scholarships/grants available. Financial award application deadline: 1/1. *Faculty research:* Clinical psychology; cognition, brain, and behavior; school psychology; social psychology. *Unit head:* Dr. Larry Lewandowski, Professor of Psychology/Interim Chair, 315-443-1015, E-mail: ljlewand@syr.edu. *Application contact:* Alecia Zema, Curriculum Coordinator, 315-443-2760, E-mail: azema@syr.edu.
Website: http://psychology.syr.edu/graduate/Clinical.html

**Syracuse University,** School of Education, Programs in School Counseling, Syracuse, NY 13244. Offers MS, CAS. *Accreditation:* APA. *Program availability:* Part-time. *Students:* Average age 24. *Degree requirements:* For master's and CAS, thesis or alternative. *Entrance requirements:* For master's, GRE or MAT, baccalaureate degree from regionally-accredited college/university, three letters of recommendation, transcripts, personal statement, interview; for CAS, master's degree in counseling; minimum of 60 credits beyond the baccalaureate, of which 30 credits must be taken at Syracuse University. Additional exam requirements/recommendations for international students: Required—TOEFL (minimum score 100 iBT). *Application deadline:* For fall admission, 6/1 priority date for domestic and international students; for spring admission, 10/15 priority date for domestic and international students; for summer admission, 1/15 priority date for domestic and international students. Applications are processed on a rolling basis. Application fee: $75. Electronic applications accepted. *Expenses:* Tuition: Full-time $25,974; part-time $1443 per credit hour. *Required fees:* $802; $50 per course. Tuition and fees vary according to course load and program. *Financial support:* Fellowships with full tuition reimbursements, research assistantships with tuition reimbursements, teaching assistantships with tuition reimbursements, career-related internships or fieldwork, and scholarships/grants available. Financial award application deadline: 1/15; financial award applicants required to submit FAFSA. *Faculty research:* Group work in counseling, social and cultural dimensions of counseling, life-span human development, counseling in the schools, assessment in counseling. *Unit head:* Dr. Nicole Hill, Professor/Chair of the Department of Counseling and Human Service, 315-443-2266, E-mail: nrhill@syr.edu. *Application contact:* Speranza Migliore, Graduate Admissions Recruiter, 315-443-2505, E-mail: gradrcrt@syr.edu.
Website: http://soeweb.syr.edu/

**Teachers College, Columbia University,** Department of Counseling and Clinical Psychology, New York, NY 10027-6696. Offers clinical psychology (PhD); counseling psychology (Ed M, Ed D, PhD); mental health counseling (ME); psychological counseling (ME, ND); psychology in education (MA, ND); school counselor (ME). *Accreditation:* APA (one or more programs are accredited). *Program availability:* Part-time. *Students:* 434 full-time (366 women), 232 part-time (184 women); includes 247 minority (62 Black or African American, non-Hispanic/Latino; 1 American Indian or Alaska Native, non-Hispanic/Latino; 80 Asian, non-Hispanic/Latino; 84 Hispanic/Latino; 20 Two or more races, non-Hispanic/Latino), 134 international. 1,470 applicants, 39% accepted, 253 enrolled. *Expenses:* Tuition: Full-time $36,288; part-time $1512 per credit. *Required fees:* $438 per semester. One-time fee: $510 full-time. Full-time tuition and fees vary according to course load. *Unit head:* Prof. Marie Miville, Head, 212-678-3343, Fax: 212-678-3275, E-mail: miville@tc.columbia.edu. *Application contact:* David Estrella, Director of Admission, 212-678-3305, E-mail: estrella@tc.columbia.edu.

**Teachers College, Columbia University,** Department of Health and Behavior Studies, New York, NY 10027-6696. Offers applied behavior analysis (MA, PhD); applied educational psychology: school psychology (Ed M, PhD); behavioral nutrition (PhD), including nutrition (Ed D, PhD); community health education (MS); community nutrition education (Ed M), including community nutrition education; education of deaf and hard of hearing (MA, PhD); health education (MA, Ed D); hearing impairment (Ed D); intellectual disability/autism (MA, Ed D, PhD); nursing education (Ed D, Advanced Certificate); nutrition and education (MS); nutrition and exercise physiology (MS); nutrition and public health (MS); nutrition education (Ed D), including nutrition (Ed D, PhD); physical disabilities (Ed D); reading specialist (MA); severe or multiple disabilities (MA); special education (Ed M, MA, Ed D); teaching of sign language (MA). *Program availability:* Part-time, evening/weekend. *Students:* 282 full-time (262 women), 262 part-time (222 women); includes 180 minority (54 Black or African American, non-Hispanic/ Latino; 1 American Indian or Alaska Native, non-Hispanic/Latino; 56 Asian, non-Hispanic/Latino; 56 Hispanic/Latino; 1 Native Hawaiian or other Pacific Islander, non-Hispanic/Latino; 12 Two or more races, non-Hispanic/Latino), 55 international. 503 applicants, 57% accepted, 146 enrolled. Terminal master's awarded for partial completion of doctoral program. *Expenses:* Tuition: Full-time $36,288; part-time $1512 per credit. *Required fees:* $438 per semester. One-time fee: $510 full-time. Full-time tuition and fees vary according to course load. *Unit head:* Prof. Stephen T. Peverly, Chair, 212-678-3964, Fax: 212-678-8259, E-mail: stp4@columbia.edu. *Application contact:* David Estrella, Director of Admission, 212-678-3305, E-mail: estrella@tc.columbia.edu.
Website: http://www.tc.columbia.edu/health-and-behavior-studies/

**Temple University,** College of Education, Department of Psychological Studies in Education, Philadelphia, PA 19122-6096. Offers adult and organizational development (Ed M); counseling psychology (Ed M, PhD), including agency counseling (Ed M), counseling psychology (PhD), school counseling (Ed M); education (PhD); educational leadership (Ed M); educational leadership and policy studies (Ed M, Ed D), including educational leadership; educational psychology (Ed M); school psychology (Ed M, PhD, Ed S); special education (Ed M). *Accreditation:* APA (one or more programs are accredited). *Program availability:* Part-time, evening/weekend. Terminal master's awarded for partial completion of doctoral program. *Degree requirements:* For master's, thesis or alternative; for doctorate, thesis/dissertation. *Entrance requirements:*

Additional exam requirements/recommendations for international students: Required—TOEFL (minimum score 550 paper-based; 79 iBT).

**Texas A&M University,** College of Education and Human Development, Department of Educational Psychology, College Station, TX 77843. Offers bilingual education (M Ed, MS); counseling psychology (PhD); educational psychology (M Ed, MS, PhD); educational technology (M Ed); school psychology (PhD); special education (M Ed, MS). *Accreditation:* APA (one or more programs are accredited). *Program availability:* Part-time, evening/weekend, blended/hybrid learning. *Faculty:* 42. *Students:* 172 full-time (139 women), 281 part-time (233 women); includes 144 minority (27 Black or African American, non-Hispanic/Latino; 1 American Indian or Alaska Native, non-Hispanic/ Latino; 19 Asian, non-Hispanic/Latino; 86 Hispanic/Latino; 1 Native Hawaiian or other Pacific Islander, non-Hispanic/Latino; 10 Two or more races, non-Hispanic/Latino), 48 international. Average age 33. 181 applicants, 44% accepted, 45 enrolled. In 2016, 99 master's, 27 doctorates awarded. *Degree requirements:* For master's, thesis optional; for doctorate, thesis/dissertation. *Entrance requirements:* For master's and doctorate, GRE General Test. Additional exam requirements/recommendations for international students: Required—TOEFL (minimum score 550 paper-based; 80 iBT), IELTS (minimum score 6), PTE (minimum score 53). *Application deadline:* For fall admission, 12/1 for domestic students; for spring admission, 10/15 for domestic students. Application fee: $50 ($90 for international students). Electronic applications accepted. *Expenses:* Contact institution. *Financial support:* In 2016–17, 231 students received support, including 8 fellowships with tuition reimbursements available (averaging $9,919 per year), 98 research assistantships with tuition reimbursements available (averaging $6,004 per year), 13 teaching assistantships with tuition reimbursements available (averaging $9,368 per year); career-related internships or fieldwork, institutionally sponsored loans, scholarships/grants, traineeships, health care benefits, tuition waivers (full and partial), and unspecified assistantships also available. Support available to part-time students. Financial award application deadline: 3/15; financial award applicants required to submit FAFSA. *Unit head:* Dr. Victor Willson, Department Head, 979-845-1394, E-mail: v-willson@tamu.edu. *Application contact:* Kristie Stramaski, Senior Academic Advisor, 979-845-1833, E-mail: epsyadvisor@tamu.edu.
Website: http://epsy.tamu.edu

**Texas A&M University–Central Texas,** Graduate Studies and Research, Killeen, TX 76549. Offers accounting (MS); business administration (MBA); clinical mental health counseling (MS); criminal justice (MCJ); curriculum and instruction (M Ed); educational administration (M Ed); educational psychology - experimental psychology (MS); history (MA); human resource management (MS); information systems (MS); liberal studies (MS); management and leadership (MS); marriage and family therapy (MS); mathematics (MS); political science (MA); school counseling (M Ed); school psychology (Ed S).

**Texas A&M University–Commerce,** College of Education and Human Services, Commerce, TX 75429-3011. Offers counseling (MS); curriculum and instruction (M Ed, MS); early childhood education (M Ed, MS); educational administration (M Ed, Ed D); educational psychology (PhD); educational technology leadership (MS); educational technology library science (MS); health, kinesiology and sports studies (MS); higher education (MS, Ed D); organization, learning, and technology (MS); psychology (MS); reading (M Ed, MS); school psychology (SSP); secondary education (M Ed, MS); social work (MSW); special education (M Ed); supervision, curriculum and instruction-elementary education (Ed D). *Program availability:* Part-time, 100% online, blended/ hybrid learning. *Faculty:* 88 full-time (52 women), 31 part-time/adjunct (24 women). *Students:* 341 full-time (276 women), 1,495 part-time (1,156 women); includes 762 minority (429 Black or African American, non-Hispanic/Latino; 4 American Indian or Alaska Native, non-Hispanic/Latino; 27 Asian, non-Hispanic/Latino; 247 Hispanic/Latino; 1 Native Hawaiian or other Pacific Islander, non-Hispanic/Latino; 54 Two or more races, non-Hispanic/Latino), 18 international. Average age 37. 1,070 applicants, 54% accepted, 452 enrolled. In 2016, 579 master's, 31 doctorates awarded. *Degree requirements:* For master's, one foreign language, comprehensive exam, thesis optional, departmental qualifying exams (for some programs); for doctorate, comprehensive exam, thesis/dissertation, departmental qualifying exam; for SSP, comprehensive exam, thesis optional. *Entrance requirements:* For master's and doctorate, GRE General Test. Additional exam requirements/recommendations for international students: Required—TOEFL (minimum score 550 paper-based; 79 iBT), IELTS (minimum score 6). *Application deadline:* For fall admission, 6/1 priority date for international students; for spring admission, 10/15 priority date for international students; for summer admission, 3/15 priority date for international students. Applications are processed on a rolling basis. Application fee: $50. Electronic applications accepted. *Expenses:* $2,254 resident; $4,744 non-resident. *Financial support:* In 2016–17, 301 students received support, including 39 research assistantships with partial tuition reimbursements available (averaging $9,000 per year), 17 teaching assistantships with partial tuition reimbursements available (averaging $9,000 per year); career-related internships or fieldwork, Federal Work-Study, institutionally sponsored loans, scholarships/grants, health care benefits, and unspecified assistantships also available. Financial award application deadline: 5/1; financial award applicants required to submit FAFSA. *Faculty research:* Cognitive and bilingual education, positive behavioral intervention, literacy, math readiness. *Total annual research expenditures:* $470,963. *Unit head:* Dr. Timothy Letzring, Dean, 903-886-5181, Fax: 903-886-5905, E-mail: tim.letzring@tamuc.edu. *Application contact:* Jennifer Faunce, Graduate Recruiter, 903-886-5030, Fax: 903-886-5905, E-mail: jennifer.faunce@tamuc.edu.
Website: http://www.tamuc.edu/academics/graduateSchool/programs/education/default.aspx

**Texas State University,** The Graduate College, College of Education, Program in School Psychology, San Marcos, TX 78666. Offers SSP. *Program availability:* Part-time. *Faculty:* 7 full-time (4 women), 5 part-time/adjunct (2 women). *Students:* 54 full-time (48 women), 20 part-time (13 women); includes 42 minority (2 Black or African American, non-Hispanic/Latino; 2 Asian, non-Hispanic/Latino; 36 Hispanic/Latino; 2 Two or more races, non-Hispanic/Latino). Average age 28. 47 applicants, 62% accepted, 17 enrolled. *Entrance requirements:* Additional exam requirements/recommendations for international students: Required—TOEFL (minimum score 550 paper-based; 78 iBT), IELTS (minimum score 6.5). *Application deadline:* For fall admission, 2/15 for domestic and international students. Applications are processed on a rolling basis. Application fee: $40 ($90 for international students). Electronic applications accepted. *Expenses:* $4,851 per semester. *Financial support:* In 2016–17, 62 students received support, including 5 research assistantships (averaging $9,385 per year), 2 teaching assistantships (averaging $6,751 per year); career-related internships or fieldwork, Federal Work-Study, institutionally sponsored loans, and scholarships/grants also available. Support available to part-time students. Financial award application deadline: 3/1; financial award applicants required to submit FAFSA. *Faculty research:* Using psychology and education in reaching bilinguals. *Unit head:* Dr. Jon Lasser, Graduate Advisor, 512-245-3413, Fax: 512-245-8872, E-mail: jl30@txstate.edu. *Application contact:* Dr. Andrea Golato, Dean of Graduate School, 512-245-2581, Fax: 512-245-8365, E-mail: gradcollege@txstate.edu.
Website: http://www.txstate.edu/clas/school-psychology-program/Program-Information.html

## School Psychology

**Texas Woman's University,** Graduate School, College of Arts and Sciences, Department of Psychology and Philosophy, Denton, TX 76201. Offers counseling psychology (MA, PhD); school psychology (PhD, SSP). *Accreditation:* APA (one or more programs are accredited). *Students:* 63 full-time (58 women), 43 part-time (39 women); includes 43 minority (11 Black or African American, non-Hispanic/Latino; 10 Asian, non-Hispanic/Latino; 19 Hispanic/Latino; 3 Two or more races, non-Hispanic/Latino). Average age 30. In 2016, 14 master's, 9 doctorates, 5 other advanced degrees awarded. Terminal master's awarded for partial completion of doctoral program. *Degree requirements:* For master's, comprehensive exam (for some programs), thesis (for some programs); for doctorate, comprehensive exam, thesis/dissertation, internship, residency. *Entrance requirements:* For master's, GRE (preferred minimum score 153 [500 old version] Verbal, 144 [500 old version] Quantitative, 4 Analytical), BA/BS or 18 hours in psychology; minimum GPA of 3.0, 3.5 in psychology classes; 3 letters of reference; curriculum vitae; essays; for doctorate, GRE (preferred minimum score 153 [500 old version] Verbal, 144 [500 old version] Quantitative, 4 Analytical), 3 letters of reference, minimum GPA of 3.0 overall and 3.5 in psychology classes, MA in psychology or related discipline with thesis, curriculum vitae, essays. Additional exam requirements/recommendations for international students: Required—TOEFL (minimum score 550 paper-based; 79 iBT). *Application deadline:* For fall admission, 12/15 priority date for domestic students, 12/15 for international students. Applications are processed on a rolling basis. Application fee: $50 ($75 for international students). Electronic applications accepted. *Expenses:* Tuition, state resident: full-time $9046; part-time $251 per credit hour. Tuition, nonresident: full-time $22,922; part-time $614 per credit hour. *International tuition:* $23,046 full-time. *Required fees:* $2690; $1285 per credit hour. One-time fee: $50. Tuition and fees vary according to course level, course load, program and reciprocity agreements. *Financial support:* Research assistantships, teaching assistantships, career-related internships or fieldwork, Federal Work-Study, institutionally sponsored loans, scholarships/grants, traineeships, health care benefits, and unspecified assistantships available. Support available to part-time students. Financial award application deadline: 3/1; financial award applicants required to submit FAFSA. *Faculty research:* Women's anger, school neuropsychological theory and assessment, body image dysfunction, traumatic stress, classical ethics, mental health and behavioral needs of adolescents in alternative education. *Unit head:* Dr. Shannon Scott, Chair, 940-898-2303, Fax: 940-898-2301, E-mail: sscott@twu.edu. *Application contact:* Dr. Samuel Wheeler, Assistant Director of Admissions, 940-898-3188, Fax: 940-898-3081, E-mail: wheelersr@twu.edu.
Website: http://www.twu.edu/psychology-philosophy/

**Towson University,** Program in Psychology, Towson, MD 21252-0001. Offers clinical psychology (MA); counseling psychology (MA); experimental psychology (MA); school psychology (MA). *Program availability:* Part-time, evening/weekend. *Students:* 104 full-time (72 women), 27 part-time (23 women); includes 34 minority (12 Black or African American, non-Hispanic/Latino; 7 Asian, non-Hispanic/Latino; 10 Hispanic/Latino; 5 Two or more races, non-Hispanic/Latino). *Degree requirements:* For master's, thesis (for some programs). *Entrance requirements:* For master's, GRE, minimum GPA of 3.0, letters of recommendation. *Application deadline:* For fall admission, 2/1 for domestic and international students. Application fee: $45. Electronic applications accepted. *Expenses:* Tuition, state resident: full-time $7580; part-time $379 per unit. Tuition, nonresident: full-time $15,700; part-time $785 per unit. *Required fees:* $2480. *Financial support:* Application deadline: 4/1. *Unit head:* Dr. Geoffrey Munro, Graduate Program Director, 410-704-2634, E-mail: psyc@towson.edu. *Application contact:* Coverley Beidleman, Assistant Director of Graduate Admissions, 410-704-2113, Fax: 410-704-3030, E-mail: grads@towson.edu.
Website: https://www.towson.edu/cla/departments/psychology/grad/

**Trinity University,** Department of Education, Master of Arts in School Psychology Program, San Antonio, TX 78212-7200. Offers MA. *Accreditation:* NCATE. *Entrance requirements:* For master's, GRE or master's degree, minimum GPA of 3.0, academic and professional references, interview with program director. Electronic applications accepted. *Expenses: Tuition:* Full-time $38,974. *Required fees:* $586.

**Tufts University,** Graduate School of Arts and Sciences, Department of Education, Program in School Psychology, Medford, MA 02155. Offers MA, Ed S. *Faculty:* 4 full-time (2 women), 6 part-time/adjunct (5 women). *Students:* 42 full-time (35 women), 1 part-time (0 women); includes 8 minority (3 Black or African American, non-Hispanic/Latino; 4 Asian, non-Hispanic/Latino; 1 Hispanic/Latino), 1 international. Average age 26. 77 applicants, 36% accepted, 16 enrolled. In 2016, 30 master's, 14 other advanced degrees awarded. *Degree requirements:* For master's, internship. *Entrance requirements:* For master's, GRE General Test. Additional exam requirements/recommendations for international students: Required—TOEFL (minimum score 550 paper-based; 80 iBT), IELTS (minimum score 6.5). *Application deadline:* For fall admission, 1/2 for domestic and international students. Applications are processed on a rolling basis. Application fee: $85. Electronic applications accepted. *Expenses:* $42,408 full-time tuition (for MA/Ed S program). *Financial support:* In 2016–17, 43 students received support. Federal Work-Study, scholarships/grants, and tuition waivers (full and partial) available. Financial award application deadline: 1/2. *Unit head:* Dr. Steve Luz-Alterman, Graduate Program Director. *Application contact:* Office of Graduate Admissions, 617-627-3395, E-mail: gradadmissions@tufts.edu.
Website: http://ase.tufts.edu/education/programs/schoolPsych/

**Union College,** Graduate Programs, Department of Psychology, Barbourville, KY 40906-1499. Offers clinical psychology (MA); counseling psychology (MA); school psychology (MA).

**The University of Akron,** Graduate School, College of Health Professions, School of Counseling, Akron, OH 44325. Offers classroom guidance for teachers (MA, MS); clinical mental health counseling (MA, MS); counseling psychology (PhD); counselor education and supervision (PhD); marriage and family counseling/therapy (MA, MS); school counseling (MA, MS). *Faculty:* 10 full-time (7 women), 19 part-time/adjunct (14 women). *Students:* 144 full-time (121 women), 152 part-time (120 women); includes 77 minority (49 Black or African American, non-Hispanic/Latino; 2 American Indian or Alaska Native, non-Hispanic/Latino; 7 Asian, non-Hispanic/Latino; 9 Hispanic/Latino; 10 Two or more races, non-Hispanic/Latino), 4 international. Average age 30. 175 applicants, 46% accepted, 53 enrolled. In 2016, 69 master's, 6 doctorates awarded. Terminal master's awarded for partial completion of doctoral program. *Degree requirements:* For master's, comprehensive exam; for doctorate, one foreign language, comprehensive exam, thesis/dissertation, written and oral exams. *Entrance requirements:* For master's, minimum GPA of 2.75, three letters of recommendation; for doctorate, GRE, interview, minimum GPA of 3.25, three letters of recommendation, resume. Additional exam requirements/recommendations for international students: Required—TOEFL (minimum score 550 paper-based; 79 iBT), IELTS (minimum score 6.5). *Application deadline:* For fall admission, 12/1 for domestic and international students; for spring admission, 10/1 for domestic and international students. Applications are processed on a rolling basis. Application fee: $45 ($70 for international students). Electronic applications accepted. *Expenses:* Tuition, state resident: full-time $8618; part-time $359 per credit hour. Tuition, nonresident: full-time $17,149; part-time $715 per credit hour. *Required fees:* $1652. *Financial support:* In 2016–17, 2 research assistantships with full tuition reimbursements, 1 teaching assistantship with full tuition

reimbursement were awarded; instructional support assistantships, administrative assistantships also available. *Faculty research:* Mindfulness, traumatology, suicidality, multiculturalism, couple and family therapy/counseling. *Total annual research expenditures:* $83,405. *Unit head:* Dr. Karin Jordan, Director, 330-972-5515.
Website: http://www.uakron.edu/soc/

**University of Alberta,** Faculty of Graduate Studies and Research, Department of Educational Psychology, Edmonton, AB T6G 2E1, Canada. Offers counseling psychology (M Ed, PhD); educational psychology (M Ed, PhD); instructional technology (M Ed); school counseling (M Ed); school psychology (M Ed, PhD); special education (M Ed, PhD); special education-deafness studies (M Ed); teaching English as a second language (M Ed). *Program availability:* Part-time. *Degree requirements:* For master's, thesis optional; for doctorate, comprehensive exam, thesis/dissertation. *Entrance requirements:* For master's and doctorate, minimum GPA of 3.0. Additional exam requirements/recommendations for international students: Required—TOEFL. *Faculty research:* Human learning, development and assessment.

**The University of Arizona,** College of Education, Department of Disability and Psychoeducational Studies, Program in School Psychology, Tucson, AZ 85721. Offers PhD, Ed S. *Program availability:* Part-time. *Entrance requirements:* For doctorate, GRE General Test; for Ed S, minimum GPA of 3.5, 3 letters of recommendation, curriculum vitae, writing sample. Additional exam requirements/recommendations for international students: Required—TOEFL (minimum score 550 paper-based; 79 iBT). Electronic applications accepted.

**The University of British Columbia,** Faculty of Education, Department of Educational and Counseling Psychology, and Special Education, Vancouver, BC V6T 1Z4, Canada. Offers counseling psychology (M Ed, MA, PhD); guidance studies (Diploma); human development, learning and culture (M Ed, MA, PhD); measurement, evaluation, and research methodology (M Ed, MA, PhD); school psychology (M Ed, MA, PhD); special education (M Ed, MA, PhD, Diploma). *Program availability:* Part-time. *Degree requirements:* For master's, thesis (for some programs); for doctorate, comprehensive exam, thesis/dissertation. *Entrance requirements:* For master's, GRE General Test (counseling psychology MA); for doctorate, GRE General Test. Additional exam requirements/recommendations for international students: Required—TOEFL. Application fee: $102 Canadian dollars ($165 Canadian dollars for international students). Electronic applications accepted. *Expenses:* $6,865 per year tuition, $10,938 per year international (for MA, M Ed); $4,802 per year tuition, $8,436 per year international (for PhD). *Financial support:* Fellowships, research assistantships, teaching assistantships, career-related internships or fieldwork, Federal Work-Study, institutionally sponsored loans, scholarships/grants, health care benefits, tuition waivers (full and partial), and unspecified assistantships available. *Faculty research:* Women, family, social problems, career transition, stress and coping problems. *Application contact:* Karen Yan, Graduate Program Assistant, 604-822-6371, Fax: 604-822-3302, E-mail: karen.yan@ubc.ca.
Website: http://ecps.educ.ubc.ca/

**University of Calgary,** Faculty of Graduate Studies, Werklund School of Education, Division of Applied Psychology, Calgary, AB T2N 1N4, Canada. Offers counseling psychology (M Sc, MC, PhD); school and applied child psychology (M Ed, M Sc, PhD). *Program availability:* Part-time. *Degree requirements:* For master's, thesis (for some programs), final oral exam; for doctorate, thesis/dissertation, candidacy exam, final oral exam. *Entrance requirements:* For master's, minimum GPA of 3.0, 3 letters of reference; for doctorate, minimum GPA of 3.5, 3 letters of reference. *Faculty research:* Counselor education, family life studies, learning and cognition.

**University of California, Riverside,** Graduate Division, Graduate School of Education, Riverside, CA 92521-0102. Offers autism (M Ed); diversity and equity (M Ed); education specialist (Credential); education, society, and culture (MA, PhD); educational psychology (MA, PhD); general education (M Ed); higher education administration and policy (M Ed, PhD); multiple subject (Credential); reading (M Ed); school psychology (PhD); single subject (Credential); special education (M Ed, MA, PhD); TESOL (M Ed). Terminal master's awarded for partial completion of doctoral program. *Degree requirements:* For master's, thesis optional, comprehensive exams or thesis (MA), case study or analytical report (M Ed); for doctorate, thesis/dissertation, written and oral qualifying exams, college teaching practicum. *Entrance requirements:* For master's, GRE General Test (for MA); CBEST and CSET (for M Ed in general education only), UCR Extension TESOL certificate (for M Ed with TESOL emphasis only); for doctorate, GRE General Test, writing sample; for Credential, CBEST, CSET. Additional exam requirements/recommendations for international students: Required—TOEFL (minimum score 550 paper-based; 80 iBT), IELTS (minimum score 7). Electronic applications accepted. *Expenses:* Tuition, state resident: full-time $16,666. Tuition, nonresident: full-time $31,768. *Required fees:* $11,055.54 per quarter. $3685.18 per quarter. Tuition and fees vary according to campus/location and program. *Faculty research:* Responsiveness to intervention, faculty core, response to intervention of English language learners, advanced modeling techniques, study on social capital, trust, and motivation.

**University of California, Santa Barbara,** Graduate Division, Gevirtz Graduate School of Education, Santa Barbara, CA 93106-9490. Offers counseling, clinical and school psychology (MA, PhD, Credential), including clinical psychology (PhD), counseling psychology (MA, PhD), pupil personnel services (Credential), school psychology (PhD); education (MA, PhD); teacher education (M Ed, Credential), including multiple subject teaching (Credential), single subject teaching (Credential), special education (Credential), teaching (M Ed); MA/PhD. *Accreditation:* APA (one or more programs are accredited). Terminal master's awarded for partial completion of doctoral program. *Degree requirements:* For master's, comprehensive exam (for some programs), thesis (for some programs); for doctorate, comprehensive exam (for some programs), thesis/dissertation. *Entrance requirements:* For master's and doctorate, GRE; for Credential, GRE or MAT, CSET, CBEST. Additional exam requirements/recommendations for international students: Required—TOEFL (minimum score 550 paper-based; 80 iBT), IELTS (minimum score 7). Electronic applications accepted. *Faculty research:* Needs of diverse students, school accountability and leadership, school violence, language learning and literacy, science/math education.

**University of Central Arkansas,** Graduate School, College of Health and Behavioral Sciences, Department of Counseling and Psychology, Program in School Psychology, Conway, AR 72035-0001. Offers MS, PhD, PMC. *Accreditation:* APA; NCATE. Terminal master's awarded for partial completion of doctoral program. *Degree requirements:* For master's, comprehensive exam, thesis optional; for doctorate, comprehensive exam, thesis/dissertation. *Entrance requirements:* For master's, GRE General Test, minimum GPA of 2.7; for doctorate, GRE General Test. Additional exam requirements/recommendations for international students: Required—TOEFL (minimum score 550 paper-based). Electronic applications accepted.

**University of Central Florida,** College of Education and Human Performance, Department of Educational and Human Sciences, Program in School Psychology, Orlando, FL 32816. Offers Ed S. *Program availability:* Part-time, evening/weekend. *Students:* 45 full-time (40 women), 1 (woman) part-time; includes 14 minority (5 Black or African American, non-Hispanic/Latino; 1 Asian, non-Hispanic/Latino; 8 Hispanic/Latino), 1 international. Average age 28. 66 applicants, 26% accepted, 16 enrolled. In

2016, 20 Ed Ss awarded. *Degree requirements:* For Ed S, thesis or alternative, practicum, internship. *Entrance requirements:* For degree, GRE General Test, minimum GPA of 3.0, resume, interview. Additional exam requirements/recommendations for international students: Required—TOEFL. *Application deadline:* For fall admission, 3/1 for domestic students. Application fee: $30. Electronic applications accepted. *Expenses:* Tuition, state resident: part-time $288.16 per credit hour. Tuition, nonresident: part-time $1071.31 per credit hour. *Financial support:* In 2016–17, 7 students received support, including 6 research assistantships with partial tuition reimbursements available (averaging $6,189 per year), 2 teaching assistantships with partial tuition reimbursements available (averaging $9,245 per year); fellowships, career-related internships or fieldwork, Federal Work-Study, institutionally sponsored loans, and tuition waivers (partial) also available. Financial award application deadline: 3/1; financial award applicants required to submit FAFSA. *Unit head:* Dr. Oliver Edwards, Program Coordinator, 407-823-2740, E-mail: oliver.edwards@ucf.edu. *Application contact:* Assistant Director, Graduate Admissions, 407-823-2766, Fax: 407-823-6442, E-mail: gradadmissions@ucf.edu.
Website: http://education.ucf.edu/schpsy/

**University of Central Oklahoma,** The Jackson College of Graduate Studies, College of Education and Professional Studies, Department of Psychology, Edmond, OK 73034-5209. Offers counseling psychology (MA); experimental psychology (MA); forensic psychology (MA); general psychology (MA); school psychology (MA). *Degree requirements:* For master's, thesis (for some programs). *Entrance requirements:* For master's, GRE. Additional exam requirements/recommendations for international students: Required—TOEFL (minimum score 550 paper-based; 79 iBT), IELTS (minimum score 6.5). Electronic applications accepted. *Faculty research:* Psychopharmacology, computer psychometrics, health psychology research.

**University of Cincinnati,** Graduate School, College of Education, Criminal Justice, and Human Services, School of Human Services, School Psychology Program, Cincinnati, OH 45221. Offers PhD, Ed S. *Accreditation:* NCATE. *Program availability:* Online only, 100% online. *Faculty:* 5 full-time (2 women), 5 part-time/adjunct (4 women). Terminal master's awarded for partial completion of doctoral program. *Degree requirements:* For doctorate, comprehensive exam, thesis/dissertation. *Entrance requirements:* For doctorate, GRE General Test, GRE Subject Test. Additional exam requirements/recommendations for international students: Required—TOEFL (minimum score 520 paper-based; 68 iBT). *Application deadline:* For fall admission, 1/15 for domestic students. Application fee: $65 ($70 for international students). Electronic applications accepted. *Expenses: Tuition, area resident:* Full-time $12,790; part-time $389 per credit hour. Tuition, state resident: full-time $13,290; part-time $419 per credit hour. Tuition, nonresident: full-time $24,532; part-time $976 per credit hour. *International tuition:* $24,832 full-time. *Required fees:* $3958; $140 per credit hour. Tuition and fees vary according to course load, degree level, program and reciprocity agreements. *Financial support:* Fellowships, research assistantships with full tuition reimbursements, teaching assistantships, career-related internships or fieldwork, scholarships/grants, health care benefits, tuition waivers (partial), and unspecified assistantships available. Financial award application deadline: 4/15. *Faculty research:* School psychology services delivery, direct assessment and intervention. *Unit head:* Dr. Renee Hawkins, Program Director, 513-556-3342, Fax: 513-556-3898, E-mail: renee.hawkins@uc.edu. *Application contact:* Amanda Carlisle, Program Coordinator, 513-556-3335, Fax: 513-556-3898, E-mail: amanda.carlisle@uc.edu.
Website: http://cech.uc.edu/human-services/graduate-programs/school-psychology-phd.html

**University of Colorado Denver,** School of Education and Human Development, Program in Counseling Psychology and Counselor Education, Denver, CO 80217. Offers counseling (MA), including clinical mental health counseling, couple and family counseling, multicultural counseling, school counseling; school counseling (MA). *Accreditation:* ACA; NCATE. *Program availability:* Part-time, evening/weekend. *Students:* 179 full-time (139 women), 42 part-time (32 women); includes 45 minority (10 Black or African American, non-Hispanic/Latino; 5 Asian, non-Hispanic/Latino; 25 Hispanic/Latino; 5 Two or more races, non-Hispanic/Latino), 1 international. Average age 30. 227 applicants, 28% accepted, 26 enrolled. In 2016, 61 master's awarded. *Degree requirements:* For master's, comprehensive exam, thesis or alternative, 63-66 hours. *Entrance requirements:* For master's, GRE or MAT (unless applicant already holds a graduate degree), letters of recommendation, interview, resume, transcripts from all colleges/universities attended. Additional exam requirements/recommendations for international students: Required—TOEFL (minimum score 525 paper-based; 71 iBT); Recommended—IELTS (minimum score 6.3). *Application deadline:* For fall admission, 1/15 for domestic students, 1/1 for international students; for spring admission, 9/15 for domestic students, 9/1 for international students. Application fee: $50 ($75 for international students). Electronic applications accepted. *Expenses:* Contact institution. *Financial support:* In 2016–17, 16 students received support. Research assistantships, Federal Work-Study, institutionally sponsored loans, scholarships/grants, and traineeships available. Financial award application deadline: 4/1; financial award applicants required to submit FAFSA. *Faculty research:* Spiritual issues in counseling, multicultural and diversity issues in counseling, adolescent suicide, career development. *Unit head:* Farah Ibrahim, Counseling Professor, 303-315-6329, E-mail: farah.ibrahim@ucdenver.edu. *Application contact:* Student Services Coordinator, 303-315-6300, Fax: 303-315-6311, E-mail: education@ucdenver.edu.
Website: http://www.ucdenver.edu/academics/colleges/SchoolOfEducation/Academics/MASTERS/counseling/Pages/default.aspx

**University of Colorado Denver,** School of Education and Human Development, Programs in Educational and School Psychology, Denver, CO 80217. Offers educational psychology (MA), including educational assessment, educational psychology, human development, human learning, research and evaluation; school psychology (Psy D, Ed S). MA program also offered in partnership with Boulder Journey School, Friends' School and Stanley British Primary School. *Program availability:* Part-time, evening/weekend. *Students:* 210 full-time (171 women), 79 part-time (71 women); includes 47 minority (5 Black or African American, non-Hispanic/Latino; 2 American Indian or Alaska Native, non-Hispanic/Latino; 5 Asian, non-Hispanic/Latino; 28 Hispanic/Latino; 7 Two or more races, non-Hispanic/Latino), 6 international. Average age 30. 179 applicants, 94% accepted, 126 enrolled. In 2016, 166 master's, 7 doctorates, 11 other advanced degrees awarded. *Degree requirements:* For master's, comprehensive exam, 9 hours of core courses, embedded within a minimum of 36 to 38 hours of relevant coursework, including an educational psychology practicum, independent study project or thesis (recommended); for Ed S, comprehensive exam, minimum of 75 semester hours (61 hours of coursework, 6 of 500-hour practicum in field, and 8 of 1200-hour internship); PRAXIS II. *Entrance requirements:* For master's, GRE if undergraduate GPA below 2.75, resume, three letters of recommendation, transcripts; for Ed S, GRE, resume, letters of recommendation, transcripts. Additional exam requirements/recommendations for international students: Required—TOEFL (minimum score 537 paper-based; 75 iBT); Recommended—IELTS (minimum score 6.5). *Application deadline:* For fall admission, 4/15 for domestic students, 4/1 for international students; for spring admission, 9/15 for domestic students, 9/1 for international students. Application fee: $50 ($75 for international students). Electronic applications accepted. *Expenses:* Contact institution. *Financial support:* In 2016–17, 90 students received

support. Research assistantships, Federal Work-Study, institutionally sponsored loans, scholarships/grants, and traineeships available. Financial award application deadline: 4/1; financial award applicants required to submit FAFSA. *Faculty research:* Crisis response and intervention, school violence prevention, immigrant experience, educational environments for English language learners, culturally competent assessment and intervention, child and youth suicide. *Unit head:* Francie Crepeau-Hobson, Associate Professor and Program Director, 303-315-6315, E-mail: franci.creapeau-hobson@ucdenver.edu. *Application contact:* 303-315-6300, E-mail: education@ucdenver.edu.
Website: http://www.ucdenver.edu/academics/colleges/SchoolOfEducation/Academics/MASTERS/EPSY/Pages/default.aspx

**University of Dayton,** Department of Counselor Education and Human Services, Dayton, OH 45469. Offers clinical mental health counseling (MS Ed); college student personnel (MS Ed); higher education administration (MS Ed); human services (MS Ed); school counseling (MS Ed); school psychology (MS Ed, Ed S). *Accreditation:* ACA; NCATE. *Program availability:* Part-time, evening/weekend. *Faculty:* 10 full-time (6 women), 24 part-time/adjunct (15 women). *Students:* 198 full-time (155 women), 95 part-time (75 women); includes 15 minority (8 Black or African American, non-Hispanic/Latino; 2 Asian, non-Hispanic/Latino; 2 Hispanic/Latino; 3 Two or more races, non-Hispanic/Latino), 3 international. Average age 36. 426 applicants, 28% accepted. In 2016, 115 master's, 9 Ed Ss awarded. *Degree requirements:* For Ed S, thesis. *Entrance requirements:* For master's, MAT or GRE (if GPA less than 2.75), essays (for some programs). Additional exam requirements/recommendations for international students: Required—TOEFL (minimum score 550 paper-based; 80 iBT); Recommended—IELTS. *Application deadline:* For fall admission, 3/10 priority date for domestic and international students; for spring admission, 9/10 priority date for domestic and international students; for summer admission, 12/1 priority date for domestic and international students. Application fee: $0 ($50 for international students). Electronic applications accepted. *Expenses:* $620 per credit hour (for master's degree programs); $740 per credit hour (for Ed S). *Financial support:* In 2016–17, 7 research assistantships with partial tuition reimbursements (averaging $8,038 per year), 4 teaching assistantships with partial tuition reimbursements (averaging $9,390 per year) were awarded; career-related internships or fieldwork, institutionally sponsored loans, health care benefits, and unspecified assistantships also available. Financial award application deadline: 1/9; financial award applicants required to submit FAFSA. *Faculty research:* School bonding, traumatic brain injuries, second-year student experience, impact of physical space on learning, integrative health and mental health care. *Total annual research expenditures:* $1,500. *Unit head:* Dr. Alan Demmitt, Chair, 937-229-3644, Fax: 937-229-1055, E-mail: ademmitt1@udayton.edu. *Application contact:* Kathleen Brown, Administrative Assistant, 937-229-3644, Fax: 937-229-1055, E-mail: kbrown1@udayton.edu.
Website: https://www.udayton.edu/education/departments_and_programs/edc/

**University of Delaware,** College of Education and Human Development, School of Education, Newark, DE 19716. Offers education (PhD); educational leadership (Ed D); higher education (M Ed); instruction (MI); reading (M Ed); school leadership (M Ed); school psychology (MA, Ed S); teaching English as a second language (TESL) (MA). *Accreditation:* NCATE. *Program availability:* Part-time, evening/weekend. Terminal master's awarded for partial completion of doctoral program. *Degree requirements:* For master's, comprehensive exam (for some programs), thesis (for some programs); for doctorate, comprehensive exam (for some programs), thesis/dissertation. *Entrance requirements:* For master's and doctorate, GRE, 3 letters of recommendation. Additional exam requirements/recommendations for international students: Required—TOEFL (minimum score 600 paper-based). Electronic applications accepted. *Faculty research:* Teacher education; curriculum theory and development; community based education models, educational leadership.

**University of Denver,** Morgridge College of Education, Denver, CO 80208. Offers child, family and school psychology (MA, PhD, Ed S); counseling psychology (MA, PhD); curriculum and instruction (MA, Ed D, PhD); curriculum instruction and teaching (Certificate); early childhood special education (MA, Certificate); educational leadership and policy studies (MA, Ed D, PhD, Certificate); higher education (Ed D, PhD); library and information science (MLIS); research methods and statistics (MA, PhD). *Accreditation:* ALA; APA (one or more programs are accredited). *Program availability:* Part-time, evening/weekend, online learning. *Faculty:* 39 full-time (29 women), 60 part-time/adjunct (42 women). *Students:* 498 full-time (392 women), 362 part-time (282 women); includes 223 minority (63 Black or African American, non-Hispanic/Latino; 6 American Indian or Alaska Native, non-Hispanic/Latino; 20 Asian, non-Hispanic/Latino; 102 Hispanic/Latino; 1 Native Hawaiian or other Pacific Islander, non-Hispanic/Latino; 31 Two or more races, non-Hispanic/Latino), 40 international. Average age 32. 1,027 applicants, 69% accepted, 386 enrolled. In 2016, 252 master's, 36 doctorates, 141 other advanced degrees awarded. Terminal master's awarded for partial completion of doctoral program. *Degree requirements:* For master's, comprehensive exam; for doctorate, 2 foreign languages, comprehensive exam, thesis/dissertation. *Entrance requirements:* For master's and doctorate, GRE General Test or GMAT. Additional exam requirements/recommendations for international students: Required—TOEFL (minimum score 550 paper-based; 80 iBT). *Application deadline:* Applications are processed on a rolling basis. Application fee: $65. Electronic applications accepted. *Expenses:* $29,022 per year full-time. *Financial support:* In 2016–17, 697 students received support, including 37 research assistantships with tuition reimbursements available (averaging $11,209 per year), 66 teaching assistantships with tuition reimbursements available (averaging $3,742 per year); career-related internships or fieldwork, Federal Work-Study, institutionally sponsored loans, scholarships/grants, and unspecified assistantships also available. Support available to part-time students. Financial award application deadline: 2/15; financial award applicants required to submit FAFSA. *Faculty research:* Early childhood education, access and equity, educational leadership, family and school partnerships, neurodevelopmental disorders. *Total annual research expenditures:* $3.3 million. *Unit head:* Dr. Karen Riley, Dean, 303-871-3665, Fax: 303-871-4456, E-mail: karen.riley@du.edu. *Application contact:* Jodi Dye, Director of Admissions, 303-871-2510, Fax: 303-871-4456, E-mail: jodi.dye@du.edu.
Website: http://morgridge.du.edu

**University of Detroit Mercy,** College of Liberal Arts and Education, Detroit, MI 48221. Offers addiction counseling (MA); addiction studies (Certificate); clinical mental health counseling (MA); clinical psychology (MA, PhD); computer and information systems (MS); criminal justice (MA); curriculum and instruction (MA); economics (MA); educational administration (MA); financial economics (MA); industrial/organizational psychology (MA); information assurance (MS); intelligence analysis (MA); liberal studies (MALS); religious studies (MA); school counseling (MA, Certificate); school psychology (Spec); security administration (MS); special education: emotionally impaired/behaviorally disordered (MA); special education: learning disabilities (MA). *Program availability:* Part-time, evening/weekend. *Degree requirements:* For doctorate, departmental qualifying exam. *Faculty research:* Psychology of aging, history of technology, Renaissance humanism, U.S. and Japanese economic relations.

**University of Florida,** Graduate School, College of Education, School of Special Education, School Psychology and Early Childhood Studies, Gainesville, FL 32611. Offers early childhood education (M Ed, MAE); school psychology (M Ed, MAE, Ed D,

PhD, Ed S); special education (M Ed, MAE, Ed D, PhD, Ed S). *Accreditation:* NCATE. *Program availability:* Part-time, evening/weekend, online learning. *Degree requirements:* For master's, comprehensive exam (for some programs), thesis (MAE); for doctorate, comprehensive exam, thesis/dissertation. *Entrance requirements:* For master's and doctorate, GRE General Test, minimum GPA of 3.0; for Ed S, GRE General Test. Additional exam requirements/recommendations for international students: Required—TOEFL (minimum score 550 paper-based; 80 iBT), IELTS (minimum score 6). Electronic applications accepted. *Faculty research:* Teacher quality/teacher education, early childhood, autism, academic and behavioral assessment and interventions.

**University of Hartford,** College of Arts and Sciences, Department of Psychology, Program in School Psychology, West Hartford, CT 06117-1599. Offers MS. *Accreditation:* NCATE. *Program availability:* Part-time. *Degree requirements:* For master's, comprehensive exam. *Entrance requirements:* For master's, GRE General Test, GRE Subject Test, minimum GPA of 3.0, 3 letters of recommendation. Additional exam requirements/recommendations for international students: Required—TOEFL (minimum score 550 paper-based). Electronic applications accepted. *Faculty research:* Family therapy, child developments, clinical supervision.

**University of Houston–Clear Lake,** School of Human Sciences and Humanities, Programs in Human Sciences, Houston, TX 77058-1002. Offers behavioral sciences (MA), including criminology, cross cultural studies, general psychology, sociology; clinical psychology (MA); criminology (MA); cross cultural studies (MA); family therapy (MA); fitness and human performance (MA); school psychology (MA). *Accreditation:* AAMFT/COAMFTE. *Program availability:* Part-time, evening/weekend, online learning. *Degree requirements:* For master's, thesis or alternative. *Entrance requirements:* For master's, GRE General Test. Additional exam requirements/recommendations for international students: Required—TOEFL (minimum score 550 paper-based). Electronic applications accepted. *Faculty research:* Smoking cessation, adolescent sexuality, white collar crime, serial murder, human factors/human computer interaction.

**University of Houston–Victoria,** School of Arts and Sciences, Program in Psychology, Victoria, TX 77901-4450. Offers counseling psychology (MA); forensic psychology (MA); school psychology (MA). *Program availability:* Part-time, evening/weekend, online learning. *Degree requirements:* For master's, project or thesis. *Entrance requirements:* For master's, GRE General Test. Additional exam requirements/recommendations for international students: Required—TOEFL (minimum score 550 paper-based). Electronic applications accepted.

**The University of Iowa,** Graduate College, College of Education, Department of Psychological and Quantitative Foundations, Iowa City, IA 52242-1316. Offers counseling psychology (PhD); educational measurement and statistics (MA, PhD); educational psychology (MA, PhD); school psychology (PhD, Ed S). *Accreditation:* APA. *Degree requirements:* For master's, thesis optional, exam; for doctorate, comprehensive exam, thesis/dissertation; for Ed S, exam. *Entrance requirements:* For master's, doctorate, and Ed S, GRE General Test, minimum GPA of 3.0. Additional exam requirements/recommendations for international students: Required—TOEFL (minimum score 550 paper-based; 81 iBT). Electronic applications accepted.

**The University of Kansas,** Graduate Studies, School of Education, Department of Educational Psychology, Program in School Psychology, Lawrence, KS 66045. Offers PhD, Ed S. *Accreditation:* APA (one or more programs are accredited); NCATE. *Students:* 28 full-time (24 women); includes 4 minority (all Hispanic/Latino), 2 international. Average age 26. 49 applicants, 45% accepted, 8 enrolled. In 2016, 4 doctorates awarded. *Entrance requirements:* For doctorate and Ed S, GRE General Test, minimum GPA of 3.0, resume, statement of purpose, official transcript, three letters of recommendation. Additional exam requirements/recommendations for international students: Required—TOEFL or IELTS. *Application deadline:* For fall admission, 12/15 for domestic and international students. Application fee: $65 ($85 for international students). Electronic applications accepted. *Financial support:* Fellowships, research assistantships, teaching assistantships, scholarships/grants, and unspecified assistantships available. Financial award application deadline: 12/15. *Faculty research:* Classroom management, anxiety in children and youth, child behavior and learning problems, behavioral and personality assessment, home/school/community partnerships. *Unit head:* Dr. Steven Lee, Chair, 785-864-3931, Fax: 785-864-3820, E-mail: swlee@ku.edu. *Application contact:* Penny Fritts, Admissions Coordinator, 785-864-9645, E-mail: fritts@ku.edu.
Website: http://epsy.ku.edu/

**University of Kentucky,** Graduate School, College of Education, Program in Educational and Counseling Psychology, Lexington, KY 40506-0032. Offers counseling psychology (MS, PhD, Ed S); educational psychology (MS, PhD); school psychology (PhD, Ed S). *Accreditation:* APA (one or more programs are accredited); NCATE. *Degree requirements:* For doctorate, comprehensive exam, thesis/dissertation; for Ed S, comprehensive exam. *Entrance requirements:* For doctorate, GRE General Test, minimum graduate GPA of 3.0; for Ed S, GRE General Test. Additional exam requirements/recommendations for international students: Required—TOEFL (minimum score 550 paper-based). Electronic applications accepted.

**University of La Verne,** LaFetra College of Education, Program in Educational Counseling, La Verne, CA 91750-4443. Offers educational counseling (MS); pupil personnel services (Credential); school psychology (MS). *Program availability:* Part-time. *Students:* 66 full-time (57 women), 98 part-time (79 women); includes 115 minority (8 Black or African American, non-Hispanic/Latino; 6 Asian, non-Hispanic/Latino; 100 Hispanic/Latino; 1 Two or more races, non-Hispanic/Latino). Average age 30. *Degree requirements:* For master's, thesis optional. *Entrance requirements:* For master's, California Basic Educational Skills Test, minimum undergraduate GPA of 2.75, graduate 3.0; interview; 1 year's experience working with children; 3 letters of reference. Additional exam requirements/recommendations for international students: Required—TOEFL (minimum score 550 paper-based). *Application deadline:* Applications are processed on a rolling basis. Application fee: $50. *Expenses:* Contact institution. *Financial support:* Scholarships/grants and traineeships available. Financial award application deadline: 3/2; financial award applicants required to submit FAFSA. *Unit head:* Laurie Schroeder, Chairperson, 909-448-4653, E-mail: lschroeder3@laverne.edu. *Application contact:* Kristen Ahn, Assistant Director of Graduate Admissions, 909-448-4480, E-mail: sahn@laverne.edu.
Website: http://www.laverne.edu/education/

**University of Louisville,** Graduate School, College of Education and Human Development, Department of Counseling and Human Development, Louisville, KY 40292-0001. Offers counseling and personnel services (M Ed, PhD), including art therapy (M Ed), clinical mental health counseling (M Ed), college student personnel, counseling psychology, counselor education and supervision (PhD), educational psychology, measurement, and evaluation (PhD), school counseling (M Ed). *Accreditation:* APA; NCATE. *Program availability:* Part-time, evening/weekend. *Students:* 148 full-time (115 women), 58 part-time (42 women); includes 52 minority (36 Black or African American, non-Hispanic/Latino; 1 American Indian or Alaska Native, non-Hispanic/Latino; 4 Asian, non-Hispanic/Latino; 7 Hispanic/Latino; 4 Two or more races, non-Hispanic/Latino), 2 international. Average age 28. 206 applicants, 56% accepted, 73 enrolled. In 2016, 38 master's, 1 doctorate awarded. *Degree requirements:* For doctorate, comprehensive exam, thesis/dissertation. *Entrance requirements:* For master's and doctorate, GRE General Test. Application fee: $60. *Expenses:* Tuition, state resident: full-time $12,246; part-time $681 per credit hour. Tuition, nonresident: full-time $25,486; part-time $1417 per credit hour. *Required fees:* $196. Tuition and fees vary according to program and reciprocity agreements. *Financial support:* Fellowships, research assistantships, teaching assistantships, career-related internships or fieldwork, Federal Work-Study, scholarships/grants, health care benefits, and unspecified assistantships available. Financial award application deadline: 6/1; financial award applicants required to submit FAFSA. *Faculty research:* Mental health services and under-served populations; health disparities and outcomes; well-being identity development; measurement and evaluation. Total annual research expenditures: $295,684. *Unit head:* Dr. Mark M. Leach, Interim Chair/Professor, 502-852-0588, Fax: 502-852-0629, E-mail: m.leach@louisville.edu. *Application contact:* Betty Hampton, Director of Graduate Student Services, 502-852-5597, Fax: 502-852-1465, E-mail: edadvise@louisville.edu.
Website: http://www.louisville.edu/education/departments/ecpy

**University of Manitoba,** Faculty of Graduate Studies, Faculty of Arts, Department of Psychology, Winnipeg, MB R3T 2N2, Canada. Offers clinical psychology (PhD); psychology (MA, PhD); school psychology (MA). *Degree requirements:* For master's, thesis; for doctorate, one foreign language, thesis/dissertation. *Entrance requirements:* For master's and doctorate, GRE General Test.

**University of Maryland, College Park,** Academic Affairs, College of Education, Department of Counseling, Higher Education and Special Education, College Park, MD 20742. Offers college student personnel (M Ed, MA); college student personnel administration (PhD); community counseling (CAGS); community/career counseling (M Ed, MA); counseling and personnel services (M Ed, MA, PhD), including art therapy (M Ed), college student personnel (M Ed), counseling and personnel services (PhD), counseling psychology (M Ed), mental health counseling (M Ed), school counseling (M Ed); counseling psychology (PhD); counselor education (PhD); rehabilitation counseling (M Ed, MA, AGSC); school counseling (M Ed, MA); school psychology (M Ed, MA, PhD). *Accreditation:* ACA (one or more programs are accredited); APA (one or more programs are accredited); NCATE. *Program availability:* Part-time, evening/weekend, online learning. *Degree requirements:* For master's, thesis (for some programs); for doctorate, thesis/dissertation. *Entrance requirements:* For master's, GRE General Test or MAT, minimum GPA of 3.0, 3 letters of recommendation; for doctorate, GRE General Test or MAT, minimum GPA of 3.5, 3 letters of recommendation. Additional exam requirements/recommendations for international students: Required—TOEFL. Electronic applications accepted. *Faculty research:* Educational psychology, counseling, health.

**University of Massachusetts Amherst,** Graduate School, College of Education, Program in Education, Amherst, MA 01003. Offers bilingual, English as a second language, and multicultural education (M Ed, Ed S); child study and early education (M Ed); children, families and schools (Ed D, Ed S); early childhood and elementary teacher education (M Ed); educational leadership (M Ed); educational policy and leadership (Ed D); higher education (M Ed); international education (M Ed); language, literacy and culture (Ed D); learning, media and technology (M Ed, Ed S); mathematics, science, and learning technologies (Ed D); reading and writing (M Ed); research, educational measurement and psychometrics (Ed D); school counselor education (M Ed, Ed S); school psychology (Ed S); science education (Ed S); secondary teacher education (M Ed); social justice education (M Ed, Ed D, Ed S); special education (M Ed, Ed D, Ed S); teacher education and school improvement (Ed D, Ed S). *Accreditation:* NCATE. *Program availability:* Part-time, online learning. Terminal master's awarded for partial completion of doctoral program. *Degree requirements:* For doctorate, comprehensive exam, thesis/dissertation. *Entrance requirements:* Additional exam requirements/recommendations for international students: Required—TOEFL (minimum score 550 paper-based; 80 iBT), IELTS (minimum score 6.5). Electronic applications accepted.

**University of Massachusetts Amherst,** Graduate School, College of Education, Program in School Psychology, Amherst, MA 01003. Offers M Ed, PhD, Ed S. *Accreditation:* APA; NCATE. *Program availability:* Part-time. Terminal master's awarded for partial completion of doctoral program. *Degree requirements:* For doctorate, comprehensive exam, thesis/dissertation. *Entrance requirements:* For doctorate, 3 letters of recommendation. Additional exam requirements/recommendations for international students: Required—TOEFL (minimum score 550 paper-based; 80 iBT), IELTS (minimum score 6.5). Electronic applications accepted.

**University of Massachusetts Boston,** College of Education and Human Development, Program in Counseling and School Psychology, Boston, MA 02125-3393. Offers PhD. *Accreditation:* ACA; CORE. *Program availability:* Part-time, evening/weekend. *Faculty:* 16 full-time (11 women), 17 part-time/adjunct (9 women). *Students:* 36 full-time (31 women), 3 part-time (all women); includes 8 minority (2 Black or African American, non-Hispanic/Latino; 4 Hispanic/Latino; 2 Two or more races, non-Hispanic/Latino), 4 international. Average age 30. 52 applicants, 27% accepted, 9 enrolled. *Application deadline:* For fall admission, 12/1 for domestic students. *Expenses:* Tuition, state resident: full-time $16,863. Tuition, nonresident: full-time $32,913. *Required fees:* $177. *Financial support:* Research assistantships with full tuition reimbursements, teaching assistantships with full tuition reimbursements, career-related internships or fieldwork, Federal Work-Study, and unspecified assistantships available. Support available to part-time students. Financial award application deadline: 3/1; financial award applicants required to submit FAFSA. *Faculty research:* Persuasion and power in the counseling process, self-efficacy for counselors and clients, career and biracial issues in family therapy. *Unit head:* Dr. Takuya Minami, Chair of the Department. *Application contact:* Peggy Roldan Patel, Graduate Admissions Coordinator, 617-287-6400, Fax: 617-287-6236, E-mail: bos.gadm@dpc.umassp.edu.

**University of Massachusetts Boston,** College of Education and Human Development, Program in School Psychology, Boston, MA 02125-3393. Offers M Ed. *Program availability:* Part-time, evening/weekend. *Students:* 16 full-time (14 women), 4 part-time (all women); includes 4 minority (1 Black or African American, non-Hispanic/Latino; 1 Asian, non-Hispanic/Latino; 2 Hispanic/Latino), 2 international. Average age 26. 77 applicants, 34% accepted, 15 enrolled. In 2016, 6 master's awarded. *Degree requirements:* For master's, comprehensive exam, practicum, final project. *Entrance requirements:* For master's, GRE General Test or MAT, minimum GPA of 3.0. *Application deadline:* For fall admission, 3/1 for domestic students; for spring admission, 11/1 for domestic students. *Expenses:* Tuition, state resident: full-time $16,863. Tuition, nonresident: full-time $32,913. *Required fees:* $177. *Financial support:* Research assistantships with full tuition reimbursements, teaching assistantships with full tuition reimbursements, career-related internships or fieldwork, Federal Work-Study, and unspecified assistantships available. Support available to part-time students. Financial award application deadline: 3/1; financial award applicants required to submit FAFSA. *Faculty research:* School psychology services, assessment of children, cultural and gender differences on psychological adjustment to disabilities. *Unit head:* Dr. Virginia Harvey, Director, 617-287-7617. *Application contact:* Peggy Roldan Patel, Graduate Admissions Coordinator, 617-287-6400, Fax: 617-287-6236, E-mail: bos.gadm@dpc.umassp.edu.

**University of Memphis,** Graduate School, College of Arts and Sciences, Department of Psychology, Memphis, TN 38152-3230. Offers clinical psychology (PhD); experimental psychology (PhD); general psychology (MS); school psychology (MA, PhD, Ed S). *Accreditation:* APA. *Faculty:* 27 full-time (12 women), 2 part-time/adjunct (0 women). *Students:* 97 full-time (70 women), 17 part-time (11 women); includes 29 minority (16 Black or African American, non-Hispanic/Latino; 5 Asian, non-Hispanic/Latino; 4 Hispanic/Latino; 4 Two or more races, non-Hispanic/Latino), 5 international. Average age 27. 278 applicants, 17% accepted, 35 enrolled. In 2016, 34 master's, 2 doctorates, 9 other advanced degrees awarded. *Degree requirements:* For master's, comprehensive exam (for some programs), thesis (for some programs), 37 credit hours (for MA); 33 credit hours with thesis or 36 with exam (for MS); for doctorate, comprehensive exam, thesis/dissertation, 80 semester hours, major area paper; 1-year placement and 1-year internship (for clinical psychology); internship (for school psychology); for Ed S, 30 credit hours. *Entrance requirements:* For master's, GRE, 3 letters of recommendation, 18 undergraduate hours in psychology; for doctorate, GRE, minimum GPA of 2.75, 18 hours of undergraduate psychology courses, transcripts, personal statement, 3 letters of recommendation, interview; for Ed S, GRE, minimum GPA of 2.75, 18 hours of undergraduate psychology courses, 3 letters of recommendation. Additional exam requirements/recommendations for international students: Required—TOEFL (minimum score 550 paper-based; 79 iBT). *Application deadline:* For fall admission, 12/5 for domestic students. Applications are processed on a rolling basis. Application fee: $35 ($60 for international students). Electronic applications accepted. *Expenses:* $5,231.50 per semester full-time in-state, $9,623.50 full-time out-of-state. *Financial support:* In 2016–17, 66 students received support, including 60 research assistantships with full tuition reimbursements available (averaging $17,582 per year), 21 teaching assistantships with full tuition reimbursements available (averaging $6,220 per year); fellowships with full tuition reimbursements available, Federal Work-Study, scholarships/grants, tuition waivers (partial), and unspecified assistantships also available. Financial award application deadline: 2/1; financial award applicants required to submit FAFSA. *Faculty research:* Clinical health; school, child and family psychology; psychotherapy; cognitive and behavioral neuroscience; industrial-organizational psychology. *Unit head:* Dr. Frank Andrasik, Chair, 901-678-2145, Fax: 901-678-2579, E-mail: rcohen@memphis.edu. *Application contact:* Dr. Robert Cohen, Coordinator of Graduate Studies, 901-678-4679, Fax: 901-678-2579, E-mail: rcohen@memphis.edu.
Website: http://www.memphis.edu/psychology

**University of Minnesota, Twin Cities Campus,** Graduate School, College of Education and Human Development, Department of Educational Psychology, Program in School Psychology, Minneapolis, MN 55455-0213. Offers MA, PhD, Ed S. *Accreditation:* APA. *Students:* 44 full-time (38 women), 17 part-time (12 women); includes 4 minority (2 Black or African American, non-Hispanic/Latino; 1 Asian, non-Hispanic/Latino; 1 Two or more races, non-Hispanic/Latino), 2 international. Average age 28. 22 applicants, 32% accepted, 7 enrolled. In 2016, 14 master's, 10 doctorates, 1 other advanced degree awarded. Application fee: $75 ($95 for international students). *Unit head:* Dr. Geoffrey Maruyama, Chair, 612-625-5861, Fax: 612-624-8241, E-mail: geoff@umn.edu. *Application contact:* Dr. Ernest Davenport, Director of Graduate Studies, 612-624-1040, E-mail: lqr6576@umn.edu.
Website: http://www.cehd.umn.edu/EdPsych/programs/SchoolPsych/

**University of Minnesota, Twin Cities Campus,** Graduate School, College of Liberal Arts, Department of Psychology, Minneapolis, MN 55455-0213. Offers biological psychopathology (PhD); clinical psychology (PhD); cognitive and biological psychology (PhD); counseling psychology (PhD); industrial/organizational psychology (PhD); personality, individual differences, and behavior genetics (PhD); quantitative/psychometric methods (PhD); school psychology (PhD); social psychology (PhD). *Accreditation:* APA. *Degree requirements:* For doctorate, comprehensive exam, thesis/dissertation. *Entrance requirements:* For doctorate, GRE General Test, GRE Subject Test (recommended), 12 credits of upper-level psychology courses, including a course in statistics or psychological measurement. Additional exam requirements/recommendations for international students: Required—TOEFL (minimum score 79 iBT).

**University of Missouri,** Office of Research and Graduate Studies, College of Education, Department of Educational, School, and Counseling Psychology, Columbia, MO 65211. Offers counseling psychology (M Ed, MA, PhD, Ed S); educational psychology (M Ed, MA, PhD, Ed S); learning and instruction (M Ed); school psychology (M Ed, MA, PhD, Ed S). *Accreditation:* APA (one or more programs are accredited). *Program availability:* Part-time. *Faculty:* 29 full-time (12 women), 1 part-time/adjunct (0 women). *Students:* 177 full-time (106 women), 204 part-time (102 women). *Degree requirements:* For doctorate, thesis/dissertation. *Entrance requirements:* For master's, doctorate, and Ed S, GRE General Test, minimum GPA of 3.0. Additional exam requirements/recommendations for international students: Required—TOEFL (minimum score 580 paper-based; 92 iBT). *Application deadline:* For fall admission, 12/1 priority date for domestic and international students. Applications are processed on a rolling basis. Application fee: $75 ($90 for international students). Electronic applications accepted. *Expenses:* Tuition, state resident: full-time $6347; part-time $352.60 per credit hour. Tuition, nonresident: full-time $17,379; part-time $965.50 per credit hour. *Required fees:* $1035. Tuition and fees vary according to course load, campus/location and program. *Financial support:* Fellowships, research assistantships, teaching assistantships, institutionally sponsored loans, traineeships, health care benefits, and unspecified assistantships available. Support available to part-time students.
Website: http://education.missouri.edu/ESCP/

**University of Missouri–St. Louis,** College of Education, Department of Education Sciences and Professional Programs, St. Louis, MO 63121. Offers adult and higher education (M Ed); educational leadership and policy studies (PhD); educational psychology (M Ed), including character and citizenship education, research and program evaluation; program evaluation (Certificate); school psychology (Ed S). *Faculty:* 36 full-time (25 women), 53 part-time/adjunct (40 women). *Students:* 47 full-time (34 women), 247 part-time (175 women); includes 107 minority (86 Black or African American, non-Hispanic/Latino; 2 American Indian or Alaska Native, non-Hispanic/Latino; 5 Asian, non-Hispanic/Latino; 10 Hispanic/Latino; 4 Two or more races, non-Hispanic/Latino), 7 international. 106 applicants, 92% accepted, 70 enrolled. *Degree requirements:* For other advanced degree, comprehensive exam, thesis or alternative, internship. *Entrance requirements:* For degree, GRE General Test, 2-4 letters of recommendation, personal interview. Additional exam requirements/recommendations for international students: Required—IELTS (minimum score 6.5); Recommended—TOEFL (minimum score 550 paper-based; 79 iBT). *Application deadline:* For fall admission, 2/15 priority date for domestic students, 2/15 for international students. Application fee: $50 ($40 for international students). Electronic applications accepted. *Financial support:* Application deadline: 4/1; applicants required to submit FAFSA. *Faculty research:* Child/adolescent psychology, quantitative and qualitative methodology, evaluation processes, measurement and assessment. *Unit head:* Dr. Donald Gouwens, Chairperson, 314-516-4773, Fax: 314-516-5784, E-mail: gouwensd@umsl.edu. *Application contact:* 314-516-5458, Fax: 314-516-6996, E-mail: gradadm@umsl.edu.
Website: https://coe.umsl.edu/dept/espp.html

**University of Montana,** Graduate School, College of Humanities and Sciences, Department of Psychology, Program in School Psychology, Missoula, MT 59812-0002. Offers MA, PhD, Ed S. *Degree requirements:* For master's, oral exam, professional paper; for Ed S, thesis. *Entrance requirements:* For master's, GRE General Test, GRE Subject Test, minimum GPA 3.25 during previous 2 years; for Ed S, GRE General Test. Additional exam requirements/recommendations for international students: Required—TOEFL. *Faculty research:* Child development and creativity, psychological measurement.

**University of Nebraska at Kearney,** College of Education, Department of Counseling and School Psychology, Kearney, NE 68849-0001. Offers clinical mental health counseling (MS Ed); school counseling (MS Ed), including elementary, secondary; school psychology (Ed S); student affairs (MS Ed). *Accreditation:* ACA; NCATE. *Program availability:* Part-time, evening/weekend, 100% online. *Faculty:* 7 full-time (3 women). *Students:* 69 full-time (56 women), 102 part-time (81 women); includes 21 minority (2 Black or African American, non-Hispanic/Latino; 2 Asian, non-Hispanic/Latino; 12 Hispanic/Latino; 5 Two or more races, non-Hispanic/Latino), 4 international. Average age 30. 43 applicants, 100% accepted, 37 enrolled. In 2016, 24 master's, 13 Ed Ss awarded. *Degree requirements:* For master's, comprehensive exam, thesis optional; for Ed S, thesis. *Entrance requirements:* For master's and Ed S, personal statement, recommendations, resume, interview. Additional exam requirements/recommendations for international students: Recommended—TOEFL (minimum score 550 paper-based; 79 iBT), IELTS (minimum score 6.5). *Application deadline:* For fall admission, 6/15 for domestic and international students; for spring admission, 10/15 for domestic and international students; for summer admission, 3/15 for domestic and international students. Application fee: $45. Electronic applications accepted. *Expenses:* Tuition, state resident: full-time $4064; part-time $225.75 per credit hour. Tuition, nonresident: full-time $8915; part-time $495.25 per credit hour. *Required fees:* $772; $23 per credit hour. Part-time tuition and fees vary according to course load, campus/location, program and reciprocity agreements. *Financial support:* In 2016–17, 7 students received support, including 7 research assistantships with full tuition reimbursements available (averaging $10,500 per year); fellowships, career-related internships or fieldwork, scholarships/grants, health care benefits, and unspecified assistantships also available. Support available to part-time students. Financial award application deadline: 2/28; financial award applicants required to submit FAFSA. *Faculty research:* Multicultural counseling and diversity issues, team decision-making, adult development, women's issues, brief therapy. *Unit head:* Dr. Grace Mims, Chair, Counseling and School Psychology, 308-865-8508, E-mail: mimsga@unk.edu. *Application contact:* Linda Johnson, Director, Graduate Admissions and Programs, 800-717-7881, Fax: 308-865-8837, E-mail: gradstudies@unk.edu.
Website: http://www.unk.edu/academics/csp/

**University of Nebraska at Omaha,** Graduate Studies, College of Arts and Sciences, Department of Psychology, Omaha, NE 68182. Offers applied behavior analysis (Certificate); human resources and training (Certificate); industrial/organizational psychology (MS); psychology (MA, PhD); school psychology (MS, Ed S). *Program availability:* Part-time. *Faculty:* 10 full-time (1 woman). *Students:* 70 full-time (52 women), 49 part-time (33 women); includes 9 minority (2 Asian, non-Hispanic/Latino; 5 Hispanic/Latino; 2 Two or more races, non-Hispanic/Latino), 1 international. Average age 27. 157 applicants, 25% accepted, 38 enrolled. In 2016, 32 master's, 6 doctorates, 10 other advanced degrees awarded. *Degree requirements:* For master's, comprehensive exam, thesis (for some programs); for doctorate, comprehensive exam, thesis/dissertation. *Entrance requirements:* For master's and doctorate, GRE, minimum GPA of 3.0, official transcripts, 3 letters of recommendation, statement of purpose, writing sample, resume. Additional exam requirements/recommendations for international students: Required—TOEFL, IELTS, PTE. *Application deadline:* For fall admission, 1/5 priority date for domestic and international students. Application fee: $45. Electronic applications accepted. *Financial support:* In 2016–17, 50 students received support, including 23 research assistantships with tuition reimbursements available, 27 teaching assistantships with tuition reimbursements available; fellowships with tuition reimbursements available, career-related internships or fieldwork, Federal Work-Study, institutionally sponsored loans, scholarships/grants, health care benefits, tuition waivers (partial), and unspecified assistantships also available. Financial award application deadline: 3/1; financial award applicants required to submit FAFSA. *Unit head:* Dr. Brigette Ryalls, Chairperson, 402-554-2341, E-mail: graduate@unomaha.edu. *Application contact:* Dr. Joseph Brown, Graduate Program Chair, 402-554-2341, E-mail: graduate@unomaha.edu.

**University of Nebraska–Lincoln,** Graduate College, College of Education and Human Sciences, Department of Educational Psychology, Lincoln, NE 68588. Offers cognition, learning and development (MA); counseling psychology (MA); educational psychology (MA, Ed S); psychological studies in education (PhD), including cognition, learning and development, counseling psychology, quantitative, qualitative, and psychometric methods, school psychology; quantitative, qualitative, and psychometric methods (MA); school psychology (MA, Ed S). *Accreditation:* APA (one or more programs are accredited); NCATE. *Degree requirements:* For master's, thesis optional. *Entrance requirements:* For master's, GRE General Test. Additional exam requirements/recommendations for international students: Required—TOEFL (minimum score 500 paper-based). Electronic applications accepted. *Faculty research:* Measurement and assessment, metacognition, academic skills, child development, multicultural education and counseling.

**The University of North Carolina at Chapel Hill,** Graduate School, School of Education, Program in School Psychology, Chapel Hill, NC 27599. Offers M Ed, MA, PhD. *Accreditation:* APA (one or more programs are accredited); NCATE. *Degree requirements:* For master's, comprehensive exam, thesis (for some programs); for doctorate, comprehensive exam, thesis/dissertation. *Entrance requirements:* For master's and doctorate, GRE General Test, minimum GPA of 3.0 during last 2 years of undergraduate course work. Additional exam requirements/recommendations for international students: Required—TOEFL (minimum score 550 paper-based). Electronic applications accepted.

**The University of North Carolina at Greensboro,** Graduate School, School of Education, Department of Counseling and Educational Development, Greensboro, NC 27412-5001. Offers advanced school counseling (PMC); counseling and counselor education (PhD); counseling and educational development (MS); couple and family counseling (PMC); school counseling (PMC); MS/Ed S. *Accreditation:* ACA (one or more programs are accredited); NCATE. *Degree requirements:* For master's, comprehensive exam, practicum, internship; for doctorate, comprehensive exam, thesis/dissertation. *Entrance requirements:* For master's, doctorate, and PMC, GRE General Test. Additional exam requirements/recommendations for international students: Required—TOEFL. Electronic applications accepted. *Faculty research:* Gerontology, invitational theory, career development, marriage and family therapy, drug and alcohol abuse prevention.

**University of Northern Colorado,** Graduate School, College of Education and Behavioral Sciences, Department of School Psychology, Greeley, CO 80639. Offers Ed S. *Accreditation:* APA; NCATE. *Program availability:* Part-time, evening/weekend. *Degree requirements:* For Ed S, comprehensive exam. *Application deadline:* For fall

## School Psychology

admission, 1/1 for domestic and international students. Applications are processed on a rolling basis. Application fee: $50 ($60 for international students). Electronic applications accepted. *Financial support:* Fellowships, research assistantships, teaching assistantships, and unspecified assistantships available. Financial award application deadline: 3/1; financial award applicants required to submit FAFSA. *Unit head:* Diane Greenshields, Program Coordinator, 970-351-2731, Fax: 970-351-2625. *Application contact:* Linda Sisson, Graduate Student Admission Coordinator, 970-351-1807, Fax: 970-351-2371, E-mail: linda.sisson@unco.edu.
Website: http://www.unco.edu/cebs/SchoolPsych/

**University of Northern Iowa,** Graduate College, College of Education, Department of Educational Psychology and Foundations; Ed S Program in School Psychology, Cedar Falls, IA 50614. Offers Ed S.

**University of Northern Iowa,** Graduate College, College of Social and Behavioral Sciences, School of Applied Human Sciences, Cedar Falls, IA 50614. Offers counseling (MA), including mental health counseling, school counseling; mental health counseling (MA); school counseling (MA). *Program availability:* Part-time. *Degree requirements:* For master's, comprehensive exam, thesis (for some programs). *Entrance requirements:* Additional exam requirements/recommendations for international students: Required—TOEFL (minimum score 550 paper-based; 79 iBT). Electronic applications accepted.

**University of Oklahoma,** Jeannine Rainbolt College of Education, Department of Educational Psychology, Program in Professional Counseling, Norman, OK 73019. Offers professional counseling (M Ed), including drug and alcohol counseling, Oklahoma licensed professional counseling, research, school counseling. *Students:* 35 full-time (26 women), 4 part-time (1 woman); includes 16 minority (3 Black or African American, non-Hispanic/Latino; 2 American Indian or Alaska Native, non-Hispanic/Latino; 1 Asian, non-Hispanic/Latino; 4 Hispanic/Latino; 6 Two or more races, non-Hispanic/Latino), 1 international. Average age 28. 29 applicants, 83% accepted, 17 enrolled. In 2016, 17 master's awarded. *Degree requirements:* For master's, comprehensive exam, internship. *Entrance requirements:* For master's, GRE. Additional exam requirements/ recommendations for international students: Required—TOEFL (minimum score 79 iBT) or IELTS (minimum score 6.5). *Application deadline:* For fall admission, 1/10 for domestic and international students. Application fee: $50 ($100 for international students). Electronic applications accepted. *Expenses:* Tuition, state resident: full-time $4886; part-time $203.60 per credit hour. Tuition, nonresident: full-time $18,989; part-time $791.20 per credit hour. *Required fees:* $3283; $126.25 per credit hour. $126.50 per semester. *Financial support:* In 2016–17, 29 students received support. Research assistantships with full and partial tuition reimbursements available and scholarships/ grants available. Financial award application deadline: 6/1; financial award applicants required to submit FAFSA. *Faculty research:* Group therapy interventions; multi and inter disciplinary collaboration; treatment of students in boarding school settings; diversity issues in counseling; applied behavior analysis. *Unit head:* Dr. Nancy E. Marchand-Martella, Chair, Department of Educational Psychology, 405-325-0624, Fax: 405-325-6655, E-mail: nmarchand-martella@ou.edu. *Application contact:* Anna Steele, Graduate Programs Specialist, 405-325-4525, Fax: 405-325-7390, E-mail: jrcoe_gps@ou.edu.
Website: http://www.ou.edu/education/edpy

**University of Phoenix–Colorado Campus,** College of Education, Lone Tree, CO 80124-5453. Offers administration and supervision (MAEd); curriculum instruction (MAEd); elementary teacher education (MAEd); school counseling (MSC); secondary teacher education (MAEd). *Program availability:* Evening/weekend. *Degree requirements:* For master's, thesis (for some programs). *Entrance requirements:* For master's, minimum undergraduate GPA of 2.5, 3 years work experience. Additional exam requirements/recommendations for international students: Required—TOEFL (minimum score 550 paper-based; 79 iBT). Electronic applications accepted.

**University of Phoenix–Colorado Springs Downtown Campus,** College of Education, Colorado Springs, CO 80903. Offers administration and supervision (MA Ed); curriculum and instruction (MA Ed); elementary teacher education (MA Ed); principal licensure certification (Certificate); school counseling (MSC); secondary teacher education (MA Ed). *Program availability:* Evening/weekend. *Degree requirements:* For master's, thesis (for some programs). *Entrance requirements:* For master's, minimum undergraduate GPA of 2.5, 3 years of work experience. Additional exam requirements/ recommendations for international students: Required—TOEFL (minimum score 550 paper-based; 79 iBT). Electronic applications accepted.

**University of Phoenix–Las Vegas Campus,** College of Education, Las Vegas, NV 89135. Offers administration and supervision (MA Ed); curriculum and instruction (MA Ed); school counseling (MSC); teacher education-elementary licensure (MA Ed). *Program availability:* Evening/weekend. *Degree requirements:* For master's, thesis (for some programs). *Entrance requirements:* For master's, minimum undergraduate GPA of 2.5, 3 years of work experience. Additional exam requirements/recommendations for international students: Required—TOEFL (minimum score 550 paper-based; 79 iBT). Electronic applications accepted.

**University of Phoenix–Utah Campus,** College of Education, Salt Lake City, UT 84123-4642. Offers administration and supervision (MA Ed); curriculum and instruction (MA Ed); elementary teacher education (MA Ed); school counseling (MSC); secondary teacher education (MA Ed); special education (MA Ed). *Program availability:* Evening/ weekend. *Degree requirements:* For master's, thesis (for some programs). *Entrance requirements:* For master's, minimum undergraduate GPA of 2.5, 3 years work experience. Additional exam requirements/recommendations for international students: Required—TOEFL (minimum score 550 paper-based; 79 iBT). Electronic applications accepted.

**University of Rhode Island,** Graduate School, College of Health Sciences, Department of Psychology, Kingston, RI 02881. Offers behavioral science (PhD); clinical psychology (PhD); school psychology (MS, PhD). *Accreditation:* APA (one or more programs are accredited). *Program availability:* Part-time. *Faculty:* 24 full-time (14 women), 2 part-time/adjunct (1 woman). *Students:* 81 full-time (62 women), 29 part-time (23 women); includes 19 minority (12 Black or African American, non-Hispanic/Latino; 2 American Indian or Alaska Native, non-Hispanic/Latino; 3 Asian, non-Hispanic/Latino; 2 Hispanic/ Latino), 6 international. In 2016, 13 master's, 17 doctorates awarded. *Degree requirements:* For master's, comprehensive exam, thesis optional; for doctorate, thesis/ dissertation. *Entrance requirements:* For master's and doctorate, GRE, 3 letters of recommendation. Additional exam requirements/recommendations for international students: Required—TOEFL. *Application deadline:* For fall admission, 12/1 for domestic and international students. Application fee: $65. Electronic applications accepted. *Expenses:* Tuition, state resident: full-time $11,796; part-time $655 per credit. Tuition, nonresident: full-time $24,206; part-time $1345 per credit. *Required fees:* $1546; $44 per credit. One-time fee: $155 full-time; $35 part-time. *Financial support:* In 2016–17, 8 research assistantships with tuition reimbursements (averaging $15,685 per year), 24 teaching assistantships with tuition reimbursements (averaging $14,504 per year) were awarded. Financial award application deadline: 12/1; financial award applicants required to submit FAFSA. *Unit head:* Dr. Mark Robbins, Chair, 401-874-5082, E-mail: markrobb@uri.edu. *Application contact:* Graduate Admission, 401-874-2872, E-mail: gradadm@etal.uri.edu.
Website: http://www.uri.edu/artsci/psy/

**University of South Carolina,** The Graduate School, College of Arts and Sciences, Department of Psychology, Program in School Psychology, Columbia, SC 29208. Offers PhD. *Accreditation:* APA; NCATE. *Degree requirements:* For doctorate, thesis/ dissertation. *Entrance requirements:* For doctorate, GRE General Test, minimum GPA of 3.0. Additional exam requirements/recommendations for international students: Required—TOEFL. Electronic applications accepted. *Faculty research:* Preschool services, families and diversity life satisfaction, ADHD intervention, attachment.

**The University of South Dakota,** Graduate School, School of Education, Division of Counseling and Psychology in Education, Vermillion, SD 57069. Offers counseling (MA, PhD, Ed S); human development and educational psychology (MA, PhD, Ed S); school psychology (PhD, Ed S). *Accreditation:* ACA (one or more programs are accredited); NCATE. *Program availability:* Part-time. *Degree requirements:* For master's and Ed S, comprehensive exam, thesis or alternative; for doctorate, comprehensive exam, thesis/ dissertation. *Entrance requirements:* For master's and doctorate, GRE General Test, minimum GPA of 3.0. Additional exam requirements/recommendations for international students: Required—TOEFL (minimum score 550 paper-based; 79 iBT). Electronic applications accepted.

**University of Southern Maine,** College of Management and Human Service, School of Education and Human Development, Program in School Psychology, Portland, ME 04103. Offers MS, Psy D. *Program availability:* Part-time, evening/weekend. *Degree requirements:* For doctorate, comprehensive exam, thesis/dissertation, dissertation defense. *Entrance requirements:* For doctorate, GRE General Test, interview. Additional exam requirements/recommendations for international students: Required—TOEFL (minimum score 550 paper-based; 79 iBT). Electronic applications accepted. *Faculty research:* Academic interventions, applied behavior analysis, assessment methods, response to intervention, school psychology practices, positive behavioral interventions and supports, multi-tier systems of support.

**University of Southern Mississippi,** Graduate School, College of Education and Psychology, Department of Child and Family Studies, Hattiesburg, MS 39406. Offers child and family studies (MS); marriage and family therapy (MS); school counseling (M Ed). *Accreditation:* AAMFT/COAMFTE (one or more programs are accredited). *Program availability:* Part-time, online learning. *Degree requirements:* For master's, comprehensive exam, thesis optional. *Entrance requirements:* For master's, GRE General Test, minimum GPA of 2.75 on last 60 hours. Additional exam requirements/ recommendations for international students: Required—TOEFL. *Application deadline:* For fall admission, 3/1 priority date for domestic students, 3/1 for international students; for spring admission, 1/1 priority date for domestic and international students. Applications are processed on a rolling basis. Application fee: $60. Electronic applications accepted. *Expenses:* Tuition, area resident: Full-time $15,708; part-time $437 per credit hour. *Financial support:* Fellowships, research assistantships with full tuition reimbursements, career-related internships or fieldwork, Federal Work-Study, institutionally sponsored loans, scholarships/grants, health care benefits, and unspecified assistantships available. Financial award application deadline: 3/15; financial award applicants required to submit FAFSA. *Faculty research:* School food service, teen pregnancy, diet and cholesterol metabolism. *Unit head:* Pat Sims, Chair, 601-266-6990, Fax: 601-266-4680. *Application contact:* Shonna Breland, Manager of Graduate Admissions, 601-266-6563, Fax: 601-266-5138.
Website: https://www.usm.edu/family-studies-child-development

**University of Southern Mississippi,** Graduate School, College of Education and Psychology, Department of Psychology, Hattiesburg, MS 39406. Offers applied behavior analysis (MS); clinical psychology (PhD); counseling psychology (MS, PhD); school psychology (PhD). *Accreditation:* APA (one or more programs are accredited). Terminal master's awarded for partial completion of doctoral program. *Degree requirements:* For master's, comprehensive exam, thesis; for doctorate, comprehensive exam, thesis/ dissertation. *Entrance requirements:* For master's, GRE General Test, minimum GPA of 3.0; for doctorate, GRE General Test, interview, minimum GPA of 3.5. Additional exam requirements/recommendations for international students: Required—TOEFL, IELTS. *Application deadline:* Applications are processed on a rolling basis. Application fee: $60. *Expenses:* Tuition, area resident: Full-time $15,708; part-time $437 per credit hour. *Financial support:* Research assistantships with full tuition reimbursements, teaching assistantships with full tuition reimbursements, career-related internships or fieldwork, Federal Work-Study, institutionally sponsored loans, scholarships/grants, health care benefits, and unspecified assistantships available. Financial award application deadline: 3/15; financial award applicants required to submit FAFSA. *Faculty research:* Psychopathology, alcohol and drug abuse, child clinical psychology, parenting, suicide, career/vocational, marine mammal, cognition, psychological psychology, behavioral interventions, positive psychology, anger/aggression, diversity issues. *Unit head:* Dr. Joe Olmi, Chair, 601-266-5693, Fax: 601-266-5580, E-mail: d.olmi@usm.edu. *Application contact:* Angela Pam, Administrative Assistant, 601-266-4592, Fax: 601-266-5580.
Website: https://www.usm.edu/psychology

**University of South Florida,** College of Education, Department of Educational and Psychological Studies, Tampa, FL 33620-9951. Offers college student affairs (M Ed); counselor education (MA, PhD, Ed S); interdisciplinary (PhD, Ed S); school psychology (PhD, Ed S). *Faculty:* 25 full-time (12 women). *Students:* 97 full-time (66 women), 94 part-time (62 women); includes 52 minority (22 Black or African American, non-Hispanic/ Latino; 8 Asian, non-Hispanic/Latino; 19 Hispanic/Latino; 3 Two or more races, non-Hispanic/Latino), 25 international. Average age 34. 132 applicants, 45% accepted, 46 enrolled. In 2016, 94 master's, 7 doctorates, 8 other advanced degrees awarded. Application fee: $30. *Expenses:* Tuition, state resident: full-time $7766; part-time $431.43 per credit hour. Tuition, nonresident: full-time $15,789; part-time $877.17 per credit hour. *Required fees:* $37 per term. *Faculty research:* College student affairs, counselor education, educational psychology, school psychology, social foundations. *Total annual research expenditures:* $11.1 million. *Unit head:* Dr. Barabara Shircliff, Chair, 813-974-4001, E-mail: shirclif@usf.edu.
Website: http://www.coedu.usf.edu/main/departments/psf/psf.html

**The University of Tennessee,** Graduate School, College of Education, Health and Human Sciences, Program in Education, Knoxville, TN 37996. Offers art education (MS); counseling education (PhD); cultural studies in education (PhD); curriculum (MS, Ed S); curriculum, educational research and evaluation (Ed D, PhD); early childhood education (PhD); early childhood special education (MS); education of deaf and hard of hearing (MS); educational administration and policy studies (Ed D, PhD); educational administration and supervision (Ed S); educational psychology (Ed D, PhD); elementary education (MS, Ed S); elementary teaching (MS); English education (MS, Ed S); exercise science (PhD); foreign language/ESL education (MS, Ed S); instructional technology (MS, Ed D, PhD, Ed S); literacy, language and ESL education (PhD); literacy, language education, and ESL education (Ed D); mathematics education (MS, Ed S); modified and comprehensive special education (MS); reading education (MS, Ed S); school counseling (Ed S); school psychology (PhD, Ed S); science education (MS, Ed S); secondary teaching (MS); social foundations (MS); social science education (MS, Ed S); socio-cultural foundations of sports and education (PhD); special education

(Ed S); teacher education (Ed D, PhD). *Accreditation:* NCATE. *Program availability:* Part-time, evening/weekend. *Degree requirements:* For master's and Ed S, thesis optional; for doctorate, variable foreign language requirement, thesis/dissertation. *Entrance requirements:* For master's, minimum GPA of 2.7; for doctorate and Ed S, GRE General Test, minimum GPA of 2.7. Additional exam requirements/recommendations for international students: Required—TOEFL. Electronic applications accepted.

**The University of Tennessee at Chattanooga,** School of Education, Chattanooga, TN 37403. Offers counseling (M Ed), including community counseling, school counseling; education (M Ed, Post-Master's Certificate), including elementary education (M Ed), school leadership, secondary education (M Ed), special education (M Ed); educational specialist (Ed S), including educational technology, school psychology; learning and leadership (Ed D), including educational leadership. *Accreditation:* ACA; NCATE. *Program availability:* Part-time. *Faculty:* 13 full-time (8 women), 2 part-time/adjunct (both women). *Students:* 50 full-time (32 women), 157 part-time (107 women); includes 42 minority (28 Black or African American, non-Hispanic/Latino; 4 Asian, non-Hispanic/Latino; 2 Hispanic/Latino; 8 Two or more races, non-Hispanic/Latino), 1 international. Average age 36. 169 applicants, 76% accepted, 49 enrolled. In 2016, 77 master's, 5 other advanced degrees awarded. *Degree requirements:* For master's, comprehensive exam, thesis optional, culminating experience; for doctorate, comprehensive exam, thesis/dissertation; for other advanced degree, internship. *Entrance requirements:* For master's, GRE General Test, PPST 1, teaching certificate; for doctorate, GRE General Test, master's degree, two years of practical work experience in organizational environment; for other advanced degree, GRE General Test, letters of reference. Additional exam requirements/recommendations for international students: Required—TOEFL (minimum score 550 paper-based; 79 iBT), IELTS (minimum score 6). *Application deadline:* For fall admission, 6/15 for domestic students, 7/1 for international students; for spring admission, 11/1 for domestic and international students. Applications are processed on a rolling basis. Application fee: $35 ($40 for international students). Electronic applications accepted. *Expenses:* $9,876 full-time in-state; $25,994 full-time out-of-state; $450 per credit part-time in-state; $1,345 per credit part-time out-of-state. *Financial support:* In 2016–17, 18 research assistantships, 5 teaching assistantships were awarded; career-related internships or fieldwork, institutionally sponsored loans, scholarships/grants, and unspecified assistantships also available. Support available to part-time students. Financial award application deadline: 7/1; financial award applicants required to submit FAFSA. *Faculty research:* School counseling, community counseling, elementary and secondary education, school leadership and administration. *Total annual research expenditures:* $247,231. *Unit head:* Dr. Renee Murley, Director, 423-425-4684, Fax: 423-425-5380, E-mail: renee-murley@utc.edu. *Application contact:* Dr. Joanne Romagni, Dean of the Graduate School, 423-425-4478, Fax: 423-425-5223, E-mail: joanne-romagni@utc.edu. Website: http://www.utc.edu/school-education/abouttheschool/gradprograms.php

**The University of Texas at Austin,** Graduate School, College of Education, Department of Educational Psychology, Austin, TX 78712-1111. Offers academic educational psychology (M Ed, MA); counseling psychology (PhD); counselor education (M Ed); human development, culture and learning sciences (PhD); program evaluation (MA); quantitative methods (M Ed, MA, PhD); school psychology (MA, PhD). *Accreditation:* APA (one or more programs are accredited). *Degree requirements:* For master's, thesis optional; for doctorate, thesis/dissertation. *Entrance requirements:* For master's and doctorate, GRE General Test, 3 letters of recommendation. Additional exam requirements/recommendations for international students: Required—TOEFL.

**The University of Texas at San Antonio,** College of Education and Human Development, Department of Educational Psychology, San Antonio, TX 78207. Offers applied behavioral analysis (Certificate); digital learning design (Certificate); language acquisition and bilingual psychoeducational assessment (Certificate); school psychology (MA). *Program availability:* Part-time. *Faculty:* 11 full-time (6 women), 1 (woman) part-time/adjunct. *Students:* 38 full-time (31 women), 29 part-time (25 women); includes 43 minority (4 Black or African American, non-Hispanic/Latino; 1 Asian, non-Hispanic/Latino; 35 Hispanic/Latino; 3 Two or more races, non-Hispanic/Latino). Average age 28. 23 applicants, 78% accepted, 13 enrolled. In 2016, 16 master's, 16 other advanced degrees awarded. *Degree requirements:* For master's, comprehensive exam, thesis (for some programs). *Entrance requirements:* For master's, GRE, bachelor's degree with 18 credit hours in field of study or in another appropriate field of study, two letters of recommendation, statement of purpose; for Certificate, 18 hours in psychology, sociology, education, or anything related (for applied behavioral analysis); minimum GPA of 2.7 in last 30 hours (for language acquisition and bilingual psychoeducational assessment). Additional exam requirements/recommendations for international students: Required—TOEFL (minimum score 550 paper-based; 79 iBT), IELTS (minimum score 6.5). *Application deadline:* For fall admission, 7/1 for domestic students, 4/1 for international students; for spring admission, 11/1 for domestic students, 9/1 for international students; for summer admission, 3/1 for international students. Applications are processed on a rolling basis. Application fee: $45 ($80 for international students). Electronic applications accepted. *Financial support:* In 2016–17, 9 research assistantships (averaging $2,829 per year) were awarded. Financial award application deadline: 3/5; financial award applicants required to submit FAFSA. *Faculty research:* Teacher consultation and culturally responsive school psychology practices, youth mentoring, cross-age peer mentoring, adolescent connectedness, pair counseling. *Total annual research expenditures:* $91,630. *Unit head:* Dr. Jeremy Sullivan, Department Chair, 210-458-2378, Fax: 210-458-2019, E-mail: jeremy.sullivan@utsa.edu. *Application contact:* Dr. John Pruiett, Development Specialist, 210-458-2721, Fax: 210-458-2019, E-mail: johnny.pruiett@utsa.edu. Website: http://education.utsa.edu/educational_psychology

**The University of Texas at Tyler,** College of Education and Psychology, Department of Psychology and Counseling, Tyler, TX 75799-0001. Offers clinical psychology (MS), including neuropsychology, school psychology; counseling psychology (MA), including general, marriage and family; interdisciplinary studies (MSIS); school counseling (MA). *Program availability:* Part-time, evening/weekend. *Degree requirements:* For master's, comprehensive exam, thesis optional. *Entrance requirements:* For master's, GRE General Test, minimum GPA of 3.0. Additional exam requirements/recommendations for international students: Required—TOEFL. Electronic applications accepted. *Faculty research:* Neuropsychology, child abuse, psychometric properties of psychological instruments, maternal behavior, clinical practice issues, victimization of women, post-traumatic stress disorder.

**The University of Texas Rio Grande Valley,** College of Education and P-16 Integration, Department of Human Development and School Services, Edinburg, TX 78539. Offers early childhood education (M Ed); early childhood special education (M Ed); educational diagnostician (M Ed); school psychology (MA). *Program availability:* Part-time, evening/weekend. *Degree requirements:* For master's, comprehensive exam (for some programs), thesis (for some programs). *Entrance requirements:* For master's, GRE General Test, interview. Tuition and fees vary according to course load and program. *Faculty research:* Reading instruction, assessment practice, behavior interventions consultation, mental retardation.

**University of the Pacific,** Gladys L. Benerd School of Education, Department of Educational and School Psychology, Stockton, CA 95211-0197. Offers educational psychology (MA, Ed D); school psychology (Ed S). *Accreditation:* NCATE. *Students:* 4 part-time (all women); includes 3 minority (all Hispanic/Latino). Average age 33. *Degree requirements:* For master's, thesis; for doctorate, thesis/dissertation. *Entrance requirements:* For master's and doctorate, GRE General Test, GRE Subject Test. Additional exam requirements/recommendations for international students: Required—TOEFL. *Application deadline:* For fall admission, 3/1 priority date for domestic students; for spring admission, 10/1 priority date for domestic students. Applications are processed on a rolling basis. Application fee: $75. *Financial support:* Teaching assistantships available. Financial award application deadline: 3/1; financial award applicants required to submit FAFSA. *Unit head:* Dr. Linda Webster, Chairperson, 209-946-2559, E-mail: lwebster@pacific.edu. *Application contact:* Office of Graduate Admissions, 209-946-2344.

**University of the Virgin Islands,** School of Education, St. Thomas, VI 00802. Offers creative leadership for innovation and change (PhD); educational leadership (MA); school counseling (MA); school psychology (Ed S). *Program availability:* Part-time, evening/weekend. *Faculty:* 8 full-time (2 women), 9 part-time/adjunct (4 women). *Students:* 9 full-time (8 women), 107 part-time (89 women); includes 69 minority (67 Black or African American, non-Hispanic/Latino; 2 Hispanic/Latino), 17 international. Average age 43. 101 applicants, 80% accepted, 69 enrolled. In 2016, 9 master's awarded. *Degree requirements:* For master's, comprehensive exam, thesis or alternative; for doctorate, comprehensive exam, thesis/dissertation, qualifying examination; for Ed S, comprehensive exam. *Entrance requirements:* For master's, GRE, minimum GPA of 2.5, BA degree from accredited institution. Additional exam requirements/recommendations for international students: Required—TOEFL (minimum score 550 paper-based). *Application deadline:* For fall admission, 4/30 for domestic and international students; for spring admission, 10/30 for domestic and international students. Application fee: $25. Electronic applications accepted. *Expenses:* Contact institution. *Financial support:* Scholarships/grants available. Financial award application deadline: 4/15; financial award applicants required to submit FAFSA. *Unit head:* Dr. Linda Thomas, Dean, 340-693-1321, Fax: 340-693-1335, E-mail: lthomas2@uvi.edu. *Application contact:* Dr. Xuri M. Allen, Director of Admissions, 340-693-1224, Fax: 340-693-1167, E-mail: xallen@uvi.edu.

**The University of Toledo,** College of Graduate Studies, College of Social Justice and Human Service, Department of School Psychology, Higher Education and Counselor Education, Toledo, OH 43606-3390. Offers counselor education (MA, PhD); higher education (ME, PhD, Certificate); school psychology (MA, Ed S). *Program availability:* Part-time. *Degree requirements:* For master's, comprehensive exam, thesis or alternative; for doctorate, comprehensive exam, thesis/dissertation; for other advanced degree, thesis optional. *Entrance requirements:* For master's, doctorate, and other advanced degree, minimum cumulative GPA of 2.7 for all previous academic work, letters of recommendation. Additional exam requirements/recommendations for international students: Required—TOEFL (minimum score 550 paper-based; 80 iBT). Electronic applications accepted.

**University of Utah,** Graduate School, College of Education, Department of Educational Psychology, Salt Lake City, UT 84112. Offers clinical mental health counseling (M Ed); counseling psychology (PhD); elementary education (M Ed); instructional design and educational technology (M Ed); instructional design and technology (MS); learning and cognition (MS, PhD); reading and literacy (M Ed, PhD); school counseling (M Ed); school psychology (M Ed, PhD, Ed S); statistics (M Stat). *Accreditation:* APA (one or more programs are accredited). *Faculty:* 23 full-time (12 women), 15 part-time/adjunct (10 women). *Students:* 119 full-time (95 women), 106 part-time (74 women); includes 37 minority (2 Black or African American, non-Hispanic/Latino; 6 Asian, non-Hispanic/Latino; 22 Hispanic/Latino; 7 Two or more races, non-Hispanic/Latino), 6 international. Average age 31. 296 applicants, 27% accepted, 73 enrolled. In 2016, 47 master's, 8 doctorates awarded. Terminal master's awarded for partial completion of doctoral program. *Degree requirements:* For master's, variable foreign language requirement, comprehensive exam (for some programs), thesis (for some programs), projects; for doctorate, variable foreign language requirement, comprehensive exam, thesis/dissertation, oral exam. *Entrance requirements:* For master's and doctorate, GRE General Test, minimum GPA of 3.0. Additional exam requirements/recommendations for international students: Required—TOEFL (minimum score 80 iBT). *Application deadline:* For fall admission, 12/15 for domestic and international students; for winter admission, 11/1 for domestic and international students; for spring admission, 3/15 for domestic and international students. Application fee: $55 ($65 for international students). Electronic applications accepted. *Expenses:* Contact institution. *Financial support:* In 2016–17, 84 students received support, including 12 fellowships with full and partial tuition reimbursements available (averaging $18,000 per year), 21 research assistantships with full and partial tuition reimbursements available (averaging $14,500 per year), 57 teaching assistantships with full and partial tuition reimbursements available (averaging $14,500 per year); career-related internships or fieldwork, Federal Work-Study, institutionally sponsored loans, scholarships/grants, traineeships, health care benefits, and unspecified assistantships also available. Financial award application deadline: 4/1; financial award applicants required to submit FAFSA. *Faculty research:* Autism, computer technology and instruction, cognitive behavior, aging, group counseling. *Total annual research expenditures:* $620,935. *Unit head:* Dr. Anne E. Cook, Chair, 801-581-7148, Fax: 801-581-5566, E-mail: anne.cook@utah.edu. *Application contact:* JoLynn N. Yates, Academic Coordinator, 801-581-7148, Fax: 801-581-5566, E-mail: jo.yates@utah.edu.
Website: http://www.ed.utah.edu/edps/

**University of Virginia,** Curry School of Education, Department of Human Services, Program in Clinical and School Psychology, Charlottesville, VA 22903. Offers PhD. *Students:* 20 full-time (19 women), 2 part-time (both women); includes 7 minority (3 Black or African American, non-Hispanic/Latino; 1 Asian, non-Hispanic/Latino; 1 Hispanic/Latino; 2 Two or more races, non-Hispanic/Latino). Average age 26. 171 applicants, 4% accepted, 5 enrolled. In 2016, 6 doctorates awarded. *Expenses:* Tuition, state resident: full-time $15,026; part-time $834 per credit hour. Tuition, nonresident: full-time $25,168; part-time $1378 per credit hour. *Required fees:* $2654. *Unit head:* Jason Downer, Program Area Director, 434-924-0792, E-mail: jdowner@virginia.edu. *Application contact:* Eric Molnar, Assistant Director, Admissions and Enrollment Reporting, 434-243-2085, E-mail: eric.molnar@virginia.edu.
Website: http://curry.virginia.edu/academics/areas-of-study/clinical-school-psychology

**University of Virginia,** Curry School of Education, Program in Education, Charlottesville, VA 22903. Offers administration and supervision (PhD); applied developmental science (PhD); counselor education (PhD); curriculum and instruction (PhD); early childhood special education (MT); education evaluation (PhD); educational psychology (PhD); educational research (PhD); elementary education (MT); English education (MT, PhD); foreign language education (MT); higher education (PhD); instructional technology (PhD); kinesiology (MT, PhD); math education (PhD); reading education (PhD); research, statistics and evaluation (PhD); school psychology (PhD); science education (PhD); social studies education (MT, PhD); special education (PhD); world languages education (MT). *Students:* 452 full-time (357 women), 18 part-time (13

## School Psychology

women); includes 100 minority (28 Black or African American, non-Hispanic/Latino; 39 Asian, non-Hispanic/Latino; 18 Hispanic/Latino; 15 Two or more races, non-Hispanic/Latino), 14 international. Average age 25. 309 applicants, 51% accepted, 87 enrolled. In 2016, 144 master's, 31 doctorates awarded. *Degree requirements:* For master's, comprehensive exam (for some programs), field project; for doctorate, comprehensive exam, thesis/dissertation. *Entrance requirements:* For doctorate, GRE General Test. Additional exam requirements/recommendations for international students: Required—TOEFL (minimum score 600 paper-based; 90 iBT), IELTS (minimum score 7). *Application deadline:* Applications are processed on a rolling basis. Application fee: $60. Electronic applications accepted. *Expenses: Tuition,* state resident: full-time $15,026; part-time $834 per credit hour. Tuition, nonresident: full-time $25,168; part-time $1378 per credit hour. *Required fees:* $2654. *Financial support:* Fellowships, research assistantships, and teaching assistantships available. Financial award application deadline: 1/5; financial award applicants required to submit FAFSA. *Unit head:* Robert C. Pianta, Dean, 434-924-3334, E-mail: pianta@virginia.edu. *Application contact:* Eric Molnar, Assistant Director, Admissions and Enrollment Reporting, 434-243-2085, E-mail: eric.molnar@virginia.edu.
Website: http://curry.virginia.edu/teacher-education

**University of Washington,** Graduate School, College of Education, Program in Educational Psychology, Seattle, WA 98195. Offers educational psychology (PhD); human development and cognition (M Ed); learning sciences (M Ed, PhD); measurement, statistics and research design (M Ed); school psychology (M Ed). Accreditation: APA. *Degree requirements:* For master's, thesis optional; for doctorate, thesis/dissertation. *Entrance requirements:* For master's and doctorate, GRE General Test, minimum GPA of 3.0. Additional exam requirements/recommendations for international students: Required—TOEFL.

**The University of West Alabama,** School of Graduate Studies, College of Education, Departments of Instructional Leadership and Support/Curriculum and Instruction, Livingston, AL 35470. Offers continuing education (MSCE), including counseling and psychology, family counseling, general, guidance and counseling, library media, student affairs in higher education; early childhood education (M Ed, Ed S), including early childhood development (M Ed), early childhood education (Ed S), early childhood education P-3 (M Ed); elementary education (M Ed, Ed S), including elementary education (Ed S), elementary education K-6 (M Ed); instructional leadership (M Ed, Ed S), including instructional leadership, teacher leader (Ed S); library media (M Ed, Ed S); school counseling (M Ed, Ed S), including guidance counseling (Ed S), school counseling; secondary education (M Ed, MAT), including biology (MAT), English language arts (MAT), high school 6-12 (M Ed), history (MAT), mathematics (MAT), science (MAT), social science (MAT); special education (M Ed, Ed S), including collaborative special education 6-12 (Ed S), collaborative special education K-6 (Ed S), special education collaborative teacher 6-12 (M Ed), special education collaborative teacher K-6 (M Ed). Accreditation: NCATE. *Program availability:* Part-time, evening/weekend, 100% online. *Faculty:* 43 full-time (27 women), 79 part-time/adjunct (50 women). *Students:* 1,868 (1,571 women); includes 689 minority (635 Black or African American, non-Hispanic/Latino; 12 American Indian or Alaska Native, non-Hispanic/Latino; 6 Asian, non-Hispanic/Latino; 12 Hispanic/Latino; 1 Native Hawaiian or other Pacific Islander, non-Hispanic/Latino; 23 Two or more races, non-Hispanic/Latino). Average age 35. 637 applicants, 87% accepted, 426 enrolled. In 2016, 498 master's, 124 other advanced degrees awarded. *Degree requirements:* For master's, comprehensive exam, thesis optional; for Ed S, comprehensive exam. *Entrance requirements:* For master's, GRE or MAT, minimum GPA of 2.75. Additional exam requirements/recommendations for international students: Required—TOEFL (minimum score 500 paper-based; 61 iBT). *Application deadline:* Applications are processed on a rolling basis. Application fee: $40. Electronic applications accepted. *Expenses: Tuition,* state resident: part-time $355 per credit hour. Tuition, nonresident: part-time $710 per credit hour. *Required fees:* $130 per semester. *Financial support:* Teaching assistantships, Federal Work-Study, scholarships/grants, and unspecified assistantships available. Support available to part-time students. Financial award application deadline: 3/1; financial award applicants required to submit FAFSA. *Unit head:* Dr. Reenay Rogers, Chair of Instructional Leadership and Support, 205-652-5423, Fax: 205-652-3706, E-mail: rrogers@uwa.edu. *Application contact:* Dr. B. J. Kimbrough, Dean of Graduate Studies, 205-652-3647, Fax: 205-652-3670, E-mail: bkimbrough@uwa.edu.

**University of Wisconsin–Eau Claire,** College of Arts and Sciences, Department of Psychology, Eau Claire, WI 54702-4004. Offers school psychology (MSE, Ed S). *Program availability:* Part-time. *Degree requirements:* For master's, comprehensive exam, thesis, National Certified School Psychologist Professional Exam, written exam, externship. *Entrance requirements:* For master's, GRE, minimum undergraduate GPA of 3.0; courses in exceptional children and youth, statistics, psychopathology, and theories of counseling. Additional exam requirements/recommendations for international students: Required—TOEFL (minimum score 79 iBT).

**University of Wisconsin–La Crosse,** College of Liberal Studies, Department of Psychology, La Crosse, WI 54601-3742. Offers school psychology (MS Ed, Ed S). *Faculty:* 5 full-time (2 women), 1 (woman) part-time/adjunct. *Students:* 24 full-time (21 women), 11 part-time (10 women); includes 1 minority (Hispanic/Latino). Average age 24. 40 applicants, 48% accepted, 12 enrolled. In 2016, 12 master's, 11 Ed Ss awarded. *Degree requirements:* For master's, thesis, seminar, or comprehensive exams. *Entrance requirements:* For master's and Ed S, GRE. Additional exam requirements/recommendations for international students: Required—TOEFL (minimum score 550 paper-based; 79 iBT). *Application deadline:* For fall admission, 1/31 for domestic and international students. Electronic applications accepted. *Financial support:* Research assistantships, Federal Work-Study, scholarships/grants, and health care benefits available. Support available to part-time students. *Unit head:* Dr. Robert Dixon, Director of the School Psychology Program, 608-785-6893, E-mail: rdixon@uwlax.edu. *Application contact:* Brandon Schaller, Senior Graduate Student Status Examiner, 608-785-8941, E-mail: admissions@uwlax.edu.
Website: https://www.uwlax.edu/Graduate-program/

**University of Wisconsin–Milwaukee,** Graduate School, School of Education, Department of Educational Psychology, Milwaukee, WI 53201-0413. Offers children's mental health for school professionals (Graduate Certificate); community counseling (MS); counseling psychology (PhD); educational statistics and measurement (MS, PhD); learning and development (MS, PhD); multicultural knowledge of mental health practices (Graduate Certificate); school counseling (MS); school counseling (Graduate Certificate); school psychology (MS, PhD, Ed S). Accreditation: APA. *Program availability:* Part-time. *Students:* 161 full-time (121 women), 53 part-time (39 women); includes 47 minority (12 Black or African American, non-Hispanic/Latino; 1 American Indian or Alaska Native, non-Hispanic/Latino; 5 Asian, non-Hispanic/Latino; 8 Hispanic/Latino; 1 Native Hawaiian or other Pacific Islander, non-Hispanic/Latino; 20 Two or more races, non-Hispanic/Latino), 6 international. Average age 30. 266 applicants, 45% accepted, 71 enrolled. In 2016, 73 master's, 9 doctorates, 18 other advanced degrees awarded. *Degree requirements:* For master's, comprehensive exam, thesis; for doctorate, thesis/dissertation. *Entrance requirements:* For master's, minimum GPA of 3.0; for doctorate, GRE General Test, minimum GPA of 3.0. Additional exam

requirements/recommendations for international students: Required—TOEFL (minimum score 550 paper-based; 79 iBT), IELTS (minimum score 6.5). *Application deadline:* For fall admission, 1/1 priority date for domestic students; for spring admission, 9/1 for domestic students. Applications are processed on a rolling basis. Application fee: $56 ($96 for international students). Electronic applications accepted. *Financial support:* In 2016–17, 14 fellowships, 1 research assistantship, 8 teaching assistantships were awarded; career-related internships or fieldwork, health care benefits, unspecified assistantships, and project assistantships also available. Support available to part-time students. Financial award application deadline: 4/15; financial award applicants required to submit FAFSA. *Application contact:* General Information Contact, 414-229-4721, E-mail: soeinfo@uwm.edu.
Website: http://uwm.edu/education/academics/educational-psychology-department/

**University of Wisconsin–River Falls,** Outreach and Graduate Studies, College of Education and Professional Studies, Department of Counseling and School Psychology, River Falls, WI 54022. Offers counseling (MSE); school psychology (MSE, Ed S). Accreditation: ACA. *Program availability:* Part-time. *Entrance requirements:* For master's, minimum GPA of 2.75, resume, 3 letters of reference, vita. Additional exam requirements/recommendations for international students: Required—TOEFL (minimum score 500 paper-based; 65 iBT), IELTS (minimum score 5.5). Electronic applications accepted.

**University of Wisconsin–Stout,** Graduate School, College of Education, Health and Human Sciences, School of Education, Program in School Psychology, Menomonie, WI 54751. Offers MS Ed, Ed S. *Program availability:* Part-time. *Degree requirements:* For master's and Ed S, thesis. *Entrance requirements:* For master's, minimum GPA of 3.0; for Ed S, minimum GPA of 3.25. Additional exam requirements/recommendations for international students: Required—TOEFL (minimum score 500 paper-based; 61 iBT). Electronic applications accepted. *Faculty research:* Intelligence assessment, eating disorders, intervention models, resilience, school violence.

**University of Wisconsin–Superior,** Graduate Division, Department of Counseling and Psychological Professions, Superior, WI 54880-4500. Offers community counseling (MSE); human relations (MSE); school counseling (MSE). *Program availability:* Part-time, evening/weekend. *Degree requirements:* For master's, position paper, practicum. *Entrance requirements:* For master's, GRE and/or MAT, minimum GPA of 2.75. Electronic applications accepted. *Faculty research:* Women and power, intrafamily dynamics.

**University of Wisconsin–Whitewater,** School of Graduate Studies, College of Letters and Sciences, Department of Psychology, Program in School Psychology, Whitewater, WI 53190-1790. Offers MSE, Ed S. *Program availability:* Evening/weekend, online learning. *Degree requirements:* For Ed S, project. *Entrance requirements:* For degree, master's degree in school psychology from an accredited school. Additional exam requirements/recommendations for international students: Required—TOEFL (minimum score 550 paper-based; 80 iBT), IELTS (minimum score 6). Electronic applications accepted.

**Utah State University,** School of Graduate Studies, Emma Eccles Jones College of Education and Human Services, Department of Psychology, Logan, UT 84322. Offers clinical/counseling/school psychology (PhD); research and evaluation methodology (PhD); school counseling (MS); school psychology (MS). Accreditation: APA (one or more programs are accredited). *Program availability:* Part-time, evening/weekend, online learning. Terminal master's awarded for partial completion of doctoral program. *Degree requirements:* For master's, thesis (for some programs); for doctorate, thesis/dissertation. *Entrance requirements:* For master's, GRE General Test (school psychology), MAT (school counseling), minimum GPA of 3.5; for doctorate, GRE General Test, minimum GPA of 3.5. Additional exam requirements/recommendations for international students: Required—TOEFL. *Faculty research:* Hearing loss detection in infancy, ADHD, eating disorders, domestic violence, neuropsychology, bilingual/Spanish speaking students/parents.

**Valparaiso University,** Graduate School and Continuing Education, Department of Education, Program in Initial Licensure, Valparaiso, IN 46383. Offers humane education (M Ed); instructional leadership (M Ed); primary education (M Ed); school psychology (M Ed, Ed S); secondary education (M Ed). *Program availability:* Part-time, evening/weekend. *Entrance requirements:* For master's, GRE General Test, Pre-Professional Skills Test (PPST), minimum GPA of 3.0. Additional exam requirements/recommendations for international students: Required—TOEFL (minimum score 550 paper-based; 80 iBT), IELTS (minimum score 6). Electronic applications accepted. *Expenses: Tuition:* Full-time $11,070; part-time $615 per credit hour. *Required fees:* $116 per semester. Tuition and fees vary according to course load, degree level and program.

**Wayne State University,** College of Education, Division of Theoretical and Behavioral Foundations, Detroit, MI 48202. Offers applied behavior analysis (Certificate); counseling (M Ed, MA, Ed D, PhD, Ed S); counseling psychology (MA); education evaluation and research (M Ed, Ed D, PhD); educational psychology (M Ed, PhD), including learning and instruction sciences (PhD); rehabilitation counseling and community inclusion (MA); school and community psychology (MA); school psychology (Certificate). Accreditation: ACA (one or more programs are accredited); CORE (one or more programs are accredited). *Program availability:* Evening/weekend. *Faculty:* 12. *Students:* 211 full-time (179 women), 237 part-time (196 women); includes 167 minority (119 Black or African American, non-Hispanic/Latino; 1 American Indian or Alaska Native, non-Hispanic/Latino; 10 Asian, non-Hispanic/Latino; 17 Hispanic/Latino; 20 Two or more races, non-Hispanic/Latino), 24 international. Average age 32. 294 applicants, 34% accepted, 72 enrolled. In 2016, 87 master's, 12 doctorates, 14 other advanced degrees awarded. *Degree requirements:* For master's, thesis (for some programs); for doctorate, thesis/dissertation. *Entrance requirements:* For master's, GRE, interview, personal statement, portfolio (art therapy); for doctorate, GRE, department-written exam, interview, curriculum vitae, references, master's degree in closely-related field with minimum GPA of 3.5, demonstration of counseling skills (counseling); for other advanced degree, master's degree in counseling and counseling license (for Ed S); good standing in school and community psychology MA program (for Certificate). Additional exam requirements/recommendations for international students: Required—TOEFL (minimum score 550 paper-based; 79 iBT), Michigan English Language Assessment Battery (minimum score 85); Recommended—IELTS (minimum score 6.5), TWE (minimum score 5.5). *Application deadline:* For fall admission, 6/1 priority date for domestic students, 5/1 priority date for international students; for winter admission, 10/1 priority date for domestic students, 9/1 priority date for international students; for spring admission, 2/1 priority date for domestic students, 1/1 priority date for international students. Applications are processed on a rolling basis. Application fee: $50. Electronic applications accepted. *Expenses:* $16,503 per year resident tuition and fees, $33,697 per year non-resident tuition and fees. *Financial support:* In 2016–17, 92 students received support, including 2 research assistantships with tuition reimbursements available (averaging $17,994 per year); fellowships with tuition reimbursements available, teaching assistantships with tuition reimbursements available, Federal Work-Study, scholarships/grants, health care benefits, and unspecified assistantships also available. Support available to part-time students. Financial award applicants required to submit FAFSA. *Faculty research:* Adolescents at risk, supervision of counseling. *Unit*

*head:* Dr. Cheryl Somers, Assistant Dean, 313-577-1670, E-mail: c.somers@wayne.edu. *Application contact:* Janice Green, Assistant Dean, 313-577-1605, E-mail: jwgreen@wayne.edu.
Website: http://coe.wayne.edu/tbf/index.php

**Western Illinois University,** School of Graduate Studies, College of Arts and Sciences, Department of Psychology, Macomb, IL 61455-1390. Offers clinical/community mental health (MS); general experimental psychology (MS); school psychology (SSP). *Program availability:* Part-time. *Students:* 37 full-time (22 women), 15 part-time (13 women); includes 6 minority (1 Black or African American, non-Hispanic/Latino; 2 Hispanic/Latino; 3 Two or more races, non-Hispanic/Latino), 2 international. Average age 25. 66 applicants, 52% accepted, 14 enrolled. In 2016, 11 master's, 7 other advanced degrees awarded. *Degree requirements:* For master's, comprehensive exam (for some programs), thesis or alternative. *Entrance requirements:* For master's and SSP, GRE General Test. Additional exam requirements/recommendations for international students: Required—TOEFL (minimum score 550 paper-based; 80 iBT). Application fee: $30. Electronic applications accepted. *Financial support:* In 2016–17, 34 students received support, including 6 research assistantships with full tuition reimbursements available (averaging $7,544 per year); unspecified assistantships also available. Financial award applicants required to submit FAFSA. *Unit head:* Dr. Karen Sears, Chairperson, 309-298-1593. *Application contact:* Dr. Nancy Parsons, Associate Provost and Director of Graduate Studies, 309-298-1806, Fax: 309-298-2345, E-mail: grad-office@wiu.edu.
Website: http://wiu.edu/psychology

**Western Kentucky University,** Graduate Studies, College of Education and Behavioral Sciences, Department of Psychology, Bowling Green, KY 42101. Offers clinical psychology (MA); experimental psychology (MA); general psychology (MA); industrial/organizational psychology (MA); school psychology (Ed S). *Degree requirements:* For master's, comprehensive exam, thesis (for some programs); for Ed S, thesis, oral exam. *Entrance requirements:* For master's, GRE General Test; for Ed S, GRE General Test, minimum GPA of 3.5. Additional exam requirements/recommendations for international students: Required—TOEFL (minimum score 555 paper-based; 79 iBT). *Faculty research:* Neural regeneration, enhancing mobility in the elderly, improvement in visual processing in older adults, lifespan development.

**Wichita State University,** Graduate School, College of Education, Department of Counseling, Educational Leadership, Educational and School Psychology, Wichita, KS 67260. Offers counseling (M Ed); educational leadership (M Ed, Ed D); educational psychology (M Ed); school psychology (Ed S). *Accreditation:* NCATE. *Program availability:* Part-time, evening/weekend. Application fee: $50 ($65 for international students). *Unit head:* Dr. Jody Fiorini, Department Head, 316-978-3325, Fax: 316-978-3102, E-mail: jody.fiorini@wichita.edu. *Application contact:* Jordan Oleson, Admissions Coordinator, 316-978-3095, Fax: 316-978-3253, E-mail: jordan.oleson@wichita.edu.
Website: http://www.wichita.edu/cles

**William James College,** Graduate Programs, Newton, MA 02459. Offers applied psychology in higher education student personnel administration (MA); clinical psychology (Psy D); counseling psychology (MA); counseling psychology and community mental health (MA); counseling psychology and global mental health (MA); executive coaching (Graduate Certificate); forensic and counseling psychology (MA); leadership psychology (Psy D); organizational psychology (MA); primary care psychology (MA); respecialization in clinical psychology (Certificate); school psychology (Psy D); MA/CAGS. *Accreditation:* APA. *Degree requirements:* For master's, comprehensive exam (for some programs); for doctorate, thesis/dissertation (for some programs). Electronic applications accepted.

**Worcester State University,** Graduate Studies, Department of Education, Program in School Psychology, Worcester, MA 01602-2597. Offers CAGS, Ed S. *Faculty:* 13 full-time (12 women), 16 part-time/adjunct (7 women). *Students:* 24 full-time (21 women), 10 part-time (all women); includes 2 minority (both Hispanic/Latino). Average age 25. 46 applicants, 54% accepted, 15 enrolled. In 2016, 8 CAGSs awarded. *Entrance requirements:* For degree, MTEL Communication and Literacy Skills test (strongly recommended), undergraduate major or concentration in psychology. Additional exam requirements/recommendations for international students: Required—TOEFL (minimum score 550 paper-based; 79 iBT). *Application deadline:* For fall admission, 3/1 priority date for domestic and international students. Applications are processed on a rolling basis. Application fee: $50. Electronic applications accepted. *Expenses:* Tuition, state resident: part-time $150 per credit. Tuition, nonresident: part-time $150 per credit. *Financial support:* Career-related internships or fieldwork, scholarships/grants, and unspecified assistantships available. Financial award application deadline: 3/1; financial award applicants required to submit FAFSA. *Unit head:* Dr. Diane Tighe Cooke, Coordinator, 508-929-8673, Fax: 508-929-8164, E-mail: dcooke@worcester.edu. *Application contact:* Sara Grady, Associate Dean for Graduate Studies and Professional Development, 508-929-8787, Fax: 508-929-8100, E-mail: sara.grady@worcester.edu.

**Yeshiva University,** Ferkauf Graduate School of Psychology, Program in School/Clinical-Child Psychology, New York, NY 10033-3201. Offers Psy D. *Accreditation:* APA. *Program availability:* Part-time. *Degree requirements:* For doctorate, comprehensive exam, thesis/dissertation. *Entrance requirements:* For doctorate, GRE General Test. *Faculty research:* Testing, early childhood intervention, child and adolescent psychotherapy, clinical child psychology.

**Youngstown State University,** Graduate School, Beeghly College of Education, Department of Counseling, Youngstown, OH 44555-0001. Offers community counseling (MS Ed); school counseling (MS Ed). *Accreditation:* ACA; NCATE. *Program availability:* Part-time, evening/weekend. *Degree requirements:* For master's, comprehensive exam. *Entrance requirements:* For master's, MAT, interview, minimum GPA of 2.7. Additional exam requirements/recommendations for international students: Required—TOEFL. *Faculty research:* Suicide, euthanasia, ethical issues, marriage and family.

# Social Psychology

**Adler University,** Programs in Psychology, Chicago, IL 60602. Offers advanced Adlerian psychotherapy (Certificate); art therapy (MA); clinical mental health counseling (MA); clinical neuropsychology (Certificate); clinical psychology (Psy D); community psychology (MA); counseling and organizational psychology (MA); counseling psychology (MA); counselor education and supervision (PhD); couple and family therapy (DCFT); criminology (MA); emergency management leadership (MA); forensic psychology (MA); marriage and family counseling (MA); marriage and family therapy (Certificate); military psychology (MA); nonprofit management (MA); organizational psychology (MA); police psychology (MA); public policy and administration (MA); rehabilitation counseling (MA); sport and health psychology (MA); substance abuse counseling (Certificate); Psy D/Certificate; Psy D/MACAT; Psy D/MACP; Psy D/MAMFC; Psy D/MASAC. *Accreditation:* APA. *Program availability:* Part-time, evening/weekend, online learning. Terminal master's awarded for partial completion of doctoral program. *Degree requirements:* For master's, thesis or alternative, oral exam, practicum; for doctorate, thesis/dissertation, clinical exam, internship, oral exam, practicum, written qualifying exam. *Entrance requirements:* For master's, 12 semester hours in psychology, minimum GPA of 3.0; for doctorate, 18 semester hours in psychology, minimum GPA of 3.25; for Certificate, appropriate master's or doctoral degree. Additional exam requirements/recommendations for international students: Required—TOEFL (minimum score 550 paper-based; 79 iBT). Electronic applications accepted.

**See Display on page 982 and Close-Up on page 1225.**

**Alliant International University–Los Angeles,** California School of Professional Psychology, Psy D Program in Clinical Psychology, Alhambra, CA 91803. Offers clinical health psychology (Psy D); family/child and couple clinical psychology (Psy D); multi-interest option (Psy D); multicultural community-clinical psychology (Psy D). *Accreditation:* APA. *Degree requirements:* For doctorate, comprehensive exam, thesis/dissertation. *Entrance requirements:* For doctorate, interview, minimum GPA of 3.0 in both psychology and overall. Additional exam requirements/recommendations for international students: Required—TOEFL (minimum score 600 paper-based), TWE. Electronic applications accepted. *Faculty research:* Child and family psychology, multicultural and community psychology, acculturation, lesbian and gay issues, women's health.

**Alvernia University,** School of Graduate Studies, Department of Psychology and Counseling, Reading, PA 19607-1799. Offers community counseling (MA). *Entrance requirements:* For master's, GRE or MAT.

**Alverno College,** School of Arts and Sciences, Milwaukee, WI 53234-3922. Offers community-based research and consultation (MSCP); professional counselor (MSCP). *Program availability:* Part-time, evening/weekend. *Faculty:* 6 full-time (all women), 7 part-time/adjunct (all women). *Students:* 78 full-time (76 women), 12 part-time (all women); includes 37 minority (24 Black or African American, non-Hispanic/Latino; 1 Asian, non-Hispanic/Latino; 11 Hispanic/Latino; 1 Two or more races, non-Hispanic/Latino), 2 international. Average age 34. 27 applicants, 93% accepted, 19 enrolled. In 2016, 19 master's awarded. *Entrance requirements:* Additional exam requirements/recommendations for international students: Required—TOEFL. *Application deadline:* For fall admission, 7/15 priority date for domestic and international students; for spring admission, 12/15 priority date for domestic and international students. Applications are processed on a rolling basis. Application fee: $0. Electronic applications accepted. *Expenses:* Contact institution. *Financial support:* In 2016–17, 2 students received support. Federal Work-Study and scholarships/grants available. Support available to part-time students. Financial award applicants required to submit FAFSA. *Unit head:* Dr. Kimberly Skerven, Associate Dean, Master of Science in Community Psychology, 414-382-6461, Fax: 414-382-6354, E-mail: kimberly.skerven@alverno.edu. *Application contact:* Katie Kipp, Graduate Admissions Counselor, 414-382-6045, Fax: 414-382-6354, E-mail: katie.kipp@alverno.edu.

**Andrews University,** School of Graduate Studies, School of Education, Department of Graduate Psychology and Counseling, Program in Community Counseling, Berrien Springs, MI 49104. Offers clinical mental health counseling (MA); community counseling (MA). *Students:* 14 full-time (8 women), 6 part-time (4 women); includes 8 minority (5 Black or African American, non-Hispanic/Latino; 3 Hispanic/Latino), 4 international. Average age 31. In 2016, 9 master's awarded. *Degree requirements:* For master's, thesis optional. *Entrance requirements:* For master's, GRE. Additional exam requirements/recommendations for international students: Required—TOEFL (minimum score 550 paper-based). Application fee: $40. *Unit head:* Dr. Nancy Carbonell, Coordinator, 269-471-3472. *Application contact:* Justina Clayburn, Supervisor of Graduate Admission, 800-253-2874, Fax: 269-471-6321, E-mail: graduate@andrews.edu.

**Argosy University, Atlanta,** Georgia School of Professional Psychology, Atlanta, GA 30328. Offers clinical psychology (MA, Psy D, Postdoctoral Respecialization Certificate), including child and family psychology (Psy D), general adult clinical (Psy D), health psychology (Psy D), neuropsychology/geropsychology (Psy D); community counseling (MA), including marriage and family therapy; counselor education and supervision (Ed D); forensic psychology (MA); industrial organizational psychology (MA); marriage and family therapy (Certificate); sport-exercise psychology (MA). *Accreditation:* APA.

**Argosy University, Chicago,** Illinois School of Professional Psychology, Chicago, IL 60601. Offers clinical psychology (MA, Psy D), including child and adolescent psychology (Psy D), client-centered and experiential psychotherapies (Psy D), diversity and multicultural psychology (Psy D), family psychology (Psy D), forensic psychology (Psy D), health psychology (Psy D), neuropsychology (Psy D), organizational consulting (Psy D), psychoanalytic psychology (Psy D), psychology and spirituality (Psy D); community counseling (MA); counseling psychology (Ed D), including counselor education and supervision; counselor education and supervision (Ed D); industrial organizational psychology (MA). *Accreditation:* APA (one or more programs are accredited). *Program availability:* Online learning.

**Argosy University, Dallas,** College of Psychology and Behavioral Sciences, Program in Community Counseling, Farmers Branch, TX 75244. Offers MA.

**Argosy University, Northern Virginia,** American School of Professional Psychology, Arlington, VA 22209. Offers clinical psychology (MA, Psy D), including child and family psychology (Psy D), diversity and multicultural psychology (Psy D), forensic psychology (Psy D), health and neuropsychology (Psy D); community counseling (MA); counseling psychology (Ed D), including counselor education and supervision; counselor education and supervision (Ed D); forensic psychology (MA).

**Argosy University, Sarasota,** College of Psychology and Behavioral Sciences, Sarasota, FL 34235. Offers community counseling (MA); counseling psychology (Ed D); counselor education and supervision (Ed D); forensic psychology (MA); marriage and family therapy (MA); mental health counseling (MA); pastoral community counseling (Ed D).

**Arizona State University at the Tempe campus,** College of Liberal Arts and Sciences, Department of Psychology, Tempe, AZ 85287-1104. Offers applied behavior analysis

## Social Psychology

(MS); behavioral neuroscience (PhD); clinical psychology (PhD); cognitive science (PhD); developmental psychology (PhD); quantitative psychology (PhD); social psychology (PhD). *Accreditation:* APA. *Degree requirements:* For doctorate, comprehensive exam, thesis/dissertation, interactive Program of Study (iPOS) submitted before completing 50 percent of required credit hours. *Entrance requirements:* For doctorate, GRE General Test, GRE Subject Test, minimum GPA of 3.0 or equivalent in last 2 years of work leading to bachelor's degree. Additional exam requirements/recommendations for international students: Required—TOEFL, IELTS, or PTE. Electronic applications accepted.

**Ball State University,** Graduate School, Teachers College, Department of Counseling Psychology and Guidance Services, Program in Social Psychology, Muncie, IN 47306. Offers social psychology (MA); social psychology and clinical mental health counseling (MA). *Entrance requirements:* For master's, GRE General Test (minimum scores 144 quantitative, 153 verbal), minimum baccalaureate GPA of 2.75 or 3.0 in latter half of baccaluareate, minimum GPA of 3.0 in psychology coursework, three letters of recommendation. Additional exam requirements/recommendations for international students: Required—TOEFL (minimum score 550 paper-based; 79 iBT), IELTS (minimum score 6.5). Electronic applications accepted.

**Becker College,** Program in Mental Health Counseling, Worcester, MA 01609. Offers community mental health (MA); school consultation (MA). *Entrance requirements:* For master's, GRE, interview, official transcript, three letters of recommendation, essay. Electronic applications accepted.

**Bowling Green State University,** Graduate College, College of Arts and Sciences, Department of Sociology, Bowling Green, OH 43403. Offers demography and population studies (MA); social psychology (MA); sociology (PhD). *Program availability:* Part-time. *Degree requirements:* For master's, thesis or alternative; for doctorate, comprehensive exam, thesis/dissertation. *Entrance requirements:* For master's and doctorate, GRE General Test. Additional exam requirements/recommendations for international students: Required—TOEFL. *Application deadline:* For fall admission, 1/15 priority date for domestic students. Application fee: $30. Electronic applications accepted. *Financial support:* Fellowships with full tuition reimbursements, research assistantships with full tuition reimbursements, teaching assistantships with full tuition reimbursements, career-related internships or fieldwork, Federal Work-Study, institutionally sponsored loans, and unspecified assistantships available. Financial award applicants required to submit FAFSA. *Faculty research:* Applied demography, criminology and deviance, family studies, population studies, social psychology. *Unit head:* Dr. Susan L. Brown, Chair, 419-372-9521, E-mail: brownsl@bgsu.edu. *Application contact:* Dr. Steve Cernkovich, Graduate Coordinator, 419-372-2743.

**Brandeis University,** Graduate School of Arts and Sciences, Department of Psychology, Waltham, MA 02454-9110. Offers brain, body and behavior (PhD); cognitive neuroscience (PhD); general psychology (MA); social/developmental psychology (PhD). *Program availability:* Part-time. *Faculty:* 14 full-time (7 women), 4 part-time/adjunct (3 women). *Students:* 40 full-time (27 women), 1 (woman) part-time; includes 5 minority (1 Black or African American, non-Hispanic/Latino; 2 Asian, non-Hispanic/Latino; 2 Hispanic/Latino), 9 international. 148 applicants, 23% accepted, 15 enrolled. In 2016, 8 master's, 3 doctorates awarded. Terminal master's awarded for partial completion of doctoral program. *Degree requirements:* For master's, thesis or alternative; for doctorate, thesis/dissertation, research reports. *Entrance requirements:* For master's and doctorate, GRE General Test; GRE Subject Test (recommended), 3 letters of recommendation, statement of purpose, transcript(s), resume. Additional exam requirements/recommendations for international students: Required—TOEFL (minimum score 600 paper-based; 100 iBT); Recommended—IELTS (minimum score 7), TSE (minimum score 68). *Application deadline:* For fall admission, 1/15 priority date for domestic and international students. Application fee: $75. Electronic applications accepted. *Financial support:* In 2016–17, 22 students received support, including 22 fellowships with full tuition reimbursements available (averaging $24,000 per year), 34 teaching assistantships with partial tuition reimbursements available (averaging $3,200 per year); Federal Work-Study, scholarships/grants, health care benefits, and tuition waivers (full and partial) also available. Support available to part-time students. Financial award application deadline: 4/15; financial award applicants required to submit FAFSA. *Faculty research:* Brain, body, and behavior across the lifespan; face perception and nonverbal communication; learning and memory; motor control and spatial orientation; neurophysiology of learning and decision making; personality and cognition in adulthood and old age; social, cultural and affective neuroscience; social relations and health physiology; speech comprehension and memory; taste physiology and psychophysics; visual perception. *Unit head:* Prof. Paul DiZio, Department Chair, 781-736-3300, Fax: 781-736-3291, E-mail: dizio@brandeis.edu. *Application contact:* Phil Gnatowski, Department Administrator, 781-736-3302, Fax: 781-736-3291, E-mail: gnat@brandeis.edu.
Website: http://www.brandeis.edu/departments/psych/

**Brock University,** Faculty of Graduate Studies, Faculty of Social Sciences, Program in Psychology, St. Catharines, ON L2S 3A1, Canada. Offers behavioral neuroscience (MA, PhD); life span development (MA, PhD); social personality (MA, PhD). *Program availability:* Part-time. *Degree requirements:* For master's, thesis; for doctorate, thesis/dissertation. *Entrance requirements:* For master's, GRE, honors degree; for doctorate, GRE, master's degree. Additional exam requirements/recommendations for international students: Required—TOEFL (minimum score 550 paper-based; 80 iBT), IELTS (minimum score 6.5), TWE (minimum score 4). Electronic applications accepted. *Faculty research:* Social personality, behavioral neuroscience, life-span development.

**Brooklyn College of the City University of New York,** School of Natural and Behavioral Sciences, Department of Psychology, Brooklyn, NY 11210-2889. Offers experimental psychology (MA); industrial and organizational psychology (MA), including human relations, organizational behavior; mental health counseling (MA); psychology (PhD). *Program availability:* Part-time. *Degree requirements:* For master's, comprehensive exam, thesis (for some programs). *Entrance requirements:* For master's, minimum GPA of 3.0, 2 letters of recommendation, essay; for doctorate, GRE. Additional exam requirements/recommendations for international students: Required—TOEFL (minimum score 520 paper-based; 69 iBT). Electronic applications accepted.

**California Institute of Integral Studies,** School of Professional Psychology and Health, San Francisco, CA 94103. Offers clinical psychology (Psy D); community mental health (MA); drama therapy (MA); expressive arts therapy (MA); human sexuality (PhD); integral counseling psychology (MA); integrative health studies (MA); psychological studies (MA); somatic psychology (MA). *Program availability:* Part-time, evening/weekend, 100% online, blended/hybrid learning. *Students:* 526 full-time (408 women), 113 part-time (96 women); includes 173 minority (34 Black or African American, non-Hispanic/Latino; 5 American Indian or Alaska Native, non-Hispanic/Latino; 31 Asian, non-Hispanic/Latino; 58 Hispanic/Latino; 1 Native Hawaiian or other Pacific Islander, non-Hispanic/Latino; 44 Two or more races, non-Hispanic/Latino), 52 international. Average age 38. 319 applicants, 85% accepted, 164 enrolled. In 2016, 157 master's, 21 doctorates awarded. *Degree requirements:* For doctorate, comprehensive exam, thesis/dissertation. *Entrance requirements:* For master's, minimum GPA of 3.0, letters of recommendation, writing sample; for doctorate, GRE, MA in psychology or social work with appropriate practical experience for advanced standing, or BA with a minimum GPA

of 3.1; letters of recommendation; writing sample. Additional exam requirements/recommendations for international students: Required—TOEFL. *Application deadline:* For fall admission, 2/1 priority date for domestic and international students; for spring admission, 10/15 priority date for domestic and international students. Applications are processed on a rolling basis. Application fee: $65. Electronic applications accepted. *Expenses:* Tuition: Full-time $19,728; part-time $1098 per semester hour. *Required fees:* $320; $320 per semester hour. *Financial support:* Research assistantships with tuition reimbursements, teaching assistantships with tuition reimbursements, career-related internships or fieldwork, Federal Work-Study, and scholarships/grants available. Support available to part-time students. Financial award application deadline: 4/15; financial award applicants required to submit FAFSA. *Faculty research:* Transpersonal psychology, somatic psychology, expressive arts therapy, drama therapy, community mental health, ecopsychology, integrative health, human sexuality. *Application contact:* Ellen Durst, Director of Admissions, 415-575-6100, Fax: 415-575-1268, E-mail: admissions@ciis.edu.

**California State University, East Bay,** Office of Graduate Studies, College of Letters, Arts, and Social Sciences, Department of Social Work, Hayward, CA 94542-3000. Offers children, youth, and family services (MSW); community mental health services (MSW). *Accreditation:* CSWE. *Students:* 129 full-time (106 women), 2 part-time (both women); includes 102 minority (33 Black or African American, non-Hispanic/Latino; 1 American Indian or Alaska Native, non-Hispanic/Latino; 20 Asian, non-Hispanic/Latino; 43 Hispanic/Latino; 5 Two or more races, non-Hispanic/Latino), 1 international. Average age 31. 394 applicants, 21% accepted, 68 enrolled. In 2016, 125 master's awarded. *Degree requirements:* For master's, comprehensive exam. *Entrance requirements:* For master's, minimum GPA of 2.8; courses in statistics and either human biology, physiology, or anatomy; liberal arts or social science baccalaureate degree; 3 letters of recommendation; personal statement; criminal background check; student professional liability insurance. Additional exam requirements/recommendations for international students: Required—TOEFL (minimum score 550 paper-based). *Application deadline:* For fall admission, 3/15 for domestic and international students. Applications are processed on a rolling basis. Application fee: $55. Electronic applications accepted. *Financial support:* Fellowships, career-related internships or fieldwork, Federal Work-Study, institutionally sponsored loans, and scholarships/grants available. Support available to part-time students. Financial award application deadline: 3/2; financial award applicants required to submit FAFSA. *Unit head:* Dr. Holly Vugia, Interim Chair, 510-885-2121, E-mail: holly.vugia@csueastbay.edu. *Application contact:* Dr. Donna Wiley, Interim Associate Vice President for Academic Programs and Graduate Studies, 510-885-3716, Fax: 510-885-4777, E-mail: donna.wiley@csueastbay.edu.
Website: http://www20.csueastbay.edu/class/departments/socialwork/

**California State University, Fullerton,** Graduate Studies, College of Health and Human Development, Department of Social Work, Fullerton, CA 92834-9480. Offers aging (MSW); child welfare (MSW); community mental health (MSW). *Accreditation:* CSWE. *Program availability:* Part-time. *Entrance requirements:* For master's, minimum GPA of 3.0 for last 60 semester or 90 quarter units. Application fee: $55. *Expenses:* Tuition, state resident: full-time $3369; part-time $1953 per unit. Tuition, nonresident: full-time $3915; part-time $2499 per unit. Tuition and fees vary according to course load, degree level and program. *Financial support:* Career-related internships or fieldwork, Federal Work-Study, institutionally sponsored loans, and scholarships/grants available. Support available to part-time students. Financial award application deadline: 3/1; financial award applicants required to submit FAFSA. *Unit head:* Dr. David Chenot, Chair, 657-278-8452, E-mail: dchenot@fullerton.edu. *Application contact:* Admissions/Applications, 657-278-2371.
Website: http://hhd.fullerton.edu/msw

**Canisius College,** Graduate Division, School of Education and Human Services, Programs in Counseling and Human Services, Buffalo, NY 14208-1098. Offers community mental health counseling (MS); counseling and human services (MS); school agency counseling (MS). *Accreditation:* ACA. *Program availability:* Part-time, evening/weekend. *Faculty:* 6 full-time (3 women), 10 part-time/adjunct (7 women). *Students:* 83 full-time (67 women), 39 part-time (33 women); includes 25 minority (13 Black or African American, non-Hispanic/Latino; 1 Asian, non-Hispanic/Latino; 6 Hispanic/Latino; 5 Two or more races, non-Hispanic/Latino), 5 international. Average age 26. 109 applicants, 86% accepted, 37 enrolled. In 2016, 48 master's awarded. *Degree requirements:* For master's, thesis, research project. *Entrance requirements:* For master's, GRE (if cumulative GPA less than 2.7), transcripts, two letters of recommendation, interview, BA. Additional exam requirements/recommendations for international students: Required—TOEFL (minimum score 550 paper-based, 79 iBT), IELTS (minimum score 6.5), or CAEL (minimum score 70). *Application deadline:* Applications are processed on a rolling basis. Application fee: $25. Electronic applications accepted. Application fee is waived when completed online. *Expenses:* Tuition: Full-time $14,742. *Required fees:* $724. *Financial support:* Career-related internships or fieldwork, Federal Work-Study, scholarships/grants, tuition waivers (partial), and unspecified assistantships available. Support available to part-time students. Financial award application deadline: 4/30; financial award applicants required to submit FAFSA. *Faculty research:* Impact of trauma on adults, long term psych-social impact on police officers. *Unit head:* Dr. Christine Moll, Chair, 716-888-3287, E-mail: moll@canisius.edu. *Application contact:* Kathleen B. Davis, Vice President of Enrollment Management, 716-888-2500, Fax: 716-888-3195, E-mail: daviskb@canisius.edu.
Website: http://www.canisius.edu/masters-counseling/

**Carnegie Mellon University,** Dietrich College of Humanities and Social Sciences, Department of Psychology, Program in Social/Personality/Health Psychology, Pittsburgh, PA 15213-3891. Offers PhD. *Degree requirements:* For doctorate, comprehensive exam, thesis/dissertation. *Entrance requirements:* For doctorate, GRE General Test. Additional exam requirements/recommendations for international students: Required—TOEFL.

**Claremont Graduate University,** Graduate Programs, School of Social Science, Policy and Evaluation, Department of Psychology, Claremont, CA 91711-6160. Offers advanced study in evaluation (Certificate); cognitive psychology (MA, PhD); developmental psychology (MA, PhD); evaluation and applied research methods (MA, PhD); health behavior research and evaluation (MA, PhD); human resource development and evaluation (MA); industrial/organizational psychology (MA, PhD); organizational behavior (MA, PhD); organizational psychology (MA, PhD); social psychology (MA, PhD); MBA/PhD. *Program availability:* Part-time. *Faculty:* 19 full-time (9 women), 1 part-time/adjunct (0 women). *Students:* 244 full-time (160 women), 66 part-time (38 women); includes 93 minority (15 Black or African American, non-Hispanic/Latino; 2 American Indian or Alaska Native, non-Hispanic/Latino; 29 Asian, non-Hispanic/Latino; 31 Hispanic/Latino; 2 Native Hawaiian or other Pacific Islander, non-Hispanic/Latino; 14 Two or more races, non-Hispanic/Latino), 41 international. Average age 30. In 2016, 61 master's, 23 doctorates, 5 other advanced degrees awarded. Terminal master's awarded for partial completion of doctoral program. *Entrance requirements:* For master's and doctorate, GRE General Test. Additional exam requirements/recommendations for international students: Required—TOEFL (minimum score 75 iBT). *Application deadline:* For fall admission, 1/15 priority date for domestic and international students. Applications are processed on a rolling basis. Application

fee: $80. Electronic applications accepted. *Expenses: Tuition:* Full-time $44,328; part-time $1847 per unit. *Required fees:* $600; $300 per semester. Tuition and fees vary according to course load and program. *Financial support:* Fellowships, research assistantships, teaching assistantships, Federal Work-Study, institutionally sponsored loans, scholarships/grants, and tuition waivers (full and partial) available. Support available to part-time students. Financial award application deadline: 2/15; financial award applicants required to submit FAFSA. *Faculty research:* Social intervention, diversity in organizations, eyewitness memory, aging and cognition, drug policy. *Unit head:* William Crano, Chair, 909-607-3311, E-mail: william.crano@cgu.edu. *Application contact:* Paige Piontkowsky, Senior Assistant Director of Admissions, 909-607-3240, E-mail: paige.piontkowsky@cgu.edu.
Website: https://www.cgu.edu/school/ssspe/programs/?areas_of_study=psychology

**Clark University,** Graduate School, Hiatt School of Psychology, Program in Social Psychology, Worcester, MA 01610-1477. Offers PhD. *Students:* 6 full-time (5 women); includes 2 minority (1 Asian, non-Hispanic/Latino; 1 Hispanic/Latino), 3 international. Average age 29. *Degree requirements:* For doctorate, thesis/dissertation. *Entrance requirements:* For doctorate, GRE General Test. Additional exam requirements/recommendations for international students: Required—TOEFL. *Application deadline:* For fall admission, 12/15 priority date for domestic and international students. Applications are processed on a rolling basis. Application fee: $75. *Expenses: Tuition:* Full-time $44,050. *Required fees:* $80. Tuition and fees vary according to course load and program. *Financial support:* In 2016–17, fellowships with full tuition reimbursements (averaging $17,325 per year), research assistantships with full tuition reimbursements (averaging $17,325 per year), teaching assistantships with full tuition reimbursements (averaging $17,325 per year) were awarded; tuition waivers (full) also available. *Faculty research:* Conceptualizing and reasoning, symbolization, psychotherapy, metaphor, emotions and personalities. *Unit head:* Dr. Johanna Ray Vollhardt, Director, 508-793-7274, E-mail: jvollhardt@clarku.edu. *Application contact:* Kelly Boulay, Graduate School Secretary, 508-793-7274, Fax: 508-793-7265, E-mail: psychology@clarku.edu.
Website: http://www.clarku.edu/departments/psychology/grad/social/index.cfm

**College of St. Joseph,** Graduate Programs, Division of Psychology and Human Services, Program in Community Counseling, Rutland, VT 05701-3899. Offers MS. *Program availability:* Part-time, evening/weekend. *Degree requirements:* For master's, comprehensive exam, thesis optional. *Entrance requirements:* For master's, official college transcripts; 2 letters of reference. Additional exam requirements/recommendations for international students: Required—TOEFL (minimum score 550 paper-based). *Application deadline:* Applications are processed on a rolling basis. Application fee: $35. Electronic applications accepted. *Expenses: Tuition, area resident:* Full-time $13,800; part-time $560 per credit. *Required fees:* $75 per semester. Full-time tuition and fees vary according to course load. *Financial support:* Career-related internships or fieldwork, Federal Work-Study, and unspecified assistantships available. Support available to part-time students. Financial award application deadline: 3/1. *Unit head:* Dr. Craig Knapp, Chair, 802-773-5900 Ext. 3219, Fax: 802-776-5258, E-mail: cknapp@csj.edu. *Application contact:* Alan Young, Dean of Admissions, 802-773-5900 Ext. 3227, Fax: 802-776-5310, E-mail: alanyoung@csj.edu.

**Cornell University,** Graduate School, Graduate Fields of Arts and Sciences, Field of Psychology, Ithaca, NY 14853. Offers biopsychology (PhD); human experimental psychology (PhD); personality and social psychology (PhD). *Degree requirements:* For doctorate, comprehensive exam, thesis/dissertation, 2 semesters of teaching experience. *Entrance requirements:* For doctorate, GRE General Test, 3 letters of recommendation. Additional exam requirements/recommendations for international students: Required—TOEFL (minimum score 550 paper-based; 77 iBT). Electronic applications accepted. *Faculty research:* Sensory and perceptual systems, social cognition, cognitive development, quantitative and computational modeling, behavioral neuroscience.

**Cornell University,** Graduate School, Graduate Fields of Arts and Sciences, Field of Sociology, Ithaca, NY 14853. Offers economy and society (MA, PhD); gender and life course (MA, PhD); methodology (MA, PhD); organizations (MA, PhD); policy analysis (MA, PhD); political sociology/social movements (MA, PhD); racial and ethnic relations (MA, PhD); social networks (MA, PhD); social psychology (MA, PhD); social stratification (MA, PhD). Terminal master's awarded for partial completion of doctoral program. *Degree requirements:* For master's, thesis; for doctorate, thesis/dissertation, 1 year of teaching experience. *Entrance requirements:* For master's and doctorate, GRE General Test, 2 letters of recommendation, writing sample. Additional exam requirements/recommendations for international students: Required—TOEFL (minimum score 550 paper-based; 77 iBT). Electronic applications accepted. *Faculty research:* Comparative societal analysis, work and family, simulations, social class and mobility, racial segregation and inequality.

**Delaware Valley University,** Program in Counseling Psychology, Doylestown, PA 18901-2697. Offers child and adolescent therapy (MA); social justice community counseling (MA).

**Florida Agricultural and Mechanical University,** Division of Graduate Studies, Research, and Continuing Education, College of Social Sciences, Arts and Humanities, Department of Psychology, Program in Community Psychology, Tallahassee, FL 32307-3200. Offers MS. *Degree requirements:* For master's, thesis, internship. *Entrance requirements:* For master's, GRE General Test, minimum GPA of 3.0, letters of recommendation (3). Additional exam requirements/recommendations for international students: Required—TOEFL. *Faculty research:* African-American personality and mental health, racism in the socialization of black children.

**Florida State University,** The Graduate School, College of Arts and Sciences, Department of Psychology, Program in Social Psychology, Tallahassee, FL 32306. Offers PhD. *Faculty:* 5 full-time (3 women). *Students:* 17 full-time (12 women); includes 3 minority (all Hispanic/Latino). Average age 28. 91 applicants, 5% accepted, 5 enrolled. In 2016, 4 doctorates awarded. Terminal master's awarded for partial completion of doctoral program. *Degree requirements:* For doctorate, comprehensive exam, thesis/dissertation. *Entrance requirements:* For doctorate, GRE General Test, minimum GPA of 3.0, research experience, letters of recommendation. Additional exam requirements/recommendations for international students: Required—TOEFL (minimum score 80 iBT). *Application deadline:* For fall admission, 12/15 for domestic and international students. Application fee: $30. Electronic applications accepted. *Expenses:* Tuition, state resident: full-time $7263; part-time $403.51 per credit hour. Tuition, nonresident: full-time $18,087; part-time $1004.85 per credit hour. *Required fees:* $1365; $75.81 per credit hour. $20 per semester. Tuition and fees vary according to campus/location. *Financial support:* In 2016–17, 16 students received support, including 2 fellowships with full tuition reimbursements available (averaging $22,815 per year), 2 research assistantships with full tuition reimbursements available (averaging $23,815 per year), 12 teaching assistantships with full tuition reimbursements available (averaging $18,315 per year); health care benefits also available. Financial award application deadline: 12/15; financial award applicants required to submit FAFSA. *Faculty research:* Self and identity, prejudice and intergroup relations, evolutionary psychology, emotion, health. *Total annual research expenditures:* $514,693. *Unit head:* Dr. Ashby Plant, Director of Social Psychology, 850-644-5533, Fax: 850-644-7739, E-mail: plant@psy.fsu.edu. *Application contact:* Lynda L. Gibson, Graduate Program Associate, 850-644-2499, Fax:

850-644-7739, E-mail: grad-info@psy.fsu.edu.
Website: http://www.psy.fsu.edu/

**Future Generations Graduate School,** Program in Applied Community Change, Franklin, WV 26807. Offers conservation (MA). *Program availability:* Blended/hybrid learning. *Degree requirements:* For master's, one foreign language, applied practicum research. *Entrance requirements:* For master's, bachelor's degree, community involvement. Additional exam requirements/recommendations for international students: Required—TOEFL. Electronic applications accepted. *Faculty research:* Sustainable communities, community engagement, peacebuilding, seed-scale community development.

**The George Washington University,** Columbian College of Arts and Sciences, Department of Psychology, Washington, DC 20052. Offers applied social psychology (PhD); clinical psychology (PhD); cognitive neuroscience (PhD). *Accreditation:* APA. *Program availability:* Part-time, evening/weekend. *Faculty:* 25 full-time (14 women). *Students:* 39 full-time (28 women), 30 part-time (21 women); includes 21 minority (9 Black or African American, non-Hispanic/Latino; 4 Asian, non-Hispanic/Latino; 6 Hispanic/Latino; 2 Two or more races, non-Hispanic/Latino), 7 international. Average age 28. 442 applicants, 5% accepted, 12 enrolled. In 2016, 12 doctorates awarded. *Degree requirements:* For doctorate, thesis/dissertation or alternative, general exam. *Entrance requirements:* For doctorate, GRE General Test, minimum GPA of 3.0. Additional exam requirements/recommendations for international students: Required—TOEFL (minimum score 550 paper-based; 80 iBT). *Application deadline:* For fall admission, 1/15 for domestic and international students. Application fee: $75. *Financial support:* In 2016–17, 62 students received support. Fellowships with tuition reimbursements available, teaching assistantships with tuition reimbursements available, career-related internships or fieldwork, Federal Work-Study, and tuition waivers available. *Unit head:* Dr. Paul Poppen, Chair, 202-994-6324, E-mail: pjp@gwu.edu. *Application contact:* Information Contact, 202-994-6320, Fax: 202-994-1602, E-mail: psydept@gwu.edu.
Website: http://psychology.columbian.gwu.edu/

**Georgia State University,** College of Arts and Sciences, Department of Psychology, Atlanta, GA 30302-3083. Offers clinical (PhD); cognitive sciences (PhD); community (PhD); developmental (PhD); neuropsychology and behavioral neuroscience (PhD). *Accreditation:* APA. *Faculty:* 40 full-time (26 women). *Students:* 101 full-time (80 women), 2 part-time (both women); includes 25 minority (8 Black or African American, non-Hispanic/Latino; 9 Asian, non-Hispanic/Latino; 3 Hispanic/Latino; 5 Two or more races, non-Hispanic/Latino), 7 international. Average age 28. 517 applicants, 6% accepted, 17 enrolled. In 2016, 19 doctorates awarded. *Degree requirements:* For doctorate, comprehensive exam, thesis/dissertation, residency year (for clinical only). *Entrance requirements:* For doctorate, GRE. Additional exam requirements/recommendations for international students: Required—TOEFL (minimum score 550 paper-based; 80 iBT). *Application deadline:* For fall admission, 12/1 for domestic and international students. Application fee: $50. Electronic applications accepted. *Expenses:* Tuition, state resident: full-time $6876; part-time $382 per credit hour. Tuition, nonresident: full-time $22,374; part-time $1243 per credit hour. *Required fees:* $2128; $1064 per term. Part-time tuition and fees vary according to course load and program. *Financial support:* In 2016–17, fellowships with full tuition reimbursements (averaging $19,282 per year), research assistantships with full tuition reimbursements (averaging $5,173 per year), teaching assistantships with full tuition reimbursements (averaging $6,389 per year) were awarded; scholarships/grants, traineeships, health care benefits, and unspecified assistantships also available. Financial award applicants required to submit FAFSA. *Faculty research:* Clinical psychology, developmental psychology, community psychology, neuropsychology and behavioral neuroscience, cognitive sciences. *Unit head:* Dr. Lisa Armistead, Chair, 404-413-6205, Fax: 404-413-6207, E-mail: lparmistead@gsu.edu. *Application contact:* Dr. Lindsey Cohen, Director of Graduate Studies, 404-413-6263, Fax: 404-413-6207, E-mail: llcohen@gsu.edu.

**The Graduate Center, City University of New York,** Graduate Studies, Program in Psychology, New York, NY 10016-4039. Offers basic applied neurocognition (PhD); biopsychology (PhD); clinical psychology (PhD); developmental psychology (PhD); environmental psychology (PhD); experimental psychology (PhD); industrial psychology (PhD); learning processes (PhD); neuropsychology (PhD); psychology (PhD); social personality (PhD). *Degree requirements:* For doctorate, one foreign language, thesis/dissertation. *Entrance requirements:* For doctorate, GRE General Test. Additional exam requirements/recommendations for international students: Required—TOEFL. Electronic applications accepted.

**Harvard University,** Graduate School of Arts and Sciences, Department of Psychology, Cambridge, MA 02138. Offers psychology (PhD), including behavior and decision analysis, cognition, developmental psychology, experimental psychology, personality, psychobiology, psychopathology; social psychology (PhD). *Accreditation:* APA. *Degree requirements:* For doctorate, thesis/dissertation, general exams. *Entrance requirements:* For doctorate, GRE General Test. Additional exam requirements/recommendations for international students: Required—TOEFL.

**Hofstra University,** College of Liberal Arts and Sciences, Programs in Psychology, Hempstead, NY 11549. Offers applied organizational psychology (PhD); clinical psychology (PhD); industrial/organizational psychology (MA); school-community psychology (Psy D). *Accreditation:* APA. *Program availability:* Part-time, evening/weekend. *Students:* 195 full-time (130 women), 32 part-time (18 women); includes 43 minority (9 Black or African American, non-Hispanic/Latino; 2 American Indian or Alaska Native, non-Hispanic/Latino; 8 Asian, non-Hispanic/Latino; 21 Hispanic/Latino; 2 Native Hawaiian or other Pacific Islander, non-Hispanic/Latino; 1 Two or more races, non-Hispanic/Latino), 21 international. Average age 27. 299 applicants, 40% accepted, 54 enrolled. In 2016, 51 master's, 36 doctorates awarded. *Degree requirements:* For master's, comprehensive exam, thesis optional, internship, minimum GPA of 3.0; for doctorate, comprehensive exam, thesis/dissertation, 1st year qualifying examination, 2nd year research project, successful practicum/externship placements, written presentation and successful oral defense of dissertation, completion of full-time internship. *Entrance requirements:* For master's, GRE General Test, minimum GPA of 3.0, essay, interview; for doctorate, GRE General Test, GRE Subject Test (psychology), 3 letters of recommendation, interview, essay, curriculum vitae. Additional exam requirements/recommendations for international students: Required—TOEFL (minimum score 550 paper-based; 80 iBT). *Application deadline:* For fall admission, 12/31 for domestic and international students. Application fee: $75. Electronic applications accepted. *Expenses: Tuition:* Full-time $1240. *Required fees:* $970. Tuition and fees vary according to program. *Financial support:* In 2016–17, 119 students received support, including 112 fellowships with full and partial tuition reimbursements available (averaging $8,418 per year), 4 research assistantships with full and partial tuition reimbursements available (averaging $5,940 per year); career-related internships or fieldwork, Federal Work-Study, institutionally sponsored loans, scholarships/grants, traineeships, tuition waivers (full and partial), and unspecified assistantships also available. Support available to part-time students. Financial award applicants required to submit FAFSA. *Faculty research:* PTSD, secondary trauma, childhood adjustment problems, the impact of exercise on emotional states treatment of anxiety disorders and depression, cognitive appraisal and emotion, evolutionary psychology - implications for

## Social Psychology

clinical psychology (evolutionary psychopathology, theory of human nature), treatment of phobic and post-traumatic stress disorders with exposure therapies, self-help and motivational interviewing. *Unit head:* Dr. Craig Johnson, Chairperson, 516-463-5636, E-mail: craig.a.johnson@hofstra.edu. *Application contact:* Sunil Samuel, Assistant Vice President of Admissions, 516-463-4723, Fax: 516-463-4664, E-mail: graduateadmission@hofstra.edu.
Website: http://www.hofstra.edu/hclas

**Howard University,** Graduate School, Department of Psychology, Washington, DC 20059-0002. Offers clinical psychology (PhD); developmental psychology (PhD); experimental psychology (PhD); neuropsychology (PhD); personality psychology (PhD); psychology (MS); social psychology (PhD). *Accreditation:* APA (one or more programs are accredited). *Program availability:* Part-time. *Degree requirements:* For master's, thesis; for doctorate, comprehensive exam, thesis/dissertation, qualifying exam. *Entrance requirements:* For master's, GRE General Test, minimum GPA of 2.5, bachelor's degree in psychology or related field; for doctorate, GRE General Test, minimum GPA of 3.0. *Faculty research:* Personality and psychophysiology, educational and social development of African-American children, child and adult psychopathology.

**Humboldt State University,** Academic Programs, College of Professional Studies, Department of Psychology, Arcata, CA 95521-8299. Offers psychology (MA), including biological psychology, counseling, developmental psychopathology, school psychology, social and environmental psychology. *Degree requirements:* For master's, thesis. *Entrance requirements:* For master's, appropriate bachelor's degree, minimum GPA of 2.5. Additional exam requirements/recommendations for international students: Required—TOEFL (minimum score 500 paper-based). *Expenses:* Tuition, state resident: full-time $6738; part-time $1953 per semester. Tuition, nonresident: full-time $13,434; part-time $3813 per semester. *Required fees:* $1738; $653 per semester. Tuition and fees vary according to program. *Faculty research:* School psychology, counseling, eating disorders, mood induction, depression.

**Husson University,** Graduate Programs in Counseling and Human Relations, Bangor, ME 04401-2999. Offers clinical mental health counseling (MS); human relations (MS); school counseling (MS). *Accreditation:* ACA. *Program availability:* Part-time, evening/weekend. *Faculty:* 3 full-time (2 women), 5 part-time/adjunct (all women). *Students:* 17 full-time (15 women), 55 part-time (48 women); includes 1 minority (Black or African American, non-Hispanic/Latino), 2 international. Average age 32. 50 applicants, 52% accepted, 20 enrolled. In 2016, 16 master's awarded. *Degree requirements:* For master's, comprehensive exam (for some programs), thesis optional. *Entrance requirements:* For master's, BS with minimum GPA of 3.0, letters of recommendation, interview. Additional exam requirements/recommendations for international students: Required—TOEFL (minimum score 550 paper-based; 80 iBT), IELTS (minimum score 6.5). *Application deadline:* For fall admission, 2/1 for priority domestic students. Application fee: $50. Electronic applications accepted. *Expenses:* $560 per credit tuition; $450 full-time fees, $220 part-time (6-9 credits), $110 part-time (less than 6 credits per year). *Financial support:* Federal Work-Study, scholarships/grants, and unspecified assistantships available. Financial award application deadline: 4/15; financial award applicants required to submit FAFSA. *Faculty research:* Challenges and rewards of counseling practice in rural, small town and neighborhood settings. *Unit head:* Dr. Deborah Drew, Director, Graduate Counseling Programs, 207-992-4912, Fax: 207-992-4952, E-mail: drewd@husson.edu. *Application contact:* Kristen Card, Director of Graduate Admissions, 207-404-5660, Fax: 207-941-7935, E-mail: cardk@husson.edu.
Website: http://www.husson.edu/college-of-health-and-education/school-of-education/graduate-programs/

**Indiana University Bloomington,** University Graduate School, College of Arts and Sciences, Department of Psychological and Brain Sciences, Bloomington, IN 47405. Offers clinical science (PhD); cognitive neuroscience (PhD); cognitive psychology (PhD); developmental psychology (PhD); methods of behavior (PhD); molecular systems neuroscience (PhD); social psychology (PhD). *Accreditation:* APA. *Degree requirements:* For doctorate, comprehensive exam, 90 credit hours, 2 advanced statistics/methods courses, 2 written research projects, the teaching of psychology course, teaching 1 semester of undergraduate methods course, qualifying examination, minor or a second major, first-year research seminar course, dissertation defense, written dissertation. *Entrance requirements:* For doctorate, GRE. Additional exam requirements/recommendations for international students: Required—TOEFL (minimum score 550 paper-based; 79 iBT). Electronic applications accepted. *Faculty research:* Clinical science, cognitive neuroscience, cognitive psychology, developmental psychology, mechanisms of behavior, molecular and systems neuroscience, social psychology.

**Indiana University of Pennsylvania,** School of Graduate Studies and Research, College of Education and Educational Technology, Department of Counseling, Program in Community Counseling, Indiana, PA 15705. Offers MA. *Program availability:* Part-time. *Faculty:* 12 full-time (10 women), 5 part-time/adjunct (all women). *Entrance requirements:* For master's, goal statement, 2 letters of recommendation. Additional exam requirements/recommendations for international students: Required—TOEFL (minimum score 540 paper-based). *Application deadline:* For fall admission, 3/17 priority date for domestic students. Application fee: $50. Electronic applications accepted. *Expenses:* Tuition, state resident: full-time $8694; part-time $483 per credit. Tuition, nonresident: full-time $13,050; part-time $725 per credit. *Required fees:* $157 per credit. $50 per term. Tuition and fees vary according to course load and program. *Financial support:* Research assistantships with full tuition reimbursements available. Financial award application deadline: 4/15; financial award applicants required to submit FAFSA. *Unit head:* Dr. Claire Dandeaneau, Chairperson/Graduate Coordinator, 724-357-2306, E-mail: candean@iup.edu.
Website: http://www.iup.edu/grad/communitycounseling/default.aspx

**Indiana Wesleyan University,** Graduate School, College of Arts and Sciences, Marion, IN 46953. Offers addictions counseling (MS); clinical mental health counseling (MS); community counseling (MS); marriage and family therapy (MS); school counseling (MS); student development counseling and administration (MS). *Accreditation:* ACA. *Program availability:* Part-time. *Degree requirements:* For master's, thesis or alternative. *Entrance requirements:* For master's, GRE General Test. Additional exam requirements/recommendations for international students: Required—TOEFL. Electronic applications accepted. *Expenses:* Contact institution. *Faculty research:* Community counseling, multicultural counseling, addictions.

**Iowa State University of Science and Technology,** Department of Psychology, Ames, IA 50011. Offers cognitive psychology (PhD); counseling psychology (PhD); psychology (MS, PhD); social psychology (PhD). *Accreditation:* APA (one or more programs are accredited). *Entrance requirements:* For doctorate, GRE General Test, GRE Subject Test (psychology), 3 letters of recommendation. Additional exam requirements/recommendations for international students: Required—TOEFL (minimum score 560 paper-based; 79 iBT), IELTS (minimum score 6.5). *Application deadline:* For fall admission, 1/2 priority date for domestic and international students. Application fee: $60 ($90 for international students). Electronic applications accepted. *Faculty research:* Counseling psychology, cognitive psychology, social psychology, health psychology, psychology and public policy. *Application contact:* Sarah Kallsen, Application Contact,

515-294-1742, Fax: 515-294-6424, E-mail: psychadm@iastate.edu.
Website: http://www.psychology.iastate.edu/

**Lesley University,** Graduate School of Arts and Social Sciences, Cambridge, MA 02138-2790. Offers clinical mental health counseling (MA), including holistic counseling, school and community counseling, trauma studies; counseling psychology (MA, CAGS), including professional counseling (MA), school counseling (MA); creative writing (MFA); expressive therapies (MA, PhD, CAGS), including art (MA), clinical mental health counseling (MA), dance (MA), expressive therapies (MA), music (MA); independent studies (CAGS); independent study (MA); intercultural relations (MA, CAGS); interdisciplinary studies (MA), including individualized studies, integrative holistic health, mindfulness studies, peace and conflict transformation, trauma sensitive assessment, intervention, and consultation, women's studies; urban environmental leadership (MA). *Program availability:* Part-time, online learning. *Degree requirements:* For master's, internship, practicum, thesis (for expressive therapies); for doctorate, thesis/dissertation, arts apprenticeship, field placement; for CAGS, thesis, internship (for counseling psychology, expressive therapies). *Entrance requirements:* For master's, MAT (counseling psychology), interview, writing samples, art portfolio; for doctorate, GRE or MAT, interview, master's degree; for CAGS, interview, master's degree. Additional exam requirements/recommendations for international students: Required—TOEFL (minimum score 550 paper-based; 80 iBT). Electronic applications accepted. *Faculty research:* Psychotherapy and culture; psychotherapy and psychological trauma; women's issues in art, teaching and psychotherapy; community-based art, psycho-spiritual inquiry.

**Loyola University Chicago,** School of Education, Program in Community Counseling, Chicago, IL 60660. Offers M Ed, MA, Ed S. MA offered through the Graduate School. *Program availability:* Part-time. *Faculty:* 4 full-time (2 women), 6 part-time/adjunct (4 women). *Students:* 11 full-time (10 women), 1 (woman) part-time; includes 7 minority (1 Black or African American, non-Hispanic/Latino; 1 American Indian or Alaska Native, non-Hispanic/Latino; 3 Asian, non-Hispanic/Latino; 2 Hispanic/Latino). Average age 25. 49 applicants, 82% accepted, 15 enrolled. In 2016, 16 master's, 4 other advanced degrees awarded. *Degree requirements:* For master's and Ed S, comprehensive exam. *Entrance requirements:* For master's, GRE General Test, minimum GPA of 3.0, letters of recommendation, resume. Additional exam requirements/recommendations for international students: Required—TOEFL (minimum score 550 paper-based; 79 iBT). *Application deadline:* For fall admission, 1/1 for domestic and international students. Application fee: $50. Electronic applications accepted. Application fee is waived when completed online. *Expenses: Tuition:* Full-time $18,594. *Required fees:* $848. Part-time tuition and fees vary according to course load, degree level and program. *Financial support:* Career-related internships or fieldwork, institutionally sponsored loans, scholarships/grants, and unspecified assistantships available. Support available to part-time students. Financial award application deadline: 2/1; financial award applicants required to submit FAFSA. *Faculty research:* Career development, prevention, group counseling, family therapy, multicultural counseling. *Unit head:* Dr. Steven Brown, Director, 312-915-6311, E-mail: sbrown@luc.edu. *Application contact:* Marie Hatland, Information Contact, 312-915-6800, E-mail: schleduc@luc.edu.

**Marquette University,** Graduate School, College of Education, Department of Counselor Education and Counseling Psychology, Milwaukee, WI 53201-1881. Offers clinical mental health counseling (MS); community counseling (MA); counseling psychology (PhD); school counseling (MA). *Accreditation:* ACA. *Program availability:* Part-time. *Faculty:* 6 full-time (3 women), 5 part-time/adjunct (3 women). *Students:* 69 full-time (53 women), 13 part-time (10 women); includes 18 minority (6 Black or African American, non-Hispanic/Latino; 3 Asian, non-Hispanic/Latino; 7 Hispanic/Latino; 2 Two or more races, non-Hispanic/Latino), 3 international. Average age 26. 122 applicants, 47% accepted, 32 enrolled. In 2016, 24 master's, 2 doctorates awarded. Terminal master's awarded for partial completion of doctoral program. *Degree requirements:* For master's, comprehensive exam, thesis (for some programs); for doctorate, thesis/dissertation, qualifying exam. *Entrance requirements:* For master's, GRE General Test or MAT, official transcripts from all current and previous colleges/universities except Marquette, three letters of recommendation, statement of purpose; for doctorate, GRE General Test, MAT, sample of written work, official transcripts from all current and previous colleges/universities except Marquette, three letters of recommendation, statement of purpose, resume/curriculum vitae. Additional exam requirements/recommendations for international students: Required—TOEFL (minimum score 530 paper-based). *Application deadline:* For fall admission, 1/15 for domestic and international students. Application fee: $50. *Financial support:* Fellowships, research assistantships, scholarships/grants, health care benefits, tuition waivers (partial), and unspecified assistantships available. Support available to part-time students. Financial award application deadline: 2/15. *Faculty research:* Ethical and legal issues in education, anxiety disorders, multicultural counseling, child psychopathology, group counseling and dynamics. *Unit head:* Dr. Alan Burkard, Chair, 414-288-3434, E-mail: alan.burkard@marquette.edu. *Application contact:* Dr. Alan Burkard.

**Martin University,** Division of Psychology, Indianapolis, IN 46218-3867. Offers community psychology (MS). *Program availability:* Part-time, evening/weekend. *Degree requirements:* For master's, thesis. *Entrance requirements:* For master's, GRE General Test, GRE Subject Test.

**Marymount California University,** Program in Community Psychology, Rancho Palos Verdes, CA 90275-6299. Offers MS.

**Missouri Valley College,** Graduate Studies, Marshall, MO 65340-3197. Offers community counseling (MA).

**Mount Aloysius College,** Program in Community Counseling, Cresson, PA 16630-1999. Offers MS. *Program availability:* Part-time. *Entrance requirements:* Additional exam requirements/recommendations for international students: Required—IELTS (minimum score 5.5); Recommended—TOEFL. *Application deadline:* For fall admission, 8/1 for domestic students; for spring admission, 12/1 for domestic students. Applications are processed on a rolling basis. Application fee: $30. Electronic applications accepted. Application fee is waived when completed online. *Expenses: Tuition:* Full-time $6750; part-time $750 per credit. *Required fees:* $285 per semester. *Financial support:* Unspecified assistantships available. *Application contact:* Matthew P. Bodenschatz, Director of Graduate and Continuing Education Admissions, 814-886-6556, Fax: 814-886-6441, E-mail: mbodenschatz@mtaloy.edu.

**The New School,** The New School for Social Research, Department of Psychology, New York, NY 10003. Offers clinical psychology (PhD); cognitive, social, and developmental psychology (PhD); psychology (MA). *Accreditation:* APA (one or more programs are accredited). *Program availability:* Part-time. *Faculty:* 16 full-time (6 women), 12 part-time/adjunct (4 women). *Students:* 115 full-time (85 women), 99 part-time (77 women); includes 36 minority (9 Black or African American, non-Hispanic/Latino; 1 American Indian or Alaska Native, non-Hispanic/Latino; 11 Asian, non-Hispanic/Latino; 12 Hispanic/Latino; 3 Two or more races, non-Hispanic/Latino), 32 international. Average age 29. 247 applicants, 84% accepted, 60 enrolled. In 2016, 57 master's, 19 doctorates awarded. Terminal master's awarded for partial completion of doctoral program. *Degree requirements:* For master's, comprehensive exam, thesis (for some programs); for doctorate, comprehensive exam, thesis/dissertation. *Entrance requirements:* For master's, GRE, letters of recommendation, writing sample, essays, unofficial transcripts; for doctorate, letters of recommendation, writing sample, essays, unofficial transcripts. Additional exam requirements/recommendations for international students: Required—TOEFL (minimum score 100 iBT), IELTS (minimum score 7), PTE (minimum score 68). *Application deadline:* For fall admission, 8/1 priority date for domestic and international students; for spring admission, 10/15 priority date for domestic and international students. Applications are processed on a rolling basis. Application fee: $50. Electronic applications accepted. *Expenses:* Contact institution. *Financial support:* Fellowships, research assistantships, teaching assistantships, career-related internships or fieldwork, Federal Work-Study, scholarships/grants, and tuition waivers (full and partial) available. Support available to part-time students. Financial award application deadline: 2/1; financial award applicants required to submit FAFSA. *Faculty research:* Cognitive, social, and developmental psychology; clinical psychology; mental health and substance abuse counseling. *Unit head:* Dr. William Milberg, Dean, The New School for Social Research, 212-229-5777, E-mail: milbergw@newschool.edu. *Application contact:* Dana Messinger, Director of Graduate Admission, 212-229-5150 Ext. 2300, E-mail: socialresearchadmit@newschool.edu.

**New York University,** Graduate School of Arts and Science, Department of Psychology, New York, NY 10012-1019. Offers cognition and perception (PhD); community psychology (PhD); general psychology (MA); industrial/organizational psychology (MA); psychotherapy and psychoanalysis (Advanced Certificate); social/personality psychology (PhD). *Program availability:* Part-time. Terminal master's awarded for partial completion of doctoral program. *Degree requirements:* For master's, comprehensive exam, thesis or alternative; for doctorate, thesis/dissertation. *Entrance requirements:* For master's and doctorate, GRE General Test. Additional exam requirements/recommendations for international students: Required—TOEFL. *Faculty research:* Vision, memory, social cognition, social and cognitive development, relationships.

**Norfolk State University,** School of Graduate Studies, School of Liberal Arts, Department of Psychology, Program in Community/Clinical Psychology, Norfolk, VA 23504. Offers MA. *Degree requirements:* For master's, comprehensive exam, thesis or alternative. *Entrance requirements:* For master's, minimum GPA of 2.7.

**North Carolina State University,** Graduate School, College of Education, Department of Curriculum and Instruction, Program in Agency Counseling, Raleigh, NC 27695. Offers M Ed, MS. *Accreditation:* APA. *Degree requirements:* For master's, thesis optional. *Entrance requirements:* For master's, GRE General Test or MAT, minimum GPA of 3.0 in major. Electronic applications accepted. *Faculty research:* Cross-cultural issues, non-cognitive variables, achievement gaps, identity development, counseling supervision.

**North Dakota State University,** College of Graduate and Interdisciplinary Studies, College of Science and Mathematics, Department of Psychology, Fargo, ND 58102. Offers clinical psychology (MS); health and social psychology (PhD); psychological clinical science (PhD); psychology (MS); visual and cognitive neuroscience (PhD). *Degree requirements:* For master's, thesis; for doctorate, thesis/dissertation. *Entrance requirements:* For master's and doctorate, GRE General Test, GRE Subject Test. Additional exam requirements/recommendations for international students: Required—TOEFL (minimum score 525 paper-based; 71 iBT). Electronic applications accepted. *Faculty research:* Cognition science, neuropsychology, group behavior, applied behavior analysis, behavior therapy.

**Northeastern Illinois University,** College of Graduate Studies and Research, College of Education, Program in Community Counseling, Chicago, IL 60625-4699. Offers MA.

**Northwestern University,** The Graduate School, Judd A. and Marjorie Weinberg College of Arts and Sciences, Department of Psychology, Evanston, IL 60208. Offers brain, behavior and cognition (PhD); clinical psychology (PhD); cognitive psychology (PhD); personality psychology (PhD); social psychology (PhD); JD/PhD. Admissions and degrees offered through The Graduate School. *Accreditation:* APA (one or more programs are accredited). *Program availability:* Part-time. *Degree requirements:* For doctorate, thesis/dissertation. *Entrance requirements:* For doctorate, GRE General Test, GRE Subject Test. Additional exam requirements/recommendations for international students: Required—TOEFL. Electronic applications accepted. *Faculty research:* Memory and higher order cognition, anxiety and depression, effectiveness of psychotherapy, social cognition, molecular basis of memory.

**The Ohio State University,** Graduate School, College of Arts and Sciences, Division of Social and Behavioral Sciences, Department of Psychology, Columbus, OH 43210. Offers behavioral neuroscience (PhD); clinical psychology (PhD); cognitive psychology (PhD); developmental psychology (PhD); intellectual and developmental disabilities psychology (PhD); quantitative psychology (PhD); social psychology (PhD). *Accreditation:* APA. *Faculty:* 57. *Students:* 156 full-time (95 women); includes 23 minority (6 Black or African American, non-Hispanic/Latino; 9 Asian, non-Hispanic/Latino; 8 Hispanic/Latino), 26 international. Average age 26. In 2016, 26 doctorates awarded. *Degree requirements:* For doctorate, thesis/dissertation. *Entrance requirements:* For doctorate, GRE General Test. Additional exam requirements/recommendations for international students: Required—TOEFL (minimum score 600 paper-based; 100 iBT); Recommended—IELTS (minimum score 8). *Application deadline:* For fall admission, 12/1 for domestic and international students. Applications are processed on a rolling basis. Application fee: $60 ($70 for international students). Electronic applications accepted. *Financial support:* Fellowships with tuition reimbursements, research assistantships with tuition reimbursements, and teaching assistantships with tuition reimbursements available. *Unit head:* Dr. John Bruno, Chair, 614-292-3038, E-mail: bruno.1@osu.edu. *Application contact:* Graduate and Professional Admissions, 614-292-9444, Fax: 614-292-3895, E-mail: gpadmissions@osu.edu.
Website: http://www.psy.ohio-state.edu/

**Oregon State University–Cascades,** Program in Counseling, Bend, OR 97701. Offers community counseling (MS); school counseling (MS).

**Penn State Harrisburg,** Graduate School, School of Behavioral Sciences and Education, Middletown, PA 17057. Offers adult education in the health and medical professions (Certificate); applied behavior analysis (MA); applied clinical psychology (MA); applied psychological research (MA); community psychology and social change (MA); English as a second language (ESL) program specialist and leadership (Certificate); folklore and ethnography (Certificate); health education (M Ed); lifelong learning and adult education (M Ed, D Ed); literacy education (M Ed); literacy leadership (Certificate); psychology: applications in clinical psychology (Certificate); psychology: health psychology (Certificate); teaching and curriculum (M Ed); training and development (M Ed, Certificate). *Program availability:* Part-time, evening/weekend. *Unit head:* Dr. Mukund S. Kulkarni, Chancellor, 717-948-6105, Fax: 717-948-6452. *Application contact:* Robert W. Coffman, Jr., Director of Enrollment Management, Recruitment and Admissions, 717-948-6250, Fax: 717-948-6325, E-mail: hbgadmit@psu.edu.
Website: https://harrisburg.psu.edu/behavioral-sciences-and-education/

**Philadelphia University,** College of Science, Health and the Liberal Arts, Program in Community and Trauma Counseling, Philadelphia, PA 19144. Offers MS.

**Queen's University at Kingston,** School of Graduate Studies, Faculty of Arts and Sciences, Department of Psychology, Kingston, ON K7L 3N6, Canada. Offers brain behavior and cognitive science (MA, PhD); clinical psychology (MA, PhD); developmental psychology (MA, PhD); social personality psychology (MA, PhD). *Degree requirements:* For master's, thesis; for doctorate, comprehensive exam, thesis/dissertation. *Entrance requirements:* For master's and doctorate, GRE General Test. Additional exam requirements/recommendations for international students: Required—TOEFL. *Faculty research:* Human development, social, personality, behavioral neuroscience, forensic.

**Rutgers University–Newark,** Graduate School, Program in Psychology, Newark, NJ 07102. Offers cognitive neuroscience (PhD); cognitive science (PhD); perception (PhD); psychobiology (PhD); social cognition (PhD). *Degree requirements:* For doctorate, comprehensive exam, thesis/dissertation. *Entrance requirements:* For doctorate, GRE General Test, GRE Subject Test, minimum undergraduate B average. Electronic applications accepted. *Faculty research:* Visual perception (luminance, motion), neuroendocrine mechanisms in behavior (reproduction, pain), attachment theory, connectionist modeling of cognition.

**Rutgers University–New Brunswick,** Graduate School-New Brunswick, Program in Psychology, Piscataway, NJ 08854-8097. Offers behavioral neuroscience (PhD); clinical psychology (PhD); cognitive psychology (PhD); interdisciplinary health psychology (PhD); social psychology (PhD). *Accreditation:* APA. *Degree requirements:* For doctorate, comprehensive exam, thesis/dissertation. *Entrance requirements:* For doctorate, GRE General Test, 3 letters of recommendation. Additional exam requirements/recommendations for international students: Required—TOEFL (minimum score 577 paper-based). Electronic applications accepted. *Faculty research:* Learning and memory, behavioral ecology, hormones and behavior, psychopharmacology, anxiety disorders.

**Sacred Heart University,** Graduate Programs, College of Arts and Sciences, Department of Psychology, Fairfield, CT 06825. Offers applied psychology (MS), including community psychology, general applied psychology, industrial-organizational psychology. *Program availability:* Part-time, evening/weekend, online learning. *Faculty:* 8 full-time (7 women). *Students:* 18 full-time (12 women), 94 part-time (75 women); includes 34 minority (19 Black or African American, non-Hispanic/Latino; 1 Asian, non-Hispanic/Latino; 12 Hispanic/Latino; 2 Two or more races, non-Hispanic/Latino), 2 international. Average age 33. 55 applicants, 65% accepted, 16 enrolled. In 2016, 50 master's awarded. *Degree requirements:* For master's, comprehensive exam, thesis optional. *Entrance requirements:* For master's, minimum overall GPA of 3.0, bachelor's degree from accredited college or university. Additional exam requirements/recommendations for international students: Required—TOEFL (minimum score 570 paper-based, 80 iBT), TWE, or IELTS (6.5); Recommended—TSE. *Application deadline:* Applications are processed on a rolling basis. Application fee: $75. Electronic applications accepted. *Expenses:* $850 per credit. *Financial support:* Unspecified assistantships available. Financial award applicants required to submit FAFSA. *Unit head:* Rachel Bowman, Interim Chair/Associate Professor, 203-396-8243, E-mail: bowmanr@sacredheart.edu. *Application contact:* William Sweeney, Director of Graduate Admissions Operations, 203-365-7916, Fax: 203-365-4732, E-mail: gradstudies@sacredheart.edu.
Website: http://www.sacredheart.edu/academics/collegeofartssciences/academicdepartments/psychology/mastersinappliedpsychology/

**Sage Graduate School,** School of Health Sciences, Department of Psychology, Program in Counseling and Community Psychology, Troy, NY 12180-4115. Offers MA. *Program availability:* Part-time, evening/weekend. *Faculty:* 3 full-time (all women), 1 (woman) part-time/adjunct. *Students:* 24 full-time (22 women), 45 part-time (36 women); includes 18 minority (8 Black or African American, non-Hispanic/Latino; 1 American Indian or Alaska Native, non-Hispanic/Latino; 4 Hispanic/Latino; 5 Two or more races, non-Hispanic/Latino). Average age 29. 85 applicants, 44% accepted, 19 enrolled. In 2016, 23 master's awarded. *Degree requirements:* For master's, externship, internship, thesis or research seminar. *Entrance requirements:* For master's, official transcripts of all previous undergraduate study; 2 letters of reference (academic or professional); undergraduate courses in statistics, history and systems of psychology; 3 other courses in behavioral science; personal prospectus statement; current resume. Additional exam requirements/recommendations for international students: Required—TOEFL (minimum score 550 paper-based). *Application deadline:* Applications are processed on a rolling basis. Application fee: $40. Electronic applications accepted. *Expenses: Tuition:* Full-time $12,240; part-time $680 per credit hour. Tuition and fees vary according to degree level and program. *Financial support:* Fellowships, research assistantships, teaching assistantships, Federal Work-Study, scholarships/grants, and unspecified assistantships available. Support available to part-time students. Financial award applicants required to submit FAFSA. *Unit head:* Dr. Theresa Hand, Dean, School of Health Sciences, 518-244-2264, Fax: 518-244-4571, E-mail: handt@sage.edu. *Application contact:* Dr. Gayle Morse, Graduate Program Director, 518-292-1819, E-mail: morseg@sage.edu.
Website: http://www.sage.edu/academics/psychology/programs/counseling/

**St. Bonaventure University,** School of Graduate Studies, School of Education, Program in Counselor Education, St. Bonaventure, NY 14778-2284. Offers community mental health counseling (MS Ed); rehabilitation counseling (MS Ed); school counseling (MS Ed); school counselor (Adv C). *Accreditation:* ACA. *Program availability:* Part-time, evening/weekend, 100% online. *Faculty:* 5 full-time (1 woman), 8 part-time/adjunct (6 women). *Students:* 53 full-time (40 women), 21 part-time (14 women); includes 6 minority (3 Black or African American, non-Hispanic/Latino; 3 Two or more races, non-Hispanic/Latino), 2 international. Average age 29. 64 applicants, 69% accepted, 29 enrolled. In 2016, 20 master's, 2 Adv Cs awarded. *Degree requirements:* For master's, comprehensive exam, thesis optional, internship, portfolio; for Adv C, internship. *Entrance requirements:* For master's, statement of intent/writing sample; transcripts from all colleges previously attended; two references; interview; minimum undergraduate GPA of 3.0; for Adv C, interview, writing sample, minimum undergraduate GPA of 3.0, two letters of recommendation, master's degree, transcripts from all colleges previously attended. Additional exam requirements/recommendations for international students: Required—TOEFL (minimum score 550 paper-based; 79 iBT). *Application deadline:* For fall admission, 3/15 priority date for domestic students, 2/1 priority date for international students; for spring admission, 11/15 priority date for domestic students, 7/1 priority date for international students. Applications are processed on a rolling basis. Application fee: $0. Electronic applications accepted. *Expenses:* $733 per credit, $100 graduation fee. *Financial support:* Career-related internships or fieldwork, Federal Work-Study, scholarships/grants, health care benefits, and unspecified assistantships available. Support available to part-time students. Financial award application deadline: 4/15; financial award applicants required to submit FAFSA. *Faculty research:* Balance between technology and personal contact in counselor education, special education and cyberbullying, school response to child abuse. *Unit head:* Dr. S. Alan Silliker, Director, 716-375-2368, Fax: 716-375-2360, E-mail: silliker@sbu.edu. *Application contact:* Bruce Campbell, Director of Graduate Admissions, 716-375-2429, Fax: 716-375-4015, E-mail: gradsch@sbu.edu.
Website: http://www.sbu.edu/academics/schools/education

## Social Psychology

**St. Cloud State University,** School of Graduate Studies, School of Health and Human Services, Department of Counseling and Community Psychology, Program in Community Counseling, St. Cloud, MN 56301-4498. Offers MS. *Degree requirements:* For master's, comprehensive exam (for some programs), thesis or alternative. *Entrance requirements:* For master's, GRE General Test, minimum GPA of 2.75. Additional exam requirements/recommendations for international students: Required—Michigan English Language Assessment Battery; Recommended—TOEFL (minimum score 550 paper-based), IELTS (minimum score 6.5). Electronic applications accepted.

**Saint Martin's University,** Office of Graduate Studies, Program in Counseling Psychology, Lacey, WA 98503. Offers MAC. *Program availability:* Part-time. *Faculty:* 3 full-time (2 women), 2 part-time/adjunct (both women). *Students:* 75 full-time (66 women), 28 part-time (25 women); includes 34 minority (5 Black or African American, non-Hispanic/Latino; 1 American Indian or Alaska Native, non-Hispanic/Latino; 2 Asian, non-Hispanic/Latino; 15 Hispanic/Latino; 2 Native Hawaiian or other Pacific Islander, non-Hispanic/Latino; 9 Two or more races, non-Hispanic/Latino). Average age 35. 36 applicants, 50% accepted, 15 enrolled. In 2016, 30 master's awarded. *Degree requirements:* For master's, clinical experience, interview. *Entrance requirements:* For master's, clinical experience. Additional exam requirements/recommendations for international students: Required—TOEFL (minimum score 550 paper-based; 79 iBT); Recommended—IELTS (minimum score 6.5). *Application deadline:* For fall admission, 4/1 priority date for domestic and international students; for spring admission, 11/1 priority date for domestic and international students. Applications are processed on a rolling basis. Application fee: $50. Electronic applications accepted. *Expenses: Tuition:* Full-time $13,800; part-time $1150 per credit hour. *Required fees:* $720; $60 per credit hour. Tuition and fees vary according to course level and program. *Financial support:* Career-related internships or fieldwork, Federal Work-Study, and institutionally sponsored loans available. Support available to part-time students. Financial award application deadline: 3/1; financial award applicants required to submit FAFSA. *Faculty research:* Alcohol studies, clinical effectiveness, social justice, parent adolescent interaction. *Unit head:* Dr. Godfrey J. Ellis, Director, 360-438-4560, E-mail: gellis@stmartin.edu. *Application contact:* Casey Caronna, Administrative Assistant, 360-412-6128, E-mail: ccaronna@stmartin.edu.
Website: https://www.stmartin.edu

**San Francisco State University,** Division of Graduate Studies, College of Science and Engineering, Department of Psychology, San Francisco, CA 94132-1722. Offers clinical psychology (MS); developmental psychology (MA); industrial/organizational psychology (MS); mind, brain, and behavior (MA); school psychology (MS, Credential); social psychology (MA). *Expenses:* Tuition, state resident: full-time $6738. Tuition, nonresident: full-time $15,666. *Required fees:* $1012. Tuition and fees vary according to degree level and program. *Financial support:* Teaching assistantships available. Financial award application deadline: 3/1. *Unit head:* Dr. Dawn Terrell, Chair, 415-338-7555, Fax: 415-338-2398, E-mail: schen9@sfsu.edu. *Application contact:* Dr. Diane Harris, Graduate Program Coordinator, 415-338-7064, Fax: 415-338-2398, E-mail: dharris@sfsu.edu.
Website: http://psychology.sfsu.edu/graduate/application.html

**Southwestern College,** Program in Transformational Ecopsychology, Santa Fe, NM 87502-4788. Offers Certificate. *Entrance requirements:* For degree, 3 letters of reference, interview.

**Stony Brook University, State University of New York,** Graduate School, College of Arts and Sciences, Department of Psychology, Program in Social and Health Psychology, Stony Brook, NY 11794. Offers PhD. *Students:* 21 full-time (all women); includes 6 minority (1 Black or African American, non-Hispanic/Latino; 4 Asian, non-Hispanic/Latino; 1 Two or more races, non-Hispanic/Latino). Average age 28. 57 applicants, 9% accepted, 5 enrolled. In 2016, 3 doctorates awarded. *Degree requirements:* For doctorate, thesis/dissertation. *Entrance requirements:* For doctorate, GRE General Test, GRE Subject Test. Additional exam requirements/recommendations for international students: Required—TOEFL (minimum score 90 iBT). *Application deadline:* For fall admission, 1/15 for domestic students; for spring admission, 10/1 for domestic students. Application fee: $100. Electronic applications accepted. *Expenses:* Contact institution. *Financial support:* In 2016–17, 1 fellowship, 1 research assistantship, 14 teaching assistantships were awarded. *Unit head:* Dr. Arthur Samuel, Chair, 631-632-7792, E-mail: arthur.samuel@stonybrook.edu. *Application contact:* Marilynn Wollmuth, Coordinator, 631-632-7855, Fax: 631-632-7876, E-mail: marilyn.wollmuth@stonybrook.edu.
Website: http://www.stonybrook.edu/commcms/psychology/social_health/overview.html

**Syracuse University,** College of Arts and Sciences, Programs in Psychology, Syracuse, NY 13244. Offers clinical psychology (PhD); cognition, brain, and behavior (PhD); school psychology (PhD); social psychology (PhD). *Accreditation:* APA. In 2016, 1 doctorate awarded. Terminal master's awarded for partial completion of doctoral program. *Degree requirements:* For doctorate, comprehensive exam, thesis/dissertation. *Entrance requirements:* For doctorate, GRE General Test, GRE Subject Test, resume, personal statement, three letters of recommendation. Additional exam requirements/recommendations for international students: Required—TOEFL (minimum score 100 iBT). *Application deadline:* For fall admission, 12/1 priority date for domestic and international students. Application fee: $75. Electronic applications accepted. *Expenses: Tuition:* Full-time $25,974; part-time $1443 per credit hour. *Required fees:* $802; $50 per course. Tuition and fees vary according to course load and program. *Financial support:* Fellowships with full tuition reimbursements, research assistantships with tuition reimbursements, teaching assistantships with tuition reimbursements, and scholarships/grants available. Financial award application deadline: 1/1. *Faculty research:* Clinical psychology; cognition, brain, and behavior; school psychology; social psychology. *Unit head:* Dr. Larry Lewandowski, Professor of Psychology/Interim Chair, 315-443-1015, E-mail: ljlewand@syr.edu. *Application contact:* Alecia Zema, Curriculum Coordinator, 315-443-2760, E-mail: azema@syr.edu.
Website: http://psychology.syr.edu/graduate/Clinical.html

**Teachers College, Columbia University,** Department of Organization and Leadership, New York, NY 10027-6696. Offers adult education guided intensive study (Ed D); adult learning and leadership (Ed M, MA, Ed D); educational leadership (Ed D); higher and postsecondary education (MA, Ed D); leadership, policy and politics (Ed D); nurse executive (MA, Ed D), including administration studies (MA), professional studies (MA); private school leadership (Ed M, MA); public school building leadership (Ed M, MA); social and organizational psychology (MA); urban education leaders (Ed D); MA/MBA. *Program availability:* Part-time, evening/weekend. *Students:* 310 full-time (214 women), 390 part-time (250 women); includes 276 minority (116 Black or African American, non-Hispanic/Latino; 3 American Indian or Alaska Native, non-Hispanic/Latino; 61 Asian, non-Hispanic/Latino; 79 Hispanic/Latino; 17 Two or more races, non-Hispanic/Latino), 93 international. 624 applicants, 57% accepted, 172 enrolled. *Degree requirements:* For doctorate, thesis/dissertation. *Expenses: Tuition:* Full-time $36,288; part-time $1512 per credit. *Required fees:* $438 per semester. One-time fee: $510 full-time. Full-time tuition and fees vary according to course load. *Unit head:* Prof. Anna Neumann, Chair, 212-678-3272, Fax: 212-678-3036, E-mail: neumann@tc.columbia.edu. *Application contact:* David Estrella, Director of Admission, 212-678-3305, E-mail: estrella@tc.columbia.edu.

**Temple University,** College of Education, Department of Psychological Studies in Education, Philadelphia, PA 19122-6096. Offers adult and organizational development (Ed M); counseling psychology (Ed M, PhD), including agency counseling (Ed M), counseling psychology (PhD), school counseling (Ed M); education (PhD); educational leadership (Ed M); educational leadership and policy studies (Ed M, Ed D), including educational leadership; educational psychology (Ed M); school psychology (Ed M, PhD, Ed S); special education (Ed M). *Accreditation:* APA (one or more programs are accredited). *Program availability:* Part-time, evening/weekend. Terminal master's awarded for partial completion of doctoral program. *Degree requirements:* For master's, thesis or alternative; for doctorate, thesis/dissertation. *Entrance requirements:* Additional exam requirements/recommendations for international students: Required—TOEFL (minimum score 550 paper-based; 79 iBT).

**Texas Christian University,** College of Science and Engineering, Department of Psychology, Fort Worth, TX 76129. Offers developmental trauma (MS); experimental psychology (PhD), including cognition/developmental, learning, neuroscience, social. *Faculty:* 12 full-time (5 women), 3 part-time/adjunct (2 women). *Students:* 33 full-time (19 women); includes 4 minority (1 Asian, non-Hispanic/Latino; 1 Hispanic/Latino; 2 Two or more races, non-Hispanic/Latino), 2 international. Average age 27. 38 applicants, 32% accepted, 12 enrolled. In 2016, 5 master's, 3 doctorates awarded. Terminal master's awarded for partial completion of doctoral program. *Degree requirements:* For master's, thesis; for doctorate, thesis/dissertation. *Entrance requirements:* For doctorate, GRE General Test. Additional exam requirements/recommendations for international students: Required—TOEFL. *Application deadline:* For fall admission, 2/1 for domestic and international students. Application fee: $60 ($0 for international students). Electronic applications accepted. *Expenses:* Contact institution. *Financial support:* In 2016–17, 23 students received support, including 23 teaching assistantships with full tuition reimbursements available (averaging $19,750 per year); scholarships/grants also available. Financial award application deadline: 2/1; financial award applicants required to submit FAFSA. *Faculty research:* Neuroscience, human and animal learning, cognition, development, experimental social psychology. *Unit head:* Dr. Mauricio R. Papini, Chair, 817-257-7410, Fax: 817-257-7681, E-mail: m.papini@tcu.edu. *Application contact:* Cindy Hayes, Administrative Assistant, 817-257-7410, Fax: 817-257-7681, E-mail: c.hayes@tcu.edu.
Website: https://psychology.tcu.edu/current-graduate-students/

**Texas State University,** The Graduate College, College of Education, Program in Professional Counseling, San Marcos, TX 78666. Offers community counseling (MA); marital, couple and family counseling (MA); school counseling (MA). *Accreditation:* ACA. *Program availability:* Part-time. *Faculty:* 13 full-time (11 women), 6 part-time/adjunct (all women). *Students:* 94 full-time (77 women), 107 part-time (89 women); includes 53 minority (4 Black or African American, non-Hispanic/Latino; 7 Asian, non-Hispanic/Latino; 34 Hispanic/Latino; 8 Two or more races, non-Hispanic/Latino), 2 international. Average age 32. 114 applicants, 52% accepted, 29 enrolled. In 2016, 54 master's awarded. *Degree requirements:* For master's, comprehensive exam, thesis single optional, internship. *Entrance requirements:* For master's, GRE General Test (minimum preferred score of 291 [150 verbal, 141 quantitative]), baccalaureate degree from regionally-accredited institution with minimum GPA of 3.0 in last 60 hours of undergraduate work; resume; statement of purpose addressing professional goals, reasoning for specified emphasis (i.e., community, school, marital), strengths and weaknesses, and perspective on diversity; 3 references. Additional exam requirements/recommendations for international students: Required—TOEFL (minimum score 550 paper-based; 78 iBT), IELTS (minimum score 6.5). *Application deadline:* For fall admission, 2/15 for domestic and international students; for spring admission, 10/1 for domestic and international students; for summer admission, 2/15 for domestic and international students. Applications are processed on a rolling basis. Application fee: $40 ($90 for international students). Electronic applications accepted. *Expenses:* $4,851 per semester. *Financial support:* In 2016–17, 105 students received support, including 8 research assistantships (averaging $8,504 per year); teaching assistantships, Federal Work-Study, institutionally sponsored loans, and scholarships/grants also available. Support available to part-time students. Financial award application deadline: 3/1; financial award applicants required to submit FAFSA. *Unit head:* Dr. Kevin Fall, Graduate Advisor, 512-245-2081, Fax: 512-245-8872, E-mail: kf22@txstate.edu. *Application contact:* Dr. Andrea Golato, Dean of Graduate School, 512-245-2581, Fax: 512-245-8365, E-mail: gradcollege@txstate.edu.

**Thomas University,** Department of Human Services, Thomasville, GA 31792-7499. Offers community counseling (MSCC); rehabilitation counseling (MRC). *Accreditation:* CORE. *Program availability:* Part-time. *Entrance requirements:* For master's, resume, 3 academic/professional references. Additional exam requirements/recommendations for international students: Required—TOEFL (minimum score 600 paper-based). Electronic applications accepted.

**Université du Québec à Rimouski,** Graduate Programs, Program in Psychosocial Studies, Rimouski, QC G5L 3A1, Canada. Offers MA.

**Université Laval,** Faculty of Social Sciences, School of Psychology, Programs in Psychology, Québec, QC G1K 7P4, Canada. Offers clinical psychology (PhD); community psychology (PhD); psychology (PhD, Psy D). *Degree requirements:* For doctorate, comprehensive exam, thesis/dissertation. *Entrance requirements:* For doctorate, comprehension of written English, knowledge of French, interview. Electronic applications accepted.

**University at Albany, State University of New York,** College of Arts and Sciences, Department of Psychology, Albany, NY 12222-0001. Offers behavioral neuroscience (PhD); clinical psychology (PhD); cognitive psychology (PhD); industrial/organizational psychology (MA, PhD); social-personality psychology (PhD). *Accreditation:* APA (one or more programs are accredited). *Faculty:* 19 full-time (6 women). *Students:* 68 full-time (42 women), 43 part-time (31 women); includes 26 minority (1 Black or African American, non-Hispanic/Latino; 11 Asian, non-Hispanic/Latino; 9 Hispanic/Latino; 5 Two or more races, non-Hispanic/Latino), 8 international. 304 applicants, 14% accepted, 24 enrolled. In 2016, 7 master's, 11 doctorates awarded. *Degree requirements:* For doctorate, thesis/dissertation. *Entrance requirements:* For doctorate, GRE General Test, GRE Subject Test. Additional exam requirements/recommendations for international students: Required—TOEFL (minimum score 550 paper-based). *Application deadline:* For fall admission, 1/15 for domestic and international students. Application fee: $75. Electronic applications accepted. *Expenses:* Tuition, state resident: full-time $10,870; part-time $453 per credit hour. Tuition, nonresident: full-time $22,210; part-time $925 per credit hour. *International tuition:* $21,550 full-time. *Required fees:* $1864; $96 per credit hour. *Financial support:* Fellowships, research assistantships, teaching assistantships, and career-related internships or fieldwork available. Financial award application deadline: 2/1. *Total annual research expenditures:* $861,900. *Unit head:* James Neely, Chair, 518-442-4820, Fax: 518-442-4867, E-mail: jneely@albany.edu. *Application contact:* Michael DeRensis, Director, Graduate Admissions, 518-442-3980, Fax: 518-442-3922, E-mail: graduate@albany.edu.
Website: http://www.albany.edu/psychology/

**University of Alaska Anchorage,** College of Arts and Sciences, Department of Psychology, Anchorage, AK 99508. Offers clinical psychology (MS); clinical-community psychology with rural-indigenous emphasis (PhD). *Accreditation:* APA. *Program* *availability:* Part-time. *Degree requirements:* For master's, thesis. *Entrance requirements:* For master's, GRE General Test, GRE Subject Test, interview, references; for doctorate, interview, bachelor's or master's degree in psychology. Additional exam requirements/recommendations for international students: Required—TOEFL (minimum score 550 paper-based). *Faculty research:* Substance abuse, childhood autism, biofeedback, psychological assessment, mental health in Native Alaskans.

**University of Alaska Fairbanks,** College of Liberal Arts, Department of Psychology, Fairbanks, AK 99775-6480. Offers clinical-community psychology (PhD). Program offered jointly with University of Alaska Anchorage. *Accreditation:* APA. *Faculty:* 8 full-time (6 women). *Students:* 6 full-time (3 women), 10 part-time (6 women); includes 8 minority (1 Black or African American, non-Hispanic/Latino; 2 Asian, non-Hispanic/Latino; 2 Hispanic/Latino; 3 Two or more races, non-Hispanic/Latino). Average age 30. In 2016, 1 doctorate awarded. *Degree requirements:* For doctorate, comprehensive exam, thesis/dissertation, oral defense of dissertation. *Entrance requirements:* For doctorate, bachelor's degree from accredited institution with minimum cumulative undergraduate and major GPA of 3.0; criminal background check; interview; course work in abnormal psychology, statistics, and research methods. Additional exam requirements/recommendations for international students: Required—TOEFL (minimum score 550 paper-based; 80 iBT), IELTS (minimum score 6.5). *Application deadline:* For fall admission, 1/15 for domestic and international students. Application fee: $60. Electronic applications accepted. *Expenses:* Tuition, state resident: full-time $7992; part-time $444 per credit. Tuition, nonresident: full-time $16,326; part-time $907 per credit. *Required fees:* $39 per credit. $322 per semester. Tuition and fees vary according to course level, course load, campus/location, program and reciprocity agreements. *Financial support:* In 2016–17, 2 research assistantships with full tuition reimbursements (averaging $13,471 per year), 5 teaching assistantships with full tuition reimbursements (averaging $6,397 per year) were awarded; fellowships with full tuition reimbursements, career-related internships or fieldwork, Federal Work-Study, scholarships/grants, health care benefits, and unspecified assistantships also available. Support available to part-time students. Financial award application deadline: 7/1; financial award applicants required to submit FAFSA. *Faculty research:* Clinical and community psychology; rural, indigenous, and cultural psychology. *Unit head:* Dr. Cecile Lardon, Department Chair, 907-474-7012, Fax: 907-474-5781, E-mail: fypsych@uaf.edu. *Application contact:* Mary Kreta, Director of Admissions, 907-474-7500, Fax: 907-474-7097, E-mail: admissions@uaf.edu.
Website: http://www.uaf.edu/psych/

**University of Alaska Fairbanks,** School of Education, Program in Counseling, Fairbanks, AK 99775. Offers community counseling (M Ed). *Program availability:* 100% online, blended/hybrid learning. *Students:* 11 full-time (9 women), 47 part-time (39 women); includes 12 minority (3 American Indian or Alaska Native, non-Hispanic/Latino; 2 Hispanic/Latino; 7 Two or more races, non-Hispanic/Latino), 1 international. Average age 38. 44 applicants, 52% accepted, 22 enrolled. In 2016, 14 master's, 1 other advanced degree awarded. *Degree requirements:* For master's, comprehensive exam, oral defense of project or thesis. *Entrance requirements:* For master's, bachelor's degree from accredited institution with minimum cumulative undergraduate and major GPA of 3.0; for Graduate Certificate, master's degree from accredited institution with minimum GPA of 3.0. Additional exam requirements/recommendations for international students: Required—TOEFL (minimum score 550 paper-based; 79 iBT), IELTS (minimum score 6.5). *Application deadline:* For fall admission, 3/1 for domestic and international students; for spring admission, 10/1 for domestic students, 9/1 for international students. Applications are processed on a rolling basis. Application fee: $60. Electronic applications accepted. *Expenses:* Tuition, state resident: full-time $7992; part-time $444 per credit. Tuition, nonresident: full-time $16,326; part-time $907 per credit. *Required fees:* $39 per credit. $322 per semester. Tuition and fees vary according to course level, course load, campus/location, program and reciprocity agreements. *Financial support:* In 2016–17, 1 teaching assistantship with full tuition reimbursement (averaging $4,247 per year) was awarded; fellowships with full tuition reimbursements, career-related internships or fieldwork, Federal Work-Study, scholarships/grants, health care benefits, and unspecified assistantships also available. Support available to part-time students. Financial award application deadline: 7/1; financial award applicants required to submit FAFSA. *Unit head:* Jane Monahan, Graduate Advisor, 907-474-5362, Fax: 907-474-5451, E-mail: jmmonahan@alaska.edu. *Application contact:* Mary Kreta, Director of Admissions, 907-474-7500, Fax: 907-474-7097, E-mail: admissions@uaf.edu.
Website: https://sites.google.com/a/alaska.edu/uaf-soe-graduate/home/potential-students——degree-programs/counseling

**University of Bridgeport,** School of Arts and Sciences, Department of Counseling, Bridgeport, CT 06604. Offers clinical mental health counseling (MS); college student personnel (MS); community counseling (MS); human resource development (MS); human service (MS). *Program availability:* Part-time, evening/weekend. *Degree requirements:* For master's, thesis, project. *Entrance requirements:* Additional exam requirements/recommendations for international students: Recommended—TOEFL (minimum score 550 paper-based; 80 iBT), IELTS (minimum score 6.5). Electronic applications accepted. *Expenses:* Contact institution.

**The University of British Columbia,** Faculty of Arts and Faculty of Graduate Studies, Department of Psychology, Vancouver, BC V6T 1Z4, Canada. Offers behavioral neuroscience (MA, PhD); clinical psychology (MA, PhD); cognitive science (MA, PhD); developmental psychology (MA, PhD); health psychology (MA, PhD); quantitative methods (MA, PhD); social/personality psychology (MA, PhD). *Accreditation:* APA (one or more programs are accredited). Terminal master's awarded for partial completion of doctoral program. *Degree requirements:* For master's, thesis; for doctorate, comprehensive exam, thesis/dissertation. *Entrance requirements:* For master's and doctorate, GRE General Test. Additional exam requirements/recommendations for international students: Required—TOEFL. *Application deadline:* Applications are processed on a rolling basis. Application fee: $100 Canadian dollars ($162 Canadian dollars for international students). Electronic applications accepted. *Expenses:* $4,802 per year tuition and fees, $8,436 per year international. *Financial support:* Fellowships, research assistantships, teaching assistantships, career-related internships or fieldwork, Federal Work-Study, institutionally sponsored loans, scholarships/grants, health care benefits, tuition waivers (full and partial), and unspecified assistantships available. Financial award application deadline: 1/1. *Faculty research:* Clinical, developmental, social/personality, cognition, behavioral neuroscience. *Application contact:* Jaclyn Shaw, 604-822-5002, Fax: 604-822-6923, E-mail: gradsec@psych.ubc.ca.
Website: http://psych.ubc.ca/

**University of Central Arkansas,** Graduate School, College of Health and Behavioral Sciences, Department of Counseling and Psychology, Program in Community Counseling, Conway, AR 72035-0001. Offers MS. *Degree requirements:* For master's, comprehensive exam, thesis optional. *Entrance requirements:* For master's, GRE General Test, minimum GPA of 2.7. Additional exam requirements/recommendations for international students: Required—TOEFL (minimum score 550 paper-based). Electronic applications accepted.

**University of Connecticut,** Graduate School, College of Liberal Arts and Sciences, Department of Psychology, Storrs, CT 06269. Offers behavioral neuroscience (PhD); biopsychology (PhD); clinical psychology (MA, PhD); cognition and instruction (PhD); developmental psychology (MA, PhD); ecological psychology (PhD); experimental psychology (PhD); general psychology (MA, PhD); industrial/organizational psychology (PhD); language and cognition (PhD); neuroscience (PhD); social psychology (MA, PhD). *Accreditation:* APA. Terminal master's awarded for partial completion of doctoral program. *Degree requirements:* For master's, comprehensive exam; for doctorate, thesis/dissertation. *Entrance requirements:* For master's and doctorate, GRE General Test, GRE Subject Test. Additional exam requirements/recommendations for international students: Required—TOEFL (minimum score 550 paper-based). Electronic applications accepted.

**University of Delaware,** College of Arts and Sciences, Department of Psychology, Newark, DE 19716. Offers behavioral neuroscience (PhD); clinical psychology (PhD); cognitive psychology (PhD); social psychology (PhD). *Accreditation:* APA. *Degree requirements:* For doctorate, thesis/dissertation. *Entrance requirements:* For doctorate, GRE General Test. Additional exam requirements/recommendations for international students: Required—TOEFL (minimum score 600 paper-based). Electronic applications accepted. *Faculty research:* Emotion development, neural and cognitive aspects of memory, neural control of feeding, intergroup relations, social cognition and communication.

**University of Denver,** Division of Arts, Humanities and Social Sciences, Department of Psychology, Denver, CO 80208. Offers affect/social psychology (PhD); clinical child psychology (PhD); cognitive psychology (PhD); developmental psychology (PhD). *Accreditation:* APA. *Faculty:* 26 full-time (13 women), 5 part-time/adjunct (3 women). *Students:* 22 full-time (16 women), 2 part-time (both women); includes 5 minority (1 Black or African American, non-Hispanic/Latino; 1 Asian, non-Hispanic/Latino; 3 Hispanic/Latino), 1 international. Average age 28. 294 applicants, 4% accepted, 8 enrolled. In 2016, 8 doctorates awarded. Terminal master's awarded for partial completion of doctoral program. *Degree requirements:* For doctorate, variable foreign language requirement, comprehensive exam (for some programs), thesis/dissertation. *Entrance requirements:* For doctorate, GRE General Test, master's degree, transcripts, biographical statement, three letters of recommendation. Additional exam requirements/recommendations for international students: Required—TOEFL (minimum score 550 paper-based; 80 iBT). *Application deadline:* For fall admission, 12/1 priority date for domestic and international students. Application fee: $65. Electronic applications accepted. *Expenses:* $29,022 per year full-time. *Financial support:* In 2016–17, 24 students received support, including 5 research assistantships with tuition reimbursements available (averaging $16,000 per year), 12 teaching assistantships with tuition reimbursements available (averaging $17,778 per year); Federal Work-Study, institutionally sponsored loans, scholarships/grants, and unspecified assistantships also available. Support available to part-time students. Financial award application deadline: 2/15; financial award applicants required to submit FAFSA. *Faculty research:* Stress and trauma, developmental science, affect science, clinical science, child psychopathology. *Unit head:* Dr. Anne DePrince, Professor and Chair, 303-871-2939, Fax: 303-871-4747, E-mail: adeprinc@du.edu. *Application contact:* Paula Houghtaling, Graduate Program Administrator, 303-871-3803, Fax: 303-871-4747, E-mail: phoughta@du.edu.
Website: http://www.du.edu/ahss/psychology

**University of Guelph,** Graduate Studies, College of Social and Applied Human Sciences, Department of Psychology, Guelph, ON N1G 2W1, Canada. Offers applied social psychology (MA, PhD); clinical psychology: applied development emphasis (PhD); clinical psychology: applied developmental emphasis (MA); industrial/organizational psychology (MA, PhD); neuroscience and applied cognitive science (MA, PhD). *Degree requirements:* For master's, thesis; for doctorate, comprehensive exam, thesis/dissertation. *Entrance requirements:* For master's, GRE General Test, GRE Subject Test, minimum B+ average during previous 2 years of course work; for doctorate, GRE General Test, GRE Subject Test, minimum A- average. Additional exam requirements/recommendations for international students: Required—TOEFL (minimum score 89 iBT). Electronic applications accepted. *Faculty research:* Organizational psychology, reading comprehension and mathematical ability, drug addiction and relapse, gender issues and culture, memory, clinical psychology.

**University of Hawaii at Manoa,** Graduate Division, College of Social Sciences, Department of Psychology, Honolulu, HI 96822. Offers clinical psychology (PhD); community and cultural psychology (PhD); community and culture (MA); psychology (MA, PhD, Graduate Certificate). *Accreditation:* APA (one or more programs are accredited). *Program availability:* Part-time. Terminal master's awarded for partial completion of doctoral program. *Degree requirements:* For master's, comprehensive exam, thesis; for doctorate, comprehensive exam, thesis/dissertation. *Entrance requirements:* For master's and doctorate, GRE General Test, GRE Subject Test. Additional exam requirements/recommendations for international students: Required—TOEFL (minimum score 600 paper-based; 100 iBT), IELTS (minimum score 7). *Faculty research:* Cross-cultural psychology, health psychology, marine mammals, child/adult psychopathology.

**University of Houston,** College of Liberal Arts and Social Sciences, Department of Psychology, Houston, TX 77204. Offers clinical psychology (PhD); developmental psychology (PhD); industrial/organizational psychology (PhD); psychology (MA); social psychology (PhD). *Accreditation:* APA (one or more programs are accredited). *Degree requirements:* For master's, comprehensive exam, thesis; for doctorate, comprehensive exam, thesis/dissertation. *Entrance requirements:* For master's, GRE General Test, career statement, 3 letters of recommendation; for doctorate, GRE General Test, 3 letters of recommendation. Additional exam requirements/recommendations for international students: Required—TOEFL (minimum score 550 paper-based; 79 iBT). Electronic applications accepted. *Faculty research:* Health psychology, depression, child/family process, organizational effectiveness, close relationships.

**The University of Kansas,** Graduate Studies, College of Liberal Arts and Sciences, Department of Psychology, Lawrence, KS 66045. Offers clinical psychology (MA, PhD); cognitive and brain sciences (MA, PhD); developmental psychology (MA, PhD); quantitative psychology (PhD); social psychology (MA, PhD). *Accreditation:* APA (one or more programs are accredited). *Program availability:* Part-time. *Students:* 69 full-time (46 women), 1 (woman) part-time; includes 11 minority (5 Black or African American, non-Hispanic/Latino; 3 Asian, non-Hispanic/Latino; 3 Two or more races, non-Hispanic/Latino), 9 international. Average age 29. 202 applicants, 10% accepted, 14 enrolled. In 2016, 12 master's, 11 doctorates awarded. Terminal master's awarded for partial completion of doctoral program. *Entrance requirements:* For doctorate, GRE General Test, three letters of recommendation, resume/curriculum vitae, statement of purpose/personal statement, writing sample. Additional exam requirements/recommendations for international students: Required—TOEFL. *Application deadline:* For fall admission, 12/1 for domestic and international students. Application fee: $65 ($85 for international students). Electronic applications accepted. *Financial support:* Fellowships, research assistantships, teaching assistantships, career-related internships or fieldwork, Federal Work-Study, scholarships/grants, health care benefits, and unspecified assistantships available. Financial award application deadline: 12/1; financial award applicants required to submit FAFSA. *Faculty research:* Origins, correlates and treatment of depression;

## Social Psychology

health and emotion; concentration on topics related to prejudice, stereotyping, and intergroup relations; memory, cognitive development, language, perception, attention, aging; psychometric methods, item response theory, structural equation modeling. *Unit head:* Ruth Anne Atchley, Chair, 785-864-4131. *Application contact:* Graduate Officer, 785-864-4195, E-mail: psycgrad@ku.edu.
Website: http://www.psych.ku.edu/

**University of Maryland, Baltimore County,** The Graduate School, College of Arts, Humanities and Social Sciences, Department of Psychology, Program in Human Services Psychology, Baltimore, MD 21250. Offers applied behavioral analysis (MA); human services psychology (PhD), including behavioral medicine, clinical psychology, community psychology. *Faculty:* 17 full-time (9 women), 11 part-time/adjunct (4 women). *Students:* 82 full-time (65 women), 1 (woman) part-time; includes 26 minority (10 Black or African American, non-Hispanic/Latino; 6 Asian, non-Hispanic/Latino; 9 Hispanic/Latino; 1 Two or more races, non-Hispanic/Latino). Average age 25. 136 applicants, 21% accepted, 18 enrolled. In 2016, 25 master's, 7 doctorates awarded. *Degree requirements:* For master's, thesis; for doctorate, comprehensive exam, thesis/dissertation. *Entrance requirements:* For master's, GRE General Test, minimum GPA of 3.0; for doctorate, GRE General Test, GRE Subject Test, minimum GPA of 3.0. Additional exam requirements/recommendations for international students: Required—TOEFL. *Application deadline:* For fall admission, 12/1 for domestic and international students. Application fee: $50. Electronic applications accepted. *Expenses:* Tuition, state resident: full-time $13,294. Tuition, nonresident: full-time $20,286. *Financial support:* In 2016–17, 43 students received support, including 3 fellowships with full tuition reimbursements available (averaging $26,000 per year), 26 research assistantships with full tuition reimbursements available (averaging $20,400 per year), 9 teaching assistantships with full tuition reimbursements available (averaging $17,250 per year); career-related internships or fieldwork, Federal Work-Study, scholarships/grants, health care benefits, tuition waivers, and unspecified assistantships also available. Financial award application deadline: 3/1; financial award applicants required to submit FAFSA. *Faculty research:* Addictive behaviors, cardiovascular and cerebrovascular disease, family violence, pediatric psychology, community prevention. *Unit head:* Dr. Lynnda Dahlquist, Director, 410-455-2567, Fax: 410-455-1055, E-mail: dahlquis@umbc.edu. *Application contact:* Nicole Mooney, Program Management Specialist, 410-455-2567, Fax: 410-455-1055, E-mail: psycdept@umbc.edu.
Website: http://psychology.umbc.edu/

**University of Maryland, College Park,** Academic Affairs, College of Behavioral and Social Sciences, Department of Psychology, College Park, MD 20742. Offers clinical psychology (PhD); developmental psychology (PhD); experimental psychology (PhD); industrial psychology (MA, MS, PhD); social psychology (PhD). *Accreditation:* APA (one or more programs are accredited). *Degree requirements:* For master's, thesis; for doctorate, variable foreign language requirement, comprehensive exam, thesis/dissertation. *Entrance requirements:* For master's and doctorate, GRE General Test, GRE Subject Test, minimum GPA of 3.5, research and/or work experience, 3 letters of recommendation. Electronic applications accepted. *Faculty research:* Social stereotyping and prejudice, anxiety disorders, auditory neuroethology, counseling and social psychology.

**University of Massachusetts Amherst,** Graduate School, College of Natural Sciences, Department of Psychological and Brain Sciences, Amherst, MA 01003. Offers clinical psychology (MS, PhD); cognitive psychology (MS, PhD); developmental science (MS, PhD); psychology of peace and violence (MS, PhD); social psychology (MS, PhD). *Accreditation:* APA (one or more programs are accredited). Terminal master's awarded for partial completion of doctoral program. *Degree requirements:* For master's, thesis; for doctorate, comprehensive exam, thesis/dissertation. *Entrance requirements:* For master's and doctorate, GRE General Test, 3 letters of recommendation. Additional exam requirements/recommendations for international students: Required—TOEFL (minimum score 550 paper-based; 80 iBT), IELTS (minimum score 6.5). Electronic applications accepted.

**University of Massachusetts Lowell,** College of Fine Arts, Humanities and Social Sciences, Department of Psychology, Lowell, MA 01854. Offers community social psychology (MA). *Program availability:* Part-time. *Degree requirements:* For master's, thesis optional. *Entrance requirements:* For master's, GRE General Test or MAT. Electronic applications accepted. *Faculty research:* Domestic violence, youth sports, teen pregnancy, substance abuse, family and work roles.

**University of Michigan,** Rackham Graduate School, College of Literature, Science, and the Arts, Department of Psychology, Ann Arbor, MI 48109. Offers biopsychology (PhD); clinical science (PhD); cognition and cognitive neuroscience (PhD); developmental psychology (PhD); personality and social contexts (PhD); social psychology (PhD). *Accreditation:* APA. *Faculty:* 60 full-time (28 women), 30 part-time/adjunct (18 women). *Students:* 147 full-time (111 women); includes 64 minority (15 Black or African American, non-Hispanic/Latino; 1 American Indian or Alaska Native, non-Hispanic/Latino; 14 Asian, non-Hispanic/Latino; 27 Hispanic/Latino; 7 Two or more races, non-Hispanic/Latino), 19 international. Average age 27. 727 applicants, 8% accepted, 34 enrolled. In 2016, 28 doctorates awarded. *Degree requirements:* For doctorate, comprehensive exam, thesis/dissertation, oral defense of dissertation, preliminary exam. *Entrance requirements:* For doctorate, GRE General Test. Additional exam requirements/recommendations for international students: Required—TOEFL. *Application deadline:* For fall admission, 12/1 for domestic and international students. Application fee: $75 ($90 for international students). Electronic applications accepted. *Expenses:* Tuition, state resident: full-time $21,466; part-time $1152 per credit hour. Tuition, nonresident: full-time $43,346; part-time $2367 per credit hour. Part-time tuition and fees vary according to course load, degree level and program. *Financial support:* In 2016–17, 104 students received support, including 64 fellowships with full tuition reimbursements available (averaging $19,800 per year), 6 research assistantships with full tuition reimbursements available (averaging $24,243 per year), 71 teaching assistantships with full tuition reimbursements available (averaging $25,136 per year); career-related internships or fieldwork, traineeships, and health care benefits also available. Financial award application deadline: 4/15. *Unit head:* Prof. Patricia Reuter-Lorenz, Department Chair, 734-764-7429. *Application contact:* Sheri M. Circele, Psychology Student Academic Affairs, 734-764-2580, Fax: 734-764-3520, E-mail: psych.saa@umich.edu.
Website: http://www.lsa.umich.edu/psych/

**University of Minnesota, Twin Cities Campus,** Graduate School, College of Liberal Arts, Department of Psychology, Program in Social Psychology, Minneapolis, MN 55455-0213. Offers PhD. *Degree requirements:* For doctorate, comprehensive exam, thesis/dissertation. *Entrance requirements:* For doctorate, GRE General Test, GRE Subject Test (recommended), 12 credits of upper-level psychology courses, including a course in statistics or psychological measurement. Additional exam requirements/recommendations for international students: Required—TOEFL (minimum score 550 paper-based; 79 iBT).

**University of Missouri–Kansas City,** College of Arts and Sciences, Department of Psychology, Kansas City, MO 64110-2499. Offers community psychology (PhD). PhD (interdisciplinary) offered through the School of Graduate Studies. *Accreditation:* APA. *Faculty:* 12 full-time (8 women). *Students:* 18 full-time (13 women), 13 part-time (9

women); includes 5 minority (1 Black or African American, non-Hispanic/Latino; 3 Hispanic/Latino; 1 Two or more races, non-Hispanic/Latino), 1 international. Average age 30. 85 applicants, 6% accepted, 5 enrolled. In 2016, 4 master's, 3 doctorates awarded. Terminal master's awarded for partial completion of doctoral program. *Degree requirements:* For master's, thesis; for doctorate, comprehensive exam, thesis/dissertation, residency. *Entrance requirements:* For master's, GRE, minimum GPA of 3.5, letter of recommendation; for doctorate, GRE, minimum GPA of 3.25. Additional exam requirements/recommendations for international students: Required—TOEFL (minimum score 550 paper-based; 80 iBT). *Application deadline:* For fall admission, 1/15 for domestic and international students. Applications are processed on a rolling basis. Application fee: $45 ($50 for international students). Electronic applications accepted. *Financial support:* In 2016–17, 1 research assistantship (averaging $12,000 per year), 14 teaching assistantships (averaging $12,684 per year) were awarded; career-related internships or fieldwork, Federal Work-Study, and institutionally sponsored loans also available. Support available to part-time students. Financial award application deadline: 3/1; financial award applicants required to submit FAFSA. *Faculty research:* HIV/AIDS research group, psycho-oncology, sensory and cognitive neuroscience, cognitive psychophysiology, obesity and related metabolic disorders. *Unit head:* Dr. Jennifer Lundgren, Department Chair, 816-235-5384, Fax: 816-235-1062, E-mail: lundgrenj@umkc.edu. *Application contact:* Dr. Cathy Rawlings, Director, Graduate Programs, 816-235-1318, Fax: 816-235-1062, E-mail: psychology@umkc.edu.
Website: http://cas.umkc.edu/psyc

**University of Nebraska–Lincoln,** Graduate College, College of Arts and Sciences, Department of Psychology, Lincoln, NE 68588. Offers biopsychology (PhD); clinical psychology (PhD); cognitive psychology (PhD); developmental psychology (PhD); psychology (MA); social/personality psychology (PhD); JD/MA; JD/PhD. *Accreditation:* APA (one or more programs are accredited). *Degree requirements:* For master's, thesis optional; for doctorate, comprehensive exam, thesis/dissertation. *Entrance requirements:* For master's and doctorate, GRE General Test. Additional exam requirements/recommendations for international students: Required—TOEFL (minimum score 550 paper-based). Electronic applications accepted. *Faculty research:* Law and psychology, rural mental health, chronic mental illness, neuropsychology, child clinical psychology.

**University of Nevada, Reno,** Graduate School, Interdisciplinary Program in Social Psychology, Reno, NV 89557. Offers PhD. *Degree requirements:* For doctorate, one foreign language, thesis/dissertation. *Entrance requirements:* For doctorate, GRE General Test, GRE Subject Test (psychology or sociology), minimum GPA of 3.0. Additional exam requirements/recommendations for international students: Required—TOEFL (minimum score 500 paper-based; 61 iBT), IELTS (minimum score 6). Electronic applications accepted. *Faculty research:* Social psychological theory, social psychology of law.

**University of New Haven,** Graduate School, College of Arts and Sciences, Program in Community Psychology, West Haven, CT 06516. Offers applications of psychology (Graduate Certificate); community clinical services (MA); community psychology (MA); forensic psychology (MA); program development (MA). *Program availability:* Part-time, evening/weekend. *Students:* 37 full-time (36 women), 6 part-time (4 women); includes 13 minority (6 Black or African American, non-Hispanic/Latino; 1 American Indian or Alaska Native, non-Hispanic/Latino; 3 Hispanic/Latino; 3 Two or more races, non-Hispanic/Latino). Average age 25. 48 applicants, 81% accepted, 21 enrolled. In 2016, 26 master's awarded. *Degree requirements:* For master's, thesis or alternative, fieldwork. *Entrance requirements:* Additional exam requirements/recommendations for international students: Required—TOEFL (minimum score 80 iBT), IELTS, PTE. *Application deadline:* Applications are processed on a rolling basis. Application fee: $50. Electronic applications accepted. Application fee is waived when completed online. *Expenses:* Tuition: Full-time $15,660; part-time $870 per credit hour. *Required fees:* $200; $85 per term. Tuition and fees vary according to program. *Financial support:* Research assistantships with partial tuition reimbursements, teaching assistantships with partial tuition reimbursements, career-related internships or fieldwork, Federal Work-Study, scholarships/grants, and unspecified assistantships available. Support available to part-time students. Financial award application deadline: 5/1; financial award applicants required to submit FAFSA. *Unit head:* Dr. Michael Morris, Coordinator, 203-932-7289, E-mail: mmorris@newhaven.edu.
Website: http://www.newhaven.edu/4725/

**The University of North Carolina at Chapel Hill,** Graduate School, College of Arts and Sciences, Department of Psychology, Chapel Hill, NC 27599-3270. Offers behavioral neuroscience psychology (PhD); clinical psychology (PhD); cognitive psychology (PhD); developmental psychology (PhD); quantitative psychology (PhD); social psychology (PhD). *Accreditation:* APA. *Degree requirements:* For doctorate, comprehensive exam, thesis/dissertation. *Entrance requirements:* For doctorate, GRE General Test, minimum GPA of 3.0. Additional exam requirements/recommendations for international students: Required—TOEFL (minimum score 550 paper-based; 79 iBT), IELTS (minimum score 7). Electronic applications accepted. *Faculty research:* Expressed emotion, cognitive development, social cognitive neuroscience, human memory personality.

**The University of North Carolina at Greensboro,** Graduate School, College of Arts and Sciences, Department of Psychology, Greensboro, NC 27412-5001. Offers clinical psychology (MA, PhD); cognitive psychology (MA, PhD); developmental psychology (MA, PhD); social psychology (MA, PhD). *Accreditation:* APA (one or more programs are accredited). Terminal master's awarded for partial completion of doctoral program. *Degree requirements:* For master's, comprehensive exam, thesis; for doctorate, one foreign language, thesis/dissertation, preliminary exam. *Entrance requirements:* For master's and doctorate, GRE General Test. Additional exam requirements/recommendations for international students: Required—TOEFL. Electronic applications accepted. *Faculty research:* Sensory and perceptual determinants; evoked potential: disorders, deafness, and development.

**University of Northern Colorado,** Graduate School, College of Natural and Health Sciences, School of Sport and Exercise Science, Greeley, CO 80639. Offers biomechanics (PhD); exercise physiology (PhD); exercise science (MS); social psychology of sport and physical activity (PhD); sport administration (MS, PhD); sport pedagogy (MS, PhD). *Program availability:* Part-time, evening/weekend. *Degree requirements:* For master's, comprehensive exam; for doctorate, comprehensive exam, thesis/dissertation. *Entrance requirements:* For master's, 2 letters of recommendation, resume; for doctorate, GRE General Test, 3 letters of recommendation, resume. *Application deadline:* Applications are processed on a rolling basis. Application fee: $50 ($60 for international students). Electronic applications accepted. *Financial support:* Fellowships, research assistantships, teaching assistantships, and unspecified assistantships available. Financial award application deadline: 3/1; financial award applicants required to submit FAFSA. *Unit head:* Dr. David Stotlar, Director, 970-351-2535, Fax: 970-351-1762. *Application contact:* Linda Sisson, Graduate Student Admission Coordinator, 970-351-1807, Fax: 970-351-2371, E-mail: linda.sisson@unco.edu. Website: http://www.unco.edu/nhs/ses/

**University of Oregon,** Graduate School, College of Arts and Sciences, Department of Psychology, Eugene, OR 97403. Offers clinical psychology (PhD); cognitive psychology (MA, MS, PhD); developmental psychology (MA, MS, PhD); physiological psychology

(MA, MS, PhD); psychology (MA, MS, PhD); social/personality psychology (MA, MS, PhD). *Accreditation:* APA (one or more programs are accredited). Terminal master's awarded for partial completion of doctoral program. *Degree requirements:* For doctorate, thesis/dissertation. *Entrance requirements:* For master's, GRE General Test, minimum GPA of 3.0; for doctorate, GRE General Test. Additional exam requirements/recommendations for international students: Required—TOEFL.

**University of Phoenix–Phoenix Campus,** College of Social Sciences, Tempe, AZ 85282-2371. Offers counseling (MS), including clinical mental health counseling, community counseling, counseling, marriage, family and child therapy; psychology (MS). *Program availability:* Evening/weekend, online learning. *Entrance requirements:* Additional exam requirements/recommendations for international students: Required—TOEFL, TOEIC (Test of English as an International Communication), Berlitz Online English Proficiency Exam, PTE, or IELTS. Electronic applications accepted. *Expenses:* Contact institution.

**University of Puerto Rico, Río Piedras Campus,** College of Social Sciences, Department of Psychology, San Juan, PR 00931-3300. Offers clinical psychology (MA); industrial organizational psychology (MA); investigative academic psychology (MA); psychology (PhD); social-community psychology (MA). *Program availability:* Part-time. *Degree requirements:* For master's, comprehensive exam, thesis; for doctorate, comprehensive exam, thesis/dissertation, internship. *Entrance requirements:* For master's, GRE or PAEG, interview, minimum GPA of 3.0; for doctorate, GRE or PAEG, interview, master's degree, minimum GPA of 3.0. *Faculty research:* Intervention on depressed Latino youth, biosychosocial training.

**University of Rochester,** Margaret Warner Graduate School of Education and Human Development, Master's Program in Counseling, Rochester, NY 14627. Offers school and community counseling (MS); school counseling (MS). *Expenses:* Tuition: Full-time $47,450; part-time $1482 per credit hour. *Required fees:* $528. Tuition and fees vary according to program.

**University of Rochester,** School of Arts and Sciences, Department of Clinical and Social Sciences in Psychology, Rochester, NY 14627. Offers clinical psychology (PhD); developmental psychology (PhD); social-personality psychology (PhD). *Accreditation:* APA. *Faculty:* 13 full-time (6 women). *Students:* 47 full-time (41 women); includes 10 minority (1 Black or African American, non-Hispanic/Latino; 3 Asian, non-Hispanic/Latino; 5 Hispanic/Latino; 1 Two or more races, non-Hispanic/Latino), 4 international. Average age 27. 257 applicants, 5% accepted, 7 enrolled. In 2016, 6 doctorates awarded. Terminal master's awarded for partial completion of doctoral program. *Degree requirements:* For doctorate, thesis/dissertation, qualifying exam. *Entrance requirements:* For doctorate, GRE General Test; GRE Subject Test (for clinical psychology, recommended for others). Additional exam requirements/recommendations for international students: Required—TOEFL. *Application deadline:* For fall admission, 4/15 for domestic and international students. Application fee: $60. Electronic applications accepted. *Expenses:* $1,538 per credit. *Financial support:* In 2016–17, 43 students received support, including 4 fellowships with full tuition reimbursements available (averaging $24,000 per year), 19 research assistantships with full tuition reimbursements available (averaging $21,000 per year), 20 teaching assistantships with full tuition reimbursements available (averaging $21,000 per year); career-related internships or fieldwork, scholarships/grants, traineeships, health care benefits, tuition waivers (full), and unspecified assistantships also available. Financial award application deadline: 2/1. *Faculty research:* Clinical psychology, social-personality psychology, developmental psychology, human motivation. *Unit head:* Loisa Bennetto, Chair, 585-275-8712, E-mail: loisa.bennetto@rochester.edu. *Application contact:* April Engram, Academic Coordinator/Analyst, 585-275-8704, E-mail: april.engram@rochester.edu. Website: http://www.psych.rochester.edu/csp/

**University of South Carolina,** The Graduate School, College of Arts and Sciences, Department of Psychology, Program in Clinical/Community Psychology, Columbia, SC 29208. Offers clinical/community psychology (PhD); general psychology (MA). *Accreditation:* APA. *Degree requirements:* For master's, comprehensive exam, thesis; for doctorate, comprehensive exam, thesis/dissertation. *Entrance requirements:* For doctorate, GRE General Test, minimum GPA of 3.2. Additional exam requirements/recommendations for international students: Required—TOEFL. Electronic applications accepted. *Faculty research:* Developmental psychopathology, health disparities, community-level interventions for psychological well being.

**University of Southern California,** Graduate School, Dana and David Dornsife College of Letters, Arts and Sciences, Department of Psychology, Los Angeles, CA 90089. Offers brain and cognitive science (PhD); clinical science (PhD); developmental psychology (PhD); human behavior (MHB); quantitative methods (PhD); social psychology (PhD). *Accreditation:* APA. *Degree requirements:* For doctorate, comprehensive exam, thesis/dissertation, one-year internship (for clinical science students). *Entrance requirements:* For doctorate, GRE. Additional exam requirements/recommendations for international students: Recommended—TOEFL (minimum score 600 paper-based; 100 iBT). Electronic applications accepted. *Faculty research:* Affective neuroscience; children and families; vision, culture and ethnicity; intergroup relations; aggression and violence; language and reading development; substance abuse.

**The University of Tennessee at Chattanooga,** School of Education, Chattanooga, TN 37403. Offers counseling (M Ed), including community counseling, school counseling; education (M Ed, Post-Master's Certificate), including elementary education (M Ed), school leadership, secondary education (M Ed), special education (M Ed); educational specialist (Ed S), including educational technology, school psychology; learning and leadership (Ed D), including educational leadership. *Accreditation:* ACA; NCATE. *Program availability:* Part-time. *Faculty:* 13 full-time (8 women), 2 part-time/adjunct (both women). *Students:* 50 full-time (32 women), 157 part-time (107 women); includes 42 minority (28 Black or African American, non-Hispanic/Latino; 4 Asian, non-Hispanic/Latino; 2 Hispanic/Latino; 8 Two or more races, non-Hispanic/Latino), 1 international. Average age 36. 169 applicants, 76% accepted, 49 enrolled. In 2016, 77 master's, 5 other advanced degrees awarded. *Degree requirements:* For master's, comprehensive exam, thesis optional, culminating experience; for doctorate, comprehensive exam, thesis/dissertation; for other advanced degree, internship. *Entrance requirements:* For master's, GRE General Test, PPST 1, teaching certificate; for doctorate, GRE General Test, master's degree, two years of practical work experience in organizational environment; for other advanced degree, GRE General Test, letters of reference. Additional exam requirements/recommendations for international students: Required—TOEFL (minimum score 550 paper-based; 79 iBT), IELTS (minimum score 6). *Application deadline:* For fall admission, 6/15 for domestic students, 7/1 for international students; for spring admission, 11/1 for domestic and international students. Applications are processed on a rolling basis. Application fee: $35 ($40 for international students). Electronic applications accepted. *Expenses:* $9,876 full-time in-state; $25,994 full-time out-of-state; $450 per credit part-time in-state; $1,345 per credit part-time out-of-state. *Financial support:* In 2016–17, 18 research assistantships, 5 teaching assistantships were awarded; career-related internships or fieldwork, institutionally sponsored loans, scholarships/grants, and unspecified assistantships also available. Support available to part-time students. Financial award application deadline: 7/1; financial award applicants required to submit FAFSA. *Faculty research:* School counseling, community counseling, elementary and secondary education, school

leadership and administration. *Total annual research expenditures:* $247,231. *Unit head:* Dr. Renee Murley, Director, 423-425-4684, Fax: 423-425-5380, E-mail: renee-murley@utc.edu. *Application contact:* Dr. Joanne Romagni, Dean of the Graduate School, 423-425-4478, Fax: 423-425-5223, E-mail: joanne-romagni@utc.edu. Website: http://www.utc.edu/school-education/abouttheschool/gradprograms.php

**The University of Tennessee at Martin,** Graduate Programs, College of Education, Health and Behavioral Sciences, Program in Counseling, Martin, TN 38238. Offers addictions counseling (MS Ed); community counseling (MS Ed); school counseling (MS Ed); student affairs and college counseling (MS Ed). *Accreditation:* NCATE. *Program availability:* Part-time, online only, 100% online. *Students:* 14 full-time (12 women), 62 part-time (59 women); includes 10 minority (6 Black or African American, non-Hispanic/Latino; 3 Hispanic/Latino; 1 Two or more races, non-Hispanic/Latino). Average age 35. 40 applicants, 48% accepted, 18 enrolled. In 2016, 17 master's awarded. *Degree requirements:* For master's, comprehensive exam. *Entrance requirements:* For master's, GRE General Test, minimum GPA of 2.5, resume, letters of reference. Additional exam requirements/recommendations for international students: Required—TOEFL (minimum score 525 paper-based; 71 iBT). *Application deadline:* For fall admission, 7/27 priority date for domestic and international students; for spring admission, 12/17 priority date for domestic and international students; for summer admission, 5/10 priority date for domestic and international students. Applications are processed on a rolling basis. Application fee: $30 ($130 for international students). Electronic applications accepted. *Expenses:* Tuition, state resident: full-time $8254; part-time $459 per credit hour. Tuition, nonresident: full-time $22,198; part-time $1234 per credit hour. *Required fees:* $79 per credit hour. Part-time tuition and fees vary according to course load and campus/location. *Financial support:* Scholarships/grants and unspecified assistantships available. Financial award application deadline: 2/1; financial award applicants required to submit FAFSA. *Unit head:* Cynthia West, Dean, 731-881-7125, Fax: 731-881-7975, E-mail: cwest@utm.edu. *Application contact:* Jolene L. Cunningham, Student Services Specialist, 731-881-7012, Fax: 731-881-7499, E-mail: jcunningham@utm.edu.

**University of Victoria,** Faculty of Graduate Studies, Faculty of Education, Department of Educational Psychology and Leadership Studies, Victoria, BC V8W 2Y2, Canada. Offers aboriginal communities counseling (M Ed); counseling (M Ed, MA); educational psychology (M Ed, MA, PhD), including counseling psychology (M Ed, MA), leadership studies (PhD), learning and development (MA, PhD), measurement and evaluation, special education (M Ed, MA); leadership studies (M Ed, MA). *Program availability:* Part-time. *Degree requirements:* For master's, thesis (for some programs), comprehensive exam (M Ed); for doctorate, comprehensive exam, thesis/dissertation, candidacy exam. *Entrance requirements:* For master's, 2 years of work experience in a relevant field; for doctorate, GRE, 2 years of work experience in a relevant field, minimum B average. Additional exam requirements/recommendations for international students: Required—TOEFL (minimum score 575 paper-based), IELTS (minimum score 7). *Faculty research:* Learning and development (child, adolescent and adult), special education and exceptional children.

**University of Victoria,** Faculty of Graduate Studies, Faculty of Social Sciences, Department of Psychology, Victoria, BC V8W 2Y2, Canada. Offers clinical psychology (PhD); clinical psychology (neuropsychology) (M Sc); cognition and brain science (M Sc, PhD); experimental neuropsychology (M Sc, PhD); individualized study (M Sc, PhD); life span development psychology (PhD); life span developmental psychology (M Sc); social psychology (M Sc, PhD). *Degree requirements:* For master's, thesis; for doctorate, thesis/dissertation, candidacy exam. *Entrance requirements:* For master's and doctorate, GRE General Test. Additional exam requirements/recommendations for international students: Required—TOEFL (minimum score 600 paper-based). Electronic applications accepted. *Faculty research:* Life span development psychology and aging, behavioral neuroscience, cognitive psychology, behavioral psychology, environmental psychology.

**University of Washington,** Graduate School, College of Arts and Sciences, Department of Psychology, Seattle, WA 98195. Offers animal behavior (PhD); child psychology (PhD); clinical psychology (PhD); cognition and perception (PhD); developmental psychology (PhD); quantitative psychology (PhD); social psychology and personality (PhD). *Accreditation:* APA. *Degree requirements:* For doctorate, thesis/dissertation. *Entrance requirements:* For doctorate, GRE General Test, minimum GPA of 3.0. Electronic applications accepted. *Faculty research:* Addictive behaviors, artificial intelligence, child psychopathology, mechanisms and development of vision, physiology of ingestive behaviors.

**University of Windsor,** Faculty of Graduate Studies, Faculty of Arts and Social Sciences, Department of Psychology, Windsor, ON N9B 3P4, Canada. Offers adult clinical (MA, PhD); applied social psychology (MA, PhD); child clinical (MA, PhD); clinical neuropsychology (MA, PhD). *Degree requirements:* For master's, thesis; for doctorate, comprehensive exam, thesis/dissertation. *Entrance requirements:* For master's, GRE General Test, GRE Subject Test in psychology, minimum B average; for doctorate, GRE General Test, GRE Subject Test in psychology, master's degree. Additional exam requirements/recommendations for international students: Required—TOEFL (minimum score 600 paper-based). Electronic applications accepted. *Faculty research:* Gambling, suicidology, emotional competence, psychotherapy and trauma.

**University of Wisconsin–Madison,** Graduate School, College of Letters and Science, Department of Psychology, Program in Social and Personality Psychology, Madison, WI 53706-1380. Offers PhD. *Degree requirements:* For doctorate, comprehensive exam, thesis/dissertation. *Entrance requirements:* For doctorate, GRE General Test, minimum undergraduate GPA of 3.0. Additional exam requirements/recommendations for international students: Required—TOEFL. Electronic applications accepted.

**University of Wisconsin–Milwaukee,** Graduate School, College of Letters and Science, Department of Psychology, Milwaukee, WI 53201-0413. Offers experimental psychology (MS, PhD), including behavior analysis, health and social psychology (PhD), health psychology (MS), neuroscience (PhD); psychology (PhD), including clinical psychology. *Accreditation:* APA (one or more programs are accredited). *Students:* 67 full-time (46 women), 19 part-time (11 women); includes 8 minority (2 Asian, non-Hispanic/Latino; 1 Hispanic/Latino; 5 Two or more races, non-Hispanic/Latino), 9 international. Average age 28. 254 applicants, 7% accepted, 16 enrolled. In 2016, 15 master's, 10 doctorates awarded. *Degree requirements:* For master's, thesis; for doctorate, variable foreign language requirement, thesis/dissertation. *Entrance requirements:* For master's and doctorate, GRE General Test, GRE Subject Test. Additional exam requirements/recommendations for international students: Required—TOEFL (minimum score 550 paper-based; 79 iBT), IELTS (minimum score 6.5). *Application deadline:* For fall admission, 1/1 priority date for domestic students; for spring admission, 9/1 for domestic students. Applications are processed on a rolling basis. Application fee: $56 ($96 for international students). Electronic applications accepted. *Financial support:* In 2016–17, 8 fellowships, 6 research assistantships, 46 teaching assistantships were awarded; career-related internships or fieldwork, unspecified assistantships, and project assistantships also available. Support available to part-time students. Financial award application deadline: 4/15; financial award applicants required to submit FAFSA. *Unit head:* Douglas Woods, Department Chair, 414-229-6636, E-mail: dwoods@uwm.edu. *Application contact:* General Information

## Social Psychology

Contact, 414-229-4982, Fax: 414-229-6967, E-mail: gradschool@uwm.edu. Website: http://www.uwm.edu/dept/psychology/

**University of Wisconsin–Milwaukee,** Graduate School, School of Education, Department of Educational Psychology, Milwaukee, WI 53201-0413. Offers children's mental health for school professionals (Graduate Certificate); community counseling (MS); counseling psychology (PhD); educational statistics and measurement (MS, PhD); learning and development (MS, PhD); multicultural knowledge of mental health practices (Graduate Certificate); school counseling (MS); school counseling (Graduate Certificate); school psychology (MS, PhD, Ed S). *Accreditation:* APA. *Program availability:* Part-time. *Students:* 161 full-time (121 women), 53 part-time (39 women); includes 47 minority (12 Black or African American, non-Hispanic/Latino; 1 American Indian or Alaska Native, non-Hispanic/Latino; 5 Asian, non-Hispanic/Latino; 8 Hispanic/Latino; 1 Native Hawaiian or other Pacific Islander, non-Hispanic/Latino; 20 Two or more races, non-Hispanic/Latino). 6 international. Average age 30. 266 applicants, 45% accepted, 71 enrolled. In 2016, 73 master's, 9 doctorates, 18 other advanced degrees awarded. *Degree requirements:* For master's, comprehensive exam, thesis; for doctorate, thesis/dissertation. *Entrance requirements:* For master's, minimum GPA of 3.0; for doctorate, GRE General Test, minimum GPA of 3.0. Additional exam requirements/recommendations for international students: Required—TOEFL (minimum score 550 paper-based; 79 iBT), IELTS (minimum score 6.5). *Application deadline:* For fall admission, 1/1 priority date for domestic students; for spring admission, 9/1 for domestic students. Applications are processed on a rolling basis. Application fee: $56 ($96 for international students). Electronic applications accepted. *Financial support:* In 2016–17, 14 fellowships, 1 research assistantship, 8 teaching assistantships were awarded; career-related internships or fieldwork, health care benefits, unspecified assistantships, and project assistantships also available. Support available to part-time students. Financial award application deadline: 4/15; financial award applicants required to submit FAFSA. *Application contact:* General Information Contact, 414-229-4721, E-mail: soeinfo@uwm.edu.
Website: http://www.uwm.edu/education/academics/educational-psychology-department/

**University of Wisconsin–Superior,** Graduate Division, Department of Counseling and Psychological Professions, Superior, WI 54880-4500. Offers community counseling (MSE); human relations (MSE); school counseling (MSE). *Program availability:* Part-time, evening/weekend. *Degree requirements:* For master's, position paper, practicum. *Entrance requirements:* For master's, GRE and/or MAT, minimum GPA of 2.75. Electronic applications accepted. *Faculty research:* Women and power, intrafamily dynamics.

**Walden University,** Graduate Programs, School of Psychology, Minneapolis, MN 55401. Offers clinical psychology (MS), including counseling, general program; forensic psychology (MS), including forensic psychology in the community, general program, mental health applications, program planning and evaluation in forensic settings, psychology and legal systems; industrial organizational (MS, PhD), including consulting psychology, forensic (MS), forensic psychology (PhD), general practice, leadership development and coaching (MS), organizational diversity and social change, research evaluation (PhD); online teaching in psychology (Post-Master's Certificate); organizational psychology and development (Postbaccalaureate Certificate); psychology (MS, PhD), including applied psychology (MS), clinical psychology (PhD), crisis management and response (MS), educational psychology, forensic psychology (PhD), general psychology (MS), general psychology research (PhD), general psychology teaching (PhD), health psychology, leadership development and coaching (MS), psychology of culture (MS), psychology, public administration, and social change (MS), social psychology, terrorism and security (MS); psychology respecialization (Post-Doctoral Certificate). *Program availability:* Part-time, evening/weekend, online only, 100% online. Terminal master's awarded for partial completion of doctoral program. *Degree requirements:* For master's, thesis optional; for doctorate, thesis/dissertation, residency. *Entrance requirements:* For master's, bachelor's degree or higher; minimum GPA of 2.5; official transcripts; goal statement (for some programs); access to computer and Internet; for doctorate, master's degree or higher; three years of related professional or academic experience (preferred); minimum GPA of 3.0; goal statement and current resume (for select programs); official transcripts; access to computer and Internet; for other advanced degree, relevant work experience; access to computer and Internet. Additional exam requirements/recommendations for international students: Required—TOEFL (minimum score 550 paper-based, 79 iBT), IELTS (minimum score 6.5), Michigan English Language Assessment Battery (minimum score 82), or PTE (minimum score 53). Electronic applications accepted.

**Wayne State University,** College of Liberal Arts and Sciences, Department of Psychology, Detroit, MI 48202. Offers behavioral and cognitive neuroscience (PhD); clinical psychology (PhD); cognitive, developmental and social psychology (PhD); industrial/organizational psychology (MA, PhD). Doctoral program admits for fall only. *Accreditation:* APA (one or more programs are accredited). *Faculty:* 36. *Students:* 98 full-time (65 women), 31 part-time (16 women); includes 19 minority (4 Black or African American, non-Hispanic/Latino; 2 Asian, non-Hispanic/Latino; 8 Hispanic/Latino; 5 Two or more races, non-Hispanic/Latino), 14 international. Average age 28. 478 applicants, 13% accepted, 33 enrolled. In 2016, 16 master's, 13 doctorates awarded. Terminal master's awarded for partial completion of doctoral program. *Degree requirements:* For master's, thesis (for some programs); for doctorate, thesis/dissertation, training assignments. *Entrance requirements:* For master's, GRE General Test, minimum undergraduate upper-division cumulative GPA of 3.0, courses in introductory psychology and statistics, two letters of recommendation, professional statement; for doctorate, GRE General Test, bachelor's, master's, or other advanced degree; at least twelve credits in psychology with minimum GPA of 3.0; courses in laboratory psychology and statistical methods in psychology; at least three letters of recommendation; statement of purpose. Additional exam requirements/recommendations for international students: Required—TOEFL (minimum score 550 paper-based; 79 iBT), TWE (minimum score 5.5), Michigan English Language Assessment Battery (minimum score 85); Recommended—IELTS (minimum score 6.5). Application fee: $50. Electronic applications accepted. *Expenses:* $16,503 per year resident tuition and fees, $33,697 per year non-resident tuition and fees. *Financial support:* In 2016–17, 90 students received support, including 12 fellowships with tuition reimbursements available (averaging $15,719 per year), 6 research assistantships with tuition reimbursements available (averaging $19,341 per year), 50 teaching assistantships with tuition reimbursements available (averaging $17,994 per year); scholarships/grants, health care benefits, and unspecified assistantships also available. Financial award applicants required to submit FAFSA. *Faculty research:* Behavioral neuroscience, cognitive/neuroscience of development and aging research, children, adolescents, and family research, cognition research, emotion research, health psychology research, homelessness and poverty research, memory research, neuropsychology research, personality/cognition, relationships research, substance use and abuse research, workplace adaptation, well-being and evaluation research. *Total annual research expenditures:* $1.4 million. *Unit head:* Boris Baltes, PhD, Chair/Professor, 313-577-2803, E-mail: b.baltes@wayne.edu. *Application contact:* Alia Allen, Academic Services Officer, 313-577-2823, E-mail: aallen@wayne.edu.
Website: http://clas.wayne.edu/psychology/

**Western Illinois University,** School of Graduate Studies, College of Arts and Sciences, Department of Psychology, Macomb, IL 61455-1390. Offers clinical/community mental health (MS); general experimental psychology (MS); school psychology (SSP). *Program availability:* Part-time. *Students:* 37 full-time (22 women), 15 part-time (13 women); includes 6 minority (1 Black or African American, non-Hispanic/Latino; 2 Hispanic/Latino; 3 Two or more races, non-Hispanic/Latino), 2 international. Average age 25. 66 applicants, 52% accepted, 14 enrolled. In 2016, 11 master's, 7 other advanced degrees awarded. *Degree requirements:* For master's, comprehensive exam (for some programs), thesis or alternative. *Entrance requirements:* For master's and SSP, GRE General Test. Additional exam requirements/recommendations for international students: Required—TOEFL (minimum score 550 paper-based; 80 iBT). Application fee: $30. Electronic applications accepted. *Financial support:* In 2016–17, 34 students received support, including 6 research assistantships with full tuition reimbursements available (averaging $7,544 per year); unspecified assistantships also available. Financial award applicants required to submit FAFSA. *Unit head:* Dr. Karen Sears, Chairperson, 309-298-1593. *Application contact:* Dr. Nancy Parsons, Associate Provost and Director of Graduate Studies, 309-298-1806, Fax: 309-298-2345, E-mail: grad-office@wiu.edu.
Website: http://wiu.edu/psychology

**Wichita State University,** Graduate School, Fairmount College of Liberal Arts and Sciences, Department of Psychology, Wichita, KS 67260. Offers clinical (PhD); community (PhD); human factors (PhD). *Accreditation:* APA. *Program availability:* Part-time. *Application deadline:* For fall admission, 12/1 for domestic and international students. Application fee: $50 ($65 for international students). *Unit head:* Dr. Rhonda K. Lewis, Chair, 316-978-3170, Fax: 316-978-3006, E-mail: rhonda.lewis@wichita.edu. *Application contact:* Jordan Oleson, Admissions Coordinator, 316-978-3095, Fax: 316-978-3253, E-mail: jordan.oleson@wichita.edu.
Website: http://www.wichita.edu/psychology

**Wilfrid Laurier University,** Faculty of Graduate and Postdoctoral Studies, Faculty of Science, Department of Psychology, Waterloo, ON N2L 3C5, Canada. Offers behavioral neuroscience (M Sc, PhD); cognitive neuroscience (M Sc, PhD); community psychology (MA, PhD); social and developmental psychology (MA, PhD). *Program availability:* Part-time. *Degree requirements:* For master's, thesis; for doctorate, thesis/dissertation. *Entrance requirements:* For master's, GRE General Test, honors BA or the equivalent in psychology, minimum B average in undergraduate course work; for doctorate, GRE General Test, master's degree, minimum A- average. Additional exam requirements/recommendations for international students: Required—TOEFL (minimum score 89 iBT). Electronic applications accepted. *Faculty research:* Brain and cognition, community psychology, social and developmental psychology.

**Yale University,** Graduate School of Arts and Sciences, Department of Psychology, New Haven, CT 06520. Offers behavioral neuroscience (PhD); clinical psychology (PhD); cognitive psychology (PhD); developmental psychology (PhD); social/personality psychology (PhD). *Accreditation:* APA. *Degree requirements:* For doctorate, thesis/dissertation. *Entrance requirements:* For doctorate, GRE General Test.

# Sport Psychology

**Adler University,** Programs in Psychology, Chicago, IL 60602. Offers advanced Adlerian psychotherapy (Certificate); art therapy (MA); clinical mental health counseling (MA); clinical neuropsychology (Certificate); clinical psychology (Psy D); community psychology (MA); counseling and organizational psychology (MA); counseling psychology (MA); counselor education and supervision (PhD); couple and family therapy (DCFT); criminology (MA); emergency management leadership (MA); forensic psychology (MA); marriage and family counseling (MA); marriage and family therapy (Certificate); military psychology (MA); nonprofit management (MA); organizational psychology (MA); police psychology (MA); public policy and administration (MA); rehabilitation counseling (MA); sport and health psychology (MA); substance abuse counseling (Certificate); Psy D/Certificate; Psy D/MACAT; Psy D/MACP; Psy D/MAMFC; Psy D/MASAC. *Accreditation:* APA. *Program availability:* Part-time, evening/weekend, online learning. Terminal master's awarded for partial completion of doctoral program. *Degree requirements:* For master's, thesis or alternative, oral exam, practicum; for doctorate, thesis/dissertation, clinical exam, internship, oral exam, practicum, written qualifying exam. *Entrance requirements:* For master's, 12 semester hours in psychology, minimum GPA of 3.0; for doctorate, 18 semester hours in psychology, minimum GPA of 3.25; for Certificate, appropriate master's or doctoral degree. Additional exam requirements/recommendations for international students: Required—TOEFL (minimum score 550 paper-based; 79 iBT). Electronic applications accepted.

See Display on page 982 and Close-Up on page 1225.

**Argosy University, Atlanta,** Georgia School of Professional Psychology, Atlanta, GA 30328. Offers clinical psychology (MA, Psy D, Postdoctoral Respecialization Certificate), including child and family psychology (Psy D), general adult clinical (Psy D), health psychology (Psy D), neuropsychology/geropsychology (Psy D); community counseling (MA), including marriage and family therapy; counselor education and supervision (Ed D); forensic psychology (MA); industrial organizational psychology (MA); marriage and family therapy (Certificate); sport-exercise psychology (MA). *Accreditation:* APA.

**Argosy University, Inland Empire,** College of Psychology and Behavioral Sciences, Ontario, CA 91761. Offers clinical psychology/marriage and family therapy (MA); counseling psychology (Ed D); counseling psychology/marriage and family therapy (MA); forensic psychology (MA); industrial organizational psychology (MA); sport-exercise psychology (MA).

**Argosy University, Orange County,** American School of Professional Psychology, Program in Sport-Exercise Psychology, Orange, CA 92868. Offers MA.

**Argosy University, Phoenix,** Arizona School of Professional Psychology, Program in Clinical Psychology, Phoenix, AZ 85021. Offers clinical psychology (MA); neuropsychology (Psy D); sports-exercise psychology (Psy D).

**Argosy University, Phoenix,** Arizona School of Professional Psychology, Program in Sport–Exercise Psychology, Phoenix, AZ 85021. Offers MA.

**Argosy University, San Francisco Bay Area,** American School of Professional Psychology, Alameda, CA 94501. Offers clinical psychology (MA, Psy D); counseling psychology (MA, Ed D); forensic psychology (MA); sport-exercise psychology (MA). *Accreditation:* APA (one or more programs are accredited).

**Argosy University, Schaumburg,** College of Behavioral Sciences, Schaumburg, IL 60173-5403. Offers clinical mental health counseling (MA); forensic psychology (MA, Post-Graduate Certificate); industrial organizational psychology (MA); sport-exercise psychology (MA). *Accreditation:* ACA; APA.

**A.T. Still University,** College of Graduate Health Studies, Kirksville, MO 63501. Offers dental public health (MPH); exercise and sport psychology (Certificate); fundamentals of education (Certificate); geriatric exercise science (Certificate); global health (Certificate); health administration (MHA, DHA); health professions (Ed D); health sciences (DH Sc); kinesiology (MS); leadership and organizational behavior (Certificate); public health (MPH); sports conditioning (Certificate). *Program availability:* Part-time, online only, 100% online, blended/hybrid learning. *Faculty:* 29 full-time (18 women), 89 part-time/adjunct (46 women). *Students:* 505 full-time (319 women), 461 part-time (276 women); includes 337 minority (151 Black or African American, non-Hispanic/Latino; 19 American Indian or Alaska Native, non-Hispanic/Latino; 70 Asian, non-Hispanic/Latino; 89 Hispanic/Latino; 1 Native Hawaiian or other Pacific Islander, non-Hispanic/Latino; 7 Two or more races, non-Hispanic/Latino), 29 international. Average age 37. 366 applicants, 98% accepted, 370 enrolled. In 2016, 113 master's, 94 doctorates, 110 other advanced degrees awarded. *Degree requirements:* For master's, thesis, integrated terminal project, practicum; for doctorate, thesis/dissertation. *Entrance requirements:* For master's, minimum GPA of 2.5, bachelor's degree or equivalent, background check, essay, three references; for doctorate, minimum GPA of 2.5, master's or terminal degree, background check, essay, three references, past experience in relevant field. Additional exam requirements/recommendations for international students: Required—TOEFL (minimum score 550 paper-based; 80 iBT). *Application deadline:* For fall admission, 5/20 for domestic and international students; for winter admission, 9/12 for domestic and international students; for spring admission, 12/12 for domestic and international students; for summer admission, 3/6 for domestic and international students. Applications are processed on a rolling basis. Application fee: $70. Electronic applications accepted. Application fee is waived when completed online. *Expenses:* Contact institution. *Financial support:* Scholarships/grants available. Financial award applicants required to submit FAFSA. *Faculty research:* Public health: influence of availability of comprehensive wellness resources online, student wellness, oral health care needs assessment of community, oral health knowledge and behaviors of Medicaid-eligible pregnant women and mothers of young children in relations to early childhood caries and tooth decay, alcohol use and alcohol related problems among college students. *Unit head:* Dr. Donald Altman, Dean, 660-626-2820, Fax: 660-626-2826, E-mail: daltman@atsu.edu. *Application contact:* Amie Waldemer, Associate Director, Online Admissions, 480-219-6146, E-mail: awaldemer@atsu.edu. Website: http://www.atsu.edu/college-of-graduate-health-studies

**Ball State University,** Graduate School, College of Applied Sciences and Technology, School of Kinesiology, Program in Physical Education and Sport, Muncie, IN 47306. Offers physical education and sport (MA, MS), including athletic coaching education, sport administration, sport and exercise psychology. *Program availability:* Part-time, 100% online. *Entrance requirements:* For master's, GRE General Test, minimum baccalaureate GPA of 2.75 or 3.0 in latter half of baccalaureate, curriculum vitae, three letters of recommendation; campus visit to meet faculty and see facilities (strongly encouraged). Additional exam requirements/recommendations for international students: Required—TOEFL (minimum score 550 paper-based; 79 iBT), IELTS (minimum score 6.5). Electronic applications accepted.

**Barry University,** School of Human Performance and Leisure Sciences, Programs in Movement Science, Specialization in Sport and Exercise Psychology, Miami Shores, FL 33161-6695. Offers MS. *Entrance requirements:* For master's, GRE.

**California State University, Fresno,** Division of Research and Graduate Studies, College of Health and Human Services, Department of Kinesiology, Fresno, CA 93740-8027. Offers exercise science (MA); general kinesiology (MA); sport administration (MA); sport psychology (MA). *Program availability:* Part-time, evening/weekend. *Degree requirements:* For master's, thesis or alternative. *Entrance requirements:* For master's, GRE General Test, minimum GPA of 2.7. Additional exam requirements/recommendations for international students: Required—TOEFL. *Application deadline:* For fall admission, 5/1 for domestic and international students; for spring admission, 10/1 for domestic and international students. Applications are processed on a rolling basis. Application fee: $55. Electronic applications accepted. *Financial support:* Teaching assistantships, career-related internships or fieldwork, Federal Work-Study, and scholarships/grants available. Support available to part-time students. Financial award application deadline: 3/1; financial award applicants required to submit FAFSA. *Faculty research:* Refugee education, homeless, geriatrics, fitness. *Unit head:* Dr. Tim Anderson, Chair, 559-278-2203, Fax: 559-278-7010, E-mail: tima@csufresno.edu. *Application contact:* Dr. Jenelle Gilbert, Coordinator, 559-278-8902, Fax: 559-278-7010, E-mail: jgilbert@csufresno.edu. Website: http://www.fresnostate.edu/chhs/kinesiology/

**California State University, Long Beach,** Graduate Studies, College of Health and Human Services, Department of Kinesiology, Long Beach, CA 90840. Offers adapted physical education (MA); coaching and student athlete development (MA); exercise physiology and nutrition (MS); exercise science (MS); individualized studies (MA); kinesiology (MA); pedagogical studies (MA); sport and exercise psychology (MS); sport management (MA); sports medicine and injury studies (MS). *Program availability:* Part-time. *Degree requirements:* For master's, oral and written comprehensive exams or thesis. *Entrance requirements:* For master's, GRE General Test, minimum GPA of 2.75 during previous 2 years of course work. *Application deadline:* For fall admission, 6/1 for domestic students. Applications are processed on a rolling basis. Application fee: $55. Electronic applications accepted. *Financial support:* Federal Work-Study, institutionally sponsored loans, and scholarships/grants available. Financial award application deadline: 3/2. *Faculty research:* Pulmonary functioning, feedback and practice structure, strength training, history and politics of sports, special population research issues. *Unit head:* Jan Schroeder, Chair, 562-985-4051.

**California University of Pennsylvania,** School of Graduate Studies and Research, College of Education and Human Services, Program in Exercise Science and Health Promotion, California, PA 15419-1394. Offers performance enhancement and injury prevention (MS); rehabilitation science (MS); sport psychology (MS); wellness and fitness (MS). *Program availability:* Part-time, evening/weekend, online learning. *Degree requirements:* For master's, comprehensive exam, thesis optional. *Entrance requirements:* For master's, minimum GPA of 3.0. Additional exam requirements/recommendations for international students: Required—TOEFL (minimum score 550

paper-based; 80 iBT). Electronic applications accepted. *Expenses:* Contact institution. *Faculty research:* Reducing obesity in children, sport performance, creating unique biomechanical assessment techniques, web-based training for fitness professionals, webcams.

**Capella University,** Harold Abel School of Social and Behavioral Science, Master's Programs in Psychology, Minneapolis, MN 55402. Offers applied behavior analysis (MS); clinical psychology (MS); counseling psychology (MS); educational psychology (MS); evaluation, research, and measurement (MS); general advanced studies in human behavior (MS); general psychology (MS); industrial/organizational psychology (MS); leadership coaching psychology (MS); school psychology (MS); sport psychology (MS).

**Chatham University,** Program in Counseling Psychology, Pittsburgh, PA 15232-2826. Offers child, adolescent and family (MSCP); counseling psychology (Psy D); health and holistic (MSCP); infant mental health (MSCP); organization and supervision (MSCP); sport and exercise (MSCP). *Accreditation:* APA. *Program availability:* Part-time, evening/weekend. *Degree requirements:* For master's, thesis optional, supervised internship; for doctorate, thesis/dissertation, internship. *Entrance requirements:* For master's, minimum GPA of 3.0; 2 letters of recommendation; resume; prerequisite coursework in statistics, biology, and psychology; for doctorate, GRE. Additional exam requirements/recommendations for international students: Required—TOEFL (minimum score 600 paper-based; 100 iBT), IELTS (minimum score 7), TWE. Electronic applications accepted. Application fee is waived when completed online. *Expenses:* Tuition: Full-time $16,254; part-time $903 per credit hour. *Required fees:* $468; $26 per credit hour. *Faculty research:* Trauma and recovery, hypnosis, psychospiritual dimensions of healing, psychotherapy of schizophrenia.

**Florida State University,** The Graduate School, College of Education, Program in Educational Psychology, Tallahassee, FL 32306. Offers learning and cognition (MS, PhD); sport psychology (MS, PhD). Terminal master's awarded for partial completion of doctoral program. *Degree requirements:* For master's, comprehensive exam, thesis optional; for doctorate, comprehensive exam, thesis/dissertation, diagnostic exam, preliminary exam, prospectus defense, dissertation defense. *Entrance requirements:* For master's and doctorate, GRE General Test, minimum upper-division GPA of 3.0. Additional exam requirements/recommendations for international students: Required—TOEFL (minimum score 550 paper-based, 80 iBT), IELTS (minimum score 6.5), Michigan English Language Assessment Battery (minimum score 77), or PTE (minimum score 55). Application fee: $30. Electronic applications accepted. *Expenses:* Tuition, state resident: full-time $7263; part-time $403.51 per credit hour. Tuition, nonresident: full-time $18,087; part-time $1004.85 per credit hour. *Required fees:* $1365; $75.81 per credit hour. $20 per semester. Tuition and fees vary according to campus/location. *Financial support:* Fellowships, research assistantships, teaching assistantships, scholarships/grants, tuition waivers (full and partial), and unspecified assistantships available. Financial award application deadline: 1/15; financial award applicants required to submit FAFSA. *Faculty research:* Motivation/emotion/cognition/critical thinking; human performance, adult learning, teacher quality; language/literacy development and instruction; evaluation of evidence-based interventions; well-being of underrepresented, high-need groups. *Unit head:* Dr. Betsy Becker, Professor/Department Chair, 850-644-2371, Fax: 850-644-8776, E-mail: bbecker@fsu.edu. *Application contact:* Eileen Sirois, Academic Program Assistant, 850-644-8786, Fax: 850-644-8776, E-mail: esirois@fsu.edu. Website: http://education.fsu.edu/degrees-and-programs/graduate-programs

**John F. Kennedy University,** Graduate School of Professional Psychology, Program in Sport Psychology, Pleasant Hill, CA 94523-4817. Offers MA. *Program availability:* Part-time, evening/weekend. *Degree requirements:* For master's, thesis or alternative. *Entrance requirements:* For master's, interview. Additional exam requirements/recommendations for international students: Required—TOEFL.

**Lock Haven University of Pennsylvania,** The Stephen Poorman College of Business, Information Systems, and Human Services, Lock Haven, PA 17745-2390. Offers clinical mental health counseling (MS); sport science (MS). *Program availability:* Online learning. *Degree requirements:* For master's, thesis. *Entrance requirements:* For master's, minimum undergraduate GPA of 3.0. Additional exam requirements/recommendations for international students: Required—TOEFL. Electronic applications accepted.

**Purdue University,** Graduate School, College of Health and Human Sciences, Department of Health and Kinesiology, West Lafayette, IN 47907. Offers athletic training education administration (MS, PhD); biomechanics (MS, PhD); exercise physiology (MS, PhD); health education (MS, PhD); history/philosophy of sport (MS, PhD); motor control and development (MS, PhD); physical education pedagogy (PhD); physical education teacher education (MS); recreation and sport management (MS, PhD); sport and exercise psychology (MS, PhD). *Program availability:* Part-time. *Faculty:* 19 full-time (7 women). *Students:* 30 full-time (13 women), 10 part-time (5 women); includes 2 minority (1 Asian, non-Hispanic/Latino; 1 Two or more races, non-Hispanic/Latino), 6 international. Average age 26. 77 applicants, 29% accepted, 18 enrolled. In 2016, 18 master's, 9 doctorates awarded. *Degree requirements:* For master's, thesis optional; for doctorate, comprehensive exam, thesis/dissertation, qualifying examination, preliminary examination. *Entrance requirements:* For master's, GRE General Test (minimum score 1000 combined verbal and quantitative), minimum undergraduate GPA of 3.0 or equivalent; for doctorate, GRE General Test (minimum score 1100 combined verbal and quantitative), minimum undergraduate GPA of 3.0 or equivalent; master's degree with minimum GPA of 3.25 (recommended). Additional exam requirements/recommendations for international students: Required—TOEFL (minimum score 77 iBT); Recommended—TWE. *Application deadline:* For fall admission, 4/30 for domestic and international students; for spring admission, 10/15 for domestic and international students. Applications are processed on a rolling basis. Application fee: $60 ($75 for international students). Electronic applications accepted. *Financial support:* Fellowships with partial tuition reimbursements, research assistantships with partial tuition reimbursements, teaching assistantships with partial tuition reimbursements, and Federal Work-Study available. Support available to part-time students. Financial award applicants required to submit FAFSA. *Faculty research:* Wellness, motivation, teaching effectiveness, learning and development. *Unit head:* Dr. Timothy P. Gavin, Head of the Graduate Program, 765-494-3178, Fax: 765-494-1239, E-mail: gavin1@purdue.edu. *Application contact:* Christy F. Daugherty, Graduate Contact, 765-494-3162, E-mail: daugher2@purdue.edu. Website: http://www.purdue.edu/hhs/hk/

**Queen's University at Kingston,** School of Graduate Studies, School of Kinesiology and Health Studies, Kingston, ON K7L 3N6, Canada. Offers applied exercise science (PhD); biomechanics/ergonomics (M Sc); exercise physiology (M Sc); social psychology of sport and exercise rehabilitation (MA); sociology of sport (MA). *Program availability:* Part-time. *Degree requirements:* For master's, thesis (for some programs); for doctorate, comprehensive exam, thesis/dissertation. *Entrance requirements:* For master's and doctorate, minimum B+ average. Additional exam requirements/recommendations for international students: Required—TOEFL. Electronic applications accepted. *Faculty research:* Expert performance ergonomics, obesity research, pregnancy and exercise, gender and sport participation.

## Sport Psychology

**Seton Hall University,** College of Education and Human Services, Department of Professional Psychology and Family Therapy, Program in Psychological Studies, South Orange, NJ 07079-2697. Offers individualized (MA); marriage and family therapy (MA); sport and exercise psychology (MA). *Program availability:* Part-time, evening/weekend. *Faculty:* 5 full-time (3 women). *Students:* 19 full-time (18 women), 17 part-time (14 women); includes 13 minority (4 Black or African American, non-Hispanic/Latino; 3 Asian, non-Hispanic/Latino; 6 Hispanic/Latino), 3 international. Average age 29. 35 applicants, 66% accepted, 9 enrolled. In 2016, 7 master's awarded. *Degree requirements:* For master's, comprehensive exam. *Entrance requirements:* For master's, GRE or MAT. *Application deadline:* Applications are processed on a rolling basis. Application fee: $75. *Financial support:* Application deadline: 2/1. *Faculty research:* Cognitive style, self-esteem anxiety in preadolescence, object relation, bonding. *Unit head:* Dr. Sandra Lee, Director, 973-275-2734, E-mail: sandra.lee@shu.edu. *Application contact:* Diana Minakakis, Director of Graduate Admissions, 973-275-2824, Fax: 973-275-2187, E-mail: diana.minakakis@shu.edu.

**Southern Illinois University Edwardsville,** Graduate School, School of Education, Health, and Human Behavior, Department of Kinesiology and Health Education, Program in Exercise and Sport Psychology, Edwardsville, IL 62026. Offers MS. *Program availability:* Part-time, evening/weekend. *Degree requirements:* For master's, comprehensive exam (for some programs), thesis (for some programs). *Entrance requirements:* Additional exam requirements/recommendations for international students: Required—TOEFL (minimum score 550 paper-based, 79 iBT), IELTS (minimum score 6.5), Michigan Test of English Language Proficiency or PTE. Electronic applications accepted.

**Springfield College,** Graduate Programs, Programs in Exercise Science and Sport Studies, Springfield, MA 01109-3797. Offers athletic training (MS); exercise physiology (MS); health promotion and disease prevention (MS); sport and exercise psychology (MS). *Program availability:* Part-time. Terminal master's awarded for partial completion of doctoral program. *Degree requirements:* For master's, comprehensive exam, research project or thesis; for doctorate, comprehensive exam, thesis/dissertation. *Entrance requirements:* For master's and doctorate, GRE General Test. Additional exam requirements/recommendations for international students: Required—TOEFL (minimum score 550 paper-based); Recommended—IELTS (minimum score 6). Electronic applications accepted. *Expenses: Tuition:* Full-time $29,640; part-time $988 per credit. *Required fees:* $195.

**Springfield College,** Graduate Programs, Programs in Psychology, Springfield, MA 01109-3797. Offers athletic counseling (MS, CAGS); clinical mental health counseling (M Ed, CAGS); counseling psychology (Psy D); industrial and organizational psychology (M Ed, CAGS); school guidance counseling (M Ed, CAGS); student personnel administration in higher education (M Ed). *Accreditation:* APA. *Program availability:* Part-time. *Degree requirements:* For master's, research project, portfolio; for doctorate, dissertation project, 1500 hours of counseling psychology practicum, full-year internship. *Entrance requirements:* Additional exam requirements/recommendations for international students: Required—TOEFL (minimum score 550 paper-based). Electronic applications accepted. *Expenses: Tuition:* Full-time $29,640; part-time $988 per credit. *Required fees:* $195.

**University of Denver,** Graduate School of Professional Psychology, Denver, CO 80208. Offers clinical psychology (Psy D); forensic psychology (MA); international disaster psychology (MA); sport and performance psychology (MA); sport coaching (MA). *Accreditation:* APA. *Faculty:* 23 full-time (13 women), 25 part-time/adjunct (14 women). *Students:* 230 full-time (187 women), 72 part-time (46 women); includes 69 minority (16 Black or African American, non-Hispanic/Latino; 1 American Indian or Alaska Native, non-Hispanic/Latino; 9 Asian, non-Hispanic/Latino; 29 Hispanic/Latino; 1 Native Hawaiian or other Pacific Islander, non-Hispanic/Latino; 13 Two or more races, non-Hispanic/Latino), 14 international. Average age 27. 800 applicants, 30% accepted, 129 enrolled. In 2016, 80 master's, 38 doctorates awarded. *Degree requirements:* For master's, comprehensive exam (for some programs); for doctorate, comprehensive exam (for some programs), paper, clinical internship. *Entrance requirements:* For master's and doctorate, GRE General Test, transcripts, resume, two letters of recommendation, essay. Additional exam requirements/recommendations for international students: Required—TOEFL (minimum score 550 paper-based; 80 iBT). *Application deadline:* For fall admission, 1/5 for domestic and international students. Application fee: $65. Electronic applications accepted. *Expenses:* $43,358 per year full-time. *Financial support:* In 2016–17, 124 students received support, including 15 teaching assistantships with tuition reimbursements available (averaging $2,708 per year); career-related internships or fieldwork, Federal Work-Study, institutionally sponsored loans, scholarships/grants, unspecified assistantships, and clinical assistantships also available. Support available to part-time students. Financial award application deadline: 2/15; financial award applicants required to submit FAFSA. *Unit head:* Dr. Shelly Smith-Acuna, Dean, 303-871-3880, Fax: 303-871-4220, E-mail: shelly.smith-acuna@du.edu. *Application contact:* Admissions Counselor, 303-871-3736, Fax: 303-871-4220, E-mail: gsppinfo@du.edu. Website: http://www.du.edu/gspp

**University of Northern Colorado,** Graduate School, College of Natural and Health Sciences, School of Sport and Exercise Science, Greeley, CO 80639. Offers biomechanics (PhD); exercise physiology (PhD); exercise science (MS); social psychology of sport and physical activity (PhD); sport administration (MS, PhD); sport pedagogy (MS, PhD). *Program availability:* Part-time, evening/weekend. *Degree requirements:* For master's, comprehensive exam; for doctorate, comprehensive exam, thesis/dissertation. *Entrance requirements:* For master's, 2 letters of recommendation, resume; for doctorate, GRE General Test, 3 letters of recommendation, resume. *Application deadline:* Applications are processed on a rolling basis. Application fee: $50 ($60 for international students). Electronic applications accepted. *Financial support:* Fellowships, research assistantships, teaching assistantships, and unspecified assistantships available. Financial award application deadline: 3/1; financial award applicants required to submit FAFSA. *Unit head:* Dr. David Stotlar, Director, 970-351-2535, Fax: 970-351-1762. *Application contact:* Linda Sisson, Graduate Student Admission Coordinator, 970-351-1807, Fax: 970-351-2371, E-mail: linda.sisson@unco.edu. Website: http://www.unco.edu/nhs/ses/

**University of Rhode Island,** Graduate School, College of Health Sciences, Department of Kinesiology, Kingston, RI 02881. Offers cultural studies of sport and physical culture (MS); exercise science (MS); psychosocial/behavioral aspects of physical activity (MS). *Accreditation:* NCATE. *Program availability:* Part-time. *Faculty:* 15 full-time (9 women). *Students:* 16 full-time (9 women), 8 part-time (5 women); includes 4 minority (1 Black or African American, non-Hispanic/Latino; 1 Asian, non-Hispanic/Latino; 2 Hispanic/Latino). In 2016, 8 master's awarded. *Degree requirements:* For master's, thesis optional. *Entrance requirements:* For master's, GRE, 2 letters of recommendation. Additional exam requirements/recommendations for international students: Required—TOEFL. *Application deadline:* For fall admission, 7/15 for domestic students, 2/1 for international students; for spring admission, 11/15 for domestic students, 7/15 for international students. Application fee: $65. Electronic applications accepted. *Expenses:* Tuition, state resident: full-time $11,796; part-time $655 per credit. Tuition, nonresident: full-time $24,206; part-time $1345 per credit. *Required fees:* $1546; $44 per credit. One-time fee: $155 full-time; $35 part-time. *Financial support:* In 2016–17, 5 teaching assistantships with tuition reimbursements (averaging $10,740 per year) were awarded; research assistantships also available. Financial award application deadline: 7/15; financial award applicants required to submit FAFSA. *Unit head:* Dr. Disa Hatfield, Interim Chair, 401-874-5183, E-mail: doch@uri.edu. *Application contact:* Dr. Matthew Delmonico, Graduate Program Director, 401-874-5440, E-mail: delmonico@uri.edu. Website: http://web.uri.edu/kinesiology/

**The University of Texas at Austin,** Graduate School, College of Education, Department of Kinesiology and Health Education, Austin, TX 78712-1111. Offers behavioral health (PhD); exercise and sport psychology (M Ed, MA); exercise science (M Ed, MS, PhD); health education (M Ed, MS, Ed D, PhD). *Program availability:* Part-time. Terminal master's awarded for partial completion of doctoral program. *Degree requirements:* For master's, thesis (for some programs); for doctorate, thesis/dissertation. *Entrance requirements:* For master's and doctorate, GRE General Test. Additional exam requirements/recommendations for international students: Required—TOEFL. Electronic applications accepted. *Faculty research:* Health promotion, human performance and exercise biochemistry, motor behavior and biomechanics, sport management, aging and pediatric development.

**West Virginia University,** College of Physical Activity and Sport Sciences, Morgantown, WV 26506-6116. Offers athletic training (MS); coaching and sport education (MS); coaching and teaching studies (Ed D); physical education/teacher education (MS, PhD), including curriculum and instruction (PhD), physical education supervision (PhD); sport and exercise psychology (MS, PhD); sport coaching (MS); sport management (MS). *Degree requirements:* For doctorate, comprehensive exam, thesis/dissertation, oral exam. *Entrance requirements:* For master's, GRE or MAT, minimum GPA of 3.0; for doctorate, GRE General Test or MAT, minimum GPA of 3.5. Additional exam requirements/recommendations for international students: Required—TOEFL (minimum score 550 paper-based). Electronic applications accepted. *Faculty research:* Sport psychosociology, teacher education, exercise psychology, counseling.

# Thanatology

**Brooklyn College of the City University of New York,** School of Natural and Behavioral Sciences, Department of Health and Nutrition Sciences, Program in Community Health, Brooklyn, NY 11210-2889. Offers community health education (MA); thanatology (MA). *Accreditation:* CEPH. *Degree requirements:* For master's, thesis or alternative. *Entrance requirements:* For master's, 2 letters of recommendation, essay. Additional exam requirements/recommendations for international students: Required—TOEFL. Electronic applications accepted. *Faculty research:* Diet restriction, religious practices in bereavement, diabetes, stress management, palliative care.

**The College of New Rochelle,** Graduate School, Division of Human Services, Program in Mental Health Counseling, New Rochelle, NY 10805-2308. Offers mental health counseling (MS); thanatology (Certificate). *Degree requirements:* For Certificate, internship.

**Marian University,** School of Nursing and Health Professions, Fond du Lac, WI 54935-4699. Offers adult nurse practitioner (MSN); nurse educator (MSN); thanatology (MS). *Accreditation:* AACN. *Program availability:* Part-time, evening/weekend. *Faculty:* 5 full-time (all women), 4 part-time/adjunct (2 women). *Students:* 12 full-time (all women), 107 part-time (94 women); includes 14 minority (7 Black or African American, non-Hispanic/Latino; 4 Asian, non-Hispanic/Latino; 3 Hispanic/Latino). Average age 41. In 2016, 28 master's awarded. *Degree requirements:* For master's, thesis, 675 clinical practicum hours. *Entrance requirements:* For master's, 3 letters of professional recommendation; undergraduate work in nursing research, statistics, health assessment. Additional exam requirements/recommendations for international students: Required—TOEFL (minimum score 525 paper-based; 70 iBT). *Application deadline:* Applications are processed on a rolling basis. Application fee: $50. Electronic applications accepted. *Expenses:* Contact institution. *Financial support:* In 2016–17, 3 students received support. Scholarships/grants available. Support available to part-time students. Financial award application deadline: 3/1; financial award applicants required to submit FAFSA. *Unit head:* Dr. Linda Matheson, Dean, 920-923-7668, Fax: 920-923-8770, E-mail: lkmatheson85@marianuniversity.edu. Website: https://www.marianuniversity.edu/degree/nursing/

**Southwestern College,** Program in Grief, Loss and Trauma Counseling, Santa Fe, NM 87502-4788. Offers MA, Certificate. *Program availability:* Part-time, evening/weekend, online learning. *Entrance requirements:* For master's, interview, references, resume; for Certificate, 3 letters of reference, interview.

**University of Maryland, Baltimore,** Graduate School, Program in Thanatology, Baltimore, MD 21201. Offers Certificate. *Students:* 10 part-time (9 women); includes 2 minority (1 Black or African American, non-Hispanic/Latino; 1 Hispanic/Latino). Average age 48. 15 applicants, 80% accepted, 7 enrolled. In 2016, 2 Certificates awarded. *Entrance requirements:* Additional exam requirements/recommendations for international students: Required—TOEFL (minimum score 80 iBT); Recommended—IELTS (minimum score 7). *Application deadline:* For fall admission, 7/15 for domestic students; for spring admission, 12/1 for domestic students. Applications are processed on a rolling basis. Application fee: $75. Electronic applications accepted. *Expenses:* $566 per credit in-state; $766 per credit out-of-state. *Financial support:* Application deadline: 3/1; applicants required to submit FAFSA. *Unit head:* Dr. Michelle Pearce, Graduate Program Director, 410-706-6164, E-mail: mpearce@som.umaryland.edu. *Application contact:* Jade Grant, Academic Program Specialist, 410-706-7131, Fax: 410-706-3473, E-mail: jgrant@umaryland.edu.

**Washington & Jefferson College,** Graduate and Continuing Studies, Washington, PA 15301. Offers applied health care economics and outcomes management (MS); professional accounting (MAC); professional writing (Graduate Certificate); thanatology (Graduate Certificate).

# Transpersonal and Humanistic Psychology

**Atlantic University,** Program in Transpersonal Psychology, Virginia Beach, VA 23451-2061. Offers applied spirituality (MA); consciousness (MA); creativity (MA); general studies (MA); leadership and conflict transformation (MA). *Program availability:* Part-time, evening/weekend, online learning. *Degree requirements:* For master's, thesis. *Entrance requirements:* For master's, official transcripts, 1000-word essay, interview. Additional exam requirements/recommendations for international students: Required—TOEFL (minimum score 550 paper-based). *Application deadline:* For fall admission, 7/19 for domestic students; for spring admission, 11/16 for domestic students; for summer admission, 3/15 for domestic students. Applications are processed on a rolling basis. Application fee: $50. Electronic applications accepted. *Expenses:* Contact institution. *Application contact:* Rachel Alvidrez, Associate Vice President of Enrollment Management Services, 757-631-8101, Fax: 757-631-8096, E-mail: info@atlanticuniv.edu.
Website: http://www.atlanticuniv.edu/MA_HistoryAndPerspective.html

**California Institute of Integral Studies,** School of Consciousness and Transformation, San Francisco, CA 94103. Offers anthropology and social change (MA, PhD); Asian philosophies and cultures (MA); creative inquiry/interdisciplinary arts (MFA); East-West psychology (MA, PhD); integral and transpersonal psychology (PhD); philosophy and religion (PhD), including ecology, spirituality, and religion, philosophy, cosmology, and consciousness, women's spirituality; theater and performance making (MFA); transformative leadership (MA); transformative studies (PhD); women, gender, spirituality and social justice (MA); writing and consciousness (MFA). *Program availability:* Part-time, evening/weekend, 100% online, blended/hybrid learning. *Students:* 390 full-time (256 women), 121 part-time (84 women); includes 135 minority (39 Black or African American, non-Hispanic/Latino; 2 American Indian or Alaska Native, non-Hispanic/Latino; 22 Asian, non-Hispanic/Latino; 40 Hispanic/Latino; 2 Native Hawaiian or other Pacific Islander, non-Hispanic/Latino; 30 Two or more races, non-Hispanic/Latino), 51 international. Average age 38. 195 applicants, 92% accepted, 124 enrolled. In 2016, 35 master's, 41 doctorates awarded. Terminal master's awarded for partial completion of doctoral program. *Degree requirements:* For master's, thesis optional; for doctorate, comprehensive exam, thesis/dissertation, 1 foreign language (for Asian philosophies and cultures). *Entrance requirements:* For master's, minimum GPA of 3.0, letters of recommendation, writing sample; for doctorate, master's degree, minimum GPA of 3.0, letters of recommendation, writing sample. Additional exam requirements/recommendations for international students: Required—TOEFL. *Application deadline:* For fall admission, 2/1 priority date for domestic and international students; for spring admission, 10/15 priority date for domestic and international students. Applications are processed on a rolling basis. Application fee: $65. Electronic applications accepted. *Expenses: Tuition:* Full-time $19,728; part-time $1098 per semester hour. *Required fees:* $320; $320 per semester hour. *Financial support:* Research assistantships, teaching assistantships, career-related internships or fieldwork, Federal Work-Study, and scholarships/grants available. Support available to part-time students. Financial award application deadline: 4/15; financial award applicants required to submit FAFSA. *Faculty research:* Ecology and sustainability, philosophy and religion, East-West psychology, integrative health, social and cultural anthropology, transformative leadership. *Application contact:* Ellen Durst, Director of Admissions, 415-575-6100, Fax: 415-575-1268, E-mail: admissions@ciis.edu.
Website: http://www.ciis.edu/

**John F. Kennedy University,** Graduate School of Holistic Studies, Department of Counseling Psychology, Program in Counseling Psychology, Pleasant Hill, CA 94523-4817. Offers holistic studies (MA); somatic psychology (MA); transpersonal psychology (MA). *Program availability:* Part-time, evening/weekend. *Degree requirements:* For master's, thesis or alternative. *Entrance requirements:* For master's, interview. Additional exam requirements/recommendations for international students: Required—TOEFL.

**John F. Kennedy University,** Graduate School of Holistic Studies, Department of Integral Studies, Program in Consciousness and Transformative Studies, Pleasant Hill, CA 94523-4817. Offers MA. *Program availability:* Part-time, evening/weekend. *Degree requirements:* For master's, thesis or alternative. *Entrance requirements:* For master's, interview. Additional exam requirements/recommendations for international students: Required—TOEFL.

**Michigan School of Professional Psychology,** MA and Psy D Programs in Clinical Psychology, Farmington Hills, MI 48334. Offers MA, Psy D. *Accreditation:* APA. *Program availability:* Part-time. *Faculty:* 8 full-time (4 women), 13 part-time/adjunct (11 women). *Students:* 84 full-time (66 women), 56 part-time (46 women); includes 42 minority (29 Black or African American, non-Hispanic/Latino; 2 Asian, non-Hispanic/Latino; 5 Hispanic/Latino; 6 Two or more races, non-Hispanic/Latino), 1 international. Average age 34. 155 applicants, 54% accepted, 61 enrolled. In 2016, 42 master's, 17 doctorates awarded. *Degree requirements:* For master's, practicum; for doctorate, comprehensive exam, thesis/dissertation, internship, practicum. *Entrance requirements:* For master's, undergraduate degree from accredited institution with minimum GPA of 2.5; major in psychology, social work, or counseling; for doctorate, GRE General Test, undergraduate degree from accredited institution with minimum GPA of 2.5; graduate degree in psychology, social work, or counseling from accredited institution with minimum GPA of 3.25; graduate-level practicum. Additional exam requirements/recommendations for international students: Required—TOEFL (minimum score 550 paper-based). *Application deadline:* For fall admission, 8/15 for domestic students; for winter admission, 12/1 for domestic students; for spring admission, 4/3 for domestic students. Applications are processed on a rolling basis. Application fee: $75. Electronic applications accepted. *Expenses:* Contact institution. *Financial support:* In 2016–17, 6 students received support, including 1 research assistantship, 5 teaching assistantships (averaging $14,436 per year); institutionally sponsored loans, scholarships/grants, and unspecified assistantships also available. Financial award application deadline: 8/30; financial award applicants required to submit FAFSA. *Faculty research:* Health psychology, trauma. *Unit head:* Dr. Frances Brown, Program Director, 248-476-1122, Fax: 248-476-1125. *Application contact:* Carrie Hauser, Coordinator of Admissions and Student Engagement, 248-476-1122 Ext. 117, Fax: 248-476-1125, E-mail: chauser@mispp.edu.
Website: http://www.mispp.edu

**Saybrook University,** School of Psychology and Interdisciplinary Inquiry, San Francisco, CA 94612. Offers human science (MA, PhD), including consciousness and spirituality, humanistic and transpersonal psychology, integrative health studies, organizational systems, social transformation; organizational systems (MA, PhD), including consciousness and spirituality, humanistic and transpersonal psychology, integrative health studies, leadership of sustainable systems (MA), organizational systems, social transformation; psychology (MA, PhD), including consciousness and spirituality, creativity studies (MA), humanistic and transpersonal psychology, integrative health studies, Jungian studies, marriage and family therapy (MA), organizational systems, social transformation. *Program availability:* Online learning. Terminal master's awarded for partial completion of doctoral program. *Degree requirements:* For master's, thesis or alternative; for doctorate, thesis/dissertation. *Entrance requirements:* Additional exam requirements/recommendations for international students: Required—TOEFL (minimum score 580 paper-based; 93 iBT). Electronic applications accepted. *Faculty research:* Humanistic theory, health studies, organizational systems, consciousness and spirituality, social transformation.

**Seattle University,** College of Arts and Sciences, Department of Psychology, Seattle, WA 98122-1090. Offers existential and phenomenological therapeutic psychology (MA Psych). *Faculty:* 57 full-time (4 women), 4 part-time/adjunct (3 women). *Students:* 32 full-time (18 women), 2 part-time (both women); includes 8 minority (1 Black or African American, non-Hispanic/Latino; 5 Asian, non-Hispanic/Latino; 1 Hispanic/Latino; 1 Two or more races, non-Hispanic/Latino), 3 international. Average age 30. 58 applicants, 50% accepted, 12 enrolled. In 2016, 26 master's awarded. *Degree requirements:* For master's, thesis optional. *Entrance requirements:* For master's, interview, minimum GPA of 3.0, previous undergraduate course work in psychology, experience (paid or volunteer) in counseling or human services. *Application deadline:* For fall admission, 1/15 for domestic and international students. Application fee: $55. Electronic applications accepted. *Financial support:* In 2016–17, 14 students received support. Career-related internships or fieldwork and Federal Work-Study available. Support available to part-time students. Financial award applicants required to submit FAFSA. *Faculty research:* Interpersonal relations, psychotherapy, qualitative research, trauma, philosophy and psychology. *Unit head:* Dr. Kevin Krycka, Director of Graduate Programs, 206-296-5398, Fax: 206-296-2141, E-mail: krycka@seattleu.edu. *Application contact:* Janet Shandley, Associate Dean of Graduate Admissions, 206-296-5900, Fax: 206-298-5656, E-mail: grad_admissions@seattleu.edu.
Website: http://www.seattleu.edu/artsci/departments/psychology/

**Sofia University,** Hybrid: Face-to-Face/Online Programs, Palo Alto, CA 94303. Offers transpersonal psychology (MA, PhD), including transpersonal psychology (PhD). *Program availability:* Online learning. *Entrance requirements:* For master's, bachelor's degree; for doctorate, bachelor's degree; master's degree. Electronic applications accepted.

**Sofia University,** Residential Programs, Palo Alto, CA 94303. Offers clinical psychology (Psy D); computer science (MS); counseling psychology (MA); transpersonal psychology (MA, PhD). *Program availability:* Part-time, evening/weekend. Terminal master's awarded for partial completion of doctoral program. *Degree requirements:* For doctorate, thesis/dissertation. *Entrance requirements:* For master's, bachelor's degree; for doctorate, bachelor's degree; master's degree (for some programs). Electronic applications accepted.

# ADLER UNIVERSITY
## Graduate Programs

★ For more information, visit http://petersons.to/adlerupsychology

**ADLER UNIVERSITY**
For a more just society

## Programs of Study

Founded in 1952, Adler University is the oldest independent school of psychology in North America. The University is named after Alfred Adler (1870–1937), the first community psychologist, whose theories and teachings of psychology emphasize the uniqueness of every individual's relationship with society. Adler University is committed to continuing Adler's pioneering work by graduating socially responsible practitioners, engaging communities, and advancing social justice. Students come from all over the world to study in a collaborative atmosphere with accomplished clinical faculty. The University offers both campus-based and online classes to accommodate recent college graduates and working professionals.

The University takes pride in its commitment to educate and train socially responsible practitioners in counseling, psychology, and policy-based fields through innovative programs that combine course work and community-based training that enable graduates to address a broad range of social issues that impact the clients they serve.

Adler University offers the following degree programs at its Chicago Campus:

The **Doctor of Psychology (Psy.D.) in Clinical Psychology** program utilizes a practitioner-scholar–based training model with an emphasis on socially responsible practice. It prepares graduates to conduct clinical interviews and psychological testing, create treatment plans, consult and collaborate with physicians and other professionals, and provide multiple forms of therapy to alleviate mental illness, behavioral problems, and emotional distress. Adler has received national recognition for its focus on socially responsible clinical practice emphasizing the broader social and systemic factors of human dysfunction. Upon completing foundational course work, students have the opportunity to be placed in internships at prestigious clinics, hospitals, mental health centers, and government agencies. Adler also offers a variety of emphasis including child and adolescent psychology, military clinical psychology, clinical neuropsychology, primary care psychology, and traumatic stress psychology. The Doctor of Psychology in Clinical Psychology program is accredited by the Committee on Accreditation of the American Psychological Association (APA), 750 First Street NE, Washington, D.C. 20002-4242; phone: 202-336-5510; website: http://www.apa.org/ed/accreditation. It also meets requirements of the National Register of Health Care providers in psychology and state licensure guidelines.

The **Doctor of Philosophy in Couple and Family Therapy** program is distinctly designed for experienced clinicians as well as recent graduates of master's degree programs. Students are prepared for careers as advanced therapists specializing in couple, marriage, and family therapy. With an emphasis on clinical practice and theoretical frameworks, our program enables students to apply comprehensive theory, research, and techniques addressed in coursework to their practicums and clinical work. The Doctor of Philosophy in Couple and Family Therapy program consists of intensive course work, clinical experiences, a dissertation, and a one-year full-time internship. Students are placed in internships at clinics, hospitals, mental health centers, schools, and social service agencies.

The **Doctor of Philosophy (Ph.D.) in Counselor Education and Supervision** program provides advanced training and academic orientation for practicing counselors to become expert clinicians, counselor educators in teaching, supervisors, and trainers of the new generation of counselors, researchers, and scholars, as well as leaders and advocates in the field of counseling. The program is designed to develop students' expertise and excellence in teaching, research, leadership and advocacy, advanced counseling, and supervision. To support the mission of Adler University, through the integration of reflective, experiential, and participant learning and social engagement, students are expected to become professionals who are also critical thinkers and courageous leaders, multiculturally competent, aware of self and the needs of others.

The **Master of Arts in Couple and Family Therapy** program prepares entry-level counselors to specialize in working with couples and families. Students complete course work and practicums focused on the understanding and integration of individual lifestyle dynamics with couple, marital, and family systems. Graduates have a theoretical understanding of marital and family systems, including developmental issues and major variations, assessment skills in lifestyle and systemic diagnosis, and intervention skills based on major models of marital and family therapy, with the theory and methods of individual psychology as the foundation.

The **Master of Arts in Counseling: Art Therapy** program combines traditional counseling theories and techniques with an understanding of the psychological aspects of the creative process and clinical training. The program, approved by the American Art Therapy Association, requires course work as well as clinical practicum experience under at least partial supervision of a registered art therapist (ATR). It provides students with the academic and clinical experiences required to apply for registration as an art therapist as well as sit for the Licensed Professional Counselor (LPC) examination in the state of Illinois.

The **Master of Arts in Counseling: Specialization in Rehabilitation Counseling** program prepares students to become certified rehabilitation counselors (CRC). It was the first program in a professional school of psychology to receive CORE—The Council on Rehabilitation Education accreditation. Rehabilitation counselors work with individuals who have mental, emotional, or physical handicaps, helping them to lead self-sufficient lives. Counselors determine the training and support their clients need to deal with the effects of their conditions. Counselors evaluate clients and arrange for rehabilitation programs that may include medical care, psychological counseling, occupational therapy, and job placement and are employed by publicly funded agencies, schools, and medical facilities.

The **Master of Arts in Counseling: Specialization in Forensic Psychology** program prepares graduates for a highly specialized career that integrates knowledge of human behavior with active participation in the criminal justice system. Specialized course work exposes students to the predominant theories and techniques of forensic evaluation, including determination of a defendant's competency to stand trial, sanity at the time of an offense, and qualification for the death penalty in the event of a capital crime conviction. Students also develop a comprehensive understanding of techniques associated with the forensic practitioner's involvement in criminal investigations: activities such as forensic hypnosis, offender and geographic profiling, and the ongoing review of police interview and witness identification procedures. Students are introduced to such specialized topics as the psychological effects of incarceration, jury selection, the evaluation of sexually dangerous persons, and the psychosocial development of the criminal personality type.

The **Master of Arts in Counseling: Specialization in Sport and Health Psychology** program prepares graduates to address individual and systemic issues that affect sport performance and health. These areas overlap in the types of interventions used to produce positive changes (goal-setting and self-monitoring to improve consistency of practice or to lose weight). Sport and health goals also share the influence of various social and community factors such as coaches, family members, culture, and access to facilities. This unique program provides training and understanding of assessment, intervention, and analysis of systems that enable graduates to work within communities, schools, and professional organizations to address the diverse needs of people with varying ages, health issues, and athletic accomplishments.

The **Master of Arts in Counseling: Specialization in Clinical Mental Health Counseling** program at Adler University is unlike any other because it provides traditional graduate training with a focus on graduating socially responsible practitioners. Through this program, students are prepared for careers as counselors in a variety of mental health fields in settings such as mental health clinics, substance abuse treatment centers, private practice, and social service agencies. Clinical mental health counselors work with individuals, couples, and families in private and public sectors. Incorporating intensive coursework with practicums that provide real-world experience in clinical settings, the flexible program allows students to choose the format that best works with their schedule.

The **Master of Arts in Public Policy and Administration** offers students an opportunity to gain multidisciplinary knowledge, skills, and attitudes that will enable them to engage in advocacy; understand government and public policy; and manage nonprofit, private, and governmental organizations. A focus on excellent communication skills will enable graduates to successfully lead organizations, advance an advocacy agenda, and problem-solve in complex situations. Students can choose from two concentrations: urban mental health and human rights advocacy.

Adler University offers the following online programs through its Online Campus:

The **Master of Arts in Criminology** program is an online program that prepares practitioners to examine the causes and consequences of criminal behavior, understand the intricacies and challenges of modern-day criminal justice systems, and apply theoretical skills to address those challenges. Graduates complete their studies ready to develop intervention and prevention strategies that are practical, effective, socially responsible, and sustainable.

The **Master of Arts in Industrial and Organizational (I/O) Psychology** program, offered entirely online, is designed to meet the guidelines for education and training provided by the Society of Industrial and Organizational Psychology (SIOP) with unique emphasis on socially responsible practice. Professionals in this field apply methods of psychology to issues of critical relevance to business and industry, including talent management, coaching, leadership development, program evaluation, training, organizational change, team building, and work-life balance. Many I/O psychology professionals also work as consultants addressing organizational challenges such as change management, workplace diversity, and employee development and engagement.

*Adler University*

The **Master of Arts in Psychology: Specialization in Military Psychology** program is designed to provide military and nonmilitary individuals and clinicians with an understanding of the theoretical evidence, scientific research, and practical aspects of the field of military psychology. Students are taught how to apply principles of military psychology to the interpersonal, managerial, and organizational dimensions of the military and support civilian environments. This allows for the development of leadership, innovation, and creativity that is required to advance social justice. Graduates are prepared for a range of positions within behavioral and medical health systems (government and non-government), enhanced private practices, advocacy and policy organizations, and community-based consumer organizations serving military personnel, veterans, retirees, and their families.

The **Masters of Arts in Nonprofit Management** is designed for professionals at all levels of nonprofit experience, from beginners to experts. Comprehensive coursework prepares students for employment in one of the fastest-growing sectors through emphasizing skills needed to build, lead, and maintain healthy organizations. Students develop skills in employee management, daily operations, relationship management, advocacy, and collaboration. Immersive hands-on community engagement projects prepare students to work in positions that influence education, philanthropy, human service, health care, public policy, and more.

The **Master of Arts in Emergency Management Leadership** program is an online program that focuses on the emergency management leader and the human side of disasters. Students are taught to address long-term psychological and mental health needs of victims and responders. The program prepares students to develop the knowledge and skills of practices in the emergency management field, with a unique focus on the human and social factors inherent in all disasters.

### Research Facilities

The Harold and Birdie Mosak Library provides resources and services to foster the educational and intellectual inquiry of students and faculty members. The Library provides on-site and remote online access to research databases in psychology, the social sciences, education, and criminal justice. In addition, the library subscribes to a growing collection of online resources, including more than 23,000 full-text electronic journals, 8,000 electronic books, and full-text collections of newspapers.

### Financial Aid

Most students rely on a combination of scholarships, student loans, and paid employment (inside or outside of the school) to finance their graduate degrees and living expenses. The Office of Financial Aid is committed to helping students identify opportunities, understand options, and make choices that are right for them. Adler offers numerous scholarships based on a variety of criteria including financial need, academic excellence, mission-based, and community involvement and service.

### Cost of Study

Tuition on the Chicago campus for 2017–18 is $1,240 per credit hour for M.A. programs and $1,445 per credit hour for the doctoral program. Tuition on the Vancouver campus for 2017–18 is Can$920 per credit hour for M.A. programs and Can$1,030 per credit hour for the doctoral program. Tuition for online programs is $855 per credit hour. Tuition costs for each year vary depending on whether the student enrolls full-time or part-time. Courses are offered during fall, spring, and summer semesters.

### Living and Housing Costs

The University does not provide housing but assists students in securing off-campus housing. Students typically live in apartments in the Chicago or Vancouver area. Living expenses vary considerably according to standard of living, housing, and transportation.

### Student Groups

Adler University's commitment to social responsibility draws both recent college graduates and working professionals from all over the world to study in a collaborative atmosphere with accomplished faculty members. Reflecting the University's cultural and professional diversity, Adler's Student Association and more than twenty student organizations represent a range of different countries and personal and professional interests through on-and off-campus learning activities.

### The Faculty

With an average class size of fewer than 12 students, faculty mentorship plays a very important role in the learning process at Adler. Faculty members are licensed professionals who combine clinical practice with their instructional duties. Many hold or have held leadership positions in professional organizations, and most present workshops and seminars throughout the United States, Europe, Canada, and other countries. Adler University's faculty members have a broad range of interest and specializations offering students a variety of expertise in the field of psychology.

### Location

Adler University is located in Chicago, Illinois and Vancouver, British Columbia. Both downtown campuses are easily accessible by public transportation and provide students with a culturally diverse learning environment as well as hundreds of opportunities for clinical training across the United States and Canada.

### The School

Adler University has provided quality education through a scholar/practitioner model for 60 years. Its mission is to train socially responsible graduates who continue the visionary work of Alfred Adler throughout the world. Enrolling more than 1,000 students in graduate programs at its campuses in Chicago, Vancouver, and Online, Adler is uniquely based on Alfred Adler's groundbreaking concept of social interest: that health resides in community life and connections. This concept is the foundation of the University's curricula, training, and community work including

partnerships with more than 700 agencies. Its Institutes and Centers advance social justice for underserved and disadvantaged communities through applied research, community outreach, and public awareness initiatives. These include the Institute on Social Exclusion, the Institute on Public Safety and Social Justice, the Adler Child Guidance Center, and the LGBT Mental Health and Inclusion Center.

### Applying

Adler employs a rolling admission process. This means that completed applications are reviewed through the year. Because most programs fill quickly, students are encouraged to begin the application process as early as possible. While applications are accepted throughout the year, February 15 is the priority deadline for the Psy.D. program (all tracks). All application materials should be submitted by this date.

### Correspondence and Information

Chicago Admissions Office:
Adler University
17 North Dearborn Street
Chicago, Illinois 60602
United States
Phone: 312-662-4100
Fax: 312-662-4099
E-mail: admissions@adler.edu
Website: http://www.adler.edu

Vancouver Admissions Office:
Adler University
520 Seymour Street
Vancouver, BC V6B 3J5
Canada
Phone: 236-521-2409
      866-874-4614 (toll-free)
Fax: 236-521-2400
E-mail: vanadmissions@adler.edu
Website: http://www.adler.edu

Online Campus Admissions Office:
Adler University
17 North Dearborn Street
Chicago, Illinois 60602
United States
Phone: 312-662-4000
E-mail: admissions@online.adler.edu
Website: http://online.adler.edu

The Harold and Birdie Mosak Library provides resources and services to foster the educational and intellectual inquiry of students and faculty members.

Adler University—for a more just society.

# PHILADELPHIA COLLEGE OF OSTEOPATHIC MEDICINE

*Graduate Programs in Clinical Psychology, Counseling and Clinical Health Psychology, and School Psychology*

 For more information, visit http://petersons.to/philiadephiacollegepsychology

## Programs of Study

The Philadelphia College of Osteopathic Medicine (PCOM) Department of Psychology offers nine graduate programs taught by an internationally renowned, highly credentialed faculty. All faculty members in PCOM's psychology department are teaching faculty members who work closely with students to help them achieve their professional goals. Students often have the opportunity to coauthor scholarly papers, books, and professional presentations with faculty members. The Department of Psychology at PCOM offers a cognitive-behavioral theoretical orientation and teaches students to apply empirically-supported approaches in delivering clinical services. PCOM has one of the only psychology departments in the country that provides a standardized patient program for student training. The standardized patient program presents authentic clinical learning and skills situations in which "patients" simulate mental health conditions. Students conduct sessions with the patients, which are videotaped and reviewed by the faculty members to help train and assess students' skills. Students in the psychology programs may also have the opportunity for clinical experience at any of the College's urban health-care centers. In addition, the department trains leadership and change practitioners in multiple sectors including the areas of public health, not-for-profit and profit sectors. The programs have an emphasis on advocacy, diversity and inclusiveness, and serving the underserved.

The 89-credit **Psy.D. in clinical psychology program** is designed to be completed in five years, including course work, practicum, internship, and dissertation. Graduates of this program are prepared to assume responsibilities in a broad range of clinical settings. Post-doctoral certificates in clinical health psychology and clinical neuropsychology will each provide one year (16 and 19 credits respectively) of post-doctoral specialty training to doctoral-level psychologists. The 107-credit **Psy.D. in school psychology program** is designed to train, develop, and prepare entry-level school psychologists with a focus on applied behavior analysis, empirically supported cognitive behavioral techniques, and advanced interventions in neuropsychology. Adopting the practitioner-scholar model of training and a competency-based model of education, the program prepares graduates to provide empirically-based and ethnically-sound direct and indirect school psychological services that promote learning and well-being of all children with sensitivity to culture and diversity. The fourteen-month, 33-credit **M.S. in school psychology program** has an applied behavior analysis emphasis and prepares professionals in community and school settings to provide mental health services to children, youth, and families. This program, taken in sequence with the Ed.S. degree program, leads to certification in school psychology and also provides the required coursework to continue to accrue supervised experience towards behavior analysis certification (BCBA). The three-year, 45-credit **Ed.S. program** provides students with the knowledge and skills to assume the role of a school psychologist in diverse settings. The two-year 60-credit **M.S. in mental health counseling program** trains graduates to offer assessment, therapy, consultation, program evaluation, social justice advocacy, and follow-up services. Students in this program may complete concentrations in addictions and offender counseling or professional counseling. This curriculum fulfills the course requirements for becoming a Licensed Professional Counselor (LPC) in many states, including Pennsylvania and New Jersey. The two-year, 48-credit **M.S. in counseling and clinical health psychology** program also trains graduates to offer assessment, therapy, consultation, program evaluation, social justice advocacy, and follow-up services. This program prepares master's-level graduates to pursue further doctoral training and/or credentialing as a licensed professional counselor to work in the mental health field. A **Certificate of Advanced Graduate Study (CAGS)** is offered for students who have already earned a master's degree and wish to complete an additional 12–18 credits at the master's level. The

36-credit **M.S. in organizational development and leadership (ODL) program** uses a unique combination of organizational theory and individual self-discovery to provide an essential leadership perspective in creating organizational change. The 36-credit **M.S. in aging and long-term care administration (ALTCA) program** is designed to address the need for leaders in critically important long-term care services, from home- and community-based care to assisted living and skilled nursing facilities. A key component of the ALTCA program is the Nursing Home Administration 120-hour program, which satisfies the educational requirement for licensure in Pennsylvania. The 36-credit **M.S. in public health management and administration program** prepares leaders in public health, advocacy and public policy who can successfully manage change in the fast-moving arena of public health organizations.

All on-site classes for the M.S., Ed.S., CAGS, and Psy.D. programs are held in the late afternoon/evening or on weekends on the Philadelphia campus, supplemented by online content. That CAGS in Applied Behavior Analysis is offered entirely online. The M.S. in public health management and administration program is offered on weekends at Public Health Management Corporations' office facilities located in the heart of Center City, Philadelphia.

## Research Facilities

The academic facilities at PCOM include state-of-the-art amphitheaters, classroom facilities, and standardized patient labs; a wireless campus and computer laboratories with extensive software, including PsycLIT and SPSS; a comfortable, sophisticated library with online access to electronic textbooks, journals, databases, and Internet guides; and access to the digital library and statistical programs through the Internet.

## Financial Aid

The Financial Aid Office at PCOM offers financial assistance to students through the Federal Direct Loan program, institutional grants, and various alternative private loan programs.

## Cost of Study

In 2017–18, the direct tuition costs of attending PCOM (including tuition, fees, books, and supplies) for the first year were approximately $25,950 for mental health counseling M.S. students, based on enrollment of 30 credits; $28,545 for school psychology M.S. students, based on enrollment of 33 credits; $7,461 for ODL M.S. students, based on enrollment of 9 credits; $19,635 for Ed.S. students, based on enrollment of 21 credits; $36,983 for Psy.D. in clinical psychology students, based on enrollment of 31 credits; and $27,680 for Psy.D. in school psychology students, based on enrollment of 32 credits.

## Living and Housing Costs

Students live off-campus within the Philadelphia metropolitan and suburban areas, as there is no on-campus housing. Room and board costs vary by individual preferences.

## Student Group

The programs seek a diverse group of students who are committed to excellence. The Psy.D. in clinical psychology program recruits in-practice professionals who have earned master's degrees in psychology, social work, counseling, psychiatric nursing, or a related field and are working in human services. This population brings to their studies a high level of maturity, established skills, diverse backgrounds, and a strong motivation to succeed. Students entering the Ed.S. program typically have completed master's degrees in psychology or education and have been working with school-aged children in some capacity. Candidates for the M.S. programs typically are working professionals and have bachelor's degrees in varying fields, having completed specific prerequisite courses, who want to be leaders in psychoeducational and mental health services to children, youth, and families.

### The Faculty

The Department of Psychology has extraordinarily committed, experienced, and dedicated faculty members who are student-centered and have themselves been trained and mentored by some of the most foremost authorities in cognitive-behavioral therapy.

Faculty members are career teachers, devoted to mentoring students and fostering their professional and personal growth.

A full listing of PCOM faculty can be found at http://www.pcom.edu/academics/faculty.

### Location

Philadelphia College of Osteopathic Medicine is one of the largest of thirty-one osteopathic colleges in the United States, with campuses in both Philadelphia and suburban Atlanta. Psychology programs are offered only on the Philadelphia campus, which is located in a suburban setting on City Avenue, minutes away from Fairmount Park, Philadelphia's historic district, art museums, theaters, restaurants, and professional sports complexes. PCOM's facilities include two large lecture halls, small classrooms, labs for teaching and research, a state-of-the-art library, and scenic landscaping, all in a suburban setting.

### The College and the Programs

PCOM, chartered in 1899, enrolls approximately 2,800 students in its various programs across both campuses. The clinical and teaching facility in Philadelphia makes an ideal home for psychology graduate programs. The graduate psychology programs at PCOM are approved by the Department of Education of the Commonwealth of Pennsylvania and the college is accredited by the Middle States Commission on Higher Education. The Psy.D. in clinical psychology program is accredited by the American Psychological Association and fulfills the requirements of the National Register for Healthcare Providers in Psychology. Clinical Psy.D. graduates qualify to take the Examination for Professional Practice of Psychology Licensure in Pennsylvania and New Jersey. The curriculum provides Psy.D. in school psychology students with the knowledge and skills to assume the role of a school psychologist, practice in a variety of settings, and be prepared for eligibility for National Certification and for Pennsylvania licensure. The school psychology M.S., Ed.S., and Psy.D. programs have been approved by the National Association of School Psychologists. The M.S. in School Psychology course sequence is approved by the Behavior Analyst Certification Board (BACB). The M.S. in school psychology and CAGS in applied behavioral analysis course sequences are approved by the Behavior Analyst Certification Board (BACB). The M.S. program in mental health counseling has been designed to fulfill the Licensed Professional Counselor curriculum requirements in Pennsylvania and New Jersey.

### Applying

M.S. applicants to the Mental Health Counseling and the Counseling and Clinical Health Psychology programs need to have a baccalaureate degree from a regionally accredited institution, with basic psychology course work (introduction to psychology, abnormal psychology or psychopathology, and statistics). Psy.D. in clinical psychology applicants must have completed a master's degree in psychology or a related field at a regionally accredited institution and also completed developmental psychology, theories of personality, abnormal psychology or psychopathology, and statistics. Those applying to the certificate of advanced graduate studies program must have completed a master's degree in psychology or related field. Candidates for the post-doctoral certificate programs must have completed a doctoral degree in clinical psychology at a regionally accredited institution. Applicants to the M.S. in school psychology program need to have a baccalaureate degree in psychology, education, or a related field from a regionally accredited institution and must have completed 6 credits each of English and math plus 15 credits in psychology or a related field. Applicants to the Psy.D. program in School Psychology program need to have a baccalaureate degree in psychology from a regionally accredited institution and must have completed statistics, introductory biology, developmental psychology, and an additional 15 credits in psychology. Applicants to the M.S. program in school psychology or mental health counseling must have taken the GRE or MAT exam. Applicants to the ODL program must have completed a bachelor's degree from a regionally accredited institution. Applicants to the Ed.S. program must have a master's degree in school psychology or a related field and must submit test scores from the GRE Psychology Subtest #81.

All applicants to Psychology Department programs must submit official college transcripts from all schools attended and as many as three letters of recommendation using either PsyCAS or the college's online application. See pcom.edu for details. Most programs require a specified writing sample and autobiographical statement. All programs utilize a rolling admissions policy. Finalists for all programs interview with the Admissions Committee and are then notified in writing of the committee's decision.

### Correspondence and Information

Office of Admissions
Philadelphia College of Osteopathic Medicine
4170 City Avenue
Philadelphia, Pennsylvania 19131-1694
Phone: 215-871-6700
       800-999-6998 (toll-free)
Fax: 215-871-6719
E-mail: Admissions@pcom.edu
Website: http://admissions.pcom.edu
Twitter: @PCOMAdmissions

PCOM provides a collaborative learning environment for students.

# Section 25
# Public, Regional, and Industrial Affairs

This section contains a directory of institutions offering graduate work in public, regional, and industrial affairs, followed by in-depth entries submitted by institutions that chose to prepare detailed program descriptions. Additional information about programs listed in the directory but not augmented by an in-depth entry may be obtained by writing directly to the dean of a graduate school or chair of a department at the address given in the directory.

For programs offering related work, see also in this book *Architecture, Area and Cultural Studies, Criminology and Forensics, Economics, Humanities, Political Science and International Affairs,* and *Sociology, Anthropology, and Archaeology.* In the other guides in this series:

**Graduate Programs in the Biological/Biomedical Sciences & Health-Related Medical Professions**
See *Public Health*
**Graduate Programs in the Physical Sciences, Mathematics, Agricultural Sciences, the Environment & Natural Resources**
See *Environmental Sciences and Management*
**Graduate Programs in Engineering & Applied Sciences**
See *Management of Engineering and Technology*
**Graduate Programs in Business, Education, Information Studies, Law & Social Work**
See *Business Administration and Management* and *Law*

## CONTENTS

# Disability Studies

**Brandeis University,** The Heller School for Social Policy and Management, Program in Social Policy, Waltham, MA 02454-9110. Offers assets and inequalities (PhD); children, youth and families (PhD); global health and development (PhD); health and behavioral health (PhD). *Degree requirements:* For doctorate, comprehensive exam, thesis/dissertation, qualifying paper, 2-year residency. *Entrance requirements:* For doctorate, GRE General Test, 3 letters of recommendation, statement of purpose, writing sample, at least 3-5 years of professional experience. Additional exam requirements/recommendations for international students: Required—TOEFL (minimum score 600 paper-based; 100 iBT). Electronic applications accepted. *Faculty research:* Health; mental health; substance abuse; children, youth, and families; aging; international and community development; disabilities; work and inequality; hunger and poverty.

**Brock University,** Faculty of Graduate Studies, Faculty of Social Sciences, Program in Applied Disability Studies, St. Catharines, ON L2S 3A1, Canada. Offers MA, MADS, Diploma. *Program availability:* Part-time. *Degree requirements:* For master's, thesis (for some programs). *Entrance requirements:* For master's, honors degree. Additional exam requirements/recommendations for international students: Required—TOEFL (minimum score 550 paper-based; 80 iBT), IELTS (minimum score 6.5). Electronic applications accepted.

**California Baptist University,** Program in Disability Studies, Riverside, CA 92503. Offers disability ministry (MA); disability policy (MA). *Program availability:* Part-time, evening/weekend, 100% online. *Faculty:* 5 full-time (2 women), 4 part-time/adjunct (2 women). *Students:* 6 part-time (all women); includes 2 minority (1 Black or African American, non-Hispanic/Latino; 1 Two or more races, non-Hispanic/Latino). Average age 43. 8 applicants. In 2016, 8 master's awarded. *Degree requirements:* For master's, research thesis or capstone project. *Entrance requirements:* For master's, minimum undergraduate GPA of 2.75; transcripts of bachelor's degree; background in disability studies through coursework, degree, or experience; three recommendations; 500-word essay; interview. Additional exam requirements/recommendations for international students: Required—TOEFL (minimum score 80 iBT). *Application deadline:* For fall admission, 8/1 priority date for domestic students, 7/1 for international students; for spring admission, 12/1 priority date for domestic students, 11/1 for international students. Applications are processed on a rolling basis. Application fee: $45. Electronic applications accepted. *Expenses:* Contact institution. *Financial support:* In 2016–17, 1 student received support. Federal Work-Study and scholarships/grants available. Financial award applicants required to submit CSS PROFILE or FAFSA. *Faculty research:* Community integration of adults with disability, models of disability, Biblical perspectives on disability, building social competence in adolescents with Asperger's syndrome. *Unit head:* Dr. David Poole, Vice President, Online and Professional Studies, 951-343-3901, E-mail: dpoole@calbaptist.edu. *Application contact:* Dr. Jeff McNair, Program Director, MA in Disability Studies, 951-343-4489, E-mail: jmcnair@calbaptist.edu.
Website: https://www.cbuonline.edu/degrees/master-of-science-in-education-specialization-in-disability-studies

**Chapman University,** College of Educational Studies, Orange, CA 92866. Offers counseling (MA), including school counseling (MA, Credential); education (PhD), including cultural and curricular studies, disability studies, leadership studies, school psychology (PhD, Credential); educational psychology (MA); leadership development (MA); multiple subjects (Credential), including Spanish/English bilingual; pupil personnel services (Credential), including school counseling (MA, Credential), school psychology (PhD, Credential); school psychology (Ed S); single subject (Credential); special education (MA, Credential), including mild/moderate (Credential), moderate/severe (Credential); teaching (MA), including elementary education, secondary education, secondary music education. *Accreditation:* TEAC. *Program availability:* Part-time, evening/weekend. *Faculty:* 29 full-time (14 women), 36 part-time/adjunct (28 women). *Students:* 186 full-time (148 women), 186 part-time (134 women); includes 144 minority (9 Black or African American, non-Hispanic/Latino; 39 Asian, non-Hispanic/Latino; 78 Hispanic/Latino; 2 Native Hawaiian or other Pacific Islander, non-Hispanic/Latino; 16 Two or more races, non-Hispanic/Latino), 8 international. Average age 29. 143 applicants, 63% accepted, 64 enrolled. In 2016, 111 master's, 24 doctorates awarded. *Degree requirements:* For doctorate, thesis/dissertation. *Entrance requirements:* Additional exam requirements/recommendations for international students: Required—TOEFL (minimum score 550 paper-based, 80 iBT), IELTS (6.5), PTE Academic (53), or CAE. *Application deadline:* Applications are processed on a rolling basis. Application fee: $60. Electronic applications accepted. *Expenses:* Contact institution. *Financial support:* Fellowships and scholarships/grants available. Financial award application deadline: 3/2; financial award applicants required to submit FAFSA. *Unit head:* Dr. Margaret Grogan, Dean, 714-516-5968, E-mail: grogan@chapman.edu. *Application contact:* Sara Simon, Graduate Admission Counselor, 714-997-6770, E-mail: simon@chapman.edu.
Website: http://www.chapman.edu/CES/

**Montclair State University,** The Graduate School, College of Education and Human Services, Developmental Models of Autism Intervention Certificate Program, Montclair, NJ 07043-1624. Offers Certificate. *Program availability:* Part-time, evening/weekend. *Entrance requirements:* Additional exam requirements/recommendations for international students: Required—TOEFL (minimum score 83 iBT), IELTS (minimum score 6.5). Electronic applications accepted. *Expenses:* Tuition, state resident: part-time $553 per credit. Tuition, nonresident: part-time $854 per credit. *Required fees:* $91 per credit. Tuition and fees vary according to program.

**Montclair State University,** The Graduate School, College of Education and Human Services, Program in Learning Disabilities, Montclair, NJ 07043-1624. Offers M Ed.

*Program availability:* Part-time, evening/weekend. *Degree requirements:* For master's, comprehensive exam, thesis or alternative. *Entrance requirements:* For master's, GRE General Test, interview, 2 letters of recommendation. Additional exam requirements/recommendations for international students: Required—TOEFL (minimum score 83 iBT), IELTS (minimum score 6.5). Electronic applications accepted. *Expenses:* Tuition, state resident: part-time $553 per credit. Tuition, nonresident: part-time $854 per credit. *Required fees:* $91 per credit. Tuition and fees vary according to program.

**Syracuse University,** School of Education, CAS Program in Disability Studies, Syracuse, NY 13244. Offers CAS. *Program availability:* Part-time. In 2016, 8 CASs awarded. *Entrance requirements:* For degree, baccalaureate degree from regionally-accredited college/university, two letters of recommendation. Additional exam requirements/recommendations for international students: Required—TOEFL (minimum score 100 iBT). *Application deadline:* For fall admission, 2/1 priority date for domestic and international students; for summer admission, 2/1 priority date for domestic and international students. Applications are processed on a rolling basis. Application fee: $75. Electronic applications accepted. *Expenses: Tuition:* Full-time $25,974; part-time $1443 per credit hour. *Required fees:* $802; $50 per course. Tuition and fees vary according to course load and program. *Financial support:* Fellowships, research assistantships, teaching assistantships, career-related internships or fieldwork, and scholarships/grants available. Financial award application deadline: 1/15. *Unit head:* Dr. Alan Foley, Program Coordinator, 315-443-5087, E-mail: disabilitystudies@syr.edu. *Application contact:* Speranza Migliore, Graduate Admissions Recruiter, 315-443-2505, E-mail: gradrcrt@syr.edu.
Website: http://disabilitystudies.syr.edu/academic-programs/cas/

**University of Hawaii at Manoa,** Graduate Division, College of Education, Program in Disability and Diversity Studies, Honolulu, HI 96822. Offers Graduate Certificate. *Program availability:* Part-time. *Entrance requirements:* Additional exam requirements/recommendations for international students: Required—TOEFL (minimum score 500 paper-based; 61 iBT), IELTS (minimum score 5).

**University of Illinois at Chicago,** College of Applied Health Sciences, Department of Disability and Human Development, Chicago, IL 60607-7128. Offers MS, PhD. *Accreditation:* AOTA. *Program availability:* Part-time. *Degree requirements:* For master's, thesis optional; for doctorate, thesis/dissertation. *Entrance requirements:* For master's and doctorate, GRE General Test. Additional exam requirements/recommendations for international students: Required—TOEFL. Electronic applications accepted. *Faculty research:* Emerging trends in disability, demography and financial structure of disability services, aging and disability, empowerment of people with disabilities, health promotion in disabilities.

**University of Manitoba,** Faculty of Graduate Studies, Interdisciplinary Programs, Program in Disability Studies, Winnipeg, MB R3T 2N2, Canada. Offers M Sc, MA.

**University of Northern British Columbia,** Office of Graduate Studies, Prince George, BC V2N 4Z9, Canada. Offers business administration (Diploma); community health science (M Sc); disability management (MA); education (M Ed); first nations studies (MA); gender studies (MA); history (MA); interdisciplinary studies (MA); international studies (MA); mathematical, computer and physical sciences (M Sc); natural resources and environmental studies (M Sc, MA, MNRES, PhD); political science (MA); psychology (M Sc, PhD); social work (MSW). *Program availability:* Part-time, evening/weekend, online learning. *Degree requirements:* For master's, thesis; for doctorate, thesis/dissertation. *Entrance requirements:* For master's, GRE, minimum B average in undergraduate course work; for doctorate, candidacy exam, minimum A average in graduate course work.

**University of Pittsburgh,** School of Law, Certificate Program in Disability Legal Studies, Pittsburgh, PA 15260. Offers Certificate. *Program availability:* Part-time. *Faculty:* 48 full-time (21 women), 104 part-time/adjunct (34 women). *Students:* 1 part-time (0 women). *Entrance requirements:* For degree, official transcript, two letters of recommendation, essay. Additional exam requirements/recommendations for international students: Required—TOEFL. *Application deadline:* Applications are processed on a rolling basis. Application fee: $0. Tuition and fees vary according to program. *Unit head:* Prof. Alan Meisel, Director, 412-648-7120, Fax: 412-648-2649, E-mail: dlcert@pitt.edu. *Application contact:* Beth Ann Pischke, Administrator, 412-648-7120, Fax: 412-648-2649, E-mail: dlcert@pitt.edu.
Website: http://law.pitt.edu/academics/programs-non-lawyers/

**Utah State University,** School of Graduate Studies, Emma Eccles Jones College of Education and Human Services, Department of Special Education and Rehabilitation, Logan, UT 84322. Offers disability disciplines (PhD); rehabilitation counselor education (MRC); special education (M Ed, MS, Ed S). *Program availability:* Part-time, online learning. *Degree requirements:* For master's, thesis (for some programs), internships (for some programs); for doctorate, comprehensive exam, thesis/dissertation. *Entrance requirements:* For master's and doctorate, GRE General Test, minimum GPA of 3.0. Additional exam requirements/recommendations for international students: Required—TOEFL (minimum score 550 paper-based). Electronic applications accepted. *Faculty research:* Applied behavior analysis, effective instructional practices, early childhood teacher training research, distance education, multicultural rehabilitation.

**York University,** Faculty of Graduate Studies, Faculty of Health, Program in Critical Disability Studies, Toronto, ON M3J 1P3, Canada. Offers MA, PhD. *Degree requirements:* For master's, thesis or alternative. *Entrance requirements:* Additional exam requirements/recommendations for international students: Required—TOEFL (minimum score 600 paper-based). Electronic applications accepted.

# Emergency Management

**Adelphi University,** University College, Graduate Certificate in Emergency Management Program, Garden City, NY 11530-0701. Offers Certificate. *Program availability:* Part-time, evening/weekend. *Students:* 3 full-time (1 woman), 15 part-time (6 women); includes 11 minority (7 Black or African American, non-Hispanic/Latino; 3 Hispanic/Latino; 1 Two or more races, non-Hispanic/Latino). Average age 37. 11 applicants, 64% accepted, 4 enrolled. In 2016, 12 Certificates awarded. *Entrance*

*requirements:* Additional exam requirements/recommendations for international students: Required—TOEFL (minimum score 550 paper-based; 80 iBT), IELTS (minimum score 6.5). *Application deadline:* For fall admission, 5/1 for international students; for spring admission, 12/1 for international students. Applications are processed on a rolling basis. Application fee: $50. Electronic applications accepted. *Expenses: Tuition:* Full-time $37,623; part-time $1179 per credit hour. *Required fees:*

$1335; $405 per semester. Tuition and fees vary according to degree level, campus/location and program. *Financial support:* Research assistantships, teaching assistantships, career-related internships or fieldwork, institutionally sponsored loans, scholarships/grants, traineeships, and unspecified assistantships available. Support available to part-time students. *Faculty research:* Emergency nursing, disaster management, disaster preparedness. *Unit head:* Shawn O'Riley, Dean, 516-877-3412, E-mail: ucinfo@adelphi.edu. *Application contact:* Christine Murphy, Director of Admissions, 516-877-3050, Fax: 516-877-3039, E-mail: graduateadmissions@adelphi.edu.
Website: http://academics.adelphi.edu/universitycollege/emergency-management-certificate.php

**Adler University,** Programs in Psychology, Chicago, IL 60602. Offers advanced Adlerian psychotherapy (Certificate); art therapy (MA); clinical mental health counseling (MA); clinical neuropsychology (Certificate); clinical psychology (Psy D); community psychology (MA); counseling and organizational psychology (MA); counseling psychology (MA); counselor education and supervision (PhD); couple and family therapy (DCFT); criminology (MA); emergency management leadership (MA); forensic psychology (MA); marriage and family counseling (MA); marriage and family therapy (Certificate); military psychology (MA); nonprofit management (MA); organizational psychology (MA); police psychology (MA); public policy and administration (MA); rehabilitation counseling (MA); sport and health psychology (MA); substance abuse counseling (Certificate); Psy D/Certificate; Psy D/MACAT; Psy D/MACP; Psy D/MAMFC; Psy D/MASAC. *Accreditation:* APA. *Program availability:* Part-time, evening/weekend, online learning. Terminal master's awarded for partial completion of doctoral program. *Degree requirements:* For master's, thesis or alternative, oral exam, practicum; for doctorate, thesis/dissertation, clinical exam, internship, oral exam, practicum, written qualifying exam. *Entrance requirements:* For master's, 12 semester hours in psychology, minimum GPA of 3.0; for doctorate, 18 semester hours in psychology, minimum GPA of 3.25; for Certificate, appropriate master's or doctoral degree. Additional exam requirements/recommendations for international students: Required—TOEFL (minimum score 550 paper-based; 79 iBT). Electronic applications accepted.

See Display on page 982 and Close-Up on page 1225.

**American Public University System,** AMU/APU Graduate Programs, Charles Town, WV 25414. Offers accounting (MBA, MS); applied business analytics (MBA, MS); criminal justice (MA), including business administration, emergency and disaster management, general (MA, MS); educational leadership (M Ed); emergency and disaster management (MA); entrepreneurship (MBA); environmental policy and management (MS), including environmental planning, environmental sustainability, fish and wildlife management, general (MA, MS), global environmental management; finance (MBA); general (MBA); government contracting and acquisition (MBA); health care administration (MBA); health information management (MS); history (MA), including American history, ancient and classical history, European history, global history, public history; homeland security (MA), including business administration, counterterrorism studies, criminal justice, cyber, emergency management and public health, intelligence studies, transportation security; homeland security resource allocation (MBA); humanities (MA); information technology (MS), including digital forensics, enterprise software development, information assurance and security, IT project management; information technology management (MBA); intelligence studies (MA), including criminal intelligence, cyber, general (MA, MS), homeland security, intelligence analysis, intelligence collection, intelligence management, intelligence operations, terrorism studies; international relations and conflict resolution (MA), including comparative and security issues, conflict resolution, international and transnational security issues, peacekeeping; legal studies (MA); management (MA), including strategic consulting; marketing (MBA); military history (MA), including American military history, American Revolution, civil war, war since 1945, World War II; military studies (MA), including joint warfare, strategic leadership; national security studies (MA), including cyber, general (MA, MS), homeland security, regional security studies, security and intelligence analysis, terrorism studies; nonprofit management (MBA); political science (MA), including American politics and government, comparative government and development, general (MA, MS), international relations, public policy; psychology (MA); public administration (MPA), including disaster management, environmental policy, health policy, human resources, national security, organizational management, security management; public health (MPH); reverse logistics management (MA); security management (MA); space studies (MS), including aerospace science, general (MA, MS), planetary science; sports and health sciences (MS); sports management (MBA); teaching (M Ed), including autism spectrum disorder, curriculum and instruction for elementary teachers, elementary reading, English language learners, instructional leadership, online learning, special education, STEAM (STEM plus the arts); transportation and logistics management (MA). *Program availability:* Part-time, evening/weekend, online only, 100% online. *Faculty:* 401 full-time (228 women), 1,678 part-time/adjunct (781 women). *Students:* 378 full-time (184 women), 8,455 part-time (3,484 women); includes 2,972 minority (1,552 Black or African American, non-Hispanic/Latino; 52 American Indian or Alaska Native, non-Hispanic/Latino; 211 Asian, non-Hispanic/Latino; 791 Hispanic/Latino; 70 Native Hawaiian or other Pacific Islander, non-Hispanic/Latino; 296 Two or more races, non-Hispanic/Latino), 109 international. Average age 37. In 2016, 3,185 master's awarded. *Degree requirements:* For master's, comprehensive exam or practicum. *Entrance requirements:* For master's, official transcript showing earned bachelor's degree from institution accredited by recognized accrediting body. Additional exam requirements/recommendations for international students: Required—TOEFL (minimum score 550 paper-based), IELTS (minimum score 6.5). *Application deadline:* Applications are processed on a rolling basis. Application fee: $0. Electronic applications accepted. *Expenses: Tuition:* Part-time $350 per credit hour. *Required fees:* $50 per course. *Financial support:* Scholarships/grants available. Financial award applicants required to submit FAFSA. *Unit head:* Dr. Karan Powell, President, 877-468-6268, Fax: 304-724-3780. *Application contact:* Terry Grant, Vice President of Enrollment Management, 877-468-6268, Fax: 304-724-3780, E-mail: info@apus.edu.
Website: http://www.apus.edu

**Anna Maria College,** Graduate Division, Program in Health Emergency Management, Paxton, MA 01612. Offers MS, Graduate Certificate. *Program availability:* Part-time, evening/weekend. *Degree requirements:* For master's, thesis. *Entrance requirements:* For master's, minimum GPA of 2.7. Additional exam requirements/recommendations for international students: Required—TOEFL (minimum score 500 paper-based). Electronic applications accepted.

**Arizona State University at the Tempe campus,** College of Public Programs, School of Public Affairs, Phoenix, AZ 85004-0687. Offers emergency management and homeland security (MA); program evaluation (MS); public administration (MPA, PhD), including nonprofit administration (MPA), urban management (MPA); public policy (MPP); MPA/MSW. *Accreditation:* NASPAA (one or more programs are accredited). *Program availability:* Part-time, evening/weekend. Terminal master's awarded for partial completion of doctoral program. *Degree requirements:* For master's, thesis or alternative, policy analysis or capstone project; interactive Program of Study (iPOS) submitted before completing 50 percent of required credit hours; for doctorate,

comprehensive exam, thesis/dissertation, interactive Program of Study (iPOS) submitted before completing 50 percent of required credit hours. *Entrance requirements:* For master's, GRE, minimum GPA of 3.0 or equivalent in last 2 years of work leading to bachelor's degree; for doctorate, GRE, minimum GPA of 3.0 or equivalent in last 2 years of work leading to bachelor's degree, 3 letters of recommendation, resume, statement of goals, samples of research reports. Additional exam requirements/recommendations for international students: Required—TOEFL (minimum score 600 paper-based; 100 iBT), IELTS (minimum score 6.5). Electronic applications accepted. *Expenses:* Contact institution.

**Arkansas State University,** Graduate School, College of Nursing and Health Professions, Disaster Preparedness Program, State University, AR 72467. Offers disaster preparedness and emergency management (MS); healthcare emergency management (Graduate Certificate). *Program availability:* Part-time. *Degree requirements:* For master's and Graduate Certificate, comprehensive exam, thesis or alternative. *Entrance requirements:* For master's, GRE General Test or MAT, appropriate bachelor's degree, TB skin test, TB mask fit test, CPR certification, liability insurance; for Graduate Certificate, bachelor's degree, TB skin test, TB mask fit test, CPR certification, liability insurance. Additional exam requirements/recommendations for international students: Required—TOEFL (minimum score 550 paper-based; 79 iBT), IELTS (minimum score 6), PTE (minimum score 56). Electronic applications accepted. *Expenses:* Contact institution.

**Arkansas Tech University,** College of Engineering and Applied Sciences, Russellville, AR 72801. Offers emergency management (MS); engineering (M Engr); information technology (MS). *Program availability:* Part-time, online learning. *Students:* 59 full-time (15 women), 63 part-time (21 women); includes 22 minority (8 Black or African American, non-Hispanic/Latino; 2 American Indian or Alaska Native, non-Hispanic/Latino; 4 Asian, non-Hispanic/Latino; 4 Hispanic/Latino; 4 Two or more races, non-Hispanic/Latino), 41 international. Average age 31. In 2016, 43 master's awarded. *Degree requirements:* For master's, comprehensive exam (for some programs), thesis (for some programs), internship. *Entrance requirements:* For master's, GRE General Test. Additional exam requirements/recommendations for international students: Required—TOEFL (minimum score 550 paper-based; 79 iBT), IELTS (minimum score 6). *Application deadline:* For fall admission, 3/1 priority date for domestic students, 5/1 priority date for international students; for spring admission, 10/1 priority date for domestic and international students. Applications are processed on a rolling basis. Application fee: $25 ($75 for international students). Electronic applications accepted. *Expenses:* Tuition, state resident: full-time $4932; part-time $274 per credit hour. Tuition, nonresident: full-time $9864; part-time $548 per credit hour. *Required fees:* $513 per semester. Tuition and fees vary according to course load. *Financial support:* In 2016–17, research assistantships with full tuition reimbursements (averaging $4,800 per year), teaching assistantships with full tuition reimbursements (averaging $4,800 per year) were awarded; career-related internships or fieldwork, Federal Work-Study, scholarships/grants, health care benefits, and unspecified assistantships also available. Support available to part-time students. Financial award application deadline: 4/15; financial award applicants required to submit FAFSA. *Unit head:* Dr. Douglas Barlow, Dean, 479-968-0353, E-mail: dbarlow@atu.edu. *Application contact:* Dr. Mary B. Gunter, Dean of Graduate College, 479-968-0398, Fax: 479-964-0542, E-mail: gradcollege@atu.edu.
Website: http://www.atu.edu/appliedsci/

**Auburn University at Montgomery,** College of Public Policy and Justice, Department of Justice and Public Safety, Montgomery, AL 36124-4023. Offers criminal studies (MSJPS); homeland security (MSJPS); homeland security and emergency management (MS); legal studies (MSJPS); organizational leadership (MSJPS); paralegal (Certificate). *Program availability:* Part-time, evening/weekend. *Degree requirements:* For master's, comprehensive exam, thesis optional. *Entrance requirements:* For master's, GRE General Test or MAT. Electronic applications accepted. *Faculty research:* Law enforcement, corrections, juvenile justice.

**Ball State University,** Graduate School, College of Sciences and Humanities, Department of Natural Resources and Environmental Management, Muncie, IN 47306. Offers emergency management and homeland security (Certificate); natural resources and environmental management (MA, MS). *Program availability:* Part-time. *Degree requirements:* For master's, thesis (for some programs). *Entrance requirements:* For master's, GRE General Test, minimum baccalaureate GPA of 2.75 or 3.0 in latter half of baccalauareate, two letters of reference. Additional exam requirements/recommendations for international students: Required—TOEFL (minimum score 550 paper-based; 79 iBT), IELTS (minimum score 6.5). Electronic applications accepted. *Faculty research:* Acid rain, indoor air pollution, land reclamation.

**Ball State University,** Graduate School, College of Sciences and Humanities, Department of Political Science, Program in Public Administration, Muncie, IN 47306. Offers public administration (MPA, Certificate), including administrative (MPA), community and economic development (MPA), criminal justice and criminology (MPA), emergency management and homeland security (MPA). *Program availability:* Part-time. *Degree requirements:* For master's, comprehensive exam. *Entrance requirements:* For master's, GRE General Test, minimum bacclaureate GPA of 2.8, two letters of recommendation. Additional exam requirements/recommendations for international students: Required—TOEFL (minimum score 550 paper-based; 79 iBT), IELTS (minimum score 6.5). Electronic applications accepted. *Faculty research:* Employment training programs, personnel and labor relations, planning.

**Benedictine University,** Graduate Programs, Program in Public Health, Lisle, IL 60532. Offers administration of health care institutions (MPH); dietetics (MPH); disaster management (MPH); health education (MPH); health information systems (MPH); MBA/MPH; MPH/MS. *Accreditation:* CEPH. *Program availability:* Part-time, evening/weekend, online learning. *Students:* 89 full-time (72 women), 462 part-time (358 women); includes 129 minority (61 Black or African American, non-Hispanic/Latino; 5 American Indian or Alaska Native, non-Hispanic/Latino; 51 Asian, non-Hispanic/Latino; 11 Hispanic/Latino; 1 Native Hawaiian or other Pacific Islander, non-Hispanic/Latino), 12 international. 195 applicants, 86% accepted, 143 enrolled. In 2016, 190 master's awarded. *Entrance requirements:* For master's, MAT, GRE, or GMAT. Additional exam requirements/recommendations for international students: Required—TOEFL (minimum score 550 paper-based). *Application deadline:* For fall admission, 9/1 for domestic students; for winter admission, 12/1 for domestic students; for spring admission, 2/15 for domestic students. Application fee: $40. *Expenses: Tuition:* Full-time $15,600; part-time $650 per hour. *Required fees:* $300. One-time fee: $125 part-time. Tuition and fees vary according to class time, course load, campus/location and program. *Financial support:* Career-related internships or fieldwork and health care benefits available. Support available to part-time students. *Unit head:* Dr. Georgeen Polyak, Director, 630-829-6217, E-mail: gpolyak@ben.edu. *Application contact:* Kari Gibbons, Associate Vice President, Enrollment Center, 630-829-6200, Fax: 630-829-6584, E-mail: kgibbons@ben.edu.

**Boston University,** School of Medicine, Division of Graduate Medical Sciences, Program in Healthcare Emergency Management, Boston, MA 02215. Offers MS. *Financial support:* Applicants required to submit FAFSA. *Unit head:* Dr. Kevin Thomas, Director, 617-414-2316, Fax: 617-414-2332, E-mail: kipthoma@bu.edu. *Application*

*Emergency Management*

*contact:* GMS Admissions Office, 617-638-5255, E-mail: askgms@bu.edu. Website: http://www.bumc.bu.edu/bmcm/

**California State University, Long Beach,** Graduate Studies, College of Health and Human Services, Department of Criminal Justice, Long Beach, CA 90840. Offers criminal justice (MS); emergency services administration (MS). *Program availability:* Part-time. *Degree requirements:* For master's, comprehensive course or thesis. *Entrance requirements:* For master's, minimum GPA of 3.0. *Application deadline:* For fall admission, 5/1 for domestic students. Applications are processed on a rolling basis. Application fee: $55. Electronic applications accepted. *Financial support:* Federal Work-Study, institutionally sponsored loans, and scholarships/grants available. Financial award application deadline: 3/2. *Unit head:* Brenda L. Vogel, Director, 562-985-8965.

**California State University Maritime Academy,** Graduate Studies, Vallejo, CA 94590. Offers transportation and engineering management (MS), including engineering management, humanitarian disaster management, transportation. *Program availability:* Evening/weekend, online only, 100% online. *Faculty:* 16 part-time/adjunct (2 women). *Students:* 49 full-time (10 women); includes 11 minority (2 Black or African American, non-Hispanic/Latino; 5 Asian, non-Hispanic/Latino; 2 Hispanic/Latino; 2 Native Hawaiian or other Pacific Islander, non-Hispanic/Latino), 1 international. Average age 32. 29 applicants, 93% accepted, 26 enrolled. In 2016, 24 master's awarded. *Degree requirements:* For master's, minimum GPA of 3.0 in 10 required courses including capstone course and project. *Entrance requirements:* For master's, GMAT/GRE (for applicants with fewer than five years of post-baccalaureate professional experience), equivalent of four-year U.S. bachelor's degree with minimum GPA of 2.5 during last two years (60 semester units or 90 quarter units) of coursework in degree program. Additional exam requirements/recommendations for international students: Required—TOEFL (minimum score 550 paper-based). *Application deadline:* Applications are processed on a rolling basis. Application fee: $55. Electronic applications accepted. *Expenses:* Contact institution. *Financial support:* Applicants required to submit FAFSA. *Unit head:* Dr. Jim Burns, Dean, Graduate Studies. *Application contact:* Kathy Arnold, Program Coordinator, 707-654-1271, Fax: 707-654-1158, E-mail: karnold@csum.edu. Website: http://www.csum.edu/web/industry/graduate-studies

**Capella University,** School of Public Service Leadership, Doctoral Programs in Healthcare, Minneapolis, MN 55402. Offers criminal justice (PhD); emergency management (PhD); epidemiology (Dr PH); general health administration (DHA); general public administration (DPA); health advocacy and leadership (Dr PH); health care administration (PhD); health care leadership (DHA); health policy advocacy (DHA); multidisciplinary human services (PhD); nonprofit management and leadership (PhD); public safety leadership (PhD); social and community services (PhD).

**Capella University,** School of Public Service Leadership, Master's Programs in Healthcare, Minneapolis, MN 55402. Offers criminal justice (MS); emergency management (MS); general public health (MPH); gerontology (MS); health administration (MHA); health care operations (MHA); health management policy (MPH); health policy (MHA); homeland security (MS); multidisciplinary human services (MS); public administration (MPA); public safety leadership (MS); social and community services (MS); social behavioral sciences (MPH); MS/MPA.

**Clemson University,** Graduate School, College of Behavioral, Social and Health Sciences, Program in Public Administration, Clemson, SC 29634. Offers public administration (MPA, Certificate), including emergency management (MPA), homeland defense and security (MPA), local government (MPA), non-profit management (MPA), sustainable development (MPA). *Program availability:* Part-time, evening/weekend, online only, 100% online. *Faculty:* 4 full-time (2 women), 11 part-time/adjunct (5 women). *Students:* 8 full-time (5 women), 54 part-time (30 women); includes 16 minority (13 Black or African American, non-Hispanic/Latino; 2 Hispanic/Latino; 1 Two or more races, non-Hispanic/Latino). Average age 36. 25 applicants, 80% accepted, 18 enrolled. In 2016, 18 master's awarded. *Degree requirements:* For master's, comprehensive exam, thesis or alternative. *Entrance requirements:* For master's, GRE General Test, two letters of recommendation, unofficial transcripts, personal statement of purpose, documentation and explanation of related professional experience, resume. Additional exam requirements/recommendations for international students: Required—TOEFL (minimum score 80 iBT), IELTS (minimum score 6.5). *Application deadline:* For fall admission, 4/1 for domestic students, 3/1 for international students; for spring admission, 11/1 for domestic students, 10/1 for international students. Applications are processed on a rolling basis. Application fee: $80 ($90 for international students). Electronic applications accepted. *Expenses:* $4,264 per semester full-time resident, $8,485 per semester full-time non-resident, $695 per credit hour. *Faculty research:* Economic development, community vitality, entrepreneurship, broadband infrastructure, public health innovations and communities. *Total annual research expenditures:* $11,485. *Unit head:* Dr. Lori Dickes, Program Coordinator, 864-656-7831, E-mail: lorid@clemson.edu. Website: https://www.clemson.edu/cbshs/departments/mpa/

**Columbia Southern University,** College of Safety and Emergency Services, Orange Beach, AL 36561. Offers criminal justice administration (MS); emergency services management (MS); occupational safety and health (MS), including environmental management. *Program availability:* Part-time, evening/weekend, online learning. *Entrance requirements:* For master's, bachelor's degree from accredited/approved institution. Additional exam requirements/recommendations for international students: Required—TOEFL. Electronic applications accepted.

**Drexel University,** College of Nursing and Health Professions, Emergency and Public Safety Services Program, Philadelphia, PA 19104-2875. Offers MS. *Program availability:* Part-time, evening/weekend. *Degree requirements:* For master's, comprehensive exam. *Entrance requirements:* For master's, GRE General Test, minimum GPA of 2.75. *Application deadline:* For fall admission, 6/1 for domestic students. Applications are processed on a rolling basis. Application fee: $50. *Expenses:* Tuition: Full-time $32,184; part-time $1192 per credit hour. *Required fees:* $280. Tuition and fees vary according to campus/location and program. *Financial support:* Career-related internships or fieldwork, Federal Work-Study, and institutionally sponsored loans available. Support available to part-time students. Financial award application deadline: 5/1; financial award applicants required to submit FAFSA. *Unit head:* Jean Will, Director, 215-762-8447, E-mail: jean.will@drexel.edu. *Application contact:* Director of Graduate Admissions, 215-895-6700, Fax: 215-895-5939, E-mail: enroll@drexel.edu.

**Excelsior College,** School of Public Service, Albany, NY 12203-5159. Offers criminal justice (MSCI); homeland security and emergency management (MSCJ); justice administration (MSCI); mediation and arbitration (MPA); public administration (MPA). *Program availability:* Part-time, evening/weekend, online learning. *Faculty:* 1 (woman) part-time/adjunct. *Students:* 181 part-time (47 women); includes 78 minority (41 Black or African American, non-Hispanic/Latino; 2 American Indian or Alaska Native, non-Hispanic/Latino; 2 Asian, non-Hispanic/Latino; 25 Hispanic/Latino; 2 Native Hawaiian or other Pacific Islander, non-Hispanic/Latino; 6 Two or more races, non-Hispanic/Latino). Average age 41. In 2016, 30 master's awarded. *Application deadline:* Applications are processed on a rolling basis. Application fee: $50. Electronic applications accepted. *Expenses: Tuition:* Part-time $645 per credit. *Required fees:* $265 per credit. *Financial support:* Scholarships/grants available. *Unit head:* Dr. Robert Waters, Dean, School of

Public Service, 518-464-8500, Fax: 518-464-8777. *Application contact:* Admissions Counselor, 888-647-2388, Fax: 518-464-8777, E-mail: gradadmissions@excelsior.edu. Website: http://www.excelsior.edu/programs/public-service

**Florida Institute of Technology,** Extended Studies Division, Melbourne, FL 32901-6975. Offers acquisition and contract management (MS); aerospace engineering (MS); business administration (MBA, DBA); computer information systems (MS); computer science (MS); electrical engineering (MS); engineering management (MS); human resources management (MS); logistics management (MS), including humanitarian and disaster relief logistics; management (MS), including acquisition and contract management, e-business, human resources management, information systems, logistics management, management, transportation management; material acquisition management (MS); mechanical engineering (MS); operations research (MS); project management (MS), including information systems, operations research; public administration (MPA); quality management (MS); software engineering (MS); space systems (MS); space systems management (MS); supply chain management (MS); systems management (MS), including information systems, operations research; technology management (MS). *Program availability:* Part-time, evening/weekend, online learning. *Faculty:* 10 full-time (3 women), 122 part-time/adjunct (29 women). *Students:* 131 full-time (58 women), 997 part-time (348 women); includes 389 minority (231 Black or African American, non-Hispanic/Latino; 9 American Indian or Alaska Native, non-Hispanic/Latino; 26 Asian, non-Hispanic/Latino; 99 Hispanic/Latino; 3 Native Hawaiian or other Pacific Islander, non-Hispanic/Latino; 21 Two or more races, non-Hispanic/Latino), 53 international. Average age 36. 962 applicants, 48% accepted, 323 enrolled. In 2016, 403 master's awarded. *Degree requirements:* For master's, comprehensive exam (for some programs). *Entrance requirements:* For master's, GMAT or resume showing 8 years of supervised experience, minimum GPA of 3.0, 2 letters of recommendation, resume. Additional exam requirements/recommendations for international students: Required—TOEFL (minimum score 550 paper-based; 79 iBT). *Application deadline:* For fall admission, 4/1 for international students; for spring admission, 9/30 for international students. Applications are processed on a rolling basis. Electronic applications accepted. *Expenses:* Contact institution. *Financial support:* Application deadline: 3/1; applicants required to submit FAFSA. *Unit head:* Dr. Theodore R. Richardson, III, Dean, 321-674-8123, Fax: 321-674-7597, E-mail: trichardson@fit.edu. *Application contact:* Carolyn Farrior, Director of Graduate Admissions, Online Learning and Off-Campus Programs, 321-674-7118, Fax: 321-674-8216, E-mail: cfarrior@fit.edu. Website: http://es.fit.edu

**Florida International University,** Steven J. Green School of International and Public Affairs, Department of Emergency Management, Miami, FL 33199. Offers disaster management (MA). *Accreditation:* AACSB. *Program availability:* Part-time, evening/weekend. *Students:* 40 full-time (21 women), 2 part-time (1 woman); includes 30 minority (12 Black or African American, non-Hispanic/Latino; 1 Asian, non-Hispanic/Latino; 15 Hispanic/Latino; 2 Two or more races, non-Hispanic/Latino), 1 international. Average age 36. 50 applicants, 90% accepted, 42 enrolled. *Entrance requirements:* For master's, minimum GPA of 3.0 in upper-level coursework; resume. Additional exam requirements/recommendations for international students: Required—TOEFL (minimum score 550 paper-based; 80 iBT) or IELTS (minimum score 6.5). *Application deadline:* For fall admission, 6/1 for domestic and international students; for spring admission, 10/1 for domestic students, 9/1 for international students. Applications are processed on a rolling basis. Application fee: $30. Electronic applications accepted. *Expenses:* Tuition, state resident: full-time $8912; part-time $446 per credit hour. Tuition, nonresident: full-time $21,393; part-time $992 per credit hour. *Required fees:* $2185; $195 per semester. Tuition and fees vary according to program. *Financial support:* Institutionally sponsored loans and scholarships/grants available. Financial award application deadline: 3/1; financial award applicants required to submit FAFSA. *Faculty research:* Emergency management, crisis intervention, disaster preparedness. *Unit head:* Amy B. Aiken, Director, 305-348-6975, E-mail: amy.aiken@fiu.edu. *Application contact:* Nanett Rojas, Manager, Admissions Operations, 305-348-7464, Fax: 305-348-7441, E-mail: nanett.rojas@fiu.edu.

**Fordham University,** Graduate School of Arts and Sciences, Program in International Humanitarian Action, New York, NY 10458. Offers MA. Program offered in collaboration with the Institute for International Humanitarian Affairs (IIHA). *Students:* 3 part-time (all women), 1 international. Average age 37. 33 applicants, 6% accepted. *Entrance requirements:* For master's, official transcripts, 3 letters of recommendation, resume, statement of interest. Application fee: $70. Electronic applications accepted. *Unit head:* Dr. Brendan Cahill, Executive Director, 212-636-6294, Fax: 212-636-7060, E-mail: iiha@fordham.edu. *Application contact:* Bernadette Valentino-Morrison, Director of Graduate Admissions, 718-817-4419, Fax: 718-817-3566, E-mail: valentinomor@fordham.edu. Website: http://www.fordham.edu/academics/programs_at_fordham_/international_humani/index.asp

**Georgetown University,** Graduate School of Arts and Sciences, School of Continuing Studies, Washington, DC 20057. Offers American studies (MALS); Catholic studies (MALS); classical civilizations (MALS); emergency and disaster management (MPS); ethics and the professions (MALS); global strategic communications (MPS); hospitality management (MPS); human resources management (MPS); humanities (MALS); individualized study (MALS); integrated marketing communications (MPS); international affairs (MALS); Islam and Muslim-Christian relations (MALS); journalism (MPS); liberal studies (DLS); literature and society (MALS); medieval and early modern European studies (MALS); public relations and corporate communications (MPS); real estate (MPS); religious studies (MALS); social and public policy (MALS); sports industry management (MPS); systems engineering management (MPS); technology management (MPS); the theory and practice of American democracy (MALS); urban and regional planning (MPS); visual culture (MALS). MPS in systems engineering management offered jointly with Stevens Institute of Technology. *Entrance requirements:* Additional exam requirements/recommendations for international students: Required—TOEFL.

**The George Washington University,** School of Medicine and Health Sciences, Health Sciences Programs, Washington, DC 20052. Offers clinical practice management (MSHS); clinical research administration (MSHS); emergency services management (MSHS); end-of-life care (MSHS); immunohematology (MSHS); immunohematology and biotechnology (MSHS); physical therapy (DPT); physician assistant (MSHS). *Program availability:* Online learning. *Faculty:* 49 full-time (40 women). *Students:* 291 full-time (211 women), 316 part-time (244 women); includes 188 minority (68 Black or African American, non-Hispanic/Latino; 1 American Indian or Alaska Native, non-Hispanic/Latino; 49 Asian, non-Hispanic/Latino; 57 Hispanic/Latino; 2 Native Hawaiian or other Pacific Islander, non-Hispanic/Latino; 11 Two or more races, non-Hispanic/Latino), 13 international. Average age 33. 2,202 applicants, 18% accepted, 237 enrolled. In 2016, 162 master's, 40 doctorates, 1 other advanced degree awarded. *Entrance requirements:* Additional exam requirements/recommendations for international students: Required—TOEFL (minimum score 550 paper-based). *Application deadline:* Applications are processed on a rolling basis. Application fee: $75. *Expenses:* Contact institution. *Unit head:* Jean E. Johnson, Senior Associate Dean, 202-994-3725, E-mail:

jejohns@gwu.edu. *Application contact:* Joke Ogundiran, Director of Admission, 202-994-1668, Fax: 202-994-0870, E-mail: jokeogun@gwu.edu.

**Georgia State University,** Andrew Young School of Policy Studies, Department of Public Management and Policy, Atlanta, GA 30303. Offers criminal justice (MPA); disaster management (Certificate); disaster policy (MPA); environmental policy (PhD); health policy (PhD); management and finance (MPA); nonprofit management (MPA, Certificate); nonprofit policy (MPA); planning and economic development (MPP, Certificate); policy analysis and evaluation (MPA), including planning and economic development; public and nonprofit management (PhD); public finance and budgeting (PhD), including science and technology policy, urban and regional economic development; public finance policy (MPA), including social policy; public health (MPA). *Accreditation:* NASPAA (one or more programs are accredited). *Program availability:* Part-time. *Faculty:* 17 full-time (9 women). *Students:* 123 full-time (77 women), 79 part-time (49 women); includes 84 minority (59 Black or African American, non-Hispanic/Latino; 5 Asian, non-Hispanic/Latino; 14 Hispanic/Latino; 6 Two or more races, non-Hispanic/Latino), 34 international. Average age 30. 237 applicants, 60% accepted, 65 enrolled. In 2016, 59 master's, 4 doctorates, 8 other advanced degrees awarded. Terminal master's awarded for partial completion of doctoral program. *Degree requirements:* For master's, thesis optional; for doctorate, comprehensive exam, thesis/dissertation. *Entrance requirements:* For master's and doctorate, GRE. Additional exam requirements/recommendations for international students: Required—TOEFL (minimum score 603 paper-based; 100 iBT) or IELTS (minimum score 7). *Application deadline:* For fall admission, 1/15 for domestic and international students. Application fee: $50. Electronic applications accepted. *Expenses:* Tuition, state resident: full-time $6876; part-time $382 per credit hour. Tuition, nonresident: full-time $22,374; part-time $1243 per credit hour. *Required fees:* $2128; $1064 per term. Part-time tuition and fees vary according to course load and program. *Financial support:* In 2016–17, fellowships (averaging $8,194 per year), research assistantships (averaging $8,068 per year), teaching assistantships (averaging $3,600 per year) were awarded; institutionally sponsored loans, scholarships/grants, health care benefits, and unspecified assistantships also available. Financial award application deadline: 2/1. *Faculty research:* Public budgeting and finance, public management, nonprofit management, performance measurement and management, urban development. *Unit head:* Dr. Carolyn Bourdeaux, Chair and Professor, 404-413-0013, Fax: 404-413-0104, E-mail: cbourdeaux@gsu.edu.
Website: http://aysps.gsu.edu/pmap/

**Grand Canyon University,** Colangelo College of Business, Phoenix, AZ 85017-1097. Offers accounting (MBA, MS); business analytics (MS); disaster preparedness and executive fire service leadership (MS); finance (MBA); general management (MBA); health systems management (MBA); information technology management (MS); leadership (MBA, MS); marketing (MBA); organizational leadership and entrepreneurship (MS); project management (MBA); sports business (MBA); strategic human resource management (MBA). *Accreditation:* ACBSP. *Program availability:* Part-time, evening/weekend, online learning. *Faculty:* 8 full-time (3 women), 147 part-time/adjunct (49 women). *Students:* 1 full-time (0 women), 2,121 part-time (1,165 women); includes 341 minority (249 Black or African American, non-Hispanic/Latino; 17 American Indian or Alaska Native, non-Hispanic/Latino; 15 Asian, non-Hispanic/Latino; 29 Hispanic/Latino; 4 Native Hawaiian or other Pacific Islander, non-Hispanic/Latino; 27 Two or more races, non-Hispanic/Latino), 20 international. Average age 38. In 2016, 569 master's awarded. *Entrance requirements:* For master's, equivalent of two years' full-time professional work experience. Additional exam requirements/recommendations for international students: Required—TOEFL (minimum score 575 paper-based; 90 iBT), IELTS (minimum score 7). *Application deadline:* For fall admission, 8/21 for domestic students, 7/2 for international students; for spring admission, 12/24 for domestic students, 11/1 for international students. Applications are processed on a rolling basis. Application fee: $0. Electronic applications accepted. *Financial support:* Federal Work-Study available. Support available to part-time students. Financial award applicants required to submit FAFSA. *Unit head:* Kim Donaldson, Dean, 602-639-6597, E-mail: kdonaldson@gcu.edu. *Application contact:* Matt Tidwell, Enrollment Manager, 602-639-6020, E-mail: mtidwell@gcu.edu.
Website: https://www.gcu.edu/colangelo-college-of-business.php

**Indiana University–Purdue University Indianapolis,** School of Public and Environmental Affairs, Indianapolis, IN 46202. Offers criminal justice and public safety (MS); homeland security and emergency management (Graduate Certificate); library management (Graduate Certificate); nonprofit management (Graduate Certificate); public affairs (MPA); public management (Graduate Certificate); social entrepreneurship: nonprofit and public benefit organizations (Graduate Certificate); JD/MPA; MLS/NMC; MLS/PMC; MPA/MA. *Accreditation:* CAHME (one or more programs are accredited); NASPAA. *Program availability:* Part-time, evening/weekend, online learning. *Entrance requirements:* For master's, GRE General Test, GMAT or LSAT, minimum GPA of 3.0 (preferred). Additional exam requirements/recommendations for international students: Required—TOEFL (minimum score 93 iBT), IELTS (minimum score 6.5). Electronic applications accepted. *Faculty research:* Nonprofit and public management, public policy, urban policy, sustainability policy, disaster preparedness and recovery, vehicular safety, homicide, offender rehabilitation and re-entry.

**Jacksonville State University,** College of Graduate Studies and Continuing Education, College of Arts and Sciences, Program in Emergency Management, Jacksonville, AL 36265-1602. Offers MS, D Sc. *Program availability:* Part-time, evening/weekend. *Faculty:* 7 full-time (2 women). *Students:* 5 full-time (3 women), 93 part-time (46 women); includes 6 minority (all Black or African American, non-Hispanic/Latino), 4 international. Average age 38. 95 applicants, 51% accepted, 39 enrolled. In 2016, 14 master's, 1 doctorate awarded. *Degree requirements:* For master's, comprehensive exam, thesis (for some programs); for doctorate, comprehensive exam, thesis/dissertation. *Entrance requirements:* Additional exam requirements/recommendations for international students: Required—TOEFL (minimum score 500 paper-based; 61 iBT). *Application deadline:* Applications are processed on a rolling basis. Application fee: $35. Electronic applications accepted. *Financial support:* In 2016–17, 9 students received support. Available to part-time students. Application deadline: 4/1; applicants required to submit FAFSA. *Unit head:* Dr. Jeff Ryan, Head, 256-782-8334, E-mail: jryan@jsu.edu. *Application contact:* Dr. Jean Pugliese, Associate Dean, 256-782-8278, Fax: 256-782-5321, E-mail: pugliese@jsu.edu.
Website: http://www.jsu.edu/emergency-management/academics/

**Lander University,** Graduate Studies, Greenwood, SC 29649-2099. Offers clinical nurse leader (MSN); emergency management (MS); Montessori education (M Ed); teaching and learning (M Ed). *Accreditation:* NCATE. *Program availability:* Part-time, online learning. *Degree requirements:* For master's, comprehensive exam, thesis or alternative. *Entrance requirements:* For master's, GRE General Test. Additional exam requirements/recommendations for international students: Required—TOEFL (minimum score 550 paper-based). Electronic applications accepted.

**Lasell College,** Graduate and Professional Studies in Criminal Justice, Newton, MA 02466. Offers emergency and crisis management (MS, Certificate); homeland security and global justice (MS, Certificate); violence prevention and advocacy (MS, Certificate). *Program availability:* Part-time, evening/weekend, online only, 100% online. *Faculty:* 1

full-time (0 women), 2 part-time/adjunct (both women). *Students:* 5 full-time (2 women), 11 part-time (5 women); includes 2 minority (1 Black or African American, non-Hispanic/Latino; 1 Asian, non-Hispanic/Latino). Average age 30. 23 applicants, 52% accepted, 8 enrolled. *Degree requirements:* For master's, minimum GPA of 3.0; internship or research paper. *Entrance requirements:* For master's, one-page personal statement, 2 letters of recommendation, resume, bachelor's degree transcript; for Certificate, bachelor's transcript, 2 letters of recommendation, 1-page statement, resume. Additional exam requirements/recommendations for international students: Required—TOEFL (minimum score 550 paper-based, 79 iBT) or IELTS (minimum score 6). *Application deadline:* For fall admission, 8/31 priority date for domestic students, 6/30 priority date for international students; for spring admission, 12/31 priority date for domestic students, 10/31 priority date for international students. Applications are processed on a rolling basis. Electronic applications accepted. *Expenses:* $600 per credit. *Financial support:* In 2016–17, 6 students received support. Federal Work-Study, scholarships/grants, and tuition discounts available. Support available to part-time students. Financial award application deadline: 8/31; financial award applicants required to submit FAFSA. *Faculty research:* Children aging out of foster care and the criminal justice system; police departments' attitudes toward the mentally ill and jail diversion programs for those offenders. *Unit head:* Dr. Joan Dolamore, Dean of Graduate and Professional Studies, 617-243-2485, Fax: 617-243-2450, E-mail: gradinfo@lasell.edu. *Application contact:* Adrienne Franciosi, Director of Graduate Enrollment, 617-243-2214, Fax: 617-243-2450, E-mail: gradinfo@lasell.edu.
Website: http://www.lasell.edu/academics/graduate-and-professional-studies/programs-of-study/master-of-science-in-criminal-justice-.html

**Liberty University,** School of Behavioral Sciences, Lynchburg, VA 24515. Offers clinical mental health counseling (MA); counselor education and supervision (PhD); human services counseling (MA), including addictions and recovery, business, child and family law, Christian ministries, criminal justice, crisis response and trauma, executive leadership, health and wellness, life coaching, marriage and family, military resilience; marriage and family therapy (MA); military resilience (Certificate); professional counseling (MA). *Program availability:* Part-time, online learning. *Students:* 2,041 full-time (1,612 women), 4,970 part-time (3,875 women); includes 1,991 minority (1,678 Black or African American, non-Hispanic/Latino; 33 American Indian or Alaska Native, non-Hispanic/Latino; 48 Asian, non-Hispanic/Latino; 80 Hispanic/Latino; 8 Native Hawaiian or other Pacific Islander, non-Hispanic/Latino; 144 Two or more races, non-Hispanic/Latino), 127 international. Average age 39. 5,496 applicants, 41% accepted, 1257 enrolled. In 2016, 2,813 master's, 11 doctorates, 20 other advanced degrees awarded. *Application deadline:* Applications are processed on a rolling basis. Application fee: $50. Electronic applications accepted. *Financial support:* Applicants required to submit FAFSA. *Unit head:* Dr. Ronald Hawkins, Founding Dean, School of Behavioral Sciences. *Application contact:* Jay Bridge, Director of Admissions, 800-424-9595, Fax: 800-628-7977, E-mail: gradadmissions@liberty.edu.

**London Metropolitan University,** Graduate Programs, London, United Kingdom. Offers applied psychology (M Sc); architecture (MA); biomedical science (M Sc); blood science (M Sc); cancer pharmacology (M Sc); computer networking and cyber security (M Sc); computing and information systems (M Sc); conference interpreting (MA); counter-terrorism studies (M Sc); creative, digital and professional writing (MA); crime, violence and prevention (M Sc); criminology (M Sc); curating contemporary art (MA); data analytics (M Sc); digital media (MA); early childhood studies (MA); education (MA, Ed D); financial services law, regulation and compliance (LL M); food science (M Sc); forensic psychology (M Sc); health and social care management and policy (M Sc); human nutrition (M Sc); human resource management (MA); human rights and international conflict (MA); information technology (M Sc); intelligence and security studies (M Sc); international oil, gas and energy law (LL M); international relations (MA); interpreting (MA); learning and teaching in higher education (MA); legal practice (LL M); media and entertainment law (LL M); organizational and consumer psychology (M Sc); psychological therapy (M Sc); psychology of mental health (M Sc); public health (M Sc); public policy and management (MPA); security studies (M Sc); social work (M Sc); spatial planning and urban design (MA); sports therapy (M Sc); supporting older children and young people with dyslexia (MA); teaching languages (MA), including Arabic, English; translation (MA); woman and child abuse (MA).

**Massachusetts Maritime Academy,** Program in Emergency Management, Buzzards Bay, MA 02532-1803. Offers MS. *Program availability:* Part-time-only, evening/weekend. Electronic applications accepted.

**Metropolitan College of New York,** Program in Public Administration, New York, NY 10006. Offers emergency and disaster management (MPA); public affairs and administration (MPA). *Program availability:* Evening/weekend. *Students:* 120 full-time (85 women), 10 part-time (4 women); includes 108 minority (76 Black or African American, non-Hispanic/Latino; 5 Asian, non-Hispanic/Latino; 26 Hispanic/Latino; 1 Native Hawaiian or other Pacific Islander, non-Hispanic/Latino), 2 international. Average age 37. In 2016, 118 master's awarded. *Degree requirements:* For master's, thesis. *Entrance requirements:* For master's, appropriate work experience, interview, minimum GPA of 2.7, internship or job in administrative setting. Additional exam requirements/recommendations for international students: Required—TOEFL (minimum score 600 paper-based). *Application deadline:* For fall admission, 7/30 priority date for domestic students, 7/1 for international students; for winter admission, 11/30 priority date for domestic students, 11/1 for international students; for spring admission, 3/30 priority date for domestic students, 3/1 for international students. Applications are processed on a rolling basis. Application fee: $45. Electronic applications accepted. *Expenses:* Contact institution. *Financial support:* Fellowships with tuition reimbursements, career-related internships or fieldwork, scholarships/grants, and tuition waivers (partial) available. Financial award application deadline: 8/15; financial award applicants required to submit FAFSA. *Faculty research:* Transnational politics and culture, women and social policy, confidentiality in the human services, concepts of marginality, ethics in social policy. *Unit head:* Prof. Humphrey Crookendale, Dean, Graduate School for Public Affairs Administration, 212-343-1234 Ext. 2209, E-mail: hcrookendale@mcny.edu. *Application contact:* Steebo Varghese, Assistant Director of Admissions, 212-343-1234 Ext. 2708, Fax: 212-343-8474, E-mail: svarghese@mcny.edu.
Website: http://www.metropolitan.edu/

**Millersville University of Pennsylvania,** College of Graduate Studies and Adult Learning, College of Science and Technology, Center for Disaster Research and Education, Millersville, PA 17551-0302. Offers emergency management (MS). *Program availability:* Part-time, evening/weekend, online only, 100% online. *Faculty:* 11 full-time (5 women). *Students:* 9 full-time (4 women), 50 part-time (17 women); includes 6 minority (2 Black or African American, non-Hispanic/Latino; 3 Hispanic/Latino; 1 Two or more races, non-Hispanic/Latino), 1 international. Average age 34. 26 applicants, 100% accepted, 20 enrolled. In 2016, 35 master's awarded. *Degree requirements:* For master's, field practicum. *Entrance requirements:* For master's, GRE or MAT (if undergraduate cumulative GPA is lower than 2.8), resume. Additional exam requirements/recommendations for international students: Required—TOEFL (minimum score 600 paper-based), IELTS (minimum score 6). *Application deadline:* Applications are processed on a rolling basis. Application fee: $40. Electronic applications accepted.

## Emergency Management

*Expenses:* $483 per credit resident tuition; $566 per credit non-resident tuition. *Financial support:* In 2016–17, 7 students received support. Unspecified assistantships available. Financial award application deadline: 3/15; financial award applicants required to submit FAFSA. *Faculty research:* Emergency management, continuity of operations, regional planning and preparedness, disaster law and policy, community preparedness and mitigation efforts. *Total annual research expenditures:* $4,000. *Unit head:* Dr. Sepideh Yalda, Director, 717-871-7433, Fax: 717-871-2429, E-mail: sepi.yalda@millersville.edu. *Application contact:* Dr. Victor S. DeSantis, Dean of College of Graduate Studies and Adult Learning/Associate Provost for Civic and Community Engagement, 717-871-7619, Fax: 717-871-7954, E-mail: victor.desantis@millersville.edu.
Website: http://www.millersville.edu/cdre/index.php

**New Jersey Institute of Technology,** Ying Wu College of Computing, Newark, NJ 07102. Offers big data management and mining (Certificate); business and information systems (Certificate); computer science (MS, PhD), including bioinformatics (MS), computer science, computing and business (MS), cyber security and privacy (MS), software engineering (MS); data mining (Certificate); information security (Certificate); information systems (MS, PhD), including business and information systems (MS), emergency management and business continuity (MS), information systems; information technology administration and security (MS); IT administration (Certificate); network security and information assurance (Certificate); software engineering analysis/design (Certificate); Web systems development (Certificate). *Program availability:* Part-time, evening/weekend. *Faculty:* 64 full-time (10 women), 38 part-time/adjunct (4 women). *Students:* 818 full-time (241 women), 225 part-time (53 women); includes 162 minority (35 Black or African American, non-Hispanic/Latino; 77 Asian, non-Hispanic/Latino; 41 Hispanic/Latino; 9 Two or more races, non-Hispanic/Latino), 772 international. Average age 27. 2,666 applicants, 51% accepted, 377 enrolled. In 2016, 398 master's, 10 doctorates, 9 other advanced degrees awarded. Terminal master's awarded for partial completion of doctoral program. *Degree requirements:* For master's, thesis optional; for doctorate, thesis/dissertation. *Entrance requirements:* For master's, GRE General Test; for doctorate, GRE General Test, minimum graduate GPA of 3.5. Additional exam requirements/recommendations for international students: Required—TOEFL (minimum score 550 paper-based; 79 iBT). *Application deadline:* For fall admission, 6/1 priority date for domestic students, 5/1 priority date for international students; for spring admission, 11/15 priority date for domestic and international students. Applications are processed on a rolling basis. Application fee: $75. Electronic applications accepted. *Expenses:* Contact institution. *Financial support:* In 2016–17, 57 students received support, including 18 research assistantships (averaging $16,073 per year), 39 teaching assistantships (averaging $20,194 per year); fellowships, career-related internships or fieldwork, Federal Work-Study, institutionally sponsored loans, and unspecified assistantships also available. Financial award application deadline: 1/15. *Faculty research:* Computer systems, communications and networking, artificial intelligence, database engineering, systems analysis, analytics and optimization in crowdsourcing. *Total annual research expenditures:* $3 million. *Unit head:* Dr. Craig Gotsman, Dean, 973-542-5488, Fax: 973-596-5777, E-mail: marek.rusinkiewicz@njit.edu. *Application contact:* Stephen Eck, Director of Admissions, 973-596-3300, Fax: 973-596-3461, E-mail: admissions@njit.edu.
Website: http://computing.njit.edu/

**New York Medical College,** School of Health Sciences and Practice, Valhalla, NY 10595. Offers behavioral sciences and health promotion (MPH); biostatistics (MS); children with special health care (Graduate Certificate); emergency preparedness (Graduate Certificate); environmental health science (MPH); epidemiology (MPH, MS); global health (Graduate Certificate); health education (Graduate Certificate); health policy and management (MPH, Dr PH); industrial hygiene (Graduate Certificate); pediatric dysphagia (Post-Graduate Certificate); physical therapy (DPT); public health (Graduate Certificate); speech-language pathology (MS). *Accreditation:* CEPH. *Program availability:* Part-time, evening/weekend, 100% online, blended/hybrid learning. *Faculty:* 42 full-time (31 women), 236 part-time/adjunct (138 women). *Students:* 235 full-time (165 women), 252 part-time (185 women); includes 188 minority (83 Black or African American, non-Hispanic/Latino; 1 American Indian or Alaska Native, non-Hispanic/Latino; 62 Asian, non-Hispanic/Latino; 36 Hispanic/Latino; 6 Two or more races, non-Hispanic/Latino), 26 international. Average age 27. In 2016, 110 master's, 37 doctorates awarded. *Degree requirements:* For master's, comprehensive exam (for some programs), thesis (for some programs); for doctorate, thesis/dissertation. *Expenses:* $1,070 per credit tuition, $105 fees. *Unit head:* Ben Watson, PhD, Vice Dean, 914-594-4531, E-mail: ben_watson@nymc.edu. *Application contact:* Veronica Jarek-Prinz, Associate Dean for Admissions and Enrollment Management, 914-594-3941, E-mail: veronica_jarekprinz@nymc.edu.
Website: http://www.nymc.edu/school-of-health-sciences-and-practice-shsp/

**Norwich University,** College of Graduate and Continuing Studies, Master of Public Administration Program, Northfield, VT 05663. Offers criminal justice and public safety (MPA); fiscal management (MPA); international development and influence (MPA); municipal governance (MPA); nonprofit management (MPA); policy analysis and analytics (MPA); public administration leadership and crisis management (MPA); public works and sustainability (MPA). *Program availability:* Evening/weekend, online only, mostly all online with a week-long residency requirement. *Faculty:* 13 part-time/adjunct (5 women). *Students:* 63 full-time (23 women); includes 9 minority (5 Black or African American, non-Hispanic/Latino; 1 Asian, non-Hispanic/Latino; 1 Hispanic/Latino; 2 Two or more races, non-Hispanic/Latino). Average age 38. 23 applicants, 100% accepted, 15 enrolled. In 2016, 38 master's awarded. *Degree requirements:* For master's, capstone. *Entrance requirements:* For master's, minimum undergraduate GPA of 2.75. Additional exam requirements/recommendations for international students: Required—TOEFL (minimum score 550 paper-based; 80 iBT), IELTS (minimum score 6.5). *Application deadline:* For fall admission, 8/14 for domestic and international students; for winter admission, 11/13 for domestic and international students; for spring admission, 2/12 for domestic and international students; for summer admission, 5/15 for domestic and international students. Electronic applications accepted. *Expenses:* Contact institution. *Financial support:* In 2016–17, 21 students received support. Scholarships/grants available. Financial award application deadline: 8/4; financial award applicants required to submit FAFSA. *Unit head:* Dr. Rosemarie Pelletier, Program Director, 802-485-2767, Fax: 802-485-2533, E-mail: rpellet2@norwich.edu. *Application contact:* Admissions Advisor, 800-460-5597 Ext. 3377, Fax: 802-485-2533, E-mail: mpa@online.norwich.edu.
Website: https://online.norwich.edu/degree-programs/masters/master-public-administration/overview

**Nova Southeastern University,** College of Osteopathic Medicine, Fort Lauderdale, FL 33328. Offers biomedical informatics (MS, Graduate Certificate), including biomedical informatics (MS), clinical informatics (Graduate Certificate); public health informatics (Graduate Certificate); disaster and emergency management (MS); medical education (MS); nutrition (MS, Graduate Certificate), including functional nutrition and herbal therapy (Graduate Certificate); osteopathic medicine (DO); public health (MPH, Graduate Certificate), including health education (Graduate Certificate); social medicine (Graduate Certificate). *Accreditation:* AOsA. *Faculty:* 126 full-time (64 women), 1,411 part-time/adjunct (352 women). *Students:* 1,040 full-time (476 women), 196 part-time (135 women); includes 635 minority (95 Black or African American, non-Hispanic/Latino;

298 Asian, non-Hispanic/Latino; 208 Hispanic/Latino; 1 Native Hawaiian or other Pacific Islander, non-Hispanic/Latino; 33 Two or more races, non-Hispanic/Latino), 54 international. Average age 27. 5,383 applicants, 7% accepted, 248 enrolled. In 2016, 94 master's, 231 doctorates, 2 other advanced degrees awarded. *Degree requirements:* For master's, comprehensive exam (for MPH); field/special projects; for doctorate, comprehensive exam, COMLEX Boards; for Graduate Certificate, thesis or alternative. *Entrance requirements:* For master's, GRE; for doctorate, MCAT, biology, chemistry, organic chemistry, physics (all with labs), biochemistry, and English. *Application deadline:* For fall admission, 1/15 for domestic students. Applications are processed on a rolling basis. Application fee: $50. Electronic applications accepted. *Expenses:* $49,639 residents, $54,806 non-residents for out-of-state students; $100 microscope/laboratory fee (for first-year students); $145 per year Health Professions Division student access fee; $1,050 per year student service fee. *Financial support:* In 2016–17, 46 students received support, including 8 fellowships (averaging $30,690 per year); research assistantships, teaching assistantships, Federal Work-Study, and scholarships/grants also available. Financial award application deadline: 6/1; financial award applicants required to submit FAFSA. *Faculty research:* Teaching strategies, simulated patient use, HIV/AIDS education, minority health issues, managed care education. *Unit head:* Elaine M. Wallace, Dean, 954-262-1457, Fax: 954-262-2250, E-mail: ewallace@nova.edu. *Application contact:* HPD Admissions, 877-640-0218, E-mail: hpdinfo@nova.edu.
Website: http://www.osteopathic.nova.edu/

**Oklahoma State University,** College of Arts and Sciences, Department of Political Science, Stillwater, OK 74078. Offers fire and emergency management administration (MS, PhD); political science (MA). *Faculty:* 23 full-time (9 women), 3 part-time/adjunct (1 woman). *Students:* 24 full-time (2 women), 46 part-time (12 women); includes 10 minority (1 Black or African American, non-Hispanic/Latino; 1 Asian, non-Hispanic/Latino; 8 Hispanic/Latino), 11 international. Average age 36. 46 applicants, 65% accepted, 20 enrolled. In 2016, 17 master's, 3 doctorates awarded. *Degree requirements:* For master's, comprehensive exam, thesis or creative component; for doctorate, comprehensive exam, thesis/dissertation. *Entrance requirements:* For master's and doctorate, GRE. Additional exam requirements/recommendations for international students: Required—TOEFL (minimum score 550 paper-based; 79 iBT). *Application deadline:* For fall admission, 3/1 priority date for international students; for spring admission, 8/1 priority date for international students. Applications are processed on a rolling basis. Application fee: $40 ($75 for international students). Electronic applications accepted. *Expenses:* Tuition, state resident: full-time $3775; part-time $209.70 per credit hour. Tuition, nonresident: full-time $14,851; part-time $825.05 per credit hour. *Required fees:* $2027; $112.60 per credit hour. Tuition and fees vary according to campus/location. *Financial support:* In 2016–17, 7 teaching assistantships (averaging $14,035 per year) were awarded; research assistantships, career-related internships or fieldwork, Federal Work-Study, scholarships/grants, health care benefits, tuition waivers (partial), and unspecified assistantships also available. Support available to part-time students. Financial award application deadline: 3/1; financial award applicants required to submit FAFSA. *Faculty research:* Fire and emergency management, environmental dispute resolution, voting and elections, women and politics, urban politics. *Unit head:* Dr. Jeanette Mendez, Department Head, 405-744-5607, E-mail: jeanette.mendez@okstate.edu.
Website: http://polsci.okstate.edu

**Pace University,** Dyson College of Arts and Sciences, MA Program in Management for Public Safety and Homeland Security Professionals, New York, NY 10038. Offers MA. *Program availability:* Evening/weekend, blended/hybrid learning. *Students:* 7 full-time (5 women), 12 part-time (4 women); includes 8 minority (4 Black or African American, non-Hispanic/Latino; 4 Hispanic/Latino). Average age 30. In 2016, 10 master's awarded. *Degree requirements:* For master's, project. *Entrance requirements:* For master's, 2 letters of recommendation, resume, personal statement, official transcripts. Additional exam requirements/recommendations for international students: Required—TOEFL. *Application deadline:* For fall admission, 8/1 for domestic students. Applications are processed on a rolling basis. Application fee: $70. Electronic applications accepted. *Expenses: Tuition:* Part-time $1195 per credit. *Required fees:* $260 per semester. Tuition and fees vary according to degree level, campus/location and program. *Financial support:* Research assistantships, scholarships/grants, and unspecified assistantships available. Financial award application deadline: 2/15; financial award applicants required to submit FAFSA. *Unit head:* Dr. Joseph Ryan, Chair, Criminal Justice and Security Department, 914-773-3814, E-mail: jryan@pace.edu. *Application contact:* Susan Ford-Goldschein, Director of Admissions, 914-422-4283, Fax: 212-346-1585, E-mail: graduateadmission@pace.edu.
Website: http://www.pace.edu/dyson/programs/ma-public-safety-homeland-security

**Park University,** School of Graduate and Professional Studies, Kansas City, MO 54105. Offers adult education (M Ed); business and government leadership (Graduate Certificate); business, government, and global society (MPA); communication and leadership (MA); creative and life writing (Graduate Certificate); disaster and emergency management (MPA, Graduate Certificate); educational leadership (M Ed); finance (MBA, Graduate Certificate); general business (MBA); global business (Graduate Certificate); healthcare administration (MHA); healthcare services management and leadership (Graduate Certificate); international business (MBA); language and literacy (M Ed), including English for speakers of other languages, special reading teacher/literacy coach; leadership of international healthcare organizations (Graduate Certificate); management information systems (MBA, Graduate Certificate); music performance (ADP, Graduate Certificate), including cello (MM, ADP), piano (MM, ADP), viola (MM, ADP), violin (MM, ADP); nonprofit and community services management (MPA); nonprofit leadership (Graduate Certificate); performance (MM), including cello (MM, ADP), piano (MM, ADP), viola (MM, ADP), violin (MM, ADP); public management (MPA); social work (MSW); teacher leadership (M Ed), including curriculum and assessment, instructional leader. *Program availability:* Part-time, evening/weekend, online learning. *Degree requirements:* For master's, comprehensive exam (for some programs), thesis (for some programs), internship (for some programs); exam (for some programs). *Entrance requirements:* For master's, GRE or GMAT (for some programs), teacher certification (for some M Ed programs), letters of recommendation, essay, resume (for some programs). Additional exam requirements/recommendations for international students: Required—TOEFL (minimum score 550 paper-based; 79 iBT), IELTS (minimum score 6). Electronic applications accepted.

**Philadelphia University,** College of Science, Health and the Liberal Arts, Program in Disaster Medicine and Management, Philadelphia, PA 19144. Offers MS. *Program availability:* Online learning.

**Regent University,** Graduate School, Robertson School of Government, Virginia Beach, VA 23464-9800. Offers government (MA), including American government, healthcare policy and ethics (MA, MPA), international relations, law and public policy, national security studies, political communication, political theory, religion and politics; public administration (MPA), including emergency management and homeland security, federal government, general public administration, healthcare policy and ethics (MA, MPA), law, nonprofit administration and faith-based organizations, public leadership and management, servant leadership. *Program availability:* Part-time, evening/weekend,

100% online, blended/hybrid learning. *Faculty:* 8 full-time (1 woman), 19 part-time/adjunct (3 women). *Students:* 40 full-time (27 women), 119 part-time (69 women); includes 73 minority (47 Black or African American, non-Hispanic/Latino; 3 Asian, non-Hispanic/Latino; 15 Hispanic/Latino; 8 Two or more races, non-Hispanic/Latino), 6 international. Average age 35. 253 applicants, 41% accepted, 70 enrolled. In 2016, 34 master's awarded. *Degree requirements:* For master's, thesis optional, internship. *Entrance requirements:* For master's, GRE General Test or LSAT, personal essay, writing sample, resume, college transcripts. Additional exam requirements/recommendations for international students: Required—TOEFL (minimum score 577 paper-based). *Application deadline:* For fall admission, 5/1 priority date for domestic students; for spring admission, 11/1 priority date for domestic students. Applications are processed on a rolling basis. Application fee: $50. Electronic applications accepted. *Expenses:* $650 per credit (MA/MPA); $250 per semester technology fee. *Financial support:* In 2016–17, 78 students received support. Career-related internships or fieldwork, scholarships/grants, and unspecified assistantships available. Support available to part-time students. *Faculty research:* International relations and politics, public administration, leadership and ethics, Biblical law, Constitutional law and Supreme Court. *Unit head:* Dr. Eric Patterson, Dean, 757-352-4616, Fax: 757-352-4735, E-mail: epatterson@regent.edu. *Application contact:* Heidi Cece, Assistant Vice President of Enrollment Management, 800-373-5504, Fax: 757-352-4381, E-mail: admissions@regent.edu.
Website: http://www.regent.edu/rsg/

**Royal Roads University,** Graduate Studies, Peace and Conflict Studies Program, Victoria, BC V9B 5Y2, Canada. Offers conflict analysis (G Dip); conflict analysis and management (MA); disaster and emergency management (MA); human security and peacebuilding (MA). *Program availability:* Online learning. *Degree requirements:* For master's, thesis. *Entrance requirements:* For master's, 5-7 years of related work experience. Additional exam requirements/recommendations for international students: Required—TOEFL (paper-based 570) or IELTS (7) recommended. Electronic applications accepted. *Faculty research:* Conflict analysis, ethno-political conflict reconciliation, international relations, displaced persons.

**Rutgers University–New Brunswick,** School of Public Health, Piscataway, NJ 08854. Offers biostatistics (MPH, MS, Dr PH, PhD); clinical epidemiology (Certificate); environmental and occupational health (MPH, Dr PH, PhD, Certificate); epidemiology (MPH, Dr PH, PhD); general public health (Certificate); health education and behavioral science (MPH, Dr PH, PhD); health systems and policy (MPH, PhD); public health (MPH, Dr PH, PhD); public health preparedness (Certificate); DO/MPH; JD/MPH; MBA/MPH; MD/MPH; MPH/MBA; MPH/MSPA; MS/MPH; Psy D/MPH. *Accreditation:* CEPH. *Program availability:* Part-time, evening/weekend. *Degree requirements:* For master's, thesis, internship; for doctorate, comprehensive exam, thesis/dissertation. *Entrance requirements:* For master's, GRE General Test; for doctorate, GRE General Test, MPH (Dr PH); MA, MPH, or MS (PhD). Additional exam requirements/recommendations for international students: Required—TOEFL. Electronic applications accepted.

**Saint Leo University,** Graduate Studies in Public Safety Administration, Saint Leo, FL 33574-6665. Offers criminal justice (MS), including corrections, criminal investigation, emergency and disaster management, forensic science, legal studies; emergency and disaster management (MS). *Program availability:* Part-time, evening/weekend, 100% online, blended/hybrid learning. *Faculty:* 7 full-time (2 women), 32 part-time/adjunct (8 women). *Students:* 3 full-time (1 woman), 667 part-time (446 women); includes 355 minority (275 Black or African American, non-Hispanic/Latino; 6 American Indian or Alaska Native, non-Hispanic/Latino; 4 Asian, non-Hispanic/Latino; 56 Hispanic/Latino; 3 Native Hawaiian or other Pacific Islander, non-Hispanic/Latino; 11 Two or more races, non-Hispanic/Latino). Average age 37. 361 applicants, 87% accepted, 177 enrolled. In 2016, 265 master's awarded. *Degree requirements:* For master's, comprehensive project. *Entrance requirements:* For master's, official transcripts, bachelor's degree from regionally-accredited university with minimum GPA of 3.0. Additional exam requirements/recommendations for international students: Required—TOEFL (minimum score 550 paper-based; 80 iBT). *Application deadline:* For fall admission, 7/1 priority date for domestic and international students; for spring admission, 11/1 priority date for domestic and international students. Applications are processed on a rolling basis. Application fee: $80. Electronic applications accepted. *Expenses:* $535 per semester hour (for MS in emergency/disaster management); $555 per semester hour (for MS in criminal justice). *Financial support:* In 2016–17, 14 students received support. Scholarships/grants and health care benefits available. Financial award application deadline: 3/1; financial award applicants required to submit FAFSA. *Unit head:* Dr. Robert Diemer, Director of Graduate Studies in Safety Administration, 352-588-8974, Fax: 352-588-8289, E-mail: graduatepublicsafety@saintleo.edu. *Application contact:* Jennifer Shelley, Senior Associate Director of Graduate Admissions, 800-707-8846, Fax: 352-588-7873, E-mail: grad.admissions@saintleo.edu.
Website: http://www.saintleo.edu/academics/graduate

**San Diego State University,** Graduate and Research Affairs, College of Health and Human Services, Graduate School of Public Health, San Diego, CA 92182. Offers environmental health (PhD); epidemiology (MPH, PhD), including biostatistics (MPH); global emergency preparedness and response (MS); global health (PhD); health behavior (PhD); health promotion (MPH); health services administration (MPH); toxicology (MS); MPH/MA; MSW/MPH. *Accreditation:* CAHME (one or more programs are accredited); CEPH (one or more programs are accredited). *Program availability:* Part-time. *Degree requirements:* For master's, comprehensive exam (for some programs), thesis (for some programs); for doctorate, thesis/dissertation. *Entrance requirements:* For master's, GMAT (MPH in health services administration), GRE General Test; for doctorate, GRE General Test. Additional exam requirements/recommendations for international students: Required—TOEFL. *Faculty research:* Evaluation of tobacco, AIDS prevalence and prevention, mammography, infant death project, Alzheimer's in elderly Chinese.

**Sul Ross State University,** College of Professional Studies, Department of Criminal Justice, Alpine, TX 79832. Offers criminal justice (MS); homeland security (MS); MS/MA. *Entrance requirements:* For master's, GRE General Test, minimum GPA of 2.5 in last 60 hours of undergraduate work.

**Syracuse University,** David B. Falk College of Sport and Human Dynamics, CAS Program in Trauma-Informed Practice, Syracuse, NY 13244. Offers CAS. *Program availability:* Part-time. *Entrance requirements:* For degree, three letters of recommendation, transcripts, personal statement, resume. Additional exam requirements/recommendations for international students: Required—TOEFL or IELTS. *Application deadline:* For fall admission, 2/15 priority date for domestic and international students; for summer admission, 11/15 priority date for domestic and international students. Application fee: $75. Electronic applications accepted. *Expenses: Tuition:* Full-time $25,974; part-time $1443 per credit hour. *Required fees:* $802; $50 per course. Tuition and fees vary according to course load and program. *Financial support:* Application deadline: 1/1. *Faculty research:* Trauma-informed practice, understanding of the vulnerabilities or triggers of trauma survivors, theoretical foundations of trauma, evidenced based approaches and techniques, trauma response and intervention. *Unit head:* Dr. Thom deLara, Department Chair/Professor of Practice, 315-443-9830, E-mail: tdelara@syr.edu. *Application contact:* Felicia Otero, Director of College Admissions,

315-443-5555, E-mail: falk@syr.edu.
Website: http://falk.syr.edu/MarriageFamilyTherapy/CAS.aspx

**Trident University International,** College of Health Sciences, Program in Health Sciences, Cypress, CA 90630. Offers clinical research administration (MS, Certificate); emergency and disaster management (MS, Certificate); environmental health science (Certificate); health care administration (PhD); health care management (MS), including health informatics; health education (MS, Certificate); health informatics (Certificate); health sciences (PhD); international health (MS); international health: educator or researcher option (PhD); international health: practitioner option (PhD); law and expert witness studies (MS, Certificate); public health (MS); quality assurance (Certificate). *Program availability:* For doctorate, comprehensive exam, thesis/dissertation, defense of dissertation. *Entrance requirements:* For master's, minimum GPA of 2.5 (students with GPA 3.0 or greater may transfer up to 30% of graduate level credits); for doctorate, minimum GPA of 3.4, curriculum vitae, course work in research methods or statistics. Additional exam requirements/recommendations for international students: Required—TOEFL. Electronic applications accepted.

**Trine University,** Program in Criminal Justice, Angola, IN 46703-1764. Offers emergency management (MS); forensic psychology (MS); law (MS); public administration (MS). *Program availability:* Part-time, evening/weekend. *Entrance requirements:* Additional exam requirements/recommendations for international students: Required—TOEFL. *Expenses: Tuition:* Full-time $13,320. *Required fees:* $460. Tuition and fees vary according to degree level, campus/location, program and student level. *Financial support:* Application deadline: 3/1; applicants required to submit FAFSA. *Unit head:* Craig Laker, Dean, College of Graduate and Professional Studies/Associate Professor, 260-665-4862, E-mail: lakerc@trine.edu.
Website: http://www.trine.edu/academics/majors-and-minors/graduate/criminal-justice/index.aspx

**Tulane University,** School of Social Work, New Orleans, LA 70118-5669. Offers city, culture and community (PhD); disaster resilience leadership (MS); social work (MSW, DSW). *Accreditation:* CSWE (one or more programs are accredited). *Program availability:* Part-time. *Degree requirements:* For master's, thesis. *Entrance requirements:* Additional exam requirements/recommendations for international students: Required—TOEFL. Electronic applications accepted. *Expenses: Tuition:* Full-time $50,920; part-time $2829 per credit hour. *Required fees:* $2040; $44.50 per credit hour. $580 per term. Tuition and fees vary according to course load, degree level and program.

**Université de Montréal,** Faculty of Medicine, Programs in Environment and Prevention, Montréal, QC H3C 3J7, Canada. Offers environment, health and disaster management (DESS). Electronic applications accepted. *Faculty research:* Health, environment, pollutants, protection, waste.

**University at Albany, State University of New York,** College of Emergency Preparedness, Homeland Security and Cybersecurity, Albany, NY 12222-0001. Offers cybersecurity (Certificate); emergency preparedness (Certificate); homeland security (Certificate). *Faculty:* 3 part-time/adjunct (0 women). *Students:* 8 part-time (5 women). 13 applicants, 100% accepted, 5 enrolled. In 2016, 5 Certificates awarded. *Entrance requirements:* Additional exam requirements/recommendations for international students: Required—TOEFL. *Expenses:* Tuition, state resident: full-time $10,870; part-time $453 per credit hour. Tuition, nonresident: full-time $22,210; part-time $925 per credit hour. *International tuition:* $21,550 full-time. *Required fees:* $1864; $96 per credit hour. *Unit head:* Dr. Robert Griffin, Dean, 518-442-5258. *Application contact:* Michael DeRensis, Director, Graduate Admissions, 518-442-3980, Fax: 518-442-3922, E-mail: graduate@albany.edu.
Website: http://www.albany.edu/cehc/

**University of Alaska Fairbanks,** School of Management, Program in Security and Disaster Management, Fairbanks, AK 99775. Offers MSDM. *Program availability:* Part-time, evening/weekend, 100% online, blended/hybrid learning. *Faculty:* 4 full-time (0 women). *Students:* 5 full-time (1 woman), 13 part-time (3 women); includes 5 minority (1 Black or African American, non-Hispanic/Latino; 4 Hispanic/Latino). Average age 34. 16 applicants, 63% accepted, 10 enrolled. *Entrance requirements:* For master's, Watson-Glaser Critical Thinking Appraisal. Additional exam requirements/recommendations for international students: Required—TOEFL (minimum score 79 iBT), IELTS (minimum score 6.5). *Application deadline:* For fall admission, 6/1 for domestic students, 3/1 for international students; for spring admission, 10/15 for domestic students, 9/1 for international students. Applications are processed on a rolling basis. Application fee: $60. Electronic applications accepted. *Expenses:* $533 per credit resident tuition, $673 per semester resident fees; $1,088 per credit non-resident tuition, $835 per semester non-resident fees. *Financial support:* In 2016–17, 1 teaching assistantship (averaging $14,820 per year) was awarded; Federal Work-Study and scholarships/grants also available. Financial award application deadline: 2/15; financial award applicants required to submit FAFSA. *Unit head:* Cameron Carlson, Director, 907-474-6537, E-mail: uaf-hsem@alaska.edu. *Application contact:* Mary Kreta, Director of Admissions, 907-474-7500, Fax: 907-474-7097, E-mail: admissions@uaf.edu.
Website: http://www.uaf.edu/som/degrees/graduate/msdm/

**University of Central Florida,** College of Health and Public Affairs, School of Public Administration, Orlando, FL 32816. Offers emergency management and homeland security (Certificate); fundraising (Certificate); non-profit management (MNM, Certificate); urban and regional planning (MS). *Accreditation:* NASPAA. *Program availability:* Part-time, evening/weekend. *Faculty:* 24 full-time (11 women), 11 part-time/adjunct (6 women). *Students:* 87 full-time (60 women), 257 part-time (190 women); includes 157 minority (83 Black or African American, non-Hispanic/Latino; 1 American Indian or Alaska Native, non-Hispanic/Latino; 9 Asian, non-Hispanic/Latino; 62 Hispanic/Latino; 2 Two or more races, non-Hispanic/Latino), 7 international. Average age 32. 192 applicants, 79% accepted, 108 enrolled. In 2016, 118 master's, 36 other advanced degrees awarded. *Degree requirements:* For master's, comprehensive exam, thesis or alternative, research report. *Entrance requirements:* For master's, GRE General Test. *Application deadline:* For fall admission, 6/15 for domestic students; for spring admission, 11/1 for domestic students. Application fee: $30. Electronic applications accepted. *Expenses:* Tuition, state resident: part-time $288.16 per credit hour. Tuition, nonresident: part-time $1071.31 per credit hour. *Financial support:* In 2016–17, 9 students received support, including 1 fellowship with partial tuition reimbursement available (averaging $4,000 per year), 9 research assistantships with partial tuition reimbursements available (averaging $6,704 per year); career-related internships or fieldwork, Federal Work-Study, institutionally sponsored loans, tuition waivers (partial), and unspecified assistantships also available. Financial award application deadline: 3/1; financial award applicants required to submit FAFSA. *Unit head:* Dr. Naim Kapucu, Director, 407-823-3693, Fax: 407-823-5651, E-mail: naim.kapucu@ucf.edu. *Application contact:* Assistant Director, Graduate Admissions, 407-823-2766, Fax: 407-823-6442, E-mail: gradadmissions@ucf.edu.
Website: https://www.cohpa.ucf.edu/publicadmin/

**University of Chicago,** Graham School of Continuing Liberal and Professional Studies, Program in Threat and Response Management, Chicago, IL 60637. Offers M Sc.

## Emergency Management

*Program availability:* Part-time, evening/weekend. *Students:* 39 part-time (16 women); includes 8 minority (4 Black or African American, non-Hispanic/Latino; 2 Asian, non-Hispanic/Latino; 2 Hispanic/Latino). 34 applicants, 88% accepted, 25 enrolled. *Entrance requirements:* Additional exam requirements/recommendations for international students: Required—TOEFL (minimum score 104 iBT), IELTS (minimum score 7). *Application deadline:* For fall admission, 6/30 for domestic and international students. Electronic applications accepted. *Application contact:* 773-834-2765, E-mail: msctrm@uchicago.edu.
Website: https://grahamschool.uchicago.edu/credit/master-science-threat-response-management/index

**University of Colorado Denver,** School of Public Affairs, Program in Criminology and Criminal Justice, Denver, CO 80217. Offers criminal justice (MCJ), including criminal justice, domestic violence, emergency management and homeland security. *Program availability:* Part-time, evening/weekend. *Students:* 23 full-time (15 women), 17 part-time (8 women); includes 5 minority (2 Black or African American, non-Hispanic/Latino; 1 Asian, non-Hispanic/Latino; 1 Hispanic/Latino; 1 Two or more races, non-Hispanic/Latino), 1 international. Average age 30. 13 applicants, 92% accepted, 7 enrolled. In 2016, 26 master's awarded. *Degree requirements:* For master's, thesis or alternative, 36-39 semester credit hours. *Entrance requirements:* For master's, GRE, GMAT, LSAT, recommendations, official transcripts, current resume, essay. Additional exam requirements/recommendations for international students: Required—TOEFL (minimum score 537 paper-based; 75 iBT); Recommended—IELTS (minimum score 6.5). *Application deadline:* For fall admission, 3/15 priority date for domestic students, 3/1 priority date for international students; for spring admission, 10/15 priority date for domestic students, 10/1 priority date for international students. Application fee: $50 ($75 for international students). Electronic applications accepted. *Expenses:* Contact institution. *Financial support:* In 2016–17, 5 students received support. Fellowships, research assistantships, teaching assistantships, Federal Work-Study, institutionally sponsored loans, scholarships/grants, traineeships, and unspecified assistantships available. Financial award application deadline: 4/1; financial award applicants required to submit FAFSA. *Faculty research:* White collar crime, women and the criminal justice system, applied family violence issues, intimate partner violence and domestic violence interventions, juvenile delinquency. *Unit head:* Dr. Callie Rennison, Program Director, 303-315-2813, Fax: 303-315-2229, E-mail: callie.rennison@ucdenver.edu. *Application contact:* Brendan Hardy, Director of Student Recruitment, 303-315-2227, Fax: 303-315-2229, E-mail: brendan.hardy@ucdenver.edu.
Website: http://ucdenver.edu/academics/colleges/SPA/Academics/programs/CriminalJustice/Pages/index.aspx

**University of Colorado Denver,** School of Public Affairs, Program in Public Affairs and Administration, Denver, CO 80127. Offers public administration (MPA), including domestic violence, emergency management and homeland security, environmental policy, management and law, homeland security and defense, local government, nonprofit management, public administration; public affairs (PhD). *Accreditation:* NASPAA. *Program availability:* Part-time, evening/weekend, online learning. *Students:* 241 full-time (146 women), 135 part-time (86 women); includes 61 minority (15 Black or African American, non-Hispanic/Latino; 1 American Indian or Alaska Native, non-Hispanic/Latino; 10 Asian, non-Hispanic/Latino; 26 Hispanic/Latino; 2 Native Hawaiian or other Pacific Islander, non-Hispanic/Latino; 7 Two or more races, non-Hispanic/Latino), 26 international. Average age 36. 240 applicants, 70% accepted, 91 enrolled. In 2016, 158 master's, 8 doctorates awarded. *Degree requirements:* For master's, thesis or alternative, 36-39 credit hours; for doctorate, comprehensive exam, thesis/dissertation, minimum of 66 semester hours, including at least 30 hours of dissertation. *Entrance requirements:* For master's, GRE, GMAT or LSAT, resume, essay, transcripts, recommendations; for doctorate, GRE, resume, essay, transcripts, recommendations. Additional exam requirements/recommendations for international students: Required—TOEFL (minimum score 550 paper-based; 80 iBT); Recommended—IELTS (minimum score 6.5). *Application deadline:* For fall admission, 2/1 priority date for domestic students, 1/15 priority date for international students; for spring admission, 10/15 priority date for domestic students, 10/1 priority date for international students. Application fee: $50 ($75 for international students). Electronic applications accepted. *Expenses:* Contact institution. *Financial support:* In 2016–17, 92 students received support. Fellowships with partial tuition reimbursements available, research assistantships with partial tuition reimbursements available, teaching assistantships with partial tuition reimbursements available, Federal Work-Study, institutionally sponsored loans, scholarships/grants, traineeships, and unspecified assistantships available. Financial award application deadline: 4/1; financial award applicants required to submit FAFSA. *Faculty research:* Housing, education and the social and economic issues of vulnerable populations; nonprofit governance and management; education finance, effectiveness and reform; P-20 education initiatives; municipal government accountability. *Unit head:* Dr. Christine Martell, Director of MPA Program, 303-315-2716, Fax: 303-315-2229, E-mail: christine.martell@ucdenver.edu. *Application contact:* Dawn Savage, Student Services Coordinator, 303-315-2743, Fax: 303-315-2229, E-mail: dawn.savage@ucdenver.edu.
Website: http://www.ucdenver.edu/academics/colleges/SPA/Academics/programs/PublicAffairsAdmin/Pages/index.aspx

**University of Delaware,** College of Arts and Sciences, School of Public Policy and Administration, Program in Disaster Science and Management, Newark, DE 19716. Offers MS, PhD.

**University of Denver,** University College, Denver, CO 80208. Offers arts and culture (MA, Certificate); communication management (MS, Certificate), including translation studies (Certificate); world history and culture (Certificate); environmental policy and management (MS); geographic information systems (MS); global affairs (MA, Certificate), including human capital in organizations (Certificate), philanthropic leadership (Certificate), project management (Certificate), strategic innovation and change (Certificate); healthcare leadership (MS); information communications and technology (MS); leadership and organizations (MS); professional creative writing (MA, Certificate), including emergency planning and response (Certificate), organizational security (Certificate); security management (MS, Certificate); strategic human resources (Certificate). *Program availability:* Part-time, evening/weekend, online learning. *Faculty:* 118 part-time/adjunct (62 women). *Students:* 59 full-time (22 women), 1,285 part-time (750 women); includes 316 minority (111 Black or African American, non-Hispanic/Latino; 8 American Indian or Alaska Native, non-Hispanic/Latino; 39 Asian, non-Hispanic/Latino; 123 Hispanic/Latino; 3 Native Hawaiian or other Pacific Islander, non-Hispanic/Latino; 32 Two or more races, non-Hispanic/Latino), 85 international. Average age 35. 703 applicants, 89% accepted, 390 enrolled. In 2016, 428 master's, 138 other advanced degrees awarded. *Degree requirements:* For master's, capstone project. *Entrance requirements:* For master's, transcripts, two letters of recommendation, personal statement, resume. Additional exam requirements/recommendations for international students: Required—TOEFL (minimum score 550 paper-based; 80 iBT). *Application deadline:* For fall admission, 6/21 priority date for domestic students, 5/1 priority date for international students; for winter admission, 9/14 priority date for domestic students, 9/19 priority date for international students; for spring admission, 1/11 priority date for domestic students, 12/12 priority date for international students; for summer admission, 3/29 priority date for domestic students, 3/6 priority date for

international students. Applications are processed on a rolling basis. Application fee: $75. Electronic applications accepted. *Expenses:* $7,236 per year full-time. *Financial support:* In 2016–17, 27 students received support, including 1 teaching assistantship (averaging $1,489 per year). Financial award applicants required to submit FAFSA. *Unit head:* Dr. Michael McGuire, Dean, 303-871-3518, Fax: 303-871-3303, E-mail: mmcguire@du.edu. *Application contact:* Information Contact, 303-871-2291, E-mail: ucoladm@du.edu.
Website: http://universitycollege.du.edu/

**University of Florida,** Graduate School, College of Design, Construction and Planning, M.E. Rinker, Sr. School of Construction Management, Gainesville, FL 32611. Offers construction management (MSCM); fire and emergency services (MFES); historic preservation (MSCM); international construction (MICM), including historic preservation; sustainable construction (MSCM); sustainable design (MSCM). *Program availability:* Part-time, online learning. *Degree requirements:* For master's, thesis. *Entrance requirements:* For master's, GRE General Test, minimum GPA of 3.0. Additional exam requirements/recommendations for international students: Required—TOEFL (minimum score 550 paper-based; 80 iBT), IELTS (minimum score 6). Electronic applications accepted. *Faculty research:* Safety, affordable housing, construction management, environmental issues, sustainable construction.

**University of Hawaii at Manoa,** Graduate Division, College of Social Sciences, Department of Urban and Regional Planning, Program in Disaster Preparedness and Emergency Management, Honolulu, HI 96822. Offers Graduate Certificate. *Program availability:* Part-time. *Entrance requirements:* Additional exam requirements/recommendations for international students: Required—TOEFL (minimum score 500 paper-based; 61 iBT), IELTS (minimum score 5).

**University of Illinois at Springfield,** Graduate Programs, College of Public Affairs and Administration, Program in Public Health, Springfield, IL 62703-5407. Offers community health education (Graduate Certificate); emergency preparedness and homeland security (Graduate Certificate); environmental health (Graduate Certificate); environmental risk assessment (Graduate Certificate); epidemiology (Graduate Certificate); public health (MPH). *Program availability:* Part-time, evening/weekend, 100% online. *Faculty:* 7 full-time (5 women). *Students:* 42 full-time (28 women), 53 part-time (32 women); includes 25 minority (14 Black or African American, non-Hispanic/Latino; 7 Asian, non-Hispanic/Latino; 3 Hispanic/Latino; 1 Two or more races, non-Hispanic/Latino), 21 international. Average age 32. 107 applicants, 40% accepted, 20 enrolled. In 2016, 38 master's, 17 other advanced degrees awarded. *Degree requirements:* For master's, comprehensive exam, internship. *Entrance requirements:* For master's, GRE, minimum undergraduate GPA of 3.0, 3 letters of recommendation, statement of personal goals. Additional exam requirements/recommendations for international students: Required—TOEFL (minimum score 500 paper-based; 61 iBT). *Application deadline:* Applications are processed on a rolling basis. Application fee: $60 ($75 for international students). Electronic applications accepted. *Expenses:* Tuition, state resident: part-time $329 per credit hour. Tuition, nonresident: part-time $675 per credit hour. *Financial support:* In 2016–17, fellowships with full tuition reimbursements (averaging $9,900 per year), research assistantships with full tuition reimbursements (averaging $9,991 per year), teaching assistantships with full tuition reimbursements (averaging $10,059 per year) were awarded; career-related internships or fieldwork, Federal Work-Study, scholarships/grants, health care benefits, and unspecified assistantships also available. Support available to part-time students. Financial award application deadline: 11/15; financial award applicants required to submit FAFSA. *Unit head:* Dr. Josiah Alamu, Program Administrator, 217-206-7874, Fax: 217-206-7279, E-mail: jalam3@uis.edu. *Application contact:* Dr. Cecelia Cornell, Associate Vice Chancellor for Graduate Education, 217-206-7230, E-mail: ccorn1@uis.edu.
Website: http://www.uis.edu/publichealth/

**University of Maryland, Baltimore County,** The Graduate School, College of Arts, Humanities and Social Sciences, Department of Emergency Health Services, Baltimore, MD 21250. Offers administration, planning, and policy (MS); education (MS); emergency health services (MS); emergency management (Postbaccalaureate Certificate); preventive medicine and epidemiology (MS); public policy (PhD), including emergency management, emergency public health. *Program availability:* Part-time, evening/weekend, 100% online, blended/hybrid learning. *Faculty:* 4 full-time (2 women), 8 part-time/adjunct (3 women). *Students:* 15 full-time (11 women), 14 part-time (6 women); includes 11 minority (5 Black or African American, non-Hispanic/Latino; 3 Asian, non-Hispanic/Latino; 2 Hispanic/Latino; 1 Two or more races, non-Hispanic/Latino), 4 international. Average age 26. 25 applicants, 88% accepted, 19 enrolled. In 2016, 22 master's awarded. *Degree requirements:* For master's, comprehensive exam (for some programs), thesis optional, capstone project. *Entrance requirements:* For master's, GRE General Test if GPA is below 3.2, minimum GPA of 3.2. Additional exam requirements/recommendations for international students: Required—TOEFL (minimum score 85 iBT) or IELTS (minimum score 6.5). *Application deadline:* For fall admission, 6/15 for domestic students, 3/1 for international students; for spring admission, 11/1 for domestic students, 10/1 for international students. Applications are processed on a rolling basis. Application fee: $50. Electronic applications accepted. *Expenses:* $13,194 in-state full-time per year, $733 per credit in-state part-time; $1,127 out-of-state per credit. *Financial support:* In 2016–17, 6 students received support, including 5 research assistantships with full tuition reimbursements available (averaging $16,875 per year); career-related internships or fieldwork, Federal Work-Study, scholarships/grants, health care benefits, and unspecified assistantships also available. Financial award application deadline: 5/30; financial award applicants required to submit FAFSA. *Faculty research:* EMS management, disaster health services, emergency management, epidemiology, risk profiles, infectious disease control, stress management for care providers, climate change and public health. *Total annual research expenditures:* $50,000. *Unit head:* Dr. J. Lee Jenkins, Department Chair, 410-455-3216, Fax: 410-455-3045, E-mail: jleejenkins@umbc.edu. *Application contact:* Dr. Rick Bissell, Program Director, 410-455-3776, Fax: 410-455-3045, E-mail: bissell@umbc.edu.
Website: http://ehs.umbc.edu/

**University of Nebraska Medical Center,** Program in Emergency Preparedness, Omaha, NE 68198. Offers MS. *Program availability:* Part-time, 100% online, blended/hybrid learning. *Students:* 2 full-time (both women), 4 part-time (2 women); includes 1 minority (Black or African American, non-Hispanic/Latino). Average age 28. 5 applicants, 60% accepted, 3 enrolled. *Degree requirements:* For master's, thesis. *Entrance requirements:* For master's, GRE. Additional exam requirements/recommendations for international students: Required—TOEFL (minimum score 550 paper-based; 80 iBT). *Application deadline:* For fall admission, 6/1 for domestic students, 4/1 for international students; for spring admission, 10/1 for domestic students, 8/1 for international students. Application fee: $45. Electronic applications accepted. *Financial support:* Scholarships/grants available. Support available to part-time students. Financial award application deadline: 2/15; financial award applicants required to submit FAFSA. *Unit head:* Dr. Sharon Medcalf, Associate Director, Center for Emergency Preparedness, 402-552-2529, E-mail: smedcalf@unmc.edu. *Application contact:* Jessica Tschirren, Coordinator, 402-561-7586, Fax: 402-561-7599, E-mail: jtschirren@unmc.edu.
Website: http://www.unmc.edu/publichealth/programs/msemergencypreparedness.html

**University of Nevada, Las Vegas,** Graduate College, Greenspun College of Urban Affairs, School of Public Policy and Leadership, Las Vegas, NV 89154-4030. Offers crisis and emergency management (MS); non-profit management (Certificate); public administration (MPA); public affairs (PhD); public management (Certificate); urban leadership (MA). *Program availability:* Part-time. *Faculty:* 13 full-time (7 women), 10 part-time/adjunct (2 women). *Students:* 76 full-time (43 women), 110 part-time (70 women); includes 81 minority (18 Black or African American, non-Hispanic/Latino; 1 American Indian or Alaska Native, non-Hispanic/Latino; 6 Asian, non-Hispanic/Latino; 38 Hispanic/Latino; 4 Native Hawaiian or other Pacific Islander, non-Hispanic/Latino; 14 Two or more races, non-Hispanic/Latino), 7 international. Average age 36. 70 applicants, 86% accepted, 43 enrolled. In 2016, 70 master's, 9 doctorates, 21 other advanced degrees awarded. *Degree requirements:* For master's, comprehensive exam (for some programs), thesis (for some programs), oral exam; for doctorate, comprehensive exam, thesis/dissertation; for Certificate, portfolio. *Entrance requirements:* For master's, GRE General Test or GMAT, bachelor's degree with minimum GPA 2.75; statement of purpose; 3 letters of recommendation; for doctorate, GRE General Test, master's degree with minimum GPA of 3.5; 3 letters of recommendation; statement of purpose; writing sample; personal interview; for Certificate, bachelor's degree; 2 letters of recommendation; writing sample. Additional exam requirements/recommendations for international students: Required—TOEFL (minimum score 550 paper-based; 80 iBT), IELTS (minimum score 7). *Application deadline:* For fall admission, 6/1 for domestic students, 5/1 for international students; for spring admission, 11/1 for domestic students, 10/1 for international students; for summer admission, 3/1 for domestic students. Application fee: $60 ($95 for international students). Electronic applications accepted. *Expenses:* $269.25 per credit, $792 per 3-credit course; $9,634 per year resident; $23,274 per year non-resident; $7,094 fees non-resident (7 credits or more); $1,307 annual health insurance fee. *Financial support:* In 2016–17, 7 research assistantships with partial tuition reimbursements (averaging $14,200 per year), 14 teaching assistantships with partial tuition reimbursements (averaging $16,411 per year) were awarded; institutionally sponsored loans, scholarships/grants, health care benefits, and unspecified assistantships also available. Financial award application deadline: 3/15. *Faculty research:* Community and organizational resilience; environmental decision-making and management; budgeting and human resource/workforce management; urban design, sustainability, and governance; public and non-profit management, public policy, governance, economic development, and urban planning. *Total annual research expenditures:* $244,881. *Unit head:* Dr. Christopher Stream, Director, 702-895-5120, Fax: 702-895-4436, E-mail: chris.stream@unlv.edu. *Application contact:* Dr. Jessica Word, Graduate Coordinator, 702-895-2684, Fax: 702-895-4436, E-mail: jessica.word@unlv.edu.
Website: https://www.unlv.edu/publicpolicy

**University of New Haven,** Graduate School, Henry C. Lee College of Criminal Justice and Forensic Sciences, Program in Emergency Management, West Haven, CT 06516. Offers MS, Graduate Certificate. *Program availability:* Part-time, online learning. *Students:* 28 full-time (7 women), 62 part-time (11 women); includes 10 minority (5 Black or African American, non-Hispanic/Latino; 1 Asian, non-Hispanic/Latino; 3 Hispanic/Latino; 1 Two or more races, non-Hispanic/Latino), 14 international. Average age 33. 56 applicants, 98% accepted, 34 enrolled. In 2016, 26 master's, 5 other advanced degrees awarded. Application fee: $50. *Expenses: Tuition:* Full-time $15,660; part-time $870 per credit hour. *Required fees:* $200; $85 per term. Tuition and fees vary according to program. *Unit head:* Wayne Sandford, Coordinator, 203-479-4891, E-mail: wsandford@newhaven.edu. *Application contact:* Michelle Mason, Director of Graduate Enrollment, 203-932-7067, E-mail: mmason@newhaven.edu.
Website: http://www.newhaven.edu/lee-college/programs/graduate/emergency-management/

**The University of North Carolina at Charlotte,** College of Liberal Arts and Sciences, Department of Political Science and Public Administration, Charlotte, NC 28223-0001. Offers emergency management (Graduate Certificate); non-profit management (Graduate Certificate); public administration (MPA), including arts administration, emergency management, non-profit management, public budgeting and finance, urban management and policy; public budgeting and finance (Graduate Certificate); urban management and policy (Graduate Certificate). *Accreditation:* NASPAA. *Program availability:* Part-time, evening/weekend. *Faculty:* 19 full-time (10 women), 3 part-time/adjunct (0 women). *Students:* 25 full-time (17 women), 57 part-time (39 women); includes 23 minority (14 Black or African American, non-Hispanic/Latino; 1 American Indian or Alaska Native, non-Hispanic/Latino; 2 Asian, non-Hispanic/Latino; 4 Hispanic/Latino; 2 Two or more races, non-Hispanic/Latino). Average age 30. 55 applicants, 73% accepted, 30 enrolled. In 2016, 31 master's, 12 other advanced degrees awarded. *Degree requirements:* For master's, research project or thesis. *Entrance requirements:* For master's, GRE General Test, bachelor's degree, or its equivalent, from accredited college or university; minimum undergraduate GPA of 3.0; 3 letters of recommendation; statement of purpose; for Graduate Certificate, statement of purpose (1-2 pages in length) explaining applicant's career goals, how the Certificate fits into achieving those goals, and any relevant work experience; official transcripts; letters of recommendation. Additional exam requirements/recommendations for international students: Required—TOEFL (minimum score 523 paper-based, 70 iBT) or IELTS (6.5). *Application deadline:* For fall admission, 8/1 for domestic and international students; for spring admission, 12/1 for domestic and international students. Applications are processed on a rolling basis. Application fee: $75. Electronic applications accepted. *Expenses:* Tuition, state resident: full-time $4252. Tuition, nonresident: full-time $17,423. *Required fees:* $3026. Tuition and fees vary according to course load and program. *Financial support:* In 2016–17, 9 students received support, including 9 research assistantships (averaging $7,117 per year); career-related internships or fieldwork, Federal Work-Study, institutionally sponsored loans, scholarships/grants, and unspecified assistantships also available. Support available to part-time students. Financial award application deadline: 3/1; financial award applicants required to submit FAFSA. *Total annual research expenditures:* $477,651. *Unit head:* Dr. Greg Weeks, Chair, 704-687-7574, E-mail: gbweeks@uncc.edu. *Application contact:* Kathy B. Giddings, Director of Graduate Admissions, 704-687-5503, Fax: 704-687-1668, E-mail: gradadm@uncc.edu.
Website: http://politicalscience.uncc.edu/

**University of North Texas,** Robert B. Toulouse School of Graduate Studies, Denton, TX 76203-5459. Offers accounting (MS); applied anthropology (MA, MS); applied behavior analysis (Certificate); applied geography (MA); applied technology and performance improvement (M Ed, MS); art education (MA); art history (MA); art museum education (Certificate); arts leadership (Certificate); audiology (Au D); behavior analysis (MS); behavioral science (PhD); biochemistry and molecular biology (MS); biology (MA, MS); biomedical engineering (MS); business analysis (MS); chemistry (MS); clinical health psychology (PhD); communication studies (MA, MS); computer engineering (MS); computer science (MS); counseling (M Ed, MS), including clinical mental health counseling (MS), college and university counseling, elementary school counseling, secondary school counseling; creative writing (MA); criminal justice (MS); curriculum and instruction (M Ed); decision sciences (MBA); design (MA, MFA), including fashion design (MFA), innovation studies, interior design (MFA); early childhood studies (MS); economics (MS); educational leadership (M Ed, Ed D); educational psychology (MS, PhD), including family studies (MS), gifted and talented (MS), human development (MS),

learning and cognition (MS), research, measurement and evaluation (MS); electrical engineering (MS); emergency management (MPA); engineering technology (MS); English (MA); English as a second language (MA); environmental science (MS); finance (MBA, MS); financial management (MPA); French (MA); health services management (MBA); higher education (M Ed, Ed D); history (MA, MS); hospitality management (MS); human resources management (MPA); information science (MS); information systems (PhD); information technologies (MBA); interdisciplinary studies (MA, MS); international studies (MA); international sustainable tourism (MS); jazz studies (MM); journalism (MA, MJ, Graduate Certificate, including interactive and virtual digital communication (Graduate Certificate), narrative journalism (Graduate Certificate), public relations (Graduate Certificate); kinesiology (MS); linguistics (MA); local government management (MPA); logistics (PhD); logistics and supply chain management (MBA); long-term care, senior housing, and aging services (MA); management (PhD); marketing (MBA); mathematics (MA, MS); mechanical and energy engineering (MS, PhD); music (MA), including ethnomusicology, music theory, musicology, performance; music composition (PhD); music education (MM Ed, PhD); nonprofit management (MPA); operations and supply chain management (MBA); performance (MM, DMA); philosophy (MA); political science (MA); professional and technical communication (MA); radio, television and film (MA, MFA); rehabilitation counseling (Certificate); sociology (MA); Spanish (MA); special education (M Ed); speech-language pathology (MA); strategic management (MBA); studio art (MFA); teaching (M Ed); MBA/MS. *Program availability:* Part-time, evening/weekend, online learning. Terminal master's awarded for partial completion of doctoral program. *Degree requirements:* For master's, variable foreign language requirement, comprehensive exam (for some programs), thesis (for some programs); for doctorate, variable foreign language requirement, comprehensive exam (for some programs), thesis/dissertation; for other advanced degree, variable foreign language requirement, comprehensive exam (for some programs). *Entrance requirements:* For master's and doctorate, GRE, GMAT. Additional exam requirements/recommendations for international students: Required—TOEFL (minimum score 550 paper-based; 79 iBT). Electronic applications accepted.

**University of South Florida,** Innovative Education, Tampa, FL 33620-9951. Offers adult, career and higher education (Graduate Certificate), including college teaching, leadership in developing human resources, leadership in higher education; Africana studies (Graduate Certificate), including diasporas and health disparities, genocide and human rights; aging studies (Graduate Certificate), including gerontology; art research (Graduate Certificate), including museum studies; business foundations (Graduate Certificate); chemical and biomedical engineering (Graduate Certificate), including materials science and engineering, water, health and sustainability; child and family studies (Graduate Certificate), including positive behavior support; civil and industrial engineering (Graduate Certificate), including transportation systems analysis; community and family health (Graduate Certificate), including maternal and child health, social marketing and public health, violence and injury: prevention and intervention, women's health; criminology (Graduate Certificate), including criminal justice administration; educational measurement and research (Graduate Certificate), including evaluation; English (Graduate Certificate), including comparative literary studies, creative writing, professional and technical communication; entrepreneurship (Graduate Certificate); environmental health (Graduate Certificate), including safety management; epidemiology and biostatistics (Graduate Certificate), including applied biostatistics, biostatistics, concepts and tools of epidemiology, epidemiology, epidemiology of infectious diseases; geography, environment and planning (Graduate Certificate), including community development, environmental policy and management, geographical information systems; geology (Graduate Certificate), including hydrogeology; global health (Graduate Certificate), including disaster management, global health and Latin American and Caribbean studies, global health practice, humanitarian assistance, infection control; government and international affairs (Graduate Certificate), including Cuban studies, globalization studies; health policy and management (Graduate Certificate), including health management and leadership, public health policy and programs; hearing specialist: early intervention (Graduate Certificate); industrial and management systems engineering (Graduate Certificate), including systems engineering, technology management; information studies (Graduate Certificate), including school library media specialist; information systems/decision sciences (Graduate Certificate), including analytics and business intelligence; instructional technology (Graduate Certificate), including distance education, Florida digital/virtual educator, instructional design, multimedia design, Web design; internal medicine, bioethics and medical humanities (Graduate Certificate), including biomedical ethics; Latin American and Caribbean studies (Graduate Certificate); mass communications (Graduate Certificate), including multimedia journalism; mathematics and statistics (Graduate Certificate), including mathematics; medicine (Graduate Certificate), including aging and neuroscience, bioinformatics, biotechnology, brain fitness and memory management, clinical investigation, health informatics, health sciences, integrative weight management, intellectual property, medicine and gender, metabolic and nutritional medicine, metabolic cardiology, pharmacy sciences; national and competitive intelligence (Graduate Certificate); psychological and social foundations (Graduate Certificate), including career counseling, college teaching, diversity in education, mental health counseling, school counseling; public affairs (Graduate Certificate), including nonprofit management, public management, research administration; public health (Graduate Certificate), including environmental health, health equity, public health generalist, translational research in adolescent behavioral health; public health practices (Graduate Certificate), including planning for healthy communities; rehabilitation and mental health counseling (Graduate Certificate), including integrative mental health care, marriage and family therapy, rehabilitation technology; secondary education (Graduate Certificate), including ESOL, foreign language education: culture and content, foreign language education: professional; social work (Graduate Certificate), including geriatric social work/clinical gerontology; special education (Graduate Certificate), including autism spectrum disorder, disabilities education: severe/profound; world languages (Graduate Certificate), including teaching English as a second language (TESL) or foreign language. *Expenses:* Tuition, state resident: full-time $7766; part-time $431.43 per credit hour. Tuition, nonresident: full-time $15,789; part-time $877.17 per credit hour. *Required fees:* $37 per term. *Unit head:* Kathy Barnes, Interdisciplinary Programs Coordinator, 813-974-8031, Fax: 813-974-7061, E-mail: barnesk@usf.edu. *Application contact:* Karen Tylinski, Metro Initiatives, 813-974-9943, Fax: 813-974-7061, E-mail: ktylinsk@usf.edu.
Website: http://www.usf.edu/innovative-education/

**The University of Toledo,** College of Graduate Studies, College of Medicine and Life Sciences, Department of Public Health and Preventative Medicine, Toledo, OH 43606-3390. Offers biostatistics and epidemiology (Certificate); contemporary gerontological practice (Certificate); environmental and occupational health and safety (MPH); epidemiology (Certificate); global public health (Certificate); health promotion and education (MPH); industrial hygiene (MSOH); medical and health science teaching and learning (Certificate); occupational health (Certificate); public health administration (MPH); public health and emergency response (Certificate); public health epidemiology (MPH); public health nutrition (MPH); MD/MPH. *Program availability:* Part-time, evening/weekend. *Degree requirements:* For master's, thesis or alternative. *Entrance requirements:* For master's, GRE, minimum undergraduate GPA of 3.0, three letters of recommendation, statement of purpose, transcripts from all prior institutions attended, resume; for Certificate, minimum undergraduate GPA of 3.0, three letters of recommendation, statement of purpose, transcripts from all prior institutions attended, resume. Additional exam requirements/recommendations for international students: Required—TOEFL (minimum score 550 paper-based; 80 iBT), IELTS (minimum score 6.5). Electronic applications accepted.

**Upper Iowa University,** Online Master's Programs, Fayette, IA 52142-1857. Offers accounting (MBA); corporate financial management (MBA); emergency management and homeland security (MPA); general management (MPA); general studies (MPA); government administration (MPA); health and human services (MPA); human resources management (MBA); nonprofit organizational management (MPA); organizational development (MBA); public management (MPA); sport administration (MSA). MBA also available at Madison, WI campus. *Program availability:* Part-time, online learning. *Degree requirements:* For master's, research project. *Entrance requirements:* For master's, GMAT, GRE, or minimum GPA of 2.7 during last 60 hours. Additional exam requirements/recommendations for international students: Required—TOEFL (minimum score 570 paper-based). Electronic applications accepted. *Faculty research:* Total quality management, teams, organization culture and climate, management.

**Virginia Commonwealth University,** Graduate School, College of Humanities and Sciences, L. Douglas Wilder School of Government and Public Affairs, Program in Homeland Security and Emergency Preparedness, Richmond, VA 23284-9005. Offers MA, Graduate Certificate. *Program availability:* Part-time, online learning. *Entrance requirements:* For master's, GRE, GMAT, MAT or LSAT, minimum GPA of 2.7; for Graduate Certificate, minimum GPA of 2.7. Additional exam requirements/recommendations for international students: Required—TOEFL (minimum score 600 paper-based; 100 iBT); Recommended—IELTS (minimum score 6.5). *Application deadline:* For fall admission, 4/1 for domestic students; for spring admission, 10/1 for domestic students. Application fee: $50. Electronic applications accepted. *Unit head:* Dr. William V. Pelfrey, Graduate Program Director, 804-828-8467, E-mail: wvpelfrey@vcu.edu. *Application contact:* Dr. Richard R. Huff, Director of Graduate Student Advising, 804-827-1430, E-mail: rrhuff@vcu.edu. Website: http://www.wilder.vcu.edu/academic/security/index.html

**Walden University,** Graduate Programs, School of Counseling, Minneapolis, MN 55401. Offers addiction counseling (MS), including addictions and public health, child and adolescent counseling, family studies and interventions, forensic counseling, general program, military families and culture, trauma and crisis counseling; clinical mental health counseling (MS), including addiction counseling, forensic counseling, military families and culture, trauma and crisis counseling; counselor education and supervision (PhD), including consultation, counseling and social change, forensic mental health counseling, leadership and program evaluation, trauma and crisis; marriage, couple, and family counseling (MS), including addiction counseling, career counseling, forensic counseling, military families and culture, trauma and crisis counseling; school counseling (MS), including addiction counseling, career counseling, crisis and trauma, military families and culture. *Accreditation:* ACA. *Program availability:* Part-time, evening/weekend, online only, 100% online. *Degree requirements:* For master's, residency, field experience, professional development plan, licensure plan; for doctorate, thesis/dissertation, residency, practicum, internship. *Entrance requirements:* For master's, bachelor's degree or higher; minimum GPA of 2.5; official transcripts; goal statement (for some programs); access to computer and Internet; for doctorate, master's degree or higher; three years of related professional or academic experience (preferred); minimum GPA of 3.0; goal statement and current resume (for select programs); official transcripts; access to computer and Internet. Additional exam requirements/recommendations for international students: Required—TOEFL (minimum score 550 paper-based, 79 iBT), IELTS (minimum score 6.5), Michigan English Language Assessment Battery (minimum score 82), or PTE (minimum score 53). Electronic applications accepted.

**Walden University,** Graduate Programs, School of Health Sciences, Minneapolis, MN 55401. Offers clinical research administration (MS, Graduate Certificate); health education and promotion (MS, PhD), including behavioral health (PhD), disease surveillance (PhD), emergency preparedness (MS), general (MHA, MS), global health (PhD), health policy (PhD), health policy and advocacy (PhD), population health (PhD); health informatics (MS); health services (PhD), including community health, healthcare administration, leadership, public health policy, self-designed; healthcare administration (MHA, DHA), including general (MHA, MS); leadership and organizational development (MHA); public health (MPH, Dr PH, PhD, Graduate Certificate), including community health education (PhD), epidemiology (PhD); systems policy (MHA). *Program availability:* Part-time, evening/weekend, online only, 100% online. *Degree requirements:* For doctorate, thesis/dissertation, residency. *Entrance requirements:* For master's, bachelor's degree or higher; minimum GPA of 2.5; official transcripts; goal statement (for some programs); access to computer and Internet; for doctorate, master's degree or higher; three years of related professional or academic experience (preferred); minimum GPA of 3.0; goal statement and current resume (for select programs); official transcripts; access to computer and Internet; for Graduate Certificate, relevant work experience; access to computer and Internet. Additional exam requirements/recommendations for international students: Required—TOEFL (minimum score 550 paper-based, 79 iBT), IELTS (minimum score 6.5), Michigan English Language Assessment Battery (minimum score 82), or PTE (minimum score 53). Electronic applications accepted.

**Walden University,** Graduate Programs, School of Public Policy and Administration, Minneapolis, MN 55401. Offers criminal justice (MPA, MPP, MS, Graduate Certificate), including emergency management (MS, PhD), general program (MS), global leadership (MS, PhD), homeland security and policy coordination (MS, PhD), law and public policy (MS, PhD), policy analysis (MS, PhD), public management and leadership (MS, PhD), self-designed (MS), terrorism, mediation, and peace (MS, PhD); criminal justice and executive management (MS), including global leadership (MS, PhD); criminal justice leadership and executive management (MS), including emergency management (MS, PhD), general program, homeland security and policy coordination (MS, PhD), law and public policy (MS, PhD), policy analysis (MS, PhD), public management and leadership (MS, PhD), self-designed, terrorism, mediation, and peace (MS, PhD); emergency management (MPA, MPP, MS), including criminal justice (MS, PhD), general program (MS), homeland security (MS), public management and leadership (MS, PhD), terrorism and emergency management (MS); general program (MPA, MPP); global leadership (MPA, MPP); government management (Graduate Certificate); health policy (MPA, MPP); homeland security (Graduate Certificate); homeland security and policy coordination (MPA, MPP); international nongovernmental organizations (MPA, MPP); law and public policy (MPA, MPP); local government management for sustainable communities (MPA, MPP); nonprofit management (Graduate Certificate); nonprofit management and leadership (MPA, MPP, MS), including global leadership (MS, PhD), international nongovernmental organization (MS), local government for sustainable communities (MS), self designed (MS); online teaching in higher education (Post-Master's Certificate); policy analysis (MPA); public management and leadership (MPA, MPP, Graduate Certificate); public policy (Graduate Certificate); public policy and administration (PhD), including criminal justice (MS, PhD), emergency management (MS, PhD), global leadership (MS, PhD), health policy, homeland security and policy coordination (MS, PhD), international nongovernmental organizations, law and public policy (MS, PhD), local government management for sustainable communities, nonprofit management and leadership, policy analysis (MS, PhD), public management and leadership (MS, PhD), terrorism, mediation, and peace (MS, PhD); strategic planning and public policy (Graduate Certificate); terrorism, mediation, and peace (MPA, MPP). *Program availability:* Part-time, evening/weekend, online only, 100% online. *Degree requirements:* For doctorate, thesis/dissertation, residency. *Entrance requirements:* For master's, bachelor's degree or higher; minimum GPA of 2.5; official transcripts; goal statement (for some programs); access to computer and Internet; for doctorate, master's degree or higher; three years of related professional or academic experience (preferred); minimum GPA of 3.0; goal statement and current resume (for select programs); official transcripts; access to computer and Internet; for other advanced degree, relevant work experience; access to computer and Internet. Additional exam requirements/recommendations for international students: Required—TOEFL (minimum score 550 paper-based, 79 iBT), IELTS (minimum score 6.5), Michigan English Language Assessment Battery (minimum score 82), or PTE (minimum score 53). Electronic applications accepted.

**Waldorf University,** Program in Organizational Leadership, Forest City, IA 50436. Offers criminal justice leadership (MA); emergency management leadership (MA); fire/rescue executive leadership (MA); human resource development (MA); public administration (MA); sport management (MA); teacher leader (MA).

**West Chester University of Pennsylvania,** College of Health Sciences, Department of Health, West Chester, PA 19383. Offers emergency preparedness (Certificate); gerontology (Certificate); health care management (Certificate); integrative health (Certificate); public health (MPH); school health (M Ed). *Accreditation:* CEPH. *Program availability:* Part-time, evening/weekend. *Faculty:* 13 full-time (8 women), 5 part-time/adjunct (3 women). *Students:* 89 full-time (70 women), 94 part-time (62 women); includes 76 minority (65 Black or African American, non-Hispanic/Latino; 6 Asian, non-Hispanic/Latino; 5 Hispanic/Latino), 17 international. Average age 30. 119 applicants, 89% accepted, 63 enrolled. In 2016, 64 master's, 2 other advanced degrees awarded. *Degree requirements:* For master's, research report (for M Ed); major project and practicum (for MPH); for Certificate, 18 credits (for gerontology). *Entrance requirements:* For master's, undergraduate introduction to statistics course; for Certificate, goal statement, two letters of recommendation, resume, and official transcripts from all previously completed coursework (for gerontology). Additional exam requirements/recommendations for international students: Required—TOEFL or IELTS. *Application deadline:* For fall admission, 5/15 for international students; for spring admission, 10/15 for international students. Applications are processed on a rolling basis. Application fee: $50. Electronic applications accepted. *Expenses:* Tuition, state resident: full-time $8694; part-time $483 per credit. Tuition, nonresident: full-time $13,050; part-time $725 per credit. *Required fees:* $2399; $119.05 per credit. Tuition and fees vary according to campus/location and program. *Financial support:* Scholarships/grants and unspecified assistantships available. Financial award application deadline: 2/15; financial award applicants required to submit FAFSA. *Faculty research:* Healthy school communities, community health issues and evidence-based programs, environment and health, nutrition and health, integrative health. *Unit head:* Dr. Bethann Cinelli, Chair, 610-436-2267, E-mail: bcinelli@wcupa.edu. *Application contact:* Dr. Lynn Carson, Graduate Coordinator, 610-436-2138, E-mail: lcarson@wcupa.edu. Website: http://www.wcupa.edu/HealthSciences/health/

**York University,** Faculty of Graduate Studies, Faculty of Liberal Arts and Professional Studies, Program in Disaster and Emergency Management, Toronto, ON M3J 1P3, Canada. Offers MA.

# Homeland Security

**American Public University System,** AMU/APU Graduate Programs, Charles Town, WV 25414. Offers accounting (MBA, MS); applied business analytics (MBA, MS); criminal justice (MA), including business administration, emergency and disaster management, general (MA, MS); educational leadership (M Ed); emergency and disaster management (MA); entrepreneurship (MBA); environmental policy and management (MS), including environmental planning, environmental sustainability, fish and wildlife management, general (MA, MS), global environmental management; finance (MBA); general (MBA); government contracting and acquisition (MBA); health care administration (MBA); health information management (MS); history (MA), including American history, ancient and classical history, European history, global history, public history; homeland security (MA), including business administration, counterterrorism studies, criminal justice, cyber, emergency management and public health, intelligence studies, transportation security; homeland security resource allocation (MA); humanities (MA); information technology (MS), including digital forensics, enterprise software development, information assurance and security, IT project management; information technology management (MBA); intelligence studies (MA), including criminal intelligence, cyber, general (MA, MS), homeland security, intelligence analysis, intelligence collection, intelligence management, intelligence operations, terrorism studies; international relations and conflict resolution (MA), including comparative and security issues, conflict resolution, international and transnational security issues, peacekeeping; legal studies (MA); management (MA), including strategic consulting; marketing (MBA); military history (MA), including American military history, American Revolution, civil war, war since 1945, World War II; military studies (MA), including joint warfare, strategic leadership; national security studies (MA), including cyber, general (MA, MS), homeland security, regional security studies, security and intelligence analysis, terrorism studies; nonprofit management (MBA); political science (MA), including American politics and government, comparative government and development, general (MA, MS), international relations, public policy; psychology (MA); public administration (MPA), including disaster management, environmental policy, health policy, human resources, national security, organizational management, security

management; public health (MPH); reverse logistics management (MA); security management (MA); space studies (MS), including aerospace science, general (MA, MS), planetary science; sports and health sciences (MS); sports management (MBA); teaching (M Ed), including autism spectrum disorder, curriculum and instruction for elementary teachers, elementary reading, English language learners, instructional leadership, online learning, special education, STEAM (STEM plus the arts); transportation and logistics management (MA). *Program availability:* Part-time, evening/weekend, online only, 100% online. *Faculty:* 401 full-time (228 women), 1,678 part-time/adjunct (781 women). *Students:* 378 full-time (184 women), 8,455 part-time (3,484 women); includes 2,972 minority (1,552 Black or African American, non-Hispanic/Latino; 52 American Indian or Alaska Native, non-Hispanic/Latino; 211 Asian, non-Hispanic/Latino; 791 Hispanic/Latino; 70 Native Hawaiian or other Pacific Islander, non-Hispanic/Latino; 296 Two or more races, non-Hispanic/Latino), 109 international. Average age 37. In 2016, 3,185 master's awarded. *Degree requirements:* For master's, comprehensive exam or practicum. *Entrance requirements:* For master's, official transcript showing earned bachelor's degree from institution accredited by recognized accrediting body. Additional exam requirements/recommendations for international students: Required—TOEFL (minimum score 550 paper-based), IELTS (minimum score 6.5). *Application deadline:* Applications are processed on a rolling basis. Application fee: $0. Electronic applications accepted. *Expenses: Tuition:* Part-time $350 per credit hour. *Required fees:* $50 per course. *Financial support:* Scholarships/grants available. Financial award applicants required to submit FAFSA. *Unit head:* Dr. Karan Powell, President, 877-468-6268, Fax: 304-724-3780. *Application contact:* Terry Grant, Vice President of Enrollment Management, 877-468-6268, Fax: 304-724-3780, E-mail: info@apus.edu.
Website: http://www.apus.edu

**Angelo State University,** College of Graduate Studies and Research, College of Arts and Humanities, Department of Security Studies and Criminal Justice, San Angelo, TX 76909. Offers criminal justice (MS); homeland security (MS); intelligence, security studies, and analysis (MSS); security studies (MSS). *Program availability:* Part-time, evening/weekend, online learning. *Students:* 75 full-time (31 women), 115 part-time (38 women); includes 65 minority (24 Black or African American, non-Hispanic/Latino; 7 Asian, non-Hispanic/Latino; 31 Hispanic/Latino; 3 Two or more races, non-Hispanic/Latino). Average age 31. *Degree requirements:* For master's, comprehensive exam. *Entrance requirements:* For master's, essay, letters of recommendation. Additional exam requirements/recommendations for international students: Required—TOEFL or IELTS. *Application deadline:* For fall admission, 7/15 priority date for domestic students, 6/10 for international students; for spring admission, 12/1 priority date for domestic students, 11/1 for international students. Applications are processed on a rolling basis. Application fee: $40 ($50 for international students). Electronic applications accepted. *Expenses:* Tuition, state resident: full-time $3726; part-time $2484 per year. Tuition, nonresident: full-time $10,746; part-time $7164 per year. *Required fees:* $2538; $1702 per unit. *Financial support:* Federal Work-Study and scholarships/grants available. Support available to part-time students. Financial award application deadline: 3/1; financial award applicants required to submit FAFSA. *Unit head:* Dr. William A. Taylor, Chair, 325-486-6689, Fax: 325-942-2544, E-mail: william.taylor@angelo.edu. *Application contact:* Dr. William A. Taylor, Chair, 325-486-6689, Fax: 325-942-2544, E-mail: william.taylor@angelo.edu.
Website: http://www.angelo.edu/dept/security_studies_criminal_justice/

**Arizona State University at the Tempe campus,** College of Public Programs, School of Public Affairs, Phoenix, AZ 85004-0687. Offers emergency management and homeland security (MA); program evaluation (MS); public administration (MPA, PhD), including nonprofit administration (MPA), urban management (MPA); public policy (MPP); MPA/MSW. *Accreditation:* NASPAA (one or more programs are accredited). *Program availability:* Part-time, evening/weekend. Terminal master's awarded for partial completion of doctoral program. *Degree requirements:* For master's, thesis or alternative, policy analysis or capstone project; interactive Program of Study (iPOS) submitted before completing 50 percent of required credit hours; for doctorate, comprehensive exam, thesis/dissertation, interactive Program of Study (iPOS) submitted before completing 50 percent of required credit hours. *Entrance requirements:* For master's, GRE, minimum GPA of 3.0 or equivalent in last 2 years of work leading to bachelor's degree; for doctorate, GRE, minimum GPA of 3.0 or equivalent in last 2 years of work leading to bachelor's degree, 3 letters of recommendation, resume, statement of goals, samples of research reports. Additional exam requirements/recommendations for international students: Required—TOEFL (minimum score 600 paper-based; 100 iBT), IELTS (minimum score 6.5). Electronic applications accepted. *Expenses:* Contact institution.

**Auburn University at Montgomery,** College of Public Policy and Justice, Department of Justice and Public Safety, Montgomery, AL 36124-4023. Offers criminal studies (MSJPS); homeland security (MSJPS); homeland security and emergency management (MS); legal studies (MSJPS); organizational leadership (MSJPS); paralegal (Certificate). *Program availability:* Part-time, evening/weekend. *Degree requirements:* For master's, comprehensive exam, thesis optional. *Entrance requirements:* For master's, GRE General Test or MAT. Electronic applications accepted. *Faculty research:* Law enforcement, corrections, juvenile justice.

**Aurora University,** College of Arts and Sciences, Aurora, IL 60506-4892. Offers homeland security (MS); mathematics (MS). *Program availability:* Part-time, evening/weekend. *Faculty:* 3 full-time (1 woman), 5 part-time/adjunct (0 women). *Students:* 24 part-time (13 women); includes 1 minority (Asian, non-Hispanic/Latino). Average age 30. 12 applicants, 100% accepted, 6 enrolled. In 2016, 11 master's awarded. *Degree requirements:* For master's, research seminars. *Entrance requirements:* For master's, bachelor's degree in mathematics or in some other field with extensive course work in mathematics. Additional exam requirements/recommendations for international students: Required—TOEFL (minimum score 550 paper-based; 79 iBT). *Application deadline:* For fall admission, 6/1 for international students; for spring admission, 10/1 for international students. Applications are processed on a rolling basis. Application fee: $0. Electronic applications accepted. *Expenses:* Contact institution. *Financial support:* Federal Work-Study, scholarships/grants, and unspecified assistantships available. Support available to part-time students. Financial award application deadline: 4/1; financial award applicants required to submit FAFSA. *Unit head:* Dr. Frank Buscher, Vice President for Academic Affairs, 630-844-5252, E-mail: fbuscher@aurora.edu. *Application contact:* Judson Curry, Dean of Adult and Graduate Studies, 630-947-8946, E-mail: jcurry@aurora.edu.

**Ball State University,** Graduate School, College of Sciences and Humanities, Department of Natural Resources and Environmental Management, Muncie, IN 47306. Offers emergency management and homeland security (Certificate); natural resources and environmental management (MA, MS). *Program availability:* Part-time. *Degree requirements:* For master's, thesis (for some programs). *Entrance requirements:* For master's, GRE General Test, minimum baccalaureate GPA of 2.75 or 3.0 in latter half of baccalaureate, two letters of reference. Additional exam requirements/recommendations for international students: Required—TOEFL (minimum score 550 paper-based; 79 iBT), IELTS (minimum score 6.5). Electronic applications accepted. *Faculty research:* Acid rain, indoor air pollution, land reclamation.

**Ball State University,** Graduate School, College of Sciences and Humanities, Department of Political Science, Program in Public Administration, Muncie, IN 47306. Offers public administration (MPA, Certificate), including administrative (MPA), community and economic development (MPA), criminal justice and criminology (MPA), emergency management and homeland security (MPA). *Program availability:* Part-time. *Degree requirements:* For master's, comprehensive exam. *Entrance requirements:* For master's, GRE General Test, minimum bacclaureate GPA of 2.8, two letters of recommendation. Additional exam requirements/recommendations for international students: Required—TOEFL (minimum score 550 paper-based; 79 iBT), IELTS (minimum score 6.5). Electronic applications accepted. *Faculty research:* Employment training programs, personnel and labor relations, planning.

**Capella University,** School of Public Service Leadership, Master's Programs in Healthcare, Minneapolis, MN 55402. Offers criminal justice (MS); emergency management (MS); general public health (MPH); gerontology (MS); health administration (MHA); health care operations (MHA); health management policy (MPH); health policy (MHA); homeland security (MS); multidisciplinary human services (MS); public administration (MPA); public safety leadership (MS); social and community services (MS); social behavioral sciences (MPH); MS/MPA.

**The Citadel, The Military College of South Carolina,** Citadel Graduate College, School of Humanities and Social Sciences, Department of Criminal Justice, Charleston, SC 29409. Offers homeland security (Graduate Certificate); intelligence analysis (Graduate Certificate); intelligence and security studies (MA). *Program availability:* Part-time, evening/weekend, 100% online, blended/hybrid learning. *Faculty:* 1 (woman) full-time. *Students:* 5 full-time (1 woman), 8 part-time (5 women); includes 1 minority (Two or more races, non-Hispanic/Latino). In 2016, 2 master's, 11 other advanced degrees awarded. *Entrance requirements:* For master's, GRE or MAT, writing sample that demonstrates strong critical thinking and communication skills. Additional exam requirements/recommendations for international students: Required—TOEFL (minimum score 550 paper-based; 79 iBT). *Application deadline:* Applications are processed on a rolling basis. Application fee: $40. Electronic applications accepted. *Expenses:* Tuition, state resident: full-time $5121; part-time $569 per credit hour. Tuition, nonresident: full-time $8613; part-time $957 per credit hour. *Required fees:* $90 per term. *Financial support:* Fellowships and unspecified assistantships available. Support available to part-time students. Financial award application deadline: 7/1; financial award applicants required to submit FAFSA. *Unit head:* Dr. Sean P. Griffin, Department Head, 843-953-0319, E-mail: sean.griffin@citadel.edu. *Application contact:* Dr. Carl Jensen, Director of Intelligence and Security Studies Program, 843-953-9680, E-mail: cjensen1@citadel.edu.
Website: http://www.citadel.edu/root/criminaljustice

**Clemson University,** Graduate School, College of Behavioral, Social and Health Sciences, Program in Public Administration, Clemson, SC 29634. Offers public administration (MPA, Certificate), including emergency management (MPA), homeland defense and security (MPA), local government (MPA), non-profit management (MPA), sustainable development (MPA). *Program availability:* Part-time, evening/weekend, online only, 100% online. *Faculty:* 4 full-time (2 women), 11 part-time/adjunct (5 women). *Students:* 8 full-time (5 women), 54 part-time (30 women); includes 16 minority (13 Black or African American, non-Hispanic/Latino; 2 Hispanic/Latino; 1 Two or more races, non-Hispanic/Latino). Average age 36. 25 applicants, 80% accepted, 18 enrolled. In 2016, 18 master's awarded. *Degree requirements:* For master's, comprehensive exam, thesis or alternative. *Entrance requirements:* For master's, GRE General Test, two letters of recommendation, unofficial transcripts, personal statement of purpose, documentation and explanation of related professional experience, resume. Additional exam requirements/recommendations for international students: Required—TOEFL (minimum score 80 iBT), IELTS (minimum score 6.5). *Application deadline:* For fall admission, 4/1 for domestic students, 3/1 for international students; for spring admission, 11/1 for domestic students, 10/1 for international students. Applications are processed on a rolling basis. Application fee: $80 ($90 for international students). Electronic applications accepted. *Expenses:* $4,264 per semester full-time resident, $8,485 per semester full-time non-resident, $695 per credit hour. *Faculty research:* Economic development, community vitality, entrepreneurship, broadband infrastructure, public health innovations and communities. *Total annual research expenditures:* $11,485. *Unit head:* Dr. Lori Dickes, Program Coordinator, 864-656-7831, E-mail: lorid@clemson.edu.
Website: https://www.clemson.edu/cbshs/departments/mpa/

**Columbus State University,** Graduate Studies, College of Letters and Sciences, Program in Public Safety Administration, Columbus, GA 31907-5645. Offers MPSA. *Program availability:* Part-time. *Faculty:* 4 part-time/adjunct (0 women). *Students:* 31 full-time (14 women), 188 part-time (49 women); includes 69 minority (61 Black or African American, non-Hispanic/Latino; 1 Asian, non-Hispanic/Latino; 4 Hispanic/Latino; 3 Two or more races, non-Hispanic/Latino). Average age 43. 44 applicants, 89% accepted, 37 enrolled. In 2016, 87 master's awarded. *Entrance requirements:* For master's, baccalaureate degree, employment in a public safety profession. Additional exam requirements/recommendations for international students: Required—TOEFL (minimum score 550 paper-based; 79 iBT). *Application deadline:* For fall admission, 6/30 for domestic students, 4/1 for international students; for spring admission, 11/1 for domestic and international students; for summer admission, 3/1 for domestic students, 2/1 for international students. Applications are processed on a rolling basis. Application fee: $50. Electronic applications accepted. *Expenses:* Tuition, state resident: full-time $4804; part-time $2412 per semester hour. Tuition, nonresident: full-time $19,218; part-time $9612 per semester hour. *Required fees:* $1850; $1850 per semester hour. Tuition and fees vary according to program. *Financial support:* Application deadline: 5/1; applicants required to submit FAFSA. *Unit head:* Dr. Dennis Rome, Dean, 706-568-2056, E-mail: rome_dennis@columbusstate.edu. *Application contact:* Kristin Williams, Director of International and Graduate Recruitment, 706-507-8848, Fax: 706-568-5091, E-mail: williams_kristin@columbusstate.edu.
Website: http://cols.columbusstate.edu

**Drexel University,** Goodwin College of Professional Studies, School of Technology and Professional Studies, Philadelphia, PA 19104-2875. Offers construction management (MS); creativity and innovation (MS); engineering technology (MS); food science (MS); hospitality management (MS); professional studies: creativity studies (MS); professional studies: e-learning leadership (MS); professional studies: homeland security management (MS); project management (MS); property management (MS); sport management (MS). *Program availability:* Part-time, evening/weekend. *Faculty:* 37 full-time (14 women). *Students:* 13 full-time, 462 part-time; includes 133 minority (86 Black or African American, non-Hispanic/Latino; 24 Asian, non-Hispanic/Latino; 23 Hispanic/Latino). In 2016, 88 master's awarded. *Entrance requirements:* Additional exam requirements/recommendations for international students: Required—TOEFL, IELTS. *Application deadline:* For fall admission, 9/1 for domestic students; for winter admission, 12/1 for domestic students; for spring admission, 3/1 for domestic students. Applications are processed on a rolling basis. Application fee: $75. Electronic applications accepted. Application fee is waived when completed online. *Expenses: Tuition:* Full-time $32,184; part-time $1192 per credit hour. *Required fees:* $280. Tuition and fees vary according to campus/location and program. *Financial support:* Applicants required to submit FAFSA.

## Homeland Security

*Unit head:* Dr. William F. Lynch, Dean, 215-895-2159, E-mail: goodwin@drexel.edu. *Application contact:* Matthew Gray, Manager, Recruitment and Enrollment, 215-895-6255, Fax: 215-895-2153, E-mail: mdg67@drexel.edu.
Website: http://drexel.edu/grad/programs/goodwin/

**Endicott College,** Van Loan School of Graduate and Professional Studies, Program in Homeland Security, Beverly, MA 01915-2096. Offers MS. *Program availability:* Part-time. *Faculty:* 5 part-time/adjunct. *Students:* 24 full-time (5 women), 1 (woman) part-time; includes 5 minority (2 Hispanic/Latino; 2 Native Hawaiian or other Pacific Islander, non-Hispanic/Latino; 1 Two or more races, non-Hispanic/Latino). Average age 27. 14 applicants, 100% accepted, 13 enrolled. In 2016, 14 master's awarded. *Degree requirements:* For master's, thesis. *Entrance requirements:* For master's, undergraduate transcript, two recommendations, personal statement. Additional exam requirements/recommendations for international students: Required—TOEFL. *Application deadline:* Applications are processed on a rolling basis. Application fee: $50. Electronic applications accepted. *Expenses:* Contact institution. *Financial support:* Applicants required to submit FAFSA. *Unit head:* Paul Joyce, Director, 978-232-2740, Fax: 978-232-3000, E-mail: pjoyce@endicott.edu. *Application contact:* Ian Menchini, Director, Graduate Enrollment and Advising, 978-232-5292, Fax: 978-232-3000, E-mail: imenchin@endicott.edu.
Website: http://www.endicott.edu/VanLoan/Graduate-Studies/Master-Science/Homeland-Security.aspx

**Excelsior College,** School of Public Service, Albany, NY 12203-5159. Offers criminal justice (MSCI); homeland security and emergency management (MSCJ); justice administration (MSCI); mediation and arbitration (MPA); public administration (MPA). *Program availability:* Part-time, evening/weekend, online learning. *Faculty:* 1 (woman) part-time/adjunct. *Students:* 181 part-time (47 women); includes 78 minority (41 Black or African American, non-Hispanic/Latino; 2 American Indian or Alaska Native, non-Hispanic/Latino; 2 Asian, non-Hispanic/Latino; 25 Hispanic/Latino; 2 Native Hawaiian or other Pacific Islander, non-Hispanic/Latino; 6 Two or more races, non-Hispanic/Latino). Average age 41. In 2016, 30 master's awarded. *Application deadline:* Applications are processed on a rolling basis. Application fee: $50. Electronic applications accepted. *Expenses: Tuition:* Part-time $645 per credit. *Required fees:* $265 per credit. *Financial support:* Scholarships/grants available. *Unit head:* Dr. Robert Waters, Dean, School of Public Service, 518-464-8500, Fax: 518-464-8777. *Application contact:* Admissions Counselor, 888-647-2388, Fax: 518-464-8777, E-mail: gradadmissions@excelsior.edu.
Website: http://www.excelsior.edu/programs/public-service

**Fairleigh Dickinson University, Metropolitan Campus,** Anthony J. Petrocelli College of Continuing Studies, School of Administrative Science, Program in Homeland Security, Teaneck, NJ 07666-1914. Offers MSHS.

**Georgian Court University,** School of Arts and Sciences, Lakewood, NJ 08701-2697. Offers applied behavior analysis (MA); clinical mental health counseling (MA); holistic health studies (MA, Certificate); homeland security (MS, Certificate); mercy spirituality (Certificate); parish business management (Certificate); professional counselor (Certificate); school psychology (MA, Certificate); theology (MA, Certificate). *Program availability:* Part-time, evening/weekend. *Faculty:* 19 full-time (11 women), 6 part-time/adjunct (3 women). *Students:* 90 full-time (75 women), 107 part-time (79 women); includes 34 minority (9 Black or African American, non-Hispanic/Latino; 20 Hispanic/Latino; 5 Two or more races, non-Hispanic/Latino), 1 international. Average age 34. 187 applicants, 49% accepted, 60 enrolled. In 2016, 66 master's, 17 other advanced degrees awarded. *Degree requirements:* For master's, comprehensive exam (for some programs), thesis (for some programs). *Entrance requirements:* For master's, GRE, GMAT, or NTE/PRAXIS, 3 letters of recommendation. Additional exam requirements/recommendations for international students: Required—TOEFL (minimum score 550 paper-based). *Application deadline:* For fall admission, 8/15 for domestic students, 5/1 for international students; for spring admission, 1/15 for domestic students, 10/1 for international students. Applications are processed on a rolling basis. Application fee: $40. Electronic applications accepted. *Expenses: Tuition:* Full-time $15,079; part-time $839 per credit. *Required fees:* $968; $496 per credit. Tuition and fees vary according to campus/location and program. *Financial support:* Scholarships/grants, health care benefits, and unspecified assistantships available. Financial award application deadline: 4/15; financial award applicants required to submit FAFSA. *Unit head:* Dr. Mary Chinery, Dean, 732-987-2493, Fax: 732-987-2007, E-mail: mchinery@georgian.edu. *Application contact:* Patrick Givens, Director of Graduate and Professional Studies Admissions, 732-987-2736, Fax: 732-987-2000, E-mail: gps@georgian.edu.
Website: http://georgian.edu/academics/school-of-arts-sciences/

**Henley-Putnam University,** Master of Science Program in Intelligence Management, San Jose, CA 95131. Offers MS. *Program availability:* Part-time, online learning. *Degree requirements:* For master's, thesis. *Entrance requirements:* For master's, bachelor's degree from an institution accredited by an agency recognized by the U.S. Department of Education and/or the Council for Higher Education Accreditation; background check. Additional exam requirements/recommendations for international students: Required—TOEFL (minimum score 650 paper-based; 79 iBT); Recommended—IELTS (minimum score 7). *Expenses:* Contact institution.

**Henley-Putnam University,** Master of Science Program in Strategic Security and Protection Management, San Jose, CA 95131. Offers extremist organizations (MS). *Program availability:* Part-time, online learning. *Degree requirements:* For master's, comprehensive exam, thesis. *Entrance requirements:* For master's, bachelor's degree from institution accredited by an agency recognized by the U.S. Department of Education and/or the Council for Higher Education Accreditation, background check. Additional exam requirements/recommendations for international students: Required—TOEFL (minimum score 650 paper-based; 79 iBT); Recommended—IELTS. *Expenses:* Contact institution.

**Henley-Putnam University,** Master of Science Program in Terrorism and Counterterrorism Studies, San Jose, CA 95131. Offers intelligence operations (MS); protective intelligence (MS). *Program availability:* Part-time, online learning. *Degree requirements:* For master's, thesis. *Entrance requirements:* For master's, bachelor's degree from institution accredited by an agency recognized by the U.S. Department of Education and/or the Council for Higher Education Accreditation. Additional exam requirements/recommendations for international students: Required—TOEFL (minimum score 650 paper-based; 79 iBT); Recommended—IELTS (minimum score 7). *Expenses:* Contact institution.

**Indiana University–Purdue University Indianapolis,** School of Public and Environmental Affairs, Indianapolis, IN 46202. Offers criminal justice and public safety (MS); homeland security and emergency management (Graduate Certificate); library management (Graduate Certificate); nonprofit management (Graduate Certificate); public affairs (MPA); public management (Graduate Certificate); social entrepreneurship: nonprofit and public benefit organizations (Graduate Certificate); JD/MPA; MLS/NMC; MLS/PMC; MPA/MA. *Accreditation:* CAHME (one or more programs are accredited); NASPAA. *Program availability:* Part-time, evening/weekend, online learning. *Entrance requirements:* For master's, GRE General Test, GMAT or LSAT, minimum GPA of 3.0 (preferred). Additional exam requirements/recommendations for international students: Required—TOEFL (minimum score 93 iBT), IELTS (minimum

score 6.5). Electronic applications accepted. *Faculty research:* Nonprofit and public management, public policy, urban policy, sustainability policy, disaster preparedness and recovery, vehicular safety, homicide, offender rehabilitation and re-entry.

**Johns Hopkins University,** Zanvyl Krieger School of Arts and Sciences, Advanced Academic Programs, Program in Government, Washington, DC 20036. Offers global security studies (MA); government (MA); national securities study (Certificate); nonprofit management (Certificate); public management (MA); research administration (MS); MA/MBA. *Program availability:* Part-time, evening/weekend, online learning. *Degree requirements:* For master's, thesis. *Entrance requirements:* For master's, minimum GPA of 3.0. Additional exam requirements/recommendations for international students: Required—TOEFL (minimum score 100 iBT). Electronic applications accepted.

**Keiser University,** MA in Criminal Justice-Homeland Security Program, Ft. Lauderdale, FL 33309. Offers MA.

**Lasell College,** Graduate and Professional Studies in Criminal Justice, Newton, MA 02466. Offers emergency and crisis management (MS, Certificate); homeland security and global justice (MS, Certificate); violence prevention and advocacy (MS, Certificate). *Program availability:* Part-time, evening/weekend, online only, 100% online. *Faculty:* 1 full-time (0 women), 2 part-time/adjunct (both women). *Students:* 5 full-time (2 women), 11 part-time (5 women); includes 2 minority (1 Black or African American, non-Hispanic/Latino; 1 Asian, non-Hispanic/Latino). Average age 30. 23 applicants, 52% accepted, 8 enrolled. *Degree requirements:* For master's, minimum GPA of 3.0; internship or research paper. *Entrance requirements:* For master's, one-page personal statement, 2 letters of recommendation, resume, bachelor's degree transcript; for Certificate, bachelor's transcript, 2 letters of recommendation, 1-page statement, resume. Additional exam requirements/recommendations for international students: Required—TOEFL (minimum score 550 paper-based, 79 iBT) or IELTS (minimum score 6). *Application deadline:* For fall admission, 8/31 priority date for domestic students, 6/30 priority date for international students; for spring admission, 12/31 priority date for domestic students, 10/31 priority date for international students. Applications are processed on a rolling basis. Electronic applications accepted. *Expenses:* $600 per credit. *Financial support:* In 2016–17, 6 students received support. Federal Work-Study, scholarships/grants, and tuition discounts available. Support available to part-time students. Financial award application deadline: 8/31; financial award applicants required to submit FAFSA. *Faculty research:* Children aging out of foster care and the criminal justice system; police departments' attitudes toward the mentally ill and jail diversion programs for those offenders. *Unit head:* Dr. Joan Dolamore, Dean of Graduate and Professional Studies, 617-243-2485, Fax: 617-243-2450, E-mail: gradinfo@lasell.edu. *Application contact:* Adrienne Franciosi, Director of Graduate Enrollment, 617-243-2214, Fax: 617-243-2450, E-mail: gradinfo@lasell.edu.
Website: http://www.lasell.edu/academics/graduate-and-professional-studies/programs-of-study/master-of-science-in-criminal-justice-.html

**London Metropolitan University,** Graduate Programs, London, United Kingdom. Offers applied psychology (M Sc); architecture (MA); biomedical science (M Sc); blood science (M Sc); cancer pharmacology (M Sc); computer networking and cyber security (M Sc); computing and information systems (M Sc); conference interpreting (MA); counter-terrorism studies (M Sc); creative, digital and professional writing (MA); crime, violence and prevention (MA); criminology (M Sc); curating contemporary art (MA); data analytics (M Sc); digital media (MA); early childhood studies (MA); education (MA, Ed D); financial services law, regulation and compliance (LL M); food science (M Sc); forensic psychology (M Sc); health and social care management and policy (M Sc); human nutrition (M Sc); human resource management (MA); human rights and international conflict (MA); information technology (M Sc); intelligence and security studies (M Sc); international oil, gas and energy law (LL M); international relations (MA); interpreting (MA); learning and teaching in higher education (MA); legal practice (LL M); media and entertainment law (LL M); organizational and consumer psychology (M Sc); psychological therapy (M Sc); psychology of mental health (M Sc); public health (M Sc); public policy and management (MPA); security studies (M Sc); social work (M Sc); spatial planning and urban design (MA); sports therapy (M Sc); supporting older children and young people with dyslexia (MA); teaching languages (MA), including Arabic, English; translation (MA); woman and child abuse (MA).

**Missouri State University,** Graduate College, College of Humanities and Public Affairs, Department of Criminology and Criminal Justice, Springfield, MO 65897. Offers community corrections (Certificate); criminology and criminal justice (MS); homeland security and defense (Certificate). *Program availability:* Part-time, 100% online, blended/hybrid learning. *Faculty:* 7 full-time (2 women). *Students:* 13 full-time (10 women), 30 part-time (15 women); includes 6 minority (3 Black or African American, non-Hispanic/Latino; 1 Asian, non-Hispanic/Latino; 1 Hispanic/Latino; 1 Two or more races, non-Hispanic/Latino). Average age 31. 38 applicants, 47% accepted, 9 enrolled. In 2016, 12 master's awarded. *Degree requirements:* For master's, comprehensive exam, thesis or alternative. *Entrance requirements:* For master's, bachelor's degree in criminology, criminal justice, or sociology; minimum undergraduate GPA of 3.0. Additional exam requirements/recommendations for international students: Required—TOEFL (minimum score 550 paper-based; 79 iBT), IELTS (minimum score 6). *Application deadline:* For fall admission, 7/20 priority date for domestic students, 5/1 for international students; for spring admission, 12/20 priority date for domestic students, 9/1 for international students; for summer admission, 5/20 priority date for domestic students. Applications are processed on a rolling basis. Application fee: $35 ($50 for international students). Electronic applications accepted. *Expenses:* Tuition, state resident: full-time $5830. Tuition, nonresident: full-time $10,708. *Required fees:* $1130. Tuition and fees vary according to class time, course level, course load and program. *Financial support:* Federal Work-Study, institutionally sponsored loans, and unspecified assistantships available. Financial award application deadline: 3/31; financial award applicants required to submit FAFSA. *Faculty research:* Homeland security initiatives, juvenile policy and programs, law enforcement and drug abuse. *Unit head:* Dr. Brett Garland, Department Head, 417-836-6954, E-mail: brettgarland@missouristate.edu. *Application contact:* Michael Edwards, Coordinator of Graduate Admissions, 417-836-5388, Fax: 417-836-6200, E-mail: michaeledwards@missouristate.edu.
Website: http://criminology.missouristate.edu/

**Missouri State University,** Graduate College, Interdisciplinary Program in Professional Studies, Springfield, MO 65897. Offers administrative studies (Certificate); applied communication (MS); criminal justice (MS); environmental management (MS); homeland security (MS); individualized (MS); screenwriting and producing (MS); sports management (MS). *Program availability:* Part-time, evening/weekend, 100% online, blended/hybrid learning. *Students:* 60 full-time (34 women), 66 part-time (29 women); includes 17 minority (7 Black or African American, non-Hispanic/Latino; 1 Asian, non-Hispanic/Latino; 5 Hispanic/Latino; 4 Two or more races, non-Hispanic/Latino), 43 international. Average age 33. 76 applicants, 58% accepted, 38 enrolled. In 2016, 48 master's awarded. *Degree requirements:* For master's, comprehensive exam, thesis or alternative. *Entrance requirements:* For master's, GRE, GMAT (if GPA less than 3.0). Additional exam requirements/recommendations for international students: Required—TOEFL (minimum score 550 paper-based; 79 iBT), IELTS (minimum score 6). *Application deadline:* For fall admission, 7/15 priority date for domestic students; for spring admission, 12/1 priority date for domestic students; for summer admission, 5/1 for

domestic students. Applications are processed on a rolling basis. Application fee: $35 ($50 for international students). Electronic applications accepted. *Expenses:* Tuition, state resident: full-time $5830. Tuition, nonresident: full-time $10,708. *Required fees:* $1130. Tuition and fees vary according to class time, course level, course load and program. *Financial support:* Career-related internships or fieldwork, Federal Work-Study, institutionally sponsored loans, scholarships/grants, and unspecified assistantships available. Support available to part-time students. Financial award application deadline: 3/31; financial award applicants required to submit FAFSA. *Unit head:* Dr. Gerald Masterson, Program Director, 417-836-5251, Fax: 417-836-6888, E-mail: mps@missouristate.edu. *Application contact:* Michael Edwards, Coordinator of Graduate Admissions, 417-836-5330, Fax: 417-836-6200, E-mail: michaeledwards@missouristate.edu.
Website: http://mps.missouristate.edu

**Monmouth University,** Graduate Studies, Department of Criminal Justice, West Long Branch, NJ 07764-1898. Offers criminal justice (MA), including homeland security; criminal justice administration (Certificate); homeland security (MS, Certificate). *Program availability:* Part-time, evening/weekend, 100% online. *Degree requirements:* For master's, comprehensive exam (for some programs), thesis (for some programs). *Entrance requirements:* For master's and Certificate, baccalaureate degree with minimum GPA of 3.0 in major, 2.5 overall; two letters of recommendation; personal essay. Additional exam requirements/recommendations for international students: Required—TOEFL (minimum score 550 paper-based; 79 iBT), IELTS (minimum score 6), Michigan English Language Assessment Battery (minimum score 77) or Certificate of Advanced English (minimum score B2). Electronic applications accepted. *Faculty research:* Violent crimes, criminal pathology, terrorism, computer crime, comparative criminal justice systems, homeland security.

**National Defense University,** College of International Security Affairs, Washington, DC 20319-5066. Offers strategic security studies (MA), including counterterrorism, homeland defense, international security studies. *Program availability:* Part-time, evening/weekend. *Degree requirements:* For master's, thesis. *Entrance requirements:* Additional exam requirements/recommendations for international students: Required—TOEFL.

**The National Graduate School of Quality Management,** Graduate Programs, Falmouth, MA 02541. Offers homeland security (MS); quality systems management (MS, DBA).

**Naval Postgraduate School,** Departments and Academic Groups, Department of National Security Affairs, Monterey, CA 93943. Offers national security affairs (MA); security studies (MA), including civil-military relations, combating terrorism: policy and strategy, defense decision-making and planning, Europe and Eurasia, Far East, Southeast Asia, the Pacific, homeland security and defense, Middle East, South Asia, Sub-Saharan Africa, stabilization and reconstruction, western hemisphere. Program only open to commissioned officers of the United States and friendly nations and selected United States federal civilian employees. *Program availability:* Part-time. *Degree requirements:* For master's, thesis (for some programs). *Faculty research:* Privatizing welfare in the Middle East; social construction of Russia's resurgence; institutions, ethnicity and political mobilization in South Africa; Hezbollah; China's strategic interests in Cambodia.

**Northeastern University,** College of Professional Studies, Boston, MA 02115-5096. Offers applied nutrition (MS); college athletics administration (MSL); commerce and economic development (MS); corporate and organizational communication (MS); criminal justice (MS); digital media (MPS); elearning and instructional design (M Ed); elementary education (MAT); geographic information technology (MPS); global studies and international relations (MS); higher education administration (M Ed); homeland security (MA); human services (MS); informatics (MPS); leadership (MS); learning analytics (M Ed); learning and instruction (M Ed); nonprofit management (MS); professional sports administration (MSL); project management (MS); regulatory affairs for drugs, biologics, and medical devices (MS); respiratory care leadership (MS); special education (M Ed); technical communication (MS). *Program availability:* Part-time, evening/weekend, 100% online, blended/hybrid learning. *Faculty:* 82 full-time (51 women), 853 part-time/adjunct (366 women). *Students:* 4,947 part-time (3,076 women). In 2016, 1,456 master's awarded. *Application deadline:* Applications are processed on a rolling basis. Application fee: $0. Electronic applications accepted. *Expenses:* Contact institution. *Financial support:* Applicants required to submit FAFSA. *Unit head:* Dr. Mary Loeffelholz, Interim Dean of the College of Professional Studies.
Website: http://www.cps.neu.edu/

**Northeastern University,** College of Social Sciences and Humanities, Boston, MA 02115. Offers criminology and criminal justice (MSCJ); criminology and justice policy (PhD); economics (MA, PhD); English (MA, PhD); international affairs (MA); law and public policy (PhD); political science (MA, PhD); public administration (MPA); public history (MA); public policy (MPP); security and resilience studies (MS); sociology (MA, PhD); urban and regional policy (MS); urban informatics (MS); world history (MA, PhD); JD/MS. *Program availability:* Online learning. *Faculty:* 234 full-time (114 women), 55 part-time/adjunct (34 women). *Students:* 427 full-time (239 women), 77 part-time (42 women). In 2016, 143 master's, 38 doctorates awarded. *Degree requirements:* For doctorate, variable foreign language requirement, comprehensive exam, thesis/dissertation. *Entrance requirements:* For master's and doctorate, GRE. Additional exam requirements/recommendations for international students: Required—TOEFL, IELTS. Application fee: $75. Electronic applications accepted. *Expenses:* $1,295 per credit. *Financial support:* Teaching assistantships, career-related internships or fieldwork, scholarships/grants, health care benefits, tuition waivers (full and partial), and unspecified assistantships available. Support available to part-time students. Financial award applicants required to submit FAFSA. *Unit head:* Dr. Uta Poiger, Dean, 617-373-5173. *Application contact:* Amber Crowe, Administrative Coordinator, 617-373-5990, Fax: 617-373-7281, E-mail: gradcssh@northeastern.edu.
Website: http://www.northeastern.edu/cssh/graduate

**Northwestern State University of Louisiana,** Graduate Studies and Research, Department of Criminal Justice, History and Social Sciences, Program in Homeland Security, Natchitoches, LA 71497. Offers MS. *Degree requirements:* For master's, comprehensive exam, thesis or alternative. *Entrance requirements:* For master's, GRE General Test. Additional exam requirements/recommendations for international students: Required—TOEFL. Electronic applications accepted.

**Notre Dame College,** Graduate Programs, South Euclid, OH 44121-4293. Offers mild/moderate needs (M Ed); reading (M Ed); security policy studies (MA, Graduate Certificate); technology (M Ed). *Program availability:* Part-time, evening/weekend. *Degree requirements:* For master's, thesis. *Entrance requirements:* For master's, GRE General Test, MAT, minimum undergraduate GPA of 2.75, valid teaching certificate, bachelor's degree in an education-related field from accredited college or university, official transcripts of most recent college work. *Faculty research:* Cognitive psychology, teaching critical thinking in the classroom.

**Pace University,** Dyson College of Arts and Sciences, MA Program in Management for Public Safety and Homeland Security Professionals, New York, NY 10038. Offers MA. *Program availability:* Evening/weekend, blended/hybrid learning. *Students:* 7 full-time (5 women), 12 part-time (4 women); includes 8 minority (4 Black or African American, non-Hispanic/Latino; 4 Hispanic/Latino). Average age 30. In 2016, 10 master's awarded. *Degree requirements:* For master's, project. *Entrance requirements:* For master's, 2 letters of recommendation, resume, personal statement, official transcripts. Additional exam requirements/recommendations for international students: Required—TOEFL. *Application deadline:* For fall admission, 8/1 for domestic students. Applications are processed on a rolling basis. Application fee: $70. Electronic applications accepted. *Expenses: Tuition:* Part-time $1195 per credit. *Required fees:* $260 per semester. Tuition and fees vary according to degree level, campus/location and program. *Financial support:* Research assistantships, scholarships/grants, and unspecified assistantships available. Financial award application deadline: 2/15; financial award applicants required to submit FAFSA. *Unit head:* Dr. Joseph Ryan, Chair, Criminal Justice and Security Department, 914-773-3814, E-mail: jryan@pace.edu. *Application contact:* Susan Ford-Goldschein, Director of Admissions, 914-422-4283, Fax: 212-346-1585, E-mail: graduateadmission@pace.edu.
Website: http://www.pace.edu/dyson/programs/ma-public-safety-homeland-security

**Penn State Harrisburg,** Graduate School, School of Public Affairs, Middletown, PA 17057. Offers criminal justice (MA); health administration (MHA); health administration: long term care (Certificate); homeland security (Certificate); public administration (MPA, PhD); public administration: non-profit administration (Certificate); public budgeting and financial management (Certificate); public sector human resource management (Certificate). *Accreditation:* NASPAA. *Unit head:* Dr. Mukund S. Kulkarni, Chancellor, 717-948-6105, Fax: 717-948-6452. *Application contact:* Robert W. Coffman, Jr., Director of Enrollment Management, Admissions, 717-948-6250, Fax: 717-948-6325, E-mail: hbgadmit@psu.edu.
Website: https://harrisburg.psu.edu/public-affairs

**Regent University,** Graduate School, Robertson School of Government, Virginia Beach, VA 23464-9800. Offers government (MA), including American government, healthcare policy and ethics (MA, MPA), international relations, law and public policy, national security studies, political communication, political theory, religion and politics; public administration (MPA), including emergency management and homeland security, federal government, general public administration, healthcare policy and ethics (MA, MPA), law, nonprofit administration and faith-based organizations, public leadership and management, servant leadership. *Program availability:* Part-time, evening/weekend, 100% online, blended/hybrid learning. *Faculty:* 8 full-time (1 woman), 19 part-time/adjunct (3 women). *Students:* 40 full-time (27 women), 119 part-time (69 women); includes 73 minority (47 Black or African American, non-Hispanic/Latino; 3 Asian, non-Hispanic/Latino; 15 Hispanic/Latino; 8 Two or more races, non-Hispanic/Latino), 6 international. Average age 35. 253 applicants, 41% accepted, 70 enrolled. In 2016, 34 master's awarded. *Degree requirements:* For master's, thesis optional, internship. *Entrance requirements:* For master's, GRE General Test or LSAT, personal essay, writing sample, resume, college transcripts. Additional exam requirements/recommendations for international students: Required—TOEFL (minimum score 577 paper-based). *Application deadline:* For fall admission, 5/1 priority date for domestic students; for spring admission, 11/1 priority date for domestic students. Applications are processed on a rolling basis. Application fee: $50. Electronic applications accepted. *Expenses:* $650 per credit (MA/MPA); $250 per semester technology fee. *Financial support:* In 2016–17, 78 students received support. Career-related internships or fieldwork, scholarships/grants, and unspecified assistantships available. Support available to part-time students. *Faculty research:* International relations and politics, public administration, leadership and ethics, Biblical law, Constitutional law and Supreme Court. *Unit head:* Dr. Eric Patterson, Dean, 757-352-4616, Fax: 757-352-4735, E-mail: epatterson@regent.edu. *Application contact:* Heidi Cece, Assistant Vice President of Enrollment Management, 800-373-5504, Fax: 757-352-4381, E-mail: admissions@regent.edu.
Website: http://www.regent.edu/rsg/

**St. Mary's University,** Graduate Studies, Program in International Relations, San Antonio, TX 78228-8507. Offers conflict transformation (Certificate); international conflict resolution (MA); international development (MA); international relations (MA); security policy (MA); JD/MA. *Program availability:* Part-time, evening/weekend, 100% online. *Faculty:* 4 full-time (2 women), 1 part-time/adjunct (0 women). *Students:* 22 full-time (14 women), 59 part-time (18 women); includes 33 minority (5 Black or African American, non-Hispanic/Latino; 2 American Indian or Alaska Native, non-Hispanic/Latino; 6 Asian, non-Hispanic/Latino; 20 Hispanic/Latino), 5 international. Average age 32. 28 applicants, 61% accepted, 6 enrolled. In 2016, 35 master's awarded. *Degree requirements:* For master's, one foreign language, comprehensive exam (for some programs), thesis (for some programs), thesis or comprehensive exam. *Entrance requirements:* For master's, minimum undergraduate cumulative GPA of 3.0. Additional exam requirements/recommendations for international students: Required—TOEFL (minimum score 550 paper-based; 80 iBT), IELTS (minimum score 6). *Application deadline:* For fall admission, 7/1 for domestic students; for spring admission, 11/15 for domestic students; for summer admission, 4/1 for domestic students. Applications are processed on a rolling basis. Application fee: $0. Electronic applications accepted. *Expenses: Tuition:* Full-time $15,600; part-time $865 per credit hour. *Required fees:* $148 per semester. *Financial support:* Research assistantships, Federal Work-Study, tuition waivers (full), unspecified assistantships, and grants for active-duty and retired military, DOD employees, and their spouses available. Financial award application deadline: 3/31; financial award applicants required to submit FAFSA. *Faculty research:* Anthropology and ethics, states in crisis and socioeconomic development, politics and society of south Asia, political psychology, international relations theory. *Unit head:* Dr. Amber Aubone, Graduate International Relations, 210-436-3111, E-mail: aaubone@stmarytx.edu. *Application contact:* Kim Thornton, Director, Graduate and Adult Enrollment Services, 210-436-3101, E-mail: kthornton@stmarytx.edu.

**Salve Regina University,** Program in Administration of Justice and Homeland Security, Newport, RI 02840-4192. Offers administration of justice and homeland security (MS); cybersecurity and intelligence (CGS); digital forensics (CGS); leadership in justice (CGS). *Program availability:* Part-time, evening/weekend, online learning. *Entrance requirements:* For master's, GMAT, GRE General Test, or MAT. Additional exam requirements/recommendations for international students: Required—TOEFL (minimum score 600 paper-based; 100 iBT). Electronic applications accepted.

**Sam Houston State University,** College of Criminal Justice, Department of Security Studies, Huntsville, TX 77341. Offers homeland security studies (MS). *Program availability:* Part-time, online learning. *Degree requirements:* For master's, thesis optional. *Entrance requirements:* For master's, undergraduate degree, official transcripts, three letters of recommendation, current resume, personal essay. Additional exam requirements/recommendations for international students: Required—TOEFL (minimum score 550 paper-based; 79 iBT); Recommended—IELTS (minimum score 6.5). Electronic applications accepted.

**Southern Illinois University Carbondale,** Graduate School, College of Applied Science, Program in Fire Service and Homeland Security, Carbondale, IL 62901-4701. Offers MS. *Program availability:* Part-time, evening/weekend, online learning. *Entrance requirements:* Additional exam requirements/recommendations for international students: Required—TOEFL. Electronic applications accepted.

*Homeland Security*

**Texas A&M University,** Bush School of Government and Public Service, College Station, TX 77840. Offers homeland security (Certificate); international affairs (MIA, Certificate); national security affairs (Certificate); non-profit management (Certificate); public service and administration (MPSA). *Accreditation:* NASPAA. *Faculty:* 68. *Students:* 324 full-time (165 women), 26 part-time (10 women); includes 89 minority (19 Black or African American, non-Hispanic/Latino; 4 Asian, non-Hispanic/Latino; 58 Hispanic/Latino; 1 Native Hawaiian or other Pacific Islander, non-Hispanic/Latino; 7 Two or more races, non-Hispanic/Latino), 44 international. Average age 27. 261 applicants, 96% accepted, 165 enrolled. In 2016, 164 master's awarded. *Degree requirements:* For master's, summer internship. *Entrance requirements:* For master's, GRE (preferred) or GMAT. Additional exam requirements/recommendations for international students: Required—TOEFL (minimum score 550 paper-based; 80 iBT), IELTS (minimum score 6), PTE (minimum score 53). *Application deadline:* For fall admission, 1/15 for domestic and international students. Application fee: $50 ($90 for international students). Electronic applications accepted. *Expenses:* Contact institution. *Financial support:* In 2016–17, 413 students received support, including 16 fellowships with tuition reimbursements available (averaging $18,236 per year), 61 research assistantships with tuition reimbursements available (averaging $5,904 per year), 1 teaching assistantship (averaging $4,025 per year); career-related internships or fieldwork, institutionally sponsored loans, scholarships/grants, traineeships, health care benefits, tuition waivers (full and partial), and unspecified assistantships also available. Support available to part-time students. Financial award application deadline: 3/15; financial award applicants required to submit FAFSA. *Faculty research:* Public policy, Presidential studies, public leadership, economic policy, social policy. *Unit head:* Dr. Mark Welsh, Dean, 979-862-8007, E-mail: mwelsh@tamu.edu. *Application contact:* Kathryn Meyer, Director of Recruitment and Admissions, 979-458-4767, Fax: 979-845-4155, E-mail: bushschooladmissions@tamu.edu.
Website: http://bush.tamu.edu/

**Thomas Edison State University,** Heavin School of Arts and Sciences, Program in Homeland Security, Trenton, NJ 08608. Offers Graduate Certificate. *Program availability:* Part-time, online learning. *Entrance requirements:* Additional exam requirements/recommendations for international students: Required—TOEFL (minimum score 550 paper-based; 79 iBT). Electronic applications accepted.

**Tiffin University,** Program in Criminal Justice, Tiffin, OH 44883-2161. Offers criminal justice (MS), including crime analysis, criminal behavior, forensic psychology, homeland security administration, justice administration. *Program availability:* Part-time, evening/weekend, 100% online, blended/hybrid learning. *Students:* 83 full-time (61 women), 191 part-time (109 women); includes 85 minority (71 Black or African American, non-Hispanic/Latino; 6 Hispanic/Latino; 1 Native Hawaiian or other Pacific Islander, non-Hispanic/Latino; 7 Two or more races, non-Hispanic/Latino), 6 international. Average age 31. In 2016, 59 master's awarded. *Degree requirements:* For master's, thesis optional. *Entrance requirements:* For master's, minimum undergraduate GPA of 2.5, work experience. Additional exam requirements/recommendations for international students: Required—TOEFL (minimum score 550 paper-based; 79 iBT). *Application deadline:* For fall admission, 9/3 for domestic students, 8/1 for international students; for spring admission, 1/9 priority date for domestic students, 12/1 for international students. Applications are processed on a rolling basis. Application fee: $50. Electronic applications accepted. *Expenses:* Contact institution. *Financial support:* Available to part-time students. Application deadline: 7/31; applicants required to submit FAFSA. *Faculty research:* Terrorism, intelligence, homeland security, guns and crime. *Unit head:* Dr. Kevin Cashen, Dean of Criminal Justice and Security Studies, 419-448-3322, Fax: 419-443-5002, E-mail: cashenk@tiffin.edu. *Application contact:* Nikki Hintze, Director of Graduate and Distance Education Academic Advising, 800-968-6446 Ext. 3596, Fax: 419-443-5002, E-mail: hintzenm@tiffin.edu
Website: http://www.tiffin.edu

**Towson University,** Program in Integrated Homeland Security Management, Towson, MD 21252-0001. Offers integrated homeland security management (MS); security assessment and management (Postbaccalaureate Certificate). *Program availability:* Part-time, evening/weekend. *Students:* 5 full-time (3 women), 27 part-time (15 women); includes 15 minority (12 Black or African American, non-Hispanic/Latino; 1 Asian, non-Hispanic/Latino; 1 Hispanic/Latino; 1 Two or more races, non-Hispanic/Latino). *Entrance requirements:* For master's and Postbaccalaureate Certificate, BA in related field, 3 years of related work experience, resume, 2 letters of reference, minimum GPA of 3.0. *Application deadline:* Applications are processed on a rolling basis. Application fee: $45. Electronic applications accepted. *Expenses:* Tuition, state resident: full-time $7580; part-time $379 per unit. Tuition, nonresident: full-time $15,700; part-time $785 per unit. *Required fees:* $2480. *Financial support:* Application deadline: 4/1. *Unit head:* Dr. Joseph Clark, Graduate Program Director, 410-704-4490, E-mail: jrclark@towson.edu. *Application contact:* Coverley Beidleman, Assistant Director of Graduate Admissions, 410-704-2113, Fax: 410-704-3030, E-mail: grads@towson.edu.
Website: http://www.towson.edu/cla/departments/interdisciplinary/grad/homelandsecurity/index.html

**University at Albany, State University of New York,** College of Emergency Preparedness, Homeland Security and Cybersecurity, Albany, NY 12222-0001. Offers cybersecurity (Certificate); emergency preparedness (Certificate); homeland security (Certificate). *Faculty:* 3 part-time/adjunct (0 women). *Students:* 8 part-time (5 women). 13 applicants, 100% accepted, 5 enrolled. In 2016, 5 Certificates awarded. *Entrance requirements:* Additional exam requirements/recommendations for international students: Required—TOEFL. *Expenses:* Tuition, state resident: full-time $10,870; part-time $453 per credit hour. Tuition, nonresident: full-time $22,210; part-time $925 per credit hour. *International tuition:* $21,550 full-time. *Required fees:* $1864; $96 per credit hour. *Unit head:* Dr. Robert Griffin, Dean, 518-442-5258. *Application contact:* Michael DeRensis, Director, Graduate Admissions, 518-442-3980, Fax: 518-442-3922, E-mail: graduate@albany.edu.
Website: http://www.albany.edu/cehc/

**University at Albany, State University of New York,** Nelson A. Rockefeller College of Public Affairs and Policy, Department of Public Administration and Policy, Albany, NY 12222-0001. Offers financial management and public economics (MPA); financial market regulation (MPA); health policy (MPA); healthcare management (MPA); homeland security (MPA); human resources management (MPA); information strategy and management (MPA); local government management (MPA); nonprofit management (MPA); nonprofit management and leadership (Certificate); organizational behavior and theory (MPA, PhD); planning and policy analysis (CAS); policy analysis (MPA); politics and administration (PhD); public finance (PhD); public management (PhD); public policy (PhD); public sector management (Certificate); women and public policy (Certificate); JD/MPA. JD/MPA offered jointly with Albany Law School. *Accreditation:* NASPAA (one or more programs are accredited). *Faculty:* 23 full-time (8 women), 14 part-time/adjunct (7 women). *Students:* 117 full-time (65 women), 95 part-time (46 women); includes 41 minority (12 Black or African American, non-Hispanic/Latino; 8 Asian, non-Hispanic/Latino; 19 Hispanic/Latino; 2 Two or more races, non-Hispanic/Latino), 38 international. 223 applicants, 70% accepted, 81 enrolled. In 2016, 52 master's, 10 doctorates, 16 other advanced degrees awarded. *Degree requirements:* For doctorate, one foreign language, thesis/dissertation. *Entrance requirements:* For doctorate, GRE General Test.

Additional exam requirements/recommendations for international students: Required—TOEFL (minimum score 550 paper-based). *Application deadline:* For fall admission, 2/1 priority date for domestic students, 5/1 for international students; for spring admission, 12/1 for domestic students. Applications are processed on a rolling basis. Application fee: $75. Electronic applications accepted. *Expenses:* Tuition, state resident: full-time $10,870; part-time $453 per credit hour. Tuition, nonresident: full-time $22,210; part-time $925 per credit hour. *International tuition:* $21,550 full-time. *Required fees:* $1864; $96 per credit hour. *Financial support:* Application deadline: 2/1. *Total annual research expenditures:* $847,949. *Unit head:* Victor Asal, Chair, 518-591-8729, E-mail: vasal@albany.edu.
Website: http://www.albany.edu/rockefeller/pad.shtml

**University of Alaska Fairbanks,** School of Management, Program in Security and Disaster Management, Fairbanks, AK 99775. Offers MSDM. *Program availability:* Part-time, evening/weekend, 100% online, blended/hybrid learning. *Faculty:* 4 full-time (0 women). *Students:* 5 full-time (1 woman), 13 part-time (3 women); includes 5 minority (1 Black or African American, non-Hispanic/Latino; 4 Hispanic/Latino). Average age 34. 16 applicants, 63% accepted, 10 enrolled. *Entrance requirements:* For master's, Watson-Glaser Critical Thinking Appraisal. Additional exam requirements/recommendations for international students: Required—TOEFL (minimum score 79 iBT), IELTS (minimum score 6.5). *Application deadline:* For fall admission, 6/1 for domestic students, 3/1 for international students; for spring admission, 10/15 for domestic students, 9/1 for international students. Applications are processed on a rolling basis. Application fee: $60. Electronic applications accepted. *Expenses:* $533 per credit resident tuition, $673 per semester resident fees; $1,088 per credit non-resident tuition, $835 per semester non-resident fees. *Financial support:* In 2016–17, 1 teaching assistantship (averaging $14,820 per year) was awarded; Federal Work-Study and scholarships/grants also available. Financial award application deadline: 2/15; financial award applicants required to submit FAFSA. *Unit head:* Cameron Carlson, Director, 907-474-6537, E-mail: uaf-hsem@alaska.edu. *Application contact:* Mary Kreta, Director of Admissions, 907-474-7500, Fax: 907-474-7097, E-mail: admissions@uaf.edu.
Website: http://www.uaf.edu/som/degrees/graduate/msdm/

**University of Central Florida,** College of Health and Public Affairs, School of Public Administration, Orlando, FL 32816. Offers emergency management and homeland security (Certificate); fundraising (Certificate); non-profit management (MNM, Certificate); urban and regional planning (MS). *Accreditation:* NASPAA. *Program availability:* Part-time, evening/weekend. *Faculty:* 24 full-time (11 women), 11 part-time/adjunct (6 women). *Students:* 87 full-time (60 women), 257 part-time (190 women); includes 157 minority (83 Black or African American, non-Hispanic/Latino; 1 American Indian or Alaska Native, non-Hispanic/Latino; 9 Asian, non-Hispanic/Latino; 62 Hispanic/Latino; 2 Two or more races, non-Hispanic/Latino), 7 international. Average age 32. 192 applicants, 79% accepted, 108 enrolled. In 2016, 118 master's, 36 other advanced degrees awarded. *Degree requirements:* For master's, comprehensive exam, thesis or alternative, research report. *Entrance requirements:* For master's, GRE General Test. *Application deadline:* For fall admission, 6/15 for domestic students; for spring admission, 11/1 for domestic students. Application fee: $30. Electronic applications accepted. *Expenses:* Tuition, state resident: part-time $288.16 per credit hour. Tuition, nonresident: part-time $1071.31 per credit hour. *Financial support:* In 2016–17, 9 students received support, including 1 fellowship with partial tuition reimbursement available (averaging $4,000 per year), 9 research assistantships with partial tuition reimbursements available (averaging $6,704 per year); career-related internships or fieldwork, Federal Work-Study, institutionally sponsored loans, tuition waivers (partial), and unspecified assistantships also available. Financial award application deadline: 3/1; financial award applicants required to submit FAFSA. *Unit head:* Dr. Naim Kapucu, Director, 407-823-3693, Fax: 407-823-5651, E-mail: naim.kapucu@ucf.edu. *Application contact:* Assistant Director, Graduate Admissions, 407-823-2766, Fax: 407-823-6442, E-mail: gradadmissions@ucf.edu.
Website: https://www.cohpa.ucf.edu/publicadmin/

**University of Colorado Denver,** School of Public Affairs, Program in Public Affairs and Administration, Denver, CO 80127. Offers public administration (MPA), including domestic violence, emergency management and homeland security, environmental policy, management and law, homeland security and defense, local government, nonprofit management, public administration; public affairs (PhD). *Accreditation:* NASPAA. *Program availability:* Part-time, evening/weekend, online learning. *Students:* 241 full-time (146 women), 135 part-time (86 women); includes 61 minority (15 Black or African American, non-Hispanic/Latino; 1 American Indian or Alaska Native, non-Hispanic/Latino; 10 Asian, non-Hispanic/Latino; 26 Hispanic/Latino; 2 Native Hawaiian or other Pacific Islander, non-Hispanic/Latino; 7 Two or more races, non-Hispanic/Latino), 26 international. Average age 36. 240 applicants, 70% accepted, 91 enrolled. In 2016, 158 master's, 8 doctorates awarded. *Degree requirements:* For master's, thesis or alternative, 36-39 credit hours; for doctorate, comprehensive exam, thesis/dissertation, minimum of 66 semester hours, including at least 30 hours of dissertation. *Entrance requirements:* For master's, GRE, GMAT or LSAT, resume, essay, transcripts, recommendations; for doctorate, GRE, resume, essay, transcripts, recommendations. Additional exam requirements/recommendations for international students: Required—TOEFL (minimum score 550 paper-based; 80 iBT); Recommended—IELTS (minimum score 6.5). *Application deadline:* For fall admission, 2/1 priority date for domestic students, 1/15 priority date for international students; for spring admission, 10/15 priority date for domestic students, 10/1 priority date for international students. Application fee: $50 ($75 for international students). Electronic applications accepted. *Expenses:* Contact institution. *Financial support:* In 2016–17, 92 students received support. Fellowships with partial tuition reimbursements available, research assistantships with partial tuition reimbursements available, teaching assistantships with partial tuition reimbursements available, Federal Work-Study, institutionally sponsored loans, scholarships/grants, traineeships, and unspecified assistantships available. Financial award application deadline: 4/1; financial award applicants required to submit FAFSA. *Faculty research:* Housing, education and the social and economic issues of vulnerable populations; nonprofit governance and management; education finance, effectiveness and reform; P-20 education initiatives; municipal government accountability. *Unit head:* Dr. Christine Martell, Director of MPA Program, 303-315-2716, Fax: 303-315-2229, E-mail: christine.martell@ucdenver.edu. *Application contact:* Dawn Savage, Student Services Coordinator, 303-315-2743, Fax: 303-315-2229, E-mail: dawn.savage@ucdenver.edu.
Website: http://www.ucdenver.edu/academics/colleges/SPA/Academics/programs/PublicAffairsAdmin/Pages/index.aspx

**University of Denver,** Josef Korbel School of International Studies, Denver, CO 80208. Offers conflict resolution (MA); global business and corporate social responsibility (Certificate); global finance, trade and economic integration (MA); global health affairs (Certificate); homeland security (Certificate); humanitarian assistance (Certificate); international administration (MA); international development (MA); international human rights (MA); international security (MA); international studies (MA, PhD); public policy studies (MPP); religion and international affairs (Certificate). *Program availability:* Part-time. *Faculty:* 46 full-time (16 women), 28 part-time/adjunct (8 women). *Students:* 368 full-time (204 women), 26 part-time (10 women); includes 82 minority (15 Black or African American, non-Hispanic/Latino; 2 American Indian or Alaska Native, non-

Hispanic/Latino; 11 Asian, non-Hispanic/Latino; 43 Hispanic/Latino; 11 Two or more races, non-Hispanic/Latino), 38 international. Average age 27. 764 applicants, 82% accepted, 138 enrolled. In 2016, 197 master's, 10 doctorates, 28 other advanced degrees awarded. *Degree requirements:* For master's, one foreign language, thesis (for some programs); for doctorate, one foreign language, comprehensive exam, thesis/dissertation, two extended research papers. *Entrance requirements:* For master's, GRE General Test, bachelor's degree, transcripts, two letters of recommendation, statement of purpose, resume or curriculum vitae; for doctorate, GRE General Test, master's degree, transcripts, three letters of recommendation, statement of purpose, resume or curriculum vitae, writing sample; for Certificate, bachelor's degree, transcripts, two letters of recommendation, statement of purpose, resume or curriculum vitae. Additional exam requirements/recommendations for international students: Required—TOEFL (minimum score 587 paper-based; 95 iBT). *Application deadline:* For fall admission, 1/15 priority date for domestic and international students; for winter admission, 11/1 for domestic and international students. Applications are processed on a rolling basis. Application fee: $65. Electronic applications accepted. *Expenses:* $43,458 per year full-time. *Financial support:* In 2016–17, 244 students received support, including 1 research assistantship with tuition reimbursement available (averaging $7,250 per year), 5 teaching assistantships with tuition reimbursements available (averaging $2,842 per year); career-related internships or fieldwork, Federal Work-Study, institutionally sponsored loans, scholarships/grants, and unspecified assistantships also available. Support available to part-time students. Financial award application deadline: 2/15; financial award applicants required to submit FAFSA. *Faculty research:* Human rights and international security, international politics and economics, economic-social and political development, international technology analysis and management. *Unit head:* Dr. Christopher R. Hill, Dean, 303-871-2359, Fax: 303-871-2456, E-mail: christopher.r.hill@du.edu. *Application contact:* Admissions Contact, E-mail: korbeladm@du.edu.
Website: http://www.du.edu/korbel

**University of Illinois at Springfield,** Graduate Programs, College of Public Affairs and Administration, Program in Public Health, Springfield, IL 62703-5407. Offers community health education (Graduate Certificate); emergency preparedness and homeland security (Graduate Certificate); environmental health (Graduate Certificate); environmental risk assessment (Graduate Certificate); epidemiology (Graduate Certificate); public health (MPH). *Program availability:* Part-time, evening/weekend, 100% online. *Faculty:* 7 full-time (5 women). *Students:* 42 full-time (28 women), 53 part-time (32 women); includes 25 minority (14 Black or African American, non-Hispanic/Latino; 7 Asian, non-Hispanic/Latino; 3 Hispanic/Latino; 1 Two or more races, non-Hispanic/Latino), 21 international. Average age 32. 107 applicants, 40% accepted, 20 enrolled. In 2016, 38 master's, 17 other advanced degrees awarded. *Degree requirements:* For master's, comprehensive exam, internship. *Entrance requirements:* For master's, GRE, minimum undergraduate GPA of 3.0, 3 letters of recommendation, statement of personal goals. Additional exam requirements/recommendations for international students: Required—TOEFL (minimum score 500 paper-based; 61 iBT). *Application deadline:* Applications are processed on a rolling basis. Application fee: $60 ($75 for international students). Electronic applications accepted. *Expenses:* Tuition, state resident: part-time $329 per credit hour. Tuition, nonresident: part-time $675 per credit hour. *Financial support:* In 2016–17, fellowships with full tuition reimbursements (averaging $9,900 per year), research assistantships with full tuition reimbursements (averaging $9,991 per year), teaching assistantships with full tuition reimbursements (averaging $10,059 per year) were awarded; career-related internships or fieldwork, Federal Work-Study, scholarships/grants, health care benefits, and unspecified assistantships also available. Support available to part-time students. Financial award application deadline: 11/15; financial award applicants required to submit FAFSA. *Unit head:* Dr. Josiah Alamu, Program Administrator, 217-206-7874, Fax: 217-206-7279, E-mail: jalam3@uis.edu. *Application contact:* Dr. Cecelia Cornell, Associate Vice Chancellor for Graduate Education, 217-206-7230, E-mail: ccorn1@uis.edu.
Website: http://www.uis.edu/publichealth/

**University of Management and Technology,** Program in Criminal Justice, Arlington, VA 22209-1609. Offers homeland security (MS). *Program availability:* Part-time, evening/weekend, online learning. *Entrance requirements:* Additional exam requirements/recommendations for international students: Required—TOEFL (minimum score 530 paper-based; 71 iBT).

**University of Management and Technology,** Program in Homeland Security, Arlington, VA 22209-1609. Offers MS. *Degree requirements:* For master's, capstone course.

**University of Oklahoma Health Sciences Center,** Graduate College, College of Public Health, Program in Preparedness and Terrorism, Oklahoma City, OK 73190. Offers MPH.

**University of Phoenix–Online Campus,** College of Justice and Security, Phoenix, AZ 85034-7209. Offers administration of justice and security (MS), including administration of justice and security, global and homeland security, law enforcement organizations; public administration (MPA). *Program availability:* Evening/weekend, online learning. *Entrance requirements:* Additional exam requirements/recommendations for international students: Required—TOEFL, TOEIC (Test of English as an International Communication), Berlitz Online English Proficiency Exam, PTE, or IELTS. Electronic applications accepted. *Expenses:* Contact institution.

**University of Phoenix–Phoenix Campus,** College of Criminal Justice and Security, Tempe, AZ 85282-2371. Offers administration of justice and security (MS); global and homeland security (MS); law enforcement organizations (MS); public administration (MPA). *Program availability:* Evening/weekend, online learning. *Entrance requirements:* Additional exam requirements/recommendations for international students: Required—TOEFL, TOEIC (Test of English as an International Communication), Berlitz Online English Proficiency Exam, PTE, or IELTS. Electronic applications accepted. *Expenses:* Contact institution.

**University of Phoenix–Southern California Campus,** College of Criminal Justice and Security, Costa Mesa, CA 92626. Offers administration of justice and security (MS), including administration of justice and security, global and homeland security, law enforcement organizations; public administration (MPA). *Program availability:* Evening/weekend, online learning. *Entrance requirements:* Additional exam requirements/recommendations for international students: Required—TOEFL, TOEIC (Test of English as an International Communication), Berlitz Online English Proficiency Exam, PTE, or IELTS. Electronic applications accepted. *Expenses:* Contact institution.

**University of Southern California,** Graduate School, School of Policy, Planning, and Development, Public Policy Programs, Los Angeles, CA 90089. Offers homeland security and public policy (Graduate Certificate); public policy (MPP, Graduate Certificate); M PI/MPP; MPP/JD. *Program availability:* Part-time. Terminal master's awarded for partial completion of doctoral program. *Degree requirements:* For master's, practicum. *Entrance requirements:* For master's, GRE. Additional exam requirements/recommendations for international students: Required—TOEFL (minimum score 600 paper-based; 100 iBT). Electronic applications accepted. *Faculty research:* Urban

political economy, community and economic development, environmental policy, transportation policy, housing policy.

**University of the District of Columbia,** College of Arts and Sciences, Program in Homeland Security, Washington, DC 20008-1175. Offers MS. *Degree requirements:* For master's, thesis or public policy paper.

**Upper Iowa University,** Online Master's Programs, Fayette, IA 52142-1857. Offers accounting (MBA); corporate financial management (MBA); emergency management and homeland security (MPA); general management (MBA); general studies (MPA); government administration (MPA); health and human services (MPA); human resources management (MBA); nonprofit organizational management (MPA); organizational development (MBA); public management (MPA); sport administration (MSA). MBA also available at Madison, WI campus. *Program availability:* Part-time, online learning. *Degree requirements:* For master's, research project. *Entrance requirements:* For master's, GMAT, GRE, or minimum GPA of 2.7 during last 60 hours. Additional exam requirements/recommendations for international students: Required—TOEFL (minimum score 570 paper-based). Electronic applications accepted. *Faculty research:* Total quality management, teams, organization culture and climate, management.

**Virginia Commonwealth University,** Graduate School, College of Humanities and Sciences, L. Douglas Wilder School of Government and Public Affairs, Program in Homeland Security and Emergency Preparedness, Richmond, VA 23284-9005. Offers MA, Graduate Certificate. *Program availability:* Part-time, online learning. *Entrance requirements:* For master's, GRE, GMAT, MAT or LSAT, minimum GPA of 2.7; for Graduate Certificate, minimum GPA of 2.7. Additional exam requirements/recommendations for international students: Required—TOEFL (minimum score 600 paper-based; 100 iBT); Recommended—IELTS (minimum score 6.5). *Application deadline:* For fall admission, 4/1 for domestic students; for spring admission, 10/1 for domestic students. Application fee: $50. Electronic applications accepted. *Unit head:* Dr. William V. Pelfrey, Graduate Program Director, 804-828-8467, E-mail: wvpelfrey@vcu.edu. *Application contact:* Dr. Richard R. Huff, Director of Graduate Student Advising, 804-827-1430, E-mail: rrhuff@vcu.edu.
Website: http://www.wilder.vcu.edu/academic/security/index.html

**Walden University,** Graduate Programs, School of Psychology, Minneapolis, MN 55401. Offers clinical psychology (MS), including counseling, general program; forensic psychology (MS), including forensic psychology in the community, general program, mental health applications, program planning and evaluation in forensic settings, psychology and legal systems; industrial organizational (MS, PhD), including consulting psychology, forensic (MS), forensic psychology (PhD), general practice, leadership development and coaching (MS), organizational diversity and social change, research evaluation (PhD); online teaching in psychology (Post-Master's Certificate); organizational psychology and development (Postbaccalaureate Certificate); psychology (MS, PhD), including applied psychology (MS), clinical psychology (PhD), crisis management and response (MS), educational psychology, forensic psychology (PhD), general psychology (MS), general psychology research (PhD), general psychology teaching (PhD), health psychology, leadership development and coaching (MS), psychology of culture (MS), psychology, public administration, and social change (MS), social psychology, terrorism and security (MS); psychology respecialization (Post-Doctoral Certificate). *Program availability:* Part-time, evening/weekend, online only, 100% online. Terminal master's awarded for partial completion of doctoral program. *Degree requirements:* For master's, thesis optional; for doctorate, thesis/dissertation, residency. *Entrance requirements:* For master's, bachelor's degree or higher; minimum GPA of 2.5; official transcripts; goal statement (for some programs); access to computer and Internet; for doctorate, master's degree or higher; three years of related professional or academic experience (preferred); minimum GPA of 3.0; goal statement and current resume (for select programs); official transcripts; access to computer and Internet; for other advanced degree, relevant work experience; access to computer and Internet. Additional exam requirements/recommendations for international students: Required—TOEFL (minimum score 550 paper-based, 79 iBT), IELTS (minimum score 6.5), Michigan English Language Assessment Battery (minimum score 82), or PTE (minimum score 53). Electronic applications accepted.

**Walden University,** Graduate Programs, School of Public Policy and Administration, Minneapolis, MN 55401. Offers criminal justice (MPA, MPP, MS, Graduate Certificate), including emergency management (MS, PhD), general program (MS), global leadership (MS, PhD), homeland security and policy coordination (MS, PhD), law and public policy (MS, PhD), policy analysis (MS, PhD), public management and leadership (MS, PhD), self-designed (MS), terrorism, mediation, and peace (MS, PhD); criminal justice and executive management (MS), including global leadership (MS, PhD); criminal justice leadership and executive management (MS), including emergency management (MS, PhD), general program, homeland security and policy coordination (MS, PhD), law and public policy (MS, PhD), policy analysis (MS, PhD), public management and leadership (MS, PhD), self-designed, terrorism, mediation, and peace (MS, PhD); emergency management (MPA, MPP, MS), including criminal justice (MS, PhD), general program (MS), homeland security (MS), public management and leadership (MS, PhD), terrorism and emergency management (MS); general program (MPA, MPP); global leadership (MPA, MPP); government management (Graduate Certificate); health policy (MPA, MPP); homeland security (Graduate Certificate); homeland security and policy coordination (MPA, MPP); international nongovernmental organizations (MPA, MPP); law and public policy (MPA, MPP); local government management for sustainable communities (MPA, MPP); nonprofit management (Graduate Certificate); nonprofit management and leadership (MPA, MPP, MS), including global leadership (MS, PhD), international nongovernmental organization (MS), local government for sustainable communities (MS), self designed (MS); online teaching in higher education (Post-Master's Certificate); policy analysis (MPA); public management and leadership (MPA, MPP, Graduate Certificate); public policy (Graduate Certificate); public policy and administration (PhD), including criminal justice (MS, PhD), emergency management (MS, PhD), global leadership (MS, PhD), health policy, homeland security and policy coordination (MS, PhD), international nongovernmental organizations, law and public policy (MS, PhD), local government management for sustainable communities, nonprofit management and leadership, policy analysis (MS, PhD), public management and leadership (MS, PhD), terrorism, mediation, and peace (MS, PhD); strategic planning and public policy (Graduate Certificate); terrorism, mediation, and peace (MPA, MPP). *Program availability:* Part-time, evening/weekend, online only, 100% online. *Degree requirements:* For doctorate, thesis/dissertation, residency. *Entrance requirements:* For master's, bachelor's degree or higher; minimum GPA of 2.5; official transcripts; goal statement (for some programs); access to computer and Internet; for doctorate, master's degree or higher; three years of related professional or academic experience (preferred); minimum GPA of 3.0; goal statement and current resume (for select programs); official transcripts; access to computer and Internet; for other advanced degree, relevant work experience; access to computer and Internet. Additional exam requirements/recommendations for international students: Required—TOEFL (minimum score 550 paper-based, 79 iBT), IELTS (minimum score 6.5), Michigan English Language Assessment Battery (minimum score 82), or PTE (minimum score 53). Electronic applications accepted.

**Wayland Baptist University,** Graduate Programs, Programs in Behavioral and Social Sciences, Plainview, TX 79072-6998. Offers counseling (MA); criminal justice (MACJ); government administration (MPA); history (MA); homeland security (MPA); humanities (MAH); justice administration (MPA). *Program availability:* Part-time, evening/weekend, online learning. *Degree requirements:* For master's, comprehensive exam. *Entrance requirements:* For master's, GRE, MAT. Additional exam requirements/recommendations for international students: Required—TOEFL (minimum score 500 paper-based; 61 iBT). Electronic applications accepted.

**Western Kentucky University,** Graduate Studies, Ogden College of Science and Engineering, Department of Physics and Astronomy, Bowling Green, KY 42101. Offers homeland security sciences (MS); physics (MA Ed).

**Western Michigan University Thomas M. Cooley Law School,** Graduate Programs, Lansing, MI 48901-3038. Offers administrative law (public law) (JD); business transactions (JD); Canadian law practice (JD); constitutional law/civil rights (public law) (JD); corporate law and finance (LL M); environmental law (public law) (JD); general practice (JD), including solo and small firm; homeland and national security law (LL M); insurance law (LL M); intellectual property (JD); intellectual property law (LL M); international law (JD); litigation (JD); self-directed (LL M, JD); tax law (LL M); taxation (JD); U.S. legal studies for foreign attorneys (LL M); JD/LL M; JD/MBA; JD/MPA; JD/MSW. *Program availability:* Part-time, evening/weekend, 100% online, blended/hybrid learning. *Degree requirements:* For master's, thesis optional; for doctorate, minimum of 3 credits of clinical experience. *Entrance requirements:* For master's, JD or LL B; for doctorate, LSAT. Additional exam requirements/recommendations for international students: Required—TOEFL (for U.S. legal studies for foreign attorneys LL M program); Recommended—TOEFL. Electronic applications accepted. *Faculty research:* Wrongful convictions, civil rights, environmental law, litigation techniques, data mining, intellectual property, practical and skills-based legal education.

**Wilmington University,** College of Business, New Castle, DE 19720-6491. Offers accounting (MBA, MS); business administration (MBA, DBA); environmental stewardship (MBA); finance (MBA); health care administration (MBA, MSM); homeland security (MBA, MSM); human resource management (MSM); management information systems (MBA, MSN); marketing (MSM); marketing management (MBA); military leadership (MSM); organizational leadership (MBA, MSM); public administration (MSM). *Program availability:* Part-time, evening/weekend. *Faculty:* 17 full-time (7 women), 106 part-time/adjunct (46 women). *Students:* 436 full-time (237 women), 1,202 part-time (739 women); includes 594 minority (474 Black or African American, non-Hispanic/Latino; 19 American Indian or Alaska Native, non-Hispanic/Latino; 64 Asian, non-Hispanic/Latino; 30 Hispanic/Latino; 3 Native Hawaiian or other Pacific Islander, non-Hispanic/Latino; 4 Two or more races, non-Hispanic/Latino), 153 international. Average age 35. 814 applicants, 98% accepted, 426 enrolled. In 2016, 594 master's, 23 doctorates awarded. *Entrance requirements:* Additional exam requirements/recommendations for international students: Required—TOEFL (minimum score 500 paper-based). *Application deadline:* Applications are processed on a rolling basis. Application fee: $35. Electronic applications accepted. *Expenses: Tuition:* Full-time $8388; part-time $466 per credit. *Required fees:* $25 per semester. Tuition and fees vary according to degree level. *Financial support:* Applicants required to submit FAFSA. *Unit head:* Dr. Robert W. Rescigno, Dean. *Application contact:* Laura Morris, Director of Admissions, 877-967-5456, E-mail: infocenter@wilmu.edu. Website: http://www.wilmu.edu/business/

**Wilmington University,** College of Social and Behavioral Sciences, New Castle, DE 19720-6491. Offers administration of human services (MS); administration of justice (MS); clinical mental health counseling (MS); homeland security (MS). *Accreditation:* ACA. *Program availability:* Part-time, evening/weekend. *Faculty:* 8 full-time (5 women), 79 part-time/adjunct (35 women). *Students:* 210 full-time (162 women), 444 part-time (325 women); includes 320 minority (285 Black or African American, non-Hispanic/Latino; 12 American Indian or Alaska Native, non-Hispanic/Latino; 9 Asian, non-Hispanic/Latino; 12 Hispanic/Latino; 1 Native Hawaiian or other Pacific Islander, non-Hispanic/Latino; 1 Two or more races, non-Hispanic/Latino), 4 international. Average age 35. 255 applicants, 100% accepted, 255 enrolled. In 2016, 248 master's awarded. *Entrance requirements:* Additional exam requirements/recommendations for international students: Required—TOEFL (minimum score 500 paper-based). *Application deadline:* Applications are processed on a rolling basis. Application fee: $35. Electronic applications accepted. *Expenses: Tuition:* Full-time $8388; part-time $466 per credit. *Required fees:* $25 per semester. Tuition and fees vary according to degree level. *Financial support:* Applicants required to submit FAFSA. *Unit head:* Dr. Edward L. Guthrie, Dean. *Application contact:* Laura Morris, Director of Admissions, 877-967-5464, E-mail: inquire@wilmcoll.edu. Website: http://www.wilmu.edu/behavioralscience/

# Industrial and Labor Relations

**Baruch College of the City University of New York,** Zicklin School of Business, Zicklin Executive Programs, Baruch Executive Master of Science in Industrial and Labor Relations Program, New York, NY 10010-5585. Offers MS. *Program availability:* Part-time, evening/weekend. *Entrance requirements:* For master's, professional experience in HR or labor relations. Additional exam requirements/recommendations for international students: Required—TOEFL. *Expenses:* Contact institution.

**Carnegie Mellon University,** Dietrich College of Humanities and Social Sciences, Department of History, Pittsburgh, PA 15213-3891. Offers African and African-American diaspora (PhD); culture and power (PhD); labor, politics and social movements (PhD); technology, environment, science and health (PhD); women, gender and the family (PhD). *Program availability:* Part-time. *Degree requirements:* For doctorate, oral and written comprehensive exams, dissertation defense. *Entrance requirements:* For doctorate, GRE General Test. Additional exam requirements/recommendations for international students: Required—TOEFL. Electronic applications accepted. *Faculty research:* Anthropology and history, African-American history, technology/environment, cultural history analysis.

**Cleveland State University,** College of Graduate Studies, Monte Ahuja College of Business, Department of Management, Cleveland, OH 44115. Offers health care administration (MBA); labor relations and human resources (MLRHR). *Program availability:* Part-time, evening/weekend. *Faculty:* 6 full-time (3 women), 8 part-time/adjunct (1 woman). *Students:* 7 full-time (5 women), 19 part-time (16 women); includes 10 minority (8 Black or African American, non-Hispanic/Latino; 2 Hispanic/Latino), 3 international. Average age 31. In 2016, 11 master's awarded. *Entrance requirements:* For master's, GMAT or GRE, minimum GPA of 3.0. Additional exam requirements/recommendations for international students: Required—TOEFL (minimum score 550 paper-based; 78 iBT). *Application deadline:* For fall admission, 7/15 for domestic students; for spring admission, 12/15 for domestic students. Applications are processed on a rolling basis. Application fee: $40. Electronic applications accepted. *Expenses:* Tuition, state resident: full-time $9565. Tuition, nonresident: full-time $17,980. Tuition and fees vary according to program. *Financial support:* In 2016–17, 3 students received support. Career-related internships or fieldwork, scholarships/grants, and unspecified assistantships available. Financial award application deadline: 5/1; financial award applicants required to submit FAFSA. *Faculty research:* Employee selection, individual differences, leadership, emotions, interviews. *Unit head:* Dr. Kenneth J. Dunegan, Chairperson, 216-687-4747, Fax: 216-687-4708, E-mail: t.degroot@csuohio.edu. *Application contact:* Lisa Marie Sample, Administrative Assistant, 216-687-4726, Fax: 216-687-6888, E-mail: l.m.sample@csuohio.edu. Website: https://www.csuohio.edu/business/management/management

**Cornell University,** Graduate School, Graduate Fields of Industrial and Labor Relations, Ithaca, NY 14853. Offers collective bargaining, labor law and labor history (MILR, MPS, MS, PhD); economic and social statistics (MILR); human resource studies (MILR, MPS, MS, PhD); industrial and labor relations problems (MILR, MPS, MS, PhD); international and comparative labor (MILR, MPS, MS, PhD); labor economics (MILR, MPS, MS, PhD); organizational behavior (MILR, MPS, MS, PhD). *Degree requirements:* For master's, thesis (MS); for doctorate, comprehensive exam, thesis/dissertation, teaching experience. *Entrance requirements:* For master's and doctorate, GMAT or GRE General Test, 2 academic recommendations. Additional exam requirements/recommendations for international students: Required—TOEFL (minimum score 550 paper-based; 77 iBT). Electronic applications accepted. *Expenses:* Contact institution.

**Georgetown University,** Graduate School of Arts and Sciences, Department of Economics, Washington, DC 20057. Offers econometrics (PhD); economic development (PhD); economic theory (PhD); industrial organization (PhD); international macro and finance (PhD); international trade (PhD); labor economics (PhD); macroeconomics (PhD); public economics and political economy (PhD); MA/PhD; MS/MA. *Degree requirements:* For doctorate, comprehensive exam, thesis/dissertation. *Entrance requirements:* For doctorate, GRE General Test. Additional exam requirements/recommendations for international students: Required—TOEFL. *Faculty research:* International economics, economic development.

**Georgia State University,** Andrew Young School of Policy Studies, Department of Economics, Atlanta, GA 30302. Offers economics (MA); environmental economics (PhD); experimental economics (PhD); labor economics (PhD); policy (MA); public finance (PhD); urban and regional economics (PhD). MA offered through the College of Arts and Sciences. *Program availability:* Part-time. *Faculty:* 26 full-time (4 women). *Students:* 112 full-time (37 women), 10 part-time (3 women); includes 17 minority (8 Black or African American, non-Hispanic/Latino; 3 Asian, non-Hispanic/Latino; 4 Hispanic/Latino; 2 Two or more races, non-Hispanic/Latino), 62 international. Average age 28. 168 applicants, 45% accepted, 31 enrolled. In 2016, 26 master's, 9 doctorates awarded. Terminal master's awarded for partial completion of doctoral program. *Degree requirements:* For master's, thesis optional; for doctorate, comprehensive exam, thesis/dissertation. *Entrance requirements:* For master's and doctorate, GRE. Additional exam requirements/recommendations for international students: Required—TOEFL (minimum score 603 paper-based; 100 iBT) or IELTS (minimum score 7). *Application deadline:* For fall admission, 1/15 for domestic and international students. Application fee: $50. Electronic applications accepted. *Expenses:* Tuition, state resident: full-time $6876; part-time $382 per credit hour. Tuition, nonresident: full-time $22,374; part-time $1243 per credit hour. *Required fees:* $2128; $1064 per term. Part-time tuition and fees vary according to course load and program. *Financial support:* In 2016–17, fellowships with full tuition reimbursements (averaging $11,333 per year), research assistantships with full tuition reimbursements (averaging $9,788 per year), teaching assistantships with full tuition reimbursements (averaging $3,000 per year) were awarded; career-related internships or fieldwork also available. Financial award application deadline: 2/15; financial award applicants required to submit FAFSA. *Faculty research:* Public, experimental, urban/environmental, labor, and health economics. *Unit head:* Dr. Rusty Tchernis, Director of the Doctoral Program, 404-413-0154, Fax: 404-413-0145, E-mail: rtchernis@gsu.edu. Website: http://economics.gsu.edu/

**Indiana University of Pennsylvania,** School of Graduate Studies and Research, College of Health and Human Services, Department of Employment and Labor Relations, Program in Employment and Labor Relations, Indiana, PA 15705. Offers MA. *Program availability:* Part-time, evening/weekend, online learning. *Faculty:* 5 full-time (1 woman). *Students:* 34 full-time (19 women), 19 part-time (13 women); includes 12 minority (4 Black or African American, non-Hispanic/Latino; 1 Asian, non-Hispanic/Latino; 3 Hispanic/Latino; 4 Two or more races, non-Hispanic/Latino), 6 international. Average age 27. 60 applicants, 80% accepted, 33 enrolled. In 2016, 48 master's awarded. *Entrance requirements:* Additional exam requirements/recommendations for international students: Required—TOEFL (minimum score 550 paper-based). *Application deadline:* Applications are processed on a rolling basis. Application fee: $50. Electronic applications accepted. *Expenses:* Tuition, state resident: full-time $8694; part-time $483 per credit. Tuition, nonresident: full-time $13,050; part-time $725 per credit. *Required fees:* $157 per credit. $50 per term. Tuition and fees vary according to course load and program. *Financial support:* In 2016–17, 15 research assistantships with tuition reimbursements (averaging $3,247 per year) were awarded; fellowships with full tuition reimbursements, career-related internships or fieldwork, Federal Work-Study, scholarships/grants, and unspecified assistantships also available. Financial award application deadline: 4/15; financial award applicants required to submit FAFSA. *Unit head:* Dr. David M. Piper, Coordinator, 724-357-4471, E-mail: david.piper@iup.edu. Website: http://www.iup.edu/elr/programs/ma/

**Inter American University of Puerto Rico, Metropolitan Campus,** Graduate Programs, Program in Labor Relations, San Juan, PR 00919-1293. Offers MA. *Degree requirements:* For master's, comprehensive exam. *Entrance requirements:* For master's, GRE or EXADEP, interview. Electronic applications accepted.

**Inter American University of Puerto Rico, Metropolitan Campus,** Graduate Programs, Program in Psychology, San Juan, PR 00919-1293. Offers counseling psychology (MA, PhD); industrial/organizational psychology (MA, PhD); labor relations (MA); school psychology (MA, PhD). *Degree requirements:* For master's, comprehensive exam. *Entrance requirements:* For master's, GRE or EXADEP, interview. Electronic applications accepted.

**McMaster University,** School of Graduate Studies, Faculty of Social Sciences, Program in Labour Studies, Hamilton, ON L8S 4M2, Canada. Offers work and society (MA).

**Memorial University of Newfoundland,** School of Graduate Studies, Interdisciplinary Program in Employment Relations, St. John's, NL A1C 5S7, Canada. Offers MER. *Program availability:* Part-time. *Degree requirements:* For master's, major supervised paper. *Entrance requirements:* For master's, undergraduate degree in related field, minimum B average. Electronic applications accepted.

**Michigan State University,** The Graduate School, College of Social Science, School of Labor and Industrial Relations, East Lansing, MI 48824. Offers human resources and labor relations (MLRHR); industrial relations and human resources (PhD). *Entrance requirements:* Additional exam requirements/recommendations for international students: Required—TOEFL.

**New York Institute of Technology,** School of Management, Department of Human Resource Management Studies, Old Westbury, NY 11568-8000. Offers human resource management (Advanced Certificate); human resource management and labor relations (MS). *Program availability:* Part-time, evening/weekend. *Faculty:* 5 full-time (1 woman), 4 part-time/adjunct (1 woman). *Students:* 33 full-time (27 women), 23 part-time (22 women); includes 21 minority (6 Black or African American, non-Hispanic/Latino; 8 Asian, non-Hispanic/Latino; 6 Hispanic/Latino; 1 Native Hawaiian or other Pacific Islander, non-Hispanic/Latino), 20 international. Average age 28. 69 applicants, 71% accepted, 20 enrolled. In 2016, 22 master's, 1 other advanced degree awarded. *Degree requirements:* For master's, seminar and comprehensive exam, or thesis. *Entrance requirements:* For master's and Advanced Certificate, bachelor's degree; minimum undergraduate GPA of 3.0. Additional exam requirements/recommendations for international students: Required—TOEFL (minimum score 79 iBT), IELTS (minimum score 6). *Application deadline:* Applications are processed on a rolling basis. Application fee: $50. Electronic applications accepted. *Expenses:* $1,215 per credit. *Financial support:* Career-related internships or fieldwork, Federal Work-Study, scholarships/grants, tuition waivers (full and partial), and unspecified assistantships available. Support available to part-time students. Financial award application deadline: 3/1; financial award applicants required to submit FAFSA. *Faculty research:* Conflict resolution, adapting human resource practices to the needs of a global workforce, the effect of leadership styles and human resource practices on employee productivity, human resource management practices as a source of competitive advantage. *Unit head:* Dr. Maya Kroumova, Chairperson, 212-261-1667, Fax: 516-686-7425, E-mail: mkroumov@nyit.edu. *Application contact:* Alice Dolitsky, Director, Graduate Admissions, 516-686-7520, Fax: 516-686-1116, E-mail: nyitgrad@nyit.edu. Website: http://www.nyit.edu/degrees/human_resources_management_labor_relations_ms

**The Ohio State University,** Graduate School, Max M. Fisher College of Business, Program in Human Resource Management, Columbus, OH 43210. Offers human resource management (MHRM, PhD); labor and human resources (PhD). *Program availability:* Part-time. *Faculty:* 21. *Students:* 100 full-time (71 women), 24 part-time (19 women); includes 12 minority (7 Black or African American, non-Hispanic/Latino; 5 Hispanic/Latino), 28 international. Average age 26. In 2016, 44 master's awarded. *Degree requirements:* For doctorate, thesis/dissertation. *Entrance requirements:* For master's and doctorate, GRE General Test or GMAT. Additional exam requirements/recommendations for international students: Required—Michigan English Language Assessment Battery (minimum score 86); Recommended—TOEFL (minimum score 600 paper-based; 100 iBT), IELTS (minimum score 7). *Application deadline:* For fall admission, 11/15 priority date for domestic and international students. Applications are processed on a rolling basis. Application fee: $60 ($70 for international students). Electronic applications accepted. *Financial support:* Fellowships with tuition reimbursements, research assistantships with tuition reimbursements, and teaching assistantships with tuition reimbursements available. *Unit head:* Dr. Bennett J. Tepper, Chair, 614-688-2129, E-mail: tepper.15@osu.edu. *Application contact:* Graduate and Professional Admissions, 614-292-9444, Fax: 614-292-3895, E-mail: gpadmissions@osu.edu. Website: http://fisher.osu.edu/departments/management-and-hr/

**Penn State University Park,** Graduate School, College of the Liberal Arts, School of Labor and Employment Relations, University Park, PA 16802. Offers human resources and employment relations (MPS, MS); labor and global workers' rights (MPS). *Unit head:* Dr. Susan Welch, Dean, 814-865-7691, Fax: 814-863-2085. *Application contact:* Lori Hawn, Director, Graduate Student Services, 814-865-1795, Fax: 814-863-4627, E-mail: l-gswww@lists.psu.edu. Website: http://lser.la.psu.edu/

**Queen's University at Kingston,** School of Graduate Studies, School of Industrial Relations, Kingston, ON K7L 3N6, Canada. Offers MIR. *Program availability:* Part-time. *Degree requirements:* For master's, research essay, skill seminars and modules. *Entrance requirements:* For master's, course work in micro-economics, macro-economics, and quantitative statistics. Additional exam requirements/recommendations for international students: Required—TOEFL (minimum score 600 paper-based). *Faculty research:* Collective bargaining and labor law, personnel and human relations, labor market analysis and policy, change management, teams.

**Rutgers University–New Brunswick,** School of Management and Labor Relations, Program in Industrial Relations and Human Resources, Piscataway, NJ 08854-8097. Offers PhD. *Program availability:* Part-time. *Degree requirements:* For doctorate, comprehensive exam, thesis/dissertation. *Entrance requirements:* For doctorate, GRE or GMAT, 3 letters of recommendation. Additional exam requirements/recommendations for international students: Required—TOEFL (minimum score 575 paper-based; 91 iBT). Electronic applications accepted. *Faculty research:* Strategic human resources, labor relations, organizational change, worker representation.

**Rutgers University–New Brunswick,** School of Management and Labor Relations, Program in Labor and Employment Relations, Piscataway, NJ 08854-8097. Offers MLER. *Program availability:* Part-time, online learning. *Degree requirements:* For master's, thesis optional. *Entrance requirements:* For master's, GRE General Test. Additional exam requirements/recommendations for international students: Required—TOEFL. Electronic applications accepted. *Expenses:* Contact institution. *Faculty research:* Labor history, women and work, labor education, comparative labor movements, labor involvement and corporate decision making.

**Southern New Hampshire University,** School of Business, Manchester, NH 03106-1045. Offers accounting (MBA, MS, Graduate Certificate); accounting finance (MS); accounting/auditing (MS); accounting/forensic accounting (MS); accounting/taxation (MS); athletic administration (MBA, Graduate Certificate); business administration (IMBA, MBA, Certificate, Graduate Certificate), including accounting (Certificate), business administration (MBA), business information systems (Graduate Certificate), human resource management (Certificate); corporate social responsibility (MBA); entrepreneurship (MBA); finance (MBA, MS, Graduate Certificate); finance/corporate finance (MS); finance/investments and securities (MS); forensic accounting (MBA); healthcare informatics (MBA); healthcare management (MBA); human resource management (Graduate Certificate); information technology (MS, Graduate Certificate);

information technology management (MBA); international business (Graduate Certificate); international business and information technology (Graduate Certificate); international finance (Graduate Certificate); international sport management (Graduate Certificate); justice studies (MBA); leadership of nonprofit organizations (Graduate Certificate); management (MS); marketing (MBA, MS, Graduate Certificate); operations and project management (MS); operations and supply chain management (MBA, Graduate Certificate); organizational leadership (MS); project management (MBA, Graduate Certificate); Six Sigma (MBA); Six Sigma quality (Graduate Certificate); social media marketing (MBA); sport management (MBA, MS, Graduate Certificate); sustainability and environmental compliance (MBA); workplace conflict management (MBA); MBA/Certificate. *Accreditation:* ACBSP. *Program availability:* Part-time, evening/weekend, online learning. Terminal master's awarded for partial completion of doctoral program. *Degree requirements:* For master's, one foreign language, comprehensive exam (for some programs), thesis or alternative. *Entrance requirements:* For master's, minimum GPA of 2.5. Additional exam requirements/recommendations for international students: Required—TOEFL (minimum score 500 paper-based). Electronic applications accepted.

**State University of New York Empire State College,** School for Graduate Studies, Program in Labor and Policy Studies, Saratoga Springs, NY 12866-4391. Offers MA. *Program availability:* Part-time, evening/weekend, online learning. *Degree requirements:* For master's, thesis, exam, final project. *Entrance requirements:* Additional exam requirements/recommendations for international students: Required—TOEFL (minimum score 600 paper-based). Electronic applications accepted. *Faculty research:* Work and technology, collective bargaining, labor law, human resources management, trade union governance.

**Université de Montréal,** Faculty of Arts and Sciences, School of Industrial Relations, Montréal, QC H3C 3J7, Canada. Offers M Sc, PhD, DESS. *Program availability:* Part-time. *Degree requirements:* For master's, thesis; for doctorate, thesis/dissertation, general exam. *Entrance requirements:* For master's, BS in industrial relations. Electronic applications accepted. *Faculty research:* Labor law, health and safety at work, stress, job satisfaction, labor economics.

**Université du Québec à Trois-Rivières,** Graduate Programs, Program in Labor Relations, Trois-Rivières, QC G9A 5H7, Canada. Offers DESS.

**Université du Québec en Outaouais,** Graduate Programs, Department of Industrial Relations, Gatineau, QC J8X 3X7, Canada. Offers M Sc, MA, PhD, Diploma. *Program availability:* Part-time. *Degree requirements:* For master's, thesis (for some programs), internship (for some programs); for doctorate, thesis/dissertation. *Entrance requirements:* For master's, appropriate bachelor's degree, proficiency in French; for doctorate, appropriate master's degree, proficiency in French.

**Université Laval,** Faculty of Social Sciences, Department of Industrial Relations, Programs in Industrial Relations, Québec, QC G1K 7P4, Canada. Offers MA, PhD. Terminal master's awarded for partial completion of doctoral program. *Degree requirements:* For master's, thesis (for some programs); for doctorate, comprehensive exam, thesis/dissertation. *Entrance requirements:* For master's and doctorate, knowledge of French, comprehension of written English. Electronic applications accepted.

**University of Alberta,** Faculty of Graduate Studies and Research, Doctoral Program in Business, Edmonton, AB T6G 2E1, Canada. Offers accounting (PhD); finance (PhD); human resources/industrial relations (PhD); management science (PhD); marketing (PhD); organizational analysis (PhD); MBA/PhD. *Accreditation:* AACSB. *Program availability:* Part-time. *Degree requirements:* For doctorate, comprehensive exam, thesis/dissertation. *Entrance requirements:* For doctorate, GMAT. Additional exam requirements/recommendations for international students: Required—TOEFL (minimum score 550 paper-based). Electronic applications accepted. *Faculty research:* Accounting, capital markets and corporate finance, organizational change and human resource management, marketing, strategic management.

**University of California, Berkeley,** Graduate Division, Haas School of Business, PhD in Business Administration Program, Berkeley, CA 94720-1500. Offers accounting (PhD); business and public policy (PhD); finance (PhD); management of organizations (PhD); marketing (PhD); real estate (PhD). *Accreditation:* AACSB. *Students:* 78 full-time (28 women); includes 34 minority (29 Asian, non-Hispanic/Latino; 5 Hispanic/Latino). Average age 27. *Degree requirements:* For doctorate, comprehensive exam, thesis/dissertation, written preliminary exams, oral qualifying exam. *Entrance requirements:* For doctorate, GMAT or GRE, minimum GPA of 3.0 in undergraduate and graduate coursework. Additional exam requirements/recommendations for international students: Required—TOEFL (minimum score 570 paper-based; 70 iBT), IELTS (minimum score 7). *Application deadline:* For fall admission, 12/1 for domestic and international students. Application fee: $90 ($110 for international students). Electronic applications accepted. *Expenses:* Contact institution. *Financial support:* Fellowships with tuition reimbursements, research assistantships with tuition reimbursements, teaching assistantships with tuition reimbursements, scholarships/grants, health care benefits, tuition waivers (full), unspecified assistantships, and transit passes, travel grants available. Financial award application deadline: 12/10. *Faculty research:* Accounting, business and public policy, entrepreneurship, finance, management of organizations, marketing, operations and information technology management, real estate. *Unit head:* Dr. Nicolae Garleanu, Director, 510-643-6349, Fax: 510-643-4255. *Application contact:* Melissa Hacker, Director, Student Affairs, 510-642-3944, Fax: 510-643-4255, E-mail: melhacker@haas.berkeley.edu. Website: http://www.haas.berkeley.edu/Phd/

**University of Cincinnati,** Graduate School, McMicken College of Arts and Sciences, Center for Organizational Leadership, Program in Labor and Employment Relations, Cincinnati, OH 45221. Offers MALER. *Program availability:* Part-time, evening/weekend. *Degree requirements:* For master's, thesis or alternative, final experience project. *Entrance requirements:* For master's, minimum undergraduate GPA of 3.0. Additional exam requirements/recommendations for international students: Required—TOEFL (minimum score 560 paper-based). Electronic applications accepted. *Expenses: Tuition, area resident:* Full-time $12,790; part-time $389 per credit hour. *Tuition, state resident:* full-time $13,290; part-time $419 per credit hour. *Tuition, nonresident:* full-time $24,532; part-time $976 per credit hour. *International tuition:* $24,832 full-time. *Required fees:* $3958; $140 per credit hour. Tuition and fees vary according to course load, degree level, program and reciprocity agreements. *Faculty research:* Human resource management, diversity, leadership.

**University of Illinois at Urbana–Champaign,** Graduate College, School of Labor and Employment Relations, Champaign, IL 61820. Offers human resources and industrial relations (MHRIR, PhD); MHRIR/JD; MHRIR/MBA. Terminal master's awarded for partial completion of doctoral program.

**The University of Manchester,** Alliance Manchester Business School, M15 6PB, United Kingdom. Offers accounting and finance (M Sc); business (M Ent); business analysis and strategic management (M Sc); business analytics: operational research and risk analysis (M Sc); business psychology (M Sc); corporate communications and reputation management (M Sc); finance (M Sc); finance and business economics (M Sc); human resource management and industrial relations (M Sc); innovation

*Industrial and Labor Relations*

management and entrepreneurship (M Sc); international business and management (M Sc); international human resource management and comparative industrial relations (M Sc); management (M Sc); marketing (M Sc); operations, project and supply chain management (M Sc); organizational psychology (M Sc); quantitative finance (M Sc). *Entrance requirements:* For master's, UK 2:1 honours degree or overseas equivalent. Additional exam requirements/recommendations for international students: Required—TOEFL (minimum score 100 iBT), IELTS (minimum score 7), PTE. Electronic applications accepted. *Faculty research:* Accounting and finance, management sciences and marketing, people management and organization, innovation management and policy, decision sciences.

**University of Massachusetts Amherst,** Graduate School, College of Social and Behavioral Sciences, The Labor Center, Amherst, MA 01003. Offers labor studies (MS); union leadership and administration (MS). *Program availability:* Part-time, online learning. *Degree requirements:* For master's, thesis or alternative. *Entrance requirements:* Additional exam requirements/recommendations for international students: Required—TOEFL (minimum score 550 paper-based; 80 iBT), IELTS (minimum score 6.5). Electronic applications accepted.

**University of Minnesota, Twin Cities Campus,** Carlson School of Management, Master of Arts Program in Human Resources and Industrial Relations, Minneapolis, MN 55455-0213. Offers MA. *Accreditation:* AACSB. *Program availability:* Part-time, evening/weekend. *Faculty:* 16 full-time (9 women), 12 part-time/adjunct (6 women). *Students:* 117 full-time (81 women), 42 part-time (35 women); includes 20 minority (9 Black or African American, non-Hispanic/Latino; 1 American Indian or Alaska Native, non-Hispanic/Latino; 5 Asian, non-Hispanic/Latino; 5 Hispanic/Latino), 56 international. Average age 25. 238 applicants, 52% accepted, 75 enrolled. In 2016, 69 master's awarded. *Degree requirements:* For master's, thesis or alternative, 48 course credits. *Entrance requirements:* For master's, GMAT or GRE General Test, undergraduate degree from accredited institution, course in microeconomics. Additional exam requirements/recommendations for international students: Required—TOEFL (minimum score 550 paper-based; 79 iBT), IELTS (minimum score 6.5). *Application deadline:* For fall admission, 6/15 for domestic and international students; for spring admission, 10/15 for domestic and international students. Applications are processed on a rolling basis. Application fee: $75 ($95 for international students). Electronic applications accepted. *Expenses:* Contact institution. *Financial support:* In 2016–17, 66 students received support, including 57 fellowships (averaging $7,500 per year), 2 research assistantships with partial tuition reimbursements available (averaging $14,500 per year), 7 teaching assistantships with partial tuition reimbursements available (averaging $9,000 per year); Federal Work-Study, institutionally sponsored loans, scholarships/grants, health care benefits, tuition waivers (full and partial), and unspecified assistantships also available. Financial award application deadline: 2/1; financial award applicants required to submit FAFSA. *Faculty research:* Staffing, training, and development; compensation and benefits; organization theory; collective bargaining. *Total annual research expenditures:* $27,000. *Unit head:* Stacy Doepner-Hove, Director, 612-625-8732, Fax: 612-624-8360, E-mail: doepn002@umn.edu. *Application contact:* Amy Danzeisen, Admissions Associate, 612-624-5704, Fax: 612-624-8360, E-mail: hrirgrad@umn.edu. Website: http://www.csom.umn.edu/chrls/

**University of New Haven,** Graduate School, Henry C. Lee College of Criminal Justice and Forensic Sciences, Program in Public Administration, West Haven, CT 06516. Offers city management (MPA); community-clinical services (MPA); health care management (MPA); long-term health care (MPA); personnel and labor relations (MPA); public administration (MPA, Graduate Certificate); MBA/MPA. *Program availability:* Part-time, evening/weekend. *Students:* 30 full-time (13 women), 15 part-time (8 women); includes 15 minority (12 Black or African American, non-Hispanic/Latino; 1 American Indian or Alaska Native, non-Hispanic/Latino; 1 Asian, non-Hispanic/Latino; 1 Hispanic/Latino), 6 international. Average age 35. 56 applicants, 98% accepted, 25 enrolled. In 2016, 31 master's, 17 other advanced degrees awarded. *Degree requirements:* For master's, thesis or alternative. *Entrance requirements:* Additional exam requirements/recommendations for international students: Required—TOEFL (minimum score 80 iBT), IELTS, PTE. *Application deadline:* Applications are processed on a rolling basis. Application fee: $50. Electronic applications accepted. Application fee is waived when completed online. *Expenses:* Contact institution. *Financial support:* Research assistantships with partial tuition reimbursements, teaching assistantships with partial tuition reimbursements, career-related internships or fieldwork, Federal Work-Study, scholarships/grants, and unspecified assistantships available. Support available to part-time students. Financial award application deadline: 5/1; financial award applicants required to submit FAFSA. *Unit head:* Dr. Cynthia Conrad, Associate Professor, 203-932-7486, E-mail: cconrad@newhaven.edu. *Application contact:* Michelle Mason, Director of Graduate Enrollment, 203-932-7067, E-mail: mmason@newhaven.edu. Website: http://www.newhaven.edu/6854/

**University of Rhode Island,** Graduate School, Schmidt Labor Research Center, Kingston, RI 02881. Offers human resources (MS, Graduate Certificate); labor relations (MS, Graduate Certificate); MS/JD. *Program availability:* Part-time, evening/weekend. *Faculty:* 1 full-time (0 women), 3 part-time/adjunct (2 women). *Students:* 3 full-time (2 women), 30 part-time (24 women); includes 6 minority (4 Black or African American, non-Hispanic/Latino; 1 American Indian or Alaska Native, non-Hispanic/Latino; 1 Hispanic/Latino). In 2016, 5 master's awarded. *Entrance requirements:* For master's, GRE, MAT, GMAT, or LSAT, 2 letters of recommendation. Additional exam requirements/recommendations for international students: Required—TOEFL. *Application deadline:* For fall admission, 7/15 for domestic students, 2/1 for international students; for spring admission, 11/15 for domestic students, 7/15 for international students; for summer admission, 4/15 for domestic students. Application fee: $65. Electronic applications accepted. *Expenses:* Tuition, state resident: full-time $11,796; part-time $655 per credit. Tuition, nonresident: full-time $24,206; part-time $1345 per credit. *Required fees:* $1546; $44 per credit. One-time fee: $155 full-time; $35 part-time. *Financial support:* In 2016–17, 2 teaching assistantships with tuition reimbursements (averaging $17,184 per year) were awarded; institutionally sponsored loans also available. Financial award application deadline: 2/1; financial award applicants required to submit FAFSA. *Unit head:* Dr. Aimee Phelps, Acting Director, 401-874-4693, E-mail: aimee@uri.edu. *Application contact:* Graduate Admission, 401-874-2872, E-mail: gradadm@etal.uri.edu. Website: http://www.uri.edu/research/lrc/

**University of Toronto,** School of Graduate Studies, Faculty of Arts and Science, Centre for Industrial Relations and Human Resources, Toronto, ON M5S 1A1, Canada. Offers MIRHR, PhD. *Program availability:* Part-time. *Degree requirements:* For doctorate, thesis/dissertation. *Entrance requirements:* For master's, GRE or GMAT (for applicants who completed degree outside of Canada), minimum B+ in final 2 years of bachelor's degree completion, 2 letters of reference, resume; for doctorate, GRE or GMAT, MIR or equivalent, minimum B+ average, 3 letters of reference, resume. Additional exam requirements/recommendations for international students: Required—TOEFL (minimum score 600 paper-based; 100 iBT), IELTS, TWE (minimum score 5), Michigan English Language Assessment Battery, or COPE. Electronic applications accepted. *Expenses:* Contact institution.

**University of Wisconsin–Milwaukee,** Graduate School, College of Letters and Science, Interdepartmental Program in Human Resources and Labor Relations, Milwaukee, WI 53201-0413. Offers human resources and labor relations (MHRLR); international human resources and labor relations (Certificate); mediation and negotiation (Certificate). *Program availability:* Part-time. *Entrance requirements:* For master's, GMAT or GRE General Test. Additional exam requirements/recommendations for international students: Required—TOEFL (minimum score 80 iBT), IELTS (minimum score 6.5). Electronic applications accepted.

**Wayne State University,** College of Liberal Arts and Sciences, Department of Economics, Detroit, MI 48202. Offers advanced macroeconomics (PhD); econometrics (MA); health economics (MA, PhD); industrial organization (MA, PhD); international economics (MA, PhD); labor and human resources (MA); labor economics (PhD); macroeconomics (MA); microeconomics (MA); JD/MA. *Faculty:* 13. *Students:* 38 full-time (11 women), 7 part-time (3 women); includes 8 minority (5 Black or African American, non-Hispanic/Latino; 1 Asian, non-Hispanic/Latino; 1 Hispanic/Latino; 1 Two or more races, non-Hispanic/Latino), 22 international. Average age 33. 97 applicants, 36% accepted, 8 enrolled. In 2016, 10 master's, 7 doctorates awarded. *Degree requirements:* For master's, comprehensive exam; for doctorate, comprehensive exam, thesis/dissertation, oral examination on research, completion of course work in quantitative methods, final lecture. *Entrance requirements:* For master's, minimum upper-division GPA of 3.0; prior coursework in intermediate microeconomic and macroeconomic theory, statistics, and elementary calculus; for doctorate, GRE, minimum upper-division GPA of 3.0, prior coursework in intermediate microeconomic and macroeconomic theory, statistics, two courses in calculus, three letters of recommendation from officials or teaching staff at institution(s) most recently attended, statement of purpose. Additional exam requirements/recommendations for international students: Required—TOEFL (minimum score 550 paper-based; 79 iBT), TWE (minimum 5.5), Michigan English Language Assessment Battery (minimum score 85); Recommended—IELTS (minimum score 6.5). *Application deadline:* For fall admission, 5/1 for domestic and international students; for winter admission, 10/1 priority date for domestic students, 9/1 priority date for international students; for spring admission, 1/1 priority date for domestic and international students. Applications are processed on a rolling basis. Application fee: $50. Electronic applications accepted. *Expenses:* $16,503 per year resident tuition and fees, $33,697 per year non-resident tuition and fees. *Financial support:* In 2016–17, 26 students received support, including 2 fellowships with tuition reimbursements available (averaging $16,000 per year), 17 teaching assistantships with tuition reimbursements available (averaging $17,994 per year); research assistantships with tuition reimbursements available, scholarships/grants, health care benefits, and unspecified assistantships also available. Support available to part-time students. Financial award applicants required to submit FAFSA. *Faculty research:* Health economics, international economics, macro economics, urban and labor economics, econometrics. *Unit head:* Dr. Stephen J. Spurr, Professor and Chair, 313-577-3232, Fax: 313-577-9564, E-mail: sspurr@wayne.edu. *Application contact:* Dr. Allen Charles Goodman, Graduate Director, 313-577-3235, Fax: 313-577-9564, E-mail: allen.goodman@wayne.edu. Website: http://clas.wayne.edu/economics/

**Wayne State University,** College of Liberal Arts and Sciences, Program in Employment and Labor Relations, Detroit, MI 48202. Offers MA. *Program availability:* Part-time, evening/weekend. *Students:* 4 full-time (3 women), 22 part-time (16 women); includes 14 minority (11 Black or African American, non-Hispanic/Latino; 3 Hispanic/Latino), 2 international. Average age 35. 18 applicants, 56% accepted, 7 enrolled. In 2016, 11 master's awarded. *Entrance requirements:* For master's, GRE or GMAT, personal statement, three letters of recommendation written by former college or university professors and/or current employers, baccalaureate degree from accredited institution, writing sample. Additional exam requirements/recommendations for international students: Required—TOEFL (minimum score 550 paper-based; 79 iBT), IELTS (minimum score 6.5), Michigan English Language Assessment Battery (minimum score 85). *Application deadline:* For fall admission, 6/1 priority date for domestic students, 5/1 priority date for international students; for winter admission, 10/1 priority date for domestic students, 9/1 priority date for international students; for spring admission, 2/1 priority date for domestic students, 1/1 priority date for international students. Application fee: $50. Electronic applications accepted. *Expenses:* $16,503 per year resident tuition and fees, $33,697 per year non-resident tuition and fees. *Financial support:* Scholarships/grants available. Financial award applicants required to submit FAFSA. *Unit head:* Dr. Marick Masters, Director, 313-577-5358, E-mail: marickm@wayne.edu. *Application contact:* Linda Johnson, Academic Services Officer, 313-577-0175, E-mail: ab1232@wayne.edu. Website: http://clas.wayne.edu/labor/maelr

**Wayne State University,** Law School, Detroit, MI 48202. Offers corporate and finance law (LL M); labor and employment law (LL M); law (JD); taxation (LL M); United States law (LL M); JD/MA; JD/MADR; JD/MBA; JD/MS. *Accreditation:* ABA. *Faculty:* 40 full-time (15 women), 27 part-time/adjunct (12 women). *Students:* 379 full-time (162 women), 58 part-time (26 women); includes 63 minority (35 Black or African American, non-Hispanic/Latino; 1 American Indian or Alaska Native, non-Hispanic/Latino; 9 Asian, non-Hispanic/Latino; 3 Hispanic/Latino; 15 Two or more races, non-Hispanic/Latino), 13 international. Average age 27. 684 applicants, 53% accepted, 138 enrolled. In 2016, 16 master's, 133 doctorates awarded. *Degree requirements:* For master's, thesis (for some programs). *Entrance requirements:* For master's, JD from ABA-accredited institution and member institution of the AALS; for doctorate, LSAT, LDAS report, bachelor's degree from accredited institution, personal statement, transcripts from all U.S. undergraduate schools attended and an analysis and summary of the transcripts; letter of recommendation (up to two are accepted). Additional exam requirements/recommendations for international students: Required—TOEFL (minimum score 600 paper-based; 100 iBT), Michigan English Language Assessment Battery (minimum score 85); Recommended—IELTS (minimum score 7). *Application deadline:* For fall admission, 7/1 for domestic students, 5/1 priority date for international students. Applications are processed on a rolling basis. Application fee: $0. Electronic applications accepted. *Expenses:* Contact institution. *Financial support:* In 2016–17, 353 students received support. Fellowships, Federal Work-Study, and scholarships/grants available. Support available to part-time students. Financial award application deadline: 6/30; financial award applicants required to submit FAFSA. *Faculty research:* Public interest law, tax law, international law, environmental law, health law. *Unit head:* Lance Gable, Interim Dean, 313-577-3933, E-mail: jbenson@wayne.edu. *Application contact:* Kathy Fox, Assistant Dean of Admissions, 313-577-3937, Fax: 313-993-8129, E-mail: lawinquire@wayne.edu. Website: http://law.wayne.edu/

**West Virginia University,** College of Business and Economics, Program in Industrial Relations, Morgantown, WV 26506. Offers MSIR. *Accreditation:* AACSB. *Entrance requirements:* For master's, GRE or GMAT, minimum GPA of 3.0. Additional exam requirements/recommendations for international students: Required—TOEFL. Electronic applications accepted. *Faculty research:* Labor relations, mediation, leadership, benefits.

# Philanthropic Studies

**Indiana University–Purdue University Indianapolis,** Lilly Family School of Philanthropy, Indianapolis, IN 46202. Offers MA, XMA, PhD. *Faculty:* 52 full-time, 10 part-time/adjunct. *Students:* 55 full-time (39 women), 63 part-time (41 women); includes 16 minority (12 Black or African American, non-Hispanic/Latino; 3 Asian, non-Hispanic/Latino; 1 Two or more races, non-Hispanic/Latino), 20 international. Average age 36. 69 applicants, 65% accepted, 27 enrolled. In 2016, 24 master's, 4 doctorates awarded. *Degree requirements:* For master's, thesis optional; for doctorate, thesis/dissertation. *Entrance requirements:* For master's, GRE General Test (minimum score 500 quantitative, 500 verbal, 4.5 analytical writing), minimum undergraduate GPA of 3.0; for doctorate, GRE General Test (minimum score 500 quantitative, 500 verbal, 4.5 analytical writing), minimum GPA of 3.0, master's degree. *Application deadline:* For fall admission, 1/15 for domestic students, 1/1 for international students. Application fee: $55 ($65 for international students). *Financial support:* In 2016–17, fellowships with partial tuition reimbursements (averaging $13,000 per year), research assistantships with partial tuition reimbursements (averaging $9,500 per year), teaching assistantships with partial tuition reimbursements (averaging $12,000 per year) were awarded; career-related internships or fieldwork, Federal Work-Study, institutionally sponsored loans, and scholarships/grants also available. Financial award application deadline: 3/1; financial award applicants required to submit FAFSA. *Unit head:* Dr. Gregory Witkowski, Director of Graduate Studies, 317-278-8970, E-mail: gwitkows@iupui.edu. Website: http://www.philanthropy.iupui.edu

**Saint Mary's University of Minnesota,** Schools of Graduate and Professional Programs, Graduate School of Business and Technology, Philanthropy and Development Program, Winona, MN 55987-1399. Offers MA. Tuition and fees vary according to degree level and program. *Unit head:* Dr. Jim Ollhoff, Director, 651-295-2454, E-mail: jollhoff@smumn.edu. *Application contact:* Jami Spitzer, Information Contact, 507-457-7500, E-mail: jspitzer@smumn.edu. Website: http://www.smumn.edu/graduate-home/areas-of-study/graduate-school-of-business-technology/ma-in-philanthropy-development

# Public Administration

**Adelphi University,** University College, Graduate Certificate in Emergency Management Program, Garden City, NY 11530-0701. Offers Certificate. *Program availability:* Part-time, evening/weekend. *Students:* 3 full-time (1 woman), 15 part-time (6 women); includes 11 minority (7 Black or African American, non-Hispanic/Latino; 3 Hispanic/Latino; 1 Two or more races, non-Hispanic/Latino). Average age 37. 11 applicants, 64% accepted, 4 enrolled. In 2016, 12 Certificates awarded. *Entrance requirements:* Additional exam requirements/recommendations for international students: Required—TOEFL (minimum score 550 paper-based; 80 iBT), IELTS (minimum score 6.5). *Application deadline:* For fall admission, 5/1 for international students; for spring admission, 12/1 for international students. Applications are processed on a rolling basis. Application fee: $50. Electronic applications accepted. *Expenses: Tuition:* Full-time $37,623; part-time $1179 per credit hour. *Required fees:* $1335; $405 per semester. Tuition and fees vary according to degree level, campus/location and program. *Financial support:* Research assistantships, teaching assistantships, career-related internships or fieldwork, institutionally sponsored loans, scholarships/grants, traineeships, and unspecified assistantships available. Support available to part-time students. *Faculty research:* Emergency nursing, disaster management, disaster preparedness. *Unit head:* Shawn O'Riley, Dean, 516-877-3412, E-mail: ucinfo@adelphi.edu. *Application contact:* Christine Murphy, Director of Admissions, 516-877-3050, Fax: 516-877-3039, E-mail: graduateadmissions@adelphi.edu. Website: http://academics.adelphi.edu/universitycollege/emergency-management-certificate.php

**Adler University,** Programs in Psychology, Chicago, IL 60602. Offers advanced Adlerian psychotherapy (Certificate); art therapy (MA); clinical mental health counseling (MA); clinical neuropsychology (Certificate); clinical psychology (Psy D); community psychology (MA); counseling and organizational psychology (MA); counseling psychology (MA); counselor education and supervision (PhD); couple and family therapy (DCFT); criminology (MA); emergency management leadership (MA); forensic psychology (MA); marriage and family counseling (MA); marriage and family therapy (Certificate); military psychology (MA); nonprofit management (MA); organizational psychology (MA); police psychology (MA); public policy and administration (MA); rehabilitation counseling (MA); sport and health psychology (MA); substance abuse counseling (Certificate); Psy D/Certificate; Psy D/MACAT; Psy D/MACP; Psy D/MAMFC; Psy D/MASAC. *Accreditation:* APA. *Program availability:* Part-time, evening/weekend, online learning. Terminal master's awarded for partial completion of doctoral program. *Degree requirements:* For master's, thesis or alternative, oral exam, practicum; for doctorate, thesis/dissertation, clinical exam, internship, oral exam, practicum, written qualifying exam. *Entrance requirements:* For master's, 12 semester hours in psychology, minimum GPA of 3.0; for doctorate, 18 semester hours in psychology, minimum GPA of 3.25; for Certificate, appropriate master's or doctoral degree. Additional exam requirements/recommendations for international students: Required—TOEFL (minimum score 550 paper-based; 79 iBT). Electronic applications accepted.

**See Display on page 982 and Close-Up on page 1225.**

**Albany State University,** College of Arts and Humanities, Albany, GA 31705-2717. Offers criminal justice (MS); English education (M Ed); public administration (MPA), including community and economic development, criminal justice administration, health administration and policy, human resources management, public management, public policy, water resources management and policy; social work (MSW). *Program availability:* Part-time. *Degree requirements:* For master's, comprehensive exam, professional portfolio (for MPA), internship, capstone report. *Entrance requirements:* For master's, GRE, MAT, minimum GPA of 3.0, official transcript, pre-medical record/certificate of immunization, letters of reference. *Application deadline:* For fall admission, 6/1 for domestic students, 5/1 for international students; for spring admission, 11/1 for domestic students, 10/1 for international students. Applications are processed on a rolling basis. Application fee: $20. Electronic applications accepted. *Financial support:* Application deadline: 4/15; applicants required to submit FAFSA. *Faculty research:* HIV prevention for minority students. *Unit head:* Dr. Rani George, Dean, 229-430-1877, Fax: 229-430-4296. *Application contact:* Jeffrey Pierce, II, Graduate Admissions Counselor, 229-430-4646, Fax: 229-430-4105, E-mail: jeffrey.pierce@asurams.edu. Website: https://www.asurams.edu/Academics/collegeofarthum/

**Albany State University,** College of Business, Albany, GA 31705-2717. Offers accounting (MBA); general business administration (MBA); healthcare (MBA); public administration (MBA); supply chain and logistics (MBA). *Accreditation:* ACBSP. *Program availability:* Part-time, evening/weekend. *Degree requirements:* For master's, comprehensive exam, internship, 3 hours of physical education. *Entrance requirements:* For master's, GMAT (minimum score of 450)/GRE (minimum score of 800) for those without earned master's degree or higher, minimum undergraduate GPA of 2.5, 2 letters of reference, official transcript, pre-entrance medical record and certificate of immunization. *Application deadline:* For fall admission, 6/1 for domestic students, 5/1 for international students; for spring admission, 11/1 for domestic students, 10/1 for international students. Applications are processed on a rolling basis. Application fee: $20. Electronic applications accepted. *Financial support:* Application deadline: 4/15; applicants required to submit FAFSA. *Faculty research:* Diversity issues, ancestry, understanding finance through use of technology. *Unit head:* Dr. Alicia Jackson, Dean, 229-430-7009, Fax: 229-430-5119. *Application contact:* Jeffrey Pierce, II, Graduate Counselor, 229-430-4646, Fax: 229-430-4105, E-mail: jeffrey.pierce@asurams.edu. Website: https://www.asurams.edu/Academics/collegeofbusiness/

**Alfred University,** Graduate School, Public Administration Program, Alfred, NY 14802-1205. Offers MPA. *Program availability:* Part-time, evening/weekend. *Students:* 49 part-time (34 women); includes 38 minority (30 Black or African American, non-Hispanic/Latino; 1 American Indian or Alaska Native, non-Hispanic/Latino; 4 Asian, non-Hispanic/Latino; 3 Hispanic/Latino). Average age 38. *Expenses: Tuition:* Full-time $38,020; part-time $810 per credit. *Required fees:* $970; $82 per semester. *Unit head:* Dr. Rick Stephens, Provost and Vice President of Academic Affairs, 607-871-2967, Fax: 607-871-2198, E-mail: stephens@alfred.edu. *Application contact:* Sara Love, Graduate Admissions Coordinator, 607-871-2115, Fax: 607-871-2198, E-mail: gradinquiry@alfred.edu.

**American Public University System,** AMU/APU Graduate Programs, Charles Town, WV 25414. Offers accounting (MBA, MS); applied business analytics (MBA, MS); criminal justice (MA), including business administration, emergency and disaster management, general (MA, MS); educational leadership (M Ed); emergency and disaster management (MA); entrepreneurship (MBA); environmental policy and management (MS), including environmental planning, environmental sustainability, fish and wildlife management, general (MA, MS), global environmental management; finance (MBA); general (MBA); government contracting and acquisition (MBA); health care administration (MBA); health information management (MS); history (MA), including American history, ancient and classical history, European history, global history, public history; homeland security (MA), including business administration, counterterrorism studies, criminal justice, cyber, emergency management and public health, intelligence studies, transportation security; homeland security resource allocation (MBA); humanities (MA); information technology (MS), including digital forensics, enterprise software development, information assurance and security, IT project management; information technology management (MBA); intelligence studies (MA), including criminal intelligence, cyber, general (MA, MS), homeland security, intelligence analysis, intelligence collection, intelligence management, intelligence operations, terrorism studies; international relations and conflict resolution (MA), including comparative and security issues, conflict resolution, international and transnational security issues, peacekeeping; legal studies (MA); management (MA), including strategic consulting; marketing (MBA); military history (MA), including American military history, American Revolution, civil war, war since 1945, World War II; military studies (MA), including joint warfare, strategic leadership; national security studies (MA), including cyber, general (MA, MS), homeland security, regional security studies, security and intelligence analysis, terrorism studies; nonprofit management (MBA); political science (MA), including American politics and government, comparative government and development, general (MA, MS), international relations, public policy; psychology (MA); public administration (MPA), including disaster management, environmental policy, health policy, human resources, national security, organizational management, security management; public health (MPH); reverse logistics management (MA); security management (MA); space studies (MS), including aerospace science, general (MA, MS), planetary science; sports and health sciences (MS); sports management (MBA); teaching (M Ed), including autism spectrum disorder, curriculum and instruction for elementary teachers, elementary reading, English language learners, instructional leadership, online learning, special education, STEAM (STEM plus the arts); transportation and logistics management (MA). *Program availability:* Part-time, evening/weekend, online only, 100% online. *Faculty:* 401 full-time (228 women), 1,678 part-time/adjunct (781 women). *Students:* 378 full-time (184 women), 8,455 part-time (3,484 women); includes 2,972 minority (1,552 Black or African American, non-Hispanic/Latino; 52 American Indian or Alaska Native, non-Hispanic/Latino; 211 Asian, non-Hispanic/Latino; 791 Hispanic/Latino; 70 Native Hawaiian or other Pacific Islander, non-Hispanic/Latino; 296 Two or more races, non-Hispanic/Latino), 109 international. Average age 37. In 2016, 3,185 master's awarded. *Degree requirements:* For master's, comprehensive exam or practicum. *Entrance requirements:* For master's, official transcript showing earned bachelor's degree from institution accredited by recognized accrediting body. Additional exam requirements/recommendations for international students: Required—TOEFL (minimum score 550 paper-based), IELTS (minimum score 6.5). *Application deadline:* Applications are processed on a rolling basis. Application fee: $0. Electronic applications accepted. *Expenses: Tuition:* Part-time $350 per credit hour. *Required fees:* $50 per course. *Financial support:* Scholarships/grants available. Financial award applicants required to submit FAFSA. *Unit head:* Dr. Karan Powell, President, 877-468-6268, Fax: 304-724-3780. *Application contact:* Terry Grant, Vice President of Enrollment Management, 877-468-6268, Fax: 304-724-3780, E-mail: info@apus.edu. Website: http://www.apus.edu

## Public Administration

**American University,** School of Public Affairs, Department of Public Administration and Policy, Program in Public Administration, Washington, DC 20016-8070. Offers MPA, PhD, Certificate. *Accreditation:* NASPAA (one or more programs are accredited). *Program availability:* Part-time, evening/weekend. *Students:* 111 full-time (70 women), 81 part-time (33 women); includes 67 minority (41 Black or African American, non-Hispanic/Latino; 1 American Indian or Alaska Native, non-Hispanic/Latino; 16 Asian, non-Hispanic/Latino; 7 Hispanic/Latino; 2 Two or more races, non-Hispanic/Latino), 13 international. Average age 31. 319 applicants, 63% accepted, 74 enrolled. In 2016, 91 master's, 6 doctorates, 6 other advanced degrees awarded. *Degree requirements:* For master's, comprehensive exam; for doctorate, comprehensive exam, thesis/dissertation. *Entrance requirements:* For master's, GRE, statement of purpose; 2 recommendations; for doctorate, GRE, 3 recommendations; for Certificate, bachelor's degree. Additional exam requirements/recommendations for international students: Required—TOEFL, IELTS (minimum score 7), PTE (minimum score 68). *Application deadline:* For fall admission, 2/1 priority date for domestic students, 5/1 for international students; for spring admission, 11/1 for domestic students. Application fee: $55. *Expenses:* $1,579 per credit tuition; $690 mandatory fees. *Financial support:* Research assistantships, teaching assistantships, institutionally sponsored loans, scholarships/grants, and unspecified assistantships available. Financial award application deadline: 2/1; financial award applicants required to submit FAFSA. *Unit head:* Dr. Alison Jacknowitz, Chair, Public Administration and Policy, 202-885-2137, Fax: 202-885-2347, E-mail: jacknowi@american.edu.
Website: http://www.american.edu/spa/dpap/

**American University,** School of Public Affairs, Department of Public Administration and Policy, Program in Public Administration and Policy, Washington, DC 20016-8001. Offers MPAP. *Program availability:* Online only, 100% online. *Students:* 1 (woman) full-time, 146 part-time (103 women); includes 19 minority (9 Black or African American, non-Hispanic/Latino; 1 American Indian or Alaska Native, non-Hispanic/Latino; 5 Asian, non-Hispanic/Latino; 1 Native Hawaiian or other Pacific Islander, non-Hispanic/Latino; 3 Two or more races, non-Hispanic/Latino), 1 international. Average age 33. 80 applicants, 93% accepted, 6 enrolled. *Degree requirements:* For master's, comprehensive exam. *Entrance requirements:* For master's, GRE General Test, two letters of recommendation, statement of purpose, resume. Additional exam requirements/recommendations for international students: Required—TOEFL (minimum score 100 iBT), IELTS (minimum score 7), PTE (minimum score 68). *Application deadline:* For fall admission, 2/1 priority date for domestic students, 5/1 for international students; for spring admission, 11/1 for domestic students. Application fee: $55. *Expenses:* $1,579 per credit tuition; $690 mandatory fees. *Financial support:* Application deadline: 2/1; applicants required to submit FAFSA. *Unit head:* Dr. Alison Jacknowitz, Department Chair, Public Administration and Policy, 202-885-2137, Fax: 202-885-2347, E-mail: jacknowi@american.edu.
Website: http://www.american.edu/spa/dpap/index.cfm

**The American University in Cairo,** School of Global Affairs and Public Policy, Cairo, Egypt. Offers gender and women's studies (MA); global affairs (MGA); international and comparative law (LL M); international human rights law (MA); journalism and mass communication (MA); Middle East studies (MA); migration and refugee studies (MA, Diploma); public administration (MPA); public policy (MPP); television and digital journalism (MA). *Program availability:* Part-time, evening/weekend. *Faculty:* 27 full-time (13 women), 5 part-time/adjunct (3 women). *Students:* 69 full-time (40 women), 194 part-time (134 women), 33 international. Average age 29. 322 applicants, 51% accepted, 86 enrolled. In 2016, 112 master's awarded. *Degree requirements:* For master's, comprehensive exam (for some programs), thesis (for some programs). *Entrance requirements:* Additional exam requirements/recommendations for international students: Required—TOEFL (minimum score 450 paper-based; 45 iBT), IELTS (minimum score 5). *Application deadline:* For fall admission, 2/1 for domestic and international students; for spring admission, 10/15 for domestic and international students. Applications are processed on a rolling basis. Application fee: $80. Electronic applications accepted. *Expenses:* Contact institution. *Financial support:* Fellowships with partial tuition reimbursements, scholarships/grants, and unspecified assistantships available. Financial award application deadline: 3/10. *Faculty research:* Law, media and journalism; public policy and public administration, gender studies, Middle East Studies, global affairs, refugees studies. *Unit head:* Dr. Nabil Fahmy, Dean, 20-2-2615-2671, E-mail: nfahmy@aucegypt.edu. *Application contact:* Maha Hegazi, Director for Graduate Admissions, 20-2-2615-1462, E-mail: mahahegazi@aucegypt.edu.
Website: http://www.aucegypt.edu/GAPP/Pages/default.aspx

**American University of Beirut,** Graduate Programs, Faculty of Arts and Sciences, Beirut, Lebanon. Offers anthropology (MA); Arab and Middle Eastern history (PhD); Arabic language and literature (MA, PhD); archaeology (MA); art history and curating (MA); biology (MS); cell and molecular biology (PhD); chemistry (MS); clinical psychology (MA); computational sciences (MS); computer science (MS); economics (MA); education (MA); English language (MA); English literature (MA); environmental policy planning (MS); financial economics (MAFE); geology (MS); history (MA); Islamic studies (MA); mathematics (MS); media studies (MA); Middle Eastern studies (MA); physics (MS); political studies (MA); psychology (MA); public administration (MA); public policy and international affairs (MA); sociology (MA); statistics (MA, MS); theoretical physics (PhD); transnational American studies (MA). *Program availability:* Part-time. *Faculty:* 133 full-time (42 women), 6 part-time/adjunct (2 women). *Students:* 240 full-time (172 women), 227 part-time (166 women). Average age 27. 286 applicants, 67% accepted, 108 enrolled. In 2016, 60 master's, 3 doctorates awarded. Terminal master's awarded for partial completion of doctoral program. *Degree requirements:* For master's, one foreign language, comprehensive exam, thesis (for some programs); for doctorate, one foreign language, comprehensive exam, thesis/dissertation. *Entrance requirements:* For master's, GRE (for some MA, MS programs), letters of recommendation; for doctorate, GRE, letters of recommendation. Additional exam requirements/recommendations for international students: Required—TOEFL (minimum score 600 paper-based; 97 iBT), IELTS (minimum score 7). *Application deadline:* For fall admission, 4/3 for domestic students; for winter admission, 11/3 for domestic students. Application fee: $50. Electronic applications accepted. *Expenses:* Contact institution. *Financial support:* In 2016–17, 4 fellowships (averaging $11,200 per year), 18 research assistantships (averaging $5,400 per year) were awarded; teaching assistantships, career-related internships or fieldwork, Federal Work-Study, institutionally sponsored loans, scholarships/grants, traineeships, health care benefits, tuition waivers (full), and unspecified assistantships also available. Support available to part-time students. *Faculty research:* Development economics, spatial econometrics, health economics, labor economics, energy economics, hydrogeology, geophysics, petrophysics, structural geology, mineralogy, petrology, geochemistry, multilingualism, comparative/world literature, translation studies, book histories/ cultures, biocatalysis, molecular recognition, photocatalysis, photophysical and biophysical chemistry, probe chemistry, machine learning, data science. *Unit head:* Dr. Nadia Maria El Cheikh, Dean, Faculty of Arts and Sciences, 961-1374374 Ext. 3800, Fax: 961-1744461, E-mail: nmcheikh@aub.edu.lb. *Application contact:* Dr. Salim Kanaan, Director, Admissions Office, 961-1350000 Ext. 2590, Fax: 961-1750775, E-mail: sk00@aub.edu.lb.
Website: http://www.aub.edu.lb/fas/

**Anabaptist Mennonite Biblical Seminary,** Graduate and Professional Programs, Elkhart, IN 46517-1999. Offers chaplaincy (M Div); Christian faith formation (M Div); Christian formation (MA); Christian spiritual formation (Certificate); divinity (M Div); pastoral ministry (M Div); pastoral theology for financial professionals (Certificate); peace studies (M Div), including environmental sustainability leadership (M Div, MA); theological studies (M Div, Certificate), including peace studies (M Div), theology and ethics (M Div); theology and peace studies (MA), including conflict transformation, environmental sustainability leadership (M Div, MA), international development administration; United Methodist leadership (M Div). Conflict transformation and environmental sustainability leadership concentrations offered in cooperation with Goshen College; international development administration offered in cooperation with Andrews University. *Accreditation:* ACIPE; ATS. *Program availability:* Part-time, 100% online, blended/hybrid learning. *Faculty:* 14 full-time (6 women), 17 part-time/adjunct (8 women). *Students:* 38 full-time (14 women), 60 part-time (33 women); includes 15 minority (4 Black or African American, non-Hispanic/Latino; 5 Asian, non-Hispanic/Latino; 5 Hispanic/Latino; 1 Two or more races, non-Hispanic/Latino), 15 international. Average age 35. 43 applicants, 70% accepted, 29 enrolled. In 2016, 16 master's, 2 other advanced degrees awarded. *Degree requirements:* For master's, variable foreign language requirement, comprehensive exam (for some programs), thesis optional, senior interview. *Entrance requirements:* For master's, undergraduate degree transcripts, 3 letters of reference, essay. Additional exam requirements/ recommendations for international students: Required—TOEFL (minimum score 90 iBT); Recommended—IELTS (minimum score 7). *Application deadline:* For fall admission, 6/1 priority date for domestic students, 5/1 priority date for international students. Applications are processed on a rolling basis. Application fee: $25. Electronic applications accepted. *Expenses: Tuition:* Full-time $13,950; part-time $5640 per year. *Required fees:* $900; $300 per unit. $50 per term. *Financial support:* In 2016–17, 40 students received support. Career-related internships or fieldwork, scholarships/grants, unspecified assistantships, and church matching grants available. Support available to part-time students. Financial award application deadline: 4/15; financial award applicants required to submit FAFSA. *Faculty research:* Biblical studies, peace studies, theology, ethics, creation care or environmental ethics, church history, church leadership, mission, ministry, preaching, pastoral leadership, social justice, peacemaking, Jesus Christ, Christianity, Anabaptism, Mennonite, Scripture, Bible, Old Testament, New Testament, spirituality, clinical pastoral education, teaching, faith formation, pastoral care, Koine Greek, Hebrew, Aramaic, Syriac, Ugaritic. *Unit head:* Sara Wenger Shenk, President, 800-964-2627, Fax: 574-295-0092. *Application contact:* Daniel Grimes, Director of Admissions, 574-296-6266, Fax: 574-295-0092, E-mail: admissions@ambs.edu.
Website: http://www.ambs.edu/

**Anna Maria College,** Graduate Division, Program in Public Administration, Paxton, MA 01612. Offers MPA.

**Appalachian State University,** Cratis D. Williams Graduate School, Department of Government and Justice Studies, Boone, NC 28608. Offers political science (MA), including American government; public administration (MPA), including public management. *Program availability:* Part-time, online learning. *Degree requirements:* For master's, variable foreign language requirement, comprehensive exam, thesis optional. *Entrance requirements:* For master's, GRE General Test, 3 letters of recommendation. Additional exam requirements/recommendations for international students: Required—TOEFL (minimum score 570 paper-based; 79 iBT), IELTS (minimum score 6.5). *Application deadline:* For fall admission, 3/15 priority date for domestic students, 2/1 for international students; for spring admission, 11/1 for domestic students, 7/1 for international students. Applications are processed on a rolling basis. Application fee: $55. Electronic applications accepted. *Expenses:* Tuition, state resident: full-time $4744. Tuition, nonresident: full-time $17,913. Full-time tuition and fees vary according to program. *Financial support:* Fellowships, research assistantships, teaching assistantships, career-related internships or fieldwork, Federal Work-Study, scholarships/grants, and unspecified assistantships available. Financial award application deadline: 4/1; financial award applicants required to submit FAFSA. *Faculty research:* Campaign finance, emerging democracies, bureaucratic politics, judicial behavior, administration of justice. *Unit head:* Dr. Brian Ellison, Chairperson, 828-262-3085, E-mail: ellisonba@appstate.edu. *Application contact:* Dr. Brad Bradbury, Program Director, 828-262-7913, E-mail: bradburymd@appstate.edu.
Website: http://www.pscj.appstate.edu

**Argosy University, Chicago,** College of Business, Chicago, IL 60601. Offers accounting (DBA); customized professional concentration (MBA, DBA); finance (MBA); fraud examination (MBA); global business sustainability (DBA); healthcare administration (MBA); information systems (DBA); information systems management (MBA); international business (MBA, DBA); management (MBA, MSM, DBA); marketing (MBA, DBA); organizational leadership (Ed D); public administration (MBA); sustainable management (MBA). *Accreditation:* ACBSP. *Program availability:* Online learning.

**Argosy University, Dallas,** College of Business, Farmers Branch, TX 75244. Offers accounting (DBA, AGC); corporate compliance (MBA, Graduate Certificate); customized professional concentration (MBA); finance (MBA, Graduate Certificate); fraud examination (MBA, Graduate Certificate); global business sustainability (DBA, AGC); healthcare administration (Graduate Certificate); healthcare management (MBA); information systems (MBA, DBA, AGC); information systems management (Graduate Certificate); international business (MBA, DBA, AGC, Graduate Certificate); management (MBA, DBA, AGC, Graduate Certificate); marketing (MBA, DBA, AGC, Graduate Certificate); public administration (MBA, Graduate Certificate); sustainable management (MBA, Graduate Certificate). *Accreditation:* ACBSP.

**Argosy University, Denver,** College of Business, Denver, CO 80231. Offers accounting (DBA); corporate compliance (MBA); customized professional concentration (MBA, DBA); finance (MBA); fraud examination (MBA); global business sustainability (DBA); healthcare administration (MBA); information systems (DBA); information systems management (MBA); international business (MBA, DBA); management (MBA, MSM, DBA); marketing (MBA, DBA); organizational leadership (Ed D); public administration (MBA); sustainable management (MBA). *Accreditation:* ACBSP.

**Argosy University, Inland Empire,** College of Business, Ontario, CA 91761. Offers accounting (DBA); corporate compliance (MBA); customized professional concentration (MBA, DBA); finance (MBA); fraud examination (MBA); global business sustainability (DBA); healthcare administration (MBA); information systems (DBA); information systems management (MBA); international business (MBA, DBA); management (MBA, MSM, DBA); marketing (MBA, DBA); organizational leadership (Ed D); public administration (MBA); sustainable management (MBA).

**Argosy University, Los Angeles,** College of Business, Santa Monica, CA 90045. Offers accounting (DBA); corporate compliance (MBA); customized professional concentration (MBA, DBA); finance (MBA); fraud examination (MBA); global business sustainability (DBA); healthcare administration (MBA); information systems (DBA); information systems management (MBA); international business (MBA, DBA); management (MBA, MSM, DBA); marketing (MBA, DBA); organizational leadership (Ed D); public administration (MBA); sustainable management (MBA).

**Argosy University, Northern Virginia,** College of Business, Arlington, VA 22209. Offers accounting (DBA); customized professional concentration (MBA, DBA); finance (MBA); fraud examination (MBA); global business sustainability (DBA); healthcare administration (MBA); information systems (DBA); information systems management (MBA); international business (MBA, DBA, Certificate); management (MBA, MSM, DBA); marketing (MBA, DBA, Certificate); organizational leadership (Ed D); public administration (MBA); sustainable management (MBA).

**Argosy University, Orange County,** College of Business, Orange, CA 92868. Offers accounting (DBA, Adv C); corporate compliance (MBA); customized professional concentration (MBA, DBA); finance (MBA, Certificate); fraud examination (MBA); global business sustainability (DBA); healthcare administration (MBA, Certificate); information systems (DBA, Adv C, Certificate); information systems management (MBA); international business (MBA, DBA, Adv C, Certificate); management (MBA, MSM, DBA, Adv C); marketing (MBA, DBA, Adv C, Certificate); organizational leadership (Ed D); public administration (MBA, Certificate); sustainable management (MBA).

**Argosy University, Phoenix,** College of Business, Phoenix, AZ 85021. Offers accounting (MBA, DBA); corporate compliance (MBA); customized professional concentration (MBA, DBA); finance (MBA); fraud examination (MBA); global business sustainability (DBA); healthcare administration (MBA); information systems (DBA); information systems management (MBA); international business (MBA, DBA); management (MBA, DBA); marketing (MBA, DBA); public administration (MBA); sustainable management (MBA).

**Argosy University, Salt Lake City,** College of Business, Draper, UT 84020. Offers accounting (DBA); corporate compliance (MBA); customized professional concentration (MBA, DBA); finance (MBA); fraud examination (MBA); global business sustainability (DBA); healthcare administration (MBA); information systems (DBA); information systems management (MBA); international business (MBA, DBA); management (MBA, DBA); marketing (MBA, DBA); public administration (MBA); sustainable management (MBA).

**Argosy University, San Diego,** College of Business, San Diego, CA 92108. Offers accounting (DBA); corporate compliance (MBA); customized professional concentration (MBA, DBA); finance (MBA); fraud examination (MBA); global business sustainability (DBA); information systems (DBA); information systems management (MBA); international business (MBA, DBA); management (MBA, MSM, DBA); marketing (MBA, DBA); organizational leadership (Ed D); public administration (MBA).

**Argosy University, San Francisco Bay Area,** College of Business, Alameda, CA 94501. Offers accounting (DBA); corporate compliance (MBA); customized professional concentration (MBA, DBA); finance (MBA); fraud examination (MBA); global business sustainability (DBA); healthcare administration (MBA); information systems (DBA); information systems management (MBA); international business (MBA, DBA); management (MBA, MSM, DBA); marketing (MBA, DBA); organizational leadership (Ed D); public administration (MBA); sustainable management (MBA).

**Argosy University, Sarasota,** College of Business, Sarasota, FL 34235. Offers accounting (DBA, Adv C); corporate compliance (MBA, DBA, Certificate); customized professional concentration (MBA, DBA); finance (MBA, Certificate); fraud examination (MBA, Certificate); global business sustainability (DBA, Adv C); healthcare administration (MBA, Certificate); information systems (DBA, Adv C, Certificate); information systems management (MBA); international business (MBA, DBA, Adv C, Certificate); management (MBA, MSM, DBA, Adv C, Certificate); marketing (MBA, DBA, Adv C, Certificate); organizational leadership (Ed D); public administration (MBA, Certificate); sustainable management (MBA, Certificate).

**Argosy University, Schaumburg,** Graduate School of Business and Management, Schaumburg, IL 60173-5403. Offers accounting (DBA, Adv C); customized professional concentration (MBA, DBA); finance (MBA, Certificate); fraud examination (MBA); healthcare administration (MBA, Certificate); human resource management (MS); information systems (Adv C, Certificate); information systems management (MBA); international business (MBA, DBA, Adv C, Certificate); management (MBA, MSM, DBA, Adv C, Certificate); marketing (MBA, DBA, Adv C, Certificate); organizational leadership (MS, Ed D); public administration (MBA); sustainable management (MBA).

**Argosy University, Seattle,** College of Business, Seattle, WA 98121. Offers accounting (DBA); corporate compliance (MBA); customized professional concentration (MBA, DBA); finance (MBA); fraud examination (MBA); global business sustainability (DBA); healthcare administration (MBA); information systems (DBA); information systems management (MBA); international business (MBA, DBA); management (MBA, MSM, DBA); marketing (MBA, DBA); organizational leadership (Ed D); public administration (MBA); sustainable management (MBA).

**Argosy University, Tampa,** College of Business, Tampa, FL 33607. Offers accounting (DBA); corporate compliance (MBA); customized professional concentration (MBA, DBA); finance (MBA); fraud examination (MBA); global business sustainability (DBA); healthcare administration (MBA); information systems (DBA); information systems management (MBA); international business (MBA, DBA); management (MBA, MSM, DBA); marketing (MBA, DBA); organizational leadership (Ed D); public administration (MBA); sustainable management (MBA).

**Argosy University, Twin Cities,** College of Business, Eagan, MN 55121. Offers accounting (DBA); customized professional concentration (MBA, DBA); finance (MBA); fraud examination (MBA); global business sustainability (DBA); healthcare administration (MBA); information systems (DBA); information systems management (MBA); international business (MBA, DBA); management (MBA, MSM, DBA); marketing (MBA, DBA); organizational leadership (Ed D); public administration (MBA); sustainable management (MBA).

**Arizona State University at the Tempe campus,** College of Public Programs, School of Public Affairs, Phoenix, AZ 85004-0687. Offers emergency management and homeland security (MA); program evaluation (MS); public administration (MPA, PhD), including nonprofit administration (MPA); urban management (MPA); public policy (MPP); MPA/MSW. *Accreditation:* NASPAA (one or more programs are accredited). *Program availability:* Part-time, evening/weekend. Terminal master's awarded for partial completion of doctoral program. *Degree requirements:* For master's, thesis or alternative, policy analysis or capstone project; interactive Program of Study (iPOS) submitted before completing 50 percent of required credit hours; for doctorate, comprehensive exam, thesis/dissertation, interactive Program of Study (iPOS) submitted before completing 50 percent of required credit hours. *Entrance requirements:* For master's, GRE, minimum GPA of 3.0 or equivalent in last 2 years of work leading to bachelor's degree; for doctorate, GRE, minimum GPA of 3.0 or equivalent in last 2 years of work leading to bachelor's degree, 3 letters of recommendation, resume, statement of goals, samples of research reports. Additional exam requirements/recommendations for international students: Required—TOEFL (minimum score 600 paper-based; 100 iBT), IELTS (minimum score 6.5). Electronic applications accepted. *Expenses:* Contact institution.

**Arkansas State University,** Graduate School, College of Humanities and Social Sciences, Department of Political Science, State University, AR 72467. Offers political science (MA); political science education (SCCT); public administration (MPA).

*Accreditation:* NASPAA (one or more programs are accredited). *Program availability:* Part-time. *Degree requirements:* For master's, comprehensive exam, thesis or alternative; for SCCT, comprehensive exam. *Entrance requirements:* For master's, GRE General Test or MAT, GMAT, appropriate bachelor's degree, letters of recommendation, official transcripts, immunization records, statement of purpose; for SCCT, GRE General Test or MAT, GMAT, interview, master's degree, official transcript, letters of recommendation, immunization records. Additional exam requirements/recommendations for international students: Required—TOEFL (minimum score 550 paper-based; 79 iBT), IELTS (minimum score 6), PTE (minimum score 56). Electronic applications accepted.

**Auburn University,** Graduate School, College of Liberal Arts, Department of Political Science, Program in Public Administration, Auburn University, AL 36849. Offers MPA, PhD, Graduate Certificate, MPA/MCP. PhD offered jointly with Auburn University Montgomery. *Accreditation:* NASPAA (one or more programs are accredited). *Program availability:* Part-time. *Faculty:* 27 full-time (14 women), 4 part-time/adjunct (2 women). *Students:* 54 full-time (33 women), 40 part-time (22 women); includes 22 minority (18 Black or African American, non-Hispanic/Latino; 2 American Indian or Alaska Native, non-Hispanic/Latino; 1 Asian, non-Hispanic/Latino; 1 Hispanic/Latino), 18 international. Average age 34. 64 applicants, 53% accepted, 22 enrolled. In 2016, 13 master's, 7 doctorates awarded. *Degree requirements:* For master's, internship or research project; for doctorate, thesis/dissertation. *Entrance requirements:* For master's, GRE General Test, sample of written work; for doctorate, GRE General Test. *Application deadline:* Applications are processed on a rolling basis. Application fee: $50 ($60 for international students). Electronic applications accepted. *Expenses:* Tuition, state resident: full-time $9072; part-time $504 per credit hour. Tuition, nonresident: full-time $27,216; part-time $1512 per credit hour. *Required fees:* $812 per semester. Tuition and fees vary according to degree level and program. *Financial support:* Fellowships, research assistantships, teaching assistantships, career-related internships or fieldwork, and Federal Work-Study available. Support available to part-time students. Financial award application deadline: 3/15; financial award applicants required to submit FAFSA. *Faculty research:* Privatization studies, policy evolution, water resources, election administration. *Unit head:* Dr. Kathleen Hale, Head, 334-844-6155. *Application contact:* Dr. George Flowers, Dean of the Graduate School, 334-844-2125. Website: http://www.cla.auburn.edu/polisci/

**Auburn University at Montgomery,** College of Public Policy and Justice, Department of Political Science and Public Administration, Montgomery, AL 36124-4023. Offers international relations (MIR); nonprofit management and leadership (Certificate); political science (MPS); public administration (MPA); public administration and public policy (PhD); public health care administration and policy (Certificate). PhD offered jointly with Auburn University. *Accreditation:* NASPAA (one or more programs are accredited). *Program availability:* Part-time, evening/weekend. *Degree requirements:* For master's, comprehensive exam; for doctorate, thesis/dissertation. *Entrance requirements:* For master's, GRE General Test or MAT; for doctorate, GRE General Test. Electronic applications accepted.

**Azusa Pacific University,** School of Business and Management, Azusa, CA 91702-7000. Offers business administration (MBA); diversity for strategic advantage (MA); entrepreneurship (MBA); finance (MBA); human and organizational development (MA); human resources and organizational development (MBA); human resources management (MA); international business (MBA); marketing (MBA); non-profit management (MA); organizational development and change (MA); performance improvement (MA); public administration (MA); strategic management (MBA). *Program availability:* Part-time, evening/weekend. *Degree requirements:* For master's, thesis (for some programs), final project. *Entrance requirements:* For master's, GMAT, minimum GPA of 3.0. Additional exam requirements/recommendations for international students: Required—TOEFL (minimum score 600 paper-based). *Expenses:* Contact institution. *Faculty research:* Gender issues, financial risk, leadership and ethics, marketing strategy.

**Ball State University,** Graduate School, College of Sciences and Humanities, Department of Political Science, Program in Public Administration, Muncie, IN 47306. Offers public administration (MPA, Certificate), including administrative (MPA), community and economic development (MPA), criminal justice and criminology (MPA), emergency management and homeland security (MPA). *Program availability:* Part-time. *Degree requirements:* For master's, comprehensive exam. *Entrance requirements:* For master's, GRE General Test, minimum bacclaureate GPA of 2.8, two letters of recommendation. Additional exam requirements/recommendations for international students: Required—TOEFL (minimum score 550 paper-based; 79 iBT), IELTS (minimum score 6.5). Electronic applications accepted. *Faculty research:* Employment training programs, personnel and labor relations, planning.

**Barry University,** School of Adult and Continuing Education, Program in Public Administration, Miami Shores, FL 33161-6695. Offers MPA. *Program availability:* Part-time, evening/weekend. *Entrance requirements:* For master's, GMAT, GRE or MAT, recommendations. Electronic applications accepted.

**Baruch College of the City University of New York,** Austin W. Marxe School of Public and International Affairs, Program in Public Administration, New York, NY 10010-5585. Offers general public administration (MPA); health care policy (MPA); nonprofit administration (MPA); policy analysis and evaluation (MPA); public management (MPA); urban development and sustainability (MPA); MS/MPA. *Accreditation:* NASPAA. *Program availability:* Part-time, evening/weekend. *Degree requirements:* For master's, thesis, capstone. *Entrance requirements:* For master's, GRE General Test. Additional exam requirements/recommendations for international students: Required—TOEFL. Electronic applications accepted. *Expenses:* Contact institution. *Faculty research:* Urbanization, population and poverty in the developing world, housing and community development, labor unions and housing, government-nongovernment relations, immigration policy, social network analysis, cross-sectoral governance, comparative welfare systems, program evaluation, social welfare policy, health outcomes, educational policy and leadership, transnationalism, infant health, welfare reform, racial/ethnic disparities in health, urban politics, homelessness, race and ethnic relations.

**See Display on page 931 and Close-Up on page 977.**

**Baylor University,** Graduate School, College of Arts and Sciences, Department of Political Science, Waco, TX 76798. Offers international studies (MA); political science (MA, PhD); public policy and administration (MPPA); JD/MPPA. *Faculty:* 18 full-time (3 women), 1 part-time/adjunct (0 women). *Students:* 29 full-time (11 women), 2 part-time (both women); includes 3 minority (all Hispanic/Latino), 2 international. Average age 26. 27 applicants, 22% accepted, 4 enrolled. In 2016, 6 master's, 2 doctorates awarded. Terminal master's awarded for partial completion of doctoral program. *Degree requirements:* For master's, variable foreign language requirement, comprehensive exam (for some programs), thesis (for some programs); for doctorate, variable foreign language requirement, comprehensive exam, thesis/dissertation. *Entrance requirements:* For master's and doctorate, GRE General Test. Additional exam requirements/recommendations for international students: Required—TOEFL. *Application deadline:* For fall admission, 12/20 for domestic and international students. Application fee: $25. Electronic applications accepted. *Expenses: Tuition:* Full-time

## Public Administration

$28,494; part-time $1583 per credit hour. *Required fees:* $167 per credit hour. Tuition and fees vary according to course load and program. *Financial support:* In 2016–17, 17 students received support, including 17 research assistantships with full tuition reimbursements available (averaging $16,000 per year); career-related internships or fieldwork, Federal Work-Study, and institutionally sponsored loans also available. Financial award application deadline: 12/20; financial award applicants required to submit FAFSA. *Unit head:* Dr. Timothy Burns, Graduate Program Director, 254-710-6237, Fax: 254-710-3122, E-mail: timothy_burns@baylor.edu. *Application contact:* Jenice Langston, Office Manager, 254-710-3161, Fax: 254-710-3122, E-mail: jenice_langston@baylor.edu.
Website: http://www.baylor.edu/political_science/

**Belhaven University,** School of Business, Jackson, MS 39202-1789. Offers business administration (MBA); health administration (MBA, MHA); human resources (MBA, MSL); leadership (MBA); public administration (MPA); sports administration (MBA, MSA). *Program availability:* Part-time, evening/weekend, 100% online. *Faculty:* 16 full-time (3 women), 82 part-time/adjunct (32 women). *Students:* 953 full-time (677 women), 392 part-time (292 women); includes 1,082 minority (1,027 Black or African American, non-Hispanic/Latino; 14 American Indian or Alaska Native, non-Hispanic/Latino; 4 Asian, non-Hispanic/Latino; 20 Hispanic/Latino; 2 Native Hawaiian or other Pacific Islander, non-Hispanic/Latino; 15 Two or more races, non-Hispanic/Latino), 11 international. Average age 35. In 2016, 235 master's awarded. *Degree requirements:* For master's, comprehensive exam (for some programs), thesis (for some programs). *Application deadline:* Applications are processed on a rolling basis. Application fee: $25. Electronic applications accepted. *Expenses:* $535 per credit hour full-time, $75 per course technology fee. *Financial support:* Applicants required to submit FAFSA. *Unit head:* Dr. Ralph Mason, Dean, 601-968-8949, Fax: 601-968-8951, E-mail: cmason@belhaven.edu. *Application contact:* Dr. Audrey Kelleher, Vice President of Adult and Graduate Marketing and Development, 407-804-1424, Fax: 407-620-5210, E-mail: akelleher@belhaven.edu.
Website: http://www.belhaven.edu/campuses/index.htm

**Bellevue University,** Graduate School, College of Professional Studies, Bellevue, NE 68005-3098. Offers instructional design and development (MS); justice administration and criminal management (MS); leadership (MA); organizational performance (MS); public administration (MPA); security management (MS).

**Binghamton University, State University of New York,** Graduate School, College of Community and Public Affairs, Department of Public Administration, Binghamton, NY 13902-6000. Offers MPA. *Accreditation:* NASPAA. *Program availability:* Part-time. *Faculty:* 32 full-time (21 women), 15 part-time/adjunct (11 women). *Students:* 87 full-time (54 women), 71 part-time (51 women); includes 38 minority (12 Black or African American, non-Hispanic/Latino; 8 Asian, non-Hispanic/Latino; 15 Hispanic/Latino; 3 Two or more races, non-Hispanic/Latino), 23 international. Average age 31. 193 applicants, 76% accepted, 63 enrolled. In 2016, 27 master's awarded. *Degree requirements:* For master's, thesis. *Entrance requirements:* Additional exam requirements/recommendations for international students: Required—TOEFL (minimum score 80 iBT). *Application deadline:* Applications are processed on a rolling basis. Application fee: $75. Electronic applications accepted. *Financial support:* In 2016–17, 62 students received support. Fellowships, research assistantships, career-related internships or fieldwork, Federal Work-Study, institutionally sponsored loans, scholarships/grants, health care benefits, tuition waivers (full and partial), and unspecified assistantships available. Financial award application deadline: 1/15; financial award applicants required to submit FAFSA. *Unit head:* Brianna King, Director of Admissions and Student Services, 607-777-2719, E-mail: bking@binghamton.edu. *Application contact:* Ben Balkaya, Assistant Dean and Director, 607-777-2151, Fax: 607-777-2501, E-mail: balkaya@binghamton.edu.

**Boise State University,** School of Public Service, Department of Public Policy and Administration, Boise, ID 83725. Offers public policy and administration (MPA, PhD, Graduate Certificate), including environmental, natural resource and energy policy and administration (MPA), general public administration (MPA), state and local government policy and administration (MPA). *Accreditation:* NASPAA. *Program availability:* Part-time. *Faculty:* 16. *Students:* 38 full-time (19 women), 85 part-time (56 women); includes 15 minority (1 American Indian or Alaska Native, non-Hispanic/Latino; 1 Asian, non-Hispanic/Latino; 12 Hispanic/Latino; 1 Two or more races, non-Hispanic/Latino), 1 international. Average age 37. 81 applicants, 43% accepted, 29 enrolled. In 2016, 22 master's awarded. Terminal master's awarded for partial completion of doctoral program. *Degree requirements:* For master's, comprehensive exam, thesis optional, directed research project, internship; for doctorate, thesis/dissertation. *Entrance requirements:* For master's, GRE General Test, minimum GPA of 3.0. Additional exam requirements/recommendations for international students: Required—TOEFL (minimum score 550 paper-based; 80 iBT), IELTS (minimum score 6). *Application deadline:* For fall admission, 2/1 for domestic and international students; for spring admission, 10/1 for domestic and international students. Application fee: $65 ($95 for international students). Electronic applications accepted. *Expenses:* Tuition, state resident: full-time $6058; part-time $358 per credit hour. Tuition, nonresident: full-time $20,108; part-time $608 per credit hour. *Required fees:* $2108. Tuition and fees vary according to program. *Financial support:* In 2016–17, 41 students received support, including 2 research assistantships (averaging $4,083 per year); scholarships/grants and unspecified assistantships also available. Financial award application deadline: 2/1; financial award applicants required to submit FAFSA. *Unit head:* Dr. Gregory Hill, Department Chair, 208-426-2917, E-mail: greghill@boisestate.edu. *Application contact:* Dr. Elizabeth Fredericksen, MPA Director, 208-426-1078, E-mail: efreder@boisestate.edu.
Website: http://sps.boisestate.edu/publicpolicy/

**Bowie State University,** Graduate Programs, Program in Public Administration, Bowie, MD 20715-9465. Offers MPA. *Accreditation:* NASPAA. *Program availability:* Part-time, evening/weekend. *Degree requirements:* For master's, comprehensive exam. *Entrance requirements:* For master's, minimum undergraduate GPA of 2.5. Electronic applications accepted.

**Bowling Green State University,** Graduate College, College of Arts and Sciences, Department of Political Science, Bowling Green, OH 43403. Offers public administration (MPA). *Degree requirements:* For master's, comprehensive exam or thesis. *Entrance requirements:* For master's, GRE General Test. Additional exam requirements/recommendations for international students: Required—TOEFL. Application fee: $30. Electronic applications accepted. *Financial support:* Research assistantships with full tuition reimbursements, teaching assistantships with full tuition reimbursements, career-related internships or fieldwork, Federal Work-Study, and unspecified assistantships available. Financial award applicants required to submit FAFSA. *Faculty research:* Public law, international relations, American government, economic development. *Unit head:* Dr. Neal Jesse, Chair, 419-372-7266. *Application contact:* Dr. Shannon Orr, Graduate Coordinator, 419-372-7593.
Website: http://www.bgsu.edu/arts-and-sciences/political-science.html

**Brandman University,** School of Business and Professional Studies, Irvine, CA 92618. Offers accounting (MBA); business administration (MBA); e-business strategic management (MBA); entrepreneurship (MBA); finance (MBA); health administration (MBA); human resources (MBA, MS); international business (MBA); marketing (MBA);

organizational leadership (MA, MBA, MPA); public administration (MPA). *Expenses:* Tuition: Full-time $14,880; part-time $620 per credit hour. Tuition and fees vary according to degree level and program. *Unit head:* Dr. Glenn Worthington, Dean, 253-861-1024, E-mail: gworthin@brandman.edu.
Website: https://www.brandman.edu/business-professional-studies

**Bridgewater State University,** College of Graduate Studies, College of Humanities and Social Sciences, Department of Political Science, Program in Public Administration, Bridgewater, MA 02325. Offers MPA. *Accreditation:* NASPAA. *Entrance requirements:* For master's, GRE General Test.

**Brigham Young University,** Graduate Studies, Marriott School of Management, Executive Master of Public Administration Program, Provo, UT 84602. Offers MPA. *Program availability:* Part-time-only, evening/weekend. *Students:* 123 part-time (48 women); includes 15 minority (1 Black or African American, non-Hispanic/Latino; 5 Asian, non-Hispanic/Latino; 5 Hispanic/Latino; 4 Native Hawaiian or other Pacific Islander, non-Hispanic/Latino), 3 international. Average age 40. 59 applicants, 83% accepted, 44 enrolled. In 2016, 57 master's awarded. *Entrance requirements:* For master's, 4 years of work experience. Additional exam requirements/recommendations for international students: Required—TOEFL (minimum score 580 paper-based; 85 iBT). *Application deadline:* For fall admission, 5/1 for domestic and international students. Application fee: $50. Electronic applications accepted. *Expenses:* Contact institution. *Financial support:* In 2016–17, 31 students received support. Application deadline: 6/15; applicants required to submit FAFSA. *Faculty research:* Taxes, budgeting, nonprofit, ethics, decision modeling, work balance, organizational behavior. *Unit head:* Dr. Jeffery Thompson, Director, 801-422-4221, Fax: 801-422-0311, E-mail: mpa@byu.edu. *Application contact:* Catherine Cooper, Associate Director, 801-422-4221, Fax: 801-422-0311, E-mail: mpa@byu.edu.
Website: http://empa.byu.edu

**Brigham Young University,** Graduate Studies, Marriott School of Management, Master of Public Administration Program, Provo, UT 84602. Offers federal government (MPA); health care (MPA); local government management (MPA); nonprofit management (MPA); JD/MPA. *Accreditation:* NASPAA. *Students:* 98 full-time (54 women); includes 16 minority (2 Black or African American, non-Hispanic/Latino; 2 Asian, non-Hispanic/Latino; 10 Hispanic/Latino; 2 Native Hawaiian or other Pacific Islander, non-Hispanic/Latino), 20 international. Average age 29. 77 applicants, 81% accepted, 49 enrolled. In 2016, 42 master's awarded. *Entrance requirements:* For master's, GMAT or GRE, minimum GPA of 3.0, MPA Excel prep course. Additional exam requirements/recommendations for international students: Required—TOEFL (minimum score 580 paper-based; 85 iBT). *Application deadline:* For fall admission, 1/15 for domestic and international students. Application fee: $50. Electronic applications accepted. *Expenses:* Contact institution. *Financial support:* In 2016–17, 99 students received support. Research assistantships, teaching assistantships, career-related internships or fieldwork, institutionally sponsored loans, and scholarships/grants available. Financial award application deadline: 4/15; financial award applicants required to submit FAFSA. *Faculty research:* Taxes, budgeting, nonprofit, ethics, decision modeling, work balance, organizational behavior. *Unit head:* Dr. Jeffery Thompson, Director, 801-422-4221, Fax: 801-422-0311, E-mail: mpa@byu.edu. *Application contact:* Catherine Cooper, Associate Director, 801-422-4221, Fax: 801-422-0311, E-mail: mpa@byu.edu.
Website: http://mpa.byu.edu

**California Baptist University,** Program in Public Administration, Riverside, CA 92504-3206. Offers public administration (MPA); strategic innovation (MPA). *Program availability:* Part-time, evening/weekend, 100% online, blended/hybrid learning. *Faculty:* 5 full-time (3 women), 3 part-time/adjunct (2 women). *Students:* 47 full-time (30 women), 26 part-time (13 women); includes 44 minority (7 Black or African American, non-Hispanic/Latino; 1 American Indian or Alaska Native, non-Hispanic/Latino; 1 Asian, non-Hispanic/Latino; 31 Hispanic/Latino; 4 Two or more races, non-Hispanic/Latino). Average age 34. 59 applicants, 56% accepted, 26 enrolled. In 2016, 47 master's awarded. *Degree requirements:* For master's, comprehensive exam or thesis. *Entrance requirements:* For master's, minimum GPA of 2.75; bachelor's degree in applicable field or any field with five years of managerial experience; three recommendations; resume; 500-word essay. Additional exam requirements/recommendations for international students: Required—TOEFL (minimum score 80 iBT). *Application deadline:* For fall admission, 8/1 priority date for domestic students, 7/1 for international students; for spring admission, 12/1 priority date for domestic students, 11/1 for international students. Applications are processed on a rolling basis. Application fee: $45. Electronic applications accepted. *Expenses:* Contact institution. *Financial support:* In 2016–17, 37 students received support. Federal Work-Study and scholarships/grants available. Financial award applicants required to submit CSS PROFILE or FAFSA. *Faculty research:* Policy networks, water policy, democratic theory, international relations, political theory and philosophy. *Unit head:* Dr. David Poole, Vice President, Online and Professional Studies, 951-343-3902, E-mail: dpoole@calbaptist.edu. *Application contact:* Dr. Elaine Ahumada, Director, MPA Program, 951-343-3929, Fax: 951-343-4661, E-mail: eahumada@calbaptist.edu.
Website: http://www.cbuonline.edu/programs/program/master-of-public-administration

**California State Polytechnic University, Pomona,** Program in Public Administration, Pomona, CA 91768-2557. Offers MPA. *Accreditation:* NASPAA. *Program availability:* Part-time, evening/weekend. *Students:* 3 full-time (2 women), 34 part-time (19 women); includes 29 minority (3 Black or African American, non-Hispanic/Latino; 4 Asian, non-Hispanic/Latino; 18 Hispanic/Latino; 4 Two or more races, non-Hispanic/Latino), 3 international. Average age 31. 17 applicants, 94% accepted, 13 enrolled. In 2016, 13 master's awarded. *Entrance requirements:* Additional exam requirements/recommendations for international students: Required—TOEFL. *Application deadline:* Applications are processed on a rolling basis. Application fee: $55. Electronic applications accepted. *Expenses:* Contact institution. *Financial support:* Application deadline: 3/2; applicants required to submit FAFSA. *Unit head:* Dr. Sandra M. Emerson, MPA Director, 909-869-3879, Fax: 909-869-6995, E-mail: smemerson@cpp.edu. *Application contact:* Andrew M. Wright, Director of Admissions, 909-869-3130, Fax: 909-869-4529, E-mail: awright@cpp.edu.
Website: http://www.cpp.edu/~class/mpa/index.shtml

**California State University, Bakersfield,** Division of Graduate Studies, School of Business and Public Administration, Program in Public Administration, Bakersfield, CA 93311. Offers MPA. *Accreditation:* NASPAA. *Students:* 42 full-time (29 women), 27 part-time (14 women); includes 40 minority (9 Black or African American, non-Hispanic/Latino; 2 Asian, non-Hispanic/Latino; 28 Hispanic/Latino; 1 Two or more races, non-Hispanic/Latino), 2 international. Average age 30. 50 applicants, 78% accepted, 31 enrolled. In 2016, 30 master's awarded. *Degree requirements:* For master's, thesis or alternative. *Entrance requirements:* For master's, minimum GPA of 3.0, official transcripts, personal statement. Additional exam requirements/recommendations for international students: Required—TOEFL (minimum score 550 paper-based; 79 iBT), IELTS (minimum score 7). *Application deadline:* Applications are processed on a rolling basis. Application fee: $55. Electronic applications accepted. *Expenses:* Tuition, state resident: full-time $2246; part-time $1302 per semester. *Financial support:* In 2016–17, fellowships (averaging $1,850 per year) were awarded; Federal Work-Study, scholarships/grants, and tuition waivers (full and partial) also available. Financial award

application deadline: 3/2; financial award applicants required to submit FAFSA. *Unit head:* Dr. Thomas Martinez, Coordinator, 661-654-3064, E-mail: tmartinez@csub.edu. *Application contact:* Debbie Blowers, Assistant Director of Admissions and Evaluations, 661-664-3381, E-mail: dblowers@csub.edu.
Website: https://bpa.csub.edu/departments/Department-of-Public-Policy-and-Administration.html

**California State University, Chico,** Office of Graduate Studies, College of Behavioral and Social Sciences, Political Science and Criminal Justice Department, Program in Public Administration, Chico, CA 95929-0722. Offers health administration (MPA); local government management (MPA). *Accreditation:* NASPAA. *Program availability:* Part-time. *Students:* 24 full-time (15 women), 12 part-time (7 women); includes 14 minority (1 American Indian or Alaska Native, non-Hispanic/Latino; 5 Asian, non-Hispanic/Latino; 5 Hispanic/Latino; 3 Two or more races, non-Hispanic/Latino). 18 applicants, 72% accepted, 9 enrolled. *Degree requirements:* For master's, thesis or culminating practicum. *Entrance requirements:* For master's, 2 letters of recommendation. Additional exam requirements/recommendations for international students: Required—TOEFL (minimum score 550 paper-based; 80 iBT), IELTS (minimum score 6.5), PTE. *Application deadline:* For fall admission, 3/1 priority date for domestic students, 3/1 for international students; for spring admission, 9/15 priority date for domestic students, 9/15 for international students. Applications are processed on a rolling basis. Application fee: $55. Electronic applications accepted. *Financial support:* Fellowships and career-related internships or fieldwork available. Financial award application deadline: 3/1; financial award applicants required to submit FAFSA. *Unit head:* Mahalley Allen, Chair, 530-898-6506, Fax: 530-898-5301, E-mail: mdallen@csuchico.edu. *Application contact:* Judy L. Morris, School of Graduate, International, and Interdisciplinary Studies, 530-898-6880, Fax: 530-898-6889, E-mail: jlmorris@csuchico.edu.
Website: http://catalog.csuchico.edu/viewer/12/POLS/PADMNONEMP.html

**California State University, Dominguez Hills,** College of Business Administration and Public Policy, Program in Public Administration, Carson, CA 90747-0001. Offers MPA. *Accreditation:* NASPAA. *Program availability:* Part-time, evening/weekend, online learning. *Degree requirements:* For master's, thesis or alternative, capstone project. *Entrance requirements:* For master's, GRE, minimum GPA of 2.75. Additional exam requirements/recommendations for international students: Required—TOEFL (minimum score 550 paper-based; 79 iBT). *Faculty research:* Applied public management.

**California State University, East Bay,** Office of Graduate Studies, College of Letters, Arts, and Social Sciences, Department of Public Affairs and Administration, Program in Public Administration, Hayward, CA 94542-3000. Offers health care administration (MPA); public management and policy analysis (MPA). *Program availability:* Part-time, evening/weekend. *Students:* 4 full-time (3 women), 143 part-time (113 women); includes 106 minority (37 Black or African American, non-Hispanic/Latino; 1 American Indian or Alaska Native, non-Hispanic/Latino; 18 Asian, non-Hispanic/Latino; 34 Hispanic/Latino; 6 Native Hawaiian or other Pacific Islander, non-Hispanic/Latino; 10 Two or more races, non-Hispanic/Latino), 8 international. Average age 33. 126 applicants, 77% accepted, 36 enrolled. In 2016, 83 master's awarded. *Degree requirements:* For master's, comprehensive exam (for some programs), comprehensive exam or thesis. *Entrance requirements:* For master's, minimum GPA of 2.5; statement of purpose; 2 letters of recommendation; professional resume/curriculum vitae. Additional exam requirements/recommendations for international students: Required—TOEFL (minimum score 550 paper-based; 79 iBT). *Application deadline:* For fall admission, 6/18 for domestic and international students. Application fee: $55. Electronic applications accepted. *Financial support:* Fellowships, teaching assistantships, career-related internships or fieldwork, Federal Work-Study, institutionally sponsored loans, and scholarships/grants available. Support available to part-time students. Financial award application deadline: 3/2; financial award applicants required to submit FAFSA. *Unit head:* Dr. Toni Fogarty, Chair, 510-885-2268, E-mail: toni.fogarty@csueastbay.edu. *Application contact:* Prof. Michael Moon, Public Administration Graduate Advisor, 510-885-2545, Fax: 510-885-3726, E-mail: michael.moon@csueastbay.edu.

**California State University, Fresno,** Division of Research and Graduate Studies, College of Social Sciences, Department of Political Science, Program in Public Administration, Fresno, CA 93740-8027. Offers MPA. *Accreditation:* NASPAA. *Program availability:* Part-time, evening/weekend. *Degree requirements:* For master's, thesis or alternative. *Entrance requirements:* For master's, GRE General Test or GMAT, minimum GPA of 3.0. Additional exam requirements/recommendations for international students: Required—TOEFL. *Application deadline:* For fall admission, 5/1 for domestic and international students; for spring admission, 10/1 for domestic and international students. Applications are processed on a rolling basis. Application fee: $55. Electronic applications accepted. *Financial support:* Career-related internships or fieldwork, Federal Work-Study, scholarships/grants, and unspecified assistantships available. Support available to part-time students. Financial award application deadline: 3/1; financial award applicants required to submit FAFSA. *Unit head:* Dr. Kurt Cline, Coordinator, 559-278-2865, Fax: 559-278-5230, E-mail: kcline@csufresno.edu.
Website: http://www.fresnostate.edu/socialsciences/polisci/degrees/ma-pubadmin.html

**California State University, Fullerton,** Graduate Studies, College of Humanities and Social Sciences, Division of Politics, Administration, and Justice, Fullerton, CA 92834-9480. Offers political science (MA); public administration (MPA). *Accreditation:* NASPAA (one or more programs are accredited). *Program availability:* Part-time. *Degree requirements:* For master's, comprehensive exam, project or thesis. *Entrance requirements:* For master's, minimum GPA of 2.5 in last 60 units of course work, 12 units of course work in social sciences. Application fee: $55. *Expenses:* Tuition, state resident: full-time $3369; part-time $1953 per unit. Tuition, nonresident: full-time $3915; part-time $2499 per unit. Tuition and fees vary according to course load, degree level and program. *Financial support:* Career-related internships or fieldwork, Federal Work-Study, institutionally sponsored loans, and scholarships/grants available. Support available to part-time students. Financial award application deadline: 3/1; financial award applicants required to submit FAFSA. *Faculty research:* Emergency management plans. *Unit head:* Dr. Stephen Stambough, Chair, 657-278-2933. *Application contact:* Admissions/Applications, 657-278-2371.

**California State University, Long Beach,** Graduate Studies, College of Health and Human Services, Graduate Center for Public Policy and Administration, Long Beach, CA 90840. Offers MPA, Graduate Certificate. *Accreditation:* NASPAA (one or more programs are accredited). *Program availability:* Part-time, evening/weekend. *Degree requirements:* For master's, comprehensive exam. *Entrance requirements:* For master's, minimum GPA of 2.75. *Application deadline:* For fall admission, 7/1 for domestic students. Applications are processed on a rolling basis. Application fee: $55. Electronic applications accepted. *Financial support:* Fellowships, career-related internships or fieldwork, Federal Work-Study, institutionally sponsored loans, and scholarships/grants available. Financial award application deadline: 3/2. *Faculty research:* Transportation access, air quality controls, coastal issues, intergovernmental relations. *Unit head:* David C. Powell, Director, 562-985-4178.

**California State University, Los Angeles,** Graduate Studies, College of Natural and Social Sciences, Department of Political Science, Los Angeles, CA 90032-8530. Offers political science (MA); public administration (MS). *Program availability:* Part-time, evening/weekend. *Degree requirements:* For master's, comprehensive exam or thesis.

*Entrance requirements:* Additional exam requirements/recommendations for international students: Required—TOEFL (minimum score 500 paper-based). Electronic applications accepted. *Faculty research:* Government; public policy and law; international, political, and economic relations; comparative politics.

★ **California State University, Northridge,** Graduate Studies, The Tseng College of Extended Learning, Northridge, CA 91330. Offers business administration (Graduate Certificate); health administration (MPA); health education (MPH); knowledge management (MKM); music industry administration (MA); nonprofit sector management (Graduate Certificate); public administration (MPA); public sector management and leadership (MPA); social work (MSW); taxation (MS); tourism, hospitality and recreation management (MS). *Faculty:* 55 part-time/adjunct (28 women). *Students:* 1 (woman) full-time, 1 (woman) part-time. Average age 40. *Entrance requirements:* For master's, GRE (if cumulative undergraduate GPA less than 3.0). *Expenses:* Tuition, state resident: full-time $4152. *Unit head:* Joyce Feucht-Haviar, Dean, 866-873-6439.
**See Display on next page and Close-Up on page 1331.**

**California State University, Sacramento,** Office of Graduate Studies, College of Social Sciences and Interdisciplinary Studies, Program in Public Policy and Administration, Sacramento, CA 95819. Offers MPPA. *Program availability:* Part-time. *Students:* 13 full-time (4 women), 39 part-time (26 women); includes 14 minority (4 Asian, non-Hispanic/Latino; 8 Hispanic/Latino; 2 Native Hawaiian or other Pacific Islander, non-Hispanic/Latino). Average age 31. 51 applicants, 80% accepted, 32 enrolled. In 2016, 13 master's awarded. *Degree requirements:* For master's, thesis or alternative, writing proficiency exam. *Entrance requirements:* For master's, GRE, minimum GPA of 3.0 for all undergraduate coursework and in last 60 units. Additional exam requirements/recommendations for international students: Required—TOEFL (minimum score 560 paper-based; 83 iBT). *Application deadline:* For fall admission, 3/1 for domestic and international students; for spring admission, 9/30 for international students. Applications are processed on a rolling basis. Application fee: $55. Electronic applications accepted. *Expenses:* $4,302 full-time tuition and fees per semester, $2,796 part-time. *Financial support:* Career-related internships or fieldwork and Federal Work-Study available. Support available to part-time students. Financial award application deadline: 3/1; financial award applicants required to submit FAFSA. *Faculty research:* Education policy, urban policy, collaborative governance, judicial administration, and California state/local governance. *Unit head:* Dr. Ted Lascher, Chair, 916-278-6557, E-mail: tedl@csus.edu. *Application contact:* Jose Martinez, Graduate Admissions Supervisor, 916-278-7871, E-mail: martinj@skymail.csus.edu.
Website: http://www.csus.edu/ppa

**California State University, San Bernardino,** Graduate Studies, College of Business and Public Administration, Program in Public Administration, San Bernardino, CA 92407. Offers MPA. *Accreditation:* NASPAA. *Program availability:* Part-time, evening/weekend. *Faculty:* 8 full-time (2 women), 5 part-time/adjunct (1 woman). *Students:* 26 full-time (10 women), 176 part-time (104 women); includes 122 minority (24 Black or African American, non-Hispanic/Latino; 12 Asian, non-Hispanic/Latino; 81 Hispanic/Latino; 1 Native Hawaiian or other Pacific Islander, non-Hispanic/Latino; 4 Two or more races, non-Hispanic/Latino), 22 international. 113 applicants, 68% accepted, 51 enrolled. In 2016, 81 master's awarded. *Degree requirements:* For master's, comprehensive exam. *Entrance requirements:* Additional exam requirements/recommendations for international students: Required—TOEFL. *Application deadline:* For fall admission, 7/16 for domestic students; for winter admission, 10/23 for domestic students; for spring admission, 1/22 for domestic students. Application fee: $55. *Expenses:* Tuition, state resident: full-time $7843; part-time $5011.20 per year. Tuition and fees vary according to course load, degree level, program and reciprocity agreements. *Financial support:* Institutionally sponsored loans available. Financial award application deadline: 3/1. *Unit head:* Dr. Jonathan Anderson, Chair, 909-537-5759, E-mail: jfanders@csusb.edu. *Application contact:* Dr. Francisca Beer, Dean of Graduate Studies, 909-537-5058, E-mail: fbeer@csusb.edu.

**California State University, Stanislaus,** College of Humanities and Social Sciences, Program in Public Administration (MPA), Turlock, CA 95382. Offers MPA. *Accreditation:* NASPAA. *Program availability:* Part-time, evening/weekend. *Degree requirements:* For master's, comprehensive exam, thesis or alternative. *Entrance requirements:* For master's, minimum GPA of 2.7, 3 letters of reference, personal statement. Additional exam requirements/recommendations for international students: Required—TOEFL (minimum score 550 paper-based), ELPT (minimum score 954). Electronic applications accepted. *Faculty research:* Blogging in the Middle East, incumbency and electoral competitiveness, legislative acceptance of gubernatorial budget proposals.

**Capella University,** School of Public Service Leadership, Doctoral Programs in Healthcare, Minneapolis, MN 55402. Offers criminal justice (PhD); emergency management (PhD); epidemiology (Dr PH); general health administration (DHA); general public administration (DPA); health advocacy and leadership (Dr PH); health care administration (PhD); health care leadership (DHA); health policy advocacy (DHA); multidisciplinary human services (PhD); nonprofit management and leadership (PhD); public safety leadership (PhD); social and community services (PhD).

**Capella University,** School of Public Service Leadership, Master's Programs in Healthcare, Minneapolis, MN 55402. Offers criminal justice (MS); emergency management (MS); general public health (MPH); gerontology (MS); health administration (MHA); health care operations (MHA); health management policy (MPH); health policy (MHA); homeland security (MS); multidisciplinary human services (MS); public administration (MPA); public safety leadership (MS); social and community services (MS); social behavioral sciences (MPH); MS/MPA.

**Carleton University,** Faculty of Graduate Studies, Faculty of Public Affairs and Management, School of Public Policy and Administration, Ottawa, ON K1S 5B6, Canada. Offers public administration (MA, DPA); public policy (PhD). *Program availability:* Part-time. *Degree requirements:* For master's, thesis optional; for doctorate, one foreign language, comprehensive exam, thesis/dissertation. *Entrance requirements:* For master's, GRE, honors degree; for doctorate, master's degree. Additional exam requirements/recommendations for international students: Required—TOEFL. *Faculty research:* Canadian public administration and policy, development administration, public policy analysis, public management.

**Carnegie Mellon University,** Heinz College, School of Public Policy and Management, Master of Public Management Program, Pittsburgh, PA 15213-3891. Offers MPM. *Accreditation:* NASPAA. *Program availability:* Part-time, evening/weekend. *Degree requirements:* For master's, internship. *Entrance requirements:* For master's, undergraduate degree; five years of full-time, relevant work experience.

**Central European University,** School of Public Policy, Budapest, Hungary. Offers public administration (MPA); public policy (MA, PhD). *Faculty:* 22 full-time (7 women), 17 part-time/adjunct (10 women). *Students:* 141 full-time (90 women). Average age 29. 931 applicants, 30% accepted, 75 enrolled. In 2016, 68 master's, 7 doctorates awarded. *Degree requirements:* For master's, one foreign language, thesis; for doctorate, one foreign language, comprehensive exam, thesis/dissertation. *Entrance requirements:* For master's and doctorate, interview. Additional exam requirements/recommendations for international students: Required—TOEFL (minimum score 570 paper-based); Recommended—IELTS (minimum score 6.5). *Application deadline:* For fall admission, 2/4 for domestic and international students. Application fee: $30. Electronic applications accepted. *Expenses: Tuition:* Full-time 13,500 euros. Tuition and fees vary according to degree level, program and student level. *Financial support:* Fellowships, career-related internships or fieldwork, scholarships/grants, health care benefits, and tuition waivers (full and partial) available. *Faculty research:* Multi-disciplinary study of public policy, innovative teaching and research, as well as meaningful engagement with policy practice, public health, law, humanitarian assistance, anti-corruption, conflict and post-conflict recovery, natural resource management. *Unit head:* Dr. Julia Buxton, Head, 36 1 327-3110, E-mail: spp@ceu.edu. *Application contact:* Zsuzsanna Jaszberenyi, Admissions Officer, 361-324-3009, Fax: 367-327-3211, E-mail: admissions@ceu.edu. Website: http://spp.ceu.edu

**Central Michigan University,** Central Michigan University Global Campus, Program in Administration, Mount Pleasant, MI 48859. Offers acquisitions administration (MSA, Certificate); engineering management administration (MSA, Certificate); general administration (MSA, Certificate); health services administration (MSA, Certificate); human resources administration (MSA, Certificate); information resource management (MSA); information resource management administration (Certificate); international administration (MSA, Certificate); leadership (MSA, Certificate); philanthropy and fundraising administration (MSA, Certificate); public administration (MSA, Certificate); recreation and park administration (MSA); research administration (MSA, Certificate). *Program availability:* Part-time, evening/weekend, online learning. *Faculty:* 21 full-time (5 women), 168 part-time/adjunct (43 women). *Students:* 3,059 (1,741 women); includes 1,392 minority (1,003 Black or African American, non-Hispanic/Latino; 27 American Indian or Alaska Native, non-Hispanic/Latino; 93 Asian, non-Hispanic/Latino; 49 Hispanic/Latino; 10 Native Hawaiian or other Pacific Islander, non-Hispanic/Latino; 210 Two or more races, non-Hispanic/Latino). Average age 38. In 2016, 289 master's awarded. *Entrance requirements:* For master's, minimum GPA of 2.7 in major. *Application deadline:* Applications are processed on a rolling basis. Application fee: $50. Electronic applications accepted. *Financial support:* Scholarships/grants available. Support available to part-time students. Financial award applicants required to submit FAFSA. *Unit head:* Dr. Patricia Chase, Director, 989-774-6525, E-mail: chase1pb@cmich.edu. *Application contact:* 877-268-4636, E-mail: cmuglobal@cmich.edu.

**Central Michigan University,** Central Michigan University Global Campus, Program in Public Administration, Mount Pleasant, MI 48859. Offers general public administration (MPA); public management (MPA); state and local government (MPA). *Accreditation:* NASPAA. *Program availability:* Part-time, evening/weekend. *Faculty:* 4 full-time (1 woman), 5 part-time/adjunct (1 woman). *Students:* 50 (31 women); includes 30 minority (22 Black or African American, non-Hispanic/Latino; 4 American Indian or Alaska Native, non-Hispanic/Latino; 1 Asian, non-Hispanic/Latino; 3 Two or more races, non-Hispanic/Latino). Average age 39. In 2016, 7 master's awarded. *Entrance requirements:* For master's, minimum GPA of 2.8. Additional exam requirements/recommendations for international students: Required—TOEFL. Electronic applications accepted. *Financial support:* Scholarships/grants available. Support available to part-time students. *Unit head:* Dr. Lawrence Sych, Program Director, 989-774-3316, E-mail: sych1l@cmich.edu. *Application contact:* 877-268-4636, E-mail: cmuglobal@cmich.edu.

**Central Michigan University,** College of Graduate Studies, College of Humanities and Social and Behavioral Sciences, Department of Political Science, Program in Public Administration, Mount Pleasant, MI 48859. Offers professional development in public administration (Graduate Certificate); public administration (MPA); public management (MPA); state and local government (MPA). *Program availability:* Part-time. *Degree requirements:* For master's, thesis or alternative. Electronic applications accepted.

**Central Michigan University,** College of Graduate Studies, Interdisciplinary Administration Programs, Mount Pleasant, MI 48859. Offers acquisitions administration (MSA, Graduate Certificate); general administration (MSA, Graduate Certificate); health services administration (MSA, Graduate Certificate); human resource administration (Graduate Certificate); human resources administration (MSA); information resource management (MSA, Graduate Certificate); international administration (MSA, Graduate Certificate); leadership (MSA, Graduate Certificate); public administration (MSA, Graduate Certificate); research administration (Graduate Certificate); sport administration (MSA). *Accreditation:* AACSB. *Program availability:* Part-time, evening/weekend, online learning. *Degree requirements:* For master's, thesis or alternative. *Entrance requirements:* For master's, bachelor's degree with minimum GPA of 2.7. Electronic applications accepted. *Faculty research:* Interdisciplinary studies in acquisitions administration, health services administration, sport administration, recreation and park administration, and international administration.

**Cheyney University of Pennsylvania,** Graduate Programs, Program in Public Administration, Cheyney, PA 19319. Offers MPA.

**City College of the City University of New York,** Graduate School, Colin Powell School for Civic and Global Leadership, New York, NY 10031-9198. Offers economics and business (MA), including economics; international relations (MA); psychology (MA, PhD), including clinical psychology (PhD), general psychology (MA), mental health counseling (MA); public service management (MPA); sociology (MA). *Program availability:* Part-time. *Entrance requirements:* For master's, GRE. Additional exam requirements/recommendations for international students: Required—TOEFL (minimum score 500 paper-based; 61 iBT). Electronic applications accepted. Tuition and fees vary according to course load, degree level and program.

**Clark Atlanta University,** School of Arts and Sciences, Department of Public Administration, Atlanta, GA 30314. Offers MPA. *Accreditation:* NASPAA. *Program availability:* Part-time. *Faculty:* 5 full-time (3 women). *Students:* 26 full-time (9 women), 23 part-time (12 women); includes 26 minority (25 Black or African American, non-Hispanic/Latino; 1 Hispanic/Latino), 12 international. Average age 30. 27 applicants, 85% accepted, 12 enrolled. In 2016, 18 master's awarded. *Degree requirements:* For master's, one foreign language, thesis or alternative. *Entrance requirements:* For master's, GRE General Test, minimum GPA of 2.5. Additional exam requirements/recommendations for international students: Required—TOEFL (minimum score 500 paper-based; 61 iBT). *Application deadline:* For fall admission, 4/1 for domestic and international students; for spring admission, 11/1 for domestic and international students. Applications are processed on a rolling basis. Application fee: $40 ($55 for international students). *Expenses: Tuition:* Full-time $15,498; part-time $861 per credit hour. *Required fees:* $1326; $1326 per credit hour. Tuition and fees vary according to course load. *Financial support:* Scholarships/grants and unspecified assistantships available. Financial award application deadline: 4/30; financial award applicants required to submit FAFSA. *Faculty research:* Nutrition education, Africa. *Unit head:* Dr. Henry Elonge, Chairperson, 404-880-6653, E-mail: helonge@cau.edu. *Application contact:* Graduate Program Admissions, 404-880-8483, E-mail: graduateadmissions@cau.edu.

**Clark University,** Graduate School, School of Professional Studies, Program in Public Administration, Worcester, MA 01610-1477. Offers MPA, Certificate. *Program availability:* Part-time, evening/weekend. *Students:* 20 full-time (14 women), 19 part-time (10 women); includes 6 minority (4 Black or African American, non-Hispanic/Latino; 2

Two or more races, non-Hispanic/Latino), 17 international. Average age 28. 80 applicants, 71% accepted, 25 enrolled. In 2016, 44 master's awarded. *Degree requirements:* For master's, thesis optional. *Entrance requirements:* Additional exam requirements/recommendations for international students: Required—TOEFL. *Application deadline:* Applications are processed on a rolling basis. Application fee: $75. Electronic applications accepted. *Expenses: Tuition:* Full-time $44,050. *Required fees:* $80. Tuition and fees vary according to course load and program. *Financial support:* Career-related internships or fieldwork available. Support available to part-time students. *Application contact:* Dr. John Chetro-Szivos, Associate Dean of Professional Studies and Online Education, 508-793-7623, E-mail: jchetroszivos@clarku.edu. Website: http://www.clarku.edu/programs/masters-public-administration

**Clemson University,** Graduate School, College of Behavioral, Social and Health Sciences, Department of Parks, Recreation, and Tourism Management, Clemson, SC 29634. Offers international parks and tourism (Certificate); parks, recreation and tourism management (MS, PhD), including recreational therapy (PhD); public administration (MPA); recreational therapy (MS); youth development leadership (MS); youth leadership development (Certificate). *Program availability:* Part-time, evening/weekend, 100% online. *Faculty:* 36 full-time (14 women), 2 part-time/adjunct (0 women). *Students:* 79 full-time (52 women), 159 part-time (100 women); includes 50 minority (36 Black or African American, non-Hispanic/Latino; 2 Asian, non-Hispanic/Latino; 6 Hispanic/Latino; 6 Two or more races, non-Hispanic/Latino), 14 international. Average age 32. 143 applicants, 62% accepted, 71 enrolled. In 2016, 37 master's, 4 doctorates, 38 other advanced degrees awarded. *Degree requirements:* For master's, comprehensive exam (for some programs), thesis (for some programs); for doctorate, comprehensive exam, thesis/dissertation; for Certificate, portfolio. *Entrance requirements:* For master's and doctorate, GRE General Test, unofficial transcripts, letter of intent, letters of reference; for Certificate, letter of recommendation, unofficial transcripts, personal statement, resume. Additional exam requirements/recommendations for international students: Required—TOEFL (minimum score 610 paper-based; 80 iBT), IELTS (minimum score 6.5). *Application deadline:* For fall admission, 1/15 priority date for domestic and international students; for spring admission, 11/15 priority date for domestic and international students. Applications are processed on a rolling basis. Application fee: $80 ($90 for international students). Electronic applications accepted. *Expenses:* $4,264 per semester full-time resident, $8,485 per semester full-time non-resident, $471 per credit hour part-time resident, $942 per credit hour part-time non-resident. *Financial support:* In 2016–17, 83 students received support, including 2 fellowships with partial tuition reimbursements available (averaging $1,750 per year), 4 research assistantships with partial tuition reimbursements available (averaging $9,219 per year), 69 teaching assistantships with partial tuition reimbursements available (averaging $10,425 per year); unspecified assistantships also available. Financial award application deadline: 1/15. *Faculty research:* Human behavior, land use, recreational therapy, sustainability, tourism. *Total annual research expenditures:* $97,805. *Unit head:* Dr. Fran McGuire, Chair, 864-656-3036, Fax: 864-656-2226, E-mail: lefty@clemson.edu. *Application contact:* Dr. Bill Norman, Graduate Coordinator, 864-656-2060, Fax: 864-656-2226, E-mail: wnorman@clemson.edu.
Website: http://www.clemson.edu/hehd/departments/prtm/

**Clemson University,** Graduate School, College of Behavioral, Social and Health Sciences, Program in Public Administration, Clemson, SC 29634. Offers public administration (MPA, Certificate), including emergency management (MPA), homeland defense and security (MPA), local government (MPA), non-profit management (MPA), sustainable development (MPA). *Program availability:* Part-time, evening/weekend, online only, 100% online. *Faculty:* 4 full-time (2 women), 11 part-time/adjunct (5 women). *Students:* 8 full-time (5 women), 54 part-time (30 women); includes 16 minority (13 Black or African American, non-Hispanic/Latino; 2 Hispanic/Latino; 1 Two or more races, non-Hispanic/Latino). Average age 36. 25 applicants, 80% accepted, 18 enrolled. In 2016, 18 master's awarded. *Degree requirements:* For master's, comprehensive exam, thesis or alternative. *Entrance requirements:* For master's, GRE General Test, two letters of recommendation, unofficial transcripts, personal statement of purpose, documentation and explanation of related professional experience, resume. Additional exam requirements/recommendations for international students: Required—TOEFL (minimum score 80 iBT), IELTS (minimum score 6.5). *Application deadline:* For fall admission, 4/1 for domestic students, 3/1 for international students; for spring admission, 11/1 for domestic students, 10/1 for international students. Applications are processed on a rolling basis. Application fee: $80 ($90 for international students). Electronic applications accepted. *Expenses:* $4,264 per semester full-time resident, $8,485 per semester full-time non-resident, $695 per credit hour. *Faculty research:* Economic development, community vitality, entrepreneurship, broadband infrastructure, public health innovations and communities. *Total annual research expenditures:* $11,485. *Unit head:* Dr. Lori Dickes, Program Coordinator, 864-656-7831, E-mail: lorid@clemson.edu.
Website: https://www.clemson.edu/cbshs/departments/mpa/

**Cleveland State University,** College of Graduate Studies, Maxine Goodman Levin College of Urban Affairs, Program in Public Administration, Cleveland, OH 44115. Offers economic development (MPA); non-profit management (MPA); public management (MPA); JD/MPA. *Accreditation:* NASPAA. *Program availability:* Part-time, evening/weekend. *Faculty:* 16 full-time (8 women), 13 part-time/adjunct (5 women). *Students:* 19 full-time (12 women), 40 part-time (24 women); includes 18 minority (14 Black or African American, non-Hispanic/Latino; 1 Asian, non-Hispanic/Latino; 1 Hispanic/Latino; 2 Two or more races, non-Hispanic/Latino), 4 international. Average age 31. 79 applicants, 77% accepted, 12 enrolled. In 2016, 29 master's awarded. *Degree requirements:* For master's, thesis or alternative, exit project. *Entrance requirements:* For master's, GRE General Test (minimum scores in 40th percentile verbal and quantitative, 4.0 writing), minimum GPA of 3.0. Additional exam requirements/recommendations for international students: Required—TOEFL (minimum score 550 paper-based; 78 iBT), IELTS (6.0), or International Test of English Proficiency (iTEP). *Application deadline:* For fall admission, 7/1 priority date for domestic students, 5/15 for international students; for spring admission, 11/15 for domestic students, 11/1 for international students; for summer admission, 4/1 for domestic students, 3/15 for international students. Applications are processed on a rolling basis. Application fee: $40. Electronic applications accepted. *Expenses:* Contact institution. *Financial support:* In 2016–17, 16 students received support, including 5 research assistantships with full tuition reimbursements available (averaging $7,200 per year), 1 teaching assistantship with partial tuition reimbursement available (averaging $2,400 per year); scholarships/grants, tuition waivers (full and partial), and unspecified assistantships also available. Support available to part-time students. Financial award application deadline: 3/1; financial award applicants required to submit FAFSA. *Faculty research:* City management, nonprofit management, health care administration, public management, economic development. *Unit head:* Dr. Nicholas Zingale, Director, 216-802-3389, Fax: 216-687-9342, E-mail: n.zingale@csuohio.edu. *Application contact:* David Arrighi, Graduate Academic Advisor, 216-523-7522, Fax: 216-687-5398, E-mail: d.arrighi@csuohio.edu.
Website: http://urban.csuohio.edu/academics/graduate/mpa/

**Cleveland State University,** College of Graduate Studies, Maxine Goodman Levin College of Urban Affairs, Program in Urban Studies and Public Affairs, Cleveland, OH 44115. Offers communication (PhD); public administration (PhD); urban policy and development (PhD). *Program availability:* Part-time, evening/weekend. *Faculty:* 16 full-time (8 women), 13 part-time/adjunct (5 women). *Students:* 8 full-time (6 women), 17 part-time (8 women); includes 5 minority (3 Black or African American, non-Hispanic/Latino; 1 Hispanic/Latino; 1 Two or more races, non-Hispanic/Latino), 6 international. Average age 43. 32 applicants, 34% accepted, 2 enrolled. In 2016, 4 doctorates awarded. *Degree requirements:* For doctorate, comprehensive exam, thesis/dissertation. *Entrance requirements:* For doctorate, GRE General Test (minimum score: verbal and quantitative 50th percentile, analytical writing 4.0), minimum GPA of 3.5. Additional exam requirements/recommendations for international students: Required—TOEFL (minimum score 550 paper-based; 78 iBT), IELTS (6.0), or International Test of English Proficiency (iTEP). *Application deadline:* For fall admission, 1/31 for domestic and international students. Application fee: $40. Electronic applications accepted. *Expenses:* Contact institution. *Financial support:* In 2016–17, 15 students received support, including 5 research assistantships with full tuition reimbursements available (averaging $11,800 per year), 1 teaching assistantship with full tuition reimbursement available (averaging $11,800 per year); scholarships/grants, tuition waivers (full and partial), and unspecified assistantships also available. Support available to part-time students. Financial award application deadline: 3/1; financial award applicants required to submit FAFSA. *Faculty research:* Urban and public policy, public affairs. *Unit head:* Dr. Bill Bowen, Professor/PhD Program Director, 216-687-9226, E-mail: w.bowen@csuohio.edu. *Application contact:* David Arrighi, Graduate Academic Advisor, 216-523-7522, Fax: 216-687-5398, E-mail: d.arrighi@csuohio.edu.
Website: http://urban.csuohio.edu/academics/graduate/phd/

**The College at Brockport, State University of New York,** School of Business and Management, Department of Public Administration, Brockport, NY 14420-2997. Offers arts administration (AGC); nonprofit management (AGC); public administration (MPA), including health care management, nonprofit management, public management. *Accreditation:* NASPAA. *Program availability:* Part-time, evening/weekend. *Faculty:* 5 full-time (3 women), 5 part-time/adjunct (1 woman). *Students:* 59 full-time (41 women), 100 part-time (60 women); includes 32 minority (16 Black or African American, non-Hispanic/Latino; 5 Asian, non-Hispanic/Latino; 8 Hispanic/Latino; 3 Two or more races, non-Hispanic/Latino), 3 international. 82 applicants, 89% accepted, 53 enrolled. In 2016, 42 master's, 10 other advanced degrees awarded. *Degree requirements:* For master's, thesis or alternative. *Entrance requirements:* For master's, GRE or minimum GPA of 3.0, letters of recommendation, statement of objectives, current resume. Additional exam requirements/recommendations for international students: Required—TOEFL (minimum score 550 paper-based; 79 iBT), IELTS (minimum score 6.5). *Application deadline:* For fall admission, 8/15 priority date for domestic and international students; for spring admission, 1/15 priority date for domestic and international students; for summer admission, 4/15 priority date for domestic and international students. Application fee: $50. Electronic applications accepted. *Expenses:* Contact institution. *Financial support:* In 2016–17, 1 fellowship with full tuition reimbursement (averaging $7,500 per year), 1 teaching assistantship with full tuition reimbursement (averaging $6,000 per year) were awarded; Federal Work-Study, scholarships/grants, and unspecified assistantships also available. Support available to part-time students. Financial award application deadline: 3/15; financial award applicants required to submit FAFSA. *Faculty research:* E-government, performance management, nonprofits and policy implementation, Medicaid and disabilities. *Unit head:* Dr. Celia Watt, Graduate Director, 585-395-5538, Fax: 585-395-2172, E-mail: cwatt@brockport.edu. *Application contact:* Danielle A. Welch, Graduate Admissions Counselor, 585-395-2525, Fax: 585-395-2515.
Website: http://www.brockport.edu/pubadmin

**College of Charleston,** Graduate School, School of Humanities and Social Sciences, Program in Public Administration, Charleston, SC 29424-0001. Offers MPA. Program offered jointly with University of South Carolina. *Accreditation:* NASPAA. *Program availability:* Part-time, evening/weekend. *Degree requirements:* For master's, thesis optional, internship, capstone seminar. *Entrance requirements:* For master's, GRE General Test, previous course work in statistics, 3 letters of recommendation, minimum GPA of 3.0. Additional exam requirements/recommendations for international students: Required—TOEFL (minimum score 81 iBT). *Application deadline:* For fall admission, 7/1 for domestic students; for spring admission, 11/1 for domestic students. Applications are processed on a rolling basis. Application fee: $45. Electronic applications accepted. *Financial support:* Research assistantships, career-related internships or fieldwork, Federal Work-Study, scholarships/grants, and unspecified assistantships available. Support available to part-time students. Financial award application deadline: 4/1; financial award applicants required to submit FAFSA. *Faculty research:* Local government, environmental policy, budgeting, ethics. *Unit head:* Phil Jos, Director, 843-953-6690. *Application contact:* Phil Jos, Director, 843-953-6690.
Website: http://www.cofc.edu/~puba/

**The College of New Rochelle,** Graduate School, Division of Human Services, Program in Public Administration, New Rochelle, NY 10805-2308. Offers long term care administration (MPA); public administration (MPA). *Degree requirements:* For master's, comprehensive exam, internship. *Entrance requirements:* For master's, minimum GPA of 3.0, personal statement, two letters of recommendation, official transcripts of all colleges/universities attended, proof of immunizations.

**College of Saint Elizabeth,** Program in Justice Administration and Public Service, Morristown, NJ 07960-6989. Offers MA. *Program availability:* Part-time. *Degree requirements:* For master's, thesis or alternative. *Entrance requirements:* For master's, GRE, bachelor's degree from accredited college or university with minimum GPA of 3.0; two letters of recommendation attesting to candidate's ability to perform a high level of academic work as a self-directed learner. Additional exam requirements/recommendations for international students: Required—TOEFL (minimum score 550 paper-based; 79 iBT), IELTS (minimum score 6.5). Electronic applications accepted. Application fee is waived when completed online. *Expenses:* Contact institution.

**Columbia University,** School of International and Public Affairs, Program in Public Policy and Administration, New York, NY 10027. Offers MPA, JD/MPA, MPA/MS, MPH/MPA. *Accreditation:* NASPAA. *Students:* Average age 27. *Entrance requirements:* For master's, GRE General Test. Additional exam requirements/recommendations for international students: Required—TOEFL (minimum score 600 paper-based; 100 iBT), IELTS (minimum score 7), PTE (minimum score 68). *Application deadline:* For fall admission, 1/5 for domestic and international students; for spring admission, 10/15 for domestic and international students. Application fee: $95. Electronic applications accepted. *Financial support:* In 2016–17, 89 students received support. Fellowships, research assistantships, teaching assistantships, career-related internships or fieldwork, Federal Work-Study, institutionally sponsored loans, and unspecified assistantships available. Financial award application deadline: 1/5; financial award applicants required to submit FAFSA. *Unit head:* Office of Admissions and Financial Aid, 212-854-6216, Fax: 212-854-3010, E-mail: sipa_admission@columbia.edu. *Application contact:* Admissions and Financial Aid, 212-854-6216, Fax: 212-854-3010, E-mail: sipa_admission@columbia.edu.
Website: http://www.columbia.edu/cu/sipa/

**Columbus State University,** Graduate Studies, College of Letters and Sciences, Department of Political Science and Public Administration, Columbus, GA 31907-5645. Offers public administration (MPA), including criminal justice, environmental policy,

## Public Administration

government administration, health services administration, political campaigning, urban policy. *Program availability:* Part-time, evening/weekend, 100% online, blended/hybrid learning. *Faculty:* 5 full-time (0 women), 5 part-time/adjunct (0 women). *Students:* 38 full-time (22 women), 61 part-time (25 women); includes 52 minority (40 Black or African American, non-Hispanic/Latino; 2 American Indian or Alaska Native, non-Hispanic/Latino; 4 Asian, non-Hispanic/Latino; 4 Hispanic/Latino; 1 Native Hawaiian or other Pacific Islander, non-Hispanic/Latino; 1 Two or more races, non-Hispanic/Latino), 2 international. Average age 32. 69 applicants, 49% accepted, 27 enrolled. In 2016, 55 master's awarded. *Degree requirements:* For master's, comprehensive exam. *Entrance requirements:* For master's, GRE General Test, minimum GPA of 2.75, three letters of recommendation. Additional exam requirements/recommendations for international students: Required—TOEFL (minimum score 550 paper-based; 79 iBT). *Application deadline:* For fall admission, 6/30 for domestic students, 5/1 for international students; for spring admission, 11/1 for domestic and international students; for summer admission, 3/1 for domestic and international students. Applications are processed on a rolling basis. Application fee: $50. Electronic applications accepted. *Expenses:* Tuition, state resident: full-time $4804; part-time $2412 per semester hour. Tuition, nonresident: full-time $19,218; part-time $9612 per semester hour. *Required fees:* $1850; $1850 per semester hour. Tuition and fees vary according to program. *Financial support:* In 2016–17, 5 students received support, including 11 research assistantships with partial tuition reimbursements available (averaging $3,000 per year); career-related internships or fieldwork, Federal Work-Study, institutionally sponsored loans, scholarships/grants, tuition waivers (partial), and unspecified assistantships also available. Support available to part-time students. Financial award application deadline: 5/1; financial award applicants required to submit FAFSA. *Unit head:* Dr. Frederick Gordon, Director, 706-565-7875, E-mail: gordon_frederick@colstate.edu. *Application contact:* Kristin Williams, Director of International and Graduate Recruitment, 706-507-8848, Fax: 706-568-5091, E-mail: williams_kristin@columbusstate.edu.
Website: http://politicalscience.columbusstate.edu/

**Concordia University,** School of Graduate Studies, Faculty of Arts and Science, Department of Political Science, Montréal, QC H3G 1M8, Canada. Offers political science (PhD); public policy and public administration (MA), including geography. *Degree requirements:* For master's, one foreign language, comprehensive exam, thesis optional, internship. *Entrance requirements:* For master's, honors degree or equivalent. Additional exam requirements/recommendations for international students: Required—TOEFL. *Faculty research:* International public policy and administration, Quebec public administration, public policy and social/political theory, geography and public policy, public administration and decision making.

**Concordia University Wisconsin,** Graduate Programs, School of Business Administration, MBA Program, Mequon, WI 53097-2402. Offers finance (MBA); health care administration (MBA); human resource management (MBA); international business (MBA); international business-bilingual English/Chinese (MBA); management (MBA); management information systems (MBA); managerial communications (MBA); marketing (MBA); public administration (MBA); risk management (MBA). *Program availability:* Online learning. *Degree requirements:* For master's, comprehensive exam, thesis or alternative. *Entrance requirements:* Additional exam requirements/recommendations for international students: Required—TOEFL. *Application deadline:* For fall admission, 8/1 priority date for domestic students; for spring admission, 1/15 for domestic students. Applications are processed on a rolling basis. Application fee: $50. *Expenses:* Contact institution. *Financial support:* Application deadline: 8/1. *Unit head:* Dr. David Borst, Director, 262-243-4298, Fax: 262-243-4428, E-mail: david.borst@cuw.edu. *Application contact:* Mary Eberhardt, Graduate Admissions, 262-243-4551, Fax: 262-243-4428, E-mail: mary.eberhardt@cuw.edu.

**Copenhagen Business School,** Graduate Programs, Copenhagen, Denmark. Offers business administration (Exec MBA, MBA, PhD); business administration and information systems (M Sc); business, language and culture (M Sc); economics and business administration (M Sc); health management (MHM); international business and politics (M Sc); public administration (MPA); shipping and logistics (Exec MBA); technology, market and organization (MBA).

**Cumberland University,** Program in Public Service Administration, Lebanon, TN 37087. Offers MS. *Program availability:* Part-time, evening/weekend. *Degree requirements:* For master's, comprehensive exam. *Entrance requirements:* For master's, MAT, 3 letters of recommendation. Additional exam requirements/recommendations for international students: Required—TOEFL (minimum score 500 paper-based).

**Dalhousie University,** Faculty of Management, School of Public Administration, Halifax, NS B3H 3J5, Canada. Offers management (MPA); public administration (MPA, GDPA); LL B/MPA; MLIS/MPA. *Program availability:* Part-time. *Entrance requirements:* For master's, GMAT. Additional exam requirements/recommendations for international students: Required—TOEFL, IELTS, CANTEST, CAEL, or Michigan English Language Assessment Battery. Electronic applications accepted. *Expenses:* Contact institution. *Faculty research:* Municipal management, policy and program management, environmental policy, economic and social policy, business and government.

**DePaul University,** College of Liberal Arts and Social Sciences, Chicago, IL 60614. Offers Arabic (MA); Chinese (MA); English (MA); French (MA); German (MA); history (MA); interdisciplinary studies (MA, MS); international public service (MS); international studies (MA); Italian (MA); Japanese (MA); leadership and policy studies (MS); liberal studies (MA); new media studies (MA); nonprofit management (MNM); public administration (MPA); public health (MPH); public service management (MS); social work (MSW); sociology (MA); Spanish (MA); sustainable urban development (MA); women and gender studies (MA); writing and publishing (MA); writing, rhetoric, and discourse (MA); MA/PhD. *Program availability:* Part-time, evening/weekend, online learning. Terminal master's awarded for partial completion of doctoral program. *Degree requirements:* For master's, variable foreign language requirement, comprehensive exam (for some programs), thesis (for some programs). Electronic applications accepted.

**DeVry University–Folsom Campus,** Graduate Programs, Folsom, CA 95630. Offers accounting (M Acc); accounting and financial management (MAFM); business administration (MBA); curriculum leadership (M Ed); educational leadership (M Ed); educational technology (M Ed); higher education leadership (M Ed); human resource management (MHRM); information systems management (MISM); network and communications management (MNCM); project management (MPM); public administration (MPA).

**Drake University,** College of Business and Public Administration, Des Moines, IA 50311-4516. Offers M Acc, MBA, MFM, MPA, JD/MBA, JD/MPA, Pharm D/MBA, Pharm D/MPA. *Program availability:* Part-time, evening/weekend. *Faculty:* 15 full-time (5 women). *Students:* 29 full-time (15 women), 199 part-time (103 women); includes 20 minority (6 Black or African American, non-Hispanic/Latino; 3 Asian, non-Hispanic/Latino; 8 Hispanic/Latino; 3 Two or more races, non-Hispanic/Latino), 12 international. Average age 32. 131 applicants, 76% accepted, 75 enrolled. In 2016, 166 master's awarded. *Degree requirements:* For master's, comprehensive exam (for some programs), thesis (for some programs), internships. *Entrance requirements:* For

master's, GMAT, letters of recommendation, resume. Additional exam requirements/recommendations for international students: Required—TOEFL (minimum score 550 paper-based). *Application deadline:* For fall admission, 8/15 priority date for domestic students; for winter admission, 12/20 priority date for domestic students; for spring admission, 12/1 priority date for domestic students. Applications are processed on a rolling basis. Application fee: $25. Electronic applications accepted. *Expenses:* Contact institution. *Financial support:* Fellowships with tuition reimbursements, teaching assistantships, career-related internships or fieldwork, and institutionally sponsored loans available. Support available to part-time students. Financial award application deadline: 3/1; financial award applicants required to submit FAFSA. *Faculty research:* Venture capital, online commerce, professional ethics, process improvement, project management. *Unit head:* Dr. Terri Vaughan, Dean, 515-271-2871, Fax: 515-271-4518, E-mail: terri.vaughan@drake.edu. *Application contact:* Danette Kenne, Assistant Dean, 515-271-2188, Fax: 515-271-4518, E-mail: cbpa.gradprograms@drake.edu.
Website: http://www.drake.edu/cbpa/

**East Carolina University,** Graduate School, Thomas Harriot College of Arts and Sciences, Department of Criminal Justice, Greenville, NC 27858-4353. Offers criminal justice (MS); criminal justice education (Certificate); public management and leadership (Certificate); security studies (Certificate). *Program availability:* Part-time, evening/weekend, online learning. *Students:* 24 full-time (12 women), 53 part-time (17 women); includes 27 minority (22 Black or African American, non-Hispanic/Latino; 1 American Indian or Alaska Native, non-Hispanic/Latino; 2 Asian, non-Hispanic/Latino; 2 Hispanic/Latino). Average age 33. 35 applicants, 91% accepted, 24 enrolled. In 2016, 11 master's awarded. *Degree requirements:* For master's, thesis, internship. *Entrance requirements:* For master's, GRE or MAT, bachelor's degree in criminal justice or related field. Additional exam requirements/recommendations for international students: Required—TOEFL. *Application deadline:* For fall admission, 1/15 priority date for domestic students. Application fee: $50. *Financial support:* Research assistantships with tuition reimbursements, career-related internships or fieldwork, Federal Work-Study, institutionally sponsored loans, scholarships/grants, tuition waivers (full), and unspecified assistantships available. Financial award application deadline: 6/1. *Faculty research:* Corrections, policing, international criminal justice, terrorism. *Unit head:* Dr. William P. Bloss, Chair, 252-328-4192, Fax: 252-328-4196, E-mail: blossw@ecu.edu. *Application contact:* Dean of Graduate School, 252-328-6012, Fax: 252-328-6071, E-mail: gradschool@ecu.edu.

**East Carolina University,** Graduate School, Thomas Harriot College of Arts and Sciences, Department of Political Science, Greenville, NC 27858-4353. Offers community health administration (Certificate); public administration (MPA); security studies (Certificate). *Accreditation:* NASPAA. *Program availability:* Part-time, evening/weekend. *Students:* 34 full-time (12 women), 92 part-time (35 women); includes 31 minority (17 Black or African American, non-Hispanic/Latino; 3 Asian, non-Hispanic/Latino; 8 Hispanic/Latino; 3 Two or more races, non-Hispanic/Latino), 2 international. Average age 33. 70 applicants, 91% accepted, 55 enrolled. In 2016, 16 master's awarded. *Degree requirements:* For master's, one foreign language, comprehensive exam. *Entrance requirements:* For master's, GRE General Test. Additional exam requirements/recommendations for international students: Required—TOEFL. *Application deadline:* For fall admission, 6/1 priority date for domestic students; for spring admission, 10/15 for domestic students. Applications are processed on a rolling basis. Application fee: $50. *Financial support:* Research assistantships with partial tuition reimbursements, teaching assistantships with partial tuition reimbursements, and Federal Work-Study available. Support available to part-time students. Financial award application deadline: 6/1. *Unit head:* Dr. Robert Thompson, Interim Chair, 252-328-5686, E-mail: thompsonro@ecu.edu. *Application contact:* Dean of Graduate School, 252-328-6012, Fax: 252-328-6071, E-mail: gradschool@ecu.edu.
Website: http://www.ecu.edu/polsci/mpa/index.html

**Eastern Kentucky University,** The Graduate School, College of Arts and Sciences, Department of Government, Program in General Public Administration, Richmond, KY 40475-3102. Offers community development (MPA); community health administration (MPA); general public administration (MPA). *Accreditation:* NASPAA. *Program availability:* Part-time, evening/weekend. *Entrance requirements:* For master's, GRE General Test, minimum GPA of 2.5.

**Eastern Michigan University,** Graduate School, College of Arts and Sciences, Department of Political Science, Programs in Public Administration, Ypsilanti, MI 48197. Offers general public management (Graduate Certificate); local government management (Graduate Certificate); management of public healthcare services (Graduate Certificate); nonprofit management (Graduate Certificate); public administration (MPA); public budget management (Graduate Certificate); public land planning and development management (Graduate Certificate); public personnel management (Graduate Certificate); public policy analysis (Graduate Certificate). *Accreditation:* NASPAA. *Students:* 11 full-time (7 women), 43 part-time (22 women); includes 19 minority (16 Black or African American, non-Hispanic/Latino; 2 Hispanic/Latino; 1 Two or more races, non-Hispanic/Latino). Average age 36. 50 applicants, 64% accepted, 17 enrolled. In 2016, 23 master's, 1 other advanced degree awarded. Application fee: $45. *Application contact:* Dr. Jeffrey L. Bernstein, Program Advisor, 734-487-6970, Fax: 734-487-3340, E-mail: jeffrey.bernstein@emich.edu.
Website: http://www.emich.edu/polisci/

**Eastern Washington University,** Graduate Studies, College of Business and Public Administration, Program in Public Administration, Cheney, WA 99004-2431. Offers MPA, MBA/MPA, MPA/MSW, MPA/MURP. *Accreditation:* NASPAA. *Program availability:* Part-time, evening/weekend. *Students:* 21 full-time (15 women), 26 part-time (20 women); includes 13 minority (2 Black or African American, non-Hispanic/Latino; 4 American Indian or Alaska Native, non-Hispanic/Latino; 1 Asian, non-Hispanic/Latino; 6 Hispanic/Latino). Average age 37. 35 applicants, 71% accepted, 17 enrolled. In 2016, 26 master's awarded. *Degree requirements:* For master's, comprehensive exam, thesis optional. *Entrance requirements:* For master's, minimum GPA of 3.0. Additional exam requirements/recommendations for international students: Required—TOEFL (minimum score 580 paper-based; 92 iBT), IELTS (minimum score 7), PTE (minimum score 63). *Application deadline:* For fall admission, 4/1 priority date for domestic students; for spring admission, 1/15 for domestic students. Applications are processed on a rolling basis. Application fee: $75. Electronic applications accepted. *Expenses:* Tuition, state resident: full-time $11,000; part-time $5500 per credit. Tuition, nonresident: full-time $24,000; part-time $12,000 per credit. *Required fees:* $1300. One-time fee: $50 full-time. Part-time tuition and fees vary according to course load, campus/location and program. *Financial support:* In 2016–17, 1 teaching assistantship with partial tuition reimbursement (averaging $10,000 per year) was awarded; career-related internships or fieldwork, Federal Work-Study, institutionally sponsored loans, scholarships/grants, health care benefits, tuition waivers (partial), and unspecified assistantships also available. Support available to part-time students. Financial award application deadline: 2/1; financial award applicants required to submit FAFSA. *Unit head:* Dr. Dick Winchell, Planning and Public Administration Department Chair, 509-828-1205, E-mail: dwinchell@ewu.edu. *Application contact:* Kathy White, Student Application Contact, E-mail: gradprograms@ewu.edu.
Website: http://www.ewu.edu/CBPA/Programs/Public-Administration.xml

**East Stroudsburg University of Pennsylvania,** Graduate and Extended Studies, College of Arts and Sciences, Department of Political Science and Economics, East Stroudsburg, PA 18301-2999. Offers management and leadership in public administration (MS); political science (MA). *Program availability:* Part-time, evening/weekend. *Students:* 15 full-time (6 women), 8 part-time (1 woman); includes 4 minority (3 Black or African American, non-Hispanic/Latino; 1 Hispanic/Latino), 3 international. *Degree requirements:* For master's, variable foreign language requirement, comprehensive exam, thesis or alternative. *Entrance requirements:* Additional exam requirements/recommendations for international students: Required—TOEFL (minimum score 560 paper-based; 83 iBT) or IELTS. *Application deadline:* For fall admission, 7/31 priority date for domestic students, 6/30 priority date for international students; for spring admission, 11/30 for domestic students, 10/31 for international students. Applications are processed on a rolling basis. Application fee: $50. Electronic applications accepted. *Expenses:* Tuition, state resident: full-time $8694; part-time $5796 per year. Tuition, nonresident: full-time $13,050; part-time $8700 per year. *Required fees:* $2550; $1690 per unit. $845 per semester. Tuition and fees vary according to course load, campus/location and program. *Financial support:* Research assistantships with tuition reimbursements, Federal Work-Study, and unspecified assistantships available. Support available to part-time students. Financial award application deadline: 3/1; financial award applicants required to submit FAFSA. *Unit head:* Samuel Quainoo, Chair, 570-422-3275, Fax: 570-422-3506. *Application contact:* Kevin Quintero, Associate Director, Graduate and Extended Studies, 570-422-3890, Fax: 570-422-2711, E-mail: kquintero@esu.edu.
Website: http://www.esu.edu/academics/departments/polisci-econ/index.cfm

**East Tennessee State University,** School of Graduate Studies, College of Arts and Sciences, Department of Political Science, International Affairs and Public Administration, Johnson City, TN 37614. Offers economic development (Postbaccalaureate Certificate); not-for-profit administration (MPA); planning and development (MPA); public financial management (MPA); urban planning (Postbaccalaureate Certificate). *Program availability:* Part-time. *Degree requirements:* For master's, internship. *Entrance requirements:* For master's, GRE General Test, three letters of recommendation; for Postbaccalaureate Certificate, GRE General Test. Additional exam requirements/recommendations for international students: Required—TOEFL (minimum score 550 paper-based; 79 iBT). Electronic applications accepted. *Faculty research:* Labor issues, presidency, public law in American politics, East Asian politics, European politics, Middle Eastern politics, development in comparative politics, international political economy, international relations, world politics in international affairs.

**The Evergreen State College,** Graduate Programs, Program in Public Administration, Olympia, WA 98505. Offers MPA. *Program availability:* Part-time, evening/weekend. *Faculty:* 5 full-time (2 women), 9 part-time/adjunct (4 women). *Students:* 76 full-time (50 women), 67 part-time (49 women); includes 50 minority (6 Black or African American, non-Hispanic/Latino; 20 American Indian or Alaska Native, non-Hispanic/Latino; 9 Hispanic/Latino; 2 Native Hawaiian or other Pacific Islander, non-Hispanic/Latino; 13 Two or more races, non-Hispanic/Latino), 1 international. Average age 35. 158 applicants, 61% accepted, 79 enrolled. In 2016, 86 master's awarded. *Degree requirements:* For master's, 6-credit capstone course or 8-credit thesis. *Entrance requirements:* For master's, minimum GPA of 3.0 in last 90 quarter hours toward BA/BS; 4 quarter credits in statistics within past 5 years; evidence of writing, analytical, and general communication skills at appropriate level for graduate study. Additional exam requirements/recommendations for international students: Required—TOEFL (minimum score 600 paper-based; 100 iBT). *Application deadline:* For fall admission, 2/1 priority date for domestic and international students. Application fee: $50. Electronic applications accepted. *Expenses:* Contact institution. *Financial support:* In 2016–17, 100 students received support, including 18 fellowships with partial tuition reimbursements available (averaging $1,254 per year); career-related internships or fieldwork, Federal Work-Study, scholarships/grants, and tuition waivers (partial) also available. Support available to part-time students. Financial award application deadline: 2/1; financial award applicants required to submit FAFSA. *Faculty research:* Public and nonprofit administration, public policy, political science, government, natural resource policy, urban studies, women's studies. *Unit head:* Dr. Doreen Swetkis, MPA Program Director, 360-867-5320, E-mail: swetkisd@evergreen.edu. *Application contact:* Randee Gibbons, Associate MPA Program Director, 360-867-6554, E-mail: gibbonsr@evergreen.edu.
Website: http://www.evergreen.edu/mpa/

**Excelsior College,** School of Public Service, Albany, NY 12203-5159. Offers criminal justice (MSCI); homeland security and emergency management (MSCJ); justice administration (MSCI); mediation and arbitration (MPA); public administration (MPA). *Program availability:* Part-time, evening/weekend, online learning. *Faculty:* 1 (woman) part-time/adjunct. *Students:* 181 part-time (47 women); includes 78 minority (41 Black or African American, non-Hispanic/Latino; 2 American Indian or Alaska Native, non-Hispanic/Latino; 2 Asian, non-Hispanic/Latino; 25 Hispanic/Latino; 2 Native Hawaiian or other Pacific Islander, non-Hispanic/Latino; 6 Two or more races, non-Hispanic/Latino). Average age 41. In 2016, 30 master's awarded. *Application deadline:* Applications are processed on a rolling basis. Application fee: $50. Electronic applications accepted. *Expenses:* Tuition: Part-time $645 per credit. *Required fees:* $265 per credit. *Financial support:* Scholarships/grants available. *Unit head:* Dr. Robert Waters, Dean, School of Public Service, 518-464-8500, Fax: 518-464-8777. *Application contact:* Admissions Counselor, 888-647-2388, Fax: 518-464-8777, E-mail: gradadmissions@excelsior.edu.
Website: http://www.excelsior.edu/programs/public-service

**Fairfield University,** College of Arts and Sciences, Fairfield, CT 06824. Offers American studies (MA); communication (MA); creative writing (MFA); mathematics (MS); public administration (MPA). *Program availability:* Part-time, evening/weekend, online learning. *Faculty:* 17 full-time (9 women), 12 part-time/adjunct (6 women). *Students:* 60 full-time (40 women), 51 part-time (28 women); includes 24 minority (9 Black or African American, non-Hispanic/Latino; 1 Asian, non-Hispanic/Latino; 11 Hispanic/Latino; 3 Two or more races, non-Hispanic/Latino), 8 international. Average age 34. 84 applicants, 74% accepted, 38 enrolled. In 2016, 68 master's awarded. *Degree requirements:* For master's, capstone research course. *Entrance requirements:* For master's, minimum GPA of 3.0, 2 letters of recommendation, resume, personal statement. Additional exam requirements/recommendations for international students: Required—TOEFL (minimum score 550 paper-based; 80 iBT) or IELTS (minimum score 6.5). *Application deadline:* For fall admission, 5/15 for international students; for spring admission, 10/15 for international students. Applications are processed on a rolling basis. Application fee: $60. Electronic applications accepted. *Expenses:* Contact institution. *Financial support:* In 2016–17, 17 students received support. Scholarships/grants and unspecified assistantships available. Financial award applicants required to submit FAFSA. *Faculty research:* Ethical theory, media industries, community-based teaching and learning, non commutative algebra and partial differential equations, cancer research in biology and physics. *Unit head:* Dr. Yohuru Williams, Dean, 203-254-4000 Ext. 2221, Fax: 203-254-4119, E-mail: ywilliams@fairfield.edu. *Application contact:* Marianne Gumpper, Director of Graduate Admission, 203-254-4184, Fax: 203-254-4073, E-mail: gradadmis@fairfield.edu.
Website: http://www.fairfield.edu/cas

**Fairleigh Dickinson University, College at Florham,** Anthony J. Petrocelli College of Continuing Studies, Public Administration Institute, Program in Public Administration, Madison, NJ 07940-1099. Offers MPA.

**Fairleigh Dickinson University, Metropolitan Campus,** Anthony J. Petrocelli College of Continuing Studies, Public Administration Institute, Program in Public Administration, Teaneck, NJ 07666-1914. Offers MPA, Certificate.

**Florida Agricultural and Mechanical University,** Division of Graduate Studies, Research, and Continuing Education, College of Social Sciences, Arts and Humanities, Department of History and Political Science, Program in Applied Social Science, Tallahassee, FL 32307-3200. Offers criminal justice (MASS); history (MASS); political science (MASS); public administration (MASS). *Program availability:* Part-time. *Degree requirements:* For master's, thesis optional. *Entrance requirements:* For master's, GRE General Test, minimum GPA of 3.0. *Faculty research:* Southern history, black history, election trends, Presidential history.

**Florida Atlantic University,** College for Design and Social Inquiry, School of Public Administration, Boca Raton, FL 33431-0991. Offers MPA, PhD. *Accreditation:* NASPAA (one or more programs are accredited). *Program availability:* Part-time, evening/weekend. *Faculty:* 10 full-time (2 women). *Students:* 44 full-time (25 women), 110 part-time (60 women); includes 74 minority (43 Black or African American, non-Hispanic/Latino; 3 Asian, non-Hispanic/Latino; 24 Hispanic/Latino; 4 Two or more races, non-Hispanic/Latino), 10 international. Average age 34. 109 applicants, 52% accepted, 32 enrolled. In 2016, 65 master's, 6 doctorates awarded. *Degree requirements:* For master's, thesis optional; for doctorate, comprehensive exam, thesis/dissertation. *Entrance requirements:* For master's, GRE General Test, minimum GPA of 3.0; for doctorate, GRE General Test, faculty reference, scholarly writing samples, letters of recommendation. Additional exam requirements/recommendations for international students: Required—TOEFL (minimum score 500 paper-based; 61 iBT), IELTS (minimum score 6). *Application deadline:* For fall admission, 5/1 priority date for domestic students, 2/15 for international students; for spring admission, 11/1 for domestic students, 7/15 for international students. Applications are processed on a rolling basis. Application fee: $30. *Expenses:* Tuition, state resident: full-time $7392; part-time $369.82 per credit hour. Tuition, nonresident: full-time $19,432; part-time $1024.81 per credit hour. *Financial support:* Fellowships with full tuition reimbursements, research assistantships with partial tuition reimbursements, teaching assistantships with partial tuition reimbursements, career-related internships or fieldwork, Federal Work-Study, institutionally sponsored loans, and tuition waivers (partial) available. Support available to part-time students. Financial award application deadline: 4/1. *Faculty research:* Public finance and budgeting, public management, evaluation, criminal justice, postmodern public administration. *Unit head:* Leslie Leip, 954-924-8818, E-mail: lleip@fau.edu.
Website: http://www.fau.edu/spa/

**Florida Gulf Coast University,** College of Arts and Sciences, Program in Public Administration, Fort Myers, FL 33965-6565. Offers environmental policy (MPA); management (MPA). *Accreditation:* NASPAA. *Program availability:* Part-time. *Faculty:* 238 full-time (97 women), 158 part-time/adjunct (62 women). *Students:* 21 full-time (15 women), 50 part-time (29 women); includes 21 minority (7 Black or African American, non-Hispanic/Latino; 14 Hispanic/Latino), 1 international. Average age 33. 30 applicants, 90% accepted, 25 enrolled. In 2016, 22 master's awarded. *Degree requirements:* For master's, thesis. *Entrance requirements:* For master's, GRE General Test, MAT, minimum GPA of 3.0. Additional exam requirements/recommendations for international students: Required—TOEFL (minimum score 550 paper-based). *Application deadline:* For fall admission, 5/1 priority date for domestic students; for spring admission, 10/1 for domestic students. Applications are processed on a rolling basis. Application fee: $30. Electronic applications accepted. *Expenses:* Tuition, state resident: full-time $6721. Tuition, nonresident: full-time $28,170. *Required fees:* $1987. Tuition and fees vary according to course load and degree level. *Financial support:* In 2016–17, 9 students received support. Research assistantships, career-related internships or fieldwork, and tuition waivers (full and partial) available. Support available to part-time students. Financial award application deadline: 3/1; financial award applicants required to submit FAFSA. *Faculty research:* Personnel, public policy, public finance, housing policy. *Unit head:* Dr. Roger Green, Chair, 239-590-7838, E-mail: rgreen@fgcu.edu. *Application contact:* Dr. Margaret Banyan, Assistant Professor/Director of MPA Program, 239-590-7850, Fax: 239-590-7846, E-mail: mbanyan@fgcu.edu.

**Florida Institute of Technology,** Extended Studies Division, Melbourne, FL 32901-6975. Offers acquisition and contract management (MS); aerospace engineering (MS); business administration (MBA, DBA); computer information systems (MS); computer science (MS); electrical engineering (MS); engineering management (MS); human resources management (MS); logistics management (MS), including humanitarian and disaster relief logistics; management (MS), including acquisition and contract management, e-business, human resources management, information systems, logistics management, management, transportation management; material acquisition management (MS); mechanical engineering (MS); operations research (MS); project management (MS), including information systems, operations research; public administration (MPA); quality management (MS); software engineering (MS); space systems (MS); space systems management (MS); supply chain management (MS); systems management (MS), including information systems, operations research; technology management (MS). *Program availability:* Part-time, evening/weekend, online learning. *Faculty:* 10 full-time (3 women), 122 part-time/adjunct (29 women). *Students:* 131 full-time (58 women), 997 part-time (348 women); includes 389 minority (231 Black or African American, non-Hispanic/Latino; 9 American Indian or Alaska Native, non-Hispanic/Latino; 26 Asian, non-Hispanic/Latino; 99 Hispanic/Latino; 3 Native Hawaiian or other Pacific Islander, non-Hispanic/Latino; 21 Two or more races, non-Hispanic/Latino), 53 international. Average age 36. 962 applicants, 48% accepted, 323 enrolled. In 2016, 403 master's awarded. *Degree requirements:* For master's, comprehensive exam (for some programs). *Entrance requirements:* For master's, GMAT or resume showing 8 years of supervised experience, minimum GPA of 3.0, 2 letters of recommendation, resume. Additional exam requirements/recommendations for international students: Required—TOEFL (minimum score 550 paper-based; 79 iBT). *Application deadline:* For fall admission, 4/1 for international students; for spring admission, 9/30 for international students. Applications are processed on a rolling basis. Electronic applications accepted. *Expenses:* Contact institution. *Financial support:* Application deadline: 3/1; applicants required to submit FAFSA. *Unit head:* Dr. Theodore R. Richardson, III, Dean, 321-674-8123, Fax: 321-674-7597, E-mail: trichardson@fit.edu. *Application contact:* Carolyn Farrior, Director of Graduate Admissions, Online Learning and Off-Campus Programs, 321-674-7118, Fax: 321-674-8216, E-mail: cfarrior@fit.edu.
Website: http://es.fit.edu

**Florida International University,** Steven J. Green School of International and Public Affairs, Department of Public Administration, Miami, FL 33199. Offers public administration (MPA); public affairs (PhD); JD/MPA; MS/MPA. *Accreditation:* NASPAA (one or more programs are accredited). *Program availability:* Part-time, evening/weekend. *Faculty:* 14 full-time (5 women), 15 part-time/adjunct (7 women). *Students:*

## Public Administration

107 full-time (61 women), 136 part-time (91 women); includes 100 minority (13 Black or African American, non-Hispanic/Latino; 5 Asian, non-Hispanic/Latino; 78 Hispanic/Latino; 4 Two or more races, non-Hispanic/Latino), 47 international. Average age 33. 149 applicants, 62% accepted, 72 enrolled. In 2016, 70 master's, 4 doctorates awarded. *Degree requirements:* For doctorate, comprehensive exam, thesis/dissertation. *Entrance requirements:* For master's, minimum undergraduate GPA of 3.0 in upper-level coursework, letter of recommendation, letter of intent; for doctorate, GRE, minimum undergraduate GPA of 3.0 in upper-level coursework, 3 letters of recommendation, samples of scholarly written work, interview (when student lives within 50 miles of campus). Additional exam requirements/recommendations for international students: Required—TOEFL (minimum score 550 paper-based; 80 iBT). *Application deadline:* For fall admission, 6/1 for domestic students, 4/1 for international students; for spring admission, 10/1 for domestic students, 9/1 for international students. Applications are processed on a rolling basis. Application fee: $30. Electronic applications accepted. *Expenses:* Tuition, state resident: full-time $8912; part-time $446 per credit hour. Tuition, nonresident: full-time $21,393; part-time $992 per credit hour. *Required fees:* $2185; $195 per semester. Tuition and fees vary according to program. *Financial support:* Institutionally sponsored loans and scholarships/grants available. Financial award application deadline: 3/1; financial award applicants required to submit FAFSA. *Unit head:* Dr. Mohamad Alkadry, Program Director, 305-348-5890, E-mail: mohamad.alkadry@fiu.edu. *Application contact:* Nanett Rojas, Manager, Admissions Operations, 305-348-7464, E-mail: gradadm@fiu.edu. Website: http://cas.fiu.edu/

**Florida National University,** Program in Business Administration, Hialeah, FL 33012. Offers finance (MBA); general management (MBA); health services administration (MBA); marketing (MBA); public management and leadership (MBA). *Program availability:* Part-time, blended/hybrid learning. *Degree requirements:* For master's, capstone. *Entrance requirements:* For master's, writing assessment, bachelor's degree from accredited institution; official undergraduate transcripts; minimum undergraduate GPA of 2.5, GMAT (minimum score of 400), or GRE (minimum score of 900); two letters of recommendation. Additional exam requirements/recommendations for international students: Required—TOEFL (minimum score 500 paper-based; 62 iBT), IELTS (minimum score 5.5). *Application deadline:* Applications are processed on a rolling basis. Electronic applications accepted. *Expenses:* Contact institution. *Financial support:* Federal Work-Study, institutionally sponsored loans, scholarships/grants, and tuition waivers available. Financial award applicants required to submit FAFSA. *Unit head:* Dr. Ernesto Gonzalez, Business Department Head, 305-821-3333 Ext. 1070, Fax: 305-362-0595, E-mail: egonzalez@fnu.edu. *Application contact:* Olga Rodriguez, Assistant Campus Dean, 305-821-3333 Ext. 1044, Fax: 305-362-0595, E-mail: orodriguez@fnu.edu.

**Florida State University,** The Graduate School, College of Social Sciences and Public Policy, Reubin O'D. Askew School of Public Administration and Policy, Tallahassee, FL 32306-2250. Offers public administration (MPA, PhD); public administration and policy (Certificate); JD/MPA; MPA/MSC; MPA/MSP; MPA/MSW. *Accreditation:* NASPAA (one or more programs are accredited). *Program availability:* Part-time, evening/weekend. *Faculty:* 10 full-time (2 women), 10 part-time/adjunct (3 women). *Students:* 78 full-time (39 women), 68 part-time (41 women); includes 74 minority (12 Black or African American, non-Hispanic/Latino; 41 Asian, non-Hispanic/Latino; 6 Hispanic/Latino; 15 Two or more races, non-Hispanic/Latino). Average age 25. 115 applicants, 67% accepted, 37 enrolled. In 2016, 82 master's, 9 doctorates awarded. *Degree requirements:* For master's, action report; for doctorate, comprehensive exam, thesis/dissertation. *Entrance requirements:* For master's, GRE General Test, GMAT, MAT, LSAT, minimum undergraduate upper-division GPA of 3.0; for doctorate, GRE General Test (minimum score of 1100 or equivalent on current grading scale); GMAT; MAT; LSAT, minimum undergraduate GPA of 3.0, graduate 3.5. Additional exam requirements/recommendations for international students: Required—TOEFL (minimum score 550 paper-based; 80 iBT), IELTS (minimum score 6.5), PTE (minimum score 55), Michigan English Language Assessment Battery (minimum score 77). *Application deadline:* For fall admission, 7/1 for domestic students, 5/1 for international students; for spring admission, 11/1 for domestic students, 9/1 for international students; for summer admission, 3/1 for domestic students, 1/1 for international students. Applications are processed on a rolling basis. Application fee: $30. Electronic applications accepted. *Expenses:* Tuition, state resident: full-time $7263; part-time $403.51 per credit hour. Tuition, nonresident: full-time $18,087; part-time $1004.85 per credit hour. *Required fees:* $1365; $75.81 per credit hour. $20 per semester. Tuition and fees vary according to campus/location. *Financial support:* In 2016–17, 22 students received support, including 8 fellowships with full tuition reimbursements available (averaging $18,000 per year), 4 research assistantships with full tuition reimbursements available (averaging $15,000 per year), 8 teaching assistantships with full tuition reimbursements available (averaging $15,000 per year); career-related internships or fieldwork, Federal Work-Study, institutionally sponsored loans, scholarships/grants, tuition waivers (full), and unspecified assistantships also available. Support available to part-time students. Financial award application deadline: 2/1; financial award applicants required to submit FAFSA. *Faculty research:* Public financial management, policy analysis and evaluation methods, leadership and strategic management, state and local government administration, public and nonprofit management, international and nongovernmental organizations. *Unit head:* Dr. Keon-Hyung Lee, Director, 850-645-8210, Fax: 850-644-7617, E-mail: klee2@fsu.edu. *Application contact:* Velda Williams, Academic Program Specialist, 850-644-3060, Fax: 850-644-7617, E-mail: vwilliams3@fsu.edu. Website: http://askew.fsu.edu/

**Framingham State University,** Continuing Education, Program in Public Administration, Framingham, MA 01701-9101. Offers MA. *Program availability:* Part-time, evening/weekend.

**Gallaudet University,** The Graduate School, Washington, DC 20002-3625. Offers American Sign Language/English bilingual early childhood deaf education: birth to 5 (Certificate); audiology (Au D); clinical psychology (PhD); deaf and hard of hearing infants, toddlers, and their families (Certificate); deaf education (MA, Ed S); deaf history (Certificate); deaf studies (Certificate); educating deaf students with disabilities (Certificate); education: teacher preparation (MA), including deaf education, early childhood education and deaf education, elementary education and deaf education, secondary education and deaf education; educational neuroscience (PhD); hearing, speech and language sciences (MS, PhD); international development (MA); interpretation (MA, PhD), including combined interpreting practice and research (MA), interpreting research (MA); linguistics (MA, PhD); mental health counseling (MA); peer mentoring (Certificate); public administration (MPA); school counseling (MA); school psychology (Psy S); sign language teaching (MA); social work (MSW); speech-language pathology (MS). *Program availability:* Part-time. *Students:* 297 full-time (231 women), 129 part-time (97 women); includes 105 minority (35 Black or African American, non-Hispanic/Latino; 20 Asian, non-Hispanic/Latino; 39 Hispanic/Latino; 11 Two or more races, non-Hispanic/Latino), 22 international. Average age 30. 471 applicants, 52% accepted, 147 enrolled. In 2016, 138 master's, 25 doctorates, 14 other advanced degrees awarded. Terminal master's awarded for partial completion of doctoral program. *Degree requirements:* For master's, comprehensive exam (for some programs), thesis optional; for doctorate, comprehensive exam, thesis/dissertation.

*Entrance requirements:* For master's and doctorate, GRE General Test or MAT, letters of recommendation, interviews, goals statement, American Sign Language proficiency interview, written English competency. Additional exam requirements/recommendations for international students: Required—TOEFL. *Application deadline:* For fall admission, 2/15 for domestic students. Applications are processed on a rolling basis. Application fee: $75. Electronic applications accepted. *Expenses: Tuition:* Full-time $17,100; part-time $950 per credit hour. *Required fees:* $3725; $276 per semester. *Financial support:* Fellowships, research assistantships, teaching assistantships, career-related internships or fieldwork, Federal Work-Study, scholarships/grants, tuition waivers (partial), and unspecified assistantships available. Support available to part-time students. Financial award application deadline: 7/1; financial award applicants required to submit FAFSA. *Faculty research:* Signing math dictionaries, telecommunications access, cancer genetics, linguistics, visual language and visual learning, integrated quantum materials, deaf legal discourse, advance recruitment and retention in geosciences. *Unit head:* Dr. Gaurav Mathur, Dean, Graduate School and Continuing Studies, 202-250-2380, Fax: 202-651-5027, E-mail: gaurav.mathur@gallaudet.edu. *Application contact:* Wednesday Luria, Coordinator of Prospective Graduate Student Services, 202-651-5400, Fax: 202-651-5295, E-mail: graduate.school@gallaudet.edu.

**Gannon University,** School of Graduate Studies, College of Engineering and Business, Dahlkemper School of Business, Program in Public Administration, Erie, PA 16541-0001. Offers MPA. *Program availability:* Part-time, evening/weekend, 100% online, blended/hybrid learning. *Students:* 21 full-time (9 women), 17 part-time (10 women); includes 3 minority (2 Black or African American, non-Hispanic/Latino; 1 Two or more races, non-Hispanic/Latino), 17 international. Average age 32. 41 applicants, 59% accepted, 5 enrolled. In 2016, 43 master's awarded. *Degree requirements:* For master's, thesis or alternative, research project. *Entrance requirements:* For master's, GRE, bachelor's degree in any discipline from accredited college or university, transcripts, 3 letters of recommendation. Additional exam requirements/recommendations for international students: Required—TOEFL (minimum score 79 iBT). *Application deadline:* Applications are processed on a rolling basis. Application fee: $25. Electronic applications accepted. Application fee is waived when completed online. *Expenses: Tuition:* Full-time $17,370. *Required fees:* $550. Tuition and fees vary according to course load and program. *Financial support:* Federal Work-Study available. Financial award application deadline: 7/1; financial award applicants required to submit FAFSA. *Unit head:* Dr. Michael Messina, Director, 814-871-5755, Fax: 814-871-7210, E-mail: messina001@gannon.edu. *Application contact:* Bridget Philip, Director of Graduate Admissions, 814-871-7412, E-mail: graduate@gannon.edu.

**George Mason University,** Schar School of Policy and Government, Program in Public Administration, Arlington, VA 22030. Offers public administration (MPA). *Accreditation:* NASPAA. *Faculty:* 18 full-time (6 women), 13 part-time/adjunct (5 women). *Students:* 75 full-time (42 women), 201 part-time (108 women); includes 101 minority (40 Black or African American, non-Hispanic/Latino; 23 Asian, non-Hispanic/Latino; 29 Hispanic/Latino; 9 Two or more races, non-Hispanic/Latino), 9 international. Average age 32. 148 applicants, 84% accepted, 66 enrolled. In 2016, 113 master's awarded. *Entrance requirements:* Additional exam requirements/recommendations for international students: Required—TOEFL, IELTS, PTE. *Application deadline:* For fall admission, 2/1 priority date for domestic students. Application fee: $75 ($80 for international students). Electronic applications accepted. *Expenses:* Contact institution. *Financial support:* In 2016–17, 6 students received support, including 6 research assistantships with tuition reimbursements available (averaging $13,982 per year); career-related internships or fieldwork, Federal Work-Study, scholarships/grants, unspecified assistantships, and health care benefits (for full-time research or teaching assistantship recipients) also available. Support available to part-time students. Financial award application deadline: 3/1; financial award applicants required to submit FAFSA. *Unit head:* Paul Posner, Director, 703-993-8138, Fax: 703-993-1399, E-mail: pposner@gmu.edu. *Application contact:* Stephanie Ellis, Graduate Admissions Coordinator, 703-993-4478, E-mail: sellis11@gmu.edu. Website: http://spgia.gmu.edu/programs/graduate-degrees/mpa-in-public-administration/

**The George Washington University,** Columbian College of Arts and Sciences, Trachtenberg School of Public Policy and Public Administration, Washington, DC 20052. Offers public administration (MPA); public policy (MPP); public policy and administration (PhD); JD/MPP; MPA/JD; PhD/MPP. *Program availability:* Part-time, evening/weekend, online learning. *Faculty:* 20 full-time (11 women), 12 part-time/adjunct (5 women). *Students:* 148 full-time (96 women), 119 part-time (73 women); includes 72 minority (25 Black or African American, non-Hispanic/Latino; 2 American Indian or Alaska Native, non-Hispanic/Latino; 21 Asian, non-Hispanic/Latino; 16 Hispanic/Latino; 1 Native Hawaiian or other Pacific Islander, non-Hispanic/Latino; 7 Two or more races, non-Hispanic/Latino), 24 international. Average age 27. 548 applicants, 80% accepted, 98 enrolled. In 2016, 122 master's, 13 doctorates awarded. *Degree requirements:* For master's, capstone project; for doctorate, comprehensive exam, thesis/dissertation. *Entrance requirements:* For master's and doctorate, minimum GPA of 3.0. Additional exam requirements/recommendations for international students: Required—TOEFL (minimum score 600 paper-based; 100 iBT). *Application deadline:* For fall admission, 1/5 priority date for domestic and international students; for spring admission, 10/1 priority date for domestic students, 10/1 for international students. Application fee: $75. Electronic applications accepted. *Expenses:* Contact institution. *Financial support:* In 2016–17, 57 students received support. Fellowships, research assistantships, teaching assistantships, Federal Work-Study, scholarships/grants, health care benefits, and unspecified assistantships available. Financial award application deadline: 1/5; financial award applicants required to submit FAFSA. *Faculty research:* Education policy, budget and finance, health policy, regulatory policy, program evaluation. *Unit head:* Dr. Kathryn E. Newcomer, Director, 202-994-3959, Fax: 202-994-6792, E-mail: newcomer@gwu.edu. *Application contact:* Denee' Bottoms, Assistant Director of Graduate Studies, 202-994-6662, Fax: 202-994-6792, E-mail: dbottoms@gwu.edu. Website: http://tspppa.gwu.edu/

**Georgia College & State University,** Graduate School, College of Arts and Sciences, Department of Government and Sociology, Program in Public Administration, Milledgeville, GA 31061. Offers MPA. *Accreditation:* NASPAA. *Program availability:* Part-time, evening/weekend. *Students:* 15 full-time (12 women), 51 part-time (32 women); includes 20 minority (17 Black or African American, non-Hispanic/Latino; 2 Hispanic/Latino; 1 Two or more races, non-Hispanic/Latino). Average age 32. 32 applicants, 97% accepted, 29 enrolled. In 2016, 14 master's awarded. *Degree requirements:* For master's, capstone project or thesis, minimum GPA of 3.0. *Entrance requirements:* For master's, GRE General Test (minimum score 290), MAT (minimum score 395), or GMAT (minimum score 450) if undergraduate GPA 2.75 - 2.99, transcript of all undergraduate and graduate work. *Application deadline:* For fall admission, 8/1 priority date for domestic students, 4/1 priority date for international students; for spring admission, 11/1 priority date for domestic students, 9/1 priority date for international students; for summer admission, 4/1 priority date for domestic students. Applications are processed on a rolling basis. Application fee: $40. Electronic applications accepted. *Expenses:* $338 per credit hour tuition; fees vary depending on hours enrolled. *Financial support:* In 2016–17, 2 students received support. Unspecified assistantships available. Financial award application deadline: 3/1; financial award applicants required to submit

FAFSA. *Unit head:* Dr. Min Kim, Graduate Coordinator for MPA Program, 478-445-7393, E-mail: min.kim@gcsu.edu. *Application contact:* Kate Marshall, Graduate Admissions Coordinator, 478-445-1184, E-mail: kate.marshall@gcsu.edu.
Website: http://www.gcsu.edu/artsandsciences/gov/public-administration-mpa

**Georgia Southern University,** Jack N. Averitt College of Graduate Studies, College of Liberal Arts and Social Sciences, Department of Non-Profit and Public Studies, Program in Public Administration, Statesboro, GA 30460. Offers MPA. *Program availability:* Part-time, evening/weekend. *Students:* 33 full-time (17 women), 17 part-time (14 women); includes 17 minority (15 Black or African American, non-Hispanic/Latino; 1 Hispanic/Latino; 1 Two or more races, non-Hispanic/Latino), 2 international. Average age 28. 35 applicants, 97% accepted, 20 enrolled. In 2016, 13 master's awarded. *Degree requirements:* For master's, comprehensive exam, internship, terminal exam. *Entrance requirements:* For master's, GRE General Test, minimum GPA of 2.5, resume, undergraduate major appropriate to field, letters of reference. Additional exam requirements/recommendations for international students: Required—TOEFL (minimum score 550 paper-based; 80 iBT), IELTS (minimum score 6). *Application deadline:* For fall admission, 3/1 priority date for domestic and international students; for spring admission, 10/1 priority date for domestic students, 10/1 for international students. Applications are processed on a rolling basis. Application fee: $50. Electronic applications accepted. *Expenses:* Tuition, state resident: full-time $7236; part-time $277 per semester hour. Tuition, nonresident: full-time $27,118; part-time $1105 per semester hour. *Required fees:* $2092. *Financial support:* In 2016–17, 9 students received support, including 3 fellowships with full tuition reimbursements available (averaging $7,750 per year); career-related internships or fieldwork, Federal Work-Study, scholarships/grants, tuition waivers (full), and unspecified assistantships also available. Support available to part-time students. Financial award application deadline: 4/15; financial award applicants required to submit FAFSA. *Faculty research:* Comparative public administration, equal employment policies, gangs, environmental policy, AIDS policy. *Unit head:* Dr. Trenton Davis, Director, 912-478-5430, Fax: 912-478-8029, E-mail: tjdavis@georgiasouthern.edu.
Website: http://centers.georgiasouthern.edu/ipns/mpa/

**Georgia State University,** Andrew Young School of Policy Studies, Department of Criminal Justice and Criminology, Atlanta, GA 30302. Offers criminal justice (MS, PhD); public administration (MS). *Program availability:* Part-time. *Faculty:* 14 full-time (5 women). *Students:* 39 full-time (30 women), 5 part-time (all women); includes 21 minority (11 Black or African American, non-Hispanic/Latino; 3 Asian, non-Hispanic/Latino; 4 Hispanic/Latino; 3 Two or more races, non-Hispanic/Latino), 1 international. Average age 29. 56 applicants, 45% accepted, 15 enrolled. In 2016, 8 master's, 2 doctorates awarded. Terminal master's awarded for partial completion of doctoral program. *Degree requirements:* For master's, thesis optional; for doctorate, comprehensive exam, thesis/dissertation. *Entrance requirements:* For master's and doctorate, GRE. Additional exam requirements/recommendations for international students: Required—TOEFL (minimum score 603 paper-based; 100 iBT) or IELTS (minimum score 7). *Application deadline:* For fall admission, 1/15 for domestic and international students. Application fee: $50. Electronic applications accepted. *Expenses:* Tuition, state resident: full-time $6876; part-time $382 per credit hour. Tuition, nonresident: full-time $22,374; part-time $1243 per credit hour. *Required fees:* $2128; $1064 per term. Part-time tuition and fees vary according to course load and program. *Financial support:* In 2016–17, fellowships with full tuition reimbursements (averaging $22,000 per year), research assistantships with full tuition reimbursements (averaging $14,000 per year), teaching assistantships with full tuition reimbursements (averaging $14,000 per year) were awarded; career-related internships or fieldwork, Federal Work-Study, scholarships/grants, traineeships, health care benefits, and unspecified assistantships also available. Financial award application deadline: 2/15. *Faculty research:* Urban violence, drugs, victimization, criminal justice, criminology. *Unit head:* Dr. Richard Wright, Professor of Criminal Justice and Criminology/Department Chair, 404-413-1015, Fax: 404-413-1030, E-mail: rwright28@gsu.edu.
Website: http://aysps.gsu.edu/cj/

**Golden Gate University,** Ageno School of Business, San Francisco, CA 94105-2968. Offers accounting (MBA); business administration (EMBA, MBA, PMBA, DBA); business analytics (MS); finance (MBA, MS, Certificate); financial planning (MS, Certificate); healthcare information systems (Certificate); human resource management (MBA, MS); human resources management (Certificate); information systems (MS); information technology (MBA); information technology management (Certificate); integrated marketing and communications (MS, Certificate); international business (MBA); management (MBA); marketing (MBA, MS, Certificate); operations supply chain management (Certificate); psychology (MA, Certificate); public administration (EMPA); public relations (MS, Certificate); technical market analysis (Certificate); JD/MBA. *Program availability:* Part-time, evening/weekend. *Faculty:* 18 full-time (3 women), 117 part-time/adjunct (44 women). *Students:* 458 full-time (254 women), 664 part-time (331 women); includes 346 minority (75 Black or African American, non-Hispanic/Latino; 2 American Indian or Alaska Native, non-Hispanic/Latino; 132 Asian, non-Hispanic/Latino; 105 Hispanic/Latino; 9 Native Hawaiian or other Pacific Islander, non-Hispanic/Latino; 23 Two or more races, non-Hispanic/Latino), 354 international. Average age 34. 905 applicants, 83% accepted, 165 enrolled. In 2016, 350 master's, 2 doctorates awarded. *Degree requirements:* For doctorate, thesis/dissertation, qualifying examination. *Entrance requirements:* For master's, GMAT (for MBA), minimum GPA of 2.5 (MS). Additional exam requirements/recommendations for international students: Required—TOEFL (minimum score 550 paper-based; 79 iBT). *Application deadline:* For fall admission, 5/15 for domestic and international students; for winter admission, 1/15 for domestic and international students; for spring admission, 9/15 for domestic and international students. Applications are processed on a rolling basis. Application fee: $70 ($110 for international students). Electronic applications accepted. *Expenses:* Contact institution. *Financial support:* In 2016–17, 372 students received support. Career-related internships or fieldwork, Federal Work-Study, institutionally sponsored loans, and scholarships/grants available. Support available to part-time students. Financial award applicants required to submit FAFSA. *Unit head:* Dr. Gordon Swartz, Dean, 415-442-7027, Fax: 415-442-6579, E-mail: gswartz@ggu.edu. *Application contact:* Angela Melero, Enrollment Services, 415-442-7800, Fax: 415-442-7807, E-mail: info@ggu.edu.
Website: http://www.ggu.edu/programs/business-and-management

**Governors State University,** College of Arts and Sciences, Program in Public Administration, University Park, IL 60484. Offers MPA. *Accreditation:* NASPAA. *Program availability:* Part-time. *Faculty:* 91 full-time (9 women), 125 part-time/adjunct (64 women). *Students:* 12 full-time (9 women), 61 part-time (43 women); includes 49 minority (45 Black or African American, non-Hispanic/Latino; 4 Hispanic/Latino), 2 international. Average age 38. 25 applicants, 60% accepted, 12 enrolled. In 2016, 13 master's awarded. *Entrance requirements:* Additional exam requirements/recommendations for international students: Required—TOEFL (minimum score 550 paper-based; 80 iBT), IELTS. *Application deadline:* For fall admission, 4/1 for domestic students. Application fee: $50. Electronic applications accepted. *Expenses:* $307 per credit hour; $88 per term or $76 per credit hour fees. *Financial support:* Application deadline: 5/1; applicants required to submit FAFSA. *Faculty research:* State and local politics. *Unit head:* Lori Montalbano, Chair, Division of Humanities and Social Science,

708-235-2802, E-mail: lmontalbano@govst.edu. *Application contact:* Yakeea Daniels, Assistant Vice President for Enrollment Services/Director of Admission, 708-534-4510, E-mail: ydaniels@govst.edu.

**Grambling State University,** School of Graduate Studies and Research, College of Arts and Sciences, Department of Political Science and Public Administration, Grambling, LA 71270. Offers health services administration (MPA); human resource management (MPA); public management (MPA); state and local government (MPA). *Accreditation:* NASPAA. *Program availability:* Part-time. *Degree requirements:* For master's, comprehensive exam (for some programs), thesis optional. *Entrance requirements:* For master's, GRE, minimum GPA of 2.75 on last degree. Additional exam requirements/recommendations for international students: Required—TOEFL (minimum score 500 paper-based; 62 iBT). Electronic applications accepted.

**Grand Valley State University,** College of Community and Public Service, School of Public, Nonprofit and Health Administration, Allendale, MI 49401-9403. Offers MHA, MPA, MPNL. *Accreditation:* NASPAA. *Program availability:* Part-time, evening/weekend. *Faculty:* 14 full-time (7 women), 5 part-time/adjunct (2 women). *Students:* 44 full-time (27 women), 100 part-time (71 women); includes 27 minority (9 Black or African American, non-Hispanic/Latino; 1 American Indian or Alaska Native, non-Hispanic/Latino; 5 Asian, non-Hispanic/Latino; 8 Hispanic/Latino; 4 Two or more races, non-Hispanic/Latino), 7 international. Average age 31. 65 applicants, 85% accepted, 32 enrolled. In 2016, 61 master's awarded. *Entrance requirements:* Additional exam requirements/recommendations for international students: Required—TOEFL. *Application deadline:* For fall admission, 5/1 priority date for domestic students; for winter admission, 11/1 priority date for domestic students. Applications are processed on a rolling basis. Application fee: $30. Electronic applications accepted. *Expenses:* Tuition, state resident: full-time $11,304; part-time $5652 per credit hour. Tuition, nonresident: full-time $11,304; part-time $5652 per credit hour. Tuition and fees vary according to degree level and program. *Financial support:* In 2016–17, 23 students received support, including 11 fellowships, 15 research assistantships with full and partial tuition reimbursements available (averaging $8,000 per year); career-related internships or fieldwork, Federal Work-Study, scholarships/grants, and unspecified assistantships also available. Financial award application deadline: 5/1. *Faculty research:* Comparative urban systems, ethics and public management, local economic development, public and nonprofit boards and governance. *Unit head:* Dr. Richard Jelier, Director, 616-331-6575, Fax: 616-331-7120, E-mail: jelierr@gvsu.edu. *Application contact:* Davia Downey, Graduate Program Director/Recruiting Contact, 616-331-6681, Fax: 616-331-7120, E-mail: downeyd@gvsu.edu.
Website: http://www.gvsu.edu/spnha

**Hamline University,** School of Business, St. Paul, MN 55104-1284. Offers business administration (MBA); nonprofit management (MNM); public administration (MPA, DPA); MBA/MNM; MBA/MPA; MPA/MNM. *Program availability:* Part-time, evening/weekend, blended/hybrid learning. *Faculty:* 21 full-time (7 women), 25 part-time/adjunct (4 women). *Students:* 272 full-time (137 women), 69 part-time (33 women); includes 76 minority (39 Black or African American, non-Hispanic/Latino; 2 American Indian or Alaska Native, non-Hispanic/Latino; 20 Asian, non-Hispanic/Latino; 10 Hispanic/Latino; 5 Two or more races, non-Hispanic/Latino), 19 international. Average age 34. 166 applicants, 64% accepted, 77 enrolled. In 2016, 191 master's, 3 doctorates awarded. *Degree requirements:* For master's, thesis (for some programs); for doctorate, comprehensive exam, thesis/dissertation. *Entrance requirements:* For master's and doctorate, personal statement, official transcripts, resume or curriculum vitae, letters of recommendation, writing sample. Additional exam requirements/recommendations for international students: Required—TOEFL (minimum score 80 iBT). *Application deadline:* For fall admission, 6/1 for domestic and international students; for spring admission, 11/1 for domestic students, 10/1 for international students; for summer admission, 3/1 for domestic students, 2/1 for international students. Applications are processed on a rolling basis. Application fee: $0 ($100 for international students). Electronic applications accepted. *Expenses:* Contact institution. *Financial support:* Career-related internships or fieldwork, Federal Work-Study, scholarships/grants, and unspecified assistantships available. Support available to part-time students. Financial award applicants required to submit FAFSA. *Faculty research:* Liberal arts-based business programs, experiential learning, organizational process/politics, gender differences, social equity. *Unit head:* Dr. Anne McCarthy, Dean, 651-523-2284, Fax: 651-523-3098, E-mail: hsb@hamline.edu. *Application contact:* Shawn Skoog, Director of Graduate Recruitment and Admission, 651-523-2900, Fax: 651-523-3058, E-mail: gradprog@hamline.edu.
Website: http://www.hamline.edu/business

**Harvard University,** John F. Kennedy School of Government, Master in Public Administration in International Development Program, Cambridge, MA 02138. Offers MPAID. *Students:* 131 full-time (55 women); includes 9 minority (1 Black or African American, non-Hispanic/Latino; 4 Asian, non-Hispanic/Latino; 1 Two or more races, non-Hispanic/Latino), 100 international. Average age 29. 241 applicants, 36% accepted, 67 enrolled. In 2016, 64 master's awarded. *Entrance requirements:* For master's, one course each in microeconomics and macroeconomics; two college-level calculus courses (one must contain multivariable calculus); bachelor's degree; 2-3 years of professional experience in development (strongly encouraged). Additional exam requirements/recommendations for international students: Required—TOEFL (minimum score 600 paper-based; 100 iBT). *Application deadline:* For fall admission, 12/1 for domestic students. Application fee: $100. Electronic applications accepted. *Financial support:* In 2016–17, 87 fellowships (averaging $42,906 per year) were awarded; research assistantships, teaching assistantships, career-related internships or fieldwork, Federal Work-Study, institutionally sponsored loans, scholarships/grants, health care benefits, and unspecified assistantships also available. Financial award application deadline: 2/24; financial award applicants required to submit CSS PROFILE or FAFSA. *Unit head:* Carol Finney, Director, 617-495-7799, E-mail: carol_finney@harvard.edu. *Application contact:* 617-495-2133, E-mail: mpaid_program@hks.harvard.edu.
Website: http://www.hks.harvard.edu/degrees/masters/mpa-id

**Harvard University,** John F. Kennedy School of Government, Mid-Career Program in Public Administration, Cambridge, MA 02138. Offers MPA. *Students:* 187 full-time (85 women), 6 part-time (4 women); includes 23 minority (11 Black or African American, non-Hispanic/Latino; 6 Asian, non-Hispanic/Latino; 5 Hispanic/Latino; 1 Two or more races, non-Hispanic/Latino), 120 international. Average age 38. 778 applicants, 30% accepted, 187 enrolled. In 2016, 206 master's awarded. *Entrance requirements:* For master's, GMAT or GRE General Test, minimum 7 years of professional experience. Additional exam requirements/recommendations for international students: Required—TOEFL (minimum score 600 paper-based; 100 iBT), TWE. *Application deadline:* For fall admission, 12/1 for domestic students. Application fee: $100. Electronic applications accepted. *Expenses:* Contact institution. *Financial support:* In 2016–17, 89 fellowships (averaging $69,820 per year) were awarded; Federal Work-Study, institutionally sponsored loans, scholarships/grants, health care benefits, and unspecified assistantships also available. Financial award application deadline: 2/24; financial award applicants required to submit CSS PROFILE or FAFSA. *Unit head:* Emma Heffern, Director, 617-496-4313, E-mail: emma_heffern@hks.harvard.edu. *Application contact:* 617-495-1155, E-mail: admissions@hks.harvard.edu.
Website: http://www.hks.harvard.edu/

*Public Administration*

**Harvard University,** John F. Kennedy School of Government, Program in Public Administration, Cambridge, MA 02138. Offers MPA. *Students:* 177 full-time (72 women); includes 34 minority (7 Black or African American, non-Hispanic/Latino; 18 Asian, non-Hispanic/Latino; 6 Hispanic/Latino; 3 Two or more races, non-Hispanic/Latino), 79 international. Average age 30. 183 applicants, 57% accepted, 90 enrolled. In 2016, 74 master's awarded. *Entrance requirements:* For master's, GMAT or GRE General Test, minimum of 3 years of work experience. Additional exam requirements/recommendations for international students: Required—TOEFL (minimum score 600 paper-based; 100 iBT), TWE. *Application deadline:* For fall admission, 12/1 for domestic students. Application fee: $100. Electronic applications accepted. *Financial support:* In 2016–17, 73 fellowships (averaging $38,797 per year) were awarded; research assistantships, teaching assistantships, career-related internships or fieldwork, Federal Work-Study, institutionally sponsored loans, scholarships/grants, health care benefits, and unspecified assistantships also available. Financial award application deadline: 2/24; financial award applicants required to submit CSS PROFILE or FAFSA. *Unit head:* Emma Heffern, Director, 617-496-4312, E-mail: emma_heffern@hks.harvard.edu. *Application contact:* 617-495-1155.
Website: http://www.hks.harvard.edu/

**Hilbert College,** Program in Public Administration, Hamburg, NY 14075-1597. Offers health administration (MPA); public administration (MPA). *Program availability:* Evening/weekend. *Faculty:* 1 full-time (0 women), 12 part-time/adjunct (6 women). *Students:* 26 full-time (21 women), 10 part-time (9 women); includes 15 minority (8 Black or African American, non-Hispanic/Latino; 2 American Indian or Alaska Native, non-Hispanic/Latino; 1 Asian, non-Hispanic/Latino; 1 Hispanic/Latino; 3 Two or more races, non-Hispanic/Latino). Average age 32. 16 applicants, 100% accepted, 14 enrolled. In 2016, 16 master's awarded. *Degree requirements:* For master's, final capstone project. *Entrance requirements:* For master's, admissions statement/essay, official transcripts from all prior colleges, two letters of recommendation, current resume, relevant work experience, baccalaureate degree from accredited college or university with minimum cumulative GPA of 3.0, personal interview. Additional exam requirements/recommendations for international students: Recommended—TOEFL. *Application deadline:* Applications are processed on a rolling basis. Application fee: $25. Electronic applications accepted. Application fee is waived when completed online. *Expenses: Tuition:* Full-time $18,600; part-time $775 per credit. *Required fees:* $160; $20 per course. One-time fee: $50. *Financial support:* In 2016–17, 25 students received support. Scholarships/grants and tuition waivers (partial) available. Financial award application deadline: 7/1; financial award applicants required to submit FAFSA. *Unit head:* Kathryn Eskew, Director of Adult and Graduate Studies, 716-649-7900 Ext. 305, Fax: 716-649-0702, E-mail: keskew@hilbert.edu. *Application contact:* Kim Chiarmonte, Director for Adult and Graduate Recruitment, 716-926-8948, Fax: 716-649-0702, E-mail: kchiarmonte@hilbert.edu.
Website: http://www.hilbert.edu/grad/mpa

**Hood College,** Graduate School, Department of Economics and Business Administration, Frederick, MD 21701-8575. Offers accounting (MBA); finance (MBA); human resource management (MBA); information systems (MBA); marketing (MBA); public management (MBA). *Accreditation:* ACBSP. *Program availability:* Part-time, evening/weekend. *Faculty:* 4 full-time, 8 part-time/adjunct. *Students:* 21 full-time (13 women), 106 part-time (60 women); includes 23 minority (12 Black or African American, non-Hispanic/Latino; 4 Asian, non-Hispanic/Latino; 6 Hispanic/Latino; 1 Two or more races, non-Hispanic/Latino), 15 international. Average age 32. 44 applicants, 91% accepted, 25 enrolled. In 2016, 45 master's awarded. *Degree requirements:* For master's, capstone/final research project. *Entrance requirements:* For master's, minimum GPA of 3.0 (or resume and two letters of recommendation), copy of official transcripts, essay. Additional exam requirements/recommendations for international students: Required—TOEFL (minimum score 575 paper-based; 89 iBT), IELTS (minimum score 6.5). *Application deadline:* For fall admission, 8/15 for domestic students, 8/5 for international students; for spring admission, 12/1 for domestic and international students; for summer admission, 5/1 for domestic students, 4/15 for international students. Applications are processed on a rolling basis. Application fee: $35. Electronic applications accepted. *Expenses:* $525 per credit; $110 comprehensive fee per semester. *Financial support:* Tuition waivers (partial) and unspecified assistantships available. Financial award applicants required to submit FAFSA. *Faculty research:* Corporate strategy and sustainable competitive advantages, business ethics, entrepreneurship, investments management, economic development. *Unit head:* April Boulton, Interim Dean of the Graduate School, 301-696-3600, Fax: 301-696-3597, E-mail: gofurther@hood.edu. *Application contact:* Spencer Berk, Assistant Director of Graduate Admissions, 301-696-3604, E-mail: gofurther@hood.edu.

**Howard University,** Graduate School, Department of Political Science, Program in Public Administration, Washington, DC 20059-0002. Offers MAPA. *Program availability:* Part-time. *Degree requirements:* For master's, comprehensive exam. *Entrance requirements:* For master's, GRE General Test, minimum GPA of 3.0.

**Idaho State University,** Office of Graduate Studies, College of Arts and Letters, Department of Political Science, Program in Public Administration, Pocatello, ID 83209-8073. Offers MPA. *Program availability:* Part-time. *Degree requirements:* For master's, comprehensive exam, thesis optional, public service internship. *Entrance requirements:* For master's, GRE General Test, course work in humanities and social sciences, 3 letters of recommendation. Additional exam requirements/recommendations for international students: Required—TOEFL (minimum score 550 paper-based; 80 iBT). Electronic applications accepted. *Faculty research:* Constitutional law, policy theory, public administration, international affairs.

**IGlobal University,** Graduate Programs, Vienna, VA 22182. Offers accounting (MBA); data management and analytics (MSIT); entrepreneurship (MBA); finance (MBA); global business management (MBA); health care management (MBA); hospitality and tourism management (MBA); human resources management (MBA); information technology (MBA); information technology systems and management (MSIT); leadership and management (MBA); project management (MBA); public service and administration (MBA); software design and management (MSIT).

**Illinois Institute of Technology,** Stuart School of Business, Program in Public Administration, Chicago, IL 60661. Offers MPA, JD/MPA, MBA/MPA. *Program availability:* Part-time, evening/weekend. *Entrance requirements:* For master's, minimum cumulative undergraduate GPA of 3.0. Additional exam requirements/recommendations for international students: Required—TOEFL (minimum score 575 paper-based; 90 iBT); Recommended—IELTS (minimum score 7). Electronic applications accepted. *Faculty research:* Comparative public administration and policy, migration and ethnic politics, social dimension and impact of science and technology, urban politics, urban ethnography.

**Indiana State University,** College of Graduate and Professional Studies, College of Arts and Sciences, Department of Political Science, Terre Haute, IN 47809. Offers public administration (MPA). *Degree requirements:* For master's, thesis (for some programs), capstone project. *Entrance requirements:* For master's, GRE or minimum undergraduate GPA of 2.75, 18 semester hours of course work in political science. Additional exam requirements/recommendations for international students: Required—TOEFL (minimum score 550 paper-based). Electronic applications accepted.

**Indiana University Bloomington,** School of Public and Environmental Affairs, Public Affairs Programs, Bloomington, IN 47405. Offers economic development (MPA); energy (MPA); environmental policy (PhD); environmental policy and natural resource management (MPA); information systems (MPA); international development (MPA); local government management (MPA); nonprofit management (MPA, Certificate); policy analysis (MPA); public budgeting and financial management (Certificate); public finance (PhD); public financial administration (MPA); public management (MPA, PhD, Certificate); public policy analysis (PhD); social entrepreneurship (Certificate); specialized public affairs (MPA); sustainability and sustainable development (MPA); JD/MPA; MPA/MA; MPA/MIS; MPA/MLS; MSES/MPA. *Accreditation:* NASPAA (one or more programs are accredited). *Program availability:* Part-time. *Degree requirements:* For master's, capstone, internship; for doctorate, comprehensive exam, thesis/dissertation. *Entrance requirements:* For master's, GRE General Test or GMAT, official transcripts, 3 letters of recommendation, resume, personal statement; for doctorate, GRE General Test, official transcripts, 3 letters of recommendation, statement of purpose. Additional exam requirements/recommendations for international students: Required—TOEFL (minimum score 600 paper-based; 96 iBT); Recommended—IELTS (minimum score 7). Electronic applications accepted. *Faculty research:* International development, environmental policy and resource management, policy analysis, public finance, public management, urban management, nonprofit management, energy policy, social policy, public finance.

**Indiana University Kokomo,** Department of Public Administration and Health Management, Kokomo, IN 46904. Offers health management (MPM, Graduate Certificate); public management (Graduate Certificate); public management and policy (MPM). *Program availability:* Part-time, evening/weekend. *Students:* 11 full-time (9 women), 15 part-time (12 women); includes 4 minority (3 Black or African American, non-Hispanic/Latino; 1 Hispanic/Latino), 2 international. Average age 34. 13 applicants, 100% accepted, 8 enrolled. In 2016, 7 master's, 2 other advanced degrees awarded. *Entrance requirements:* For master's, GRE/GMAT for GPAs lower than 3.0, letters of recommendation. Additional exam requirements/recommendations for international students: Required—TOEFL (minimum score 550 paper-based; 73 iBT). *Application deadline:* For fall admission, 6/15 for domestic students, 6/1 for international students; for spring admission, 11/1 for domestic students, 10/1 for international students; for summer admission, 3/1 for domestic students. Application fee: $40 ($60 for international students). Electronic applications accepted. *Expenses:* $329.79 per credit hour in-state; $739.85 per credit hour out-of-state. *Financial support:* Scholarships/grants available. Financial award application deadline: 3/10; financial award applicants required to submit FAFSA. *Unit head:* Alan Krabbenhoff, Dean, 765-455-9275, E-mail: agkrabbe@iuk.edu. *Application contact:* Gloria Preece, Director of the MPM Program, 765-455-9269, E-mail: gpreece@iuk.edu.
Website: http://www.iuk.edu/public-administration-and-health-management/index.php

**Indiana University Northwest,** School of Public and Environmental Affairs, Gary, IN 46408. Offers criminal justice (MPA); environmental affairs (Graduate Certificate); health services (MPA); nonprofit management (Certificate); public management (MPA, Graduate Certificate). *Accreditation:* NASPAA (one or more programs are accredited). *Program availability:* Part-time. *Faculty:* 5 full-time (3 women). *Students:* 10 full-time (8 women), 39 part-time (28 women); includes 25 minority (18 Black or African American, non-Hispanic/Latino; 7 Hispanic/Latino), 1 international. Average age 37. 31 applicants, 97% accepted, 16 enrolled. In 2016, 13 master's, 9 other advanced degrees awarded. *Entrance requirements:* For master's, GRE General Test (minimum combined verbal and quantitative score of 280), GMAT, or LSAT, letters of recommendation. *Application deadline:* For fall admission, 8/15 priority date for domestic students. Applications are processed on a rolling basis. Application fee: $40 ($60 for international students). Electronic applications accepted. *Financial support:* Career-related internships or fieldwork, Federal Work-Study, and tuition waivers (partial) available. Support available to part-time students. Financial award application deadline: 3/1; financial award applicants required to submit FAFSA. *Faculty research:* Employment in income security policies, evidence in criminal justice, equal employment law, social welfare policy and welfare reform, public finance in developing countries. *Unit head:* Dr. Karl Besel, Assistant Dean and Director, 219-980-6554, Fax: 219-980-6737, E-mail: kbesel@iun.edu.
Website: http://www.iun.edu/spea/index.htm

**Indiana University–Purdue University Indianapolis,** School of Public and Environmental Affairs, Indianapolis, IN 46202. Offers criminal justice and public safety (MS); homeland security and emergency management (Graduate Certificate); library management (Graduate Certificate); nonprofit management (Graduate Certificate); public affairs (MPA); public management (Graduate Certificate); social entrepreneurship: nonprofit and public benefit organizations (Graduate Certificate); JD/MPA; MLS/NMC; MLS/PMC; MPA/MA. *Accreditation:* CAHME (one or more programs are accredited); NASPAA. *Program availability:* Part-time, evening/weekend, online learning. *Entrance requirements:* For master's, GRE General Test, GMAT or LSAT, minimum GPA of 3.0 (preferred). Additional exam requirements/recommendations for international students: Required—TOEFL (minimum score 93 iBT), IELTS (minimum score 6.5). Electronic applications accepted. *Faculty research:* Nonprofit and public management, public policy, urban policy, sustainability policy, disaster preparedness and recovery, vehicular safety, homicide, offender rehabilitation and re-entry.

**Indiana University South Bend,** College of Liberal Arts and Sciences, South Bend, IN 46634-7111. Offers advanced computer programming (Graduate Certificate); applied informatics (Graduate Certificate); applied mathematics and computer science (MS); behavior modification (Graduate Certificate); computer applications (Graduate Certificate); computer programming (Graduate Certificate); correctional management and supervision (Graduate Certificate); English (MA); health systems management (Graduate Certificate); international studies (Graduate Certificate); liberal studies (MLS); nonprofit management (Graduate Certificate); paralegal studies (Graduate Certificate); professional writing (Graduate Certificate); public affairs (MPA); public management (Graduate Certificate); social and cultural diversity (Graduate Certificate); strategic sustainability leadership (Graduate Certificate); technology for administration (Graduate Certificate). *Program availability:* Part-time, evening/weekend. *Faculty:* 79 full-time (33 women). *Students:* 31 full-time (11 women), 92 part-time (53 women); includes 28 minority (9 Black or African American, non-Hispanic/Latino; 8 Asian, non-Hispanic/Latino; 5 Hispanic/Latino; 6 Two or more races, non-Hispanic/Latino), 19 international. Average age 38. 51 applicants, 84% accepted, 31 enrolled. In 2016, 30 master's, 6 other advanced degrees awarded. *Degree requirements:* For master's, variable foreign language requirement, thesis (for some programs). *Entrance requirements:* For master's, minimum GPA of 3.0. Additional exam requirements/recommendations for international students: Required—TOEFL (minimum score 550 paper-based; 80 iBT). *Application deadline:* For fall admission, 7/31 priority date for domestic students, 7/1 priority date for international students; for spring admission, 3/31 priority date for domestic students, 11/1 priority date for international students. Applications are processed on a rolling basis. Application fee: $40 ($60 for international students). *Expenses:* $276.98 per credit hour in-state; $652.54 per credit hour out-of-state. *Financial support:* In 2016–17, 5 teaching assistantships were awarded; Federal Work-Study also available. Support available to part-time students. Financial award application deadline: 3/10. *Faculty research:* Artificial intelligence, bioinformatics,

English language and literature, creative writing, computer networks. *Total annual research expenditures:* $127,000. *Unit head:* Dr. Elizabeth E. Dunn, Dean, 574-520-4290, E-mail: elizdunn@iusb.edu. *Application contact:* Admissions Counselor, 574-520-4839, Fax: 574-520-4834, E-mail: graduate@iusb.edu.
Website: https://www.iusb.edu/clas/

**Institute of Public Administration,** Programs in Public Administration, Dublin, Ireland. Offers healthcare management (MA); local government management (MA); public management (MA, Diploma).

**Instituto Tecnológico y de Estudios Superiores de Monterrey, Campus Ciudad Juárez,** Program in Applied Public Management, Ciudad Juárez, Mexico. Offers MPM.

**International University in Geneva,** Leadership Programs, Geneva, Switzerland. Offers international relations and diplomacy (MIRD); media and communication (MA); public administration (DPA). *Degree requirements:* For master's, comprehensive exam. *Entrance requirements:* Additional exam requirements/recommendations for international students: Required—TOEFL. Electronic applications accepted.

**Iowa State University of Science and Technology,** Department of Political Science, Ames, IA 50011. Offers political science (MA); public administration (MPA); JD/MA. JD/MA offered jointly with Drake University. *Degree requirements:* For master's, thesis (for some programs). *Entrance requirements:* For master's, GRE General Test, GMAT or LSAT. Additional exam requirements/recommendations for international students: Required—TOEFL (minimum score 570 paper-based; 80 iBT), IELTS (minimum score 6.5). *Application deadline:* For fall admission, 1/1 priority date for domestic and international students; for spring admission, 10/1 for domestic and international students. Application fee: $60 ($90 for international students). Electronic applications accepted. *Application contact:* Alex Tuckness, Application Contact, 515-294-8910, Fax: 515-294-1003, E-mail: tuckness@iastate.edu.
Website: http://www.pols.iastate.edu

**Jackson State University,** Graduate School, College of Public Service, Department of Public Policy and Administration, Jackson, MS 39217. Offers public administration (PhD); public policy and administration (MPPA). *Accreditation:* NASPAA (one or more programs are accredited). *Program availability:* Evening/weekend. *Degree requirements:* For master's, comprehensive exam, thesis optional; for doctorate, comprehensive exam, thesis/dissertation. *Entrance requirements:* For master's, GRE General Test; for doctorate, GRE, GMAT, MAT. Additional exam requirements/recommendations for international students: Required—TOEFL (minimum score 520 paper-based; 67 iBT). *Application deadline:* For fall admission, 3/1 for domestic and international students; for spring admission, 10/1 for domestic and international students. Application fee: $25. *Expenses:* Tuition, state resident: full-time $7141. Tuition, nonresident: full-time $17,494. *Required fees:* $1080. Tuition and fees vary according to class time, course level, course load, degree level, campus/location, program and student level. *Financial support:* Career-related internships or fieldwork, Federal Work-Study, scholarships/grants, tuition waivers (full and partial), and unspecified assistantships available. Support available to part-time students. Financial award application deadline: 3/1; financial award applicants required to submit FAFSA. *Unit head:* Dr. Johnny Gilleylen, Sr., Chair, 601-432-6277, Fax: 601-432-6322, E-mail: ppa@jsums.edu. *Application contact:* Fatoumatta Sisay, Manager of Graduate Admissions, 601-979-0342, Fax: 601-979-4325, E-mail: fatoumatta.sisay@jsums.edu.
Website: http://www.jsums.edu/publicpolicy/

**James Madison University,** The Graduate School, College of Arts and Letters, Program in Public Administration, Harrisonburg, VA 22807. Offers individualized (MPA); public management (MPA), including international stabilization and recovery, management in international non-governmental organizations, nonprofit management, public management. Public and nonprofit management program offered in Roanoke. *Accreditation:* NASPAA. *Program availability:* Part-time. *Students:* 26 full-time (10 women), 19 part-time (8 women); includes 9 minority (6 Black or African American, non-Hispanic/Latino; 1 Hispanic/Latino; 2 Two or more races, non-Hispanic/Latino). Average age 30. 27 applicants, 89% accepted, 12 enrolled. In 2016, 9 master's awarded. Application fee: $55. Electronic applications accepted. *Financial support:* Federal Work-Study and 16 assistantships (averaging $7911) available. Financial award application deadline: 3/1; financial award applicants required to submit FAFSA. *Unit head:* Dr. Charles Blake, Department Head, 540-568-6149, E-mail: blakech@jmu.edu. *Application contact:* Lynette D. Michael, Director of Graduate Admissions, 540-568-6131, Fax: 540-568-7860, E-mail: michaeld@jmu.edu.
Website: http://www.jmu.edu/mpa

**John Jay College of Criminal Justice of the City University of New York,** Graduate Studies, Program in Public Administration, New York, NY 10019. Offers MPA. *Accreditation:* NASPAA. *Program availability:* Part-time, evening/weekend. *Degree requirements:* For master's, thesis or alternative. *Entrance requirements:* For master's, minimum B average. Additional exam requirements/recommendations for international students: Required—TOEFL (minimum score 500 paper-based).

**Johns Hopkins University,** Zanvyl Krieger School of Arts and Sciences, Advanced Academic Programs, Program in Government, Washington, DC 20036. Offers global security studies (MA); government (MA); national securities study (Certificate); nonprofit management (Certificate); public management (MA); research administration (MS); MA/MBA. *Program availability:* Part-time, evening/weekend, online learning. *Degree requirements:* For master's, thesis. *Entrance requirements:* For master's, minimum GPA of 3.0. Additional exam requirements/recommendations for international students: Required—TOEFL (minimum score 100 iBT). Electronic applications accepted.

**Kansas State University,** Graduate School, College of Arts and Sciences, Department of Political Science, Manhattan, KS 66506. Offers political science (MA), including political science; public administration (MPA). *Program availability:* Part-time. *Faculty:* 18 full-time (5 women). *Students:* 6 full-time (4 women), 1 part-time (1 woman); includes 1 minority (Black or African American, non-Hispanic/Latino), 1 international. Average age 35. 6 applicants, 67% accepted, 2 enrolled. In 2016, 1 master's awarded. *Degree requirements:* For master's, comprehensive exam, thesis or alternative. *Entrance requirements:* For master's, GRE (recommended), minimum GPA of 3.0. Additional exam requirements/recommendations for international students: Required—TOEFL (minimum score 550 paper-based; 79 iBT); Recommended—IELTS (minimum score 6.5), TSE (minimum score 58). *Application deadline:* For fall admission, 2/1 priority date for domestic and international students; for spring admission, 8/1 priority date for domestic and international students. Applications are processed on a rolling basis. Application fee: $50 ($75 for international students). Electronic applications accepted. *Expenses:* Tuition, state resident: full-time $9670. Tuition, nonresident: full-time $21,828. *Required fees:* $862. *Financial support:* In 2016–17, 14 students received support, including 9 teaching assistantships with tuition reimbursements available (averaging $14,000 per year); fellowships, research assistantships, career-related internships or fieldwork, Federal Work-Study, institutionally sponsored loans, and scholarships/grants also available. Support available to part-time students. Financial award application deadline: 3/1; financial award applicants required to submit FAFSA. *Faculty research:* Armed conflict, civil military relations, comparative public administration and policy, electoral competition, legislative studies. *Unit head:* Dr. Jeff Pickering, Head, 785-532-0454, Fax: 785-532-2339, E-mail: jjp@ksu.edu. *Application*

*contact:* Dr. James Franke, Director, 785-532-0451, Fax: 785-532-2339, E-mail: jfranke@ksu.edu.
Website: http://www.k-state.edu/polsci/

**Kean University,** College of Business and Public Management, Program in Public Administration, Union, NJ 07083. Offers health services administration (MPA); non-profit management (MPA); public administration (MPA). *Accreditation:* NASPAA. *Program availability:* Part-time. *Faculty:* 14 full-time (4 women). *Students:* 70 full-time (46 women), 51 part-time (37 women); includes 90 minority (63 Black or African American, non-Hispanic/Latino; 8 Asian, non-Hispanic/Latino; 18 Hispanic/Latino; 1 Two or more races, non-Hispanic/Latino), 4 international. Average age 31. 73 applicants, 42% accepted, 28 enrolled. In 2016, 56 master's awarded. *Degree requirements:* For master's, thesis, internship, research seminar. *Entrance requirements:* For master's, minimum cumulative GPA of 3.0, official transcripts from all institutions attended, two letters of recommendation, personal statement, writing sample, professional resume/curriculum vitae. Additional exam requirements/recommendations for international students: Required—TOEFL (minimum score 550 paper-based; 79 iBT), IELTS (minimum score 6.5). *Application deadline:* For fall admission, 6/1 for domestic and international students; for spring admission, 12/1 for domestic and international students. Applications are processed on a rolling basis. Application fee: $75. Electronic applications accepted. *Expenses:* Tuition, state resident: full-time $13,156; part-time $640 per credit. Tuition, nonresident: full-time $17,831; part-time $785 per credit. *Required fees:* $3316; $151 per credit. Tuition and fees vary according to course level, course load, degree level and program. *Financial support:* Scholarships/grants and unspecified assistantships available. Financial award applicants required to submit FAFSA. *Unit head:* Dr. Patricia Moore, Program Coordinator, 908-737-4314, E-mail: pmoore@kean.edu. *Application contact:* Pedro Lopes, Admissions Counselor, 908-737-7100, E-mail: grad-adm@kean.edu.
Website: http://grad.kean.edu/masters-programs/public-administration

**Kennesaw State University,** College of Humanities and Social Sciences, Program in Public Administration, Kennesaw, GA 30144. Offers MPA. *Accreditation:* NASPAA. *Program availability:* Part-time, evening/weekend. *Degree requirements:* For master's, thesis optional. *Entrance requirements:* For master's, GRE General Test, minimum GPA of 2.75. Additional exam requirements/recommendations for international students: Required—TOEFL (minimum score 550 paper-based; 80 iBT), IELTS (minimum score 6.5). Electronic applications accepted.

**Kent State University,** College of Arts and Sciences, Department of Political Science, Kent, OH 44242-0001. Offers political science (MA, PhD), including American politics and policy, conflict analysis and management, transnational and comparative politics and policy; public administration (MPA). *Program availability:* Part-time, online learning. *Faculty:* 18 full-time (5 women). *Students:* 34 full-time (14 women), 62 part-time (31 women); includes 12 minority (5 Black or African American, non-Hispanic/Latino; 1 American Indian or Alaska Native, non-Hispanic/Latino; 2 Asian, non-Hispanic/Latino; 2 Hispanic/Latino; 2 Two or more races, non-Hispanic/Latino), 9 international. Average age 30. 65 applicants, 57% accepted, 21 enrolled. In 2016, 20 master's, 1 doctorate awarded. *Degree requirements:* For master's, thesis (for some programs); for doctorate, comprehensive exam, thesis/dissertation. *Entrance requirements:* For master's and doctorate, GRE, statement of purpose, transcripts, writing sample, 3 letters of recommendation. *Application deadline:* For fall admission, 1/31 for domestic and international students. Applications are processed on a rolling basis. Application fee: $45 ($70 for international students). Electronic applications accepted. *Expenses:* Tuition, state resident: full-time $10,864; part-time $495 per credit hour. Tuition, nonresident: full-time $18,380; part-time $837 per credit hour. *Financial support:* Research assistantships with full tuition reimbursements, teaching assistantships with full tuition reimbursements, health care benefits, and unspecified assistantships available. Financial award application deadline: 1/31. *Unit head:* Dr. Andrew Barnes, Associate Professor and Chair, 330-672-2060, E-mail: abarnes3@kent.edu. *Application contact:* Dr. Ryan L. Claassen, Graduate Coordinator, 330-672-2060, E-mail: rclaasse@kent.edu.
Website: http://www.kent.edu/polisci

**Kentucky State University,** College of Professional Studies, Frankfort, KY 40601. Offers nursing (DNP); public administration (MPA), including human resource management; special education (MA). *Program availability:* Part-time, evening/weekend, 100% online, blended/hybrid learning. *Faculty:* 6 full-time (3 women), 7 part-time/adjunct (6 women). *Students:* 32 full-time (22 women), 37 part-time (30 women); includes 48 minority (47 Black or African American, non-Hispanic/Latino; 1 Asian, non-Hispanic/Latino). Average age 34. 42 applicants, 79% accepted, 24 enrolled. In 2016, 19 master's awarded. *Degree requirements:* For master's, comprehensive exam, thesis optional; for doctorate, comprehensive exam, thesis/dissertation optional, 180 clinical hours. *Entrance requirements:* For master's, GMAT, GRE, transcript, essay, letters of recommendation; for doctorate, RN license; resume; graduate research and statistics courses (strongly recommended). Additional exam requirements/recommendations for international students: Required—TOEFL (minimum score 525 paper-based). *Application deadline:* For fall admission, 7/1 for domestic students, 4/1 for international students; for spring admission, 11/15 for domestic students, 8/15 for international students; for summer admission, 5/1 for domestic students, 2/1 for international students. Applications are processed on a rolling basis. Application fee: $30 ($100 for international students). Electronic applications accepted. *Expenses:* Tuition, state resident: full-time $7524; part-time $418 per credit hour. Tuition, nonresident: full-time $11,322; part-time $629 per credit hour. Tuition and fees vary according to course load. *Financial support:* In 2016–17, 57 students received support, including 3 research assistantships (averaging $10,083 per year); scholarships/grants, tuition waivers (partial), and unspecified assistantships also available. Financial award application deadline: 4/15; financial award applicants required to submit FAFSA. *Faculty research:* Risk assessment and failure modeling for the public sector implication of property rights on economic development, the social stability of communities, civil peace of nations. *Total annual research expenditures:* $129,604. *Unit head:* Dr. Candice L. Jackson, Vice President of Academic Affairs, 502-597-6442, E-mail: candice.jackson@kysu.edu. *Application contact:* Dr. James Obielodan, Director of Graduate Studies, 502-597-4723, E-mail: james.obielodan@kysu.edu.
Website: http://kysu.edu/academics/college-of-professional-studies/

**Kutztown University of Pennsylvania,** College of Liberal Arts and Sciences, Program in Public Administration, Kutztown, PA 19530-0730. Offers MPA. *Program availability:* Part-time, evening/weekend. *Faculty:* 3 full-time (1 woman). *Students:* 10 full-time (4 women), 19 part-time (13 women); includes 10 minority (6 Black or African American, non-Hispanic/Latino; 2 Hispanic/Latino; 2 Two or more races, non-Hispanic/Latino). Average age 31. 21 applicants, 86% accepted, 7 enrolled. In 2016, 12 master's awarded. *Degree requirements:* For master's, comprehensive exam, thesis optional. *Entrance requirements:* For master's, GRE, GMAT, MAT, or LSAT, 3 letters of recommendation. Additional exam requirements/recommendations for international students: Required—TOEFL (minimum score 550 paper-based, 79 iBT) or IELTS (minimum score 6.5). *Application deadline:* For fall admission, 8/1 for domestic and international students; for spring admission, 12/1 for domestic and international students. Application fee: $35. Electronic applications accepted. *Expenses:* Tuition,

## Public Administration

state resident: full-time $4347; part-time $483 per credit. Tuition, nonresident: full-time $6525; part-time $725 per credit. *Required fees:* $88 per credit. One-time fee: $50 full-time. *Financial support:* Career-related internships or fieldwork, Federal Work-Study, scholarships/grants, and unspecified assistantships available. Financial award application deadline: 3/1; financial award applicants required to submit FAFSA. *Faculty research:* Structure of code enforcement offices in smaller developing communities. *Unit head:* Dr. Steve Lem, Chairperson, 610-683-4471, Fax: 610-683-4603, E-mail: lem@kutztown.edu. *Application contact:* Carol Dignazio, Academic Department Secretary, 610-683-4449, E-mail: dignazio@kutztown.edu.
Website: https://www.kutztown.edu/academics/graduate-programs/public-administration.htm

**Lamar University,** College of Graduate Studies, College of Arts and Sciences, Department of Political Science, Beaumont, TX 77710. Offers public administration (MPA). *Program availability:* Part-time. *Faculty:* 3 full-time (2 women). *Students:* 5 full-time (1 woman), 9 part-time (4 women); includes 9 minority (8 Black or African American, non-Hispanic/Latino; 1 Hispanic/Latino), 3 international. Average age 31. 8 applicants, 100% accepted, 5 enrolled. In 2016, 5 master's awarded. *Entrance requirements:* For master's, GRE General Test. Additional exam requirements/recommendations for international students: Required—TOEFL (minimum score 550 paper-based; 79 iBT), IELTS (minimum score 6.5). *Application deadline:* For fall admission, 8/10 for domestic students, 7/1 for international students; for spring admission, 1/5 for domestic students, 12/1 for international students. Applications are processed on a rolling basis. Application fee: $25 ($50 for international students). Electronic applications accepted. *Expenses:* $8,134 in-state full-time, $5,574 in-state part-time; $15,604 out-of-state full-time, $10,554 out-of-state part-time per year. *Financial support:* Fellowships, research assistantships, teaching assistantships, career-related internships or fieldwork, Federal Work-Study, and institutionally sponsored loans available. Financial award application deadline: 4/1; financial award applicants required to submit FAFSA. *Faculty research:* Political activities of administrators, administrative response to Hurricane Rita, budgeting, environmental politics, urban planning. *Unit head:* Dr. Terri Davis, Chair, 409-880-8285, Fax: 409-880-8710. *Application contact:* Deidre Mayer, Interim Director, Admissions and Academic Services, 409-880-8888, Fax: 409-880-7419, E-mail: gradmissions@lamar.edu.
Website: http://artssciences.lamar.edu/political-science

**Liberty University,** Helms School of Government, Lynchburg, VA 24515. Offers public administration (MS). *Program availability:* Part-time, online learning. *Students:* 279 full-time (128 women), 626 part-time (233 women); includes 223 minority (163 Black or African American, non-Hispanic/Latino; 10 American Indian or Alaska Native, non-Hispanic/Latino; 10 Asian, non-Hispanic/Latino; 11 Hispanic/Latino; 1 Native Hawaiian or other Pacific Islander, non-Hispanic/Latino; 28 Two or more races, non-Hispanic/Latino), 12 international. Average age 35. 713 applicants, 51% accepted, 182 enrolled. In 2016, 256 master's awarded. *Entrance requirements:* For master's, minimum undergraduate GPA of 3.0. Additional exam requirements/recommendations for international students: Required—TOEFL (minimum score 500 paper-based; 100 iBT). *Application deadline:* Applications are processed on a rolling basis. Application fee: $50. Electronic applications accepted. *Unit head:* Shawn D. Akers, Dean, 434-592-4986. *Application contact:* Jay Bridge, Director of Admissions, 800-424-9595, Fax: 800-628-7977, E-mail: gradadmissions@liberty.edu.

**Liberty University,** School of Business, Lynchburg, VA 24515. Offers accounting (MBA, MS); business administration (MBA); criminal justice (MBA); cyber security (MS); executive leadership (MA); information systems (MS), including information assurance, technology management; international business (MBA, DBA); leadership (DBA); marketing (MBA, MS, DBA), including digital marketing and advertising (MS), project management (MS), public relations (MS), sports marketing and media (MS); project management (MBA, DBA); public administration (MBA); public relations (MBA). *Program availability:* Part-time, online learning. *Students:* 1,458 full-time (807 women), 4,188 part-time (2,041 women); includes 1,372 minority (1,060 Black or African American, non-Hispanic/Latino; 19 American Indian or Alaska Native, non-Hispanic/Latino; 85 Asian, non-Hispanic/Latino; 75 Hispanic/Latino; 10 Native Hawaiian or other Pacific Islander, non-Hispanic/Latino; 123 Two or more races, non-Hispanic/Latino), 124 international. Average age 35. 5,424 applicants, 45% accepted, 1242 enrolled. In 2016, 1,859 master's, 87 other advanced degrees awarded. *Entrance requirements:* For master's, minimum undergraduate GPA of 3.0, 15 hours of upper-level business courses. Additional exam requirements/recommendations for international students: Required—TOEFL (minimum score 600 paper-based; 100 iBT). *Application deadline:* Applications are processed on a rolling basis. Application fee: $50. Electronic applications accepted. *Expenses:* Contact institution. *Financial support:* Applicants required to submit FAFSA. *Unit head:* Dr. Scott Hicks, Dean, 434-592-4808, Fax: 434-582-2366, E-mail: smhicks@liberty.edu. *Application contact:* Jay Bridge, Director of Graduate Admissions, 800-424-9595, Fax: 800-628-7977, E-mail: gradadmissions@liberty.edu.
Website: http://www.liberty.edu/academics/business/index.cfm?PID=149

**Lincoln University,** Graduate Studies, Jefferson City, MO 65101. Offers business administration (MBA), including accounting, management, management information systems, public administration/policy; elementary teaching (M Ed); environmental science (MS); guidance and counseling (M Ed), including community/agency counseling, elementary school, secondary school; higher education (MA); history (MA); integrated agricultural systems (MS); middle school (M Ed); natural sciences (MS); secondary teaching (M Ed); sociology (MA); sociology/criminal justice (MA). *Program availability:* Part-time, evening/weekend, 100% online, blended/hybrid learning. *Students:* 50 full-time (29 women), 68 part-time (39 women); includes 40 minority (37 Black or African American, non-Hispanic/Latino; 1 Asian, non-Hispanic/Latino; 2 Two or more races, non-Hispanic/Latino), 14 international. Average age 33. 75 applicants, 80% accepted, 34 enrolled. In 2016, 51 master's awarded. *Degree requirements:* For master's, comprehensive exam, thesis optional. *Entrance requirements:* For master's, GRE, MAT or GMAT, minimum GPA of 2.75 overall, 3.0 in courses related to specialization; 3 letters of recommendation; minimum C average in English composition; personal statement of purpose. Additional exam requirements/recommendations for international students: Required—TOEFL (minimum score 500 paper-based; 61 iBT), IELTS (minimum score 5.5), Michigan English Language Assessment Battery (minimum score 80). *Application deadline:* For fall admission, 7/1 priority date for domestic students, 5/1 priority date for international students; for spring admission, 11/1 priority date for domestic students, 10/1 priority date for international students; for summer admission, 6/1 priority date for domestic students. Applications are processed on a rolling basis. Application fee: $30. Electronic applications accepted. *Expenses:* Tuition, state resident: full-time $6840; part-time $5130 per year. Tuition, nonresident: full-time $12,720; part-time $9540 per year. *Required fees:* $852; $811 per unit. Tuition and fees vary according to course load. *Financial support:* In 2016–17, 2 fellowships with tuition reimbursements, 8 research assistantships with tuition reimbursements were awarded; Federal Work-Study, scholarships/grants, and unspecified assistantships also available. Support available to part-time students. Financial award application deadline: 3/1; financial award applicants required to submit FAFSA. *Unit head:* Dr. Rolundus R. Rice, Dean, 573-681-5247, Fax: 573-681-5106, E-mail: gradschool@lincolnu.edu. *Application contact:* Irasema Steck, Administrative Assistant, 573-681-5247, Fax: 573-681-5106,

E-mail: gradschool@lincolnu.edu.
Website: http://www.lincolnu.edu/web/graduate-studies/graduate-studies

**Lindenwood University,** Graduate Programs, Plaster School of Business and Entrepreneurship, St. Charles, MO 63301-1695. Offers accountancy (M Acc); accounting (MBA); business administration (MBA); entrepreneurial studies (MBA); finance (MBA, MS); human resource management (MBA); international business (MBA); leadership (MA); management (MBA); marketing (MBA, MS); nonprofit administration (MA); public administration (MBA); sport management (MA); supply chain management (MBA). *Accreditation:* ACBSP. *Program availability:* Part-time, evening/weekend, 100% online. *Faculty:* 15 full-time (6 women), 25 part-time/adjunct (7 women). *Students:* 197 full-time (97 women), 213 part-time (132 women); includes 81 minority (62 Black or African American, non-Hispanic/Latino; 1 American Indian or Alaska Native, non-Hispanic/Latino; 4 Asian, non-Hispanic/Latino; 9 Hispanic/Latino; 5 Two or more races, non-Hispanic/Latino), 83 international. Average age 31. 279 applicants, 54% accepted, 133 enrolled. In 2016, 269 master's awarded. *Degree requirements:* For master's, comprehensive exam (for some programs), thesis (for some programs), minimum GPA of 3.0. *Entrance requirements:* For master's, interview, minimum undergraduate cumulative GPA of 3.0, letter of recommendation. Additional exam requirements/recommendations for international students: Required—TOEFL (minimum score 550 paper-based; 80 iBT); Recommended—IELTS (minimum score 6.5). *Application deadline:* For fall admission, 8/28 priority date for domestic and international students; for winter admission, 1/8 priority date for domestic and international students; for spring admission, 3/5 for domestic students, 3/5 priority date for international students; for summer admission, 6/4 priority date for domestic and international students. Applications are processed on a rolling basis. Application fee: $30 ($100 for international students). Electronic applications accepted. *Expenses:* Contact institution. *Financial support:* In 2016–17, 256 students received support. Career-related internships or fieldwork, Federal Work-Study, institutionally sponsored loans, scholarships/grants, tuition waivers (partial), and unspecified assistantships available. Financial award application deadline: 6/30; financial award applicants required to submit FAFSA. *Unit head:* Roger Ellis, Dean, School of Business and Entrepreneurship, 636-949-4839, E-mail: rellis@lindenwood.edu. *Application contact:* Tyler Kostich, Director, Evening and Graduate Admissions, 636-949-4138, Fax: 636-949-4109, E-mail: adultadmissions@lindenwood.edu.
Website: http://www.lindenwood.edu/academics/academic-schools/robert-w-plaster-school-of-business-entrepreneurship/

**Lipscomb University,** School of Public Policy, Nashville, TN 37204-3951. Offers leadership and public service (MA). *Faculty:* 6 full-time (2 women), 3 part-time/adjunct (1 woman). *Students:* 22 full-time (15 women); includes 8 minority (7 Black or African American, non-Hispanic/Latino; 1 Hispanic/Latino). Average age 28. *Entrance requirements:* For master's, GRE or GMAT, references, resume, goals statement. Additional exam requirements/recommendations for international students: Required—TOEFL (minimum score 550 paper-based). *Application deadline:* Applications are processed on a rolling basis. Application fee: $50 ($75 for international students). Electronic applications accepted. *Expenses:* $1,290 per hour. *Faculty research:* African American family strengths and their relationship to health and mental health prevention and intervention, application of hope theories, systems theories and positive psychology principles in systems and organizations at multiples levels. *Unit head:* Dr. Kristine LaLonde, Academic Director, 615-966-6692, E-mail: kristine.lalonde@lipscomb.edu. *Application contact:* Amy Goode, New Student Enrollment Manager, 615-966-6691, E-mail: amy.goode@lipscomb.edu.

**London Metropolitan University,** Graduate Programs, London, United Kingdom. Offers applied psychology (M Sc); architecture (MA); biomedical science (M Sc); blood science (M Sc); cancer pharmacology (M Sc); computer networking and cyber security (M Sc); computing and information systems (M Sc); conference interpreting (MA); counter-terrorism studies (M Sc); creative, digital and professional writing (MA); crime, violence and prevention (M Sc); criminology (M Sc); curating contemporary art (MA); data analytics (M Sc); digital media (MA); early childhood studies (MA); education (MA, Ed D); financial services law, regulation and compliance (LL M); food science (M Sc); forensic psychology (M Sc); health and social care management and policy (M Sc); human nutrition (M Sc); human resource management (MA); human rights and international conflict (MA); information technology (M Sc); intelligence and security studies (M Sc); international oil, gas and energy law (LL M); international relations (MA); interpreting (MA); learning and teaching in higher education (MA); legal practice (LL M); media and entertainment law (LL M); organizational and consumer psychology (M Sc); psychological therapy (M Sc); psychology of mental health (M Sc); public health (M Sc); public policy and management (MPA); security studies (M Sc); social work (M Sc); spatial planning and urban design (MA); sports therapy (M Sc); supporting older children and young people with dyslexia (MA); teaching languages (MA), including Arabic, English; translation (MA); woman and child abuse (MA).

**Long Island University–Hudson,** Graduate School, Purchase, NY 10577. Offers autism (Advanced Certificate); childhood education (MS Ed); early childhood education (MS Ed); educational leadership (MS Ed); finance (MBA); health administration (MPA); healthcare sector management (MBA); literacy (MS Ed); management (MBA); marriage and family therapy (MS); mental health counseling (MS), including credentialed alcoholism and substance abuse counselor; middle childhood and adolescence education (MS Ed); pharmaceutics (MS), including cosmetic science, industrial pharmacy; public administration (MPA); school counseling (MS Ed, Advanced Certificate); school psychology (MS Ed); special education (MS Ed); TESOL (all grades) (Advanced Certificate); TESOL and bilingual education (MS Ed); the business of pharmaceutics and biotechnology (MBA). *Program availability:* Part-time, evening/weekend, online learning. *Faculty:* 7 full-time (5 women), 42 part-time/adjunct (25 women). *Students:* 55 full-time (41 women), 158 part-time (123 women); includes 40 minority (8 Black or African American, non-Hispanic/Latino; 1 Asian, non-Hispanic/Latino; 31 Hispanic/Latino). Average age 35. *Entrance requirements:* Additional exam requirements/recommendations for international students: Required—TOEFL (minimum score 550 paper-based; 79 iBT). *Application deadline:* Applications are processed on a rolling basis. Application fee: $50. Electronic applications accepted. *Expenses:* Contact institution. *Unit head:* Dr. Sylvia Blake, Dean and Chief Operating Officer, 914-831-2700, E-mail: westchester@liu.edu. *Application contact:* Cindy Pagnotta, Director of Marketing and Enrollment, 914-831-2701, Fax: 914-251-5959, E-mail: cindy.pagnotta@liu.edu.

**Long Island University–LIU Brooklyn,** School of Business, Public Administration and Information Sciences, Brooklyn, NY 11201-8423. Offers accounting (MBA); accounting (MS); business administration (MBA); computer science (MS); gerontology (Advanced Certificate); health administration (MPA); human resources management (MS); not-for-profit management (Advanced Certificate); public administration (MPA); taxation (MS). *Program availability:* Part-time, evening/weekend, blended/hybrid learning. *Faculty:* 18 full-time (9 women), 32 part-time/adjunct (10 women). *Students:* 275 full-time (150 women), 238 part-time (161 women); includes 281 minority (200 Black or African American, non-Hispanic/Latino; 2 American Indian or Alaska Native, non-Hispanic/Latino; 38 Asian, non-Hispanic/Latino; 36 Hispanic/Latino; 1 Native Hawaiian or other Pacific Islander, non-Hispanic/Latino; 4 Two or more races, non-Hispanic/Latino), 140 international. 796 applicants, 66% accepted, 143 enrolled. In 2016, 185 master's, 17

other advanced degrees awarded. *Entrance requirements:* Additional exam requirements/recommendations for international students: Required—TOEFL (minimum score 527 paper-based; 75 iBT). *Application deadline:* Applications are processed on a rolling basis. Application fee: $50. Electronic applications accepted. *Expenses: Tuition:* Full-time $28,272; part-time $1178 per credit. *Required fees:* $451 per term. Tuition and fees vary according to degree level, program and student level. *Financial support:* In 2016–17, 94 students received support. Career-related internships or fieldwork, Federal Work-Study, institutionally sponsored loans, scholarships/grants, and unspecified assistantships available. Support available to part-time students. Financial award application deadline: 2/15; financial award applicants required to submit FAFSA. *Faculty research:* Corporate social responsibility; executive compensation and corporate governance; combinatorics; secure mobile coding; social equity and justice, particularly among the Latino population; public and healthcare finance. *Unit head:* Dr. Edward Rogoff, Dean, 718-488-1159, E-mail: edward.rogoff@liu.edu. *Application contact:* Gabrielle Gannon, Director of Graduate Admissions, 718-488-1011, Fax: 718-780-6110, E-mail: bkln-admissions@liu.edu.
Website: http://liu.edu/Brooklyn/Academics/School-of-Business-Public-Administration-and-Information-Sciences

**Long Island University–LIU Post,** School of Health Professions and Nursing, Brookville, NY 11548-1300. Offers cardiovascular perfusion (MS); clinical lab sciences (MS); clinical laboratory management (MS); dietetic internship (Advanced Certificate); family nurse practitioner (MS, Advanced Certificate); forensic social work (Advanced Certificate); gerontology (Advanced Certificate); health administration (MPA); medical biology (MS); non-profit management (Advanced Certificate); nursing education (MS); nutrition (MS); public administration (MPA); social work (MSW). *Program availability:* Part-time, evening/weekend, blended/hybrid learning. *Faculty:* 27 full-time (20 women), 43 part-time/adjunct (32 women). *Students:* 251 full-time (184 women), 243 part-time (197 women); includes 179 minority (76 Black or African American, non-Hispanic/Latino; 55 Asian, non-Hispanic/Latino; 42 Hispanic/Latino; 1 Native Hawaiian or other Pacific Islander, non-Hispanic/Latino; 5 Two or more races, non-Hispanic/Latino), 79 international. 581 applicants, 67% accepted, 168 enrolled. In 2016, 185 master's, 29 other advanced degrees awarded. *Degree requirements:* For master's, comprehensive exam (for some programs), thesis (for some programs); for Advanced Certificate, comprehensive exam (for some programs). *Entrance requirements:* Additional exam requirements/recommendations for international students: Required—TOEFL (minimum score 550 paper-based, 75 iBT) or IELTS. *Application deadline:* Applications are processed on a rolling basis. Application fee: $50. Electronic applications accepted. *Expenses: Tuition:* Full-time $28,272; part-time $1178 per credit. *Required fees:* $451 per term. Tuition and fees vary according to degree level and program. *Financial support:* In 2016–17, 5 research assistantships with partial tuition reimbursements (averaging $725 per year), 3 teaching assistantships with partial tuition reimbursements (averaging $800 per year) were awarded; career-related internships or fieldwork, Federal Work-Study, institutionally sponsored loans, scholarships/grants, and unspecified assistantships also available. Support available to part-time students. Financial award application deadline: 2/15; financial award applicants required to submit FAFSA. *Faculty research:* Cancer gene regulation, childhood obesity, host-pathogen interaction, interprofessional simulation, interstitial cystitis. *Total annual research expenditures:* $35,000. *Unit head:* Dr. Stacy Gropack, Dean, 516-299-2485, Fax: 516-299-2527, E-mail: post-shpn@liu.edu. *Application contact:* Carol Zerah, Director of Graduate Admissions, 516-299-2900, Fax: 516-299-2137, E-mail: post-enroll@liu.edu.
Website: http://liu.edu/post/health

**Louisiana State University and Agricultural & Mechanical College,** Graduate School, E. J. Ourso College of Business, Public Administration Institute, Baton Rouge, LA 70803. Offers MPA, JD/MPA. *Accreditation:* NASPAA.

**Louisiana State University and Agricultural & Mechanical College,** Graduate School, Manship School of Mass Communication, Baton Rouge, LA 70803. Offers MMC, PhD, JD/MMC. *Accreditation:* ACEJMC.

**Marist College,** Graduate Programs, School of Management, Program in Public Administration, Poughkeepsie, NY 12601-1387. Offers MPA. *Accreditation:* NASPAA. *Program availability:* Part-time, evening/weekend, online learning. *Entrance requirements:* For master's, GRE General Test, resume. Additional exam requirements/recommendations for international students: Required—TOEFL (minimum score 550 paper-based; 80 iBT); Recommended—IELTS (minimum score 6.5). Electronic applications accepted. *Faculty research:* Public policy analysis, health administration.

**Marshall University,** Academic Affairs Division, College of Liberal Arts, Department of Political Science, Huntington, WV 25755. Offers MA, MPA. *Degree requirements:* For master's, thesis optional. *Entrance requirements:* For master's, GRE General Test.

**Marywood University,** Academic Affairs, College of Health and Human Services, School of Social Work, Program in Public Administration, Scranton, PA 18509-1598. Offers MPA. *Program availability:* Part-time. Electronic applications accepted.

**McMaster University,** School of Graduate Studies, Faculty of Social Sciences, Department of Political Science, Hamilton, ON L8S 4M2, Canada. Offers international relations (PhD); political science (MA); public and the global economy (MA); public policy (PhD); public policy and administration (MA). MA program in public policy and administration offered jointly with University of Guelph. *Program availability:* Part-time. *Degree requirements:* For master's, thesis or alternative. *Entrance requirements:* For master's, minimum B+ average. Additional exam requirements/recommendations for international students: Required—TOEFL (minimum score 580 paper-based). *Faculty research:* Organizational theory, internationalization of public policy, water resource policies, political interest intermediation, comparative politics.

**Metropolitan College of New York,** Program in Public Administration, New York, NY 10006. Offers emergency and disaster management (MPA); public affairs and administration (MPA). *Program availability:* Evening/weekend. *Students:* 120 full-time (85 women), 10 part-time (4 women); includes 108 minority (76 Black or African American, non-Hispanic/Latino; 5 Asian, non-Hispanic/Latino; 26 Hispanic/Latino; 1 Native Hawaiian or other Pacific Islander, non-Hispanic/Latino), 2 international. Average age 37. In 2016, 118 master's awarded. *Degree requirements:* For master's, thesis. *Entrance requirements:* For master's, appropriate work experience, interview, minimum GPA of 2.7, internship or job in administrative setting. Additional exam requirements/recommendations for international students: Required—TOEFL (minimum score 600 paper-based). *Application deadline:* For fall admission, 7/30 priority date for domestic students, 7/1 for international students; for winter admission, 11/30 priority date for domestic students, 11/1 for international students; for spring admission, 3/30 priority date for domestic students, 3/1 for international students. Applications are processed on a rolling basis. Application fee: $45. Electronic applications accepted. *Expenses:* Contact institution. *Financial support:* Fellowships with tuition reimbursements, career-related internships or fieldwork, scholarships/grants, and tuition waivers (partial) available. Financial award application deadline: 8/15; financial award applicants required to submit FAFSA. *Faculty research:* Transnational politics and culture, women and social policy, confidentiality in the human services, concepts of marginality, ethics in social policy. *Unit head:* Prof. Humphrey Crookendale, Dean, Graduate School for Public Affairs Administration, 212-343-1234 Ext. 2209, E-mail: hcrookendale@mcny.edu. *Application contact:* Steebo Varghese, Assistant Director of Admissions, 212-343-1234 Ext. 2708, Fax: 212-343-8474, E-mail: svarghese@mcny.edu.
Website: http://www.metropolitan.edu/

**Metropolitan State University,** College of Management, St. Paul, MN 55106-5000. Offers business administration (MBA, DBA); database administration (Graduate Certificate); healthcare information technology management (Graduate Certificate); information assurance security (Graduate Certificate); management information systems (MMIS); MIS generalist (Graduate Certificate); MIS systems analysis and design (Graduate Certificate); project management (Graduate Certificate); public and nonprofit administration (MPNA). *Program availability:* Part-time, evening/weekend. *Degree requirements:* For master's, thesis optional, computer language (MMIS). *Entrance requirements:* For master's, GMAT (for MBA), resume. Additional exam requirements/recommendations for international students: Required—TOEFL (minimum score 550 paper-based). Electronic applications accepted. *Faculty research:* Yugoslav economic system, workers' cooperatives, participative management and job enrichment, global business systems.

**Mid-America Christian University,** Program in Public Administration, Oklahoma City, OK 73170-4504. Offers MA. *Entrance requirements:* For master's, bachelor's degree from a regionally accredited college or university, minimum overall cumulative GPA of 2.75 of bachelor course work. Additional exam requirements/recommendations for international students: Required—TOEFL (minimum score 550 paper-based).

**Middlebury Institute of International Studies at Monterey,** Graduate School of International Policy and Management, Program in Public Administration, Monterey, CA 93940-2691. Offers MPA. *Degree requirements:* For master's, one foreign language. *Entrance requirements:* For master's, minimum GPA of 3.0, proficiency in a foreign language. Additional exam requirements/recommendations for international students: Required—TOEFL (minimum score 550 paper-based; 80 iBT). Electronic applications accepted. *Expenses: Tuition:* Full-time $38,250; part-time $1820 per credit. *Required fees:* $78 per semester.

**Minnesota State University Mankato,** College of Graduate Studies and Research, College of Social and Behavioral Sciences, Department of Government, Program in Public Administration, Mankato, MN 56001. Offers MPA. *Accreditation:* NASPAA. *Students:* 12 full-time (7 women), 19 part-time (7 women). *Degree requirements:* For master's, one foreign language, comprehensive exam, thesis or alternative. *Entrance requirements:* For master's, minimum GPA of 3.0 during previous 2 years. Additional exam requirements/recommendations for international students: Required—TOEFL. *Application deadline:* For fall admission, 3/1 for domestic students. Applications are processed on a rolling basis. Application fee: $40. Electronic applications accepted. *Financial support:* Research assistantships with full tuition reimbursements, teaching assistantships with full tuition reimbursements, and unspecified assistantships available. Financial award application deadline: 3/15; financial award applicants required to submit FAFSA. *Unit head:* Kevin Parsneau, Director, 507-389-5232, Fax: 507-389-6377, E-mail: kevin.parsneau@mnsu.edu.
Website: http://sbs.mnsu.edu/government/graduate/publicadmin/

**Mississippi State University,** College of Arts and Sciences, Department of Political Science and Public Administration, Mississippi State, MS 39762. Offers political science (MA); public policy and administration (MPPA, PhD). *Accreditation:* NASPAA (one or more programs are accredited). *Program availability:* Evening/weekend, blended/hybrid learning. *Faculty:* 14 full-time (4 women), 1 part-time/adjunct (0 women). *Students:* 34 full-time (18 women), 35 part-time (18 women); includes 26 minority (22 Black or African American, non-Hispanic/Latino; 1 American Indian or Alaska Native, non-Hispanic/Latino; 3 Hispanic/Latino), 4 international. Average age 31. 33 applicants, 61% accepted, 18 enrolled. In 2016, 22 master's, 7 doctorates awarded. *Degree requirements:* For master's, thesis optional, comprehensive oral or written exam; for doctorate, thesis/dissertation, comprehensive oral and written exam. *Entrance requirements:* For master's, GRE, minimum GPA of 3.0 on the last two years of undergraduate courses or graduate work; for doctorate, GRE General Test, minimum graduate GPA of 3.35. Additional exam requirements/recommendations for international students: Required—TOEFL (minimum score 600 paper-based; 100 iBT); Recommended—IELTS (minimum score 7.5). *Application deadline:* For fall admission, 8/1 priority date for domestic students, 5/1 for international students; for spring admission, 12/1 priority date for domestic students, 9/1 for international students. Applications are processed on a rolling basis. Application fee: $60. Electronic applications accepted. *Expenses:* Tuition, state resident: full-time $7670; part-time $852.50 per credit hour. Tuition, nonresident: full-time $20,790; part-time $2310.50 per credit hour. Part-time tuition and fees vary according to course load. *Financial support:* In 2016–17, 6 research assistantships with full tuition reimbursements (averaging $9,085 per year), 2 teaching assistantships with full tuition reimbursements (averaging $8,920 per year) were awarded; Federal Work-Study, institutionally sponsored loans, scholarships/grants, and unspecified assistantships also available. Financial award application deadline: 4/1; financial award applicants required to submit FAFSA. *Faculty research:* American politics, international relations, state and local government, comparative government, public administration. *Total annual research expenditures:* $977,000. *Unit head:* Dr. P. Edward French, Interim Department Head, 662-325-2711, Fax: 662-325-2716, E-mail: efrench@pspa.msstate.edu. *Application contact:* Nathan Drake, Admissions and Enrollment Assistant, 662-325-3804, E-mail: ndrake@grad.msstate.edu.
Website: http://www.pspa.msstate.edu/

**Missouri State University,** Graduate College, College of Humanities and Public Affairs, Department of Political Science, Program in Public Administration, Springfield, MO 65897. Offers MPA. *Accreditation:* NASPAA. *Program availability:* Part-time. *Students:* 11 full-time (4 women), 6 part-time (4 women), 4 international. Average age 31. 14 applicants, 71% accepted, 7 enrolled. In 2016, 10 master's awarded. *Degree requirements:* For master's, comprehensive exam, thesis or alternative, internship. *Entrance requirements:* For master's, GRE, minimum GPA of 3.0. Additional exam requirements/recommendations for international students: Required—TOEFL (minimum score 550 paper-based; 79 iBT), IELTS (minimum score 6). *Application deadline:* For fall admission, 7/20 priority date for domestic students, 5/1 for international students; for spring admission, 12/20 priority date for domestic students, 9/1 for international students; for summer admission, 5/20 priority date for domestic students. Applications are processed on a rolling basis. Application fee: $35 ($50 for international students). Electronic applications accepted. *Expenses:* Tuition, state resident: full-time $5830. Tuition, nonresident: full-time $10,708. *Required fees:* $1130. Tuition and fees vary according to class time, course level, course load and program. *Financial support:* Career-related internships or fieldwork, Federal Work-Study, institutionally sponsored loans, scholarships/grants, and unspecified assistantships available. Support available to part-time students. Financial award application deadline: 3/31; financial award applicants required to submit FAFSA. *Faculty research:* Public management, environmental policy, health care policy, law and religion. *Unit head:* Dr. George Connor, Department Head, 417-836-5630, Fax: 417-836-6655, E-mail: georgeconnor@missouristate.edu. *Application contact:* Michael Edwards, Coordinator of Graduate Admissions, 417-836-5330, Fax: 417-836-6200, E-mail:

## Public Administration

michaeledwards@missouristate.edu.
Website: http://polsci.missouristate.edu/mpa/

**Missouri State University,** Graduate College, Interdisciplinary Program in Professional Studies, Springfield, MO 65897. Offers administrative studies (Certificate); applied communication (MS); criminal justice (MS); environmental management (MS); homeland security (MS); individualized (MS); screenwriting and producing (MS); sports management (MS). *Program availability:* Part-time, evening/weekend, 100% online, blended/hybrid learning. *Students:* 60 full-time (34 women), 66 part-time (29 women); includes 17 minority (7 Black or African American, non-Hispanic/Latino; 1 Asian, non-Hispanic/Latino; 5 Hispanic/Latino; 4 Two or more races, non-Hispanic/Latino), 43 international. Average age 33. 76 applicants, 58% accepted, 38 enrolled. In 2016, 48 master's awarded. *Degree requirements:* For master's, comprehensive exam, thesis or alternative. *Entrance requirements:* For master's, GRE, GMAT (if GPA less than 3.0). Additional exam requirements/recommendations for international students: Required—TOEFL (minimum score 550 paper-based; 79 iBT), IELTS (minimum score 6). *Application deadline:* For fall admission, 7/15 priority date for domestic students; for spring admission, 12/1 priority date for domestic students; for summer admission, 5/1 for domestic students. Applications are processed on a rolling basis. Application fee: $35 ($50 for international students). Electronic applications accepted. *Expenses:* Tuition, state resident: full-time $5830. Tuition, nonresident: full-time $10,708. *Required fees:* $1130. Tuition and fees vary according to class time, course level, course load and program. *Financial support:* Career-related internships or fieldwork, Federal Work-Study, institutionally sponsored loans, scholarships/grants, and unspecified assistantships available. Support available to part-time students. Financial award application deadline: 3/31; financial award applicants required to submit FAFSA. *Unit head:* Dr. Gerald Masterson, Program Director, 417-836-5251, Fax: 417-836-6888, E-mail: mps@missouristate.edu. *Application contact:* Michael Edwards, Coordinator of Graduate Admissions, 417-836-5330, Fax: 417-836-6200, E-mail: michaeledwards@missouristate.edu
Website: http://mps.missouristate.edu

**Montana State University,** The Graduate School, College of Letters and Science, Department of Political Science, Bozeman, MT 59717. Offers public administration (MPA). Program offered jointly with The University of Montana. *Program availability:* Part-time. *Degree requirements:* For master's, comprehensive exam, thesis (for some programs). *Entrance requirements:* For master's, GRE General Test. Additional exam requirements/recommendations for international students: Required—TOEFL (minimum score 550 paper-based). Electronic applications accepted. *Faculty research:* National resource policy, political economy of agriculture, qualitative methods, organizational theory.

**Morehead State University,** Graduate Programs, Institute for Regional Analysis and Public Policy, Morehead, KY 40351. Offers public administration (MPA). *Entrance requirements:* For master's, GRE. Additional exam requirements/recommendations for international students: Required—TOEFL (minimum score 500 paper-based). Electronic applications accepted.

**National University,** Academic Affairs, School of Professional Studies, La Jolla, CA 92037-1011. Offers criminal justice (MCJ); digital cinema (MFA); digital journalism (MA); juvenile justice (MS); public administration (MPA), including human resource management. *Program availability:* Part-time, evening/weekend, 100% online, blended/hybrid learning. *Faculty:* 21 full-time (8 women), 35 part-time/adjunct (9 women). *Students:* 280 full-time (155 women), 100 part-time (54 women); includes 226 minority (76 Black or African American, non-Hispanic/Latino; 1 American Indian or Alaska Native, non-Hispanic/Latino; 27 Asian, non-Hispanic/Latino; 102 Hispanic/Latino; 3 Native Hawaiian or other Pacific Islander, non-Hispanic/Latino; 17 Two or more races, non-Hispanic/Latino), 3 international. Average age 37. In 2016, 21 master's awarded. *Degree requirements:* For master's, thesis (for some programs). *Entrance requirements:* For master's, interview, minimum GPA of 2.5. Additional exam requirements/recommendations for international students: Required—TOEFL (minimum score 550 paper-based; 79 iBT), IELTS (minimum score 6). *Application deadline:* Applications are processed on a rolling basis. Application fee: $60 ($65 for international students). Electronic applications accepted. *Financial support:* Career-related internships or fieldwork, institutionally sponsored loans, scholarships/grants, and tuition waivers (partial) available. Support available to part-time students. Financial award application deadline: 6/30; financial award applicants required to submit FAFSA. *Unit head:* School of Professional Studies, 800-628-8648, E-mail: sops@nu.edu. *Application contact:* Brandon Jouganatos, Vice President for Enrollment Services, 800-628-8648, E-mail: advisor@nu.edu.
Website: http://www.nu.edu/OurPrograms/School-of-Professional-Studies.html

**New Charter University,** College of Public Policy and Administration, Program in Public Administration, Salt Lake City, UT 84101. Offers MPA. *Program availability:* Part-time, evening/weekend, online learning. *Entrance requirements:* For master's, course work in calculus, statistics. Additional exam requirements/recommendations for international students: Required—TOEFL (minimum score 550 paper-based). Electronic applications accepted.

**New Mexico State University,** College of Arts and Sciences, Department of Government, Las Cruces, NM 88003. Offers government (MA); public administration (MPA). *Accreditation:* NASPAA (one or more programs are accredited). *Program availability:* Part-time. *Faculty:* 8 full-time (4 women), 1 (woman) part-time/adjunct. *Students:* 22 full-time (9 women), 13 part-time (7 women); includes 22 minority (3 Black or African American, non-Hispanic/Latino; 18 Hispanic/Latino; 1 Two or more races, non-Hispanic/Latino), 1 international. Average age 31. 17 applicants, 65% accepted, 7 enrolled. In 2016, 14 master's awarded. *Degree requirements:* For master's, comprehensive exam (for some programs), thesis optional. *Entrance requirements:* For master's, GRE (if GPA less than 3.0), writing sample, 3 letters of recommendation, resume. Additional exam requirements/recommendations for international students: Required—TOEFL (minimum score 550 paper-based; 79 iBT), IELTS (minimum score 6.5). *Application deadline:* For fall admission, 10/1 for domestic and international students; for spring admission, 3/1 for domestic and international students; for summer admission, 3/1 for domestic and international students. Application fee: $40 ($50 for international students). Electronic applications accepted. *Expenses:* Tuition, state resident: full-time $4086. Tuition, nonresident: full-time $14,254. *Required fees:* $853. Tuition and fees vary according to course load. *Financial support:* In 2016–17, 15 students received support, including 10 teaching assistantships (averaging $12,723 per year); career-related internships or fieldwork, Federal Work-Study, scholarships/grants, health care benefits, and unspecified assistantships also available. Support available to part-time students. Financial award application deadline: 3/1. *Faculty research:* U.S.-Mexico border studies, public administration and policy, international relations, Latin America, American politics and theory. *Total annual research expenditures:* $6,605. *Unit head:* Dr. Neil Harvey, Department Head, 575-646-4935, Fax: 575-646-2052, E-mail: nharvey@nmsu.edu. *Application contact:* Dr. Neil Harvey, Director, Master of Arts in Government Program, 575-646-4935, Fax: 575-646-2052, E-mail: nharvey@nmsu.edu.
Website: http://deptofgov.nmsu.edu

**New York University,** Robert F. Wagner Graduate School of Public Service, Executive Master of Public Administration Program, New York, NY 10010. Offers global public

policy and management (EMPA); MSW/EMPA. EMPA in global public policy and management offered jointly with University College London. *Accreditation:* AACSB. *Program availability:* Part-time. *Entrance requirements:* Additional exam requirements/recommendations for international students: Required—TOEFL (minimum score 100 iBT), IELTS (minimum score 7.5), TWE. Electronic applications accepted. *Expenses:* Contact institution.

**New York University,** Robert F. Wagner Graduate School of Public Service, Program in Public Administration, New York, NY 10010. Offers public administration (PhD); public and nonprofit management and policy (MPA, Advanced Certificate), including financial management and public finance (MPA), international policy and management (MPA), management for public and nonprofit organizations, public policy analysis, social impact, innovation, and investment (MPA); JD/MPA; MBA/MPA; MPA/MA. *Accreditation:* NASPAA (one or more programs are accredited). *Program availability:* Part-time. *Degree requirements:* For master's, thesis or alternative, capstone end event; for doctorate, one foreign language, comprehensive exam, thesis/dissertation, preliminary qualifying examination. *Entrance requirements:* Additional exam requirements/recommendations for international students: Required—TOEFL (minimum score 100 iBT), IELTS (minimum score 7.5), TWE. Electronic applications accepted. *Expenses:* Contact institution.

**North Carolina Central University,** College of Behavioral and Social Sciences, Department of Public Administration, Durham, NC 27707-3129. Offers MPA. *Program availability:* Part-time, evening/weekend. *Degree requirements:* For master's, one foreign language, comprehensive exam, thesis or alternative. *Entrance requirements:* For master's, GRE, minimum GPA of 3.0 in major, 2.5 overall. Additional exam requirements/recommendations for international students: Required—TOEFL.

**North Carolina State University,** Graduate School, College of Humanities and Social Sciences, School of Public and International Affairs, Program in Public Administration, Raleigh, NC 27695. Offers MPA, PhD. *Accreditation:* NASPAA. *Degree requirements:* For master's, thesis optional; for doctorate, thesis/dissertation. *Entrance requirements:* For master's, GRE General Test, minimum GPA of 3.0 during previous 2 years; for doctorate, GRE General Test. Electronic applications accepted. *Faculty research:* Public budgeting, human resources, public information technology, nonprofit management, environmental policy.

**Northeastern University,** College of Social Sciences and Humanities, Boston, MA 02115. Offers criminology and criminal justice (MSCJ); criminology and justice policy (PhD); economics (MA, PhD); English (MA, PhD); international affairs (MA); law and public policy (PhD); political science (MA, PhD); public administration (MPA); public history (MA); public policy (MPP); security and resilience studies (MS); sociology (MA, PhD); urban and regional policy (MS); urban informatics (MS); world history (MA, PhD); JD/MS. *Program availability:* Online learning. *Faculty:* 234 full-time (114 women), 55 part-time/adjunct (34 women). *Students:* 427 full-time (239 women), 77 part-time (42 women). In 2016, 143 master's, 38 doctorates awarded. *Degree requirements:* For doctorate, variable foreign language requirement, comprehensive exam, thesis/dissertation. *Entrance requirements:* For master's and doctorate, GRE. Additional exam requirements/recommendations for international students: Required—TOEFL, IELTS. Application fee: $75. Electronic applications accepted. *Expenses:* $1,295 per credit. *Financial support:* Teaching assistantships, career-related internships or fieldwork, scholarships/grants, health care benefits, tuition waivers (full and partial), and unspecified assistantships available. Support available to part-time students. Financial award applicants required to submit FAFSA. *Unit head:* Dr. Uta Poiger, Dean, 617-373-5173. *Application contact:* Amber Crowe, Administrative Coordinator, 617-373-5990, Fax: 617-373-7281, E-mail: gradcssh@northeastern.edu.
Website: http://www.northeastern.edu/cssh/graduate

**Northern Arizona University,** Graduate College, College of Social and Behavioral Sciences, Department of Politics and International Affairs, Flagstaff, AZ 86011. Offers political science (MA, PhD); public administration (MPA); public management (Certificate). *Program availability:* Part-time. *Degree requirements:* For master's, comprehensive exam (for some programs), thesis optional; for doctorate, one foreign language, comprehensive exam, thesis/dissertation. *Entrance requirements:* For master's, GRE (minimum 70th percentile ranking in each testing area preferred); for doctorate, GRE (minimum score in 70th percentile in each testing area preferred). Additional exam requirements/recommendations for international students: Required—TOEFL (minimum score 550 paper-based; 80 iBT), IELTS (minimum score 7). Electronic applications accepted. *Expenses:* Tuition, state resident: full-time $8971; part-time $444 per credit hour. Tuition, nonresident: full-time $20,958; part-time $1164 per credit hour. *Required fees:* $1018; $644 per credit hour. Tuition and fees vary according to course load, campus/location and program.

**Northern Illinois University,** Graduate School, College of Liberal Arts and Sciences, Department of Public Administration, De Kalb, IL 60115-2854. Offers MPA. *Accreditation:* NASPAA. *Program availability:* Part-time, evening/weekend. *Faculty:* 5 full-time (1 woman), 3 part-time/adjunct (1 woman). *Students:* 49 full-time (19 women), 36 part-time (14 women); includes 19 minority (6 Black or African American, non-Hispanic/Latino; 1 Asian, non-Hispanic/Latino; 10 Hispanic/Latino; 2 Two or more races, non-Hispanic/Latino), 4 international. Average age 30. 62 applicants, 60% accepted, 27 enrolled. In 2016, 24 master's awarded. *Degree requirements:* For master's, comprehensive exam, internship, research paper. *Entrance requirements:* For master's, GRE General Test, minimum GPA of 2.75, 9 hours in social science. Additional exam requirements/recommendations for international students: Required—TOEFL (minimum score 550 paper-based). *Application deadline:* For fall admission, 3/1 priority date for domestic students, 5/1 for international students; for spring admission, 10/1 priority date for domestic students, 10/1 for international students. Applications are processed on a rolling basis. Application fee: $40. Electronic applications accepted. *Financial support:* In 2016–17, 18 research assistantships with full tuition reimbursements, 2 teaching assistantships were awarded; fellowships with full tuition reimbursements, career-related internships or fieldwork, Federal Work-Study, scholarships/grants, tuition waivers (full), and unspecified assistantships also available. Support available to part-time students. Financial award applicants required to submit FAFSA. *Faculty research:* Urban service and management, manpower public policy, performance appraisal, bureaucratic politics. *Unit head:* Dr. Kurt Thurmaier, Chair, 815-753-0311, Fax: 815-753-2539, E-mail: kthur@niu.edu. *Application contact:* Graduate School Office, 815-753-0395, E-mail: gradsch@niu.edu.
Website: http://www.niu.edu/pub_ad/

**Northern Kentucky University,** Office of Graduate Programs, College of Arts and Sciences, Program in Public Administration, Highland Heights, KY 41099. Offers non-profit management (Certificate); public administration (MPA). *Accreditation:* NASPAA. *Program availability:* Part-time. *Degree requirements:* For master's, 39 semester hours, including completion of the capstone course. *Entrance requirements:* For master's, GRE, minimum GPA of 2.5, letters of references, portfolios; for Certificate, minimum GPA of 2.0. Additional exam requirements/recommendations for international students: Required—TOEFL (minimum score 79 iBT); Recommended—IELTS (minimum score 6.5). Electronic applications accepted. *Faculty research:* Nonprofit management, human resource management, urban planning, service-learning, homeland security.

**Northern Michigan University,** Office of Graduate Education and Research, College of Health Sciences and Professional Studies, School of Education, Leadership and Public Service, Marquette, MI 49855-5301. Offers administration and supervision (MAE); elementary education (MAE); higher education in student affairs (MA); instruction (MAE); learning disabilities (MAE); public administration (MPA), including criminal justice administration, human resource administration, public administration, public management, state and local government; reading education (MAE), including reading, reading specialist; science education (MS); secondary education (MAE). *Accreditation:* TEAC. *Program availability:* Part-time, online learning. *Degree requirements:* For master's, thesis, (for some programs). *Entrance requirements:* For master's, minimum GPA of 3.0. Additional exam requirements/recommendations for international students: Required—TOEFL (minimum score 550 paper-based; 79 iBT), IELTS (minimum score 6.5). Electronic applications accepted.

**Northwestern University,** School of Professional Studies, Program in Public Policy and Administration, Evanston, IL 60208. Offers global policy (MA); health services policy (MA); public administration (MA); public policy (MA). *Program availability:* Online learning.

**Norwich University,** College of Graduate and Continuing Studies, Master of Public Administration Program, Northfield, VT 05663. Offers criminal justice and public safety (MPA); fiscal management (MPA); international development and influence (MPA); municipal governance (MPA); nonprofit management (MPA); policy analysis and analytics (MPA); public administration leadership and crisis management (MPA); public works and sustainability (MPA). *Program availability:* Evening/weekend, online only, mostly all online with a week-long residency requirement. *Faculty:* 13 part-time/adjunct (5 women). *Students:* 63 full-time (23 women); includes 9 minority (5 Black or African American, non-Hispanic/Latino; 1 Asian, non-Hispanic/Latino; 1 Hispanic/Latino; 2 Two or more races, non-Hispanic/Latino). Average age 38. 23 applicants, 100% accepted, 15 enrolled. In 2016, 38 master's awarded. *Degree requirements:* For master's, capstone. *Entrance requirements:* For master's, minimum undergraduate GPA of 2.75. Additional exam requirements/recommendations for international students: Required—TOEFL (minimum score 550 paper-based; 80 iBT), IELTS (minimum score 6.5). *Application deadline:* For fall admission, 8/14 for domestic and international students; for winter admission, 11/13 for domestic and international students; for spring admission, 2/12 for domestic and international students; for summer admission, 5/15 for domestic and international students. Electronic applications accepted. *Expenses:* Contact institution. *Financial support:* In 2016–17, 21 students received support. Scholarships/grants available. Financial award application deadline: 8/4; financial award applicants required to submit FAFSA. *Unit head:* Dr. Rosemarie Pelletier, Program Director, 802-485-2767, Fax: 802-485-2533, E-mail: rpellet2@norwich.edu. *Application contact:* Admissions Advisor, 800-460-5597 Ext. 3377, Fax: 802-485-2533, E-mail: mpa@online.norwich.edu.
Website: https://online.norwich.edu/degree-programs/masters/master-public-administration/overview

**Notre Dame de Namur University,** Division of Academic Affairs, School of Business and Management, Program in Public Administration, Belmont, CA 94002-1908. Offers human resource management (MPA); public administration (MPA); public affairs administration (MPA); social enterprise (MPA). *Program availability:* Part-time, evening/weekend, online learning. *Entrance requirements:* For master's, interview, minimum GPA of 2.5. Additional exam requirements/recommendations for international students: Required—TOEFL (minimum score 550 paper-based; 79 iBT). Electronic applications accepted.

**Nova Southeastern University,** H. Wayne Huizenga College of Business and Entrepreneurship, Fort Lauderdale, FL 33314-7796. Offers accounting (M Acc); business intelligence/analytics (MBA); entrepreneurship (MBA); finance (MBA); human resource management (MBA); international business (MBA); management (MBA); marketing (MBA); process improvement (MBA); public administration (MPA); real estate development (MS); sport revenue generation (MBA); supply chain management (MBA); taxation (M Tax). *Program availability:* Part-time, evening/weekend, 100% online, blended/hybrid learning. *Faculty:* 65 full-time (26 women), 111 part-time/adjunct (74 women). *Students:* 2,242 full-time (1,400 women), 425 part-time (239 women); includes 1,798 minority (734 Black or African American, non-Hispanic/Latino; 5 American Indian or Alaska Native, non-Hispanic/Latino; 110 Asian, non-Hispanic/Latino; 890 Hispanic/Latino; 2 Native Hawaiian or other Pacific Islander, non-Hispanic/Latino; 57 Two or more races, non-Hispanic/Latino), 255 international. Average age 34. 1,422 applicants, 64% accepted, 672 enrolled. In 2016, 971 master's awarded. *Degree requirements:* For master's, thesis optional. *Entrance requirements:* For master's, GMAT or GRE (depending on undergraduate GPA), official transcripts from all schools attended while in pursuit of bachelor's degree; minimum GPA of 2.5 from regionally-accredited institution. Additional exam requirements/recommendations for international students: Required—TOEFL (minimum score 550 paper-based; 79 iBT), IELTS (minimum score 6), PTE (minimum score 54). *Application deadline:* For fall admission, 8/5 priority date for domestic students, 7/29 priority date for international students; for winter admission, 12/16 priority date for domestic students, 12/9 priority date for international students; for summer admission, 4/21 priority date for domestic and international students. Applications are processed on a rolling basis. Application fee: $50. Electronic applications accepted. *Expenses:* Contact institution. *Financial support:* In 2016–17, 325 students received support. Federal Work-Study and scholarships/grants available. Support available to part-time students. Financial award application deadline: 4/15; financial award applicants required to submit FAFSA. *Faculty research:* Reputation management, call centers, international social capital, corporate earnings guidance, corporate governance. *Unit head:* Dr. J. Preston Jones, Dean, 954-262-5127, E-mail: prestonj@nova.edu. *Application contact:* Zeida Rodriquez, Associate Director of Enrollment Services, 954-262-5163, Fax: 954-262-3822, E-mail: zeida@nova.edu.
Website: http://www.huizenga.nova.edu

**Oakland University,** Graduate Study and Lifelong Learning, College of Arts and Sciences, Department of Political Science, Rochester, MI 48309-4401. Offers local government management (Graduate Certificate); non-profit and organizational management (PMC); public administration (MPA). *Accreditation:* NASPAA. *Program availability:* Part-time, evening/weekend. *Entrance requirements:* For master's, minimum GPA of 3.0. Additional exam requirements/recommendations for international students: Required—TOEFL (minimum score 550 paper-based). Electronic applications accepted.

**The Ohio State University,** Graduate School, John Glenn College of Public Affairs, Columbus, OH 43210. Offers public administration (MA, MPA); public policy and management (PhD). *Accreditation:* NASPAA (one or more programs are accredited). *Program availability:* Part-time. *Faculty:* 20. *Students:* 122 full-time (58 women), 41 part-time (30 women). Average age 31. In 2016, 78 master's, 2 doctorates awarded. *Degree requirements:* For doctorate, thesis/dissertation. *Entrance requirements:* For master's, GRE General Test (for MPA), minimum GPA of 3.0 (for MA); for doctorate, GRE General Test. Additional exam requirements/recommendations for international students: Required—TOEFL (minimum score 600 paper-based; 100 iBT); Recommended—IELTS (minimum score 7.5). *Application deadline:* For fall admission, 12/1 priority date for domestic students, 11/30 priority date for international students; for spring admission, 11/15 for domestic and international students; for summer admission, 4/1 for domestic

and international students. Applications are processed on a rolling basis. Application fee: $60 ($70 for international students). Electronic applications accepted. *Financial support:* Fellowships, research assistantships, teaching assistantships, Federal Work-Study, institutionally sponsored loans, and unspecified assistantships available. Support available to part-time students. *Unit head:* Dr. Trevor Brown, Dean, 614-292-4533, Fax: 614-292-4868, E-mail: brown.2296@osu.edu. *Application contact:* Graduate and Professional Admissions, 614-292-6031, Fax: 614-292-3656, E-mail: gpadmissions@osu.edu.
Website: http://glenn.osu.edu/

**Ohio University,** Graduate College, Voinovich School of Leadership and Public Affairs, Athens, OH 45701-2979. Offers environmental studies (MS, Certificate); public administration (MPA). Application fee: $50 ($55 for international students). Electronic applications accepted. *Unit head:* Dr. Mark Weinberg, Head, 740-593-4390, Fax: 740-593-9758, E-mail: weinberm@ohio.edu. *Application contact:* Dr. Ani Ruhil, Associate Director of Academic Affairs, 740-597-1949, E-mail: ruhil@ohio.edu.
Website: http://www.voinovichschool.ohio.edu/

**Old Dominion University,** Strome College of Business, Doctoral Program in Public Administration and Urban Policy, Norfolk, VA 23529. Offers PhD. *Program availability:* Part-time, evening/weekend. *Faculty:* 9 full-time (3 women). *Students:* 9 full-time (6 women), 22 part-time (11 women); includes 10 minority (5 Black or African American, non-Hispanic/Latino; 1 Asian, non-Hispanic/Latino; 4 Hispanic/Latino), 6 international. Average age 38. 9 applicants, 89% accepted, 8 enrolled. In 2016, 3 doctorates awarded. *Degree requirements:* For doctorate, comprehensive exam, thesis/dissertation. *Entrance requirements:* For doctorate, GMAT, GRE General Test, master's degree, minimum graduate GPA of 3.25. Additional exam requirements/recommendations for international students: Required—TOEFL (minimum score 550 paper-based; 79 iBT). *Application deadline:* For fall admission, 3/15 priority date for domestic and international students. Application fee: $50. Electronic applications accepted. *Expenses:* Contact institution. *Financial support:* In 2016–17, 14 students received support, including 4 fellowships with full tuition reimbursements available (averaging $7,500 per year), 8 research assistantships with full tuition reimbursements available (averaging $6,000 per year), 2 teaching assistantships with full tuition reimbursements available (averaging $7,500 per year); unspecified assistantships also available. Financial award application deadline: 3/15; financial award applicants required to submit FAFSA. *Faculty research:* Multi-sectoral cooperation; policy analysis and administration, public-private partnerships, public finance and budgeting, economic development and sustainability. *Total annual research expenditures:* $60,000. *Unit head:* Dr. Meagan Jordan, Graduate Program Director, 757-683-3961, Fax: 757-683-4886, E-mail: mmjordan@odu.edu. *Application contact:* Megan S. Jones, Graduate Program Manager, 757-683-3961, Fax: 757-683-4886, E-mail: mmjones@odu.edu.
Website: http://www.odu.edu/business/departments/sps/academics/paup

**Old Dominion University,** Strome College of Business, Master of Public Administration Program, Norfolk, VA 23529. Offers multi sector public service (MPA); public administration (MPA). *Accreditation:* NASPAA. *Program availability:* Part-time, evening/weekend, 100% online, blended/hybrid learning. *Faculty:* 9 full-time (3 women), 10 part-time/adjunct (7 women). *Students:* 38 full-time (20 women), 114 part-time (68 women); includes 69 minority (51 Black or African American, non-Hispanic/Latino; 1 Asian, non-Hispanic/Latino; 6 Hispanic/Latino; 11 Two or more races, non-Hispanic/Latino), 2 international. Average age 37. 61 applicants, 85% accepted, 37 enrolled. In 2016, 44 master's awarded. *Degree requirements:* For master's, thesis optional, capstone seminar. *Entrance requirements:* For master's, GRE or work experience. Additional exam requirements/recommendations for international students: Required—TOEFL (minimum score 550 paper-based; 79 iBT). *Application deadline:* For fall admission, 7/15 for domestic and international students; for spring admission, 11/15 for domestic and international students. Applications are processed on a rolling basis. Application fee: $50. Electronic applications accepted. *Expenses:* $478 per credit hour in-state, $66 fees. *Financial support:* In 2016–17, 5 students received support, including 5 research assistantships (averaging $10,000 per year); unspecified assistantships also available. Financial award application deadline: 4/15; financial award applicants required to submit FAFSA. *Faculty research:* Environmental administration, personnel policy analysis, non-profit management, transportation policy, public budgeting. *Unit head:* Dr. David W. Chapman, Graduate Program Director, 757-683-7053, Fax: 757-683-5639, E-mail: mpa@odu.edu. *Application contact:* Megan S. Jones, Graduate Program Manager, 757-683-3961, Fax: 757-683-4886, E-mail: mmjones@odu.edu.
Website: http://www.odu.edu/mpa

**Pace University,** Dyson College of Arts and Sciences, Department of Public Administration, New York, NY 10038. Offers government management (MPA); health care administration (MPA); not-for-profit management (MPA); JD/MPA. *Program availability:* Part-time, evening/weekend. *Faculty:* 6 full-time (4 women), 4 part-time/adjunct (1 woman). *Students:* 65 full-time (43 women), 78 part-time (42 women); includes 62 minority (40 Black or African American, non-Hispanic/Latino; 10 Asian, non-Hispanic/Latino; 11 Hispanic/Latino; 1 Two or more races, non-Hispanic/Latino), 21 international. Average age 30. In 2016, 54 master's awarded. *Degree requirements:* For master's, comprehensive exam, thesis (for some programs), capstone project. *Entrance requirements:* For master's, 2 letters of recommendation, resume, personal statement, official transcripts, essay. Additional exam requirements/recommendations for international students: Required—TOEFL (minimum score 88 iBT), IELTS (minimum score 7) or PTE (minimum score 60). *Application deadline:* For fall admission, 8/1 priority date for domestic students, 6/1 for international students; for spring admission, 12/1 priority date for domestic students, 10/1 for international students. Applications are processed on a rolling basis. Application fee: $70. Electronic applications accepted. *Expenses: Tuition:* Part-time $1195 per credit. *Required fees:* $260 per semester. Tuition and fees vary according to degree level, campus/location and program. *Financial support:* Research assistantships, career-related internships or fieldwork, Federal Work-Study, and tuition waivers (partial) available. Support available to part-time students. Financial award application deadline: 2/15; financial award applicants required to submit FAFSA. *Unit head:* Dr. Hillary Knepper, Chairperson, 914-773-3140, E-mail: hknepper@pace.edu. *Application contact:* Susan Ford-Goldschein, Director of Admissions, 914-422-4283, Fax: 212-346-1585, E-mail: graduateadmission@pace.edu.
Website: http://www.pace.edu/dyson/academic-departments-and-programs/public-admin

**Park University,** School of Graduate and Professional Studies, Kansas City, MO 54105. Offers adult education (M Ed); business and government leadership (Graduate Certificate); business, government, and global society (MPA); communication and leadership (MA); creative and life writing (Graduate Certificate); disaster and emergency management (MPA, Graduate Certificate); educational leadership (M Ed); finance (MBA, Graduate Certificate); general business (MBA); global business (Graduate Certificate); healthcare administration (MHA); healthcare services management and leadership (Graduate Certificate); international business (MBA); language and literacy (M Ed), including English for speakers of other languages, special reading teacher/literacy coach; leadership of international healthcare organizations (Graduate Certificate); management information systems (MBA, Graduate Certificate); music performance (ADP, Graduate Certificate), including cello (MM, ADP), piano (MM, ADP),

## Public Administration

viola (MM, ADP), violin (MM, ADP); nonprofit and community services management (MPA); nonprofit leadership (Graduate Certificate); performance (MM), including cello (MM, ADP), piano (MM, ADP), viola (MM, ADP), violin (MM, ADP); public management (MPA); social work (MSW); teacher leadership (M Ed), including curriculum and assessment, instructional leader. *Program availability:* Part-time, evening/weekend, online learning. *Degree requirements:* For master's, comprehensive exam (for some programs), thesis (for some programs), internship (for some programs); exam (for some programs). *Entrance requirements:* For master's, GRE or GMAT (for some programs), teacher certification (for some M Ed programs), letters of recommendation, essay, resume (for some programs). Additional exam requirements/recommendations for international students: Required—TOEFL (minimum score 550 paper-based; 79 iBT), IELTS (minimum score 6). Electronic applications accepted.

**Penn State Harrisburg,** Graduate School, School of Public Affairs, Middletown, PA 17057. Offers criminal justice (MA); health administration (MHA); health administration: long term care (Certificate); homeland security (Certificate); public administration (MPA, PhD); public administration: non-profit administration (Certificate); public budgeting and financial management (Certificate); public sector human resource management (Certificate). *Accreditation:* NASPAA. *Unit head:* Dr. Mukund S. Kulkarni, Chancellor, 717-948-6105, Fax: 717-948-6452. *Application contact:* Robert W. Coffman, Jr., Director of Enrollment Management, Admissions, 717-948-6250, Fax: 717-948-6325, E-mail: hbgadmit@psu.edu.
Website: https://harrisburg.psu.edu/public-affairs

**Pontifical Catholic University of Puerto Rico,** College of Graduate Studies in Behavioral Science and Community Affairs, Program in Public Administration, Ponce, PR 00717-0777. Offers MSS. *Program availability:* Part-time, evening/weekend. *Degree requirements:* For master's, thesis. *Entrance requirements:* For master's, EXADEP, 3 letters of recommendation, interview, minimum GPA of 2.75.

**Portland State University,** Graduate Studies, College of Urban and Public Affairs, Hatfield School of Government, Division of Public Administration, Portland, OR 97207-0751. Offers public administration (MPA); public affairs and policy (PhD). *Accreditation:* NASPAA (one or more programs are accredited). *Program availability:* Part-time, evening/weekend. *Faculty:* 14 full-time (6 women), 9 part-time/adjunct (6 women). *Students:* 99 full-time (68 women), 122 part-time (82 women); includes 48 minority (5 Black or African American, non-Hispanic/Latino; 4 American Indian or Alaska Native, non-Hispanic/Latino; 7 Asian, non-Hispanic/Latino; 23 Hispanic/Latino; 9 Two or more races, non-Hispanic/Latino), 14 international. Average age 35. 143 applicants, 74% accepted, 68 enrolled. In 2016, 60 master's, 2 doctorates awarded. *Degree requirements:* For master's, internship (MPA), practicum (MPH); for doctorate, comprehensive exam, thesis/dissertation. *Entrance requirements:* For master's, GRE (minimum scores: verbal 150, quantitative 149, and analytic writing 4.5), minimum GPA of 3.0, 3 recommendation letters, resume, 500-word statement of intent; for doctorate, GRE, 3 recommendation letters, resume, 500-word personal essay. Additional exam requirements/recommendations for international students: Required—TOEFL (minimum score 550 paper-based; 80 iBT), IELTS (minimum score 7). *Application deadline:* For fall admission, 4/1 for domestic students, 3/1 for international students; for winter admission, 9/1 for domestic students, 8/1 for international students; for spring admission, 11/1 for domestic and international students. Application fee: $65. *Expenses:* Contact institution. *Financial support:* In 2016–17, 5 research assistantships with full tuition reimbursements (averaging $8,341 per year), 4 teaching assistantships with full tuition reimbursements (averaging $7,291 per year) were awarded; career-related internships or fieldwork, Federal Work-Study, scholarships/grants, tuition waivers (partial), and unspecified assistantships also available. Support available to part-time students. Financial award application deadline: 3/1; financial award applicants required to submit FAFSA. *Faculty research:* Public budgeting, program evaluation, nonprofit management, natural resources policy and administration. *Total annual research expenditures:* $819,192. *Unit head:* Dr. Masami Nishishiba, Chair, 503-725-5151, E-mail: nishism@pdx.edu.
Website: https://www.pdx.edu/hatfieldschool/public-administration

**Post University,** Program in Public Administration, Waterbury, CT 06723-2540. Offers MPA. *Program availability:* Online learning.

**Regent University,** Graduate School, Robertson School of Government, Virginia Beach, VA 23464-9800. Offers government (MA), including American government, healthcare policy and ethics (MA, MPA), international relations, law and public policy, national security studies, political communication, political theory, religion and politics; public administration (MPA), including emergency management and homeland security, federal government, general public administration, healthcare policy and ethics (MA, MPA), law, nonprofit administration and faith-based organizations, public leadership and management, servant leadership. *Program availability:* Part-time, evening/weekend, 100% online, blended/hybrid learning. *Faculty:* 8 full-time (1 woman), 19 part-time/adjunct (3 women). *Students:* 40 full-time (27 women), 119 part-time (69 women); includes 73 minority (47 Black or African American, non-Hispanic/Latino; 3 Asian, non-Hispanic/Latino; 15 Hispanic/Latino; 8 Two or more races, non-Hispanic/Latino), 6 international. Average age 35. 253 applicants, 41% accepted, 70 enrolled. In 2016, 34 master's awarded. *Degree requirements:* For master's, thesis optional, internship. *Entrance requirements:* For master's, GRE General Test or LSAT, personal essay, writing sample, resume, college transcripts. Additional exam requirements/recommendations for international students: Required—TOEFL (minimum score 577 paper-based). *Application deadline:* For fall admission, 5/1 priority date for domestic students; for spring admission, 11/1 priority date for domestic students. Applications are processed on a rolling basis. Application fee: $50. Electronic applications accepted. *Expenses:* $650 per credit (MA/MPA); $250 per semester technology fee. *Financial support:* In 2016–17, 78 students received support. Career-related internships or fieldwork, scholarships/grants, and unspecified assistantships available. Support available to part-time students. *Faculty research:* International relations and politics, public administration, leadership and ethics, Biblical law, Constitutional law and Supreme Court. *Unit head:* Dr. Eric Patterson, Dean, 757-352-4616, Fax: 757-352-4735, E-mail: epatterson@regent.edu. *Application contact:* Heidi Cece, Assistant Vice President of Enrollment Management, 800-373-5504, Fax: 757-352-4381, E-mail: admissions@regent.edu.
Website: http://www.regent.edu/rsg/

**Rhode Island College,** School of Graduate Studies, Faculty of Arts and Sciences, Department of Political Science, Providence, RI 02908-1991. Offers public administration (MPA). *Program availability:* Part-time, evening/weekend. *Faculty:* 4 full-time (1 woman). *Entrance requirements:* For master's, GRE, GMAT, or MAT. Additional exam requirements/recommendations for international students: Recommended—TOEFL (minimum score 550 paper-based; 79 iBT). *Application deadline:* For fall admission, 3/1 for domestic students; for spring admission, 11/1 for domestic students. Applications are processed on a rolling basis. *Expenses:* Tuition, state resident: full-time $8928; part-time $372 per credit. Tuition, nonresident: full-time $17,376; part-time $724 per credit. *Required fees:* $604; $22 per credit. One-time fee: $74. *Financial support:* Career-related internships or fieldwork, Federal Work-Study, scholarships/grants, health care benefits, and unspecified assistantships available. Support available to part-time students. Financial award application deadline: 5/15; financial award

applicants required to submit FAFSA. *Unit head:* Dr. Thomas Schmeling, Chair, 401-456-8056. *Application contact:* Graduate Studies, 401-456-8700.
Website: http://www.ric.edu/politicalscience/index.php

**Roger Williams University,** School of Justice Studies, Bristol, RI 02809. Offers criminal justice (MS); cybersecurity (MS); leadership (MS), including health care administration (MPA, MS), public management (MPA, MS), public administration (MPA), including health care administration (MPA, MS), public management (MPA, MS); MS/JD. *Program availability:* Part-time, evening/weekend, 100% online, blended/hybrid learning. *Faculty:* 10 full-time (5 women), 4 part-time/adjunct (0 women). *Students:* 63 full-time (37 women), 67 part-time (30 women); includes 30 minority (13 Black or African American, non-Hispanic/Latino; 1 American Indian or Alaska Native, non-Hispanic/Latino; 2 Asian, non-Hispanic/Latino; 13 Hispanic/Latino; 1 Native Hawaiian or other Pacific Islander, non-Hispanic/Latino), 3 international. Average age 36. 67 applicants, 96% accepted, 34 enrolled. In 2016, 27 master's awarded. *Degree requirements:* For master's, thesis optional. *Entrance requirements:* For master's, 2 letters of recommendation, college transcript, and resume (for MS in leadership and MPA programs); criminal background check (for MS in cybersecurity). Additional exam requirements/recommendations for international students: Required—TOEFL (minimum score 85 iBT), IELTS (minimum score 6.5). *Application deadline:* For fall admission, 8/1 for domestic students; for spring admission, 1/1 for domestic students. Applications are processed on a rolling basis. Application fee: $50. Electronic applications accepted. Application fee is waived when completed online. *Expenses:* $552 per credit hour tuition (for MS in leadership and MPA); $843 per credit hour tuition (for MS in criminal justice and MS in cybersecurity). *Financial support:* Research assistantships, scholarships/grants, and unspecified assistantships available. Financial award application deadline: 4/1; financial award applicants required to submit FAFSA. *Unit head:* Dr. Stephanie Manzi, Dean, 401-254-3021, Fax: 401-254-3431, E-mail: smanzi@rwu.edu. *Application contact:* Marcus Hanscom, Director of Graduate Admissions, 401-254-6200, Fax: 401-254-3557, E-mail: gradadmit@rwu.edu.
Website: http://www.rwu.edu/academics/departments/criminaljustice.htm#graduate

**Roosevelt University,** Graduate Division, College of Arts and Sciences, Department of Political Science and Public Administration, Program in Public Administration, Chicago, IL 60605. Offers MPA. *Program availability:* Part-time, evening/weekend. *Degree requirements:* For master's, thesis optional. *Entrance requirements:* For master's, minimum undergraduate GPA of 3.0. *Faculty research:* Health policy issues, environmental policy, local government administration.

**Rutgers University–Camden,** Graduate School of Arts and Sciences, Department of Public Policy and Administration, Camden, NJ 08102. Offers education policy and leadership (MPA); international public service and development (MPA); public management (MPA); JD/MPA; MPA/MA. *Accreditation:* NASPAA. *Program availability:* Part-time, evening/weekend. *Degree requirements:* For master's, directed study, research workshop, 42 credits. *Entrance requirements:* For master's, GRE General Test, GMAT or LSAT, 3 letters of recommendation; resume. Additional exam requirements/recommendations for international students: Required—TOEFL (minimum score 550 paper-based), IELTS. Electronic applications accepted. *Faculty research:* Nonprofit management, county and municipal administration, health and human services, government communication, administrative law, educational finance.

**Rutgers University–Newark,** Graduate School, Program in Public Administration, Newark, NJ 07102. Offers health care administration (MPA); human resources administration (MPA); public administration (PhD); public management (MPA); public policy analysis (MPA); urban systems and issues (MPA). *Accreditation:* NASPAA (one or more programs are accredited). *Program availability:* Part-time, evening/weekend. *Degree requirements:* For master's, comprehensive exam, thesis or alternative; for doctorate, thesis/dissertation. *Entrance requirements:* For master's, GRE, minimum undergraduate B average; for doctorate, GRE, MPA, minimum B average. Electronic applications accepted. *Faculty research:* Government finance, municipal and state government, public productivity.

**Saginaw Valley State University,** College of Arts and Behavioral Sciences, Program in Public Administration, University Center, MI 48710. Offers MA. *Program availability:* Part-time, evening/weekend. *Students:* 13 full-time (7 women), 24 part-time (15 women); includes 9 minority (7 Black or African American, non-Hispanic/Latino; 1 Asian, non-Hispanic/Latino; 1 Two or more races, non-Hispanic/Latino), 1 international. Average age 30. 23 applicants, 91% accepted, 17 enrolled. In 2016, 23 master's awarded. *Degree requirements:* For master's, thesis optional. *Entrance requirements:* For master's, minimum GPA of 2.75. Additional exam requirements/recommendations for international students: Required—TOEFL (minimum score 580 paper-based; 92 iBT). *Application deadline:* For fall admission, 7/15 for international students; for winter admission, 11/15 for international students; for spring admission, 4/15 for international students. Applications are processed on a rolling basis. Application fee: $30 ($90 for international students). Electronic applications accepted. *Expenses:* Tuition, state resident: full-time $9652; part-time $536 per credit hour. Tuition, nonresident: full-time $12,259; part-time $1022 per credit hour. *Required fees:* $263; $14.60 per credit hour. Tuition and fees vary according to degree level. *Financial support:* Federal Work-Study and scholarships/grants available. Support available to part-time students. Financial award application deadline: 4/1; financial award applicants required to submit FAFSA. *Unit head:* Dr. Joseph Jaksa, Program Coordinator, 989-964-2178, E-mail: jjjaksa@svsu.edu. *Application contact:* Jenna Briggs, Director, Graduate and International Admissions, 989-964-6096, Fax: 989-964-2788, E-mail: gradadm@svsu.edu.

**St. John's University,** St. John's College of Liberal Arts and Sciences, Department of Government and Politics, Program in Government and Politics, Queens, NY 11439. Offers government and politics (MA); public administration (Adv C); JD/MA. *Program availability:* Part-time, evening/weekend. *Degree requirements:* For master's, comprehensive exam, thesis optional. *Entrance requirements:* For master's, minimum GPA of 3.0, 18 credits at undergraduate level in government and politics. Additional exam requirements/recommendations for international students: Required—TOEFL (minimum score 600 paper-based; 100 iBT), IELTS (minimum score 7). Electronic applications accepted.

**Saint Louis University,** Graduate Education, College of Education and Public Service, Department of Public Policy Studies, St. Louis, MO 63103. Offers geographic information systems (Certificate); organizational development (Certificate); public administration (MAPA); public policy analysis (PhD); urban affairs (MAUA); urban planning and real estate development (MUPRED). *Program availability:* Part-time. *Degree requirements:* For master's, comprehensive exam (for some programs), thesis (for some programs); for doctorate, comprehensive exam, thesis/dissertation, preliminary exams. *Entrance requirements:* For master's, GMAT, GRE General Test, or LSAT, letters of recommendation, resume; for doctorate, GMAT, GRE General Test, or LSAT, letters of recommendation, resumé, interview, transcripts, goal statement. Additional exam requirements/recommendations for international students: Required—TOEFL (minimum score 525 paper-based). Electronic applications accepted. *Faculty research:* Urban politics, brown fields, e-government, and administration, evaluation research, community development, electronic government and governance.

**St. Mary's University,** Graduate Studies, Program in Public Administration, San Antonio, TX 78228-8507. Offers public administration (MPA); public communication, public policy and public leadership (Certificate); JD/MPA. *Program availability:* Part-time, evening/weekend, online learning. *Faculty:* 3 full-time (0 women), 4 part-time/adjunct (1 woman). *Students:* 17 full-time (10 women), 5 part-time (3 women); includes 10 minority (2 Black or African American, non-Hispanic/Latino; 8 Hispanic/Latino), 6 international. Average age 32. 39 applicants, 62% accepted. In 2016, 18 master's awarded. *Degree requirements:* For master's, comprehensive exam, 6-hour internship or applied public service. *Entrance requirements:* For master's, GRE General Test, letters of recommendation, writing sample, essay. Additional exam requirements/ recommendations for international students: Required—TOEFL (minimum score 550 paper-based; 80 iBT), IELTS (minimum score 6). *Application deadline:* For fall admission, 7/1 for domestic students; for spring admission, 11/15 for domestic students; for summer admission, 4/1 for domestic students. Applications are processed on a rolling basis. Application fee: $0. Electronic applications accepted. *Expenses: Tuition:* Full-time $15,600; part-time $865 per credit hour. *Required fees:* $148 per semester. *Financial support:* Career-related internships or fieldwork, Federal Work-Study, and institutionally sponsored loans available. Financial award application deadline: 3/31; financial award applicants required to submit FAFSA. *Faculty research:* Municipal service delivery, election systems, urban management and planning. *Unit head:* Dr. Henry Flores, Director, Graduate Public Administration, 210-436-3110, E-mail: hflores@stmarytx.edu. *Application contact:* Kim Thornton, Director, Graduate and Adult Enrollment Services, 210-436-3101, E-mail: kthornton@stmarytx.edu.
Website: https://www.stmarytx.edu/academics/graduate/masters/mpa/

**Saint Peter's University,** Program in Public Administration, Jersey City, NJ 07306-5997. Offers MPA. *Degree requirements:* For master's, capstone project.

**St. Thomas University,** School of Business, Department of Management, Miami Gardens, FL 33054-6459. Offers accounting (MBA); general management (MSM, Certificate); health management (MBA, MSM, Certificate); human resource management (MBA, MSM, Certificate); international business (MBA, MIB, MSM, Certificate); justice administration (MSM, Certificate); management accounting (MSM, Certificate); public management (MSM, Certificate); sports administration (MS). *Program availability:* Part-time, evening/weekend. *Degree requirements:* For master's, comprehensive exam. *Entrance requirements:* For master's, interview, minimum GPA of 3.0 or GMAT. Additional exam requirements/recommendations for international students: Required—TOEFL (minimum score 550 paper-based; 79 iBT). Electronic applications accepted.

**Sam Houston State University,** College of Humanities and Social Sciences, Department of Political Science, Huntsville, TX 77341. Offers political science (MA); public administration (MPA). *Program availability:* Part-time, online learning. *Degree requirements:* For master's, comprehensive exam, thesis optional, internship. *Entrance requirements:* For master's, GRE General Test, GMAT, writing sample of scholarly work, letters of recommendation, statement of purpose, resume. Additional exam requirements/recommendations for international students: Required—TOEFL (minimum score 550 paper-based; 79 iBT), IELTS (minimum score 6.5). Electronic applications accepted.

**San Diego State University,** Graduate and Research Affairs, College of Professional Studies and Fine Arts, School of Public Affairs, Program in Public Administration, San Diego, CA 92182. Offers MPA. *Accreditation:* NASPAA. *Program availability:* Part-time. *Entrance requirements:* For master's, GRE General Test, 2 letters of reference. Additional exam requirements/recommendations for international students: Required—TOEFL. Electronic applications accepted.

**San Francisco State University,** Division of Graduate Studies, College of Health and Social Sciences, Public Administration Program, San Francisco, CA 94132-1722. Offers criminal justice administration (MPA); environmental administration and policy (MPA); gerontology (MPA); nonprofit administration (MPA); public management (MPA); public policy (MPA); urban administration (MPA). *Accreditation:* NASPAA. *Expenses:* Tuition, state resident: full-time $6738. Tuition, nonresident: full-time $15,666. *Required fees:* $1012. Tuition and fees vary according to degree level and program. *Unit head:* Dr. Elizabeth Brown, Director of the School of Public Affairs and Civic Engagement, 415-817-4455, Fax: 415-817-4464, E-mail: mpa@sfsu.edu. *Application contact:* Dr. Jennifer Shea, Graduate Coordinator, 415-817-4462, Fax: 415-817-4464, E-mail: jshea@sfsu.edu.
Website: http://mpa.sfsu.edu/

**San Jose State University,** Graduate Studies and Research, College of Social Sciences, San Jose, CA 95192-0001. Offers applications of technology in planning (Certificate); applied anthropology (MA); communication studies (MS); community design and development (Certificate); economics (MA), including applied economics, social sciences; environmental planning (Certificate); geographic information science (Certificate); geography (MA); global citizenship (Certificate); history (MA), including history education, social sciences; Mexican American studies (MA); psychology (MA, MS), including clinical psychology (MS), industrial/organizational psychology (MS); research and experimental psychology (MA); public administration (MA); real estate development (Certificate); social sciences (MPA, MS); sociology (MA); transportation and land use planning (Certificate). *Program availability:* Part-time, evening/weekend. *Entrance requirements:* For master's, minimum GPA of 3.0. Electronic applications accepted.

**Savannah State University,** Master of Public Administration Program, Savannah, GA 31404. Offers city management (MPA); human resources (MPA). *Accreditation:* NASPAA. *Program availability:* Part-time. *Degree requirements:* For master's, comprehensive exam, thesis, public service internship, capstone seminar. *Entrance requirements:* For master's, GRE General Test, GMAT, or MAT, minimum cumulative GPA of 2.5, 3 letters of recommendation, essay, official transcripts, resume, essay of 500-1000 words detailing reasons for pursuing degree. Additional exam requirements/ recommendations for international students: Required—TOEFL. Electronic applications accepted. *Expenses:* Contact institution. *Faculty research:* Community development, human resources, leadership, conflict resolution, city management, non-profit management.

**Seattle University,** College of Arts and Sciences, Institute of Public Service, Seattle, WA 98122-1090. Offers MNPL, MPA. *Accreditation:* NASPAA. *Program availability:* Part-time, evening/weekend. *Faculty:* 11 full-time (6 women), 4 part-time/adjunct (2 women). *Students:* 19 full-time (11 women), 127 part-time (91 women); includes 56 minority (16 Black or African American, non-Hispanic/Latino; 2 American Indian or Alaska Native, non-Hispanic/Latino; 16 Asian, non-Hispanic/Latino; 11 Hispanic/Latino; 11 Two or more races, non-Hispanic/Latino), 8 international. Average age 31. 64 applicants, 72% accepted, 31 enrolled. In 2016, 58 master's awarded. *Degree requirements:* For master's, thesis. *Entrance requirements:* For master's, minimum GPA of 3.0, letters of recommendation, current resume reflecting two years of relevant professional experience in nonprofit organization (preferred). Additional exam requirements/recommendations for international students: Required—TOEFL, IELTS. *Application deadline:* For fall admission, 7/20 priority date for domestic students, 7/20 for international students; for winter admission, 10/20 priority date for domestic students,

10/20 for international students; for spring admission, 2/20 priority date for domestic students, 2/20 for international students. Applications are processed on a rolling basis. Application fee: $55. Electronic applications accepted. *Financial support:* In 2016–17, 22 students received support. Career-related internships or fieldwork, Federal Work-Study, and unspecified assistantships available. Support available to part-time students. Financial award applicants required to submit FAFSA. *Faculty research:* Leadership development, decision-making, and advocacy; government and nonprofit management, processes, and program analysis; organizational theory and structure; policy formation and analysis, financial analysis and planning. *Unit head:* Dr. John Collins, Interim Director, Institute of Public Service, 206-296-5442, Fax: 206-296-5997, E-mail: collinsj@seattleu.edu. *Application contact:* Janet Shandley, Associate Dean of Graduate Admissions, 206-296-5900, Fax: 206-298-5656, E-mail: grad_admissions@seattleu.edu.
Website: http://www.seattleu.edu/artsci/departments/ips/

**Seton Hall University,** College of Arts and Sciences, Department of Political Science and Public Affairs, South Orange, NJ 07079-2697. Offers nonprofit organization management (Graduate Certificate); public administration (MPA), including health policy and management, nonprofit organization management, public service: leadership, governance, and policy. *Accreditation:* CAHME; NASPAA. *Program availability:* Part-time, evening/weekend. *Degree requirements:* For master's, alternative, internship or practicum. *Entrance requirements:* Additional exam requirements/ recommendations for international students: Required—TOEFL. Electronic applications accepted.

**Shippensburg University of Pennsylvania,** School of Graduate Studies, College of Arts and Sciences, Department of Political Science, Shippensburg, PA 17257-2299. Offers public administration (MPA). *Program availability:* Part-time, evening/weekend. *Faculty:* 5 full-time (2 women). *Students:* 12 full-time (4 women), 17 part-time (7 women); includes 3 minority (2 Black or African American, non-Hispanic/Latino; 1 Hispanic/Latino), 1 international. Average age 31. 22 applicants, 82% accepted, 9 enrolled. In 2016, 12 master's awarded. *Degree requirements:* For master's, thesis or internship. *Entrance requirements:* For master's, current resume, official transcript showing minimum cumulative GPA of 2.75 or sufficient work experience. Additional exam requirements/recommendations for international students: Required—TOEFL (minimum score 550 paper-based, 68 iBT) or IELTS (minimum score 6). *Application deadline:* For fall admission, 4/30 for international students; for spring admission, 9/30 for international students. Applications are processed on a rolling basis. Application fee: $45. Electronic applications accepted. *Expenses:* Tuition, state resident: part-time $483 per credit. Tuition, nonresident: part-time $725 per credit. *Required fees:* $141 per credit. *Financial support:* In 2016–17, 3 students received support. Career-related internships or fieldwork, scholarships/grants, unspecified assistantships, and resident hall director and student payroll positions available. Support available to part-time students. Financial award application deadline: 3/1; financial award applicants required to submit FAFSA. *Unit head:* Dr. C. Niel Brasher, Department Chair and Program Coordinator, 717-477-1718, Fax: 717-477-4030, E-mail: cnbras@ship.edu. *Application contact:* Megan N. Luft, Assistant Dean of Graduate Admissions, 717-477-1231, Fax: 717-477-4016, E-mail: mnluft@ship.edu.
Website: http://www.ship.edu/political_science/

**Sonoma State University,** School of Social Sciences, Department of Political Science, Rohnert Park, CA 94928. Offers administration of nonprofit agencies (Certificate); public administration (MPA). *Program availability:* Part-time, evening/weekend. *Degree requirements:* For master's, thesis or alternative. *Entrance requirements:* For master's, GRE General Test, minimum GPA of 3.0. Additional exam requirements/ recommendations for international students: Required—TOEFL (minimum score 500 paper-based). *Application deadline:* For fall admission, 11/30 for domestic students; for spring admission, 8/31 for domestic students. Application fee: $55. *Expenses:* Tuition, state resident: full-time $6738; part-time $3906 per unit. *Required fees:* $1916; $1916 per year. Tuition and fees vary according to course load, degree level and program. *Financial support:* Research assistantships, teaching assistantships, career-related internships or fieldwork, and Federal Work-Study available. Support available to part-time students. Financial award application deadline: 3/2; financial award applicants required to submit FAFSA. *Unit head:* Catherine Nelson, Chair, 707-664-2179, E-mail: catherine.nelson@sonoma.edu. *Application contact:* Diane Brown, Graduate Program Coordinator, 707-664-2875, Fax: 707-664-3920, E-mail: diane.brown@sonoma.edu.
Website: http://www.sonoma.edu/polisci

**Southeast Missouri State University,** School of Graduate Studies, Department of Political Science, Philosophy and Religion, Cape Girardeau, MO 63701-4799. Offers MPA. *Program availability:* Part-time, evening/weekend, 100% online, blended/hybrid learning. *Faculty:* 5 full-time (1 woman). *Students:* 9 full-time (4 women), 27 part-time (14 women); includes 2 minority (both Black or African American, non-Hispanic/Latino), 9 international. Average age 28. 11 applicants, 73% accepted, 8 enrolled. In 2016, 10 master's awarded. *Degree requirements:* For master's, thesis or alternative, internship paper. *Entrance requirements:* For master's, statement of interest, minimum GPA of 2.7. Additional exam requirements/recommendations for international students: Required—TOEFL (minimum score 550 paper-based; 79 iBT), IELTS (minimum score 6), PTE (minimum score 53). *Application deadline:* For fall admission, 8/1 for domestic students, 6/1 for international students; for spring admission, 11/21 for domestic students, 10/1 for international students; for summer admission, 5/15 for domestic students. Applications are processed on a rolling basis. Application fee: $30 ($40 for international students). Electronic applications accepted. *Expenses:* Tuition, state resident: full-time $3130; part-time $260.80 per credit hour. Tuition, nonresident: full-time $5842; part-time $486.80 per credit hour. *Required fees:* $33.70 per credit hour. *Financial support:* In 2016–17, 18 students received support. Career-related internships or fieldwork, Federal Work-Study, scholarships/grants, traineeships, tuition waivers (full), and unspecified assistantships available. Financial award application deadline: 6/30; financial award applicants required to submit FAFSA. *Faculty research:* Rural public administration, public policy analysis, budgeting, emergency management. *Unit head:* Dr. Hamner Hill, Chairperson, Department of Political Science, Philosophy, and Religion, 573-651-2816, Fax: 573-651-2695, E-mail: hhill@semo.edu. *Application contact:* Dr. Rick Althaus, Graduate Coordinator, Department of Political Science, Philosophy, and Religion, 573-651-2700, Fax: 573-651-2695, E-mail: ralthaus@semo.edu.
Website: http://www.semo.edu/polisci

**Southern Arkansas University–Magnolia,** School of Graduate Studies, Magnolia, AR 71753. Offers agriculture (MS); business administration (MBA), including agri-business, social entrepreneurship, supply chain management; clinical and mental health counseling (MS); computer and information sciences (MS), including cyber security and privacy, data science, information technology; gifted and talented (M Ed), including curriculum and instruction, educational administration and supervision, gifted and talented P-8/7-12, instructional specialist P-4; higher, adult and lifelong education (M Ed); kinesiology (M Ed), including coaching; library media and information specialist (M Ed); public administration (MPA); school counseling K-12 (M Ed); student affairs and college counseling (M Ed); teaching (MAT). *Accreditation:* NCATE. *Program availability:* Part-time, 100% online, blended/hybrid learning. *Faculty:* 36 full-time (19 women), 33 part-time/adjunct (14 women). *Students:* 605 full-time (143 women), 879 part-time (352

## Public Administration

women); includes 130 minority (113 Black or African American, non-Hispanic/Latino; 7 American Indian or Alaska Native, non-Hispanic/Latino; 2 Asian, non-Hispanic/Latino; 2 Hispanic/Latino; 6 Two or more races, non-Hispanic/Latino), 1,048 international. Average age 28. 904 applicants, 81% accepted, 262 enrolled. In 2016, 278 master's awarded. *Degree requirements:* For master's, comprehensive exam (for some programs), thesis optional. *Entrance requirements:* For master's, GRE, MAT or GMAT, minimum GPA of 2.5. Additional exam requirements/recommendations for international students: Required—TOEFL (minimum score 550 paper-based), IELTS (minimum score 6). *Application deadline:* For fall admission, 7/20 for domestic students, 7/10 for international students; for spring admission, 12/1 for domestic students, 11/15 for international students; for summer admission, 4/1 for domestic students, 5/1 for international students. Applications are processed on a rolling basis. Application fee: $25 ($50 for international students). Electronic applications accepted. *Expenses:* Tuition, state resident: full-time $2511; part-time $279 per credit hour. Tuition, nonresident: full-time $3726; part-time $414 per credit hour. *Required fees:* $307 per semester. Tuition and fees vary according to course load and program. *Financial support:* Career-related internships or fieldwork, Federal Work-Study, scholarships/grants, tuition waivers (full), and unspecified assistantships available. Financial award applicants required to submit FAFSA. *Faculty research:* Alternative certification for teachers, supervision of instruction, instructional leadership, counseling. *Unit head:* Dr. Kim Bloss, Dean, School of Graduate Studies, 870-235-4150, Fax: 870-235-5227, E-mail: kkbloss@saumag.edu. *Application contact:* Shrijana Malakar, Admissions Specialist, 870-235-4150, Fax: 870-235-5227, E-mail: smalakar@saumag.edu. Website: http://www.saumag.edu/graduate

**Southern Illinois University Carbondale,** Graduate School, College of Liberal Arts, Department of Political Science, Public Administration Program, Carbondale, IL 62901-4701. Offers MPA, JD/MPA. *Accreditation:* NASPAA. *Program availability:* Part-time. *Degree requirements:* For master's, thesis or alternative. *Entrance requirements:* For master's, minimum GPA of 3.0. Additional exam requirements/recommendations for international students: Required—TOEFL (minimum score 600 paper-based; 100 iBT). *Faculty research:* Natural resources and environmental management, intergovernmental relations, state mandates, rural administration, economic development policy, nonprofit management.

**Southern Illinois University Edwardsville,** Graduate School, College of Arts and Sciences, Department of Public Administration and Policy Analysis, Edwardsville, IL 62026. Offers public administration (MPA). *Accreditation:* NASPAA. *Program availability:* Part-time, evening/weekend. *Degree requirements:* For master's, comprehensive exam. *Entrance requirements:* Additional exam requirements/recommendations for international students: Required—TOEFL (minimum score 550 paper-based; 79 iBT), IELTS (minimum score 6.5). Electronic applications accepted.

**Southern University and Agricultural and Mechanical College,** Graduate School, Nelson Mandela School of Public Policy and Urban Affairs, Department of Public Administration, Baton Rouge, LA 70813. Offers MPA. *Accreditation:* NASPAA. *Program availability:* Part-time, evening/weekend. *Degree requirements:* For master's, thesis. *Entrance requirements:* For master's, GRE General Test. Additional exam requirements/recommendations for international students: Required—TOEFL (minimum score 525 paper-based). *Faculty research:* Fiscal policy, public finance policy and practitioner interests; minority politics, healthcare and political economy.

**Southern Utah University,** Program in Public Administration, Cedar City, UT 84720-2498. Offers MPA. *Accreditation:* NASPAA. *Program availability:* Part-time, evening/weekend, 100% online. *Faculty:* 8 full-time (2 women), 1 part-time/adjunct. *Students:* 38 full-time (14 women), 61 part-time (27 women); includes 11 minority (2 Black or African American, non-Hispanic/Latino; 1 American Indian or Alaska Native, non-Hispanic/Latino; 3 Asian, non-Hispanic/Latino; 3 Hispanic/Latino; 2 Native Hawaiian or other Pacific Islander, non-Hispanic/Latino), 2 international. Average age 34. 53 applicants, 66% accepted, 35 enrolled. In 2016, 39 master's awarded. *Entrance requirements:* For master's, GMAT, GRE, MAT, or LSAT. Additional exam requirements/recommendations for international students: Required—TOEFL (minimum score 550 paper-based, 79 iBT) or IELTS (minimum score 6). *Application deadline:* For fall admission, 7/15 for domestic and international students; for spring admission, 11/15 for domestic and international students; for summer admission, 4/15 for domestic and international students. Applications are processed on a rolling basis. Application fee: $60 ($65 for international students). Electronic applications accepted. *Expenses:* $7,692 per year resident or online full-time; $23,384 per year on-campus non-resident full-time. *Financial support:* Tuition waivers (full and partial) and unspecified assistantships available. Financial award application deadline: 5/31. *Unit head:* Dr. Angela Pool-Funai, MPA Program Director, 435-865-8153, Fax: 435-586-1925, E-mail: angelapoolfunai@suu.edu. Website: https://www.suu.edu/hss/polscj/mpa/

**South University,** Graduate Programs, College of Business, Program in Public Administration, Savannah, GA 31406. Offers MPA.

**South University,** Program in Public Administration, Montgomery, AL 36116-1120. Offers MPA.

**South University,** Program in Public Administration, Royal Palm Beach, FL 33411. Offers MPA.

**Stephen F. Austin State University,** Graduate School, College of Liberal Arts, Department of Political Science and Geography, Nacogdoches, TX 75962. Offers public administration (MPA). *Degree requirements:* For master's, thesis optional. *Entrance requirements:* For master's, GRE General Test. Additional exam requirements/recommendations for international students: Required—TOEFL.

**Strayer University,** Graduate Studies, Washington, DC 20005-2603. Offers accounting (MS); acquisition (MBA); business administration (MBA); communications technology (MS); educational management (M Ed); finance (MBA); health services administration (MHSA); hospitality and tourism management (MBA); human resource management (MBA); information systems (MS), including computer security management, decision support system management, enterprise resource management, network management, software engineering management, systems development management; management (MBA); management information systems (MS); marketing (MBA); professional accounting (MS), including accounting information systems, controllership, taxation; public administration (MPA); supply chain management (MBA); technology in education (M Ed). Programs also offered at campus locations in Birmingham, AL; Chamblee, GA; Cobb County, GA; Morrow, GA; White Marsh, MD; Charleston, SC; Columbia, SC; Greensboro, NC; Greenville, SC; Lexington, KY; Louisville, KY; Nashville, TN; North Raleigh, NC; Washington, DC. *Accreditation:* ACBSP. *Program availability:* Part-time, evening/weekend, online learning. *Degree requirements:* For master's, thesis. *Entrance requirements:* For master's, GMAT, GRE General Test, bachelor's degree from an accredited college or university, minimum undergraduate GPA of 2.75. Electronic applications accepted.

**Suffolk University,** Sawyer Business School, Department of Public Administration, Boston, MA 02108-2770. Offers community health (MPA); information systems, performance management, and big data analytics (MPA); nonprofit management (MPA); state and local government (MPA); JD/MPA; MPA/MS; MPA/MSCJ; MPA/MSMHC; MPA/MSPS. *Accreditation:* NASPAA (one or more programs are accredited). *Program availability:* Part-time, evening/weekend. *Faculty:* 4 full-time (1 woman), 2 part-time/adjunct (both women). *Students:* 26 full-time (13 women), 96 part-time (58 women); includes 42 minority (18 Black or African American, non-Hispanic/Latino; 5 Asian, non-Hispanic/Latino; 18 Hispanic/Latino; 1 Two or more races, non-Hispanic/Latino), 4 international. Average age 34. 133 applicants, 85% accepted, 53 enrolled. In 2016, 47 degrees awarded. *Entrance requirements:* Additional exam requirements/recommendations for international students: Required—TOEFL (minimum score 550 paper-based; 80 iBT). *Application deadline:* For fall admission, 3/15 priority date for domestic and international students; for spring admission, 10/15 priority date for domestic and international students. Applications are processed on a rolling basis. Application fee: $50. Electronic applications accepted. *Expenses:* Tuition: Full-time $41,490; part-time $1383 per credit hour. *Required fees:* $52; $52 per credit hour. Part-time tuition and fees vary according to course load and program. *Financial support:* In 2016–17, 82 students received support, including 78 fellowships (averaging $6,546 per year); career-related internships or fieldwork, Federal Work-Study, institutionally sponsored loans, and scholarships/grants also available. Support available to part-time students. Financial award application deadline: 4/1; financial award applicants required to submit FAFSA. *Faculty research:* Local government, health care, federal policy, mental health, HIV/AIDS. *Unit head:* Brenda Bond, Director/Department Chair, 617-305-1768, E-mail: bbond@suffolk.edu. *Application contact:* Mara Marzocchi, Associate Director of Graduate Admissions, 617-573-8302, Fax: 617-305-1733, E-mail: grad.admission@suffolk.edu. Website: http://www.suffolk.edu/mpa

**Syracuse University,** Maxwell School of Citizenship and Public Affairs, Dual MPA/IR Program in Public Administration and International Relations, Syracuse, NY 13244. Offers MPA/MA. *Students:* Average age 27. *Entrance requirements:* Additional exam requirements/recommendations for international students: Required—TOEFL (minimum score 100 iBT). *Application deadline:* For fall admission, 2/1 priority date for domestic and international students. Application fee: $75. Electronic applications accepted. *Expenses:* Tuition: Full-time $25,974; part-time $1443 per credit hour. *Required fees:* $802; $50 per course. Tuition and fees vary according to course load and program. *Financial support:* Fellowships with full tuition reimbursements, research assistantships with tuition reimbursements, and teaching assistantships with tuition reimbursements available. Financial award application deadline: 1/1; financial award applicants required to submit FAFSA. *Faculty research:* Economics for public decisions, comparative foreign policy, international and development administration, public and nonprofit management, quantitative analysis. *Unit head:* Dr. Robert Bifulco, Associate Dean and Chair, Department of Public Administration and International Affairs, 315-443-3232, E-mail: rbifulco@maxwell.syr.edu. *Application contact:* Christine Omolino, 315-443-4000, E-mail: comolino@syr.edu. Website: http://www.maxwell.syr.edu/

**Syracuse University,** Maxwell School of Citizenship and Public Affairs, EMPA Program of Public Administration Program, Syracuse, NY 13244. Offers EMPA. *Program availability:* Part-time. *Entrance requirements:* For master's, 7 years of mid-level professional experience, resume, personal statement, official transcripts, three letters of recommendation. Additional exam requirements/recommendations for international students: Required—TOEFL (minimum score 100 iBT). *Application deadline:* For fall admission, 2/1 for domestic and international students; for spring admission, 8/15 for domestic and international students. Applications are processed on a rolling basis. Application fee: $75. Electronic applications accepted. *Expenses:* Tuition: Full-time $25,974; part-time $1443 per credit hour. *Required fees:* $802; $50 per course. Tuition and fees vary according to course load and program. *Financial support:* Application deadline: 2/1. *Unit head:* Steven Lux, Director, Executive Education Programs, 315-443-3759, E-mail: sjlux@maxwell.syr.edu. *Application contact:* Margaret Lane, Assistant Director, Executive Education Programs, 315-443-8708, E-mail: melane02@maxwell.syr.edu. Website: http://www.maxwell.syr.edu/

**Syracuse University,** Maxwell School of Citizenship and Public Affairs, Programs in Public Administration, Syracuse, NY 13244. Offers MPA, PhD, JD/MPA, MPA/MA. *Accreditation:* NASPAA (one or more programs are accredited). *Program availability:* Part-time. In 2016, 124 master's awarded. *Degree requirements:* For doctorate, comprehensive exam, thesis/dissertation. *Entrance requirements:* For master's and doctorate, GRE General Test, resume, three letters of recommendation, personal statement, official transcripts. Additional exam requirements/recommendations for international students: Required—TOEFL (minimum score 100 iBT). *Application deadline:* For fall admission, 2/1 priority date for domestic and international students. Application fee: $75. Electronic applications accepted. *Expenses:* Tuition: Full-time $25,974; part-time $1443 per credit hour. *Required fees:* $802; $50 per course. Tuition and fees vary according to course load and program. *Financial support:* Fellowships with full tuition reimbursements, research assistantships with tuition reimbursements, teaching assistantships with tuition reimbursements, scholarships/grants, and unspecified assistantships available. Financial award application deadline: 1/1; financial award applicants required to submit FAFSA. *Faculty research:* Public and nonprofit management, government contracting, public-private partnerships, policy implementation, strategic management. *Unit head:* Dr. Robert Bifulco, Associate Dean and Chair, Public Administration and International Affairs, 315-443-3232, E-mail: rbifulco@maxwell.syr.edu. *Application contact:* Christine Omolino, Associate Director, 315-443-3712, Fax: 315-443-5330, E-mail: comolino@syr.edu. Website: http://www.maxwell.syr.edu/

**Tarleton State University,** College of Graduate Studies, College of Liberal and Fine Arts, Master of Public Administration Program, Stephenville, TX 76402. Offers MPA. *Program availability:* Part-time, evening/weekend, 100% online, blended/hybrid learning. *Faculty:* 1 full-time (0 women). *Students:* 8 full-time (6 women), 50 part-time (27 women); includes 23 minority (17 Black or African American, non-Hispanic/Latino; 6 Hispanic/Latino), 2 international. 44 applicants, 93% accepted, 31 enrolled. In 2016, 7 master's awarded. *Degree requirements:* For master's, thesis optional. *Entrance requirements:* Additional exam requirements/recommendations for international students: Required—TOEFL (minimum score 550 paper-based; 80 iBT). *Application deadline:* Applications are processed on a rolling basis. Application fee: $45 ($145 for international students). Electronic applications accepted. *Expenses:* $3,672 tuition; $2,437 fees. *Financial support:* Applicants required to submit FAFSA. *Unit head:* Dr. Alex del Carmen, Executive Director of School of Criminology, Criminal Justice, and Strategic Studies, 817-717-3669, E-mail: delcarmen@tarleton.edu. *Application contact:* Information Contact, 254-968-9104, Fax: 254-968-9670, E-mail: gradoffice@tarleton.edu. Website: http://www.tarleton.edu/degrees/masters/mpa/

**Tennessee State University,** The School of Graduate Studies and Research, College of Public Service, Nashville, TN 37209-1561. Offers human resource management (MPS); public administration (MPA, PhD); social work (MSW); strategic leadership (MPS); training and development (MPS). *Accreditation:* NASPAA (one or more programs are accredited). *Program availability:* Part-time, evening/weekend. *Degree requirements:* For master's, comprehensive exam, thesis optional; for doctorate, comprehensive exam, thesis/dissertation. *Entrance requirements:* For master's, GRE

General Test, minimum GPA of 2.5, writing sample; for doctorate, GRE General Test, minimum GPA of 3.25, writing sample. *Faculty research:* Total quality management and process improvement, national health care policy and administration, starting non-profit ventures, public service ethics, state education financing across the U.S. public.

**Texas A&M International University,** Office of Graduate Studies and Research, College of Arts and Sciences, Department of Public Affairs and Social Research, Laredo, TX 78041-1900. Offers criminal justice (MS); history and political thought (MA); political science (MA); public administration (MPA). *Degree requirements:* For master's, comprehensive exam (for some programs), thesis (for some programs). *Entrance requirements:* For master's, GRE General Test. Additional exam requirements/recommendations for international students: Required—TOEFL (minimum score 550 paper-based; 79 iBT).

**Texas A&M University,** Bush School of Government and Public Service, College Station, TX 77840. Offers homeland security (Certificate); international affairs (MIA, Certificate); national security affairs (Certificate); non-profit management (Certificate); public service and administration (MPSA). *Accreditation:* NASPAA. *Faculty:* 68. *Students:* 324 full-time (165 women), 26 part-time (10 women); includes 89 minority (19 Black or African American, non-Hispanic/Latino; 4 Asian, non-Hispanic/Latino; 58 Hispanic/Latino; 1 Native Hawaiian or other Pacific Islander, non-Hispanic/Latino; 7 Two or more races, non-Hispanic/Latino), 44 international. Average age 27. 261 applicants, 96% accepted, 165 enrolled. In 2016, 164 master's awarded. *Degree requirements:* For master's, summer internship. *Entrance requirements:* For master's, GRE (preferred) or GMAT. Additional exam requirements/recommendations for international students: Required—TOEFL (minimum score 550 paper-based; 80 iBT), IELTS (minimum score 6), PTE (minimum score 53). *Application deadline:* For fall admission, 1/15 for domestic and international students. Application fee: $50 ($90 for international students). Electronic applications accepted. *Expenses:* Contact institution. *Financial support:* In 2016–17, 413 students received support, including 16 fellowships with tuition reimbursements available (averaging $18,236 per year), 61 research assistantships with tuition reimbursements available (averaging $5,904 per year), 1 teaching assistantship (averaging $4,025 per year); career-related internships or fieldwork, institutionally sponsored loans, scholarships/grants, traineeships, health care benefits, tuition waivers (full and partial), and unspecified assistantships also available. Support available to part-time students. Financial award application deadline: 3/15; financial award applicants required to submit FAFSA. *Faculty research:* Public policy, Presidential studies, public leadership, economic policy, social policy. *Unit head:* Dr. Mark Welsh, Dean, 979-862-8007, E-mail: mwelsh@tamu.edu. *Application contact:* Kathryn Meyer, Director of Recruitment and Admissions, 979-458-4767, Fax: 979-845-4155, E-mail: bushschooladmissions@tamu.edu.
Website: http://bush.tamu.edu/

**Texas A&M University–Corpus Christi,** College of Graduate Studies, College of Liberal Arts, Corpus Christi, TX 78412-5503. Offers communication (MA); English (MA); history (MA); psychology (MA), including clinical psychology, general psychology; public administration (MPA); studio art (MFA). *Program availability:* Part-time, evening/weekend. *Faculty:* 76 full-time (39 women), 9 part-time/adjunct (4 women). *Students:* 81 full-time (49 women), 102 part-time (71 women); includes 90 minority (8 Black or African American, non-Hispanic/Latino; 2 Asian, non-Hispanic/Latino; 76 Hispanic/Latino; 4 Two or more races, non-Hispanic/Latino), 13 international. Average age 32. 134 applicants, 56% accepted, 57 enrolled. In 2016, 48 master's awarded. *Degree requirements:* For master's, comprehensive exam (for some programs), thesis (for some programs). *Entrance requirements:* For master's, portfolio. Additional exam requirements/recommendations for international students: Required—TOEFL (minimum score 550 paper-based; 79 iBT), IELTS (minimum score 6.5). *Application deadline:* For fall admission, 7/15 for domestic students, 5/1 for international students; for spring admission, 11/15 priority date for domestic students, 9/1 priority date for international students. Applications are processed on a rolling basis. Application fee: $50 ($70 for international students). Electronic applications accepted. *Financial support:* Research assistantships, teaching assistantships, career-related internships or fieldwork, Federal Work-Study, institutionally sponsored loans, scholarships/grants, health care benefits, and unspecified assistantships available. Support available to part-time students. Financial award application deadline: 3/15; financial award applicants required to submit FAFSA. *Unit head:* Dr. Mark Hartlaub, Interim Dean, 361-825-2659, Fax: 361-825-5844, E-mail: mark.hartlaub@tamucc.edu. *Application contact:* Graduate Admissions Coordinator, 361-825-2177, Fax: 361-825-2755, E-mail: gradweb@tamucc.edu.
Website: http://cla.tamucc.edu/

**Texas Southern University,** School of Public Affairs, Program in Public Administration, Houston, TX 77004-4584. Offers MPA. *Accreditation:* NASPAA. *Degree requirements:* For master's, comprehensive exam, thesis optional. *Entrance requirements:* For master's, GRE General Test, minimum GPA of 2.5. Additional exam requirements/recommendations for international students: Required—TOEFL. Electronic applications accepted.

**Texas State University,** The Graduate College, College of Liberal Arts, Program in Public Administration, San Marcos, TX 78666. Offers international relations (MPA); legal and judicial administration (MPA). *Accreditation:* NASPAA. *Program availability:* Part-time, evening/weekend. *Faculty:* 9 full-time (4 women). *Students:* 36 full-time (14 women), 59 part-time (29 women); includes 53 minority (15 Black or African American, non-Hispanic/Latino; 4 Asian, non-Hispanic/Latino; 32 Hispanic/Latino; 2 Two or more races, non-Hispanic/Latino), 1 international. Average age 31. 41 applicants, 78% accepted, 19 enrolled. In 2016, 22 master's awarded. *Degree requirements:* For master's, comprehensive exam, applied research project. *Entrance requirements:* For master's, baccalaureate degree from regionally-accredited university with minimum GPA of 3.0 on last 60 undergraduate semester hours. Additional exam requirements/recommendations for international students: Required—TOEFL (minimum score 550 paper-based; 78 iBT), IELTS (minimum score 6.5). *Application deadline:* For fall admission, 2/1 priority date for domestic and international students; for spring admission, 10/15 for domestic students, 10/1 for international students; for summer admission, 4/15 for domestic students, 3/15 for international students. Applications are processed on a rolling basis. Application fee: $40 ($90 for international students). Electronic applications accepted. *Expenses:* $4,851 per semester. *Financial support:* In 2016–17, 53 students received support, including 4 research assistantships (averaging $13,336 per year), 10 teaching assistantships (averaging $13,718 per year); career-related internships or fieldwork, Federal Work-Study, institutionally sponsored loans, scholarships/grants, and unspecified assistantships also available. Support available to part-time students. Financial award application deadline: 3/1; financial award applicants required to submit FAFSA. *Unit head:* Dr. Patricia Shields, Graduate Advisor, 512-245-3256, Fax: 512-245-7815, E-mail: ps07@txstate.edu. *Application contact:* Dr. Andrea Golato, Dean of Graduate School, 512-245-2581, Fax: 512-245-8365, E-mail: gradcollege@txstate.edu.
Website: http://www.polisci.txstate.edu/degrees-programs/graduate/MPA.html

**Texas Tech University,** Graduate School, College of Arts and Sciences, Department of Political Science, Lubbock, TX 79409-1015. Offers political science (MA, PhD); public administration (MPA); JD/MPA. *Accreditation:* NASPAA (one or more programs are

accredited). *Program availability:* Online learning. *Faculty:* 32 full-time (7 women). *Students:* 53 full-time (21 women), 25 part-time (11 women); includes 13 minority (3 Black or African American, non-Hispanic/Latino; 1 Asian, non-Hispanic/Latino; 8 Hispanic/Latino; 1 Two or more races, non-Hispanic/Latino), 20 international. Average age 31. 66 applicants, 61% accepted, 27 enrolled. In 2016, 17 master's, 5 doctorates awarded. *Degree requirements:* For master's, thesis or alternative; for doctorate, thesis/dissertation. *Entrance requirements:* For master's and doctorate, GRE General Test, 3 letters of reference. Additional exam requirements/recommendations for international students: Required—TOEFL (minimum score 550 paper-based; 79 iBT). *Application deadline:* For fall admission, 6/1 priority date for domestic students, 1/15 priority date for international students; for spring admission, 9/1 priority date for domestic students, 6/15 priority date for international students. Applications are processed on a rolling basis. Application fee: $75. Electronic applications accepted. *Expenses:* $300 per credit hour full-time resident tuition, $708 per credit hour full-time non-resident tuition; $50.50 per credit hour fee plus $608 per term fee. *Financial support:* In 2016–17, 60 students received support, including 46 fellowships (averaging $2,133 per year), 4 research assistantships (averaging $8,661 per year), 51 teaching assistantships (averaging $11,454 per year); tuition waivers and grader positions also available. Financial award application deadline: 4/15; financial award applicants required to submit FAFSA. *Faculty research:* State politics, American institutions and behavior, Asian politics, international and comparative political relations and economics, public administration and organizations. *Total annual research expenditures:* $177,690. *Unit head:* Dr. Dennis Patterson, Chair, 806-742-3121, Fax: 806-742-0850, E-mail: dennis.patterson@ttu.edu. *Application contact:* Dr. David Lektzian, Associate Chair, 806-742-3121, Fax: 806-742-0850, E-mail: david.lektzian@ttu.edu.
Website: http://www.depts.ttu.edu/politicalscience/

**Thomas Edison State University,** John S. Watson School of Public Service and Continuing Studies, Trenton, NJ 08608. Offers public service leadership (MPSL). *Program availability:* Part-time, online learning. *Entrance requirements:* Additional exam requirements/recommendations for international students: Required—TOEFL (minimum score 550 paper-based; 79 iBT). Electronic applications accepted.

**Trident University International,** College of Business Administration, Program in Business Administration, Cypress, CA 90630. Offers business administration (PhD); conflict and negotiation management (MBA); criminal justice administration (MBA); entrepreneurship (MBA); finance (MBA); general management (MBA); government accounting (MBA); human resource management (MBA); information security and digital assurance management (MBA); information technology management (MBA); international business (MBA); logistics management (MBA); marketing (MBA); project management (MBA); public management (MBA); quality management (MBA); strategic leadership (MBA). *Program availability:* Part-time, evening/weekend, online learning. *Degree requirements:* For doctorate, comprehensive exam, thesis/dissertation, defense of dissertation. *Entrance requirements:* For master's, minimum GPA of 2.5 (students with GPA 3.0 or greater may transfer up to 30% of graduate level credits); for doctorate, minimum GPA of 3.4, curriculum vitae, course work in research methods or statistics. Additional exam requirements/recommendations for international students: Required—TOEFL. Electronic applications accepted.

**Trine University,** Program in Criminal Justice, Angola, IN 46703-1764. Offers emergency management (MS); forensic psychology (MS); law (MS); public administration (MS). *Program availability:* Part-time, evening/weekend. *Entrance requirements:* Additional exam requirements/recommendations for international students: Required—TOEFL. *Expenses:* Tuition: Full-time $13,320. *Required fees:* $460. Tuition and fees vary according to degree level, campus/location, program and student level. *Financial support:* Application deadline: 3/1; applicants required to submit FAFSA. *Unit head:* Craig Laker, Dean, College of Graduate and Professional Studies/Associate Professor, 260-665-4862, E-mail: lakerc@trine.edu.
Website: http://www.trine.edu/academics/majors-and-minors/graduate/criminal-justice/index.aspx

**Troy University,** Graduate School, College of Arts and Sciences, Program in Public Administration, Troy, AL 36082. Offers government contracting (MPA). *Accreditation:* NASPAA. *Program availability:* Part-time, evening/weekend, online learning. *Faculty:* 16 full-time (11 women), 4 part-time/adjunct (2 women). *Students:* 37 full-time (21 women), 193 part-time (124 women); includes 119 minority (104 Black or African American, non-Hispanic/Latino; 1 American Indian or Alaska Native, non-Hispanic/Latino; 3 Asian, non-Hispanic/Latino; 8 Hispanic/Latino; 3 Two or more races, non-Hispanic/Latino). Average age 33. 231 applicants, 76% accepted, 17 enrolled. In 2016, 77 master's awarded. *Degree requirements:* For master's, capstone course with minimum B grade, minimum GPA of 3.0, admission to candidate. *Entrance requirements:* For master's, GRE (minimum score of 920 on old exam or 294 on new exam), MAT (minimum score of 400) or GMAT (minimum score of 490), bachelor's degree, minimum undergraduate GPA of 2.5 or 3.0 on last 30 semester hours, letter of recommendation, essay, resume. Additional exam requirements/recommendations for international students: Required—TOEFL (minimum score 523 paper-based; 70 iBT), IELTS (minimum score 6). *Application deadline:* Applications are processed on a rolling basis. Application fee: $50. Electronic applications accepted. *Expenses:* Tuition, state resident: full-time $7146; part-time $397 per credit hour. Tuition, nonresident: full-time $14,292; part-time $794 per credit hour. *Required fees:* $802; $50 per semester. Tuition and fees vary according to campus/location and program. *Financial support:* Fellowships, career-related internships or fieldwork, and scholarships/grants available. Support available to part-time students. Financial award applicants required to submit FAFSA. *Unit head:* Dr. Terry Anderson, Director, 850-301-2144, E-mail: tanderson@troy.edu. *Application contact:* Jessica A. Kimbro, Director of Graduate Admissions, 334-670-3178, E-mail: jacord@troy.edu.

**Tufts University,** Graduate School of Arts and Sciences, Graduate Certificate Programs, Program Evaluation Program, Medford, MA 02155. Offers Certificate. *Program availability:* Part-time, evening/weekend. Electronic applications accepted. *Expenses:* Contact institution.

**Université de Moncton,** Faculty of Arts and Social Sciences, Department of Public Administration, Moncton, NB E1A 3E9, Canada. Offers MPA, LL B/MPA. *Program availability:* Part-time, evening/weekend. *Degree requirements:* For master's, one foreign language. *Entrance requirements:* For master's, minimum GPA of 3.0. *Faculty research:* Public sector reform, privatization, economic modeling, public policy.

**Université de Sherbrooke,** Faculty of Administration, Program in Public Management, Sherbrooke, QC J1K 2R1, Canada. Offers M Adm. *Degree requirements:* For master's, one foreign language, thesis. *Entrance requirements:* For master's, bachelor's degree in related field, minimum GPA of 3.0 (on 4.3 scale). Electronic applications accepted.

**Université du Québec à Montréal,** Graduate Programs, Program in Urban Analysis and Management, Montréal, QC H3C 3P8, Canada. Offers MA. Program offered jointly with Université du Québec, École nationale d'administration publique and Université du Québec, Institut National de la Recherche Scientifique. *Program availability:* Part-time. *Entrance requirements:* For master's, appropriate bachelor's degree or equivalent and proficiency in French.

## Public Administration

**Université du Québec, École nationale d'administration publique,** Graduate Programs in Public Administration, Diploma Program in Public Administration, Quebec, QC G1K 9E5, Canada. Offers Diploma.

**Université du Québec, École nationale d'administration publique,** Graduate Programs in Public Administration, Doctorate Program in Public Administration, Quebec, QC G1K 9E5, Canada. Offers PhD.

**University at Albany, State University of New York,** Nelson A. Rockefeller College of Public Affairs and Policy, Department of Public Administration and Policy, Albany, NY 12222-0001. Offers financial management and public economics (MPA); financial market regulation (MPA); health policy (MPA); healthcare management (MPA); homeland security (MPA); human resources management (MPA); information strategy and management (MPA); local government management (MPA); nonprofit management (MPA); nonprofit management and leadership (Certificate); organizational behavior and theory (MPA, PhD); planning and policy analysis (CAS); policy analysis (MPA); politics and administration (PhD); public finance (PhD); public management (PhD); public policy (PhD); public sector management (Certificate); women and public policy (Certificate); JD/MPA. JD/MPA offered jointly with Albany Law School. *Accreditation:* NASPAA (one or more programs are accredited). *Faculty:* 23 full-time (8 women), 14 part-time/adjunct (7 women). *Students:* 117 full-time (65 women), 95 part-time (46 women); includes 41 minority (12 Black or African American, non-Hispanic/Latino; 8 Asian, non-Hispanic/Latino; 19 Hispanic/Latino; 2 Two or more races, non-Hispanic/Latino), 38 international. 223 applicants, 70% accepted, 81 enrolled. In 2016, 52 master's, 10 doctorates, 16 other advanced degrees awarded. *Degree requirements:* For doctorate, one foreign language, thesis/dissertation. *Entrance requirements:* For doctorate, GRE General Test. Additional exam requirements/recommendations for international students: Required—TOEFL (minimum score 550 paper-based). *Application deadline:* For fall admission, 2/1 priority date for domestic students, 5/1 for international students; for spring admission, 12/1 for domestic students. Applications are processed on a rolling basis. Application fee: $75. Electronic applications accepted. *Expenses:* Tuition, state resident: full-time $10,870; part-time $453 per credit hour. Tuition, nonresident: full-time $22,210; part-time $925 per credit hour. *International tuition:* $21,550 full-time. *Required fees:* $1864; $96 per credit hour. *Financial support:* Application deadline: 2/1. *Total annual research expenditures:* $847,949. *Unit head:* Victor Asal, Chair, 518-591-8729, E-mail: vasal@albany.edu.
Website: http://www.albany.edu/rockefeller/pad.shtml

**The University of Akron,** Graduate School, Buchtel College of Arts and Sciences, Department of Public Administration and Urban Studies, Program in Public Administration, Akron, OH 44325. Offers MPA; JD/MPA. *Students:* 35 full-time (21 women), 23 part-time (16 women); includes 20 minority (16 Black or African American, non-Hispanic/Latino; 1 Hispanic/Latino; 3 Two or more races, non-Hispanic/Latino), 9 international. Average age 34. 40 applicants, 95% accepted, 20 enrolled. In 2016, 22 master's awarded. *Entrance requirements:* For master's, GRE, GMAT, LSAT, MAT (if undergraduate cumulative GPA less than 3.0), minimum GPA of 3.0, resume, one-page personal essay, three letters of recommendation. Additional exam requirements/recommendations for international students: Required—TOEFL (minimum score 550 paper-based; 79 iBT). *Application deadline:* For fall admission, 7/1 priority date for domestic and international students; for spring admission, 11/15 priority date for domestic and international students; for summer admission, 4/1 priority date for domestic and international students. Applications are processed on a rolling basis. Application fee: $45 ($70 for international students). Electronic applications accepted. *Expenses:* Tuition, state resident: full-time $8618; part-time $359 per credit hour. Tuition, nonresident: full-time $17,149; part-time $715 per credit hour. *Required fees:* $1652. *Unit head:* Dr. Nancy Marion, Interim Chair, 330-972-5551, E-mail: nmarion@uakron.edu.
Website: http://www.uakron.edu/paus/academics/

**The University of Alabama,** Graduate School, College of Arts and Sciences, Department of Political Science, Tuscaloosa, AL 35487. Offers political science (MA, PhD); public administration (MPA). *Program availability:* Part-time. *Faculty:* 16 full-time (4 women). *Students:* 48 full-time (16 women), 17 part-time (3 women); includes 12 minority (9 Black or African American, non-Hispanic/Latino; 1 American Indian or Alaska Native, non-Hispanic/Latino; 1 Asian, non-Hispanic/Latino; 1 Two or more races, non-Hispanic/Latino), 6 international. Average age 30. 44 applicants, 70% accepted, 16 enrolled. In 2016, 16 master's, 4 doctorates awarded. Terminal master's awarded for partial completion of doctoral program. *Degree requirements:* For master's, comprehensive exam, thesis optional; for doctorate, comprehensive exam, thesis/dissertation. *Entrance requirements:* For master's and doctorate, GRE, minimum undergraduate GPA of 3.0. Additional exam requirements/recommendations for international students: Required—TOEFL. *Application deadline:* For fall admission, 6/30 for domestic and international students; for spring admission, 10/15 for domestic and international students. Applications are processed on a rolling basis. Application fee: $50 ($60 for international students). Electronic applications accepted. *Expenses:* Tuition, state resident: full-time $10,470. Tuition, nonresident: full-time $26,950. *Financial support:* In 2016–17, 15 students received support, including 3 fellowships with full tuition reimbursements available (averaging $15,000 per year), teaching assistantships with full tuition reimbursements available (averaging $12,500 per year); career-related internships or fieldwork and Federal Work-Study also available. Financial award application deadline: 2/15. *Faculty research:* American politics, comparative politics, international relations, public policy and administration, political theory. *Total annual research expenditures:* $5,000. *Unit head:* Dr. Joseph Smith, Chair and Professor, 205-348-5981, E-mail: josmith@bama.ua.edu. *Application contact:* Dr. Douglas Gibler, Graduate Advisor, 205-348-5528, Fax: 205-348-5298, E-mail: dmgibler@bama.ua.edu.
Website: http://www.as.ua.edu/psc/

**The University of Alabama at Birmingham,** College of Arts and Sciences, Master of Public Administration Program, Birmingham, AL 35233. Offers MPA, MPA/JD, MPA/MPH, MPA/MSCJ. *Accreditation:* NASPAA (one or more programs are accredited). *Program availability:* Part-time, evening/weekend, 100% online, blended/hybrid learning. *Degree requirements:* For master's, portfolio or thesis. *Entrance requirements:* For master's, GRE General Test (preferred), references. Additional exam requirements/recommendations for international students: Required—TOEFL (minimum score 500 paper-based; 70 iBT), IELTS (minimum score 6.5). Electronic applications accepted. *Expenses:* Contact institution. *Faculty research:* Information management and technology, nonprofit management, education policy and planning, political philosophy, program evaluation, Geographic Information System, administrative ethics, administrative theory and behavior.

**University of Alaska Anchorage,** College of Business and Public Policy, Program in Public Administration, Anchorage, AK 99508. Offers MPA. *Program availability:* Part-time. *Degree requirements:* For master's, comprehensive exam, thesis or alternative, capstone project. *Entrance requirements:* For master's, GRE General Test. Additional exam requirements/recommendations for international students: Required—TOEFL (minimum score 550 paper-based). *Faculty research:* Policy analysis, policy and administration issues in the North, hypothetical government policies, public management in health care.

**University of Alaska Southeast,** Graduate Programs, Program in Public Administration, Juneau, AK 99801. Offers MPA. *Program availability:* Part-time, evening/weekend, online learning. *Degree requirements:* For master's, capstone course or thesis. *Entrance requirements:* For master's, minimum GPA of 3.0, resume or curriculum vitae, three letters of reference. Additional exam requirements/recommendations for international students: Recommended—TOEFL. *Application deadline:* Applications are processed on a rolling basis. Application fee: $60. Electronic applications accepted. *Expenses:* Tuition, state resident: part-time $466 per credit. Tuition, nonresident: part-time $979 per credit. *Required fees:* $19 per credit. Part-time tuition and fees vary according to course level, campus/location and reciprocity agreements. *Financial support:* Federal Work-Study, scholarships/grants, and tuition waivers (full and partial) available. Support available to part-time students. Financial award applicants required to submit FAFSA. *Faculty research:* Democratic governance, public administrative theory, local government. *Unit head:* Kathy DiLorenzo, Director, 907-796-6418, Fax: 907-796-6383, E-mail: kathy.dilorenzo@uas.alaska.edu.
Website: http://www.uas.alaska.edu/mpa

**The University of Arizona,** College of Social and Behavioral Sciences, Program in Public Administration, Tucson, AZ 85721. Offers public administration (MPA); public administration and policy (PhD). *Accreditation:* NASPAA. *Degree requirements:* For master's, internship of 400 hours; for doctorate, comprehensive exam, thesis/dissertation. *Entrance requirements:* For doctorate, GMAT or GRE, minimum graduate GPA of 3.5, letter of interest, 3 letters of recommendation, resume. Additional exam requirements/recommendations for international students: Required—TOEFL (minimum score 650 paper-based; 115 iBT). Electronic applications accepted. *Expenses:* Contact institution.

**University of Arkansas,** Graduate School, J. William Fulbright College of Arts and Sciences, Department of Political Science, Program in Public Administration, Fayetteville, AR 72701. Offers MPA. In 2016, 10 master's awarded. *Degree requirements:* For master's, comprehensive exam, thesis or alternative. *Entrance requirements:* For master's, GRE General Test. *Application deadline:* For fall admission, 4/1 for international students; for spring admission, 10/1 for international students. Applications are processed on a rolling basis. Application fee: $40 ($50 for international students). Electronic applications accepted. *Financial support:* In 2016–17, 2 research assistantships, 1 teaching assistantship were awarded; fellowships with tuition reimbursements, career-related internships or fieldwork, and Federal Work-Study also available. Support available to part-time students. Financial award application deadline: 4/1; financial award applicants required to submit FAFSA. *Unit head:* Dr. John Gaber, 479-575-3356, Fax: 479-575-6432, E-mail: jgaber@uark.edu. *Application contact:* Dr. Pearl Dowe, Graduate Coordinator, 479-575-3356, Fax: 479-575-6432, E-mail: pkford@uark.edu.
Website: http://plsc.uark.edu/

**University of Arkansas at Little Rock,** Graduate School, College of Social Sciences and Communication, Program in Public Administration, Little Rock, AR 72204-1099. Offers MPA. *Accreditation:* NASPAA. *Program availability:* Part-time, evening/weekend. *Degree requirements:* For master's, comprehensive exam. *Entrance requirements:* For master's, GRE General Test or MAT, minimum GPA of 2.7. *Faculty research:* State and local administration, nonprofit management.

**University of Baltimore,** Graduate School, College of Public Affairs, Doctoral Program in Public Administration, Baltimore, MD 21201-5779. Offers DPA. *Program availability:* Part-time, evening/weekend. *Degree requirements:* For doctorate, thesis/dissertation. *Entrance requirements:* For doctorate, GRE. Additional exam requirements/recommendations for international students: Required—TOEFL.

**University of Baltimore,** Graduate School, College of Public Affairs, Master's Program in Public Administration, Baltimore, MD 21201-5779. Offers MPA, JD/MPA. *Accreditation:* NASPAA. *Program availability:* Part-time, evening/weekend, online learning. *Entrance requirements:* For master's, interview, minimum GPA of 3.0. Additional exam requirements/recommendations for international students: Required—TOEFL (minimum score 550 paper-based). Electronic applications accepted. *Expenses:* Contact institution. *Faculty research:* Welfare policy, public administration ethics, bureaucratic politics, public sector budgeting, program evaluation.

**University of Central Florida,** College of Health and Public Affairs, School of Public Administration, Orlando, FL 32816. Offers emergency management and homeland security (Certificate); fundraising (Certificate); non-profit management (MNM, Certificate); urban and regional planning (MS). *Accreditation:* NASPAA. *Program availability:* Part-time, evening/weekend. *Faculty:* 24 full-time (11 women), 11 part-time/adjunct (6 women). *Students:* 87 full-time (60 women), 257 part-time (190 women); includes 157 minority (83 Black or African American, non-Hispanic/Latino; 1 American Indian or Alaska Native, non-Hispanic/Latino; 9 Asian, non-Hispanic/Latino; 62 Hispanic/Latino; 2 Two or more races, non-Hispanic/Latino), 7 international. Average age 32. 192 applicants, 79% accepted, 108 enrolled. In 2016, 118 master's, 36 other advanced degrees awarded. *Degree requirements:* For master's, comprehensive exam, thesis or alternative, research report. *Entrance requirements:* For master's, GRE General Test. *Application deadline:* For fall admission, 6/15 for domestic students; for spring admission, 11/1 for domestic students. Application fee: $30. Electronic applications accepted. *Expenses:* Tuition, state resident: part-time $288.16 per credit hour. Tuition, nonresident: part-time $1071.31 per credit hour. *Financial support:* In 2016–17, 9 students received support, including 1 fellowship with partial tuition reimbursement available (averaging $4,000 per year), 9 research assistantships with partial tuition reimbursements available (averaging $6,704 per year); career-related internships or fieldwork, Federal Work-Study, institutionally sponsored loans, tuition waivers (partial), and unspecified assistantships also available. Financial award application deadline: 3/1; financial award applicants required to submit FAFSA. *Unit head:* Dr. Naim Kapucu, Director, 407-823-3693, Fax: 407-823-5651, E-mail: naim.kapucu@ucf.edu. *Application contact:* Assistant Director, Graduate Admissions, 407-823-2766, Fax: 407-823-6442, E-mail: gradadmissions@ucf.edu.
Website: https://www.cohpa.ucf.edu/publicadmin/

**University of Central Oklahoma,** The Jackson College of Graduate Studies, College of Liberal Arts, Department of Political Science, Edmond, OK 73034-5209. Offers international affairs (MA); political science (MA); public administration (MPA). *Program availability:* Part-time. *Degree requirements:* For master's, comprehensive exam (for some programs), thesis (for some programs). *Entrance requirements:* For master's, GRE, 18 undergraduate hours in political science. Additional exam requirements/recommendations for international students: Required—TOEFL (minimum score 550 paper-based; 79 iBT), IELTS (minimum score 6.5). Electronic applications accepted.

**University of Colorado Colorado Springs,** School of Public Affairs, Colorado Springs, CO 80918. Offers criminal justice (MCJ); public administration (MPA). *Accreditation:* NASPAA. *Program availability:* Part-time, evening/weekend, 100% online, blended/hybrid learning. *Faculty:* 11 full-time (4 women), 5 part-time/adjunct (3 women). *Students:* 22 full-time (12 women), 142 part-time (79 women); includes 44 minority (6 Black or African American, non-Hispanic/Latino; 1 American Indian or Alaska Native, non-Hispanic/Latino; 4 Asian, non-Hispanic/Latino; 25 Hispanic/Latino; 8 Two or more races, non-Hispanic/Latino). Average age 35. 62 applicants, 94% accepted, 44 enrolled.

In 2016, 32 master's awarded. *Degree requirements:* For master's, internship, capstone project, or thesis. *Entrance requirements:* For master's, GRE General Test, GMAT, LSAT, minimum GPA of 3.0. Additional exam requirements/recommendations for international students: Recommended—TOEFL (minimum score 550 paper-based; 80 iBT), IELTS (minimum score 6.5). *Application deadline:* Applications are processed on a rolling basis. Application fee: $60 ($100 for international students). Electronic applications accepted. *Expenses:* Contact institution. *Financial support:* In 2016–17, 36 students received support. Career-related internships or fieldwork, scholarships/grants, and tuition waivers available. Support available to part-time students. Financial award application deadline: 3/1; financial award applicants required to submit FAFSA. *Faculty research:* Antiquated prison environments; public management; intersections of gender, class, race and crime; national security/U.S. foreign policy; leadership, ethics, organizational theory and behavior. *Total annual research expenditures:* $513,691. *Unit head:* Dr. George Reed, Dean, 719-255-4109, E-mail: george.reed@uccs.edu. *Application contact:* Crista Hill, Outreach Student Services Specialist, 719-255-4993, Fax: 719-255-4183, E-mail: chill12@uccs.edu.
Website: http://www.uccs.edu/spa/

**University of Colorado Denver,** School of Public Affairs, Program in Public Affairs and Administration, Denver, CO 80127. Offers public administration (MPA), including domestic violence, emergency management and homeland security, environmental policy, management and law, homeland security and defense, local government, nonprofit management, public administration; public affairs (PhD). *Accreditation:* NASPAA. *Program availability:* Part-time, evening/weekend, online learning. *Students:* 241 full-time (146 women), 135 part-time (86 women); includes 61 minority (15 Black or African American, non-Hispanic/Latino; 1 American Indian or Alaska Native, non-Hispanic/Latino; 10 Asian, non-Hispanic/Latino; 26 Hispanic/Latino; 2 Native Hawaiian or other Pacific Islander, non-Hispanic/Latino; 7 Two or more races, non-Hispanic/Latino), 26 international. Average age 36. 240 applicants, 70% accepted, 91 enrolled. In 2016, 158 master's, 8 doctorates awarded. *Degree requirements:* For master's, thesis or alternative, 36-39 credit hours; for doctorate, comprehensive exam, thesis/dissertation, minimum of 66 semester hours, including at least 30 hours of dissertation. *Entrance requirements:* For master's, GRE, GMAT or LSAT, resume, essay, transcripts, recommendations; for doctorate, GRE, resume, essay, transcripts, recommendations. Additional exam requirements/recommendations for international students: Required—TOEFL (minimum score 550 paper-based; 80 iBT); Recommended—IELTS (minimum score 6.5). *Application deadline:* For fall admission, 2/1 priority date for domestic students, 1/15 priority date for international students; for spring admission, 10/15 priority date for domestic students, 10/1 priority date for international students. Application fee: $50 ($75 for international students). Electronic applications accepted. *Expenses:* Contact institution. *Financial support:* In 2016–17, 92 students received support. Fellowships with partial tuition reimbursements available, research assistantships with partial tuition reimbursements available, teaching assistantships with partial tuition reimbursements available, Federal Work-Study, institutionally sponsored loans, scholarships/grants, traineeships, and unspecified assistantships available. Financial award application deadline: 4/1; financial award applicants required to submit FAFSA. *Faculty research:* Housing, education and the social and economic issues of vulnerable populations; nonprofit governance and management; education finance, effectiveness and reform; P-20 education initiatives; municipal government accountability. *Unit head:* Dr. Christine Martell, Director of MPA Program, 303-315-2716, Fax: 303-315-2229, E-mail: christine.martell@ucdenver.edu. *Application contact:* Dawn Savage, Student Services Coordinator, 303-315-2743, Fax: 303-315-2229,
E-mail: dawn.savage@ucdenver.edu.
Website: http://www.ucdenver.edu/academics/colleges/SPA/Academics/programs/PublicAffairsAdmin/Pages/index.aspx

**University of Connecticut,** Graduate School, College of Liberal Arts and Sciences, Department of Public Policy, Field of Public Administration, Storrs, CT 06269. Offers MPA. *Accreditation:* NASPAA. *Degree requirements:* For master's, comprehensive exam, internship. *Entrance requirements:* For master's, GRE General Test. Additional exam requirements/recommendations for international students: Required—TOEFL (minimum score 550 paper-based). Electronic applications accepted.

**University of Dayton,** Master of Public Administration Program, Dayton, OH 45469. Offers MPA. *Accreditation:* NASPAA. *Program availability:* Part-time, evening/weekend. *Faculty:* 6 full-time (2 women), 4 part-time/adjunct (2 women). *Students:* 19 full-time (12 women), 8 part-time (5 women); includes 3 minority (1 Black or African American, non-Hispanic/Latino; 2 Two or more races, non-Hispanic/Latino), 1 international. Average age 31. 39 applicants, 21% accepted. In 2016, 7 master's awarded. *Degree requirements:* For master's, internship or public service project. *Entrance requirements:* For master's, GRE General Test. Additional exam requirements/recommendations for international students: Required—TOEFL (minimum score 550 paper-based; 85 iBT). *Application deadline:* Applications are processed on a rolling basis. Application fee: $0 ($50 for international students). Electronic applications accepted. *Expenses:* $620 per credit hour, $25 registration fee per term. *Financial support:* In 2016–17, 5 research assistantships with full tuition reimbursements (averaging $11,700 per year) were awarded; health care benefits and unspecified assistantships also available. Financial award application deadline: 3/1; financial award applicants required to submit FAFSA. *Faculty research:* Environmental policy and regulation, state politics, NGOs advocacy, urban politics. *Unit head:* Dr. Michelle Pautz, Director, MPA Program, 937-229-3651, Fax: 937-229-1400, E-mail: mpautz1@udayton.edu. *Application contact:* Dr. Michelle Pautz, Director, MPA Program, 937-229-3651, Fax: 937-229-1400,
E-mail: graduateadmission@udayton.edu.
Website: https://www.udayton.edu/artssciences/academics/politicalscience/grad/index.php

**University of Delaware,** College of Arts and Sciences, School of Public Policy and Administration, Program in Public Administration, Newark, DE 19716. Offers MPA. *Accreditation:* NASPAA. *Program availability:* Part-time, evening/weekend. *Degree requirements:* For master's, internship or thesis. *Entrance requirements:* For master's, GRE General Test. Additional exam requirements/recommendations for international students: Required—TOEFL. Electronic applications accepted. *Faculty research:* State and local management, community development and nonprofit leadership, drug and alcohol epidemiology, fiscal and financial policy, transportation impacts and management.

**See Display below and Close-Up on page 1333.**

**University of Evansville,** Center for Adult Education, Evansville, IN 47722. Offers public service administration (MS). *Program availability:* Part-time, evening/weekend. *Entrance requirements:* For master's, GRE or MAT, minimum undergraduate GPA of 3.0, resume, minimum of 3 years' work experience, 2 letters of reference. Additional exam requirements/recommendations for international students: Required—TOEFL (minimum score 79 iBT), IELTS (minimum score 6.5). *Application deadline:* For fall admission, 7/15 for domestic students; for spring admission, 11/30 for domestic students. Application fee: $35. *Expenses:* Contact institution. *Financial support:* Unspecified assistantships available. Financial award application deadline: 6/1; financial award applicants required to submit FAFSA. *Unit head:* Lindsay Roberts, Director, 812-488-3101, Fax: 812-488-2432, E-mail: cae@evansville.edu.
Website: http://www.evansville.edu/adulteducation/

**The University of Findlay,** Office of Graduate Admissions, Findlay, OH 45840-3653. Offers applied security and analytics (MSAS); athletic training (MAT); business (MBA), including certified management accountant, certified public accountant, health care

## Public Administration

management, hospitality management; education (MA Ed, Ed D), including children's literature (MA Ed), curriculum and teaching (MA Ed), education (MA Ed), educational administration (MA Ed), human resource development (MA Ed), reading (MA Ed), science education (MA Ed), superintendent (Ed D), teaching (Ed D), technology (MA Ed); environmental, safety and health management (MSEM); health informatics (MS); occupational therapy (MOT); pharmacy (Pharm D); physical therapy (DPT); physician assistant (MPA); rhetoric and writing (MA); teaching English to speakers of other languages (TESOL) and bilingual education (MA). *Program availability:* Part-time, evening/weekend, 100% online, blended/hybrid learning. *Faculty:* 114 full-time (63 women), 44 part-time/adjunct (18 women). *Students:* 751 full-time (452 women), 573 part-time (323 women); includes 164 minority (82 Black or African American, non-Hispanic/Latino; 1 American Indian or Alaska Native, non-Hispanic/Latino; 27 Asian, non-Hispanic/Latino; 37 Hispanic/Latino; 17 Two or more races, non-Hispanic/Latino), 280 international. Average age 28. 661 applicants, 52% accepted, 288 enrolled. In 2016, 366 master's, 137 doctorates awarded. *Degree requirements:* For master's, comprehensive exam (for some programs), thesis, cumulative project, capstone project; for doctorate, thesis/dissertation. *Entrance requirements:* For master's, GRE (for some programs), bachelor's degree from accredited institution, minimum undergraduate GPA of 3.0 in last 64 hours of course work; for doctorate, MAT, minimum cumulative GPA of 3.0, master's degree. Additional exam requirements/recommendations for international students: Recommended—TOEFL (minimum score 79 iBT), IELTS (minimum score 7). *Application deadline:* For fall admission, 6/15 for international students; for spring admission, 12/1 for international students; for summer admission, 4/1 for international students. Applications are processed on a rolling basis. Electronic applications accepted. *Expenses:* Contact institution. *Financial support:* In 2016–17, 139 students received support, including 15 research assistantships with partial tuition reimbursements available (averaging $7,200 per year), 25 teaching assistantships with partial tuition reimbursements available (averaging $7,200 per year); Federal Work-Study, institutionally sponsored loans, and unspecified assistantships also available. Financial award application deadline: 4/1; financial award applicants required to submit FAFSA. *Unit head:* Christopher M. Harris, Director of Admissions, 419-434-4347, E-mail: harrisc1@findlay.edu. *Application contact:* Madeline Fauser Brennan, Graduate Admissions Counselor, 419-434-4636, Fax: 419-434-4898, E-mail: fauserbrennan@findlay.edu.
Website: http://www.findlay.edu/admissions/graduate/Pages/default.aspx

**University of Georgia,** School of Public and International Affairs, Department of Public Administration and Policy, Athens, GA 30602. Offers public administration (MPA, PhD). *Accreditation:* NASPAA (one or more programs are accredited). *Degree requirements:* For master's, internship; for doctorate, thesis/dissertation. *Entrance requirements:* For master's and doctorate, GRE General Test. *Application deadline:* For fall admission, 7/1 priority date for domestic students; for spring admission, 11/15 for domestic students. Application fee: $50. Electronic applications accepted. *Financial support:* Fellowships, research assistantships, teaching assistantships, and unspecified assistantships available. *Unit head:* Dr. J. Edward Kellough, Head, 706-542-0488, E-mail: kellough@uga.edu. *Application contact:* Dr. Vicky M. Wilkins, Graduate Coordinator, 706-542-2648, Fax: 706-583-4421, E-mail: vwilkins@uga.edu.

**University of Guam,** Office of Graduate Studies, School of Business and Public Administration, Public Administration Program, Mangilao, GU 96923. Offers MPA. *Entrance requirements:* For master's, GRE General Test. Additional exam requirements/recommendations for international students: Required—TOEFL.

**University of Guelph,** Graduate Studies, College of Social and Applied Human Sciences, Department of Political Science, Guelph, ON N1G 2W1, Canada. Offers comparative politics (MA); international development (MA); political science (MA); public policy and public administration (MA); the Americas (Canada emphasis) (MA). MA in public policy and public administration offered in collaboration with Department of Political Science of McMaster University. *Degree requirements:* For master's, thesis or paper. *Entrance requirements:* For master's, minimum B average during previous 2 years of course work, 4 year Honours Degree in Political Science. Additional exam requirements/recommendations for international students: Required—TOEFL. Electronic applications accepted. *Faculty research:* Political ethics, constitutional power.

**University of Hawaii at Manoa,** Graduate Division, College of Social Sciences, Department of Public Administration, Honolulu, HI 96822. Offers MPA, Graduate Certificate. *Program availability:* Part-time. *Degree requirements:* For master's, thesis optional, practicum. *Entrance requirements:* Additional exam requirements/recommendations for international students: Required—TOEFL (minimum score 540 paper-based; 76 iBT), IELTS (minimum score 5). *Faculty research:* Public sector finance and the budget process, collaboration between sectors, organizational problem solving and communication processes, system reform in government organizations, public policy analysis.

**University of Houston,** College of Liberal Arts and Social Sciences, Department of Political Science, Houston, TX 77204. Offers political science (MA, PhD); public administration (MA). *Program availability:* Part-time. Terminal master's awarded for partial completion of doctoral program. *Degree requirements:* For master's, thesis optional; for doctorate, thesis/dissertation. *Entrance requirements:* For master's and doctorate, GRE. Additional exam requirements/recommendations for international students: Required—TOEFL (minimum score 550 paper-based; 79 iBT). *Faculty research:* American politics, political theory, judicial process, public policy, comparative politics.

**University of Idaho,** College of Graduate Studies, College of Letters, Arts and Social Sciences, Department of Politics and Philosophy, Moscow, ID 83844. Offers political science (MA, PhD); public administration (MPA). *Faculty:* 9 full-time. *Students:* 8 full-time, 12 part-time. Average age 35. In 2016, 7 master's awarded. *Entrance requirements:* For master's, minimum GPA of 3.0. Additional exam requirements/recommendations for international students: Required—TOEFL. *Expenses:* Tuition, state resident: full-time $6460; part-time $414 per credit hour. Tuition, nonresident: full-time $21,268; part-time $1237 per credit hour. *Required fees:* $2070; $60 per credit hour. Full-time tuition and fees vary according to course load and reciprocity agreements. *Unit head:* Dr. Brian Ellison, Chair, 208-885-6328, E-mail: politicsphilosophy@uidaho.edu. *Application contact:* Sean Scoggin, Graduate Recruitment Coordinator, 208-885-4723, E-mail: graduateadmissions@uidaho.edu.
Website: https://www.uidaho.edu/class/politics-and-philosophy

**University of Illinois at Chicago,** College of Urban Planning and Public Affairs, Department of Public Administration, Chicago, IL 60607-7128. Offers MPA, PhD. *Accreditation:* NASPAA (one or more programs are accredited). *Program availability:* Part-time, evening/weekend. Terminal master's awarded for partial completion of doctoral program. *Degree requirements:* For master's, internship/project. *Entrance requirements:* For master's, GRE General Test, minimum GPA of 3.0. Additional exam requirements/recommendations for international students: Required—TOEFL. Electronic applications accepted. *Expenses:* Contact institution. *Faculty research:* E-government, science and technology policy, financial management, urban policy, nonprofit management, public management.

**University of Illinois at Springfield,** Graduate Programs, College of Public Affairs and Administration, Program in Public Administration, Springfield, IL 62703-5407. Offers management of nonprofit organizations (Graduate Certificate); public administration (MPA, DPA). *Accreditation:* NASPAA. *Program availability:* Part-time, evening/weekend, 100% online, blended/hybrid learning. *Faculty:* 13 full-time (6 women), 7 part-time/ adjunct (4 women). *Students:* 46 full-time (26 women), 168 part-time (105 women); includes 68 minority (40 Black or African American, non-Hispanic/Latino; 8 Asian, non-Hispanic/Latino; 13 Hispanic/Latino; 1 Native Hawaiian or other Pacific Islander, non-Hispanic/Latino; 6 Two or more races, non-Hispanic/Latino), 7 international. Average age 35. 167 applicants, 50% accepted, 64 enrolled. In 2016, 69 master's, 1 doctorate, 15 other advanced degrees awarded. *Degree requirements:* For master's, capstone seminar; for doctorate, comprehensive exam, thesis/dissertation. *Entrance requirements:* For master's, minimum undergraduate GPA of 2.5; completion of prerequisites that include undergraduate coursework in political science in American national government, microeconomics or a market-based economics survey course, basic statistics, and competence in one computer spreadsheet application package; resume; career goals statement; for doctorate, GRE, master's degree with minimum GPA of 3.25; educational and professional goals statement of at least 600 words, including possible research interest; evidence of significant work experience in public affairs field; at least one sample of professional writing; current vitae; 3 letters of recommendation. Additional exam requirements/recommendations for international students: Required—TOEFL (minimum score 550 paper-based). *Application deadline:* Applications are processed on a rolling basis. Application fee: $60 ($75 for international students). Electronic applications accepted. *Expenses:* $409.75 per hour in-state, $775.75 per hour out-of-state (for DPA); $453 per hour (for online MPA). *Financial support:* In 2016–17, fellowships with full tuition reimbursements (averaging $9,900 per year), research assistantships with full tuition reimbursements (averaging $9,991 per year), teaching assistantships with full tuition reimbursements (averaging $10,059 per year) were awarded; career-related internships or fieldwork, Federal Work-Study, scholarships/grants, health care benefits, and unspecified assistantships also available. Support available to part-time students. Financial award application deadline: 11/15; financial award applicants required to submit FAFSA. *Unit head:* Dr. Robert Blankenberger, Program Administrator, 217-206-8327, E-mail: rblan2@uis.edu. *Application contact:* Dr. Cecelia Cornell, Associate Vice Chancellor for Graduate Education, 217-206-7230, E-mail: ccorn1@uis.edu.
Website: http://www.uis.edu/publicadministration/

**The University of Kansas,** Graduate Studies, College of Liberal Arts and Sciences, School of Public Affairs and Administration, Lawrence, KS 66045-3177. Offers city and county management (Graduate Certificate); performance management (Graduate Certificate); public administration (MPA, PhD); JD/MPA; MUP/MPA. *Accreditation:* NASPAA. *Program availability:* Part-time, evening/weekend. *Students:* 45 full-time (21 women), 67 part-time (39 women); includes 18 minority (8 Black or African American, non-Hispanic/Latino; 3 American Indian or Alaska Native, non-Hispanic/Latino; 2 Asian, non-Hispanic/Latino; 5 Hispanic/Latino), 5 international. Average age 34. 85 applicants, 46% accepted, 29 enrolled. In 2016, 33 master's, 1 other advanced degree awarded. Terminal master's awarded for partial completion of doctoral program. *Entrance requirements:* For master's and doctorate, GRE General Test, official transcript, current resume, personal statement, writing sample, three letters of recommendation. Additional exam requirements/recommendations for international students: Required—TOEFL or IELTS. *Application deadline:* For fall admission, 1/25 priority date for domestic and international students; for spring admission, 5/1 priority date for domestic and international students; for summer admission, 2/1 for domestic and international students. Application fee: $65 ($85 for international students). Electronic applications accepted. *Financial support:* Fellowships, research assistantships, teaching assistantships, career-related internships or fieldwork, institutionally sponsored loans, scholarships/grants, and unspecified assistantships available. Financial award application deadline: 1/25. *Faculty research:* Collaboration, law and society, social equity, performance management, sustainability. *Unit head:* Reggie Robinson, Director, 785-864-3527, E-mail: rlrobinson@ku.edu. *Application contact:* Angie Soden, Graduate Admissions Contact, 785-864-3527, E-mail: padept@ku.edu.
Website: http://www.kupa.ku.edu/

**University of Kentucky,** Graduate School, Martin School of Public Policy and Administration, Lexington, KY 40506-0027. Offers public administration (MPA); public financial management (MPFM, Graduate Certificate); public policy (MPP); public policy and administration (PhD). *Accreditation:* NASPAA (one or more programs are accredited). *Program availability:* Part-time, evening/weekend, 100% online. *Faculty:* 10 full-time (2 women), 3 part-time/adjunct (1 woman). *Students:* 74 full-time (26 women), 15 part-time (7 women); includes 7 minority (3 Black or African American, non-Hispanic/ Latino; 4 Asian, non-Hispanic/Latino), 27 international. Average age 30. 98 applicants, 63% accepted, 33 enrolled. In 2016, 22 master's, 4 doctorates awarded. Terminal master's awarded for partial completion of doctoral program. *Degree requirements:* For master's, thesis; for doctorate, comprehensive exam, thesis/dissertation. *Entrance requirements:* For master's, GMAT or GRE General Test, minimum undergraduate GPA of 2.75; for doctorate, GMAT or GRE General Test, minimum graduate GPA of 3.0. Additional exam requirements/recommendations for international students: Required— TOEFL (minimum score 550 paper-based; 79 iBT); Recommended—IELTS (minimum score 6.5). *Application deadline:* For fall admission, 7/15 priority date for domestic students, 3/15 priority date for international students; for spring admission, 12/15 priority date for domestic students, 8/15 priority date for international students. Applications are processed on a rolling basis. Application fee: $65 ($75 for international students). Electronic applications accepted. *Expenses:* Contact institution. *Financial support:* In 2016–17, 22 students received support, including 4 fellowships with full tuition reimbursements available (averaging $10,000 per year), 13 research assistantships with full tuition reimbursements available (averaging $12,500 per year); career-related internships or fieldwork, scholarships/grants, health care benefits, and unspecified assistantships also available. Financial award application deadline: 2/1. *Faculty research:* Public financial management, education finance and policy, tax policy, environmental policy, public organizations and management. *Unit head:* Dr. Ron W. Zimmer, Director of the Martin School, 859-323-5413, Fax: 859-323-1937, E-mail: ron.zimmer@uky.edu. *Application contact:* Jackie McCuddy, Student Affairs Officer, 859-257-5594, Fax: 859-323-1937, E-mail: jackie.mccuddy@uky.edu.
Website: http://www.martin.uky.edu/

**University of La Verne,** College of Business and Public Management, Doctoral Program in Public Administration, La Verne, CA 91750-4443. Offers DPA. *Program availability:* Part-time. *Students:* 61 part-time (31 women); includes 38 minority (11 Black or African American, non-Hispanic/Latino; 2 Asian, non-Hispanic/Latino; 23 Hispanic/ Latino; 1 Native Hawaiian or other Pacific Islander, non-Hispanic/Latino; 1 Two or more races, non-Hispanic/Latino), 6 international. Average age 41. *Degree requirements:* For doctorate, thesis/dissertation. *Entrance requirements:* For doctorate, MAT, GMAT or GRE, minimum undergraduate GPA of 3.25, interview, 3 letters of recommendation, statement of purpose. Additional exam requirements/recommendations for international students: Required—TOEFL (minimum score 550 paper-based). Application fee: $75. *Expenses:* Contact institution. *Financial support:* Institutionally sponsored loans and scholarships/grants available. Financial award application deadline: 3/2; financial award

applicants required to submit FAFSA. *Unit head:* Dr. Suzanne Beaumaster, Chairperson, 909-448-4166, E-mail: sbeaumaster@laverne.edu. *Application contact:* Cathy Cook, Associate Director of Graduate Admission, 909-448-4719, Fax: 909-971-2295, E-mail: ccook2@laverne.edu.
Website: http://laverne.edu/business-and-public-administration/doctor-of-public-administration/

**University of La Verne,** College of Business and Public Management, Master's Program in Public Administration, La Verne, CA 91750-4443. Offers nonprofit (MPA); urban management and affairs (MPA). *Accreditation:* NASPAA. *Program availability:* Part-time. *Students:* 16 full-time (14 women), 44 part-time (25 women); includes 46 minority (1 Asian, non-Hispanic/Latino; 45 Hispanic/Latino), 1 international. Average age 32. *Entrance requirements:* For master's, minimum undergraduate GPA of 3.0, statement of purpose, 2 letters of recommendation, resume. Additional exam requirements/recommendations for international students: Required—TOEFL (minimum score 550 paper-based). *Application deadline:* Applications are processed on a rolling basis. Application fee: $50. *Expenses:* Contact institution. *Financial support:* Institutionally sponsored loans and scholarships/grants available. Financial award application deadline: 3/2; financial award applicants required to submit FAFSA. *Unit head:* Marcia Godwin, Chairperson, 909-448-4103, E-mail: mgodwin@laverne.edu. *Application contact:* Cathy Cook, Associate Director of Graduate Admissions, 909-448-4719, Fax: 909-971-2295, E-mail: ccook2@laverne.edu.
Website: http://laverne.edu/business-and-public-administration/master-of-public-administration/

**University of Louisiana at Monroe,** Graduate School, College of Business and Social Sciences, Program in Public Administration, Monroe, LA 71209-0001. Offers MPA. *Program availability:* Online learning. *Faculty:* 2 full-time (1 woman). *Students:* 3 full-time (2 women), 40 part-time (28 women); includes 26 minority (20 Black or African American, non-Hispanic/Latino; 2 American Indian or Alaska Native, non-Hispanic/Latino; 1 Asian, non-Hispanic/Latino; 2 Hispanic/Latino; 1 Two or more races, non-Hispanic/Latino). Average age 30. 92 applicants, 57% accepted, 16 enrolled. *Entrance requirements:* For master's, GRE. *Expenses:* Tuition, state resident: full-time $6489. Tuition, nonresident: full-time $18,589. *Required fees:* $8984. Tuition and fees vary according to course level, course load, degree level and program. *Unit head:* Dr. Leigh Hersey, Director, 318-342-1332, E-mail: hersey@ulm.edu.
Website: http://www.ulm.edu/onlinedegrees/m_pa.html

**University of Louisville,** Graduate School, College of Arts and Sciences, Department of Urban and Public Affairs, Louisville, KY 40208. Offers public administration (MPA), including human resources management, non-profit management, public policy and administration; urban and public affairs (PhD), including urban planning and development, urban policy and administration; urban planning (MUP), including administration of planning organizations, housing and community development, land use and environmental planning, spatial analysis. *Program availability:* Part-time, evening/weekend. *Faculty:* 12 full-time (5 women), 3 part-time/adjunct (1 woman). *Students:* 59 full-time (23 women), 32 part-time (19 women); includes 19 minority (13 Black or African American, non-Hispanic/Latino; 1 Asian, non-Hispanic/Latino; 2 Hispanic/Latino; 3 Two or more races, non-Hispanic/Latino), 5 international. Average age 30. 75 applicants, 65% accepted, 25 enrolled. In 2016, 22 master's, 2 doctorates awarded. Terminal master's awarded for partial completion of doctoral program. *Degree requirements:* For master's, internship; for doctorate, comprehensive exam, thesis/dissertation. *Entrance requirements:* For master's, GRE General Test, minimum GPA of 3.0; for doctorate, GRE General Test, master's degree in appropriate field. Additional exam requirements/recommendations for international students: Required—TOEFL (minimum score 550 paper-based; 79 iBT). *Application deadline:* Applications are processed on a rolling basis. Application fee: $60. *Expenses:* Contact institution. *Financial support:* Fellowships, research assistantships, tuition waivers (full and partial), and unspecified assistantships available. Financial award application deadline: 2/1. *Faculty research:* Urban theory, sustainability, public administration, urban planning, urban management. *Total annual research expenditures:* $240,308. *Unit head:* Dr. David Simpson, Chair, 502-852-8019, Fax: 502-852-4558, E-mail: dave.simpson@louisville.edu. *Application contact:* Libby Leggett, Director, Graduate Admissions, 502-852-3101, Fax: 502-852-4558, E-mail: gradadm@louisville.edu.
Website: http://supa.louisville.edu

**University of Management and Technology,** Program in Public Administration, Arlington, VA 22209-1609. Offers MPA, Advanced Certificate.

**University of Manitoba,** Faculty of Graduate Studies, Faculty of Arts, Department of Political Studies, Program in Public Administration, Winnipeg, MB R3T 2N2, Canada. Offers MPA. Program offered jointly with The University of Winnipeg. *Degree requirements:* For master's, thesis or alternative.

**University of Maryland, College Park,** Academic Affairs, Joint Program in Business and Management/Public Policy, College Park, MD 20742. Offers MBA/MPM. *Accreditation:* AACSB. Electronic applications accepted.

**University of Maryland, College Park,** Academic Affairs, School of Public Policy, Joint Program in Public Policy/Law, College Park, MD 20742. Offers JD/MPM. Electronic applications accepted.

**University of Maryland, College Park,** Academic Affairs, School of Public Policy, Public Management Program, College Park, MD 20742. Offers MPM. *Degree requirements:* For master's, internship. *Entrance requirements:* For master's, GRE General Test, minimum GPA of 3.0. Additional exam requirements/recommendations for international students: Required—TOEFL. Electronic applications accepted. *Faculty research:* International security, economic policy, financial management, social policy.

**University of Massachusetts Amherst,** Graduate School, College of Social and Behavioral Sciences, Center for Public Policy and Administration, Amherst, MA 01003. Offers MPP, MPPA, MPH/MPPA, MPPA/M Ed, MPPA/MBA, MRP/MPPA. *Program availability:* Part-time. *Degree requirements:* For master's, thesis or alternative. *Entrance requirements:* For master's, GRE General Test. Additional exam requirements/recommendations for international students: Required—TOEFL (minimum score 550 paper-based; 80 iBT), IELTS (minimum score 6.5). Electronic applications accepted.

**University of Massachusetts Amherst,** Graduate School, Interdisciplinary Programs, Dual Degree Program in Education and Public Policy and Administration, Amherst, MA 01003. Offers MPPA/M Ed. *Entrance requirements:* Additional exam requirements/recommendations for international students: Required—TOEFL (minimum score 550 paper-based; 80 iBT), IELTS (minimum score 6.5). Electronic applications accepted.

**University of Massachusetts Amherst,** Graduate School, Interdisciplinary Programs, Dual Degree Program in Management and Public Policy and Administration, Amherst, MA 01003. Offers MPPA/MBA. *Accreditation:* AACSB. *Program availability:* Part-time. *Entrance requirements:* Additional exam requirements/recommendations for international students: Required—TOEFL (minimum score 600 paper-based; 100 iBT), IELTS (minimum score 7). Electronic applications accepted.

**University of Massachusetts Amherst,** Graduate School, Interdisciplinary Programs, Dual Degree Program in Public Policy and Administration and Public Health, Amherst, MA 01003. Offers MPH/MPPA. *Entrance requirements:* Additional exam requirements/

recommendations for international students: Required—TOEFL (minimum score 550 paper-based; 80 iBT), IELTS (minimum score 6.5). Electronic applications accepted.

**University of Massachusetts Amherst,** Graduate School, Interdisciplinary Programs, Dual Degree Program in Regional Planning and Public Policy and Administration, Amherst, MA 01003. Offers MPPA/MRP. *Entrance requirements:* Additional exam requirements/recommendations for international students: Required—TOEFL (minimum score 550 paper-based; 80 iBT), IELTS (minimum score 6.5). Electronic applications accepted.

**University of Massachusetts Boston,** John W. McCormack Graduate School of Policy and Global Studies, Program in Global Comparative Public Administration, Boston, MA 02125-3393. Offers MPA. *Program availability:* Online learning. *Students:* 9 full-time (8 women), 6 part-time (4 women); includes 5 minority (3 Black or African American, non-Hispanic/Latino; 2 Asian, non-Hispanic/Latino), 4 international. Average age 28. 22 applicants, 82% accepted, 14 enrolled. *Application deadline:* For fall admission, 5/1 for domestic students. *Expenses:* Tuition, state resident: full-time $16,863. Tuition, nonresident: full-time $32,913. *Required fees:* $177. *Unit head:* Dr. Aroon Manoharan, Director, 617-287-5935, E-mail: aroon.manoharan@umb.edu. *Application contact:* Peggy Roldan Patel, Graduate Admissions Coordinator, 617-287-6400, Fax: 617-287-6236, E-mail: bos.gadm@dpc.umassp.edu.

**University of Massachusetts Boston,** John W. McCormack Graduate School of Policy and Global Studies, Program in Public Administration, Boston, MA 02125-3393. Offers MPA. *Program availability:* Part-time, evening/weekend. *Faculty:* 10 full-time (3 women), 4 part-time/adjunct (2 women). *Students:* 17 full-time (9 women), 49 part-time (23 women); includes 12 minority (5 Black or African American, non-Hispanic/Latino; 7 Hispanic/Latino), 9 international. Average age 31. 75 applicants, 57% accepted, 34 enrolled. In 2016, 28 master's awarded. *Degree requirements:* For master's, final project. *Entrance requirements:* For master's, GRE General Test or MAT, minimum GPA of 2.75. *Application deadline:* For fall admission, 3/1 for domestic students. *Expenses:* Tuition, state resident: full-time $16,863. Tuition, nonresident: full-time $32,913. *Required fees:* $177. *Financial support:* Research assistantships with full tuition reimbursements, teaching assistantships with full tuition reimbursements, career-related internships or fieldwork, Federal Work-Study, and unspecified assistantships available. Support available to part-time students. Financial award application deadline: 3/1; financial award applicants required to submit FAFSA. *Faculty research:* Leadership and policy implementation, public management, disability; human services and sound policy. *Unit head:* Dr. David Cash, Dean. *Application contact:* Peggy Roldan Patel, Graduate Admissions Coordinator, 617-287-6400, Fax: 617-287-6236, E-mail: bos.gadm@dpc.umassp.edu.

**University of Massachusetts Dartmouth,** Graduate School, College of Arts and Sciences, Department of Public Policy, North Dartmouth, MA 02747-2300. Offers educational policy (Graduate Certificate); environmental policy (Graduate Certificate); public management (Graduate Certificate); public policy (MPP). *Program availability:* Part-time, 100% online. *Faculty:* 4 full-time (0 women), 1 part-time/adjunct (0 women). *Students:* 7 full-time (5 women), 70 part-time (43 women); includes 14 minority (5 Black or African American, non-Hispanic/Latino; 1 Asian, non-Hispanic/Latino; 5 Hispanic/Latino; 3 Two or more races, non-Hispanic/Latino). Average age 36. 66 applicants, 94% accepted, 40 enrolled. In 2016, 15 master's, 17 other advanced degrees awarded. *Degree requirements:* For master's, e-portfolio. *Entrance requirements:* For master's, GRE (waived if applicant has already earned a master's degree or higher, has successfully completed the educational policy or environmental policy post baccalaureate certificates, or is submitting LSAT scores as a joint JD/MPP program applicant), statement of purpose (minimum of 300 words), resume, 2 letters of recommendation, official transcripts; for Graduate Certificate, statement of purpose (minimum of 300 words), resume, official transcripts. Additional exam requirements/recommendations for international students: Required—TOEFL (minimum score 600 paper-based). *Application deadline:* Applications are processed on a rolling basis. Application fee: $60. Electronic applications accepted. *Expenses:* Tuition, state resident: full-time $14,994; part-time $624.75 per credit. Tuition, nonresident: full-time $27,068; part-time $1127.83 per credit. *Required fees:* $405; $25.88 per credit. Tuition and fees vary according to course load and reciprocity agreements. *Financial support:* In 2016–17, 3 research assistantships (averaging $3,400 per year) were awarded; career-related internships or fieldwork, institutionally sponsored loans, scholarships/grants, and unspecified assistantships also available. Support available to part-time students. Financial award application deadline: 3/1; financial award applicants required to submit FAFSA. *Faculty research:* Demographic analysis, legal and regulatory framework, human rights policy, globalization policies, women's public policy issues, educational leadership, environmental law, effects of evaluation models, international trade and finance, corporate social responsibility. *Total annual research expenditures:* $3,000. *Unit head:* Michael Goodman, Graduate Program Director, Public Policy, 508-910-6986, Fax: 508-999-8374, E-mail: mgoodman@umassd.edu. *Application contact:* Steven Briggs, Director of Marketing and Recruitment for Graduate Studies, 508-999-8604, Fax: 508-999-8183, E-mail: graduate@umassd.edu.
Website: http://www.umassd.edu/cas/departmentsanddegreeprograms/publicpolicy/

**University of Memphis,** Graduate School, College of Arts and Sciences, Division of Public and Nonprofit Administration, Memphis, TN 38103. Offers local government management (Graduate Certificate); philanthropy and nonprofit leadership (Graduate Certificate). *Accreditation:* NASPAA. *Program availability:* Part-time, evening/weekend, blended/hybrid learning. *Faculty:* 5 full-time (3 women), 2 part-time/adjunct (1 woman). *Students:* 17 full-time (12 women), 25 part-time (15 women); includes 23 minority (21 Black or African American, non-Hispanic/Latino; 1 Asian, non-Hispanic/Latino; 1 Hispanic/Latino), 1 international. Average age 32. 21 applicants, 90% accepted, 14 enrolled. In 2016, 39 master's, 36 other advanced degrees awarded. *Degree requirements:* For master's, comprehensive exam, thesis or alternative, internship. *Entrance requirements:* For master's, GRE General Test, GMAT, MAT, or LSAT, minimum GPA of 3.0, resume, two references, statement of interest. Additional exam requirements/recommendations for international students: Required—TOEFL. *Application deadline:* For fall admission, 7/1 for domestic students, 5/1 for international students; for spring admission, 12/1 for domestic students, 9/15 for international students; for summer admission, 5/1 for domestic students, 2/1 for international students. Applications are processed on a rolling basis. Application fee: $35 ($60 for international students). Electronic applications accepted. *Expenses:* $5,231.50 per semester full-time in-state, $9,623.50 full-time out-of-state. *Financial support:* In 2016–17, 37 students received support, including 5 fellowships (averaging $9,000 per year); research assistantships with full tuition reimbursements available, career-related internships or fieldwork, Federal Work-Study, scholarships/grants, health care benefits, and unspecified assistantships also available. Support available to part-time students. Financial award application deadline: 2/1; financial award applicants required to submit FAFSA. *Faculty research:* Nonprofit organization governance, local government management, community collaboration, urban problems, accountability. *Unit head:* Dr. Michael Howell-Moroney, Chair, 901-678-3360, Fax: 901-678-2981, E-mail: mhwllmrn@memphis.edu. *Application contact:* Dr. Sharon Wrobel, MPA Coordinator, 901-678-4720, Fax: 901-678-2981, E-mail: swrobel@memphis.edu.
Website: http://www.memphis.edu/padm/

*Public Administration*

**University of Michigan–Dearborn,** College of Arts, Sciences, and Letters, Master of Public Administration Program, Dearborn, MI 48128. Offers MPA. *Program availability:* Part-time, evening/weekend. *Faculty:* 10 full-time (5 women), 10 part-time/adjunct (5 women). *Students:* 8 full-time (5 women), 47 part-time (29 women); includes 24 minority (14 Black or African American, non-Hispanic/Latino; 4 Asian, non-Hispanic/Latino; 3 Hispanic/Latino; 3 Two or more races, non-Hispanic/Latino). Average age 38. 33 applicants, 48% accepted, 8 enrolled. In 2016, 14 master's awarded. *Degree requirements:* For master's, assessment seminar. *Entrance requirements:* For master's, GRE or minimum undergraduate GPA of 3.0, 3 letters of recommendation. Additional exam requirements/recommendations for international students: Required—TOEFL (minimum score 560 paper-based; 84 iBT), IELTS (minimum score 6.5). *Application deadline:* For fall admission, 8/1 priority date for domestic students, 5/1 priority date for international students; for winter admission, 12/1 priority date for domestic students, 9/1 priority date for international students; for spring admission, 4/1 priority date for domestic students, 1/1 priority date for international students. Applications are processed on a rolling basis. Application fee: $60. Electronic applications accepted. *Expenses:* Contact institution. *Financial support:* In 2016–17, 15 students received support. Career-related internships or fieldwork, scholarships/grants, and non-resident tuition scholarships available. Financial award application deadline: 3/1; financial award applicants required to submit FAFSA. *Faculty research:* Human resources management, organizational theory, public policy, urban development, nonprofit administration. *Unit head:* Dr. Georgina Hickey, Director, 313-583-6405, E-mail: ghickey@umich.edu. *Application contact:* Carol Ligienza, Coordinator, CASL Graduate Programs, 313-593-1183, Fax: 313-583-6700, E-mail: caslgrad@umich.edu.
Website: http://umdearborn.edu/casl/mpad/

**University of Michigan–Flint,** Graduate Programs, Program in Public Administration, Flint, MI 48502. Offers administration of non-profit agencies (MPA); criminal justice administration (MPA); educational administration (MPA); general public administration (MPA); healthcare administration (MPA). *Program availability:* Part-time. *Faculty:* 1 full-time (0 women), 3 part-time/adjunct (all women). *Students:* 13 full-time (10 women), 97 part-time (59 women); includes 45 minority (35 Black or African American, non-Hispanic/Latino; 1 Asian, non-Hispanic/Latino; 3 Hispanic/Latino; 1 Native Hawaiian or other Pacific Islander, non-Hispanic/Latino; 5 Two or more races, non-Hispanic/Latino), 5 international. Average age 35. 60 applicants, 78% accepted, 38 enrolled. In 2016, 52 master's awarded. *Degree requirements:* For master's, thesis or alternative, internship. *Entrance requirements:* For master's, bachelor's degree from regionally-accredited institution, minimum overall undergraduate GPA of 3.0. Additional exam requirements/recommendations for international students: Required—TOEFL (minimum score 84 iBT), IELTS (minimum score 6.5). *Application deadline:* For fall admission, 8/1 for domestic students, 5/1 for international students; for winter admission, 11/15 for domestic students, 9/1 for international students; for spring admission, 3/15 for domestic students, 1/1 for international students; for summer admission, 5/15 for domestic students. Applications are processed on a rolling basis. Application fee: $55. Electronic applications accepted. *Expenses:* Contact institution. *Financial support:* Career-related internships or fieldwork, Federal Work-Study, and scholarships/grants available. Support available to part-time students. Financial award application deadline: 3/1; financial award applicants required to submit FAFSA. *Unit head:* Dr. Kathryn Schellenberg, Director, 810-762-3340, E-mail: kathsch@umflint.edu. *Application contact:* Bradley T. Maki, Director of Graduate Admissions, 810-762-3171, Fax: 810-766-6789, E-mail: bmaki@umflint.edu.
Website: http://www.umflint.edu/graduateprograms/public-administration-mpa

**University of Missouri,** Office of Research and Graduate Studies, Harry S Truman School of Public Affairs, Columbia, MO 65211. Offers grantsmanship (Graduate Certificate); nonprofit management (Graduate Certificate); organizational change (Graduate Certificate); public affairs (MPA, PhD); public management (Graduate Certificate); science and public policy (Graduate Certificate). *Accreditation:* NASPAA. *Faculty:* 10 full-time (7 women), 2 part-time/adjunct (0 women). *Students:* 76 full-time (37 women), 168 part-time (88 women); includes 36 minority (21 Black or African American, non-Hispanic/Latino; 1 American Indian or Alaska Native, non-Hispanic/Latino; 2 Asian, non-Hispanic/Latino; 6 Hispanic/Latino; 6 Two or more races, non-Hispanic/Latino), 24 international. Average age 34. *Entrance requirements:* For master's, GRE General Test, minimum GPA of 3.0. Additional exam requirements/recommendations for international students: Required—TOEFL (minimum score 550 paper-based; 80 iBT), IELTS (minimum score 6.5). *Application deadline:* For fall admission, 2/1 priority date for domestic and international students. Applications are processed on a rolling basis. Application fee: $75 ($90 for international students). Electronic applications accepted. *Expenses:* Tuition, state resident: full-time $6347; part-time $352.60 per credit hour. Tuition, nonresident: full-time $17,379; part-time $965.50 per credit hour. *Required fees:* $1035. Tuition and fees vary according to course load, campus/location and program. *Financial support:* Fellowships, research assistantships, teaching assistantships, institutionally sponsored loans, scholarships/grants, traineeships, health care benefits, and unspecified assistantships available. Support available to part-time students.
Website: http://truman.missouri.edu/

**University of Missouri–Kansas City,** Henry W. Bloch School of Management, Kansas City, MO 64110-2499. Offers accounting (MS); finance (MS); public affairs (MPA, PhD); JD/MBA; LL M/MPA. PhD (interdisciplinary) offered through the School of Graduate Studies. *Accreditation:* AACSB; NASPAA. *Program availability:* Part-time, evening/weekend. *Faculty:* 60 full-time (19 women), 40 part-time/adjunct (11 women). *Students:* 204 full-time (97 women), 308 part-time (151 women); includes 70 minority (29 Black or African American, non-Hispanic/Latino; 1 American Indian or Alaska Native, non-Hispanic/Latino; 17 Asian, non-Hispanic/Latino; 18 Hispanic/Latino; 5 Two or more races, non-Hispanic/Latino), 82 international. Average age 30. 389 applicants, 49% accepted, 190 enrolled. In 2016, 248 master's, 2 doctorates awarded. Terminal master's awarded for partial completion of doctoral program. *Entrance requirements:* For master's, GMAT, GRE, 2 essays, 3 references, support of employer; for doctorate, GRE, minimum GPA of 3.0. Additional exam requirements/recommendations for international students: Required—TOEFL (minimum score 550 paper-based; 80 iBT). *Application deadline:* For fall admission, 5/1 priority date for domestic and international students; for spring admission, 10/1 priority date for domestic and international students. Applications are processed on a rolling basis. Application fee: $45 ($50 for international students). Electronic applications accepted. *Financial support:* In 2016–17, 31 research assistantships with partial tuition reimbursements (averaging $10,597 per year), 10 teaching assistantships with partial tuition reimbursements (averaging $14,592 per year) were awarded; career-related internships or fieldwork, Federal Work-Study, institutionally sponsored loans, scholarships/grants, tuition waivers (full and partial), and unspecified assistantships also available. Support available to part-time students. Financial award application deadline: 3/1; financial award applicants required to submit FAFSA. *Faculty research:* Entrepreneurship, finance, non-profit, risk management. *Unit head:* Dr. David Donnelly, Dean, 816-235-1333, Fax: 816-235-2206, E-mail: donnellyd@umkc.edu. *Application contact:* 816-235-1111, E-mail: admit@umkc.edu.
Website: http://www.bloch.umkc.edu

**University of Missouri–St. Louis,** College of Arts and Sciences, Department of Political Science, St. Louis, MO 63121. Offers American politics (MA); comparative politics (MA); international politics (MA); political process and behavior (MA); political science (PhD); public administration and public policy (MA); urban and regional politics (MA). *Program availability:* Part-time, evening/weekend. *Faculty:* 17 full-time (5 women), 8 part-time/adjunct (4 women). *Students:* 28 full-time (8 women), 30 part-time (12 women); includes 8 minority (7 Black or African American, non-Hispanic/Latino; 1 Two or more races, non-Hispanic/Latino), 5 international. 17 applicants, 82% accepted, 9 enrolled. Terminal master's awarded for partial completion of doctoral program. *Degree requirements:* For master's, thesis optional; for doctorate, thesis/dissertation. *Entrance requirements:* For master's, GRE General Test, 2 letters of recommendation, statement of purpose; for doctorate, GRE General Test, 3 letters of recommendation, statement of purpose. Additional exam requirements/recommendations for international students: Required—TOEFL (minimum score 550 paper-based; 79 iBT), IELTS (minimum score 6.5). *Application deadline:* For fall admission, 2/15 priority date for domestic and international students; for winter admission, 10/15 for domestic and international students; for spring admission, 10/15 priority date for domestic and international students. Applications are processed on a rolling basis. Application fee: $50 ($40 for international students). Electronic applications accepted. *Financial support:* Fellowships, research assistantships with tuition reimbursements, teaching assistantships with tuition reimbursements, and career-related internships or fieldwork available. Support available to part-time students. Financial award application deadline: 3/15; financial award applicants required to submit FAFSA. *Faculty research:* Public policy, urban politics and administration, American government. *Unit head:* Dave Robertson, Chair, 314-516-5521, Fax: 314-516-7236. *Application contact:* 314-516-5458, Fax: 314-516-6996, E-mail: gradadm@umsl.edu.
Website: http://www.umsl.edu/~polisci/

**University of Missouri–St. Louis,** Graduate School, Program in Public Policy Administration, St. Louis, MO 63121. Offers local government management (MPPA, Certificate); nonprofit management and leadership (MPPA, Certificate); policy and program evaluation (MPPA, Certificate). *Accreditation:* NASPAA. *Program availability:* Part-time, evening/weekend. *Faculty:* 2 full-time (both women), 6 part-time/adjunct (2 women). *Students:* 10 full-time (5 women), 43 part-time (26 women); includes 14 minority (12 Black or African American, non-Hispanic/Latino; 2 Asian, non-Hispanic/Latino). Average age 33. 28 applicants, 89% accepted, 17 enrolled. *Degree requirements:* For master's, exit project. *Entrance requirements:* For master's, 3 letters of recommendation, personal statement. Additional exam requirements/recommendations for international students: Recommended—TOEFL (minimum score 550 paper-based), IELTS (minimum score 6.5). *Application deadline:* For fall admission, 7/1 priority date for domestic and international students; for spring admission, 12/1 priority date for domestic and international students. Applications are processed on a rolling basis. Application fee: $50 ($40 for international students). Electronic applications accepted. *Financial support:* Research assistantships with tuition reimbursements and career-related internships or fieldwork available. Financial award application deadline: 4/1; financial award applicants required to submit FAFSA. *Faculty research:* Urban policy, public finance, evaluation. *Unit head:* Dr. Deborah Balser, Director, 314-516-5146, Fax: 314-516-5210, E-mail: balserd@umsl.edu. *Application contact:* 314-516-5458, Fax: 314-516-6996, E-mail: gradadm@umsl.edu.
Website: http://www.umsl.edu/gradschool/ppa/

**University of Montana,** Graduate School, College of Humanities and Sciences, Department of Political Science, Program in Public Administration, Missoula, MT 59812-0002. Offers MPA, JD/MPA. MPA offered jointly with Montana State University. *Degree requirements:* For master's, professional paper. *Entrance requirements:* For master's, GRE General Test.

**University of Nebraska at Omaha,** Graduate Studies, College of Public Affairs and Community Service, School of Public Administration, Omaha, NE 68182. Offers public administration (MPA, PhD); public management (Certificate); urban studies (MS). *Accreditation:* NASPAA (one or more programs are accredited). *Program availability:* Part-time, evening/weekend, online learning. *Faculty:* 14 full-time (7 women). *Students:* 38 full-time (25 women), 200 part-time (106 women); includes 39 minority (11 Black or African American, non-Hispanic/Latino; 1 Asian, non-Hispanic/Latino; 18 Hispanic/Latino; 1 Native Hawaiian or other Pacific Islander, non-Hispanic/Latino; 8 Two or more races, non-Hispanic/Latino), 14 international. Average age 33. 165 applicants, 67% accepted, 82 enrolled. In 2016, 52 master's, 4 doctorates, 2 other advanced degrees awarded. *Degree requirements:* For master's, comprehensive exam (for some programs), thesis (for some programs); for doctorate, comprehensive exam, thesis/dissertation. *Entrance requirements:* For master's, GRE General Test, minimum GPA of 3.0, 2 letters of recommendation, statement of purpose, resume, official transcripts; for doctorate, GRE General Test, master's degree, minimum GPA of 3.2, 3 letters of recommendation, statement of purpose, resume, official transcripts; for Certificate, 3 years of work experience in the public sector, official transcripts, resume, statement of purpose, minimum undergraduate GPA of 3.0. Additional exam requirements/recommendations for international students: Required—TOEFL (minimum score 550 paper-based; 80 iBT), IELTS (minimum score 5.5), PTE (minimum score 44). *Application deadline:* For fall admission, 6/1 for domestic and international students; for spring admission, 10/1 for domestic and international students. Applications are processed on a rolling basis. Application fee: $45. Electronic applications accepted. *Financial support:* In 2016–17, 25 students received support, including 16 research assistantships with tuition reimbursements available, 9 teaching assistantships with tuition reimbursements available; career-related internships or fieldwork, Federal Work-Study, institutionally sponsored loans, scholarships/grants, health care benefits, tuition waivers (partial), and unspecified assistantships also available. Support available to part-time students. Financial award application deadline: 3/1; financial award applicants required to submit FAFSA. *Unit head:* Dr. Ethel Williams, Director, 402-554-2341, E-mail: graduate@unomaha.edu. *Application contact:* Dr. Meagan Van Gelder, Graduate Program Chair, 402-554-2341, E-mail: graduate@unomaha.edu.

**University of Nevada, Las Vegas,** Graduate College, Greenspun College of Urban Affairs, School of Public Policy and Leadership, Las Vegas, NV 89154-4030. Offers crisis and emergency management (MS); non-profit management (Certificate); public administration (MPA); public affairs (PhD); public management (Certificate); urban leadership (MA). *Program availability:* Part-time. *Faculty:* 13 full-time (7 women), 10 part-time/adjunct (2 women). *Students:* 76 full-time (43 women), 110 part-time (70 women); includes 81 minority (18 Black or African American, non-Hispanic/Latino; 1 American Indian or Alaska Native, non-Hispanic/Latino; 6 Asian, non-Hispanic/Latino; 38 Hispanic/Latino; 4 Native Hawaiian or other Pacific Islander, non-Hispanic/Latino; 14 Two or more races, non-Hispanic/Latino), 7 international. Average age 36. 70 applicants, 86% accepted, 43 enrolled. In 2016, 70 master's, 9 doctorates, 21 other advanced degrees awarded. *Degree requirements:* For master's, comprehensive exam (for some programs), thesis (for some programs), oral exam; for doctorate, comprehensive exam, thesis/dissertation; for Certificate, portfolio. *Entrance requirements:* For master's, GRE General Test or GMAT, bachelor's degree with minimum GPA 2.75; statement of purpose; 3 letters of recommendation; for doctorate, GRE General Test, master's degree with minimum GPA of 3.5; 3 letters of recommendation; statement of purpose; writing sample; personal interview; for Certificate, bachelor's degree; 2 letters of recommendation; writing sample. Additional exam requirements/recommendations for international students: Required—TOEFL (minimum score 550 paper-based; 80 iBT), IELTS (minimum score 7). *Application deadline:* For fall admission, 6/1 for domestic students, 5/1 for international students; for spring admission, 11/1 for domestic students, 10/1 for international students; for summer admission, 3/1 for domestic students. Application fee: $60 ($95 for international students). Electronic applications accepted. *Expenses:* $269.25 per credit, $792 per 3-credit course; $9,634 per year resident; $23,274 per year non-resident; $7,094 fees non-resident (7 credits or more); $1,307 annual health insurance fee. *Financial support:* In 2016–17, 7 research assistantships with partial tuition reimbursements (averaging $14,200 per year), 14 teaching assistantships with partial tuition reimbursements (averaging $16,411 per year) were awarded; institutionally sponsored loans, scholarships/grants, health care benefits, and unspecified assistantships also available. Financial award application deadline: 3/15. *Faculty research:* Community and organizational resilience; environmental decision-making and management; budgeting and human resource/workforce management; urban design, sustainability, and governance; public and non-profit management, public policy, governance, economic development, and urban planning. *Total annual research expenditures:* $244,881. *Unit head:* Dr. Christopher Stream, Director, 702-895-5120, Fax: 702-895-4436, E-mail: chris.stream@unlv.edu. *Application contact:* Dr. Jessica Word, Graduate Coordinator, 702-895-2684, Fax: 702-895-4436, E-mail: jessica.word@unlv.edu. Website: https://www.unlv.edu/publicpolicy

**University of Nevada, Reno,** Graduate School, College of Liberal Arts, Department of Political Science, Program in Public Administration and Policy, Reno, NV 89557. Offers public administration (MPA). *Degree requirements:* For master's, comprehensive exam, oral exam/thesis or professional paper. *Entrance requirements:* For master's, GRE General Test, GMAT, or LSAT, minimum GPA of 2.75. Additional exam requirements/recommendations for international students: Required—TOEFL (minimum score 500 paper-based; 61 iBT), IELTS (minimum score 6). Electronic applications accepted. *Faculty research:* Administrative processes and problems, public policy issues.

**University of New Brunswick Fredericton,** School of Graduate Studies, Faculty of Business Administration, Fredericton, NB E3B 5A3, Canada. Offers business administration (MBA); engineering management (MBA); entrepreneurship (MBA); sports and recreation management (MBA); MBA/LL B. *Program availability:* Part-time. *Degree requirements:* For master's, thesis optional. *Entrance requirements:* For master's, GMAT (minimum score 550), minimum GPA of 3.0; 3-5 years of work experience; 3 letters of reference with at least one academic reference. Additional exam requirements/recommendations for international students: Required—TOEFL (minimum score 580 paper-based; 92 iBT) or IELTS (minimum score 7). Electronic applications accepted. *Faculty research:* Entrepreneurship, finance, law, sport and recreation management, engineering management.

**University of New Hampshire,** Graduate School, College of Liberal Arts, Department of Political Science, Program in Public Administration, Durham, NH 03824. Offers MPA. *Program availability:* Part-time. *Entrance requirements:* For master's, GMAT or GRE General Test. Additional exam requirements/recommendations for international students: Required—TOEFL (minimum score 550 paper-based; 80 iBT). Electronic applications accepted.

**University of New Hampshire,** Graduate School Manchester Campus, Manchester, NH 03101. Offers business administration (MBA); educational administration and supervision (Ed S); educational studies (M Ed); elementary teacher education (M Ed); information technology (MS); public administration (MPA); public health (MPH, Certificate); secondary teacher education (M Ed, MAT); social work (MSW); substance use disorders (Certificate). *Program availability:* Part-time, evening/weekend. *Degree requirements:* For master's, thesis or alternative. *Entrance requirements:* Additional exam requirements/recommendations for international students: Required—TOEFL (minimum score 550 paper-based; 80 iBT). Electronic applications accepted.

**University of New Haven,** Graduate School, Henry C. Lee College of Criminal Justice and Forensic Sciences, Program in Fire Science, West Haven, CT 06516. Offers fire administration (MS); fire science (MS); fire/arson investigation (MS, Graduate Certificate); public safety management (MS, Graduate Certificate). *Program availability:* Part-time, evening/weekend. *Students:* 15 full-time (4 women), 2 part-time (0 women); includes 2 minority (1 Asian, non-Hispanic/Latino; 1 Hispanic/Latino), 10 international. Average age 28. 13 applicants, 100% accepted, 7 enrolled. In 2016, 10 master's, 7 other advanced degrees awarded. *Degree requirements:* For master's, thesis or alternative, research project or internship. *Entrance requirements:* Additional exam requirements/recommendations for international students: Required—TOEFL (minimum score 80 iBT), IELTS, PTE (minimum score 53). *Application deadline:* Applications are processed on a rolling basis. Application fee: $50. Electronic applications accepted. Application fee is waived when completed online. *Expenses:* Tuition: Full-time $15,660; part-time $870 per credit hour. *Required fees:* $200; $85 per term. Tuition and fees vary according to program. *Financial support:* Research assistantships with partial tuition reimbursements, teaching assistantships with partial tuition reimbursements, career-related internships or fieldwork, Federal Work-Study, scholarships/grants, and unspecified assistantships available. Support available to part-time students. Financial award applicants required to submit FAFSA. *Unit head:* Dr. Sorin Iliescu, Director, 203-932-7239, E-mail: silliescu@newhaven.edu. *Application contact:* Michelle Mason, Director of Graduate Enrollment, 203-932-7067, E-mail: mmason@newhaven.edu. Website: http://www.newhaven.edu/5922/

**University of New Haven,** Graduate School, Henry C. Lee College of Criminal Justice and Forensic Sciences, Program in National Security, West Haven, CT 06516. Offers information protection and security (MS); national security (MS, Graduate Certificate); national security administration (Graduate Certificate). *Program availability:* Part-time, evening/weekend. *Students:* 43 full-time (20 women), 34 part-time (13 women); includes 19 minority (6 Black or African American, non-Hispanic/Latino; 1 Asian, non-Hispanic/Latino; 9 Hispanic/Latino; 3 Two or more races, non-Hispanic/Latino), 6 international. Average age 31. 41 applicants, 98% accepted, 27 enrolled. In 2016, 27 master's, 2 other advanced degrees awarded. *Degree requirements:* For master's, thesis or alternative, research project or internship. *Entrance requirements:* Additional exam requirements/recommendations for international students: Required—TOEFL (minimum score 70 iBT), IELTS, or PTE (minimum score of 53). *Application deadline:* Applications are processed on a rolling basis. Application fee: $50. Electronic applications accepted. Application fee is waived when completed online. *Expenses:* Tuition: Full-time $15,660; part-time $870 per credit hour. *Required fees:* $200; $85 per term. Tuition and fees vary according to program. *Financial support:* Research assistantships with partial tuition reimbursements, teaching assistantships with partial tuition reimbursements, career-related internships or fieldwork, Federal Work-Study, scholarships/grants, and unspecified assistantships available. Support available to part-time students. Financial award applicants required to submit FAFSA. *Unit head:* Dr. Jibey Asthappan, Director, 203-479-4147, E-mail: jasthappan@newhaven.edu. *Application contact:* Michelle Mason, Director of Graduate Enrollment, 203-932-7067, E-mail: mmason@newhaven.edu. Website: http://www.newhaven.edu/5924/

**University of New Haven,** Graduate School, Henry C. Lee College of Criminal Justice and Forensic Sciences, Program in Public Administration, West Haven, CT 06516. Offers city management (MPA); community-clinical services (MPA); health care

management (MPA); long-term health care (MPA); personnel and labor relations (MPA); public administration (MPA, Graduate Certificate); MBA/MPA. *Program availability:* Part-time, evening/weekend. *Students:* 30 full-time (13 women), 15 part-time (8 women); includes 15 minority (12 Black or African American, non-Hispanic/Latino; 1 American Indian or Alaska Native, non-Hispanic/Latino; 1 Asian, non-Hispanic/Latino; 1 Hispanic/Latino), 6 international. Average age 35. 56 applicants, 98% accepted, 25 enrolled. In 2016, 31 master's, 17 other advanced degrees awarded. *Degree requirements:* For master's, thesis or alternative. *Entrance requirements:* Additional exam requirements/recommendations for international students: Required—TOEFL (minimum score 80 iBT), IELTS, PTE. *Application deadline:* Applications are processed on a rolling basis. Application fee: $50. Electronic applications accepted. Application fee is waived when completed online. *Expenses:* Contact institution. *Financial support:* Research assistantships with partial tuition reimbursements, teaching assistantships with partial tuition reimbursements, career-related internships or fieldwork, Federal Work-Study, scholarships/grants, and unspecified assistantships available. Support available to part-time students. Financial award application deadline: 5/1; financial award applicants required to submit FAFSA. *Unit head:* Dr. Cynthia Conrad, Associate Professor, 203-932-7486, E-mail: cconrad@newhaven.edu. *Application contact:* Michelle Mason, Director of Graduate Enrollment, 203-932-7067, E-mail: mmason@newhaven.edu. Website: http://www.newhaven.edu/6854/

**University of New Mexico,** Graduate Studies, School of Public Administration, Program in Public Administration, Albuquerque, NM 87131-2039. Offers MPA. *Accreditation:* NASPAA. *Faculty:* 10 full-time (3 women), 2 part-time/adjunct (0 women). *Students:* 50 full-time (36 women), 83 part-time (59 women); includes 78 minority (3 Black or African American, non-Hispanic/Latino; 20 American Indian or Alaska Native, non-Hispanic/Latino; 2 Asian, non-Hispanic/Latino; 51 Hispanic/Latino; 2 Two or more races, non-Hispanic/Latino), 9 international. Average age 37. 51 applicants, 61% accepted, 26 enrolled. In 2016, 94 master's awarded. *Entrance requirements:* For master's, baccalaureate degree from accredited college or university with minimum undergraduate GPA of 3.0 for last 60 hours or overall major; letter of intent; three letters of recommendation; resume; official transcripts. *Application deadline:* For fall admission, 4/1 for domestic students, 3/1 for international students; for spring admission, 10/1 for domestic students, 8/1 for international students. Application fee: $50. Electronic applications accepted. *Unit head:* Dr. Uday Desai, Director, 505-277-1092, Fax: 505-277-2529, E-mail: ucdesai@unm.edu. *Application contact:* Gene V. Henley, Associate Director and Graduate Academic Advisor, 505-277-9196, Fax: 505-277-2529, E-mail: spadvise@unm.edu. Website: http://spa.unm.edu/mpa-graduate-program/

**University of New Orleans,** Graduate School, College of Liberal Arts, Department of Political Science, Program in Public Administration, New Orleans, LA 70148. Offers MPA. *Accreditation:* NASPAA. *Degree requirements:* For master's, thesis. *Entrance requirements:* For master's, GRE General Test. Additional exam requirements/recommendations for international students: Required—TOEFL (minimum score 550 paper-based; 79 iBT), IELTS (minimum score 6.5). Electronic applications accepted.

**The University of North Carolina at Chapel Hill,** Graduate School, School of Government, Chapel Hill, NC 27599. Offers MPA, JD/MPA, MPA/MRP, MPA/MSW. *Accreditation:* NASPAA. *Degree requirements:* For master's, comprehensive exam. *Entrance requirements:* For master's, GRE General Test, minimum GPA of 3.0. Additional exam requirements/recommendations for international students: Required—TOEFL. Electronic applications accepted. *Faculty research:* Local government management, nonprofit management.

**The University of North Carolina at Charlotte,** College of Liberal Arts and Sciences, Department of Political Science and Public Administration, Charlotte, NC 28223-0001. Offers emergency management (Graduate Certificate); non-profit management (Graduate Certificate); public administration (MPA), including arts administration, emergency management, non-profit management, public budgeting and finance, urban management and policy; public budgeting and finance (Graduate Certificate); urban management and policy (Graduate Certificate). *Accreditation:* NASPAA. *Program availability:* Part-time, evening/weekend. *Faculty:* 19 full-time (10 women), 3 part-time/adjunct (0 women). *Students:* 25 full-time (17 women), 57 part-time (39 women); includes 23 minority (14 Black or African American, non-Hispanic/Latino; 1 American Indian or Alaska Native, non-Hispanic/Latino; 2 Asian, non-Hispanic/Latino; 4 Hispanic/Latino; 2 Two or more races, non-Hispanic/Latino). Average age 30. 55 applicants, 73% accepted, 30 enrolled. In 2016, 31 master's, 12 other advanced degrees awarded. *Degree requirements:* For master's, research project or thesis. *Entrance requirements:* For master's, GRE General Test, bachelor's degree, or its equivalent, from accredited college or university; minimum undergraduate GPA of 3.0; 3 letters of recommendation; statement of purpose; for Graduate Certificate, statement of purpose (1-2 pages in length) explaining applicant's career goals, how the Certificate fits into achieving those goals, and any relevant work experience; official transcripts; letters of recommendation. Additional exam requirements/recommendations for international students: Required—TOEFL (minimum score 523 paper-based, 70 iBT) or IELTS (6.5). *Application deadline:* For fall admission, 8/1 for domestic and international students; for spring admission, 12/1 for domestic and international students. Applications are processed on a rolling basis. Application fee: $75. Electronic applications accepted. *Expenses:* Tuition, state resident: full-time $4252. Tuition, nonresident: full-time $17,423. *Required fees:* $3026. Tuition and fees vary according to course load and program. *Financial support:* In 2016–17, 9 students received support, including 9 research assistantships (averaging $7,117 per year); career-related internships or fieldwork, Federal Work-Study, institutionally sponsored loans, scholarships/grants, and unspecified assistantships also available. Support available to part-time students. Financial award application deadline: 3/1; financial award applicants required to submit FAFSA. *Total annual research expenditures:* $477,651. *Unit head:* Dr. Greg Weeks, Chair, 704-687-7574, E-mail: gbweeks@uncc.edu. *Application contact:* Kathy B. Giddings, Director of Graduate Admissions, 704-687-5503, Fax: 704-687-1668, E-mail: gradadm@uncc.edu. Website: http://politicalscience.uncc.edu/

**The University of North Carolina at Pembroke,** The Graduate School, Public Administration Program, Pembroke, NC 28372-1510. Offers MPA. *Program availability:* Part-time, evening/weekend, online learning. *Degree requirements:* For master's, comprehensive exam, thesis optional. *Entrance requirements:* For master's, GRE General Test or MAT, minimum GPA of 3.0 in major, 2.5 overall; interview. Additional exam requirements/recommendations for international students: Required—TOEFL.

**The University of North Carolina Wilmington,** College of Arts and Sciences, Department of Public and International Affairs, Wilmington, NC 28403-3297. Offers coastal and ocean policy (MS); conflict management and resolution (MA); public administration (MPA), including coastal management. *Accreditation:* NASPAA. *Program availability:* Part-time. *Faculty:* 17 full-time (8 women). *Students:* 71 full-time (40 women), 63 part-time (38 women); includes 29 minority (16 Black or African American, non-Hispanic/Latino; 1 American Indian or Alaska Native, non-Hispanic/Latino; 2 Asian, non-Hispanic/Latino; 5 Hispanic/Latino; 5 Two or more races, non-Hispanic/Latino), 2 international. Average age 32. 55 applicants, 85% accepted, 32 enrolled. In 2016, 47 master's awarded. *Degree requirements:* For master's, comprehensive exam (for some programs), thesis or alternative, internship, practicum, capstone project. *Entrance* *requirements:* For master's, GRE, GMAT, 3 letters of recommendation, statement of interest, resume, essay. Additional exam requirements/recommendations for international students: Required—TOEFL (minimum score 79 iBT), IELTS (minimum score 6.5). *Application deadline:* For fall admission, 4/15 for domestic students; for spring admission, 11/15 for domestic students. Applications are processed on a rolling basis. Application fee: $60. Electronic applications accepted. *Expenses:* Contact institution. *Financial support:* Scholarships/grants and unspecified assistantships available. Financial award application deadline: 3/15; financial award applicants required to submit FAFSA. *Unit head:* Dr. Daniel Masters, Chair, 910-962-7583, Fax: 910-962-3286, E-mail: mastersd@uncw.edu. *Application contact:* Dr. Mark Imperial, MPA Program Director, 910-962-7928, Fax: 910-962-3286, E-mail: imperialm@uncw.edu. Website: http://www.uncw.edu/pia/graduate/index.html

**University of North Dakota,** Graduate School, College of Business and Public Administration, Program in Public Administration, Grand Forks, ND 58202. Offers MPA, MPA/JD. *Accreditation:* NASPAA. *Program availability:* Part-time, online learning. *Degree requirements:* For master's, comprehensive exam, thesis or alternative, final exam. *Entrance requirements:* For master's, GRE General Test, GMAT or LSAT, minimum GPA of 3.0. Additional exam requirements/recommendations for international students: Required—TOEFL (minimum score 550 paper-based; 79 iBT), IELTS (minimum score 6.5). *Application deadline:* For fall admission, 8/1 priority date for domestic students, 5/1 priority date for international students; for spring admission, 12/1 priority date for domestic students, 9/1 priority date for international students. Applications are processed on a rolling basis. Application fee: $35. Electronic applications accepted. *Financial support:* Fellowships with full and partial tuition reimbursements, research assistantships with full and partial tuition reimbursements, teaching assistantships with full and partial tuition reimbursements, Federal Work-Study, institutionally sponsored loans, scholarships/grants, health care benefits, tuition waivers (full and partial), and unspecified assistantships available. Support available to part-time students. Financial award application deadline: 3/15; financial award applicants required to submit FAFSA. *Unit head:* Dr. Jason Jensen, Director, 701-777-3831, Fax: 701-777-5099, E-mail: jason_jensen2@und.nodak.edu. *Application contact:* Matt Anderson, Admissions Specialist, 701-777-2947, Fax: 701-777-3619, E-mail: matthew.anderson@gradschool.und.edu. Website: http://business.und.edu/mpa/

**University of North Florida,** College of Arts and Sciences, Department of Political Science and Public Administration, Jacksonville, FL 32224. Offers nonprofit management (Graduate Certificate); public administration (MPA). *Accreditation:* NASPAA. *Program availability:* Part-time. *Faculty:* 13 full-time (5 women). *Students:* 19 full-time (11 women), 40 part-time (19 women); includes 15 minority (9 Black or African American, non-Hispanic/Latino; 1 Asian, non-Hispanic/Latino; 4 Hispanic/Latino; 1 Two or more races, non-Hispanic/Latino), 2 international. Average age 32. 53 applicants, 43% accepted, 17 enrolled. In 2016, 19 master's awarded. *Degree requirements:* For master's, thesis or alternative, internship. *Entrance requirements:* For master's, GRE General Test, minimum GPA of 3.0 in last 60 hours, 2 letters of recommendation, interview. Additional exam requirements/recommendations for international students: Required—TOEFL (minimum score 500 paper-based; 61 iBT). *Application deadline:* For fall admission, 8/1 priority date for domestic students, 5/1 for international students; for spring admission, 12/1 priority date for domestic students, 10/1 for international students; for summer admission, 3/15 priority date for domestic students, 2/1 for international students. Application fee: $30. Electronic applications accepted. Tuition and fees vary according to course load, campus/location and program. *Financial support:* In 2016–17, 7 students received support, including 1 teaching assistantship (averaging $4,590 per year); research assistantships, career-related internships or fieldwork, Federal Work-Study, scholarships/grants, tuition waivers (partial), and unspecified assistantships also available. Financial award application deadline: 4/1; financial award applicants required to submit FAFSA. *Faculty research:* America's usage of the Internet, use of information communication technologies by educators and children. *Total annual research expenditures:* $3,643. *Unit head:* Dr. Matthew T. Corrigan, Chair, 904-620-2997, Fax: 904-620-2979, E-mail: mcorriga@unf.edu. *Application contact:* Dr. Amanda Pascale, Director, The Graduate School, 904-620-1360, Fax: 907-620-1362, E-mail: graduateschool@unf.edu. Website: http://www.unf.edu/coas/pspa/

**University of North Georgia,** Program in Public Administration, Dahlonega, GA 30597. Offers MPA. *Program availability:* Part-time, online only, 100% online. *Faculty:* 9 full-time (1 woman). *Students:* 9 full-time (8 women), 1 (woman) part-time; includes 1 minority (Hispanic/Latino), 2 international. Average age 29. 8 applicants, 50% accepted, 3 enrolled. In 2016, 10 master's awarded. *Degree requirements:* For master's, comprehensive exam. *Entrance requirements:* For master's, GRE or GMAT, official transcripts, three recommendation forms, certificate of immunizations, baccalaureate degree with minimum cumulative GPA of 2.75; proof of lawful presence in the United States (if applying for in-state tuition). Additional exam requirements/recommendations for international students: Required—TOEFL (minimum score 550 paper-based; 79 iBT), IELTS (minimum score 6.5). *Application deadline:* For fall admission, 8/10 for domestic students; for spring admission, 12/10 for domestic students; for summer admission, 5/10 for domestic students. Application fee: $40. Electronic applications accepted. *Expenses:* Contact institution. *Financial support:* Research assistantships and teaching assistantships available. Financial award application deadline: 3/17; financial award applicants required to submit FAFSA. *Unit head:* Dr. Luisa Diaz-Kope, Program Coordinator, 706-864-1699, E-mail: luisa.diazkope@ung.edu. *Application contact:* Melinda Maxwell, Director of Graduate Admissions, 706-864-1543, E-mail: melinda.maxwell@ung.edu. Website: http://ung.catalog.acalog.com/preview_program.php?catoid=21&poid=2696&returnto=618

**University of North Texas,** Robert B. Toulouse School of Graduate Studies, Denton, TX 76203-5459. Offers accounting (MS); applied anthropology (MA, MS); applied behavior analysis (Certificate); applied geography (MA); applied technology and performance improvement (M Ed, MS); art education (MA); art history (MA); art museum education (Certificate); arts leadership (Certificate); audiology (Au D); behavior analysis (MS); behavioral science (PhD); biochemistry and molecular biology (MS); biology (MA, MS); biomedical engineering (MS); business analysis (MS); chemistry (MS); clinical health psychology (PhD); communication studies (MA, MS); computer engineering (MS); computer science (MS); counseling (M Ed, MS), including clinical mental health counseling (MS), college and university counseling, elementary school counseling, secondary school counseling; creative writing (MA); criminal justice (MS); curriculum and instruction (M Ed); decision sciences (MBA); design (MA, MFA), including fashion design (MFA), innovation studies, interior design (MFA); early childhood studies (MS); economics (MS); educational leadership (M Ed, Ed D); educational psychology (MS, PhD), including family studies (MS), gifted and talented (MS), human development (MS), learning and cognition (MS), research, measurement and evaluation (MS); electrical engineering (MS); emergency management (MPA); engineering technology (MS); English (MA); English as a second language (MA); environmental science (MS); finance (MBA, MS); financial management (MPA); French (MA); health services management (MBA); higher education (M Ed, Ed D); history (MA, MS); hospitality management (MS); human resources management (MPA); information science (MS); information systems

(PhD); information technologies (MBA); interdisciplinary studies (MA, MS); international studies (MA); international sustainable tourism (MS); jazz studies (MM); journalism (MA, MJ, Graduate Certificate), including interactive and virtual digital communication (Graduate Certificate), narrative journalism (Graduate Certificate), public relations (Graduate Certificate); kinesiology (MS); linguistics (MA); local government management (MPA); logistics (PhD); logistics and supply chain management (MBA); long-term care, senior housing, and aging services (MA); management (PhD); marketing (MBA); mathematics (MA, MS); mechanical and energy engineering (MS, PhD); music (MA), including ethnomusicology, music theory, musicology, performance; music composition (PhD); music education (MM Ed, PhD); nonprofit management (MPA); operations and supply chain management (MBA); performance (DM, DMA); philosophy (MA); political science (MA); professional and technical communication (MA); radio, television and film (MA, MFA); rehabilitation counseling (Certificate); sociology (MA); Spanish (MA); special education (M Ed); speech-language pathology (MA); strategic management (MBA); studio art (MFA); teaching (M Ed); MBA/MS. *Program availability:* Part-time, evening/weekend, online learning. Terminal master's awarded for partial completion of doctoral program. *Degree requirements:* For master's, variable foreign language requirement, comprehensive exam (for some programs), thesis (for some programs); for doctorate, variable foreign language requirement, comprehensive exam (for some programs), thesis/dissertation; for other advanced degree, variable foreign language requirement, comprehensive exam (for some programs). *Entrance requirements:* For master's and doctorate, GRE, GMAT. Additional exam requirements/recommendations for international students: Required—TOEFL (minimum score 550 paper-based; 79 iBT). Electronic applications accepted.

**University of North Texas at Dallas,** Graduate School, Dallas, TX 75241. Offers accounting (MBA); counseling (M Ed, MS); criminal justice (MS); curriculum and instruction (M Ed); educational administration (M Ed); human resources and organizational behavior (MBA); public leadership (MS); strategic management (MBA).

**University of Oklahoma,** College of Arts and Sciences, Department of Political Science, Program in Public Administration, Norman, OK 73019. Offers general (MPA); individualized intensive study (MPA); nonprofit management (MPA). *Program availability:* Part-time, evening/weekend. *Students:* 28 full-time (17 women), 48 part-time (26 women); includes 16 minority (5 Black or African American, non-Hispanic/Latino; 3 American Indian or Alaska Native, non-Hispanic/Latino; 1 Asian, non-Hispanic/Latino; 5 Hispanic/Latino; 2 Two or more races, non-Hispanic/Latino), 1 international. Average age 29. 42 applicants, 88% accepted, 31 enrolled. In 2016, 24 master's awarded. Terminal master's awarded for partial completion of doctoral program. *Degree requirements:* For master's, comprehensive exam, thesis or alternative, 36 hours. *Entrance requirements:* For master's, GRE, statement of purpose, resume, two letters of recommendation. Additional exam requirements/recommendations for international students: Required—TOEFL (minimum score 100 iBT) or IELTS (minimum score 7). *Application deadline:* For fall admission, 4/1 priority date for international students; for spring admission, 9/1 for international students. Applications are processed on a rolling basis. Application fee: $50 ($100 for international students). Electronic applications accepted. *Expenses:* Tuition, state resident: full-time $4886; part-time $203.60 per credit hour. Tuition, nonresident: full-time $18,989; part-time $791.20 per credit hour. *Required fees:* $3283; $126.25 per credit hour. $126.50 per semester. *Financial support:* In 2016–17, 40 students received support. Research assistantships with full tuition reimbursements available, teaching assistantships with full tuition reimbursements available, career-related internships or fieldwork, scholarships/grants, health care benefits, unspecified assistantships, and travel and conference attendance funding available. Financial award application deadline: 6/1; financial award applicants required to submit FAFSA. *Faculty research:* Public and nonprofit management, public policy analysis, program evaluation, public finance and budgeting. *Unit head:* Prof. Keith Gaddie, Chair, 405-325-2061, Fax: 405-325-0718, E-mail: pscgradprog@ou.edu. *Application contact:* Jeff Alexander, Graduate Programs Coordinator, 405-325-1845, Fax: 405-325-0718, E-mail: pscgradprog@ou.edu. Website: http://psc.ou.edu/mpa

**University of Ottawa,** Faculty of Graduate and Postdoctoral Studies, Interdisciplinary Programs, Ottawa, ON K1N 6N5, Canada. Offers e-business (Certificate); e-commerce (Certificate); finance (Certificate); health services and policies research (Diploma); population health (PhD); population health risk assessment and management (Certificate); public management and governance (Certificate); systems science (Certificate).

**University of Pennsylvania,** School of Arts and Sciences, Fels Institute of Government, Philadelphia, PA 19104. Offers economic development and growth (Certificate); government administration (MGA); nonprofit administration (Certificate); organization dynamics (MS); politics (Certificate); public administration (MPA); public finance (Certificate). *Program availability:* Part-time, evening/weekend. *Students:* 49 full-time (29 women), 65 part-time (35 women); includes 28 minority (13 Black or African American, non-Hispanic/Latino; 6 Asian, non-Hispanic/Latino; 6 Hispanic/Latino; 3 Two or more races, non-Hispanic/Latino), 18 international. Average age 30. 371 applicants, 39% accepted, 71 enrolled. In 2016, 52 master's, 17 other advanced degrees awarded. *Expenses:* Tuition: Full-time $31,068; part-time $5762 per course. *Required fees:* $3200; $336 per course. Full-time tuition and fees vary according to degree level, program and student level. Part-time tuition and fees vary according to course load, degree level and program. *Financial support:* Application deadline: 1/1. Website: http://www.fels.upenn.edu/

**University of Phoenix–Atlanta Campus,** School of Business, Sandy Springs, GA 30350-4147. Offers accounting (MBA); business administration (MBA); global management (MBA); human resources management (MBA, MM); management (MM); marketing (MBA); public administration (MM). *Accreditation:* ACBSP. *Program availability:* Evening/weekend, online learning. *Degree requirements:* For master's, thesis (for some programs). *Entrance requirements:* For master's, minimum undergraduate GPA of 3.0, 3 years of work experience. Additional exam requirements/recommendations for international students: Required—TOEFL (minimum score 550 paper-based; 79 iBT).

**University of Phoenix–Augusta Campus,** School of Business, Augusta, GA 30909-4583. Offers accounting (MBA); business administration (MBA); business and management (MBA, MM); global management (MBA); human resources management (MBA, MM); management (MM); marketing (MBA); public administration (MBA, MM). *Accreditation:* ACBSP. *Program availability:* Online learning.

**University of Phoenix–Bay Area Campus,** School of Business, San Jose, CA 95134-1805. Offers accountancy (MS); accounting (MBA); business administration (MBA, DBA); energy management (MBA); global management (MBA); health care management (MBA); human resource management (MBA); human resources management (MM); management (MM); marketing (MBA); organizational leadership (DM); project management (MBA); public administration (MPA); technology management (MBA). *Accreditation:* ACBSP. *Program availability:* Evening/weekend, online learning. *Degree requirements:* For master's, thesis (for some programs). *Entrance requirements:* For master's, minimum undergraduate GPA of 3.0, 3 years of work experience. Additional exam requirements/recommendations for international students: Required—TOEFL (minimum score 550 paper-based; 79 iBT). Electronic applications accepted.

**University of Phoenix–Central Valley Campus,** School of Business, Fresno, CA 93720-1552. Offers accounting (MBA); business administration (MBA); global management (MBA); human resources management (MBA, MM); management (MM); marketing (MBA); public administration (MBA, MM). *Accreditation:* ACBSP.

**University of Phoenix–Colorado Campus,** School of Business, Lone Tree, CO 80124-5453. Offers accountancy (MSA); accounting (MBA); business administration (MBA); e-business (MBA); global management (MBA); human resources management (MBA, MM); management (MM); marketing (MBA); public administration (MBA, MM). *Accreditation:* ACBSP. *Program availability:* Evening/weekend, online learning. *Degree requirements:* For master's, thesis (for some programs). *Entrance requirements:* For master's, minimum undergraduate GPA of 3.0, 3 years work experience. Additional exam requirements/recommendations for international students: Required—TOEFL (minimum score 550 paper-based; 79 iBT). Electronic applications accepted.

**University of Phoenix–Colorado Springs Downtown Campus,** School of Business, Colorado Springs, CO 80903. Offers accounting (MBA); business administration (MBA); global management (MBA); human resources management (MBA, MM); management (MM); marketing (MBA); public administration (MM). *Program availability:* Evening/weekend. *Degree requirements:* For master's, thesis (for some programs). *Entrance requirements:* For master's, minimum undergraduate GPA of 3.0, 3 years of work experience. Additional exam requirements/recommendations for international students: Required—TOEFL (minimum score 550 paper-based; 79 iBT). Electronic applications accepted.

**University of Phoenix–Columbus Georgia Campus,** School of Business, Columbus, GA 31909. Offers accounting (MBA); business administration (MBA); global management (MBA); human resources management (MBA, MM); management (MM); marketing (MBA); public administration (MBA). *Accreditation:* ACBSP. *Program availability:* Evening/weekend. *Degree requirements:* For master's, thesis (for some programs). *Entrance requirements:* For master's, minimum undergraduate GPA of 3.0, 3 years of work experience. Additional exam requirements/recommendations for international students: Required—TOEFL (minimum score 550 paper-based; 79 iBT). Electronic applications accepted.

**University of Phoenix–Dallas Campus,** School of Business, Dallas, TX 75251. Offers accounting (MBA); business administration (MBA); global management (MBA); human resources management (MBA, MM); management (MM); marketing (MBA); public administration (MBA, MM). *Accreditation:* ACBSP. *Program availability:* Evening/weekend, online learning. *Degree requirements:* For master's, thesis (for some programs). *Entrance requirements:* For master's, 3 years of work experience, minimum undergraduate GPA of 3.0. Additional exam requirements/recommendations for international students: Required—TOEFL (minimum score 550 paper-based; 79 iBT). Electronic applications accepted.

**University of Phoenix–Hawaii Campus,** School of Business, Honolulu, HI 96813-3800. Offers accounting (MBA); business administration (MBA); global management (MBA); human resources management (MBA, MM); management (MM); marketing (MBA); public administration (MBA, MM). *Accreditation:* ACBSP. *Program availability:* Evening/weekend. *Degree requirements:* For master's, thesis (for some programs). *Entrance requirements:* For master's, minimum undergraduate GPA of 3.0, 3 years of work experience. Additional exam requirements/recommendations for international students: Required—TOEFL (minimum score 550 paper-based; 79 iBT). Electronic applications accepted.

**University of Phoenix–Houston Campus,** School of Business, Houston, TX 77079-2004. Offers accounting (MBA); business administration (MBA); global management (MBA); human resources management (MBA, MM); management (MM); marketing (MBA); public administration (MBA, MM). *Accreditation:* ACBSP. *Program availability:* Evening/weekend, online learning. *Degree requirements:* For master's, thesis (for some programs). *Entrance requirements:* For master's, 3 years of work experience, minimum undergraduate GPA of 3.0. Additional exam requirements/recommendations for international students: Required—TOEFL (minimum score 550 paper-based; 79 iBT). Electronic applications accepted.

**University of Phoenix–Jersey City Campus,** School of Business, Jersey City, NJ 07310. Offers accounting (MBA); business administration (MBA); global management (MBA); human resources management (MBA, MM); management (MM); marketing (MBA); public administration (MBA, MM). *Accreditation:* ACBSP.

**University of Phoenix–Las Vegas Campus,** School of Business, Las Vegas, NV 89135. Offers accounting (MBA); business administration (MBA); global management (MBA); human resources management (MBA, MM); management (MM); marketing (MBA); public administration (MM). *Accreditation:* ACBSP. *Program availability:* Evening/weekend, online learning. *Degree requirements:* For master's, thesis (for some programs). *Entrance requirements:* For master's, minimum undergraduate GPA of 3.0, 3 years of work experience. Additional exam requirements/recommendations for international students: Required—TOEFL (minimum score 550 paper-based; 79 iBT). Electronic applications accepted.

**University of Phoenix–North Florida Campus,** School of Business, Jacksonville, FL 32216-0959. Offers accounting (MBA); business administration (MBA); global management (MBA); human resources management (MBA, MM); management (MM); marketing (MBA); public administration (MBA, MM). *Accreditation:* ACBSP. *Program availability:* Evening/weekend. *Degree requirements:* For master's, thesis (for some programs). *Entrance requirements:* For master's, minimum undergraduate GPA of 3.0, 3 years work experience. Additional exam requirements/recommendations for international students: Required—TOEFL (minimum score 550 paper-based; 79 iBT). Electronic applications accepted.

**University of Phoenix–Online Campus,** College of Justice and Security, Phoenix, AZ 85034-7209. Offers administration of justice and security (MS), including administration of justice and security, global and homeland security, law enforcement organizations; public administration (MPA). *Program availability:* Evening/weekend, online learning. *Entrance requirements:* Additional exam requirements/recommendations for international students: Required—TOEFL, TOEIC (Test of English as an International Communication), Berlitz Online English Proficiency Exam, PTE, or IELTS. Electronic applications accepted. *Expenses:* Contact institution.

**University of Phoenix–Online Campus,** School of Business, Phoenix, AZ 85034-7209. Offers accountancy (MS); accounting (MBA, Certificate); business administration (MBA); energy management (MBA); global management (MBA); health care management (MBA); human resource management (MBA, Certificate); human resources management (MM); management (MM); marketing (MBA, Certificate); project management (MBA, Certificate); public administration (MBA, MM); technology management (MBA). *Program availability:* Evening/weekend, online learning. *Entrance requirements:* Additional exam requirements/recommendations for international students: Required—TOEFL, TOEIC (Test of English as an International Communication), Berlitz Online English Proficiency Exam, PTE, or IELTS. Electronic applications accepted. *Expenses:* Contact institution.

**University of Phoenix–Phoenix Campus,** College of Criminal Justice and Security, Tempe, AZ 85282-2371. Offers administration of justice and security (MS); global and homeland security (MS); law enforcement organizations (MS); public administration (MPA). *Program availability:* Evening/weekend, online learning. *Entrance requirements:* Additional exam requirements/recommendations for international students: Required—TOEFL, TOEIC (Test of English as an International Communication), Berlitz Online English Proficiency Exam, PTE, or IELTS. Electronic applications accepted. *Expenses:* Contact institution.

**University of Phoenix–Sacramento Valley Campus,** School of Business, Sacramento, CA 95833-4334. Offers accounting (MBA); business administration (MBA); global management (MBA); human resources management (MBA, MM); management (MM); marketing (MBA); public administration (MBA, MM). *Accreditation:* ACBSP. *Program availability:* Evening/weekend. *Degree requirements:* For master's, thesis (for some programs). *Entrance requirements:* For master's, minimum undergraduate GPA of 3.0, 3 years work experience. Additional exam requirements/recommendations for international students: Required—TOEFL (minimum score 550 paper-based; 79 iBT). Electronic applications accepted.

**University of Phoenix–San Antonio Campus,** School of Business, San Antonio, TX 78230. Offers accounting (MBA); business administration (MBA); e-business (MBA); global management (MBA); human resources management (MBA, MM); management (MM); marketing (MBA); public administration (MBA, MM). *Accreditation:* ACBSP.

**University of Phoenix–San Diego Campus,** School of Business, San Diego, CA 92123. Offers accounting (MBA); business administration (MBA); global management (MBA); human resources management (MBA, MM); management (MM); marketing (MBA); public administration (MBA). *Accreditation:* ACBSP. *Program availability:* Evening/weekend. *Degree requirements:* For master's, thesis (for some programs). *Entrance requirements:* For master's, 3 years of work experience, minimum undergraduate GPA of 3.0. Additional exam requirements/recommendations for international students: Required—TOEFL (minimum score 550 paper-based; 79 iBT). Electronic applications accepted.

**University of Phoenix–Southern California Campus,** College of Criminal Justice and Security, Costa Mesa, CA 92626. Offers administration of justice and security (MS), including administration of justice and security, global and homeland security, law enforcement organizations; public administration (MPA). *Program availability:* Evening/weekend, online learning. *Entrance requirements:* Additional exam requirements/recommendations for international students: Required—TOEFL, TOEIC (Test of English as an International Communication), Berlitz Online English Proficiency Exam, PTE, or IELTS. Electronic applications accepted. *Expenses:* Contact institution.

**University of Phoenix–South Florida Campus,** School of Business, Miramar, FL 33027-4145. Offers accounting (MBA); business administration (MBA); global management (MBA); human resource management (MBA); human resources management (MM); management (MM); marketing (MBA); public administration (MBA, MM). *Accreditation:* ACBSP. *Program availability:* Evening/weekend. *Degree requirements:* For master's, thesis (for some programs). *Entrance requirements:* For master's, minimum undergraduate GPA of 3.0, 3 years work experience. Additional exam requirements/recommendations for international students: Required—TOEFL (minimum score 550 paper-based; 79 iBT). Electronic applications accepted.

**University of Phoenix–Washington D.C. Campus,** School of Business, Washington, DC 20001. Offers accountancy (MS); business administration (MBA, DBA); human resources management (MM); management (MM); organizational leadership (DM); public administration (MPA). *Accreditation:* ACBSP.

**University of Pittsburgh,** Graduate School of Public and International Affairs, Doctoral Program in Public and International Affairs, Pittsburgh, PA 15260. Offers international affairs (PhD); international development (PhD); public administration (PhD); public policy (PhD). *Program availability:* Part-time, evening/weekend. *Faculty:* 34 full-time (12 women), 17 part-time/adjunct (5 women). *Students:* 29 full-time (12 women), 1 part-time (0 women); includes 4 minority (2 Asian, non-Hispanic/Latino; 2 Hispanic/Latino), 14 international. Average age 37. 60 applicants, 18% accepted, 5 enrolled. In 2016, 3 doctorates awarded. *Degree requirements:* For doctorate, comprehensive exam, thesis/dissertation, mid-term evaluation, preliminary exam, annual review. *Entrance requirements:* For doctorate, GRE or GMAT, 2 letters of recommendation, resume, undergraduate transcripts, personal statement, writing sample. Additional exam requirements/recommendations for international students: Required—TOEFL (minimum score 80 iBT); Recommended—IELTS (minimum score 7). *Application deadline:* For fall admission, 1/15 for domestic and international students. Application fee: $50. Electronic applications accepted. *Expenses:* $22,578 per year in-state; $36,734 per year out-of-state. *Financial support:* In 2016–17, 16 students received support, including 16 research assistantships with partial tuition reimbursements available (averaging $14,620 per year); fellowships also available. Financial award application deadline: 1/15; financial award applicants required to submit FAFSA. *Faculty research:* International development, international security and intelligence, human rights, urban affairs and planning, energy and environmental policy, nonprofit management, public management. *Total annual research expenditures:* $1.3 million. *Unit head:* Dr. John T.S. Keeler, Dean, 412-648-7605, Fax: 412-648-2605, E-mail: keeler@pitt.edu. *Application contact:* Dr. Michael T. Rizzi, Director of Student Services, 412-648-7640, Fax: 412-648-7641, E-mail: rizzim@pitt.edu.
Website: http://www.gspia.pitt.edu/

**University of Pittsburgh,** Graduate School of Public and International Affairs, Master of Public Administration Program, Pittsburgh, PA 15260. Offers energy and environment (MPA); governance and international public management (MPA); policy research and analysis (MPA); public and nonprofit management (MPA); urban affairs and planning (MPA); JD/MPA; MPH/MPA; MSIS/MPA; MSW/MPA. *Accreditation:* NASPAA. *Program availability:* Part-time, evening/weekend. *Faculty:* 34 full-time (12 women), 17 part-time/adjunct (5 women). *Students:* 93 full-time (66 women), 21 part-time (16 women); includes 8 minority (4 Black or African American, non-Hispanic/Latino; 1 Asian, non-Hispanic/Latino; 3 Hispanic/Latino), 61 international. Average age 26. 200 applicants, 81% accepted, 49 enrolled. In 2016, 62 master's awarded. *Degree requirements:* For master's, thesis optional, capstone seminar. *Entrance requirements:* For master's, GRE General Test or GMAT, 2 letters of recommendation, resume, undergraduate transcripts, personal statement. Additional exam requirements/recommendations for international students: Required—TOEFL (minimum score 80 iBT); Recommended—IELTS (minimum score 7). *Application deadline:* For fall admission, 2/1 priority date for domestic students, 1/15 for international students; for spring admission, 11/1 for domestic students, 8/1 for international students. Application fee: $50. Electronic applications accepted. *Expenses:* $22,578 per year in-state; $36,734 per year out-of-state. *Financial support:* In 2016–17, 10 students received support, including 2 research assistantships with full tuition reimbursements available (averaging $14,620 per year); fellowships with full tuition reimbursements available, career-related internships or fieldwork, scholarships/grants, health care benefits, and unspecified assistantships also available. Financial award application deadline: 2/1; financial award applicants required to submit FAFSA. *Faculty research:* Urban affairs and planning, governance and international public management, nonprofit management, policy research and analysis,

## Public Administration

energy and environmental policy. *Total annual research expenditures:* $1.3 million. *Unit head:* Dr. John T.S. Keeler, Dean, 412-648-7605, Fax: 412-648-2605, E-mail: keeler@pitt.edu. *Application contact:* Dr. Michael T. Rizzi, Director of Student Services, 412-648-7640, Fax: 412-648-7641, E-mail: rizzim@pitt.edu.
Website: http://www.gspia.pitt.edu/

**University of Puerto Rico, Río Piedras Campus,** College of Social Sciences, School of Public Administration, San Juan, PR 00931-3300. Offers MPA. *Accreditation:* NASPAA. *Program availability:* Part-time. *Degree requirements:* For master's, comprehensive exam, thesis. *Entrance requirements:* For master's, GRE or PAEG, interview, minimum GPA of 3.0, letter of recommendation.

**University of Regina,** Faculty of Graduate Studies and Research, Johnson-Shoyama Graduate School of Public Policy, Regina, SK S4S 0A2, Canada. Offers economic analysis for public policy (Master's Certificate); health administration (MHA); health systems management (Master's Certificate); public management (MPA, Master's Certificate); public policy (MPA, MPP, PhD); public policy analysis (Master's Certificate). *Program availability:* Part-time. *Faculty:* 9 full-time (4 women), 15 part-time/adjunct (4 women). *Students:* 88 full-time (56 women), 159 part-time (103 women). 202 applicants, 43% accepted. In 2016, 43 master's, 20 other advanced degrees awarded. *Degree requirements:* For master's, thesis (for some programs); for doctorate, thesis/dissertation. *Entrance requirements:* For doctorate, master's degree, intended research program in an area of public policy. Additional exam requirements/recommendations for international students: Required—TOEFL (minimum score 580 paper-based; 80 iBT), IELTS (minimum score 6.5), PTE (minimum score 59). *Application deadline:* For fall admission, 2/1 for domestic and international students. Application fee: $100. Electronic applications accepted. *Expenses:* Contact institution. *Financial support:* In 2016–17, 17 fellowships (averaging $6,059 per year), 19 teaching assistantships (averaging $2,507 per year) were awarded; career-related internships or fieldwork and scholarships/grants also available. Financial award application deadline: 6/15. *Faculty research:* Governance and administration, public finance, public policy analysis, non-governmental organizations and alternative service delivery, micro-economics for policy analysis. *Unit head:* Dr. Kathleen McNutt, Executive Director, Main Campus, 306-585-4759, Fax: 306-585-5461, E-mail: kathy.mcnutt@uregina.ca. *Application contact:* Constance Heshka-Argue, Manager, Main Campus, 306-585-5462, Fax: 306-585-5461, E-mail: connie.heska-argue@uregina.ca.
Website: http://www.schoolofpublicpolicy.sk.ca/

**University of Rhode Island,** Graduate School, College of Arts and Sciences, Department of Political Science, Kingston, RI 02881. Offers political science (MA), including American politics, comparative government, international relations, public policy; public policy and administration (MPA). *Program availability:* Part-time. *Faculty:* 12 full-time (5 women). *Students:* 20 full-time (9 women), 37 part-time (20 women); includes 11 minority (4 Black or African American, non-Hispanic/Latino; 2 American Indian or Alaska Native, non-Hispanic/Latino; 1 Asian, non-Hispanic/Latino; 3 Hispanic/Latino; 1 Two or more races, non-Hispanic/Latino), 1 international. In 2016, 15 master's awarded. *Degree requirements:* For master's, comprehensive exam (for some programs), thesis optional. *Entrance requirements:* For master's, GRE, GMAT, or MAT if undergraduate GPA below 3.0, 2 letters of recommendation. Additional exam requirements/recommendations for international students: Required—TOEFL. *Application deadline:* For fall admission, 2/1 for international students; for spring admission, 7/15 for international students. Application fee: $65. Electronic applications accepted. *Expenses:* Tuition, state resident: full-time $11,796; part-time $655 per credit. Tuition, nonresident: full-time $24,206; part-time $1345 per credit. *Required fees:* $1546; $44 per credit. One-time fee: $155 full-time; $35 part-time. *Financial support:* In 2016–17, 6 teaching assistantships with tuition reimbursements (averaging $15,753 per year) were awarded; research assistantships also available. Financial award application deadline: 7/15; financial award applicants required to submit FAFSA. *Unit head:* Dr. Brian Krueger, Department Chair, 401-874-4058, Fax: 401-874-4072, E-mail: bkrueger@uri.edu. *Application contact:* Dr. Marc Hutchison, Director/Associate Professor, 401-874-4054, Fax: 401-874-4072, E-mail: mlhutch@uri.edu.
Website: http://www.uri.edu/artsci/psc/

**University of St. Thomas,** School of Arts and Sciences, Houston, TX 77006-4696. Offers public policy administration (MPPA); sacred music (MSM). *Program availability:* Part-time. *Faculty:* 2 full-time (0 women), 4 part-time/adjunct (all women). *Students:* 9 full-time (6 women), 17 part-time (10 women); includes 16 minority (3 Black or African American, non-Hispanic/Latino; 1 Asian, non-Hispanic/Latino; 12 Hispanic/Latino). Average age 33. 14 applicants, 86% accepted, 9 enrolled. In 2016, 7 master's awarded. *Entrance requirements:* Additional exam requirements/recommendations for international students: Required—TOEFL (minimum score 79 iBT), IELTS (minimum score 6.5), PTE (minimum score 53). *Application deadline:* For fall admission, 7/15 priority date for domestic and international students; for spring admission, 12/1 priority date for domestic and international students; for summer admission, 5/1 priority date for domestic and international students. Applications are processed on a rolling basis. Application fee: $35. Electronic applications accepted. *Expenses:* Tuition: Full-time $20,934; part-time $1163 per credit hour. *Required fees:* $81 per semester. One-time fee: $100. Part-time tuition and fees vary according to course level, course load, campus/location and program. *Financial support:* In 2016–17, 23 students received support. Federal Work-Study, scholarships/grants, and state work-study, institutional employment available. Support available to part-time students. Financial award application deadline: 4/15; financial award applicants required to submit FAFSA. *Unit head:* Dr. John W. Starner, Jr., Interim Dean, School of Arts and Sciences, 713-525-3527, E-mail: starner@stthom.edu. *Application contact:* Todd Boutte, Director of Graduate Admissions, 713-942-3403, E-mail: bouttet@stthom.edu.
Website: http://www.stthom.edu/Academics/School_of_Arts_and_Sciences/Index.aqf

**University of San Francisco,** School of Management, Master of Public Administration Program, San Francisco, CA 94117. Offers health services administration (MPA); public administration (MPA). *Program availability:* Part-time, evening/weekend, online learning. *Faculty:* 11 full-time (2 women), 7 part-time/adjunct (2 women). *Students:* 218 full-time (139 women), 14 part-time (10 women); includes 150 minority (31 Black or African American, non-Hispanic/Latino; 43 Asian, non-Hispanic/Latino; 65 Hispanic/Latino; 3 Native Hawaiian or other Pacific Islander, non-Hispanic/Latino; 8 Two or more races, non-Hispanic/Latino), 1 international. Average age 33. 145 applicants, 81% accepted, 84 enrolled. In 2016, 74 master's awarded. *Entrance requirements:* For master's, resume demonstrating minimum of two years of professional work experience, transcripts from each college or university attended, two letters of recommendation, personal statement. Additional exam requirements/recommendations for international students: Required—TOEFL (minimum score 600 paper-based, 100 iBT), IELTS (minimum score 7) or PTE (minimum score 68). *Application deadline:* For fall admission, 6/15 for domestic students, 5/15 for international students. Application fee: $55. Electronic applications accepted. *Expenses:* Tuition: Full-time $23,310; part-time $1295 per credit. Tuition and fees vary according to course load, degree level, campus/location and program. *Financial support:* In 2016–17, 17 students received support. Scholarships/grants available. Financial award application deadline: 3/2; financial award applicants required to submit FAFSA. *Unit head:* Dr. Catherine Horiuchi, Director, 415-422-2221, E-mail: management@usfca.edu. *Application contact:* Office of Graduate Recruiting and Admissions, 415-422-2221, Fax: 415-422-6315, E-mail: management@usfca.edu.
Website: http://www.usfca.edu/mpa

**University of South Africa,** College of Economic and Management Sciences, Pretoria, South Africa. Offers accounting (D Admin, D Com); accounting science (DA); auditing (D Admin, D Com); business administration (M Tech); business economics (D Admin); business leadership (DBL); business management (D Admin, D Com); economic management analysis (M Tech); economics (D Admin, D Com, PhD); human resource development (M Tech); industrial psychology (D Admin, D Com, PhD); logistics (D Com); marketing (M Tech); public administration (D Admin, D Com, DPA, PhD); public management (M Tech); quantitative management (D Admin, D Com); real estate (M Tech); statistics (D Admin, PhD); tourism management (D Admin, D Com); transport economics (D Admin, D Com).

**University of South Alabama,** College of Arts and Sciences, Department of Political Science and Criminal Justice, Mobile, AL 36688. Offers public administration (MPA). *Program availability:* Part-time, evening/weekend. *Faculty:* 4 full-time (1 woman). *Students:* 19 full-time (14 women), 4 part-time (all women); includes 12 minority (8 Black or African American, non-Hispanic/Latino; 1 American Indian or Alaska Native, non-Hispanic/Latino; 1 Asian, non-Hispanic/Latino; 1 Hispanic/Latino; 1 Two or more races, non-Hispanic/Latino). Average age 27. 23 applicants, 57% accepted, 4 enrolled. In 2016, 10 master's awarded. *Degree requirements:* For master's, comprehensive exam, thesis optional. *Entrance requirements:* For master's, GRE, minimum GPA of 3.0. Additional exam requirements/recommendations for international students: Required—TOEFL. *Application deadline:* For fall admission, 7/1 priority date for domestic students, 6/1 priority date for international students; for spring admission, 12/1 priority date for domestic students, 11/1 priority date for international students; for summer admission, 5/1 priority date for domestic students. Applications are processed on a rolling basis. Application fee: $35. Electronic applications accepted. *Expenses:* Tuition, state resident: full-time $9768; part-time $407 per credit hour. Tuition, nonresident: full-time $19,536; part-time $814 per credit hour. *Financial support:* Fellowships, research assistantships, teaching assistantships, career-related internships or fieldwork, Federal Work-Study, institutionally sponsored loans, scholarships/grants, and unspecified assistantships available. Support available to part-time students. Financial award application deadline: 5/31; financial award applicants required to submit FAFSA. *Unit head:* Dr. Nader Entessar, Chair, Political Science/Criminal Justice, 251-460-7161, E-mail: nentessar@southalabama.edu. *Application contact:* Dr. Samuel Fisher, Director of Graduate Studies, Political Science/Criminal Justice, 251-460-7204, Fax: 251-460-7928, E-mail: sfisher@southalabama.edu.
Website: http://www.southalabama.edu/colleges/artsandsci/poliscie/

**University of South Carolina,** The Graduate School, College of Arts and Sciences, Department of Political Science, Program in Public Administration, Columbia, SC 29208. Offers MPA, JD/MPA, MSW/MPA. MPA offered jointly with Clemson University, The Graduate School of the College of Charleston. *Accreditation:* NASPAA. *Program availability:* Part-time, evening/weekend. *Degree requirements:* For master's, capstone seminar. *Entrance requirements:* For master's, GRE General Test, minimum GPA of 3.0. Additional exam requirements/recommendations for international students: Required—TOEFL. Electronic applications accepted. *Faculty research:* Public policy, organizational theory, personnel administration, budgeting, finance.

**The University of South Dakota,** Graduate School, College of Arts and Sciences, Department of Political Science, Vermillion, SD 57069. Offers American political institutions (PhD); American politics and public policy (MA); political science (EMPA, MA); public administration (MPA, PhD); public policy (PhD); JD/MA. *Accreditation:* NASPAA (one or more programs are accredited). *Program availability:* Part-time, online learning. *Degree requirements:* For master's, comprehensive exam, thesis (for some programs). *Entrance requirements:* For master's, GRE or LSAT (for MPA), GRE General Test (for MA), minimum GPA of 3.0. Additional exam requirements/recommendations for international students: Required—TOEFL (minimum score 550 paper-based; 79 iBT). Electronic applications accepted.

**University of Southern California,** Graduate School, School of Policy, Planning, and Development, Master of Public Administration Program, Los Angeles, CA 90089. Offers nonprofit management and policy (Graduate Certificate); political management (Graduate Certificate); public administration (MPA); public management (Graduate Certificate); MPA/JD; MPA/M Pl; MPA/MA; MPA/MAJCS; MPA/MS; MPA/MSW. *Accreditation:* NASPAA (one or more programs are accredited). *Program availability:* Part-time, evening/weekend, online learning. Terminal master's awarded for partial completion of doctoral program. *Degree requirements:* For master's, capstone, internship. *Entrance requirements:* For master's, GRE, GMAT. Additional exam requirements/recommendations for international students: Required—TOEFL (minimum score 600 paper-based; 100 iBT). Electronic applications accepted. *Faculty research:* Collaborative governance and decision-making, nonprofit management, environmental management, institutional analysis, local government, civic engagement.

**University of Southern Indiana,** Graduate Studies, College of Liberal Arts, Program in Public Administration, Evansville, IN 47712-3590. Offers nonprofit administration (MPA); public sector administration (MPA). *Program availability:* Part-time, evening/weekend. *Faculty:* 5 full-time (2 women). *Students:* 25 full-time (14 women), 4 part-time (3 women); includes 2 minority (both Black or African American, non-Hispanic/Latino), 4 international. Average age 29. In 2016, 12 master's awarded. *Entrance requirements:* For master's, resume, 2 letters of reference, personal statement, minimum GPA of 3.0. Additional exam requirements/recommendations for international students: Required—TOEFL (minimum score 550 paper-based; 79 iBT), IELTS (minimum score 6). *Application deadline:* For fall admission, 8/15 priority date for domestic students, 3/1 priority date for international students; for spring admission, 1/5 for domestic students, 11/15 for international students. Applications are processed on a rolling basis. Application fee: $40. Electronic applications accepted. *Expenses:* Tuition, state resident: full-time $8497. Tuition, nonresident: full-time $16,691. *Required fees:* $500. *Financial support:* In 2016–17, 4 students received support. Federal Work-Study, scholarships/grants, tuition waivers (full and partial), and unspecified assistantships available. Financial award application deadline: 3/1; financial award applicants required to submit FAFSA. *Unit head:* Dr. Matthew J. Hanka, Director, 812-461-5204, E-mail: mjhanka@usi.edu. *Application contact:* Dr. Mayola Rowser, Director, Graduate Studies, 812-465-7015, E-mail: mrowser@usi.edu.
Website: http://www.usi.edu/liberal-arts/master-of-public-administration

**University of South Florida,** College of Arts and Sciences, Department of Government and International Affairs, Tampa, FL 33620-9951. Offers government (PhD); Latin American, Caribbean and Latino studies (MA); political science (MA), including comparative government and politics; public administration (MPA). *Program availability:* Part-time, evening/weekend. *Faculty:* 15 full-time (3 women). *Students:* 47 full-time (26 women), 40 part-time (22 women); includes 15 minority (6 Black or African American, non-Hispanic/Latino; 1 Asian, non-Hispanic/Latino; 7 Hispanic/Latino; 1 Two or more races, non-Hispanic/Latino), 15 international. Average age 32. 59 applicants, 58% accepted, 21 enrolled. In 2016, 30 master's, 3 doctorates awarded. *Degree requirements:* For master's, comprehensive exam, thesis; for doctorate, comprehensive exam, thesis/dissertation. *Entrance requirements:* For master's, GRE General Test,

minimum GPA of 3.0 in upper-division undergraduate course work; letters of recommendation (2 for MPA, 3 for MS); 500-word personal statement and undergraduate background in political science or related fields (for MS); one-page career statement (for MPA); for doctorate, GRE General Test, 500-word personal statement, three letters of recommendation, transcripts of MA/BA coursework, writing sample. Additional exam requirements/recommendations for international students: Required—TOEFL (minimum score 550 paper-based; 79 iBT) or IELTS (minimum score 6.5). *Application deadline:* For fall admission, 1/5 for domestic and international students; for spring admission, 10/15 for domestic students, 9/15 for international students. Applications are processed on a rolling basis. Application fee: $30. Electronic applications accepted. *Expenses:* Tuition, state resident: full-time $7766; part-time $431.43 per credit hour. Tuition, nonresident: full-time $15,789; part-time $877.17 per credit hour. *Required fees:* $37 per term. *Financial support:* In 2016–17, 1 student received support, including 18 teaching assistantships with tuition reimbursements available (averaging $12,390 per year); unspecified assistantships also available. Financial award application deadline: 4/1. *Faculty research:* Citizenship and identity, social movements, global governance, American politics, public policy. *Total annual research expenditures:* $222,648. *Unit head:* Dr. Steven Tauber, Associate Professor/Interim Chair, 813-974-2278, Fax: 813-974-0832, E-mail: stauber@usf.edu. *Application contact:* Dr. Bernd Reiter, Associate Professor and Director of Graduate Studies, 813-974-3583, Fax: 813-974-0832, E-mail: breiter@usf.edu.
Website: http://gia.usf.edu/

**University of South Florida,** Innovative Education, Tampa, FL 33620-9951. Offers adult, career and higher education (Graduate Certificate), including college teaching, leadership in developing human resources, leadership in higher education; Africana studies (Graduate Certificate), including diasporas and health disparities, genocide and human rights; aging studies (Graduate Certificate), including gerontology; art research (Graduate Certificate), including museum studies; business foundations (Graduate Certificate); chemical and biomedical engineering (Graduate Certificate), including materials science and engineering, water, health and sustainability; child and family studies (Graduate Certificate), including positive behavior support; civil and industrial engineering (Graduate Certificate), including transportation systems analysis; community and family health (Graduate Certificate), including maternal and child health, social marketing and public health, violence and injury: prevention and intervention, women's health; criminology (Graduate Certificate), including criminal justice administration; educational measurement and research (Graduate Certificate), including evaluation; English (Graduate Certificate), including comparative literary studies, creative writing, professional and technical communication; entrepreneurship (Graduate Certificate); environmental health (Graduate Certificate), including safety management; epidemiology and biostatistics (Graduate Certificate), including applied biostatistics, biostatistics, concepts and tools of epidemiology, epidemiology, epidemiology of infectious diseases; geography, environment and planning (Graduate Certificate), including community development, environmental policy and management, geographical information systems; geology (Graduate Certificate), including hydrogeology; global health (Graduate Certificate), including disaster management, global health and Latin American and Caribbean studies, global health practice, humanitarian assistance, infection control; government and international affairs (Graduate Certificate), including Cuban studies, globalization studies; health policy and management (Graduate Certificate), including health management and leadership, public health policy and programs; hearing specialist: early intervention (Graduate Certificate); industrial and management systems engineering (Graduate Certificate), including systems engineering, technology management; information studies (Graduate Certificate), including school library media specialist; information systems/decision sciences (Graduate Certificate), including analytics and business intelligence; instructional technology (Graduate Certificate), including distance education, Florida digital/virtual educator, instructional design, multimedia design, Web design; internal medicine, bioethics and medical humanities (Graduate Certificate), including biomedical ethics; Latin American and Caribbean studies (Graduate Certificate); mass communications (Graduate Certificate), including multimedia journalism; mathematics and statistics (Graduate Certificate), including mathematics; medicine (Graduate Certificate), including aging and neuroscience, bioinformatics, biotechnology, brain fitness and memory management, clinical investigation, health informatics, health sciences, integrative weight management, intellectual property, medicine and gender, metabolic and nutritional medicine, metabolic cardiology, pharmacy sciences; national and competitive intelligence (Graduate Certificate); psychological and social foundations (Graduate Certificate), including career counseling, college teaching, diversity in education, mental health counseling, school counseling; public affairs (Graduate Certificate), including nonprofit management, public management, research administration; public health (Graduate Certificate), including environmental health, health equity, public health generalist, translational research in adolescent behavioral health; public health practices (Graduate Certificate), including planning for healthy communities; rehabilitation and mental health counseling (Graduate Certificate), including integrative mental health care, marriage and family therapy, rehabilitation technology; secondary education (Graduate Certificate), including ESOL, foreign language education: culture and content, foreign language education: professional; social work (Graduate Certificate), including geriatric social work/clinical gerontology; special education (Graduate Certificate), including autism spectrum disorder, disabilities education: severe/profound; world languages (Graduate Certificate), including teaching English as a second language (TESL) or foreign language. *Expenses:* Tuition, state resident: full-time $7766; part-time $431.43 per credit hour. Tuition, nonresident: full-time $15,789; part-time $877.17 per credit hour. *Required fees:* $37 per term. *Unit head:* Kathy Barnes, Interdisciplinary Programs Coordinator, 813-974-8031, Fax: 813-974-7061, E-mail: barnesk@usf.edu. *Application contact:* Karen Tylinski, Metro Initiatives, 813-974-9943, Fax: 813-974-7061, E-mail: ktylinsk@usf.edu.
Website: http://www.usf.edu/innovative-education/

**The University of Tennessee,** Graduate School, College of Arts and Sciences, Department of Political Science, Program in Public Administration, Knoxville, TN 37996. Offers MPA, JD/MPA. *Accreditation:* NASPAA. *Program availability:* Part-time. *Degree requirements:* For master's, thesis or alternative. *Entrance requirements:* For master's, GRE General Test, minimum GPA of 2.7. Additional exam requirements/recommendations for international students: Required—TOEFL. Electronic applications accepted.

**The University of Tennessee at Chattanooga,** Department of Political Science and Public Service, Chattanooga, TN 37403. Offers local government management (MPA); non profit management (MPA); public administration (MPA); public administration and non-profit management (Postbaccalaureate Certificate). *Program availability:* Part-time, evening/weekend. *Faculty:* 5 full-time (2 women). *Students:* 8 full-time (2 women), 14 part-time (11 women); includes 6 minority (4 Black or African American, non-Hispanic/Latino; 1 Asian, non-Hispanic/Latino; 1 Two or more races, non-Hispanic/Latino). Average age 31. 14 applicants, 86% accepted, 7 enrolled. In 2016, 11 master's awarded. *Degree requirements:* For master's, comprehensive exam, thesis or alternative, internship. *Entrance requirements:* For master's, GRE General Test. Additional exam requirements/recommendations for international students: Required—TOEFL (minimum score 550 paper-based; 79 iBT), IELTS (minimum score 6).

*Application deadline:* For fall admission, 6/15 priority date for domestic students, 7/1 for international students; for spring admission, 11/1 priority date for domestic students, 11/1 for international students. Applications are processed on a rolling basis. Application fee: $35 ($40 for international students). Electronic applications accepted. *Expenses:* $9,876 full-time in-state; $25,994 full-time out-of-state; $450 per credit part-time in-state; $1,345 per credit part-time out-of-state. *Financial support:* In 2016–17, 2 research assistantships were awarded; career-related internships or fieldwork, scholarships/grants, and unspecified assistantships also available. Support available to part-time students. Financial award application deadline: 7/1; financial award applicants required to submit FAFSA. *Faculty research:* Organizational cultures and renewal, management theory, public policy, policy analysis, nonprofit organization. *Total annual research expenditures:* $1,700. *Unit head:* Dr. Michelle D. Deardorf, Department Head, 423-425-4231, Fax: 423-425-2373, E-mail: michelle-deardorff@utc.edu. *Application contact:* Dr. Joanne Romagni, Dean of the Graduate School, 423-425-4478, Fax: 423-425-5223, E-mail: joanne-romagni@utc.edu.
Website: http://www.utc.edu/political-science-public-service/

**The University of Texas at Arlington,** Graduate School, College of Architecture, Planning and Public Affairs, Program in Public Administration, Arlington, TX 76019. Offers MPA. *Accreditation:* NASPAA. *Program availability:* Part-time, evening/weekend, online learning. *Degree requirements:* For master's, comprehensive exam, thesis or alternative. *Entrance requirements:* For master's, GRE General Test, three letters of recommendation, essay (approximately 250 words), minimum GPA of 3.0. Additional exam requirements/recommendations for international students: Required—TOEFL (minimum score 550 paper-based). *Application deadline:* For fall admission, 6/1 for domestic students, 4/1 for international students; for spring admission, 10/15 for domestic students, 9/15 for international students. Applications are processed on a rolling basis. Application fee: $35 ($50 for international students). Electronic applications accepted. *Financial support:* Fellowships, research assistantships, and career-related internships or fieldwork available. Financial award application deadline: 6/1; financial award applicants required to submit FAFSA. *Faculty research:* Environment, statistics, public administration, social welfare, economic development, economics, budgeting, planning. *Unit head:* Dr. David Coursey, Program Director, 817-272-4061, Fax: 817-272-3415, E-mail: dcoursey@uta.edu. *Application contact:* Tangie Fields, Academic Advisor, 817-272-3340, Fax: 817-272-3415, E-mail: nfields@uta.edu.
Website: http://www.uta.edu/supa

**The University of Texas at Austin,** Graduate School, Lyndon B. Johnson School of Public Affairs, Austin, TX 78712-1111. Offers global policy studies (MGPS); public affairs (MP Aff); public leadership (EMPL); public policy (PhD); JD/MP Aff; MBA/MP Aff; MP Aff/MA; MP Aff/MSE. *Accreditation:* NASPAA (one or more programs are accredited). *Program availability:* Part-time. *Degree requirements:* For master's, thesis, summer internship; for doctorate, thesis/dissertation. *Entrance requirements:* For master's, GRE General Test (for MP Aff and MGPS), minimum GPA of 3.0 in upper-division classes, seven years of experience in the public sector, and interview (for EMPL); for doctorate, GRE General Test, master's degree in policy-related field. Additional exam requirements/recommendations for international students: Required—TOEFL. Electronic applications accepted. *Faculty research:* Human resource development, health and social policy, philanthropy and community service, ethical leadership, urban and international policy, science and technology policy.

**The University of Texas at Dallas,** School of Economic, Political and Policy Sciences, Program in Public and Nonprofit Management, Richardson, TX 75080. Offers applied sociology (MS); public affairs (MPA, PhD). *Accreditation:* NASPAA. *Program availability:* Part-time, evening/weekend. *Faculty:* 12 full-time (5 women), 2 part-time/adjunct (0 women). *Students:* 30 full-time (25 women), 89 part-time (55 women); includes 45 minority (17 Black or African American, non-Hispanic/Latino; 6 Asian, non-Hispanic/Latino; 18 Hispanic/Latino; 4 Two or more races, non-Hispanic/Latino), 16 international. Average age 37. 79 applicants, 67% accepted, 45 enrolled. In 2016, 34 master's, 6 doctorates awarded. *Degree requirements:* For master's, internship; for doctorate, thesis/dissertation. *Entrance requirements:* For master's and doctorate, GRE (minimum combined score of 1000 on verbal and quantitative), minimum GPA of 3.0 in upper-level course work in field. Additional exam requirements/recommendations for international students: Required—TOEFL (minimum score 550 paper-based). *Application deadline:* For fall admission, 7/15 for domestic students, 5/1 priority date for international students; for spring admission, 11/15 for domestic students, 9/1 priority date for international students. Applications are processed on a rolling basis. Application fee: $50 ($100 for international students). Electronic applications accepted. *Expenses:* Tuition, state resident: full-time $12,418; part-time $690 per semester hour. Tuition, nonresident: full-time $24,150; part-time $1342 per semester hour. Tuition and fees vary according to course load. *Financial support:* In 2016–17, 46 students received support, including 1 research assistantship with partial tuition reimbursement available (averaging $15,600 per year), 7 teaching assistantships with partial tuition reimbursements available (averaging $13,157 per year); career-related internships or fieldwork, Federal Work-Study, institutionally sponsored loans, and scholarships/grants also available. Support available to part-time students. Financial award application deadline: 4/30; financial award applicants required to submit FAFSA. *Faculty research:* Corporate citizenship and urban problem solving, policy analysis, presidential decision-making, hazardous material safety, emergency management. *Unit head:* Dr. Doug Goodman, Program Head, 972-883-4969, Fax: 972-883-2735, E-mail: doug.goodman@utdallas.edu. *Application contact:* Katie Doctor, Graduate Program Administrator, 972-883-4936, Fax: 972-883-2735, E-mail: kdoctor@utdallas.edu.
Website: http://www.utdallas.edu/epps/public-affairs/

**The University of Texas at San Antonio,** College of Public Policy, Department of Public Administration, San Antonio, TX 78207. Offers MPA. *Accreditation:* NASPAA. *Program availability:* Part-time, evening/weekend. *Faculty:* 8 full-time (4 women), 6 part-time/adjunct (2 women). *Students:* 30 full-time (15 women), 147 part-time (86 women); includes 119 minority (23 Black or African American, non-Hispanic/Latino; 1 American Indian or Alaska Native, non-Hispanic/Latino; 4 Asian, non-Hispanic/Latino; 87 Hispanic/Latino; 4 Two or more races, non-Hispanic/Latino), 6 international. Average age 33. 73 applicants, 86% accepted, 53 enrolled. In 2016, 34 master's awarded. *Degree requirements:* For master's, comprehensive exam, final exit paper. *Entrance requirements:* For master's, bachelor's degree with 18 credit hours in field of study or in another appropriate field of study, two letters of recommendation, statement of purpose. Additional exam requirements/recommendations for international students: Required—TOEFL (minimum score 550 paper-based; 79 iBT), IELTS (minimum score 6.5). *Application deadline:* For fall admission, 7/1 for domestic students, 4/1 for international students; for spring admission, 11/1 for domestic students, 9/1 for international students; for summer admission, 5/1 for domestic students, 3/1 for international students. Application fee: $45 ($80 for international students). Electronic applications accepted. *Financial support:* Scholarships/grants and unspecified assistantships available. Financial award application deadline: 2/15. *Faculty research:* Public administration, public policy, nonprofit management, urban and regional planning, urban and regional management. *Total annual research expenditures:* $1,266. *Unit head:* Dr. Christopher G. Reddick, Department Chair, 210-458-2533, Fax: 210-458-2536, E-mail: chris.reddick@utsa.edu. *Application contact:* Dr. Jennifer K. Alexander, Graduate Advisor of Record, 210-458-2532, Fax: 210-458-2536, E-mail:

## Public Administration

jennifer.alexander@utsa.edu.
Website: http://copp.utsa.edu/public-administration/

**The University of Texas at Tyler,** College of Arts and Sciences, Department of Social Sciences, Tyler, TX 75799-0001. Offers criminal justice (MS); public administration (MPA); sociology (MS). *Program availability:* Part-time, evening/weekend. *Degree requirements:* For master's, comprehensive exam, thesis optional. *Entrance requirements:* For master's, GRE General Test, minimum GPA of 3.0. Additional exam requirements/recommendations for international students: Required—TOEFL. *Faculty research:* Urban segregation, minority business, violent crime, gender discrimination.

**The University of Texas Rio Grande Valley,** College of Liberal Arts, Department of Public Affairs and Security Studies, Edinburg, TX 78539. Offers global security studies and leadership (MPA); public administration (MPA); public policy and management (MPA). *Program availability:* Part-time, evening/weekend. *Degree requirements:* For master's, comprehensive exam (for some programs), thesis optional. *Entrance requirements:* For master's, minimum undergraduate GPA of 3.0, official transcripts, personal statement, three recommendations. Additional exam requirements/recommendations for international students: Required—TOEFL (minimum score 550 paper-based; 79 iBT). Electronic applications accepted. Tuition and fees vary according to course load and program. *Faculty research:* Immigration policy reform, agriculture food policy, social service delivery systems, community development, social welfare policy reform, urban/city management.

**University of the District of Columbia,** School of Business and Public Administration, Program in Public Administration, Washington, DC 20008-1175. Offers MPA. *Program availability:* Part-time, evening/weekend. *Degree requirements:* For master's, comprehensive exam, thesis optional. *Entrance requirements:* For master's, GMAT or GRE General Test, writing proficiency exam. Additional exam requirements/recommendations for international students: Required—TOEFL. *Faculty research:* Government management, public personnel management, urban management, management information systems, public financial management.

**The University of Toledo,** College of Graduate Studies, College of Languages, Literature and Social Sciences, Department of Political Science and Public Administration, Toledo, OH 43606-3390. Offers health care policy and administration (Certificate); management of non-profit organizations (Certificate); municipal administration (Certificate); political science (MA); public administration (MPA); JD/MPA. *Accreditation:* NASPAA. *Program availability:* Part-time. *Degree requirements:* For master's, comprehensive exam (for some programs), thesis. *Entrance requirements:* For master's, GRE General Test, minimum cumulative point-hour ratio of 2.7 (3.0 for MPA) for all previous academic work, three letters of recommendation, statement of purpose, transcripts from all prior institutions attended; for Certificate, minimum cumulative point-hour ratio of 2.7 for all previous academic work, three letters of recommendation, statement of purpose, transcripts from all prior institutions attended. Additional exam requirements/recommendations for international students: Required—TOEFL (minimum score 550 paper-based; 80 iBT). Electronic applications accepted. *Faculty research:* Economic development, health care, Third World, criminal justice, Eastern Europe.

**University of Utah,** Graduate School, College of Social and Behavioral Science, Department of Political Science, Program in Political Science, Salt Lake City, UT 84112. Offers American politics (MA, MS, PhD); comparative politics (MA, MS, PhD); international relations (MA, MS, PhD); political theory (MA, MS, PhD); public administration (MA, MS, PhD). *Faculty:* 31 full-time (8 women), 10 part-time/adjunct (3 women). *Students:* 45 full-time (16 women), 19 part-time (9 women); includes 6 minority (2 Asian, non-Hispanic/Latino; 2 Hispanic/Latino; 2 Two or more races, non-Hispanic/Latino), 4 international. Average age 35. 37 applicants, 49% accepted, 7 enrolled. In 2016, 2 master's, 4 doctorates awarded. Terminal master's awarded for partial completion of doctoral program. *Degree requirements:* For master's, variable foreign language requirement, thesis or research paper; for doctorate, comprehensive exam, thesis/dissertation. *Entrance requirements:* For master's and doctorate, GRE General Test, minimum GPA of 3.2. Additional exam requirements/recommendations for international students: Required—TOEFL (minimum score 580 paper-based; 61 iBT), IELTS (minimum score 6). *Application deadline:* For fall admission, 1/15 priority date for domestic and international students. Application fee: $55 ($65 for international students). Electronic applications accepted. *Expenses:* Contact institution. *Financial support:* In 2016–17, 10 students received support, including 5 fellowships with full tuition reimbursements available (averaging $15,250 per year), 13 teaching assistantships with full tuition reimbursements available (averaging $15,000 per year); career-related internships or fieldwork, scholarships/grants, health care benefits, and unspecified assistantships also available. Financial award application deadline: 1/15; financial award applicants required to submit FAFSA. *Faculty research:* International politics, comparative politics, political theory, American politics, public administration. *Total annual research expenditures:* $15,000. *Unit head:* Mark Button, Chair, 801-585-7987, Fax: 801-585-6492, E-mail: mark.button@poli-sci.utah.edu. *Application contact:* Sandy Hiskey, Graduate Academic Advisor, 801-581-8608, Fax: 801-585-6492, E-mail: sandy.hiskey@utah.edu.
Website: http://www.poli-sci.utah.edu/

**University of Utah,** Graduate School, College of Social and Behavioral Science, Department of Political Science, Program in Public Administration, Salt Lake City, UT 84112. Offers Exec MPA, MPA, JD/MPA, MHA/MPA, MPA/Ed D, MPA/MPH, MPA/MSW, MPA/PhD. *Accreditation:* NASPAA (one or more programs are accredited). *Program availability:* Part-time, evening/weekend. *Students:* 44 full-time (25 women), 97 part-time (54 women); includes 22 minority (1 American Indian or Alaska Native, non-Hispanic/Latino; 5 Asian, non-Hispanic/Latino; 13 Hispanic/Latino; 3 Two or more races, non-Hispanic/Latino). Average age 33. 76 applicants, 88% accepted, 62 enrolled. In 2016, 63 master's awarded. *Degree requirements:* For master's, internship, research paper. *Entrance requirements:* For master's, GMAT, GRE General Test, LSAT, MAT, minimum GPA of 3.2. Additional exam requirements/recommendations for international students: Required—TOEFL (minimum score 580 paper-based; 92 iBT), IELTS (minimum score 7). *Application deadline:* For fall admission, 2/1 priority date for domestic and international students. Application fee: $55 ($65 for international students). *Expenses:* Contact institution. *Financial support:* In 2016–17, 4 students received support, including 4 fellowships with full tuition reimbursements available; unspecified assistantships also available. Financial award application deadline: 3/1. *Faculty research:* Non-profit organizations, health policy, environmental policy and natural resources, law and ethics, human resource management, local government, education, conflict resolution, organization theory and behavior, crisis management, policy analysis and program evaluation. *Unit head:* Lina Svedin, MPA Director, 801-581-7031, E-mail: lina.svedin@poli-sci.utah.edu. *Application contact:* Clint Curry, Program Assistant, 801-581-6781, Fax: 801-585-6492, E-mail: clint.curry@utah.edu.
Website: http://www.mpa.utah.edu

**University of Vermont,** Graduate College, College of Agriculture and Life Sciences, Department of Community Development and Applied Economics, Program in Public Administration, Burlington, VT 05405. Offers MPA. *Accreditation:* NASPAA. *Students:* 20 full-time (14 women); includes 1 minority (Black or African American, non-Hispanic/Latino). Average age 30. 15 applicants, 80% accepted, 6 enrolled. In 2016, 16 master's awarded. *Entrance requirements:* For master's, GRE General Test. Additional exam

requirements/recommendations for international students: Required—TOEFL (minimum score 550 paper-based; 80 iBT). *Application deadline:* For fall admission, 4/1 priority date for domestic students, 4/1 for international students. Applications are processed on a rolling basis. Application fee: $65. Electronic applications accepted. *Expenses:* Tuition, state resident: full-time $5814. Tuition, nonresident: full-time $14,670. *Financial support:* Fellowships and teaching assistantships available. Financial award application deadline: 3/1. *Unit head:* Dr. Christopher Koliba, Coordinator, 802-656-0009, E-mail: christopher.koliba@uvm.edu.

**University of Victoria,** Faculty of Graduate Studies, Faculty of Human and Social Development, School of Public Administration, Victoria, BC V8W 2Y2, Canada. Offers dispute resolution (MADR); public administration (MPA, PhD); MPA/LL B. *Program availability:* Part-time, evening/weekend, online learning. *Degree requirements:* For master's, thesis (for some programs), report; for doctorate, thesis/dissertation, candidacy exam. *Entrance requirements:* For master's, GMAT or GRE General Test, professional resume; for doctorate, GMAT or GRE General Test. Additional exam requirements/recommendations for international students: Required—TOEFL (minimum score 610 paper-based). Electronic applications accepted. *Faculty research:* Policy analysis, local government, performance management, energy markets, labor markets.

**University of Washington,** Graduate School, Evans School of Public Policy and Governance, Seattle, WA 98195. Offers public administration (MPA); public policy and management (PhD); JD/MPA; MPA/MAIS; MPA/MPH; MPA/MS; MPA/MUP. *Accreditation:* NASPAA. *Program availability:* Part-time, evening/weekend. *Degree requirements:* For master's, thesis, internship or cooperative experience. *Entrance requirements:* For master's and doctorate, GRE General Test, minimum GPA of 3.0. Additional exam requirements/recommendations for international students: Required—TOEFL (minimum score 580 paper-based; 92 iBT). Electronic applications accepted. *Faculty research:* Environmental policy, education and social policy, nonprofit management, international affairs, urban and regional development.

**University of West Georgia,** College of Social Sciences, Carrollton, GA 30118. Offers criminology (MA); data analysis and evaluation methods (Postbaccalaureate Certificate); European Union studies (Postbaccalaureate Certificate); integrative health systems (Postbaccalaureate Certificate); nonprofit management and community development (Postbaccalaureate Certificate); psychology (MA, PhD), including consciousness and society (PhD); public administration (MPA); public management (Postbaccalaureate Certificate); sociology (MA). *Program availability:* Part-time, evening/weekend, 100% online, blended/hybrid learning. *Faculty:* 45 full-time (21 women). *Students:* 107 full-time (67 women), 73 part-time (46 women); includes 47 minority (39 Black or African American, non-Hispanic/Latino; 4 Asian, non-Hispanic/Latino; 4 Hispanic/Latino), 10 international. Average age 31. 83 applicants, 88% accepted, 60 enrolled. In 2016, 56 master's, 7 doctorates, 5 other advanced degrees awarded. *Entrance requirements:* Additional exam requirements/recommendations for international students: Required—TOEFL (minimum score 523 paper-based; 69 iBT); Recommended—IELTS (minimum score 6.5). *Application deadline:* For fall admission, 7/15 for domestic students, 6/1 for international students; for spring admission, 11/30 for domestic students, 10/15 for international students; for summer admission, 5/15 for domestic students, 3/30 for international students. Applications are processed on a rolling basis. Application fee: $40. Electronic applications accepted. *Expenses:* Tuition, state resident: full-time $5316; part-time $222 per semester hour. Tuition, nonresident: full-time $20,658; part-time $861 per semester hour. *Required fees:* $1962. Tuition and fees vary according to course load, degree level and program. *Financial support:* Fellowships, research assistantships, teaching assistantships, career-related internships or fieldwork, Federal Work-Study, institutionally sponsored loans, scholarships/grants, and unspecified assistantships available. Support available to part-time students. Financial award application deadline: 4/1; financial award applicants required to submit FAFSA. *Unit head:* Dr. N. Jane McCandless, Dean of Social Sciences, 678-839-5170, Fax: 678-839-5171, E-mail: jmccandl@westga.edu. *Application contact:* Dr. Toby Ziglar, Assistant Dean of the Graduate School, 678-839-1394, Fax: 678-839-1395, E-mail: graduate@westga.edu.
Website: https://www.westga.edu/coss

**The University of Winnipeg,** Graduate Studies, Program in Public Administration, Winnipeg, MB R3B 2E9, Canada. Offers MPA. Program offered jointly with University of Manitoba. *Program availability:* Part-time. *Degree requirements:* For master's, comprehensive exam, thesis optional. *Entrance requirements:* For master's, minimum GPA of 3.0 in last 60 credit hours. *Faculty research:* Policy evaluation, federalism, administrative innovation, administrative ethics, economic development/administration.

**University of Wisconsin–Milwaukee,** Graduate School, College of Letters and Science, Department of Public and Nonprofit Administration, Milwaukee, WI 53201-0413. Offers public administration (MPA), including general public administration, municipal management, non-profit management. *Program availability:* Part-time. *Students:* 12 full-time (8 women), 10 part-time (3 women); includes 3 minority (all Two or more races, non-Hispanic/Latino), 1 international. Average age 33. 16 applicants, 63% accepted, 5 enrolled. In 2016, 11 master's awarded. *Degree requirements:* For master's, thesis or alternative. *Entrance requirements:* For master's, GRE General Test, minimum GPA of 3.0. Additional exam requirements/recommendations for international students: Required—TOEFL (minimum score 550 paper-based; 79 iBT), IELTS (minimum score 6.5). *Application deadline:* For fall admission, 1/1 priority date for domestic students; for spring admission, 9/1 for domestic students. Applications are processed on a rolling basis. Application fee: $56 ($96 for international students). Electronic applications accepted. *Financial support:* In 2016–17, 20 teaching assistantships were awarded; fellowships, research assistantships, career-related internships or fieldwork, health care benefits, and unspecified assistantships also available. Support available to part-time students. Financial award application deadline: 4/15; financial award applicants required to submit FAFSA. *Unit head:* Douglas Ihrke, Department Chair, 414-229-4732, E-mail: dihrke@uwm.edu. *Application contact:* General Information Contact, 414-229-4982, Fax: 414-229-6967, E-mail: gradschool@uwm.edu.
Website: https://uwm.edu/public-nonprofit-administration/

**University of Wisconsin–Oshkosh,** Graduate Studies, College of Letters and Science, Department of Public Administration, Oshkosh, WI 54901. Offers general agency (MPA); health care (MPA). *Program availability:* Part-time, evening/weekend. *Degree requirements:* For master's, thesis or alternative. *Entrance requirements:* For master's, public service-related experience, resume, sample of written work. Additional exam requirements/recommendations for international students: Required—TOEFL (minimum score 550 paper-based; 79 iBT). Electronic applications accepted. *Faculty research:* Drug policy, local government state revenues and expenditures, health care regulation.

**University of Wyoming,** College of Arts and Sciences, Department of Political Science, Program in Public Administration, Laramie, WY 82071. Offers MPA. *Program availability:* Part-time, online learning. *Degree requirements:* For master's, comprehensive exam (for some programs), thesis (for some programs). *Entrance requirements:* For master's, GRE General Test, minimum GPA of 3.0. Additional exam requirements/recommendations for international students: Required—TOEFL (minimum score 525 paper-based). Electronic applications accepted. *Faculty research:* Public policy, public ethics, administrative theory, natural resource policy.

**Upper Iowa University,** Online Master's Programs, Fayette, IA 52142-1857. Offers accounting (MBA); corporate financial management (MBA); emergency management and homeland security (MPA); general management (MBA); general studies (MPA); government administration (MPA); health and human services (MPA); human resources management (MBA); nonprofit organizational management (MPA); organizational development (MBA); public management (MPA); sport administration (MSA). MBA also available at Madison, WI campus. *Program availability:* Part-time, online learning. *Degree requirements:* For master's, research project. *Entrance requirements:* For master's, GMAT, GRE, or minimum GPA of 2.7 during last 60 hours. Additional exam requirements/recommendations for international students: Required—TOEFL (minimum score 570 paper-based). Electronic applications accepted. *Faculty research:* Total quality management, teams, organization culture and climate, management.

**Villanova University,** Graduate School of Liberal Arts and Sciences, Department of Public Administration, Villanova, PA 19085-1699. Offers city management (Certificate); nonprofit management (Certificate); public administration (MPA, Certificate). *Accreditation:* NASPAA. *Program availability:* Part-time, evening/weekend, 100% online. *Faculty:* 26. *Students:* 133 full-time (70 women), 81 part-time (38 women); includes 67 minority (35 Black or African American, non-Hispanic/Latino; 3 American Indian or Alaska Native, non-Hispanic/Latino; 5 Asian, non-Hispanic/Latino; 17 Hispanic/Latino; 1 Native Hawaiian or other Pacific Islander, non-Hispanic/Latino; 6 Two or more races, non-Hispanic/Latino), 1 international. Average age 35. 48 applicants, 77% accepted, 26 enrolled. In 2016, 106 master's, 26 other advanced degrees awarded. *Degree requirements:* For master's, comprehensive exam. *Entrance requirements:* For master's, GRE General Test, minimum GPA of 3.0, statement of goals, 3 letters of recommendation. Additional exam requirements/recommendations for international students: Required—TOEFL. *Application deadline:* For fall admission, 5/1 for international students; for spring admission, 10/15 for international students. Applications are processed on a rolling basis. Application fee: $50. Electronic applications accepted. *Financial support:* Career-related internships or fieldwork, scholarships/grants, and unspecified assistantships available. Financial award application deadline: 3/15; financial award applicants required to submit FAFSA. *Unit head:* Dr. Catherine Wilson, Program Director, 610-519-7851. Website: http://www1.villanova.edu/villanova/artsci/publicadmin.html

**Virginia Commonwealth University,** Graduate School, College of Humanities and Sciences, L. Douglas Wilder School of Government and Public Affairs, Department of Political Science and Public Administration, Richmond, VA 23284-9005. Offers financial management (MPA). *Accreditation:* NASPAA. *Program availability:* Part-time. *Entrance requirements:* For master's, GRE, GMAT or LSAT. Additional exam requirements/recommendations for international students: Required—TOEFL (minimum score 600 paper-based; 100 iBT); Recommended—IELTS (minimum score 6.5). *Application deadline:* For fall admission, 4/1 for domestic students; for spring admission, 10/1 for domestic students. Applications are processed on a rolling basis. Application fee: $50. Electronic applications accepted. *Financial support:* Fellowships, career-related internships or fieldwork, Federal Work-Study, institutionally sponsored loans, and tuition waivers (full and partial) available. Support available to part-time students. Financial award application deadline: 3/1. *Faculty research:* Environmental policy, executive leadership, human resource management, local government management, nonprofit management, public financial management, public policy analysis and evaluation. *Unit head:* Dr. Niraj Verma, Director, L. Douglas Wilder School of Government and Public Affairs, 804-828-2292. *Application contact:* Dr. Richard R. Huff, Graduate Program Director, 804-827-9813, E-mail: rrhuff@vcu.edu. Website: http://www.wilder.vcu.edu/academic/pubadmin.html

**Virginia International University,** School of Public and International Affairs, Fairfax, VA 22030. Offers international relations (MS); public administration (MPA).

**Virginia Polytechnic Institute and State University,** Graduate School, College of Architecture and Urban Studies, Blacksburg, VA 24061. Offers architecture (MS Arch); architecture and design research (PhD); building/construction science and management (MS); creative technologies (MFA); environmental design and planning (PhD); landscape architecture (MLA); planning, governance, and globalization (PhD); public administration (MPA); public administration/public affairs (PhD, Certificate); public and international affairs (MPIA); urban and regional planning (MURP). *Accreditation:* ASLA (one or more programs are accredited). *Faculty:* 136 full-time (53 women). *Students:* 371 full-time (185 women), 210 part-time (104 women); includes 118 minority (49 Black or African American, non-Hispanic/Latino; 1 American Indian or Alaska Native, non-Hispanic/Latino; 30 Asian, non-Hispanic/Latino; 32 Hispanic/Latino; 6 Two or more races, non-Hispanic/Latino), 137 international. Average age 31. 566 applicants, 55% accepted, 160 enrolled. In 2016, 137 master's, 24 doctorates awarded. *Degree requirements:* For master's, comprehensive exam (for some programs), thesis (for some programs); for doctorate, comprehensive exam (for some programs), thesis/dissertation (for some programs). *Entrance requirements:* For master's and doctorate, GRE/GMAT. Additional exam requirements/recommendations for international students: Required—TOEFL (minimum score 80 iBT). *Application deadline:* For fall admission, 8/1 for domestic students, 4/1 for international students; for spring admission, 1/1 for domestic students, 9/1 for international students. Applications are processed on a rolling basis. Application fee: $75. Electronic applications accepted. *Expenses:* Tuition, state resident: full-time $12,467; part-time $692.50 per credit hour. Tuition, nonresident: full-time $25,095; part-time $1394.25 per credit hour. *Required fees:* $2669; $491.50 per semester. Tuition and fees vary according to course load, campus/location and program. *Financial support:* In 2016–17, 11 research assistantships with full tuition reimbursements (averaging $19,474 per year), 45 teaching assistantships with full tuition reimbursements (averaging $16,014 per year) were awarded. Financial award application deadline: 3/1; financial award applicants required to submit FAFSA. *Total annual research expenditures:* $3.6 million. *Unit head:* Dr. A. J. Davis, Dean, 540-231-6416, Fax: 540-231-6332, E-mail: davisa@vt.edu. *Application contact:* Christine Mattsson-Coon, Executive Assistant, 540-231-6416, Fax: 540-231-6332, E-mail: cmattsso@vt.edu. Website: http://www.caus.vt.edu/

**Walden University,** Graduate Programs, School of Public Policy and Administration, Minneapolis, MN 55401. Offers criminal justice (MPA, MPP, MS, Graduate Certificate), including emergency management (MS, PhD), general program (MS), global leadership (MS, PhD), homeland security and policy coordination (MS, PhD), law and public policy (MS, PhD), policy analysis (MS, PhD), public management and leadership (MS, PhD), self-designed (MS), terrorism, mediation, and peace (MS, PhD); criminal justice and executive management (MS), including global leadership (MS, PhD); criminal justice leadership and executive management (MS), including emergency management (MS, PhD), general program, homeland security and policy coordination (MS, PhD), law and public policy (MS, PhD), policy analysis (MS, PhD), public management and leadership (MS, PhD), self-designed, terrorism, mediation, and peace (MS, PhD); emergency management (MPA, MPP, MS), including criminal justice (MS, PhD), general program (MS), homeland security (MS), public management and leadership (MS, PhD), terrorism and emergency management (MS); general program (MPA, MPP); global leadership (MPA, MPP); government management (Graduate Certificate); health policy (MPA, MPP); homeland security (Graduate Certificate); homeland security and policy

coordination (MPA, MPP); international nongovernmental organizations (MPA, MPP); law and public policy (MPA, MPP); local government management for sustainable communities (MPA, MPP); nonprofit management (Graduate Certificate); nonprofit management and leadership (MPA, MPP, MS), including global leadership (MS, PhD), international nongovernmental organization (MS), local government for sustainable communities (MS), self designed (MS); online teaching in higher education (Post-Master's Certificate); policy analysis (MPA); public management and leadership (MPA, MPP, Graduate Certificate); public policy (Graduate Certificate); public policy and administration (PhD), including criminal justice (MS, PhD), emergency management (MS, PhD), global leadership (MS, PhD), health policy, homeland security and policy coordination (MS, PhD), international nongovernmental organizations, law and public policy (MS, PhD), local government management for sustainable communities, nonprofit management and leadership, policy analysis (MS, PhD), public management and leadership (MS, PhD), terrorism, mediation, and peace (MS, PhD); strategic planning and public policy (Graduate Certificate); terrorism, mediation, and peace (MPA, MPP). *Program availability:* Part-time, evening/weekend, online only, 100% online. *Degree requirements:* For doctorate, thesis/dissertation, residency. *Entrance requirements:* For master's, bachelor's degree or higher; minimum GPA of 2.5; official transcripts; goal statement (for some programs); access to computer and Internet; for doctorate, master's degree or higher; three years of related professional or academic experience (preferred); minimum GPA of 3.0; goal statement and current resume (for select programs); official transcripts; access to computer and Internet; for other advanced degree, relevant work experience; access to computer and Internet. Additional exam requirements/recommendations for international students: Required—TOEFL (minimum score 550 paper-based, 79 iBT), IELTS (minimum score 6.5), Michigan English Language Assessment Battery (minimum score 82), or PTE (minimum score 53). Electronic applications accepted.

**Waldorf University,** Program in Organizational Leadership, Forest City, IA 50436. Offers criminal justice leadership (MA); emergency management leadership (MA); fire/rescue executive leadership (MA); human resource development (MA); public administration (MA); sport management (MA); teacher leader (MA).

**Washington Adventist University,** Program in Public Administration, Takoma Park, MD 20912. Offers MPA. *Program availability:* Part-time. *Entrance requirements:* Additional exam requirements/recommendations for international students: Required—TOEFL (minimum score 550 paper-based), IELTS (minimum score 5).

**Wayne State University,** College of Liberal Arts and Sciences, Department of Political Science, Detroit, MI 48202. Offers political science (MA, PhD); public administration (MPA), including economic development policy and management, health and human services policy and management, human and fiscal resource management, nonprofit policy and management, organizational behavior and management, urban and metropolitan policy and management; JD/MA. *Accreditation:* NASPAA. *Faculty:* 20. *Students:* 64 full-time (20 women), 75 part-time (45 women); includes 48 minority (32 Black or African American, non-Hispanic/Latino; 5 Asian, non-Hispanic/Latino; 4 Hispanic/Latino; 7 Two or more races, non-Hispanic/Latino), 7 international. Average age 33. 105 applicants, 50% accepted, 27 enrolled. In 2016, 25 master's, 5 doctorates awarded. *Degree requirements:* For master's, comprehensive exam (for some programs), thesis (for some programs); for doctorate, thesis/dissertation. *Entrance requirements:* For master's, GRE General Test, substantial undergraduate preparation in the social sciences, minimum upper-division undergraduate GPA of 3.0, two letters of recommendation, personal statement; for doctorate, GRE General Test, 3 letters of recommendation; personal statement; interview. Additional exam requirements/recommendations for international students: Required—TOEFL (minimum score 550 paper-based; 79 iBT), TWE (minimum score 5.5), Michigan English Language Assessment Battery (minimum score 85); Recommended—IELTS (minimum score 6.5). *Application deadline:* For fall admission, 5/15 for domestic students, 5/1 priority date for international students; for winter admission, 10/15 for domestic students, 9/1 priority date for international students. Applications are processed on a rolling basis. Application fee: $50. Electronic applications accepted. *Expenses:* $16,503 per year resident tuition and fees, $33,697 per year non-resident tuition and fees. *Financial support:* In 2016–17, 48 students received support, including 3 fellowships with tuition reimbursements available (averaging $17,333 per year), 13 teaching assistantships with tuition reimbursements available (averaging $18,067 per year); research assistantships with tuition reimbursements available, scholarships/grants, health care benefits, and unspecified assistantships also available. Financial award applicants required to submit FAFSA. *Faculty research:* American government and politics, comparative politics, political methodology, political theory, public administration, public law, public policy, world politics/international relations, formal theory/modeling, gender and politics, international law, peace research, political economy, political psychology, politics of developing countries, race, religion, and ethnicity, urban politics. *Unit head:* Dr. Daniel Geller, Professor and Chair, 313-577-6328, E-mail: dgeller@wayne.edu. *Application contact:* Dr. Sharon Lean, Graduate Director, 313-577-2630, E-mail: gradpolisci@wayne.edu. Website: http://clas.wayne.edu/politicalscience/

**Webster University,** George Herbert Walker School of Business and Technology, Department of Management, St. Louis, MO 63119-3194. Offers business and organizational security management (MA); digital marketing management (Graduate Certificate); government contracting (Graduate Certificate); health administration (MHA); health care management (MA); health services management (MA); human resources development (MA); human resources management (MA); information technology management (MA, MS); management (D Mgt); management and leadership (MA); marketing (MA); nonprofit leadership (MA); nonprofit revenue development (Graduate Certificate); organizational development (Graduate Certificate); procurement and acquisitions management (MA); public administration (MPA); space systems operations management (MS). *Program availability:* Part-time, evening/weekend, online learning. *Degree requirements:* For master's, thesis (for some programs); for doctorate, thesis/dissertation, written exam. *Entrance requirements:* For doctorate, GMAT, 3 years of work experience, MBA. Additional exam requirements/recommendations for international students: Required—TOEFL. *Application deadline:* Applications are processed on a rolling basis. Application fee: $25 ($50 for international students). *Expenses: Tuition:* Full-time $21,900; part-time $730 per credit hour. Tuition and fees vary according to campus/location and program. *Financial support:* Federal Work-Study available. Support available to part-time students. Financial award application deadline: 4/1; financial award applicants required to submit FAFSA. *Unit head:* Barrett Baebler, Chair, 314-246-7940, E-mail: baeblerb@webster.edu. *Application contact:* Sarah Nandor, Director, Graduate and Transfer Admissions, 314-968-7109, E-mail: gadmit@webster.edu.

**West Chester University of Pennsylvania,** College of Business and Public Management, Department of Public Policy and Administration, West Chester, PA 19383. Offers administration (Certificate); human resource management (MPA, Certificate); human resources management (DPA); non profit administration (Certificate); nonprofit administration (MPA); public administration (MPA); public policy and administration (MPA). *Accreditation:* NASPAA. *Program availability:* Part-time, evening/weekend, 100% online. *Faculty:* 6 full-time (4 women), 3 part-time/adjunct (2 women). *Students:*

*Public Administration*

62 full-time (35 women), 144 part-time (80 women); includes 72 minority (60 Black or African American, non-Hispanic/Latino; 1 American Indian or Alaska Native, non-Hispanic/Latino; 3 Asian, non-Hispanic/Latino; 7 Hispanic/Latino; 1 Two or more races, non-Hispanic/Latino), 6 international. Average age 33. 133 applicants, 92% accepted, 97 enrolled. In 2016, 58 master's, 1 other advanced degree awarded. *Degree requirements:* For master's, capstone project. *Entrance requirements:* For master's and other advanced degree, statement of professional goals, resume, two letters of reference, academic transcripts. Additional exam requirements/recommendations for international students: Required—TOEFL or IELTS. *Application deadline:* For fall admission, 5/15 for international students; for spring admission, 10/15 for international students. Applications are processed on a rolling basis. Application fee: $50. Electronic applications accepted. *Expenses:* Tuition, state resident: full-time $8694; part-time $483 per credit. Tuition, nonresident: full-time $13,050; part-time $725 per credit. *Required fees:* $2399; $119.05 per credit. Tuition and fees vary according to campus/location and program. *Financial support:* Scholarships/grants and unspecified assistantships available. Financial award application deadline: 2/15; financial award applicants required to submit FAFSA. *Faculty research:* Public policy, economic development, research methodology, public administration, nonprofit administration. *Unit head:* Dr. Allison Turner, Department Chair/Director of MPA Program, 610-436-2438, E-mail: aturner@wcupa.edu. *Application contact:* Dr. Jeremy Phillips, DPA Graduate Coordinator, 610-436-2016, E-mail: jphillips@wcupa.edu.
Website: http://www.wcupa.edu/business-publicManagement/mpa/

**Western Kentucky University,** Graduate Studies, Potter College of Arts and Letters, Department of Political Science, Bowling Green, KY 42101. Offers MPA. *Accreditation:* NASPAA. *Program availability:* Part-time, evening/weekend. *Degree requirements:* For master's, comprehensive exam, final exam. *Entrance requirements:* For master's, GRE General Test, minimum GPA of 2.75. Additional exam requirements/recommendations for international students: Required—TOEFL (minimum score 555 paper-based; 79 iBT). *Faculty research:* Role of non-profits, comparative policy analysis, social welfare policy, rural administration, ethics and bureaucracy.

**Western Michigan University,** Graduate College, College of Arts and Sciences, Department of Political Science, Kalamazoo, MI 49008. Offers international development administration (MIDA), including Peace Corps; political science (MA, PhD). *Degree requirements:* For master's, thesis optional; for doctorate, thesis/dissertation.

**Western Michigan University,** Graduate College, College of Arts and Sciences, School of Public Affairs and Administration, Kalamazoo, MI 49008. Offers health care administration (MPA, Graduate Certificate); nonprofit leadership and administration (Graduate Certificate); public administration (PhD). *Accreditation:* NASPAA (one or more programs are accredited). *Degree requirements:* For doctorate, thesis/dissertation.

**Westfield State University,** College of Graduate and Continuing Education, Department of Political Science, Westfield, MA 01086. Offers criminal justice administration (MPA); non-profit management (MPA); public management (MPA). *Program availability:* Part-time, evening/weekend. *Faculty:* 2 full-time (1 woman), 4 part-time/adjunct (2 women). *Students:* 13 full-time (6 women), 38 part-time (17 women); includes 11 minority (2 American Indian or Alaska Native, non-Hispanic/Latino; 8 Hispanic/Latino; 1 Two or more races, non-Hispanic/Latino). Average age 29. 16 applicants, 88% accepted, 13 enrolled. In 2016, 17 master's awarded. *Degree requirements:* For master's, comprehensive exam, thesis (for some programs). *Entrance requirements:* For master's, GRE General Test or MAT, minimum undergraduate GPA of 2.8. Additional exam requirements/recommendations for international students: Recommended—TOEFL (minimum score 550 paper-based; 79 iBT). *Application deadline:* For fall admission, 6/30 for domestic students; for spring admission, 10/31 for domestic students; for summer admission, 3/31 for domestic students. Applications are processed on a rolling basis. Application fee: $50. *Expenses:* Tuition, state resident: part-time $318 per semester hour. Tuition, nonresident: part-time $318 per semester hour. *Required fees:* $75 per semester. Tuition and fees vary according to course load and program. *Financial support:* Unspecified assistantships available. Financial award application deadline: 3/1; financial award applicants required to submit FAFSA. *Unit head:* Dr. Hugh Jo, Chair, 413-572-8806, Fax: 413-572-8168, E-mail: hjo@westfield.ma.edu. *Application contact:* Shelly Henrichon, Admissions Coordinator, 413-572-8022, Fax: 413-572-5227, E-mail: mhenrichon@westfield.ma.edu.

**West Virginia University,** Eberly College of Arts and Sciences, Department of Public Administration, Morgantown, WV 26506. Offers legal studies (MLS); public administration (MPA); JD/MPA; MSW/MPA. *Accreditation:* NASPAA. *Program availability:* Part-time. *Degree requirements:* For master's, internship. *Entrance requirements:* For master's, GRE General Test, minimum GPA of 2.75. Additional exam requirements/recommendations for international students: Required—TOEFL.

Electronic applications accepted. *Faculty research:* Public management and organization, conflict resolution, work satisfaction, health administration, social policy and welfare.

**Wichita State University,** Graduate School, Fairmount College of Liberal Arts and Sciences, Hugo Wall School of Public Affairs, Wichita, KS 67260. Offers public administration (MPA). *Accreditation:* NASPAA. *Program availability:* Part-time, 100% online, blended/hybrid learning. *Unit head:* Dr. Samuel L. Brown, Director, 316-978-7240, Fax: 316-978-6533, E-mail: sam.brown@wichita.edu. *Application contact:* Jordan Oleson, Admissions Coordinator, 316-978-3095, E-mail: jordan.oleson@wichita.edu.

**Widener University,** College of Arts and Sciences, Program in Public Administration, Chester, PA 19013-5792. Offers MPA, Psy D/MPA. *Program availability:* Part-time, evening/weekend. *Faculty:* 1 full-time (0 women), 3 part-time/adjunct (0 women). *Students:* 7 part-time (4 women); includes 2 minority (1 Black or African American, non-Hispanic/Latino; 1 Hispanic/Latino). Average age 31. 21 applicants, 86% accepted. In 2016, 9 master's awarded. *Degree requirements:* For master's, thesis or comprehensive exam. *Entrance requirements:* For master's, minimum undergraduate GPA of 3.0. *Application deadline:* For fall admission, 8/1 priority date for domestic students; for spring admission, 12/1 priority date for domestic students. Applications are processed on a rolling basis. Application fee: $25 ($300 for international students). Electronic applications accepted. *Expenses:* Contact institution. *Financial support:* In 2016–17, 8 students received support. Career-related internships or fieldwork and institutionally sponsored loans available. Support available to part-time students. Financial award application deadline: 5/1. *Faculty research:* Intergovernmental relations, nonprofit organizations, public policy, political economy, bureaucratic politics. *Unit head:* Dr. James E. Vike, Director, 610-499-1120, Fax: 610-499-4603, E-mail: james.vike@widener.edu.
Website: http://www.widener.edu/academics/schools/arts_sciences/public_admin/default.aspx

**Wilmington University,** College of Business, New Castle, DE 19720-6491. Offers accounting (MBA, MS); business administration (MBA, DBA); environmental stewardship (MBA); finance (MBA); health care administration (MBA, MSM); homeland security (MBA, MSM); human resource management (MSM); management information systems (MBA, MSN); marketing (MSM); marketing management (MBA); military leadership (MSM); organizational leadership (MBA, MSM); public administration (MSM). *Program availability:* Part-time, evening/weekend. *Faculty:* 17 full-time (7 women), 106 part-time/adjunct (46 women). *Students:* 436 full-time (237 women), 1,202 part-time (739 women); includes 594 minority (474 Black or African American, non-Hispanic/Latino; 19 American Indian or Alaska Native, non-Hispanic/Latino; 64 Asian, non-Hispanic/Latino; 30 Hispanic/Latino; 3 Native Hawaiian or other Pacific Islander, non-Hispanic/Latino; 4 Two or more races, non-Hispanic/Latino), 153 international. Average age 35. 814 applicants, 98% accepted, 426 enrolled. In 2016, 594 master's, 23 doctorate awarded. *Entrance requirements:* Additional exam requirements/recommendations for international students: Required—TOEFL (minimum score 500 paper-based). *Application deadline:* Applications are processed on a rolling basis. Application fee: $35. Electronic applications accepted. *Expenses: Tuition:* Full-time $8388; part-time $466 per credit. *Required fees:* $25 per semester. Tuition and fees vary according to degree level. *Financial support:* Applicants required to submit FAFSA. *Unit head:* Dr. Robert W. Rescigno, Dean. *Application contact:* Laura Morris, Director of Admissions, 877-967-5456, E-mail: infocenter@wilmu.edu.
Website: http://www.wilmu.edu/business

**Wright State University,** Graduate School, College of Liberal Arts, Department of Urban Affairs and Geography, Dayton, OH 45435. Offers public administration (MPA). *Accreditation:* NASPAA. *Degree requirements:* For master's, thesis optional. *Entrance requirements:* For master's, interview, minimum GPA of 2.7. Additional exam requirements/recommendations for international students: Required—TOEFL. Application fee: $25. *Expenses:* Tuition, state resident: full-time $9952; part-time $622 per credit hour. Tuition, nonresident: full-time $16,960; part-time $1060 per credit hour. *Financial support:* Fellowships and unspecified assistantships available. Support available to part-time students. Financial award applicants required to submit FAFSA. *Faculty research:* Strategic planning, economic development, housing and public management. *Unit head:* Dr. Jack L. Dustin, Chair, 937-775-4451, Fax: 937-775-2422, E-mail: jack.dustin@wright.edu. *Application contact:* John Kimble, Associate Director of Graduate Admissions and Records, 937-775-2957, Fax: 937-775-2453, E-mail: john.kimble@wright.edu.

**York University,** Faculty of Graduate Studies, Faculty of Liberal Arts and Professional Studies, Program in Public Policy, Administration and Law, Toronto, ON M3J 1P3, Canada. Offers MPPAL.

# Public Affairs

**American University,** School of Communication, Program in Journalism and Public Affairs, Washington, DC 20016-8001. Offers broadcast journalism (MA); international journalism (MA); investigative journalism (MA). *Accreditation:* ACEJMC. *Faculty:* 13 full-time (5 women), 4 part-time/adjunct (all women). *Students:* 28 full-time (20 women); includes 13 minority (7 Black or African American, non-Hispanic/Latino; 1 Asian, non-Hispanic/Latino; 4 Hispanic/Latino; 1 Two or more races, non-Hispanic/Latino), 4 international. 110 applicants, 73% accepted, 28 enrolled. In 2016, 28 master's awarded. *Degree requirements:* For master's, comprehensive exam, thesis or alternative. *Entrance requirements:* Additional exam requirements/recommendations for international students: Required—TOEFL (minimum score 600 paper-based; 100 iBT), IELTS (minimum score 7). *Application deadline:* For fall admission, 2/1 priority date for domestic and international students. Applications are processed on a rolling basis. Application fee: $55. Electronic applications accepted. *Expenses: Tuition:* Full-time $28,422; part-time $1579 per credit hour. *Required fees:* $690; $200 per term. Tuition and fees vary according to course load, degree level and program. *Financial support:* In 2016–17, 3 fellowships with tuition reimbursements (averaging $27,000 per year), 14 research assistantships with partial tuition reimbursements (averaging $7,000 per year), 3 teaching assistantships with partial tuition reimbursements (averaging $7,000 per year) were awarded; career-related internships or fieldwork, Federal Work-Study, institutionally sponsored loans, scholarships/grants, tuition waivers (partial), and unspecified assistantships also available. Financial award application deadline: 2/1; financial award applicants required to submit FAFSA. *Faculty research:* Government and media effects of journalistic practices and policies; race, gender, and the media; investigative reporting; computer-assisted reporting; data driven journalism. *Unit head:* Prof. John Watson, Division Director, 202-885-2083, Fax: 202-885-2099, E-mail: jwatson@american.edu. *Application contact:* Christine Rials, Assistant Director for Graduate Admissions, 202-885-2040, Fax: 202-885-2019, E-mail: crials@american.edu.
Website: http://www.american.edu/soc/journalism/index.cfm

**Arizona State University at the Tempe campus,** College of Public Programs, School of Public Affairs, Phoenix, AZ 85004-0687. Offers emergency management and homeland security (MA); program evaluation (MS); public administration (MPA, PhD), including nonprofit administration (MPA); urban management (MPA); public policy (MPP); MPA/MSW. *Accreditation:* NASPAA (one or more programs are accredited). *Program availability:* Part-time, evening/weekend. Terminal master's awarded for partial completion of doctoral program. *Degree requirements:* For master's, thesis or alternative, policy analysis or capstone project; interactive Program of Study (iPOS) submitted before completing 50 percent of required credit hours; for doctorate, comprehensive exam, thesis/dissertation, interactive Program of Study (iPOS) submitted before completing 50 percent of required credit hours. *Entrance requirements:* For master's, GRE, minimum GPA of 3.0 or equivalent in last 2 years of work leading to bachelor's degree; for doctorate, GRE, minimum GPA of 3.0 or equivalent in last 2 years of work leading to bachelor's degree, 3 letters of recommendation, resume, statement of goals, samples of research reports. Additional exam requirements/recommendations for international students: Required—TOEFL (minimum score 600 paper-based; 100 iBT), IELTS (minimum score 6.5). Electronic applications accepted. *Expenses:* Contact institution.

**Cleveland State University,** College of Graduate Studies, Maxine Goodman Levin College of Urban Affairs, Program in Urban Studies and Public Affairs, Cleveland, OH 44115. Offers communication (PhD); public administration (PhD); urban policy and development (PhD). *Program availability:* Part-time, evening/weekend. *Faculty:* 16 full-time (8 women), 13 part-time/adjunct (5 women). *Students:* 8 full-time (6 women), 17 part-time (8 women); includes 5 minority (3 Black or African American, non-Hispanic/Latino; 1 Hispanic/Latino; 1 Two or more races, non-Hispanic/Latino), 6 international. Average age 43. 32 applicants, 34% accepted, 2 enrolled. In 2016, 4 doctorates awarded. *Degree requirements:* For doctorate, comprehensive exam, thesis/dissertation. *Entrance requirements:* For doctorate, GRE General Test (minimum score: verbal and quantitative 50th percentile, analytical writing 4.0), minimum GPA of 3.5. Additional exam requirements/recommendations for international students: Required—TOEFL (minimum score 550 paper-based; 78 iBT), IELTS (6.0), or International Test of English Proficiency (iTEP). *Application deadline:* For fall admission, 1/31 for domestic and international students. Application fee: $40. Electronic applications accepted. *Expenses:* Contact institution. *Financial support:* In 2016–17, 15 students received support, including 5 research assistantships with full tuition reimbursements available (averaging $11,800 per year), 1 teaching assistantship with full tuition reimbursement available (averaging $11,800 per year); scholarships/grants, tuition waivers (full and partial), and unspecified assistantships also available. Support available to part-time students. Financial award application deadline: 3/1; financial award applicants required to submit FAFSA. *Faculty research:* Urban and public policy, public affairs. *Unit head:* Dr. Bill Bowen, Professor/PhD Program Director, 216-687-9226, E-mail: w.bowen@csuohio.edu. *Application contact:* David Arrighi, Graduate Academic Advisor, 216-523-7522, Fax: 216-687-5398, E-mail: d.arrighi@csuohio.edu. Website: http://urban.csuohio.edu/academics/graduate/phd/

**Concordia University,** School of Graduate Studies, Faculty of Arts and Science, School of Community and Public Affairs, Montréal, QC H3G 1M8, Canada. Offers community economic development (Diploma).

**Cornell University,** Graduate School, Graduate Fields of Human Ecology, Field of Public Affairs, Ithaca, NY 14853. Offers MA. *Degree requirements:* For master's, thesis, research project, paper. *Entrance requirements:* For master's, GRE General Test, 2 letters of recommendation. Additional exam requirements/recommendations for international students: Required—TOEFL (minimum score 550 paper-based; 77 iBT). Electronic applications accepted.

**Florida International University,** Steven J. Green School of International and Public Affairs, Department of Public Administration, Miami, FL 33199. Offers public administration (MPA); public affairs (PhD); JD/MPA; MS/MPA. *Accreditation:* NASPAA (one or more programs are accredited). *Program availability:* Part-time, evening/weekend. *Faculty:* 14 full-time (5 women), 15 part-time/adjunct (7 women). *Students:* 107 full-time (61 women), 136 part-time (91 women); includes 100 minority (13 Black or African American, non-Hispanic/Latino; 5 Asian, non-Hispanic/Latino; 78 Hispanic/Latino; 4 Two or more races, non-Hispanic/Latino), 47 international. Average age 33. 149 applicants, 62% accepted, 72 enrolled. In 2016, 70 master's, 4 doctorates awarded. *Degree requirements:* For doctorate, comprehensive exam, thesis/dissertation. *Entrance requirements:* For master's, minimum undergraduate GPA of 3.0 in upper-level coursework, letter of recommendation, letter of intent; for doctorate, GRE, minimum undergraduate GPA of 3.0 in upper-level coursework, 3 letters of recommendation, samples of scholarly written work, interview (when student lives within 50 miles of campus). Additional exam requirements/recommendations for international students: Required—TOEFL (minimum score 550 paper-based; 80 iBT). *Application deadline:* For fall admission, 6/1 for domestic students, 4/1 for international students; for spring admission, 10/1 for domestic students, 9/1 for international students. Applications are processed on a rolling basis. Application fee: $30. Electronic applications accepted. *Expenses:* Tuition, state resident: full-time $8912; part-time $446 per credit hour. Tuition, nonresident: full-time $21,393; part-time $992 per credit hour. *Required fees:* $2185; $195 per semester. Tuition and fees vary according to program. *Financial support:* Institutionally sponsored loans and scholarships/grants available. Financial award application deadline: 3/1; financial award applicants required to submit FAFSA. *Unit head:* Dr. Mohamad Alkadry, Program Director, 305-348-5890, E-mail: mohamad.alkadry@fiu.edu. *Application contact:* Nanett Rojas, Manager, Admissions Operations, 305-348-7464, E-mail: gradadm@fiu.edu. Website: http://cas.fiu.edu/

**George Mason University,** College of Humanities and Social Sciences, Department of Philosophy, Fairfax, VA 22030. Offers ethics and public affairs (MA). *Faculty:* 12 full-time (3 women), 7 part-time/adjunct (0 women). *Students:* 3 full-time (2 women), 11 part-time (3 women); includes 3 minority (1 Hispanic/Latino; 2 Two or more races, non-Hispanic/Latino). Average age 35. 6 applicants, 83% accepted, 2 enrolled. In 2016, 4 master's awarded. *Degree requirements:* For master's, thesis optional. *Entrance requirements:* For master's, 3 letters of recommendation; official transcript; expanded goals statement; writing sample; resume. Additional exam requirements/recommendations for international students: Required—TOEFL (minimum score 575 paper-based; 88 iBT), IELTS (minimum score 6.5), PTE (minimum score 59). *Application deadline:* For fall admission, 3/1 for domestic students. Electronic applications accepted. *Expenses:* Tuition, state resident: full-time $10,628; part-time $443 per credit. Tuition, nonresident: full-time $29,306; part-time $1221 per credit. *Required fees:* $3096; $129 per credit. Tuition and fees vary according to program. *Financial support:* In 2016–17, 2 students received support, including 1 research assistantship with tuition reimbursement available (averaging $6,500 per year), 1 teaching assistantship with tuition reimbursement available (averaging $7,000 per year); career-related internships or fieldwork, Federal Work-Study, scholarships/grants, unspecified assistantships, and health care benefits (for full-time research or teaching assistantship recipients) also available. Financial award application deadline: 3/1; financial award applicants required to submit FAFSA. *Faculty research:* Cultural studies, political theory philosophy, social and political philosophy, feminist theory, analytical and Continental philosophy, philosophy of science. *Total annual research expenditures:* $36,365. *Unit head:* Ted Kinnaman, Chair/Associate Professor, 703-993-4328, Fax: 703-993-1297, E-mail: tkinnama@gmu.edu. *Application contact:* Rose Cherubin, Associate Professor and Graduate Coordinator, 703-993-1332, Fax: 703-993-1297, E-mail: rcherubi@gmu.edu. Website: http://philosophy.gmu.edu/

**The George Washington University,** Columbian College of Arts and Sciences, School of Media and Public Affairs, Washington, DC 20052. Offers MA, Graduate Certificate. *Faculty:* 22 full-time (10 women). *Students:* 31 full-time (20 women), 19 part-time (15 women); includes 10 minority (7 Black or African American, non-Hispanic/Latino; 1 Asian, non-Hispanic/Latino; 1 Hispanic/Latino; 1 Native Hawaiian or other Pacific Islander, non-Hispanic/Latino), 9 international. Average age 27. 86 applicants, 59% accepted, 24 enrolled. In 2016, 22 master's, 13 other advanced degrees awarded. *Degree requirements:* For master's, thesis optional. *Entrance requirements:* For master's, GRE General Test. Additional exam requirements/recommendations for international students: Required—TOEFL (minimum score 550 paper-based; 80 iBT). *Application deadline:* For fall admission, 4/1 priority date for domestic students, 1/15 priority date for international students; for spring admission, 10/1 priority date for domestic students, 9/1 priority date for international students. Applications are processed on a rolling basis. Application fee: $75. Electronic applications accepted. *Financial support:* In 2016–17, fellowships with tuition reimbursements (averaging $10,000 per year), teaching assistantships with tuition reimbursements (averaging $5,000 per year) were awarded. Financial award application deadline: 1/15. *Unit head:*

Frank Sesno, Director, 202-994-9553, E-mail: sesno@gwu.edu. *Application contact:* Information Contact, 202-994-6227, Fax: 202-994-5806, E-mail: smpa@gwu.edu. Website: http://smpa.gwu.edu/

**Indiana University Bloomington,** School of Public and Environmental Affairs, Public Affairs Programs, Bloomington, IN 47405. Offers economic development (MPA); energy (MPA); environmental policy (PhD); environmental policy and natural resource management (MPA); information systems (MPA); international development (MPA); local government management (MPA); nonprofit management (MPA, Certificate); policy analysis (MPA); public budgeting and financial management (Certificate); public finance (PhD); public financial administration (MPA); public management (MPA, PhD, Certificate); public policy analysis (PhD); social entrepreneurship (Certificate); specialized public affairs (MPA); sustainability and sustainable development (MPA); JD/MPA; MPA/MA; MPA/MIS; MPA/MLS; MSES/MPA. *Accreditation:* NASPAA (one or more programs are accredited). *Program availability:* Part-time. *Degree requirements:* For master's, capstone, internship; for doctorate, comprehensive exam, thesis/dissertation. *Entrance requirements:* For master's, GRE General Test or GMAT, official transcripts, 3 letters of recommendation, resume, personal statement; for doctorate, GRE General Test, official transcripts, 3 letters of recommendation, statement of purpose. Additional exam requirements/recommendations for international students: Required—TOEFL (minimum score 600 paper-based; 96 iBT), Recommended—IELTS (minimum score 7). Electronic applications accepted. *Faculty research:* International development, environmental policy and resource management, policy analysis, public finance, public management, urban management, nonprofit management, energy policy, social policy, public finance.

**Indiana University Northwest,** School of Public and Environmental Affairs, Gary, IN 46408. Offers criminal justice (MPA); environmental affairs (Graduate Certificate); health services (MPA); nonprofit management (Certificate); public management (MPA, Graduate Certificate). *Accreditation:* NASPAA (one or more programs are accredited). *Program availability:* Part-time. *Faculty:* 5 full-time (3 women). *Students:* 10 full-time (8 women), 39 part-time (28 women); includes 25 minority (18 Black or African American, non-Hispanic/Latino; 7 Hispanic/Latino), 1 international. Average age 37. 31 applicants, 97% accepted, 16 enrolled. In 2016, 13 master's, 9 other advanced degrees awarded. *Entrance requirements:* For master's, GRE General Test (minimum combined verbal and quantitative score of 280), GMAT, or LSAT, letters of recommendation. *Application deadline:* For fall admission, 8/15 priority date for domestic students. Applications are processed on a rolling basis. Application fee: $40 ($60 for international students). Electronic applications accepted. *Financial support:* Career-related internships or fieldwork, Federal Work-Study, and tuition waivers (partial) available. Support available to part-time students. Financial award application deadline: 3/1; financial award applicants required to submit FAFSA. *Faculty research:* Employment in income security policies, evidence in criminal justice, equal employment law, social welfare policy and welfare reform, public finance in developing countries. *Unit head:* Dr. Karl Besel, Assistant Dean and Director, 219-980-6554, Fax: 219-980-6737, E-mail: kbesel@iun.edu. Website: http://www.iun.edu/spea/index.htm

**Indiana University of Pennsylvania,** School of Graduate Studies and Research, College of Humanities and Social Sciences, Department of Political Science, Program in Public Affairs, Indiana, PA 15705. Offers MA. *Program availability:* Part-time. *Faculty:* 7 full-time (4 women). *Students:* 15 full-time (5 women), 7 part-time (4 women); includes 2 minority (1 Black or African American, non-Hispanic/Latino; 1 Hispanic/Latino), 8 international. Average age 26. 21 applicants, 76% accepted, 10 enrolled. In 2016, 7 master's awarded. *Degree requirements:* For master's, thesis optional. *Entrance requirements:* For master's, 2 letters of recommendation. Additional exam requirements/recommendations for international students: Required—TOEFL (minimum score 550 paper-based). *Application deadline:* Applications are processed on a rolling basis. Application fee: $50. Electronic applications accepted. *Expenses:* Tuition, state resident: full-time $8694; part-time $483 per credit. Tuition, nonresident: full-time $13,050; part-time $725 per credit. *Required fees:* $157 per credit. $50 per term. Tuition and fees vary according to course load and program. *Financial support:* In 2016–17, 10 research assistantships with tuition reimbursements (averaging $2,748 per year) were awarded; fellowships with full tuition reimbursements, career-related internships or fieldwork, Federal Work-Study, scholarships/grants, and unspecified assistantships also available. Support available to part-time students. Financial award application deadline: 4/15; financial award applicants required to submit FAFSA. *Unit head:* Dr. Sarah Wheeler, Graduate Coordinator, 724-357-2290, E-mail: wheeler@iup.edu. Website: http://www.iup.edu/grad/publicaffairs/default.aspx

**Indiana University–Purdue University Indianapolis,** School of Public and Environmental Affairs, Indianapolis, IN 46202. Offers criminal justice and public safety (MS); homeland security and emergency management (Graduate Certificate); library management (Graduate Certificate); nonprofit management (Graduate Certificate); public affairs (MPA); public management (Graduate Certificate); social entrepreneurship: nonprofit and public benefit organizations (Graduate Certificate); JD/MPA; MLS/NMC; MLS/PMC; MPA/MA. *Accreditation:* CAHME (one or more programs are accredited); NASPAA. *Program availability:* Part-time, evening/weekend, online learning. *Entrance requirements:* For master's, GRE General Test, GMAT or LSAT, minimum GPA of 3.0 (preferred). Additional exam requirements/recommendations for international students: Required—TOEFL (minimum score 93 iBT), IELTS (minimum score 6.5). Electronic applications accepted. *Faculty research:* Nonprofit and public management, public policy, urban policy, sustainability policy, disaster preparedness and recovery, vehicular safety, homicide, offender rehabilitation and re-entry.

**Indiana University South Bend,** College of Liberal Arts and Sciences, South Bend, IN 46634-7111. Offers advanced computer programming (Graduate Certificate); applied informatics (Graduate Certificate); applied mathematics and computer science (MS); behavior modification (Graduate Certificate); computer applications (Graduate Certificate); computer programming (Graduate Certificate); correctional management and supervision (Graduate Certificate); English (MA); health systems management (Graduate Certificate); international studies (Graduate Certificate); liberal studies (MLS); nonprofit management (Graduate Certificate); paralegal studies (Graduate Certificate); professional writing (Graduate Certificate); public affairs (MPA); public management (Graduate Certificate); social and cultural diversity (Graduate Certificate); strategic sustainability leadership (Graduate Certificate); technology for administration (Graduate Certificate). *Program availability:* Part-time, evening/weekend. *Faculty:* 79 full-time (33 women). *Students:* 31 full-time (11 women), 92 part-time (53 women); includes 28 minority (9 Black or African American, non-Hispanic/Latino; 8 Asian, non-Hispanic/Latino; 5 Hispanic/Latino; 6 Two or more races, non-Hispanic/Latino), 19 international. Average age 38. 51 applicants, 84% accepted, 31 enrolled. In 2016, 30 master's, 6 other advanced degrees awarded. *Degree requirements:* For master's, variable foreign language requirement, thesis (for some programs). *Entrance requirements:* For master's, minimum GPA of 3.0. Additional exam requirements/recommendations for international students: Required—TOEFL (minimum score 550 paper-based; 80 iBT). *Application deadline:* For fall admission, 7/31 priority date for domestic students, 7/1 priority date for international students; for spring admission, 3/31 priority date for domestic students, 11/1 priority date for international students. Applications are

*Public Affairs*

processed on a rolling basis. Application fee: $40 ($60 for international students). *Expenses:* $276.98 per credit hour in-state; $652.54 per credit hour out-of-state. *Financial support:* In 2016–17, 5 teaching assistantships were awarded; Federal Work-Study also available. Support available to part-time students. Financial award application deadline: 3/10. *Faculty research:* Artificial intelligence, bioinformatics, English language and literature, creative writing, computer networks. *Total annual research expenditures:* $127,000. *Unit head:* Dr. Elizabeth E. Dunn, Dean, 574-520-4290, E-mail: elizdunn@iusb.edu. *Application contact:* Admissions Counselor, 574-520-4839, Fax: 574-520-4834, E-mail: graduate@iusb.edu.
Website: https://www.iusb.edu/clas/

**The Institute of World Politics,** Graduate Programs in National Security, Intelligence, and International Affairs, Washington, DC 20036. Offers American foreign policy (Certificate); comparative political culture (Certificate); counterintelligence (Certificate); democracy building (Certificate); intelligence (Certificate); international politics (Certificate); national security affairs (Certificate); public diplomacy and political warfare (Certificate); statecraft and national security affairs (MA); statecraft and world politics (MA); strategic intelligence studies (MA). *Program availability:* Part-time, evening/weekend. *Degree requirements:* For master's, comprehensive exam, thesis optional. *Entrance requirements:* For master's, GRE General Test. Additional exam requirements/recommendations for international students: Required—TOEFL. Electronic applications accepted. *Faculty research:* Intelligence, national security, statecraft.

**Jackson State University,** Graduate School, College of Public Service, Jackson, MS 39217. Offers MA, MPPA, MSW, PhD. *Degree requirements:* For master's, comprehensive exam. *Entrance requirements:* For master's, GRE General Test. Additional exam requirements/recommendations for international students: Required—TOEFL. *Application deadline:* For fall admission, 3/1 for domestic and international students; for spring admission, 10/1 for domestic and international students. Application fee: $25. *Expenses:* Tuition, state resident: full-time $7141. Tuition, nonresident: full-time $17,494. *Required fees:* $1080. Tuition and fees vary according to class time, course level, course load, degree level, campus/location, program and student level. *Financial support:* Career-related internships or fieldwork, Federal Work-Study, scholarships/grants, tuition waivers (full), and unspecified assistantships available. Support available to part-time students. Financial award application deadline: 3/1; financial award applicants required to submit FAFSA. *Unit head:* Dr. Ricardo A. Brown, Dean, 601-979-8836, Fax: 601-979-3360, E-mail: deanofcps@jsums.edu. *Application contact:* Fatoumatta Sisay, Manager of Graduate Admissions, 601-979-0342, Fax: 601-979-4325, E-mail: fatoumatta.sisay@jsums.edu.
Website: http://www.jsums.edu/publicservice/

**McMaster University,** School of Graduate Studies, Faculty of Social Sciences, Department of Political Science, Hamilton, ON L8S 4M2, Canada. Offers international relations (PhD); political science (MA); public and the global economy (MA); public policy (PhD); public policy and administration (MA). MA program in public policy and administration offered jointly with University of Guelph. *Program availability:* Part-time. *Degree requirements:* For master's, thesis or alternative. *Entrance requirements:* For master's, minimum B+ average. Additional exam requirements/recommendations for international students: Required—TOEFL (minimum score 580 paper-based). *Faculty research:* Organizational theory, internationalization of public policy, water resource policies, political interest intermediation, comparative politics.

**Merrimack College,** School of Liberal Arts, North Andover, MA 01845-5800. Offers clinical mental health counseling (MS); public affairs (MPA). *Program availability:* Part-time, evening/weekend. *Faculty:* 6 full-time, 4 part-time/adjunct. *Students:* 22 full-time (16 women), 2 part-time (0 women); includes 3 minority (2 Black or African American, non-Hispanic/Latino; 1 Hispanic/Latino), 1 international. Average age 32. 22 applicants, 95% accepted, 16 enrolled. *Degree requirements:* For master's, internship/strategic capstone. *Entrance requirements:* For master's, official college transcripts, resume, personal statement, 2 recommendations. Additional exam requirements/recommendations for international students: Required—TOEFL (minimum score 84 iBT), IELTS (minimum score 6.5), PTE (minimum score 56). *Application deadline:* For fall admission, 8/14 for domestic students, 7/14 for international students; for spring admission, 1/10 for domestic students, 12/10 for international students; for summer admission, 5/10 for domestic students, 4/10 for international students. Applications are processed on a rolling basis. Electronic applications accepted. *Expenses:* Contact institution. *Financial support:* Career-related internships or fieldwork, scholarships/grants, and health care benefits available. Support available to part-time students. Financial award application deadline: 5/1; financial award applicants required to submit FAFSA. *Faculty research:* Resilience, bereavement and grief, cultural competency training in counseling, government spending and taxation, applied ethics. *Application contact:* Jennifer Greenwood, Graduate Admissions Counselor, 978-837-3563, E-mail: greenwoodjl@merrimack.edu.

**Metropolitan College of New York,** Program in Public Administration, New York, NY 10006. Offers emergency and disaster management (MPA); public affairs and administration (MPA). *Program availability:* Evening/weekend. *Students:* 120 full-time (85 women), 10 part-time (4 women); includes 108 minority (76 Black or African American, non-Hispanic/Latino; 5 Asian, non-Hispanic/Latino; 26 Hispanic/Latino; 1 Native Hawaiian or other Pacific Islander, non-Hispanic/Latino), 2 international. Average age 37. In 2016, 118 master's awarded. *Degree requirements:* For master's, thesis. *Entrance requirements:* For master's, appropriate work experience, interview, minimum GPA of 2.7, internship or job in administrative setting. Additional exam requirements/recommendations for international students: Required—TOEFL (minimum score 600 paper-based). *Application deadline:* For fall admission, 7/30 priority date for domestic students, 7/1 for international students; for winter admission, 11/30 priority date for domestic students, 11/1 for international students; for spring admission, 3/30 priority date for domestic students, 3/1 for international students. Applications are processed on a rolling basis. Application fee: $45. Electronic applications accepted. *Expenses:* Contact institution. *Financial support:* Fellowships with tuition reimbursements, career-related internships or fieldwork, scholarships/grants, and tuition waivers (partial) available. Financial award application deadline: 8/15; financial award applicants required to submit FAFSA. *Faculty research:* Transnational politics and culture, women and social policy, confidentiality in the human services, concepts of marginality, ethics in social policy. *Unit head:* Prof. Humphrey Crookendale, Dean, Graduate School for Public Affairs Administration, 212-343-1234 Ext. 2209, E-mail: hcrookendale@mcny.edu. *Application contact:* Steebo Varghese, Assistant Director of Admissions, 212-343-1234 Ext. 2708, Fax: 212-343-8474, E-mail: svarghese@mcny.edu.
Website: http://www.metropolitan.edu/

**Murray State University,** College of Humanities and Fine Arts, Department of Government, Laws and International Affairs, Program in Public Administration, Murray, KY 42071. Offers public affairs (MPA). *Program availability:* Part-time, online learning. *Degree requirements:* For master's, capstone course. *Entrance requirements:* For master's, GRE General Test. Additional exam requirements/recommendations for international students: Required—TOEFL.

**New Mexico Highlands University,** Graduate Studies, College of Arts and Sciences, Department of History, Political Science, and Languages and Culture, Las Vegas, NM

87701. Offers public affairs (MA), including historical and cross-cultural perspectives, history/political science, political and governmental processes. *Degree requirements:* For master's, comprehensive exam, thesis or alternative. *Entrance requirements:* Additional exam requirements/recommendations for international students: Required—TOEFL (minimum score 540 paper-based).

**New Mexico Highlands University,** Graduate Studies, College of Arts and Sciences, Department of Social and Behavioral Sciences, Las Vegas, NM 87701. Offers psychology (MS), including clinical psychology/counseling, general psychology; public affairs (MA), including applied sociology; Southwest studies (MA), including anthropology. *Program availability:* Part-time. *Degree requirements:* For master's, comprehensive exam, thesis or alternative. *Entrance requirements:* For master's, minimum undergraduate GPA of 3.0. Additional exam requirements/recommendations for international students: Required—TOEFL (minimum score 540 paper-based). *Faculty research:* Southwest Native American resettlement development, community-level interventions, neurochemistry of personality, comparative criminal justice, social theory and activism.

**Notre Dame de Namur University,** Division of Academic Affairs, School of Business and Management, Program in Public Administration, Belmont, CA 94002-1908. Offers human resource management (MPA); public administration (MPA); public affairs administration (MPA); social enterprise (MPA). *Program availability:* Part-time, evening/weekend, online learning. *Entrance requirements:* For master's, interview, minimum GPA of 2.5. Additional exam requirements/recommendations for international students: Required—TOEFL (minimum score 550 paper-based; 79 iBT). Electronic applications accepted.

**The Ohio State University,** Graduate School, John Glenn College of Public Affairs, Columbus, OH 43210. Offers public administration (MA, MPA); public policy and management (PhD). *Accreditation:* NASPAA (one or more programs are accredited). *Program availability:* Part-time. *Faculty:* 20. *Students:* 122 full-time (58 women), 41 part-time (30 women). Average age 31. In 2016, 78 master's, 2 doctorates awarded. *Degree requirements:* For doctorate, thesis/dissertation. *Entrance requirements:* For master's, GRE General Test (for MPA), minimum GPA of 3.0 (for MA); for doctorate, GRE General Test. Additional exam requirements/recommendations for international students: Required—TOEFL (minimum score 600 paper-based; 100 iBT); Recommended—IELTS (minimum score 7.5). *Application deadline:* For fall admission, 12/1 priority date for domestic students, 11/30 priority date for international students; for spring admission, 11/15 for domestic and international students; for summer admission, 4/1 for domestic and international students. Applications are processed on a rolling basis. Application fee: $60 ($70 for international students). Electronic applications accepted. *Financial support:* Fellowships, research assistantships, teaching assistantships, Federal Work-Study, institutionally sponsored loans, and unspecified assistantships available. Support available to part-time students. *Unit head:* Dr. Trevor Brown, Dean, 614-292-4533, Fax: 614-292-4868, E-mail: brown.2296@osu.edu. *Application contact:* Graduate and Professional Admissions, 614-292-6031, Fax: 614-292-3656, E-mail: gpadmissions@osu.edu.
Website: http://glenn.osu.edu/

**Park University,** School of Graduate and Professional Studies, Kansas City, MO 54105. Offers adult education (M Ed); business and government leadership (Graduate Certificate); business, government, and global society (MPA); communication and leadership (MA); creative and life writing (Graduate Certificate); disaster and emergency management (MPA, Graduate Certificate); educational leadership (M Ed); finance (MBA, Graduate Certificate); general business (MBA); global business (Graduate Certificate); healthcare administration (MHA); healthcare services management and leadership (Graduate Certificate); international business (MBA); language and literacy (M Ed), including English for speakers of other languages, special reading teacher/literacy coach; leadership of international healthcare organizations (Graduate Certificate); management information systems (MBA, Graduate Certificate); music performance (ADP, Graduate Certificate), including cello (MM, ADP), piano (MM, ADP), viola (MM, ADP), violin (MM, ADP); nonprofit and community services management (MPA); nonprofit leadership (Graduate Certificate); performance (MM), including cello (MM, ADP), piano (MM, ADP), viola (MM, ADP), violin (MM, ADP); public management (MPA); social work (MSW); teacher leadership (M Ed), including curriculum and assessment, instructional leader. *Program availability:* Part-time, evening/weekend, online learning. *Degree requirements:* For master's, comprehensive exam (for some programs), thesis (for some programs), internship (for some programs); exam (for some programs). *Entrance requirements:* For master's, GRE or GMAT (for some programs), teacher certification (for some M Ed programs), letters of recommendation, essay, resume (for some programs). Additional exam requirements/recommendations for international students: Required—TOEFL (minimum score 550 paper-based; 79 iBT), IELTS (minimum score 6). Electronic applications accepted.

**Penn State Harrisburg,** Graduate School, School of Public Affairs, Middletown, PA 17057. Offers criminal justice (MA); health administration (MHA); health administration: long term care (Certificate); homeland security (Certificate); public administration (MPA, PhD); public administration: non-profit administration (Certificate); public budgeting and financial management (Certificate); public sector human resource management (Certificate). *Accreditation:* NASPAA. *Unit head:* Dr. Mukund S. Kulkarni, Chancellor, 717-948-6105, Fax: 717-948-6452. *Application contact:* Robert W. Coffman, Jr., Director of Enrollment Management, Admissions, 717-948-6250, Fax: 717-948-6325, E-mail: hbgadmit@psu.edu.
Website: https://harrisburg.psu.edu/public-affairs

**Portland State University,** Graduate Studies, College of Urban and Public Affairs, Hatfield School of Government, Division of Public Administration, Portland, OR 97207-0751. Offers public administration (MPA); public affairs and policy (PhD). *Accreditation:* NASPAA (one or more programs are accredited). *Program availability:* Part-time, evening/weekend. *Faculty:* 14 full-time (6 women), 9 part-time/adjunct (6 women). *Students:* 99 full-time (68 women), 122 part-time (82 women); includes 48 minority (5 Black or African American, non-Hispanic/Latino; 4 American Indian or Alaska Native, non-Hispanic/Latino; 7 Asian, non-Hispanic/Latino; 23 Hispanic/Latino; 9 Two or more races, non-Hispanic/Latino), 14 international. Average age 35. 143 applicants, 74% accepted, 68 enrolled. In 2016, 60 master's, 2 doctorates awarded. *Degree requirements:* For master's, internship (MPA), practicum (MPH); for doctorate, comprehensive exam, thesis/dissertation. *Entrance requirements:* For master's, GRE (minimum scores: verbal 150, quantitative 149, and analytic writing 4.5), minimum GPA of 3.0, 3 recommendation letters, resume, 500-word statement of intent; for doctorate, GRE, 3 recommendation letters, resume, 500-word personal essay. Additional exam requirements/recommendations for international students: Required—TOEFL (minimum score 550 paper-based; 80 iBT), IELTS (minimum score 7). *Application deadline:* For fall admission, 4/1 for domestic students, 3/1 for international students; for winter admission, 9/1 for domestic students, 8/1 for international students; for spring admission, 11/1 for domestic and international students. Application fee: $65. *Expenses:* Contact institution. *Financial support:* In 2016–17, 5 research assistantships with full tuition reimbursements (averaging $8,341 per year), 4 teaching assistantships with full tuition reimbursements (averaging $7,291 per year) were awarded; career-related internships or fieldwork, Federal Work-Study, scholarships/grants, tuition waivers (partial), and

unspecified assistantships also available. Support available to part-time students. Financial award application deadline: 3/1; financial award applicants required to submit FAFSA. *Faculty research:* Public budgeting, program evaluation, nonprofit management, natural resources policy and administration. *Total annual research expenditures:* $819,192. *Unit head:* Dr. Masami Nishishiba, Chair, 503-725-5151, E-mail: nishism@pdx.edu.
Website: https://www.pdx.edu/hatfieldschool/public-administration

**Princeton University,** Graduate School, Program in Population Studies, Princeton, NJ 08544-1019. Offers demography (PhD, Certificate); economics and demography (PhD); public affairs and demography (PhD); sociology and demography (PhD). *Degree requirements:* For doctorate, thesis/dissertation. *Entrance requirements:* For doctorate, GRE General Test. Additional exam requirements/recommendations for international students: Required—TOEFL (minimum score 600 paper-based). Electronic applications accepted. *Faculty research:* Models, fertility, infant and child mortality, migration.

**Princeton University,** Graduate School, Woodrow Wilson School of Public and International Affairs, Princeton, NJ 08544-1019. Offers public affairs (MPA, PhD); public policy (MPP); JD/MPA. JD/MPA offered jointly with Columbia University, New York University, Stanford University. Terminal master's awarded for partial completion of doctoral program. *Degree requirements:* For master's, internship; for doctorate, one foreign language, thesis/dissertation. *Entrance requirements:* For master's, GRE General Test, original policy memo; for doctorate, GRE General Test. Additional exam requirements/recommendations for international students: Required—TOEFL (minimum score 600 paper-based). Electronic applications accepted.

**Regis College,** Program in Heritage Studies for a Global Society, Weston, MA 02493. Offers heritage studies for a global society (MA). *Program availability:* Part-time, blended/hybrid learning. *Degree requirements:* For master's, capstone. *Entrance requirements:* Additional exam requirements/recommendations for international students: Required—TOEFL; Recommended—IELTS. *Application deadline:* Applications are processed on a rolling basis. Application fee: $65. Electronic applications accepted. *Financial support:* Federal Work-Study and unspecified assistantships available. Financial award applicants required to submit FAFSA. *Unit head:* Kathryn Edney, Director, 781-768-7196.

**Syracuse University,** Maxwell School of Citizenship and Public Affairs, MA/MS Program in Public Diplomacy, Syracuse, NY 13244. Offers MS/MA. *Students:* Average age 26. *Entrance requirements:* Additional exam requirements/recommendations for international students: Required—TOEFL (minimum score 100 iBT). *Application deadline:* For fall admission, 2/1 for domestic students, 2/1 priority date for international students. Application fee: $75. Electronic applications accepted. *Expenses: Tuition:* Full-time $25,974; part-time $1443 per credit hour. *Required fees:* $802; $50 per course. Tuition and fees vary according to course load and program. *Financial support:* Fellowships with full tuition reimbursements, research assistantships, and teaching assistantships available. Financial award application deadline: 1/1. *Faculty research:* Public diplomacy and communications, economic dimensions of global power, comparative foreign policy, development and sustainability, culture in world affairs. *Unit head:* Dr. Robert Bifulco, Associate Dean and Chair, Public Administration and International Affairs, 315-443-3232, E-mail: rbifulco@maxwell.syr.edu. *Application contact:* Martha Coria, Program Contact, 315-443-5749, Fax: 315-443-1834, E-mail: pcgrad@syr.edu.
Website: http://www.maxwell.syr.edu/

**Syracuse University,** S. I. Newhouse School of Public Communications, MS/MA in Public Diplomacy Program, Syracuse, NY 13244. Offers MS/MA. *Students:* Average age 26. *Entrance requirements:* Additional exam requirements/recommendations for international students: Required—TOEFL (minimum score 100 iBT). *Application deadline:* For fall admission, 2/1 priority date for domestic and international students. Application fee: $45. Electronic applications accepted. *Expenses: Tuition:* Full-time $25,974; part-time $1443 per credit hour. *Required fees:* $802; $50 per course. Tuition and fees vary according to course load and program. *Financial support:* Fellowships with full tuition reimbursements, research assistantships with partial tuition reimbursements, and teaching assistantships with partial tuition reimbursements available. Financial award application deadline: 1/15. *Faculty research:* Media law, public diplomacy, public relation theory, international relations. *Unit head:* Dr. Dennis Kinsey, Director, 315-443-3801, E-mail: publicdiplomacy@syr.edu. *Application contact:* Martha Coria, Graduate Records Office, 315-443-4039, Fax: 315-443-1834, E-mail: pcgrad@syr.edu.
Website: http://newhouse.syr.edu/

**Texas A&M University,** Bush School of Government and Public Service, College Station, TX 77840. Offers homeland security (Certificate); international affairs (MIA, Certificate); national security affairs (Certificate); non-profit management (Certificate); public service and administration (MPSA). *Accreditation:* NASPAA. *Faculty:* 68. *Students:* 324 full-time (165 women), 26 part-time (10 women); includes 89 minority (19 Black or African American, non-Hispanic/Latino; 4 Asian, non-Hispanic/Latino; 58 Hispanic/Latino; 1 Native Hawaiian or other Pacific Islander, non-Hispanic/Latino; 7 Two or more races, non-Hispanic/Latino), 44 international. Average age 27. 261 applicants, 96% accepted, 165 enrolled. In 2016, 164 master's awarded. *Degree requirements:* For master's, summer internship. *Entrance requirements:* For master's, GRE (preferred) or GMAT. Additional exam requirements/recommendations for international students: Required—TOEFL (minimum score 550 paper-based; 80 iBT), IELTS (minimum score 6), PTE (minimum score 53). *Application deadline:* For fall admission, 1/15 for domestic and international students. Application fee: $50 ($90 for international students). Electronic applications accepted. *Expenses:* Contact institution. *Financial support:* In 2016–17, 413 students received support, including 16 fellowships with tuition reimbursements available (averaging $18,236 per year), 61 research assistantships with tuition reimbursements available (averaging $5,904 per year), 1 teaching assistantship (averaging $4,025 per year); career-related internships or fieldwork, institutionally sponsored loans, scholarships/grants, traineeships, health care benefits, tuition waivers (full and partial), and unspecified assistantships also available. Support available to part-time students. Financial award application deadline: 3/15; financial award applicants required to submit FAFSA. *Faculty research:* Public policy, Presidential studies, public leadership, economic policy, social policy. *Unit head:* Dr. Mark Welsh, Dean, 979-862-8007, E-mail: mwelsh@tamu.edu. *Application contact:* Kathryn Meyer, Director of Recruitment and Admissions, 979-458-4767, Fax: 979-845-4155, E-mail: bushschooladmissions@tamu.edu.
Website: http://bush.tamu.edu/

**The University of Alabama in Huntsville,** School of Graduate Studies, College of Arts, Humanities, and Social Sciences, Program in Public Affairs, Huntsville, AL 35899. Offers MA. *Program availability:* Part-time, evening/weekend. *Degree requirements:* For master's, comprehensive exam, thesis or alternative, oral and written exams. *Entrance requirements:* For master's, GRE General Test, minimum GPA of 3.0. Additional exam requirements/recommendations for international students: Required—TOEFL (minimum score 500 paper-based; 80 iBT), IELTS (minimum score 6.5). Electronic applications accepted. *Expenses:* Tuition, state resident: full-time $9834; part-time $600 per credit hour. Tuition, nonresident: full-time $21,830; part-time $1325 per credit hour. *Faculty research:* Public policy and the law, middle eastern engagements, globalization, American politics, politics in south and central America.

**University of Arkansas at Little Rock,** Graduate School, Clinton School of Public Service, Little Rock, AR 72204-1099. Offers MPS, Graduate Certificate.

**University of Baltimore,** Graduate School, College of Public Affairs, Baltimore, MD 21201-5779. Offers MPA, MS, DPA, JD/MPA, JD/MS.

**University of California, Berkeley,** Graduate Division, Graduate School of Public Policy, Program in Public Affairs, Berkeley, CA 94720-1500. Offers MPA. *Program availability:* Part-time-only. *Students:* 25 full-time (7 women); includes 5 minority (1 Black or African American, non-Hispanic/Latino; 1 Asian, non-Hispanic/Latino; 3 Hispanic/Latino), 9 international. 98 applicants, 25 enrolled. Application fee: $105 ($125 for international students). *Financial support:* Institutionally sponsored loans and health care benefits available. *Unit head:* Prof. Henry Brady, Dean, 510-642-4670, E-mail: mpa@berkeley.edu. *Application contact:* 510-642-4670, Fax: 510-643-9657, E-mail: mpa@berkeley.edu.
Website: http://gspp.berkeley.edu/programs/masters-of-public-affairs-mpa

**University of Central Florida,** College of Health and Public Affairs, Program in Public Affairs, Orlando, FL 32816. Offers public affairs (PhD); research administration (MRA, Certificate). *Program availability:* Part-time, evening/weekend. *Faculty:* 24 full-time (11 women), 11 part-time/adjunct (6 women). *Students:* 33 full-time (14 women), 56 part-time (44 women); includes 30 minority (14 Black or African American, non-Hispanic/Latino; 1 American Indian or Alaska Native, non-Hispanic/Latino; 4 Asian, non-Hispanic/Latino; 9 Hispanic/Latino; 2 Two or more races, non-Hispanic/Latino), 12 international. Average age 37. 59 applicants, 59% accepted, 27 enrolled. In 2016, 13 master's, 12 doctorates awarded. *Degree requirements:* For doctorate, thesis/dissertation, candidacy and qualifying exams. *Entrance requirements:* For doctorate, GRE General Test or minimum GPA of 3.0 during final 60 hours. Additional exam requirements/recommendations for international students: Required—TOEFL. *Application deadline:* For fall admission, 3/1 for domestic students. Application fee: $30. Electronic applications accepted. *Expenses:* Tuition, state resident: part-time $288.16 per credit hour. Tuition, nonresident: part-time $1071.31 per credit hour. *Financial support:* In 2016–17, 22 students received support, including 15 fellowships with partial tuition reimbursements available (averaging $8,710 per year), 10 research assistantships with partial tuition reimbursements available (averaging $6,512 per year), 9 teaching assistantships with partial tuition reimbursements available (averaging $9,814 per year); career-related internships or fieldwork, Federal Work-Study, institutionally sponsored loans, tuition waivers (partial), and unspecified assistantships also available. Financial award application deadline: 3/1; financial award applicants required to submit FAFSA. *Unit head:* Dr. Robyne Stevenson, Interim Director, 407-823-3459, Fax: 407-823-0822, E-mail: robyne.stevenson@ucf.edu. *Application contact:* Assistant Director, Graduate Admissions, 407-823-2766, Fax: 407-823-6442, E-mail: gradadmissions@ucf.edu.
Website: http://www.ucf.edu/academics/public-affairs-phd/

**University of Colorado Colorado Springs,** School of Public Affairs, Colorado Springs, CO 80918. Offers criminal justice (MCJ); public administration (MPA). *Accreditation:* NASPAA. *Program availability:* Part-time, evening/weekend, 100% online, blended/hybrid learning. *Faculty:* 11 full-time (4 women), 5 part-time/adjunct (3 women). *Students:* 22 full-time (12 women), 142 part-time (79 women); includes 44 minority (6 Black or African American, non-Hispanic/Latino; 1 American Indian or Alaska Native, non-Hispanic/Latino; 4 Asian, non-Hispanic/Latino; 25 Hispanic/Latino; 8 Two or more races, non-Hispanic/Latino). Average age 35. 62 applicants, 94% accepted, 44 enrolled. In 2016, 32 master's awarded. *Degree requirements:* For master's, internship, capstone project, or thesis. *Entrance requirements:* For master's, GRE General Test, GMAT, LSAT, minimum GPA of 3.0. Additional exam requirements/recommendations for international students: Recommended—TOEFL (minimum score 550 paper-based; 80 iBT), IELTS (minimum score 6.5). *Application deadline:* Applications are processed on a rolling basis. Application fee: $60 ($100 for international students). Electronic applications accepted. *Expenses:* Contact institution. *Financial support:* In 2016–17, 36 students received support. Career-related internships or fieldwork, scholarships/grants, and tuition waivers available. Support available to part-time students. Financial award application deadline: 3/1; financial award applicants required to submit FAFSA. *Faculty research:* Antiquated prison environments; public management; intersections of gender, class, race and crime; national security/U.S. foreign policy; leadership, ethics, organizational theory and behavior. *Total annual research expenditures:* $513,691. *Unit head:* Dr. George Reed, Dean, 719-255-4109, E-mail: george.reed@uccs.edu. *Application contact:* Crista Hill, Outreach Student Services Specialist, 719-255-4993, Fax: 719-255-4183, E-mail: chill12@uccs.edu.
Website: http://www.uccs.edu/spa/

**University of Colorado Denver,** School of Public Affairs, Program in Public Affairs and Administration, Denver, CO 80127. Offers public administration (MPA), including domestic violence, emergency management and homeland security, environmental policy, management and law, homeland security and defense, local government, nonprofit management, public administration; public affairs (PhD). *Accreditation:* NASPAA. *Program availability:* Part-time, evening/weekend, online learning. *Students:* 241 full-time (146 women), 135 part-time (86 women); includes 61 minority (15 Black or African American, non-Hispanic/Latino; 1 American Indian or Alaska Native, non-Hispanic/Latino; 10 Asian, non-Hispanic/Latino; 26 Hispanic/Latino; 2 Native Hawaiian or other Pacific Islander, non-Hispanic/Latino; 7 Two or more races, non-Hispanic/Latino), 26 international. Average age 36. 240 applicants, 70% accepted, 91 enrolled. In 2016, 158 master's, 8 doctorates awarded. *Degree requirements:* For master's, thesis or alternative, 36-39 credit hours; for doctorate, comprehensive exam, thesis/dissertation, minimum of 66 semester hours, including at least 30 hours of dissertation. *Entrance requirements:* For master's, GRE, GMAT or LSAT, resume, essay, transcripts, recommendations; for doctorate, GRE, resume, essay, transcripts, recommendations. Additional exam requirements/recommendations for international students: Required—TOEFL (minimum score 550 paper-based; 80 iBT); Recommended—IELTS (minimum score 6.5). *Application deadline:* For fall admission, 2/1 priority date for domestic students, 1/15 priority date for international students; for spring admission, 10/15 priority date for domestic students, 10/1 priority date for international students. Application fee: $50 ($75 for international students). Electronic applications accepted. *Expenses:* Contact institution. *Financial support:* In 2016–17, 92 students received support. Fellowships with partial tuition reimbursements available, research assistantships with partial tuition reimbursements available, teaching assistantships with partial tuition reimbursements available, Federal Work-Study, institutionally sponsored loans, scholarships/grants, traineeships, and unspecified assistantships available. Financial award application deadline: 4/1; financial award applicants required to submit FAFSA. *Faculty research:* Housing, education and the social and economic issues of vulnerable populations; nonprofit governance and management; education finance, effectiveness and reform; P-20 education initiatives; municipal government accountability. *Unit head:* Dr. Christine Martell, Director of MPA Program, 303-315-2716, Fax: 303-315-2229, E-mail: christine.martell@ucdenver.edu. *Application contact:* Dawn Savage, Student Services Coordinator, 303-315-2743, Fax: 303-315-2229, E-mail: dawn.savage@ucdenver.edu.

## Public Affairs

Website: http://www.ucdenver.edu/academics/colleges/SPA/Academics/programs/PublicAffairsAdmin/Pages/index.aspx

**University of Florida,** Graduate School, College of Liberal Arts and Sciences, Department of Political Science, Gainesville, FL 32611. Offers educational policy (PhD); international development policy and administration (MA, Certificate); international relations (MA, MAT); political campaigning (MA, Certificate); political science (MA, PhD); public affairs (MA, Certificate); tropical conservation and development (MA, PhD); JD/MA. Terminal master's awarded for partial completion of doctoral program. *Degree requirements:* For master's, variable foreign language requirement, comprehensive exam (for some programs), thesis or alternative, internship (for some programs); for doctorate, variable foreign language requirement, comprehensive exam, thesis/dissertation. *Entrance requirements:* For master's and doctorate, GRE General Test (minimum score: 308 combined verbal/quantitative), minimum GPA of 3.5. Additional exam requirements/recommendations for international students: Required—TOEFL (minimum score 550 paper-based; 80 iBT), IELTS (minimum score 6). Electronic applications accepted. *Faculty research:* American electoral politics and political institutions, comparative democratization and development, theories of international relation, and political theory.

**University of Louisville,** Graduate School, College of Arts and Sciences, Department of Urban and Public Affairs, Louisville, KY 40208. Offers public administration (MPA), including human resources management, non-profit management, public policy and administration; urban and public affairs (PhD), including urban planning and development, urban policy and administration; urban planning (MUP), including administration of planning organizations, housing and community development, land use and environmental planning, spatial analysis. *Program availability:* Part-time, evening/weekend. *Faculty:* 12 full-time (5 women), 3 part-time/adjunct (1 woman). *Students:* 59 full-time (23 women), 32 part-time (19 women); includes 19 minority (13 Black or African American, non-Hispanic/Latino; 1 Asian, non-Hispanic/Latino; 2 Hispanic/Latino; 3 Two or more races, non-Hispanic/Latino), 5 international. Average age 30. 75 applicants, 65% accepted, 25 enrolled. In 2016, 22 master's, 2 doctorates awarded. Terminal master's awarded for partial completion of doctoral program. *Degree requirements:* For master's, internship; for doctorate, comprehensive exam, thesis/dissertation. *Entrance requirements:* For master's, GRE General Test, minimum GPA of 3.0; for doctorate, GRE General Test, master's degree in appropriate field. Additional exam requirements/recommendations for international students: Required—TOEFL (minimum score 550 paper-based; 79 iBT). *Application deadline:* Applications are processed on a rolling basis. Application fee: $60. *Expenses:* Contact institution. *Financial support:* Fellowships, research assistantships, tuition waivers (full and partial), and unspecified assistantships available. Financial award application deadline: 2/1. *Faculty research:* Urban theory, sustainability, public administration, urban planning, urban management. *Total annual research expenditures:* $240,308. *Unit head:* Dr. David Simpson, Chair, 502-852-8019, Fax: 502-852-4558, E-mail: dave.simpson@louisville.edu. *Application contact:* Libby Leggett, Director, Graduate Admissions, 502-852-3101, Fax: 502-852-4558, E-mail: gradadm@louisville.edu.
Website: http://supa.louisville.edu

**University of Minnesota, Twin Cities Campus,** Graduate School, Hubert H. Humphrey School of Public Affairs, PhD Program in Public Affairs, Minneapolis, MN 55455. Offers management and governance (PhD); public policy (PhD); science, technology, and environmental policy (PhD); urban planning (PhD). *Program availability:* Part-time. *Degree requirements:* For doctorate, comprehensive exam, thesis/dissertation. *Entrance requirements:* For doctorate, GRE General Test. Additional exam requirements/recommendations for international students: Required—TOEFL (minimum score 650 paper-based; 100 iBT), IELTS (minimum score 7). Electronic applications accepted. *Expenses:* Contact institution. *Faculty research:* Public policy, urban/regional planning, public/nonprofit management and governance, science/technology/environmental policy.

**University of Minnesota, Twin Cities Campus,** Graduate School, Hubert H. Humphrey School of Public Affairs, Program in Public Affairs, Minneapolis, MN 55455. Offers MPA. *Program availability:* Part-time-only, evening/weekend. *Entrance requirements:* For master's, 10 years of work experience, minimum undergraduate GPA of 3.0. Additional exam requirements/recommendations for international students: Required—TOEFL (minimum score 600 paper-based; 100 iBT), IELTS (minimum score 7). Electronic applications accepted. *Expenses:* Contact institution. *Faculty research:* Public and non-profit leadership and management, social policy, urban and regional planning, economic and community development, foreign policy and international affairs.

**University of Missouri,** Office of Research and Graduate Studies, Harry S Truman School of Public Affairs, Columbia, MO 65211. Offers grantsmanship (Graduate Certificate); nonprofit management (Graduate Certificate); organizational change (Graduate Certificate); public affairs (MPA, PhD); public management (Graduate Certificate); science and public policy (Graduate Certificate). *Accreditation:* NASPAA. *Faculty:* 10 full-time (7 women), 2 part-time/adjunct (0 women). *Students:* 76 full-time (37 women), 168 part-time (88 women); includes 36 minority (21 Black or African American, non-Hispanic/Latino; 1 American Indian or Alaska Native, non-Hispanic/Latino; 2 Asian, non-Hispanic/Latino; 6 Hispanic/Latino; 6 Two or more races, non-Hispanic/Latino), 24 international. Average age 34. *Entrance requirements:* For master's, GRE General Test, minimum GPA of 3.0. Additional exam requirements/recommendations for international students: Required—TOEFL (minimum score 550 paper-based; 80 iBT), IELTS (minimum score 6.5). *Application deadline:* For fall admission, 2/1 priority date for domestic and international students. Applications are processed on a rolling basis. Application fee: $75 ($90 for international students). Electronic applications accepted. *Expenses:* Tuition, state resident: full-time $6347; part-time $352.60 per credit hour. Tuition, nonresident: full-time $17,379; part-time $965.50 per credit hour. *Required fees:* $1035. Tuition and fees vary according to course load, campus/location and program. *Financial support:* Fellowships, research assistantships, teaching assistantships, institutionally sponsored loans, scholarships/grants, traineeships, health care benefits, and unspecified assistantships available. Support available to part-time students.
Website: http://truman.missouri.edu/

**University of Missouri–Kansas City,** Henry W. Bloch School of Management, Kansas City, MO 64110-2499. Offers accounting (MS); finance (MS); public affairs (MPA, PhD); JD/MBA; LL M/MPA. PhD (interdisciplinary) offered through the School of Graduate Studies. *Accreditation:* AACSB; NASPAA. *Program availability:* Part-time, evening/weekend. *Faculty:* 60 full-time (19 women), 40 part-time/adjunct (11 women). *Students:* 204 full-time (97 women), 308 part-time (151 women); includes 70 minority (29 Black or African American, non-Hispanic/Latino; 1 American Indian or Alaska Native, non-Hispanic/Latino; 17 Asian, non-Hispanic/Latino; 18 Hispanic/Latino; 5 Two or more races, non-Hispanic/Latino), 82 international. Average age 30. 389 applicants, 49% accepted, 190 enrolled. In 2016, 248 master's, 2 doctorates awarded. Terminal master's awarded for partial completion of doctoral program. *Entrance requirements:* For master's, GMAT, GRE, 2 essays, 2 references, support of employer; for doctorate, GRE, minimum GPA of 3.0. Additional exam requirements/recommendations for international students: Required—TOEFL (minimum score 550 paper-based; 80 iBT). *Application deadline:* For fall admission, 5/1 priority date for domestic and international students; for

spring admission, 10/1 priority date for domestic and international students. Applications are processed on a rolling basis. Application fee: $45 ($50 for international students). Electronic applications accepted. *Financial support:* In 2016–17, 31 research assistantships with partial tuition reimbursements (averaging $10,597 per year), 10 teaching assistantships with partial tuition reimbursements (averaging $14,592 per year) were awarded; career-related internships or fieldwork, Federal Work-Study, institutionally sponsored loans, scholarships/grants, tuition waivers (full and partial), and unspecified assistantships also available. Support available to part-time students. Financial award application deadline: 3/1; financial award applicants required to submit FAFSA. *Faculty research:* Entrepreneurship, finance, non-profit, risk management. *Unit head:* Dr. David Donnelly, Dean, 816-235-1333, Fax: 816-235-2206, E-mail: donnellyd@umkc.edu. *Application contact:* 816-235-1111, E-mail: admit@umkc.edu.
Website: http://www.bloch.umkc.edu

**University of Nevada, Las Vegas,** Graduate College, Greenspun College of Urban Affairs, School of Public Policy and Leadership, Las Vegas, NV 89154-4030. Offers crisis and emergency management (MS); non-profit management (Certificate); public administration (MPA); public affairs (PhD); public management (Certificate); urban leadership (MA). *Program availability:* Part-time. *Faculty:* 13 full-time (7 women), 10 part-time/adjunct (2 women). *Students:* 76 full-time (43 women), 110 part-time (70 women); includes 81 minority (18 Black or African American, non-Hispanic/Latino; 1 American Indian or Alaska Native, non-Hispanic/Latino; 6 Asian, non-Hispanic/Latino; 38 Hispanic/Latino; 4 Native Hawaiian or other Pacific Islander, non-Hispanic/Latino; 14 Two or more races, non-Hispanic/Latino), 7 international. Average age 36. 70 applicants, 86% accepted, 43 enrolled. In 2016, 70 master's, 9 doctorates, 21 other advanced degrees awarded. *Degree requirements:* For master's, comprehensive exam (for some programs), thesis (for some programs), oral exam; for doctorate, comprehensive exam, thesis/dissertation; for Certificate, portfolio. *Entrance requirements:* For master's, GRE General Test or GMAT, bachelor's degree with minimum GPA 2.75; statement of purpose; 3 letters of recommendation; for doctorate, GRE General Test, master's degree with minimum GPA of 3.5; 3 letters of recommendation; statement of purpose; writing sample; personal interview; for Certificate, bachelor's degree; 2 letters of recommendation; writing sample. Additional exam requirements/recommendations for international students: Required—TOEFL (minimum score 550 paper-based; 80 iBT), IELTS (minimum score 7). *Application deadline:* For fall admission, 6/1 for domestic students, 5/1 for international students; for spring admission, 11/1 for domestic students, 10/1 for international students; for summer admission, 3/1 for domestic students. Application fee: $60 ($95 for international students). Electronic applications accepted. *Expenses:* $269.25 per credit, $792 per 3-credit course; $9,634 per year resident; $23,274 per year non-resident; $7,094 fees non-resident (7 credits or more); $1,307 annual health insurance fee. *Financial support:* In 2016–17, 7 research assistantships with partial tuition reimbursements (averaging $14,200 per year), 14 teaching assistantships with partial tuition reimbursements (averaging $16,411 per year) were awarded; institutionally sponsored loans, scholarships/grants, health care benefits, and unspecified assistantships also available. Financial award application deadline: 3/15. *Faculty research:* Community and organizational resilience; environmental decision-making and management; budgeting and human resource/workforce management; urban design, sustainability, and governance; public and non-profit management, public policy, governance, economic development, and urban planning. *Total annual research expenditures:* $244,881. *Unit head:* Dr. Christopher Stream, Director, 702-895-5120, Fax: 702-895-4436, E-mail: chris.stream@unlv.edu. *Application contact:* Dr. Jessica Word, Graduate Coordinator, 702-895-2684, Fax: 702-895-4436, E-mail: jessica.word@unlv.edu.
Website: https://www.unlv.edu/publicpolicy

**The University of North Carolina at Greensboro,** Graduate School, College of Arts and Sciences, Department of Political Science, Greensboro, NC 27412-5001. Offers nonprofit management (Certificate); public affairs (MPA); urban and economic development (Certificate). *Accreditation:* NASPAA. *Degree requirements:* For master's, comprehensive exam. *Entrance requirements:* For master's, GRE General Test. Additional exam requirements/recommendations for international students: Required—TOEFL. Electronic applications accepted. *Faculty research:* U.S. Constitution, Canadian parliament, public management, ethical challenge of public service.

**University of San Francisco,** College of Arts and Sciences, Public Affairs Program, San Francisco, CA 94117-1080. Offers MPA. *Accreditation:* NASPAA. *Program availability:* Part-time. *Faculty:* 4 full-time (2 women), 4 part-time/adjunct (0 women). *Students:* 24 full-time (18 women), 2 part-time (1 woman); includes 15 minority (4 Black or African American, non-Hispanic/Latino; 9 Hispanic/Latino; 2 Two or more races, non-Hispanic/Latino), 2 international. Average age 27. 32 applicants, 69% accepted, 9 enrolled. In 2016, 10 master's awarded. *Degree requirements:* For master's, internship, capstone project. *Entrance requirements:* Additional exam requirements/recommendations for international students: Required—TOEFL, IELTS, PTE. *Application deadline:* For fall admission, 3/1 for domestic and international students. Electronic applications accepted. *Expenses:* Tuition: Full-time $23,310; part-time $1295 per credit. Tuition and fees vary according to course load, degree level, campus/location and program. *Financial support:* In 2016–17, 14 students received support. Scholarships/grants available. Financial award applicants required to submit FAFSA. *Unit head:* Kresten Froistad-Martin, Program Manager, 415-422-5683, E-mail: upa@usfca.edu. *Application contact:* Mark Landerghini, Information Contact, 415-422-5101, Fax: 415-422-2217, E-mail: asgraduate@usfca.edu.
Website: https://www.usfca.edu/arts-sciences/graduate-programs/urban-public-affairs

**University of Saskatchewan,** College of Graduate Studies and Research, School of Public Policy, Saskatoon, SK S7N 5A2, Canada. Offers MIT, MPA, MPP, PhD.

**University of South Florida,** Innovative Education, Tampa, FL 33620-9951. Offers adult, career and higher education (Graduate Certificate), including college teaching, leadership in developing human resources, leadership in higher education; Africana studies (Graduate Certificate), including diasporas and health disparities, genocide and human rights; aging studies (Graduate Certificate), including gerontology; art research (Graduate Certificate), including museum studies; business foundations (Graduate Certificate); chemical and biomedical engineering (Graduate Certificate), including materials science and engineering, water, health and sustainability; child and family studies (Graduate Certificate), including positive behavior support; civil and industrial engineering (Graduate Certificate), including transportation systems analysis; community and family health (Graduate Certificate), including maternal and child health, social marketing and public health, violence and injury: prevention and intervention, women's health; criminology (Graduate Certificate), including criminal justice administration; educational measurement and research (Graduate Certificate), including evaluation; English (Graduate Certificate), including comparative literary studies, creative writing, professional and technical communication; entrepreneurship (Graduate Certificate), including safety management; epidemiology and biostatistics (Graduate Certificate), including applied biostatistics, biostatistics, concepts and tools of epidemiology, epidemiology, epidemiology of infectious diseases; geography, environment and planning (Graduate Certificate), including community development, environmental policy and management, geographical information systems; geology (Graduate Certificate), including

hydrogeology; global health (Graduate Certificate), including disaster management, global health and Latin American and Caribbean studies, global health practice, humanitarian assistance, infection control; government and international affairs (Graduate Certificate), including Cuban studies, globalization studies; health policy and management (Graduate Certificate), including health management and leadership, public health policy and programs; hearing specialist: early intervention (Graduate Certificate); industrial and management systems engineering (Graduate Certificate), including systems engineering, technology management; information studies (Graduate Certificate), including school library media specialist; information systems/decision sciences (Graduate Certificate), including analytics and business intelligence; instructional technology (Graduate Certificate), including distance education, Florida digital/virtual educator, instructional design, multimedia design, Web design; internal medicine, bioethics and medical humanities (Graduate Certificate), including biomedical ethics; Latin American and Caribbean studies (Graduate Certificate); mass communications (Graduate Certificate), including multimedia journalism; mathematics and statistics (Graduate Certificate), including mathematics; medicine (Graduate Certificate), including aging and neuroscience, bioinformatics, biotechnology, brain fitness and memory management, clinical investigation, health informatics, health sciences, integrative weight management, intellectual property, medicine and gender, metabolic and nutritional medicine, metabolic cardiology, pharmacy sciences; national and competitive intelligence (Graduate Certificate); psychological and social foundations (Graduate Certificate), including career counseling, college teaching, diversity in education, mental health counseling, school counseling; public affairs (Graduate Certificate), including nonprofit management, public management, research administration; public health (Graduate Certificate), including environmental health, health equity, public health generalist, translational research in adolescent behavioral health; public health practices (Graduate Certificate), including planning for healthy communities; rehabilitation and mental health counseling (Graduate Certificate), including integrative mental health care, marriage and family therapy, rehabilitation technology; secondary education (Graduate Certificate), including ESOL, foreign language education: culture and content, foreign language education: professional; social work (Graduate Certificate), including geriatric social work/clinical gerontology; special education (Graduate Certificate), including autism spectrum disorder, disabilities education: severe/profound; world languages (Graduate Certificate), including teaching English as a second language (TESL) or foreign language. *Expenses:* Tuition, state resident: full-time $7766; part-time $431.43 per credit hour. Tuition, nonresident: full-time $15,789; part-time $877.17 per credit hour. *Required fees:* $37 per term. *Unit head:* Kathy Barnes, Interdisciplinary Programs Coordinator, 813-974-8031, Fax: 813-974-7061, E-mail: barnesk@usf.edu. *Application contact:* Karen Tylinski, Metro Initiatives, 813-974-9943, Fax: 813-974-7061, E-mail: ktylinsk@usf.edu.
Website: http://www.usf.edu/innovative-education/

**The University of Texas at Austin,** Graduate School, Lyndon B. Johnson School of Public Affairs, Austin, TX 78712-1111. Offers global policy studies (MGPS); public affairs (MP Aff); public leadership (EMPL); public policy (PhD); JD/MP Aff; MBA/MP Aff; MP Aff/MA; MP Aff/MSE. *Accreditation:* NASPAA (one or more programs are accredited). *Program availability:* Part-time. *Degree requirements:* For master's, thesis, summer internship; for doctorate, thesis/dissertation. *Entrance requirements:* For master's, GRE General Test (for MP Aff and MGPS), minimum GPA of 3.0 in upper-division classes, seven years of experience in the public sector, and interview (for EMPL); for doctorate, GRE General Test, master's degree in policy-related field. Additional exam requirements/recommendations for international students: Required—TOEFL. Electronic applications accepted. *Faculty research:* Human resource development, health and social policy, philanthropy and community service, ethical leadership, urban and international policy, science and technology policy.

**The University of Texas Rio Grande Valley,** College of Liberal Arts, Department of Public Affairs and Security Studies, Edinburg, TX 78539. Offers global security studies and leadership (MPA); public administration (MPA); public policy and management (MPA). *Program availability:* Part-time, evening/weekend. *Degree requirements:* For master's, comprehensive exam (for some programs), thesis optional. *Entrance requirements:* For master's, minimum undergraduate GPA of 3.0, official transcripts, personal statement, three recommendations. Additional exam requirements/recommendations for international students: Required—TOEFL (minimum score 550 paper-based; 79 iBT). Electronic applications accepted. Tuition and fees vary according to course load and program. *Faculty research:* Immigration policy reform, agriculture food policy, social service delivery systems, community development, social welfare policy reform, urban/city management.

**University of Washington,** Graduate School, Evans School of Public Policy and Governance, Seattle, WA 98195. Offers public administration (MPA); public policy and management (PhD); JD/MPA; MPA/MAIS; MPA/MPH; MPA/MS; MPA/MUP. *Accreditation:* NASPAA. *Program availability:* Part-time, evening/weekend. *Degree requirements:* For master's, thesis, internship or cooperative experience. *Entrance requirements:* For master's and doctorate, GRE General Test, minimum GPA of 3.0. Additional exam requirements/recommendations for international students: Required—TOEFL (minimum score 580 paper-based; 92 iBT). Electronic applications accepted. *Faculty research:* Environmental policy, education and social policy, nonprofit management, international affairs, urban and regional development.

**University of Waterloo,** Graduate Studies, Faculty of Arts, Department of Anthropology, Waterloo, ON N2L 3G1, Canada. Offers anthropology (MA); public issues (MA). *Entrance requirements:* Additional exam requirements/recommendations for international students: Required—TOEFL, IELTS, PTE. Electronic applications accepted. *Faculty research:* Applied socio-cultural anthropology and archaeology.

**University of Wisconsin–Madison,** Graduate School, College of Letters and Science, Robert M. La Follette School of Public Affairs, Public Policy and Administration Program, Madison, WI 53706-1380. Offers MIPA, MPA. *Program availability:* Part-time. Electronic applications accepted.

**Virginia Commonwealth University,** Graduate School, College of Humanities and Sciences, L. Douglas Wilder School of Government and Public Affairs, Richmond, VA 23284-9005. Offers MA, MPA, MS, MURP, PhD, Certificate, Graduate Certificate, Postbaccalaureate Certificate. *Unit head:* Dr. Niraj Verma, Director, L. Douglas Wilder School of Government and Public Affairs, 804-828-2292. *Application contact:* Dr. Sarah

J. Brubaker, Associate Director, 804-827-2400, E-mail: sbrubaker@vcu.edu. Website: http://www.wilder.vcu.edu/

**Virginia Polytechnic Institute and State University,** Graduate School, College of Architecture and Urban Studies, Blacksburg, VA 24061. Offers architecture (MS Arch); architecture and design research (PhD); building/construction science and management (MS); creative technologies (MFA); environmental design and planning (PhD); landscape architecture (MLA); planning, governance, and globalization (PhD); public administration (MPA); public administration/public affairs (PhD, Certificate); public and international affairs (MPIA); urban and regional planning (MURP). *Accreditation:* ASLA (one or more programs are accredited). *Faculty:* 136 full-time (53 women). *Students:* 371 full-time (185 women), 210 part-time (104 women); includes 118 minority (49 Black or African American, non-Hispanic/Latino; 1 American Indian or Alaska Native, non-Hispanic/Latino; 30 Asian, non-Hispanic/Latino; 32 Hispanic/Latino; 6 Two or more races, non-Hispanic/Latino), 137 international. Average age 31. 566 applicants, 55% accepted, 160 enrolled. In 2016, 137 master's, 24 doctorates awarded. *Degree requirements:* For master's, comprehensive exam (for some programs), thesis (for some programs); for doctorate, comprehensive exam (for some programs), thesis/dissertation (for some programs). *Entrance requirements:* For master's and doctorate, GRE/GMAT. Additional exam requirements/recommendations for international students: Required—TOEFL (minimum score 80 iBT). *Application deadline:* For fall admission, 8/1 for domestic students, 4/1 for international students; for spring admission, 1/1 for domestic students, 9/1 for international students. Applications are processed on a rolling basis. Application fee: $75. Electronic applications accepted. *Expenses:* Tuition, state resident: full-time $12,467; part-time $692.50 per credit hour. Tuition, nonresident: full-time $25,095; part-time $1394.25 per credit hour. *Required fees:* $2669; $491.50 per semester. Tuition and fees vary according to course load, campus/location and program. *Financial support:* In 2016–17, 11 research assistantships with full tuition reimbursements (averaging $19,474 per year), 45 teaching assistantships with full tuition reimbursements (averaging $16,014 per year) were awarded. Financial award application deadline: 3/1; financial award applicants required to submit FAFSA. *Total annual research expenditures:* $3.6 million. *Unit head:* Dr. A. J. Davis, Dean, 540-231-6416, Fax: 540-231-6332, E-mail: davisa@vt.edu. *Application contact:* Christine Mattsson-Coon, Executive Assistant, 540-231-6416, Fax: 540-231-6332, E-mail: cmattsso@vt.edu.
Website: http://www.caus.vt.edu/

**Washington State University,** College of Arts and Sciences, School of Politics, Philosophy and Public Affairs, Pullman, WA 99164-4880. Offers bioethics (Graduate Certificate); political science (MA, PhD); public affairs (MPA). MPA, MA, and PhD programs also offered at the Vancouver campus; Graduate Certificate offered through Global (online) campus. *Accreditation:* NASPAA. *Program availability:* Online learning. Terminal master's awarded for partial completion of doctoral program. *Degree requirements:* For master's, comprehensive exam (for some programs), thesis, oral exam; for doctorate, comprehensive exam, thesis/dissertation, oral exam, written exam. *Entrance requirements:* For master's, GRE General Test, minimum GPA of 3.0; for doctorate, GRE General Test, minimum GPA of 3.5. Additional exam requirements/recommendations for international students: Required—TOEFL. Electronic applications accepted. *Faculty research:* Political psychology and image theory, grass roots environmental policy, federal juvenile policy.

**West Chester University of Pennsylvania,** College of Business and Public Management, West Chester, PA 19383. Offers MA, MBA, MPA, MS, MSA, MURP, Certificate, DPA. *Program availability:* Part-time, evening/weekend, 100% online, blended/hybrid learning. *Faculty:* 30 full-time (14 women), 8 part-time/adjunct (6 women). *Students:* 133 full-time (72 women), 416 part-time (198 women); includes 140 minority (101 Black or African American, non-Hispanic/Latino; 1 American Indian or Alaska Native, non-Hispanic/Latino; 14 Asian, non-Hispanic/Latino; 19 Hispanic/Latino; 5 Two or more races, non-Hispanic/Latino), 9 international. Average age 32. 397 applicants, 86% accepted, 252 enrolled. In 2016, 125 master's, 18 other advanced degrees awarded. *Degree requirements:* For master's, comprehensive exam (for some programs), thesis (for some programs). *Entrance requirements:* Additional exam requirements/recommendations for international students: Required—TOEFL or IELTS. *Application deadline:* For fall admission, 5/15 for international students; for spring admission, 10/15 for international students. Applications are processed on a rolling basis. Application fee: $50. Electronic applications accepted. *Expenses:* Tuition, state resident: full-time $8694; part-time $483 per credit. Tuition, nonresident: full-time $13,050; part-time $725 per credit. *Required fees:* $2399; $119.05 per credit. Tuition and fees vary according to campus/location and program. *Financial support:* Scholarships/grants and unspecified assistantships available. Financial award application deadline: 2/15; financial award applicants required to submit FAFSA. *Unit head:* Dr. Jeffery L. Osgood, Jr., Interim Dean, 610-436-2930, Fax: 610-436-3170, E-mail: josgood@wcupa.edu. *Application contact:* Office of Graduate Studies and Extended Education, 610-436-2943, Fax: 610-436-2763, E-mail: gradstudy@wcupa.edu.
Website: http://www.wcupa.edu/business-publicManagement/

**Western Carolina University,** Graduate School, College of Arts and Sciences, Department of Political Science and Public Affairs, Cullowhee, NC 28723. Offers MPA. *Accreditation:* NASPAA. *Program availability:* Part-time, evening/weekend. *Degree requirements:* For master's, comprehensive exam. *Entrance requirements:* For master's, GRE General Test, appropriate undergraduate degree, 3 letters of recommendation. Additional exam requirements/recommendations for international students: Required—TOEFL (minimum score 550 paper-based; 79 iBT). *Expenses:* Tuition, state resident: full-time $2174. Tuition, nonresident: full-time $7377. *Required fees:* $1442. Part-time tuition and fees vary according to course load. *Faculty research:* Press-government relations, comparative governments, gender in politics, Latin American political systems, foreign policy, trust in government, zoning.

**Western Michigan University,** Graduate College, College of Arts and Sciences, School of Public Affairs and Administration, Kalamazoo, MI 49008. Offers health care administration (MPA, Graduate Certificate); nonprofit leadership and administration (Graduate Certificate); public administration (PhD). *Accreditation:* NASPAA (one or more programs are accredited). *Degree requirements:* For doctorate, thesis/dissertation.

**York University,** Faculty of Graduate Studies, Glendon Campus, Program in Public and International Affairs, Toronto, ON M3J 1P3, Canada. Offers MA.

# Public Policy

**Adler University,** Programs in Psychology, Chicago, IL 60602. Offers advanced Adlerian psychotherapy (Certificate); art therapy (MA); clinical mental health counseling (MA); clinical neuropsychology (Certificate); clinical psychology (Psy D); community psychology (MA); counseling and organizational psychology (MA); counseling

## Public Policy

psychology (MA); counselor education and supervision (PhD); couple and family therapy (DCFT); criminology (MA); emergency management leadership (MA); forensic psychology (MA); marriage and family counseling (MA); marriage and family therapy (Certificate); military psychology (MA); nonprofit management (MA); organizational psychology (MA); police psychology (MA); public policy and administration (MA); rehabilitation counseling (MA); sport and health psychology (MA); substance abuse counseling (Certificate); Psy D/Certificate; Psy.D/MACAT; Psy D/MACP; Psy D/MAMFC; Psy D/MASAC. *Accreditation:* APA. *Program availability:* Part-time, evening/weekend, online learning. Terminal master's awarded for partial completion of doctoral program. *Degree requirements:* For master's, thesis or alternative, oral exam, practicum; for doctorate, thesis/dissertation, clinical exam, internship, oral exam, practicum, written qualifying exam. *Entrance requirements:* For master's, 12 semester hours in psychology, minimum GPA of 3.0; for doctorate, 18 semester hours in psychology, minimum GPA of 3.25; for Certificate, appropriate master's or doctoral degree. Additional exam requirements/recommendations for international students: Required—TOEFL (minimum score 550 paper-based; 79 iBT). Electronic applications accepted.

**See Display on page 982 and Close-Up on page 1225.**

**Albany State University,** College of Arts and Humanities, Albany, GA 31705-2717. Offers criminal justice (MS); English education (M Ed); public administration (MPA), including community and economic development, criminal justice administration, health administration and policy, human resources management, public management, public policy, water resources management and policy; social work (MSW). *Program availability:* Part-time. *Degree requirements:* For master's, comprehensive exam, professional portfolio (for MPA), internship, capstone report. *Entrance requirements:* For master's, GRE, MAT, minimum GPA of 3.0, official transcript, pre-medical record/certificate of immunization, letters of reference. *Application deadline:* For fall admission, 6/1 for domestic students, 5/1 for international students; for spring admission, 11/1 for domestic students, 10/1 for international students. Applications are processed on a rolling basis. Application fee: $20. Electronic applications accepted. *Financial support:* Application deadline: 4/15; applicants required to submit FAFSA. *Faculty research:* HIV prevention for minority students. *Unit head:* Dr. Rani George, Dean, 229-430-1877, Fax: 229-430-4296. *Application contact:* Jeffrey Pierce, II, Graduate Admissions Counselor, 229-430-4646, Fax: 229-430-4105, E-mail: jeffrey.pierce@asurams.edu.
Website: https://www.asurams.edu/Academics/collegeofarthum/

**American Public University System,** AMU/APU Graduate Programs, Charles Town, WV 25414. Offers accounting (MBA, MS); applied business analytics (MBA, MS); criminal justice (MA), including business administration, emergency and disaster management, general (MA, MS); educational leadership (M Ed); emergency and disaster management (MA); entrepreneurship (MBA); environmental policy and management (MS), including environmental planning, environmental sustainability, fish and wildlife management, general (MA, MS); global environmental management; finance (MBA); general (MBA); government contracting and acquisition (MBA); health care administration (MBA); health information management (MS); history (MA), including American history, ancient and classical history, European history, global history, public history; homeland security (MA), including business administration, counterterrorism studies, criminal justice, cyber, emergency management and public health, intelligence studies, transportation security; homeland security resource allocation (MBA); humanities (MA); information technology (MS), including digital forensics, enterprise software development, information assurance and security, IT project management; information technology management (MBA); intelligence studies (MA), including criminal intelligence, cyber, general (MA, MS), homeland security, intelligence analysis, intelligence collection, intelligence management, intelligence operations, terrorism studies; international relations and conflict resolution (MA), including comparative and security issues, conflict resolution, international and transnational security issues, peacekeeping; legal studies (MA); management (MA), including strategic consulting; marketing (MBA); military history (MA), including American military history, American Revolution, civil war, war since 1945, World War II; military studies (MA), including joint warfare, strategic leadership; national security studies (MA), including cyber, general (MA, MS), homeland security, regional security studies, security and intelligence analysis, terrorism studies; nonprofit management (MBA); political science (MA), including American politics and government, comparative government and development, general (MA, MS), international relations, public policy; psychology (MA); public administration (MPA), including disaster management, environmental policy, health policy, human resources, national security, organizational management, security management; public health (MPH); reverse logistics management (MA); security management (MA); space studies (MS), including aerospace science, general (MA, MS), planetary science; sports and health sciences (MS); sports management (MBA); teaching (M Ed), including autism spectrum disorder, curriculum and instruction for elementary teachers, elementary reading, English language learners, instructional leadership, online learning, special education, STEAM (STEM plus the arts); transportation and logistics management (MA). *Program availability:* Part-time, evening/weekend, online only, 100% online. *Faculty:* 401 full-time (228 women), 1,678 part-time/adjunct (781 women). *Students:* 378 full-time (184 women), 8,455 part-time (3,484 women); includes 2,972 minority (1,552 Black or African American, non-Hispanic/Latino; 52 American Indian or Alaska Native, non-Hispanic/Latino; 211 Asian, non-Hispanic/Latino; 791 Hispanic/Latino; 70 Native Hawaiian or other Pacific Islander, non-Hispanic/Latino; 296 Two or more races, non-Hispanic/Latino), 109 international. Average age 37. In 2016, 3,185 master's awarded. *Degree requirements:* For master's, comprehensive exam or practicum. *Entrance requirements:* For master's, official transcript showing earned bachelor's degree from institution accredited by recognized accrediting body. Additional exam requirements/recommendations for international students: Required—TOEFL (minimum score 550 paper-based), IELTS (minimum score 6.5). *Application deadline:* Applications are processed on a rolling basis. Application fee: $0. Electronic applications accepted. *Expenses:* Tuition: Part-time $350 per credit hour. *Required fees:* $50 per course. *Financial support:* Scholarships/grants available. Financial award applicants required to submit FAFSA. *Unit head:* Dr. Karan Powell, President, 877-468-6268, Fax: 304-724-3780. *Application contact:* Terry Grant, Vice President of Enrollment Management, 877-468-6268, Fax: 304-724-3780, E-mail: info@apus.edu.
Website: http://www.apus.edu

**American University,** School of Public Affairs, Department of Public Administration and Policy, Program in Public Administration and Policy, Washington, DC 20016-8001. Offers MPAP. *Program availability:* Online only, 100% online. *Students:* 1 (woman) full-time, 146 part-time (103 women); includes 19 minority (9 Black or African American, non-Hispanic/Latino; 1 American Indian or Alaska Native, non-Hispanic/Latino; 5 Asian, non-Hispanic/Latino; 1 Native Hawaiian or other Pacific Islander, non-Hispanic/Latino; 3 Two or more races, non-Hispanic/Latino), 1 international. Average age 33. 80 applicants, 93% accepted, 6 enrolled. *Degree requirements:* For master's, comprehensive exam. *Entrance requirements:* For master's, GRE General Test, two letters of recommendation, statement of purpose, resume. Additional exam requirements/recommendations for international students: Required—TOEFL (minimum score 100 iBT), IELTS (minimum score 7), PTE (minimum score 68). *Application deadline:* For fall admission, 2/1 priority date for domestic students, 5/1 for international

students; for spring admission, 11/1 for domestic students. Application fee: $55. *Expenses:* $1,579 per credit tuition; $690 mandatory fees. *Financial support:* Application deadline: 2/1; applicants required to submit FAFSA. *Unit head:* Dr. Alison Jacknowitz, Department Chair, Public Administration and Policy, 202-885-2137, Fax: 202-885-2347, E-mail: jacknowi@american.edu.
Website: http://www.american.edu/spa/dpap/index.cfm

**American University,** School of Public Affairs, Department of Public Administration and Policy, Program in Public Policy, Washington, DC 20016-8070. Offers public policy (MPP); public policy analysis (Certificate); MPP/JD; MPP/LL M. *Accreditation:* NASPAA. *Students:* 47 full-time (24 women), 30 part-time (18 women); includes 44 minority (27 Black or African American, non-Hispanic/Latino; 1 American Indian or Alaska Native, non-Hispanic/Latino; 8 Asian, non-Hispanic/Latino; 6 Hispanic/Latino; 2 Two or more races, non-Hispanic/Latino), 21 international. Average age 27. 252 applicants, 79% accepted, 33 enrolled. In 2016, 43 master's awarded. *Degree requirements:* For master's, comprehensive exam. *Entrance requirements:* For master's, GRE, 2 recommendations, statement of purpose, resume. Additional exam requirements/recommendations for international students: Required—TOEFL. *Application deadline:* For fall admission, 2/1 for domestic students; for spring admission, 11/1 for domestic students. Application fee: $55. *Expenses:* $1,579 per credit tuition; $690 mandatory fees. *Financial support:* Research assistantships, teaching assistantships, institutionally sponsored loans, scholarships/grants, and unspecified assistantships available. Financial award application deadline: 2/1; financial award applicants required to submit FAFSA. *Unit head:* Dr. Alison Jacknowitz, Department Chair, Public Administration and Policy, 202-885-2137, Fax: 202-885-2347, E-mail: jacknowi@american.edu.
Website: http://www.american.edu/spa/dpap/

**American University of Beirut,** Graduate Programs, Faculty of Arts and Sciences, Beirut, Lebanon. Offers anthropology (MA); Arab and Middle Eastern history (PhD); Arabic language and literature (MA, PhD); archaeology (MA); art history and curating (MA); biology (MS); cell and molecular biology (PhD); chemistry (MS); clinical psychology (MA); computational sciences (MS); computer science (MS); economics (MA); education (MA); English language (MA); English literature (MA); environmental policy planning (MS); financial economics (MAFE); geology (MS); history (MA); Islamic studies (MA); mathematics (MS); media studies (MA); Middle Eastern studies (MA); physics (MS); political studies (MA); psychology (MA); public administration (MA); public policy and international affairs (MA); sociology (MA); statistics (MA, MS); theoretical physics (PhD); transnational American studies (MA). *Program availability:* Part-time. *Faculty:* 133 full-time (42 women), 6 part-time/adjunct (2 women). *Students:* 240 full-time (172 women), 227 part-time (166 women). Average age 27. 286 applicants, 67% accepted, 108 enrolled. In 2016, 60 master's, 3 doctorates awarded. Terminal master's awarded for partial completion of doctoral program. *Degree requirements:* For master's, one foreign language, comprehensive exam, thesis (for some programs); for doctorate, one foreign language, comprehensive exam, thesis/dissertation. *Entrance requirements:* For master's, GRE (for some MA, MS programs), letters of recommendation; for doctorate, GRE, letters of recommendation. Additional exam requirements/recommendations for international students: Required—TOEFL (minimum score 600 paper-based; 97 iBT), IELTS (minimum score 7). *Application deadline:* For fall admission, 4/3 for domestic students; for winter admission, 11/3 for domestic students. Application fee: $50. Electronic applications accepted. *Expenses:* Contact institution. *Financial support:* In 2016–17, 4 fellowships (averaging $11,200 per year), 18 research assistantships (averaging $5,400 per year) were awarded; teaching assistantships, career-related internships or fieldwork, Federal Work-Study, institutionally sponsored loans, scholarships/grants, traineeships, health care benefits, tuition waivers (full), and unspecified assistantships also available. Support available to part-time students. *Faculty research:* Development economics, spatial econometrics, health economics, labor economics, energy economics, hydrogeology, geophysics, petrophysics, structural geology, mineralogy, petrology, geochemistry, multilingualism, comparative/world literature, translation studies, book histories/ cultures, biocatalysis, molecular recognition, photocatalysis, photophysical and biophysical chemistry, probe chemistry, machine learning, data science. *Unit head:* Dr. Nadia Maria El Cheikh, Dean, Faculty of Arts and Sciences, 961-1374374 Ext. 3800, Fax: 961-1744461, E-mail: nmcheikh@aub.edu.lb. *Application contact:* Dr. Salim Kanaan, Director, Admissions Office, 961-1350000 Ext. 2590, Fax: 961-1750775, E-mail: sk00@aub.edu.lb.
Website: http://www.aub.edu.lb/fas/

**The American University of Paris,** Graduate Programs, Paris, France. Offers cross-cultural and sustainable business management (MA); cultural translation (MA); global communications (MA); global communications and civil society (MA); international affairs (MA); international affairs, conflict resolution and civil society development (MA); Middle East and Islamic studies (MA); Middle East and Islamic studies and international affairs (MA); public policy and international affairs (MA); public policy and international law (MA). *Degree requirements:* For master's, thesis (for some programs). *Entrance requirements:* For master's, minimum undergraduate GPA of 3.0. Additional exam requirements/recommendations for international students: Recommended—TOEFL, IELTS. Electronic applications accepted.

**Arizona State University at the Tempe campus,** College of Public Programs, School of Public Affairs, Phoenix, AZ 85004-0687. Offers emergency management and homeland security (MA); program evaluation (MS); public administration (MPA, PhD), including nonprofit administration (MPA), urban management (MPA); public policy (MPP); MPA/MSW. *Accreditation:* NASPAA (one or more programs are accredited). *Program availability:* Part-time, evening/weekend. Terminal master's awarded for partial completion of doctoral program. *Degree requirements:* For master's, thesis or alternative, policy analysis or capstone project; interactive Program of Study (iPOS) submitted before completing 50 percent of required credit hours; for doctorate, comprehensive exam, thesis/dissertation, interactive Program of Study (iPOS) submitted before completing 50 percent of required credit hours. *Entrance requirements:* For master's, GRE, minimum GPA of 3.0 or equivalent in last 2 years of work leading to bachelor's degree; for doctorate, GRE, minimum GPA of 3.0 or equivalent in last 2 years of work leading to bachelor's degree, 3 letters of recommendation, resume, statement of goals, samples of research reports. Additional exam requirements/recommendations for international students: Required—TOEFL (minimum score 600 paper-based; 100 iBT), IELTS (minimum score 6.5). Electronic applications accepted. *Expenses:* Contact institution.

**Arizona State University at the Tempe campus,** Sandra Day O'Connor College of Law, Phoenix, AZ 85004-4467. Offers biotechnology and genomics (LL M); law (JD); legal studies (MLS); patent practice (MLS); sports law and business (MSLB); tribal policy, law and government (LL M); JD/MBA; JD/MD; JD/MSW; JD/PhD. *Accreditation:* ABA. *Program availability:* 100% online. *Faculty:* 71 full-time (31 women), 67 part-time/adjunct (16 women). *Students:* 718 full-time (300 women); includes 195 minority (17 Black or African American, non-Hispanic/Latino; 14 American Indian or Alaska Native, non-Hispanic/Latino; 27 Asian, non-Hispanic/Latino; 98 Hispanic/Latino; 3 Native Hawaiian or other Pacific Islander, non-Hispanic/Latino; 36 Two or more races, non-Hispanic/Latino), 13 international. Average age 28. 1,860 applicants, 42% accepted, 228 enrolled. In 2016, 52 master's, 190 doctorates awarded. *Entrance requirements:* For master's, bachelor's degree and JD (for LL M); for doctorate, LSAT, bachelor's degree.

Additional exam requirements/recommendations for international students: Required—TOEFL (minimum score 550 paper-based; 80 iBT). *Application deadline:* For fall admission, 3/1 priority date for domestic and international students. Applications are processed on a rolling basis. Application fee: $65. Electronic applications accepted. *Expenses:* Contact institution. *Financial support:* In 2016–17, 432 students received support. Institutionally sponsored loans and scholarships/grants available. Financial award application deadline: 3/15; financial award applicants required to submit FAFSA. *Faculty research:* Emerging technologies and the law, Indian law, international law, intellectual property, health law, sports law and business. *Total annual research expenditures:* $1.9 million. *Unit head:* Douglas Sylvester, Dean/Professor, 480-965-6188, Fax: 480-965-6521, E-mail: douglas.sylvester@asu.edu. *Application contact:* Chitra Damania, Director of Operations, 480-965-1474, Fax: 480-727-7930, E-mail: law.admissions@asu.edu.
Website: http://www.law.asu.edu/

**Arizona State University at the Tempe campus,** School of Letters and Sciences, Program in Applied Ethics, Tempe, AZ 85287-4503. Offers biomedical and health ethics (MA); ethics and emerging technologies (MA); public administration, policy and ethics (MA); science, technology and ethics (MA). *Program availability:* Part-time, evening/weekend. *Degree requirements:* For master's, thesis or alternative, applied project, interactive Program of Study (iPOS) submitted before completing 50 percent of required credit hours. *Entrance requirements:* For master's, GRE (for ethics and emerging technologies concentration), minimum GPA of 3.0 or equivalent in last 2 years of work leading to bachelor's degree, 2 letters of recommendation, resume, personal statement of interest and qualifications. Additional exam requirements/recommendations for international students: Required—TOEFL (minimum score 550 paper-based; 80 iBT). Electronic applications accepted.

**Auburn University at Montgomery,** College of Public Policy and Justice, Department of Political Science and Public Administration, Montgomery, AL 36124-4023. Offers international relations (MIR); nonprofit management and leadership (Certificate); political science (MPS); public administration (MPA); public administration and public policy (PhD); public health care administration and policy (Certificate). PhD offered jointly with Auburn University. *Accreditation:* NASPAA (one or more programs are accredited). *Program availability:* Part-time, evening/weekend. *Degree requirements:* For master's, comprehensive exam; for doctorate, thesis/dissertation. *Entrance requirements:* For master's, GRE General Test or MAT; for doctorate, GRE General Test. Electronic applications accepted.

**Aurora University,** Dunham School of Business and Public Policy, Aurora, IL 60506-4892. Offers accountancy (MS); business (MBA); digital marketing and analytics (MS). *Program availability:* Part-time, evening/weekend, 100% online. *Faculty:* 8 full-time (1 woman), 19 part-time/adjunct (9 women). *Students:* 67 full-time (42 women), 186 part-time (98 women); includes 76 minority (32 Black or African American, non-Hispanic/Latino; 2 Asian, non-Hispanic/Latino; 35 Hispanic/Latino; 7 Two or more races, non-Hispanic/Latino), 5 international. Average age 33. 123 applicants, 99% accepted, 21 enrolled. In 2016, 99 master's awarded. *Entrance requirements:* For master's, minimum GPA of 2.75, 2 years of work experience. Additional exam requirements/recommendations for international students: Required—TOEFL (minimum score 550 paper-based; 79 iBT). *Application deadline:* For fall admission, 6/1 for international students; for spring admission, 10/1 for international students. Applications are processed on a rolling basis. Application fee: $0. Electronic applications accepted. *Expenses:* Contact institution. *Financial support:* In 2016–17, 58 students received support. Federal Work-Study, scholarships/grants, and unspecified assistantships available. Support available to part-time students. Financial award applicants required to submit FAFSA. *Unit head:* Dr. Toby Arquette, Executive Director of School of Business and Policy, 630-844-5614, E-mail: tarquett@aurora.edu. *Application contact:* Ed Miranda, Senior Recruiter for Adult and Graduate Programs, 630-947-8923, E-mail: emiranda@aurora.edu.

**Baruch College of the City University of New York,** Austin W. Marxe School of Public and International Affairs, Program in Public Administration, New York, NY 10010-5585. Offers general public administration (MPA); health care policy (MPA); nonprofit administration (MPA); policy analysis and evaluation (MPA); public management (MPA); urban development and sustainability (MPA); MS/MPA. *Accreditation:* NASPAA. *Program availability:* Part-time, evening/weekend. *Degree requirements:* For master's, thesis, capstone. *Entrance requirements:* For master's, GRE General Test. Additional exam requirements/recommendations for international students: Required—TOEFL. Electronic applications accepted. *Expenses:* Contact institution. *Faculty research:* Urbanization, population and poverty in the developing world, housing and community development, labor unions and housing, government-nongovernment relations, immigration policy, social network analysis, cross-sectoral governance, comparative healthcare systems, program evaluation, social welfare policy, health outcomes, educational policy and leadership, transnationalism, infant health, welfare reform, racial/ethnic disparities in health, urban politics, homelessness, race and ethnic relations.

**See Display on page 931 and Close-Up on page 977.**

**Baylor University,** Graduate School, College of Arts and Sciences, Department of Political Science, Waco, TX 76798. Offers international studies (MA); political science (MA, PhD); public policy and administration (MPPA); JD/MPPA. *Faculty:* 18 full-time (3 women), 1 part-time/adjunct (0 women). *Students:* 29 full-time (11 women), 2 part-time (both women); includes 3 minority (all Hispanic/Latino), 2 international. Average age 26. 27 applicants, 22% accepted, 4 enrolled. In 2016, 6 master's, 2 doctorates awarded. Terminal master's awarded for partial completion of doctoral program. *Degree requirements:* For master's, variable foreign language requirement, comprehensive exam (for some programs), thesis (for some programs); for doctorate, variable foreign language requirement, comprehensive exam, thesis/dissertation. *Entrance requirements:* For master's and doctorate, GRE General Test. Additional exam requirements/recommendations for international students: Required—TOEFL. *Application deadline:* For fall admission, 12/20 for domestic and international students. Application fee: $25. Electronic applications accepted. *Expenses:* Tuition: Full-time $28,494; part-time $1583 per credit hour. *Required fees:* $167 per credit hour. Tuition and fees vary according to course load and program. *Financial support:* In 2016–17, 17 students received support, including 17 research assistantships with full tuition reimbursements available (averaging $16,000 per year); career-related internships or fieldwork, Federal Work-Study, and institutionally sponsored loans also available. Financial award application deadline: 12/20; financial award applicants required to submit FAFSA. *Unit head:* Dr. Timothy Burns, Graduate Program Director, 254-710-6237, Fax: 254-710-3122, E-mail: timothy_burns@baylor.edu. *Application contact:* Jenice Langston, Office Manager, 254-710-3161, Fax: 254-710-3122, E-mail: jenice_langston@baylor.edu.
Website: http://www.baylor.edu/political_science

**Boise State University,** School of Public Service, Department of Public Policy and Administration, Boise, ID 83725. Offers public policy and administration (MPA, PhD, Graduate Certificate), including environmental, natural resource and energy policy and administration (MPA), general public administration (MPA), state and local government policy and administration (MPA). *Accreditation:* NASPAA. *Program availability:* Part-

time. *Faculty:* 16. *Students:* 38 full-time (19 women), 85 part-time (56 women); includes 15 minority (1 American Indian or Alaska Native, non-Hispanic/Latino; 1 Asian, non-Hispanic/Latino; 12 Hispanic/Latino; 1 Two or more races, non-Hispanic/Latino), 1 international. Average age 37. 81 applicants, 43% accepted, 29 enrolled. In 2016, 22 master's awarded. Terminal master's awarded for partial completion of doctoral program. *Degree requirements:* For master's, comprehensive exam, thesis optional, directed research project, internship; for doctorate, thesis/dissertation. *Entrance requirements:* For master's, GRE General Test, minimum GPA of 3.0. Additional exam requirements/recommendations for international students: Required—TOEFL (minimum score 550 paper-based; 80 iBT), IELTS (minimum score 6). *Application deadline:* For fall admission, 2/1 for domestic and international students; for spring admission, 10/1 for domestic and international students. Application fee: $65 ($95 for international students). Electronic applications accepted. *Expenses:* Tuition, state resident: full-time $6058; part-time $358 per credit hour. Tuition, nonresident: full-time $20,108; part-time $608 per credit hour. *Required fees:* $2108. Tuition and fees vary according to program. *Financial support:* In 2016–17, 41 students received support, including 2 research assistantships (averaging $4,083 per year); scholarships/grants and unspecified assistantships also available. Financial award application deadline: 2/1; financial award applicants required to submit FAFSA. *Unit head:* Dr. Gregory Hill, Department Chair, 208-426-2917, E-mail: greghill@boisestate.edu. *Application contact:* Dr. Elizabeth Fredericksen, MPA Director, 208-426-1078, E-mail: efreder@boisestate.edu.
Website: http://sps.boisestate.edu/publicpolicy/

**Brandeis University,** Graduate School of Arts and Sciences, Joint Master's Programs in Women's, Gender, and Sexuality Studies, Waltham, MA 02454-9110. Offers anthropology and women's, gender, and sexuality studies (MA); English and women's, gender, and sexuality studies (MA); near Eastern and Judaic studies and women's, gender, and sexuality studies (MA); public policy and women's, gender, and sexuality studies (MA); sociology and women's, gender, and sexuality studies (MA); sustainable international development and women's, gender, and sexuality studies (MA). *Degree requirements:* For master's, thesis. *Entrance requirements:* For master's, GRE, sample of written work, resume, statement of purpose, transcript(s), two letters of recommendation. Additional exam requirements/recommendations for international students: Required—TOEFL (minimum score 600 paper-based; 100 iBT), PTE (minimum score 68); Recommended—IELTS (minimum score 7). *Application deadline:* For fall admission, 1/15 for domestic students. Application fee: $75. Electronic applications accepted. *Financial support:* Fellowships with full tuition reimbursements and teaching assistantships with partial tuition reimbursements available. Financial award application deadline: 4/15; financial award applicants required to submit FAFSA. *Faculty research:* Anthropology, English, history, music, Near Eastern and Judaic studies, public policy, psychology, sociology, and sustainable international development. *Unit head:* Elizabeth Brainerd, Director of Graduate Study, 781-736-4816, E-mail: ebrainer@brandeis.edu. *Application contact:* Shannon Hunt, Program Administrator, 781-736-3045, Fax: 781-736-3044, E-mail: shunt@brandeis.edu.
Website: http://www.brandeis.edu/gsas

**Brandeis University,** The Heller School for Social Policy and Management, Program in Public Policy, Waltham, MA 02454-9110. Offers aging (MPP); behavioral health (MPP); children, youth and families (MPP); general social policy (MPP); health (MPP); poverty alleviation and development (MPP); MPP/MA. *Degree requirements:* For master's, thesis. *Entrance requirements:* For master's, GRE, 3 letters of recommendation, statement of purpose, 3 to 5 years of professional experience. Additional exam requirements/recommendations for international students: Required—TOEFL (minimum score 600 paper-based; 100 iBT). Electronic applications accepted. *Faculty research:* Health and behavioral health, children and families, disabilities, aging policy, substance abuse, work, inequality and social change, women/gender, poverty alleviation.

**Brock University,** Faculty of Graduate Studies, Faculty of Social Sciences, Program in Political Science, St. Catharines, ON L2S 3A1, Canada. Offers Canadian politics (MA); comparative politics (MA); international relations (MA); political theory or philosophy (MA); public policy (MA). *Program availability:* Part-time. *Degree requirements:* For master's, thesis optional. *Entrance requirements:* For master's, honors degree. Additional exam requirements/recommendations for international students: Required—TOEFL (minimum score 550 paper-based; 80 iBT), IELTS (minimum score 6.5), TWE (minimum score 4). Electronic applications accepted. *Faculty research:* Public administration reform, economic and social justice, politics of societies, Canadian politics, international relations.

**Brooklyn College of the City University of New York,** School of Humanities and Social Sciences, Department of Political Science, Brooklyn, NY 11210-2889. Offers international affairs (MA); political science (MA); urban policy and administration (MA). *Program availability:* Part-time, evening/weekend. *Degree requirements:* For master's, comprehensive exam (for some programs), thesis or alternative, foreign language exam (for international affairs program). *Entrance requirements:* For master's, 2 letters of recommendation, personal statement. Additional exam requirements/recommendations for international students: Required—TOEFL (minimum score 500 paper-based; 61 iBT). *Faculty research:* Ethics and politics, politics of criminal justice, Western Europe, international law and politics, labor politics.

**Brown University,** Graduate School, A. Alfred Taubman Center for Public Policy and American Institutions, Providence, RI 02912. Offers MPA, MPP, MD/MPP. *Entrance requirements:* For master's, GRE, 3 letters of recommendation. Additional exam requirements/recommendations for international students: Required—TOEFL.

**California Lutheran University,** Graduate Studies, School of Management, Thousand Oaks, CA 91360-2787. Offers business (IMBA); computer science (MS); econometrics (MBA); economics (MS); entrepreneurship (MBA, Certificate); finance (MBA, Certificate); financial planning (MBA, Certificate); information systems and technology (MS); information technology management (MBA, Certificate); international business (MBA, Certificate); management and organization behavior (MBA); management and organizational behavior (Certificate); marketing (MBA, Certificate); microeconomics (MBA); nonprofit and social enterprise (MBA); public policy and administration (MPPA). *Program availability:* Part-time, evening/weekend, 100% online, blended/hybrid learning. *Faculty:* 55 full-time (10 women), 36 part-time/adjunct (12 women). *Students:* 427 full-time (172 women), 189 part-time (87 women); includes 120 minority (14 Black or African American, non-Hispanic/Latino; 2 American Indian or Alaska Native, non-Hispanic/Latino; 19 Asian, non-Hispanic/Latino; 37 Hispanic/Latino; 48 Two or more races, non-Hispanic/Latino), 338 international. Average age 30. 591 applicants, 64% accepted, 131 enrolled. In 2016, 305 master's awarded. *Entrance requirements:* For master's, GMAT, interview, minimum GPA of 3.0. *Application deadline:* Applications are processed on a rolling basis. Application fee: $50. Electronic applications accepted. *Expenses:* Contact institution. *Unit head:* Dr. Gerhard Apfelthaler, Dean, 805-493-3360. *Application contact:* 805-493-3325, Fax: 805-493-3861, E-mail: clugrad@callutheran.edu.
Website: http://www.callutheran.edu/management/

**California State University, East Bay,** Office of Graduate Studies, College of Letters, Arts, and Social Sciences, Department of Public Affairs and Administration, Program in Public Administration, Hayward, CA 94542-3000. Offers health care administration (MPA); public management and policy analysis (MPA). *Program availability:* Part-time, evening/weekend. *Students:* 4 full-time (3 women), 143 part-time (113 women); includes

## Public Policy

106 minority (37 Black or African American, non-Hispanic/Latino; 1 American Indian or Alaska Native, non-Hispanic/Latino; 18 Asian, non-Hispanic/Latino; 34 Hispanic/Latino; 6 Native Hawaiian or other Pacific Islander, non-Hispanic/Latino; 10 Two or more races, non-Hispanic/Latino), 8 international. Average age 33. 126 applicants, 77% accepted, 36 enrolled. In 2016, 83 master's awarded. *Degree requirements:* For master's, comprehensive exam (for some programs), comprehensive exam or thesis. *Entrance requirements:* For master's, minimum GPA of 2.5; statement of purpose; 2 letters of recommendation; professional resume/curriculum vitae. Additional exam requirements/recommendations for international students: Required—TOEFL (minimum score 550 paper-based; 79 iBT). *Application deadline:* For fall admission, 6/18 for domestic and international students. Application fee: $55. Electronic applications accepted. *Financial support:* Fellowships, teaching assistantships, career-related internships or fieldwork, Federal Work-Study, institutionally sponsored loans, and scholarships/grants available. Support available to part-time students. Financial award application deadline: 3/2; financial award applicants required to submit FAFSA. *Unit head:* Dr. Toni Fogarty, Chair, 510-885-2268, E-mail: toni.fogarty@csueastbay.edu. *Application contact:* Prof. Michael Moon, Public Administration Graduate Advisor, 510-885-2545, Fax: 510-885-3726, E-mail: michael.moon@csueastbay.edu.

**California State University, Long Beach,** Graduate Studies, College of Health and Human Services, Graduate Center for Public Policy and Administration, Long Beach, CA 90840. Offers MPA, Graduate Certificate. *Accreditation:* NASPAA (one or more programs are accredited). *Program availability:* Part-time, evening/weekend. *Degree requirements:* For master's, comprehensive exam. *Entrance requirements:* For master's, minimum GPA of 2.75. *Application deadline:* For fall admission, 7/1 for domestic students. Applications are processed on a rolling basis. Application fee: $55. Electronic applications accepted. *Financial support:* Fellowships, career-related internships or fieldwork, Federal Work-Study, institutionally sponsored loans, and scholarships/grants available. Financial award application deadline: 3/2. *Faculty research:* Transportation access, air quality controls, coastal issues, intergovernmental relations. *Unit head:* David C. Powell, Director, 562-985-4178.

**California State University, Sacramento,** Office of Graduate Studies, College of Social Sciences and Interdisciplinary Studies, Program in Public Policy and Administration, Sacramento, CA 95819. Offers MPPA. *Program availability:* Part-time. *Students:* 13 full-time (4 women), 39 part-time (26 women); includes 14 minority (4 Asian, non-Hispanic/Latino; 8 Hispanic/Latino; 2 Native Hawaiian or other Pacific Islander, non-Hispanic/Latino). Average age 31. 51 applicants, 80% accepted, 32 enrolled. In 2016, 13 master's awarded. *Degree requirements:* For master's, thesis or alternative, writing proficiency exam. *Entrance requirements:* For master's, GRE, minimum GPA of 3.0 for all undergraduate coursework and in last 60 units. Additional exam requirements/recommendations for international students: Required—TOEFL (minimum score 560 paper-based; 83 iBT). *Application deadline:* For fall admission, 3/1 for domestic and international students; for spring admission, 9/30 for international students. Applications are processed on a rolling basis. Application fee: $55. Electronic applications accepted. *Expenses:* $4,302 full-time tuition and fees per semester, $2,796 part-time. *Financial support:* Career-related internships or fieldwork and Federal Work-Study available. Support available to part-time students. Financial award application deadline: 3/1; financial award applicants required to submit FAFSA. *Faculty research:* Education policy, urban policy, collaborative governance, judicial administration, and California state/local governance. *Unit head:* Dr. Ted Lascher, Chair, 916-278-6557, E-mail: tedl@csus.edu. *Application contact:* Jose Martinez, Graduate Admissions Supervisor, 916-278-7871, E-mail: martinj@skymail.csus.edu.
Website: http://www.csus.edu/ppa

**Carleton University,** Faculty of Graduate Studies, Faculty of Public Affairs and Management, School of Public Policy and Administration, Ottawa, ON K1S 5B6, Canada. Offers public administration (MA, DPA); public policy (PhD). *Program availability:* Part-time. *Degree requirements:* For master's, thesis optional; for doctorate, one foreign language, comprehensive exam, thesis/dissertation. *Entrance requirements:* For master's, GRE, honors degree; for doctorate, master's degree. Additional exam requirements/recommendations for international students: Required—TOEFL. *Faculty research:* Canadian public administration and policy, development administration, public policy analysis, public management.

**Carnegie Mellon University,** Dietrich College of Humanities and Social Sciences, Department of Statistics, Pittsburgh, PA 15213-3891. Offers machine learning and statistics (PhD); mathematical finance (PhD); statistics (MS, PhD), including applied statistics (PhD), computational statistics (PhD), theoretical statistics (PhD); statistics and public policy (PhD). Terminal master's awarded for partial completion of doctoral program. *Degree requirements:* For doctorate, comprehensive exam, thesis/dissertation. *Entrance requirements:* For master's and doctorate, GRE General Test. Additional exam requirements/recommendations for international students: Required—TOEFL. *Faculty research:* Stochastic processes, Bayesian statistics, statistical computing, decision theory, psychiatric statistics.

**Carnegie Mellon University,** Heinz College Australia, Master of Science in Public Policy and Management Program (Adelaide, South Australia), Adelaide SA 5000, Australia. Offers MS. *Entrance requirements:* For master's, GRE or GMAT, college-level course in advanced algebra/pre-calculus; college-level courses in economics and statistics (recommended). Additional exam requirements/recommendations for international students: Required—TOEFL or IELTS.

**Carnegie Mellon University,** Heinz College, School of Public Policy and Management, Master of Science in Public Policy and Management Program, Pittsburgh, PA 15213-3891. Offers MS. Program also offered with second-year study in Washington, DC. *Accreditation:* NASPAA. *Degree requirements:* For master's, internship. *Entrance requirements:* For master's, GRE or GMAT, college-level course in advanced algebra/pre-calculus; college-level courses in economics and statistics (recommended). Additional exam requirements/recommendations for international students: Required—TOEFL or IELTS. Electronic applications accepted.

**Carnegie Mellon University,** Heinz College, School of Public Policy and Management, PhD in Public Policy and Management Program, Pittsburgh, PA 15213-3891. Offers PhD. *Entrance requirements:* For doctorate, GRE or GMAT. Additional exam requirements/recommendations for international students: Required—TOEFL or IELTS.

**The Catholic University of America,** School of Arts and Sciences, Department of Sociology, Washington, DC 20064. Offers crime and justice studies (MA); global and comparative sociology (MA); public policy (MA). *Program availability:* Part-time. *Faculty:* 3 full-time (2 women), 4 part-time/adjunct (0 women). *Students:* 2 full-time (both women), 1 (woman) part-time; includes 2 minority (1 Black or African American, non-Hispanic/Latino; 1 Hispanic/Latino). Average age 22. 7 applicants, 29% accepted, 2 enrolled. In 2016, 2 master's awarded. *Degree requirements:* For master's, comprehensive exam, thesis or alternative, two seminar papers. *Entrance requirements:* For master's, GRE General Test, statement of purpose, official copies of academic transcripts, three letters of recommendation. Additional exam requirements/recommendations for international students: Required—TOEFL (minimum score 550 paper-based; 80 iBT). *Application deadline:* For fall admission, 7/15 priority date for domestic students, 7/1 for international students; for spring admission, 11/15 priority

date for domestic students, 11/1 for international students. Applications are processed on a rolling basis. Application fee: $55. Electronic applications accepted. *Expenses:* $42,850 per year; $1,170 per credit; $200 per semester part-time fees. *Financial support:* Fellowships, research assistantships, teaching assistantships, Federal Work-Study, scholarships/grants, tuition waivers (full and partial), and unspecified assistantships available. Financial award application deadline: 2/1; financial award applicants required to submit FAFSA. *Faculty research:* Social movements, gender structure, political sociology, race and ethnic relations, evaluation methodologies. *Total annual research expenditures:* $2,586. *Unit head:* Dr. Enrique S. Pumar, Chair, 202-319-5445, Fax: 202-319-4980, E-mail: pumar@cua.edu. *Application contact:* Director of Graduate Admissions, 202-319-5057, Fax: 202-319-6533, E-mail: cua-admissions@cua.edu.
Website: http://sociology.cua.edu/

**Central European University,** School of Public Policy, Budapest, Hungary. Offers public administration (MPA); public policy (MA, PhD). *Faculty:* 22 full-time (7 women), 17 part-time/adjunct (10 women). *Students:* 141 full-time (90 women). Average age 29. 931 applicants, 30% accepted, 75 enrolled. In 2016, 68 master's, 7 doctorates awarded. *Degree requirements:* For master's, one foreign language, thesis; for doctorate, one foreign language, comprehensive exam, thesis/dissertation. *Entrance requirements:* For master's and doctorate, interview. Additional exam requirements/recommendations for international students: Required—TOEFL (minimum score 570 paper-based); Recommended—IELTS (minimum score 6.5). *Application deadline:* For fall admission, 2/4 for domestic and international students. Application fee: $30. Electronic applications accepted. *Expenses:* Tuition: Full-time 13,500 euros. Tuition and fees vary according to degree level, program and student level. *Financial support:* Fellowships, career-related internships or fieldwork, scholarships/grants, health care benefits, and tuition waivers (full and partial) available. *Faculty research:* Multi-disciplinary study of public policy, innovative teaching and research, as well as meaningful engagement with policy practice, public health, law, humanitarian assistance, anti-corruption, conflict and post-conflict recovery, natural resource management. *Unit head:* Dr. Julia Buxton, Head, 36 1 327-3110, E-mail: spp@ceu.edu. *Application contact:* Zsuzsanna Jaszberenyi, Admissions Officer, 361-324-3009, Fax: 367-327-3211, E-mail: admissions@ceu.edu.
Website: http://spp.ceu.edu

**Claremont Graduate University,** Graduate Programs, School of Social Science, Policy and Evaluation, Department of Economics, Claremont, CA 91711-6160. Offers behavioral economics and neuroeconomics (PhD); business and financial economics (MA, PhD); economic development (Certificate); international economic and development policy (PhD); international economics policy and development (MA); international money and finance (PhD); political economy and public economics (PhD); political economy and public policy (MA); MBA/PhD. *Program availability:* Part-time. *Faculty:* 5 full-time (1 woman), 2 part-time/adjunct (0 women). *Students:* 92 full-time (31 women), 34 part-time (15 women); includes 14 minority (4 Black or African American, non-Hispanic/Latino; 7 Asian, non-Hispanic/Latino; 2 Hispanic/Latino; 1 Two or more races, non-Hispanic/Latino), 67 international. Average age 33. In 2016, 20 master's, 16 doctorates awarded. *Entrance requirements:* For master's and doctorate, GRE General Test or GMAT. Additional exam requirements/recommendations for international students: Required—TOEFL (minimum score 75 iBT). *Application deadline:* For fall admission, 2/1 priority date for domestic and international students. Applications are processed on a rolling basis. Application fee: $80. Electronic applications accepted. *Expenses:* Tuition: Full-time $44,328; part-time $1847 per unit. *Required fees:* $600; $300 per semester. Tuition and fees vary according to course load and program. *Financial support:* Fellowships, research assistantships, teaching assistantships, Federal Work-Study, institutionally sponsored loans, and scholarships/grants available. Support available to part-time students. Financial award application deadline: 2/15; financial award applicants required to submit FAFSA. *Faculty research:* International and financial economics, law and economics, regulation, public choice economics. *Unit head:* Paul Zak, Chair, 909-621-8788, E-mail: paul.zak@cgu.edu. *Application contact:* Paige Piontkowsky, Senior Assistant Director of Admissions, 909-607-3240, E-mail: paige.piontkowsky@cgu.edu.
Website: https://www.cgu.edu/school/ssspe/programs/?areas_of_study=economics

**Claremont Graduate University,** Graduate Programs, School of Social Science, Policy and Evaluation, Department of Politics and Policy, Claremont, CA 91711-6160. Offers American politics (MA, PhD); comparative politics (PhD); international political economy (MA); international studies (MA); political philosophy (PhD); political science (PhD); politics, economics and business (MA); public policy (MA, PhD); world politics (PhD); MBA/PhD. *Program availability:* Part-time. *Faculty:* 6 full-time (4 women), 3 part-time/adjunct (0 women). *Students:* 107 full-time (37 women), 32 part-time (10 women); includes 41 minority (6 Black or African American, non-Hispanic/Latino; 10 Asian, non-Hispanic/Latino; 17 Hispanic/Latino; 8 Two or more races, non-Hispanic/Latino), 31 international. Average age 36. In 2016, 21 master's, 14 doctorates awarded. Terminal master's awarded for partial completion of doctoral program. *Entrance requirements:* For master's and doctorate, GRE General Test. Additional exam requirements/recommendations for international students: Required—TOEFL (minimum score 75 iBT). *Application deadline:* For fall admission, 2/1 priority date for domestic and international students. Applications are processed on a rolling basis. Application fee: $80. Electronic applications accepted. *Expenses:* Tuition: Full-time $44,328; part-time $1847 per unit. *Required fees:* $600; $300 per semester. Tuition and fees vary according to course load and program. *Financial support:* Fellowships, research assistantships, teaching assistantships, Federal Work-Study, institutionally sponsored loans, and scholarships/grants available. Support available to part-time students. Financial award application deadline: 2/15; financial award applicants required to submit FAFSA. *Faculty research:* Environmental policy, international debt, global democratization, Third World development, public sector discrimination. *Unit head:* Heather Campbell, Chair, 909-621-8689, E-mail: heather.campbell@cgu.edu. *Application contact:* Paige Piontkowsky, Senior Assistant Director of Admissions, 909-607-3240, E-mail: paige.piontkowsky@cgu.edu.
Website: https://www.cgu.edu/school/ssspe/programs/?areas_of_study=politics-and-government

**Claremont Graduate University,** Graduate Programs, School of Social Science, Policy and Evaluation, Program in Public Policy and Evaluation, Claremont, CA 91711-6160. Offers MA. *Entrance requirements:* For master's, GRE General Test. Additional exam requirements/recommendations for international students: Required—TOEFL (minimum score 75 iBT). *Application deadline:* For fall admission, 2/1 priority date for domestic and international students. Application fee: $80. Electronic applications accepted. *Expenses:* Tuition: Full-time $44,328; part-time $1847 per unit. *Required fees:* $600; $300 per semester. Tuition and fees vary according to course load and program. *Financial support:* Fellowships, Federal Work-Study, institutionally sponsored loans, and scholarships/grants available. Support available to part-time students. Financial award application deadline: 2/15; financial award applicants required to submit FAFSA. *Unit head:* Stewart Donaldson, Dean, 909-607-8235, E-mail: stewart.donaldson@cgu.edu. *Application contact:* Paige Piontkowsky, Senior Assistant Director of Admissions, 909-607-3240, E-mail: paige.piontkowsky@cgu.edu.
Website: https://www.cgu.edu/academics/program/public-policy-evaluation/

**Clemson University,** Graduate School, College of Behavioral, Social and Health Sciences, Program in Policy Studies, Clemson, SC 29634. Offers PhD, Certificate. *Program availability:* Part-time, 100% online. *Faculty:* 7 full-time (2 women). *Students:* 7 full-time (1 woman), 10 part-time (5 women), 5 international. Average age 38. 7 applicants, 43% accepted, 2 enrolled. In 2016, 3 doctorates awarded. *Degree requirements:* For doctorate, comprehensive exam, thesis/dissertation. *Entrance requirements:* For doctorate, GRE General Test, letters of recommendation, unofficial transcripts, biographical statement, statement of interest. Additional exam requirements/recommendations for international students: Required—TOEFL (minimum score 80 iBT), IELTS (minimum score 6.5). *Application deadline:* For fall admission, 7/15 for domestic students, 5/1 for international students; for spring admission, 12/15 for domestic students, 10/1 for international students. Applications are processed on a rolling basis. Application fee: $80 ($90 for international students). Electronic applications accepted. *Expenses:* $3,431 per semester full-time resident, $6,875 per semester full-time non-resident, $387 per credit hour part-time resident, $770 per credit hour part-time non-resident; $3,428 per credit hour (for online courses). *Financial support:* In 2016–17, 7 students received support, including 1 fellowship with partial tuition reimbursement available (averaging $5,000 per year), 5 research assistantships with partial tuition reimbursements available (averaging $15,000 per year); unspecified assistantships also available. Financial award application deadline: 4/1. *Unit head:* Dr. Bruce Ransom, II, Program Chair, 864-656-0214, E-mail: bii@clemson.edu. *Application contact:* Carolyn Benson, Administrative Specialist, 864-656-4463, E-mail: cbenson@clemson.edu. Website: http://sti.clemson.edu/policy-studies-home-psmainmenu-173

**The College of William and Mary,** Faculty of Arts and Sciences, William and Mary Public Policy Program, Williamsburg, VA 23187-8795. Offers MPP, JD/MPP, MBA/MPP, MS/MPP. *Faculty:* 32 full-time (11 women), 4 part-time/adjunct (1 woman). *Students:* 31 full-time (12 women); includes 7 minority (1 Black or African American, non-Hispanic/Latino; 1 American Indian or Alaska Native, non-Hispanic/Latino; 4 Hispanic/Latino; 1 Two or more races, non-Hispanic/Latino). Average age 24. 61 applicants, 64% accepted, 17 enrolled. In 2016, 20 master's awarded. *Entrance requirements:* For master's, GRE General Test. Additional exam requirements/recommendations for international students: Required—TOEFL (minimum score 600 paper-based; 100 iBT), IELTS (minimum score 7.5). *Application deadline:* For fall admission, 2/15 priority date for domestic and international students. Application fee: $45. Electronic applications accepted. *Expenses:* Tuition, state resident: full-time $9000; part-time $500 per credit hour. Tuition, nonresident: full-time $24,686; part-time $1200 per credit hour. *Required fees:* $5258. One-time fee: $400 full-time. *Financial support:* In 2016–17, 33 students received support, including 20 research assistantships with partial tuition reimbursements available (averaging $7,000 per year), 15 teaching assistantships with partial tuition reimbursements available (averaging $8,000 per year); career-related internships or fieldwork and unspecified assistantships also available. Financial award application deadline: 1/15; financial award applicants required to submit FAFSA. *Faculty research:* Social policy, international development, health care policy, environmental policy, state and local policy, education policy, regulatory policy. *Total annual research expenditures:* $225,421. *Unit head:* Dr. John Gilmour, Director, 757-221-2368, Fax: 757-221-1175, E-mail: slstaf@wm.edu. *Application contact:* Katherine French, Director of Admissions, 757-221-2384, Fax: 757-221-2390, E-mail: krfrench@wm.edu. Website: http://www.wm.edu/publicpolicy

**Columbia University,** School of International and Public Affairs, Program in Public Policy and Administration, New York, NY 10027. Offers MPA, JD/MPA, MPA/MS, MPH/MPA. *Accreditation:* NASPAA. *Students:* Average age 27. *Entrance requirements:* For master's, GRE General Test. Additional exam requirements/recommendations for international students: Required—TOEFL (minimum score 600 paper-based; 100 iBT), IELTS (minimum score 7), PTE (minimum score 68). *Application deadline:* For fall admission, 1/5 for domestic and international students; for spring admission, 10/15 for domestic and international students. Application fee: $95. Electronic applications accepted. *Financial support:* In 2016–17, 89 students received support. Fellowships, research assistantships, teaching assistantships, career-related internships or fieldwork, Federal Work-Study, institutionally sponsored loans, and unspecified assistantships available. Financial award application deadline: 1/5; financial award applicants required to submit FAFSA. *Unit head:* Office of Admissions and Financial Aid, 212-854-6216, Fax: 212-854-3010, E-mail: sipa_admission@columbia.edu. *Application contact:* Admissions and Financial Aid, 212-854-6216, Fax: 212-854-3010, E-mail: sipa_admission@columbia.edu. Website: http://www.columbia.edu/cu/sipa/

**Concordia University,** School of Graduate Studies, Faculty of Arts and Science, Department of Political Science, Montréal, QC H3G 1M8, Canada. Offers political science (PhD); public policy and public administration (MA), including geography. *Degree requirements:* For master's, one foreign language, comprehensive exam, thesis optional, internship. *Entrance requirements:* For master's, honors degree or equivalent. Additional exam requirements/recommendations for international students: Required—TOEFL. *Faculty research:* International public policy and administration, Quebec public administration, public policy and social/political theory, geography and public policy, public administration and decision making.

**Cornell University,** Graduate School, Graduate Fields of Arts and Sciences, Field of Government, Ithaca, NY 14853. Offers American politics (PhD); comparative politics (PhD); international relations (PhD); political methodology (PhD); political thought (PhD); public policy (PhD). *Degree requirements:* For doctorate, comprehensive exam, thesis/dissertation. *Entrance requirements:* For doctorate, GRE General Test, sample of written work, 3 letters of recommendation. Additional exam requirements/recommendations for international students: Required—TOEFL (minimum score 550 paper-based; 77 iBT). Electronic applications accepted. *Faculty research:* Political theory, American politics, comparative politics, international relations, methodology.

**Cornell University,** Graduate School, Graduate Fields of Human Ecology, Field of Policy Analysis and Management, Ithaca, NY 14853. Offers consumer policy (PhD); family and social welfare policy (PhD); health administration (MHA); health management and policy (PhD); public policy (PhD). *Degree requirements:* For master's, thesis; for doctorate, thesis/dissertation. *Entrance requirements:* For master's, GRE General Test or GMAT, 2 letters of recommendation; for doctorate, GRE General Test, 2 letters of recommendation. Additional exam requirements/recommendations for international students: Required—TOEFL (minimum score 550 paper-based; 77 iBT). Electronic applications accepted. *Faculty research:* Health policy, family policy, social welfare policy, program evaluation, consumer policy.

**DePaul University,** College of Liberal Arts and Social Sciences, Chicago, IL 60614. Offers Arabic (MA); Chinese (MA); English (MA); French (MA); German (MA); history (MA); interdisciplinary studies (MA, MS); international public service (MS); international studies (MA); Italian (MA); Japanese (MA); leadership and policy studies (MS); liberal studies (MA); new media studies (MA); nonprofit management (MNM); public administration (MPA); public health (MPH); public service management (MS); social work (MSW); sociology (MA); Spanish (MA); sustainable urban development (MA); women and gender studies (MA); writing and publishing (MA); writing, rhetoric, and discourse (MA); MA/PhD. *Program availability:* Part-time, evening/weekend, online learning. Terminal master's awarded for partial completion of doctoral program. *Degree*

*requirements:* For master's, variable foreign language requirement, comprehensive exam (for some programs), thesis (for some programs). Electronic applications accepted.

**Duke University,** Graduate School, PhD Program in Public Policy, Durham, NC 27708. Offers PhD. *Entrance requirements:* For doctorate, GRE General Test. Additional exam requirements/recommendations for international students: Required—TOEFL (minimum score 577 paper-based; 90 iBT) or IELTS. Electronic applications accepted.

**Duke University,** Sanford School of Public Policy, MPP Program, Durham, NC 27708. Offers MPP, MBA/MPP, MD/MPP, MEM/MPP, MPP/JD, MPP/M Div. MPP/JD offered with North Carolina Central University; MBA/MPP with The University of North Carolina at Chapel Hill. *Faculty:* 70 full-time (25 women), 18 part-time/adjunct (6 women). *Students:* 139 full-time (82 women); includes 38 minority (11 Black or African American, non-Hispanic/Latino; 1 American Indian or Alaska Native, non-Hispanic/Latino; 17 Asian, non-Hispanic/Latino; 8 Hispanic/Latino; 1 Native Hawaiian or other Pacific Islander, non-Hispanic/Latino), 18 international. Average age 26. 401 applicants, 61 enrolled. In 2016, 63 master's awarded. *Degree requirements:* For master's, thesis, internship. *Entrance requirements:* For master's, GRE. Additional exam requirements/recommendations for international students: Required—TOEFL (minimum score 105 iBT), IELTS. *Application deadline:* For fall admission, 1/5 for domestic and international students. Application fee: $80. Electronic applications accepted. *Expenses:* $46,939 per year. *Financial support:* Fellowships, research assistantships, teaching assistantships, career-related internships or fieldwork, Federal Work-Study, scholarships/grants, and unspecified assistantships available. Financial award application deadline: 1/5; financial award applicants required to submit FAFSA. *Unit head:* Mac McCorkle, Director of Graduate Studies, 919-613-9206, E-mail: mac.mccorkle@duke.edu. *Application contact:* Jessica Pan, Director of Admissions and Scholarships, 919-613-9205, E-mail: mppadmit@duke.edu. Website: https://www.sanford.duke.edu

**Eastern Michigan University,** Graduate School, College of Arts and Sciences, Department of Political Science, Programs in Public Administration, Ypsilanti, MI 48197. Offers general public management (Graduate Certificate); local government management (Graduate Certificate); management of public healthcare services (Graduate Certificate); nonprofit management (Graduate Certificate); public administration (MPA); public budget management (Graduate Certificate); public land planning and development management (Graduate Certificate); public personnel management (Graduate Certificate); public policy analysis (Graduate Certificate). *Accreditation:* NASPAA. *Students:* 11 full-time (7 women), 43 part-time (22 women); includes 19 minority (16 Black or African American, non-Hispanic/Latino; 2 Hispanic/Latino; 1 Two or more races, non-Hispanic/Latino). Average age 36. 50 applicants, 64% accepted, 17 enrolled. In 2016, 23 master's, 1 other advanced degree awarded. Application fee: $45. *Application contact:* Dr. Jeffrey L. Bernstein, Program Advisor, 734-487-6970, Fax: 734-487-3340, E-mail: jeffrey.bernstein@emich.edu. Website: http://www.emich.edu/polisci/

**Eastern University,** Palmer Theological Seminary, St. Davids, PA 19087-3696. Offers Biblical studies and theology (MTS); Christian counseling (MTS); Christian faith and public policy (MTS); divinity (M Div); general studies (MTS); leadership of missional church renewal (D Min); theological studies (MTS); M Div/MA; M Div/MSW. *Accreditation:* ACIPE; ATS; MSA/CIHE. *Program availability:* Part-time, online learning. *Students:* 93 full-time (43 women), 135 part-time (66 women); includes 120 minority (105 Black or African American, non-Hispanic/Latino; 2 Asian, non-Hispanic/Latino; 12 Hispanic/Latino; 1 Two or more races, non-Hispanic/Latino), 4 international. Average age 47. In 2016, 42 master's, 9 doctorates awarded. *Entrance requirements:* Additional exam requirements/recommendations for international students: Required—TOEFL (minimum score 550 paper-based; 79 iBT). *Application deadline:* Applications are processed on a rolling basis. Application fee: $30. Electronic applications accepted. Application fee is waived when completed online. *Expenses:* $370 - $520 per credit (based on program and number of credits per semester). *Unit head:* Michael Dziedziak, Executive Director of Enrollment, 800-452-0996, E-mail: semadmis@eastern.edu. Website: http://palmerseminary.edu/

**Florida State University,** The Graduate School, College of Social Sciences and Public Policy, Reubin O'D. Askew School of Public Administration and Policy, Tallahassee, FL 32306-2250. Offers public administration (MPA, PhD); public administration and policy (Certificate); JD/MPA; MPA/MSC; MPA/MSP; MPA/MSW. *Accreditation:* NASPAA (one or more programs are accredited). *Program availability:* Part-time, evening/weekend. *Faculty:* 10 full-time (2 women), 10 part-time/adjunct (3 women). *Students:* 78 full-time (39 women), 68 part-time (41 women); includes 74 minority (12 Black or African American, non-Hispanic/Latino; 41 Asian, non-Hispanic/Latino; 6 Hispanic/Latino; 15 Two or more races, non-Hispanic/Latino). Average age 25. 115 applicants, 67% accepted, 37 enrolled. In 2016, 82 master's, 9 doctorates awarded. *Degree requirements:* For master's, action report; for doctorate, comprehensive exam, thesis/dissertation. *Entrance requirements:* For master's, GRE General Test, GMAT, MAT, LSAT, minimum undergraduate upper-division GPA of 3.0; for doctorate, GRE General Test (minimum score of 1100 or equivalent on current grading scale); GMAT; MAT; LSAT, minimum undergraduate GPA of 3.0, graduate 3.5. Additional exam requirements/recommendations for international students: Required—TOEFL (minimum score 550 paper-based; 80 iBT), IELTS (minimum score 6.5), PTE (minimum score 55), Michigan English Language Assessment Battery (minimum score 77). *Application deadline:* For fall admission, 7/1 for domestic students, 5/1 for international students; for spring admission, 11/1 for domestic students, 9/1 for international students; for summer admission, 3/1 for domestic students, 1/1 for international students. Applications are processed on a rolling basis. Application fee: $30. Electronic applications accepted. *Expenses:* Tuition, state resident: full-time $7263; part-time $403.51 per credit hour. Tuition, nonresident: full-time $18,087; part-time $1004.85 per credit hour. *Required fees:* $1365; $75.81 per credit hour. $20 per semester. Tuition and fees vary according to campus/location. *Financial support:* In 2016–17, 22 students received support, including 8 fellowships with full tuition reimbursements available (averaging $18,000 per year), 4 research assistantships with full tuition reimbursements available (averaging $15,000 per year), 8 teaching assistantships with full tuition reimbursements available (averaging $15,000 per year); career-related internships or fieldwork, Federal Work-Study, institutionally sponsored loans, scholarships/grants, tuition waivers (full), and unspecified assistantships also available. Support available to part-time students. Financial award application deadline: 2/1; financial award applicants required to submit FAFSA. *Faculty research:* Public financial management, policy analysis and evaluation methods, leadership and strategic management, state and local government administration, public and nonprofit management, international and nongovernmental organizations. *Unit head:* Dr. Keon-Hyung Lee, Director, 850-645-8210, Fax: 850-644-7617, E-mail: klee2@fsu.edu. *Application contact:* Velda Williams, Academic Program Specialist, 850-644-3060, Fax: 850-644-7617, E-mail: vwilliams3@fsu.edu. Website: http://askew.fsu.edu/

**Frederick S. Pardee RAND Graduate School,** Program in Policy Analysis, Santa Monica, CA 90407-2138. Offers PhD. *Faculty:* 229 part-time/adjunct (80 women). *Students:* 107 full-time (51 women); includes 20 minority (3 Black or African American, non-Hispanic/Latino; 9 Asian, non-Hispanic/Latino; 8 Hispanic/Latino), 38 international.

*Public Policy*

Average age 31. 136 applicants, 29% accepted, 22 enrolled. In 2016, 19 doctorates awarded. *Degree requirements:* For doctorate, comprehensive exam, thesis/dissertation. *Entrance requirements:* For doctorate, GMAT or GRE General Test, resume or curriculum vitae, three essays, three letters of recommendation. Additional exam requirements/recommendations for international students: Required—TOEFL (minimum score 100 iBT). *Application deadline:* For fall admission, 1/10 for domestic and international students. Application fee: $50. Electronic applications accepted. *Expenses:* Contact institution. *Financial support:* In 2016–17, 107 students received support, including 107 fellowships (averaging $46,000 per year), 30 teaching assistantships (averaging $2,000 per year); scholarships/grants and health care benefits also available. Financial award application deadline: 7/1. *Faculty research:* Education, defense policy, health, labor and population, justice. *Unit head:* Dr. Susan L. Marquis, Dean, 310-393-0411 Ext. 7075, Fax: 310-451-6978. *Application contact:* Mary Parker, Registrar/Admissions Manager, 310-393-0411 Ext. 7690, Fax: 310-451-6978, E-mail: mfparker@prgs.edu.
Website: http://www.prgs.edu

**George Mason University,** Schar School of Policy and Government, Program in Public Policy, Arlington, VA 22201. Offers MPP, PhD. *Faculty:* 26 full-time (11 women), 7 part-time/adjunct (2 women). *Students:* 109 full-time (52 women), 199 part-time (92 women); includes 98 minority (37 Black or African American, non-Hispanic/Latino; 19 Asian, non-Hispanic/Latino; 30 Hispanic/Latino; 1 Native Hawaiian or other Pacific Islander, non-Hispanic/Latino; 11 Two or more races, non-Hispanic/Latino), 34 international. Average age 32. 184 applicants, 82% accepted, 60 enrolled. In 2016, 115 master's, 15 doctorates awarded. *Degree requirements:* For master's, thesis or alternative, professional experience; for doctorate, comprehensive exam, thesis/dissertation, field studies. *Entrance requirements:* For master's, GRE/GMAT (for students seeking merit-based scholarships), bachelor's degree with minimum GPA of 3.0, current resume, 2 letters of recommendation, expanded goals statement, 2 copies of official transcripts; for doctorate, GMAT or GRE General Test, master's degree with minimum GPA of 3.0; current resume; expanded goals statement; 2 official copies of transcripts; writing sample. Additional exam requirements/recommendations for international students: Required—TOEFL (minimum score 575 paper-based; 88 iBT), IELTS (minimum score 6.5), PTE (minimum score 59). Application fee: $75 ($80 for international students). Electronic applications accepted. *Expenses:* Contact institution. *Financial support:* In 2016–17, 30 students received support, including 1 fellowship (averaging $1,300 per year), 28 research assistantships with tuition reimbursements available (averaging $18,948 per year); career-related internships or fieldwork, Federal Work-Study, scholarships/grants, unspecified assistantships, and health care benefits (for full-time research or teaching assistantship recipients) also available. Support available to part-time students. Financial award application deadline: 3/1; financial award applicants required to submit FAFSA. *Unit head:* Siona Listokin-Smith, Director, Master of Public Policy, 703-703-9756, Fax: 703-993-8215, E-mail: slistoki@gmu.edu. *Application contact:* Stephanie Ellis, Graduate Admissions Coordinator, 703-993-4478, E-mail: sellis11@gmu.edu.
Website: http://spgia.gmu.edu/programs/graduate-degrees/master-of-public-policy-mpp/

**Georgetown University,** Graduate School of Arts and Sciences, Department of Government, Washington, DC 20057. Offers American government (MA); conflict resolution (MA); democracy and governance (MA); development, management and policy (MA); government (PhD); MA/PhD. Terminal master's awarded for partial completion of doctoral program. *Degree requirements:* For master's, one foreign language, comprehensive exam; for doctorate, one foreign language, comprehensive exam, thesis/dissertation. *Entrance requirements:* For master's, GRE General Test, minimum B average; for doctorate, GRE General Test, MA. Additional exam requirements/recommendations for international students: Required—TOEFL. *Faculty research:* Western Europe, Latin America, the Middle East, political theory, international relations and law, methodology, American politics and institutions.

**Georgetown University,** Graduate School of Arts and Sciences, McCourt School of Public Policy, Washington, DC 20057. Offers data science for public policy (MDSPP); international development policy (MIDP); policy leadership (EMPL); policy management (MPM); public policy (MPP); MBA/MPP; MPP/JD; MPP/MA; MPP/MSFS; MPP/PhD. *Entrance requirements:* For master's, GRE General Test, minimum B average. Additional exam requirements/recommendations for international students: Required—TOEFL. *Faculty research:* Social policy, government, private sector.

**Georgetown University,** Graduate School of Arts and Sciences, School of Continuing Studies, Washington, DC 20057. Offers American studies (MALS); Catholic studies (MALS); classical civilizations (MALS); emergency and disaster management (MPS); ethics and the professions (MALS); global strategic communications (MPS); hospitality management (MPS); human resources management (MPS); humanities (MALS); individualized study (MALS); integrated marketing communications (MPS); international affairs (MALS); Islam and Muslim-Christian relations (MALS); journalism (MPS); liberal studies (DLS); literature and society (MALS); medieval and early modern European studies (MALS); public relations and corporate communications (MPS); real estate (MPS); religious studies (MALS); social and public policy (MALS); sports industry management (MPS); systems engineering management (MPS); technology management (MPS); the theory and practice of American democracy (MALS); urban and regional planning (MPS); visual culture (MALS). MPS in systems engineering management offered jointly with Stevens Institute of Technology. *Entrance requirements:* Additional exam requirements/recommendations for international students: Required—TOEFL.

**The George Washington University,** Columbian College of Arts and Sciences, Department of Philosophy, Washington, DC 20052. Offers philosophy and social policy (MA). *Faculty:* 12 full-time (4 women). *Students:* 5 full-time (1 woman), 1 part-time. Average age 26. 25 applicants, 80% accepted, 6 enrolled. *Degree requirements:* For master's, comprehensive exam, thesis or alternative. *Entrance requirements:* For master's, GRE General Test, interview, minimum GPA of 3.0. Additional exam requirements/recommendations for international students: Required—TOEFL (minimum score 600 paper-based; 100 iBT). *Application deadline:* For fall admission, 4/1 priority date for domestic and international students; for spring admission, 10/1 priority date for domestic students, 9/1 priority date for international students. Applications are processed on a rolling basis. Application fee: $60. Electronic applications accepted. *Financial support:* Fellowships with tuition reimbursements, Federal Work-Study, and institutionally sponsored loans available. Financial award application deadline: 1/15. *Unit head:* Tad Zawidzki, Chair, 202-994-6444, E-mail: zawidzki@gwu.edu. *Application contact:* Amanda McLaughlin, Executive Aide, 202-994-6265, Fax: 202-994-8683, E-mail: philosop@gwu.edu.
Website: https://philosophy.columbian.gwu.edu/

**The George Washington University,** Columbian College of Arts and Sciences, Trachtenberg School of Public Policy and Public Administration, Washington, DC 20052. Offers public administration (MPA); public policy (MPP); public policy and administration (PhD); JD/MPP; MPA/JD; PhD/MPP. *Program availability:* Part-time, evening/weekend, online learning. *Faculty:* 20 full-time (11 women), 12 part-time/adjunct (5 women). *Students:* 148 full-time (96 women), 119 part-time (73 women); includes 72 minority (25 Black or African American, non-Hispanic/Latino; 2 American Indian or Alaska Native,

non-Hispanic/Latino; 21 Asian, non-Hispanic/Latino; 16 Hispanic/Latino; 1 Native Hawaiian or other Pacific Islander, non-Hispanic/Latino; 7 Two or more races, non-Hispanic/Latino), 24 international. Average age 27. 548 applicants, 80% accepted, 98 enrolled. In 2016, 122 master's, 13 doctorates awarded. *Degree requirements:* For master's, capstone project; for doctorate, comprehensive exam, thesis/dissertation. *Entrance requirements:* For master's and doctorate, minimum GPA of 3.0. Additional exam requirements/recommendations for international students: Required—TOEFL (minimum score 600 paper-based; 100 iBT). *Application deadline:* For fall admission, 1/5 priority date for domestic and international students; for spring admission, 10/1 priority date for domestic students, 10/1 for international students. Application fee: $75. Electronic applications accepted. *Financial support:* In 2016–17, 57 students received support. Fellowships, research assistantships, teaching assistantships, Federal Work-Study, scholarships/grants, health care benefits, and unspecified assistantships available. Financial award application deadline: 1/5; financial award applicants required to submit FAFSA. *Faculty research:* Education policy, budget and finance, health policy, regulatory policy, program evaluation. *Unit head:* Dr. Kathyrn E. Newcomer, Director, 202-994-3959, Fax: 202-994-6792, E-mail: newcomer@gwu.edu. *Application contact:* Denee' Bottoms, Assistant Director of Graduate Studies, 202-994-6662, Fax: 202-994-6792, E-mail: dbottoms@gwu.edu. Website: http://www.tspppa.gwu.edu/

**The George Washington University,** School of Business, Department of Strategic Management and Public Policy, Washington, DC 20052. Offers MBA, PhD. *Accreditation:* NASPAA. *Program availability:* Part-time, evening/weekend. *Faculty:* 13 full-time (4 women). *Students:* 178 full-time (71 women), 1 (woman) part-time; includes 34 minority (8 Black or African American, non-Hispanic/Latino; 1 American Indian or Alaska Native, non-Hispanic/Latino; 11 Asian, non-Hispanic/Latino; 9 Hispanic/Latino; 5 Two or more races, non-Hispanic/Latino), 86 international. Average age 29. 522 applicants, 51% accepted, 89 enrolled. In 2016, 93 master's awarded. *Degree requirements:* For doctorate, thesis/dissertation. *Entrance requirements:* For master's, GMAT; for doctorate, GMAT or GRE. Additional exam requirements/recommendations for international students: Required—TOEFL. *Application deadline:* For fall admission, 4/1 priority date for domestic students; for spring admission, 10/1 for domestic students. Applications are processed on a rolling basis. Application fee: $75. *Financial support:* In 2016–17, 1 student received support. Fellowships, teaching assistantships, career-related internships or fieldwork, Federal Work-Study, and institutionally sponsored loans available. Financial award application deadline: 4/1. *Unit head:* Dr. Jennifer Griffin, Chair, 202-994-2536, E-mail: jgriffin@gwu.edu. *Application contact:* Christopher Storer, Executive Director, Graduate Admissions, 202-994-1212, E-mail: gwmba@gwu.edu. Website: http://business.gwu.edu/smpp/

**Georgia Institute of Technology,** Graduate Studies, Ivan Allen College of Liberal Arts, School of Public Policy, Atlanta, GA 30332-0001. Offers MS, PhD. *Program availability:* Part-time. Terminal master's awarded for partial completion of doctoral program. *Degree requirements:* For master's, professional paper, public policy workshop or thesis; internship; minimum overall GPA of 3.0; for doctorate, comprehensive exam, thesis/dissertation, minimum overall GPA of 3.0, one year of full-time residency. *Entrance requirements:* For master's and doctorate, GRE, three letters of recommendation, transcripts from each college/university attended, essays. Additional exam requirements/recommendations for international students: Required—TOEFL (minimum score 600 paper-based; 100 iBT). Electronic applications accepted. *Faculty research:* National/regional science and technology policy, environmental policy, urban policy and planning, telecommunications policy.

**Georgia State University,** Andrew Young School of Policy Studies, Department of Public Management and Policy, Atlanta, GA 30303. Offers criminal justice (MPA); disaster management (Certificate); disaster policy (MPA); environmental policy (PhD); health policy (PhD); management and finance (MPA); nonprofit management (MPA, Certificate); nonprofit policy (MPA); planning and economic development (MPP, Certificate); policy analysis and evaluation (MPA), including planning and economic development; public and nonprofit management (PhD); public finance and budgeting (PhD), including science and technology policy, urban and regional economic development; public finance policy (MPA), including social policy; public health (MPA). *Accreditation:* NASPAA (one or more programs are accredited). *Program availability:* Part-time. *Faculty:* 17 full-time (9 women). *Students:* 123 full-time (77 women), 79 part-time (49 women); includes 84 minority (59 Black or African American, non-Hispanic/Latino; 5 Asian, non-Hispanic/Latino; 14 Hispanic/Latino; 6 Two or more races, non-Hispanic/Latino), 34 international. Average age 30. 237 applicants, 60% accepted, 65 enrolled. In 2016, 59 master's, 4 doctorates, 8 other advanced degrees awarded. Terminal master's awarded for partial completion of doctoral program. *Degree requirements:* For master's, thesis optional; for doctorate, comprehensive exam, thesis/dissertation. *Entrance requirements:* For master's and doctorate, GRE. Additional exam requirements/recommendations for international students: Required—TOEFL (minimum score 603 paper-based; 100 iBT) or IELTS (minimum score 7). *Application deadline:* For fall admission, 1/15 for domestic and international students. Application fee: $50. Electronic applications accepted. *Expenses:* Tuition, state resident: full-time $6876; part-time $382 per credit hour. Tuition, nonresident: full-time $22,374; part-time $1243 per credit hour. *Required fees:* $2128; $1064 per term. Part-time tuition and fees vary according to course load and program. *Financial support:* In 2016–17, fellowships (averaging $8,194 per year), research assistantships (averaging $8,068 per year), teaching assistantships (averaging $3,600 per year) were awarded; institutionally sponsored loans, scholarships/grants, health care benefits, and unspecified assistantships also available. Financial award application deadline: 2/1. *Faculty research:* Public budgeting and finance, public management, nonprofit management, performance measurement and management, urban development. *Unit head:* Dr. Carolyn Bourdeaux, Chair and Professor, 404-413-0013, Fax: 404-413-0104, E-mail: cbourdeaux@gsu.edu.
Website: http://aysps.gsu.edu/pmap/

**The Graduate Center, City University of New York,** Graduate Studies, Interdisciplinary Studies, New York, NY 10016-4039. Offers language in social context (PhD); medieval studies (PhD); public policy (MA, PhD); urban studies (MA, PhD); women's studies (MA, PhD). Terminal master's awarded for partial completion of doctoral program. *Degree requirements:* For master's, thesis; for doctorate, comprehensive exam, thesis/dissertation. *Entrance requirements:* For master's and doctorate, GRE General Test.

**Harvard University,** Graduate School of Arts and Sciences and John F. Kennedy School of Government, Committee on Public Policy, Cambridge, MA 02138. Offers PhD. *Degree requirements:* For doctorate, thesis/dissertation, exams. *Entrance requirements:* For doctorate, GRE General Test or GMAT, Harvard MPP degree. Additional exam requirements/recommendations for international students: Required—TOEFL.

**Harvard University,** Graduate School of Arts and Sciences, Program in Social Policy, Cambridge, MA 02138. Offers PhD.

**Harvard University,** John F. Kennedy School of Government, Doctoral Programs in Government, Cambridge, MA 02138. Offers political economy and government (PhD); public policy (PhD). *Students:* 20 full-time (11 women); includes 3 minority (all Two or more races, non-Hispanic/Latino), 6 international. Average age 27. 243 applicants, 7%

accepted, 12 enrolled. *Degree requirements:* For doctorate, comprehensive exam, thesis/dissertation. *Entrance requirements:* For doctorate, GRE General Test, course work in macroeconomics, multi-variable calculus. Additional exam requirements/recommendations for international students: Required—TOEFL (minimum score 600 paper-based; 100 iBT), TWE. *Application deadline:* For fall admission, 12/1 for domestic students. Application fee: $100. Electronic applications accepted. *Financial support:* Fellowships, research assistantships, teaching assistantships, Federal Work-Study, institutionally sponsored loans, scholarships/grants, health care benefits, and unspecified assistantships available. *Unit head:* Nicole Tateosian, Director, 617-495-1190, E-mail: nicole_tateosian@harvard.edu. *Application contact:* 617-495-1155, Fax: 617-496-1165, E-mail: ksg_admissions@harvard.edu.
Website: http://www.hks.harvard.edu/

**Harvard University,** John F. Kennedy School of Government, Program in Public Policy, Cambridge, MA 02138. Offers MPP, JD/MPP, MBA/MPP, MD/MPP. *Students:* 432 full-time (204 women); includes 93 minority (15 Black or African American, non-Hispanic/Latino; 1 American Indian or Alaska Native, non-Hispanic/Latino; 41 Asian, non-Hispanic/Latino; 23 Hispanic/Latino; 1 Native Hawaiian or other Pacific Islander, non-Hispanic/Latino; 12 Two or more races, non-Hispanic/Latino), 131 international. Average age 27. 1,656 applicants, 24% accepted, 254 enrolled. In 2016, 196 master's awarded. *Entrance requirements:* For master's, GMAT or GRE General Test. Additional exam requirements/recommendations for international students: Required—TOEFL (minimum score 600 paper-based; 100 iBT), TWE. *Application deadline:* For fall admission, 12/1 for domestic students. Application fee: $100. Electronic applications accepted. *Financial support:* In 2016–17, 200 fellowships (averaging $37,373 per year) were awarded; research assistantships, teaching assistantships, career-related internships or fieldwork, Federal Work-Study, institutionally sponsored loans, scholarships/grants, health care benefits, and unspecified assistantships also available. Financial award application deadline: 2/24; financial award applicants required to submit CSS PROFILE or FAFSA. *Unit head:* Eleni Cortis, Director, 617-496-8593, E-mail: eleni_cortis@hks.harvard.edu. *Application contact:* 617-495-1155. Website: http://www.hks.harvard.edu/

**Indiana University Bloomington,** School of Public and Environmental Affairs, Public Affairs Programs, Bloomington, IN 47405. Offers economic development (MPA); energy (MPA); environmental policy (PhD); environmental policy and natural resource management (MPA); information systems (MPA); international development (MPA); local government management (MPA); nonprofit management (MPA, Certificate); policy analysis (MPA); public budgeting and financial management (Certificate); public finance (PhD); public financial administration (MPA); public management (MPA, PhD, Certificate); public policy analysis (PhD); social entrepreneurship (Certificate); specialized public affairs (MPA); sustainability and sustainable development (MPA); JD/MPA; MPA/MA; MPA/MIS; MPA/MLS; MSES/MPA. *Accreditation:* NASPAA (one or more programs are accredited). *Program availability:* Part-time. *Degree requirements:* For master's, capstone, internship; for doctorate, comprehensive exam, thesis/dissertation. *Entrance requirements:* For master's, GRE General Test or GMAT, official transcripts, 3 letters of recommendation, resume, personal statement; for doctorate, GRE General Test, official transcripts, 3 letters of recommendation, statement of purpose. Additional exam requirements/recommendations for international students: Required—TOEFL (minimum score 600 paper-based; 96 iBT); Recommended—IELTS (minimum score 7). Electronic applications accepted. *Faculty research:* International development, environmental policy and resource management, policy analysis, public finance, public management, urban management, nonprofit management, energy policy, social policy, public finance.

**Indiana University Kokomo,** Department of Public Administration and Health Management, Kokomo, IN 46904. Offers health management (MPM, Graduate Certificate); public management (Graduate Certificate); public management and policy (MPM). *Program availability:* Part-time, evening/weekend. *Students:* 11 full-time (9 women), 15 part-time (12 women); includes 4 minority (3 Black or African American, non-Hispanic/Latino; 1 Hispanic/Latino), 2 international. Average age 34. 13 applicants, 100% accepted, 8 enrolled. In 2016, 7 master's, 2 other advanced degrees awarded. *Entrance requirements:* For master's, GRE/GMAT for GPAs lower than 3.0, letters of recommendation. Additional exam requirements/recommendations for international students: Required—TOEFL (minimum score 550 paper-based; 73 iBT). *Application deadline:* For fall admission, 6/15 for domestic students, 6/1 for international students; for spring admission, 11/1 for domestic students, 10/1 for international students; for summer admission, 3/1 for domestic students. Application fee: $40 ($60 for international students). Electronic applications accepted. *Expenses:* $329.79 per credit hour in-state; $739.85 per credit hour out-of-state. *Financial support:* Scholarships/grants available. Financial award application deadline: 3/10; financial award applicants required to submit FAFSA. *Unit head:* Alan Krabbenhoft, Dean, 765-455-9275, E-mail: akrabbe@iuk.edu. *Application contact:* Gloria Preece, Director of the MPM Program, 765-455-9269, E-mail: gpreece@iuk.edu.
Website: http://www.iuk.edu/public-administration-and-health-management/index.php

**Indiana University–Purdue University Fort Wayne,** College of Education and Public Policy, Department of Public Policy, Fort Wayne, IN 46805-1499. Offers public management (MPM, Certificate). *Program availability:* Part-time. *Degree requirements:* For master's, internship. *Entrance requirements:* For master's, GRE General Test or GMAT, minimum GPA of 3.0, 3 letters of reference. Additional exam requirements/recommendations for international students: Required—TOEFL (minimum score 550 paper-based; 79 iBT). *Faculty research:* Opioid safety, homeless and stigma.

**The Institute of World Politics,** Graduate Programs in National Security, Intelligence, and International Affairs, Washington, DC 20036. Offers American foreign policy (Certificate); comparative political culture (Certificate); counterintelligence (Certificate); democracy building (Certificate); intelligence (Certificate); international politics (Certificate); national security affairs (Certificate); public diplomacy and political warfare (Certificate); statecraft and national security affairs (MA); statecraft and world politics (MA); strategic intelligence studies (MA). *Program availability:* Part-time, evening/weekend. *Degree requirements:* For master's, comprehensive exam, thesis optional. *Entrance requirements:* For master's, GRE General Test. Additional exam requirements/recommendations for international students: Required—TOEFL. Electronic applications accepted. *Faculty research:* Intelligence, national security, statecraft.

**Jackson State University,** Graduate School, College of Public Service, Department of Public Policy and Administration, Jackson, MS 39217. Offers public administration (PhD); public policy and administration (MPPA). *Accreditation:* NASPAA (one or more programs are accredited). *Program availability:* Evening/weekend. *Degree requirements:* For master's, comprehensive exam, thesis optional; for doctorate, comprehensive exam, thesis/dissertation. *Entrance requirements:* For master's, GRE General Test; for doctorate, GRE, GMAT, MAT. Additional exam requirements/recommendations for international students: Required—TOEFL (minimum score 520 paper-based; 67 iBT). *Application deadline:* For fall admission, 3/1 for domestic and international students; for spring admission, 10/1 for domestic and international students. Application fee: $25. *Expenses:* Tuition, state resident: full-time $7141. Tuition, nonresident: full-time $17,494. *Required fees:* $1080. Tuition and fees vary according to class time, course level, course load, degree level, campus/location, program and student level. *Financial support:* Career-related internships or fieldwork,

Federal Work-Study, scholarships/grants, tuition waivers (full and partial), and unspecified assistantships available. Support available to part-time students. Financial award application deadline: 3/1; financial award applicants required to submit FAFSA. *Unit head:* Dr. Johnny Gilleylen, Sr., Chair, 601-432-6277, Fax: 601-432-6322, E-mail: ppa@jsums.edu. *Application contact:* Fatoumatta Sisay, Manager of Graduate Admissions, 601-979-0342, Fax: 601-979-4325, E-mail: fatoumatta.sisay@jsums.edu. Website: http://www.jsums.edu/publicpolicy/

**Jacksonville University,** Public Policy Institute, Jacksonville, FL 32211. Offers MPP, MBA/MPP, MPP/JD, MPP/MS. MPP/JD offered in partnership with Florida Coastal School of Law; MBA/MPP with Davis College of Business; MPP/MS with Marine Science Research Institute. *Program availability:* Part-time, evening/weekend. *Faculty:* 2 part-time/adjunct (0 women). *Students:* 10 full-time (4 women), 19 part-time (10 women); includes 6 minority (2 Black or African American, non-Hispanic/Latino; 1 Asian, non-Hispanic/Latino; 2 Hispanic/Latino; 1 Two or more races, non-Hispanic/Latino). Average age 36. 43 applicants, 51% accepted, 19 enrolled. In 2016, 10 master's awarded. *Degree requirements:* For master's, thesis, internship, capstone project. *Entrance requirements:* For master's, GRE, GMAT, LSAT, resume, essay, transcripts, 2 references. Additional exam requirements/recommendations for international students: Recommended—TOEFL (minimum score 540 paper-based; 76 iBT). *Application deadline:* For fall admission, 4/1 priority date for domestic students. Applications are processed on a rolling basis. Application fee: $50. Electronic applications accepted. *Expenses:* $740 per credit hour. *Financial support:* In 2016–17, 11 students received support. Career-related internships or fieldwork, scholarships/grants, and unspecified assistantships available. Financial award application deadline: 4/1. *Unit head:* Richard A. Mullaney, Director, 904-256-7342, E-mail: rmullan1@ju.edu. *Application contact:* Allana Forte, Director of Admissions and Recruitment, 904-256-7000, E-mail: admiss@ju.edu. Website: http://www.ju.edu/ppi/

**John Jay College of Criminal Justice of the City University of New York,** Graduate Studies, Programs in Criminal Justice, New York, NY 10019. Offers criminal justice (MA, PhD); criminology and deviance (PhD); forensic psychology (PhD); forensic science (PhD); international crime and justice (MA); law and philosophy (PhD); organizational behavior (PhD); public policy (PhD). *Program availability:* Part-time, evening/weekend. Terminal master's awarded for partial completion of doctoral program. *Degree requirements:* For master's, thesis or alternative; for doctorate, one foreign language, thesis/dissertation. *Entrance requirements:* For master's, GRE General Test, minimum B average; for doctorate, GRE General Test. Additional exam requirements/recommendations for international students: Required—TOEFL (minimum score 500 paper-based).

**Johns Hopkins University,** Bloomberg School of Public Health, Department of Health Policy and Management, Baltimore, MD 21205-1996. Offers bioethics and policy (PhD); health and public policy (PhD); health care management and leadership (Dr PH); health economics (MHS); health economics and policy (PhD); health finance and management (MHA); health policy (MSPH); health services research and policy (PhD); public policy (MPP). *Accreditation:* CAHME (one or more programs are accredited). *Program availability:* Part-time. *Degree requirements:* For master's, thesis (for some programs), internship (for some programs); for doctorate, comprehensive exam, thesis/dissertation, 1-year full-time residency (for some programs), oral and written exams. *Entrance requirements:* For master's, GRE General Test or GMAT, 3 letters of recommendation, curriculum vitae/resume; for doctorate, GRE General Test or GMAT, 3 letters of recommendation, curriculum vitae, transcripts. Additional exam requirements/recommendations for international students: Recommended—TOEFL (minimum score 600 paper-based; 100 iBT), IELTS. Electronic applications accepted. *Faculty research:* Quality of care and health outcomes, health care finance and technology, health disparities and vulnerable populations, injury prevention, health policy and health care policy.

**Liberty University,** Helms School of Government, Lynchburg, VA 24515. Offers public administration (MS). *Program availability:* Part-time, online learning. *Students:* 279 full-time (128 women), 626 part-time (233 women); includes 259 minority (163 Black or African American, non-Hispanic/Latino; 10 American Indian or Alaska Native, non-Hispanic/Latino; 10 Asian, non-Hispanic/Latino; 11 Hispanic/Latino; 1 Native Hawaiian or other Pacific Islander, non-Hispanic/Latino; 28 Two or more races, non-Hispanic/Latino), 12 international. Average age 35. 713 applicants, 51% accepted, 182 enrolled. In 2016, 256 master's awarded. *Entrance requirements:* For master's, minimum undergraduate GPA of 3.0. Additional exam requirements/recommendations for international students: Required—TOEFL (minimum score 600 paper-based; 100 iBT). *Application deadline:* Applications are processed on a rolling basis. Application fee: $50. Electronic applications accepted. *Unit head:* Shawn D. Akers, Dean, 434-592-4986. *Application contact:* Jay Bridge, Director of Admissions, 800-424-9595, Fax: 800-628-7977, E-mail: gradadmissions@liberty.edu.

**Lincoln University,** Graduate Studies, Jefferson City, MO 65101. Offers business administration (MBA), including accounting, management, management information systems, public administration/policy; elementary teaching (M Ed); environmental science (MS); guidance and counseling (M Ed), including community/agency counseling, elementary school, secondary school; higher education (MA); history (MA); integrated agricultural systems (MS); middle school (M Ed); natural sciences (MS); secondary teaching (M Ed); sociology (MA); sociology/criminal justice (MA). *Program availability:* Part-time, evening/weekend, 100% online, blended/hybrid learning. *Students:* 50 full-time (29 women), 68 part-time (39 women); includes 40 minority (37 Black or African American, non-Hispanic/Latino; 1 Asian, non-Hispanic/Latino; 2 Two or more races, non-Hispanic/Latino), 14 international. Average age 39. 75 applicants, 80% accepted, 34 enrolled. In 2016, 51 master's awarded. *Degree requirements:* For master's, comprehensive exam, thesis optional. *Entrance requirements:* For master's, GRE, MAT or GMAT, minimum GPA of 2.75 overall, 3.0 in courses related to specialization; 3 letters of recommendation; minimum C average in English composition; personal statement of purpose. Additional exam requirements/recommendations for international students: Required—TOEFL (minimum score 500 paper-based; 61 iBT), IELTS (minimum score 5.5), Michigan English Language Assessment Battery (minimum score 80). *Application deadline:* For fall admission, 7/1 priority date for domestic students, 5/1 priority date for international students; for spring admission, 11/1 priority date for domestic students, 10/1 priority date for international students; for summer admission, 6/1 priority date for domestic students. Applications are processed on a rolling basis. Application fee: $30. Electronic applications accepted. *Expenses:* Tuition, state resident: full-time $6840; part-time $5130 per year. Tuition, nonresident: full-time $12,720; part-time $9540 per year. *Required fees:* $852; $811 per unit. Tuition and fees vary according to course load. *Financial support:* In 2016–17, 2 fellowships with tuition reimbursements, 8 research assistantships with tuition reimbursements were awarded; Federal Work-Study, scholarships/grants, and unspecified assistantships also available. Support available to part-time students. Financial award application deadline: 3/1; financial award applicants required to submit FAFSA. *Unit head:* Dr. Rolundus R. Rice, Dean, 573-681-5247, Fax: 573-681-5106, E-mail: gradschool@lincolnu.edu. *Application contact:* Irasema Steck, Administrative Assistant, 573-681-5247, Fax: 573-681-5106, E-mail: gradschool@lincolnu.edu.
Website: http://www.lincolnu.edu/web/graduate-studies/graduate-studies

## Public Policy

**Lipscomb University,** School of Public Policy, Nashville, TN 37204-3951. Offers leadership and public service (MA). *Faculty:* 6 full-time (2 women), 3 part-time/adjunct (1 woman). *Students:* 22 full-time (15 women); includes 8 minority (7 Black or African American, non-Hispanic/Latino; 1 Hispanic/Latino). Average age 28. *Entrance requirements:* For master's, GRE or GMAT, references, resume, goals statement. Additional exam requirements/recommendations for international students: Required— TOEFL (minimum score 550 paper-based). *Application deadline:* Applications are processed on a rolling basis. Application fee: $50 ($75 for international students). Electronic applications accepted. *Expenses:* $1,290 per hour. *Faculty research:* African American family strengths and their relationship to health and mental health prevention and intervention, application of hope theories, systems theories and positive psychology principles in systems and organizations at multiples levels. *Unit head:* Dr. Kristine LaLonde, Academic Director, 615-966-6692, E-mail: kristine.lalonde@lipscomb.edu. *Application contact:* Amy Goode, New Student Enrollment Manager, 615-966-6691, E-mail: amy.goode@lipscomb.edu.

**London Metropolitan University,** Graduate Programs, London, United Kingdom. Offers applied psychology (M Sc); architecture (MA); biomedical science (M Sc); blood science (M Sc); cancer pharmacology (M Sc); computer networking and cyber security (M Sc); computing and information systems (M Sc); conference interpreting (MA); counter-terrorism studies (M Sc); creative, digital and professional writing (MA); crime, violence and prevention (M Sc); criminology (M Sc); curating contemporary art (MA); data analytics (M Sc); digital media (MA); early childhood studies (MA); education (MA, Ed D); financial services law, regulation and compliance (LL M); food science (M Sc); forensic psychology (M Sc); health and social care management and policy (M Sc); human nutrition (M Sc); human resource management (MA); human rights and international conflict (MA); information technology (M Sc); intelligence and security studies (M Sc); international oil, gas and energy law (LL M); international relations (MA); interpreting (MA); learning and teaching in higher education (MA); legal practice (LL M); media and entertainment law (LL M); organizational and consumer psychology (M Sc); psychological therapy (M Sc); psychology of mental health (M Sc); public health (M Sc); public policy and management (MPA); security studies (M Sc); social work (M Sc); spatial planning and urban design (MA); sports therapy (M Sc); supporting older children and young people with dyslexia (MA); teaching languages (MA), including Arabic, English; translation (MA); woman and child abuse (MA).

**Loyola University Chicago,** Graduate School, Program in Public Policy, Chicago, IL 60660. Offers MPP. *Program availability:* Part-time, evening/weekend. *Faculty:* 2 full-time (both women), 3 part-time/adjunct (1 woman). *Students:* 8 full-time (4 women), 5 part-time (2 women); includes 4 minority (1 American Indian or Alaska Native, non-Hispanic/Latino; 1 Asian, non-Hispanic/Latino; 2 Hispanic/Latino), 1 international. Average age 27. 24 applicants, 71% accepted, 7 enrolled. In 2016, 13 master's awarded. *Degree requirements:* For master's, internship or capstone experience. *Entrance requirements:* For master's, GRE, three letters of recommendation, transcripts, statement of purpose. Additional exam requirements/recommendations for international students: Required—TOEFL. *Application deadline:* For fall admission, 6/30 for domestic students. Applications are processed on a rolling basis. Application fee: $0. Electronic applications accepted. *Expenses: Tuition:* Full-time $18,594. *Required fees:* $848. Part-time tuition and fees vary according to course load, degree level and program. *Financial support:* In 2016–17, 5 students received support, including 5 fellowships (averaging $5,000 per year), 1 research assistantship with partial tuition reimbursement available (averaging $12,000 per year); unspecified assistantships and Fulbright scholarships also available. Financial award application deadline: 2/15; financial award applicants required to submit FAFSA. *Faculty research:* Urban public policy. *Unit head:* Dr. Annette Steinacker, Director, 773-508-3396. *Application contact:* Ron Martin, Assistant Director of Enrollment Management, 312-915-8950, Fax: 312-915-8905, E-mail: gradapp@luc.edu.

**McMaster University,** School of Graduate Studies, Faculty of Social Sciences, Department of Political Science, Hamilton, ON L8S 4M2, Canada. Offers international relations (PhD); political science (MA); public and the global economy (MA); public policy (PhD); public policy and administration (MA). MA program in public policy and administration offered jointly with University of Guelph. *Program availability:* Part-time. *Degree requirements:* For master's, thesis or alternative. *Entrance requirements:* For master's, minimum B+ average. Additional exam requirements/recommendations for international students: Required—TOEFL (minimum score 580 paper-based). *Faculty research:* Organizational theory, internationalization of public policy, water resource policies, political interest intermediation, comparative politics.

**Mills College,** Graduate Studies, Joint MBA/MPP Program, Oakland, CA 94613-1000. Offers MBA/MPP. *Faculty:* 4 full-time (3 women), 14 part-time/adjunct (8 women). *Students:* 12 full-time (10 women), 3 part-time (all women); includes 8 minority (2 Black or African American, non-Hispanic/Latino; 5 Hispanic/Latino; 1 Two or more races, non-Hispanic/Latino). Average age 33. 12 applicants, 83% accepted, 6 enrolled. *Entrance requirements:* Additional exam requirements/recommendations for international students: Required—TOEFL (minimum score 550 paper-based; 80 iBT) or IELTS (minimum score 6). *Application deadline:* For winter admission, 2/1 priority date for domestic students, 12/15 priority date for international students. Application fee: $50. Electronic applications accepted. *Expenses:* Contact institution. *Financial support:* In 2016–17, 17 students received support, including 17 fellowships (averaging $10,220 per year). Financial award application deadline: 2/1; financial award applicants required to submit FAFSA. *Faculty research:* Diversity and inclusion, applied econometrics, non-profit management, business communication and effective public speaking, social media, Internet marketing, organizational and cultural chance, economics of the family, urbanization and land conservation, gender and science, comparative race and ethnic relations. *Unit head:* Lori Bamberger, Professor of Public Policy, 510-430-3375, Fax: 510-430-2159, E-mail: lbamberger@mills.edu. *Application contact:* Robynne Lofton, Director of Admissions, 510-430-3295, Fax: 510-430-2159, E-mail: grad-admission@mills.edu. Website: http://www.mills.edu/academics/graduate/ppol/program/joint_MPPMBA.php

**Mills College,** Graduate Studies, Program in Public Policy, Oakland, CA 94613-1000. Offers MPP. *Faculty:* 1 full-time (0 women), 7 part-time/adjunct (5 women). *Students:* 28 full-time (25 women); includes 11 minority (2 Black or African American, non-Hispanic/Latino; 1 American Indian or Alaska Native, non-Hispanic/Latino; 1 Asian, non-Hispanic/Latino; 6 Hispanic/Latino; 1 Two or more races, non-Hispanic/Latino). Average age 33. 37 applicants, 92% accepted, 18 enrolled. In 2016, 15 master's awarded. *Degree requirements:* For master's, thesis. *Entrance requirements:* For master's, GRE, SAT, or ACT, statement of purpose, resume. Additional exam requirements/recommendations for international students: Required—TOEFL (minimum score 550 paper-based; 80 iBT) or IELTS (minimum score 6). *Application deadline:* For fall admission, 1/15 for domestic students, 12/15 for international students. Applications are processed on a rolling basis. Application fee: $50. Electronic applications accepted. *Expenses: Tuition:* Full-time $31,620. *Required fees:* $1118. Tuition and fees vary according to course load, degree level and program. *Financial support:* In 2016–17, 32 students received support, including 32 fellowships with tuition reimbursements available (averaging $8,607 per year), 6 teaching assistantships with tuition reimbursements available (averaging $1,900 per year); scholarships/grants also available. Financial award application deadline: 2/1;

financial award applicants required to submit FAFSA. *Faculty research:* Organizational culture and change, economics of the family, urbanization and land conservation, gender and science, comparative race and ethnic relations. *Unit head:* Lori Bamberger, Department Chair, 510-430-3375, E-mail: lbamberger@mills.edu. *Application contact:* Robynne Lofton, Director of Admissions, 510-430-3295, Fax: 510-430-2159, E-mail: grad-admission@mills.edu.
Website: http://www.mills.edu/publicpolicy

**Mississippi State University,** College of Arts and Sciences, Department of Political Science and Public Administration, Mississippi State, MS 39762. Offers political science (MA); public policy and administration (MPPA, PhD). *Accreditation:* NASPAA (one or more programs are accredited). *Program availability:* Evening/weekend, blended/hybrid learning. *Faculty:* 14 full-time (4 women), 1 part-time/adjunct (0 women). *Students:* 34 full-time (18 women), 35 part-time (18 women); includes 26 minority (22 Black or African American, non-Hispanic/Latino; 1 American Indian or Alaska Native, non-Hispanic/Latino; 3 Hispanic/Latino), 4 international. Average age 31. 33 applicants, 61% accepted, 18 enrolled. In 2016, 22 master's, 7 doctorates awarded. *Degree requirements:* For master's, thesis optional, comprehensive oral or written exam; for doctorate, thesis/dissertation, comprehensive oral and written exam. *Entrance requirements:* For master's, GRE, minimum GPA of 3.0 on the last two years of undergraduate courses or graduate work; for doctorate, GRE General Test, minimum graduate GPA of 3.35. Additional exam requirements/recommendations for international students: Required—TOEFL (minimum score 600 paper-based; 100 iBT); Recommended—IELTS (minimum score 7.5). *Application deadline:* For fall admission, 8/1 priority date for domestic students, 5/1 for international students; for spring admission, 12/1 priority date for domestic students, 9/1 for international students. Applications are processed on a rolling basis. Application fee: $60. Electronic applications accepted. *Expenses:* Tuition, state resident: full-time $7670; part-time $852.50 per credit hour. Tuition, nonresident: full-time $20,790; part-time $2310.50 per credit hour. Part-time tuition and fees vary according to course load. *Financial support:* In 2016–17, 6 research assistantships with full tuition reimbursements (averaging $9,085 per year), 2 teaching assistantships with full tuition reimbursements (averaging $8,920 per year) were awarded; Federal Work-Study, institutionally sponsored loans, scholarships/grants, and unspecified assistantships also available. Financial award application deadline: 4/1; financial award applicants required to submit FAFSA. *Faculty research:* American politics, international relations, state and local government, comparative government, public administration. *Total annual research expenditures:* $977,000. *Unit head:* Dr. P. Edward French, Interim Department Head, 662-325-2711, Fax: 662-325-2716, E-mail: efrench@pspa.msstate.edu. *Application contact:* Nathan Drake, Admissions and Enrollment Assistant, 662-325-3804, E-mail: ndrake@grad.msstate.edu.
Website: http://www.pspa.msstate.edu/

**Monmouth University,** Graduate Studies, Department of Public Policy, West Long Branch, NJ 07764-1898. Offers MA. *Program availability:* Part-time, evening/weekend. *Degree requirements:* For master's, comprehensive exam (for some programs), thesis (for some programs). *Entrance requirements:* For master's, minimum overall GPA of 2.75, personal statement (500 words maximum) on goals and interests in field, two letters of recommendation. Additional exam requirements/recommendations for international students: Required—TOEFL (minimum score 550 paper-based, 79 iBT), IELTS (minimum score 6), Michigan English Language Assessment Battery (minimum score 77) or Certificate of Advanced English(minimum score B2). Electronic applications accepted. *Faculty research:* Political theory, international relations and comparative politics, globalization, politics of language, family sociology, race-class-gender studies, the U.S. Senate and impact of domestic politics on U.S. foreign policy.

**Morehead State University,** Graduate Programs, College of Business and Public Affairs, School of Public Affairs, Morehead, KY 40351. Offers public policy (MPA). *Accreditation:* NASPAA. *Program availability:* Part-time, evening/weekend. *Degree requirements:* For master's, comprehensive exam, thesis. *Entrance requirements:* For master's, GRE, thesis (two-page paper to be used as writing sample on personal, education or career goals). Additional exam requirements/recommendations for international students: Required—TOEFL (minimum score 500 paper-based). Electronic applications accepted.

**National Louis University,** College of Arts and Sciences, Chicago, IL 60603. Offers adult education (Ed D); counseling and human services (MS); language and academic development (M Ed, Certificate); psychology (MA, PhD, Certificate); public policy (MA); written communication (MS, Certificate). *Program availability:* Part-time, evening/weekend, online learning. *Degree requirements:* For master's and Certificate, comprehensive exam (for some programs), thesis (for some programs); for doctorate, thesis/dissertation. *Entrance requirements:* For master's, MAT or GRE, 3 professional or academic references, interview, minimum GPA of 3.0; for doctorate, GRE General Test, MAT, or Watson-Glaser Critical Thinking Appraisal, three professional or academic references, statement of academic and professional goals, 3 years of experience in field, interview, master's degree, resume, writing sample; for Certificate, GRE, MAT, or Watson-Glaser Critical Thinking Appraisal, three professional or academic references, statement of academic and professional goals, interview, minimum GPA of 3.0. Additional exam requirements/recommendations for international students: Required— Department of Language Studies Assessment or TOEFL (minimum score 550 paper-based; 79 iBT). Electronic applications accepted.

**New England College,** Program in Public Policy, Henniker, NH 03242-3293. Offers MA. *Program availability:* Part-time, evening/weekend, online learning. *Degree requirements:* For master's, thesis. *Entrance requirements:* Additional exam requirements/recommendations for international students: Recommended—TOEFL (minimum score 600 paper-based). Electronic applications accepted.

**The New School,** Schools of Public Engagement, Program in Public and Urban Policy, New York, NY 10011. Offers public and urban policy (PhD). *Accreditation:* NASPAA. *Program availability:* Part-time, evening/weekend. *Faculty:* 34 full-time (16 women), 8 part-time/adjunct (3 women). *Students:* 50 full-time (39 women), 90 part-time (56 women); includes 63 minority (28 Black or African American, non-Hispanic/Latino; 8 Asian, non-Hispanic/Latino; 22 Hispanic/Latino; 5 Two or more races, non-Hispanic/Latino), 28 international. Average age 32. 146 applicants, 64% accepted, 29 enrolled. In 2016, 6 doctorates awarded. Terminal master's awarded for partial completion of doctoral program. *Degree requirements:* For doctorate, comprehensive exam, thesis/dissertation. *Entrance requirements:* For doctorate, transcripts, recommendation letters, resume, statement of goals and purpose, example of scholarly work. Additional exam requirements/recommendations for international students: Required—TOEFL (minimum score 100 iBT), IELTS (minimum score 7), PTE (minimum score 68). *Application deadline:* For fall admission, 1/15 priority date for domestic and international students. Applications are processed on a rolling basis. Application fee: $50. Electronic applications accepted. *Expenses:* Contact institution. *Financial support:* Fellowships, research assistantships, teaching assistantships, career-related internships or fieldwork, Federal Work-Study, scholarships/grants, and unspecified assistantships available. Support available to part-time students. Financial award application deadline: 2/1; financial award applicants required to submit FAFSA. *Unit head:* Darrick Hamilton, Director, 212-229-5400 Ext. 1514, E-mail: hamiltod@newschool.edu. *Application*

contact: Sharon Greenidge, Assistant Director, 212-229-5400 Ext. 1103, E-mail: greenids@newschool.edu/
Website: http://www.newschool.edu/

**New York University,** Robert F. Wagner Graduate School of Public Service, Executive Master of Public Administration Program, New York, NY 10010. Offers global public policy and management (EMPA); MSW/EMPA. EMPA in global public policy and management offered jointly with University College London. *Accreditation:* AACSB. *Program availability:* Part-time. *Entrance requirements:* Additional exam requirements/recommendations for international students: Required—TOEFL (minimum score 100 iBT), IELTS (minimum score 7.5), TWE. Electronic applications accepted. *Expenses:* Contact institution.

**Northeastern University,** College of Engineering, Boston, MA 02115-5096. Offers bioengineering (MS, PhD); chemical engineering (MS, PhD); civil engineering (MS, PhD); computer engineering (PhD); computer systems engineering (MS); electrical and computer engineering (MS); electrical and computer engineering leadership (MS); electrical engineering (PhD); energy systems (MS); engineering and public policy (MS); engineering management (MS, Certificate); environmental engineering (MS); industrial engineering (MS, PhD); information assurance (PhD); information systems (MS); interdisciplinary engineering (PhD); mechanical engineering (PhD); operations research (MS); telecommunication systems management (MS). *Program availability:* Part-time, online learning. *Faculty:* 202 full-time (59 women), 53 part-time/adjunct (9 women). *Students:* 2,982 full-time (954 women), 192 part-time (38 women). In 2016, 851 master's, 74 doctorates awarded. Application fee: $75. Electronic applications accepted. *Expenses:* $1,471 per credit. *Financial support:* Fellowships, research assistantships, teaching assistantships, career-related internships or fieldwork, scholarships/grants, health care benefits, tuition waivers, and unspecified assistantships available. Support available to part-time students. Financial award applicants required to submit FAFSA. *Unit head:* Dr. Nadine Aubry, Dean, College of Engineering. *Application contact:* Jeffery Hengel, Director of Graduate Admissions, 617-373-2711, E-mail: j.hengel@northeastern.edu.
Website: http://www.coe.neu.edu/academics/graduate-school-engineering

**Northeastern University,** College of Social Sciences and Humanities, Boston, MA 02115. Offers criminology and criminal justice (MSCJ); criminology and justice policy (PhD); economics (MA, PhD); English (MA, PhD); international affairs (MA); law and public policy (PhD); political science (MA, PhD); public administration (MPA); public history (MA); public policy (MPP); security and resilience studies (MS); sociology (MA, PhD); urban and regional policy (MS); urban informatics (MS); world history (MA, PhD); JD/MS. *Program availability:* Online learning. *Faculty:* 234 full-time (114 women), 55 part-time/adjunct (34 women). *Students:* 427 full-time (239 women), 77 part-time (42 women). In 2016, 143 master's, 38 doctorates awarded. *Degree requirements:* For doctorate, variable foreign language requirement, comprehensive exam, thesis/dissertation. *Entrance requirements:* For master's and doctorate, GRE. Additional exam requirements/recommendations for international students: Required—TOEFL, IELTS. Application fee: $75. Electronic applications accepted. *Expenses:* $1,295 per credit. *Financial support:* Teaching assistantships, career-related internships or fieldwork, scholarships/grants, health care benefits, tuition waivers (full and partial), and unspecified assistantships available. Support available to part-time students. Financial award applicants required to submit FAFSA. *Unit head:* Dr. Uta Poiger, Dean, 617-373-5173. *Application contact:* Amber Crowe, Administrative Coordinator, 617-373-5990, Fax: 617-373-7281, E-mail: gradcssh@northeastern.edu.
Website: http://www.northeastern.edu/cssh/graduate

**Northwestern University,** The Graduate School, School of Education and Social Policy, Program in Human Development and Social Policy, Evanston, IL 60208. Offers PhD. Admissions and degrees offered through The Graduate School. *Degree requirements:* For doctorate, comprehensive exam, thesis/dissertation. *Entrance requirements:* For doctorate, GRE General Test. Additional exam requirements/recommendations for international students: Required—TOEFL (minimum score 600 paper-based; 100 iBT). Electronic applications accepted. *Faculty research:* Individual development and the personal narrative; the life course and culture; development, intervention and culture; the life course and policy; analysis of policy effects on lives.

**Northwestern University,** School of Professional Studies, Program in Public Policy and Administration, Evanston, IL 60208. Offers global policy (MA); health services policy (MA); public administration (MA); public policy (MA). *Program availability:* Online learning.

**Norwich University,** College of Graduate and Continuing Studies, Master of Public Administration Program, Northfield, VT 05663. Offers criminal justice and public safety (MPA); fiscal management (MPA); international development and influence (MPA); municipal governance (MPA); nonprofit management (MPA); policy analysis and analytics (MPA); public administration leadership and crisis management (MPA); public works and sustainability (MPA). *Program availability:* Evening/weekend, online only, mostly all online with a week-long residency requirement. *Faculty:* 13 part-time/adjunct (5 women). *Students:* 63 full-time (23 women); includes 9 minority (5 Black or African American, non-Hispanic/Latino; 1 Asian, non-Hispanic/Latino; 1 Hispanic/Latino; 2 Two or more races, non-Hispanic/Latino). Average age 38. 23 applicants, 100% accepted, 15 enrolled. In 2016, 38 master's awarded. *Degree requirements:* For master's, capstone. *Entrance requirements:* For master's, minimum undergraduate GPA of 2.75. Additional exam requirements/recommendations for international students: Required—TOEFL (minimum score 550 paper-based; 80 iBT), IELTS (minimum score 6.5). *Application deadline:* For fall admission, 8/14 for domestic and international students; for winter admission, 11/13 for domestic and international students; for spring admission, 2/12 for domestic and international students; for summer admission, 5/15 for domestic and international students. Electronic applications accepted. *Expenses:* Contact institution. *Financial support:* In 2016-17, 21 students received support. Scholarships/grants available. Financial award application deadline: 8/4; financial award applicants required to submit FAFSA. *Unit head:* Dr. Rosemarie Pelletier, Program Director, 802-485-2767, Fax: 802-485-2533, E-mail: rpellet2@norwich.edu. *Application contact:* Admissions Advisor, 800-460-5597 Ext. 3377, Fax: 802-485-2533, E-mail: mpa@online.norwich.edu.
Website: https://online.norwich.edu/degree-programs/masters/master-public-administration/overview

**The Ohio State University,** Graduate School, John Glenn College of Public Affairs, Columbus, OH 43210. Offers public administration (MA, MPA); public policy and management (PhD). *Accreditation:* NASPAA (one or more programs are accredited). *Program availability:* Part-time. *Faculty:* 20. *Students:* 122 full-time (58 women), 41 part-time (30 women). Average age 31. In 2016, 78 master's, 2 doctorates awarded. *Degree requirements:* For doctorate, comprehensive exam, thesis/dissertation. *Entrance requirements:* For master's, GRE General Test (for MPA), minimum GPA of 3.0 (for MA); for doctorate, GRE General Test. Additional exam requirements/recommendations for international students: Required—TOEFL (minimum score 600 paper-based; 100 iBT); Recommended—IELTS (minimum score 7.5). *Application deadline:* For fall admission, 12/1 priority date for domestic students, 11/30 priority date for international students; for spring admission, 11/15 for domestic and international students; for summer admission, 4/1 for domestic and international students. Applications are processed on a rolling basis. Application

fee: $60 ($70 for international students). Electronic applications accepted. *Financial support:* Fellowships, research assistantships, teaching assistantships, Federal Work-Study, institutionally sponsored loans, and unspecified assistantships available. Support available to part-time students. *Unit head:* Dr. Trevor Brown, Dean, 614-292-4533, Fax: 614-292-4868, E-mail: brown.2296@osu.edu. *Application contact:* Graduate and Professional Admissions, 614-292-6031, Fax: 614-292-3656, E-mail: gpadmissions@osu.edu.
Website: http://glenn.osu.edu/

**Oregon State University,** College of Liberal Arts, Program in Public Policy, Corvallis, OR 97331. Offers energy policy (MPP, PhD); environmental policy (MPP, PhD); international policy (MPP, PhD); law, crime, and policy (MPP, PhD); rural policy (MPP, PhD); science and technology policy (MPP, PhD); social policy (MPP, PhD). *Accreditation:* NASPAA. *Program availability:* Part-time, 100% online. *Faculty:* 37 full-time (16 women), 2 part-time/adjunct (1 woman). *Students:* 59 full-time (41 women); includes 11 minority (1 Black or African American, non-Hispanic/Latino; 2 Asian, non-Hispanic/Latino; 4 Hispanic/Latino; 1 Native Hawaiian or other Pacific Islander, non-Hispanic/Latino; 3 Two or more races, non-Hispanic/Latino), 23 international. Average age 30. 65 applicants, 37% accepted, 14 enrolled. In 2016, 24 master's, 1 doctorate awarded. *Degree requirements:* For doctorate, thesis/dissertation. *Entrance requirements:* For master's and doctorate, GRE. Additional exam requirements/recommendations for international students: Required—TOEFL, IELTS (minimum score 6.5). *Application deadline:* For fall admission, 8/1 for domestic students, 4/1 for international students; for winter admission, 12/1 for domestic students, 7/1 for international students; for spring admission, 2/1 for domestic students, 10/1 for international students; for summer admission, 5/1 for domestic students, 1/1 for international students. Application fee: $75 ($85 for international students). *Expenses:* Tuition, state resident: full-time $12,150; part-time $450 per credit. Tuition, nonresident: full-time $21,789; part-time $807 per credit. *Required fees:* $1651; $1507 per credit. One-time fee: $350. Tuition and fees vary according to course load, campus/location and program. *Financial support:* Application deadline: 1/15. *Unit head:* Dr. Denise Lach, Director. *Application contact:* Dr. Brent Steel, Professor and Director, Public Policy Graduate Program, 541-737-6133, E-mail: schoolofpublicpolicy@oregonstate.edu.
Website: http://oregonstate.edu/cla/spp/

**Pepperdine University,** School of Public Policy, Malibu, CA 90263. Offers American politics (MPP); economics (MPP); international relations (MPP); state and local policy (MPP); JD/MPP; MBA/MPP; MDR/MPP. *Faculty:* 4 full-time (1 woman), 5 part-time/adjunct (0 women). *Students:* 57 full-time (27 women), 7 part-time (5 women); includes 22 minority (9 Black or African American, non-Hispanic/Latino; 2 American Indian or Alaska Native, non-Hispanic/Latino; 6 Asian, non-Hispanic/Latino; 4 Hispanic/Latino; 1 Two or more races, non-Hispanic/Latino), 10 international. Average age 25. 174 applicants, 55% accepted, 29 enrolled. In 2016, 34 master's awarded. *Entrance requirements:* For master's, GRE or GMAT, 2 letters of recommendation, resume, two essays. Additional exam requirements/recommendations for international students: Required—TOEFL. *Application deadline:* For fall admission, 6/15 for domestic students. Applications are processed on a rolling basis. Application fee: $50. Electronic applications accepted. *Expenses:* $47,710 per academic year; $1,525 per unit (for master's). *Financial support:* Institutionally sponsored loans and scholarships/grants available. Financial award application deadline: 5/1; financial award applicants required to submit FAFSA. *Unit head:* Dr. Pete Peterson, Dean, School of Public Policy, 310-506-7490, Fax: 310-506-7494, E-mail: pete.n.peterson@pepperdine.edu. *Application contact:* Carson Bruno, Assistant Dean for Admission and Program Relations, 310-506-7493, E-mail: carson.bruno@pepperdine.edu.
Website: http://publicpolicy.pepperdine.edu/

**Portland State University,** Graduate Studies, College of Urban and Public Affairs, Hatfield School of Government, Division of Public Administration, Portland, OR 97207-0751. Offers public administration (MPA); public affairs and policy (PhD). *Accreditation:* NASPAA (one or more programs are accredited). *Program availability:* Part-time, evening/weekend. *Faculty:* 14 full-time (6 women), 9 part-time/adjunct (6 women). *Students:* 99 full-time (68 women), 122 part-time (82 women); includes 48 minority (5 Black or African American, non-Hispanic/Latino; 4 American Indian or Alaska Native, non-Hispanic/Latino; 7 Asian, non-Hispanic/Latino; 23 Hispanic/Latino; 9 Two or more races, non-Hispanic/Latino), 14 international. Average age 35. 143 applicants, 74% accepted, 68 enrolled. In 2016, 60 master's, 2 doctorates awarded. *Degree requirements:* For master's, internship (MPA), practicum (MPH); for doctorate, comprehensive exam, thesis/dissertation. *Entrance requirements:* For master's, GRE (minimum scores: verbal 150, quantitative 149, and analytic writing 4.5), minimum GPA of 3.0, 3 recommendation letters, resume, 500-word statement of intent; for doctorate, GRE, 3 recommendation letters, resume, 500-word personal essay. Additional exam requirements/recommendations for international students: Required—TOEFL (minimum score 550 paper-based; 80 iBT), IELTS (minimum score 7). *Application deadline:* For fall admission, 4/1 for domestic students, 3/1 for international students; for winter admission, 9/1 for domestic students, 8/1 for international students; for spring admission, 11/1 for domestic and international students. Application fee: $65. *Expenses:* Contact institution. *Financial support:* In 2016-17, 5 research assistantships with full tuition reimbursements (averaging $8,341 per year), 4 teaching assistantships with full tuition reimbursements (averaging $7,291 per year) were awarded; career-related internships or fieldwork, Federal Work-Study, scholarships/grants, tuition waivers (partial), and unspecified assistantships also available. Support available to part-time students. Financial award application deadline: 3/1; financial award applicants required to submit FAFSA. *Faculty research:* Public budgeting, program evaluation, nonprofit management, natural resources policy and administration. *Total annual research expenditures:* $819,192. *Unit head:* Dr. Masami Nishishiba, Chair, 503-725-5151, E-mail: nishism@pdx.edu.
Website: https://www.pdx.edu/hatfieldschool/public-administration

**Princeton University,** Graduate School, Woodrow Wilson School of Public and International Affairs, Princeton, NJ 08544-1019. Offers public affairs (MPA, PhD); public policy (MPP); JD/MPA. JD/MPA offered jointly with Columbia University, New York University, Stanford University. Terminal master's awarded for partial completion of doctoral program. *Degree requirements:* For master's, internship; for doctorate, one foreign language, thesis/dissertation. *Entrance requirements:* For master's, GRE General Test, original policy memo; for doctorate, GRE General Test. Additional exam requirements/recommendations for international students: Required—TOEFL (minimum score 600 paper-based). Electronic applications accepted.

**Queen's University at Kingston,** School of Graduate Studies, School of Policy Studies, Kingston, ON K7L 3N6, Canada. Offers MIR, MPA. *Program availability:* Part-time. *Entrance requirements:* For master's, minimum B+ average. Additional exam requirements/recommendations for international students: Required—TOEFL. *Faculty research:* Public management, social policy, defense management, health policy, the third sector.

**Regent University,** Graduate School, Robertson School of Government, Virginia Beach, VA 23464-9800. Offers government (MA), including American government, healthcare policy and ethics (MA, MPA), international relations, law and public policy, national security studies, political communication, political theory, religion and politics;

*Public Policy*

public administration (MPA), including emergency management and homeland security, federal government, general public administration, healthcare policy and ethics (MA, MPA), law, nonprofit administration and faith-based organizations, public leadership and management, servant leadership. *Program availability:* Part-time, evening/weekend, 100% online, blended/hybrid learning. *Faculty:* 8 full-time (1 woman), 19 part-time/adjunct (3 women). *Students:* 40 full-time (27 women), 119 part-time (69 women); includes 73 minority (47 Black or African American, non-Hispanic/Latino; 3 Asian, non-Hispanic/Latino; 15 Hispanic/Latino; 8 Two or more races, non-Hispanic/Latino), 6 international. Average age 35. 253 applicants, 41% accepted, 70 enrolled. In 2016, 34 master's awarded. *Degree requirements:* For master's, thesis optional, internship. *Entrance requirements:* For master's, GRE General Test or LSAT, personal essay, writing sample, resume, college transcripts. Additional exam requirements/recommendations for international students: Required—TOEFL (minimum score 577 paper-based). *Application deadline:* For fall admission, 5/1 priority date for domestic students; for spring admission, 11/1 priority date for domestic students. Applications are processed on a rolling basis. Application fee: $50. Electronic applications accepted. *Expenses:* $650 per credit (MA/MPA); $250 per semester technology fee. *Financial support:* In 2016–17, 78 students received support. Career-related internships or fieldwork, scholarships/grants, and unspecified assistantships available. Support available to part-time students. *Faculty research:* International relations and politics, public administration, leadership and ethics, Biblical law, Constitutional law and Supreme Court. *Unit head:* Dr. Eric Patterson, Dean, 757-352-4616, Fax: 757-352-4735, E-mail: epatterson@regent.edu. *Application contact:* Heidi Cece, Assistant Vice President of Enrollment Management, 800-373-5504, Fax: 757-352-4381, E-mail: admissions@regent.edu.
Website: http://www.regent.edu/rsg/

**Rochester Institute of Technology,** Graduate Enrollment Services, College of Liberal Arts, Department of Public Policy, MS Program in Science, Technology and Public Policy, Rochester, NY 14623. Offers MS. *Program availability:* Part-time. *Students:* 1 (woman) full-time, 2 part-time (1 woman). Average age 27. 5 applicants, 20% accepted, 1 enrolled. In 2016, 2 master's awarded. *Degree requirements:* For master's, thesis. *Entrance requirements:* For master's, GRE, minimum GPA of 3.0 (recommended). Additional exam requirements/recommendations for international students: Required—TOEFL (minimum score 570 paper-based; 88 iBT), IELTS (minimum score 6.5), PTE (minimum score 61). *Application deadline:* For fall admission, 2/15 priority date for domestic and international students; for spring admission, 12/15 priority date for domestic and international students. Applications are processed on a rolling basis. Application fee: $60. Electronic applications accepted. *Expenses:* $1,742 per credit hour. *Financial support:* In 2016–17, 4 students received support. Research assistantships with partial tuition reimbursements available, teaching assistantships with partial tuition reimbursements available, career-related internships or fieldwork, scholarships/grants, and unspecified assistantships available. Support available to part-time students. Financial award applicants required to submit FAFSA. *Faculty research:* Environmental management, innovation, and policy; technological innovation, environmental economics and policy; alternative energy and climate change; cybersecurity economics and Internet policy; e-democracy and digital government. *Unit head:* Franz Foltz, Graduate Program Director, 585-475-5368, E-mail: fafgsh@rit.edu. *Application contact:* Diane Ellison, Associate Vice President, Graduate Enrollment Services, 585-475-2229, Fax: 585-475-7164, E-mail: gradinfo@rit.edu.
Website: http://www.rit.edu/cla/publicpolicy/academics/science-technology-and-public-policy-ms

**Rutgers University–Camden,** Graduate School of Arts and Sciences, Department of Public Policy and Administration, Camden, NJ 08102. Offers education policy and leadership (MPA); international public service and development (MPA); public management (MPA); JD/MPA; MPA/MA. *Accreditation:* NASPAA. *Program availability:* Part-time, evening/weekend. *Degree requirements:* For master's, directed study, research workshop, 42 credits. *Entrance requirements:* For master's, GRE General Test, GMAT or LSAT, 3 letters of recommendation; resume. Additional exam requirements/recommendations for international students: Required—TOEFL (minimum score 550 paper-based), IELTS. Electronic applications accepted. *Faculty research:* Nonprofit management, county and municipal administration, health and human services, government communication, administrative law, educational finance.

**Rutgers University–Newark,** Graduate School, Program in Public Administration, Newark, NJ 07102. Offers health care administration (MPA); human resources administration (MPA); public administration (PhD); public management (MPA); public policy analysis (MPA); urban systems and issues (MPA). *Accreditation:* NASPAA (one or more programs are accredited). *Program availability:* Part-time, evening/weekend. *Degree requirements:* For master's, comprehensive exam, thesis or alternative; for doctorate, thesis/dissertation. *Entrance requirements:* For master's, GRE, minimum undergraduate B average; for doctorate, GRE, MPA, minimum B average. Electronic applications accepted. *Faculty research:* Government finance, municipal and state government, public productivity.

**Rutgers University–Newark,** School of Public Health, Newark, NJ 07107-1709. Offers clinical epidemiology (Certificate); dental public health (MPH); general public health (Certificate); public policy and oral health services administration (Certificate); quantitative methods (MPH); urban health (MPH); DMD/MPH; MD/MPH; MS/MPH. *Accreditation:* CEPH. *Program availability:* Part-time, evening/weekend. *Degree requirements:* For master's, thesis, internship. *Entrance requirements:* For master's, GRE General Test. Additional exam requirements/recommendations for international students: Required—TOEFL. Electronic applications accepted.

**Rutgers University–New Brunswick,** Edward J. Bloustein School of Planning and Public Policy, Doctoral Program in Planning and Public Policy, New Brunswick, NJ 08901. Offers PhD. *Program availability:* Part-time. *Degree requirements:* For doctorate, comprehensive exam, thesis/dissertation. *Entrance requirements:* For doctorate, GRE, master's degree. Additional exam requirements/recommendations for international students: Required—TOEFL (minimum score 575 paper-based; 88 iBT). Electronic applications accepted. *Faculty research:* Housing and community development, land use and transportation, politics and policy analysis, urban and regional economics, international development.

**Rutgers University–New Brunswick,** Edward J. Bloustein School of Planning and Public Policy, Program in Public Policy, New Brunswick, NJ 08901. Offers MPAP, MPP, JD/MPAP, MBA/MPP, MCRP/MPP. JD/MPAP offered jointly with Rutgers, The State University of New Jersey, Camden. *Accreditation:* NASPAA. *Program availability:* Part-time, evening/weekend. *Entrance requirements:* For master's, GRE General Test. Additional exam requirements/recommendations for international students: Required—TOEFL (minimum score 575 paper-based; 88 iBT). Electronic applications accepted. *Faculty research:* Environment, social and health policy, public opinion, economics, education policy, community development.

**Saint Louis University,** Graduate Education, College of Education and Public Service, Department of Public Policy Studies, St. Louis, MO 63103. Offers geographic information systems (Certificate); organizational development (Certificate); public administration (MAPA); public policy analysis (PhD); urban affairs (MAUA); urban planning and real estate development (MUPRED). *Program availability:* Part-time.

*Degree requirements:* For master's, comprehensive exam (for some programs), thesis (for some programs); for doctorate, comprehensive exam, thesis/dissertation, preliminary exams. *Entrance requirements:* For master's, GMAT, GRE General Test, or LSAT, letters of recommendation, resume; for doctorate, GMAT, GRE General Test, or LSAT, letters of recommendation, resumé, interview, transcripts, goal statement. Additional exam requirements/recommendations for international students: Required—TOEFL (minimum score 525 paper-based). Electronic applications accepted. *Faculty research:* Urban politics, brown fields, e-government, and administration, evaluation research, community development, electronic government and governance.

**St. Mary's University,** Graduate Studies, Program in Communication Studies, San Antonio, TX 78228-8507. Offers communication studies (MA); public communication, public policy and public leadership (Certificate); JD/MA. *Program availability:* Part-time, evening/weekend, online learning. *Faculty:* 7 full-time (3 women), 3 part-time/adjunct (2 women). *Students:* 15 full-time (9 women); includes 13 minority (4 Black or African American, non-Hispanic/Latino; 9 Hispanic/Latino), 2 international. Average age 30. 14 applicants, 43% accepted, 2 enrolled. In 2016, 5 master's awarded. *Degree requirements:* For master's, thesis (for some programs). *Entrance requirements:* For master's, GRE General Test, MAT, minimum GPA of 3.1; professional experience. Additional exam requirements/recommendations for international students: Required—TOEFL (minimum score 550 paper-based; 80 iBT), IELTS (minimum score 6). *Application deadline:* For fall admission, 7/1 priority date for domestic students; for spring admission, 11/15 for domestic students; for summer admission, 4/1 for domestic students. Applications are processed on a rolling basis. Application fee: $0. Electronic applications accepted. *Expenses: Tuition:* Full-time $15,600; part-time $865 per credit hour. *Required fees:* $148 per semester. *Financial support:* Research assistantships, career-related internships or fieldwork, Federal Work-Study, institutionally sponsored loans, scholarships/grants, and health care benefits available. Financial award application deadline: 3/31; financial award applicants required to submit FAFSA. *Faculty research:* Interpersonal communication, rhetorical communication. *Unit head:* Dr. William Israel, Graduate Program Director, 210-436-3650, E-mail: bisreal@stmarytx.edu. *Application contact:* Kim Thornton, Director, Graduate and Adult Enrollment Services, 210-436-3101, E-mail: kthornton@stmarytx.edu.
Website: https://www.stmarytx.edu/academics/graduate/masters/communication/

**San Francisco State University,** Division of Graduate Studies, College of Health and Social Sciences, Public Administration Program, San Francisco, CA 94132-1722. Offers criminal justice administration (MPA); environmental administration and policy (MPA); gerontology (MPA); nonprofit administration (MPA); public management (MPA); public policy (MPA); urban administration (MPA). *Accreditation:* NASPAA. *Expenses: Tuition,* state resident: full-time $6738. Tuition, nonresident: full-time $15,666. *Required fees:* $1012. Tuition and fees vary according to degree level and program. *Unit head:* Dr. Elizabeth Brown, Director of the School of Public Affairs and Civic Engagement, 415-817-4455, Fax: 415-817-4464, E-mail: mpa@sfsu.edu. *Application contact:* Dr. Jennifer Shea, Graduate Coordinator, 415-817-4462, Fax: 415-817-4464, E-mail: jshea@sfsu.edu.
Website: http://mpa.sfsu.edu/

**Seton Hall University,** College of Arts and Sciences, Department of Political Science and Public Affairs, South Orange, NJ 07079-2697. Offers nonprofit organization management (Graduate Certificate); public administration (MPA), including health policy and management, nonprofit organization management, public service: leadership, governance, and policy. *Accreditation:* CAHME; NASPAA. *Program availability:* Part-time, evening/weekend. *Degree requirements:* For master's, thesis or alternative, internship or practicum. *Entrance requirements:* Additional exam requirements/recommendations for international students: Required—TOEFL. Electronic applications accepted.

**Simmons College,** College of Arts and Sciences, Boston, MA 02115. Offers elementary education (MAT); English (MA); gender/cultural studies (MA); history (MA); public health (MPH); public policy (MPP). *Program availability:* Part-time. *Faculty:* 19 full-time (12 women), 1 (woman) part-time/adjunct. *Students:* 6 full-time (all women), 38 part-time (27 women); includes 10 minority (4 Black or African American, non-Hispanic/Latino; 1 Asian, non-Hispanic/Latino; 2 Hispanic/Latino; 3 Two or more races, non-Hispanic/Latino), 1 international. Average age 26. 50 applicants, 88% accepted, 17 enrolled. In 2016, 19 master's awarded. Terminal master's awarded for partial completion of doctoral program. *Degree requirements:* For master's, thesis (for some programs). *Entrance requirements:* For master's, GRE. Additional exam requirements/recommendations for international students: Required—TOEFL (minimum score 600 paper-based; 100 iBT). *Application deadline:* For fall admission, 8/1 for domestic and international students; for spring admission, 12/15 for domestic and international students; for summer admission, 5/1 for domestic and international students. Applications are processed on a rolling basis. Application fee: $35. Electronic applications accepted. *Expenses:* $1,050 per credit, $4,200 per course, $52 activity fee per semester. *Financial support:* In 2016–17, 4 fellowships with partial tuition reimbursements, 22 teaching assistantships with partial tuition reimbursements were awarded; scholarships/grants and unspecified assistantships also available. Support available to part-time students. Financial award applicants required to submit FAFSA. *Unit head:* Dr. Renee White, Dean, 617-521-2079. *Application contact:* Patricia Flaherty, Director, Graduate Studies Admission, 617-521-3902, Fax: 617-521-3058, E-mail: gsa@simmons.edu.
Website: http://www.simmons.edu/gradstudies/

**Simon Fraser University,** Office of Graduate Studies and Postdoctoral Fellows, Faculty of Arts and Social Sciences, School of Public Policy, Vancouver, BC V6B 5K3, Canada. Offers MPP. *Faculty:* 8 full-time (4 women). *Students:* 56 full-time (32 women), 2 part-time (0 women). 154 applicants, 38% accepted, 28 enrolled. In 2016, 29 master's awarded. *Degree requirements:* For master's, thesis or alternative, internship. *Entrance requirements:* For master's, GRE (for applicants with non-Canadian degrees), minimum GPA of 3.0 on scale of 4.33) or 3.33 based on last 60 credits of undergraduate courses. Additional exam requirements/recommendations for international students: Recommended—TOEFL (minimum score 580 paper-based; 93 iBT), IELTS (minimum score 7), TWE (minimum score 5). *Application deadline:* For fall admission, 2/1 for domestic and international students. Application fee: $90 ($125 for international students). Electronic applications accepted. *Expenses:* Contact institution. *Financial support:* In 2016–17, 40 students received support, including 31 fellowships (averaging $3,250 per year), teaching assistantships (averaging $5,608 per year); research assistantships, career-related internships or fieldwork, and scholarships/grants also available. *Faculty research:* Health policy, labor market and immigration, gender and discrimination, taxation policy, environmental policy. *Unit head:* Rhys Kesselman, Graduate Chair, 778-782-5035, Fax: 778-782-5288, E-mail: mpp-grad-chair@sfu.ca. *Application contact:* Dawn Geil Allison, Manager, Academic and Administrative Resources, 778-782-5289, Fax: 778-782-5288, E-mail: mpp@sfu.ca.
Website: http://www.sfu.ca/mpp/

**Southern University and Agricultural and Mechanical College,** Graduate School, Nelson Mandela School of Public Policy and Urban Affairs, Program in Public Policy, Baton Rouge, LA 70813. Offers PhD. *Degree requirements:* For doctorate, comprehensive exam, thesis/dissertation. *Entrance requirements:* For doctorate, GRE

General Test. Additional exam requirements/recommendations for international students: Required—TOEFL (minimum score 525 paper-based).

**State University of New York Empire State College,** School for Graduate Studies, Program in Social Policy, Saratoga Springs, NY 12866-4391. Offers MA. *Program availability:* Part-time, evening/weekend, online learning. *Degree requirements:* For master's, thesis, exam, final project. *Entrance requirements:* Additional exam requirements/recommendations for international students: Required—TOEFL (minimum score 600 paper-based). Electronic applications accepted. *Faculty research:* Study of culture, society and mass communications, urban culture and policy, social decision-making processes.

**Stony Brook University, State University of New York,** Graduate School, College of Arts and Sciences, Department of Political Science, Program in Public Policy and Urban Development, Stony Brook, NY 11794. Offers MA. *Students:* 23 full-time (10 women), 15 part-time (4 women); includes 8 minority (4 Black or African American, non-Hispanic/Latino; 2 Asian, non-Hispanic/Latino; 2 Hispanic/Latino), 7 international. 49 applicants, 73% accepted, 23 enrolled. In 2016, 28 master's awarded. *Entrance requirements:* For master's, GRE, three letters of recommendation, statement of purpose. Additional exam requirements/recommendations for international students: Required—TOEFL (minimum score 85 iBT). *Application deadline:* For fall admission, 7/1 for domestic students, 5/15 for international students; for spring admission, 12/5 for domestic students, 10/15 for international students. Application fee: $100. Electronic applications accepted. *Expenses:* Contact institution. *Unit head:* Dr. Jeffrey Segal, Chair, 631-632-7662, Fax: 631-632-4116, E-mail: jeffrey.segal@stonybrook.edu. *Application contact:* Carri Ann Horner, Graduate Program Coordinator, 631-632-7667, Fax: 631-632-4116, E-mail: carri.horner@stonybrook.edu.

**Suffolk University,** College of Arts and Sciences, Department of Philosophy, Boston, MA 02108-2770. Offers administration of higher education (M Ed, CAGS); ethics and public policy (MS). *Program availability:* Part-time, evening/weekend. *Faculty:* 4 full-time (0 women), 2 part-time/adjunct (0 women). *Students:* 22 full-time (16 women), 29 part-time (24 women); includes 10 minority (1 Black or African American, non-Hispanic/Latino; 6 Hispanic/Latino; 3 Two or more races, non-Hispanic/Latino), 1 international. Average age 28. 56 applicants, 75% accepted, 19 enrolled. In 2016, 34 master's awarded. *Degree requirements:* For master's, internship or thesis; practicum (for M Ed). *Entrance requirements:* For master's, GRE General Test, MAT, GMAT, statement of professional goals, official transcripts, 2 letters of recommendation, resume. Additional exam requirements/recommendations for international students: Required—TOEFL (minimum score 550 paper-based; 80 iBT). *Application deadline:* For fall admission, 3/15 priority date for domestic and international students; for spring admission, 10/15 priority date for domestic and international students. Applications are processed on a rolling basis. Application fee: $50. Electronic applications accepted. *Expenses:* Contact institution. *Financial support:* In 2016–17, 38 students received support, including 30 fellowships (averaging $6,556 per year); career-related internships or fieldwork, Federal Work-Study, institutionally sponsored loans, and unspecified assistantships also available. Support available to part-time students. Financial award application deadline: 4/1; financial award applicants required to submit FAFSA. *Faculty research:* Predicting competent Head Start preschoolers, cultural differences, school counseling technology, sibling attachment in divorce cases, consequences of ethical breaches by human resource professionals. *Unit head:* Dr. Greg Fried, Chair of Philosophy Department, 617-573-8109, E-mail: gfried@suffolk.edu. *Application contact:* Mara Marzocchi, Associate Director of Graduate Admissions, 617-573-8302, Fax: 617-305-1733, E-mail: grad.admission@suffolk.edu.
Website: http://www.suffolk.edu/college/graduate/69296.php

**Trinity College,** Graduate Programs, Program in Public Policy, Hartford, CT 06106-3100. Offers health care policy (MA); public policy studies (MA). *Program availability:* Part-time, evening/weekend. *Degree requirements:* For master's, thesis optional, departmental qualifying exam. *Entrance requirements:* For master's, minimum GPA of 3.0, two letters of recommendation, statement of purpose.

**Tufts University,** Graduate School of Arts and Sciences, Department of Urban and Environmental Policy and Planning, Medford, MA 02155. Offers community development (MA); environmental policy (MA); health and human welfare (MA); housing policy (MA); international environment/development policy (MA); public policy (MPP); MA/JD; MA/MBA; MA/MPH; MA/MS; MALD/MA. MALD/MA offered in connection with The Fletcher School of Law and Diplomacy; MA/MPH with School of Medicine; MA/MS with School of Nutrition Science and Policy or School of Engineering; MA/MBA with Boston College, Carroll School of Management; MA/JD with Boston College Law School. *Accreditation:* ACSP (one or more programs are accredited). *Program availability:* Part-time. *Students:* 94 full-time (73 women), 18 part-time (14 women); includes 29 minority (11 Black or African American, non-Hispanic/Latino; 9 Asian, non-Hispanic/Latino; 6 Hispanic/Latino; 3 Two or more races, non-Hispanic/Latino), 18 international. Average age 30. 153 applicants, 78% accepted, 51 enrolled. In 2016, 20 master's awarded. *Degree requirements:* For master's, thesis or alternative, internship. *Entrance requirements:* For master's, GRE General Test. Additional exam requirements/recommendations for international students: Required—TOEFL (minimum score 550 paper-based; 80 iBT), IELTS (minimum score 6.5). *Application deadline:* For fall admission, 1/15 for domestic and international students. Applications are processed on a rolling basis. Application fee: $85. Electronic applications accepted. *Expenses:* $49,982 full-time tuition (for MPP); $34,932 full-time tuition (for MA). *Financial support:* Fellowships, research assistantships, teaching assistantships, career-related internships or fieldwork, Federal Work-Study, scholarships/grants, tuition waivers (full and partial), and unspecified assistantships available. Support available to part-time students. Financial award application deadline: 1/15. *Unit head:* Dr. Mary Davis, Graduate Program Director. *Application contact:* Office of Graduate Admissions, 617-627-3395, E-mail: gradadmissions@tufts.edu.
Website: http://ase.tufts.edu/uep/

**Union Institute & University,** Master of Arts Program, Cincinnati, OH 45206-1925. Offers creativity studies (MA); health and wellness (MA); history and culture (MA); leadership, public policy, and social issues (MA); literature and writing (MA). *Program availability:* Part-time, online only, 100% online. *Faculty:* 2 full-time (both women), 9 part-time/adjunct (7 women). *Students:* 9 full-time (7 women), 70 part-time (56 women); includes 33 minority (22 Black or African American, non-Hispanic/Latino; 1 American Indian or Alaska Native, non-Hispanic/Latino; 6 Hispanic/Latino; 4 Two or more races, non-Hispanic/Latino). Average age 40. In 2016, 45 master's awarded. *Degree requirements:* For master's, thesis. *Entrance requirements:* For master's, transcript, essay, 3 letters of recommendation, resume. Additional exam requirements/recommendations for international students: Recommended—TOEFL. *Application deadline:* For spring admission, 3/13 for domestic students. Applications are processed on a rolling basis. Application fee: $50. Electronic applications accepted. *Expenses:* Contact institution. *Financial support:* Career-related internships or fieldwork and tuition waivers available. Financial award applicants required to submit FAFSA. *Unit head:* Elden Golden, Director, 513-487-1153, E-mail: elden.golden@myunion.edu. *Application contact:* Director of Admissions, 800-861-6400.

**Universidad Autonoma de Guadalajara,** Graduate Programs, Guadalajara, Mexico. Offers administrative law and justice (LL M); advertising and corporate communications (MA); architecture (M Arch); business (MBA); computational science (MCC); education (Ed M, Ed D); English-Spanish translation (MA); entrepreneurship and management (MBA); integrated management of digital animation (MA); international business (MIB); international corporate law (LL M); internet technologies (MS); manufacturing systems (MMS); occupational health (MS); philosophy (MA, PhD); power electronics (MS); quality systems (MQS); renewable energy (MS); social evaluation of projects (MBA); strategic market research (MBA); tax law (MA); teaching mathematics (MA).

**Universidad del Este,** Graduate School, Carolina, PR 00984. Offers accounting (MBA); adult education (M Ed); agribusiness (MBA); criminal justice and criminology (MA); curriculum and instruction - early education (M Ed); curriculum and instruction - elementary (M Ed); curriculum and instruction - English (M Ed); curriculum and instruction - Spanish (M Ed); human resources (MBA); information security management (MBA); information technology and Web business development (MBA); management (MBA); public policy (MPA); social work (MA), including clinical social work; special education (M Ed); strategic leadership (MBA).

**Université de Montréal,** Faculty of Arts and Sciences, Program in Societies, Public Policies and Health, Montréal, QC H3C 3J7, Canada. Offers DESS.

**University at Albany, State University of New York,** Nelson A. Rockefeller College of Public Affairs and Policy, Department of Public Administration and Policy, Albany, NY 12222-0001. Offers financial management and public economics (MPA); financial market regulation (MPA); health policy (MPA); healthcare management (MPA); homeland security (MPA); human resources management (MPA); information strategy and management (MPA); local government management (MPA); nonprofit management (MPA); nonprofit management and leadership (Certificate); organizational behavior and theory (MPA, PhD); planning and policy analysis (CAS); policy analysis (MPA); politics and administration (PhD); public finance (PhD); public management (PhD); public policy (PhD); public sector management (Certificate); women and public policy (Certificate); JD/MPA. JD/MPA offered jointly with Albany Law School. *Accreditation:* NASPAA (one or more programs are accredited). *Faculty:* 23 full-time (8 women), 14 part-time/adjunct (7 women). *Students:* 117 full-time (65 women), 95 part-time (46 women); includes 41 minority (12 Black or African American, non-Hispanic/Latino; 8 Asian, non-Hispanic/Latino; 19 Hispanic/Latino; 2 Two or more races, non-Hispanic/Latino), 38 international. 223 applicants, 70% accepted, 81 enrolled. In 2016, 52 master's, 10 doctorates, 16 other advanced degrees awarded. *Degree requirements:* For doctorate, one foreign language, thesis/dissertation. *Entrance requirements:* For doctorate, GRE General Test. Additional exam requirements/recommendations for international students: Required—TOEFL (minimum score 550 paper-based). *Application deadline:* For fall admission, 2/1 priority date for domestic students, 5/1 for international students; for spring admission, 12/1 for domestic students. Applications are processed on a rolling basis. Application fee: $75. Electronic applications accepted. *Expenses:* Tuition, state resident: full-time $10,870; part-time $453 per credit hour. Tuition, nonresident: full-time $22,210; part-time $925 per credit hour. *International tuition:* $21,550 full-time. *Required fees:* $1864; $96 per credit hour. *Financial support:* Application deadline: 2/1. *Total annual research expenditures:* $847,949. *Unit head:* Victor Asal, Chair, 518-591-8729, E-mail: vasal@albany.edu.
Website: http://www.albany.edu/rockefeller/pad.shtml

**The University of Arizona,** College of Social and Behavioral Sciences, Program in Public Administration, Tucson, AZ 85721. Offers public administration (MPA); public administration and policy (PhD). *Accreditation:* NASPAA. *Degree requirements:* For master's, internship of 400 hours; for doctorate, comprehensive exam, thesis/dissertation. *Entrance requirements:* For doctorate, GMAT or GRE, minimum graduate GPA of 3.5, letter of interest, 3 letters of recommendation, resume. Additional exam requirements/recommendations for international students: Required—TOEFL (minimum score 650 paper-based; 115 iBT). Electronic applications accepted. *Expenses:* Contact institution.

**University of Arkansas,** Graduate School, Interdisciplinary Program in Public Policy, Fayetteville, AR 72701. Offers PhD. In 2016, 8 doctorates awarded. *Degree requirements:* For doctorate, thesis/dissertation. *Application deadline:* For fall admission, 4/1 for international students; for spring admission, 10/1 for international students. Applications are processed on a rolling basis. Application fee: $40 ($50 for international students). Electronic applications accepted. *Financial support:* In 2016–17, 10 research assistantships, 1 teaching assistantship were awarded; fellowships with tuition reimbursements also available. Financial award application deadline: 4/1; financial award applicants required to submit FAFSA. *Unit head:* Dr. Brinck Kerr, Head, 479-575-3356, Fax: 479-575-5908, E-mail: jbkerr@uark.edu. *Application contact:* Graduate Admissions, 479-575-6246, Fax: 479-575-5908, E-mail: gradinfo@uark.edu.
Website: http://policy.uark.edu/

**The University of British Columbia,** Institute of Asian Research, Vancouver, BC V6T 1Z2, Canada. Offers Asia Pacific policy studies (MAAPPS); public policy and global affairs (MPPGA). *Degree requirements:* For master's, thesis optional. *Entrance requirements:* Additional exam requirements/recommendations for international students: Required—TOEFL. Application fee: $100 ($162 for international students). Electronic applications accepted. *Expenses:* $26,842 per year tuition and fees, $42,648 per year international. *Financial support:* Fellowships with tuition reimbursements, research assistantships, career-related internships or fieldwork, institutionally sponsored loans, scholarships/grants, and tuition waivers (partial) available. *Faculty research:* Social cohesion, globalization, social safety nets, policy research, research and development alliances, knowledge-based workshops on Asia-Pacific studies. *Application contact:* Kerry Ross, Graduate Program Staff, 604-822-4571, E-mail: mppga.program@ubc.ca.
Website: http://iar.ubc.ca/

**University of California, Berkeley,** Graduate Division, Graduate School of Public Policy, Program in Public Policy, Berkeley, CA 94720-1500. Offers MPP, PhD. *Students:* 199 full-time (124 women); includes 63 minority (12 Black or African American, non-Hispanic/Latino; 2 American Indian or Alaska Native, non-Hispanic/Latino; 31 Asian, non-Hispanic/Latino; 17 Hispanic/Latino; 1 Native Hawaiian or other Pacific Islander, non-Hispanic/Latino), 27 international. 656 applicants, 94 enrolled. In 2016, 89 master's awarded. *Application deadline:* For fall admission, 12/1 for domestic students. Application fee: $105 ($125 for international students). Electronic applications accepted. *Financial support:* Fellowships, research assistantships, teaching assistantships, institutionally sponsored loans, health care benefits, and unspecified assistantships available. *Unit head:* Prof. Henry Brady, Dean, 510-642-4670, E-mail: gsppadm@berkeley.edu. *Application contact:* 510-642-4670, Fax: 510-643-9657, E-mail: gsppadm@berkeley.edu.
Website: https://gspp.berkeley.edu

**University of California, Berkeley,** Graduate Division, Haas School of Business, PhD in Business Administration Program, Berkeley, CA 94720-1500. Offers accounting (PhD); business and public policy (PhD); finance (PhD); management of organizations (PhD); marketing (PhD); real estate (PhD). *Accreditation:* AACSB. *Students:* 78 full-time (28 women); includes 34 minority (29 Asian, non-Hispanic/Latino; 5 Hispanic/Latino). Average age 27. *Degree requirements:* For doctorate, comprehensive exam, thesis/dissertation, written preliminary exams, oral qualifying exam. *Entrance requirements:*

## Public Policy

For doctorate, GMAT or GRE, minimum GPA of 3.0 in undergraduate and graduate coursework. Additional exam requirements/recommendations for international students: Required—TOEFL (minimum score 570 paper-based; 70 iBT), IELTS (minimum score 7). *Application deadline:* For fall admission, 12/1 for domestic and international students. Application fee: $90 ($110 for international students). Electronic applications accepted. *Expenses:* Contact institution. *Financial support:* Fellowships with tuition reimbursements, research assistantships with tuition reimbursements, teaching assistantships with tuition reimbursements, scholarships/grants, health care benefits, tuition waivers (full), unspecified assistantships, and transit passes, travel grants available. Financial award application deadline: 12/10. *Faculty research:* Accounting, business and public policy, entrepreneurship, finance, management of organizations, marketing, operations and information technology management, real estate. *Unit head:* Dr. Nicolae Garleanu, Director, 510-643-6349, Fax: 510-643-4255. *Application contact:* Melissa Hacker, Director, Student Affairs, 510-642-3944, Fax: 510-643-4255, E-mail: melhacker@haas.berkeley.edu.
Website: http://www.haas.berkeley.edu/Phd/

**University of California, Los Angeles,** Graduate Division, School of Public Affairs, Program in Public Policy, Los Angeles, CA 90095. Offers MPP. *Accreditation:* NASPAA. *Entrance requirements:* For master's, GRE General Test, minimum GPA of 3.0. Additional exam requirements/recommendations for international students: Required—TOEFL. Electronic applications accepted.

**University of California, Riverside,** Graduate Division, School of Public Policy, Riverside, CA 92521-0102. Offers global media (MS); public policy (MPP, PhD); MD/MPP. MD/MPP offered in partnership with School of Medicine. *Expenses:* Tuition, state resident: full-time $16,666. Tuition, nonresident: full-time $31,768. *Required fees:* $11,055.54 per quarter. $3685.18 per quarter. Tuition and fees vary according to campus/location and program.

**University of California, San Diego,** Graduate Division, School of Global Policy and Strategy, Master of Public Policy Program, La Jolla, CA 92093. Offers American policy in global context (MPP); business, government and regulation (MPP); energy and environmental policy (MPP); health policy (MPP); program design and evaluation (MPP); security policy (MPP). *Faculty:* 33 full-time (9 women), 20 part-time/adjunct (4 women). *Students:* 300 full-time (150 women). 460 applicants, 120 enrolled. *Entrance requirements:* For master's, GMAT or GRE General Test. Additional exam requirements/recommendations for international students: Required—TOEFL (minimum score 90 iBT), IELTS (minimum score 7). *Application deadline:* For fall admission, 1/15 for domestic and international students. Applications are processed on a rolling basis. Application fee: $105 ($125 for international students). Electronic applications accepted. *Expenses:* Contact institution. *Financial support:* Fellowships, research assistantships, teaching assistantships, career-related internships or fieldwork, scholarships/grants, and unspecified assistantships available. Financial award application deadline: 1/15. *Unit head:* Sonja Steinbrech, Director of Enrollment, 858-534-7162, E-mail: ssteinbrech@ucsd.edu. *Application contact:* Admissions Representative, 858-534-5914, E-mail: gps-apply@uscd.edu.
Website: http://gps.ucsd.edu/academics/mpp.html

**University of Chicago,** Harris School of Public Policy, Master of Arts in Public Policy Program, Chicago, IL 60637. Offers public policy studies (AM). *Students:* 10 full-time (2 women); includes 1 minority (Black or African American, non-Hispanic/Latino), 5 international. 29 applicants, 66% accepted, 9 enrolled. *Entrance requirements:* For master's, GRE General Test, graduate degree. Additional exam requirements/recommendations for international students: Required—TOEFL (minimum score 600 paper-based; 104 iBT), IELTS (minimum score 7). *Application deadline:* For fall admission, 1/10 for domestic and international students. Application fee: $75. Electronic applications accepted. *Financial support:* Fellowships, Federal Work-Study, institutionally sponsored loans, and scholarships/grants available. Financial award application deadline: 1/10; financial award applicants required to submit FAFSA. *Application contact:* Allison Bevan, Director of Admissions, 773-702-8401, E-mail: harrisadmissions@uchicago.edu.
Website: http://harris.uchicago.edu/academics/programs-degrees/degrees/ma-public-policy-ma

**University of Chicago,** Harris School of Public Policy, Master of Public Policy Program, Chicago, IL 60637. Offers MPP. *Students:* 274 full-time (138 women), 11 part-time (6 women); includes 49 minority (14 Black or African American, non-Hispanic/Latino; 19 Asian, non-Hispanic/Latino; 14 Hispanic/Latino; 2 Two or more races, non-Hispanic/Latino), 132 international. 737 applicants, 57% accepted, 129 enrolled. *Entrance requirements:* For master's, GRE General Test. Additional exam requirements/recommendations for international students: Required—TOEFL (minimum score 600 paper-based; 104 iBT), IELTS (minimum score 7). *Application deadline:* For fall admission, 1/10 priority date for domestic and international students. Application fee: $75. Electronic applications accepted. *Financial support:* Federal Work-Study, institutionally sponsored loans, and scholarships/grants available. Financial award application deadline: 1/10; financial award applicants required to submit FAFSA. *Unit head:* Daniel Deirmeier, Dean, 773-702-8400. *Application contact:* Allison Bevan, Director of Admissions, 773-702-8401, E-mail: harrisadmissions@uchicago.edu.
Website: http://harris.uchicago.edu/academics/programs-degrees/degrees/master-public-policy-mpp

**University of Chicago,** Harris School of Public Policy, PhD Program in Public Policy, Chicago, IL 60637. Offers PhD. *Students:* 36 full-time (16 women); includes 4 minority (2 Asian, non-Hispanic/Latino; 1 Hispanic/Latino; 1 Two or more races, non-Hispanic/Latino), 22 international. 212 applicants, 12% accepted, 4 enrolled. *Degree requirements:* For doctorate, comprehensive exam, thesis/dissertation, four qualifying examinations. *Entrance requirements:* For doctorate, GRE General Test. Additional exam requirements/recommendations for international students: Required—TOEFL (minimum score 600 paper-based; 104 iBT), IELTS (minimum score 7). *Application deadline:* For fall admission, 12/3 for domestic and international students. Application fee: $75. Electronic applications accepted. *Financial support:* Fellowships, teaching assistantships, institutionally sponsored loans, and scholarships/grants available. Financial award application deadline: 12/3; financial award applicants required to submit FAFSA. *Faculty research:* Health policy, municipal finance, cultural policy, urban policy, data science. *Unit head:* Scott Ashworth, Director, 773-251-9563, E-mail: sashwort@uchicago.edu. *Application contact:* Allison Bevan, Director of Admissions, 773-702-8401, E-mail: harrisadmissions@uchicago.edu.
Website: http://harris.uchicago.edu/academics/programs-degrees/degrees/phd

**University of Delaware,** Center for Energy and Environmental Policy, Newark, DE 19716. Offers energy and environmental policy (MA, MEEP, PhD); urban affairs and public policy (PhD), including technology, environment, and society. *Degree requirements:* For master's, analytical paper or thesis; for doctorate, comprehensive exam, thesis/dissertation. *Entrance requirements:* For master's, GRE General Test, minimum GPA of 3.0; for doctorate, GRE General Test, minimum GPA of 3.5. Additional exam requirements/recommendations for international students: Required—TOEFL. Electronic applications accepted. *Faculty research:* Sustainable development, renewable energy, climate change, environmental policy, environmental justice, disaster policy.

**University of Delaware,** College of Arts and Sciences, School of Public Policy and Administration, Program in Urban Affairs and Public Policy, Newark, DE 19716. Offers governance planning and management (PhD); historic preservation (MA); social and urban policy (PhD); technology, environment and society (PhD); urban affairs and public policy (MA). *Program availability:* Part-time. Terminal master's awarded for partial completion of doctoral program. *Degree requirements:* For master's, analytical paper or thesis; for doctorate, thesis/dissertation. *Entrance requirements:* For master's, GRE General Test, minimum GPA of 3.0; for doctorate, GRE General Test, minimum GPA of 3.5. Additional exam requirements/recommendations for international students: Required—TOEFL. Electronic applications accepted. *Faculty research:* Political economy; social policy analysis; technology and society; historic preservation; urban policy.

**University of Denver,** Josef Korbel School of International Studies, Institute for Public Policy Studies, Denver, CO 80208. Offers MPP. *Faculty:* 10 full-time (5 women), 4 part-time/adjunct (2 women). *Students:* 16 full-time (8 women), 3 part-time (1 woman); includes 2 minority (both Hispanic/Latino), 1 international. Average age 26. 21 applicants, 81% accepted, 4 enrolled. In 2016, 9 master's awarded. *Degree requirements:* For master's, thesis or alternative, policy memorandum capstone. *Entrance requirements:* For master's, GRE General Test, bachelor's degree, transcripts, personal statement, three letters of recommendation, interview. Additional exam requirements/recommendations for international students: Required—TOEFL (minimum score 570 paper-based; 88 iBT). *Application deadline:* For fall admission, 7/1 priority date for domestic and international students; for winter admission, 11/15 priority date for domestic and international students. Applications are processed on a rolling basis. Application fee: $65. Electronic applications accepted. *Expenses:* $29,022 per year full-time. *Financial support:* In 2016–17, 17 students received support, including 2 teaching assistantships with tuition reimbursements available (averaging $3,750 per year); Federal Work-Study, scholarships/grants, and unspecified assistantships also available. Financial award application deadline: 2/15; financial award applicants required to submit FAFSA. *Faculty research:* Health policy, politics of mobility and migration, aging and later life migration, immigration policy. *Unit head:* Dr. Richard Caldwell, Co-Director, 303-871-2468, Fax: 303-871-3066, E-mail: richard.caldwell@du.edu.
Website: http://www.du.edu/korbel/ipps/index.html

**University of Georgia,** School of Public and International Affairs, Department of Public Administration and Policy, Athens, GA 30602. Offers public administration (MPA, PhD). *Accreditation:* NASPAA (one or more programs are accredited). *Degree requirements:* For master's, internship; for doctorate, thesis/dissertation. *Entrance requirements:* For master's and doctorate, GRE General Test. *Application deadline:* For fall admission, 7/1 priority date for domestic students; for spring admission, 11/15 for domestic students. Application fee: $50. Electronic applications accepted. *Financial support:* Fellowships, research assistantships, teaching assistantships, and unspecified assistantships available. *Unit head:* Dr. J. Edward Kellough, Head, 706-542-0488, E-mail: kellough@uga.edu. *Application contact:* Dr. Vicky M. Wilkins, Graduate Coordinator, 706-542-2648, Fax: 706-583-4421, E-mail: vwilkins@uga.edu.

**University of Guelph,** Graduate Studies, College of Social and Applied Human Sciences, Department of Political Science, Guelph, ON N1G 2W1, Canada. Offers comparative politics (MA); international development (MA); political science (MA); public policy and public administration (MA); the Americas (Canada emphasis) (MA). MA in public policy and public administration offered in collaboration with Department of Political Science of McMaster University. *Degree requirements:* For master's, thesis or paper. *Entrance requirements:* For master's, minimum B average during previous 2 years of course work, 4 year Honours Degree in Political Science. Additional exam requirements/recommendations for international students: Required—TOEFL. Electronic applications accepted. *Faculty research:* Political ethics, constitutional power.

**University of Hawaii at Manoa,** Graduate Division, College of Social Sciences, Public Policy Center, Honolulu, HI 96822. Offers Graduate Certificate. *Program availability:* Part-time. *Entrance requirements:* Additional exam requirements/recommendations for international students: Required—TOEFL (minimum score 500 paper-based; 61 iBT), IELTS (minimum score 5).

**University of Houston,** College of Liberal Arts and Social Sciences, Hobby School of Public Affairs, Houston, TX 77204. Offers public policy (MPP). *Program availability:* Part-time. *Entrance requirements:* For master's, GRE General Test.

**University of Kentucky,** Graduate School, Martin School of Public Policy and Administration, Lexington, KY 40506-0027. Offers public administration (MPA); public financial management (MPFM, Graduate Certificate); public policy (MPP); public policy and administration (PhD). *Accreditation:* NASPAA (one or more programs are accredited). *Program availability:* Part-time, evening/weekend, 100% online. *Faculty:* 10 full-time (2 women), 3 part-time/adjunct (1 woman). *Students:* 74 full-time (26 women), 15 part-time (7 women); includes 7 minority (3 Black or African American, non-Hispanic/Latino; 4 Asian, non-Hispanic/Latino), 27 international. Average age 30. 98 applicants, 63% accepted, 33 enrolled. In 2016, 22 master's, 4 doctorates awarded. Terminal master's awarded for partial completion of doctoral program. *Degree requirements:* For master's, thesis; for doctorate, comprehensive exam, thesis/dissertation. *Entrance requirements:* For master's, GMAT or GRE General Test, minimum undergraduate GPA of 2.75; for doctorate, GMAT or GRE General Test, minimum graduate GPA of 3.0. Additional exam requirements/recommendations for international students: Required—TOEFL (minimum score 550 paper-based; 79 iBT); Recommended—IELTS (minimum score 6.5). *Application deadline:* For fall admission, 7/15 priority date for domestic students, 3/15 priority date for international students; for spring admission, 12/15 priority date for domestic students, 8/15 priority date for international students. Applications are processed on a rolling basis. Application fee: $65 ($75 for international students). Electronic applications accepted. *Expenses:* Contact institution. *Financial support:* In 2016–17, 22 students received support, including 4 fellowships with full tuition reimbursements available (averaging $10,000 per year), 13 research assistantships with full tuition reimbursements available (averaging $12,500 per year); career-related internships or fieldwork, scholarships/grants, health care benefits, and unspecified assistantships also available. Financial award application deadline: 2/1. *Faculty research:* Public financial management, education finance and policy, tax policy, environmental policy, public organizations and management. *Unit head:* Dr. Ron W. Zimmer, Director of the Martin School, 859-323-5413, Fax: 859-323-1937, E-mail: ron.zimmer@uky.edu. *Application contact:* Jackie McCuddy, Student Affairs Officer, 859-257-5594, Fax: 859-323-1937, E-mail: jackie.mccuddy@uky.edu.
Website: http://www.martin.uky.edu/

**University of Louisville,** Graduate School, College of Arts and Sciences, Department of Urban and Public Affairs, Louisville, KY 40208. Offers public administration (MPA), including human resources management, non-profit management, public policy and administration; urban and public affairs (PhD), including urban planning and development, urban policy and administration; urban planning (MUP), including administration of planning organizations, housing and community development, land use and environmental planning, spatial analysis. *Program availability:* Part-time, evening/weekend. *Faculty:* 12 full-time (5 women), 3 part-time/adjunct (1 woman). *Students:* 59 full-time (23 women), 32 part-time (19 women); includes 19 minority (13 Black or African American, non-Hispanic/Latino; 1 Asian, non-Hispanic/Latino; 2 Hispanic/Latino; 3 Two

or more races, non-Hispanic/Latino), 5 international. Average age 30. 75 applicants, 65% accepted, 25 enrolled. In 2016, 22 master's, 2 doctorates awarded. Terminal master's awarded for partial completion of doctoral program. *Degree requirements:* For master's, internship; for doctorate, comprehensive exam, thesis/dissertation. *Entrance requirements:* For master's, GRE General Test, minimum GPA of 3.0; for doctorate, GRE General Test, master's degree in appropriate field. Additional exam requirements/recommendations for international students: Required—TOEFL (minimum score 550 paper-based; 79 iBT). *Application deadline:* Applications are processed on a rolling basis. Application fee: $60. *Expenses:* Contact institution. *Financial support:* Fellowships, research assistantships, tuition waivers (full and partial), and unspecified assistantships available. Financial award application deadline: 2/1. *Faculty research:* Urban theory, sustainability, public administration, urban planning, urban management. *Total annual research expenditures:* $240,308. *Unit head:* Dr. David Simpson, Chair, 502-852-8019, Fax: 502-852-4558, E-mail: dave.simpson@louisville.edu. *Application contact:* Libby Leggett, Director, Graduate Admissions, 502-852-3101, Fax: 502-852-4558, E-mail: gradadm@louisville.edu.
Website: http://supa.louisville.edu

**University of Maryland, Baltimore County,** The Graduate School, College of Arts, Humanities and Social Sciences, Department of Economics, Program in Economic Policy Analysis, Baltimore, MD 21250. Offers MA. *Program availability:* Part-time. *Faculty:* 17 full-time (6 women), 4 part-time/adjunct (2 women). *Students:* 5 full-time (2 women), 6 part-time (3 women); includes 2 minority (1 Black or African American, non-Hispanic/Latino; 1 Asian, non-Hispanic/Latino), 4 international. Average age 29. 16 applicants, 63% accepted, 5 enrolled. In 2016, 6 master's awarded. *Degree requirements:* For master's, comprehensive exam, capstone research project. *Entrance requirements:* For master's, GRE General Test, undergraduate coursework in economic theory, econometrics, and calculus; letters of reference; statement of purpose; transcripts. Additional exam requirements/recommendations for international students: Required—TOEFL. *Application deadline:* For fall admission, 7/1 priority date for domestic students, 3/1 priority date for international students; for spring admission, 1/1 priority date for domestic students, 9/15 priority date for international students. Applications are processed on a rolling basis. Application fee: $45. Electronic applications accepted. *Expenses:* Tuition, state resident: full-time $13,294. Tuition, nonresident: full-time $20,286. *Financial support:* In 2016–17, 6 students received support, including 5 research assistantships with tuition reimbursements available (averaging $12,560 per year), 1 teaching assistantship with partial tuition reimbursement available (averaging $6,500 per year); Federal Work-Study, health care benefits, tuition waivers (full and partial), and unspecified assistantships also available. Support available to part-time students. Financial award application deadline: 4/15; financial award applicants required to submit FAFSA. *Faculty research:* Health and hospital policy evaluation, environmental policy analysis, economics of education, economic growth and development, cost-benefit and risk analysis. *Total annual research expenditures:* $28,539. *Unit head:* Dr. David F. Mitch, Chair, 410-455-2157, Fax: 410-455-1054, E-mail: mitch@umbc.edu. *Application contact:* Dr. Tim H. Gindling, Graduate Program Director, 410-455-3629, Fax: 410-455-1054,
E-mail: econ-masters@umbc.edu.
Website: http://www.umbc.edu/economics/grad_intro.html

**University of Maryland, Baltimore County,** The Graduate School, College of Arts, Humanities and Social Sciences, Department of Emergency Health Services, Baltimore, MD 21250. Offers administration, planning, and policy (MS); education (MS); emergency health services (MS); emergency management (Postbaccalaureate Certificate); preventive medicine and epidemiology (MS); public policy (PhD), including emergency management, emergency public health. *Program availability:* Part-time, evening/weekend, 100% online, blended/hybrid learning. *Faculty:* 4 full-time (2 women), 8 part-time/adjunct (3 women). *Students:* 15 full-time (11 women), 14 part-time (6 women); includes 11 minority (5 Black or African American, non-Hispanic/Latino; 3 Asian, non-Hispanic/Latino; 2 Hispanic/Latino; 1 Two or more races, non-Hispanic/Latino), 4 international. Average age 26. 25 applicants, 88% accepted, 19 enrolled. In 2016, 22 master's awarded. *Degree requirements:* For master's, comprehensive exam (for some programs), thesis optional, capstone project. *Entrance requirements:* For master's, GRE General Test if GPA is below 3.2, minimum GPA of 3.2. Additional exam requirements/recommendations for international students: Required—TOEFL (minimum score 85 iBT) or IELTS (minimum score 6.5). *Application deadline:* For fall admission, 6/15 for domestic students, 3/1 for international students; for spring admission, 11/1 for domestic students, 10/1 for international students. Applications are processed on a rolling basis. Application fee: $50. Electronic applications accepted. *Expenses:* $13,194 in-state full-time per year, $733 per credit in-state part-time; $1,127 out-of-state per credit. *Financial support:* In 2016–17, 6 students received support, including 5 research assistantships with full tuition reimbursements available (averaging $16,875 per year); career-related internships or fieldwork, Federal Work-Study, scholarships/grants, health care benefits, and unspecified assistantships also available. Financial award application deadline: 5/30; financial award applicants required to submit FAFSA. *Faculty research:* EMS management, disaster health services, emergency management, epidemiology, risk profiles, infectious disease control, stress management for care providers, climate change and public health. *Total annual research expenditures:* $50,000. *Unit head:* Dr. J. Lee Jenkins, Department Chair, 410-455-3216, Fax: 410-455-3045, E-mail: jleejenkins@umbc.edu. *Application contact:* Dr. Rick Bissell, Program Director, 410-455-3776, Fax: 410-455-3045, E-mail: bissell@umbc.edu.
Website: http://ehs.umbc.edu/

**University of Maryland, Baltimore County,** The Graduate School, College of Arts, Humanities and Social Sciences, School of Public Policy, Baltimore, MD 21250. Offers public policy (MPP, PhD), including economics (PhD), educational policy, emergency services (PhD), environmental policy, evaluation and analytical methods, health policy, policy history (PhD), public management, urban policy. *Program availability:* Part-time, evening/weekend. *Faculty:* 10 full-time (4 women), 1 part-time/adjunct (0 women). *Students:* 48 full-time (23 women), 66 part-time (36 women); includes 23 minority (14 Black or African American, non-Hispanic/Latino; 4 Asian, non-Hispanic/Latino; 3 Hispanic/Latino; 1 Native Hawaiian or other Pacific Islander, non-Hispanic/Latino; 1 Two or more races, non-Hispanic/Latino), 6 international. Average age 37. 49 applicants, 65% accepted, 16 enrolled. In 2016, 15 master's, 6 doctorates awarded. Terminal master's awarded for partial completion of doctoral program. *Degree requirements:* For master's, thesis, policy analysis paper, internship for pre-service; for doctorate, thesis/dissertation, comprehensive and field qualifying exams. *Entrance requirements:* For master's and doctorate, GRE General Test, 3 academic letters of reference, resume, research paper, official transcripts. Additional exam requirements/recommendations for international students: Required—TOEFL (minimum score 550 paper-based; 80 iBT). *Application deadline:* For fall admission, 1/15 priority date for domestic students, 1/1 priority date for international students; for spring admission, 11/1 priority date for domestic students, 5/1 priority date for international students. Applications are processed on a rolling basis. Application fee: $50. Electronic applications accepted. *Expenses:* $733 per credit hour in-state tuition and fees, $1,127 per credit hour out-of-state; $27,321 tuition and fees in-state, $41,899 out-of-state (for MPP); $38,316 tuition and fees in-state, $58,804 out-of-state (PhD). *Financial support:* In 2016–17, 25 students received support, including 2 fellowships with full tuition reimbursements

available (averaging $14,000 per year), 23 research assistantships with full tuition reimbursements available (averaging $20,000 per year); career-related internships or fieldwork, Federal Work-Study, scholarships/grants, health care benefits, and unspecified assistantships also available. Financial award application deadline: 1/15; financial award applicants required to submit FAFSA. *Faculty research:* Education policy, health policy, urban policy, public management, evaluation and analytical method. *Unit head:* Dr. Donald F. Norris, Director, 410-455-3201, Fax: 410-455-1172, E-mail: norris@umbc.edu. *Application contact:* Sally F. Helms, Administrator of Academic Affairs, 410-455-3202, Fax: 410-455-1172, E-mail: gradpubpol@umbc.edu.
Website: http://publicpolicy.umbc.edu/

**University of Maryland, College Park,** Academic Affairs, A. James Clark School of Engineering and School of Public Policy, Program in Engineering and Public Policy, College Park, MD 20742. Offers MS.

**University of Maryland, College Park,** Academic Affairs, School of Public Policy, Policy Studies Program, College Park, MD 20742. Offers PhD. *Degree requirements:* For doctorate, comprehensive exam, thesis/dissertation, written and oral exams. *Entrance requirements:* For doctorate, GRE General Test, writing sample. Electronic applications accepted.

**University of Maryland, College Park,** Academic Affairs, School of Public Policy, Programs in Public Policy, College Park, MD 20742. Offers MPP. *Accreditation:* NASPAA. *Entrance requirements:* Additional exam requirements/recommendations for international students: Required—TOEFL. Electronic applications accepted.

**University of Massachusetts Amherst,** Graduate School, College of Social and Behavioral Sciences, Center for Public Policy and Administration, Amherst, MA 01003. Offers MPP, MPPA, MPH/MPPA, MPPA/M Ed, MPPA/MBA, MRP/MPPA. *Program availability:* Part-time. *Degree requirements:* For master's, thesis or alternative. *Entrance requirements:* For master's, GRE General Test. Additional exam requirements/recommendations for international students: Required—TOEFL (minimum score 550 paper-based; 80 iBT), IELTS (minimum score 6.5). Electronic applications accepted.

**University of Massachusetts Amherst,** Graduate School, Interdisciplinary Programs, Dual Degree Program in Education and Public Policy and Administration, Amherst, MA 01003. Offers MPPA/M Ed. *Entrance requirements:* Additional exam requirements/recommendations for international students: Required—TOEFL (minimum score 550 paper-based; 80 iBT), IELTS (minimum score 6.5). Electronic applications accepted.

**University of Massachusetts Amherst,** Graduate School, Interdisciplinary Programs, Dual Degree Program in Management and Public Policy and Administration, Amherst, MA 01003. Offers MPPA/MBA. *Accreditation:* AACSB. *Program availability:* Part-time. *Entrance requirements:* Additional exam requirements/recommendations for international students: Required—TOEFL (minimum score 600 paper-based; 100 iBT), IELTS (minimum score 7). Electronic applications accepted.

**University of Massachusetts Amherst,** Graduate School, Interdisciplinary Programs, Dual Degree Program in Public Policy and Administration and Public Health, Amherst, MA 01003. Offers MPH/MPPA. *Entrance requirements:* Additional exam requirements/recommendations for international students: Required—TOEFL (minimum score 550 paper-based; 80 iBT), IELTS (minimum score 6.5). Electronic applications accepted.

**University of Massachusetts Amherst,** Graduate School, Interdisciplinary Programs, Dual Degree Program in Regional Planning and Public Policy and Administration, Amherst, MA 01003. Offers MPPA/MRP. *Entrance requirements:* Additional exam requirements/recommendations for international students: Required—TOEFL (minimum score 550 paper-based; 80 iBT), IELTS (minimum score 6.5). Electronic applications accepted.

**University of Massachusetts Boston,** John W. McCormack Graduate School of Policy and Global Studies, Program in Public Policy, Boston, MA 02125-3393. Offers MS, PhD. *Program availability:* Evening/weekend. *Faculty:* 10 full-time (3 women), 2 part-time/adjunct (1 woman). *Students:* 16 full-time (8 women), 31 part-time (21 women); includes 4 minority (2 Asian, non-Hispanic/Latino; 2 Hispanic/Latino), 14 international. Average age 34. 33 applicants, 30% accepted, 7 enrolled. In 2016, 1 master's, 2 doctorates awarded. *Degree requirements:* For doctorate, comprehensive exam, thesis/dissertation, practicum, oral exam. *Entrance requirements:* For doctorate, GRE General Test. *Application deadline:* For fall admission, 1/15 for domestic students. *Expenses:* Tuition, state resident: full-time $16,863. Tuition, nonresident: full-time $32,913. *Required fees:* $177. *Financial support:* Research assistantships with full tuition reimbursements, teaching assistantships with full tuition reimbursements, career-related internships or fieldwork, Federal Work-Study, and unspecified assistantships available. Support available to part-time students. Financial award application deadline: 3/1; financial award applicants required to submit FAFSA. *Faculty research:* Political economy, public managerial control, healthcare policy, planning and public policy theory, economic development. *Unit head:* Dr. David Cash, Dean. *Application contact:* Peggy Roldan Patel, Graduate Admissions Coordinator, 617-287-6400, Fax: 617-287-6236, E-mail: bos.gadm@dpc.umassp.edu.

**University of Massachusetts Dartmouth,** Graduate School, College of Arts and Sciences, Department of Public Policy, North Dartmouth, MA 02747-2300. Offers educational policy (Graduate Certificate); environmental policy (Graduate Certificate); public management (Graduate Certificate); public policy (MPP). *Program availability:* Part-time, 100% online. *Faculty:* 4 full-time (0 women), 1 part-time/adjunct (0 women). *Students:* 7 full-time (5 women), 70 part-time (43 women); includes 14 minority (5 Black or African American, non-Hispanic/Latino; 1 Asian, non-Hispanic/Latino; 5 Hispanic/Latino; 3 Two or more races, non-Hispanic/Latino). Average age 36. 66 applicants, 94% accepted, 40 enrolled. In 2016, 15 master's, 17 other advanced degrees awarded. *Degree requirements:* For master's, e-portfolio. *Entrance requirements:* For master's, GRE (waived if applicant has already earned a master's degree or higher, has successfully completed the educational policy or environmental policy post baccalaureate certificates, or is submitting LSAT scores as a joint JD/MPP program applicant), statement of purpose (minimum of 300 words), resume, 2 letters of recommendation, official transcripts; for Graduate Certificate, statement of purpose (minimum of 300 words), resume, official transcripts. Additional exam requirements/recommendations for international students: Required—TOEFL (minimum score 600 paper-based). *Application deadline:* Applications are processed on a rolling basis. Application fee: $60. Electronic applications accepted. *Expenses:* Tuition, state resident: full-time $14,994; part-time $624.75 per credit. Tuition, nonresident: full-time $27,068; part-time $1127.83 per credit. *Required fees:* $405; $25.88 per credit. Tuition and fees vary according to course load and reciprocity agreements. *Financial support:* In 2016–17, 3 research assistantships (averaging $3,400 per year) were awarded; career-related internships or fieldwork, institutionally sponsored loans, scholarships/grants, and unspecified assistantships also available. Support available to part-time students. Financial award application deadline: 3/1; financial award applicants required to submit FAFSA. *Faculty research:* Demographic analysis, legal and regulatory framework, human rights policy, globalization policies, women's public policy issues, educational leadership, environmental law, effects of evaluation models, international trade and finance, corporate social responsibility. *Total annual research expenditures:* $3,000. *Unit head:* Michael Goodman, Graduate Program Director, Public Policy, 508-910-6986, Fax: 508-999-8374, E-mail: mgoodman@umassd.edu. *Application contact:*

## Public Policy

Steven Briggs, Director of Marketing and Recruitment for Graduate Studies, 508-999-8604, Fax: 508-999-8183, E-mail: graduate@umassd.edu. Website: http://www.umassd.edu/cas/departmentsanddegreeprograms/publicpolicy/

**University of Memphis,** Graduate School, College of Arts and Sciences, Division of Public and Nonprofit Administration, Memphis, TN 38103. Offers local government management (Graduate Certificate); philanthropy and nonprofit leadership (Graduate Certificate). *Accreditation:* NASPAA. *Program availability:* Part-time, evening/weekend, blended/hybrid learning. *Faculty:* 5 full-time (3 women), 2 part-time/adjunct (1 woman). *Students:* 17 full-time (12 women), 25 part-time (15 women); includes 23 minority (21 Black or African American, non-Hispanic/Latino; 1 Asian, non-Hispanic/Latino; 1 Hispanic/Latino), 1 international. Average age 32. 21 applicants, 90% accepted, 14 enrolled. In 2016, 39 master's, 36 other advanced degrees awarded. *Degree requirements:* For master's, comprehensive exam, thesis or alternative, internship. *Entrance requirements:* For master's, GRE General Test, GMAT, MAT, or LSAT, minimum GPA of 3.0, resume, two references, statement of interest. Additional exam requirements/recommendations for international students: Required—TOEFL. *Application deadline:* For fall admission, 7/1 for domestic students, 5/1 for international students; for spring admission, 12/1 for domestic students, 9/15 for international students; for summer admission, 5/1 for domestic students, 2/1 for international students. Applications are processed on a rolling basis. Application fee: $35 ($60 for international students). Electronic applications accepted. *Expenses:* $5,231.50 per semester full-time in-state, $9,623.50 full-time out-of-state. *Financial support:* In 2016–17, 37 students received support, including 5 fellowships (averaging $9,000 per year), research assistantships with full tuition reimbursements available, career-related internships or fieldwork, Federal Work-Study, scholarships/grants, health care benefits, and unspecified assistantships also available. Support available to part-time students. Financial award application deadline: 2/1; financial award applicants required to submit FAFSA. *Faculty research:* Nonprofit organization governance, local government management, community collaboration, urban problems, accountability. *Unit head:* Dr. Michael Howell-Moroney, Chair, 901-678-3360, Fax: 901-678-2981, E-mail: mhwllmrn@memphis.edu. *Application contact:* Dr. Sharon Wrobel, MPA Coordinator, 901-678-4720, Fax: 901-678-2981, E-mail: swrobel@memphis.edu. Website: http://www.memphis.edu/padm

**University of Michigan,** Gerald R. Ford School of Public Policy, Ann Arbor, MI 48109. Offers MPA, MPP, PhD, JD/MPP, MBA/MPP, MD/MPP, MHSA/MPP, MPH/MPP, MPP/AM, MPP/MA, MPP/MIS, MPP/MS, MPP/MUP, MSW/MPP. *Faculty:* 36 full-time (13 women), 37 part-time/adjunct (16 women). *Students:* 262 full-time (133 women); includes 72 minority (24 Black or African American, non-Hispanic/Latino; 1 American Indian or Alaska Native, non-Hispanic/Latino; 21 Asian, non-Hispanic/Latino; 17 Hispanic/Latino; 9 Two or more races, non-Hispanic/Latino), 56 international. Average age 28. 631 applicants, 65% accepted, 114 enrolled. In 2016, 103 master's, 7 doctorates awarded. *Degree requirements:* For doctorate, comprehensive exam, thesis/dissertation. *Entrance requirements:* For master's and doctorate, GRE. Additional exam requirements/recommendations for international students: Required—TOEFL (minimum score 560 paper-based; 84 iBT). *Application deadline:* For fall admission, 1/15 priority date for domestic students, 1/15 for international students. Application fee: $75 ($90 for international students). Electronic applications accepted. *Expenses:* $24,480 per year, in-state, $44,386 per year, out-of-state (for master's); $11,422 (for PhD). *Financial support:* In 2016–17, 205 students received support, including 181 fellowships with tuition reimbursements available, 27 teaching assistantships with tuition reimbursements available; research assistantships, career-related internships or fieldwork, traineeships, health care benefits, and unspecified assistantships also available. Financial award application deadline: 1/15; financial award applicants required to submit FAFSA. *Faculty research:* Quantitative policy analysis; U.S. social policy; international economic policy; environmental policy; health policy. *Total annual research expenditures:* $2.4 million. *Unit head:* Dr. Susan M. Collins, Dean, 734-764-3490. *Application contact:* Beth Soboleski, Director, Admissions and Recruiting, 734-764-0453, Fax: 734-647-7486, E-mail: fspp-admissions@umich.edu. Website: http://www.fordschool.umich.edu/

**University of Michigan,** Rackham Graduate School, College of Literature, Science, and the Arts, Department of Economics, Ann Arbor, MI 48109. Offers applied economics (AM); economics (AM, PhD); public policy and economics (PhD); social work and economics (PhD); JD/PhD; MPP/AM. Terminal master's awarded for partial completion of doctoral program. *Degree requirements:* For doctorate, comprehensive exam, thesis/dissertation, oral defense of dissertation; preliminary exams in microeconomics, macroeconomics, and 2 fields. *Entrance requirements:* For master's and doctorate, GRE General Test. Additional exam requirements/recommendations for international students: Required—TOEFL (minimum score 600 paper-based; 100 iBT). Electronic applications accepted. *Expenses:* Tuition, state resident: full-time $21,466; part-time $1152 per credit hour. Tuition, nonresident: full-time $43,346; part-time $2367 per credit hour. Part-time tuition and fees vary according to course load, degree level and program. *Faculty research:* Econometric analysis, finance, industrial organization, international trade, public finance, economic development, economic history, health, labor, natural resources, population studies, macro theory, micro theory.

**University of Michigan,** Rackham Graduate School, College of Literature, Science, and the Arts, Department of Political Science, Ann Arbor, MI 48109. Offers political science (PhD); political science and public policy (PhD); social work and political science (PhD). *Faculty:* 48 full-time (17 women), 6 part-time/adjunct (4 women). *Students:* 104 full-time (42 women); includes 17 minority (5 Black or African American, non-Hispanic/Latino; 4 Asian, non-Hispanic/Latino; 6 Hispanic/Latino; 2 Two or more races, non-Hispanic/Latino), 29 international. Average age 29. 397 applicants, 12% accepted, 17 enrolled. In 2016, 27 doctorates awarded. Terminal master's awarded for partial completion of doctoral program. *Degree requirements:* For doctorate, comprehensive exam, thesis/dissertation, oral defense of dissertation, preliminary exams. *Entrance requirements:* For doctorate, GRE General Test. Additional exam requirements/recommendations for international students: Required—TOEFL. *Application deadline:* For fall admission, 12/15 for domestic and international students. Application fee: $75 ($90 for international students). Electronic applications accepted. *Expenses:* Tuition, state resident: full-time $21,466; part-time $1152 per credit hour. Tuition, nonresident: full-time $43,346; part-time $2367 per credit hour. Part-time tuition and fees vary according to course load, degree level and program. *Financial support:* In 2016–17, 100 students received support, including 17 fellowships with full tuition reimbursements available (averaging $19,737 per year), 12 research assistantships with full tuition reimbursements available (averaging $19,737 per year), 35 teaching assistantships with full tuition reimbursements available (averaging $19,737 per year); health care benefits, tuition waivers (full), and unspecified assistantships also available. Financial award application deadline: 12/15. *Faculty research:* Political theory; American politics; world politics; comparative politics; research methods; law, courts, and politics. *Unit head:* Nancy Burns, Chair, 734-764-6313, Fax: 734-764-3522. *Application contact:* Nicole Rutherford, Academic Program Manager, 734-764-6313, Fax: 734-764-3522, E-mail: psgradinfo@umich.edu. Website: http://www.lsa.umich.edu/polisci

**University of Michigan,** Rackham Graduate School, College of Literature, Science, and the Arts, Department of Sociology, Ann Arbor, MI 48109. Offers public policy and sociology (PhD); social work and sociology (PhD); sociology (PhD). *Degree requirements:* For doctorate, comprehensive exam, thesis/dissertation, oral defense of dissertation, preliminary exam. *Entrance requirements:* For doctorate, GRE General Test, letters of recommendation, writing sample, academic statement of purpose, personal statement, transcript. Additional exam requirements/recommendations for international students: Required—TOEFL (minimum score 560 paper-based; 84 iBT). Electronic applications accepted. *Expenses:* Tuition, state resident: full-time $21,466; part-time $1152 per credit hour. Tuition, nonresident: full-time $43,346; part-time $2367 per credit hour. Part-time tuition and fees vary according to course load, degree level and program. *Faculty research:* Power, history and social change; gender and sexuality; race and ethnicity; economic sociology; social demography.

**University of Minnesota, Twin Cities Campus,** Graduate School, Hubert H. Humphrey School of Public Affairs, PhD Program in Public Affairs, Minneapolis, MN 55455. Offers management and governance (PhD); public policy (PhD); science, technology, and environmental policy (PhD); urban planning (PhD). *Program availability:* Part-time. *Degree requirements:* For doctorate, comprehensive exam, thesis/dissertation. *Entrance requirements:* For doctorate, GRE General Test. Additional exam requirements/recommendations for international students: Required—TOEFL (minimum score 650 paper-based; 100 iBT), IELTS (minimum score 7). Electronic applications accepted. *Expenses:* Contact institution. *Faculty research:* Public policy, urban/regional planning, public/nonprofit management and governance, science/technology/environmental policy.

**University of Minnesota, Twin Cities Campus,** Graduate School, Hubert H. Humphrey School of Public Affairs, Program in Public Policy, Minneapolis, MN 55455. Offers MPP, JD/MPP, MBA/MPP, MPP/MPH, MSW/MPP. *Accreditation:* NASPAA. *Program availability:* Part-time. *Degree requirements:* For master's, thesis or alternative, internship or equivalent work experience. *Entrance requirements:* For master's, GRE General Test, minimum undergraduate GPA of 3.0. Additional exam requirements/recommendations for international students: Required—TOEFL (minimum score 600 paper-based; 100 iBT), IELTS (minimum score 7). Electronic applications accepted. *Expenses:* Contact institution. *Faculty research:* Social policy, public and non-profit management and leadership, community and economic development, foreign policy and international affairs, women and public policy.

**University of Missouri,** Office of Research and Graduate Studies, Harry S Truman School of Public Affairs, Columbia, MO 65211. Offers grantsmanship (Graduate Certificate); nonprofit management (Graduate Certificate); organizational change (Graduate Certificate); public affairs (MPA, PhD); public management (Graduate Certificate); science and public policy (Graduate Certificate). *Accreditation:* NASPAA. *Faculty:* 10 full-time (7 women), 2 part-time/adjunct (0 women). *Students:* 76 full-time (37 women), 168 part-time (88 women); includes 36 minority (21 Black or African American, non-Hispanic/Latino; 1 American Indian or Alaska Native, non-Hispanic/Latino; 2 Asian, non-Hispanic/Latino; 6 Hispanic/Latino; 6 Two or more races, non-Hispanic/Latino), 24 international. Average age 34. *Entrance requirements:* For master's, GRE General Test, minimum GPA of 3.0. Additional exam requirements/recommendations for international students: Required—TOEFL (minimum score 550 paper-based; 80 iBT), IELTS (minimum score 6.5). *Application deadline:* For fall admission, 2/1 priority date for domestic and international students. Applications are processed on a rolling basis. Application fee: $75 ($90 for international students). Electronic applications accepted. *Expenses:* Tuition, state resident: full-time $6347; part-time $352.60 per credit hour. Tuition, nonresident: full-time $17,379; part-time $965.50 per credit hour. *Required fees:* $1035. Tuition and fees vary according to course load, campus/location and program. *Financial support:* Fellowships, research assistantships, teaching assistantships, institutionally sponsored loans, scholarships/grants, traineeships, health care benefits, and unspecified assistantships available. Support available to part-time students. Website: http://truman.missouri.edu/

**University of Missouri–St. Louis,** College of Arts and Sciences, Department of Political Science, St. Louis, MO 63121. Offers American politics (MA); comparative politics (MA); international politics (MA); political process and behavior (MA); political science (PhD); public administration and public policy (MA); urban and regional politics (MA). *Program availability:* Part-time, evening/weekend. *Faculty:* 17 full-time (5 women), 8 part-time/adjunct (4 women). *Students:* 28 full-time (8 women), 30 part-time (12 women); includes 8 minority (7 Black or African American, non-Hispanic/Latino; 1 Two or more races, non-Hispanic/Latino), 5 international. 17 applicants, 82% accepted, 9 enrolled. Terminal master's awarded for partial completion of doctoral program. *Degree requirements:* For master's, thesis optional; for doctorate, thesis/dissertation. *Entrance requirements:* For master's, GRE General Test, 2 letters of recommendation, statement of purpose; for doctorate, GRE General Test, 3 letters of recommendation, statement of purpose. Additional exam requirements/recommendations for international students: Required—TOEFL (minimum score 550 paper-based; 79 iBT), IELTS (minimum score 6.5). *Application deadline:* For fall admission, 2/15 priority date for domestic and international students; for winter admission, 10/15 for domestic and international students; for spring admission, 10/15 priority date for domestic and international students. Applications are processed on a rolling basis. Application fee: $50 ($40 for international students). Electronic applications accepted. *Financial support:* Fellowships, research assistantships with tuition reimbursements, teaching assistantships with tuition reimbursements, and career-related internships or fieldwork available. Support available to part-time students. Financial award application deadline: 3/15; financial award applicants required to submit FAFSA. *Faculty research:* Public policy, urban politics and administration, American government. *Unit head:* Dave Robertson, Chair, 314-516-5521, Fax: 314-516-7236. *Application contact:* 314-516-5458, Fax: 314-516-6996, E-mail: gradadm@umsl.edu. Website: http://www.umsl.edu/~polisci/

**University of Missouri–St. Louis,** Graduate School, Program in Public Policy Administration, St. Louis, MO 63121. Offers local government management (MPPA, Certificate); nonprofit management and leadership (MPPA, Certificate); policy and program evaluation (MPPA, Certificate). *Accreditation:* NASPAA. *Program availability:* Part-time, evening/weekend. *Faculty:* 2 full-time (both women), 6 part-time/adjunct (2 women). *Students:* 10 full-time (5 women), 43 part-time (26 women); includes 14 minority (12 Black or African American, non-Hispanic/Latino; 2 Asian, non-Hispanic/Latino). Average age 33. 28 applicants, 89% accepted, 17 enrolled. *Degree requirements:* For master's, exit project. *Entrance requirements:* For master's, 3 letters of recommendation, personal statement. Additional exam requirements/recommendations for international students: Recommended—TOEFL (minimum score 550 paper-based), IELTS (minimum score 6.5). *Application deadline:* For fall admission, 7/1 priority date for domestic and international students; for spring admission, 12/1 priority date for domestic and international students. Applications are processed on a rolling basis. Application fee: $50 ($40 for international students). Electronic applications accepted. *Financial support:* Research assistantships with tuition reimbursements and career-related internships or fieldwork available. Financial award application deadline: 4/1; financial award applicants required to submit FAFSA. *Faculty research:* Urban policy,

public finance, evaluation. *Unit head:* Dr. Deborah Balser, Director, 314-516-5146, Fax: 314-516-5210, E-mail: balserd@umsl.edu. *Application contact:* 314-516-5458, Fax: 314-516-6996, E-mail: gradadm@umsl.edu.
Website: http://www.umsl.edu/gradschool/ppa/

**University of Nebraska–Lincoln,** Graduate College, College of Arts and Sciences, Department of Political Science, Lincoln, NE 68588. Offers political science (MA, PhD); public policy analysis (Graduate Certificate). *Degree requirements:* For master's, thesis optional; for doctorate, variable foreign language requirement, comprehensive exam, thesis/dissertation. *Entrance requirements:* For master's and doctorate, GRE General Test, writing sample. Additional exam requirements/recommendations for international students: Required—TOEFL (minimum score 600 paper-based). Electronic applications accepted. *Faculty research:* Public policy; comparative politics; international relations; political theory, behavior, and methodology; American politics.

**University of Nevada, Las Vegas,** Graduate College, Greenspun College of Urban Affairs, School of Public Policy and Leadership, Las Vegas, NV 89154-4030. Offers crisis and emergency management (MS); non-profit management (Certificate); public administration (MPA); public affairs (PhD); public management (Certificate); urban leadership (MA). *Program availability:* Part-time. *Faculty:* 13 full-time (7 women), 10 part-time/adjunct (2 women). *Students:* 76 full-time (43 women), 110 part-time (70 women); includes 81 minority (18 Black or African American, non-Hispanic/Latino; 1 American Indian or Alaska Native, non-Hispanic/Latino; 6 Asian, non-Hispanic/Latino; 38 Hispanic/Latino; 4 Native Hawaiian or other Pacific Islander, non-Hispanic/Latino; 14 Two or more races, non-Hispanic/Latino), 7 international. Average age 36. 70 applicants, 86% accepted, 43 enrolled. In 2016, 70 master's, 9 doctorates, 21 other advanced degrees awarded. *Degree requirements:* For master's, comprehensive exam (for some programs), thesis (for some programs), oral exam; for doctorate, comprehensive exam, thesis/dissertation; for Certificate, portfolio. *Entrance requirements:* For master's, GRE General Test or GMAT, bachelor's degree with minimum GPA 2.75; statement of purpose; 3 letters of recommendation; for doctorate, GRE General Test, master's degree with minimum GPA of 3.5; 3 letters of recommendation; statement of purpose; writing sample; personal interview; for Certificate, bachelor's degree; 2 letters of recommendation; writing sample. Additional exam requirements/recommendations for international students: Required—TOEFL (minimum score 550 paper-based; 80 iBT), IELTS (minimum score 7). *Application deadline:* For fall admission, 6/1 for domestic students, 5/1 for international students; for spring admission, 11/1 for domestic students, 10/1 for international students; for summer admission, 3/1 for domestic students. Application fee: $60 ($95 for international students). Electronic applications accepted. *Expenses:* $269.25 per credit, $792 per 3-credit course; $9,634 per year resident; $23,274 per year non-resident; $7,094 fees non-resident (7 credits or more); $1,307 annual health insurance fee. *Financial support:* In 2016–17, 7 research assistantships with partial tuition reimbursements (averaging $14,200 per year), 14 teaching assistantships with partial tuition reimbursements (averaging $16,411 per year) were awarded; institutionally sponsored loans, scholarships/grants, health care benefits, and unspecified assistantships also available. Financial award application deadline: 3/15. *Faculty research:* Community and organizational resilience; environmental decision-making and management; budgeting and human resource/workforce management; urban design, sustainability, and governance; public and non-profit management, public policy, governance, economic development, and urban planning. *Total annual research expenditures:* $244,881. *Unit head:* Dr. Christopher Stream, Director, 702-895-5120, Fax: 702-895-4436, E-mail: chris.stream@unlv.edu. *Application contact:* Dr. Jessica Word, Graduate Coordinator, 702-895-2684, Fax: 702-895-4436, E-mail: jessica.word@unlv.edu.
Website: https://www.unlv.edu/publicpolicy

**University of New Brunswick Fredericton,** School of Graduate Studies, Policy Studies Program, Fredericton, NB E3B 5A3, Canada. Offers citizen engagement/dispute resolution (M Phil); community development (M Phil); international development (M Phil); leadership (M Phil); sustainability/environmental issues (M Phil); worldviews (M Phil). *Program availability:* Part-time. *Degree requirements:* For master's, thesis, report. *Entrance requirements:* For master's, minimum GPA of 3.5. Additional exam requirements/recommendations for international students: Required—TWE (minimum score 5.5), TOEFL (minimum score 600 paper-based; 100 iBT) or IELTS (minimum score 7). Electronic applications accepted. *Faculty research:* International development, worldviews, citizenship/dispute resolution, sustainability/environmental issues, leadership, community development.

**University of New Hampshire,** Graduate School, Carsey School of Public Policy, Durham, NH 03824. Offers community development policy and practice (MA); public policy (MPP). *Students:* 4 part-time. *Degree requirements:* For master's, project. *Entrance requirements:* Additional exam requirements/recommendations for international students: Required—TOEFL (minimum score 550 paper-based; 80 iBT). *Application deadline:* For fall admission, 2/15 for domestic students. Applications are processed on a rolling basis. Application fee: $65. Electronic applications accepted. *Financial support:* Fellowships, research assistantships, teaching assistantships, and scholarships/grants available. *Unit head:* Michael Ettlinger, Director, 603-862-3201, Fax: 603-862-0275, E-mail: michael.ettlinger@unh.edu. *Application contact:* Robin Husslage, Program Manager, 603-862-2338, E-mail: robin.husslage@unh.edu.
Website: http://carsey.unh.edu/

**The University of North Carolina at Chapel Hill,** Graduate School, College of Arts and Sciences, Department of Public Policy, Chapel Hill, NC 27599. Offers PhD. *Degree requirements:* For doctorate, thesis/dissertation. *Entrance requirements:* For doctorate, GRE General Test. Electronic applications accepted. *Faculty research:* Environmental policy; energy policy; economic development and science and technology policy; social policy; welfare, education and low-income communities.

**The University of North Carolina at Charlotte,** College of Liberal Arts and Sciences, Department of Political Science and Public Administration, Charlotte, NC 28223-0001. Offers emergency management (Graduate Certificate); non-profit management (Graduate Certificate); public administration (MPA), including arts administration, emergency management, non-profit management, public budgeting and finance, urban management and policy; public budgeting and finance (Graduate Certificate); urban management and policy (Graduate Certificate). *Accreditation:* NASPAA. *Program availability:* Part-time, evening/weekend. *Faculty:* 19 full-time (10 women), 3 part-time/adjunct (0 women). *Students:* 25 full-time (17 women), 57 part-time (39 women); includes 23 minority (14 Black or African American, non-Hispanic/Latino; 1 American Indian or Alaska Native, non-Hispanic/Latino; 2 Asian, non-Hispanic/Latino; 4 Hispanic/Latino; 2 Two or more races, non-Hispanic/Latino). Average age 30. 55 applicants, 73% accepted, 30 enrolled. In 2016, 31 master's, 12 other advanced degrees awarded. *Degree requirements:* For master's, research project or thesis. *Entrance requirements:* For master's, GRE General Test, bachelor's degree, or its equivalent, from accredited college or university; minimum undergraduate GPA of 3.0; 3 letters of recommendation; statement of purpose; for Graduate Certificate, statement of purpose (1-2 pages in length) explaining applicant's career goals, how the Certificate fits into achieving those goals, and any relevant work experience; official transcripts; letters of recommendation. Additional exam requirements/recommendations for international students: Required—TOEFL (minimum score 523 paper-based, 70 iBT) or IELTS (6.5). *Application deadline:*

For fall admission, 8/1 for domestic and international students; for spring admission, 12/1 for domestic and international students. Applications are processed on a rolling basis. Application fee: $75. Electronic applications accepted. *Expenses:* Tuition, state resident: full-time $4252. Tuition, nonresident: full-time $17,423. *Required fees:* $3026. Tuition and fees vary according to course load and program. *Financial support:* In 2016–17, 9 students received support, including 9 research assistantships (averaging $7,117 per year); career-related internships or fieldwork, Federal Work-Study, institutionally sponsored loans, scholarships/grants, and unspecified assistantships also available. Support available to part-time students. Financial award application deadline: 3/1; financial award applicants required to submit FAFSA. *Total annual research expenditures:* $477,651. *Unit head:* Dr. Greg Weeks, Chair, 704-687-7574, E-mail: gbweeks@uncc.edu. *Application contact:* Kathy B. Giddings, Director of Graduate Admissions, 704-687-5503, Fax: 704-687-1668, E-mail: gradadm@uncc.edu.
Website: http://politicalscience.uncc.edu/

**The University of North Carolina at Charlotte,** College of Liberal Arts and Sciences, Interdisciplinary Liberal Arts and Sciences Programs, Charlotte, NC 28223-0001. Offers gender, sexuality, and women's studies (Graduate Certificate); gerontology (MA, Graduate Certificate); Latin American studies (MA); liberal studies (MA); organizational science (PhD); public policy (PhD). *Program availability:* Part-time, evening/weekend. *Faculty:* 1 (woman) part-time/adjunct. *Students:* 65 full-time (49 women), 61 part-time (50 women); includes 31 minority (11 Black or African American, non-Hispanic/Latino; 1 American Indian or Alaska Native, non-Hispanic/Latino; 2 Asian, non-Hispanic/Latino; 16 Hispanic/Latino; 1 Two or more races, non-Hispanic/Latino), 15 international. Average age 32. 128 applicants, 41% accepted, 40 enrolled. In 2016, 15 master's, 12 doctorates, 7 other advanced degrees awarded. *Degree requirements:* For master's, comprehensive exam (for some programs), thesis (for some programs), practicum, project; for doctorate, comprehensive exam, thesis/dissertation; for Graduate Certificate, practicum (for gerontology). *Entrance requirements:* For master's, GRE General Test or MAT, bachelor's degree from accredited college or university; official transcripts of all previous academic work attempted beyond high school; minimum overall GPA of 3.0 on applicant's previous work beyond high school; statement of purpose; recommendation letters; for doctorate, GRE or GMAT, statement of purpose discussing interest in program and objectives for pursuing degree, current resume or curriculum vitae, unofficial transcripts; for Graduate Certificate, bachelor's degree from accredited university and either be enrolled in and in good standing in a graduate degree program at UNC Charlotte or have a minimum undergraduate GPA of 3.0. Additional exam requirements/recommendations for international students: Required—TOEFL (minimum score 523 paper-based, 70 iBT) or IELTS (6.5). *Application deadline:* For fall admission, 2/15 for domestic and international students; for spring admission, 10/1 for domestic and international students; for summer admission, 4/1 for domestic and international students. Applications are processed on a rolling basis. Application fee: $75. Electronic applications accepted. *Expenses:* Tuition, state resident: full-time $4252. Tuition, nonresident: full-time $17,423. *Required fees:* $3026. Tuition and fees vary according to course load and program. *Financial support:* In 2016–17, 26 students received support, including 17 research assistantships (averaging $12,840 per year), 7 teaching assistantships (averaging $14,442 per year); career-related internships or fieldwork, institutionally sponsored loans, scholarships/grants, unspecified assistantships, and administrative assistantships also available. Support available to part-time students. Financial award application deadline: 3/1; financial award applicants required to submit FAFSA. *Unit head:* Dr. Nancy A. Gutierrez, Dean, 704-687-0081, E-mail: ngutierr@uncc.edu. *Application contact:* Kathy B. Giddings, Director of Graduate Admissions, 704-687-5503, Fax: 704-687-3279, E-mail: gradadm@uncc.edu.
Website: http://clas.uncc.edu/academics

**University of Northern Iowa,** Graduate College, College of Social and Behavioral Sciences, MPP Program in Public Policy, Cedar Falls, IA 50614. Offers MPP. *Program availability:* Part-time. *Degree requirements:* For master's, comprehensive exam (for some programs). *Entrance requirements:* For master's, minimum GPA of 3.0. Additional exam requirements/recommendations for international students: Required—TOEFL (minimum score 500 paper-based; 61 iBT). Electronic applications accepted.

**University of Oregon,** Graduate School, School of Architecture and Allied Arts, Department of Planning, Public Policy, and Management, Program in Public Policy and Management, Eugene, OR 97403. Offers MA, MPA, MS. *Accreditation:* NASPAA. *Program availability:* Part-time, evening/weekend. *Degree requirements:* For master's, thesis. *Entrance requirements:* For master's, minimum GPA of 3.0. Additional exam requirements/recommendations for international students: Required—TOEFL. *Faculty research:* Community economic development, families in poverty, health services.

**University of Pennsylvania,** Wharton School, Department of Business and Public Policy, Philadelphia, PA 19104. Offers MBA, PhD. *Degree requirements:* For doctorate, thesis/dissertation. *Entrance requirements:* For doctorate, GRE General Test. *Expenses:* Tuition: Full-time $31,068; part-time $5762 per course. *Required fees:* $3200; $336 per course. Full-time tuition and fees vary according to degree level, program and student level. Part-time tuition and fees vary according to course load, degree level and program. *Faculty research:* International policy, business and government, regulation, urban development and policy, transportation.

**University of Pittsburgh,** Graduate School of Public and International Affairs, Doctoral Program in Public and International Affairs, Pittsburgh, PA 15260. Offers international affairs (PhD); international development (PhD); public administration (PhD); public policy (PhD). *Program availability:* Part-time, evening/weekend. *Faculty:* 34 full-time (12 women), 17 part-time/adjunct (5 women). *Students:* 29 full-time (12 women), 1 part-time (0 women); includes 4 minority (2 Asian, non-Hispanic/Latino; 2 Hispanic/Latino), 14 international. Average age 37. 60 applicants, 18% accepted, 5 enrolled. In 2016, 3 doctorates awarded. *Degree requirements:* For doctorate, comprehensive exam, thesis/dissertation, mid-term evaluation, preliminary exam, annual review. *Entrance requirements:* For doctorate, GRE or GMAT, 2 letters of recommendation, resume, undergraduate transcripts, personal statement, writing sample. Additional exam requirements/recommendations for international students: Required—TOEFL (minimum score 80 iBT); Recommended—IELTS (minimum score 7). *Application deadline:* For fall admission, 1/15 for domestic and international students. Application fee: $50. Electronic applications accepted. *Expenses:* $22,578 per year in-state; $36,734 per year out-of-state. *Financial support:* In 2016–17, 16 students received support, including 16 research assistantships with partial tuition reimbursements available (averaging $14,620 per year); fellowships also available. Financial award application deadline: 1/15; financial award applicants required to submit FAFSA. *Faculty research:* International development, international security and intelligence, human rights, urban affairs and planning, energy and environmental policy, nonprofit management, public management. *Total annual research expenditures:* $1.3 million. *Unit head:* Dr. John T.S. Keeler, Dean, 412-648-7605, Fax: 412-648-2605, E-mail: keeler@pitt.edu. *Application contact:* Dr. Michael T. Rizzi, Director of Student Services, 412-648-7640, Fax: 412-648-7641, E-mail: rizzim@pitt.edu.
Website: http://www.gspia.pitt.edu/

**University of Pittsburgh,** Graduate School of Public and International Affairs, Master of Public Administration Program, Pittsburgh, PA 15260. Offers energy and environment (MPA); governance and international public management (MPA); policy research and

analysis (MPA); public and nonprofit management (MPA); urban affairs and planning (MPA); JD/MPA; MPH/MPA; MSIS/MPA; MSW/MPA. *Accreditation:* NASPAA. *Program availability:* Part-time, evening/weekend. *Faculty:* 34 full-time (12 women), 17 part-time/adjunct (5 women). *Students:* 93 full-time (66 women), 21 part-time (16 women); includes 8 minority (4 Black or African American, non-Hispanic/Latino; 1 Asian, non-Hispanic/Latino; 3 Hispanic/Latino), 61 international. Average age 26. 200 applicants, 81% accepted, 49 enrolled. In 2016, 62 master's awarded. *Degree requirements:* For master's, thesis optional, capstone seminar. *Entrance requirements:* For master's, GRE General Test or GMAT, 2 letters of recommendation, resume, undergraduate transcripts, personal statement. Additional exam requirements/recommendations for international students: Required—TOEFL (minimum score 80 iBT); Recommended—IELTS (minimum score 7). *Application deadline:* For fall admission, 2/1 priority date for domestic students, 1/15 for international students; for spring admission, 11/1 for domestic students, 8/1 for international students. Application fee: $50. Electronic applications accepted. *Expenses:* $22,578 per year in-state; $36,734 per year out-of-state. *Financial support:* In 2016–17, 10 students received support, including 2 research assistantships with full tuition reimbursements available (averaging $14,620 per year); fellowships with full tuition reimbursements available, career-related internships or fieldwork, scholarships/grants, health care benefits, and unspecified assistantships also available. Financial award application deadline: 2/1; financial award applicants required to submit FAFSA. *Faculty research:* Urban affairs and planning, governance and international public management, nonprofit management, policy research and analysis, energy and environmental policy. *Total annual research expenditures:* $1.3 million. *Unit head:* Dr. John T.S. Keeler, Dean, 412-648-7605, Fax: 412-648-2605, E-mail: keeler@pitt.edu. *Application contact:* Dr. Michael T. Rizzi, Director of Student Services, 412-648-7640, Fax: 412-648-7641, E-mail: rizzim@pitt.edu.
Website: http://www.gspia.pitt.edu/

**University of Pittsburgh,** Graduate School of Public and International Affairs, Master of Public Policy and Management Program, Pittsburgh, PA 15236. Offers MPPM. *Program availability:* Part-time, evening/weekend, 100% online. *Faculty:* 34 full-time (12 women), 17 part-time/adjunct (5 women). *Students:* 17 full-time (4 women), 98 part-time (63 women); includes 17 minority (6 Black or African American, non-Hispanic/Latino; 2 Asian, non-Hispanic/Latino; 2 Hispanic/Latino; 7 Two or more races, non-Hispanic/Latino), 11 international. Average age 41. 78 applicants, 79% accepted, 47 enrolled. In 2016, 16 master's awarded. *Entrance requirements:* For master's, 2 letters of recommendation, resume, personal statement, 5 years of full-time supervisory or budgetary experience. Additional exam requirements/recommendations for international students: Required—TOEFL (minimum score 80 iBT); Recommended—IELTS (minimum score 7). *Application deadline:* For fall admission, 6/1 priority date for domestic students, 1/15 for international students; for spring admission, 11/1 for domestic students, 8/1 for international students; for summer admission, 3/1 for domestic students, 1/15 for international students. Application fee: $50. Electronic applications accepted. *Expenses:* $877 per credit in-state tuition, $1,468 per credit out-of-state tuition; $265 per term part-time fees, $830 per term full-time fees. *Financial support:* In 2016–17, 18 students received support. Scholarships/grants available. Financial award application deadline: 1/1; financial award applicants required to submit FAFSA. *Faculty research:* Public and nonprofit management, policy research and analysis. *Total annual research expenditures:* $1.3 million. *Unit head:* Dr. John T.S. Keeler, Dean, 412-648-7605, Fax: 412-648-2605. *Application contact:* Dr. Michael T. Rizzi, Director of Student Services, 412-648-7640, Fax: 412-648-7641, E-mail: rizzim@pitt.edu.
Website: http://www.gspia.pitt.edu/

**University of Puerto Rico, Río Piedras Campus,** Graduate School of Planning, San Juan, PR 00931-3300. Offers economic planning systems (MP); environmental planning (MP); social policy and planning (MP); urban and territorial planning (MP). *Accreditation:* ACSP. *Program availability:* Part-time. *Degree requirements:* For master's, comprehensive exam, thesis, planning project defense. *Entrance requirements:* For master's, PAEG, GRE, minimum GPA of 3.0, 2 letters of recommendation. *Faculty research:* Municipalities, historic Atlas, Puerto Rico, economic future.

**University of Regina,** Faculty of Graduate Studies and Research, Johnson-Shoyama Graduate School of Public Policy, Regina, SK S4S 0A2, Canada. Offers economic analysis for public policy (Master's Certificate); health administration (MHA); health systems management (Master's Certificate); public management (MPA, Master's Certificate); public policy (MPA, MPP, PhD); public policy analysis (Master's Certificate). *Program availability:* Part-time. *Faculty:* 9 full-time (4 women), 15 part-time/adjunct (4 women). *Students:* 88 full-time (56 women), 159 part-time (103 women). 202 applicants, 43% accepted. In 2016, 43 master's, 20 other advanced degrees awarded. *Degree requirements:* For master's, thesis (for some programs); for doctorate, thesis/dissertation. *Entrance requirements:* For doctorate, master's degree, intended research program in an area of public policy. Additional exam requirements/recommendations for international students: Required—TOEFL (minimum score 580 paper-based; 80 iBT), IELTS (minimum score 6.5), PTE (minimum score 59). *Application deadline:* For fall admission, 2/1 for domestic and international students. Application fee: $100. Electronic applications accepted. *Expenses:* Contact institution. *Financial support:* In 2016–17, 17 fellowships (averaging $6,059 per year), 19 teaching assistantships (averaging $2,507 per year) were awarded; career-related internships or fieldwork and scholarships/grants also available. Financial award application deadline: 6/15. *Faculty research:* Governance and administration, public finance, public policy analysis, non-governmental organizations and alternative service delivery, micro-economics for policy analysis. *Unit head:* Dr. Kathleen McNutt, Executive Director, Main Campus, 306-585-4759, Fax: 306-585-5461, E-mail: kathy.mcnutt@uregina.ca. *Application contact:* Constance Heshka-Argue, Manager, Main Campus, 306-585-5462, Fax: 306-585-5461, E-mail: connie.heska-argue@uregina.ca.
Website: http://www.schoolofpublicpolicy.sk.ca/

**University of Rhode Island,** Graduate School, College of Arts and Sciences, Department of Political Science, Kingston, RI 02881. Offers political science (MA), including American politics, comparative government, international relations, public policy; public policy and administration (MPA). *Program availability:* Part-time. *Faculty:* 12 full-time (5 women). *Students:* 20 full-time (9 women), 37 part-time (20 women); includes 11 minority (4 Black or African American, non-Hispanic/Latino; 2 American Indian or Alaska Native, non-Hispanic/Latino; 1 Asian, non-Hispanic/Latino; 3 Hispanic/Latino; 1 Two or more races, non-Hispanic/Latino), 1 international. In 2016, 15 master's awarded. *Degree requirements:* For master's, comprehensive exam (for some programs), thesis optional. *Entrance requirements:* For master's, GRE, GMAT, or MAT if undergraduate GPA below 3.0, 2 letters of recommendation. Additional exam requirements/recommendations for international students: Required—TOEFL. *Application deadline:* For fall admission, 2/1 for international students; for spring admission, 7/15 for international students. Application fee: $65. Electronic applications accepted. *Expenses:* Tuition, state resident: full-time $11,796; part-time $655 per credit. Tuition, nonresident: full-time $24,206; part-time $1345 per credit. *Required fees:* $1546; $44 per credit. One-time fee: $155 full-time; $35 part-time. *Financial support:* In 2016–17, 6 teaching assistantships with tuition reimbursements (averaging $15,753 per year) were awarded; research assistantships also available. Financial award application deadline: 7/15; financial award applicants required to submit FAFSA. *Unit head:* Dr.

Brian Krueger, Department Chair, 401-874-4058, Fax: 401-874-4072, E-mail: bkrueger@uri.edu. *Application contact:* Dr. Marc Hutchison, Director/Associate Professor, 401-874-4054, Fax: 401-874-4072, E-mail: mlhutch@uri.edu.
Website: http://www.uri.edu/artsci/psc/

**University of St. Thomas,** School of Arts and Sciences, Houston, TX 77006-4696. Offers public policy administration (MPPA); sacred music (MSM). *Program availability:* Part-time. *Faculty:* 2 full-time (0 women), 4 part-time/adjunct (all women). *Students:* 9 full-time (6 women), 17 part-time (10 women); includes 16 minority (3 Black or African American, non-Hispanic/Latino; 1 Asian, non-Hispanic/Latino; 12 Hispanic/Latino). Average age 33. 14 applicants, 86% accepted, 9 enrolled. In 2016, 7 master's awarded. *Entrance requirements:* Additional exam requirements/recommendations for international students: Required—TOEFL (minimum score 79 iBT), IELTS (minimum score 6.5), PTE (minimum score 53). *Application deadline:* For fall admission, 7/15 priority date for domestic and international students; for spring admission, 12/1 priority date for domestic and international students; for summer admission, 5/1 priority date for domestic and international students. Applications are processed on a rolling basis. Application fee: $35. Electronic applications accepted. *Expenses:* Tuition: Full-time $20,934; part-time $1163 per credit hour. *Required fees:* $81 per semester. One-time fee: $100. Part-time tuition and fees vary according to course level, course load, campus/location and program. *Financial support:* In 2016–17, 23 students received support. Federal Work-Study, scholarships/grants, and state work-study, institutional employment available. Support available to part-time students. Financial award application deadline: 4/15; financial award applicants required to submit FAFSA. *Unit head:* Dr. John W. Starner, Jr., Interim Dean, School of Arts and Sciences, 713-525-3527, E-mail: starner@stthom.edu. *Application contact:* Todd Boutte, Director of Graduate Admissions, 713-942-3403, E-mail: boutet@stthom.edu.
Website: http://www.stthom.edu/Academics/School_of_Arts_and_Sciences/Index.aqf

**University of Saskatchewan,** College of Graduate Studies and Research, School of Public Policy, Saskatoon, SK S7N 5A2, Canada. Offers MIT, MPA, MPP, PhD.

**The University of South Dakota,** Graduate School, College of Arts and Sciences, Department of Political Science, Vermillion, SD 57069. Offers American political institutions (PhD); American politics and public policy (MA); political science (EMPA, MA); public administration (MPA, PhD); public policy (PhD); JD/MA. *Accreditation:* NASPAA (one or more programs are accredited). *Program availability:* Part-time, online learning. *Degree requirements:* For master's, comprehensive exam, thesis (for some programs). *Entrance requirements:* For master's, GRE or LSAT (for MPA), GRE General Test (for MA), minimum GPA of 3.0. Additional exam requirements/recommendations for international students: Required—TOEFL (minimum score 550 paper-based; 79 iBT). Electronic applications accepted.

**University of Southern California,** Graduate School, School of Policy, Planning, and Development, Doctor of Philosophy in Public Policy and Management Program, Los Angeles, CA 90089. Offers PhD. *Degree requirements:* For doctorate, thesis/dissertation. *Entrance requirements:* For doctorate, GRE. Additional exam requirements/recommendations for international students: Required—TOEFL (minimum score 600 paper-based; 100 iBT). Electronic applications accepted. *Faculty research:* Governance: effective institutions, leadership, management, community and economic development, institutional analysis, civic engagement.

**University of Southern California,** Graduate School, School of Policy, Planning, and Development, Public Policy Programs, Los Angeles, CA 90089. Offers homeland security and public policy (Graduate Certificate); public policy (MPP, Graduate Certificate); M PI/MPP; MPP/JD. *Program availability:* Part-time. Terminal master's awarded for partial completion of doctoral program. *Degree requirements:* For master's, practicum. *Entrance requirements:* For master's, GRE. Additional exam requirements/recommendations for international students: Required—TOEFL (minimum score 600 paper-based; 100 iBT). Electronic applications accepted. *Faculty research:* Urban political economy, community and economic development, environmental policy, transportation policy, housing policy.

**University of Southern Maine,** College of Management and Human Service, Muskie School of Public Service, Program in Public Policy and Management, Portland, ME 04103. Offers MPPM, JD/MPPM. *Program availability:* Part-time, evening/weekend, online learning. *Degree requirements:* For master's, thesis, capstone project, field experience. *Entrance requirements:* For master's, GRE General Test or LSAT. Additional exam requirements/recommendations for international students: Required—TOEFL. Electronic applications accepted. *Faculty research:* State and local public finance, education finance, applied social science methodology, nonprofit and higher education organizational management, public service ethics, comparative public policy.

**The University of Texas at Arlington,** Graduate School, College of Architecture, Planning and Public Affairs, Program in Public Policy, Arlington, TX 76019. Offers MPP. *Program availability:* Part-time, evening/weekend. *Application deadline:* For fall admission, 2/1 for domestic and international students. Application fee: $35 ($50 for international students). Electronic applications accepted. *Financial support:* Fellowships, research assistantships, and teaching assistantships with full tuition reimbursements available. Financial award application deadline: 6/1; financial award applicants required to submit FAFSA. *Faculty research:* Environment urban policy personnel, research theoretical foundations, urban problems. *Unit head:* Dr. David Coursey, Program Director/Academic Advisor, 817-272-0416, Fax: 817-272-3415, E-mail: dcoursey@uta.edu. *Application contact:* Tangie Fields, Academic Advisor, 817-272-3340, Fax: 817-272-3415, E-mail: nfields@uta.edu.
Website: http://www.uta.edu/cappa/academics/public-affairs/public-policy/mpp.php

**The University of Texas at Arlington,** Graduate School, College of Architecture, Planning and Public Affairs, Program in Urban Planning and Public Policy, Arlington, TX 76019. Offers PhD. *Accreditation:* ACSP. *Program availability:* Part-time, evening/weekend. *Entrance requirements:* Additional exam requirements/recommendations for international students: Required—TOEFL (minimum score 550 paper-based). *Application deadline:* For fall admission, 6/1 for domestic students, 4/1 for international students; for spring admission, 10/15 for domestic students, 9/15 for international students. Applications are processed on a rolling basis. Application fee: $35 ($50 for international students). Electronic applications accepted. *Financial support:* Fellowships, research assistantships, and career-related internships or fieldwork available. Financial award application deadline: 6/1; financial award applicants required to submit FAFSA. *Faculty research:* Urban structure, GIS environmental resolutions, qualitative methods, planning history/theory. *Unit head:* Dr. Ivonne Audirac, Program Director, 817-272-3338, Fax: 817-272-5008, E-mail: audirac@uta.edu. *Application contact:* Christa Barreras, Academic Advisor, 817-272-5631, Fax: 817-272-5631, E-mail: christab@uta.edu.
Website: http://www.uta.edu/cappa/academics/planning-landscape-architecture/phd-uppp.php

**The University of Texas at Austin,** Graduate School, Lyndon B. Johnson School of Public Affairs, Austin, TX 78712-1111. Offers global policy studies (MGPS); public affairs (MP Aff); public leadership (EMPL); public policy (PhD); JD/MP Aff; MBA/MP Aff; MP Aff/MA; MP Aff/MSE. *Accreditation:* NASPAA (one or more programs are accredited). *Program availability:* Part-time. *Degree requirements:* For master's, thesis, summer internship; for doctorate, thesis/dissertation. *Entrance requirements:* For master's, GRE General Test (for MP Aff and MGPS), minimum GPA of 3.0 in upper-division classes, seven years of experience in the public sector, and interview (for EMPL); for doctorate, GRE General Test, master's degree in policy-related field. Additional exam requirements/recommendations for international students: Required—TOEFL. Electronic applications accepted. *Faculty research:* Human resource development, health and social policy, philanthropy and community service, ethical leadership, urban and international policy, science and technology policy.

**The University of Texas at Dallas,** School of Economic, Political and Policy Sciences, Program in Public Policy and Political Economy, Richardson, TX 75080. Offers international political economy (MS); public policy (MPP); public policy and political economy (PhD); social data analytics and research (MS). *Program availability:* Part-time, evening/weekend. *Faculty:* 24 full-time (2 women), 2 part-time/adjunct (1 woman). *Students:* 47 full-time (24 women), 30 part-time (14 women); includes 20 minority (4 Black or African American, non-Hispanic/Latino; 1 American Indian or Alaska Native, non-Hispanic/Latino; 3 Asian, non-Hispanic/Latino; 11 Hispanic/Latino; 1 Two or more races, non-Hispanic/Latino), 25 international. Average age 35. 55 applicants, 55% accepted, 12 enrolled. In 2016, 13 master's, 9 doctorates awarded. *Degree requirements:* For doctorate, thesis/dissertation. *Entrance requirements:* For master's and doctorate, GRE General Test, minimum GPA of 3.0 in upper-level course work in field. Additional exam requirements/recommendations for international students: Required—TOEFL (minimum score 550 paper-based). *Application deadline:* For fall admission, 7/15 for domestic students, 5/1 priority date for international students; for spring admission, 11/15 for domestic students, 9/1 priority date for international students. Applications are processed on a rolling basis. Application fee: $50 ($100 for international students). Electronic applications accepted. *Expenses:* Tuition, state resident: full-time $12,418; part-time $690 per semester hour. Tuition, nonresident: full-time $24,150; part-time $1342 per semester hour. Tuition and fees vary according to course load. *Financial support:* In 2016–17, 45 students received support, including 13 research assistantships with partial tuition reimbursements available (averaging $18,538 per year), 14 teaching assistantships with partial tuition reimbursements available (averaging $13,100 per year); career-related internships or fieldwork, Federal Work-Study, institutionally sponsored loans, scholarships/grants, and unspecified assistantships also available. Support available to part-time students. Financial award application deadline: 4/30; financial award applicants required to submit FAFSA. *Faculty research:* Ethnicity, community and local public good provision; community mental health policy; Texas Schools Project; biological and chemical arms control; cross-disciplinary applications of quantitative methodology. *Unit head:* Dr. Jennifer Holmes, Program Head, 972-883-6843, Fax: 972-883-6297, E-mail: jholmes@utdallas.edu. *Application contact:* Betsy Albritton, Graduate Program Administrator, 972-883-6406, Fax: 972-883-6297, E-mail: betsy.albritton@utdallas.edu.
Website: http://www.utdallas.edu/epps/public-policy-and-political-economy/

**The University of Texas Rio Grande Valley,** College of Liberal Arts, Department of Public Affairs and Security Studies, Edinburg, TX 78539. Offers global security studies and leadership (MPA); public administration (MPA); public policy and management (MPA). *Program availability:* Part-time, evening/weekend. *Degree requirements:* For master's, comprehensive exam (for some programs), thesis optional. *Entrance requirements:* For master's, minimum undergraduate GPA of 3.0, official transcripts, personal statement, three recommendations. Additional exam requirements/recommendations for international students: Required—TOEFL (minimum score 550 paper-based; 79 iBT). Electronic applications accepted. Tuition and fees vary according to course load and program. *Faculty research:* Immigration policy reform, agriculture food policy, social service delivery systems, community development, social welfare policy reform, urban/city management.

**University of the Pacific,** McGeorge School of Law, Sacramento, CA 95817. Offers advocacy (JD); international water resources law (JSD); public policy and law (LL M); JD/MBA; JD/MPPA. *Accreditation:* ABA. *Program availability:* Part-time, evening/weekend. *Faculty:* 38 full-time (17 women), 40 part-time/adjunct (11 women). *Students:* 365 full-time (195 women), 188 part-time (105 women); includes 187 minority (24 Black or African American, non-Hispanic/Latino; 3 American Indian or Alaska Native, non-Hispanic/Latino; 43 Asian, non-Hispanic/Latino; 114 Hispanic/Latino; 1 Native Hawaiian or other Pacific Islander, non-Hispanic/Latino; 2 Two or more races, non-Hispanic/Latino), 1 international. Average age 28. In 2016, 4 master's, 158 doctorates awarded. *Degree requirements:* For master's, thesis (for some programs); for doctorate, thesis/dissertation (for some programs). *Entrance requirements:* For master's, JD; for doctorate, LSAT (for JD), LL M (for JSD). Additional exam requirements/recommendations for international students: Required—TOEFL (minimum score 600 paper-based; 100 iBT). *Application deadline:* For fall admission, 3/15 priority date for domestic students. Applications are processed on a rolling basis. Application fee: $50. Electronic applications accepted. *Expenses:* Contact institution. *Financial support:* Fellowships, research assistantships, teaching assistantships, career-related internships or fieldwork, Federal Work-Study, institutionally sponsored loans, and scholarships/grants available. Support available to part-time students. Financial award applicants required to submit FAFSA. *Faculty research:* International legal studies, public policy and law, advocacy, intellectual property law, taxation, criminal law. *Unit head:* Francis Jay Mootz, III, Dean, 916-739-7151, E-mail: jmootz@pacific.edu. *Application contact:* 916-739-7105, Fax: 916-739-7301, E-mail: mcgeorge@pacific.edu.
Website: http://www.mcgeorge.edu/

**University of Utah,** Graduate School, College of Social and Behavioral Science, Department of Political Science, Program in Public Policy, Salt Lake City, UT 84112. Offers MPP, MPP/JD, MPP/MPH, MPP/PhD. *Program availability:* Part-time, evening/weekend. *Students:* 9 full-time (7 women), 9 part-time (8 women); includes 1 minority (Hispanic/Latino). Average age 34. 26 applicants, 88% accepted, 11 enrolled. In 2016, 8 master's awarded. *Degree requirements:* For master's, project. *Entrance requirements:* For master's, GRE, LSAT, GMAT, or MAT. Additional exam requirements/recommendations for international students: Required—TOEFL (minimum score 583 paper-based; 93 iBT). *Application deadline:* For fall admission, 3/1 for domestic and international students. Application fee: $55 ($65 for international students). Electronic applications accepted. *Expenses:* Contact institution. *Financial support:* In 2016–17, 5 students received support, including 3 fellowships with partial tuition reimbursements available (averaging $1,500 per year); unspecified assistantships also available. Financial award application deadline: 2/15. *Unit head:* Lina Svedin, Director, 801-581-7031, E-mail: lina.svedin@poli-sci.utah.edu. *Application contact:* Elizabeth Henke, Program Manager, 801-585-7834, E-mail: elizabeth.henke@cppa.utah.edu.
Website: http://www.mpp.utah.edu

**University of Virginia,** Frank Batten Sr. School of Leadership and Public Policy, Charlottesville, VA 22903. Offers MPP, JD/MPP, MBA/MPP, MPP/MPH, MPP/MUEP, MPP/PhD. *Faculty:* 20 full-time (7 women), 3 part-time/adjunct (1 woman). *Students:* 108 full-time (70 women); includes 21 minority (3 Black or African American, non-Hispanic/Latino; 5 Asian, non-Hispanic/Latino; 5 Hispanic/Latino; 8 Two or more races, non-Hispanic/Latino), 7 international. Average age 24. 200 applicants, 79% accepted, 73 enrolled. In 2016, 70 master's awarded. *Entrance requirements:* Additional exam requirements/recommendations for international students: Required—TOEFL, IELTS.

*Application deadline:* For fall admission, 2/20 for domestic and international students. Applications are processed on a rolling basis. Electronic applications accepted. *Expenses:* $23,904 tuition, $2,654 fees in-state; $44,792 tuition, $3,336 fees out-of-state. *Unit head:* Allan C. Stam, Dean, 434-924-0812, Fax: 434-243-2318, E-mail: stam@virginia.edu. *Application contact:* Patti Edson, Assistant Director of Admissions, 434-982-2583, Fax: 434-243-2318, E-mail: patti.edson@virginia.edu.
Website: http://batten.virginia.edu/

**University of Washington,** Graduate School, Evans School of Public Policy and Governance, Seattle, WA 98195. Offers public administration (MPA); public policy and management (PhD); JD/MPA; MPA/MAIS; MPA/MPH; MPA/MS; MPA/MUP. *Accreditation:* NASPAA. *Program availability:* Part-time, evening/weekend. *Degree requirements:* For master's, thesis, internship or cooperative experience. *Entrance requirements:* For master's and doctorate, GRE General Test, minimum GPA of 3.0. Additional exam requirements/recommendations for international students: Required—TOEFL (minimum score 580 paper-based; 92 iBT). Electronic applications accepted. *Faculty research:* Environmental policy, education and social policy, nonprofit management, international affairs, urban and regional development.

**University of Washington, Bothell,** Master of Arts in Policy Studies Program, Bothell, WA 98011. Offers MA. *Program availability:* Evening/weekend. *Degree requirements:* For master's, thesis. *Entrance requirements:* For master's, GRE, statistics and micro-economics courses. Additional exam requirements/recommendations for international students: Required—TOEFL. Electronic applications accepted. *Faculty research:* Policy studies, cultural studies, cultural and environmental politics, disability studies, public policy.

**Vanderbilt University,** Program in Community Research and Action, Nashville, TN 37240-1001. Offers PhD. *Faculty:* 18 full-time (10 women). *Students:* 23 full-time (16 women); includes 8 minority (3 Black or African American, non-Hispanic/Latino; 1 Asian, non-Hispanic/Latino; 1 Hispanic/Latino; 3 Two or more races, non-Hispanic/Latino), 3 international. Average age 30. 95 applicants, 7% accepted, 4 enrolled. In 2016, 8 doctorates awarded. *Degree requirements:* For doctorate, thesis/dissertation, internship, fundable grant proposal. *Entrance requirements:* For doctorate, GRE General Test. Additional exam requirements/recommendations for international students: Required—TOEFL (minimum score 570 paper-based; 88 iBT). *Application deadline:* For fall admission, 12/1 for domestic and international students. Application fee: $0. Electronic applications accepted. *Expenses:* Contact institution. *Financial support:* In 2016–17, 16 students received support. Fellowships with tuition reimbursements available, research assistantships with full tuition reimbursements available, teaching assistantships with full tuition reimbursements available, Federal Work-Study, scholarships/grants, health care benefits, tuition waivers, and unspecified assistantships available. Financial award application deadline: 1/15; financial award applicants required to submit FAFSA. *Faculty research:* Applied psychological research, community theory, mental health, public policy, race dynamics. *Unit head:* Dr. Douglas Perkins, Director of Graduate Studies, 615-322-7213, Fax: 615-322-1769, E-mail: douglas.d.perkins@vanderbilt.edu. *Application contact:* Sherrie Lane, Administrative Assistant, 615-322-8484, Fax: 615-322-1141, E-mail: sherrie.a.lane@vanderbilt.edu.
Website: http://peabody.vanderbilt.edu/departments/hod/graduate-programs/phd_in_community_research_and_action/community_research_and_action_program.php

**Virginia Commonwealth University,** Graduate School, College of Humanities and Sciences, L. Douglas Wilder School of Government and Public Affairs, Center for Public Policy, Richmond, VA 23284-9005. Offers public policy and administration (PhD). *Degree requirements:* For doctorate, thesis/dissertation. *Entrance requirements:* For doctorate, GMAT, GRE General Test, LSAT, or MAT. Additional exam requirements/recommendations for international students: Required—TOEFL (minimum score 600 paper-based; 100 iBT); Recommended—IELTS (minimum score 6.5). *Application deadline:* For fall admission, 3/15 for domestic students. Application fee: $50. Electronic applications accepted. *Financial support:* Fellowships, career-related internships or fieldwork, and Federal Work-Study available. Support available to part-time students. Financial award applicants required to submit FAFSA. *Unit head:* Dr. Sarah J. Brubaker, Associate Director, 804-827-2400, E-mail: sbrubaker@vcu.edu. *Application contact:* Dr. Richard R. Huff, Coordinator, Public Policy and Administration, 804-827-1430, E-mail: rrhuff@vcu.edu.
Website: http://www.wilder.vcu.edu/academic/pubpolicy.html

**Virginia Polytechnic Institute and State University,** Graduate School, College of Science, Blacksburg, VA 24061. Offers biological sciences (MS, PhD); biomedical technology development and management (MS); chemistry (MS, PhD); data analysis and applied statistics (MA); economics (MA, PhD); geosciences (MS, PhD); mathematics (MS, PhD); physics (MS, PhD); psychology (MS, PhD); statistics (MS, PhD). *Faculty:* 299 full-time (92 women), 1 part-time/adjunct (0 women). *Students:* 567 full-time (222 women), 47 part-time (19 women); includes 66 minority (14 Black or African American, non-Hispanic/Latino; 12 Asian, non-Hispanic/Latino; 29 Hispanic/Latino; 11 Two or more races, non-Hispanic/Latino), 247 international. Average age 27. 956 applicants, 17% accepted, 118 enrolled. In 2016, 75 master's, 71 doctorates awarded. *Degree requirements:* For master's, comprehensive exam (for some programs), thesis (for some programs); for doctorate, comprehensive exam (for some programs), thesis/dissertation (for some programs). *Entrance requirements:* For master's and doctorate, GRE/GMAT. Additional exam requirements/recommendations for international students: Required—TOEFL (minimum score 80 iBT). *Application deadline:* For fall admission, 8/1 for domestic students, 4/1 for international students; for spring admission, 1/1 for domestic students, 9/1 for international students. Applications are processed on a rolling basis. Application fee: $75. Electronic applications accepted. *Expenses:* Tuition, state resident: full-time $12,467; part-time $692.50 per credit hour. Tuition, nonresident: full-time $25,095; part-time $1394.25 per credit hour. *Required fees:* $2669; $491.50 per semester. Tuition and fees vary according to course load, campus/location and program. *Financial support:* In 2016–17, 156 research assistantships with full tuition reimbursements (averaging $21,863 per year), 379 teaching assistantships with full tuition reimbursements (averaging $18,980 per year) were awarded. Financial award application deadline: 3/1; financial award applicants required to submit FAFSA. *Total annual research expenditures:* $22.3 million. *Unit head:* Dr. Sally C. Morton, Dean, 540-231-5422, Fax: 540-231-3380, E-mail: scmorton@vt.edu. *Application contact:* Teresa Price, Executive Assistant to the Dean and Grants Specialist, 540-231-6394, Fax: 540-231-3380, E-mail: tfprice@vt.edu.
Website: http://www.science.vt.edu/

**Walden University,** Graduate Programs, Richard W. Riley College of Education and Leadership, Minneapolis, MN 55401. Offers adult education (Post-Master's Certificate); adult learning (Graduate Certificate); college teaching and learning (Graduate Certificate); community college leadership (Ed D); curriculum, instruction and assessment (Ed D, Ed S, Graduate Certificate); developmental education (Graduate Certificate); early childhood administration, management, and leadership (Graduate Certificate); early childhood education (Ed D, Ed S); early childhood public policy and advocacy (Graduate Certificate); early childhood studies (MS), including administration, management and leadership, early childhood public policy and advocacy, teaching adults in the early childhood field, teaching and diversity in early childhood education;

## Public Policy

education (MS, PhD), including adolescent literacy and learning (MS), curriculum, instruction, and assessment (grades K-12) (MS), curriculum, instruction, assessment, and evaluation (PhD), early childhood leadership and advocacy (PhD), early childhood special education (PhD), educational leadership, educational leadership and administration (principal preparation) (MS), educational technology and design (PhD), elementary reading and literacy (PreK-6) (MS), elementary reading and mathematics (grades K-6) (MS), global and comparative education (PhD), higher education leadership management and policy (PhD), integrating technology in the classroom (grades K-12) (MS), learning, instruction and innovation (PhD), mathematics (grades 5-8) (MS), mathematics (grades K-6) (MS), mathematics and science (grades K-8) (MS), organizational research, assessment, and evaluation (PhD), reading and literacy with a reading K-12 endorsement (MS), reading literacy assessment and evaluation (PhD), science (grades K-8) (MS), special education (non-licensure) (grades K-12) (MS), teacher leadership (grades K-12) (MS), teaching English language learners (grades K-12) (MS); educational administration and leadership (Ed D); educational leadership and administration (principal preparation) (Ed S); educational technology (Ed D, Ed S, Post Master's Certificate); elementary reading and literacy (Graduate Certificate); engaging culturally diverse learners (Graduate Certificate); enrollment management and institutional marketing (Graduate Certificate); higher education (MS), including adult learning, college teaching and learning, enrollment management and institutional marketing, global higher education, leadership for student success, online and distance learning; higher education and adult learning (Ed D); higher education leadership and management (Ed D); higher education leadership for student success (Graduate Certificate); instructional design and technology (MS, Postbaccalaureate Certificate), including general program (MS), online learning (MS), training and performance improvement (MS); integrating technology in the classroom (Graduate Certificate); mathematics 5-8 (Graduate Certificate); mathematics K-6 (Graduate Certificate); online teaching for adult educators (Graduate Certificate); reading, literacy, and assessment (Ed D, Ed S); science K-8 (Graduate Certificate); special education (Ed D, Ed S, Graduate Certificate); special education (K-age 21) (MAT); teacher leadership (Graduate Certificate); teaching adults English as a second language (Graduate Certificate); teaching adults in the early childhood field (Graduate Certificate); teaching and diversity in early childhood education (Graduate Certificate); teaching English language learners (grades K-12) (Graduate Certificate); teaching K-12 students online (Graduate Certificate). *Accreditation:* NCATE. *Program availability:* Part-time, evening/weekend, online only, 100% online. *Degree requirements:* For doctorate, thesis/dissertation (for some programs), residency; for other advanced degree, residency for some programs). *Entrance requirements:* For master's, bachelor's degree or higher; minimum GPA of 2.5; official transcripts; goal statement (for some programs); access to computer and Internet; for doctorate, master's degree or higher; three years of related professional or academic experience (preferred); minimum GPA of 3.0; goal statement and current resume (for select programs); official transcripts; access to computer and Internet; for other advanced degree, relevant work experience; access to computer and Internet. Additional exam requirements/recommendations for international students: Required—TOEFL (minimum score 550 paper-based, 79 iBT), IELTS (minimum score 6.5), Michigan English Language Assessment Battery (minimum score 82), or PTE (minimum score 53). Electronic applications accepted.

**Walden University,** Graduate Programs, School of Public Policy and Administration, Minneapolis, MN 55401. Offers criminal justice (MPA, MPP, MS, Graduate Certificate), including emergency management (MS, PhD), general program (MS), global leadership (MS, PhD), homeland security and policy coordination (MS, PhD), law and public policy (MS, PhD), policy analysis (MS, PhD), public management and leadership (MS, PhD), self-designed (MS), terrorism, mediation, and peace (MS, PhD); criminal justice and executive management (MS), including global leadership (MS, PhD); criminal justice leadership and executive management (MS), including emergency management (MS, PhD), general program, homeland security and policy coordination (MS, PhD), law and public policy (MS, PhD), policy analysis (MS, PhD), public management and leadership (MS, PhD), self-designed, terrorism, mediation, and peace (MS, PhD); emergency management (MPA, MPP, MS), including criminal justice (MS, PhD), general program (MS), homeland security (MS), public management and leadership (MS, PhD), terrorism and emergency management (MS); general program (MPA, MPP); global leadership (MPA, MPP); government management (Graduate Certificate); health policy (MPA, MPP); homeland security (Graduate Certificate); homeland security and policy coordination (MPA, MPP); international nongovernmental organizations (MPA, MPP); law and public policy (MPA, MPP); local government management for sustainable communities (MPA, MPP); nonprofit management (Graduate Certificate); nonprofit management and leadership (MPA, MPP, MS), including global leadership (MS, PhD), international nongovernmental organization (MS), local government for sustainable communities (MS), self designed (MS); online teaching in higher education (Post-Master's Certificate); policy analysis (MPA); public management and leadership (MPA, MPP, Graduate Certificate); public policy (Graduate Certificate); public policy and administration (PhD), including criminal justice (MS, PhD), emergency management (MS, PhD), global leadership (MS, PhD), health policy, homeland security and policy coordination (MS, PhD), international nongovernmental organizations, law and public policy (MS, PhD), local government management for sustainable communities, nonprofit management and leadership, policy analysis (MS, PhD), public management and leadership (MS, PhD), terrorism, mediation, and peace (MS, PhD); strategic planning and public policy (Graduate Certificate); terrorism, mediation, and peace (MPA, MPP). *Program availability:* Part-time, evening/weekend, online only, 100% online. *Degree requirements:* For doctorate, thesis/dissertation, residency. *Entrance requirements:* For master's, bachelor's degree or higher; minimum GPA of 2.5; official transcripts; goal statement (for some programs); access to computer and Internet; for doctorate, master's degree or higher; three years of related professional or academic experience (preferred); minimum GPA of 3.0; goal statement and current resume (for select programs); official transcripts; access to computer and Internet; for other advanced degree, relevant work experience; access to computer and Internet. Additional exam requirements/recommendations for international students: Required—TOEFL (minimum score 550 paper-based, 79 iBT), IELTS (minimum score 6.5), Michigan English Language Assessment Battery (minimum score 82), or PTE (minimum score 53). Electronic applications accepted.

**Walden University,** Graduate Programs, School of Social Work and Human Services, Minneapolis, MN 55401. Offers addictions and social work (DSW); advanced clinical practice (MSW); clinical expertise (DSW); criminal justice (DSW); disaster, crisis, and intervention (DSW); family studies and interventions (DSW); human and social services (PhD), including advanced research, community and social services, community intervention and leadership, conflict management, criminal justice, disaster crisis and intervention, family studies and intervention, gerontology, global social services, higher education, human services and nonprofit administration, mental health facilitation; medical social work (DSW); military social work (MSW); policy practice (DSW); social work (PhD), including addictions and social work, clinical expertise, criminal justice, disaster, crisis and intervention, family studies and interventions, medical social work, policy practice, social work administration; social work administration (DSW); social work in healthcare (MSW); social work with children and families (MSW). *Accreditation:* CSWE. *Program availability:* Part-time, evening/weekend, online only, 100% online.

*Degree requirements:* For master's, residency (for some programs); for doctorate, thesis/dissertation, residency. *Entrance requirements:* For master's, bachelor's degree or higher; minimum GPA of 2.5; official transcripts; goal statement (for some programs); access to computer and Internet; for doctorate, master's degree or higher; three years of related professional or academic experience (preferred); minimum GPA of 3.0; goal statement and current resume (for select programs); official transcripts; access to computer and Internet. Additional exam requirements/recommendations for international students: Required—TOEFL (minimum score 550 paper-based, 79 iBT), IELTS (minimum score 6.5), Michigan English Language Assessment Battery (minimum score 82), or PTE (minimum score 53). Electronic applications accepted.

**Wayne State University,** College of Liberal Arts and Sciences, Department of Political Science, Detroit, MI 48202. Offers political science (MA, PhD); public administration (MPA), including economic development policy and management, health and human services policy and management, human and fiscal resource management, nonprofit policy and management, organizational behavior and management, urban and metropolitan policy and management; JD/MA. *Accreditation:* NASPAA. *Faculty:* 20. *Students:* 64 full-time (20 women), 75 part-time (45 women); includes 48 minority (32 Black or African American, non-Hispanic/Latino; 5 Asian, non-Hispanic/Latino; 4 Hispanic/Latino; 7 Two or more races, non-Hispanic/Latino), 7 international. Average age 33. 105 applicants, 50% accepted, 27 enrolled. In 2016, 25 master's, 5 doctorates awarded. *Degree requirements:* For master's, comprehensive exam (for some programs), thesis (for some programs); for doctorate, thesis/dissertation. *Entrance requirements:* For master's, GRE General Test, substantial undergraduate preparation in the social sciences, minimum upper-division undergraduate GPA of 3.0, two letters of recommendation, personal statement; for doctorate, GRE General Test, 3 letters of recommendation; personal statement; interview. Additional exam requirements/recommendations for international students: Required—TOEFL (minimum score 550 paper-based; 79 iBT), TWE (minimum score 5.5), Michigan English Language Assessment Battery (minimum score 85); Recommended—IELTS (minimum score 6.5). *Application deadline:* For fall admission, 5/15 for domestic students, 5/1 priority date for international students; for winter admission, 10/15 for domestic students, 9/1 priority date for international students. Applications are processed on a rolling basis. Application fee: $50. Electronic applications accepted. *Expenses:* $16,503 per year resident tuition and fees, $33,697 per year non-resident tuition and fees. *Financial support:* In 2016–17, 48 students received support, including 3 fellowships with tuition reimbursements available (averaging $17,333 per year), 13 teaching assistantships with tuition reimbursements available (averaging $18,067 per year); research assistantships with tuition reimbursements available, scholarships/grants, health care benefits, and unspecified assistantships also available. Financial award applicants required to submit FAFSA. *Faculty research:* American government and politics, comparative politics, political methodology, political theory, public administration, public law, public policy, world politics/international relations, formal theory/modeling, gender and politics, international law, peace research, political economy, political psychology, politics of developing countries, race, religion, and ethnicity, urban politics. *Unit head:* Dr. Daniel Geller, Professor and Chair, 313-577-6328, E-mail: dgeller@wayne.edu. *Application contact:* Dr. Sharon Lean, Graduate Director, 313-577-2630, E-mail: gradpolisci@wayne.edu.
Website: http://clas.wayne.edu/politicalscience/

**West Virginia University,** Eberly College of Arts and Sciences, Department of Political Science, Morgantown, WV 26506. Offers American public policy and politics (MA); international and comparative public policy and politics (MA); political science (PhD); public policy analysis (PhD). Terminal master's awarded for partial completion of doctoral program. *Degree requirements:* For master's, thesis optional; for doctorate, comprehensive exam, thesis/dissertation. *Entrance requirements:* For master's, GRE General Test, minimum GPA of 2.75; for doctorate, GRE General Test, minimum GPA of 3.0. Additional exam requirements/recommendations for international students: Required—TOEFL. *Faculty research:* Public policy, research methods, foreign policy analysis, judicial politics, environmental and energy policy.

**Wilfrid Laurier University,** Faculty of Graduate and Postdoctoral Studies, School of International Policy and Governance, International Public Policy Program, Waterloo, ON N2L 3C5, Canada. Offers global governance (MIPP); human security (MIPP); international economic relations (MIPP); international environmental policy (MIPP). Offered jointly with University of Waterloo. *Entrance requirements:* For master's, honours BA with minimum B average. Additional exam requirements/recommendations for international students: Required—TOEFL (minimum score 89 iBT). Electronic applications accepted. *Faculty research:* International environmental policy, international economic relations, human security, global governance.

**William Paterson University of New Jersey,** College of Humanities and Social Sciences, Wayne, NJ 07470-8420. Offers applied sociology (MA); clinical and counseling psychology (MA); clinical psychology (Psy D); creative and professional writing (MFA); English (MA); history (MA); political science and public policy (MA); public policy and international affairs (MA). *Program availability:* Part-time, evening/weekend. *Faculty:* 35 full-time (19 women), 8 part-time/adjunct (5 women). *Students:* 58 full-time (38 women), 62 part-time (46 women); includes 40 minority (9 Black or African American, non-Hispanic/Latino; 6 Asian, non-Hispanic/Latino; 21 Hispanic/Latino; 4 Two or more races, non-Hispanic/Latino), 4 international. Average age 32. 160 applicants, 55% accepted, 50 enrolled. In 2016, 56 master's awarded. *Degree requirements:* For master's, thesis (for some programs), internship (for some programs). *Entrance requirements:* For master's, GRE/MAT, minimum GPA of 3.0; 2 letters of recommendation; writing sample/personal statement. Additional exam requirements/recommendations for international students: Required—TOEFL (minimum score 500 paper-based; 79 iBT), IELTS (minimum score 6). *Application deadline:* For fall admission, 8/1 for domestic students, 4/1 for international students; for spring admission, 12/1 for domestic students, 11/1 for international students; for summer admission, 5/1 for domestic students, 2/1 for international students. Applications are processed on a rolling basis. Application fee: $50. Electronic applications accepted. *Expenses:* Tuition, state resident: full-time $12,480; part-time $611 per credit. Tuition, nonresident: full-time $20,263; part-time $992 per credit. *Required fees:* $1573; $77 per credit. Tuition and fees vary according to course load, degree level and program. *Financial support:* Career-related internships or fieldwork, Federal Work-Study, scholarships/grants, and unspecified assistantships available. Support available to part-time students. Financial award applicants required to submit FAFSA. *Faculty research:* Relationship violence among adolescents; autism in young children; game theory; gender, governance and empowerment in India; Chinese development policies concerning Africa. *Total annual research expenditures:* $162,900. *Unit head:* Dr. Kara Rabbitt, Dean, 973-720-2180, Fax: 973-720-2955, E-mail: rabbittk@wpunj.edu. *Application contact:* Tinu Adeniran, Associate Director, Graduate Admissions, 973-720-2764, Fax: 973-720-2035, E-mail: adenirant@wpunj.edu.
Website: http://www.wpunj.edu/cohss

**York University,** Faculty of Graduate Studies, Faculty of Liberal Arts and Professional Studies, Program in Public Policy, Administration and Law, Toronto, ON M3J 1P3, Canada. Offers MPPAL.

# Rural Planning and Studies

**Brandon University,** Department of Rural Development, Brandon, MB R7A 6A9, Canada. Offers MRD, Diploma. *Degree requirements:* For master's, thesis. *Entrance requirements:* For master's, minimum GPA of 3.0, 2 letters of reference. Additional exam requirements/recommendations for international students: Required—TOEFL (minimum score 580 paper-based). Electronic applications accepted. *Faculty research:* Regional development, healthy communities, economic impact analysis, rural tourism, resource management.

**Dalhousie University,** Faculty of Architecture and Planning, School of Planning, Halifax, NS B3J 2X4, Canada. Offers M Eng, M Plan, MPS. *Degree requirements:* For master's, thesis. *Entrance requirements:* Additional exam requirements/recommendations for international students: Required—TOEFL, IELTS, CANTEST, CAEL, or Michigan English Language Assessment Battery. Electronic applications accepted.

**East Carolina University,** Graduate School, Thomas Harriot College of Arts and Sciences, Department of Geography, Planning, and Environment, Greenville, NC 27858-4353. Offers economic development (Certificate); geographic information science and technology (Certificate); geography (MA), including geography, planning, rural development. *Program availability:* Part-time, evening/weekend. *Students:* 15 full-time (8 women), 11 part-time (5 women); includes 6 minority (2 Black or African American, non-Hispanic/Latino; 1 Asian, non-Hispanic/Latino; 3 Hispanic/Latino). Average age 28. 17 applicants, 94% accepted, 9 enrolled. In 2016, 1 master's awarded. *Degree requirements:* For master's, one foreign language, comprehensive exam, thesis optional. *Entrance requirements:* For master's, GRE General Test. Additional exam requirements/recommendations for international students: Required—TOEFL. *Application deadline:* For fall admission, 6/1 priority date for domestic students; for spring admission, 10/15 for domestic students. Applications are processed on a rolling basis. Application fee: $50. *Financial support:* Research assistantships with partial tuition reimbursements, teaching assistantships with partial tuition reimbursements, and Federal Work-Study available. Support available to part-time students. Financial award application deadline: 6/1. *Unit head:* Dr. Burrell Montz, Chair, 252-328-6086, E-mail: montzb@ecu.edu. *Application contact:* Dean of Graduate School, 252-328-6012, Fax: 252-328-6071, E-mail: gradschool@ecu.edu. Website: http://www.ecu.edu/geog/

**Iowa State University of Science and Technology,** Rural, Agricultural, Technological, and Environmental History Program, Ames, IA 50011-1054. Offers PhD. *Entrance requirements:* Additional exam requirements/recommendations for international students: Required—TOEFL (minimum score 600 paper-based; 79 iBT), IELTS (minimum score 7). *Application deadline:* For fall admission, 1/1 for domestic and international students. Electronic applications accepted. *Application contact:* Michael Bailey, Application Contact, 515-294-1284, E-mail: mdbailey@iastate.edu. Website: https://history.iastate.edu/graduate-study/rate-ph-d/

**Université Laval,** Faculty of Agricultural and Food Sciences, Program in Integrated Rural Development, Québec, QC G1K 7P4, Canada. Offers Diploma. *Entrance requirements:* For degree, good knowledge of French. Electronic applications accepted.

**University of Alaska Fairbanks,** College of Rural and Community Development, Department of Alaska Native Studies and Rural Development, Fairbanks, AK 99775. Offers rural development (MA). *Program availability:* Part-time, online only, blended/hybrid learning. *Faculty:* 8 full-time (all women). *Students:* 5 full-time (3 women), 15 part-time (10 women); includes 10 minority (8 American Indian or Alaska Native, non-Hispanic/Latino; 2 Two or more races, non-Hispanic/Latino), 1 international. Average age 38. 11 applicants, 64% accepted, 6 enrolled. In 2016, 7 master's awarded. *Degree requirements:* For master's, comprehensive exam, oral defense of project or thesis. *Entrance requirements:* For master's, bachelor's degree from accredited institution with minimum cumulative undergraduate and major GPA of 3.0. Additional exam requirements/recommendations for international students: Required—TOEFL (minimum score 550 paper-based; 79 iBT). *Application deadline:* For fall admission, 6/1 for domestic students, 3/1 for international students; for spring admission, 10/15 for domestic students, 9/1 for international students. Applications are processed on a rolling

basis. Application fee: $60. Electronic applications accepted. *Expenses:* Tuition, state resident: full-time $7992; part-time $444 per credit. Tuition, nonresident: full-time $16,326; part-time $907 per credit. *Required fees:* $39 per credit. $322 per semester. Tuition and fees vary according to course level, course load, campus/location, program and reciprocity agreements. *Financial support:* In 2016–17, 1 teaching assistantship with full tuition reimbursement (averaging $5,034 per year) was awarded; fellowships with full tuition reimbursements, research assistantships with full tuition reimbursements, Federal Work-Study, scholarships/grants, and health care benefits also available. Support available to part-time students. Financial award application deadline: 2/15; financial award applicants required to submit FAFSA. *Faculty research:* International indigenous leadership development, interrelationships between rural communities and global economy. *Unit head:* Cathy Brooks, Department Co-Chair, 907-474-6528, Fax: 907-474-6325, E-mail: fydanrd@uaf.edu. *Application contact:* Mary Kreta, Director of Admissions, 907-474-7500, Fax: 907-474-7097, E-mail: admissions@uaf.edu. Website: http://www.uaf.edu/danrd/

**University of Guelph,** Graduate Studies, Ontario Agricultural College, School of Environmental Design and Rural Development, Interdisciplinary Program in Rural Studies, Guelph, ON N1G 2W1, Canada. Offers PhD. Offered in cooperation with the Department of Food, Agricultural and Resource Economics, and the Department of Geography. *Program availability:* Part-time. *Degree requirements:* For master's, thesis/dissertation, qualifying exam. *Entrance requirements:* Additional exam requirements/recommendations for international students: Required—TOEFL (minimum score 600 paper-based), IELTS (minimum score 7). Electronic applications accepted. *Faculty research:* Sustainable rural communities, human resource development, rural planning and development.

**University of Guelph,** Graduate Studies, Ontario Agricultural College, School of Environmental Design and Rural Development, Program in Capacity Development and Extension, Guelph, ON N1G 2W1, Canada. Offers M Sc. *Program availability:* Part-time. *Degree requirements:* For master's, thesis optional. *Entrance requirements:* For master's, minimum B- average in previous 2 years of course work. Additional exam requirements/recommendations for international students: Required—TOEFL (minimum score 550 paper-based; 89 iBT), IELTS (minimum score 6.5). Electronic applications accepted. *Faculty research:* Adult learning in non-formal settings, communication technology for remote areas, rural quality of life.

**University of Guelph,** Graduate Studies, Ontario Agricultural College, School of Environmental Design and Rural Development, Program in Rural Planning and Development, Guelph, ON N1G 2W1, Canada. Offers international rural planning and development (M Sc); rural planning and development in Canada (M Sc). M Sc offered in cooperation with Departments of Food, Agricultural and Resource Economics; Geography; Land Resource Science; and others by arrangement. *Program availability:* Part-time. *Degree requirements:* For master's, thesis or alternative. *Entrance requirements:* For master's, minimum B- average during previous 2 years of course work. Additional exam requirements/recommendations for international students: Required—TOEFL (minimum score 550 paper-based), IELTS (minimum score 6.5). Electronic applications accepted. *Faculty research:* Canadian and international rural planning, resource and economic development, tourism.

**University of Montana,** Graduate School, College of Humanities and Sciences, Department of Geography, Missoula, MT 59812-0002. Offers community and environmental planning (MA); geography (MA, MS). *Entrance requirements:* For master's, GRE General Test. Additional exam requirements/recommendations for international students: Required—TOEFL.

**University of Wyoming,** College of Arts and Sciences, Department of Geography, Program in Rural Planning and Natural Resources, Laramie, WY 82071. Offers community and regional planning and natural resources (MP). *Degree requirements:* For master's, thesis or alternative. *Entrance requirements:* For master's, GRE General Test, minimum GPA of 3.0. Additional exam requirements/recommendations for international students: Required—TOEFL. *Faculty research:* Rural and small town planning, public land management.

# Sustainable Development

**Acadia University,** Faculty of Professional Studies, School of Recreation Management and Community Development, Wolfville, NS B4P 2R6, Canada. Offers MR. *Degree requirements:* For master's, thesis. *Entrance requirements:* Additional exam requirements/recommendations for international students: Required—TOEFL (minimum score 630 paper-based; 93 iBT), IELTS (minimum score 6.5).

**American University,** School of International Service, Washington, DC 20016-8071. Offers comparative and regional studies (Certificate); cross-cultural communication (Certificate); development management (MS); ethics, peace, and global affairs (MA); European studies (Certificate); global environmental policy (MA, Certificate); global information technology (Certificate); international affairs (MA), including comparative and international disability policy, comparative and regional studies, international economic relations, international politics, natural resources and sustainable development, U.S. foreign policy; international arts management (Certificate); international communication (MA, Certificate); international development (MA); international economic policy (Certificate); international economic relations (Certificate); international economics (MA); international media (MA); international peace and conflict resolution (MA, Certificate); international politics (Certificate); international relations (MA, PhD); international service (MIS); peacebuilding (Certificate); social enterprise (MA); the Americas (Certificate); United States foreign policy (Certificate); JD/MA. *Program availability:* Part-time, evening/weekend, 100% online. *Faculty:* 116 full-time (53 women), 57 part-time/adjunct (19 women). *Students:* 575 full-time (360 women), 491 part-time (277 women); includes 287 minority (100 Black or African American, non-Hispanic/Latino; 6 American Indian or Alaska Native, non-Hispanic/Latino; 58 Asian, non-Hispanic/Latino; 92 Hispanic/Latino; 1 Native Hawaiian or other Pacific Islander, non-Hispanic/Latino; 30 Two or more races, non-Hispanic/Latino), 151 international. Average age 29. 1,504 applicants, 84% accepted, 403 enrolled. In 2016, 374 master's, 3 doctorates, 1 other advanced degree awarded. Terminal master's awarded for partial completion of doctoral program. *Degree requirements:* For master's, one foreign

language, comprehensive exam, thesis or alternative; for doctorate, one foreign language, comprehensive exam, thesis/dissertation. *Entrance requirements:* For master's, GRE; GMAT or GRE (for MA in social enterprise), transcripts, resume, 2 letters of recommendation, statement of purpose; for doctorate, GRE, transcripts, resume, 3 letters of recommendation, statement of purpose. Additional exam requirements/recommendations for international students: Required—TOEFL (minimum score 600 paper-based, 100 iBT), IELTS (minimum score 7 ), or PTE (minimum score of 68). Application fee: $55. Electronic applications accepted. *Expenses:* $1,579 per credit tuition; $1,930 mandatory fees. *Financial support:* Research assistantships, teaching assistantships, institutionally sponsored loans, scholarships/grants, and unspecified assistantships available. Financial award application deadline: 1/15; financial award applicants required to submit FAFSA. *Unit head:* Dr. James Goldgeier, Dean, 202-885-1603, Fax: 202-885-2494, E-mail: goldgeier@american.edu. *Application contact:* Jia Jiang, Associate Director, Graduate Education Enrollment, 202-885-1689, Fax: 202-885-1109, E-mail: jiang@american.edu. Website: http://www.american.edu/sis/

**The American University in Cairo,** School of Sciences and Engineering, Cairo, Egypt. Offers biotechnology (MS); chemistry (MS); computer science (MS); computing (M Comp); construction engineering (M Eng, MS); electronics and communications engineering (M Eng); environmental engineering (MS); environmental system design (M Eng); mechanical engineering (M Eng, MS); nanotechnology (MS); physics (MS); robotics, control and smart systems (MS); sciences and engineering (PhD); sustainable development (MS, Graduate Diploma). *Program availability:* Part-time, evening/weekend. *Faculty:* 43 full-time (4 women), 12 part-time/adjunct (1 woman). *Students:* 50 full-time (21 women), 262 part-time (128 women), 13 international. Average age 28. 193 applicants, 46% accepted, 55 enrolled. In 2016, 71 master's, 5 doctorates awarded. *Degree requirements:* For master's, comprehensive exam (for some programs), thesis (for some programs); for doctorate, comprehensive exam (for some programs), thesis/

## Sustainable Development

dissertation. *Entrance requirements:* Additional exam requirements/recommendations for international students: Required—TOEFL (minimum score 450 paper-based; 45 iBT), IELTS (minimum score 5). *Application deadline:* For fall admission, 2/1 priority date for domestic and international students; for spring admission, 10/15 priority date for domestic and international students. Applications are processed on a rolling basis. Application fee: $80. Electronic applications accepted. *Expenses:* Contact institution. *Financial support:* Fellowships with partial tuition reimbursements, scholarships/grants, and unspecified assistantships available. Financial award application deadline: 3/10. *Faculty research:* Construction, mechanical and electronics engineering, physics, computer science, biotechnology and nanotechnology. *Unit head:* Dr. Hassan El Fawal, Dean, 20-2-2615-2926, E-mail: hassan.elfawal@aucegypt.edu. *Application contact:* Maha Hegazi, Director for Graduate Admissions, 20-2-2615-1462, E-mail: mahahegazi@aucegypt.edu.
Website: http://www.aucegypt.edu/sse/Pages/default.aspx

**Antioch University Los Angeles,** Graduate Programs, Program in Urban Sustainability, Culver City, CA 90230. Offers MA.

**Antioch University New England,** Graduate School, Department of Education, Experienced Educators Program, Keene, NH 03431-3552. Offers foundations of education (M Ed), including applied behavioral analysis, autism spectrum disorders, educating for sustainability, next-generation learning using technology, problem-based learning using critical skills, teacher leadership; principal certification (PMC). *Degree requirements:* For master's, thesis, practicum. *Entrance requirements:* For master's, previous course work and work experience in education. Additional exam requirements/recommendations for international students: Required—TOEFL (minimum score 550 paper-based). Electronic applications accepted. *Expenses:* Contact institution. *Faculty research:* Classroom action research, school restructuring, problem-based learning, brain-based learning.

**Antioch University New England,** Graduate School, Department of Environmental Studies, Program in Advocacy for Social Justice and Sustainability, Keene, NH 03431-3552. Offers MS. *Degree requirements:* For master's, practicum, seminar. *Entrance requirements:* For master's, samples of written work, portfolio, letters of recommendation, interview. Additional exam requirements/recommendations for international students: Required—TOEFL (minimum score 550 paper-based). Electronic applications accepted.

**Arizona State University at the Tempe campus,** School of Sustainability, Tempe, AZ 85287-5502. Offers sustainability (MA, MS, PhD); sustainable technology and management (Graduate Certificate). *Program availability:* Part-time, evening/weekend. Terminal master's awarded for partial completion of doctoral program. *Degree requirements:* For master's, thesis, interactive Program of Study (iPOS) submitted before completing 50 percent of required credit hours; for doctorate, comprehensive exam, thesis/dissertation, interactive Program of Study (iPOS) submitted before completing 50 percent of required credit hours. *Entrance requirements:* For master's, GRE; for doctorate, GRE, minimum GPA of 3.0 or equivalent in last 2 years of work leading to bachelor's degree. Additional exam requirements/recommendations for international students: Required—TOEFL, IELTS, or PTE. Electronic applications accepted.

**Baruch College of the City University of New York,** Austin W. Marxe School of Public and International Affairs, Program in Public Administration, New York, NY 10010-5585. Offers general public administration (MPA); health care policy (MPA); nonprofit administration (MPA); policy analysis and evaluation (MPA); public management (MPA); urban development and sustainability (MPA); MS/MPA. *Accreditation:* NASPAA. *Program availability:* Part-time, evening/weekend. *Degree requirements:* For master's, thesis, capstone. *Entrance requirements:* For master's, GRE General Test. Additional exam requirements/recommendations for international students: Required—TOEFL. Electronic applications accepted. *Expenses:* Contact institution. *Faculty research:* Urbanization, population and poverty in the developing world, housing and community development, labor unions and housing, government-nongovernment relations, immigration policy, social network analysis, cross-sectoral governance, comparative healthcare systems, program evaluation, social welfare policy, health outcomes, educational policy and leadership, transnationalism, infant health, welfare reform, racial/ethnic disparities in health, urban politics, homelessness, race and ethnic relations.

See Display on page 931 and Close-Up on page 977.

**Binghamton University, State University of New York,** Graduate School, Program in Sustainable Communities, Binghamton, NY 13902-6000. Offers MA, MS. *Program availability:* Part-time. *Faculty:* 12 full-time (11 women). *Students:* 5 full-time (4 women), 1 (woman) part-time; includes 2 minority (1 Black or African American, non-Hispanic/Latino; 1 Asian, non-Hispanic/Latino). Average age 24. 15 applicants, 73% accepted, 6 enrolled. *Entrance requirements:* For master's, undergraduate transcripts, minimum GPA of 3.0, personal statement, resume or curriculum vitae, two letters of recommendation, professional writing sample or essay. Additional exam requirements/recommendations for international students: Required—TOEFL, IELTS, or PTE. *Application deadline:* Applications are processed on a rolling basis. *Unit head:* George Homsy, Program Advisor, 607-777-9184, E-mail: ghomsy@binghamton.edu. *Application contact:* Ben Balkaya, Assistant Dean and Director, 607-777-2151, Fax: 607-777-2501, E-mail: balkaya@binghamton.edu.
Website: https://www.binghamton.edu/sustainable-communities/

**Boston Architectural College,** Graduate Programs, Boston, MA 02115-2795. Offers architecture (M Arch); historic preservation (MDS); interior design (MID); landscape architecture (MLA); sustainable design (MDS). *Accreditation:* CIDA. *Degree requirements:* For master's, thesis. *Entrance requirements:* For master's, portfolio (recommended). Electronic applications accepted.

**Brandeis University,** The Heller School for Social Policy and Management, Program in Nonprofit Management, Waltham, MA 02454-9110. Offers child, youth, and family management (MBA); health care management (MBA); social impact management (MBA); social policy and management (MBA); sustainable development (MBA); MBA/MA; MBA/MD. MBA/MD program offered in conjunction with Tufts University School of Medicine. *Accreditation:* AACSB. *Program availability:* Part-time. *Degree requirements:* For master's, team consulting project. *Entrance requirements:* For master's, GMAT (preferred) or GRE, 2 letters of recommendation, problem statement analysis, 3-5 years of professional experience. Additional exam requirements/recommendations for international students: Required—TOEFL (minimum score 600 paper-based; 100 iBT). Electronic applications accepted. *Expenses:* Contact institution. *Faculty research:* Health care; children and families; elder and disabled services; social impact management; organizations in the non-profit, for-profit, or public sector.

**Brandeis University,** The Heller School for Social Policy and Management, Program in Sustainable International Development, Waltham, MA 02454-9110. Offers international development (MA); MA/JD; MA/MA; MBA/MA. MA/JD program offered in conjunction with Northeastern University School of Law. *Degree requirements:* For master's, 2nd year fieldwork or internship; capstone paper and presentation. *Entrance requirements:* For master's, 3 letters of recommendation, curriculum vitae or resume, 3 years of development experience (international experience preferred). Additional exam

requirements/recommendations for international students: Required—TOEFL (minimum score 600 paper-based; 100 iBT). Electronic applications accepted. *Faculty research:* Water resource management, human rights, biosphere management, rural development, public policy and governance, gender, conservation, civil society, poverty eradication, project planning and implementation, evaluation, organizational management.

**California State University, Stanislaus,** College of Natural Sciences, Program in Ecology and Sustainability (MS), Turlock, CA 95382. Offers ecological conservation (MS); ecological economics (MS). *Program availability:* Part-time. *Degree requirements:* For master's, thesis. *Entrance requirements:* For master's, GRE, minimum GPA of 3.0, 3 letters of recommendation, personal statement. Additional exam requirements/recommendations for international students: Required—TOEFL (minimum score 550 paper-based). Electronic applications accepted.

**Carnegie Mellon University,** Carnegie Institute of Technology, Department of Civil and Environmental Engineering, Pittsburgh, PA 15213. Offers advanced infrastructure systems (MS, PhD); advanced infrastructure systems technology development and application (MS); air quality engineering and science (MS); civil and environmental engineering (MS, PhD); civil and environmental engineering/engineering and public policy (PhD); civil engineering (MS, PhD); computational mechanics (MS, PhD); computational modeling and monitoring for resilient structural and material systems (MS); energy infrastructure systems (MS); environmental engineering (MS, PhD); environmental management and science (MS, PhD); IT-based sustainable global infrastructure and construction management (MS); sustainability and green design (MS); water quality engineering and science (MS). *Program availability:* Part-time. *Faculty:* 23 full-time (5 women), 12 part-time/adjunct (3 women). *Students:* 230 full-time (87 women), 4 part-time (0 women); includes 17 minority (4 Black or African American, non-Hispanic/Latino; 12 Asian, non-Hispanic/Latino; 1 Two or more races, non-Hispanic/Latino), 179 international. Average age 25. 653 applicants, 60% accepted, 107 enrolled. In 2016, 145 master's, 15 doctorates awarded. Terminal master's awarded for partial completion of doctoral program. *Degree requirements:* For master's, thesis optional; for doctorate, comprehensive exam, thesis/dissertation, two-part qualifying exam, public defense of dissertation. *Entrance requirements:* For master's, GRE General Test, BS in engineering, science or mathematics; for doctorate, GRE General Test, BS or MS in engineering, science or mathematics. Additional exam requirements/recommendations for international students: Required—TOEFL (minimum score 84 iBT) or IELTS (6.0). *Application deadline:* For fall admission, 1/5 priority date for domestic and international students; for spring admission, 9/15 priority date for domestic and international students. Applications are processed on a rolling basis. Application fee: $65. Electronic applications accepted. *Expenses:* Contact institution. *Financial support:* In 2016–17, 129 students received support. Fellowships with tuition reimbursements available, research assistantships with tuition reimbursements available, scholarships/grants, tuition waivers (full and partial), unspecified assistantships, and service assistantships available. Financial award application deadline: 1/5. *Faculty research:* Advanced infrastructure systems; environmental engineering, sustainability, and science; mechanics, materials, and computing. *Total annual research expenditures:* $7.4 million. *Unit head:* Dr. David A. Dzombak, Professor and Department Head, 412-268-2941, Fax: 412-268-7813, E-mail: dzombak@cmu.edu. *Application contact:* David A. Vey, Graduate Admissions Manager, 412-268-2292, Fax: 412-268-7813, E-mail: dvey@andrew.cmu.edu.
Website: http://www.cmu.edu/cee/

**The Catholic University of America,** School of Architecture and Planning, Washington, DC 20064. Offers architecture and planning (M Arch, MS Arch St); city and regional planning (M Arch); facilities management (MS Arch); regional development (Certificate); sustainable design (M Arch, Certificate). *Program availability:* Part-time. *Faculty:* 20 full-time (7 women), 15 part-time/adjunct (1 woman). *Students:* 69 full-time (28 women), 21 part-time (13 women); includes 35 minority (11 Black or African American, non-Hispanic/Latino; 5 Asian, non-Hispanic/Latino; 11 Hispanic/Latino; 8 Two or more races, non-Hispanic/Latino), 13 international. Average age 28. 73 applicants, 84% accepted, 24 enrolled. In 2016, 42 master's awarded. *Degree requirements:* For master's, thesis. *Entrance requirements:* For master's, GRE (minimum score: 1000), minimum GPA of 2.8, portfolio, statement of purpose, official copies of academic transcripts, three letters of recommendation. Additional exam requirements/recommendations for international students: Required—TOEFL (minimum score 550 paper-based; 80 iBT). *Application deadline:* For fall admission, 1/15 priority date for domestic students, 7/1 for international students; for spring admission, 10/15 priority date for domestic students, 11/1 for international students. Applications are processed on a rolling basis. Application fee: $55. Electronic applications accepted. *Expenses:* $43,380 per year; $1,170 per credit; $200 per semester part-time fees. *Financial support:* Fellowships, research assistantships, teaching assistantships, Federal Work-Study, scholarships/grants, tuition waivers (full and partial), and unspecified assistantships available. Financial award application deadline: 2/1; financial award applicants required to submit FAFSA. *Faculty research:* Architectural history, cultural studies/sacred space, design technologies, digital media, real estate development, urban design. *Total annual research expenditures:* $93,903. *Unit head:* Randall Ott, Dean, 202-319-5784, Fax: 202-319-2023, E-mail: ott@cua.edu. *Application contact:* Director of Graduate Admissions, 202-319-5057, Fax: 202-319-6533, E-mail: cua-admissions@cua.edu.
Website: http://architecture.cua.edu/

**City College of the City University of New York,** Graduate School, Program in Sustainability in the Urban Environment, New York, NY 10031-9198. Offers MS. *Degree requirements:* For master's, capstone project. Tuition and fees vary according to course load, degree level and program.

**Clarkson University,** Institute for a Sustainable Environment, Potsdam, NY 13699. Offers MS, PhD. *Faculty:* 4 full-time (2 women), 6 part-time/adjunct (2 women). *Students:* 21 full-time (7 women), 12 international. *Expenses:* Tuition: Full-time $23,400; part-time $1300 per credit hour. Tuition and fees vary according to campus/location and program. *Unit head:* Dr. Susan Powers, Interim Director of the Institute for a Sustainable Environment/Associate Director of Sustainability, 315-268-6542, E-mail: spowers@clarkson.edu. *Application contact:* Dan Capogna, Graduate Admissions Contact, 518-631-9910, E-mail: graduate@clarkson.edu.
Website: http://graduate.clarkson.edu

**Clark University,** Graduate School, Department of International Development, Community, and Environment, Worcester, MA 01610-1477. Offers community and global health (MHS); community development and planning (MA); environmental science and policy (MS); geographic information science for development and environment (MS); international development and social change (MA); MA/MBA; MBA/MS. *Faculty:* 16 full-time (8 women), 8 part-time/adjunct (2 women). *Students:* 161 full-time (97 women), 21 part-time (7 women); includes 31 minority (13 Black or African American, non-Hispanic/Latino; 1 American Indian or Alaska Native, non-Hispanic/Latino; 8 Asian, non-Hispanic/Latino; 7 Hispanic/Latino; 2 Two or more races, non-Hispanic/Latino), 47 international. Average age 27. 364 applicants, 86% accepted, 113 enrolled. In 2016, 115 master's awarded. *Degree requirements:* For master's, thesis. *Entrance requirements:* For master's, 3 references, resume or curriculum vitae.

Additional exam requirements/recommendations for international students: Required—TOEFL (minimum score 575 paper-based; 90 iBT) or IELTS (minimum score 6.5). *Application deadline:* For fall admission, 1/15 for domestic students. Application fee: $75. *Expenses: Tuition:* Full-time $44,050. *Required fees:* $80. Tuition and fees vary according to course load and program. *Financial support:* Fellowships with partial tuition reimbursements, research assistantships with partial tuition reimbursements, teaching assistantships with partial tuition reimbursements, institutionally sponsored loans, and scholarships/grants available. *Faculty research:* Community action research, gender analysis, environmental risk assessment, land-use planning, geographic information systems, HIV and AIDS, global health and social justice, environmental health, climate change and sustainability. *Total annual research expenditures:* $140,000. *Unit head:* Dr. Ed Carr, Director, 508-421-3895, Fax: 508-793-8820, E-mail: edcarr@clarku.edu. *Application contact:* Erika Paradis, Student and Academic Services Director, 508-793-7201, Fax: 508-793-8820, E-mail: eparadis@clarku.edu.
Website: http://www2.clarku.edu/departments/international-development-community-environment/

**Clemson University,** Graduate School, College of Behavioral, Social and Health Sciences, Program in Public Administration, Clemson, SC 29634. Offers public administration (MPA, Certificate), including emergency management (MPA), homeland defense and security (MPA), local government (MPA), non-profit management (MPA), sustainable development (MPA). *Program availability:* Part-time, evening/weekend, online only, 100% online. *Faculty:* 4 full-time (2 women), 11 part-time/adjunct (5 women). *Students:* 8 full-time (5 women), 54 part-time (30 women); includes 16 minority (13 Black or African American, non-Hispanic/Latino; 2 Hispanic/Latino; 1 Two or more races, non-Hispanic/Latino). Average age 36. 25 applicants, 80% accepted, 18 enrolled. In 2016, 18 master's awarded. *Degree requirements:* For master's, comprehensive exam, thesis or alternative. *Entrance requirements:* For master's, GRE General Test, two letters of recommendation, unofficial transcripts, personal statement of purpose, documentation and explanation of related professional experience, resume. Additional exam requirements/recommendations for international students: Required—TOEFL (minimum score 80 iBT), IELTS (minimum score 6.5). *Application deadline:* For fall admission, 4/1 for domestic students, 3/1 for international students; for spring admission, 11/1 for domestic students, 10/1 for international students. Applications are processed on a rolling basis. Application fee: $80 ($90 for international students). Electronic applications accepted. *Expenses:* $4,264 per semester full-time resident, $8,485 per semester full-time non-resident, $695 per credit hour. *Faculty research:* Economic development, community vitality, entrepreneurship, broadband infrastructure, public health innovations and communities. *Total annual research expenditures:* $11,485. *Unit head:* Dr. Lori Dickes, Program Coordinator, 864-656-7831, E-mail: lorid@clemson.edu.
Website: https://www.clemson.edu/cbshs/departments/mpa/

**Cleveland State University,** College of Graduate Studies, Maxine Goodman Levin College of Urban Affairs, Program in Urban Planning, Design, and Development, Cleveland, OH 44115. Offers environmental sustainability (MUPDD); housing and neighborhood development (MUPDD); urban economic development (Certificate); JD/MUPDD. *Accreditation:* ACSP. *Program availability:* Part-time, evening/weekend. *Faculty:* 16 full-time (8 women), 13 part-time/adjunct (5 women). *Students:* 8 full-time (4 women), 26 part-time (15 women); includes 4 minority (2 Black or African American, non-Hispanic/Latino; 1 Asian, non-Hispanic/Latino; 1 Two or more races, non-Hispanic/Latino), 2 international. Average age 28. 48 applicants, 56% accepted, 14 enrolled. In 2016, 21 master's awarded. *Degree requirements:* For master's, thesis or alternative, exit project. *Entrance requirements:* For master's, GRE General Test (minimum score: 50th percentile combined verbal and quantitative, 4.0 analytical writing), minimum GPA of 3.0. Additional exam requirements/recommendations for international students: Required—TOEFL (minimum score 550 paper-based; 78 iBT), IELTS (6.0), or International Test of English Proficiency (iTEP). *Application deadline:* For fall admission, 7/1 priority date for domestic students, 5/15 for international students; for spring admission, 11/15 for domestic students, 11/1 for international students; for summer admission, 4/1 for domestic students, 3/15 for international students. Applications are processed on a rolling basis. Application fee: $40. Electronic applications accepted. *Expenses:* Contact institution. *Financial support:* In 2016–17, 10 students received support, including 5 research assistantships with full tuition reimbursements available (averaging $7,200 per year), 3 teaching assistantships with partial tuition reimbursements available (averaging $2,400 per year); scholarships/grants, tuition waivers (full and partial), and unspecified assistantships also available. Support available to part-time students. Financial award application deadline: 3/1; financial award applicants required to submit FAFSA. *Faculty research:* Housing and neighborhood development, urban housing policy, environmental sustainability, economic development, GIS and planning decision support. *Unit head:* Dr. Stephanie Ryberg-Webster, Assistant Professor/Director of MUPD Program, 216-802-3386, Fax: 216-687-2013, E-mail: s.ryberg@csuohio.edu. *Application contact:* David Arrighi, Graduate Academic Advisor, 216-523-7522, Fax: 216-687-5398, E-mail: d.arrighi@csuohio.edu.
Website: http://urban.csuohio.edu/academics/graduate/mupdd/

**Colorado State University,** Warner College of Natural Resources, Department of Ecosystem Science and Sustainability, Fort Collins, CO 80523-1476. Offers greenhouse gas management and accounting (MGMA); watershed science (MS). *Faculty:* 9 full-time (2 women), 3 part-time/adjunct (2 women). *Students:* 14 full-time (8 women), 13 part-time (8 women); includes 5 minority (3 Hispanic/Latino; 2 Two or more races, non-Hispanic/Latino), 2 international. Average age 28. 34 applicants, 47% accepted, 11 enrolled. In 2016, 4 master's awarded. *Degree requirements:* For master's, thesis (for some programs), internship. *Entrance requirements:* For master's, GRE (70th percentile or higher), minimum GPA of 3.0. Additional exam requirements/recommendations for international students: Required—TOEFL (minimum score 550 paper-based; 80 iBT), IELTS (minimum score 6.5). *Application deadline:* For fall admission, 2/1 priority date for domestic and international students. Application fee: $60 ($70 for international students). Electronic applications accepted. *Expenses:* Contact institution. *Financial support:* In 2016–17, 9 students received support, including 1 fellowship (averaging $61,080 per year), 4 research assistantships (averaging $23,138 per year), 7 teaching assistantships (averaging $13,932 per year). *Faculty research:* Watershed/snow/alpine/land use hydrology, geographic information systems and remote sensing, greenhouse gas emissions, climate change, environmental accounting. *Total annual research expenditures:* $2.2 million. *Unit head:* Dr. John Moore, Department Head, 970-491-5589, Fax: 970-491-1965, E-mail: john.moore@colostate.edu. *Application contact:* Nikki Foxley, Graduate Admissions Coordinator, 970-491-5589, Fax: 970-491-1965, E-mail: nikki.foxley@colostate.edu.
Website: http://warnercnr.colostate.edu/departments/ess

**Columbia University,** Graduate School of Arts and Sciences, New York, NY 10027. Offers African-American studies (MA); American studies (MA); anthropology (MA, PhD); art history and archaeology (MA, PhD); astronomy (PhD); biological sciences (PhD); biotechnology (MA); chemical physics (PhD); chemistry (PhD); classical studies (MA, PhD); classics (MA, PhD); climate and society (MA); conservation biology (MA); earth and environmental sciences (PhD); East Asia: regional studies (MA); East Asian languages and cultures (MA, PhD); ecology, evolution and environmental biology (MA), including conservation biology; ecology, evolution, and environmental biology (PhD), including ecology and evolutionary biology, evolutionary primatology; economics (MA, PhD); English and comparative literature (MA, PhD); French and Romance philology (MA, PhD); Germanic languages (MA, PhD); global French studies (MA); global thought (MA); Hispanic cultural studies (MA); history (PhD); history and literature (MA); human rights studies (MA); Islamic studies (MA); Italian (MA, PhD); Japanese pedagogy (MA); Jewish studies (MA); Latin America and the Caribbean: regional studies (MA); Latin American and Iberian cultures (PhD); mathematics (MA, PhD), including finance (MA); medieval and Renaissance studies (MA); Middle Eastern, South Asian, and African studies (MA, PhD); modern art: critical and curatorial studies (MA); modern European studies (MA); museum anthropology (MA); music (DMA, PhD); oral history (MA); philosophical foundations of physics (MA); philosophy (MA, PhD); physics (PhD); political science (MA, PhD); psychology (PhD); quantitative methods in the social sciences (MA); religion (MA, PhD); Russia, Eurasia and East Europe: regional studies (MA); Russian translation (MA); Slavic cultures (MA); Slavic languages (MA, PhD); sociology (MA, PhD); South Asian studies (MA); statistics (MA, PhD); theatre (PhD). Dual-degree programs require admission to both Graduate School of Arts and Sciences and another Columbia school. *Program availability:* Part-time. Terminal master's awarded for partial completion of doctoral program. *Degree requirements:* For master's, variable foreign language requirement, comprehensive exam (for some programs), thesis (for some programs); for doctorate, variable foreign language requirement, comprehensive exam (for some programs), thesis/dissertation. *Entrance requirements:* For master's and doctorate, GRE General Test, GRE Subject Test (for some programs). Additional exam requirements/recommendations for international students: Required—TOEFL, IELTS. Electronic applications accepted.

**Columbia University,** School of International and Public Affairs, Program in Development Practice, New York, NY 10027. Offers MPA. Offered through The Earth Institute. *Entrance requirements:* For master's, GRE. Additional exam requirements/recommendations for international students: Required—TOEFL (minimum score 100 iBT), IELTS (minimum score 7), PTE (minimum score 68). *Application deadline:* For fall admission, 1/5 for domestic students. *Unit head:* Glenn Denning, Program Director, 212-854-2636, E-mail: gd2147@columbia.edu. *Application contact:* Grace Han, Executive Director of Admissions and Financial Aid, 212-854-6216, Fax: 212-854-3010, E-mail: sipa_admission@columbia.edu.
Website: http://www.sipa.columbia.edu

**Cornell University,** Graduate School, Graduate Fields of Agriculture and Life Sciences and Graduate Fields of Engineering, Field of Biological and Environmental Engineering, Ithaca, NY 14853. Offers bioenergy and integrated energy systems (M Eng, MPS, MS, PhD); biological engineering (M Eng, MPS, MS, PhD); bioprocess engineering (M Eng, MPS, MS, PhD); ecohydrology (M Eng, MPS, MS, PhD); environmental engineering (M Eng, MPS, MS, PhD); environmental management (MPS); food engineering (M Eng, MPS, MS, PhD); industrial biotechnology (M Eng, MPS, MS, PhD); nanobiotechnology (M Eng, MPS, MS, PhD); sustainable systems (M Eng, MPS, MS, PhD); synthetic biology (MS); syntheticbiology (M Eng, MPS, PhD). Terminal master's awarded for partial completion of doctoral program. *Degree requirements:* For master's, thesis (MS); for doctorate, comprehensive exam, thesis/dissertation. *Entrance requirements:* For master's, letters of recommendation (3 for MS, 2 for M Eng and MPS); for doctorate, GRE General Test, 3 letters of recommendation. Additional exam requirements/recommendations for international students: Required—TOEFL (minimum score 550 paper-based; 77 iBT). Electronic applications accepted. *Faculty research:* Biological and food engineering, environmental, soil and water engineering, international agricultural engineering, structures and controlled environments, machine systems and energy.

**DePaul University,** College of Liberal Arts and Social Sciences, Chicago, IL 60614. Offers Arabic (MA); Chinese (MA); English (MA); French (MA); German (MA); history (MA); interdisciplinary studies (MA, MS); international public service (MS); international studies (MA); Italian (MA); Japanese (MA); leadership and policy studies (MS); liberal studies (MA); new media studies (MA); nonprofit management (MNM); public administration (MPA); public health (MPH); public service management (MS); social work (MSW); sociology (MA); Spanish (MA); sustainable urban development (MA); women and gender studies (MA); writing and publishing (MA); writing, rhetoric, and discourse (MA); MA/PhD. *Program availability:* Part-time, evening/weekend, online learning. Terminal master's awarded for partial completion of doctoral program. *Degree requirements:* For master's, variable foreign language requirement, comprehensive exam (for some programs), thesis (for some programs). Electronic applications accepted.

**Eastern Illinois University,** Graduate School, Lumpkin College of Business and Applied Sciences, School of Technology, Program in Sustainable Energy, Charleston, IL 61920. Offers MS, MS/MBA, MS/MS. *Program availability:* Part-time, evening/weekend. *Degree requirements:* For master's, comprehensive exam. *Entrance requirements:* For master's, GMAT or GRE. Additional exam requirements/recommendations for international students: Required—TOEFL (minimum score 500 paper-based; 61 iBT), IELTS (minimum score 6). Electronic applications accepted.

**Eastern Michigan University,** Graduate School, College of Technology, School of Visual and Built Environments, Programs in Construction Management, Ypsilanti, MI 48197. Offers construction (Certificate); construction management (MS); project leadership (Certificate); sustainable construction (Certificate). *Program availability:* Part-time, evening/weekend, online learning. *Students:* 18 full-time (1 woman), 12 part-time (3 women); includes 5 minority (2 Black or African American, non-Hispanic/Latino; 1 Asian, non-Hispanic/Latino; 2 Two or more races, non-Hispanic/Latino), 17 international. Average age 30. 49 applicants, 61% accepted, 9 enrolled. In 2016, 4 master's, 1 other advanced degree awarded. *Entrance requirements:* Additional exam requirements/recommendations for international students: Required—TOEFL. *Application deadline:* Applications are processed on a rolling basis. Application fee: $45. *Financial support:* Fellowships, research assistantships with full tuition reimbursements, teaching assistantships with full tuition reimbursements, career-related internships or fieldwork, Federal Work-Study, institutionally sponsored loans, scholarships/grants, tuition waivers (partial), and unspecified assistantships available. Support available to part-time students. Financial award applicants required to submit FAFSA. *Application contact:* Dr. Suleiman Ashur, Director, 734-487-0354, Fax: 734-487-8755, E-mail: sashur@emich.edu.

**Emory University,** Laney Graduate School, Program in Development Practice, Atlanta, GA 30322-1100. Offers MDP. *Entrance requirements:* Additional exam requirements/recommendations for international students: Recommended—TOEFL.

**Future Generations Graduate School,** Program in Applied Community Change, Franklin, WV 26807. Offers conservation (MA). *Program availability:* Blended/hybrid learning. *Degree requirements:* For master's, one foreign language, applied practicum research. *Entrance requirements:* For master's, bachelor's degree, community involvement. Additional exam requirements/recommendations for international students: Required—TOEFL. Electronic applications accepted. *Faculty research:* Sustainable communities, community engagement, peacebuilding, seed-scale community development.

*Sustainable Development*

**Hawai`i Pacific University,** College of Liberal Arts, Program in Global Leadership and Sustainable Development, Honolulu, HI 96813. Offers MA. *Program availability:* Part-time, evening/weekend. *Faculty:* 5 full-time (0 women), 2 part-time/adjunct (0 women). *Students:* 19 full-time (13 women), 3 part-time (2 women); includes 6 minority (1 Black or African American, non-Hispanic/Latino; 2 Hispanic/Latino; 3 Two or more races, non-Hispanic/Latino), 2 international. Average age 30. 31 applicants, 84% accepted, 14 enrolled. In 2016, 12 master's awarded. *Entrance requirements:* Additional exam requirements/recommendations for international students: Recommended—TOEFL (minimum score 550 paper-based; 80 iBT), IELTS (minimum score 6), TWE (minimum score 5). *Application deadline:* For fall admission, 2/15 priority date for domestic students; for spring admission, 10/15 priority date for domestic students. Applications are processed on a rolling basis. Application fee: $50. Electronic applications accepted. *Expenses: Tuition:* Full-time $17,190; part-time $955 per credit. *Required fees:* $150; $26 per credit. Tuition and fees vary according to course load and program. *Financial support:* In 2016–17, 10 students received support. Career-related internships or fieldwork, Federal Work-Study, scholarships/grants, tuition waivers, and unspecified assistantships available. Financial award application deadline: 3/1; financial award applicants required to submit FAFSA. *Unit head:* Dr. Regina Ostergaard-Klem, Program Chair, 808-236-2492, E-mail: rostergaardklem@hpu.edu. *Application contact:* Danny Lam, Assistant Director of Graduate Admissions, 808-544-1135, E-mail: graduate@hpu.edu.
Website: http://www.hpu.edu/CHSS/SocialSciences/GLSD/

**HEC Montreal,** School of Business Administration, Graduate Diploma Programs in Administration, Program in Management and Sustainable Development, Montréal, QC H3T 2A7, Canada. Offers Graduate Diploma. All courses are given in French. *Students:* 18 full-time (15 women), 39 part-time (24 women). 45 applicants, 69% accepted, 24 enrolled. In 2016, 19 Graduate Diplomas awarded. *Degree requirements:* For Graduate Diploma, one foreign language. *Entrance requirements:* For degree, bachelor's degree (not in administration). *Application deadline:* For fall admission, 4/15 for domestic and international students; for winter admission, 9/15 for domestic and international students. Application fee: $86. Electronic applications accepted. *Expenses: Tuition, area resident:* Part-time $77.80 Canadian dollars per credit. Tuition, state resident: full-time $2797 Canadian dollars; part-time $240.92 Canadian dollars per credit. Tuition, nonresident: full-time $8673 Canadian dollars; part-time $531.43 Canadian dollars per credit. *International tuition:* $19,131 Canadian dollars full-time. *Required fees:* $1699 Canadian dollars; $40.58 Canadian dollars per credit. $67.32 Canadian dollars per term. Tuition and fees vary according to degree level and program. *Financial support:* In 2016–17, 814 students received support. Research assistantships, teaching assistantships, and scholarships/grants available. Financial award application deadline: 9/2. *Unit head:* Renaud Lachance, Director, 514-340-7165, E-mail: renaud.lachance@hec.ca. *Application contact:* Anny Caron, Administrative Director, 514-340-3598, Fax: 514-340-6411, E-mail: anny.caron@hec.ca.
Website: http://www.hec.ca/programmes/dess/dess-gestion-developpement-durable/index.html

**Hofstra University,** College of Liberal Arts and Sciences, Program in Sustainability Studies, Hempstead, NY 11549. Offers MA. *Accreditation:* APA; NCATE. *Program availability:* Part-time, evening/weekend. *Students:* 6 full-time (2 women), 4 part-time (3 women); includes 2 minority (1 Black or African American, non-Hispanic/Latino; 1 Asian, non-Hispanic/Latino), 1 international. Average age 29. 9 applicants, 89% accepted, 4 enrolled. *Entrance requirements:* For master's, minimum GPA of 3.0, essay, 3 letters of recommendation. Additional exam requirements/recommendations for international students: Required—TOEFL (minimum score 550 paper-based; 80 iBT) *Application deadline:* Applications are processed on a rolling basis. Application fee: $75. Electronic applications accepted. *Expenses: Tuition:* Full-time $1240. *Required fees:* $970. Tuition and fees vary according to program. *Financial support:* In 2016–17, 8 students received support, including 5 fellowships with full and partial tuition reimbursements available (averaging $4,331 per year), 1 research assistantship with full and partial tuition reimbursement available (averaging $8,775 per year); career-related internships or fieldwork, Federal Work-Study, institutionally sponsored loans, scholarships/grants, tuition waivers (full and partial), and unspecified assistantships also available. Support available to part-time students. Financial award applicants required to submit FAFSA. *Faculty research:* Human impacts on climate; geographic information systems (GIS); energy analysis; greenhouse gas accounting; water policy. *Unit head:* Dr. Sandra Garren, Program Director, 516-463-5565, Fax: 516-463-5120, E-mail: sandra.j.garren@hofstra.edu. *Application contact:* Sunil Samuel, Assistant Vice President of Admissions, 516-463-4723, Fax: 516-463-4664, E-mail: graduateadmission@hofstra.edu.
Website: http://www.hofstra.edu/hclas

**Hunter College of the City University of New York,** Graduate School, School of Arts and Sciences, Department of Psychology, New York, NY 10065-5085. Offers animal behavior and conservation (MA, Certificate); general psychology (MA). *Program availability:* Part-time, evening/weekend. *Students:* 6 full-time (5 women), 79 part-time (59 women); includes 17 minority (5 Black or African American, non-Hispanic/Latino; 5 Asian, non-Hispanic/Latino; 7 Hispanic/Latino), 5 international. Average age 29. 145 applicants, 42% accepted, 38 enrolled. In 2016, 27 master's, 11 other advanced degrees awarded. *Degree requirements:* For master's, comprehensive exam, thesis. *Entrance requirements:* For master's, GRE General Test, minimum 12 credits of course work in psychology, including statistics and experimental psychology; 2 letters of recommendation. Additional exam requirements/recommendations for international students: Required—TOEFL. *Application deadline:* For fall admission, 4/1 for domestic students, 2/1 for international students; for spring admission, 11/1 for domestic students, 9/1 for international students. Applications are processed on a rolling basis. *Financial support:* Federal Work-Study, scholarships/grants, and tuition waivers (partial) available. Support available to part-time students. *Faculty research:* Personality, cognitive and linguistic development, hormonal and neural control of behavior, gender and culture, social cognition of health and attitudes. *Unit head:* Christopher B. Braun, Chair, 212-772-5554, Fax: 212-772-5620, E-mail: psychadv@hunter.cuny.edu. *Application contact:* Milena Solo, Graduate Admissions Director, 212-772-4288, Fax: 212-650-3336, E-mail: milena.solo@hunter.cuny.edu.
Website: http://www.hunter.cuny.edu/psychology/

**Instituto Centroamericano de Administración de Empresas,** Graduate Programs, La Garita, Costa Rica. Offers agribusiness management (MIAM); business administration (EMBA); finance (MBA); real estate management (MGREM); sustainable development (MBA); technology (MBA). *Degree requirements:* For master's, comprehensive exam, essay. *Entrance requirements:* For master's, GMAT or GRE General Test, fluency in Spanish, interview, letters of recommendation, minimum 1 year of work experience. Additional exam requirements/recommendations for international students: Recommended—TOEFL. Electronic applications accepted. *Faculty research:* Competitiveness, production.

**Instituto Tecnologico de Santo Domingo,** Graduate School, Area of Humanities and Social Sciences, Santo Domingo, Dominican Republic. Offers accounting (Certificate); adult education (Certificate); applied linguistics (MA); economics (MA); education (M Ed); educational psychology (MA, Certificate); gender and development (MA,

Certificate); humanistic studies (MA); international marketing management (Certificate); international relations in the Caribbean basin (Certificate); intervention systems in family therapy (MA); linguistic and literary communication (Certificate); pedagogical support (MA); social science education (M Ed); sustainable human development (MA); terminal illness and death psychology (Certificate); youth and adult education (M Ed).

**Iowa State University of Science and Technology,** Program in Sustainable Agriculture, Ames, IA 50011. Offers MS, PhD. *Entrance requirements:* For master's and doctorate, GRE General Test. Additional exam requirements/recommendations for international students: Required—TOEFL (minimum score 570 paper-based; 80 iBT), IELTS (minimum score 6.5). *Application deadline:* For fall admission, 2/1 for domestic and international students; for spring admission, 6/1 priority date for domestic and international students. Application fee: $60 ($90 for international students). Electronic applications accepted. *Application contact:* Angela Stone, Application Contact, 515-294-1191, Fax: 515-294-6390, E-mail: susag@iastate.edu.
Website: http://www.sust.ag.iastate.edu/gpsa/application.html

**Judson University,** Master of Architecture Program, Elgin, IL 60123-1498. Offers architecture (M Arch); sustainable design (M Arch); traditional architecture and urbanism (M Arch). *Program availability:* Part-time. *Faculty:* 9 full-time (3 women), 3 part-time/adjunct (1 woman). *Students:* 19 full-time (5 women); includes 5 minority (1 Black or African American, non-Hispanic/Latino; 3 Hispanic/Latino; 1 Two or more races, non-Hispanic/Latino). Average age 22. 24 applicants, 83% accepted, 19 enrolled. In 2016, 16 master's awarded. *Degree requirements:* For master's, thesis optional, 1600-hour practicum/preceptorship completed prior to enrollment. *Entrance requirements:* For master's, GRE, Judson BA in architecture or equivalent; minimum cumulative undergraduate GPA of 2.75, 3.0 in architecture; comprehensive portfolio; letter of intent. Additional exam requirements/recommendations for international students: Required—TOEFL (minimum score 550 paper-based), IELTS (minimum score 6.5). *Application deadline:* For fall admission, 2/15 priority date for domestic and international students; for winter admission, 11/15 for domestic students; for spring admission, 11/15 for domestic and international students. Applications are processed on a rolling basis. Application fee: $100. Electronic applications accepted. *Expenses:* Contact institution. *Financial support:* In 2016–17, 19 students received support, including 1 fellowship with partial tuition reimbursement available (averaging $5,000 per year), 1 research assistantship with partial tuition reimbursement available (averaging $5,000 per year), 12 teaching assistantships with partial tuition reimbursements available (averaging $2,500 per year); unspecified assistantships also available. Financial award application deadline: 7/1; financial award applicants required to submit FAFSA. *Faculty research:* Sustainable design, urbanism, daylighting, acoustics, digital media and fabrication. *Unit head:* Ian Hoffman, Chair, 847-628-1014, E-mail: ihoffman@judsonu.edu. *Application contact:* Molly Smith, Director of Admissions, 847-628-2521, E-mail: molly.smith@judsonu.edu.
Website: http://www.judsonu.edu/ArchMaster/

**Lehigh University,** College of Arts and Sciences, Environmental Policy Design Program, Bethlehem, PA 18015. Offers environmental policy and law (Graduate Certificate); environmental policy design (MA); sustainable development (Graduate Certificate); urban environmental policy (Graduate Certificate). *Program availability:* Part-time. *Faculty:* 11 full-time (4 women). *Students:* 5 full-time (3 women), 2 part-time (both women); includes 2 minority (1 Black or African American, non-Hispanic/Latino; 1 Hispanic/Latino). Average age 30. 8 applicants, 88% accepted, 3 enrolled. In 2016, 4 master's awarded. *Degree requirements:* For master's, thesis or additional course work. *Entrance requirements:* For master's, GRE, minimum GPA of 2.75, 3.0 for last two undergraduate semesters; essay; 2 letters of recommendation. Additional exam requirements/recommendations for international students: Required—TOEFL (minimum score 85 iBT). *Application deadline:* For fall admission, 1/1 for domestic and international students; for spring admission, 12/1 for domestic and international students. Applications are processed on a rolling basis. Application fee: $75. *Expenses:* $1,240 per credit. *Financial support:* Fellowships, scholarships/grants, tuition waivers (partial), and community fellowship and tuition remission available. Financial award application deadline: 1/1. *Faculty research:* Environmental policy, environmental law, urban policy, urban politics, urban environmental policy, sustainability, sustainable development, international environmental law, international environmental policy, environmental justice, social justice. *Unit head:* Dr. Donald P. Morris, Director, 610-758-5175, E-mail: dpm2@lehigh.edu. *Application contact:* Gary Burgess, Academic Coordinator, 610-758-4281, Fax: 610-758-6232, E-mail: glb215@lehigh.edu.
Website: http://ei.cas2.lehigh.edu/

**Lenoir-Rhyne University,** Graduate Programs, School of Natural Sciences, Program in Sustainability Studies, Hickory, NC 28601. Offers MS. *Program availability:* Part-time, evening/weekend, online learning. *Entrance requirements:* For master's, GRE General Test or MAT, official transcripts, essay. Additional exam requirements/recommendations for international students: Required—TOEFL (minimum score 600 paper-based). Electronic applications accepted. *Expenses:* Contact institution.

**Lesley University,** Graduate School of Arts and Social Sciences, Cambridge, MA 02138-2790. Offers clinical mental health counseling (MA), including holistic counseling, school and community counseling, trauma studies; counseling psychology (MA, CAGS), including professional counseling (MA), school counseling (MA); creative writing (MFA); expressive therapies (MA, PhD, CAGS), including art (MA), clinical mental health counseling (MA), dance (MA), expressive therapies (MA), music (MA); independent studies (CAGS); independent study (MA); intercultural relations (MA, CAGS); interdisciplinary studies (MA), including individualized studies, integrative holistic studies, mindfulness studies, peace and conflict transformation, trauma sensitive assessment, intervention, and consultation, women's studies; urban environmental leadership (MA). *Program availability:* Part-time, online learning. *Degree requirements:* For master's, internship, practicum, thesis (for expressive therapies); for doctorate, thesis/dissertation, arts apprenticeship, field placement; for CAGS, thesis, internship (for counseling psychology, expressive therapies). *Entrance requirements:* For master's, MAT (counseling psychology), interview, writing samples, art portfolio; for doctorate, GRE or MAT, interview, master's degree; for CAGS, interview, master's degree. Additional exam requirements/recommendations for international students: Required—TOEFL (minimum score 550 paper-based; 80 iBT). Electronic applications accepted. *Faculty research:* Psychotherapy and culture; psychotherapy and psychological trauma; women's issues in art, teaching and psychotherapy; community-based art, psycho-spiritual inquiry.

**Lipscomb University,** Institute for Sustainable Practice, Nashville, TN 37204-3951. Offers MS, Certificate, MBA/MS. *Program availability:* Part-time, evening/weekend, online learning. *Faculty:* 2 full-time (0 women), 3 part-time/adjunct (1 woman). *Students:* 8 full-time (5 women), 10 part-time (7 women); includes 5 minority (3 Black or African American, non-Hispanic/Latino; 2 Hispanic/Latino). Average age 31. 24 applicants, 71% accepted, 8 enrolled. In 2016, 13 master's awarded. *Degree requirements:* For master's, capstone project. *Entrance requirements:* For master's, GRE or GMAT, 2 references, interview. Additional exam requirements/recommendations for international students: Required—TOEFL (minimum score 570 paper-based; 80 iBT). *Application deadline:* For fall admission, 7/15 for domestic students; for spring admission, 12/15 for domestic students. Applications are processed on a rolling basis. Application fee: $50 ($75 for international students). Electronic applications accepted. *Expenses:* $1,312 per hour.

*Financial support:* Unspecified assistantships available. Financial award applicants required to submit FAFSA. *Faculty research:* Water and energy sustainability practices, sociology of conversation and natural resource management, new sustainability practices in forestry. *Unit head:* G. Dodd Galbreath, Executive Director, 615-966-1771, E-mail: dodd.galbreath@lipscomb.edu. *Application contact:* Emily Stutzman Jones, Academic Director, 615-966-5076, E-mail: emily.jones@lipscomb.edu. Website: http://lipscomb.edu/sustainability

**Long Island University–LIU Post,** College of Liberal Arts and Sciences, Brookville, NY 11548-1300. Offers applied mathematics (MS); behavior analysis (MA); biology (MS); criminal justice (MS); earth science (MS); English (MA); environmental sustainability (MS); genetic counseling (MS); history (MA); interdisciplinary studies (MA, MS); mathematics for secondary school teachers (MS); mobile GIS application development (Advanced Certificate); political science (MA); psychology (MA). *Program availability:* Part-time, evening/weekend, blended/hybrid learning. *Faculty:* 68 full-time (30 women), 20 part-time/adjunct (13 women). *Students:* 155 full-time (117 women), 125 part-time (82 women); includes 65 minority (17 Black or African American, non-Hispanic/Latino; 14 Asian, non-Hispanic/Latino; 27 Hispanic/Latino; 7 Two or more races, non-Hispanic/Latino), 19 international. 485 applicants, 36% accepted, 77 enrolled. In 2016, 91 master's, 15 other advanced degrees awarded. *Degree requirements:* For master's, comprehensive exam (for some programs), thesis (for some programs). *Entrance requirements:* Additional exam requirements/recommendations for international students: Required—PTE, TOEFL (minimum score 550 paper-based, 75 iBT) or IELTS (6.5). *Application deadline:* Applications are processed on a rolling basis. Application fee: $50. Electronic applications accepted. *Expenses: Tuition:* Full-time $28,272; part-time $1178 per credit. *Required fees:* $451 per term. Tuition and fees vary according to degree level and program. *Financial support:* In 2016–17, 24 teaching assistantships with partial tuition reimbursements (averaging $410 per year) were awarded; fellowships, research assistantships, career-related internships or fieldwork, Federal Work-Study, institutionally sponsored loans, scholarships/grants, tuition waivers (partial), and unspecified assistantships also available. Support available to part-time students. Financial award application deadline: 2/15; financial award applicants required to submit FAFSA. *Faculty research:* Biology, criminal justice, environmental sustainability, mathematics, psychology. *Total annual research expenditures:* $218,000. *Unit head:* Dr. Jeffrey Belnap, Acting Dean, 516-299-2233, Fax: 516-299-4140, E-mail: jeffrey.belnap@liu.edu. *Application contact:* Carol Zerah, Director of Graduate Admissions, 516-299-2900, Fax: 516-299-2137, E-mail: post-enroll@liu.edu. Website: http://liu.edu/CWPost/Academics/Schools/CLAS

**Minneapolis College of Art and Design,** Certificate Programs, Minneapolis, MN 55404-4347. Offers design (Certificate); fine arts (Certificate); graphic design (Certificate); media (Certificate); sustainable design (Certificate). *Program availability:* Part-time, online learning. *Degree requirements:* For Certificate, final project. *Entrance requirements:* For degree, resume, portfolio, letter of recommendation. Additional exam requirements/recommendations for international students: Required—TOEFL (minimum score 550 paper-based; 79 iBT). Electronic applications accepted. *Faculty research:* Visual arts.

**Mississippi State University,** College of Forest Resources, Department of Sustainable Bioproducts, Mississippi State, MS 39762. Offers MS, PhD. *Faculty:* 11 full-time (3 women), 1 part-time/adjunct (0 women). *Students:* 28 full-time (17 women), 4 part-time (1 woman); includes 4 minority (2 Black or African American, non-Hispanic/Latino; 1 Asian, non-Hispanic/Latino; 1 Two or more races, non-Hispanic/Latino), 24 international. Average age 29. 38 applicants, 89% accepted, 33 enrolled. In 2016, 6 master's, 4 doctorates awarded. *Degree requirements:* For master's, thesis optional; for doctorate, comprehensive exam, thesis/dissertation. *Entrance requirements:* For master's, GRE (if undergraduate GPA of last two years less than 3.0); for doctorate, GRE if undergraduate GPA of last two years is below 3.0. Additional exam requirements/recommendations for international students: Required—TOEFL (minimum score 550 paper-based; 79 iBT); Recommended—IELTS (minimum score 6.5). *Application deadline:* For fall admission, 7/1 for domestic students, 5/1 for international students; for spring admission, 11/1 for domestic students, 9/1 for international students. Applications are processed on a rolling basis. Application fee: $60. Electronic applications accepted. *Expenses:* Tuition, state resident: full-time $7670; part-time $852.50 per credit hour. Tuition, nonresident: full-time $20,790; part-time $2310.50 per credit hour. Part-time tuition and fees vary according to course load. *Financial support:* In 2016–17, 100 students received support, including 24 research assistantships with full tuition reimbursements available (averaging $16,415 per year); Federal Work-Study, institutionally sponsored loans, and unspecified assistantships also available. Financial award application deadline: 4/1; financial award applicants required to submit FAFSA. *Faculty research:* Wood property enhancement and durability, environmental science and chemistry, wood-based composites, primary wood production, furniture manufacturing and management. *Unit head:* Dr. Rubin Shmulsky, Professor/Head/Associate Director, 662-325-2116, Fax: 662-325-8126, E-mail: rshmulsky@cfr.msstate.edu. *Application contact:* Nathan Drake, Admissions and Enrollment Assistant, 662-325-3804, E-mail: ndrake@grad.msstate.edu. Website: http://www.cfr.msstate.edu/forestp//index.asp

**Montclair State University,** The Graduate School, College of Science and Mathematics, Program in Sustainability Science, Montclair, NJ 07043-1624. Offers MS. *Expenses:* Tuition, state resident: part-time $553 per credit. Tuition, nonresident: part-time $854 per credit. *Required fees:* $91 per credit. Tuition and fees vary according to program.

**New Jersey Institute of Technology,** College of Science and Liberal Arts, Newark, NJ 07102. Offers applied mathematics (MS); applied physics (M Sc, PhD); applied statistics (MS, Certificate); biology (MS, PhD); biostatistics (MS); chemistry (MS, PhD); computational biology (MS); environmental and sustainability policy (MS); environmental science (MS, PhD); history (MA, MAT); materials science and engineering (MS, PhD); mathematical and computational finance (MS); mathematics science (PhD); pharmaceutical chemistry (MS); practice of technical communications (Certificate); professional and technical communications (MS). *Program availability:* Part-time, evening/weekend. *Faculty:* 166 full-time (39 women), 87 part-time/adjunct (32 women). *Students:* 196 full-time (71 women), 68 part-time (33 women); includes 55 minority (15 Black or African American, non-Hispanic/Latino; 19 Asian, non-Hispanic/Latino; 15 Hispanic/Latino; 6 Two or more races, non-Hispanic/Latino), 140 international. Average age 28. 504 applicants, 64% accepted, 65 enrolled. In 2016, 81 master's, 18 doctorates, 1 other advanced degree awarded. Terminal master's awarded for partial completion of doctoral program. *Degree requirements:* For master's, thesis optional; for doctorate, thesis/dissertation. *Entrance requirements:* For master's, GRE General Test; for doctorate, GRE General Test, minimum graduate GPA of 3.5. Additional exam requirements/recommendations for international students: Required—TOEFL (minimum score 550 paper-based; 79 iBT). *Application deadline:* For fall admission, 6/1 priority date for domestic students, 5/1 priority date for international students; for spring admission, 11/15 priority date for domestic and international students. Applications are processed on a rolling basis. Application fee: $75. Electronic applications accepted. *Expenses:* Contact institution. *Financial support:* In 2016–17, 106 students received support, including 32 research assistantships (averaging $17,108 per year), 74 teaching

assistantships (averaging $21,368 per year); fellowships, scholarships/grants, traineeships, and unspecified assistantships also available. Financial award application deadline: 1/15. *Faculty research:* Biophotonics and bioimaging, morphogenetic patterning, embryogenesis, biological fluid dynamics, applied research in the mathematical sciences. *Unit head:* Dr. Kevin Belfield, Dean, 973-596-3676, Fax: 973-565-0586, E-mail: kevin.d.belfield@njit.edu. *Application contact:* Stephen Eck, Director of Admissions, 973-596-3300, Fax: 973-596-3461, E-mail: admissions@njit.edu. Website: http://csla.njit.edu/

**New York School of Interior Design,** Program in Sustainable Interior Environments, New York, NY 10021-5110. Offers MPS. *Entrance requirements:* For master's, degree in interior design, architecture, or closely-related field; portfolio. Additional exam requirements/recommendations for international students: Required—TOEFL (minimum score 550 paper-based; 79 iBT). Electronic applications accepted.

**New York University,** Graduate School of Arts and Science, Program in Historical and Sustainable Architecture, New York, NY 10012-1019. Offers MA. *Entrance requirements:* For master's, GRE, writing sample.

**New York University,** School of Continuing and Professional Studies, Schack Institute of Real Estate, Program in Real Estate Development, New York, NY 10012-1019. Offers global real estate (MS); sustainable development (MS); the business of development (MS). *Program availability:* Part-time, evening/weekend. *Degree requirements:* For master's, thesis, capstone project. *Entrance requirements:* For master's, GRE or GMAT (only upon request), bachelor's degree, resume with relevant professional work, internship or volunteer experience, two letters of recommendation, statement of purpose. Additional exam requirements/recommendations for international students: Required—TOEFL (minimum score 600 paper-based; 100 iBT), IELTS (minimum score 7). Electronic applications accepted. *Faculty research:* Valuation, real estate capital markets, regional economics, real estate investment trusts.

**Northern Arizona University,** Graduate College, College of Social and Behavioral Sciences, Program in Sustainable Communities, Flagstaff, AZ 86011. Offers MA. *Program availability:* Part-time. *Degree requirements:* For master's, thesis. *Entrance requirements:* For master's, minimum GPA of 3.0. Additional exam requirements/recommendations for international students: Required—TOEFL (minimum score 550 paper-based; 80 iBT), IELTS (minimum score 7). Electronic applications accepted. *Expenses:* Tuition, state resident: full-time $8971; part-time $444 per credit hour. Tuition, nonresident: full-time $20,958; part-time $1164 per credit hour. *Required fees:* $1018; $644 per credit hour. Tuition and fees vary according to course load, campus/location and program.

**Pace University,** Elisabeth Haub School of Law, White Plains, NY 10603. Offers comparative legal studies (LL M); environmental law (LL M, SJD), including climate change (LL M), land use and sustainability (LL M); law (JD); JD/LL M; JD/MA; JD/MBA; JD/MEM; JD/MPA; JD/MS. JD/MA offered jointly with Sarah Lawrence College; JD/MEM offered jointly with Yale University School of Forestry and Environmental Studies. *Accreditation:* ABA. *Program availability:* Part-time. *Faculty:* 26 full-time (11 women), 52 part-time/adjunct (19 women). *Students:* 516 full-time (274 women), 63 part-time (36 women); includes 150 minority (30 Black or African American, non-Hispanic/Latino; 2 American Indian or Alaska Native, non-Hispanic/Latino; 23 Asian, non-Hispanic/Latino; 58 Hispanic/Latino; 37 Two or more races, non-Hispanic/Latino), 2 international. Average age 26. 1,423 applicants, 56% accepted, 206 enrolled. In 2016, 20 master's, 171 doctorates awarded. *Degree requirements:* For master's, writing sample; for doctorate, thesis/dissertation (for some programs), extensive thesis proposal (for SJD). *Entrance requirements:* For doctorate, LSAT (for JD). Additional exam requirements/recommendations for international students: Required—TOEFL (minimum score 100 iBT); Recommended—TWE. *Application deadline:* For fall admission, 6/1 priority date for domestic students; for winter admission, 11/15 priority date for domestic students. Applications are processed on a rolling basis. Application fee: $65. Electronic applications accepted. *Expenses:* Contact institution. *Financial support:* In 2016–17, 430 students received support. Fellowships, research assistantships, career-related internships or fieldwork, Federal Work-Study, institutionally sponsored loans, scholarships/grants, and unspecified assistantships available. Support available to part-time students. Financial award application deadline: 2/1; financial award applicants required to submit FAFSA. *Faculty research:* Reform of energy regulations, international law, land use law, prosecutorial misconduct, corporation law, international sale of goods. *Total annual research expenditures:* $2.2 million. *Unit head:* David Yassky, Dean, 914-422-4407, E-mail: dyassky@law.pace.edu. *Application contact:* Cathy Alexander, Assistant Dean, 914-422-4210, Fax: 914-989-8714, E-mail: calexander@law.pace.edu. Website: http://www.law.pace.edu/

**Penn State University Park,** Graduate School, Intercollege Graduate Programs, Intercollege Program in Renewable Energy and Sustainability Systems, University Park, PA 16802. Offers MPS. *Unit head:* Dr. Regina Vasilatos-Younken, Dean, 814-865-2516, Fax: 814-863-4627. *Application contact:* Lori Hawn, Director, Graduate Student Services, 814-865-1795, Fax: 814-863-4627, E-mail: l-gswww@lists.psu.edu. Website: https://www.ress.psu.edu/

**Philadelphia University,** College of Architecture and the Built Environment, Program in Sustainable Design, Philadelphia, PA 19144. Offers MS. *Program availability:* Part-time, online learning.

**Pratt Institute,** School of Architecture, Program in Sustainable Environmental Systems, Brooklyn, NY 11205-3899. Offers MS. *Program availability:* Part-time. *Faculty:* 5 part-time/adjunct (3 women). *Students:* 28 full-time (20 women), 3 part-time (1 woman); includes 3 minority (1 Black or African American, non-Hispanic/Latino; 2 Asian, non-Hispanic/Latino), 16 international. Average age 28. 42 applicants, 60% accepted, 3 enrolled. In 2016, 5 master's awarded. *Degree requirements:* For master's, thesis. *Entrance requirements:* For master's, portfolio or writing sample, letters of recommendation. Additional exam requirements/recommendations for international students: Required—TOEFL (minimum score 550 paper-based; 79 iBT). *Application deadline:* For fall admission, 1/5 for domestic and international students; for spring admission, 10/1 for domestic and international students. Application fee: $50 ($90 for international students). Electronic applications accepted. *Expenses:* $29,646 full-time tuition, $1,938 fees. *Financial support:* Career-related internships or fieldwork, Federal Work-Study, institutionally sponsored loans, scholarships/grants, health care benefits, and unspecified assistantships available. Support available to part-time students. Financial award application deadline: 2/1; financial award applicants required to submit FAFSA. *Unit head:* Jaime Stein, Chairperson, 718-399-4323, E-mail: jstein9@pratt.edu. *Application contact:* Natalie Capannelli, Director of Graduate Admissions, 718-636-3551, Fax: 718-399-4242, E-mail: ncapanne@pratt.edu. Website: https://www.pratt.edu/academics/architecture/sustainable-environmental-systems/

See Display on page 114 and Close-Up on page 137.

**Rochester Institute of Technology,** Graduate Enrollment Services, Golisano Institute for Sustainability, Architecture and Sustainability Department, MS Program in Sustainable Systems, Rochester, NY 14623. Offers MS. *Program availability:* Part-time. *Students:* 17 full-time (6 women), 6 part-time (1 woman); includes 2 minority (1 Black or

## Sustainable Development

African American, non-Hispanic/Latino; 1 Hispanic/Latino), 14 international. Average age 29. 34 applicants, 85% accepted, 9 enrolled. In 2016, 6 master's awarded. *Degree requirements:* For master's, thesis or project. *Entrance requirements:* For master's, GRE, minimum GPA of 3.0 (recommended). Additional exam requirements/recommendations for international students: Required—TOEFL (minimum score 600 paper-based; 100 iBT), IELTS (minimum score 6.5), PTE (minimum score 68). *Application deadline:* For fall admission, 2/15 priority date for domestic and international students; for spring admission, 12/15 priority date for domestic and international students. Applications are processed on a rolling basis. Application fee: $60. Electronic applications accepted. *Expenses:* $1,742 per credit hour. *Financial support:* In 2016–17, 3 students received support. Research assistantships with partial tuition reimbursements available, teaching assistantships with partial tuition reimbursements available, career-related internships or fieldwork, scholarships/grants, and unspecified assistantships available. Financial award applicants required to submit FAFSA. *Faculty research:* Renewable energy and energy policy; food systems; material extraction and recycling; green transportation and logistics; eco-design and circular economy. *Unit head:* Prof. Thomas Trabold, Graduate Director, 585-475-4696, E-mail: info@sustainability.rit.edu. *Application contact:* Diane Ellison, Associate Vice President, Graduate Enrollment Services, 585-475-2229, Fax: 585-475-7164, E-mail: gradinfo@rit.edu.
Website: http://www.rit.edu/gis/academics/ms-sustainability/

**Rochester Institute of Technology,** Graduate Enrollment Services, Golisano Institute for Sustainability, Architecture and Sustainability Department, PhD Program in Sustainability, Rochester, NY 14623. Offers PhD. *Students:* 15 full-time (7 women), 4 part-time (2 women), 12 international. Average age 31. 48 applicants, 15% accepted, 3 enrolled. In 2016, 4 doctorates awarded. *Degree requirements:* For doctorate, comprehensive exam, thesis/dissertation. *Entrance requirements:* For doctorate, GRE, minimum GPA of 3.0 (recommended). Additional exam requirements/recommendations for international students: Required—TOEFL (minimum score 600 paper-based; 100 iBT), IELTS (minimum score 6.5), PTE (minimum score 68). *Application deadline:* For fall admission, 1/15 priority date for domestic and international students. Applications are processed on a rolling basis. Application fee: $60. Electronic applications accepted. *Expenses:* $1,742 per credit hour. *Financial support:* In 2016–17, 19 students received support. Research assistantships with full tuition reimbursements available, teaching assistantships with full tuition reimbursements available, career-related internships or fieldwork, scholarships/grants, health care benefits, and unspecified assistantships available. Financial award applicants required to submit FAFSA. *Faculty research:* Renewable energy and energy policy; food systems; material extraction and recycling; green transportation and logistics; eco-design and circular economy. *Unit head:* Prof. Thomas Trabold, Head, Sustainability Department/Associate Professor, 585-475-4696, E-mail: info@sustainability.rit.edu. *Application contact:* Diane Ellison, Associate Vice President, Graduate Enrollment Services, 585-475-2229, Fax: 585-475-7164, E-mail: gradinfo@rit.edu.
Website: https://www.rit.edu/gis/academics/sustainability-phd/overview

**Rochester Institute of Technology,** Graduate Enrollment Services, Kate Gleason College of Engineering, Industrial and Systems Engineering Department, ME Program in Sustainable Engineering, Rochester, NY 14623-5603. Offers ME. *Program availability:* Part-time. *Students:* 6 full-time (4 women), 2 part-time (1 woman); includes 1 minority (Two or more races, non-Hispanic/Latino), 3 international. Average age 24. 15 applicants, 53% accepted, 5 enrolled. In 2016, 2 master's awarded. *Degree requirements:* For master's, capstone project. *Entrance requirements:* For master's, minimum GPA of 3.0 (recommended). Additional exam requirements/recommendations for international students: Required—TOEFL (minimum score 550 paper-based; 79 iBT), IELTS (minimum score 6.5), PTE (minimum score 58). *Application deadline:* For fall admission, 2/15 priority date for domestic and international students; for spring admission, 12/15 priority date for domestic and international students. Applications are processed on a rolling basis. Application fee: $60. Electronic applications accepted. *Expenses:* $1,742 per credit hour. *Financial support:* In 2016–17, 1 student received support. Research assistantships with partial tuition reimbursements available, teaching assistantships with partial tuition reimbursements available, career-related internships or fieldwork, scholarships/grants, and unspecified assistantships available. Support available to part-time students. Financial award applicants required to submit FAFSA. *Faculty research:* Renewable and alternative energies; grid optimization and Smart Grid applications; life cycle assessment; product/process design methodologies; sanitation, water supply, soil fertility; off grid energy applications; human centered design. *Unit head:* Dr. Brian Thorn, Associate Professor, 585-475-6166, E-mail: bkteie@rit.edu. *Application contact:* Diane Ellison, Associate Vice President, Graduate Enrollment Services, 585-475-2229, Fax: 585-475-7164, E-mail: gradinfo@rit.edu.
Website: http://www.rit.edu/kgcoe/ise/program/master-engineering-degrees/master-engineering-sustainable-engineering

**Rochester Institute of Technology,** Graduate Enrollment Services, Kate Gleason College of Engineering, Industrial and Systems Engineering Department, MS Program in Sustainable Engineering, Rochester, NY 14623-5603. Offers MS. *Program availability:* Part-time. *Students:* 5 full-time (2 women), 3 part-time (2 women); includes 1 minority (Hispanic/Latino), 3 international. Average age 25. 14 applicants, 43% accepted, 1 enrolled. In 2016, 3 master's awarded. *Degree requirements:* For master's, thesis. *Entrance requirements:* For master's, GRE, minimum GPA of 3.0 (recommended). Additional exam requirements/recommendations for international students: Required—TOEFL (minimum score 550 paper-based; 79 iBT), IELTS (minimum score 6.5), PTE (minimum score 58). *Application deadline:* For fall admission, 2/15 priority date for domestic and international students; for spring admission, 12/15 priority date for domestic and international students. Applications are processed on a rolling basis. Application fee: $60. Electronic applications accepted. *Expenses:* $1,742 per credit hour. *Financial support:* In 2016–17, 5 students received support. Research assistantships with partial tuition reimbursements available, teaching assistantships with partial tuition reimbursements available, career-related internships or fieldwork, scholarships/grants, and unspecified assistantships available. Support available to part-time students. Financial award applicants required to submit FAFSA. *Faculty research:* Renewable and alternative energies; grid optimization and Smart Grid applications; life cycle assessment; product/process design methodologies; sanitation, water supply, soil fertility; off grid energy applications; human centered design. *Unit head:* Dr. Brian Thorn, Associate Professor, 585-475-6166, E-mail: bkteie@rit.edu. *Application contact:* Diane Ellison, Associate Vice President, Graduate Enrollment Services, 585-475-2229, Fax: 585-475-7164, E-mail: gradinfo@rit.edu.
Website: http://www.rit.edu/kgcoe/ise/program/master-science-degrees/master-science-sustainable-engineering

**St. Edward's University,** School of Behavioral and Social Sciences, Austin, TX 78704. Offers environmental management and sustainability (PSM). *Students:* 33 full-time (26 women); includes 9 minority (1 Asian, non-Hispanic/Latino; 7 Hispanic/Latino; 1 Native Hawaiian or other Pacific Islander, non-Hispanic/Latino). Average age 26. 75 applicants, 51% accepted, 14 enrolled. In 2016, 15 master's awarded. *Degree requirements:* For master's, 36 hours of coursework with minimum cumulative GPA of 3.0. *Entrance requirements:* For master's, GRE or GMAT, 2 letters of recommendation, resume or curriculum vitae, essay, minimum GPA of 3.0 in last 60 hours of course work. Additional

exam requirements/recommendations for international students: Required—TOEFL (minimum score 79 iBT), IELTS (minimum score 6). *Application deadline:* For fall admission, 2/15 priority date for domestic and international students. Applications are processed on a rolling basis. Application fee: $50. Electronic applications accepted. *Expenses:* $11,889 tuition per semester, $3,000 field course program fee. *Unit head:* Dr. Peter Beck, Program Director/Associate Professor, 512-428-1249, Fax: 512-233-1664, E-mail: peterab@stedwards.edu. *Application contact:* Dave Bralower, Director of Graduate Admission, 512-233-1424, Fax: 512-464-8877, E-mail: davidcb@stedwards.edu.
Website: http://www.stedwards.edu

**San Jose State University,** Graduate Studies and Research, College of Science, San Jose, CA 95192-0001. Offers biological sciences (MA, MS), including molecular biology and microbiology (MS), organismal biology, conservation and ecology (MS), physiology (MS); biotechnology (MBT); chemistry (MA, MS); computer science (MS); cybersecurity (Certificate); cybersecurity: core technologies (Certificate); geology (MS); marine science (MS); mathematics (MA, MS), including mathematics education (MA), science; meteorology (MS); physics (MS), including computational physics, modern optics, science (MA, MS); science education (MA); statistics (MS); Unix system administration (Certificate). *Program availability:* Part-time, evening/weekend. *Entrance requirements:* For master's, GRE. Electronic applications accepted. *Faculty research:* Radiochemistry/environmental analysis, health physics, radiation effects.

**Savannah College of Art and Design,** Graduate School, Program in Design for Sustainability, Savannah, GA 31402-3146. Offers MA, MFA. *Program availability:* Part-time. *Students:* 13 full-time (9 women), 1 part-time (0 women); includes 2 minority (both Hispanic/Latino), 5 international. Average age 26. 27 applicants, 56% accepted, 8 enrolled. In 2016, 1 master's awarded. *Degree requirements:* For master's, final project (for MA); thesis (for MFA). *Entrance requirements:* For master's, GRE (recommended), portfolio (submitted in digital format), audition or writing submission, resume, statement of purpose, two letters of recommendation. Additional exam requirements/recommendations for international students: Required—TOEFL (minimum score 550 paper-based, 85 iBT), IELTS (minimum score 6.5), or ACTFL. *Application deadline:* For fall admission, 4/1 for domestic and international students. Applications are processed on a rolling basis. Application fee: $40. Electronic applications accepted. *Expenses:* Tuition: Full-time $36,045. Tuition and fees vary according to course load. *Financial support:* Career-related internships or fieldwork, Federal Work-Study, and scholarships/grants available. Financial award application deadline: 4/1; financial award applicants required to submit FAFSA. *Unit head:* Victor Ermoli, Dean, School of Design. *Application contact:* Jenny Jaquillard, Executive Director of Admissions, Recruitment and Events, 912-525-5100, Fax: 912-525-5985, E-mail: admission@scad.edu.
Website: http://www.scad.edu/academics/programs/design-sustainability

**Saybrook University,** School of Psychology and Interdisciplinary Inquiry, San Francisco, CA 94612. Offers human science (MA, PhD), including consciousness and spirituality, humanistic and transpersonal psychology, integrative health studies, organizational systems, social transformation; organizational systems (MA, PhD), including consciousness and spirituality, humanistic and transpersonal psychology, integrative health studies, leadership of sustainable systems (MA), organizational systems, social transformation; psychology (MA, PhD), including consciousness and spirituality, creativity studies (MA), humanistic and transpersonal psychology, integrative health studies, Jungian studies, marriage and family therapy (MA), organizational systems, social transformation. *Program availability:* Online learning. Terminal master's awarded for partial completion of doctoral program. *Degree requirements:* For master's, thesis or alternative; for doctorate, thesis/dissertation. *Entrance requirements:* Additional exam requirements/recommendations for international students: Required—TOEFL (minimum score 580 paper-based; 93 iBT). Electronic applications accepted. *Faculty research:* Humanistic theory, health studies, organizational systems, consciousness and spirituality, social transformation.

**SIT Graduate Institute,** Graduate Programs, Master's Programs in Intercultural Service, Leadership, and Management, Program in Sustainable Development, Washington, DC 20005. Offers MA.

**Southern Illinois University Edwardsville,** Graduate School, Program in Integrative Studies, Edwardsville, IL 62026. Offers cultural heritage and resources management (MA, MS); diversity training (MA, MS); organizational design thinking (MS); sustainability (MS). *Program availability:* Part-time, evening/weekend. *Degree requirements:* For master's, variable foreign language requirement, comprehensive exam (for some programs), thesis (for some programs). *Entrance requirements:* Additional exam requirements/recommendations for international students: Required—TOEFL (minimum score 550 paper-based; 79 iBT), IELTS (minimum score 6.5). Electronic applications accepted.

**Southern Methodist University,** Bobby B. Lyle School of Engineering, Department of Environmental and Civil Engineering, Dallas, TX 75275-0340. Offers air pollution control and atmospheric sciences (PhD); civil engineering (MS); environmental engineering (MS); environmental science (PhD); structural engineering (PhD); sustainability and development (MA); water and wastewater engineering (PhD). *Program availability:* Part-time, evening/weekend, online learning. Terminal master's awarded for partial completion of doctoral program. *Degree requirements:* For master's, thesis optional; for doctorate, thesis/dissertation, oral and written qualifying exams. *Entrance requirements:* For master's, GRE General Test, minimum GPA of 3.0 in last 2 years; bachelor's degree in engineering, mathematics, or sciences; for doctorate, GRE, BS and MS in related field, minimum GPA of 3.3. Additional exam requirements/recommendations for international students: Required—TOEFL. Electronic applications accepted. *Faculty research:* Human and environmental health effects of endocrine disrupters, development of air pollution control systems for diesel engines, structural analysis and design, modeling and design of waste treatment systems.

**Stanford University,** School of Engineering, Department of Civil and Environmental Engineering, Stanford, CA 94305-2004. Offers atmosphere and energy (MS, PhD); construction (MS), including construction engineering and management, design-construction integration, sustainable design and construction; environmental engineering and science (MS, PhD, Eng); environmental fluid mechanics and hydrology (PhD); geomechanics (MS); structural engineering (MS). Terminal master's awarded for partial completion of doctoral program. *Degree requirements:* For doctorate, thesis/dissertation, qualifying exam; for Eng, thesis. *Entrance requirements:* For master's, doctorate, and Eng, GRE General Test. Additional exam requirements/recommendations for international students: Required—TOEFL. Electronic applications accepted. *Expenses:* Tuition: Full-time $47,331. Required fees: $609.

**State University of New York College of Environmental Science and Forestry,** Department of Paper and Bioprocess Engineering, Syracuse, NY 13210-2779. Offers biomaterials engineering (MS, PhD); bioprocess engineering (MPS, MS, PhD); bioprocessing (Advanced Certificate); paper science and engineering (MPS, MS, PhD); sustainable engineering management (MPS). *Faculty:* 13 full-time (2 women), 4 part-time/adjunct (0 women). *Students:* 28 full-time (14 women), 3 part-time (2 women); includes 1 minority (Asian, non-Hispanic/Latino), 19 international. Average age 29. 19 applicants, 89% accepted, 6 enrolled. In 2016, 6 master's, 1 doctorate, 4 other

advanced degrees awarded. *Degree requirements:* For master's, thesis; for doctorate, comprehensive exam, thesis/dissertation; for Advanced Certificate, 15 credit hours. *Entrance requirements:* For master's and doctorate, GRE General Test, minimum GPA of 3.0; for Advanced Certificate, BS, calculus plus science major. Additional exam requirements/recommendations for international students: Required—TOEFL (minimum score 550 paper-based; 80 iBT), IELTS (minimum score 6). *Application deadline:* For fall admission, 2/1 priority date for domestic and international students; for spring admission, 11/1 priority date for domestic and international students. Applications are processed on a rolling basis. Application fee: $60. *Expenses:* Tuition, state resident: full-time $10,870; part-time $453 per credit. Tuition, nonresident: full-time $22,210; part-time $925 per credit. *Required fees:* $1075; $89.22 per credit. *Financial support:* In 2016–17, 14 students received support. Application deadline: 6/30; applicants required to submit FAFSA. *Faculty research:* Sustainable products and processes, biorefinery, pulping and papermaking, nanocellulose, bioconversions, process control and modeling. *Unit head:* Dr. Gary M. Scott, Chair, 315-470-6501, Fax: 315-470-6945, E-mail: gscott@esf.edu. *Application contact:* Scott Shannon, Associate Provost and Dean, Instruction and Graduate Studies, 315-470-6599, Fax: 315-470-6978, E-mail: esfgrad@esf.edu.
Website: http://www.esf.edu/pbe/

**State University of New York College of Environmental Science and Forestry,** Department of Sustainable Construction Management and Engineering, Syracuse, NY 13210-2779. Offers construction management (MPS, MS, PhD); sustainable construction (MPS, MS, PhD); wood science (MPS, MS, PhD). *Students:* 8 full-time (5 women), 4 part-time (1 woman); includes 1 minority (Hispanic/Latino), 5 international. Average age 29. 5 applicants, 80% accepted, 1 enrolled. In 2016, 1 master's awarded. *Degree requirements:* For master's, thesis (for some programs); for doctorate, comprehensive exam, thesis/dissertation. *Entrance requirements:* For master's and doctorate, GRE General Test, minimum GPA of 3.0. Additional exam requirements/recommendations for international students: Required—TOEFL (minimum score 550 paper-based; 80 iBT), IELTS (minimum score 6). *Application deadline:* For fall admission, 2/1 priority date for domestic and international students; for spring admission, 11/1 priority date for domestic and international students. Applications are processed on a rolling basis. Application fee: $60. *Expenses:* Tuition, state resident: full-time $10,870; part-time $453 per credit. Tuition, nonresident: full-time $22,210; part-time $925 per credit. *Required fees:* $1075; $89.22 per credit. *Financial support:* In 2016–17, 2 students received support. Application deadline: 6/30; applicants required to submit FAFSA. *Unit head:* Dr. Susan E. Anagnost, Chair, 315-470-6880, Fax: 315-470-6879, E-mail: seanagno@esf.edu. *Application contact:* Scott Shannon, Associate Provost for Instruction/Dean of the Graduate School, 315-470-6599, Fax: 315-470-6879, E-mail: esfgrad@esf.edu.
Website: http://www.esf.edu/scme/

**Temple University,** Tyler School of Art, Department of Planning and Community Development, Ambler, PA 19122. Offers city and regional planning (MS); sustainable community planning (Graduate Certificate); transportation planning (Graduate Certificate). *Accreditation:* ACSP. *Program availability:* Part-time, evening/weekend. *Entrance requirements:* For master's, GRE or GMAT, 2 letters of recommendation, minimum undergraduate GPA of 3.0, statement of goals. Additional exam requirements/recommendations for international students: Required—TOEFL (minimum score 550 paper-based; 79 iBT). *Faculty research:* Regional environmental planning, collaboration, management community development through sustainable food systems, storm water management and floodplain mapping, land use policy innovations, community planning for aging.

**Texas A&M University–Kingsville,** College of Graduate Studies, Frank H. Dotterweich College of Engineering, Program in Sustainable Energy Systems Engineering, Kingsville, TX 78363. Offers PhD. *Degree requirements:* For doctorate, variable foreign language requirement, comprehensive exam, thesis/dissertation (for some programs). *Entrance requirements:* For doctorate, GRE, MAT, GMAT, bachelor's or master's degree in engineering or science, curriculum vitae, official transcripts, statement of purpose, three letters of recommendation. Additional exam requirements/recommendations for international students: Required—TOEFL (minimum score 550 paper-based; 79 iBT). Electronic applications accepted.

**Texas State University,** The Graduate College, College of Liberal Arts, Interdisciplinary Studies Program in Sustainability, San Marcos, TX 78666. Offers MA, MS. *Program availability:* Part-time. *Faculty:* 6 full-time (2 women). *Students:* 11 full-time (9 women), 11 part-time (7 women); includes 5 minority (1 Asian, non-Hispanic/Latino; 3 Hispanic/Latino; 1 Two or more races, non-Hispanic/Latino), 2 international. Average age 32. 15 applicants, 67% accepted, 6 enrolled. In 2016, 7 master's awarded. *Degree requirements:* For master's, comprehensive exam, thesis optional. *Entrance requirements:* For master's, bachelor's degree from accredited institution, minimum GPA of 3.0 on last 60 hours of undergraduate work, statement of personal goals, letter of intent to mentor from faculty member who will serve as research advisor and chair the master's committee. Additional exam requirements/recommendations for international students: Required—TOEFL (minimum score 550 paper-based; 78 iBT), IELTS (minimum score 6.5). *Application deadline:* For fall admission, 1/15 priority date for domestic students, 1/1 priority date for international students; for spring admission, 10/15 for domestic students, 10/1 for international students; for summer admission, 5/15 for domestic students, 3/15 for international students. Applications are processed on a rolling basis. Application fee: $40 ($90 for international students). Electronic applications accepted. *Expenses:* $4,851 per semester. *Financial support:* In 2016–17, 1 student received support, including 1 research assistantship (averaging $13,170 per year), 7 teaching assistantships (averaging $13,502 per year); Federal Work-Study and scholarships/grants also available. Support available to part-time students. Financial award application deadline: 3/1; financial award applicants required to submit FAFSA. *Faculty research:* Climate change, sustainable clothing, drought related tree mortality. *Total annual research expenditures:* $26,762. *Unit head:* Dr. Patti Giuffre, Graduate Advisor, 512-245-8983, E-mail: pg07@txstate.edu. *Application contact:* Dr. Andrea Golato, Dean of Graduate School, 512-245-2581, Fax: 512-245-8365, E-mail: gradcollege@txstate.edu.

**Texas Tech University,** Graduate School, Interdisciplinary Programs, Lubbock, TX 79409. Offers arid land studies (MS); biotechnology (MS); interdisciplinary studies (MA, MS); museum science (MA); wind science and engineering (PhD); JD/MS. *Program availability:* Part-time. *Faculty:* 10 full-time (4 women). *Students:* 122 full-time (56 women), 83 part-time (46 women); includes 78 minority (25 Black or African American, non-Hispanic/Latino; 1 American Indian or Alaska Native, non-Hispanic/Latino; 2 Asian, non-Hispanic/Latino; 41 Hispanic/Latino; 1 Native Hawaiian or other Pacific Islander, non-Hispanic/Latino; 8 Two or more races, non-Hispanic/Latino), 32 international. Average age 29. 114 applicants, 71% accepted, 60 enrolled. In 2016, 55 master's, 1 doctorate awarded. Terminal master's awarded for partial completion of doctoral program. *Degree requirements:* For master's, comprehensive exam (for some programs), thesis (for some programs); for doctorate, comprehensive exam, thesis/dissertation (for some programs). *Entrance requirements:* Additional exam requirements/recommendations for international students: Required—TOEFL (minimum score 550 paper-based; 79 iBT), IELTS (minimum score 6.5), PTE (minimum score 60),

Cambridge Advanced (B), Cambridge Proficiency (C), ELS English for Academic Purposes (Level 112). *Application deadline:* For fall admission, 6/1 priority date for domestic students, 1/15 priority date for international students; for spring admission, 9/1 priority date for domestic students, 6/15 priority date for international students. Applications are processed on a rolling basis. Application fee: $75. Electronic applications accepted. *Expenses:* Tuition, state resident: full-time $7200; part-time $300 per credit hour. Tuition, nonresident: full-time $16,992; part-time $708 per credit hour. *Required fees:* $2428; $50.50 per credit hour. $608 per semester. Tuition and fees vary according to program. *Financial support:* In 2016–17, 116 students received support, including 107 fellowships (averaging $4,360 per year), 10 research assistantships (averaging $10,619 per year), 7 teaching assistantships (averaging $9,152 per year); scholarships/grants and unspecified assistantships also available. Financial award application deadline: 4/15; financial award applicants required to submit FAFSA. *Total annual research expenditures:* $2 million. *Unit head:* Dr. Mark Sheridan, Vice Provost for Graduate and Postdoctoral Affairs/Dean of the Graduate School, 806-742-2787, Fax: 806-742-1746, E-mail: mark.sheridan@ttu.edu. *Application contact:* Amanda Wysinger, Academic Advisor, 806-834-0822, Fax: 806-742-4038, E-mail: amanda.wysinger@ttu.edu.
Website: http://www.depts.ttu.edu/gradschool/about/INDS/index.php

**Unity College,** Program in Professional Science, Unity, ME 04988. Offers sustainability science (MS); sustainable natural resource management (MS). *Program availability:* Online learning.

**University of Alaska Fairbanks,** School of Natural Resources and Extension, Fairbanks, AK 99775-7140. Offers natural resources and sustainability (PhD); natural resources management (MS). *Program availability:* Part-time. *Faculty:* 12 full-time (3 women), 3 part-time/adjunct (2 women). *Students:* 16 full-time (12 women), 19 part-time (9 women); includes 2 minority (1 Hispanic/Latino; 1 Two or more races, non-Hispanic/Latino), 1 international. Average age 37. 20 applicants, 45% accepted, 5 enrolled. In 2016, 6 master's, 4 doctorates awarded. *Degree requirements:* For master's, comprehensive exam, thesis (for some programs), oral defense of project or thesis; for doctorate, comprehensive exam, thesis/dissertation, defense of the dissertation. *Entrance requirements:* For master's, GRE General Test, bachelor's degree from accredited institution with minimum cumulative undergraduate and major GPA of 3.0; for doctorate, minimum cumulative GPA of 3.0. Additional exam requirements/recommendations for international students: Required—TOEFL (minimum score 550 paper-based; 89 iBT), IELTS (minimum score 6.5). *Application deadline:* For fall admission, 6/1 for domestic students, 3/1 for international students; for spring admission, 10/15 for domestic students, 9/1 for international students. Applications are processed on a rolling basis. Application fee: $60. Electronic applications accepted. *Expenses:* Tuition, state resident: full-time $7992; part-time $444 per credit. Tuition, nonresident: full-time $16,326; part-time $907 per credit. *Required fees:* $39 per credit. $322 per semester. Tuition and fees vary according to course level, course load, campus/location, program and reciprocity agreements. *Financial support:* In 2016–17, 5 research assistantships with full tuition reimbursements (averaging $16,539 per year), 6 teaching assistantships with full tuition reimbursements (averaging $5,874 per year) were awarded; fellowships with full tuition reimbursements, career-related internships or fieldwork, Federal Work-Study, scholarships/grants, health care benefits, and unspecified assistantships also available. Support available to part-time students. Financial award application deadline: 2/15; financial award applicants required to submit FAFSA. *Faculty research:* Conservation biology, soil/water conservation, land use policy and planning in the arctic and subarctic, forest ecosystem management, subarctic agricultural production. *Total annual research expenditures:* $2.9 million. *Unit head:* Stephen Sparrow, Dean, 907-474-9450, Fax: 907-474-6268, E-mail: fysnras@uaf.edu. *Application contact:* Mary Kreta, Director of Admissions, 907-474-7500, Fax: 907-474-7097, E-mail: admissions@uaf.edu.
Website: http://www.uaf.edu/snre/

**University of Calgary,** Faculty of Graduate Studies, Faculty of Environmental Design, Calgary, AB T2N 1N4, Canada. Offers architecture (M Arch); environmental design (M Env Des, PhD); planning (M Plan). *Degree requirements:* For master's, thesis; for doctorate, thesis/dissertation. *Entrance requirements:* For master's, minimum GPA of 3.0; for doctorate, minimum GPA of 3.5. Additional exam requirements/recommendations for international students: Required—TOEFL (minimum score 550 paper-based). *Faculty research:* Sustainable development in architecture, planning and product design, energy and environment, impact assessment, ecotourism.

**University of California, Berkeley,** Graduate Division, Master of Development Practice Program, Berkeley, CA 94720-1500. Offers MDP. *Students:* 49 full-time (29 women); includes 10 minority (1 Black or African American, non-Hispanic/Latino; 7 Asian, non-Hispanic/Latino; 2 Hispanic/Latino), 20 international. 129 applicants, 24 enrolled. In 2016, 27 master's awarded. *Application deadline:* For fall admission, 1/6 for domestic students. Application fee: $105 ($125 for international students). *Financial support:* Fellowships, research assistantships, teaching assistantships, institutionally sponsored loans, health care benefits, and unspecified assistantships available. Financial award applicants required to submit FAFSA. *Unit head:* David Zilberman, Executive Director, 510-642-6570, Fax: 510-643-8911, E-mail: info-mdp@berkeley.edu. *Application contact:* 510-642-7405.
Website: http://mdp.berkeley.edu

**University of California, Berkeley,** UC Berkeley Extension, Certificate Programs in Sustainability Studies, Berkeley, CA 94720-1500. Offers leadership in sustainability and environmental management (Professional Certificate); solar energy and green building (Professional Certificate); sustainable design (Professional Certificate).

**University of California, Santa Barbara,** Graduate Division, College of Letters and Sciences, Division of Social Sciences, Department of Global Studies, Santa Barbara, CA 93106-7065. Offers global culture, ideology, and religion (MA, PhD); global government, human rights, and civil society (MA, PhD); political economy, sustainable development, and the environment (MA, PhD). *Degree requirements:* For master's, one foreign language, thesis, 2 years of a second language; for doctorate, one foreign language, thesis/dissertation, reading proficiency in at least one language other than English. *Entrance requirements:* For master's, GRE, 2 years of a second language with minimum B grade in the final term, statement of purpose, resume or curriculum vitae, 3 letters of recommendation, transcripts (from all post-secondary institutions attended), writing sample (15-20 pages); for doctorate, GRE, statement of purpose, personal achievements/contributions statement, resume or curriculum vitae, 3 letters of recommendation, transcripts from all post-secondary institutions attended, writing sample (15-20 pages). Additional exam requirements/recommendations for international students: Required—TOEFL (minimum score 600 paper-based; 94 iBT), IELTS (minimum score 7). Electronic applications accepted.

**University of Colorado Denver,** College of Architecture and Planning, Program in Design and Planning, Denver, CO 80217. Offers history of architecture, landscape and urbanism (PhD); sustainable and healthy environments (PhD). *Program availability:* Part-time. *Faculty:* 8 full-time (3 women), 9 part-time/adjunct (1 woman). *Students:* 6 full-time (2 women), 9 part-time (4 women); includes 1 minority (Hispanic/Latino), 5 international. Average age 35. 21 applicants, 14% accepted, 3 enrolled. In 2016, 3 doctorates awarded. *Degree requirements:* For doctorate, comprehensive exam, thesis/

## Sustainable Development

dissertation. *Entrance requirements:* For doctorate, GRE (minimum score of 158 for both verbal and quantitative; writing 4.0), minimum undergraduate GPA of 3.0, graduate 3.5; writing sample; three letters of recommendation; statement of personal and professional goals. Additional exam requirements/recommendations for international students: Required—TOEFL (minimum score 80 iBT); Recommended—IELTS (minimum score 6.8). *Application deadline:* For fall admission, 2/2 for domestic students, 1/2 for international students; for spring admission, 10/1 for domestic students. Application fee: $50 ($75 for international students). Electronic applications accepted. *Expenses:* Contact institution. *Financial support:* In 2016–17, 6 students received support. Fellowships, research assistantships, teaching assistantships, Federal Work-Study, institutionally sponsored loans, scholarships/grants, traineeships, and unspecified assistantships available. Financial award application deadline: 4/1; financial award applicants required to submit FAFSA. *Faculty research:* Land use and environmental planning and design; design and planning processes and practices; history, theory, and criticism of the built environment. *Unit head:* Dr. Osman Attmann, Director, 303-315-0032, E-mail: o.attmann@ucdenver.edu. *Application contact:* Rachael Kuroiwa, Manager of Admissions and Outreach, 303-315-2325, E-mail: rachael.kuroiwa@ucdenver.edu.
Website: http://www.ucdenver.edu/academics/colleges/ArchitecturePlanning/Academics/DegreePrograms/PhD/Pages/PhD.aspx

**University of Colorado Denver,** College of Engineering and Applied Science, Department of Civil Engineering, Denver, CO 80217. Offers civil engineering (EASPh D); civil engineering systems (PhD); environmental and sustainability engineering (MS, PhD); geographic information systems (MS); geotechnical engineering (MS, PhD); hydrology and hydraulics (MS, PhD); structural engineering (MS, PhD); transportation engineering (MS, PhD). *Program availability:* Part-time, evening/weekend. *Faculty:* 15 full-time (3 women), 9 part-time/adjunct (0 women). *Students:* 50 full-time (15 women), 33 part-time (7 women); includes 10 minority (1 Black or African American, non-Hispanic/Latino; 2 Asian, non-Hispanic/Latino; 6 Hispanic/Latino; 1 Two or more races, non-Hispanic/Latino), 31 international. Average age 30. 105 applicants, 51% accepted, 14 enrolled. In 2016, 29 master's, 2 doctorates awarded. *Degree requirements:* For master's, comprehensive exam, 30 credit hours, project or thesis; for doctorate, comprehensive exam, thesis/dissertation, 60 credit hours (30 of which are dissertation research). *Entrance requirements:* For master's, GRE, statement of purpose, transcripts, three references; for doctorate, GRE, statement of purpose, transcripts, references, letter of support from faculty stating willingness to serve as dissertation advisor and outlining plan for financial support. Additional exam requirements/recommendations for international students: Required—TOEFL (minimum score 537 paper-based; 75 iBT); Recommended—IELTS (minimum score 6.5). *Application deadline:* For fall admission, 5/1 for domestic students, 4/1 for international students; for spring admission, 10/1 for domestic students, 9/1 for international students; for summer admission, 2/15 for domestic students, 1/15 for international students. Application fee: $50 ($75 for international students). Electronic applications accepted. *Expenses:* Contact institution. *Financial support:* In 2016–17, 62 students received support. Fellowships, research assistantships, teaching assistantships, career-related internships or fieldwork, Federal Work-Study, institutionally sponsored loans, scholarships/grants, traineeships, and unspecified assistantships available. Financial award application deadline: 4/1; financial award applicants required to submit FAFSA. *Faculty research:* Earthquake source physics, environmental biotechnology, hydrologic and hydraulic engineering, sustainability assessments, transportation energy use and greenhouse gas emissions. *Unit head:* Dr. Kevin Rens, Chair, 303-556-8017, E-mail: kevin.rens@ucdenver.edu. *Application contact:* Roxanne Pizano, Program Coordinator, 303-556-6274, E-mail: roxanne.pizano@ucdenver.edu.
Website: http://www.ucdenver.edu/academics/colleges/Engineering/Programs/Civil-Engineering/Pages/CivilEngineering.aspx

**University of Colorado Denver,** College of Liberal Arts and Sciences, Department of Anthropology, Denver, CO 80217. Offers archaeological studies (MA); biological anthropology (MA); medical anthropology (MA); sustainable development and political ecology (MA). *Program availability:* Part-time, evening/weekend. *Faculty:* 9 full-time (3 women), 1 part-time/adjunct (0 women). *Students:* 30 full-time (22 women), 5 part-time (3 women); includes 9 minority (2 Black or African American, non-Hispanic/Latino; 1 American Indian or Alaska Native, non-Hispanic/Latino; 4 Hispanic/Latino; 2 Two or more races, non-Hispanic/Latino), 1 international. Average age 28. 40 applicants, 53% accepted, 11 enrolled. In 2016, 13 master's awarded. *Degree requirements:* For master's, comprehensive exam, thesis or alternative, 30-36 credit hours. *Entrance requirements:* For master's, GRE General Test, minimum GPA of 3.0 for all undergraduate studies, transcripts from all undergraduate/graduate institutions attended, prior training in anthropology, three letters of recommendation, statement of purpose. Additional exam requirements/recommendations for international students: Required—TOEFL (minimum score 537 paper-based; 75 iBT); Recommended—IELTS (minimum score 6.5). *Application deadline:* For fall admission, 2/15 for domestic students, 1/15 for international students. Application fee: $50 ($75 for international students). Electronic applications accepted. *Expenses:* Tuition, state resident: full-time $11,006; part-time $474 per credit. Tuition, nonresident: full-time $28,212; part-time $1264 per credit hour. *Required fees:* $256 per semester. One-time fee: $94.32. Tuition and fees vary according to campus/location and program. *Financial support:* In 2016–17, 3 students received support. Fellowships, research assistantships, teaching assistantships, Federal Work-Study, institutionally sponsored loans, scholarships/grants, and traineeships available. Financial award application deadline: 4/1; financial award applicants required to submit FAFSA. *Faculty research:* Applied medical anthropology, primate social behavior, environmental anthropology, Southwestern and Mexican archaeology, human ecology. *Application contact:* Connie Turner, Program Assistant, 303-556-3554, E-mail: connie.turner@ucdenver.edu.
Website: http://www.ucdenver.edu/academics/colleges/CLAS/Departments/anthropology/Programs/Masters/Pages/Masters.aspx

**University of Florida,** Graduate School, College of Liberal Arts and Sciences, Center for Latin American Studies, Gainesville, FL 32611. Offers Latin American studies (MA, Certificate); sustainable development practice (MDP); tropical conservation and development (MA); JD/MA. *Program availability:* Part-time. *Degree requirements:* For master's, thesis. *Entrance requirements:* For master's, GRE General Test, minimum GPA of 3.0. Additional exam requirements/recommendations for international students: Required—TOEFL (minimum score 550 paper-based; 80 iBT), IELTS (minimum score 6). Electronic applications accepted. *Faculty research:* Tropical conservation and development; ethnicity in the Americas, Brazil, and Cuba; North American Free Trade Agreement (NAFTA).

**University of Georgia,** Eugene P. Odum School of Ecology, Athens, GA 30602. Offers conservation ecology and sustainable development (MS); ecology (PhD). *Degree requirements:* For master's, thesis; for doctorate, one foreign language, thesis/dissertation. *Entrance requirements:* For master's and doctorate, GRE General Test. *Application deadline:* For fall admission, 7/1 priority date for domestic students; for spring admission, 11/15 for domestic students. Application fee: $50. Electronic applications accepted. *Financial support:* Fellowships, research assistantships, teaching assistantships, and unspecified assistantships available. *Unit head:* Dr. John L. Gittleman, Dean, 706-542-2968, Fax: 706-542-4819, E-mail: ecohead@uga.edu.

*Application contact:* Ford Ballantyne, Graduate Coordinator, 706-542-3404, E-mail: fb4@uga.edu.
Website: http://www.ecology.uga.edu/

**University of Hawaii at Manoa,** Graduate Division, College of Social Sciences, Department of Urban and Regional Planning, Honolulu, HI 96822. Offers community planning (MURP); disaster management and humanitarian assistance (Graduate Certificate); environmental planning and sustainability (MURP); international development planning (MURP); land use, transportation and infrastructure planning (MURP); planning studies (Graduate Certificate); urban and regional planning (PhD, Graduate Certificate). *Accreditation:* ACSP. *Program availability:* Part-time. *Entrance requirements:* For master's, GRE General Test, minimum GPA of 3.0; for doctorate, GRE General Test. Additional exam requirements/recommendations for international students: Required—TOEFL (minimum score 500 paper-based; 61 iBT), IELTS (minimum score 5).

**University of Maryland, College Park,** Academic Affairs, College of Computer, Mathematical and Natural Sciences, Department of Biology, Program in Sustainable Development and Conservation Biology, College Park, MD 20742. Offers MS. *Program availability:* Part-time, evening/weekend. *Degree requirements:* For master's, internship, scholarly paper. *Entrance requirements:* For master's, GRE General Test, minimum GPA of 3.0, 3 letters of recommendation. Electronic applications accepted. *Faculty research:* Biodiversity, global change, conservation.

**University of Massachusetts Amherst,** Graduate School, College of Natural Sciences, Department of Environmental Conservation, Program in Sustainability Science, Amherst, MA 01003. Offers MS. *Program availability:* Part-time. *Degree requirements:* For master's, internship. *Entrance requirements:* Additional exam requirements/recommendations for international students: Required—TOEFL (minimum score 550 paper-based; 80 iBT), IELTS (minimum score 6.5). Electronic applications accepted.

**University of Michigan,** School for Environment and Sustainability, Program in Natural Resources and Environment, Ann Arbor, MI 48109. Offers behavior, education and communication (MS); conservation ecology (MS); environmental informatics (MS); environmental justice (MS); environmental policy and planning (MS); natural resources and environment (PhD); sustainable systems (MS); MS/JD; MS/MBA; MS/MPH; MS/MPP; MS/MSE; MS/MURP. *Faculty:* 31 full-time (12 women), 40 part-time/adjunct (10 women). *Students:* 337 full-time (199 women); includes 51 minority (3 Black or African American, non-Hispanic/Latino; 15 Asian, non-Hispanic/Latino; 20 Hispanic/Latino; 1 Native Hawaiian or other Pacific Islander, non-Hispanic/Latino; 12 Two or more races, non-Hispanic/Latino), 72 international. Average age 27. 486 applicants. In 2016, 129 master's, 8 doctorates awarded. Terminal master's awarded for partial completion of doctoral program. *Degree requirements:* For master's, practicum or group project; for doctorate, comprehensive exam, thesis/dissertation, oral defense of dissertation, preliminary exam. *Entrance requirements:* For master's, GRE General Test; for doctorate, GRE General Test, master's degree. Additional exam requirements/recommendations for international students: Required—TOEFL (minimum score 560 paper-based; 84 iBT), IELTS (minimum score 6.5). *Application deadline:* For fall admission, 4/30 for domestic and international students. Application fee: $75 ($90 for international students). Electronic applications accepted. *Expenses:* Tuition, state resident: full-time $21,466; part-time $1152 per credit hour. Tuition, nonresident: full-time $43,346; part-time $2367 per credit hour. Part-time tuition and fees vary according to course load, degree level and program. *Financial support:* Fellowships, research assistantships, teaching assistantships, career-related internships or fieldwork, Federal Work-Study, scholarships/grants, and health care benefits available. Financial award application deadline: 1/6; financial award applicants required to submit FAFSA. *Faculty research:* Ecological science, social sciences, and sustainable systems. *Unit head:* Dr. Daniel Brown, Interim Dean, 734-764-2550, E-mail: danbrown@umich.edu. *Application contact:* Sara O'Brien, Director of Academic Programs, 734-764-6453, Fax: 734-936-2195, E-mail: seas-admissions@umich.edu.

**University of New Brunswick Fredericton,** School of Graduate Studies, Policy Studies Program, Fredericton, NB E3B 5A3, Canada. Offers citizen engagement/dispute resolution (M Phil); community development (M Phil); international development (M Phil); leadership (M Phil); sustainability/environmental issues (M Phil); worldviews (M Phil). *Program availability:* Part-time. *Degree requirements:* For master's, thesis, report. *Entrance requirements:* For master's, minimum GPA of 3.5. Additional exam requirements/recommendations for international students: Required—TWE (minimum score 5.5), TOEFL (minimum score 600 paper-based; 100 iBT) or IELTS (minimum score 7). Electronic applications accepted. *Faculty research:* International development, worldviews, citizenship/dispute resolution, sustainability/environmental issues, leadership, community development.

**University of North Carolina at Asheville,** Master of Liberal Arts and Sciences Program, Asheville, NC 28804-3299. Offers climate change and society (Graduate Certificate); environmental and cultural sustainability (Graduate Certificate). *Program availability:* Part-time, evening/weekend. *Faculty:* 5 full-time (1 woman), 4 part-time/adjunct (0 women). *Students:* 2 full-time (1 woman), 19 part-time (9 women); includes 2 minority (1 Black or African American, non-Hispanic/Latino; 1 Asian, non-Hispanic/Latino). Average age 43. 18 applicants, 83% accepted, 8 enrolled. In 2016, 19 master's awarded. *Degree requirements:* For master's, thesis. *Entrance requirements:* For master's and Graduate Certificate, essay, 3 letters of recommendation, official transcripts. Additional exam requirements/recommendations for international students: Required—TOEFL (minimum score 85 iBT) or IELTS (6.5). *Application deadline:* For fall admission, 4/15 for domestic students; for spring admission, 11/15 for domestic students. Applications are processed on a rolling basis. Application fee: $75. Electronic applications accepted. *Expenses:* Tuition, state resident: full-time $4818. Tuition, nonresident: full-time $20,820. *Required fees:* $2936. Part-time tuition and fees vary according to course load. *Financial support:* Health care benefits available. Financial award application deadline: 5/1; financial award applicants required to submit FAFSA. *Unit head:* Gerard Voos, Director, Master of Liberal Arts and Sciences Program and the Asheville Graduate Center, 828-232-5040, E-mail: gvoos@unca.edu. *Application contact:* Jordan Dolfi, Program Associate, Master of Liberal Arts and Sciences Program and the Asheville Graduate Center, 828-251-6099, E-mail: jdolfi@unca.edu.
Website: https://mlas.unca.edu/

**University of Notre Dame,** Graduate School, Keough School of Global Affairs, Notre Dame, IN 46556. Offers global affairs (MGA); international peace studies (MGA); sustainable development (MGA).

**University of Oklahoma,** College of Atmospheric and Geographic Sciences, Department of Geography and Environmental Sustainability, Norman, OK 73019. Offers environmental sustainability (MS); geography (MA, MS, PhD), including geospatial technologies (MS), physical geography (MS). *Program availability:* Part-time. *Faculty:* 23 full-time (7 women). *Students:* 22 full-time (18 women), 10 part-time (3 women); includes 4 minority (1 American Indian or Alaska Native, non-Hispanic/Latino; 2 Hispanic/Latino; 1 Two or more races, non-Hispanic/Latino), 4 international. Average age 29. 16 applicants, 31% accepted, 4 enrolled. In 2016, 7 master's, 6 doctorates awarded. *Degree requirements:* For master's, comprehensive exam (for some programs), thesis (for some programs); for doctorate, comprehensive exam (for some programs), thesis/

dissertation (for some programs). *Entrance requirements:* For master's and doctorate, GRE, personal statement, transcripts, two letters of recommendation, writing sample. Additional exam requirements/recommendations for international students: Required—TOEFL (minimum score 79 iBT) or IELTS (minimum score 6.5). *Application deadline:* For fall admission, 1/15 for domestic and international students; for spring admission, 9/1 for domestic students, 11/1 for international students. Application fee: $50 ($100 for international students). Electronic applications accepted. *Expenses:* Tuition, state resident: full-time $4886; part-time $203.60 per credit hour. Tuition, nonresident: full-time $18,989; part-time $791.20 per credit hour. *Required fees:* $3283; $126.25 per credit hour. $126.50 per semester. *Financial support:* In 2016–17, 36 students received support, including 2 fellowships with full tuition reimbursements available (averaging $3,500 per year), 8 research assistantships with full tuition reimbursements available (averaging $14,928 per year), 11 teaching assistantships with full tuition reimbursements available (averaging $13,952 per year); Federal Work-Study, scholarships/grants, and unspecified assistantships also available. Financial award application deadline: 6/1; financial award applicants required to submit FAFSA. *Faculty research:* Land cover land use change; economic geography; landscape ecology; environmental economics; renewable energy. *Total annual research expenditures:* $1.2 million. *Unit head:* Dr. Kristen de Beurs, Associate Professor and Chair, 405-325-5325, E-mail: kdebeurs@ou.edu. *Application contact:* Travis Gliedt, Graduate Liaison, 405-325-5325, E-mail: tgliedt@ou.edu.
Website: http://geography.ou.edu

**University of Southern California,** Graduate School, School of Policy, Planning, and Development, Master of Planning Program, Los Angeles, CA 90089. Offers sustainable cities (Graduate Certificate); transportation systems (Graduate Certificate); urban planning (M Pl); M Arch/M Pl; M Pl/MA; M Pl/MPP; M Pl/MRED; M Pl/MS; M Pl/MSW; MBA/M Pl; ML Arch/M Pl; MPA/M Pl. *Accreditation:* ACSP. *Program availability:* Part-time. *Degree requirements:* For master's, comprehensive exam, internship. *Entrance requirements:* For master's, GRE, GMAT. Additional exam requirements/recommendations for international students: Required—TOEFL (minimum score 600 paper-based; 100 iBT). Electronic applications accepted. *Faculty research:* Transportation and infrastructure, comparative international development, healthy communities, social economic development, sustainable community planning.

**University of Southern California,** Graduate School, Viterbi School of Engineering, Sonny Astani Department of Civil Engineering, Los Angeles, CA 90089. Offers applied mechanics (MS); civil engineering (MS, PhD); computer-aided engineering (ME, Graduate Certificate); construction management (MCM); engineering technology commercialization (Graduate Certificate); environmental engineering (MS, PhD); environmental quality management (ME); structural design (ME); sustainable cities (Graduate Certificate); transportation systems (MS, Graduate Certificate); water and waste management (MS). *Program availability:* Part-time, evening/weekend. Terminal master's awarded for partial completion of doctoral program. *Degree requirements:* For master's, thesis optional; for doctorate, thesis/dissertation. *Entrance requirements:* For master's and doctorate, GRE General Test. Additional exam requirements/recommendations for international students: Recommended—TOEFL. Electronic applications accepted. *Faculty research:* Geotechnical engineering, transportation engineering, structural engineering, construction management, environmental engineering, water resources.

**University of South Florida,** College of Global Sustainability, Tampa, FL 33620-9951. Offers energy, global, water and sustainable tourism (Graduate Certificate); global sustainability (MA), including building sustainable enterprise, climate change and sustainability, coastal sustainability, entrepreneurship, food sustainability and security, sustainable energy, sustainable tourism, sustainable transportation, water. *Faculty:* 4 full-time (0 women). *Students:* 59 full-time (35 women), 51 part-time (29 women); includes 25 minority (3 Black or African American, non-Hispanic/Latino; 1 American Indian or Alaska Native, non-Hispanic/Latino; 2 Asian, non-Hispanic/Latino; 16 Hispanic/Latino; 3 Two or more races, non-Hispanic/Latino), 30 international. Average age 28. 134 applicants, 59% accepted, 55 enrolled. In 2016, 36 master's awarded. *Degree requirements:* For master's, comprehensive exam (for some programs), thesis or alternative, internship. *Entrance requirements:* For master's, minimum GPA of 3.0 in undergraduate coursework; at least two letters of recommendation (one must be academic); 200-250 word essay on student's background, professional goals, and reasons for seeking degree. Additional exam requirements/recommendations for international students: Required—TOEFL (minimum score 550 paper-based; 79 iBT). *Application deadline:* For fall admission, 6/1 for domestic students, 5/1 for international students; for spring admission, 10/15 for domestic students, 9/15 for international students. Electronic applications accepted. *Expenses:* Tuition, state resident: full-time $7766; part-time $431.43 per credit hour. Tuition, nonresident: full-time $15,789; part-time $877.17 per credit hour. *Required fees:* $37 per term. *Financial support:* In 2016–17, 20 students received support. *Faculty research:* Global sustainability, integrated resource management, systems thinking, green communities, entrepreneurship, ecotourism. *Total annual research expenditures:* $208,988. *Unit head:* Dr. Rafael Perez, Interim Dean, 813-974-9694, E-mail: perez@usf.edu.
Website: http://psgs.usf.edu/

**University of South Florida,** Innovative Education, Tampa, FL 33620-9951. Offers adult, career and higher education (Graduate Certificate), including college teaching, leadership in developing human resources, leadership in higher education; Africana studies (Graduate Certificate), including diasporas and health disparities, genocide and human rights; aging studies (Graduate Certificate), including gerontology; art research (Graduate Certificate), including museum studies; business foundations (Graduate Certificate); chemical and biomedical engineering (Graduate Certificate), including materials science and engineering, water, health and sustainability; child and family studies (Graduate Certificate), including positive behavior support; civil and industrial engineering (Graduate Certificate), including transportation systems analysis; community and family health (Graduate Certificate), including maternal and child health, social marketing and public health, violence and injury: prevention and intervention, women's health; criminology (Graduate Certificate), including criminal justice administration; educational measurement and research (Graduate Certificate), including evaluation; English (Graduate Certificate), including comparative literary studies, creative writing, professional and technical communication; entrepreneurship (Graduate Certificate); environmental health (Graduate Certificate), including safety management; epidemiology and biostatistics (Graduate Certificate), including applied biostatistics, biostatistics, concepts and tools of epidemiology, epidemiology, epidemiology of infectious diseases; geography, environment and planning (Graduate Certificate), including community development, environmental policy and management, geographical information systems; geology (Graduate Certificate), including hydrogeology; global health (Graduate Certificate), including disaster management, global health and Latin American and Caribbean studies, global health practice, humanitarian assistance, infection control; government and international affairs (Graduate Certificate), including Cuban studies, globalization studies; health policy and management (Graduate Certificate), including health management and leadership, public health policy and programs; hearing specialist: early intervention (Graduate Certificate); industrial and management systems engineering (Graduate Certificate), including systems engineering, technology management; information studies (Graduate

Certificate), including school library media specialist; information systems/decision sciences (Graduate Certificate), including analytics and business intelligence; instructional technology (Graduate Certificate), including distance education, Florida digital/virtual educator, instructional design, multimedia design, Web design; internal medicine, bioethics and medical humanities (Graduate Certificate), including biomedical ethics; Latin American and Caribbean studies (Graduate Certificate); mass communications (Graduate Certificate), including multimedia journalism; mathematics and statistics (Graduate Certificate), including mathematics; medicine (Graduate Certificate), including aging and neuroscience, bioinformatics, biotechnology, brain fitness and memory management, clinical investigation, health informatics, health sciences, integrative weight management, intellectual property, medicine and gender, metabolic and nutritional medicine, metabolic cardiology, pharmacy sciences; national and competitive intelligence (Graduate Certificate); psychological and social foundations (Graduate Certificate), including career counseling, college teaching, diversity in education, mental health counseling, school counseling; public affairs (Graduate Certificate), including nonprofit management, public management, research administration; public health (Graduate Certificate), including environmental health, health equity, public health generalist, translational research in adolescent behavioral health; public health practices (Graduate Certificate), including planning for healthy communities; rehabilitation and mental health counseling (Graduate Certificate), including integrative mental health care, marriage and family therapy, rehabilitation technology; secondary education (Graduate Certificate), including ESOL, foreign language education: culture and content, foreign language education: professional; social work (Graduate Certificate), including geriatric social work/clinical gerontology; special education (Graduate Certificate), including autism spectrum disorder, disabilities education: severe/profound; world languages (Graduate Certificate), including teaching English as a second language (TESL) or foreign language. *Expenses:* Tuition, state resident: full-time $7766; part-time $431.43 per credit hour. Tuition, nonresident: full-time $15,789; part-time $877.17 per credit hour. *Required fees:* $37 per term. *Unit head:* Kathy Barnes, Interdisciplinary Programs Coordinator, 813-974-8031, Fax: 813-974-7061, E-mail: barnesk@usf.edu. *Application contact:* Karen Tylinski, Metro Initiatives, 813-974-9943, Fax: 813-974-7061, E-mail: ktylinsk@usf.edu.
Website: http://www.usf.edu/innovative-education/

**The University of Texas at Austin,** Graduate School, School of Architecture, Program in Sustainable Design, Austin, TX 78712-1111. Offers M Arch I, M Arch II, MSSD.

**University of Washington,** Graduate School, College of the Environment, School of Environmental and Forest Sciences, Seattle, WA 98195. Offers bioresource science and engineering (MS, PhD); environmental horticulture (MEH); forest ecology (MS, PhD); forest management (MFR); forest soils (MS, PhD); restoration ecology (MS, PhD); restoration ecology and environmental horticulture (MS, PhD); social sciences (MS, PhD); sustainable resource management (MS, PhD); wildlife science (MS, PhD); MFR/MAIS; MPA/MS. *Accreditation:* SAF. *Program availability:* Part-time. *Degree requirements:* For master's, thesis; for doctorate, comprehensive exam, thesis/dissertation. *Entrance requirements:* For master's and doctorate, GRE, minimum GPA of 3.0. Additional exam requirements/recommendations for international students: Required—TOEFL. Electronic applications accepted. *Faculty research:* Ecosystem analysis, silviculture and forest protection, paper science and engineering, environmental horticulture and urban forestry, natural resource policy and economics, restoration ecology and environment horticulture, conservation, human dimensions, wildlife, bioresource science and engineering.

**University of Washington,** Graduate School, School of Law, Seattle, WA 98195-3020. Offers Asian law (LL M, PhD); intellectual property law and policy (LL M); law (JD); law of sustainable international development (LL M); taxation (LL M); JD/LL M; JD/MA; JD/MAIS; JD/MBA; JD/MPA; JD/MS; JD/PhD. *Accreditation:* ABA. *Degree requirements:* For master's, thesis; for doctorate, thesis/dissertation (for some programs). *Entrance requirements:* For master's, language proficiency (LL M in Asian law); for doctorate, LSAT (for JD). Additional exam requirements/recommendations for international students: Required—TOEFL. *Expenses:* Contact institution. *Faculty research:* Asian, international and comparative law, intellectual property law, health law, environmental law, taxation.

**The University of Western Ontario,** Faculty of Graduate Studies, Physical Sciences Division, Department of Earth Sciences, London, ON N6A 5B8, Canada. Offers environment and sustainability (MES); geology (M Sc, PhD); geology and environmental science (M Sc, PhD); geophysics (M Sc, PhD); geophysics and environmental science (M Sc, PhD). *Degree requirements:* For master's, thesis; for doctorate, thesis/dissertation, qualifying exam. *Entrance requirements:* For master's, honors in B Sc; for doctorate, M Sc. Additional exam requirements/recommendations for international students: Required—TOEFL. *Faculty research:* Geophysics, geochemistry, paleontology, sedimentology/stratigraphy, glaciology/quaternary.

**University of Wisconsin–Madison,** Graduate School, Gaylord Nelson Institute for Environmental Studies, Environmental Conservation Program, Madison, WI 53706-1380. Offers MS. *Faculty:* 4 full-time (1 woman), 5 part-time/adjunct (2 women). *Students:* 22 full-time (16 women); includes 2 minority (1 Asian, non-Hispanic/Latino; 1 Hispanic/Latino), 2 international. Average age 29. 52 applicants, 77% accepted, 23 enrolled. In 2016, 21 master's awarded. *Degree requirements:* For master's, thesis or alternative, spring/summer leadership (internship) experience. *Entrance requirements:* For master's, GRE General Test (recommended for potential scholarship consideration). Additional exam requirements/recommendations for international students: Required—TOEFL (minimum score 550 paper-based, 80 iBT) or IELTS (6.5). *Application deadline:* For summer admission, 12/1 for domestic and international students. Applications are processed on a rolling basis. Application fee: $75 ($81 for international students). Electronic applications accepted. *Expenses:* Contact institution. *Financial support:* In 2016–17, 16 students received support. Career-related internships or fieldwork and scholarships/grants available. Financial award application deadline: 12/1. *Faculty research:* Geographic information systems, forestry, wildlife ecology, agroecology, landscape architecture, sociology, rural sociology, plant ecology, biodiversity, sustainability, sustainable development, conservation biology, conservation planning/management, land tenure. *Unit head:* Dr. Janet M. Silbernagel, Chair, 608-262-4510, Fax: 608-262-2273, E-mail: jmsilber@wisc.edu. *Application contact:* Nathan Schulfer, Senior Student Services Coordinator, 608-263-7771, Fax: 608-262-2273, E-mail: schulfer@wisc.edu.
Website: http://nelson.wisc.edu/graduate/environmental-conservation/index.php

**Walden University,** Graduate Programs, School of Public Policy and Administration, Minneapolis, MN 55401. Offers criminal justice (MPA, MPP, MS, Graduate Certificate), including emergency management (MS, PhD), general program (MS), global leadership (MS, PhD), homeland security and policy coordination (MS, PhD), law and public policy (MS, PhD), policy analysis (MS, PhD), public management and leadership (MS, PhD), self-designed (MS), terrorism, mediation, and peace (MS, PhD); criminal justice and executive management (MS), including global leadership (MS, PhD); criminal justice leadership and executive management (MS), including emergency management (MS, PhD), general program, homeland security and policy coordination (MS, PhD), law and public policy (MS, PhD), policy analysis (MS, PhD), public management and leadership (MS, PhD), self-designed, terrorism, mediation, and peace (MS, PhD); emergency management (MPA, MPP, MS), including criminal justice (MS, PhD), general program (MS), homeland security (MS), public management and leadership (MS, PhD), terrorism and emergency management (MS); general program (MPA, MPP); global leadership (MPA, MPP); government management (Graduate Certificate); health policy (MPA, MPP); homeland security (Graduate Certificate); homeland security and policy coordination (MPA, MPP); international nongovernmental organizations (MPA, MPP); law and public policy (MPA, MPP); local government management for sustainable communities (MPA, MPP); nonprofit management (Graduate Certificate); nonprofit management and leadership (MPA, MPP, MS), including global leadership (MS, PhD), international nongovernmental organization (MS), local government for sustainable communities (MS), self designed (MS); online teaching in higher education (Post-Master's Certificate); policy analysis (MPA); public management and leadership (MPA, MPP, Graduate Certificate); public policy (Graduate Certificate); public policy and administration (PhD), including criminal justice (MS, PhD), emergency management (MS, PhD), global leadership (MS, PhD), health policy, homeland security and policy coordination (MS, PhD), international nongovernmental organizations, law and public policy (MS, PhD), local government management for sustainable communities, nonprofit management and leadership, policy analysis (MS, PhD), public management and leadership (MS, PhD), terrorism, mediation, and peace (MS, PhD); strategic planning and public policy (Graduate Certificate); terrorism, mediation, and peace (MPA, MPP). *Program availability:* Part-time, evening/weekend, online only, 100% online. *Degree requirements:* For doctorate, thesis/dissertation, residency. *Entrance requirements:* For master's, bachelor's degree or higher; minimum GPA of 2.5; official transcripts; goal statement (for some programs); access to computer and Internet; for doctorate, master's degree or higher; three years of related professional or academic experience (preferred); minimum GPA of 3.0; goal statement and current resume (for select programs); official transcripts; access to computer and Internet; for other advanced degree, relevant work experience; access to computer and Internet. Additional exam requirements/recommendations for international students: Required—TOEFL (minimum score 550 paper-based, 79 iBT), IELTS (minimum score 6.5), Michigan English Language Assessment Battery (minimum score 82), or PTE (minimum score 53). Electronic applications accepted.

**West Chester University of Pennsylvania,** College of Education and Social Work, Department of Professional and Secondary Education, West Chester, PA 19383. Offers education for sustainability (Certificate); educational technology (Certificate); entrepreneurial education (Certificate); transformative education and social change (MS). *Program availability:* Part-time. *Faculty:* 10 full-time (3 women). *Students:* 6 full-time (5 women), 35 part-time (22 women); includes 2 minority (1 Hispanic/Latino; 1 Two or more races, non-Hispanic/Latino). Average age 30. 24 applicants, 88% accepted, 17 enrolled. In 2016, 7 master's, 3 other advanced degrees awarded. *Degree requirements:* For master's, comprehensive exam (for some programs), thesis, 36 credits. *Entrance requirements:* For master's, teaching certification (strongly recommended); for Certificate, minimum GPA of 3.0. Additional exam requirements/recommendations for international students: Required—TOEFL or IELTS. *Application deadline:* For fall admission, 5/15 for international students; for spring admission, 10/15 for international

students. Applications are processed on a rolling basis. Application fee: $50. Electronic applications accepted. *Expenses:* Tuition, state resident: full-time $8694; part-time $483 per credit. Tuition, nonresident: full-time $13,050; part-time $725 per credit. *Required fees:* $2399; $119.05 per credit. Tuition and fees vary according to campus/location and program. *Financial support:* Scholarships/grants and unspecified assistantships available. Financial award application deadline: 2/15; financial award applicants required to submit FAFSA. *Faculty research:* Technology integration: preparing our teachers for the twenty-first century, critical pedagogy. *Unit head:* Dr. John Elmore, Chair, 610-436-6934, Fax: 610-436-3102, E-mail: jelmore@wcupa.edu. *Application contact:* Dr. Matthew Kruger-Ross, Graduate Coordinator, 610-436-2106, Fax: 610-436-3102, E-mail: mkruger-ross@wcupa.edu.
Website: http://www.wcupa.edu/education-socialWork/profsecedu/

**Western Illinois University,** School of Graduate Studies, College of Arts and Sciences, Department of Geography, Macomb, IL 61455-1390. Offers community development and planning (Certificate); geography (MA); GIS analysis: GIS applications (Certificate). *Program availability:* Part-time. *Students:* 7 full-time (2 women), 5 part-time (2 women); includes 3 minority (2 Black or African American, non-Hispanic/Latino; 1 Asian, non-Hispanic/Latino), 1 international. Average age 30. 10 applicants, 80% accepted, 4 enrolled. In 2016, 9 master's, 3 other advanced degrees awarded. *Degree requirements:* For master's, thesis or alternative. *Entrance requirements:* Additional exam requirements/recommendations for international students: Required—TOEFL (minimum score 550 paper-based; 80 iBT). *Application deadline:* Applications are processed on a rolling basis. Application fee: $30. Electronic applications accepted. *Financial support:* In 2016–17, 6 students received support, including research assistantships with full tuition reimbursements available (averaging $7,544 per year); unspecified assistantships also available. Financial award applicants required to submit FAFSA. *Unit head:* Dr. Sam Thompson, Chairperson, 309-298-1648. *Application contact:* Dr. Nancy Parsons, Associate Provost and Director of Graduate School, 309-298-1806, Fax: 309-298-2345, E-mail: grad-office@wiu.edu. Website: http://www.wiu.edu/cas/geography/

**West Virginia University,** Davis College of Agriculture, Forestry and Consumer Sciences, Division of Resource Management and Sustainable Development, Program in Resource Management and Sustainable Development, Morgantown, WV 26506. Offers PhD. *Program availability:* Part-time. *Degree requirements:* For doctorate, thesis/dissertation. *Entrance requirements:* For doctorate, GRE General Test. Additional exam requirements/recommendations for international students: Required—TOEFL.

**Xavier University,** College of Arts and Sciences, Department of Interdisciplinary Studies, Cincinnati, OH 45207. Offers urban sustainability and resilience (MA). *Degree requirements:* For master's, thesis (for some programs), internship. *Entrance requirements:* For master's, MAT or GRE, official transcript, resume, 500-word statement of purpose, two letters of reference. Additional exam requirements/recommendations for international students: Required—TOEFL (minimum score 550 paper-based; 79 iBT). Electronic applications accepted. Application fee is waived when completed online. *Expenses:* Contact institution.

# Urban and Regional Planning

**Alabama Agricultural and Mechanical University,** School of Graduate Studies, College of Agricultural, Life and Natural Sciences, Department of Community and Regional Planning, Huntsville, AL 35811. Offers urban and regional planning (MURP). *Accreditation:* ACSP. *Program availability:* Part-time, evening/weekend. *Degree requirements:* For master's, comprehensive exam. *Entrance requirements:* For master's, GRE General Test. Additional exam requirements/recommendations for international students: Required—TOEFL (minimum score 500 paper-based; 61 iBT). *Application deadline:* For fall admission, 5/1 for domestic students. Applications are processed on a rolling basis. Application fee: $25. Electronic applications accepted. *Expenses:* Tuition, nonresident: part-time $826 per credit hour. Full-time tuition and fees vary according to course load and program. *Financial support:* Fellowships, research assistantships with full tuition reimbursements, and career-related internships or fieldwork available. Support available to part-time students. Financial award application deadline: 4/1. *Faculty research:* Urban and rural research, needs assessment and community trends through analysis of social indicators, fiscal impact studies, rural transportation, health care. *Unit head:* Dr. Berneece Herbert, Interim Chair, 256-372-4988, Fax: 256-372-5906.
Website: http://www.aamu.edu/academics/alns/crp/

**American University of Beirut,** Graduate Programs, Faculty of Agricultural and Food Sciences, Beirut, Lebanon. Offers agricultural economics (MS); animal science (MS); ecosystem management (MSES); food security (MS); food technology (MS); irrigation (MS); nutrition (MS); plant protection (MS); plant science (MS); poultry science (MS); rural community development (MS). *Program availability:* Part-time. *Faculty:* 15 full-time (2 women), 1 part-time/adjunct (0 women). *Students:* 11 full-time (10 women), 63 part-time (46 women); includes 1 minority (Asian, non-Hispanic/Latino). Average age 26. 108 applicants, 76% accepted, 28 enrolled. In 2016, 23 master's awarded. *Degree requirements:* For master's, one foreign language, comprehensive exam, thesis (for some programs). *Entrance requirements:* Additional exam requirements/recommendations for international students: Required—TOEFL (minimum score 600 paper-based; 100 iBT), IELTS (minimum score 7.5). *Application deadline:* For fall admission, 2/10 for domestic and international students; for spring admission, 11/2 for domestic and international students. Application fee: $50. Electronic applications accepted. *Expenses:* Tuition: Full-time $16,740; part-time $930 per credit. *Required fees:* $716. Tuition and fees vary according to course load and program. *Financial support:* In 2016–17, 5 research assistantships with full and partial tuition reimbursements (averaging $1,800 per year), 58 teaching assistantships with full and partial tuition reimbursements (averaging $1,400 per year) were awarded; scholarships/grants, health care benefits, and unspecified assistantships also available. Financial award application deadline: 2/2. *Faculty research:* Noncommunicable disease epidemic; evapotranspiration; rapid poverty assessment; green house biological control strategies; integrated energy planning. *Total annual research expenditures:* $500,000. *Unit head:* Prof. Nahla Chawkat Hwalla, Dean, 961-1350000 Ext. 4400, Fax: 961-1744460, E-mail: nahla@aub.edu.lb. *Application contact:* Dr. Rabih Talhouk, Director, Graduate Council, 961-1350000 Ext. 4386, Fax: 961-1374374, E-mail: graduate.council@aub.edu.lb.
Website: http://www.aub.edu.lb/fafs/fafs_home/Pages/index.aspx

**American University of Beirut,** Graduate Programs, Faculty of Engineering and Architecture, 11-0236, Lebanon. Offers applied energy (ME); civil engineering (PhD); electrical and computer engineering (PhD); energy studies (MS); engineering management (MEM); environmental and water resources (ME); environmental

technology (MSES); mechanical engineering (ME, PhD); urban design (MUD); urban planning and policy (MUPP). *Program availability:* Part-time, evening/weekend, 100% online. *Faculty:* 99 full-time (22 women), 1 part-time/adjunct (0 women). *Students:* 308 full-time (143 women), 86 part-time (39 women). Average age 26. 430 applicants, 69% accepted, 125 enrolled. In 2016, 103 master's, 7 doctorates awarded. Terminal master's awarded for partial completion of doctoral program. *Degree requirements:* For master's, comprehensive exam, thesis optional; for doctorate, comprehensive exam, thesis/dissertation. *Entrance requirements:* For doctorate, GRE. Additional exam requirements/recommendations for international students: Required—TOEFL (minimum score 573 paper-based; 88 iBT); Recommended—IELTS (minimum score 7). *Application deadline:* For fall admission, 2/10 priority date for domestic and international students; for spring admission, 11/2 priority date for domestic students, 11/2 for international students. Application fee: $50. Electronic applications accepted. *Expenses:* Contact institution. *Financial support:* In 2016–17, 22 students received support, including 94 fellowships with full tuition reimbursements available (averaging $18,200 per year), 44 research assistantships with full tuition reimbursements available (averaging $7,596 per year), 124 teaching assistantships with full tuition reimbursements available (averaging $1,056 per year); career-related internships or fieldwork, Federal Work-Study, institutionally sponsored loans, scholarships/grants, traineeships, health care benefits, tuition waivers, and unspecified assistantships also available. Support available to part-time students. Financial award application deadline: 12/20. *Total annual research expenditures:* $1.5 million. *Unit head:* Prof. Alan Shihadeh, Interim Dean, 961-1350000 Ext. 3400, Fax: 961-1744462, E-mail: as20@aub.edu.lb. *Application contact:* Dr. Salim Kanaan, Director, Admissions Office, 961-1350000 Ext. 2594, Fax: 961-1750775, E-mail: sk00@aub.edu.lb.
Website: http://www.aub.edu.lb/fea/fea_home/Pages/index.aspx

**American University of Sharjah,** Graduate Programs, Sharjah, United Arab Emirates. Offers accounting (MS); business (EMBA, MBA); chemical engineering (MS Ch E); civil engineering (MSCE); computer engineering (MS); electrical engineering (MSEE); engineering systems management (MS); mathematics (MS); mechanical engineering (MSME); mechatronics engineering (MS); teaching English to speakers of other languages (MA); translation and interpreting (MA); urban planning (MUP). *Program availability:* Part-time, evening/weekend. *Degree requirements:* For master's, thesis (for some programs). *Entrance requirements:* For master's, GMAT (for MBA). Additional exam requirements/recommendations for international students: Required—TOEFL (minimum score 550 paper-based; 80 iBT), TWE (minimum score 5); Recommended—IELTS (minimum score 6.5). Electronic applications accepted. *Faculty research:* Water pollution, management and waste water treatment, energy and sustainability, air pollution, Islamic finance, family business and small and medium enterprises.

**Andrews University,** School of Graduate Studies, College of Arts and Sciences, Department of Behavioral Science, Program in International Development, Berrien Springs, MI 49104. Offers community and international development (MSCID). *Program availability:* Online learning. *Faculty:* 10 full-time (2 women), 1 part-time/adjunct (0 women). *Students:* 15 full-time (13 women), 6 part-time (3 women); includes 9 minority (4 Black or African American, non-Hispanic/Latino; 2 Asian, non-Hispanic/Latino; 3 Hispanic/Latino), 8 international. Average age 32. In 2016, 12 master's awarded. *Entrance requirements:* For master's, GRE General Test. Additional exam requirements/recommendations for international students: Required—TOEFL (minimum score 550 paper-based). Application fee: $40. *Unit head:* Dr. Duane C. McBride, Director, 269-471-

3152. *Application contact:* Justina Clayburn, Supervisor of Graduate Admission, 800-253-2874, Fax: 269-471-6321, E-mail: graduate@andrews.edu.
Website: http://www.andrews.edu/grad/programs/community-and-international-development-off-campus.html

**Arizona State University at the Tempe campus,** College of Liberal Arts and Sciences, School of Geographical Sciences and Urban Planning, Tempe, AZ 85287-5302. Offers geographic information systems (MAS); geographical information science (Graduate Certificate); geography (MA, PhD); transportation systems (Graduate Certificate); urban and environmental planning (MUEP); urban planning (PhD). *Accreditation:* ACSP. Terminal master's awarded for partial completion of doctoral program. *Degree requirements:* For master's, thesis, interactive Program of Study (iPOS) submitted before completing 50 percent of required credit hours; for doctorate, comprehensive exam, thesis/dissertation, interactive Program of Study (iPOS) submitted before completing 50 percent of required credit hours. *Entrance requirements:* For master's and doctorate, GRE, minimum GPA of 3.0 or equivalent in last 2 years of work leading to bachelor's degree. Additional exam requirements/recommendations for international students: Required—TOEFL, IELTS, or PTE. Electronic applications accepted. *Expenses:* Contact institution.

**Arizona State University at the Tempe campus,** College of Public Programs, School of Community Resources and Development, Phoenix, AZ 85004-0685. Offers community resources and development (MS, PhD); nonprofit leadership and management (Graduate Certificate); nonprofit studies (MNpS); sustainable tourism (MAS). *Program availability:* Part-time, evening/weekend. Terminal master's awarded for partial completion of doctoral program. *Degree requirements:* For master's, thesis or alternative, interactive Program of Study (iPOS) submitted before completing 50 percent of required credit hours; for doctorate, comprehensive exam, thesis/dissertation, interactive Program of Study (iPOS) submitted before completing 50 percent of required credit hours. *Entrance requirements:* For master's and doctorate, GRE, minimum GPA of 3.0 or equivalent in last 2 years of work leading to bachelor's degree. Additional exam requirements/recommendations for international students: Required—TOEFL, IELTS, or PTE. Electronic applications accepted. *Expenses:* Contact institution.

**Arizona State University at the Tempe campus,** College of Public Programs, School of Public Affairs, Phoenix, AZ 85004-0687. Offers emergency management and homeland security (MA); program evaluation (MS); public administration (MPA, PhD), including nonprofit administration (MPA), urban management (MPA); public policy (MPP); MPA/MSW. *Accreditation:* NASPAA (one or more programs are accredited). *Program availability:* Part-time, evening/weekend. Terminal master's awarded for partial completion of doctoral program. *Degree requirements:* For master's, thesis or alternative, policy analysis or capstone project; interactive Program of Study (iPOS) submitted before completing 50 percent of required credit hours; for doctorate, comprehensive exam, thesis/dissertation, interactive Program of Study (iPOS) submitted before completing 50 percent of required credit hours. *Entrance requirements:* For master's, GRE, minimum GPA of 3.0 or equivalent in last 2 years of work leading to bachelor's degree; for doctorate, GRE, minimum GPA of 3.0 or equivalent in last 2 years of work leading to bachelor's degree, 3 letters of recommendation, resume, statement of goals, samples of research reports. Additional exam requirements/recommendations for international students: Required—TOEFL (minimum score 600 paper-based; 100 iBT), IELTS (minimum score 6.5). Electronic applications accepted. *Expenses:* Contact institution.

**Auburn University,** Graduate School, College of Architecture, Design, and Construction, Program in Community Planning, Auburn University, AL 36849. Offers MCP, MPA/MCP. *Program availability:* Part-time. *Faculty:* 24 full-time (7 women), 5 part-time/adjunct (0 women). *Students:* 6 full-time (4 women); includes 2 minority (both Black or African American, non-Hispanic/Latino), 1 international. Average age 29. 8 applicants, 88% accepted. In 2016, 10 master's awarded. *Degree requirements:* For master's, oral exam, project. *Entrance requirements:* For master's, GRE General Test. *Application deadline:* Applications are processed on a rolling basis. Application fee: $50 ($60 for international students). Electronic applications accepted. *Expenses:* Tuition, state resident: full-time $9072; part-time $504 per credit hour. Tuition, nonresident: full-time $27,216; part-time $1512 per credit hour. *Required fees:* $812 per semester. Tuition and fees vary according to degree level and program. *Financial support:* Federal Work-Study available. Support available to part-time students. Financial award application deadline: 3/15; financial award applicants required to submit FAFSA. *Unit head:* Dr. David Hinson, Head, 334-844-4516. *Application contact:* Dr. George Flowers, Dean of the Graduate School, 334-844-2125.
Website: http://cadc.auburn.edu/studentservices/Pages/APLA/APLA_MCP_Degree.aspx

**Ball State University,** Graduate School, College of Architecture and Planning, Department of Urban Planning, Muncie, IN 47306. Offers urban and regional planning (MURP). *Accreditation:* ACSP. *Program availability:* Part-time. *Degree requirements:* For master's, thesis. *Entrance requirements:* For master's, minimum baccalaureate GPA of 2.75 or 3.0 in latter half of baccalaureate; at least three letters of recommendation (minimum of two from instructors) and two-page personal statement (if GPA is below 3.0). Additional exam requirements/recommendations for international students: Required—TOEFL (minimum score 550 paper-based; 79 iBT), IELTS (minimum score 6.5). Electronic applications accepted. *Expenses:* Contact institution. *Faculty research:* Computer-assisted land-use analysis.

**Ball State University,** Graduate School, Miller College of Business, Interdepartmental Program in Business Administration, Muncie, IN 47306. Offers business administration (MBA); business essentials (Graduate Certificate); community and economic development (Certificate). *Accreditation:* AACSB. *Program availability:* Part-time, 100% online, blended/hybrid learning. *Entrance requirements:* For master's, GMAT or GRE, minimum baccalaureate GPA of 2.75 or 3.0 in latter half of baccalaureate, resume or curriculum vitae, four professional letters of recommendation. Additional exam requirements/recommendations for international students: Required—TOEFL (minimum score 550 paper-based; 79 iBT), IELTS (minimum score 6.5). Electronic applications accepted. *Expenses:* Contact institution.

**Boston University,** Metropolitan College, Program in City Planning, Boston, MA 02215. Offers MCP. *Program availability:* Part-time, evening/weekend. *Faculty:* 2 full-time (1 woman), 6 part-time/adjunct (2 women). *Students:* 10 full-time (5 women), 20 part-time (14 women); includes 4 minority (1 Black or African American, non-Hispanic/Latino; 1 Asian, non-Hispanic/Latino; 2 Hispanic/Latino), 11 international. Average age 29. 45 applicants, 87% accepted, 9 enrolled. In 2016, 8 master's awarded. *Degree requirements:* For master's, thesis optional. *Entrance requirements:* Additional exam requirements/recommendations for international students: Required—TOEFL (minimum score 84 iBT). *Application deadline:* For fall admission, 7/15 priority date for international students; for spring admission, 11/15 priority date for international students. Applications are processed on a rolling basis. Application fee: $85. Electronic applications accepted. *Expenses:* Contact institution. *Financial support:* In 2016–17, 4 research assistantships (averaging $4,200 per year) were awarded; career-related internships or fieldwork and unspecified assistantships also available. Support available to part-time students. Financial award applicants required to submit FAFSA. *Faculty research:* Housing, community development and land use planning, environmental management and planning, international comparative development planning. *Unit head:* Dr. Daniel P. LeClair, Chair, 617-353-3025, Fax: 617-358-3595, E-mail: dleclair@bu.edu. *Application contact:* Dr. Madhu Dutta-Koehler, Assistant Professor and Faculty Coordinator, 617-358-3264, Fax: 617-358-3595, E-mail: duttam@bu.edu.
Website: http://www.bu.edu/cityplanning/

**California Polytechnic State University, San Luis Obispo,** College of Architecture and Environmental Design, Department of City and Regional Planning, San Luis Obispo, CA 93407. Offers MCRP, MCRP/MS. *Accreditation:* ACSP. *Program availability:* Part-time. *Faculty:* 7 full-time (3 women). *Students:* 28 full-time (13 women); includes 2 minority (1 Asian, non-Hispanic/Latino; 1 Hispanic/Latino), 2 international. Average age 25. 50 applicants, 58% accepted, 13 enrolled. In 2016, 26 master's awarded. *Degree requirements:* For master's, comprehensive exam (for some programs), thesis. *Entrance requirements:* For master's, GRE. Additional exam requirements/recommendations for international students: Required—TOEFL (minimum score 80 iBT). *Application deadline:* For fall admission, 2/1 for domestic and international students; for winter admission, 11/1 for domestic students, 6/30 for international students. Applications are processed on a rolling basis. Application fee: $55. Electronic applications accepted. *Expenses:* Tuition, state resident: full-time $6738; part-time $3906 per year. Tuition, nonresident: full-time $15,666; part-time $8370 per year. *Required fees:* $3603; $3141 per unit. $1047 per term. *Financial support:* Fellowships, research assistantships, career-related internships or fieldwork, institutionally sponsored loans, and unspecified assistantships available. Financial award application deadline: 3/2; financial award applicants required to submit FAFSA. *Faculty research:* Community sustainability, climate action planning, natural hazards, small town and rural planning, subdivision site design. *Unit head:* Cornelius Nuworsoo, Graduate Coordinator, E-mail: cnuworso@calpoly.edu.
Website: http://www.planning.calpoly.edu/

**California State Polytechnic University, Pomona,** Program in Urban and Regional Planning, Pomona, CA 91768-2557. Offers MURP. *Accreditation:* ACSP. *Program availability:* Part-time, evening/weekend. *Students:* 29 full-time (16 women), 11 part-time (6 women); includes 30 minority (3 Black or African American, non-Hispanic/Latino; 7 Asian, non-Hispanic/Latino; 20 Hispanic/Latino), 2 international. Average age 27. 21 applicants, 100% accepted, 19 enrolled. In 2016, 18 master's awarded. *Entrance requirements:* Additional exam requirements/recommendations for international students: Required—TOEFL. *Application deadline:* Applications are processed on a rolling basis. Application fee: $55. Electronic applications accepted. *Expenses:* Contact institution. *Financial support:* Application deadline: 3/2; applicants required to submit FAFSA. *Unit head:* Dr. Courtney Knapp, Graduate Coordinator, 909-869-4507, E-mail: ceknapp@cpp.edu. *Application contact:* Andrew M. Wright, Director of Admissions, 909-869-3130, Fax: 909-869-4529, E-mail: awright@cpp.edu.
Website: https://env.cpp.edu/urp/degree/master-urban-and-regional-planning

**The Catholic University of America,** School of Architecture and Planning, Washington, DC 20064. Offers architecture and planning (M Arch, MS Arch St); city and regional planning (M Arch); facilities management (MS Arch); regional development (Certificate); sustainable design (M Arch, Certificate). *Program availability:* Part-time. *Faculty:* 20 full-time (7 women), 15 part-time/adjunct (1 woman). *Students:* 69 full-time (28 women), 21 part-time (13 women); includes 35 minority (11 Black or African American, non-Hispanic/Latino; 5 Asian, non-Hispanic/Latino; 11 Hispanic/Latino; 8 Two or more races, non-Hispanic/Latino), 13 international. Average age 28. 73 applicants, 84% accepted, 24 enrolled. In 2016, 42 master's awarded. *Degree requirements:* For master's, thesis. *Entrance requirements:* For master's, GRE (minimum score: 1000), minimum GPA of 2.8, portfolio, statement of purpose, official copies of academic transcripts, three letters of recommendation. Additional exam requirements/recommendations for international students: Required—TOEFL (minimum score 550 paper-based; 80 iBT). *Application deadline:* For fall admission, 1/15 priority date for domestic students, 7/1 for international students; for spring admission, 10/15 priority date for domestic students, 11/1 for international students. Applications are processed on a rolling basis. Application fee: $55. Electronic applications accepted. *Expenses:* $43,380 per year; $1,170 per credit; $200 per semester part-time fees. *Financial support:* Fellowships, research assistantships, teaching assistantships, Federal Work-Study, scholarships/grants, tuition waivers (full and partial), and unspecified assistantships available. Financial award application deadline: 2/1; financial award applicants required to submit FAFSA. *Faculty research:* Architectural history, cultural studies/sacred space, design technologies, digital media, real estate development, urban design. *Total annual research expenditures:* $93,903. *Unit head:* Randall Ott, Dean, 202-319-5784, Fax: 202-319-2023, E-mail: ott@cua.edu. *Application contact:* Director of Graduate Admissions, 202-319-5057, Fax: 202-319-6533, E-mail: cua-admissions@cua.edu.
Website: http://architecture.cua.edu/

**Clark University,** Graduate School, Department of International Development, Community, and Environment, Program in Community Development and Planning, Worcester, MA 01610-1477. Offers MA, MA/MBA. *Students:* 39 full-time (29 women), 4 part-time (3 women); includes 11 minority (4 Black or African American, non-Hispanic/Latino; 3 Asian, non-Hispanic/Latino; 4 Hispanic/Latino), 1 international. Average age 25. 72 applicants, 83% accepted, 34 enrolled. In 2016, 29 master's awarded. *Degree requirements:* For master's, thesis. *Entrance requirements:* For master's, 3 references, resume or curriculum vitae. Additional exam requirements/recommendations for international students: Required—TOEFL (minimum score 575 paper-based; 90 iBT) or IELTS (minimum score 6.5). *Application deadline:* For fall admission, 1/15 for domestic students. Application fee: $75. *Expenses:* Tuition: Full-time $44,050. *Required fees:* $80. Tuition and fees vary according to course load and program. *Financial support:* Fellowships with partial tuition reimbursements, research assistantships with partial tuition reimbursements, teaching assistantships with partial tuition reimbursements, institutionally sponsored loans, and scholarships/grants available. *Faculty research:* Urban revitalization, youth and gang violence, amenities, systemic education reform, housing for disabled residents, economic development in neighborhood planning. *Unit head:* Dr. Ramon Borges-Mendez, Coordinator, 508-421-3838, Fax: 508-793-8820. *Application contact:* Sawsan Berjawi, Manager of Academic and Student Affairs, 508-421-3846, Fax: 508-793-8820, E-mail: sberjawi@clarku.edu.
Website: http://www.clarku.edu/programs/masters-community-development-and-planning

**Clemson University,** Graduate School, College of Architecture, Arts, and Humanities, Department of City Planning and Real Estate Development, Program in City and Regional Planning, Clemson, SC 29634. Offers MCRP. *Accreditation:* ACSP. *Faculty:* 8 full-time (1 woman). *Students:* 43 full-time (20 women), 3 part-time (2 women); includes 3 minority (1 Black or African American, non-Hispanic/Latino; 1 Asian, non-Hispanic/Latino; 1 Hispanic/Latino), 13 international. Average age 26. 74 applicants, 74% accepted, 23 enrolled. In 2016, 11 master's awarded. *Degree requirements:* For master's, departmental paper or thesis. *Entrance requirements:* For master's, GRE General Test, unofficial transcripts, letters of recommendation. Additional exam requirements/recommendations for international students: Required—TOEFL (minimum score 80 iBT), IELTS (minimum score 6.5). *Application deadline:* For fall admission, 2/15 priority date for domestic and international students. Applications are processed on a rolling basis. Application fee: $80 ($90 for international students). Electronic applications

## Urban and Regional Planning

accepted. *Expenses:* $4,841 per semester full-time resident, $9,640 per semester full-time non-resident, $612 per credit hour part-time resident, $1,223 per credit hour part-time non-resident. *Financial support:* In 2016–17, 25 students received support, including 1 fellowship with partial tuition reimbursement available (averaging $5,000 per year), 12 research assistantships with partial tuition reimbursements available (averaging $4,950 per year); career-related internships or fieldwork and unspecified assistantships also available. Financial award application deadline: 2/15. *Faculty research:* Coastal planning, transportation, land use and urban design, economic development, geographic information systems. *Unit head:* Dr. James Spencer, Department Chair, 864-656-1527, E-mail: jhspenc@clemson.edu. *Application contact:* Dr. Cliff Ellis, Program Director, 864-656-2477, E-mail: cliffoe@clemson.edu. Website: http://www.clemson.edu/caah/departments/city-and-regional-planning/

**Cleveland State University,** College of Graduate Studies, Maxine Goodman Levin College of Urban Affairs, Program in Urban Planning, Design, and Development, Cleveland, OH 44115. Offers environmental sustainability (MUPDD); housing and neighborhood development (MUPDD); urban economic development (Certificate); JD/MUPDD. *Accreditation:* ACSP. *Program availability:* Part-time, evening/weekend. *Faculty:* 16 full-time (8 women), 13 part-time/adjunct (5 women). *Students:* 8 full-time (3 women), 26 part-time (15 women); includes 4 minority (2 Black or African American, non-Hispanic/Latino; 1 Asian, non-Hispanic/Latino; 1 Two or more races, non-Hispanic/Latino), 2 international. Average age 28. 48 applicants, 56% accepted, 14 enrolled. In 2016, 21 master's awarded. *Degree requirements:* For master's, thesis or alternative, exit project. *Entrance requirements:* For master's, GRE General Test (minimum score: 50th percentile combined verbal and quantitative, 4.0 analytical writing), minimum GPA of 3.0. Additional exam requirements/recommendations for international students: Required—TOEFL (minimum score 550 paper-based; 78 iBT), IELTS (6.0), or International Test of English Proficiency (iTEP). *Application deadline:* For fall admission, 7/1 priority date for domestic students; 5/15 for international students; for spring admission, 11/15 for domestic students, 11/1 for international students; for summer admission, 4/1 for domestic students, 3/15 for international students. Applications are processed on a rolling basis. Application fee: $40. Electronic applications accepted. *Expenses:* Contact institution. *Financial support:* In 2016–17, 10 students received support, including 5 research assistantships with full tuition reimbursements available (averaging $7,200 per year), 3 teaching assistantships with partial tuition reimbursements available (averaging $2,400 per year); scholarships/grants, tuition waivers (full and partial), and unspecified assistantships also available. Support available to part-time students. Financial award application deadline: 3/1; financial award applicants required to submit FAFSA. *Faculty research:* Housing and neighborhood development, urban housing policy, environmental sustainability, economic development, GIS and planning decision support. *Unit head:* Dr. Stephanie Ryberg-Webster, Assistant Professor/Director of MUPD Program, 216-802-3386, Fax: 216-687-2013, E-mail: s.ryberg@csuohio.edu. *Application contact:* David Arrighi, Graduate Academic Advisor, 216-523-7522, Fax: 216-687-5398, E-mail: d.arrighi@csuohio.edu. Website: http://urban.csuohio.edu/academics/graduate/mupdd/

**College of Charleston,** Graduate School, School of Humanities and Social Sciences, Program in Urban and Regional Planning, Charleston, SC 29424-0001. Offers Certificate. *Program availability:* Part-time, evening/weekend. *Entrance requirements:* Additional exam requirements/recommendations for international students: Required—TOEFL (minimum score 81 iBT). *Application deadline:* For fall admission, 4/1 for domestic students; for spring admission, 11/1 for domestic students. Application fee: $45. Electronic applications accepted. *Unit head:* Dr. Kevin Keenan, Program Director, 843-953-5679, E-mail: keenank@cofc.edu. *Application contact:* Susan Hallatt, Director of Graduate Admissions, 843-953-5614, Fax: 843-953-1434, E-mail: hallatts@cofc.edu. Website: http://spinner.cofc.edu/~puba/URBP_certificate.html

**Columbia University,** Graduate School of Architecture, Planning, and Preservation, Program in Urban Planning, New York, NY 10027. Offers MS, PhD, JD/MS, M Arch/MS, MBA/MS, MIA/MS, MPH/MS, MS/MS. PhD offered through the Graduate School of Arts and Sciences. *Accreditation:* ACSP (one or more programs are accredited). *Degree requirements:* For master's, thesis. *Entrance requirements:* For master's, GRE General Test.

**Concordia University,** School of Graduate Studies, Faculty of Arts and Science, School of Community and Public Affairs, Montréal, QC H3G 1M8, Canada. Offers community economic development (Diploma).

**Cornell University,** Graduate School, Graduate Fields of Architecture, Art and Planning, Field of City and Regional Planning, Ithaca, NY 14853. Offers city and regional planning (MRP, PhD); environmental planning and design (MRP, PhD); historic preservation planning (MA); international development planning (MRP, PhD); planning theory and systems analysis (MRP, PhD); regional economics and development planning (MRP, PhD); regional science (MRP, PhD); social and health systems planning (MRP, PhD); urban and regional theory (MRP, PhD); urban planning history (MRP, PhD). *Accreditation:* ACSP (one or more programs are accredited). *Degree requirements:* For master's, thesis (MA); for doctorate, comprehensive exam, thesis/dissertation. *Entrance requirements:* For master's and doctorate, GRE General Test, 2 letters of recommendation. Additional exam requirements/recommendations for international students: Required—TOEFL (minimum score 600 paper-based; 77 iBT). Electronic applications accepted. *Faculty research:* Land use planning, economic development, international development, historic preservation, community development.

**Cornell University,** Graduate School, Graduate Fields of Architecture, Art and Planning, Field of Regional Science, Ithaca, NY 14853. Offers environmental studies (MA, MS, PhD); international spatial problems (MA, MS, PhD); location theory (MA, MS, PhD); multiregional economic analysis (MA, MS, PhD); peace science (MA, MS, PhD); planning methods (MA, MS, PhD); urban and regional economics (MA, MS, PhD). Terminal master's awarded for partial completion of doctoral program. *Degree requirements:* For master's, thesis; for doctorate, comprehensive exam, thesis/dissertation. *Entrance requirements:* For master's and doctorate, GRE General Test, 2 letters of recommendation. Additional exam requirements/recommendations for international students: Required—TOEFL (minimum score 600 paper-based; 77 iBT). Electronic applications accepted. *Faculty research:* Urban and regional growth, spatial economics, formation of spatial patterns by socioeconomic systems, non-linear dynamics and complex systems, environmental-economic systems.

**Dalhousie University,** Faculty of Architecture and Planning, School of Planning, Halifax, NS B3J 2X4, Canada. Offers M Eng, M Plan, MPS. *Degree requirements:* For master's, thesis. *Entrance requirements:* Additional exam requirements/recommendations for international students: Required—TOEFL, IELTS, CANTEST, CAEL, or Michigan English Language Assessment Battery. Electronic applications accepted.

**Delta State University,** Graduate Programs, College of Arts and Sciences, Division of Social Sciences and History, Program in Community Development, Cleveland, MS 38733-0001. Offers MS. *Program availability:* Part-time. *Degree requirements:* For master's, thesis or alternative.

**East Carolina University,** Graduate School, Thomas Harriot College of Arts and Sciences, Department of Geography, Planning, and Environment, Greenville, NC 27858-4353. Offers economic development (Certificate); geographic information science and technology (Certificate); geography (MA), including geography, planning, rural development. *Program availability:* Part-time, evening/weekend. *Students:* 15 full-time (8 women), 11 part-time (5 women); includes 6 minority (2 Black or African American, non-Hispanic/Latino; 1 Asian, non-Hispanic/Latino; 3 Hispanic/Latino). Average age 28. 17 applicants, 94% accepted, 9 enrolled. In 2016, 1 master's awarded. *Degree requirements:* For master's, one foreign language, comprehensive exam, thesis optional. *Entrance requirements:* For master's, GRE General Test. Additional exam requirements/recommendations for international students: Required—TOEFL. *Application deadline:* For fall admission, 6/1 priority date for domestic students; for spring admission, 10/15 for domestic students. Applications are processed on a rolling basis. Application fee: $50. *Financial support:* Research assistantships with partial tuition reimbursements, teaching assistantships with partial tuition reimbursements, and Federal Work-Study available. Support available to part-time students. Financial award application deadline: 6/1. *Unit head:* Dr. Burrell Montz, Chair, 252-328-6086, E-mail: montzb@ecu.edu. *Application contact:* Dean of Graduate School, 252-328-6012, Fax: 252-328-6071, E-mail: gradschool@ecu.edu. Website: http://www.ecu.edu/geog/

**Eastern Kentucky University,** The Graduate School, College of Arts and Sciences, Department of Government, Program in General Public Administration, Richmond, KY 40475-3102. Offers community development (MPA); community health administration (MPA); general public administration (MPA). *Accreditation:* NASPAA. *Program availability:* Part-time, evening/weekend. *Entrance requirements:* For master's, GRE General Test, minimum GPA of 2.5.

**Eastern Michigan University,** Graduate School, College of Arts and Sciences, Department of Geography and Geology, Programs in Urban and Regional Planning, Ypsilanti, MI 48197. Offers transportation planning and modeling (Graduate Certificate); urban and regional planning (MS). *Students:* 5 full-time (all women), 8 part-time (5 women); includes 4 minority (3 Black or African American, non-Hispanic/Latino; 1 Hispanic/Latino), 3 international. Average age 27. 19 applicants, 68% accepted, 5 enrolled. In 2016, 6 master's, 1 other advanced degree awarded. Application fee: $45. *Application contact:* Dr. Heather Khan, Program Advisor, 734-487-8021, Fax: 734-487-6979, E-mail: hkhan3@emich.edu.

**Eastern University,** Department of Urban Studies, St. Davids, PA 19087-3696. Offers urban studies (MA), including community development, juvenile justice ministry, youth leadership. *Program availability:* Part-time, evening/weekend, online learning. *Students:* 8 full-time (all women), 32 part-time (27 women); includes 21 minority (16 Black or African American, non-Hispanic/Latino; 1 Asian, non-Hispanic/Latino; 3 Hispanic/Latino; 1 Two or more races, non-Hispanic/Latino), 2 international. Average age 33. In 2016, 12 master's awarded. *Entrance requirements:* Additional exam requirements/recommendations for international students: Required—TOEFL (minimum score 550 paper-based; 79 iBT). *Application deadline:* Applications are processed on a rolling basis. Application fee: $35. Electronic applications accepted. Application fee is waived when completed online. *Expenses:* $690 per credit. *Financial support:* Applicants required to submit FAFSA. *Unit head:* Michael Dziedziak, Executive Director of Enrollment, 800-452-0996, E-mail: gpsadmissions@eastern.edu. Website: http://www.eastern.edu/academics/programs/urban-studies-department

**Eastern University,** School of Leadership and Development, St. Davids, PA 19087-3696. Offers economic development (MBA), including international development, urban development (MA, MBA); international development (MA), including global development, urban development (MA, MBA); nonprofit management (MS); organizational leadership (MA); M Div/MBA. *Program availability:* Part-time, evening/weekend, online learning. *Students:* 59 full-time (32 women), 67 part-time (35 women); includes 40 minority (32 Black or African American, non-Hispanic/Latino; 1 Asian, non-Hispanic/Latino; 5 Hispanic/Latino; 2 Two or more races, non-Hispanic/Latino), 22 international. Average age 33. In 2016, 44 master's awarded. *Entrance requirements:* Additional exam requirements/recommendations for international students: Required—TOEFL (minimum score 550 paper-based; 79 iBT). *Application deadline:* Applications are processed on a rolling basis. Application fee: $35. Electronic applications accepted. Application fee is waived when completed online. *Expenses:* $690 per credit. *Faculty research:* Micro-level economic development, China welfare and economic development, macroethics, micro- and macro-level economic development in transitional economics, organizational effectiveness. *Unit head:* Michael Dziedziak, Executive Director of Enrollment, 800-452-0996, E-mail: gpsadmissions@eastern.edu. Website: http://www.eastern.edu/academics/programs/graduate-programs-leadership-development

**Eastern Washington University,** Graduate Studies, College of Business and Public Administration, Program in Urban and Regional Planning, Cheney, WA 99004-2431. Offers MURP, MPA/MURP. *Accreditation:* ACSP. *Faculty:* 2 full-time (0 women). *Students:* 15 full-time (10 women); includes 5 minority (4 American Indian or Alaska Native, non-Hispanic/Latino; 1 Hispanic/Latino). Average age 33. 20 applicants, 65% accepted, 7 enrolled. In 2016, 9 master's awarded. *Degree requirements:* For master's, comprehensive exam, thesis or alternative. *Entrance requirements:* For master's, GRE, minimum GPA of 3.0. Additional exam requirements/recommendations for international students: Required—TOEFL (minimum score 580 paper-based; 92 iBT), IELTS (minimum score 7), PTE (minimum score 63). *Application deadline:* For fall admission, 4/1 priority date for domestic students; for spring admission, 1/15 for domestic students. Applications are processed on a rolling basis. Application fee: $75. Electronic applications accepted. *Expenses:* Tuition, state resident: full-time $11,000; part-time $5500 per credit. Tuition, nonresident: full-time $24,000; part-time $12,000 per credit. *Required fees:* $1300. One-time fee: $50 full-time. Part-time tuition and fees vary according to course load, campus/location and program. *Financial support:* In 2016–17, teaching assistantships with partial tuition reimbursements (averaging $10,000 per year) were awarded; career-related internships or fieldwork, Federal Work-Study, institutionally sponsored loans, scholarships/grants, health care benefits, tuition waivers (partial), and unspecified assistantships also available. Financial award application deadline: 2/1; financial award applicants required to submit FAFSA. *Unit head:* Dr. Dick Winchell, Planning and Public Administration Department Chair, 509-828-1205, E-mail: dwinchell@ewu.edu. *Application contact:* Lorene Winters, Program Coordinator for MBA Program, 509-828-1232, E-mail: mbaprogram@ewu.edu. Website: http://www.ewu.edu/CBPA/Programs/Urban-Regional-Planning.xml

**East Tennessee State University,** School of Graduate Studies, College of Arts and Sciences, Department of Political Science, International Affairs and Public Administration, Johnson City, TN 37614. Offers economic development (Postbaccalaureate Certificate); not-for-profit administration (MPA); planning and development (MPA); public financial management (MPA); urban planning (Postbaccalaureate Certificate). *Program availability:* Part-time. *Degree requirements:* For master's, internship. *Entrance requirements:* For master's, GRE General Test, three letters of recommendation; for Postbaccalaureate Certificate, GRE General Test. Additional exam requirements/recommendations for international students: Required—TOEFL (minimum score 550 paper-based; 79 iBT). Electronic applications accepted.

*Faculty research:* Labor issues, presidency, public law in American politics, East Asian politics, European politics, Middle Eastern politics, development in comparative politics, international political economy, international relations, world politics in international affairs.

**Florida Atlantic University,** College for Design and Social Inquiry, School of Urban and Regional Planning, Boca Raton, FL 33431-0991. Offers MURP. *Accreditation:* ACSP. *Program availability:* Part-time, evening/weekend. *Faculty:* 4 full-time (1 woman). *Students:* 28 full-time (14 women), 12 part-time (4 women); includes 16 minority (8 Black or African American, non-Hispanic/Latino; 7 Hispanic/Latino; 1 Two or more races, non-Hispanic/Latino), 3 international. Average age 29. 27 applicants, 48% accepted, 8 enrolled. In 2016, 11 master's awarded. *Entrance requirements:* For master's, GRE General Test, minimum GPA of 3.0. Additional exam requirements/recommendations for international students: Required—TOEFL (minimum score 500 paper-based; 61 iBT), IELTS (minimum score 6). *Application deadline:* For fall admission, 5/1 priority date for domestic students, 2/15 for international students; for spring admission, 11/1 priority date for domestic students, 7/15 for international students. Applications are processed on a rolling basis. Application fee: $30. *Expenses:* Tuition, state resident: full-time $7392; part-time $369.82 per credit hour. Tuition, nonresident: full-time $19,432; part-time $1024.81 per credit hour. *Financial support:* Fellowships with full tuition reimbursements, research assistantships, career-related internships or fieldwork, Federal Work-Study, institutionally sponsored loans, and tuition waivers (partial) available. Financial award application deadline: 4/1. *Faculty research:* Growth management, urban design, computer applications/geographical information systems, environmental planning. *Unit head:* 954-762-5652, E-mail: durp@fau.edu. Website: http://www.fau.edu/durp/

**Florida State University,** The Graduate School, College of Social Sciences and Public Policy, Department of Urban and Regional Planning, Tallahassee, FL 32306. Offers planning (MSP); urban and regional planning (PhD); JD/MSP; MA/MSP; MPH/MSP; MSP/MS. *Accreditation:* ACSP (one or more programs are accredited). *Program availability:* Part-time. *Faculty:* 10 full-time (4 women), 16 part-time/adjunct (4 women). *Students:* 74 full-time (40 women), 14 part-time (6 women); includes 33 minority (14 Black or African American, non-Hispanic/Latino; 6 Asian, non-Hispanic/Latino; 1 Hispanic/Latino; 12 Two or more races, non-Hispanic/Latino), 11 international. Average age 28. 105 applicants, 59% accepted, 33 enrolled. In 2016, 31 master's, 1 doctorate awarded. *Degree requirements:* For master's, capstone project, internship; for doctorate, thesis/dissertation. *Entrance requirements:* For master's and doctorate, GRE General Test, minimum GPA of 3.0. Additional exam requirements/recommendations for international students: Required—TOEFL (minimum score 600 paper-based; 100 iBT); Recommended—IELTS (minimum score 7). *Application deadline:* For fall admission, 2/15 priority date for domestic students, 11/15 priority date for international students; for spring admission, 11/1 for domestic students, 9/1 for international students. Applications are processed on a rolling basis. Application fee: $30. Electronic applications accepted. *Expenses:* Contact institution. *Financial support:* In 2016–17, 45 students received support, including 5 fellowships with full tuition reimbursements available (averaging $17,200 per year), 28 research assistantships with full tuition reimbursements available (averaging $9,600 per year), 6 teaching assistantships with full tuition reimbursements available (averaging $17,000 per year); career-related internships or fieldwork, Federal Work-Study, institutionally sponsored loans, and tuition waivers (partial) also available. Financial award application deadline: 2/15; financial award applicants required to submit FAFSA. *Faculty research:* Land use planning, environmental planning, developing countries, transportation, sustainable and healthy communities, neighborhood planning, climate change. *Total annual research expenditures:* $560,000. *Unit head:* Dr. Jeffrey R. Brown, Professor and Chairperson, 850-644-4510, Fax: 850-645-4841, E-mail: jrbrown3@fsu.edu. *Application contact:* Susan A. Taylor, Admissions Coordinator, 850-644-4510, Fax: 850-644-4841, E-mail: durp@coss.fsu.edu. Website: http://www.coss.fsu.edu/durp/

**Future Generations Graduate School,** Program in Applied Community Change, Franklin, WV 26807. Offers conservation (MA). *Program availability:* Blended/hybrid learning. *Degree requirements:* For master's, one foreign language, applied practicum research. *Entrance requirements:* For master's, bachelor's degree, community involvement. Additional exam requirements/recommendations for international students: Required—TOEFL. Electronic applications accepted. *Faculty research:* Sustainable communities, community engagement, peacebuilding, seed-scale community development.

**Georgetown University,** Graduate School of Arts and Sciences, School of Continuing Studies, Washington, DC 20057. Offers American studies (MALS); Catholic studies (MALS); classical civilizations (MALS); emergency and disaster management (MPS); ethics and the professions (MALS); global strategic communications (MPS); hospitality management (MPS); human resources management (MPS); humanities (MALS); individualized study (MALS); integrated marketing communications (MPS); international affairs (MALS); Islam and Muslim-Christian relations (MALS); journalism (MPS); liberal studies (DLS); literature and society (MALS); medieval and early modern European studies (MALS); public relations and corporate communications (MPS); real estate (MPS); religious studies (MALS); social and public policy (MALS); sports industry management (MPS); systems engineering management (MPS); technology management (MPS); the theory and practice of American democracy (MALS); urban and regional planning (MPS); visual culture (MALS). MPS in systems engineering management offered jointly with Stevens Institute of Technology. *Entrance requirements:* Additional exam requirements/recommendations for international students: Required—TOEFL.

**Georgia Institute of Technology,** Graduate Studies, College of Architecture, School of City and Regional Planning, Atlanta, GA 30332-0001. Offers city and regional planning (PhD); economic development (MCRP); environmental planning and management (MCRP); geographic information systems (MCRP); land and community development (MCRP); land use planning (MCRP); transportation (MCRP); urban design (MCRP); MCP/MSCE. *Accreditation:* ACSP. *Degree requirements:* For master's, thesis, internship. *Entrance requirements:* For master's, GRE General Test, minimum GPA of 2.7. Additional exam requirements/recommendations for international students: Required—TOEFL. Electronic applications accepted.

**Georgia State University,** Andrew Young School of Policy Studies, Department of Public Management and Policy, Atlanta, GA 30303. Offers criminal justice (MPA); disaster management (Certificate); disaster policy (MPA); environmental policy (PhD); health policy (PhD); management and finance (MPA); nonprofit management (MPA, Certificate); nonprofit policy (MPA); planning and economic development (MPP, Certificate); policy analysis and evaluation (MPA), including planning and economic development; public and nonprofit management (PhD); public finance and budgeting (PhD), including science and technology policy, urban and regional economic development; public finance policy (MPA), including social policy; public health (MPA). *Accreditation:* NASPAA (one or more programs are accredited). *Program availability:* Part-time. *Faculty:* 17 full-time (9 women). *Students:* 123 full-time (77 women), 79 part-time (49 women); includes 84 minority (59 Black or African American, non-Hispanic/Latino; 5 Asian, non-Hispanic/Latino; 14 Hispanic/Latino; 6 Two or more races, non-Hispanic/Latino), 34 international. Average age 30. 237 applicants, 60% accepted, 65 enrolled. In 2016, 59 master's, 4 doctorates, 8 other advanced degrees awarded. Terminal master's awarded for partial completion of doctoral program. *Degree requirements:* For master's, thesis optional; for doctorate, comprehensive exam, thesis/dissertation. *Entrance requirements:* For master's and doctorate, GRE. Additional exam requirements/recommendations for international students: Required—TOEFL (minimum score 603 paper-based; 100 iBT) or IELTS (minimum score 7). *Application deadline:* For fall admission, 1/15 for domestic and international students. Application fee: $50. Electronic applications accepted. *Expenses:* Tuition, state resident: full-time $6876; part-time $382 per credit hour. Tuition, nonresident: full-time $22,374; part-time $1243 per credit hour. *Required fees:* $2128; $1064 per term. Part-time tuition and fees vary according to course load and program. *Financial support:* In 2016–17, fellowships (averaging $8,194 per year), research assistantships (averaging $8,068 per year), teaching assistantships (averaging $3,600 per year) were awarded; institutionally sponsored loans, scholarships/grants, health care benefits, and unspecified assistantships also available. Financial award application deadline: 2/1. *Faculty research:* Public budgeting and finance, public management, nonprofit management, performance measurement and management, urban development. *Unit head:* Dr. Carolyn Bourdeaux, Chair and Professor, 404-413-0013, Fax: 404-413-0104, E-mail: cbourdeaux@gsu.edu. Website: http://aysps.gsu.edu/pmap/

**Harvard University,** Graduate School of Arts and Sciences, Committee on Architecture, Landscape Architecture, and Urban Planning, Cambridge, MA 02138. Offers architecture (PhD); landscape architecture (PhD); urban planning (PhD). *Accreditation:* ACSP. *Degree requirements:* For doctorate, one foreign language, thesis/dissertation, oral exam. *Entrance requirements:* For doctorate, GRE General Test. Additional exam requirements/recommendations for international students: Required—TOEFL.

**Harvard University,** Graduate School of Design, Department of Urban Planning and Design, Cambridge, MA 02138. Offers urban planning (MUP); urban planning and design (MAUD, MLAUD). *Accreditation:* ACSP (one or more programs are accredited). *Entrance requirements:* For master's, GRE General Test. Additional exam requirements/recommendations for international students: Required—TOEFL (minimum score 600 paper-based; 104 iBT). Electronic applications accepted.

**Hunter College of the City University of New York,** Graduate School, School of Arts and Sciences, Department of Urban Affairs and Planning, Program in Urban Planning, New York, NY 10065-5085. Offers MUP, JD/MUP. JD/MUP offered jointly with Brooklyn Law School. *Accreditation:* ACSP. *Program availability:* Part-time. *Students:* 37 full-time (20 women), 104 part-time (59 women); includes 51 minority (19 Black or African American, non-Hispanic/Latino; 12 Asian, non-Hispanic/Latino; 20 Hispanic/Latino), 6 international. Average age 30. 153 applicants, 70% accepted, 45 enrolled. In 2016, 35 master's awarded. *Degree requirements:* For master's, planning studio and internship. *Entrance requirements:* For master's, minimum 12 credits of course work in social sciences, 2 letters of recommendation. Additional exam requirements/recommendations for international students: Required—TOEFL. *Application deadline:* For fall admission, 4/1 for domestic students, 2/1 for international students; for spring admission, 11/1 for domestic students, 9/1 for international students. *Financial support:* Fellowships with full tuition reimbursements, research assistantships, teaching assistantships, career-related internships or fieldwork, Federal Work-Study, and tuition waivers (partial) available. Support available to part-time students. *Faculty research:* Community and economic development, transportation planning and policy, geographic information systems, housing, land use. *Unit head:* Dr. John Chin, Program Director, 212-772-5603, E-mail: john.chin@hunter.cuny.edu. *Application contact:* Milena Solo, Director for Graduate Admissions, 212-772-4480, E-mail: admissions@hunter.cuny.edu.

**Indiana University of Pennsylvania,** School of Graduate Studies and Research, College of Humanities and Social Sciences, Department of Geography and Regional Planning, Regional Planning Track, Indiana, PA 15705. Offers MS. *Program availability:* Part-time. *Faculty:* 9 full-time (2 women). *Students:* 2 full-time (1 woman). Average age 26. 2 applicants, 50% accepted. In 2016, 3 master's awarded. *Degree requirements:* For master's, thesis optional. *Entrance requirements:* Additional exam requirements/recommendations for international students: Required—TOEFL (minimum score 550 paper-based). *Application deadline:* Applications are processed on a rolling basis. Application fee: $50. Electronic applications accepted. *Expenses:* Tuition, state resident: full-time $8694; part-time $483 per credit. Tuition, nonresident: full-time $13,050; part-time $725 per credit. *Required fees:* $157 per credit. $50 per term. Tuition and fees vary according to course load and program. *Financial support:* In 2016–17, 2 research assistantships with tuition reimbursements (averaging $2,970 per year) were awarded; fellowships with full tuition reimbursements, career-related internships or fieldwork, Federal Work-Study, scholarships/grants, and unspecified assistantships also available. Financial award application deadline: 4/15; financial award applicants required to submit FAFSA. *Unit head:* Dr. Richard Hoch, Graduate Coordinator, 724-357-5990, E-mail: richard.hoch@iup.edu. Website: http://www.iup.edu/georegionalplan/grad/default.aspx

**Iowa State University of Science and Technology,** Department of Community and Regional Planning, Ames, IA 50011. Offers community and regional planning (MCRP); transportation (MS); M Arch/MCRP; MBA/MCRP; MCRP/MLA; MCRP/MPA. *Accreditation:* ACSP (one or more programs are accredited). *Degree requirements:* For master's, thesis or alternative. *Entrance requirements:* For master's, GRE General Test. Additional exam requirements/recommendations for international students: Required—TOEFL (minimum score 550 paper-based; 79 iBT), IELTS (minimum score 6.5). *Application deadline:* For fall admission, 1/1 priority date for domestic and international students. Applications are processed on a rolling basis. Application fee: $60 ($90 for international students). Electronic applications accepted. *Financial support:* Tuition waivers (partial) available. Financial award applicants required to submit FAFSA. *Faculty research:* Economic development, housing, land use, geographic information systems planning in developing nations, regional and community revitalization, transportation planning in developing countries. *Application contact:* Meredith Foley, Director of Graduate Education, 515-294-0816, Fax: 515-294-2348, E-mail: merfoley@iastate.edu. Website: http://www.design.iastate.edu/CRP/graduateprograms.php

**Jackson State University,** Graduate School, College of Public Service, Department of Urban and Regional Planning, Jackson, MS 39217. Offers MA, PhD. *Degree requirements:* For master's, comprehensive exam. *Entrance requirements:* For master's, GRE General Test. Additional exam requirements/recommendations for international students: Required—TOEFL (minimum score 520 paper-based; 67 iBT). *Application deadline:* For fall admission, 3/1 for domestic and international students; for spring admission, 10/1 for domestic and international students. Application fee: $25. *Expenses:* Tuition, state resident: full-time $7141. Tuition, nonresident: full-time $17,494. *Required fees:* $1080. Tuition and fees vary according to class time, course level, course load, degree level, campus/location, program and student level. *Financial support:* Application deadline: 3/1. *Unit head:* Chair, 601-432-6865. *Application contact:* Fatoumatta Sisay, Manager of Graduate Admissions, 601-979-0342, Fax: 601-979-4325, E-mail: fatoumatta.sisay@jsums.edu. Website: http://www.jsums.edu/planning/

## Urban and Regional Planning

**Kansas State University,** Graduate School, College of Architecture, Planning and Design, Department of Interior Architecture and Product Design, Manhattan, KS 66506. Offers MIAPD. *Faculty:* 13 full-time (5 women). *Students:* 50 full-time (35 women); includes 8 minority (3 Asian, non-Hispanic/Latino; 5 Hispanic/Latino), 2 international. Average age 22. 37 applicants, 81% accepted, 30 enrolled. In 2016, 15 master's awarded. *Degree requirements:* For master's, thesis, oral exam, culminating project. *Entrance requirements:* For master's, minimum GPA of 3.0, portfolio. Additional exam requirements/recommendations for international students: Required—TOEFL (minimum score 600 paper-based; 95 iBT) or IELTS (minimum score 7). *Application deadline:* For fall admission, 12/1 priority date for domestic students, 12/1 for international students; for summer admission, 12/1 for domestic and international students. Applications are processed on a rolling basis. Application fee: $65 ($75 for international students). Electronic applications accepted. *Expenses:* Tuition, state resident: full-time $9670. Tuition, nonresident: full-time $21,828. *Required fees:* $862. *Financial support:* In 2016–17, 8 teaching assistantships with full tuition reimbursements (averaging $7,500 per year) were awarded; career-related internships or fieldwork, Federal Work-Study, institutionally sponsored loans, and scholarships/grants also available. Support available to part-time students. Financial award application deadline: 3/1; financial award applicants required to submit FAFSA. *Faculty research:* Planning interior spaces for exhibition; residential and commercial spaces; design of objects such as furniture, lighting, equipment, finishing treatments and accessories. *Total annual research expenditures:* $1,523. *Unit head:* Nathan Howe, Head, 785-532-5992, Fax: 785-532-6722, E-mail: nhowe@ksu.edu. *Application contact:* Neal Hubbell, Associate Professor, 785-532-5992, Fax: 785-532-6722, E-mail: nhubbel@ksu.edu.
Website: http://apdesign.k-state.edu/iapd/

**Kansas State University,** Graduate School, College of Architecture, Planning and Design, Department of Landscape Architecture and Regional and Community Planning, Manhattan, KS 66506. Offers community development (MS); landscape architecture (MLA); regional and community planning (MRCP). MS offered online through the Great Plains Interactive Distance Education Alliance: Iowa State University, University of Nebraska, North Dakota State University, South Dakota State University. *Accreditation:* ACSP; ASLA. *Program availability:* Part-time, 100% online. *Faculty:* 17 full-time (6 women), 1 (woman) part-time/adjunct. *Students:* 41 full-time (25 women), 18 part-time (11 women); includes 9 minority (2 Black or African American, non-Hispanic/Latino; 1 Asian, non-Hispanic/Latino; 3 Hispanic/Latino; 3 Two or more races, non-Hispanic/Latino), 4 international. Average age 26. 47 applicants, 62% accepted, 20 enrolled. In 2016, 27 master's awarded. Terminal master's awarded for partial completion of doctoral program. *Degree requirements:* For master's, thesis, oral exam. *Entrance requirements:* Additional exam requirements/recommendations for international students: Required—TOEFL (minimum score 600 paper-based), IELTS (minimum score 6.5). *Application deadline:* For fall admission, 2/1 priority date for domestic and international students; for spring admission, 8/1 priority date for domestic and international students. Applications are processed on a rolling basis. Application fee: $80. Electronic applications accepted. *Expenses:* Tuition, state resident: full-time $9670. Tuition, nonresident: full-time $21,828. *Required fees:* $862. *Financial support:* In 2016–17, 2 research assistantships (averaging $9,500 per year), 10 teaching assistantships with full tuition reimbursements (averaging $7,366 per year) were awarded; fellowships, career-related internships or fieldwork, Federal Work-Study, institutionally sponsored loans, and scholarships/grants also available. Support available to part-time students. Financial award application deadline: 3/15; financial award applicants required to submit FAFSA. *Faculty research:* Community planning and design, design and implementation, geospatial modeling, fluvial and green systems, transportation systems. *Total annual research expenditures:* $110,033. *Unit head:* Prof. Stephanie Rolley, Head, 785-532-5961, Fax: 785-532-6722, E-mail: srolley@ksu.edu. *Application contact:* Jody Hodges, Application Contact, 785-532-5961, Fax: 785-532-6722, E-mail: jodyhodges@ksu.edu.
Website: http://apdesign.k-state.edu/larcp/

**Lesley University,** Graduate School of Arts and Social Sciences, Cambridge, MA 02138-2790. Offers clinical mental health counseling (MA), including holistic counseling, school and community counseling, trauma studies; counseling psychology (MA, CAGS), including professional counseling (MA), school counseling (MA); creative writing (MFA); expressive therapies (MA, PhD, CAGS), including art (MA), clinical mental health counseling (MA), dance (MA), expressive therapies (MA), music (MA); independent studies (CAGS); independent study (MA); intercultural relations (MA, CAGS); interdisciplinary studies (MA), including individualized studies, integrative holistic health, mindfulness studies, peace and conflict transformation, trauma sensitive assessment, intervention, and consultation, women's studies; urban environmental leadership (MA). *Program availability:* Part-time, online learning. *Degree requirements:* For master's, internship, practicum, thesis (for expressive therapies); for doctorate, thesis/dissertation, arts apprenticeship, field placement; for CAGS, thesis, internship (for counseling psychology, expressive therapies). *Entrance requirements:* For master's, MAT (counseling psychology), interview, writing samples, art portfolio; for doctorate, GRE or MAT, interview, master's degree; for CAGS, interview, master's degree. Additional exam requirements/recommendations for international students: Required—TOEFL (minimum score 550 paper-based; 80 iBT). Electronic applications accepted. *Faculty research:* Psychotherapy and culture; psychotherapy and psychological trauma; women's issues in art, teaching and psychotherapy; community-based art, psycho-spiritual inquiry.

**Massachusetts Institute of Technology,** School of Architecture and Planning, Department of Urban Studies and Planning, Cambridge, MA 02139. Offers city planning (MCP); urban and regional planning (PhD); urban and regional studies (PhD); urban studies and planning (SM). *Accreditation:* ACSP (one or more programs are accredited). *Faculty:* 25 full-time (6 women). *Students:* 208 full-time (116 women); includes 48 minority (11 Black or African American, non-Hispanic/Latino; 17 Asian, non-Hispanic/Latino; 16 Hispanic/Latino; 4 Two or more races, non-Hispanic/Latino), 74 international. Average age 29. 542 applicants, 21% accepted, 83 enrolled. In 2016, 62 master's, 10 doctorates awarded. *Degree requirements:* For master's, thesis; for doctorate, comprehensive exam, thesis/dissertation. *Entrance requirements:* For master's and doctorate, GRE General Test. Additional exam requirements/recommendations for international students: Required—TOEFL, IELTS. *Application deadline:* For fall admission, 1/3 for domestic and international students. Application fee: $75. Electronic applications accepted. *Expenses:* Tuition: Full-time $46,400; part-time $725 per credit. One-time fee: $312 full-time. Full-time tuition and fees vary according to course load and program. *Financial support:* In 2016–17, 188 students received support, including 85 fellowships (averaging $26,800 per year), 85 research assistantships (averaging $25,400 per year), 22 teaching assistantships (averaging $37,200 per year); Federal Work-Study, institutionally sponsored loans, scholarships/grants, traineeships, health care benefits, unspecified assistantships, and resident tutors also available. Support available to part-time students. Financial award application deadline: 5/1; financial award applicants required to submit FAFSA. *Faculty research:* City design and regional development; housing, community, and economic development; environmental policy; international development; infrastructure systems and climate change planning; spatial modeling and urban analytics. *Total annual research expenditures:* $4.8 million. *Unit head:* Prof. Eran Ben-Joseph, Department Head, 617-253-9403, E-mail: duspinfo@mit.edu. *Application contact:* 617-253-4543, E-mail: duspapply@mit.edu.
Website: http://dusp.mit.edu/

**McGill University,** Faculty of Graduate and Postdoctoral Studies, Faculty of Engineering, School of Urban Planning, Montréal, QC H3A 2T5, Canada. Offers environmental planning (MUP); housing (MUP); transportation (MUP); urban design (MUP); urban planning, policy and design (PhD).

**Michigan State University,** The Graduate School, College of Agriculture and Natural Resources and College of Social Science, School of Planning, Design and Construction, East Lansing, MI 48824. Offers construction management (MS, PhD); environmental design (MA); interior design and facilities management (MA); international planning studies (MIPS); urban and regional planning (MURP). *Degree requirements:* For master's, thesis or alternative. *Entrance requirements:* Additional exam requirements/recommendations for international students: Required—TOEFL. Electronic applications accepted.

**Minnesota State University Mankato,** College of Graduate Studies and Research, College of Social and Behavioral Sciences, Department of Urban and Regional Studies, Mankato, MN 56001. Offers local government management (Certificate); non-profit leadership (Certificate); urban and regional studies (MA); urban planning (MA, Certificate). *Students:* 9 full-time (7 women), 12 part-time (4 women). *Degree requirements:* For master's, one foreign language, comprehensive exam, thesis or alternative. *Entrance requirements:* For master's, minimum GPA of 3.0 during previous 2 years, 2 letters of recommendation. Additional exam requirements/recommendations for international students: Required—TOEFL. *Application deadline:* For fall admission, 7/1 priority date for domestic students; for spring admission, 11/1 for domestic students. Applications are processed on a rolling basis. Application fee: $40. Electronic applications accepted. *Financial support:* Fellowships with partial tuition reimbursements, research assistantships with full tuition reimbursements, teaching assistantships with full tuition reimbursements, career-related internships or fieldwork, Federal Work-Study, institutionally sponsored loans, and unspecified assistantships available. Support available to part-time students. Financial award application deadline: 3/15; financial award applicants required to submit FAFSA.
Website: http://sbs.mnsu.edu/ursi/graduate/

**Missouri State University,** Graduate College, College of Natural and Applied Sciences, Department of Geography, Geology, and Planning, Springfield, MO 65897. Offers natural and applied science (MNAS), including geography, geology and planning; secondary education (MS Ed), including earth science, physical geography. *Program availability:* Part-time, evening/weekend. *Faculty:* 18 full-time (4 women), 1 part-time/adjunct (0 women). *Students:* 18 full-time (6 women), 15 part-time (9 women); includes 2 minority (both Hispanic/Latino), 4 international. Average age 30. 36 applicants, 67% accepted, 19 enrolled. In 2016, 5 master's awarded. *Degree requirements:* For master's, comprehensive exam, thesis (for some programs). *Entrance requirements:* For master's, GRE General Test (MS, MNAS), minimum undergraduate GPA of 3.0 (MS, MNAS), 9-12 teacher certification (MS Ed). Additional exam requirements/recommendations for international students: Required—TOEFL (minimum score 550 paper-based; 79 iBT), IELTS (minimum score 6). *Application deadline:* For fall admission, 7/20 priority date for domestic students, 5/1 for international students; for spring admission, 12/20 priority date for domestic students, 9/1 for international students. Applications are processed on a rolling basis. Application fee: $35 ($50 for international students). Electronic applications accepted. *Expenses:* Tuition, state resident: full-time $5830. Tuition, nonresident: full-time $10,708. *Required fees:* $1130. Tuition and fees vary according to class time, course level, course load and program. *Financial support:* In 2016–17, 3 research assistantships with full tuition reimbursements (averaging $11,574 per year), 15 teaching assistantships with full tuition reimbursements (averaging $9,365 per year) were awarded; career-related internships or fieldwork, Federal Work-Study, institutionally sponsored loans, scholarships/grants, and unspecified assistantships also available. Financial award application deadline: 3/31; financial award applicants required to submit FAFSA. *Faculty research:* Stratigraphy and ancient meteorite impacts, environmental geochemistry of karst, hyperspectral image processing, water quality, small town planning. *Unit head:* Dr. Toby Dogwiler, Department Head, 417-836-5800, Fax: 417-836-6934, E-mail: tobydogwiler@missouristate.edu. *Application contact:* Michael Edwards, Coordinator of Graduate Admissions, 417-836-5330, Fax: 417-836-6200, E-mail: michaeledwards@missouristate.edu.
Website: http://geosciences.missouristate.edu/

**Morgan State University,** School of Graduate Studies, Institute of Architecture and Planning, Program in City and Regional Planning, Baltimore, MD 21251. Offers MCRP. *Accreditation:* ACSP. *Degree requirements:* For master's, thesis. *Entrance requirements:* Additional exam requirements/recommendations for international students: Required—TOEFL (minimum score 550 paper-based). *Faculty research:* Nonprofit organizations, community development, urban design, transportation, international planning.

**New York University,** Polytechnic School of Engineering, Department of Civil and Urban Engineering, Major in Urban Systems Engineering and Management, New York, NY 10012-1019. Offers MS.

**New York University,** Robert F. Wagner Graduate School of Public Service, Program in Urban Planning, New York, NY 10012-1019. Offers MUP, JD/MUP. *Accreditation:* ACSP (one or more programs are accredited). *Program availability:* Part-time. *Degree requirements:* For master's, thesis or alternative, end event capstone program. *Entrance requirements:* Additional exam requirements/recommendations for international students: Required—TOEFL (minimum score 100 iBT), IELTS (minimum score 7.5), TWE. Electronic applications accepted.

**North Dakota State University,** College of Graduate and Interdisciplinary Studies, College of Arts, Humanities and Social Sciences, Department of Sociology and Anthropology, Program in Community Development, Fargo, ND 58102. Offers MA, MS. Electronic applications accepted.

**Northern Arizona University,** Graduate College, College of Social and Behavioral Sciences, Department of Geography, Planning, and Recreation, Flagstaff, AZ 86011. Offers applied geospatial sciences (MS); community planning (Certificate); geographic information systems (Certificate). *Program availability:* Online learning. *Degree requirements:* For master's, thesis optional. *Entrance requirements:* For master's, GRE General Test. Additional exam requirements/recommendations for international students: Required—TOEFL (minimum score 550 paper-based; 80 iBT), IELTS (minimum score 7). Electronic applications accepted. *Expenses:* Tuition, state resident: full-time $8971; part-time $444 per credit hour. Tuition, nonresident: full-time $20,958; part-time $1164 per credit hour. *Required fees:* $1018; $644 per credit hour. Tuition and fees vary according to course load, campus/location and program.

**Northwest University,** College of Social and Behavioral Sciences, Kirkland, WA 98033. Offers counseling psychology (MA, Psy D); international community development (MA). *Program availability:* Evening/weekend. *Entrance requirements:* For master's, 3 character references. Additional exam requirements/recommendations for international students: Required—TOEFL (minimum score 580 paper-based). *Expenses:* Contact institution.

**The Ohio State University,** Graduate School, College of Engineering, Austin E. Knowlton School of Architecture, Columbus, OH 43210. Offers architecture (M Arch); city and regional planning (MCRP, PhD); landscape architecture (M Land Arch). *Accreditation:* ACSP; ASLA. *Faculty:* 41. *Students:* 191 full-time (83 women), 4 part-time. Average age 26. In 2016, 60 master's, 2 doctorates awarded. *Degree requirements:* For doctorate, thesis/dissertation. *Entrance requirements:* For master's, GRE or GMAT (city and regional planning), portfolio (for architecture and landscape architecture); for doctorate, GRE or GMAT (city and regional planning), example of research or written work. Additional exam requirements/recommendations for international students: Required—TOEFL (minimum score 600 paper-based; 100 iBT), Michigan English Language Assessment Battery (minimum score 86); Recommended—IELTS (minimum score 8). *Application deadline:* For fall admission, 1/1 priority date for domestic students, 11/30 priority date for international students. Applications are processed on a rolling basis. Application fee: $60 ($70 for international students). Electronic applications accepted. *Financial support:* Fellowships with tuition reimbursements, research assistantships with tuition reimbursements, Federal Work-Study, institutionally sponsored loans, and unspecified assistantships available. Support available to part-time students. *Unit head:* Michael B. Cadwell, Professor/Director, 614-292-3174, E-mail: cadwell.1@osu.edu. *Application contact:* Graduate and Professional Admissions, 614-292-9444, Fax: 614-292-3895, E-mail: gpadmissions@osu.edu. Website: http://knowlton.osu.edu/

**Penn State University Park,** Graduate School, College of Agricultural Sciences, Department of Agricultural Economics, Sociology, and Education, University Park, PA 16802. Offers agricultural and extension education (M Ed, MS, PhD, Certificate); agricultural, environmental and regional economics (MS, PhD); applied youth, family and community education (M Ed); community and economic development (MPS); rural sociology (MS, PhD). *Unit head:* Dr. Richard T. Roush, Dean, 814-865-2541, Fax: 814-865-3103. *Application contact:* Lori Hawn, Director, Graduate Student Services, 814-865-1795, Fax: 814-863-4627, E-mail: l-gswww@lists.psu.edu. Website: http://aese.psu.edu/

**Philadelphia University,** College of Architecture and the Built Environment, Program in Geodesign, Philadelphia, PA 19144. Offers MS. *Program availability:* Part-time.

**Portland State University,** Graduate Studies, College of Urban and Public Affairs, Nohad A. Toulan School of Urban Studies and Planning, Program in Urban and Regional Planning, Portland, OR 97207-0751. Offers MURP. *Accreditation:* ACSP. *Program availability:* Part-time. *Faculty:* 17 full-time (8 women), 10 part-time/adjunct (3 women). *Students:* 106 full-time (47 women), 46 part-time (21 women); includes 29 minority (4 Black or African American, non-Hispanic/Latino; 5 Asian, non-Hispanic/Latino; 12 Hispanic/Latino; 8 Two or more races, non-Hispanic/Latino), 19 international. Average age 33. 221 applicants, 45% accepted, 81 enrolled. In 2016, 56 master's awarded. *Degree requirements:* For master's, workshop. *Entrance requirements:* For master's, GRE (recommended), minimum GPA of 3.0, transcripts, statement of purpose, 3 letters of recommendation, resume. Additional exam requirements/recommendations for international students: Required—TOEFL (minimum score 550 paper-based; 80 iBT). *Application deadline:* For fall admission, 1/15 for domestic and international students. Application fee: $65. *Expenses:* Contact institution. *Financial support:* In 2016–17, 30 research assistantships with full tuition reimbursements (averaging $6,879 per year) were awarded; teaching assistantships, career-related internships or fieldwork, Federal Work-Study, and unspecified assistantships also available. Support available to part-time students. Financial award application deadline: 3/1; financial award applicants required to submit FAFSA. *Faculty research:* Policy planning and administration, community development, land-use and environment, transportation, urban and regional analysis. *Total annual research expenditures:* $323,031. *Unit head:* Jennifer Dill, Director, 503-725-5173, E-mail: jdill@pdx.edu. *Application contact:* Tracy Braden, Office Coordinator, 503-725-5477, Fax: 503-725-8770, E-mail: tbraden@pdx.edu. Website: https://www.pdx.edu/usp/

**Pratt Institute,** School of Architecture, Program in City and Regional Planning, Brooklyn, NY 11205-3899. Offers MSCRP. *Accreditation:* ACSP. *Program availability:* Part-time. *Faculty:* 5 full-time (2 women), 31 part-time/adjunct (9 women). *Students:* 76 full-time (49 women), 2 part-time (1 woman); includes 25 minority (12 Black or African American, non-Hispanic/Latino; 3 Asian, non-Hispanic/Latino; 8 Hispanic/Latino; 2 Two or more races, non-Hispanic/Latino), 16 international. Average age 27. 98 applicants, 78% accepted, 18 enrolled. In 2016, 32 master's awarded. *Degree requirements:* For master's, thesis. *Entrance requirements:* For master's, writing sample, bachelor's degree, transcripts, letters of recommendation, portfolio. Additional exam requirements/recommendations for international students: Required—TOEFL (minimum score 575 paper-based; 90 iBT). *Application deadline:* For fall admission, 1/5 for domestic and international students; for spring admission, 10/1 for domestic and international students. Application fee: $50 ($90 for international students). Electronic applications accepted. *Expenses:* $29,646 full-time tuition, $1,938 fees. *Financial support:* Career-related internships or fieldwork, Federal Work-Study, institutionally sponsored loans, scholarships/grants, health care benefits, and unspecified assistantships available. Support available to part-time students. Financial award application deadline: 2/1; financial award applicants required to submit FAFSA. *Faculty research:* Advocacy planning, community development, comprehensive physical planning, transportation planning, real estate development. *Unit head:* Eve Baron, Chairperson, 718-687-5641, Fax: 718-636-3709, E-mail: ebaron@pratt.edu. *Application contact:* Natalie Capannelli, Director of Graduate Admissions, 718-636-3551, Fax: 718-399-4242, E-mail: ncapanne@pratt.edu.
Website: https://www.pratt.edu/academics/architecture/city-and-regional-planning/

**See Display on page 114 and Close-Up on page 137.**

**Pratt Institute,** School of Architecture, Program in Urban Placemaking and Management, Brooklyn, NY 11205-3899. Offers MS. *Students:* 20 full-time (13 women), 8 part-time (3 women); includes 7 minority (1 Black or African American, non-Hispanic/Latino; 5 Asian, non-Hispanic/Latino; 1 Hispanic/Latino), 9 international. Average age 30. 37 applicants, 86% accepted, 14 enrolled. *Degree requirements:* For master's, thesis. *Entrance requirements:* For master's, resume, writing sample, work sample or portfolio. Additional exam requirements/recommendations for international students: Required—TOEFL (minimum score 575 paper-based; 90 iBT). *Application deadline:* For fall admission, 1/5 for domestic and international students; for spring admission, 10/1 for domestic and international students. Application fee: $50 ($90 for international students). Electronic applications accepted. *Expenses:* $29,646 full-time tuition, $1,938 fees. *Financial support:* Career-related internships or fieldwork, Federal Work-Study, institutionally sponsored loans, scholarships/grants, health care benefits, and unspecified assistantships available. Support available to part-time students. Financial award application deadline: 2/1; financial award applicants required to submit FAFSA. *Unit head:* Thomas Hanrahan, Dean, 718-399-4304, Fax: 718-399-4315, E-mail: hanrahan@pratt.edu. *Application contact:* Natalie Capannelli, Director of Graduate Admissions, 718-636-3551, Fax: 718-399-4242, E-mail: ncapanne@pratt.edu.
Website: https://www.pratt.edu/academics/architecture/urban-placemaking-and-management/

**Queen's University at Kingston,** School of Graduate Studies, School of Urban and Regional Planning, Kingston, ON K7L 3N6, Canada. Offers M Pl. *Program availability:* Part-time. *Degree requirements:* For master's, thesis optional. *Entrance requirements:* Additional exam requirements/recommendations for international students: Required—TOEFL (minimum score 580 paper-based). *Faculty research:* Housing, real estate development, human services, environmental services, land use planning.

**Rutgers University–New Brunswick,** Edward J. Bloustein School of Planning and Public Policy, Doctoral Program in Planning and Public Policy, New Brunswick, NJ 08901. Offers PhD. *Program availability:* Part-time. *Degree requirements:* For doctorate, comprehensive exam, thesis/dissertation. *Entrance requirements:* For doctorate, GRE, master's degree. Additional exam requirements/recommendations for international students: Required—TOEFL (minimum score 575 paper-based; 88 iBT). Electronic applications accepted. *Faculty research:* Housing and community development, land use and transportation, politics and policy analysis, urban and regional economics, international development.

**Rutgers University–New Brunswick,** Edward J. Bloustein School of Planning and Public Policy, Program in Urban Planning and Policy Development, New Brunswick, NJ 08901. Offers MCRP, MCRS, JD/MCRP, MBA/MCRP. *Accreditation:* ACSP (one or more programs are accredited). *Program availability:* Part-time, evening/weekend. *Entrance requirements:* For master's, GRE General Test. Additional exam requirements/recommendations for international students: Required—TOEFL (minimum score 575 paper-based; 88 iBT). Electronic applications accepted. *Faculty research:* Land use, transportation, housing, environmental planning, urban redevelopment, international development.

**St. Francis Xavier University,** Graduate Studies, Department of Adult Education, Antigonish, NS B2G 2W5, Canada. Offers adult education (M Ad Ed); community development (M Ad Ed). *Program availability:* Part-time, online learning. *Degree requirements:* For master's, thesis. *Entrance requirements:* For master's, minimum undergraduate B average, 2 years of work experience in field. Additional exam requirements/recommendations for international students: Required—TOEFL (minimum score 580 paper-based). *Application deadline:* Applications are processed on a rolling basis. Application fee: $40. *Expenses: Tuition:* Full-time $9060 Canadian dollars; part-time $725 Canadian dollars per credit. *Required fees:* $789 Canadian dollars; $78.84 Canadian dollars per credit. Tuition and fees vary according to course load, degree level and program. *Faculty research:* Adult learning and development, religious education, women's issues, literacy, action research. *Unit head:* Dr. Maureen Coady, Chair, 902-867-3244, Fax: 902-867-3765, E-mail: mjcoady@stfx.ca. *Application contact:* 902-867-2219, Fax: 902-867-2329, E-mail: admit@stfx.ca.
Website: http://sites.stfx.ca/adult_education_graduate_studies/

**San Diego State University,** Graduate and Research Affairs, College of Professional Studies and Fine Arts, School of Public Affairs, Program in City Planning, San Diego, CA 92182. Offers MCP. *Program availability:* Part-time. *Entrance requirements:* For master's, GRE General Test. Additional exam requirements/recommendations for international students: Required—TOEFL. Electronic applications accepted. *Faculty research:* Community development, housing, sustainable development, visioning.

**Savannah State University,** Master of Public Administration Program, Savannah, GA 31404. Offers city management (MPA); human resources (MPA). *Accreditation:* NASPAA. *Program availability:* Part-time. *Degree requirements:* For master's, comprehensive exam, thesis, public service internship, capstone seminar. *Entrance requirements:* For master's, GRE General Test, GMAT, or MAT, minimum cumulative GPA of 2.5, 3 letters of recommendation, essay, official transcripts, resume, essay of 500-1000 words detailing reasons for pursuing degree. Additional exam requirements/recommendations for international students: Required—TOEFL. Electronic applications accepted. *Expenses:* Contact institution. *Faculty research:* Community development, human resources, leadership, conflict resolution, city management, non-profit management.

**Southeastern University,** College of Behavioral and Social Sciences, Lakeland, FL 33801-6099. Offers human services (MA); international community development (MA); marriage and family counseling (MS); professional counseling (MS); school counseling (MS); social work (MSW). *Program availability:* Evening/weekend. *Expenses: Tuition:* Full-time $9450; part-time $6300 per credit. *Required fees:* $500; $250 per semester. One-time fee: $150. Tuition and fees vary according to degree level, campus/location and program. *Unit head:* Erica H. Sirrine, Dean, 863-667-5341, E-mail: ehsirrine@seu.edu.
Website: http://www.seu.edu/behavior/

**State University of New York College of Environmental Science and Forestry,** Department of Landscape Architecture, Syracuse, NY 13210-2779. Offers community design and planning (MLA, MS); cultural landscape studies and conservation (MLA, MS); landscape and urban ecology (MLA, MS). *Accreditation:* ASLA (one or more programs are accredited). *Faculty:* 11 full-time (4 women), 9 part-time/adjunct (3 women). *Students:* 31 full-time (17 women), 3 part-time (2 women); includes 4 minority (2 Black or African American, non-Hispanic/Latino; 1 Asian, non-Hispanic/Latino; 1 Hispanic/Latino), 6 international. Average age 26. 53 applicants, 72% accepted, 12 enrolled. In 2016, 9 master's awarded. *Degree requirements:* For master's, comprehensive exam (for some programs), thesis (for some programs). *Entrance requirements:* For master's, GRE General Test, minimum GPA of 3.0. Additional exam requirements/recommendations for international students: Required—TOEFL (minimum score 550 paper-based; 80 iBT), IELTS (minimum score 6), or STEP Eiken (grade 1). *Application deadline:* For fall admission, 2/1 priority date for domestic and international students; for spring admission, 11/1 priority date for domestic and international students. Applications are processed on a rolling basis. Application fee: $60. *Expenses:* Tuition, state resident: full-time $10,870; part-time $453 per credit. Tuition, nonresident: full-time $22,210; part-time $925 per credit. *Required fees:* $1075; $89.22 per credit. *Financial support:* In 2016–17, 16 students received support. *Application deadline:* 6/30; applicants required to submit FAFSA. *Faculty research:* Site analysis and design, city and regional planning, community environments. *Total annual research expenditures:* $437,597. *Unit head:* Dr. Douglas Johnston, Chair, 315-470-6544, Fax: 315-470-6540, E-mail: dmjohnst@esf.edu. *Application contact:* Scott Shannon, Associate Provost for Instruction/Dean of the Graduate School, 315-470-6599, Fax: 315-470-6978, E-mail: esfgrad@esf.edu. Website: http://www.esf.edu/la/

**State University of New York College of Environmental Science and Forestry,** Program in Environmental Science, Syracuse, NY 13210-2779. Offers biophysical and ecological economics (MPS); coupled natural and human systems (MPS); ecosystem restoration (MPS); environmental and community land planning (MPS, MS); environmental and natural resources policy (PhD); environmental communication and participatory processes (PhD); environmental monitoring and modeling (MPS); water and wetland resource studies (MPS, MS). *Program availability:* Part-time. *Faculty:* 1 full-time (0 women), 1 (woman) part-time/adjunct. *Students:* 59 full-time (39 women), 16 part-time (10 women); includes 6 minority (1 Black or African American, non-Hispanic/Latino; 1 Asian, non-Hispanic/Latino; 3 Hispanic/Latino; 1 Two or more races, non-Hispanic/Latino), 25 international. Average age 30. 70 applicants, 59% accepted, 20 enrolled. In 2016, 13 master's, 8 doctorates awarded. *Degree requirements:* For

master's, thesis (for some programs); for doctorate, comprehensive exam, thesis/dissertation. *Entrance requirements:* For master's and doctorate, GRE General Test, minimum GPA of 3.0. Additional exam requirements/recommendations for international students: Required—TOEFL (minimum score 550 paper-based; 80 iBT), IELTS (minimum score 6). *Application deadline:* For fall admission, 2/1 priority date for domestic and international students; for spring admission, 11/1 priority date for domestic and international students. Applications are processed on a rolling basis. Application fee: $60. *Expenses:* Tuition, state resident: full-time $10,870; part-time $453 per credit. Tuition, nonresident: full-time $22,210; part-time $925 per credit. *Required fees:* $1075; $89.22 per credit. *Financial support:* In 2016–17, 32 students received support. Application deadline: 6/30; applicants required to submit FAFSA. *Faculty research:* Environmental education/communications, water resources, land resources, waste management. *Unit head:* Dr. Ruth Yanai, Coordinator, 315-470-6955, Fax: 315-470-6700, E-mail: rdyanai@esf.edu. *Application contact:* Scott Shannon, Associate Provost for Instruction/Dean of the Graduate School, 315-470-6599, Fax: 315-470-6978, E-mail: esfgrad@esf.edu.
Website: http://www.esf.edu/environmentalscience/graduate/

**Syracuse University,** Maxwell School of Citizenship and Public Affairs, CAS Program in Public Infrastructure Management and Leadership, Syracuse, NY 13244. Offers CAS. *Program availability:* Part-time. *Entrance requirements:* For degree, personal statement, resume, three letters of recommendation, official transcripts. Additional exam requirements/recommendations for international students: Required—TOEFL. *Application deadline:* For fall admission, 2/1 priority date for domestic students; for spring admission, 8/15 priority date for domestic and international students. Application fee: $75. *Expenses: Tuition:* Full-time $25,974; part-time $1443 per credit hour. *Required fees:* $802; $50 per course. Tuition and fees vary according to course load and program. *Financial support:* Application deadline: 1/1. *Faculty research:* Managerial leadership, public budgeting, financial management, engineering economics, infrastructure engineering and management. *Unit head:* Margaret Lane, Assistant Director, Executive Education Programs, 315-443-8708, E-mail: melane02@maxwell.syr.edu. *Application contact:* Margaret Lane, Assistant Director, Executive Education Programs, 315-443-8708, E-mail: melane02@maxwell.syr.edu.
Website: http://www.maxwell.syr.edu/

**Temple University,** Tyler School of Art, Department of Planning and Community Development, Ambler, PA 19122. Offers city and regional planning (MS); sustainable community planning (Graduate Certificate); transportation planning (Graduate Certificate). *Accreditation:* ACSP. *Program availability:* Part-time, evening/weekend. *Entrance requirements:* For master's, GRE or GMAT, 2 letters of recommendation, minimum undergraduate GPA of 3.0, statement of goals. Additional exam requirements/recommendations for international students: Required—TOEFL (minimum score 550 paper-based; 79 iBT). *Faculty research:* Regional environmental planning, collaboration, management community development through sustainable food systems, storm water management and floodplain mapping, land use policy innovations, community planning for aging.

**Texas A&M University,** College of Architecture, Department of Landscape Architecture and Urban Planning, College Station, TX 77843. Offers land and property development (MLPD); landscape architecture (MLA); urban and regional planning (MUP); urban and regional science (PhD). *Accreditation:* ACSP (one or more programs are accredited), ASLA (one or more programs are accredited). *Faculty:* 28. *Students:* 161 full-time (88 women), 14 part-time (7 women); includes 21 minority (2 Black or African American, non-Hispanic/Latino; 5 Asian, non-Hispanic/Latino; 13 Hispanic/Latino; 1 Native Hawaiian or other Pacific Islander, non-Hispanic/Latino), 102 international. Average age 28. 186 applicants, 66% accepted, 56 enrolled. In 2016, 69 master's, 10 doctorates awarded. Terminal master's awarded for partial completion of doctoral program. *Degree requirements:* For master's, thesis optional, professional internship; for doctorate, comprehensive exam, thesis/dissertation, seminar. *Entrance requirements:* For master's, GMAT or GRE General Test, portfolio (MLA), minimum GPA of 3.0; for doctorate, GMAT or GRE General Test. Additional exam requirements/recommendations for international students: Required—TOEFL (minimum score 550 paper-based; 80 iBT), IELTS (minimum score 6), PTE (minimum score 53). *Application deadline:* For fall admission, 12/1 priority date for domestic and international students; for spring admission, 8/1 for domestic students. Applications are processed on a rolling basis. Application fee: $50 ($90 for international students). Electronic applications accepted. *Expenses:* Contact institution. *Financial support:* In 2016–17, 123 students received support, including 3 fellowships with tuition reimbursements available (averaging $6,298 per year), 43 research assistantships with tuition reimbursements available (averaging $4,626 per year), 12 teaching assistantships with tuition reimbursements available (averaging $7,956 per year); career-related internships or fieldwork, institutionally sponsored loans, scholarships/grants, traineeships, health care benefits, tuition waivers (full and partial), and unspecified assistantships also available. Support available to part-time students. Financial award application deadline: 3/15; financial award applicants required to submit FAFSA. *Faculty research:* Erosion control/water quality, geographic information systems/spatial information technology, transport hazards, international sustainable development. *Unit head:* Dr. Forster Ndubisi, Head, 979-845-1019, Fax: 979-862-1784. *Application contact:* Thena Morris, Administrative Assistant, 979-458-4306, E-mail: t-morris@tamu.edu.
Website: http://laup.arch.tamu.edu/

**Texas Southern University,** School of Public Affairs, Program in Urban Planning and Environmental Policy, Houston, TX 77004-4584. Offers MS, PhD. *Accreditation:* ACSP. *Program availability:* Part-time, evening/weekend. *Degree requirements:* For master's, comprehensive exam, thesis optional. *Entrance requirements:* For master's, GRE General Test, minimum GPA of 2.5. Additional exam requirements/recommendations for international students: Required—TOEFL. Electronic applications accepted.

**Tufts University,** Graduate School of Arts and Sciences, Department of Urban and Environmental Policy and Planning, Medford, MA 02155. Offers community development (MA); environmental policy (MA); health and human welfare (MA); housing policy (MA); international environment/development policy (MA); public policy (MPP); MA/MBA; MA/MPH; MA/MS; MALD/MA. MALD/MA offered in connection with The Fletcher School of Law and Diplomacy; MA/MPH with School of Medicine; MA/MS with School of Nutrition Science and Policy or School of Engineering; MA/MBA with Boston College, Carroll School of Management; MA/JD with Boston College Law School. *Accreditation:* ACSP (one or more programs are accredited). *Program availability:* Part-time. *Students:* 94 full-time (73 women), 18 part-time (14 women); includes 29 minority (11 Black or African American, non-Hispanic/Latino; 9 Asian, non-Hispanic/Latino; 6 Hispanic/Latino; 3 Two or more races, non-Hispanic/Latino), 18 international. Average age 30. 153 applicants, 78% accepted, 51 enrolled. In 2016, 20 master's awarded. *Degree requirements:* For master's, thesis or alternative, internship. *Entrance requirements:* For master's, GRE General Test. Additional exam requirements/recommendations for international students: Required—TOEFL (minimum score 550 paper-based; 80 iBT), IELTS (minimum score 6.5). *Application deadline:* For fall admission, 1/15 for domestic and international students. Applications are processed on a rolling basis. Application fee: $85. Electronic applications accepted. *Expenses:* $49,982 full-time tuition (for MPP); $34,932 full-time tuition (for MA). *Financial support:*

Fellowships, research assistantships, teaching assistantships, career-related internships or fieldwork, Federal Work-Study, scholarships/grants, tuition waivers (full and partial), and unspecified assistantships available. Support available to part-time students. Financial award application deadline: 1/15. *Unit head:* Dr. Mary Davis, Graduate Program Director. *Application contact:* Office of Graduate Admissions, 617-627-3395, E-mail: gradadmissions@tufts.edu.
Website: http://ase.tufts.edu/uep/

**Université de Montréal,** Faculty of Environmental Design and Planning, Montréal, QC H3C 3J7, Canada. Offers environmental design and planning (M Sc A, PhD); environmental planning and design projects (DESS); game design (DESS); urban management for developing countries (DESS); urban planning (M Urb). DESS programs offered jointly with HEC Montreal and École Polytechnique de Montréal. *Accreditation:* ACSP. *Degree requirements:* For doctorate, thesis/dissertation, general exam. Electronic applications accepted. *Expenses:* Contact institution. *Faculty research:* Wayfinding, environmental evaluation, housing studies, urban design, urban and regional planning.

**Université du Québec à Rimouski,** Graduate Programs, Program in Regional Development, Rimouski, QC G5L 3A1, Canada. Offers MA, PhD, Diploma. PhD offered jointly with Université du Québec à Chicoutimi; Diploma with Université du Québec, École nationale d'administration publique. *Program availability:* Part-time. *Degree requirements:* For master's, thesis. *Entrance requirements:* For master's, appropriate bachelor's degree, proficiency in French.

**Université du Québec en Outaouais,** Graduate Programs, Program in Regional Development, Gatineau, QC J8X 3X7, Canada. Offers MA. *Program availability:* Part-time. *Degree requirements:* For master's, thesis (for some programs).

**Université Laval,** Faculty of Architecture, Planning and Visual Arts, Department of Regional Planning, Programs in Planning and Regional Development, Québec, QC G1K 7P4, Canada. Offers MATDR, PhD. Terminal master's awarded for partial completion of doctoral program. *Degree requirements:* For master's, thesis (for some programs); for doctorate, comprehensive exam, thesis/dissertation. *Entrance requirements:* For master's and doctorate, knowledge of French and English. Electronic applications accepted.

**University at Albany, State University of New York,** College of Arts and Sciences, Department of Geography and Planning, Program in Regional Planning, Albany, NY 12222-0001. Offers MRP. *Accreditation:* ACSP. *Program availability:* Part-time. *Degree requirements:* For master's, thesis optional. *Entrance requirements:* Additional exam requirements/recommendations for international students: Required—TOEFL (minimum score 550 paper-based). *Application deadline:* For fall admission, 3/1 for domestic students, 5/1 for international students; for spring admission, 11/1 for international students. Applications are processed on a rolling basis. Application fee: $75. Electronic applications accepted. *Expenses:* Tuition, state resident: full-time $10,870; part-time $453 per credit hour. Tuition, nonresident: full-time $22,210; part-time $925 per credit hour. *International tuition:* $21,550 full-time. *Required fees:* $1864; $96 per credit hour. *Financial support:* Fellowships, teaching assistantships, career-related internships or fieldwork, Federal Work-Study, and institutionally sponsored loans available. Financial award application deadline: 6/1. *Faculty research:* Urban planning, Third World development, political and social aspects of planning, urban housing and employment, environmental planning. *Unit head:* Catherine Lawson, Chair, 518-442-4775, E-mail: lawsone@albany.edu. *Application contact:* Michael DeRensis, Director, Graduate Admissions, 518-442-3980, Fax: 518-442-3922, E-mail: graduate@albany.edu.
Website: http://www.albany.edu/gp/masters_regional_planning.php

**University at Buffalo, the State University of New York,** Graduate School, School of Architecture and Planning, Department of Urban and Regional Planning, Buffalo, NY 14214. Offers historic preservation (Certificate); urban and regional planning (PhD); JD/MUP; M Arch/MUP. *Accreditation:* ACSP. *Program availability:* Part-time. *Faculty:* 14 full-time (6 women), 12 part-time/adjunct (3 women). *Students:* 78 full-time (29 women), 12 part-time (7 women); includes 19 minority (11 Black or African American, non-Hispanic/Latino; 1 Asian, non-Hispanic/Latino; 5 Hispanic/Latino; 2 Two or more races, non-Hispanic/Latino), 24 international. Average age 27. 216 applicants, 23% accepted, 36 enrolled. In 2016, 34 master's awarded. *Degree requirements:* For master's, thesis or alternative, project; for doctorate, thesis/dissertation. *Entrance requirements:* For master's, minimum GPA of 3.0, resume, 3 letters of recommendation, 500-word personal statement, transcripts; for doctorate, GRE, transcripts, 3 letters of recommendation, minimum GPA of 3.0, resume, research statement, writing sample. Additional exam requirements/recommendations for international students: Required—TOEFL (minimum score 79 iBT), IELTS (minimum score 6.5). *Application deadline:* For fall admission, 3/1 priority date for domestic and international students; for spring admission, 10/31 priority date for domestic students, 10/1 priority date for international students. Applications are processed on a rolling basis. Application fee: $75. Electronic applications accepted. *Expenses:* Contact institution. *Financial support:* In 2016–17, 3 students received support, including 3 fellowships with full tuition reimbursements available (averaging $10,400 per year), 5 research assistantships with tuition reimbursements available (averaging $8,751 per year), 15 teaching assistantships with partial tuition reimbursements available (averaging $3,684 per year); career-related internships or fieldwork, Federal Work-Study, institutionally sponsored loans, scholarships/grants, health care benefits, and unspecified assistantships also available. Financial award application deadline: 3/1; financial award applicants required to submit FAFSA. *Faculty research:* Economic and international development, environmental and land use planning, GIS and spatial analysis, urban design and physical planning, neighborhood planning and community development, historic preservation. *Total annual research expenditures:* $3.8 million. *Unit head:* Dr. Ernest Sternberg, Professor, 716-829-3671 Ext. 109, Fax: 716-829-3256, E-mail: ezs@buffalo.edu. *Application contact:* Norma Everett, Assistant to the Chair, 716-829-3283, Fax: 716-829-3256, E-mail: norma.everett@buffalo.edu.
Website: http://www.ap.buffalo.edu/planning/

**The University of Arizona,** College of Architecture, Planning, and Landscape Architecture, Planning Program, Tucson, AZ 85721. Offers MS. *Accreditation:* ACSP. *Entrance requirements:* For master's, GRE, 3 letters of recommendation, letter of intent. Additional exam requirements/recommendations for international students: Required—TOEFL (minimum score 573 paper-based; 80 iBT). Electronic applications accepted.

**The University of British Columbia,** Faculty of Applied Science, School of Community and Regional Planning, Vancouver, BC V6T 1Z2, Canada. Offers M Sc P, MAP, MCRP, PhD. *Accreditation:* ACSP. *Degree requirements:* For master's, thesis; for doctorate, thesis/dissertation, oral exam. *Entrance requirements:* For master's, GRE (recommended); for doctorate, MCRP or equivalent. Additional exam requirements/recommendations for international students: Required—TOEFL. Application fee: $100 Canadian dollars ($162 Canadian dollars for international students). Electronic applications accepted. *Expenses:* Contact institution. *Financial support:* Fellowships with partial tuition reimbursements, research assistantships, teaching assistantships, career-related internships or fieldwork, Federal Work-Study, institutionally sponsored loans, scholarships/grants, tuition waivers (full and partial), and research travel bursaries available. *Faculty research:* Natural resources management, international

development, urban spatial, urban policy and community development planning. *Application contact:* Laura Keith, Graduate Program Staff, 604-822-4422, Fax: 604-822-3787, E-mail: grad.scarp@ubc.ca.
Website: https://scarp.ubc.ca/

**University of California, Berkeley,** Graduate Division, College of Environmental Design, Department of City and Regional Planning, Berkeley, CA 94720-1500. Offers MCP, PhD, JD/MCP, M Arch/MCP, MCP/MPH, MCP/MS, MLA/MCP. JD/MCP offered jointly with School of Law. *Accreditation:* ACSP. *Students:* 129 full-time (73 women); includes 37 minority (9 Black or African American, non-Hispanic/Latino; 13 Asian, non-Hispanic/Latino; 15 Hispanic/Latino), 24 international. Average age 30. 467 applicants, 43 enrolled. In 2016, 51 master's, 11 doctorates awarded. *Degree requirements:* For master's, comprehensive exam (for some programs), thesis (for some programs), professional project or thesis; for doctorate, thesis/dissertation, qualifying exam. *Entrance requirements:* For master's and doctorate, GRE General Test, minimum GPA of 3.0, 3 letters of recommendation. Additional exam requirements/recommendations for international students: Required—TOEFL (minimum score 570 paper-based; 90 iBT). *Application deadline:* For fall admission, 12/7 for domestic students. Application fee: $105 ($125 for international students). Electronic applications accepted. *Financial support:* Fellowships, research assistantships, teaching assistantships, career-related internships or fieldwork, institutionally sponsored loans, health care benefits, and unspecified assistantships available. *Faculty research:* Housing and project development, physical planning and design, community and economic development, geographic information systems, transportation. *Unit head:* Prof. Teresa Caldeira, 510-642-3619, Fax: 510-642-1641. *Application contact:* 510-643-9440, Fax: 510-642-1641, E-mail: dcrpgrad@berkeley.edu.
Website: http://dcrp.ced.berkeley.edu/

**University of California, Davis,** Graduate Studies, Graduate Group in Community Development, Davis, CA 95616. Offers MS. *Degree requirements:* For master's, comprehensive exam (for some programs), thesis (for some programs). *Entrance requirements:* For master's, GRE General Test, minimum GPA of 3.0. Additional exam requirements/recommendations for international students: Required—TOEFL (minimum score 550 paper-based). Electronic applications accepted. *Faculty research:* Globalization; community economic change; urban and regional development; community planning design and sustainability; race, ethnic, and gender roles; community organization and political mobilization.

**University of California, Irvine,** School of Social Ecology, Department of Planning, Policy and Design, Irvine, CA 92697. Offers planning, policy and design (PhD); urban and regional planning (MURP). *Accreditation:* ACSP (one or more programs are accredited). *Students:* 120 full-time (68 women), 3 part-time (1 woman); includes 59 minority (3 Black or African American, non-Hispanic/Latino; 1 American Indian or Alaska Native, non-Hispanic/Latino; 21 Asian, non-Hispanic/Latino; 25 Hispanic/Latino; 9 Two or more races, non-Hispanic/Latino), 29 international. Average age 28. 323 applicants, 52% accepted, 47 enrolled. In 2016, 57 master's, 5 doctorates awarded. *Degree requirements:* For doctorate, thesis/dissertation, research project. *Entrance requirements:* For master's and doctorate, GRE General Test, minimum GPA of 3.0. Additional exam requirements/recommendations for international students: Required—TOEFL (minimum score 550 paper-based). *Application deadline:* For fall admission, 1/15 priority date for domestic and international students. Application fee: $105 ($125 for international students). Electronic applications accepted. *Financial support:* Fellowships with tuition reimbursements, research assistantships with full tuition reimbursements, teaching assistantships with tuition reimbursements, institutionally sponsored loans, traineeships, health care benefits, and unspecified assistantships available. Financial award application deadline: 1/15; financial award applicants required to submit FAFSA. *Faculty research:* Community and social policy, economic development, land-use and growth management, transportation planning, environmental policy. *Unit head:* David L. Feldman, Chair, 949-824-4384, Fax: 949-824-3056, E-mail: feldmand@uci.edu. *Application contact:* Janet Gallagher, Graduate Coordinator, 949-824-9849, Fax: 949-824-8566, E-mail: janetg@uci.edu.
Website: http://www.seweb.uci.edu/ppd/

**University of California, Los Angeles,** Graduate Division, School of Public Affairs, Department of Urban Planning, Los Angeles, CA 90095. Offers MA, PhD, JD/MA, MA/MA, MBA/MA. *Accreditation:* ACSP (one or more programs are accredited). *Degree requirements:* For master's, comprehensive exam or thesis; for doctorate, thesis/dissertation, oral and written qualifying exams. *Entrance requirements:* For master's, GRE General Test (recommended); for doctorate, GRE General Test, master's degree in urban planning or related field. Additional exam requirements/recommendations for international students: Required—TOEFL. Electronic applications accepted. *Faculty research:* Industrial hazards, political economy of South and Southeast Asia, historic preservation, flexible production in U.S. and Western Europe, land-use controls.

**University of Central Arkansas,** Graduate School, College of Liberal Arts, Department of Geography, Conway, AR 72035-0001. Offers community and economic development (MS); geographic information systems (MGIS, Certificate). *Program availability:* Part-time, online learning. *Entrance requirements:* Additional exam requirements/recommendations for international students: Required—TOEFL (minimum score 550 paper-based). Electronic applications accepted.

**University of Central Florida,** College of Health and Public Affairs, School of Public Administration, Orlando, FL 32816. Offers emergency management and homeland security (Certificate); fundraising (Certificate); non-profit management (MNM, Certificate); urban and regional planning (MS). *Accreditation:* NASPAA. *Program availability:* Part-time, evening/weekend. *Faculty:* 24 full-time (11 women), 11 part-time/adjunct (6 women). *Students:* 87 full-time (60 women), 257 part-time (190 women); includes 157 minority (83 Black or African American, non-Hispanic/Latino; 1 American Indian or Alaska Native, non-Hispanic/Latino; 9 Asian, non-Hispanic/Latino; 62 Hispanic/Latino; 2 Two or more races, non-Hispanic/Latino), 7 international. Average age 32. 192 applicants, 79% accepted, 108 enrolled. In 2016, 118 master's, 36 other advanced degrees awarded. *Degree requirements:* For master's, comprehensive exam, thesis or alternative, research report. *Entrance requirements:* For master's, GRE General Test. *Application deadline:* For fall admission, 6/15 for domestic students; for spring admission, 11/1 for domestic students. Application fee: $30. Electronic applications accepted. *Expenses:* Tuition, state resident: part-time $288.16 per credit hour. Tuition, nonresident: part-time $1071.31 per credit hour. *Financial support:* In 2016–17, 9 students received support, including 1 fellowship with partial tuition reimbursement available (averaging $4,000 per year), 9 research assistantships with partial tuition reimbursements available (averaging $6,704 per year); career-related internships or fieldwork, Federal Work-Study, institutionally sponsored loans, tuition waivers (partial), and unspecified assistantships also available. Financial award application deadline: 3/1; financial award applicants required to submit FAFSA. *Unit head:* Dr. Naim Kapucu, Director, 407-823-3693, Fax: 407-823-5651, E-mail: naim.kapucu@ucf.edu. *Application contact:* Assistant Director, Graduate Admissions, 407-823-2766, Fax: 407-823-6442, E-mail: gradadmissions@ucf.edu.
Website: https://www.cohpa.ucf.edu/publicadmin/

**University of Cincinnati,** Graduate School, College of Design, Architecture, Art, and Planning, School of Planning, Program in Community Planning, Cincinnati, OH 45221.

Offers MCP, JD/MCP. *Accreditation:* ACSP. *Degree requirements:* For master's, thesis. *Entrance requirements:* For master's, GRE General Test. Additional exam requirements/recommendations for international students: Required—TOEFL. *Expenses: Tuition, area resident:* Full-time $12,790; part-time $389 per credit hour. Tuition, state resident: full-time $13,290; part-time $419 per credit hour. Tuition, nonresident: full-time $24,532; part-time $976 per credit hour. *International tuition:* $24,832 full-time. *Required fees:* $3958; $140 per credit hour. Tuition and fees vary according to course load, degree level, program and reciprocity agreements.

**University of Colorado Denver,** College of Architecture and Planning, Program in Design and Planning, Denver, CO 80217. Offers history of architecture, landscape and urbanism (PhD); sustainable and healthy environments (PhD). *Program availability:* Part-time. *Faculty:* 8 full-time (3 women), 9 part-time/adjunct (1 woman). *Students:* 6 full-time (2 women), 9 part-time (6 women); includes 1 minority (Hispanic/Latino), 5 international. Average age 35. 21 applicants, 14% accepted, 3 enrolled. In 2016, 3 doctorates awarded. *Degree requirements:* For doctorate, comprehensive exam, thesis/dissertation. *Entrance requirements:* For doctorate, GRE (minimum score of 158 for both verbal and quantitative; writing 4.0), minimum undergraduate GPA of 3.0, graduate 3.5; writing sample; three letters of recommendation; statement of personal and professional goals. Additional exam requirements/recommendations for international students: Required—TOEFL (minimum score 80 iBT); Recommended—IELTS (minimum score 6.8). *Application deadline:* For fall admission, 2/2 for domestic students, 1/2 for international students; for spring admission, 10/1 for domestic students. Application fee: $50 ($75 for international students). Electronic applications accepted. *Expenses:* Contact institution. *Financial support:* In 2016–17, 6 students received support. Fellowships, research assistantships, teaching assistantships, Federal Work-Study, institutionally sponsored loans, scholarships/grants, traineeships, and unspecified assistantships available. Financial award application deadline: 4/1; financial award applicants required to submit FAFSA. *Faculty research:* Land use and environmental planning and design; design and planning processes and practices; history, theory, and criticism of the built environment. *Unit head:* Dr. Osman Attmann, Director, 303-315-0032, E-mail: o.attmann@ucdenver.edu. *Application contact:* Rachael Kuroiwa, Manager of Admissions and Outreach, 303-315-2325, E-mail: rachael.kuroiwa@ucdenver.edu.
Website: http://www.ucdenver.edu/academics/colleges/ArchitecturePlanning/Academics/DegreePrograms/PhD/Pages/PhD.aspx

**University of Colorado Denver,** College of Architecture and Planning, Program in Urban and Regional Planning, Denver, CO 80217. Offers economic and community development planning (MURP); land use and environmental planning (MURP); urban place making (MURP). *Accreditation:* ACSP. *Program availability:* Part-time. *Students:* 93 full-time (62 women), 7 part-time (3 women); includes 27 minority (5 Black or African American, non-Hispanic/Latino; 5 Asian, non-Hispanic/Latino; 14 Hispanic/Latino; 3 Two or more races, non-Hispanic/Latino). Average age 30. 139 applicants, 38% accepted, 39 enrolled. In 2016, 54 master's awarded. *Degree requirements:* For master's, thesis, minimum of 51 semester hours. *Entrance requirements:* For master's, GRE (for students with an undergraduate GPA below 3.0), sample of writing or work project; statement of interest; resume; three letters of recommendation. Additional exam requirements/recommendations for international students: Required—TOEFL (minimum score 75 iBT). *Application deadline:* For fall admission, 2/1 priority date for domestic students, 1/1 priority date for international students; for spring admission, 10/1 for domestic students. Application fee: $50 ($75 for international students). Electronic applications accepted. *Expenses:* Contact institution. *Financial support:* In 2016–17, 37 students received support. Fellowships, research assistantships, teaching assistantships, Federal Work-Study, institutionally sponsored loans, scholarships/grants, and traineeships available. Financial award application deadline: 4/1; financial award applicants required to submit FAFSA. *Faculty research:* Physical planning, environmental planning, economic development planning. *Unit head:* Austin Troy, Professor/Chair, 303-315-1006, E-mail: austin.troy@ucdenver.edu. *Application contact:* Rachael Kuroiwa, Manager of Admissions and Outreach, 303-315-2325, E-mail: rachael.kuroiwa@ucdenver.edu.
Website: http://www.ucdenver.edu/academics/colleges/ArchitecturePlanning/Academics/DegreePrograms/MURP/Pages/MURP.aspx

**University of Detroit Mercy,** School of Architecture, Detroit, MI 48221. Offers architecture (M Arch); community development (MA). *Entrance requirements:* For master's, BS in architecture, minimum GPA of 3.0, portfolio.

**University of Florida,** Graduate School, College of Design, Construction and Planning, Department of Urban and Regional Planning, Gainesville, FL 32611. Offers geographic information systems (MAURP); historic preservation (MAURP); sustainable design (MAURP); tropical conservation and development (MAURP); urban and regional planning (MAURP, MURP); wetland sciences (MAURP); JD/MAURP. *Accreditation:* ACSP (one or more programs are accredited). *Program availability:* Online learning. *Entrance requirements:* For master's, GRE General Test, minimum GPA of 3.0. Additional exam requirements/recommendations for international students: Required—TOEFL (minimum score 550 paper-based; 80 iBT), IELTS (minimum score 6). Electronic applications accepted. *Faculty research:* Planning and information systems, urban and environmental design, community and economic development, transportation and growth management.

**University of Florida,** Graduate School, College of Design, Construction and Planning, Doctoral Program in Design, Construction and Planning, Gainesville, FL 32611. Offers construction management (PhD); design, construction and planning (PhD); geographic information systems (PhD); historic preservation (PhD); interior design (PhD); landscape architecture (PhD); urban and regional planning (PhD). *Degree requirements:* For doctorate, thesis/dissertation. *Entrance requirements:* For doctorate, GRE General Test, minimum GPA of 3.0. Additional exam requirements/recommendations for international students: Required—TOEFL (minimum score 550 paper-based; 80 iBT), IELTS (minimum score 6). Electronic applications accepted. *Faculty research:* Architecture, building construction, urban and regional planning.

**University of Hawaii at Manoa,** Graduate Division, College of Social Sciences, Department of Urban and Regional Planning, Honolulu, HI 96822. Offers community planning (MURP); disaster management and humanitarian assistance (Graduate Certificate); environmental planning and sustainability (MURP); international development planning (MURP); land use, transportation and infrastructure planning (MURP); planning studies (Graduate Certificate); urban and regional planning (PhD, Graduate Certificate). *Accreditation:* ACSP. *Program availability:* Part-time. *Entrance requirements:* For master's, GRE General Test, minimum GPA of 3.0; for doctorate, GRE General Test. Additional exam requirements/recommendations for international students: Required—TOEFL (minimum score 500 paper-based; 61 iBT), IELTS (minimum score 5).

**University of Idaho,** College of Graduate Studies, College of Art and Architecture, Program in Bioregional Planning and Community Design, Moscow, ID 83844. Offers MS. *Faculty:* 2 full-time. *Students:* 3 full-time, 2 part-time. Average age 28. In 2016, 2 master's awarded. *Entrance requirements:* For master's, GRE, minimum GPA of 3.0. Additional exam requirements/recommendations for international students: Required—TOEFL. *Application deadline:* Applications are processed on a rolling basis. Application fee: $60. Electronic applications accepted. *Expenses:* Tuition, state resident: full-time

## Urban and Regional Planning

$6460; part-time $414 per credit hour. Tuition, nonresident: full-time $21,268; part-time $1237 per credit hour. *Required fees:* $2070; $60 per credit hour. Full-time tuition and fees vary according to course load and reciprocity agreements. *Financial support:* Applicants required to submit FAFSA. *Faculty research:* Environment and behavior interaction, geographic trade, design development, economic development, natural resource policy. *Unit head:* Dr. Shauna Corry, Interim Dean, 208-885-4409, E-mail: bioregionalplanning@uidaho.edu. *Application contact:* Sean Scoggin, Graduate Recruitment Coordinator, 208-885-4001, Fax: 208-805-4406, E-mail: graduateadmissions@uidaho.edu.
Website: http://www.uidaho.edu/caa/programs/biop

**University of Illinois at Chicago,** College of Urban Planning and Public Affairs, Department of Urban Planning and Policy, Chicago, IL 60607-7128. Offers MUPP, PhD. *Accreditation:* ACSP (one or more programs are accredited). *Program availability:* Part-time. *Degree requirements:* For master's, thesis or alternative, internship; for doctorate, thesis/dissertation. *Entrance requirements:* For master's and doctorate, GRE General Test, minimum GPA of 2.75, writing sample. Additional exam requirements/recommendations for international students: Required—TOEFL. Electronic applications accepted. *Expenses:* Contact institution. *Faculty research:* Urban and regional economic and workforce development issues, current policy issues and social trends, racial justice and related issues of poverty, quality of life of people living in Chicago and other great cities of the world.

**University of Illinois at Urbana–Champaign,** Graduate College, College of Fine and Applied Arts, Department of Urban and Regional Planning, Champaign, IL 61820. Offers regional planning (PhD); urban planning (MUP); JD/MUP; M Arch/MUP; MLA/MUP. *Accreditation:* ACSP (one or more programs are accredited).

**The University of Iowa,** Graduate College, Program in Urban and Regional Planning, Iowa City, IA 52242-1316. Offers MA, MS, JD/MA, MHA/MA, MHA/MS, MS/MA, MS/MS, MSW/MA, MSW/MS. *Accreditation:* ACSP. *Degree requirements:* For master's, thesis optional, portfolio. *Entrance requirements:* For master's, GRE General Test, minimum GPA of 3.0. Additional exam requirements/recommendations for international students: Required—TOEFL (minimum score 600 paper-based; 100 iBT). Electronic applications accepted.

**The University of Kansas,** Graduate Studies, School of Architecture, Design, and Planning, Department of Urban Planning, Lawrence, KS 66045. Offers MUP. *Accreditation:* ACSP. *Program availability:* Part-time. *Students:* 32 full-time (14 women), 1 part-time (0 women); includes 3 minority (1 Black or African American, non-Hispanic/Latino; 2 Hispanic/Latino), 11 international. Average age 28. 39 applicants, 77% accepted, 10 enrolled. In 2016, 21 master's awarded. *Entrance requirements:* For master's, GRE, three letters of reference, resume, statement of career goals and substantive interests in urban planning, official transcripts. Additional exam requirements/recommendations for international students: Required—TOEFL (minimum score 570 paper-based). *Application deadline:* For fall admission, 7/1 for domestic students, 6/1 for international students; for spring admission, 12/1 for domestic students, 11/1 for international students. Application fee: $65 ($85 for international students). Electronic applications accepted. *Financial support:* Fellowships, research assistantships, teaching assistantships, career-related internships or fieldwork, scholarships/grants, and unspecified assistantships available. Financial award application deadline: 2/15; financial award applicants required to submit FAFSA. *Faculty research:* Environmental land use, housing and economic development, community development and transportation, urban mass transportation, urban sprawl. *Unit head:* Stacey M. Swearingen White, Chair, 785-864-3530, E-mail: sswhite@ku.edu. *Application contact:* Pat Owens, Graduate Admission Contact, 785-864-4184, E-mail: ubpl@ku.edu.
Website: http://urbanplanning.ku.edu/

**University of Louisville,** Graduate School, College of Arts and Sciences, Department of Urban and Public Affairs, Louisville, KY 40208. Offers public administration (MPA), including human resources management, non-profit management, public policy and administration; urban and public affairs (PhD), including urban planning and development, urban policy and administration; urban planning (MUP), including administration of planning organizations, housing and community development, land use and environmental planning, spatial analysis. *Program availability:* Part-time, evening/weekend. *Faculty:* 12 full-time (5 women), 3 part-time/adjunct (1 woman). *Students:* 59 full-time (23 women), 32 part-time (19 women); includes 19 minority (13 Black or African American, non-Hispanic/Latino; 1 Asian, non-Hispanic/Latino; 2 Hispanic/Latino; 3 Two or more races, non-Hispanic/Latino), 5 international. Average age 30. 75 applicants, 65% accepted, 25 enrolled. In 2016, 22 master's, 2 doctorates awarded. Terminal master's awarded for partial completion of doctoral program. *Degree requirements:* For master's, internship; for doctorate, comprehensive exam, thesis/dissertation. *Entrance requirements:* For master's, GRE General Test, minimum GPA of 3.0; for doctorate, GRE General Test, master's degree in appropriate field. Additional exam requirements/recommendations for international students: Required—TOEFL (minimum score 550 paper-based; 79 iBT). *Application deadline:* Applications are processed on a rolling basis. Application fee: $60. *Expenses:* Contact institution. *Financial support:* Fellowships, research assistantships, tuition waivers (full and partial), and unspecified assistantships available. Financial award application deadline: 2/1. *Faculty research:* Urban theory, sustainability, public administration, urban planning, urban management. *Total annual research expenditures:* $240,308. *Unit head:* Dr. David Simpson, Chair, 502-852-8019, Fax: 502-852-4558, E-mail: dave.simpson@louisville.edu. *Application contact:* Libby Leggett, Director, Graduate Admissions, 502-852-3101, Fax: 502-852-4558, E-mail: gradadm@louisville.edu.
Website: http://supa.louisville.edu

**University of Manitoba,** Faculty of Graduate Studies, Faculty of Architecture, Department of City Planning, Winnipeg, MB R3T 2N2, Canada. Offers MCP. *Degree requirements:* For master's, thesis.

**University of Maryland, College Park,** Academic Affairs, School of Architecture, Planning and Preservation, Program in Urban Studies and Planning, College Park, MD 20742. Offers urban and regional planning/design (PhD); urban studies and planning (MCP). *Accreditation:* ACSP. *Program availability:* Part-time, evening/weekend. *Entrance requirements:* For master's and doctorate, GRE General Test, minimum GPA of 3.0, 3 letters of recommendation. Additional exam requirements/recommendations for international students: Required—TOEFL. Electronic applications accepted. *Faculty research:* Policy analysis, urban planning, program planning and management, economic development planning.

**University of Massachusetts Amherst,** Graduate School, College of Social and Behavioral Sciences, Department of Landscape Architecture and Regional Planning, Dual Degree Program in Landscape Architecture and Regional Planning, Amherst, MA 01003. Offers MLA/MRP. *Accreditation:* ACSP; ASLA. *Program availability:* Part-time. *Entrance requirements:* Additional exam requirements/recommendations for international students: Required—TOEFL (minimum score 550 paper-based; 80 iBT), IELTS (minimum score 6.5). Electronic applications accepted.

**University of Massachusetts Amherst,** Graduate School, College of Social and Behavioral Sciences, Department of Landscape Architecture and Regional Planning, Program in Regional Planning, Amherst, MA 01003. Offers MRP, PhD, M Arch/MRP, MRP/MPPA. *Accreditation:* ACSP (one or more programs are accredited). *Program availability:* Part-time. Terminal master's awarded for partial completion of doctoral program. *Degree requirements:* For master's, thesis or alternative; for doctorate, comprehensive exam, thesis/dissertation. *Entrance requirements:* For master's and doctorate, GRE General Test. Additional exam requirements/recommendations for international students: Required—TOEFL (minimum score 550 paper-based; 80 iBT), IELTS (minimum score 6.5). Electronic applications accepted.

**University of Massachusetts Amherst,** Graduate School, Interdisciplinary Programs, Dual Degree Program in Regional Planning and Public Policy and Administration, Amherst, MA 01003. Offers MPPA/MRP. *Entrance requirements:* Additional exam requirements/recommendations for international students: Required—TOEFL (minimum score 550 paper-based; 80 iBT), IELTS (minimum score 6.5). Electronic applications accepted.

**University of Massachusetts Boston,** College of Science and Mathematics, Program in Urban Planning and Community Development, Boston, MA 02125-3393. Offers MS. *Students:* 6 full-time (3 women), 6 part-time (3 women); includes 5 minority (3 Black or African American, non-Hispanic/Latino; 1 Hispanic/Latino; 1 Two or more races, non-Hispanic/Latino), 2 international. Average age 31. 20 applicants, 75% accepted, 8 enrolled. *Expenses:* Tuition, state resident: full-time $16,863. Tuition, nonresident: full-time $32,913. *Required fees:* $177. *Unit head:* Dr. William Hagar, Interim Dean, 617-287-5777. *Application contact:* Peggy Roldan Patel, Graduate Admissions Coordinator, 617-287-6400, Fax: 617-287-6236, E-mail: bos.gadm@dpc.umassp.edu.

**University of Massachusetts Lowell,** College of Fine Arts, Humanities and Social Sciences, Program in Regional Economic and Social Development, Lowell, MA 01854. Offers MA, Graduate Certificate. *Program availability:* Part-time. *Entrance requirements:* For master's, GRE. Electronic applications accepted.

**University of Memphis,** Graduate School, College of Arts and Sciences, Department of City and Regional Planning, Memphis, TN 38103. Offers MCRP. *Accreditation:* ACSP. *Faculty:* 5 full-time (2 women), 1 part-time/adjunct (0 women). *Students:* 21 full-time (14 women), 4 part-time (1 woman); includes 5 minority (4 Black or African American, non-Hispanic/Latino; 1 Hispanic/Latino). Average age 29. 22 applicants, 95% accepted, 11 enrolled. In 2016, 8 master's awarded. *Degree requirements:* For master's, comprehensive exam, thesis or alternative, terminal project. *Entrance requirements:* For master's, GRE General Test or MAT, personal statement, resume. Additional exam requirements/recommendations for international students: Required—TOEFL (minimum score 550 paper-based; 79 iBT). *Application deadline:* For fall admission, 4/15 priority date for domestic students; for spring admission, 12/1 for domestic students. Applications are processed on a rolling basis. Application fee: $35 ($60 for international students). Electronic applications accepted. *Expenses:* $5,231.50 per semester full-time in-state, $9,623.50 full-time out-of-state. *Financial support:* In 2016–17, 14 students received support. Research assistantships with full tuition reimbursements available, career-related internships or fieldwork, Federal Work-Study, scholarships/grants, and unspecified assistantships available. Financial award application deadline: 2/1; financial award applicants required to submit FAFSA. *Faculty research:* Growth planning, site design, economic development, housing, smart growth. *Unit head:* Dr. Charles Santo, Chair, 901-678-2161, Fax: 901-678-4162, E-mail: casanto@memphis.edu. *Application contact:* Dr. Charles Santo, Director of Graduate Program, 901-678-2161, Fax: 901-678-4162, E-mail: casanto@memphis.edu.
Website: http://www.memphis.edu/planning/

**University of Michigan,** Taubman College of Architecture and Urban Planning, Master of Urban and Regional Planning Program, Ann Arbor, MI 48109. Offers Graduate Certificate. *Accreditation:* ACSP. *Faculty:* 11 full-time (6 women), 9 part-time/adjunct (2 women). *Students:* 100 full-time (59 women); includes 21 minority (6 Black or African American, non-Hispanic/Latino; 5 Asian, non-Hispanic/Latino; 6 Hispanic/Latino; 4 Two or more races, non-Hispanic/Latino), 27 international. 184 applicants, 89% accepted, 45 enrolled. *Entrance requirements:* Additional exam requirements/recommendations for international students: Required—TOEFL (minimum score 83 iBT), GRE. *Application deadline:* For fall admission, 1/15 for domestic and international students. Application fee: $75 ($90 for international students). Electronic applications accepted. *Expenses:* Contact institution. *Financial support:* In 2016–17, 56 students received support, including 20 teaching assistantships with full tuition reimbursements available (averaging $21,000 per year); scholarships/grants also available. Financial award application deadline: 1/15; financial award applicants required to submit FAFSA. *Faculty research:* Housing community and economic development, transportation planning, physical planning and urban design, planning in developing countries, land use and environmental planning. *Unit head:* Joe Grengs, Urban and Regional Planning Chair, 734-764-1300, E-mail: grengs@umich.edu. *Application contact:* Mike Smith, Admissions Officer, 734-647-2187, E-mail: taubmancollegestudentservices@umich.edu.
Website: http://taubmancollege.umich.edu/urbanplanning/degrees/master-urban-planning

**University of Michigan,** Taubman College of Architecture and Urban Planning, Urban and Regional Planning PhD Program, Ann Arbor, MI 48109. Offers PhD. *Faculty:* 21 full-time (9 women). *Students:* 17 full-time (5 women); includes 3 minority (1 Black or African American, non-Hispanic/Latino; 2 Hispanic/Latino), 5 international. 67 applicants, 9% accepted, 4 enrolled. In 2016, 1 doctorate awarded. *Degree requirements:* For doctorate, comprehensive exam, thesis/dissertation. *Entrance requirements:* Additional exam requirements/recommendations for international students: Required—TOEFL (minimum score 83 iBT), GRE. *Application deadline:* For fall admission, 1/15 for domestic and international students. Application fee: $75 ($90 for international students). Electronic applications accepted. *Expenses:* Tuition, state resident: full-time $21,466; part-time $1152 per credit hour. Tuition, nonresident: full-time $43,346; part-time $2367 per credit hour. Part-time tuition and fees vary according to course load, degree level and program. *Financial support:* In 2016–17, 2 students received support, including 5 teaching assistantships with full tuition reimbursements available (averaging $21,050 per year); health care benefits and tuition waivers (full) also available. Financial award application deadline: 1/15; financial award applicants required to submit FAFSA. *Unit head:* Joe Grengs, Urban and Regional Planning Chair, 734-763-1300, E-mail: grengs@umich.edu. *Application contact:* Lisa Hauser, Assistant Director for Admissions and Recruiting, 734-763-1275, E-mail: taubmancollegestudentservices@umich.edu.

**University of Minnesota, Twin Cities Campus,** Graduate School, Hubert H. Humphrey School of Public Affairs, PhD Program in Public Affairs, Minneapolis, MN 55455. Offers management and governance (PhD); public policy (PhD); science, technology, and environmental policy (PhD); urban planning (PhD). *Program availability:* Part-time. *Degree requirements:* For doctorate, comprehensive exam, thesis/dissertation. *Entrance requirements:* For doctorate, GRE General Test. Additional exam requirements/recommendations for international students: Required—TOEFL (minimum score 650 paper-based; 100 iBT), IELTS (minimum score 7). Electronic applications accepted. *Expenses:* Contact institution. *Faculty research:* Public policy, urban/regional planning, public/nonprofit management and governance, science/technology/environmental policy.

**University of Minnesota, Twin Cities Campus,** Graduate School, Hubert H. Humphrey School of Public Affairs, Program in Urban and Regional Planning, Minneapolis, MN 55455. Offers MURP, JD/MURP, MURP/MPH, MURP/MS, MURP/MSW. *Accreditation:* ACSP (one or more programs are accredited). *Program availability:* Part-time. *Degree requirements:* For master's, thesis or alternative, internship or equivalent work experience. *Entrance requirements:* For master's, GRE General Test, minimum undergraduate GPA of 3.0. Additional exam requirements/recommendations for international students: Required—TOEFL (minimum score 600 paper-based; 100 iBT), IELTS (minimum score 7). Electronic applications accepted. *Expenses:* Contact institution. *Faculty research:* Policy planning, resource allocation planning, regulatory planning, program planning, project planning.

**University of Nebraska–Lincoln,** Graduate College, College of Agricultural Sciences and Natural Resources, Department of Agricultural Economics, Lincoln, NE 68588. Offers agribusiness (MBA); agricultural economics (MS, PhD); community development (M Ag). *Degree requirements:* For master's, thesis optional; for doctorate, comprehensive exam, thesis/dissertation. *Entrance requirements:* For master's and doctorate, GRE General Test. Additional exam requirements/recommendations for international students: Required—TOEFL (minimum score 550 paper-based). Electronic applications accepted. *Faculty research:* Marketing and agribusiness, production economics, resource law, international trade and development, rural policy and revitalization.

**University of Nebraska–Lincoln,** Graduate College, College of Architecture, Department of Community and Regional Planning, Lincoln, NE 68588. Offers MCRP, JD/MCRP, M Arch/MCRP, MCRP/MSCE. *Accreditation:* ACSP. *Degree requirements:* For master's, thesis optional. *Entrance requirements:* For master's, GRE General Test. Additional exam requirements/recommendations for international students: Required—TOEFL (minimum score 550 paper-based). Electronic applications accepted. *Faculty research:* Economic development, community development and improvement, social planning, land use planning, physical planning, environmental planning.

**University of New Brunswick Fredericton,** School of Graduate Studies, Policy Studies Program, Fredericton, NB E3B 5A3, Canada. Offers citizen engagement/dispute resolution (M Phil); community development (M Phil); international development (M Phil); leadership (M Phil); sustainability/environmental issues (M Phil); worldviews (M Phil). *Program availability:* Part-time. *Degree requirements:* For master's, thesis, report. *Entrance requirements:* For master's, minimum GPA of 3.5. Additional exam requirements/recommendations for international students: Required—TWE (minimum score 5.5), TOEFL (minimum score 600 paper-based; 100 iBT) or IELTS (minimum score 7). Electronic applications accepted. *Faculty research:* International development, worldviews, citizenship/dispute resolution, sustainability/environmental issues, leadership, community development.

**University of New Haven,** Graduate School, Henry C. Lee College of Criminal Justice and Forensic Sciences, Program in Public Administration, West Haven, CT 06516. Offers city management (MPA); community-clinical services (MPA); health care management (MPA); long-term health care (MPA); personnel and labor relations (MPA); public administration (MPA, Graduate Certificate); MBA/MPA. *Program availability:* Part-time, evening/weekend. *Students:* 30 full-time (13 women), 15 part-time (8 women); includes 15 minority (12 Black or African American, non-Hispanic/Latino; 1 American Indian or Alaska Native, non-Hispanic/Latino; 1 Asian, non-Hispanic/Latino; 1 Hispanic/Latino), 6 international. Average age 35. 56 applicants, 98% accepted, 25 enrolled. In 2016, 31 master's, 17 other advanced degrees awarded. *Degree requirements:* For master's, thesis or alternative. *Entrance requirements:* Additional exam requirements/recommendations for international students: Required—TOEFL (minimum score 80 iBT), IELTS, PTE. *Application deadline:* Applications are processed on a rolling basis. Application fee: $50. Electronic applications accepted. Application fee is waived when completed online. *Expenses:* Contact institution. *Financial support:* Research assistantships with partial tuition reimbursements, teaching assistantships with partial tuition reimbursements, career-related internships or fieldwork, Federal Work-Study, scholarships/grants, and unspecified assistantships available. Support available to part-time students. Financial award application deadline: 5/1; financial award applicants required to submit FAFSA. *Unit head:* Dr. Cynthia Conrad, Associate Professor, 203-932-7486, E-mail: cconrad@newhaven.edu. *Application contact:* Michelle Mason, Director of Graduate Enrollment, 203-932-7067, E-mail: mmason@newhaven.edu. Website: http://www.newhaven.edu/6854/

**University of New Mexico,** Graduate Studies, School of Architecture and Planning, Program in Community and Regional Planning, Albuquerque, NM 87131-2039. Offers MCRP, MCRP/MA, MPA/MCRP. *Accreditation:* ACSP. *Program availability:* Part-time. *Faculty:* 13 full-time (6 women), 3 part-time/adjunct (0 women). *Students:* 48 full-time (29 women), 20 part-time (11 women); includes 36 minority (1 American Indian or Alaska Native, non-Hispanic/Latino; 21 Hispanic/Latino; 4 Two or more races, non-Hispanic/Latino), 3 international. Average age 34. 36 applicants, 67% accepted, 19 enrolled. In 2016, 21 master's awarded. *Degree requirements:* For master's, thesis. *Entrance requirements:* For master's, minimum GPA of 3.0 in last two years of graduate study, 3 letters of recommendation, letter of intent, resume, copies of all official transcripts. Additional exam requirements/recommendations for international students: Required—TOEFL (minimum score 550 paper-based; 79 iBT). *Application deadline:* For fall admission, 1/30 priority date for domestic students, 1/30 for international students. Application fee: $50. Electronic applications accepted. *Financial support:* Fellowships, research assistantships with partial tuition reimbursements, teaching assistantships with partial tuition reimbursements, career-related internships or fieldwork, Federal Work-Study, institutionally sponsored loans, scholarships/grants, health care benefits, tuition waivers (full), and unspecified assistantships available. Support available to part-time students. Financial award application deadline: 3/1; financial award applicants required to submit FAFSA. *Faculty research:* Community development, urban and ecological design, land economics, community-based planning, environmental dispute resolution, environmental justice, indigenous planning, watershed management. *Unit head:* Dr. Teresa L. Cordova, Program Director, 505-277-3922, Fax: 505-277-0076, E-mail: tcordova@unm.edu. *Application contact:* Elizabeth M. Rowe, Senior Academic Advisor, 505-277-1303, Fax: 505-277-0076, E-mail: erowe@unm.edu. Website: http://www.unm.edu/~crp

**University of New Orleans,** Graduate School, College of Liberal Arts, Department of Planning and Urban Studies, Program in Urban and Regional Planning, New Orleans, LA 70148. Offers MURP. *Accreditation:* ACSP. *Degree requirements:* For master's, thesis. *Entrance requirements:* For master's, GRE General Test. Additional exam requirements/recommendations for international students: Required—TOEFL (minimum score 550 paper-based; 79 iBT), IELTS (minimum score 6.5). Electronic applications accepted. *Faculty research:* Urban economic development, environmental planning and analysis, social and cultural change.

**The University of North Carolina at Chapel Hill,** Graduate School, College of Arts and Sciences, Department of City and Regional Planning, Chapel Hill, NC 27599-3140. Offers city and regional planning (MCRP); planning (PhD); public policy analysis (PhD); JD/MCRP; MBA/MCRP; MPA/MCRP. *Accreditation:* ACSP (one or more programs are accredited). *Degree requirements:* For master's, project; for doctorate, comprehensive exam, thesis/dissertation. *Entrance requirements:* For master's and doctorate, GRE General Test. Additional exam requirements/recommendations for international students: Required—TOEFL (minimum score 550 paper-based). Electronic applications accepted. *Faculty research:* Developing areas, transportation, affordable housing, growth management, coastal zone management.

**The University of North Carolina at Charlotte,** College of Liberal Arts and Sciences, Department of Political Science and Public Administration, Charlotte, NC 28223-0001. Offers emergency management (Graduate Certificate); non-profit management (Graduate Certificate); public administration (MPA), including arts administration, emergency management, non-profit management, public budgeting and finance, urban management and policy; public budgeting and finance (Graduate Certificate); urban management and policy (Graduate Certificate). *Accreditation:* NASPAA. *Program availability:* Part-time, evening/weekend. *Faculty:* 19 full-time (10 women), 3 part-time/adjunct (0 women). *Students:* 25 full-time (17 women), 57 part-time (39 women); includes 23 minority (14 Black or African American, non-Hispanic/Latino; 1 American Indian or Alaska Native, non-Hispanic/Latino; 2 Asian, non-Hispanic/Latino; 4 Hispanic/Latino; 2 Two or more races, non-Hispanic/Latino). Average age 30. 55 applicants, 73% accepted, 30 enrolled. In 2016, 31 master's, 12 other advanced degrees awarded. *Degree requirements:* For master's, research project or thesis. *Entrance requirements:* For master's, GRE General Test, bachelor's degree, or its equivalent, from accredited college or university; minimum undergraduate GPA of 3.0; 3 letters of recommendation; statement of purpose; for Graduate Certificate, statement of purpose (1-2 pages in length) explaining applicant's career goals, how the Certificate fits into achieving those goals, and any relevant work experience; official transcripts; letters of recommendation. Additional exam requirements/recommendations for international students: Required—TOEFL (minimum score 523 paper-based, 70 iBT) or IELTS (6.5). *Application deadline:* For fall admission, 8/1 for domestic and international students; for spring admission, 12/1 for domestic and international students. Applications are processed on a rolling basis. Application fee: $75. Electronic applications accepted. *Expenses:* Tuition, state resident: full-time $4252. Tuition, nonresident: full-time $17,423. *Required fees:* $3026. Tuition and fees vary according to course load and program. *Financial support:* In 2016–17, 9 students received support, including 9 research assistantships (averaging $7,117 per year); career-related internships or fieldwork, Federal Work-Study, institutionally sponsored loans, scholarships/grants, and unspecified assistantships also available. Support available to part-time students. Financial award application deadline: 3/1; financial award applicants required to submit FAFSA. *Total annual research expenditures:* $477,651. *Unit head:* Dr. Greg Weeks, Chair, 704-687-7574, E-mail: gbweeks@uncc.edu. *Application contact:* Kathy B. Giddings, Director of Graduate Admissions, 704-687-5503, Fax: 704-687-1668, E-mail: gradadm@uncc.edu. Website: http://politicalscience.uncc.edu/

**University of Oklahoma,** College of Architecture, Division of Regional and City Planning, Norman, OK 73019. Offers community and economic development (MRCP); physical planning (MRCP); MRCP/MLA. *Accreditation:* ACSP. *Program availability:* Part-time. *Students:* 20 full-time (13 women), 4 part-time (3 women); includes 6 minority (2 Black or African American, non-Hispanic/Latino; 1 American Indian or Alaska Native, non-Hispanic/Latino; 1 Hispanic/Latino; 2 Two or more races, non-Hispanic/Latino), 3 international. Average age 28. 12 applicants, 67% accepted, 5 enrolled. In 2016, 13 master's awarded. Terminal master's awarded for partial completion of doctoral program. *Degree requirements:* For master's, comprehensive exam or thesis. *Entrance requirements:* Additional exam requirements/recommendations for international students: Required—TOEFL (minimum iBT score 79) or IELTS (minimum score 6.5). *Application deadline:* For fall admission, 4/1 priority date for international students. Applications are processed on a rolling basis. Application fee: $50 ($100 for international students). Electronic applications accepted. *Expenses:* Tuition, state resident: full-time $4886; part-time $203.60 per credit hour. Tuition, nonresident: full-time $18,989; part-time $791.20 per credit hour. *Required fees:* $3283; $126.25 per credit hour. $126.50 per semester. *Financial support:* In 2016–17, 26 students received support, including 2 fellowships (averaging $3,750 per year), 3 research assistantships with tuition reimbursements available (averaging $11,915 per year); teaching assistantships, career-related internships or fieldwork, Federal Work-Study, scholarships/grants, health care benefits, tuition waivers, and unspecified assistantships also available. Financial award application deadline: 6/1; financial award applicants required to submit FAFSA. *Faculty research:* Food systems planning, the built environment and public health, community revitalization and minority communities, freight modeling. *Unit head:* Dr. Charles Warnken, Director, 405-325-2444, Fax: 405-325-7558, E-mail: cwarnken@ou.edu. Website: http://rcpl.ou.edu

**University of Oregon,** Graduate School, School of Architecture and Allied Arts, Department of Planning, Public Policy, and Management, Program in Community and Regional Planning, Eugene, OR 97403. Offers MCRP. *Accreditation:* ACSP. *Program availability:* Part-time. *Degree requirements:* For master's, thesis or alternative. *Entrance requirements:* For master's, minimum GPA of 3.0. Additional exam requirements/recommendations for international students: Required—TOEFL. *Faculty research:* Community economic development, tourism, families in poverty.

**University of Pennsylvania,** School of Design, Department of City and Regional Planning, Philadelphia, PA 19104. Offers city and regional planning (PhD); city planning (MCP); GIS and spatial analysis (Certificate); land preservation (Certificate); urban design (Certificate); urban redevelopment (Certificate); urban spatial analytics (MUSA). *Accreditation:* ACSP (one or more programs are accredited). *Program availability:* Part-time. *Faculty:* 13 full-time (5 women), 4 part-time/adjunct (0 women). *Students:* 136 full-time (77 women), 15 part-time (11 women); includes 22 minority (5 Black or African American, non-Hispanic/Latino; 8 Asian, non-Hispanic/Latino; 6 Hispanic/Latino; 1 Native Hawaiian or other Pacific Islander, non-Hispanic/Latino; 2 Two or more races, non-Hispanic/Latino), 56 international. Average age 27. 419 applicants, 58% accepted, 90 enrolled. In 2016, 76 master's, 8 doctorates awarded. *Degree requirements:* For doctorate, thesis/dissertation. *Entrance requirements:* Additional exam requirements/recommendations for international students: Required—TOEFL (minimum score 100 iBT); Recommended—IELTS (minimum score 7), TSE (minimum score 68). *Application deadline:* For spring admission, 1/12 for domestic students. Application fee: $80. Electronic applications accepted. *Expenses:* Tuition: Full-time $31,068; part-time $5762 per course. *Required fees:* $3200; $336 per course. Full-time tuition and fees vary according to degree level, program and student level. Part-time tuition and fees vary according to course load, degree level and program. *Financial support:* In 2016–17, 39 teaching assistantships (averaging $2,000 per year) were awarded; fellowships, research assistantships, and Federal Work-Study also available. Financial award application deadline: 2/15; financial award applicants required to submit FAFSA. *Faculty research:* Transportation planning, community and economic development, public private development, land use and environmental planning, urban design. *Unit head:* Dr. John Landis, Department Chair, 215-746-2340, E-mail: jlan@design.upenn.edu. *Application contact:* Roslynne Carter, Administrative Assistant, 215-898-8330, Fax: 215-898-5730, E-mail: admissions@design.upenn.edu. Website: https://www.design.upenn.edu/city-regional-planning

**University of Pittsburgh,** Graduate School of Public and International Affairs, Master of International Development Program, Pittsburgh, PA 15260. Offers energy and

environment (MID); governance and international public management (MID); human security (MID); nongovernmental organizations and civil society (MID); urban affairs and planning (MID); MID/JD; MID/MBA; MID/MPH; MID/MSIS; MID/MSW. *Program availability:* Part-time, evening/weekend. *Faculty:* 34 full-time (12 women), 17 part-time/ adjunct (5 women). *Students:* 47 full-time (32 women), 10 part-time (8 women); includes 13 minority (7 Black or African American, non-Hispanic/Latino; 3 Asian, non-Hispanic/ Latino; 2 Hispanic/Latino; 1 Two or more races, non-Hispanic/Latino), 12 international. Average age 28. 107 applicants, 87% accepted, 29 enrolled. In 2016, 29 master's awarded. *Degree requirements:* For master's, thesis optional, capstone seminar. *Entrance requirements:* For master's, GRE General Test or GMAT, 2 letters of recommendation; undergraduate transcripts; resume; personal statement. Additional exam requirements/recommendations for international students: Required—TOEFL (minimum score 80 iBT); Recommended—IELTS (minimum score 7). *Application deadline:* For fall admission, 2/1 priority date for domestic students, 1/15 for international students; for spring admission, 11/1 priority date for domestic students, 8/1 for international students. Application fee: $50. Electronic applications accepted. *Expenses:* $22,578 per year in-state; $36,734 per year out-of-state. *Financial support:* In 2016–17, 28 students received support, including 4 fellowships with full tuition reimbursements available (averaging $18,000 per year), 4 research assistantships with full tuition reimbursements available (averaging $14,620 per year); career-related internships or fieldwork, scholarships/grants, health care benefits, and unspecified assistantships also available. Financial award application deadline: 2/1; financial award applicants required to submit FAFSA. *Faculty research:* Nongovernmental organizations, energy and environmental policy, human security, urban affairs and planning, governance and international management. *Total annual research expenditures:* $1.3 million. *Unit head:* Dr. John T.S. Keeler, Dean, 412-648-7605, Fax: 412-648-2605, E-mail: keeler@pitt.edu. *Application contact:* Dr. Michael T. Rizzi, Director of Student Services, 412-648-7640, Fax: 412-648-7641, E-mail: rizzim@pitt.edu.
Website: http://www.gspia.pitt.edu/

**University of Pittsburgh,** Graduate School of Public and International Affairs, Master of Public Administration Program, Pittsburgh, PA 15260. Offers energy and environment (MPA); governance and international public management (MPA); policy research and analysis (MPA); public and nonprofit management (MPA); urban affairs and planning (MPA); JD/MPA; MPH/MPA; MSIS/MPA; MSW/MPA. *Accreditation:* NASPAA. *Program availability:* Part-time, evening/weekend. *Faculty:* 34 full-time (12 women), 17 part-time/ adjunct (5 women). *Students:* 93 full-time (66 women), 21 part-time (16 women); includes 8 minority (4 Black or African American, non-Hispanic/Latino; 1 Asian, non-Hispanic/Latino; 3 Hispanic/Latino), 61 international. Average age 26. 200 applicants, 81% accepted, 49 enrolled. In 2016, 62 master's awarded. *Degree requirements:* For master's, thesis optional, capstone seminar. *Entrance requirements:* For master's, GRE General Test or GMAT, 2 letters of recommendation, resume, undergraduate transcripts, personal statement. Additional exam requirements/recommendations for international students: Required—TOEFL (minimum score 80 iBT); Recommended—IELTS (minimum score 7). *Application deadline:* For fall admission, 2/1 priority date for domestic students, 1/15 for international students; for spring admission, 11/1 for domestic students, 8/1 for international students. Application fee: $50. Electronic applications accepted. *Expenses:* $22,578 per year in-state; $36,734 per year out-of-state. *Financial support:* In 2016–17, 10 students received support, including 2 research assistantships with full tuition reimbursements available (averaging $14,620 per year); fellowships with full tuition reimbursements available, career-related internships or fieldwork, scholarships/grants, health care benefits, and unspecified assistantships also available. Financial award application deadline: 2/1; financial award applicants required to submit FAFSA. *Faculty research:* Urban affairs and planning, governance and international public management, nonprofit management, policy research and analysis, energy and environmental policy. *Total annual research expenditures:* $1.3 million. *Unit head:* Dr. John T.S. Keeler, Dean, Fax: 412-648-2605, E-mail: keeler@pitt.edu. *Application contact:* Dr. Michael T. Rizzi, Director of Student Services, 412-648-7640, Fax: 412-648-7641, E-mail: rizzim@pitt.edu.
Website: http://www.gspia.pitt.edu/

**University of Puerto Rico, Río Piedras Campus,** Graduate School of Planning, San Juan, PR 00931-3300. Offers economic planning systems (MP); environmental planning (MP); social policy and planning (MP); urban and territorial planning (MP). *Accreditation:* ACSP. *Program availability:* Part-time. *Degree requirements:* For master's, comprehensive exam, thesis, planning project defense. *Entrance requirements:* For master's, PAEG, GRE, minimum GPA of 3.0, 2 letters of recommendation. *Faculty research:* Municipalities, historic Atlas, Puerto Rico, economic future.

**University of Southern California,** Graduate School, School of Policy, Planning, and Development, Doctor of Philosophy in Urban Planning and Development Program, Los Angeles, CA 90089. Offers PhD. *Accreditation:* ACSP. *Degree requirements:* For doctorate, thesis/dissertation. *Entrance requirements:* For doctorate, GRE. Additional exam requirements/recommendations for international students: Required—TOEFL (minimum score 600 paper-based; 100 iBT). Electronic applications accepted. *Faculty research:* Transportation and infrastructure, healthy urban and place development, social economic development, sustainable community planning.

**University of Southern California,** Graduate School, School of Policy, Planning, and Development, Doctor of Policy, Planning, and Development Program, Los Angeles, CA 90089. Offers DPPD. *Accreditation:* ACSP. *Program availability:* Part-time. *Degree requirements:* For doctorate, project. *Entrance requirements:* Additional exam requirements/recommendations for international students: Required—TOEFL (minimum score 600 paper-based; 100 iBT). Electronic applications accepted. *Faculty research:* Governance: effective institutions, leadership, management, healthy urban and place development, sustainability, community, public policy and planning, societal problem solving and analysis.

**University of Southern California,** Graduate School, School of Policy, Planning, and Development, Master of Planning Program, Los Angeles, CA 90089. Offers sustainable cities (Graduate Certificate); transportation systems (Graduate Certificate); urban planning (M Pl); M Arch/M Pl; M Pl/MA; M Pl/MPP; M Pl/MRED; M Pl/MS; M Pl/MSW; MBA/M Pl; ML Arch/M Pl; MPA/M Pl. *Accreditation:* ACSP. *Program availability:* Part-time. *Degree requirements:* For master's, comprehensive exam, internship. *Entrance requirements:* For master's, GRE, GMAT. Additional exam requirements/ recommendations for international students: Required—TOEFL (minimum score 600 paper-based; 100 iBT). Electronic applications accepted. *Faculty research:* Transportation and infrastructure, comparative international development, healthy communities, social economic development, sustainable community planning.

**University of Southern Maine,** College of Management and Human Service, Muskie School of Public Service, Program in Community Planning and Development, Portland, ME 04103. Offers MCPD, CGS, JD/MCPD. *Program availability:* Part-time, evening/ weekend. *Degree requirements:* For master's, thesis, capstone project, field experience. *Entrance requirements:* For master's, GRE General Test or LSAT. Additional exam requirements/recommendations for international students: Required—TOEFL. Electronic applications accepted. *Faculty research:* Urban and regional growth and change, sustainability, responses to climate and environmental risks, food systems planning and policy, transportation, energy, landscape modeling and simulation.

**University of South Florida,** College of Arts and Sciences, School of Geosciences, Tampa, FL 33620-9951. Offers environmental science and policy (MS); geography (MA), including environmental geography, geographic information science and spatial analysis, human geography; geography and environmental science and policy (PhD); geology (MS, PhD); urban and regional planning (MURP). *Program availability:* Part-time, evening/weekend. *Faculty:* 31 full-time (6 women). *Students:* 88 full-time (42 women), 44 part-time (17 women); includes 16 minority (7 Black or African American, non-Hispanic/Latino; 5 Asian, non-Hispanic/Latino; 3 Hispanic/Latino; 1 Two or more races, non-Hispanic/Latino), 34 international. Average age 32. 133 applicants, 51% accepted, 34 enrolled. In 2016, 28 master's, 7 doctorates awarded. *Degree requirements:* For master's, comprehensive exam, thesis (for some programs); for doctorate, comprehensive exam, thesis/dissertation. *Entrance requirements:* For master's, GRE General Test, minimum GPA of 3.0 for last 60 credits of undergraduate degree, letter of intent, letters of recommendation; for doctorate, GRE General Test, minimum GPA of 3.0 (for geology), 3.2 (for environmental science and policy and geography); letter of intent; letters of recommendation. Additional exam requirements/ recommendations for international students: Required—TOEFL (minimum score 550 paper-based; 79 iBT) or IELTS (minimum score 6.5) for MA and MURP; TOEFL (minimum score 600 paper-based) for MS and PhD. *Application deadline:* For fall admission, 2/15 for domestic and international students; for spring admission, 10/15 for domestic students, 9/15 for international students. Application fee: $30. Electronic applications accepted. *Expenses:* Tuition, state resident: full-time $7766; part-time $431.43 per credit hour. Tuition, nonresident: full-time $15,789; part-time $877.17 per credit hour. *Required fees:* $37 per term. *Financial support:* In 2016–17, 47 students received support, including 3 research assistantships (averaging $12,345 per year), 25 teaching assistantships with tuition reimbursements available (averaging $12,807 per year); unspecified assistantships also available. Financial award application deadline: 3/ 1. *Faculty research:* Geography: human geography, environmental geography, geographic information science and spatial analysis, urban geography, social theory; environmental science, policy, and planning: water resources, wildlife ecology, Karst and wetland environments, natural hazards, soil contamination, meteorology and climatology, environmental sustainability and policy, urban and regional planning. *Total annual research expenditures:* $3.3 million. *Unit head:* Dr. Jayajit Chakraborty, Professor and Chair, Geography Division, 813-974-8188, Fax: 813-974-5911, E-mail: jchakrab@usf.edu. *Application contact:* Dr. Jennifer Collins, Associate Professor and Graduate Program Coordinator, 813-974-4242, Fax: 813-974-5911, E-mail: collinsjm@usf.edu.
Website: http://hennarot.forest.usf.edu/main/depts/geosci/

**University of South Florida,** Innovative Education, Tampa, FL 33620-9951. Offers adult, career and higher education (Graduate Certificate), including college teaching, leadership in developing human resources, leadership in higher education; Africana studies (Graduate Certificate), including diasporas and health disparities, genocide and human rights; aging studies (Graduate Certificate), including gerontology; art research (Graduate Certificate), including museum studies; business foundations (Graduate Certificate); chemical and biomedical engineering (Graduate Certificate), including materials science and engineering, water, health and sustainability; child and family studies (Graduate Certificate), including positive behavior support; civil and industrial engineering (Graduate Certificate), including transportation systems analysis; community and family health (Graduate Certificate), including maternal and child health, social marketing and public health, violence and injury: prevention and intervention, women's health; criminology (Graduate Certificate), including criminal justice administration; educational measurement and research (Graduate Certificate), including evaluation; English (Graduate Certificate), including comparative literary studies, creative writing, professional and technical communication; entrepreneurship (Graduate Certificate); environmental health (Graduate Certificate), including safety management; epidemiology and biostatistics (Graduate Certificate), including applied biostatistics, biostatistics, concepts and tools of epidemiology, epidemiology, epidemiology of infectious diseases; geography, environment and planning (Graduate Certificate), including community development, environmental policy and management, geographical information systems; geology (Graduate Certificate), including hydrogeology; global health (Graduate Certificate), including disaster management, global health and Latin American and Caribbean studies, global health practice, humanitarian assistance, infection control; government and international affairs (Graduate Certificate), including Cuban studies, globalization studies; health policy and management (Graduate Certificate), including health management and leadership, public health policy and programs; hearing specialist: early intervention (Graduate Certificate); industrial and management systems engineering (Graduate Certificate), including systems engineering, technology management; information studies (Graduate Certificate), including school library media specialist; information systems/decision sciences (Graduate Certificate), including analytics and business intelligence; instructional technology (Graduate Certificate), including distance education, Florida digital/virtual educator, instructional design, multimedia design, Web design; internal medicine, bioethics and medical humanities (Graduate Certificate), including biomedical ethics; Latin American and Caribbean studies (Graduate Certificate); mass communications (Graduate Certificate), including multimedia journalism; mathematics and statistics (Graduate Certificate), including mathematics; medicine (Graduate Certificate), including aging and neuroscience, bioinformatics, biotechnology, brain fitness and memory management, clinical investigation, health informatics, health sciences, integrative weight management, intellectual property, medicine and gender, metabolic and nutritional medicine, metabolic cardiology, pharmacy sciences; national and competitive intelligence (Graduate Certificate); psychological and social foundations (Graduate Certificate), including career counseling, college teaching, diversity in education, mental health counseling, school counseling; public affairs (Graduate Certificate), including nonprofit management, public management, research administration; public health (Graduate Certificate), including environmental health, health equity, public health generalist, translational research in adolescent behavioral health; public health practices (Graduate Certificate), including planning for healthy communities; rehabilitation and mental health counseling (Graduate Certificate), including integrative mental health care, marriage and family therapy, rehabilitation technology; secondary education (Graduate Certificate), including ESOL, foreign language education; social work (Graduate Certificate), including culture and content, foreign language education: professional; social work (Graduate Certificate), including geriatric social work/clinical gerontology; special education (Graduate Certificate), including autism spectrum disorder, disabilities education: severe/profound; world languages (Graduate Certificate), including teaching English as a second language (TESL) or foreign language. *Expenses:* Tuition, state resident: full-time $7766; part-time $431.43 per credit hour. Tuition, nonresident: full-time $15,789; part-time $877.17 per credit hour. *Required fees:* $37 per term. *Unit head:* Kathy Barnes, Interdisciplinary Programs Coordinator, 813-974-8031, Fax: 813-974-7061, E-mail: barnesk@usf.edu. *Application contact:* Karen Tylinski, Metro Initiatives, 813-974-9943, Fax: 813-974-7061, E-mail: ktylinsk@usf.edu.
Website: http://www.usf.edu/innovative-education/

**The University of Texas at Arlington,** Graduate School, College of Architecture, Planning and Public Affairs, Program in Public and Urban Administration, Arlington, TX 76019. Offers PhD. *Program availability:* Part-time, evening/weekend. *Entrance*

*requirements:* Additional exam requirements/recommendations for international students: Required—TOEFL (minimum score 550 paper-based). *Application deadline:* For fall admission, 6/1 for domestic students, 4/1 for international students; for spring admission, 10/15 for domestic students. Application fee: $35 ($50 for international students). *Financial support:* Research assistantships and career-related internships or fieldwork available. Financial award application deadline: 6/1; financial award applicants required to submit FAFSA. *Faculty research:* Personnel, non-profit organizational change, welfare policy, urban research. *Unit head:* Dr. David Coursey, Program Director, 817-272-0416, Fax: 817-272-3415, E-mail: dcoursey@uta.edu. *Application contact:* Tangie Fields, Graduate Advisor, 817-272-3340, Fax: 817-272-3415, E-mail: nfields@uta.edu.
Website: http://www.uta.edu/supa

**The University of Texas at Arlington,** Graduate School, College of Architecture, Planning and Public Affairs, Program in Urban Planning and Public Policy, Arlington, TX 76019. Offers PhD. *Accreditation:* ACSP. *Program availability:* Part-time, evening/weekend. *Entrance requirements:* Additional exam requirements/recommendations for international students: Required—TOEFL (minimum score 550 paper-based). *Application deadline:* For fall admission, 6/1 for domestic students, 4/1 for international students; for spring admission, 10/15 for domestic students, 9/15 for international students. Applications are processed on a rolling basis. Application fee: $35 ($50 for international students). Electronic applications accepted. *Financial support:* Fellowships, research assistantships, and career-related internships or fieldwork available. Financial award application deadline: 6/1; financial award applicants required to submit FAFSA. *Faculty research:* Urban structure, GIS environmental resolutions, qualitative methods, planning history/theory. *Unit head:* Dr. Ivonne Audirac, Program Director, 817-272-3338, Fax: 817-272-5008, E-mail: audirac@uta.edu. *Application contact:* Christa Barreras, Academic Advisor, 817-272-5631, Fax: 817-272-5631, E-mail: christab@uta.edu.
Website: http://www.uta.edu/cappa/academics/planning-landscape-architecture/phd-uppp.php

**The University of Texas at Austin,** Graduate School, School of Architecture, Program in Community and Regional Planning, Austin, TX 78712-1111. Offers MSCRP, PhD, JD/MSCRP, MSCRP/MA. *Accreditation:* ACSP. *Degree requirements:* For master's, thesis; for doctorate, thesis/dissertation. *Entrance requirements:* For master's and doctorate, GRE General Test. Electronic applications accepted.

**The University of Texas at San Antonio,** College of Architecture, Program in Urban and Regional Planning, San Antonio, TX 78249-0617. Offers MS. *Program availability:* Part-time. *Faculty:* 2 full-time (1 woman), 2 part-time/adjunct (0 women). *Students:* 7 full-time (2 women), 13 part-time (6 women); includes 10 minority (2 Black or African American, non-Hispanic/Latino; 8 Hispanic/Latino), 2 international. Average age 33. 11 applicants, 45% accepted, 4 enrolled. In 2016, 13 master's awarded. *Entrance requirements:* For master's, GRE, transcripts, two letters of recommendation, letter of intent. Additional exam requirements/recommendations for international students: Required—TOEFL (minimum score 550 paper-based; 79 iBT), IELTS (minimum score 6.5). Application fee: $45 ($80 for international students). *Total annual research expenditures:* $140,273. *Unit head:* Dr. Richard Tangum, Program Coordinator, Department of Architecture, 210-458-3137, Fax: 210-458-3016, E-mail: richard.tangum@utsa.edu. *Application contact:* Dr. Hazem Rashed-Ali, Associate Dean, College of Architecture, 210-458-3088, Fax: 210-458-3088, E-mail: hazem.rashedali@utsa.edu.
Website: http://architecture.utsa.edu/academic-programs/urban-and-regional-planning/

**The University of Toledo,** College of Graduate Studies, College of Languages, Literature and Social Sciences, Department of Geography and Planning, Toledo, OH 43606-3390. Offers geographic information science and applied geographics (Certificate); geography and planning (MA); spatially-integrated social science (PhD). *Program availability:* Part-time. *Degree requirements:* For master's, comprehensive exam, thesis; for doctorate, thesis/dissertation. *Entrance requirements:* For master's and doctorate, GRE General Test, minimum cumulative point-hour ratio of 2.7 for all previous academic work, three letters of recommendation; for Certificate, minimum cumulative point-hour ratio of 2.7 for all previous academic work, three letters of recommendation. Additional exam requirements/recommendations for international students: Required—TOEFL (minimum score 550 paper-based; 80 iBT). Electronic applications accepted.

**University of Toronto,** School of Graduate Studies, Faculty of Arts and Science, Department of Geography, Program in Planning, Toronto, ON M5S 1A1, Canada. Offers M Sc Pl, MUDS, PhD. *Program availability:* Part-time. *Degree requirements:* For master's, summer internship. *Entrance requirements:* For master's, bachelor's degree in planning, geography, social science or a closely related professional field, minimum B+ average in final year, 3 letters of reference; for doctorate, minimum A- or equivalent standing in previous master's program. Additional exam requirements/recommendations for international students: Required—TOEFL (minimum score 580 paper-based; 93 iBT), TWE (minimum score 5). Electronic applications accepted. *Expenses:* Contact institution.

**University of Utah,** Graduate School, College of Architecture and Planning, Department of City and Metropolitan Planning, Salt Lake City, UT 84112. Offers city and metropolitan planning (MCMP), including ecological planning, small town and resort planning, smart growth and transportation, urban design; metropolitan planning, policy and design (PhD). *Program availability:* Part-time. *Faculty:* 7 full-time (3 women), 25 part-time/adjunct (9 women). *Students:* 42 full-time (21 women), 14 part-time (4 women); includes 9 minority (6 Asian, non-Hispanic/Latino; 1 Hispanic/Latino; 2 Two or more races, non-Hispanic/Latino), 11 international. Average age 30. 33 applicants, 100% accepted, 16 enrolled. In 2016, 15 master's, 3 doctorates awarded. *Degree requirements:* For master's, thesis or alternative, comprehensive project; for doctorate, thesis/dissertation. *Entrance requirements:* For master's, GRE, minimum undergraduate GPA of 3.0; for doctorate, GRE, minimum GPA of 3.5. Additional exam requirements/recommendations for international students: Required—TOEFL (minimum score 500 paper-based; 61 iBT); Recommended—IELTS (minimum score 6). *Application deadline:* For fall admission, 1/15 priority date for domestic and international students; for spring admission, 11/1 for domestic and international students. Applications are processed on a rolling basis. Application fee: $55 ($65 for international students). Electronic applications accepted. *Expenses:* Contact institution. *Financial support:* In 2016–17, 25 students received support, including 1 fellowship with full tuition reimbursement available (averaging $25,000 per year), 3 research assistantships with tuition reimbursements available (averaging $16,000 per year), 21 teaching assistantships with tuition reimbursements available (averaging $10,000 per year); career-related internships or fieldwork, Federal Work-Study, scholarships/grants, health care benefits, and unspecified assistantships also available. Financial award application deadline: 1/15; financial award applicants required to submit FAFSA. *Faculty research:* Transportation, land-use, smart growth, public health, climate change, urban design, sustainable communities, community-based decision-making process, urban morphology, theory and practice in scenario-planning techniques, community-engaged teaching methodologies, interactions between federal environmental policies and state/local community development patterns, values in architecture and planning practices.

*Total annual research expenditures:* $689,627. *Unit head:* Reid Ewing, Chair, 801-585-3745, Fax: 801-581-8217, E-mail: ewing@arch.utah.edu. *Application contact:* Saolo Utu, Recruitment and Admissions Advisor, 801-581-2361, Fax: 801-581-8217, E-mail: recruitment@arch.utah.edu.
Website: http://www.plan.utah.edu/

**University of Virginia,** School of Architecture, Department of Urban and Environmental Planning, Charlottesville, VA 22903. Offers MUEP, JD/MUEP, MPP/MUEP. *Accreditation:* ACSP (one or more programs are accredited). *Faculty:* 9 full-time (6 women). *Students:* 45 full-time (30 women), 2 part-time (0 women); includes 7 minority (4 Black or African American, non-Hispanic/Latino; 2 Asian, non-Hispanic/Latino; 1 Two or more races, non-Hispanic/Latino), 12 international. Average age 26. 89 applicants, 91% accepted, 30 enrolled. In 2016, 27 master's awarded. *Entrance requirements:* For master's, GRE General Test, previous course work in statistics, 3 letters of recommendation. Additional exam requirements/recommendations for international students: Required—TOEFL (minimum score 600 paper-based; 90 iBT). *Application deadline:* For fall admission, 1/15 for domestic students, 1/16 for international students. Applications are processed on a rolling basis. Application fee: $60. Electronic applications accepted. *Expenses:* Tuition, state resident: full-time $15,026; part-time $834 per credit hour. Tuition, nonresident: full-time $25,168; part-time $1378 per credit hour. *Required fees:* $2654. *Financial support:* Applicants required to submit FAFSA. *Faculty research:* Urban development, land use, environment, policy analysis, historic preservation. *Unit head:* Timothy Beatley, Chair, 434-924-6457, Fax: 434-982-2678, E-mail: tb6d@virginia.edu. *Application contact:* Kristine Nelson, Director of Admissions and Financial Aid, 434-924-6442, Fax: 434-982-2678, E-mail: arch-admissions@virginia.edu.
Website: http://www.arch.virginia.edu/academics/disciplines/planning

**University of Washington,** Graduate School, College of Built Environments, Department of Urban Design and Planning, Seattle, WA 98195. Offers urban design and planning (PhD); urban planning (MUP). *Accreditation:* ACSP (one or more programs are accredited). *Degree requirements:* For master's, thesis or alternative; for doctorate, thesis/dissertation. *Entrance requirements:* For master's and doctorate, GRE General Test, minimum GPA of 3.0. Additional exam requirements/recommendations for international students: Required—TOEFL. *Faculty research:* Land-use and growth management, urban form and travel behavior, geographic information systems/remote sensing, historic preservation, urban ecology and environmental planning.

**University of Waterloo,** Graduate Studies, Faculty of Environment, Program in Local Economic Development, Waterloo, ON N2L 3G1, Canada. Offers MAES. *Program availability:* Part-time. *Degree requirements:* For master's, internship, research paper. *Entrance requirements:* Additional exam requirements/recommendations for international students: Required—TOEFL, IELTS, PTE. Electronic applications accepted.

**University of Waterloo,** Graduate Studies, Faculty of Environment, School of Planning, Waterloo, ON N2L 3G1, Canada. Offers M Plan, MA, MAES, MES, PhD. *Program availability:* Part-time. *Degree requirements:* For master's, thesis (for some programs); for doctorate, comprehensive exam, thesis/dissertation. *Entrance requirements:* For master's, honors degree, minimum B+ average; for doctorate, master's degree, minimum A- average, resume. Additional exam requirements/recommendations for international students: Required—TOEFL, IELTS, PTE. Electronic applications accepted. *Faculty research:* Environmental planning, planning for resource development, urban planning and information systems, social planning, urban design.

**University of West Georgia,** College of Social Sciences, Carrollton, GA 30118. Offers criminology (MA); data analysis and evaluation methods (Postbaccalaureate Certificate); European Union studies (Postbaccalaureate Certificate); integrative health systems (Postbaccalaureate Certificate); nonprofit management and community development (Postbaccalaureate Certificate); psychology (MA, PhD), including consciousness and society (PhD); public administration (MPA); public management (Postbaccalaureate Certificate); sociology (MA). *Program availability:* Part-time, evening/weekend, 100% online, blended/hybrid learning. *Faculty:* 45 full-time (21 women). *Students:* 107 full-time (67 women), 73 part-time (46 women); includes 47 minority (39 Black or African American, non-Hispanic/Latino; 4 Asian, non-Hispanic/Latino; 4 Hispanic/Latino), 10 international. Average age 31. 83 applicants, 88% accepted, 60 enrolled. In 2016, 56 master's, 7 doctorates, 5 other advanced degrees awarded. *Entrance requirements:* Additional exam requirements/recommendations for international students: Required—TOEFL (minimum score 523 paper-based; 69 iBT); Recommended—IELTS (minimum score 6.5). *Application deadline:* For fall admission, 7/15 for domestic students, 6/1 for international students; for spring admission, 11/30 for domestic students, 10/15 for international students; for summer admission, 5/15 for domestic students, 3/30 for international students. Applications are processed on a rolling basis. Application fee: $40. Electronic applications accepted. *Expenses:* Tuition, state resident: full-time $5316; part-time $222 per semester hour. Tuition, nonresident: full-time $20,658; part-time $861 per semester hour. *Required fees:* $1962. Tuition and fees vary according to course load, degree level and program. *Financial support:* Fellowships, research assistantships, teaching assistantships, career-related internships or fieldwork, Federal Work-Study, institutionally sponsored loans, scholarships/grants, and unspecified assistantships available. Support available to part-time students. Financial award application deadline: 4/1; financial award applicants required to submit FAFSA. *Unit head:* Dr. N. Jane McCandless, Dean of Social Sciences, 678-839-5170, Fax: 678-839-5171, E-mail: jmccandl@westga.edu. *Application contact:* Dr. Toby Ziglar, Assistant Dean of the Graduate School, 678-839-1394, Fax: 678-839-1395, E-mail: graduate@westga.edu.
Website: https://www.westga.edu/coss

**University of Wisconsin–Madison,** Graduate School, College of Letters and Science and College of Agricultural and Life Sciences, Department of Urban and Regional Planning, Madison, WI 53706-1380. Offers MS, PhD. *Accreditation:* ACSP (one or more programs are accredited). *Program availability:* Part-time. *Degree requirements:* For master's, thesis optional, internship; for doctorate, thesis/dissertation, 3 preliminary exams. *Entrance requirements:* For master's, GRE, minimum GPA of 3.0, previous course work in statistics; for doctorate, 1 year of experience, master's degree in related field. Electronic applications accepted. *Faculty research:* Land use, environmental planning, community development, economic development planning.

**University of Wisconsin–Milwaukee,** Graduate School, School of Architecture and Urban Planning, Department of Urban Planning, Milwaukee, WI 53201-0413. Offers MUP. *Accreditation:* ACSP. *Program availability:* Part-time. *Students:* 14 full-time (5 women), 4 part-time (1 woman); includes 3 minority (1 Hispanic/Latino; 2 Two or more races, non-Hispanic/Latino), 1 international. Average age 29. 22 applicants, 73% accepted, 3 enrolled. In 2016, 29 master's awarded. *Degree requirements:* For master's, comprehensive exam, thesis or alternative. *Entrance requirements:* For master's, GRE General Test. Additional exam requirements/recommendations for international students: Required—TOEFL (minimum score 550 paper-based; 79 iBT), IELTS (minimum score 6.5). *Application deadline:* For fall admission, 1/1 priority date for domestic students; for spring admission, 9/1 for domestic students. Applications are processed on a rolling basis. Application fee: $56 ($96 for international students). Electronic applications accepted. *Financial support:* Fellowships, research

assistantships, teaching assistantships, career-related internships or fieldwork, health care benefits, and unspecified assistantships available. Support available to part-time students. Financial award application deadline: 4/15; financial award applicants required to submit FAFSA. *Unit head:* Robert Greenstreet. *Application contact:* Student Advising Office, 414-229-4015, E-mail: sarup-grad@uwm.edu.
Website: https://uwm.edu/sarup/urban-planning/

**Utah State University,** School of Graduate Studies, College of Humanities, Arts and Social Sciences, Department of Landscape Architecture and Environmental Planning, Logan, UT 84322. Offers bioregional planning (MS); landscape architecture (MLA). *Accreditation:* ASLA (one or more programs are accredited). *Degree requirements:* For master's, thesis. *Entrance requirements:* For master's, GRE General Test, minimum GPA of 3.0. Additional exam requirements/recommendations for international students: Required—TOEFL. *Faculty research:* Visual resource management, planning for wildlife, agricultural land preservation, watershed planning, community planning and design.

**Utah State University,** School of Graduate Studies, College of Natural Resources, Department of Environment and Society, Logan, UT 84322. Offers bioregional planning (MS); geography (MA, MS); human dimensions of ecosystem science and management (MS, PhD); recreation resource management (MS, PhD). *Degree requirements:* For master's, comprehensive exam, thesis (for some programs). *Entrance requirements:* For master's and doctorate, GRE General Test, minimum GPA of 3.0. Additional exam requirements/recommendations for international students: Required—TOEFL. Electronic applications accepted. *Faculty research:* Geographic information systems/geographic and environmental education, bioregional planning, natural resource and environmental policy, outdoor recreation and tourism, natural resource and environmental management.

**Vanderbilt University,** Peabody College, Department of Human and Organizational Development, Nashville, TN 37240-1001. Offers community development and action (M Ed); human development counseling (M Ed). *Accreditation:* ACA; NCATE. *Program availability:* Part-time. *Faculty:* 30 full-time (18 women), 38 part-time/adjunct (26 women). *Students:* 113 full-time (94 women), 12 part-time (10 women); includes 19 minority (7 Black or African American, non-Hispanic/Latino; 2 Asian, non-Hispanic/Latino; 6 Hispanic/Latino; 4 Two or more races, non-Hispanic/Latino), 5 international. Average age 25. 217 applicants, 48% accepted, 53 enrolled. In 2016, 60 master's awarded. *Degree requirements:* For master's, comprehensive exam, thesis optional. *Entrance requirements:* For master's, GRE General Test, MAT. Additional exam requirements/recommendations for international students: Required—TOEFL (minimum score 550 paper-based; 80 iBT). *Application deadline:* For fall admission, 12/31 priority date for domestic and international students; for spring admission, 11/1 priority date for domestic and international students. Applications are processed on a rolling basis. Application fee: $0. Electronic applications accepted. *Expenses:* Tuition: Part-time $1854 per credit hour. *Financial support:* Fellowships with partial tuition reimbursements, research assistantships with partial tuition reimbursements, teaching assistantships with partial tuition reimbursements, Federal Work-Study, institutionally sponsored loans, scholarships/grants, tuition waivers (partial), and unspecified assistantships available. Support available to part-time students. Financial award application deadline: 1/15; financial award applicants required to submit FAFSA. *Faculty research:* Community psychology and community development; counseling and mental health services, prevention and positive youth development; organizational and community change; youth physical and behavioral health in schools and communities. *Unit head:* Dr. Paul Speer, Chair, 615-322-6881, Fax: 615-322-1141, E-mail: paul.w.speer@vanderbilt.edu. *Application contact:* Sherrie Lane, Educational Coordinator, 615-322-8484, Fax: 615-322-1141, E-mail: sherrie.a.lane@vanderbilt.edu.

**Virginia Commonwealth University,** Graduate School, College of Humanities and Sciences, L. Douglas Wilder School of Government and Public Affairs, Department of Urban Studies and Planning, Program in Urban and Regional Planning, Richmond, VA 23284-9005. Offers urban and regional planning (MURP). *Degree requirements:* For master's, thesis optional, internship. *Entrance requirements:* For master's, GRE General Test, GMAT, or LSAT, minimum GPA of 2.7. Additional exam requirements/recommendations for international students: Required—TOEFL (minimum score 600 paper-based; 100 iBT); Recommended—IELTS (minimum score 6.5). *Application deadline:* For fall admission, 4/1 for domestic students; for spring admission, 10/1 for domestic students. Applications are processed on a rolling basis. Application fee: $50. Electronic applications accepted. *Unit head:* Dr. Meghan Z. Gough, Program Director, 804-827-0869, E-mail: mzgough@vcu.edu. *Application contact:* Dr. Richard R. Huff, Director of Graduate Advising, 804-827-1430, E-mail: rrhuff@vcu.edu.
Website: http://www.wilder.vcu.edu/academic/urban/index.html

**Virginia Polytechnic Institute and State University,** Graduate School, College of Architecture and Urban Studies, Blacksburg, VA 24061. Offers architecture (MS Arch); architecture and design research (PhD); building/construction science and management (MS); creative technologies (MFA); environmental design and planning (PhD); landscape architecture (MLA); planning, governance, and globalization (PhD); public administration (MPA); public administration/public affairs (PhD, Certificate); public and international affairs (MPIA); urban and regional planning (MURP). *Accreditation:* ASLA (one or more programs are accredited). *Faculty:* 136 full-time (53 women). *Students:* 371 full-time (185 women), 210 part-time (104 women); includes 118 minority (49 Black or African American, non-Hispanic/Latino; 1 American Indian or Alaska Native, non-Hispanic/Latino; 30 Asian, non-Hispanic/Latino; 32 Hispanic/Latino; 6 Two or more races, non-Hispanic/Latino), 137 international. Average age 31. 566 applicants, 55% accepted, 160 enrolled. In 2016, 137 master's, 24 doctorates awarded. *Degree requirements:* For master's, comprehensive exam (for some programs), thesis (for some programs); for doctorate, comprehensive exam (for some programs), thesis/dissertation (for some programs). *Entrance requirements:* For master's and doctorate, GRE/GMAT. Additional exam requirements/recommendations for international students: Required—TOEFL (minimum score 80 iBT). *Application deadline:* For fall admission, 8/1 for domestic students, 4/1 for international students; for spring admission, 1/1 for domestic students, 9/1 for international students. Applications are processed on a rolling basis. Application fee: $75. Electronic applications accepted. *Expenses:* Tuition, state resident: full-time $12,467; part-time $692.50 per credit hour. Tuition, nonresident: full-

time $25,095; part-time $1394.25 per credit hour. *Required fees:* $2669; $491.50 per semester. Tuition and fees vary according to course load, campus/location and program. *Financial support:* In 2016–17, 11 research assistantships with full tuition reimbursements (averaging $19,474 per year), 45 teaching assistantships with full tuition reimbursements (averaging $16,014 per year) were awarded. Financial award application deadline: 3/1; financial award applicants required to submit FAFSA. *Total annual research expenditures:* $3.6 million. *Unit head:* Dr. A. J. Davis, Dean, 540-231-6416, Fax: 540-231-6332, E-mail: davisa@vt.edu. *Application contact:* Christine Mattsson-Coon, Executive Assistant, 540-231-6416, Fax: 540-231-6332, E-mail: cmattsso@vt.edu.
Website: http://www.caus.vt.edu/

**Wayne State University,** College of Liberal Arts and Sciences, Department of Urban Studies and Planning, Detroit, MI 48202. Offers economic development (Graduate Certificate); urban studies and planning (MUP). *Accreditation:* ACSP. *Program availability:* Evening/weekend. *Students:* 17 full-time (7 women), 41 part-time (25 women); includes 23 minority (16 Black or African American, non-Hispanic/Latino; 1 Asian, non-Hispanic/Latino; 3 Hispanic/Latino; 3 Two or more races, non-Hispanic/Latino), 2 international. Average age 29. 67 applicants, 51% accepted, 22 enrolled. In 2016, 15 master's awarded. *Degree requirements:* For master's, thesis or essay. *Entrance requirements:* For degree, graduate degree or actively pursuing a graduate degree at WSU; personal statement of interest. Additional exam requirements/recommendations for international students: Required—TOEFL (minimum score 550 paper-based; 79 iBT), TWE (minimum score 5.5), Michigan English Language Assessment Battery (minimum score 85); Recommended—IELTS (minimum score 6.5). *Application deadline:* For fall admission, 6/1 priority date for domestic students, 5/1 priority date for international students; for winter admission, 10/1 priority date for domestic students, 9/1 priority date for international students; for spring admission, 2/1 priority date for domestic students, 1/1 priority date for international students. Applications are processed on a rolling basis. Application fee: $50. Electronic applications accepted. *Expenses:* $16,503 per year resident tuition and fees, $33,697 per year non-resident tuition and fees. *Financial support:* In 2016–17, 14 students received support, including 2 research assistantships (averaging $14,244 per year); scholarships/grants and unspecified assistantships also available. Financial award applicants required to submit FAFSA. *Faculty research:* Community development, economic development, environmental planning, housing policy, land use planning and policy, local fiscal policy, local planning practices, neighborhood change, sustainable food systems. *Unit head:* Dr. Kami Pothukuchi, Associate Professor and Chair, 313-577-4296, E-mail: k.pothukuchi@wayne.edu. *Application contact:* E-mail: dusp@wayne.edu.
Website: http://clas.wayne.edu/dusp/

**West Chester University of Pennsylvania,** College of Business and Public Management, Department of Geography and Planning, West Chester, PA 19383. Offers geographic information systems (Certificate); geography (MS); geography and planning (MURP); urban and regional planning (MPA, Certificate). *Program availability:* Part-time, evening/weekend. *Faculty:* 5 full-time (2 women). *Students:* 8 full-time (4 women), 13 part-time (5 women); includes 2 minority (both Black or African American, non-Hispanic/Latino), 2 international. Average age 32. 14 applicants, 100% accepted, 8 enrolled. In 2016, 8 master's, 1 other advanced degree awarded. *Degree requirements:* For master's, thesis optional, 48 credits: 27 credits required, 21 credits electives (for MURP); 33 credits or 11 courses (for MS); for Certificate, 12 credits or 4 courses (for geographic information systems); 18 credits or 6 courses (for urban and regional planning). *Entrance requirements:* For master's and Certificate, minimum GPA of 2.8, resume, two letters of recommendation. Additional exam requirements/recommendations for international students: Required—TOEFL or IELTS. *Application deadline:* For fall admission, 5/15 for international students; for spring admission, 10/15 for international students. Applications are processed on a rolling basis. Application fee: $50. Electronic applications accepted. *Expenses:* Tuition, state resident: full-time $8694; part-time $483 per credit. Tuition, nonresident: full-time $13,050; part-time $725 per credit. *Required fees:* $2399; $119.05 per credit. Tuition and fees vary according to campus/location and program. *Financial support:* Scholarships/grants and unspecified assistantships available. Financial award application deadline: 2/15; financial award applicants required to submit FAFSA. *Faculty research:* Sustainability and environmental conservation, land use/suburban planning, geographic information systems, transportation planning, housing, economic development. *Unit head:* Dr. Dottie Ives Dewey, Chair/Graduate Coordinator for GIS Certificate Program, 610-436-2746, Fax: 610-436-2889, E-mail: divesdewey@wcupa.edu. *Application contact:* Dr. Matin Katirai, Graduate Coordinator, 610-436-2392, Fax: 610-436-2889, E-mail: mkatirai@wcupa.edu.
Website: http://www.wcupa.edu/business-publicManagement/geographyPlanning/

**West Virginia University,** Davis College of Agriculture, Forestry and Consumer Sciences, Division of Resource Management and Sustainable Development, Morgantown, WV 26506. Offers agricultural and extension education (MS, PhD), including agricultural and extension education, teaching vocational-agriculture (MS); agricultural and resource economics (MS); human and community development (PhD); natural resource economics (PhD); resource management (PhD); resource management and sustainable development (PhD). *Program availability:* Part-time. *Degree requirements:* For master's, thesis; for doctorate, comprehensive exam, thesis/dissertation. *Entrance requirements:* For master's, GRE General Test. Additional exam requirements/recommendations for international students: Required—TOEFL. *Faculty research:* Environmental economics, energy economics, agriculture.

**West Virginia University,** Eberly College of Arts and Sciences, Department of Geology and Geography, Program in Geography, Morgantown, WV 26506. Offers energy and environmental resources (MA); geographic information systems (PhD); geography-regional development (PhD); GIS/cartographic analysis (MA); regional development (MA). *Program availability:* Part-time. *Degree requirements:* For master's, thesis, oral and written exams; for doctorate, comprehensive exam, thesis/dissertation, oral and written exams. *Entrance requirements:* For master's and doctorate, GRE General Test, minimum GPA of 3.0. Additional exam requirements/recommendations for international students: Required—TOEFL. Electronic applications accepted. *Faculty research:* Space, place and development, geographic information science, environmental geography.

# Urban Studies

---

**Arizona State University at the Tempe campus,** College of Liberal Arts and Sciences, School of Human Evolution and Social Change, Tempe, AZ 85287-2402. Offers anthropology (MA, PhD), including anthropology (PhD), archaeology (PhD), bioarchaeology (PhD), evolutionary (PhD), museum studies (MA), sociocultural (PhD);

applied mathematics for the life and social sciences (PhD); environmental social science (PhD), including environmental social science, urbanism; global health (MA, PhD), including complex adaptive systems science (PhD), evolutionary global health sciences (PhD), health and culture (PhD), urbanism (PhD); immigration studies (Graduate

Certificate). Terminal master's awarded for partial completion of doctoral program. *Degree requirements:* For master's, thesis or alternative, interactive Program of Study (iPOS) submitted before completing 50 percent of required credit hours; for doctorate, comprehensive exam, thesis/dissertation, interactive Program of Study (iPOS) submitted before completing 50 percent of required credit hours. *Entrance requirements:* For master's and doctorate, GRE, minimum GPA of 3.0 or equivalent in last 2 years of work leading to bachelor's degree. Additional exam requirements/recommendations for international students: Required—TOEFL, IELTS, or PTE. Electronic applications accepted.

**Azusa Pacific University,** Haggard Graduate School of Theology, Program in Pastoral Studies, Concentration in Urban Studies, Azusa, CA 91702-7000. Offers MAPS.

**Boston University,** Metropolitan College, Program in Urban Affairs, Boston, MA 02215. Offers MUA. *Program availability:* Part-time, evening/weekend. *Faculty:* 2 full-time (1 woman), 6 part-time/adjunct (2 women). *Students:* 5 full-time (1 woman), 36 part-time (18 women); includes 18 minority (10 Black or African American, non-Hispanic/Latino; 2 Asian, non-Hispanic/Latino; 6 Hispanic/Latino), 5 international. Average age 32. 9 applicants, 89% accepted, 5 enrolled. In 2016, 8 master's awarded. *Degree requirements:* For master's, thesis optional. *Entrance requirements:* Additional exam requirements/recommendations for international students: Required—TOEFL. *Application deadline:* For fall admission, 7/15 priority date for domestic and international students; for spring admission, 12/15 for domestic students, 11/15 priority date for international students. Applications are processed on a rolling basis. Application fee: $85. Electronic applications accepted. *Expenses:* Contact institution. *Financial support:* In 2016–17, 4 research assistantships (averaging $4,200 per year) were awarded; career-related internships or fieldwork, Federal Work-Study, and unspecified assistantships also available. Support available to part-time students. Financial award applicants required to submit FAFSA. *Faculty research:* Housing, community development and land use planning, environmental management and planning, international comparative development planning, sustainability. *Unit head:* Dr. Daniel P. LeClair, Chair, 617-353-3025, Fax: 617-358-3595, E-mail: dleclair@bu.edu. *Application contact:* Dr. Madhu Dutta-Koehler, 617-358-2364, E-mail: duttam@bu.edu.

**Brooklyn College of the City University of New York,** School of Humanities and Social Sciences, Department of Political Science, Brooklyn, NY 11210-2889. Offers international affairs (MA); political science (MA); urban policy and administration (MA). *Program availability:* Part-time, evening/weekend. *Degree requirements:* For master's, comprehensive exam (for some programs), thesis or alternative, foreign language exam (for international affairs program). *Entrance requirements:* For master's, 2 letters of recommendation, personal statement. Additional exam requirements/recommendations for international students: Required—TOEFL (minimum score 500 paper-based; 61 iBT). *Faculty research:* Ethics and politics, politics of criminal justice, Western Europe, international law and politics, labor politics.

**Cleveland State University,** College of Graduate Studies, Maxine Goodman Levin College of Urban Affairs, Program in Urban Studies, Cleveland, OH 44115. Offers MS, Certificate. *Program availability:* Part-time, evening/weekend. *Faculty:* 23 full-time (11 women), 23 part-time/adjunct (6 women). *Students:* 3 full-time (1 woman), 8 part-time (3 women), 1 international. Average age 27. 21 applicants, 29% accepted, 4 enrolled. In 2016, 7 master's awarded. *Degree requirements:* For master's, thesis or alternative, exit project. *Entrance requirements:* For master's, GRE General Test (minimum score: verbal and quantitative combined 40th percentile, analytical writing 4.0), minimum GPA of 3.0. Additional exam requirements/recommendations for international students: Required—TOEFL (minimum score 550 paper-based; 78 iBT), IELTS (6.0), or International Test of English Proficiency (iTEP). *Application deadline:* For fall admission, 7/1 priority date for domestic students, 5/15 for international students; for spring admission, 11/15 for domestic students, 11/1 for international students; for summer admission, 4/1 for domestic students, 3/15 for international students. Applications are processed on a rolling basis. Application fee: $40. Electronic applications accepted. *Expenses:* Contact institution. *Financial support:* In 2016–17, 4 students received support, including 4 research assistantships with full tuition reimbursements available (averaging $7,200 per year), 2 teaching assistantships with tuition reimbursements available (averaging $4,800 per year); scholarships/grants, tuition waivers (full and partial), and unspecified assistantships also available. Support available to part-time students. Financial award application deadline: 3/1; financial award applicants required to submit FAFSA. *Faculty research:* Environmental issues, economic development, urban and public policy, public management, community and neighborhood development. *Unit head:* Dr. Brian Mikelbank, Associate Professor/Program Director, 216-875-9980, Fax: 216-687-9342, E-mail: b.mikelbank@csuohio.edu. *Application contact:* David Arrighi, Graduate Academic Advisor, 216-523-7522, Fax: 216-687-5398, E-mail: d.arrighi@csuohio.edu.
Website: http://urban.csuohio.edu/academics/graduate/msus/

**Cleveland State University,** College of Graduate Studies, Maxine Goodman Levin College of Urban Affairs, Program in Urban Studies and Public Affairs, Cleveland, OH 44115. Offers communication (PhD); public administration (PhD); urban policy and development (PhD). *Program availability:* Part-time, evening/weekend. *Faculty:* 16 full-time (8 women), 13 part-time/adjunct (5 women). *Students:* 8 full-time (6 women), 17 part-time (8 women); includes 5 minority (3 Black or African American, non-Hispanic/Latino; 1 Hispanic/Latino; 1 Two or more races, non-Hispanic/Latino), 6 international. Average age 43. 32 applicants, 34% accepted, 2 enrolled. In 2016, 4 doctorates awarded. *Degree requirements:* For doctorate, comprehensive exam, thesis/dissertation. *Entrance requirements:* For doctorate, GRE General Test (minimum score: verbal and quantitative 50th percentile, analytical writing 4.0), minimum GPA of 3.5. Additional exam requirements/recommendations for international students: Required—TOEFL (minimum score 550 paper-based; 78 iBT), IELTS (6.0), or International Test of English Proficiency (iTEP). *Application deadline:* For fall admission, 1/31 for domestic and international students. Application fee: $40. Electronic applications accepted. *Expenses:* Contact institution. *Financial support:* In 2016–17, 15 students received support, including 5 research assistantships with full tuition reimbursements available (averaging $11,800 per year), 1 teaching assistantship with full tuition reimbursement available (averaging $11,800 per year); scholarships/grants, tuition waivers (full and partial), and unspecified assistantships also available. Support available to part-time students. Financial award application deadline: 3/1; financial award applicants required to submit FAFSA. *Faculty research:* Urban and public policy, public affairs. *Unit head:* Dr. Bill Bowen, Professor/PhD Program Director, 216-687-9226, E-mail: w.bowen@csuohio.edu. *Application contact:* David Arrighi, Graduate Academic Advisor, 216-523-7522, Fax: 216-687-5398, E-mail: d.arrighi@csuohio.edu.
Website: http://urban.csuohio.edu/academics/graduate/phd/

**Columbus State University,** Graduate Studies, College of Letters and Sciences, Department of Political Science and Public Administration, Columbus, GA 31907-5645. Offers public administration (MPA), including criminal justice, environmental policy, government administration, health services administration, political campaigning, urban policy. *Program availability:* Part-time, evening/weekend, 100% online, blended/hybrid learning. *Faculty:* 5 full-time (0 women), 5 part-time/adjunct (0 women). *Students:* 38 full-time (22 women), 61 part-time (25 women); includes 52 minority (40 Black or African American, non-Hispanic/Latino; 2 American Indian or Alaska Native, non-Hispanic/

Latino; 4 Asian, non-Hispanic/Latino; 4 Hispanic/Latino; 1 Native Hawaiian or other Pacific Islander, non-Hispanic/Latino; 1 Two or more races, non-Hispanic/Latino), 2 international. Average age 36. 69 applicants, 49% accepted, 27 enrolled. In 2016, 55 master's awarded. *Degree requirements:* For master's, comprehensive exam. *Entrance requirements:* For master's, GRE General Test, minimum GPA of 2.75, three letters of recommendation. Additional exam requirements/recommendations for international students: Required—TOEFL (minimum score 550 paper-based; 79 iBT). *Application deadline:* For fall admission, 6/30 for domestic students, 5/1 for international students; for spring admission, 11/1 for domestic and international students; for summer admission, 3/1 for domestic and international students. Applications are processed on a rolling basis. Application fee: $50. Electronic applications accepted. *Expenses:* Tuition, state resident: full-time $4804; part-time $2412 per semester hour. Tuition, nonresident: full-time $19,218; part-time $9612 per semester hour. *Required fees:* $1850; $1850 per semester hour. Tuition and fees vary according to program. *Financial support:* In 2016–17, 5 students received support, including 11 research assistantships with partial tuition reimbursements available (averaging $3,000 per year); career-related internships or fieldwork, Federal Work-Study, institutionally sponsored loans, scholarships/grants, tuition waivers (partial), and unspecified assistantships also available. Support available to part-time students. Financial award application deadline: 5/1; financial award applicants required to submit FAFSA. *Unit head:* Dr. Frederick Gordon, Director, 706-565-7875, E-mail: gordon_frederick@colstate.edu. *Application contact:* Kristin Williams, Director of International and Graduate Recruitment, 706-507-8848, Fax: 706-568-5091, E-mail: williams_kristin@columbusstate.edu.
Website: http://politicalscience.columbusstate.edu/

**Concordia University,** School of Graduate Studies, Faculty of Arts and Science, Department of Geography, Planning and Environment, Montréal, QC H3G 1M8, Canada. Offers environmental assessment (M Env, Diploma); geography, urban and environmental studies (M Sc, PhD).

**Eastern University,** Department of Urban Studies, St. Davids, PA 19087-3696. Offers urban studies (MA), including community development, juvenile justice ministry, youth leadership. *Program availability:* Part-time, evening/weekend, online learning. *Students:* 8 full-time (all women), 32 part-time (27 women); includes 21 minority (16 Black or African American, non-Hispanic/Latino; 1 Asian, non-Hispanic/Latino; 3 Hispanic/Latino; 1 Two or more races, non-Hispanic/Latino), 2 international. Average age 33. In 2016, 12 master's awarded. *Entrance requirements:* Additional exam requirements/recommendations for international students: Required—TOEFL (minimum score 550 paper-based; 79 iBT). *Application deadline:* Applications are processed on a rolling basis. Application fee: $35. Electronic applications accepted. Application fee is waived when completed online. *Expenses:* $690 per credit. *Financial support:* Applicants required to submit FAFSA. *Unit head:* Michael Dziedziak, Executive Director of Enrollment, 800-452-0996, E-mail: gpsadmissions@eastern.edu.
Website: http://www.eastern.edu/academics/programs/urban-studies-department

**Fordham University,** Graduate School of Arts and Sciences, Program in Urban Studies, New York, NY 10458. Offers MA. *Students:* 7 full-time (1 woman), 9 part-time (3 women); includes 5 minority (4 Black or African American, non-Hispanic/Latino; 1 Asian, non-Hispanic/Latino), 5 international. Average age 28. 49 applicants, 51% accepted, 10 enrolled. In 2016, 1 master's awarded. *Degree requirements:* For master's, internship or field work, research project. Application fee: $70. *Financial support:* Tuition waivers (partial) available. *Unit head:* Dr. Annika Hinze, Director, 718-817-3960, E-mail: rwakeman@fordham.edu. *Application contact:* Bernadette Valentino-Morrison, Director of Graduate Admissions, 718-817-4419, Fax: 718-817-3566, E-mail: valentinomor@fordham.edu.

**Fresno Pacific University,** Biblical Seminary, Program in Community Leadership and Transformation, Fresno, CA 93702-4709. Offers MA. Program offered in partnership with the Center for Community Transformation (CCT). *Entrance requirements:* For master's, bachelor's degree, minimum GPA of 2.5, personal profile statement, three letters of references, writing sample.

**The Graduate Center, City University of New York,** Graduate Studies, Interdisciplinary Studies, New York, NY 10016-4039. Offers language in social context (PhD); medieval studies (PhD); public policy (MA, PhD); urban studies (MA, PhD); women's studies (MA, PhD). Terminal master's awarded for partial completion of doctoral program. *Degree requirements:* For master's, thesis; for doctorate, comprehensive exam, thesis/dissertation. *Entrance requirements:* For master's and doctorate, GRE General Test.

**Hunter College of the City University of New York,** Graduate School, School of Arts and Sciences, Department of Urban Affairs and Planning, Program in Urban Affairs, New York, NY 10065-5085. Offers MS. *Program availability:* Part-time. *Students:* 19 part-time (14 women); includes 7 minority (3 Black or African American, non-Hispanic/Latino; 4 Hispanic/Latino), 1 international. Average age 34. In 2016, 13 master's awarded. *Degree requirements:* For master's, thesis or alternative, 2 formal reports, internship. *Entrance requirements:* For master's, minimum 12 credits of course work in social sciences. Additional exam requirements/recommendations for international students: Required—TOEFL. *Application deadline:* For fall admission, 4/1 priority date for domestic students, 2/1 for international students; for spring admission, 11/1 priority date for domestic students, 9/1 for international students. Applications are processed on a rolling basis. *Financial support:* Fellowships, research assistantships, teaching assistantships, career-related internships or fieldwork, Federal Work-Study, scholarships/grants, and unspecified assistantships available. *Faculty research:* Women, tourism, youth, immigration, employment. *Unit head:* Dr. Owen D. Gutfreund, Director, 212-396-6248, E-mail: owen.gutfreund@hunter.cuny.edu. *Application contact:* Milena Solo, Director for Graduate Admissions, 212-772-4480, E-mail: admissions@hunter.cuny.edu.

**Indiana University Northwest,** College of Arts and Sciences, Gary, IN 46408. Offers clinical counseling (MS), including drug and alcohol counseling; community development/urban studies (Graduate Certificate); computer information systems (Graduate Certificate); liberal studies (MLS); race-ethnic studies (Graduate Certificate); women's and gender studies (Graduate Certificate). *Program availability:* Part-time, evening/weekend. *Students:* 4 full-time (all women), 18 part-time (10 women); includes 10 minority (9 Black or African American, non-Hispanic/Latino; 1 Hispanic/Latino). Average age 39. 22 applicants, 77% accepted, 13 enrolled. In 2016, 6 master's awarded. *Entrance requirements:* For master's, GRE (recommended for MS), minimum undergraduate GPA of 3.0, bachelor's degree from accredited university (for MS). *Application deadline:* For fall admission, 7/1 priority date for domestic and international students; for spring admission, 12/1 priority date for domestic and international students. Application fee: $40 ($60 for international students). Electronic applications accepted. *Expenses:* $276.98 per credit hour in-state; $652.54 per credit hour out-of-state. *Financial support:* Applicants required to submit FAFSA. *Unit head:* Mark Hoyert, Dean, E-mail: mhoyert@iun.edu. Website: http://www.iun.edu/coas/

**Le Moyne College,** Department of Education, Syracuse, NY 13214. Offers adolescent education (MS Ed, MST); adolescent education/special education (MS Ed, MST); adolescent English (MST), including grades 7-12; adolescent English/special education (MST), including grades 7-12; adolescent foreign language (MST), including grades 7-

## Urban Studies

12; adolescent history (MST), including grades 7-12; childhood education (MS Ed); childhood education/special education (MS Ed); elementary education (MS Ed); general education (MS Ed); inclusive childhood education (MST); literacy education (MS Ed), including birth to grade 6, grades 5-12; school building leader (MS Ed); school building leadership (CAS); school district business leader (MS Ed, CAS); school district leader (MS Ed); school district leadership (CAS); secondary education (MS Ed); special education (MS Ed); teaching English to speakers of other languages (MS Ed); urban studies (MS Ed). *Accreditation:* TEAC. *Program availability:* Part-time, evening/weekend. *Faculty:* 8 full-time (5 women), 20 part-time/adjunct (12 women). *Students:* 66 full-time (40 women), 155 part-time (117 women); includes 13 minority (4 Black or African American, non-Hispanic/Latino; 2 American Indian or Alaska Native, non-Hispanic/Latino; 2 Asian, non-Hispanic/Latino; 5 Hispanic/Latino), 3 international. Average age 30. 74 applicants, 99% accepted, 66 enrolled. In 2016, 81 master's, 53 CASs awarded. *Degree requirements:* For master's, thesis. *Entrance requirements:* For master's, bachelor's degree with minimum undergraduate GPA of 3.0, 2 letters of recommendation, transcripts. Additional exam requirements/recommendations for international students: Required—TOEFL (minimum score 550 paper-based; 79 iBT); Recommended—IELTS (minimum score 6.5). *Application deadline:* For fall admission, 4/1 priority date for domestic and international students; for spring admission, 10/1 priority date for domestic and international students; for summer admission, 3/1 priority date for domestic and international students. Applications are processed on a rolling basis. Application fee: $50. Electronic applications accepted. *Expenses:* $700 per credit hour. *Financial support:* In 2016–17, 21 students received support. Career-related internships or fieldwork, scholarships/grants, and health care benefits available. Support available to part-time students. Financial award applicants required to submit FAFSA. *Faculty research:* Minority teachers, special education, multiculturalism, literacy, technology, media literacy learning, autism, school district organization, service-learning, higher level problem solving, teacher leadership. *Unit head:* Dr. Stephen C. Fleury, Chair, Department of Education, 315-445-4376, Fax: 315-445-4744, E-mail: fleurysc@lemoyne.edu. *Application contact:* Kristen P. Richards, Senior Director of Enrollment Management, 315-445-5444, Fax: 315-445-6092, E-mail: trapaskp@lemoyne.edu.
Website: http://www.lemoyne.edu/education

**Long Island University–LIU Brooklyn,** Richard L. Conolly College of Liberal Arts and Sciences, Brooklyn, NY 11201-8423. Offers biology (MS); chemistry (MS); clinical psychology (PhD); communication sciences and disorders (MS); creative writing (MFA); English (MA); media arts (MA, MFA); political science (MA); psychology (MA); social science (MS); sociology (MA); speech-language pathology (MS); United Nations (Advanced Certificate); urban studies (MA); writing and production for television (MFA). *Program availability:* Part-time, evening/weekend. *Faculty:* 90 full-time (35 women), 125 part-time/adjunct (67 women). *Students:* 355 full-time (276 women), 220 part-time (161 women); includes 245 minority (119 Black or African American, non-Hispanic/Latino; 32 Asian, non-Hispanic/Latino; 80 Hispanic/Latino; 1 Native Hawaiian or other Pacific Islander, non-Hispanic/Latino; 13 Two or more races, non-Hispanic/Latino), 85 international. 792 applicants, 41% accepted, 141 enrolled. In 2016, 154 master's, 18 doctorates, 4 other advanced degrees awarded. *Degree requirements:* For master's, comprehensive exam (for some programs), thesis (for some programs); for doctorate, comprehensive exam (for some programs), thesis/dissertation (for some programs). *Entrance requirements:* For master's and doctorate, GRE. Additional exam requirements/recommendations for international students: Recommended—TOEFL (minimum score 550 paper-based; 79 iBT). *Application deadline:* Applications are processed on a rolling basis. Application fee: $50. Electronic applications accepted. *Expenses:* Tuition: Full-time $28,272; part-time $1178 per credit. *Required fees:* $451 per term. Tuition and fees vary according to degree level, program and student level. *Financial support:* In 2016–17, 120 fellowships with full and partial tuition reimbursements (averaging $915 per year), 5 research assistantships with full and partial tuition reimbursements (averaging $2,300 per year), 136 teaching assistantships with full and partial tuition reimbursements (averaging $2,300 per year) were awarded; career-related internships or fieldwork, Federal Work-Study, institutionally sponsored loans, scholarships/grants, tuition waivers (full and partial), and unspecified assistantships also available. Support available to part-time students. Financial award application deadline: 2/15; financial award applicants required to submit FAFSA. *Faculty research:* Nanocrystal polymerization of cellulose using electron microscopy. *Unit head:* Dr. Kevin Lauth, Acting Dean, 718-488-1347, E-mail: kevin.lauth@liu.edu. *Application contact:* Gabrielle Gannon, Director of Graduate Admissions, 718-488-1011, Fax: 718-780-6110, E-mail: bkln-admissions@liu.edu.

**Loyola University Chicago,** Graduate School, Program in Urban Affairs, Chicago, IL 60660. Offers MA. *Program availability:* Part-time, evening/weekend. *Faculty:* 2 full-time (both women), 3 part-time/adjunct (1 woman). *Students:* 1 (woman) part-time. Average age 32. 7 applicants, 57% accepted, 2 enrolled. In 2016, 1 master's awarded. *Degree requirements:* For master's, internship or capstone experience. *Entrance requirements:* For master's, GRE, three letters of recommendation, transcripts, statement of purpose. Additional exam requirements/recommendations for international students: Required—TOEFL. *Application deadline:* For fall admission, 6/30 for domestic students. Applications are processed on a rolling basis. Application fee: $0. Electronic applications accepted. *Expenses:* Tuition: Full-time $18,594. *Required fees:* $848. Part-time tuition and fees vary according to course load, degree level and program. *Financial support:* Fellowships, research assistantships, unspecified assistantships, and Fulbright scholarships available. Financial award application deadline: 2/15; financial award applicants required to submit FAFSA. *Faculty research:* Urban public policy. *Unit head:* Dr. Annette Steinacker, Director, 773-508-3396. *Application contact:* Ron Martin, Assistant Director of Enrollment Management, 312-915-8950, Fax: 312-915-8905, E-mail: gradapp@luc.edu.

**Massachusetts Institute of Technology,** School of Architecture and Planning, Department of Urban Studies and Planning, Cambridge, MA 02139. Offers city planning (MCP); urban and regional planning (PhD); urban and regional studies (PhD); urban studies and planning (SM). *Accreditation:* ACSP (one or more programs are accredited). *Faculty:* 25 full-time (6 women). *Students:* 208 full-time (116 women); includes 48 minority (11 Black or African American, non-Hispanic/Latino; 17 Asian, non-Hispanic/Latino; 16 Hispanic/Latino; 4 Two or more races, non-Hispanic/Latino), 74 international. Average age 29. 542 applicants, 21% accepted, 83 enrolled. In 2016, 62 master's, 10 doctorates awarded. *Degree requirements:* For master's, thesis; for doctorate, comprehensive exam, thesis/dissertation. *Entrance requirements:* For master's and doctorate, GRE General Test. Additional exam requirements/recommendations for international students: Required—TOEFL, IELTS. *Application deadline:* For fall admission, 1/3 for domestic and international students. Application fee: $75. Electronic applications accepted. *Expenses:* Tuition: Full-time $46,400; part-time $725 per credit. One-time fee: $312 full-time. Full-time tuition and fees vary according to course load and program. *Financial support:* In 2016–17, 188 students received support, including 85 fellowships (averaging $26,800 per year), 85 research assistantships (averaging $25,400 per year), 22 teaching assistantships (averaging $37,200 per year); Federal Work-Study, institutionally sponsored loans, scholarships/grants, traineeships, health care benefits, unspecified assistantships, and resident tutors also available. Support available to part-time students. Financial award application deadline: 5/1; financial award applicants required to submit FAFSA. *Faculty research:* City design and regional development; housing, community, and economic development; environmental policy; international development; infrastructure systems and climate change planning; spatial modeling and urban analytics. *Total annual research expenditures:* $4.8 million. *Unit head:* Prof. Eran Ben-Joseph, Department Head, 617-253-9403, E-mail: duspinfo@mit.edu. *Application contact:* 617-253-4543, E-mail: duspapply@mit.edu.
Website: http://dusp.mit.edu/

**Minnesota State University Mankato,** College of Graduate Studies and Research, College of Social and Behavioral Sciences, Department of Urban and Regional Studies, Mankato, MN 56001. Offers local government management (Certificate); non-profit leadership (Certificate); urban and regional studies (MA); urban planning (MA, Certificate). *Students:* 9 full-time (7 women), 12 part-time (4 women). *Degree requirements:* For master's, one foreign language, comprehensive exam, thesis or alternative. *Entrance requirements:* For master's, minimum GPA of 3.0 during previous 2 years, 2 letters of recommendation. Additional exam requirements/recommendations for international students: Required—TOEFL. *Application deadline:* For fall admission, 7/1 priority date for domestic students; for spring admission, 11/1 for domestic students. Applications are processed on a rolling basis. Application fee: $40. Electronic applications accepted. *Financial support:* Fellowships with partial tuition reimbursements, research assistantships with full tuition reimbursements, teaching assistantships with full tuition reimbursements, career-related internships or fieldwork, Federal Work-Study, institutionally sponsored loans, and unspecified assistantships available. Support available to part-time students. Financial award application deadline: 3/15; financial award applicants required to submit FAFSA.
Website: http://sbs.mnsu.edu/ursi/graduate/

**Moody Bible Institute,** Graduate School, Chicago, IL 60610-3284. Offers biblical studies (MABS, Graduate Certificate); intercultural studies (MAIS, Graduate Certificate); ministry (M Div, M Min); spiritual formation and discipleship (MASF, Graduate Certificate); urban studies (MA, Graduate Certificate). *Program availability:* Part-time. *Degree requirements:* For master's, 2 foreign languages, fieldwork (MABS); colloquium, field research project (MA Min). *Entrance requirements:* For master's, 30 hours in Bible/theology, 2 years of ministry experience (MA Min).

**New Jersey City University,** Debra Cannon Partridge Wolfe College of Education, Department of Educational Leadership and Counseling, Jersey City, NJ 07305-1597. Offers counselor education (MA); educational administration and supervision (MA); urban education (MA). *Accreditation:* TEAC. *Program availability:* Part-time, evening/weekend. *Entrance requirements:* Additional exam requirements/recommendations for international students: Required—TOEFL (minimum score 79 iBT).

**New Jersey Institute of Technology,** College of Architecture and Design, Newark, NJ 07102. Offers architecture (M Arch, MS Arch); infrastructure planning (MIP); urban systems (PhD). *Program availability:* Part-time, evening/weekend. *Faculty:* 31 full-time (8 women), 37 part-time/adjunct (14 women). *Students:* 40 full-time (23 women), 6 part-time (0 women); includes 16 minority (1 Black or African American, non-Hispanic/Latino; 3 Asian, non-Hispanic/Latino; 5 Hispanic/Latino; 1 Two or more races, non-Hispanic/Latino), 19 international. Average age 30. 129 applicants, 37% accepted, 10 enrolled. In 2016, 16 master's, 4 doctorates awarded. Terminal master's awarded for partial completion of doctoral program. *Degree requirements:* For master's, thesis (for some programs). *Entrance requirements:* For master's, GRE General Test, minimum GPA of 3.0. Additional exam requirements/recommendations for international students: Required—TOEFL (minimum score 550 paper-based; 79 iBT). *Application deadline:* For fall admission, 6/1 priority date for domestic students, 5/1 priority date for international students; for spring admission, 11/15 priority date for domestic and international students. Applications are processed on a rolling basis. Application fee: $75. Electronic applications accepted. *Expenses:* Contact institution. *Financial support:* In 2016–17, 31 students received support, including 6 teaching assistantships (averaging $22,500 per year); fellowships, career-related internships or fieldwork, Federal Work-Study, institutionally sponsored loans, scholarships/grants, traineeships, unspecified assistantships, and studio assistantships (1 averaging $10,000) also available. Financial award application deadline: 1/15. *Faculty research:* Building sciences, community and urban design history and theory, computer-aided architecture, material dynamics. *Unit head:* Anthony W. Schuman, Interim Dean, 973-596-6370, E-mail: anthony.w.schuman@njit.edu. *Application contact:* Stephen Eck, Director of Admissions, 973-596-3300, Fax: 973-596-3461, E-mail: admissions@njit.edu.
Website: http://architecture.njit.edu/

**The New School,** Schools of Public Engagement, Program in Urban Policy Analysis and Management, New York, NY 10011. Offers MS. *Accreditation:* NASPAA. *Program availability:* Part-time. *Faculty:* 34 full-time (16 women), 8 part-time/adjunct (3 women). *Students:* 50 full-time (39 women), 90 part-time (56 women); includes 63 minority (28 Black or African American, non-Hispanic/Latino; 8 Asian, non-Hispanic/Latino; 22 Hispanic/Latino; 5 Two or more races, non-Hispanic/Latino), 28 international. Average age 32. 146 applicants, 64% accepted, 29 enrolled. In 2016, 39 degrees awarded. *Degree requirements:* For master's, capstone project: Professional Decision Report (PDR). *Entrance requirements:* For master's, two letters of recommendation, statement of purpose, resume, transcripts. Additional exam requirements/recommendations for international students: Required—TOEFL (minimum score 100 iBT), IELTS (minimum score 7), PTE (minimum score 68). *Application deadline:* For fall admission, 1/15 priority date for domestic and international students; for spring admission, 10/15 priority date for domestic and international students. Applications are processed on a rolling basis. Application fee: $50. Electronic applications accepted. *Expenses:* Contact institution. *Financial support:* Research assistantships, career-related internships or fieldwork, Federal Work-Study, scholarships/grants, and unspecified assistantships available. Support available to part-time students. Financial award application deadline: 2/1; financial award applicants required to submit FAFSA. *Faculty research:* Community and economic development, national urban policy, social welfare policy, management of low-income housing, race and gender issues. *Unit head:* Suzanne Bostwick, Chair, 212-229-5400 Ext. 1601, E-mail: bostwics@newschool.edu. *Application contact:* Sharon Greenidge, Assistant Director of Admission, 212-229-5400 Ext. 1103, E-mail: greenids@newschool.edu.

**New York University,** Polytechnic School of Engineering, Department of Civil and Urban Engineering, Major in Urban Systems Engineering and Management, New York, NY 10012-1019. Offers MS.

**Norfolk State University,** School of Graduate Studies, School of Liberal Arts, Department of Sociology, Program in Urban Affairs, Norfolk, VA 23504. Offers MA. *Program availability:* Part-time. *Degree requirements:* For master's, thesis. *Entrance requirements:* For master's, minimum GPA of 2.5.

**North Dakota State University,** College of Graduate and Interdisciplinary Studies, Interdisciplinary Program in Transportation and Logistics, Fargo, ND 58102. Offers managerial logistics (MML); transportation and logistics (PhD); transportation and urban systems (MS). *Entrance requirements:* For doctorate, 1 year of calculus, statistics and probability, minimum GPA of 3.0. Additional exam requirements/recommendations for international students: Required—TOEFL (minimum score 550 paper-based; 79 iBT).

*Faculty research:* Supply chain optimization, spatial analysis of transportation networks, advanced traffic analysis, transportation demand, railroad/intermodal freight.

**Northeastern University,** College of Social Sciences and Humanities, Boston, MA 02115. Offers criminology and criminal justice (MSCJ); criminology and justice policy (PhD); economics (MA, PhD); English (MA, PhD); international affairs (MA); law and public policy (PhD); political science (MA, PhD); public administration (MPA); public history (MA); public policy (MPP); security and resilience studies (MS); sociology (MA, PhD); urban and regional policy (MS); urban informatics (MS); world history (MA, PhD); JD/MS. *Program availability:* Online learning. *Faculty:* 234 full-time (114 women), 55 part-time/adjunct (34 women). *Students:* 427 full-time (239 women), 77 part-time (42 women). In 2016, 143 master's, 38 doctorates awarded. *Degree requirements:* For doctorate, variable foreign language requirement, comprehensive exam, thesis/dissertation. *Entrance requirements:* For master's and doctorate, GRE. Additional exam requirements/recommendations for international students: Required—TOEFL, IELTS. Application fee: $75. Electronic applications accepted. *Expenses:* $1,295 per credit. *Financial support:* Teaching assistantships, career-related internships or fieldwork, scholarships/grants, health care benefits, tuition waivers (full and partial), and unspecified assistantships available. Support available to part-time students. Financial award applicants required to submit FAFSA. *Unit head:* Dr. Uta Poiger, Dean, 617-373-5173. *Application contact:* Amber Crowe, Administrative Coordinator, 617-373-5990, Fax: 617-373-7281, E-mail: gradcssh@northeastern.edu.
Website: http://www.northeastern.edu/cssh/graduate

**Old Dominion University,** Strome College of Business, Doctoral Program in Public Administration and Urban Policy, Norfolk, VA 23529. Offers PhD. *Program availability:* Part-time, evening/weekend. *Faculty:* 9 full-time (3 women). *Students:* 9 full-time (6 women), 22 part-time (11 women); includes 10 minority (5 Black or African American, non-Hispanic/Latino; 1 Asian, non-Hispanic/Latino; 4 Hispanic/Latino), 6 international. Average age 38. 9 applicants, 89% accepted, 8 enrolled. In 2016, 3 doctorates awarded. *Degree requirements:* For doctorate, comprehensive exam, thesis/dissertation. *Entrance requirements:* For doctorate, GMAT, GRE General Test, master's degree, minimum graduate GPA of 3.25. Additional exam requirements/recommendations for international students: Required—TOEFL (minimum score 550 paper-based; 79 iBT). *Application deadline:* For fall admission, 3/15 priority date for domestic and international students. Application fee: $50. Electronic applications accepted. *Expenses:* Contact institution. *Financial support:* In 2016–17, 14 students received support, including 4 fellowships with full tuition reimbursements available (averaging $7,500 per year), 8 research assistantships with full tuition reimbursements available (averaging $6,000 per year), 2 teaching assistantships with full tuition reimbursements available (averaging $7,500 per year); unspecified assistantships also available. Financial award application deadline: 3/15; financial award applicants required to submit FAFSA. *Faculty research:* Multi-sectoral cooperation; policy analysis and administration; public-private partnerships, public finance and budgeting, economic development and sustainability. *Total annual research expenditures:* $60,000. *Unit head:* Dr. Meagan Jordan, Graduate Program Director, 757-683-3961, Fax: 757-683-4886, E-mail: mmjordan@odu.edu. *Application contact:* Megan S. Jones, Graduate Program Manager, 757-683-3961, Fax: 757-683-4886, E-mail: mmjones@odu.edu.
Website: http://www.odu.edu/business/departments/sps/academics/paup

**Portland State University,** Graduate Studies, College of Urban and Public Affairs, Nohad A. Toulan School of Urban Studies and Planning, Program in Urban Studies, Portland, OR 97207-0751. Offers MUS, PhD. *Degree requirements:* For doctorate, comprehensive exam, thesis/dissertation, residency. *Entrance requirements:* For master's and doctorate, GRE General Test, minimum GPA of 3.0, 3 letters of recommendation, resume, statement of purpose, transcripts. Additional exam requirements/recommendations for international students: Required—TOEFL (minimum score 550 paper-based; 80 iBT). *Application deadline:* For fall admission, 1/15 for domestic and international students; for winter admission, 9/1 for domestic and international students. Application fee: $50. Electronic applications accepted. *Expenses:* Contact institution. *Financial support:* In 2016–17, 15 research assistantships with full tuition reimbursements (averaging $8,694 per year) were awarded. Financial award application deadline: 3/1. *Application contact:* Bryony Mangan, Administrative Program Assistant, 503-725-4068, Fax: 503-725-8770, E-mail: bmangan@pdx.edu.

**Queens College of the City University of New York,** Division of Social Sciences, Department of Urban Studies, Queens, NY 11367-1597. Offers urban affairs (MA). *Program availability:* Part-time, evening/weekend. *Faculty:* 21 full-time (8 women), 28 part-time/adjunct (13 women). *Students:* 7 full-time (4 women), 95 part-time (65 women); includes 76 minority (36 Black or African American, non-Hispanic/Latino; 16 Asian, non-Hispanic/Latino; 22 Hispanic/Latino; 2 Two or more races, non-Hispanic/Latino), 9 international. Average age 36. 65 applicants, 95% accepted, 36 enrolled. In 2016, 53 master's awarded. *Degree requirements:* For master's, thesis. *Entrance requirements:* For master's, minimum GPA of 3.0. Additional exam requirements/recommendations for international students: Required—TOEFL (minimum score 61 iBT), IELTS (minimum score 5). *Application deadline:* For fall admission, 8/15 for domestic students; for spring admission, 1/15 for domestic students. Applications are processed on a rolling basis. Application fee: $125. Electronic applications accepted. *Expenses:* Tuition, state resident: full-time $5065; part-time $425 per credit. Tuition, nonresident: part-time $780 per credit. *Required fees:* $522; $397 per credit. Part-time tuition and fees vary according to course load and program. *Financial support:* Career-related internships or fieldwork and unspecified assistantships available. Financial award application deadline: 4/1; financial award applicants required to submit FAFSA. *Unit head:* Dr. Leonard S. Rodberg, Chairperson, 718-997-5130, E-mail: leonard.rodberg@qc.cuny.edu.

**Rutgers University–Newark,** Graduate School, Program in Public Administration, Newark, NJ 07102. Offers health care administration (MPA); human resources administration (MPA); public administration (PhD); public management (MPA); public policy analysis (MPA); urban systems and issues (MPA). *Accreditation:* NASPAA (one or more programs are accredited). *Program availability:* Part-time, evening/weekend. *Degree requirements:* For master's, comprehensive exam, thesis or alternative; for doctorate, thesis/dissertation. *Entrance requirements:* For master's, GRE, minimum undergraduate B average; for doctorate, GRE, MPA, minimum B average. Electronic applications accepted. *Faculty research:* Government finance, municipal and state government, public productivity.

**Rutgers University–Newark,** Graduate School, Program in Urban Systems, Newark, NJ 07102. Offers PhD. Program offered jointly with New Jersey Institute of Technology.

**Saint Louis University,** Graduate Education, College of Education and Public Service, Department of Public Policy Studies, St. Louis, MO 63103. Offers geographic information systems (Certificate); organizational development (Certificate); public administration (MAPA); public policy analysis (PhD); urban affairs (MAUA); urban planning and real estate development (MUPRED). *Program availability:* Part-time. *Degree requirements:* For master's, comprehensive exam (for some programs), thesis (for some programs); for doctorate, comprehensive exam, thesis/dissertation, preliminary exams. *Entrance requirements:* For master's, GMAT, GRE General Test, or LSAT, letters of recommendation, resume; for doctorate, GMAT, GRE General Test, or LSAT, letters of recommendation, resumé, interview, transcripts, goal statement. Additional exam requirements/recommendations for international students: Required—

TOEFL (minimum score 525 paper-based). Electronic applications accepted. *Faculty research:* Urban politics, brown fields, e-government, and administration, evaluation research, community development, electronic government and governance.

**Savannah State University,** Master of Science in Urban Studies and Planning Program, Savannah, GA 31404. Offers MSUS. *Program availability:* Part-time. *Degree requirements:* For master's, thesis or capstone project. *Entrance requirements:* For master's, GRE or MAT, minimum cumulative GPA of 2.6, 3 letters of recommendation, statement of interest, official transcripts, curriculum vitae. Additional exam requirements/recommendations for international students: Required—TOEFL. Electronic applications accepted. *Expenses:* Contact institution.

**Simon Fraser University,** Office of Graduate Studies and Postdoctoral Fellows, Faculty of Arts and Social Sciences, Urban Studies Program, Vancouver, BC V6B 5K3, Canada. Offers M Urb, Graduate Diploma. *Program availability:* Part-time. *Faculty:* 5 full-time (2 women). *Students:* 22 full-time (12 women), 37 part-time (18 women). 87 applicants, 32% accepted, 14 enrolled. In 2016, 16 master's, 3 other advanced degrees awarded. *Degree requirements:* For master's, project. *Entrance requirements:* For master's, minimum GPA of 3.0 (on scale of 4.33) or 3.33 based on last 60 credits of undergraduate courses; for Graduate Diploma, minimum GPA of 2.5 (on scale of 4.33) or 2.67 based on last 60 credits of undergraduate courses. Additional exam requirements/recommendations for international students: Recommended—TOEFL (minimum score 580 paper-based; 93 iBT), IELTS (minimum score 7), TWE (minimum score 5). *Application deadline:* For fall admission, 2/10 for domestic and international students. Application fee: $90 ($125 for international students). Electronic applications accepted. *Financial support:* In 2016–17, 9 students received support, including 7 fellowships (averaging $6,036 per year); research assistantships and scholarships/grants also available. *Faculty research:* Urban history; public policy and culture; environmental, transportation, and energy policy; urban governance and administration; urban sustainability. *Unit head:* Dr. Peter Hall, Graduate Chair, 778-782-6691, Fax: 778-782-5297, E-mail: urb-grad-chair@sfu.ca. *Application contact:* Terri Evans, Graduate Secretary, 778-782-7914, Fax: 778-782-5297, E-mail: urban@sfu.ca.
Website: http://www.urban.sfu.ca/

**Temple University,** College of Liberal Arts, Department of Geography and Urban Studies, Philadelphia, PA 19122-6096. Offers geographic information systems (PSM, Graduate Certificate); geography and urban studies (MA, PhD). *Degree requirements:* For master's, comprehensive exam, thesis or alternative. *Entrance requirements:* For master's, GRE General Test, minimum GPA of 3.0, 3 letters of recommendation; for doctorate, GRE, minimum GPA of 3.0, 3 letters of recommendation. Additional exam requirements/recommendations for international students: Required—TOEFL (minimum score 575 paper-based; 88 iBT). Electronic applications accepted. *Faculty research:* Social justice, sustainability, globalization, geographic methods, urban processes.

**Tufts University,** Graduate School of Arts and Sciences, Department of Urban and Environmental Policy and Planning, Medford, MA 02155. Offers community development (MA); environmental policy (MA); health and human welfare (MA); housing policy (MA); international environment/development policy (MA); public policy (MPP); MA/JD; MA/MBA; MA/MPH; MA/MS; MALD/MA. MALD/MA offered in connection with The Fletcher School of Law and Diplomacy; MA/MPH with School of Medicine; MA/MS with School of Nutrition Science and Policy or School of Engineering; MA/MBA with Boston College, Carroll School of Management; MA/JD with Boston College Law School. *Accreditation:* ACSP (one or more programs are accredited). *Program availability:* Part-time. *Students:* 94 full-time (73 women), 18 part-time (14 women); includes 29 minority (11 Black or African American, non-Hispanic/Latino; 9 Asian, non-Hispanic/Latino; 6 Hispanic/Latino; 3 Two or more races, non-Hispanic/Latino), 18 international. Average age 30. 153 applicants, 78% accepted, 51 enrolled. In 2016, 20 master's awarded. *Degree requirements:* For master's, thesis or alternative, internship. *Entrance requirements:* For master's, GRE General Test. Additional exam requirements/recommendations for international students: Required—TOEFL (minimum score 550 paper-based; 80 iBT), IELTS (minimum score 6.5). *Application deadline:* For fall admission, 1/15 for domestic and international students. Applications are processed on a rolling basis. Application fee: $85. Electronic applications accepted. *Expenses:* $49,982 full-time tuition (for MPP); $34,932 full-time tuition (for MA). *Financial support:* Fellowships, research assistantships, teaching assistantships, career-related internships or fieldwork, Federal Work-Study, scholarships/grants, tuition waivers (full and partial), and unspecified assistantships available. Support available to part-time students. Financial award application deadline: 1/15. *Unit head:* Dr. Mary Davis, Graduate Program Director. *Application contact:* Office of Graduate Admissions, 617-627-3395, E-mail: gradadmissions@tufts.edu.
Website: http://ase.tufts.edu/uep/

**Université du Québec à Montréal,** Graduate Programs, Program in Urban Analysis and Management, Montréal, QC H3C 3P8, Canada. Offers MA. Program offered jointly with Université du Québec, École nationale d'administration publique and Université du Québec, Institut National de la Recherche Scientifique. *Program availability:* Part-time. *Entrance requirements:* For master's, appropriate bachelor's degree or equivalent and proficiency in French.

**Université du Québec à Montréal,** Graduate Programs, Program in Urban Studies, Montréal, QC H3C 3P8, Canada. Offers MA, PhD. *Program availability:* Part-time. *Degree requirements:* For doctorate, thesis/dissertation. *Entrance requirements:* For doctorate, appropriate master's degree or equivalent, proficiency in French.

**Université du Québec, École nationale d'administration publique,** Graduate Programs in Public Administration, Program in Urban Analysis and Management, Quebec, QC G1K 9E5, Canada. Offers MAGU. *Program availability:* Part-time. *Entrance requirements:* For master's, appropriate bachelor's degree, proficiency in French.

**Université du Québec, Institut National de la Recherche Scientifique,** Graduate Programs, Centre for Urbanisation Culture Societe, Montreal, QC G1K 9A9, Canada. Offers demography (M Sc, PhD); research practices and action (MA, DESS); urban studies (M Sc, PhD). *Program availability:* Part-time. *Faculty:* 34 full-time. *Students:* 79 full-time (43 women), 14 part-time (10 women), 13 international. Average age 32. 40 applicants, 88% accepted, 20 enrolled. In 2016, 17 master's, 5 doctorates awarded. *Degree requirements:* For master's, thesis (for some programs); for doctorate, thesis/dissertation. *Entrance requirements:* For master's, appropriate bachelor's degree, proficiency in French; for doctorate, appropriate master's degree, proficiency in French; for DESS, proficiency in French. *Application deadline:* For fall admission, 3/30 for domestic and international students; for winter admission, 11/1 for domestic and international students; for spring admission, 3/1 for domestic and international students. Application fee: $45. Electronic applications accepted. *Financial support:* In 2016–17, fellowships (averaging $16,500 per year) were awarded; research assistantships also available. *Faculty research:* Mobility and migration, cultural policies, knowledge mobilization, spatial analysis of data, social demography. *Unit head:* Claire Poitras, Director, 514-499-4002, E-mail: claire.poitras@ucs.inrs.ca. *Application contact:* Sylvie Richard, Registrar, 418-654-2518, Fax: 418-654-3858, E-mail: sylvie.richard@adm.inrs.ca.
Website: http://www.ucs.inrs.ca

## Urban Studies

**University at Albany, State University of New York,** College of Arts and Sciences, Department of Sociology, Albany, NY 12222-0001. Offers demography (Certificate); sociology (MA, PhD); urban policy (Certificate). *Faculty:* 8 full-time (6 women). *Students:* 25 full-time (19 women), 63 part-time (46 women); includes 17 minority (4 Black or African American, non-Hispanic/Latino; 1 American Indian or Alaska Native, non-Hispanic/Latino; 5 Asian, non-Hispanic/Latino; 5 Hispanic/Latino; 2 Two or more races, non-Hispanic/Latino), 27 international. 85 applicants, 39% accepted, 11 enrolled. In 2016, 2 master's, 15 doctorates awarded. Terminal master's awarded for partial completion of doctoral program. *Degree requirements:* For master's, thesis; for doctorate, thesis/dissertation, 2 specialization exams, research tool. *Entrance requirements:* For master's and doctorate, GRE General Test. Additional exam requirements/recommendations for international students: Required—TOEFL. *Application deadline:* For fall admission, 1/15 for domestic students, 5/1 for international students. Applications are processed on a rolling basis. Application fee: $75. Electronic applications accepted. *Expenses:* Tuition, state resident: full-time $10,870; part-time $453 per credit hour. Tuition, nonresident: full-time $22,210; part-time $925 per credit hour. *International tuition:* $21,550 full-time. *Required fees:* $1864; $96 per credit hour. *Financial support:* Fellowships, research assistantships, teaching assistantships, career-related internships or fieldwork, and Federal Work-Study available. Financial award application deadline: 3/15. *Faculty research:* Gender and equality, crime and deviance, aging, work and organizations, social demography. *Total annual research expenditures:* $418,522. *Unit head:* Nancy Denton, Chair, 518-442-4666, Fax: 518-442-4936, E-mail: ndenton@albany.edu. *Application contact:* Michael DeRensis, Director, Graduate Admissions, 518-442-3980, Fax: 518-442-3922, E-mail: graduate@albany.edu.
Website: http://www.albany.edu/sociology/index.html

**University of California, Irvine,** School of Social Ecology, Department of Planning, Policy and Design, Irvine, CA 92697. Offers planning, policy and design (PhD); urban and regional planning (MURP). *Accreditation:* ACSP (one or more programs are accredited). *Students:* 120 full-time (68 women), 3 part-time (1 woman); includes 59 minority (3 Black or African American, non-Hispanic/Latino; 1 American Indian or Alaska Native, non-Hispanic/Latino; 21 Asian, non-Hispanic/Latino; 25 Hispanic/Latino; 9 Two or more races, non-Hispanic/Latino), 29 international. Average age 28. 323 applicants, 52% accepted, 47 enrolled. In 2016, 57 master's, 5 doctorates awarded. *Degree requirements:* For doctorate, thesis/dissertation, research project. *Entrance requirements:* For master's and doctorate, GRE General Test, minimum GPA of 3.0. Additional exam requirements/recommendations for international students: Required—TOEFL (minimum score 550 paper-based). *Application deadline:* For fall admission, 1/15 priority date for domestic and international students. Application fee: $105 ($125 for international students). Electronic applications accepted. *Financial support:* Fellowships with tuition reimbursements, research assistantships with full tuition reimbursements, teaching assistantships with tuition reimbursements, institutionally sponsored loans, traineeships, health care benefits, and unspecified assistantships available. Financial award application deadline: 1/15; financial award applicants required to submit FAFSA. *Faculty research:* Community and social policy, economic development, land-use and growth management, transportation planning, environmental policy. *Unit head:* David L. Feldman, Chair, 949-824-4384, Fax: 949-824-3056, E-mail: feldmand@uci.edu. *Application contact:* Janet Gallagher, Graduate Coordinator, 949-824-9849, Fax: 949-824-8566, E-mail: janetg@uci.edu.
Website: http://www.seweb.uci.edu/ppd/

**University of Delaware,** Center for Energy and Environmental Policy, Newark, DE 19716. Offers energy and environmental policy (MA, MEEP, PhD); urban affairs and public policy (PhD), including technology, environment, and society. *Degree requirements:* For master's, analytical paper or thesis; for doctorate, comprehensive exam, thesis/dissertation. *Entrance requirements:* For master's, GRE General Test, minimum GPA of 3.0; for doctorate, GRE General Test, minimum GPA of 3.5. Additional exam requirements/recommendations for international students: Required—TOEFL. Electronic applications accepted. *Faculty research:* Sustainable development, renewable energy, climate change, environmental policy, environmental justice, disaster policy.

**University of Delaware,** College of Arts and Sciences, School of Public Policy and Administration, Program in Urban Affairs and Public Policy, Newark, DE 19716. Offers governance planning and management (PhD); historic preservation (MA); social and urban policy (PhD); technology, environment and society (PhD); urban affairs and public policy (MA). *Program availability:* Part-time. Terminal master's awarded for partial completion of doctoral program. *Degree requirements:* For master's, analytical paper or thesis; for doctorate, thesis/dissertation. *Entrance requirements:* For master's, GRE General Test, minimum GPA of 3.0; for doctorate, GRE General Test, minimum GPA of 3.5. Additional exam requirements/recommendations for international students: Required—TOEFL. Electronic applications accepted. *Faculty research:* Political economy; social policy analysis; technology and society; historic preservation; urban policy.

**University of Lethbridge,** School of Graduate Studies, Lethbridge, AB T1K 3M4, Canada. Offers addictions counseling (M Sc); agricultural biotechnology (M Sc); agricultural studies (M Sc, MA); anthropology (MA); archaeology (M Sc, MA); art (MA, MFA); biochemistry (M Sc); biological sciences (M Sc); biomolecular science (PhD); biosystems and biodiversity (PhD); Canadian studies (MA); chemistry (M Sc); computer science (M Sc); computer science and geographical information science (M Sc); counseling (MC); counseling psychology (M Ed); dramatic arts (MA); earth, space, and physical science (PhD); economics (MA); education (MA, PhD); educational leadership (M Ed); English (MA); environmental science (M Sc); evolution and behavior (PhD); exercise science (M Sc); French (MA); French/German (MA); French/Spanish (MA); general education (M Ed); geography (M Sc, MA); German (MA); health sciences (M Sc); individualized multidisciplinary (M Sc, MA); kinesiology (M Sc, MA); management (M Sc), including accounting, finance, human resource management and labor relations, information systems, international management, marketing, policy and strategy; mathematics (M Sc); music (M Mus, MA); Native American studies (MA); neuroscience (M Sc, PhD); new media (MA, MFA); nursing (M Sc, MN); philosophy (MA); physics (M Sc); political science (MA); psychology (M Sc, MA); religious studies (MA); sociology (MA); theatre and dramatic arts (MFA); theoretical and computational science (PhD); urban and regional studies (MA); women and gender studies (MA). *Program availability:* Part-time, evening/weekend. *Degree requirements:* For master's, thesis (for some programs); for doctorate, comprehensive exam, thesis/dissertation. *Entrance requirements:* For master's, GMAT (for M Sc in management), bachelor's degree in related field, minimum GPA of 3.0 during previous 20 graded semester courses, 2 years' teaching or related experience (M Ed); for doctorate, master's degree, minimum graduate GPA of 3.5. Additional exam requirements/recommendations for international students: Required—TOEFL (minimum score 580 paper-based; 93 iBT). Electronic applications accepted. *Faculty research:* Movement and brain plasticity, gibberellin physiology, photosynthesis, carbon cycling, molecular properties of main-group ring components.

**University of Louisville,** Graduate School, College of Arts and Sciences, Department of Urban and Public Affairs, Louisville, KY 40208. Offers public administration (MPA),

including human resources management, non-profit management, public policy and administration; urban and public affairs (PhD), including urban planning and development, urban policy and administration; urban planning (MUP), including administration of planning organizations, housing and community development, land use and environmental planning, spatial analysis. *Program availability:* Part-time, evening/weekend. *Faculty:* 12 full-time (5 women), 3 part-time/adjunct (1 woman). *Students:* 59 full-time (23 women), 32 part-time (19 women); includes 19 minority (13 Black or African American, non-Hispanic/Latino; 1 Asian, non-Hispanic/Latino; 2 Hispanic/Latino; 3 Two or more races, non-Hispanic/Latino), 5 international. Average age 30. 75 applicants, 65% accepted, 25 enrolled. In 2016, 22 master's, 2 doctorates awarded. Terminal master's awarded for partial completion of doctoral program. *Degree requirements:* For master's, internship; for doctorate, comprehensive exam, thesis/dissertation. *Entrance requirements:* For master's, GRE General Test, minimum GPA of 3.0; for doctorate, GRE General Test, master's degree in appropriate field. Additional exam requirements/recommendations for international students: Required—TOEFL (minimum score 550 paper-based; 79 iBT). *Application deadline:* Applications are processed on a rolling basis. Application fee: $60. *Expenses:* Contact institution. *Financial support:* Fellowships, research assistantships, tuition waivers (full and partial), and unspecified assistantships available. Financial award application deadline: 2/1. *Faculty research:* Urban theory, sustainability, public administration, urban planning, urban management. *Total annual research expenditures:* $240,308. *Unit head:* Dr. David Simpson, Chair, 502-852-8019, Fax: 502-852-4558, E-mail: dave.simpson@louisville.edu. *Application contact:* Libby Leggett, Director, Graduate Admissions, 502-852-3101, Fax: 502-852-4558, E-mail: gradadm@louisville.edu.
Website: http://supa.louisville.edu

**University of Maryland, Baltimore County,** The Graduate School, College of Arts, Humanities and Social Sciences, School of Public Policy, Baltimore, MD 21250. Offers public policy (MPP, PhD), including economics (PhD), educational policy, emergency services (PhD), environmental policy, evaluation and analytical methods, health policy, policy history (PhD), public management, urban policy. *Program availability:* Part-time, evening/weekend. *Faculty:* 10 full-time (4 women), 1 part-time/adjunct (0 women). *Students:* 48 full-time (23 women), 66 part-time (36 women); includes 23 minority (14 Black or African American, non-Hispanic/Latino; 4 Asian, non-Hispanic/Latino; 3 Hispanic/Latino; 1 Native Hawaiian or other Pacific Islander, non-Hispanic/Latino; 1 Two or more races, non-Hispanic/Latino), 6 international. Average age 37. 49 applicants, 65% accepted, 16 enrolled. In 2016, 15 master's, 6 doctorates awarded. Terminal master's awarded for partial completion of doctoral program. *Degree requirements:* For master's, thesis, policy analysis paper, internship for pre-service; for doctorate, thesis/dissertation, comprehensive and field qualifying exams. *Entrance requirements:* For master's and doctorate, GRE General Test, 3 academic letters of reference, resume, research paper, official transcripts. Additional exam requirements/recommendations for international students: Required—TOEFL (minimum score 550 paper-based; 80 iBT). *Application deadline:* For fall admission, 1/15 priority date for domestic students, 1/1 priority date for international students; for spring admission, 11/1 priority date for domestic students, 5/1 priority date for international students. Applications are processed on a rolling basis. Application fee: $50. Electronic applications accepted. *Expenses:* $733 per credit hour in-state tuition and fees, $1,127 per credit hour out-of-state; $27,321 tuition and fees in-state, $41,899 out-of-state (for MPP); $38,316 tuition and fees in-state, $58,804 out-of-state (PhD). *Financial support:* In 2016–17, 25 students received support, including 2 fellowships with full tuition reimbursements available (averaging $14,000 per year), 23 research assistantships with full tuition reimbursements available (averaging $20,000 per year); career-related internships or fieldwork, Federal Work-Study, scholarships/grants, health care benefits, and unspecified assistantships also available. Financial award application deadline: 1/15; financial award applicants required to submit FAFSA. *Faculty research:* Education policy, health policy, urban policy, public management, evaluation and analytical method. *Unit head:* Dr. Donald F. Norris, Director, 410-455-3201, Fax: 410-455-1172, E-mail: norris@umbc.edu. *Application contact:* Sally F. Helms, Administrator of Academic Affairs, 410-455-3202, Fax: 410-455-1172, E-mail: gradpubpol@umbc.edu.
Website: http://publicpolicy.umbc.edu/

**University of New Orleans,** Graduate School, College of Liberal Arts, Department of Planning and Urban Studies, Program in Urban Studies, New Orleans, LA 70148. Offers MS, PhD. *Degree requirements:* For master's, thesis; for doctorate, thesis/dissertation. *Entrance requirements:* For master's, GRE General Test. Additional exam requirements/recommendations for international students: Required—TOEFL (minimum score 550 paper-based; 79 iBT), IELTS (minimum score 6.5). Electronic applications accepted. *Faculty research:* Urban economic development, environmental planning and analysis, social and cultural change.

**University of San Francisco,** College of Arts and Sciences, Urban and Public Affairs Program, San Francisco, CA 94117. Offers MA. *Program availability:* Part-time. *Faculty:* 2 full-time (1 woman), 3 part-time/adjunct (1 woman). *Students:* 21 full-time (10 women); includes 14 minority (2 Black or African American, non-Hispanic/Latino; 2 Asian, non-Hispanic/Latino; 8 Hispanic/Latino; 2 Two or more races, non-Hispanic/Latino), 1 international. Average age 27. 26 applicants, 85% accepted, 5 enrolled. In 2016, 5 master's awarded. *Entrance requirements:* Additional exam requirements/recommendations for international students: Required—TOEFL, IELTS, PTE. *Application deadline:* For fall admission, 3/1 for domestic and international students. Electronic applications accepted. *Expenses: Tuition:* Full-time $23,310; part-time $1295 per credit. Tuition and fees vary according to course load, degree level, campus/location and program. *Financial support:* In 2016–17, 10 students received support. Applicants required to submit FAFSA. *Unit head:* Kresten Froistad-Martin, Program Manager, 415-422-5683, E-mail: upa@usfca.edu. *Application contact:* Mark Landerghini, Information Contact, 415-422-5101, Fax: 415-422-2217, E-mail: asgraduate@usfca.edu.
Website: https://www.usfca.edu/arts-sciences/graduate-programs/urban-public-affairs

**Virginia Polytechnic Institute and State University,** Graduate School, College of Architecture and Urban Studies, Blacksburg, VA 24061. Offers architecture (MS Arch); architecture and design research (PhD); building/construction science and management (MS); creative technologies (MFA); environmental design and planning (PhD); landscape architecture (MLA); planning, governance, and globalization (PhD); public administration (MPA); public administration/public affairs (PhD, Certificate); public and international affairs (MPIA); urban and regional planning (MURP). *Accreditation:* ASLA (one or more programs are accredited). *Faculty:* 136 full-time (53 women). *Students:* 371 full-time (185 women), 210 part-time (104 women); includes 118 minority (49 Black or African American, non-Hispanic/Latino; 1 American Indian or Alaska Native, non-Hispanic/Latino; 30 Asian, non-Hispanic/Latino; 32 Hispanic/Latino; 6 Two or more races, non-Hispanic/Latino), 137 international. Average age 31. 566 applicants, 55% accepted, 160 enrolled. In 2016, 137 master's, 24 doctorates awarded. *Degree requirements:* For master's, comprehensive exam (for some programs), thesis (for some programs); for doctorate, comprehensive exam (for some programs), thesis/dissertation (for some programs). *Entrance requirements:* For master's and doctorate, GRE/GMAT. Additional exam requirements/recommendations for international students: Required—TOEFL (minimum score 80 iBT). *Application deadline:* For fall admission, 8/1 for domestic students, 4/1 for international students; for spring admission, 1/1 for domestic students, 9/1 for international students. Applications are processed on a rolling basis.

Application fee: $75. Electronic applications accepted. *Expenses:* Tuition, state resident: full-time $12,467; part-time $692.50 per credit hour. Tuition, nonresident: full-time $25,095; part-time $1394.25 per credit hour. *Required fees:* $2669; $491.50 per semester. Tuition and fees vary according to course load, campus/location and program. *Financial support:* In 2016–17, 11 research assistantships with full tuition reimbursements (averaging $19,474 per year), 45 teaching assistantships with full tuition reimbursements (averaging $16,014 per year) were awarded. Financial award application deadline: 3/1; financial award applicants required to submit FAFSA. *Total annual research expenditures:* $3.6 million. *Unit head:* Dr. A. J. Davis, Dean, 540-231-6416, Fax: 540-231-6332, E-mail: davisa@vt.edu. *Application contact:* Christine Mattsson-Coon, Executive Assistant, 540-231-6416, Fax: 540-231-6332, E-mail: cmattsso@vt.edu.
Website: http://www.caus.vt.edu/

**Wayne State University,** College of Liberal Arts and Sciences, Department of Political Science, Detroit, MI 48202. Offers political science (MA, PhD); public administration (MPA), including economic development policy and management, health and human services policy and management, human and fiscal resource management, nonprofit policy and management, organizational behavior and management, urban and metropolitan policy and management; JD/MA. *Accreditation:* NASPAA. *Faculty:* 20. *Students:* 64 full-time (20 women), 75 part-time (45 women); includes 48 minority (32 Black or African American, non-Hispanic/Latino; 5 Asian, non-Hispanic/Latino; 4 Hispanic/Latino; 7 Two or more races, non-Hispanic/Latino), 7 international. Average age 33. 105 applicants, 50% accepted, 27 enrolled. In 2016, 25 master's, 5 doctorates awarded. *Degree requirements:* For master's, comprehensive exam (for some programs), thesis (for some programs); for doctorate, thesis/dissertation. *Entrance requirements:* For master's, GRE General Test, substantial undergraduate preparation in the social sciences, minimum upper-division undergraduate GPA of 3.0, two letters of recommendation, personal statement; for doctorate, GRE General Test, 3 letters of recommendation; personal statement; interview. Additional exam requirements/recommendations for international students: Required—TOEFL (minimum score 550 paper-based; 79 iBT), TWE (minimum score 5.5), Michigan English Language Assessment Battery (minimum score 85); Recommended—IELTS (minimum score 6.5). *Application deadline:* For fall admission, 5/15 for domestic students, 5/1 priority date for international students; for winter admission, 10/15 for domestic students, 9/1 priority date for international students. Applications are processed on a rolling basis. Application fee: $50. Electronic applications accepted. *Expenses:* $16,503 per year resident tuition and fees, $33,697 per year non-resident tuition and fees. *Financial support:* In 2016–17, 48 students received support, including 3 fellowships with tuition reimbursements available (averaging $17,333 per year), 13 teaching assistantships with tuition reimbursements available (averaging $18,067 per year); research assistantships with tuition reimbursements available, scholarships/grants, health care benefits, and unspecified assistantships also available. Financial award applicants required to submit FAFSA. *Faculty research:* American government and politics, comparative politics, political methodology, political theory, public administration, public law, public policy, world politics/international relations, formal theory/modeling, gender and politics, international law, peace research, political economy, political psychology, politics of developing countries, race, religion, and ethnicity, urban politics. *Unit head:* Dr. Daniel Geller, Professor and Chair, 313-577-6328, E-mail: dgeller@wayne.edu. *Application contact:* Dr. Sharon Lean, Graduate Director, 313-577-2630, E-mail: gradpolisci@wayne.edu.
Website: http://clas.wayne.edu/politicalscience/

**Wright State University,** Graduate School, College of Liberal Arts, Department of Urban Affairs and Geography, Dayton, OH 45435. Offers public administration (MPA). *Accreditation:* NASPAA. *Degree requirements:* For master's, thesis optional. *Entrance requirements:* For master's, interview, minimum GPA of 2.7. Additional exam requirements/recommendations for international students: Required—TOEFL. Application fee: $25. *Expenses:* Tuition, state resident: full-time $9952; part-time $622 per credit hour. Tuition, nonresident: full-time $16,960; part-time $1060 per credit hour. *Financial support:* Fellowships and unspecified assistantships available. Support available to part-time students. Financial award applicants required to submit FAFSA. *Faculty research:* Strategic planning, economic development, housing and public management. *Unit head:* Dr. Jack L. Dustin, Chair, 937-775-4451, Fax: 937-775-2422, E-mail: jack.dustin@wright.edu. *Application contact:* John Kimble, Associate Director of Graduate Admissions and Records, 937-775-2957, Fax: 937-775-2453, E-mail: john.kimble@wright.edu.

# CALIFORNIA STATE UNIVERSITY, NORTHRIDGE

*The Tseng College of Extended Learning,*
*Master of Public Administration*

 For more information, visit http://petersons.to/csunmpa

## Program of Study

California State University, Northridge (CSUN) offers a highly regarded Master of Public Administration (M.P.A.) degree program at state-university rates. The university is the top provider of M.P.A. degrees in the State of California and the third leading provider in the country (following Harvard and Columbia universities).

The program is ideal for professionals in the public and nonprofit sectors. It includes three delivery formats: on-campus (open enrollment format), off-campus (cohort format) and online (cohort format). Each format delivers an advanced M.P.A. degree curriculum, personalized student attention, superior instruction, and comprehensive support services.

**Public Sector Management and Leadership Option:** This specialization, within CSUN's M.P.A. program, develops and enhances management skills, enabling graduates to function more effectively within all types of public organizations. This specialization in management and leadership emphasizes both the quantitative aspects of management (i.e., decisions based on analytical data) and the human dynamics of leadership. By emphasizing conceptual and professional development, the program offers a well-rounded perspective of the field and develops leaders with a broad understanding at both the organizational and theoretical levels.

Most participants come to the program with highly specialized knowledge that reflects their experience within a particular area of expertise. The program's integrated curriculum provides graduates with a broader perspective as well as a conceptual vocabulary for leading agencies through increasingly complex issues. The program also emphasizes systems thinking, which gives participants an understanding of the external and internal forces that impact decision-making and problem solving at their agencies. Graduates are prepared to excel in senior positions in local, state, and national government; regional planning agencies; and nonprofit organizations.

**Online Option:** Convenience, flexibility in the when and where of completing weekly assignments, and easy access to the support of fellow students make this program the right choice for many participants. The online Master of Public Administration degree program meets the same rigorous standards as the on-campus and off-campus programs. Online program accreditation and evaluation standards, on-time graduation rates, and students' success rates on licensing exams are comparable to those in the face-to-face programs.

The program's cohesive learning environment includes exceptional support services, accessible faculty members, and close interaction among students who move through the program as a group. It also provides asynchronous course meetings that allow students to attend classes and access course materials according to their schedules.

The course of study includes five core courses (15 credits), six courses in management and leadership (18 credits), and a graduate project (3 credits).

**On-Campus Program:** Students who choose to study on campus have access to CSUN's many campus resources such as face-to-face interaction with students and faculty, and also have the ability to customize the duration of the program by choosing the number of courses they take each semester. The on-campus M.P.A. degree program is ideal for working adults who can attend in-person classes. Classes generally meet evenings and weekends, and students can take courses in any sequence at their own pace.

The course of study includes five core courses (15 credits), six courses in management and leadership (18 credits), and a graduate project (3 credits).

**Off-Campus Program:** To better serve the region, CSUN offers its M.P.A. degree program at sites in several cities across Los Angeles, including Glendale, Downtown Los Angeles, Santa Clarita, Ventura and other areas.

The curriculum includes five core courses (15 credits), six courses in management and leadership (18 credits), and a graduate project (3 credits).

**Graduate Certificate Programs:** CSUN offers graduate certificate programs in management and leadership, health administration, and nonprofit sector management that can be completed in only one year of study. These certificate programs allow professionals in the public and nonprofit sectors to strengthen their professional skills and leadership abilities without expending the cost and time required to earn a Master of Public Administration degree.

The curricula, which are offered in the cohort format, consist of five to six courses.

## Support Services

California State University, Northridge offers exceptional support services designed for working professionals. From application to graduation, students have one-on-one support from a designated program manager and a CSUN faculty member assigned to coordinate the efforts of all teaching in the program. This personalized support frees working professionals to focus on their studies without university- or program-related administrative distractions. In addition, program managers automatically enroll students in all required courses.

## Financial Aid

Several financial aid options are available to M.P.A. students. To be considered, students must be admitted to CSUN and must also complete the Free Application for Federal Student Aid (FAFSA). CSUN's Federal School Code is 001153.

Graduate students may qualify for the Unsubsidized Stafford Loan. Students must officially maintain at least half-time enrollment to remain eligible for loan(s).

U.S. military veterans and military dependents who are approved for VA Educational Benefits should contact the CSUN Veterans Affairs Office at 818-677-5928 or email veteransmail@csun.edu.

Sponsorship is another option. Fees on student accounts can be sponsored (paid for) by an organization, such as an employer, the military, department of vocational rehabilitation, or a foreign government.

Additional details regarding CSUN financial aid offerings can be found at http://tsengcollege.csun.edu/studentinfo/financialaid#req.

## Cost of Study

In the 2017–18 academic year for the M.P.A. Public Sector Management and Leadership program, the cost per unit is $562 for a total tuition cost of $20,232 for the on-campus and off-campus locations. The cost per unit is $723 for a total tuition cost of $26,028 for the online offering. These amounts are for tuition only and do not include books, supplies, or fees. Tuition is subject to change.

## Living and Housing

There are housing options available for students who choose to study on campus. The majority of student housing is managed by the CSUN campus housing office. On-campus housing is available at the University Park Apartments, located at the north end of campus. Spacious two-bedroom apartments are fully furnished and have recreational facilities including swimming pools, a jogging track and basketball and sand volleyball courts. Computer labs are available to residents. In-room data connections also are available to residents who own their own computers.

## Location

Cal State Northridge's campus is situated on 356-acres in Northridge, California in the western region of the United States.

## The College and the University

The Tseng College at CSUN provides programs for midcareer professionals, international students, and regional employers. It specializes in graduate and certificate programs that prepare students for career advancement in emerging fields. Programs are designed to meet the needs of working adults with busy schedules and are offered online, on-campus, and off-campus as well as in blended formats. Classes typically meet evenings and weekends; and courses are offered year-round.

Established in 1958, California State University, Northridge is committed to helping students achieve their educational and professional goals. It offers nearly 40,000 students 64 bachelor's, 58 master's, and 2 doctoral programs as well as 55 teaching credential programs.

One of the nation's largest single-campus universities, CSUN encourages students to combine academic pursuits with hands-on experience. It also serves as the intellectual, economic and cultural heart of the San Fernando Valley and beyond.

## Faculty

The MPA program is taught by CSUN faculty who also work in the field in a range of settings and roles. The program focuses on an evidence-based approach to learning and problem solving. The study of real-world cases brings current knowledge into the classroom and provides students with an optimal combination of theory and practice. Faculty members for the M.P.A. degree program include accomplished professors from various departments within the university as well as talented practicing professionals.

For example, Dr. James David Ballard, professor of sociology, has authored more than 50 articles, book chapters and governmental documents regarding terrorist attacks on radioactive waste facilities and nuclear waste shipments.

Dr. Paul D. Krivonos, professor of communication studies, has written books and articles on topics concerning communication and management. He is also a communication and management consultant who has presented seminars and workshops in countries that include Australia, Fiji, South Africa, and the United States.

Additional information regarding the Tseng College faculty and staff is available at http://tsengcollege.csun.edu/contactus/staffdirectory.

## Applying

The registration process is outlined with complete information online at http://tsengcollege.csun.edu/studentinfo/howtoregister.

## Correspondence and Information

The Tseng College California State University Northridge
18111 Nordhoff Street Northridge, California 91330-8383
United States
Phone: 818-677-3332
Fax:
E-mail: exl@csun.edu
Website: http://tsengcollege.csun.edu/programs/MPA

# UNIVERSITY OF DELAWARE
## School of Public Policy and Administration

 For more information, visit http://petersons.to/delawarepublicadministration

## Programs of Study

The School of Public Policy and Administration offers five graduate degree programs: a Master of Public Administration (M.P.A.), a Master of Arts (M.A.) in urban affairs and public policy, a Ph.D. in urban affairs and public policy, a Master of Science in Disaster Science and Management, and a Ph.D. in Disaster Science and Management.

The M.P.A. is a 36-credit, two-year professional degree program that prepares students for leadership positions in public affairs. It is the preferred professional degree for anyone whose ambition is a career in public or nonprofit management. The program boasts a strong, collaborative, faculty-student research environment and has been accredited by the Network of Schools of Public Policy, Affairs, and Administration (NASPAA) since 1982. Areas of specialization include nonprofit management, public policy analysis, emergency management, public management, or a student-designed area (with faculty approval).

The M.A. in urban affairs and public policy is a 36-credit program that typically involves four semesters of full-time study. It offers students a strong foundation in public policy theory and analysis with a strong focus on solving a variety of societal problems. The program is particularly strong in providing students with many opportunities to apply their new theoretical knowledge and analytical skills to real-world issues. This is done through the careful selection of elective courses, participation in a policy analysis studio, or writing a thesis. Most importantly, this application of skills occurs in the close collaboration with faculty and professional staff in conducting research and public service projects that have clear policy impact. These projects tend to be in the areas of disaster science and management, health policy, historic preservation, housing and community development, media and public policy, nonprofits and philanthropy, and urban and regional planning. The program also has a vibrant international component with study trips, organized and led by the faculty and professional staff, to various places in Europe, Asia, Latin America, and Africa.

The Ph.D. is an interdisciplinary, research-oriented degree that focuses on analysis of the critical policy challenges of our times. The program prepares scholars to create usable knowledge that can inform decision-making and improve the quality of life in communities at all scales, from cities to nations. The doctoral program prepares scholars to approach these multifaceted challenges from creative vantage points, reflecting diverse, international perspectives that transcend disciplinary views and embody the highest research standards. A concern for the global policy challenges and opportunities of an urbanizing world cuts across all research. Students work alongside faculty and researchers to create new knowledge and develop innovative approaches to expand the possibilities for community enhancement and policy improvement.

The School offers a nationally recognized internship program that places students in paid professional positions in international, national, state, and local government. All students in the School are eligible; the internship is a requirement for preservice M.P.A. students.

The M.S. and Ph.D. program in disaster science and management covers the theories, research methodologies, and policies informing efforts focused on emergency preparedness, mitigation, management and response. The M.S. degree requires 30 credits (non-thesis requires 24 credits). The Ph.D. degree requires 42 credits of graduate-level course work beyond the master's degree and 9 credits of dissertation.

## Research Facilities

The School is centrally located in its own building, with its own classrooms and student offices. One of the most distinguishing characteristics of the School of Public Policy and Administration is the integration of theory and practice through applied research projects with the affiliated research and public service centers. Some full-time students are awarded research assistantships on projects in these centers.

The Center for Applied Demography and Survey Research provides demographic and survey data and information on important public issues to researchers and policy makers at all levels (http://www.cadsr.udel.edu). The Center for Community Research and Service helps public, nonprofit, and private organizations in Delaware to design, implement, and evaluate policies and programs that address the needs of low- and moderate-income families and communities related to economic development, housing, and social services. The center also focuses on issues that are vital to the physical and emotional well-being of the world's population. These questions concern the delivery and financing of health care and the outcomes of health care provided (http://www.udel.edu/CCRS). The Center for Historic Architecture and Design focuses on shaping historic preservation planning and policy, reconstructing historic landscapes, documenting threatened historic properties, and advocating for the preservation of historic resources (http://www.udel.edu/CHAD). The Institute for Public Administration links the resources of the University of Delaware (UD) with the management and policy information needs of public and nonprofit organizations (http://www.ipa.udel.edu).

## Financial Aid

The School has competitive financial aid programs, including fellowships, research assistantships, and scholarships. Aid is awarded on merit and is limited by the various restrictions established by the sources of aid. Stipends for 2017–18 are $19,000 for the full academic year. Additional special assistantships, fellowships, and internships are available to students through the University Graduate Scholar's Program, for both newly admitted and graduate students currently enrolled. Awards are competitive and are based on many criteria, including challenging social, economic, educational, cultural, or other life circumstances; academic achievements; first generation graduate student status; and/or need as determined by federal income guidelines (FAFSA). Funds are also available through the Delaware Legislative Fellows Program.

## Cost of Study

Graduate students will be billed by the credit. The 2017–18 rate is $1,770 per credit. Fully-matriculated students are automatically assessed nonrefundable charges of $454 for the health services fee, $238 for student-sponsored activities, and a $100 recreational fee.

## Living and Housing Costs

The University provides some graduate apartments, and there is plenty of off-campus housing in the surrounding community in many price ranges. For more information, students should contact the Housing Assignment Services Office (302-831-2491; http://www.udel.edu/has).

## Student Group

The School has 54 students in the M.P.A. program, 25 in the M.A. and 40 in the Ph.D. Urban Affairs and Public Policy program, and 8 in the M.S. and 17 in the Ph.D. Disaster Science and Management program.

## Student Outcomes

Graduates find career positions in government and nonprofit organizations and occasionally in the private sector with consulting firms. With UD's proximity to Washington, D.C.; Philadelphia; and New York, many graduates pursue positions in nearby metropolitan areas, as well as positions in state and local government in the region and in the nation. Several recent graduates have been successful in the highly competitive federal Presidential Management Fellowship Program.

## Location

Located midway between Philadelphia and Baltimore, the main campus of the University of Delaware is in Newark, conveniently near New York City; Washington, D.C.; and the seashore. A community of 30,000, with a vibrant Main Street of coffeehouses, restaurants, and small shops, Newark is about 14 miles from Wilmington, Delaware's largest city.

## The University

The University is a comprehensive land-, sea-, space-, and urban-grant institution of higher education with an enrollment of approximately 3,750 graduate students in 2016–17. The University offers 134 programs leading to a master's degree and 67 programs leading to a doctoral degree. In 2016, the University awarded 274 doctoral degrees and 889 master's degrees.

*University of Delaware*

## Applying

SPPA welcomes informal inquiries. Students seeking priority consideration for financial aid or admission to any of the graduate programs should apply by January 15. For the master's programs, candidates must have an undergraduate GPA above 3.0 (on a 4.0 scale). Admission to the Ph.D. program requires a master's degree with at least a 3.5 GPA. A GRE score in the 69th or higher percentile is normally expected; competitive scores for admission are 160 for the verbal section and 155 for the quantitative section. Complete applications contain three letters of recommendation, a personal statement of academic and career objectives (for the Ph.D., include a statement of the applicant's research interests), and academic transcripts. For nonnative speakers of English, a demonstrated proficiency in English is required, with a TOEFL score of at least 105.

## Correspondence and Information

School of Public Policy and Administration Admissions
University of Delaware
Newark, Delaware 19716-7310
Phone: 302-831-1687
Fax: 302-831-3296
E-mail: sppa@udel.edu
Website: http://www.sppa.udel.edu

## THE FACULTY AND THEIR RESEARCH

At the core of the School of Public Policy and Administration are the dedicated faculty members, who are challenging teachers, seasoned researchers, and experienced practitioners. With interdisciplinary backgrounds as skilled executives, managers, and community leaders, they bring practical experience to the classroom and successfully blend a solid academic base with stimulating practical experience.

Maria P. Aristigueta, Charles P. Messick Professor in Public Administration; Director, School of Public Policy and Administration; and Senior Policy Fellow, Institute for Public Administration; D.P.A., USC, 1997. Administrative behavior, performance management, policy analysis, strategic management.

Philip J. Barnes, Assistant Professor, Ph.D., Delaware, 2015. Energy, environment.

Jane Case-Lilly, Assistant Professor of Instruction; Ph.D., Delaware, 2008. Organizational leadership, ethics, communication, decision making.

Nina P. David, Assistant Professor; Ph.D., Michigan, 2008. Land use planning and policy, regional planning and cooperation, growth management, architecture and urban design.

Robert B. Denhardt, Visiting Scholar; Ph.D., Kentucky, 1968. Public sector management, strategic planning and public productivity.

Eric D. Jacobson, Associate Professor and Policy Scientist, Institute for Public Administration; M.P.A., Delaware, 1981. Public economics, health policy, employee compensation and benefits, tourism development and research, analytical methods.

Jonathan Justice, Professor; Ph.D., Rutgers, 2003. Public financial management, nongovernmental public administration, urban policy and administration.

Gerald Kauffman, Assistant Professor and Project Director, Water Resources Agency; Ph.D., Delaware. Watershed policy, planning, and management; water resources government and finance; water resources engineering; hydrology and hydraulics.

James Kendra, Professor, Director, Disaster Research Center; Ph.D., Rutgers, 2000. Disasters, hurricanes, environment.

Erin Knight, Assistant Professor; Ph.D., Delaware, 2011. Equity, public health, evaluation.

Jerome R. Lewis, Associate Professor; Director, Institute for Public Administration; Ph.D., NYU, 1968. Public administration, personnel management, urban planning, political leadership.

John G. McNutt, Professor; Ph.D., Tennessee, 1991. Technology, nonprofit management, advocacy and government relations, community organization and planning.

Anthony E. Middlebrooks, Associate Professor; Ph.D., Wisconsin, 1999. Leadership formation and development, creativity and leadership, service and social justice, research methods.

James L. Morrison, Professor; Ed.D., Temple, 1971. Telecommunications and consumer policy, consumer environmental issues, consumer protection.

K. C. Morrison, Professor; Ph.D., Wisconsin, 1977. Comparative public administration, public administration, public policy and comparative politics.

Kathleen M. Murphy, Instructor and Coordinator, Conflict Resolution Program; M.P.A., Delaware. Conflict resolution, mediation, organizational and leadership development.

Steven W. Peuquet, Associate Professor and Director, Center for Community Research and Service; Ph.D., Pennsylvania, 1996. Strategic planning, housing, homelessness, electronic community networks, public policy analysis and evaluation.

Edward C. Ratledge, Associate Professor and Director, Center for Applied Demography and Survey Research; M.A., Delaware, 1972. Management information systems, econometrics, criminal justice systems.

Chandra Reedy, Professor and Interim Director, Center for Historic Architecture and Design; Ph.D., California, 2011. Preservation, conservation, archaeology.

Daniel Rich, University Professor of Public Policy; Director, Urban Affairs and Public Policy Ph.D. Program; Director, Community Engagement Initiative; Ph.D., MIT, 1972. Public policy and public management.

Breck Robinson, Associate Professor and Director, Public Policy Undergraduate Program; Ph.D., Tennessee, 1994. Financial institutions, public policy, development.

Andrea Sarzynski, Associate Professor; Ph.D., George Washington, 2006. Urbanization and environmental change; environmental policy and politics; urban and regional planning; science and policymaking.

Daniel Smith, Associate Professor and Director, Master of Public Administration Program; Ph.D., Georgia, 2008. Public budgeting and finance, public management, public policy.

Karen F. Stein, Associate Professor and Director, Organizational and Community Leadership Undergraduate Program; Ph.D., Delaware, 1984. Domestic elder abuse and neglect, leadership studies, consumer and family economic policy analysis.

Tibor Tóth, Assistant Professor; Ph.D., Delaware, 2005. Environment, health.

Joseph Trainor, Associate Professor; Ph.D., Delaware, 2008. Disasters, health, human behavior, organizations, evacuation.

Leland Ware, Louis L. Redding Chair for the Study of Law and Public Policy and Associate Director, School of Public Policy and Administration; J.D., Boston College, 1973. Employment discrimination law, civil rights law, civil procedure.

Harvey White, Professor of Practice; Ph.D., North Carolina at Chapel Hill, 1985. Human talent development and management, international development and management, social equity and environmental justice, health policy.

Danilo Yanich, Professor; Director, Urban Affairs and Public Policy Master's Program; and Associate Policy Scientist, Center for Community Research and Service; Ph.D., Delaware, 1980. Criminal justice policy, media and public policy, international comparative governance.

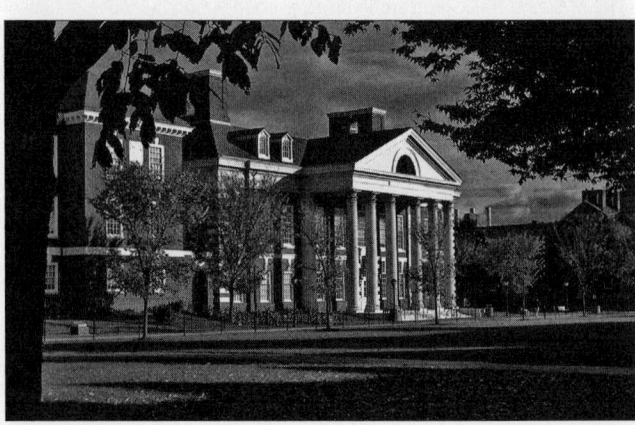

# Section 26
# Social Sciences

This section contains a directory of institutions offering graduate work in social sciences. Additional information about programs listed in the directory may be obtained by writing directly to the dean of a graduate school or chair of a department at the address given in the directory.

For programs offering related work, see also in this book *Area and Cultural Studies, Communication and Media, Criminology and Forensics, Economics, Geography, Family and Consumer Sciences, Political Science and International Affairs, Psychology and Counseling,* and *Sociology, Anthropology, and Archaeology.*

## CONTENTS

**Program Directory**

# Social Sciences

**Antioch University Midwest,** Graduate Programs, Individualized Interdisciplinary Studies and Social Sciences Program, Yellow Springs, OH 45387-1609. Offers applied psychology (MA); conflict studies (MA); health and human development (MA); integral studies (MA); peace studies (MA); systems and organizations (MA). *Program availability:* Part-time, evening/weekend, online learning. *Degree requirements:* For master's, thesis or alternative. *Entrance requirements:* For master's, resume, goal statement, interview. *Application deadline:* For fall admission, 8/1 for domestic students; for winter admission, 12/1 for domestic students; for spring admission, 3/10 for domestic students. Applications are processed on a rolling basis. Application fee: $50. Electronic applications accepted. *Expenses:* $799 per credit hour. *Financial support:* Federal Work-Study available. Financial award applicants required to submit FAFSA. *Application contact:* Deena Kent-Hummel, Director of Admissions, 937-769-1800, Fax: 937-769-1804, E-mail: dkent@antioch.edu.
Website: https://www.antioch.edu/midwest/degrees-programs/business-management-leadership/individualized-master-of-arts-ma/interdisciplinary-studies-and-social-

**Assumption College,** Resiliency in the Helping Professions Program, Worcester, MA 01609-1296. Offers CAGS, CGS. *Program availability:* Part-time, evening/weekend. *Entrance requirements:* For degree, bachelor's degree with minimum GPA of 3.0 (for CGS); master's degree (for CAGS); 2 letters of recommendation, official transcripts, personal statement, current resume. Additional exam requirements/recommendations for international students: Required—TOEFL (minimum score 540 paper-based; 76 iBT), IELTS (minimum score 6). *Application deadline:* Applications are processed on a rolling basis. Application fee: $30. *Expenses: Tuition:* Full-time $11,610; part-time $645 per credit. *Required fees:* $70 per term. Tuition and fees vary according to course load and program. *Unit head:* Lea Christo, Director, 508-767-7503, Fax: 508-798-2872, E-mail: l.christo@assumption.edu. *Application contact:* Karen Stoyanoff, Director of Recruitment for Graduate Enrollment, 508-767-7442, Fax: 508-799-4412, E-mail: graduate@assumption.edu.
Website: http://graduate.assumption.edu/resiliency-helping-professions/resiliency-helping-professions

**Augusta University,** College of Allied Health Sciences, Program in Public Health, Augusta, GA 30912. Offers environmental health (MPH); health informatics (MPH); health management (MPH); social and behavioral sciences (MPH). *Accreditation:* CEPH. *Program availability:* Part-time. *Degree requirements:* For master's, thesis (for some programs). *Entrance requirements:* For master's, GRE General Test, three letters of recommendation. Additional exam requirements/recommendations for international students: Required—TOEFL. Electronic applications accepted.

**California Institute of Technology,** Division of the Humanities and Social Sciences, Social Science Program, Pasadena, CA 91125-0001. Offers MS, PhD. Terminal master's awarded for partial completion of doctoral program. *Degree requirements:* For doctorate, thesis/dissertation. *Entrance requirements:* For doctorate, GRE General Test. Additional exam requirements/recommendations for international students: Required—TOEFL (minimum score 90 iBT); Recommended—TWE. Electronic applications accepted. *Faculty research:* Theoretical and applied microeconomics, experimental social science, political science, quantitative history, behavioral economics and neuroscience.

**California State University, Chico,** Office of Graduate Studies, College of Behavioral and Social Sciences, Social Science Program, Chico, CA 95929-0722. Offers MA. *Faculty:* 5 full-time (2 women), 8 part-time/adjunct (2 women). *Degree requirements:* For master's, thesis or project. *Entrance requirements:* For master's, GRE General Test or MAT, two letters of recommendation, statement of purpose. Additional exam requirements/recommendations for international students: Required—TOEFL (minimum score 550 paper-based; 80 iBT), IELTS (minimum score 6.5), PTE (minimum score 59). *Application deadline:* For fall admission, 3/1 priority date for domestic students, 3/1 for international students; for spring admission, 9/15 priority date for domestic students, 9/15 for international students. Application fee: $55. Electronic applications accepted. *Financial support:* Fellowships, teaching assistantships, career-related internships or fieldwork, institutionally sponsored loans, traineeships, and unspecified assistantships available. Financial award application deadline: 3/1; financial award applicants required to submit FAFSA. *Unit head:* Dr. Eugenie Rovai, Coordinator, 530-895-5688, Fax: 530-898-6781, E-mail: erovai@csuchico.edu. *Application contact:* Judy L. Rice, Graduate Admissions Counselor, 530-898-5416, Fax: 530-898-3342, E-mail: jlmorris@csuchico.edu.
Website: http://www.csuchico.edu/sosc/

**California State University, San Bernardino,** Graduate Studies, College of Social and Behavioral Sciences, Program in Social Sciences and Globalization, San Bernardino, CA 92407. Offers MA. *Students:* 2 full-time (1 woman), 22 part-time (12 women); includes 14 minority (12 Hispanic/Latino; 2 Two or more races, non-Hispanic/Latino), 1 international. 21 applicants, 57% accepted, 11 enrolled. In 2016, 11 master's awarded. *Entrance requirements:* Additional exam requirements/recommendations for international students: Required—TOEFL. *Application deadline:* For fall admission, 5/15 for domestic students. Application fee: $55. *Expenses:* Tuition, state resident: full-time $7843; part-time $5011.20 per year. Tuition and fees vary according to course load, degree level, program and reciprocity agreements. *Financial support:* Fellowships, research assistantships, teaching assistantships, and institutionally sponsored loans available. Financial award application deadline: 5/1. *Unit head:* Dr. Cherstyn Lyon, Coordinator, 909-537-3836, E-mail: clyon@csusb.edu. *Application contact:* Dr. Francisca Beer, Dean of Graduate Studies, 909-537-5058, E-mail: fbeer@csusb.edu.

**Campbellsville University,** College of Arts and Sciences, Campbellsville, KY 42718-2799. Offers social science (MA). *Program availability:* Part-time, evening/weekend, 100% online, blended/hybrid learning. *Faculty:* 6 full-time (2 women), 3 part-time/adjunct (1 woman). *Students:* 1 full-time (0 women), 23 part-time (13 women); includes 4 minority (1 Black or African American, non-Hispanic/Latino; 1 Asian, non-Hispanic/Latino; 2 Hispanic/Latino), 5 international. Average age 25. 28 applicants, 71% accepted, 17 enrolled. In 2016, 4 master's awarded. *Degree requirements:* For master's, comprehensive exam. *Entrance requirements:* For master's, GRE General Test, minimum GPA of 2.9, letters of recommendation, college transcripts. Additional exam requirements/recommendations for international students: Recommended—TOEFL, IELTS. *Application deadline:* Applications are processed on a rolling basis. Application fee: $25. Electronic applications accepted. *Expenses:* $499 per credit hour (for MASM); $399 per credit hour (for MTESL). *Financial support:* Unspecified assistantships available. Financial award application deadline: 6/1; financial award applicants required to submit FAFSA. *Unit head:* Dr. Mike Page, Dean, 270-789-5394. *Application contact:* Monica Bamwine, Assistant Director of Graduate Admissions, 270-789-5221, Fax: 270-789-5071, E-mail: mkbamwine@campbellsville.edu.
Website: http://www.campbellsville.edu/

**Carnegie Mellon University,** Dietrich College of Humanities and Social Sciences, Department of Social and Decision Sciences, Pittsburgh, PA 15213-3891. Offers behavioral decision research (PhD); social and decision science (PhD); strategy, entrepreneurship, and technological change (PhD). Terminal master's awarded for partial completion of doctoral program. *Degree requirements:* For doctorate, comprehensive exam, thesis/dissertation, research paper. *Entrance requirements:* For doctorate, GRE General Test. Additional exam requirements/recommendations for international students: Required—TOEFL. Electronic applications accepted. *Faculty research:* Organization theory, political science, sociology, technology studies.

**The Citadel, The Military College of South Carolina,** Citadel Graduate College, School of Humanities and Social Sciences, Department of Political Science, Charleston, SC 29409. Offers international politics and military affairs (MA); social science (MA). *Program availability:* Part-time, evening/weekend, 100% online, blended/hybrid learning. *Faculty:* 5 full-time (1 woman). *Students:* 19 full-time (7 women), 22 part-time (14 women); includes 11 minority (9 Black or African American, non-Hispanic/Latino; 1 Hispanic/Latino; 1 Two or more races, non-Hispanic/Latino). 24 applicants, 79% accepted, 9 enrolled. In 2016, 6 master's awarded. *Entrance requirements:* For master's, GRE (minimum combined score of 290 verbal and quantitative), MAT (minimum raw score of 396), written statement of purpose setting forth intentions, goals, and preparation for graduate study; at least 2 academic letters of recommendation addressing ability to undertake coursework at graduate level. Additional exam requirements/recommendations for international students: Required—TOEFL (minimum score 550 paper-based; 79 iBT). *Application deadline:* Applications are processed on a rolling basis. Application fee: $40. Electronic applications accepted. *Expenses:* Tuition, state resident: full-time $5121; part-time $569 per credit hour. Tuition, nonresident: full-time $8613; part-time $957 per credit hour. *Required fees:* $90 per term. *Financial support:* Fellowships and unspecified assistantships available. Support available to part-time students. Financial award application deadline: 7/1; financial award applicants required to submit FAFSA. *Unit head:* Dr. DuBose Kapeluck, Department Head, 843-953-2037, E-mail: dubose.kapeluck@citadel.edu. *Application contact:* Dr. Terry Mays, Associate Professor, 843-953-5069, E-mail: terry.mays@citadel.edu.
Website: http://www.citadel.edu/root/politicalscience

**Columbia University,** Graduate School of Arts and Sciences, New York, NY 10027. Offers African-American studies (MA); American studies (MA); anthropology (MA, PhD); art history and archaeology (MA, PhD); astronomy (PhD); biological sciences (PhD); biotechnology (MA); chemical physics (PhD); chemistry (PhD); classical studies (MA, PhD); classics (MA, PhD); climate and society (MA); conservation biology (MA); earth and environmental sciences (PhD); East Asia: regional studies (MA); East Asian languages and cultures (MA, PhD); ecology, evolution and environmental biology (MA), including conservation biology; ecology, evolution, and environmental biology (PhD), including ecology and evolutionary biology, evolutionary primatology; economics (MA, PhD); English and comparative literature (MA, PhD); French and Romance philology (MA, PhD); Germanic languages (MA, PhD); global French studies (MA); global thought (MA); Hispanic cultural studies (MA); history (PhD); history and literature (MA); human rights studies (MA); Islamic studies (MA); Italian (MA, PhD); Japanese pedagogy (MA); Jewish studies (MA); Latin America and the Caribbean: regional studies (MA); Latin American and Iberian cultures (PhD); mathematics (MA, PhD), including finance (MA); medieval and Renaissance studies (MA); Middle Eastern, South Asian, and African studies (MA, PhD); modern art: critical and curatorial studies (MA); modern European studies (MA); museum anthropology (MA); music (DMA, PhD); oral history (MA); philosophical foundations of physics (MA); philosophy (MA, PhD); physics (PhD); political science (MA, PhD); psychology (PhD); quantitative methods in the social sciences (MA); religion (MA, PhD); Russia, Eurasia and East Europe: regional studies (MA); Russian translation (MA); Slavic cultures (MA); Slavic languages (MA, PhD); sociology (MA, PhD); South Asian studies (MA); statistics (MA, PhD); theatre (PhD). Dual-degree programs require admission to both Graduate School of Arts and Sciences and another Columbia school. *Program availability:* Part-time. Terminal master's awarded for partial completion of doctoral program. *Degree requirements:* For master's, variable foreign language requirement, comprehensive exam (for some programs), thesis (for some programs); for doctorate, variable foreign language requirement, comprehensive exam (for some programs), thesis/dissertation. *Entrance requirements:* For master's and doctorate, GRE General Test, GRE Subject Test (for some programs). Additional exam requirements/recommendations for international students: Required—TOEFL, IELTS. Electronic applications accepted.

**Eastern Michigan University,** Graduate School, College of Arts and Sciences, Department of History and Philosophy, Program in Social Science, Ypsilanti, MI 48197. Offers MA. *Program availability:* Part-time, evening/weekend, online learning. *Students:* 5 part-time (2 women); includes 3 minority (2 Black or African American, non-Hispanic/Latino; 1 Hispanic/Latino). Average age 38. 2 applicants, 100% accepted, 1 enrolled. In 2016, 3 master's awarded. *Degree requirements:* For master's, thesis optional. *Entrance requirements:* Additional exam requirements/recommendations for international students: Required—TOEFL. *Application deadline:* Applications are processed on a rolling basis. Application fee: $45. *Financial support:* Fellowships, research assistantships with full tuition reimbursements, teaching assistantships with full tuition reimbursements, career-related internships or fieldwork, Federal Work-Study, institutionally sponsored loans, scholarships/grants, tuition waivers (partial), and unspecified assistantships available. Support available to part-time students. Financial award applicants required to submit FAFSA. *Application contact:* Dr. Ronald Delph, Director, 734-487-1018, Fax: 734-487-6835, E-mail: rdelph@emich.edu.

**Florida Agricultural and Mechanical University,** Division of Graduate Studies, Research, and Continuing Education, College of Social Sciences, Arts and Humanities, Department of History and Political Science, Program in Applied Social Science, Tallahassee, FL 32307-3200. Offers criminal justice (MASS); history (MASS); political science (MASS); public administration (MASS). *Program availability:* Part-time. *Degree requirements:* For master's, thesis optional. *Entrance requirements:* For master's, GRE General Test, minimum GPA of 3.0. *Faculty research:* Southern history, black history, election trends, Presidential history.

**Graduate Theological Union,** Graduate Programs, Berkeley, CA 94709-1212. Offers art and religion (MA, PhD, Th D); biblical languages (MA); biblical studies (MA); Biblical studies (PhD, Th D); Buddhist studies (MA); Christian spirituality (MA, PhD, Th D); cultural and historical studies of religions (MA, PhD, Th D); ethics and social theory (PhD, Th D); history (MA, PhD, Th D); homiletics (MA, PhD, Th D); interdisciplinary studies (PhD, Th D); Jewish studies (MA, PhD, Th D, Certificate); liturgical studies (MA, PhD, Th D); Near Eastern religions (PhD, Th D); Orthodox Christian studies (MA); religion and psychology (MA, PhD, Th D); religion and society/ethics and social theory (MA); systematic and philosophical theology (MA, PhD, Th D). PhD programs in Jewish studies and Near Eastern religions offered jointly with University of California, Berkeley.

*Accreditation:* ATS. Terminal master's awarded for partial completion of doctoral program. *Degree requirements:* For master's, one foreign language, thesis; for doctorate, one foreign language, comprehensive exam, thesis/dissertation. *Entrance requirements:* For master's, GRE General Test; for doctorate, GRE General Test, MA or M Div. Additional exam requirements/recommendations for international students: Required—TOEFL. Electronic applications accepted.

**Harrison Middleton University,** Graduate Program, Tempe, AZ 85282. Offers education (MA, Ed D); humanities (MA); imaginative literature (MA); interdisciplinary studies (DA); jurisprudence (MA); natural science (MA); philosophy and religion (MA); social science (MA). *Program availability:* Part-time, evening/weekend, online learning. *Degree requirements:* For master's and doctorate, capstone project. *Entrance requirements:* For master's, interview; for doctorate, 2 academic letters of reference, interview, essay. Additional exam requirements/recommendations for international students: Required—TOEFL (minimum score 550 paper-based; 80 iBT). Electronic applications accepted. *Faculty research:* Japanese animation, educational leadership, war art, John Muir's wilderness.

**Hollins University,** Graduate Programs, Program in Liberal Studies, Roanoke, VA 24020. Offers humanities (MALS); interdisciplinary studies (MALS); leadership (MALS); social sciences (MALS); visual and performing arts (MALS). *Program availability:* Part-time, evening/weekend. *Degree requirements:* For master's, thesis. *Entrance requirements:* For master's, three letters of recommendation, interview, bachelor's degree, undergraduate transcripts, statement of educational objectives. Additional exam requirements/recommendations for international students: Required—TOEFL (minimum score 550 paper-based; 80 iBT), IELTS (minimum score 6.5). *Application deadline:* Applications are processed on a rolling basis. Application fee: $40. Electronic applications accepted. *Expenses:* $395 per credit hour. *Financial support:* Fellowships and scholarships/grants available. Support available to part-time students. Financial award application deadline: 7/15; financial award applicants required to submit FAFSA. *Faculty research:* Diversity, gender and women's studies, political science, leadership. *Unit head:* Director, 540-362-6576, Fax: 540-362-6288, E-mail: hugrad@hollins.edu. *Application contact:* Cathy S. Koon, Manager of Graduate Programs, 540-362-6326, Fax: 540-362-6288, E-mail: ckoon@hollins.edu. Website: http://www.hollins.edu/academics/graduate-degrees/liberal-studies/

**Humboldt State University,** Academic Programs, College of Arts, Humanities, and Social Sciences, Program in Environment and Community, Arcata, CA 95521-8299. Offers MA. *Degree requirements:* For master's, thesis or alternative, qualifying exam. *Entrance requirements:* For master's, minimum GPA of 2.5, 3 letters of recommendation. Additional exam requirements/recommendations for international students: Required—TOEFL (minimum score 500 paper-based). *Expenses:* Tuition, state resident: full-time $6738; part-time $1953 per semester. Tuition, nonresident: full-time $13,434; part-time $3813 per semester. *Required fees:* $1738; $653 per semester. Tuition and fees vary according to program. *Faculty research:* Geography, political science, ethnic studies, anthropology, economics.

**Indiana University Bloomington,** Maurer School of Law, Bloomington, IN 47405-7000. Offers comparative law (MCL); juridical science (SJD); law (LL M, JD); law and social sciences (PhD); legal studies (Certificate); JD/MA; JD/MBA; JD/MLS; JD/MPA; JD/MS; JD/MSES. PhD offered through University Graduate School. *Accreditation:* ABA. *Degree requirements:* For master's, thesis or practicum; for doctorate, thesis/dissertation (for some programs), research seminar (for JD). *Entrance requirements:* For master's, LSAT, 3 letters of recommendation, law degree or license to practice; for doctorate, LSAT. Additional exam requirements/recommendations for international students: Required—TOEFL (minimum score 560 paper-based; 80 iBT). Electronic applications accepted. *Faculty research:* Environmental risk assessment and policy analysis, information privacy and security, judicial independence, accountability, ethics.

**Indiana University–Purdue University Indianapolis,** School of Public Health, Indianapolis, IN 46202. Offers biostatistics (MPH); environmental health science (MPH); epidemiology (MPH, PhD); health administration (MHA); health policy and management (MPH, PhD); social and behavioral sciences (MPH). *Accreditation:* CEPH. *Expenses:* Contact institution.

**Johns Hopkins University,** Bloomberg School of Public Health, Department of Health, Behavior and Society, Baltimore, MD 21218. Offers genetic counseling (Sc M); health education and health communication (MSPH); social and behavioral sciences (Dr PH, PhD); social factors in health (MHS). *Degree requirements:* For master's, comprehensive exam (for some programs), thesis (for some programs); for doctorate, comprehensive exam, thesis/dissertation. *Entrance requirements:* For master's, GRE, curriculum vitae, 3 letters of recommendation; for doctorate, GRE, transcripts, curriculum vitae, 3 recommendation letters. Additional exam requirements/recommendations for international students: Required—TOEFL (minimum score 600 paper-based; 100 iBT). Electronic applications accepted. *Faculty research:* Social determinants of health and structural and community-level inventions to improve health, communication and health education, behavioral and social aspects of genetic counseling.

**Massachusetts Institute of Technology,** School of Humanities, Arts, and Social Sciences, Program in Science, Technology, and Society, Cambridge, MA 02139. Offers history, anthropology, and science, technology and society (PhD). *Faculty:* 13 full-time (5 women). *Students:* 31 full-time (22 women); includes 5 minority (1 American Indian or Alaska Native, non-Hispanic/Latino; 2 Asian, non-Hispanic/Latino; 2 Hispanic/Latino), 8 international. Average age 31. 160 applicants, 5% accepted, 5 enrolled. In 2016, 3 doctorates awarded. *Degree requirements:* For doctorate, one foreign language, comprehensive exam, thesis/dissertation. *Entrance requirements:* For doctorate, GRE General Test. Additional exam requirements/recommendations for international students: Required—TOEFL, IELTS. *Application deadline:* For fall admission, 12/15 for domestic and international students. Application fee: $75. Electronic applications accepted. *Expenses:* Tuition: Full-time $46,400; part-time $725 per credit. One-time fee: $312 full-time. Full-time tuition and fees vary according to course load and program. *Financial support:* In 2016–17, 30 students received support, including 21 fellowships (averaging $38,600 per year), 1 research assistantship (averaging $39,300 per year), 4 teaching assistantships (averaging $40,200 per year); Federal Work-Study, institutionally sponsored loans, scholarships/grants, traineeships, health care benefits, unspecified assistantships, and resident tutors also available. Support available to part-time students. Financial award application deadline: 5/1; financial award applicants required to submit FAFSA. *Faculty research:* History of science; history of technology; sociology of science and technology; anthropology of science and technology; science, technology, and society. *Total annual research expenditures:* $186,000. *Unit head:* Prof. Jenniger Light, Program Director, 617-253-4062, Fax: 617-258-8118, E-mail: stsprogram@mit.edu. *Application contact:* 617-253-9759, E-mail: hasts@mit.edu. Website: http://sts-program.mit.edu/

**Mississippi College,** Graduate School, College of Arts and Sciences, School of Humanities and Social Sciences, Department of History, Political Science, Administration of Justice, and Paralegal Studies, Clinton, MS 39058. Offers administration of justice (MSS); history (M Ed, MA, MSS); paralegal studies (Certificate); political science (MSS); social sciences (M Ed, MSS). *Program availability:* Part-time.

*Degree requirements:* For master's, one foreign language, comprehensive exam, thesis (for some programs). *Entrance requirements:* For master's, GRE or NTE, minimum GPA of 2.5. Additional exam requirements/recommendations for international students: Recommended—TOEFL, IELTS. Electronic applications accepted.

**Montclair State University,** The Graduate School, College of Education and Human Services, MAT Program in Teaching, Montclair, NJ 07043-1624. Offers art (MAT); biology (MAT); chemistry (MAT); earth science (MAT); English (MAT); French (MAT); health and physical education (MAT); health education (MAT); mathematics (MAT); music (MAT); physical education (MAT); physical science (MAT); social studies (MAT); Spanish (MAT); teacher of English as a second language (MAT). *Degree requirements:* For master's, comprehensive exam, thesis or alternative. *Entrance requirements:* For master's, .interview, 2 letters of recommendation. Additional exam requirements/recommendations for international students: Required—TOEFL (minimum score 83 iBT), IELTS (minimum score 6.5). Electronic applications accepted. *Expenses:* Tuition, state resident: part-time $553 per credit. Tuition, nonresident: part-time $854 per credit. *Required fees:* $91 per credit. Tuition and fees vary according to program.

**The New School,** The New School for Social Research, New York, NY 10003. Offers M Phil, MA, MS, PhD. *Program availability:* Part-time. *Faculty:* 50 full-time (18 women), 12 part-time/adjunct (4 women). *Students:* 606 full-time (309 women), 184 part-time (107 women); includes 116 minority (24 Black or African American, non-Hispanic/Latino; 1 American Indian or Alaska Native, non-Hispanic/Latino; 24 Asian, non-Hispanic/Latino; 48 Hispanic/Latino; 19 Two or more races, non-Hispanic/Latino), 266 international. Average age 31. 979 applicants, 76% accepted, 161 enrolled. In 2016, 195 master's, 57 doctorates awarded. Terminal master's awarded for partial completion of doctoral program. *Degree requirements:* For master's, comprehensive exam (for some programs), thesis (for some programs); for doctorate, variable foreign language requirement, comprehensive exam (for some programs), thesis/dissertation. *Entrance requirements:* For master's, letters of recommendation, writing sample, essays, official transcripts. Additional exam requirements/recommendations for international students: Required—TOEFL (minimum score 100 iBT), IELTS (minimum score 7), PTE (minimum score 68). *Application deadline:* For fall admission, 8/1 priority date for domestic students, 6/1 priority date for international students; for spring admission, 10/15 priority date for domestic and international students. Applications are processed on a rolling basis. Application fee: $50. Electronic applications accepted. *Expenses:* Contact institution. *Financial support:* Fellowships, research assistantships, teaching assistantships, career-related internships or fieldwork, Federal Work-Study, scholarships/grants, and tuition waivers (full and partial) available. Support available to part-time students. Financial award application deadline: 3/1; financial award applicants required to submit FAFSA. *Faculty research:* Critical political and social inquiry; empirical, historical, and ethnographic scholarship; continental philosophy; heterodox economics; cognitive, social, developmental and clinical psychology. *Total annual research expenditures:* $60,000. *Unit head:* Dr. William Milberg, Dean, 212-229-5777, E-mail: milbergw@newschool.edu. *Application contact:* Dana Messinger, Director of Graduate Admission, 212-229-5150 Ext. 2300, E-mail: messingd@newschool.edu. Website: http://www.newschool.edu/

**New York University,** College of Global Public Health, New York, NY 10003. Offers biological basis of public health (PhD); community and international health (MPH); global health leadership (MPH); health systems and health services research (PhD); population and community health (PhD); public health nutrition (MPH); social and behavioral sciences (MPH); socio-behavioral health (PhD). *Accreditation:* CEPH. *Program availability:* Part-time, online learning. *Degree requirements:* For master's, thesis (for some programs); for doctorate, thesis/dissertation. *Entrance requirements:* For master's and doctorate, GRE. Additional exam requirements/recommendations for international students: Required—TOEFL. Electronic applications accepted.

**North Dakota State University,** College of Graduate and Interdisciplinary Studies, College of Arts, Humanities and Social Sciences, Department of Sociology and Anthropology, Fargo, ND 58102. Offers anthropology (MA, MS); community development (MA, MS); social science (MA, MS); sociology (MS). *Program availability:* Part-time. *Degree requirements:* For master's, thesis. *Entrance requirements:* For master's, GRE (for emergency management), course work in sociology, minimum GPA of 3.2. Additional exam requirements/recommendations for international students: Required—TOEFL. Electronic applications accepted. *Faculty research:* Medical sociology, demography, ethnology, archaeology.

**Nova Southeastern University,** College of Arts, Humanities, and Social Sciences, Fort Lauderdale, FL 33314-7796. Offers advanced conflict resolution practice (Graduate Certificate); college student affairs (MS); conflict analysis and resolution (MS, PhD); cross-disciplinary studies (MA); family studies (Graduate Certificate); family systems health care (Graduate Certificate); family therapy (MS, PhD); marriage and family therapy (DMFT); peace studies (Graduate Certificate); qualitative research (Graduate Certificate); solution focused coaching (Graduate Certificate). *Accreditation:* AAMFT/COAMFTE (one or more programs are accredited). *Program availability:* Part-time, evening/weekend, 100% online, blended/hybrid learning. *Faculty:* 29 full-time (18 women), 27 part-time/adjunct (21 women). *Students:* 306 full-time (242 women), 889 part-time (683 women); includes 677 minority (403 Black or African American, non-Hispanic/Latino; 2 American Indian or Alaska Native, non-Hispanic/Latino; 20 Asian, non-Hispanic/Latino; 224 Hispanic/Latino; 1 Native Hawaiian or other Pacific Islander, non-Hispanic/Latino; 27 Two or more races, non-Hispanic/Latino), 53 international. Average age 37. 624 applicants, 61% accepted, 285 enrolled. In 2016, 303 master's, 71 doctorates, 34 other advanced degrees awarded. *Degree requirements:* For master's, thesis optional, comprehensive exams, portfolios (for some programs), table-top exams (for some programs); for doctorate, comprehensive exam, thesis/dissertation, qualifying exams, portfolios (for some programs). *Entrance requirements:* For master's, interview, minimum GPA of 3.0, writing sample; for doctorate, interview, minimum GPA of 3.5, master's degree in related field, writing sample; for Graduate Certificate, minimum GPA of 3.0. Additional exam requirements/recommendations for international students: Required—TOEFL. *Application deadline:* For fall admission, 5/17 priority date for domestic and international students; for winter admission, 12/1 priority date for domestic and international students; for spring admission, 4/1 priority date for domestic and international students. Applications are processed on a rolling basis. Application fee: $50. Electronic applications accepted. *Expenses:* $1,005. *Financial support:* In 2016–17, 170 students received support. Career-related internships or fieldwork, Federal Work-Study, scholarships/grants, and unspecified assistantships available. Financial award application deadline: 4/1; financial award applicants required to submit CSS PROFILE. *Faculty research:* Conflict resolution, family therapy, peace research, international conflict, multi-disciplinary studies, college student affairs, national security affairs, health care conflict resolution, family systems health care, advanced family systems, qualitative research, solution-focused coaching. *Unit head:* Dr. Honggang Yang, Dean, 954-262-3016, Fax: 954-262-3968, E-mail: yangh@nova.edu. *Application contact:* Marcia Arango, Student Recruitment Coordinator, 954-262-3006, Fax: 954-262-3968, E-mail: marango@nsu.nova.edu. Website: http://cahss.nova.edu/

**The Ohio State University,** Graduate School, College of Food, Agricultural, and Environmental Sciences, School of Environment and Natural Resources, Columbus, OH

## Social Sciences

43210. Offers ecological restoration (MS, PhD); ecosystem science (MS, PhD); environment and natural resources (MENR); environmental social sciences (MS, PhD); fisheries and wildlife science (MS, PhD); forest science (MS, PhD); rural sociology (MS, PhD); soil science (MS, PhD). *Faculty:* 38. *Students:* 94 full-time (59 women), 8 part-time (4 women); includes 12 minority (7 Hispanic/Latino; 5 Two or more races, non-Hispanic/Latino), 6 international. Average age 28. In 2016, 19 master's, 8 doctorates awarded. *Degree requirements:* For master's, thesis; for doctorate, thesis/dissertation. *Entrance requirements:* For master's and doctorate, GRE. Additional exam requirements/recommendations for international students: Required—TOEFL (minimum score 550 paper-based; 79 iBT), Michigan English Language Assessment Battery (minimum score 82); Recommended—IELTS (minimum score 7). *Application deadline:* For fall admission, 1/1 priority date for domestic students, 12/15 priority date for international students; for spring admission, 11/1 for domestic students, 9/15 for international students. Applications are processed on a rolling basis. Application fee: $60 ($70 for international students). Electronic applications accepted. *Financial support:* Fellowships with tuition reimbursements, research assistantships with tuition reimbursements, teaching assistantships with tuition reimbursements, health care benefits, and unspecified assistantships available. *Unit head:* Dr. Jeff S. Sharp, Director, 614-292-9410, E-mail: sharp.123@osu.edu. *Application contact:* Graduate and Professional Admissions, 614-292-9444, Fax: 614-292-3895, E-mail: gpadmissions@osu.edu.
Website: http://senr.osu.edu/

**Ohio University,** Graduate College, College of Arts and Sciences, Program in Social Sciences, Athens, OH 45701-2979. Offers MSS. *Program availability:* Online learning. *Degree requirements:* For master's, oral exam. *Entrance requirements:* For master's, minimum GPA of 2.75. Additional exam requirements/recommendations for international students: Required—TOEFL (minimum score 600 paper-based). Application fee: $50 ($55 for international students). Electronic applications accepted. *Financial support:* Institutionally sponsored loans available. Financial award application deadline: 3/15; financial award applicants required to submit FAFSA. *Unit head:* Dr. Robert Frank, Dean, E-mail: frank@ohio.edu. *Application contact:* Brenda K. Nelson, Administrative Assistant, 740-593-4332, E-mail: nelsonb1@ohio.edu.
Website: http://www.ohio.edu/history/graduate/master-social-science.html

**Oregon State University,** Interdisciplinary/Institutional Programs, Program in Environmental Sciences, Corvallis, OR 97331. Offers biogeochemistry (MA, MS, PhD); ecology (MA, MS, PhD); environmental education (MA, MS, PhD); environmental sciences (PSM); natural resources (MA, MS, PhD); quantitative analysis (MA, MS, PhD); social science (MA, MS, PhD); water resources (MA, MS, PhD). *Program availability:* Part-time. *Students:* 22 full-time (16 women), 10 part-time (4 women); includes 5 minority (2 Asian, non-Hispanic/Latino; 1 Hispanic/Latino; 2 Two or more races, non-Hispanic/Latino), 4 international. Average age 33. 51 applicants, 33% accepted, 8 enrolled. In 2016, 4 master's, 6 doctorates awarded. *Degree requirements:* For master's, variable foreign language requirement, thesis; for doctorate, thesis/dissertation. *Entrance requirements:* For master's and doctorate, GRE. Additional exam requirements/recommendations for international students: Required—TOEFL (minimum score 80 iBT), IELTS (minimum score 6.5). *Application deadline:* For fall admission, 1/15 priority date for domestic and international students. Application fee: $75 ($85 for international students). *Expenses:* Tuition, state resident: full-time $12,150; part-time $450 per credit. Tuition, nonresident: full-time $21,789; part-time $807 per credit. *Required fees:* $1651; $1507 per credit. One-time fee: $350. Tuition and fees vary according to course load, campus/location and program. *Unit head:* Dr. Carolyn Fonyo Boggess, Interim Director, 541-760-4196, E-mail: carolyn.fonyo@oregonstate.edu.
Website: http://gradschool.oregonstate.edu/environmental-sciences-graduate-program-esgp

**Southern University and Agricultural and Mechanical College,** Graduate School, College of Arts and Humanities, Department of History, Baton Rouge, LA 70813. Offers social sciences (MA). *Program availability:* Part-time. *Degree requirements:* For master's, thesis. *Entrance requirements:* For master's, GRE General Test. Additional exam requirements/recommendations for international students: Required—TOEFL (minimum score 525 paper-based).

**Syracuse University,** Maxwell School of Citizenship and Public Affairs, Programs in Social Sciences, Syracuse, NY 13244. Offers MA, PhD. *Program availability:* Part-time, evening/weekend, online learning. *Degree requirements:* For doctorate, comprehensive exam, thesis/dissertation. *Entrance requirements:* For master's, resume, personal statement, official transcripts, three letters of recommendation; for doctorate, GRE General Test, resume, personal statement, official transcripts, three letters of recommendation. Additional exam requirements/recommendations for international students: Required—TOEFL (minimum score 100 iBT). *Application deadline:* For fall admission, 3/15 priority date for domestic and international students. Application fee: $75. Electronic applications accepted. *Expenses:* Tuition: Full-time $25,974; part-time $1443 per credit hour. *Required fees:* $802; $50 per course. Tuition and fees vary according to course load and program. *Financial support:* Fellowships with full tuition reimbursements, research assistantships with tuition reimbursements, and teaching assistantships with tuition reimbursements available. Financial award application deadline: 1/1. *Faculty research:* Social and political theory and social policy, intergenerational relationships and social support systems, philanthropy. *Unit head:* Dr. Vernon Greene, Chair, 315-443-2275, Fax: 315-443-1463, E-mail: vgreene@maxwell.syr.edu. *Application contact:* Tammy Salisbury, Graduate Contact, 315-443-2275, E-mail: mtsalisb@maxwell.syr.edu.
Website: http://www.maxwell.syr.edu/

**Texas A&M International University,** Office of Graduate Studies and Research, College of Arts and Sciences, Department of Public Affairs and Social Research, Laredo, TX 78041-1900. Offers criminal justice (MS); history and political thought (MA); political science (MA); public administration (MPA). *Degree requirements:* For master's, comprehensive exam (for some programs), thesis (for some programs). *Entrance requirements:* For master's, GRE General Test. Additional exam requirements/recommendations for international students: Required—TOEFL (minimum score 550 paper-based; 79 iBT).

**Towson University,** Program in Social Science, Towson, MD 21252-0001. Offers MS. *Program availability:* Part-time, evening/weekend. *Students:* 7 full-time (4 women), 9 part-time (7 women); includes 8 minority (5 Black or African American, non-Hispanic/Latino; 1 Hispanic/Latino; 2 Two or more races, non-Hispanic/Latino). *Entrance requirements:* For master's, minimum GPA of 3.0, 3 letters of recommendation, statement of intent. *Application deadline:* For fall admission, 10/15 for domestic and international students; for spring admission, 4/15 for domestic and international students. Applications are processed on a rolling basis. Application fee: $45. Electronic applications accepted. *Expenses:* Tuition, state resident: full-time $7580; part-time $379 per unit. Tuition, nonresident: full-time $15,700; part-time $785 per unit. *Required fees:* $2480. *Financial support:* Application deadline: 4/1. *Unit head:* Dr. Paul McCartney, Graduate Program Director, 410-704-5218, E-mail: pmccartney@towson.edu. *Application contact:* Coverley Beidleman, Assistant Director of Graduate Admissions, 410-704-2113, Fax: 410-704-3030, E-mail: grads@towson.edu.
Website: http://www.towson.edu/cla/departments/interdisciplinary/grad/socialscience/

**Troy University,** Graduate School, College of Arts and Sciences, Program in Social Science, Troy, AL 36082. Offers MS Sc. *Program availability:* Part-time, evening/weekend. *Faculty:* 2 full-time (both women), 1 part-time/adjunct (0 women). *Students:* 14 full-time (9 women), 81 part-time (67 women); includes 50 minority (43 Black or African American, non-Hispanic/Latino; 5 Hispanic/Latino; 2 Two or more races, non-Hispanic/Latino). Average age 35. 16 applicants, 94% accepted, 14 enrolled. In 2016, 2 master's awarded. *Degree requirements:* For master's, comprehensive exam, thesis optional. *Entrance requirements:* For master's, GRE (minimum score of 850 on old exam or 290 on new exam), MAT (minimum score of 385), or GMAT (minimum score of 380), bachelor's degree, minimum undergraduate GPA of 2.5 or 3.0 on last 30 semester hours, letter of recommendation. Additional exam requirements/recommendations for international students: Required—TOEFL (minimum score 523 paper-based; 70 iBT), IELTS (minimum score 6). *Application deadline:* For fall admission, 6/1 for international students; for spring admission, 10/15 for international students. Applications are processed on a rolling basis. Application fee: $50. Electronic applications accepted. *Expenses:* Tuition, state resident: full-time $7146; part-time $397 per credit hour. Tuition, nonresident: full-time $14,292; part-time $794 per credit hour. *Required fees:* $802; $50 per semester. Tuition and fees vary according to campus/location and program. *Financial support:* Fellowships, career-related internships or fieldwork, and scholarships/grants available. Support available to part-time students. *Unit head:* Dr. Annette Allen, Chairman, Social Science, 334-808-6595, Fax: 334-670-3753, E-mail: aallen40379@troy.edu. *Application contact:* Jessica A. Kimbro, Director of Graduate Admissions, 334-670-3178, E-mail: jacord@troy.edu.

**University at Buffalo, the State University of New York,** Graduate School, College of Arts and Sciences, Program in Interdisciplinary Studies, Buffalo, NY 14260. Offers humanities (MA); natural sciences (MS); social sciences (MS). *Program availability:* Part-time. *Entrance requirements:* Additional exam requirements/recommendations for international students: Required—TOEFL (minimum score 550 paper-based; 79 iBT). *Application deadline:* For fall admission, 2/1 priority date for domestic students, 1/1 priority date for international students; for spring admission, 11/1 priority date for domestic students, 10/1 priority date for international students. Applications are processed on a rolling basis. Electronic applications accepted. *Expenses:* Contact institution. *Financial support:* Fellowships, research assistantships, and teaching assistantships available. *Unit head:* Danielle Lewis, Graduate Interdisciplinary Program Coordinator, 716-645-1457, E-mail: dvegas@buffalo.edu.
Website: http://gradidp.buffalo.edu/

**University of California, Merced,** Graduate Division, School of Social Sciences, Humanities and Arts, Merced, CA 95343. Offers cognitive and information sciences (PhD); interdisciplinary humanities (MA, PhD); psychological sciences (MA, PhD); social sciences (MA, PhD); sociology (MA, PhD). *Faculty:* 93 full-time (41 women), 3 part-time/adjunct (all women). *Students:* 172 full-time (112 women), 3 part-time (2 women); includes 69 minority (4 Black or African American, non-Hispanic/Latino; 15 Asian, non-Hispanic/Latino; 43 Hispanic/Latino; 7 Two or more races, non-Hispanic/Latino), 25 international. Average age 31. 195 applicants, 50% accepted, 52 enrolled. In 2016, 13 master's, 11 doctorates awarded. Terminal master's awarded for partial completion of doctoral program. *Degree requirements:* For master's, variable foreign language requirement, comprehensive exam, thesis or alternative; for doctorate, variable foreign language requirement, comprehensive exam, thesis/dissertation. *Entrance requirements:* For master's and doctorate, GRE. Additional exam requirements/recommendations for international students: Required—TOEFL (minimum score 550 paper-based; 80 iBT); Recommended—IELTS (minimum score 7). *Application deadline:* For fall admission, 1/15 for domestic and international students. Application fee: $90 ($110 for international students). Electronic applications accepted. *Expenses:* Contact institution. *Financial support:* In 2016–17, 167 students received support, including 12 fellowships with full tuition reimbursements available (averaging $20,237 per year), 12 research assistantships with full tuition reimbursements available (averaging $18,842 per year), 121 teaching assistantships with full tuition reimbursements available (averaging $19,655 per year); scholarships/grants, traineeships, and health care benefits also available. Financial award application deadline: 1/15. *Faculty research:* Social inequality, critical race and ethnic studies, public health and health sciences, cognitive science and language acquisition, political institutions. *Total annual research expenditures:* $1.2 million. *Unit head:* Dr. Jill Robbins, Dean, E-mail: jillrobbins@ucmerced.edu. *Application contact:* Tsu Ya, Director of Admissions and Academic Services, 209-228-4521, Fax: 209-228-6906, E-mail: tya@ucmerced.edu.

**University of California, Santa Barbara,** Graduate Division, College of Letters and Sciences, Division of Mathematics, Life, and Physical Sciences, Department of Psychological and Brain Sciences, Santa Barbara, CA 93106-9660. Offers cognitive science (PhD); psychology (PhD); quantitative methods in the social sciences (PhD); technology and society (PhD). Terminal master's awarded for partial completion of doctoral program. *Degree requirements:* For doctorate, comprehensive exam, thesis/dissertation, teaching assistant training, progress report, papers, mini-convention presentation, 1 quarter of student teaching or teaching assistant class with section lab, continued participation in research and weekly area meetings. *Entrance requirements:* For doctorate, GRE General Test. Additional exam requirements/recommendations for international students: Required—TOEFL (minimum score 550 paper-based; 80 iBT) or IELTS (minimum score 7). Electronic applications accepted. *Faculty research:* Social psychology; developmental and evolutionary psychology; neuroscience and behavior; cognition, perception and cognitive neuroscience.

**University of California, Santa Barbara,** Graduate Division, College of Letters and Sciences, Division of Social Sciences, Department of Communication, Santa Barbara, CA 93106-4020. Offers cognitive science (PhD); communication (PhD); feminist studies (PhD); language, interaction and social organization (PhD); quantitative methods in the social sciences (PhD); society and technology (PhD); MA/PhD. Terminal master's awarded for partial completion of doctoral program. *Degree requirements:* For doctorate, comprehensive exam, thesis/dissertation. *Entrance requirements:* For doctorate, GRE. Additional exam requirements/recommendations for international students: Required—TOEFL (minimum score 80 iBT), IELTS (minimum score 7). Electronic applications accepted. *Faculty research:* Interpersonal, intergroup, intercultural, organizational, health, media.

**University of California, Santa Cruz,** Division of Graduate Studies, Division of Humanities, Program in the History of Consciousness, Santa Cruz, CA 95064. Offers PhD. *Degree requirements:* For doctorate, one foreign language, thesis/dissertation, qualifying exam. *Entrance requirements:* For doctorate, GRE General Test. Additional exam requirements/recommendations for international students: Required—TOEFL (minimum score 550 paper-based; 83 iBT); Recommended—IELTS (minimum score 8). Electronic applications accepted. *Faculty research:* Interdisciplinary humanities and social sciences, political theory, cultural theory, feminist studies, literary theory.

**University of Chicago,** Division of the Social Sciences, The John U. Nef Committee on Social Thought, Chicago, IL 60637. Offers PhD. *Students:* 44 full-time (15 women); includes 4 minority (1 Black or African American, non-Hispanic/Latino; 1 American Indian or Alaska Native, non-Hispanic/Latino; 1 Asian, non-Hispanic/Latino; 1 Hispanic/Latino), 13 international. 110 applicants, 6% accepted, 6 enrolled. In 2016, 3 doctorates awarded. *Degree requirements:* For doctorate, one foreign language, thesis/

dissertation, exam. *Entrance requirements:* For doctorate, GRE General Test. Additional exam requirements/recommendations for international students: Required—TOEFL (minimum score 104 iBT), IELTS (minimum score 7). *Application deadline:* For fall admission, 12/15 for domestic and international students. Application fee: $90. Electronic applications accepted. *Financial support:* In 2016–17, 6 students received support, including 5 fellowships with full tuition reimbursements available (averaging $23,000 per year); career-related internships or fieldwork, Federal Work-Study, institutionally sponsored loans, scholarships/grants, health care benefits, and tuition waivers (full) also available. Financial award application deadline: 12/15. *Unit head:* Prof. Robert Pippin, Chair, 773-702-5453, Fax: 773-834-1968, E-mail: r-pippin@uchicago.edu. *Application contact:* Office of the Dean of Students, 773-702-8415, E-mail: admissions@ssd.uchicago.edu.
Website: http://socialthought.uchicago.edu

**University of Chicago,** Division of the Social Sciences, Master of Arts Program in Computational Social Science, Chicago, IL 60637. Offers MA. *Degree requirements:* For master's, thesis. *Entrance requirements:* For master's, GRE General Test. Additional exam requirements/recommendations for international students: Required—TOEFL (minimum score 104 iBT), IELTS (minimum score 7). *Application deadline:* For fall admission, 1/5 priority date for domestic students, 1/5 for international students. Application fee: $90. Electronic applications accepted. *Financial support:* Federal Work-Study, institutionally sponsored loans, and scholarships/grants available. Financial award application deadline: 1/5. *Faculty research:* Social science data analytics, modeling social systems, cognitive neuroimaging, quantitative social science. *Unit head:* Dr. James Evans, Director, 773-702-9168, E-mail: jevans@uchicago.edu. *Application contact:* Office of the Dean of Students, 773-702-8415, E-mail: admissions@ssd.uchicago.edu.
Website: http://macss.uchicago.edu/

**University of Chicago,** Division of the Social Sciences, Master of Arts Program in the Social Sciences, Chicago, IL 60637. Offers MA. *Program availability:* Part-time. *Students:* 195 full-time (99 women); includes 36 minority (5 Black or African American, non-Hispanic/Latino; 1 American Indian or Alaska Native, non-Hispanic/Latino; 12 Asian, non-Hispanic/Latino; 17 Hispanic/Latino; 1 Two or more races, non-Hispanic/Latino), 55 international. Average age 25. 236 applicants, 79% accepted, 78 enrolled. In 2016, 157 master's awarded. *Degree requirements:* For master's, thesis. *Entrance requirements:* For master's, GRE General Test. Additional exam requirements/recommendations for international students: Required—TOEFL (minimum score 104 iBT), IELTS (minimum score 7). *Application deadline:* For fall admission, 1/5 priority date for domestic and international students. Application fee: $90. Electronic applications accepted. *Financial support:* In 2016–17, 172 students received support. Federal Work-Study, institutionally sponsored loans, and scholarships/grants available. Financial award application deadline: 1/5. *Unit head:* Prof. Dain Borges, Director, 773-702-8317, E-mail: mapssstaff@uchicago.edu. *Application contact:* Office of the Dean of Students, 773-702-8415, E-mail: admissions@ssd.uchicago.edu.
Website: http://mapss.uchicago.edu

**University of Florida,** Graduate School, College of Public Health and Health Professions, Programs in Public Health, Gainesville, FL 32611. Offers biostatistics (MPH); clinical and translational science (PhD); environmental health (MPH); epidemiology (MPH); health management and policy (MPH); public health (MPH, PhD, Certificate); public health practice (MPH); rehabilitation science (PhD); social and behavioral sciences (MPH); DPT/MPH; DVM/MPH; JD/MPH; MD/MPH; Pharm D/MPH. *Accreditation:* CEPH. *Program availability:* Online learning. *Degree requirements:* For master's, internship. *Entrance requirements:* For master's, GRE General Test, minimum GPA of 3.0. Additional exam requirements/recommendations for international students: Required—TOEFL (minimum score 550 paper-based; 80 iBT), IELTS (minimum score 6).

**University of Illinois at Springfield,** Graduate Programs, College of Education and Human Services, Program in Human Services, Springfield, IL 62703-5407. Offers alcohol and substance abuse (Graduate Certificate); alcoholism and substance abuse (MA); child and family services (MA); gerontology (MA); social services administration (MA). *Program availability:* Part-time, evening/weekend, 100% online, blended/hybrid learning. *Faculty:* 4 full-time (all women), 2 part-time/adjunct (1 woman). *Students:* 10 full-time (8 women), 62 part-time (53 women); includes 28 minority (23 Black or African American, non-Hispanic/Latino; 3 Hispanic/Latino; 2 Two or more races, non-Hispanic/Latino). Average age 34. 37 applicants, 46% accepted, 16 enrolled. In 2016, 32 master's, 3 other advanced degrees awarded. *Degree requirements:* For master's, internship; capstone project or thesis. *Entrance requirements:* For master's, minimum undergraduate GPA of 3.0, 2 letters of recommendation from professional or academic sources, statement of intent, interview. Additional exam requirements/recommendations for international students: Required—TOEFL (minimum score 500 paper-based; 61 iBT). *Application deadline:* Applications are processed on a rolling basis. Application fee: $60 ($75 for international students). Electronic applications accepted. *Expenses:* Tuition, state resident: part-time $329 per credit hour. Tuition, nonresident: part-time $675 per credit hour. *Financial support:* In 2016–17, fellowships with full tuition reimbursements (averaging $9,900 per year), research assistantships with full tuition reimbursements (averaging $9,991 per year), teaching assistantships with full tuition reimbursements (averaging $10,059 per year) were awarded; career-related internships or fieldwork, Federal Work-Study, scholarships/grants, health care benefits, and unspecified assistantships also available. Support available to part-time students. Financial award application deadline: 11/15; financial award applicants required to submit FAFSA. *Unit head:* Dr. Carolyn Peck, Program Administrator, 217-206-7577, Fax: 217-206-6775, E-mail: peck.carolyn@uis.edu. *Application contact:* Dr. Cecelia Cornell, Associate Vice Chancellor for Graduate Education, 217-206-7230, E-mail: ccorn1@uis.edu.
Website: http://www.uis.edu/humanservices

**The University of Manchester,** School of Social Sciences, Manchester, United Kingdom. Offers ethnographic documentary (M Phil); interdisciplinary study of culture (PhD); philosophy (PhD); politics (PhD); social anthropology (PhD); social anthropology with visual media (PhD); social change (PhD); social statistics (PhD); sociology (PhD); visual anthropology (M Phil).

**University of Maryland, Baltimore County,** The Graduate School, College of Arts, Humanities and Social Sciences, Doctoral Program in Gerontology at UMB/UMBC, Baltimore, MD 21201. Offers aging policy issues (PhD); epidemiology of aging (PhD); social, cultural, and behavioral sciences (PhD); MA/PhD; MS/PhD. Program offered with University of Maryland, Baltimore. *Program availability:* Part-time. *Faculty:* 17 part-time/adjunct (13 women). *Students:* 9 full-time (8 women), 12 part-time (10 women); includes 7 minority (3 Black or African American, non-Hispanic/Latino; 2 Asian, non-Hispanic/Latino; 2 Hispanic/Latino), 3 international. Average age 35. 13 applicants, 31% accepted, 3 enrolled. In 2016, 4 doctorates awarded. *Degree requirements:* For doctorate, comprehensive exam, thesis/dissertation. *Entrance requirements:* For doctorate, GRE General Test. Additional exam requirements/recommendations for international students: Required—TOEFL, TWE. *Application deadline:* For spring admission, 1/15 for domestic and international students. Application fee: $45. Electronic applications accepted. *Expenses:* Tuition, state resident: full-time $13,294. Tuition, nonresident: full-time $20,286. *Financial support:* Dissertation awards available.

Financial award application deadline: 2/1; financial award applicants required to submit FAFSA. *Faculty research:* Aging and health policy, behavioral aspects of aging, epidemiology of aging. *Total annual research expenditures:* $13.5 million. *Unit head:* Dr. John Schumacher, Co-Director, UMBC Campus, 410-455-2074, Fax: 410-455-3184, E-mail: jschuma@umbc.edu. *Application contact:* Justine Golden, Academic Coordinator, 410-706-4926, Fax: 410-706-4433, E-mail: jgold002@umaryland.edu.
Website: http://lifesciences.umaryland.edu/gerontologyphd/

**University of Memphis,** Graduate School, School of Public Health, Memphis, TN 38152. Offers biostatistics (MPH); environmental health (MPH); epidemiology (MPH, PhD); health systems and policy (PhD); health systems management (MPH); public health (MHA); social and behavioral sciences (MPH, PhD). *Accreditation:* CEPH. *Program availability:* Part-time, evening/weekend. *Faculty:* 20 full-time (7 women), 6 part-time/adjunct (2 women). *Students:* 116 full-time (74 women), 60 part-time (46 women); includes 84 minority (54 Black or African American, non-Hispanic/Latino; 18 Asian, non-Hispanic/Latino; 8 Hispanic/Latino; 4 Two or more races, non-Hispanic/Latino), 19 international. Average age 31. 121 applicants, 92% accepted, 76 enrolled. In 2016, 72 master's, 3 doctorates awarded. *Degree requirements:* For master's, comprehensive exam, thesis (for some programs), practicum/field experience; for doctorate, comprehensive exam, thesis/dissertation, residency. *Entrance requirements:* For master's, GRE or GMAT, letters of recommendation; letter of intent; for doctorate, GRE, letters of recommendation; personal statement. Additional exam requirements/recommendations for international students: Required—TOEFL (minimum score 550 paper-based; 79 iBT). *Application deadline:* For fall admission, 4/1 for domestic students; for spring admission, 11/1 for domestic students. Application fee: $35 ($60 for international students). Electronic applications accepted. *Expenses:* $5,231.50 per semester full-time in-state, $9,623.50 full-time out-of-state. *Financial support:* In 2016–17, 46 students received support, including 11 research assistantships with full tuition reimbursements available (averaging $13,000 per year); Federal Work-Study, scholarships/grants, and unspecified assistantships also available. Financial award application deadline: 2/1; financial award applicants required to submit FAFSA. *Faculty research:* Health and medical savings accounts, adoption rates, health informatics, Telehealth technologies, biostatistics, environmental health, epidemiology, health systems management, social and behavioral sciences. *Unit head:* Dr. Lisa M. Klesges, Dean, 901-678-4501, E-mail: lmklsges@memphis.edu. *Application contact:* Dr. Marian Levy, Assistant Dean, 901-678-4514, Fax: 901-678-5023, E-mail: sph-admin@memphis.edu.
Website: http://www.memphis.edu/sph/

**University of Michigan,** School of Social Work, Interdisciplinary PhD Program in Social Work and Social Science, Ann Arbor, MI 48109-1106. Offers social work and anthropology (PhD); social work and economics (PhD); social work and political science (PhD); social work and psychology (PhD); social work and sociology (PhD). Programs offered through the Rackham Graduate School. *Faculty:* 50 full-time (29 women), 62 part-time/adjunct (48 women). *Students:* 59 full-time (42 women); includes 30 minority (14 Black or African American, non-Hispanic/Latino; 9 Asian, non-Hispanic/Latino; 7 Hispanic/Latino). Average age 32. 114 applicants, 7% accepted, 8 enrolled. In 2016, 8 doctorates awarded. *Degree requirements:* For doctorate, thesis/dissertation, oral defense of dissertation, preliminary exam. *Entrance requirements:* For doctorate, GRE General Test. Additional exam requirements/recommendations for international students: Required—TOEFL (minimum score 620 paper-based, 88 iBT) or IELTS. *Application deadline:* For fall admission, 12/1 for domestic and international students. Application fee: $75 ($90 for international students). Electronic applications accepted. *Expenses:* $42,016 fall/winter tuition. *Financial support:* In 2016–17, 59 students received support, including 20 fellowships with full tuition reimbursements available (averaging $15,200 per year), 8 research assistantships with full tuition reimbursements available (averaging $19,737 per year), 17 teaching assistantships with full tuition reimbursements available (averaging $19,737 per year); career-related internships or fieldwork, scholarships/grants, traineeships, health care benefits, tuition waivers (full and partial), and unspecified assistantships also available. Financial award application deadline: 12/1; financial award applicants required to submit FAFSA. *Faculty research:* Children and family, aging, community organization, health and mental health, police and evaluation. *Total annual research expenditures:* $3.8 million. *Unit head:* Dr. Daphne C. Watkins, Director, 734-763-5768, E-mail: daphnew@umich.edu. *Application contact:* Todd Huynh, Graduate Coordinator, 734-647-2554, Fax: 734-615-3192, E-mail: ssw.phd.info@umich.edu.
Website: https://ssw.umich.edu/offices/phd

**University of Michigan–Flint,** College of Arts and Sciences, Program in Social Sciences, Flint, MI 48502-1950. Offers gender studies (MA); global studies (MA); U.S. history and politics (MA). *Program availability:* Part-time. *Faculty:* 9 full-time (1 woman), 1 (woman) part-time/adjunct. *Students:* 4 full-time (1 woman), 21 part-time (14 women); includes 12 minority (9 Black or African American, non-Hispanic/Latino; 2 Hispanic/Latino; 1 Two or more races, non-Hispanic/Latino). Average age 39. 17 applicants, 82% accepted, 7 enrolled. In 2016, 7 master's awarded. *Entrance requirements:* For master's, bachelor's degree from regionally-accredited institution, minimum overall undergraduate GPA of 3.0. Additional exam requirements/recommendations for international students: Required—TOEFL (minimum score 84 iBT), IELTS (minimum score 6.5). *Application deadline:* For fall admission, 8/1 for domestic students, 5/1 for international students; for winter admission, 11/1 for domestic students, 9/1 for international students; for spring admission, 3/15 for domestic students, 1/1 for international students; for summer admission, 5/15 for domestic students. Applications are processed on a rolling basis. Application fee: $55. Electronic applications accepted. *Financial support:* Federal Work-Study, scholarships/grants, and unspecified assistantships available. Support available to part-time students. Financial award application deadline: 3/1; financial award applicants required to submit FAFSA. *Unit head:* Dr. Adam Lutzker, Director, 810-762-3470, Fax: 810-762-3281, E-mail: alutzker@umflint.edu. *Application contact:* Bradley T. Maki, Director of Graduate Admissions, 810-762-3171, Fax: 810-766-6789, E-mail: bmaki@umflint.edu.
Website: http://www.umflint.edu/graduateprograms/social-sciences-ma

**University of Northern Iowa,** Graduate College, College of Social and Behavioral Sciences, MA Program in Social Science, Cedar Falls, IA 50614. Offers MA. *Entrance requirements:* For master's, minimum GPA of 3.0. Additional exam requirements/recommendations for international students: Required—TOEFL (minimum score 500 paper-based; 61 iBT).

**University of Regina,** Faculty of Graduate Studies and Research, Faculty of Arts, Department of Sociology and Social Studies, Regina, SK S4S 0A2, Canada. Offers social studies (MA); sociology (MA). *Program availability:* Part-time. *Faculty:* 9 full-time (4 women), 7 part-time/adjunct (all women). *Students:* 6 full-time (4 women), 6 part-time (3 women). 10 applicants, 20% accepted. In 2016, 7 master's awarded. *Degree requirements:* For master's, thesis. *Entrance requirements:* Additional exam requirements/recommendations for international students: Required—TOEFL (minimum score 580 paper-based; 80 iBT), IELTS (minimum score 6.5), PTE (minimum score 59). *Application deadline:* Applications are processed on a rolling basis. Application fee: $100. Electronic applications accepted. *Financial support:* In 2016–17, 1 fellowship (averaging $6,000 per year), 5 teaching assistantships (averaging $2,501 per year) were

## Social Sciences

awarded; scholarships/grants also available. Financial award application deadline: 6/15. *Faculty research:* Social justice, international development, globalization, social policy, political economy. *Unit head:* Dr. John Conway, Department Head, 306-585-4052, Fax: 306-585-4815, E-mail: john.conway@uregina.ca. *Application contact:* Dr. Henry Chow, Graduate Coordinator, 306-585-5604, Fax: 306-585-4815, E-mail: henry.chow@uregina.ca.
Website: http://www.uregina.ca/arts/sociology-social-studies

**University of South Florida Sarasota-Manatee,** College of Liberal Arts and Social Sciences, Sarasota, FL 34243. Offers criminal justice (MA); education (MA); educational leadership (M Ed), including curriculum leadership, K-12 public school leadership, non-public/charter school leadership; elementary education (MAT); English education (MA); social work (MSW). *Program availability:* Part-time, 100% online, blended/hybrid learning. *Faculty:* 11 full-time (9 women), 7 part-time/adjunct (5 women). *Students:* 11 full-time (all women), 55 part-time (41 women); includes 18 minority (5 Black or African American, non-Hispanic/Latino; 1 American Indian or Alaska Native, non-Hispanic/Latino; 2 Asian, non-Hispanic/Latino; 10 Hispanic/Latino). Average age 36. 40 applicants, 43% accepted, 17 enrolled. In 2016, 28 master's awarded. *Degree requirements:* For master's, comprehensive exam (for some programs). *Entrance requirements:* Additional exam requirements/recommendations for international students: Required—TOEFL (minimum score 550 paper-based; 79 iBT), IELTS (minimum score 6.5). *Application deadline:* For fall admission, 3/1 priority date for domestic students, 3/1 for international students; for spring admission, 10/1 priority date for domestic students, 10/1 for international students. Applications are processed on a rolling basis. Application fee: $30. Electronic applications accepted. *Expenses:* Contact institution. *Financial support:* In 2016–17, 9 students received support. Career-related internships or fieldwork, institutionally sponsored loans, scholarships/grants, health care benefits, and unspecified assistantships available. Support available to part-time students. Financial award application deadline: 3/1; financial award applicants required to submit FAFSA. *Faculty research:* Educational leadership, secondary education, elementary education, criminal justice, social work. *Unit head:* Dr. Jane Rose, Dean, 941-359-4469, Fax: 941-359-4778, E-mail: jane.rose@sar.usf.edu. *Application contact:* Brandon Avery, Assistant Director, Admissions, 941-359-4331, E-mail: bavery@sar.usf.edu.
Website: http://usfsm.edu/college-of-liberal-arts-sciences/

**The University of Texas at Tyler,** College of Arts and Sciences, Department of Social Sciences, Tyler, TX 75799-0001. Offers criminal justice (MS); public administration (MPA); sociology (MS). *Program availability:* Part-time, evening/weekend. *Degree requirements:* For master's, comprehensive exam, thesis optional. *Entrance requirements:* For master's, GRE General Test, minimum GPA of 3.0. Additional exam requirements/recommendations for international students: Required—TOEFL. *Faculty research:* Urban segregation, minority business, violent crime, gender discrimination.

**University of the Virgin Islands,** College of Liberal Arts and Social Sciences, St. Thomas, VI 00802. Offers M Psych, MPA. *Program availability:* Part-time, evening/weekend. *Faculty:* 7 full-time (5 women), 4 part-time/adjunct (0 women). *Students:* 23 full-time (19 women), 13 part-time (9 women); includes 27 minority (24 Black or African American, non-Hispanic/Latino; 1 Asian, non-Hispanic/Latino; 1 Hispanic/Latino; 1 Two or more races, non-Hispanic/Latino), 6 international. Average age 34. 13 applicants, 85% accepted, 10 enrolled. In 2016, 4 master's awarded. *Degree requirements:* For master's, comprehensive exam, thesis or alternative. *Entrance requirements:* For master's, GRE, minimum GPA of 2.5. Additional exam requirements/recommendations for international students: Required—TOEFL (minimum score 550 paper-based). *Application deadline:* For fall admission, 4/30 for domestic and international students; for spring admission, 10/30 for domestic and international students. Application fee: $30. Electronic applications accepted. *Expenses:* Contact institution. *Financial support:* Career-related internships or fieldwork and scholarships/grants available. Financial award application deadline: 4/15; financial award applicants required to submit FAFSA. *Faculty research:* Ethical issues of arbitration, spiritual leadership, accountability. *Unit head:* Dr. Emily Allen-Williams, Dean, 340-693-1261, Fax: 340-693-1265, E-mail: emily.allenwilliams@uvi.edu. *Application contact:* Dr. Xuri M. Allen, Director of Admissions, 340-693-1224, Fax: 340-693-1167, E-mail: xallen@uvi.edu.

**University of Toronto,** School of Graduate Studies, Department of Public Health Sciences, Toronto, ON M5S 1A1, Canada. Offers biostatistics (M Sc, PhD); community health (M Sc); community nutrition (MPH), including nutrition and dietetics; epidemiology (MPH, PhD); family and community medicine (MPH); occupational and environmental health (MPH); social and behavioral health science (PhD); social and behavioral health sciences (MPH), including health promotion. *Accreditation:* CAHME (one or more programs are accredited). *Program availability:* Part-time. *Degree requirements:* For master's, thesis (for some programs), practicum; for doctorate, comprehensive exam, thesis/dissertation, oral thesis defense. *Entrance requirements:* For master's, 2 letters of reference, relevant professional/research experience, minimum B average in final year; for doctorate, 2 letters of reference, relevant professional/research experience, minimum B+ average. Additional exam requirements/recommendations for international students: Required—TOEFL (minimum score 580 paper-based; 93 iBT), TWE (minimum score 5). Electronic applications accepted. *Expenses:* Contact institution.

**University of Washington,** Graduate School, School of Public Health, Department of Health Services, Seattle, WA 98195. Offers clinical research (MS); community-oriented public health practice (MPH); evaluative sciences and statistics (PhD); health behavior and social determinants of health (PhD); health economics (PhD); health informatics and health information management (MHIHIM); health services (MS, PhD); health services administration (EMHA, MHA); health systems and policy (MPH); health systems research (PhD); maternal and child health (MPH); social and behavioral sciences (MPH); JD/MHA; MHA/MBA; MHA/MD; MHA/MPA; MPH/JD; MPH/MD; MPH/MN; MPH/MPA; MPH/MS; MPH/MSD; MPH/MSW; MPH/PhD. *Program availability:* Online

learning. Terminal master's awarded for partial completion of doctoral program. *Degree requirements:* For master's, thesis (for some programs), practicum (MPH); for doctorate, comprehensive exam, thesis/dissertation. *Entrance requirements:* For master's and doctorate, GRE General Test, minimum GPA of 3.0. Additional exam requirements/recommendations for international students: Required—TOEFL (minimum score 580 paper-based; 92 iBT), IELTS (minimum score 7). Electronic applications accepted. *Expenses:* Contact institution. *Faculty research:* Public health practice, health promotion and disease prevention, maternal and child health, organizational behavior and culture, health policy.

**Wilfrid Laurier University,** Faculty of Graduate and Postdoctoral Studies, Faculty of Arts, Cultural Analysis and Social Theory Program, Waterloo, ON N2L 3C5, Canada. Offers body politics (MA); cultural representation and social theory (MA); gender, sexuality and embodiment (MA); globalization, identity and social movements (MA). *Program availability:* Part-time. *Entrance requirements:* For master's, honours BA in humanities, social science or interdisciplinary program with social theory, minimum B+ in final year of full-time study. Additional exam requirements/recommendations for international students: Required—TOEFL (minimum score 89 iBT). Electronic applications accepted. *Faculty research:* Globalization; identity and social movements; body politics: gender, sexuality and embodiment; cultural representation and social theory.

**Worcester Polytechnic Institute,** Graduate Studies and Research, Department of Social Science and Policy Studies, Worcester, MA 01609-2280. Offers interdisciplinary social science (PhD); system dynamics (MS, Graduate Certificate). *Program availability:* Part-time, evening/weekend, 100% online. *Faculty:* 3 full-time (1 woman), 4 part-time/adjunct (1 woman). *Students:* 2 full-time (1 woman), 7 part-time (0 women), 2 international. 5 applicants, 100% accepted, 2 enrolled. In 2016, 2 master's awarded. *Entrance requirements:* For master's and doctorate, GRE General Test, 3 letters of recommendation, statement of purpose. Additional exam requirements/recommendations for international students: Required—TOEFL (minimum score 563 paper-based; 84 iBT), IELTS (minimum score 7). *Application deadline:* For fall admission, 1/1 priority date for domestic students, 1/1 for international students; for spring admission, 10/1 priority date for domestic students, 10/1 for international students. Applications are processed on a rolling basis. Application fee: $70. Electronic applications accepted. *Financial support:* Research assistantships, teaching assistantships, career-related internships or fieldwork, institutionally sponsored loans, scholarships/grants, and unspecified assistantships available. Financial award application deadline: 1/1; financial award applicants required to submit FAFSA. *Unit head:* Dr. James K. Doyle, Head, 508-831-5296, Fax: 508-831-5896, E-mail: doyle@wpi.edu. *Application contact:* Dr. Khalid Saeed, Graduate Coordinator, 508-831-5296, Fax: 508-831-5896, E-mail: saeed@wpi.edu.
Website: http://www.wpi.edu/academics/ssps

**Worcester Polytechnic Institute,** Graduate Studies and Research, Programs in Interdisciplinary Studies, Worcester, MA 01609-2280. Offers bioscience administration (MS); impact engineering (MS); manufacturing engineering management (MS); power systems management (MS); social science (PhD); systems modeling (MS). *Program availability:* Part-time, evening/weekend. *Faculty:* 1 part-time/adjunct (0 women). *Students:* 5 full-time (2 women), 54 part-time (21 women); includes 14 minority (3 Black or African American, non-Hispanic/Latino; 5 Asian, non-Hispanic/Latino; 5 Hispanic/Latino; 1 Two or more races, non-Hispanic/Latino), 4 international. 18 applicants, 89% accepted, 8 enrolled. *Degree requirements:* For master's, thesis; for doctorate, comprehensive exam, thesis/dissertation. *Entrance requirements:* For master's and doctorate, 3 letters of recommendation. Additional exam requirements/recommendations for international students: Required—TOEFL (minimum score 563 paper-based; 84 iBT), IELTS (minimum score 7). *Application deadline:* For fall admission, 1/1 priority date for domestic students, 1/1 for international students; for spring admission, 10/1 priority date for domestic students, 10/1 for international students. Applications are processed on a rolling basis. Application fee: $70. Electronic applications accepted. *Financial support:* Institutionally sponsored loans, scholarships/grants, and unspecified assistantships available. Financial award application deadline: 1/1; financial award applicants required to submit FAFSA. *Unit head:* Dr. Fred J. Looft, Head, 508-831-5231, Fax: 508-831-5491, E-mail: fjlooft@wpi.edu. *Application contact:* Lynne Dougherty, Administrative Assistant, 508-831-5301, Fax: 508-831-5717, E-mail: grad@wpi.edu.

**Yale University,** Yale School of Medicine, Yale School of Public Health, New Haven, CT 06520. Offers applied biostatistics and epidemiology (APMPH); biostatistics (MPH, MS, PhD), including global health (MPH); chronic disease epidemiology (MPH, PhD), including global health (MPH); environmental health sciences (MPH, PhD), including global health (MPH); epidemiology of microbial diseases (MPH, PhD), including global health (MPH); global health (APMPH); health management (MPH), including global health; health policy (MPH), including global health; health policy and administration (APMPH, PhD); occupational and environmental medicine (APMPH); preventive medicine (APMPH); social and behavioral sciences (APMPH, MPH), including global health (MPH); JD/MPH; M Div/MPH; MBA/MPH; MD/MPH; MEM/MPH; MFS/MPH; MM Sc/MPH; MPH/MA; MSN/MPH. MS and PhD offered through the Graduate School. *Accreditation:* CEPH. *Program availability:* Part-time. Terminal master's awarded for partial completion of doctoral program. *Degree requirements:* For master's, thesis, summer internship; for doctorate, comprehensive exam, thesis/dissertation, residency. *Entrance requirements:* For master's, GMAT, GRE, or MCAT, two years of undergraduate coursework in math and science; for doctorate, GRE General Test. Additional exam requirements/recommendations for international students: Required—TOEFL (minimum score 100 iBT). Electronic applications accepted. *Expenses:* Contact institution. *Faculty research:* Genetic and emerging infections epidemiology, virology, cost/quality, vector biology, quantitative methods, aging, asthma, cancer.

# Section 27
# Sociology, Anthropology, and Archaeology

This section contains a directory of institutions offering graduate work in sociology, anthropology, and archaeology. Additional information about programs listed in the directory may be obtained by writing directly to the dean of a graduate school or chair of a department at the address given in the directory.

For programs offering related work, see also in this book *Area and Cultural Studies, Art and Art History, History, Humanities, Language and Literature,* and *Psychology and Counseling.*

## CONTENTS

**Program Directories**

# Anthropology

**American University,** College of Arts and Sciences, Department of Anthropology, Washington, DC 20016-8003. Offers MA, PhD, Certificate. *Program availability:* Part-time, evening/weekend. *Faculty:* 11 full-time (7 women), 3 part-time/adjunct (all women). *Students:* 64 full-time (44 women), 21 part-time (18 women); includes 21 minority (8 Black or African American, non-Hispanic/Latino; 1 Asian, non-Hispanic/Latino; 9 Hispanic/Latino; 3 Two or more races, non-Hispanic/Latino), 7 international. Average age 32. 95 applicants, 69% accepted, 37 enrolled. In 2016, 10 master's, 5 doctorates awarded. Terminal master's awarded for partial completion of doctoral program. *Degree requirements:* For master's, comprehensive exam, thesis or alternative; for doctorate, 2 foreign languages, comprehensive exam, thesis/dissertation. *Entrance requirements:* For master's, GRE, sample of written work, personal statement, two letters of recommendation, transcripts, resume; for doctorate, GRE, sample of written work, personal statement, three letters of recommendation, resume, transcripts; for Certificate, statement of purpose, transcripts. Additional exam requirements/recommendations for international students: Required—TOEFL (minimum score 100 iBT), IELTS (minimum score 7), PTE (minimum score 68). *Application deadline:* For fall admission, 2/1 priority date for domestic students; for spring admission, 11/1 for domestic students. Application fee: $55. *Expenses:* $1,579 per credit tuition; $690 mandatory fees. *Financial support:* Research assistantships, teaching assistantships, institutionally sponsored loans, and unspecified assistantships available. Financial award application deadline: 1/15; financial award applicants required to submit FAFSA. *Faculty research:* Poverty and race, lesbian and gay studies, class and culture, developing countries. *Unit head:* Dr. Daniel Sayers, Department Chair, 202-885-1833, Fax: 202-885-1837, E-mail: sayers@american.edu. *Application contact:* Kathleen Clowery, Associate Director, Graduate Admissions, 202-885-3620, Fax: 202-885-1344, E-mail: clowery@american.edu.
Website: http://www.american.edu/cas/anthropology/

**American University of Beirut,** Graduate Programs, Faculty of Arts and Sciences, Beirut, Lebanon. Offers anthropology (MA); Arab and Middle Eastern history (PhD); Arabic language and literature (MA, PhD); archaeology (MA); art history and curating (MA); biology (MS); cell and molecular biology (PhD); chemistry (MS); clinical psychology (MA); computational science (MS); computer science (MS); economics (MA); education (MA); English language (MA); English literature (MA); environmental policy planning (MS); financial economics (MAFE); geology (MS); history (MA); Islamic studies (MA); mathematics (MS); media studies (MA); Middle Eastern studies (MA); physics (MS); political studies (MA); psychology (MA); public administration (MA); public policy and international affairs (MA); sociology (MA); statistics (MA, MS); theoretical physics (PhD); transnational American studies (MA). *Program availability:* Part-time. *Faculty:* 133 full-time (42 women), 6 part-time/adjunct (2 women). *Students:* 240 full-time (172 women), 227 part-time (166 women). Average age 27. 286 applicants, 67% accepted, 108 enrolled. In 2016, 60 master's, 3 doctorates awarded. Terminal master's awarded for partial completion of doctoral program. *Degree requirements:* For master's, one foreign language, comprehensive exam, thesis (for some programs); for doctorate, one foreign language, comprehensive exam, thesis/dissertation. *Entrance requirements:* For master's, GRE (for some MA, MS programs), letters of recommendation; for doctorate, GRE, letters of recommendation. Additional exam requirements/recommendations for international students: Required—TOEFL (minimum score 600 paper-based; 97 iBT), IELTS (minimum score 7). *Application deadline:* For fall admission, 4/3 for domestic students; for winter admission, 11/3 for domestic students. Application fee: $50. Electronic applications accepted. *Expenses:* Contact institution. *Financial support:* In 2016–17, 4 fellowships (averaging $11,200 per year), 18 research assistantships (averaging $5,400 per year) were awarded; teaching assistantships, career-related internships or fieldwork, Federal Work-Study, institutionally sponsored loans, scholarships/grants, traineeships, health care benefits, tuition waivers (full), and unspecified assistantships also available. Support available to part-time students. *Faculty research:* Development economics, spatial econometrics, health economics, labor economics, energy economics, hydrogeology, geophysics, petrophysics, structural geology, mineralogy, petrology, geochemistry, multilingualism, comparative/world literature, translation studies, book histories/ cultures, biocatalysis, molecular recognition, photocatalysis, photophysical and biophysical chemistry, probe chemistry, machine learning, data science. *Unit head:* Dr. Nadia Maria El Cheikh, Dean, Faculty of Arts and Sciences, 961-1374374 Ext. 3800, Fax: 961-1744461, E-mail: nmcheikh@aub.edu.lb. *Application contact:* Dr. Salim Kanaan, Director, Admissions Office, 961-1350000 Ext. 2590, Fax: 961-1750775, E-mail: sk00@aub.edu.lb.
Website: http://www.aub.edu.lb/fas/

**Arizona State University at the Tempe campus,** College of Liberal Arts and Sciences, School of Human Evolution and Social Change, Tempe, AZ 85287-2402. Offers anthropology (MA, PhD), including anthropology (PhD), archaeology (PhD); bioarchaeology (PhD), evolutionary (PhD), museum studies (MA), sociocultural (PhD); applied mathematics for the life and social sciences (PhD); environmental social science (PhD), including environmental social science, urbanism; global health (MA, PhD), including complex adaptive systems science (PhD), evolutionary global health sciences (PhD), health and culture (PhD), urbanism (PhD); immigration studies (Graduate Certificate). Terminal master's awarded for partial completion of doctoral program. *Degree requirements:* For master's, thesis or alternative, interactive Program of Study (iPOS) submitted before completing 50 percent of required credit hours; for doctorate, comprehensive exam, thesis/dissertation, interactive Program of Study (iPOS) submitted before completing 50 percent of required credit hours. *Entrance requirements:* For master's and doctorate, GRE, minimum GPA of 3.0 or equivalent in last 2 years of work leading to bachelor's degree. Additional exam requirements/recommendations for international students: Required—TOEFL, IELTS, or PTE. Electronic applications accepted.

**Ball State University,** Graduate School, College of Sciences and Humanities, Department of Anthropology, Muncie, IN 47306. Offers anthropology (MA); interpretive ethnography (Certificate). *Program availability:* Part-time. *Entrance requirements:* For master's, GRE General Test, minimum baccalaureate GPA of 2.75 or 3.0 in latter half of baccalauareate, official transcripts, goals statement, resume, three letters of recommendation. Additional exam requirements/recommendations for international students: Required—TOEFL (minimum score 550 paper-based; 79 iBT), IELTS (minimum score 6.5). Electronic applications accepted.

**Binghamton University, State University of New York,** Graduate School, Harpur College of Arts and Sciences, Department of Anthropology, Binghamton, NY 13902-6000. Offers anthropology (MA, PhD); biomedical anthropology (MS). *Program availability:* Part-time. *Faculty:* 20 full-time (8 women), 3 part-time/adjunct (1 woman). *Students:* 62 full-time (38 women), 93 part-time (71 women); includes 25 minority (1 Black or African American, non-Hispanic/Latino; 3 American Indian or Alaska Native, non-Hispanic/Latino; 4 Asian, non-Hispanic/Latino; 12 Hispanic/Latino; 1 Native Hawaiian or other Pacific Islander, non-Hispanic/Latino; 4 Two or more races, non-Hispanic/Latino), 23 international. Average age 31. 92 applicants, 79% accepted, 32 enrolled. In 2016, 12 master's, 4 doctorates awarded. Terminal master's awarded for partial completion of doctoral program. *Degree requirements:* For master's, variable foreign language requirement, comprehensive exam (for some programs), thesis (for some programs); for doctorate, variable foreign language requirement, comprehensive exam, thesis/dissertation. *Entrance requirements:* For master's and doctorate, GRE General Test. Additional exam requirements/recommendations for international students: Required—TOEFL (minimum score 550 paper-based; 80 iBT). *Application deadline:* For fall admission, 4/15 priority date for domestic and international students; for spring admission, 10/15 priority date for domestic and international students. Application fee: $75. Electronic applications accepted. *Financial support:* In 2016–17, 47 students received support, including 1 fellowship with full tuition reimbursement available (averaging $5,000 per year), 1 research assistantship with full tuition reimbursement available (averaging $17,000 per year), 30 teaching assistantships with full tuition reimbursements available (averaging $15,000 per year); career-related internships or fieldwork, Federal Work-Study, institutionally sponsored loans, scholarships/grants, health care benefits, tuition waivers (full and partial), and unspecified assistantships also available. Financial award application deadline: 1/15; financial award applicants required to submit FAFSA. *Unit head:* Kathleen Sterling, Graduate Director, 607-777-2100, E-mail: sterling@binghamton.edu. *Application contact:* Ben Balkaya, Assistant Dean and Director, 607-777-2151, Fax: 607-777-2501, E-mail: balkaya@binghamton.edu.
Website: http://www.binghamton.edu/anthropology/

**Biola University,** Cook School of Intercultural Studies, La Mirada, CA 90639-0001. Offers anthropology (MA); applied linguistics (MA); intercultural education (PhD); intercultural studies (MA, PhD); linguistics (Certificate); linguistics and Biblical languages (MA); missiology (D Miss); missions (MA); teaching English to speakers of other languages (MA, Certificate); teaching English to speakers of other languages (online) (MA). *Program availability:* Part-time, 100% online. *Entrance requirements:* For master's, minimum undergraduate GPA of 3.0; for doctorate, master's degree or equivalent, 3 years of cross-cultural experience, minimum graduate GPA of 3.3. Additional exam requirements/recommendations for international students: Required—TOEFL. Electronic applications accepted. *Faculty research:* Linguistics, anthropology, intercultural studies, teaching English to speakers of other languages, missions, missiology.

**Boise State University,** College of Arts and Sciences, Department of Anthropology, Boise, ID 83725. Offers anthropology (MA); applied anthropology (MAA). *Program availability:* Part-time. *Faculty:* 6. *Students:* 12 full-time (7 women), 3 part-time (2 women); includes 2 minority (both Hispanic/Latino), 1 international. Average age 31. 10 applicants, 80% accepted, 4 enrolled. In 2016, 4 master's awarded. *Degree requirements:* For master's, comprehensive exam, thesis and project (MAA). *Entrance requirements:* For master's, GRE General Test. Additional exam requirements/recommendations for international students: Required—TOEFL (minimum score 550 paper-based; 80 iBT), IELTS (minimum score 6). *Application deadline:* For fall admission, 5/1 for domestic and international students. Application fee: $65 ($95 for international students). Electronic applications accepted. *Expenses:* Tuition, state resident: full-time $6058; part-time $358 per credit hour. Tuition, nonresident: full-time $20,108; part-time $608 per credit hour. *Required fees:* $2108. Tuition and fees vary according to program. *Financial support:* In 2016–17, 3 students received support. Scholarships/grants and unspecified assistantships available. Financial award application deadline: 2/15; financial award applicants required to submit FAFSA. *Unit head:* Dr. John Ziker, Department Chair, 208-426-2121, E-mail: jziker@boisestate.edu. *Application contact:* Dr. Mark Plew, Graduate Program Coordinator, 208-426-3444, E-mail: mplew@boisestate.edu.
Website: http://anthropology.boisestate.edu/

**Boston University,** Graduate School of Arts and Sciences, Department of Anthropology, Boston, MA 02215. Offers anthropology (PhD); applied anthropology (MA). *Students:* 41 full-time (28 women), 1 (woman) part-time; includes 2 minority (1 Black or African American, non-Hispanic/Latino; 1 Two or more races, non-Hispanic/Latino), 14 international. Average age 30. 92 applicants, 11% accepted, 6 enrolled. In 2016, 3 master's, 3 doctorates awarded. Terminal master's awarded for partial completion of doctoral program. *Degree requirements:* For master's, one foreign language, comprehensive exam, thesis or alternative; for doctorate, one foreign language, thesis/dissertation. *Entrance requirements:* For master's and doctorate, GRE General Test, 3 letters of recommendation, transcripts, personal statement. Additional exam requirements/recommendations for international students: Required—TOEFL (minimum score 550 paper-based; 84 iBT). *Application deadline:* For fall admission, 1/15 for domestic and international students. Application fee: $95. Electronic applications accepted. *Financial support:* In 2016–17, 33 students received support, including 11 fellowships with full tuition reimbursements available (averaging $21,500 per year), 14 teaching assistantships with full tuition reimbursements available (averaging $21,500 per year); Federal Work-Study, scholarships/grants, health care benefits, and unspecified assistantships also available. Support available to part-time students. Financial award application deadline: 1/15. *Unit head:* Thomas Barfield, Chair, 617-353-5028, Fax: 617-353-2610, E-mail: barfield@bu.edu. *Application contact:* Martin Wraga, Administrator, 617-353-2195, Fax: 617-353-2610, E-mail: mwraga@bu.edu.
Website: http://www.bu.edu/ANTHROP/

**Boston University,** School of Medicine, Division of Graduate Medical Sciences, Program in Forensic Anthropology, Boston, MA 02215. Offers MS. *Financial support:* Applicants required to submit FAFSA. *Unit head:* Dr. Tara L. Moore, Co-Director, 617-638-4054, Fax: 617-638-4922, E-mail: tlmoore@bu.edu. *Application contact:* GMS Admissions Office, 617-638-5255, E-mail: askgms@bu.edu.
Website: http://www.bumc.bu.edu/gms/forensicanthro-masters-program/

**Boston University,** School of Medicine, Division of Graduate Medical Sciences, Program in Medical Anthropology and Cross Cultural Practice, Boston, MA 02215. Offers MA. *Unit head:* Dr. Linda Barnes, Director, 617-414-4534, Fax: 617-414-5511, E-mail: linda.barnes@bmc.org. *Application contact:* GMS Admissions Office, 617-638-5255, E-mail: askgms@bu.edu.
Website: http://www.bu.edu/academics/gms/programs/medical-anthropology-and-cross-cultural-practice/

**Brandeis University,** Graduate School of Arts and Sciences, Department of Anthropology, Waltham, MA 02454. Offers anthropology (MA, PhD); anthropology/women's, gender, and sexuality studies (PhD). *Program availability:* Part-time. *Faculty:* 9 full-time (5 women), 4 part-time/adjunct (1 woman). *Students:* 38 full-time (25 women), 1 part-time (0 women); includes 7 minority (2 Black or African American, non-Hispanic/

Latino; 3 Hispanic/Latino; 2 Two or more races, non-Hispanic/Latino), 6 international. 62 applicants, 48% accepted, 15 enrolled. In 2016, 14 master's, 2 doctorates awarded. *Degree requirements:* For master's, thesis or alternative; for doctorate, one foreign language, comprehensive exam, thesis/dissertation. *Entrance requirements:* For master's and doctorate, GRE General Test, sample of written work, resume, letters of recommendation. Additional exam requirements/recommendations for international students: Required—TOEFL (minimum score 600 paper-based; 100 iBT); Recommended—IELTS (minimum score 7), TSE (minimum score 68). *Application deadline:* For fall admission, 1/15 for domestic students. Application fee: $75. Electronic applications accepted. *Financial support:* In 2016–17, 39 students received support, including 11 fellowships with full tuition reimbursements available (averaging $24,000 per year), 20 teaching assistantships with partial tuition reimbursements available (averaging $3,200 per year); scholarships/grants, health care benefits, and tuition waivers (partial) also available. Support available to part-time students. Financial award application deadline: 4/15; financial award applicants required to submit FAFSA. *Faculty research:* Sociocultural anthropology, archaeology, gender and sexuality, linguistic anthropology, physical anthropology. *Unit head:* Dr. Sarah Lamb, Director of Graduate Studies, 781-736-2210, Fax: 781-736-2232, E-mail: lamb@brandeis.edu. *Application contact:* Laurel Carpenter, Academic Administrator, 781-736-2210, Fax: 781-736-2232, E-mail: lcarpenter@brandeis.edu.
Website: http://www.brandeis.edu/gsas

**Brigham Young University,** Graduate Studies, College of Family, Home, and Social Sciences, Department of Anthropology, Provo, UT 84602. Offers MA. *Faculty:* 11 full-time (1 woman). *Students:* 16 full-time (13 women); includes 1 minority (Asian, non-Hispanic/Latino). Average age 29. 5 applicants, 80% accepted, 3 enrolled. In 2016, 2 master's awarded. *Degree requirements:* For master's, comprehensive exam, thesis. *Entrance requirements:* For master's, GRE General Test, minimum GPA of 3.0 in last 60 hours. Additional exam requirements/recommendations for international students: Required—TOEFL (minimum score 580 paper-based). *Application deadline:* For fall admission, 2/1 for domestic and international students. Application fee: $50. Electronic applications accepted. *Expenses:* Contact institution. *Financial support:* In 2016–17, 16 students received support, including 10 research assistantships (averaging $10,000 per year), 3 teaching assistantships (averaging $7,500 per year); fellowships, career-related internships or fieldwork, institutionally sponsored loans, and tuition waivers (partial) also available. Financial award application deadline: 3/1; financial award applicants required to submit FAFSA. *Faculty research:* Archaeology of the Southwest, Near East, South America, and Mesoamerica; Mayan glyphs. *Total annual research expenditures:* $52,000. *Unit head:* Dr. James R. Allison, Chair, 801-422-3059, Fax: 801-422-7942, E-mail: jallison@byu.edu.
Website: http://anthropology.byu.edu/

**Brown University,** Graduate School, Department of Anthropology, Providence, RI 02912. Offers MA, PhD. *Degree requirements:* For doctorate, one foreign language, thesis/dissertation, preliminary exam.

**California State University, Bakersfield,** Division of Graduate Studies, School of Social Sciences and Education, Program in Anthropology, Bakersfield, CA 93311. Offers MA. *Students:* 1 full-time (0 women), 1 (woman) part-time. Average age 38. *Degree requirements:* For master's, thesis optional. *Entrance requirements:* For master's, GRE, minimum GPA of 2.5, 3 letters of recommendation. Additional exam requirements/recommendations for international students: Required—TOEFL (minimum score 550 paper-based). *Application deadline:* For fall admission, 5/1 for domestic students. Application fee: $55. *Expenses:* Tuition, state resident: full-time $2246; part-time $1302 per semester. *Financial support:* In 2016–17, fellowships (averaging $1,850 per year) were awarded; Federal Work-Study, scholarships/grants, and tuition waivers (full and partial) also available. Financial award application deadline: 3/2; financial award applicants required to submit FAFSA. *Faculty research:* Human services, social science teaching. *Unit head:* Dr. Robert Yohe, Graduate Coordinator, 661-654-3457, Fax: 661-654-6909, E-mail: ryohe@csub.edu. *Application contact:* Debbie Blowers, Assistant Director of Admissions and Evaluations, 661-664-3381, E-mail: dblowers@csub.edu.
Website: https://www.csub.edu/anthropology/index.html

**California State University, Chico,** Office of Graduate Studies, College of Behavioral and Social Sciences, Department of Anthropology, Chico, CA 95929-0722. Offers anthropology (MA); museum studies (MA). *Faculty:* 11 full-time (4 women), 6 part-time/adjunct (5 women). *Students:* 12 full-time (8 women), 12 part-time (10 women); includes 5 minority (3 Hispanic/Latino; 2 Two or more races, non-Hispanic/Latino). 58 applicants, 16% accepted, 5 enrolled. In 2016, 9 master's awarded. *Degree requirements:* For master's, comprehensive exam, thesis, oral evaluation. *Entrance requirements:* For master's, GRE General Test, two letters of recommendation, statement of purpose, curriculum vitae, writing sample. Additional exam requirements/recommendations for international students: Required—TOEFL (minimum score 550 paper-based; 80 iBT), IELTS (minimum score 6.5), PTE (minimum score 59). *Application deadline:* For fall admission, 1/15 for domestic and international students. Application fee: $55. Electronic applications accepted. *Financial support:* Fellowships, career-related internships or fieldwork, institutionally sponsored loans, scholarships/grants, and unspecified assistantships available. Financial award application deadline: 3/1; financial award applicants required to submit FAFSA. *Unit head:* Jesse Dizard, Chair, 530-898-6193, Fax: 530-898-6143, E-mail: anth@csuchico.edu. *Application contact:* Judy L. Morris, Graduate Admissions Coordinator, 530-898-6880, Fax: 530-898-6889, E-mail: jlmorris@csuchico.edu.
Website: http://www.csuchico.edu/anth/

**California State University, East Bay,** Office of Graduate Studies, College of Letters, Arts, and Social Sciences, Department of Anthropology, Geography and Environmental Studies, Hayward, CA 94542-3000. Offers anthropology (MA); geography (MA). *Program availability:* Part-time. *Students:* 1 (woman) full-time (all women); includes 3 minority (all Hispanic/Latino). Average age 38. In 2016, 5 master's awarded. *Degree requirements:* For master's, variable foreign language requirement, project or thesis. *Entrance requirements:* For master's, minimum GPA of 3.0 in field. Additional exam requirements/recommendations for international students: Required—TOEFL (minimum score 550 paper-based). *Application deadline:* For fall admission, 6/30 for domestic and international students. Applications are processed on a rolling basis. Application fee: $55. Electronic applications accepted. *Financial support:* Fellowships, teaching assistantships, career-related internships or fieldwork, Federal Work-Study, institutionally sponsored loans, and scholarships/grants available. Support available to part-time students. Financial award application deadline: 3/2; financial award applicants required to submit FAFSA. *Faculty research:* Sustainability, water resources, geographic information systems (GIS), mapping. *Unit head:* Dr. David Larson, Chair, 510-885-3192, E-mail: david.larson@csueastbay.edu. *Application contact:* Prof. David Woo, Graduate Advisor for Geography, 510-885-3160, Fax: 510-885-2353, E-mail: david.woo@csueastbay.edu.
Website: http://www20.csueastbay.edu/class/departments/ages/index.html

**California State University, Fullerton,** Graduate Studies, College of Humanities and Social Sciences, Department of Anthropology, Fullerton, CA 92834-9480. Offers MA. *Program availability:* Part-time. *Degree requirements:* For master's, project or thesis. *Entrance requirements:* For master's, minimum GPA of 2.5 in last 60 hours of course

work. Application fee: $55. *Expenses:* Tuition, state resident: full-time $3369; part-time $1953 per unit. Tuition, nonresident: full-time $3915; part-time $2499 per unit. Tuition and fees vary according to course load, degree level and program. *Financial support:* Career-related internships or fieldwork, Federal Work-Study, institutionally sponsored loans, and scholarships/grants available. Support available to part-time students. Financial award application deadline: 3/1; financial award applicants required to submit FAFSA. *Unit head:* Dr. Mitch Avila, Chair, 657-278-2272. *Application contact:* Admissions/Applications, 657-278-2371.

**California State University, Long Beach,** Graduate Studies, College of Liberal Arts, Department of Anthropology, Long Beach, CA 90840. Offers anthropology (MA); applied anthropology (MA). *Program availability:* Part-time. *Degree requirements:* For master's, one foreign language, comprehensive exam or thesis. *Application deadline:* For fall admission, 4/15 for domestic students. Applications are processed on a rolling basis. Application fee: $55. Electronic applications accepted. *Financial support:* Research assistantships, Federal Work-Study, institutionally sponsored loans, and scholarships/grants available. Financial award application deadline: 3/2. *Faculty research:* Archeology of California, Fiji, and Ireland; cultures of American Indians and Mexico. *Unit head:* Karen Quintiliani, Chair, 562-985-5171, Fax: 562-985-4379.

**California State University, Los Angeles,** Graduate Studies, College of Natural and Social Sciences, Department of Anthropology, Los Angeles, CA 90032-8530. Offers MA. *Program availability:* Part-time, evening/weekend. *Degree requirements:* For master's, one foreign language, comprehensive exam or thesis. *Entrance requirements:* Additional exam requirements/recommendations for international students: Required—TOEFL (minimum score 500 paper-based). *Faculty research:* Archaeology, folklore, petroglyphs, symbolism, medical anthropology.

**California State University, Northridge,** Graduate Studies, College of Social and Behavioral Sciences, Department of Anthropology, Northridge, CA 91330. Offers general anthropology (MA); public archaeology (MA). *Faculty:* 11 full-time (2 women), 9 part-time/adjunct (6 women). *Students:* 5 full-time (4 women), 13 part-time (9 women); includes 3 minority (1 Black or African American, non-Hispanic/Latino; 2 Asian, non-Hispanic/Latino), 6 international. Average age 30. 20 applicants, 20% accepted, 3 enrolled. *Degree requirements:* For master's, thesis or alternative. *Entrance requirements:* For master's, GRE General Test or minimum GPA of 3.0. Additional exam requirements/recommendations for international students: Required—TOEFL. *Application deadline:* For fall admission, 11/30 for domestic students. Application fee: $55. *Expenses:* Tuition, state resident: full-time $4152. *Financial support:* Career-related internships or fieldwork, Federal Work-Study, and institutionally sponsored loans available. Financial award application deadline: 3/1. *Unit head:* Dr. Sabina Magliocco, Chair, 818-677-3331.
Website: http://www.csun.edu/csbs/departments/anthropology/index.html

**California State University, Sacramento,** Office of Graduate Studies, College of Social Sciences and Interdisciplinary Studies, Department of Anthropology, Sacramento, CA 95819. Offers MA. *Program availability:* Part-time. *Students:* 3 full-time (2 women), 12 part-time (7 women); includes 2 minority (1 American Indian or Alaska Native, non-Hispanic/Latino; 1 Hispanic/Latino). Average age 37. 15 applicants, 33% accepted, 3 enrolled. In 2016, 4 master's awarded. *Degree requirements:* For master's, thesis, departmental qualifying exam, writing proficiency exam. *Entrance requirements:* For master's, minimum GPA of 3.0 during previous 2 years. Additional exam requirements/recommendations for international students: Required—TOEFL (minimum score 550 paper-based; 80 iBT). *Application deadline:* For fall admission, 3/1 for domestic and international students; for spring admission, 9/30 for international students. Applications are processed on a rolling basis. Application fee: $55. Electronic applications accepted. *Expenses:* $4,302 full-time tuition and fees per semester, $2,796 part-time. *Financial support:* Career-related internships or fieldwork and Federal Work-Study available. Support available to part-time students. Financial award application deadline: 3/1; financial award applicants required to submit FAFSA. *Unit head:* Dr. Raghuraman Trichur, Chair, 916-278-4789, E-mail: rtrichur@csus.edu. *Application contact:* Jose Martinez, Graduate Admissions Supervisor, 916-278-7871, E-mail: martinj@skymail.csus.edu.
Website: http://www.csus.edu/anth

**Canisius College,** Graduate Division, College of Arts and Sciences, Department of Animal Behavior, Ecology and Conservation, Buffalo, NY 14208-1098. Offers anthrozoology (MS). Applicants accepted in fall only. *Program availability:* Part-time, evening/weekend, blended/hybrid learning. *Faculty:* 5 full-time (3 women), 2 part-time/adjunct (both women). *Students:* 14 full-time (13 women), 34 part-time (27 women); includes 4 minority (1 Black or African American, non-Hispanic/Latino; 1 Asian, non-Hispanic/Latino; 1 Hispanic/Latino; 1 Two or more races, non-Hispanic/Latino), 3 international. Average age 33. 81 applicants, 32% accepted, 25 enrolled. In 2016, 12 master's awarded. *Entrance requirements:* For master's, GRE (recommended), official transcript of all college work, bachelor's degree, minimum GPA of 3.0, three essays. Additional exam requirements/recommendations for international students: Required—TOEFL (minimum score 550 paper-based, 80 iBT), IELTS (minimum score 6.5), or CAEL (minimum score 70). *Application deadline:* For fall admission, 3/1 for domestic and international students. Applications are processed on a rolling basis. Application fee: $25. Electronic applications accepted. Application fee is waived when completed online. *Expenses:* Tuition: Full-time $14,742. *Required fees:* $724. *Financial support:* Career-related internships or fieldwork, Federal Work-Study, scholarships/grants, tuition waivers (partial), and unspecified assistantships available. Support available to part-time students. Financial award application deadline: 4/30; financial award applicants required to submit FAFSA. *Faculty research:* Human animal relations; advocacy of animal welfare and conservation. *Unit head:* Dr. Michael Noonan, Program Director, 716-888-2770, E-mail: noonan@canisius.edu. *Application contact:* Kathleen B. Davis, Vice President of Enrollment Management, 716-888-2500, Fax: 716-888-3195, E-mail: daviskb@canisius.edu.
Website: http://www.canisius.edu/abec/

**Carleton University,** Faculty of Graduate Studies, Faculty of Arts and Social Sciences, Department of Sociology and Anthropology, Program in Anthropology, Ottawa, ON K1S 5B6, Canada. Offers MA. *Degree requirements:* For master's, comprehensive exam, thesis optional. *Entrance requirements:* For master's, honors degree. Additional exam requirements/recommendations for international students: Required—TOEFL. *Faculty research:* Culture, symbols and mind, anthropology of signs and symbols, Indigenous studies, anthropology of development and underdevelopment.

**Case Western Reserve University,** School of Graduate Studies, Department of Anthropology, Cleveland, OH 44106. Offers MA, PhD, MD/MA, MD/PhD, MPH/MA, MSN/MA, PhD/MPH. *Program availability:* Part-time. *Faculty:* 11 full-time (6 women), 7 part-time/adjunct (3 women). *Students:* 29 full-time (21 women), 1 (woman) part-time; includes 4 minority (1 Black or African American, non-Hispanic/Latino; 3 Asian, non-Hispanic/Latino), 5 international. Average age 31. 22 applicants, 59% accepted, 6 enrolled. In 2016, 7 master's, 2 doctorates awarded. Terminal master's awarded for partial completion of doctoral program. *Degree requirements:* For master's, comprehensive exam, thesis optional; for doctorate, thesis/dissertation. *Entrance requirements:* For master's and doctorate, GRE General Test, statement of purpose; 3 letters of recommendation; official transcripts. Additional exam requirements/

recommendations for international students: Required—TOEFL (minimum score 577 paper-based; 90 iBT), IELTS (minimum score 7). *Application deadline:* For fall admission, 3/1 priority date for domestic students; for spring admission, 11/1 for domestic students. Applications are processed on a rolling basis. Application fee: $50. Electronic applications accepted. *Expenses: Tuition:* Full-time $42,576; part-time $1774 per credit hour. *Required fees:* $34. Tuition and fees vary according to course load and program. *Financial support:* Research assistantships with tuition reimbursements, teaching assistantships with tuition reimbursements, career-related internships or fieldwork, and unspecified assistantships available. Support available to part-time students. Financial award application deadline: 3/1; financial award applicants required to submit CSS PROFILE or FAFSA. *Faculty research:* Medical anthropology, psychological anthropology, cross-cultural aging, physical anthropology, international health. *Unit head:* Lawrence P. Greksa, Professor and Chair, 216-368-6777, Fax: 216-368-5334, E-mail: lawrence.greksa@case.edu. *Application contact:* Linda LaPinta, Department Administrator, 216-368-2264, Fax: 216-368-5334, E-mail: linda.lapinta@case.edu.
Website: http://anthropology.case.edu/

**The Catholic University of America,** School of Arts and Sciences, Department of Anthropology, Washington, DC 20064. Offers MA. *Program availability:* Part-time. *Faculty:* 2 full-time (1 woman), 5 part-time/adjunct (3 women). *Students:* 1 applicant. *Degree requirements:* For master's, one foreign language, comprehensive exam, thesis or alternative. *Entrance requirements:* For master's, GRE General Test, statement of purpose, official copies of academic transcripts, three letters of recommendation. Additional exam requirements/recommendations for international students: Required—TOEFL (minimum score 550 paper-based; 80 iBT). *Application deadline:* For fall admission, 2/1 priority date for domestic students, 7/1 for international students; for spring admission, 11/15 priority date for domestic students, 11/1 for international students. Applications are processed on a rolling basis. Application fee: $55. Electronic applications accepted. *Expenses:* $42,850 per year; $1,170 per credit; $200 per semester part-time fees. *Financial support:* Fellowships, research assistantships, teaching assistantships, Federal Work-Study, scholarships/grants, tuition waivers (full and partial), and unspecified assistantships available. Financial award application deadline: 2/1; financial award applicants required to submit FAFSA. *Faculty research:* Medical anthropology, Latin American studies, ancient states and empires; political anthropology, cultural heritage studies, Middle East studies, Andean archaeology. *Unit head:* Dr. Anita Cook, Chair, 202-319-5080, Fax: 202-319-4782, E-mail: cook@cua.edu. *Application contact:* Director of Graduate Admissions, 202-319-5057, Fax: 202-319-6533, E-mail: cua-admissions@cua.edu.
Website: http://anthropology.cua.edu/

**Central European University,** Department of Sociology and Social Anthropology, Budapest, Hungary. Offers MA. *Faculty:* 11 full-time (4 women), 4 part-time/adjunct (1 woman). *Students:* 77 full-time (47 women). Average age 28. 339 applicants, 14% accepted, 39 enrolled. In 2016, 27 master's, 8 doctorates awarded. *Degree requirements:* For master's, one foreign language, thesis; for doctorate, one foreign language, comprehensive exam, thesis/dissertation. *Entrance requirements:* For master's and doctorate, interview. Additional exam requirements/recommendations for international students: Required—TOEFL (minimum score 570 paper-based); Recommended—IELTS (minimum score 6.5). *Application deadline:* For fall admission, 2/4 for domestic and international students. Application fee: $30. Electronic applications accepted. *Expenses: Tuition:* Full-time 13,500 euros. Tuition and fees vary according to degree level, program and student level. *Financial support:* Fellowships, career-related internships or fieldwork, scholarships/grants, health care benefits, and tuition waivers (full and partial) available. *Faculty research:* Migration studies, post colonialism, studies of globalization, political and economic sociology, urban studies and sociologies of culture. *Unit head:* Dr. Andreas Dafinger, Head of Department, 36 1 327-3000 Ext. 2131, E-mail: sociology@ceu.edu. *Application contact:* Zsuzsanna Jaszberenyi, Admissions Officer, 361-324-3009, Fax: 367-327-3211, E-mail: admissions@ceu.edu.
Website: http://sociology.ceu.edu/

**The College of William and Mary,** Faculty of Arts and Sciences, Department of Anthropology, Williamsburg, VA 23187-8795. Offers MA. *Faculty:* 15 full-time (7 women), 5 part-time/adjunct (3 women). *Students:* 23 full-time (13 women), 1 part-time (0 women); includes 4 minority (1 Hispanic/Latino; 3 Two or more races, non-Hispanic/Latino), 3 international. Average age 29. 45 applicants, 18% accepted, 5 enrolled. In 2016, 6 master's, 1 doctorate awarded. Terminal master's awarded for partial completion of doctoral program. *Degree requirements:* For master's, thesis, fieldwork; for doctorate, one foreign language, comprehensive exam, thesis/dissertation, fieldwork. *Entrance requirements:* For master's and doctorate, GRE, course work in anthropology or history. Additional exam requirements/recommendations for international students: Required—TOEFL. *Application deadline:* For fall admission, 1/15 for domestic and international students. Application fee: $45. Electronic applications accepted. *Expenses:* Tuition, state resident: full-time $9000; part-time $500 per credit hour. Tuition, nonresident: full-time $24,686; part-time $1200 per credit hour. *Required fees:* $5258. One-time fee: $400 full-time. *Financial support:* In 2016–17, 16 students received support. Research assistantships with full tuition reimbursements available, teaching assistantships with full tuition reimbursements available, career-related internships or fieldwork, institutionally sponsored loans, and scholarships/grants available. Financial award application deadline: 1/15; financial award applicants required to submit FAFSA. *Faculty research:* Historical archaeology, comparative colonialism, biocultural anthropology, African diaspora, historical archaeology of native America. *Total annual research expenditures:* $877,506. *Unit head:* Dr. Brad L. Weiss, Chair, 757-221-1067, Fax: 757-221-1209, E-mail: blweis@wm.edu. *Application contact:* Dr. Neil L. Norman, Director of Graduate Studies, 757-221-1960, Fax: 757-221-1066, E-mail: nlnorman@wm.edu.
Website: http://www.wm.edu/anthropology/

**Colorado State University,** College of Liberal Arts, Department of Anthropology, Fort Collins, CO 80523-1787. Offers anthropology of health and well-being (MA); humans and the environment (MA); international development (MA); professional methods and techniques (MA). *Program availability:* Part-time. *Faculty:* 9 full-time (3 women), 1 (woman) part-time/adjunct. *Students:* 25 full-time (15 women), 21 part-time (14 women); includes 3 minority (1 Asian, non-Hispanic/Latino; 2 Hispanic/Latino), 6 international. Average age 29. 50 applicants, 54% accepted, 17 enrolled. In 2016, 10 master's awarded. *Degree requirements:* For master's, thesis (for some programs), professional portfolio. *Entrance requirements:* For master's, GRE General Test, minimum GPA of 3.0, BA/BS, transcripts, statement of purpose, writing sample, 3 letters of recommendation. Additional exam requirements/recommendations for international students: Required—TOEFL (minimum score 550 paper-based; 80 iBT). *Application deadline:* For fall admission, 2/1 for domestic and international students. Application fee: $60 ($70 for international students). Electronic applications accepted. *Expenses:* Tuition, state resident: full-time $9628. Tuition, nonresident: full-time $23,603. *Required fees:* $2253; $528.14 per credit hour. $264.07 per semester. Tuition and fees vary according to course load and program. *Financial support:* In 2016–17, 15 students received support, including 14 teaching assistantships with full and partial tuition reimbursements available (averaging $13,932 per year); scholarships/grants and unspecified assistantships also available. Financial award application deadline: 3/1;

financial award applicants required to submit FAFSA. *Faculty research:* Archaeology, cultural anthropology, biological anthropology, geography. *Total annual research expenditures:* $329,999. *Unit head:* Dr. Michelle M. Glantz, Professor and Chair, 970-491-4635, Fax: 970-491-7597, E-mail: mica.glantz@colostate.edu. *Application contact:* Dr. Mary Van Buren, Graduate Program Coordinator, 970-491-3781, Fax: 970-491-7597, E-mail: mary.vanburen@colostate.edu.
Website: http://anthropology.colostate.edu/

**Columbia University,** Graduate School of Arts and Sciences, New York, NY 10027. Offers African-American studies (MA); American studies (MA); anthropology (MA, PhD); art history and archaeology (MA, PhD); astronomy (PhD); biological sciences (PhD); biotechnology (MA); chemical physics (PhD); chemistry (PhD); classical studies (MA, PhD); classics (MA, PhD); climate and society (MA); conservation biology (MA); earth and environmental sciences (PhD); East Asia: regional studies (MA); East Asian languages and cultures (MA, PhD); ecology, evolution and environmental biology (MA), including conservation biology; ecology, evolution, and environmental biology (PhD), including ecology and evolutionary biology, evolutionary primatology; economics (MA, PhD); English and comparative literature (MA, PhD); French and Romance philology (MA, PhD); Germanic languages (MA, PhD); global French studies (MA); global thought (MA); Hispanic cultural studies (MA); history (PhD); history and literature (MA); human rights studies (MA); Islamic studies (MA); Italian studies (MA, PhD); Japanese pedagogy (MA); Jewish studies (MA); Latin America and the Caribbean: regional studies (MA); Latin American and Iberian cultures (PhD); mathematics (MA, PhD), including finance (MA); medieval and Renaissance studies (MA); Middle Eastern, South Asian, and African studies (MA, PhD); modern art: critical and curatorial studies (MA); modern European studies (MA); museum anthropology (MA); music (DMA, PhD); oral history (MA); philosophical foundations of physics (MA); philosophy (MA, PhD); physics (PhD); political science (MA, PhD); psychology (PhD); quantitative methods in the social sciences (MA); religion (MA, PhD); Russia, Eurasia and East Europe: regional studies (MA); Russian translation (MA); Slavic cultures (MA); Slavic languages (MA, PhD); sociology (MA, PhD); South Asian studies (MA); statistics (MA, PhD); theatre (PhD). Dual-degree programs require admission to both Graduate School of Arts and Sciences and another Columbia school. *Program availability:* Part-time. Terminal master's awarded for partial completion of doctoral program. *Degree requirements:* For master's, variable foreign language requirement, comprehensive exam (for some programs), thesis (for some programs); for doctorate, variable foreign language requirement, comprehensive exam (for some programs), thesis/dissertation. *Entrance requirements:* For master's and doctorate, GRE General Test, GRE Subject Test (for some programs). Additional exam requirements/recommendations for international students: Required—TOEFL, IELTS. Electronic applications accepted.

**Concordia University,** School of Graduate Studies, Faculty of Arts and Science, Department of Sociology and Anthropology, Montréal, QC H3G 1M8, Canada. Offers social and cultural analysis (PhD); social and cultural anthropology (MA); sociology (MA). *Degree requirements:* For master's, comprehensive exam or thesis. *Entrance requirements:* For master's, honors degree in sociology or equivalent. *Faculty research:* Community and ethnic relations, popular culture, regional development in Canada, industrial and social movements, social problems and policies.

**Cornell University,** Graduate School, Graduate Fields of Arts and Sciences, Field of Anthropology, Ithaca, NY 14853. Offers archaeological anthropology (PhD); biological anthropology (PhD); sociocultural anthropology (PhD). *Degree requirements:* For doctorate, one foreign language, comprehensive exam, thesis/dissertation, teaching experience. *Entrance requirements:* For doctorate, GRE General Test, 3 letters of recommendation, sample of written work. Additional exam requirements/recommendations for international students: Required—TOEFL (minimum score 550 paper-based; 77 iBT). Electronic applications accepted. *Faculty research:* Culture, engaged anthropology, political economy, area studies: Asia, Americas, Europe; interdisciplinary and ethnic studies: Asian-American studies.

**Creighton University,** Graduate School, College of Arts and Sciences, Program in Medical Anthropology, Omaha, NE 68178-0001. Offers MA. *Program availability:* Part-time, online only, blended/hybrid learning. *Faculty:* 13 full-time (8 women). *Students:* 3 full-time (all women), 16 part-time (12 women); includes 1 minority (American Indian or Alaska Native, non-Hispanic/Latino), 3 international. Average age 37. In 2016, 5 master's awarded. *Degree requirements:* For master's, thesis optional. *Entrance requirements:* For master's, three recommendations; resume; statement of purpose; writing sample. Additional exam requirements/recommendations for international students: Required—TOEFL (minimum score 90 iBT). *Application deadline:* For summer admission, 1/15 for domestic and international students. Applications are processed on a rolling basis. Application fee: $50. Electronic applications accepted. *Expenses: Tuition:* Full-time $14,400; part-time $800 per credit hour. *Required fees:* $158 per semester. Tuition and fees vary according to course load, campus/location, program, reciprocity agreements and student's religious affiliation. *Financial support:* Teaching assistantships and scholarships/grants available. Financial award application deadline: 3/15; financial award applicants required to submit FAFSA. *Unit head:* Dr. Alex Roedlach, Program Director, 402-280-2567, E-mail: alexanderroedlach@creighton.edu. *Application contact:* Lindsay Johnson, Director of Graduate and Adult Recruitment, 402-280-2703, Fax: 402-280-2423, E-mail: gradschool@creighton.edu.

**Dalhousie University,** Faculty of Arts and Social Science, Department of Sociology and Social Anthropology, Halifax, NS B3H 4R2, Canada. Offers social anthropology (MA, PhD); sociology (MA, PhD). *Entrance requirements:* Additional exam requirements/recommendations for international students: Required—TOEFL, IELTS, CANTEST, CAEL, or Michigan English Language Assessment Battery. Electronic applications accepted. *Faculty research:* Social inequality and social injustice; work, industry, and development (regional and international perspectives); health and illness.

**East Carolina University,** Graduate School, Thomas Harriot College of Arts and Sciences, Department of Anthropology, Greenville, NC 27858-4353. Offers MA. *Program availability:* Part-time. *Students:* 22 full-time (16 women), 8 part-time (6 women); includes 4 minority (1 Black or African American, non-Hispanic/Latino; 2 Hispanic/Latino; 1 Two or more races, non-Hispanic/Latino). Average age 29. 35 applicants, 46% accepted, 10 enrolled. In 2016, 3 master's awarded. *Degree requirements:* For master's, one foreign language, comprehensive exam, thesis. *Entrance requirements:* For master's, GRE General Test. Additional exam requirements/recommendations for international students: Required—TOEFL. *Application deadline:* For fall admission, 6/1 priority date for domestic students; for spring admission, 10/15 for domestic students. Applications are processed on a rolling basis. Application fee: $50. *Financial support:* Research assistantships with partial tuition reimbursements available. Financial award application deadline: 6/1. *Unit head:* Dr. Randolph Daniel, Jr., Interim Chair, 252-328-9455, E-mail: danieli@ecu.edu. *Application contact:* Dean of Graduate School, 252-328-6012, Fax: 252-328-6071, E-mail: gradschool@ecu.edu.

**Eastern New Mexico University,** Graduate School, College of Liberal Arts and Sciences, Department of Anthropology and Applied Archaeology, Portales, NM 88130. Offers anthropology (MA). *Program availability:* Part-time. *Degree requirements:* For master's, variable foreign language requirement, comprehensive exam, thesis. *Entrance requirements:* For master's, minimum GPA of 3.0, letters of recommendation, curriculum vitae, writing sample. Additional exam requirements/recommendations for international students: Required—TOEFL (minimum score 550 paper-based; 79 iBT), IELTS (minimum score 6). Electronic applications accepted. *Faculty research:* Paleobotany, remote sensing, conservation archaeology, obsidian hydration.

**Edinboro University of Pennsylvania,** Department of History, Politics, Languages and Cultures, Edinboro, PA 16444. Offers social sciences (MA), including anthropology, history. *Program availability:* Part-time, evening/weekend. *Degree requirements:* For master's, thesis or alternative, competency exam. *Entrance requirements:* For master's, GRE or MAT, minimum QPA of 2.5. Electronic applications accepted.

**Emory University,** Laney Graduate School, Department of Anthropology, Atlanta, GA 30322-1100. Offers PhD. *Degree requirements:* For doctorate, thesis/dissertation, qualifying exams. *Entrance requirements:* For doctorate, GRE General Test. Additional exam requirements/recommendations for international students: Required—TOEFL. Electronic applications accepted. *Faculty research:* Primate behavioral ecology, comparative human biology, human growth and development, medical anthropology, globalization, gender and sexuality.

**Florida Atlantic University,** Dorothy F. Schmidt College of Arts and Letters, Department of Anthropology, Boca Raton, FL 33431-0991. Offers MA, MAT. *Program availability:* Part-time. *Faculty:* 8 full-time (5 women). *Students:* 28 full-time (16 women), 15 part-time (8 women); includes 11 minority (1 Asian, non-Hispanic/Latino; 8 Hispanic/Latino; 2 Two or more races, non-Hispanic/Latino). Average age 30. 23 applicants, 74% accepted, 14 enrolled. In 2016, 12 master's awarded. *Degree requirements:* For master's, one foreign language, thesis. *Entrance requirements:* For master's, GRE General Test, minimum GPA of 3.0. Additional exam requirements/recommendations for international students: Required—TOEFL (minimum score 500 paper-based; 61 iBT), IELTS (minimum score 6). *Application deadline:* For fall admission, 7/1 priority date for domestic students, 2/15 for international students; for spring admission, 11/1 for domestic students, 7/15 for international students. Applications are processed on a rolling basis. Application fee: $30. Electronic applications accepted. *Expenses:* Tuition, state resident: full-time $7392; part-time $369.82 per credit hour. Tuition, nonresident: full-time $19,432; part-time $1024.81 per credit hour. *Financial support:* Fellowships, research assistantships with tuition reimbursements, teaching assistantships with tuition reimbursements, Federal Work-Study, and unspecified assistantships available. *Faculty research:* Archaeological, ethnological, ethnographical, osteological, paleoanthropological, and zoo-archaeological research. *Unit head:* Dr. Michael S. Harris, Chairman, 561-297-3233, Fax: 561-297-0084, E-mail: mharris@fau.edu. *Website:* http://www.fau.edu/anthro/

**George Mason University,** College of Humanities and Social Sciences, Department of Sociology and Anthropology, Fairfax, VA 22030. Offers anthropology (MA); sociology (PhD). *Faculty:* 23 full-time (12 women), 8 part-time/adjunct (6 women). *Students:* 36 full-time (27 women), 59 part-time (35 women); includes 23 minority (7 Black or African American, non-Hispanic/Latino; 4 Asian, non-Hispanic/Latino; 11 Hispanic/Latino; 1 Two or more races, non-Hispanic/Latino), 5 international. Average age 33. 60 applicants, 53% accepted, 18 enrolled. In 2016, 22 master's, 4 doctorates awarded. *Degree requirements:* For master's, thesis; for doctorate, comprehensive exam, thesis/dissertation. *Entrance requirements:* For master's, official transcript; expanded goals statement; 3 letters of recommendation; writing sample; resume; 3 credits in undergraduate sociology theory, statistics and research methods (for sociology); 3 credits of sociocultural anthropology (for anthropology); for doctorate, GRE General Test, expanded goals statement; 3 letters of recommendation; writing sample; official transcript. Additional exam requirements/recommendations for international students: Required—TOEFL (minimum score 575 paper-based; 88 iBT), IELTS (minimum score 6.5), PTE (minimum score 59). Application fee: $75 ($80 for international students). Electronic applications accepted. *Expenses:* Tuition, state resident: full-time $10,628; part-time $443 per credit. Tuition, nonresident: full-time $29,306; part-time $1221 per credit. *Required fees:* $3096; $129 per credit. Tuition and fees vary according to program. *Financial support:* In 2016–17, 30 students received support, including 5 fellowships (averaging $12,400 per year), 10 research assistantships with tuition reimbursements available (averaging $17,800 per year), 16 teaching assistantships with tuition reimbursements available (averaging $12,534 per year); career-related internships or fieldwork, Federal Work-Study, scholarships/grants, unspecified assistantships, and health care benefits (for full-time research or teaching assistantship recipients) also available. Support available to part-time students. Financial award application deadline: 3/1; financial award applicants required to submit FAFSA. *Faculty research:* Africa, American teenagers, black entrepreneurs, human rights, gambling. *Total annual research expenditures:* $128,824. *Unit head:* Amy Best, Department Chair, 703-993-1426, Fax: 703-993-1446, E-mail: abest@gmu.edu. *Application contact:* Nancy Hanrahan, Graduate Director, 703-993-1433, Fax: 703-993-1446, E-mail: nhanraha@gmu.edu.
*Website:* http://soan.gmu.edu

**The George Washington University,** Columbian College of Arts and Sciences, Department of Anthropology, Washington, DC 20052. Offers anthropology (MA, PhD); international development (MA); medical anthropology (MA); museum training (MA). *Program availability:* Part-time, evening/weekend. *Faculty:* 15 full-time (6 women). *Students:* 27 full-time (20 women), 11 part-time (8 women); includes 12 minority (1 Black or African American, non-Hispanic/Latino; 2 Asian, non-Hispanic/Latino; 5 Hispanic/Latino; 4 Two or more races, non-Hispanic/Latino), 6 international. Average age 28. 86 applicants, 33% accepted, 9 enrolled. In 2016, 10 master's awarded. *Degree requirements:* For master's, one foreign language, comprehensive exam, thesis or alternative. *Entrance requirements:* For master's, GRE General Test, minimum GPA of 3.0. Additional exam requirements/recommendations for international students: Required—TOEFL (minimum score 550 paper-based; 80 iBT). *Application deadline:* For fall admission, 1/15 priority date for international students; for spring admission, 9/15 priority date for domestic students, 9/1 priority date for international students. Applications are processed on a rolling basis. Application fee: $75. Electronic applications accepted. *Financial support:* In 2016–17, 8 students received support. Fellowships, teaching assistantships, career-related internships or fieldwork, and Federal Work-Study available. Financial award application deadline: 1/15. *Unit head:* Richard Grinker, Chair, 202-994-6984, E-mail: rgrink@email.gwu.edu. *Application contact:* Information Contact, 202-994-6075, E-mail: anth@gwu.edu.
*Website:* http://anthropology.columbian.gwu.edu/

**Georgia State University,** College of Arts and Sciences, Department of Anthropology, Atlanta, GA 30302. Offers MA. *Program availability:* Part-time. *Faculty:* 10 full-time (7 women). *Students:* 32 full-time (23 women), 11 part-time (9 women); includes 9 minority (1 Black or African American, non-Hispanic/Latino; 1 Asian, non-Hispanic/Latino; 3 Hispanic/Latino; 4 Two or more races, non-Hispanic/Latino), 5 international. Average age 31. 22 applicants, 86% accepted, 11 enrolled. In 2016, 12 master's awarded. *Degree requirements:* For master's, one foreign language, comprehensive exam, 33 to 36 credit hours, thesis/practicum defense. *Entrance requirements:* For master's, GRE, statement of purpose, writing sample, official transcripts, two letters of recommendation, curriculum vitae. Additional exam requirements/recommendations for international students: Required—TOEFL (minimum score 550 paper-based; 80 iBT), IELTS (minimum score 6.5). *Application deadline:* For fall admission, 3/15 for domestic and international students; for spring admission, 10/15 for domestic and international

students. Applications are processed on a rolling basis. Application fee: $50. Electronic applications accepted. *Expenses:* Tuition, state resident: full-time $6876; part-time $382 per credit hour. Tuition, nonresident: full-time $22,374; part-time $1243 per credit hour. *Required fees:* $2128; $1064 per term. Part-time tuition and fees vary according to course load and program. *Financial support:* In 2016–17, research assistantships with full tuition reimbursements (averaging $4,000 per year) were awarded. Financial award applicants required to submit FAFSA. *Faculty research:* Archaeology, medical anthropology, linguistic anthropology, biological/physical anthropology, cultural anthropology. *Unit head:* Dr. Frank L. Williams, Chair, 404-413-5154, Fax: 404-413-5159, E-mail: frankwilliams@gsu.edu. *Application contact:* Dr. Emanuela Guano, Director of Graduate Studies, 404-413-5152, Fax: 404-413-5159, E-mail: eguano@gsu.edu.
*Website:* http://www.cas.gsu.edu/anthropology/

**The Graduate Center, City University of New York,** Graduate Studies, Program in Anthropology, New York, NY 10016-4039. Offers anthropological linguistics (PhD); archaeology (PhD); cultural anthropology (PhD); physical anthropology (PhD). *Degree requirements:* For doctorate, one foreign language, thesis/dissertation. *Entrance requirements:* For doctorate, GRE General Test. Additional exam requirements/recommendations for international students: Required—TOEFL. Electronic applications accepted.

**Harvard University,** Graduate School of Arts and Sciences, Committee on Middle Eastern Studies, Cambridge, MA 02138. Offers anthropology and Middle Eastern studies (PhD); economics and Middle Eastern studies (PhD); fine arts and Middle Eastern studies (PhD); history and Middle Eastern studies (PhD); regional studies–Middle East (AM). Terminal master's awarded for partial completion of doctoral program. *Degree requirements:* For master's, one foreign language; for doctorate, 2 foreign languages, thesis/dissertation. *Entrance requirements:* For master's, GRE General Test; for doctorate, GRE General Test, 1 year of course work in Middle Eastern regional studies, proficiency in a related language. Additional exam requirements/recommendations for international students: Required—TOEFL.

**Harvard University,** Graduate School of Arts and Sciences, Department of Anthropology, Cambridge, MA 02138. Offers archaeology (PhD); biological anthropology (PhD); legal anthropology (AM); medical anthropology (AM); social anthropology (AM, PhD); social change and development (AM). Terminal master's awarded for partial completion of doctoral program. *Degree requirements:* For master's, 2 foreign languages, thesis (for some programs); for doctorate, 2 foreign languages, thesis/dissertation, laboratory and/or fieldwork; general, qualifying, or special exams. *Entrance requirements:* For master's and doctorate, GRE General Test. Additional exam requirements/recommendations for international students: Required—TOEFL.

**Humboldt State University,** Academic Programs, College of Arts, Humanities, and Social Sciences, Department of Anthropology, Arcata, CA 95521-8299. Offers applied anthropology (MA). *Program availability:* Part-time, online learning. *Degree requirements:* For master's, comprehensive exam, thesis, 180 hours of field placement/internship. *Entrance requirements:* For master's, three letters of recommendation. Electronic applications accepted. *Expenses:* Tuition, state resident: full-time $6738; part-time $1953 per semester. Tuition, nonresident: full-time $13,434; part-time $3813 per semester. *Required fees:* $1738; $653 per semester. Tuition and fees vary according to program.

**Hunter College of the City University of New York,** Graduate School, School of Arts and Sciences, Department of Anthropology, New York, NY 10065-5085. Offers MA. *Program availability:* Part-time, evening/weekend. *Students:* 1 (woman) full-time, 43 part-time (28 women); includes 16 minority (4 Black or African American, non-Hispanic/Latino; 6 Asian, non-Hispanic/Latino; 6 Hispanic/Latino), 1 international. Average age 34. 24 applicants, 63% accepted, 9 enrolled. In 2016, 14 master's awarded. *Degree requirements:* For master's, comprehensive exam, thesis, language or statistics exam. *Entrance requirements:* For master's, GRE General Test, minimum 9 credits of course work in anthropology or a related field. Additional exam requirements/recommendations for international students: Required—TOEFL. *Application deadline:* For fall admission, 4/1 for domestic students, 2/1 for international students; for spring admission, 11/1 for domestic students, 9/1 for international students. *Financial support:* Research assistantships and tuition waivers (full and partial) available. *Faculty research:* Primatology, human ecology, archeology, political anthropology, primate and human evolution. *Unit head:* Jonathan Shannon, Chair, 212-772-5410, Fax: 212-772-5423, E-mail: jshanno@hunter.cuny.edu. *Application contact:* William Zlata, Director for Graduate Admissions, 212-772-4482, Fax: 212-650-3336, E-mail: admissions@hunter.cuny.edu.
*Website:* http://www.hunter.cuny.edu/anthropology

**Idaho State University,** Office of Graduate Studies, College of Arts and Letters, Department of Anthropology, Pocatello, ID 83209-8005. Offers MA, MS. *Program availability:* Part-time. *Degree requirements:* For master's, one foreign language, comprehensive exam, thesis, 4 semesters foreign language, oral defense. *Entrance requirements:* For master's, GRE General Test, GMAT or MAT, minimum GPA of 3.0 in all upper-division classes, 3 letters of recommendation. Additional exam requirements/recommendations for international students: Required—TOEFL (minimum score 550 paper-based; 80 iBT). Electronic applications accepted. *Faculty research:* Native American studies: health care, language/ethnopoetics, prehistory, art, resource environmental management.

**Indiana University Bloomington,** University Graduate School, College of Arts and Sciences, Department of Anthropology, Bloomington, IN 47405. Offers anthropology (MA, PhD), including archaeology (PhD); bioanthropology (PhD); linguistic anthropology (PhD); social-cultural anthropology (PhD). *Faculty:* 35 full-time (23 women). *Students:* 101 full-time (76 women); includes 16 minority (2 Black or African American, non-Hispanic/Latino; 2 American Indian or Alaska Native, non-Hispanic/Latino; 1 Asian, non-Hispanic/Latino; 6 Hispanic/Latino; 5 Two or more races, non-Hispanic/Latino), 15 international. Average age 33. 81 applicants, 15% accepted, 6 enrolled. In 2016, 8 master's, 10 doctorates awarded. *Degree requirements:* For master's, comprehensive exam (for some programs), thesis or alternative; for doctorate, 2 foreign languages, comprehensive exam, thesis/dissertation. *Entrance requirements:* For master's and doctorate, GRE General Test, minimum GPA of 3.0. Additional exam requirements/recommendations for international students: Required—TOEFL (minimum score 550 paper-based; 79 iBT) or IELTS. *Application deadline:* For fall admission, 12/1 for domestic and international students. Application fee: $55 ($65 for international students). Electronic applications accepted. *Expenses:* $3,429 per course non-resident; $990 per course resident. *Financial support:* In 2016–17, 68 students received support, including 22 fellowships with full tuition reimbursements available (averaging $18,000 per year), 4 research assistantships with full tuition reimbursements available (averaging $15,750 per year), 46 teaching assistantships with full tuition reimbursements available (averaging $15,750 per year); Federal Work-Study, scholarships/grants, health care benefits, and unspecified assistantships also available. *Faculty research:* Archaeology in social context; bio anthropology; anthropology of food and ecology; gender studies; communication, media and performance. *Total annual research expenditures:* $170,905. *Unit head:* Dr. Jeanne Sept, Chair, 812-855-2555, Fax: 812-855-4358, E-mail: sept@indiana.edu. *Application contact:* Debra Wilkerson, Administrative

## Anthropology

Secretary, 812-855-1203, Fax: 812-855-4358, E-mail: dwilkers@indiana.edu. Website: http://www.indiana.edu/~anthro/index.shtml

**Iowa State University of Science and Technology,** Department of Anthropology, Ames, IA 50011. Offers MA. *Degree requirements:* For master's, thesis. *Entrance requirements:* For master's, GRE General Test. Additional exam requirements/recommendations for international students: Required—TOEFL (minimum score 550 paper-based; 79 iBT), IELTS (minimum score 6.5). *Application deadline:* For fall admission, 1/15 priority date for domestic and international students; for spring admission, 10/1 for domestic and international students. Applications are processed on a rolling basis. Application fee: $60 ($90 for international students). Electronic applications accepted. *Application contact:* Amanda Runyan, Application Contact, 515-294-4910, E-mail: runyan@iastate.edu.
Website: http://www.anthr.iastate.edu

**Johns Hopkins University,** Zanvyl Krieger School of Arts and Sciences, Department of Anthropology, Baltimore, MD 21218. Offers PhD. *Degree requirements:* For doctorate, one foreign language, thesis/dissertation. *Entrance requirements:* For doctorate, GRE General Test. Additional exam requirements/recommendations for international students: Required—TOEFL, IELTS. Electronic applications accepted. *Faculty research:* Social and cultural anthropology of complex societies, gender politics, economic anthropology, religion.

**Kent State University,** College of Arts and Sciences, Department of Anthropology, Kent, OH 44242-0001. Offers MA. *Program availability:* Part-time. *Faculty:* 8 full-time (2 women). *Students:* 10 full-time (8 women), 11 part-time (5 women); includes 4 minority (1 Black or African American, non-Hispanic/Latino; 1 Hispanic/Latino; 2 Two or more races, non-Hispanic/Latino). Average age 30. 15 applicants, 53% accepted, 5 enrolled. In 2016, 3 master's awarded. *Degree requirements:* For master's, thesis, thesis defense. *Entrance requirements:* For master's, GRE, goal statement, 3 letters of recommendation, transcript. Additional exam requirements/recommendations for international students: Required—TOEFL (minimum score of 525 paper-based, 71 iBT), IELTS (minimum score of 6), Michigan English Language Assessment Battery (minimum score of 75), or PTE (minimum score of 48). *Application deadline:* For fall admission, 2/1 for domestic and international students. Applications are processed on a rolling basis. Application fee: $45 ($70 for international students). Electronic applications accepted. *Expenses:* Tuition, state resident: full-time $10,864; part-time $495 per credit hour. Tuition, nonresident: full-time $18,380; part-time $837 per credit hour. *Financial support:* Research assistantships with full tuition reimbursements, teaching assistantships with full tuition reimbursements, career-related internships or fieldwork, Federal Work-Study, scholarships/grants, and unspecified assistantships available. Financial award application deadline: 2/1; financial award applicants required to submit FAFSA. *Unit head:* Dr. Mary Ann Raghanti, Associate Professor and Interim Chair, 330-672-9354, E-mail: mraghant@kent.edu. *Application contact:* Dr. Richard S. Meindl, Professor, 330-672-7998, E-mail: rmeindl@kent.edu.
Website: https://www.kent.edu/anthropology

**Louisiana State University and Agricultural & Mechanical College,** Graduate School, College of Humanities and Social Sciences, Department of Geography and Anthropology, Baton Rouge, LA 70803. Offers geography (MA, MS); geography and anthropology (PhD).

**McGill University,** Faculty of Graduate and Postdoctoral Studies, Faculty of Arts, Department of Anthropology, Montréal, QC H3A 2T5, Canada. Offers anthropology (MA, PhD); medical anthropology (MA).

**McGill University,** Faculty of Graduate and Postdoctoral Studies, Faculty of Medicine, Department of Social Studies in Medicine, Montréal, QC H3A 2T5, Canada. Offers medical anthropology (MA, PhD); medical history (MA, PhD); medical sociology (MA, PhD).

**McMaster University,** School of Graduate Studies, Faculty of Social Sciences, Department of Anthropology, Hamilton, ON L8S 4M2, Canada. Offers MA, PhD. *Program availability:* Part-time. *Degree requirements:* For master's, thesis or alternative; for doctorate, one foreign language, comprehensive exam, thesis/dissertation, fieldwork. *Entrance requirements:* Additional exam requirements/recommendations for international students: Required—TOEFL (minimum score 580 paper-based). *Faculty research:* Medical anthropology, contemporary ethnography in an interdisciplinary perspective, archaeological and social theory, linguistics, folklore.

**Memorial University of Newfoundland,** School of Graduate Studies, Department of Anthropology, St. John's, NL A1C 5S7, Canada. Offers archaeology and physical anthropology (MA, PhD); social and cultural anthropology (MA, PhD). *Program availability:* Part-time. *Degree requirements:* For master's, comprehensive exam (for some programs), thesis (for some programs); for doctorate, comprehensive exam, thesis/dissertation, oral defense of thesis. *Entrance requirements:* For master's, 2nd class degree in related field. Electronic applications accepted. *Faculty research:* Early European settlements, ethnoarchaeology, economic/political anthropology, land claims and aboriginal rights, marine anthropology.

**Mercyhurst University,** Graduate Studies, Program in Anthropology, Erie, PA 16546. Offers archaeology and geological archaeology (MS); forensic and biological anthropology (MS). *Entrance requirements:* For master's, GRE or MAT, undergraduate degree in related field, interview, resume, essay, three professional references, transcripts. Additional exam requirements/recommendations for international students: Required—TOEFL.

**Michigan State University,** The Graduate School, College of Social Science, Department of Anthropology, East Lansing, MI 48824. Offers anthropology (MA, PhD); professional applications in anthropology (MA). Terminal master's awarded for partial completion of doctoral program. *Degree requirements:* For master's, comprehensive exam (for some programs); for doctorate, annual evaluation. *Entrance requirements:* Additional exam requirements/recommendations for international students: Required—TOEFL. Electronic applications accepted.

**Minnesota State University Mankato,** College of Graduate Studies and Research, College of Social and Behavioral Sciences, Department of Anthropology, Mankato, MN 56001. Offers applied anthropology (MS). *Program availability:* Part-time. *Students:* 1 (woman) full-time, 21 part-time (14 women). *Degree requirements:* For master's, comprehensive exam, thesis. *Entrance requirements:* For master's, GRE. Additional exam requirements/recommendations for international students: Required—TOEFL. *Application deadline:* For fall admission, 7/1 priority date for domestic students; for spring admission, 11/1 for domestic students. Applications are processed on a rolling basis. Application fee: $40. Electronic applications accepted. *Financial support:* Fellowships, scholarships/grants, and unspecified assistantships available. Financial award application deadline: 3/15; financial award applicants required to submit FAFSA. *Unit head:* Dr. Kathleen Blue, Chair, 507-389-6370, Fax: 507-389-6769, E-mail: kathleen.blue@mnsu.edu. *Application contact:* Dr. Kathryn Elliott, Graduate Coordinator, 507-389-6590, Fax: 507-389-6769, E-mail: kathryn.elliott@mnsu.edu.
Website: http://sbs.mnsu.edu/anthropology/

**Mississippi State University,** College of Arts and Sciences, Department of Anthropology and Middle Eastern Cultures, Mississippi State, MS 39762. Offers MA.

*Program availability:* Part-time. *Faculty:* 9 full-time (4 women). *Students:* 20 full-time (12 women), 24 part-time (14 women); includes 5 minority (2 Black or African American, non-Hispanic/Latino; 1 Asian, non-Hispanic/Latino; 2 Hispanic/Latino), 4 international. Average age 30. 10 applicants, 90% accepted, 6 enrolled. In 2016, 13 master's awarded. *Degree requirements:* For master's, thesis. *Entrance requirements:* For master's, GRE, minimum GPA of 3.0 on last 60 hours of undergraduate courses. Additional exam requirements/recommendations for international students: Required—TOEFL (minimum score 477 paper-based; 53 iBT); Recommended—IELTS (minimum score 4.5). *Application deadline:* For fall admission, 4/15 priority date for domestic students, 4/15 for international students; for spring admission, 11/1 priority date for domestic students, 9/1 for international students. Applications are processed on a rolling basis. Application fee: $60. Electronic applications accepted. *Expenses:* Tuition, state resident: full-time $7670; part-time $852.50 per credit hour. Tuition, nonresident: full-time $20,790; part-time $2310.50 per credit hour. Part-time tuition and fees vary according to course load. *Financial support:* In 2016–17, 8 teaching assistantships with partial tuition reimbursements (averaging $9,392 per year) were awarded; Federal Work-Study, institutionally sponsored loans, scholarships/grants, and unspecified assistantships also available. Financial award application deadline: 3/15; financial award applicants required to submit FAFSA. *Faculty research:* Archaeology and bioarchaeology, environmental archaeology, cultural archaeology, research projects in Southeastern archaeology and bioarcheology. *Unit head:* Dr. Michael Galaty, Department Head, 662-325-7525, Fax: 662-325-8690, E-mail: mgalaty@anthro.msstate.edu. *Application contact:* Nathan Drake, Admissions and Enrollment Assistant, 662-325-3804, E-mail: ndrake@grad.msstate.edu.
Website: http://www.amec.msstate.edu

**Monmouth University,** Graduate Studies, Program in Anthropology, West Long Branch, NJ 07764-1898. Offers MA. *Program availability:* Part-time, evening/weekend. *Degree requirements:* For master's, comprehensive exam (for some programs), thesis (for some programs). *Entrance requirements:* For master's, minimum undergraduate GPA of 3.0, 500-word essay highlighting personal and/or professional goals and objectives for graduate anthropology study, two professional letters of recommendation. Additional exam requirements/recommendations for international students: Required—TOEFL (minimum score 550 paper-based; 79 iBT), IELTS (minimum score 6), Michigan English Language Assessment Battery (minimum score 77) or Certificate of Advanced English (minimum score B2). Electronic applications accepted. *Faculty research:* Historical archeology, early America, Native Americans, historic preservation, archeology of NJ and Northeast.

**New Mexico Highlands University,** Graduate Studies, College of Arts and Sciences, Department of Social and Behavioral Sciences, Las Vegas, NM 87701. Offers psychology (MS), including clinical psychology/counseling, general psychology; public affairs (MA), including applied sociology; Southwest studies (MA), including anthropology. *Program availability:* Part-time. *Degree requirements:* For master's, comprehensive exam, thesis or alternative. *Entrance requirements:* For master's, minimum undergraduate GPA of 3.0. Additional exam requirements/recommendations for international students: Required—TOEFL (minimum score 540 paper-based). *Faculty research:* Southwest Native American resettlement development, community-level interventions, neurochemistry of personality, comparative criminal justice, social theory and activism.

**New Mexico State University,** College of Arts and Sciences, Department of Anthropology, Las Cruces, NM 88003. Offers anthropology (MA); cultural resource management (Graduate Certificate); museum studies (Graduate Certificate). *Program availability:* Part-time. *Faculty:* 9 full-time (5 women), 1 part-time/adjunct (0 women). *Students:* 35 full-time (23 women), 22 part-time (16 women); includes 20 minority (2 Black or African American, non-Hispanic/Latino; 1 American Indian or Alaska Native, non-Hispanic/Latino; 15 Hispanic/Latino; 2 Two or more races, non-Hispanic/Latino), 2 international. Average age 32. 27 applicants, 67% accepted, 12 enrolled. In 2016, 16 master's, 7 other advanced degrees awarded. *Degree requirements:* For master's, comprehensive exam (for some programs), thesis or internship. *Entrance requirements:* For master's, minimum undergraduate GPA of 3.0. Additional exam requirements/recommendations for international students: Required—TOEFL (minimum score 550 paper-based; 79 iBT), IELTS (minimum score 6.5). *Application deadline:* For fall admission, 2/1 priority date for domestic and international students; for spring admission, 10/1 priority date for domestic and international students. Applications are processed on a rolling basis. Application fee: $40 ($50 for international students). Electronic applications accepted. *Expenses:* Tuition, state resident: full-time $4086. Tuition, nonresident: full-time $14,254. *Required fees:* $853. Tuition and fees vary according to course load. *Financial support:* In 2016–17, 27 students received support, including 5 fellowships (averaging $4,088 per year), 2 research assistantships (averaging $8,482 per year), 11 teaching assistantships (averaging $10,097 per year); career-related internships or fieldwork, Federal Work-Study, scholarships/grants, traineeships, health care benefits, and unspecified assistantships also available. Support available to part-time students. Financial award application deadline: 3/1. *Faculty research:* Native American culture and society, Latin America and border studies, prehistoric and historic archaeology, medical anthropology, applied anthropology, museum studies. *Total annual research expenditures:* $31,819. *Unit head:* Dr. Rani Alexander, Department Head, 575-646-2725, E-mail: raalexan@nmsu.edu. *Application contact:* Dr. Lois Stanford, Graduate Advisor, 575-646-6092, E-mail: lstanfor@nmsu.edu.
Website: http://anthropology.nmsu.edu

**The New School,** The New School for Social Research, Department of Anthropology, New York, NY 10003. Offers M Phil, MA, PhD. *Program availability:* Part-time. *Faculty:* 2 full-time (1 woman), 12 part-time/adjunct (4 women). *Students:* 42 full-time (28 women), 9 part-time (6 women); includes 8 minority (1 Black or African American, non-Hispanic/Latino; 3 Asian, non-Hispanic/Latino; 3 Hispanic/Latino; 1 Two or more races, non-Hispanic/Latino), 22 international. Average age 32. 62 applicants, 76% accepted, 10 enrolled. In 2016, 17 master's, 2 doctorates awarded. Terminal master's awarded for partial completion of doctoral program. *Degree requirements:* For master's, variable foreign language requirement, comprehensive exam; for doctorate, one foreign language, comprehensive exam, thesis/dissertation. *Entrance requirements:* For master's, GRE, letters of recommendation, writing sample, essays, unofficial transcript; for doctorate, letters of recommendation, writing sample, essays, unofficial transcript. Additional exam requirements/recommendations for international students: Required—TOEFL (minimum score 100 iBT), IELTS (minimum score 7), PTE (minimum score 68). *Application deadline:* For fall admission, 8/1 priority date for domestic students, 6/1 priority date for international students; for spring admission, 10/15 priority date for domestic and international students. Applications are processed on a rolling basis. Application fee: $50. Electronic applications accepted. *Expenses:* Contact institution. *Financial support:* Fellowships, research assistantships, teaching assistantships, Federal Work-Study, scholarships/grants, and tuition waivers (full and partial) available. Support available to part-time students. Financial award application deadline: 2/1; financial award applicants required to submit FAFSA. *Faculty research:* Theoretical and methodological foundations of social and cultural anthropology; critical ethnography. *Unit head:* Dr. William Milberg, Dean, The New School for Social Research, 212-229-5777, E-mail: milbergw@newschool.edu. *Application contact:* Dana Messinger, Director

of Graduate Admission, 212-229-5150 Ext. 2300, E-mail: socialresearchadmit@newschool.edu.
Website: http://www.newschool.edu/

**New York University,** Graduate School of Arts and Science, Department of Anthropology, New York, NY 10012-1019. Offers anthropology (MA, PhD), including archaeological anthropology, linguistic anthropology, physical anthropology, socio-cultural anthropology; anthropology and French studies (PhD); MA/Advanced Certificate; PhD/Advanced Certificate. *Program availability:* Part-time. *Degree requirements:* For master's, thesis; for doctorate, one foreign language, comprehensive exam, thesis/dissertation. *Entrance requirements:* For master's and doctorate, GRE General Test. Additional exam requirements/recommendations for international students: Required—TOEFL. *Faculty research:* Sociocultural anthropology, archaeology, biological anthropology, linguistic anthropology.

**North Carolina State University,** Graduate School, College of Humanities and Social Sciences, Department of Sociology and Anthropology, Program in Anthropology, Raleigh, NC 27695. Offers bioarchaeology (MA); cultural anthropology (MA); environmental anthropology (MA).

**North Dakota State University,** College of Graduate and Interdisciplinary Studies, College of Arts, Humanities and Social Sciences, Department of Sociology and Anthropology, Fargo, ND 58102. Offers anthropology (MA, MS); community development (MA, MS); social science (MA, MS); sociology (MS). *Program availability:* Part-time. *Degree requirements:* For master's, thesis. *Entrance requirements:* For master's, GRE (for emergency management), course work in sociology, minimum GPA of 3.2. Additional exam requirements/recommendations for international students: Required—TOEFL. Electronic applications accepted. *Faculty research:* Medical sociology, demography, ethnology, archaeology.

**Northern Arizona University,** Graduate College, College of Social and Behavioral Sciences, Department of Anthropology, Flagstaff, AZ 86011. Offers archaeology (MA); linguistic anthropology (MA); sociocultural anthropology (MA). *Degree requirements:* For master's, thesis (for some programs), internship paper. *Entrance requirements:* For master's, 12 undergraduate hours in anthropology. Additional exam requirements/recommendations for international students: Required—TOEFL (minimum score 550 paper-based; 80 iBT), IELTS (minimum score 7). Electronic applications accepted. *Expenses:* Tuition, state resident: full-time $8971; part-time $444 per credit hour. Tuition, nonresident: full-time $20,958; part-time $1164 per credit hour. *Required fees:* $1018; $644 per credit hour. Tuition and fees vary according to course load, campus/location and program. *Faculty research:* Economic development, culture change, ethnohistory, archaeology of the Southwest, small town networks and HIV.

**Northern Illinois University,** Graduate School, College of Liberal Arts and Sciences, Department of Anthropology, De Kalb, IL 60115-2854. Offers MA. *Program availability:* Part-time. *Faculty:* 12 full-time (6 women). *Students:* 14 full-time (9 women), 9 part-time (8 women); includes 2 minority (1 Asian, non-Hispanic/Latino; 1 Hispanic/Latino), 3 international. Average age 31. 21 applicants, 62% accepted, 5 enrolled. In 2016, 9 master's awarded. *Degree requirements:* For master's, one foreign language, comprehensive exam, thesis optional. *Entrance requirements:* For master's, GRE General Test, minimum GPA of 2.75, 15 hours of course work in anthropology, course work in statistics. Additional exam requirements/recommendations for international students: Required—TOEFL (minimum score 550 paper-based). *Application deadline:* For fall admission, 6/1 for domestic students, 5/1 for international students; for spring admission, 11/1 for domestic students, 10/1 for international students. Applications are processed on a rolling basis. Application fee: $40. Electronic applications accepted. *Financial support:* In 2016–17, 3 research assistantships with full tuition reimbursements, 8 teaching assistantships with full tuition reimbursements were awarded; fellowships with full tuition reimbursements, career-related internships or fieldwork, Federal Work-Study, scholarships/grants, tuition waivers (full), and unspecified assistantships also available. Support available to part-time students. Financial award applicants required to submit FAFSA. *Faculty research:* Linguistic anthropology of Oceania, Mayan languages, human paleontology, primate evolution, dental anthropology. *Unit head:* Dr. Kendall Thu, Chair, 815-753-0479, Fax: 815-753-7027, E-mail: kthu@niu.edu. *Application contact:* Graduate School Office, 815-753-0395, E-mail: gradsch@niu.edu.
Website: http://www.niu.edu/anthro/

**Northwestern University,** The Graduate School, Judd A. and Marjorie Weinberg College of Arts and Sciences, Department of Anthropology, Evanston, IL 60208. Offers PhD, JD/PhD. Admissions and degrees offered through The Graduate School. *Degree requirements:* For doctorate, thesis/dissertation. *Entrance requirements:* For doctorate, GRE General Test. Additional exam requirements/recommendations for international students: Required—TOEFL. Electronic applications accepted. *Faculty research:* Archaeology of complex societies, gender, political/urban anthropology, linguistic anthropology, African studies.

**The Ohio State University,** Graduate School, College of Arts and Sciences, Division of Social and Behavioral Sciences, Department of Anthropology, Columbus, OH 43210. Offers MA, PhD. *Faculty:* 17. *Students:* 61 full-time (47 women); includes 5 minority (all Hispanic/Latino). Average age 31. In 2016, 3 master's, 2 doctorates awarded. *Degree requirements:* For master's, thesis optional; for doctorate, one foreign language, thesis/dissertation. *Entrance requirements:* For master's and doctorate, GRE General Test, minimum GPA of 3.3 in undergraduate work, 3.5 in all previous graduate work (recommended). Additional exam requirements/recommendations for international students: Required—TOEFL (minimum score 550 paper-based; 79 iBT), Michigan English Language Assessment Battery (minimum score 82); Recommended—IELTS (minimum score 7). *Application deadline:* For fall admission, 11/19 priority date for domestic and international students. Applications are processed on a rolling basis. Application fee: $60 ($70 for international students). Electronic applications accepted. *Financial support:* Fellowships with tuition reimbursements, research assistantships with tuition reimbursements, teaching assistantships with tuition reimbursements, Federal Work-Study, institutionally sponsored loans, and unspecified assistantships available. Support available to part-time students. *Unit head:* Dr. Kristen Gremillion, Chair and Professor, 614-292-4388, Fax: 614-292-4155, E-mail: gremillion.1@osu.edu. *Application contact:* Graduate and Professional Admissions, 614-292-9444, Fax: 614-292-3895, E-mail: gpadmissions@osu.edu.
Website: http://anthropology.osu.edu/

**Oregon State University,** College of Liberal Arts, Program in Applied Anthropology, Corvallis, OR 97331. Offers MA, PhD. *Faculty:* 18 full-time (9 women). *Students:* 44 full-time (26 women), 12 part-time (9 women); includes 18 minority (3 Black or African American, non-Hispanic/Latino; 1 American Indian or Alaska Native, non-Hispanic/Latino; 10 Hispanic/Latino; 4 Two or more races, non-Hispanic/Latino), 1 international. Average age 33. 37 applicants, 57% accepted, 13 enrolled. In 2016, 8 master's, 2 doctorates awarded. *Degree requirements:* For master's, one foreign language, thesis. *Entrance requirements:* Additional exam requirements/recommendations for international students: Required—TOEFL (minimum score 80 iBT), IELTS (minimum score 6.5). *Application deadline:* For fall admission, 1/1 for domestic and international students. Application fee: $75 ($85 for international students). *Expenses:* Tuition, state

resident: full-time $12,150; part-time $450 per credit. Tuition, nonresident: full-time $21,789; part-time $807 per credit. *Required fees:* $1651; $1507 per credit. One-time fee: $350. Tuition and fees vary according to course load, campus/location and program. *Financial support:* Research assistantships and teaching assistantships available. Financial award application deadline: 1/1. *Faculty research:* Historical anthropology, evolutionary anthropology, medical anthropology, anthropology of food, environmental anthropology. *Unit head:* Dr. Larry Roper, Director of School of Language, Culture and Society. *Application contact:* Dr. Kenneth Maes, Assistant Professor, 541-737-7870, E-mail: kenneth.maes@oregonstate.edu.
Website: http://liberalarts.oregonstate.edu/slcs/anthropology

**Penn State University Park,** Graduate School, College of the Liberal Arts, Department of Anthropology, University Park, PA 16802. Offers MA, PhD. *Unit head:* Dr. Susan Welch, Dean, 814-865-7691, Fax: 814-863-2085. *Application contact:* Lori Hawn, Director, Graduate Student Services, 814-865-1795, Fax: 814-863-4627, E-mail: l-gswww@lists.psu.edu.
Website: http://anth.la.psu.edu/

**Portland State University,** Graduate Studies, College of Liberal Arts and Sciences, Department of Anthropology, Portland, OR 97207-0751. Offers MA. *Faculty:* 9 full-time (6 women), 7 part-time/adjunct (4 women). *Students:* 11 full-time (9 women), 11 part-time (7 women); includes 1 minority (Two or more races, non-Hispanic/Latino). Average age 31. 29 applicants, 31% accepted, 5 enrolled. In 2016, 5 master's awarded. *Degree requirements:* For master's, one foreign language, thesis. *Entrance requirements:* For master's, GRE General Test, minimum GPA of 3.25 in upper-division anthropology course work, 3.0 overall; 3 letters of recommendation. Additional exam requirements/recommendations for international students: Required—TOEFL (minimum score 550 paper-based; 80 iBT), IELTS (minimum score 6.5). *Application deadline:* For fall admission, 2/1 for domestic and international students. Application fee: $65. *Expenses:* Contact institution. *Financial support:* In 2016–17, 1 research assistantship (averaging $6,390 per year), 3 teaching assistantships with full tuition reimbursements (averaging $3,508 per year) were awarded; career-related internships or fieldwork, Federal Work-Study, and unspecified assistantships also available. Support available to part-time students. Financial award application deadline: 3/1; financial award applicants required to submit FAFSA. *Faculty research:* Forensic anthropology, Northwest Coast prehistory, Native Americans, applied anthropology, urban anthropology. *Total annual research expenditures:* $924,447. *Unit head:* Dr. Michele Gamburd, Chair, 503-725-3317, E-mail: gamburdm@pdx.edu. *Application contact:* Connie Cash, Office Coordinator, 503-725-3361, Fax: 503-725-3905, E-mail: cashc@pdx.edu.
Website: http://www.pdx.edu/anthropology/

**Portland State University,** Graduate Studies, College of Liberal Arts and Sciences, Systems Science Program, Portland, OR 97207-0751. Offers computational intelligence (Certificate); computer modeling and simulation (Certificate); systems science (MS); systems science/anthropology (PhD); systems science/business administration (PhD); systems science/civil engineering (PhD); systems science/economics (PhD); systems science/engineering management (PhD); systems science/general (PhD); systems science/mathematical sciences (PhD); systems science/mechanical engineering (PhD); systems science/psychology (PhD); systems science/sociology (PhD). *Faculty:* 2 full-time (0 women), 3 part-time/adjunct (1 woman). *Students:* 12 full-time (3 women), 21 part-time (5 women); includes 5 minority (1 Black or African American, non-Hispanic/Latino; 2 Hispanic/Latino; 2 Two or more races, non-Hispanic/Latino). Average age 39. 16 applicants, 69% accepted, 9 enrolled. In 2016, 4 master's, 6 doctorates awarded. *Degree requirements:* For master's, comprehensive exam (for some programs), thesis optional; for doctorate, variable foreign language requirement, comprehensive exam (for some programs), thesis/dissertation. *Entrance requirements:* For master's, GRE/GMAT (recommended), minimum GPA of 3.0 undergraduate or graduate work, 2 letters of recommendation, statement of interest; for doctorate, GMAT, GRE General Test, minimum GPA of 3.0 undergraduate, 3.25 graduate; 2 letters of recommendation; statement of interest. Additional exam requirements/recommendations for international students: Required—TOEFL (minimum score 550 paper-based; 80 iBT). *Application deadline:* For fall admission, 1/15 for domestic and international students; for spring admission, 11/1 for domestic students. Application fee: $65. Electronic applications accepted. *Expenses:* Contact institution. *Financial support:* In 2016–17, 2 research assistantships with tuition reimbursements (averaging $7,830 per year) were awarded; teaching assistantships, career-related internships or fieldwork, Federal Work-Study, scholarships/grants, and unspecified assistantships also available. Support available to part-time students. Financial award application deadline: 3/1; financial award applicants required to submit FAFSA. *Faculty research:* Systems theory and methodology, artificial intelligence neural networks, information theory, nonlinear dynamics/chaos, modeling and simulation. *Unit head:* Dr. Wayne Wakeland, Chair, 503-725-4975, E-mail: wakeland@pdx.edu.
Website: http://www.pdx.edu/sysc/

**Princeton University,** Graduate School, Department of Anthropology, Princeton, NJ 08544-1019. Offers PhD. *Degree requirements:* For doctorate, variable foreign language requirement, thesis/dissertation. *Entrance requirements:* For doctorate, GRE General Test, sample of written work. Additional exam requirements/recommendations for international students: Required—TOEFL (minimum score 600 paper-based). Electronic applications accepted. *Faculty research:* Symbolic anthropology, social theory, gender studies, law and society, political and social anthropology.

**Purdue University,** Graduate School, College of Liberal Arts, Department of Anthropology, West Lafayette, IN 47907. Offers MS, PhD. *Faculty:* 16 full-time (11 women), 1 part-time/adjunct. *Students:* 21 full-time (17 women), 3 part-time (0 women); includes 5 minority (1 Asian, non-Hispanic/Latino; 3 Hispanic/Latino; 1 Two or more races, non-Hispanic/Latino), 3 international. Average age 28. 27 applicants, 30% accepted, 4 enrolled. In 2016, 5 master's, 3 doctorates awarded. Terminal master's awarded for partial completion of doctoral program. *Degree requirements:* For master's, thesis; for doctorate, comprehensive exam, thesis/dissertation. *Entrance requirements:* For master's, GRE General Test, minimum undergraduate GPA of 3.0 or equivalent; for doctorate, GRE General Test, minimum undergraduate GPA of 3.0 or equivalent; master's degree. Additional exam requirements/recommendations for international students: Required—TOEFL (minimum score 550 paper-based; 77 iBT), TWE. *Application deadline:* For fall admission, 12/1 for domestic and international students. Applications are processed on a rolling basis. Application fee: $60 ($75 for international students). Electronic applications accepted. *Financial support:* In 2016–17, 27 students received support. Fellowships, research assistantships, teaching assistantships, and tuition waivers (full) available. Support available to part-time students. Financial award application deadline: 2/15; financial award applicants required to submit FAFSA. *Faculty research:* Communiversity survey project, risk, fear, constrained behavior, archaeological services. *Unit head:* Ellen R. Gruenbaum, Head, 765-496-7422, E-mail: gruenbaum@purdue.edu. *Application contact:* Talin M. Lindsay, Graduate Contact, 765-496-7428, E-mail: tlindsay@purdue.edu.
Website: http://www.cla.purdue.edu/anthropology/

**Rice University,** Graduate Programs, School of Social Sciences, Department of Anthropology, Houston, TX 77251-1892. Offers archaeology (MA, PhD); social-cultural anthropology (MA, PhD). Terminal master's awarded for partial completion of doctoral

*Anthropology*

program. *Degree requirements:* For master's, one foreign language, 3 major papers, dissertation proposal and language exam or thesis; for doctorate, one foreign language, thesis/dissertation. *Entrance requirements:* For master's and doctorate, research proposal. Additional exam requirements/recommendations for international students: Required—TOEFL (minimum score 90 iBT). Electronic applications accepted.

**Roosevelt University,** Graduate Division, College of Arts and Sciences, Department of Sociology and Anthropology, Chicago, IL 60605. Offers anthropology (MA); sociology (MA). *Program availability:* Part-time, evening/weekend. *Degree requirements:* For master's, comprehensive exam, thesis. *Faculty research:* Social theory, urban sociology, gerontology, social organizations.

**Rutgers University–New Brunswick,** Graduate School-New Brunswick, Program in Anthropology, Piscataway, NJ 08854-8097. Offers MA, PhD. Terminal master's awarded for partial completion of doctoral program. *Degree requirements:* For master's, thesis or alternative; for doctorate, comprehensive exam, thesis/dissertation. *Entrance requirements:* For master's and doctorate, GRE General Test, writing sample. Additional exam requirements/recommendations for international students: Required—TOEFL. Electronic applications accepted. *Faculty research:* Human evolution, lithic technology, behavioral ecology, ethnicity, gender.

**San Diego State University,** Graduate and Research Affairs, College of Arts and Letters, Department of Anthropology, San Diego, CA 92182. Offers MA. *Degree requirements:* For master's, one foreign language, thesis. *Entrance requirements:* For master's, GRE General Test, 3 letters of recommendation, typed writing sample. Additional exam requirements/recommendations for international students: Required—TOEFL. Electronic applications accepted. *Faculty research:* Meso-American archaeology, cognitive anthropology, ethnomusicology, primate conservation, biomedical anthropology.

**San Francisco State University,** Division of Graduate Studies, College of Liberal and Creative Arts, Department of Anthropology, San Francisco, CA 94132-1722. Offers archaeology (MA); biological/physical anthropology (MA); social/cultural anthropology (MA); visual anthropology (MA). *Expenses:* Tuition, state resident: full-time $6738. Tuition, nonresident: full-time $15,666. *Required fees:* $1012. Tuition and fees vary according to degree level and program. *Faculty research:* Immigration, ethnicity, urban anthropology, Californian and Latin American archaeology. *Unit head:* Dr. James Quesada, Chair, 415-338-1633, Fax: 415-338-6159, E-mail: jquesada@sfsu.edu. *Application contact:* Dr. Douglass Bailey, Graduate Coordinator, 415-338-1427, Fax: 415-338-6159, E-mail: dwbailey@sfsu.edu.
Website: http://anthropology.sfsu.edu/

**San Jose State University,** Graduate Studies and Research, College of Social Sciences, San Jose, CA 95192-0001. Offers applications of technology in planning (Certificate); applied anthropology (MA); communication studies (MS); community design and development (Certificate); economics (MA), including applied economics, social sciences; environmental planning (Certificate); geographic information science (Certificate); geography (MA); global citizenship (Certificate); history (MA), including history education, social sciences; Mexican American studies (MA); psychology (MA, MS), including clinical psychology (MS), industrial/organizational psychology (MS); research and experimental psychology (MA); public administration (MA); real estate development (Certificate); social sciences (MPA, MS); sociology (MA); transportation and land use planning (Certificate). *Program availability:* Part-time, evening/weekend. *Entrance requirements:* For master's, minimum GPA of 3.0. Electronic applications accepted.

**Simon Fraser University,** Office of Graduate Studies and Postdoctoral Fellows, Faculty of Arts and Social Sciences, Department of Sociology and Anthropology, Burnaby, BC V5A 1S6, Canada. Offers anthropology (MA, PhD); sociology (MA, PhD). *Faculty:* 21 full-time (17 women). *Students:* 50 full-time (35 women). 48 applicants, 50% accepted, 18 enrolled. In 2016, 2 master's, 2 doctorates awarded. *Degree requirements:* For master's, thesis; for doctorate, comprehensive exam, thesis/dissertation, cooperative education. *Entrance requirements:* For master's, minimum GPA of 3.0 (on scale of 4.33) or 3.33 based on last 60 credits of undergraduate courses; for doctorate, minimum GPA of 3.5 (on scale of 4.33). Additional exam requirements/recommendations for international students: Recommended—TOEFL (minimum score 580 paper-based; 93 iBT), IELTS (minimum score 7), TWE (minimum score 5). *Application deadline:* For fall admission, 12/15 for domestic and international students; for winter admission, 2/1 for domestic students. Application fee: $90 ($125 for international students). Electronic applications accepted. *Financial support:* In 2016–17, 29 students received support, including 11 fellowships (averaging $5,909 per year), teaching assistantships (averaging $5,608 per year); research assistantships, career-related internships or fieldwork, and scholarships/grants also available. Financial award application deadline: 3/15. *Faculty research:* Globalization and development, health, environment and science, knowledge, culture and power, social justice, policy, law and society, women, gender and sexuality. *Unit head:* Dr. Dara Culhane, Graduate Chair, 778-782-4469, Fax: 778-782-5799, E-mail: sa-grad-chair@sfu.ca. *Application contact:* Chantelle Ryerson, Graduate Secretary, 778-782-3518, Fax: 778-782-5799, E-mail: gradsecsa@sfu.ca.
Website: http://www.sfu.ca/sociology-anthropology.html

**Sonoma State University,** School of Social Sciences, Program in Cultural Resources Management, Rohnert Park, CA 94928. Offers MA. *Program availability:* Part-time. *Degree requirements:* For master's, thesis. *Entrance requirements:* For master's, minimum GPA of 3.0. Additional exam requirements/recommendations for international students: Required—TOEFL (minimum score 500 paper-based). *Application deadline:* For fall admission, 1/31 for domestic students. Application fee: $55. *Expenses:* Tuition, state resident: full-time $6738; part-time $3906 per unit. *Required fees:* $1916; $1916 per year. Tuition and fees vary according to course load, degree level and program. *Financial support:* Career-related internships or fieldwork, scholarships/grants, traineeships, and unspecified assistantships available. Financial award application deadline: 3/2; financial award applicants required to submit FAFSA. *Unit head:* Margaret Purser, Chair, Anthropology Department, 707-664-3164, Fax: 707-664-2505, E-mail: margaret.purser@sonoma.edu.
Website: http://www.sonoma.edu/anthropology/graduate/master.html

**Southern Illinois University Carbondale,** Graduate School, College of Liberal Arts, Department of Anthropology, Carbondale, IL 62901-4701. Offers MA, PhD. *Degree requirements:* For master's, one foreign language, thesis; for doctorate, one foreign language, thesis/dissertation. *Entrance requirements:* For master's, GRE General Test, minimum GPA of 2.7; for doctorate, GRE General Test, minimum GPA of 3.25. Additional exam requirements/recommendations for international students: Required—TOEFL (minimum score 600 paper-based; 100 iBT). *Faculty research:* Archaeology, human variability, evolution, cultural ecology, social anthropology.

**Southern Methodist University,** Dedman College of Humanities and Sciences, Department of Anthropology, Dallas, TX 75205. Offers anthropology (PhD); medical anthropology (MA). Terminal master's awarded for partial completion of doctoral program. *Degree requirements:* For master's, one foreign language, comprehensive exam, thesis or alternative; for doctorate, one foreign language, comprehensive exam, thesis/dissertation, qualifying exam, defense of dissertation. *Entrance requirements:* For master's and doctorate, GRE General Test, minimum GPA of 3.0. Additional exam

requirements/recommendations for international students: Required—TOEFL (minimum score 550 paper-based). *Faculty research:* Health and gender, Paleo-Indians, Mesoamerica, American southwest, migration and ethnicity.

**Stanford University,** School of Humanities and Sciences, Department of Anthropology, Stanford, CA 94305-2004. Offers anthropology (MA); archaeology (PhD); culture and society (PhD); ecology and environment (PhD). Terminal master's awarded for partial completion of doctoral program. *Degree requirements:* For master's, thesis; for doctorate, one foreign language, thesis/dissertation. *Entrance requirements:* For master's and doctorate, GRE General Test. Additional exam requirements/ recommendations for international students: Required—TOEFL. Electronic applications accepted. *Expenses: Tuition:* Full-time $47,331. *Required fees:* $609.

**Stony Brook University, State University of New York,** Graduate School, College of Arts and Sciences, Department of Anthropology, Stony Brook, NY 11794. Offers MA, PhD. *Program availability:* Part-time. *Faculty:* 13 full-time (7 women), 2 part-time/adjunct (1 woman). *Students:* 28 full-time (19 women), 1 part-time (0 women); includes 6 minority (1 Black or African American, non-Hispanic/Latino; 2 Hispanic/Latino; 3 Two or more races, non-Hispanic/Latino), 5 international. Average age 29. 59 applicants, 19% accepted, 5 enrolled. In 2016, 3 master's, 8 doctorates awarded. *Degree requirements:* For master's, fieldwork; for doctorate, thesis/dissertation. *Entrance requirements:* For master's and doctorate, GRE General Test. Additional exam requirements/ recommendations for international students: Required—TOEFL (minimum score 90 iBT). *Application deadline:* For fall admission, 1/15 for domestic students; for spring admission, 10/1 for domestic students. Application fee: $100. *Expenses:* Contact institution. *Financial support:* In 2016–17, 1 fellowship, 3 research assistantships, 20 teaching assistantships were awarded; career-related internships or fieldwork also available. *Faculty research:* Anthropology, archaeology, human evolution, paleontology, Africa. *Total annual research expenditures:* $108,852. *Unit head:* Dr. David Hicks, Chair, 631-632-7617, E-mail: david.hicks@stonybrook.edu. *Application contact:* Tara J. Powers, Coordinator, 631-632-7606, E-mail: tara.powers@stonybrook.edu.
Website: http://www.stonybrook.edu/commcms/anthropology/

**Stony Brook University, State University of New York,** Graduate School, College of Arts and Sciences, Interdepartmental Doctoral Program in Anthropological Sciences (IDPAS), Stony Brook, NY 11794. Offers PhD. *Students:* 28 full-time (19 women); includes 6 minority (1 Black or African American, non-Hispanic/Latino; 2 Hispanic/ Latino; 3 Two or more races, non-Hispanic/Latino), 5 international. 42 applicants, 21% accepted, 5 enrolled. In 2016, 8 doctorates awarded. *Degree requirements:* For doctorate, one foreign language, thesis/dissertation, fieldwork. *Entrance requirements:* For doctorate, GRE General Test. Additional exam requirements/recommendations for international students: Required—TOEFL (minimum score 90 iBT). *Application deadline:* For fall admission, 1/15 for domestic students; for spring admission, 10/1 for domestic students. Application fee: $100. Electronic applications accepted. *Expenses:* Tuition, state resident: full-time $10,870; part-time $453 per credit hour. Tuition, nonresident: full-time $22,210; part-time $925 per credit hour. *Financial support:* In 2016–17, 1 fellowship, 3 research assistantships, 20 teaching assistantships were awarded. *Unit head:* Prof. Andreas Koenig, Director, 631-632-1513, E-mail: andreas.koenig@stonybrook.edu. *Application contact:* Tara J. Powers, Coordinator, 631-632-7606, Fax: 631-632-9165, E-mail: tara.powers@stonybrook.edu.
Website: https://www.grad.stonybrook.edu/brochure/anthropologysciences/

**Syracuse University,** Maxwell School of Citizenship and Public Affairs, Programs in Anthropology, Syracuse, NY 13244. Offers MA, PhD. In 2016, 5 master's, 4 doctorates awarded. *Degree requirements:* For master's, thesis or alternative; for doctorate, one foreign language, comprehensive exam, thesis/dissertation. *Entrance requirements:* For master's and doctorate, GRE General Test, resume, three letters of recommendation, personal statement, official transcripts. Additional exam requirements/recommendations for international students: Required—TOEFL (minimum score 100 iBT). *Application deadline:* For fall admission, 12/15 priority date for domestic and international students. Application fee: $75. Electronic applications accepted. *Expenses: Tuition:* Full-time $25,974; part-time $1443 per credit hour. *Required fees:* $802; $50 per course. Tuition and fees vary according to course load and program. *Financial support:* Fellowships with full tuition reimbursements, research assistantships with tuition reimbursements, and teaching assistantships with tuition reimbursements available. Financial award application deadline: 1/1. *Faculty research:* Human diversity, globalization, ethnology, sociolinguistics, osteology. *Unit head:* Dr. John Burdick, Professor and Chair, Anthropology, 315-443-3822, E-mail: jsburdic@maxwell.syr.edu. *Application contact:* Prof. Douglas Armstrong, Professor, Anthropology, 315-443-2405, E-mail: dvarmstr@maxwell.syr.edu.
Website: http://www.maxwell.syr.edu/

**Teachers College, Columbia University,** Department of International and Transcultural Studies, New York, NY 10027-6696. Offers anthropology and education (MA, Ed D, PhD); applied anthropology (PhD); comparative and international education (MA, Ed D, PhD); international educational development (Ed M, MA, Ed D, PhD). *Program availability:* Part-time. *Students:* 151 full-time (128 women), 119 part-time (95 women); includes 83 minority (17 Black or African American, non-Hispanic/Latino; 32 Asian, non-Hispanic/Latino; 23 Hispanic/Latino; 11 Two or more races, non-Hispanic/ Latino), 97 international. 422 applicants, 67% accepted, 138 enrolled. *Degree requirements:* For doctorate, thesis/dissertation. *Expenses: Tuition:* Full-time $36,288; part-time $1512 per credit. *Required fees:* $438 per semester. One-time fee: $510 full-time. Full-time tuition and fees vary according to course load. *Unit head:* Prof. Herve Varenne, Chair, 212-678-3190, E-mail: varenne@tc.columbia.edu. *Application contact:* David Estrella, Director of Admission, 212-678-3305, E-mail: estrella@tc.columbia.edu.

**Temple University,** College of Liberal Arts, Department of Anthropology, Philadelphia, PA 19122-6096. Offers PhD. *Program availability:* Part-time. Terminal master's awarded for partial completion of doctoral program. *Degree requirements:* For doctorate, one foreign language, thesis/dissertation. *Entrance requirements:* For doctorate, GRE General Test, minimum GPA of 3.0; 3 letters of recommendation. Additional exam requirements/recommendations for international students: Required—TOEFL (minimum score 550 paper-based; 79 iBT). Electronic applications accepted. *Faculty research:* Anthropology of visual communication, political economy of language, historical archaeology, bicultural adaptation.

**Texas A&M University,** College of Liberal Arts, Department of Anthropology, College Station, TX 77843. Offers anthropology (MA, PhD); maritime archaeology and conservation (MS). *Faculty:* 25. *Students:* 55 full-time (35 women), 34 part-time (19 women); includes 15 minority (3 Black or African American, non-Hispanic/Latino; 1 American Indian or Alaska Native, non-Hispanic/Latino; 3 Asian, non-Hispanic/Latino; 5 Hispanic/Latino; 3 Two or more races, non-Hispanic/Latino), 9 international. Average age 32. 66 applicants, 44% accepted, 20 enrolled. In 2016, 6 master's, 9 doctorates awarded. *Degree requirements:* For doctorate, thesis/dissertation. *Entrance requirements:* For master's and doctorate, GRE General Test. Additional exam requirements/recommendations for international students: Required—TOEFL (minimum score 550 paper-based; 80 iBT), IELTS (minimum score 6), PTE (minimum score 53). *Application deadline:* For fall admission, 12/1 for domestic students. Application fee: $50 ($90 for international students). *Expenses:* Contact institution. *Financial support:* In 2016–17, 73 students received support, including 7 fellowships with tuition

reimbursements available (averaging $13,398 per year), 9 research assistantships with tuition reimbursements available (averaging $5,273 per year), 31 teaching assistantships with tuition reimbursements available (averaging $9,951 per year); career-related internships or fieldwork, institutionally sponsored loans, scholarships/grants, traineeships, health care benefits, tuition waivers (full and partial), and unspecified assistantships also available. Support available to part-time students. Financial award application deadline: 3/15; financial award applicants required to submit FAFSA. *Faculty research:* Nautical archaeology, archaeological conservation, archaeological palynology, paleo ethnobotany, folklore. *Unit head:* Dr. Ted Goebel, Interim Department Head, 979-845-5242, E-mail: goebel@tamu.edu. *Application contact:* Marco Valadez, Academic Advisor, 979-845-9333, Fax: 979-845-4070, E-mail: mlvaladez@tamu.edu.
Website: http://anthropology.tamu.edu/html/home.html

**Texas State University,** The Graduate College, College of Liberal Arts, Program in Anthropology, San Marcos, TX 78666. Offers MA. *Program availability:* Part-time. *Faculty:* 16 full-time (7 women), 4 part-time/adjunct (3 women). *Students:* 34 full-time (27 women), 18 part-time (12 women); includes 13 minority (2 Black or African American, non-Hispanic/Latino; 2 Asian, non-Hispanic/Latino; 6 Hispanic/Latino; 3 Two or more races, non-Hispanic/Latino). Average age 27. 140 applicants, 27% accepted, 21 enrolled. In 2016, 15 master's awarded. *Degree requirements:* For master's, comprehensive exam, thesis. *Entrance requirements:* For master's, GRE (minimum score 300 verbal and quantitative preferred), baccalaureate degree from regionally-accredited university with minimum GPA of 3.0 on last 60 undergraduate semester hours. Additional exam requirements/recommendations for international students: Required—TOEFL (minimum score 550 paper-based; 78 iBT), IELTS (minimum score 6.5). *Application deadline:* For fall admission, 1/15 priority date for domestic and international students. Applications are processed on a rolling basis. Application fee: $40 ($90 for international students). Electronic applications accepted. *Expenses:* $4,851 per semester. *Financial support:* In 2016–17, 44 students received support, including 9 research assistantships (averaging $10,424 per year), 21 teaching assistantships (averaging $7,312 per year); Federal Work-Study, institutionally sponsored loans, scholarships/grants, and unspecified assistantships also available. Support available to part-time students. Financial award application deadline: 3/1; financial award applicants required to submit FAFSA. *Faculty research:* Graphical user interface for a multi-factorial age-at-death estimation method, MRI: acquisition of high-res computed tomography system for research and education, sociocultural elements of emergency communication about medical countermeasures, Riverside Drive reconstruction monitoring, off-site data recovery at Spring Lake. *Total annual research expenditures:* $240,208. *Unit head:* Dr. Emily Brunson, Graduate Advisor, 512-245-6753, E-mail: grad-anthropology@txstate.edu. *Application contact:* Dr. Andrea Golato, Dean of Graduate School, 512-245-2581, Fax: 512-245-8365, E-mail: gradcollege@txstate.edu.
Website: http://www.txstate.edu/anthropology/

**Texas Tech University,** Graduate School, College of Arts and Sciences, Department of Sociology, Anthropology and Social Work, Lubbock, TX 79409. Offers anthropology (MA); social work (MSW); sociology (MA). *Program availability:* Part-time. *Faculty:* 28 full-time (16 women), 8 part-time/adjunct (4 women). *Students:* 49 full-time (38 women), 11 part-time (6 women); includes 20 minority (4 Black or African American, non-Hispanic/Latino; 14 Hispanic/Latino; 2 Two or more races, non-Hispanic/Latino), 5 international. Average age 27. 63 applicants, 52% accepted, 24 enrolled. In 2016, 19 master's awarded. *Degree requirements:* For master's, one foreign language, comprehensive exam (for some programs), thesis (for some programs). *Entrance requirements:* For master's, GRE (for MA in anthropology), two letters of recommendation, statement of purpose, writing sample, curriculum vitae; minimum GPA of 3.0 and coursework in sociology or closely-related fields (for MA in sociology); coursework in anthropology (for MA in anthropology). Additional exam requirements/recommendations for international students: Required—TOEFL (minimum score 550 paper-based; 79 iBT). *Application deadline:* For fall admission, 6/1 priority date for domestic students, 1/15 priority date for international students; for spring admission, 9/1 priority date for domestic students, 6/15 priority date for international students. Applications are processed on a rolling basis. Application fee: $75. Electronic applications accepted. *Expenses:* $300 per credit hour full-time resident tuition, $708 per credit hour full-time non-resident tuition; $50.50 per credit hour fee plus $608 per term fee. *Financial support:* In 2016–17, 53 students received support, including 42 fellowships (averaging $4,678 per year), 33 teaching assistantships (averaging $12,439 per year); research assistantships, Federal Work-Study, scholarships/grants, tuition waivers (partial), and unspecified assistantships also available. Financial award application deadline: 2/1; financial award applicants required to submit FAFSA. *Faculty research:* Sociology of criminology/deviance, population/migration, forensic anthropology, archaeology, social work (advanced generalist). *Total annual research expenditures:* $122,652. *Unit head:* Dr. Brett A. Houk, Chair and Associate Professor, 806-834-8107, Fax: 806-742-1088, E-mail: brett.houk@ttu.edu. *Application contact:* Dr. Cristina Bradatan, Associate Professor/Sociology Graduate Program Director, 806-834-1796, E-mail: cristina.bradatan@ttu.edu.
Website: http://www.depts.ttu.edu/sasw/

**Trent University,** Graduate Studies, Program in Anthropology, Peterborough, ON K9J 7B8, Canada. Offers MA. *Program availability:* Part-time. *Degree requirements:* For master's, thesis. *Entrance requirements:* For master's, honors degree. *Faculty research:* Paleoecology, trade and fortification networks, pre-Columbian art.

**Tulane University,** School of Liberal Arts, Department of Anthropology, New Orleans, LA 70118-5669. Offers PhD. Terminal master's awarded for partial completion of doctoral program. *Degree requirements:* For doctorate, 2 foreign languages, thesis/dissertation. *Entrance requirements:* For doctorate, GRE General Test. Additional exam requirements/recommendations for international students: Required—TOEFL. Electronic applications accepted. *Expenses: Tuition:* Full-time $50,920; part-time $2829 per credit hour. *Required fees:* $2040; $44.50 per credit hour. $580 per term. Tuition and fees vary according to course load, degree level and program. *Faculty research:* Linguistics, physical anthropology, sociocultural archaeology, Mesoamerica.

**Universidad de las Américas Puebla,** Division of Graduate Studies, School of Social Sciences, Program in Anthropology, Puebla, Mexico. Offers anthropology (MA); archaeology (MA). *Program availability:* Part-time, evening/weekend. *Degree requirements:* For master's, one foreign language, thesis. *Entrance requirements:* For master's, bachelor's degree in anthropology or equivalent. *Faculty research:* Archaeology, ethnography, and ethnohistory of Mesoamerica.

**Université de Montréal,** Faculty of Arts and Sciences, Department of Anthropology, Montréal, QC H3C 3J7, Canada. Offers M Sc, PhD. *Program availability:* Part-time. *Degree requirements:* For master's, thesis; for doctorate, thesis/dissertation, general exam. Electronic applications accepted. *Faculty research:* Archaeology, ethnolinguistics, ethnology.

**Université Laval,** Faculty of Social Sciences, Department of Anthropology, Programs in Anthropology, Québec, QC G1K 7P4, Canada. Offers MA, PhD. Terminal master's awarded for partial completion of doctoral program. *Degree requirements:* For master's, thesis; for doctorate, thesis/dissertation. *Entrance requirements:* For master's, knowledge of French, interview; for doctorate, knowledge of French, comprehensive of written English, knowledge of a third language. Electronic applications accepted.

**University at Albany, State University of New York,** College of Arts and Sciences, Department of Anthropology, Albany, NY 12222-0001. Offers MA, PhD. *Faculty:* 12 full-time (5 women). *Students:* 30 full-time (18 women), 37 part-time (28 women); includes 10 minority (3 Black or African American, non-Hispanic/Latino; 2 Asian, non-Hispanic/Latino; 4 Hispanic/Latino; 1 Native Hawaiian or other Pacific Islander, non-Hispanic/Latino), 6 international. Average age 29. 44 applicants, 68% accepted, 12 enrolled. In 2016, 8 master's, 6 doctorates awarded. Terminal master's awarded for partial completion of doctoral program. *Degree requirements:* For master's, comprehensive exam, thesis; for doctorate, 2 foreign languages, thesis/dissertation, field exams. *Entrance requirements:* For master's and doctorate, GRE. Additional exam requirements/recommendations for international students: Required—TOEFL (minimum score 550 paper-based). *Application deadline:* For fall admission, 3/15 priority date for domestic students, 4/1 for international students; for spring admission, 11/1 for international students. Applications are processed on a rolling basis. Application fee: $75. Electronic applications accepted. *Expenses:* Tuition, state resident: full-time $10,870; part-time $453 per credit hour. Tuition, nonresident: full-time $22,210; part-time $925 per credit hour. *International tuition:* $21,550 full-time. *Required fees:* $1864; $96 per credit hour. *Financial support:* Fellowships, research assistantships, teaching assistantships, and career-related internships or fieldwork available. Financial award application deadline: 3/15. *Faculty research:* Economic and ecological anthropology; language, culture, and cognition; symbolic and interpretive anthropology; human evolution, morphology, demography, and medical anthropology; spatial and settlement archaeology. *Total annual research expenditures:* $171,199. *Unit head:* Lee Bickmore, Chair, 518-442-4700, Fax: 518-442-5710, E-mail: lbickmore@albany.edu. *Application contact:* Michael DeRensis, Director, Graduate Studies, 518-442-3980, Fax: 518-442-3922, E-mail: graduate@albany.edu.
Website: http://www.albany.edu/anthro/

**University at Buffalo, the State University of New York,** Graduate School, College of Arts and Sciences, Department of Anthropology, Buffalo, NY 14260. Offers MA, PhD. *Faculty:* 17 full-time (7 women), 1 part-time/adjunct (0 women). *Students:* 82 full-time (56 women), 4 part-time (3 women); includes 8 minority (2 Black or African American, non-Hispanic/Latino; 1 American Indian or Alaska Native, non-Hispanic/Latino; 1 Asian, non-Hispanic/Latino; 4 Hispanic/Latino), 3 international. Average age 30. 53 applicants, 68% accepted, 15 enrolled. In 2016, 9 master's, 7 doctorates awarded. Terminal master's awarded for partial completion of doctoral program. *Degree requirements:* For master's, project; for doctorate, one foreign language, comprehensive exam, thesis/dissertation, exam. *Entrance requirements:* For master's, GRE General Test, minimum GPA of 3.0; for doctorate, GRE General Test, minimum GPA 3.2. Additional exam requirements/recommendations for international students: Required—TOEFL (minimum score 600 paper-based; 79 iBT). *Application deadline:* For fall admission, 12/15 priority date for domestic and international students; for winter admission, 5/1 for domestic students, 3/15 for international students. Applications are processed on a rolling basis. Application fee: $75. Electronic applications accepted. *Financial support:* In 2016–17, 7 fellowships with full tuition reimbursements (averaging $19,616 per year), 1 research assistantship with full tuition reimbursement (averaging $13,896 per year), 14 teaching assistantships with full tuition reimbursements (averaging $13,896 per year) were awarded; career-related internships or fieldwork, Federal Work-Study, and institutionally sponsored loans also available. Financial award application deadline: 12/15; financial award applicants required to submit FAFSA. *Faculty research:* Old and New World archaeology, medical anthropology, primatology/human biology, cognition, bioarcheology. *Total annual research expenditures:* $800,000. *Unit head:* Dr. Peter Biehl, Chair, 716-645-2414, Fax: 716-645-3808. *Application contact:* Maria Portera, Graduate Coordinator, 716-645-2414, Fax: 716-645-3808, E-mail: mportera@buffalo.edu.
Website: http://www.buffalo.edu/cas/anthropology

**The University of Alabama,** Graduate School, College of Arts and Sciences, Department of Anthropology, Tuscaloosa, AL 35487. Offers MA, PhD. *Faculty:* 14 full-time (6 women), 2 part-time/adjunct (0 women). *Students:* 33 full-time (22 women), 2 part-time (both women); includes 1 minority (Black or African American, non-Hispanic/Latino), 2 international. Average age 28. 41 applicants, 56% accepted, 10 enrolled. In 2016, 8 master's, 3 doctorates awarded. *Degree requirements:* For master's, one foreign language, comprehensive exam, thesis optional; for doctorate, one foreign language, comprehensive exam, thesis/dissertation. *Entrance requirements:* For master's, GRE, bachelor's degree in anthropology or closely-related discipline, undergraduate coursework in at least three of four anthropology subdisciplines; for doctorate, master's degree in anthropology or closely-related discipline, undergraduate or graduate coursework in at least three of four anthropology subdisciplines. Additional exam requirements/recommendations for international students: Required—TOEFL. *Application deadline:* For fall admission, 1/31 for domestic and international students. Application fee: $50 ($60 for international students). Electronic applications accepted. *Expenses:* Tuition, state resident: full-time $10,470. Tuition, nonresident: full-time $26,950. *Financial support:* In 2016–17, 25 students received support, including 4 fellowships with full tuition reimbursements available (averaging $15,000 per year), 1 research assistantship with full tuition reimbursement available (averaging $13,500 per year), 21 teaching assistantships with full tuition reimbursements available (averaging $14,720 per year); Federal Work-Study and health care benefits also available. Financial award application deadline: 1/31. *Faculty research:* Medical anthropology, southeastern archaeology, Latin American archaeology, biological anthropology, cultural anthropology. *Total annual research expenditures:* $451,365. *Unit head:* Dr. Ian W. Brown, Chair and Professor, 205-348-9758, Fax: 205-348-7937, E-mail: ibrown@ua.edu. *Application contact:* Dr. Jason A. DeCaro, Associate Professor and Director of Graduate Studies, 205-348-9061, Fax: 205-348-7937, E-mail: jdecaro@ua.edu.
Website: http://anthropology.ua.edu

**The University of Alabama at Birmingham,** College of Arts and Sciences, Program in Anthropology, Birmingham, AL 35294. Offers MA. Program offered jointly with The University of Alabama (Tuscaloosa). *Degree requirements:* For master's, one foreign language, thesis (for some programs). *Entrance requirements:* For master's, GRE General Test. Additional exam requirements/recommendations for international students: Required—TOEFL, TWE. Electronic applications accepted. Full-time tuition and fees vary according to course load and program. *Faculty research:* Ethnicity, medical anthropology, primate conservation, pastoral systems, Southeastern archaeology.

**University of Alaska Anchorage,** College of Arts and Sciences, Department of Anthropology, Anchorage, AK 99508. Offers MA. *Degree requirements:* For master's, comprehensive exam, thesis (for some programs), practicum. *Entrance requirements:* For master's, GRE General Test. Additional exam requirements/recommendations for international students: Required—TOEFL (minimum score 550 paper-based).

**University of Alaska Fairbanks,** College of Liberal Arts, Department of Anthropology, Fairbanks, AK 99775-7720. Offers MA, PhD. *Program availability:* Part-time. *Faculty:* 10 full-time (6 women). *Students:* 16 full-time (10 women), 17 part-time (9 women); includes

## Anthropology

2 minority (1 American Indian or Alaska Native, non-Hispanic/Latino; 1 Two or more races, non-Hispanic/Latino), 4 international. Average age 34. 15 applicants, 60% accepted, 7 enrolled. In 2016, 6 master's, 2 doctorates awarded. *Degree requirements:* For master's, one foreign language, comprehensive exam, oral defense of project or thesis; for doctorate, one foreign language, comprehensive exam, thesis/dissertation, oral defense of dissertation. *Entrance requirements:* For master's, GRE General Test, bachelor's degree in anthropology with minimum cumulative undergraduate and major GPA of 3.0; for doctorate, GRE General Test, master's degree in anthropology. Additional exam requirements/recommendations for international students: Required—TOEFL (minimum score 550 paper-based; 79 iBT), IELTS (minimum score 6.5). *Application deadline:* For fall admission, 1/15 for domestic and international students; for spring admission, 10/1 for domestic students, 9/1 for international students. Applications are processed on a rolling basis. Application fee: $60. Electronic applications accepted. *Expenses:* Tuition, state resident: full-time $7992; part-time $444 per credit. Tuition, nonresident: full-time $16,326; part-time $907 per credit. *Required fees:* $39 per credit. $322 per semester. Tuition and fees vary according to course level, course load, campus/location, program and reciprocity agreements. *Financial support:* In 2016–17, 1 research assistantship with full tuition reimbursement (averaging $17,664 per year), 14 teaching assistantships with full tuition reimbursements (averaging $4,511 per year) were awarded; fellowships with full tuition reimbursements, Federal Work-Study, scholarships/grants, health care benefits, and unspecified assistantships also available. Support available to part-time students. Financial award application deadline: 7/1; financial award applicants required to submit FAFSA. *Faculty research:* Circumpolar archaeology and population biology; rural subsistence; arctic physical, biological and social anthropology; arctic ethno history; arctic linguistics. *Total annual research expenditures:* $155,000. *Unit head:* David Koester, Department Chair, 907-474-7288, Fax: 907-474-7453, E-mail: uaf-anthropology@alaska.edu. *Application contact:* Mary Kreta, Director of Admissions, 907-474-7500, Fax: 907-474-7097, E-mail: admissions@uaf.edu.
Website: http://www.uaf.edu/anthro/

**University of Alberta,** Faculty of Graduate Studies and Research, Department of Anthropology, Edmonton, AB T6G 2E1, Canada. Offers MA, PhD. *Degree requirements:* For master's, thesis; for doctorate, one foreign language, thesis/dissertation. *Entrance requirements:* For master's and doctorate, minimum GPA of 7.0 on a 9.0 scale in last 2 years. Additional exam requirements/recommendations for international students: Required—TOEFL. *Faculty research:* Cultural anthropology of North America, South East Asia; physical anthropology in osteology, forensic primatology; archaeology of North America, South America, Old World/Africa.

**The University of Arizona,** College of Social and Behavioral Sciences, School of Anthropology, Tucson, AZ 85721. Offers MA, MS, PhD, Graduate Certificate. *Program availability:* Part-time. Terminal master's awarded for partial completion of doctoral program. *Degree requirements:* For master's, thesis or alternative; for doctorate, one foreign language, thesis/dissertation. *Entrance requirements:* For master's and doctorate, GRE General Test, minimum GPA of 3.5, 2 letters of recommendation. Additional exam requirements/recommendations for international students: Required—TOEFL (minimum score 550 paper-based; 79 iBT). Electronic applications accepted. *Faculty research:* Archaeology of pre-Han China, cultural ecology, health and illness-related behavior, interaction of linguistic and social processes, human growth and development under stress.

**University of Arkansas,** Graduate School, J. William Fulbright College of Arts and Sciences, Department of Anthropology, Fayetteville, AR 72701. Offers MA, PhD. *Program availability:* Part-time, evening/weekend. In 2016, 8 master's awarded. *Degree requirements:* For master's, comprehensive exam. *Entrance requirements:* For master's, GRE General Test, minimum GPA of 3.0; for doctorate, GRE General Test. *Application deadline:* For fall admission, 4/1 for international students; for spring admission, 10/1 for international students. Applications are processed on a rolling basis. Application fee: $40 ($50 for international students). Electronic applications accepted. *Financial support:* In 2016–17, 6 research assistantships, 21 teaching assistantships were awarded; fellowships with tuition reimbursements, career-related internships or fieldwork, and Federal Work-Study also available. Support available to part-time students. Financial award application deadline: 4/1; financial award applicants required to submit FAFSA. *Unit head:* Dr. Justin Nolan, Department Chairperson, 479-575-2508, Fax: 479-575-6595, E-mail: jmnolan@uark.edu. *Application contact:* Dr. JoAnn D'Alisera, Graduate Coordinator, 479-575-4460, Fax: 479-575-6595, E-mail: daliser@uark.edu.
Website: http://anthropology.uark.edu/

**The University of British Columbia,** Faculty of Arts, Department of Anthropology, Vancouver, BC V6T 1Z1, Canada. Offers MA, PhD. *Program availability:* Part-time. *Degree requirements:* For master's, thesis; for doctorate, comprehensive exam, thesis/dissertation. *Entrance requirements:* For master's, BA in anthropology or equivalent with minimum B+ average in upper-level courses; for doctorate, MA in anthropology or equivalent. Additional exam requirements/recommendations for international students: Required—TOEFL. Application fee: $100 Canadian dollars ($162 Canadian dollars for international students). Electronic applications accepted. *Expenses:* $4,802 per year tuition and fees, $8,436 per year international. *Financial support:* Fellowships, research assistantships, teaching assistantships, Federal Work-Study, institutionally sponsored loans, scholarships/grants, health care benefits, tuition waivers (full and partial), and unspecified assistantships available. Financial award application deadline: 10/1. *Faculty research:* Cultures of North America, East Asia, Oceania; museum studies; archaeology. *Application contact:* Adam Wright, Graduate Program Assistant, 604-822-1617, Fax: 604-822-6161, E-mail: anth.grad@ubc.ca.
Website: http://anth.ubc.ca/graduate/

**University of Calgary,** Faculty of Graduate Studies, Faculty of Arts, Department of Anthropology, Calgary, AB T2N 1N4, Canada. Offers MA, PhD. *Degree requirements:* For master's, thesis; for doctorate, one foreign language, comprehensive exam, thesis/dissertation, candidacy exam. *Entrance requirements:* Additional exam requirements/recommendations for international students: Required—TOEFL. *Faculty research:* Primatology, culture and society, biosocial anthropology, political anthropology, evolutionary theory.

**University of California, Berkeley,** Graduate Division, College of Letters and Science, Department of Anthropology, Program in Anthropology, Berkeley, CA 94720-1500. Offers PhD. *Students:* 78 full-time (41 women); includes 22 minority (1 Black or African American, non-Hispanic/Latino; 2 American Indian or Alaska Native, non-Hispanic/Latino; 9 Asian, non-Hispanic/Latino; 10 Hispanic/Latino), 11 international. Average age 31. 247 applicants, 11 enrolled. In 2016, 9 doctorates awarded. *Degree requirements:* For doctorate, thesis/dissertation. *Entrance requirements:* For doctorate, GRE General Test, minimum GPA of 3.0, 3 letters of recommendation. Additional exam requirements/recommendations for international students: Required—TOEFL (minimum score 570 paper-based; 90 iBT). *Application deadline:* For fall admission, 12/1 for domestic students. Application fee: $105 ($125 for international students). Electronic applications accepted. *Financial support:* Fellowships, research assistantships, teaching assistantships, institutionally sponsored loans, health care benefits, and unspecified assistantships available. *Unit head:* Daniel Fisher, Chair, 510-642-3392, Fax: 510-643-

8557, E-mail: anthro_chair@berkeley.edu. *Application contact:* Ned Garrett, Student Affairs Officer, 510-642-3406, Fax: 510-643-8557, E-mail: ned@berkeley.edu.
Website: http://anthropology.berkeley.edu.

**University of California, Berkeley,** Graduate Division, College of Letters and Science, Department of Anthropology, Program in Medical Anthropology, Berkeley, CA 94720-1500. Offers PhD. Program held jointly with University of California, San Francisco. *Students:* 12 full-time (4 women); includes 4 minority (1 American Indian or Alaska Native, non-Hispanic/Latino; 1 Asian, non-Hispanic/Latino; 2 Hispanic/Latino), 2 international. Average age 33. 28 applicants, 2 enrolled. In 2016, 1 doctorate awarded. *Degree requirements:* For doctorate, thesis/dissertation. *Entrance requirements:* For doctorate, GRE General Test, minimum GPA of 3.0, 3 letters of recommendation. Additional exam requirements/recommendations for international students: Required—TOEFL (minimum score 570 paper-based; 90 iBT). *Application deadline:* For fall admission, 12/1 for domestic students. Application fee: $105 ($125 for international students). Electronic applications accepted. *Financial support:* Fellowships, research assistantships, teaching assistantships, Federal Work-Study, institutionally sponsored loans, health care benefits, and unspecified assistantships available. Financial award applicants required to submit FAFSA. *Unit head:* Prof. Nancy Scheper-Hughes, Chair, 510-642-3392, E-mail: anthro@berkeley.edu. *Application contact:* Ned Garrett, Student Affairs Officer, 510-642-3406, Fax: 510-643-8557, E-mail: ned@berkeley.edu.
Website: http://anthropology.berkeley.edu/programs/graduate/medical.php

**University of California, Davis,** Graduate Studies, Program in Anthropology, Davis, CA 95616. Offers MA, PhD. Terminal master's awarded for partial completion of doctoral program. *Degree requirements:* For master's, one foreign language; for doctorate, one foreign language, thesis/dissertation. *Entrance requirements:* For master's and doctorate, GRE General Test, minimum GPA of 3.0. Additional exam requirements/recommendations for international students: Required—TOEFL (minimum score 550 paper-based). Electronic applications accepted. *Faculty research:* Archaeology, linguistics, biological and sociocultural anthropology.

**University of California, Irvine,** School of Social Sciences, Department of Anthropology, Irvine, CA 92697. Offers MA, PhD. *Students:* 57 full-time (37 women), 3 part-time (all women); includes 17 minority (2 American Indian or Alaska Native, non-Hispanic/Latino; 2 Asian, non-Hispanic/Latino; 9 Hispanic/Latino; 4 Two or more races, non-Hispanic/Latino), 9 international. Average age 30. 89 applicants, 26% accepted, 13 enrolled. In 2016, 6 master's, 7 doctorates awarded. *Degree requirements:* For doctorate, thesis/dissertation. *Entrance requirements:* For master's, GRE, minimum GPA of 3.0; for doctorate, GRE General Test, minimum GPA of 3.0. Additional exam requirements/recommendations for international students: Required—TOEFL (minimum score 550 paper-based). *Application deadline:* For fall admission, 1/15 priority date for domestic and international students. Applications are processed on a rolling basis. Application fee: $105 ($125 for international students). Electronic applications accepted. *Financial support:* Fellowships, research assistantships with full tuition reimbursements, teaching assistantships, institutionally sponsored loans, traineeships, health care benefits, and unspecified assistantships available. Financial award application deadline: 3/1; financial award applicants required to submit FAFSA. *Faculty research:* Cognitive anthropology, sociology of culture, social structure, family and gender. *Unit head:* George Marcus, Chair, 949-824-5345, Fax: 949-824-6046, E-mail: gmarcus@uci.edu. *Application contact:* Tom Boellstorff, Graduate Program Director, 949-824-9944, Fax: 949-824-0646, E-mail: tboellst@uci.edu.
Website: http://www.anthropology.uci.edu

**University of California, Los Angeles,** Graduate Division, College of Letters and Science, Department of Anthropology, Los Angeles, CA 90095. Offers MA, PhD. Terminal master's awarded for partial completion of doctoral program. *Degree requirements:* For master's, thesis; for doctorate, thesis/dissertation, oral and written qualifying exams. *Entrance requirements:* For master's and doctorate, GRE General Test, bachelor's degree; minimum undergraduate GPA of 3.0 (or its equivalent if letter grade system not used); writing sample. Additional exam requirements/recommendations for international students: Required—TOEFL. Electronic applications accepted.

**University of California, Riverside,** Graduate Division, Department of Anthropology, Riverside, CA 92521-0102. Offers MA, MS, PhD. *Program availability:* Part-time. Terminal master's awarded for partial completion of doctoral program. *Degree requirements:* For master's, comprehensive exams or thesis; for doctorate, one foreign language, comprehensive exam, thesis/dissertation, qualifying exams. *Entrance requirements:* For master's and doctorate, GRE General Test, sample of written work, minimum GPA of 3.2, 3 letters of recommendation. Additional exam requirements/recommendations for international students: Required—TOEFL (minimum score 550 paper-based; 80 iBT). Electronic applications accepted. *Expenses:* Tuition, state resident: full-time $16,666. Tuition, nonresident: full-time $31,768. *Required fees:* $11,055.54 per quarter. $3685.18 per quarter. Tuition and fees vary according to campus/location and program. *Faculty research:* Transnational processes, border communities, political and cultural ecology, Mesoamerican and Western U.S. archaeology, applied anthropology.

**University of California, San Diego,** Graduate Division, Department of Anthropology, La Jolla, CA 92093. Offers PhD. *Students:* 59 full-time (42 women), 1 part-time (0 women). 88 applicants, 20% accepted, 9 enrolled. In 2016, 9 doctorates awarded. *Degree requirements:* For doctorate, variable foreign language requirement, comprehensive exam, thesis/dissertation, 1-quarter teaching assistantship. *Entrance requirements:* For doctorate, GRE General Test, 3 letters of recommendation, statement of purpose. Additional exam requirements/recommendations for international students: Required—TOEFL (minimum score 550 paper-based; 80 iBT), IELTS (minimum score 7), PTE. *Application deadline:* For fall admission, 1/26 for domestic students. Application fee: $105 ($125 for international students). Electronic applications accepted. *Expenses:* Tuition, state resident: full-time $11,220. Tuition, nonresident: full-time $26,322. *Required fees:* $1864. *Financial support:* Fellowships, research assistantships, teaching assistantships, and scholarships/grants available. Financial award applicants required to submit FAFSA. *Faculty research:* Anthropological archaeology, biological anthropology, sociocultural anthropology, psychological anthropology, linguistic anthropology, anthropogony. *Unit head:* Thomas Csordas, Department Chair, 858-534-4145, E-mail: tcsordas@ucsd.edu. *Application contact:* Nikki Gee, Graduate Coordinator, 858-534-0107, E-mail: ngee@ucsd.edu.
Website: http://anthropology.ucsd.edu/

**University of California, San Francisco,** Graduate Division, Program in Medical Anthropology, San Francisco, CA 94143. Offers PhD. Program offered jointly with University of California, Berkeley. *Degree requirements:* For doctorate, one foreign language, thesis/dissertation, 3 field statements. *Entrance requirements:* For doctorate, GRE General Test, master's degree in anthropology or a related social or health science. *Faculty research:* Ethnicity, gender, aging, international health, health policy.

**University of California, Santa Barbara,** Graduate Division, College of Letters and Sciences, Division of Social Sciences, Department of Anthropology, Santa Barbara, CA 93106-2014. Offers sociocultural anthropology (PhD); MA/PhD. Terminal master's awarded for partial completion of doctoral program. *Degree requirements:* For master's, comprehensive exam (for some programs), thesis (for some programs); for doctorate, comprehensive exam (for some programs), thesis/dissertation. *Entrance requirements:* For master's and doctorate, GRE General Test, statement of purpose, personal achievements statement, transcripts, writing sample, curriculum vitae, letters of recommendation. Additional exam requirements/recommendations for international students: Required—TOEFL (minimum score 550 paper-based; 80 iBT), IELTS (minimum score 7). Electronic applications accepted. *Faculty research:* Archaeology, bioarchaeology, biosocial anthropology, evolutionary ecology, evolutionary psychology, sociocultural anthropology.

**University of California, Santa Cruz,** Division of Graduate Studies, Division of Social Sciences, Department of Anthropology, Santa Cruz, CA 95064. Offers cultural anthropology (PhD). *Degree requirements:* For doctorate, thesis/dissertation, qualifying exam. *Entrance requirements:* For doctorate, GRE General Test. Additional exam requirements/recommendations for international students: Required—TOEFL (minimum score 550 paper-based; 83 iBT); Recommended—IELTS (minimum score 8). Electronic applications accepted. *Faculty research:* Culture and power, women's roles, AIDS, folklore.

**University of Central Florida,** College of Sciences, Department of Anthropology, Orlando, FL 32816. Offers anthropology (MA); Maya studies (Certificate). *Faculty:* 20 full-time (10 women), 1 part-time/adjunct (0 women). *Students:* 32 full-time (23 women), 6 part-time (4 women); includes 3 minority (2 Hispanic/Latino; 1 Native Hawaiian or other Pacific Islander, non-Hispanic/Latino), 1 international. Average age 29. 29 applicants, 72% accepted, 16 enrolled. In 2016, 17 master's awarded. *Degree requirements:* For master's, thesis or alternative. *Entrance requirements:* For master's, GRE General Test. Additional exam requirements/recommendations for international students: Required—TOEFL. *Application deadline:* For fall admission, 2/15 for domestic students; for spring admission, 11/1 for domestic students. Application fee: $30. Electronic applications accepted. *Expenses:* Tuition, state resident: part-time $288.16 per credit hour. Tuition, nonresident: part-time $1071.31 per credit hour. *Financial support:* In 2016–17, 23 students received support, including 5 fellowships with partial tuition reimbursements available (averaging $2,600 per year), 2 research assistantships with partial tuition reimbursements available (averaging $10,355 per year), 21 teaching assistantships with partial tuition reimbursements available (averaging $9,174 per year); institutionally sponsored loans and scholarships/grants also available. Financial award application deadline: 3/1; financial award applicants required to submit FAFSA. *Unit head:* Dr. Tosha Dupras, Chair, 407-823-2227, Fax: 407-823-3498, E-mail: tosha.dupras@ucf.edu. *Application contact:* Assistant Director, Graduate Admissions, 407-823-2766, Fax: 407-823-6442, E-mail: gradadmissions@ucf.edu.
Website: http://anthropology.cos.ucf.edu/

**University of Chicago,** Division of the Humanities, Department of Linguistics, Chicago, IL 60637. Offers anthropology and linguistics (PhD); linguistics (PhD). *Students:* 46 full-time (22 women); includes 11 minority (1 Black or African American, non-Hispanic/Latino; 1 American Indian or Alaska Native, non-Hispanic/Latino; 4 Asian, non-Hispanic/Latino; 5 Hispanic/Latino), 13 international. 103 applicants, 13% accepted, 9 enrolled. In 2016, 4 doctorates awarded. Terminal master's awarded for partial completion of doctoral program. *Degree requirements:* For doctorate, 3 foreign languages, thesis/dissertation. *Entrance requirements:* For doctorate, GRE General Test. Additional exam requirements/recommendations for international students: Required—TOEFL (minimum score 104 iBT), IELTS (minimum score 7). *Application deadline:* For fall admission, 12/15 for domestic and international students. Application fee: $90. Electronic applications accepted. *Financial support:* Fellowships with full tuition reimbursements, teaching assistantships with full tuition reimbursements, Federal Work-Study, institutionally sponsored loans, scholarships/grants, and health care benefits available. Financial award application deadline: 12/15; financial award applicants required to submit FAFSA. *Unit head:* Dr. Lenore Grenoble, Chair, 773-702-0927, E-mail: grenoble@uchicago.edu. *Application contact:* Michael Beetley, Assistant Dean of Students, Admissions and Fellowships, 773-702-1552, Fax: 773-834-9148, E-mail: humanitiesadmissions@uchicago.edu.
Website: http://linguistics.uchicago.edu/

**University of Chicago,** Division of the Social Sciences, Department of Anthropology, Chicago, IL 60637. Offers archaeology (PhD); sociocultural and linguistic anthropology (PhD). *Students:* 146 full-time (80 women); includes 25 minority (5 Black or African American, non-Hispanic/Latino; 2 American Indian or Alaska Native, non-Hispanic/Latino; 3 Asian, non-Hispanic/Latino; 5 Hispanic/Latino; 10 Two or more races, non-Hispanic/Latino), 48 international. 271 applicants, 10% accepted, 16 enrolled. In 2016, 15 doctorates awarded. *Degree requirements:* For doctorate, one foreign language, thesis/dissertation, exams. *Entrance requirements:* For doctorate, GRE General Test. Additional exam requirements/recommendations for international students: Required—TOEFL (minimum score 104 iBT), IELTS (minimum score 7). *Application deadline:* For fall admission, 12/15 for domestic and international students. Application fee: $90. Electronic applications accepted. *Financial support:* In 2016–17, 16 students received support, including 12 fellowships with full tuition reimbursements available (averaging $23,000 per year); career-related internships or fieldwork, Federal Work-Study, institutionally sponsored loans, scholarships/grants, and health care benefits also available. Financial award application deadline: 12/15. *Unit head:* Dr. William Mazzarella, Chair, 773-834-4873, E-mail: mazzarel@uchicago.edu. *Application contact:* Office of the Dean of Students, 773-702-8415, E-mail: admissions@ssd.uchicago.edu.
Website: http://anthropology.uchicago.edu

**University of Cincinnati,** Graduate School, McMicken College of Arts and Sciences, Department of Anthropology, Cincinnati, OH 45221. Offers MA. *Program availability:* Part-time. *Degree requirements:* For master's, thesis or alternative. *Entrance requirements:* For master's, GRE General Test. Additional exam requirements/recommendations for international students: Required—TOEFL; Recommended—TWE. Electronic applications accepted. *Expenses: Tuition, area resident:* Full-time $12,790; part-time $389 per credit hour. Tuition, state resident: full-time $13,290; part-time $419 per credit hour. Tuition, nonresident: full-time $24,532; part-time $976 per credit hour. *International tuition:* $24,832 full-time. *Required fees:* $3958; $140 per credit hour. Tuition and fees vary according to course load, degree level, program and reciprocity agreements. *Faculty research:* Medical anthropology, Mayan prehistory, southwestern U.S. prehistory, skeletal biology and paleoanthropology; immigrants; Mexico.

**University of Colorado Boulder,** Graduate School, College of Arts and Sciences, Department of Anthropology, Boulder, CO 80309. Offers MA, PhD. *Faculty:* 23 full-time (12 women). *Students:* 55 full-time (38 women), 3 part-time (2 women); includes 11 minority (1 American Indian or Alaska Native, non-Hispanic/Latino; 2 Asian, non-Hispanic/Latino; 5 Hispanic/Latino; 3 Two or more races, non-Hispanic/Latino), 2 international. Average age 30. 73 applicants, 22% accepted, 6 enrolled. In 2016, 5 master's, 5 doctorates awarded. Terminal master's awarded for partial completion of doctoral program. *Degree requirements:* For master's, comprehensive exam, thesis or alternative; for doctorate, one foreign language, thesis/dissertation. *Entrance requirements:* For master's, GRE General Test, minimum undergraduate GPA of 3.0; for doctorate, GRE General Test, minimum undergraduate GPA of 3.0, master's degree in anthropology. *Application deadline:* For fall admission, 1/9 for domestic students, 12/1 for international students. Applications are processed on a rolling basis. Application fee:

$60 ($80 for international students). Electronic applications accepted. Application fee is waived when completed online. *Financial support:* In 2016–17, 140 students received support, including 28 fellowships (averaging $9,096 per year), 4 research assistantships with full and partial tuition reimbursements available (averaging $21,504 per year), 43 teaching assistantships with full and partial tuition reimbursements available (averaging $32,234 per year); institutionally sponsored loans, scholarships/grants, health care benefits, and unspecified assistantships also available. Financial award application deadline: 1/15; financial award applicants required to submit FAFSA. *Faculty research:* Anthropology, cultural/social anthropology, archaeology, ethnography, physical anthropology. *Total annual research expenditures:* $745,091. *Application contact:* E-mail: anthro@colorado.edu.
Website: http://www.colorado.edu/anthropology

**University of Colorado Denver,** College of Liberal Arts and Sciences, Department of Anthropology, Denver, CO 80217. Offers archaeological studies (MA); biological anthropology (MA); medical anthropology (MA); sustainable development and political ecology (MA). *Program availability:* Part-time, evening/weekend. *Faculty:* 9 full-time (3 women), 1 part-time/adjunct (0 women). *Students:* 30 full-time (22 women), 5 part-time (3 women); includes 9 minority (2 Black or African American, non-Hispanic/Latino; 1 American Indian or Alaska Native, non-Hispanic/Latino; 4 Hispanic/Latino; 2 Two or more races, non-Hispanic/Latino), 1 international. Average age 28. 40 applicants, 53% accepted, 11 enrolled. In 2016, 13 master's awarded. *Degree requirements:* For master's, comprehensive exam, thesis or alternative, 30-36 credit hours. *Entrance requirements:* For master's, GRE General Test, minimum GPA of 3.0 for all undergraduate studies, transcripts from all undergraduate/graduate institutions attended, prior training in anthropology, three letters of recommendation, statement of purpose. Additional exam requirements/recommendations for international students: Required—TOEFL (minimum score 537 paper-based; 75 iBT); Recommended—IELTS (minimum score 6.5). *Application deadline:* For fall admission, 2/15 for domestic students, 1/15 for international students. Application fee: $50 ($75 for international students). Electronic applications accepted. *Expenses:* Tuition, state resident: full-time $11,006; part-time $474 per credit. Tuition, nonresident: full-time $28,212; part-time $1264 per credit hour. *Required fees:* $256 per semester. One-time fee: $94.32. Tuition and fees vary according to campus/location and program. *Financial support:* In 2016–17, 3 students received support. Fellowships, research assistantships, teaching assistantships, Federal Work-Study, institutionally sponsored loans, scholarships/grants, and traineeships available. Financial award application deadline: 4/1; financial award applicants required to submit FAFSA. *Faculty research:* Applied medical anthropology, primate social behavior, environmental anthropology, Southwestern and Mexican archaeology, human ecology. *Application contact:* Connie Turner, Program Assistant, 303-556-3554, E-mail: connie.turner@ucdenver.edu.
Website: http://www.ucdenver.edu/academics/colleges/CLAS/Departments/anthropology/Programs/Masters/Pages/Masters.aspx

**University of Connecticut,** Graduate School, College of Liberal Arts and Sciences, Department of Anthropology, Storrs, CT 06269. Offers MA, PhD. Terminal master's awarded for partial completion of doctoral program. *Degree requirements:* For master's, comprehensive exam; for doctorate, thesis/dissertation. *Entrance requirements:* For master's and doctorate, GRE General Test. Additional exam requirements/recommendations for international students: Required—TOEFL (minimum score 550 paper-based). Electronic applications accepted.

**University of Denver,** Division of Arts, Humanities and Social Sciences, Department of Anthropology, Denver, CO 80208. Offers archaeology (MA); cultural anthropology (MA); museum and heritage studies (MA). *Program availability:* Part-time. *Faculty:* 8 full-time (2 women). *Students:* 3 full-time (all women), 17 part-time (16 women); includes 2 minority (1 American Indian or Alaska Native, non-Hispanic/Latino; 1 Hispanic/Latino). Average age 25. 47 applicants, 43% accepted, 11 enrolled. In 2016, 11 master's awarded. *Degree requirements:* For master's, one foreign language, comprehensive exam, thesis (for some programs), tool, foreign language literacy, or course work. *Entrance requirements:* For master's, GRE General Test, bachelor's degree, transcripts, personal statement, two letters of recommendation. Additional exam requirements/recommendations for international students: Required—TOEFL (minimum score 550 paper-based; 80 iBT). *Application deadline:* For fall admission, 2/4 priority date for domestic and international students. Applications are processed on a rolling basis. Application fee: $65. Electronic applications accepted. *Expenses:* $29,022 per year full-time. *Financial support:* In 2016–17, 19 students received support, including 6 teaching assistantships with tuition reimbursements available (averaging $6,667 per year); career-related internships or fieldwork, Federal Work-Study, institutionally sponsored loans, scholarships/grants, and unspecified assistantships also available. Support available to part-time students. Financial award application deadline: 2/15; financial award applicants required to submit FAFSA. *Faculty research:* Human diversity, human rights, historic archaeology, museums and heritage, high-tech field methods. *Unit head:* Dr. Larry Conyers, Professor and Chair, 303-871-2684, Fax: 303-871-2437, E-mail: lconyers@du.edu. *Application contact:* Dr. Larry Conyers, Professor and Director of Graduate Program, 303-871-2684, Fax: 303-871-2437, E-mail: lconyers@du.edu.
Website: http://www.du.edu/ahss/anthropology

**University of Florida,** Graduate School, College of Liberal Arts and Sciences, Department of Anthropology, Gainesville, FL 32611. Offers anthropology (MA, MAT, PhD), including historic preservation (MA, PhD), tropical conservation and development, women's and gender studies (PhD). *Program availability:* Part-time. *Degree requirements:* For master's, thesis optional; for doctorate, comprehensive exam, thesis/dissertation. *Entrance requirements:* For master's and doctorate, GRE General Test, minimum GPA of 3.2. Additional exam requirements/recommendations for international students: Required—TOEFL (minimum score 550 paper-based; 80 iBT), IELTS (minimum score 6). Electronic applications accepted. *Faculty research:* Social and cultural anthropology, archaeology, biological anthropology, medical anthropology, linguistic anthropology.

**University of Georgia,** Franklin College of Arts and Sciences, Department of Anthropology, Athens, GA 30602. Offers anthropology (MA, PhD). *Degree requirements:* For master's, one foreign language, thesis; for doctorate, one foreign language, thesis/dissertation. *Entrance requirements:* For master's and doctorate, GRE General Test. *Application deadline:* For fall admission, 7/1 priority date for domestic students; for spring admission, 11/15 for domestic students. Application fee: $50. Electronic applications accepted. *Financial support:* Fellowships, research assistantships, teaching assistantships, and unspecified assistantships available. *Unit head:* Dr. Ted Gragson, Head, 706-542-1479, Fax: 706-542-3998, E-mail: tgragso@uga.edu. *Application contact:* Susan Turner, Graduate Coordinator, 706-542-1483, E-mail: stanner1@uga.edu.
Website: http://anthropology.uga.edu/

**University of Guelph,** Graduate Studies, College of Social and Applied Human Sciences, Department of Sociology and Anthropology, Guelph, ON N1G 2W1, Canada. Offers anthropology (MA); crime and criminal justice policy (MA); sociology (MA, PhD). *Degree requirements:* For master's, thesis or major paper; for doctorate, comprehensive exam, thesis/dissertation. *Entrance requirements:* For master's, minimum B+ average during previous 2 years of course work, honors BA or equivalent; for doctorate, must

## Anthropology

have an MA in Sociology, must have 80% or higher in graduate level studies. Additional exam requirements/recommendations for international students: Required—TOEFL (minimum score 550 paper-based; 89 iBT) or IELTS (minimum score 6.5). Electronic applications accepted. *Faculty research:* Rural and development sociology; education, employment, and the workplace; race, ethnicity, and native studies; criminology and deviance; social psychology.

**University of Hawaii at Manoa,** Graduate Division, College of Social Sciences, Department of Anthropology, Honolulu, HI 96822. Offers MA, PhD. *Program availability:* Part-time. *Degree requirements:* For master's, thesis optional; for doctorate, comprehensive exam, thesis/dissertation. *Entrance requirements:* For master's and doctorate, GRE General Test. Additional exam requirements/recommendations for international students: Required—TOEFL (minimum score 560 paper-based; 83 iBT), IELTS (minimum score 5). *Faculty research:* Evolution of social complexity, ethnopharmacology, social interaction, faunal analysis, human ecology.

**University of Houston,** College of Liberal Arts and Social Sciences, Department of Anthropology, Houston, TX 77204. Offers MA. *Program availability:* Part-time. *Degree requirements:* For master's, comprehensive exam, thesis. *Entrance requirements:* For master's, GRE General Test (minimum 500 verbal, 500 quantitative), minimum GPA of 3.0 in last 60 undergraduate hours. Additional exam requirements/recommendations for international students: Required—TOEFL (minimum score 550 paper-based; 79 iBT). Electronic applications accepted.

**University of Idaho,** College of Graduate Studies, College of Letters, Arts and Social Sciences, Department of Sociology and Anthropology, Moscow, ID 83844. Offers anthropology (MA). *Faculty:* 9 full-time. *Students:* 11 full-time, 8 part-time. Average age 35. In 2016, 7 master's awarded. *Degree requirements:* For master's, variable foreign language requirement. *Entrance requirements:* For master's, minimum GPA of 3.0. *Application deadline:* For fall admission, 8/1 for domestic students; for spring admission, 12/15 for domestic students. Applications are processed on a rolling basis. Application fee: $60. Electronic applications accepted. *Expenses:* Tuition, state resident: full-time $6460; part-time $414 per credit hour. Tuition, nonresident: full-time $21,268; part-time $1237 per credit hour. *Required fees:* $2070; $60 per credit hour. Full-time tuition and fees vary according to course load and reciprocity agreements. *Financial support:* Research assistantships and teaching assistantships available. Financial award applicants required to submit FAFSA. *Unit head:* Dr. Mark Warner, Chair, 208-885-6751, E-mail: socanth@uidaho.edu. *Application contact:* Sean Scoggin, Graduate Recruitment Coordinator, 208-885-4723, Fax: 208-885-4406, E-mail: graduateadmissions@uidaho.edu.
Website: https://www.uidaho.edu/class/soc-anthro

**University of Illinois at Chicago,** College of Liberal Arts and Sciences, Department of Anthropology, Chicago, IL 60607-7128. Offers anthropology (MA, PhD); environmental and urban geography (MA), including environmental studies, urban geography. *Program availability:* Part-time. *Degree requirements:* For doctorate, comprehensive exam. *Entrance requirements:* For master's and doctorate, minimum GPA of 2.75. Additional exam requirements/recommendations for international students: Required—TOEFL. Electronic applications accepted. *Faculty research:* Archaeological, physical, and cultural anthropology; environmental and urban geography.

**University of Illinois at Urbana–Champaign,** Graduate College, College of Liberal Arts and Sciences, Department of Anthropology, Champaign, IL 61820. Offers MA, PhD. Terminal master's awarded for partial completion of doctoral program.

**University of Indianapolis,** Graduate Programs, College of Arts and Sciences, Department of Anthropology, Indianapolis, IN 46227-3697. Offers MS. *Entrance requirements:* For master's, GRE General Test (minimum score of 500 on both the verbal and quantitative sections), bachelor's degree with major or minor in anthropology or closely-related field; undergraduate or graduate coursework in anthropology and the natural sciences with minimum C grade (ideally, semester in cultural anthropology, biological anthropology, archeology, statistics, and geology); minimum cumulative undergraduate GPA of 3.2. Additional exam requirements/recommendations for international students: Required—TOEFL (minimum score 550 paper-based; 79 iBT).

**The University of Iowa,** Graduate College, College of Liberal Arts and Sciences, Department of Anthropology, Iowa City, IA 52242-1316. Offers MA, PhD. *Degree requirements:* For master's, thesis optional, exam; for doctorate, comprehensive exam, thesis/dissertation. *Entrance requirements:* For master's and doctorate, GRE General Test, minimum GPA of 3.0. Additional exam requirements/recommendations for international students: Required—TOEFL (minimum score 550 paper-based; 81 iBT). Electronic applications accepted.

**The University of Kansas,** Graduate Studies, College of Liberal Arts and Sciences, Department of Anthropology, Lawrence, KS 66045. Offers MA, PhD. *Students:* 30 full-time (17 women), 5 part-time (4 women); includes 3 minority (2 Black or African American, non-Hispanic/Latino; 1 Two or more races, non-Hispanic/Latino), 6 international. Average age 32. 36 applicants, 56% accepted, 9 enrolled. In 2016, 5 master's, 3 doctorates awarded. *Entrance requirements:* For master's, GRE (for university fellowship), letter stating academic objectives and clearly indicating disciplinary track of interest; copy of curriculum vitae; transcripts of undergraduate and graduate study completed; three letters of recommendation; for doctorate, GRE (for university fellowship), letter stating academic objectives and clearly indicating disciplinary track of interest; copy of curriculum vitae; transcripts of undergraduate and graduate study completed; three letters of recommendation; professional writing sample. Additional exam requirements/recommendations for international students: Required—TOEFL. *Application deadline:* For fall admission, 1/5 for domestic and international students. Application fee: $65 ($85 for international students). Electronic applications accepted. *Financial support:* Fellowships, research assistantships, teaching assistantships, career-related internships or fieldwork, institutionally sponsored loans, and unspecified assistantships available. Financial award application deadline: 1/5; financial award applicants required to submit FAFSA. *Faculty research:* Archaeological, biological, cultural, linguistic, and applied anthropology. *Unit head:* Joane P. Nagel, Chair, 785-864-4114, E-mail: nagel@ku.edu. *Application contact:* Le-Thu Erazmus, Graduate Officer, 785-864-2630, E-mail: lerazmus@ku.edu.
Website: http://anthropology.ku.edu/

**University of Kentucky,** Graduate School, College of Arts and Sciences, Program in Anthropology, Lexington, KY 40506-0032. Offers MA, PhD. *Program availability:* Part-time. *Degree requirements:* For master's, comprehensive exam, thesis optional; for doctorate, one foreign language, comprehensive exam, thesis/dissertation. *Entrance requirements:* For master's, GRE General Test, minimum undergraduate GPA of 2.75; for doctorate, GRE General Test, minimum graduate GPA of 3.0. Additional exam requirements/recommendations for international students: Required—TOEFL (minimum score 550 paper-based). Electronic applications accepted. *Faculty research:* Applied social anthropology, developmental change, medical anthropology, culture history, ethnohistory.

**University of Lethbridge,** School of Graduate Studies, Lethbridge, AB T1K 3M4, Canada. Offers addictions counseling (M Sc); agricultural biotechnology (M Sc); agricultural studies (M Sc, MA); anthropology (MA); archaeology (M Sc, MA); art (MA, MFA); biochemistry (M Sc); biological sciences (M Sc); biomolecular science (PhD);

biosystems and biodiversity (PhD); Canadian studies (MA); chemistry (M Sc); computer science (M Sc); computer science and geographical information science (M Sc); counseling (MC); counseling psychology (M Ed); dramatic arts (MA); earth, space, and physical science (PhD); economics (MA); education (MA, PhD); educational leadership (M Ed); English (MA); environmental science (M Sc); evolution and behavior (PhD); exercise science (M Sc); French (MA); French/German (MA); French/Spanish (MA); general education (M Ed); geography (M Sc, MA); German (MA); health sciences (M Sc); individualized multidisciplinary (M Sc, MA); kinesiology (M Sc, MA); management (M Sc), including accounting, finance, human resource management and labor relations, information systems, international management, marketing, policy and strategy; mathematics (M Sc); music (M Mus, MA); Native American studies (MA); neuroscience (M Sc, PhD); new media (MA, MFA); nursing (M Sc, MN); philosophy (MA); physics (M Sc); political science (MA); psychology (M Sc, MA); religious studies (MA); sociology (MA); theatre and dramatic arts (MFA); theoretical and computational science (PhD); urban and regional studies (MA); women and gender studies (MA). *Program availability:* Part-time, evening/weekend. *Degree requirements:* For master's, thesis (for some programs); for doctorate, comprehensive exam, thesis/dissertation. *Entrance requirements:* For master's, GMAT (for M Sc in management), bachelor's degree in related field, minimum GPA of 3.0 during previous 20 graded semester courses, 2 years' teaching or related experience (M Ed); for doctorate, master's degree, minimum graduate GPA of 3.5. Additional exam requirements/recommendations for international students: Required—TOEFL (minimum score 580 paper-based; 93 iBT). Electronic applications accepted. *Faculty research:* Movement and brain plasticity, gibberellin physiology, photosynthesis, carbon cycling, molecular properties of main-group ring components.

**University of Louisville,** Graduate School, College of Arts and Sciences, Department of Anthropology, Louisville, KY 40292-0001. Offers MA. *Program availability:* Part-time, evening/weekend, online learning. *Faculty:* 11 full-time (5 women), 1 (woman) part-time/adjunct. *Students:* 7 full-time (6 women), 12 part-time (6 women). Average age 27. 6 applicants, 100% accepted, 5 enrolled. In 2016, 3 master's awarded. *Degree requirements:* For master's, variable foreign language requirement, comprehensive exam (for some programs), thesis (for some programs). *Entrance requirements:* For master's, GRE. Additional exam requirements/recommendations for international students: Recommended—TOEFL (minimum score 550 paper-based; 79 iBT), IELTS. *Application deadline:* Applications are processed on a rolling basis. Application fee: $60. Electronic applications accepted. *Expenses:* Tuition, state resident: full-time $12,246; part-time $681 per credit hour. Tuition, nonresident: full-time $25,486; part-time $1417 per credit hour. *Required fees:* $196. Tuition and fees vary according to program and reciprocity agreements. *Financial support:* Teaching assistantships with full tuition reimbursements, career-related internships or fieldwork, and scholarships/grants available. *Faculty research:* Evolutionary anthropology, cultural diaspora studies, archaeology, political economy, violence and the state. *Total annual research expenditures:* $115,533. *Unit head:* Dr. Lisa Markowitz, Chair, 502-852-2426, Fax: 502-852-4560, E-mail: lisam@louisville.edu. *Application contact:* Libby Leggett, Director, Graduate Admissions, 502-852-3101, Fax: 502-852-6536, E-mail: gradadm@louisville.edu.
Website: http://louisville.edu/anthropology

**University of Maine,** Graduate School, College of Liberal Arts and Sciences, Department of Anthropology, Orono, ME 04469. Offers anthropology and environmental policy (PhD). *Faculty:* 10 full-time (4 women). *Students:* 7 full-time (6 women), 1 part-time (0 women). Average age 30. 12 applicants, 33% accepted, 1 enrolled. In 2016, 1 doctorate awarded. *Degree requirements:* For doctorate, comprehensive exam, thesis/dissertation. *Entrance requirements:* For doctorate, GRE General Test. Additional exam requirements/recommendations for international students: Required—TOEFL. *Application deadline:* For fall admission, 1/15 for domestic students. Application fee: $65. Electronic applications accepted. *Expenses:* Tuition, state resident: full-time $7524; part-time $2508 per credit. Tuition, nonresident: full-time $24,498; part-time $8166 per credit. *Required fees:* $1148; $571 per credit. *Financial support:* In 2016–17, 8 students received support, including 1 fellowship (averaging $25,000 per year), 5 research assistantships (averaging $20,100 per year), 1 teaching assistantship (averaging $14,600 per year). Financial award application deadline: 3/1. *Faculty research:* Culture change, archeology, environmental policy, climate change, economic anthropology, natural resources. *Unit head:* Gregory Zaro, Chair, 207-581-1857, Fax: 207-581-1823, E-mail: gregory.zaro@umit.maine.edu. *Application contact:* Scott G. Delcourt, Assistant Vice President for Graduate Studies and Senior Associate Dean, 207-581-3291, Fax: 207-581-3232, E-mail: graduate@maine.edu.
Website: http://www.umaine.edu/anthropology/graduate-programs/

**The University of Manchester,** School of Arts, Histories and Cultures, Manchester, United Kingdom. Offers anthropology, media and performance (PhD); applied theatre professional (PhD); archaeology (PhD); art history and visual studies (PhD); arts management and cultural policy (PhD); classics and ancient history (PhD); composition (PhD); creative writing (PhD); drama (PhD); economic and social history (PhD); electroacoustic composition (PhD); English and American studies (PhD); history (PhD); humanitarianism and conflict response (PhD); museology (PhD); music (PhD); musicology (PhD); religions and theology (PhD).

**The University of Manchester,** School of Social Sciences, Manchester, United Kingdom. Offers ethnographic documentary (M Phil); interdisciplinary study of culture (PhD); philosophy (PhD); politics (PhD); social anthropology (PhD); social anthropology with visual media (PhD); social change (PhD); social statistics (PhD); sociology (PhD); visual anthropology (M Phil).

**University of Manitoba,** Faculty of Graduate Studies, Faculty of Arts, Department of Anthropology, Winnipeg, MB R3T 2N2, Canada. Offers MA, PhD. *Degree requirements:* For master's, thesis or alternative.

**University of Maryland, College Park,** Academic Affairs, College of Behavioral and Social Sciences, Department of Anthropology, College Park, MD 20742. Offers applied anthropology (MAA). *Program availability:* Part-time, evening/weekend. *Degree requirements:* For master's, internship. *Entrance requirements:* For master's, GRE General Test, minimum GPA of 3.0, 3 letters of recommendation. Additional exam requirements/recommendations for international students: Required—TOEFL. Electronic applications accepted. *Faculty research:* Archaeology, human biodiversity, cultural and resource management.

**University of Massachusetts Amherst,** Graduate School, College of Social and Behavioral Sciences, Department of Anthropology, Amherst, MA 01003. Offers MA, PhD. *Program availability:* Part-time. Terminal master's awarded for partial completion of doctoral program. *Degree requirements:* For master's, thesis or alternative; for doctorate, comprehensive exam, thesis/dissertation. *Entrance requirements:* Additional exam requirements/recommendations for international students: Required—TOEFL (minimum score 550 paper-based; 80 iBT), IELTS (minimum score 6.5). Electronic applications accepted.

**University of Memphis,** Graduate School, College of Arts and Sciences, Department of Anthropology, Memphis, TN 38152. Offers medical anthropology (MA). *Program availability:* Part-time. *Faculty:* 7 full-time (5 women), 2 part-time/adjunct (1 woman).

*Students:* 18 full-time (15 women), 2 part-time (1 woman); includes 5 minority (4 Black or African American, non-Hispanic/Latino; 1 Asian, non-Hispanic/Latino), 3 international. Average age 28. 15 applicants, 87% accepted, 8 enrolled. In 2016, 13 master's awarded. *Degree requirements:* For master's, comprehensive exam, practicum. *Entrance requirements:* For master's, GRE General Test, minimum GPA of 3.0, letter of intent, 3 letters of recommendation. *Application deadline:* For fall admission, 1/31 priority date for domestic students; for spring admission, 9/1 priority date for domestic students. Applications are processed on a rolling basis. Application fee: $35 ($60 for international students). Electronic applications accepted. *Expenses:* $5,231.50 per semester full-time in-state, $9,623.50 full-time out-of-state. *Financial support:* In 2016–17, 9 research assistantships with full tuition reimbursements (averaging $8,289 per year) were awarded; fellowships, teaching assistantships with full tuition reimbursements, career-related internships or fieldwork, Federal Work-Study, scholarships/grants, and unspecified assistantships also available. Financial award application deadline: 2/1; financial award applicants required to submit FAFSA. *Faculty research:* Community development, medical anthropology, environmental justice, health disparities, cultural identity and heritage. *Unit head:* Dr. Ruthbeth Finerman, Chair, 901-678-2080, Fax: 901-678-2069, E-mail: finerman@memphis.edu. *Application contact:* Dr. Katheryn Hicks, Coordinator of Graduate Studies, 901-678-3328, Fax: 901-678-2069, E-mail: kahicks2@memphis.edu.
Website: http://www.memphis.edu/anthropology

**University of Michigan,** Rackham Graduate School, College of Literature, Science, and the Arts, Department of Anthropology, Ann Arbor, MI 48109. Offers anthropological archaeology (PhD); biological anthropology (PhD); linguistic anthropology (PhD); sociocultural anthropology (PhD). *Faculty:* 41 full-time (18 women), 5 part-time/adjunct (2 women). *Students:* 149 full-time (89 women); includes 41 minority (3 Black or African American, non-Hispanic/Latino; 3 American Indian or Alaska Native, non-Hispanic/Latino; 16 Asian, non-Hispanic/Latino; 14 Hispanic/Latino; 5 Two or more races, non-Hispanic/Latino), 16 international. Average age 28. 209 applicants, 9% accepted, 13 enrolled. In 2016, 17 doctorates awarded. *Degree requirements:* For doctorate, one foreign language, comprehensive exam, thesis/dissertation, preliminary examination, oral defense of dissertation. *Entrance requirements:* For doctorate, GRE General Test. Additional exam requirements/recommendations for international students: Required—TOEFL (minimum score 560 paper-based; 84 iBT). *Application deadline:* For fall admission, 12/15 for domestic and international students. Application fee: $75 ($90 for international students). Electronic applications accepted. *Expenses:* Tuition, state resident: full-time $21,466; part-time $1152 per credit hour. Tuition, nonresident: full-time $43,346; part-time $2367 per credit hour. Part-time tuition and fees vary according to course load, degree level and program. *Financial support:* In 2016–17, 76 students received support, including 54 fellowships with full tuition reimbursements available (averaging $19,350 per year), 9 research assistantships with full tuition reimbursements available (averaging $19,350 per year), 30 teaching assistantships with full tuition reimbursements available (averaging $19,350 per year); institutionally sponsored loans, scholarships/grants, traineeships, health care benefits, tuition waivers (full), and unspecified assistantships also available. Financial award application deadline: 3/1; financial award applicants required to submit FAFSA. *Faculty research:* Sociocultural, linguistic, biological and archaeological anthropology. *Unit head:* Dr. Andrew Shryock, Chair, 734-764-7274, Fax: 734-763-6077. *Application contact:* Katia Kitchen, Graduate Program Assistant, 734-936-7933, Fax: 734-763-6077, E-mail: kitchenk@umich.edu.
Website: http://www.lsa.umich.edu/anthro/

**University of Michigan,** Rackham Graduate School, College of Literature, Science, and the Arts, Doctoral Program in Anthropology and History, Ann Arbor, MI 48109. Offers PhD. *Degree requirements:* For doctorate, 2 foreign languages, thesis/dissertation, oral defense of dissertation, preliminary exam. *Entrance requirements:* For doctorate, GRE General Test, writing sample. Additional exam requirements/recommendations for international students: Required—TOEFL. Electronic applications accepted. *Expenses:* Tuition, state resident: full-time $21,466; part-time $1152 per credit hour. Tuition, nonresident: full-time $43,346; part-time $2367 per credit hour. Part-time tuition and fees vary according to course load, degree level and program. *Faculty research:* Historical anthropology.

**University of Michigan,** School of Social Work, Interdisciplinary PhD Program in Social Work and Social Science, Ann Arbor, MI 48109-1106. Offers social work and anthropology (PhD); social work and economics (PhD); social work and political science (PhD); social work and psychology (PhD); social work and sociology (PhD). Programs offered through the Rackham Graduate School. *Faculty:* 50 full-time (29 women), 62 part-time/adjunct (48 women). *Students:* 59 full-time (42 women); includes 30 minority (14 Black or African American, non-Hispanic/Latino; 9 Asian, non-Hispanic/Latino; 7 Hispanic/Latino). Average age 32. 114 applicants, 7% accepted, 8 enrolled. In 2016, 8 doctorates awarded. *Degree requirements:* For doctorate, thesis/dissertation, oral defense of dissertation, preliminary exam. *Entrance requirements:* For doctorate, GRE General Test. Additional exam requirements/recommendations for international students: Required—TOEFL (minimum score 620 paper-based, 88 iBT) or IELTS. *Application deadline:* For fall admission, 12/1 for domestic and international students. Application fee: $75 ($90 for international students). Electronic applications accepted. *Expenses:* $42,016 fall/winter tuition. *Financial support:* In 2016–17, 59 students received support, including 20 fellowships with full tuition reimbursements available (averaging $15,200 per year), 8 research assistantships with full tuition reimbursements available (averaging $19,737 per year), 17 teaching assistantships with full tuition reimbursements available (averaging $19,737 per year); career-related internships or fieldwork, scholarships/grants, traineeships, health care benefits, tuition waivers (full and partial), and unspecified assistantships also available. Financial award application deadline: 12/1; financial award applicants required to submit FAFSA. *Faculty research:* Children and family, aging, community organization, health and mental health, police and evaluation. *Total annual research expenditures:* $3.8 million. *Unit head:* Dr. Daphne C. Watkins, Director, 734-763-5768, E-mail: daphnew@umich.edu. *Application contact:* Todd Huynh, Graduate Coordinator, 734-647-2554, Fax: 734-615-3192, E-mail: ssw.phd.info@umich.edu.
Website: https://ssw.umich.edu/offices/phd

**University of Minnesota, Duluth,** Graduate School, College of Liberal Arts, Department of Sociology/Anthropology, Duluth, MN 55812-2496. Offers criminology (MA); liberal studies (MLS). *Program availability:* Part-time. *Degree requirements:* For master's, thesis or alternative. *Entrance requirements:* For master's, interview, minimum GPA of 3.0, letters of recommendation. Additional exam requirements/recommendations for international students: Required—TOEFL. *Faculty research:* Nature of knowledge, philosophy of science, ecology, cultural studies, language.

**University of Minnesota, Twin Cities Campus,** Graduate School, College of Liberal Arts, Department of Anthropology, Minneapolis, MN 55455-0213. Offers MA, PhD. Terminal master's awarded for partial completion of doctoral program. *Degree requirements:* For master's, thesis optional; for doctorate, comprehensive exam, thesis/dissertation. *Entrance requirements:* For master's and doctorate, GRE. Additional exam requirements/recommendations for international students: Recommended—TOEFL. Electronic applications accepted. *Faculty research:* Psychological/psychoanalytic

anthropology, gender and feminist anthropology, economic anthropology, medical anthropology, paleoanthropology.

**University of Mississippi,** Graduate School, College of Liberal Arts, University, MS 38677. Offers anthropology (MA); biology (MS, PhD); chemistry (MS, PhD); economics (MA, PhD); English (MA, PhD); experimental psychology (PhD); history (MA, PhD); mathematics (MS, PhD); modern languages (MA); music (MM); philosophy (MA); physics (MA, MS, PhD); political science (MA, PhD); studio art (MFA). *Program availability:* Part-time. *Faculty:* 472 full-time (263 women), 75 part-time/adjunct (35 women). *Students:* 415 full-time (210 women), 57 part-time (20 women); includes 70 minority (35 Black or African American, non-Hispanic/Latino; 13 Asian, non-Hispanic/Latino; 14 Hispanic/Latino; 8 Two or more races, non-Hispanic/Latino), 102 international. Average age 27. *Degree requirements:* For doctorate, thesis/dissertation. *Entrance requirements:* For master's, GRE General Test, minimum GPA of 3.0; for doctorate, GRE General Test. Additional exam requirements/recommendations for international students: Required—TOEFL. *Application deadline:* For fall admission, 4/1 for domestic students; for spring admission, 10/1 for domestic students. Applications are processed on a rolling basis. Application fee: $40. Electronic applications accepted. *Financial support:* Fellowships, research assistantships, teaching assistantships, career-related internships or fieldwork, Federal Work-Study, institutionally sponsored loans, scholarships/grants, and unspecified assistantships available. Financial award application deadline: 3/1; financial award applicants required to submit FAFSA. *Unit head:* Dr. Lee Michael Cohen, Dean, 662-915-7177, Fax: 662-915-5792, E-mail: libarts@olemiss.edu. *Application contact:* Dr. Christy M. Wyandt, Associate Dean of Graduate School, 662-915-7474, Fax: 662-915-7577, E-mail: cwyandt@olemiss.edu.
Website: https://www.olemiss.edu

**University of Missouri,** Office of Research and Graduate Studies, College of Arts and Science, Department of Anthropology, Columbia, MO 65211. Offers MA, PhD. *Faculty:* 12 full-time (4 women). *Students:* 33 full-time (19 women), 5 part-time (3 women); includes 6 minority (1 Black or African American, non-Hispanic/Latino; 1 Asian, non-Hispanic/Latino; 2 Hispanic/Latino; 2 Two or more races, non-Hispanic/Latino), 1 international. Average age 31. *Degree requirements:* For master's, thesis (for some programs); for doctorate, one foreign language, comprehensive exam, thesis/dissertation. *Entrance requirements:* For master's, GRE General Test (minimum score 1000 verbal and quantitative), minimum GPA of 3.25 in last 60 hours and in all anthropology courses; for doctorate, GRE General Test (minimum score 1000 verbal and quantitative), minimum GPA of 3.5 in previous graduate work. Additional exam requirements/recommendations for international students: Required—TOEFL (minimum score 500 paper-based; 61 iBT), IELTS (minimum score 5.5). *Application deadline:* For fall admission, 1/10 priority date for domestic and international students; for winter admission, 10/15 for domestic and international students. Applications are processed on a rolling basis. Application fee: $75 ($90 for international students). Electronic applications accepted. *Expenses:* Tuition, state resident: full-time $6347; part-time $352.60 per credit hour. Tuition, nonresident: full-time $17,379; part-time $965.50 per credit hour. *Required fees:* $1035. Tuition and fees vary according to course load, campus/location and program. *Financial support:* Fellowships with full tuition reimbursements, research assistantships with full tuition reimbursements, teaching assistantships with full tuition reimbursements, institutionally sponsored loans, scholarships/grants, health care benefits, and unspecified assistantships available. Support available to part-time students. *Faculty research:* Social/cultural anthropology, biological anthropology, archaeology.
Website: http://anthropology.missouri.edu/

**University of Montana,** Graduate School, College of Humanities and Sciences, Department of Anthropology, Missoula, MT 59812-0002. Offers anthropology (MA, PhD); applied anthropology (PhD); applied medical anthropology (MA); cultural heritage (MA, PhD); forensic anthropology (MA); linguistic anthropology (MA). *Degree requirements:* For master's, thesis (for some programs). *Entrance requirements:* For master's, GRE General Test. Additional exam requirements/recommendations for international students: Required—TOEFL. *Faculty research:* Historical preservation, plateau-plains archaeology and ethnohistory.

**University of Nebraska–Lincoln,** Graduate College, College of Arts and Sciences, Department of Anthropology and Geography, Program in Anthropology, Lincoln, NE 68588. Offers MA. *Degree requirements:* For master's, thesis optional. *Entrance requirements:* For master's, GRE General Test. Additional exam requirements/recommendations for international students: Required—TOEFL (minimum score 500 paper-based). Electronic applications accepted. *Faculty research:* Cultural, archaeologic, linguistic, and physical anthropology.

**University of Nevada, Las Vegas,** Graduate College, College of Liberal Arts, Department of Anthropology, Las Vegas, NV 89154-5003. Offers MA, PhD. *Program availability:* Part-time. *Faculty:* 13 full-time (4 women). *Students:* 29 full-time (16 women), 14 part-time (8 women); includes 12 minority (2 Asian, non-Hispanic/Latino; 7 Hispanic/Latino; 3 Two or more races, non-Hispanic/Latino). Average age 32. 48 applicants, 31% accepted, 10 enrolled. In 2016, 11 master's awarded. *Degree requirements:* For master's, thesis, oral defense of thesis; for doctorate, comprehensive exam, thesis/dissertation, oral defense of dissertation. *Entrance requirements:* For master's, GRE General Test, 18 semester credit hours in anthropology with minimum GPA of 3.0; research paper; letter of intent; 3 letters of recommendation; for doctorate, GRE General Test, minimum GPA of 3.5 for previous graduate work; example of previous work; statement of intent; 3 letters of recommendation. Additional exam requirements/recommendations for international students: Required—TOEFL (minimum score 550 paper-based; 80 iBT), IELTS (minimum score 7). *Application deadline:* For fall admission, 2/1 for domestic students. Application fee: $60 ($95 for international students). Electronic applications accepted. *Expenses:* $269.25 per credit, $792 per 3-credit course; $9,634 per year resident; $23,274 per year non-resident; $7,094 fees non-resident (7 credits or more); $1,307 annual health insurance fee. *Financial support:* In 2016–17, 3 fellowships with partial tuition reimbursements (averaging $18,333 per year), 7 research assistantships with partial tuition reimbursements (averaging $14,500 per year), 14 teaching assistantships with partial tuition reimbursements (averaging $15,250 per year) were awarded; institutionally sponsored loans, scholarships/grants, health care benefits, and unspecified assistantships also available. Financial award application deadline: 3/15. *Faculty research:* Food and nutrition, adaptive strategies, childhood and parenting, sexuality, gender and identity. *Total annual research expenditures:* $127,206. *Unit head:* Dr. Barbara Roth, Chair/Professor, 702-895-3646, Fax: 702-895-4823, E-mail: barbara.roth@unlv.edu. *Application contact:* Dr. Peter Gray, Graduate Coordinator, 702-895-3586, Fax: 702-895-4823, E-mail: peter.gray@unlv.edu.
Website: http://anthro.unlv.edu/

**University of Nevada, Reno,** Graduate School, College of Liberal Arts, Department of Anthropology, Reno, NV 89557. Offers MA, PhD. Terminal master's awarded for partial completion of doctoral program. *Degree requirements:* For master's, thesis; for doctorate, thesis/dissertation. *Entrance requirements:* For master's, GRE, minimum GPA of 2.75; for doctorate, GRE, minimum GPA of 3.0. Additional exam requirements/recommendations for international students: Required—TOEFL (minimum score 500 paper-based; 61 iBT), IELTS (minimum score 6). Electronic applications accepted.

*Anthropology*

*Faculty research:* Ethnology, linguistics, cultural/medical/religious/ethnic relations, ecological anthropology, historical anthropology.

**University of New Brunswick Fredericton,** School of Graduate Studies, Faculty of Arts, Department of Anthropology, Fredericton, NB E3B 5A3, Canada. Offers MA. *Program availability:* Part-time. *Degree requirements:* For master's, thesis. *Entrance requirements:* For master's, minimum GPA of 3.0. Additional exam requirements/recommendations for international students: Required—TOEFL. Electronic applications accepted. *Faculty research:* Medical anthropology, anthropology of education, community-based fisheries, maritime archaeology, world prehistory, geoarchaeology, zooarchaeology socio-cultural anthropology, bioarchaeology, forensics, globalization, legal anthropology.

**University of New Mexico,** Graduate Studies, College of Arts and Sciences, Program in Anthropology, Albuquerque, NM 87131-2039. Offers archaeology (MA, MS, PhD); ethnology (MA, MS, PhD); evolutionary anthropology (PhD); public archaeology (MA, MS, PhD). *Faculty:* 24 full-time (13 women). *Students:* 38 full-time (29 women), 68 part-time (39 women); includes 24 minority (3 American Indian or Alaska Native, non-Hispanic/Latino; 2 Asian, non-Hispanic/Latino; 14 Hispanic/Latino; 5 Two or more races, non-Hispanic/Latino), 9 international. Average age 33. 67 applicants, 46% accepted, 18 enrolled. In 2016, 18 master's, 14 doctorates awarded. Terminal master's awarded for partial completion of doctoral program. *Degree requirements:* For master's, comprehensive exam (for some programs), thesis or alternative, 1-2 exams; for doctorate, one foreign language, comprehensive exam, thesis/dissertation, exam, proposal, oral defense, skill and/or second language. *Entrance requirements:* For master's and doctorate, GRE General Test, 3 letters of recommendation, letter of interest, transcripts. Additional exam requirements/recommendations for international students: Required—TOEFL (minimum score 550 paper-based), IELTS (minimum score 7). *Application deadline:* For fall admission, 1/4 for domestic and international students. Application fee: $50. Electronic applications accepted. *Financial support:* Fellowships, research assistantships with partial tuition reimbursements, teaching assistantships with partial tuition reimbursements, career-related internships or fieldwork, Federal Work-Study, institutionally sponsored loans, scholarships/grants, traineeships, health care benefits, tuition waivers (partial), and unspecified assistantships available. Support available to part-time students. Financial award application deadline: 3/1; financial award applicants required to submit FAFSA. *Faculty research:* Ethnology, archaeology, evolutionary anthropology, environment, water and land use, gender and social frameworks, Greater Southwest, Latin America, political economy, public anthropology. *Total annual research expenditures:* $875,790. *Unit head:* Michael W. Graves, Chair, 505-277-4524, Fax: 505-277-0874, E-mail: mwgraves@unm.edu. *Application contact:* Erika E. Gerety, Program Advisement Coordinator, 505-277-2732, Fax: 505-277-0874, E-mail: erika@unm.edu.
Website: http://www.unm.edu/~anthro/

**The University of North Carolina at Chapel Hill,** Graduate School, College of Arts and Sciences, Department of Anthropology, Chapel Hill, NC 27599-3115. Offers MA, PhD. Terminal master's awarded for partial completion of doctoral program. *Degree requirements:* For master's, variable foreign language requirement, thesis; for doctorate, variable foreign language requirement, comprehensive exam, thesis/dissertation. *Entrance requirements:* For master's and doctorate, GRE General Test, minimum GPA of 3.0. Additional exam requirements/recommendations for international students: Required—TOEFL. Electronic applications accepted. *Faculty research:* Archeology, ecology and evolution, medical anthropology, social systems, anthropology of meaning.

**The University of North Carolina at Charlotte,** College of Liberal Arts and Sciences, Department of Anthropology, Charlotte, NC 28223-0001. Offers MA. *Program availability:* Part-time. *Faculty:* 12 full-time (8 women), 1 part-time/adjunct (0 women). *Students:* 9 full-time (4 women), 9 part-time (8 women); includes 3 minority (1 Black or African American, non-Hispanic/Latino; 1 Hispanic/Latino; 1 Two or more races, non-Hispanic/Latino). Average age 29. 13 applicants, 92% accepted, 9 enrolled. In 2016, 4 master's awarded. *Degree requirements:* For master's, thesis or alternative, research thesis or applied practicum and project report. *Entrance requirements:* For master's, GRE, three letters of recommendation from individuals who can comment on candidate's academic and professional promise, at least two from academic referees; statement of purpose that discusses applicant's specific interests in anthropology and professional goals; transcripts from all colleges or universities attended. Additional exam requirements/recommendations for international students: Required—TOEFL (minimum score 523 paper-based, 70 iBT) or IELTS (6.5). *Application deadline:* For fall admission, 3/1 priority date for domestic and international students. Applications are processed on a rolling basis. Application fee: $75. Electronic applications accepted. *Expenses:* Tuition, state resident: full-time $4252. Tuition, nonresident: full-time $17,423. *Required fees:* $3026. Tuition and fees vary according to course load and program. *Financial support:* In 2016–17, 7 students received support, including 2 research assistantships (averaging $10,500 per year), 5 teaching assistantships (averaging $8,130 per year); institutionally sponsored loans, scholarships/grants, and unspecified assistantships also available. Support available to part-time students. Financial award application deadline: 3/1. *Faculty research:* Impact of environment on the social strategies and reproductive careers of Sifaka; molecular anthropology: the application of genetic data; family abuse and women's health; aging cross-culturally; production and circulation of knowledge in material form; the relationship among knowledge, power, policy and practice as they pertain to health and health care; the development of ranked societies in prehistory. *Total annual research expenditures:* $118,543. *Unit head:* Dr. Steven Falconer, Chair, 704-687-7459, E-mail: sfalcon1@uncc.edu. *Application contact:* Kathy B. Giddings, Director of Graduate Admissions, 704-687-5503, Fax: 704-687-1668, E-mail: gradadm@uncc.edu.
Website: http://anthropology.uncc.edu/

**University of North Georgia,** Department of History, Anthropology and Philosophy, Dahlonega, GA 30597. Offers history (MA), including American history, military history, world history. *Program availability:* Part-time, evening/weekend. *Faculty:* 11 full-time (4 women), 1 part-time/adjunct. *Students:* 4 full-time (0 women), 11 part-time (5 women); includes 1 minority (Two or more races, non-Hispanic/Latino). Average age 32. 12 applicants, 92% accepted, 11 enrolled. In 2016, 2 master's awarded. *Degree requirements:* For master's, thesis optional. *Entrance requirements:* For master's, GRE, 3 recommendations, writing sample, letter of intent, minimum GPA of 2.75. Additional exam requirements/recommendations for international students: Required—TOEFL (minimum score 550 paper-based; 79 iBT), IELTS (minimum score 6.5). *Application deadline:* For fall admission, 4/15 priority date for domestic students, 7/1 priority date for international students. Applications are processed on a rolling basis. Application fee: $40. Electronic applications accepted. *Expenses:* Contact institution. *Financial support:* Unspecified assistantships available. Financial award application deadline: 3/17; financial award applicants required to submit FAFSA. *Unit head:* Dr. Jeff Pardue, Department Head, 678-717-3867. *Application contact:* Melinda Maxwell, Director of Graduate Admissions, 706-864-1543, E-mail: melinda.maxwell@ung.edu.
Website: http://ung.edu/history-anthropology-philosophy/

**University of North Texas,** Robert B. Toulouse School of Graduate Studies, Denton, TX 76203-5459. Offers accounting (MS); applied anthropology (MA, MS); applied behavior analysis (Certificate); applied geography (MA); applied technology and performance improvement (M Ed, MS); art education (MA); art history (MA); art museum education (Certificate); arts leadership (Certificate); audiology (Au D); behavior analysis (MS); behavioral science (PhD); biochemistry and molecular biology (MS); biology (MA, MS); biomedical engineering (MS); business analysis (MS); chemistry (MS); clinical health psychology (PhD); communication studies (MA, MS); computer engineering (MS); computer science (MS); counseling (M Ed, MS), including clinical mental health counseling (MS), college and university counseling, elementary school counseling, secondary school counseling; creative writing (MA); criminal justice (MS); curriculum and instruction (M Ed); decision sciences (MBA); design (MA, MFA), including fashion design (MFA), innovation studies, interior design (MFA); early childhood studies (MS); economics (MS); educational leadership (M Ed, Ed D); educational psychology (MS, PhD), including family studies (MS), gifted and talented (MS), human development (MS), learning and cognition (MS), research, measurement and evaluation (MS); electrical engineering (MS); emergency management (MPA); engineering technology (MS); English (MA); English as a second language (MA); environmental science (MS); finance (MBA, MS); financial management (MPA); French (MA); health services management (MBA); higher education (M Ed, Ed D); history (MA, MS); hospitality management (MS); human resources management (MPA); information science (MS); information systems (PhD); information technologies (MBA); interdisciplinary studies (MA, MS); international studies (MA); international sustainable tourism (MS); jazz studies (MM); journalism (MA, MJ, Graduate Certificate), including interactive and virtual digital communication (Graduate Certificate), narrative journalism (Graduate Certificate), public relations (Graduate Certificate); kinesiology (MS); linguistics (MA); local government management (MPA); logistics (PhD); logistics and supply chain management (MBA); long-term care, senior housing, and aging services (MA); management (PhD); marketing (MBA); mathematics (MA, MS); mechanical and energy engineering (MS, PhD); music (MA), including ethnomusicology, music theory, musicology, performance; music composition (PhD); music education (MM Ed, PhD); nonprofit management (MPA); operations and supply chain management (MBA); performance (MM, DMA); philosophy (MA); political science (MA); professional and technical communication (MA); radio, television and film (MA, MFA); rehabilitation counseling (Certificate); sociology (MA); Spanish (MA); special education (M Ed); speech-language pathology (MA); strategic management (MBA); studio art (MFA); teaching (M Ed); MBA/MS. *Program availability:* Part-time, evening/weekend, online learning. Terminal master's awarded for partial completion of doctoral program. *Degree requirements:* For master's, variable foreign language requirement, comprehensive exam (for some programs), thesis (for some programs); for doctorate, variable foreign language requirement, comprehensive exam (for some programs), thesis/dissertation; for other advanced degree, variable foreign language requirement, comprehensive exam (for some programs). *Entrance requirements:* For master's and doctorate, GRE, GMAT. Additional exam requirements/recommendations for international students: Required—TOEFL (minimum score 550 paper-based; 79 iBT). Electronic applications accepted.

**University of Oklahoma,** College of Arts and Sciences, Department of Anthropology, Norman, OK 73019. Offers anthropology (MA, PhD); applied linguistic anthropology (MA); archaeology (PhD); health and human biology (PhD); socio-cultural and linguistics (PhD); socio-cultural anthropology (MA). *Faculty:* 29 full-time (12 women). *Students:* 22 full-time (15 women), 27 part-time (19 women); includes 9 minority (6 American Indian or Alaska Native, non-Hispanic/Latino; 1 Hispanic/Latino; 2 Two or more races, non-Hispanic/Latino), 2 international. Average age 32. 36 applicants, 36% accepted, 7 enrolled. In 2016, 9 master's, 4 doctorates awarded. *Degree requirements:* For master's, one foreign language, thesis; for doctorate, comprehensive exam, thesis/dissertation. *Entrance requirements:* For master's and doctorate, GRE, minimum undergraduate GPA of 3.0; statement of purpose; 2 letters of recommendation. Additional exam requirements/recommendations for international students: Required—TOEFL (minimum score 79 iBT) or IELTS (minimum score 6.5). *Application deadline:* For spring admission, 2/15 for domestic and international students. Application fee: $50 ($100 for international students). Electronic applications accepted. *Expenses:* Tuition, state resident: full-time $4886; part-time $203.60 per credit hour. Tuition, nonresident: full-time $18,989; part-time $791.20 per credit hour. *Required fees:* $3283; $126.25 per credit hour. $126.50 per semester. *Financial support:* In 2016–17, 44 students received support, including 1 fellowship (averaging $5,000 per year), 2 research assistantships with full tuition reimbursements available (averaging $14,670 per year), 8 teaching assistantships with full tuition reimbursements available (averaging $15,295 per year); career-related internships or fieldwork, Federal Work-Study, institutionally sponsored loans, health care benefits, and unspecified assistantships also available. Financial award application deadline: 6/1; financial award applicants required to submit FAFSA. *Faculty research:* North American archaeology; linguistics including applied; health and human biology; sociocultural anthropology; native North America. *Total annual research expenditures:* $657,637. *Unit head:* Dr. Diane Warren, Associate Professor and Department Chair, 405-325-7609, Fax: 405-325-7386, E-mail: dmwarren@ou.edu. *Application contact:* Dr. Patrick Livingood, Associate Professor/Graduate Liaison, 405-397-0215, Fax: 405-325-7386, E-mail: patrickl@ou.edu.
Website: http://cas.ou.edu/anthropology

**University of Oregon,** Graduate School, College of Arts and Sciences, Department of Anthropology, Eugene, OR 97403. Offers MA, MS, PhD. Terminal master's awarded for partial completion of doctoral program. *Degree requirements:* For master's, one foreign language; for doctorate, 2 foreign languages, thesis/dissertation. *Entrance requirements:* For master's and doctorate, GRE General Test. Additional exam requirements/recommendations for international students: Required—TOEFL. *Faculty research:* Prehistory, primatology, cultural anthropology of Native Americans, human evolution, Africa.

**University of Ottawa,** Faculty of Graduate and Postdoctoral Studies, Faculty of Social Sciences, Department of Sociology and Anthropology, Ottawa, ON K1N 6N5, Canada. Offers MA. *Degree requirements:* For master's, thesis or alternative. *Entrance requirements:* For master's, honors bachelor's degree or equivalent, minimum B average. Electronic applications accepted. *Faculty research:* Inter-ethnic relations, development, political policies.

**University of Pennsylvania,** School of Arts and Sciences, Graduate Group in Anthropology, Philadelphia, PA 19104. Offers AM, MS, PhD. *Faculty:* 18 full-time (6 women), 11 part-time/adjunct (7 women). *Students:* 59 full-time (38 women), 5 part-time (4 women); includes 8 minority (3 Black or African American, non-Hispanic/Latino; 1 Asian, non-Hispanic/Latino; 2 Hispanic/Latino; 2 Two or more races, non-Hispanic/Latino), 12 international. Average age 30. 158 applicants, 7% accepted, 8 enrolled. In 2016, 1 master's, 10 doctorates awarded. Terminal master's awarded for partial completion of doctoral program. *Expenses: Tuition:* Full-time $31,068; part-time $5762 per course. *Required fees:* $3200; $336 per course. Full-time tuition and fees vary according to degree level, program and student level. Part-time tuition and fees vary according to course load, degree level and program.
Website: http://www.sas.upenn.edu/graduate-division

**University of Pittsburgh,** Dietrich School of Arts and Sciences, Department of Anthropology, Pittsburgh, PA 15260. Offers MA, PhD. *Program availability:* Part-time, evening/weekend, online learning. *Faculty:* 20 full-time (9 women), 5 part-time/adjunct (1 woman). *Students:* 62 full-time (41 women), 1 (woman) part-time; includes 4 minority (2

Black or African American, non-Hispanic/Latino; 2 Hispanic/Latino), 32 international. Average age 24. 107 applicants, 11% accepted, 5 enrolled. In 2016, 4 doctorates awarded. Terminal master's awarded for partial completion of doctoral program. *Degree requirements:* For master's, one foreign language, thesis or alternative; for doctorate, thesis/dissertation. *Entrance requirements:* For master's and doctorate, GRE General Test. Additional exam requirements/recommendations for international students: Required—TOEFL (minimum score 550 paper-based; 90 iBT), IELTS (minimum score 6.5). *Application deadline:* For fall admission, 1/15 for domestic and international students. Applications are processed on a rolling basis. Application fee: $50. Electronic applications accepted. Tuition and fees vary according to program. *Financial support:* In 2016–17, 49 students received support, including 23 fellowships with full tuition reimbursements available (averaging $22,042 per year), 2 research assistantships with full tuition reimbursements available (averaging $14,620 per year), 24 teaching assistantships with full tuition reimbursements available (averaging $18,620 per year); career-related internships or fieldwork, Federal Work-Study, scholarships/grants, health care benefits, tuition waivers (full), and unspecified assistantships also available. Financial award application deadline: 1/15. *Faculty research:* Conflict studies; ethnicity, nationalism, and the state; Latin American archaeology; human evolutionary biology. *Total annual research expenditures:* $94,617. *Unit head:* Dr. Bryan Hanks, Chair, 412-648-7530, E-mail: bkh5@pitt.edu. *Application contact:* Phyllis J. Deasy, Graduate Administrator, 412-648-7504, E-mail: pdeasy@pitt.edu.
Website: http://www.anthropology.pitt.edu

**University of Regina,** Faculty of Graduate Studies and Research, Faculty of Arts, Department of Anthropology, Regina, SK S4S 0A2, Canada. Offers MA. Offered as a special case program. *Program availability:* Part-time. *Faculty:* 6 full-time (2 women), 1 part-time/adjunct (0 women). *Students:* 1 full-time (0 women). 1 applicant, 100% accepted. *Degree requirements:* For master's, thesis. *Entrance requirements:* Additional exam requirements/recommendations for international students: Required—TOEFL (minimum score 580 paper-based; 80 iBT), IELTS (minimum score 6.5), PTE (minimum score 59). *Application deadline:* Applications are processed on a rolling basis. Application fee: $100. Electronic applications accepted. *Financial support:* Fellowships, teaching assistantships, and scholarships/grants available. Financial award application deadline: 6/15. *Unit head:* Dr. Tabias Sperlich, Department Head, 306-585-4773, E-mail: tobias.sperlich@uregina.ca.
Website: http://www.uregina.ca/arts/anthropology/

**University of Rhode Island,** Graduate School, College of Arts and Sciences, Department of History, Kingston, RI 02881. Offers archaeology and anthropology (MA); history (MA), including European history, United States history; MLIS/MA. *Program availability:* Part-time. *Faculty:* 16 full-time (7 women). *Students:* 11 full-time (5 women), 3 part-time (2 women). In 2016, 7 master's awarded. *Degree requirements:* For master's, comprehensive exam (for some programs), thesis optional. *Entrance requirements:* For master's, GRE, 2 letters of recommendation. Additional exam requirements/recommendations for international students: Required—TOEFL. *Application deadline:* For fall admission, 7/15 for domestic students, 2/1 for international students; for spring admission, 11/15 for domestic students, 7/15 for international students; for summer admission, 4/15 for domestic students. Application fee: $65. Electronic applications accepted. *Expenses:* Tuition, state resident: full-time $11,796; part-time $655 per credit. Tuition, nonresident: full-time $24,206; part-time $1345 per credit. *Required fees:* $1546; $44 per credit. One-time fee: $155 full-time; $35 part-time. *Financial support:* In 2016–17, 4 teaching assistantships with tuition reimbursements (averaging $15,036 per year) were awarded. Financial award application deadline: 2/1; financial award applicants required to submit FAFSA. *Unit head:* Dr. Rod Mather, Chair, 401-874-4093, E-mail: rodmather@uri.edu. *Application contact:* Dr. Erik Loomis, Acting Director of Graduate Studies, 401-874-4078, E-mail: eloomis@uri.edu.
Website: http://www.uri.edu/artsci/his/

**University of Saskatchewan,** College of Graduate Studies and Research, College of Arts and Science, Department of Religion and Culture, Saskatoon, SK S7N 5A2, Canada. Offers MA. *Degree requirements:* For master's, thesis. *Entrance requirements:* Additional exam requirements/recommendations for international students: Required—TOEFL (minimum score 80 iBT); Recommended—IELTS (minimum score 6.5). Electronic applications accepted.

**University of South Africa,** College of Human Sciences, Pretoria, South Africa. Offers adult education (M Ed); African languages (MA, PhD); African politics (MA, PhD); Afrikaans (MA, PhD); ancient history (MA, PhD); ancient Near Eastern studies (MA, PhD); anthropology (MA, PhD); applied linguistics (MA); Arabic (MA, PhD); archaeology (MA); art history (MA); Biblical archaeology (MA); Biblical studies (M Th, D Th, PhD); Christian spirituality (M Th, D Th); church history (M Th, D Th); classical studies (MA, PhD); clinical psychology (MA); communication (MA, PhD); comparative education (M Ed, Ed D); consulting psychology (D Admin, D Com, PhD); curriculum studies (M Ed, Ed D); development studies (M Admin, MA, D Admin, PhD); didactics (M Ed, Ed D); education (M Tech); education management (M Ed, Ed D); educational psychology (M Ed); English (MA); environmental education (M Ed); French (MA, PhD); German (MA, PhD); Greek (MA); guidance and counseling (M Ed); health studies (MA, PhD), including health sciences education (MA), health services management (MA), medical and surgical nursing science (critical care general) (MA), midwifery and neonatal nursing science (MA), trauma and emergency care (MA); history (MA, PhD); history of education (Ed D); inclusive education (M Ed, Ed D); information and communications technology policy and regulation (MA); information science (MA, MIS, PhD); international politics (MA, PhD); Islamic studies (MA, PhD); Italian (MA, PhD); Judaica (MA, PhD); linguistics (MA, PhD); mathematical education (M Ed); mathematics education (MA); missiology (M Th, D Th); modern Hebrew (MA, PhD); musicology (MA, MMus, D Mus, PhD); natural science education (M Ed); New Testament (M Th, D Th); Old Testament (D Th); pastoral therapy (M Th, D Th); philosophy (MA); philosophy of education (M Ed, Ed D); politics (MA, PhD); Portuguese (MA, PhD); practical theology (M Th, D Th); psychology (MA, MS, PhD); psychology of education (M Ed, Ed D); public health (MA); religious studies (MA, D Th, PhD); Romance languages (MA); Russian (MA, PhD); Semitic languages (MA, PhD); social behavior studies in HIV/AIDS (MA); social science (mental health) (MA); social science in development studies (MA); social science in psychology (MA); social science in social work (MA); social science in sociology (MA); social work (MSW, DSW, PhD); socio-education (M Ed, Ed D); sociolinguistics (MA); sociology (MA, PhD); Spanish (MA, PhD); systematic theology (M Th, D Th); TESOL (teaching English to speakers of other languages) (MA); theological ethics (M Th, D Th); theory of literature (MA, PhD); urban ministries (D Th); urban ministry (M Th).

**University of South Carolina,** The Graduate School, College of Arts and Sciences, Department of Anthropology, Columbia, SC 29208. Offers MA, PhD. Terminal master's awarded for partial completion of doctoral program. *Degree requirements:* For master's, comprehensive exam, thesis; for doctorate, comprehensive exam, thesis/dissertation. *Entrance requirements:* For master's and doctorate, GRE General Test, letters of reference. Additional exam requirements/recommendations for international students: Required—TOEFL. Electronic applications accepted. *Faculty research:* Biocultural anthropology, archaeology, cultural anthropology.

**University of Southern Mississippi,** Graduate School, College of Arts and Letters, Department of Anthropology and Sociology, Hattiesburg, MS 39406. Offers

anthropology (MA). *Program availability:* Part-time. *Degree requirements:* For master's, one foreign language, comprehensive exam, thesis (for some programs). *Entrance requirements:* For master's, GRE General Test, minimum GPA of 2.75 in last 2 years, 3.0 in field of study. Additional exam requirements/recommendations for international students: Required—TOEFL, IELTS. *Application deadline:* For fall admission, 3/15 priority date for domestic students, 3/1 for international students. Applications are processed on a rolling basis. Application fee: $60. *Expenses:* Tuition, area resident: Full-time $15,708; part-time $437 per credit hour. *Financial support:* Research assistantships with full tuition reimbursements, teaching assistantships with full tuition reimbursements, career-related internships or fieldwork, Federal Work-Study, institutionally sponsored loans, scholarships/grants, and unspecified assistantships available. Financial award application deadline: 3/15; financial award applicants required to submit FAFSA. *Faculty research:* Archaeology of North America, historic archaeology, bio archaeology, ethnography of Europe, ethnography of Africa. *Unit head:* Ann Marie Kinnell, Chair, 601-266-4306, Fax: 601-266-6373, E-mail: ann.kinnell@usm.edu.
Website: https://www.usm.edu/anthropology-sociology

**University of South Florida,** College of Arts and Sciences, Department of Anthropology, Tampa, FL 33620-9951. Offers applied anthropology (MA, PhD), including archaeological and forensic sciences, biocultural medical anthropology, cultural resource management, heritage studies; medical anthropology (Graduate Certificate). *Program availability:* Part-time. *Faculty:* 23 full-time (14 women). *Students:* 70 full-time (52 women), 41 part-time (28 women); includes 28 minority (6 Black or African American, non-Hispanic/Latino; 2 Asian, non-Hispanic/Latino; 16 Hispanic/Latino; 1 Native Hawaiian or other Pacific Islander, non-Hispanic/Latino; 3 Two or more races, non-Hispanic/Latino), 6 international. Average age 31. 130 applicants, 34% accepted, 18 enrolled. In 2016, 15 master's, 11 doctorates awarded. *Degree requirements:* For master's, one foreign language, comprehensive exam, thesis; for doctorate, one foreign language, comprehensive exam, thesis/dissertation. *Entrance requirements:* For master's and doctorate, GRE, minimum GPA of 3.0, 3 letters of recommendation, statement of purpose, signed research ethics statement, resume or curriculum vitae; for Graduate Certificate, bachelor's degree with minimum GPA of 3.0. Additional exam requirements/recommendations for international students: Required—TOEFL (minimum score 550 paper-based; 79 iBT) or IELTS (minimum score 6.5). *Application deadline:* For fall admission, 12/15 for domestic and international students. Application fee: $30. Electronic applications accepted. *Expenses:* Tuition, state resident: full-time $7766; part-time $431.43 per credit hour. Tuition, nonresident: full-time $15,789; part-time $877.17 per credit hour. *Required fees:* $37 per term. *Financial support:* In 2016–17, 32 students received support, including 14 research assistantships with tuition reimbursements available (averaging $14,475 per year), 52 teaching assistantships with partial tuition reimbursements available (averaging $12,540 per year); scholarships/grants and tuition waivers (partial) also available. Financial award application deadline: 1/15; financial award applicants required to submit FAFSA. *Faculty research:* Biocultural medical anthropology; archaeology and culture resource management in the Americas; community identity and heritage; urban community issues; verbal and nonverbal communications in media and education; global dynamics of sustainable resource management and economic development; social and cultural constructions of race, ethnicity, and gender. *Total annual research expenditures:* $1.1 million. *Unit head:* Dr. David Himmelgreen, Professor/Department Chairperson, 813-974-2138, Fax: 813-974-2668, E-mail: dhimmelg@usf.edu. *Application contact:* Dr. Heide Castaneda, Assistant Professor and Graduate Director, 813-974-2138, Fax: 813-974-2668, E-mail: hcastaneda@usf.edu.
Website: http://anthropology.usf.edu/graduate/

**The University of Tennessee,** Graduate School, College of Arts and Sciences, Department of Anthropology, Knoxville, TN 37996. Offers archaeology (MA, PhD); biological anthropology (MA, PhD); cultural anthropology (MA, PhD); zoo-archaeology (MA, PhD). *Degree requirements:* For master's, thesis; for doctorate, one foreign language, thesis/dissertation. *Entrance requirements:* For master's and doctorate, GRE General Test, minimum GPA of 2.7. Additional exam requirements/recommendations for international students: Required—TOEFL. Electronic applications accepted.

**The University of Texas at Arlington,** Graduate School, College of Liberal Arts, Department of Sociology and Anthropology, Program in Anthropology, Arlington, TX 79019. Offers MA. *Program availability:* Part-time, evening/weekend. *Degree requirements:* For master's, comprehensive exam, thesis or alternative. *Entrance requirements:* For master's, GRE General Test, minimum GPA of 3.0, 3 letters of recommendation. Additional exam requirements/recommendations for international students: Required—TOEFL (minimum score 550 paper-based). *Application deadline:* For fall admission, 6/15 priority date for domestic students. Applications are processed on a rolling basis. Application fee: $35 ($50 for international students). Electronic applications accepted. *Financial support:* Fellowships, teaching assistantships, Federal Work-Study, and institutionally sponsored loans available. Financial award application deadline: 6/1; financial award applicants required to submit FAFSA. *Unit head:* Dr. Shelley Smith, Chairman, 817-272-2650, Fax: 817-272-3759, E-mail: slsmith@uta.edu. *Application contact:* Dr. Joci Ryan, Graduate Advisor, 817-272-3765, Fax: 817-272-3759, E-mail: jcryan@uta.edu.
Website: http://www.uta.edu/sociology-anthropology

**The University of Texas at Austin,** Graduate School, College of Liberal Arts, Department of Anthropology, Austin, TX 78712-1111. Offers archaeology (MA, PhD); cultural forms (MA, PhD); linguistic anthropology (MA, PhD); physical anthropology (MA, PhD); social anthropology (MA, PhD). *Program availability:* Part-time. Terminal master's awarded for partial completion of doctoral program. *Degree requirements:* For master's, thesis; for doctorate, one foreign language, thesis/dissertation. *Entrance requirements:* For master's and doctorate, GRE General Test. Additional exam requirements/recommendations for international students: Required—TOEFL. Electronic applications accepted.

**The University of Texas at El Paso,** Graduate School, College of Liberal Arts, Department of Sociology and Anthropology, El Paso, TX 79968-0001. Offers applied anthropology (Certificate); applied social sciences (Certificate); sociology (MA). *Program availability:* Part-time, evening/weekend. *Degree requirements:* For master's, thesis. *Entrance requirements:* For master's, GRE General Test, minimum GPA of 3.0. Additional exam requirements/recommendations for international students: Required—TOEFL. Electronic applications accepted. *Faculty research:* U.S.-Mexico border, social inequality, immigration, Chicano culture, Mexico.

**The University of Texas at San Antonio,** College of Liberal and Fine Arts, Department of Anthropology, San Antonio, TX 78249-0617. Offers MA, PhD. *Program availability:* Part-time. *Faculty:* 11 full-time (5 women), 2 part-time/adjunct (0 women). *Students:* 9 full-time (6 women), 48 part-time (33 women); includes 16 minority (1 Asian, non-Hispanic/Latino; 14 Hispanic/Latino; 1 Two or more races, non-Hispanic/Latino), 3 international. Average age 33. 24 applicants, 54% accepted, 5 enrolled. In 2016, 8 master's, 2 doctorates awarded. Terminal master's awarded for partial completion of doctoral program. *Degree requirements:* For master's, comprehensive exam, thesis; for doctorate, comprehensive exam, thesis/dissertation, proficiency in foreign language, statistics, or computer programming. *Entrance requirements:* For master's, GRE

*Anthropology*

General Test, minimum GPA of 3.3 during last 60 hours (preferred), 18 hours in major field, three letters of recommendation, statement of purpose, writing sample; for doctorate, GRE General Test, minimum GPA of 3.3 (preferred), transcripts from all colleges and universities attended, 3 letters of recommendation, statement of purpose, writing sample. Additional exam requirements/recommendations for international students: Required—TOEFL (minimum score 550 paper-based; 79 iBT), IELTS (minimum score 6.5). *Application deadline:* For fall admission, 7/1 for domestic students, 4/1 for international students; for spring admission, 11/1 for domestic students, 9/1 for international students. Application fee: $45 ($80 for international students). Electronic applications accepted. *Expenses:* Contact institution. *Financial support:* In 2016–17, 30 students received support, including 3 fellowships (averaging $20,000 per year), 1 research assistantship (averaging $9,600 per year), 14 teaching assistantships (averaging $8,750 per year); scholarships/grants and unspecified assistantships also available. *Faculty research:* Political and cultural ecology, the archaeology of complexity, indigenous and environmental politics, primate and evolutionary ecology, medical anthropology. *Total annual research expenditures:* $853,580. *Unit head:* Dr. Jason Yaeger, Chair and Professor of Anthropology, 210-458-4075, Fax: 210-458-7811, E-mail: jason.yeager@utsa.edu.
Website: http://colfa.utsa.edu/ant/

**The University of Texas Rio Grande Valley,** College of Liberal Arts, Department of Sociology and Anthropology, Edinburg, TX 78539. Offers MS. *Program availability:* Part-time, evening/weekend, online learning. *Entrance requirements:* For master's, GRE General Test, minimum undergraduate GPA of 3.0, bachelor's degree, official transcripts, personal statement, two letters of recommendation. Tuition and fees vary according to course load and program. *Faculty research:* Sociology of education, sociology of health, sociology of religion, migration, race and ethnicity, gender, border studies, disaster studies.

**University of Toronto,** School of Graduate Studies, Faculty of Arts and Science, Department of Anthropology, Toronto, ON M5S 1A1, Canada. Offers M Sc, MA, PhD. *Program availability:* Part-time. *Degree requirements:* For master's, research paper; for doctorate, one foreign language, thesis/dissertation, comprehensive exam, thesis defense. *Entrance requirements:* For master's, minimum B+ average, 5 full-year anthropology courses, 2 letters of reference, statement of interest; for doctorate, minimum B+ average, master's degree in relevant area, resume, 2 letters of reference, statement of interest. Additional exam requirements/recommendations for international students: Required—TOEFL (minimum score 580 paper-based; 93 iBT), IELTS (minimum score 7), TWE (minimum score 5), Michigan English Language Assessment Battery (minimum score 85), or COPE (minimum score 4). Electronic applications accepted.

**The University of Tulsa,** Graduate School, Kendall College of Arts and Sciences, Department of Anthropology, Tulsa, OK 74104-3189. Offers MA, PhD, JD/MA. *Program availability:* Part-time. *Faculty:* 9 full-time (1 woman), 2 part-time/adjunct (0 women). *Students:* 14 full-time (11 women), 3 part-time (all women); includes 4 minority (1 Black or African American, non-Hispanic/Latino; 1 American Indian or Alaska Native, non-Hispanic/Latino; 2 Two or more races, non-Hispanic/Latino), 2 international. Average age 33. 9 applicants, 56% accepted, 4 enrolled. In 2016, 5 master's awarded. Terminal master's awarded for partial completion of doctoral program. *Degree requirements:* For master's, thesis (for some programs); for doctorate, comprehensive exam, thesis/dissertation. *Entrance requirements:* For master's, GRE General Test. Additional exam requirements/recommendations for international students: Required—TOEFL (minimum score 577 paper-based; 91 iBT), IELTS (minimum score 6.5). *Application deadline:* Applications are processed on a rolling basis. Application fee: $55. Electronic applications accepted. *Expenses: Tuition:* Full-time $22,230; part-time $1235 per credit hour. *Required fees:* $990 per semester. Tuition and fees vary according to course load. *Financial support:* In 2016–17, 16 students received support, including 3 fellowships with full tuition reimbursements available (averaging $1,479 per year), 1 research assistantship with full tuition reimbursement available (averaging $9,226 per year), 10 teaching assistantships with full tuition reimbursements available (averaging $12,467 per year); career-related internships or fieldwork, Federal Work-Study, scholarships/grants, health care benefits, tuition waivers (full and partial), and unspecified assistantships also available. Support available to part-time students. Financial award application deadline: 2/1; financial award applicants required to submit FAFSA. *Faculty research:* Archaeology, paleoanthropology, zoo archaeology, Native American studies, ecological archaeology, lithic analysis, cultural anthropology. *Total annual research expenditures:* $144,476. *Unit head:* Dr. Peter Stromberg, Chairperson, 918-631-2370, Fax: 918-631-2540, E-mail: peter-stromberg@utulsa.edu. *Application contact:* Dr. Thomas Foster, Advisor, 918-631-3082, Fax: 918-631-2540, E-mail: thomas-foster@utulsa.edu.
Website: http://artsandsciences.utulsa.edu/academics/departments-schools/anthropology/

**University of Utah,** Graduate School, College of Social and Behavioral Science, Department of Anthropology, Salt Lake City, UT 84112. Offers M Phil, MA, MS, PhD. *Program availability:* Part-time. *Faculty:* 15 full-time (5 women), 8 part-time/adjunct (5 women). *Students:* 17 full-time (11 women), 12 part-time (4 women); includes 5 minority (2 Hispanic/Latino; 3 Two or more races, non-Hispanic/Latino), 2 international. Average age 37. 39 applicants, 28% accepted, 11 enrolled. In 2016, 6 doctorates awarded. *Degree requirements:* For master's, variable foreign language requirement, comprehensive exam, thesis optional; for doctorate, variable foreign language requirement, comprehensive exam (for some programs), thesis/dissertation. *Entrance requirements:* For master's, GRE General Test, minimum undergraduate GPA of 3.0; for doctorate, GRE General Test, minimum GPA of 3.0. Additional exam requirements/recommendations for international students: Required—TOEFL (minimum score 500 paper-based). *Application deadline:* For fall admission, 1/15 for domestic and international students. Application fee: $55 ($65 for international students). Electronic applications accepted. *Expenses:* Contact institution. *Financial support:* In 2016–17, 18 students received support, including 12 fellowships with full tuition reimbursements available, 1 research assistantship with full tuition reimbursement available (averaging $18,000 per year), 16 teaching assistantships with full tuition reimbursements available (averaging $12,500 per year); career-related internships or fieldwork, health care benefits, and unspecified assistantships also available. Financial award application deadline: 11/15. *Faculty research:* Evolutionary ecology, anthropological genetics, hunter-gatherers, North American archaeology. *Total annual research expenditures:* $288,569. *Unit head:* Dr. Leslie Ann Knapp, Chair, 801-581-6251, Fax: 801-581-6252, E-mail: leslie.knapp@anthro.utah.edu. *Application contact:* Linda K. Morgan, Administrative Assistant, 801-581-6251, Fax: 801-581-6252, E-mail: linda.morgan@anthro.utah.edu.
Website: http://www.anthro.utah.edu/

**University of Victoria,** Faculty of Graduate Studies, Faculty of Social Sciences, Department of Anthropology, Victoria, BC V8W 2Y2, Canada. Offers MA. *Program availability:* Part-time. *Degree requirements:* For master's, comprehensive exam (for some programs), thesis (for some programs). *Entrance requirements:* For master's, minimum B+ average in last 2 years of undergraduate course work, writing sample. Additional exam requirements/recommendations for international students: Required—TOEFL (minimum score 575 paper-based), IELTS (minimum score 7).

**University of Virginia,** College and Graduate School of Arts and Sciences, Department of Anthropology, Charlottesville, VA 22903. Offers MA, PhD. *Faculty:* 22 full-time (10 women), 1 (woman) part-time/adjunct. *Students:* 38 full-time (25 women), 2 part-time (0 women); includes 5 minority (1 Black or African American, non-Hispanic/Latino; 1 Asian, non-Hispanic/Latino; 1 Hispanic/Latino; 2 Two or more races, non-Hispanic/Latino), 8 international. Average age 30. 69 applicants, 22% accepted, 6 enrolled. In 2016, 3 master's, 3 doctorates awarded. *Degree requirements:* For master's, one foreign language, thesis; for doctorate, 2 foreign languages, thesis/dissertation. *Entrance requirements:* For master's and doctorate, GRE General Test, GRE Subject Test, 3 letters of recommendation. Additional exam requirements/recommendations for international students: Required—TOEFL (minimum score 600 paper-based; 90 iBT), IELTS (minimum score 7). *Application deadline:* For fall admission, 12/15 for domestic and international students. Applications are processed on a rolling basis. Application fee: $60. Electronic applications accepted. *Expenses:* Tuition, state resident: full-time $15,026; part-time $834 per credit hour. Tuition, nonresident: full-time $25,168; part-time $1378 per credit hour. *Required fees:* $2654. *Financial support:* Application deadline: 3/15; applicants required to submit FAFSA. *Unit head:* Eve Danziger, Chair, 434-924-3002, Fax: 434-924-1350, E-mail: danziger@virginia.edu. *Application contact:* Frederick Damon, Director of Graduate Admissions, 434-982-6826, Fax: 434-924-1350, E-mail: fhd@virginia.edu.
Website: http://anthropology.virginia.edu/

**University of Washington,** Graduate School, College of Arts and Sciences, Department of Anthropology, Seattle, WA 98195. Offers MA, PhD. *Faculty:* 32 full-time (16 women), 5 part-time/adjunct (3 women). *Students:* 52 full-time (32 women), 4 part-time (3 women); includes 16 minority (4 Black or African American, non-Hispanic/Latino; 2 American Indian or Alaska Native, non-Hispanic/Latino; 3 Asian, non-Hispanic/Latino; 4 Hispanic/Latino; 1 Native Hawaiian or other Pacific Islander, non-Hispanic/Latino; 2 Two or more races, non-Hispanic/Latino), 12 international. Average age 32. 63 applicants, 13% accepted, 3 enrolled. In 2016, 11 master's, 10 doctorates awarded. Terminal master's awarded for partial completion of doctoral program. *Degree requirements:* For master's, comprehensive exam, thesis or alternative; for doctorate, variable foreign language requirement, comprehensive exam, thesis/dissertation. *Entrance requirements:* For doctorate, GRE General Test, minimum GPA of 3.6. Additional exam requirements/recommendations for international students: Recommended—TOEFL (minimum score 500 paper-based; 61 iBT). *Application deadline:* For fall admission, 12/15 for domestic and international students. Application fee: $85. Electronic applications accepted. *Financial support:* In 2016–17, 45 students received support, including 3 fellowships with full tuition reimbursements available (averaging $20,000 per year), 6 research assistantships with full tuition reimbursements available (averaging $21,000 per year), 23 teaching assistantships with full tuition reimbursements available (averaging $21,000 per year); institutionally sponsored loans, scholarships/grants, traineeships, health care benefits, tuition waivers (full and partial), and unspecified assistantships also available. Financial award application deadline: 1/15; financial award applicants required to submit FAFSA. *Faculty research:* Sociocultural anthropology, biocultural anthropology, archaeology, environmental anthropology, medical anthropology. *Unit head:* Dr. Patricia Ann Kramer, Chair, 206-543-5240, Fax: 206-543-3285, E-mail: pakramer@uw.edu. *Application contact:* Catherine M. Zeigler, Graduate Program Advisor, 206-685-1562, Fax: 206-543-3285, E-mail: gradanth@uw.edu.
Website: https://anthropology.washington.edu

**University of Waterloo,** Graduate Studies, Faculty of Arts, Department of Anthropology, Waterloo, ON N2L 3G1, Canada. Offers anthropology (MA); public issues (MA). *Entrance requirements:* Additional exam requirements/recommendations for international students: Required—TOEFL, IELTS, PTE. Electronic applications accepted. *Faculty research:* Applied socio-cultural anthropology and archaeology.

**The University of Western Ontario,** Faculty of Graduate Studies, Social Sciences Division, Department of Anthropology, London, ON N6A 5B8, Canada. Offers MA, PhD. *Degree requirements:* For master's, thesis; for doctorate, thesis/dissertation. *Entrance requirements:* For master's, minimum B average, honors BA. Additional exam requirements/recommendations for international students: Required—TOEFL. Electronic applications accepted. *Faculty research:* Sociocultural anthropology, bioarchaeology, linguistics.

**University of West Florida,** College of Arts, Social Sciences, and Humanities, Division of Anthropology and Archaeology, Pensacola, FL 32514-5750. Offers anthropology (MA); historical archaeology (MA). *Degree requirements:* For master's, internship or thesis. *Entrance requirements:* For master's, GRE, transcripts, minimum GPA of 3.0, 3 letters of recommendation, writing sample, letter of intent describing background, study interests, and professional goals. Additional exam requirements/recommendations for international students: Required—TOEFL (minimum score 550 paper-based). *Application deadline:* For fall admission, 6/1 for domestic and international students; for spring admission, 10/1 for domestic and international students. Application fee: $30. *Expenses:* Tuition, state resident: full-time $5316.12. Tuition, nonresident: full-time $11,308. *Required fees:* $583.92. Tuition and fees vary according to course load and program. *Financial support:* Research assistantships with partial tuition reimbursements, teaching assistantships with partial tuition reimbursements, and unspecified assistantships available. Financial award application deadline: 4/15; financial award applicants required to submit FAFSA. *Unit head:* Dr. John Bratten, Chair, 850-474-2706, E-mail: jbratten@uwf.edu. *Application contact:* Terry McCray, Assistant Director of Graduate Admissions, 850-473-7718, Fax: 850-473-7714, E-mail: gradadmissions@uwf.edu.
Website: http://uwf.edu/anthropology/

**University of Wisconsin–Madison,** Graduate School, College of Letters and Science, Department of Anthropology, Madison, WI 53706-1380. Offers archaeology (PhD); biological anthropology (PhD); cultural anthropology (PhD). Terminal master's awarded for partial completion of doctoral program. *Degree requirements:* For doctorate, thesis/dissertation. *Entrance requirements:* For doctorate, qualifying exam. Electronic applications accepted. *Faculty research:* Archaeology, biological, anthropology, cultural anthropology.

**University of Wisconsin–Milwaukee,** Graduate School, College of Letters and Science, Department of Anthropology, Milwaukee, WI 53201-0413. Offers anthropology (MS, PhD), including archaeology (MS), biological anthropology (MS), cultural anthropology (MS); museum studies (Graduate Certificate). *Students:* 58 full-time (43 women), 36 part-time (29 women); includes 8 minority (1 American Indian or Alaska Native, non-Hispanic/Latino; 2 Hispanic/Latino; 5 Two or more races, non-Hispanic/Latino), 1 international. Average age 32. 46 applicants, 100% accepted, 20 enrolled. In 2016, 17 master's, 2 doctorates, 14 other advanced degrees awarded. *Degree requirements:* For master's, thesis or alternative; for doctorate, one foreign language, thesis/dissertation, departmental qualifying exam. *Entrance requirements:* For master's, GRE; for doctorate, GRE, minimum GPA of 3.0, master's degree. Additional exam requirements/recommendations for international students: Required—TOEFL (minimum score 550 paper-based; 79 iBT), IELTS (minimum score 6.5). *Application deadline:* For fall admission, 1/1 priority date for domestic students; for spring admission, 9/1 for domestic students. Applications are processed on a rolling basis. Application fee: $56

($96 for international students). *Financial support:* In 2016–17, 4 fellowships, 2 research assistantships, 26 teaching assistantships were awarded; career-related internships or fieldwork, unspecified assistantships, and project assistantships also available. Support available to part-time students. Financial award application deadline: 4/15; financial award applicants required to submit FAFSA. *Unit head:* Thomas Malaby, Department Chair, 414-229-5247, E-mail: malaby@uwm.edu. *Application contact:* General Information Contact, 414-229-4982, Fax: 414-229-6967, E-mail: gradschool@uwm.edu. Website: https://uwm.edu/letters-science/programs/?discipline-Anthropology

**University of Wyoming,** College of Arts and Sciences, Department of Anthropology, Laramie, WY 82071. Offers MA, PhD. *Program availability:* Part-time. Terminal master's awarded for partial completion of doctoral program. *Degree requirements:* For master's, one foreign language, comprehensive exam, thesis optional; for doctorate, one foreign language, comprehensive exam, thesis/dissertation. *Entrance requirements:* For master's and doctorate, GRE General Test, minimum GPA of 3.0. Electronic applications accepted. *Faculty research:* Paleo-Indian archaeology, osteology, faunal analysis, lithic analysis, hunter-gatherers.

**Vanderbilt University,** Department of Anthropology, Nashville, TN 37240-1001. Offers MA, PhD. *Faculty:* 13 full-time (4 women). *Students:* 27 full-time (20 women); includes 6 minority (all Hispanic/Latino), 9 international. Average age 33. 71 applicants, 8% accepted, 5 enrolled. In 2016, 3 master's, 2 doctorates awarded. *Degree requirements:* For master's, comprehensive exam, thesis or alternative; for doctorate, one foreign language, comprehensive exam, thesis/dissertation, general, qualifying, and final exams. *Entrance requirements:* For master's and doctorate, GRE General Test. Additional exam requirements/recommendations for international students: Required—TOEFL (minimum score 570 paper-based; 88 iBT). *Application deadline:* 1/15 for domestic and international students. Application fee: $0. Electronic applications accepted. *Expenses: Tuition:* Part-time $1854 per credit hour. *Financial support:* Fellowships with tuition reimbursements, research assistantships with full tuition reimbursements, teaching assistantships with full tuition reimbursements, career-related internships or fieldwork, Federal Work-Study, institutionally sponsored loans, scholarships/grants, and health care benefits available. Financial award application deadline: 1/15; financial award applicants required to submit CSS PROFILE or FAFSA. *Faculty research:* Archaeology, ethnohistory and ethnography, epigraphy, conflict theory, Latin America. *Unit head:* Dr. Beth Conklin, Chair, 615-343-6120, Fax: 615-343-0230, E-mail: beth.a.conklin@vanderbilt.edu. *Application contact:* John Janusek, Director of Graduate Studies, 615-343-6120, E-mail: john.w.janusek@vanderbilt.edu. Website: http://as.vanderbilt.edu/anthropology/

**Washington State University,** College of Arts and Sciences, Department of Anthropology, Pullman, WA 99164. Offers archaeology (MA, PhD); cultural anthropology (PhD); evolutionary anthropology (MA, PhD). Program applications must be made through the Pullman campus. *Degree requirements:* For master's, one foreign language, comprehensive exam (for some programs), thesis; for doctorate, one foreign language, comprehensive exam, thesis/dissertation, written and oral preliminary exam. *Entrance requirements:* For master's and doctorate, GRE General Test, curriculum vitae, statement of intent, official transcripts, 3 letters of recommendation, one or two undergraduate papers (from BA/BS applicants), minimum GPA of 3.0. Additional exam requirements/recommendations for international students: Required—TOEFL (minimum score 550 paper-based), IELTS. Electronic applications accepted. *Faculty research:* Quantitative analysis of archaeological data, simulation of aspects of prehistoric behavior, subsistence strategies, language use, inequality and poverty, gender, pedagogy, Mexico/U.S. border region, childhood, infectious and parasitic diseases, the analysis of mitochondrial DNA (mtDNA) and Y-chromosomal DNA.

**Washington University in St. Louis,** The Graduate School, Department of Anthropology, St. Louis, MO 63130-4899. Offers PhD. *Students:* 56 full-time (36 women); includes 13 minority (3 Black or African American, non-Hispanic/Latino; 3 American Indian or Alaska Native, non-Hispanic/Latino; 1 Asian, non-Hispanic/Latino; 6 Hispanic/Latino), 11 international. 106 applicants, 22% accepted, 12 enrolled. In 2016, 6 doctorates awarded. Terminal master's awarded for partial completion of doctoral program. *Degree requirements:* For doctorate, thesis/dissertation. *Entrance requirements:* Additional exam requirements/recommendations for international students: Required—TOEFL. *Application deadline:* For fall admission, 12/1 for domestic and international students. Application fee: $45. Electronic applications accepted. *Financial support:* Fellowships with tuition reimbursements available. Financial award application deadline: 1/15. *Faculty research:* Sociocultural anthropology (including medical anthropology); archaeology; physical anthropology (including primate studies, paleontology and human biology). *Unit head:* Dr. T.R. Kidder, Chair, 314-935-5252. *Application contact:* Bridget Coleman, Director of Admissions, 314-935-6880, Fax: 314-935-4887.
Website: http://anthropology.artsci.wustl.edu/

**Wayne State University,** College of Liberal Arts and Sciences, Department of Anthropology, Detroit, MI 48202. Offers anthropology (MA, PhD); social work (PhD). Doctoral program admits for fall only. *Program availability:* Part-time. *Faculty:* 12. *Students:* 41 full-time (30 women), 22 part-time (13 women); includes 10 minority (4 Black or African American, non-Hispanic/Latino; 3 Two or more races, non-Hispanic/Latino), 2 international. Average age 35. 48 applicants, 46% accepted, 17 enrolled. In 2016, 7 master's, 2 doctorates awarded. *Degree requirements:* For master's, thesis (for some programs); for doctorate, one foreign language, thesis/dissertation. *Entrance requirements:* For master's, three letters of recommendation, completion of introduction to anthropology, letter of intent, writing sample, minimum undergraduate GPA of 3.2; for doctorate, GRE, bachelor's degree in anthropology or a related field, three letters of recommendation, completion of introduction to anthropology, letter of intent, writing sample, minimum undergraduate GPA of 3.2. Additional exam requirements/recommendations for international students: Required—TOEFL (minimum score 550 paper-based; 79 iBT), TWE (minimum score 5.5), Michigan English Language Assessment Battery (minimum score 85); Recommended—IELTS (minimum score 6.5). *Application deadline:* For fall admission, 1/10 for domestic and international students; for winter admission, 10/1 for domestic and international students. Application fee: $50. Electronic applications accepted. *Expenses:* $16,503 per year resident tuition and fees,

$33,697 per year non-resident tuition and fees. *Financial support:* In 2016–17, 28 students received support, including 2 fellowships with tuition reimbursements available (averaging $13,500 per year), 5 teaching assistantships with tuition reimbursements available (averaging $18,394 per year); research assistantships, scholarships/grants, and unspecified assistantships also available. Financial award applicants required to submit FAFSA. *Faculty research:* Business anthropology and organizational culture, African and African-American religions, medical anthropology, Latin American anthropology and archaeology, urban anthropology and historical archaeology. *Unit head:* Dr. Andrea Sankar, Professor and Chair, E-mail: asankar@wayne.edu. *Application contact:* Dr. Stephen Chrisomalis, Director of Graduate Studies, 313-577-9922, E-mail: chrisomalis@wayne.edu.
Website: http://clas.wayne.edu/anthropology/

**Wayne State University,** School of Social Work, Detroit, MI 48202. Offers alcohol and drug abuse studies (Certificate); clinical social work theory and practice (Certificate); disabilities (Certificate); gerontology (Certificate); social welfare research and evaluation (Certificate); social work (MSW, PhD); social work and anthropology (PhD); social work and gerontology (PhD); social work and infant mental health (MSW, PhD); social work practice with families and couples (Certificate). Application deadlines: April 1 for MSW, December 19 for PhD. *Accreditation:* CSWE (one or more programs are accredited). *Program availability:* Part-time, evening/weekend. *Faculty:* 24. *Students:* 515 full-time (442 women), 150 part-time (128 women); includes 251 minority (179 Black or African American, non-Hispanic/Latino; 4 American Indian or Alaska Native, non-Hispanic/Latino; 11 Asian, non-Hispanic/Latino; 29 Hispanic/Latino; 1 Native Hawaiian or other Pacific Islander, non-Hispanic/Latino; 27 Two or more races, non-Hispanic/Latino), 17 international. Average age 31. 809 applicants, 36% accepted, 200 enrolled. In 2016, 356 master's, 2 doctorates, 20 other advanced degrees awarded. *Degree requirements:* For master's, filed work; for doctorate, variable foreign language requirement, comprehensive exam, thesis/dissertation. *Entrance requirements:* For master's, personal interest statement, resume, 3 references; for doctorate, GRE (minimum combined score of 1000 on Verbal and Quantitative components), minimum undergraduate GPA of 3.5, MSW from CSWE-accredited institution (or working towards one), resume, three letters of reference, personal statement, summary of relevant research and professional experience, writing sample, interview; for Certificate, MSW or actively enrolled in advanced portion of MSW program. Additional exam requirements/recommendations for international students: Required—TOEFL (minimum score 550 paper-based; 79 iBT), TWE (minimum score 5.5), Michigan English Language Assessment Battery (minimum score 85); Recommended—IELTS (minimum score 6.5). *Application deadline:* Applications are processed on a rolling basis. Application fee: $50. Electronic applications accepted. *Expenses:* $16,503 per year resident tuition and fees, $33,697 per year non-resident tuition and fees. *Financial support:* In 2016–17, 119 students received support, including 5 fellowships with tuition reimbursements available (averaging $18,800 per year), 2 research assistantships with tuition reimbursements available (averaging $21,593 per year), 2 teaching assistantships with tuition reimbursements available (averaging $17,994 per year); scholarships/grants and unspecified assistantships also available. Financial award applicants required to submit FAFSA. *Faculty research:* Aging, child welfare, health and behavioral health, interpersonal violence, community development, policy and program development. *Unit head:* Dr. Jerrold Brandell, Interim Dean, 313-577-4409, E-mail: aa4537@wayne.edu. *Application contact:* Shantalea Johns, Interim Director of Admissions, 313-577-4409, E-mail: shantalea@wayne.edu.
Website: http://socialwork.wayne.edu/

**Western Kentucky University,** Graduate Studies, Potter College of Arts and Letters, Department of Folk Studies and Anthropology, Bowling Green, KY 42101. Offers folk studies (MA). *Degree requirements:* For master's, comprehensive exam, thesis optional, written exam. *Entrance requirements:* For master's, GRE General Test, minimum GPA of 3.0. Additional exam requirements/recommendations for international students: Required—TOEFL (minimum score 555 paper-based; 79 iBT). *Faculty research:* Public folklore, folklore and education, vernacular belief, music and culture, historic presentation.

**Western Michigan University,** Graduate College, College of Arts and Sciences, Department of Anthropology, Kalamazoo, MI 49008. Offers MA. *Degree requirements:* For master's, comprehensive exam, thesis.

**Western Washington University,** Graduate School, College of Humanities and Social Sciences, Department of Anthropology, Bellingham, WA 98225-5996. Offers MA. *Program availability:* Part-time. *Degree requirements:* For master's, thesis. *Entrance requirements:* For master's, GRE General Test, minimum GPA of 3.0 in last 60 semester hours or last 90 quarter hours. Additional exam requirements/recommendations for international students: Required—TOEFL (minimum score 567 paper-based). Electronic applications accepted. *Faculty research:* Peoples and culture of the Pacific Rim; prehistory of North America; applied health; community-based action research; globalization and human rights.

**Wichita State University,** Graduate School, Fairmount College of Liberal Arts and Sciences, Department of Anthropology, Wichita, KS 67260. Offers MA. *Program availability:* Part-time. *Entrance requirements:* For master's, minimum GPA of 2.75 in last 60 hours, 3.0 in anthropology. *Unit head:* Dr. Peer H. Moore-Jansen, Chair, 316-978-3195, E-mail: pmojan@wichita.edu. *Application contact:* Jordan Oleson, Admission Coordinator, 316-978-3095, E-mail: jordan.oleson@wichita.edu.
Website: http://www.wichita.edu/anthropology

**Yale University,** Graduate School of Arts and Sciences, Department of Anthropology, New Haven, CT 06520. Offers M Phil, MA, PhD. *Degree requirements:* For doctorate, thesis/dissertation. *Entrance requirements:* For master's and doctorate, GRE General Test. *Faculty research:* Linguistics, national identity.

**York University,** Faculty of Graduate Studies, Faculty of Liberal Arts and Professional Studies, Program in Social Anthropology, Toronto, ON M3J 1P3, Canada. Offers MA, PhD. *Program availability:* Part-time. *Degree requirements:* For master's, thesis or alternative; for doctorate, comprehensive exam, thesis/dissertation. Electronic applications accepted.

# Applied Social Research

---

**American University,** College of Arts and Sciences, Department of Sociology, Washington, DC 22016-8072. Offers public sociology (Certificate); social research (Certificate); sociology (MA). *Program availability:* Part-time, evening/weekend. *Faculty:* 14 full-time (10 women), 8 part-time/adjunct (5 women). *Students:* 3 full-time (all women), 6 part-time (4 women); includes 6 minority (3 Black or African American, non-

Hispanic/Latino; 1 Hispanic/Latino; 2 Two or more races, non-Hispanic/Latino). Average age 27. 22 applicants, 86% accepted, 6 enrolled. In 2016, 8 master's awarded. *Degree requirements:* For master's, comprehensive exam, thesis or alternative. *Entrance requirements:* For master's, GRE, statement of purpose, transcripts, 2 letters of recommendation, resume; for Certificate, bachelor's degree, statement of purpose,

*Applied Social Research*

transcripts, resume. Additional exam requirements/recommendations for international students: Required—TOEFL, IELTS (minimum score 7), PTE (minimum score 68). *Application deadline:* For fall admission, 2/1 priority date for domestic students; for spring admission, 11/1 for domestic students. Application fee: $55. *Expenses:* $1,579 per credit tuition; $690 mandatory fees. *Financial support:* Research assistantships, teaching assistantships, institutionally sponsored loans, scholarships/grants, and unspecified assistantships available. Financial award application deadline: 2/1; financial award applicants required to submit FAFSA. *Unit head:* Dr. Gloria Young, Department Chair, 202-885-2254, Fax: 202-885-2477, E-mail: gyoung@american.edu. *Application contact:* Kathleen Clowery, Associate Director, Graduate Admissions, 202-885-3620, Fax: 202-885-1344, E-mail: clowery@american.edu.
Website: http://www.american.edu/cas/sociology/

**California State University, Dominguez Hills,** College of Natural and Behavioral Sciences, Program in Sociology, Carson, CA 90747-0001. Offers social research (Certificate); sociology (MA). *Program availability:* Part-time, evening/weekend. *Degree requirements:* For master's, comprehensive exam, thesis. *Entrance requirements:* For master's, minimum GPA of 2.85. *Faculty research:* Community studies, social movements, criminology.

**Concordia University Irvine,** School of Theology, Irvine, CA 92612-3299. Offers Christian leadership (MA); research in theology (MA); theology and culture (MA). *Program availability:* Part-time, evening/weekend. *Degree requirements:* For master's, project/thesis or vicarage. *Entrance requirements:* For master's, official college transcript(s), statement of intent, 2 references, interview. Additional exam requirements/recommendations for international students: Required—TOEFL. Electronic applications accepted. *Expenses:* Contact institution.

**Florida State University,** The Graduate School, College of Social Sciences and Public Policy, Department of Sociology, Tallahassee, FL 32306. Offers applied social research (MS); sociology (MA, MS, PhD); sociology of health and aging (MS). *Faculty:* 18 full-time (9 women). *Students:* 50 full-time (32 women), 10 part-time (7 women); includes 18 minority (9 Black or African American, non-Hispanic/Latino; 2 Asian, non-Hispanic/Latino; 2 Hispanic/Latino; 5 Two or more races, non-Hispanic/Latino). Average age 28. 57 applicants, 35% accepted, 11 enrolled. In 2016, 13 master's, 9 doctorates awarded. *Degree requirements:* For doctorate, comprehensive exam, thesis/dissertation. *Entrance requirements:* For master's and doctorate, GRE General Test, minimum GPA of 3.0. Additional exam requirements/recommendations for international students: Required—TOEFL (minimum score 550 paper-based; 80 iBT). *Application deadline:* For fall admission, 12/15 priority date for domestic students, 12/15 for international students. Applications are processed on a rolling basis. Application fee: $30. Electronic applications accepted. *Expenses:* Contact institution. *Financial support:* In 2016–17, 57 students received support, including 3 fellowships with full tuition reimbursements available (averaging $25,115 per year), 4 research assistantships with full tuition reimbursements available (averaging $21,150 per year), 50 teaching assistantships with full tuition reimbursements available (averaging $21,150 per year); institutionally sponsored loans, scholarships/grants, health care benefits, and unspecified assistantships also available. Financial award application deadline: 12/15; financial award applicants required to submit FAFSA. *Faculty research:* Aging and health, demography, inequality (gender/race and social movements/politics). *Total annual research expenditures:* $428,302. *Unit head:* Dr. John Reynolds, Chair, 850-644-6416, Fax: 850-644-6208, E-mail: john.reynolds@fsu.edu. *Application contact:* Jamie Yeargan, Graduate Program Coordinator, 850-644-6506, Fax: 850-644-6208, E-mail: jdyeargan@fsu.edu.
Website: http://coss.fsu.edu/sociology/

**Hunter College of the City University of New York,** Graduate School, School of Arts and Sciences, Department of Sociology, Program in Applied Social Research, New York, NY 10065-5085. Offers MS. *Program availability:* Part-time, evening/weekend. *Students:* 13 full-time (8 women), 20 part-time (17 women); includes 10 minority (5 Black or African American, non-Hispanic/Latino; 2 Asian, non-Hispanic/Latino; 3 Hispanic/Latino), 4 international. Average age 31. 18 applicants, 94% accepted, 14 enrolled. In 2016, 2 master's awarded. *Degree requirements:* For master's, internship, research reports. *Entrance requirements:* For master's, GRE General Test or GMAT, 3 credits of course work in statistics, research methods, background in sociology or related social science. Additional exam requirements/recommendations for international students: Required—TOEFL. *Application deadline:* For fall admission, 4/1 for domestic students, 2/1 for international students; for spring admission, 11/1 for domestic students, 9/1 for international students. Applications are processed on a rolling basis. *Financial support:* Fellowships, research assistantships, teaching assistantships, career-related internships or fieldwork, Federal Work-Study, institutionally sponsored loans, scholarships/grants, and tuition waivers (full and partial) available. Support available to part-time students. *Faculty research:* Consumer behavior, new electronic media, voting behavior, policy analysis, sociomedicine. *Unit head:* Dr. Howard Lune, Director, 212-772-5641, E-mail: hlune@hunter.cuny.edu. *Application contact:* Milena Solo, Director of Graduate Admissions, 212-772-4480, E-mail: admissions@hunter.cuny.edu.
Website: http://www.hunter.cuny.edu/sociology/graduate

**Laurentian University,** School of Graduate Studies and Research, Programme in Sociology, Sudbury, ON P3E 2C6, Canada. Offers applied social research (MA). *Program availability:* Part-time. *Entrance requirements:* For master's, honors degree in sociology or equivalent. *Faculty research:* Work foundations, managing AIDS organization, tracking laid-off mine workers.

**Loma Linda University,** School of Behavioral Health, Department of Social Work and Social Ecology, Loma Linda, CA 92350. Offers criminal justice (MS); gerontology (MS); social policy and social research (PhD); social work (MSW). *Accreditation:* CSWE. *Degree requirements:* For master's, comprehensive exam, thesis optional; for doctorate, comprehensive exam, thesis/dissertation. *Entrance requirements:* For master's and doctorate, GRE General Test. Additional exam requirements/recommendations for international students: Required—TOEFL, Michigan English Language Assessment Battery. Electronic applications accepted.

**The New School,** The New School for Social Research, New York, NY 10003. Offers M Phil, MA, MS, PhD. *Program availability:* Part-time. *Faculty:* 50 full-time (18 women), 12 part-time/adjunct (4 women). *Students:* 606 full-time (309 women), 184 part-time (107 women); includes 116 minority (24 Black or African American, non-Hispanic/Latino; 1 American Indian or Alaska Native, non-Hispanic/Latino; 24 Asian, non-Hispanic/Latino; 48 Hispanic/Latino; 19 Two or more races, non-Hispanic/Latino), 266 international. Average age 31. 979 applicants, 76% accepted, 161 enrolled. In 2016, 195 master's, 57 doctorates awarded. Terminal master's awarded for partial completion of doctoral program. *Degree requirements:* For master's, comprehensive exam (for some programs), thesis (for some programs); for doctorate, variable foreign language requirement, comprehensive exam (for some programs), thesis/dissertation. *Entrance requirements:* For master's, letters of recommendation, writing sample, essays, official transcripts. Additional exam requirements/recommendations for international students: Required—TOEFL (minimum score 100 iBT), IELTS (minimum score 7), PTE (minimum score 68). *Application deadline:* For fall admission, 8/1 priority date for domestic students, 6/1 priority date for international students; for spring admission, 10/15 priority date for domestic and international students. Applications are processed on a rolling basis. Application fee: $50. Electronic applications accepted. *Expenses:* Contact institution. *Financial support:* Fellowships, research assistantships, teaching assistantships, career-related internships or fieldwork, Federal Work-Study, scholarships/grants, and tuition waivers (full and partial) available. Support available to part-time students. Financial award application deadline: 3/1; financial award applicants required to submit FAFSA. *Faculty research:* Critical political and social inquiry; empirical, historical, and ethnographic scholarship; continental philosophy; heterodox economics; cognitive, social, developmental and clinical psychology. *Total annual research expenditures:* $60,000. *Unit head:* Dr. William Milberg, Dean, 212-229-5777, E-mail: milbergw@newschool.edu. *Application contact:* Dana Messinger, Director of Graduate Admission, 212-229-5150 Ext. 2300, E-mail: messingd@newschool.edu.
Website: http://www.newschool.edu/

**New York University,** Steinhardt School of Culture, Education, and Human Development, Department of Humanities and Social Sciences in the Professions, Program in Applied Statistics for Social Science Research, New York, NY 10012-1019. Offers MS. *Entrance requirements:* For master's, GRE, statement of purpose, resume/curriculum vitae, two letters of recommendation, transcripts. Additional exam requirements/recommendations for international students: Required—TOEFL. Electronic applications accepted. *Faculty research:* Causal inference, multi-level models, multivariate analysis, psychometrics, survey research and design.

**Portland State University,** Graduate Studies, School of Social Work, Portland, OR 97207-0751. Offers social work (MSW); social work and social research (PhD). *Accreditation:* CSWE (one or more programs are accredited). *Program availability:* Part-time. *Faculty:* 35 full-time (26 women), 41 part-time/adjunct (32 women). *Students:* 358 full-time (284 women), 270 part-time (222 women); includes 188 minority (33 Black or African American, non-Hispanic/Latino; 22 American Indian or Alaska Native, non-Hispanic/Latino; 20 Asian, non-Hispanic/Latino; 75 Hispanic/Latino; 1 Native Hawaiian or other Pacific Islander, non-Hispanic/Latino; 37 Two or more races, non-Hispanic/Latino), 2 international. Average age 35. 794 applicants, 33% accepted, 239 enrolled. In 2016, 221 master's, 6 doctorates awarded. *Degree requirements:* For doctorate, comprehensive exam, thesis/dissertation, residency. *Entrance requirements:* For master's, minimum GPA of 3.0 in upper-division course work or 2.75 overall; for doctorate, GRE General Test, 4 references. Additional exam requirements/recommendations for international students: Required—TOEFL (minimum score 550 paper-based; 80 iBT). *Application deadline:* For fall admission, 2/1 for domestic and international students. Application fee: $65. *Expenses:* Contact institution. *Financial support:* In 2016–17, 6 research assistantships with tuition reimbursements (averaging $7,366 per year), 5 teaching assistantships with tuition reimbursements (averaging $5,621 per year) were awarded; career-related internships or fieldwork, Federal Work-Study, scholarships/grants, tuition waivers (partial), and unspecified assistantships also available. Support available to part-time students. Financial award application deadline: 3/1; financial award applicants required to submit FAFSA. *Faculty research:* Child welfare; child mental health; social welfare policies and services; work, family, and dependent care; adult mental health. *Total annual research expenditures:* $14.7 million. *Unit head:* Dr. Laura B. Nissen, Dean, 503-725-3997, Fax: 503-725-5545, E-mail: nissen@pdx.edu. *Application contact:* Prof. Sarah Bradley, Director of MSW Program, 503-725-8028, Fax: 503-725-5545, E-mail: bradles@pdx.edu.
Website: https://www.pdx.edu/ssw/

**Queens College of the City University of New York,** Division of Social Sciences, Department of Sociology, Queens, NY 11367-1597. Offers data analytics and applied social research (MA); sociology (MA). *Program availability:* Part-time, evening/weekend. *Faculty:* 30 full-time (15 women), 40 part-time/adjunct (22 women). *Students:* 7 full-time (4 women), 27 part-time (15 women); includes 17 minority (1 Black or African American, non-Hispanic/Latino; 6 Asian, non-Hispanic/Latino; 10 Hispanic/Latino), 4 international. Average age 27. 40 applicants, 75% accepted, 16 enrolled. In 2016, 11 master's awarded. *Degree requirements:* For master's, thesis optional. *Entrance requirements:* For master's, minimum GPA of 3.0. Additional exam requirements/recommendations for international students: Required—TOEFL (minimum score 100 iBT), IELTS (minimum score 7). *Application deadline:* For fall admission, 5/15 for domestic students; for spring admission, 12/1 for domestic students. Applications are processed on a rolling basis. Application fee: $125. Electronic applications accepted. *Expenses:* Tuition, state resident: full-time $5065; part-time $425 per credit. Tuition, nonresident: part-time $780 per credit. *Required fees:* $522; $397 per credit. Part-time tuition and fees vary according to course load and program. *Financial support:* Career-related internships or fieldwork and unspecified assistantships available. Financial award application deadline: 4/1; financial award applicants required to submit FAFSA. *Unit head:* Dr. Andrew Beveridge, Chairperson, 718-997-2800, E-mail: andrew.beveridge@qc.cuny.edu.

**University of California, Los Angeles,** Graduate Division, School of Public Affairs, Los Angeles, CA 90095. Offers MA, MPP, MSW, PhD, JD/MA, JD/MSW, MA/MA, MBA/MA, MD/PhD. *Accreditation:* CSWE. *Degree requirements:* For doctorate, thesis/dissertation, oral and written qualifying exams. *Entrance requirements:* For master's, minimum GPA of 3.0; for doctorate, minimum undergraduate GPA of 3.0. Additional exam requirements/recommendations for international students: Required—TOEFL. Electronic applications accepted.

# Archaeology

**American University of Beirut,** Graduate Programs, Faculty of Arts and Sciences, Beirut, Lebanon. Offers anthropology (MA); Arab and Middle Eastern history (PhD); Arabic language and literature (MA, PhD); archaeology (MA); art history and curating (MA); biology (MS); cell and molecular biology (PhD); chemistry (MS); clinical psychology (MA); computational sciences (MS); computer science (MS); economics (MA); education (MA); English language (MA); English literature (MA); environmental policy planning (MS); financial economics (MAFE); geology (MS); history (MA); Islamic studies (MA); mathematics (MS); media studies (MA); Middle Eastern studies (MA); physics (MS); political studies (MA); psychology (MA); public administration (MA); public policy and international affairs (MA); sociology (MA); statistics (MA, MS); theoretical physics (PhD); transnational American studies (MA). *Program availability:* Part-time. *Faculty:* 133 full-time (42 women), 6 part-time/adjunct (2 women). *Students:* 240 full-time (172 women), 227 part-time (166 women). Average age 27. 286 applicants, 67% accepted, 108 enrolled. In 2016, 60 master's, 3 doctorates awarded. Terminal master's awarded for partial completion of doctoral program. *Degree requirements:* For master's, one foreign language, comprehensive exam, thesis (for some programs); for doctorate, one foreign language, comprehensive exam, thesis/dissertation. *Entrance requirements:* For master's, GRE (for some MA, MS programs), letters of recommendation; for doctorate, GRE, letters of recommendation. Additional exam requirements/recommendations for international students: Required—TOEFL (minimum score 600 paper-based; 97 iBT), IELTS (minimum score 7). *Application deadline:* For fall admission, 4/3 for domestic students; for winter admission, 11/3 for domestic students. Application fee: $50. Electronic applications accepted. *Expenses:* Contact institution. *Financial support:* In 2016–17, 4 fellowships (averaging $11,200 per year), 18 research assistantships (averaging $5,400 per year) were awarded; teaching assistantships, career-related internships or fieldwork, Federal Work-Study, institutionally sponsored loans, scholarships/grants, traineeships, health care benefits, tuition waivers (full), and unspecified assistantships also available. Support available to part-time students. *Faculty research:* Development economics, spatial econometrics, health economics, labor economics, energy economics, hydrogeology, geophysics, petrophysics, structural geology, mineralogy, petrology, geochemistry, multilingualism, comparative/world literature, translation studies, book histories/ cultures, biocatalysis, molecular recognition, photocatalysis, photophysical and biophysical chemistry, probe chemistry, machine learning, data science. *Unit head:* Dr. Nadia Maria El Cheikh, Dean, Faculty of Arts and Sciences, 961-1374374 Ext. 3800, Fax: 961-1744461, E-mail: nmcheikh@aub.edu.lb. *Application contact:* Dr. Salim Kanaan, Director, Admissions Office, 961-1350000 Ext. 2590, Fax: 961-1750775, E-mail: sk00@aub.edu.lb. Website: http://www.aub.edu.lb/fas/

**Arizona State University at the Tempe campus,** College of Liberal Arts and Sciences, School of Human Evolution and Social Change, Tempe, AZ 85287-2402. Offers anthropology (MA, PhD), including anthropology (PhD), archaeology (PhD), bioarchaeology (PhD), evolutionary (PhD), museum studies (MA), sociocultural (PhD); applied mathematics for the life and social sciences (PhD); environmental social science (PhD), including environmental social science, urbanism; global health (MA, PhD), including complex adaptive systems science (PhD), evolutionary global health sciences (PhD), health and culture (PhD), urbanism (PhD); immigration studies (Graduate Certificate). Terminal master's awarded for partial completion of doctoral program. *Degree requirements:* For master's, thesis or alternative, interactive Program of Study (iPOS) submitted before completing 50 percent of required credit hours; for doctorate, comprehensive exam, thesis/dissertation, interactive Program of Study (iPOS) submitted before completing 50 percent of required credit hours. *Entrance requirements:* For master's and doctorate, GRE, minimum GPA of 3.0 or equivalent in last 2 years of work leading to bachelor's degree. Additional exam requirements/recommendations for international students: Required—TOEFL, IELTS, or PTE. Electronic applications accepted.

**Boston University,** Graduate School of Arts and Sciences, Department of Archaeology, Boston, MA 02215. Offers MA, PhD. *Students:* 27 full-time (19 women), 2 part-time (0 women); includes 3 minority (2 Hispanic/Latino; 1 Two or more races, non-Hispanic/Latino), 7 international. Average age 30. 40 applicants, 53% accepted, 2 enrolled. In 2016, 6 master's, 5 doctorates awarded. Terminal master's awarded for partial completion of doctoral program. *Degree requirements:* For master's, one foreign language, comprehensive exam, thesis or alternative; for doctorate, 2 foreign languages, comprehensive exam, thesis/dissertation. *Entrance requirements:* For master's and doctorate, GRE General Test, 3 letters of recommendation, transcripts, personal statement, scholarly writing sample. Additional exam requirements/ recommendations for international students: Required—TOEFL (minimum score 550 paper-based; 84 iBT). *Application deadline:* For fall admission, 1/5 for domestic and international students. Application fee: $95. Electronic applications accepted. *Financial support:* In 2016–17, 26 students received support, including 1 fellowship with full tuition reimbursement available (averaging $21,500 per year), 4 research assistantships with full tuition reimbursements available (averaging $21,500 per year), 15 teaching assistantships with full tuition reimbursements available (averaging $21,500 per year); career-related internships or fieldwork, Federal Work-Study, scholarships/grants, and health care benefits also available. Support available to part-time students. Financial award application deadline: 1/5. *Unit head:* Curtis Runnels, Chair, 617-358-1647, Fax: 617-353-6800, E-mail: runnels@bu.edu. *Application contact:* Maria Sousa, Senior Program Coordinator, 617-353-3415, Fax: 617-353-6800, E-mail: mhsousa@bu.edu. Website: http://www.bu.edu/ARCHAEOLOGY/

**Brown University,** Graduate School, Department of Egyptology and Ancient Western Asian Studies, Providence, RI 02912. Offers ancient western Asian studies (PhD); Egyptology (PhD); history of the exact sciences in antiquity (PhD). *Degree requirements:* For doctorate, 2 foreign languages, comprehensive exam, thesis/dissertation. *Entrance requirements:* For doctorate, GRE General Test.

**Brown University,** Graduate School, Joukowsky Institute for Archaeology and the Ancient World, Providence, RI 02912. Offers PhD. *Degree requirements:* For doctorate, thesis/dissertation.

**Bryn Mawr College,** Graduate School of Arts and Sciences, Department of Classical and Near Eastern Archaeology, Bryn Mawr, PA 19010-2899. Offers MA, PhD. *Program availability:* Part-time. *Faculty:* 4 full-time (3 women), 2 part-time/adjunct (1 woman). *Students:* 12 full-time (10 women), 4 part-time (3 women); includes 1 minority (Hispanic/Latino). Average age 30. 17 applicants, 29% accepted, 3 enrolled. In 2016, 5 master's, 2 doctorates awarded. *Degree requirements:* For master's, 2 foreign languages, thesis; for doctorate, 3 foreign languages, comprehensive exam, thesis/dissertation. *Entrance requirements:* For master's and doctorate, GRE General Test, transcripts, three letters of recommendation, statement of interest, resume or curriculum vitae, writing sample. Additional exam requirements/recommendations for international students: Required—TOEFL (minimum score 600 paper-based; 100 iBT), IELTS (minimum score 7). *Application deadline:* For fall admission, 12/15 for domestic and international students. Application fee: $50. Electronic applications accepted. *Expenses: Tuition:* Full-time $40,620; part-time $6770 per unit. Tuition and fees vary according to program. *Financial support:* In 2016–17, 16 students received support, including 12 fellowships with tuition reimbursements available (averaging $18,764 per year), 2 teaching assistantships with tuition reimbursements available (averaging $19,000 per year); Federal Work-Study and scholarships/grants also available. Support available to part-time students. Financial award application deadline: 12/15. *Unit head:* Maria Dantis, Graduate Program Administrator, 610-526-5074, E-mail: gsas@brynmawr.edu.

**California State University, Northridge,** Graduate Studies, College of Social and Behavioral Sciences, Department of Anthropology, Northridge, CA 91330. Offers general anthropology (MA); public archaeology (MA). *Faculty:* 11 full-time (2 women), 9 part-time/adjunct (6 women). *Students:* 5 full-time (4 women), 13 part-time (9 women); includes 3 minority (1 Black or African American, non-Hispanic/Latino; 2 Asian, non-Hispanic/Latino), 6 international. Average age 30. 20 applicants, 20% accepted, 3 enrolled. *Degree requirements:* For master's, thesis or alternative. *Entrance requirements:* For master's, GRE General Test or minimum GPA of 3.0. Additional exam requirements/recommendations for international students: Required—TOEFL. *Application deadline:* For fall admission, 11/30 for domestic students. Application fee: $55. *Expenses:* Tuition, state resident: full-time $4152. *Financial support:* Career-related internships or fieldwork, Federal Work-Study, and institutionally sponsored loans available. Financial award application deadline: 3/1. *Unit head:* Dr. Sabina Magliocco, Chair, 818-677-3331. Website: http://www.csun.edu/csbs/departments/anthropology/index.html

**California State University, San Bernardino,** Graduate Studies, College of Social and Behavioral Sciences, Program in Applied Archaeology, San Bernardino, CA 92407. Offers clinical psychology (MS). *Students:* 1 (woman) full-time, 17 part-time (8 women); includes 5 minority (1 Black or African American, non-Hispanic/Latino; 1 American Indian or Alaska Native, non-Hispanic/Latino; 1 Hispanic/Latino; 2 Two or more races, non-Hispanic/Latino). 8 applicants, 100% accepted, 6 enrolled. *Entrance requirements:* Additional exam requirements/recommendations for international students: Required—TOEFL. *Application deadline:* For fall admission, 5/20 for domestic students. Application fee: $55. *Expenses:* Tuition, state resident: full-time $7843; part-time $5011.20 per year. Tuition and fees vary according to course load, degree level, program and reciprocity agreements. *Financial support:* Application deadline: 3/1. *Unit head:* Dr. Robert Ricco, Chair, 909-537-5485, Fax: 909-537-7003, E-mail: rricco@csusb.edu. *Application contact:* Dr. Amy Gusick, Program Coordinator, 909-537-5520, E-mail: amy.gusick@csusb.edu.

**Columbia University,** Graduate School of Arts and Sciences, New York, NY 10027. Offers African-American studies (MA); American studies (MA); anthropology (MA, PhD); art history and archaeology (MA, PhD); astronomy (PhD); biological sciences (PhD); biotechnology (MA); chemical physics (PhD); chemistry (PhD); classical studies (MA, PhD); classics (MA, PhD); climate and society (MA); conservation biology (MA); earth and environmental sciences (PhD); East Asia: regional studies (MA); East Asian languages and cultures (MA, PhD); ecology, evolution and environmental biology (MA), including conservation biology; ecology, evolution, and environmental biology (PhD), including ecology and evolutionary biology, evolutionary primatology; economics (MA, PhD); English and comparative literature (MA, PhD); French and Romance philology (MA, PhD); Germanic languages (MA, PhD); global French studies (MA); global thought (MA); Hispanic cultural studies (MA); history (PhD); history and literature (MA); human rights studies (MA); Islamic studies (MA); Italian (MA, PhD); Japanese pedagogy (MA); Jewish studies (MA); Latin America and the Caribbean: regional studies (MA); Latin American and Iberian cultures (PhD); mathematics (MA, PhD), including finance (MA); medieval and Renaissance studies (MA); Middle Eastern, South Asian, and African studies (MA, PhD); modern art: critical and curatorial studies (MA); modern European studies (MA); museum anthropology (MA); music (DMA, PhD); oral history (MA); philosophical foundations of physics (MA); philosophy (MA, PhD); physics (PhD); political science (MA, PhD); psychology (PhD); quantitative methods in the social sciences (MA); religion (MA, PhD); Russia, Eurasia and East Europe: regional studies (MA); Russian translation (MA); Slavic cultures (MA); Slavic languages (MA, PhD); sociology (MA, PhD); South Asian studies (MA); statistics (MA, PhD); theatre (PhD). Dual-degree programs require admission to both Graduate School of Arts and Sciences and another Columbia school. *Program availability:* Part-time. Terminal master's awarded for partial completion of doctoral program. *Degree requirements:* For master's, variable foreign language requirement, comprehensive exam (for some programs), thesis (for some programs); for doctorate, variable foreign language requirement, comprehensive exam (for some programs), thesis/dissertation. *Entrance requirements:* For master's and doctorate, GRE General Test, GRE Subject Test (for some programs). Additional exam requirements/recommendations for international students: Required—TOEFL, IELTS. Electronic applications accepted.

**Cornell University,** Graduate School, Graduate Fields of Arts and Sciences, Field of Archaeology, Ithaca, NY 14853. Offers environmental archaeology (MA); historical archaeology (MA); Latin American archaeology (MA); medieval archaeology (MA); Mediterranean and Near Eastern archaeology (MA); Stone Age archaeology (MA). *Degree requirements:* For master's, one foreign language, thesis. *Entrance requirements:* For master's, GRE General Test, 3 letters of recommendation, sample of written work. Additional exam requirements/recommendations for international students: Required—TOEFL (minimum score 550 paper-based; 77 iBT). Electronic applications accepted. *Faculty research:* Anatolia, Lydia, Sardis, classical and Hellenistic Greece, science in archaeology, North American Indians, Stone Age Africa, Mayan trade.

**Cornell University,** Graduate School, Graduate Fields of Arts and Sciences, Field of History of Art, Archaeology and Visual Studies, Ithaca, NY 14853. Offers 19th century art (PhD); African, African American and African diaspora (PhD); American art (PhD); ancient art and archaeology (PhD); Asian American art (PhD); Baroque art (PhD); comparative modernities (PhD); digital art (PhD); East Asian art (PhD); history of photography (PhD); Islamic art (PhD); Latin American art (PhD); medieval art (PhD); modern art (PhD); Renaissance art (PhD); Southeast Asian art (PhD); theory and criticism (PhD); visual studies (PhD). *Degree requirements:* For doctorate, one foreign language, comprehensive exam, thesis/dissertation, general exams in 3 areas. *Entrance requirements:* For doctorate, GRE General Test, sample of written work, 3 letters of recommendation. Additional exam requirements/recommendations for international students: Required—TOEFL (minimum score 550 paper-based; 77 iBT). Electronic applications accepted.

**Florida State University,** The Graduate School, College of Arts and Sciences, Department of Classics, Tallahassee, FL 32306-1510. Offers ancient history (MA); classical archaeology (MA); classical civilization (MA); classics (PhD), including classical archaeology, classics; Greek (MA); Greek and Latin (MA); Latin (MA). *Faculty:* 17 full-time (7 women), 2 part-time/adjunct (1 woman). *Students:* 47 full-time (29 women); includes 3 minority (1 Black or African American, non-Hispanic/Latino; 1 Asian, non-Hispanic/Latino; 1 Hispanic/Latino). Average age 25. 50 applicants, 40% accepted, 12 enrolled. In 2016, 4 master's, 3 doctorates awarded. Terminal master's awarded for partial completion of doctoral program. *Degree requirements:* For master's, 2 foreign languages, comprehensive exam, thesis or alternative; for doctorate, 4 foreign languages, comprehensive exam, thesis/dissertation. *Entrance requirements:* For master's, GRE General Test, minimum GPA of 3.0; for doctorate, GRE General Test, minimum GPA of 3.5. Additional exam requirements/recommendations for international students: Required—TOEFL (minimum score 550 paper-based; 80 iBT). *Application deadline:* For fall admission, 12/15 priority date for domestic students, 12/15 for international students. Applications are processed on a rolling basis. Application fee: $30. Electronic applications accepted. *Expenses:* Tuition, state resident: full-time $7263; part-time $403.51 per credit hour. Tuition, nonresident: full-time $18,087; part-time $1004.85 per credit hour. *Required fees:* $1365; $75.81 per credit hour. $20 per semester. Tuition and fees vary according to campus/location. *Financial support:* In 2016–17, 45 students received support, including 2 fellowships with full tuition reimbursements available (averaging $18,000 per year), 3 research assistantships with full tuition reimbursements available (averaging $12,000 per year), 25 teaching assistantships with full tuition reimbursements available (averaging $14,000 per year); Federal Work-Study, scholarships/grants, tuition waivers (full), and unspecified assistantships also available. Financial award application deadline: 1/15; financial award applicants required to submit FAFSA. *Faculty research:* Greek and Latin literature, classical archaeology, mythology, ancient history, religion. *Total annual research expenditures:* $100,000. *Unit head:* Dr. Daniel J. Pullen, Chairman, 850-644-0304, Fax: 850-644-4073, E-mail: dpullen@fsu.edu. *Application contact:* Dr. Timothy Stover, Admissions Director, 850-644-4259, Fax: 850-644-4073, E-mail: tstover@fsu.edu. Website: http://classics.fsu.edu/

**Gordon-Conwell Theological Seminary,** Graduate and Professional Programs, South Hamilton, MA 01982. Offers Biblical languages (MABL); church history (MACH); counseling (MACO); ministry (D Min); missions/evangelism (MAME); New Testament (MANT); Old Testament (MAOT); religion (MAR); theology (M Div, MATH, Th M, Th D). *Accreditation:* ACIPE; ATS (one or more programs are accredited). *Program availability:* Part-time, evening/weekend. *Degree requirements:* For master's, one foreign language, thesis optional; for doctorate, 2 foreign languages, thesis/dissertation. *Entrance requirements:* For master's, minimum GPA of 2.5; for doctorate, minimum GPA of 3.0.

**The Graduate Center, City University of New York,** Graduate Studies, Program in Anthropology, New York, NY 10016-4039. Offers anthropological linguistics (PhD); archaeology (PhD); cultural anthropology (PhD); physical anthropology (PhD). *Degree requirements:* For doctorate, one foreign language, thesis/dissertation. *Entrance requirements:* For doctorate, GRE General Test. Additional exam requirements/ recommendations for international students: Required—TOEFL. Electronic applications accepted.

**Harvard University,** Graduate School of Arts and Sciences, Department of Anthropology, Cambridge, MA 02138. Offers archaeology (PhD); biological anthropology (PhD); legal anthropology (AM); medical anthropology (AM); social anthropology (AM, PhD); social change and development (AM). Terminal master's awarded for partial completion of doctoral program. *Degree requirements:* For master's, 2 foreign languages, thesis (for some programs); for doctorate, 2 foreign languages, thesis/dissertation, laboratory and/or fieldwork; general, qualifying, or special exams. *Entrance requirements:* For master's and doctorate, GRE General Test. Additional exam requirements/recommendations for international students: Required—TOEFL.

**Harvard University,** Graduate School of Arts and Sciences, Department of Near Eastern Languages and Civilizations, Cambridge, MA 02138. Offers Akkadian and Sumerian (AM, PhD); Arabic (AM, PhD); Armenian (AM, PhD); biblical history (AM, PhD); Hebrew (AM, PhD); Indo-Muslim culture (AM, PhD); Iranian (AM, PhD); Jewish history and literature (AM, PhD); Persian (AM, PhD); Semitic philology (AM, PhD); Syro-Palestinian archaeology (AM, PhD); Turkish (AM, PhD). *Degree requirements:* For doctorate, variable foreign language requirement, thesis/dissertation, general exams. *Entrance requirements:* For master's, GRE General Test; for doctorate, GRE General Test, proficiency in a Near Eastern language. Additional exam requirements/ recommendations for international students: Required—TOEFL.

**Harvard University,** Graduate School of Arts and Sciences, Department of the Classics, Cambridge, MA 02138. Offers Byzantine Greek (PhD); classical archaeology (PhD); classical philology (PhD); classical philosophy (PhD); medieval Latin (PhD). *Degree requirements:* For doctorate, 4 foreign languages, thesis/dissertation, preliminary and special exams. *Entrance requirements:* For doctorate, GRE General Test. Additional exam requirements/recommendations for international students: Required—TOEFL.

**Illinois State University,** Graduate School, College of Arts and Sciences, Department of Sociology, Program in Historical Archaeology, Normal, IL 61790-2200. Offers MA, MS.

**Indiana University Bloomington,** University Graduate School, College of Arts and Sciences, Department of Anthropology, Bloomington, IN 47405. Offers anthropology (MA, PhD), including archaeology (PhD), bioanthropology (PhD), linguistic anthropology (PhD), social-cultural anthropology (PhD). *Faculty:* 35 full-time (23 women). *Students:* 101 full-time (76 women); includes 16 minority (2 Black or African American, non-Hispanic/Latino; 2 American Indian or Alaska Native, non-Hispanic/Latino; 1 Asian, non-Hispanic/Latino; 6 Hispanic/Latino; 5 Two or more races, non-Hispanic/Latino), 15 international. Average age 33. 81 applicants, 15% accepted, 6 enrolled. In 2016, 8 master's, 10 doctorates awarded. *Degree requirements:* For master's, comprehensive exam (for some programs), thesis or alternative; for doctorate, 2 foreign languages, comprehensive exam, thesis/dissertation. *Entrance requirements:* For master's and doctorate, GRE General Test, minimum GPA of 3.0. Additional exam requirements/ recommendations for international students: Required—TOEFL (minimum score 550 paper-based, 79 iBT) or IELTS. *Application deadline:* For fall admission, 12/1 for domestic and international students. Application fee: $55 ($65 for international students). Electronic applications accepted. *Expenses:* $3,429 per course non-resident, $990 per course resident. *Financial support:* In 2016–17, 68 students received support, including 22 fellowships with full tuition reimbursements available (averaging $18,000 per year), 4 research assistantships with full tuition reimbursements available (averaging $15,750 per year), 46 teaching assistantships with full tuition reimbursements available (averaging $15,750 per year); Federal Work-Study, scholarships/grants, health care benefits, and unspecified assistantships also available. *Faculty research:* Archaeology in social context; bio anthropology; anthropology of food and ecology; gender studies; communication, media and performance. *Total annual research expenditures:* $170,905. *Unit head:* Dr. Jeanne Sept, Chair, 812-855-2555, Fax: 812-855-4358, E-mail: sept@indiana.edu. *Application contact:* Debra Wilkerson, Administrative Secretary, 812-855-1203, Fax: 812-855-4358, E-mail: dwilkers@indiana.edu. Website: http://www.indiana.edu/~anthro/index.shtml

**Indiana University of Pennsylvania,** School of Graduate Studies and Research, College of Humanities and Social Sciences, Department of Anthropology, Indiana, PA 15705. Offers applied archaeology (MA). *Program availability:* Part-time. *Faculty:* 6 full-time (2 women). *Students:* 15 full-time (8 women), 1 part-time (0 women), 1 international. Average age 24. 23 applicants, 65% accepted, 11 enrolled. In 2016, 5 master's awarded. *Degree requirements:* For master's, thesis and/or internship. *Entrance requirements:* For master's, GRE, 2 letters of recommendation. Additional exam requirements/recommendations for international students: Required—TOEFL (minimum score 540 paper-based). *Application deadline:* Applications are processed on a rolling basis. Application fee: $50. Electronic applications accepted. *Expenses:* Tuition, state resident: full-time $8694; part-time $483 per credit. Tuition, nonresident: full-time $13,050; part-time $725 per credit. *Required fees:* $157 per credit. $50 per term. Tuition and fees vary according to course load and program. *Financial support:* In 2016–17, 8 research assistantships with tuition reimbursements (averaging $3,095 per year) were awarded; fellowships with partial tuition reimbursements, Federal Work-Study, scholarships/grants, and unspecified assistantships also available. Financial award application deadline: 4/15; financial award applicants required to submit FAFSA. *Unit head:* Dr. Phillip Neusius, Chair, 724-357-2841, Fax: 724-357-7637, E-mail: phillip.neusius@iup.edu. Website: http://www.iup.edu/anthropology/

**Johns Hopkins University,** Zanvyl Krieger School of Arts and Sciences, Department of Near Eastern Studies, Baltimore, MD 21218. Offers archaeology (PhD); Assyriology (PhD); Egyptology (PhD); Hebrew Bible/Northwest Semitics (PhD). *Degree requirements:* For doctorate, 2 foreign languages, comprehensive exam, thesis/ dissertation. *Entrance requirements:* For doctorate, GRE. Additional exam requirements/recommendations for international students: Required—TOEFL (minimum score 600 paper-based; 100 iBT); Recommended—IELTS. Electronic applications accepted. *Faculty research:* Egyptology, Assyriology, Hebrew Bible/Northwest Semitic languages, Demotic Egyptian, archaeology.

**Massachusetts Institute of Technology,** School of Engineering, Department of Materials Science and Engineering, Cambridge, MA 02139. Offers archaeological materials (PhD, Sc D); materials engineering (Mat E); materials science and engineering (SM, PhD, Sc D). *Faculty:* 32 full-time (10 women). *Students:* 170 full-time (43 women); includes 29 minority (1 Black or African American, non-Hispanic/Latino; 17 Asian, non-Hispanic/Latino; 6 Hispanic/Latino; 5 Two or more races, non-Hispanic/Latino), 93 international. Average age 26. 463 applicants, 12% accepted, 28 enrolled. In 2016, 5 master's, 39 doctorates awarded. *Degree requirements:* For master's, thesis; for doctorate, comprehensive exam, thesis/dissertation; for Mat E, comprehensive exam, thesis. *Entrance requirements:* For master's and doctorate, GRE General Test. Additional exam requirements/recommendations for international students: Required—IELTS. *Application deadline:* For fall admission, 12/1 for domestic and international students. Application fee: $75. Electronic applications accepted. *Expenses: Tuition:* Full-time $46,400; part-time $725 per credit. One-time fee: $312 full-time. Full-time tuition and fees vary according to course load and program. *Financial support:* In 2016–17, 159 students received support, including fellowships (averaging $34,000 per year), 103 research assistantships (averaging $37,500 per year), 16 teaching assistantships (averaging $39,800 per year); Federal Work-Study, institutionally sponsored loans, scholarships/grants, traineeships, health care benefits, unspecified assistantships, and resident tutors also available. Support available to part-time students. Financial award application deadline: 5/1; financial award applicants required to submit FAFSA. *Faculty research:* Thermodynamics and kinetics of materials; structure, processing and properties of materials; electronic, structural and biological materials engineering; computational materials science; materials in energy, medicine, nanotechnology and the environment. *Total annual research expenditures:* $25.5 million. *Unit head:* Prof. Christopher Schuh, Department Head, 617-253-3300, Fax: 617-252-1775, E-mail: dmse@mit.edu. *Application contact:* 617-253-3302, E-mail: dmse-admissions@mit.edu. Website: http://dmse.mit.edu/

**Memorial University of Newfoundland,** School of Graduate Studies, Department of Anthropology, St. John's, NL A1C 5S7, Canada. Offers archaeology and physical anthropology (MA, PhD); social and cultural anthropology (MA, PhD). *Program availability:* Part-time. *Degree requirements:* For master's, comprehensive exam (for some programs), thesis (for some programs); for doctorate, comprehensive exam, thesis/dissertation, oral defense of thesis. *Entrance requirements:* For master's, 2nd class degree in related field. Electronic applications accepted. *Faculty research:* Early European settlements, ethnoarchaeology, economic/political anthropology, land claims and aboriginal rights, marine anthropology.

**Mercyhurst University,** Graduate Studies, Program in Anthropology, Erie, PA 16546. Offers archaeology and geological archaeology (MS); forensic and biological anthropology (MS). *Entrance requirements:* For master's, GRE or MAT, undergraduate degree in related field, interview, resume, essay, three professional references, transcripts. Additional exam requirements/recommendations for international students: Required—TOEFL.

**Michigan Technological University,** Graduate School, College of Sciences and Arts, Department of Social Sciences, Houghton, MI 49931. Offers environmental and energy policy (MS, PhD); industrial archaeology (MS); industrial heritage and archaeology (PhD). *Faculty:* 31 full-time (15 women), 20 part-time/adjunct (5 women). *Students:* 18 full-time (10 women), 14 part-time (5 women); includes 2 minority (both American Indian or Alaska Native, non-Hispanic/Latino), 7 international. Average age 36. 66 applicants, 17% accepted, 7 enrolled. In 2016, 13 master's, 3 doctorates awarded. Terminal master's awarded for partial completion of doctoral program. *Degree requirements:* For master's, thesis; for doctorate, comprehensive exam, thesis/dissertation. *Entrance requirements:* For master's and doctorate, GRE, statement of purpose, official transcripts, 3 letters of recommendation, writing sample, resume/curriculum vitae. Additional exam requirements/recommendations for international students: Required—TOEFL (recommended minimum score 100 iBT) or IELTS. *Application deadline:* For fall admission, 1/15 priority date for domestic students, 2/1 priority date for international students; for spring admission, 10/1 for domestic students. Applications are processed on a rolling basis. Application fee: $0. Electronic applications accepted. *Expenses:* Tuition, state resident: full-time $16,290; part-time $905 per credit. Tuition, nonresident: full-time $16,290; part-time $905 per credit. *Required fees:* $248; $124 per term. Tuition and fees vary according to course load and program. *Financial support:* In 2016–17, 22 students received support, including 2 fellowships with full tuition reimbursements available (averaging $15,242 per year), 5 research assistantships with full tuition reimbursements available (averaging $15,242 per year), 10 teaching assistantships with full tuition reimbursements available (averaging $15,242 per year); career-related internships or fieldwork, scholarships/grants, health care benefits, unspecified assistantships, and cooperative program also available. Financial award application deadline: 1/15. *Faculty research:* Industrial archeology, mining history, environmental and energy policy, land-use policy, environmental decision-making, sustainability. *Total annual research expenditures:* $984,488. *Unit head:* Dr. Hugh S. Gorman, Chair, 906-487-2116, E-mail: hsgorman@mtu.edu. *Application contact:* Amy Spahn, Office Assistant, 906-487-2113, Fax: 906-487-2284, E-mail: gradadms@mtu.edu. Website: http://www.mtu.edu/social-sciences/

**New York University,** Graduate School of Arts and Science, Institute of Fine Arts, Program in Art History and Archaeology, New York, NY 10012-1019. Offers architectural studies (PhD); art history and archaeology (MA, PhD); classical art and archaeology (PhD); curatorial studies (PhD); East and South Asian art (PhD); Near Eastern art and archaeology (PhD); MA/Diploma; PhD/Certificate. *Program availability:* Part-time. Terminal master's awarded for partial completion of doctoral program. *Degree requirements:* For master's, 2 foreign languages, thesis or alternative, 2 qualifying papers; for doctorate, 2 foreign languages, thesis/dissertation. *Entrance requirements:* For master's, GRE General Test; for doctorate, GRE General Test, MA. Additional exam requirements/recommendations for international students: Required—TOEFL.

**Northern Arizona University,** Graduate College, College of Social and Behavioral Sciences, Department of Anthropology, Flagstaff, AZ 86011. Offers archaeology (MA); linguistic anthropology (MA); sociocultural anthropology (MA). *Degree requirements:* For master's, thesis (for some programs), internship paper. *Entrance requirements:* For master's, 12 undergraduate hours in anthropology. Additional exam requirements/ recommendations for international students: Required—TOEFL (minimum score 550 paper-based; 80 iBT), IELTS (minimum score 7). Electronic applications accepted. *Expenses:* Tuition, state resident: full-time $8971; part-time $444 per credit hour. Tuition, nonresident: full-time $20,958; part-time $1164 per credit hour. *Required fees:* $1018; $644 per credit hour. Tuition and fees vary according to course load, campus/

location and program. *Faculty research:* Economic development, culture change, ethnohistory, archaeology of the Southwest, small town networks and HIV.

**Princeton University,** Graduate School, Department of Art and Archaeology, Princeton, NJ 08544-1019. Offers classical art and archaeology (PhD); East Asian art and archaeology (PhD). *Degree requirements:* For doctorate, 2 foreign languages, thesis/ dissertation. *Entrance requirements:* For doctorate, GRE General Test. Additional exam requirements/recommendations for international students: Required—TOEFL (minimum score 600 paper-based). Electronic applications accepted.

**Rice University,** Graduate Programs, School of Social Sciences, Department of Anthropology, Houston, TX 77251-1892. Offers archaeology (MA, PhD); social-cultural anthropology (MA, PhD). Terminal master's awarded for partial completion of doctoral program. *Degree requirements:* For master's, one foreign language, 3 major papers, dissertation proposal and language exam or thesis; for doctorate, one foreign language, thesis/dissertation. *Entrance requirements:* For master's and doctorate, research proposal. Additional exam requirements/recommendations for international students: Required—TOEFL (minimum score 90 iBT). Electronic applications accepted.

**St. Cloud State University,** School of Graduate Studies, College of Social Sciences, Program in Cultural Resource Management Archeology, St. Cloud, MN 56301-4498. Offers MS. *Entrance requirements:* For master's, GRE General Test, minimum GPA of 2.75. Additional exam requirements/recommendations for international students: Required—Michigan English Language Assessment Battery; Recommended—TOEFL (minimum score 550 paper-based).

**San Francisco State University,** Division of Graduate Studies, College of Liberal and Creative Arts, Department of Anthropology, San Francisco, CA 94132-1722. Offers archaeology (MA); biological/physical anthropology (MA); social/cultural anthropology (MA); visual anthropology (MA). *Expenses:* Tuition, state resident: full-time $6738. Tuition, nonresident: full-time $15,666. *Required fees:* $1012. Tuition and fees vary according to degree level and program. *Faculty research:* Immigration, ethnicity, urban anthropology, Californian and Latin American archaeology. *Unit head:* Dr. James Quesada, Chair, 415-338-1633, Fax: 415-338-6159, E-mail: jquesada@sfsu.edu. *Application contact:* Dr. Douglass Bailey, Graduate Coordinator, 415-338-1427, Fax: 415-338-6159, E-mail: dwbailey@sfsu.edu.
Website: http://anthropology.sfsu.edu/

**Simon Fraser University,** Office of Graduate Studies and Postdoctoral Fellows, Faculty of Environment, Department of Archaeology, Burnaby, BC V5A 1S6, Canada. Offers MA, PhD. *Faculty:* 15 full-time (3 women). *Students:* 53 full-time (34 women), 1 part-time. 56 applicants, 45% accepted, 21 enrolled. In 2016, 5 master's, 6 doctorates awarded. *Degree requirements:* For master's, one foreign language, thesis; for doctorate, one foreign language, comprehensive exam, thesis/dissertation. *Entrance requirements:* For master's, minimum GPA of 3.0 (on scale of 4.33) or 3.33 based on last 60 credits of undergraduate courses; for doctorate, minimum GPA of 3.5 (on scale of 4.33). Additional exam requirements/recommendations for international students: Recommended—TOEFL (minimum score 580 paper-based; 93 iBT), IELTS (minimum score 7), TWE (minimum score 5). *Application deadline:* For fall admission, 2/15 for domestic and international students; for spring admission, 2/1 for domestic students. Application fee: $90 ($125 for international students). Electronic applications accepted. *Financial support:* In 2016–17, 29 students received support, including 13 fellowships (averaging $6,500 per year), teaching assistantships (averaging $5,608 per year); research assistantships and scholarships/grants also available. *Faculty research:* Archaeometry, cultural resource management, ethnoarchaeology, forensic anthropology, palaeoethnobotany, skeletal biology, zoo archaeology. *Unit head:* Dr. Dana Lepofsky, Graduate Chair, 778-782-5403, Fax: 778-782-5666, E-mail: arch-grad-chair@sfu.ca. *Application contact:* Merrill Farmer, Graduate Secretary, 778-782-4727, Fax: 778-782-5666, E-mail: arch-grad-secretary@sfu.ca.
Website: http://www.sfu.ca/archaeology/

**Stanford University,** School of Humanities and Sciences, Department of Anthropology, Stanford, CA 94305-2004. Offers anthropology (MA); archaeology (PhD); culture and society (PhD); ecology and environment (PhD). Terminal master's awarded for partial completion of doctoral program. *Degree requirements:* For master's, thesis; for doctorate, one foreign language, thesis/dissertation. *Entrance requirements:* For master's and doctorate, GRE General Test. Additional exam requirements/recommendations for international students: Required—TOEFL. Electronic applications accepted. *Expenses:* Tuition: Full-time $47,331. *Required fees:* $609.

**Trinity International University,** Trinity Evangelical Divinity School, Deerfield, IL 60015-1284. Offers academic ministry (M Div); Biblical and Near Eastern archaeology and languages (MA); chaplaincy and ministry care (MA); Christian studies (Certificate); church and parachurch ministry (M Div); church history (MA, Th M); counseling (Th M); educational ministries (MA); educational ministry (Th M); educational studies (PhD); intercultural studies (MA, PhD); leadership and management (D Min); mental health counseling (MA); military chaplaincy (D Min); ministry (MA); missions (Th M); missions and evangelism (D Min); New Testament (MA, Th M); Old Testament (Th M); Old Testament and Semitic languages (MA); pastoral ministry and care (D Min); pastoral theology (Th M); preaching and teaching (D Min); spiritual formation and education (D Min); systematic theology (MA, Th M); theological studies (MA, PhD); urban ministry (MA). *Program availability:* Part-time, online learning. *Students:* 578 full-time (141 women), 711 part-time (202 women). *Degree requirements:* For master's, comprehensive exam, thesis, fieldwork; for doctorate, comprehensive exam (for some programs), thesis/dissertation; for Certificate, comprehensive exam, integrative papers. *Entrance requirements:* For master's, GRE, MAT, minimum cumulative undergraduate GPA of 3.0; for doctorate, GRE, minimum cumulative graduate GPA of 3.2; for Certificate, GRE, MAT, minimum undergraduate GPA of 2.5. Additional exam requirements/recommendations for international students: Required—TOEFL (minimum score 580 paper-based), TWE (minimum score 4). *Application deadline:* For fall admission, 7/15 priority date for domestic and international students. Applications are processed on a rolling basis. Application fee: $25. Electronic applications accepted. *Expenses:* Tuition, area resident: Full-time $19,898. *Required fees:* $200. *Financial support:* Fellowships with partial tuition reimbursements, teaching assistantships with partial tuition reimbursements, career-related internships or fieldwork, Federal Work-Study, scholarships/grants, and tuition waivers (partial) available. Financial award application deadline: 4/1; financial award applicants required to submit FAFSA. *Unit head:* Dr. Tite Tienou, Academic Dean, 847-317-8086, Fax: 847-317-8014, E-mail: ttienou@teds.edu. *Application contact:* Ron Campbell, Director of Admissions, 800-345-8337, Fax: 847-317-8097, E-mail: rcampbel@tiu.edu.
Website: https://divinity.tiu.edu/

**Tufts University,** Graduate School of Arts and Sciences, Department of Classics, Medford, MA 02155. Offers classical archaeology (MA); classics (MA); classics with teaching licensure (MA). *Program availability:* Part-time. *Students:* 9 full-time (6 women); includes 3 minority (1 Black or African American, non-Hispanic/Latino; 1 Asian, non-Hispanic/Latino; 1 Hispanic/Latino), 3 international. Average age 24. 32 applicants, 53% accepted, 7 enrolled. In 2016, 4 master's awarded. *Degree requirements:* For master's, 2 foreign languages, comprehensive exam, thesis or alternative. *Entrance requirements:* For master's, GRE General Test, writing sample. Additional exam requirements/

recommendations for international students: Required—TOEFL (minimum score 550 paper-based; 80 iBT), IELTS (minimum score 6.5). *Application deadline:* For fall admission, 2/15 for domestic and international students; for spring admission, 10/15 for domestic and international students. Applications are processed on a rolling basis. Application fee: $85. Electronic applications accepted. *Expenses:* $49,982 full-time tuition (for MA). *Financial support:* In 2016–17, 9 students received support. Teaching assistantships, Federal Work-Study, scholarships/grants, tuition waivers (full and partial), and unspecified assistantships available. Financial award application deadline: 1/15; financial award applicants required to submit FAFSA. *Unit head:* Dr. Marie-Claire Beaulieu, Graduate Program Director. *Application contact:* Office of Graduate Admissions, 617-627-3395, E-mail: gradadmissions@tufts.edu.
Website: http://www.ase.tufts.edu/classics/

**Universidad de las Américas Puebla,** Division of Graduate Studies, School of Social Sciences, Program in Anthropology, Puebla, Mexico. Offers anthropology (MA); archaeology (MA). *Program availability:* Part-time, evening/weekend. *Degree requirements:* For master's, one foreign language, thesis. *Entrance requirements:* For master's, bachelor's degree in anthropology or equivalent. *Faculty research:* Archaeology, ethnography, and ethnohistory of Mesoamerica.

**Université Laval,** Faculty of Letters, Department of History, Programs in Archaeology, Québec, QC G1K 7P4, Canada. Offers MA, PhD. Terminal master's awarded for partial completion of doctoral program. *Degree requirements:* For master's, thesis; for doctorate, comprehensive exam, thesis/dissertation. *Entrance requirements:* For master's and doctorate, English test, knowledge of French. Electronic applications accepted.

**University of Alberta,** Faculty of Graduate Studies and Research, Department of History and Classics, Edmonton, AB T6G 2E1, Canada. Offers ancient history (PhD); classical archaeology (MA, PhD); classical literature (PhD); classics (MA); history (MA, PhD). *Program availability:* Part-time, evening/weekend. *Degree requirements:* For master's, one foreign language, thesis (for some programs); for doctorate, one foreign language, thesis/dissertation. *Entrance requirements:* For master's, minimum B+ average; for doctorate, minimum A- average. Additional exam requirements/recommendations for international students: Required—TOEFL (minimum score 580 paper-based). Electronic applications accepted. *Faculty research:* Western Canada, classical archaeology, Britain, Eastern Europe, East Asia.

**The University of British Columbia,** Faculty of Arts, Department of Classical, Near Eastern and Religious Studies, Vancouver, BC V6T 1Z1, Canada. Offers ancient culture, religion, and ethnicity (MA); classical and Near eastern archaeology (MA); classics (MA, PhD), including classics; religious studies (MA). *Program availability:* Part-time. *Degree requirements:* For master's, 2 foreign languages, comprehensive exam, thesis optional; for doctorate, 2 foreign languages, comprehensive exam, thesis/dissertation. *Entrance requirements:* For master's, BA; for doctorate, MA. Additional exam requirements/recommendations for international students: Required—TOEFL, IELTS. *Application deadline:* Applications are processed on a rolling basis. Application fee: $100 Canadian dollars ($162 Canadian dollars for international students). Electronic applications accepted. *Expenses:* $4,802 per year tuition and fees, $8,436 per year international. *Financial support:* Fellowships, teaching assistantships, scholarships/grants, and health care benefits available. *Faculty research:* Classical literature, ancient history, Biblical studies, archaeology, classical languages, Judaic studies. *Application contact:* Odessa Cadieux-Rey, Graduate Program Staff, 604-822-2515, Fax: 604-822-9431, E-mail: cners.gradsec@ubc.ca.
Website: http://cnrs.ubc.ca/

**University of Calgary,** Faculty of Graduate Studies, Faculty of Arts, Department of Archaeology, Calgary, AB T2N 1N4, Canada. Offers MA. *Degree requirements:* For master's, thesis. *Entrance requirements:* For master's, BA or B Sc in anthropology or archaeology; statement of intent; sample of written work; curriculum vitae. Additional exam requirements/recommendations for international students: Required—TOEFL. Electronic applications accepted. *Faculty research:* Pre-history, ethnoarchaeology, Africa, Latin America, biological anthropology.

**University of California, Berkeley,** Graduate Division, College of Letters and Science, Department of Classics, Berkeley, CA 94720-1500. Offers classical archaeology (MA, PhD); classics (MA, PhD); Greek (MA); Latin (MA). *Faculty:* 19 full-time, 3 part-time/adjunct. *Students:* 27 full-time (11 women); includes 7 minority (3 Asian, non-Hispanic/Latino; 4 Hispanic/Latino), 2 international. Average age 29. 64 applicants, 4 enrolled. In 2016, 4 master's, 5 doctorates awarded. Terminal master's awarded for partial completion of doctoral program. *Degree requirements:* For master's, one foreign language, exams; for doctorate, 2 foreign languages, thesis/dissertation, qualifying exam. *Entrance requirements:* For master's and doctorate, GRE General Test, minimum GPA of 3.0, 3 letters of recommendation. Additional exam requirements/recommendations for international students: Required—TOEFL (minimum score 570 paper-based; 90 iBT), TWE. *Application deadline:* For fall admission, 12/9 for domestic students. Application fee: $105 ($125 for international students). Electronic applications accepted. *Financial support:* Fellowships, research assistantships, teaching assistantships, Federal Work-Study, institutionally sponsored loans, health care benefits, and unspecified assistantships available. *Faculty research:* Greek and Latin literature, textual criticism, history, archaeology and philosophy. *Unit head:* Prof. Ellen Oliensis, Chair, 510-642-4218, Fax: 510-643-2959. *Application contact:* Cassandra Dunn, 510-642-3672, Fax: 510-643-2959, E-mail: cassandrajj@berkeley.edu.
Website: http://classics.berkeley.edu/

**University of California, Berkeley,** Graduate Division, College of Letters and Science, Group in Ancient History and Mediterranean Archaeology, Berkeley, CA 94720-1500. Offers MA, PhD. *Students:* 14 full-time (8 women); includes 2 minority (1 Asian, non-Hispanic/Latino; 1 Hispanic/Latino). Average age 30. 45 applicants, 3 enrolled. In 2016, 1 master's, 3 doctorates awarded. Terminal master's awarded for partial completion of doctoral program. *Degree requirements:* For master's, one foreign language, exam or thesis; for doctorate, 2 foreign languages, thesis/dissertation, qualifying exam. *Entrance requirements:* For master's and doctorate, GRE General Test, minimum GPA of 3.0, 3 letters of recommendation. Additional exam requirements/recommendations for international students: Required—TOEFL (minimum score 570 paper-based; 90 iBT), TWE. *Application deadline:* For fall admission, 12/9 for domestic students. Application fee: $105 ($125 for international students). Electronic applications accepted. *Financial support:* Fellowships, research assistantships, teaching assistantships, career-related internships or fieldwork, institutionally sponsored loans, health care benefits, and unspecified assistantships available. *Unit head:* Prof. Carlos Norena, Chair, 510-643-8741, E-mail: casmaadm@berkeley.edu. *Application contact:* Miguel Valencia, Student Affairs Officer, 510-643-8741, Fax: 510-643-2959, E-mail: casmaadm@berkeley.edu.
Website: http://ahma.berkeley.edu

**University of California, Los Angeles,** Graduate Division, College of Letters and Science, Interdepartmental Program in Archaeology, Los Angeles, CA 90095. Offers MA, PhD. Terminal master's awarded for partial completion of doctoral program. *Degree requirements:* For master's, one foreign language, comprehensive exam, field experience; for doctorate, 2 foreign languages, thesis/dissertation, oral and written qualifying exams. *Entrance requirements:* For doctorate, GRE General Test, bachelor's degree; minimum undergraduate GPA of 3.0 (or its equivalent if letter grade system not used); writing sample. Additional exam requirements/recommendations for international students: Required—TOEFL. Electronic applications accepted.

**University of California, Los Angeles,** Graduate Division, College of Letters and Science, Interdepartmental Program in Conservation of Archaeological and Ethnographic Materials, Los Angeles, CA 90095. Offers MA. *Degree requirements:* For master's, one foreign language, thesis, eleven-month internship. *Entrance requirements:* For master's, GRE General Test, bachelor's degree; minimum undergraduate GPA of 3.0 (or its equivalent if letter grade system not used); proficiency in one foreign language; portfolio; writing sample; documented practical experience; interview. Additional exam requirements/recommendations for international students: Required—TOEFL.

**University of Chicago,** Division of the Social Sciences, Department of Anthropology, Chicago, IL 60637. Offers archaeology (PhD); sociocultural and linguistic anthropology (PhD). *Students:* 146 full-time (80 women); includes 25 minority (5 Black or African American, non-Hispanic/Latino; 2 American Indian or Alaska Native, non-Hispanic/Latino; 3 Asian, non-Hispanic/Latino; 10 Two or more races, non-Hispanic/Latino), 48 international. 271 applicants, 10% accepted, 16 enrolled. In 2016, 15 doctorates awarded. *Degree requirements:* For doctorate, one foreign language, thesis/dissertation, exams. *Entrance requirements:* For doctorate, GRE General Test. Additional exam requirements/recommendations for international students: Required—TOEFL (minimum score 104 iBT), IELTS (minimum score 7). *Application deadline:* For fall admission, 12/15 for domestic and international students. Application fee: $90. Electronic applications accepted. *Financial support:* In 2016–17, 16 students received support, including 12 fellowships with full tuition reimbursements available (averaging $23,000 per year); career-related internships or fieldwork, Federal Work-Study, institutionally sponsored loans, scholarships/grants, and health care benefits also available. Financial award application deadline: 12/15. *Unit head:* Dr. William Mazzarella, Chair, 773-834-4873, E-mail: mazzarel@uchicago.edu. *Application contact:* Office of the Dean of Students, 773-702-8415, E-mail: admissions@ssd.uchicago.edu. Website: http://anthropology.uchicago.edu

**University of Colorado Denver,** College of Liberal Arts and Sciences, Department of Anthropology, Denver, CO 80217. Offers archaeological studies (MA); biological anthropology (MA); medical anthropology (MA); sustainable development and political ecology (MA). *Program availability:* Part-time, evening/weekend. *Faculty:* 9 full-time (3 women), 1 part-time/adjunct (0 women). *Students:* 30 full-time (22 women), 5 part-time (3 women); includes 9 minority (2 Black or African American, non-Hispanic/Latino; 1 American Indian or Alaska Native, non-Hispanic/Latino; 4 Hispanic/Latino; 2 Two or more races, non-Hispanic/Latino), 1 international. Average age 28. 40 applicants, 53% accepted, 11 enrolled. In 2016, 13 master's awarded. *Degree requirements:* For master's, comprehensive exam, thesis or alternative, 30-36 credit hours. *Entrance requirements:* For master's, GRE General Test, minimum GPA of 3.0 for all undergraduate studies, transcripts from all undergraduate/graduate institutions attended, prior training in anthropology, three letters of recommendation, statement of purpose. Additional exam requirements/recommendations for international students: Required—TOEFL (minimum score 537 paper-based; 75 iBT); Recommended—IELTS (minimum score 6.5). *Application deadline:* For fall admission, 2/15 for domestic students, 1/15 for international students. Application fee: $50 ($75 for international students). Electronic applications accepted. *Expenses:* Tuition, state resident: full-time $11,006; part-time $474 per credit. Tuition, nonresident: full-time $28,212; part-time $1264 per credit hour. *Required fees:* $256 per semester. One-time fee: $94.32. Tuition and fees vary according to campus/location and program. *Financial support:* In 2016–17, 3 students received support. Fellowships, research assistantships, teaching assistantships, Federal Work-Study, institutionally sponsored loans, scholarships/grants, and traineeships available. Financial award application deadline: 4/1; financial award applicants required to submit FAFSA. *Faculty research:* Applied medical anthropology, primate social behavior, environmental anthropology, Southwestern and Mexican archaeology, human ecology. *Application contact:* Connie Turner, Program Assistant, 303-556-3554, E-mail: connie.turner@ucdenver.edu.
Website: http://www.ucdenver.edu/academics/colleges/CLAS/Departments/anthropology/Programs/Masters/Pages/Masters.aspx

**University of Denver,** Division of Arts, Humanities and Social Sciences, Department of Anthropology, Denver, CO 80208. Offers archaeology (MA); cultural anthropology (MA); museum and heritage studies (MA). *Program availability:* Part-time. *Faculty:* 8 full-time (2 women). *Students:* 3 full-time (all women), 17 part-time (16 women); includes 2 minority (1 American Indian or Alaska Native, non-Hispanic/Latino; 1 Hispanic/Latino). Average age 25. 47 applicants, 43% accepted, 11 enrolled. In 2016, 11 master's awarded. *Degree requirements:* For master's, one foreign language, comprehensive exam, thesis (for some programs), tool, foreign language literacy, or course work. *Entrance requirements:* For master's, GRE General Test, bachelor's degree, transcripts, personal statement, two letters of recommendation. Additional exam requirements/recommendations for international students: Required—TOEFL (minimum score 550 paper-based; 80 iBT). *Application deadline:* For fall admission, 2/4 priority date for domestic and international students. Applications are processed on a rolling basis. Application fee: $65. Electronic applications accepted. *Expenses:* $29,022 per year full-time. *Financial support:* In 2016–17, 19 students received support, including 6 teaching assistantships with tuition reimbursements available (averaging $6,667 per year); career-related internships or fieldwork, Federal Work-Study, institutionally sponsored loans, scholarships/grants, and unspecified assistantships also available. Support available to part-time students. Financial award application deadline: 2/15; financial award applicants required to submit FAFSA. *Faculty research:* Human diversity, human rights, historic archaeology, museums and heritage, high-tech field methods. *Unit head:* Dr. Larry Conyers, Professor and Chair, 303-871-2684, Fax: 303-871-2437, E-mail: lconyers@du.edu. *Application contact:* Dr. Larry Conyers, Professor and Director of Graduate Program, 303-871-2684, Fax: 303-871-2437, E-mail: lconyers@du.edu. Website: http://www.du.edu/ahss/anthropology

**University of Lethbridge,** School of Graduate Studies, Lethbridge, AB T1K 3M4, Canada. Offers addictions counseling (M Sc); agricultural biotechnology (M Sc); agricultural studies (M Sc, MA); anthropology (MA); archaeology (M Sc, MA); art (MA, MFA); biochemistry (M Sc); biological sciences (M Sc); biomolecular science (PhD); biosystems and biodiversity (PhD); Canadian studies (MA); chemistry (M Sc); computer science (M Sc); computer science and geographical information science (M Sc); counseling (MC); counseling psychology (M Ed); dramatic arts (MA); earth, space, and physical science (M Sc); economics (MA); education (MA, PhD); educational leadership (M Ed); English (MA); environmental science (M Sc); evolution and behavior (PhD); exercise science (M Sc); French (MA); French/German (MA); French/Spanish (MA); general education (M Ed); geography (M Sc, MA); German (MA); health sciences (M Sc); individualized multidisciplinary (M Sc, MA); kinesiology (M Sc, MA); management (M Sc), including accounting, finance, human resource management and labor relations, information systems, international management, marketing, policy and strategy; mathematics (M Sc); music (M Mus, MA); Native American studies (MA); neuroscience (M Sc, PhD); new media (MA, MFA); nursing (M Sc, MN); philosophy (MA); physics (M Sc); political science (MA); psychology (M Sc, MA); religious studies

(MA); sociology (MA); theatre and dramatic arts (MFA); theoretical and computational science (PhD); urban and regional studies (MA); women and gender studies (MA). *Program availability:* Part-time, evening/weekend. *Degree requirements:* For master's, thesis (for some programs); for doctorate, comprehensive exam, thesis/dissertation. *Entrance requirements:* For master's, GMAT (for M Sc in management), bachelor's degree in related field, minimum GPA of 3.0 during previous 20 graded semester courses, 2 years' teaching or related experience (M Ed); for doctorate, master's degree, minimum graduate GPA of 3.5. Additional exam requirements/recommendations for international students: Required—TOEFL (minimum score 580 paper-based; 93 iBT). Electronic applications accepted. *Faculty research:* Movement and brain plasticity, gibberellin physiology, photosynthesis, carbon cycling, molecular properties of main-group ring components.

**The University of Manchester,** Faculty of Life Sciences, Manchester, United Kingdom. Offers adaptive organismal biology (M Phil, PhD); animal biology (M Phil, PhD); biochemistry (M Phil, PhD); bioinformatics (M Phil, PhD); biomolecular sciences (M Phil, PhD); biotechnology (M Phil, PhD); cell biology (M Phil, PhD); cell matrix research (M Phil, PhD); channels and transporters (M Phil, PhD); developmental biology (M Phil, PhD); Egyptology (M Phil, PhD); environmental biology (M Phil, PhD); evolutionary biology (M Phil, PhD); gene expression (M Phil, PhD); genetics (M Phil, PhD); history of science, technology and medicine (M Phil, PhD); immunology (M Phil, PhD); integrative neurobiology and behavior (M Phil, PhD); membrane trafficking (M Phil, PhD); microbiology (M Phil, PhD); molecular and cellular neuroscience (M Phil, PhD); molecular biology (M Phil, PhD); molecular cancer studies (M Phil, PhD); neuroscience (M Phil, PhD); ophthalmology (M Phil, PhD); optometry (M Phil, PhD); organelle function (M Phil, PhD); pharmacology (M Phil, PhD); physiology (M Phil, PhD); plant sciences (M Phil, PhD); stem cell research (M Phil, PhD); structural biology (M Phil, PhD); systems neuroscience (M Phil, PhD); toxicology (M Phil, PhD).

**The University of Manchester,** School of Arts, Histories and Cultures, Manchester, United Kingdom. Offers anthropology, media and performance (PhD); applied theatre professional (PhD); archaeology (PhD); art history and visual studies (PhD); arts management and cultural policy (PhD); classics and ancient history (PhD); composition (PhD); creative writing (PhD); drama (PhD); economic and social history (PhD); electroacoustic composition (PhD); English and American studies (PhD); history (PhD); humanitarianism and conflict response (PhD); museology (PhD); music (PhD); musicology (PhD); religions and theology (PhD).

**University of Massachusetts Boston,** College of Liberal Arts, Program in Historical Archaeology, Boston, MA 02125-3393. Offers MA. *Program availability:* Part-time, evening/weekend. *Students:* 11 full-time (7 women), 38 part-time (25 women); includes 4 minority (1 Black or African American, non-Hispanic/Latino; 1 Hispanic/Latino; 2 Two or more races, non-Hispanic/Latino), 1 international. Average age 27. 27 applicants, 48% accepted, 10 enrolled. In 2016, 3 master's awarded. *Degree requirements:* For master's, thesis, oral exams, practicum. *Entrance requirements:* For master's, GRE General Test, minimum GPA of 2.75. *Application deadline:* For fall admission, 3/1 for domestic students; for spring admission, 11/1 for domestic students. *Expenses:* Tuition, state resident: full-time $16,863. Tuition, nonresident: full-time $32,913. *Required fees:* $177. *Financial support:* Research assistantships with full tuition reimbursements, teaching assistantships, career-related internships or fieldwork, Federal Work-Study, and unspecified assistantships available. Support available to part-time students. Financial award application deadline: 3/1; financial award applicants required to submit FAFSA. *Faculty research:* New World Colonialism, New England archeology, historical and urban archeology, archeological botany, ethnology. *Unit head:* Dr. Stephen Silliman, Associate Director, 617-287-6850, E-mail: stephen.silliman@umb.edu. *Application contact:* Peggy Roldan Patel, Graduate Admissions Coordinator, 617-287-6400, Fax: 617-287-6236, E-mail: bos.gadm@dpc.umassp.edu.

**University of Memphis,** Graduate School, College of Arts and Sciences, Department of Earth Sciences, Memphis, TN 38152. Offers earth sciences (MA, MS, PhD), including archaeology (MS), geography (MS), geology (MS), geophysics (MS), interdisciplinary studies (MS); geographic information systems (Graduate Certificate), including geographic information systems, GIS educator, GIS planning, GIS professional. *Program availability:* Part-time, evening/weekend. *Faculty:* 17 full-time (3 women), 5 part-time/adjunct (0 women). *Students:* 37 full-time (10 women), 25 part-time (6 women); includes 3 minority (2 Black or African American, non-Hispanic/Latino; 1 Two or more races, non-Hispanic/Latino), 22 international. Average age 33. 30 applicants, 60% accepted, 12 enrolled. In 2016, 21 master's, 5 doctorates, 6 other advanced degrees awarded. Terminal master's awarded for partial completion of doctoral program. *Degree requirements:* For master's, comprehensive exam, thesis, seminar presentation; for doctorate, comprehensive exam, thesis/dissertation, qualifying exam, submission of two manuscripts for publication in peer-reviewed journal or books. *Entrance requirements:* For master's, GRE General Test, 3 letters of recommendation, statement of research interests; for doctorate, GRE General Test, 2 letters of recommendation, resume, personal statement. Additional exam requirements/recommendations for international students: Required—TOEFL (minimum score 550 paper-based; 79 iBT). *Application deadline:* For fall admission, 1/15 for domestic students; for spring admission, 11/1 for domestic students. Applications are processed on a rolling basis. Application fee: $35 ($60 for international students). Electronic applications accepted. *Expenses:* $5,231.50 per semester full-time in-state, $9,623.50 full-time out-of-state. *Financial support:* In 2016–17, 18 students received support, including 4 research assistantships with full tuition reimbursements available (averaging $13,960 per year), 11 teaching assistantships with full tuition reimbursements available (averaging $18,864 per year); fellowships with full tuition reimbursements available, Federal Work-Study, scholarships/grants, and unspecified assistantships also available. Financial award application deadline: 2/1; financial award applicants required to submit FAFSA. *Faculty research:* Hazards, active tectonics, geophysics, hydrology and water resources, spatial analysis. *Unit head:* Dr. Daniel Larsen, Chair, 901-678-4538, Fax: 901-678-2178, E-mail: dlarsen@memphis.edu. *Application contact:* Dr. Randel T. Cox, Graduate Coordinator, 901-678-4361, Fax: 901-678-2178, E-mail: randycox@memphis.edu. Website: http://www.memphis.edu/earthsciences/

**University of Michigan,** Rackham Graduate School, College of Literature, Science, and the Arts, Department of Anthropology, Ann Arbor, MI 48109. Offers anthropological archaeology (PhD); biological anthropology (PhD); linguistic anthropology (PhD); sociocultural anthropology (PhD). *Faculty:* 41 full-time (18 women), 5 part-time/adjunct (2 women). *Students:* 149 full-time (89 women); includes 41 minority (3 Black or African American, non-Hispanic/Latino; 3 American Indian or Alaska Native, non-Hispanic/Latino; 16 Asian, non-Hispanic/Latino; 14 Hispanic/Latino; 5 Two or more races, non-Hispanic/Latino), 16 international. Average age 28. 209 applicants, 9% accepted, 13 enrolled. In 2016, 17 doctorates awarded. *Degree requirements:* For doctorate, one foreign language, comprehensive exam, thesis/dissertation, preliminary examination, oral defense of dissertation. *Entrance requirements:* For doctorate, GRE General Test. Additional exam requirements/recommendations for international students: Required—TOEFL (minimum score 560 paper-based; 84 iBT). *Application deadline:* For fall admission, 12/15 for domestic and international students. Application fee: $75 ($90 for international students). Electronic applications accepted. *Expenses:* Tuition, state resident: full-time $21,466; part-time $1152 per credit hour. Tuition, nonresident: full-time $43,346; part-time $2367 per credit hour. Part-time tuition and fees vary according to course load, degree level and program. *Financial support:* In 2016–17, 76 students received support, including 54 fellowships with full tuition reimbursements available (averaging $19,350 per year), 9 research assistantships with full tuition reimbursements available (averaging $19,350 per year), 30 teaching assistantships with full tuition reimbursements available (averaging $19,350 per year); institutionally sponsored loans, scholarships/grants, traineeships, health care benefits, tuition waivers (full), and unspecified assistantships also available. Financial award application deadline: 3/1; financial award applicants required to submit FAFSA. *Faculty research:* Sociocultural, linguistic, biological and archaeological anthropology. *Unit head:* Dr. Andrew Shryock, Chair, 734-764-7274, Fax: 734-763-6077. *Application contact:* Katia Kitchen, Graduate Program Assistant, 734-936-7933, Fax: 734-763-6077, E-mail: kitchenk@umich.edu. Website: http://www.lsa.umich.edu/anthro/

**University of Michigan,** Rackham Graduate School, College of Literature, Science, and the Arts, Interdepartmental Program in Classical Art and Archaeology, Ann Arbor, MI 48109-1390. Offers MA, PhD. *Faculty:* 17 full-time (8 women), 4 part-time/adjunct (2 women). *Students:* 28 full-time (19 women); includes 4 minority (1 Black or African American, non-Hispanic/Latino; 1 Asian, non-Hispanic/Latino; 2 Hispanic/Latino), 2 international. 59 applicants, 15% accepted, 3 enrolled. In 2016, 3 doctorates awarded. *Degree requirements:* For doctorate, 4 foreign languages, comprehensive exam, thesis/ dissertation, ancient history exam, qualifying exam, preliminary exam. *Entrance requirements:* For doctorate, GRE General Test. Additional exam requirements/ recommendations for international students: Required—TOEFL (minimum score 560 paper-based; 84 iBT). *Application deadline:* For fall admission, 12/1 for domestic and international students. Application fee: $75 ($90 for international students). Electronic applications accepted. *Expenses:* Tuition, state resident: full-time $21,466; part-time $1152 per credit hour. Tuition, nonresident: full-time $43,346; part-time $2367 per credit hour. Part-time tuition and fees vary according to course load, degree level and program. *Financial support:* In 2016–17, 22 students received support, including 9 fellowships with full tuition reimbursements available (averaging $19,737 per year), 1 research assistantship with full tuition reimbursement available (averaging $19,304 per year), 9 teaching assistantships with full tuition reimbursements available (averaging $19,737 per year); career-related internships or fieldwork, health care benefits, and summer research funding, ad hoc conference travel funding also available. Financial award application deadline: 4/15. *Faculty research:* Prehistoric art and archaeology, Greek art and archaeology, Roman art and archaeology, Near Eastern art and archaeology, archaeological theory and methodology. *Total annual research expenditures:* $13,500. *Unit head:* Prof. Lisa Nevett, Graduate Program Director, 734-764-8581, Fax: 734-763-8976, E-mail: lcnevett@umich.edu. *Application contact:* Alexander Zwinak, Graduate Program Coordinator, 734-764-6323, Fax: 734-763-8976, E-mail: ipcaa.office@umich.edu.
Website: http://lsa.umich.edu/ipcaa/

**University of Minnesota, Twin Cities Campus,** Graduate School, College of Liberal Arts, Department of Classical and Near Eastern Studies, Minneapolis, MN 55455-0213. Offers ancient and medieval art and archaeology (MA, PhD); classics (MA, PhD); Greek (MA, PhD); Latin (MA, PhD); religions in antiquity (MA). *Program availability:* Part-time. Terminal master's awarded for partial completion of doctoral program. *Degree requirements:* For master's, 2 foreign languages, comprehensive exam, thesis or alternative; for doctorate, variable foreign language requirement, comprehensive exam, thesis/dissertation. *Entrance requirements:* For master's and doctorate, GRE, 3 letters of recommendation, writing sample, copies of transcripts, personal statement. Additional exam requirements/recommendations for international students: Required—TOEFL. Electronic applications accepted. *Faculty research:* Greek and Latin literature, religions in antiquity, ancient Near East.

**University of Missouri,** Office of Research and Graduate Studies, College of Arts and Science, Department of Art History and Archaeology, Columbia, MO 65211. Offers MA, PhD. *Students:* 26 full-time (23 women), 1 (woman) part-time; includes 2 minority (both Hispanic/Latino), 1 international. Average age 32. Terminal master's awarded for partial completion of doctoral program. *Degree requirements:* For master's, 2 foreign languages, thesis; for doctorate, 2 foreign languages, thesis/dissertation. *Entrance requirements:* For master's, GRE General Test (minimum score 1000 verbal and quantitative, 4.5 analytical), minimum GPA of 3.0, 3.3 in major field; at least 3 semesters in appropriate foreign language; for doctorate, GRE General Test, minimum GPA of 3.0; MA or equivalent in art history or classical archaeology; master's thesis. Additional exam requirements/recommendations for international students: Required—TOEFL (minimum score 500 paper-based; 61 iBT), IELTS (minimum score 5.5). *Application deadline:* For fall admission, 1/18 priority date for domestic students. Applications are processed on a rolling basis. Application fee: $75 ($90 for international students). Electronic applications accepted. *Expenses:* Tuition, state resident: full-time $6347; part-time $352.60 per credit hour. Tuition, nonresident: full-time $17,379; part-time $965.50 per credit hour. *Required fees:* $1035. Tuition and fees vary according to course load, campus/location and program. *Financial support:* Fellowships with full tuition reimbursements, research assistantships with full tuition reimbursements, teaching assistantships with full tuition reimbursements, institutionally sponsored loans, health care benefits, and unspecified assistantships available. *Faculty research:* Classical Mediterranean archaeology, medieval and Renaissance art, art and architecture of modern Europe and the Americas.
Website: http://aha.missouri.edu/

**University of Nebraska–Lincoln,** Graduate College, College of Arts and Sciences, Department of Anthropology and Geography, Lincoln, NE 68588. Offers anthropology (MA); geography (MA, PhD); professional archaeology (MA). *Degree requirements:* For master's, thesis optional. *Entrance requirements:* For master's, GRE General Test. Additional exam requirements/recommendations for international students: Required—TOEFL. Electronic applications accepted.

**University of New Mexico,** Graduate Studies, College of Arts and Sciences, Program in Anthropology, Albuquerque, NM 87131-2039. Offers archaeology (MA, MS, PhD); ethnology (MA, MS, PhD); evolutionary anthropology (PhD); public archaeology (MA, MS, PhD). *Faculty:* 24 full-time (13 women). *Students:* 38 full-time (29 women), 68 part-time (39 women); includes 24 minority (3 American Indian or Alaska Native, non-Hispanic/Latino; 2 Asian, non-Hispanic/Latino; 14 Hispanic/Latino; 5 Two or more races, non-Hispanic/Latino), 9 international. Average age 33. 67 applicants, 46% accepted, 18 enrolled. In 2016, 18 master's, 14 doctorates awarded. Terminal master's awarded for partial completion of doctoral program. *Degree requirements:* For master's, comprehensive exam (for some programs), thesis or alternative, 1-2 exams; for doctorate, one foreign language, comprehensive exam, thesis/dissertation, exam, proposal, oral defense, skill and/or second language. *Entrance requirements:* For master's and doctorate, GRE General Test, 3 letters of recommendation, letter of interest, transcripts. Additional exam requirements/recommendations for international students: Required—TOEFL (minimum score 550 paper-based), IELTS (minimum score 7). *Application deadline:* For fall admission, 1/4 for domestic and international students. Application fee: $50. Electronic applications accepted. *Financial support:* Fellowships, research assistantships with partial tuition reimbursements, teaching assistantships with partial tuition reimbursements, career-related internships or fieldwork, Federal Work-

Study, institutionally sponsored loans, scholarships/grants, traineeships, health care benefits, tuition waivers (partial), and unspecified assistantships available. Support available to part-time students. Financial award application deadline: 3/1; financial award applicants required to submit FAFSA. *Faculty research:* Ethnology, archaeology, evolutionary anthropology, environment, water and land use, gender and social frameworks, Greater Southwest, Latin America, political economy, public anthropology. *Total annual research expenditures:* $875,790. *Unit head:* Michael W. Graves, Chair, 505-277-4524, Fax: 505-277-0874, E-mail: mwgraves@unm.edu. *Application contact:* Erika E. Gerety, Program Advisement Coordinator, 505-277-2732, Fax: 505-277-0874, E-mail: erika@unm.edu.
Website: http://www.unm.edu/~anthro/

**The University of North Carolina at Chapel Hill,** Graduate School, College of Arts and Sciences, Department of Classics, Chapel Hill, NC 27599. Offers classical archaeology (MA, PhD); classics (MA, PhD). Terminal master's awarded for partial completion of doctoral program. *Degree requirements:* For master's, one foreign language, comprehensive exam, thesis; for doctorate, 2 foreign languages, comprehensive exam, thesis/dissertation. *Entrance requirements:* For master's and doctorate, GRE General Test, minimum GPA of 3.0. Electronic applications accepted.

**University of Oklahoma,** College of Arts and Sciences, Department of Anthropology, Norman, OK 73019. Offers anthropology (MA, PhD); applied linguistic anthropology (MA); archaeology (PhD); health and human biology (PhD); socio-cultural and linguistics (PhD); socio-cultural anthropology (MA). *Faculty:* 29 full-time (12 women). *Students:* 22 full-time (15 women), 27 part-time (19 women); includes 9 minority (6 American Indian or Alaska Native, non-Hispanic/Latino; 1 Hispanic/Latino; 2 Two or more races, non-Hispanic/Latino), 2 international. Average age 32. 36 applicants, 36% accepted, 7 enrolled. In 2016, 9 master's, 4 doctorates awarded. *Degree requirements:* For master's, one foreign language, thesis; for doctorate, comprehensive exam, thesis/dissertation. *Entrance requirements:* For master's and doctorate, GRE, minimum undergraduate GPA of 3.0; statement of purpose; 2 letters of recommendation. Additional exam requirements/recommendations for international students: Required—TOEFL (minimum score 79 iBT) or IELTS (minimum score 6.5). *Application deadline:* For spring admission, 2/15 for domestic and international students. Application fee: $50 ($100 for international students). Electronic applications accepted. *Expenses:* Tuition, state resident: full-time $4886; part-time $203.60 per credit hour. Tuition, nonresident: full-time $18,989; part-time $791.20 per credit hour. *Required fees:* $3283; $126.25 per credit hour. $126.50 per semester. *Financial support:* In 2016–17, 44 students received support, including 1 fellowship (averaging $5,000 per year), 2 research assistantships with full tuition reimbursements available (averaging $14,670 per year), 8 teaching assistantships with full tuition reimbursements available (averaging $15,295 per year); career-related internships or fieldwork, Federal Work-Study, institutionally sponsored loans, health care benefits, and unspecified assistantships also available. Financial award application deadline: 6/1; financial award applicants required to submit FAFSA. *Faculty research:* North American archaeology; linguistics including applied; health and human biology; sociocultural anthropology; native North America. *Total annual research expenditures:* $657,637. *Unit head:* Dr. Diane Warren, Associate Professor and Department Chair, 405-325-7609, Fax: 405-325-7386, E-mail: dmwarren@ou.edu. *Application contact:* Dr. Patrick Livingood, Associate Professor/Graduate Liaison, 405-397-0215, Fax: 405-325-7386, E-mail: patrickl@ou.edu.
Website: http://cas.ou.edu/anthropology

**University of Pennsylvania,** School of Arts and Sciences, Graduate Group in Art and Archaeology of the Mediterranean World, Philadelphia, PA 19104. Offers AM, PhD. *Program availability:* Part-time. *Faculty:* 16 full-time (8 women), 5 part-time/adjunct (4 women). *Students:* 20 full-time (12 women), 3 part-time (all women); includes 2 minority (both Two or more races, non-Hispanic/Latino), 3 international. Average age 31. 66 applicants, 11% accepted, 2 enrolled. In 2016, 1 master's, 2 doctorates awarded. Terminal master's awarded for partial completion of doctoral program. *Expenses:* Tuition: Full-time $31,068; part-time $5762 per course. *Required fees:* $3200; $336 per course. Full-time tuition and fees vary according to degree level, program and student level. Part-time tuition and fees vary according to course load, degree level and program.
Website: http://www.sas.upenn.edu/graduate-division

**University of Rhode Island,** Graduate School, College of Arts and Sciences, Department of History, Kingston, RI 02881. Offers archaeology and anthropology (MA); history (MA), including European history, United States history; MLIS/MA. *Program availability:* Part-time. *Faculty:* 16 full-time (7 women). *Students:* 11 full-time (5 women), 3 part-time (2 women). In 2016, 7 master's awarded. *Degree requirements:* For master's, comprehensive exam (for some programs), thesis optional. *Entrance requirements:* For master's, GRE, 2 letters of recommendation. Additional exam requirements/recommendations for international students: Required—TOEFL. *Application deadline:* For fall admission, 7/15 for domestic students, 2/1 for international students; for spring admission, 11/15 for domestic students, 7/15 for international students; for summer admission, 4/15 for domestic students. Application fee: $65. Electronic applications accepted. *Expenses:* Tuition, state resident: full-time $11,796; part-time $655 per credit. Tuition, nonresident: full-time $24,206; part-time $1345 per credit. *Required fees:* $1546; $44 per credit. One-time fee: $155 full-time; $35 part-time. *Financial support:* In 2016–17, 4 teaching assistantships with tuition reimbursements (averaging $15,036 per year) were awarded. Financial award application deadline: 2/1; financial award applicants required to submit FAFSA. *Unit head:* Dr. Rod Mather, Chair, 401-874-4093, E-mail: rodmather@uri.edu. *Application contact:* Dr. Erik Loomis, Acting Director of Graduate Studies, 401-874-4078, E-mail: eloomis@uri.edu.
Website: http://www.uri.edu/artsci/his/

**University of Saskatchewan,** College of Graduate Studies and Research, College of Arts and Science, Department of Archaeology, Saskatoon, SK S7N 5A2, Canada. Offers MA, PhD. *Program availability:* Part-time. *Degree requirements:* For master's, thesis; for doctorate, comprehensive exam (for some programs), thesis/dissertation. *Entrance requirements:* Additional exam requirements/recommendations for international students: Required—TOEFL (minimum score 80 iBT); Recommended—IELTS (minimum score 6.5).

**University of South Africa,** College of Human Sciences, Pretoria, South Africa. Offers adult education (M Ed); African languages (MA, PhD); African politics (MA, PhD); Afrikaans (MA, PhD); ancient history (MA, PhD); ancient Near Eastern studies (MA, PhD); anthropology (MA, PhD); applied linguistics (MA); Arabic (MA, PhD); archaeology (MA); art history (MA); Biblical archaeology (MA); Biblical studies (M Th, D Th, PhD); Christian spirituality (M Th, D Th); church history (M Th, D Th); classical studies (MA, PhD); clinical psychology (MA); communication (MA, PhD); comparative education (M Ed, Ed D); consulting psychology (D Admin, D Com, PhD); curriculum studies (M Ed, Ed D); development studies (M Admin, MA, D Admin, PhD); didactics (M Ed, Ed D); education (M Tech); education management (M Ed, Ed D); educational psychology (M Ed); English (MA); environmental education (M Ed); French (MA, PhD); German (MA, PhD); Greek (MA); guidance and counseling (M Ed); health studies (MA, PhD), including health sciences education (MA), health services management (MA), medical and surgical nursing science (critical care general) (MA), midwifery and neonatal nursing science (MA), trauma and emergency care (MA); history (MA, PhD); history of education

*Archaeology*

(Ed D); inclusive education (M Ed, Ed D); information and communications technology policy and regulation (MA); information science (MA, MIS, PhD); international politics (MA, PhD); Islamic studies (MA, PhD); Italian (MA, PhD); Judaica (MA, PhD); linguistics (MA, PhD); mathematical education (M Ed); mathematics education (MA); missiology (M Th, D Th); modern Hebrew (MA, PhD); musicology (MA, MMus, D Mus, PhD); natural science education (M Ed); New Testament (M Th, D Th); Old Testament (D Th); pastoral therapy (M Th, D Th); philosophy (MA); philosophy of education (M Ed, Ed D); politics (MA, PhD); Portuguese (MA, PhD); practical theology (M Th, D Th); psychology (MA, MS, PhD); psychology of education (M Ed, Ed D); public health (MA); religious studies (MA, D Th, PhD); Romance languages (MA); Russian (MA, PhD); Semitic languages (MA, PhD); social behavior studies in HIV/AIDS (MA); social science (mental health) (MA); social science in development studies (MA); social science in psychology (MA); social science in social work (MA); social science in sociology (MA); social work (MSW, DSW, PhD); socio-education (M Ed, Ed D); sociolinguistics (MA); sociology (MA, PhD); Spanish (MA, PhD); systematic theology (M Th, D Th); TESOL (teaching English to speakers of other languages) (MA); theological ethics (M Th, D Th); theory of literature (MA, PhD); urban ministries (D Th); urban ministry (M Th).

**University of South Florida,** College of Arts and Sciences, Department of Anthropology, Tampa, FL 33620-9951. Offers applied anthropology (MA, PhD), including archaeological and forensic sciences, biocultural medical anthropology, cultural resource management, heritage studies; medical anthropology (Graduate Certificate). *Program availability:* Part-time. *Faculty:* 23 full-time (14 women). *Students:* 70 full-time (52 women), 41 part-time (28 women); includes 28 minority (6 Black or African American, non-Hispanic/Latino; 2 Asian, non-Hispanic/Latino; 16 Hispanic/Latino; 1 Native Hawaiian or other Pacific Islander, non-Hispanic/Latino; 3 Two or more races, non-Hispanic/Latino), 6 international. Average age 31. 130 applicants, 34% accepted, 18 enrolled. In 2016, 15 master's, 11 doctorates awarded. *Degree requirements:* For master's, one foreign language, comprehensive exam, thesis; for doctorate, one foreign language, comprehensive exam, thesis/dissertation. *Entrance requirements:* For master's and doctorate, GRE, minimum GPA of 3.0, 3 letters of recommendation, statement of purpose, signed research ethics statement, resume or curriculum vitae; for Graduate Certificate, bachelor's degree with minimum GPA of 3.0. Additional exam requirements/recommendations for international students: Required—TOEFL (minimum score 550 paper-based; 79 iBT) or IELTS (minimum score 6.5). *Application deadline:* For fall admission, 12/15 for domestic and international students. Application fee: $30. Electronic applications accepted. *Expenses:* Tuition, state resident: full-time $7766; part-time $431.43 per credit hour. Tuition, nonresident: full-time $15,789; part-time $877.17 per credit hour. *Required fees:* $37 per term. *Financial support:* In 2016–17, 32 students received support, including 14 research assistantships with tuition reimbursements available (averaging $14,475 per year), 52 teaching assistantships with partial tuition reimbursements available (averaging $12,540 per year); scholarships/grants and tuition waivers (partial) also available. Financial award application deadline: 1/15; financial award applicants required to submit FAFSA. *Faculty research:* Biocultural medical anthropology; archaeology and culture resource management in the Americas; community identity and heritage; urban community issues; verbal and nonverbal communications in media and education; global dynamics of sustainable resource management and economic development; social and cultural constructions of race, ethnicity, and gender. *Total annual research expenditures:* $1.1 million. *Unit head:* Dr. David Himmelgreen, Professor/Department Chairperson, 813-974-2138, Fax: 813-974-2668, E-mail: dhimmelg@usf.edu. *Application contact:* Dr. Heide Castaneda, Assistant Professor and Graduate Director, 813-974-2138, Fax: 813-974-2668, E-mail: hcastaneda@usf.edu.
Website: http://anthropology.usf.edu/graduate/

**The University of Tennessee,** Graduate School, College of Arts and Sciences, Department of Anthropology, Knoxville, TN 37996. Offers archaeology (MA, PhD); biological anthropology (MA, PhD); cultural anthropology (MA, PhD); zoo-archaeology (MA, PhD). *Degree requirements:* For master's, thesis; for doctorate, one foreign language, thesis/dissertation. *Entrance requirements:* For master's and doctorate, GRE General Test, minimum GPA of 2.7. Additional exam requirements/recommendations for international students: Required—TOEFL. Electronic applications accepted.

**The University of Texas at Austin,** Graduate School, College of Liberal Arts, Department of Anthropology, Austin, TX 78712-1111. Offers archaeology (MA, PhD); cultural forms (MA, PhD); linguistic anthropology (MA, PhD); physical anthropology (MA, PhD); social anthropology (MA, PhD). *Program availability:* Part-time. Terminal master's awarded for partial completion of doctoral program. *Degree requirements:* For master's, thesis; for doctorate, one foreign language, thesis/dissertation. *Entrance requirements:* For master's and doctorate, GRE General Test. Additional exam requirements/recommendations for international students: Required—TOEFL. Electronic applications accepted.

**University of West Florida,** College of Arts, Social Sciences, and Humanities, Division of Anthropology and Archaeology, Pensacola, FL 32514-5750. Offers anthropology (MA); historical archaeology (MA). *Degree requirements:* For master's, internship or thesis. *Entrance requirements:* For master's, GRE, transcripts, minimum GPA of 3.0, 3 letters of recommendation, writing sample, letter of intent describing background, study interests, and professional goals. Additional exam requirements/recommendations for international students: Required—TOEFL (minimum score 550 paper-based). *Application deadline:* For fall admission, 6/1 for domestic and international students; for spring admission, 10/1 for domestic and international students. Application fee: $30. *Expenses:* Tuition, state resident: full-time $5316.12. Tuition, nonresident: full-time $11,308. *Required fees:* $583.92. Tuition and fees vary according to course load and program. *Financial support:* Research assistantships with partial tuition reimbursements, teaching assistantships with partial tuition reimbursements, and unspecified assistantships available. Financial award application deadline: 4/15; financial award applicants required to submit FAFSA. *Unit head:* Dr. John Bratten, Chair, 850-474-2706, E-mail: jbratten@uwf.edu. *Application contact:* Terry McCray, Assistant Director of Graduate Admissions, 850-473-7718, Fax: 850-473-7714, E-mail: gradadmissions@uwf.edu.
Website: http://uwf.edu/anthropology/

**University of Wisconsin–Madison,** Graduate School, College of Letters and Science, Department of Anthropology, Madison, WI 53706-1380. Offers archaeology (PhD); biological anthropology (PhD); cultural anthropology (PhD). Terminal master's awarded for partial completion of doctoral program. *Degree requirements:* For doctorate, thesis/dissertation. *Entrance requirements:* For doctorate, qualifying exam. Electronic applications accepted. *Faculty research:* Archaeology, biological, anthropology, cultural anthropology.

**University of Wisconsin–Milwaukee,** Graduate School, College of Letters and Science, Department of Anthropology, Milwaukee, WI 53201-0413. Offers anthropology (MS, PhD), including archaeology (MS), biological anthropology (MS), cultural anthropology (MS); museum studies (Graduate Certificate). *Students:* 58 full-time (43 women), 36 part-time (29 women); includes 8 minority (1 American Indian or Alaska Native, non-Hispanic/Latino; 2 Hispanic/Latino; 5 Two or more races, non-Hispanic/Latino), 1 international. Average age 32. 46 applicants, 100% accepted, 20 enrolled. In 2016, 17 master's, 2 doctorates, 14 other advanced degrees awarded. *Degree requirements:* For master's, thesis or alternative; for doctorate, one foreign language, thesis/dissertation, departmental qualifying exam. *Entrance requirements:* For master's, GRE; for doctorate, GRE, minimum GPA of 3.0, master's degree. Additional exam requirements/recommendations for international students: Required—TOEFL (minimum score 550 paper-based; 79 iBT), IELTS (minimum score 6.5). *Application deadline:* For fall admission, 1/1 priority date for domestic students; for spring admission, 9/1 for domestic students. Applications are processed on a rolling basis. Application fee: $56 ($96 for international students). *Financial support:* In 2016–17, 4 fellowships, 2 research assistantships, 26 teaching assistantships were awarded; career-related internships or fieldwork, unspecified assistantships, and project assistantships also available. Support available to part-time students. Financial award application deadline: 4/15; financial award applicants required to submit FAFSA. *Unit head:* Thomas Malaby, Department Chair, 414-229-5247, E-mail: malaby@uwm.edu. *Application contact:* General Information Contact, 414-229-4982, Fax: 414-229-6967, E-mail: gradschool@uwm.edu.
Website: https://uwm.edu/letters-science/programs/?discipline-Anthropology

**Washington State University,** College of Arts and Sciences, Department of Anthropology, Pullman, WA 99164. Offers archaeology (MA, PhD); cultural anthropology (PhD); evolutionary anthropology (MA, PhD). Program applications must be made through the Pullman campus. *Degree requirements:* For master's, one foreign language, comprehensive exam (for some programs), thesis; for doctorate, one foreign language, comprehensive exam, thesis/dissertation, written and oral preliminary exam. *Entrance requirements:* For master's and doctorate, GRE General Test, curriculum vitae, statement of intent, official transcripts, 3 letters of recommendation, one or two undergraduate papers (from BA/BS applicants), minimum GPA of 3.0. Additional exam requirements/recommendations for international students: Required—TOEFL (minimum score 550 paper-based), IELTS. Electronic applications accepted. *Faculty research:* Quantitative analysis of archaeological data, simulation of aspects of prehistoric behavior, subsistence strategies, language use, inequality and poverty, gender, pedagogy, Mexico/U.S. border region, childhood, infectious and parasitic diseases, the analysis of mitochondrial DNA (mtDNA) and Y-chromosomal DNA.

**Washington University in St. Louis,** The Graduate School, Department of Art History and Archaeology, St. Louis, MO 63130-4899. Offers AM, PhD. *Degree requirements:* For doctorate, 2 foreign languages, comprehensive exam, thesis/dissertation. *Entrance requirements:* For master's and doctorate, GRE General Test, sample of written work. Electronic applications accepted. *Faculty research:* Ancient, medieval, Renaissance, early modern European, modern and contemporary European and American, and Asian art history; classical archaeology.

**Wheaton College,** Graduate School, Department of Biblical and Theological Studies, Wheaton, IL 60187-5593. Offers Biblical and theological studies (PhD); Biblical archaeology (MA); Biblical exegesis (MA); Biblical studies (MA); general theological studies (MA); historical and systematic theology (MA), including biblical and theological studies; history of Christianity (MA), including Biblical and theological studies. *Program availability:* Part-time. *Faculty:* 8 full-time (1 woman), 1 part-time/adjunct (0 women). *Students:* 53 full-time (12 women), 48 part-time (20 women); includes 14 minority (3 Black or African American, non-Hispanic/Latino; 5 Asian, non-Hispanic/Latino; 3 Hispanic/Latino; 3 Two or more races, non-Hispanic/Latino), 18 international. Average age 34. 116 applicants, 63% accepted, 35 enrolled. In 2016, 32 master's, 2 doctorates awarded. *Degree requirements:* For doctorate, thesis/dissertation. *Entrance requirements:* For master's, GRE General Test. Additional exam requirements/recommendations for international students: Required—TOEFL (minimum score 550 paper-based; 80 iBT), IELTS (minimum score 6.5), TOEFL (minimum score 600 paper-based; 90 iBT) or IELTS (minimum score 7.5) for PhD. *Application deadline:* For fall admission, 1/1 priority date for domestic students, 1/1 for international students; for spring admission, 11/1 for domestic students. Applications are processed on a rolling basis. Application fee: $30. Electronic applications accepted. *Expenses:* Tuition: Full-time $19,080; part-time $795 per credit hour. Tuition and fees vary according to degree level and program. *Financial support:* Scholarships/grants and unspecified assistantships available. Financial award application deadline: 3/1; financial award applicants required to submit FAFSA. *Unit head:* Dr. Lynn Cohick, Interim Associate Dean, 630-752-5054. *Application contact:* Dusty Di Santo, Director of Graduate Admissions, 630-752-5195, Fax: 630-752-7047, E-mail: graduate.admissions@wheaton.edu.
Website: http://www.wheaton.edu/academics/departments/theology

**Yale University,** Graduate School of Arts and Sciences, Department of Near Eastern Languages and Civilizations, New Haven, CT 06520. Offers Arabic and Islamic studies (MA, PhD); archaeology of the ancient Near East (MA, PhD); Assyriology (MA, PhD); Egyptology (MA, PhD); Graeco-Arabic studies (MA, PhD); Northwest Semitic, Bible, comparative Semitics (MA, PhD). *Degree requirements:* For doctorate, 2 foreign languages, thesis/dissertation. *Entrance requirements:* For doctorate, GRE General Test.

**Yale University,** Graduate School of Arts and Sciences, Interdisciplinary Program in Archaeological Studies, New Haven, CT 06520. Offers MA. *Degree requirements:* For master's, thesis. *Entrance requirements:* For master's, GRE General Test.

# Biological Anthropology

**Duke University,** Graduate School, Department of Evolutionary Anthropology, Durham, NC 27708. Offers cellular and molecular biology (PhD); gross anatomy and physical anthropology (PhD), including comparative morphology of human and non-human primates, primate social behavior, vertebrate paleontology; neuroanatomy (PhD).

*Degree requirements:* For doctorate, one foreign language, thesis/dissertation. *Entrance requirements:* For doctorate, GRE General Test. Additional exam requirements/recommendations for international students: Required—TOEFL (minimum score 577 paper-based; 90 iBT) or IELTS (minimum score 7). Electronic applications accepted.

**Kent State University,** College of Arts and Sciences, School of Biomedical Sciences, Kent, OH 44242-0001. Offers biological anthropology (PhD); biomedical mathematics (MS, PhD); cellular and molecular biology (MS, PhD), including cellular biology and structures, molecular biology and genetics; neurosciences (MS, PhD); pharmacology (MS, PhD); physiology (MS, PhD). *Students:* 72 full-time (47 women), 1 part-time (0 women); includes 6 minority (2 Asian, non-Hispanic/Latino; 1 Hispanic/Latino; 3 Two or more races, non-Hispanic/Latino), 25 international. Average age 30. 111 applicants, 22% accepted, 16 enrolled. In 2016, 2 master's, 19 doctorates awarded. Terminal master's awarded for partial completion of doctoral program. *Degree requirements:* For master's, thesis; for doctorate, comprehensive exam, thesis/dissertation. *Entrance requirements:* For master's and doctorate, GRE, minimum GPA of 3.0, transcripts, goal statement, 3 letters of recommendation. Additional exam requirements/recommendations for international students: Required—TOEFL (minimum score of 600 paper-based, 100 iBT), IELTS (minimum score of 7.0), Michigan English Language Assessment Battery (minimum score of 85), or PTE (minimum score of 68). *Application deadline:* For fall admission, 1/1 for domestic and international students. Applications are processed on a rolling basis. Application fee: $45 ($70 for international students). Electronic applications accepted. *Expenses:* Tuition, state resident: full-time $10,864; part-time $495 per credit hour. Tuition, nonresident: full-time $18,380; part-time $837 per credit hour. *Financial support:* Research assistantships with full tuition reimbursements, teaching assistantships, health care benefits, and unspecified assistantships available. Financial award application deadline: 1/1. *Unit head:* Dr. Ernest J. Freeman, Director, School of Biomedical Sciences, 330-672-2363, E-mail: efreema2@kent.edu. *Application contact:* School of Biomedical Sciences, 330-672-2263, Fax: 330-672-9391, E-mail: efreema2@kent.edu.
Website: http://www.kent.edu/biomedical/

**Mercyhurst University,** Graduate Studies, Program in Anthropology, Erie, PA 16546. Offers archaeology and geological archaeology (MS); forensic and biological anthropology (MS). *Entrance requirements:* For master's, GRE or MAT, undergraduate degree in related field, interview, resume, essay, three professional references, transcripts. Additional exam requirements/recommendations for international students: Required—TOEFL.

**University of Wisconsin–Milwaukee,** Graduate School, College of Letters and Science, Department of Anthropology, Milwaukee, WI 53201-0413. Offers anthropology (MS, PhD), including archaeology (MS), biological anthropology (MS), cultural anthropology (MS); museum studies (Graduate Certificate). *Students:* 58 full-time (43 women), 36 part-time (29 women); includes 8 minority (1 American Indian or Alaska Native, non-Hispanic/Latino; 2 Hispanic/Latino; 5 Two or more races, non-Hispanic/Latino), 1 international. Average age 32. 46 applicants, 100% accepted, 20 enrolled. In 2016, 17 master's, 2 doctorates, 14 other advanced degrees awarded. *Degree requirements:* For master's, thesis or alternative; for doctorate, one foreign language, thesis/dissertation, departmental qualifying exam. *Entrance requirements:* For master's, GRE; for doctorate, GRE, minimum GPA of 3.0, master's degree. Additional exam requirements/recommendations for international students: Required—TOEFL (minimum score 550 paper-based; 79 iBT), IELTS (minimum score 6.5). *Application deadline:* For fall admission, 1/1 priority date for domestic students; for spring admission, 9/1 for domestic students. Applications are processed on a rolling basis. Application fee: $56 ($96 for international students). *Financial support:* In 2016–17, 4 fellowships, 2 research assistantships, 26 teaching assistantships were awarded; career-related internships or fieldwork, unspecified assistantships, and project assistantships also available. Support available to part-time students. Financial award application deadline: 4/15; financial award applicants required to submit FAFSA. *Unit head:* Thomas Malaby, Department Chair, 414-229-5247, E-mail: malaby@uwm.edu. *Application contact:* General Information Contact, 414-229-4982, Fax: 414-229-6967, E-mail: gradschool@uwm.edu.
Website: https://uwm.edu/letters-science/programs/?discipline-Anthropology

# Cultural Anthropology

**California Institute of Integral Studies,** School of Consciousness and Transformation, San Francisco, CA 94103. Offers anthropology and social change (MA, PhD); Asian philosophies and cultures (MA); creative inquiry/interdisciplinary arts (MFA); East-West psychology (MA, PhD); integral and transpersonal psychology (PhD); philosophy and religion (PhD), including ecology, spirituality, and religion, philosophy, cosmology, and consciousness, women's spirituality; theater and performance making (MFA); transformative leadership (MA); transformative studies (PhD); women, gender, spirituality and social justice (MA); writing and consciousness (MFA). *Program availability:* Part-time, evening/weekend, 100% online, blended/hybrid learning. *Students:* 390 full-time (256 women), 121 part-time (84 women); includes 135 minority (39 Black or African American, non-Hispanic/Latino; 2 American Indian or Alaska Native, non-Hispanic/Latino; 22 Asian, non-Hispanic/Latino; 40 Hispanic/Latino; 2 Native Hawaiian or other Pacific Islander, non-Hispanic/Latino; 30 Two or more races, non-Hispanic/Latino), 51 international. Average age 38. 195 applicants, 92% accepted, 124 enrolled. In 2016, 35 master's, 41 doctorates awarded. Terminal master's awarded for partial completion of doctoral program. *Degree requirements:* For master's, thesis optional; for doctorate, comprehensive exam, thesis/dissertation, 1 foreign language (for Asian philosophies and cultures). *Entrance requirements:* For master's, minimum GPA of 3.0, letters of recommendation, writing sample; for doctorate, master's degree, minimum GPA of 3.0, letters of recommendation, writing sample. Additional exam requirements/recommendations for international students: Required—TOEFL. *Application deadline:* For fall admission, 2/1 priority date for domestic and international students; for spring admission, 10/15 priority date for domestic and international students. Applications are processed on a rolling basis. Application fee: $65. Electronic applications accepted. *Expenses: Tuition:* Full-time $19,728; part-time $1098 per semester hour. *Required fees:* $320; $320 per semester hour. *Financial support:* Research assistantships, teaching assistantships, career-related internships or fieldwork, Federal Work-Study, and scholarships/grants available. Support available to part-time students. Financial award application deadline: 4/15; financial award applicants required to submit FAFSA. *Faculty research:* Ecology and sustainability, philosophy and religion, East-West psychology, integrative health, social and cultural anthropology, transformative leadership. *Application contact:* Ellen Durst, Director of Admissions, 415-575-6100, Fax: 415-575-1268, E-mail: admissions@ciis.edu.
Website: http://www.ciis.edu/

**Concordia University,** School of Graduate Studies, Faculty of Arts and Science, Department of Sociology and Anthropology, Montréal, QC H3G 1M8, Canada. Offers social and cultural analysis (PhD); social and cultural anthropology (MA); sociology (MA). *Degree requirements:* For master's, comprehensive exam or thesis. *Entrance requirements:* For master's, honors degree in sociology or equivalent. *Faculty research:* Community and ethnic relations, popular culture, regional development in Canada, industrial and social movements, social problems and policies.

**Cornell University,** Graduate School, Graduate Fields of Arts and Sciences, Field of Anthropology, Ithaca, NY 14853. Offers archaeological anthropology (PhD); biological anthropology (PhD); sociocultural anthropology (PhD). *Degree requirements:* For doctorate, one foreign language, comprehensive exam, thesis/dissertation, teaching experience. *Entrance requirements:* For doctorate, GRE General Test, 3 letters of recommendation, sample of written work. Additional exam requirements/recommendations for international students: Required—TOEFL (minimum score 550 paper-based; 77 iBT). Electronic applications accepted. *Faculty research:* Culture, engaged anthropology, political economy, area studies: Asia, Americas, Europe; interdisciplinary and ethnic studies: Asian-American studies.

**Duke University,** Graduate School, Department of Cultural Anthropology, Durham, NC 27708. Offers physical anthropology (PhD), including comparative morphology of human and non-human primates, primate social behavior; social/cultural anthropology (PhD); JD/AM. *Degree requirements:* For doctorate, one foreign language, thesis/dissertation. *Entrance requirements:* For doctorate, GRE General Test. Additional exam requirements/recommendations for international students: Required—TOEFL (minimum score 577 paper-based; 90 iBT) or IELTS (minimum score 7).

**Eastern University,** Program in Theological and Cultural Anthropology, St. Davids, PA 19087-3696. Offers MA. *Students:* 2 full-time (1 woman), 9 part-time (7 women); includes 3 minority (1 Black or African American, non-Hispanic/Latino; 2 Hispanic/Latino). Average age 32. In 2016, 3 master's awarded. *Entrance requirements:* Additional exam requirements/recommendations for international students: Required—TOEFL. *Application deadline:* Applications are processed on a rolling basis. Application fee: $35. Electronic applications accepted. Application fee is waived when completed online. *Expenses:* $690 per credit. *Unit head:* Michael Dziedziak, Executive Director of Enrollment, 800-452-0996, E-mail: gpsadmissions@eastern.edu.
Website: http://www.eastern.edu/academics/programs/missiology-and-anthropology-department/ma-theological-and-cultural-anthropology

**The Graduate Center, City University of New York,** Graduate Studies, Program in Anthropology, New York, NY 10016-4039. Offers anthropological linguistics (PhD); archaeology (PhD); cultural anthropology (PhD); physical anthropology (PhD). *Degree requirements:* For doctorate, one foreign language, thesis/dissertation. *Entrance requirements:* For doctorate, GRE General Test. Additional exam requirements/recommendations for international students: Required—TOEFL. Electronic applications accepted.

**Memorial University of Newfoundland,** School of Graduate Studies, Department of Anthropology, St. John's, NL A1C 5S7, Canada. Offers archaeology and physical anthropology (MA, PhD); social and cultural anthropology (MA, PhD). *Program availability:* Part-time. *Degree requirements:* For master's, comprehensive exam (for some programs), thesis (for some programs); for doctorate, comprehensive exam, thesis/dissertation, oral defense of thesis. *Entrance requirements:* For master's, 2nd class degree in related field. Electronic applications accepted. *Faculty research:* Early European settlements, ethnoarchaeology, economic/political anthropology, land claims and aboriginal rights, marine anthropology.

**North Carolina State University,** Graduate School, College of Humanities and Social Sciences, Department of Sociology and Anthropology, Program in Anthropology, Raleigh, NC 27695. Offers bioarchaeology (MA); cultural anthropology (MA); environmental anthropology (MA).

**Northern Arizona University,** Graduate College, College of Social and Behavioral Sciences, Department of Anthropology, Flagstaff, AZ 86011. Offers archaeology (MA); linguistic anthropology (MA); sociocultural anthropology (MA). *Degree requirements:* For master's, thesis (for some programs), internship paper. *Entrance requirements:* For master's, 12 undergraduate hours in anthropology. Additional exam requirements/recommendations for international students: Required—TOEFL (minimum score 550 paper-based; 80 iBT), IELTS (minimum score 7). Electronic applications accepted. *Expenses:* Tuition, state resident: full-time $8971; part-time $444 per credit hour. Tuition, nonresident: full-time $20,958; part-time $1164 per credit hour. *Required fees:* $1018; $644 per credit hour. Tuition and fees vary according to course load, campus/location and program. *Faculty research:* Economic development, culture change, ethnohistory, archaeology of the Southwest, small town networks and HIV.

**Rice University,** Graduate Programs, School of Social Sciences, Department of Anthropology, Houston, TX 77251-1892. Offers archaeology (MA, PhD); social-cultural anthropology (MA, PhD). Terminal master's awarded for partial completion of doctoral program. *Degree requirements:* For master's, one foreign language, 3 major papers, dissertation proposal and language exam or thesis; for doctorate, one foreign language, thesis/dissertation. *Entrance requirements:* For master's and doctorate, research proposal. Additional exam requirements/recommendations for international students: Required—TOEFL (minimum score 90 iBT). Electronic applications accepted.

**San Francisco State University,** Division of Graduate Studies, College of Liberal and Creative Arts, Department of Anthropology, San Francisco, CA 94132-1722. Offers archaeology (MA); biological/physical anthropology (MA); social/cultural anthropology (MA); visual anthropology (MA). *Expenses:* Tuition, state resident: full-time $6738. Tuition, nonresident: full-time $15,666. *Required fees:* $1012. Tuition and fees vary according to degree level and program. *Faculty research:* Immigration, ethnicity, urban anthropology, Californian and Latin American archaeology. *Unit head:* Dr. James Quesada, Chair, 415-338-1633, Fax: 415-338-6159, E-mail: jquesada@sfsu.edu. *Application contact:* Dr. Douglass Bailey, Graduate Coordinator, 415-338-1427, Fax: 415-338-6159, E-mail: dwbailey@sfsu.edu.
Website: http://anthropology.sfsu.edu/

**Southern Illinois University Edwardsville,** Graduate School, Program in Integrative Studies, Edwardsville, IL 62026. Offers cultural heritage and resources management (MA, MS); diversity training (MA, MS); organizational design thinking (MS); sustainability (MS). *Program availability:* Part-time, evening/weekend. *Degree requirements:* For master's, variable foreign language requirement, comprehensive exam (for some programs), thesis (for some programs). *Entrance requirements:* Additional exam requirements/recommendations for international students: Required—TOEFL (minimum score 550 paper-based; 79 iBT), IELTS (minimum score 6.5). Electronic applications accepted.

*Cultural Anthropology*

**University of California, Santa Barbara,** Graduate Division, College of Letters and Sciences, Division of Social Sciences, Department of Anthropology, Santa Barbara, CA 93106-2014. Offers sociocultural anthropology (PhD); MA/PhD. Terminal master's awarded for partial completion of doctoral program. *Degree requirements:* For master's, comprehensive exam (for some programs), thesis (for some programs); for doctorate, comprehensive exam (for some programs), thesis/dissertation. *Entrance requirements:* For master's and doctorate, GRE General Test, statement of purpose, personal achievements statement, transcripts, writing sample, curriculum vitae, letters of recommendation. Additional exam requirements/recommendations for international students: Required—TOEFL (minimum score 550 paper-based; 80 iBT), IELTS (minimum score 7). Electronic applications accepted. *Faculty research:* Archaeology, bioarchaeology, biosocial anthropology, evolutionary ecology, evolutionary psychology, sociocultural anthropology.

**University of California, Santa Cruz,** Division of Graduate Studies, Division of Social Sciences, Department of Anthropology, Santa Cruz, CA 95064. Offers cultural anthropology (PhD). *Degree requirements:* For doctorate, thesis/dissertation, qualifying exam. *Entrance requirements:* For doctorate, GRE General Test. Additional exam requirements/recommendations for international students: Required—TOEFL (minimum score 550 paper-based; 83 iBT); Recommended—IELTS (minimum score 8). Electronic applications accepted. *Faculty research:* Culture and power, women's roles, AIDS, folklore.

**University of Denver,** Division of Arts, Humanities and Social Sciences, Department of Anthropology, Denver, CO 80208. Offers archaeology (MA); cultural anthropology (MA); museum and heritage studies (MA). *Program availability:* Part-time. *Faculty:* 8 full-time (2 women). *Students:* 3 full-time (all women), 17 part-time (16 women); includes 2 minority (1 American Indian or Alaska Native, non-Hispanic/Latino; 1 Hispanic/Latino). Average age 25. 47 applicants, 43% accepted, 11 enrolled. In 2016, 11 master's awarded. *Degree requirements:* For master's, one foreign language, comprehensive exam, thesis (for some programs), tool, foreign language literacy, or course work. *Entrance requirements:* For master's, GRE General Test, bachelor's degree, transcripts, personal statement, two letters of recommendation. Additional exam requirements/recommendations for international students: Required—TOEFL (minimum score 550 paper-based; 80 iBT). *Application deadline:* For fall admission, 2/4 priority date for domestic and international students. Applications are processed on a rolling basis. Application fee: $65. Electronic applications accepted. *Expenses:* $29,022 per year full-time. *Financial support:* In 2016–17, 19 students received support, including 6 teaching assistantships with tuition reimbursements available (averaging $6,667 per year); career-related internships or fieldwork, Federal Work-Study, institutionally sponsored loans, scholarships/grants, and unspecified assistantships also available. Support available to part-time students. Financial award application deadline: 2/15; financial award applicants required to submit FAFSA. *Faculty research:* Human diversity, human rights, historic archaeology, museums and heritage, high-tech field methods. *Unit head:* Dr. Larry Conyers, Professor and Chair, 303-871-2684, Fax: 303-871-2437, E-mail: lconyers@du.edu. *Application contact:* Dr. Larry Conyers, Professor and Director of Graduate Program, 303-871-2684, Fax: 303-871-2437, E-mail: lconyers@du.edu. Website: http://www.du.edu/ahss/anthropology

**University of Michigan,** Rackham Graduate School, College of Literature, Science, and the Arts, Department of Anthropology, Ann Arbor, MI 48109. Offers anthropological archaeology (PhD); biological anthropology (PhD); linguistic anthropology (PhD); sociocultural anthropology (PhD). *Faculty:* 41 full-time (18 women), 5 part-time/adjunct (2 women). *Students:* 149 full-time (89 women); includes 41 minority (3 Black or African American, non-Hispanic/Latino; 3 American Indian or Alaska Native, non-Hispanic/Latino; 16 Asian, non-Hispanic/Latino; 14 Hispanic/Latino; 5 Two or more races, non-Hispanic/Latino), 16 international. Average age 28. 209 applicants, 9% accepted, 13 enrolled. In 2016, 17 doctorates awarded. *Degree requirements:* For doctorate, one foreign language, comprehensive exam, thesis/dissertation, preliminary examination, oral defense of dissertation. *Entrance requirements:* For doctorate, GRE General Test. Additional exam requirements/recommendations for international students: Required—TOEFL (minimum score 560 paper-based; 84 iBT). *Application deadline:* For fall admission, 12/15 for domestic and international students. Application fee: $75 ($90 for international students). Electronic applications accepted. *Expenses:* Tuition, state resident: full-time $21,466; part-time $1152 per credit hour. Tuition, nonresident: full-time $43,346; part-time $2367 per credit hour. Part-time tuition and fees vary according to course load, degree level and program. *Financial support:* In 2016–17, 76 students received support, including 54 fellowships with full tuition reimbursements available (averaging $19,350 per year), 9 research assistantships with full tuition reimbursements available (averaging $19,350 per year), 30 teaching assistantships with full tuition reimbursements available (averaging $19,350 per year); institutionally sponsored loans, scholarships/grants, traineeships, health care benefits, tuition waivers (full), and unspecified assistantships also available. Financial award application deadline: 3/1; financial award applicants required to submit FAFSA. *Faculty research:* Sociocultural, linguistic, biological and archaeological anthropology. *Unit head:* Dr. Andrew Shryock, Chair, 734-764-7274, Fax: 734-763-6077. *Application contact:* Katia Kitchen, Graduate Program Assistant, 734-936-7933, Fax: 734-763-6077, E-mail: kitchenk@umich.edu. Website: http://www.lsa.umich.edu/anthro/

**The University of Tennessee,** Graduate School, College of Arts and Sciences, Department of Anthropology, Knoxville, TN 37996. Offers archaeology (MA, PhD); biological anthropology (MA, PhD); cultural anthropology (MA, PhD); zoo-archaeology (MA, PhD). *Degree requirements:* For master's, thesis; for doctorate, one foreign language, thesis/dissertation. *Entrance requirements:* For master's and doctorate, GRE General Test, minimum GPA of 2.7. Additional exam requirements/recommendations for international students: Required—TOEFL. Electronic applications accepted.

**University of Wisconsin–Madison,** Graduate School, College of Letters and Science, Department of Anthropology, Madison, WI 53706-1380. Offers archaeology (PhD); biological anthropology (PhD); cultural anthropology (PhD). Terminal master's awarded for partial completion of doctoral program. *Degree requirements:* For doctorate, thesis/dissertation. *Entrance requirements:* For doctorate, qualifying exam. Electronic applications accepted. *Faculty research:* Archaeology, biological, anthropology, cultural anthropology.

**University of Wisconsin–Milwaukee,** Graduate School, College of Letters and Science, Department of Anthropology, Milwaukee, WI 53201-0413. Offers anthropology (MS, PhD), including archaeology (MS), biological anthropology (MS), cultural anthropology (MS); museum studies (Graduate Certificate). *Students:* 58 full-time (43 women), 36 part-time (29 women); includes 8 minority (1 American Indian or Alaska Native, non-Hispanic/Latino; 2 Hispanic/Latino; 5 Two or more races, non-Hispanic/Latino), 1 international. Average age 32. 46 applicants, 100% accepted, 20 enrolled. In 2016, 17 master's, 2 doctorates, 14 other advanced degrees awarded. *Degree requirements:* For master's, thesis or alternative; for doctorate, one foreign language, thesis/dissertation, departmental qualifying exam. *Entrance requirements:* For master's, GRE; for doctorate, GRE, minimum GPA of 3.0, master's degree. Additional exam requirements/recommendations for international students: Required—TOEFL (minimum score 550 paper-based; 79 iBT), IELTS (minimum score 6.5). *Application deadline:* For fall admission, 1/1 priority date for domestic students; for spring admission, 9/1 for domestic students. Applications are processed on a rolling basis. Application fee: $56 ($96 for international students). *Financial support:* In 2016–17, 4 fellowships, 2 research assistantships, 26 teaching assistantships were awarded; career-related internships or fieldwork, unspecified assistantships, and project assistantships also available. Support available to part-time students. Financial award application deadline: 4/15; financial award applicants required to submit FAFSA. *Unit head:* Thomas Malaby, Department Chair, 414-229-5247, E-mail: malaby@uwm.edu. *Application contact:* General Information Contact, 414-229-4982, Fax: 414-229-6967, E-mail: gradschool@uwm.edu. Website: https://uwm.edu/letters-science/programs/?discipline-Anthropology

**Washington State University,** College of Arts and Sciences, Department of Anthropology, Pullman, WA 99164. Offers archaeology (MA, PhD); cultural anthropology (PhD); evolutionary anthropology (MA, PhD). Program applications must be made through the Pullman campus. *Degree requirements:* For master's, one foreign language, comprehensive exam (for some programs), thesis; for doctorate, one foreign language, comprehensive exam, thesis/dissertation, written and oral preliminary exam. *Entrance requirements:* For master's and doctorate, GRE General Test, curriculum vitae, statement of intent, official transcripts, 3 letters of recommendation, one or two undergraduate papers (from BA/BS applicants), minimum GPA of 3.0. Additional exam requirements/recommendations for international students: Required—TOEFL (minimum score 550 paper-based), IELTS. Electronic applications accepted. *Faculty research:* Quantitative analysis of archaeological data, simulation of aspects of prehistoric behavior, subsistence strategies, language use, inequality and poverty, gender, pedagogy, Mexico/U.S. border region, childhood, infectious and parasitic diseases, the analysis of mitochondrial DNA (mtDNA) and Y-chromosomal DNA.

# Demography and Population Studies

**Bowling Green State University,** Graduate College, College of Arts and Sciences, Department of Sociology, Bowling Green, OH 43403. Offers demography and population studies (MA); social psychology (MA); sociology (PhD). *Program availability:* Part-time. *Degree requirements:* For master's, thesis or alternative; for doctorate, comprehensive exam, thesis/dissertation. *Entrance requirements:* For master's and doctorate, GRE General Test. Additional exam requirements/recommendations for international students: Required—TOEFL. *Application deadline:* For fall admission, 1/15 priority date for domestic students. Application fee: $30. Electronic applications accepted. *Financial support:* Fellowships with full tuition reimbursements, research assistantships with full tuition reimbursements, teaching assistantships with full tuition reimbursements, career-related internships or fieldwork, Federal Work-Study, institutionally sponsored loans, and unspecified assistantships available. Financial award applicants required to submit FAFSA. *Faculty research:* Applied demography, criminology and deviance, family studies, population studies, social psychology. *Unit head:* Dr. Susan L. Brown, Chair, 419-372-9521, E-mail: brownsl@bgsu.edu. *Application contact:* Dr. Steve Cernkovich, Graduate Coordinator, 419-372-2743.

**Cornell University,** Graduate School, Graduate Fields of Agriculture and Life Sciences, Field of Development Sociology, Ithaca, NY 14853. Offers population and development (MS, PhD); rural and environmental sociology (MS, PhD); state, economy, and society (MS, PhD). *Degree requirements:* For doctorate, comprehensive exam, thesis/dissertation. *Entrance requirements:* For master's and doctorate, GRE General Test, 3 letters of recommendation. Additional exam requirements/recommendations for international students: Required—TOEFL (minimum score 550 paper-based; 77 iBT). Electronic applications accepted. *Faculty research:* Demography (population and development), environmental sociology, international and rural community development, political economy and ecology, sustainable agriculture.

**Cornell University,** Graduate School, Graduate Fields of Agriculture and Life Sciences, Field of Global Development, Ithaca, NY 14853. Offers development policy (MPS); international agriculture and development (MPS); international development (MPS); international nutrition (MPS); international planning (MPS); international population (MPS); science and technology policy (MPS). *Degree requirements:* For master's, project paper. *Entrance requirements:* For master's, GRE General Test (recommended), 2 years of development experience, 2 letters of recommendation. Additional exam requirements/recommendations for international students: Required—TOEFL (minimum score 550 paper-based; 77 iBT). Electronic applications accepted.

**Florida State University,** The Graduate School, College of Social Sciences and Public Policy, Center for Demography and Population Health, Tallahassee, FL 32306-2240. Offers demography (MS). *Program availability:* Part-time. *Faculty:* 10 full-time (5 women). *Students:* 6 full-time (1 woman), 2 part-time (both women); includes 2 minority (both Black or African American, non-Hispanic/Latino). Average age 22. 9 applicants, 100% accepted, 6 enrolled. In 2016, 6 master's awarded. *Degree requirements:* For master's, thesis. *Entrance requirements:* For master's, GRE General Test, minimum upper-division GPA of 3.0. Additional exam requirements/recommendations for international students: Required—TOEFL (minimum score 550 paper-based; 80 iBT). *Application deadline:* For fall admission, 6/1 for domestic and international students; for spring admission, 11/1 for domestic and international students. Application fee: $30. Electronic applications accepted. *Expenses:* Contact institution. *Financial support:* Career-related internships or fieldwork, Federal Work-Study, institutionally sponsored loans, scholarships/grants, and tuition waivers (partial) available. Financial award applicants required to submit FAFSA. *Faculty research:* Aging and life course; families, children, youth; fertility and sexual behavior; mortality, morbidity, and health; mathematical demography. *Unit head:* Dr. Karin L. Brewster, Director, 850-644-7106, Fax: 850-644-8818, E-mail: karin.brewster@fsu.edu. *Application contact:* Barbara G. Rousseau, Program Assistant, 850-644-1762, Fax: 850-644-8818, E-mail: brousseau@fsu.edu. Website: http://popcenter.fsu.edu

**Harvard University,** Harvard T.H. Chan School of Public Health, Department of Global Health and Population, Boston, MA 02115. Offers SM, SD. *Accreditation:* CEPH.

*Program availability:* Part-time. *Degree requirements:* For master's, thesis; for doctorate, thesis/dissertation, qualifying exam. *Entrance requirements:* For master's, GRE, MCAT; for doctorate, GRE. Additional exam requirements/recommendations for international students: Recommended—TOEFL (minimum score 600 paper-based; 100 iBT), IELTS (minimum score 7). Electronic applications accepted. *Faculty research:* Health systems, international health policy, economics, population and reproductive health, ecology.

**Johns Hopkins University,** Bloomberg School of Public Health, Department of Population, Family and Reproductive Health, Baltimore, MD 21205. Offers child and adolescent health and development (MHS, Dr PH, PhD); demography (MHS); population and health (Dr PH, PhD); reproductive, perinatal and women's health (MHS, Dr PH, PhD). *Program availability:* Part-time. *Degree requirements:* For master's, essay, fieldwork; for doctorate, thesis/dissertation, 1-year full-time residency, oral and written exams. *Entrance requirements:* For master's and doctorate, GRE General Test, 3 letters of recommendation, curriculum vitae. Additional exam requirements/recommendations for international students: Required—TOEFL (minimum score 600 paper-based). Electronic applications accepted. *Faculty research:* Child and adolescent health and development, population and health and reproductive, perinatal and women's health.

**Miami University,** College of Arts and Science, Department of Sociology and Gerontology, Oxford, OH 45056. Offers gerontology (MGS); population and social gerontology (MPSG); social gerontology (PhD). *Students:* 29 full-time (25 women), 11 part-time (8 women); includes 3 minority (1 Black or African American, non-Hispanic/Latino; 1 Asian, non-Hispanic/Latino; 1 Hispanic/Latino), 12 international. Average age 33. In 2016, 14 master's, 3 doctorates awarded. *Expenses:* Tuition, state resident: full-time $12,890; part-time $564 per credit hour. Tuition, nonresident: full-time $29,604; part-time $1260 per credit hour. *Required fees:* $638. Part-time tuition and fees vary according to course load and program. *Unit head:* Dr. Stephen Lippman, Chair and Associate Professor, 513-529-8515, E-mail: lippmas@miamioh.edu. *Application contact:* Dr. Jennifer Kinney, Director of Graduate Studies, 513-529-2915, E-mail: kinneyjm@miamioh.edu.
Website: http://www.MiamiOH.edu/sociology/

**New York University,** College of Global Public Health, New York, NY 10003. Offers biological basis of public health (PhD); community and international health (MPH); global health leadership (MPH); health systems and health services research (PhD); population and community health (PhD); public health nutrition (MPH); social and behavioral sciences (MPH); socio-behavioral health (PhD). *Accreditation:* CEPH. *Program availability:* Part-time, online learning. *Degree requirements:* For master's, thesis (for some programs); for doctorate, thesis/dissertation. *Entrance requirements:* For master's and doctorate, GRE. Additional exam requirements/recommendations for international students: Required—TOEFL. Electronic applications accepted.

**Princeton University,** Graduate School, Department of Sociology, Princeton, NJ 08544-1019. Offers sociology (PhD); sociology and demography (PhD). *Degree requirements:* For doctorate, variable foreign language requirement, thesis/dissertation. *Entrance requirements:* For doctorate, GRE General Test, GRE Subject Test (recommended), sample of written work. Additional exam requirements/recommendations for international students: Required—TOEFL (minimum score 600 paper-based). Electronic applications accepted.

**Princeton University,** Graduate School, Program in Population Studies, Princeton, NJ 08544-1019. Offers demography (PhD, Certificate); economics and demography (PhD); public affairs and demography (PhD); sociology and demography (PhD). *Degree requirements:* For doctorate, thesis/dissertation. *Entrance requirements:* For doctorate, GRE General Test. Additional exam requirements/recommendations for international students: Required—TOEFL (minimum score 600 paper-based). Electronic applications accepted. *Faculty research:* Models, fertility, infant and child mortality, migration.

**Université de Montréal,** Faculty of Arts and Sciences, Department of Demography, Montréal, QC H3C 3J7, Canada. Offers M Sc, PhD. Terminal master's awarded for partial completion of doctoral program. *Degree requirements:* For master's, one foreign language, thesis; for doctorate, one foreign language, thesis/dissertation, general exam. *Entrance requirements:* For master's, minimum GPA of 2.7. Electronic applications accepted. *Faculty research:* Historical demography, population and development, ethnic and linguistic groups, aging of population, family demography.

**Université du Québec, Institut National de la Recherche Scientifique,** Graduate Programs, Centre for Urbanisation Culture Societe, Montreal, QC G1K 9A9, Canada. Offers demography (M Sc, PhD); research practices and public action (MA, DESS); urban studies (M Sc, PhD). *Program availability:* Part-time. *Faculty:* 34 full-time. *Students:* 79 full-time (43 women), 14 part-time (10 women), 13 international. Average age 32. 40 applicants, 88% accepted, 20 enrolled. In 2016, 17 master's, 5 doctorates awarded. *Degree requirements:* For master's, thesis (for some programs); for doctorate, thesis/dissertation. *Entrance requirements:* For master's, appropriate bachelor's degree, proficiency in French; for doctorate, appropriate master's degree, proficiency in French; for DESS, proficiency in French. *Application deadline:* For fall admission, 3/30 for domestic and international students; for winter admission, 11/1 for domestic and international students; for spring admission, 3/1 for domestic and international students. Application fee: $45. Electronic applications accepted. *Financial support:* In 2016–17, fellowships (averaging $16,500 per year) were awarded; research assistantships also available. *Faculty research:* Mobility and migration, cultural policies, knowledge mobilization, spatial analysis of data, social demography. *Unit head:* Claire Poitras, Director, 514-499-4002, E-mail: claire.poitras@ucs.inrs.ca. *Application contact:* Sylvie Richard, Registrar, 418-654-2518, Fax: 418-654-3858,
E-mail: sylvie.richard@adm.inrs.ca.
Website: http://www.ucs.inrs.ca

**University at Albany, State University of New York,** College of Arts and Sciences, Department of Sociology, Albany, NY 12222-0001. Offers demography (Certificate); sociology (MA, PhD); urban policy (Certificate). *Faculty:* 8 full-time (6 women). *Students:* 25 full-time (19 women), 63 part-time (46 women); includes 17 minority (4 Black or African American, non-Hispanic/Latino; 1 American Indian or Alaska Native, non-Hispanic/Latino; 5 Asian, non-Hispanic/Latino; 5 Hispanic/Latino; 2 Two or more races, non-Hispanic/Latino), 27 international. 85 applicants, 39% accepted, 11 enrolled. In 2016, 2 master's, 15 doctorates awarded. Terminal master's awarded for partial completion of doctoral program. *Degree requirements:* For master's, thesis; for doctorate, thesis/dissertation, 2 specialization exams, research tool. *Entrance requirements:* For master's and doctorate, GRE General Test. Additional exam requirements/recommendations for international students: Required—TOEFL. *Application deadline:* For fall admission, 1/15 for domestic students, 5/1 for international students. Applications are processed on a rolling basis. Application fee: $75. Electronic applications accepted. *Expenses:* Tuition, state resident: full-time $10,870; part-time $453 per credit hour. Tuition, nonresident: full-time $22,210; part-time $925 per credit hour. *International tuition:* $21,550 full-time. *Required fees:* $1864; $96 per credit hour. *Financial support:* Fellowships, research assistantships, teaching assistantships, career-related internships or fieldwork, and Federal Work-Study available. Financial award application deadline: 3/15. *Faculty research:* Gender and equality, crime and deviance, aging, work and organizations, social demography. *Total annual research expenditures:* $418,522. *Unit head:* Nancy Denton, Chair, 518-442-4666, Fax: 518-442-

4936, E-mail: ndenton@albany.edu. *Application contact:* Michael DeRensis, Director, Graduate Admissions, 518-442-3980, Fax: 518-442-3922,
E-mail: graduate@albany.edu.
Website: http://www.albany.edu/sociology/index.html

**University of Alberta,** Faculty of Graduate Studies and Research, Department of Sociology, Edmonton, AB T6G 2E1, Canada. Offers criminal justice (MA); demography (MA, PhD); sociology (MA, PhD). *Program availability:* Part-time. *Degree requirements:* For master's, thesis (for some programs); for doctorate, thesis/dissertation. *Faculty research:* Criminology, knowledge and culture, methods and theory, population studies, stratification.

**University of California, Berkeley,** Graduate Division, College of Letters and Science, Department of Demography, Berkeley, CA 94720-1500. Offers PhD. *Students:* 9 full-time (6 women); includes 1 minority (Asian, non-Hispanic/Latino), 4 international. Average age 30. 20 applicants, 3 enrolled. In 2016, 2 doctorates awarded. *Degree requirements:* For doctorate, thesis/dissertation, qualifying exam. *Entrance requirements:* For doctorate, GRE General Test, minimum GPA of 3.0, 3 letters of recommendation. Additional exam requirements/recommendations for international students: Required—TOEFL (minimum score 570 paper-based; 90 iBT). *Application deadline:* For fall admission, 12/15 for domestic students. Application fee: $105 ($125 for international students). Electronic applications accepted. *Financial support:* Fellowships with full and partial tuition reimbursements, research assistantships with full and partial tuition reimbursements, teaching assistantships with full and partial tuition reimbursements, institutionally sponsored loans, health care benefits, and unspecified assistantships available. Financial award applicants required to submit FAFSA. *Unit head:* Prof. Josh Goldstein, Chair, 510-642-9800. *Application contact:* Monique Marie Verrier, Student Affairs Officer, 510-642-9800, Fax: 510-643-8558, E-mail: applications@demog.berkeley.edu.
Website: http://www.demog.berkeley.edu/

**University of California, Berkeley,** Graduate Division, College of Letters and Science, Group in Sociology and Demography, Berkeley, CA 94720-1500. Offers MA, PhD. *Students:* 6 full-time (3 women); includes 1 minority (Hispanic/Latino), 2 international. Average age 30. 20 applicants, 1 enrolled. *Degree requirements:* For doctorate, thesis/dissertation, qualifying exam. *Entrance requirements:* For master's and doctorate, GRE General Test, minimum GPA of 3.0, 3 letters of recommendation. *Application deadline:* For fall admission, 12/15 for domestic students. Application fee: $105 ($125 for international students). Electronic applications accepted. *Financial support:* Fellowships with full and partial tuition reimbursements, research assistantships with full and partial tuition reimbursements, teaching assistantships with full and partial tuition reimbursements, traineeships, and unspecified assistantships available. *Unit head:* Prof. Josh Goldstein, Chair, 510-642-9800. *Application contact:* Monique Marie Verrier, Student Affairs Officer, 510-642-9800, Fax: 510-643-8558, E-mail: applications@demog.berkeley.edu.
Website: http://www.demog.berkeley.edu/students/socdemog.shtml

**University of California, Irvine,** School of Social Sciences and School of Social Ecology, Program in Demographic and Social Analysis, Irvine, CA 92697. Offers MA. *Students:* 13 full-time (7 women); includes 8 minority (1 Black or African American, non-Hispanic/Latino; 2 Asian, non-Hispanic/Latino; 4 Hispanic/Latino; 1 Two or more races, non-Hispanic/Latino), 4 international. Average age 25. 30 applicants, 70% accepted, 13 enrolled. In 2016, 14 master's awarded. *Entrance requirements:* For master's, GRE, minimum GPA of 3.0. Additional exam requirements/recommendations for international students: Required—TOEFL (minimum score 550 paper-based). *Application deadline:* For fall admission, 1/15 priority date for domestic and international students. Application fee: $105 ($125 for international students). *Financial support:* Application deadline: 3/1. *Unit head:* Susan Brown, Graduate Director, 949-824-9382, Fax: 949-824-4717, E-mail: skbrown@uci.edu. *Application contact:* John Sommerhauser, Director of Graduate Affairs, 949-824-4074, E-mail: john.sommerhauser@uci.edu.
Website: http://www.demography.uci.edu/

**University of Guelph,** Ontario Veterinary College and Graduate Studies, Graduate Programs in Veterinary Sciences, Department of Population Medicine, Guelph, ON N1G 2W1, Canada. Offers epidemiology (M Sc, DV Sc, PhD); health management (DV Sc); population medicine and management (M Sc); swine health management (M Sc); theriogenology (M Sc, DV Sc). *Degree requirements:* For master's, thesis; for doctorate, comprehensive exam, thesis/dissertation. *Entrance requirements:* Additional exam requirements/recommendations for international students: Required—TOEFL.

**University of Hawaii at Manoa,** John A. Burns School of Medicine, Department of Public Health Sciences and Epidemiology, Global Health and Population Studies Program, Honolulu, HI 96822. Offers Graduate Certificate. *Program availability:* Part-time. *Entrance requirements:* For degree, GRE General Test. Additional exam requirements/recommendations for international students: Required—TOEFL (minimum score 550 paper-based; 79 iBT), IELTS (minimum score 5).

**University of Pennsylvania,** School of Arts and Sciences, Graduate Group in Demography, Philadelphia, PA 19104. Offers AM, PhD. *Faculty:* 38 full-time (17 women), 8 part-time/adjunct (3 women). *Students:* 21 full-time (8 women); includes 5 minority (1 Black or African American, non-Hispanic/Latino; 3 Asian, non-Hispanic/Latino; 1 Hispanic/Latino), 12 international. Average age 29. 27 applicants, 19% accepted, 4 enrolled. In 2016, 1 master's, 5 doctorates awarded. Terminal master's awarded for partial completion of doctoral program. *Expenses: Tuition:* Full-time $31,068; part-time $5762 per course. *Required fees:* $3200; $336 per course. Full-time tuition and fees vary according to degree level, program and student level. Part-time tuition and fees vary according to course load, degree level and program. *Unit head:* Dr. Ralph M. Rosen, Associate Dean for Graduate Studies, 215-898-7156, Fax: 215-573-8068, E-mail: grad-dean@sas.upenn.edu. *Application contact:* Arts and Sciences Graduate Admissions, 215-573-5816, Fax: 215-573-8068,
E-mail: gdasadmis@sas.upenn.edu.
Website: http://demog.pop.upenn.edu

**University of Puerto Rico, Medical Sciences Campus,** Graduate School of Public Health, Department of Social Sciences, Program in Demography, San Juan, PR 00936-5067. Offers MS. *Program availability:* Part-time. *Degree requirements:* For master's, thesis. *Entrance requirements:* For master's, GRE, previous course work in algebra and statistics.

**The University of Texas at San Antonio,** College of Public Policy, Department of Demography, San Antonio, TX 78207. Offers applied demography (PhD). *Program availability:* Part-time, evening/weekend. *Faculty:* 6 full-time (3 women). *Students:* 16 full-time (6 women), 18 part-time (11 women); includes 21 minority (4 Black or African American, non-Hispanic/Latino; 3 Asian, non-Hispanic/Latino; 14 Hispanic/Latino), 8 international. Average age 38. 13 applicants, 92% accepted, 8 enrolled. In 2016, 7 doctorates awarded. *Degree requirements:* For doctorate, comprehensive exam, thesis/dissertation, dissertation proposal defense. *Entrance requirements:* For doctorate, GRE, three letters of recommendation, statement of purpose, MA/MS. Additional exam requirements/recommendations for international students: Required—TOEFL (minimum score 550 paper-based; 79 iBT), IELTS (minimum score 6.5). *Application deadline:* For fall admission, 2/1 for domestic students. Application fee: $45 ($80 for international

students). Electronic applications accepted. *Financial support:* In 2016–17, 1 fellowship (averaging $5,000 per year), 10 research assistantships (averaging $22,500 per year), 1 teaching assistantship (averaging $5,500 per year) were awarded. *Faculty research:* International migration, health disparities and inequality, food security, poverty, demographic change in communities, demographics of energy use. *Total annual research expenditures:* $369,707. *Unit head:* Dr. Joachim Singelmann, Department Chair, 210-458-3163, Fax: 210-458-3164, E-mail: joachim.singelmann@utsa.edu. *Application contact:* Corey Sparks, Graduate Advisor of Record, 210-458-3166, Fax: 210-458-3164, E-mail: johnelle.sparks@utsa.edu.
Website: http://copp.utsa.edu/demography/

**The University of Texas Medical Branch,** Graduate School of Biomedical Sciences, Program in Population Health Sciences, Galveston, TX 77555. Offers PhD.

**University of Wisconsin–Madison,** School of Medicine and Public Health, Population Health and Epidemiology Program, Madison, WI 53726. Offers epidemiology (MS, PhD); population health (MS, PhD). *Program availability:* Part-time. *Faculty:* 25 full-time (14 women). *Students:* 40 full-time (32 women), 10 part-time (9 women); includes 7 minority (2 Black or African American, non-Hispanic/Latino; 3 Asian, non-Hispanic/Latino; 2 Hispanic/Latino), 3 international. Average age 31. 66 applicants, 26% accepted, 13 enrolled. In 2016, 8 master's, 5 doctorates awarded. Terminal master's awarded for partial completion of doctoral program. *Degree requirements:* For master's, thesis, thesis defense; for doctorate, comprehensive exam, thesis/dissertation, qualifying exam, preliminary exam, dissertation defense. *Entrance requirements:* For master's and doctorate, GRE taken within the last 5 years (MCAT or LSAT acceptable for those with doctoral degrees), minimum GPA of 3.0, quantitative preparation (calculus, statistics, or other) with minimum B average. Additional exam requirements/recommendations for international students: Required—TOEFL (minimum score 580 paper-based; 92 iBT). *Application deadline:* For fall admission, 1/15 for domestic and international students. Application fee: $75. Electronic applications accepted. *Expenses:* $5,971 per semester full-time resident tuition, $12,634 per semester full-time non-resident tuition; $607 per semester fees. *Financial support:* Fellowships with full tuition reimbursements, research assistantships with full tuition reimbursements, teaching assistantships with full tuition reimbursements, scholarships/grants, traineeships, health care benefits, and unspecified assistantships available. Support available to part-time students. *Faculty research:* Epidemiology (cancer, environmental, aging, infectious and genetic disease), determinants of population health, health services research, social and behavioral health sciences, biostatistics. *Total annual research expenditures:* $12 million. *Unit head:* Mari Palta, Graduate Program Chair, 608-263-4029, Fax: 608-263-2820, E-mail: mpalta@wisc.edu. *Application contact:* Quinn H. Fullenkamp, Graduate Program Coordinator, 608-265-8108, Fax: 608-263-2820, E-mail: pophealth@mailplus.wisc.edu.
Website: https://pophealth.wisc.edu/grad

# Rural Sociology

**Cornell University,** Graduate School, Graduate Fields of Agriculture and Life Sciences, Field of Development Sociology, Ithaca, NY 14853. Offers population and development (MS, PhD); rural and environmental sociology (MS, PhD); state, economy, and society (MS, PhD). *Degree requirements:* For doctorate, comprehensive exam, thesis/dissertation. *Entrance requirements:* For master's and doctorate, GRE General Test, 3 letters of recommendation. Additional exam requirements/recommendations for international students: Required—TOEFL (minimum score 550 paper-based; 77 iBT). Electronic applications accepted. *Faculty research:* Demography (population and development), environmental sociology, international and rural community development, political economy and ecology, sustainable agriculture.

**Iowa State University of Science and Technology,** Department of Sociology, Ames, IA 50011. Offers rural sociology (MS, PhD); sociology (MS, PhD). *Degree requirements:* For master's, thesis; for doctorate, thesis/dissertation. *Entrance requirements:* For master's and doctorate, GRE General Test. Additional exam requirements/recommendations for international students: Required—TOEFL (minimum score 550 paper-based; 79 iBT), IELTS (minimum score 6.5). *Application deadline:* For fall admission, 1/10 priority date for domestic and international students; for spring admission, 10/1 for domestic and international students. Application fee: $60 ($90 for international students). Electronic applications accepted. *Application contact:* Rachel Burlingame, Application Contact, 515-294-2506, Fax: 515-294-8649, E-mail: rmb@iastate.edu.
Website: http://www.soc.iastate.edu/graduate/index.html

**Iowa State University of Science and Technology,** Program in Rural Sociology, Ames, IA 50011. Offers MS, PhD. *Degree requirements:* For master's, thesis; for doctorate, thesis/dissertation. *Entrance requirements:* For master's, GRE General Test; for doctorate, GRE General Test, master's degree. Additional exam requirements/recommendations for international students: Required—TOEFL (minimum score 550 paper-based; 79 iBT), IELTS (minimum score 6.5). *Application deadline:* For fall admission, 1/10 priority date for domestic and international students; for spring admission, 10/1 for domestic and international students. Application fee: $60 ($90 for international students). Electronic applications accepted. *Application contact:* Rachel Burlingame, Application Contact, 515-294-2506, Fax: 515-294-8649, E-mail: rmb@iastate.edu.
Website: http://www.soc.iastate.edu/graduate/index.html

**The Ohio State University,** Graduate School, College of Food, Agricultural, and Environmental Sciences, School of Environment and Natural Resources, Columbus, OH 43210. Offers ecological restoration (MS, PhD); ecosystem science (MS, PhD); environment and natural resources (MENR); environmental social sciences (MS, PhD); fisheries and wildlife science (MS, PhD); forest science (MS, PhD); rural sociology (MS, PhD); soil science (MS, PhD). *Faculty:* 38. *Students:* 94 full-time (59 women), 8 part-time (4 women); includes 12 minority (7 Hispanic/Latino; 5 Two or more races, non-Hispanic/Latino), 6 international. Average age 28. In 2016, 19 master's, 8 doctorates awarded. *Degree requirements:* For master's, thesis; for doctorate, thesis/dissertation. *Entrance requirements:* For master's and doctorate, GRE. Additional exam requirements/recommendations for international students: Required—TOEFL (minimum score 550 paper-based; 79 iBT), Michigan English Language Assessment Battery (minimum score 82); Recommended—IELTS (minimum score 7). *Application deadline:* For fall admission, 1/1 priority date for domestic students, 12/15 priority date for international students; for spring admission, 11/1 for domestic students, 9/15 for international students. Applications are processed on a rolling basis. Application fee: $60 ($70 for international students). Electronic applications accepted. *Financial support:* Fellowships with tuition reimbursements, research assistantships with tuition reimbursements, teaching assistantships with tuition reimbursements, health care benefits, and unspecified assistantships available. *Unit head:* Dr. Jeff S. Sharp, Director, 614-292-9410, E-mail: sharp.123@osu.edu. *Application contact:* Graduate and Professional Admissions, 614-292-9444, Fax: 614-292-3895, E-mail: gpadmissions@osu.edu.
Website: http://senr.osu.edu/

**Penn State University Park,** Graduate School, College of Agricultural Sciences, Department of Agricultural Economics, Sociology, and Education, University Park, PA 16802. Offers agricultural and extension education (M Ed, MS, PhD, Certificate); agricultural, environmental and regional economics (MS, PhD); applied youth, family and community education (M Ed); community and economic development (MPS); rural sociology (MS, PhD). *Unit head:* Dr. Richard T. Roush, Dean, 814-865-2541, Fax: 814-865-3103. *Application contact:* Lori Hawn, Director, Graduate Student Services, 814-865-1795, Fax: 814-863-4627, E-mail: l-gswww@lists.psu.edu.
Website: http://aese.psu.edu/

**University of Alberta,** Faculty of Graduate Studies and Research, Department of Rural Economy, Edmonton, AB T6G 2E1, Canada. Offers agricultural economics (M Ag, M Sc, PhD); forest economics (M Ag, M Sc, PhD); rural sociology (M Ag, M Sc); MBA/M Ag. *Program availability:* Part-time. *Degree requirements:* For doctorate, thesis/dissertation. *Entrance requirements:* Additional exam requirements/recommendations for international students: Required—TOEFL. *Faculty research:* Agroforestry, development, extension education, marketing and trade, natural resources and environment, policy, production economics.

**University of Missouri,** Office of Research and Graduate Studies, College of Agriculture, Food and Natural Resources, Department of Rural Sociology, Columbia, MO 65211. Offers MS, PhD. *Program availability:* Part-time. *Faculty:* 6 full-time (2 women). *Students:* 18 full-time (12 women), 6 part-time (4 women); includes 1 minority (Two or more races, non-Hispanic/Latino), 6 international. Average age 39. *Degree requirements:* For doctorate, comprehensive exam, thesis/dissertation. *Entrance requirements:* For master's and doctorate, GRE General Test, minimum GPA of 3.0. Additional exam requirements/recommendations for international students: Required—TOEFL (minimum score 570 paper-based; 89 iBT). *Application deadline:* Applications are processed on a rolling basis. Application fee: $75 ($90 for international students). Electronic applications accepted. *Expenses:* Tuition, state resident: full-time $6347; part-time $352.60 per credit hour. Tuition, nonresident: full-time $17,379; part-time $965.50 per credit hour. *Required fees:* $1035. Tuition and fees vary according to course load, campus/location and program. *Financial support:* Fellowships with tuition reimbursements, research assistantships with tuition reimbursements, teaching assistantships with tuition reimbursements, institutionally sponsored loans, scholarships/grants, health care benefits, and unspecified assistantships available. Support available to part-time students. *Faculty research:* Rural social organization; social change and development; sociology of agriculture; natural resource management; sociology of consumption, culture and organization; science, technology and society studies; social inequality; survey research; entrepreneurship; state and local public finance; community economics; rural development.
Website: http://dass.missouri.edu/ruralsoc/grad/

**University of Montana,** Graduate School, College of Humanities and Sciences, Department of Sociology, Missoula, MT 59812-0002. Offers criminology (MA); inequality and social justice (MA); rural and environmental change (MA); sociology (MA). *Entrance requirements:* For master's, GRE General Test. Additional exam requirements/recommendations for international students: Required—TOEFL. *Faculty research:* Housing, homelessness, hunger, infant mortality, work safety.

**University of Puerto Rico, Mayagüez Campus,** Graduate Studies, College of Agricultural Sciences, Department of Agricultural Economics and Rural Sociology, Mayagüez, PR 00681-9000. Offers MS. *Program availability:* Part-time. *Faculty:* 15 full-time (7 women). *Students:* 20 full-time (12 women), 2 part-time (0 women); all minorities (all Hispanic/Latino). Average age 25. 8 applicants, 50% accepted, 3 enrolled. In 2016, 1 master's awarded. *Degree requirements:* For master's, comprehensive exam, thesis. *Entrance requirements:* For master's, bachelor's degree in agricultural economics or its equivalent. *Application deadline:* For fall admission, 2/15 for domestic and international students; for spring admission, 9/15 for domestic and international students. Applications are processed on a rolling basis. Application fee: $25. Electronic applications accepted. *Expenses: Tuition, area resident:* Full-time $2466. *International tuition:* $7166 full-time. *Required fees:* $210. One-time fee: $5 full-time. Tuition and fees vary according to course level, campus/location, program and student level. *Financial support:* In 2016–17, 18 students received support, including 15 research assistantships with tuition reimbursements available (averaging $2,477 per year), 10 teaching assistantships with tuition reimbursements available (averaging $2,066 per year); scholarships/grants and unspecified assistantships also available. *Faculty research:* Farm management, agricultural development, agrimarketing, natural resource economics. *Unit head:* Alwin J. Jiménez, PhD, Director, 787-265-3855 Ext. 3860, Fax: 787-265-3860, E-mail: alwin.jimenez@upr.edu. *Application contact:* Margarita Olivencia, Secretary, 787-832-4040 Ext. 2471, Fax: 787-265-3860, E-mail: margarita.olivencia@upr.edu.
Website: http://economia.cca.uprm.edu/

**University of Wisconsin–Madison,** Graduate School, College of Letters and Science, Department of Sociology, Madison, WI 53706-1380. Offers rural sociology (MS); sociology (MS, PhD). *Program availability:* Part-time. Terminal master's awarded for partial completion of doctoral program. *Degree requirements:* For master's, thesis, oral exam; for doctorate, thesis/dissertation, preliminary and final oral exams, 4 seminars. *Entrance requirements:* For master's and doctorate, GRE General Test. Additional exam requirements/recommendations for international students: Required—TOEFL. Electronic applications accepted.

# Sociology

**Acadia University,** Faculty of Arts, Department of Sociology, Wolfville, NS B4P 2R6, Canada. Offers MA. *Degree requirements:* For master's, thesis. *Entrance requirements:* For master's, honors degree, minimum GPA of 3.25. Additional exam requirements/ recommendations for international students: Required—TOEFL (minimum score 630 paper-based; 93 iBT), IELTS (minimum score 6.5). *Faculty research:* Atlantic cultures, class analysis, gender and women's studies, religion, symbolism, development studies.

**American University,** College of Arts and Sciences, Department of Sociology, Washington, DC 22016-8072. Offers public sociology (Certificate); social research (Certificate); sociology (MA). *Program availability:* Part-time, evening/weekend. *Faculty:* 14 full-time (10 women), 8 part-time/adjunct (5 women). *Students:* 3 full-time (all women), 6 part-time (4 women); includes 6 minority (3 Black or African American, non-Hispanic/Latino; 1 Hispanic/Latino; 2 Two or more races, non-Hispanic/Latino). Average age 27. 22 applicants, 86% accepted, 6 enrolled. In 2016, 8 master's awarded. *Degree requirements:* For master's, comprehensive exam, thesis or alternative. *Entrance requirements:* For master's, GRE, statement of purpose, transcripts, 2 letters of recommendation, resume; for Certificate, bachelor's degree, statement of purpose, transcripts, resume. Additional exam requirements/recommendations for international students: Required—TOEFL, IELTS (minimum score 7), PTE (minimum score 68). *Application deadline:* For fall admission, 2/1 priority date for domestic students; for spring admission, 11/1 for domestic students. Application fee: $55. *Expenses:* $1,579 per credit tuition; $690 mandatory fees. *Financial support:* Research assistantships, teaching assistantships, institutionally sponsored loans, scholarships/grants, and unspecified assistantships available. Financial award application deadline: 2/1; financial award applicants required to submit FAFSA. *Unit head:* Dr. Gloria Young, Department Chair, 202-885-2254, Fax: 202-885-2477, E-mail: gyoung@american.edu. *Application contact:* Kathleen Clowery, Associate Director, Graduate Admissions, 202-885-3620, Fax: 202-885-1344, E-mail: clowery@american.edu.
Website: http://www.american.edu/cas/sociology/

**American University of Beirut,** Graduate Programs, Faculty of Arts and Sciences, Beirut, Lebanon. Offers anthropology (MA); Arab and Middle Eastern history (PhD); Arabic language and literature (MA, PhD); archaeology (MA); art history and curating (MA); biology (MS); cell and molecular biology (PhD); chemistry (MS); clinical psychology (MA); computational sciences (MS); computer science (MS); economics (MA); education (MA); English language (MA); English literature (MA); environmental policy planning (MS); financial economics (MAFE); geology (MS); history (MA); Islamic studies (MA); mathematics (MS); media studies (MA); Middle Eastern studies (MA); physics (MS); political studies (MA); psychology (MA); public administration (MA); public policy and international affairs (MA); sociology (MA); statistics (MA, MS); theoretical physics (PhD); transnational American studies (MA). *Program availability:* Part-time. *Faculty:* 133 full-time (42 women), 6 part-time/adjunct (2 women). *Students:* 240 full-time (172 women), 227 part-time (166 women). Average age 27. 286 applicants, 67% accepted, 108 enrolled. In 2016, 60 master's, 3 doctorates awarded. Terminal master's awarded for partial completion of doctoral program. *Degree requirements:* For master's, one foreign language, comprehensive exam, thesis (for some programs); for doctorate, one foreign language, comprehensive exam, thesis/dissertation. *Entrance requirements:* For master's, GRE (for some MA, MS programs), letters of recommendation; for doctorate, GRE, letters of recommendation. Additional exam requirements/ recommendations for international students: Required—TOEFL (minimum score 600 paper-based; 97 iBT), IELTS (minimum score 7). *Application deadline:* For fall admission, 4/3 for domestic students; for winter admission, 11/3 for domestic students. Application fee: $50. Electronic applications accepted. *Expenses:* Contact institution. *Financial support:* In 2016–17, 4 fellowships (averaging $11,200 per year), 18 research assistantships (averaging $5,400 per year) were awarded; teaching assistantships, career-related internships or fieldwork, Federal Work-Study, institutionally sponsored loans, scholarships/grants, traineeships, health care benefits, tuition waivers (full), and unspecified assistantships also available. Support available to part-time students. *Faculty research:* Development economics, spatial econometrics, health economics, labor economics, energy economics, hydrogeology, geophysics, petrophysics, structural geology, mineralogy, petrology, geochemistry, multilingualism, comparative/world literature, translation studies, book histories/ cultures, biocatalysis, molecular recognition, photocatalysis, photophysical and biophysical chemistry, probe chemistry, machine learning, data science. *Unit head:* Dr. Nadia Maria El Cheikh, Dean, Faculty of Arts and Sciences, 961-1374374 Ext. 3800, Fax: 961-1744461, E-mail: nmcheikh@aub.edu.lb. *Application contact:* Dr. Salim Kanaan, Director, Admissions Office, 961-1350000 Ext. 2590, Fax: 961-1750775, E-mail: sk00@aub.edu.lb.
Website: http://www.aub.edu.lb/fas/

**Arizona State University at the Tempe campus,** College of Liberal Arts and Sciences, School of Social and Family Dynamics, Tempe, AZ 85287-3701. Offers family and human development (MS, PhD); infant-family practice (MAS); marriage and family therapy (MAS); sociology (MA, PhD). Terminal master's awarded for partial completion of doctoral program. *Degree requirements:* For master's, thesis or alternative, interactive Program of Study (iPOS) submitted before completing 50 percent of required credit hours; for doctorate, thesis/dissertation, interactive Program of Study (iPOS) submitted before completing 50 percent of required credit hours. *Entrance requirements:* For master's and doctorate, GRE, minimum GPA of 3.0 or equivalent in last 2 years of work leading to bachelor's degree. Additional exam requirements/recommendations for international students: Required—TOEFL, IELTS, or PTE. Electronic applications accepted. *Expenses:* Contact institution.

**Arkansas State University,** Graduate School, College of Humanities and Social Sciences, Department of Criminology, Sociology, and Geography, State University, AR 72467. Offers criminal justice (MA); sociology (MA); sociology education (SCCT). *Program availability:* Part-time. *Degree requirements:* For master's, one foreign language, comprehensive exam, thesis or alternative; for SCCT, comprehensive exam. *Entrance requirements:* For master's, GRE General Test or MAT, appropriate bachelor's degree, letters of recommendation, official transcripts, immunization records; for SCCT, GRE General Test or MAT, interview, master's degree, official transcript, immunization records. Additional exam requirements/recommendations for international students: Required—TOEFL (minimum score 550 paper-based; 79 iBT), IELTS (minimum score 6), PTE (minimum score 56). Electronic applications accepted.

**Arkansas Tech University,** College of Arts and Humanities, Russellville, AR 72801. Offers applied sociology (MS); English (M Ed, MA); history (MA); liberal arts (MLA); multi-media journalism (MA); psychology (MS); teaching English as a second language (MA). *Program availability:* Part-time. *Students:* 56 full-time (42 women), 121 part-time (85 women); includes 23 minority (7 Black or African American, non-Hispanic/Latino; 1 Asian, non-Hispanic/Latino; 11 Hispanic/Latino; 4 Two or more races, non-Hispanic/Latino), 34 international. Average age 32. In 2016, 90 master's awarded. *Degree requirements:* For master's, comprehensive exam (for some programs), thesis (for some

programs), project. *Entrance requirements:* For master's, GRE General Test or GMAT. Additional exam requirements/recommendations for international students: Required— TOEFL (minimum score 550 paper-based; 79 iBT), IELTS (minimum score 6). *Application deadline:* For fall admission, 3/1 priority date for domestic students, 5/1 priority date for international students; for spring admission, 10/1 priority date for domestic and international students. Applications are processed on a rolling basis. Application fee: $25 ($75 for international students). Electronic applications accepted. *Expenses:* Tuition, state resident: full-time $4932; part-time $274 per credit hour. Tuition, nonresident: full-time $9864; part-time $548 per credit hour. *Required fees:* $513 per semester. Tuition and fees vary according to course load. *Financial support:* In 2016–17, research assistantships with full tuition reimbursements (averaging $4,800 per year), teaching assistantships with full tuition reimbursements (averaging $4,800 per year) were awarded; career-related internships or fieldwork, Federal Work-Study, scholarships/grants, health care benefits, and unspecified assistantships also available. Support available to part-time students. Financial award application deadline: 4/15; financial award applicants required to submit FAFSA. *Unit head:* Dr. Jeffrey Woods, Dean, 479-968-0274, Fax: 479-964-0812, E-mail: jwoods@atu.edu. *Application contact:* Dr. Mary B. Gunter, Dean of Graduate College, 479-968-0398, Fax: 479-964-0542, E-mail: gradcollege@atu.edu.
Website: http://www.atu.edu/humanities/

**Auburn University,** Graduate School, Interdepartmental Programs, Graduate Programs in Sociology and Rural Sociology, Auburn University, AL 36849. Offers MA, MS. *Program availability:* Part-time. *Faculty:* 17 full-time (12 women), 1 part-time/adjunct (0 women). *Students:* 11 full-time (5 women), 3 part-time (2 women); includes 2 minority (1 Black or African American, non-Hispanic/Latino; 1 Hispanic/Latino), 1 international. Average age 32. 16 applicants, 63% accepted, 5 enrolled. In 2016, 2 master's awarded. *Degree requirements:* For master's, thesis, computer language (MS), foreign language (MA). *Entrance requirements:* For master's, GRE General Test. *Application deadline:* Applications are processed on a rolling basis. Application fee: $50 ($60 for international students). *Expenses:* Tuition, state resident: full-time $9072; part-time $504 per credit hour. Tuition, nonresident: full-time $27,216; part-time $1512 per credit hour. *Required fees:* $812 per semester. Tuition and fees vary according to degree level and program. *Financial support:* Research assistantships and teaching assistantships available. Financial award application deadline: 3/15; financial award applicants required to submit FAFSA. *Unit head:* Deacue Fields, Chair, 334-844-5049. *Application contact:* Dr. George Flowers, Dean of the Graduate School, 334-844-4700.

**Ball State University,** Graduate School, College of Sciences and Humanities, Department of Sociology, Muncie, IN 47306. Offers MA. *Program availability:* Part-time. *Entrance requirements:* For master's, GRE General Test, minimum baccalaureate GPA of 2.75 or 3.0 in latter half of baccalauareate, three letters of recommendation. Additional exam requirements/recommendations for international students: Required—TOEFL (minimum score 550 paper-based; 79 iBT), IELTS (minimum score 6.5). Electronic applications accepted. *Faculty research:* Retention policies for secondary education, community mental health.

**Baylor University,** Graduate School, College of Arts and Sciences, Department of Sociology, Waco, TX 76798-7326. Offers community analytics (PhD); sociology (MA); sociology of religion (PhD). *Faculty:* 13 full-time (3 women). *Students:* 19 full-time (7 women); includes 3 minority (1 Black or African American, non-Hispanic/Latino; 1 Hispanic/Latino; 1 Two or more races, non-Hispanic/Latino), 3 international. 20 applicants, 25% accepted, 4 enrolled. In 2016, 3 master's, 4 doctorates awarded. Terminal master's awarded for partial completion of doctoral program. *Degree requirements:* For master's, thesis; for doctorate, comprehensive exam, thesis/ dissertation. *Entrance requirements:* For master's and doctorate, GRE General Test. Additional exam requirements/recommendations for international students: Required— TOEFL. *Application deadline:* For fall admission, 1/15 priority date for domestic and international students. Applications are processed on a rolling basis. Electronic applications accepted. *Expenses: Tuition:* Full-time $28,494; part-time $1583 per credit hour. *Required fees:* $167 per credit hour. Tuition and fees vary according to course load and program. *Financial support:* In 2016–17, 23 students received support, including 23 teaching assistantships with full tuition reimbursements available; research assistantships, career-related internships or fieldwork, Federal Work-Study, institutionally sponsored loans, scholarships/grants, health care benefits, and unspecified assistantships also available. Financial award applicants required to submit FAFSA. *Faculty research:* Applied sociology, family, community, rural sociology, collective behavior/social movements, demography, racial and ethnic relations, criminology/delinquency, religion, health/medicine, aging. *Unit head:* Dr. Kevin D. Dougherty, Associate Professor and Graduate Program Director, 254-710-6232, Fax: 254-710-1175, E-mail: kevin_dougherty@baylor.edu. *Application contact:* Sharon Tate, Office Manager, 254-710-1165, Fax: 254-710-1175, E-mail: sharon_tate@baylor.edu.
Website: http://www.baylor.edu/sociology/

**Binghamton University, State University of New York,** Graduate School, Harpur College of Arts and Sciences, Department of Sociology, Binghamton, NY 13902-6000. Offers MA, PhD. *Program availability:* Part-time. *Faculty:* 17 full-time (7 women), 1 (woman) part-time/adjunct. *Students:* 12 full-time (5 women), 56 part-time (26 women); includes 7 minority (3 Black or African American, non-Hispanic/Latino; 2 Asian, non-Hispanic/Latino; 2 Hispanic/Latino), 35 international. Average age 36. 41 applicants, 24% accepted, 6 enrolled. In 2016, 4 master's, 1 doctorate awarded. Terminal master's awarded for partial completion of doctoral program. *Degree requirements:* For doctorate, comprehensive exam, thesis/dissertation. *Entrance requirements:* For master's and doctorate, GRE General Test, writing sample. Additional exam requirements/ recommendations for international students: Required—TOEFL (minimum score 550 paper-based; 80 iBT). *Application deadline:* For fall admission, 1/15 priority date for domestic and international students. Application fee: $75. Electronic applications accepted. *Financial support:* In 2016–17, 27 students received support, including 1 research assistantship (averaging $13,500 per year), 20 teaching assistantships with full tuition reimbursements available (averaging $15,000 per year); career-related internships or fieldwork, Federal Work-Study, institutionally sponsored loans, scholarships/grants, health care benefits, tuition waivers (full and partial), and unspecified assistantships also available. Financial award applicants required to submit FAFSA. *Unit head:* Dr. Michael O. West, Chairperson, 607-777-2629, E-mail: mwest@binghamton.edu. *Application contact:* Ben Balkaya, Assistant Dean and Director, 607-777-2151, Fax: 607-777-2501, E-mail: balkaya@binghamton.edu.

**Boston College,** Graduate School of Arts and Sciences, Department of Sociology, Chestnut Hill, MA 02467-3800. Offers MA, PhD, MBA/MA, MBA/PhD. *Faculty:* 18 full-time. *Students:* 45 full-time (26 women); includes 8 minority (4 Black or African American, non-Hispanic/Latino; 1 Asian, non-Hispanic/Latino; 2 Hispanic/Latino; 1 Two or more races, non-Hispanic/Latino), 6 international. 112 applicants, 50% accepted, 11

## Sociology

enrolled. In 2016, 8 master's, 9 doctorates awarded. Terminal master's awarded for partial completion of doctoral program. *Degree requirements:* For master's, thesis optional; for doctorate, thesis/dissertation. *Entrance requirements:* For master's and doctorate, GRE General Test. Additional exam requirements/recommendations for international students: Required—TOEFL (minimum score 600 paper-based; 100 iBT), IELTS (minimum score 8). *Application deadline:* For fall admission, 1/2 for domestic and international students. Application fee: $75. Electronic applications accepted. Tuition and fees vary according to program. *Financial support:* In 2016–17, fellowships with full tuition reimbursements (averaging $21,400 per year), research assistantships with full tuition reimbursements (averaging $20,900 per year), teaching assistantships with full tuition reimbursements (averaging $20,900 per year) were awarded; Federal Work-Study, health care benefits, and unspecified assistantships also available. Support available to part-time students. Financial award application deadline: 3/1; financial award applicants required to submit FAFSA. *Faculty research:* Social theory, race, gender studies, aging, global and transnational sociology, economic sociology, environmental sociology, political sociology, quantitative and statistical methodology. *Unit head:* Dr. Sarah Babb, Chairperson, 617-552-2930, E-mail: sarah.babb@bc.edu. *Application contact:* Dr. Natasha Sarkisian, Graduate Program Director, 617-552-4209, E-mail: natalia.sarkisian@bc.edu.
Website: http://www.bc.edu/sociology

**Boston University,** Graduate School of Arts and Sciences, Department of Sociology, Boston, MA 02215. Offers MA, PhD. *Students:* 41 full-time (29 women), 2 part-time (both women); includes 8 minority (2 Black or African American, non-Hispanic/Latino; 3 Hispanic/Latino; 3 Two or more races, non-Hispanic/Latino), 11 international. Average age 30. 166 applicants, 13% accepted, 6 enrolled. In 2016, 1 master's, 2 doctorates awarded. Terminal master's awarded for partial completion of doctoral program. *Degree requirements:* For master's, comprehensive exam, thesis; for doctorate, comprehensive exam, thesis/dissertation. *Entrance requirements:* For master's and doctorate, GRE General Test, 3 letters of recommendation, transcripts, personal statement, academic writing sample. Additional exam requirements/recommendations for international students: Required—TOEFL (minimum score 550 paper-based; 84 iBT). *Application deadline:* For fall admission, 1/15 for domestic and international students. Application fee: $95. Electronic applications accepted. *Financial support:* In 2016–17, 32 students received support, including 17 fellowships with full tuition reimbursements available (averaging $21,500 per year), research assistantships with full tuition reimbursements available (averaging $21,500 per year), 11 teaching assistantships with full tuition reimbursements available (averaging $21,500 per year); career-related internships or fieldwork, Federal Work-Study, scholarships/grants, and health care benefits also available. Financial award application deadline: 1/15. *Unit head:* Nazli Kibria, Chair, 617-358-0634, Fax: 617-353-4837, E-mail: nkibria@bu.edu. *Application contact:* Anna Bakanova, Department Administrator, 617-353-2594, Fax: 617-353-4837, E-mail: bakanova@bu.edu.
Website: http://www.bu.edu/sociology/

**Bowling Green State University,** Graduate College, College of Arts and Sciences, Department of Sociology, Bowling Green, OH 43403. Offers demography and population studies (MA); social psychology (MA); sociology (PhD). *Program availability:* Part-time. *Degree requirements:* For master's, thesis or alternative; for doctorate, comprehensive exam, thesis/dissertation. *Entrance requirements:* For master's and doctorate, GRE General Test. Additional exam requirements/recommendations for international students: Required—TOEFL. *Application deadline:* For fall admission, 1/15 priority date for domestic students. Application fee: $30. Electronic applications accepted. *Financial support:* Fellowships with full tuition reimbursements, research assistantships with full tuition reimbursements, teaching assistantships with full tuition reimbursements, career-related internships or fieldwork, Federal Work-Study, institutionally sponsored loans, and unspecified assistantships available. Financial award applicants required to submit FAFSA. *Faculty research:* Applied demography, criminology and deviance, family studies, population studies, social psychology. *Unit head:* Dr. Susan L. Brown, Chair, 419-372-9521, E-mail: brownsl@bgsu.edu. *Application contact:* Dr. Steve Cernkovich, Graduate Coordinator, 419-372-2743.

**Brandeis University,** Graduate School of Arts and Sciences, Department of Sociology, Waltham, MA 02454-9110. Offers social policy and sociology (PhD); sociology (PhD); sociology and women's, gender, and sexuality studies (MA). *Program availability:* Part-time. *Faculty:* 8 full-time (6 women), 7 part-time/adjunct (5 women). *Students:* 19 full-time (17 women), 3 part-time (2 women); includes 6 minority (3 Asian, non-Hispanic/Latino; 2 Hispanic/Latino; 1 Two or more races, non-Hispanic/Latino), 2 international. 70 applicants, 20% accepted, 2 enrolled. In 2016, 2 master's, 3 doctorates awarded. Terminal master's awarded for partial completion of doctoral program. *Degree requirements:* For master's, thesis, project or exam; for doctorate, comprehensive exam, thesis/dissertation, qualifying exam. *Entrance requirements:* For master's and doctorate, GRE, resume, letters of recommendation, statement of purpose, writing sample, transcript(s). Additional exam requirements/recommendations for international students: Required—TOEFL (minimum score 600 paper-based; 100 iBT); Recommended—IELTS (minimum score 7), TSE (minimum score 68). *Application deadline:* For fall admission, 12/15 for domestic and international students. Application fee: $75. Electronic applications accepted. *Financial support:* In 2016–17, 12 students received support, including 11 fellowships with full tuition reimbursements available (averaging $24,000 per year), 9 teaching assistantships with partial tuition reimbursements available (averaging $3,200 per year); Federal Work-Study, scholarships/grants, health care benefits, and tuition waivers (full and partial) also available. Support available to part-time students. Financial award application deadline: 4/15; financial award applicants required to submit FAFSA. *Faculty research:* Gender and feminist studies; medical sociology; politics and social change; culture and religion. *Unit head:* Dr. Laura Miller, Director of Graduate Studies, 781-736-2630, Fax: 781-736-2653, E-mail: lamiller@brandeis.edu. *Application contact:* Lauren Jordahl, Graduate Program Administrator, 781-736-2644, Fax: 781-736-2653, E-mail: ljordahl@brandeis.edu.
Website: http://www.brandeis.edu/gsas/

**Brigham Young University,** Graduate Studies, College of Family, Home, and Social Sciences, Department of Sociology, Provo, UT 84602. Offers MS. *Faculty:* 17 full-time (4 women). *Students:* 15 full-time (11 women); includes 4 minority (1 Asian, non-Hispanic/Latino; 3 Hispanic/Latino). Average age 25. 14 applicants, 79% accepted, 8 enrolled. In 2016, 2 master's awarded. Terminal master's awarded for partial completion of doctoral program. *Degree requirements:* For master's, thesis. *Entrance requirements:* For master's, GRE General Test, minimum GPA of 3.0 in last 60 hours, writing sample, bachelor's degree in sociology or related field, 3 letters of recommendation, Honor Code commitment. Additional exam requirements/recommendations for international students: Required—TOEFL (minimum score 580 paper-based; 85 iBT), IELTS (minimum score 7). *Application deadline:* For fall admission, 1/15 for domestic and international students. Application fee: $50. Electronic applications accepted. *Expenses:* Contact institution. *Financial support:* In 2016–17, 15 students received support, including 13 research assistantships (averaging $16,750 per year); institutionally sponsored loans and unspecified assistantships also available. Financial award application deadline: 4/15. *Faculty research:* Demography, race and ethnicity, gender, rural and community, international development, comparative family. *Total annual research expenditures:* $33,500. *Unit head:* Dr. Richard B. Miller, Department Chair, 801-422-2860, Fax: 801-

422-0625, E-mail: rick_miller@byu.edu. *Application contact:* Dr. Mikaela J. Dufur, Graduate Coordinator, 801-422-1720, Fax: 801-422-0625, E-mail: mikaela_dufur@byu.edu.
Website: http://sociology.byu.edu/

**Brock University,** Faculty of Graduate Studies, Faculty of Social Sciences, Program in Critical Sociology, St. Catharines, ON L2S 3A1, Canada. Offers MA.

**Brooklyn College of the City University of New York,** School of Humanities and Social Sciences, Department of Sociology, Brooklyn, NY 11210-2889. Offers MA, PhD. *Program availability:* Part-time, evening/weekend. *Degree requirements:* For master's, comprehensive exam or research essay. *Entrance requirements:* For master's, 12 upper-level credits in sociology, 2 letters of recommendation, essay. Additional exam requirements/recommendations for international students: Required—TOEFL (minimum score 500 paper-based; 61 iBT). Electronic applications accepted. *Faculty research:* Urbanization, religion, family, gender, research methods.

**Brown University,** Graduate School, Department of Sociology, Providence, RI 02912. Offers MA, PhD. *Degree requirements:* For master's, thesis; for doctorate, thesis/dissertation, oral exam. *Entrance requirements:* For master's and doctorate, GRE General Test.

**California State University, Bakersfield,** Division of Graduate Studies, School of Social Sciences and Education, Program in Sociology, Bakersfield, CA 93311. Offers MA. *Students:* 1 full-time (0 women), 5 part-time (3 women); includes 4 minority (2 Black or African American, non-Hispanic/Latino; 2 Hispanic/Latino). Average age 31. In 2016, 21 master's awarded. *Entrance requirements:* For master's, baccalaureate degree; minimum GPA of 2.5 overall, 3.0 in major. Additional exam requirements/recommendations for international students: Required—TOEFL (minimum score 500 paper-based). *Application deadline:* Applications are processed on a rolling basis. Application fee: $55. Electronic applications accepted. *Expenses:* Tuition, state resident: full-time $2246; part-time $1302 per semester. *Financial support:* In 2016–17, fellowships (averaging $1,850 per year) were awarded; Federal Work-Study, scholarships/grants, and tuition waivers (full and partial) also available. Financial award application deadline: 3/2; financial award applicants required to submit FAFSA. *Unit head:* Dr. Rhonda Dugan, Graduate Coordinator, 661-654-6613, E-mail: rdugan2@csub.edu. *Application contact:* Debbie Blowers, Assistant Director of Admissions and Evaluations, 661-654-3381, E-mail: dblowers@csub.edu.
Website: https://www.csub.edu/sociology/index.html

**California State University, Dominguez Hills,** College of Natural and Behavioral Sciences, Program in Sociology, Carson, CA 90747-0001. Offers social research (Certificate); sociology (MA). *Program availability:* Part-time, evening/weekend. *Degree requirements:* For master's, comprehensive exam, thesis. *Entrance requirements:* For master's, minimum GPA of 2.85. *Faculty research:* Community studies, social movements, criminology.

**California State University, Fullerton,** Graduate Studies, College of Humanities and Social Sciences, Department of Sociology, Fullerton, CA 92834-9480. Offers MA. *Program availability:* Part-time. *Degree requirements:* For master's, thesis. *Entrance requirements:* For master's, minimum GPA of 3.0 in sociology, 2.5 in last 60 units. Application fee: $55. *Expenses:* Tuition, state resident: full-time $3369; part-time $1953 per unit. Tuition, nonresident: full-time $3915; part-time $2499 per unit. Tuition and fees vary according to course load, degree level and program. *Financial support:* Career-related internships or fieldwork, Federal Work-Study, institutionally sponsored loans, and scholarships/grants available. Support available to part-time students. Financial award application deadline: 3/1; financial award applicants required to submit FAFSA. *Faculty research:* Gerontology wellness clinic. *Unit head:* Eileen Walsh, Chair, 657-278-3188, E-mail: ewalsh@fullerton.edu. *Application contact:* Admissions/Applications, 657-278-2371.

**California State University, Los Angeles,** Graduate Studies, College of Natural and Social Sciences, Department of Sociology, Los Angeles, CA 90032-8530. Offers MA. *Program availability:* Part-time, evening/weekend. *Degree requirements:* For master's, comprehensive exam or thesis. *Entrance requirements:* For master's, minimum GPA of 2.5 in last 90 units of course work. Additional exam requirements/recommendations for international students: Required—TOEFL (minimum score 500 paper-based). Electronic applications accepted. *Faculty research:* Criminal and delinquent careers, family and sex, ethnic minorities, demographic trends, human socialization and aging.

**California State University, Northridge,** Graduate Studies, College of Social and Behavioral Sciences, Department of Sociology, Northridge, CA 91330. Offers MA. *Accreditation:* CSWE. *Program availability:* Part-time, evening/weekend. *Faculty:* 15 full-time (6 women), 29 part-time/adjunct (13 women). *Students:* 8 full-time (3 women), 12 part-time (10 women); includes 12 minority (2 Black or African American, non-Hispanic/Latino; 1 Asian, non-Hispanic/Latino; 9 Hispanic/Latino), 1 international. Average age 32. 35 applicants, 31% accepted, 6 enrolled. *Degree requirements:* For master's, thesis or alternative. *Entrance requirements:* For master's, GRE General Test. Additional exam requirements/recommendations for international students: Required—TOEFL. *Application deadline:* For fall admission, 3/27 for domestic students; for spring admission, 10/10 for domestic students. Application fee: $55. *Expenses:* Tuition, state resident: full-time $4152. *Financial support:* Career-related internships or fieldwork, Federal Work-Study, and institutionally sponsored loans available. Support available to part-time students. Financial award application deadline: 3/1. *Faculty research:* Crime and corrections, relationships between adult children and parents. *Unit head:* Karen Morgaine, Chair, 818-677-3591, E-mail: sociology@csun.edu.
Website: http://www.csun.edu/csbs/departments/sociology/index.html

**California State University, Sacramento,** Office of Graduate Studies, College of Social Sciences and Interdisciplinary Studies, Department of Sociology, Sacramento, CA 95819. Offers MA. *Program availability:* Part-time. *Students:* 10 full-time (8 women), 33 part-time (18 women); includes 26 minority (7 Black or African American, non-Hispanic/Latino; 1 American Indian or Alaska Native, non-Hispanic/Latino; 6 Asian, non-Hispanic/Latino; 12 Hispanic/Latino). Average age 29. 49 applicants, 63% accepted, 25 enrolled. In 2016, 8 master's awarded. *Degree requirements:* For master's, thesis or project; writing proficiency exam. *Entrance requirements:* For master's, minimum GPA of 3.0 during previous 2 years; completion of 18 undergraduate units in sociology. Additional exam requirements/recommendations for international students: Required—TOEFL (minimum score 550 paper-based; 80 iBT). *Application deadline:* For fall admission, 3/1 for domestic and international students; for spring admission, 9/30 for international students. Applications are processed on a rolling basis. Application fee: $55. Electronic applications accepted. *Expenses:* $4,302 full-time tuition and fees per semester, $2,796 part-time. *Financial support:* Career-related internships or fieldwork and Federal Work-Study available. Support available to part-time students. Financial award application deadline: 3/1; financial award applicants required to submit FAFSA. *Unit head:* Dr. Bohsiu Wu, Chair, 916-278-6678, E-mail: bwu@csus.edu. *Application contact:* Jose Martinez, Graduate Admissions Supervisor, 916-278-7871, E-mail: martinj@skymail.csus.edu.
Website: http://www.csus.edu/soc

**California State University, San Marcos,** College of Humanities, Arts, Behavioral and Social Sciences, Program in Sociological Practice, San Marcos, CA 92096-0001. Offers

MA. *Program availability:* Part-time, evening/weekend. *Degree requirements:* For master's, thesis. *Entrance requirements:* For master's, minimum GPA of 3.0, statement of purpose, writing sample, official transcripts, three letters of recommendation. Electronic applications accepted. *Expenses:* Tuition, state resident: full-time $6738. Tuition, nonresident: full-time $13,434. *Required fees:* $1906. Tuition and fees vary according to campus/location and program. *Faculty research:* Organized crime, juvenile detention, counseling services for minorities, mental-health facilities.

**Carleton University,** Faculty of Graduate Studies, Faculty of Arts and Social Sciences, Department of Sociology and Anthropology, Program in Sociology, Ottawa, ON K1S 5B6, Canada. Offers MA, PhD. *Degree requirements:* For master's, thesis optional; for doctorate, one foreign language, comprehensive exam, thesis/dissertation. *Entrance requirements:* For master's, honors degree; for doctorate, master's degree. Additional exam requirements/recommendations for international students: Required—TOEFL. *Faculty research:* Canadian society and policy, inequality and mobility, race/ethnic relations, cultural studies, gender studies.

**Case Western Reserve University,** School of Graduate Studies, Department of Sociology, Cleveland, OH 44106. Offers MA, PhD. *Faculty:* 9 full-time (5 women), 6 part-time/adjunct (3 women). *Students:* 32 full-time (24 women), 1 (woman) part-time; includes 7 minority (4 Black or African American, non-Hispanic/Latino; 1 Asian, non-Hispanic/Latino; 2 Two or more races, non-Hispanic/Latino), 6 international. Average age 31. 14 applicants, 64% accepted, 4 enrolled. In 2016, 1 master's, 4 doctorates awarded. Terminal master's awarded for partial completion of doctoral program. *Degree requirements:* For master's, comprehensive exam; for doctorate, comprehensive exam, thesis/dissertation. *Entrance requirements:* For master's and doctorate, GRE, cuuriculum vitae, writing sample, letter of intent, three letters of recommendation. Additional exam requirements/recommendations for international students: Required—TOEFL (minimum score 577 paper-based; 90 iBT); Recommended—IELTS (minimum score 7). *Application deadline:* For fall admission, 2/1 priority date for domestic students. Applications are processed on a rolling basis. Application fee: $50. Electronic applications accepted. *Expenses: Tuition:* Full-time $42,576; part-time $1774 per credit hour. *Required fees:* $34. Tuition and fees vary according to course load and program. *Financial support:* Research assistantships, tuition waivers (full and partial), and student employment available. Financial award application deadline: 1/15; financial award applicants required to submit FAFSA. *Faculty research:* Sociology of aging and the life course, health and medical sociology, research design and methods. *Unit head:* Dr. Dale Dannefer, Professor and Chair, Department of Sociology, 216-368-2703, Fax: 216-368-2676, E-mail: dale.dannefer@case.edu. *Application contact:* Michelle Rizzuto, Department Administrator, 216-368-2214, Fax: 216-368-2676, E-mail: michelle.rizzuto@case.edu.
Website: http://sociology.case.edu/

**The Catholic University of America,** School of Arts and Sciences, Department of Sociology, Washington, DC 20064. Offers crime and justice studies (MA); global and comparative sociology (MA); public policy (MA). *Program availability:* Part-time. *Faculty:* 3 full-time (2 women), 4 part-time/adjunct (0 women). *Students:* 2 full-time (both women), 1 (woman) part-time; includes 2 minority (1 Black or African American, non-Hispanic/Latino; 1 Hispanic/Latino). Average age 22. 7 applicants, 29% accepted, 2 enrolled. In 2016, 2 master's awarded. *Degree requirements:* For master's, comprehensive exam, thesis or alternative, two seminar papers. *Entrance requirements:* For master's, GRE General Test, statement of purpose, official copies of academic transcripts, three letters of recommendation. Additional exam requirements/recommendations for international students: Required—TOEFL (minimum score 550 paper-based; 80 iBT). *Application deadline:* For fall admission, 7/15 priority date for domestic students, 7/1 for international students; for spring admission, 11/15 priority date for domestic students, 11/1 for international students. Applications are processed on a rolling basis. Application fee: $55. Electronic applications accepted. *Expenses:* $42,850 per year; $1,170 per credit; $200 per semester part-time fees. *Financial support:* Fellowships, research assistantships, teaching assistantships, Federal Work-Study, scholarships/grants, tuition waivers (full and partial), and unspecified assistantships available. Financial award application deadline: 2/1; financial award applicants required to submit FAFSA. *Faculty research:* Social movements, gender structure, political sociology, race and ethnic relations, evaluation methodologies. *Total annual research expenditures:* $2,586. *Unit head:* Dr. Enrique S. Pumar, Chair, 202-319-5445, Fax: 202-319-4980, E-mail: pumar@cua.edu. *Application contact:* Director of Graduate Admissions, 202-319-5057, Fax: 202-319-6533, E-mail: cua-admissions@cua.edu.
Website: http://sociology.cua.edu/

**Central European University,** Department of Sociology and Social Anthropology, Budapest, Hungary. Offers MA, PhD. *Faculty:* 11 full-time (4 women), 4 part-time/adjunct (1 woman). *Students:* 77 full-time (47 women). Average age 28. 339 applicants, 14% accepted, 39 enrolled. In 2016, 27 master's, 8 doctorates awarded. *Degree requirements:* For master's, one foreign language, thesis; for doctorate, one foreign language, comprehensive exam, thesis/dissertation. *Entrance requirements:* For master's and doctorate, interview. Additional exam requirements/recommendations for international students: Required—TOEFL (minimum score 570 paper-based); Recommended—IELTS (minimum score 6.5). *Application deadline:* For fall admission, 2/4 for domestic and international students. Application fee: $30. Electronic applications accepted. *Expenses: Tuition:* Full-time 13,500 euros. Tuition and fees vary according to degree level, program and student level. *Financial support:* Fellowships, career-related internships or fieldwork, scholarships/grants, health care benefits, and tuition waivers (full and partial) available. *Faculty research:* Migration studies, post colonialism, studies of globalization, political and economic sociology, urban studies and sociologies of culture. *Unit head:* Dr. Andreas Dafinger, Head of Department, 36 1 327-3000 Ext. 2131, E-mail: sociology@ceu.edu. *Application contact:* Zsuzsanna Jaszberenyi, Admissions Officer, 361-324-3009, Fax: 367-327-3211, E-mail: admissions@ceu.edu.
Website: http://sociology.ceu.edu/

**City College of the City University of New York,** Graduate School, Colin Powell School for Civic and Global Leadership, Department of Sociology, New York, NY 10031-9198. Offers MA. *Degree requirements:* For master's, one foreign language, comprehensive exam, thesis. *Entrance requirements:* Additional exam requirements/recommendations for international students: Required—TOEFL (minimum score 500 paper-based; 61 iBT). Electronic applications accepted. Tuition and fees vary according to course load, degree level and program. *Faculty research:* Urban sociology, criminology and deviance, race and ethnicity.

**Clark Atlanta University,** School of Arts and Sciences, Department of Sociology, Atlanta, GA 30314. Offers MA. *Program availability:* Part-time. *Faculty:* 2 full-time (1 woman), 1 part-time/adjunct (0 women). *Students:* 6 full-time (2 women), 4 part-time (3 women); includes 5 minority (4 Black or African American, non-Hispanic/Latino; 1 Asian, non-Hispanic/Latino), 3 international. Average age 28. 7 applicants, 100% accepted, 5 enrolled. In 2016, 1 master's awarded. *Degree requirements:* For master's, one foreign language, comprehensive exam, thesis. *Entrance requirements:* For master's, GRE General Test, minimum GPA of 2.5. Additional exam requirements/recommendations for international students: Required—TOEFL (minimum score 500 paper-based; 61 iBT). *Application deadline:* For fall admission, 4/1 for domestic and international students; for

spring admission, 11/1 for domestic and international students. Applications are processed on a rolling basis. Application fee: $40 ($55 for international students). Electronic applications accepted. *Expenses: Tuition:* Full-time $15,498; part-time $861 per credit hour. *Required fees:* $1326; $1326 per credit hour. Tuition and fees vary according to course load. *Financial support:* Scholarships/grants and unspecified assistantships available. Financial award application deadline: 4/30; financial award applicants required to submit FAFSA. *Faculty research:* Gerontology, geriatric education. *Unit head:* Dr. Obie Clayton, Chairperson, 404-880-8681, E-mail: oclayton@cau.edu. *Application contact:* Graduate Program Admissions, 404-880-8483, E-mail: graduateadmissions@cau.edu.

**Clemson University,** Graduate School, College of Behavioral, Social and Health Sciences, Department of Sociology and Anthropology, Clemson, SC 29634. Offers applied sociology (MS). *Program availability:* Part-time. *Faculty:* 22 full-time (14 women). *Students:* 8 full-time (6 women); includes 1 minority (Black or African American, non-Hispanic/Latino), 2 international. Average age 31. 7 applicants, 43% accepted, 3 enrolled. In 2016, 2 master's awarded. *Degree requirements:* For master's, thesis optional. *Entrance requirements:* For master's, GRE General Test, unofficial transcripts, letters of recommendation. Additional exam requirements/recommendations for international students: Required—TOEFL (minimum score 80 iBT), IELTS (minimum score 6.5). *Application deadline:* For fall admission, 2/1 priority date for domestic and international students. Applications are processed on a rolling basis. Application fee: $80 ($90 for international students). Electronic applications accepted. *Expenses:* $4,264 per semester full-time resident, $8,485 per semester full-time non-resident, $471 per credit hour part-time resident, $942 per credit hour part-time non-resident. *Financial support:* In 2016–17, 7 students received support, including 6 teaching assistantships with partial tuition reimbursements available (averaging $10,000 per year); career-related internships or fieldwork and unspecified assistantships also available. Financial award application deadline: 2/1. *Faculty research:* Environmental issues; social inequalities; health and medical development; sociology of food, nutrition, and food security. *Total annual research expenditures:* $36,371. *Unit head:* Dr. Catherine Mobley, Interim Department Chair, 864-656-3815, Fax: 864-656-1252, E-mail: camoble@clemson.edu. *Application contact:* Dr. William Haller, Graduate Program Coordinator, 864-656-3814, E-mail: whaller@clemson.edu.
Website: http://www.clemson.edu/cbshs/departments/sociology/

**Colorado State University,** College of Liberal Arts, Department of Sociology, Fort Collins, CO 80523-1784. Offers MA, PhD. *Program availability:* Part-time. *Faculty:* 8 full-time (5 women). *Students:* 12 full-time (7 women), 35 part-time (24 women); includes 2 minority (both Hispanic/Latino), 6 international. Average age 32. 42 applicants, 26% accepted, 8 enrolled. In 2016, 5 master's, 2 doctorates awarded. Terminal master's awarded for partial completion of doctoral program. *Degree requirements:* For master's, comprehensive exam (for some programs), thesis (for some programs), practicum, professional paper; for doctorate, comprehensive exam, thesis/dissertation. *Entrance requirements:* For master's, GRE General Test, minimum GPA of 3.0, BA coursework in sociology, three letters of recommendation, official transcripts, statement of purpose; for doctorate, GRE General Test, minimum GPA of 3.0, BA and MA coursework in sociology, three letters of recommendation, official transcripts, statement of purpose. Additional exam requirements/recommendations for international students: Required—TOEFL (minimum score 550 paper-based; 80 iBT), IELTS (minimum score 6.5). *Application deadline:* For fall admission, 1/15 priority date for domestic and international students. Application fee: $60 ($70 for international students). Electronic applications accepted. *Expenses:* Tuition, state resident: full-time $9628. Tuition, nonresident: full-time $23,603. *Required fees:* $2253; $528.14 per credit hour. $264.07 per semester. Tuition and fees vary according to course load and program. *Financial support:* In 2016–17, 20 students received support, including 1 research assistantship with full and partial tuition reimbursement available (averaging $24,214 per year), 21 teaching assistantships with full and partial tuition reimbursements available (averaging $14,909 per year); scholarships/grants and unspecified assistantships also available. Financial award application deadline: 1/15; financial award applicants required to submit FAFSA. *Faculty research:* Environment/natural resources; food, agriculture and development; crime, law and deviance; social inequality, social justice and governance. *Total annual research expenditures:* $327,247. *Unit head:* Pete Taylor, Chair, 970-491-6044, Fax: 970-491-2191, E-mail: pete.taylor@colostate.edu. *Application contact:* Dr. Mike Lacy, Director of Graduate Studies, 970-491-6044, Fax: 970-491-2191, E-mail: gradsoc@lamar.colostate.edu.
Website: http://sociology.colostate.edu/

**Columbia University,** Graduate School of Arts and Sciences, New York, NY 10027. Offers African-American studies (MA); American studies (MA); anthropology (MA, PhD); art history and archaeology (MA, PhD); astronomy (PhD); biological sciences (PhD); biotechnology (MA); chemical physics (PhD); chemistry (PhD); classical studies (MA, PhD); classics (MA, PhD); climate and society (MA); conservation biology (MA); earth and environmental sciences (PhD); East Asia: regional studies (MA); East Asian languages and cultures (MA, PhD); ecology, evolution and environmental biology (MA), including conservation biology; ecology, evolution, and environmental biology (PhD), including ecology and evolutionary biology, evolutionary primatology; economics (MA, PhD); English and comparative literature (MA, PhD); French and Romance philology (MA, PhD); Germanic languages (MA, PhD); global French studies (MA); global thought (MA); Hispanic cultural studies (MA); history (PhD); history and literature (MA); human rights studies (MA); Islamic studies (MA); Italian (MA, PhD); Japanese pedagogy (MA); Jewish studies (MA); Latin America and the Caribbean: regional studies (MA); Latin American and Iberian cultures (PhD); mathematics (MA, PhD), including finance (MA); medieval and Renaissance studies (MA); Middle Eastern, South Asian, and African studies (MA, PhD); modern art: critical and curatorial studies (MA); modern European studies (MA); museum anthropology (MA); music (DMA, PhD); oral history (MA); philosophical foundations of physics (MA); philosophy (MA, PhD); physics (PhD); political science (MA, PhD); psychology (PhD); quantitative methods in the social sciences (MA); religion (MA, PhD); Russia, Eurasia and East Europe: regional studies (MA); Russian translation (MA); Slavic cultures (MA); Slavic languages (MA, PhD); sociology (MA, PhD); South Asian studies (MA); statistics (MA, PhD); theatre (PhD). Dual-degree programs require admission to both Graduate School of Arts and Sciences and another Columbia school. *Program availability:* Part-time. Terminal master's awarded for partial completion of doctoral program. *Degree requirements:* For master's, variable foreign language requirement, comprehensive exam (for some programs), thesis (for some programs); for doctorate, variable foreign language requirement, comprehensive exam (for some programs), thesis/dissertation. *Entrance requirements:* For master's and doctorate, GRE General Test, GRE Subject Test (for some programs). Additional exam requirements/recommendations for international students: Required—TOEFL, IELTS. Electronic applications accepted.

**Concordia University,** School of Graduate Studies, Faculty of Arts and Science, Department of Sociology and Anthropology, Montréal, QC H3G 1M8, Canada. Offers social and cultural analysis (PhD); social and cultural anthropology (MA); sociology (MA). *Degree requirements:* For master's, comprehensive exam or thesis. *Entrance requirements:* For master's, honors degree in sociology or equivalent. *Faculty research:* Community and ethnic relations, popular culture, regional development in Canada, industrial and social movements, social problems and policies.

*Sociology*

**Cornell University,** Graduate School, Graduate Fields of Agriculture and Life Sciences, Field of Development Sociology, Ithaca, NY 14853. Offers population and development (MS, PhD); rural and environmental sociology (MS, PhD); state, economy, and society (MS, PhD). *Degree requirements:* For doctorate, comprehensive exam, thesis/dissertation. *Entrance requirements:* For master's and doctorate, GRE General Test, 3 letters of recommendation. Additional exam requirements/recommendations for international students: Required—TOEFL (minimum score 550 paper-based; 77 iBT). Electronic applications accepted. *Faculty research:* Demography (population and development), environmental sociology, international and rural community development, political economy and ecology, sustainable agriculture.

**Cornell University,** Graduate School, Graduate Fields of Arts and Sciences, Field of Sociology, Ithaca, NY 14853. Offers economy and society (MA, PhD); gender and life course (MA, PhD); methodology (MA, PhD); organizations (MA, PhD); policy analysis (MA, PhD); political sociology/social movements (MA, PhD); racial and ethnic relations (MA, PhD); social networks (MA, PhD); social psychology (MA, PhD); social stratification (MA, PhD). Terminal master's awarded for partial completion of doctoral program. *Degree requirements:* For master's, thesis; for doctorate, thesis/dissertation, 1 year of teaching experience. *Entrance requirements:* For master's and doctorate, GRE General Test, 2 letters of recommendation, writing sample. Additional exam requirements/recommendations for international students: Required—TOEFL (minimum score 550 paper-based; 77 iBT). Electronic applications accepted. *Faculty research:* Comparative societal analysis, work and family, simulations, social class and mobility, racial segregation and inequality.

**Dalhousie University,** Faculty of Arts and Social Science, Department of Sociology and Social Anthropology, Halifax, NS B3H 4R2, Canada. Offers social anthropology (MA, PhD); sociology (MA, PhD). *Entrance requirements:* Additional exam requirements/recommendations for international students: Required—TOEFL, IELTS, CANTEST, CAEL, or Michigan English Language Assessment Battery. Electronic applications accepted. *Faculty research:* Social inequality and social injustice; work, industry, and development (regional and international perspectives); health and illness.

**DePaul University,** College of Liberal Arts and Social Sciences, Chicago, IL 60614. Offers Arabic (MA); Chinese (MA); English (MA); French (MA); German (MA); history (MA); interdisciplinary studies (MA, MS); international public service (MS); international studies (MA); Italian (MA); Japanese (MA); leadership and policy studies (MS); liberal studies (MA); new media studies (MA); nonprofit management (MNM); public administration (MPA); public health (MPH); public service management (MS); social work (MSW); sociology (MA); Spanish (MA); sustainable urban development (MA); women and gender studies (MA); writing and publishing (MA); writing, rhetoric, and discourse (MA); MA/PhD. *Program availability:* Part-time, evening/weekend, online learning. Terminal master's awarded for partial completion of doctoral program. *Degree requirements:* For master's, variable foreign language requirement, comprehensive exam (for some programs), thesis (for some programs). Electronic applications accepted.

**Duke University,** Graduate School, Department of Sociology, Durham, NC 27708. Offers AM, PhD. Terminal master's awarded for partial completion of doctoral program. *Degree requirements:* For doctorate, thesis/dissertation. *Entrance requirements:* For master's and doctorate, GRE General Test. Additional exam requirements/recommendations for international students: Required—TOEFL (minimum score 577 paper-based; 90 iBT) or IELTS (minimum score 7). Electronic applications accepted.

**East Carolina University,** Graduate School, Thomas Harriot College of Arts and Sciences, Department of Sociology, Greenville, NC 27858-4353. Offers MA. *Program availability:* Part-time, evening/weekend. *Students:* 12 full-time (8 women), 3 part-time (2 women); includes 5 minority (all Black or African American, non-Hispanic/Latino). Average age 30. 8 applicants, 100% accepted, 7 enrolled. In 2016, 4 master's awarded. *Degree requirements:* For master's, one foreign language, comprehensive exam, thesis. *Entrance requirements:* For master's, GRE General Test. Additional exam requirements/recommendations for international students: Required—TOEFL. *Application deadline:* For fall admission, 6/1 priority date for domestic students; for spring admission, 10/15 for domestic students. Applications are processed on a rolling basis. Application fee: $50. *Financial support:* Fellowships with partial tuition reimbursements, research assistantships with partial tuition reimbursements, teaching assistantships with partial tuition reimbursements, and Federal Work-Study available. Support available to part-time students. Financial award application deadline: 6/1. *Unit head:* Marieke Van Willigen, Interim Chair, 252-328-6092, E-mail: vanwilligenm@ecu.edu. *Application contact:* Dean of Graduate School, 252-328-6012, Fax: 252-328-6071, E-mail: gradschool@ecu.edu.
Website: http://www.ecu.edu/soci/

**Eastern Michigan University,** Graduate School, College of Arts and Sciences, Department of Sociology, Anthropology and Criminology, Programs in Sociology, Ypsilanti, MI 48197. Offers sociology (MA); sociology - applied research specialty (MA). *Students:* 3 full-time (2 women), 10 part-time (8 women); includes 5 minority (3 Black or African American, non-Hispanic/Latino; 2 Two or more races, non-Hispanic/Latino), 1 international. Average age 31. 14 applicants, 71% accepted, 4 enrolled. In 2016, 3 master's awarded. Application fee: $45. *Application contact:* Dr. Solage Simoes, Graduate Coordinator, 734-487-0012, Fax: 734-487-9666, E-mail: ssimoes@emich.edu.
Website: http://www.emich.edu/sac/

**East Tennessee State University,** School of Graduate Studies, College of Arts and Sciences, Department of Sociology and Anthropology, Johnson City, TN 37614. Offers MA. *Program availability:* Part-time, evening/weekend. *Degree requirements:* For master's, comprehensive exam, internship or thesis. *Entrance requirements:* For master's, GRE General Test, minimum GPA of 3.0 in sociology major, three letters of recommendation. Additional exam requirements/recommendations for international students: Required—TOEFL (minimum score 550 paper-based; 79 iBT). Electronic applications accepted. *Faculty research:* Survey research methodologies, religion, sociology of sport, sociology of emotions, race and gender studies.

**Emory University,** Laney Graduate School, Department of Sociology, Atlanta, GA 30322-1100. Offers PhD. Terminal master's awarded for partial completion of doctoral program. *Degree requirements:* For doctorate, comprehensive exam, thesis/dissertation, 2 preliminary exams, research paper, paper presentation. *Entrance requirements:* For doctorate, GRE General Test, minimum GPA of 3.0. Additional exam requirements/recommendations for international students: Required—TOEFL. Electronic applications accepted. *Faculty research:* Political economy and global analysis, culture, social psychology, criminology, stratification.

**Fayetteville State University,** Graduate School, Program in Sociology, Fayetteville, NC 28301-4298. Offers MA. *Program availability:* Part-time, evening/weekend. *Faculty:* 11 full-time (3 women). *Students:* 1 (woman) full-time, 8 part-time (6 women); includes 7 minority (5 Black or African American, non-Hispanic/Latino; 1 American Indian or Alaska Native, non-Hispanic/Latino; 1 Two or more races, non-Hispanic/Latino). Average age 35. 1 applicant, 1 enrolled. In 2016, 6 master's awarded. *Degree requirements:* For master's, comprehensive exam, internship. *Entrance requirements:* For master's, GRE. Additional exam requirements/recommendations for international students: Required—TOEFL. *Application deadline:* For fall admission, 4/15 for domestic students; for spring

admission, 10/15 for domestic students. Applications are processed on a rolling basis. Application fee: $40. Electronic applications accepted. *Financial support:* Application deadline: 3/1; applicants required to submit FAFSA. *Faculty research:* Research methodology, African demography, urban sociology, aging and health, divided social problems, medical sociology, social change. *Unit head:* Dr. Nicole Lucas, Chairperson, 910-672-1122, Fax: 910-672-1378, E-mail: nlucas2@uncfsu.edu. *Application contact:* Latoya Parker, Academic Advisor, 910-672-2322, Fax: 910-672-1378, E-mail: lmparker01@uncfsu.edu.

**Florida Atlantic University,** Dorothy F. Schmidt College of Arts and Letters, Department of Sociology, Boca Raton, FL 33431-0991. Offers MA. *Program availability:* Part-time, evening/weekend. *Faculty:* 10 full-time (4 women). *Students:* 18 full-time (9 women), 3 part-time (2 women); includes 11 minority (8 Black or African American, non-Hispanic/Latino; 3 Hispanic/Latino). Average age 33. 12 applicants, 67% accepted, 7 enrolled. In 2016, 8 master's awarded. *Degree requirements:* For master's, thesis (for some programs). *Entrance requirements:* For master's, GRE General Test, minimum GPA of 3.0. Additional exam requirements/recommendations for international students: Required—TOEFL, IELTS. *Application deadline:* For fall admission, 5/1 priority date for domestic and international students. Applications are processed on a rolling basis. Application fee: $30. Electronic applications accepted. *Expenses:* Tuition, state resident: full-time $7392; part-time $369.82 per credit hour. Tuition, nonresident: full-time $19,432; part-time $1024.81 per credit hour. *Financial support:* Teaching assistantships with tuition reimbursements and Federal Work-Study available. *Faculty research:* Gender/race/class, globalization, theory, social control, social movements. *Unit head:* Cathy King, Program Administrator, 561-297-3270, E-mail: cking11@fau.edu.
Website: http://www.fau.edu/sociology/

**Florida International University,** Steven J. Green School of International and Public Affairs, Department of Global and Sociocultural Studies, Miami, FL 33199. Offers MA, PhD. *Program availability:* Part-time, evening/weekend. *Faculty:* 31 full-time (10 women), 13 part-time/adjunct (5 women). *Students:* 33 full-time (20 women), 26 part-time (18 women); includes 35 minority (9 Black or African American, non-Hispanic/Latino; 1 Asian, non-Hispanic/Latino; 23 Hispanic/Latino; 2 Two or more races, non-Hispanic/Latino), 4 international. Average age 35. 42 applicants, 60% accepted, 8 enrolled. In 2016, 2 master's, 2 doctorates awarded. *Degree requirements:* For master's, thesis; for doctorate, comprehensive exam, thesis/dissertation. *Entrance requirements:* For master's, GRE General Test, 3 letters of recommendation; minimum undergraduate GPA of 3.25, 3.5 on any previous graduate work; written examples of academic or other relevant professional work; for doctorate, GRE General Test, letter of intent; 3 letters of recommendation; minimum undergraduate GPA of 3.25, 3.5 on any previous graduate work; written examples of academic or other relevant professional work. Additional exam requirements/recommendations for international students: Required—TOEFL (minimum score 550 paper-based; 80 iBT). *Application deadline:* For fall admission, 6/1 for domestic students, 4/1 for international students; for spring admission, 10/1 for domestic students, 9/1 for international students. Applications are processed on a rolling basis. Application fee: $30. Electronic applications accepted. *Expenses:* Tuition, state resident: full-time $8912; part-time $446 per credit hour. Tuition, nonresident: full-time $21,393; part-time $992 per credit hour. *Required fees:* $2185; $195 per semester. Tuition and fees vary according to program. *Financial support:* Institutionally sponsored loans and scholarships/grants available. Financial award application deadline: 3/1; financial award applicants required to submit FAFSA. *Unit head:* Dr. Rod Neumann, Chair, 305-348-2936, Fax: 305-348-3605, E-mail: roderick.neumann@fiu.edu. *Application contact:* Nanett Rojas, Manager, Admissions Operations, 305-348-7464, Fax: 305-348-7441, E-mail: gradadm@fiu.edu.

**Florida State University,** The Graduate School, College of Social Sciences and Public Policy, Department of Sociology, Tallahassee, FL 32306. Offers applied social research (MS); sociology (MA, MS, PhD); sociology of health and aging (MS). *Faculty:* 18 full-time (9 women). *Students:* 50 full-time (32 women), 10 part-time (7 women); includes 18 minority (9 Black or African American, non-Hispanic/Latino; 2 Asian, non-Hispanic/Latino; 2 Hispanic/Latino; 5 Two or more races, non-Hispanic/Latino). Average age 28. 57 applicants, 35% accepted, 11 enrolled. In 2016, 13 master's, 9 doctorates awarded. *Degree requirements:* For doctorate, comprehensive exam, thesis/dissertation. *Entrance requirements:* For master's and doctorate, GRE General Test, minimum GPA of 3.0. Additional exam requirements/recommendations for international students: Required—TOEFL (minimum score 550 paper-based; 80 iBT). *Application deadline:* For fall admission, 12/15 priority date for domestic students, 12/15 for international students. Applications are processed on a rolling basis. Application fee: $30. Electronic applications accepted. *Expenses:* Contact institution. *Financial support:* In 2016–17, 57 students received support, including 3 fellowships with full tuition reimbursements available (averaging $25,115 per year), 4 research assistantships with full tuition reimbursements available (averaging $21,150 per year), 50 teaching assistantships with full tuition reimbursements available (averaging $21,150 per year); institutionally sponsored loans, scholarships/grants, health care benefits, and unspecified assistantships also available. Financial award application deadline: 12/15; financial award applicants required to submit FAFSA. *Faculty research:* Aging and health, demography, inequality (gender/race and social movements/politics). *Total annual research expenditures:* $428,302. *Unit head:* Dr. John Reynolds, Chair, 850-644-6416, Fax: 850-644-6208, E-mail: john.reynolds@fsu.edu. *Application contact:* Jamie Yeargan, Graduate Program Coordinator, 850-644-6506, Fax: 850-644-6208, E-mail: jdyeargan@fsu.edu.
Website: http://coss.fsu.edu/sociology/

**George Mason University,** College of Humanities and Social Sciences, Department of Sociology and Anthropology, Fairfax, VA 22030. Offers anthropology (MA); sociology (PhD). *Faculty:* 23 full-time (12 women), 8 part-time/adjunct (6 women). *Students:* 36 full-time (27 women), 59 part-time (35 women); includes 23 minority (7 Black or African American, non-Hispanic/Latino; 4 Asian, non-Hispanic/Latino; 11 Hispanic/Latino; 1 Two or more races, non-Hispanic/Latino), 5 international. Average age 33. 60 applicants, 53% accepted, 18 enrolled. In 2016, 22 master's, 4 doctorates awarded. *Degree requirements:* For master's, thesis; for doctorate, comprehensive exam, thesis/dissertation. *Entrance requirements:* For master's, official transcript; expanded goals statement; 3 letters of recommendation; writing sample; resume; 3 credits in undergraduate sociology theory, statistics and research methods (for sociology); 3 credits of sociocultural anthropology (for anthropology); for doctorate, GRE General Test, expanded goals statement; 3 letters of recommendation; writing sample; official transcript. Additional exam requirements/recommendations for international students: Required—TOEFL (minimum score 575 paper-based; 88 iBT), IELTS (minimum score 6.5), PTE (minimum score 59). Application fee: $75 ($80 for international students). Electronic applications accepted. *Expenses:* Tuition, state resident: full-time $10,628; part-time $443 per credit. Tuition, nonresident: full-time $29,306; part-time $1221 per credit. *Required fees:* $3096; $129 per credit. Tuition and fees vary according to program. *Financial support:* In 2016–17, 30 students received support, including 5 fellowships (averaging $12,400 per year), 10 research assistantships with tuition reimbursements available (averaging $17,800 per year), 16 teaching assistantships with tuition reimbursements available (averaging $12,534 per year); career-related internships or fieldwork, Federal Work-Study, scholarships/grants, unspecified

assistantships, and health care benefits (for full-time research or teaching assistantship recipients) also available. Support available to part-time students. Financial award application deadline: 3/1; financial award applicants required to submit FAFSA. *Faculty research:* Africa, American teenagers, black entrepreneurs, human rights, gambling. *Total annual research expenditures:* $128,824. *Unit head:* Amy Best, Department Chair, 703-993-1426, Fax: 703-993-1446, E-mail: abest@gmu.edu. *Application contact:* Nancy Hanrahan, Graduate Director, 703-993-1433, Fax: 703-993-1446, E-mail: nhanraha@gmu.edu.
Website: http://soan.gmu.edu

**The George Washington University,** Columbian College of Arts and Sciences, Department of Sociology, Washington, DC 20052. Offers criminology (MA); sociology (MA). *Program availability:* Part-time, evening/weekend. *Faculty:* 11 full-time (6 women). *Students:* 21 full-time (18 women), 4 part-time (all women); includes 12 minority (9 Black or African American, non-Hispanic/Latino; 1 Hispanic/Latino; 2 Two or more races, non-Hispanic/Latino), 4 international. Average age 25. 43 applicants, 77% accepted, 14 enrolled. In 2016, 7 master's awarded. *Degree requirements:* For master's, comprehensive exam, thesis or alternative. *Entrance requirements:* For master's, GRE General Test, minimum GPA of 3.0. Additional exam requirements/recommendations for international students: Required—TOEFL (minimum score 550 paper-based; 80 iBT). *Application deadline:* For fall admission, 6/1 priority date for domestic students, 1/15 priority date for international students; for spring admission, 11/1 priority date for domestic students, 9/1 priority date for international students. Applications are processed on a rolling basis. Application fee: $75. Electronic applications accepted. *Financial support:* In 2016–17, 7 students received support. Fellowships with full tuition reimbursements available, teaching assistantships with tuition reimbursements available, career-related internships or fieldwork, Federal Work-Study, and tuition waivers available. Financial award application deadline: 1/15. *Unit head:* Dr. Greg Squires, Chair, 202-994-7466, E-mail: squires@gwu.edu. *Application contact:* Information Contact, 202-994-6345, Fax: 202-994-3239, E-mail: soc@gwu.edu.
Website: http://sociology.columbian.gwu.edu/

**Georgia Southern University,** Jack N. Averitt College of Graduate Studies, College of Liberal Arts and Social Sciences, Program in Social Science, Statesboro, GA 30460. Offers MA. *Program availability:* Part-time, evening/weekend. *Students:* 35 full-time (27 women), 11 part-time (8 women); includes 22 minority (15 Black or African American, non-Hispanic/Latino; 3 Hispanic/Latino; 4 Two or more races, non-Hispanic/Latino), 1 international. Average age 27. 26 applicants, 100% accepted, 13 enrolled. In 2016, 22 master's awarded. *Degree requirements:* For master's, thesis optional. *Entrance requirements:* For master's, GRE General Test. Additional exam requirements/recommendations for international students: Required—TOEFL (minimum score 550 paper-based; 80 iBT), IELTS (minimum score 6). *Application deadline:* For fall admission, 3/1 priority date for domestic and international students; for spring admission, 10/1 priority date for domestic students, 10/1 for international students. Applications are processed on a rolling basis. Application fee: $50. Electronic applications accepted. *Expenses:* Tuition, state resident: full-time $7236; part-time $277 per semester hour. Tuition, nonresident: full-time $27,118; part-time $1105 per semester hour. *Required fees:* $2092. *Financial support:* In 2016–17, 14 students received support, including 7 fellowships with full tuition reimbursements available (averaging $7,750 per year); career-related internships or fieldwork, Federal Work-Study, scholarships/grants, tuition waivers (full), and unspecified assistantships also available. Support available to part-time students. Financial award application deadline: 4/15; financial award applicants required to submit FAFSA. *Faculty research:* Anthropology, sociology, criminal justice, history, political science. *Total annual research expenditures:* $40,162. *Unit head:* Dr. Marieke VanWilligen, Department Chair, 912-478-5621, Fax: 912-478-0703, E-mail: mvanwilligen@georgiasouthern.edu.
Website: http://class.georgiasouthern.edu/socianth/

**Georgia State University,** College of Arts and Sciences, Department of Sociology, Atlanta, GA 30302-3083. Offers MA, PhD, MA/PhD. *Program availability:* Part-time, evening/weekend. *Faculty:* 23 full-time (15 women). *Students:* 71 full-time (53 women), 22 part-time (16 women); includes 51 minority (35 Black or African American, non-Hispanic/Latino; 1 American Indian or Alaska Native, non-Hispanic/Latino; 2 Asian, non-Hispanic/Latino; 5 Hispanic/Latino; 8 Two or more races, non-Hispanic/Latino), 3 international. Average age 34. 58 applicants, 55% accepted, 16 enrolled. In 2016, 11 master's, 5 doctorates awarded. Terminal master's awarded for partial completion of doctoral program. *Degree requirements:* For master's, thesis; for doctorate, comprehensive exam, thesis/dissertation. *Entrance requirements:* For master's and doctorate, GRE. Additional exam requirements/recommendations for international students: Required—TOEFL (minimum score 600 paper-based; 100 iBT). *Application deadline:* For fall admission, 4/15 for domestic students, 2/1 for international students; for spring admission, 4/15 for domestic and international students. Applications are processed on a rolling basis. Application fee: $50. Electronic applications accepted. *Expenses:* Tuition, state resident: full-time $6876; part-time $382 per credit hour. Tuition, nonresident: full-time $22,374; part-time $1243 per credit hour. *Required fees:* $2128; $1064 per term. Part-time tuition and fees vary according to course load and program. *Financial support:* In 2016–17, fellowships with tuition reimbursements (averaging $5,000 per year), research assistantships with tuition reimbursements (averaging $17,500 per year), teaching assistantships with tuition reimbursements (averaging $13,000 per year) were awarded; scholarships/grants and unspecified assistantships also available. Financial award application deadline: 2/1; financial award applicants required to submit FAFSA. *Faculty research:* Race and urban studies, gender and sexuality, family, health, life course. *Unit head:* Dr. Donald C. Reitzes, Department Chair, 404-413-6506, Fax: 404-413-6505, E-mail: dreitzes@gsu.edu. *Application contact:* Dr. Leslie Reid, Director of Graduate Studies, 404-413-6521, Fax: 404-413-6505, E-mail: lesleyreid@gsu.edu.
Website: http://cas.gsu.edu/graduate-studies/admissions/

**The Graduate Center, City University of New York,** Graduate Studies, Program in Sociology, New York, NY 10016-4039. Offers PhD. *Degree requirements:* For doctorate, one foreign language, thesis/dissertation. *Entrance requirements:* For doctorate, GRE General Test, writing sample. Additional exam requirements/recommendations for international students: Required—TOEFL. Electronic applications accepted.

**Harvard University,** Graduate School of Arts and Sciences, Department of Sociology, Cambridge, MA 02138. Offers PhD. *Degree requirements:* For doctorate, thesis/dissertation, oral exams in 2 subfields. *Entrance requirements:* For doctorate, GRE General Test. Additional exam requirements/recommendations for international students: Required—TOEFL. *Faculty research:* Sociological theory, political theories, quantitative approaches to methodology.

**Howard University,** Graduate School, Department of Health, Human Performance and Leisure Studies, Washington, DC 20059-0002. Offers exercise physiology (MS); health education (MS); sports studies (MS), including sociology of sports, sports management; urban recreation (MS), including leisure studies. *Program availability:* Part-time, evening/weekend. *Degree requirements:* For master's, comprehensive exam, thesis. *Entrance requirements:* For master's, BS in human performance or related field. Additional exam requirements/recommendations for international students: Recommended—TOEFL. Electronic applications accepted. *Faculty research:* Health

promotion, cardiovascular hypertension, physical activity, sport and human rights issues.

**Howard University,** Graduate School, Department of Sociology and Anthropology, Washington, DC 20059-0002. Offers sociology (MA, PhD). *Program availability:* Part-time, evening/weekend. *Degree requirements:* For master's, thesis; for doctorate, one foreign language, comprehensive exam, thesis/dissertation, RCR, writing exam. *Entrance requirements:* For master's, GRE General Test, minimum GPA of 3.0; for doctorate, GRE General Test, minimum GPA of 3.5. Additional exam requirements/recommendations for international students: Required—TOEFL. Electronic applications accepted. *Faculty research:* Medical sociology; criminology; race, class and gender; urban sociology.

**Humboldt State University,** Academic Programs, College of Arts, Humanities, and Social Sciences, Department of Sociology, Arcata, CA 95521-8299. Offers MA. *Degree requirements:* For master's, thesis or alternative, qualifying exam. *Entrance requirements:* For master's, minimum GPA of 2.5, 3 letters of recommendation. Additional exam requirements/recommendations for international students: Required—TOEFL (minimum score 500 paper-based). *Expenses:* Tuition, state resident: full-time $6738; part-time $1953 per semester. Tuition, nonresident: full-time $13,434; part-time $3813 per semester. *Required fees:* $1738; $653 per semester. Tuition and fees vary according to program. *Faculty research:* Sociology of women political activists, environmental dispute resolution, prosocial behavior.

**Hunter College of the City University of New York,** Graduate School, School of Arts and Sciences, Department of Sociology, New York, NY 10065-5085. Offers applied social research (MS). *Students:* 13 full-time (8 women), 20 part-time (17 women); includes 10 minority (5 Black or African American, non-Hispanic/Latino; 2 Asian, non-Hispanic/Latino; 3 Hispanic/Latino), 4 international. Average age 31. 18 applicants, 94% accepted, 14 enrolled. In 2016, 2 master's awarded. *Degree requirements:* For master's, internship. *Entrance requirements:* For master's, GRE General Test or GMAT, 3 credits of course work in statistics, 2 letters of recommendation. Additional exam requirements/recommendations for international students: Required—TOEFL. *Application deadline:* For fall admission, 4/1 for domestic students, 2/1 for international students; for spring admission, 11/1 for domestic students, 9/1 for international students. *Financial support:* Federal Work-Study and tuition waivers (partial) available. Support available to part-time students. *Unit head:* Lynn Chancer, Chair, 212-772-5585, Fax: 212-772-5645. *Application contact:* Milena Solo, Graduate Admissions Director, 212-772-4480, E-mail: admissions@hunter.cuny.edu.
Website: http://www.hunter.cuny.edu/sociology

**Idaho State University,** Office of Graduate Studies, College of Arts and Letters, Department of Sociology, Pocatello, ID 83209-8114. Offers MA. *Program availability:* Part-time. *Degree requirements:* For master's, comprehensive exam, thesis, oral defense of thesis. *Entrance requirements:* For master's, GRE General Test (minimum 40th percentile in one of 3 sections), minimum undergraduate GPA of 3.0, 3 letters of recommendation. Additional exam requirements/recommendations for international students: Required—TOEFL (minimum score 550 paper-based; 80 iBT). Electronic applications accepted. *Faculty research:* Terrorism, social organization, family social work.

**Illinois State University,** Graduate School, College of Arts and Sciences, Department of Sociology, Normal, IL 61790-2200. Offers historical archaeology (MA, MS); sociology (MA, MS). *Degree requirements:* For master's, thesis. *Entrance requirements:* For master's, GRE General Test, GRE Subject Test, minimum GPA of 2.4 in last 60 hours of course work. *Faculty research:* Japanese Saturday School (Kato).

**Indiana University Bloomington,** University Graduate School, College of Arts and Sciences, Department of Sociology, Bloomington, IN 47405-7000. Offers MA, PhD. Terminal master's awarded for partial completion of doctoral program. *Degree requirements:* For master's, thesis; for doctorate, comprehensive exam, thesis/dissertation. *Entrance requirements:* For master's and doctorate, GRE General Test. Additional exam requirements/recommendations for international students: Required—TOEFL. Electronic applications accepted. *Faculty research:* Social psychology, political sociology, sociological research methods, stratification/mobility, education.

**Indiana University of Pennsylvania,** School of Graduate Studies and Research, College of Humanities and Social Sciences, Department of Sociology, Program in Sociology, Indiana, PA 15705. Offers MA. *Program availability:* Part-time. *Faculty:* 13 full-time (9 women). *Students:* 11 full-time (8 women), 1 international. Average age 26. 21 applicants, 48% accepted, 6 enrolled. In 2016, 1 master's awarded. *Degree requirements:* For master's, thesis optional. *Entrance requirements:* For master's, GRE, 2 letters of recommendation. Additional exam requirements/recommendations for international students: Required—TOEFL (minimum score 550 paper-based). *Application deadline:* Applications are processed on a rolling basis. Application fee: $50. Electronic applications accepted. *Expenses:* Tuition, state resident: full-time $8694; part-time $483 per credit. Tuition, nonresident: full-time $13,050; part-time $725 per credit. *Required fees:* $157 per credit. $50 per term. Tuition and fees vary according to course load and program. *Financial support:* In 2016–17, 8 research assistantships with tuition reimbursements (averaging $5,796 per year) were awarded; fellowships with full tuition reimbursements, career-related internships or fieldwork, Federal Work-Study, scholarships/grants, and unspecified assistantships also available. Financial award application deadline: 4/15; financial award applicants required to submit FAFSA. *Unit head:* Dr. Diane Shinberg, Coordinator, 724-357-4769, E-mail: shinberg@iup.edu.
Website: http://www.iup.edu/grad/sociology/default.aspx

**Indiana University–Purdue University Indianapolis,** School of Liberal Arts, Department of Sociology, Indianapolis, IN 46202. Offers family/gender studies (MA); medical sociology (MA); work/occupations (MA).

**Iowa State University of Science and Technology,** Department of Sociology, Ames, IA 50011. Offers rural sociology (MS, PhD); sociology (MS, PhD). *Degree requirements:* For master's, thesis; for doctorate, thesis/dissertation. *Entrance requirements:* For master's and doctorate, GRE General Test. Additional exam requirements/recommendations for international students: Required—TOEFL (minimum score 550 paper-based; 79 iBT), IELTS (minimum score 6.5). *Application deadline:* For fall admission, 1/10 priority date for domestic and international students; for spring admission, 10/1 for domestic and international students. Electronic applications accepted. *Application contact:* Rachel Burlingame, Application Contact, 515-294-2506, Fax: 515-294-8649, E-mail: rmb@iastate.edu.
Website: http://www.soc.iastate.edu/graduate/index.html

**Jackson State University,** Graduate School, College of Liberal Arts, Department of Criminal Justice and Sociology, Jackson, MS 39217. Offers criminology and justice services (MA); sociology (MA). *Program availability:* Part-time, evening/weekend. *Degree requirements:* For master's, comprehensive exam, thesis or alternative. *Entrance requirements:* For master's, GRE General Test. Additional exam requirements/recommendations for international students: Required—TOEFL (minimum score 520 paper-based; 67 iBT). *Application deadline:* For fall admission, 3/1 priority date for domestic students, 3/1 for international students; for spring admission, 10/1 for domestic students. Applications are processed on a rolling basis. Application fee: $25. *Expenses:*

## Sociology

Tuition, state resident: full-time $7141. Tuition, nonresident: full-time $17,494. *Required fees:* $1080. Tuition and fees vary according to class time, course level, course load, degree level, campus/location, program and student level. *Financial support:* Career-related internships or fieldwork, Federal Work-Study, scholarships/grants, and unspecified assistantships available. Support available to part-time students. Financial award application deadline: 3/1; financial award applicants required to submit FAFSA. *Unit head:* Dr. Etta F. Morgan, Chair, 601-979-2626, E-mail: etta.morgan@jsums.edu. *Application contact:* Fatoumatta Sisay, Manager of Graduate Admissions, 601-979-0342, Fax: 601-979-4325, E-mail: fatoumatta.sisay@jsums.edu.
Website: http://www.jsums.edu/criminaljustice/

**Johns Hopkins University,** Bloomberg School of Public Health, Department of Health, Behavior and Society, Baltimore, MD 21218. Offers genetic counseling (Sc M); health education and health communication (MSPH); social and behavioral sciences (Dr PH, PhD); social factors in health (MHS). *Degree requirements:* For master's, comprehensive exam (for some programs), thesis (for some programs); for doctorate, comprehensive exam, thesis/dissertation. *Entrance requirements:* For master's, GRE, curriculum vitae, 3 letters of recommendation; for doctorate, GRE, transcripts, curriculum vitae, 3 recommendation letters. Additional exam requirements/recommendations for international students: Required—TOEFL (minimum score 600 paper-based; 100 iBT). Electronic applications accepted. *Faculty research:* Social determinants of health and structural and community-level inventions to improve health, communication and health education, behavioral and social aspects of genetic counseling.

**Johns Hopkins University,** Zanvyl Krieger School of Arts and Sciences, Department of Sociology, Baltimore, MD 21218. Offers PhD. *Degree requirements:* For doctorate, one foreign language, thesis/dissertation. *Entrance requirements:* For doctorate, GRE General Test. Additional exam requirements/recommendations for international students: Required—TOEFL (minimum score 600 paper-based; 100 iBT), IELTS; Recommended—TWE. Electronic applications accepted. *Faculty research:* Education, immigration, race and gender, world systems, social policy.

**Kansas State University,** Graduate School, College of Arts and Sciences, Department of Sociology, Anthropology and Social Work, Manhattan, KS 66506. Offers sociology (MA, PhD). *Program availability:* Part-time. *Faculty:* 15 full-time (6 women). *Students:* 25 full-time (14 women), 14 part-time (8 women); includes 8 minority (3 Black or African American, non-Hispanic/Latino; 2 Asian, non-Hispanic/Latino; 1 Hispanic/Latino; 2 Two or more races, non-Hispanic/Latino), 5 international. Average age 34. 20 applicants, 80% accepted, 8 enrolled. In 2016, 4 master's, 4 doctorates awarded. *Degree requirements:* For master's, thesis or alternative; for doctorate, comprehensive exam, thesis/dissertation. *Entrance requirements:* For master's, GRE, minimum undergraduate GPA of 3.0; for doctorate, GRE, master's degree in sociology or related field. Additional exam requirements/recommendations for international students: Required—TOEFL (minimum score 550 paper-based; 79 iBT), IELTS (minimum score 6.5). *Application deadline:* For fall admission, 1/15 priority date for domestic students, 1/1 priority date for international students; for spring admission, 10/1 priority date for domestic students, 8/1 priority date for international students. Applications are processed on a rolling basis. Application fee: $50 ($75 for international students). Electronic applications accepted. *Expenses:* Tuition, state resident: full-time $9670. Tuition, nonresident: full-time $21,828. *Required fees:* $862. *Financial support:* In 2016–17, 3 research assistantships, 14 teaching assistantships with full tuition reimbursements (averaging $12,100 per year) were awarded; institutionally sponsored loans, scholarships/grants, health care benefits, and unspecified assistantships also available. Support available to part-time students. Financial award application deadline: 1/15; financial award applicants required to submit FAFSA. *Faculty research:* Politics and development; criminology; community, agriculture, food, and environment; social inequalities. *Total annual research expenditures:* $337,838. *Unit head:* Dr. Laszlo Kulcsar, Department Head, 785-532-6865, E-mail: kulcsar@ksu.edu. *Application contact:* Dr. Lisa Melander, Graduate Program Director, 785-532-4970, E-mail: lmeland@ksu.edu.
Website: http://www.k-state.edu/sasw/

**Kent State University,** College of Arts and Sciences, Department of Sociology, Kent, OH 44242-0001. Offers criminology and criminal justice (MA), including corrections, global security, policing, victimology; sociology (MA, PhD). PhD offered jointly with The University of Akron. *Program availability:* Part-time, 100% online. *Faculty:* 31 full-time (18 women). *Students:* 44 full-time (25 women), 53 part-time (36 women); includes 27 minority (19 Black or African American, non-Hispanic/Latino; 1 Asian, non-Hispanic/Latino; 5 Hispanic/Latino; 2 Two or more races, non-Hispanic/Latino). Average age 30. 71 applicants, 39% accepted, 18 enrolled. In 2016, 4 master's awarded. Terminal master's awarded for partial completion of doctoral program. *Degree requirements:* For master's, capstone project; for doctorate, comprehensive exam, thesis/dissertation. *Entrance requirements:* For master's, minimum GPA of 3.0, transcripts, resume/curriculum vitae, goal statement, 3 letters of recommendation; for doctorate, GRE, minimum GPA of 3.0, transcripts, personal statement, 3 letters of recommendation. Additional exam requirements/recommendations for international students: Required—TOEFL (minimum score of 525 paper-based, 71 iBT), IELTS (minimum score of 6), Michigan English Language Assessment Battery (minimum score of 75), or PTE (minimum score of 48). *Application deadline:* For fall admission, 12/15 for domestic students, 12/1 for international students. Applications are processed on a rolling basis. Application fee: $45 ($70 for international students). Electronic applications accepted. *Expenses:* Tuition, state resident: full-time $10,864; part-time $495 per credit hour. Tuition, nonresident: full-time $18,380; part-time $837 per credit hour. *Financial support:* Research assistantships with full tuition reimbursements, teaching assistantships with full tuition reimbursements, health care benefits, and unspecified assistantships available. Financial award application deadline: 12/15. *Unit head:* Dr. Richard T. Serpe, Professor and Chair, 330-672-2562, E-mail: rserpe@kent.edu. *Application contact:* Dr. William Kalkhoff, Professor and Graduate Coordinator, 330-672-3712, E-mail: wkalkhof@kent.edu.
Website: http://www.kent.edu/sociology/

**Lakehead University,** Graduate Studies, Faculty of Social Sciences and Humanities, Department of Sociology, Thunder Bay, ON P7B 5E1, Canada. Offers gerontology (MA); health services and policy research (MA); sociology (MA); women's studies (MA). *Program availability:* Part-time, evening/weekend. *Degree requirements:* For master's, research project or thesis. *Entrance requirements:* For master's, minimum B average. Additional exam requirements/recommendations for international students: Required—TOEFL. *Faculty research:* Sociology of medicine, cultural and social change, health human resources, gerontology, women's studies.

**Laurentian University,** School of Graduate Studies and Research, Programme in Sociology, Sudbury, ON P3E 2C6, Canada. Offers applied social research (MA). *Program availability:* Part-time. *Entrance requirements:* For master's, honors degree in sociology or equivalent. *Faculty research:* Work foundations, managing AIDS organization, tracking laid-off mine workers.

**Lehigh University,** College of Arts and Sciences, Department of Sociology and Anthropology, Bethlehem, PA 18015. Offers sociology (MA). *Program availability:* Part-time, evening/weekend. *Faculty:* 11 full-time (8 women), 1 part-time/adjunct (0 women). *Students:* 8 full-time (5 women); includes 4 minority (2 Black or African American, non-Hispanic/Latino; 2 Hispanic/Latino). Average age 25. 14 applicants, 71% accepted, 6 enrolled. In 2016, 9 master's awarded. *Degree requirements:* For master's, comprehensive exam, thesis optional. *Entrance requirements:* For master's, GRE General Test. Additional exam requirements/recommendations for international students: Required—TOEFL (minimum score 650 paper-based; 96 iBT). *Application deadline:* For fall admission, 1/15 for domestic and international students. Application fee: $75. Electronic applications accepted. *Expenses:* $1,420 per credit. *Financial support:* In 2016–17, 9 students received support, including 3 fellowships with full tuition reimbursements available, 6 teaching assistantships with full tuition reimbursements available; scholarships/grants also available. Financial award application deadline: 1/1. *Faculty research:* Urban sociology, medical sociology, policy studies, globalization. *Total annual research expenditures:* $14,858. *Unit head:* Dr. John Gatewood, Chair/Professor, 610-758-3814, Fax: 610-758-6552, E-mail: jbg1@lehigh.edu. *Application contact:* Prof. Yuping Zhang, Graduate Program Director, 610-758-3820, Fax: 610-758-6552, E-mail: yuz307@lehigh.edu.
Website: http://cas.lehigh.edu/socanthro

**Lincoln University,** Graduate Studies, Jefferson City, MO 65101. Offers business administration (MBA), including accounting, management, management information systems, public administration/policy; elementary teaching (M Ed); environmental science (MS); guidance and counseling (M Ed), including community/agency counseling, elementary school, secondary school; higher education (MA); history (MA); integrated agricultural systems (MS); middle school (M Ed); natural sciences (MS); secondary teaching (M Ed); sociology (MA); sociology/criminal justice (MA). *Program availability:* Part-time, evening/weekend, 100% online, blended/hybrid learning. *Students:* 50 full-time (29 women), 68 part-time (39 women); includes 40 minority (37 Black or African American, non-Hispanic/Latino; 1 Asian, non-Hispanic/Latino; 2 Two or more races, non-Hispanic/Latino), 14 international. Average age 33. 75 applicants, 80% accepted, 34 enrolled. In 2016, 51 master's awarded. *Degree requirements:* For master's, comprehensive exam, thesis optional. *Entrance requirements:* For master's, GRE, MAT or GMAT, minimum GPA of 2.75 overall, 3.0 in courses related to specialization; 3 letters of recommendation; minimum C average in English composition; personal statement of purpose. Additional exam requirements/recommendations for international students: Required—TOEFL (minimum score 500 paper-based; 61 iBT), IELTS (minimum score 5.5), Michigan English Language Assessment Battery (minimum score 80). *Application deadline:* For fall admission, 7/1 priority date for domestic students, 5/1 priority date for international students; for spring admission, 11/1 priority date for domestic students, 10/1 priority date for international students; for summer admission, 6/1 priority date for domestic students. Applications are processed on a rolling basis. Application fee: $30. Electronic applications accepted. *Expenses:* Tuition, state resident: full-time $6840; part-time $5130 per year. Tuition, nonresident: full-time $12,720; part-time $9540 per year. *Required fees:* $852; $811 per unit. Tuition and fees vary according to course load. *Financial support:* In 2016–17, 2 fellowships with tuition reimbursements, 8 research assistantships with tuition reimbursements were awarded; Federal Work-Study, scholarships/grants, and unspecified assistantships also available. Support available to part-time students. Financial award application deadline: 3/1; financial award applicants required to submit FAFSA. *Unit head:* Dr. Rolundus R. Rice, Dean, 573-681-5247, Fax: 573-681-5106, E-mail: gradschool@lincolnu.edu. *Application contact:* Irasema Steck, Administrative Assistant, 573-681-5247, Fax: 573-681-5106, E-mail: gradschool@lincolnu.edu.
Website: http://www.lincolnu.edu/web/graduate-studies/graduate-studies

**Long Island University–LIU Brooklyn,** Richard L. Conolly College of Liberal Arts and Sciences, Brooklyn, NY 11201-8423. Offers biology (MS); chemistry (MS); clinical psychology (PhD); communication sciences and disorders (MS); creative writing (MFA); English (MA); media arts (MA, MFA); political science (MA); psychology (MA); social science (MS); sociology (MA); speech-language pathology (MS); United Nations (Advanced Certificate); urban studies (MA); writing and production for television (MFA). *Program availability:* Part-time, evening/weekend. *Faculty:* 90 full-time (35 women), 125 part-time/adjunct (67 women). *Students:* 355 full-time (276 women), 220 part-time (161 women); includes 245 minority (119 Black or African American, non-Hispanic/Latino; 32 Asian, non-Hispanic/Latino; 80 Hispanic/Latino; 1 Native Hawaiian or other Pacific Islander, non-Hispanic/Latino; 13 Two or more races, non-Hispanic/Latino), 85 international. 792 applicants, 41% accepted, 141 enrolled. In 2016, 154 master's, 18 doctorates, 4 other advanced degrees awarded. *Degree requirements:* For master's, comprehensive exam (for some programs), thesis (for some programs); for doctorate, comprehensive exam (for some programs), thesis/dissertation (for some programs). *Entrance requirements:* For master's and doctorate, GRE. Additional exam requirements/recommendations for international students: Recommended—TOEFL (minimum score 550 paper-based; 79 iBT). *Application deadline:* Applications are processed on a rolling basis. Application fee: $50. Electronic applications accepted. *Expenses:* Tuition: Full-time $28,272; part-time $1178 per credit. *Required fees:* $451 per term. Tuition and fees vary according to degree level, program and student level. *Financial support:* In 2016–17, 120 fellowships with full and partial tuition reimbursements (averaging $915 per year), 5 research assistantships with full and partial tuition reimbursements (averaging $2,300 per year), 136 teaching assistantships with full and partial tuition reimbursements (averaging $2,300 per year) were awarded; career-related internships or fieldwork, Federal Work-Study, institutionally sponsored loans, scholarships/grants, tuition waivers (full and partial), and unspecified assistantships also available. Support available to part-time students. Financial award application deadline: 2/15; financial award applicants required to submit FAFSA. *Faculty research:* Nanocrystal polymerization of cellulose using electron microscopy. *Unit head:* Dr. Kevin Lauth, Acting Dean, 718-488-1347, E-mail: kevin.lauth@liu.edu. *Application contact:* Gabrielle Gannon, Director of Graduate Admissions, 718-488-1011, Fax: 718-780-6110, E-mail: bkln-admissions@liu.edu.

**Louisiana State University and Agricultural & Mechanical College,** Graduate School, College of Humanities and Social Sciences, Department of Sociology, Baton Rouge, LA 70803. Offers MA, PhD.

**Loyola University Chicago,** Graduate School, Department of Sociology, Chicago, IL 60660. Offers applied and public sociology (MA); sociology (MA, PhD). *Program availability:* Part-time, evening/weekend. *Faculty:* 17 full-time (10 women). *Students:* 39 full-time (21 women), 3 part-time (all women); includes 15 minority (5 Black or African American, non-Hispanic/Latino; 5 Asian, non-Hispanic/Latino; 3 Hispanic/Latino; 2 Two or more races, non-Hispanic/Latino), 3 international. Average age 30. 53 applicants, 25% accepted, 9 enrolled. In 2016, 8 master's, 5 doctorates awarded. Terminal master's awarded for partial completion of doctoral program. *Degree requirements:* For master's, thesis or alternative; for doctorate, comprehensive exam, thesis/dissertation. *Entrance requirements:* For master's, GRE General Test (recommended); for doctorate, GRE General Test. Additional exam requirements/recommendations for international students: Required—TOEFL (minimum score 550 paper-based; 79 iBT), IELTS (minimum score 6.5). *Application deadline:* For fall admission, 1/5 for domestic and international students; for winter admission, 1/5 for domestic students, 1/4 for international students. Electronic applications accepted. *Expenses:* Contact institution. *Financial support:* In 2016–17, 14 students received support, including 4 fellowships with full tuition reimbursements available (averaging $18,000 per year), 6 research assistantships with full tuition reimbursements available (averaging $18,000 per year), 4 teaching assistantships with full tuition reimbursements available (averaging $18,000 per year); Federal Work-Study, health care benefits, and tuition waivers (full and partial) also available. Financial award application deadline: 1/5; financial award applicants required to submit FAFSA. *Faculty research:* Medical, religion, urban, knowledge, culture. *Total annual research expenditures:* $160,000. *Unit head:* Dr. Anne Figert, Chair, 773-508-3431, Fax: 773-508-7099, E-mail: afigert@luc.edu. *Application contact:* Dr. Marilyn Krogh, Graduate Program Director, 773-508-3445, Fax: 773-508-7099, E-mail: mkrogh@luc.edu.

**Marshall University,** Academic Affairs Division, College of Liberal Arts, Department of Sociology and Anthropology, Huntington, WV 25755. Offers sociology (MA). *Degree requirements:* For master's, thesis optional. *Entrance requirements:* For master's, GRE.

**McGill University,** Faculty of Graduate and Postdoctoral Studies, Faculty of Arts, Department of Sociology, Montréal, QC H3A 2T5, Canada. Offers medical sociology (MA); neo-tropical environment (MA); social statistics (MA); sociology (MA, PhD, Diploma).

**McGill University,** Faculty of Graduate and Postdoctoral Studies, Faculty of Medicine, Department of Social Studies in Medicine, Montréal, QC H3A 2T5, Canada. Offers medical anthropology (MA, PhD); medical history (MA, PhD); medical sociology (MA, PhD).

**McMaster University,** School of Graduate Studies, Faculty of Social Sciences, Department of Sociology, Hamilton, ON L8S 4M2, Canada. Offers MA, PhD. *Program availability:* Part-time. *Degree requirements:* For master's, thesis; for doctorate, comprehensive exam, thesis/dissertation. *Entrance requirements:* For master's and doctorate, minimum B+ average. Additional exam requirements/recommendations for international students: Required—TOEFL (minimum score 580 paper-based). *Faculty research:* Socialization and conversion, ethnic relations, international migration, racism, social implications of the Internet.

**Memorial University of Newfoundland,** School of Graduate Studies, Department of Sociology, St. John's, NL A1C 5S7, Canada. Offers gender (PhD); maritime sociology (PhD); sociology (M Phil, MA); work and development (PhD). *Program availability:* Part-time. *Degree requirements:* For master's, comprehensive exam, thesis optional, program journal (M Phil); for doctorate, one foreign language, comprehensive exam, thesis/dissertation, oral defense of thesis. *Entrance requirements:* For master's, 2nd class degree from university of recognized standing in area of study; for doctorate, MA, M Phil, or equivalent. Electronic applications accepted. *Faculty research:* Work and development, gender, maritime sociology.

**Michigan State University,** The Graduate School, College of Social Science, Department of Sociology, East Lansing, MI 48824. Offers MA, PhD. *Program availability:* Part-time. *Entrance requirements:* Additional exam requirements/recommendations for international students: Required—TOEFL (minimum score 550 paper-based), Michigan State University ELT (minimum score 85), Michigan English Language Assessment Battery (minimum score 83). Electronic applications accepted.

**Middle Tennessee State University,** College of Graduate Studies, College of Liberal Arts, Department of Sociology and Anthropology, Murfreesboro, TN 37132. Offers sociology (MA). *Program availability:* Part-time, evening/weekend, online learning. *Degree requirements:* For master's, comprehensive exam, thesis. *Entrance requirements:* For master's, GRE. Additional exam requirements/recommendations for international students: Required—TOEFL (minimum score 525 paper-based; 71 iBT) or IELTS (minimum score 6). Electronic applications accepted. *Faculty research:* Women's and gender studies, crime and deviance, aging studies, social organizations.

**Minnesota State University Mankato,** College of Graduate Studies and Research, College of Social and Behavioral Sciences, Department of Sociology and Corrections, Mankato, MN 56001. Offers sociology (MA); sociology: college teaching (MA); sociology: corrections (MS); sociology: human services planning and administration (MS). *Program availability:* Part-time. *Students:* 9 full-time (5 women), 19 part-time (16 women). *Degree requirements:* For master's, comprehensive exam, thesis or alternative. *Entrance requirements:* For master's, minimum GPA of 3.0 during previous 2 years, 3 letters of reference, resume. Additional exam requirements/recommendations for international students: Required—TOEFL. *Application deadline:* For fall admission, 7/1 priority date for domestic students; for spring admission, 11/1 for domestic students. Applications are processed on a rolling basis. Application fee: $40. Electronic applications accepted. *Financial support:* Research assistantships with full tuition reimbursements, teaching assistantships with full tuition reimbursements, career-related internships or fieldwork, Federal Work-Study, institutionally sponsored loans, and unspecified assistantships available. Support available to part-time students. Financial award application deadline: 3/15; financial award applicants required to submit FAFSA. *Unit head:* Dr. Luis Posas, Chair, 507-389-2257, E-mail: luis.posas@mnsu.edu. *Application contact:* Donald Ebel, Graduate Studies Coordinator, 507-389-5188, Fax: 507-389-5615, E-mail: donald.ebel@mnsu.edu. Website: http://sbs.mnsu.edu/soccorr/

**Mississippi State University,** College of Arts and Sciences, Department of Sociology, Mississippi State, MS 39762. Offers MS, PhD. *Program availability:* Part-time. *Faculty:* 18 full-time (14 women). *Students:* 26 full-time (17 women), 8 part-time (5 women); includes 9 minority (6 Black or African American, non-Hispanic/Latino; 1 Asian, non-Hispanic/Latino; 2 Hispanic/Latino), 2 international. Average age 30. 23 applicants, 43% accepted, 6 enrolled. In 2016, 3 master's, 2 doctorates awarded. *Degree requirements:* For master's, thesis optional, comprehensive oral or written exam; for doctorate, thesis/dissertation, comprehensive oral and written exam. *Entrance requirements:* For master's, minimum GPA of 3.0 on last two years of undergraduate courses or GRE; academic writing sample in English (student's choice); for doctorate, GRE, academic writing sample in English (student's choice). Additional exam requirements/recommendations for international students: Required—TOEFL (minimum score 477 paper-based; 53 iBT); Recommended—IELTS (minimum score 4.5). *Application deadline:* For fall admission, 4/15 priority date for domestic students, 5/1 for international students; for spring admission, 10/15 priority date for domestic students, 9/1 for international students. Applications are processed on a rolling basis. Application fee: $60. Electronic applications accepted. *Expenses:* Tuition, state resident: full-time $7670; part-time $852.50 per credit hour. Tuition, nonresident: full-time $20,790; part-time $2310.50 per credit hour. Part-time tuition and fees vary according to course load. *Financial support:* In 2016–17, 2 research assistantships with full tuition reimbursements (averaging $15,866 per year), 12 teaching assistantships with partial tuition reimbursements (averaging $13,294 per year) were awarded; Federal Work-Study, institutionally sponsored loans, scholarships/grants, and unspecified assistantships also available. Financial award application deadline: 2/15; financial award applicants required to submit FAFSA. *Faculty research:* Community and regional development, criminology, natural resource development, family sociology, gender. *Total annual research expenditures:* $1.6 million. *Unit head:* Dr. Leslie Hossfeld, Professor and Department Head, 662-325-7868, Fax: 662-325-4564, E-mail: lh401@msstate.edu. *Application contact:* Lakan Drinker, Admissions and Enrollment Assistant, 662-325-8951, E-mail: ldrinker@grad.msstate.edu. Website: http://www.sociology.msstate.edu/

**Morehead State University,** Graduate Programs, Caudill College of Arts, Humanities and Social Sciences, Department of Sociology, Social Work and Criminology, Morehead, KY 40351. Offers criminology (MA); general sociology (MA); gerontology (MA); sociology regional analysis (MA); sociology/chemical dependency (MA). *Program availability:* Part-time, evening/weekend. *Degree requirements:* For master's, comprehensive exam, thesis (for some programs). *Entrance requirements:* For master's, GRE General Test, minimum GPA of 3.0 in sociology, 2.75 overall; 18 hours of course work in sociology, writing sample. Additional exam requirements/recommendations for international students: Required—TOEFL (minimum score 500 paper-based). Electronic applications accepted. *Faculty research:* Death and dying; aging, drinking, and drugs; economic development; adult children of alcoholics.

**Morgan State University,** School of Graduate Studies, College of Liberal Arts, Department of Sociology and Anthropology, Baltimore, MD 21251. Offers sociology (MA, MS). *Program availability:* Part-time, evening/weekend. *Degree requirements:* For master's, comprehensive exam. *Entrance requirements:* Additional exam requirements/recommendations for international students: Required—TOEFL (minimum score 550 paper-based). *Faculty research:* Domestic violence, homelessness, social movements, marriage and family.

**New Mexico Highlands University,** Graduate Studies, College of Arts and Sciences, Department of Social and Behavioral Sciences, Las Vegas, NM 87701. Offers psychology (MS), including clinical psychology/counseling, general psychology; public affairs (MA), including applied sociology; Southwest studies (MA), including anthropology. *Program availability:* Part-time. *Degree requirements:* For master's, comprehensive exam, thesis or alternative. *Entrance requirements:* For master's, minimum undergraduate GPA of 3.0. Additional exam requirements/recommendations for international students: Required—TOEFL (minimum score 540 paper-based). *Faculty research:* Southwest Native American resettlement development, community-level interventions, neurochemistry of personality, comparative criminal justice, social theory and activism.

**New Mexico State University,** College of Arts and Sciences, Department of Sociology, Las Cruces, NM 88003. Offers MA. *Program availability:* Part-time, 100% online. *Faculty:* 9 full-time (6 women). *Students:* 11 full-time (7 women), 45 part-time (30 women); includes 15 minority (5 Black or African American, non-Hispanic/Latino; 1 Asian, non-Hispanic/Latino; 7 Hispanic/Latino; 1 Native Hawaiian or other Pacific Islander, non-Hispanic/Latino; 1 Two or more races, non-Hispanic/Latino), 2 international. Average age 39. 32 applicants, 78% accepted, 18 enrolled. In 2016, 12 master's awarded. *Degree requirements:* For master's, comprehensive exam (for some programs), thesis (for some programs). *Entrance requirements:* Additional exam requirements/recommendations for international students: Required—TOEFL (minimum score 550 paper-based; 79 iBT), IELTS (minimum score 6.5). *Application deadline:* For fall admission, 3/15 for domestic and international students. Application fee: $40 ($50 for international students). Electronic applications accepted. *Expenses:* Tuition, state resident: full-time $4086. Tuition, nonresident: full-time $14,254. *Required fees:* $853. Tuition and fees vary according to course load. *Financial support:* In 2016–17, 12 students received support, including 2 fellowships (averaging $4,088 per year), 4 teaching assistantships (averaging $8,482 per year); career-related internships or fieldwork, Federal Work-Study, scholarships/grants, traineeships, health care benefits, and unspecified assistantships also available. Support available to part-time students. Financial award application deadline: 3/1. *Faculty research:* Environmental sociology, borderland issues, sexualities, race and ethnicity, inequality. *Total annual research expenditures:* $6,147. *Unit head:* Dr. David G. LoConto, Department Head, 575-646-3448, Fax: 575-646-7601, E-mail: dloconto@nmsu.edu. *Application contact:* Dr. Sandra M. Way, Director of Graduate Studies, 575-646-3448, Fax: 575-646-7601, E-mail: sway@nmsu.edu. Website: http://sociology.nmsu.edu/

**The New School,** The New School for Social Research, Department of Sociology, New York, NY 10003. Offers historical studies (PhD); sociology (MA). *Program availability:* Part-time. *Faculty:* 7 full-time (3 women), 12 part-time/adjunct (4 women). *Students:* 92 full-time (50 women), 4 part-time (1 woman); includes 13 minority (2 Black or African American, non-Hispanic/Latino; 2 Asian, non-Hispanic/Latino; 5 Hispanic/Latino; 4 Two or more races, non-Hispanic/Latino), 49 international. Average age 34. 109 applicants, 69% accepted, 9 enrolled. In 2016, 21 master's, 11 doctorates awarded. Terminal master's awarded for partial completion of doctoral program. *Degree requirements:* For master's, comprehensive exam; for doctorate, one foreign language, thesis/dissertation. *Entrance requirements:* For master's and doctorate, GRE, letters of recommendation, writing sample, essays, unofficial transcripts. Additional exam requirements/recommendations for international students: Required—TOEFL (minimum score 100 iBT), IELTS (minimum score 7), PTE (minimum score 68). *Application deadline:* For fall admission, 5/5 priority date for domestic students, 6/1 priority date for international students; for spring admission, 10/15 priority date for domestic and international students. Applications are processed on a rolling basis. Application fee: $50. Electronic applications accepted. *Expenses:* Contact institution. *Financial support:* Fellowships, research assistantships, teaching assistantships, Federal Work-Study, scholarships/grants, and tuition waivers (full and partial) available. Support available to part-time students. Financial award application deadline: 2/1; financial award applicants required to submit FAFSA. *Faculty research:* Social inequalities; culture and politics; law, rights, and citizenship; historical and comparative sociology; and cities and publics. *Unit head:* Dr. William Milberg, Dean, The New School for Social Research, 212-229-5777, E-mail: milbergw@newschool.edu. *Application contact:* Dana Messinger, Director of Graduate Admission, 212-229-5150 Ext. 2300, E-mail: socialresearchadmit@newschool.edu. Website: http://www.newschool.edu/

**New York University,** Graduate School of Arts and Science, Department of Sociology, New York, NY 10012-1019. Offers French studies and sociology (PhD); sociology (MA, PhD); JD/MA. *Program availability:* Part-time. Terminal master's awarded for partial completion of doctoral program. *Degree requirements:* For master's, thesis or alternative; for doctorate, comprehensive exam, thesis/dissertation. *Entrance requirements:* For master's and doctorate, GRE General Test. Additional exam requirements/recommendations for international students: Required—TOEFL. *Faculty research:* Political sociology and social movements; gender and inequality; deviance, law, and crime; education; stratification and theory.

**New York University,** Steinhardt School of Culture, Education, and Human Development, Department of Humanities and Social Sciences in the Professions, Program in Sociology of Education, New York, NY 10003. Offers education policy (MA); social and cultural studies of education (MA); sociology of education (PhD). *Program availability:* Part-time. *Degree requirements:* For master's, thesis (for some programs); for doctorate, thesis/dissertation. *Entrance requirements:* For master's, letters of recommendation; for doctorate, GRE General Test, interview. Additional exam requirements/recommendations for international students: Required—TOEFL (minimum score 100 iBT). Electronic applications accepted. *Faculty research:* Legal and institutional environments of schools; social inequality; high school reform and achievement; urban schooling, economics and education, educational policy.

**North Carolina State University,** Graduate School, College of Humanities and Social Sciences, Department of Sociology and Anthropology, Program in Sociology, Raleigh,

*Sociology*

NC 27695. Offers M Soc, MS, PhD. *Program availability:* Part-time. *Degree requirements:* For master's, practicum (M Soc), thesis (MS); for doctorate, comprehensive exam, thesis/dissertation. *Entrance requirements:* For master's and doctorate, GRE General Test, sample of written work. Electronic applications accepted. *Faculty research:* Inequity: gender, race and class; crime and social control; work and organizations; rural sociology; family and intimate relations.

**North Dakota State University,** College of Graduate and Interdisciplinary Studies, College of Arts, Humanities and Social Sciences, Department of Sociology and Anthropology, Fargo, ND 58102. Offers anthropology (MA, MS); community development (MA, MS); social science (MA, MS); sociology (MS). *Program availability:* Part-time. *Degree requirements:* For master's, thesis. *Entrance requirements:* For master's, GRE (for emergency management), course work in sociology, minimum GPA of 3.2. Additional exam requirements/recommendations for international students: Required—TOEFL. Electronic applications accepted. *Faculty research:* Medical sociology, demography, ethnology, archaeology.

**Northeastern University,** College of Social Sciences and Humanities, Boston, MA 02115. Offers criminology and criminal justice (MSCJ); criminology and justice policy (PhD); economics (MA, PhD); English (MA, PhD); international affairs (MA); law and public policy (PhD); political science (MA, PhD); public administration (MPA); public history (MA); public policy (MPP); security and resilience studies (MS); sociology (MA, PhD); urban and regional policy (MS); urban informatics (MS); world history (MA, PhD); JD/MS. *Program availability:* Online learning. *Faculty:* 234 full-time (114 women), 55 part-time/adjunct (34 women). *Students:* 427 full-time (239 women), 77 part-time (42 women). In 2016, 143 master's, 38 doctorates awarded. *Degree requirements:* For doctorate, variable foreign language requirement, comprehensive exam, thesis/dissertation. *Entrance requirements:* For master's and doctorate, GRE. Additional exam requirements/recommendations for international students: Required—TOEFL, IELTS. Application fee: $75. Electronic applications accepted. *Expenses:* $1,295 per credit. *Financial support:* Teaching assistantships, career-related internships or fieldwork, scholarships/grants, health care benefits, tuition waivers (full and partial), and unspecified assistantships available. Support available to part-time students. Financial award applicants required to submit FAFSA. *Unit head:* Dr. Uta Poiger, Dean, 617-373-5173. *Application contact:* Amber Crowe, Administrative Coordinator, 617-373-5990, Fax: 617-373-7281, E-mail: gradcssh@northeastern.edu.
Website: http://www.northeastern.edu/cssh/graduate

**Northern Arizona University,** Graduate College, College of Social and Behavioral Sciences, Department of Sociology and Social Work, Flagstaff, AZ 86011. Offers applied sociology (MA). *Program availability:* Part-time. *Degree requirements:* For master's, thesis or internship. *Entrance requirements:* For master's, minimum GPA of 3.0. Additional exam requirements/recommendations for international students: Required—TOEFL (minimum score 550 paper-based; 80 iBT), IELTS (minimum score 7). Electronic applications accepted. *Expenses:* Tuition, state resident: full-time $8971; part-time $444 per credit hour. Tuition, nonresident: full-time $20,958; part-time $1164 per credit hour. *Required fees:* $1018; $644 per credit hour. Tuition and fees vary according to course load, campus/location and program. *Faculty research:* Demography, death and dying, criminology, social policy, divorce.

**Northern Illinois University,** Graduate School, College of Liberal Arts and Sciences, Department of Sociology, De Kalb, IL 60115-2854. Offers MA. *Program availability:* Part-time. *Faculty:* 14 full-time (3 women). *Students:* 9 full-time (5 women), 7 part-time (2 women); includes 3 minority (all Hispanic/Latino). Average age 28. 20 applicants, 65% accepted, 8 enrolled. In 2016, 2 master's awarded. *Degree requirements:* For master's, comprehensive exam, thesis optional. *Entrance requirements:* For master's, GRE General Test, minimum GPA of 2.75; course work in social theory, social methods, and statistics. Additional exam requirements/recommendations for international students: Required—TOEFL (minimum score 550 paper-based). *Application deadline:* For fall admission, 6/1 for domestic students, 5/1 for international students; for spring admission, 11/1 for domestic students, 10/1 for international students. Applications are processed on a rolling basis. Application fee: $40. Electronic applications accepted. *Financial support:* In 2016–17, 1 research assistantship with full tuition reimbursement, 16 teaching assistantships with full tuition reimbursements were awarded; fellowships with full tuition reimbursements, career-related internships or fieldwork, Federal Work-Study, scholarships/grants, tuition waivers (full), and unspecified assistantships also available. Support available to part-time students. Financial award applicants required to submit FAFSA. *Faculty research:* Welfare reform, interpersonal disputes, multicultural education, race and ethnicism, social control. *Unit head:* Dr. Kirk Miller, Chair, 815-753-1194, Fax: 815-753-6302, E-mail: kmiller7@niu.edu. *Application contact:* Dr. Keri B. Burchfield, Director, Graduate Studies, 815-753-0302, E-mail: kburchfield@niu.edu.
Website: http://www.sociology.niu.edu/

**Northwestern University,** The Graduate School, Judd A. and Marjorie Weinberg College of Arts and Sciences, Department of Sociology, Evanston, IL 60208. Offers PhD, JD/PhD. Admissions and degrees offered through The Graduate School. *Degree requirements:* For doctorate, thesis/dissertation. *Entrance requirements:* For doctorate, GRE General Test. Additional exam requirements/recommendations for international students: Required—TOEFL. Electronic applications accepted. *Faculty research:* Sociology of culture, social organizations, social inequality, comparative/historical sociology, economic sociology.

**Northwestern University,** The Graduate School, Kellogg School of Management, Management Programs, Evanston, IL 60208. Offers accounting information and management (MBA, PhD); analytical finance (MBA); business administration (MBA); decision sciences (MBA); entrepreneurship and innovation (MBA); finance (MBA, PhD); health enterprise management (MBA); human resources management (MBA); international business (MBA); management and organizations (MBA, PhD); management and organizations and sociology (PhD); management and strategy (MBA); management studies (MS); managerial analytics (MBA); managerial economics (MBA); managerial economics and strategy (PhD); marketing (MBA, PhD); marketing management (MBA); media management (MBA); operations management (MBA, PhD); real estate (MBA); social enterprise at Kellogg (MBA); JD/MBA. *Program availability:* Part-time, evening/weekend. Terminal master's awarded for partial completion of doctoral program. *Degree requirements:* For doctorate, thesis/dissertation, 2 years of coursework, qualifying (field) exam and candidacy, summer research papers and presentations to faculty, proposal defense, final exam/defense. *Entrance requirements:* For master's, GMAT, GRE, interview, 2 letters of recommendation, college transcripts, resume, essays, Kellogg honor code; for doctorate, GMAT, GRE, statement of purpose, transcripts, 2 letters of recommendation, resume, interview. Additional exam requirements/recommendations for international students: Required—TOEFL, IELTS. Electronic applications accepted. *Expenses:* Contact institution. *Faculty research:* Business cycles and international finance, health policy, networks, non-market strategy, consumer psychology.

**The Ohio State University,** Graduate School, College of Arts and Sciences, Division of Social and Behavioral Sciences, Department of Sociology, Columbus, OH 43210. Offers PhD. *Faculty:* 29. *Students:* 61 full-time (37 women), 1 (woman) part-time; includes 13 minority (5 Black or African American, non-Hispanic/Latino; 8 Hispanic/Latino), 7 international. Average age 28. In 2016, 9 doctorates awarded. *Degree requirements:* For

doctorate, thesis/dissertation. *Entrance requirements:* For doctorate, GRE General Test. Additional exam requirements/recommendations for international students: Required—TOEFL (minimum score 600 paper-based; 100 iBT); Recommended—IELTS (minimum score 7). *Application deadline:* For fall admission, 12/1 for domestic students, 11/30 for international students. Applications are processed on a rolling basis. Application fee: $60 ($70 for international students). Electronic applications accepted. *Financial support:* Fellowships with tuition reimbursements, research assistantships with tuition reimbursements, teaching assistantships with tuition reimbursements, Federal Work-Study, and institutionally sponsored loans available. Support available to part-time students. *Unit head:* Dr. Claudia Buchmann, Professor and Chair, 614-292-5452, E-mail: buchmann.4@osu.edu. *Application contact:* Graduate and Professional Admissions, 614-292-9444, Fax: 614-292-3895, E-mail: gpadmissions@osu.edu.
Website: http://sociology.osu.edu/

**Ohio University,** Graduate College, College of Arts and Sciences, Department of Sociology and Anthropology, Athens, OH 45701-2979. Offers sociology (MA). *Program availability:* Part-time. *Degree requirements:* For master's, thesis or alternative. *Entrance requirements:* For master's, minimum GPA of 3.0; minimum of 20 hours in sociology including statistics, theory, and research methods. Additional exam requirements/recommendations for international students: Required—TOEFL (minimum score 550 paper-based; 80 iBT) or IELTS (minimum score 6.5). *Application deadline:* For fall admission, 6/1 for domestic students, 3/1 priority date for international students; for winter admission, 10/1 for domestic and international students; for spring admission, 1/1 for domestic and international students. Application fee: $50 ($55 for international students). Electronic applications accepted. *Financial support:* Research assistantships with full and partial tuition reimbursements, teaching assistantships with full tuition reimbursements, career-related internships or fieldwork, Federal Work-Study, and unspecified assistantships available. Financial award application deadline: 3/1. *Faculty research:* Criminology/deviance, gender studies, inequality, social psychology and rural poverty. *Unit head:* Dr. Christine Mattley, Department Chair, 740-593-1381, Fax: 740-593-1365, E-mail: mattley@ohio.edu. *Application contact:* Dr. Debra A. Henderson, Graduate Chair, 740-593-1382, Fax: 740-593-1365, E-mail: henderd2@ohio.edu.
Website: http://www.ohio.edu/socanth/

**Oklahoma City University,** Petree College of Arts and Sciences, Oklahoma City, OK 73106-1402. Offers applied behavioral studies (M Ed); applied sociology: nonprofit leadership (MA); creative writing (MFA); criminology (MS); early childhood education (M Ed); elementary education (M Ed); general studies (MLA); leadership/management (MLA); moving image arts (MFA); professional counseling (M Ed); teaching (MA); teaching English to speakers of other languages (MA). *Program availability:* Part-time, evening/weekend. *Faculty:* 11 full-time (5 women), 15 part-time/adjunct (6 women). *Students:* 77 full-time (55 women), 46 part-time (30 women); includes 32 minority (13 Black or African American, non-Hispanic/Latino; 1 American Indian or Alaska Native, non-Hispanic/Latino; 2 Asian, non-Hispanic/Latino; 12 Hispanic/Latino; 4 Two or more races, non-Hispanic/Latino), 37 international. Average age 34. 92 applicants, 74% accepted, 46 enrolled. In 2016, 72 master's awarded. *Degree requirements:* For master's, capstone/practicum. *Entrance requirements:* For master's, bachelor's degree from accredited institution with minimum GPA of 3.0, essay, recommendation letters. Additional exam requirements/recommendations for international students: Required—TOEFL (minimum score 550 paper-based; 80 iBT). *Application deadline:* Applications are processed on a rolling basis. Application fee: $50. Electronic applications accepted. *Expenses:* Contact institution. *Financial support:* In 2016–17, 16 students received support. Federal Work-Study, institutionally sponsored loans, scholarships/grants, and tuition waivers (full and partial) available. Support available to part-time students. Financial award application deadline: 6/1; financial award applicants required to submit FAFSA. *Unit head:* Dr. Amy Cataldi, Dean, 405-208-5446, Fax: 405-208-5447, E-mail: acataldi@okcu.edu. *Application contact:* Michael Harrington, Director of Graduate Admissions, 800-633-7242, Fax: 405-208-5356, E-mail: gadmissions@okcu.edu.
Website: http://www.okcu.edu/petree/

**Oklahoma State University,** College of Arts and Sciences, Department of Sociology, Stillwater, OK 74078. Offers MS, PhD. *Faculty:* 16 full-time (7 women), 3 part-time/adjunct (2 women). *Students:* 9 full-time (4 women), 16 part-time (10 women); includes 2 minority (1 Black or African American, non-Hispanic/Latino; 1 Hispanic/Latino), 4 international. Average age 29. 29 applicants, 31% accepted, 7 enrolled. In 2016, 8 master's, 1 doctorate awarded. *Degree requirements:* For master's, thesis; for doctorate, comprehensive exam, thesis/dissertation. *Entrance requirements:* For master's and doctorate, GRE General Test. Additional exam requirements/recommendations for international students: Required—TOEFL (minimum score 550 paper-based; 79 iBT). *Application deadline:* For fall admission, 3/1 priority date for international students; for spring admission, 8/1 priority date for international students. Applications are processed on a rolling basis. Application fee: $40 ($75 for international students). Electronic applications accepted. *Expenses:* Tuition, state resident: full-time $3775; part-time $209.70 per credit hour. Tuition, nonresident: full-time $14,851; part-time $825.05 per credit hour. *Required fees:* $2027; $112.60 per credit hour. Tuition and fees vary according to campus/location. *Financial support:* In 2016–17, 4 research assistantships (averaging $15,015 per year), 18 teaching assistantships (averaging $15,224 per year) were awarded; career-related internships or fieldwork, Federal Work-Study, scholarships/grants, health care benefits, tuition waivers (partial), and unspecified assistantships also available. Support available to part-time students. Financial award application deadline: 3/1; financial award applicants required to submit FAFSA. *Faculty research:* Criminology/correction/legal issues; race, ethnicity, and gender in American society; environmental conflict and population problems; international comparative research; social change and social movement in American culture. *Unit head:* Dr. Sharon Bird, Department Head, 405-744-6104, Fax: 405-744-5780, E-mail: sharon.bird@okstate.edu.
Website: http://sociology.okstate.edu

**Old Dominion University,** College of Arts and Letters, Program in Applied Sociology, Norfolk, VA 23529. Offers criminal justice (MA); general sociology (MA); women's studies (MA). *Program availability:* Part-time, evening/weekend. *Faculty:* 19 full-time (11 women). *Students:* 11 full-time (8 women), 2 part-time (1 woman); includes 6 minority (3 Black or African American, non-Hispanic/Latino; 3 Two or more races, non-Hispanic/Latino). Average age 23. 26 applicants, 65% accepted, 12 enrolled. In 2016, 4 master's awarded. *Degree requirements:* For master's, thesis. *Entrance requirements:* For master's, GRE General Test, minimum GPA of 3.0; 12 credits in criminal justice, sociology, or women's studies. Additional exam requirements/recommendations for international students: Required—TOEFL. *Application deadline:* For fall admission, 3/1 for domestic and international students. Application fee: $50. Electronic applications accepted. *Expenses:* Contact institution. *Financial support:* In 2016–17, 8 students received support, including 2 research assistantships (averaging $10,000 per year), 6 teaching assistantships (averaging $10,000 per year); career-related internships or fieldwork, scholarships/grants, and unspecified assistantships also available. Financial award application deadline: 2/15. *Faculty research:* Quantitative methodology, theory, family, gender/class/race, crime. *Total annual research expenditures:* $350,000. *Unit head:* Dr. Ingrid Whitaker, Graduate Program Director, 757-683-3811, Fax: 757-683-5634, E-mail: iwhitake@odu.edu. *Application contact:* Dr. David C. Earnest, Associate

Dean, 757-683-6077, Fax: 757-683-5746, E-mail: dearnest@odu.edu. Website: http://al.odu.edu/sociology/gradprogram/graduatehome.shtml

**Our Lady of the Lake University,** School of Professional Studies, Program in Sociology, San Antonio, TX 78207-4689. Offers MA. *Program availability:* Part-time, evening/weekend, online learning. *Faculty:* 2 full-time (1 woman). *Students:* 11 full-time (9 women), 2 part-time (1 woman); includes 9 minority (3 Black or African American, non-Hispanic/Latino; 6 Hispanic/Latino). Average age 32. 9 applicants, 100% accepted, 7 enrolled. In 2016, 1 master's awarded. *Entrance requirements:* For master's, official transcripts showing minimum B grade in undergraduate statistics course, personal statement, two letters of recommendation, interview. Additional exam requirements/recommendations for international students: Required—TOEFL. *Application deadline:* For fall admission, 6/15 for domestic and international students. Application fee: $40 ($50 for international students). Electronic applications accepted. *Expenses:* Tuition: Full-time $14,796. Tuition and fees vary according to course load, degree level, campus/location and program. *Financial support:* In 2016–17, 5 students received support. Federal Work-Study, scholarships/grants, unspecified assistantships, and tuition discounts available. Support available to part-time students. Financial award application deadline: 5/1; financial award applicants required to submit FAFSA. *Faculty research:* Community based population health. *Unit head:* Dr. Steve Blanchard, Professor of Sociology, 210-528-7119, E-mail: steveblanchard@ollusa.edu. *Application contact:* Office of Graduate Admissions, 210-431-3995 Ext. 2314, Fax: 210-431-3945, E-mail: gradadm@lake.ollusa.edu. Website: http://www.ollusa.edu/s/1190/hybrid/default-hybrid-ollu.aspx?sid-1190&gid-1&pgid-7989

**Oxford Graduate School,** Graduate Programs, Dayton, TN 37321-6736. Offers family life education (M Litt); integration of religion and society (D Phil); organizational leadership (M Litt). *Faculty:* 10 full-time (2 women), 22 part-time/adjunct (7 women). *Students:* 105 full-time (40 women). *Entrance requirements:* For master's, official transcripts, three letters of recommendation, bachelor's degree or its equivalent, minimum undergraduate GPA of 3.0, minimum of 3 years of professional experience; for doctorate, official transcripts, three letters of recommendation, master's degree with minimum GPA of 3.0, minimum of 5 years of professional experience. *Expenses:* $7,875 per year (for D Phil); $6,000 per year (for M Litt). *Application contact:* Gwen Ballant, Director of Admissions, 423-775-6596, Fax: 423-775-6599, E-mail: oxfordgraduateschool@ogs.edu.

**Penn State University Park,** Graduate School, College of the Liberal Arts, Department of Sociology and Criminology, University Park, PA 16802. Offers criminology (MA, PhD); sociology (MA, PhD). *Unit head:* Dr. Susan Welch, Dean, 814-865-7691, Fax: 814-863-2085. *Application contact:* Lori Hawn, Director, Graduate Student Services, 814-865-1795, Fax: 814-863-4627, E-mail: l-gswww@lists.psu.edu. Website: http://sociology.la.psu.edu/

**Portland State University,** Graduate Studies, College of Liberal Arts and Sciences, Department of Sociology, Portland, OR 97207-0751. Offers MA, MS, PhD. *Program availability:* Part-time. *Faculty:* 16 full-time (9 women), 8 part-time/adjunct (4 women). *Students:* 24 full-time (15 women), 14 part-time (10 women); includes 10 minority (3 Black or African American, non-Hispanic/Latino; 2 Asian, non-Hispanic/Latino; 4 Hispanic/Latino; 1 Two or more races, non-Hispanic/Latino), 3 international. Average age 35. 43 applicants, 23% accepted, 9 enrolled. In 2016, 8 master's, 1 doctorate awarded. *Degree requirements:* For master's, variable foreign language requirement, thesis, written exam; for doctorate, thesis/dissertation. *Entrance requirements:* For master's, GRE General Test, GRE Subject Test, minimum GPA of 3.0 in upper-division course work or 2.75 overall, 3 letters of recommendation. Additional exam requirements/recommendations for international students: Required—TOEFL (minimum score 550 paper-based; 80 iBT), IELTS (minimum score 6.5). *Application deadline:* For fall admission, 1/15 for domestic and international students. Applications are processed on a rolling basis. Application fee: $65. *Expenses:* Contact institution. *Financial support:* In 2016–17, 2 research assistantships with full tuition reimbursements (averaging $5,064 per year), 18 teaching assistantships with tuition reimbursements (averaging $7,908 per year) were awarded; fellowships with full tuition reimbursements, career-related internships or fieldwork, Federal Work-Study, and unspecified assistantships also available. Support available to part-time students. Financial award application deadline: 3/1; financial award applicants required to submit FAFSA. *Faculty research:* Urban sociology, gender and class, development, social change, race/ethnic/minority relations. *Total annual research expenditures:* $289,852. *Unit head:* Melissa Thompson, Chair, 503-725-3614, Fax: 503-725-3957, E-mail: mthomp@pdx.edu. *Application contact:* Ginny Garcia-Alexander, Professor/Graduate Committee Chair, 503-725-9572, E-mail: gin5@pdx.edu. Website: https://www.pdx.edu/sociology/

**Portland State University,** Graduate Studies, College of Liberal Arts and Sciences, Systems Science Program, Portland, OR 97207-0751. Offers computational intelligence (Certificate); computer modeling and simulation (Certificate); systems science (MS); systems science/anthropology (PhD); systems science/business administration (PhD); systems science/civil engineering (PhD); systems science/economics (PhD); systems science/engineering management (PhD); systems science/general (PhD); systems science/mathematical sciences (PhD); systems science/mechanical engineering (PhD); systems science/psychology (PhD); systems science/sociology (PhD). *Faculty:* 2 full-time (0 women), 3 part-time/adjunct (1 woman). *Students:* 12 full-time (3 women), 21 part-time (5 women); includes 5 minority (1 Black or African American, non-Hispanic/Latino; 2 Hispanic/Latino; 2 Two or more races, non-Hispanic/Latino). Average age 39. 16 applicants, 69% accepted, 9 enrolled. In 2016, 4 master's, 6 doctorates awarded. *Degree requirements:* For master's, comprehensive exam (for some programs), thesis optional; for doctorate, variable foreign language requirement, comprehensive exam (for some programs), thesis/dissertation. *Entrance requirements:* For master's, GRE/GMAT (recommended), minimum GPA of 3.0 undergraduate or graduate work, 2 letters of recommendation, statement of interest; for doctorate, GMAT, GRE General Test, minimum GPA of 3.0 undergraduate, 3.25 graduate; 2 letters of recommendation; statement of interest. Additional exam requirements/recommendations for international students: Required—TOEFL (minimum score 550 paper-based; 80 iBT). *Application deadline:* For fall admission, 1/15 for domestic and international students; for spring admission, 11/1 for domestic students. Application fee: $65. Electronic applications accepted. *Expenses:* Contact institution. *Financial support:* In 2016–17, 2 research assistantships with tuition reimbursements (averaging $7,830 per year) were awarded; teaching assistantships, career-related internships or fieldwork, Federal Work-Study, scholarships/grants, and unspecified assistantships also available. Support available to part-time students. Financial award application deadline: 3/1; financial award applicants required to submit FAFSA. *Faculty research:* Systems theory and methodology, artificial intelligence neural networks, information theory, nonlinear dynamics/chaos, modeling and simulation. *Unit head:* Dr. Wayne Wakeland, Chair, 503-725-4975, E-mail: wakeland@pdx.edu. Website: http://www.pdx.edu/sysc/

**Prairie View A&M University,** College of Arts and Sciences, Division of Social Work, Behavioral and Political Sciences, Prairie View, TX 77446. Offers sociology (MA). *Program availability:* Part-time, evening/weekend. *Faculty:* 4 full-time (1 woman).

*Students:* 2 full-time (both women), 1 part-time (0 women); all minorities (all Black or African American, non-Hispanic/Latino). Average age 41. 3 applicants, 100% accepted, 2 enrolled. In 2016, 7 master's awarded. *Degree requirements:* For master's, comprehensive exam, thesis (for some programs). *Entrance requirements:* For master's, GRE General Test. Additional exam requirements/recommendations for international students: Required—TOEFL (minimum score 550 paper-based; 79 iBT). *Application deadline:* For fall admission, 5/1 priority date for domestic and international students; for spring admission, 10/1 priority date for domestic students, 9/1 priority date for international students; for summer admission, 3/1 priority date for domestic students, 2/1 priority date for international students. Applications are processed on a rolling basis. Application fee: $50. Electronic applications accepted. *Expenses:* Tuition, state resident: full-time $4362; part-time $273.48 per credit hour. Tuition, nonresident: full-time $12,390; part-time $534.10 per credit hour. *Required fees:* $2782; $178.26 per credit hour. *Financial support:* Career-related internships or fieldwork, Federal Work-Study, institutionally sponsored loans, and tuition waivers available. Financial award application deadline: 4/1; financial award applicants required to submit FAFSA. *Faculty research:* Social theory, political and military sociology, sociology of religion and education, media studies, African-American status attainment. *Unit head:* Dr. Walle Engedayehu, Division Head, 936-261-3202, Fax: 936-261-3229, E-mail: waengedayehu@pvamu.edu. *Application contact:* Pauline Walker, Administrative Assistant II, Research and Graduate Studies, 936-261-3521, Fax: 936-261-3529, E-mail: gradadmissions@pvamu.edu. Website: http://www.pvamu.edu/swbps/

**Princeton University,** Graduate School, Department of Sociology, Princeton, NJ 08544-1019. Offers sociology (PhD); sociology and demography (PhD). *Degree requirements:* For doctorate, variable foreign language requirement, thesis/dissertation. *Entrance requirements:* For doctorate, GRE General Test, GRE Subject Test (recommended), sample of written work. Additional exam requirements/recommendations for international students: Required—TOEFL (minimum score 600 paper-based). Electronic applications accepted.

**Princeton University,** Graduate School, Program in Population Studies, Princeton, NJ 08544-1019. Offers demography (PhD, Certificate); economics and demography (PhD); public affairs and demography (PhD); sociology and demography (PhD). *Degree requirements:* For doctorate, thesis/dissertation. *Entrance requirements:* For doctorate, GRE General Test. Additional exam requirements/recommendations for international students: Required—TOEFL (minimum score 600 paper-based). Electronic applications accepted. *Faculty research:* Models, fertility, infant and child mortality, migration.

**Purdue University,** Graduate School, College of Liberal Arts, Department of Sociology, West Lafayette, IN 47907. Offers MS, PhD. *Faculty:* 25 full-time (9 women), 1 part-time/adjunct (0 women). *Students:* 27 full-time (15 women), 5 part-time (1 woman); includes 3 minority (1 Black or African American, non-Hispanic/Latino; 1 Hispanic/Latino; 1 Two or more races, non-Hispanic/Latino), 8 international. Average age 29. 36 applicants, 39% accepted, 10 enrolled. In 2016, 2 master's, 6 doctorates awarded. *Degree requirements:* For master's, thesis; for doctorate, comprehensive exam, thesis/dissertation. *Entrance requirements:* For master's, GRE General Test, minimum undergraduate GPA of 3.0 or equivalent; for doctorate, GRE General Test, minimum undergraduate GPA of 3.0 or equivalent; master's degree in sociology with minimum GPA of 3.25 or equivalent. Additional exam requirements/recommendations for international students: Required—TOEFL (minimum score 78 iBT). *Application deadline:* For fall admission, 12/15 for domestic and international students. Application fee: $60 ($75 for international students). *Unit head:* Daniel V.A. Olson, Head, 765-496-3141, E-mail: dolson@purdue.edu. *Application contact:* Nicole A. Remley, Graduate Contact, 765-494-4673, E-mail: ncavanau@purdue.edu. Website: http://www.cla.purdue.edu/sociology/

**Queens College of the City University of New York,** Division of Social Sciences, Department of Sociology, Queens, NY 11367-1597. Offers data analytics and applied social research (MA); sociology (MA). *Program availability:* Part-time, evening/weekend. *Faculty:* 30 full-time (15 women), 40 part-time/adjunct (22 women). *Students:* 7 full-time (4 women), 27 part-time (15 women); includes 17 minority (1 Black or African American, non-Hispanic/Latino; 6 Asian, non-Hispanic/Latino; 10 Hispanic/Latino), 4 international. Average age 27. 40 applicants, 75% accepted, 16 enrolled. In 2016, 11 master's awarded. *Degree requirements:* For master's, thesis optional. *Entrance requirements:* For master's, minimum GPA of 3.0. Additional exam requirements/recommendations for international students: Required—TOEFL (minimum score 100 iBT), IELTS (minimum score 7). *Application deadline:* For fall admission, 5/15 for domestic students; for spring admission, 12/1 for domestic students. Applications are processed on a rolling basis. Application fee: $125. Electronic applications accepted. *Expenses:* Tuition, state resident: full-time $5065; part-time $425 per credit. Tuition, nonresident: part-time $780 per credit. *Required fees:* $522; $397 per credit. Part-time tuition and fees vary according to course load and program. *Financial support:* Career-related internships or fieldwork and unspecified assistantships available. Financial award application deadline: 4/1; financial award applicants required to submit FAFSA. *Unit head:* Dr. Andrew Beveridge, Chairperson, 718-997-2800, E-mail: andrew.beveridge@qc.cuny.edu.

**Queen's University at Kingston,** School of Graduate Studies, Faculty of Arts and Sciences, Department of Sociology, Kingston, ON K7L 3N6, Canada. Offers communication and Information technology (MA, PhD); feminist sociology (MA, PhD); socio-legal studies (MA, PhD); sociological theory (MA, PhD). *Program availability:* Part-time. *Degree requirements:* For master's, thesis; for doctorate, comprehensive exam, thesis/dissertation. *Entrance requirements:* For master's, honors bachelors degree in sociology; for doctorate, honors bachelors degree, masters degree in sociology. Additional exam requirements/recommendations for international students: Required—TOEFL. *Faculty research:* Social change and modernization, social control, deviance and criminology, surveillance.

**Rice University,** Graduate Programs, School of Social Sciences, Department of Sociology, Houston, TX 77251-1892. Offers PhD.

**Roosevelt University,** Graduate Division, College of Arts and Sciences, Department of Sociology and Anthropology, Chicago, IL 60605. Offers anthropology (MA); sociology (MA). *Program availability:* Part-time, evening/weekend. *Degree requirements:* For master's, comprehensive exam, thesis. *Faculty research:* Social theory, urban sociology, gerontology, social organizations.

**Rutgers University–New Brunswick,** Graduate School-New Brunswick, Program in Sociology, Piscataway, NJ 08854-8097. Offers MA, PhD. Terminal master's awarded for partial completion of doctoral program. *Degree requirements:* For master's, qualifying paper; for doctorate, thesis/dissertation, qualifying exam, qualifying papers. *Entrance requirements:* For master's, GRE General Test; for doctorate, GRE General Test, sample of written work. Additional exam requirements/recommendations for international students: Required—TOEFL. Electronic applications accepted. *Faculty research:* Comparative-historical, sex and gender, organizations and work, culture and cognition, economics, occupations/professions, religion.

**St. John's University,** St. John's College of Liberal Arts and Sciences, Department of Sociology and Anthropology, Queens, NY 11439. Offers criminology and justice (MA); sociology (MA). *Program availability:* Part-time, evening/weekend. *Degree*

*Sociology*

*requirements:* For master's, comprehensive exam, thesis optional. *Entrance requirements:* For master's, 18 undergraduate credits in social sciences, minimum GPA of 3.0, bachelor's degree. Additional exam requirements/recommendations for international students: Required—TOEFL (minimum score 600 paper-based; 100 iBT), IELTS (minimum score 7). Electronic applications accepted. *Faculty research:* Community studies and gentrification, global financial crisis, insurance fraud, globalization, immigration and human rights.

**Sam Houston State University,** College of Humanities and Social Sciences, Department of Sociology, Huntsville, TX 77341. Offers MA. *Program availability:* Part-time, evening/weekend, online learning. *Degree requirements:* For master's, comprehensive exam, thesis optional, professional paper. *Entrance requirements:* For master's, GRE General Test, minimum GPA of 3.0, letter of intent, letters of recommendation. Additional exam requirements/recommendations for international students: Required—TOEFL (minimum score 550 paper-based; 79 iBT), IELTS (minimum score 6.5). Electronic applications accepted.

**San Diego State University,** Graduate and Research Affairs, College of Arts and Letters, Department of Sociology, San Diego, CA 92182. Offers MA. *Degree requirements:* For master's, thesis. *Entrance requirements:* For master's, GRE General Test, 3 letters of recommendation, writing sample. Additional exam requirements/recommendations for international students: Required—TOEFL. Electronic applications accepted. *Faculty research:* The homeless and mentally ill, medical data relating to the homeless.

**San Jose State University,** Graduate Studies and Research, College of Social Sciences, San Jose, CA 95192-0001. Offers applications of technology in planning (Certificate); applied anthropology (MA); communication studies (MS); community design and development (Certificate); economics (MA), including applied economics, social sciences; environmental planning (Certificate); geographic information science (Certificate); geography (MA); global citizenship (Certificate); history (MA), including history education, social sciences; Mexican American studies (MA); psychology (MA, MS), including clinical psychology (MS), industrial/organizational psychology (MS), research and experimental psychology (MA); public administration (MA); real estate development (Certificate); social sciences (MPA, MS); sociology (MA); transportation and land use planning (Certificate). *Program availability:* Part-time, evening/weekend. *Entrance requirements:* For master's, minimum GPA of 3.0. Electronic applications accepted.

**Shippensburg University of Pennsylvania,** School of Graduate Studies, College of Arts and Sciences, Department of Sociology and Anthropology, Shippensburg, PA 17257-2299. Offers organizational development and leadership (MS), including business, higher education structure and policy, historical administration, leadership in society, management information systems, public organizations. *Program availability:* Part-time, evening/weekend. *Faculty:* 4 full-time (3 women). *Students:* 11 full-time (6 women), 29 part-time (18 women); includes 9 minority (7 Black or African American, non-Hispanic/Latino; 1 Hispanic/Latino; 1 Two or more races, non-Hispanic/Latino). Average age 29. 58 applicants, 67% accepted, 21 enrolled. In 2016, 24 master's awarded. *Degree requirements:* For master's, capstone experience including internship. *Entrance requirements:* For master's, interview (if GPA less than 2.75), current resume, personal goals statement. Additional exam requirements/recommendations for international students: Required—TOEFL (minimum score 550 paper-based, 68 iBT) or IELTS (minimum score 6). *Application deadline:* For fall admission, 4/30 for international students; for spring admission, 9/30 for international students. Applications are processed on a rolling basis. Application fee: $45. Electronic applications accepted. *Expenses:* Tuition, state resident: part-time $483 per credit. Tuition, nonresident: part-time $725 per credit. *Required fees:* $141 per credit. *Financial support:* In 2016–17, 9 students received support. Career-related internships or fieldwork, scholarships/grants, unspecified assistantships, and resident hall director and student payroll positions available. Support available to part-time students. Financial award application deadline: 3/1; financial award applicants required to submit FAFSA. *Unit head:* Dr. Barbara J. Denison, Departmental Chair and Program Coordinator, 717-477-1735, Fax: 717-477-4011, E-mail: bjdeni@ship.edu. *Application contact:* Megan N. Luft, Assistant Dean of Graduate Admissions, 717-477-1231, Fax: 717-477-4016, E-mail: mnluft@ship.edu. Website: http://www.ship.edu/odl/

**Simon Fraser University,** Office of Graduate Studies and Postdoctoral Fellows, Faculty of Arts and Social Sciences, Department of Sociology and Anthropology, Burnaby, BC V5A 1S6, Canada. Offers anthropology (MA, PhD); sociology (MA, PhD). *Faculty:* 21 full-time (17 women). *Students:* 50 full-time (35 women). 48 applicants, 50% accepted, 18 enrolled. In 2016, 2 master's, 2 doctorates awarded. *Degree requirements:* For master's, thesis; for doctorate, comprehensive exam, thesis/dissertation, cooperative education. *Entrance requirements:* For master's, minimum GPA of 3.0 (on scale of 4.33) or 3.33 based on last 60 credits of undergraduate courses; for doctorate, minimum GPA of 3.5 (on scale of 4.33). Additional exam requirements/recommendations for international students: Recommended—TOEFL (minimum score 580 paper-based; 93 iBT), IELTS (minimum score 7), TWE (minimum score 5). *Application deadline:* For fall admission, 12/15 for domestic and international students; for winter admission, 2/1 for domestic students. Application fee: $90 ($125 for international students). Electronic applications accepted. *Financial support:* In 2016–17, 29 students received support, including 11 fellowships (averaging $5,909 per year), teaching assistantships (averaging $5,608 per year); research assistantships, career-related internships or fieldwork, and scholarships/grants also available. Financial award application deadline: 3/15. *Faculty research:* Globalization and development, health, environment and science, knowledge, culture and power, social justice, policy, law and society, women, gender and sexuality. *Unit head:* Dr. Dara Culhane, Graduate Chair, 778-782-4469, Fax: 778-782-5799, E-mail: sa-grad-chair@sfu.ca. *Application contact:* Chantelle Ryerson, Graduate Secretary, 778-782-3518, Fax: 778-782-5799, E-mail: gradsecsa@sfu.ca. Website: http://www.sfu.ca/sociology-anthropology.html

**South Dakota State University,** Graduate School, College of Agriculture and Biological Sciences, Department of Sociology and Rural Studies, Brookings, SD 57007. Offers sociology (MS, PhD). *Program availability:* Part-time, online learning. *Degree requirements:* For master's, comprehensive exam (for some programs), thesis, oral and written exams; for doctorate, comprehensive exam, thesis/dissertation, preliminary oral and written exams. *Entrance requirements:* Additional exam requirements/recommendations for international students: Required—TOEFL (minimum score 550 paper-based; 79 iBT). *Faculty research:* Demography, rural families, rural development, Native Americans, rural poverty, sociology of agriculture.

**Southeastern Louisiana University,** College of Arts, Humanities and Social Sciences, Department of Sociology and Criminal Justice, Hammond, LA 70402. Offers applied sociology (MS). *Program availability:* Part-time, evening/weekend. *Faculty:* 3 full-time (2 women), 1 (woman) part-time/adjunct. *Students:* 12 full-time (9 women), 10 part-time (4 women); includes 6 minority (3 Black or African American, non-Hispanic/Latino; 1 Asian, non-Hispanic/Latino; 2 Two or more races, non-Hispanic/Latino), 1 international. Average age 28. 11 applicants, 73% accepted, 8 enrolled. In 2016, 8 master's awarded. *Degree requirements:* For master's, comprehensive exam, thesis (for some programs), internship research (for those who select an internship track). *Entrance requirements:* For master's, GRE General Test (verbal and quantitative). Additional exam

requirements/recommendations for international students: Required—TOEFL (minimum score 500 paper-based; 61 iBT). *Application deadline:* For fall admission, 7/15 priority date for domestic students, 6/1 priority date for international students; for spring admission, 12/1 priority date for domestic students, 10/1 priority date for international students. Applications are processed on a rolling basis. Application fee: $20 ($30 for international students). Electronic applications accepted. *Expenses:* Tuition, state resident: full-time $6540; part-time $465 per credit hour. Tuition, nonresident: full-time $19,017; part-time $1158 per credit hour. *Required fees:* $1829. *Financial support:* In 2016–17, 3 students received support, including 3 research assistantships (averaging $10,100 per year); career-related internships or fieldwork, Federal Work-Study, institutionally sponsored loans, scholarships/grants, and unspecified assistantships also available. Support available to part-time students. Financial award application deadline: 5/1; financial award applicants required to submit FAFSA. *Faculty research:* Criminology, environmental sociology, globalization, sociology of disasters, sociology of religion. *Unit head:* Dr. Kenneth Bolton, Department Head, 985-549-2110, Fax: 985-549-5961, E-mail: kbolton@southeastern.edu. *Application contact:* Amanda Harper, Graduate Admissions Analyst, 985-549-5620, Fax: 985-549-5632, E-mail: admissions@southeastern.edu. Website: http://www.southeastern.edu/acad_research/depts/soc_cj/grad_degree/index.html

**Southern Connecticut State University,** School of Graduate Studies, School of Arts and Sciences, Department of Sociology, New Haven, CT 06515-1355. Offers MS. *Program availability:* Part-time, evening/weekend. *Faculty:* 4 full-time (1 woman). *Students:* 5 full-time (4 women), 7 part-time (6 women); includes 5 minority (3 Black or African American, non-Hispanic/Latino; 2 Hispanic/Latino). Average age 27. 19 applicants, 32% accepted, 3 enrolled. In 2016, 6 master's awarded. *Degree requirements:* For master's, thesis or alternative. *Entrance requirements:* For master's, interview. *Application deadline:* For fall admission, 7/15 priority date for domestic students. Applications are processed on a rolling basis. Application fee: $50. Electronic applications accepted. *Expenses:* Tuition, state resident: full-time $6497; part-time $519 per credit hour. Tuition, nonresident: full-time $18,102; part-time $535 per credit hour. *Required fees:* $4722; $55 per semester. Tuition and fees vary according to program. *Financial support:* Career-related internships or fieldwork, scholarships/grants, and unspecified assistantships available. Financial award application deadline: 4/15; financial award applicants required to submit FAFSA. *Unit head:* Dr. Gregory Adams, Chairperson, 203-392-5641, Fax: 203-392-5670, E-mail: adamsg1@southernct.edu. *Application contact:* Lisa Galvin, Director of Graduate Admissions, 203-392-5240, Fax: 203-392-5235, E-mail: galvinl1@southernct.edu.

**Southern Illinois University Carbondale,** Graduate School, College of Liberal Arts, Department of Sociology, Carbondale, IL 62901-4701. Offers MA, PhD. *Program availability:* Part-time. *Degree requirements:* For master's, thesis; for doctorate, thesis/dissertation. *Entrance requirements:* For master's, GRE, minimum GPA of 2.7; for doctorate, GRE, minimum GPA of 3.25. Additional exam requirements/recommendations for international students: Required—TOEFL. *Faculty research:* Deviance, family, social stratification, social change, theory methodology, culture.

**Southern Illinois University Edwardsville,** Graduate School, College of Arts and Sciences, Department of Sociology and Criminal Justice Studies, Edwardsville, IL 62026. Offers sociology (MA). *Program availability:* Part-time. *Degree requirements:* For master's, thesis (for some programs), internship. *Entrance requirements:* Additional exam requirements/recommendations for international students: Required—TOEFL (minimum score 550 paper-based; 79 iBT), IELTS (minimum score 6.5). Electronic applications accepted.

**Stanford University,** School of Humanities and Sciences, Department of Sociology, Stanford, CA 94305-2004. Offers PhD. *Degree requirements:* For doctorate, thesis/dissertation, oral exam. *Entrance requirements:* For doctorate, GRE General Test. Additional exam requirements/recommendations for international students: Required—TOEFL. Electronic applications accepted. *Expenses: Tuition:* Full-time $47,331. *Required fees:* $609.

**Stony Brook University, State University of New York,** Graduate School, College of Arts and Sciences, Department of Sociology, Stony Brook, NY 11794. Offers MA, PhD. *Faculty:* 19 full-time (9 women), 2 part-time/adjunct (both women). *Students:* 49 full-time (29 women), 1 (woman) part-time; includes 13 minority (1 Black or African American, non-Hispanic/Latino; 5 Asian, non-Hispanic/Latino; 3 Hispanic/Latino; 4 Two or more races, non-Hispanic/Latino), 14 international. Average age 31. 56 applicants, 32% accepted, 9 enrolled. In 2016, 3 master's, 8 doctorates awarded. *Degree requirements:* For doctorate, thesis/dissertation, comprehensive exam or professional papers, field exam, teaching practicum. *Entrance requirements:* For doctorate, GRE General Test, minimum GPA of 3.0. Additional exam requirements/recommendations for international students: Required—TOEFL (minimum score 90 iBT). *Application deadline:* For fall admission, 1/15 for domestic students; for spring admission, 10/1 for domestic students. Application fee: $100. *Expenses:* Contact institution. *Financial support:* In 2016–17, 1 fellowship, 27 teaching assistantships were awarded; research assistantships also available. *Faculty research:* Adolescents, disability studies, globalization, sociology, sociology of sex and gender. *Total annual research expenditures:* $63,570. *Unit head:* Dr. Daniel Levy, Chair, 631-632-7755, E-mail: daniel.levy@stonybrook.edu. *Application contact:* Wanda Vega, Coordinator, 631-632-7730, Fax: 631-632-8203, E-mail: wanda.olivera@stonybrook.edu. Website: http://www.sunysb.edu/sociology/

**Syracuse University,** Maxwell School of Citizenship and Public Affairs, Programs in Sociology, Syracuse, NY 13244. Offers MA, PhD. *Degree requirements:* For master's, thesis; for doctorate, comprehensive exam, thesis/dissertation. *Entrance requirements:* For master's and doctorate, GRE General Test, three letters of recommendation, resume, personal statement, official transcripts. Additional exam requirements/recommendations for international students: Required—TOEFL (minimum score 100 iBT). *Application deadline:* For fall admission, 1/10 priority date for domestic and international students. Application fee: $75. Electronic applications accepted. *Expenses: Tuition:* Full-time $25,974; part-time $1443 per credit hour. *Required fees:* $802; $50 per course. Tuition and fees vary according to course load and program. *Financial support:* Fellowships with full tuition reimbursements, research assistantships with tuition reimbursements, teaching assistantships with tuition reimbursements, tuition waivers, and unspecified assistantships available. Financial award application deadline: 1/1. *Faculty research:* Qualitative methods and feminist methods, inequality studies, aging and the life course, sociological theory. *Unit head:* Dr. Madonna Harrington Meyer, Professor and Chair, Sociology, 315-443-6755, E-mail: mhm@maxwell.syr.edu. *Application contact:* Janet Coria, Recruiting Contact, 315-443-2347, E-mail: jmcoria@syr.edu. Website: http://www.maxwell.syr.edu/soc/

**Teachers College, Columbia University,** Department of Education Policy and Social Analysis, New York, NY 10027. Offers economics and education (Ed M, MA, PhD); education policy (Ed M, MA, Ed D, PhD); politics and education (Ed M, MA, Ed D, PhD); sociology and education (Ed M, MA, Ed D, PhD). *Students:* 148 full-time (110 women), 107 part-time (85 women); includes 95 minority (40 Black or African American, non-Hispanic/Latino; 23 Asian, non-Hispanic/Latino; 26 Hispanic/Latino; 6 Two or more

races, non-Hispanic/Latino), 74 international. 516 applicants, 54% accepted, 98 enrolled. *Expenses: Tuition:* Full-time $36,288; part-time $1512 per credit. *Required fees:* $438 per semester. One-time fee: $510 full-time. Full-time tuition and fees vary according to course load. *Unit head:* Dr. Jeffrey Henig, Chair, 212-678-8313, Fax: 212-678-3589, E-mail: henig@tc.columbia.edu. *Application contact:* David Estrella, Director of Admissions, 212-678-3305, E-mail: estrella@tc.columbia.edu.
Website: http://www.tc.columbia.edu/education-policy-and-social-analysis/

**Temple University,** College of Liberal Arts, Department of Sociology, Philadelphia, PA 19122-6096. Offers MA, PhD. *Program availability:* Part-time, evening/weekend. Terminal master's awarded for partial completion of doctoral program. *Degree requirements:* For doctorate, thesis/dissertation. *Entrance requirements:* For master's and doctorate, GRE General Test, minimum GPA of 3.0, 3 letters of recommendation. Additional exam requirements/recommendations for international students: Required—TOEFL (minimum score 600 paper-based; 100 iBT). Electronic applications accepted. *Faculty research:* Urban sociology, gender and sexuality, race and ethnicity, globalization, medical sociology.

**Texas A&M University,** College of Liberal Arts, Department of Sociology, College Station, TX 77843. Offers sociology (MS, PhD). *Faculty:* 28. *Students:* 66 full-time (44 women), 13 part-time (9 women); includes 40 minority (14 Black or African American, non-Hispanic/Latino; 1 American Indian or Alaska Native, non-Hispanic/Latino; 1 Asian, non-Hispanic/Latino; 24 Hispanic/Latino), 12 international. Average age 32. 46 applicants, 78% accepted, 12 enrolled. In 2016, 4 master's, 9 doctorates awarded. *Degree requirements:* For master's, thesis or alternative; for doctorate, thesis/dissertation. *Entrance requirements:* For master's and doctorate, GRE General Test. Additional exam requirements/recommendations for international students: Required—TOEFL (minimum score 550 paper-based; 80 iBT), IELTS (minimum score 6), PTE. *Application deadline:* For fall admission, 12/15 for domestic students. Applications are processed on a rolling basis. Application fee: $50 ($90 for international students). Electronic applications accepted. *Expenses:* Contact institution. *Financial support:* In 2016–17, 69 students received support, including 6 fellowships with tuition reimbursements available (averaging $17,293 per year), 14 research assistantships with tuition reimbursements available (averaging $5,691 per year), 48 teaching assistantships with tuition reimbursements available (averaging $9,786 per year); career-related internships or fieldwork, institutionally sponsored loans, scholarships/grants, traineeships, health care benefits, tuition waivers (full and partial), and unspecified assistantships also available. Support available to part-time students. Financial award application deadline: 3/15; financial award applicants required to submit FAFSA. *Faculty research:* Crime, deviance, and law; culture; demography and human ecology; political and economic sociology; racial and ethnic relations; social psychology; Latino sociology; gender; Asian studies. *Unit head:* Dr. Jane Sell, Department Head, 979-845-6120, Fax: 979-862-4057, E-mail: j-sell@tamu.edu. *Application contact:* Dr. Wendy Leo Moore, Graduate Advisor, 979-845-5133, Fax: 979-862-4057, E-mail: wlmoore@tamu.edu.
Website: http://sociology.tamu.edu/

**Texas A&M University–Commerce,** College of Humanities, Social Sciences and Arts, Commerce, TX 75429-3011. Offers applied criminology (MS); applied linguistics (MA, MS); art (MA, MFA); Christianity in history (Graduate Certificate); computational linguistics (Graduate Certificate); creative writing (Graduate Certificate); English (MA, MS, PhD); film studies (Graduate Certificate); history (MA, MS); music (MM); political science (MA, MS); public history (Graduate Certificate); sociology (MS); Spanish (MA); studies in children's and adolescent literature and culture (Graduate Certificate); teaching English to speakers of other languages (Graduate Certificate); theater (MA, MS). *Program availability:* Part-time. *Faculty:* 53 full-time (26 women), 7 part-time/adjunct (2 women). *Students:* 87 full-time (55 women), 528 part-time (362 women); includes 198 minority (86 Black or African American, non-Hispanic/Latino; 2 American Indian or Alaska Native, non-Hispanic/Latino; 8 Asian, non-Hispanic/Latino; 84 Hispanic/Latino; 18 Two or more races, non-Hispanic/Latino), 27 international. Average age 37. 333 applicants, 56% accepted, 149 enrolled. In 2016, 66 master's, 8 doctorates awarded. *Degree requirements:* For master's, one foreign language, comprehensive exam, thesis (for some programs); for doctorate, one foreign language, comprehensive exam, thesis/dissertation, departmental qualifying exam. *Entrance requirements:* For master's and doctorate, GRE General Test. Additional exam requirements/recommendations for international students: Required—TOEFL (minimum score 550 paper-based; 79 iBT), IELTS (minimum score 6). *Application deadline:* Applications are processed on a rolling basis. Application fee: $50. Electronic applications accepted. *Expenses:* Contact institution. *Financial support:* In 2016–17, 255 students received support, including 9 research assistantships with partial tuition reimbursements available (averaging $9,000 per year), 68 teaching assistantships with partial tuition reimbursements available (averaging $9,000 per year); Federal Work-Study, institutionally sponsored loans, scholarships/grants, health care benefits, and unspecified assistantships also available. Financial award application deadline: 5/1; financial award applicants required to submit FAFSA. *Unit head:* Dr. Salvatore Attardo, Dean, 903-886-5166, Fax: 903-886-5774, E-mail: salvatore.attardo@tamuc.edu. *Application contact:* Shelby Miller, Graduate Recruiter, 903-468-8123, Fax: 903-886-5774, E-mail: shelby.miller@tamuc.edu.
Website: http://www.tamuc.edu/academics/graduateSchool/programs/humanitiesSocialScienceArts/default.aspx

**Texas A&M University–Kingsville,** College of Graduate Studies, College of Arts and Sciences, Department of Psychology and Sociology, Program in Sociology, Kingsville, TX 78363. Offers MA, MS. *Entrance requirements:* Additional exam requirements/recommendations for international students: Required—TOEFL (minimum score 550 paper-based; 79 iBT); Recommended—IELTS. Electronic applications accepted.

**Texas Southern University,** College of Liberal Arts and Behavioral Sciences, Department of Sociology, Houston, TX 77004-4584. Offers MA. *Program availability:* Part-time, evening/weekend. *Degree requirements:* For master's, comprehensive exam, thesis. *Entrance requirements:* For master's, GRE General Test, minimum GPA of 2.5. Additional exam requirements/recommendations for international students: Required—TOEFL. Electronic applications accepted. *Faculty research:* Sociocultural systems, ethnic and regional studies, community sociology.

**Texas State University,** The Graduate College, College of Liberal Arts, Program in Applied Sociology, San Marcos, TX 78666. Offers MS. *Program availability:* Part-time, evening/weekend. *Faculty:* 13 full-time (5 women), 2 part-time/adjunct (0 women). *Students:* 4 full-time, 6 part-time (5 women); includes 4 minority (2 Black or African American, non-Hispanic/Latino; 1 Asian, non-Hispanic/Latino; 1 Hispanic/Latino). Average age 32. 10 applicants, 50% accepted, 3 enrolled. In 2016, 5 master's awarded. *Degree requirements:* For master's, comprehensive exam. *Entrance requirements:* For master's, baccalaureate degree from regionally-accredited university with minimum GPA of 3.0 on last 60 undergraduate semester hours. Additional exam requirements/recommendations for international students: Required—TOEFL (minimum score 550 paper-based; 78 iBT), IELTS (minimum score 6.5). *Application deadline:* For fall admission, 3/1 priority date for domestic and international students; for spring admission, 10/15 priority date for domestic students, 10/1 for international students; for summer admission, 4/15 for domestic students, 3/15 for international students.

Applications are processed on a rolling basis. Application fee: $40 ($90 for international students). Electronic applications accepted. *Expenses:* $4,851 per semester. *Financial support:* In 2016–17, 9 students received support, including 1 teaching assistantship (averaging $13,849 per year); research assistantships, Federal Work-Study, institutionally sponsored loans, scholarships/grants, health care benefits, and unspecified assistantships also available. Support available to part-time students. Financial award application deadline: 3/1; financial award applicants required to submit FAFSA. *Faculty research:* Evaluation of Harris County Protective Services' integrated behavioral health. *Total annual research expenditures:* $8,169. *Unit head:* Dr. Patti Giuffre, Graduate Advisor, 512-245-8983, E-mail: pg07@txstate.edu. *Application contact:* Dr. Andrea Golato, Dean of Graduate School, 512-245-2581, Fax: 512-245-8365, E-mail: gradcollege@txstate.edu.
Website: http://www.soci.txstate.edu

**Texas State University,** The Graduate College, College of Liberal Arts, Program in Sociology, San Marcos, TX 78666. Offers MA. *Program availability:* Part-time, evening/weekend. *Faculty:* 13 full-time (5 women), 2 part-time/adjunct (0 women). *Students:* 19 full-time (16 women), 11 part-time (8 women); includes 18 minority (4 Black or African American, non-Hispanic/Latino; 11 Hispanic/Latino; 3 Two or more races, non-Hispanic/Latino), 1 international. Average age 28. 16 applicants, 50% accepted, 3 enrolled. In 2016, 19 master's awarded. *Degree requirements:* For master's, comprehensive exam, thesis optional. *Entrance requirements:* For master's, baccalaureate degree from regionally-accredited university with minimum GPA of 3.0 on last 60 undergraduate semester hours. Additional exam requirements/recommendations for international students: Required—TOEFL (minimum score 550 paper-based; 78 iBT), IELTS (minimum score 6.5). *Application deadline:* For fall admission, 3/1 priority date for domestic and international students; for spring admission, 10/15 for domestic students, 10/1 for international students; for summer admission, 4/15 for domestic students, 3/15 for international students. Applications are processed on a rolling basis. Application fee: $40 ($90 for international students). Electronic applications accepted. *Expenses:* $4,851 per semester. *Financial support:* In 2016–17, 23 students received support, including 1 research assistantship (averaging $13,509 per year), 12 teaching assistantships (averaging $13,774 per year); Federal Work-Study, institutionally sponsored loans, scholarships/grants, health care benefits, and unspecified assistantships also available. Support available to part-time students. Financial award application deadline: 3/1; financial award applicants required to submit FAFSA. *Unit head:* Dr. Patti Giuffre, Graduate Advisor, 512-245-8983, Fax: 512-245-2174, E-mail: pg07@txstate.edu. *Application contact:* Dr. Andrea Golato, Dean of Graduate School, 512-245-2581, Fax: 512-245-8365, E-mail: gradcollege@txstate.edu.
Website: http://www.soci.txstate.edu/Graduate-Degree/MASoc

**Texas Tech University,** Graduate School, College of Arts and Sciences, Department of Sociology, Anthropology and Social Work, Lubbock, TX 79409. Offers anthropology (MA); social work (MSW); sociology (MA). *Program availability:* Part-time. *Faculty:* 28 full-time (16 women), 8 part-time/adjunct (4 women). *Students:* 49 full-time (38 women), 11 part-time (6 women); includes 20 minority (4 Black or African American, non-Hispanic/Latino; 14 Hispanic/Latino; 2 Two or more races, non-Hispanic/Latino), 5 international. Average age 27. 63 applicants, 52% accepted, 24 enrolled. In 2016, 19 master's awarded. *Degree requirements:* For master's, one foreign language, comprehensive exam (for some programs), thesis (for some programs). *Entrance requirements:* For master's, GRE (or MA in anthropology), two letters of recommendation, statement of purpose, writing sample, curriculum vitae; minimum GPA of 3.0 and coursework in sociology or closely-related fields (for MA in sociology); coursework in anthropology (for MA in anthropology). Additional exam requirements/recommendations for international students: Required—TOEFL (minimum score 550 paper-based; 79 iBT). *Application deadline:* For fall admission, 6/1 priority date for domestic students, 1/15 priority date for international students; for spring admission, 9/1 priority date for domestic students, 6/15 priority date for international students. Applications are processed on a rolling basis. Application fee: $75. Electronic applications accepted. *Expenses:* $300 per credit hour full-time resident tuition; $708 per credit hour full-time non-resident tuition; $50.50 per credit hour fee plus $608 per term fee. *Financial support:* In 2016–17, 53 students received support, including 42 fellowships (averaging $4,678 per year), 33 teaching assistantships (averaging $12,439 per year); research assistantships, Federal Work-Study, scholarships/grants, tuition waivers (partial), and unspecified assistantships also available. Financial award application deadline: 2/1; financial award applicants required to submit FAFSA. *Faculty research:* Sociology of criminology/deviance, population/migration, forensic anthropology, archaeology, social work (advanced generalist). *Total annual research expenditures:* $122,652. *Unit head:* Dr. Brett A. Houk, Chair and Associate Professor, 806-834-8107, Fax: 806-742-1088, E-mail: brett.houk@ttu.edu. *Application contact:* Dr. Cristina Bradatan, Associate Professor/Sociology Graduate Program Director, 806-834-1796, E-mail: cristina.bradatan@ttu.edu.
Website: http://www.depts.ttu.edu/sasw/

**Texas Woman's University,** Graduate School, College of Arts and Sciences, Department of Sociology and Social Work, Denton, TX 76201. Offers sociology (MA, PhD). *Program availability:* Evening/weekend. *Students:* 3 full-time (2 women), 50 part-time (34 women); includes 20 minority (12 Black or African American, non-Hispanic/Latino; 1 Asian, non-Hispanic/Latino; 7 Hispanic/Latino), 2 international. Average age 38. In 2016, 7 master's, 6 doctorates awarded. Terminal master's awarded for partial completion of doctoral program. *Degree requirements:* For master's, comprehensive exam, thesis (for some programs); for doctorate, comprehensive exam, thesis/dissertation. *Entrance requirements:* For master's, 2 letters of reference, 2-3 page statement of interest; for doctorate, GRE General Test, minimum GPA of 3.5 on last 60 undergraduate hours and all graduate coursework, graduate statistics and social sciences research methods, 3 letters of reference, 2-3 page statement of interest. Additional exam requirements/recommendations for international students: Required—TOEFL (minimum score 550 paper-based; 79 iBT). *Application deadline:* For fall admission, 6/1 priority date for domestic students, 3/1 for international students; for spring admission, 11/1 priority date for domestic students, 7/1 for international students. Applications are processed on a rolling basis. Application fee: $50 ($75 for international students). Electronic applications accepted. *Expenses: Tuition,* state resident: full-time $9046; part-time $251 per credit hour. *Tuition,* nonresident: full-time $22,922; part-time $614 per credit hour. *International tuition:* $23,046 full-time. *Required fees:* $2690; $1285 per credit hour. One-time fee: $50. Tuition and fees vary according to course level, course load, program and reciprocity agreements. *Financial support:* Research assistantships, teaching assistantships, career-related internships or fieldwork, Federal Work-Study, institutionally sponsored loans, scholarships/grants, traineeships, health care benefits, and unspecified assistantships available. Support available to part-time students. Financial award application deadline: 3/1; financial award applicants required to submit FAFSA. *Faculty research:* Pre-impact evaluation planning for families of law enforcement, disasters, criminology, immigration, sociological theory, race/ethnicity, culture of breast cancer. *Unit head:* Dr. Philip Yang, Professor and Graduate Program Director, 940-898-2054, Fax: 940-898-2067, E-mail: pyang@twu.edu. *Application contact:* Dr. Samuel Wheeler, Assistant Director of Admissions, 940-898-3188, Fax: 940-898-3081, E-mail: wheelersr@twu.edu.
Website: http://www.twu.edu/sociology/

## Sociology

**Tulane University,** School of Liberal Arts, Department of Sociology, New Orleans, LA 70118-5669. Offers MA. Terminal master's awarded for partial completion of doctoral program. *Degree requirements:* For master's, thesis. *Entrance requirements:* For master's, GRE General Test, minimum B average in undergraduate course work. Additional exam requirements/recommendations for international students: Required—TOEFL. Electronic applications accepted. *Expenses: Tuition:* Full-time $50,920; part-time $2829 per credit hour. *Required fees:* $2040; $44.50 per credit hour. $580 per term. Tuition and fees vary according to course load, degree level and program.

**Université de Montréal,** Faculty of Arts and Sciences, Department of Sociology, Montréal, QC H3C 3J7, Canada. Offers M Sc, PhD. *Degree requirements:* For master's, thesis; for doctorate, thesis/dissertation, general exam. *Entrance requirements:* For master's, minimum GPA of 3.0; for doctorate, minimum GPA of 3.5, proficiency in French. Electronic applications accepted. *Faculty research:* Sociological theory, economy, state and social movements, work, social politics and health.

**Université du Québec à Montréal,** Graduate Programs, Program in Social Intervention, Montréal, QC H3C 3P8, Canada. Offers MA. *Program availability:* Part-time. *Degree requirements:* For master's, thesis. *Entrance requirements:* For master's, appropriate bachelor's degree or equivalent, proficiency in French.

**Université du Québec à Montréal,** Graduate Programs, Program in Sociology, Montréal, QC H3C 3P8, Canada. Offers MA, PhD. *Program availability:* Part-time. *Degree requirements:* For master's, thesis optional; for doctorate, thesis/dissertation. *Entrance requirements:* For master's, appropriate bachelor's degree or equivalent, proficiency in French; for doctorate, appropriate master's degree or equivalent, proficiency in French.

**Université Laval,** Faculty of Social Sciences, Department of Sociology, Programs in Sociology, Québec, QC G1K 7P4, Canada. Offers MA, PhD. Terminal master's awarded for partial completion of doctoral program. *Degree requirements:* For master's, thesis; for doctorate, comprehensive exam, thesis/dissertation. *Entrance requirements:* For master's, English exam (comprehension of written English), French exam (for some), knowledge of French; for doctorate, English exam (comprehension of written English), French exam may be required, knowledge of French. Electronic applications accepted.

**University at Albany, State University of New York,** College of Arts and Sciences, Department of Communication, Albany, NY 12222-0001. Offers communication (MA); sociology and communication (PhD). *Program availability:* Part-time. *Faculty:* 15 full-time (6 women), 26 part-time/adjunct (16 women). *Students:* 25 full-time (19 women), 33 part-time (21 women); includes 13 minority (8 Black or African American, non-Hispanic/Latino; 2 Asian, non-Hispanic/Latino; 2 Hispanic/Latino; 1 Two or more races, non-Hispanic/Latino), 12 international. 70 applicants, 56% accepted, 16 enrolled. In 2016, 21 master's awarded. *Degree requirements:* For master's, comprehensive exam, thesis or alternative; for doctorate, comprehensive exam, thesis/dissertation. *Entrance requirements:* For master's, minimum GPA of 3.0; for doctorate, GRE, minimum GPA of 3.0. Additional exam requirements/recommendations for international students: Required—TOEFL (minimum score 550 paper-based). *Application deadline:* For fall admission, 2/20 priority date for domestic students, 5/1 for international students. Applications are processed on a rolling basis. Application fee: $75. Electronic applications accepted. *Expenses:* Tuition, state resident: full-time $10,870; part-time $453 per credit hour. Tuition, nonresident: full-time $22,210; part-time $925 per credit hour. *International tuition:* $21,550 full-time. *Required fees:* $1864; $96 per credit hour. *Financial support:* Fellowships, teaching assistantships, career-related internships or fieldwork, and institutionally sponsored loans available. Financial award application deadline: 3/1. *Faculty research:* Language and social interaction, campaign communication, media agenda-setting, high-speed management, organizational boundary-spanning. *Total annual research expenditures:* $25,868. *Unit head:* Annis Golden, Chair, 518-442-4871, Fax: 518-442-3884, E-mail: agolden@albany.edu. *Application contact:* Michael DeRensis, Director, Graduate Admissions, 518-442-3980, Fax: 518-442-3922, E-mail: graduate@albany.edu.
Website: http://www.albany.edu/communication/

**University at Albany, State University of New York,** College of Arts and Sciences, Department of Sociology, Albany, NY 12222-0001. Offers demography (Certificate); sociology (MA, PhD); urban policy (Certificate). *Faculty:* 8 full-time (6 women). *Students:* 25 full-time (19 women), 63 part-time (46 women); includes 17 minority (4 Black or African American, non-Hispanic/Latino; 1 American Indian or Alaska Native, non-Hispanic/Latino; 5 Asian, non-Hispanic/Latino; 5 Hispanic/Latino; 2 Two or more races, non-Hispanic/Latino), 27 international. 85 applicants, 39% accepted, 11 enrolled. In 2016, 2 master's, 15 doctorates awarded. Terminal master's awarded for partial completion of doctoral program. *Degree requirements:* For master's, thesis; for doctorate, thesis/dissertation, 2 specialization exams, research tool. *Entrance requirements:* For master's and doctorate, GRE General Test. Additional exam requirements/recommendations for international students: Required—TOEFL. *Application deadline:* For fall admission, 1/15 for domestic students, 5/1 for international students. Applications are processed on a rolling basis. Application fee: $75. Electronic applications accepted. *Expenses:* Tuition, state resident: full-time $10,870; part-time $453 per credit hour. Tuition, nonresident: full-time $22,210; part-time $925 per credit hour. *International tuition:* $21,550 full-time. *Required fees:* $1864; $96 per credit hour. *Financial support:* Fellowships, research assistantships, teaching assistantships, career-related internships or fieldwork, and Federal Work-Study available. Financial award application deadline: 3/15. *Faculty research:* Gender and equality, crime and deviance, aging, work and organizations, social demography. *Total annual research expenditures:* $418,522. *Unit head:* Nancy Denton, Chair, 518-442-4666, Fax: 518-442-4936, E-mail: ndenton@albany.edu. *Application contact:* Michael DeRensis, Director, Graduate Admissions, 518-442-3980, Fax: 518-442-3922, E-mail: graduate@albany.edu.
Website: http://www.albany.edu/sociology/index.html

**University at Buffalo, the State University of New York,** Graduate School, College of Arts and Sciences, Department of Sociology, Buffalo, NY 14260. Offers MA, PhD. *Program availability:* Part-time. *Faculty:* 15 full-time (8 women), 4 part-time/adjunct (3 women). *Students:* 53 full-time (28 women), 7 part-time (3 women); includes 23 minority (4 Black or African American, non-Hispanic/Latino; 1 American Indian or Alaska Native, non-Hispanic/Latino; 16 Asian, non-Hispanic/Latino; 1 Hispanic/Latino; 1 Two or more races, non-Hispanic/Latino). Average age 30. 57 applicants, 68% accepted, 12 enrolled. In 2016, 9 master's, 2 doctorates awarded. Terminal master's awarded for partial completion of doctoral program. *Degree requirements:* For master's, project or thesis; for doctorate, thesis/dissertation, qualifying paper. *Entrance requirements:* For master's and doctorate, GRE General Test. Additional exam requirements/recommendations for international students: Required—TOEFL (minimum score 550 paper-based; 79 iBT), IELTS (minimum score 6.5). *Application deadline:* For fall admission, 8/1 priority date for domestic students, 4/1 priority date for international students. Applications are processed on a rolling basis. Application fee: $75. Electronic applications accepted. *Financial support:* In 2016–17, 15 students received support, including 6 fellowships with full tuition reimbursements available (averaging $6,100 per year), 15 teaching assistantships with full tuition reimbursements available (averaging $14,100 per year); scholarships/grants, health care benefits, and tuition waivers (full) also available. Financial award application deadline: 1/15; financial award applicants required to submit

FAFSA. *Faculty research:* Family and the life course, health, law and social policy, social inequalities, work and organizations. *Unit head:* Dr. Debra Street, Chair, 716-645-8475, Fax: 716-645-3934, E-mail: dastreet@buffalo.edu. *Application contact:* Dr. Mary Nell Trautner, Director of Graduate Studies, 716-645-8477, Fax: 716-645-3934, E-mail: trautner@buffalo.edu.

**The University of Akron,** Graduate School, Buchtel College of Arts and Sciences, Department of Sociology, Akron, OH 44325. Offers MA, PhD. PhD offered jointly with Kent State University. *Program availability:* Part-time. *Faculty:* 10 full-time (5 women), 2 part-time/adjunct (both women). *Students:* 23 full-time (13 women), 11 part-time (9 women); includes 10 minority (6 Black or African American, non-Hispanic/Latino; 3 Asian, non-Hispanic/Latino; 1 Hispanic/Latino), 2 international. Average age 32. 28 applicants, 57% accepted, 9 enrolled. In 2016, 1 master's, 4 doctorates awarded. Terminal master's awarded for partial completion of doctoral program. *Degree requirements:* For master's, thesis optional, oral defense of thesis, paper or oral exam; for doctorate, one foreign language, comprehensive exam, thesis/dissertation. *Entrance requirements:* For master's, GRE General Test, minimum GPA of 3.0, three letters of recommendation, writing sample, statement of purpose outlining educational and career objectives; for doctorate, GRE General Test, minimum GPA of 3.5, three letters of recommendation, writing sample, statement of purpose outlining educational and career objectives. Additional exam requirements/recommendations for international students: Required—TOEFL (minimum score 550 paper-based; 79 iBT), IELTS (minimum score 6.5). *Application deadline:* For fall admission, 1/15 priority date for domestic and international students. Application fee: $45 ($70 for international students). Electronic applications accepted. *Expenses:* Tuition, state resident: full-time $8618; part-time $359 per credit hour. Tuition, nonresident: full-time $17,149; part-time $715 per credit hour. *Required fees:* $1652. *Financial support:* In 2016–17, 8 teaching assistantships with full tuition reimbursements were awarded; instructional support assistantships also available. *Faculty research:* Medical sociology, inequality, social psychology, criminology, mental health. *Total annual research expenditures:* $21,113. *Unit head:* Dr. William Lyons, Interim Chair, 330-972-5855, E-mail: wtlyons@uakron.edu. *Application contact:* Dr. John Zipp, Director of Graduate Studies, 330-972-6893, E-mail: jzipp@uakron.edu.
Website: http://www.uakron.edu/sociology/

**The University of Alabama at Birmingham,** College of Arts and Sciences, Program in Medical Sociology, Birmingham, AL 35294. Offers PhD. *Program availability:* Part-time. Terminal master's awarded for partial completion of doctoral program. *Degree requirements:* For doctorate, comprehensive exam, thesis/dissertation, student teaching, manuscript review. *Entrance requirements:* For doctorate, GRE, minimum GPA of 3.0 overall and in all previous graduate coursework, 3.2 on last 60 semester hours of baccalaureate work. Additional exam requirements/recommendations for international students: Required—TOEFL, TWE; Recommended—IELTS. Electronic applications accepted. Full-time tuition and fees vary according to course load and program. *Faculty research:* Health disparities; aging and life course; gender, race, and mental health; family sociology; social psychology.

**University of Alberta,** Faculty of Graduate Studies and Research, Department of Sociology, Edmonton, AB T6G 2E1, Canada. Offers criminal justice (MA); demography (MA, PhD); sociology (MA, PhD). *Program availability:* Part-time. *Degree requirements:* For master's, thesis (for some programs); for doctorate, thesis/dissertation. *Faculty research:* Criminology, knowledge and culture, methods and theory, population studies, stratification.

**The University of Arizona,** College of Social and Behavioral Sciences, Department of Sociology, Tucson, AZ 85721. Offers MA, PhD. *Degree requirements:* For master's, publishable paper/oral; for doctorate, thesis/dissertation, 2 preliminary exams. *Entrance requirements:* For doctorate, GRE General Test, 3 letters of recommendation, writing samples. Additional exam requirements/recommendations for international students: Required—TOEFL (minimum score 630 paper-based). Electronic applications accepted. *Faculty research:* Organizations, social psychology, social movement, stratification, religion.

**University of Arkansas,** Graduate School, J. William Fulbright College of Arts and Sciences, Department of Sociology, Fayetteville, AR 72701. Offers MA. *Program availability:* Part-time. In 2016, 6 master's awarded. *Degree requirements:* For master's, thesis. *Application deadline:* For fall admission, 4/1 for international students; for spring admission, 10/1 for international students. Applications are processed on a rolling basis. Application fee: $40 ($50 for international students). Electronic applications accepted. *Financial support:* In 2016–17, 5 research assistantships, 10 teaching assistantships were awarded; fellowships with tuition reimbursements, career-related internships or fieldwork, and Federal Work-Study also available. Support available to part-time students. Financial award application deadline: 4/1; financial award applicants required to submit FAFSA. *Unit head:* Dr. Anna Zajicek, Department Chairperson, 479-575-3205, Fax: 479-575-7981, E-mail: azajicek@uark.edu. *Application contact:* Shauna Morimoto, 479-575-3205, Fax: 479-575-7981, E-mail: smorimot@uark.edu.
Website: http://sociology.uark.edu/

**The University of British Columbia,** Faculty of Arts, Department of Sociology, Vancouver, BC V6T 1Z1, Canada. Offers MA, PhD. *Degree requirements:* For master's, thesis; for doctorate, comprehensive exam, thesis/dissertation. *Entrance requirements:* For master's, BA in sociology or equivalent with minimum B+ average in upper-level courses; for doctorate, master's degree in sociology or equivalent. Additional exam requirements/recommendations for international students: Required—TOEFL. Application fee: $100 Canadian dollars ($162 Canadian dollars for international students). Electronic applications accepted. *Expenses:* $4,802 per year tuition and fees, $8,436 per year international. *Financial support:* Fellowships, research assistantships, teaching assistantships, Federal Work-Study, institutionally sponsored loans, scholarships/grants, health care benefits, tuition waivers (full and partial), and unspecified assistantships available. *Faculty research:* Social and cultural theories and methods; gender, race, class and sexuality; environment economy and development politics; law and social movements. *Application contact:* May Chan, Graduate Program Staff, 604-822-0503, Fax: 604-822-6161, E-mail: soci.grad@ubc.ca.
Website: http://soci.ubc.ca/

**University of Calgary,** Faculty of Graduate Studies, Faculty of Arts, Department of Sociology, Calgary, AB T2N 1N4, Canada. Offers MA, PhD. Terminal master's awarded for partial completion of doctoral program. *Degree requirements:* For master's, thesis, prospectus; for doctorate, comprehensive exam, thesis/dissertation, oral and written candidacy exams, prospectus, qualifying paper. *Entrance requirements:* For master's, minimum GPA of 3.2; for doctorate, minimum GPA of 3.5. Additional exam requirements/recommendations for international students: Required—TOEFL or IELTS. Electronic applications accepted. *Faculty research:* Deviance, gender, medical, religion, ethnicity.

**University of California, Berkeley,** Graduate Division, College of Letters and Science, Department of Sociology, Berkeley, CA 94720-1500. Offers PhD. *Faculty:* 16 full-time, 9 part-time/adjunct. *Students:* 116 full-time (51 women); includes 50 minority (17 Black or African American, non-Hispanic/Latino; 13 Asian, non-Hispanic/Latino; 20 Hispanic/Latino), 9 international. Average age 31. 338 applicants, 15 enrolled. In 2016, 14

doctorates awarded. *Degree requirements:* For doctorate, thesis/dissertation, qualifying exam. *Entrance requirements:* For doctorate, GRE General Test, minimum GPA of 3.0, sample of academic written work, 3 letters of recommendation. Additional exam requirements/recommendations for international students: Required—TOEFL (minimum score 570 paper-based) or IELTS. *Application deadline:* For fall admission, 12/5 for domestic students. Application fee: $105 ($125 for international students). Electronic applications accepted. *Financial support:* Fellowships with full tuition reimbursements, research assistantships with partial tuition reimbursements, teaching assistantships with partial tuition reimbursements, Federal Work-Study, institutionally sponsored loans, health care benefits, and unspecified assistantships available. Financial award applicants required to submit FAFSA. *Faculty research:* Race, gender, political, stratification theory. *Unit head:* Prof. Mara Loveman, Chair, 510-642-4766, E-mail: sociology@berkeley.edu. *Application contact:* Information Contact, 510-642-1445, E-mail: socgrad_admit@berkeley.edu.
Website: http://sociology.berkeley.edu/

**University of California, Davis,** Graduate Studies, Program in Sociology, Davis, CA 95616. Offers MA, PhD. Terminal master's awarded for partial completion of doctoral program. *Degree requirements:* For master's, written exam; for doctorate, thesis/dissertation, professional paper, qualifying exam. *Entrance requirements:* For master's and doctorate, GRE General Test, minimum GPA of 3.0, writing sample. Additional exam requirements/recommendations for international students: Required—TOEFL (minimum score 550 paper-based). Electronic applications accepted. *Faculty research:* Collective behavior, social movements, comparative sociology, historical sociology, culture development, inequality.

**University of California, Irvine,** School of Social Sciences, Department of Sociology, Irvine, CA 92697. Offers social networks (PhD); social science (PhD); sociology and social relations (PhD). *Students:* 86 full-time (50 women), 1 part-time (0 women); includes 41 minority (7 Black or African American, non-Hispanic/Latino; 10 Asian, non-Hispanic/Latino; 18 Hispanic/Latino; 6 Two or more races, non-Hispanic/Latino), 5 international. Average age 30. 144 applicants, 28% accepted, 16 enrolled. In 2016, 17 doctorates awarded. *Degree requirements:* For doctorate, thesis/dissertation. *Entrance requirements:* For doctorate, GRE General Test, minimum GPA of 3.0. *Application deadline:* For fall admission, 1/15 priority date for domestic students, 1/15 for international students. Applications are processed on a rolling basis. Application fee: $105 ($125 for international students). Electronic applications accepted. *Financial support:* Fellowships, research assistantships with full tuition reimbursements, teaching assistantships, institutionally sponsored loans, traineeships, health care benefits, and unspecified assistantships available. Financial award application deadline: 3/1; financial award applicants required to submit FAFSA. *Faculty research:* Cognitive anthropology, sociology of culture, social structure, family and gender. *Unit head:* Prof. Matt Huffman, Chair, 949-824-5341, E-mail: mhuffman@uci.edu. *Application contact:* Ann Hironaka, Graduate Program Director, 949-824-3504, E-mail: hironaka@uci.edu.
Website: http://www.sociology.uci.edu/

**University of California, Los Angeles,** Graduate Division, College of Letters and Science, Department of Sociology, Los Angeles, CA 90095. Offers MA, PhD. Terminal master's awarded for partial completion of doctoral program. *Degree requirements:* For master's, thesis or alternative, paper; for doctorate, thesis/dissertation, oral and written qualifying exams. *Entrance requirements:* For doctorate, GRE General Test, bachelor's degree; minimum undergraduate GPA of 3.0 (or its equivalent if letter grade system not used); writing sample. Additional exam requirements/recommendations for international students: Required—TOEFL. Electronic applications accepted.

**University of California, Merced,** Graduate Division, School of Social Sciences, Humanities and Arts, Merced, CA 95343. Offers cognitive and information sciences (PhD); interdisciplinary humanities (MA, PhD); psychological sciences (MA, PhD); social sciences (MA, PhD); sociology (MA, PhD). *Faculty:* 93 full-time (41 women), 3 part-time/adjunct (all women). *Students:* 172 full-time (112 women), 3 part-time (2 women); includes 69 minority (4 Black or African American, non-Hispanic/Latino; 15 Asian, non-Hispanic/Latino; 43 Hispanic/Latino; 7 Two or more races, non-Hispanic/Latino), 25 international. Average age 31. 195 applicants, 50% accepted, 52 enrolled. In 2016, 13 master's, 11 doctorates awarded. Terminal master's awarded for partial completion of doctoral program. *Degree requirements:* For master's, variable foreign language requirement, comprehensive exam, thesis or alternative; for doctorate, variable foreign language requirement, comprehensive exam, thesis/dissertation. *Entrance requirements:* For master's and doctorate, GRE. Additional exam requirements/recommendations for international students: Required—TOEFL (minimum score 550 paper-based; 80 iBT); Recommended—IELTS (minimum score 7). *Application deadline:* For fall admission, 1/15 for domestic and international students. Application fee: $90 ($110 for international students). Electronic applications accepted. *Expenses:* Contact institution. *Financial support:* In 2016–17, 167 students received support, including 12 fellowships with full tuition reimbursements available (averaging $20,237 per year), 12 research assistantships with full tuition reimbursements available (averaging $18,842 per year), 121 teaching assistantships with full tuition reimbursements available (averaging $19,655 per year); scholarships/grants, traineeships, and health care benefits also available. Financial award application deadline: 1/15. *Faculty research:* Social inequality, critical race and ethnic studies, public health and health sciences, cognitive science and language acquisition, political institutions. *Total annual research expenditures:* $1.2 million. *Unit head:* Dr. Jill Robbins, Dean, E-mail: jillrobbins@ucmerced.edu. *Application contact:* Tsu Ya, Director of Admissions and Academic Services, 209-228-4521, Fax: 209-228-6906, E-mail: tya@ucmerced.edu.

**University of California, Riverside,** Graduate Division, Department of Sociology, Riverside, CA 92521-0102. Offers MA, PhD. *Degree requirements:* For doctorate, thesis/dissertation, 1 quarter of teaching experience, professional paper. *Entrance requirements:* For doctorate, GRE General Test, minimum GPA of 3.2. Additional exam requirements/recommendations for international students: Required—TOEFL (minimum score 550 paper-based; 80 iBT). Electronic applications accepted. *Expenses:* Tuition, state resident: full-time $16,666. Tuition, nonresident: full-time $31,768. *Required fees:* $11,055.54 per quarter. $3685.18 per quarter. Tuition and fees vary according to campus/location and program. *Faculty research:* Crime/deviance, race/ethnic relations, family/gender, political economy/globalization, theory.

**University of California, San Diego,** Graduate Division, Department of Sociology, La Jolla, CA 92093. Offers PhD. *Students:* 51 full-time (28 women), 2 part-time (both women). 147 applicants, 18% accepted, 9 enrolled. In 2016, 11 doctorates awarded. *Degree requirements:* For doctorate, comprehensive exam, thesis/dissertation. *Entrance requirements:* For doctorate, GRE General Test, minimum GPA of 3.0, writing sample, statement of purpose, 3 letters of recommendation. Additional exam requirements/recommendations for international students: Required—TOEFL (minimum score 550 paper-based; 80 iBT), IELTS (minimum score 7). *Application deadline:* For fall admission, 1/9 for domestic students. Application fee: $105 ($125 for international students). Electronic applications accepted. *Expenses:* Tuition, state resident: full-time $11,220. Tuition, nonresident: full-time $26,322. *Required fees:* $1864. *Financial support:* Fellowships, teaching assistantships, scholarships/grants, and readerships, research and travel funds available. Financial award applicants required to submit FAFSA. *Faculty research:* Comparative and historical sociology; sociology of culture;

sociology of science, technology, and medicine; social inequalities. *Unit head:* Akos Rona-Tas, Chair, 858-534-2779, E-mail: aronatas@ucsd.edu. *Application contact:* Teresa Eckert, Graduate Coordinator, 858-534-4627, E-mail: socphd@ucsd.edu.
Website: http://sociology.ucsd.edu/

**University of California, San Francisco,** Graduate Division, School of Nursing, Department of Social and Behavioral Sciences, San Francisco, CA 94143. Offers sociology (PhD). *Degree requirements:* For doctorate, one foreign language, thesis/dissertation. *Entrance requirements:* For doctorate, GRE General Test, statement of purpose, official transcripts, two letters of recommendation, scholarly writing example, curriculum vitae or resume. Additional exam requirements/recommendations for international students: Required—TOEFL (minimum score 84 iBT). *Faculty research:* Urban social relations; sociology of women's role in healing; sociology of work, occupations, and professions.

**University of California, Santa Barbara,** Graduate Division, College of Letters and Sciences, Division of Social Sciences, Department of Sociology, Santa Barbara, CA 93106-9430. Offers interdisciplinary emphasis: Black studies (PhD); interdisciplinary emphasis: environment and society (PhD); interdisciplinary emphasis: feminist studies (PhD); interdisciplinary emphasis: global studies (PhD); interdisciplinary emphasis: language, interaction and social organization (PhD); interdisciplinary emphasis: quantitative methods in the social sciences (PhD); interdisciplinary emphasis: technology and society (PhD); sociology (PhD); MA/PhD. Terminal master's awarded for partial completion of doctoral program. *Degree requirements:* For doctorate, comprehensive exam, thesis/dissertation. *Entrance requirements:* For doctorate, GRE General Test. Additional exam requirements/recommendations for international students: Required—TOEFL (minimum score 550 paper-based; 80 iBT), IELTS (minimum score 7). Electronic applications accepted. *Faculty research:* Gender and sexualities, race/ethnicity, social movements, conversation analysis, global sociology.

**University of California, Santa Cruz,** Division of Graduate Studies, Division of Social Sciences, Department of Sociology, Santa Cruz, CA 95064. Offers PhD. *Degree requirements:* For doctorate, thesis/dissertation, qualifying exam. *Entrance requirements:* For doctorate, GRE General Test. Additional exam requirements/recommendations for international students: Required—TOEFL (minimum score 550 paper-based; 83 iBT); Recommended—IELTS (minimum score 8). Electronic applications accepted. *Faculty research:* Globalization, political economy, and environment; inequality and identity; culture, knowledge, and power.

**University of Central Florida,** College of Sciences, Department of Sociology, Orlando, FL 32816. Offers applied sociology (MA); sociology (PhD). *Program availability:* Part-time, evening/weekend. *Faculty:* 23 full-time (10 women), 6 part-time/adjunct (all women). *Students:* 48 full-time (35 women), 15 part-time (12 women); includes 24 minority (9 Black or African American, non-Hispanic/Latino; 1 American Indian or Alaska Native, non-Hispanic/Latino; 2 Asian, non-Hispanic/Latino; 12 Hispanic/Latino), 1 international. Average age 31. 47 applicants, 66% accepted, 19 enrolled. In 2016, 11 master's, 9 doctorates awarded. *Degree requirements:* For master's, thesis or alternative; for doctorate, comprehensive exam, thesis/dissertation. *Entrance requirements:* For master's, GRE General Test, minimum GPA of 3.0 in last 60 hours of course work; for doctorate, GRE General Test. Additional exam requirements/recommendations for international students: Required—TOEFL. Application fee: $30. Electronic applications accepted. *Expenses:* Tuition, state resident: part-time $288.16 per credit hour. Tuition, nonresident: part-time $1071.31 per credit hour. *Financial support:* In 2016–17, 36 students received support, including 12 fellowships with partial tuition reimbursements available (averaging $5,679 per year), 8 research assistantships with partial tuition reimbursements available (averaging $12,237 per year), 25 teaching assistantships with partial tuition reimbursements available (averaging $12,748 per year); career-related internships or fieldwork, Federal Work-Study, institutionally sponsored loans, tuition waivers (partial), and unspecified assistantships also available. Financial award application deadline: 3/1; financial award applicants required to submit FAFSA. *Faculty research:* Criminology/domestic violence, social inequalities, health, families and communities, social and behavioral sciences. *Unit head:* Dr. Elizabeth Mustaine, Chair, 407-823-6568, E-mail: elizabeth.mustaine@ucf.edu. *Application contact:* Assistant Director, Graduate Admissions, 407-823-2766, Fax: 407-823-6442, E-mail: gradadmissions@ucf.edu.
Website: http://sociology.cos.ucf.edu/

**University of Central Missouri,** The Graduate School, Warrensburg, MO 64093. Offers accountancy (MA); accounting (MBA); applied mathematics (MS); aviation safety (MA); biology (MS); business administration (MBA); career and technical education leadership (MS); college student personnel administration (MS); communication (MA); computer science (MS); counseling (MS); criminal justice (MS); educational leadership (Ed D); educational technology (MS); elementary and early childhood education (MSE); English (MA); environmental studies (MA); finance (MBA); history (MA); human services/educational technology (Ed S); human services/learning resources (Ed S); human services/professional counseling (Ed S); industrial hygiene (MS); industrial management (MS); information systems (MBA); information technology (MS); kinesiology (MS); library science and information services (MS); literacy education (MSE); marketing (MBA); mathematics (MS); music (MA); occupational safety management (MS); psychology (MS); rural family nursing (MS); school administration (MSE); social gerontology (MS); sociology (MA); special education (MSE); speech language pathology (MS); superintendency (Ed S); teaching (MAT); teaching English as a second language (MA); technology (MS); technology management (PhD); theatre (MA). *Program availability:* Part-time, 100% online, blended/hybrid learning. *Degree requirements:* For master's and Ed S, comprehensive exam (for some programs), thesis (for some programs). *Entrance requirements:* Additional exam requirements/recommendations for international students: Required—TOEFL (minimum score 550 paper-based; 79 iBT). Electronic applications accepted.

**University of Central Oklahoma,** The Jackson College of Graduate Studies, College of Liberal Arts, Department of Sociology, Gerontology, and Substance Abuse Studies, Edmond, OK 73034-5209. Offers gerontology (MA); sociology (MA), including substance abuse studies. *Program availability:* Part-time. *Degree requirements:* For master's, variable foreign language requirement, comprehensive exam (for some programs), thesis (for some programs). *Entrance requirements:* For master's, GRE. Additional exam requirements/recommendations for international students: Required—TOEFL (minimum score 550 paper-based; 79 iBT), IELTS (minimum score 6.5). Electronic applications accepted.

**University of Chicago,** Division of the Social Sciences, Department of Sociology, Chicago, IL 60637. Offers PhD. *Students:* 120 full-time (65 women); includes 31 minority (9 Black or African American, non-Hispanic/Latino; 2 American Indian or Alaska Native, non-Hispanic/Latino; 7 Asian, non-Hispanic/Latino; 8 Hispanic/Latino; 5 Two or more races, non-Hispanic/Latino), 38 international. 212 applicants, 15% accepted, 15 enrolled. In 2016, 10 doctorates awarded. *Degree requirements:* For doctorate, one foreign language, comprehensive exam, thesis/dissertation, 2 field exams. *Entrance requirements:* For doctorate, GRE General Test. Additional exam requirements/recommendations for international students: Required—TOEFL (minimum score 104 iBT), IELTS (minimum score 7). *Application deadline:* For fall admission, 12/15 for domestic and international students. Application fee: $90. Electronic applications

accepted. *Financial support:* In 2016–17, 14 students received support, including 14 fellowships with full tuition reimbursements available (averaging $23,000 per year); career-related internships or fieldwork, Federal Work-Study, institutionally sponsored loans, scholarships/grants, and health care benefits also available. Financial award application deadline: 12/15. *Unit head:* Karin Knorr Cetina, Chair, 773-834-3312, E-mail: knorr@uchicago.edu. *Application contact:* Office of the Dean of Students, 773-702-8415, E-mail: admissions@ssd.uchicago.edu.
Website: http://sociology.uchicago.edu

**University of Cincinnati,** Graduate School, McMicken College of Arts and Sciences, Department of Sociology, Cincinnati, OH 45221-0378. Offers MA, PhD. *Program availability:* Part-time. *Faculty:* 9 full-time (5 women). *Students:* 33 full-time (18 women), 15 part-time (9 women); includes 16 minority (14 Black or African American, non-Hispanic/Latino; 2 Asian, non-Hispanic/Latino), 8 international. 40 applicants, 40% accepted, 13 enrolled. In 2016, 3 master's, 3 doctorates awarded. Terminal master's awarded for partial completion of doctoral program. *Degree requirements:* For master's, comprehensive exam (for some programs), thesis (for some programs); for doctorate, comprehensive exam, thesis/dissertation. *Entrance requirements:* For master's and doctorate, GRE General Test. Additional exam requirements/recommendations for international students: Required—TOEFL (minimum score 600 paper-based; 100 iBT), IELTS (minimum score 7). *Application deadline:* For fall admission, 4/1 for domestic and international students. Application fee: $65 ($70 for international students). Electronic applications accepted. *Expenses:* Contact institution. *Financial support:* In 2016–17, 22 students received support. Tuition waivers (full and partial) and unspecified assistantships available. Financial award application deadline: 1/15. *Faculty research:* Urban, race, education, health, and methods. *Total annual research expenditures:* $72,600. *Unit head:* Dr. Steven Carlton-Ford, Department Head, 513-556-4716, Fax: 513-556-0057, E-mail: carltosl@ucmail.uc.edu. *Application contact:* Dr. Jeffrey M. Timberlake, Graduate Program Director, 513-556-4704, Fax: 513-556-0057, E-mail: timberjm@ucmail.uc.edu.
Website: http://www.artsci.uc.edu/sociology

**University of Colorado Boulder,** Graduate School, College of Arts and Sciences, Department of Sociology, Boulder, CO 80309. Offers PhD. *Faculty:* 22 full-time (13 women). *Students:* 55 full-time (40 women); includes 9 minority (1 Asian, non-Hispanic/Latino; 4 Hispanic/Latino; 4 Two or more races, non-Hispanic/Latino), 4 international. Average age 30. 95 applicants, 26% accepted, 10 enrolled. In 2016, 8 doctorates awarded. *Degree requirements:* For doctorate, comprehensive exam, thesis/dissertation. *Entrance requirements:* For doctorate, GRE General Test, GRE Subject Test, minimum undergraduate GPA of 2.75. *Application deadline:* For fall admission, 12/1 for domestic and international students. Application fee: $60 ($80 for international students). Electronic applications accepted. Application fee is waived when completed online. *Financial support:* In 2016–17, 155 students received support, including 33 fellowships (averaging $7,776 per year), 9 research assistantships with full and partial tuition reimbursements available (averaging $30,178 per year), 44 teaching assistantships with full and partial tuition reimbursements available (averaging $40,775 per year); institutionally sponsored loans, scholarships/grants, health care benefits, and unspecified assistantships also available. Financial award application deadline: 1/1; financial award applicants required to submit FAFSA. *Faculty research:* Sociology, minorities and disadvantaged, medical sociology, criminology, demography. *Total annual research expenditures:* $2 million. *Application contact:* E-mail: sociology@colorado.edu.
Website: http://SOCSCI.colorado.edu/SOC/

**University of Colorado Colorado Springs,** College of Letters, Arts and Sciences, Department of Sociology, Colorado Springs, CO 80918. Offers MA. *Program availability:* Part-time, blended/hybrid learning. *Faculty:* 12 full-time (7 women), 3 part-time/adjunct (all women). *Students:* 5 full-time (3 women), 31 part-time (24 women); includes 9 minority (2 Black or African American, non-Hispanic/Latino; 1 Asian, non-Hispanic/Latino; 5 Hispanic/Latino; 1 Two or more races, non-Hispanic/Latino). Average age 34. 17 applicants, 94% accepted, 9 enrolled. In 2016, 9 master's awarded. *Degree requirements:* For master's, thesis optional. *Entrance requirements:* For master's, minimum GPA of 3.0 or GRE. Additional exam requirements/recommendations for international students: Recommended—TOEFL (minimum score 550 paper-based; 100 iBT), IELTS (minimum score 7). *Application deadline:* For fall admission, 2/1 priority date for domestic and international students; for spring admission, 11/15 priority date for domestic and international students. Applications are processed on a rolling basis. Application fee: $60 ($100 for international students). Electronic applications accepted. *Expenses:* Tuition, state resident: full-time $9983. Tuition, nonresident: full-time $20,153. Tuition and fees vary according to course load, degree level, program and reciprocity agreements. *Financial support:* In 2016–17, 8 students received support. Career-related internships or fieldwork, Federal Work-Study, scholarships/grants, and unspecified assistantships available. Support available to part-time students. Financial award application deadline: 3/1; financial award applicants required to submit FAFSA. *Faculty research:* Intersectionality, culture, justice studies and globalization and development. *Unit head:* Dr. Heather Albanesi, Department Chair, 719-255-4137, Fax: 719-255-4450, E-mail: halbanes@uccs.edu. *Application contact:* Rosemary Kelbel, Program Assistant, 719-255-4153, Fax: 719-255-4450, E-mail: rkelbel@uccs.edu.
Website: http://www.uccs.edu/~soc/

**University of Colorado Denver,** College of Liberal Arts and Sciences, Department of Sociology, Denver, CO 80217. Offers MA. *Program availability:* Part-time, evening/weekend. *Faculty:* 9 full-time (7 women). *Students:* 16 full-time (12 women), 7 part-time (4 women); includes 5 minority (2 Black or African American, non-Hispanic/Latino; 2 Hispanic/Latino; 1 Two or more races, non-Hispanic/Latino). Average age 32. 23 applicants, 74% accepted, 11 enrolled. In 2016, 1 master's awarded. *Degree requirements:* For master's, 36 credit hours, project or thesis. *Entrance requirements:* For master's, GRE (recommended), minimum combined GPA of 3.3 for all courses taken at undergraduate or graduate level, 3.5 for all sociology courses; writing sample; statement of intent; three letters of recommendation. Additional exam requirements/recommendations for international students: Required—TOEFL (minimum score 537 paper-based; 75 iBT); Recommended—IELTS (minimum score 6.5). *Application deadline:* For fall admission, 3/1 for domestic students, 2/15 for international students. Application fee: $50 ($75 for international students). Electronic applications accepted. *Expenses:* Tuition, state resident: full-time $11,006; part-time $474 per credit. Tuition, nonresident: full-time $28,212; part-time $1264 per credit hour. *Required fees:* $256 per semester. One-time fee: $94.32. Tuition and fees vary according to campus/location and program. *Financial support:* In 2016–17, 8 students received support. Fellowships, research assistantships, teaching assistantships, Federal Work-Study, institutionally sponsored loans, scholarships/grants, and traineeships available. Financial award application deadline: 4/1; financial award applicants required to submit FAFSA. *Faculty research:* Domestic violence, elderly and housing, family demography, immigrants and immigration, social determinants of health behaviors. *Unit head:* Kari Alexander, Sociology Graduate Program Director, 303-315-2137, E-mail: kari.alexander@ucdenver.edu. *Application contact:* Rachel Gallegos, Program Assistant, 303-315-2148, E-mail: rachel.gallegos@ucdenver.edu.
Website: http://www.ucdenver.edu/academics/colleges/CLAS/Departments/sociology/Programs/MasterofArts/Pages/MasterofArts.aspx

**University of Colorado Denver,** College of Liberal Arts and Sciences, Program in Humanities, Denver, CO 80217. Offers community health science (MSS); humanities (MH); international studies (MSS); philosophy and theory (MH); social justice (MSS); society and the environment (MSS); visual studies (MH); women's and gender studies (MSS). *Program availability:* Part-time, evening/weekend. *Faculty:* 3 full-time (1 woman). *Students:* 12 full-time (6 women), 15 part-time (7 women); includes 6 minority (1 American Indian or Alaska Native, non-Hispanic/Latino; 3 Hispanic/Latino; 2 Two or more races, non-Hispanic/Latino). Average age 41. 4 applicants, 100% accepted, 4 enrolled. In 2016, 5 master's awarded. *Degree requirements:* For master's, 36 credit hours, project or thesis. *Entrance requirements:* For master's, writing sample, statement of purpose/letter of intent, three letters of recommendation. Additional exam requirements/recommendations for international students: Required—TOEFL (minimum score 537 paper-based; 75 iBT); Recommended—IELTS (minimum score 6.5). *Application deadline:* For fall admission, 5/15 for domestic students, 5/15 priority date for international students; for spring admission, 10/15 for domestic students, 10/15 priority date for international students; for summer admission, 3/15 for domestic and international students. Application fee: $50 ($75 for international students). Electronic applications accepted. *Expenses:* Tuition, state resident: full-time $11,006; part-time $474 per credit. Tuition, nonresident: full-time $28,212; part-time $1264 per credit hour. *Required fees:* $256 per semester. One-time fee: $94.32. Tuition and fees vary according to campus/location and program. *Financial support:* In 2016–17, 2 students received support. Fellowships, research assistantships, teaching assistantships, Federal Work-Study, institutionally sponsored loans, scholarships/grants, and traineeships available. Financial award application deadline: 4/1; financial award applicants required to submit FAFSA. *Faculty research:* Women and gender in the classical Mediterranean, communication theory and democracy, relationship between psychology and philosophy. *Unit head:* Margaret Woodhull, Director of Humanities, 303-315-3568, E-mail: margaret.woodhull@ucdenver.edu. *Application contact:* Angela Beale, Program Assistant, 303-315-3565, E-mail: mastershs@ucdenver.edu.
Website: http://www.ucdenver.edu/academics/colleges/CLAS/Programs/HumanitiesSocialSciences/Programs/Pages/MasterofHumanities.aspx

**University of Connecticut,** Graduate School, College of Liberal Arts and Sciences, Department of Sociology, Storrs, CT 06269. Offers MA, PhD. Terminal master's awarded for partial completion of doctoral program. *Degree requirements:* For master's, comprehensive exam; for doctorate, thesis/dissertation. *Entrance requirements:* For master's and doctorate, GRE General Test. Additional exam requirements/recommendations for international students: Required—TOEFL (minimum score 550 paper-based). Electronic applications accepted.

**University of Delaware,** College of Arts and Sciences, Department of Sociology and Criminal Justice, Newark, DE 19716. Offers criminology (MA, PhD); sociology (MA, PhD). *Degree requirements:* For master's, thesis; for doctorate, comprehensive exam, thesis/dissertation. *Entrance requirements:* For master's and doctorate, GRE, 3 letters of recommendation. Additional exam requirements/recommendations for international students: Required—TOEFL. Electronic applications accepted. *Faculty research:* Sex and gender, criminology/deviance, theory, methods, collective behavior.

**University of Florida,** Graduate School, College of Liberal Arts and Sciences, Department of Sociology and Criminology and Law, Gainesville, FL 32611. Offers criminology, law, and society (MA, PhD); sociology (MA, PhD), including sociology, tropical conservation and development, women's and gender studies (PhD); MA/JD. *Program availability:* Part-time. Terminal master's awarded for partial completion of doctoral program. *Degree requirements:* For master's, thesis optional; for doctorate, comprehensive exam, thesis/dissertation. *Entrance requirements:* For master's and doctorate, GRE, minimum GPA of 3.0. Additional exam requirements/recommendations for international students: Required—TOEFL (minimum score 550 paper-based; 80 iBT), IELTS (minimum score 6). Electronic applications accepted. *Faculty research:* Law and society, juvenile justice, criminal investigation procedures, deviance, biosocial criminology, environmental sociology, comparative race and ethnic studies, health and aging, families and gender.

**University of Georgia,** Franklin College of Arts and Sciences, Department of Sociology, Athens, GA 30602. Offers MA, PhD. *Degree requirements:* For master's, thesis; for doctorate, thesis/dissertation. *Entrance requirements:* For master's and doctorate, GRE General Test. Additional exam requirements/recommendations for international students: Required—TOEFL. *Application deadline:* For fall admission, 2/1 priority date for domestic students, 1/1 for international students. Application fee: $50. Electronic applications accepted. *Financial support:* Research assistantships, teaching assistantships with full tuition reimbursements, and unspecified assistantships available. Financial award application deadline: 1/1. *Faculty research:* Race, deviance, gender, culture. *Unit head:* Dr. William Finlay, Head, 706-542-3175, Fax: 706-542-4320, E-mail: wfinlay@uga.edu. *Application contact:* Justine Tinkler, Graduate Coordinator, 706-542-5497, E-mail: jtinkler@uga.edu.
Website: http://www.uga.edu/~soc/

**University of Guelph,** Graduate Studies, College of Social and Applied Human Sciences, Department of Sociology and Anthropology, Guelph, ON N1G 2W1, Canada. Offers anthropology (MA); crime and criminal justice policy (MA); sociology (MA, PhD). *Degree requirements:* For master's, thesis or major paper; for doctorate, comprehensive exam, thesis/dissertation. *Entrance requirements:* For master's, minimum B+ average during previous 2 years of course work, honors BA or equivalent; for doctorate, must have an MA in Sociology, must have 80% or higher in graduate level studies. Additional exam requirements/recommendations for international students: Required—TOEFL (minimum score 550 paper-based; 89 iBT) or IELTS (minimum score 6.5). Electronic applications accepted. *Faculty research:* Rural and development sociology; education, employment, and the workplace; race, ethnicity, and native studies; criminology and deviance; social psychology.

**University of Hawaii at Manoa,** Graduate Division, College of Social Sciences, Department of Sociology, Honolulu, HI 96822. Offers MA, PhD. *Program availability:* Part-time. *Degree requirements:* For master's, thesis optional; for doctorate, comprehensive exam, thesis/dissertation. *Entrance requirements:* For master's and doctorate, GRE General Test. Additional exam requirements/recommendations for international students: Required—TOEFL (minimum score 500 paper-based; 61 iBT), IELTS (minimum score 5). *Faculty research:* Comparative sociology of Asia; population studies; crime, law, and deviance; health; aging and medical sociology.

**University of Houston,** College of Liberal Arts and Social Sciences, Department of Sociology, Houston, TX 77204. Offers MA. *Program availability:* Part-time. *Degree requirements:* For master's, thesis, 4 core courses, 36 hours. *Entrance requirements:* For master's, GRE (minimum score 1000), minimum GPA of 3.0; letters of recommendation, resume. Additional exam requirements/recommendations for international students: Required—TOEFL (minimum score 550 paper-based; 79 iBT). Electronic applications accepted. *Faculty research:* Immigration, public education, HIV/AIDS.

**University of Houston–Clear Lake,** School of Human Sciences and Humanities, Programs in Human Sciences, Houston, TX 77058-1002. Offers behavioral sciences (MA), including criminology, cross cultural studies, general psychology, sociology;

clinical psychology (MA); criminology (MA); cross cultural studies (MA); family therapy (MA); fitness and human performance (MA); school psychology (MA). *Accreditation:* AAMFT/COAMFTE. *Program availability:* Part-time, evening/weekend, online learning. *Degree requirements:* For master's, thesis or alternative. *Entrance requirements:* For master's, GRE General Test. Additional exam requirements/recommendations for international students: Required—TOEFL (minimum score 550 paper-based). Electronic applications accepted. *Faculty research:* Smoking cessation, adolescent sexuality, white collar crime, serial murder, human factors/human computer interaction.

**University of Illinois at Chicago,** College of Liberal Arts and Sciences, Department of Sociology, Chicago, IL 60607-7128. Offers MA, PhD. Terminal master's awarded for partial completion of doctoral program. *Degree requirements:* For master's, comprehensive exam, thesis; for doctorate, thesis/dissertation, qualifying exam. *Entrance requirements:* For master's and doctorate, GRE General Test, minimum GPA of 3.0. Additional exam requirements/recommendations for international students: Required—TOEFL. Electronic applications accepted. *Faculty research:* Social psychology, social organization, applied sociology, demography and human ecology.

**University of Illinois at Urbana–Champaign,** Graduate College, College of Liberal Arts and Sciences, Department of Sociology, Champaign, IL 61820. Offers MA, PhD.

**University of Indianapolis,** Graduate Programs, College of Arts and Sciences, Department of Social Sciences, Indianapolis, IN 46227-3697. Offers applied sociology (MA). *Program availability:* Part-time, evening/weekend. *Degree requirements:* For master's, thesis optional. *Entrance requirements:* For master's, GRE Subject Test, minimum GPA of 3.0, letter of intent, 3 letters of recommendation. Additional exam requirements/recommendations for international students: Required—TOEFL (minimum score 550 paper-based). Electronic applications accepted.

**The University of Iowa,** Graduate College, College of Liberal Arts and Sciences, Department of Sociology, Iowa City, IA 52242-1316. Offers MA, PhD. *Degree requirements:* For master's, thesis optional, exam; for doctorate, comprehensive exam, thesis/dissertation. *Entrance requirements:* For master's and doctorate, GRE General Test, minimum GPA of 3.0. Additional exam requirements/recommendations for international students: Required—TOEFL (minimum score 600 paper-based; 100 iBT). Electronic applications accepted.

**The University of Kansas,** Graduate Studies, College of Liberal Arts and Sciences, Department of Sociology, Lawrence, KS 66045. Offers PhD. *Program availability:* Part-time. *Students:* 39 full-time (19 women), 1 (woman) part-time; includes 3 minority (2 Hispanic/Latino; 1 Two or more races, non-Hispanic/Latino), 4 international. Average age 32. 28 applicants, 57% accepted, 8 enrolled. In 2016, 8 doctorates awarded. *Entrance requirements:* For doctorate, GRE General Test, current resume, statement of academic interests and professional goals, writing sample of academic work, three recommendation letters, official transcripts. Additional exam requirements/recommendations for international students: Required—TOEFL or IELTS. *Application deadline:* For fall admission, 12/15 for domestic and international students. Application fee: $65 ($85 for international students). Electronic applications accepted. *Financial support:* Fellowships, research assistantships, teaching assistantships, scholarships/grants, and unspecified assistantships available. Financial award application deadline: 12/15. *Faculty research:* Culture, demography, environment, gender and sexuality, globalization, immigration and migration, life course, aging and family, medicine and health, political sociology, race and ethnicity, religion, social inequality and stratification, social theory. *Unit head:* Kelly H. Chong, Director, 785-864-4111, Fax: 785-864-5280, E-mail: socdept@ku.edu. *Application contact:* Corinne Butler, Graduate Secretary, 785-864-9419, Fax: 785-864-5280, E-mail: cleg@ku.edu.
Website: http://www.sociology.ku.edu/

**University of Kentucky,** Graduate School, College of Arts and Sciences, Program in Sociology, Lexington, KY 40506-0032. Offers MA, MS, PhD. *Program availability:* Part-time. *Degree requirements:* For master's, comprehensive exam, thesis optional; for doctorate, comprehensive exam, thesis/dissertation. *Entrance requirements:* For master's, GRE General Test, minimum undergraduate GPA of 2.75; for doctorate, GRE General Test, minimum graduate GPA of 3.0. Additional exam requirements/recommendations for international students: Required—TOEFL (minimum score 550 paper-based). Electronic applications accepted. *Faculty research:* Work organizations, social inequalities, rural sociology, criminology/deviance, medical sociology.

**University of Lethbridge,** School of Graduate Studies, Lethbridge, AB T1K 3M4, Canada. Offers addictions counseling (M Sc); agricultural biotechnology (M Sc); agricultural studies (M Sc, MA); anthropology (MA); archaeology (M Sc, MA); art (MA, MFA); biochemistry (M Sc); biological sciences (M Sc); biomolecular science (PhD); biosystems and biodiversity (PhD); Canadian studies (MA); chemistry (M Sc); computer science (M Sc); computer science and geographical information science (M Sc); counseling (MC); counseling psychology (M Ed); dramatic arts (MA); earth, space, and physical science (PhD); economics (MA); education (MA, PhD); educational leadership (M Ed); English (MA); environmental science (M Sc); evolution and behavior (PhD); exercise science (M Sc); French (MA); French/German (MA); French/Spanish (MA); general education (M Ed); geography (M Sc, MA); German (MA); health sciences (M Sc); individualized multidisciplinary (M Sc, MA); kinesiology (M Sc, MA); management (M Sc), including accounting, finance, human resource management and labor relations, information systems, international management, marketing, policy and strategy; mathematics (M Sc); music (M Mus, MA); Native American studies (MA); neuroscience (M Sc, PhD); new media (MA, MFA); nursing (M Sc, MN); philosophy (MA); physics (M Sc); political science (MA); psychology (M Sc, MA); religious studies (MA); sociology (MA); theatre and dramatic arts (MFA); theoretical and computational science (PhD); urban and regional studies (MA); women and gender studies (MA). *Program availability:* Part-time, evening/weekend. *Degree requirements:* For master's, thesis (for some programs); for doctorate, comprehensive exam, thesis/dissertation. *Entrance requirements:* For master's, GMAT (for M Sc in management), bachelor's degree in related field, minimum GPA of 3.0 during previous 20 graded semester courses, 2 years' teaching or related experience (M Ed); for doctorate, master's degree, minimum graduate GPA of 3.5. Additional exam requirements/recommendations for international students: Required—TOEFL (minimum score 580 paper-based; 93 iBT). Electronic applications accepted. *Faculty research:* Movement and brain plasticity, gibberellin physiology, photosynthesis, carbon cycling, molecular properties of main-group ring components.

**University of Louisville,** Graduate School, College of Arts and Sciences, Department of Sociology, Louisville, KY 40292. Offers applied sociology (PhD); sociology (MA). *Program availability:* Part-time, evening/weekend. *Faculty:* 17 full-time (9 women), 5 part-time/adjunct (all women). *Students:* 16 full-time (8 women), 10 part-time (8 women); includes 3 minority (2 Black or African American, non-Hispanic/Latino; 1 Hispanic/Latino). Average age 34. 12 applicants, 75% accepted, 4 enrolled. In 2016, 3 master's awarded. Terminal master's awarded for partial completion of doctoral program. *Degree requirements:* For master's, thesis (for some programs), thesis or practicum; for doctorate, comprehensive exam, thesis/dissertation. *Entrance requirements:* For master's, GRE (minimum combined quantitative/verbal score of 1000, if tested prior to August 2011, or 300, if tested since August 2011), official copies of transcripts from all colleges attended; two references (preferably from former instructors); for doctorate,

GRE (minimum combined quantitative/verbal score of 1000, if tested prior to August 2011, or 300, if tested since August 2011), official copies of transcripts from all colleges attended, three references (preferably from former instructors). Additional exam requirements/recommendations for international students: Required—TOEFL (minimum score 550 paper-based; 79 iBT), IELTS (minimum score 6.5). *Application deadline:* For fall admission, 6/1 for domestic and international students; for spring admission, 11/1 for domestic and international students. Application fee: $65. Electronic applications accepted. *Expenses:* Contact institution. *Financial support:* In 2016–17, 2 fellowships with full tuition reimbursements (averaging $18,000 per year), 2 research assistantships with full tuition reimbursements (averaging $18,000 per year), 4 teaching assistantships with full tuition reimbursements (averaging $18,000 per year) were awarded; tuition waivers (full) also available. Financial award application deadline: 1/5. *Faculty research:* Applied sociology/evaluation research; family; sex and gender; race, class, and gender; medical sociology. *Total annual research expenditures:* $6,821. *Unit head:* Dr. Ryan D. Schroeder, Associate Professor and Chair, 502-852-8010, Fax: 502-852-0099, E-mail: ryan.schroeder@louisville.edu. *Application contact:* Libby Leggett, Director, Graduate Admissions, 502-852-3101, Fax: 502-852-6536, E-mail: gradadm@louisville.edu.
Website: http://louisville.edu/sociology

**The University of Manchester,** School of Social Sciences, Manchester, United Kingdom. Offers ethnographic documentary (M Phil); interdisciplinary study of culture (PhD); philosophy (PhD); politics (PhD); social anthropology (PhD); social anthropology with visual media (PhD); social change (PhD); social statistics (PhD); sociology (PhD); visual anthropology (M Phil).

**University of Manitoba,** Faculty of Graduate Studies, Faculty of Arts, Department of Sociology, Winnipeg, MB R3T 2N2, Canada. Offers MA, PhD. *Degree requirements:* For master's, thesis.

**University of Maryland, Baltimore County,** The Graduate School, College of Arts, Humanities and Social Sciences, Department of Sociology, Anthropology, and Health Administration and Policy, Program in Applied Sociology, Baltimore, MD 21250. Offers MA. *Program availability:* Part-time, evening/weekend. *Faculty:* 16 full-time (13 women), 2 part-time/adjunct (0 women). *Students:* 11 full-time (6 women), 17 part-time (11 women); includes 11 minority (4 Black or African American, non-Hispanic/Latino; 3 Asian, non-Hispanic/Latino; 3 Hispanic/Latino; 1 Two or more races, non-Hispanic/Latino). Average age 29. 7 applicants, 86% accepted, 5 enrolled. In 2016, 13 master's awarded. *Degree requirements:* For master's, thesis or alternative. *Entrance requirements:* For master's, minimum GPA of 3.0. Additional exam requirements/recommendations for international students: Required—TOEFL. *Application deadline:* For fall admission, 4/1 priority date for domestic students, 1/1 for international students; for spring admission, 11/15 for domestic students, 9/1 for international students. Application fee: $70. Electronic applications accepted. *Expenses:* Tuition, state resident: full-time $13,294. Tuition, nonresident: full-time $20,286. *Financial support:* In 2016–17, 10 students received support, including 1 research assistantship with tuition reimbursement available, 9 teaching assistantships with tuition reimbursements available; health care benefits, unspecified assistantships, and tuition remission also available. *Faculty research:* Sociology of aging; sociology of health; diversity, gender, and culture; research methods. *Unit head:* Dr. Marina Adler, Graduate Program Director, 410-455-3155, Fax: 410-455-1154, E-mail: adler@umbc.edu. *Application contact:* Faith Dinh, Graduate Program Coordinator, 410-455-3365, Fax: 410-455-1154, E-mail: fdinh1@umbc.edu.
Website: http://sociology.umbc.edu/ma-in-applied-sociology/

**University of Maryland, College Park,** Academic Affairs, College of Behavioral and Social Sciences, Department of Sociology, College Park, MD 20742. Offers MA, PhD. *Degree requirements:* For master's, thesis; for doctorate, thesis/dissertation, 2 qualifying exams. *Entrance requirements:* For master's, GRE General Test, minimum GPA of 3.0, 3 letters of recommendation; for doctorate, GRE General Test, 3 letters of recommendation. Additional exam requirements/recommendations for international students: Required—TOEFL. Electronic applications accepted. *Faculty research:* Social psychology, sociology of work, sociology of the military, population studies, stratification.

**University of Massachusetts Amherst,** Graduate School, College of Social and Behavioral Sciences, Department of Sociology, Amherst, MA 01003. Offers MA, PhD. *Program availability:* Part-time. Terminal master's awarded for partial completion of doctoral program. *Degree requirements:* For master's, thesis or alternative; for doctorate, comprehensive exam, thesis/dissertation. *Entrance requirements:* For master's and doctorate, GRE General Test, writing sample, 3 letters of recommendation. Additional exam requirements/recommendations for international students: Required—TOEFL (minimum score 550 paper-based; 80 iBT), IELTS (minimum score 6.5). Electronic applications accepted.

**University of Massachusetts Boston,** College of Liberal Arts, Program in Applied Sociology, Boston, MA 02125-3393. Offers MA. *Program availability:* Part-time, evening/weekend. *Students:* 10 full-time (7 women), 3 part-time (2 women); includes 5 minority (1 Asian, non-Hispanic/Latino; 3 Hispanic/Latino; 1 Two or more races, non-Hispanic/Latino). Average age 27. 16 applicants, 69% accepted, 5 enrolled. In 2016, 10 master's awarded. *Degree requirements:* For master's, comprehensive exam, thesis. *Entrance requirements:* For master's, GRE or MAT, minimum GPA of 2.75. *Application deadline:* For fall admission, 3/1 for domestic students; for spring admission, 11/1 for domestic students. *Expenses:* Tuition, state resident: full-time $16,863. Tuition, nonresident: full-time $32,913. *Required fees:* $177. *Financial support:* Research assistantships with full tuition reimbursements, teaching assistantships with full tuition reimbursements, career-related internships or fieldwork, Federal Work-Study, and unspecified assistantships available. Support available to part-time students. Financial award application deadline: 3/1; financial award applicants required to submit FAFSA. *Faculty research:* Sociology of education, social deviance and control, women and development, race and ethnic group relations, criminology. *Unit head:* Dr. Russell Schutt, Director, 617-287-6250, E-mail: russell.schutt@umb.edu. *Application contact:* Peggy Roldan Patel, Graduate Admissions Coordinator, 617-287-6400, Fax: 617-287-6236, E-mail: bos.gadm@dpc.umassp.edu.

**University of Massachusetts Boston,** College of Liberal Arts, Program in Sociology, Boston, MA 02125-3393. Offers PhD. *Faculty:* 28 full-time (14 women), 18 part-time/adjunct (12 women). *Students:* 8 full-time (6 women), 20 part-time (17 women); includes 5 minority (1 Black or African American, non-Hispanic/Latino; 1 American Indian or Alaska Native, non-Hispanic/Latino; 1 Asian, non-Hispanic/Latino; 1 Hispanic/Latino; 1 Two or more races, non-Hispanic/Latino), 1 international. Average age 34. 22 applicants, 45% accepted, 6 enrolled. *Expenses:* Tuition, state resident: full-time $16,863. Tuition, nonresident: full-time $32,913. *Required fees:* $177. *Financial support:* Teaching assistantships and unspecified assistantships available. *Unit head:* Dr. Reef Youngreen, Director, 617-287-3909, E-mail: reef.youngreen@umb.edu. *Application contact:* Peggy Roldan Patel, Graduate Admissions Coordinator, 617-287-6400, Fax: 617-287-6236, E-mail: bos.gadm@dpc.umassp.edu.
Website: http://www.umb.edu/academics/cla/sociology/graduate_programs/phd_in_sociology

**University of Massachusetts Lowell,** College of Fine Arts, Humanities and Social Sciences, Program in Regional Economic and Social Development, Lowell, MA 01854.

Offers MA, Graduate Certificate. *Program availability:* Part-time. *Entrance requirements:* For master's, GRE. Electronic applications accepted.

**University of Memphis,** Graduate School, College of Arts and Sciences, Department of Sociology, Memphis, TN 38103. Offers MA. *Program availability:* Part-time. *Faculty:* 5 full-time (2 women). *Students:* 10 full-time (7 women), 2 part-time (both women); includes 7 minority (2 Black or African American, non-Hispanic/Latino; 1 Asian, non-Hispanic/Latino; 2 Hispanic/Latino; 2 Two or more races, non-Hispanic/Latino). Average age 29. 6 applicants, 100% accepted, 4 enrolled. In 2016, 6 master's awarded. *Degree requirements:* For master's, comprehensive exam, thesis (for some programs). *Entrance requirements:* For master's, GRE General Test, 12 undergraduate hours in sociology, letters of reference, writing sample. Additional exam requirements/recommendations for international students: Required—TOEFL (minimum score 550 paper-based; 79 iBT). *Application deadline:* For fall admission, 7/1 for domestic students, 5/1 for international students; for spring admission, 12/1 for domestic students, 9/15 for international students. Applications are processed on a rolling basis. Application fee: $35 ($60 for international students). Electronic applications accepted. *Expenses:* $5,231.50 per semester full-time in-state, $9,623.50 full-time out-of-state. *Financial support:* In 2016–17, 12 students received support, including 12 research assistantships with full tuition reimbursements available (averaging $14,528 per year); teaching assistantships with full tuition reimbursements available, Federal Work-Study, scholarships/grants, and unspecified assistantships also available. Financial award application deadline: 2/1; financial award applicants required to submit FAFSA. *Faculty research:* Globalization, medical, inequality, religion, urban. *Unit head:* Dr. Gretchen Peterson, Chair, Fax: 901-678-2525, E-mail: gpterson@memphis.edu. *Application contact:* Dr. Wesley James, Coordinator of Graduate Studies, 901-678-1631, Fax: 901-678-2525, E-mail: wes.james@memphis.edu.
Website: http://sociology.memphis.edu

**University of Miami,** Graduate School, College of Arts and Sciences, Department of Sociology, Coral Gables, FL 33124. Offers MA, PhD. *Program availability:* Part-time. Terminal master's awarded for partial completion of doctoral program. *Degree requirements:* For master's, thesis; for doctorate, comprehensive exam, thesis/dissertation. *Entrance requirements:* For master's and doctorate, GRE General Test. Additional exam requirements/recommendations for international students: Required—TOEFL (minimum score 515 paper-based). Electronic applications accepted. *Faculty research:* Crime, violence, mental health, ethnic relations, health.

**University of Miami,** Graduate School, School of Education and Human Development, Department of Educational and Psychological Studies, Program in Community and Social Change, Coral Gables, FL 33124. Offers MS Ed. *Program availability:* Part-time, evening/weekend. *Faculty:* 5 full-time (4 women). *Students:* 19 full-time (18 women), 8 part-time (all women); includes 22 minority (6 Black or African American, non-Hispanic/Latino; 15 Hispanic/Latino; 1 Native Hawaiian or other Pacific Islander, non-Hispanic/Latino), 1 international. Average age 27. 35 applicants, 80% accepted, 15 enrolled. In 2016, 14 master's awarded. *Degree requirements:* For master's, thesis optional, capstone project or comprehensive exam. *Entrance requirements:* For master's, GRE General Test. Additional exam requirements/recommendations for international students: Required—TOEFL (minimum score 550 paper-based; 80 iBT); Recommended—IELTS (minimum score 6.5). *Application deadline:* For fall admission, 3/1 for domestic students, 10/1 for international students. Application fee: $65. Electronic applications accepted. *Financial support:* In 2016–17, 27 students received support. Institutionally sponsored loans and scholarships/grants available. Support available to part-time students. Financial award application deadline: 3/1; financial award applicants required to submit FAFSA. *Unit head:* Dr. Ashmeet Oberoi, Assistant Professor of Professional Practice/Program Director, 305-284-5956, E-mail: a.oberoi@miami.edu. *Application contact:* Lois Heffernan, Graduate Admissions Coordinator, 305-284-2167, Fax: 305-284-9395, E-mail: lheffernan@miami.edu.
Website: http://www.education.miami.edu

**University of Miami,** Graduate School, School of Education and Human Development, Department of Teaching and Learning, Program in Education and Social Change, Coral Gables, FL 33124. Offers MS Ed. *Program availability:* Part-time, evening/weekend. *Faculty:* 9 full-time (3 women), 9 part-time/adjunct (3 women). *Students:* 6 full-time (5 women), 8 part-time (all women); includes 6 minority (2 Black or African American, non-Hispanic/Latino; 4 Hispanic/Latino), 1 international. Average age 24. 2 applicants, 100% accepted, 2 enrolled. In 2016, 22 master's awarded. *Degree requirements:* For master's, electronic portfolio. *Entrance requirements:* For master's, GRE General Test. Additional exam requirements/recommendations for international students: Required—TOEFL (minimum score 550 paper-based; 80 iBT); Recommended—IELTS (minimum score 6.5). *Application deadline:* For fall admission, 2/1 for domestic students. Application fee: $65. Electronic applications accepted. *Financial support:* Application deadline: 3/1; applicants required to submit FAFSA. *Unit head:* Dr. Mary Avalos, Assistant Research Professor and Program Director, 305-284-6467, Fax: 305-284-3003, E-mail: mavalos@miami.edu. *Application contact:* Lois Heffernan, Graduate Admissions Coordinator, 305-284-2167, Fax: 305-284-9395, E-mail: lheffernan@miami.edu.
Website: http://www.education.miami.edu

**University of Michigan,** Rackham Graduate School, College of Literature, Science, and the Arts, Department of Sociology, Ann Arbor, MI 48109. Offers public policy and sociology (PhD); social work and sociology (PhD); sociology (PhD). *Degree requirements:* For doctorate, comprehensive exam, thesis/dissertation, oral defense of dissertation, preliminary exam. *Entrance requirements:* For doctorate, GRE General Test, letters of recommendation, writing sample, academic statement of purpose, personal statement, transcript. Additional exam requirements/recommendations for international students: Required—TOEFL (minimum score 560 paper-based; 84 iBT). Electronic applications accepted. *Expenses:* Tuition, state resident: full-time $21,466; part-time $1152 per credit hour. Tuition, nonresident: full-time $43,346; part-time $2367 per credit hour. Part-time tuition and fees vary according to course load, degree level and program. *Faculty research:* Power, history and social change; gender and sexuality; race and ethnicity; economic sociology; social demography.

**University of Michigan,** School of Social Work, Interdisciplinary PhD Program in Social Work and Social Science, Ann Arbor, MI 48109-1106. Offers social work and anthropology (PhD); social work and economics (PhD); social work and political science (PhD); social work and psychology (PhD); social work and sociology (PhD). Programs offered through the Rackham Graduate School. *Faculty:* 50 full-time (29 women), 62 part-time/adjunct (48 women). *Students:* 59 full-time (42 women); includes 30 minority (14 Black or African American, non-Hispanic/Latino; 9 Asian, non-Hispanic/Latino; 7 Hispanic/Latino). Average age 32. 114 applicants, 7% accepted, 8 enrolled. In 2016, 8 doctorates awarded. *Degree requirements:* For doctorate, thesis/dissertation, oral defense of dissertation, preliminary exam. *Entrance requirements:* For doctorate, GRE General Test. Additional exam requirements/recommendations for international students: Required—TOEFL (minimum score 620 paper-based, 88 iBT) or IELTS. *Application deadline:* For fall admission, 12/1 for domestic and international students. Application fee: $75 ($90 for international students). Electronic applications accepted. *Expenses:* $42,016 fall/winter tuition. *Financial support:* In 2016–17, 59 students received support, including 20 fellowships with full tuition reimbursements available (averaging $15,200 per year), 8 research assistantships with full tuition reimbursements

available (averaging $19,737 per year), 17 teaching assistantships with full tuition reimbursements available (averaging $19,737 per year); career-related internships or fieldwork, scholarships/grants, traineeships, health care benefits, tuition waivers (full and partial), and unspecified assistantships also available. Financial award application deadline: 12/1; financial award applicants required to submit FAFSA. *Faculty research:* Children and family, aging, community organization, health and mental health, police and evaluation. *Total annual research expenditures:* $3.8 million. *Unit head:* Dr. Daphne C. Watkins, Director, 734-763-5768, E-mail: daphnew@umich.edu. *Application contact:* Todd Huynh, Graduate Coordinator, 734-647-2554, Fax: 734-615-3192, E-mail: ssw.phd.info@umich.edu.
Website: https://ssw.umich.edu/offices/phd

**University of Minnesota, Duluth,** Graduate School, College of Liberal Arts, Department of Sociology/Anthropology, Duluth, MN 55812-2496. Offers criminology (MA); liberal studies (MLS). *Program availability:* Part-time. *Degree requirements:* For master's, thesis or alternative. *Entrance requirements:* For master's, interview, minimum GPA of 3.0, letters of recommendation. Additional exam requirements/recommendations for international students: Required—TOEFL. *Faculty research:* Nature of knowledge, philosophy of science, ecology, cultural studies, language.

**University of Minnesota, Twin Cities Campus,** Graduate School, College of Liberal Arts, Department of Sociology, Minneapolis, MN 55455. Offers MA, PhD. Terminal master's awarded for partial completion of doctoral program. *Degree requirements:* For master's, thesis optional; for doctorate, comprehensive exam, thesis/dissertation, preliminary written and oral exam, prospectus hearing, final oral defense and dissertation. *Entrance requirements:* For doctorate, GRE General Test, bachelor's degree, transcripts, minimum GPA of 3.0, personal statement, three letters of recommendation, writing sample. Additional exam requirements/recommendations for international students: Required—TOEFL (minimum score 587 paper-based; 95 iBT). Electronic applications accepted. *Faculty research:* Organizations, work, and markets; inequality: race, class, and gender; law, crime and deviance; family and life course; political sociology and social movements.

**University of Missouri,** Office of Research and Graduate Studies, College of Arts and Science, Department of Sociology, Columbia, MO 65211. Offers PhD. *Faculty:* 11 full-time (5 women). *Students:* 47 full-time (25 women), 2 part-time (1 woman); includes 14 minority (6 Black or African American, non-Hispanic/Latino; 1 American Indian or Alaska Native, non-Hispanic/Latino; 5 Hispanic/Latino; 2 Two or more races, non-Hispanic/Latino), 6 international. Average age 33. *Degree requirements:* For doctorate, one foreign language, comprehensive exam, thesis/dissertation. *Entrance requirements:* For doctorate, GRE General Test, minimum GPA of 3.0; 15 hours of undergraduate sociology with minimum B average, including one course each in sociological theory and basic statistics. Additional exam requirements/recommendations for international students: Required—TOEFL (minimum score 500 paper-based; 61 iBT). *Application deadline:* For fall admission, 1/15 priority date for domestic students. Applications are processed on a rolling basis. Application fee: $75 ($90 for international students). Electronic applications accepted. *Expenses:* Tuition, state resident: full-time $6347; part-time $352.60 per credit hour. Tuition, nonresident: full-time $17,379; part-time $965.50 per credit hour. *Required fees:* $1035. Tuition and fees vary according to course load, campus/location and program. *Financial support:* Fellowships with full tuition reimbursements, research assistantships with full tuition reimbursements, teaching assistantships with full tuition reimbursements, institutionally sponsored loans, health care benefits, and unspecified assistantships available.
Website: http://sociology.missouri.edu/graduate/requirements.shtml

**University of Missouri–Kansas City,** College of Arts and Sciences, Department of Sociology, Kansas City, MO 64110-2499. Offers MA. PhD (interdisciplinary) offered through the School of Graduate Studies. *Program availability:* Part-time, evening/weekend. *Faculty:* 7 full-time (5 women). *Students:* 6 part-time (5 women). Average age 29. 10 applicants, 50% accepted, 5 enrolled. *Degree requirements:* For master's, thesis optional. *Entrance requirements:* For master's, GRE, minimum GPA of 3.0 in major, 2.7 overall. Additional exam requirements/recommendations for international students: Required—TOEFL (minimum score 550 paper-based; 80 iBT). *Application deadline:* For fall admission, 3/1 for domestic and international students; for spring admission, 11/1 for domestic and international students. Applications are processed on a rolling basis. Application fee: $45 ($50 for international students). Electronic applications accepted. *Financial support:* In 2016–17, 4 teaching assistantships with tuition reimbursements (averaging $11,200 per year) were awarded; research assistantships with full tuition reimbursements, career-related internships or fieldwork, Federal Work-Study, institutionally sponsored loans, and tuition waivers (partial) also available. Support available to part-time students. Financial award application deadline: 3/1; financial award applicants required to submit FAFSA. *Faculty research:* Gerontology, religious movements, urban community and neighborhoods. *Unit head:* Dr. Deborah Smith, Chair, 816-235-2529, Fax: 816-235-1117, E-mail: smithde@umkc.edu. *Application contact:* Tamara Byland, Director of Admissions, 816-235-1111, Fax: 816-235-5544, E-mail: admit@umkc.edu.
Website: http://cas.umkc.edu/soc/

**University of Montana,** Graduate School, College of Humanities and Sciences, Department of Sociology, Missoula, MT 59812-0002. Offers criminology (MA); inequality and social justice (MA); rural and environmental change (MA); sociology (MA). *Entrance requirements:* For master's, GRE General Test. Additional exam requirements/recommendations for international students: Required—TOEFL. *Faculty research:* Housing, homelessness, hunger, infant mortality, work safety.

**University of Nebraska at Omaha,** Graduate Studies, College of Arts and Sciences, Department of Sociology and Anthropology, Omaha, NE 68182. Offers sociology (MA). *Program availability:* Part-time. *Faculty:* 9 full-time (6 women). *Students:* 5 full-time (4 women), 20 part-time (12 women); includes 4 minority (1 Black or African American, non-Hispanic/Latino; 3 Hispanic/Latino), 2 international. Average age 30. 19 applicants, 68% accepted, 12 enrolled. In 2016, 6 master's awarded. *Degree requirements:* For master's, comprehensive exam (for some programs), thesis optional. *Entrance requirements:* For master's, 3 letters of recommendation, resume, statement of purpose, writing sample, minimum GPA of 3.0, official transcripts. Additional exam requirements/recommendations for international students: Required—TOEFL, IELTS, PTE. *Application deadline:* For fall admission, 4/15 for domestic and international students; for spring admission, 11/15 for domestic and international students. Applications are processed on a rolling basis. Application fee: $45. Electronic applications accepted. *Financial support:* In 2016–17, 4 students received support, including 2 research assistantships with tuition reimbursements available, 2 teaching assistantships with tuition reimbursements available; Federal Work-Study, institutionally sponsored loans, scholarships/grants, health care benefits, tuition waivers (partial), and unspecified assistantships also available. Support available to part-time students. Financial award application deadline: 3/1; financial award applicants required to submit FAFSA. *Unit head:* Dr. Mary Ann Powell, Chairperson, 402-554-2341, E-mail: graduate@unomaha.edu. *Application contact:* Dr. Daniel Hawkins, Graduate Program Chair, 402-554-2341, E-mail: graduate@unomaha.edu.

**University of Nebraska–Lincoln,** Graduate College, College of Arts and Sciences, Department of Sociology, Lincoln, NE 68588. Offers MA, PhD. *Degree requirements:*

For master's, thesis optional; for doctorate, comprehensive exam, thesis/dissertation. *Entrance requirements:* For master's and doctorate, GRE General Test, writing sample. Additional exam requirements/recommendations for international students: Required—TOEFL (minimum score 550 paper-based). Electronic applications accepted. *Faculty research:* Family, deviance and social control, ethnic studies, inequality (gender, race, and class).

**University of Nevada, Las Vegas,** Graduate College, College of Liberal Arts, Department of Sociology, Las Vegas, NV 89154-5003. Offers MA, PhD. *Program availability:* Part-time. *Faculty:* 10 full-time (3 women), 1 part-time/adjunct (0 women). *Students:* 34 full-time (20 women), 15 part-time (10 women); includes 11 minority (2 Black or African American, non-Hispanic/Latino; 1 Asian, non-Hispanic/Latino; 6 Hispanic/Latino; 2 Two or more races, non-Hispanic/Latino), 3 international. Average age 34. 35 applicants, 66% accepted, 14 enrolled. In 2016, 2 master's, 6 doctorates awarded. Terminal master's awarded for partial completion of doctoral program. *Degree requirements:* For doctorate, comprehensive exam, thesis/dissertation, oral defense. *Entrance requirements:* For doctorate, GRE General Test, 3 letters of recommendation; statement of purpose; writing samples. Additional exam requirements/recommendations for international students: Required—TOEFL (minimum score 550 paper-based; 80 iBT), IELTS (minimum score 7). *Application deadline:* For fall admission, 2/1 for domestic students. Application fee: $60 ($95 for international students). Electronic applications accepted. *Expenses:* $269.25 per credit, $792 per 3-credit course; $9,634 per year resident; $23,274 per year non-resident; $7,094 fees non-resident (7 credits or more); $1,307 annual health insurance fee. *Financial support:* In 2016–17, 1 fellowship with partial tuition reimbursement (averaging $20,000 per year), 11 research assistantships with partial tuition reimbursements (averaging $16,648 per year), 19 teaching assistantships with partial tuition reimbursements (averaging $16,230 per year) were awarded; institutionally sponsored loans, scholarships/grants, health care benefits, and unspecified assistantships also available. Financial award application deadline: 3/15. *Faculty research:* Urban and community studies, culture, sex and gender, health and environment, theory and social psychology. *Unit head:* Dr. Robert Futrell, Chair/Professor, 702-895-0270, Fax: 702-895-4800, E-mail: robert.futrell@unlv.edu. *Application contact:* Dr. Barbara Brents, Graduate Coordinator, 702-895-0261, Fax: 702-895-4800, E-mail: barb.brents@unlv.edu.
Website: http://www.unlv.edu/sociology

**University of Nevada, Reno,** Graduate School, College of Liberal Arts, School of Social Research and Justice Studies, Department of Sociology, Reno, NV 89557. Offers MA. *Degree requirements:* For master's, thesis optional. *Entrance requirements:* For master's, GRE General Test, minimum GPA of 2.75. Additional exam requirements/recommendations for international students: Required—TOEFL (minimum score 500 paper-based; 61 iBT), IELTS (minimum score 6). Electronic applications accepted. *Faculty research:* Statistics, politics and economics, religion and law, industry, theory stratification.

**University of New Brunswick Fredericton,** School of Graduate Studies, Faculty of Arts, Department of Sociology, Fredericton, NB E3B 5A3, Canada. Offers MA, PhD. *Program availability:* Part-time. *Degree requirements:* For master's, thesis; for doctorate, comprehensive exam, thesis/dissertation, 6 courses. *Entrance requirements:* For master's, minimum GPA of 3.5; for doctorate, MA in sociology with thesis or equivalent, curriculum vitae, statement of interest about intended research and why UNB was selected. Additional exam requirements/recommendations for international students: Required—TOEFL. Electronic applications accepted. *Faculty research:* Social policy, media, sociology and cooperative economy, charities and philanthropy, gender health and entrepreneurship, reproductive health and women, international development, criminology, environment, science and technology, family and domestic violence, sociology of health, health policy and social determinants of health, law and social policy.

**University of New Hampshire,** Graduate School, College of Liberal Arts, Department of Sociology, Durham, NH 03824. Offers MA, PhD. *Program availability:* Part-time. *Degree requirements:* For master's, thesis; for doctorate, one foreign language, thesis/dissertation. *Entrance requirements:* For master's and doctorate, GRE General Test. Additional exam requirements/recommendations for international students: Required—TOEFL (minimum score 550 paper-based; 80 iBT). Electronic applications accepted. *Faculty research:* Deviance, conflict and control, social psychology, comparative institutional analysis, family.

**University of New Mexico,** Graduate Studies, College of Arts and Sciences, Program in Sociology, Albuquerque, NM 87131. Offers MA, PhD. *Program availability:* Part-time. *Faculty:* 12 full-time (6 women), 1 (woman) part-time/adjunct. *Students:* 19 full-time (12 women), 15 part-time (11 women); includes 13 minority (1 Black or African American, non-Hispanic/Latino; 1 American Indian or Alaska Native, non-Hispanic/Latino; 2 Asian, non-Hispanic/Latino; 9 Hispanic/Latino), 3 international. Average age 33. 25 applicants, 40% accepted, 3 enrolled. In 2016, 4 master's awarded. Terminal master's awarded for partial completion of doctoral program. *Degree requirements:* For master's, thesis; for doctorate, comprehensive exam, thesis/dissertation. *Entrance requirements:* For master's and doctorate, GRE General Test, 2 writing samples, 3 letters of reference, letter of intent. Additional exam requirements/recommendations for international students: Required—TOEFL (minimum score 550 paper-based; 79 iBT), IELTS (minimum score 7). *Application deadline:* For fall admission, 1/15 priority date for domestic and international students; for spring admission, 9/30 for domestic students. Application fee: $50. Electronic applications accepted. *Financial support:* Fellowships, research assistantships, teaching assistantships with partial tuition reimbursements, institutionally sponsored loans, scholarships/grants, health care benefits, tuition waivers (partial), and unspecified assistantships available. Support available to part-time students. Financial award application deadline: 1/15; financial award applicants required to submit FAFSA. *Faculty research:* Criminology/crime/law/social control, sociology of health and medicine, social movements, race and ethnicity, comparative sociology, Latin American comparative sociology, political sociology, sociology of science and knowledge, sociology of education. *Unit head:* Dr. Richard Santos, Interim Departmental Chair, 505-277-2501, Fax: 505-277-8805, E-mail: santos@unm.edu. *Application contact:* Shannon Kindilien, Academic Advisor, 505-277-2501, Fax: 505-277-8805, E-mail: sadvisor@unm.edu.
Website: http://www.unm.edu/~socdept/

**University of New Orleans,** Graduate School, College of Liberal Arts, Department of Sociology, New Orleans, LA 70148. Offers MA. *Program availability:* Part-time, evening/weekend. *Degree requirements:* For master's, thesis (for some programs). *Entrance requirements:* For master's, GRE General Test. Additional exam requirements/recommendations for international students: Required—TOEFL (minimum score 550 paper-based; 79 iBT), IELTS (minimum score 6.5). Electronic applications accepted. *Faculty research:* Environment and gender.

**The University of North Carolina at Chapel Hill,** Graduate School, College of Arts and Sciences, Department of Sociology, Chapel Hill, NC 27599. Offers MA, PhD. *Degree requirements:* For master's, comprehensive exam, thesis; for doctorate, comprehensive exam, thesis/dissertation. *Entrance requirements:* For master's and doctorate, GRE General Test, minimum GPA of 3.0. Additional exam requirements/recommendations for international students: Required—TOEFL (minimum score 550 paper-based). Electronic

applications accepted. *Faculty research:* Comparative historical, work/organizations, religion, demography, stratification.

**The University of North Carolina at Charlotte,** College of Liberal Arts and Sciences, Department of Sociology, Charlotte, NC 28223-0001. Offers MA. *Program availability:* Part-time, evening/weekend. *Faculty:* 17 full-time (10 women). *Students:* 9 full-time (7 women), 10 part-time (3 women); includes 6 minority (5 Black or African American, non-Hispanic/Latino; 1 Hispanic/Latino). Average age 31. 10 applicants, 70% accepted, 4 enrolled. In 2016, 3 master's awarded. *Degree requirements:* For master's, thesis or practicum. *Entrance requirements:* For master's, GRE, minimum undergraduate GPA of 3.0; minimum of 18 hours of undergraduate course work in the social sciences, including social theory; demonstrated undergraduate competence in research methods and statistics. Additional exam requirements/recommendations for international students: Required—TOEFL (minimum score 523 paper-based, 70 iBT) or IELTS (6.5). *Application deadline:* For fall admission, 3/1 priority date for domestic and international students; for spring admission, 10/1 priority date for domestic and international students; for summer admission, 4/1 priority date for domestic and international students. Applications are processed on a rolling basis. Application fee: $75. Electronic applications accepted. *Expenses:* Tuition, state resident: full-time $4252. Tuition, nonresident: full-time $17,423. *Required fees:* $3026. Tuition and fees vary according to course load and program. *Financial support:* In 2016–17, 14 students received support, including 8 research assistantships (averaging $10,455 per year), 6 teaching assistantships (averaging $10,000 per year); career-related internships or fieldwork, institutionally sponsored loans, scholarships/grants, and unspecified assistantships also available. Support available to part-time students. Financial award application deadline: 3/1; financial award applicants required to submit FAFSA. *Total annual research expenditures:* $456,383. *Unit head:* Dr. Stephanie Moller, Chair, 704-687-7824, Fax: 704-687-1397, E-mail: smoller@uncc.edu. *Application contact:* Kathy B. Giddings, Director of Graduate Admissions, 704-687-5503, Fax: 704-687-1668, E-mail: gradadm@uncc.edu.
Website: http://sociology.uncc.edu/

**The University of North Carolina at Greensboro,** Graduate School, College of Arts and Sciences, Department of Sociology, Greensboro, NC 27412-5001. Offers criminology (MA); sociology (MA). *Program availability:* Part-time. *Degree requirements:* For master's, comprehensive exam, thesis. *Entrance requirements:* For master's, GRE General Test. Additional exam requirements/recommendations for international students: Required—TOEFL. Electronic applications accepted.

**The University of North Carolina Wilmington,** College of Arts and Sciences, Department of Sociology and Criminology, Wilmington, NC 28403-3297. Offers MA. *Program availability:* Part-time. *Faculty:* 15 full-time (9 women). *Students:* 21 full-time (14 women), 6 part-time (5 women); includes 5 minority (1 Black or African American, non-Hispanic/Latino; 2 Hispanic/Latino; 2 Two or more races, non-Hispanic/Latino). Average age 25. 30 applicants, 83% accepted, 16 enrolled. In 2016, 4 master's awarded. *Degree requirements:* For master's, thesis or internship. *Entrance requirements:* For master's, GRE General Test, 3 letters of recommendation, statement of interest, writing sample, minimum GPA of 3.0 in undergraduate work. Additional exam requirements/recommendations for international students: Required—TOEFL (minimum score 79 iBT), IELTS (minimum score 6.5). *Application deadline:* For fall admission, 2/15 for domestic students. Applications are processed on a rolling basis. Application fee: $60. Electronic applications accepted. *Expenses:* Contact institution. *Financial support:* Teaching assistantships, scholarships/grants, and out-of-state tuition award available. Financial award application deadline: 3/15; financial award applicants required to submit FAFSA. *Unit head:* Dr. Mike Maume, Chair, 910-962-7749, Fax: 910-962-7385, E-mail: maume@uncw.edu. *Application contact:* Dr. Daniel Buffington, Graduate Coordinator, 910-962-3434, Fax: 910-962-7385, E-mail: buffingtond@uncw.edu.
Website: http://www.uncw.edu/socgrad/index.html

**University of North Dakota,** Graduate School, College of Arts and Sciences, Department of Sociology, Grand Forks, ND 58202. Offers MA. *Degree requirements:* For master's, thesis, final examination. *Entrance requirements:* For master's, minimum GPA of 3.0. Additional exam requirements/recommendations for international students: Required—TOEFL (minimum score 550 paper-based; 79 iBT), IELTS (minimum score 6.5). *Application deadline:* For fall admission, 8/1 priority date for domestic students, 5/1 priority date for international students; for spring admission, 12/1 priority date for domestic students, 9/1 priority date for international students. Applications are processed on a rolling basis. Application fee: $35. Electronic applications accepted. *Financial support:* Fellowships with full and partial tuition reimbursements, research assistantships with full and partial tuition reimbursements, teaching assistantships with full and partial tuition reimbursements, Federal Work-Study, institutionally sponsored loans, scholarships/grants, health care benefits, tuition waivers (full and partial), and unspecified assistantships available. Support available to part-time students. Financial award application deadline: 3/15; financial award applicants required to submit FAFSA. *Faculty research:* Criminal justice studies, social psychology, research methods, corrections, social theory. *Unit head:* Dr. Abdallah Badahdah, Graduate Director, 701-777-4424, Fax: 701-777-2468, E-mail: abdallah.badahdah@und.nodak.edu. *Application contact:* Matt Anderson, Admissions Specialist, 701-777-2947, Fax: 701-777-3619, E-mail: matthew.anderson@gradschool.und.edu.
Website: http://www.und.edu/dept/soc/

**University of Northern Colorado,** Graduate School, College of Humanities and Social Sciences, Department of Sociology, Greeley, CO 80639. Offers MA. *Program availability:* Part-time. *Degree requirements:* For master's, comprehensive exam. *Entrance requirements:* For master's, 2 letters of recommendation. *Application deadline:* Applications are processed on a rolling basis. Application fee: $50 ($60 for international students). Electronic applications accepted. *Financial support:* Fellowships, research assistantships, teaching assistantships, and unspecified assistantships available. Financial award application deadline: 3/1; financial award applicants required to submit FAFSA. *Unit head:* Dr. Kyle Anne Nelson, Associate Professor and Chair, 970-351-2592, Fax: 970-351-1527, E-mail: kyle.nelson@unco.edu. *Application contact:* Linda Sisson, Graduate Student Admission Coordinator, 970-351-1807, Fax: 970-351-2371, E-mail: linda.sisson@unco.edu.
Website: http://www.unco.edu/hss/sociology/

**University of North Texas,** Robert B. Toulouse School of Graduate Studies, Denton, TX 76203-5459. Offers accounting (MS); applied anthropology (MA, MS); applied behavior analysis (Certificate); applied geography (MA); applied technology and performance improvement (M Ed, MS); art education (MA); art history (MA); art museum education (Certificate); arts leadership (Certificate); audiology (Au D); behavior analysis (MS); behavioral science (PhD); biochemistry and molecular biology (MS); biology (MA, MS); biomedical engineering (MS); business analysis (MS); chemistry (MS); clinical health psychology (PhD); communication studies (MA, MS); computer engineering (MS); computer science (MS); counseling (M Ed, MS), including clinical mental health counseling (MS), college and university counseling, elementary school counseling, secondary school counseling; creative writing (MA); criminal justice (MS); curriculum and instruction (M Ed); decision sciences (MBA); design (MA, MFA), including fashion design (MFA), innovation studies, interior design (MFA); early childhood studies (MS); economics (MS); educational leadership (M Ed, Ed D); educational psychology (MS,

## Sociology

PhD), including family studies (MS), gifted and talented (MS), human development (MS), learning and cognition (MS), research, measurement and evaluation (MS); electrical engineering (MS); emergency management (MPA); engineering technology (MS); English (MA); English as a second language (MA); environmental science (MS); finance (MBA, MS); financial management (MPA); French (MA); health services management (MBA); higher education (M Ed, Ed D); history (MA, MS); hospitality management (MS); human resources management (MPA); information science (MS); information systems (PhD); information technologies (MBA); interdisciplinary studies (MA, MS); international studies (MA); international sustainable tourism (MS); jazz studies (MM); journalism (MA, MJ, Graduate Certificate), including interactive and virtual digital communication (Graduate Certificate), narrative journalism (Graduate Certificate), public relations (Graduate Certificate); kinesiology (MS); linguistics (MA); local government management (MPA); logistics (PhD); logistics and supply chain management (MBA); long-term care, senior housing, and aging services (MA); management (PhD); marketing (MBA); mathematics (MA, MS); mechanical and energy engineering (MS, PhD); music (MA), including ethnomusicology, music theory, musicology, performance; music composition (PhD); music education (MM Ed, PhD); nonprofit management (MPA); operations and supply chain management (MBA); performance (MM, DMA); philosophy (MA); political science (MA); professional and technical communication (MA); radio, television and film (MA, MFA); rehabilitation counseling (Certificate); sociology (MA); Spanish (MA); special education (M Ed); speech-language pathology (MA); strategic management (MBA); studio art (MFA); teaching (M Ed); MBA/MS. *Program availability:* Part-time, evening/weekend, online learning. Terminal master's awarded for partial completion of doctoral program. *Degree requirements:* For master's, variable foreign language requirement, comprehensive exam (for some programs), thesis (for some programs); for doctorate, variable foreign language requirement, comprehensive exam (for some programs), thesis/dissertation; for other advanced degree, variable foreign language requirement, comprehensive exam (for some programs). *Entrance requirements:* For master's and doctorate, GRE, GMAT. Additional exam requirements/recommendations for international students: Required—TOEFL (minimum score 550 paper-based; 79 iBT). Electronic applications accepted.

**University of Notre Dame,** Graduate School, College of Arts and Letters, Division of Social Science, Department of Sociology, Notre Dame, IN 46556. Offers PhD. *Degree requirements:* For doctorate, thesis/dissertation, 2 area specialty exams. *Entrance requirements:* For doctorate, GRE General Test, GRE Subject Test (strongly recommended). Additional exam requirements/recommendations for international students: Required—TOEFL (minimum score 600 paper-based; 80 iBT). Electronic applications accepted. *Faculty research:* Cultural sociology, development, family, education, historical/comparative sociology.

**University of Oklahoma,** College of Arts and Sciences, Department of Sociology, Norman, OK 73019. Offers MA, PhD. *Program availability:* Part-time. *Faculty:* 16 full-time (8 women). *Students:* 16 full-time (11 women), 9 part-time (5 women), 2 international. Average age 31. 18 applicants, 78% accepted, 9 enrolled. In 2016, 8 master's, 4 doctorates awarded. Terminal master's awarded for partial completion of doctoral program. *Degree requirements:* For master's, thesis, three semesters of statistics; one semester each of theory, research methods, and professionalization seminar; for doctorate, comprehensive exam, thesis/dissertation, three semesters of statistics; two semesters of theory; one semester each research methods and professionalization/teaching seminar. *Entrance requirements:* For master's and doctorate, GRE. Additional exam requirements/recommendations for international students: Required—TOEFL (minimum score 79 iBT) or IELTS (minimum score 6.5). *Application deadline:* For fall admission, 1/1 for domestic and international students. Application fee: $50 ($100 for international students). Electronic applications accepted. *Expenses:* Tuition, state resident: full-time $4886; part-time $203.60 per credit hour. Tuition, nonresident: full-time $18,989; part-time $791.20 per credit hour. *Required fees:* $3283; $126.25 per credit hour. $126.50 per semester. *Financial support:* In 2016–17, 19 students received support, including 6 fellowships with full tuition reimbursements available (averaging $3,417 per year), 18 teaching assistantships with full tuition reimbursements available (averaging $14,635 per year); health care benefits also available. Financial award application deadline: 6/1; financial award applicants required to submit FAFSA. *Faculty research:* Criminology; LGBTQ issues; aging; international/cross-national sociology; environmental sociology; sociology of religion. *Total annual research expenditures:* $6,878. *Unit head:* Dr. Craig St. John, Professor and Chair, 405-325-1751, Fax: 405-325-7825, E-mail: cstjohn@ou.edu. *Application contact:* Dr. Trina Hope, Graduate Liaison, 405-325-3647, Fax: 405-325-7825, E-mail: thope@ou.edu. Website: http://soc.ou.edu

**University of Oregon,** Graduate School, College of Arts and Sciences, Department of Sociology, Eugene, OR 97403. Offers MA, MS, PhD. *Program availability:* Part-time. Terminal master's awarded for partial completion of doctoral program. *Degree requirements:* For doctorate, thesis/dissertation. *Entrance requirements:* For master's and doctorate, GRE General Test, minimum GPA of 3.0. Additional exam requirements/recommendations for international students: Required—TOEFL. *Faculty research:* Criminology, environment, gender, labor, political economy.

**University of Ottawa,** Faculty of Graduate and Postdoctoral Studies, Faculty of Social Sciences, Department of Sociology and Anthropology, Ottawa, ON K1N 6N5, Canada. Offers MA. *Degree requirements:* For master's, thesis or alternative. *Entrance requirements:* For master's, honors bachelor's degree or equivalent, minimum B average. Electronic applications accepted. *Faculty research:* Inter-ethnic relations, development, political policies.

**University of Pennsylvania,** School of Arts and Sciences, Graduate Group in Sociology, Philadelphia, PA 19104. Offers AM, PhD. *Faculty:* 38 full-time (17 women), 8 part-time/adjunct (3 women). *Students:* 51 full-time (37 women); includes 15 minority (6 Black or African American, non-Hispanic/Latino; 1 Asian, non-Hispanic/Latino; 8 Hispanic/Latino), 16 international. Average age 29. 266 applicants, 7% accepted, 7 enrolled. In 2016, 4 master's, 5 doctorates awarded. Terminal master's awarded for partial completion of doctoral program. *Expenses:* Tuition: Full-time $31,068; part-time $5762 per course. *Required fees:* $3200; $336 per course. Full-time tuition and fees vary according to degree level, program and student level. Part-time tuition and fees vary according to course load, degree level and program. Website: http://sociology.sas.upenn.edu/graduate_resources

**University of Pittsburgh,** Dietrich School of Arts and Sciences, Department of Sociology, Pittsburgh, PA 15260. Offers MA, PhD. *Program availability:* Part-time, evening/weekend, online learning. *Faculty:* 13 full-time (6 women). *Students:* 31 full-time (18 women), 1 (woman) part-time; includes 7 minority (3 Black or African American, non-Hispanic/Latino; 2 Asian, non-Hispanic/Latino; 2 Hispanic/Latino), 4 international. Average age 33. 45 applicants, 13% accepted, 5 enrolled. In 2016, 4 master's, 8 doctorates awarded. Terminal master's awarded for partial completion of doctoral program. *Degree requirements:* For master's, thesis; for doctorate, comprehensive exam, thesis/dissertation, preliminary exam. *Entrance requirements:* For master's and doctorate, GRE General Test, writing sample. Additional exam requirements/recommendations for international students: Required—TOEFL (minimum score 550 paper-based; 90 iBT), IELTS (minimum score 7). *Application deadline:* For fall admission, 1/15 for domestic and international students. Application fee: $50. Electronic

applications accepted. Tuition and fees vary according to program. *Financial support:* In 2016–17, 7 fellowships with full tuition reimbursements, 9 research assistantships with full tuition reimbursements, 15 teaching assistantships with full tuition reimbursements were awarded; Federal Work-Study, scholarships/grants, health care benefits, tuition waivers (full and partial), unspecified assistantships, and part-time instructor positions also available. Financial award application deadline: 1/15. *Faculty research:* Collective behavior/social movements, comparative sociology/historical sociology, cultural sociology, political sociology, qualitative methodology, quantitative methodology, sex and gender, social change, theory. *Total annual research expenditures:* $63,912. *Unit head:* Dr. Suzanne Staggenborg, Chair, 412-648-7582, Fax: 412-648-2799, E-mail: suzstagg@pitt.edu. *Application contact:* Graduate Coordinator, 412-648-7585, Fax: 412-648-2799. Website: http://www.sociology.pitt.edu/graduate/

**University of Puerto Rico, Río Piedras Campus,** College of Social Sciences, Department of Sociology, San Juan, PR 00931-3300. Offers MA. *Degree requirements:* For master's, comprehensive exam, thesis. *Entrance requirements:* For master's, GRE or PAEG, interview, minimum GPA of 3.0, letter of recommendation.

**University of Regina,** Faculty of Graduate Studies and Research, Faculty of Arts, Department of Sociology and Social Studies, Regina, SK S4S 0A2, Canada. Offers social studies (MA); sociology (MA). *Program availability:* Part-time. *Faculty:* 9 full-time (4 women), 7 part-time/adjunct (all women). *Students:* 6 full-time (4 women), 6 part-time (3 women). 10 applicants, 20% accepted. In 2016, 7 master's awarded. *Degree requirements:* For master's, thesis. *Entrance requirements:* Additional exam requirements/recommendations for international students: Required—TOEFL (minimum score 580 paper-based; 80 iBT), IELTS (minimum score 6.5), PTE (minimum score 59). *Application deadline:* Applications are processed on a rolling basis. Application fee: $100. Electronic applications accepted. *Financial support:* In 2016–17, 1 fellowship (averaging $6,000 per year), 5 teaching assistantships (averaging $2,501 per year) were awarded; scholarships/grants also available. Financial award application deadline: 6/15. *Faculty research:* Social justice, international development, globalization, social policy, political economy. *Unit head:* Dr. John Conway, Department Head, 306-585-4052, Fax: 306-585-4815, E-mail: john.conway@uregina.ca. *Application contact:* Dr. Henry Chow, Graduate Coordinator, 306-585-5604, Fax: 306-585-4815, E-mail: henry.chow@uregina.ca. Website: http://www.uregina.ca/arts/sociology-social-studies

**University of Saskatchewan,** College of Graduate Studies and Research, College of Arts and Science, Department of Sociology, Saskatoon, SK S7N 5A2, Canada. Offers MA, PhD. *Degree requirements:* For master's, thesis; for doctorate, comprehensive exam (for some programs), thesis/dissertation. *Entrance requirements:* Additional exam requirements/recommendations for international students: Required—TOEFL (minimum score 80 iBT); Recommended—IELTS (minimum score 6.5). Electronic applications accepted.

**University of South Africa,** College of Human Sciences, Pretoria, South Africa. Offers adult education (M Ed); African languages (MA, PhD); African politics (MA, PhD); Afrikaans (MA, PhD); ancient history (MA, PhD); ancient Near Eastern studies (MA, PhD); anthropology (MA, PhD); applied linguistics (MA); Arabic (MA, PhD); archaeology (MA); art history (MA); Biblical archaeology (MA); Biblical studies (M Th, D Th, PhD); Christian spirituality (M Th, D Th); church history (M Th, D Th); classical studies (MA, PhD); clinical psychology (MA); communication (MA, PhD); comparative education (M Ed, Ed D); consulting psychology (D Admin, D Com, PhD); curriculum studies (M Ed, Ed D); development studies (M Admin, MA, D Admin, PhD); didactics (M Ed, Ed D); education (M Tech); education management (M Ed, Ed D); educational psychology (M Ed); English (MA); environmental education (M Ed); French (MA, PhD); German (MA, PhD); Greek (MA); guidance and counseling (M Ed); health studies (MA, PhD), including health sciences education (MA), health services management (MA), medical and surgical nursing science (critical care general) (MA), midwifery and neonatal nursing science (MA), trauma and emergency care (MA); history (MA, PhD); history of education (Ed D); inclusive education (M Ed, Ed D); information and communications technology policy and regulation (MA); information science (MA, MIS, PhD); international politics (MA, PhD); Islamic studies (MA, PhD); Italian (MA, PhD); Judaica (MA, PhD); linguistics (MA, PhD); mathematical education (M Ed); mathematics education (MA); missiology (M Th, D Th); modern Hebrew (MA); musicology (MA, MMus, D Mus, PhD); natural science education (M Ed); New Testament (M Th, D Th); Old Testament (D Th); pastoral therapy (M Th, D Th); philosophy (MA); philosophy of education (M Ed, Ed D); politics (MA, PhD); Portuguese (MA, PhD); practical theology (M Th, D Th); psychology (MA, MS, PhD); psychology of education (M Ed, Ed D); public health (MA); religious studies (MA, D Th, PhD); Romance languages (MA); Russian (MA, PhD); Semitic languages (MA, PhD); social behavior studies in HIV/AIDS (MA); social science (mental health) (MA); social science in development studies (MA); social science in psychology (MA); social science in social work (MA); social science in sociology (MA); social work (MSW, DSW, PhD); socio-education (M Ed, Ed D); sociolinguistics (MA); sociology (MA, PhD); Spanish (MA, PhD); systematic theology (M Th, D Th); TESOL (teaching English to speakers of other languages) (MA); theological ethics (M Th, D Th); theory of literature (MA, PhD); urban ministries (D Th); urban ministry (M Th).

**University of South Alabama,** College of Arts and Sciences, Department of Sociology, Anthropology and Social Work, Mobile, AL 36688. Offers sociology (MA). *Program availability:* Part-time, evening/weekend. *Faculty:* 3 full-time (0 women). *Students:* 4 full-time (3 women); includes 1 minority (Black or African American, non-Hispanic/Latino). Average age 28. 7 applicants, 29% accepted, 1 enrolled. In 2016, 5 master's awarded. *Degree requirements:* For master's, comprehensive exam, thesis optional. *Entrance requirements:* For master's, GRE General Test, minimum GPA of 3.0. Additional exam requirements/recommendations for international students: Required—TOEFL (minimum score 525 paper-based; 71 iBT). *Application deadline:* For fall admission, 7/1 priority date for domestic students, 6/1 priority date for international students; for spring admission, 12/1 priority date for domestic students, 5/1 priority date for international students; for summer admission, 5/1 for domestic students. Applications are processed on a rolling basis. Application fee: $35. Electronic applications accepted. *Expenses:* Tuition, state resident: full-time $9768; part-time $407 per credit hour. Tuition, nonresident: full-time $19,536; part-time $814 per credit hour. *Financial support:* Fellowships, research assistantships, teaching assistantships, career-related internships or fieldwork, Federal Work-Study, institutionally sponsored loans, scholarships/grants, and unspecified assistantships available. Support available to part-time students. Financial award application deadline: 5/31; financial award applicants required to submit FAFSA. *Faculty research:* Cultural adaptation, child welfare, social inequality. *Unit head:* Dr. Roma S. Hanks, Chair, 251-460-6347, Fax: 251-460-7925, E-mail: rhanks@southalabama.edu. *Application contact:* Dr. Christopher Freed, Graduate Coordinator, Sociology, 251-460-6348, Fax: 251-460-7925, E-mail: cfreed@southalabama.edu. Website: http://www.southalabama.edu/colleges/artsandsci/syansw

**University of South Carolina,** The Graduate School, College of Arts and Sciences, Department of Sociology, Columbia, SC 29208. Offers MA, PhD. *Program availability:* Part-time. Terminal master's awarded for partial completion of doctoral program. *Degree requirements:* For master's, thesis; for doctorate, comprehensive exam, thesis/

dissertation. *Entrance requirements:* For master's and doctorate, GRE General Test. Additional exam requirements/recommendations for international students: Required—TOEFL (minimum score 570 paper-based; 75 iBT). Electronic applications accepted. *Faculty research:* Social psychology, social inequality.

**University of Southern California,** Graduate School, Dana and David Dornsife College of Letters, Arts, and Sciences, Department of Sociology, Los Angeles, CA 90089. Offers PhD. *Degree requirements:* For doctorate, comprehensive exam, thesis/dissertation. *Entrance requirements:* For doctorate, GRE. Additional exam requirements/recommendations for international students: Required—TOEFL. Electronic applications accepted. *Faculty research:* Family, immigration, gender, culture, race.

**University of South Florida,** College of Arts and Sciences, Department of Sociology, Tampa, FL 33620-9951. Offers MA, PhD. *Program availability: Faculty:* 10 full-time (8 women). *Students:* 35 full-time (23 women), 4 part-time (2 women); includes 13 minority (3 Black or African American, non-Hispanic/Latino; 3 Asian, non-Hispanic/Latino; 4 Hispanic/Latino; 3 Two or more races, non-Hispanic/Latino), 6 international. Average age 30. 42 applicants, 45% accepted, 11 enrolled. In 2016, 8 master's, 4 doctorates awarded. *Degree requirements:* For master's, comprehensive exam, thesis; for doctorate, comprehensive exam, thesis/dissertation. *Entrance requirements:* For master's, GRE General Test, minimum GPA of 3.25 in undergraduate coursework, three letters of recommendation, personal statement (1-3 pages), academic writing sample; for doctorate, GRE General Test, minimum GPA of 3.5 in graduate work, three letters of recommendation, personal statement, writing sample. Additional exam requirements/recommendations for international students: Required—TOEFL (minimum score 550 paper-based; 79 iBT) or IELTS (minimum score 6.5) for PhD; TOEFL (minimum score 600 paper-based) for MA. *Application deadline:* For fall admission, 2/15 priority date for domestic students, 1/15 priority date for international students; for spring admission, 10/15 for domestic students, 9/15 priority date for international students. Application fee: $30. Electronic applications accepted. *Expenses:* Tuition, state resident: full-time $7766; part-time $431.43 per credit hour. Tuition, nonresident: full-time $15,789; part-time $877.17 per credit hour. *Required fees:* $37 per term. *Financial support:* In 2016–17, 16 students received support, including 21 teaching assistantships with tuition reimbursements available (averaging $12,581 per year); unspecified assistantships also available. Financial award application deadline: 3/1. *Faculty research:* Urban development and culture; social inequalities; identities and communities; social problems and social movements; globalization, power, and politics; immigration and migration; community, networks, and wellbeing. *Total annual research expenditures:* $320,911. *Unit head:* Dr. Elizabeth Aranda, Associate Professor and Chairperson, 813-974-7690, Fax: 813-974-6455, E-mail: earanda@usf.edu. *Application contact:* Dr. Margarethe Kusenbach, Associate Professor, 813-974-2595, Fax: 813-974-6455, E-mail: mkusenba@usf.edu.
Website: http://sociology.usf.edu

**The University of Tennessee,** Graduate School, College of Arts and Sciences, Department of Sociology, Knoxville, TN 37996. Offers criminology (MA, PhD); energy, environment, and resource policy (MA, PhD); political economy (MA, PhD). *Program availability:* Part-time. *Degree requirements:* For master's, thesis or alternative; for doctorate, thesis/dissertation. *Entrance requirements:* For master's, GRE General Test, minimum GPA of 3.0; for doctorate, GRE General Test, minimum GPA of 3.5. Additional exam requirements/recommendations for international students: Required—TOEFL. Electronic applications accepted.

**The University of Texas at Arlington,** Graduate School, College of Liberal Arts, Department of Sociology and Anthropology, Program in Sociology, Arlington, TX 76019. Offers MA. *Program availability:* Part-time, evening/weekend. *Degree requirements:* For master's, comprehensive exam, thesis or alternative. *Entrance requirements:* For master's, GRE General Test, 12 hours of undergraduate course work in sociology. Additional exam requirements/recommendations for international students: Required—TOEFL (minimum score 550 paper-based). *Application deadline:* For fall admission, 6/15 for domestic students. Applications are processed on a rolling basis. Application fee: $35 ($50 for international students). Electronic applications accepted. *Financial support:* Fellowships with full tuition reimbursements, research assistantships, teaching assistantships, career-related internships or fieldwork, Federal Work-Study, and scholarships/grants available. Financial award application deadline: 4/1. *Unit head:* Dr. Shelley Smith, Chairman, 817-272-2650, Fax: 817-272-3759, E-mail: slsmith@uta.edu. *Application contact:* Dr. Bob Kunovich, Graduate Advisor, 817-272-2650, Fax: 817-272-3759, E-mail: kunovich@uta.edu.
Website: http://www.uta.edu/sociology-anthropology

**The University of Texas at Austin,** Graduate School, College of Liberal Arts, Department of Sociology, Austin, TX 78712-1111. Offers MA, PhD. *Degree requirements:* For master's, thesis; for doctorate, thesis/dissertation. *Entrance requirements:* For master's and doctorate, GRE General Test. Additional exam requirements/recommendations for international students: Required—TOEFL. Electronic applications accepted. *Faculty research:* Criminology, demography, Latin America, health, political sociology.

**The University of Texas at El Paso,** Graduate School, College of Liberal Arts, Department of Sociology and Anthropology, El Paso, TX 79968-0001. Offers applied anthropology (Certificate); applied social sciences (Certificate); sociology (MA). *Program availability:* Part-time, evening/weekend. *Degree requirements:* For master's, thesis. *Entrance requirements:* For master's, GRE General Test, minimum GPA of 3.0. Additional exam requirements/recommendations for international students: Required—TOEFL. Electronic applications accepted. *Faculty research:* U.S.-Mexico border, social inequality, immigration, Chicano culture, Mexico.

**The University of Texas at San Antonio,** College of Liberal and Fine Arts, Department of Sociology, San Antonio, TX 78249-0617. Offers MS. *Program availability:* Part-time. *Faculty:* 11 full-time (4 women). *Students:* 18 full-time (11 women), 24 part-time (15 women); includes 17 minority (6 Black or African American, non-Hispanic/Latino; 11 Hispanic/Latino), 1 international. Average age 30. 19 applicants, 84% accepted, 14 enrolled. In 2016, 13 master's awarded. *Degree requirements:* For master's, comprehensive exam, internship or thesis. *Entrance requirements:* For master's, GRE (waived if GPA 3.5 or above), BA/BS with 18 credit hours in field of study or other appropriate field of study; official transcripts; statement of purpose; academic writing sample; 3 letters of recommendation; minimum GPA of 3.0. Additional exam requirements/recommendations for international students: Required—TOEFL (minimum score 550 paper-based; 79 iBT), IELTS (minimum score 6.5). *Application deadline:* For fall admission, 7/1 for domestic students, 4/1 for international students; for spring admission, 11/1 for domestic students, 9/1 for international students. Application fee: $45 ($80 for international students). *Expenses:* Contact institution. *Financial support:* In 2016–17, 1 fellowship (averaging $2,500 per year), 8 research assistantships (averaging $20,000 per year), 3 teaching assistantships (averaging $2,500 per year) were awarded; career-related internships or fieldwork, scholarships/grants, and unspecified assistantships also available. Financial award application deadline: 4/1; financial award applicants required to submit FAFSA. *Faculty research:* Border studies, Latino studies, race and ethnicity, cultural media, communications studies, family and child development, health and illness, religion. *Total annual research expenditures:* $960,343. *Unit head:* Dr. Xiaohe Xu, Chair, 210-458-4620, Fax: 210-458-4619, E-mail: xiaohe.xu@utsa.edu. *Application contact:* Dr. Terri Earnest, Graduate Advisor of Record, 210-458-6239, Fax: 210-458-6239, E-mail: terri.earnest@utsa.edu.
Website: http://colfa.utsa.edu/Sociology/

**The University of Texas at Tyler,** College of Arts and Sciences, Department of Social Sciences, Tyler, TX 75799-0001. Offers criminal justice (MS); public administration (MPA); sociology (MS). *Program availability:* Part-time, evening/weekend. *Degree requirements:* For master's, comprehensive exam, thesis optional. *Entrance requirements:* For master's, GRE General Test, minimum GPA of 3.0. Additional exam requirements/recommendations for international students: Required—TOEFL. *Faculty research:* Urban segregation, minority business, violent crime, gender discrimination.

**The University of Texas Rio Grande Valley,** College of Liberal Arts, Department of Sociology and Anthropology, Edinburg, TX 78539. Offers MS. *Program availability:* Part-time, evening/weekend, online learning. *Entrance requirements:* For master's, GRE General Test, minimum undergraduate GPA of 3.0, bachelor's degree, official transcripts, personal statement, two letters of recommendation. Tuition and fees vary according to course load and program. *Faculty research:* Sociology of education, sociology of health, sociology of religion, migration, race and ethnicity, gender, border studies, disaster studies.

**The University of Toledo,** College of Graduate Studies, College of Languages, Literature and Social Sciences, Department of Sociology and Anthropology, Toledo, OH 43606-3390. Offers sociology (MA). *Program availability:* Part-time. *Degree requirements:* For master's, thesis or alternative. *Entrance requirements:* For master's, GRE, minimum cumulative point-hour ratio of 2.7 for all previous academic work, three letters of recommendation, statement of purpose, transcripts from all prior institutions attended. Additional exam requirements/recommendations for international students: Required—TOEFL (minimum score 550 paper-based; 80 iBT). Electronic applications accepted. *Faculty research:* Medical and social gerontology, population, social movements, socioeconomic development, corporations and work, race and ethnicity.

**University of Toronto,** School of Graduate Studies, Faculty of Arts and Science, Department of Sociology, Toronto, ON M5S 1A1, Canada. Offers MA, PhD. *Program availability:* Part-time. *Degree requirements:* For doctorate, thesis/dissertation. *Entrance requirements:* For master's, GRE (for applicants from non-Canadian universities, recommended for those from Canadian universities), 5 full-year courses in sociology, basic research and statistical skills; 2 letters of reference; minimum B+ average in each of last two years of post-secondary education; for doctorate, GRE (for applicants from non-Canadian universities; recommended for those from Canadian universities), MA in sociology, minimum A- average, 2 letters of reference, statement of interest. Additional exam requirements/recommendations for international students: Required—TOEFL (minimum score 580 paper-based; 93 iBT), TWE (minimum score 5). Electronic applications accepted.

**University of Utah,** Graduate School, College of Social and Behavioral Science, Department of Sociology, Salt Lake City, UT 84112-1107. Offers M Stat, MA, MS, PhD. *Faculty:* 11 full-time (8 women), 5 part-time/adjunct (2 women). *Students:* 14 full-time (12 women), 8 part-time (5 women); includes 4 minority (1 Black or African American, non-Hispanic/Latino; 1 Asian, non-Hispanic/Latino; 2 Hispanic/Latino), 5 international. Average age 32. 25 applicants, 40% accepted, 6 enrolled. In 2016, 1 master's, 4 doctorates awarded. *Degree requirements:* For master's, comprehensive exam (for some programs), thesis; for doctorate, comprehensive exam, thesis/dissertation. *Entrance requirements:* For master's and doctorate, GRE, minimum undergraduate GPA of 3.0. Additional exam requirements/recommendations for international students: Required—TOEFL (minimum score 550 paper-based). *Application deadline:* For fall admission, 2/1 priority date for domestic and international students. Application fee: $55 ($65 for international students). Electronic applications accepted. *Expenses:* Contact institution. *Financial support:* In 2016–17, 2 students received support, including 1 research assistantship with full tuition reimbursement available (averaging $15,000 per year), 15 teaching assistantships with full tuition reimbursements available (averaging $15,000 per year); scholarships/grants, health care benefits, tuition waivers (full), and unspecified assistantships also available. Financial award application deadline: 2/1; financial award applicants required to submit FAFSA. *Faculty research:* Comparative international sociology, population studies, health disparities, environment, gender. *Total annual research expenditures:* $9,900. *Unit head:* Dr. Ming Wen, Chair, 801-581-6153, Fax: 801-585-3784, E-mail: ming.wen@soc.utah.edu. *Application contact:* Dr. Rebecca Utz, Director of Graduate Studies, 801-581-7922, Fax: 801-585-3784, E-mail: rebecca.utz@soc.utah.edu.
Website: http://www.soc.utah.edu/

**University of Utah,** Graduate School, Interdepartmental Program in Statistics, Salt Lake City, UT 84112-1107. Offers biostatistics (M Stat); econometrics (M Stat); educational psychology (M Stat); mathematics (M Stat); sociology (M Stat). *Program availability:* Part-time. *Students:* 30 full-time (9 women), 29 part-time (8 women); includes 10 minority (7 Asian, non-Hispanic/Latino; 3 Hispanic/Latino), 12 international. Average age 31. 50 applicants, 70% accepted, 27 enrolled. In 2016, 20 master's awarded. *Degree requirements:* For master's, comprehensive exam (for some programs), projects. *Entrance requirements:* For master's, GRE General Test (for all but biostatistics); GRE Subject Test (for mathematics), minimum GPA of 3.0; course work in calculus, matrix theory, statistics. Additional exam requirements/recommendations for international students: Required—TOEFL (minimum score 500 paper-based; 61 iBT). *Application deadline:* For fall admission, 7/1 for domestic students, 4/1 for international students. Applications are processed on a rolling basis. Application fee: $55 ($65 for international students). Electronic applications accepted. *Expenses:* Tuition, state resident: full-time $7011; part-time $3918.24 per credit hour. Tuition, nonresident: full-time $22,154; part-time $11,665.42 per credit hour. *Financial support:* In 2016–17, 10 students received support, including 10 research assistantships with tuition reimbursements available (averaging $1,000 per year); career-related internships or fieldwork, scholarships/grants, and unspecified assistantships also available. *Faculty research:* Biostatistics, sociology, economics, educational psychology, mathematics. *Unit head:* Xiaoming Sheng, Chair, University Statistics Committee, 801-213-3729, E-mail: xiaoming.sheng@utah.edu. *Application contact:* Laura Egbert, Coordinator, 801-585-6853, E-mail: laura.egbert@utah.edu.
Website: http://www.mstat.utah.edu

**University of Victoria,** Faculty of Graduate Studies, Faculty of Social Sciences, Department of Sociology, Victoria, BC V8W 2Y2, Canada. Offers MA, PhD. PhD by special arrangement. *Program availability:* Part-time. *Degree requirements:* For master's, thesis; for doctorate, thesis/dissertation, candidacy exam. *Entrance requirements:* For master's, minimum B+ average. Additional exam requirements/recommendations for international students: Required—TOEFL (minimum score 575 paper-based), IELTS (minimum score 7), TWE (minimum score 4). *Faculty research:* Social and political thought, social justice, health and aging, globalization and social psychology.

**University of Virginia,** College and Graduate School of Arts and Sciences, Department of Sociology, Charlottesville, VA 22903. Offers MA, PhD. *Faculty:* 15 full-time (7 women), 2 part-time/adjunct (1 woman). *Students:* 33 full-time (24 women); includes 5 minority (2 Black or African American, non-Hispanic/Latino; 1 Asian, non-Hispanic/

## Sociology

Latino; 1 Hispanic/Latino; 1 Two or more races, non-Hispanic/Latino), 9 international. Average age 29. 58 applicants, 22% accepted, 7 enrolled. In 2016, 5 master's, 6 doctorates awarded. *Degree requirements:* For master's, thesis; for doctorate, comprehensive exam, thesis/dissertation. *Entrance requirements:* For master's and doctorate, GRE General Test, GRE Subject Test, 2 letters of recommendation. Additional exam requirements/recommendations for international students: Required—TOEFL (minimum score 600 paper-based; 90 iBT), IELTS (minimum score 7). *Application deadline:* For fall admission, 1/1 for domestic and international students. Applications are processed on a rolling basis. Application fee: $60. Electronic applications accepted. *Expenses:* Tuition, state resident: full-time $15,026; part-time $834 per credit hour. Tuition, nonresident: full-time $25,168; part-time $1378 per credit hour. *Required fees:* $2654. *Financial support:* Applicants required to submit FAFSA. *Unit head:* Jeffrey Olick, Chair, 434-924-3526, Fax: 434-924-7028, E-mail: sociology@virginia.edu. *Application contact:* Isaac Reed, Director of Graduate Admissions, 434-982-7794, Fax: 434-924-7028, E-mail: iar2c@virginia.edu.
Website: http://www.virginia.edu/sociology/

**University of Washington,** Graduate School, College of Arts and Sciences, Department of Sociology, Seattle, WA 98195. Offers MA, PhD. *Degree requirements:* For master's, thesis; for doctorate, thesis/dissertation. *Entrance requirements:* For master's and doctorate, GRE General Test, minimum GPA of 3.0. Additional exam requirements/recommendations for international students: Required—TOEFL. Electronic applications accepted. *Faculty research:* Demography, criminology, social psychology, race/ethnicity/inequality, family.

**University of Waterloo,** Graduate Studies, Faculty of Arts, Department of Sociology, Waterloo, ON N2L 3G1, Canada. Offers MA, PhD. *Program availability:* Part-time. *Degree requirements:* For master's, thesis (for some programs); for doctorate, one foreign language, thesis/dissertation. *Entrance requirements:* For master's, honors degree, minimum B+ average, resume, writing sample; for doctorate, master's degree, minimum A- average, resume, writing sample. Additional exam requirements/recommendations for international students: Required—TOEFL, IELTS, PTE. Electronic applications accepted. *Faculty research:* Theory, methods, stratification deviance, political sociology.

**The University of Western Ontario,** Faculty of Graduate Studies, Social Sciences Division, Department of Sociology, London, ON N6A 5B8, Canada. Offers MA, PhD. Terminal master's awarded for partial completion of doctoral program. *Degree requirements:* For master's, thesis (for some programs); for doctorate, one foreign language, comprehensive exam, thesis/dissertation. *Entrance requirements:* For master's, minimum B+ average, honors degree; for doctorate, minimum A- average. Additional exam requirements/recommendations for international students: Required—TOEFL. Electronic applications accepted. *Faculty research:* Social demography, class and change, health and aging, theory, methods.

**University of West Georgia,** College of Social Sciences, Carrollton, GA 30118. Offers criminology (MA); data analysis and evaluation methods (Postbaccalaureate Certificate); European Union studies (Postbaccalaureate Certificate); integrative health systems (Postbaccalaureate Certificate); nonprofit management and community development (Postbaccalaureate Certificate); psychology (MA, PhD), including consciousness and society (PhD); public administration (MPA); public management (Postbaccalaureate Certificate); sociology (MA). *Program availability:* Part-time, evening/weekend, 100% online, blended/hybrid learning. *Faculty:* 45 full-time (21 women). *Students:* 107 full-time (67 women), 73 part-time (46 women); includes 47 minority (39 Black or African American, non-Hispanic/Latino; 4 Asian, non-Hispanic/Latino; 4 Hispanic/Latino), 10 international. Average age 31. 83 applicants, 88% accepted, 60 enrolled. In 2016, 56 master's, 7 doctorates, 5 other advanced degrees awarded. *Entrance requirements:* Additional exam requirements/recommendations for international students: Required—TOEFL (minimum score 523 paper-based; 69 iBT); Recommended—IELTS (minimum score 6.5). *Application deadline:* For fall admission, 7/15 for domestic students, 6/1 for international students; for spring admission, 11/30 for domestic students, 10/15 for international students; for summer admission, 5/15 for domestic students, 3/30 for international students. Applications are processed on a rolling basis. Application fee: $40. Electronic applications accepted. *Expenses:* Tuition, state resident: full-time $5316; part-time $222 per semester hour. Tuition, nonresident: full-time $20,658; part-time $861 per semester hour. *Required fees:* $1962. Tuition and fees vary according to course load, degree level and program. *Financial support:* Fellowships, research assistantships, teaching assistantships, career-related internships or fieldwork, Federal Work-Study, institutionally sponsored loans, scholarships/grants, and unspecified assistantships available. Support available to part-time students. Financial award application deadline: 4/1; financial award applicants required to submit FAFSA. *Unit head:* Dr. N. Jane McCandless, Dean of Social Sciences, 678-839-5170, Fax: 678-839-5171, E-mail: jmccandl@westga.edu. *Application contact:* Dr. Toby Ziglar, Assistant Dean of the Graduate School, 678-839-1394, Fax: 678-839-1395, E-mail: graduate@westga.edu.
Website: https://www.westga.edu/coss

**University of Windsor,** Faculty of Graduate Studies, Faculty of Arts and Social Sciences, Department of Sociology and Anthropology, Windsor, ON N9B 3P4, Canada. Offers criminology (MA); sociology (MA); sociology-social justice (PhD). *Program availability:* Part-time. *Degree requirements:* For master's, thesis; for doctorate, comprehensive exam, thesis/dissertation. *Entrance requirements:* For master's, minimum B+ average; for doctorate, writing sample, minimum B+ average. Additional exam requirements/recommendations for international students: Required—TOEFL (minimum score 560 paper-based). Electronic applications accepted. *Faculty research:* Power and social change; criminology/deviance; social psychology; comparative development; race and ethnic relations; family, sex, and gender, social justice.

**University of Wisconsin–Madison,** Graduate School, College of Letters and Science, Department of Sociology, Madison, WI 53706-1380. Offers rural sociology (MS); sociology (MS, PhD). *Program availability:* Part-time. Terminal master's awarded for partial completion of doctoral program. *Degree requirements:* For master's, thesis, oral exam; for doctorate, thesis/dissertation, preliminary and final oral exams, 4 seminars. *Entrance requirements:* For master's and doctorate, GRE General Test. Additional exam requirements/recommendations for international students: Required—TOEFL. Electronic applications accepted.

**University of Wisconsin–Milwaukee,** Graduate School, College of Letters and Science, Department of Sociology, Milwaukee, WI 53201-0413. Offers MA, PhD. *Program availability:* Part-time. *Students:* 20 full-time (9 women), 8 part-time (6 women); includes 8 minority (4 Black or African American, non-Hispanic/Latino; 1 Asian, non-Hispanic/Latino; 3 Two or more races, non-Hispanic/Latino), 2 international. Average age 32. 29 applicants, 48% accepted, 9 enrolled. In 2016, 6 master's awarded. *Degree requirements:* For master's, thesis. *Entrance requirements:* For master's, GRE. *Application deadline:* For fall admission, 1/1 priority date for domestic students; for spring admission, 9/1 for domestic students. Applications are processed on a rolling basis. Application fee: $56 ($96 for international students). Electronic applications accepted. *Financial support:* Fellowships, teaching assistantships, career-related internships or fieldwork, unspecified assistantships, and project assistantships available. Support available to part-time students. Financial award application deadline: 4/15;

financial award applicants required to submit FAFSA. *Unit head:* Donald Green, Department Chair, 414-229-4259, E-mail: dgreen@uwm.edu. *Application contact:* General Information Contact, 414-229-4982, Fax: 414-229-6967, E-mail: gradschool@uwm.edu.
Website: http://www.uwm.edu/dept/sociology/

**University of Wyoming,** College of Arts and Sciences, Department of Sociology, Laramie, WY 82071. Offers MA. *Program availability:* Part-time. *Degree requirements:* For master's, thesis. *Entrance requirements:* For master's, GRE General Test, minimum GPA of 3.0. Additional exam requirements/recommendations for international students: Required—TOEFL (minimum score 525 paper-based). Electronic applications accepted. *Faculty research:* Gender, theory, international studies, law, social inequality.

**Utah State University,** School of Graduate Studies, College of Humanities, Arts and Social Sciences, Department of Sociology, Logan, UT 84322. Offers MA, MS, MSS, PhD. *Degree requirements:* For master's, thesis; for doctorate, comprehensive exam, thesis/dissertation. *Entrance requirements:* For master's, GRE General Test, minimum GPA of 3.0, recommendation letters; for doctorate, GRE General Test, minimum GPA of 3.0, recommendation letters, transcripts, personal statement, MS degree. Additional exam requirements/recommendations for international students: Required—TOEFL; Recommended—TWE. *Faculty research:* Demography, environmental/natural resource sociology, rural community change, international development, health studies.

**Vanderbilt University,** Department of Sociology, Nashville, TN 37240-1001. Offers MA, PhD. *Faculty:* 15 full-time (5 women). *Students:* 37 full-time (30 women); includes 13 minority (5 Black or African American, non-Hispanic/Latino; 4 Asian, non-Hispanic/Latino; 4 Hispanic/Latino), 4 international. Average age 28. 124 applicants, 6% accepted, 6 enrolled. In 2016, 3 master's, 6 doctorates awarded. *Degree requirements:* For master's, thesis; for doctorate, comprehensive exam, thesis/dissertation, area, qualifying, and final exams. *Entrance requirements:* For master's and doctorate, GRE General Test. Additional exam requirements/recommendations for international students: Required—TOEFL (minimum score 570 paper-based; 88 iBT). *Application deadline:* For fall admission, 1/15 for domestic and international students. Electronic applications accepted. *Expenses: Tuition:* Part-time $1854 per credit hour. *Financial support:* Fellowships with full tuition reimbursements, research assistantships, teaching assistantships with full tuition reimbursements, Federal Work-Study, institutionally sponsored loans, scholarships/grants, and health care benefits available. Financial award application deadline: 1/15; financial award applicants required to submit CSS PROFILE or FAFSA. *Faculty research:* Criminology; cultural sociology; gender, race, and ethics relations; deviant behavior and social control. *Unit head:* Dr. Larry Isaac, Chair, 615-322-7626, Fax: 615-322-7505, E-mail: larry.isaac@vanderbilt.edu. *Application contact:* Richard Pitt, Director of Graduate Studies, 615-322-7530, Fax: 615-322-7505, E-mail: r.pitt@vanderbilt.edu.
Website: http://www.vanderbilt.edu/sociology/VDOS_Home.shtml

**Virginia Commonwealth University,** Graduate School, College of Humanities and Sciences, Department of Sociology, Richmond, VA 23284-9005. Offers digital sociology (MS). *Degree requirements:* For master's, thesis optional. *Entrance requirements:* For master's, GRE General Test. Additional exam requirements/recommendations for international students: Required—TOEFL (minimum score 600 paper-based; 100 iBT); Recommended—IELTS (minimum score 6.5). *Application deadline:* For fall admission, 4/1 for domestic students; for spring admission, 10/1 for domestic students. Application fee: $50. Electronic applications accepted. *Financial support:* Teaching assistantships, career-related internships or fieldwork, Federal Work-Study, institutionally sponsored loans, and tuition waivers (full and partial) available. Support available to part-time students. *Unit head:* Dr. Julia A. Honnold, Graduate Program Director, 804-828-6680, E-mail: jhonn@vcu.edu. *Application contact:* Dr. Jennifer A. Johnson, Program Chair, 804-828-6826, Fax: 804-828-1027, E-mail: jajohnson3@vcu.edu.
Website: http://sociology.vcu.edu/

**Virginia Polytechnic Institute and State University,** Graduate School, College of Liberal Arts and Human Sciences, Blacksburg, VA 24061. Offers career and technical education (MS Ed, Ed D, PhD, Ed S); communication (MA); counselor education (MA Ed, Ed D, PhD, Ed S); creative writing (MFA); curriculum and instruction (MA Ed, Ed D, PhD, Ed S); educational leadership and policy studies (MA Ed, Ed D, PhD, Ed S); educational research and evaluation (PhD); English (MA); foreign languages, cultures, and literatures (MA); higher education (PhD); higher education and student affairs (MA Ed); history (MA); human development (MS, PhD); material culture and public humanities (MA); philosophy (MA); political science (MA); rhetoric and writing (PhD); science and technology studies (MS, PhD); social, political, ethical, and cultural thought (PhD); sociology (MS, PhD); theater arts (MFA). *Faculty:* 408 full-time (204 women), 3 part-time/adjunct (2 women). *Students:* 657 full-time (446 women), 457 part-time (292 women); includes 213 minority (114 Black or African American, non-Hispanic/Latino; 3 American Indian or Alaska Native, non-Hispanic/Latino; 29 Asian, non-Hispanic/Latino; 44 Hispanic/Latino; 23 Two or more races, non-Hispanic/Latino), 93 international. Average age 33. 805 applicants, 55% accepted, 328 enrolled. In 2016, 270 master's, 91 doctorates awarded. *Degree requirements:* For master's, comprehensive exam (for some programs), thesis (for some programs); for doctorate, comprehensive exam (for some programs), thesis/dissertation (for some programs). *Entrance requirements:* For master's and doctorate, GRE/GMAT. Additional exam requirements/recommendations for international students: Required—TOEFL (minimum score 80 iBT). *Application deadline:* For fall admission, 8/1 for domestic students, 4/1 for international students; for spring admission, 1/1 for domestic students, 9/1 for international students. Applications are processed on a rolling basis. Application fee: $75. Electronic applications accepted. *Expenses:* Tuition, state resident: full-time $12,467; part-time $692.50 per credit hour. Tuition, nonresident: full-time $25,095; part-time $1394.25 per credit hour. *Required fees:* $2669; $491.50 per semester. Tuition and fees vary according to course load, campus/location and program. *Financial support:* In 2016–17, 21 research assistantships with full tuition reimbursements (averaging $19,817 per year), 237 teaching assistantships with full tuition reimbursements (averaging $15,497 per year) were awarded. Financial award application deadline: 3/1; financial award applicants required to submit FAFSA. *Total annual research expenditures:* $6.6 million. *Unit head:* Rosemary Blieszner, Interim Dean, 540-231-6779, Fax: 540-231-7157, E-mail: liberalartsdean@vt.edu. *Application contact:* Chelsea Blanchet, Executive Assistant, 540-231-6779, Fax: 540-231-7157, E-mail: bchels1@vt.edu.
Website: http://www.liberalarts.vt.edu/

**Washington State University,** College of Arts and Sciences, Department of Sociology, Pullman, WA 99164. Offers MA, PhD. Program applications must be made through the Pullman campus. *Program availability:* Part-time. Terminal master's awarded for partial completion of doctoral program. *Degree requirements:* For master's, thesis; for doctorate, comprehensive exam, thesis/dissertation. *Entrance requirements:* For master's, bachelor's degree, minimum GPA of 3.0; for doctorate, MA in sociology, minimum GPA of 3.0. Additional exam requirements/recommendations for international students: Required—TOEFL (minimum score 550 paper-based). Electronic applications accepted. *Faculty research:* Criminology, environmental sociology, family, gender, social inequality.

**Wayne State University,** College of Liberal Arts and Sciences, Department of Sociology, Detroit, MI 48202. Offers applied sociological research methodology (MA);

sociology (MA, PhD). *Faculty:* 11 full-time (7 women). *Students:* 32 full-time (23 women), 4 part-time (all women); includes 11 minority (9 Black or African American, non-Hispanic/Latino; 1 Hispanic/Latino; 1 Two or more races, non-Hispanic/Latino), 3 international. Average age 39. 38 applicants, 24% accepted, 7 enrolled. In 2016, 4 master's, 8 doctorates awarded. *Degree requirements:* For master's, comprehensive exam (for some programs), thesis (for some programs), oral exam, public defense of thesis/essay; for doctorate, comprehensive exam, thesis/dissertation. *Entrance requirements:* For master's, GRE General Test, minimum GPA of 3.3 in upper-division courses; substantial background in sociology, social science research methods, sociological theory, and basic statistics; three letters of reference (at least 2 from college/university faculty); writing sample; statement of interest; for doctorate, GRE General Test, minimum GPA of 3.5 in master's work; three letters of reference (at least 2 from college/university faculty); statement of interest; sample of written work. Additional exam requirements/recommendations for international students: Required—TOEFL (minimum score 600 paper-based; 100 iBT), TWE, Michigan English Language Assessment Battery (minimum score 85); Recommended—IELTS. *Application deadline:* For fall admission, 1/15 for domestic and international students. Application fee: $50. Electronic applications accepted. *Expenses:* $16,503 per year resident tuition and fees, $33,697 per year non-resident tuition and fees. *Financial support:* In 2016–17, 20 students received support, including 5 fellowships with tuition reimbursements available (averaging $14,000 per year), 7 teaching assistantships with tuition reimbursements available (averaging $17,994 per year); research assistantships with tuition reimbursements available, scholarships/grants, health care benefits, and unspecified assistantships also available. Financial award applicants required to submit FAFSA. *Faculty research:* Medical sociology, inequality, mental health and immigration, labor, women's menopause and midlife experiences. *Unit head:* Dr. Jeffrey Kentor, Chair and Professor, E-mail: jeffrey.kentor@wayne.edu. *Application contact:* Dr. Krista Brumley, Director of Graduate Studies, 313-577-1418, E-mail: kbrumley@wayne.edu. Website: http://clas.wayne.edu/Sociology/

**Western Illinois University,** School of Graduate Studies, College of Arts and Sciences, Department of Sociology and Anthropology, Macomb, IL 61455-1390. Offers sociology (MA). *Program availability:* Part-time. *Students:* 12 full-time (8 women), 4 part-time (3 women); includes 7 minority (3 Black or African American, non-Hispanic/Latino; 2 Hispanic/Latino; 2 Two or more races, non-Hispanic/Latino), 2 international. Average age 31. 15 applicants, 93% accepted, 7 enrolled. In 2016, 5 master's awarded. *Degree requirements:* For master's, thesis or alternative. *Entrance requirements:* Additional exam requirements/recommendations for international students: Required—TOEFL (minimum score 550 paper-based; 80 iBT). *Application deadline:* Applications are processed on a rolling basis. Application fee: $30. Electronic applications accepted. *Financial support:* In 2016–17, 10 students received support. Unspecified assistantships available. Financial award applicants required to submit FAFSA. *Unit head:* Dr. John Wozniak, Chairperson, 309-298-1056. *Application contact:* Dr. Nancy Parsons, Associate Provost and Director of Graduate Studies, 309-298-1806, Fax: 309-298-2345, E-mail: grad-office@wiu.edu. Website: http://wiu.edu/sociology

**Western Kentucky University,** Graduate Studies, Potter College of Arts and Letters, Department of Sociology, Bowling Green, KY 42101. Offers criminology (MA); sociology (MA). *Program availability:* Online learning. *Degree requirements:* For master's, comprehensive exam, thesis optional, final exam. *Entrance requirements:* For master's, GRE General Test, minimum GPA of 3.0. Additional exam requirements/recommendations for international students: Required—TOEFL (minimum score 555 paper-based; 79 iBT). *Faculty research:* Criminology/delinquency, quantitative and survey research methodology, occupations/professions, sex and gender, demography.

**Western Michigan University,** Graduate College, College of Arts and Sciences, Department of Sociology, Kalamazoo, MI 49008. Offers MA, PhD. *Degree requirements:* For master's, thesis; for doctorate, one foreign language, thesis/dissertation.

**West Virginia University,** Eberly College of Arts and Sciences, Department of Sociology and Anthropology, Morgantown, WV 26506. Offers sociology (MA, PhD), including community (PhD), crime (PhD), culture (PhD). *Program availability:* Part-time. *Degree requirements:* For master's, thesis or alternative. *Entrance requirements:* For master's, GRE General Test, minimum GPA of 2.75. Additional exam requirements/ recommendations for international students: Required—TOEFL. *Faculty research:*

Applied sociology, stratification, social/complex organization, research methodology criminology.

**Wichita State University,** Graduate School, Fairmount College of Liberal Arts and Sciences, Department of Sociology, Wichita, KS 67260. Offers MA. *Program availability:* Part-time. *Unit head:* Dr. Jodie Hertzog, Chair, 316-978-3280, Fax: 316-978-3281, E-mail: jodie.hertzog@wichita.edu. *Application contact:* Jordan Oleson, Admissions Coordinator, 316-978-3095, Fax: 316-978-3253, E-mail: jordan.oleson@wichita.edu. Website: http://www.wichita.edu/sociology

**Wilfrid Laurier University,** Faculty of Graduate and Postdoctoral Studies, Faculty of Arts, Department of Sociology, Waterloo, ON N2L 3C5, Canada. Offers health, family and well-being (MA); internationalization, migration and human rights (MA). *Entrance requirements:* For master's, honours BA with minimum B+ average and major in sociology. Additional exam requirements/recommendations for international students: Required—TOEFL (minimum score 89 iBT). Electronic applications accepted. *Faculty research:* Internationalization, migration and human rights, health, families, and well-being.

**William Paterson University of New Jersey,** College of Humanities and Social Sciences, Wayne, NJ 07470-8420. Offers applied sociology (MA); clinical and counseling psychology (MA); clinical psychology (Psy D); creative and professional writing (MFA); English (MA); history (MA); political science and public policy (MA); public policy and international affairs (MA). *Program availability:* Part-time, evening/weekend. *Faculty:* 35 full-time (19 women), 8 part-time/adjunct (5 women). *Students:* 58 full-time (38 women), 62 part-time (46 women); includes 40 minority (9 Black or African American, non-Hispanic/Latino; 6 Asian, non-Hispanic/Latino; 21 Hispanic/Latino; 4 Two or more races, non-Hispanic/Latino), 4 international. Average age 32. 160 applicants, 55% accepted, 50 enrolled. In 2016, 56 master's awarded. *Degree requirements:* For master's, thesis (for some programs), internship (for some programs). *Entrance requirements:* For master's, GRE/MAT, minimum GPA of 3.0; 2 letters of recommendation; writing sample/personal statement. Additional exam requirements/ recommendations for international students: Required—TOEFL (minimum score 550 paper-based; 79 iBT), IELTS (minimum score 6). *Application deadline:* For fall admission, 8/1 for domestic students, 4/1 for international students; for spring admission, 12/1 for domestic students, 11/1 for international students; for summer admission, 5/1 for domestic students, 2/1 for international students. Applications are processed on a rolling basis. Application fee: $50. Electronic applications accepted. *Expenses:* Tuition, state resident: full-time $12,480; part-time $611 per credit. Tuition, nonresident: full-time $20,263; part-time $992 per credit. *Required fees:* $1573; $77 per credit. Tuition and fees vary according to course load, degree level and program. *Financial support:* Career-related internships or fieldwork, Federal Work-Study, scholarships/grants, and unspecified assistantships available. Support available to part-time students. Financial award applicants required to submit FAFSA. *Faculty research:* Relationship violence among adolescents; autism in young children; game theory; gender, governance and empowerment in India; Chinese development policies concerning Africa. *Total annual research expenditures:* $162,900. *Unit head:* Dr. Kara Rabbitt, Dean, 973-720-2180, Fax: 973-720-2955, E-mail: rabbittk@wpunj.edu. *Application contact:* Tinu Adeniran, Associate Director, Graduate Admissions, 973-720-2764, Fax: 973-720-2035, E-mail: adenirant@wpunj.edu. Website: http://www.wpunj.edu/cohss

**Yale University,** Graduate School of Arts and Sciences, Department of Sociology, New Haven, CT 06520. Offers comparative and historical sociology (PhD); cultural sociology and social theory (PhD); social stratification and the life course (PhD). *Degree requirements:* For doctorate, thesis/dissertation. *Entrance requirements:* For doctorate, GRE General Test.

**York University,** Faculty of Graduate Studies, Faculty of Liberal Arts and Professional Studies, Program in Sociology, Toronto, ON M3J 1P3, Canada. Offers MA, PhD. *Program availability:* Part-time. *Degree requirements:* For master's, thesis or alternative; for doctorate, one foreign language, comprehensive exam, thesis/dissertation, analytical paper. Electronic applications accepted.

**York University,** Faculty of Graduate Studies, Program in Social and Political Thought, Toronto, ON M3J 1P3, Canada. Offers MA, PhD. *Program availability:* Part-time. *Degree requirements:* For master's, one foreign language, thesis or alternative, oral exams; for doctorate, one foreign language, comprehensive exam, thesis/dissertation. Electronic applications accepted.

# Survey Methodology

---

**University of Maryland, College Park,** Academic Affairs, College of Behavioral and Social Sciences, Joint Program in Survey Methodology, College Park, MD 20742. Offers MS, PhD. Program offered with University of Michigan and Westat. *Degree requirements:* For master's, thesis (for some programs), scholarly paper; for doctorate, thesis/dissertation. *Entrance requirements:* For master's, GRE General Test (recommended), minimum GPA of 3.0, 3 letters of recommendation; for doctorate, GRE General Test, minimum GPA of 3.0, 3 letters of recommendation. Electronic applications accepted.

**University of Michigan,** Rackham Graduate School, Program in Survey Methodology, Ann Arbor, MI 48106. Offers data science (MS, PhD); social and psychological (MS, PhD); statistical (MS, PhD); survey methodology (Certificate). *Program availability:* Part-time. Terminal master's awarded for partial completion of doctoral program. *Degree requirements:* For master's, internships; for doctorate, comprehensive exam, thesis/ dissertation. *Entrance requirements:* For master's and doctorate, GRE, 3 letters of

recommendation, academic statement of purpose, personal statement, resume or curriculum vitae, academic transcripts; for Certificate, 3 letters of recommendation, academic statement of purpose, personal statement, resume or curriculum vitae, academic transcripts. Additional exam requirements/recommendations for international students: Required—TOEFL (minimum score 560 paper-based; 84 iBT). Electronic applications accepted. *Expenses:* Contact institution. *Faculty research:* Survey methodology, web surveys, survey non-response, sample design methods, adaptive survey design.

**University of Nebraska–Lincoln,** Graduate College, Interdepartmental Area of Survey Research and Methodology, Lincoln, NE 68588. Offers MS, PhD. *Degree requirements:* For master's, comprehensive exam. *Entrance requirements:* For master's, GRE General Test or GMAT. Additional exam requirements/recommendations for international students: Required—TOEFL (minimum score 550 paper-based). Electronic applications accepted. *Faculty research:* Survey research and data analysis.

# APPENDIXES

# Institutional Changes
# Since the 2017 Edition

Following is an alphabetical listing of institutions that have recently closed, merged with other institutions, or changed their names or status. In the case of a name change, the former name appears first, followed by the new name.

Alliant International University–México City (Mexico City, Mexico): *closed.*

The American College (Bryn Mawr, PA): *name changed to The American College of Financial Services.*

Andover Newton Theological School (Newton Centre, MA): *now affiliated with Yale Divinity School.*

Argosy University, Washington DC (Arlington, VA): *name changed to Argosy University, Northern Virginia.*

The Art Institute of Dallas, a campus of South University (Dallas, TX): *name changed to The Art Institute of Dallas, a branch of Miami International University of Art & Design.*

Bard Graduate Center: Decorative Arts, Design History, Material Culture (New York, NY): *name changed to Bard Graduate Center.*

Bexley Hall Episcopal Seminary (Columbus, OH): *merged into a single entry for Bexley Seabury Seminary (Chicago, IL).*

Blessing-Rieman College of Nursing (Quincy, IL): *name changed to Blessing-Rieman College of Nursing & Health Sciences.*

California Maritime Academy (Vallejo, CA): *name changed to California State University Maritime Academy.*

California National University for Advanced Studies (Northridge, CA): *closed.*

California School of Podiatric Medicine at Samuel Merritt University (Oakland, CA): *merged as a unit into Samuel Merritt University (Oakland, CA).*

Calvary Bible College and Theological Seminary (Kansas City, MO): *name changed to Calvary University.*

Carolina Graduate School of Divinity (Greensboro, NC): *closed.*

Centenary College (Hackettstown, NJ): *name changed to Centenary University.*

Charlotte School of Law (Charlotte, NC): *will not be enrolling new students for the fall 2017 term.*

Colorado Heights University (Denver, CO): *closed.*

Colorado Technical University Denver South (Aurora, CO): *name changed to Colorado Technical University Aurora.*

The Commonwealth Medical College (Scranton, PA): *name changed to Geisinger Commonwealth School of Medicine.*

Connecticut College (New London, CT): *will not be accepting graduate program applications for the 2017-18 academic year.*

Daniel Webster College (Nashua, NH): *merged into Southern New Hampshire University (Manchester, NH).*

DeVry College of New York (New York, NY): *name changed to DeVry College of New York–Midtown Manhattan Campus.*

DeVry University (Glendale, AZ): *now a DeVry University center and no longer profiled separately.*

DeVry University (Mesa, AZ): *now a DeVry University center and no longer profiled separately.*

DeVry University (Phoenix, AZ): *name changed to DeVry University–Phoenix Campus.*

DeVry University (Alhambra, CA): *closed.*

DeVry University (Anaheim, CA): *now a DeVry University center and no longer profiled separately.*

DeVry University (Fremont, CA): *name changed to DeVry University–Fremont Campus.*

DeVry University (Long Beach, CA): *name changed to DeVry University–Long Beach Campus.*

DeVry University (Oakland, CA): *now a DeVry University center and no longer profiled separately.*

DeVry University (Oxnard, CA): *closed.*

DeVry University (Palmdale, CA): *now a DeVry University center and no longer profiled separately.*

DeVry University (Pomona, CA): *name changed to DeVry University–Pomona Campus.*

DeVry University (San Diego, CA): *name changed to DeVry University–San Diego Campus.*

DeVry University (Colorado Springs, CO): *now a DeVry University center and no longer profiled separately.*

DeVry University (Jacksonville, FL): *name changed to DeVry University–Jacksonville Campus.*

DeVry University (Miramar, FL): *name changed to DeVry University–Miramar Campus.*

DeVry University (Orlando, FL): *name changed to DeVry University–Orlando Campus.*

DeVry University (Alpharetta, GA): *name changed to DeVry University–Alpharetta Campus.*

DeVry University (Decatur, GA): *name changed to DeVry University–Decatur Campus.*

DeVry University (Duluth, GA): *now a DeVry University center and no longer profiled separately.*

DeVry University (Chicago, IL): *name changed to DeVry University–Chicago Campus.*

DeVry University (Downers Grove, IL): *now a DeVry University center and no longer profiled separately.*

DeVry University (Elgin, IL): *now a DeVry University center and no longer profiled separately.*

DeVry University (Gurnee, IL): *now a DeVry University center and no longer profiled separately.*

DeVry University (Naperville, IL): *now a DeVry University center and no longer profiled separately.*

DeVry University (Tinley Park, IL): *name changed to DeVry University–Tinley Park Campus.*

DeVry University (Merrillville, IN): *now a DeVry University center and no longer profiled separately.*

DeVry University (Henderson, NV): *name changed to DeVry University–Henderson Campus.*

DeVry University (North Brunswick, NJ): *name changed to DeVry University–North Brunswick Campus.*

DeVry University (Paramus, NJ): *now a DeVry University center and no longer profiled separately.*

DeVry University (Charlotte, NC): *name changed to DeVry University–Charlotte Campus.*

DeVry University (Columbus, OH): *name changed to DeVry University–Columbus Campus.*

DeVry University (Seven Hills, OH): *name changed to DeVry University–Seven Hills Campus.*

DeVry University (Fort Washington, PA): *name changed to DeVry University–Ft. Washington Campus.*

DeVry University (King of Prussia, PA): *closed.*

DeVry University (Nashville, TN): *name changed to DeVry University–Nashville Campus.*

DeVry University (Irving, TX): *name changed to DeVry University–Irving Campus.*

DeVry University (Arlington, VA): *name changed to DeVry University–Arlington Campus.*

DeVry University (Chesapeake, VA): *name changed to DeVry University–Chesapeake Campus.*

DeVry University (Manassas, VA): *closed.*

Ellis University (Oakbrook Terrace, IL): *closed.*

Everest University (Largo, FL): *closed.*

Everest University (Orlando, FL): *closed.*

Hillsdale Free Will Baptist College (Moore, OK): *name changed to Randall University.*

Houston College of Law (Houston, TX): *name changed to South Texas College of Law Houston.*

Humphreys College (Stockton, CA): *name changed to Humphreys University.*

ITT Technical Institute (Indianapolis, IN): *closed.*

John Marshall Law School (Chicago, IL): *name changed to The John Marshall Law School.*

Lakehead University–Orillia (Orillia, ON, Canada): *name changed to Lakehead University.*

Long Island University–Hudson at Rockland (Orangeburg, NY): *merged into a single entry for Long Island University–Hudson (Purchase, NY) by request from the institution.*

Mary Baldwin College (Staunton, VA): *name changed to Mary Baldwin University.*

The Master's College and Seminary (Santa Clarita, CA): *name changed to The Master's University.*

Mayo Graduate School (Rochester, MN): *name changed to Mayo Clinic Graduate School of Biomedical Sciences.*

Mayo Medical School (Rochester, MN): *name changed to Mayo Clinic School of Medicine.*

Mayo School of Health Sciences (Rochester, MN): *name changed to Mayo Clinic School of Health Sciences.*

National College of Natural Medicine (Portland, OR): *name changed to National University of Natural Medicine.*

Oregon College of Art & Craft (Portland, OR): *name changed to Oregon College of Art and Craft.*

Our Lady of the Lake University of San Antonio (San Antonio, TX): *name changed to Our Lady of the Lake University.*

Phillips Graduate Institute (Encino, CA): *name changed to Phillips Graduate University.*

Pinchot University (Seattle, WA): *acquired by Presidio Graduate School (San Francisco, CA).*

Purdue University Northwest (Westville, IN): *merged into a single entry for Purdue University Northwest (Hammond, IN).*

Rabbi Isaac Elchanan Theological Seminary (New York, NY): *merged into Yeshiva University (New York, NY).*

Saint Joseph's College (Rensselaer, IN): *closed.*

School of the Museum of Fine Arts, Boston (Boston, MA): *merged as a unit into Tufts University (Medford, MA).*

Seabury-Western Theological Seminary (Evanston, IL): *name changed to Bexley Seabury Seminary.*

Seminary of the Immaculate Conception (Huntington, NY): *no longer degree granting.*

Summit University (Clarks Summit, PA): *name changed to Clarks Summit University.*

Tennessee Wesleyan College (Athens, TN): *name changed to Tennessee Wesleyan University.*

Texas A&M University at Galveston (Galveston, TX): *merged as a unit into Texas A&M University (College Station, TX).*

Waldorf College (Forest City, IA): name changed to *Waldorf University.*

# Abbreviations Used in the Guides

The following list includes abbreviations of degree names used in the profiles in the 2018 edition of the guides. Because some degrees (e.g., Doctor of Education) can be abbreviated in more than one way (e.g., D.Ed. or Ed.D.), and because the abbreviations used in the guides reflect the preferences of the individual colleges and universities, the list may include two or more abbreviations for a single degree.

## DEGREES

| | |
|---|---|
| A Mus D | Doctor of Musical Arts |
| AC | Advanced Certificate |
| AD | Artist's Diploma |
| | Doctor of Arts |
| ADP | Artist's Diploma |
| Adv C | Advanced Certificate |
| AGC | Advanced Graduate Certificate |
| AGSC | Advanced Graduate Specialist Certificate |
| ALM | Master of Liberal Arts |
| AM | Master of Arts |
| AMBA | Accelerated Master of Business Administration |
| AMRS | Master of Arts in Religious Studies |
| APC | Advanced Professional Certificate |
| APMPH | Advanced Professional Master of Public Health |
| App Sc | Applied Scientist |
| App Sc D | Doctor of Applied Science |
| AstE | Astronautical Engineer |
| ATC | Advanced Training Certificate |
| Au D | Doctor of Audiology |
| B Th | Bachelor of Theology |
| BN | Bachelor of Naturopathy |
| CAES | Certificate of Advanced Educational Specialization |
| CAGS | Certificate of Advanced Graduate Studies |
| CAL | Certificate in Applied Linguistics |
| CAPS | Certificate of Advanced Professional Studies |
| CAS | Certificate of Advanced Studies |
| CASPA | Certificate of Advanced Study in Public Administration |
| CASR | Certificate in Advanced Social Research |
| CATS | Certificate of Achievement in Theological Studies |
| CBHS | Certificate in Basic Health Sciences |
| CCJA | Certificate in Criminal Justice Administration |
| CCTS | Certificate in Clinical and Translational Science |
| CE | Civil Engineer |
| CEM | Certificate of Environmental Management |
| CET | Certificate in Educational Technologies |
| CGS | Certificate of Graduate Studies |
| Ch E | Chemical Engineer |
| Clin Sc D | Doctor of Clinical Science |
| CM | Certificate in Management |
| CMH | Certificate in Medical Humanities |
| CMM | Master of Church Ministries |
| CMS | Certificate in Ministerial Studies |
| CNM | Certificate in Nonprofit Management |
| CPASF | Certificate Program for Advanced Study in Finance |
| CPC | Certificate in Professional Counseling |
| | Certificate in Publication and Communication |
| CPH | Certificate in Public Health |
| CPM | Certificate in Public Management |
| CPS | Certificate of Professional Studies |
| CScD | Doctor of Clinical Science |
| CSD | Certificate in Spiritual Direction |
| CSS | Certificate of Special Studies |
| CTS | Certificate of Theological Studies |
| CURP | Certificate in Urban and Regional Planning |
| D Admin | Doctor of Administration |
| D Arch | Doctor of Architecture |
| D Be | Doctor in Bioethics |
| D Com | Doctor of Commerce |
| D Couns | Doctor of Counseling |
| D Des | Doctorate of Design |
| D Div | Doctor of Divinity |
| D Ed | Doctor of Education |
| D Ed Min | Doctor of Educational Ministry |
| D Eng | Doctor of Engineering |
| D Engr | Doctor of Engineering |
| D Ent | Doctor of Enterprise |
| D Env | Doctor of Environment |
| D Law | Doctor of Law |
| D Litt | Doctor of Letters |
| D Med Sc | Doctor of Medical Science |
| D Min | Doctor of Ministry |
| D Miss | Doctor of Missiology |
| D Mus | Doctor of Music |
| D Mus A | Doctor of Musical Arts |
| D Phil | Doctor of Philosophy |
| D Prof | Doctor of Professional Studies |
| D Ps | Doctor of Psychology |
| D Sc | Doctor of Science |
| D Sc D | Doctor of Science in Dentistry |
| D Sc IS | Doctor of Science in Information Systems |
| D Sc PA | Doctor of Science in Physician Assistant Studies |
| D Th | Doctor of Theology |
| D Th P | Doctor of Practical Theology |
| DA | Doctor of Accounting |
| | Doctor of Arts |
| DAH | Doctor of Arts in Humanities |
| DAOM | Doctorate in Acupuncture and Oriental Medicine |
| DAT | Doctorate of Athletic Training |
| | Professional Doctor of Art Therapy |
| DBA | Doctor of Business Administration |
| DBH | Doctor of Behavioral Health |
| DBL | Doctor of Business Leadership |
| DC | Doctor of Chiropractic |
| DCC | Doctor of Computer Science |
| DCD | Doctor of Communications Design |
| DCL | Doctor of Civil Law |
| | Doctor of Comparative Law |
| DCM | Doctor of Church Music |
| DCN | Doctor of Clinical Nutrition |
| DCS | Doctor of Computer Science |
| DDN | Diplôme du Droit Notarial |
| DDS | Doctor of Dental Surgery |
| DE | Doctor of Education |
| | Doctor of Engineering |
| DED | Doctor of Economic Development |
| DEIT | Doctor of Educational Innovation and Technology |
| DEL | Doctor of Executive Leadership |
| DEM | Doctor of Educational Ministry |
| DEPD | Diplôme Études Spécialisées |
| DES | Doctor of Engineering Science |
| DESS | Diplôme Études Supérieures Spécialisées |
| DET | Doctor of Educational Technology |
| DFA | Doctor of Fine Arts |
| DGP | Diploma in Graduate and Professional Studies |
| DH Ed | Doctor of Health Education |

| | | | | |
|---|---|---|---|---|
| DH Sc | Doctor of Health Sciences | | EDB | Executive Doctorate in Business |
| DHA | Doctor of Health Administration | | EDBA | Executive Doctor of Business Administration |
| DHCE | Doctor of Health Care Ethics | | EDM | Executive Doctorate in Management |
| DHL | Doctor of Hebrew Letters | | EE | Electrical Engineer |
| DHPE | Doctorate of Health Professionals Education | | EJD | Executive Juris Doctor |
| DHS | Doctor of Health Science | | EMBA | Executive Master of Business Administration |
| DHSc | Doctor of Health Science | | EMFA | Executive Master of Forensic Accounting |
| Dip CS | Diploma in Christian Studies | | EMHA | Executive Master of Health Administration |
| DIT | Doctor of Industrial Technology | | EMIB | Executive Master of International Business |
| | Doctor of Information Technology | | EML | Executive Master of Leadership |
| DJS | Doctor of Jewish Studies | | EMPA | Executive Master of Public Administration |
| DLS | Doctor of Liberal Studies | | EMPL | Executive Master in Public Leadership |
| DM | Doctor of Management | | EMS | Executive Master of Science |
| | Doctor of Music | | EMTM | Executive Master of Technology Management |
| DMA | Doctor of Musical Arts | | Eng | Engineer |
| DMD | Doctor of Dental Medicine | | Eng Sc D | Doctor of Engineering Science |
| DME | Doctor of Manufacturing Management | | Engr | Engineer |
| | Doctor of Music Education | | Exec M Tax | Executive Master of Taxation |
| DMEd | Doctor of Music Education | | Exec MAC | Executive Master of Accounting |
| DMFT | Doctor of Marital and Family Therapy | | Exec Ed D | Executive Doctor of Education |
| DMH | Doctor of Medical Humanities | | Exec MBA | Executive Master of Business Administration |
| DML | Doctor of Modern Languages | | Exec MPA | Executive Master of Public Administration |
| DMP | Doctorate in Medical Physics | | Exec MPH | Executive Master of Public Health |
| DMPNA | Doctor of Management Practice in Nurse Anesthesia | | Exec MS | Executive Master of Science |
| | | | Executive Fellows MBA | Executive Fellows Master of Business Administration |
| DN Sc | Doctor of Nursing Science | | | |
| DNAP | Doctor of Nurse Anesthesia Practice | | G Dip | Graduate Diploma |
| DNP | Doctor of Nursing Practice | | GBC | Graduate Business Certificate |
| DNP-A | Doctor of Nursing Practice - Anesthesia | | GDM | Graduate Diploma in Management |
| DNS | Doctor of Nursing Science | | GDPA | Graduate Diploma in Public Administration |
| DO | Doctor of Osteopathy | | GDRE | Graduate Diploma in Religious Education |
| DOT | Doctor of Occupational Therapy | | GEMBA | Global Executive Master of Business Administration |
| DPA | Doctor of Public Administration | | | |
| DPDS | Doctor of Planning and Development Studies | | GMBA | Global Master of Business Administration |
| DPH | Doctor of Public Health | | GP LL M | Global Professional Master of Laws |
| DPM | Doctor of Plant Medicine | | GPD | Graduate Performance Diploma |
| | Doctor of Podiatric Medicine | | GSS | Graduate Special Certificate for Students in Special Situations |
| DPPD | Doctor of Policy, Planning, and Development | | | |
| DPS | Doctor of Professional Studies | | IEMBA | International Executive Master of Business Administration |
| DPT | Doctor of Physical Therapy | | | |
| DPTSc | Doctor of Physical Therapy Science | | IMA | Interdisciplinary Master of Arts |
| Dr DES | Doctor of Design | | IMBA | International Master of Business Administration |
| Dr NP | Doctor of Nursing Practice | | | |
| Dr OT | Doctor of Occupational Therapy | | IMES | International Master's in Environmental Studies |
| Dr PH | Doctor of Public Health | | | |
| Dr Sc PT | Doctor of Science in Physical Therapy | | Ingeniero | Engineer |
| DrAP | Doctor of Anesthesia Practice | | JCD | Doctor of Canon Law |
| DRSc | Doctor of Regulatory Science | | JCL | Licentiate in Canon Law |
| DS | Doctor of Science | | JD | Juris Doctor |
| DS Sc | Doctor of Social Science | | JM | Juris Master |
| DSJS | Doctor of Science in Jewish Studies | | JSD | Doctor of Juridical Science |
| DSL | Doctor of Strategic Leadership | | | Doctor of Jurisprudence |
| DSS | Doctor of Strategic Security | | | Doctor of the Science of Law |
| DSW | Doctor of Social Work | | JSM | Master of the Science of Law |
| DTL | Doctor of Talmudic Law | | L Th | Licenciate in Theology |
| | Doctor of Transformational Leadership | | LL B | Bachelor of Laws |
| DV Sc | Doctor of Veterinary Science | | LL CM | Master of Comparative Law |
| DVM | Doctor of Veterinary Medicine | | LL D | Doctor of Laws |
| DWS | Doctor of Worship Studies | | LL M | Master of Laws |
| EAA | Engineer in Aeronautics and Astronautics | | LL M in Tax | Master of Laws in Taxation |
| EASPh D | Engineering and Applied Science Doctor of Philosophy | | LL M CL | Master of Laws in Common Law |
| | | | M Ac | Master of Accountancy |
| ECS | Engineer in Computer Science | | | Master of Accounting |
| Ed D | Doctor of Education | | | Master of Acupuncture |
| Ed DCT | Doctor of Education in College Teaching | | M Ac OM | Master of Acupuncture and Oriental Medicine |
| Ed L D | Doctor of Education Leadership | | M Acc | Master of Accountancy |
| Ed M | Master of Education | | | Master of Accounting |
| Ed S | Specialist in Education | | M Acct | Master of Accountancy |
| Ed Sp | Specialist in Education | | | Master of Accounting |

| | |
|---|---|
| M Accy | Master of Accountancy |
| M Actg | Master of Accounting |
| M Acy | Master of Accountancy |
| M Ad | Master of Administration |
| M Ad Ed | Master of Adult Education |
| M Adm | Master of Administration |
| M Adm Mgt | Master of Administrative Management |
| M Admin | Master of Administration |
| M ADU | Master of Architectural Design and Urbanism |
| M Adv | Master of Advertising |
| M AEST | Master of Applied Environmental Science and Technology |
| M Ag | Master of Agriculture |
| M Ag Ed | Master of Agricultural Education |
| M Agr | Master of Agriculture |
| M Anesth Ed | Master of Anesthesiology Education |
| M App Comp Sc | Master of Applied Computer Science |
| M App St | Master of Applied Statistics |
| M Appl Stat | Master of Applied Statistics |
| M Aq | Master of Aquaculture |
| M Arc | Master of Architecture |
| M Arch | Master of Architecture |
| M Arch I | Master of Architecture I |
| M Arch II | Master of Architecture II |
| M Arch E | Master of Architectural Engineering |
| M Arch H | Master of Architectural History |
| M Bioethics | Master in Bioethics |
| M Biomath | Master of Biomathematics |
| M Ch E | Master of Chemical Engineering |
| M Chem | Master of Chemistry |
| M Cl D | Master of Clinical Dentistry |
| M Cl Sc | Master of Clinical Science |
| M Comp | Master of Computing |
| M Comp Sc | Master of Computer Science |
| M Coun | Master of Counseling |
| M Dent | Master of Dentistry |
| M Dent Sc | Master of Dental Sciences |
| M Des | Master of Design |
| M Des S | Master of Design Studies |
| M Div | Master of Divinity |
| M E Sci | Master of Earth Science |
| M Ec | Master of Economics |
| M Econ | Master of Economics |
| M Ed | Master of Education |
| M Ed T | Master of Education in Teaching |
| M En | Master of Engineering |
| M En S | Master of Environmental Sciences |
| M Eng | Master of Engineering |
| M Eng Mgt | Master of Engineering Management |
| M Engr | Master of Engineering |
| M Ent | Master of Enterprise |
| M Env | Master of Environment |
| M Env Des | Master of Environmental Design |
| M Env E | Master of Environmental Engineering |
| M Env Sc | Master of Environmental Science |
| M Fin | Master of Finance |
| M FSc | Master of Fisheries Science |
| M Geo E | Master of Geological Engineering |
| M Geoenv E | Master of Geoenvironmental Engineering |
| M Geog | Master of Geography |
| M Hum | Master of Humanities |
| M IDST | Master's in Interdisciplinary Studies |
| M Kin | Master of Kinesiology |
| M Land Arch | Master of Landscape Architecture |
| M Litt | Master of Letters |
| M Mat SE | Master of Material Science and Engineering |
| M Math | Master of Mathematics |
| M Mech E | Master of Mechanical Engineering |
| M Med Sc | Master of Medical Science |
| M Mgmt | Master of Management |
| M Mgt | Master of Management |
| M Min | Master of Ministries |
| M Mtl E | Master of Materials Engineering |
| M Mu | Master of Music |
| M Mus | Master of Music |
| M Mus Ed | Master of Music Education |
| M Music | Master of Music |
| M Nat Sci | Master of Natural Science |
| M Pet E | Master of Petroleum Engineering |
| M Pharm | Master of Pharmacy |
| M Phil | Master of Philosophy |
| M Phil F | Master of Philosophical Foundations |
| M Pl | Master of Planning |
| M Plan | Master of Planning |
| M Pol | Master of Political Science |
| M Pr Met | Master of Professional Meteorology |
| M Prob S | Master of Probability and Statistics |
| M Psych | Master of Psychology |
| M Pub | Master of Publishing |
| M Rel | Master of Religion |
| M Sc | Master of Science |
| M Sc A | Master of Science (Applied) |
| M Sc AC | Master of Science in Applied Computing |
| M Sc AHN | Master of Science in Applied Human Nutrition |
| M Sc BMC | Master of Science in Biomedical Communications |
| M Sc CS | Master of Science in Computer Science |
| M Sc E | Master of Science in Engineering |
| M Sc Eng | Master of Science in Engineering |
| M Sc Engr | Master of Science in Engineering |
| M Sc F | Master of Science in Forestry |
| M Sc FE | Master of Science in Forest Engineering |
| M Sc Geogr | Master of Science in Geography |
| M Sc N | Master of Science in Nursing |
| M Sc OT | Master of Science in Occupational Therapy |
| M Sc P | Master of Science in Planning |
| M Sc Pl | Master of Science in Planning |
| M Sc PT | Master of Science in Physical Therapy |
| M Sc T | Master of Science in Teaching |
| M SEM | Master of Sustainable Environmental Management |
| M Serv Soc | Master of Social Service |
| M Soc | Master of Sociology |
| M Sp Ed | Master of Special Education |
| M St | Master of Studies |
| M Stat | Master of Statistics |
| M Sys E | Master of Systems Engineering |
| M Sys Sc | Master of Systems Science |
| M Tax | Master of Taxation |
| M Tech | Master of Technology |
| M Th | Master of Theology |
| M Tox | Master of Toxicology |
| M Trans E | Master of Transportation Engineering |
| M U Ed | Master of Urban Education |
| M Urb | Master of Urban Planning |
| M Vet Sc | Master of Veterinary Science |
| MA | Master of Accounting |
| | Master of Administration |
| | Master of Arts |
| MA Comm | Master of Arts in Communication |
| MA Ed | Master of Arts in Education |
| MA Ed/HD | Master of Arts in Education and Human Development |
| MA Ext | Master of Agricultural Extension |
| MA Min | Master of Arts in Ministry |
| MA Past St | Master of Arts in Pastoral Studies |
| MA Ph | Master of Arts in Philosophy |

| | |
|---|---|
| MA Psych | Master of Arts in Psychology |
| MA Sc | Master of Applied Science |
| MA Sp | Master of Arts (Spirituality) |
| MA Th | Master of Arts in Theology |
| MA-R | Master of Arts (Research) |
| MAA | Master of Administrative Arts |
| | Master of Applied Anthropology |
| | Master of Applied Arts |
| | Master of Arts in Administration |
| MAAA | Master of Arts in Arts Administration |
| MAAAP | Master of Arts Administration and Policy |
| MAAD | Master of Advanced Architectural Design |
| MAAE | Master of Arts in Art Education |
| MAAPPS | Master of Arts in Asia Pacific Policy Studies |
| MAAS | Master of Arts in Aging and Spirituality |
| MAASJ | Master of Arts in Applied Social Justice |
| MAAT | Master of Arts in Applied Theology |
| | Master of Arts in Art Therapy |
| MAB | Master of Agribusiness |
| MABC | Master of Arts in Biblical Counseling |
| MABE | Master of Arts in Bible Exposition |
| MABL | Master of Arts in Biblical Languages |
| MABM | Master of Agribusiness Management |
| MABS | Master of Arts in Biblical Studies |
| MABT | Master of Arts in Bible Teaching |
| MAC | Master of Accountancy |
| | Master of Accounting |
| | Master of Arts in Communication |
| | Master of Arts in Counseling |
| MACC | Master of Arts in Christian Counseling |
| | Master of Arts in Clinical Counseling |
| MACCT | Master of Accounting |
| MACD | Master of Arts in Christian Doctrine |
| MACE | Master of Arts in Christian Education |
| MACH | Master of Arts in Church History |
| MACI | Master of Arts in Curriculum and Instruction |
| MACIS | Master of Accounting and Information Systems |
| MACJ | Master of Arts in Criminal Justice |
| MACL | Master of Arts in Christian Leadership |
| | Master of Arts in Community Leadership |
| MACM | Master of Arts in Christian Ministries |
| | Master of Arts in Christian Ministry |
| | Master of Arts in Church Music |
| | Master of Arts in Counseling Ministries |
| MACN | Master of Arts in Counseling |
| MACO | Master of Arts in Counseling |
| MAcOM | Master of Acupuncture and Oriental Medicine |
| MACP | Master of Arts in Christian Practice |
| | Master of Arts in Church Planting |
| | Master of Arts in Counseling Psychology |
| MACS | Master of Applied Computer Science |
| | Master of Arts in Catholic Studies |
| | Master of Arts in Christian Studies |
| MACSE | Master of Arts in Christian School Education |
| MACT | Master of Arts in Communications and Technology |
| MAD | Master in Educational Institution Administration |
| | Master of Art and Design |
| MADR | Master of Arts in Dispute Resolution |
| MADS | Master of Animal and Dairy Science |
| | Master of Applied Disability Studies |
| MAE | Master of Aerospace Engineering |
| | Master of Agricultural Economics |
| | Master of Agricultural Education |
| | Master of Applied Economics |
| | Master of Architectural Engineering |
| | Master of Art Education |

| | |
|---|---|
| | Master of Arts in Education |
| | Master of Arts in English |
| MAEd | Master of Arts Education |
| MAEL | Master of Arts in Educational Leadership |
| MAEM | Master of Arts in Educational Ministries |
| MAEP | Master of Arts in Economic Policy |
| | Master of Arts in Educational Psychology |
| MAES | Master of Arts in Environmental Sciences |
| MAET | Master of Arts in English Teaching |
| MAF | Master of Arts in Finance |
| MAFE | Master of Arts in Financial Economics |
| MAFLL | Master of Arts in Foreign Language and Literature |
| MAFM | Master of Accounting and Financial Management |
| MAFS | Master of Arts in Family Studies |
| MAG | Master of Applied Geography |
| MAGS | Master of Arts in Global Service |
| MAGU | Master of Urban Analysis and Management |
| MAH | Master of Arts in Humanities |
| MAHA | Master of Arts in Humanitarian Assistance |
| MAHCM | Master of Arts in Health Care Mission |
| MAHG | Master of American History and Government |
| MAHL | Master of Arts in Hebrew Letters |
| MAHN | Master of Applied Human Nutrition |
| MAHR | Master of Applied Historical Research |
| MAHS | Master of Arts in Human Services |
| MAHSR | Master in Applied Health Services Research |
| MAIA | Master of Arts in International Administration |
| | Master of Arts in International Affairs |
| MAIDM | Master of Arts in Interior Design and Merchandising |
| MAIH | Master of Arts in Interdisciplinary Humanities |
| MAIOP | Master of Applied Industrial/Organizational Psychology |
| MAIPCR | Master of Arts in International Peace and Conflict Management |
| MAIS | Master of Arts in Intercultural Studies |
| | Master of Arts in Interdisciplinary Studies |
| | Master of Arts in International Studies |
| MAIT | Master of Administration in Information Technology |
| MAJ | Master of Arts in Journalism |
| MAJ Ed | Master of Arts in Jewish Education |
| MAJCS | Master of Arts in Jewish Communal Service |
| MAJE | Master of Arts in Jewish Education |
| MAJPS | Master of Arts in Jewish Professional Studies |
| MAJS | Master of Arts in Jewish Studies |
| MAL | Master in Agricultural Leadership |
| MALA | Master of Arts in Liberal Arts |
| MALD | Master of Arts in Law and Diplomacy |
| MALER | Master of Arts in Labor and Employment Relations |
| MALL | Master of Arts in Language Learning |
| MALP | Master of Arts in Language Pedagogy |
| MALS | Master of Arts in Liberal Studies |
| MAM | Master of Acquisition Management |
| | Master of Agriculture and Management |
| | Master of Applied Mathematics |
| | Master of Arts in Management |
| | Master of Arts in Ministry |
| | Master of Arts Management |
| | Master of Avian Medicine |
| MAMB | Master of Applied Molecular Biology |
| MAMC | Master of Arts in Mass Communication |
| | Master of Arts in Ministry and Culture |
| | Master of Arts in Ministry for a Multicultural Church |
| | Master of Arts in Missional Christianity |
| MAME | Master of Arts in Missions/Evangelism |

| | | | |
|---|---|---|---|
| MAMFC | Master of Arts in Marriage and Family Counseling | | Master's in Administration of Telecommunications |
| MAMFT | Master of Arts in Marriage and Family Therapy | Mat E | Materials Engineer |
| MAMHC | Master of Arts in Mental Health Counseling | MATCM | Master of Acupuncture and Traditional Chinese Medicine |
| MAMS | Master of Applied Mathematical Sciences | MATDE | Master of Arts in Theology, Development, and Evangelism |
| | Master of Applied Meditation Studies | | |
| | Master of Arts in Ministerial Studies | MATDR | Master of Territorial Management and Regional Development |
| | Master of Arts in Ministry and Spirituality | MATE | Master of Arts for the Teaching of English |
| MAMT | Master of Arts in Mathematics Teaching | MATESL | Master of Arts in Teaching English as a Second Language |
| MAN | Master of Applied Nutrition | | |
| MANT | Master of Arts in New Testament | MATESOL | Master of Arts in Teaching English to Speakers of Other Languages |
| MAOL | Master of Arts in Organizational Leadership | | |
| MAOM | Master of Acupuncture and Oriental Medicine | MATF | Master of Arts in Teaching English as a Foreign Language/Intercultural Studies |
| MAOT | Master of Arts in Old Testament | | |
| MAP | Master of Applied Politics | MATFL | Master of Arts in Teaching Foreign Language |
| | Master of Applied Psychology | MATH | Master of Arts in Therapy |
| | Master of Arts in Planning | MATI | Master of Administration of Information Technology |
| | Master of Psychology | | |
| | Master of Public Administration | MATL | Master of Arts in Teacher Leadership |
| MAP Min | Master of Arts in Pastoral Ministry | | Master of Arts in Teaching of Languages |
| MAPA | Master of Arts in Public Administration | | Master of Arts in Transformational Leadership |
| MAPC | Master of Arts in Pastoral Counseling | MATM | Master of Arts in Teaching of Mathematics |
| MAPE | Master of Arts in Physics Education | MATS | Master of Arts in Theological Studies |
| | Master of Arts in Political Economy | | Master of Arts in Transforming Spirituality |
| MAPM | Master of Arts in Pastoral Ministry | MATSL | Master of Arts in Teaching a Second Language |
| | Master of Arts in Pastoral Music | MAUA | Master of Arts in Urban Affairs |
| | Master of Arts in Practical Ministry | MAUD | Master of Arts in Urban Design |
| MAPP | Master of Arts in Public Policy | MAURP | Master of Arts in Urban and Regional Planning |
| MAPS | Master of Arts in Pastoral Studies | MAW | Master of Arts in Worship |
| | Master of Arts in Public Service | MAWSHP | Master of Arts in Worship |
| MAPT | Master of Practical Theology | MAYM | Master of Arts in Youth Ministry |
| MAPW | Master of Arts in Professional Writing | MB | Master of Bioinformatics |
| MAR | Master of Arts in Reading | MBA | Master of Business Administration |
| | Master of Arts in Religion | MBA-AM | Master of Business Administration in Aviation Management |
| Mar Eng | Marine Engineer | | |
| MARC | Master of Arts in Rehabilitation Counseling | MBA-EP | Master of Business Administration–Experienced Professionals |
| MARE | Master of Arts in Religious Education | | |
| MARL | Master of Arts in Religious Leadership | MBAA | Master of Business Administration in Aviation |
| MARS | Master of Arts in Religious Studies | MBAE | Master of Biological and Agricultural Engineering |
| MAS | Master of Accounting Science | | |
| | Master of Actuarial Science | | Master of Biosystems and Agricultural Engineering |
| | Master of Administrative Science | MBAH | Master of Business Administration in Health |
| | Master of Advanced Study | MBAi | Master of Business Administration–International |
| | Master of Aeronautical Science | | |
| | Master of American Studies | MBAICT | Master of Business Administration in Information and Communication Technology |
| | Master of Animal Science | | |
| | Master of Applied Science | MBATM | Master of Business Administration in Technology Management |
| | Master of Applied Statistics | | |
| | Master of Archival Studies | MBC | Master of Building Construction |
| MASA | Master of Advanced Studies in Architecture | MBE | Master of Bilingual Education |
| MASD | Master of Arts in Spiritual Direction | | Master of Bioengineering |
| MASE | Master of Arts in Special Education | | Master of Bioethics |
| MASF | Master of Arts in Spiritual Formation | | Master of Biomedical Engineering |
| MASJ | Master of Arts in Systems of Justice | | Master of Business Economics |
| MASLA | Master of Advanced Studies in Landscape Architecture | | Master of Business Education |
| | | MBEE | Master in Biotechnology Enterprise and Entrepreneurship |
| MASM | Master of Aging Services Management | | |
| | Master of Arts in Specialized Ministries | MBET | Master of Business, Entrepreneurship and Technology |
| MASP | Master of Applied Social Psychology | | |
| | Master of Arts in School Psychology | MBID | Master of Biomedical Innovation and Development |
| MASPAA | Master of Arts in Sports and Athletic Administration | | |
| | | MBIOT | Master of Biotechnology |
| MASS | Master of Applied Social Science | MBiotech | Master of Biotechnology |
| | Master of Arts in Social Science | MBL | Master of Business Law |
| | | | Master of Business Leadership |
| MAST | Master of Arts in Science Teaching | MBLE | Master in Business Logistics Engineering |
| MAT | Master of Arts in Teaching | MBME | Master's in Biomedical Engineering |
| | Master of Arts in Theology | MBMSE | Master of Business Management and Software Engineering |
| | Master of Athletic Training | | |

| | |
|---|---|
| MBOE | Master of Business Operational Excellence |
| MBS | Master of Biblical Studies |
| | Master of Biological Science |
| | Master of Biomedical Sciences |
| | Master of Bioscience |
| | Master of Building Science |
| | Master of Business and Science |
| MBST | Master of Biostatistics |
| MBT | Master of Biomedical Technology |
| | Master of Biotechnology |
| | Master of Business Taxation |
| MBV | Master of Business for Veterans |
| MC | Master of Communication |
| | Master of Counseling |
| | Master of Cybersecurity |
| MC Ed | Master of Continuing Education |
| MC Sc | Master of Computer Science |
| MCA | Master in Collegiate Athletics |
| | Master of Commercial Aviation |
| | Master of Criminology (Applied) |
| MCAM | Master of Computational and Applied Mathematics |
| MCC | Master of Computer Science |
| MCD | Master of Communications Disorders |
| | Master of Community Development |
| MCE | Master in Electronic Commerce |
| | Master of Christian Education |
| | Master of Civil Engineering |
| | Master of Control Engineering |
| MCEM | Master of Construction Engineering Management |
| MCHE | Master of Chemical Engineering |
| MCIS | Master of Communication and Information Studies |
| | Master of Computer and Information Science |
| | Master of Computer Information Systems |
| MCIT | Master of Computer and Information Technology |
| MCJ | Master of Criminal Justice |
| MCL | Master in Communication Leadership |
| | Master of Canon Law |
| | Master of Comparative Law |
| MCM | Master of Christian Ministry |
| | Master of Church Music |
| | Master of City Management |
| | Master of Communication Management |
| | Master of Community Medicine |
| | Master of Construction Management |
| | Master of Contract Management |
| MCMin | Master of Christian Ministry |
| MCMP | Master of City and Metropolitan Planning |
| MCMS | Master of Clinical Medical Science |
| MCN | Master of Clinical Nutrition |
| MCOL | Master of Arts in Community and Organizational Leadership |
| MCP | Master of City Planning |
| | Master of Community Planning |
| | Master of Counseling Psychology |
| | Master of Cytopathology Practice |
| | Master of Science in Quality Systems and Productivity |
| MCPC | Master of Arts in Chaplaincy and Pastoral Care |
| MCPD | Master of Community Planning and Development |
| MCR | Master in Clinical Research |
| MCRP | Master of City and Regional Planning |
| | Master of Community and Regional Planning |
| MCRS | Master of City and Regional Studies |
| MCS | Master of Chemical Sciences |
| | Master of Christian Studies |

| | |
|---|---|
| | Master of Clinical Science |
| | Master of Combined Sciences |
| | Master of Communication Studies |
| | Master of Computer Science |
| | Master of Consumer Science |
| MCSE | Master of Computer Science and Engineering |
| MCSL | Master of Catholic School Leadership |
| MCSM | Master of Construction Science and Management |
| MCTM | Master of Clinical Translation Management |
| MCTP | Master of Communication Technology and Policy |
| MCTS | Master of Clinical and Translational Science |
| MCVS | Master of Cardiovascular Science |
| MD | Doctor of Medicine |
| MDA | Master of Dietetic Administration |
| MDB | Master of Design-Build |
| MDE | Master of Developmental Economics |
| | Master of Distance Education |
| | Master of the Education of the Deaf |
| MDH | Master of Dental Hygiene |
| MDM | Master of Design Methods |
| | Master of Digital Media |
| MDP | Master in Sustainable Development Practice |
| | Master of Development Practice |
| MDR | Master of Dispute Resolution |
| MDS | Master of Dental Surgery |
| | Master of Design Studies |
| | Master of Digital Sciences |
| ME | Master of Education |
| | Master of Engineering |
| | Master of Entrepreneurship |
| ME Sc | Master of Engineering Science |
| ME-PD | Master of Education–Professional Development |
| MEA | Master of Educational Administration |
| | Master of Engineering Administration |
| MEAE | Master of Entertainment Arts and Engineering |
| MEAP | Master of Environmental Administration and Planning |
| MEB | Master of Energy Business |
| MEBD | Master in Environmental Building Design |
| MEBT | Master in Electronic Business Technologies |
| MEC | Master of Electronic Commerce |
| Mech E | Mechanical Engineer |
| MED | Master of Education of the Deaf |
| MEDS | Master of Environmental Design Studies |
| MEE | Master in Education |
| | Master of Electrical Engineering |
| | Master of Energy Engineering |
| | Master of Environmental Engineering |
| MEEM | Master of Environmental Engineering and Management |
| MEENE | Master of Engineering in Environmental Engineering |
| MEEP | Master of Environmental and Energy Policy |
| MEERM | Master of Earth and Environmental Resource Management |
| MEH | Master in Humanistic Studies |
| | Master of Environmental Health |
| | Master of Environmental Horticulture |
| MEHS | Master of Environmental Health and Safety |
| MEIM | Master of Entertainment Industry Management |
| | Master of Equine Industry Management |
| MEL | Master of Educational Leadership |
| | Master of English Literature |
| MELP | Master of Environmental Law and Policy |
| MEM | Master of Engineering Management |
| | Master of Environmental Management |
| | Master of Marketing |

| | | | |
|---|---|---|---|
| MEME | Master of Engineering in Manufacturing Engineering | MGE | Master of Geotechnical Engineering |
| | Master of Engineering in Mechanical Engineering | MGEM | Master of Global Entrepreneurship and Management |
| MENR | Master of Environment and Natural Resources | MGIS | Master of Geographic Information Science |
| MENVEGR | Master of Environmental Engineering | | Master of Geographic Information Systems |
| MEP | Master of Engineering Physics | MGM | Master of Global Management |
| MEPC | Master of Environmental Pollution Control | MGP | Master of Gestion de Projet |
| MEPD | Master of Environmental Planning and Design | MGPS | Master of Global Policy Studies |
| MER | Master of Employment Relations | MGREM | Master of Global Real Estate Management |
| MERE | Master of Entrepreneurial Real Estate | MGS | Master of Gerontological Studies |
| MERL | Master of Energy Regulation and Law | | Master of Global Studies |
| MES | Master of Education and Science | MGsc | Master of Geoscience |
| | Master of Engineering Science | MH | Master of Humanities |
| | Master of Environment and Sustainability | MH Sc | Master of Health Sciences |
| | Master of Environmental Science | MHA | Master of Health Administration |
| | Master of Environmental Studies | | Master of Healthcare Administration |
| | Master of Environmental Systems | | Master of Hospital Administration |
| | Master of Special Education | | Master of Hospitality Administration |
| MESM | Master of Environmental Science and Management | MHB | Master of Human Behavior |
| | | MHC | Master of Mental Health Counseling |
| MET | Master of Educational Technology | MHCA | Master of Health Care Administration |
| | Master of Engineering Technology | MHCD | Master of Health Care Design |
| | Master of Entertainment Technology | MHCI | Master of Human-Computer Interaction |
| | Master of Environmental Toxicology | MHCL | Master of Health Care Leadership |
| METM | Master of Engineering and Technology Management | MHE | Master of Health Education |
| | | | Master of Human Ecology |
| MEVE | Master of Environmental Engineering | MHE Ed | Master of Home Economics Education |
| MF | Master of Finance | MHEA | Master of Higher Education Administration |
| | Master of Forestry | MHHS | Master of Health and Human Services |
| MFA | Master of Fine Arts | MHI | Master of Health Informatics |
| MFALP | Master of Food and Agriculture Law and Policy | | Master of Healthcare Innovation |
| MFAM | Master's of Food Animal Medicine | MHIHIM | Master of Health Informatics and Health Information Management |
| MFAS | Master of Fisheries and Aquatic Science | | |
| MFAW | Master of Fine Arts in Writing | MHIIM | Master of Health Informatics and Information Management |
| MFC | Master of Forest Conservation | | |
| MFCS | Master of Family and Consumer Sciences | MHIS | Master of Health Information Systems |
| MFE | Master of Financial Economics | MHK | Master of Human Kinetics |
| | Master of Financial Engineering | MHM | Master of Healthcare Management |
| | Master of Forest Engineering | MHMS | Master of Health Management Systems |
| MFES | Master of Fire and Emergency Services | MHP | Master of Health Physics |
| MFG | Master of Functional Genomics | | Master of Heritage Preservation |
| MFHD | Master of Family and Human Development | | Master of Historic Preservation |
| MFM | Master of Financial Management | MHPA | Master of Heath Policy and Administration |
| | Master of Financial Mathematics | MHPE | Master of Health Professions Education |
| MFPE | Master of Food Process Engineering | MHR | Master of Human Resources |
| MFR | Master of Forest Resources | MHRD | Master in Human Resource Development |
| MFRC | Master of Forest Resources and Conservation | MHRIR | Master of Human Resources and Industrial Relations |
| MFRE | Master of Food and Resource Economics | | |
| MFS | Master of Food Science | MHRLR | Master of Human Resources and Labor Relations |
| | Master of Forensic Sciences | | |
| | Master of Forest Science | MHRM | Master of Human Resources Management |
| | Master of Forest Studies | MHS | Master of Health Science |
| | Master of French Studies | | Master of Health Sciences |
| MFST | Master of Food Safety and Technology | | Master of Health Studies |
| MFT | Master of Family Therapy | | Master of Hispanic Studies |
| | Master of Food Technology | | Master of Human Services |
| MFWB | Master of Fishery and Wildlife Biology | | Master of Humanistic Studies |
| MFWCB | Master of Fish, Wildlife and Conservation Biology | MHSA | Master of Health Services Administration |
| | | MHSE | Master of Health Science Education |
| MFWS | Master of Fisheries and Wildlife Sciences | MHSM | Master of Health Systems Management |
| MFYCS | Master of Family, Youth and Community Sciences | MI | Master of Information |
| | | | Master of Instruction |
| MG | Master of Genetics | MI Arch | Master of Interior Architecture |
| MGA | Master of Global Affairs | MIA | Master of Interior Architecture |
| | Master of Government Administration | | Master of International Affairs |
| | Master of Governmental Administration | MIAA | Master of International Affairs and Administration |
| MGC | Master of Genetic Counseling | | |
| MGD | Master of Graphic Design | MIAM | Master of International Agribusiness Management |

| | | | |
|---|---|---|---|
| MIAPD | Master of Interior Architecture and Product Design | | Master of Juridical Studies |
| MIB | Master of International Business | MK | Master of Kinesiology |
| MIBA | Master of International Business Administration | MKM | Master of Knowledge Management |
| MICM | Master of International Construction Management | ML | Master of Latin |
| | | ML Arch | Master of Landscape Architecture |
| MID | Master of Industrial Design | MLA | Master of Landscape Architecture |
| | Master of Industrial Distribution | | Master of Liberal Arts |
| | Master of Interior Design | MLAS | Master of Laboratory Animal Science |
| | Master of International Development | | Master of Liberal Arts and Sciences |
| MIDA | Master of International Development Administration | MLAUD | Master of Landscape Architecture in Urban Development |
| MIDC | Master of Integrated Design and Construction | MLD | Master of Leadership Development |
| MIDP | Master of International Development Policy | | Master of Leadership Studies |
| MIE | Master of Industrial Engineering | MLE | Master of Applied Linguistics and Exegesis |
| MIHTM | Master of International Hospitality and Tourism Management | MLER | Master of Labor and Employment Relations |
| | | MLI Sc | Master of Library and Information Science |
| MIJ | Master of International Journalism | MLIS | Master of Library and Information Science |
| MILR | Master of Industrial and Labor Relations | | Master of Library and Information Studies |
| MIM | Master in Ministry | MLM | Master of Leadership in Ministry |
| | Master of Information Management | MLPD | Master of Land and Property Development |
| | Master of International Management | MLRHR | Master of Labor Relations and Human Resources |
| MIMLAE | Master of International Management for Latin American Executives | MLS | Master of Leadership Studies |
| MIMS | Master of Information Management and Systems | | Master of Legal Studies |
| | | | Master of Liberal Studies |
| | Master of Integrated Manufacturing Systems | | Master of Library Science |
| MIP | Master of Infrastructure Planning | | Master of Life Sciences |
| | Master of Intellectual Property | MLSCM | Master of Logistics and Supply Chain Management |
| | Master of International Policy | MLSP | Master of Law and Social Policy |
| MIPA | Master of International Public Affairs | MLT | Master of Language Technologies |
| MIPD | Master of Integrated Product Design | MLTCA | Master of Long Term Care Administration |
| MIPM | Master of International Policy Management | MLW | Master of Studies in Law |
| MIPP | Master of International Policy and Practice | MLWS | Master of Land and Water Systems |
| | Master of International Public Policy | MM | Master of Management |
| MIPS | Master of International Planning Studies | | Master of Ministry |
| MIR | Master of Industrial Relations | | Master of Missiology |
| | Master of International Relations | | Master of Music |
| MIRHR | Master of Industrial Relations and Human Resources | MM Ed | Master of Music Education |
| | | MM Sc | Master of Medical Science |
| MIS | Master of Imaging Science | MM St | Master of Museum Studies |
| | Master of Industrial Statistics | MMA | Master of Marine Affairs |
| | Master of Information Science | | Master of Media Arts |
| | Master of Information Systems | | Master of Ministry Administration |
| | Master of Integrated Science | | Master of Musical Arts |
| | Master of Interdisciplinary Studies | MMAL | Master of Maritime Administration and Logistics |
| | Master of International Service | MMAS | Master of Military Art and Science |
| | Master of International Studies | MMB | Master of Microbial Biotechnology |
| MISE | Master of Industrial and Systems Engineering | MMC | Master of Manufacturing Competitiveness |
| MISKM | Master of Information Sciences and Knowledge Management | | Master of Mass Communications |
| | | | Master of Music Conducting |
| MISM | Master of Information Systems Management | MMCM | Master of Music in Church Music |
| MISW | Master of Indigenous Social Work | MMCSS | Master of Mathematical Computational and Statistical Sciences |
| MIT | Master in Teaching | | |
| | Master of Industrial Technology | MME | Master of Manufacturing Engineering |
| | Master of Information Technology | | Master of Mathematics Education |
| | Master of Initial Teaching | | Master of Mathematics for Educators |
| | Master of International Trade | | Master of Mechanical Engineering |
| | Master of Internet Technology | | Master of Mining Engineering |
| MITA | Master of Information Technology Administration | | Master of Music Education |
| | | MMF | Master of Mathematical Finance |
| MITM | Master of Information Technology and Management | MMFT | Master of Marriage and Family Therapy |
| | | MMH | Master of Management in Hospitality |
| MJ | Master of Journalism | | Master of Medical Humanities |
| | Master of Jurisprudence | MMI | Master of Management of Innovation |
| MJ Ed | Master of Jewish Education | MMIS | Master of Management Information Systems |
| MJA | Master of Justice Administration | MML | Master of Managerial Logistics |
| MJM | Master of Justice Management | MMM | Master of Manufacturing Management |
| MJS | Master of Judicial Studies | | |

|  |  |  |  |
|---|---|---|---|
|  | Master of Marine Management |  | Master of Physician Assistant |
|  | Master of Medical Management |  | Master of Professional Accountancy |
| MMP | Master of Management Practice |  | Master of Professional Accounting |
|  | Master of Marine Policy |  | Master of Public Administration |
|  | Master of Medical Physics |  | Master of Public Affairs |
|  | Master of Music Performance | MPAC | Master of Professional Accounting |
| MMPA | Master of Management and Professional Accounting | MPAID | Master of Public Administration and International Development |
| MMQM | Master of Manufacturing Quality Management | MPAP | Master of Physician Assistant Practice |
| MMR | Master of Marketing Research |  | Master of Public Administration and  Policy |
| MMRM | Master of Marine Resources Management |  | Master of Public Affairs and Politics |
| MMS | Master of Management Science | MPAS | Master of Physician Assistant Science |
|  | Master of Management Studies |  | Master of Physician Assistant Studies |
|  | Master of Manufacturing Systems | MPC | Master of Professional Communication |
|  | Master of Marine Studies |  | Master of Professional Counseling |
|  | Master of Materials Science | MPD | Master of Product Development |
|  | Master of Mathematical Sciences |  | Master of Public Diplomacy |
|  | Master of Medical Science | MPDS | Master of Planning and Development Studies |
|  | Master of Medieval Studies | MPE | Master of Physical Education |
| MMSE | Master of Manufacturing Systems Engineering | MPEM | Master of Project Engineering and Management |
| MMSM | Master of Music in Sacred Music | MPH | Master of Public Health |
| MMT | Master in Marketing | MPHE | Master of Public Health Education |
|  | Master of Music Teaching | MPHM | Master in Plant Health Management |
|  | Master of Music Therapy | MPHS | Master of Population Health Sciences |
|  | Master's in Marketing Technology | MPHTM | Master of Public Health and Tropical Medicine |
| MMus | Master of Music | MPI | Master of Product Innovation |
| MN | Master of Nursing | MPIA | Master of Public and International Affairs |
|  | Master of Nutrition | MPM | Master of Pastoral Ministry |
| MN NP | Master of Nursing in Nurse Practitioner |  | Master of Pest Management |
| MNA | Master of Nonprofit Administration |  | Master of Policy Management |
|  | Master of Nurse Anesthesia |  | Master of Practical Ministries |
| MNAL | Master of Nonprofit Administration and Leadership |  | Master of Project Management |
| MNAS | Master of Natural and Applied Science |  | Master of Public Management |
| MNCM | Master of Network and Communications Management | MPNA | Master of Public and Nonprofit Administration |
| MNE | Master of Nuclear Engineering | MPNL | Master of Philanthropy and Nonprofit Leadership |
| MNL | Master in International Business for Latin America | MPO | Master of Prosthetics and Orthotics |
| MNM | Master of Nonprofit Management | MPOD | Master of Positive Organizational Development |
| MNO | Master of Nonprofit Organization | MPP | Master of Public Policy |
| MNPL | Master of Not-for-Profit Leadership | MPPA | Master of Public Policy Administration |
| MNpS | Master of Nonprofit Studies |  | Master of Public Policy and Administration |
| MNR | Master of Natural Resources | MPPAL | Master of Public Policy, Administration and Law |
| MNRD | Master of Natural Resources Development | MPPM | Master of Public and Private Management |
| MNRES | Master of Natural Resources and Environmental Studies |  | Master of Public Policy and Management |
| MNRM | Master of Natural Resource Management | MPPPM | Master of Plant Protection and Pest Management |
| MNRMG | Master of Natural Resource Management and Geography | MPRTM | Master of Parks, Recreation, and Tourism Management |
| MNRS | Master of Natural Resource Stewardship | MPS | Master of Pastoral Studies |
| MNS | Master of Natural Science |  | Master of Perfusion Science |
| MO | Master of Oceanography |  | Master of Planning Studies |
| MOD | Master of Organizational Development |  | Master of Political Science |
| MOGS | Master of Oil and Gas Studies |  | Master of Preservation Studies |
| MOL | Master of Organizational Leadership |  | Master of Prevention Science |
| MOM | Master of Organizational Management |  | Master of Professional Studies |
|  | Master of Oriental Medicine |  | Master of Public Service |
| MOR | Master of Operations Research | MPSA | Master of Public Service Administration |
| MOT | Master of Occupational Therapy | MPSG | Master of Population and Social Gerontology |
| MP | Master of Physiology | MPSIA | Master of Political Science and International Affairs |
|  | Master of Planning | MPSL | Master of Public Safety Leadership |
| MP Ac | Master of Professional Accountancy | MPSRE | Master of Professional Studies in Real Estate |
| MP Acc | Master of Professional Accountancy | MPT | Master of Pastoral Theology |
|  | Master of Professional Accounting |  | Master of Physical Therapy |
|  | Master of Public Accounting |  | Master of Practical Theology |
| MP Aff | Master of Public Affairs | MPVM | Master of Preventive Veterinary Medicine |
| MP Th | Master of Pastoral Theology | MPW | Master of Professional Writing |
| MPA | Master of Performing Arts |  | Master of Public Works |

| | |
|---|---|
| MQM | Master of Quality Management |
| MQS | Master of Quality Systems |
| MR | Master of Recreation |
| | Master of Retailing |
| MRA | Master in Research Administration |
| MRC | Master of Rehabilitation Counseling |
| MRCP | Master of Regional and City Planning |
| | Master of Regional and Community Planning |
| MRD | Master of Rural Development |
| MRE | Master of Real Estate |
| | Master of Religious Education |
| MRED | Master of Real Estate Development |
| MREM | Master of Resource and Environmental Management |
| MRLS | Master of Resources Law Studies |
| MRM | Master of Resources Management |
| MRP | Master of Regional Planning |
| MRRD | Master in Recreation Resource Development |
| MRS | Master of Religious Studies |
| MRSc | Master of Rehabilitation Science |
| MRTP | Master of Rural and Town Planning |
| MS | Master of Science |
| MS Cmp E | Master of Science in Computer Engineering |
| MS Kin | Master of Science in Kinesiology |
| MS Acct | Master of Science in Accounting |
| MS Accy | Master of Science in Accountancy |
| MS Aero E | Master of Science in Aerospace Engineering |
| MS Ag | Master of Science in Agriculture |
| MS Arch | Master of Science in Architecture |
| MS Arch St | Master of Science in Architectural Studies |
| MS Bio E | Master of Science in Bioengineering |
| MS Bm E | Master of Science in Biomedical Engineering |
| MS Ch E | Master of Science in Chemical Engineering |
| MS Cp E | Master of Science in Computer Engineering |
| MS Eco | Master of Science in Economics |
| MS Econ | Master of Science in Economics |
| MS Ed | Master of Science in Education |
| MS El | Master of Science in Educational Leadership and Administration |
| MS En E | Master of Science in Environmental Engineering |
| MS Eng | Master of Science in Engineering |
| MS Engr | Master of Science in Engineering |
| MS Env E | Master of Science in Environmental Engineering |
| MS Exp Surg | Master of Science in Experimental Surgery |
| MS Mat E | Master of Science in Materials Engineering |
| MS Mat SE | Master of Science in Material Science and Engineering |
| MS Met E | Master of Science in Metallurgical Engineering |
| MS Mgt | Master of Science in Management |
| MS Min | Master of Science in Mining |
| MS Min E | Master of Science in Mining Engineering |
| MS Mt E | Master of Science in Materials Engineering |
| MS Otol | Master of Science in Otolaryngology |
| MS Pet E | Master of Science in Petroleum Engineering |
| MS Sc | Master of Social Science |
| MS Sp Ed | Master of Science in Special Education |
| MS Stat | Master of Science in Statistics |
| MS Surg | Master of Science in Surgery |
| MS Tax | Master of Science in Taxation |
| MS Tc E | Master of Science in Telecommunications Engineering |
| MS-R | Master of Science (Research) |
| MSA | Master of School Administration |
| | Master of Science in Accountancy |
| | Master of Science in Accounting |
| | Master of Science in Administration |
| | Master of Science in Aeronautics |

| | |
|---|---|
| | Master of Science in Agriculture |
| | Master of Science in Analytics |
| | Master of Science in Anesthesia |
| | Master of Science in Architecture |
| | Master of Science in Aviation |
| | Master of Sports Administration |
| | Master of Surgical Assisting |
| MSAA | Master of Science in Astronautics and Aeronautics |
| MSAAE | Master of Science in Aeronautical and Astronautical Engineering |
| MSABE | Master of Science in Agricultural and Biological Engineering |
| MSAC | Master of Science in Acupuncture |
| MSACC | Master of Science in Accounting |
| MSACS | Master of Science in Applied Computer Science |
| MSAE | Master of Science in Aeronautical Engineering |
| | Master of Science in Aerospace Engineering |
| | Master of Science in Applied Economics |
| | Master of Science in Applied Engineering |
| | Master of Science in Architectural Engineering |
| MSAEM | Master of Science in Aerospace Engineering and Mechanics |
| MSAF | Master of Science in Aviation Finance |
| MSAG | Master of Science in Applied Geosciences |
| MSAH | Master of Science in Allied Health |
| MSAL | Master of Sport Administration and Leadership |
| MSAM | Master of Science in Applied Mathematics |
| MSANR | Master of Science in Agriculture and Natural Resources |
| MSAPM | Master of Security Analysis and Portfolio Management |
| MSAS | Master of Science in Applied Statistics |
| | Master of Science in Architectural Studies |
| MSAT | Master of Science in Accounting and Taxation |
| | Master of Science in Advanced Technology |
| | Master of Science in Athletic Training |
| MSB | Master of Science in Biotechnology |
| | Master of Sustainable Business |
| MSBA | Master of Science in Business Administration |
| | Master of Science in Business Analysis |
| MSBAE | Master of Science in Biological and Agricultural Engineering |
| | Master of Science in Biosystems and Agricultural Engineering |
| MSBC | Master of Science in Building Construction |
| | Master of Science in Business Communication |
| MSBCB | Master's in Bioinformatics and Computational Biology |
| MSBE | Master of Science in Biological Engineering |
| | Master of Science in Biomedical Engineering |
| MSBENG | Master of Science in Bioengineering |
| MSBH | Master of Science in Behavioral Health |
| MSBIT | Master of Science in Business Information Technology |
| MSBM | Master of Sport Business Management |
| MSBME | Master of Science in Biomedical Engineering |
| MSBMS | Master of Science in Basic Medical Science |
| MSBS | Master of Science in Biomedical Sciences |
| MSBTM | Master of Science in Biotechnology and Management |
| MSC | Master of Science in Commerce |
| | Master of Science in Communication |
| | Master of Science in Computers |
| | Master of Science in Counseling |
| | Master of Science in Criminology |
| | Master of Strategic Communication |
| MSCC | Master of Science in Community Counseling |
| MSCD | Master of Science in Communication Disorders |
| | Master of Science in Community Development |

| | |
|---|---|
| MSCE | Master of Science in Civil Engineering |
| | Master of Science in Clinical Epidemiology |
| | Master of Science in Computer Engineering |
| | Master of Science in Continuing Education |
| MSCEE | Master of Science in Civil and Environmental Engineering |
| MSCF | Master of Science in Computational Finance |
| MSCH | Master of Science in Chemical Engineering |
| MSChE | Master of Science in Chemical Engineering |
| MSCI | Master of Science in Clinical Investigation |
| MSCIS | Master of Science in Computer and Information Science |
| | Master of Science in Computer and Information Systems |
| | Master of Science in Computer Information Science |
| | Master of Science in Computer Information Systems |
| MSCIT | Master of Science in Computer Information Technology |
| MSCJ | Master of Science in Criminal Justice |
| MSCJA | Master of Science in Criminal Justice Administration |
| MSCJS | Master of Science in Crime and Justice Studies |
| MSCLS | Master of Science in Clinical Laboratory Studies |
| MSCM | Master of Science in Church Management |
| | Master of Science in Conflict Management |
| | Master of Science in Construction Management |
| | Master of Supply Chain Management |
| MSCNU | Master of Science in Clinical Nutrition |
| MSCP | Master of Science in Clinical Psychology |
| | Master of Science in Community Psychology |
| | Master of Science in Computer Engineering |
| | Master of Science in Counseling Psychology |
| MSCPE | Master of Science in Computer Engineering |
| MSCPharm | Master of Science in Pharmacy |
| MSCR | Master of Science in Clinical Research |
| MSCRP | Master of Science in City and Regional Planning |
| | Master of Science in Community and Regional Planning |
| MSCS | Master of Science in Clinical Science |
| | Master of Science in Computer Science |
| | Master of Science in Cyber Security |
| MSCSD | Master of Science in Communication Sciences and Disorders |
| MSCSE | Master of Science in Computer Science and Engineering |
| MSCTE | Master of Science in Career and Technical Education |
| MSD | Master of Science in Dentistry |
| | Master of Science in Design |
| | Master of Science in Dietetics |
| MSE | Master of Science Education |
| | Master of Science in Economics |
| | Master of Science in Education |
| | Master of Science in Engineering |
| | Master of Science in Engineering Management |
| | Master of Software Engineering |
| | Master of Special Education |
| | Master of Structural Engineering |
| MSECE | Master of Science in Electrical and Computer Engineering |
| MSED | Master of Sustainable Economic Development |
| MSEE | Master of Science in Electrical Engineering |
| | Master of Science in Environmental Engineering |
| MSEH | Master of Science in Environmental Health |
| MSEL | Master of Science in Educational Leadership |
| MSEM | Master of Science in Engineering Management |
| | Master of Science in Engineering Mechanics |

| | |
|---|---|
| | Master of Science in Environmental Management |
| MSENE | Master of Science in Environmental Engineering |
| MSEO | Master of Science in Electro-Optics |
| MSEP | Master of Science in Economic Policy |
| MSES | Master of Science in Embedded Software Engineering |
| | Master of Science in Engineering Science |
| | Master of Science in Environmental Science |
| | Master of Science in Environmental Studies |
| | Master of Science in Exercise Science |
| MSET | Master of Science in Educational Technology |
| | Master of Science in Engineering Technology |
| MSEV | Master of Science in Environmental Engineering |
| MSF | Master of Science in Finance |
| | Master of Science in Forestry |
| | Master of Spiritual Formation |
| MSFA | Master of Science in Financial Analysis |
| MSFCS | Master of Science in Family and Consumer Science |
| MSFE | Master of Science in Financial Engineering |
| MSFM | Master of Sustainable Forest Management |
| MSFOR | Master of Science in Forestry |
| MSFP | Master of Science in Financial Planning |
| MSFS | Master of Science in Financial Sciences |
| | Master of Science in Forensic Science |
| MSFSB | Master of Science in Financial Services and Banking |
| MSFT | Master of Science in Family Therapy |
| MSGC | Master of Science in Genetic Counseling |
| MSH | Master of Science in Health |
| | Master of Science in Hospice |
| MSHA | Master of Science in Health Administration |
| MSHCA | Master of Science in Health Care Administration |
| MSHCI | Master of Science in Human Computer Interaction |
| MSHCPM | Master of Science in Health Care Policy and Management |
| MSHE | Master of Science in Health Education |
| MSHES | Master of Science in Human Environmental Sciences |
| MSHFID | Master of Science in Human Factors in Information Design |
| MSHFS | Master of Science in Human Factors and Systems |
| MSHI | Master of Science in Health Informatics |
| MSHP | Master of Science in Health Professions |
| | Master of Science in Health Promotion |
| MSHR | Master of Science in Human Resources |
| MSHRL | Master of Science in Human Resource Leadership |
| MSHRM | Master of Science in Human Resource Management |
| MSHROD | Master of Science in Human Resources and Organizational Development |
| MSHS | Master of Science in Health Science |
| | Master of Science in Health Services |
| | Master of Science in Homeland Security |
| MSI | Master of Science in Information |
| | Master of Science in Instruction |
| | Master of System Integration |
| MSIA | Master of Science in Industrial Administration |
| | Master of Science in Information Assurance |
| MSIB | Master of Science in International Business |
| MSIDM | Master of Science in Interior Design and Merchandising |
| MSIE | Master of Science in Industrial Engineering |
| | Master of Science in International Economics |

| | |
|---|---|
| MSIEM | Master of Science in Information Engineering and Management |
| MSIID | Master of Science in Information and Instructional Design |
| MSIM | Master of Science in Information Management |
| | Master of Science in International Management |
| MSIMC | Master of Science in Integrated Marketing Communications |
| MSIR | Master of Science in Industrial Relations |
| MSIS | Master of Science in Information Science |
| | Master of Science in Information Studies |
| | Master of Science in Information Systems |
| | Master of Science in Interdisciplinary Studies |
| MSISE | Master of Science in Infrastructure Systems Engineering |
| MSISM | Master of Science in Information Systems Management |
| MSISPM | Master of Science in Information Security Policy and Management |
| MSIST | Master of Science in Information Systems Technology |
| MSIT | Master of Science in Industrial Technology |
| | Master of Science in Information Technology |
| | Master of Science in Instructional Technology |
| MSITM | Master of Science in Information Technology Management |
| MSJ | Master of Science in Journalism |
| | Master of Science in Jurisprudence |
| MSJC | Master of Social Justice and Criminology |
| MSJE | Master of Science in Jewish Education |
| MSJFP | Master of Science in Juvenile Forensic Psychology |
| MSJJ | Master of Science in Juvenile Justice |
| MSJPS | Master of Science in Justice and Public Safety |
| MSJS | Master of Science in Jewish Studies |
| MSL | Master of School Leadership |
| | Master of Science in Leadership |
| | Master of Science in Limnology |
| | Master of Strategic Leadership |
| | Master of Studies in Law |
| MSLA | Master of Science in Legal Administration |
| MSLFS | Master of Science in Life Sciences |
| MSLP | Master of Speech-Language Pathology |
| MSLS | Master of Science in Library Science |
| MSLSCM | Master of Science in Logistics and Supply Chain Management |
| MSLT | Master of Second Language Teaching |
| MSM | Master of Sacred Ministry |
| | Master of Sacred Music |
| | Master of School Mathematics |
| | Master of Science in Management |
| | Master of Science in Medicine |
| | Master of Science in Organization Management |
| | Master of Security Management |
| MSMA | Master of Science in Marketing Analysis |
| MSMAE | Master of Science in Materials Engineering |
| MSMC | Master of Science in Mass Communications |
| MSME | Master of Science in Mathematics Education |
| | Master of Science in Mechanical Engineering |
| MSMFT | Master of Science in Marriage and Family Therapy |
| MSMHC | Master of Science in Mental Health Counseling |
| MSMIS | Master of Science in Management Information Systems |
| MSMIT | Master of Science in Management and Information Technology |
| MSMLS | Master of Science in Medical Laboratory Science |
| MSMOT | Master of Science in Management of Technology |
| MSMP | Master of Science in Medical Physics |

| | |
|---|---|
| MSMS | Master of Science in Management Science |
| | Master of Science in Marine Science |
| | Master of Science in Medical Sciences |
| MSMSE | Master of Science in Manufacturing Systems Engineering |
| | Master of Science in Material Science and Engineering |
| | Master of Science in Mathematics and Science Education |
| MSMT | Master of Science in Management and Technology |
| MSMus | Master of Sacred Music |
| MSN | Master of Science in Nursing |
| MSNA | Master of Science in Nurse Anesthesia |
| MSNE | Master of Science in Nuclear Engineering |
| MSNED | Master of Science in Nurse Education |
| MSNM | Master of Science in Nonprofit Management |
| MSNS | Master of Science in Natural Science |
| | Master of Science in Nutritional Science |
| MSOD | Master of Science in Organization Development |
| | Master of Science in Organizational Development |
| MSOEE | Master of Science in Outdoor and Environmental Education |
| MSOES | Master of Science in Occupational Ergonomics and Safety |
| MSOH | Master of Science in Occupational Health |
| MSOL | Master of Science in Organizational Leadership |
| MSOM | Master of Science in Operations Management |
| | Master of Science in Oriental Medicine |
| MSOR | Master of Science in Operations Research |
| MSOT | Master of Science in Occupational Technology |
| | Master of Science in Occupational Therapy |
| MSP | Master of Science in Pharmacy |
| | Master of Science in Planning |
| | Master of Speech Pathology |
| MSPA | Master of Science in Physician Assistant |
| | Master of Science in Professional Accountancy |
| MSPAS | Master of Science in Physician Assistant Studies |
| MSPC | Master of Science in Professional Communications |
| MSPE | Master of Science in Petroleum Engineering |
| MSPH | Master of Science in Public Health |
| MSPHR | Master of Science in Pharmacy |
| MSPM | Master of Science in Professional Management |
| | Master of Science in Project Management |
| MSPNGE | Master of Science in Petroleum and Natural Gas Engineering |
| MSPO | Master of Science in Prosthetics and Orthotics |
| MSPPM | Master of Science in Public Policy and Management |
| MSPS | Master of Science in Pharmaceutical Science |
| | Master of Science in Political Science |
| | Master of Science in Psychological Services |
| MSPT | Master of Science in Physical Therapy |
| MSpVM | Master of Specialized Veterinary Medicine |
| MSR | Master of Science in Radiology |
| | Master of Science in Reading |
| MSRA | Master of Science in Recreation Administration |
| MSRE | Master of Science in Real Estate |
| | Master of Science in Religious Education |
| MSRED | Master of Science in Real Estate Development |
| | Master of Sustainable Real Estate Development |
| MSRLS | Master of Science in Recreation and Leisure Studies |
| MSRM | Master of Science in Risk Management |
| MSRMP | Master of Science in Radiological Medical Physics |
| MSRS | Master of Science in Radiological Sciences |
| | Master of Science in Rehabilitation Science |

| | | | |
|---|---|---|---|
| MSS | Master of Security Studies | MTHM | Master of Tourism and Hospitality Management |
| | Master of Social Science | MTI | Master of Information Technology |
| | Master of Social Services | MTID | Master of Tangible Interaction Design |
| | Master of Software Systems | MTL | Master of Talmudic Law |
| | Master of Sports Science | MTM | Master of Technology Management |
| | Master of Strategic Studies | | Master of Telecommunications Management |
| | Master's in Statistical Science | | Master of the Teaching of Mathematics |
| MSSA | Master of Science in Social Administration | MTMH | Master of Tropical Medicine and Hygiene |
| MSSCM | Master of Science in Supply Chain Management | MTMS | Master in Teaching Mathematics and Science |
| MSSD | Master of Arts in Software Driven Systems Design | MTOM | Master of Traditional Oriental Medicine |
| | Master of Science in Sustainable Design | MTPC | Master of Technical and Professional Communication |
| MSSE | Master of Science in Software Engineering | MTR | Master of Translational Research |
| | Master of Science in Special Education | MTS | Master of Theatre Studies |
| MSSEM | Master of Science in Systems and Engineering Management | | Master of Theological Studies |
| | | MTWM | Master of Trust and Wealth Management |
| MSSI | Master of Science in Security Informatics | MTX | Master of Taxation |
| | Master of Science in Strategic Intelligence | MUA | Master of Urban Affairs |
| MSSL | Master of Science in School Leadership | MUCD | Master of Urban and Community Design |
| | Master of Science in Strategic Leadership | MUD | Master of Urban Design |
| MSSLP | Master of Science in Speech-Language Pathology | MUDS | Master of Urban Design Studies |
| MSSM | Master of Science in Sports Medicine | MUEP | Master of Urban and Environmental Planning |
| MSSP | Master of Science in Social Policy | MUP | Master of Urban Planning |
| MSSPA | Master of Science in Student Personnel Administration | MUPDD | Master of Urban Planning, Design, and Development |
| MSSS | Master of Science in Safety Science | MUPP | Master of Urban Planning and Policy |
| | Master of Science in Systems Science | MUPRED | Master of Urban Planning and Real Estate Development |
| MSST | Master of Science in Security Technologies | MURP | Master of Urban and Regional Planning |
| MSSW | Master of Science in Social Work | | Master of Urban and Rural Planning |
| MSSWE | Master of Science in Software Engineering | MUS | Master of Urban Studies |
| MST | Master of Science and Technology | MUSA | Master of Urban Spatial Analytics |
| | Master of Science in Taxation | MVP | Master of Voice Pedagogy |
| | Master of Science in Teaching | MVPH | Master of Veterinary Public Health |
| | Master of Science in Technology | MVS | Master of Visual Studies |
| | Master of Science in Telecommunications | MWC | Master of Wildlife Conservation |
| | Master of Science Teaching | MWM | Master of Water Management |
| MSTC | Master of Science in Technical Communication | MWPS | Master of Wood and Paper Science |
| | Master of Science in Telecommunications | MWR | Master of Water Resources |
| MSTCM | Master of Science in Traditional Chinese Medicine | MWS | Master of Women's Studies |
| | | | Master of Worship Studies |
| MSTE | Master of Science in Telecommunications Engineering | MWSc | Master of Wildlife Science |
| | Master of Science in Transportation Engineering | MZS | Master of Zoological Science |
| | | Nav Arch | Naval Architecture |
| MSTL | Master of Science in Teacher Leadership | Naval E | Naval Engineer |
| MSTM | Master of Science in Technology Management | ND | Doctor of Naturopathic Medicine |
| | Master of Science in Transfusion Medicine | NE | Nuclear Engineer |
| MSTOM | Master of Science in Traditional Oriental Medicine | Nuc E | Nuclear Engineer |
| | | OD | Doctor of Optometry |
| MSUASE | Master of Science in Unmanned and Autonomous Systems Engineering | OTD | Doctor of Occupational Therapy |
| | | PBME | Professional Master of Biomedical Engineering |
| MSUD | Master of Science in Urban Design | PC | Performer's Certificate |
| MSUS | Master of Science in Urban Studies | PD | Professional Diploma |
| MSW | Master of Social Work | PGC | Post-Graduate Certificate |
| MSWE | Master of Software Engineering | PGD | Postgraduate Diploma |
| MSWREE | Master of Science in Water Resources and Environmental Engineering | Ph L | Licentiate of Philosophy |
| | | Pharm D | Doctor of Pharmacy |
| MT | Master of Taxation | PhD | Doctor of Philosophy |
| | Master of Teaching | PhD Otol | Doctor of Philosophy in Otolaryngology |
| | Master of Technology | PhD Surg | Doctor of Philosophy in Surgery |
| | Master of Textiles | PhDEE | Doctor of Philosophy in Electrical Engineering |
| MTA | Master of Tax Accounting | PMBA | Professional Master of Business Administration |
| | Master of Teaching Arts | PMC | Post Master Certificate |
| | Master of Tourism Administration | PMD | Post-Master's Diploma |
| MTCM | Master of Traditional Chinese Medicine | PMS | Professional Master of Science |
| MTD | Master of Training and Development | | Professional Master's |
| MTE | Master in Educational Technology | Post-Doctoral MS | Post-Doctoral Master of Science |
| MTESOL | Master in Teaching English to Speakers of Other Languages | Post-MSN Certificate | Post-Master of Science in Nursing Certificate |
| | | PPDPT | Postprofessional Doctor of Physical Therapy |

| | | | |
|---|---|---|---|
| Pro-MS | Professional Science Master's | SMACT | Master of Science in Art, Culture and Technology |
| Professional MA | Professional Master of Arts | SMBT | Master of Science in Building Technology |
| Professional MBA | Professional Master of Business Administration | SP | Specialist Degree |
| Professional MS | Professional Master of Science | Sp Ed | Specialist in Education |
| PSM | Professional Master of Science | Sp LIS | Specialist in Library and Information Science |
| | Professional Science Master's | SPA | Specialist in Arts |
| Psy D | Doctor of Psychology | Spec | Specialist's Certificate |
| Psy M | Master of Psychology | Spec M | Specialist in Music |
| Psy S | Specialist in Psychology | Spt | Specialist Degree |
| Psya D | Doctor of Psychoanalysis | SSP | Specialist in School Psychology |
| S Psy S | Specialist in Psychological Services | STB | Bachelor of Sacred Theology |
| Sc D | Doctor of Science | STD | Doctor of Sacred Theology |
| Sc M | Master of Science | STL | Licentiate of Sacred Theology |
| SCCT | Specialist in Community College Teaching | STM | Master of Sacred Theology |
| ScDPT | Doctor of Physical Therapy Science | TDPT | Transitional Doctor of Physical Therapy |
| SD | Doctor of Science | Th D | Doctor of Theology |
| | Specialist Degree | Th M | Master of Theology |
| SJD | Doctor of Juridical Sciences | TOTD | Transitional Doctor of Occupational Therapy |
| SLPD | Doctor of Speech-Language Pathology | VMD | Doctor of Veterinary Medicine |
| SM | Master of Science | WEMBA | Weekend Executive Master of Business Administration |
| SM Arch S | Master of Science in Architectural Studies | XMA | Executive Master of Arts |

# INDEXES

# Displays and Close-Ups

# Directories and Subject Areas

Following is an alphabetical listing of directories and subject areas. Also listed are cross-references for subject area names not used in the directory structure of the guides, for example, "City and Regional Planning (*see* Urban and Regional Planning)."

## Graduate Programs in the Humanities, Arts & Social Sciences

Addictions/Substance Abuse Counseling
Administration (*see* Arts Administration; Public Administration)
African-American Studies
African Languages and Literatures (*see* African Studies)
African Studies
Agribusiness (*see* Agricultural Economics and Agribusiness)
Agricultural Economics and Agribusiness
Alcohol Abuse Counseling (*see* Addictions/Substance Abuse Counseling)
American Indian/Native American Studies
American Studies
Anthropology
Applied Arts and Design—General
Applied Behavior Analysis
Applied Economics
Applied History (*see* Public History)
Applied Psychology
Applied Social Research
Arabic (*see* Near and Middle Eastern Languages)
Arab Studies (*see* Near and Middle Eastern Studies)
Archaeology
Architectural History
Architecture
Archives Administration (*see* Public History)
Area and Cultural Studies (*see* African-American Studies; African Studies; American Indian/Native American Studies; American Studies; Asian-American Studies; Asian Studies; Canadian Studies; Cultural Studies; East European and Russian Studies; Ethnic Studies; Folklore; Gender Studies; Hispanic Studies; Holocaust Studies; Jewish Studies; Latin American Studies; Near and Middle Eastern Studies; Northern Studies; Pacific Area/Pacific Rim Studies; Western European Studies; Women's Studies)
Art/Fine Arts
Art History
Arts Administration
Arts Journalism
Art Therapy
Asian-American Studies
Asian Languages
Asian Studies
Behavioral Sciences (*see* Psychology)
Bible Studies (*see* Religion; Theology)
Biological Anthropology
Black Studies (*see* African-American Studies)
Broadcasting (*see* Communication; Film, Television, and Video Production)
Broadcast Journalism
Building Science
Canadian Studies
Celtic Languages
Ceramics (*see* Art/Fine Arts)
Child and Family Studies
Child Development
Chinese
Chinese Studies (*see* Asian Languages; Asian Studies)
Christian Studies (*see* Missions and Missiology; Religion; Theology)
Cinema (*see* Film, Television, and Video Production)
City and Regional Planning (*see* Urban and Regional Planning)
Classical Languages and Literatures (*see* Classics)
Classics
Clinical Psychology
Clothing and Textiles

Cognitive Psychology (*see* Psychology—General; Cognitive Sciences)
Cognitive Sciences
Communication—General
Community Affairs (*see* Urban and Regional Planning; Urban Studies)
Community Planning (*see* Architecture; Environmental Design; Urban and Regional Planning; Urban Design; Urban Studies)
Community Psychology (*see* Social Psychology)
Comparative and Interdisciplinary Arts
Comparative Literature
Composition (*see* Music)
Computer Art and Design
Conflict Resolution and Mediation/Peace Studies
Consumer Economics
Corporate and Organizational Communication
Corrections (*see* Criminal Justice and Criminology)
Counseling (*see* Counseling Psychology; Pastoral Ministry and Counseling)
Counseling Psychology
Crafts (*see* Art/Fine Arts)
Creative Arts Therapies (*see* Art Therapy; Therapies—Dance, Drama, and Music)
Criminal Justice and Criminology
Cultural Anthropology
Cultural Studies
Dance
Decorative Arts
Demography and Population Studies
Design (*see* Applied Arts and Design; Architecture; Art/Fine Arts; Environmental Design; Graphic Design; Industrial Design; Interior Design; Textile Design; Urban Design)
Developmental Psychology
Diplomacy (*see* International Affairs)
Disability Studies
Drama Therapy (*see* Therapies—Dance, Drama, and Music)
Dramatic Arts (*see* Theater)
Drawing (*see* Art/Fine Arts)
Drug Abuse Counseling (*see* Addictions/Substance Abuse Counseling)
Drug and Alcohol Abuse Counseling (*see* Addictions/Substance Abuse Counseling)
East Asian Studies (*see* Asian Studies)
East European and Russian Studies
Economic Development
Economics
Educational Theater (*see* Theater; Therapies—Dance, Drama, and Music)
Emergency Management
English
Environmental Design
Ethics
Ethnic Studies
Ethnomusicology (*see* Music)
Experimental Psychology
Family and Consumer Sciences—General
Family Studies (*see* Child and Family Studies)
Family Therapy (*see* Child and Family Studies; Clinical Psychology; Counseling Psychology; Marriage and Family Therapy)
Filmmaking (*see* Film, Television, and Video Production)
Film Studies (*see* Film, Television, and Video Production)
Film, Television, and Video Production
Film, Television, and Video Theory and Criticism
Fine Arts (*see* Art/Fine Arts)
Folklore
Foreign Languages (*see* specific language)
Foreign Service (*see* International Affairs; International Development)
Forensic Psychology
Forensic Sciences
Forensics (*see* Speech and Interpersonal Communication)
French
Gender Studies
General Studies (*see* Liberal Studies)
Genetic Counseling
Geographic Information Systems

Geography
German
Gerontology
Graphic Design
Greek (*see* Classics)
Health Communication
Health Psychology
Hebrew (*see* Near and Middle Eastern Languages)
Hebrew Studies (*see* Jewish Studies)
Hispanic and Latin American Languages
Hispanic Studies
Historic Preservation
History
History of Art (*see* Art History)
History of Medicine
History of Science and Technology
Holocaust and Genocide Studies
Home Economics (*see* Family and Consumer Sciences—General)
Homeland Security
Household Economics, Sciences, and Management (*see* Family and Consumer Sciences—General)
Human Development
Humanities
Illustration
Industrial and Labor Relations
Industrial and Organizational Psychology
Industrial Design
Interdisciplinary Studies
Interior Design
International Affairs
International Development
International Economics
International Service (*see* International Affairs; International Development)
International Trade Policy
Internet and Interactive Multimedia
Interpersonal Communication (*see* Speech and Interpersonal Communication)
Interpretation (*see* Translation and Interpretation)
Islamic Studies (*see* Near and Middle Eastern Studies; Religion)
Italian
Japanese
Japanese Studies (*see* Asian Languages; Asian Studies; Japanese)
Jewelry (*see* Art/Fine Arts)
Jewish Studies
Journalism
Judaic Studies (*see* Jewish Studies; Religion)
Labor Relations (*see* Industrial and Labor Relations)
Landscape Architecture
Latin American Studies
Latin (*see* Classics)
Law Enforcement (*see* Criminal Justice and Criminology)
Liberal Studies
Lighting Design
Linguistics
Literature (*see* Classics; Comparative Literature; specific language)
Marriage and Family Therapy
Mass Communication
Media Studies
Medical Illustration
Medieval and Renaissance Studies
Metalsmithing (*see* Art/Fine Arts)
Middle Eastern Studies (*see* Near and Middle Eastern Studies)
Military and Defense Studies
Mineral Economics
Ministry (*see* Pastoral Ministry and Counseling; Theology)
Missions and Missiology
Motion Pictures (*see* Film, Television, and Video Production)
Museum Studies
Music
Musicology (*see* Music)
Music Therapy (*see* Therapies—Dance, Drama, and Music)
National Security
Native American Studies (*see* American Indian/Native American Studies)
Near and Middle Eastern Languages

Near and Middle Eastern Studies
Near Environment (*see* Family and Consumer Sciences)
Northern Studies
Organizational Psychology (*see* Industrial and Organizational Psychology)
Oriental Languages (*see* Asian Languages)
Oriental Studies (*see* Asian Studies)
Pacific Area/Pacific Rim Studies
Painting (*see* Art/Fine Arts)
Pastoral Ministry and Counseling
Philanthropic Studies
Philosophy
Photography
Playwriting (*see* Theater; Writing)
Policy Studies (*see* Public Policy)
Political Science
Population Studies (*see* Demography and Population Studies)
Portuguese
Printmaking (*see* Art/Fine Arts)
Product Design (*see* Industrial Design)
Psychoanalysis and Psychotherapy
Psychology—General
Public Administration
Public Affairs
Public History
Public Policy
Public Speaking (*see* Mass Communication; Rhetoric; Speech and Interpersonal Communication)
Publishing
Regional Planning (*see* Architecture; Urban and Regional Planning; Urban Design; Urban Studies)
Rehabilitation Counseling
Religion
Renaissance Studies (*see* Medieval and Renaissance Studies)
Rhetoric
Romance Languages
Romance Literatures (*see* Romance Languages)
Rural Planning and Studies
Rural Sociology
Russian
Scandinavian Languages
School Psychology
Sculpture (*see* Art/Fine Arts)
Security Administration (*see* Criminal Justice and Criminology)
Slavic Languages
Slavic Studies (*see* East European and Russian Studies; Slavic Languages)
Social Psychology
Social Sciences
Sociology
Southeast Asian Studies (*see* Asian Studies)
Soviet Studies (*see* East European and Russian Studies; Russian)
Spanish
Speech and Interpersonal Communication
Sport Psychology
Studio Art (*see* Art/Fine Arts)
Substance Abuse Counseling (*see* Addictions/Substance Abuse Counseling)
Survey Methodology
Sustainable Development
Technical Communication
Technical Writing
Telecommunications (*see* Film, Television, and Video Production)
Television (*see* Film, Television, and Video Production)
Textile Design
Textiles (*see* Clothing and Textiles; Textile Design)
Thanatology
Theater
Theater Arts (*see* Theater)
Theology
Therapies—Dance, Drama, and Music
Translation and Interpretation
Transpersonal and Humanistic Psychology
Urban and Regional Planning
Urban Design

Urban Planning (*see* Architecture; Urban and Regional Planning; Urban Design; Urban Studies)
Urban Studies
Video (*see* Film, Television, and Video Production)
Visual Arts (*see* Applied Arts and Design; Art/Fine Arts; Film, Television, and Video Production; Graphic Design; Illustration; Photography)
Western European Studies
Women's Studies
World Wide Web (*see* Internet and Interactive Multimedia)
Writing

# Graduate Programs in the Biological/ Biomedical Sciences & Health-Related Medical Professions

Acupuncture and Oriental Medicine
Acute Care/Critical Care Nursing Administration (*see* Health Services Management and Hospital Administration; Nursing and Healthcare Administration; Pharmaceutical Administration)
Adult Nursing
Advanced Practice Nursing (*see* Family Nurse Practitioner Studies)
Allied Health—General
Allied Health Professions (*see* Clinical Laboratory Sciences/Medical Technology; Clinical Research; Communication Disorders; Dental Hygiene; Emergency Medical Services; Occupational Therapy; Physical Therapy; Physician Assistant Studies; Rehabilitation Sciences)
Allopathic Medicine
Anatomy
Anesthesiologist Assistant Studies
Animal Behavior
Bacteriology
Behavioral Sciences (*see* Biopsychology; Neuroscience; Zoology)
Biochemistry
Bioethics
Biological and Biomedical Sciences—General Biological Chemistry (*see* Biochemistry)
Biological Oceanography (*see* Marine Biology)
Biophysics
Biopsychology
Botany
Breeding (*see* Botany; Plant Biology; Genetics)
Cancer Biology/Oncology
Cardiovascular Sciences
Cell Biology
Cellular Physiology (*see* Cell Biology; Physiology)
Child-Care Nursing (*see* Maternal and Child/Neonatal Nursing)
Chiropractic
Clinical Laboratory Sciences/Medical Technology
Clinical Research
Community Health
Community Health Nursing
Computational Biology
Conservation (*see* Conservation Biology; Environmental Biology)
Conservation Biology
Crop Sciences (*see* Botany; Plant Biology)
Cytology (*see* Cell Biology)
Dental and Oral Surgery (*see* Oral and Dental Sciences)
Dental Assistant Studies (*see* Dental Hygiene)
Dental Hygiene
Dental Services (*see* Dental Hygiene)
Dentistry
Developmental Biology Dietetics (*see* Nutrition)
Ecology
Embryology (*see* Developmental Biology)
Emergency Medical Services
Endocrinology (*see* Physiology)
Entomology
Environmental Biology
Environmental and Occupational Health

Epidemiology
Evolutionary Biology
Family Nurse Practitioner Studies
Foods (*see* Nutrition)
Forensic Nursing
Genetics
Genomic Sciences
Gerontological Nursing
Health Physics/Radiological Health
Health Promotion
Health-Related Professions (*see* individual allied health professions)
Health Services Management and Hospital Administration
Health Services Research
Histology (*see* Anatomy; Cell Biology)
HIV/AIDS Nursing
Hospice Nursing
Hospital Administration (*see* Health Services Management and Hospital Administration)
Human Genetics
Immunology
Industrial Hygiene
Infectious Diseases
International Health
Laboratory Medicine (*see* Clinical Laboratory Sciences/Medical Technology; Immunology; Microbiology; Pathology)
Life Sciences (*see* Biological and Biomedical Sciences)
Marine Biology
Maternal and Child Health
Maternal and Child/Neonatal Nursing
Medical Imaging
Medical Microbiology
Medical Nursing (*see* Medical/Surgical Nursing)
Medical Physics
Medical/Surgical Nursing
Medical Technology (*see* Clinical Laboratory Sciences/Medical Technology)
Medical Sciences (*see* Biological and Biomedical Sciences)
Medical Science Training Programs (*see* Biological and Biomedical Sciences)
Medicinal and Pharmaceutical Chemistry
Medicinal Chemistry (*see* Medicinal and Pharmaceutical Chemistry)
Medicine (*see* Allopathic Medicine; Naturopathic Medicine; Osteopathic Medicine; Podiatric Medicine)
Microbiology
Midwifery (*see* Nurse Midwifery)
Molecular Biology
Molecular Biophysics
Molecular Genetics
Molecular Medicine
Molecular Pathogenesis
Molecular Pathology
Molecular Pharmacology
Molecular Physiology
Molecular Toxicology
Naturopathic Medicine
Neural Sciences (*see* Biopsychology; Neurobiology; Neuroscience)
Neurobiology
Neuroendocrinology (*see* Biopsychology; Neurobiology; Neuroscience; Physiology)
Neuropharmacology (*see* Biopsychology; Neurobiology; Neuroscience; Pharmacology)
Neurophysiology (*see* Biopsychology; Neurobiology; Neuroscience; Physiology)
Neuroscience
Nuclear Medical Technology (*see* Clinical Laboratory Sciences/ Medical Technology)
Nurse Anesthesia
Nurse Midwifery
Nurse Practitioner Studies (*see* Family Nurse Practitioner Studies)
Nursing Administration (*see* Nursing and Healthcare Administration)
Nursing and Healthcare Administration
Nursing Education
Nursing—General
Nursing Informatics
Nutrition

Occupational Health (*see* Environmental and Occupational Health; Occupational Health Nursing)
Occupational Health Nursing
Occupational Therapy
Oncology (*see* Cancer Biology/Oncology)
Oncology Nursing
Optometry
Oral and Dental Sciences
Oral Biology (*see* Oral and Dental Sciences)
Oral Pathology (*see* Oral and Dental Sciences)
Organismal Biology (*see* Biological and Biomedical Sciences; Zoology)
Oriental Medicine and Acupuncture (*see* Acupuncture and Oriental Medicine)
Orthodontics (*see* Oral and Dental Sciences)
Osteopathic Medicine
Parasitology
Pathobiology
Pathology
Pediatric Nursing
Pedontics (*see* Oral and Dental Sciences)
Perfusion
Pharmaceutical Administration
Pharmaceutical Chemistry (*see* Medicinal and Pharmaceutical Chemistry)
Pharmaceutical Sciences
Pharmacology
Pharmacy
Photobiology of Cells and Organelles (*see* Botany; Cell Biology; Plant Biology)
Physical Therapy
Physician Assistant Studies
Physiological Optics (*see* Vision Sciences)
Podiatric Medicine
Preventive Medicine (*see* Community Health and Public Health)
Physiological Optics (*see* Physiology)
Physiology
Plant Biology
Plant Molecular Biology
Plant Pathology
Plant Physiology
Pomology (*see* Botany; Plant Biology)
Psychiatric Nursing
Public Health—General
Public Health Nursing (*see* Community Health Nursing)
Psychiatric Nursing
Psychobiology (*see* Biopsychology)
Psychopharmacology (*see* Biopsychology; Neuroscience; Pharmacology)
Radiation Biology
Radiological Health (*see* Health Physics/Radiological Health)
Rehabilitation Nursing
Rehabilitation Sciences
Rehabilitation Therapy (*see* Physical Therapy)
Reproductive Biology
School Nursing
Sociobiology (*see* Evolutionary Biology)
Structural Biology
Surgical Nursing (*see* Medical/Surgical Nursing)
Systems Biology
Teratology
Therapeutics
Theoretical Biology (*see* Biological and Biomedical Sciences)
Therapeutics (*see* Pharmaceutical Sciences; Pharmacology; Pharmacy)
Toxicology
Transcultural Nursing
Translational Biology
Tropical Medicine (*see* Parasitology)
Veterinary Medicine
Veterinary Sciences
Virology
Vision Sciences
Wildlife Biology (*see* Zoology)
Women's Health Nursing
Zoology

# Graduate Programs in the Physical Sciences, Mathematics, Agricultural Sciences, the Environment & Natural Resources

Acoustics
Agricultural Sciences
Agronomy and Soil Sciences
Analytical Chemistry
Animal Sciences
Applied Mathematics
Applied Physics
Applied Statistics
Aquaculture
Astronomy
Astrophysical Sciences (*see* Astrophysics; Atmospheric Sciences; Meteorology; Planetary and Space Sciences)
Astrophysics
Atmospheric Sciences
Biological Oceanography (*see* Marine Affairs; Marine Sciences; Oceanography)
Biomathematics
Biometry
Biostatistics
Chemical Physics
Chemistry
Computational Sciences
Condensed Matter Physics
Dairy Science (*see* Animal Sciences)
Earth Sciences (*see* Geosciences)
Environmental Management and Policy
Environmental Sciences
Environmental Studies (*see* Environmental Management and Policy)
Experimental Statistics (*see* Statistics)
Fish, Game, and Wildlife Management
Food Science and Technology
Forestry
General Science (*see* specific topics)
Geochemistry
Geodetic Sciences
Geological Engineering (*see* Geology)
Geological Sciences (*see* Geology)
Geology
Geophysical Fluid Dynamics (*see* Geophysics)
Geophysics
Geosciences
Horticulture
Hydrogeology
Hydrology
Inorganic Chemistry
Limnology
Marine Affairs
Marine Geology
Marine Sciences
Marine Studies (*see* Marine Affairs; Marine Geology; Marine Sciences; Oceanography)
Mathematical and Computational Finance
Mathematical Physics
Mathematical Statistics (*see* Applied Statistics; Statistics)
Mathematics
Meteorology
Mineralogy
Natural Resource Management (*see* Environmental Management and Policy; Natural Resources)
Natural Resources
Nuclear Physics (*see* Physics)
Ocean Engineering (*see* Marine Affairs; Marine Geology; Marine Sciences; Oceanography)
Oceanography
Optical Sciences
Optical Technologies (*see* Optical Sciences)
Optics (*see* Applied Physics; Optical Sciences; Physics)
Organic Chemistry

Paleontology
Paper Chemistry (*see* Chemistry)
Photonics
Physical Chemistry
Physics
Planetary and Space Sciences
Plant Sciences
Plasma Physics
Poultry Science (*see* Animal Sciences)
Radiological Physics (*see* Physics)
Range Management (*see* Range Science)
Range Science
Resource Management (*see*   Environmental Management and Policy;
   Natural Resources)
Solid-Earth Sciences (*see* Geosciences)
Space Sciences (*see* Planetary and Space Sciences)
Statistics
Theoretical Chemistry
Theoretical Physics
Viticulture and Enology
Water Resources

# Graduate Programs in Engineering & Applied Sciences

Aeronautical Engineering (*see* Aerospace/Aeronautical Engineering)
Aerospace/Aeronautical Engineering
Aerospace Studies (*see* Aerospace/Aeronautical Engineering)
Agricultural Engineering
Applied Mechanics (*see* Mechanics)
Applied Science and Technology
Architectural Engineering
Artificial Intelligence/Robotics
Astronautical Engineering (*see* Aerospace/Aeronautical Engineering)
Automotive Engineering
Aviation
Biochemical Engineering
Bioengineering
Bioinformatics
Biological Engineering (*see* Bioengineering)
Biomedical Engineering
Biosystems Engineering
Biotechnology
Ceramic Engineering (*see* Ceramic Sciences and Engineering)
Ceramic Sciences and Engineering
Ceramics (*see* Ceramic Sciences and Engineering)
Chemical Engineering
Civil Engineering
Computer and Information Systems Security
Computer Engineering
Computer Science
Computing Technology (*see* Computer Science)
Construction Engineering
Construction Management
Database Systems
Electrical Engineering
Electronic Materials
Electronics Engineering (*see* Electrical Engineering)
Energy and Power Engineering
Energy Management and Policy
Engineering and Applied Sciences
Engineering and Public Affairs (*see* Technology and Public Policy)
Engineering and Public Policy (*see* Energy Management and Policy;
   Technology and Public Policy)
Engineering Design
Engineering Management
Engineering Mechanics (*see* Mechanics)
Engineering Metallurgy (*see* Metallurgical Engineering and
   Metallurgy)
Engineering Physics
Environmental Design (*see* Environmental Engineering)
Environmental Engineering
Ergonomics and Human Factors

Financial Engineering
Fire Protection Engineering
Food Engineering (*see* Agricultural Engineering)
Game Design and Development
Gas Engineering (*see* Petroleum Engineering)
Geological Engineering
Geophysics Engineering (*see* Geological Engineering)
Geotechnical Engineering
Hazardous Materials Management
Health Informatics
Health Systems (*see* Safety Engineering; Systems Engineering)
Highway Engineering (*see* Transportation and Highway Engineering)
Human-Computer Interaction
Human Factors (*see* Ergonomics and Human Factors)
Hydraulics
Hydrology (*see* Water Resources Engineering)
Industrial Engineering (*see* Industrial/Management Engineering)
Industrial/Management Engineering
Information Science
Internet Engineering
Macromolecular Science (*see* Polymer Science and Engineering)
Management Engineering (*see* Engineering Management; Industrial/
   Management Engineering)
Management of Technology
Manufacturing Engineering
Marine Engineering (*see* Civil Engineering)
Materials Engineering
Materials Sciences
Mechanical Engineering
Mechanics
Medical Informatics
Metallurgical Engineering and Metallurgy
Metallurgy (*see* Metallurgical Engineering and Metallurgy)
Mineral/Mining Engineering
Modeling and Simulation
Nanotechnology
Nuclear Engineering
Ocean Engineering
Operations Research
Paper and Pulp Engineering
Petroleum Engineering
Pharmaceutical Engineering
Plastics Engineering (*see* Polymer Science and Engineering)
Polymer Science and Engineering
Public Policy (*see* Energy Management and Policy; Technology and
   Public Policy)
Reliability Engineering
Robotics (*see* Artificial Intelligence/Robotics)
Safety Engineering
Software Engineering
Solid-State Sciences (*see* Materials Sciences)
Structural Engineering
Surveying Science and Engineering
Systems Analysis (*see* Systems Engineering)
Systems Engineering
Systems Science
Technology and Public Policy
Telecommunications
Telecommunications Management
Textile Sciences and Engineering
Textiles (*see* Textile Sciences and Engineering)
Transportation and Highway Engineering
Urban Systems Engineering (*see* Systems Engineering)
Waste Management (*see* Hazardous Materials Management)
Water Resources Engineering

# Graduate Programs in Business, Education, Information Studies, Law & Social Work

Accounting

Actuarial Science
Adult Education
Advertising and Public Relations
Agricultural Education
Alcohol Abuse Counseling (*see* Counselor Education)
Archival Management and Studies
Art Education
Athletics Administration (*see* Kinesiology and Movement Studies)
Athletic Training and Sports Medicine
Audiology (*see* Communication Disorders)
Aviation Management
Banking (*see* Finance and Banking)
Business Administration and Management—General
Business Education
Communication Disorders
Community College Education
Computer Education
Continuing Education (*see* Adult Education)
Counseling (*see* Counselor Education)
Counselor Education
Curriculum and Instruction
Developmental Education
Distance Education Development
Drug Abuse Counseling (*see* Counselor Education)
Early Childhood Education
Educational Leadership and Administration
Educational Measurement and Evaluation
Educational Media/Instructional Technology
Educational Policy
Educational Psychology
Education—General
Education of the Blind (*see* Special Education)
Education of the Deaf (*see* Special Education)
Education of the Gifted
Education of the Hearing Impaired (*see* Special Education)
Education of the Learning Disabled (*see* Special Education)
Education of the Mentally Retarded (*see* Special Education)
Education of the Physically Handicapped (*see* Special Education)
Education of Students with Severe/Multiple Disabilities
Education of the Visually Handicapped (*see* Special Education)
Electronic Commerce
Elementary Education
English as a Second Language
English Education
Entertainment Management
Entrepreneurship
Environmental Education
Environmental Law
Exercise and Sports Science
Exercise Physiology (*see* Kinesiology and Movement Studies)
Facilities and Entertainment Management
Finance and Banking
Food Services Management (*see* Hospitality Management)
Foreign Languages Education
Foundations and Philosophy of Education
Guidance and Counseling (*see* Counselor Education)
Health Education
Health Law
Hearing Sciences (*see* Communication Disorders)
Higher Education
Home Economics Education
Hospitality Management
Hotel Management (*see* Travel and Tourism)
Human Resources Development
Human Resources Management
Human Services
Industrial Administration (*see* Industrial and Manufacturing Management)
Industrial and Manufacturing Management
Industrial Education (*see* Vocational and Technical Education)
Information Studies
Instructional Technology (*see* Educational Media/Instructional Technology)
Insurance
Intellectual Property Law
International and Comparative Education

International Business
International Commerce (*see* International Business)
International Economics (*see* International Business)
International Trade (*see* International Business)
Investment and Securities (*see* Business Administration and Management; Finance and Banking; Investment Management)
Investment Management
Junior College Education (*see* Community College Education)
Kinesiology and Movement Studies
Law
Legal and Justice Studies
Leisure Services (*see* Recreation and Park Management)
Leisure Studies
Library Science
Logistics
Management (*see* Business Administration and Management)
Management Information Systems
Management Strategy and Policy
Marketing
Marketing Research
Mathematics Education
Middle School Education
Movement Studies (*see* Kinesiology and Movement Studies)
Multilingual and Multicultural Education
Museum Education
Music Education
Nonprofit Management
Nursery School Education (*see* Early Childhood Education)
Occupational Education (*see* Vocational and Technical Education)
Organizational Behavior
Organizational Management
Parks Administration (*see* Recreation and Park Management)
Personnel (*see* Human Resources Development; Human Resources Management; Organizational Behavior; Organizational Management; Student Affairs)
Philosophy of Education (*see* Foundations and Philosophy of Education)
Physical Education
Project Management
Public Relations (*see* Advertising and Public Relations)
Quality Management
Quantitative Analysis
Reading Education
Real Estate
Recreation and Park Management
Recreation Therapy (*see* Recreation and Park Management)
Religious Education
Remedial Education (*see* Special Education)
Restaurant Administration (*see* Hospitality Management)
Science Education
Secondary Education
Social Sciences Education
Social Studies Education (*see* Social Sciences Education)
Social Work
Special Education
Speech-Language Pathology and Audiology (*see* Communication Disorders)
Sports Management
Sports Medicine (*see* Athletic Training and Sports Medicine)
Sports Psychology and Sociology (*see* Kinesiology and Movement Studies)
Student Affairs
Substance Abuse Counseling (*see* Counselor Education)
Supply Chain Management
Sustainability Management
Systems Management (*see* Management Information Systems)
Taxation
Teacher Education (*see* specific subject areas)
Teaching English as a Second Language (*see* English as a Second Language)
Technical Education (*see* Vocational and Technical Education)
Transportation Management
Travel and Tourism
Urban Education
Vocational and Technical Education
Vocational Counseling (*see* Counselor Education)

# Directories and Subject Areas in This Book

**NOTES**

**NOTES**

**NOTES**

**NOTES**

# NOTES

**NOTES**

**NOTES**

**NOTES**

**NOTES**

**NOTES**

**NOTES**